GW00836325

This
Holy Bible
Presented to

____

____

By

____

____

Date

____

HOLY BIBLE

CONTAINING THE OLD AND NEW TESTAMENTS

NKJV
NEW
KING
JAMES
VERSION™

TRANSLATED OUT OF THE ORIGINAL TONGUES
AND WITH THE FORMER TRANSLATIONS
DILIGENTLY COMPARED AND REVISED

REFERENCE EDITION
with center-column references, concordance,
translation notes, significant textual variants, and
special study helps

WORDS OF CHRIST IN RED

BIBLE PUBLISHERS, INC.
Iowa Falls, IA 50126 U.S.A.

Printed in the Republic of Korea

1 2 3 4 5 05 04 03 02 01

PREFACE

Purpose

In the preface to the 1611 edition, the translators of the Authorized Version, known popularly as the King James Bible, state that it was not their purpose "to make a new translation . . . but to make a good one better." Indebted to the earlier work of William Tyndale and others, they saw their best contribution to consist in revising and enhancing the excellence of the English versions which had sprung from the Reformation of the sixteenth century. In harmony with the purpose of the King James scholars, the translators and editors of the present work have not pursued a goal of innovation. They have perceived the Holy Bible, New King James Version, as a continuation of the labors of the earlier translators, thus unlocking for today's readers the spiritual treasures found especially in the Authorized Version of the Holy Scriptures.

A Living Legacy

For nearly four hundred years, and throughout several revisions of its English form, the King James Bible has been deeply revered among the English-speaking peoples of the world. The precision of translation for which it is historically renowned, and its majesty of style, have enabled that monumental version of the Word of God to become the mainspring of the religion, language, and legal foundations of our civilization.

Although the Elizabethan period and our own era share in zeal for technical advance, the former period was more aggressively devoted to classical learning. Along with this awakened concern for the classics came a flourishing companion interest in the Scriptures, an interest that was enlivened by the conviction that the manuscripts were providentially handed down and were a trustworthy record of the inspired Word of God. The King James translators were committed to producing an English Bible that would be a precise translation, and by no means a paraphrase or a broadly approximate rendering. On the one hand, the scholars were almost as familiar with the original languages of the Bible as with their native English. On the other hand, their reverence for the divine Author and His Word assured a translation of the Scriptures in which only a principle of utmost accuracy could be accepted.

In 1786 Catholic scholar Alexander Geddes said of the King James Bible, "If accuracy and strictest attention to the letter of the text be supposed to constitute an excellent version, this is of all versions the most excellent." George Bernard Shaw became a literary legend in our century because of his severe and often humorous criticisms of our most cherished values. Surprisingly, however, Shaw pays the following tribute to the scholars commissioned by King James: "The translation was extraordinarily well done because to the translators what they were translating was not merely a curious collection of ancient books written by different authors in different stages of culture, but the Word of God divinely revealed through His chosen and expressly inspired scribes. In this conviction they carried out their work with boundless reverence and care and achieved a beautifully artistic result." History agrees with these estimates. Therefore, while seeking to unveil the excellent *form* of the traditional English Bible, special care has also been taken in the present edition to preserve the work of *precision* which is the legacy of the 1611 translators.

Complete Equivalence in Translation

Where new translation has been necessary in the New King James Version, the most complete representation of the original has been rendered by considering the history of usage and etymology of words in their contexts. This principle of complete equivalence seeks to preserve *all* of the information in the text, while presenting it in good literary form. Dynamic equivalence, a recent procedure in Bible translation, commonly results in paraphrasing where a more literal rendering is needed to reflect a specific and vital sense. For example, complete equivalence truly renders the original text in expressions such as "lifted her voice and wept" (Gen. 21:16); "I gave you cleanness of teeth" (Amos 4:6); "Jesus met them, saying, 'Rejoice!' " (Matt. 28:9); and " 'Woman, what does your concern have to do with Me?' " (John 2:4). Complete equivalence translates fully, in order to provide an English text that is both accurate and readable.

In keeping with the principle of complete equivalence, it is the policy to translate interjections which are commonly omitted in modern language renderings of the Bible. As an example, the interjection *behold*, in the older King James editions, continues to have a place in English usage, especially in dramatically calling attention to a spectacular scene, or an event of profound importance such as the Immanuel prophecy of Isaiah 7:14. Consequently, *behold* is retained for these occasions in the present edition. However, the Hebrew and Greek originals for this word can be translated variously, depending on the circumstances in the passage. Therefore, in addition to *behold*, words such as *indeed, look, see,* and *surely* are also rendered to convey the appropriate sense suggested by the context in each case.

In faithfulness to God and to our readers, it was deemed appropriate that all participating scholars sign a statement affirming their belief in the verbal and plenary inspiration of Scripture, and in the inerrancy of the original autographs.

Devotional Quality

The King James scholars readily appreciated the intrinsic beauty of divine revelation. They accordingly disciplined their talents to render well-chosen English words of their time, as well as a graceful, often musical arrangement of language, which has stirred the hearts of Bible readers through the years. The translators, the committees, and the editors of the present edition, while sensitive to the late-twentieth-century English idiom, and while adhering faithfully to the Hebrew, Aramaic, and Greek texts, have sought to maintain those lyrical and devotional qualities that are so highly regarded in the Authorized Version. This devotional quality is especially apparent in the poetic and prophetic books, although even the relatively plain style of the Gospels and Epistles cannot strictly be likened, as sometimes suggested, to modern newspaper style. The Koine Greek of the New Testament is influenced by the Hebrew background of the writers, for whom even the gospel narratives were not merely flat utterance, but often song in various degrees of rhythm.

The Style

Students of the Bible applaud the timeless devotional character of our historic Bible. Yet it is also universally understood that our language, like all living languages, has undergone profound change since 1611. Subsequent revisions of the King James Bible have sought to keep abreast of changes in English speech. The present work is a further step toward this objective. Where obsolescence and other reading difficulties exist, present-day vocabulary, punctuation, and grammar have been carefully integrated. Words representing ancient objects, such as *chariot* and *phylactery*, have no modern substitutes and are therefore retained.

A special feature of the New King James Version is its conformity to the thought flow of the 1611 Bible. The reader discovers that the sequence and selection of words, phrases, and clauses of the new edition, while much clearer, are so close to the traditional that there is remarkable ease in listening to the reading of either edition while following with the other.

In the discipline of translating biblical and other ancient languages, a standard method of transliteration, that is, the English spelling of untranslated words, such as names of persons and places, has never been commonly adopted. In keeping with the design of the present work, the King James spelling of untranslated words is retained, although made uniform throughout. For example, instead of the spellings *Isaiah* and *Elijah* in the Old Testament, and *Esaias* and *Elias* in the New Testament, *Isaiah* and *Elijah* now appear in both Testaments.

King James doctrinal and theological terms, for example, *propitiation, justification,* and *sanctification,* are generally familiar to English-speaking peoples. Such terms have been retained except where the original language indicates need for a more precise translation.

Readers of the Authorized Version will immediately be struck by the absence of several pronouns: *thee, thou,* and *ye* are replaced by the simple *you,* while *your* and *yours* are substituted for *thy* and *thine* as applicable. *Thee, thou, thy,* and *thine* were once forms of address to express a special relationship to human as well as divine persons. These pronouns are no longer part of our language. However, reverence for God in the present work is preserved by capitalizing pronouns, including *You, Your,* and *Yours,* which refer to Him. Additionally, capitalization of these pronouns benefits the reader by clearly distinguishing divine and human persons referred to in a passage. Without such capitalization the distinction is often obscure, because the antecedent of a pronoun is not always clear in the English translation.

In addition to the pronoun usages of the seventeenth century, the *-eth* and *-est* verb endings, so familiar in the earlier King James editions, are now obsolete. Unless a speaker is schooled in these verb endings, there is common difficulty in selecting the correct form to be used with a given subject of the verb in vocal prayer. That is, should we use *love, loveth,* or *lovest? do, doeth, doest,* or *dost? have, hath,* or *hast?* Because these forms are obsolete, contemporary English usage has been substituted for the previous verb endings.

In older editions of the King James Version, the frequency of the connective *and* far exceeded the limits of present English usage. Also, biblical linguists agree that the Hebrew and Greek original words for this conjunction may commonly be translated otherwise, depending on the immediate context. Therefore, instead of *and,* alternatives such as *also, but, however, now, so, then,* and *thus* are accordingly rendered in the present edition, when the original language permits.

The real character of the Authorized Version does not reside in its archaic pronouns or verbs or other grammatical forms of the seventeenth century, but rather in the care taken by its scholars to impart the letter and spirit of the original text in a majestic and reverent style.

The Format

The format of the New King James Version is designed to enhance the vividness and devotional quality of the Holy Scriptures:

- Subject headings assist the reader to identify topics and transitions in the biblical content.
- Words or phrases in *italics* indicate expressions in the original language which require clarification by additional English words, as also done throughout the history of the King James Bible.
- Verse numbers in **bold** type indicate the beginning of a paragraph.
- *Oblique type* in the New Testament indicates a quotation from the Old Testament.
- Poetry is structured as contemporary verse to reflect the poetic form and beauty of the passage in the original language.
- The covenant name of God was usually translated from the Hebrew as "LORD" or "GOD" (using capital letters as shown) in the King James Old Testament. This tradition is maintained. In the present edition the name is so capitalized whenever the covenant name is quoted in the New Testament from a passage in the Old Testament.

The Old Testament Text

The Hebrew Bible has come down to us through the scrupulous care of ancient scribes who copied the original text in successive generations. By the sixth century A.D. the scribes were succeeded by a group known as the Masoretes, who continued to preserve the sacred Scriptures for another five hundred years in a form known as the Masoretic Text. Babylonia, Palestine, and Tiberias were the main centers of Masoretic activity; but by the tenth century A.D. the Masoretes of Tiberias, led by the family of ben Asher, gained the ascendancy. Through subsequent editions, the ben Asher text became in the twelfth century the only recognized form of the Hebrew Scriptures.

Daniel Bomberg printed the first Rabbinic Bible in 1516–17; that work was followed in 1524–25 by a second edition prepared by Jacob ben Chayyim and also published by Bomberg. The text of ben Chayyim was adopted in most subsequent Hebrew Bibles, including those used by the King James translators. The ben Chayyim text was also used for the first two editions of Rudolph Kittel's *Biblia Hebraica* of 1906 and 1912. In 1937 Paul Kahle published a third edition of *Biblia Hebraica*. This edition was based on the oldest dated manuscript of the ben Asher text, the Leningrad Manuscript B19a (A.D. 1008), which Kahle regarded as superior to that used by ben Chayyim.

For the New King James Version the text used was the 1967/1977 Stuttgart edition of the *Biblia Hebraica*, with frequent comparisons being made with the Bomberg edition of 1524–25. The Septuagint (Greek) Version of the Old Testament and the Latin Vulgate also were consulted. In addition to referring to a variety of ancient versions of the Hebrew Scriptures, the

New King James Version draws on the resources of relevant manuscripts from the Dea Sea caves. In the few places where the Hebrew was so obscure that the 1611 King James was compelled to follow one of the versions, but where information is now available to resolve the problems, the New King James Version follows the Hebrew text. Significant variations are recorded in the center reference column.

The New Testament Text

There is more manuscript support for the New Testament than for any other body of ancient literature. Over five thousand Greek, eight thousand Latin, and many more manuscripts in other languages attest the integrity of the New Testament. There is only one basic New Testament used by Protestants, Roman Catholics, and Orthodox, by conservatives and liberals. Minor variations in hand copying have appeared through the centuries, before mechanical printing began about A.D. 1450.

Some variations exist in the spelling of Greek words, in word order, and in similar details. These ordinarily do not show up in translation and do not affect the sense of the text in any way.

Other manuscript differences such as omission or inclusion of a word or a clause, and two paragraphs in the Gospels, should not overshadow the overwhelming degree of *agreement* which exists among the ancient records. Bible readers may be assured that the most important differences in English New Testaments of today are due, not to manuscript divergence, but to the way in which translators view the task of translation: How literally should the text be rendered? How does the translator view the matter of biblical inspiration? Does the translator adopt a paraphrase when a literal rendering would be quite clear and more to the point? The New King James Version follows the historic precedent of the Authorized Version in maintaining a literal approach to translation, except where the idiom of the original language cannot be translated directly into our tongue.

The King James New Testament was based on the traditional text of the Greek-speaking churches, first published in 1516, and later called the Textus Receptus or Received Text. Although based on the relatively few available manuscripts, these were representative of many more which existed at the time but only became known later. In the late nineteenth century, B. Westcott and F. Hort taught that this text had been officially edited by the fourth-century church, but a total lack of historical evidence for this event has forced a revision of the theory. It is now widely held that the Byzantine Text that largely supports the Textus Receptus has as much right as the Alexandrian or any other tradition to be weighed in determining the text of the New Testament. Those readings in the Textus Receptus which have weak support are indicated in the center reference column as being opposed by both Critical and Majority Texts (see "Center-Column Notes").

Since the 1880s most contemporary translations of the New Testament have relied upon a relatively few manuscripts discovered chiefly in the late nineteenth and early twentieth centuries. Such translations depend primarily on two manuscripts, Codex Vaticanus and Codex Sinaiticus, because of their greater age. The Greek text obtained by using these sources and the related papyri (our most ancient manuscripts) is known as the Alexandrian Text. However, some scholars have grounds for doubting the faithfulness of Vaticanus and Sinaiticus, since they often disagree with one another, and Sinaiticus exhibits excessive omission.

A third viewpoint of New Testament scholarship holds that the best text is based on the consensus of the majority of existing Greek manuscripts. This text is called the Majority Text. Most of these manuscripts are in substantial agreement. Even though many are late, and none is earlier than the fifth century, usually their readings are verified by papyri, ancient versions, quotations from the early church fathers, or a combination of these. The Majority Text is similar to the Textus Receptus, but it corrects those readings which have little or no support in the Greek manuscript tradition.

Today, scholars agree that the science of New Testament textual criticism is in a state of flux. Very few scholars still favor the Textus Receptus as such, and then often for its historical prestige as the text of Luther, Calvin, Tyndale, and the King James Version. For about a century most have followed a Critical Text (so called because it is edited according to specific principles of textual criticism) which depends heavily upon the Alexandrian type of text. More recently many have abandoned this Critical Text (which is quite similar to the one edited by Westcott and Hort) for one that is more eclectic. Finally, a small but growing number of scholars prefer the Majority Text, which is close to the traditional text except in the Revelation.

In light of these facts, and also because the New King James Version is the fifth revision of a historic document translated from specific Greek texts, the editors decided to retain the traditional text in the body of the New Testament and to indicate major Critical and Majority Text variant readings in the center reference column. Although these variations are duly indicated in the center-column notes of the present edition, it is most important to emphasize that fully eighty-five percent of the New Testament text is the same in the Textus Receptus, the Alexandrian Text, and the Majority Text.

Center-Column Notes

Significant explanatory notes, alternate translations, and cross-references, as well as New Testament citations of Old Testament passages, are supplied in the center reference column. Cross-references enclosed in square brackets identify passages similar in concept to the referenced passage in the text.

Important textual variants in the Old Testament are identified in a standard form.

The textual notes in the present edition of the New Testament make no evaluation of readings, but do clearly indicate the manuscript sources of readings. They objectively present the facts without such tendentious remarks as "the best manuscripts omit" or "the most reliable manuscripts read." Such notes are value judgments that differ according to varying viewpoints on the text. By giving a clearly defined set of variants the New King James Version benefits readers of all textual persuasions.

Where significant variations occur in the New Testament Greek manuscripts, textual notes are classified as follows:

1. NU-Text
   These variations from the traditional text generally represent the Alexandrian or Egyptian type of text described previously in "The New Testament Text." They are found in the Critical Text published in the twenty-sixth edition of the Nestle-Aland Greek New Testament (N) and in the United Bible Societies' third edition (U), hence the acronym, "NU-Text."

2. M-Text
   This symbol indicates points of variation in the Majority Text from the traditional text, as also previously discussed in "The New Testament Text." It should be noted that M stands for whatever reading is printed in the published *Greek New Testament According to the Majority Text,* whether supported by overwhelming, strong, or only a divided majority textual tradition.

The textual notes reflect the scholarship of the past 150 years and will assist the reader to observe the variations between the different manuscript traditions of the New Testament. Such information is generally not available in English translations of the New Testament.

Special Abbreviations

Arab.	Arabic
Aram.	Aramaic
Bg.	the 1524–25 edition of the Hebrew Old Testament published by Daniel Bomberg (see Preface, "The Old Testament Text")
cf.	compare
ch., chs.	chapter, chapters
DSS	Dead Sea Scrolls
e.g.	for example
et al.	and others
etc.	and so forth
fem.	feminine
f., ff.	following verse, following verses
Gr.	Greek
Heb.	Hebrew
i.e.	that is
Kt.	Kethib (literally, in Aramaic, "written")—the written words of the Hebrew Old Testament preserved by the Masoretes (see "Qr.")
Lat.	Latin
lit.	literally
LXX	Septuagint—an ancient translation of the Old Testament into Greek
M	Majority Text (see Preface, "The New Testament Text")
ms., mss.	manuscript, manuscripts
masc.	masculine
MT	Masoretic Text—the traditional Hebrew Old Testament (see Preface, "The Old Testament Text")
NU	the most prominent modern Critical Text of the Greek New Testament, published in the twenty-sixth edition of the Nestle-Aland Greek New Testament and in the third edition of the United Bible Societies' Greek New Testament (see Preface, "The New Testament Text")
pl.	plural
Qr.	Qere (literally, in Aramaic, "read")—certain words read aloud, differing from the written words, in the Masoretic tradition of the Hebrew Old Testament (see "Kt.")
Sam.	Samaritan Pentateuch—a variant Hebrew edition of the books of Moses, used by the Samaritan community
sing.	singular
Syr.	Syriac
Tg.	Targum—an Aramaic paraphrase of the Old Testament
TR	Textus Receptus or Received Text (see Preface, "The New Testament Text")
v., vv.	verse, verses
vss.	versions—ancient translations of the Bible
Vg.	Vulgate—an ancient translation of the Bible into Latin, translated and edited by Jerome

How to Use This Reference Bible

A BOLD-FACE NUMERAL in the center column indicates the verse to which an entry applies.

A SUPERIOR LETTER (usually preceding the referenced word or phrase in the text as space permits) indicates cross-references.

SQUARE BRACKETS indicate a conceptual cross-reference, which identifies a passage similar in *concept* to the referenced passage in the text.

A SUPERIOR NUMERAL indicates an equivalent translation, alternate translation, literal translation, language note, explanatory note, or textual note.

An EQUIVALENT TRANSLATION is *similar* in meaning to the translation in the text. It helps you understand the text by showing you a synonym.

An ALTERNATE TRANSLATION is *different* in meaning from the words in the text, but is justified by the original languages. That is, the translators could have understood the original word or phrase this way, although they felt their choice was more appropriate.

An EXPLANATORY NOTE explains the word or phrase. Words set in roman type in translation notes are explanatory only and are not translated from the original languages.

Greeting

PAUL, [a]called *to be* an apostle
of Jesus Christ [b]through the
will of God, and [c]Sosthenes
our brother,

2 To the church of God which is
at Corinth, to those who [a]are
[1]sanctified in Christ Jesus, [b]called
to be saints, with all who in every
place call on the name of Jesus
Christ [c]our Lord, [d]both theirs and
ours:

3 [a]Grace to you and peace from
God our Father and the Lord Jesus
Christ.

Spiritual Gifts at Corinth

4 [a]I thank my God always concerning
you for the grace of God
which was given to you by Christ
Jesus,
5 that you were enriched in every
thing by Him [a]in all [1]utterance and
all knowledge,
6 even as [a]the testimony of
Christ was confirmed [1]in you,

CHAPTER 1

1 [a]Rom. 1:1 [b]2 Cor. 1:1 [c]Acts 18:17
2 [a][Acts 15:9] [b]Rom. 1:7 [c][1 Cor. 8:6] [d][Rom. 3:22] [1]*set apart*
3 [a]Rom. 1:7
4 [a]Rom. 1:8
5 [a][1 Cor. 12:8] [1]*speech*
6 [a]2 Tim. 1:8 [1]Or *among*
7 [a]Phil. 3:20
8 [a]1 Thess. 3:13; 5:23 [b]Col. 1:22; 2:7
9 [a]Is. 49:7 [b][John 15:4]
10 [a]2 Cor. 13:11 [1]Have a uniform testimony [2]*schisms* or *dissensions*
11 [1]*quarrels*
12 [a]1 Cor. 3:4 [b]Acts 18:24 [c]John 1:42

CHAPTER 1

1 [a]Rom. 1:1 [b]2 Cor. 1:1 [c]Acts 18:17
2 [a][Acts 15:9] [b]Rom. 1:7 [c][1 Cor. 8:6] [d][Rom. 3:22] [1]*set apart*
3 [a]Rom. 1:7
4 [a]Rom. 1:8
5 [a][1 Cor. 12:8] [1]*speech*
6 [a]2 Tim. 1:8 [1]Or *among*
7 [a]Phil. 3:20
8 [a]1 Thess. 3:13; 5:23 [b]Col. 1:22; 2:7
9 [a]Is. 49:7 [b][John 15:4]
10 [a]2 Cor. 13:11 [1]Have a uniform testimony [2]*schisms* or *dissensions*
11 [1]*quarrels*
12 [a]1 Cor. 3:4

less in the day of our Lord Jesus
Christ.
9 [a]God *is* faithful, by whom you
were called into [b]the fellowship of
His Son, Jesus Christ our Lord.

Sectarianism Is Sin

10 Now I plead with you, brethren,
by the name of our Lord Jesus
Christ, [a]that you all [1]speak the
same thing, and *that* there be no
[2]divisions among you, but *that*
you be perfectly joined together in
the same mind and in the same
judgment.
11 For it has been declared to me
concerning you, my brethren, by
those of Chloe's *household*, that
there are [1]contentions among you.
12 Now I say this, that [a]each of
you says, "I am of Paul," or "I am
of [b]Apollos," or "I am of [c]Cephas,"
or "I am of Christ."
13 [a]Is Christ divided? Was Paul
crucified for you? Or were you
baptized in the name of Paul?

not know whether I baptized any
other.
17 For Christ did not send me to
baptize, but to preach the gospel,
[a]not with wisdom of words, lest
the cross of Christ should be made
of no effect.

Christ the Power and Wisdom of God

18 For the [1]message of the cross
is [a]foolishness to [b]those who are
perishing, but to us [c]who are being
saved it is the [d]power of God.
19 For it is written:

> [a]*"I will destroy the wisdom of the*
> *wise,*
> *And bring to nothing the*
> *understanding of the prudent."*

20 [a]Where is the wise? Where *is*
the scribe? Where *is* the [1]disputer
of this age? [b]Has not God made
foolish the wisdom of this world?
21 For since, in the [a]wisdom of
God, the world through wisdom
did not know God, it pleased God
through the foolishness of the
message preached to save those
who believe.
22 For [a]Jews request a sign, and
Greeks seek after wisdom;
23 but we preach Christ crucified,
[a]to the Jews a [1]stumbling block
and to the [2]Greeks [b]foolishness,
24 but to those who are called,
both Jews and Greeks, Christ [a]the
power of God and [b]the wisdom of
God.
25 Because the foolishness of God
is wiser than men, and the weak-
ness of God is stronger than men.

Glory Only in the Lord

26 For [1]you see your calling,
brethren, [a]that not many wise ac-
cording to the flesh, not many
mighty, not many [2]noble, *are*
called.
27 But [a]God has chosen the fool-
ish things of the world to put to
shame the wise, and God has cho-
sen the weak things of the world
to put to shame the things which
are mighty;
28 and the [1]base things of the
world and the things which are de-
spised God has chosen, and the
things which are not, to bring to
nothing the things that are,

17 [a][1 Cor. 2:1, 4, 13]
18 [a]1 Cor. 2:14 [b]2 Cor. 2:15 [c][1 Cor. 15:2] [d]Rom. 1:16; 1 Cor. 1:24 [1]Lit. *word*
19 [a]Is. 29:14
20 [a]Is. 19:12; 33:18 [b]Job 12:17; Matt. 13:22; 1 Cor. 2:6, 8; 3:18, 19 [1]*debater*
21 [a]Dan. 2:20; [Rom. 11:33]
22 [a]Matt. 12:38; Mark 8:11; John 2:18; 4:48
23 [a]Is. 8:14; Luke 2:34; John 6:60; Gal. 5:11; [1 Pet. 2:8] [b][1 Cor. 2:14] [1]Gr. *skandalon, offense* [2]NU *Gentiles*
24 [a][Rom. 1:4] [b]Col. 2:3
26 [a]John 7:48 [1]*consider* [2]*well-born*
27 [a]Ps. 8:2; Matt. 11:25
28 [1]*insignificant* or *lowly*
30 [a]Jer. 23:5; 33:16; [2 Cor. 5:21; Phil. 3:9]
31 [a]Jer. 9:23, 24; 2 Cor. 10:17

CHAPTER 2

1 [1]NU *mystery*
2 [a]1 Cor. 1:23; Gal. 6:14
3 [a]Acts 18:1 [b][2 Cor. 4:7]
4 [a]2 Pet. 1:16 [b]Rom. 15:19; 1 Cor. 4:20 [1]NU omits *human*
5 [a]Rom. 1:16; 1 Thess. 1:5
7 [1]*predetermined*
8 [a]Luke 23:34 [b]Matt. 27:33–50
9 [a][Is. 64:4; 65:17]
10 [a]Matt. 11:25; 13:11; 16:17; [Gal. 1:12; Eph. 3:3, 5]
11 [a]Job 32:8; Eccl. 12:7; [1 Cor. 6:20; James 2:26] [b]Rom. 11:33

A LITERAL TRANSLATION gives the literal meaning of the word or phrase.

A LANGUAGE NOTE gives the Hebrew, Greek, or Aramaic word or phrase that underlies the English translation.

A TEXTUAL NOTE points out one or more significant textual variants. The sources of the variant readings are identified by abbreviations listed on page ix.

The notes in the present edition of the New Testament do not evaluate readings (and so they avoid terms such as "better manuscripts"), but they do clearly indicate the sources of readings that diverge from the traditional text. Thus this edition does not take sides, but presents a clearly defined statement of the variants, representing all textual persuasions.

Readings labeled "NU" are from the modern eclectic or "critical" text, which depends heavily upon the Alexandrian type of text. Readings labeled "M" are from the Majority Text. (See the Preface, "The New Testament Text," for an explanation of these terms.)

OBLIQUE TYPE in the New Testament indicates a quotation from the Old Testament. The sources of the quotations are found in cross-references.

ITALIC TYPE in the text indicates words that the original texts do not contain but which English requires for clarity.

SUBJECT HEADINGS have been added to help you follow the flow of thought in the biblical material.

A BOLD-FACE VERSE NUMERAL in the text indicates a paragraph break. When a new paragraph begins within a verse, the new paragraph is indented (see, for example, Nehemiah 13:22).

QUOTATION MARKS in the text follow modern English usage. For easier reading, only the marks denoting the most recently opened quotation are repeated in a new paragraph.

PERSONAL PRONOUNS and certain nouns are capitalized when they refer to Deity.

POETRY is structured as contemporary verse to reflect the poetic form and beauty of the original language.

THE COVENANT NAME OF GOD in the Old Testament, represented by the Hebrew consonants YHWH, is translated "LORD" or "GOD" (using capital letters as shown), as it has been throughout the history of the King James Bible. In this edition the capitalized form is also used whenever the covenant name is quoted in the New Testament from a passage in the Old Testament.

31 "But concerning the resurrection of the dead, have you not read what was spoken to you by God, saying,
32 [a]*'I am the God of Abraham, the God of Isaac, and the God of Jacob'*? God is not the God of the dead, but of the living."
33 And when the multitudes heard *this,* [a]they were astonished at His teaching.

The Scribes: Which Is the First Commandment of All?

34 [a]But when the Pharisees heard that He had silenced the Sadducees, they gathered together.
35 Then one of them, [a]a lawyer, asked *Him a question,* testing Him, and saying,
36 "Teacher, which *is* the great commandment in the law?"
37 Jesus said to him, "'*You shall love the LORD your God with all your heart, with all your soul, and with all your mind.*'
38 "This is *the* first and great commandment.
39 "And *the* second *is* like it: [a]*'You shall love your neighbor as yourself.'*
40 [a]"On these two commandments hang all the Law and the Prophets."

Jesus: How Can David Call His Descendant Lord?

41 [a]While the Pharisees were gathered together, Jesus asked them,
42 saying, "What do you think about the Christ? Whose Son is He?" They said to Him, "The [a]Son of David."
43 He said to them, "How then does David in the Spirit call Him 'Lord,' saying:

44 *'The LORD said to my Lord,*
"Sit at My right hand,
Till I make Your enemies Your footstool"'?

45 "If David then calls Him 'Lord,' how is He his Son?"
46 [a]And no one was able to answer Him a word, [b]nor from that day on did anyone dare question Him anymore.

32 [a]Ex. 3:6, 15
33 [a]Matt. 7:28
34 [a]Mark 12:28–31
35 [a]Luke 7:30; 10:25; 11:45, 46, 52; 14:3
37 [a]Deut. 6:5; 10:12; 30:6
39 [a]Lev. 19:18
40 [a][Matt. 7:12]
41 [a]Luke 20:41–44
42 [a]Matt. 1:1; 21:9
44 [a]Ps. 110:1
46 [a]Luke 14:6 [b]Mark 12:34

CHAPTER 23

2 [a]Neh. 8:4, 8
3 [a][Rom. 2:19] [1]NU omits *to observe*
4 [a]Luke 11:46
5 [a][Matt. 6:1–6, 16–18]
6 [a]Luke 11:43; 20:46 [1]Or *place of honor*
8 [a][James 3:1] [1]*Leader* [2]NU omits *the* Christ
9 [a][Mal. 1:6]
11 [a]Matt. 20:26, 27
12 [a]Luke 14:11; 18:14 [1]*put down* [2]*lifted up*
13 [a]Luke 11:52
14 [a]Mark 12:40 [1]NU omits v. 14.
15 [1]Gr. *Gehenna*
16 [a]Matt. 15:14; 23:24

Books of the Old and New Testaments and Their Abbreviations

The Old Testament

The New Testament

The Old Testament

The First Book of Moses Called

Genesis

THE first part of Genesis focuses on the beginning and spread of sin in the world and culminates in the devastating flood in the days of Noah. The second part of the book focuses on God's dealings with one man, Abraham, through whom God promises to bring salvation and blessing to the world. Abraham and his descendants learn firsthand that it is always safe to trust the Lord in times of famine and feasting, blessing and bondage. From Abraham . . . to Isaac . . . to Jacob . . . to Joseph . . . God's promises begin to come to fruition in a great nation possessing a great land.

Genesis is a Greek word meaning "origin," "source," "generation," or "beginning." The original Hebrew title *Bereshith* means "In the Beginning."

The literary structure of Genesis is clear and is built around eleven separate units, each including the word *genealogy* in the phrase "This is the genealogy" or "The book of the genealogy": (1) Introduction to the Genealogies (1:1—2:3); (2) Heaven and Earth (2:4—4:26); (3) Adam (5:1—6:8); (4) Noah (6:9—9:29); (5) Sons of Noah (10:1—11:9); (6) Shem (11:10–26); (7) Terah (11:27—25:11); (8) Ishmael (25:12–18); (9) Isaac (25:19—35:29); (10) Esau (36:1—37:1); (11) Jacob (37:2—50:26).

The History of Creation

IN the [a]beginning [b]God created
the heavens and the earth.
2 The earth was [a]without
form, and void; and darkness [1]*was*
on the face of the deep. [b]And the
Spirit of God was hovering over
the face of the waters.
3 [a]Then God said, [b]"Let there be
[c]light"; and there was light.
4 And God saw the light, that *it*
was good; and God divided the
light from the darkness.
5 God called the light Day, and
the [a]darkness He called Night. [1]So
the evening and the morning were
the first day.
6 Then God said, [a]"Let there be
a [1]firmament in the midst of the
waters, and let it divide the waters
from the waters."
7 Thus God made the firmament,
[a]and divided the waters which
were under the firmament from
the waters which *were* [b]above the
firmament; and it was so.
8 And God called the firmament
Heaven. So the evening and the
morning were the second day.
9 Then God said, [a]"Let the wa-
ters under the heavens be gathered
together into one place, and [b]let
the dry *land* appear"; and it was
so.
10 And God called the dry *land*
Earth, and the gathering together
of the waters He called Seas. And
God saw that *it was* good.
11 Then God said, "Let the earth
[a]bring forth grass, the herb *that*
yields seed, *and* the [b]fruit tree *that*
yields fruit according to its kind,
whose seed *is* in itself, on the
earth"; and it was so.
12 And the earth brought forth
grass, the herb *that* yields seed ac-
cording to its kind, and the tree
that yields fruit, whose seed *is* in
itself according to its kind. And
God saw that *it was* good.
13 So the evening and the morn-
ing were the third day.
14 Then God said, "Let there be
[a]lights in the firmament of the
heavens to divide the day from the
night; and let them be for signs
and [b]seasons, and for days and
years;
15 "and let them be for lights in

CHAPTER 1

1 [a][John 1:1–3] [b]Acts 17:24
2 [a]Jer. 4:23 [b]Is. 40:13, 14 [1]Words in italic type have been added for clarity. They are not found in the original Hebrew or Aramaic.
3 [a]Ps. 33:6, 9 [b]2 Cor. 4:6 [c][Heb. 11:3]
5 [a]Ps. 19:2; 33:6; 74:16; 104:20; 136:5 [1]Lit. *And evening was, and morning was, a day, one.*
6 [a]Jer. 10:12 [1]*expanse*
7 [a]Prov. 8:27–29 [b]Ps. 148:4
9 [a]Job 26:10 [b]Ps. 24:1, 2; 33:7; 95:5
11 [a]Heb. 6:7 [b]2 Sam. 16:1
14 [a]Ps. 74:16; 136:5–9 [b]Ps. 104:19

the firmament of the heavens to
give light on the earth"; and it was
so.
16 Then God made two great
[1]lights: the [a]greater light to rule
the day, and the [b]lesser light to
rule the night. *He made* [c]the stars
also.
17 God set them in the firmament
of the [a]heavens to give light on the
earth,
18 and to [a]rule over the day and
over the night, and to divide the
light from the darkness. And God
saw that *it was* good.
19 So the evening and the morn-
ing were the fourth day.
20 Then God said, "Let the waters
abound with an abundance of liv-
ing [1]creatures, and let birds fly
above the earth across the face of
the [2]firmament of the heavens."
21 So [a]God created great sea crea-
tures and every living thing that
moves, with which the waters
abounded, according to their kind,
and every winged bird according
to its kind. And God saw that *it
was* good.
22 And God blessed them, saying,
[a]"Be fruitful and multiply, and fill
the waters in the seas, and let birds
multiply on the earth."
23 So the evening and the morn-
ing were the fifth day.
24 Then God said, "Let the earth
bring forth the living creature ac-
cording to its kind: cattle and
creeping thing and beast of the
earth, *each* according to its kind";
and it was so.
25 And God made the beast of the
earth according to its kind, cattle
according to its kind, and every-
thing that creeps on the earth ac-
cording to its kind. And God saw
that *it was* good.
26 Then God said, [a]"Let Us make
man in Our image, according to
Our likeness; [b]let them have do-
minion over the fish of the sea,
over the birds of the air, and over
the cattle, over [1]all the earth and
over every creeping thing that
creeps on the earth."
27 So God created man [a]in His
own image; in the image of God
He created him; [b]male and female
He created them.
28 Then God blessed them, and
God said to them, [a]"Be fruitful and

16 [a]Ps. 136:8 [b]Deut. 17:3; Ps. 8:3 [c]Deut. 4:19; Job 38:7; Is. 40:26 [1]*luminaries*
17 [a]Gen. 15:5; Jer. 33:20, 25
18 [a]Jer. 31:35
20 [1]*souls* [2]*expanse*
21 [a]Ps. 104:25–28
22 [a]Gen. 8:17
26 [a]Gen. 9:6; Ps. 100:3; Eccl. 7:29; [Eph. 4:24]; James 3:9 [b]Gen. 9:2; Ps. 8:6–8 [1]Syr. *all the wild animals of*
27 [a]Gen. 5:2; 1 Cor. 11:7 [b]Matt. 19:4; [Mark 10:6–8]
28 [a]Gen. 9:1, 7; Lev. 26:9 [b]1 Cor. 9:27 [1]*moves about on*
29 [a]Gen. 9:3; Ps. 104:14, 15
30 [a]Ps. 145:15 [b]Job 38:41 [1]*a living soul*
31 [a][Ps. 104:24; 1 Tim. 4:4]

CHAPTER 2

1 [a]Ps. 33:6
2 [a]Ex. 20:9–11; 31:17; Heb. 4:4, 10
3 [a][Is. 58:13]
4 [a]Gen. 1:1; Ps. 90:1, 2 [1]Heb. *toledoth,* lit. *generations*
5 [a]Gen. 1:11, 12 [b]Gen. 7:4; Job 5:10; 38:26–28 [c]Gen. 3:23
7 [a]Gen. 3:19, 23; Ps. 103:14 [b]Job 33:4 [c]Gen. 7:22 [d]1 Cor. 15:45
8 [a]Is. 51:3 [b]Gen. 3:23, 24 [c]Gen. 4:16
9 [a]Ezek. 31:8

multiply; fill the earth and [b]subdue
it; have dominion over the fish of
the sea, over the birds of the air,
and over every living thing that
[1]moves on the earth."
29 And God said, "See, I have
given you every herb *that* yields
seed which *is* on the face of all the
earth, and every tree whose fruit
yields seed; [a]to you it shall be for
food.
30 "Also, to [a]every beast of the
earth, to every [b]bird of the air, and
to everything that creeps on the
earth, in which *there is* [1]life, *I have
given* every green herb for food";
and it was so.
31 Then [a]God saw everything that
He had made, and indeed *it was*
very good. So the evening and the
morning were the sixth day.

2 Thus the heavens and the
earth, and [a]all the host of them,
were finished.
2 [a]And on the seventh day God
ended His work which He had
done, and He rested on the seventh
day from all His work which He
had done.
3 Then God [a]blessed the seventh
day and sanctified it, because in
it He rested from all His work
which God had created and made.
4 [a]This *is* the [1]history of the
heavens and the earth when they
were created, in the day that the
LORD God made the earth and the
heavens,
5 before any [a]plant of the field
was in the earth and before any
herb of the field had grown. For
the LORD God had not [b]caused it
to rain on the earth, and *there was*
no man [c]to till the ground;
6 but a mist went up from the
earth and watered the whole face
of the ground.
7 And the LORD God formed man
of the [a]dust of the ground, and
[b]breathed into his [c]nostrils the
breath of life; and [d]man became a
living being.

Life in God's Garden

8 The LORD God planted [a]a gar-
den [b]eastward in [c]Eden, and there
He put the man whom He had
formed.
9 And out of the ground the LORD
God made [a]every tree grow that
is pleasant to the sight and good

for food. [b]The tree of life *was* also
in the midst of the garden, and the
tree of the knowledge of good and
[c]evil.
10 Now a river went out of Eden
to water the garden, and from
there it parted and became four
riverheads.
11 The name of the first *is* Pishon;
it *is* the one which skirts [a]the
whole land of Havilah, where
there is gold.
12 And the gold of that land *is*
good. [a]Bdellium and the onyx
stone *are* there.
13 The name of the second river
is Gihon; it *is* the one which goes
around the whole land of Cush.
14 The name of the third river *is*
[a]Hiddekel;[1] it *is* the one which
goes toward the east of [2]Assyria.
The fourth river *is* the Euphrates.
15 Then the LORD God took [1]the
man and put him in the garden of
Eden to [2]tend and keep it.
16 And the LORD God commanded
the man, saying, "Of every tree of
the garden you may freely eat;
17 "but of the tree of the knowl-
edge of good and evil [a]you shall
not eat, for in the day that you eat
of it [b]you[1] shall surely [c]die."
18 And the LORD God said, "*It is*
not good that man should be
alone; [a]I will make him a helper
comparable to him."
19 [a]Out of the ground the LORD
God formed every beast of the
field and every bird of the air, and
[b]brought *them* to [1]Adam to see
what he would call them. And
whatever Adam called each living
creature, that *was* its name.
20 So Adam gave names to all cat-
tle, to the birds of the air, and to
every beast of the field. But for
Adam there was not found a
helper comparable to him.
21 And the LORD God caused a
[a]deep sleep to fall on Adam, and
he slept; and He took one of his
ribs, and closed up the flesh in its
place.
22 Then the rib which the LORD
God had taken from man He
[1]made into a woman, [a]and He
[b]brought her to the man.
23 And Adam said:

"This *is* now [a]bone of my bones
And flesh of my flesh;
She shall be called [1]Woman,
Because she was [b]taken out of
[2]Man."

24 [a]Therefore a man shall leave
his father and mother and [b]be[1]
joined to his wife, and they shall
become one flesh.
25 [a]And they were both naked, the
man and his wife, and were not
[b]ashamed.

The Temptation and Fall of Man

3 Now [a]the serpent was [b]more
cunning than any beast of the
field which the LORD God had
made. And he said to the woman,
"Has God indeed said, 'You shall
not eat of every tree of the gar-
den'?"
2 And the woman said to the ser-
pent, "We may eat the [a]fruit of the
trees of the garden;
3 "but of the fruit of the tree
which *is* in the midst of the garden,
God has said, 'You shall not eat
it, nor shall you [a]touch it, lest you
die.'"
4 [a]Then the serpent said to the
woman, "You will not surely die.
5 "For God knows that in the day
you eat of it your eyes will be
opened, and you will be like God,
knowing good and evil."
6 So when the woman [a]saw that
the tree *was* good for food, that it
was [1]pleasant to the eyes, and a
tree desirable to make *one* wise,
she took of its fruit [b]and ate. She
also gave to her husband with her,
and he ate.
7 Then the eyes of both of them
were opened, [a]and they knew that
they *were* naked; and they sewed
fig leaves together and made
themselves [1]coverings.
8 And they heard [a]the [1]sound of
the LORD God walking in the gar-
den in the [2]cool of the day, and
Adam and his wife [b]hid them-
selves from the presence of the
LORD God among the trees of the
garden.
9 Then the LORD God called to
Adam and said to him, "Where *are*
you?"
10 So he said, "I heard Your voice
in the garden, [a]and I was afraid
because I was naked; and I hid my-
self."
11 And He said, "Who told you

9 [b][Gen. 3:22; Rev. 2:7; 22:2, 14] [c][Deut. 1:39]
11 [a]Gen. 25:18
12 [a]Num. 11:7
14 [a]Dan. 10:4 [1]Or *Tigris* [2]Heb. *Ashshur*
15 [1]Or *Adam* [2]*cultivate*
17 [a]Gen. 3:1, 3, 11, 17 [b]Gen. 3:3, 19; [Rom. 6:23] [c]Rom. 5:12; 1 Cor. 15:21, 22 [1]Lit. *dying you shall die*
18 [a]1 Cor. 11:8, 9; 1 Tim. 2:13
19 [a]Gen. 1:20, 24 [b]Ps. 8:6 [1]Or *the man*
21 [a]Gen. 15:12; 1 Sam. 26:12
22 [a]Gen. 3:20; 1 Tim. 2:13 [b]Heb. 13:4 [1]Lit. *built*
23 [a]Gen. 29:14; Eph. 5:28–30 [b]1 Cor. 11:8, 9 [1]Heb. *Ishshah* [2]Heb. *Ish*
24 [a]Matt. 19:5; Eph. 5:31 [b]Mark 10:6–8; 1 Cor. 6:16 [1]Lit. *cling*
25 [a]Gen. 3:7, 10 [b]Is. 47:3

CHAPTER 3

1 [a]1 Chr. 21:1; [Rev. 12:9; 20:2, 10] [b]2 Cor. 11:3
2 [a]Gen. 2:16, 17
3 [a]Ex. 19:12, 13; Rev. 22:14
4 [a]John 8:44; [2 Cor. 11:3; 1 Tim. 2:14]
6 [a]1 John 2:16 [b]1 Tim. 2:14 [1]Lit. *a desirable thing*
7 [a]Gen. 2:25 [1]*girding coverings*
8 [a]Job 38:1 [b]Job 31:33; Jer. 23:24 [1]Or *voice* [2]Or *wind, breeze*
10 [a]Gen. 2:25; Ex. 3:6; Deut. 9:19; 1 John 3:20

that you *were* naked? Have you eaten from the tree of which I commanded you that you should not eat?"

12 Then the man said, [a]"The woman whom You gave *to be* with me, she gave me of the tree, and I ate."

13 And the LORD God said to the woman, "What *is* this you have done?" The woman said, [a]"The serpent deceived me, and I ate."

14 So the LORD God said to the serpent:

"Because you have done this,
You *are* cursed more than all
cattle,
And more than every beast of the
field;
On your belly you shall go,
And [a]you shall eat dust
All the days of your life.
15 And I will put enmity
Between you and the woman,
And between [a]your seed and [b]her
Seed;
[c]He shall bruise your head,
And you shall bruise His heel."

16 To the woman He said:

"I will greatly multiply your
sorrow and your conception;
[a]In pain you shall bring forth
children;
[b]Your desire *shall be* [1]for your
husband,
And he shall [c]rule over you."

17 Then to Adam He said, [a]"Because you have heeded the voice of your wife, and have eaten from the tree [b]of which I commanded you, saying, 'You shall not eat of it':

[c]"Cursed *is* the ground for your
sake;
[d]In toil you shall eat *of* it
All the days of your life.
18 Both thorns and thistles it shall
[1]bring forth for you,
And [a]you shall eat the herb of the
field.
19 [a]In the sweat of your face you
shall eat bread
Till you return to the ground,
For out of it you were taken;
[b]For dust you *are*,
And [c]to dust you shall return."

20 And Adam called his wife's name [a]Eve,[1] because she was the mother of all living.

12 [a][Prov. 28:13]

13 [a]2 Cor. 11:3

14 [a]Deut. 28:15–20

15 [a]John 8:44 [b]Is. 7:14 [c]Rom. 16:20

16 [a]John 16:21 [b]Gen. 4:7 [c]1 Cor. 11:3 [1]Lit. *toward*

17 [a]1 Sam. 15:23 [b]Gen. 2:17 [c]Rom. 8:20–22 [d]Eccl. 2:23

18 [a]Ps. 104:14 [1]*cause to grow*

19 [a]2 Thess. 3:10 [b]Gen. 2:7; 5:5 [c]Job 21:26

20 [a]2 Cor. 11:3 [1]Lit. *Life* or *Living*

23 [a]Gen. 4:2; 9:20

24 [a]Ezek. 31:3, 11 [b]Ps. 104:4 [c]Gen. 2:8 [d]Gen. 2:9

CHAPTER 4

1 [1]Lit. *Acquire*

2 [a]Luke 11:50, 51 [1]Lit. *Breath* or *Nothing*

3 [a]Num. 18:12 [1]Lit. *at the end of days*

4 [a]Num. 18:17 [b]Lev. 3:16 [c]Heb. 11:4

7 [1]Lit. *toward*

8 [a][1 John 3:12–15] [1]Lit. *said to* [2]Sam., LXX, Syr., Vg. add *"Let us go out to the field."*

9 [a]John 8:44 [b]1 Cor. 8:11–13

10 [a]Heb. 12:24

21 Also for Adam and his wife the LORD God made tunics of skin, and clothed them.

22 Then the LORD God said, "Behold, the man has become like one of Us, to know good and evil. And now, lest he put out his hand and take also of the tree of life, and eat, and live forever"—

23 therefore the LORD God sent him out of the garden of Eden [a]to till the ground from which he was taken.

24 So [a]He drove out the man; and He placed [b]cherubim [c]at the east of the garden of Eden, and a flaming sword which turned every way, to guard the way to the tree of [d]life.

Cain Murders Abel

4 Now Adam knew Eve his wife, and she conceived and bore [1]Cain, and said, "I have acquired a man from the LORD."

2 Then she bore again, this time his brother [1]Abel. Now [a]Abel was a keeper of sheep, but Cain was a tiller of the ground.

3 And [1]in the process of time it came to pass that Cain brought an offering of the fruit [a]of the ground to the LORD.

4 Abel also brought of [a]the firstborn of his flock and of [b]their fat. And the LORD [c]respected Abel and his offering,

5 but He did not respect Cain and his offering. And Cain was very angry, and his countenance fell.

6 So the LORD said to Cain, "Why are you angry? And why has your countenance fallen?

7 "If you do well, will you not be accepted? And if you do not do well, sin lies at the door. And its desire *is* [1]for you, but you should rule over it."

8 Now Cain [1]talked with Abel his [2]brother; and it came to pass, when they were in the field, that Cain rose up against Abel his brother and [a]killed him.

9 Then the LORD said to Cain, "Where *is* Abel your brother?" He said, [a]"I do not know. *Am* I [b]my brother's keeper?"

10 And He said, "What have you done? The voice of your brother's blood [a]cries out to Me from the ground.

11 "So now [a]you *are* cursed from the earth, which has opened its mouth to receive your brother's blood from your hand.

12 "When you till the ground, it shall no longer yield its strength to you. A fugitive and a vagabond you shall be on the earth."

13 And Cain said to the LORD, "My [1]punishment *is* greater than I can bear!

14 "Surely You have driven me out this day from the face of the ground; [a]I shall be [b]hidden from Your face; I shall be a fugitive and a vagabond on the earth, and it will happen *that* [c]anyone who finds me will kill me."

15 And the LORD said to him, [1]"Therefore, whoever kills Cain, vengeance shall be taken on him [a]sevenfold." And the LORD set a [b]mark on Cain, lest anyone finding him should kill him.

The Family of Cain

16 Then Cain [a]went out from the [b]presence of the LORD and dwelt in the land of [1]Nod on the east of Eden.

17 And Cain knew his wife, and she conceived and bore Enoch. And he built a city, [a]and called the name of the city after the name of his son—Enoch.

18 To Enoch was born Irad; and Irad begot Mehujael, and Mehujael begot Methushael, and Methushael begot Lamech.

19 Then Lamech took for himself [a]two wives: the name of one *was* Adah, and the name of the second *was* Zillah.

20 And Adah bore Jabal. He was the father of those who dwell in tents and have livestock.

21 His brother's name *was* Jubal. He was the father of all those who play the harp and [1]flute.

22 And as for Zillah, she also bore Tubal-Cain, an instructor of every craftsman in bronze and iron. And the sister of Tubal-Cain *was* Naamah.

23 Then Lamech said to his wives:

"Adah and Zillah, hear my voice;
Wives of Lamech, listen to my
speech!
For I have [1]killed a man for
wounding me,
Even a young man [2]for hurting
me.
24 [a]If Cain shall be avenged
sevenfold,
Then Lamech seventy-
sevenfold."

A New Son

25 And Adam knew his wife again, and she bore a son and [a]named him [1]Seth, "For God has appointed another seed for me instead of Abel, whom Cain killed."

26 And as for Seth, [a]to him also a son was born; and he named him [1]Enosh. Then *men* began [b]to call on the name of the LORD.

The Family of Adam

5 This is the book of the [a]genealogy of Adam. In the day that God created man, He made him in [b]the likeness of God.

2 He created them [a]male and female, and [b]blessed them and called them Mankind in the day they were created.

3 And Adam lived one hundred and thirty years, and begot *a son* [a]in his own likeness, after his image, and [b]named him Seth.

4 After he begot Seth, [a]the days of Adam were eight hundred years; [b]and he had sons and daughters.

5 So all the days that Adam lived were nine hundred and thirty years; [a]and he died.

6 Seth lived one hundred and five years, and begot [a]Enosh.

7 After he begot Enosh, Seth lived eight hundred and seven years, and had sons and daughters.

8 So all the days of Seth were nine hundred and twelve years; and he died.

9 Enosh lived ninety years, and begot [1]Cainan.

10 After he begot Cainan, Enosh lived eight hundred and fifteen years, and had sons and daughters.

11 So all the days of Enosh were nine hundred and five years; and he died.

12 Cainan lived seventy years, and begot Mahalalel.

13 After he begot Mahalalel, Cainan lived eight hundred and

---

11 [a]Gen. 3:14; Deut. 11:28; 28:15–20; Gal. 3:10
13 [1]*iniquity*
14 [a]Ps. 51:11 [b]Deut. 31:18; Is. 1:15 [c]Gen. 9:6; Num. 35:19, 21, 27
15 [a]Gen. 4:24; Ps. 79:12 [b]Gen. 9:6; Ezek. 9:4, 6 [1]So with MT, Tg.; LXX, Syr., Vg. *Not so;*
16 [a]2 Kin. 13:23; 24:20; Jer. 23:39; 52:3 [b]Jon. 1:3 [1]Lit. *Wandering*
17 [a]Ps. 49:11
19 [a]Gen. 2:24; 16:3; 1 Tim. 3:2
21 [1]*pipe*
23 [1]*slain a man for my wound* [2]*for my hurt*
24 [a]Gen. 4:15
25 [a]Gen. 5:3 [1]Lit. *Appointed*
26 [a]Gen. 5:6 [b]Gen. 12:8; 26:25; 1 Kin. 18:24; Ps. 116:17; Joel 2:32; Zeph. 3:9; 1 Cor. 1:2 [1]Gr. *Enos,* Luke 3:38

CHAPTER 5

1 [a]Gen. 2:4; 6:9; 1 Chr. 1:1; Matt. 1:1 [b]Gen. 1:26; 9:6; [Eph. 4:24; Col. 3:10]
2 [a]Gen. 1:27; Deut. 4:32; Matt. 19:4; Mark 10:6 [b]Gen. 1:28; 9:1
3 [a]1 Cor. 15:48, 49 [b]Gen. 4:25
4 [a]1 Chr. 1:1–4; Luke 3:36–38 [b]Gen. 1:28; 4:25
5 [a]Gen. 2:17; 3:19; 6:17; [Heb. 9:27]
6 [a]Gen. 4:26
9 [1]Heb. *Qenan*

forty years, and had sons and
daughters.
14 So all the days of Cainan were
nine hundred and ten years; and
he died.
15 Mahalalel lived sixty-five
years, and begot Jared.
16 After he begot Jared, Mahalalel
lived eight hundred and thirty
years, and had sons and daugh-
ters.
17 So all the days of Mahalalel
were eight hundred and ninety-
five years; and he died.
18 Jared lived one hundred and
sixty-two years, and begot [a]Enoch.
19 After he begot Enoch, Jared
lived eight hundred years, and had
sons and daughters.
20 So all the days of Jared were
nine hundred and sixty-two years;
and he died.
21 Enoch lived sixty-five years,
and begot Methuselah.
22 After he begot Methuselah,
Enoch [a]walked with God three
hundred years, and had sons and
daughters.
23 So all the days of Enoch were
three hundred and sixty-five years.
24 And [a]Enoch walked with God;
and he *was* not, for God [b]took him.
25 Methuselah lived one hundred
and eighty-seven years, and begot
Lamech.
26 After he begot Lamech, Methu-
selah lived seven hundred and
eighty-two years, and had sons
and daughters.
27 So all the days of Methuselah
were nine hundred and sixty-nine
years; and he died.
28 Lamech lived one hundred and
eighty-two years, and had a son.
29 And he called his name [a]Noah,[1]
saying, "This *one* will comfort us
concerning our work and the toil
of our hands, because of the
ground [b]which the LORD has
cursed."
30 After he begot Noah, Lamech
lived five hundred and ninety-five
years, and had sons and daugh-
ters.
31 So all the days of Lamech were
seven hundred and seventy-seven
years; and he died.
32 And Noah was five hundred
years old, and Noah begot [a]Shem,
Ham, [b]and Japheth.

The Wickedness and Judgment of Man

6 Now it came to pass, [a]when
men began to multiply on the
face of the earth, and daughters
were born to them,
2 that the sons of God saw the
daughters of men, that they *were*
beautiful; and they [a]took wives for
themselves of all whom they
chose.
3 And the LORD said, [a]"My Spirit
shall not [b]strive[1] with man forever,
[c]for he *is* indeed flesh; yet his days
shall be one hundred and twenty
years."
4 There were [1]giants on the earth
in those [a]days, and also afterward,
when the sons of God came in to
the daughters of men and they
bore *children* to them. Those *were*
the mighty men who *were* of old,
men of renown.
5 Then [1]the LORD saw that the
wickedness of man *was* great in
the earth, and *that* every [a]intent[2]
of the thoughts of his heart *was*
only evil [3]continually.
6 And [a]the LORD was sorry that
He had made man on the earth,
and [b]He was grieved in His [c]heart.
7 So the LORD said, "I will [a]de-
stroy man whom I have created
from the face of the earth, both
man and beast, creeping thing and
birds of the air, for I am sorry that
I have made them."
8 But Noah [a]found grace in the
eyes of the LORD.

Noah Pleases God

9 This is the genealogy of Noah.
[a]Noah was a just man, [1]perfect in
his generations. Noah [b]walked
with God.
10 And Noah begot three sons:
[a]Shem, Ham, and Japheth.
11 The earth also was corrupt [a]be-
fore God, and the earth was [b]filled
with violence.
12 So God [a]looked upon the earth,
and indeed it was corrupt; for [b]all
flesh had corrupted their way on
the earth.

The Ark Prepared

13 And God said to Noah, [a]"The
end of all flesh has come before
Me, for the earth is filled with vio-
lence through them; [b]and behold,
[c]I will destroy them with the earth.

18 [a]Jude 14, 15
22 [a]Gen. 6:9; 17:1; 24:40; 48:15
24 [a]2 Kin. 2:11 [b]Heb. 11:5
29 [a]Luke 3:36 [b]Gen. 3:17–19; 4:11 [1]Lit. *Rest*
32 [a]Gen. 6:10; 7:13 [b]Gen. 10:21

CHAPTER 6

1 [a]Gen. 1:28
2 [a]Deut. 7:3, 4
3 [a][Gal. 5:16, 17] [b]2 Thess. 2:7 [c]Ps. 78:39 [1]LXX, Syr., Tg., Vg. *abide*
4 [a]Num. 13:32, 33 [1]Heb. *nephilim, fallen* or *mighty ones*
5 [a]Gen. 8:21 [1]So with MT, Tg.; Vg. *God;* LXX *LORD God* [2]*thought* [3]*all the day*
6 [a]1 Sam. 15:11, 29 [b]Is. 63:10 [c]Mark 3:5
7 [a]Gen. 7:4, 23
8 [a]Gen. 19:19
9 [a]2 Pet. 2:5 [b]Gen. 5:22, 24 [1]*blameless* or *having integrity*
10 [a]Gen. 5:32; 7:13
11 [a]Rom. 2:13 [b]Ezek. 8:17
12 [a]Ps. 14:2; 53:2, 3 [b]Ps. 14:1–3
13 [a]1 Pet. 4:7 [b]Gen. 6:17 [c]2 Pet. 2:4–10

14 "Make yourself an ark of
gopherwood; make [1]rooms in the
ark, and cover it inside and outside
with pitch.
15 "And this is how you shall
make it: The length of the ark *shall
be* three hundred [1]cubits, its width
fifty cubits, and its height thirty
cubits.
16 "You shall make a window for
the ark, and you shall finish it to
a cubit from above; and set the
door of the ark in its side. You
shall make it *with* lower, second,
and third *decks*.
17 [a]"And behold, I Myself am
bringing [b]floodwaters on the
earth, to destroy from under
heaven all flesh in which *is* the
breath of life; everything that *is* on
the earth shall [c]die.
18 "But I will establish My [a]cov-
enant with you; and [b]you shall go
into the ark—you, your sons, your
wife, and your sons' wives with
you.
19 "And of every living thing of
all flesh you shall bring [a]two of
every *sort* into the ark, to keep
them alive with you; they shall be
male and female.
20 "Of the birds after their kind,
of animals after their kind, and of
every creeping thing of the earth
after its kind, two of every *kind*
[a]will come to you to keep *them*
alive.
21 "And you shall take for your-
self of all food that is eaten, and
you shall gather *it* to yourself; and
it shall be food for you and for
them."
22 [a]Thus Noah did; [b]according to
all that [c]God commanded him, so
he did.

The Great Flood

7 Then the [a]LORD said to Noah,
[b]"Come into the ark, you and
all your household, because I have
seen *that* [c]you *are* righteous be-
fore Me in this generation.
2 "You shall take with you seven
each of every [a]clean animal, a
male and his female; [b]two each of
animals that *are* unclean, a male
and his female;
3 "also seven each of birds of the
air, male and female, to keep [1]the
species alive on the face of all
the earth.
4 "For after [a]seven more days I
will cause it to rain on the earth
[b]forty days and forty nights, and
I will [1]destroy from the face of the
earth all living things that I have
made."
5 [a]And Noah did according to all
that the LORD commanded him.
6 Noah *was* [a]six hundred years
old when the floodwaters were on
the earth.
7 [a]So Noah, with his sons, his
wife, and his sons' wives, went
into the ark because of the waters
of the flood.
8 Of clean animals, of animals
that *are* unclean, of birds, and of
everything that creeps on the
earth,
9 two by two they went into the
ark to Noah, male and female, as
God had commanded Noah.
10 And it came to pass after seven
days that the waters of the flood
were on the earth.
11 In the six hundredth year of
Noah's life, in the second month,
the seventeenth day of the month,
on [a]that day all [b]the fountains of
the great deep were broken up,
and the [c]windows of heaven were
opened.
12 [a]And the rain was on the earth
forty days and forty nights.
13 On the very same day Noah
and Noah's sons, Shem, Ham, and
Japheth, and Noah's wife and the
three wives of his sons with them,
entered the ark—
14 [a]they and every beast after its
kind, all cattle after their kind,
every creeping thing that creeps
on the earth after its kind, and
every bird after its kind, every bird
of every [b]sort.
15 And they [a]went into the ark to
Noah, two by two, of all flesh in
which *is* the breath of life.
16 So those that entered, male and
female of all flesh, went in [a]as God
had commanded him; and the
LORD shut him in.
17 [a]Now the flood was on the
earth forty days. The waters in-
creased and lifted up the ark, and
it rose high above the earth.
18 The waters prevailed and
greatly increased on the earth,
[a]and the ark moved about on the
surface of the waters.
19 And the waters prevailed

14 [1]Lit. *compartments* or *nests*
15 [1]A cubit is about 18 inches.
17 [a]Gen. 7:4, 21–23; 2 Pet. 2:5 [b]2 Pet. 3:6 [c]Luke 16:22
18 [a]Gen. 8:20—9:17; 17:7 [b]Gen. 7:1, 7, 13; 1 Pet. 3:20; 2 Pet. 2:5
19 [a]Gen. 7:2, 8, 9, 14–16
20 [a]Gen. 7:9, 15
22 [a]Gen. 7:5; 12:4, 5; Heb. 11:7 [b]Gen. 7:5, 9, 16 [c][1 John 5:3]

CHAPTER 7

1 [a]Matt. 11:28 [b]Matt. 24:38; Luke 17:26; Heb. 11:7; 1 Pet. 3:20; 2 Pet. 2:5 [c]Gen. 6:9; Ps. 33:18; Prov. 10:9; 2 Pet. 2:9
2 [a]Lev. 11; Deut. 14:3–20 [b]Lev. 10:10; Ezek. 44:23
3 [1]Lit. *seed*
4 [a]Gen. 7:10; Ex. 7:25 [b]Gen. 7:12, 17 [1]Lit. *blot out*
5 [a]Gen. 6:22
6 [a]Gen. 5:4, 32
7 [a]Gen. 6:18; 7:1, 13; Matt. 24:38; Luke 17:27
11 [a]Matt. 24:39; Luke 17:27; 2 Pet. 2:5; 3:6 [b]Gen. 8:2; Prov. 8:28; Is. 51:10; Ezek. 26:19 [c]Gen. 8:2; Ps. 78:23
12 [a]Gen. 7:4, 17; 1 Sam. 12:18
14 [a]Gen. 6:19 [b]Gen. 1:21
15 [a]Gen. 6:19, 20; 7:9
16 [a]Gen. 7:2, 3
17 [a]Gen. 7:4, 12; 8:6
18 [a]Ps. 104:26

exceedingly on the earth, and all
the high hills under the whole
heaven were covered.
20 The waters prevailed fifteen
cubits upward, and the mountains
were covered.
21 [a]And all flesh died that moved
on [1]the earth: birds and cattle and
beasts and every creeping thing
that creeps on the earth, and every
man.
22 All in [a]whose nostrils *was* the
breath [1]of the spirit of life, all that
was on the dry *land*, died.
23 So He destroyed all living
things which were on the face of
the ground: both man and cattle,
creeping thing and bird of the air.
They were destroyed from the
earth. Only [a]Noah and those who
were with him in the ark remained
alive.
24 [a]And the waters prevailed on
the earth one hundred and fifty
days.

Noah's Deliverance

8 Then God [a]remembered Noah,
and every living thing, and all
the animals that *were* with him in
the ark. [b]And God made a wind
to pass over the earth, and the wa-
ters subsided.
2 [a]The fountains of the deep and
the windows of heaven were also
[b]stopped, and [c]the rain from
heaven was restrained.
3 And the waters receded contin-
ually from the earth. At the end
[a]of the hundred and fifty days the
waters decreased.
4 Then the ark rested in the sev-
enth month, the seventeenth day
of the month, on the mountains of
Ararat.
5 And the waters decreased con-
tinually until the tenth month. In
the tenth *month*, on the first *day*
of the month, the tops of the moun-
tains were seen.
6 So it came to pass, at the end
of forty days, that Noah opened
[a]the window of the ark which he
had made.
7 Then he sent out a raven,
which kept going to and fro until
the waters had dried up from the
earth.
8 He also sent out from himself
a dove, to see if the waters had re-
ceded from the face of the ground.

21 [a]Gen. 6:7, 13, 17; 7:4 [1]*the land*
22 [a]Gen. 2:7 [1]LXX, Vg. omit *of the spirit*
23 [a]2 Pet. 2:5
24 [a]Gen. 8:3, 4

CHAPTER 8

1 [a]Gen. 19:29 [b]Ex. 14:21; 15:10
2 [a]Gen. 7:11 [b]Deut. 11:17 [c]Job 38:37
3 [a]Gen. 7:24
6 [a]Gen. 6:16
16 [a]Gen. 7:13
17 [a]Gen. 1:22, 28; 9:1, 7
20 [a]Gen. 12:7 [b]Lev. 11 [c]Ex. 10:25
21 [a]Ex. 29:18, 25

9 But the dove found no resting
place for the sole of her foot, and
she returned into the ark to him,
for the waters *were* on the face of
the whole earth. So he put out his
hand and took her, and drew her
into the ark to himself.
10 And he waited yet another
seven days, and again he sent the
dove out from the ark.
11 Then the dove came to him in
the evening, and behold, a freshly
plucked olive leaf *was* in her
mouth; and Noah knew that the
waters had receded from the
earth.
12 So he waited yet another seven
days and sent out the dove, which
did not return again to him any-
more.
13 And it came to pass in the six
hundred and first year, in the first
month, the first *day* of the month,
that the waters were dried up from
the earth; and Noah removed the
covering of the ark and looked,
and indeed the surface of the
ground was dry.
14 And in the second month, on
the twenty-seventh day of the
month, the earth was dried.
15 Then God spoke to Noah, say-
ing,
16 "Go out of the ark, [a]you and
your wife, and your sons and your
sons' wives with you.
17 "Bring out with you every liv-
ing thing of all flesh that *is* with
you: birds and cattle and every
creeping thing that creeps on the
earth, so that they may abound on
the earth, and [a]be fruitful and mul-
tiply on the earth."
18 So Noah went out, and his sons
and his wife and his sons' wives
with him.
19 Every animal, every creeping
thing, every bird, *and* whatever
creeps on the earth, according
to their families, went out of the
ark.

God's Covenant with Creation

20 Then Noah built an [a]altar to the
LORD, and took of [b]every clean ani-
mal and of every clean bird, and
offered [c]burnt offerings on the al-
tar.
21 And the LORD smelled [a]a sooth-
ing aroma. Then the LORD said in
His heart, "I will never again

[b]curse the ground for man's sake,
although the [c]imagination[1] of
man's heart *is* evil from his youth;
[d]nor will I again destroy every liv-
ing thing as I have done.

22 "While the earth [a]remains,
Seedtime and harvest,
Cold and heat,
Winter and summer,
And [b]day and night
Shall not cease."

9

So God blessed Noah and his
sons, and said to them: [a]"Be
fruitful and multiply, and fill the
earth.
2 [a]"And the fear of you and the
dread of you shall be on every
beast of the earth, on every bird
of the air, on all that move *on* the
earth, and on all the fish of the sea.
They are given into your hand.
3 [a]"Every moving thing that lives
shall be food for you. I have given
you [b]all things, even as the [c]green
herbs.
4 [a]"But you shall not eat flesh
with its life, *that is,* its blood.
5 "Surely for your lifeblood I will
demand *a reckoning;* [a]from the
hand of every beast I will require
it, and [b]from the hand of man.
From the hand of every [c]man's
brother I will require the life of
man.

6 "Whoever [a]sheds man's blood,
By man his blood shall be shed;
[b]For in the image of God
He made man.
7 And as for you, [a]be fruitful and
multiply;
Bring forth abundantly in the
earth
And multiply in it."

8 Then God spoke to Noah and
to his sons with him, saying:
9 "And as for Me, [a]behold, I es-
tablish [b]My covenant with you
and with your [1]descendants after
you,
10 [a]"and with every living crea-
ture that *is* with you: the birds, the
cattle, and every beast of the earth
with you, of all that go out of the
ark, every beast of the earth.
11 "Thus [a]I establish My covenant
with you: Never again shall all
flesh be cut off by the waters of
the flood; never again shall there
be a flood to destroy the earth."

21 [b]Gen. 3:17; 6:7, 13, 17 [c]Gen. 6:5; 11:6 [d]Gen. 9:11, 15 [1]*intent* or *thought*
22 [a]Is. 54:9 [b]Jer. 33:20, 25

CHAPTER 9

1 [a]Gen. 1:28, 29; 8:17; 9:7, 19; 10:32
2 [a]Ps. 8:6
3 [a]Deut. 12:15; 14:3, 9, 11 [b]Rom. 14:14, 20 [c]Gen. 1:29
4 [a]1 Sam. 14:33, 34
5 [a]Ex. 21:28 [b]Gen. 4:9, 10 [c]Acts 17:26
6 [a]Lev. 24:17 [b]Gen. 1:26, 27
7 [a]Gen. 9:1, 19
9 [a]Gen. 6:18 [b]Is. 54:9 [1]Lit. *seed*
10 [a]Ps. 145:9
11 [a]Is. 54:9
12 [a]Gen. 9:13, 17; 17:11
13 [a]Ezek. 1:28
15 [a]Lev. 26:42, 45
16 [a]Gen. 17:13, 19
18 [a]Gen. 9:25–27; 10:6
19 [a]Gen. 5:32 [b]1 Chr. 1:4
20 [a]Gen. 3:19, 23; 4:2
21 [a]Prov. 20:1
23 [a]Ex. 20:12 [1]Lit. *backwards*
25 [a]Deut. 27:16 [b]Josh. 9:23

12 And God said: [a]"This *is* the
sign of the covenant which I make
between Me and you, and every
living creature that *is* with you, for
perpetual generations:
13 "I set [a]My rainbow in the cloud,
and it shall be for the sign of the
covenant between Me and the
earth.
14 "It shall be, when I bring a
cloud over the earth, that the rain-
bow shall be seen in the cloud;
15 "and [a]I will remember My cov-
enant which *is* between Me and
you and every living creature of
all flesh; the waters shall never
again become a flood to destroy
all flesh.
16 "The rainbow shall be in the
cloud, and I will look on it to re-
member [a]the everlasting covenant
between God and every living
creature of all flesh that *is* on the
earth."
17 And God said to Noah, "This
is the sign of the covenant which
I have established between Me and
all flesh that *is* on the earth."

Noah and His Sons

18 Now the sons of Noah who
went out of the ark were Shem,
Ham, and Japheth. [a]And Ham *was*
the father of Canaan.
19 [a]These three *were* the sons of
Noah, [b]and from these the whole
earth was populated.
20 And Noah began *to be* [a]a
farmer, and he planted a vineyard.
21 Then he drank of the wine [a]and
was drunk, and became uncovered
in his tent.
22 And Ham, the father of Ca-
naan, saw the nakedness of his fa-
ther, and told his two brothers out-
side.
23 [a]But Shem and Japheth took a
garment, laid *it* on both their
shoulders, and went backward
and covered the nakedness of their
father. Their faces *were* [1]turned
away, and they did not see their
father's nakedness.
24 So Noah awoke from his wine,
and knew what his younger son
had done to him.
25 Then he said:

[a]"Cursed *be* Canaan;
A [b]servant of servants
He shall be to his brethren."

26 And he said:

[a]"Blessed *be* the LORD,
The God of Shem,
And may Canaan be his servant.
27 May God [a]enlarge Japheth,
[b]And may he dwell in the tents of
Shem;
And may Canaan be his servant."

28 And Noah lived after the flood
three hundred and fifty years.
29 So all the days of Noah were
nine hundred and fifty years; and
he died.

Nations Descended from Noah

10 Now this *is* the genealogy
of the sons of Noah: Shem,
Ham, and Japheth. [a]And sons
were born to them after the
flood.
2 [a]The sons of Japheth *were*
Gomer, Magog, Madai, Javan, Tu-
bal, Meshech, and Tiras.
3 The sons of Gomer *were* Ash-
kenaz, [1]Riphath, and Togarmah.
4 The sons of Javan *were* Eli-
shah, Tarshish, Kittim, and
[1]Dodanim.
5 From these [a]the coastland *peo-
ples* of the Gentiles were separated
into their lands, everyone accord-
ing to his language, according to
their families, into their nations.
6 [a]The sons of Ham *were* Cush,
Mizraim, [1]Put, and Canaan.
7 The sons of Cush *were* Seba,
Havilah, Sabtah, Raamah, and
Sabtechah; and the sons of
Raamah *were* Sheba and Dedan.
8 Cush begot [a]Nimrod; he began
to be a mighty one on the earth.
9 He was a mighty [a]hunter [b]be-
fore the LORD; therefore it is said,
"Like Nimrod the mighty hunter
before the LORD."
10 [a]And the beginning of his king-
dom was [b]Babel, Erech, Accad,
and Calneh, in the land of Shinar.
11 From that land he went [a]to As-
syria and built Nineveh, Rehoboth
Ir, Calah,
12 and Resen between Nineveh
and Calah (that *is* the principal
city).
13 Mizraim begot Ludim, An-
amim, Lehabim, Naphtuhim,
14 Pathrusim, and Casluhim
[a](from whom came the Philistines
and Caphtorim).
15 Canaan begot Sidon his first-
born, and [a]Heth;
16 [a]the Jebusite, the Amorite, and
the Girgashite;
17 the Hivite, the Arkite, and the
Sinite;
18 the Arvadite, the Zemarite, and
the Hamathite. Afterward the fam-
ilies of the Canaanites were dis-
persed.
19 [a]And the border of the Canaan-
ites was from Sidon as you go to-
ward Gerar, as far as Gaza; then
as you go toward Sodom, Gomor-
rah, Admah, and Zeboiim, as far
as Lasha.
20 These *were* the sons of Ham,
according to their families, accord-
ing to their languages, in their
lands *and* in their nations.
21 And *children* were born also to
Shem, the father of all the children
of Eber, [1]the brother of Japheth
the elder.
22 The [a]sons of Shem *were* Elam,
Asshur, [b]Arphaxad, Lud, and
Aram.
23 The sons of Aram *were* Uz,
Hul, Gether, and [1]Mash.
24 [1]Arphaxad begot [a]Salah, and
Salah begot Eber.
25 [a]To Eber were born two sons:
the name of one *was* [1]Peleg, for
in his days the earth was divided;
and his brother's name *was* Jok-
tan.
26 Joktan begot Almodad, She-
leph, Hazarmaveth, Jerah,
27 Hadoram, Uzal, Diklah,
28 [1]Obal, Abimael, Sheba,
29 Ophir, Havilah, and Jobab. All
these *were* the sons of Joktan.
30 And their dwelling place was
from Mesha as you go toward Se-
phar, the mountain of the east.
31 These *were* the sons of Shem,
according to their families, ac-
cording to their languages, in
their lands, according to their na-
tions.
32 [a]These *were* the families of the
sons of Noah, according to their
generations, in their nations; [b]and
from these the nations were di-
vided on the earth after the flood.

The Tower of Babel

11 Now the whole earth had
one language and one
[1]speech.
2 And it came to pass, as they

26 [a]Gen. 14:20; 24:27; Ps. 144:15; Heb. 11:16
27 [a]Gen. 10:2–5; 39:3; Is. 66:19 [b]Luke 3:36; John 1:14; Eph. 2:13, 14; 3:6

CHAPTER 10

1 [a]Gen. 9:1, 7, 19
2 [a]1 Chr. 1:5–7
3 [1]*Diphath,* 1 Chr. 1:6
4 [1]Sam. *Rodanim* and 1 Chr. 1:7
5 [a]Gen. 11:8; Ps. 72:10; Jer. 2:10; 25:22
6 [a]1 Chr. 1:8–16 [1]Or *Phut*
8 [a]Mic. 5:6
9 [a]Jer. 16:16; Mic. 7:2 [b]Gen. 21:20
10 [a]Mic. 5:6 [b]Gen. 11:9
11 [a]Gen. 25:18; 2 Kin. 19:36; Mic. 5:6
14 [a]1 Chr. 1:12
15 [a]Gen. 23:3
16 [a]Gen. 14:7; 15:19–21; Deut. 7:1; Neh. 9:8
19 [a]Gen. 13:12, 14, 15, 17; 15:18–21; Num. 34:2–12
21 [1]Or *the older brother of Japheth*
22 [a]Gen. 11:10–26; 1 Chr. 1:17–28 [b]Gen. 10:24; 11:10; Luke 3:36
23 [1]LXX *Meshech* and 1 Chr. 1:17
24 [a]Gen. 11:12; Luke 3:35 [1]So with MT, Vg., Tg.; LXX *Arphaxad begot Cainan, and Cainan begot Salah* (cf. Luke 3:35, 36)
25 [a]1 Chr. 1:19 [1]Lit. *Division*
28 [1]*Ebal,* 1 Chr. 1:22
32 [a]Gen. 10:1 [b]Gen. 9:19; 11:8

CHAPTER 11

1 [1]Lit. *lip*

journeyed from the east, that they
found a plain in the land [a]of Shi-
nar, and they dwelt there.
3 Then they said to one another,
"Come, let us make bricks and
[1]bake *them* thoroughly." They had
brick for stone, and they had as-
phalt for mortar.
4 And they said, "Come, let us
build ourselves a city, and a tower
[a]whose top *is* in the heavens; let
us make a [b]name for ourselves,
lest we [c]be scattered abroad over
the face of the whole earth."
5 [a]But the LORD came down to
see the city and the tower which
the sons of men had built.
6 And the LORD said, "Indeed
[a]the people *are* one and they all
have [b]one language, and this is
what they begin to do; now noth-
ing that they [c]propose to do will
be withheld from them.
7 "Come, [a]let Us go down and
there [b]confuse their language, that
they may not understand one an-
other's speech."
8 So [a]the LORD scattered them
abroad from there [b]over the face
of all the earth, and they ceased
building the city.
9 Therefore its name is called
[1]Babel, [a]because there the LORD
confused the language of all the
earth; and from there the LORD
scattered them abroad over the
face of all the earth.

Shem's Descendants

10 [a]This *is* the genealogy of Shem:
Shem *was* one hundred years old,
and begot Arphaxad two years af-
ter the flood.
11 After he begot Arphaxad,
Shem lived five hundred years,
and begot sons and daughters.
12 Arphaxad lived thirty-five
years, [a]and begot Salah.
13 After he begot Salah, Ar-
phaxad lived four hundred and
three years, and begot sons and
daughters.
14 Salah lived thirty years, and
begot Eber.
15 After he begot Eber, Salah
lived four hundred and three
years, and begot sons and daugh-
ters.
16 [a]Eber lived thirty-four years,
and begot [b]Peleg.
17 After he begot Peleg, Eber lived
four hundred and thirty years, and
begot sons and daughters.
18 Peleg lived thirty years, and be-
got Reu.
19 After he begot Reu, Peleg lived
two hundred and nine years, and
begot sons and daughters.
20 Reu lived thirty-two years, and
begot [a]Serug.
21 After he begot Serug, Reu lived
two hundred and seven years, and
begot sons and daughters.
22 Serug lived thirty years, and
begot Nahor.
23 After he begot Nahor, Serug
lived two hundred years, and be-
got sons and daughters.
24 Nahor lived twenty-nine years,
and begot [a]Terah.
25 After he begot Terah, Nahor
lived one hundred and nineteen
years, and begot sons and daugh-
ters.
26 Now Terah lived seventy years,
and [a]begot [1]Abram, Nahor, and
Haran.

Terah's Descendants

27 This *is* the genealogy of Terah:
Terah begot [a]Abram, Nahor, and
Haran. Haran begot Lot.
28 And Haran died before his fa-
ther Terah in his native land, in
Ur of the Chaldeans.
29 Then Abram and Nahor took
wives: the name of Abram's wife
was [a]Sarai,[1] and the name of Na-
hor's wife, [b]Milcah, the daughter
of Haran the father of Milcah and
the father of Iscah.
30 But [a]Sarai was barren; she had
no child.
31 And Terah [a]took his son
Abram and his grandson Lot, the
son of Haran, and his daughter-in-
law Sarai, his son Abram's wife,
and they went out with them from
[b]Ur of the Chaldeans to go to [c]the
land of Canaan; and they came to
Haran and dwelt there.
32 So the days of Terah were two
hundred and five years, and Terah
died in Haran.

Promises to Abram

12 Now the [a]LORD had said to
Abram:

"Get [b]out of your country,
From your family

2 [a]Gen. 10:10; 14:1; Dan. 1:2
3 [1]Lit. *burn*
4 [a]Deut. 1:28; 9:1; Ps. 107:26 [b]Gen. 6:4; 2 Sam. 8:13 [c]Deut. 4:27
5 [a]Gen. 18:21; Ex. 3:8; 19:11, 18, 20
6 [a]Gen. 9:19; Acts 17:26 [b]Gen. 11:1 [c]Deut. 31:21; Ps. 2:1
7 [a]Gen. 1:26 [b]Gen. 42:23; Ex. 4:11; Deut. 28:49; Is. 33:19; Jer. 5:15
8 [a]Gen. 11:4; Deut. 32:8; Ps. 92:9; [Luke 1:51] [b]Gen. 10:25, 32
9 [a]1 Cor. 14:23 [1]Lit. *Confusion*, Babylon
10 [a]Gen. 10:22–25; 1 Chr. 1:17
12 [a]Luke 3:35
16 [a]1 Chr. 1:19 [b]Luke 3:35
20 [a]Luke 3:35
24 [a]Gen. 11:31; Josh. 24:2; Luke 3:34
26 [a]Josh. 24:2; 1 Chr. 1:26 [1]*Abraham*, Gen. 17:5
27 [a]Gen. 11:31; 17:5
29 [a]Gen. 17:15; 20:12 [b]Gen. 22:20, 23; 24:15 [1]*Sarah*, Gen. 17:15
30 [a]Gen. 16:1, 2; Luke 1:36
31 [a]Gen. 12:1 [b]Gen. 15:7; Neh. 9:7; Acts 7:4 [c]Gen. 10:19

CHAPTER 12
1 [a]Gen. 15:7; Acts 7:2, 3; [Heb. 11:8] [b]Gen. 13:9

And from your father's house,
To a land that I will show you.
2 [a]I will make you a great nation;
[b]I will bless you
And make your name great;
[c]And you shall be a blessing.
3 [a]I will bless those who bless you,
And I will curse him who curses
you;
And in [b]you all the families of the
earth shall be [c]blessed."

4 So Abram departed as the
LORD had spoken to him, and Lot
went with him. And Abram *was*
seventy-five years old when he de-
parted from Haran.
5 Then Abram took Sarai his
wife and Lot his brother's son, and
all their possessions that they had
gathered, and [a]the [1]people whom
they had acquired [b]in Haran, and
they [c]departed to go to the land of
Canaan. So they came to the land
of Canaan.
6 Abram [a]passed through the
land to the place of Shechem, [b]as
far as [1]the terebinth tree of Moreh.
[c]And the Canaanites *were* then in
the land.
7 [a]Then the LORD appeared to
Abram and said, [b]"To your [1]de-
scendants I will give this land."
And there he built an [c]altar to
the LORD, who had appeared to
him.
8 And he moved from there to
the mountain east of Bethel, and
he pitched his tent *with* Bethel on
the west and Ai on the east; there
he built an altar to the LORD and
[a]called on the name of the LORD.
9 So Abram journeyed, [a]going on
still toward the [1]South.

Abram in Egypt

10 Now there was [a]a famine in the
land, and Abram [b]went down to
Egypt to dwell there, for the fam-
ine *was* [c]severe in the land.
11 And it came to pass, when he
was close to entering Egypt, that
he said to Sarai his wife, "Indeed
I know that you *are* [a]a woman of
beautiful countenance.
12 "Therefore it will happen,
when the Egyptians see you, that
they will say, 'This *is* his wife'; and
they [a]will kill me, but they will let
you live.
13 [a]"Please say you *are* my [b]sister,
that it may be well with me for
your sake, and that [1]I may live be-
cause of you."
14 So it was, when Abram came
into Egypt, that the Egyptians saw
the woman, that she *was* very
beautiful.
15 The princes of Pharaoh also
saw her and commended her to
Pharaoh. And the woman was
taken to Pharaoh's house.
16 He [a]treated Abram well for her
sake. He [b]had sheep, oxen, male
donkeys, male and female ser-
vants, female donkeys, and cam-
els.
17 But the LORD [a]plagued Pharaoh
and his house with great plagues
because of Sarai, Abram's wife.
18 And Pharaoh called Abram
and said, [a]"What *is* this you have
done to me? Why did you not tell
me that she *was* your wife?
19 "Why did you say, 'She *is* my
sister'? I might have taken her as
my wife. Now therefore, here is
your wife; take *her* and go your
way."
20 [a]So Pharaoh commanded *his*
men concerning him; and they
sent him away, with his wife and
all that he had.

Abram Inherits Canaan

13 Then Abram went up from
Egypt, he and his wife and
all that he had, and [a]Lot with him,
[b]to the [1]South.
2 [a]Abram *was* very rich in live-
stock, in silver, and in gold.
3 And he went on his journey
[a]from the South as far as Bethel,
to the place where his tent had
been at the beginning, between
Bethel and Ai,
4 to the [a]place of the altar which
he had made there at first. And
there Abram [b]called on the name
of the LORD.
5 Lot also, who went with
Abram, had flocks and herds and
tents.
6 Now [a]the land was not able to
[1]support them, that they might
dwell together, for their posses-
sions were so great that they could
not dwell together.
7 And there was [a]strife between
the herdsmen of Abram's livestock
and the herdsmen of Lot's live-
stock. [b]The Canaanites and the
Perizzites then dwelt in the land.

2 [a]Deut. 26:5 [b]Gen. 22:17; 24:35 [c]Gen. 28:4
3 [a]Num. 24:9 [b]Acts 3:25 [c]Is. 41:27
5 [a]Gen. 14:14 [b]Gen. 11:31 [c]Gen. 13:18 [1]Lit. *souls*
6 [a]Heb. 11:9 [b]Deut. 11:30 [c]Gen. 10:18, 19 [1]Heb. *Alon Moreh*
7 [a]Gen. 17:1; 18:1 [b]Gen. 13:15; 15:18; 17:8 [c]Gen. 13:4, 18; 22:9 [1]Lit. *seed*
8 [a]Gen. 4:26; 13:4; 21:33
9 [a]Gen. 13:1, 3; 20:1; 24:62 [1]Heb. *Negev*
10 [a]Gen. 26:1 [b]Ps. 105:13 [c]Gen. 43:1
11 [a]Gen. 12:14; 26:7; 29:17
12 [a]Gen. 20:11; 26:7
13 [a]Gen. 20:1–18; 26:6–11 [b]Gen. 20:12 [1]Lit. *my soul*
16 [a]Gen. 20:14 [b]Gen. 13:2
17 [a]1 Chr. 16:21
18 [a]Gen. 20:9, 10; 26:10
20 [a][Prov. 21:1]

CHAPTER 13

1 [a]Gen. 12:4; 14:12, 16 [b]Gen. 12:9 [1]Heb. *Negev*
2 [a]Gen. 24:35; 26:14
3 [a]Gen. 12:8, 9
4 [a]Gen. 12:7, 8; 21:33 [b]Ps. 116:17
6 [a]Gen. 36:7 [1]Lit. *bear*
7 [a]Gen. 26:20 [b]Gen. 12:6; 15:20, 21

8 So Abram said to Lot, [a]"Please
let there be no strife between you
and me, and between my herds-
men and your herdsmen; for we
are brethren.
9 [a]"*Is* not the whole land before
you? Please [b]separate from me. [c]If
you take the left, then I will go to
the right; or, if *you go* to the right,
then I will go to the left."
10 And Lot lifted his eyes and saw
all [a]the plain of Jordan, that it *was*
well watered everywhere (before
the LORD [b]destroyed Sodom and
Gomorrah) [c]like the garden of the
LORD, like the land of Egypt as you
go toward [d]Zoar.
11 Then Lot chose for himself all
the plain of Jordan, and Lot jour-
neyed east. And they separated
from each other.
12 Abram dwelt in the land of Ca-
naan, and Lot [a]dwelt in the cities
of the plain and [b]pitched *his* tent
even as far as Sodom.
13 But the men of Sodom [a]*were*
exceedingly wicked and [b]sinful
against the LORD.
14 And the LORD said to Abram,
after Lot [a]had separated from him:
"Lift your eyes now and look from
the place where you are—[b]north-
ward, southward, eastward, and
westward;
15 "for all the land which you see
[a]I give to you and [b]your [1]descen-
dants forever.
16 "And [a]I will make your de-
scendants as the dust of the
earth; so that if a man could num-
ber the dust of the earth, *then* your
descendants also could be num-
bered.
17 "Arise, walk in the land
through its length and its width,
for I give it to you."
18 [a]Then Abram moved *his* tent,
and went and [b]dwelt by [1]the tere-
binth trees of Mamre, [c]which *are*
in Hebron, and built an [d]altar there
to the LORD.

Lot's Captivity and Rescue

14 And it came to pass in the
days of Amraphel king [a]of
Shinar, Arioch king of Ellasar,
Chedorlaomer king of [b]Elam, and
Tidal king of [1]nations,
2 *that* they made war with Bera
king of Sodom, Birsha king of Go-
morrah, Shinab king of [a]Admah,

8 [a]1 Cor. 6:7
9 [a]Gen. 20:15; 34:10 [b]Gen. 13:11, 14 [c][Rom. 12:18]
10 [a]Gen. 19:17–29 [b]Gen. 19:24 [c]Gen. 2:8, 10 [d]Deut. 34:3
12 [a]Gen. 19:24, 25, 29 [b]Gen. 14:12; 19:1
13 [a]Gen. 18:20, 21 [b]Gen. 6:11; 39:9
14 [a]Gen. 13:11 [b]Gen. 28:14
15 [a]Acts 7:5 [b]2 Chr. 20:7 [1]Lit. *seed*
16 [a]Gen. 22:17
18 [a]Gen. 26:17 [b]Gen. 14:13 [c]Gen. 23:2; 35:27 [d]Gen. 8:20; 22:8, 9 [1]Heb. *Alon Mamre*

CHAPTER 14

1 [a]Gen. 10:10; 11:2 [b]Is. 11:11; 21:2 [1]Heb. *goyim*
2 [a]Deut. 29:23 [b]Gen. 13:10; 19:22
3 [a]Num. 34:12
4 [a]Gen. 9:26
5 [a]Gen. 15:20 [b]Deut. 2:20 [c]Deut. 2:10
6 [a]Deut. 2:12, 22
7 [a]2 Chr. 20:2
9 [1]Heb. *goyim*
10 [a]Gen. 11:3 [b]Gen. 19:17, 30
11 [a]Gen. 14:16, 21
12 [a]Gen. 11:27; 12:5 [b]Gen. 13:12
13 [a]Gen. 39:14; 40:15 [b]Gen. 13:18 [c]Gen. 14:24; 21:27, 32 [1]Heb. *Alon Mamre*
14 [a]Gen. 19:29 [b]Gen. 13:8; 14:12 [c]Gen. 12:5; 15:3; 17:27 [d]Deut. 34:1

Shemeber king of Zeboiim, and
the king of Bela (that is, [b]Zoar).
3 All these joined together in the
Valley of Siddim [a](that is, the Salt
Sea).
4 Twelve years [a]they served
Chedorlaomer, and in the thir-
teenth year they rebelled.
5 In the fourteenth year Chedor-
laomer and the kings that *were*
with him came and attacked [a]the
Rephaim in Ashteroth Karnaim,
[b]the Zuzim in Ham, [c]the Emim in
Shaveh Kiriathaim,
6 [a]and the Horites in their moun-
tain of Seir, as far as El Paran,
which *is* by the wilderness.
7 Then they turned back and
came to En Mishpat (that *is*, Ka-
desh), and attacked all the country
of the Amalekites, and also the
Amorites who dwelt [a]in Hazezon
Tamar.
8 And the king of Sodom, the
king of Gomorrah, the king of Ad-
mah, the king of Zeboiim, and the
king of Bela (that *is*, Zoar) went
out and joined together in battle
in the Valley of Siddim
9 against Chedorlaomer king of
Elam, Tidal king of [1]nations, Am-
raphel king of Shinar, and Arioch
king of Ellasar—four kings against
five.
10 Now the Valley of Siddim *was*
full of [a]asphalt pits; and the kings
of Sodom and Gomorrah fled;
some fell there, and the remainder
fled [b]to the mountains.
11 Then they took [a]all the goods
of Sodom and Gomorrah, and all
their provisions, and went their
way.
12 They also took Lot, Abram's
[a]brother's son [b]who dwelt in
Sodom, and his goods, and de-
parted.
13 Then one who had escaped
came and told Abram the [a]He-
brew, for [b]he dwelt by [1]the tere-
binth trees of Mamre the Amorite,
brother of Eshcol and brother of
Aner; [c]and they *were* allies with
Abram.
14 Now [a]when Abram heard that
[b]his brother was taken captive, he
armed his three hundred and eigh-
teen trained *servants* who were
[c]born in his own house, and went
in pursuit [d]as far as Dan.
15 He divided his forces against

them by night, and he and his ser-
vants [a]attacked them and pursued
them as far as Hobah, which *is*
[1]north of Damascus.
16 So he [a]brought back all the
goods, and also brought back his
brother Lot and his goods, as well
as the women and the people.
17 And the king of Sodom [a]went
out to meet him at the Valley of
Shaveh (that *is,* the [b]King's Val-
ley), [c]after his return from [1]the de-
feat of Chedorlaomer and the
kings who *were* with him.

Abram and Melchizedek

18 Then [a]Melchizedek king of Sa-
lem brought out [b]bread and wine;
he *was* [c]the priest of [d]God Most
High.
19 And he blessed him and said:

[a]"Blessed be Abram of God Most
High,
[b]Possessor of heaven and earth;
20 And [a]blessed be God Most High,
Who has delivered your enemies
into your hand."

And he [b]gave him [1]a tithe of all.
21 Now the king of Sodom said to
Abram, "Give me the [1]persons,
and take the goods for yourself."
22 But Abram [a]said to the king of
Sodom, "I [b]have raised my hand
to the LORD, God Most High, [c]the
Possessor of heaven and earth,
23 "that [a]I *will take* nothing, from
a thread to a sandal strap, and that
I will not take anything that *is*
yours, lest you should say, 'I have
made Abram rich'—
24 "except only what the young
men have eaten, and the portion
of the men who went with me:
Aner, Eshcol, and Mamre; let them
take their portion."

God's Covenant with Abram

15 After these things the word
of the LORD came to Abram
[a]in a vision, saying, [b]"Do not be
afraid, Abram. I *am* your [c]shield,
[1]your exceedingly [d]great reward."
2 [a]But Abram said, "Lord GOD,
what will You give me, [b]seeing I
[1]go childless, and the heir of my
house *is* Eliezer of Damascus?"
3 Then Abram said, "Look, You
have given me no offspring; in-

15 [a]Is. 4:2, 3 [1]Lit. *on the left hand of*
16 [a]Gen. 31:18
17 [a]1 Sam. 18:6 [b]2 Sam. 18:18 [c]Heb. 7:1 [1]Lit. *striking*
18 [a]Heb. 7:1–10 [b]Gen. 18:5 [c]Ps. 110:4 [d]Acts 16:17
19 [a]Ruth 3:10 [b]Gen. 14:22
20 [a]Gen. 24:27 [b]Heb. 7:4 [1]*one-tenth*
21 [1]Lit. *souls*
22 [a]Gen. 14:2, 8, 10 [b]Dan. 12:7 [c]Gen. 14:19
23 [a]2 Kin. 5:16

CHAPTER 15

1 [a]Dan. 10:1 [b]Gen. 21:17; 26:24 [c]Deut. 33:29 [d]Prov. 11:18 [1]Or *your reward shall be very great*
2 [a]Gen. 17:18 [b]Acts 7:5 [1]*am childless*
3 [a]Gen. 14:14 [1]*a servant*
4 [a]2 Sam. 7:12
5 [a]Ps. 147:4 [b]Jer. 33:22 [c]Ex. 32:13 [d]Gen. 17:19
6 [a]Rom. 4:3, 9, 22 [b]Ps. 32:2; 106:31
7 [a]Gen. 12:1 [b]Gen. 11:28, 31 [c]Ps. 105:42, 44
8 [a]Luke 1:18
10 [a]Jer. 34:18 [b]Lev. 1:17
12 [a]Gen. 2:21; 28:11
13 [a]Ex. 1:11 [b]Ex. 12:40
14 [a]Ex. 6:6 [b]Ex. 12:36
15 [a]Job 5:26 [b]Gen. 25:8; 47:30 [c]Gen. 25:8 [1]Die and join your ancestors
16 [a]Ex. 12:41 [b]1 Kin. 21:26 [c]Matt. 23:32
17 [a]Jer. 34:18, 19

deed [a]one[1] born in my house is my
heir!"
4 And behold, the word of the
LORD *came* to him, saying, "This
one shall not be your heir, but one
who [a]will come from your own
body shall be your heir."
5 Then He brought him outside
and said, "Look now toward
heaven, and [a]count the [b]stars if
you are able to number them."
And He said to him, [c]"So shall
your [d]descendants be."
6 And he [a]believed in the LORD,
and He [b]accounted it to him for
righteousness.
7 Then He said to him, "I *am* the
LORD, who [a]brought you out of [b]Ur
of the Chaldeans, [c]to give you this
land to inherit it."
8 And he said, "Lord GOD, [a]how
shall I know that I will inherit it?"
9 So He said to him, "Bring Me
a three-year-old heifer, a three-
year-old female goat, a three-year-
old ram, a turtledove, and a young
pigeon."
10 Then he brought all these to
Him and [a]cut them in two, down
the middle, and placed each piece
opposite the other; but he did not
cut [b]the birds in two.
11 And when the vultures came
down on the carcasses, Abram
drove them away.
12 Now when the sun was going
down, [a]a deep sleep fell upon
Abram; and behold, horror *and*
great darkness fell upon him.
13 Then He said to Abram: "Know
certainly [a]that your descendants
will be strangers in a land *that is*
not theirs, and will serve them, and
[b]they will afflict them four hun-
dred years.
14 "And also the nation whom
they serve [a]I will judge; afterward
[b]they shall come out with great
possessions.
15 "Now as for you, [a]you shall [1]go
[b]to your fathers in peace; [c]you
shall be buried at a good old age.
16 "But [a]in the fourth generation
they shall return here, for the
iniquity [b]of the Amorites [c]*is* not
yet complete."
17 And it came to pass, when the
sun went down and it was dark,
that behold, there appeared a
smoking oven and a burning torch
that [a]passed between those pieces.

18 On the same day the LORD
[a]made a covenant with Abram,
saying:
[b]"To your descendants I have
given this land, from the river of
Egypt to the great river, the River
Euphrates—
19 "the Kenites, the Kenezzites,
the Kadmonites,
20 "the Hittites, the Perizzites, the
Rephaim,
21 "the Amorites, the Canaanites,
the Girgashites, and the Jebu-
sites."

Hagar and Ishmael

16 Now Sarai, Abram's wife,
[a]had borne him no *children*.
And she had [b]an Egyptian
maidservant whose name was
[c]Hagar.
2 [a]So Sarai said to Abram, "See
now, the LORD [b]has restrained me
from bearing *children*. Please, [c]go
in to my maid; perhaps I shall [1]ob-
tain children by her." And Abram
[d]heeded the voice of Sarai.
3 Then Sarai, Abram's wife, took
Hagar her maid, the Egyptian, and
gave her to her husband Abram to
be his wife, after Abram [a]had
dwelt ten years in the land of Ca-
naan.
4 So he went in to Hagar, and she
conceived. And when she saw that
she had conceived, her mistress
became [a]despised in her [1]eyes.
5 Then Sarai said to Abram,
[1]"My wrong *be* upon you! I gave
my maid into your embrace; and
when she saw that she had con-
ceived, I became despised in her
eyes. [a]The LORD judge between
you and me."
6 [a]So Abram said to Sarai, "In-
deed your maid *is* in your hand;
do to her as you please." And
when Sarai dealt harshly with her,
[b]she fled from her presence.
7 Now the [a]Angel of the LORD
found her by a spring of water in
the wilderness, [b]by the spring on
the way to [c]Shur.
8 And He said, "Hagar, Sarai's
maid, where have you come from,
and where are you going?" She
said, "I am fleeing from the pres-
ence of my mistress Sarai."
9 The Angel of the LORD said to
her, "Return to your mistress, and
[a]submit yourself under her hand."

18 [a]Gen. 24:7 [b]Gen. 12:7; 17:8

CHAPTER 16

1 [a]Gen. 11:30; 15:2, 3 [b]Gen. 12:16; 21:9 [c]Gal. 4:24
2 [a]Gen. 30:3 [b]Gen. 20:18 [c]Gen. 30:3, 9 [d]Gen. 3:17 [1]Lit. *be built up from*
3 [a]Gen. 12:4, 5
4 [a][Prov. 30:21, 23] [1]*sight*
5 [a]Gen. 31:53 [1]*The wrong done to me be*
6 [a]1 Pet. 3:7 [b]Ex. 2:15
7 [a]Gen. 21:17, 18; 22:11, 15; 31:11 [b]Gen. 20:1; 25:18 [c]Ex. 15:22
9 [a][Titus 2:9]
10 [a]Gen. 17:20
11 [a]Luke 1:13, 31 [1]Lit. *God Hears*
12 [a]Gen. 21:20 [b]Gen. 25:18
13 [a]Gen. 31:42 [1]Heb. *El Roi* [2]Seen the back of
14 [a]Gen. 24:62 [b]Num. 13:26 [1]Lit. *Well of the One Who Lives and Sees Me*
15 [a]Gal. 4:22

CHAPTER 17

1 [a]Gen. 12:7; 18:1 [b]Gen. 28:3; 35:11 [c]2 Kin. 20:3 [d]Deut. 18:13 [1]Heb. *El Shaddai*
2 [a]Gen. 15:18 [b]Gen. 12:2; 13:16; 15:5; 18:18
4 [a][Rom. 4:11, 12, 16] [1]Lit. *multitude of nations*
5 [a]Neh. 9:7 [b]Rom. 4:17 [1]Lit. *Exalted Father* [2]Lit. *Father of a Multitude* [3]*a multitude of*
6 [a]Gen. 17:16; 35:11 [b]Matt. 1:6
7 [a][Gal. 3:17]

10 Then the Angel of the LORD
said to her, [a]"I will multiply your
descendants exceedingly, so that
they shall not be counted for multi-
tude."
11 And the Angel of the LORD said
to her:

"Behold, you *are* with child,
[a]And you shall bear a son.
You shall call his name [1]Ishmael,
Because the LORD has heard your
affliction.
12 [a]He shall be a wild man;
His hand *shall be* against every
man,
And every man's hand against
him.
[b]And he shall dwell in the
presence of all his brethren."

13 Then she called the name of the
LORD who spoke to her, You-Are-
[1]the-God-Who-Sees; for she said,
"Have I also here [2]seen Him [a]who
sees me?"
14 Therefore the well was called
[a]Beer Lahai Roi;[1] observe, *it is* [b]be-
tween Kadesh and Bered.
15 So [a]Hagar bore Abram a son;
and Abram named his son, whom
Hagar bore, Ishmael.
16 Abram *was* eighty-six years
old when Hagar bore Ishmael to
Abram.

The Sign of the Covenant

17 When Abram was ninety-
nine years old, the LORD
[a]appeared to Abram and said to
him, [b]"I *am* [1]Almighty God; [c]walk
before Me and be [d]blameless.
2 "And I will make My [a]covenant
between Me and you, and [b]will
multiply you exceedingly."
3 Then Abram fell on his face,
and God talked with him, saying:
4 "As for Me, behold, My cov-
enant is with you, and you shall
be [a]a father of [1]many nations.
5 "No longer shall [a]your name be
called [1]Abram, but your name
shall be [2]Abraham; [b]for I have
made you a father of [3]many na-
tions.
6 "I will make you exceedingly
fruitful; and I will make [a]nations
of you, and [b]kings shall come from
you.
7 "And I will [a]establish My cov-
enant between Me and you and
your descendants after you in their

generations, for an everlasting
covenant, [b]to be God to you and
[c]your descendants after you.
8 "Also [a]I give to you and your
descendants after you the land [b]in[1]
which you are a stranger, all the
land of Canaan, as an everlasting
possession; and [c]I will be their
God."
9 And God said to Abraham: "As
for you, [a]you shall keep My cov-
enant, you and your descendants
after you throughout their gen-
erations.
10 "This *is* My covenant which
you shall keep, between Me and
you and your descendants after
you: [a]Every male child among you
shall be circumcised;
11 "and you shall be circumcised
in the flesh of your foreskins, and
it shall be [a]a sign of the covenant
between Me and you.
12 "He who is eight days old
among you [a]shall be circumcised,
every male child in your genera-
tions, he who is born in your house
or bought with money from any
foreigner who is not your de-
scendant.
13 "He who is born in your house
and he who is bought with your
money must be circumcised, and
My covenant shall be in your flesh
for an everlasting covenant.
14 "And the uncircumcised male
child, who is not circumcised in
the flesh of his foreskin, that per-
son [a]shall be cut off from his peo-
ple; he has broken My covenant."
15 Then God said to Abraham,
"As for Sarai your wife, you shall
not call her name Sarai, but [1]Sarah
shall be her name.
16 "And I will bless her [a]and also
give you a son by her; then I will
bless her, and she shall be *a
mother* [b]*of* nations; [c]kings of peo-
ples shall be from her."
17 Then Abraham fell on his face
[a]and laughed, and said in his
heart, "Shall *a child* be born to a
man who is one hundred years
old? And shall Sarah, who is
ninety years old, bear *a child?*"
18 And Abraham [a]said to God,
"Oh, that Ishmael might live be-
fore You!"
19 Then God said: "No, [a]Sarah
your wife shall bear you a son, and
you shall call his name Isaac; I will
establish My [b]covenant with him
for an everlasting covenant, *and*
with his descendants after him.
20 "And as for Ishmael, I have
heard you. Behold, I have blessed
him, and will make him fruitful,
and [a]will multiply him exceed-
ingly. He shall beget [b]twelve
princes, [c]and I will make him a
great nation.
21 "But My [a]covenant I will estab-
lish with Isaac, [b]whom Sarah shall
bear to you at this [c]set time next
year."
22 Then He finished talking with
him, and God went up from Abra-
ham.
23 So Abraham took Ishmael his
son, all who were born in his
house and all who were bought
with his money, every male among
the men of Abraham's house, and
circumcised the flesh of their fore-
skins that very same day, as God
had said to him.
24 Abraham *was* ninety-nine
years old when he was circum-
cised in the flesh of his foreskin.
25 And Ishmael his son *was* thir-
teen years old when he was cir-
cumcised in the flesh of his fore-
skin.
26 That very same day Abraham
was circumcised, and his son Ish-
mael;
27 and [a]all the men of his house,
born in the house or bought with
money from a foreigner, were cir-
cumcised with him.

The Son of Promise

18 Then the LORD appeared to
him by [1]the [a]terebinth trees
of Mamre, as he was sitting in
the tent door in the heat of the
day.
2 [a]So he lifted his eyes and
looked, and behold, three men
were standing by him; [b]and when
he saw *them*, he ran from the tent
door to meet them, and bowed
himself to the ground,
3 and said, "My Lord, if I have
now found favor in Your sight, do
not pass on by Your servant.
4 "Please let [a]a little water be
brought, and wash your feet, and
rest yourselves under the tree.
5 "And [a]I will bring a morsel of
bread, that [b]you may refresh your
hearts. After that you may pass by,

---

7 [b]Gen. 26:24; 28:13; Lev. 11:45; 26:12, 45; Heb. 11:16 [c]Rom. 9:8; Gal. 3:16
8 [a]Gen. 12:7; 13:15, 17; Acts 7:5 [b]Gen. 23:4; 28:4 [c]Ex. 6:7; 29:45; Lev. 26:12; Deut. 29:13; Rev. 21:7 [1]Lit. *of your sojournings*
9 [a]Ex. 19:5
10 [a]John 7:22; Acts 7:8
11 [a]Ex. 12:13, 48; [Rom. 4:11]
12 [a]Lev. 12:3
14 [a]Ex. 4:24–26
15 [1]Lit. *Princess*
16 [a]Gen. 18:10 [b]Gen. 35:11; Gal. 4:31; 1 Pet. 3:6 [c]Gen. 17:6; 36:31; 1 Sam. 8:22
17 [a]Gen. 17:3; 18:12; 21:6
18 [a]Gen. 18:23
19 [a]Gen. 18:10; 21:2; [Gal. 4:28] [b]Gen. 22:16; Matt. 1:2; Luke 3:34
20 [a]Gen. 16:10 [b]Gen. 25:12–16 [c]Gen. 21:13, 18
21 [a]Gen. 26:2–5 [b]Gen. 21:2 [c]Gen. 18:14
27 [a]Gen. 18:19

CHAPTER 18

1 [a]Gen. 13:18; 14:13 [1]Heb. *Alon Mamre*
2 [a]Gen. 18:16, 22; 32:24; Josh. 5:13; Judg. 13:6–11; Heb. 13:2 [b]Gen. 19:1; 1 Pet. 4:9
4 [a]Gen. 19:2; 24:32; 43:24
5 [a]Judg. 6:18, 19; 13:15, 16 [b]Judg. 19:5; Ps. 104:15

[c]inasmuch as you have come to
your servant." They said, "Do as
you have said."
6 So Abraham hurried into the
tent to Sarah and said, "Quickly,
make ready three measures of fine
meal; knead *it* and make cakes."
7 And Abraham ran to the herd,
took a tender and good calf, gave
it to a young man, and he hastened
to prepare it.
8 So [a]he took butter and milk
and the calf which he had pre-
pared, and set *it* before them; and
he stood by them under the tree
as they ate.
9 Then they said to him, "Where
is Sarah your wife?" So he said,
"Here, [a]in the tent."
10 And He said, "I will certainly
return to you [a]according to the
time of life, and behold, [b]Sarah
your wife shall have a son." (Sarah
was listening in the tent door
which *was* behind him.)
11 Now [a]Abraham and Sarah
were old, well advanced in age;
and [1]Sarah [b]had passed the age of
childbearing.
12 Therefore Sarah [a]laughed
within herself, saying, [b]"After I
have grown old, shall I have plea-
sure, my [c]lord being old also?"
13 And the LORD said to Abraham,
"Why did Sarah laugh, saying,
'Shall I surely bear *a child,* since
I am old?'
14 [a]"Is anything too hard for the
LORD? [b]At the appointed time I will
return to you, according to the
time of life, and Sarah shall have
a son."
15 But Sarah denied *it,* saying, "I
did not laugh," for she was afraid.
And He said, "No, but you did
laugh!"

Abraham Intercedes for Sodom

16 Then the men rose from there
and looked toward Sodom, and
Abraham went with them [a]to send
them on the way.
17 And the LORD said, [a]"Shall I
hide from Abraham what I am do-
ing,
18 "since Abraham shall surely
become a great and mighty nation,
and all the nations of the earth
shall be [a]blessed in him?
19 "For I have known him, in or-
der [a]that he may command his
children and his household after
him, that they keep the way of the
LORD, to do righteousness and jus-
tice, that the LORD may bring to
Abraham what He has spoken to
him."
20 And the LORD said, "Because
[a]the outcry against Sodom and Go-
morrah is great, and because their
[b]sin is very grave,
21 [a]"I will go down now and see
whether they have done altogether
according to the outcry against it
that has come to Me; and if not,
[b]I will know."
22 Then the men turned away
from there [a]and went toward
Sodom, but Abraham still stood
before the LORD.
23 And Abraham [a]came near and
said, [b]"Would You also [c]destroy
the [d]righteous with the wicked?
24 "Suppose there were fifty righ-
teous within the city; would You
also destroy the place and not
spare *it* for the fifty righteous that
were in it?
25 "Far be it from You to do such
a thing as this, to slay the righ-
teous with the wicked, so [a]that the
righteous should be as the wicked;
far be it from You! [b]Shall not
the Judge of all the earth do
right?"
26 So the LORD said, [a]"If I find in
Sodom fifty righteous within the
city, then I will spare all the place
for their sakes."
27 Then Abraham answered and
said, "Indeed now, I who *am* [a]*but*
dust and ashes have taken it upon
myself to speak to the Lord:
28 "Suppose there were five less
than the fifty righteous; would You
destroy all of the city for *lack of*
five?" So He said, "If I find there
forty-five, I will not destroy *it.*"
29 And he spoke to Him yet again
and said, "Suppose there should
be forty found there?" So He said,
"I will not do *it* for the sake of
forty."
30 Then he said, "Let not the Lord
be angry, and I will speak: Sup-
pose thirty should be found
there?" So He said, "I will not do
it if I find thirty there."
31 And he said, "Indeed now, I
have taken it upon myself to speak
to the Lord: Suppose twenty
should be found there?" So He

5 [c]Gen. 19:8; 33:10
8 [a]Gen. 19:3
9 [a]Gen. 24:67
10 [a]2 Kin. 4:16 [b]Gen. 17:19, 21; 21:2; Rom. 9:9
11 [a]Gen. 17:17; Luke 1:18; Rom. 4:19; Heb. 11:11, 12, 19 [b]Gen. 31:35 [1]Lit. *the manner of women had ceased to be with Sarah*
12 [a]Gen. 17:17 [b]Luke 1:18 [c]1 Pet. 3:6
14 [a]Num. 11:23; Jer. 32:17; Zech. 8:6; Matt. 3:9; 19:26; Luke 1:37; Rom. 4:21 [b]Gen. 17:21; 18:10; 2 Kin. 4:16
16 [a]Acts 15:3; Rom. 15:24
17 [a]Gen. 18:22, 26, 33; Ps. 25:14; Amos 3:7; [John 15:15]
18 [a][Gen. 12:3; 22:18]; Matt. 1:1; Luke 3:34; [Acts 3:25, 26; Gal. 3:8]
19 [a][Deut. 4:9, 10; 6:6, 7]
20 [a]Gen. 4:10; 19:13; Ezek. 16:49, 50 [b]Gen. 13:13
21 [a]Gen. 11:5; Ex. 3:8; Ps. 14:2 [b]Deut. 8:2; 13:3; Josh. 22:22; Luke 16:15; 2 Cor. 11:11
22 [a]Gen. 18:16; 19:1
23 [a][Heb. 10:22] [b]Ex. 23:7; Num. 16:22; 2 Sam. 24:17; Ps. 11:4–7 [c]Job 9:22 [d]Gen. 20:4
25 [a]Job 8:20; Is. 3:10, 11 [b]Deut. 1:16, 17; 32:4; Job 8:3, 20; 34:17; Ps. 58:11; 94:2; Is. 3:10, 11; Rom. 3:5, 6
26 [a]Jer. 5:1; Ezek. 22:30
27 [a][Gen. 3:19]; Job 4:19; 30:19; 42:6; [1 Cor. 15:47, 48]

said, "I will not destroy *it* for the
sake of twenty."
32 Then he said, [a]"Let not the
Lord be angry, and I will speak but
once more: Suppose ten should be
found there?" [b]And He said, "I will
not destroy *it* for the sake of ten."
33 So the LORD went His way as
soon as He had finished speaking
with Abraham; and Abraham re-
turned to his place.

Sodom's Depravity

19 Now [a]the two angels came
to Sodom in the evening,
and [b]Lot was sitting in the gate of
Sodom. When Lot saw *them*, he
rose to meet them, and he bowed
himself with his face toward the
ground.
2 And he said, "Here now, my
lords, please [a]turn in to your ser-
vant's house and spend the night,
and [b]wash your feet; then you may
rise early and go on your way."
And they said, [c]"No, but we will
spend the night in the open
square."
3 But he insisted strongly; so
they turned in to him and entered
his house. [a]Then he made them a
feast, and baked [b]unleavened
bread, and they ate.
4 Now before they lay down, the
men of the city, the men of Sodom,
both old and young, all the people
from every quarter, surrounded
the house.
5 [a]And they called to Lot and
said to him, "Where are the men
who came to you tonight? [b]Bring
them out to us that we [c]may know
them *carnally*."
6 So [a]Lot went out to them
through the doorway, shut the
door behind him,
7 and said, "Please, my brethren,
do not do so wickedly!
8 [a]"See now, I have two daugh-
ters who have not known a man;
please, let me bring them out to
you, and you may do to them as
you wish; only do nothing to these
men, [b]since this is the reason they
have come under the shadow of
my roof."
9 And they said, "Stand back!"
Then they said, "This one [a]came
in to [1]stay *here*, [b]and he keeps act-
ing as a judge; now we will deal
worse with you than with them."
So they pressed hard against the
man Lot, and came near to break
down the door.
10 But the men reached out their
hands and pulled Lot into the
house with them, and shut the
door.
11 And they [a]struck the men who
were at the doorway of the house
with blindness, both small and
great, so that they became weary
trying to find the door.

Sodom and Gomorrah Destroyed

12 Then the men said to Lot,
"Have you anyone else here? Son-
in-law, your sons, your daughters,
and whomever you have in the
city—[a]take *them* out of this
place!
13 "For we will destroy this place,
because the [a]outcry against them
has grown great before the face of
the LORD, and [b]the LORD has sent
us to destroy it."
14 So Lot went out and spoke to
his sons-in-law, [a]who had married
his daughters, and said, [b]"Get up,
get out of this place; for the LORD
will destroy this city!" [c]But to his
sons-in-law he seemed to be jok-
ing.
15 When the morning dawned, the
angels urged Lot to hurry, saying,
[a]"Arise, take your wife and your
two daughters who are here, lest
you be consumed in the punish-
ment of the city."
16 And while he lingered, the men
[a]took hold of his hand, his wife's
hand, and the hands of his two
daughters, the [b]LORD being merci-
ful to him, [c]and they brought
him out and set him outside the
city.
17 So it came to pass, when they
had brought them outside, that [1]he
said, [a]"Escape for your life! [b]Do
not look behind you nor stay any-
where in the plain. Escape [c]to
the mountains, lest you be [2]de-
stroyed."
18 Then Lot said to them, "Please,
[a]no, my lords!
19 "Indeed now, your servant has
found favor in your sight, and you
have increased your mercy which
you have shown me by saving my
life; but I cannot escape to the
mountains, lest some evil overtake
me and I die.

32 [a]Judg. 6:39 [b]James 5:16

CHAPTER 19

1 [a]Gen. 18:2, 16, 22 [b]Gen. 18:1–5
2 [a][Heb. 13:2] [b]Gen. 18:4; 24:32 [c]Luke 24:28
3 [a]Gen. 18:6–8 [b]Ex. 12:8
5 [a]Is. 3:9 [b]Judg. 19:22 [c]Gen. 4:1
6 [a]Judg. 19:23
8 [a]Judg. 19:24 [b]Gen. 18:5
9 [a]2 Pet. 2:7, 8 [b]Ex. 2:14 [1]As a resident alien
11 [a]Gen. 20:17, 18
12 [a]2 Pet. 2:7, 9
13 [a]Gen. 18:20 [b]1 Chr. 21:15
14 [a]Matt. 1:18 [b]Num. 16:21, 24, 26, 45 [c]Ex. 9:21
15 [a]Rev. 18:4
16 [a]2 Pet. 2:7 [b]Luke 18:13 [c]Ps. 34:22
17 [a]Jer. 48:6 [b]Matt. 24:16–18 [c]Gen. 14:10 [1]LXX, Syr., Vg. *they* [2]Lit. *swept away*
18 [a]Acts 10:14

20 "See now, this city *is* near *enough* to flee to, and it *is* a little one; please let me escape there (*is* it not a little one?) and my soul shall live."

21 And he said to him, "See, [a]I have favored you concerning this thing also, in that I will not overthrow this city for which you have spoken.

22 "Hurry, escape there. For [a]I cannot do anything until you arrive there." Therefore [b]the name of the city was called [1]Zoar.

23 The sun had risen upon the earth when Lot entered Zoar.

24 Then the LORD rained [a]brimstone and [b]fire on Sodom and Gomorrah, from the LORD out of the heavens.

25 So He [1]overthrew those cities, all the plain, all the inhabitants of the cities, and [a]what grew on the ground.

26 But his wife looked back behind him, and she became [a]a pillar of salt.

27 And Abraham went early in the morning to the place where [a]he had stood before the LORD.

28 Then he looked toward Sodom and Gomorrah, and toward all the land of the plain; and he saw, and behold, [a]the smoke of the land which went up like the smoke of a furnace.

29 And it came to pass, when God destroyed the cities of the plain, that God [a]remembered Abraham, and sent Lot out of the midst of the overthrow, when He overthrew the cities in which Lot had dwelt.

The Descendants of Lot

30 Then Lot went up out of Zoar and [a]dwelt in the mountains, and his two daughters were with him; for he was afraid to dwell in Zoar. And he and his two daughters dwelt in a cave.

31 Now the firstborn said to the younger, "Our father *is* old, and *there is* no man on the earth [a]to come in to us as is the custom of all the earth.

32 "Come, let us make our father drink wine, and we will lie with him, that we [a]may preserve the [1]lineage of our father."

33 So they made their father drink wine that night. And the firstborn went in and lay with her father, and he did not know when she lay down or when she arose.

34 It happened on the next day that the firstborn said to the younger, "Indeed I lay with my father last night; let us make him drink wine tonight also, and you go in *and* lie with him, that we may preserve the [1]lineage of our father."

35 Then they made their father drink wine that night also. And the younger arose and lay with him, and he did not know when she lay down or when she arose.

36 Thus both the daughters of Lot were with child by their father.

37 The firstborn bore a son and called his name Moab; [a]he *is* the father of the Moabites to this day.

38 And the younger, she also bore a son and called his name Ben-Ammi; [a]he *is* the father of the people of Ammon to this day.

Abraham and Abimelech

20 And Abraham journeyed from [a]there to the South, and dwelt between [b]Kadesh and Shur, and [c]stayed in Gerar.

2 Now Abraham said of Sarah his wife, [a]"She *is* my sister." And Abimelech king of Gerar sent and [b]took Sarah.

3 But [a]God came to Abimelech [b]in a dream by night, and said to him, [c]"Indeed you *are* a dead man because of the woman whom you have taken, for she *is* [1]a man's wife."

4 But Abimelech had not come near her; and he said, "Lord, [a]will You slay a righteous nation also?

5 "Did he not say to me, 'She *is* my sister'? And she, even she herself said, 'He *is* my brother.' [a]In the [1]integrity of my heart and innocence of my hands I have done this."

6 And God said to him in a dream, "Yes, I know that you did this in the integrity of your heart. For [a]I also withheld you from sinning [b]against Me; therefore I did not let you touch her.

7 "Now therefore, restore the man's wife; [a]for he *is* a prophet, and he will pray for you and you shall live. But if you do not restore *her*, [b]know that you shall surely

21 [a]Job 42:8, 9
22 [a]Ex. 32:10 [b]Gen. 13:10; 14:2 [1]Lit. *Little* or *Insignificant*
24 [a]Deut. 29:23 [b]Lev. 10:2
25 [a]Ps. 107:34 [1]*devastated*
26 [a]Luke 17:32
27 [a]Gen. 18:22
28 [a]Rev. 9:2; 18:9
29 [a]Gen. 8:1; 18:23
30 [a]Gen. 19:17, 19
31 [a]Gen. 16:2, 4; 38:8, 9
32 [a][Mark 12:19] [1]Lit. *seed*
34 [1]Lit. *seed*
37 [a]Deut. 2:9
38 [a]Deut. 2:19

CHAPTER 20

1 [a]Gen. 18:1 [b]Gen. 12:9; 16:7, 14 [c]Gen. 26:1, 6
2 [a]Gen. 12:11–13; 26:7 [b]Gen. 12:15
3 [a]Ps. 105:14 [b]Job 33:15 [c]Gen. 20:7 [1]Lit. *married to a husband*
4 [a]Gen. 18:23–25
5 [a]2 Kin. 20:3 [1]*innocence*
6 [a]1 Sam. 25:26, 34 [b]Gen. 39:9
7 [a]1 Sam. 7:5 [b]Gen. 2:17

die, you [c]and all who *are* yours."
8 So Abimelech rose early in the
morning, called all his servants,
and told all these things in their
hearing; and the men were very
much afraid.
9 And Abimelech called Abra-
ham and said to him, "What have
you done to us? How have I [1]of-
fended you, [a]that you have
brought on me and on my king-
dom a great sin? You have done
deeds to me [b]that ought not to be
done."
10 Then Abimelech said to Abra-
ham, "What did you have in view,
that you have done this thing?"
11 And Abraham said, "Because
I thought, surely [a]the fear of God
is not in this place; and [b]they will
kill me on account of my wife.
12 "But indeed [a]*she is* truly my
sister. She *is* the daughter of my
father, but not the daughter of
my mother; and she became my
wife.
13 "And it came to pass, when
[a]God caused me to wander from
my father's house, that I said to
her, 'This *is* your kindness that you
should do for me: in every place,
wherever we go, [b]say of me, "He
is my brother." ' "
14 Then Abimelech [a]took sheep,
oxen, and male and female ser-
vants, and gave *them* to Abraham;
and he restored Sarah his wife to
him.
15 And Abimelech said, "See, [a]my
land *is* before you; dwell where it
pleases you."
16 Then to Sarah he said, "Be-
hold, I have given your brother a
thousand *pieces* of silver; [a]indeed
this [1]vindicates you [b]before all
who *are* with you and before
everybody." Thus she was [2]re-
buked.
17 So Abraham [a]prayed to God;
and God [b]healed Abimelech, his
wife, and his female servants.
Then they bore *children;*
18 for the LORD [a]had closed up all
the wombs of the house of Abime-
lech because of Sarah, Abraham's
wife.

Isaac Is Born

21 And the LORD [a]visited Sarah
as He had said, and the LORD
did for Sarah [b]as He had spoken.

7 [c]Num. 16:32, 33
9 [a]Gen. 26:10; 39:9 [b]Gen. 34:7 [1]*sinned against*
11 [a]Prov. 16:6 [b]Gen. 12:12; 26:7
12 [a]Gen. 11:29
13 [a]Gen. 12:1–9, 11 [b]Gen. 12:13; 20:5
14 [a]Gen. 12:16
15 [a]Gen. 13:9; 34:10; 47:6
16 [a]Gen. 26:11 [b]Mal. 2:9 [1]Lit. *is a covering of the eyes for you to all* [2]Or *justified*
17 [a]Job 42:9 [b]Gen. 21:2
18 [a]Gen. 12:17
CHAPTER 21
1 [a]1 Sam. 2:21 [b][Gal. 4:23, 28]
2 [a]Heb. 11:11, 12 [b]Gen. 17:21; 18:10, 14
3 [a]Gen. 17:19, 21 [1]Lit. *Laughter*
4 [a]Acts 7:8 [b]Gen. 17:10, 12
5 [a]Gen. 17:1, 17
6 [a]Is. 54:1 [b]Luke 1:58 [1]Lit. *made laughter for me*
7 [a]Gen. 18:11, 12
9 [a]Gen. 16:1, 4, 15 [b][Gal. 4:29] [1]Lit. *laughing*
10 [a]Gal. 3:18; 4:30
11 [a]Gen. 17:18 [1]*distressing*
12 [a][Rom. 9:7, 8]
13 [a]Gen. 16:10; 17:20; 21:18; 25:12–18 [1]*descendant*
14 [a]John 8:35 [1]A water bottle made of skins

2 For Sarah [a]conceived and bore
Abraham a son in his old age, [b]at
the set time of which God had spo-
ken to him.
3 And Abraham called the name
of his son who was born to him—
whom Sarah bore to him—[a]Isaac.[1]
4 Then Abraham [a]circumcised
his son Isaac when he was eight
days old, [b]as God had commanded
him.
5 Now [a]Abraham was one hun-
dred years old when his son Isaac
was born to him.
6 And Sarah said, [a]"God has
[1]made me laugh, *and* all who hear
[b]will laugh with me."
7 She also said, "Who would
have said to Abraham that Sarah
would nurse children? [a]For I have
borne *him* a son in his old age."

Hagar and Ishmael Depart

8 So the child grew and was
weaned. And Abraham made a
great feast on the same day that
Isaac was weaned.
9 And Sarah saw the son of Ha-
gar [a]the Egyptian, whom she had
borne to Abraham, [b]scoffing.[1]
10 Therefore she said to Abra-
ham, [a]"Cast out this bondwoman
and her son; for the son of this
bondwoman shall not be heir with
my son, *namely* with Isaac."
11 And the matter was very [1]dis-
pleasing in Abraham's sight [a]be-
cause of his son.
12 But God said to Abraham, "Do
not let it be displeasing in your
sight because of the lad or because
of your bondwoman. Whatever
Sarah has said to you, listen to her
voice; for [a]in Isaac your seed shall
be called.
13 "Yet I will also make [a]a nation
of the son of the bondwoman, be-
cause he *is* your [1]seed."
14 So Abraham rose early in the
morning, and took bread and [1]a
skin of water; and putting *it* on her
shoulder, he gave *it* and the boy
to Hagar, and [a]sent her away.
Then she departed and wandered
in the Wilderness of Beersheba.
15 And the water in the skin was
used up, and she placed the boy
under one of the shrubs.
16 Then she went and sat down
across from *him* at a distance of
about a bowshot; for she said to

herself, "Let me not see the death
of the boy." So she sat opposite
him, and lifted her voice and wept.
17 And [a]God heard the voice of
the lad. Then the [b]angel of God
called to Hagar out of heaven, and
said to her, "What ails you, Hagar?
Fear not, for God has heard the
voice of the lad where he *is.*
18 "Arise, lift up the lad and hold
him with your hand, for [a]I will
make him a great nation."
19 Then [a]God opened her eyes,
and she saw a well of water. And
she went and filled the skin with
water, and gave the lad a drink.
20 So God [a]was with the lad; and
he grew and dwelt in the wilder-
ness, [b]and became an archer.
21 He dwelt in the Wilderness of
Paran; and his mother [a]took a wife
for him from the land of Egypt.

A Covenant with Abimelech

22 And it came to pass at that time
that [a]Abimelech and Phichol, the
commander of his army, spoke to
Abraham, saying, [b]"God *is* with
you in all that you do.
23 "Now therefore, [a]swear[1] to me
by God that you will not deal
falsely with me, with my offspring,
or with my posterity; but that ac-
cording to the kindness that I have
done to you, you will do to me and
to the land in which you have
dwelt."
24 And Abraham said, "I will
swear."
25 Then Abraham rebuked Abim-
elech because of a well of water
which Abimelech's servants [a]had
seized.
26 And Abimelech said, "I do not
know who has done this thing; you
did not tell me, nor had I heard *of
it* until today."
27 So Abraham took sheep and
oxen and gave them to Abimelech,
and the two of them [a]made a
[1]covenant.
28 And Abraham set seven ewe
lambs of the flock by themselves.
29 Then Abimelech asked Abra-
ham, [a]"What *is the meaning of*
these seven ewe lambs which you
have set by themselves?"
30 And he said, "You will take
these seven ewe lambs from my
hand, that [a]they may be my wit-
ness that I have dug this well."

17 [a]Ex. 3:7 [b]Gen. 22:11
18 [a]Gen. 16:10; 21:13; 25:12–16
19 [a]Num. 22:31
20 [a]Gen. 28:15; 39:2, 3, 21 [b]Gen. 16:12
21 [a]Gen. 24:4
22 [a]Gen. 20:2, 14; 26:26 [b]Gen. 26:28
23 [a]Josh. 2:12 [1]*take an oath*
25 [a]Gen. 26:15, 18, 20–22
27 [a]Gen. 26:31; 31:44 [1]*treaty*
29 [a]Gen. 33:8
30 [a]Gen. 31:48, 52
31 [a]Gen. 21:14; 26:33 [1]Lit. *Well of the Oath* or *Well of the Seven*
33 [a]Gen. 4:26; 12:8; 13:4; 26:25 [b]Deut. 32:40; 33:27

CHAPTER 22

1 [a]Heb. 11:17
2 [a]Gen. 22:12, 16 [b]John 5:20 [c]2 Chr. 3:1 [d]Gen. 8:20; 31:54
5 [a][Heb. 11:19] [1]Or *young man*
6 [a]John 19:17
7 [1]Or *goat*
8 [a]John 1:29, 36 [b]Ex. 12:3–6

31 Therefore he [a]called that place
[1]Beersheba, because the two of
them swore an oath there.
32 Thus they made a covenant at
Beersheba. So Abimelech rose
with Phichol, the commander of
his army, and they returned to the
land of the Philistines.
33 Then *Abraham* planted a tam-
arisk tree in Beersheba, and
[a]there called on the name of the
LORD, [b]the Everlasting God.
34 And Abraham stayed in the
land of the Philistines many days.

Abraham's Faith Confirmed

22 Now it came to pass after
these things that [a]God tested
Abraham, and said to him, "Abra-
ham!" And he said, "Here I am."
2 Then He said, "Take now your
son, [a]your only *son* Isaac, whom
you [b]love, and go [c]to the land of
Moriah, and offer him there as a
[d]burnt offering on one of the
mountains of which I shall tell
you."
3 So Abraham rose early in the
morning and saddled his donkey,
and took two of his young men
with him, and Isaac his son; and
he split the wood for the burnt of-
fering, and arose and went to the
place of which God had told him.
4 Then on the third day Abraham
lifted his eyes and saw the place
afar off.
5 And Abraham said to his
young men, "Stay here with the
donkey; the [1]lad and I will go yon-
der and worship, and we will
[a]come back to you."
6 So Abraham took the wood of
the burnt offering and [a]laid *it* on
Isaac his son; and he took the fire
in his hand, and a knife, and the
two of them went together.
7 But Isaac spoke to Abraham
his father and said, "My father!"
And he said, "Here I am, my son."
Then he said, "Look, the fire and
the wood, but where *is* the [1]lamb
for a burnt offering?"
8 And Abraham said, "My son,
God will provide for Himself the
[a]lamb for a [b]burnt offering." So
the two of them went together.
9 Then they came to the place of
which God had told him. And
Abraham built an altar there and
placed the wood in order; and he

bound Isaac his son and [a]laid him on the altar, upon the wood.

10 And Abraham stretched out his hand and took the knife to slay his son.

11 But the [a]Angel of the LORD called to him from heaven and said, "Abraham, Abraham!" So he said, "Here I am."

12 And He said, [a]"Do not lay your hand on the lad, or do anything to him; for [b]now I know that you fear God, since you have not [c]withheld your son, your only *son*, from Me."

13 Then Abraham lifted his eyes and looked, and there behind *him was* a ram caught in a thicket by its horns. So Abraham went and took the ram, and offered it up for a burnt offering instead of his son.

14 And Abraham called the name of the place, [1]The-LORD-Will-Provide; as it is said *to* this day, "In the Mount of the LORD it shall be provided."

15 Then the Angel of the LORD called to Abraham a second time out of heaven,

16 and said: [a]"By Myself I have sworn, says the LORD, because you have done this thing, and have not withheld your son, your only *son*—

17 "blessing I will [a]bless you, and multiplying I will multiply your descendants [b]as the stars of the heaven [c]and as the sand which *is* on the seashore; and [d]your descendants shall possess the gate of their enemies.

18 [a]"In your seed all the nations of the earth shall be blessed, [b]because you have obeyed My voice."

19 So Abraham returned to his young men, and they rose and went together to [a]Beersheba; and Abraham dwelt at Beersheba.

The Family of Nahor

20 Now it came to pass after these things that it was told Abraham, saying, "Indeed [a]Milcah also has borne children to your brother Nahor:

21 [a]"Huz his firstborn, Buz his brother, Kemuel the father [b]of Aram,

22 "Chesed, Hazo, Pildash, Jidlaph, and Bethuel."

23 And [a]Bethuel begot [1]Rebekah. These eight Milcah bore to Nahor, Abraham's brother.

24 His concubine, whose name was Reumah, also bore Tebah, Gaham, Thahash, and Maachah.

Sarah's Death and Burial

23 Sarah lived one hundred and twenty-seven years; *these were* the years of the life of Sarah.

2 So Sarah died in [a]Kirjath Arba (that *is*, [b]Hebron) in the land of Canaan, and Abraham came to mourn for Sarah and to weep for her.

3 Then Abraham stood up from before his dead, and spoke to the sons of [a]Heth, saying,

4 [a]"I *am* a foreigner and a visitor among you. [b]Give me property for a burial place among you, that I may bury my dead out of my sight."

5 And the sons of Heth answered Abraham, saying to him,

6 "Hear us, my lord: You *are* [a]a [1]mighty prince among us; bury your dead in the choicest of our burial places. None of us will withhold from you his burial place, that you may bury your dead."

7 Then Abraham stood up and bowed himself to the people of the land, the sons of Heth.

8 And he spoke with them, saying, "If it is your wish that I bury my dead out of my sight, hear me, and [1]meet with Ephron the son of Zohar for me,

9 "that he may give me the cave of [a]Machpelah which he has, which *is* at the end of his field. Let him give it to me at the full price, as property for a burial place among you."

10 Now Ephron dwelt among the sons of Heth; and Ephron the Hittite answered Abraham in the presence of the sons of Heth, all who [a]entered at the gate of his city, saying,

11 [a]"No, my lord, hear me: I give you the field and the cave that *is* in it; I give it to you in the presence of the sons of my people. I give it to you. Bury your dead!"

12 Then Abraham bowed himself down before the people of the land;

9 [a][Heb. 11:17–19]
11 [a]Gen. 16:7–11; 21:17, 18; 31:11
12 [a]1 Sam. 15:22 [b]Gen. 26:5; James 2:21, 22 [c]Gen. 22:2, 16; John 3:16
14 [1]Heb. *YHWH Yireh*
16 [a]Ps. 105:9; Luke 1:73; [Heb. 6:13, 14]
17 [a]Gen. 17:16; 26:3, 24 [b]Gen. 15:5; 26:4; Deut. 1:10; Jer. 33:22; Heb. 11:12 [c]Gen. 13:16; 32:12; 1 Kin. 4:20 [d]Gen. 24:60
18 [a]Gen. 12:3; 18:18; 26:4; Matt. 1:1; Luke 3:34; [Acts 3:25, 26]; Gal. 3:8, 9, 16, 18 [b]Gen. 18:19; 22:3, 10; 26:5
19 [a]Gen. 21:31
20 [a]Gen. 11:29; 24:15
21 [a]Job 1:1 [b]Job 32:2
23 [a]Gen. 24:15 [1]*Rebecca*, Rom. 9:10

CHAPTER 23

2 [a]Gen. 35:27; Josh. 14:15; 15:13; 21:11 [b]Gen. 13:18; 23:19
3 [a]Gen. 10:15; 15:20; 2 Kin. 7:6
4 [a][Gen. 17:8]; Lev. 25:23; 1 Chr. 29:15; Ps. 39:12; 105:12; 119:19; [Heb. 11:9, 13] [b]Acts 7:5, 16
6 [a]Gen. 13:2; 14:14; 24:35 [1]Lit. *prince of God*
8 [1]*entreat*
9 [a]Gen. 25:9
10 [a]Gen. 23:18; 34:20, 24; Ruth 4:1, 4, 11
11 [a]2 Sam. 24:21–24

13 and he spoke to Ephron in the
hearing of the people of the land,
saying, "If you *will give it*, please
hear me. I will give you money for
the field; take *it* from me and I will
bury my dead there."
14 And Ephron answered Abra-
ham, saying to him,
15 "My lord, listen to me; the land
is worth four hundred [a]shekels of
silver. What *is* that between you
and me? So bury your dead."
16 And Abraham listened to
Ephron; and Abraham [a]weighed
out the silver for Ephron which he
had named in the hearing of the
sons of Heth, four hundred shek-
els of silver, currency of the mer-
chants.
17 So [a]the field of Ephron which
was in Machpelah, which *was* be-
fore Mamre, the field and the cave
which *was* in it, and all the trees
that *were* in the field, which *were*
within all the surrounding borders,
were deeded
18 to Abraham as a possession in
the presence of the sons of Heth,
before all who went in at the gate
of his city.
19 And after this, Abraham buried
Sarah his wife in the cave of the
field of Machpelah, before Mamre
(that *is*, Hebron) in the land of Ca-
naan.
20 So the field and the cave that
is in it [a]were deeded to Abraham
by the sons of Heth as property for
a burial place.

A Bride for Isaac

24 Now Abraham [a]was old,
well advanced in age; and
the LORD [b]had blessed Abraham in
all things.
2 So Abraham said [a]to the oldest
servant of his house, who [b]ruled
over all that he had, "Please, [c]put
your hand under my thigh,
3 "and I will make you [a]swear[1]
by the LORD, the God of heaven
and the God of the earth, that [b]you
will not take a wife for my son
from the daughters of the Canaan-
ites, among whom I dwell;
4 [a]"but you shall go [b]to my coun-
try and to my family, and take a
wife for my son Isaac."
5 And the servant said to him,
"Perhaps the woman will not be
willing to follow me to this land.
Must I take your son back to the
land from which you came?"
6 But Abraham said to him, "Be-
ware that you do not take my son
back there.
7 "The LORD God of heaven, who
[a]took me from my father's house
and from the land of my family,
and who spoke to me and swore
to me, saying, [b]'To your [1]descen-
dants I give this land,' [c]He will send
His angel before you, and you
shall take a wife for my son from
there.
8 "And if the woman is not will-
ing to follow you, then [a]you will
be released from this oath; only do
not take my son back there."
9 So the servant put his hand un-
der the thigh of Abraham his mas-
ter, and swore to him concerning
this matter.
10 Then the servant took ten of his
master's camels and departed, [a]for
all his master's goods *were in* his
hand. And he arose and went to
Mesopotamia, to [b]the city of Na-
hor.
11 And he made his camels kneel
down outside the city by a well of
water at evening time, the time
[a]when women go out to draw *wa-
ter*.
12 Then he [a]said, "O LORD God of
my master Abraham, please [b]give
me success this day, and show
kindness to my master Abraham.
13 "Behold, *here* [a]I stand by the
well of water, and [b]the daughters
of the men of the city are coming
out to draw water.
14 "Now let it be that the young
woman to whom I say, 'Please let
down your pitcher that I may
drink,' and she says, 'Drink, and I
will also give your camels a
drink'—*let* her *be the one* You
have appointed for Your servant
Isaac. And [a]by this I will know that
You have shown kindness to my
master."
15 And it happened, [a]before he
had finished speaking, that be-
hold, [b]Rebekah,[1] who was born to
Bethuel, son of [c]Milcah, the wife
of Nahor, Abraham's brother,
came out with her pitcher on her
shoulder.
16 Now the young woman [a]*was*
very beautiful to behold, a virgin;
no man had known her. And she

---

15 [a]Ex. 30:13
16 [a]Jer. 32:9, 10
17 [a]Gen. 25:9; 49:29–32; 50:13
20 [a]Jer. 32:10, 11

CHAPTER 24

1 [a]Gen. 18:11; 21:5 [b]Gen. 12:2; 13:2; 24:35
2 [a]Gen. 15:2 [b]Gen. 24:10; 39:4–6 [c]Gen. 47:29
3 [a]Gen. 14:19, 22 [b]Deut. 7:3 [1]*take an oath*
4 [a]Gen. 28:2 [b]Gen. 12:1
7 [a]Gen. 12:1; 24:3 [b]Gen. 12:7; 13:15; 15:18; 17:8 [c]Ex. 23:20, 23; 33:2 [1]Lit. *seed*
8 [a]Josh. 2:17–20
10 [a]Gen. 24:2, 22 [b]Gen. 11:31, 32; 22:20; 27:43; 29:5
11 [a]Ex. 2:16
12 [a]Ex. 3:6, 15 [b]Neh. 1:11
13 [a]Gen. 24:43 [b]Ex. 2:16
14 [a]Judg. 6:17, 37
15 [a]Is. 65:24 [b]Gen. 24:45; 25:20 [c]Gen. 22:20, 23 [1]*Rebecca*, Rom. 9:10
16 [a]Gen. 12:11; 26:7; 29:17

went down to the well, filled her
pitcher, and came up.
17 And the servant ran to meet her
and said, "Please let me drink a
little water from your pitcher."
18 [a]So she said, "Drink, my lord."
Then she quickly let her pitcher
down to her hand, and gave him
a drink.
19 And when she had finished giv-
ing him a drink, she said, "I will
draw *water* for your camels also,
until they have finished drinking."
20 Then she quickly emptied her
pitcher into the trough, ran back
to the well to draw *water*, and
drew for all his camels.
21 And the man, wondering at
her, remained silent so as to know
whether [a]the LORD had made his
journey prosperous or not.
22 So it was, when the camels had
finished drinking, that the man
took a golden [a]nose ring weighing
half a shekel, and two bracelets for
her wrists weighing ten *shekels* of
gold,
23 and said, "Whose daughter *are*
you? Tell me, please, is there room
in your father's house for us [1]to
lodge?"
24 So she said to him, [a]"I *am* the
daughter of Bethuel, Milcah's son,
whom she bore to Nahor."
25 Moreover she said to him, "We
have both straw and feed enough,
and room to lodge."
26 Then the man [a]bowed down his
head and worshiped the LORD.
27 And he said, [a]"Blessed *be* the
LORD God of my master Abraham,
who has not forsaken [b]His mercy
and His truth toward my master.
As for me, being on the way, the
LORD [c]led me to the house of my
master's brethren."
28 So the young woman ran and
told her mother's household these
things.
29 Now Rebekah had a brother
whose name *was* [a]Laban, and La-
ban ran out to the man by the well.
30 So it came to pass, when he
saw the nose ring, and the brace-
lets on his sister's wrists, and
when he heard the words of his
sister Rebekah, saying, "Thus the
man spoke to me," that he went
to the man. And there he stood by
the camels at the well.
31 And he said, "Come in, [a]O
blessed of the LORD! Why do you
stand outside? For I have prepared
the house, and a place for the cam-
els."
32 Then the man came to the
house. And he unloaded the cam-
els, and [a]provided straw and feed
for the camels, and water to [b]wash
his feet and the feet of the men
who *were* with him.
33 *Food* was set before him to eat,
but he said, [a]"I will not eat until I
have told about my errand." And
he said, "Speak on."
34 So he said, "I *am* Abraham's
servant.
35 "The LORD [a]has blessed my
master greatly, and he has become
great; and He has given him flocks
and herds, silver and gold, male
and female servants, and camels
and donkeys.
36 "And Sarah my master's wife
[a]bore a son to my master when she
was old; and [b]to him he has given
all that he has.
37 "Now my master [a]made me
swear, saying, 'You shall not take
a wife for my son from the daugh-
ters of the Canaanites, in whose
land I dwell;
38 [a]'but you shall go to my father's
house and to my family, and take
a wife for my son.'
39 [a]"And I said to my master, 'Per-
haps the woman will not follow
me.'
40 [a]"But he said to me, 'The LORD,
[b]before whom I walk, will send His
angel with you and [1]prosper your
way; and you shall take a wife for
my son from my family and from
my father's house.
41 [a]'You will be clear from this
oath when you arrive among my
family; for if they will not give *her*
to you, then you will be released
from my oath.'
42 "And this day I came to the
well and said, [a]'O LORD God of my
master Abraham, if You will now
prosper the way in which I go,
43 [a]'behold, I stand by the well of
water; and it shall come to pass
that when the virgin comes out to
draw *water*, and I say to her,
"Please give me a little water from
your pitcher to drink,"
44 'and she says to me, "Drink,
and I will draw for your camels
also,"—*let* her *be* the woman

18 [a]Gen. 24:14, 46; [1 Pet. 3:8, 9]
21 [a]Gen. 24:12–14, 27, 52
22 [a]Gen. 24:47; Ex. 32:2, 3; Is. 3:19–21
23 [1]*to spend the night*
24 [a]Gen. 22:23; 24:15
26 [a]Gen. 24:48, 52; Ex. 4:31
27 [a]Gen. 24:12, 42, 48; Ex. 18:10; Ruth 4:14; 1 Sam. 25:32, 39; 2 Sam. 18:28; Luke 1:68 [b]Gen. 32:10; Ps. 98:3 [c]Gen. 24:21, 48
29 [a]Gen. 29:5, 13
31 [a]Gen. 26:29; Judg. 17:2; Ruth 3:10; Ps. 115:15
32 [a]Gen. 43:24; Judg. 19:21 [b]Gen. 19:2; John 13:5, 13–15
33 [a]Job 23:12; John 4:34; Eph. 6:5–7
35 [a]Gen. 13:2; 24:1
36 [a]Gen. 21:1–7 [b]Gen. 21:10; 25:5
37 [a]Gen. 24:2–4
38 [a]Gen. 24:4
39 [a]Gen. 24:5
40 [a]Gen. 24:7 [b]Gen. 5:22, 24; 17:1; 1 Kin. 8:23 [1]*make your way successful*
41 [a]Gen. 24:8
42 [a]Gen. 24:12
43 [a]Gen. 24:13

whom the LORD has appointed for
my master's son.'
45 [a]"But before I had finished
[b]speaking in my heart, there was
Rebekah, coming out with her
pitcher on her shoulder; and she
went down to the well and drew
water. And I said to her, 'Please
let me drink.'
46 "And she made haste and let
her pitcher down from her *shoul-*
der, and said, 'Drink, and I will
give your camels a drink also.' So
I drank, and she gave the camels
a drink also.
47 "Then I asked her, and said,
'Whose daughter *are* you?' And
she said, 'The daughter of Bethuel,
Nahor's son, whom Milcah bore to
him.' So I put the nose ring on her
nose and the bracelets on her
wrists.
48 [a]"And I bowed my head and
worshiped the LORD, and blessed
the LORD God of my master Abra-
ham, who had led me in the way
of truth to [b]take the daughter of
my master's brother for his son.
49 "Now if you will [a]deal kindly
and truly with my master, tell me.
And if not, tell me, that I may turn
to the right hand or to the left."
50 Then Laban and Bethuel an-
swered and said, [a]"The thing
comes from the LORD; we cannot
[b]speak to you either bad or good.
51 [a]"Here *is* Rebekah before you;
take *her* and go, and let her be
your master's son's wife, as the
LORD has spoken."
52 And it came to pass, when
Abraham's servant heard their
words, that [a]he worshiped the
LORD, *bowing himself* to the earth.
53 Then the servant brought out
[a]jewelry of silver, jewelry of gold,
and clothing, and gave *them* to
Rebekah. He also gave [b]precious
things to her brother and to her
mother.
54 And he and the men who *were*
with him ate and drank and stayed
all night. Then they arose in the
morning, and he said, [a]"Send me
away to my master."
55 But her brother and her mother
said, "Let the young woman stay
with us *a few* days, at least ten;
after that she may go."
56 And he said to them, "Do not
[1]hinder me, since the LORD has

45 [a]Gen. 24:15 [b]1 Sam. 1:13
48 [a]Gen. 24:26, 52 [b]Gen. 22:23; 24:27; Ps. 32:8; 48:14; Is. 48:17
49 [a]Gen. 47:29; Josh. 2:14
50 [a]Ps. 118:23; Matt. 21:42; Mark 12:11 [b]Gen. 31:24, 29
51 [a]Gen. 20:15
52 [a]Gen. 24:26, 48
53 [a]Gen. 24:10, 22; Ex. 3:22; 11:2; 12:35 [b]2 Chr. 21:3; Ezra 1:6
54 [a]Gen. 24:56, 59; 30:25
56 [1]*delay*
59 [a]Gen. 35:8
60 [a]Gen. 17:16 [b]Gen. 22:17; 28:14
62 [a]Gen. 16:14; 25:11
63 [a]Josh. 1:8; Ps. 1:2; 77:12; 119:15, 27, 48; 143:5; 145:5
64 [a]Josh. 15:18
67 [a]Gen. 25:20; 29:20; Prov. 18:22 [b]Gen. 23:1, 2; 38:12

CHAPTER 25

1 [a]1 Chr. 1:32, 33
2 [a]1 Chr. 1:32, 33

prospered my way; send me away
so that I may go to my master."
57 So they said, "We will call the
young woman and ask her per-
sonally."
58 Then they called Rebekah and
said to her, "Will you go with this
man?" And she said, "I will go."
59 So they sent away Rebekah
their sister [a]and her nurse, and
Abraham's servant and his men.
60 And they blessed Rebekah and
said to her:

"Our sister, *may* you *become*
[a]*The mother of* thousands of ten
thousands;
[b]And may your descendants
possess
The gates of those who hate
them."

61 Then Rebekah and her maids
arose, and they rode on the camels
and followed the man. So the ser-
vant took Rebekah and departed.
62 Now Isaac came from the way
of [a]Beer Lahai Roi, for he dwelt
in the South.
63 And Isaac went out [a]to medi-
tate in the field in the evening; and
he lifted his eyes and looked, and
there, the camels *were* coming.
64 Then Rebekah lifted her eyes,
and when she saw Isaac [a]she dis-
mounted from her camel;
65 for she had said to the servant,
"Who *is* this man walking in the
field to meet us?" The servant said,
"It *is* my master." So she took a
veil and covered herself.
66 And the servant told Isaac all
the things that he had done.
67 Then Isaac brought her into his
mother Sarah's tent; and he [a]took
Rebekah and she became his wife,
and he loved her. So Isaac [b]was
comforted after his mother's
death.

Abraham and Keturah

25 Abraham again took a wife,
and her name *was* [a]Keturah.
2 And [a]she bore him Zimran,
Jokshan, Medan, Midian, Ishbak,
and Shuah.
3 Jokshan begot Sheba and De-
dan. And the sons of Dedan were
Asshurim, Letushim, and Leum-
mim.
4 And the sons of Midian *were*

Ephah, Epher, Hanoch, Abidah,
and Eldaah. All these *were* the
children of Keturah.
5 And [a]Abraham gave all that he
had to Isaac.
6 But Abraham gave gifts to the
sons of the concubines which
Abraham had; and while he was
still living he [a]sent them eastward,
away from Isaac his son, to [b]the
country of the east.

Abraham's Death and Burial

7 This *is* the sum of the years of
Abraham's life which he lived: one
hundred and seventy-five years.
8 Then Abraham breathed his
last and [a]died in a good old age,
an old man and full *of years,* and
[b]was gathered to his people.
9 And [a]his sons Isaac and Ish-
mael buried him in the cave of
[b]Machpelah, which *is* before
Mamre, in the field of Ephron the
son of Zohar the Hittite,
10 [a]the field which Abraham pur-
chased from the sons of Heth.
[b]There Abraham was buried, and
Sarah his wife.
11 And it came to pass, after the
death of Abraham, that God
blessed his son Isaac. And Isaac
dwelt at [a]Beer Lahai Roi.

The Families of Ishmael and Isaac

12 Now this *is* the [a]genealogy of
Ishmael, Abraham's son, whom
Hagar the Egyptian, Sarah's
maidservant, bore to Abraham.
13 And [a]these *were* the names of
the sons of Ishmael, by their
names, according to their genera-
tions: The firstborn of Ishmael,
Nebajoth; then Kedar, Adbeel,
Mibsam,
14 Mishma, Dumah, Massa,
15 [1]Hadar, Tema, Jetur, Naphish,
and Kedemah.
16 These *were* the sons of Ishmael
and these *were* their names, by
their towns and their [1]settlements,
[a]twelve princes according to their
nations.
17 These *were* the years of the life
of Ishmael: one hundred and
thirty-seven years; and [a]he
breathed his last and died, and was
gathered to his people.
18 [a](They dwelt from Havilah as
far as Shur, which *is* east of Egypt
as you go toward Assyria.) He
[1]died [b]in the presence of all his
brethren.
19 This *is* the [a]genealogy of Isaac,
Abraham's son. [b]Abraham begot
Isaac.
20 Isaac was forty years old when
he took Rebekah as wife, [a]the
daughter of Bethuel the Syrian of
Padan Aram, [b]the sister of Laban
the Syrian.
21 Now Isaac pleaded with the
LORD for his wife, because she *was*
barren; [a]and the LORD granted his
plea, [b]and Rebekah his wife con-
ceived.
22 But the children struggled to-
gether within her; and she said, "If
all is well, why *am I like* this?" [a]So
she went to inquire of the LORD.
23 And the LORD said to her:

[a]"Two nations *are* in your womb,
Two peoples shall be separated
from your body;
One people shall be stronger than
[b]the other,
[c]And the older shall serve the
younger."

24 So when her days were fulfilled
for her to give birth, indeed *there*
were twins in her womb.
25 And the first came out red. *He*
was [a]like a hairy garment all over;
so they called his name [1]Esau.
26 Afterward his brother came
out, and [a]his hand took hold of
Esau's heel; so [b]his name was
called [1]Jacob. Isaac *was* sixty
years old when she bore them.
27 So the boys grew. And Esau
was [a]a skillful hunter, a man of the
field; but Jacob was [b]a [1]mild man,
[c]dwelling in tents.
28 And Isaac loved Esau because
he [a]ate *of his* game, [b]but Rebekah
loved Jacob.

Esau Sells His Birthright

29 Now Jacob cooked a stew; and
Esau came in from the field, and
he *was* weary.
30 And Esau said to Jacob,
"Please feed me with that same
red *stew,* for I *am* weary." There-
fore his name was called [1]Edom.
31 But Jacob said, "Sell me your
birthright as of this day."
32 And Esau said, "Look, I *am*
about to die; so [a]what is this birth-
right to me?"

5 [a]Gen. 24:35, 36
6 [a]Gen. 21:14 [b]Judg. 6:3
8 [a]Gen. 15:15; 47:8, 9 [b]Gen. 25:17; 35:29; 49:29, 33
9 [a]Gen. 35:29; 50:13 [b]Gen. 23:9, 17; 49:30
10 [a]Gen. 23:3–16 [b]Gen. 49:31
11 [a]Gen. 16:14
12 [a]Gen. 11:10, 27; 16:15
13 [a]1 Chr. 1:29–31
15 [1]MT *Hadad*
16 [a]Gen. 17:20 [1]*camps*
17 [a]Gen. 25:8; 49:33
18 [a]Gen. 20:1; 1 Sam. 15:7 [b]Gen. 16:12 [1]*fell*
19 [a]Gen. 36:1, 9 [b]Matt. 1:2
20 [a]Gen. 22:23; 24:15, 29, 67 [b]Gen. 24:29
21 [a]1 Sam. 1:17; 1 Chr. 5:20; 2 Chr. 33:13; Ezra 8:23; Ps. 127:3 [b]Rom. 9:10–13
22 [a]1 Sam. 1:15; 9:9; 10:22
23 [a]Gen. 17:4–6, 16; 24:60; Num. 20:14; Deut. 2:4–8 [b]2 Sam. 8:14 [c]Gen. 27:29, 40; Mal. 1:2, 3; Rom. 9:12
25 [a]Gen. 27:11, 16, 23 [1]Lit. *Hairy*
26 [a]Hos. 12:3 [b]Gen. 27:36 [1]*Supplanter* or *Deceitful,* lit. *One Who Takes the Heel*
27 [a]Gen. 27:3, 5 [b]Job 1:1, 8 [c]Heb. 11:9 [1]Lit. *complete*
28 [a]Gen. 27:4, 19, 25, 31 [b]Gen. 27:6–10
30 [1]Lit. *Red*
32 [a]Matt. 16:26; Mark 8:36, 37

33 Then Jacob said, [1]"Swear to
me as of this day." So he swore
to him, and [a]sold his birthright to
Jacob.
34 And Jacob gave Esau bread
and stew of lentils; then [a]he ate
and drank, arose, and went his
way. Thus Esau [b]despised *his*
birthright.

Isaac and Abimelech

26 There was a famine in the
land, besides [a]the first fam-
ine that was in the days of Abra-
ham. And Isaac went to [b]Abime-
lech king of the Philistines, in
Gerar.
2 Then the LORD appeared to him
and said: [a]"Do not go down to
Egypt; live in [b]the land of which I
shall tell you.
3 [a]"Dwell in this land, and [b]I will
be with you and [c]bless you; for to
you and your descendants [d]I give
all these lands, and I will perform
[e]the oath which I swore to Abra-
ham your father.
4 "And [a]I will make your descen-
dants multiply as the stars of
heaven; I will give to your descen-
dants all these lands; [b]and in your
seed all the nations of the earth
shall be blessed;
5 [a]"because Abraham obeyed
My voice and kept My charge, My
commandments, My statutes, and
My laws."
6 So Isaac dwelt in Gerar.
7 And the men of the place asked
about his wife. And [a]he said, "She
is my sister"; for [b]he was afraid
to say, "*She is* my wife," *because
he thought,* "lest the men of the
place kill me for Rebekah, because
she *is* [c]beautiful to behold."
8 Now it came to pass, when he
had been there a long time, that
Abimelech king of the Philistines
looked through a window, and
saw, and there was Isaac, [1]show-
ing endearment to Rebekah his
wife.
9 Then Abimelech called Isaac
and said, "Quite obviously she *is*
your wife; so how could you say,
'She *is* my sister'?" Isaac said to
him, "Because I said, 'Lest I die on
account of her.'"
10 And Abimelech said, "What *is*
this you have done to us? One of
the people might soon have lain
with your wife, and [a]you would
have brought guilt on us."
11 So Abimelech charged all *his*
people, saying, "He who [a]touches
this man or his wife shall surely
be put to death."
12 Then Isaac sowed in that land,
and reaped in the same year
[a]a hundredfold; and the LORD
[b]blessed him.
13 The man [a]began to prosper,
and continued prospering until he
became very prosperous;
14 for he had possessions of flocks
and possessions of herds and a
great number of servants. So the
Philistines [a]envied him.
15 Now the Philistines had
stopped up all the wells [a]which his
father's servants had dug in the
days of Abraham his father, and
they had filled them with earth.
16 And Abimelech said to Isaac,
"Go away from us, for [a]you are
much mightier than we."
17 Then Isaac departed from there
and [1]pitched his tent in the Valley
of Gerar, and dwelt there.
18 And Isaac dug again the wells
of water which they had dug in the
days of Abraham his father, for the
Philistines had stopped them up
after the death of Abraham. [a]He
called them by the names which
his father had called them.
19 Also Isaac's servants dug in the
valley, and found a well of running
water there.
20 But the herdsmen of Gerar
[a]quarreled with Isaac's herdsmen,
saying, "The water *is* ours." So he
called the name of the well [1]Esek,
because they quarreled with
him.
21 Then they dug another well,
and they quarreled over that *one*
also. So he called its name [1]Sitnah.
22 And he moved from there and
dug another well, and they did not
quarrel over it. So he called its
name [1]Rehoboth, because he said,
"For now the LORD has made room
for us, and we shall [a]be fruitful in
the land."
23 Then he went up from there to
Beersheba.
24 And the LORD [a]appeared to him
the same night and said, [b]"I *am*
the God of your father Abraham;
[c]do not fear, for [d]I *am* with you. I
will bless you and multiply your

33 [a]Heb. 12:16 [1]*Take an oath*
34 [a]Eccl. 8:15 [b]Heb. 12:16, 17

CHAPTER 26

1 [a]Gen. 12:10 [b]Gen. 20:1, 2
2 [a]Gen. 12:7; 17:1; 18:1; 35:9 [b]Gen. 12:1
3 [a]Heb. 11:9 [b]Gen. 28:13, 15 [c]Gen. 12:2 [d]Gen. 12:7; 13:15; 15:18 [e]Gen. 22:16
4 [a]Gen. 15:5; 22:17 [b]Gen. 12:3; 22:18
5 [a]Gen. 22:16, 18
7 [a]Gen. 12:13; 20:2, 12, 13 [b]Prov. 29:25 [c]Gen. 12:11; 24:16; 29:17
8 [1]*caressing*
10 [a]Gen. 20:9
11 [a]Ps. 105:15
12 [a]Matt. 13:8, 23 [b]Gen. 24:1; 25:8, 11; 26:3
13 [a][Prov. 10:22]
14 [a]Gen. 37:11
15 [a]Gen. 21:25, 30
16 [a]Ex. 1:9
17 [1]*camped*
18 [a]Gen. 21:31
20 [a]Gen. 21:25 [1]Lit. *Quarrel*
21 [1]Lit. *Enmity*
22 [a]Gen. 17:6; 28:3; 41:52 [1]Lit. *Spaciousness*
24 [a]Gen. 26:2 [b]Gen. 17:7, 8; 24:12 [c]Gen. 15:1 [d]Gen. 26:3, 4

descendants for My servant Abra-
ham's sake."
25 So he [a]built an altar there and
[b]called on the name of the LORD,
and he pitched his tent there;
and there Isaac's servants dug a
well.
26 Then Abimelech came to him
from Gerar with Ahuzzath, one of
his friends, [a]and Phichol the com-
mander of his army.
27 And Isaac said to them, "Why
have you come to me, [a]since you
hate me and have [b]sent me away
from you?"
28 But they said, "We have cer-
tainly seen that the LORD [a]is with
you. So we said, 'Let there now be
an oath between us, between you
and us; and let us make a [1]cov-
enant with you,
29 'that you will do us no harm,
since we have not touched you,
and since we have done nothing
to you but good and have sent you
away in peace. [a]You *are* now the
blessed of the LORD.' "
30 [a]So he made them a feast, and
they ate and drank.
31 Then they arose early in the
morning and [a]swore an oath with
one another; and Isaac sent them
away, and they departed from him
in peace.
32 It came to pass the same day
that Isaac's servants came and told
him about the well which they had
dug, and said to him, "We have
found water."
33 So he called it [1]Shebah. [a]There-
fore the name of the city *is* [2]Beer-
sheba to this day.
34 [a]When Esau was forty years
old, he took as wives Judith the
daughter of Beeri the Hittite, and
Basemath the daughter of Elon the
Hittite.
35 And [a]they were a grief of mind
to Isaac and Rebekah.

Isaac Blesses Jacob

27 Now it came to pass, when
Isaac was [a]old and [b]his eyes
were so dim that he could not see,
that he called Esau his older son
and said to him, "My son." And
he answered him, "Here I am."
2 Then he said, "Behold now, I
am old. I [a]do not know the day of
my death.
3 [a]"Now therefore, please take

25 [a]Gen. 12:7, 8; 13:4, 18; 22:9; 33:20 [b]Gen. 21:33; Ps. 116:17
26 [a]Gen. 21:22
27 [a]Judg. 11:7 [b]Gen. 26:16
28 [a]Gen. 21:22, 23 [1]*treaty*
29 [a]Gen. 24:31; Ps. 115:15
30 [a]Gen. 19:3
31 [a]Gen. 21:31
33 [a]Gen. 21:31; 28:10 [1]Lit. *Oath* or *Seven* [2]Lit. *Well of the Oath* or *Well of the Seven*
34 [a]Gen. 28:8; 36:2
35 [a]Gen. 27:46; 28:1, 8

CHAPTER 27

1 [a]Gen. 35:28 [b]Gen. 48:10; 1 Sam. 3:2
2 [a][Prov. 27:1; James 4:14]
3 [a]Gen. 25:27, 28
4 [a]Gen. 27:19, 25, 27, 31; 48:9, 15, 16; 49:28; Deut. 33:1; Heb. 11:20 [1]*tasty*
7 [1]*tasty*
8 [a]Gen. 27:13, 43
9 [a]Gen. 27:4
10 [a]Gen. 27:4; 48:16
11 [a]Gen. 25:25
12 [a]Gen. 27:21, 22 [b]Gen. 9:25; Deut. 27:18
13 [a]Gen. 43:9; 1 Sam. 25:24; 2 Sam. 14:9; Matt. 27:25
14 [a]Prov. 23:3; Luke 21:34 [1]*tasty*
15 [a]Gen. 27:27

your weapons, your quiver and
your bow, and go out to the field
and hunt game for me.
4 "And make me [1]savory food,
such as I love, and bring *it* to me
that I may eat, that my soul [a]may
bless you before I die."
5 Now Rebekah was listening
when Isaac spoke to Esau his son.
And Esau went to the field to hunt
game and to bring *it*.
6 So Rebekah spoke to Jacob her
son, saying, "Indeed I heard your
father speak to Esau your brother,
saying,
7 'Bring me game and make [1]sa-
vory food for me, that I may eat it
and bless you in the presence of
the LORD before my death.'
8 "Now therefore, my son, [a]obey
my voice according to what I com-
mand you.
9 "Go now to the flock and bring
me from there two choice kids of
the goats, and I will make [a]savory
food from them for your father,
such as he loves.
10 "Then you shall take *it* to your
father, that he may eat *it*, and that
he [a]may bless you before his
death."
11 And Jacob said to Rebekah his
mother, "Look, [a]Esau my brother
is a hairy man, and I *am* a smooth-
skinned man.
12 "Perhaps my father will [a]feel
me, and I shall seem to be a de-
ceiver to him; and I shall bring
[b]a curse on myself and not a bless-
ing."
13 But his mother said to him,
[a]"*Let* your curse *be* on me, my son;
only obey my voice, and go, get
them for me."
14 And he went and got *them* and
brought *them* to his mother, and
his mother [a]made [1]savory food,
such as his father loved.
15 Then Rebekah took [a]the choice
clothes of her elder son Esau,
which *were* with her in the house,
and put them on Jacob her
younger son.
16 And she put the skins of the
kids of the goats on his hands and
on the smooth part of his neck.
17 Then she gave the savory food
and the bread, which she had pre-
pared, into the hand of her son Ja-
cob.
18 So he went to his father and

said, "My father." And he said,
"Here I am. Who *are* you, my
son?"
19 Jacob said to his father, "I *am*
Esau your firstborn; I have done
just as you told me; please arise,
sit and eat of my game, [a]that your
soul may bless me."
20 But Isaac said to his son, "How
is it that you have found *it* so
quickly, my son?" And he said,
"Because the LORD your God
brought *it* to me."
21 Then Isaac said to Jacob,
"Please come near, that I [a]may feel
you, my son, whether you *are* re-
ally my son Esau or not."
22 So Jacob went near to Isaac
his father, and he felt him and
said, "The voice *is* Jacob's voice,
but the hands *are* the hands of
Esau."
23 And he did not recognize him,
because [a]his hands were hairy like
his brother Esau's hands; so he
blessed him.
24 Then he said, "*Are* you really
my son Esau?" He said, "I *am*."
25 He said, "Bring *it* near to me,
and I will eat of my son's game,
so [a]that my soul may bless you."
So he brought *it* near to him, and
he ate; and he brought him wine,
and he drank.
26 Then his father Isaac said to
him, "Come near now and kiss me,
my son."
27 And he came near and [a]kissed
him; and he smelled the smell of
his clothing, and blessed him and
said:

"Surely, [b]the smell of my son
Is like the smell of a field
Which the LORD has blessed.
28 Therefore may [a]God give you
Of [b]the dew of heaven,
Of [c]the fatness of the earth,
And [d]plenty of grain and wine.
29 [a]Let peoples serve you,
And nations bow down to you.
Be master over your brethren,
And [b]let your mother's sons bow
down to you.
[c]Cursed *be* everyone who curses
you,
And blessed *be* those who bless
you!"

Esau's Lost Hope

30 Now it happened, as soon as
Isaac had finished blessing Jacob,

19 [a]Gen. 27:4
21 [a]Gen. 27:12
23 [a]Gen. 27:16
25 [a]Gen. 27:4, 10, 19, 31
27 [a]Gen. 29:13 [b]Song 4:11; Hos. 14:6
28 [a]Heb. 11:20 [b]Gen. 27:39; Deut. 33:13, 28; 2 Sam. 1:21; Ps. 133:3; Prov. 3:20; Mic. 5:7; Zech. 8:12 [c]Gen. 45:18; Num. 18:12 [d]Deut. 7:13; 33:28
29 [a]Gen. 9:25; 25:23; Is. 45:14; 49:7; 60:12, 14 [b]Gen. 37:7, 10; 49:8 [c]Gen. 12:2, 3; Zeph. 2:8, 9
31 [a]Gen. 27:4 [1]*tasty*
33 [a]Gen. 25:23; 28:3, 4; Num. 23:20; Rom. 11:29
34 [a][Heb. 12:17]
36 [a]Gen. 25:26, 32–34 [1]*Supplanter* or *Deceitful*, lit. *One Who Takes the Heel*
37 [a]2 Sam. 8:14 [b]Gen. 27:28, 29 [1]*provided support for*
38 [a]Heb. 12:17
39 [a]Gen. 27:28; Heb. 11:20 [1]*fertility*
40 [a]Gen. 25:23; 27:29; 2 Sam. 8:14; [Obad. 18–20] [b]2 Kin. 8:20–22

and Jacob had scarcely gone out
from the presence of Isaac his fa-
ther, that Esau his brother came
in from his hunting.
31 He also had made [1]savory food,
and brought it to his father, and
said to his father, "Let my father
arise and [a]eat of his son's game,
that your soul may bless me."
32 And his father Isaac said to
him, "Who *are* you?" So he said,
"I *am* your son, your firstborn,
Esau."
33 Then Isaac trembled exceed-
ingly, and said, "Who? Where *is*
the one who hunted game and
brought *it* to me? I ate all *of it* be-
fore you came, and I have blessed
him—[a]*and* indeed he shall be
blessed."
34 When Esau heard the words of
his father, [a]he cried with an ex-
ceedingly great and bitter cry, and
said to his father, "Bless me—me
also, O my father!"
35 But he said, "Your brother
came with deceit and has taken
away your blessing."
36 And *Esau* said, [a]"Is he not
rightly named [1]Jacob? For he has
supplanted me these two times.
He took away my birthright, and
now look, he has taken away my
blessing!" And he said, "Have
you not reserved a blessing for
me?"
37 Then Isaac answered and said
to Esau, [a]"Indeed I have made him
your master, and all his brethren
I have given to him as servants;
with [b]grain and wine I have [1]sus-
tained him. What shall I do now
for you, my son?"
38 And Esau said to his father,
"Have you only one blessing, my
father? Bless me—me also, O my
father!" And Esau lifted up his
voice [a]and wept.
39 Then Isaac his father answered
and said to him:

"Behold, [a]your dwelling shall be
of the [1]fatness of the earth,
And of the dew of heaven from
above.
40 By your sword you shall live,
And [a]you shall serve your
brother;
And [b]it shall come to pass, when
you become restless,
That you shall break his yoke
from your neck."

Jacob Escapes from Esau

41 So Esau [a]hated Jacob because
of the blessing with which his fa-
ther blessed him, and Esau said in
his heart, [b]"The days of mourning
for my father [1]are at hand; [c]then
I will kill my brother Jacob."
42 And the words of Esau her
older son were told to Rebekah. So
she sent and called Jacob her
younger son, and said to him,
"Surely your brother Esau [a]com-
forts himself concerning you *by in-
tending* to kill you.
43 "Now therefore, my son, obey
my voice: arise, flee to my brother
Laban [a]in Haran.
44 "And stay with him a [a]few
days, until your brother's fury
turns away,
45 "until your brother's anger
turns away from you, and he for-
gets what you have done to him;
then I will send and bring you from
there. Why should I be bereaved
also of you both in one day?"
46 And Rebekah said to Isaac, [a]"I
am weary of my life because of the
daughters of Heth; [b]if Jacob takes
a wife of the daughters of Heth,
like these *who are* the daughters
of the land, what good will my life
be to me?"

28 Then Isaac called Jacob and
[a]blessed him, and [1]charged
him, and said to him: [b]"You shall
not take a wife from the daughters
of Canaan.
2 [a]"Arise, go to [b]Padan Aram,
to the house of [c]Bethuel your
mother's father; and take your-
self a wife from there of the
daughters of [d]Laban your mother's
brother.

3 "May [a]God Almighty bless you,
And make you [b]fruitful and
multiply you,
That you may be an assembly of
peoples;
4 And give you [a]the blessing of
Abraham,
To you and your descendants
with you,
That you may inherit the land
[b]In[1] which you are a stranger,
Which God gave to Abraham."

5 So Isaac sent Jacob away, and
he went to Padan Aram, to Laban
the son of Bethuel the Syrian, the

41 [a]Gen. 26:27; 32:3–11; 37:4, 5, 8 [b]Gen. 50:2–4, 10 [c]Obad. 10 [1]*are soon here*
42 [a]Ps. 64:5
43 [a]Gen. 11:31; 25:20; 28:2, 5
44 [a]Gen. 31:41
46 [a]Gen. 26:34, 35; 28:8 [b]Gen. 24:3

CHAPTER 28
1 [a]Gen. 27:33 [b]Gen. 24:3 [1]*commanded*
2 [a]Hos. 12:12 [b]Gen. 25:20 [c]Gen. 22:23 [d]Gen. 24:29; 27:43; 29:5
3 [a]Gen. 17:16; 35:11; 48:3 [b]Gen. 26:4, 24
4 [a]Gen. 12:2, 3; 22:17 [b]Gen. 17:8; 23:4; 36:7 [1]Lit. *Of your sojournings*
8 [a]Gen. 24:3; 26:34, 35; 27:46
9 [a]Gen. 26:34, 35 [b]Gen. 36:2, 3 [c]Gen. 25:13
10 [a]Hos. 12:12 [b]Gen. 12:4, 5; 27:43; 29:4
12 [a]Gen. 31:10; 41:1 [b]John 1:51
13 [a]Gen. 35:1; 48:3 [b]Gen. 26:24 [c]Gen. 13:15, 17; 26:3; 35:12
14 [a]Gen. 13:16; 22:17 [b]Gen. 13:14, 15 [c]Gen. 12:3; 18:18; 22:18; 26:4
15 [a]Gen. 26:3, 24; 31:3 [b]Gen. 48:16 [c]Gen. 35:6; 48:21 [d]Deut. 7:9; 31:6, 8 [e]Num. 23:19 [1]*protect*
16 [a]Ex. 3:5

brother of Rebekah, the mother of
Jacob and Esau.

Esau Marries Mahalath

6 Esau saw that Isaac had
blessed Jacob and sent him away
to Padan Aram to take himself a
wife from there, *and that* as he
blessed him he gave him a charge,
saying, "You shall not take a wife
from the daughters of Canaan,"
7 and that Jacob had obeyed his
father and his mother and had
gone to Padan Aram.
8 Also Esau saw [a]that the daugh-
ters of Canaan did not please his
father Isaac.
9 So Esau went to Ishmael and
[a]took [b]Mahalath the daughter of
Ishmael, Abraham's son, [c]the sis-
ter of Nebajoth, to be his wife in
addition to the wives he had.

Jacob's Vow at Bethel

10 Now Jacob [a]went out from
Beersheba and went toward [b]Ha-
ran.
11 So he came to a certain place
and stayed there all night, because
the sun had set. And he took one
of the stones of that place and put
it at his head, and he lay down in
that place to sleep.
12 Then he [a]dreamed, and behold,
a ladder *was* set up on the earth,
and its top reached to heaven; and
there [b]the angels of God were as-
cending and descending on it.
13 [a]And behold, the LORD stood
above it and said: [b]"I *am* the LORD
God of Abraham your father and
the God of Isaac; [c]the land on
which you lie I will give to you and
your descendants.
14 "Also your [a]descendants shall
be as the dust of the earth; you
shall spread abroad [b]to the west
and the east, to the north and the
south; and in you and [c]in your seed
all the families of the earth shall
be blessed.
15 "Behold, [a]I *am* with you and
will [b]keep[1] you wherever you go,
and will [c]bring you back to this
land; for [d]I will not leave you [e]until
I have done what I have spoken
to you."
16 Then Jacob awoke from his
sleep and said, "Surely the LORD
is in [a]this place, and I did not know
it."

17 And he was afraid and said,
"How awesome *is* this place! This
is none other than the house of
God, and this *is* the gate of
heaven!"
18 Then Jacob rose early in the
morning, and took the stone that
he had put at his head, [a]set it up
as a pillar, [b]and poured oil on top
of it.
19 And he called the name of [a]that
place [1]Bethel; but the name of that
city had been Luz previously.
20 [a]Then Jacob made a vow, say-
ing, "If [b]God will be with me, and
keep me in this way that I am go-
ing, and give me [c]bread to eat and
clothing to put on,
21 "so that [a]I come back to my fa-
ther's house in peace, [b]then the
LORD shall be my God.
22 "And this stone which I have
set as a pillar [a]shall be God's
house, [b]and of all that You give me
I will surely give a [1]tenth to You."

Jacob Meets Rachel

29 So Jacob went on his jour-
ney [a]and came to the land
of the people of the East.
2 And he looked, and saw a [a]well
in the field; and behold, there *were*
three flocks of sheep lying by it;
for out of that well they watered
the flocks. A large stone *was* on
the well's mouth.
3 Now all the flocks would be
gathered there; and they would
roll the stone from the well's
mouth, water the sheep, and put
the stone back in its place on the
well's mouth.
4 And Jacob said to them, "My
brethren, where *are* you from?"
And they said, "We *are* from
[a]Haran."
5 Then he said to them, "Do you
know [a]Laban the son of Nahor?"
And they said, "We know him."
6 So he said to them, [a]"Is he
well?" And they said, "*He is* well.
And look, his daughter Rachel [b]is
coming with the sheep."
7 Then he said, "Look, *it is* still
[1]high day; *it is* not time for the
cattle to be gathered together.
Water the sheep, and go and feed
them."
8 But they said, "We cannot until
all the flocks are gathered to-
gether, and they have rolled the
stone from the well's mouth; then
we water the sheep."
9 Now while he was still speak-
ing with them, [a]Rachel came with
her father's sheep, for she was a
shepherdess.
10 And it came to pass, when Ja-
cob saw Rachel the daughter of
Laban his mother's brother, and
the sheep of Laban his mother's
brother, that Jacob went near and
[a]rolled the stone from the well's
mouth, and watered the flock of
Laban his mother's brother.
11 Then Jacob [a]kissed Rachel,
and lifted up his voice and wept.
12 And Jacob told Rachel that he
was [a]her father's relative and that
he *was* Rebekah's son. [b]So she ran
and told her father.
13 Then it came to pass, when La-
ban heard the report about Jacob
his sister's son, that [a]he ran to
meet him, and embraced him and
kissed him, and brought him to his
house. So he told Laban all these
things.
14 And Laban said to him,
[a]"Surely you *are* my bone and my
flesh." And he stayed with him for
a month.

Jacob Marries Leah and Rachel

15 Then Laban said to Jacob, "Be-
cause you *are* my relative, should
you therefore serve me for noth-
ing? Tell me, [a]what *should* your
wages *be*?"
16 Now Laban had two daughters:
the name of the elder *was* Leah,
and the name of the younger *was*
Rachel.
17 Leah's eyes *were* [1]delicate, but
Rachel was [a]beautiful of form and
appearance.
18 Now Jacob loved Rachel; so
he said, [a]"I will serve you seven
years for Rachel your younger
daughter."
19 And Laban said, "*It is* better
that I give her to you than that I
should give her to another man.
Stay with me."
20 So Jacob [a]served seven years
for Rachel, and they seemed *only*
a few days to him because of the
love he had for her.
21 Then Jacob said to Laban,
"Give *me* my wife, for my days are
fulfilled, that I may [a]go in to her."
22 And Laban gathered together

18 [a]Gen. 31:13, 45 [b]Lev. 8:10–12
19 [a]Judg. 1:23, 26 [1]Lit. *House of God*
20 [a]Judg. 11:30 [b]Gen. 28:15 [c]1 Tim. 6:8
21 [a]Judg. 11:31 [b]Deut. 26:17
22 [a]Gen. 35:7, 14 [b]Gen. 14:20 [1]*tithe*

CHAPTER 29

1 [a]Num. 23:7
2 [a]Gen. 24:10, 11
4 [a]Gen. 11:31; 28:10
5 [a]Gen. 24:24, 29; 28:2
6 [a]Gen. 43:27 [b]Ex. 2:16, 17
7 [1]*early in the day*
9 [a]Ex. 2:16
10 [a]Ex. 2:17
11 [a]Gen. 33:4; 45:14, 15
12 [a]Gen. 13:8; 14:14, 16; 28:5 [b]Gen. 24:28
13 [a]Gen. 24:29–31
14 [a]Gen. 2:23; 37:27
15 [a]Gen. 30:28; 31:41
17 [a]Gen. 12:11, 14; 26:7 [1]Or *weak*
18 [a]Gen. 31:41
20 [a]Gen. 30:26
21 [a]Judg. 15:1

all the men of the place and [a]made
a feast.
23 Now it came to pass in the eve-
ning, that he took Leah his daugh-
ter and brought her to Jacob; and
he went in to her.
24 And Laban gave his maid [a]Zil-
pah to his daughter Leah *as* a
maid.
25 So it came to pass in the morn-
ing, that behold, it *was* Leah. And
he said to Laban, "What is this you
have done to me? Was it not for
Rachel that I served you? Why
then have you [a]deceived me?"
26 And Laban said, "It must not
be done so in our [1]country, to give
the younger before the firstborn.
27 [a]"Fulfill her week, and we will
give you this one also for the ser-
vice which you will serve with me
still another seven years."
28 Then Jacob did so and fulfilled
her week. So he gave him his
daughter Rachel as wife also.
29 And Laban gave his maid [a]Bil-
hah to his daughter Rachel as a
maid.
30 Then *Jacob* also went in to Ra-
chel, and he also [a]loved Rachel
more than Leah. And he served
with Laban [b]still another seven
years.

The Children of Jacob

31 When the LORD [a]saw that Leah
was [1]unloved, He [b]opened her
womb; but Rachel *was* barren.
32 So Leah conceived and bore a
son, and she called his name [1]Reu-
ben; for she said, "The LORD has
surely [a]looked on my affliction.
Now therefore, my husband will
love me."
33 Then she conceived again and
bore a son, and said, "Because the
LORD has heard that I *am* [1]unloved,
He has therefore given me this *son*
also." And she called his name
[2]Simeon.
34 She conceived again and bore
a son, and said, "Now this time my
husband will become attached to
me, because I have borne him
three sons." Therefore his name
was called [1]Levi.
35 And she conceived again and
bore a son, and said, "Now I will
praise the LORD." Therefore she
called his name [a]Judah.[1] Then she
stopped bearing.

30 Now when Rachel saw that
[a]she bore Jacob no children,
Rachel [b]envied her sister, and said
to Jacob, "Give me children, [c]or
else I die!"
2 And Jacob's anger was aroused
against Rachel, and he said, [a]"*Am*
I in the place of God, who has
withheld from you the fruit of the
womb?"
3 So she said, "Here is [a]my maid
Bilhah; go in to her, [b]and she will
bear *a child* on my knees, [c]that I
also may [1]have children by her."
4 Then she gave him Bilhah her
maid [a]as wife, and Jacob went in
to her.
5 And Bilhah conceived and bore
Jacob a son.
6 Then Rachel said, "God has
[a]judged my case; and He has also
heard my voice and given me a
son." Therefore she called his
name [1]Dan.
7 And Rachel's maid Bilhah con-
ceived again and bore Jacob a sec-
ond son.
8 Then Rachel said, "With [1]great
wrestlings I have wrestled with my
sister, *and* indeed I have pre-
vailed." So she called his name
[2]Naphtali.
9 When Leah saw that she had
stopped bearing, she took Zilpah
her maid and [a]gave her to Jacob
as wife.
10 And Leah's maid Zilpah bore
Jacob a son.
11 Then Leah said, [1]"A troop
comes!" So she called his name
[2]Gad.
12 And Leah's maid Zilpah bore
Jacob a second son.
13 Then Leah said, "I am happy,
for the daughters [a]will call me
blessed." So she called his name
[1]Asher.
14 Now Reuben went in the days
of wheat harvest and found man-
drakes in the field, and brought
them to his mother Leah. Then Ra-
chel said to Leah, [a]"Please give me
some of your son's mandrakes."
15 But she said to her, [a]"*Is it* a
small matter that you have taken
away my husband? Would you
take away my son's mandrakes
also?" And Rachel said, "There-
fore he will lie with you tonight for
your son's mandrakes."
16 When Jacob came out of the

22 [a]John 2:1, 2
24 [a]Gen. 30:9, 10
25 [a]Gen. 27:35; 31:7; 1 Sam. 28:12
26 [1]Lit. *place*
27 [a]Gen. 31:41; Judg. 14:2
29 [a]Gen. 30:3–5
30 [a]Gen. 29:17–20; Deut. 21:15–17 [b]Gen. 30:26; 31:41; Hos. 12:12
31 [a]Ps. 127:3 [b]Gen. 30:1 [1]Lit. *hated*
32 [a]Gen. 16:11; 31:42; Ex. 3:7; 4:31; Deut. 26:7; Ps. 25:18 [1]Lit. *See, a Son*
33 [1]Lit. *hated* [2]Lit. *Heard*
34 [1]Lit. *Attached*
35 [a]Gen. 49:8; Matt. 1:2 [1]Lit. *Praise*

CHAPTER 30
1 [a]Gen. 16:1, 2; 29:31 [b]Gen. 37:11 [c]1 Sam. 1:5, 6; [Job 5:2]
2 [a]Gen. 16:2; 1 Sam. 1:5
3 [a]Gen. 16:2 [b]Gen. 50:23; Job 3:12 [c]Gen. 16:2, 3 [1]Lit. *be built up by her*
4 [a]Gen. 16:3, 4
6 [a]Gen. 18:25; Ps. 35:24; 43:1; Lam. 3:59 [1]Lit. *Judge*
8 [1]Lit. *wrestlings of God* [2]Lit. *My Wrestling*
9 [a]Gen. 30:4
11 [1]So with Qr., Syr., Tg.; Kt., LXX, Vg. *in fortune* [2]Lit. *Troop* or *Fortune*
13 [a]Prov. 31:28; Luke 1:48 [1]Lit. *Happy*
14 [a]Gen. 25:30
15 [a][Num. 16:9, 13]

field in the evening, Leah went out
to meet him and said, "You must
come in to me, for I have surely
hired you with my son's man-
drakes." And he lay with her that
night.
17 And God listened to Leah, and
she conceived and bore Jacob a
fifth son.
18 Leah said, "God has given me
my wages, because I have given
my maid to my husband." So she
called his name [1]Issachar.
19 Then Leah conceived again
and bore Jacob a sixth son.
20 And Leah said, "God has en-
dowed me *with* a good endow-
ment; now my husband will dwell
with me, because I have borne him
six sons." So she called his name
[1]Zebulun.
21 Afterward she bore a [a]daugh-
ter, and called her name [1]Dinah.
22 Then God [a]remembered Ra-
chel, and God listened to her and
[b]opened her womb.
23 And she conceived and bore a
son, and said, "God has taken
away [a]my reproach."
24 So she called his name [1]Joseph,
and said, [a]"The LORD shall add to
me another son."

Jacob's Agreement with Laban

25 And it came to pass, when Ra-
chel had borne Joseph, that Jacob
said to Laban, [a]"Send me away,
that I may go to [b]my own place
and to my country.
26 "Give *me* my wives and my
children [a]for whom I have served
you, and let me go; for you know
my service which I have done for
you."
27 And Laban said to him, "Please
stay, if I have found favor in your
eyes, *for* [a]I have learned by experi-
ence that the LORD has blessed me
for your sake."
28 Then he said, [a]"Name me your
wages, and I will give *it*."
29 So *Jacob* said to him, [a]"You
know how I have served you and
how your livestock has been with
me.
30 "For what you had before I
came was little, and it has in-
creased to a great amount; the
LORD has blessed you [1]since my
coming. And now, when shall I
also [a]provide for my own house?"
31 So he said, "What shall I give
you?" And Jacob said, "You shall
not give me anything. If you will
do this thing for me, I will again
feed and keep your flocks:
32 "Let me pass through all your
flock today, removing from there
all the speckled and spotted sheep,
and all the brown ones among the
lambs, and the spotted and speck-
led among the goats; and [a]*these*
shall be my wages.
33 "So my [a]righteousness will an-
swer for me in time to come, when
the subject of my wages comes be-
fore you: every one that *is* not
speckled and spotted among the
goats, and brown among the
lambs, will be considered stolen,
if *it is* with me."
34 And Laban said, "Oh, that it
were according to your word!"
35 So he removed that day the
male goats that were [a]speckled
and spotted, all the female goats
that were speckled and spotted,
every one that had *some* white in
it, and all the brown ones among
the lambs, and gave *them* into the
hand of his sons.
36 Then he put three days' jour-
ney between himself and Jacob,
and Jacob fed the rest of Laban's
flocks.
37 Now [a]Jacob took for himself
rods of green poplar and of the al-
mond and chestnut trees, peeled
white strips in them, and exposed
the white which *was* in the
rods.
38 And the rods which he had
peeled, he set before the flocks in
the gutters, in the watering
troughs where the flocks came to
drink, so that they should conceive
when they came to drink.
39 So the flocks conceived before
the rods, and the flocks brought
forth streaked, speckled, and spot-
ted.
40 Then Jacob separated the
lambs, and made the flocks face
toward the streaked and all the
brown in the flock of Laban; but
he put his own flocks by them-
selves and did not put them with
Laban's flock.
41 And it came to pass, whenever
the stronger livestock conceived,
that Jacob placed the rods before
the eyes of the livestock in the

18 [1]Lit. *Wages*
20 [1]Lit. *Dwelling*
21 [a]Gen. 34:1 [1]Lit. *Judgment*
22 [a]Gen. 19:29; 1 Sam. 1:19, 20 [b]Gen. 29:31
23 [a]1 Sam. 1:6; Is. 4:1; Luke 1:25
24 [a]Gen. 35:16–18 [1]Lit. *He Will Add*
25 [a]Gen. 24:54, 56 [b]Gen. 18:33
26 [a]Gen. 29:18–20, 27, 30; Hos. 12:12
27 [a]Gen. 26:24; 39:3; Is. 61:9
28 [a]Gen. 29:15; 31:7, 41
29 [a]Gen. 31:6, 38–40; Matt. 24:45; Titus 2:10
30 [a][1 Tim. 5:8] [1]Lit. *at my foot*
32 [a]Gen. 31:8
33 [a]Ps. 37:6
35 [a]Gen. 31:9–12
37 [a]Gen. 31:9–12

gutters, that they might conceive
among the rods.
42 But when the flocks were fee-
ble, he did not put *them* in; so the
feebler were Laban's and the
stronger Jacob's.
43 Thus the man [a]became exceed-
ingly prosperous, and [b]had large
flocks, female and male servants,
and camels and donkeys.

Jacob Flees from Laban

31 Now *Jacob* heard the words
of Laban's sons, saying, "Ja-
cob has taken away all that was
our father's, and from what was
our father's he has acquired all
this [a]wealth."
2 And Jacob saw the [a]counte-
nance of Laban, and indeed it *was*
not [b]*favorable* toward him as be-
fore.
3 Then the LORD said to Jacob,
[a]"Return to the land of your fa-
thers and to your family, and I will
[b]be with you."
4 So Jacob sent and called Ra-
chel and Leah to the field, to his
flock,
5 and said to them, [a]"I see your
father's [1]countenance, that it *is* not
favorable toward me as before; but
the God of my father [b]has been
with me.
6 "And [a]you know that with all
my might I have served your fa-
ther.
7 "Yet your father has deceived
me and [a]changed my wages [b]ten
times, but God [c]did not allow him
to hurt me.
8 "If he said thus: [a]'The speckled
shall be your wages,' then all the
flocks bore speckled. And if he
said thus: 'The streaked shall be
your wages,' then all the flocks
bore streaked.
9 "So God has [a]taken away the
livestock of your father and given
them to me.
10 "And it happened, at the time
when the flocks conceived, that I
lifted my eyes and saw in a dream,
and behold, the rams which leaped
upon the flocks *were* streaked,
speckled, and gray-spotted.
11 "Then [a]the Angel of God spoke
to me in a dream, saying, 'Jacob.'
And I said, 'Here I am.'
12 "And He said, 'Lift your eyes
now and see, all the rams which
leap on the flocks *are* streaked,
speckled, and gray-spotted; for [a]I
have seen all that Laban is doing
to you.
13 'I *am* the God of Bethel, [a]where
you anointed the pillar *and* where
you made a vow to Me. Now
[b]arise, get out of this land, and re-
turn to the land of your family.'"
14 Then Rachel and Leah an-
swered and said to him, [a]"Is there
still any portion or inheritance for
us in our father's house?
15 "Are we not considered strang-
ers by him? For [a]he has sold us,
and also completely consumed our
money.
16 "For all these riches which God
has taken from our father are *re-*
ally ours and our children's; now
then, whatever God has said to
you, do it."
17 Then Jacob rose and set his
sons and his wives on camels.
18 And he carried away all his
livestock and all his possessions
which he had gained, his acquired
livestock which he had gained in
Padan Aram, to go to his father
Isaac in the land of [a]Canaan.
19 Now Laban had gone to shear
his sheep, and Rachel had stolen
the [a]household[1] idols that were her
father's.
20 And Jacob stole away, un-
known to Laban the Syrian, in that
he did not tell him that he intended
to flee.
21 So he fled with all that he had.
He arose and crossed the river,
and [a]headed[1] toward the moun-
tains of Gilead.

Laban Pursues Jacob

22 And Laban was told on the
third day that Jacob had fled.
23 Then he took [a]his brethren
with him and pursued him for
seven days' journey, and he over-
took him in the mountains of
Gilead.
24 But God [a]had come to Laban
the Syrian in a dream by night,
and said to him, "Be careful that
you [b]speak to Jacob neither good
nor bad."
25 So Laban overtook Jacob. Now
Jacob had pitched his tent in the
mountains, and Laban with his
brethren pitched in the mountains
of Gilead.

43 [a]Gen. 12:16; 30:30 [b]Gen. 13:2; 24:35; 26:13, 14

CHAPTER 31

1 [a]Ps. 49:16
2 [a]Gen. 4:5 [b]Deut. 28:54
3 [a]Gen. 28:15, 20, 21; 32:9 [b]Gen. 46:4
5 [a]Gen. 31:2, 3 [b]Gen. 21:22; 28:13, 15; 31:29, 42, 53; Is. 41:10; Heb. 13:5 [1]Lit. *face*
6 [a]Gen. 30:29; 31:38–41
7 [a]Gen. 29:25; 31:41 [b]Num. 14:22; Neh. 4:12; Job 19:3; Zech. 8:23 [c]Gen. 15:1; 20:6; 31:29; Job 1:10; Ps. 37:28; 105:14
8 [a]Gen. 30:32
9 [a]Gen. 31:1, 16
11 [a]Gen. 16:7–11; 22:11, 15; 31:13; 48:16
12 [a]Gen. 31:42; Ex. 3:7; Ps. 139:3; Eccl. 5:8
13 [a]Gen. 28:16–22; 35:1, 6, 15 [b]Gen. 31:3; 32:9
14 [a]Gen. 2:24
15 [a]Gen. 29:15, 20, 23, 27; Neh. 5:8
18 [a]Gen. 17:8; 33:18; 35:27
19 [a]Gen. 31:30, 34; 35:2; Judg. 17:5; 1 Sam. 19:13; Hos. 3:4 [1]Heb. *teraphim*
21 [a]Gen. 46:28; 2 Kin. 12:17; Luke 9:51, 53 [1]Lit. *set his face toward*
23 [a]Gen. 13:8
24 [a]Gen. 20:3; 31:29; 46:2–4; Job 33:15; Matt. 1:20 [b]Gen. 24:50; 31:7, 29

26 And Laban said to Jacob:
"What have you done, that you
have stolen away unknown to
me, and [a]carried away my daugh-
ters like captives *taken* with the
sword?
27 "Why did you flee away se-
cretly, and steal away from me,
and not tell me; for I might have
sent you away with joy and songs,
with timbrel and harp?
28 "And you did not allow me [a]to
kiss my sons and my daughters.
Now [b]you have done foolishly in
so doing.
29 "It is in my power to do you
harm, but the [a]God of your father
spoke to me [b]last night, saying, 'Be
careful that you speak to Jacob
neither good nor bad.'
30 "And now you have surely
gone because you greatly long for
your father's house, *but* why did
you [a]steal my gods?"
31 Then Jacob answered and said
to Laban, "Because I was [a]afraid,
for I said, 'Perhaps you would take
your daughters from me by
force.'
32 "With whomever you find your
gods, [a]do not let him live. In the
presence of our brethren, identify
what I have of yours and take *it*
with you." For Jacob did not know
that Rachel had stolen them.
33 And Laban went into Jacob's
tent, into Leah's tent, and into the
two maids' tents, but he did not
find *them*. Then he went out of
Leah's tent and entered Rachel's
tent.
34 Now Rachel had taken the
[1]household idols, put them in the
camel's saddle, and sat on them.
And Laban [2]searched all about the
tent but did not find *them*.
35 And she said to her father, "Let
it not displease my lord that I can-
not [a]rise before you, for the man-
ner of women *is* with me." And he
searched but did not find the
[1]household idols.
36 Then Jacob was angry and re-
buked Laban, and Jacob answered
and said to Laban: "What *is* my
[1]trespass? What *is* my sin, that you
have so hotly pursued me?
37 "Although you have searched
all my things, what part of your
household things have you found?
Set *it* here before my brethren and
your brethren, that they may judge
between us both!
38 "These twenty years I *have
been* with you; your ewes and your
female goats have not miscarried
their young, and I have not eaten
the rams of your flock.
39 [a]"That which was torn *by
beasts* I did not bring to you; I bore
the loss of it. [b]You required it from
my hand, *whether* stolen by day
or stolen by night.
40 "*There* I was! In the day the
drought consumed me, and the
frost by night, and my sleep de-
parted from my eyes.
41 "Thus I have been in your
house twenty years; I [a]served you
fourteen years for your two daugh-
ters, and six years for your flock,
and [b]you have changed my wages
ten times.
42 [a]"Unless the God of my father,
the God of Abraham and [b]the Fear
of Isaac, had been with me, surely
now you would have sent me away
empty-handed. [c]God has seen my
affliction and the labor of my
hands, and [d]rebuked *you* last
night."

Laban's Covenant with Jacob

43 And Laban answered and said
to Jacob, "*These* daughters *are* my
daughters, and *these* children *are*
my children, and *this* flock *is* my
flock; all that you see *is* mine. But
what can I do this day to these my
daughters or to their children
whom they have borne?
44 "Now therefore, come, [a]let us
make a [1]covenant, [b]you and I, and
let it be a witness between you and
me."
45 So Jacob [a]took a stone and set
it up *as* a pillar.
46 Then Jacob said to his breth-
ren, "Gather stones." And they
took stones and made a heap, and
they ate there on the heap.
47 Laban called it [1]Jegar Sahadu-
tha, but Jacob called it [2]Galeed.
48 And Laban said, [a]"This heap *is*
a witness between you and me this
day." Therefore its name was
called Galeed,
49 also [a]Mizpah,[1] because he said,
"May the LORD watch between you
and me when we are absent one
from another.
50 "If you afflict my daughters, or

26 [a]1 Sam. 30:2
28 [a]Gen. 31:55; Ruth 1:9, 14; 1 Kin. 19:20; Acts 20:37 [b]1 Sam. 13:13
29 [a]Gen. 28:13; 31:5, 24, 42, 53 [b]Gen. 31:24
30 [a]Gen. 31:19; Josh. 24:2; Judg. 17:5; 18:24
31 [a]Gen. 26:7; 32:7, 11
32 [a]Gen. 44:9
34 [1]Heb. *teraphim* [2]Lit. *felt*
35 [a]Ex. 20:12; Lev. 19:32 [1]Heb. *teraphim*
36 [1]*transgression*
39 [a]Ex. 22:10 [b]Ex. 22:10–13
41 [a]Gen. 29:20, 27–30 [b]Gen. 31:7
42 [a]Gen. 31:5, 29, 53; Ps. 124:1, 2 [b]Gen. 31:53; Is. 8:13 [c]Gen. 29:32; Ex. 3:7 [d]Gen. 31:24, 29; 1 Chr. 12:17
44 [a]Gen. 21:27, 32; 26:28 [b]Josh. 24:27 [1]*treaty*
45 [a]Gen. 28:18; 35:14; Josh. 24:26, 27
47 [1]Lit., in Aram., *Heap of Witness* [2]Lit., in Heb., *Heap of Witness*
48 [a]Josh. 24:27
49 [a]Judg. 10:17; 11:29; 1 Sam. 7:5, 6 [1]Lit. *Watch*

if you take *other* wives besides my
daughters, *although* no man *is*
with us—see, God *is* witness be-
tween you and me!"
51 Then Laban said to Jacob,
"Here is this heap and here is *this*
pillar, which I have placed be-
tween you and me.
52 "This heap *is* a witness, and
this pillar *is* a witness, that I will
not pass beyond this heap to you,
and you will not pass beyond this
heap and this pillar to me, for
harm.
53 "The God of Abraham, the God
of Nahor, and the God of their fa-
ther [a]judge between us." And Ja-
cob [b]swore by [c]the [1]Fear of his fa-
ther Isaac.
54 Then Jacob offered a sacrifice
on the mountain, and called his
brethren to eat bread. And they ate
bread and stayed all night on the
mountain.
55 And early in the morning La-
ban arose, and [a]kissed his sons
and daughters and [b]blessed them.
Then Laban departed and [c]re-
turned to his place.

Esau Comes to Meet Jacob

32 So Jacob went on his way,
and [a]the angels of God met
him.
2 When Jacob saw them, he said,
"This *is* God's [a]camp." And he
called the name of that place
[1]Mahanaim.
3 Then Jacob sent messengers
before him to Esau his brother [a]in
the land of Seir, [b]the [1]country of
Edom.
4 And he commanded them, say-
ing, [a]"Speak thus to my lord Esau,
'Thus your servant Jacob says: "I
have dwelt with Laban and stayed
there until now.
5 [a]"I have oxen, donkeys, flocks,
and male and female servants; and
I have sent to tell my lord, that [b]I
may find favor in your sight." ' "
6 Then the messengers returned
to Jacob, saying, "We came to
your brother Esau, and [a]he also is
coming to meet you, and four hun-
dred men *are* with him."
7 So Jacob was greatly afraid
and [a]distressed; and he divided the
people that *were* with him, and the
flocks and herds and camels, into
two companies.
8 And he said, "If Esau comes to
the one company and [1]attacks it,
then the other company which is
left will escape."
9 [a]Then Jacob said, [b]"O God of
my father Abraham and God of my
father Isaac, the LORD [c]who said
to me, 'Return to your country and
to your family, and I will deal well
with you':
10 "I am not worthy of the least
of all the [a]mercies and of all the
truth which You have shown Your
servant; for I crossed over this Jor-
dan with [b]my staff, and now I have
become two companies.
11 [a]"Deliver me, I pray, from the
hand of my brother, from the hand
of Esau; for I fear him, lest he
come and [1]attack me *and* [b]the
mother with the children.
12 "For [a]You said, 'I will surely
treat you well, and make your de-
scendants as the [b]sand of the sea,
which cannot be numbered for
multitude.' "
13 So he lodged there that same
night, and took what [1]came to his
hand as [a]a present for Esau his
brother:
14 two hundred female goats and
twenty male goats, two hundred
ewes and twenty rams,
15 thirty milk camels with their
colts, forty cows and ten bulls,
twenty female donkeys and ten
foals.
16 Then he delivered *them* to the
hand of his servants, every drove
by itself, and said to his servants,
"Pass over before me, and put
some distance between successive
droves."
17 And he commanded the first
one, saying, "When Esau my
brother meets you and asks you,
saying, 'To whom do you belong,
and where are you going? Whose
are these in front of you?'
18 "then you shall say, 'They *are*
your servant Jacob's. It *is* a pres-
ent sent to my lord Esau; and be-
hold, he also *is* behind us.' "
19 So he commanded the second,
the third, and all who followed the
droves, saying, "In this manner
you shall speak to Esau when you
find him;
20 "and also say, 'Behold, your
servant Jacob *is* behind us.' " For
he said, "I will [a]appease him with

53 [a]Gen. 16:5 [b]Gen. 21:23 [c]Gen. 31:42 [1]A reference to God
55 [a]Gen. 29:11, 13; 31:28, 43 [b]Gen. 28:1 [c]Gen. 18:33; 30:25; Num. 24:25

CHAPTER 32

1 [a]Num. 22:31; 2 Kin. 6:16, 17; [Ps. 34:7; 91:1; Heb. 1:14]
2 [a]Josh. 5:14; Ps. 103:21; 148:2; Luke 2:13 [1]Lit. *Double Camp*
3 [a]Gen. 14:6; 33:14, 16 [b]Gen. 25:30; 36:6–9; Deut. 2:5; Josh. 24:4 [1]Lit. *field*
4 [a]Prov. 15:1
5 [a]Gen. 30:43 [b]Gen. 33:8, 15
6 [a]Gen. 33:1
7 [a]Gen. 32:11; 35:3
8 [1]Lit. *strikes*
9 [a][Ps. 50:15] [b]Gen. 28:13; 31:42 [c]Gen. 31:3, 13
10 [a]Gen. 24:27 [b]Job 8:7
11 [a]Ps. 59:1, 2 [b]Hos. 10:14 [1]Lit. *strike*
12 [a]Gen. 28:13–15 [b]Gen. 22:17
13 [a]Gen. 43:11 [1]*he had received*
20 [a][Prov. 21:14]

the present that goes before me,
and afterward I will see his face;
perhaps he will accept me."
21 So the present went on over be-
fore him, but he himself lodged
that night in the camp.

Wrestling with God

22 And he arose that night and
took his two wives, his two female
servants, and his eleven sons, [a]and
crossed over the ford of Jabbok.
23 He took them, sent them [1]over
the brook, and sent over what he
had.
24 Then Jacob was left alone; and
[a]a Man wrestled with him until the
[1]breaking of day.
25 Now when He saw that He
did not prevail against him, He
[1]touched the socket of his hip; and
[a]the socket of Jacob's hip was out
of joint as He wrestled with him.
26 And [a]He said, "Let Me go, for
the day breaks." But he said, [b]"I
will not let You go unless You
bless me!"
27 So He said to him, "What *is*
your name?" He said, "Jacob."
28 And He said, [a]"Your name
shall no longer be called Jacob, but
[1]Israel; for you have [b]struggled
with God and [c]with men, and have
prevailed."
29 Then Jacob asked, saying,
"Tell *me* Your name, I pray." And
He said, [a]"Why *is* it *that* you ask
about My name?" And He [b]blessed
him there.
30 So Jacob called the name of the
place [1]Peniel: "For [a]I have seen
God face to face, and my life is pre-
served."
31 Just as he crossed over [1]Penuel
the sun rose on him, and he limped
on his hip.
32 Therefore to this day the chil-
dren of Israel do not eat the muscle
that shrank, which *is* on the hip
socket, because He [1]touched the
socket of Jacob's hip in the muscle
that shrank.

Jacob and Esau Meet

33 Now Jacob lifted his eyes
and looked, and there, [a]Esau
was coming, and with him were
four hundred men. So he divided
the children among Leah, Rachel,
and the two maidservants.
2 And he put the maidservants
and their children in front, Leah
and her children behind, and Ra-
chel and Joseph last.
3 Then he crossed over before
them and [a]bowed himself to the
ground seven times, until he came
near to his brother.
4 [a]But Esau ran to meet him, and
embraced him, [b]and fell on his
neck and kissed him, and they
wept.
5 And he lifted his eyes and saw
the women and children, and said,
"Who *are* these with you?" So he
said, "The children [a]whom God
has graciously given your ser-
vant."
6 Then the maidservants came
near, they and their children, and
bowed down.
7 And Leah also came near with
her children, and they bowed
down. Afterward Joseph and Ra-
chel came near, and they bowed
down.
8 Then Esau said, "What *do* you
mean by [a]all this company which
I met?" And he said, "*These are*
[b]to find favor in the sight of my
lord."
9 But Esau said, "I have enough,
my brother; keep what you have
for yourself."
10 And Jacob said, "No, please, if
I have now found favor in your
sight, then receive my present
from my hand, inasmuch as I
[a]have seen your face as though I
had seen the face of God, and you
were pleased with me.
11 "Please, take [a]my blessing that
is brought to you, because God has
dealt [b]graciously with me, and be-
cause I have [1]enough." [c]So he
urged him, and he took *it*.
12 Then Esau said, "Let us take
our journey; let us go, and I will
go before you."
13 But Jacob said to him, "My lord
knows that the children *are* weak,
and the flocks and herds which are
nursing *are* with me. And if the
men should drive them hard one
day, all the flock will die.
14 "Please let my lord go on ahead
before his servant. I will lead on
slowly at a pace which the live-
stock that go before me, and the
children, [1]are able to endure, until
I come to my lord [a]in Seir."
15 And Esau said, "Now let me

22 [a]Num. 21:24; Deut. 3:16; Josh. 12:2
23 [1]*across*
24 [a]Josh. 5:13–15; Hos. 12:2–4 [1]*dawn*
25 [a]Matt. 26:41; 2 Cor. 12:7 [1]*struck*
26 [a]Luke 24:28 [b]Hos. 12:4
28 [a]Gen. 35:10; 1 Kin. 18:31; 2 Kin. 17:34 [b]Hos. 12:3, 4 [c]Gen. 25:31; 27:33 [1]Lit. *Prince with God*
29 [a]Judg. 13:17, 18 [b]Gen. 35:9
30 [a]Gen. 16:13; Ex. 24:10, 11; 33:20; Num. 12:8; Deut. 5:24; Judg. 6:22; Is. 6:5; [Matt. 5:8; 1 Cor. 13:12] [1]Lit. *Face of God*
31 [1]Lit. *Face of God;* same as *Peniel,* v. 30
32 [1]*struck*

CHAPTER 33

1 [a]Gen. 32:6
3 [a]Gen. 18:2; 42:6
4 [a]Gen. 32:28 [b]Gen. 45:14, 15
5 [a]Gen. 48:9; [Ps. 127:3]; Is. 8:18
8 [a]Gen. 32:13–16 [b]Gen. 32:5
10 [a]Gen. 43:3; 2 Sam. 3:13; 14:24, 28, 32
11 [a]Judg. 1:15; 1 Sam. 25:27; 30:26 [b]Gen. 30:43; Ex. 33:19 [c]2 Kin. 5:23 [1]Lit. *all*
14 [a]Gen. 32:3; 36:8 [1]*can stand*

leave with you *some* of the people
who *are* with me." But he said,
"What need is there? [a]Let me find
favor in the sight of my lord."
16 So Esau returned that day on
his way to Seir.
17 And Jacob journeyed to [a]Suc-
coth, built himself a house, and
made [1]booths for his livestock.
Therefore the name of the place
is called [2]Succoth.

Jacob Comes to Canaan

18 Then Jacob came [1]safely to
[a]the city of [b]Shechem, which *is* in
the land of Canaan, when he came
from Padan Aram; and he pitched
his tent before the city.
19 And [a]he bought the parcel of
[1]land, where he had pitched his
tent, from the children of Hamor,
Shechem's father, for one hundred
pieces of money.
20 Then he erected an altar there
and called it [a]El[1] Elohe Israel.

The Dinah Incident

34 Now [a]Dinah the daughter of
Leah, whom she had borne
to Jacob, went out to see the
daughters of the land.
2 And when Shechem the son of
Hamor the Hivite, prince of the
country, saw her, he [a]took her and
lay with her, and violated her.
3 His soul [1]was strongly at-
tracted to Dinah the daughter of
Jacob, and he loved the young
woman and spoke [2]kindly to the
young woman.
4 So Shechem [a]spoke to his fa-
ther Hamor, saying, "Get me this
young woman as a wife."
5 And Jacob heard that he had
defiled Dinah his daughter. Now
his sons were with his livestock in
the field; so Jacob [a]held[1] his peace
until they came.
6 Then Hamor the father of She-
chem went out to Jacob to speak
with him.
7 And the sons of Jacob came in
from the field when they heard *it;*
and the men were grieved and
very angry, because he [a]had done
a disgraceful thing in Israel by ly-
ing with Jacob's daughter, [b]a thing
which ought not to be done.
8 But Hamor spoke with them,
saying, "The soul of my son She-
chem longs for your daughter.
Please give her to him as a wife.
9 "And make marriages with us;
give your daughters to us, and take
our daughters to yourselves.
10 "So you shall dwell with us,
and the land shall be before you.
Dwell and trade in it, and acquire
possessions for yourselves in it."
11 Then Shechem said to her fa-
ther and her brothers, "Let me find
favor in your eyes, and whatever
you say to me I will give.
12 "Ask me ever so much [a]dowry[1]
and gift, and I will give according
to what you say to me; but give
me the young woman as a wife."
13 But the sons of Jacob answered
Shechem and Hamor his father,
and spoke [a]deceitfully, because he
had defiled Dinah their sister.
14 And they said to them, "We
cannot do this thing, to give our
sister to one who is [a]uncircum-
cised, for [b]that *would be* a re-
proach to us.
15 "But on this *condition* we will
consent to you: If you will become
as we *are,* if every male of you is
circumcised,
16 "then we will give our daugh-
ters to you, and we will take your
daughters to us; and we will dwell
with you, and we will become one
people.
17 "But if you will not heed us and
be circumcised, then we will take
our daughter and be gone."
18 And their words pleased Ha-
mor and Shechem, Hamor's son.
19 So the young man did not delay
to do the thing, because he de-
lighted in Jacob's daughter. He
was [a]more honorable than all the
household of his father.
20 And Hamor and Shechem his
son came to the [a]gate of their city,
and spoke with the men of their
city, saying:
21 "These men *are* at peace with
us. Therefore let them dwell in the
land and trade in it. For indeed the
land *is* large enough for them. Let
us take their daughters to us as
wives, and let us give them our
daughters.
22 "Only on this *condition* will the
men consent to dwell with us, to
be one people: if every male
among us is circumcised as they
are circumcised.
23 "*Will* not their livestock, their

15 [a]Gen. 34:11; 47:25; Ruth 2:13
17 [a]Josh. 13:27; Judg. 8:5; Ps. 60:6 [1]*shelters* [2]Lit. *Booths*
18 [a]John 3:23 [b]Gen. 12:6; 35:4; Josh. 24:1; Judg. 9:1; Ps. 60:6 [1]Or *to Shalem, a city of*
19 [a]Josh. 24:32; John 4:5 [1]Lit. *the field*
20 [a]Gen. 35:7 [1]Lit. *God, the God of Israel*

CHAPTER 34

1 [a]Gen. 30:21
2 [a]Gen. 20:2
3 [1]Lit. *clung to* [2]*tenderly*
4 [a]Judg. 14:2
5 [a]2 Sam. 13:22 [1]*kept silent*
7 [a]Deut. 22:20–30; Josh. 7:15; Judg. 20:6 [b]Deut. 23:17; 2 Sam. 13:12
12 [a]Ex. 22:16, 17; Deut. 22:29 [1]*bride-price*
13 [a]Gen. 31:7; Ex. 8:29
14 [a]Ex. 12:48 [b]Josh. 5:2–9
19 [a]1 Chr. 4:9
20 [a]Gen. 19:1; 23:10; Ruth 4:1, 11; 2 Sam. 15:2

property, and every animal of
theirs *be* ours? Only let us consent
to them, and they will dwell with
us."
24 And all who went out of the
gate of his city heeded Hamor and
Shechem his son; every male was
circumcised, all who [a]went out of
the gate of his city.
25 Now it came to pass on the
third day, when they were in
pain, that two of the sons of
Jacob, [a]Simeon and Levi, Dinah's
brothers, each took his sword and
came boldly upon the city and
killed all the males.
26 And they [a]killed Hamor and
Shechem his son with the edge of
the sword, and took Dinah from
Shechem's house, and went out.
27 The sons of Jacob came upon
the slain, and plundered the city,
because their sister had been de-
filed.
28 They took their sheep, their
oxen, and their donkeys, what *was*
in the city and what *was* in the
field,
29 and all their wealth. All their
little ones and their wives they
took captive; and they plundered
even all that *was* in the houses.
30 Then Jacob said to Simeon and
Levi, [a]"You have [b]troubled me [c]by
making me obnoxious among the
inhabitants of the land, among the
Canaanites and the Perizzites;
[d]and since I *am* few in number,
they will gather themselves to-
gether against me and kill me. I
shall be destroyed, my household
and I."
31 But they said, "Should he treat
our sister like a harlot?"

Jacob's Return to Bethel

35 Then God said to Jacob,
"Arise, go up to [a]Bethel and
dwell there; and make an altar
there to God, [b]who appeared to
you [c]when you fled from the face
of Esau your brother."
2 And Jacob said to his [a]house-
hold and to all who *were* with him,
"Put away [b]the foreign gods that
are among you, [c]purify yourselves,
and change your garments.
3 "Then let us arise and go up
to Bethel; and I will make an altar
there to God, [a]who answered me
in the day of my distress [b]and has
been with me in the way which I
have gone."
4 So they gave Jacob all the for-
eign [1]gods which *were* in their
hands, and the [a]earrings which
were in their ears; and Jacob hid
them under [b]the terebinth tree
which *was* by Shechem.
5 And they journeyed, and [a]the
terror of God was upon the cities
that *were* all around them, and
they did not pursue the sons of Ja-
cob.
6 So Jacob came to [a]Luz (that *is,*
Bethel), which *is* in the land of Ca-
naan, he and all the people who
were with him.
7 And he [a]built an altar there and
called the place [1]El Bethel, be-
cause [b]there God appeared to him
when he fled from the face of his
brother.
8 Now [a]Deborah, Rebekah's
nurse, died, and she was buried
below Bethel under the terebinth
tree. So the name of it was called
[1]Allon Bachuth.
9 Then [a]God appeared to Jacob
again, when he came from Padan
Aram, and [b]blessed him.
10 And God said to him, "Your
name *is* Jacob; [a]your name shall
not be called Jacob anymore, [b]but
Israel shall be your name." So He
called his name Israel.
11 Also God said to him: [a]"I *am*
God Almighty. [b]Be fruitful and
multiply; [c]a nation and a company
of nations shall proceed from you,
and kings shall come from your
body.
12 "The [a]land which I gave Abra-
ham and Isaac I give to you; and
to your descendants after you I
give this land."
13 Then God [a]went[1] up from him
in the place where He talked with
him.
14 So Jacob [a]set up a pillar in the
place where He talked with him,
a pillar of stone; and he poured a
drink offering on it, and he poured
oil on it.
15 And Jacob called the name of
the place where God spoke with
him, [a]Bethel.

Death of Rachel

16 Then they journeyed from
Bethel. And when there was but a
little distance to go to Ephrath,

24 [a]Gen. 23:10, 18
25 [a]Gen. 29:33, 34; 42:24; 49:5–7
26 [a]Gen. 49:5, 6
30 [a]Gen. 49:6 [b]Josh. 7:25 [c]Ex. 5:21; 1 Sam. 13:4; 2 Sam. 10:6 [d]Gen. 46:26, 27; Deut. 4:27; 1 Chr. 16:19; Ps. 105:12

CHAPTER 35

1 [a]Gen. 28:19; 31:13 [b]Gen. 28:13 [c]Gen. 27:43
2 [a]Gen. 18:19; Josh. 24:15 [b]Gen. 31:19, 30, 34; Josh. 24:2, 14, 23 [c]Ex. 19:10, 14; Lev. 13:6
3 [a]Gen. 32:7, 24; Ps. 107:6 [b]Gen. 28:15, 20; 31:3, 42
4 [a]Hos. 2:13 [b]Josh. 24:26; Judg. 9:6 [1]*idols*
5 [a]Ex. 15:16; 23:27; [Deut. 2:25; 11:25]; Josh. 2:9; 1 Sam. 14:15
6 [a]Gen. 28:19, 22; 48:3
7 [a]Gen. 33:20; 35:3; Eccl. 5:4 [b]Gen. 28:13 [1]Lit. *God of the House of God*
8 [a]Gen. 24:59 [1]Lit. *Terebinth of Weeping*
9 [a]Josh. 5:13; Dan. 10:5 [b]Gen. 32:29; Hos. 12:4
10 [a]Gen. 17:5 [b]Gen. 32:28
11 [a]Gen. 17:1; 28:3; 48:3, 4; Ex. 6:3 [b]Gen. 9:1, 7 [c]Gen. 17:5, 6, 16; 28:3; 48:4
12 [a]Gen. 12:7; 13:15; 26:3, 4; 28:13; 48:4; Ex. 32:13
13 [a]Gen. 17:22; 18:33 [1]*departed*
14 [a]Gen. 28:18, 19; 31:45
15 [a]Gen. 28:19

Rachel labored *in childbirth*, and
she had hard labor.
17 Now it came to pass, when she
was in hard labor, that the midwife
said to her, "Do not fear; [a]you will
have this son also."
18 And so it was, as her soul was
departing (for she died), that she
called his name [1]Ben-Oni; but his
father called him [2]Benjamin.
19 So [a]Rachel died and was buried
on the way to [b]Ephrath (that *is*,
Bethlehem).
20 And Jacob set a pillar on her
grave, which *is* the pillar of Ra-
chel's grave [a]to this day.
21 Then Israel journeyed and
pitched his tent beyond [a]the tower
of Eder.
22 And it happened, when Israel
dwelt in that land, that Reuben
went and [a]lay with Bilhah his fa-
ther's concubine; and Israel heard
about it.

Jacob's Twelve Sons

Now the sons of Jacob were
twelve:
23 the sons of Leah *were* [a]Reuben,
Jacob's firstborn, and Simeon,
Levi, Judah, Issachar, and Zeb-
ulun;
24 the sons of Rachel *were* Joseph
and Benjamin;
25 the sons of Bilhah, Rachel's
maidservant, *were* Dan and Naph-
tali;
26 and the sons of Zilpah, Leah's
maidservant, *were* Gad and Asher.
These *were* the sons of Jacob who
were born to him in Padan Aram.

Death of Isaac

27 Then Jacob came to his father
Isaac at [a]Mamre, or [b]Kirjath Arba[1]
(that *is*, Hebron), where Abraham
and Isaac had dwelt.
28 Now the days of Isaac were one
hundred and eighty years.
29 So Isaac breathed his last and
died, and [a]was [1]gathered to his
people, *being* old and full of days.
And [b]his sons Esau and Jacob bur-
ied him.

The Family of Esau

36 Now this *is* the genealogy of
Esau, [a]who is Edom.
2 [a]Esau took his wives from the
daughters of Canaan: Adah the
daughter of Elon the [b]Hittite;
[c]Aholibamah[1] the daughter of
Anah, the daughter of Zibeon the
Hivite;
3 and [a]Basemath, Ishmael's
daughter, sister of Nebajoth.
4 Now [a]Adah bore Eliphaz to
Esau, and Basemath bore Reuel.
5 And [1]Aholibamah bore Jeush,
Jaalam, and Korah. These *were*
the sons of Esau who were born
to him in the land of Canaan.
6 Then Esau took his wives, his
sons, his daughters, and all the
persons of his household, his cattle
and all his animals, and all his
goods which he had gained in the
land of Canaan, and went to a
country away from the presence of
his brother Jacob.
7 [a]For their possessions were too
great for them to dwell together,
and [b]the land where they were
strangers could not support them
because of their livestock.
8 So Esau dwelt in [a]Mount Seir.
[b]Esau *is* Edom.
9 And this *is* the genealogy of
Esau the father of the Edomites in
Mount Seir.
10 These *were* the names of
Esau's sons: [a]Eliphaz the son of
Adah the wife of Esau, and Reuel
the son of Basemath the wife of
Esau.
11 And the sons of Eliphaz were
Teman, Omar, [1]Zepho, Gatam, and
Kenaz.
12 Now Timna was the concubine
of Eliphaz, Esau's son, and she
bore [a]Amalek to Eliphaz. These
were the sons of Adah, Esau's
wife.
13 These *were* the sons of Reuel:
Nahath, Zerah, Shammah, and
Mizzah. These were the sons of
Basemath, Esau's wife.
14 These were the sons of [1]Aholi-
bamah, Esau's wife, the daughter
of Anah, the daughter of Zibeon.
And she bore to Esau: Jeush, Jaa-
lam, and Korah.

The Chiefs of Edom

15 These *were* the chiefs of the
sons of Esau. The sons of Eliphaz,
the firstborn *son* of Esau, were
Chief Teman, Chief Omar, Chief
Zepho, Chief Kenaz,
16 [1]Chief Korah, Chief Gatam,
and Chief Amalek. These *were* the
chiefs of Eliphaz in the land of

17 [a]Gen. 30:24; 1 Sam. 4:20
18 [1]Lit. *Son of My Sorrow* [2]Lit. *Son of the Right Hand*
19 [a]Gen. 48:7 [b]Ruth 1:2; 4:11; Mic. 5:2; Matt. 2:6
20 [a]1 Sam. 10:2
21 [a]Mic. 4:8
22 [a]Gen. 49:4; 1 Chr. 5:1
23 [a]Gen. 29:31–35; 30:18–20; 46:8; Ex. 1:1–4
27 [a]Gen. 13:18; 18:1; 23:19 [b]Josh. 14:15 [1]Lit. *Town* or *City of Arba*
29 [a]Gen. 15:15; 25:8; 49:33 [b]Gen. 25:9; 49:31 [1]Joined his ancestors

CHAPTER 36

1 [a]Gen. 25:30
2 [a]Gen. 26:34; 28:9 [b]2 Kin. 7:6 [c]Gen. 36:25 [1]Or *Oholibamah*
3 [a]Gen. 28:9
4 [a]1 Chr. 1:35
5 [1]Or *Oholibamah*
7 [a]Gen. 13:6, 11 [b]Gen. 17:8; 28:4; Heb. 11:9
8 [a]Gen. 32:3; Deut. 2:5; Josh. 24:4 [b]Gen. 36:1, 19
10 [a]1 Chr. 1:35
11 [1]*Zephi,* 1 Chr. 1:36
12 [a]Ex. 17:8–16; Num. 24:20; Deut. 25:17–19; 1 Sam. 15:2, 3
14 [1]Or *Oholibamah*
16 [1]Sam. omits *Chief Korah*

Edom. They *were* the sons of
Adah.
17 These *were* the sons of Reuel,
Esau's son: Chief Nahath, Chief
Zerah, Chief Shammah, and Chief
Mizzah. These *were* the chiefs of
Reuel in the land of Edom. These
were the sons of Basemath, Esau's
wife.
18 And these *were* the sons of
[1]Aholibamah, Esau's wife: Chief
Jeush, Chief Jaalam, and Chief
Korah. These *were* the chiefs *who*
descended from Aholibamah,
Esau's wife, the daughter of Anah.
19 These *were* the sons of Esau,
who is Edom, and these *were* their
chiefs.

The Sons of Seir

20 [a]These *were* the sons of Seir
[b]the Horite who inhabited the
land: Lotan, Shobal, Zibeon,
Anah,
21 Dishon, Ezer, and Dishan.
These *were* the chiefs of the Ho-
rites, the sons of Seir, in the land
of Edom.
22 And the sons of Lotan were
Hori and [1]Hemam. Lotan's sister
was Timna.
23 These *were* the sons of Shobal:
[1]Alvan, Manahath, Ebal, [2]Shepho,
and Onam.
24 These *were* the sons of Zibeon:
both Ajah and Anah. This *was*
the Anah who found the [1]water
in the wilderness as he pastured
[a]the donkeys of his father Zib-
eon.
25 These *were* the children of
Anah: Dishon and [1]Aholibamah
the daughter of Anah.
26 These *were* the sons of [1]Di-
shon: [2]Hemdan, Eshban, Ithran,
and Cheran.
27 These *were* the sons of Ezer:
Bilhan, Zaavan, and [1]Akan.
28 These *were* the sons of Dishan:
[a]Uz and Aran.
29 These *were* the chiefs of the
Horites: Chief Lotan, Chief Sho-
bal, Chief Zibeon, Chief Anah,
30 Chief Dishon, Chief Ezer, and
Chief Dishan. These *were* the
chiefs of the Horites, according to
their chiefs in the land of Seir.

The Kings of Edom

31 [a]Now these *were* the kings who
reigned in the land of Edom before
any king reigned over the children
of Israel:
32 Bela the son of Beor reigned in
Edom, and the name of his city
was Dinhabah.
33 And when Bela died, Jobab the
son of Zerah of Bozrah reigned in
his place.
34 When Jobab died, Husham of
the land of the Temanites reigned
in his place.
35 And when Husham died, Ha-
dad the son of Bedad, who at-
tacked Midian in the field of Moab,
reigned in his place. And the name
of his city *was* Avith.
36 When Hadad died, Samlah of
Masrekah reigned in his place.
37 And when Samlah died, Saul
of [a]Rehoboth-*by*-the-River reigned
in his place.
38 When Saul died, Baal-Hanan
the son of Achbor reigned in his
place.
39 And when Baal-Hanan the son
of Achbor died, [1]Hadar reigned in
his place; and the name of his city
was [2]Pau. His wife's name *was*
Mehetabel, the daughter of Ma-
tred, the daughter of Mezahab.

The Chiefs of Esau

40 And these *were* the names of
the chiefs of Esau, according to
their families and their places, by
their names: Chief Timnah, Chief
[1]Alvah, Chief Jetheth,
41 Chief [1]Aholibamah, Chief Elah,
Chief Pinon,
42 Chief Kenaz, Chief Teman,
Chief Mibzar,
43 Chief Magdiel, and Chief Iram.
These *were* the chiefs of Edom, ac-
cording to their dwelling places in
the land of their possession. Esau
was the father of [1]the Edomites.

Joseph Dreams of Greatness

37 Now Jacob dwelt in the land
[a]where his father was a
[1]stranger, in the land of Canaan.
2 This *is* the history of Jacob. Jo-
seph, *being* seventeen years old,
was feeding the flock with his
brothers. And the lad *was* with the
sons of Bilhah and the sons of Zil-
pah, his father's wives; and Joseph
brought [a]a bad report of them to
his father.
3 Now Israel loved Joseph more
than all his children, because he

18 [1]Or *Oholibamah*
20 [a]1 Chr. 1:38–42 [b]Gen. 14:6; Deut. 2:12, 22
22 [1]*Homam*, 1 Chr. 1:39
23 [1]*Alian*, 1 Chr. 1:40 [2]*Shephi*, 1 Chr. 1:40
24 [a]Lev. 19:19 [1]So with MT, Vg. (*hot springs*); LXX *Jamin;* Tg. *mighty men;* Talmud *mules*
25 [1]Or *Oholibamah*
26 [1]Heb. *Dishan* [2]*Hamran*, 1 Chr. 1:41
27 [1]*Jaakan*, 1 Chr. 1:42
28 [a]Job 1:1
31 [a]Gen. 17:6, 16; 35:11; 1 Chr. 1:43
37 [a]Gen. 10:11
39 [1]Sam., Syr. *Hadad* and 1 Chr. 1:50 [2]*Pai*, 1 Chr. 1:50
40 [1]*Aliah*, 1 Chr. 1:51
41 [1]Or *Oholibamah*
43 [1]Heb. *Edom*

CHAPTER 37

1 [a]Gen. 17:8; 23:4; 28:4; 36:7; Heb. 11:9 [1]*sojourner*, temporary resident
2 [a]Gen. 35:25, 26; 1 Sam. 2:22–24

was [a]the son of his old age. Also
he [b]made him a tunic of *many* col-
ors.
4 But when his brothers saw that
their father loved him more than
all his brothers, they [a]hated him
and could not speak peaceably to
him.
5 Now Joseph had a dream, and
he told *it* to his brothers; and they
hated him even more.
6 So he said to them, "Please
hear this dream which I have
dreamed:
7 [a]"There we were, binding
sheaves in the field. Then behold,
my sheaf arose and also stood
upright; and indeed your sheaves
stood all around and bowed down
to my sheaf."
8 And his brothers said to him,
"Shall you indeed reign over us?
Or shall you indeed have dominion
over us?" So they hated him even
more for his dreams and for his
words.
9 Then he dreamed still another
dream and told it to his brothers,
and said, "Look, I have dreamed
another dream. And this time, [a]the
sun, the moon, and the eleven stars
bowed down to me."
10 So he told *it* to his father and
his brothers; and his father re-
buked him and said to him, "What
is this dream that you have
dreamed? Shall your mother and
I and [a]your brothers indeed come
to bow down to the earth before
you?"
11 And [a]his brothers envied him,
but his father [b]kept the matter *in
mind.*

Joseph Sold by His Brothers

12 Then his brothers went to feed
their father's flock in [a]Shechem.
13 And Israel said to Joseph, "Are
not your brothers feeding *the flock*
in Shechem? Come, I will send you
to them." So he said to him, "Here
I am."
14 Then he said to him, "Please
go and see if it is well with
your brothers and well with the
flocks, and bring back word to
me." So he sent him out of the Val-
ley of [a]Hebron, and he went to
Shechem.
15 Now a certain man found him,
and there he was, wandering in the
field. And the man asked him, say-
ing, "What are you seeking?"
16 So he said, "I am seeking my
brothers. [a]Please tell me where
they are feeding *their flocks.*"
17 And the man said, "They have
departed from here, for I heard
them say, 'Let us go to Dothan.' "
So Joseph went after his brothers
and found them in [a]Dothan.
18 Now when they saw him afar
off, even before he came near
them, [a]they conspired against him
to kill him.
19 Then they said to one another,
"Look, this [1]dreamer is coming!
20 [a]"Come therefore, let us now
kill him and cast him into some pit;
and we shall say, 'Some wild beast
has devoured him.' We shall see
what will become of his dreams!"
21 But [a]Reuben heard *it,* and he
delivered him out of their hands,
and said, "Let us not kill him."
22 And Reuben said to them,
"Shed no blood, *but* cast him into
this pit which *is* in the wilderness,
and do not lay a hand on him"—
that he might deliver him out of
their hands, and bring him back
to his father.
23 So it came to pass, when Jo-
seph had come to his brothers, that
they [a]stripped Joseph *of* his tunic,
the tunic of *many* colors that *was*
on him.
24 Then they took him and cast
him into a pit. And the pit *was*
empty; *there was* no water in it.
25 [a]And they sat down to eat a
meal. Then they lifted their eyes
and looked, and there was a com-
pany of [b]Ishmaelites, coming from
Gilead with their camels, bearing
spices, [c]balm, and myrrh, on their
way to carry *them* down to Egypt.
26 So Judah said to his brothers,
"What profit *is there* if we kill our
brother and [a]conceal his blood?
27 "Come and let us sell him to
the Ishmaelites, and [a]let not our
hand be upon him, for he *is* [b]our
brother *and* [c]our flesh." And his
brothers listened.
28 Then [a]Midianite traders passed
by; so *the brothers* pulled Joseph
up and lifted him out of the pit,
[b]and sold him to the Ishmaelites
for [c]twenty *shekels* of silver. And
they took Joseph to Egypt.
29 Then Reuben returned to the

3 [a]Gen. 44:20 [b]Gen. 37:23, 32; Judg. 5:30; 1 Sam. 2:19
4 [a]Gen. 27:41; 49:23; 1 Sam. 17:28; John 15:18–20
7 [a]Gen. 42:6, 9; 43:26; 44:14
9 [a]Gen. 46:29; 47:25
10 [a]Gen. 27:29
11 [a]Matt. 27:17, 18; Acts 7:9 [b]Dan. 7:28; Luke 2:19, 51
12 [a]Gen. 33:18–20
14 [a]Gen. 13:18; 23:2, 19; 35:27; Josh. 14:14, 15; Judg. 1:10
16 [a]Song 1:7
17 [a]2 Kin. 6:13
18 [a]1 Sam. 19:1; Ps. 31:13; 37:12, 32; Matt. 21:38; 26:3, 4; 27:1; Mark 14:1; John 11:53; Acts 23:12
19 [1]Lit. *master of dreams*
20 [a]Gen. 37:22; Prov. 1:11
21 [a]Gen. 42:22
23 [a]Matt. 27:28
25 [a]Prov. 30:20 [b]Gen. 16:11, 12; 37:28, 36; 39:1 [c]Jer. 8:22
26 [a]Gen. 37:20
27 [a]1 Sam. 18:17 [b]Gen. 42:21 [c]Gen. 29:14
28 [a]Gen. 37:25; Judg. 6:1–3; 8:22, 24 [b]Gen. 45:4, 5; Ps. 105:17; Acts 7:9 [c]Matt. 27:9

pit, and indeed Joseph *was* not in
the pit; and he [a]tore his clothes.
30 And he returned to his brothers
and said, "The lad [a]*is* no *more;* and
I, where shall I go?"
31 So they took [a]Joseph's tunic,
killed a kid of the goats, and
dipped the tunic in the blood.
32 Then they sent the tunic of
many colors, and they brought *it*
to their father and said, "We have
found this. Do you know whether
it *is* your son's tunic or not?"
33 And he recognized it and said,
"*It is* my son's tunic. A [a]wild beast
has devoured him. Without doubt
Joseph is torn to pieces."
34 Then Jacob [a]tore his clothes,
put sackcloth on his waist, and
[b]mourned for his son many days.
35 And all his sons and all his
daughters [a]arose to comfort him;
but he refused to be comforted,
and he said, "For [b]I shall go down
into the grave to my son in mourn-
ing." Thus his father wept for him.
36 Now [a]the [1]Midianites had sold
him in Egypt to Potiphar, an offi-
cer of Pharaoh *and* captain of the
guard.

Judah and Tamar

38 It came to pass at that time
that Judah departed from
his brothers, and [a]visited a certain
Adullamite whose name *was*
Hirah.
2 And Judah [a]saw there a daugh-
ter of a certain Canaanite whose
name *was* [b]Shua, and he married
her and went in to her.
3 So she conceived and bore a
son, and he called his name [a]Er.
4 She conceived again and bore
a son, and she called his name
[a]Onan.
5 And she conceived yet again
and bore a son, and called his
name [a]Shelah. He was at Chezib
when she bore him.
6 Then Judah [a]took a wife for Er
his firstborn, and her name *was*
[b]Tamar.
7 But [a]Er, Judah's firstborn, was
wicked in the sight of the LORD,
[b]and the LORD killed him.
8 And Judah said to Onan, "Go
in to [a]your brother's wife and
marry her, and raise up an heir to
your brother."
9 But Onan knew that the heir

29 [a]Gen. 37:34; 44:13; Job 1:20
30 [a]Gen. 42:13, 36
31 [a]Gen. 37:3, 23
33 [a]Gen. 37:20
34 [a]Gen. 37:29; 2 Sam. 3:31 [b]Gen. 50:10
35 [a]2 Sam. 12:17 [b]Gen. 25:8; 35:29; 42:38; 44:29, 31
36 [a]Gen. 39:1 [1]MT *Medanites*

CHAPTER 38

1 [a]2 Kin. 4:8
2 [a]Gen. 34:2 [b]1 Chr. 2:3
3 [a]Gen. 46:12; Num. 26:19
4 [a]Gen. 46:12; Num. 26:19
5 [a]Num. 26:20
6 [a]Gen. 21:21 [b]Ruth 4:12
7 [a]Gen. 46:12; Num. 26:19 [b]1 Chr. 2:3
8 [a]Deut. 25:5, 6; Matt. 22:24
9 [a]Deut. 25:6
10 [a]Gen. 46:12; Num. 26:19 [1]Lit. *was evil in the eyes of*
11 [a]Ruth 1:12, 13 [b]Lev. 22:13
12 [a]2 Sam. 13:39
13 [a]Josh. 15:10, 57; Judg. 14:1
14 [a]Prov. 7:12 [b]Gen. 38:11, 26
17 [a]Judg. 15:1; Ezek. 16:33 [b]Gen. 38:20
18 [a]Gen. 38:25; 41:42
19 [a]Gen. 38:14
21 [1]*in full view*

would not be [a]his; and it came
to pass, when he went in to his
brother's wife, that he emitted on
the ground, lest he should give an
heir to his brother.
10 And the thing which he did
[1]displeased the LORD; therefore He
killed [a]him also.
11 Then Judah said to Tamar his
daughter-in-law, [a]"Remain a
widow in your father's house till
my son Shelah is grown." For he
said, "Lest he also die like his
brothers." And Tamar went and
dwelt [b]in her father's house.
12 Now in the process of time the
daughter of Shua, Judah's wife,
died; and Judah [a]was comforted,
and went up to his sheepshearers
at Timnah, he and his friend Hirah
the Adullamite.
13 And it was told Tamar, saying,
"Look, your father-in-law is going
up [a]to Timnah to shear his sheep."
14 So she took off her widow's
garments, covered *herself* with a
veil and wrapped herself, and [a]sat
in an open place which *was* on the
way to Timnah; for she saw [b]that
Shelah was grown, and she was
not given to him as a wife.
15 When Judah saw her, he
thought she *was* a harlot, because
she had covered her face.
16 Then he turned to her by the
way, and said, "Please let me come
in to you"; for he did not know that
she *was* his daughter-in-law. So
she said, "What will you give me,
that you may come in to me?"
17 And he said, [a]"I will send a
young goat from the flock." So she
said, [b]"Will you give *me* a pledge
till you send *it?*"
18 Then he said, "What pledge
shall I give you?" So she said,
[a]"Your signet and cord, and your
staff that *is* in your hand." Then
he gave *them* to her, and went in
to her, and she conceived by him.
19 So she arose and went away,
and [a]laid aside her veil and put on
the garments of her widowhood.
20 And Judah sent the young goat
by the hand of his friend the Adul-
lamite, to receive *his* pledge from
the woman's hand, but he did not
find her.
21 Then he asked the men of
that place, saying, "Where is the
harlot who *was* [1]openly by the

roadside?" And they said, "There
was no harlot in this *place*."
22 So he returned to Judah and
said, "I cannot find her. Also, the
men of the place said there was
no harlot in this *place*."
23 Then Judah said, "Let her take
them for herself, lest we be
shamed; for I sent this young goat
and you have not found her."
24 And it came to pass, about
three months after, that Judah
was told, saying, "Tamar your
daughter-in-law has [a]played the
harlot; furthermore she *is* [1]with
child by harlotry." So Judah said,
"Bring her out [b]and let her be
burned!"
25 When she *was* brought out, she
sent to her father-in-law, saying,
"By the man to whom these be-
long, I *am* with child." And she
said, [a]"Please determine whose
these *are*—the signet and cord,
and staff."
26 So Judah [a]acknowledged *them*
and said, [b]"She has been more
righteous than I, because [c]I did not
give her to Shelah my son." And
he [d]never knew her again.
27 Now it came to pass, at the time
for giving birth, that behold, twins
were in her womb.
28 And so it was, when she was
giving birth, that *the one* put out
his hand; and the midwife took a
scarlet *thread* and bound it on his
hand, saying, "This one came out
first."
29 Then it happened, as he drew
back his hand, that his brother
came out unexpectedly; and she
said, "How did you break through?
This breach *be* upon you!" There-
fore his name was called [a]Perez.[1]
30 Afterward his brother came out
who had the scarlet *thread* on his
hand. And his name was called
[a]Zerah.

Joseph a Slave in Egypt

39 Now Joseph had been taken
[a]down to Egypt. And [b]Poti-
phar, an officer of Pharaoh, cap-
tain of the guard, an Egyptian,
[c]bought him from the Ishmaelites
who had taken him down there.
2 [a]The LORD was with Joseph,
and he was a successful man; and
he was in the house of his master
the Egyptian.
3 And his master saw that the
LORD *was* with him and that the
LORD [a]made all he did [1]to prosper
in his hand.
4 So Joseph [a]found favor in his
sight, and served him. Then he
made him [b]overseer of his house,
and all *that* he had he put [1]under
his authority.
5 So it was, from the time *that*
he had made him overseer of his
house and all that he had, that [a]the
LORD blessed the Egyptian's house
for Joseph's sake; and the blessing
of the LORD was on all that he had
in the house and in the field.
6 Thus he left all that he had in
Joseph's [1]hand, and he did not
know what he had except for the
[2]bread which he ate. Now Joseph
[a]was handsome in form and ap-
pearance.
7 And it came to pass after these
things that his master's wife [1]cast
longing eyes on Joseph, and she
said, [a]"Lie with me."
8 But he refused and said to his
master's wife, "Look, my master
does not know what *is* with me in
the house, and he has committed
all that he has to my hand.
9 "*There is* no one greater in this
house than I, nor has he kept back
anything from me but you, be-
cause you *are* his wife. [a]How then
can I do this great wickedness, and
[b]sin against God?"
10 So it was, as she spoke to Jo-
seph day by day, that he [a]did not
heed her, to lie with her *or* to be
with her.
11 But it happened about this
time, when Joseph went into the
house to do his work, and none of
the men of the house *was* inside,
12 that she [a]caught him by his gar-
ment, saying, "Lie with me." But
he left his garment in her hand,
and fled and ran outside.
13 And so it was, when she saw
that he had left his garment in her
hand and fled outside,
14 that she called to the men of
her house and spoke to them, say-
ing, "See, he has brought in to us
a [a]Hebrew to [1]mock us. He came
in to me to lie with me, and I cried
out with a loud voice.
15 "And it happened, when he
heard that I lifted my voice and
cried out, that he left his garment

24 [a]Judg. 19:2 [b]Lev. 20:14; 21:9; Deut. 22:21 [1]*pregnant*

25 [a]Gen. 37:32; 38:18

26 [a]Gen. 37:33 [b]1 Sam. 24:17 [c]Gen. 38:14 [d]Job 34:31, 32

29 [a]Gen. 46:12; Num. 26:20; Ruth 4:12; 1 Chr. 2:4; Matt. 1:3 [1]Lit. *Breach* or *Breakthrough*

30 [a]Gen. 46:12; 1 Chr. 2:4; Matt. 1:3

CHAPTER 39

1 [a]Gen. 12:10; 43:15 [b]Gen. 37:36; Ps. 105:17 [c]Gen. 37:28; 45:4

2 [a]Gen. 26:24, 28; 28:15; 35:3; 39:3, 21, 23; 1 Sam. 16:18; 18:14, 28; Acts 7:9

3 [a]Ps. 1:3 [1]*to be a success*

4 [a]Gen. 18:3; 19:19; 39:21 [b]Gen. 24:2, 10; 39:8, 22; 41:40 [1]Lit. *in his hand*

5 [a]Gen. 18:26; 30:27; 2 Sam. 6:11

6 [a]Gen. 29:17; 1 Sam. 16:12 [1]Care [2]Food

7 [a]2 Sam. 13:11 [1]Lit. *lifted up her eyes toward*

9 [a]Lev. 20:10; Prov. 6:29, 32 [b]Gen. 20:6; 42:18; 2 Sam. 12:13; Ps. 51:4

10 [a]Prov. 1:10

12 [a]Prov. 7:13

14 [a]Gen. 14:13; 41:12 [1]*laugh at*

with me, and fled and went out-
side."
16 So she kept his garment with
her until his master came home.
17 Then she [a]spoke to him with
words like these, saying, "The He-
brew servant whom you brought
to us came in to me to mock me;
18 "so it happened, as I lifted my
voice and cried out, that he left
his garment with me and fled out-
side."
19 So it was, when his master
heard the words which his wife
spoke to him, saying, "Your ser-
vant did to me after this manner,"
that his [a]anger was aroused.
20 Then Joseph's master took him
and [a]put him into the [b]prison, a
place where the king's prisoners
were confined. And he was there
in the prison.
21 But the LORD was with Joseph
and showed him mercy, and He
[a]gave[1] him favor in the sight of the
keeper of the prison.
22 And the keeper of the prison
[a]committed to Joseph's hand all
the prisoners who *were* in the
prison; whatever they did there, it
was his doing.
23 The keeper of the prison did
not look into anything *that was*
under [1]*Joseph's* authority, because
[a]the LORD was with him; and what-
ever he did, the LORD made *it* pros-
per.

The Prisoners' Dreams

40 It came to pass after these
things *that* the [a]butler and
the baker of the king of Egypt of-
fended their lord, the king of
Egypt.
2 And Pharaoh was [a]angry with
his two officers, the chief butler
and the chief baker.
3 [a]So he put them in custody in
the house of the captain of the
guard, in the prison, the place
where Joseph *was* confined.
4 And the captain of the guard
charged Joseph with them, and he
served them; so they were in cus-
tody for a while.
5 Then the butler and the baker
of the king of Egypt, who *were*
confined in the prison, [a]had a
dream, both of them, each man's
dream in one night *and* each man's
dream with its *own* interpretation.

17 [a]Ex. 23:1; Ps. 120:3; Prov. 26:28
19 [a]Prov. 6:34, 35
20 [a]Ps. 105:18; [1 Pet. 2:19] [b]Gen. 40:3, 15; 41:14
21 [a]Gen. 39:2; Ex. 3:21; Ps. 105:19; [Prov. 16:7]; Dan. 1:9; Acts 7:9, 10 [1]Caused him to be viewed with favor by
22 [a]Gen. 39:4; 40:3, 4
23 [a]Gen. 39:2, 3 [1]Lit. *his hand*

CHAPTER 40
1 [a]Gen. 40:11, 13; Neh. 1:11
2 [a]Prov. 16:14
3 [a]Gen. 39:1, 20, 23; 41:10
5 [a]Gen. 37:5; 41:1
6 [1]*dejected*
7 [a]Neh. 2:2
8 [a]Gen. 41:15 [b][Gen. 41:16; Dan. 2:11, 20–22, 27, 28, 47]
12 [a]Gen. 40:18; 41:12, 25; Judg. 7:14; Dan. 2:36; 4:18, 19 [b]Gen. 40:18; 42:17
13 [a]2 Kin. 25:27; Ps. 3:3; Jer. 52:31 [1]*position*
14 [a]1 Sam. 25:31; Luke 23:42 [b]Gen. 24:49; 47:29; Josh. 2:12; 1 Sam. 20:14, 15; 2 Sam. 9:1; 1 Kin. 2:7
15 [a]Gen. 37:26–28 [b]Gen. 39:20
16 [1]Or *baskets of white bread*
18 [a]Gen. 40:12
19 [a]Gen. 40:13 [b]Deut. 21:22 [1]Lit. *up*

6 And Joseph came in to them in
the morning and looked at them,
and saw that they *were* [1]sad.
7 So he asked Pharaoh's officers
who *were* with him in the custody
of his lord's house, saying, [a]"Why
do you look *so* sad today?"
8 And they said to him, [a]"We
each have had a dream, and *there
is* no interpreter of it." So Joseph
said to them, [b]"Do not interpreta-
tions belong to God? Tell *them* to
me, please."
9 Then the chief butler told his
dream to Joseph, and said to him,
"Behold, in my dream a vine *was*
before me,
10 "and in the vine *were* three
branches; it *was* as though it
budded, its blossoms shot forth,
and its clusters brought forth ripe
grapes.
11 "Then Pharaoh's cup *was* in
my hand; and I took the grapes
and pressed them into Pharaoh's
cup, and placed the cup in Pha-
raoh's hand."
12 And Joseph said to him, [a]"This
is the interpretation of it: The three
branches [b]*are* three days.
13 "Now within three days Pha-
raoh will [a]lift up your head and re-
store you to your [1]place, and you
will put Pharaoh's cup in his hand
according to the former manner,
when you were his butler.
14 "But [a]remember me when it is
well with you, and [b]please show
kindness to me; make mention of
me to Pharaoh, and get me out of
this house.
15 "For indeed I was [a]stolen away
from the land of the Hebrews; [b]and
also I have done nothing here that
they should put me into the dun-
geon."
16 When the chief baker saw that
the interpretation was good, he
said to Joseph, "I also *was* in my
dream, and there *were* three
[1]white baskets on my head.
17 "In the uppermost basket *were*
all kinds of baked goods for Pha-
raoh, and the birds ate them out
of the basket on my head."
18 So Joseph answered and said,
[a]"This *is* the interpretation of it:
The three baskets *are* three days.
19 [a]"Within three days Pharaoh
will lift [1]off your head from you
and [b]hang you on a tree; and the

birds will eat your flesh from
you."
20 Now it came to pass on the
third day, *which was* Pharaoh's
[a]birthday, that he [b]made a feast for
all his servants; and he [c]lifted up
the head of the chief butler and
of the chief baker among his ser-
vants.
21 Then he [a]restored the chief but-
ler to his butlership again, and [b]he
placed the cup in Pharaoh's hand.
22 But he [a]hanged the chief baker,
as Joseph had interpreted to them.
23 Yet the chief butler did not re-
member Joseph, but [a]forgot him.

Pharaoh's Dreams

41 Then it came to pass, at the
end of two full years, that
[a]Pharaoh had a dream; and be-
hold, he stood by the river.
2 Suddenly there came up out of
the river seven cows, fine looking
and fat; and they fed in the
meadow.
3 Then behold, seven other cows
came up after them out of the
river, ugly and gaunt, and stood
by the *other* cows on the bank of
the river.
4 And the ugly and gaunt cows
ate up the seven fine looking and
fat cows. So Pharaoh awoke.
5 He slept and dreamed a second
time; and suddenly seven heads of
grain came up on one stalk, plump
and good.
6 Then behold, seven thin heads,
blighted by the [a]east wind, sprang
up after them.
7 And the seven thin heads de-
voured the seven plump and full
heads. So Pharaoh awoke, and in-
deed, *it was* a dream.
8 Now it came to pass in the
morning [a]that his spirit was trou-
bled, and he sent and called for all
[b]the magicians of Egypt and all its
[c]wise men. And Pharaoh told them
his dreams, but *there was* no one
who could interpret them for Pha-
raoh.
9 Then the [a]chief butler spoke to
Pharaoh, saying: "I remember my
faults this day.
10 "When Pharaoh was [a]angry
with his servants, [b]and put me in
custody in the house of the captain
of the guard, *both* me and the chief
baker,

20 [a]Matt. 14:6–10 [b]Mark 6:21 [c]Gen. 40:13, 19; 2 Kin. 25:27; Jer. 52:31; Matt. 25:19

21 [a]Gen. 40:13 [b]Neh. 2:1

22 [a]Gen. 40:19; Deut. 21:23; Esth. 7:10

23 [a]Job 19:14; Ps. 31:12; Eccl. 9:15, 16; Is. 49:15; Amos 6:6

CHAPTER 41

1 [a]Gen. 40:5; Judg. 7:13

6 [a]Ex. 10:13; Ezek. 17:10

8 [a]Dan. 2:1, 3; 4:5, 19 [b]Ex. 7:11, 22; Is. 29:14; Dan. 1:20; 2:2; 4:7 [c]Matt. 2:1

9 [a]Gen. 40:1, 14, 23

10 [a]Gen. 40:2, 3 [b]Gen. 39:20

11 [a]Gen. 40:5; Judg. 7:15

12 [a]Gen. 39:14; 43:32 [b]Gen. 37:36 [c]Gen. 40:12

13 [a]Gen. 40:21, 22

14 [a]Ps. 105:20 [b]Dan. 2:25 [c][1 Sam. 2:8] [d]2 Kin. 25:27–29

15 [a]Gen. 41:8, 12; Dan. 5:16

16 [a]Dan. 2:30; Acts 3:12; [2 Cor. 3:5] [b]Gen. 40:8; 41:25, 28, 32; Deut. 29:29; Dan. 2:22, 28, 47

17 [a]Gen. 41:1

22 [1]Heads of grain

24 [a]Gen. 41:8; Ex. 7:11; Is. 8:19; Dan. 4:7

11 [a]"we each had a dream in one
night, he and I. Each of us
dreamed according to the interpre-
tation of his *own* dream.
12 "Now there *was* a young [a]He-
brew man with us there, a [b]servant
of the captain of the guard. And
we told him, and he [c]interpreted
our dreams for us; to each man he
interpreted according to his *own*
dream.
13 "And it came to pass, just [a]as
he interpreted for us, so it hap-
pened. He restored me to my of-
fice, and he hanged him."
14 [a]Then Pharaoh sent and called
Joseph, and they [b]brought him
quickly [c]out of the dungeon; and
he shaved, [d]changed his clothing,
and came to Pharaoh.
15 And Pharaoh said to Joseph, "I
have had a dream, and *there is* no
one who can interpret it. [a]But I
have heard it said of you *that* you
can understand a dream, to inter-
pret it."
16 So Joseph answered Pharaoh,
saying, [a]"*It is* not in me; [b]God will
give Pharaoh an answer of peace."
17 Then Pharaoh said to Joseph:
"Behold, [a]in my dream I stood on
the bank of the river.
18 "Suddenly seven cows came up
out of the river, fine looking and
fat; and they fed in the meadow.
19 "Then behold, seven other
cows came up after them, poor and
very ugly and gaunt, such ugliness
as I have never seen in all the land
of Egypt.
20 "And the gaunt and ugly cows
ate up the first seven, the fat cows.
21 "When they had eaten them up,
no one would have known that
they had eaten them, for they *were*
just as ugly as at the beginning.
So I awoke.
22 "Also I saw in my dream, and
suddenly seven [1]heads came up on
one stalk, full and good.
23 "Then behold, seven heads,
withered, thin, *and* blighted by
the east wind, sprang up after
them.
24 "And the thin heads devoured
the seven good heads. So [a]I told
this to the magicians, but *there
was* no one who could explain *it*
to me."
25 Then Joseph said to Pharaoh,
"The dreams of Pharaoh *are* one;

[a]God has shown Pharaoh what He
is about to do:
26 "The seven good cows *are*
seven years, and the seven good
[1]heads *are* seven years; the
dreams *are* one.
27 "And the seven thin and ugly
cows which came up after them
are seven years, and the seven
empty heads blighted by the east
wind are [a]seven years of famine.
28 [a]"This *is* the thing which I have
spoken to Pharaoh. God has
shown Pharaoh what He *is* about
to do.
29 "Indeed [a]seven years of great
plenty will come throughout all the
land of Egypt;
30 "but after them seven years of
famine will [a]arise, and all the
plenty will be forgotten in the land
of Egypt; and the famine [b]will de-
plete the land.
31 "So the plenty will not be
known in the land because of the
famine following, for it *will be* very
severe.
32 "And the dream was repeated
to Pharaoh twice because the
[a]thing *is* established by God, and
God will shortly bring it to pass.
33 "Now therefore, let Pharaoh
select a discerning and wise
man, and set him over the land of
Egypt.
34 "Let Pharaoh do *this*, and let
him appoint [1]officers over the
land, [a]to collect one-fifth *of the
produce* of the land of Egypt in
the seven plentiful years.
35 "And [a]let them gather all the
food of those good years that are
coming, and store up grain under
the [1]authority of Pharaoh, and let
them keep food in the cities.
36 "Then that food shall be as a
[1]reserve for the land for the seven
years of famine which shall be in
the land of Egypt, that the land
[a]may not [2]perish during the fam-
ine."

Joseph's Rise to Power

37 So [a]the advice was good in the
eyes of Pharaoh and in the eyes
of all his servants.
38 And Pharaoh said to his ser-
vants, "Can we find *such a one* as
this, a man [a]in whom *is* the Spirit
of God?"
39 Then Pharaoh said to Joseph,
"Inasmuch as God has shown you
all this, *there is* no one as discern-
ing and wise as you.
40 [a]"You shall be [1]over my house,
and all my people shall be ruled
according to your word; only in re-
gard to the throne will I be greater
than you."
41 And Pharaoh said to Joseph,
"See, I have [a]set you over all the
land of Egypt."
42 Then Pharaoh [a]took his signet
ring off his hand and put it on Jo-
seph's hand; and he [b]clothed him
in garments of fine linen [c]and put
a gold chain around his neck.
43 And he had him ride in the sec-
ond [a]chariot which he had; [b]and
they cried out before him, "Bow
the knee!" So he set him [c]over all
the land of Egypt.
44 Pharaoh also said to Joseph, "I
am Pharaoh, and without your
consent no man may lift his hand
or foot in all the land of Egypt."
45 And Pharaoh called Joseph's
name [1]Zaphnath-Paaneah. And he
gave him as a wife [a]Asenath, the
daughter of Poti-Pherah priest of
On. So Joseph went out over *all*
the land of Egypt.
46 Joseph was thirty years old
when he [a]stood before Pharaoh
king of Egypt. And Joseph went
out from the presence of Pharaoh,
and went throughout all the land
of Egypt.
47 Now in the seven plentiful
years the ground brought forth
[1]abundantly.
48 So he gathered up all the food
of the seven years which were in
the land of Egypt, and laid up the
food in the cities; he laid up in
every city the food of the fields
which surrounded them.
49 Joseph gathered very much
grain, [a]as the sand of the sea, until
he stopped counting, for *it was* im-
measurable.
50 [a]And to Joseph were born two
sons before the years of famine
came, whom Asenath, the daugh-
ter of Poti-Pherah priest of On,
bore to him.
51 Joseph called the name of the
firstborn [1]Manasseh: "For God has
made me forget all my toil and all
my [a]father's house."
52 And the name of the second he
called [1]Ephraim: "For God has

25 [a]Gen. 41:28, 32; Dan. 2:28, 29, 45; Rev. 4:1
26 [1]Heads of grain
27 [a]2 Kin. 8:1
28 [a][Gen. 41:25, 32; Dan. 2:28]
29 [a]Gen. 41:47
30 [a]Gen. 41:54, 56 [b]Gen. 47:13; Ps. 105:16
32 [a]Gen. 41:25, 28; Num. 23:19; Is. 46:10, 11
34 [a][Prov. 6:6–8] [1]*overseers*
35 [a]Gen. 41:48 [1]Lit. *hand*
36 [a]Gen. 47:15, 19 [1]Lit. *supply* [2]*be cut off*
37 [a]Ps. 105:19; Acts 7:10
38 [a]Num. 27:18; [Job 32:8; Prov. 2:6]; Dan. 4:8, 9, 18; 5:11, 14; 6:3
40 [a]Ps. 105:21; Acts 7:10 [1]In charge of
41 [a]Gen. 42:6; Ps. 105:21; Dan. 6:3; Acts 7:10
42 [a]Esth. 3:10 [b]Esth. 8:2, 15 [c]Dan. 5:7, 16, 29
43 [a]Gen. 46:29 [b]Esth. 6:9 [c]Gen. 42:6
45 [a]Gen. 46:20 [1]Probably Egyptian for *God Speaks and He Lives*
46 [a]1 Sam. 16:21; 1 Kin. 12:6, 8; Dan. 1:19
47 [1]Lit. *by handfuls*
49 [a]Gen. 22:17; Judg. 7:12; 1 Sam. 13:5
50 [a]Gen. 46:20; 48:5
51 [a]Ps. 45:10 [1]Lit. *Making Forgetful*
52 [1]Lit. *Fruitfulness*

caused me to be [a]fruitful in the
land of my affliction."
53 Then the seven years of plenty
which were in the land of Egypt
ended,
54 [a]and the seven years of famine
began to come, [b]as Joseph had
said. The famine was in all lands,
but in all the land of Egypt there
was bread.
55 So when all the land of Egypt
was famished, the people cried to
Pharaoh for bread. Then Pharaoh
said to all the Egyptians, "Go to
Joseph; [a]whatever he says to you,
do."
56 The famine was over all the
face of the earth, and Joseph
opened [1]all the storehouses and
[a]sold to the Egyptians. And the
famine became severe in the land
of Egypt.
57 [a]So all countries came to Jo-
seph in Egypt to [b]buy *grain*, be-
cause the famine was severe in all
lands.

Joseph's Brothers Go to Egypt

42 When [a]Jacob saw that there
was grain in Egypt, Jacob
said to his sons, "Why do you look
at one another?"
2 And he said, "Indeed I have
heard that there is grain in Egypt;
go down to that place and buy for
us there, that we may [a]live and not
die."
3 So Joseph's ten brothers went
down to buy grain in Egypt.
4 But Jacob did not send Jo-
seph's brother Benjamin with his
brothers, for he said, [a]"Lest some
calamity befall him."
5 And the sons of Israel went to
buy *grain* among those who jour-
neyed, for the famine was [a]in the
land of Canaan.
6 Now Joseph *was* governor
[a]over the land; and it was he who
sold to all the people of the land.
And Joseph's brothers came and
[b]bowed down before him with
their faces to the earth.
7 Joseph saw his brothers and
recognized them, but he acted as
[a]a stranger to them and spoke
[1]roughly to them. Then he said to
them, "Where do you come from?"
And they said, "From the land of
Canaan to buy food."
8 So Joseph recognized his

52 [a]Gen. 17:6; 28:3; 49:22
54 [a]Ps. 105:16; Acts 7:11 [b]Gen. 41:30
55 [a]John 2:5
56 [a]Gen. 42:6 [1]Lit. *all that was in them*
57 [a]Ezek. 29:12 [b]Gen. 27:28, 37; 42:3

CHAPTER 42

1 [a]Acts 7:12
2 [a]Gen. 43:8; Ps. 33:18, 19; Is. 38:1
4 [a]Gen. 42:38
5 [a]Gen. 12:10; 26:1; 41:57; Acts 7:11
6 [a]Gen. 41:41, 55 [b]Gen. 37:7–10; 41:43; Is. 60:14
7 [a]Gen. 45:1, 2 [1]*harshly*
9 [a]Gen. 37:5–9 [1]Exposed parts
13 [a]Gen. 37:30; 42:32; 44:20; Lam. 5:7
15 [a]1 Sam. 1:26; 17:55
16 [1]Lit. *bound*
17 [a]Gen. 40:4, 7, 12 [1]Lit. *gathered*
18 [a]Gen. 22:12; 39:9; Ex. 1:17; Lev. 25:43; Neh. 5:15; Prov. 1:7; 9:10
20 [a]Gen. 42:34; 43:5; 44:23
21 [a]Gen. 37:26–28; 44:16; 45:3; Job 36:8, 9; Hos. 5:15 [b]Prov. 21:13; Matt. 7:2
22 [a]Gen. 37:21, 22, 29

brothers, but they did not recog-
nize him.
9 Then Joseph [a]remembered the
dreams which he had dreamed
about them, and said to them,
"You *are* spies! You have come to
see the [1]nakedness of the land!"
10 And they said to him, "No, my
lord, but your servants have come
to buy food.
11 "We *are* all one man's sons; we
are honest *men;* your servants are
not spies."
12 But he said to them, "No, but
you have come to see the naked-
ness of the land."
13 And they said, "Your servants
are twelve brothers, the sons of
one man in the land of Canaan;
and in fact, the youngest *is* with
our father today, and one [a]*is* no
more."
14 But Joseph said to them, "It *is*
as I spoke to you, saying, 'You *are*
spies!'
15 "In this *manner* you shall be
tested: [a]By the life of Pharaoh, you
shall not leave this place unless
your youngest brother comes here.
16 "Send one of you, and let him
bring your brother; and you shall
be [1]kept in prison, that your words
may be tested to see whether *there*
is any truth in you; or else, by the
life of Pharaoh, surely you *are*
spies!"
17 So he [1]put them all together in
prison [a]three days.
18 Then Joseph said to them the
third day, "Do this and live, [a]*for* I
fear God:
19 "If you *are* honest *men*, let one
of your brothers be confined to
your prison house; but you, go and
carry grain for the famine of your
houses.
20 "And [a]bring your youngest
brother to me; so your words will
be verified, and you shall not die."
And they did so.
21 Then they said to one another,
[a]"We *are* truly guilty concerning
our brother, for we saw the an-
guish of his soul when he pleaded
with us, and we would not hear;
[b]therefore this distress has come
upon us."
22 And Reuben answered them,
saying, [a]"Did I not speak to you,
saying, 'Do not sin against the
boy'; and you would not listen?

Therefore behold, his blood is now
[b]required of us."
23 But they did not know that Jo-
seph understood *them*, for he
spoke to them through an in-
terpreter.
24 And he turned himself away
from them and [a]wept. Then he re-
turned to them again, and talked
with them. And he took [b]Simeon
from them and bound him before
their eyes.

The Brothers Return to Canaan

25 Then Joseph [a]gave a command
to fill their sacks with grain, to [b]re-
store every man's money to his
sack, and to give them provisions
for the journey. [c]Thus he did for
them.
26 So they loaded their donkeys
with the grain and departed from
there.
27 But as [a]one *of them* opened his
sack to give his donkey feed at the
encampment, he saw his money;
and there it was, in the mouth of
his sack.
28 So he said to his brothers, "My
money has been restored, and
there it is, in my sack!" Then their
hearts [1]failed *them* and they were
afraid, saying to one another,
"What *is* this *that* God has done
to us?"
29 Then they went to Jacob their
father in the land of Canaan and
told him all that had happened to
them, saying:
30 "The man *who is* lord of the
land [a]spoke [1]roughly to us, and
took us for spies of the country.
31 "But we said to him, 'We *are*
honest *men;* we are not spies.
32 'We *are* twelve brothers, sons
of our father; one *is* no *more*, and
the youngest *is* with our father this
day in the land of Canaan.'
33 "Then the man, the lord of the
country, said to us, [a]'By this I will
know that you *are* honest *men:*
Leave one of your brothers *here*
with me, take *food for* the famine
of your households, and be gone.
34 'And bring your [a]youngest
brother to me; so I shall know that
you *are* not spies, but *that* you *are*
honest *men.* I will grant your
brother to you, and you may [b]trade
in the land.'"
35 Then it happened as they emp-

22 [b]Gen. 9:5, 6; 1 Kin. 2:32; 2 Chr. 24:22; Ps. 9:12; Luke 11:50, 51
24 [a]Gen. 43:30; 45:14, 15 [b]Gen. 34:25, 30; 43:14, 23
25 [a]Gen. 44:1 [b]Gen. 43:12 [c][Matt. 5:44; Rom. 12:17, 20, 21; 1 Pet. 3:9]
27 [a]Gen. 43:21, 22
28 [1]*sank*
30 [a]Gen. 42:7 [1]*harshly*
33 [a]Gen. 42:15, 19, 20
34 [a]Gen. 42:20; 43:3, 5 [b]Gen. 34:10
35 [a]Gen. 43:12, 15, 21
36 [a]Gen. 43:14 [b]Gen. 35:18; [Rom. 8:28, 31]
38 [a]Gen. 37:22; 42:13; 44:20, 28 [b]Gen. 42:4; 44:29 [c]Gen. 37:35; 44:31

CHAPTER 43

1 [a]Gen. 41:54, 57; 42:5; 45:6, 11
2 [a]Gen. 42:2; 44:25
3 [a]Gen. 42:20; 43:5; 44:23
6 [1]Lit. *wickedly*

tied their sacks, that surprisingly
[a]each man's bundle of money *was*
in his sack; and when they and
their father saw the bundles of
money, they were afraid.
36 And Jacob their father said to
them, "You have [a]bereaved me:
Joseph is no *more*, Simeon is no
more, and you want to take [b]Ben-
jamin. All these things are against
me."
37 Then Reuben spoke to his fa-
ther, saying, "Kill my two sons if
I do not bring him *back* to you;
put him in my hands, and I will
bring him back to you."
38 But he said, "My son shall not
go down with you, for [a]his brother
is dead, and he is left alone. [b]If any
calamity should befall him along
the way in which you go, then you
would [c]bring down my gray hair
with sorrow to the grave."

Joseph's Brothers Return with Benjamin

43 Now the famine *was* [a]severe
in the land.
2 And it came to pass, when they
had eaten up the grain which they
had brought from Egypt, that their
father said to them, "Go [a]back,
buy us a little food."
3 But Judah spoke to him, say-
ing, "The man solemnly warned
us, saying, 'You shall not see my
face unless your [a]brother *is* with
you.'
4 "If you send our brother with
us, we will go down and buy you
food.
5 "But if you will not send *him*,
we will not go down; for the man
said to us, 'You shall not see my
face unless your brother *is* with
you.'"
6 And Israel said, "Why did you
deal *so* [1]wrongfully with me *as* to
tell the man whether you had still
another brother?"
7 But they said, "The man asked
us pointedly about ourselves and
our family, saying, '*Is* your father
still alive? Have you *another*
brother?' And we told him accord-
ing to these words. Could we pos-
sibly have known that he would
say, 'Bring your brother down'?"
8 Then Judah said to Israel his
father, "Send the lad with me, and
we will arise and go, that we may

[a]live and not die, both we and you
and also our little ones.
9 "I myself will be surety for him;
from my hand you shall require
him. [a]If I do not bring him *back*
to you and set him before you, then
let me bear the blame forever.
10 "For if we had not lingered,
surely by now we would have re-
turned this second time."
11 And their father Israel said to
them, "If *it must be* so, then do
this: Take some of the best fruits
of the land in your vessels and
[a]carry down a present for the
man—a little [b]balm and a little
honey, spices and myrrh, pistachio
nuts and almonds.
12 "Take double money in your
hand, and take back in your hand
the money [a]that was returned in
the mouth of your sacks; perhaps
it was an oversight.
13 "Take your brother also, and
arise, go back to the man.
14 "And may God [a]Almighty [b]give
you mercy before the man, that he
may release your other brother
and Benjamin. [c]If I am bereaved,
I am bereaved!"
15 So the men took that present
and Benjamin, and they took dou-
ble money in their hand, and arose
and went [a]down to Egypt; and they
stood before Joseph.
16 When Joseph saw Benjamin
with them, he said to the [a]steward
of his house, "Take *these* men to
my home, and slaughter [1]an ani-
mal and make ready; for *these*
men will dine with me at noon."
17 Then the man did as Joseph or-
dered, and the man brought the
men into Joseph's house.
18 Now the men were [a]afraid be-
cause they were brought into Jo-
seph's house; and they said, "*It is*
because of the money, which was
returned in our sacks the first time,
that we are brought in, so that he
may [1]make a case against us and
seize us, to take us as slaves with
our donkeys."
19 When they drew near to the
steward of Joseph's house, they
talked with him at the door of the
house,
20 and said, "O sir, [a]we indeed
came down the first time to buy
food;
21 "but [a]it happened, when we
came to the encampment, that we
opened our sacks, and there, *each*
man's money *was* in the mouth of
his sack, our money in full weight;
so we have brought it back in our
hand.
22 "And we have brought down
other money in our hands to buy
food. We do not know who put our
money in our sacks."
23 But he said, "Peace *be* with
you, do not be afraid. Your God
and the God of your father has
given you treasure in your sacks;
I had your money." Then he
brought [a]Simeon out to them.
24 So the man brought the men
into Joseph's house and [a]gave
them water, and they washed their
feet; and he gave their donkeys
feed.
25 Then they made the present
ready for Joseph's coming at noon,
for they heard that they would eat
bread there.
26 And when Joseph came home,
they brought him the present
which *was* in their hand into the
house, and [a]bowed down before
him to the earth.
27 Then he asked them about
their well-being, and said, "*Is* your
father well, the old man [a]of whom
you spoke? *Is* he still alive?"
28 And they answered, "Your ser-
vant our father *is* in good health;
he *is* still alive." [a]And they bowed
their heads down and prostrated
themselves.
29 Then he lifted his eyes and
saw his brother Benjamin, [a]his
mother's son, and said, "*Is* this
your younger brother [b]of whom
you spoke to me?" And he said,
"God be gracious to you, my son."
30 Now [a]his heart yearned for his
brother; so Joseph made haste and
sought *somewhere* to weep. And
he went into *his* chamber and
[b]wept there.
31 Then he washed his face and
came out; and he restrained him-
self, and said, "Serve the [a]bread."
32 So they set him a place by him-
self, and them by themselves, and
the Egyptians who ate with him by
themselves; because the Egyptians
could not eat food with the [a]He-
brews, for that *is* [b]an abomination
to the Egyptians.
33 And they sat before him, the

8 [a]Gen. 42:2; 47:19
9 [a]Gen. 42:37; 44:32; Philem. 18, 19
11 [a]Gen. 32:20; 33:10; 43:25, 26; [Prov. 18:16] [b]Gen. 37:25; Jer. 8:22; Ezek. 27:17
12 [a]Gen. 42:25, 35; 43:21, 22
14 [a]Gen. 17:1; 28:3; 35:11; 48:3 [b]Gen. 39:21; Ps. 106:46 [c]Gen. 42:36; Esth. 4:16
15 [a]Gen. 39:1; 46:3, 6
16 [a]Gen. 24:2; 39:4; 44:1 [1]Lit. *a slaughter*
18 [a]Gen. 42:28 [1]Lit. *roll himself upon us*
20 [a]Gen. 42:3, 10
21 [a]Gen. 42:27, 35
23 [a]Gen. 42:24
24 [a]Gen. 18:4; 19:2; 24:32
26 [a]Gen. 37:7, 10; 42:6; 44:14
27 [a]Gen. 29:6; 42:11, 13; 43:7; 45:3; 2 Kin. 4:26
28 [a]Gen. 37:7, 10
29 [a]Gen. 35:17, 18 [b]Gen. 42:13
30 [a]1 Kin. 3:26 [b]Gen. 42:24; 45:2, 14, 15; 46:29
31 [a]Gen. 43:25
32 [a]Gen. 41:12; Ex. 1:15 [b]Gen. 46:34; Ex. 8:26

firstborn according to his [a]birth-
right and the youngest according
to his youth; and the men looked
in astonishment at one another.
34 Then he took servings to them
from before him, but Benjamin's
serving was [a]five times as much
as any of theirs. So they drank and
were merry with him.

Joseph's Cup

44 And he commanded [1]the
[a]steward of his house, say-
ing, [b]"Fill the men's sacks with
food, as much as they can carry,
and put each man's money in the
mouth of his sack.
2 "Also put my cup, the silver
cup, in the mouth of the sack of
the youngest, and his grain
money." So he did according to the
word that Joseph had spoken.
3 As soon as the morning
dawned, the men were sent away,
they and their donkeys.
4 When they had gone out of the
city, *and* were not *yet* far off, Jo-
seph said to his steward, "Get up,
follow the men; and when you
overtake them, say to them, 'Why
have you [a]repaid evil for good?
5 '*Is* not this *the one* from which
my lord drinks, and with which he
indeed practices divination? You
have done evil in so doing.' "
6 So he overtook them, and he
spoke to them these same words.
7 And they said to him, "Why
does my lord say these words? Far
be it from us that your servants
should do such a thing.
8 "Look, we brought back to you
from the land of Canaan [a]the
money which we found in the
mouth of our sacks. How then
could we steal silver or gold from
your lord's house?
9 "With whomever of your ser-
vants it is found, [a]let him die, and
we also will be my lord's slaves."
10 And he said, "Now also *let* it
be according to your words; he
with whom it is found shall be my
slave, and you shall be blameless."
11 Then each man speedily let
down his sack to the ground, and
each opened his sack.
12 So he searched. He began with
the oldest and [1]left off with the
youngest; and the cup was found
in Benjamin's sack.

33 [a]Gen. 27:36; 42:7; Deut. 21:16, 17
34 [a]Gen. 35:24; 45:22
CHAPTER 44
1 [a]Gen. 43:16 [b]Gen. 42:25 [1]Lit. *the one over*
4 [a]1 Sam. 25:21
8 [a]Gen. 43:21
9 [a]Gen. 31:32
12 [1]*finished with*
13 [a]Gen. 37:29, 34; Num. 14:6; 2 Sam. 1:11
14 [a]Gen. 37:7, 10
16 [a][Num. 32:23] [b]Gen. 44:9
17 [a]Prov. 17:15
18 [a]Gen. 18:30, 32; Ex. 32:22
20 [a]Gen. 37:3; 43:8; 44:30 [b]Gen. 42:38 [c]Gen. 46:19 [d]Gen. 42:4
21 [a]Gen. 42:15, 20
23 [a]Gen. 43:3, 5
25 [a]Gen. 43:2

13 Then they [a]tore their clothes,
and each man loaded his donkey
and returned to the city.
14 So Judah and his brothers
came to Joseph's house, and he
was still there; and they [a]fell be-
fore him on the ground.
15 And Joseph said to them,
"What deed *is* this you have done?
Did you not know that such a man
as I can certainly practice divi-
nation?"
16 Then Judah said, "What shall
we say to my lord? What shall we
speak? Or how shall we clear our-
selves? God has [a]found out the
iniquity of your servants; here
[b]we are, my lord's slaves, both we
and *he* also with whom the cup
was found."
17 But he said, [a]"Far be it from me
that I should do so; the man in
whose hand the cup was found, he
shall be my slave. And as for you,
go up in peace to your father."

Judah Intercedes for Benjamin

18 Then Judah came near to him
and said: "O my lord, please let
your servant speak a word in my
lord's hearing, and [a]do not let your
anger burn against your servant;
for you *are* even like Pharaoh.
19 "My lord asked his servants,
saying, 'Have you a father or a
brother?'
20 "And we said to my lord, 'We
have a father, an old man, and [a]a
child of *his* old age, *who is* young;
his brother is [b]dead, and he [c]alone
is left of his mother's children, and
his [d]father loves him.'
21 "Then you said to your ser-
vants, [a]'Bring him down to me,
that I may set my eyes on him.'
22 "And we said to my lord, 'The
lad cannot leave his father, for *if*
he should leave his father, *his fa-
ther* would die.'
23 "But you said to your servants,
[a]'Unless your youngest brother
comes down with you, you shall
see my face no more.'
24 "So it was, when we went up
to your servant my father, that we
told him the words of my lord.
25 "And [a]our father said, 'Go back
and buy us a little food.'
26 "But we said, 'We cannot go
down; if our youngest brother is
with us, then we will go down; for

we may not see the man's face un-
less our youngest brother *is* with
us.'
27 "Then your servant my father
said to us, 'You know that [a]my
wife bore me two sons;
28 'and the one went out from me,
and I said, [a]"Surely he is torn to
pieces"; and I have not seen him
since.
29 'But if you [a]take this one also
from me, and calamity befalls him,
you shall bring down my gray hair
with sorrow to the grave.'
30 "Now therefore, when I come
to your servant my father, and the
lad *is* not with us, since [a]his life
is bound up in the lad's life,
31 "it will happen, when he sees
that the lad *is* not *with us,* that he
will die. So your servants will
bring down the gray hair of your
servant our father with sorrow to
the grave.
32 "For your servant became
surety for the lad to my father, say-
ing, [a]'If I do not bring him *back*
to you, then I shall bear the blame
before my father forever.'
33 "Now therefore, please [a]let
your servant remain instead of the
lad as a slave to my lord, and let
the lad go up with his brothers.
34 "For how shall I go up to my
father if the lad *is* not with me, lest
perhaps I see the evil that would
[1]come upon my father?"

Joseph Revealed to His Brothers

45 Then Joseph could not re-
strain himself before all
those who stood by him, and he
cried out, "Make everyone go out
from me!" So no one stood with
him [a]while Joseph made himself
known to his brothers.
2 And he [a]wept aloud, and the
Egyptians and the house of Pha-
raoh heard *it.*
3 Then Joseph said to his
brothers, [a]"I *am* Joseph; does my
father still live?" But his brothers
could not answer him, for they
were dismayed in his presence.
4 And Joseph said to his
brothers, "Please come near to
me." So they came near. Then he
said: "I *am* Joseph your brother,
[a]whom you sold into Egypt.
5 "But now, do not therefore be
grieved or angry with yourselves
because you sold me here; [a]for
God sent me before you to pre-
serve life.
6 "For these two years the [a]fam-
ine *has been* in the land, and *there*
are still five years in which *there*
will be neither plowing nor har-
vesting.
7 "And God [a]sent me before you
to preserve a [1]posterity for you in
the earth, and to save your lives
by a great deliverance.
8 "So now *it was* not you *who*
sent me here, but [a]God; and He has
made me [b]a father to Pharaoh, and
lord of all his house, and a [c]ruler
throughout all the land of Egypt.
9 "Hurry and go up to my father,
and say to him, 'Thus says your
son Joseph: "God has made me
lord of all Egypt; come down to
me, do not [1]tarry.
10 [a]"You shall dwell in the land
of Goshen, and you shall be near
to me, you and your children, your
children's children, your flocks
and your herds, and all that you
have.
11 "There I will [a]provide for you,
lest you and your household, and
all that you have, come to poverty;
for *there are* still five years of fam-
ine." '
12 "And behold, your eyes and the
eyes of my brother Benjamin see
that *it is* [a]my mouth that speaks
to you.
13 "So you shall tell my father of
all my glory in Egypt, and of all
that you have seen; and you shall
hurry and [a]bring my father down
here."
14 Then he fell on his brother Ben-
jamin's neck and wept, and Benja-
min wept on his neck.
15 Moreover he [a]kissed all his
brothers and wept over them, and
after that his brothers talked with
him.
16 Now the report of it was heard
in Pharaoh's house, saying, "Jo-
seph's brothers have come." So it
pleased Pharaoh and his servants
well.
17 And Pharaoh said to Joseph,
"Say to your brothers, 'Do this:
Load your animals and depart; go
to the land of Canaan.
18 'Bring your father and your
households and come to me; I will
give you the best of the land of

27 [a]Gen. 30:22–24; 35:16–18; 46:19
28 [a]Gen. 37:31–35
29 [a]Gen. 42:36, 38; 44:31
30 [a][1 Sam. 18:1; 25:29]
32 [a]Gen. 43:9
33 [a]Ex. 32:32
34 [1]Lit. *find*

CHAPTER 45

1 [a]Acts 7:13
2 [a]Gen. 43:30; 46:29
3 [a]Gen. 43:27; Acts 7:13
4 [a]Gen. 37:28; 39:1; Ps. 105:17
5 [a]Gen. 45:7, 8; 50:20; Ps. 105:16, 17
6 [a]Gen. 43:1; 47:4, 13
7 [a]Gen. 45:5; 50:20 [1]*remnant*
8 [a][Rom. 8:28] [b]Judg. 17:10; Is. 22:21 [c]Gen. 41:43; 42:6
9 [1]*delay*
10 [a]Gen. 46:28, 34; 47:1, 6; Ex. 9:26
11 [a]Gen. 47:12
12 [a]Gen. 42:23
13 [a]Gen. 46:6–28; Acts 7:14
15 [a]Gen. 48:10

Egypt, and you will eat [a]the [1]fat
of the land.
19 'Now you are commanded—do
this: Take carts out of the land of
Egypt for your little ones and your
wives; bring your father and come.
20 'Also do not be concerned
about your goods, for the best of
all the land of Egypt *is* yours.' "
21 Then the sons of Israel did so;
and Joseph gave them [a]carts,[1] ac-
cording to the command of Pha-
raoh, and he gave them provisions
for the journey.
22 He gave to all of them, to each
man, [a]changes of garments; but to
Benjamin he gave three hundred
pieces of silver and [b]five changes
of garments.
23 And he sent to his father these
things: ten donkeys loaded with
the good things of Egypt, and ten
female donkeys loaded with grain,
bread, and food for his father for
the journey.
24 So he sent his brothers away,
and they departed; and he said to
them, "See that you do not become
troubled along the way."
25 Then they went up out of
Egypt, and came to the land of Ca-
naan to Jacob their father.
26 And they told him, saying, "Jo-
seph *is* still alive, and he *is* gover-
nor over all the land of Egypt."
[a]And Jacob's heart stood still, be-
cause he did not believe them.
27 But when they told him all the
words which Joseph had said to
them, and when he saw the carts
which Joseph had sent to carry
him, the spirit [a]of Jacob their fa-
ther revived.
28 Then Israel said, "*It is* enough.
Joseph my son *is* still alive. I will
go and see him before I die."

Jacob's Journey to Egypt

46 So Israel took his journey
with all that he had, and
came to [a]Beersheba, and offered
sacrifices [b]to the God of his father
Isaac.
2 Then God spoke to Israel [a]in
the visions of the night, and said,
"Jacob, Jacob!" And he said,
"Here I am."
3 So He said, "I *am* God, [a]the
God of your father; do not fear to
go down to Egypt, for I will [b]make
of you a great nation there.
4 [a]"I will go down with you to
Egypt, and I will also surely [b]bring
you up *again;* and [c]Joseph [1]will
put his hand on your eyes."
5 Then [a]Jacob arose from Beer-
sheba; and the sons of Israel car-
ried their father Jacob, their little
ones, and their wives, in the [1]carts
[b]which Pharaoh had sent to carry
him.
6 So they took their livestock and
their goods, which they had ac-
quired in the land of Canaan, and
went to Egypt, [a]Jacob and all his
descendants with him.
7 His sons and his sons' sons, his
daughters and his sons' daughters,
and all his descendants he brought
with him to Egypt.
8 Now [a]these *were* the names of
the children of Israel, Jacob and
his sons, who went to Egypt: [b]Reu-
ben *was* Jacob's firstborn.
9 The [a]sons of Reuben *were* Ha-
noch, Pallu, Hezron, and Carmi.
10 [a]The sons of Simeon *were*
[1]Jemuel, Jamin, Ohad, [2]Jachin,
[3]Zohar, and Shaul, the son of a Ca-
naanite woman.
11 The sons of [a]Levi *were* Ger-
shon, Kohath, and Merari.
12 The sons of [a]Judah *were* [b]Er,
Onan, Shelah, Perez, and Zerah
(but Er and Onan died in the land
of Canaan). [c]The sons of Perez
were Hezron and Hamul.
13 The sons of Issachar *were* Tola,
[1]Puvah, [2]Job, and Shimron.
14 The [a]sons of Zebulun *were*
Sered, Elon, and Jahleel.
15 These *were* the [a]sons of Leah,
whom she bore to Jacob in Padan
Aram, with his daughter Dinah.
All the persons, his sons and his
daughters, *were* thirty-three.
16 The sons of Gad *were* [1]Ziphion,
Haggi, Shuni, [2]Ezbon, Eri, [3]Arodi,
and Areli.
17 [a]The sons of Asher *were* Jim-
nah, Ishuah, Isui, Beriah, and
Serah, their sister. And the sons
of Beriah *were* Heber and Mal-
chiel.
18 [a]These *were* the sons of Zilpah,
[b]whom Laban gave to Leah his
daughter; and these she bore to Ja-
cob: sixteen persons.
19 The [a]sons of Rachel, [b]Jacob's
wife, *were* Joseph and Benjamin.
20 [a]And to Joseph in the land of
Egypt were born Manasseh and

18 [a]Gen. 27:28; 47:6; Deut. 32:9–14 [1]The choicest produce
21 [a]Gen. 45:19; 46:5 [1]*wagons*
22 [a]2 Kin. 5:5 [b]Gen. 43:34
26 [a]Job 29:24
27 [a]Judg. 15:19

CHAPTER 46

1 [a]Gen. 21:31, 33; 26:32, 33; 28:10 [b]Gen. 26:24, 25; 28:13; 31:42; 32:9
2 [a]Gen. 15:1; 22:11; 31:11
3 [a]Gen. 17:1; 28:13 [b]Deut. 26:5
4 [a]Gen. 28:15; 31:3; 48:21 [b]Gen. 15:16; 50:12, 24, 25 [c]Gen. 50:1 [1]Will close your eyes when you die
5 [a]Acts 7:15 [b]Gen. 45:19–21 [1]*wagons*
6 [a]Deut. 26:5
8 [a]Ex. 1:1–4 [b]Num. 26:4, 5
9 [a]Ex. 6:14
10 [a]Ex. 6:15 [1]*Nemuel,* 1 Chr. 4:24 [2]*Jarib,* 1 Chr. 4:24 [3]*Zerah,* 1 Chr. 4:24
11 [a]1 Chr. 6:1, 16
12 [a]1 Chr. 2:3; 4:21 [b]Gen. 38:3, 7, 10 [c]Gen. 38:29
13 [1]*Puah,* Num. 26:23; 1 Chr. 7:1 [2]*Jashub,* Num. 26:24; 1 Chr. 7:1
14 [a]Num. 26:26
15 [a]Gen. 35:23; 49:31
16 [1]Sam., LXX *Zephon* and Num. 26:15 [2]*Ozni,* Num. 26:16 [3]*Arod,* Num. 26:17
17 [a]1 Chr. 7:30
18 [a]Gen. 30:10; 37:2 [b]Gen. 29:24
19 [a]Gen. 35:24 [b]Gen. 44:27
20 [a]Gen. 41:45, 50–52; 48:1

Ephraim, whom Asenath, the
daughter of Poti-Pherah priest of
On, bore to him.
21 [a]The sons of Benjamin *were*
Belah, Becher, Ashbel, Gera, Naa-
man, [b]Ehi, Rosh, [c]Muppim,
[1]Huppim, and Ard.
22 These *were* the sons of Rachel,
who were born to Jacob: fourteen
persons in all.
23 The son of Dan *was* [1]Hushim.
24 [a]The sons of Naphtali *were*
[1]Jahzeel, Guni, Jezer, and [2]Shil-
lem.
25 [a]These *were* the sons of Bilhah,
[b]whom Laban gave to Rachel his
daughter, and she bore these to Ja-
cob: seven persons in all.
26 [a]All the persons who went with
Jacob to Egypt, who came from his
body, [b]besides Jacob's sons' wives,
were sixty-six persons in all.
27 And the sons of Joseph who
were born to him in Egypt *were*
two persons. [a]All the persons of
the house of Jacob who went to
Egypt were seventy.

Jacob Settles in Goshen

28 Then he sent Judah before him
to Joseph, [a]to point out before him
the way to Goshen. And they came
[b]to the land of Goshen.
29 So Joseph made ready his
[a]chariot and went up to Goshen to
meet his father Israel; and he pre-
sented himself to him, and [b]fell on
his neck and wept on his neck a
good while.
30 And Israel said to Joseph,
[a]"Now let me die, since I have seen
your face, because you *are* still
alive."
31 Then Joseph said to his
brothers and to his father's house-
hold, [a]"I will go up and tell Pha-
raoh, and say to him, 'My brothers
and those of my father's house,
who *were* in the land of Canaan,
have come to me.
32 'And the men *are* [a]shepherds,
for their occupation has been to
feed livestock; and they have
brought their flocks, their herds,
and all that they have.'
33 "So it shall be, when Pharaoh
calls you and says, [a]'What is your
occupation?'
34 "that you shall say, 'Your ser-
vants' [a]occupation has been with
livestock [b]from our youth even till
now, both we *and* also our fathers,'
that you may dwell in the land of
Goshen; for every shepherd *is* [c]an[1]
abomination to the Egyptians."

47 Then Joseph [a]went and told
Pharaoh, and said, "My fa-
ther and my brothers, their flocks
and their herds and all that they
possess, have come from the land
of Canaan; and indeed they *are* in
[b]the land of Goshen."
2 And he took five men from
among his brothers and [a]pre-
sented them to Pharaoh.
3 Then Pharaoh said to his
brothers, [a]"What *is* your occupa-
tion?" And they said to Pharaoh,
[b]"Your servants *are* shepherds,
both we *and* also our fathers."
4 And they said to Pharaoh,
[a]"We have come to dwell in the
land, because your servants have
no pasture for their flocks, [b]for the
famine *is* severe in the land of Ca-
naan. Now therefore, please let
your servants [c]dwell in the land of
Goshen."
5 Then Pharaoh spoke to Joseph,
saying, "Your father and your
brothers have come to you.
6 [a]"The land of Egypt *is* be-
fore you. Have your father and
brothers dwell in the best of the
land; let them dwell [b]in the land
of Goshen. And if you know *any*
competent men among them, then
make them chief herdsmen over
my livestock."
7 Then Joseph brought in his fa-
ther Jacob and set him before
Pharaoh; and Jacob [a]blessed Pha-
raoh.
8 Pharaoh said to Jacob, "How
old *are* you?"
9 And Jacob said to Pharaoh,
[a]"The days of the years of my [1]pil-
grimage *are* [b]one hundred and
thirty years; [c]few and evil have
been the days of the years of my
life, and [d]they have not attained
to the days of the years of the life
of my fathers in the days of their
pilgrimage."
10 So Jacob [a]blessed Pharaoh,
and went out from before Pharaoh.
11 And Joseph situated his father
and his brothers, and gave them
a possession in the land of Egypt,
in the best of the land, in the land
of [a]Rameses, [b]as Pharaoh had
commanded.

---

21 [a]1 Chr. 7:6; 8:1 [b]Num. 26:38 [c]Num. 26:39; 1 Chr. 7:12 [1]*Hupham,* Num. 26:39
23 [1]*Shuham,* Num. 26:42
24 [a]Num. 26:48 [1]*Jahziel,* 1 Chr. 7:13 [2]*Shallum,* 1 Chr. 7:13
25 [a]Gen. 30:5, 7 [b]Gen. 29:29
26 [a]Ex. 1:5 [b]Gen. 35:11
27 [a]Ex. 1:5; Deut. 10:22; Acts 7:14
28 [a]Gen. 31:21 [b]Gen. 47:1
29 [a]Gen. 41:43 [b]Gen. 45:14, 15
30 [a]Luke 2:29, 30
31 [a]Gen. 47:1
32 [a]Gen. 47:3
33 [a]Gen. 47:2, 3
34 [a]Gen. 47:3 [b]Gen. 30:35; 34:5; 37:17 [c]Gen. 43:32; Ex. 8:26 [1]*loathsome*

CHAPTER 47

1 [a]Gen. 46:31 [b]Gen. 45:10; 46:28; 50:8
2 [a]Acts 7:13
3 [a]Gen. 46:33; Jon. 1:8 [b]Gen. 46:32, 34; Ex. 2:17, 19
4 [a]Gen. 15:13; Deut. 26:5; Ps. 105:23 [b]Gen. 43:1; Acts 7:11 [c]Gen. 46:34
6 [a]Gen. 20:15; 45:10, 18; 47:11 [b]Gen. 47:4
7 [a]Gen. 47:10; 48:15, 20; 2 Sam. 14:22; 1 Kin. 8:66; Heb. 7:7
9 [a]Ps. 39:12; [Heb. 11:9, 13] [b]Gen. 47:28 [c][Job 14:1] [d]Gen. 5:5; 11:10, 11; 25:7, 8; 35:28 [1]Lit. *sojourning*
10 [a]Gen. 47:7
11 [a]Ex. 1:11; 12:37 [b]Gen. 47:6, 27

12 Then Joseph provided [a]his fa-
ther, his brothers, and all his fa-
ther's household with bread, ac-
cording to the number in *their*
families.

Joseph Deals with the Famine

13 Now *there was* no bread in all
the land; for the famine *was* very
severe, [a]so that the land of Egypt
and the land of Canaan languished
because of the famine.
14 [a]And Joseph gathered up all
the money that was found in the
land of Egypt and in the land of
Canaan, for the grain which they
bought; and Joseph brought the
money into Pharaoh's house.
15 So when the money failed in
the land of Egypt and in the land
of Canaan, all the Egyptians came
to Joseph and said, "Give us bread,
for [a]why should we die in your
presence? For the money has
failed."
16 Then Joseph said, "Give your
livestock, and I will give you *bread*
for your livestock, if the money is
gone."
17 So they brought their livestock
to Joseph, and Joseph gave them
bread *in exchange* for the horses,
the flocks, the cattle of the herds,
and for the donkeys. Thus he [1]fed
them with bread *in exchange* for
all their livestock that year.
18 When that year had ended,
they came to him the next year and
said to him, "We will not hide from
my lord that our money is gone;
my lord also has our herds of live-
stock. There is nothing left in the
sight of my lord but our bodies and
our lands.
19 "Why should we die before
your eyes, both we and our land?
Buy us and our land for bread, and
we and our land will be servants
of Pharaoh; give *us* seed, that we
may [a]live and not die, that the land
may not be desolate."
20 Then Joseph [a]bought all the
land of Egypt for Pharaoh; for
every man of the Egyptians sold
his field, because the famine was
severe upon them. So the land be-
came Pharaoh's.
21 And as for the people, he
[1]moved them into the cities, from
one end of the borders of Egypt
to the *other* end.

12 [a]Gen. 45:11; 50:21
13 [a]Gen. 41:30; Acts 7:11
14 [a]Gen. 41:56; 42:6
15 [a]Gen. 47:19
17 [1]*supplied*
19 [a]Gen. 43:8
20 [a]Jer. 32:43
21 [1]So with MT, Tg.; Sam., LXX, Vg. *made the people virtual slaves*
22 [a]Lev. 25:34; Ezra 7:24 [b]Gen. 41:45
25 [a]Gen. 33:15
26 [a]Gen. 47:22
27 [a]Gen. 47:11 [b]Gen. 17:6; 26:4; 35:11; 46:3; Ex. 1:7; Deut. 26:5; Acts 7:17
29 [a]Deut. 31:14; 1 Kin. 2:1 [b]Gen. 24:2–4 [c]Gen. 24:49; Josh. 2:14 [d]Gen. 50:25
30 [a]2 Sam. 19:37 [b]Gen. 49:29; 50:5–13; Heb. 11:21
31 [a]Gen. 48:2; 1 Kin. 1:47; Heb. 11:21

22 [a]Only the land of the [b]priests
he did not buy; for the priests had
rations *allotted to them* by Pha-
raoh, and they ate their rations
which Pharaoh gave them; there-
fore they did not sell their
lands.
23 Then Joseph said to the people,
"Indeed I have bought you and
your land this day for Pharaoh.
Look, *here is* seed for you, and you
shall sow the land.
24 "And it shall come to pass in
the harvest that you shall give one-
fifth to Pharaoh. Four-fifths shall
be your own, as seed for the field
and for your food, for those of your
households and as food for your
little ones."
25 So they said, "You have saved
[a]our lives; let us find favor in the
sight of my lord, and we will be
Pharaoh's servants."
26 And Joseph made it a law over
the land of Egypt to this day, *that*
Pharaoh should have one-fifth,
[a]except for the land of the priests
only, *which* did not become Pha-
raoh's.

Joseph's Vow to Jacob

27 So Israel [a]dwelt in the land of
Egypt, in the country of Goshen;
and they had possessions there
and [b]grew and multiplied ex-
ceedingly.
28 And Jacob lived in the land of
Egypt seventeen years. So the
length of Jacob's life was one hun-
dred and forty-seven years.
29 When the time [a]drew near that
Israel must die, he called his son
Joseph and said to him, "Now if I
have found favor in your sight,
please [b]put your hand under my
thigh, and [c]deal kindly and truly
with me. [d]Please do not bury me
in Egypt,
30 "but [a]let me lie with my fa-
thers; you shall carry me out of
Egypt and [b]bury me in their burial
place." And he said, "I will do as
you have said."
31 Then he said, "Swear to me."
And he swore to him. So [a]Israel
bowed himself on the head of the
bed.

Jacob Blesses Joseph's Sons

48 Now it came to pass after
these things that Joseph was

told, "Indeed your father *is* sick"; and he took with him his two sons, [a]Manasseh and Ephraim.
2 And Jacob was told, "Look, your son Joseph is coming to you"; and Israel [1]strengthened himself and sat up on the bed.
3 Then Jacob said to Joseph: "God [a]Almighty appeared to me at [b]Luz in the land of Canaan and blessed me,
4 "and said to me, 'Behold, I will [a]make you fruitful and multiply you, and I will make of you a multitude of people, and [b]give this land to your descendants after you [c]*as* an everlasting possession.'
5 "And now your [a]two sons, Ephraim and Manasseh, who were born to you in the land of Egypt before I came to you in Egypt, *are* mine; as Reuben and Simeon, they shall be mine.
6 "Your [1]offspring [2]whom you beget after them shall be yours; they will be called by the name of their brothers in their inheritance.
7 "But as for me, when I came from Padan, [a]Rachel died beside me in the land of Canaan on the way, when *there was* but a little distance to go to Ephrath; and I buried her there on the way to Ephrath (that is, Bethlehem)."
8 Then Israel saw Joseph's sons, and said, "Who *are* these?"
9 And Joseph said to his father, "They *are* my sons, whom God has given me in this *place*." And he said, "Please bring them to me, and [a]I will bless them."
10 Now [a]the eyes of Israel were dim with age, *so that* he could not see. Then Joseph brought them near him, and he [b]kissed them and embraced them.
11 And Israel said to Joseph, [a]"I had not thought to see your face; but in fact, God has also shown me your offspring!"
12 So Joseph brought them from beside his knees, and he bowed down with his face to the earth.
13 And Joseph took them both, Ephraim with his right hand toward Israel's left hand, and Manasseh with his left hand toward Israel's right hand, and brought *them* near him.
14 Then Israel stretched out his right hand and [a]laid *it* on Ephraim's head, who *was* the younger, and his left hand on Manasseh's head, [b]guiding his hands knowingly, for Manasseh *was* the [c]firstborn.
15 And [a]he blessed Joseph, and said:

"God, [b]before whom my fathers
Abraham and Isaac walked,
The God who has fed me all my
life long to this day,
16 The Angel [a]who has redeemed
me from all evil,
Bless the lads;
Let [b]my name be named upon
them,
And the name of my fathers
Abraham and Isaac;
And let them [c]grow into a
multitude in the midst of the
earth."

17 Now when Joseph saw that his father [a]laid his right hand on the head of Ephraim, it displeased him; so he took hold of his father's hand to remove it from Ephraim's head to Manasseh's head.
18 And Joseph said to his father, "Not so, my father, for this *one is* the firstborn; put your right hand on his head."
19 But his father refused and said, [a]"I know, my son, I know. He also shall become a people, and he also shall be great; but truly [b]his younger brother shall be greater than he, and his descendants shall become a multitude of nations."
20 So he blessed them that day, saying, [a]"By you Israel will bless, saying, 'May God make you as Ephraim and as Manasseh!'" And thus he set Ephraim before Manasseh.
21 Then Israel said to Joseph, "Behold, I am dying, but [a]God will be with you and bring you back to the land of your fathers.
22 "Moreover [a]I have given to you one [1]portion above your brothers, which I took from the hand [b]of the Amorite with my sword and my bow."

Jacob's Last Words to His Sons

49 And Jacob called his sons and said, "Gather together, that I may [a]tell you what shall befall you [b]in the last days:

CHAPTER 48

1 [a]Gen. 41:51, 56; 46:20; 50:23; Josh. 14:4
2 [1]Collected his strength
3 [a]Gen. 43:14; 49:25 [b]Gen. 28:13, 19; 35:6, 9
4 [a]Gen. 46:3 [b]Gen. 35:12; Ex. 6:8 [c]Gen. 17:8
5 [a]Gen. 41:50; 46:20; 48:8; Josh. 13:7; 14:4
6 [1]*children* [2]Who are born to you
7 [a]Gen. 35:9, 16, 19, 20
9 [a]Gen. 27:4; 47:15
10 [a]Gen. 27:1; 1 Sam. 3:2 [b]Gen. 27:27; 45:15; 50:1
11 [a]Gen. 45:26
14 [a]Matt. 19:15; Mark 10:16 [b]Gen. 48:19 [c]Gen. 41:51, 52; Josh. 17:1
15 [a]Gen. 47:7, 10; 49:24; [Heb. 11:21] [b]Gen. 17:1; 24:40; 2 Kin. 20:3
16 [a]Gen. 22:11, 15–18; 28:13–15; 31:11; [Ps. 34:22; 121:7] [b]Amos 9:12; Acts 15:17 [c]Num. 26:34, 37
17 [a]Gen. 48:14
19 [a]Gen. 48:14 [b]Num. 1:33, 35; Deut. 33:17
20 [a]Ruth 4:11, 12
21 [a]Gen. 28:15; 46:4; 50:24
22 [a]Gen. 14:7; Josh. 24:32; John 4:5 [b]Gen. 34:28 [1]Lit. *shoulder*

CHAPTER 49

1 [a]Deut. 33:1, 6–25; [Amos 3:7] [b]Num. 24:14; [Deut. 4:30]; Is. 2:2; 39:6; Jer. 23:20; Heb. 1:2

2 "Gather together and hear, you
sons of Jacob,
And listen to Israel your father.

3 "Reuben, you are [a]my firstborn,
My might and the beginning of
my strength,
The excellency of dignity and the
excellency of power.
4 Unstable as water, you shall not
excel,
Because you [a]went up to your
father's bed;
Then you defiled *it*—
He went up to my couch.

5 "Simeon and Levi *are* brothers;
Instruments of [1]cruelty *are in*
their dwelling place.
6 [a]Let not my soul enter their
council;
Let not my honor be united [b]to
their assembly;
[c]For in their anger they slew a
man,
And in their self-will they
[1]hamstrung an ox.
7 Cursed *be* their anger, for *it is*
fierce;
And their wrath, for it is cruel!
[a]I will divide them in Jacob
And scatter them in Israel.

8 "Judah,[a] you *are he* whom your
brothers shall praise;
[b]Your hand *shall be* on the neck
of your enemies;
[c]Your father's children shall bow
down before you.
9 Judah *is* [a]a lion's whelp;
From the prey, my son, you have
gone up.
[b]He [1]bows down, he lies down as
a lion;
And as a lion, who shall rouse
him?
10 [a]The [1]scepter shall not depart
from Judah,
Nor [b]a lawgiver from between his
feet,
[c]Until Shiloh comes;
[d]And to Him *shall be* the
obedience of the people.
11 Binding his donkey to the vine,
And his donkey's colt to the
choice vine,
He washed his garments in wine,
And his clothes in the blood of
grapes.
12 His eyes *are* darker than wine,
And his teeth whiter than milk.

13 "Zebulun[a] shall dwell by the
haven of the sea;
He *shall become* a haven for
ships,
And his border shall [b]adjoin
Sidon.

14 "Issachar[a] is a strong donkey,
Lying down between two
burdens;
15 He saw that rest *was* good,
And that the land *was* pleasant;
He bowed [a]his shoulder to bear
a burden,
And became a band of slaves.

16 "Dan[a] shall judge his people
As one of the tribes of Israel.
17 [a]Dan shall be a serpent by the
way,
A viper by the path,
That bites the horse's heels
So that its rider shall fall
backward.
18 [a]I have waited for your salvation,
O LORD!

19 "Gad,[a1] a troop shall [2]tramp upon
him,
But he shall [2]triumph at last.

20 "Bread from [a]Asher *shall be* rich,
And he shall yield royal
dainties.

21 "Naphtali[a] *is* a deer let loose;
He uses beautiful words.

22 "Joseph *is* a fruitful bough,
A fruitful bough by a well;
His branches run over the wall.
23 The archers have [a]bitterly
grieved him,
Shot *at him* and hated him.
24 But his [a]bow remained in
strength,
And the arms of his hands were
[1]made strong
By the hands of [b]the Mighty *God*
of Jacob
[c](From there [d]*is* the Shepherd, [e]the
Stone of Israel),
25 [a]By the God of your father who
will help you,
[b]And by the Almighty [c]who will
bless you
With blessings of heaven above,
Blessings of the deep that lies
beneath,
Blessings of the breasts and of
the womb.
26 The blessings of your father
Have excelled the blessings of my
ancestors,
[a]Up to the utmost bound of the
everlasting hills.

3 [a]Gen. 29:32
4 [a]Gen. 35:22
5 [1]*violence*
6 [a]Prov. 1:15, 16 [b]Ps. 26:9 [c]Gen. 34:26 [1]*lamed*
7 [a]Josh. 19:1, 9; 21:1–42
8 [a]Deut. 33:7 [b]Ps. 18:40 [c]1 Chr. 5:2
9 [a][Rev. 5:5] [b]Num. 23:24; 24:9 [1]*couches*
10 [a]Num. 24:17 [b]Ps. 60:7 [c]Is. 11:1 [d]Ps. 2:6–9; 72:8–11 [1]A symbol of kingship
13 [a]Deut. 33:18, 19 [b]Gen. 10:19
14 [a]1 Chr. 12:32
15 [a]1 Sam. 10:9
16 [a]Deut. 33:22
17 [a]Judg. 18:27
18 [a]Is. 25:9
19 [a]Deut. 33:20 [1]Lit. *Troop* [2]Lit. *raid*
20 [a]Deut. 33:24
21 [a]Deut. 33:23
23 [a]Gen. 37:4, 24
24 [a]Job 29:20 [b]Ps. 132:2, 5 [c]Gen. 45:11; 47:12 [d][Ps. 23:1; 80:1] [e]Is. 28:16 [1]Or *supple*
25 [a]Gen. 28:13; 32:9; 35:3; 43:23; 50:17 [b]Gen. 17:1; 35:11 [c]Deut. 33:13
26 [a]Deut. 33:15

[b]They shall be on the head of
Joseph,
And on the crown of the head of
him who was separate from his
brothers.

27 "Benjamin is a [a]ravenous wolf;
In the morning he shall devour
the prey,
[b]And at night he shall divide the
spoil."

28 All these *are* the twelve tribes
of Israel, and this *is* what their fa-
ther spoke to them. And he blessed
them; he blessed each one accord-
ing to his own blessing.

Jacob's Death and Burial

29 Then he charged them and said
to them: "I [a]am to be gathered to
my people; [b]bury me with my fa-
thers [c]in the cave that *is* in the field
of Ephron the Hittite,
30 "in the cave that *is* in the field
of Machpelah, which *is* before
Mamre in the land of Canaan,
[a]which Abraham bought with the
field of Ephron the Hittite as a pos-
session for a burial place.
31 [a]"There they buried Abraham
and Sarah his wife, [b]there they
buried Isaac and Rebekah his wife,
and there I buried Leah.
32 "The field and the cave that *is*
there *were* purchased from the
sons of Heth."
33 And when Jacob had finished
commanding his sons, he drew his
feet up into the bed and breathed
his last, and was gathered to his
people.

50 Then Joseph [a]fell on his fa-
ther's face, and [b]wept over
him, and kissed him.
2 And Joseph commanded his
servants the physicians to [a]em-
balm his father. So the physicians
embalmed Israel.
3 Forty days were required for
him, for such are the days required
for those who are embalmed; and
the Egyptians [a]mourned[1] for him
seventy days.
4 Now when the days of his
mourning were past, Joseph spoke
to [a]the household of Pharaoh, say-
ing, "If now I have found favor in
your eyes, please speak in the
hearing of Pharaoh, saying,
5 [a]'My father made me swear,
saying, "Behold, I am dying; in my
grave [b]which I dug for myself in
the land of Canaan, there you shall
bury me." Now therefore, please
let me go up and bury my father,
and I will come back.'"
6 And Pharaoh said, "Go up and
bury your father, as he made you
swear."
7 So Joseph went up to bury his
father; and with him went up all
the servants of Pharaoh, the elders
of his house, and all the elders of
the land of Egypt,
8 as well as all the house of Jo-
seph, his brothers, and his father's
house. Only their little ones, their
flocks, and their herds they left in
the land of Goshen.
9 And there went up with him
both chariots and horsemen, and
it was a very great gathering.
10 Then they came to the thresh-
ing floor of Atad, which *is* beyond
the Jordan, and they [a]mourned
there with a great and very solemn
lamentation. [b]He observed seven
days of mourning for his father.
11 And when the inhabitants of
the land, the Canaanites, saw the
mourning at the threshing floor of
Atad, they said, "This *is* a deep
mourning of the Egyptians."
Therefore its name was called
[1]Abel Mizraim, which *is* beyond
the Jordan.
12 So his sons did for him just as
he had commanded them.
13 For [a]his sons carried him to the
land of Canaan, and buried him in
the cave of the field of Machpelah,
before Mamre, which Abraham
[b]bought with the field from
Ephron the Hittite as property for
a burial place.
14 And after he had buried his
father, Joseph returned to Egypt,
he and his brothers and all who
went up with him to bury his fa-
ther.

Joseph Reassures His Brothers

15 When Joseph's brothers saw
that their father was dead, [a]they
said, "Perhaps Joseph will hate
us, and may [1]actually repay us
for all the evil which we did to
him."
16 So they sent *messengers* to Jo-
seph, saying, "Before your father
died he commanded, saying,

26 [b]Deut. 33:16
27 [a]Judg. 20:21, 25 [b]Num. 23:24; Esth. 8:11; Ezek. 39:10; Zech. 14:1
29 [a]Gen. 15:15; 25:8; 35:29 [b]Gen. 47:30; 2 Sam. 19:37 [c]Gen. 23:16–20; 50:13
30 [a]Gen. 23:3–20
31 [a]Gen. 23:19, 20; 25:9 [b]Gen. 35:29; 50:13

CHAPTER 50

1 [a]Gen. 46:4, 29 [b]2 Kin. 13:14
2 [a]Gen. 50:26; 2 Chr. 16:14; Matt. 26:12; Mark 16:1; Luke 24:1; John 19:39, 40
3 [a]Gen. 37:34; Num. 20:29; Deut. 34:8 [1]Lit. *wept*
4 [a]Esth. 4:2
5 [a]Gen. 47:29–31 [b]2 Chr. 16:14; Is. 22:16; Matt. 27:60
10 [a]Acts 8:2 [b]1 Sam. 31:13; Job 2:13
11 [1]Lit. *Mourning of Egypt*
13 [a]Gen. 49:29–31; Acts 7:16 [b]Gen. 23:16–20
15 [a][Job 15:21] [1]*fully*

17 'Thus you shall say to Joseph:
"I beg you, please forgive the tres-
pass of your brothers and their sin;
[a]for they did evil to you."' Now,
please, forgive the trespass of the
servants of [b]the God of your fa-
ther." And Joseph wept when they
spoke to him.
18 Then his brothers also went
and [a]fell down before his face, and
they said, "Behold, we *are* your
servants."
19 Joseph said to them, [a]"Do not
be afraid, [b]for *am* I in the place
of God?
20 [a]"But as for you, you meant
evil against me; *but* [b]God meant
it for good, in order to bring it
about as *it is* this day, to save
many people alive.
21 "Now therefore, do not be
afraid; [a]I will provide for you and
your little ones." And he com-
forted them and spoke [1]kindly to
them.

Death of Joseph

22 So Joseph dwelt in Egypt, he
and his father's household. And
Joseph lived one hundred and ten
years.
23 Joseph saw Ephraim's children
[a]to the third *generation.* [b]The chil-
dren of Machir, the son of Manas-
seh, [c]were also brought up on Jo-
seph's knees.
24 And Joseph said to his breth-
ren, "I am dying; but [a]God will
surely visit you, and bring you out
of this land to the land [b]of which
He swore to Abraham, to Isaac,
and to Jacob."
25 Then [a]Joseph took an oath
from the children of Israel, saying,
"God will surely [1]visit you, and
[b]you shall carry up my [c]bones
from here."
26 So Joseph died, *being* one hun-
dred and ten years old; and they
embalmed him, and he was put in
a coffin in Egypt.

17 [a][Prov. 28:13] [b]Gen. 49:25
18 [a]Gen. 37:7–10; 41:43; 44:14
19 [a]Gen. 45:5 [b]2 Kin. 5:7
20 [a]Ps. 56:5 [b][Acts 3:13–15]
21 [a][Matt. 5:44] [1]Lit. *to their hearts*
23 [a]Job 42:16 [b]Num. 26:29; 32:39 [c]Gen. 30:3
24 [a]Ex. 3:16, 17 [b]Gen. 26:3; 35:12; 46:4
25 [a]Ex. 13:19 [b]Deut. 1:8; 30:1–8 [c]Ex. 13:19 [1]*give attention to*

The Second Book of Moses Called

Exodus

EXODUS is the record of Israel's birth as a nation. Within the protective "womb" of Egypt, the Jewish family of seventy rapidly multiplies. At the right time, accompanied with severe "birth pains," an infant nation, numbering between two and three million people, is brought into the world where it is divinely protected, fed, and nurtured.

The Hebrew title, *We'elleh Shemoth,* "Now These *Are* the Names," comes from the first phrase in 1:1. Exodus begins with "Now" to show it as a continuation of Genesis. The Greek title is *Exodus,* a word meaning "exit," "departure," or "going out." The Septuagint uses this word to describe the book by its key event (see 19:1, "gone out"). In Luke 9:31 and in Second Peter 1:15, the word *exodus* speaks of physical death (Jesus and Peter). This embodies Exodus's theme of redemption, because redemption is accomplished only through death. The Latin title is *Liber Exodus,* "Book of Departure," taken from the Greek title.

Israel's Suffering in Egypt

NOW [a]these *are* the names of
the children of Israel who
came to Egypt; each man and
his household came with Jacob:
2 Reuben, Simeon, Levi, and Ju-
dah;
3 Issachar, Zebulun, and Benja-
min;
4 Dan, Naphtali, Gad, and Asher.
5 All those [1]who were descen-
dants of Jacob were [a]seventy[2] per-
sons (for Joseph was in Egypt *al-
ready*).
6 And [a]Joseph died, all his broth-
ers, and all that generation.
7 [a]But the children of Israel were
fruitful and increased abundantly,
multiplied and [1]grew exceedingly
mighty; and the land was filled
with them.
8 Now there arose a new king
over Egypt, [a]who did not know Jo-
seph.
9 And he said to his people,
"Look, the people of the children
of Israel *are* more and [a]mightier
than we;
10 [a]"come, let us [b]deal shrewdly
with them, lest they multiply, and
it happen, in the event of war, that
they also join our enemies and
fight against us, and *so* go up out
of the land."
11 Therefore they set taskmasters
over them [a]to afflict them with
their [b]burdens. And they built for
Pharaoh [c]supply cities, Pithom
[d]and Raamses.
12 But the more they afflicted
them, the more they multiplied
and grew. And they were in dread
of the children of Israel.
13 So the Egyptians made the chil-
dren of Israel [a]serve with [1]rigor.
14 And they [a]made their lives bit-
ter with hard bondage—[b]in mor-
tar, in brick, and in all manner of
service in the field. All their ser-
vice in which they made them
serve *was* with rigor.
15 Then the king of Egypt spoke
to the [a]Hebrew midwives, of whom
the name of one *was* Shiphrah and
the name of the other Puah;
16 and he said, "When you do the
duties of a midwife for the Hebrew
women, and see *them* on the birth-
stools, if it *is* a [a]son, then you shall
kill him; but if it *is* a daughter, then
she shall live."
17 But the midwives [a]feared God,
and did not do [b]as the king of
Egypt commanded them, but
saved the male children alive.
18 So the king of Egypt called for
the midwives and said to them,
"Why have you done this thing,
and saved the male children
alive?"
19 And [a]the midwives said to

CHAPTER 1

1 [a]Gen. 46:8–27
5 [a]Gen. 46:26, 27 [1]Lit. *who came from the loins of* [2]DSS, LXX *seventy-five;* cf. Acts 7:14
6 [a]Gen. 50:26
7 [a]Acts 7:17 [1]*became very numerous*
8 [a]Acts 7:18, 19
9 [a]Gen. 26:16
10 [a]Ps. 83:3, 4 [b]Acts 7:19
11 [a]Ex. 3:7; 5:6 [b]Ex. 1:14; 2:11; 5:4–9; 6:6 [c]1 Kin. 9:19 [d]Gen. 47:11
13 [a]Gen. 15:13 [1]*harshness*
14 [a]Num. 20:15 [b]Ps. 81:6
15 [a]Ex. 2:6
16 [a]Acts 7:19
17 [a]Prov. 16:6 [b]Dan. 3:16, 18
19 [a]Josh. 2:4

Pharaoh, "Because the Hebrew
women *are* not like the Egyptian
women; for they [1]*are* lively and
give birth before the midwives
come to them."
20 [a]Therefore God dealt well with
the midwives, and the people mul-
tiplied and [1]grew very mighty.
21 And so it was, because the mid-
wives feared God, [a]that He [1]pro-
vided households for them.
22 So Pharaoh commanded all his
people, saying, [a]"Every son who
is [1]born you shall cast into the
river, and every daughter you shall
save alive."

Moses Is Born

2 And [a]a man of the house of
Levi went and took *as wife* a
daughter of Levi.
2 So the woman conceived and
bore a son. And [a]when she saw
that he *was* a beautiful *child,* she
hid him three months.
3 But when she could no longer
hide him, she took an ark of [a]bul-
rushes for him, daubed it with [b]as-
phalt and [c]pitch, put the child in
it, and laid *it* in the reeds [d]by the
river's bank.
4 [a]And his sister stood afar off,
to know what would be done to
him.
5 Then the [a]daughter of Pharaoh
came down to bathe at the river.
And her maidens walked along the
riverside; and when she saw the
ark among the reeds, she sent her
maid to get it.
6 And when she opened *it,* she
saw the child, and behold, the
baby wept. So she had compassion
on him, and said, "This is one of
the Hebrews' children."
7 Then his sister said to Pha-
raoh's daughter, "Shall I go and
call a nurse for you from the He-
brew women, that she may nurse
the child for you?"
8 And Pharaoh's daughter said
to her, "Go." So the maiden went
and called the child's mother.
9 Then Pharaoh's daughter said
to her, "Take this child away and
nurse him for me, and I will give
you your wages." So the woman
took the child and nursed him.
10 And the child grew, and she
brought him to Pharaoh's daugh-
ter, and he became [a]her son. So

19 [1]*have vigor of life,* bear quickly, easily
20 [a][Prov. 11:18] [1]*became very numerous*
21 [a]1 Sam. 2:35 [1]*gave them families*
22 [a]Acts 7:19 [1]Sam., LXX, Tg. add *to the Hebrews*

CHAPTER 2

1 [a]Ex. 6:16–20
2 [a]Acts 7:20
3 [a]Is. 18:2 [b]Gen. 14:10 [c]Gen. 6:14 [d]Is. 19:6
4 [a]Num. 26:59
5 [a]Acts 7:21
10 [a]Acts 7:21 [1]Heb. *Mosheh,* lit. *Drawn Out*
11 [a]Heb. 11:24–26
12 [a]Acts 7:24, 25
13 [a]Acts 7:26–28 [b]Prov. 25:8
14 [a]Acts 7:27, 28 [b]Judg. 6:27
15 [a]Acts 7:29 [b]Ex. 3:1 [c]Gen. 24:11; 29:2 [1]*the presence of Pharaoh*
16 [a]Ex. 3:1; 4:18; 18:12 [b]Gen. 24:11, 13, 19; 29:6–10 [c]Gen. 30:38
17 [a]Gen. 47:3 [b]Gen. 26:19–21 [c]Gen. 29:3, 10
18 [a]Num. 10:29 [b]Ex. 3:1; 4:18 [1]*Jethro,* Ex. 3:1
20 [a]Gen. 31:54; 43:25
21 [a]Ex. 4:25; 18:2
22 [a]Ex. 4:20; 18:3, 4 [b]Acts 7:29 [1]Lit. *Stranger There* [2]*sojourner,* temporary resident

she called his name [1]Moses, say-
ing, "Because I drew him out of
the water."

Moses Flees to Midian

11 Now it came to pass in those
days, [a]when Moses was grown,
that he went out to his brethren
and looked at their burdens. And
he saw an Egyptian beating a He-
brew, one of his brethren.
12 So he looked this way and that
way, and when he saw no one, he
[a]killed the Egyptian and hid him
in the sand.
13 And [a]when he went out the sec-
ond day, behold, two Hebrew men
[b]were fighting, and he said to the
one who did the wrong, "Why are
you striking your companion?"
14 Then he said, [a]"Who made you
a prince and a judge over us? Do
you intend to kill me as you killed
the Egyptian?" So Moses [b]feared
and said, "Surely this thing is
known!"
15 When Pharaoh heard of this
matter, he sought to kill Moses.
But [a]Moses fled from [1]the face of
Pharaoh and dwelt in the land of
[b]Midian; and he sat down by [c]a
well.
16 [a]Now the priest of Midian had
seven daughters. [b]And they came
and drew water, and they filled the
[c]troughs to water their father's
flock.
17 Then the [a]shepherds came and
[b]drove them away; but Moses
stood up and helped them, and
[c]watered their flock.
18 When they came to [a]Reuel[1]
their father, [b]he said, "How *is it*
that you have come so soon to-
day?"
19 And they said, "An Egyptian
delivered us from the hand of the
shepherds, and he also drew
enough water for us and watered
the flock."
20 So he said to his daughters,
"And where *is* he? Why *is* it *that*
you have left the man? Call him,
that he may [a]eat bread."
21 Then Moses was content to live
with the man, and he gave [a]Zippo-
rah his daughter to Moses.
22 And she bore *him* a son. He
called his name [a]Gershom,[1] for he
said, "I have been [b]a [2]stranger in
a foreign land."

23 Now it happened [a]in the pro-
cess of time that the king of Egypt
died. Then the children of Israel
[b]groaned because of the bondage,
and they cried out; and [c]their cry
came up to God because of the
bondage.
24 So God [a]heard their groaning,
and God [b]remembered His [c]cov-
enant with Abraham, with Isaac,
and with Jacob.
25 And God [a]looked upon the chil-
dren of Israel, and God [b]acknowl-
edged *them.*

Moses at the Burning Bush

3 Now Moses was tending the
flock of [a]Jethro his father-in-
law, [b]the priest of Midian. And he
led the flock to the back of the
desert, and came to [c]Horeb, [d]the
mountain of God.
2 And [a]the Angel of the LORD ap-
peared to him in a flame of fire
from the midst of a bush. So he
looked, and behold, the bush was
burning with fire, but the bush *was*
not consumed.
3 Then Moses said, "I will now
turn aside and see this [a]great sight,
why the bush does not burn."
4 So when the LORD saw that he
turned aside to look, God called [a]to
him from the midst of the bush and
said, "Moses, Moses!" And he
said, "Here I am."
5 Then He said, "Do not draw
near this place. [a]Take your sandals
off your feet, for the place where
you stand *is* holy ground."
6 Moreover He said, [a]"I *am* the
God of your father—the God of
Abraham, the God of Isaac, and
the God of Jacob." And Moses hid
his face, for [b]he was afraid to look
upon God.
7 And the LORD said: [a]"I have
surely seen the oppression of My
people who *are* in Egypt, and have
heard their cry [b]because of their
taskmasters, [c]for I know their
[1]sorrows.
8 "So [a]I have come down to [b]de-
liver them out of the hand of the
Egyptians, and to bring them up
from that land [c]to a good and large
land, to a land [d]flowing with milk
and honey, to the place of [e]the Ca-
naanites and the Hittites and the
Amorites and the Perizzites and
the Hivites and the Jebusites.

23 [a]Acts 7:34 [b]Deut. 26:7 [c]James 5:4

24 [a]Ex. 6:5 [b]Gen. 15:13; 22:16–18; 26:2–5; 28:13–15 [c]Gen. 12:1–3; 15:14; 17:1–14

25 [a]Ex. 4:31 [b]Ex. 3:7

CHAPTER 3

1 [a]Ex. 4:18 [b]Ex. 2:16 [c]Ex. 17:6 [d]Ex. 18:5

2 [a]Deut. 33:16

3 [a]Acts 7:31

4 [a]Deut. 33:16

5 [a]Josh. 5:15

6 [a][Matt. 22:32] [b]1 Kin. 19:13

7 [a]Ex. 2:23–25 [b]Ex. 1:11 [c]Ex. 2:25 [1]*pain*

8 [a]Gen. 15:13–16; 46:4; 50:24, 25 [b]Ex. 6:6–8; 12:51 [c]Deut. 1:25; 8:7–9 [d]Jer. 11:5 [e]Gen. 15:19–21

9 [a]Ex. 2:23 [b]Ex. 1:11, 13, 14

10 [a][Mic. 6:4]

11 [a]Ex. 4:10; 6:12

12 [a]Gen. 31:3 [b]Ex. 4:8; 19:3

14 [a][John 8:24, 28, 58]

15 [a]Ps. 30:4; 97:12; 102:12; 135:13

16 [a]Ex. 4:29 [b]Ex. 2:25; 4:31

17 [a]Gen. 15:13–21; 46:4; 50:24, 25

18 [a]Ex. 4:31 [b]Ex. 5:1, 3 [c]Num. 23:3, 4, 15, 16

9 "Now therefore, behold, [a]the
cry of the children of Israel has
come to Me, and I have also seen
the [b]oppression with which the
Egyptians oppress them.
10 [a]"Come now, therefore, and I
will send you to Pharaoh that you
may bring My people, the children
of Israel, out of Egypt."
11 But Moses said to God, [a]"Who
am I that I should go to Pharaoh,
and that I should bring the chil-
dren of Israel out of Egypt?"
12 So He said, [a]"I will certainly be
with you. And this *shall be* a [b]sign
to you that I have sent you: When
you have brought the people out
of Egypt, you shall serve God on
this mountain."
13 Then Moses said to God, "In-
deed, *when* I come to the children
of Israel and say to them, 'The God
of your fathers has sent me to you,'
and they say to me, 'What *is* His
name?' what shall I say to them?"
14 And God said to Moses, "I AM
WHO I AM." And He said, "Thus
you shall say to the children of Is-
rael, [a]'I AM has sent me to you.' "
15 Moreover God said to Moses,
"Thus you shall say to the children
of Israel: 'The LORD God of your
fathers, the God of Abraham, the
God of Isaac, and the God of Ja-
cob, has sent me to you. This *is*
[a]My name forever, and this *is* My
memorial to all generations.'
16 "Go and [a]gather the elders of
Israel together, and say to them,
'The LORD God of your fathers, the
God of Abraham, of Isaac, and of
Jacob, appeared to me, saying, [b]"I
have surely visited you and *seen*
what is done to you in Egypt;
17 "and I have said [a]I will bring
you up out of the affliction of
Egypt to the land of the Canaan-
ites and the Hittites and the Amo-
rites and the Perizzites and the
Hivites and the Jebusites, to a land
flowing with milk and honey." '
18 "Then [a]they will heed your
voice; and [b]you shall come, you
and the elders of Israel, to the king
of Egypt; and you shall say to him,
'The LORD God of the Hebrews has
[c]met with us; and now, please, let
us go three days' journey into the
wilderness, that we may sacrifice
to the LORD our God.'
19 "But I am sure that the king of

Egypt [a]will not let you go, no, not
even by a mighty hand.
20 "So I will [a]stretch out My hand
and strike Egypt with [b]all My won-
ders which I will do in its midst;
and [c]after that he will let you go.
21 "And [a]I will give this people fa-
vor in the sight of the Egyptians;
and it shall be, when you go, that
you shall not go empty-handed.
22 [a]"But every woman shall ask
of her neighbor, namely, of her
who dwells near her house, [b]arti-
cles of silver, articles of gold, and
clothing; and you shall put *them*
on your sons and on your daugh-
ters. So [c]you shall plunder the
Egyptians."

Miraculous Signs for Pharaoh

4 Then Moses answered and
said, "But suppose they will
not believe me or listen to my
voice; suppose they say, 'The LORD
has not appeared to you.'"
2 So the LORD said to him, "What
is that in your hand?" He said, "A
rod."
3 And He said, "Cast it on the
ground." So he cast it on the
ground, and it became a serpent;
and Moses fled from it.
4 Then the LORD said to Moses,
"Reach out your hand and take *it*
by the tail" (and he reached out
his hand and caught it, and it be-
came a rod in his hand),
5 "that they may [a]believe that the
[b]LORD God of their fathers, the
God of Abraham, the God of Isaac,
and the God of Jacob, has ap-
peared to you."
6 Furthermore the LORD said to
him, "Now put your hand in your
bosom." And he put his hand in
his bosom, and when he took it
out, behold, his hand *was* leprous,
[a]like snow.
7 And He said, "Put your hand
in your bosom again." So he put
his hand in his bosom again, and
drew it out of his bosom, and be-
hold, [a]it was restored like his *other*
flesh.
8 "Then it will be, if they do not
believe you, nor heed the message
of the [a]first sign, that they may be-
lieve the message of the latter sign.
9 "And it shall be, if they do not
believe even these two signs, or lis-
ten to your voice, that you shall

19 [a]Ex. 5:2
20 [a]Ex. 6:6; 9:15 [b]Deut. 6:22 [c]Ex. 11:1; 12:31–37
21 [a]Ex. 11:3; 12:36
22 [a]Ex. 11:2 [b]Ex. 33:6 [c]Job 27:17

CHAPTER 4

5 [a]Ex. 4:31; 19:9 [b]Ex. 3:6, 15
6 [a]Num. 12:10
7 [a]Deut. 32:39
8 [a]Ex. 7:6–13
9 [a]Ex. 7:19, 20 [1]The Nile
10 [a]Ex. 3:11; 4:1; 6:12 [1]*heavy* or *dull of tongue;* cannot talk very well
11 [a]Ps. 94:9; 146:8
12 [a]Is. 50:4
13 [a]Jon. 1:3
14 [a]Num. 11:1, 33 [b]Num. 26:59 [c]Ex. 4:27
15 [a]Ex. 4:12, 30; 7:1, 2 [b]Num. 23:5, 12 [c]Deut. 5:31
16 [a]Ex. 7:1, 2
18 [a]Ex. 2:21; 3:1; 4:18 [b]Judg. 18:6
19 [a]Ex. 3:1; 18:1 [b]Gen. 46:3, 6 [c]Ex. 2:15, 23
20 [a]Ex. 18:2–5 [b]Num. 20:8, 9, 11
21 [a]Ex. 3:20; 11:9, 10

take water from [1]the river and
pour *it* on the dry *land.* [a]The water
which you take from the river will
become blood on the dry *land.*"
10 Then Moses said to the LORD,
"O my Lord, I *am* not eloquent,
neither before nor since You have
spoken to Your servant; but [a]I *am*
slow of speech and [1]slow of
tongue."
11 So the LORD said to him, [a]"Who
has made man's mouth? Or who
makes the mute, the deaf, the see-
ing, or the blind? *Have* not I, the
LORD?
12 "Now therefore, go, and I will
be [a]with your mouth and teach you
what you shall say."
13 But he said, "O my Lord,
[a]please send by the hand of
whomever *else* You may send."
14 So [a]the anger of the LORD was
kindled against Moses, and He
said: "Is not Aaron the Levite your
[b]brother? I know that he can speak
well. And look, [c]he is also coming
out to meet you. When he sees you,
he will be glad in his heart.
15 "Now [a]you shall speak to him
and [b]put the words in his mouth.
And I will be with your mouth and
with his mouth, and [c]I will teach
you what you shall do.
16 "So he shall be your spokes-
man to the people. And he himself
shall be as a mouth for you, and
[a]you shall be to him as God.
17 "And you shall take this rod in
your hand, with which you shall
do the signs."

Moses Goes to Egypt

18 So Moses went and returned to
[a]Jethro his father-in-law, and said
to him, "Please let me go and re-
turn to my brethren who *are* in
Egypt, and see whether they are
still alive." And Jethro said to Mo-
ses, [b]"Go in peace."
19 Now the LORD said to Moses in
[a]Midian, "Go, return to [b]Egypt; for
[c]all the men who sought your life
are dead."
20 Then Moses [a]took his wife and
his sons and set them on a donkey,
and he returned to the land of
Egypt. And Moses took [b]the rod
of God in his hand.
21 And the LORD said to Moses,
"When you go back to Egypt, see
that you do all those [a]wonders

before Pharaoh which I have put
in your hand. But [b]I will harden
his heart, so that he will not let the
people go.
22 "Then you shall [a]say to Pha-
raoh, 'Thus says the LORD: [b]"Israel
is My son, [c]My firstborn.
23 "So I say to you, let My son go
that he may serve Me. But if you
refuse to let him go, indeed [a]I will
kill your son, your firstborn." ' "
24 And it came to pass on the way,
at the [a]encampment, that the LORD
[b]met him and sought to [c]kill him.
25 Then [a]Zipporah took [b]a sharp
stone and cut off the foreskin of
her son and [1]cast *it* at [2]*Moses'* feet,
and said, "Surely you *are* a hus-
band of blood to me!"
26 So He let him go. Then she
said, "*You are* a [1]husband of
blood!"—because of the circum-
cision.
27 And the LORD said to Aaron,
"Go into the wilderness [a]to meet
Moses." So he went and met him
on [b]the mountain of God, and
kissed him.
28 So Moses [a]told Aaron all the
words of the LORD who had sent
him, and all the [b]signs which He
had commanded him.
29 Then Moses and Aaron [a]went
and gathered together all the el-
ders of the children of Israel.
30 [a]And Aaron spoke all the
words which the LORD had spoken
to Moses. Then he did the signs
in the sight of the people.
31 So the people [a]believed; and
when they heard that the LORD had
[b]visited the children of Israel and
that He [c]had looked on their afflic-
tion, then [d]they bowed their heads
and worshiped.

First Encounter with Pharaoh

5 Afterward Moses and Aaron
went in and told Pharaoh,
"Thus says the LORD God of Israel:
'Let My people go, that they may
[1]hold [a]a feast to Me in the wil-
derness.' "
2 And Pharaoh said, [a]"Who *is*
the LORD, that I should obey His
voice to let Israel go? I do not
know the LORD, [b]nor will I let Is-
rael go."
3 So they said, [a]"The God of the
Hebrews has [b]met with us. Please,
let us go three days' journey into

21 [b]Ex. 7:3, 13; 9:12, 35; 10:1, 20, 27; 14:4, 8; Deut. 2:30; Josh. 11:20; 1 Sam. 6:6; Is. 63:17; John 12:40; Rom. 9:18
22 [a]Ex. 5:1 [b]Is. 63:16; 64:8; Hos. 11:1; [Rom. 9:4; 2 Cor. 6:16, 18] [c]Jer. 31:9; [James 1:18]
23 [a]Ex. 11:5; 12:29; Ps. 105:36; 135:8; 136:10
24 [a]Gen. 42:27 [b]Ex. 3:18; 5:3; Num. 22:22 [c]Gen. 17:14
25 [a]Ex. 2:21; 18:2 [b]Gen. 17:14; Josh. 5:2, 3 [1]Lit. *made it touch* [2]Lit. *his*
26 [1]*bride-groom*
27 [a]Ex. 4:14 [b]Ex. 3:1; 18:5; 24:13
28 [a]Ex. 4:15, 16 [b]Ex. 4:8, 9
29 [a]Ex. 3:16; 12:21
30 [a]Ex. 4:15, 16
31 [a]Ex. 3:18; 4:8, 9; 19:9 [b]Gen. 50:24; Ex. 3:16 [c]Ex. 2:25; 3:7 [d]Gen. 24:26; Ex. 12:27; 1 Chr. 29:20

CHAPTER 5

1 [a]Ex. 3:18; 7:16; 10:9 [1]*keep a pilgrim-feast*
2 [a]2 Kin. 18:35; 2 Chr. 32:14; Job 21:15 [b]Ex. 3:19; 7:14
3 [a]Ex. 3:18; 7:16 [b]Ex. 4:24; Num. 23:3 [c]Ex. 9:15
4 [a]Ex. 1:11; 2:11; 6:6
5 [a]Ex. 1:7, 9
6 [a]Ex. 1:11; 3:7; 5:10, 13, 14
7 [a]Ex. 1:14
14 [a]Ex. 5:6 [b]Is. 10:24

the desert and sacrifice to the LORD
our God, lest He fall upon us with
[c]pestilence or with the sword."
4 Then the king of Egypt said to
them, "Moses and Aaron, why
do you take the people from
their work? Get *back* to your [a]la-
bor."
5 And Pharaoh said, "Look, the
people of the land *are* [a]many now,
and you make them rest from their
labor!"
6 So the same day Pharaoh com-
manded the [a]taskmasters of the
people and their officers, saying,
7 "You shall no longer give the
people straw to make [a]brick as be-
fore. Let them go and gather straw
for themselves.
8 "And you shall lay on them the
quota of bricks which they made
before. You shall not reduce it. For
they are idle; therefore they cry
out, saying, 'Let us go *and* sacrifice
to our God.'
9 "Let more work be laid on the
men, that they may labor in it, and
let them not regard false words."
10 And the taskmasters of the
people and their officers went out
and spoke to the people, saying,
"Thus says Pharaoh: 'I will not
give you straw.
11 'Go, get yourselves straw
where you can find it; yet none of
your work will be reduced.' "
12 So the people were scattered
abroad throughout all the land of
Egypt to gather stubble instead of
straw.
13 And the taskmasters forced
them to hurry, saying, "Fulfill your
work, *your* daily quota, as when
there was straw."
14 Also the [a]officers of the chil-
dren of Israel, whom Pharaoh's
taskmasters had set over them,
were [b]beaten *and* were asked,
"Why have you not fulfilled your
task in making brick both yester-
day and today, as before?"
15 Then the officers of the chil-
dren of Israel came and cried out
to Pharaoh, saying, "Why are you
dealing thus with your servants?
16 "There is no straw given to
your servants, and they say to us,
'Make brick!' And indeed your ser-
vants *are* beaten, but the fault *is*
in your *own* people."
17 But he said, "You *are* idle! Idle!

Therefore you say, 'Let us go *and*
sacrifice to the LORD.'
18 "Therefore go now *and* work;
for no straw shall be given you,
yet you shall deliver the quota of
bricks."
19 And the officers of the children
of Israel saw *that* they *were* in
trouble after it was said, "You
shall not reduce *any* bricks from
your daily quota."
20 Then, as they came out from
Pharaoh, they met Moses and
Aaron who stood there to meet
them.
21 [a]And they said to them, "Let
the LORD look on you and judge,
because you have made [1]us abhor-
rent in the sight of Pharaoh and
in the sight of his servants, to
put a sword in their hand to kill
us."

Israel's Deliverance Assured

22 So Moses returned to the LORD
and said, "Lord, why have You
brought trouble on this people?
Why *is* it You have sent me?
23 "For since I came to Pharaoh
to speak in Your name, he has
done evil to this people; neither
have You delivered Your people at
all."

6 Then the LORD said to Moses,
"Now you shall see what I will
do to Pharaoh. For [a]with a strong
hand he will let them go, and with
a strong hand [b]he will drive them
out of his land."
2 And God spoke to Moses and
said to him: "I *am* [1]the LORD.
3 [a]"I appeared to Abraham, to
Isaac, and to Jacob, as [b]God Al-
mighty, but *by* My name [c]LORD[1] I
was not known to them.
4 [a]"I have also [1]established My
covenant with them, [b]to give them
the land of Canaan, the land of
their [2]pilgrimage, [c]in which they
were [3]strangers.
5 "And [a]I have also heard the
groaning of the children of Israel
whom the Egyptians keep in bond-
age, and I have remembered My
covenant.
6 "Therefore say to the children
of Israel: [a]'I *am* the LORD; [b]I will
bring you out from under the bur-
dens of the Egyptians, I will [c]res-
cue you from their bondage, and I
will redeem you with [1]an out-
stretched arm and with great judg-
ments.
7 'I will [a]take you as My people,
and [b]I will be your God. Then you
shall know that I *am* the LORD your
God who brings you out [c]from un-
der the burdens of the Egyptians.
8 'And I will bring you into the
land which I [a]swore[1] to give to
Abraham, Isaac, and Jacob; and I
will give it to you *as* a heritage: I
am the LORD.'"
9 So Moses spoke thus to the
children of Israel; [a]but they did not
heed Moses, because of [b]anguish[1]
of spirit and cruel bondage.
10 And the LORD spoke to Moses,
saying,
11 "Go in, tell Pharaoh king of
Egypt to let the children of Israel
go out of his land."
12 And Moses spoke before the
LORD, saying, "The children of Is-
rael have not heeded me. How
then shall Pharaoh heed me, for
[a]I *am* [1]of uncircumcised lips?"
13 Then the LORD spoke to Moses
and Aaron, and gave them a
[a]command[1] for the children of Is-
rael and for Pharaoh king of
Egypt, to bring the children of Is-
rael out of the land of Egypt.

The Family of Moses and Aaron

14 These *are* the heads of their fa-
thers' houses: [a]The sons of Reu-
ben, the firstborn of Israel, *were*
Hanoch, Pallu, Hezron, and Carmi.
These are the families of Reu-
ben.
15 [a]And the sons of Simeon *were*
[1]Jemuel, Jamin, Ohad, Jachin, Zo-
har, and Shaul the son of a Ca-
naanite woman. These *are* the
families of Simeon.
16 These *are* the names of [a]the
sons of Levi according to their
generations: Gershon, Kohath,
and Merari. And the years of the
life of Levi *were* one hundred and
thirty-seven.
17 [a]The sons of Gershon *were*
Libni and Shimi according to their
families.
18 And [a]the sons of Kohath *were*
Amram, Izhar, Hebron, and Uz-
ziel. And the years of the life of
Kohath *were* one hundred and
thirty-three.
19 [a]The sons of Merari *were* Mahli
and Mushi. These *are* the families

21 [a]Ex. 6:9; 14:11; 15:24; 16:2 [1]Lit. *our scent to stink before*

CHAPTER 6

1 [a]Ex. 3:19 [b]Ex. 12:31, 33, 39

2 [1]Heb. *YHWH*

3 [a]Gen. 17:1; 35:9; 48:3 [b]Gen. 28:3; 35:11 [c]Ps. 68:4; 83:18 [1]Heb. *YHWH*, traditionally *Jehovah*

4 [a]Gen. 12:7; 15:18; 17:4, 7, 8; 26:3; 28:4, 13 [b]Lev. 25:23 [c]Gen. 28:4 [1]*made* or *ratified* [2]*sojournings* [3]*sojourners*, temporary residents

5 [a]Ex. 2:24

6 [a]Deut. 6:12 [b]Deut. 26:8 [c]Deut. 7:8 [1]Mighty power

7 [a]2 Sam. 7:24 [b]Ex. 29:45, 46 [c]Ex. 5:4, 5

8 [a]Gen. 15:18; 26:3 [1]*promised*, lit. *lifted up My hand*

9 [a]Ex. 5:21 [b]Ex. 2:23 [1]Lit. *shortness*

12 [a]Jer. 1:6 [1]One who does not speak well

13 [a]Deut. 31:14 [1]*charge*

14 [a]Gen. 46:9

15 [a]Gen. 46:10 [1]*Nemuel*, Num. 26:12

16 [a]Gen. 46:11

17 [a]1 Chr. 6:17

18 [a]1 Chr. 6:2, 18

19 [a]1 Chr. 6:19; 23:21

of Levi according to their gen-
erations.
20 Now [a]Amram took for himself
[b]Jochebed, his father's sister, as
wife; and she bore him [c]Aaron and
Moses. And the years of the life
of Amram *were* one hundred and
thirty-seven.
21 [a]The sons of Izhar *were* Korah,
Nepheg, and Zichri.
22 And [a]the sons of Uzziel *were*
Mishael, Elzaphan, and Zithri.
23 Aaron took to himself Elish-
eba, daughter of [a]Amminadab, sis-
ter of Nahshon, as wife; and she
bore him [b]Nadab, Abihu, [c]Eleazar,
and Ithamar.
24 And [a]the sons of Korah *were*
Assir, Elkanah, and Abiasaph.
These are the families of the Ko-
rahites.
25 Eleazar, Aaron's son, took for
himself one of the daughters of Pu-
tiel as wife; and [a]she bore him
Phinehas. These *are* the heads of
the fathers' houses of the Levites
according to their families.
26 These *are the same* Aaron and
Moses to whom the LORD said,
"Bring out the children of Israel
from the land of Egypt according
to their [a]armies."[1]
27 These *are* the ones who spoke
to Pharaoh king of Egypt, [a]to bring
out the children of Israel from
Egypt. These *are the same* Moses
and Aaron.

Aaron Is Moses' Spokesman

28 And it came to pass, on the day
the LORD spoke to Moses in the
land of Egypt,
29 that the LORD spoke to Moses,
saying, "I *am* the LORD. [a]Speak to
Pharaoh king of Egypt all that I
say to you."
30 But Moses said before the
LORD, "Behold, [a]I *am* [1]of uncir-
cumcised lips, and how shall Pha-
raoh heed me?"

7 So the LORD said to Moses:
"See, I have made you [a]*as* God
to Pharaoh, and Aaron your
brother shall be [b]your prophet.
2 "You [a]shall speak all that I
command you. And Aaron your
brother shall tell Pharaoh to send
the children of Israel out of his
land.
3 "And [a]I will harden Pharaoh's
heart, and [b]multiply My [c]signs and
My wonders in the land of Egypt.
4 "But [a]Pharaoh will not heed
you, so [b]that I may lay My hand
on Egypt and bring My [1]armies
and My people, the children of Is-
rael, out of the land of Egypt [c]by
great judgments.
5 "And the Egyptians [a]shall
know that I *am* the LORD, when I
[b]stretch out My hand on Egypt and
[c]bring out the children of Israel
from among them."
6 Then Moses and Aaron [a]did *so;*
just as the LORD commanded them,
so they did.
7 And Moses *was* [a]eighty years
old and [b]Aaron eighty-three years
old when they spoke to Pharaoh.

Aaron's Miraculous Rod

8 Then the LORD spoke to Moses
and Aaron, saying,
9 "When Pharaoh speaks to you,
saying, [a]'Show a miracle for your-
selves,' then you shall say to
Aaron, [b]'Take your rod and cast
it before Pharaoh, *and* let it be-
come a serpent.' "
10 So Moses and Aaron went in
to Pharaoh, and they did so, just
[a]as the LORD commanded. And
Aaron cast down his rod before
Pharaoh and before his servants,
and it [b]became a serpent.
11 But Pharaoh also [a]called the
wise men and [b]the [1]sorcerers; so
the magicians of Egypt, they also
[c]did in like manner with their [2]en-
chantments.
12 For every man threw down his
rod, and they became serpents.
But Aaron's rod swallowed up
their rods.
13 And Pharaoh's heart grew
hard, and he did not heed them,
as the LORD had said.

The First Plague: Waters Become Blood

14 So the LORD said to Moses:
[a]"Pharaoh's heart *is* hard; he re-
fuses to let the people go.
15 "Go to Pharaoh in the morning,
when he goes out to the [a]water,
and you shall stand by the river's
bank to meet him; and [b]the rod
which was turned to a serpent you
shall take in your hand.
16 "And you shall say to him,
[a]'The LORD God of the Hebrews
has sent me to you, saying, "Let

---

20 [a]Ex. 2:1, 2 [b]Num. 26:59 [c]Num. 26:59
21 [a]1 Chr. 6:37, 38
22 [a]Lev. 10:4
23 [a]Ruth 4:19, 20 [b]Lev. 10:1 [c]Ex. 28:1
24 [a]Num. 26:11
25 [a]Num. 25:7, 11
26 [a]Ex. 7:4; 12:17, 51 [1]*hosts*
27 [a]Ps. 77:20
29 [a]Ex. 6:11; 7:2
30 [a]Ex. 4:10; 6:12 [1]One who does not speak well

CHAPTER 7

1 [a]Ex. 4:16 [b]Ex. 4:15, 16
2 [a]Ex. 4:15
3 [a]Ex. 4:21; 9:12 [b]Ex. 11:9 [c]Deut. 4:34
4 [a]Ex. 3:19, 20; 10:1; 11:9 [b]Ex. 9:14 [c]Ex. 6:6; 12:12 [1]*hosts*
5 [a]Ps. 9:16 [b]Ex. 9:15 [c]Ex. 3:20; 6:6; 12:51
6 [a]Ex. 7:2
7 [a]Deut. 29:5; 31:2; 34:7 [b]Num. 33:39
9 [a]Is. 7:11 [b]Ex. 4:2, 3, 17
10 [a]Ex. 7:9 [b]Ex. 4:3
11 [a]Gen. 41:8 [b]2 Tim. 3:8 [c]Ex. 7:22; 8:7, 18 [1]*soothsayers* [2]*secret arts*
14 [a]Ex. 8:15; 10:1, 20, 27
15 [a]Ex. 2:5; 8:20 [b]Ex. 4:2, 3; 7:10
16 [a]Ex. 3:13, 18; 4:22

My people go, [b]that they may
[1]serve Me in the wilderness"; but
indeed, until now you would not
hear!
17 'Thus says the LORD: "By this
[a]you shall know that I *am* the
LORD. Behold, I will strike the wa-
ters which *are* in the river with the
rod that *is* in my hand, and [b]they
shall be turned [c]to blood.
18 "And the fish that *are* in the
river shall die, the river shall stink,
and the Egyptians will [a]loathe[1] to
drink the water of the river." ' "
19 Then the LORD spoke to Moses,
"Say to Aaron, 'Take your rod and
[a]stretch out your hand over the
waters of Egypt, over their
streams, over their rivers, over
their ponds, and over all their
pools of water, that they may be-
come blood. And there shall be
blood throughout all the land of
Egypt, both in *buckets of* wood
and *pitchers of* stone.' "
20 And Moses and Aaron did so,
just as the LORD commanded. So
he [a]lifted up the rod and struck the
waters that *were* in the river, in
the sight of Pharaoh and in the
sight of his servants. And all the
[b]waters that *were* in the river were
turned to blood.
21 The fish that *were* in the river
died, the river stank, and the Egyp-
tians [a]could not drink the water of
the river. So there was blood
throughout all the land of Egypt.
22 [a]Then the magicians of Egypt
did [b]so with their [1]enchantments;
and Pharaoh's heart grew hard,
and he did not heed them, [c]as the
LORD had said.
23 And Pharaoh turned and went
into his house. Neither was his
heart moved by this.
24 So all the Egyptians dug all
around the river for water to drink,
because they could not drink the
water of the river.
25 And seven days passed after
the LORD had struck the river.

The Second Plague: Frogs

8 And the LORD spoke to Moses,
"Go to Pharaoh and say to him,
'Thus says the LORD: "Let My peo-
ple go, [a]that they may serve Me.
2 "But if you [a]refuse to let *them*
go, behold, I will smite all your ter-
ritory with [b]frogs.
3 "So the river shall bring forth
frogs abundantly, which shall go
up and come into your house, into
your [a]bedroom, on your bed, into
the houses of your servants, on
your people, into your ovens, and
into your kneading bowls.
4 "And the frogs shall come up
on you, on your people, and on all
your servants." ' "
5 Then the LORD spoke to Moses,
"Say to Aaron, [a]'Stretch out your
hand with your rod over the
streams, over the rivers, and over
the ponds, and cause frogs to come
up on the land of Egypt.' "
6 So Aaron stretched out his
hand over the waters of Egypt, and
[a]the frogs came up and covered
the land of Egypt.
7 [a]And the magicians did so with
their [1]enchantments, and brought
up frogs on the land of Egypt.
8 Then Pharaoh called for Moses
and Aaron, and said, [a]"Entreat[1]
the LORD that He may take away
the frogs from me and from my
people; and I will let the people
[b]go, that they may sacrifice to the
LORD."
9 And Moses said to Pharaoh,
"Accept the honor of saying when
I shall intercede for you, for your
servants, and for your people, to
destroy the frogs from you and
your houses, *that* they may re-
main in the river only."
10 So he said, "Tomorrow." And
he said, "*Let it be* according to
your word, that you may know
that [a]*there is* no one like the LORD
our God.
11 "And the frogs shall depart
from you, from your houses, from
your servants, and from your peo-
ple. They shall remain in the river
only."
12 Then Moses and Aaron went
out from Pharaoh. And Moses
[a]cried out to the LORD concerning
the frogs which He had brought
against Pharaoh.
13 So the LORD did according to
the word of Moses. And the frogs
died out of the houses, out of
the courtyards, and out of the
fields.
14 They gathered them together in
heaps, and the land stank.
15 But when Pharaoh saw that
there was [a]relief, [b]he hardened his

16 [b]Ex. 3:12, 18; 4:23; 5:1, 3; 8:1 [1]*worship*
17 [a]Ex. 5:2; 7:5; 10:2; Ps. 9:16; Ezek. 25:17 [b]Ex. 4:9; 7:20 [c]Rev. 11:6; 16:4, 6
18 [a]Ex. 7:24 [1]*be weary of drinking*
19 [a]Ex. 8:5, 6, 16; 9:22; 10:12, 21; 14:21, 26
20 [a]Ex. 17:5 [b]Ps. 78:44; 105:29, 30
21 [a]Ex. 7:18
22 [a]Ex. 7:11 [b]Ex. 8:7 [c]Ex. 3:19; 7:3 [1]*secret arts*

CHAPTER 8

1 [a]Ex. 3:12, 18; 4:23; 5:1, 3
2 [a]Ex. 7:14; 9:2 [b]Rev. 16:13
3 [a]Ps. 105:30
5 [a]Ex. 7:19
6 [a]Ps. 78:45; 105:30
7 [a]Ex. 7:11, 22 [1]*secret arts*
8 [a]Ex. 8:28; 9:28; 10:17; Num. 21:7; 1 Kin. 13:6 [b]Ex. 10:8, 24 [1]*Pray to, Make supplication to*
10 [a]Ex. 9:14; 15:11; Deut. 4:35, 39; 33:26; 2 Sam. 7:22; 1 Chr. 17:20; Ps. 86:8; Is. 46:9; [Jer. 10:6, 7]
12 [a]Ex. 8:30; 9:33; 10:18; 32:11; [James 5:16–18]
15 [a]Eccl. 8:11 [b]Ex. 7:14, 22; 9:34; 1 Sam. 6:6

heart and did not heed them, as
the LORD had said.

The Third Plague: Lice

16 So the LORD said to Moses,
"Say to Aaron, 'Stretch out your
rod, and strike the dust of the land,
so that it may become [1]lice
throughout all the land of Egypt.' "
17 And they did so. For Aaron
stretched out his hand with his rod
and struck the dust of the earth,
and [a]it became lice on man and
beast. All the dust of the land be-
came lice throughout all the land
of Egypt.
18 Now [a]the magicians so worked
with their [1]enchantments to bring
forth lice, but they [b]could not. So
there were lice on man and beast.
19 Then the magicians said to
Pharaoh, "This *is* [a]the[1] finger of
God." But Pharaoh's [b]heart grew
hard, and he did not heed them,
just as the LORD had said.

The Fourth Plague: Flies

20 And the LORD said to Moses,
[a]"Rise early in the morning and
stand before Pharaoh as he comes
out to the water. Then say to him,
'Thus says the LORD: [b]"Let My
people go, that they may serve Me.
21 "Or else, if you will not let My
people go, behold, I will send
swarms *of flies* on you and your
servants, on your people and into
your houses. The houses of the
Egyptians shall be full of swarms
of flies, and also the ground on
which they *stand.*
22 "And in that day [a]I will set
apart the land of [b]Goshen, in
which My people dwell, that no
swarms *of flies* shall be there, in
order that you may [c]know that I
am the LORD in the midst of the
[d]land.
23 "I will [1]make a difference be-
tween My people and your people.
Tomorrow this [a]sign shall be." ' "
24 And the LORD did so. [a]Thick
swarms *of flies* came into the
house of Pharaoh, *into* his ser-
vants' houses, and into all the land
of Egypt. The land was corrupted
because of the swarms *of flies.*
25 Then Pharaoh called for Moses
and Aaron, and said, "Go, sacrifice
to your God in the land."
26 And Moses said, "It is not right
to do so, for we would be sacrific-
ing [a]the abomination of the Egyp-
tians to the LORD our God. If we
sacrifice the abomination of the
Egyptians before their eyes, then
will they not [1]stone us?
27 "We will go [a]three days' jour-
ney into the wilderness and sacri-
fice to the LORD our God as [b]He
will command us."
28 So Pharaoh said, "I will let you
go, that you may sacrifice to the
LORD your God in the wilderness;
only you shall not go very far
away. [a]Intercede for me."
29 Then Moses said, "Indeed I am
going out from you, and I will en-
treat the LORD, that the swarms *of
flies* may depart tomorrow from
Pharaoh, from his servants, and
from his people. But let Pharaoh
not [a]deal deceitfully anymore in
not letting the people go to sacri-
fice to the LORD."
30 So Moses went out from Pha-
raoh and [a]entreated the LORD.
31 And the LORD did according to
the word of Moses; He removed
the swarms *of flies* from Pharaoh,
from his servants, and from his
people. Not one remained.
32 But Pharaoh [a]hardened his
heart at this time also; neither
would he let the people go.

The Fifth Plague: Livestock Diseased

9 Then the LORD said to Moses,
[a]"Go in to Pharaoh and tell
him, 'Thus says the LORD God of
the Hebrews: "Let My people go,
that they may [b]serve Me.
2 "For if you [a]refuse to let *them*
go, and still hold them,
3 "behold, the [a]hand of the LORD
will be on your cattle in the field,
on the horses, on the donkeys, on
the camels, on the oxen, and on
the sheep—a very severe pesti-
lence.
4 "And [a]the LORD will make a dif-
ference between the livestock of
Israel and the livestock of Egypt.
So nothing shall die of all *that*
belongs to the children of Is-
rael." ' "
5 Then the LORD appointed a set
time, saying, "Tomorrow the LORD
will do this thing in the land."
6 So the LORD did this thing on
the next day, and [a]all the livestock
of Egypt died; but of the livestock

16 [1]*gnats*

17 [a]Ps. 105:31

18 [a]Ex. 7:11, 12; 8:7 [b]Dan. 5:8; 2 Tim. 3:8, 9 [1]*secret arts*

19 [a]Ex. 7:5; 10:7; 1 Sam. 6:3, 9; Ps. 8:3; Luke 11:20 [b]Ex. 8:15 [1]An act of God

20 [a]Ex. 7:15; 9:13 [b]Ex. 3:18; 4:23; 5:1, 3; 8:1

22 [a]Ex. 9:4, 6, 26; 10:23; 11:6, 7; 12:13 [b]Gen. 50:8 [c]Ex. 7:5, 17; 10:2; 14:4 [d]Ex. 9:29

23 [a]Ex. 4:8 [1]Lit. *set a ransom,* Ex. 9:4; 11:7

24 [a]Ps. 78:45; 105:31

26 [a]Gen. 43:32; 46:34; [Deut. 7:25, 26; 12:31] [1]Put us to death by stoning

27 [a]Ex. 3:18; 5:3 [b]Ex. 3:12

28 [a]Ex. 8:8, 15, 29, 32; 9:28; 1 Kin. 13:6

29 [a]Ex. 8:8, 15

30 [a]Ex. 8:12

32 [a]Ex. 4:21; 8:8, 15; Ps. 52:2

CHAPTER 9

1 [a]Ex. 4:23; 8:1 [b]Ex. 7:16

2 [a]Ex. 8:2

3 [a]Ex. 7:4; 1 Sam. 5:6; Ps. 39:10; Acts 13:11

4 [a]Ex. 8:22

6 [a]Ex. 9:19, 20, 25; Ps. 78:48, 50

of the children of Israel, not one
died.
7 Then Pharaoh sent, and in-
deed, not even one of the livestock
of the Israelites was dead. But the
[a]heart of Pharaoh became hard,
and he did not let the people go.

The Sixth Plague: Boils

8 So the LORD said to Moses and
Aaron, "Take for yourselves hand-
fuls of ashes from a furnace, and
let Moses scatter it toward the
heavens in the sight of Pharaoh.
9 "And it will become fine dust
in all the land of Egypt, and it will
cause [a]boils that break out in sores
on man and beast throughout all
the land of Egypt."
10 Then they took ashes from the
furnace and stood before Pharaoh,
and Moses scattered *them* toward
heaven. And *they* caused [a]boils
that break out in sores on man and
beast.
11 And the [a]magicians could not
stand before Moses because of the
[b]boils, for the boils were on the
magicians and on all the Egyp-
tians.
12 But the LORD hardened the
heart of Pharaoh; and he [a]did not
heed them, just [b]as the LORD had
spoken to Moses.

The Seventh Plague: Hail

13 Then the LORD said to Moses,
[a]"Rise early in the morning and
stand before Pharaoh, and say to
him, 'Thus says the LORD God of
the Hebrews: "Let My people go,
that they may [b]serve Me,
14 "for at this time I will send all
My plagues to your very heart,
and on your servants and on your
people, [a]that you may know that
there is none like Me in all the
earth.
15 "Now if I had [a]stretched out My
hand and struck you and your peo-
ple with [b]pestilence, then you
would have been cut off from the
earth.
16 "But indeed for [a]this *purpose* I
have raised you up, that I may
[b]show My power *in* you, and that
My [c]name may be declared in all
the earth.
17 "As yet you exalt yourself
against My people in that you will
not let them go.
18 "Behold, tomorrow about this
time I will cause very heavy hail
to rain down, such as has not been
in Egypt since its founding until
now.
19 "Therefore send now *and*
gather your livestock and all that
you have in the field, for the hail
shall come down on every man
and every animal which is found
in the field and is not brought
home; and they shall die." ' "
20 He who [a]feared the word of the
LORD among the [b]servants of Pha-
raoh made his servants and his
livestock flee to the houses.
21 But he who did not regard the
word of the LORD left his servants
and his livestock in the field.
22 Then the LORD said to Moses,
"Stretch out your hand toward
heaven, that there may be [a]hail in
all the land of Egypt—on man, on
beast, and on every herb of the
field, throughout the land of
Egypt."
23 And Moses stretched out his
rod toward heaven; and [a]the LORD
sent thunder and hail, and fire
darted to the ground. And the
LORD rained hail on the land of
Egypt.
24 So there was hail, and fire min-
gled with the hail, so very heavy
that there was none like it in all
the land of Egypt since it became
a nation.
25 And the [a]hail struck through-
out the whole land of Egypt, all
that *was* in the field, both man and
beast; and the hail struck every
herb of the field and broke every
tree of the field.
26 [a]Only in the land of Goshen,
where the children of Israel *were*,
there was no hail.
27 And Pharaoh sent and [a]called
for Moses and Aaron, and said to
them, [b]"I have sinned this time.
[c]The LORD *is* righteous, and my
people and I *are* wicked.
28 [a]"Entreat[1] the LORD, that there
may be no *more* [2]mighty thunder-
ing and hail, for *it is* enough. I will
let you [b]go, and you shall stay no
longer."
29 So Moses said to him, "As soon
as I have gone out of the city, I
will [a]spread out my hands to the
LORD; the thunder will cease, and
there will be no more hail, that you

7 [a]Ex. 7:14; 8:32
9 [a]Deut. 28:27; Rev. 16:2
10 [a]Deut. 28:27
11 [a][Ex. 8:18, 19; 2 Tim. 3:9] [b]Deut. 28:27; Job 2:7; Rev. 16:1, 2
12 [a]Ex. 7:13 [b]Ex. 4:21
13 [a]Ex. 8:20 [b]Ex. 9:1
14 [a]Ex. 8:10; Deut. 3:24; 2 Sam. 7:22; 1 Chr. 17:20; Ps. 86:8; Is. 45:5–8; 46:9; Jer. 10:6, 7
15 [a]Ex. 3:20; 7:5 [b]Ex. 5:3
16 [a]Ex. 14:17; Prov. 16:4; [Rom. 9:17, 18; 1 Pet. 2:8, 9] [b]Ex. 7:4, 5; 10:1; 11:9; 14:17 [c]1 Kin. 8:43
20 [a]Ex. 1:17; 14:31; [Prov. 13:13] [b]Ex. 8:19; 10:7
22 [a]Rev. 16:21
23 [a]Gen. 19:24; Josh. 10:11; Ps. 18:13; 78:47; 105:32; 148:8; Is. 30:30; Ezek. 38:22; Rev. 8:7
25 [a]Ex. 9:19; Ps. 78:47, 48; 105:32, 33
26 [a]Ex. 8:22, 23; 9:4, 6; 10:23; 11:7; 12:13; Is. 32:18, 19
27 [a]Ex. 8:8 [b]Ex. 9:34; 10:16, 17 [c]2 Chr. 12:6; Ps. 129:4; 145:17; Lam. 1:18
28 [a]Ex. 8:8, 28; 10:17; Acts 8:24 [b]Ex. 8:25; 10:8, 24 [1]*Pray to, Make supplication to* [2]Lit. *voices of God* or *sounds of God*
29 [a]1 Kin. 8:22, 38; Ps. 143:6; Is. 1:15

may know that the [b]earth *is* the
LORD's.
30 "But as for you and your ser-
vants, [a]I know that you will not yet
fear the LORD God."
31 Now the flax and the barley
were struck, [a]for the barley *was*
in the head and the flax *was* in
bud.
32 But the wheat and the spelt
were not struck, for they *are* [1]late
crops.
33 So Moses went out of the city
from Pharaoh and [a]spread out his
hands to the LORD; then the thun-
der and the hail ceased, and
the rain was not poured on the
earth.
34 And when Pharaoh saw that
the rain, the hail, and the thunder
had ceased, he sinned yet more;
and he hardened his heart, he and
his servants.
35 So [a]the heart of Pharaoh was
hard; neither would he let the chil-
dren of Israel go, as the LORD had
spoken by Moses.

The Eighth Plague: Locusts

10 Now the LORD said to Moses,
"Go in to Pharaoh; [a]for I
have hardened his heart and the
hearts of his servants, [b]that I may
show these signs of Mine before
him,
2 "and that [a]you may tell in the
hearing of your son and your son's
son the mighty things I have done
in Egypt, and My signs which I
have done among them, that you
may [b]know that I *am* the LORD."
3 So Moses and Aaron came in
to Pharaoh and said to him, "Thus
says the LORD God of the Hebrews:
'How long will you refuse to
[a]humble yourself before Me? Let
My people go, that they may
[b]serve Me.
4 'Or else, if you refuse to let My
people go, behold, tomorrow I
will bring [a]locusts into your terri-
tory.
5 'And they shall cover the face
of the earth, so that no one will
be able to see the earth; and [a]they
shall eat the residue of what is left,
which remains to you from the
hail, and they shall eat every tree
which grows up for you out of the
field.
6 'They shall [a]fill your houses,
the houses of all your servants,
and the houses of all the Egyp-
tians—which neither your fathers
nor your fathers' fathers have
seen, since the day that they were
on the earth to this day.'" And he
turned and went out from Pha-
raoh.
7 Then Pharaoh's [a]servants said
to him, "How long shall this man
be [b]a snare to us? Let the men go,
that they may serve the LORD their
God. Do you not yet know that
Egypt is destroyed?"
8 So Moses and Aaron were
brought again to Pharaoh, and he
said to them, "Go, serve the LORD
your God. Who *are* the ones that
are going?"
9 And Moses said, "We will go
with our young and our old; with
our sons and our daughters, with
our flocks and our herds we will
go, for [a]we must hold a feast to
the LORD."
10 Then he said to them, "The
LORD had better be with you when
I let you and your little ones
go! Beware, for evil is ahead of
you.
11 "Not so! Go now, you *who are*
men, and serve the LORD, for that
is what you desired." And they
were driven [a]out from Pharaoh's
presence.
12 Then the LORD said to Moses,
[a]"Stretch out your hand over the
land of Egypt for the locusts, that
they may come upon the land
of Egypt, and [b]eat every herb of
the land—all that the hail has
left."
13 So Moses stretched out his rod
over the land of Egypt, and the
LORD brought an east wind on the
land all that day and all *that* night.
When it was morning, the east
wind brought the locusts.
14 And [a]the locusts went up over
all the land of Egypt and rested on
all the territory of Egypt. *They
were* very severe; [b]previously
there had been no such locusts as
they, nor shall there be such after
them.
15 For they [a]covered the face of
the whole earth, so that the land
was darkened; and they [b]ate every
herb of the land and all the fruit
of the trees which the hail had left.
So there remained nothing green

---

29 [b]Ex. 8:22; 19:5; 20:11; Ps. 24:1; 1 Cor. 10:26, 28
30 [a]Ex. 8:29; [Is. 26:10]
31 [a]Ruth 1:22; 2:23
32 [1]Lit. *darkened*
33 [a]Ex. 8:12; 9:29
35 [a]Ex. 4:21

CHAPTER 10

1 [a]Ex. 4:21; 7:14; 9:12; 10:27; 11:10; 14:4; Josh. 11:20; John 12:40; Rom. 9:18 [b]Ex. 7:4; 9:16
2 [a]Ex. 12:26; 13:8, 14; Deut. 4:9; 6:7; 11:19; Ps. 44:1; 78:5; Joel 1:3 [b]Ex. 7:5, 17; 8:22
3 [a][1 Kin. 21:29; 2 Chr. 34:27]; Job 42:6; [James 4:10; 1 Pet. 5:6] [b]Ex. 4:23; 8:1; 9:1
4 [a]Prov. 30:27; Rev. 9:3
5 [a]Ex. 9:32; Joel 1:4; 2:25
6 [a]Ex. 8:3, 21
7 [a]Ex. 7:5; 8:19; 9:20; 12:33 [b]Ex. 23:33; Josh. 23:13; 1 Sam. 18:21; Eccl. 7:26; 1 Cor. 7:35
9 [a]Ex. 5:1; 7:16
11 [a]Ex. 10:28
12 [a]Ex. 7:19 [b]Ex. 10:5, 15
14 [a]Deut. 28:38; Ps. 78:46; 105:34 [b]Joel 1:4, 7; 2:1–11; Rev. 9:3
15 [a]Ex. 10:5 [b]Ps. 105:35

on the trees or on the plants of the
field throughout all the land of
Egypt.
16 Then Pharaoh called [a]for Mo-
ses and Aaron in haste, and said,
[b]"I have sinned against the LORD
your God and against you.
17 "Now therefore, please forgive
my sin only this once, and [a]en-
treat[1] the LORD your God, that He
may take away from me this death
only."
18 So he [a]went out from Pharaoh
and entreated the LORD.
19 And the LORD turned a very
strong west wind, which took the
locusts away and blew them [a]into
the Red Sea. There remained not
one locust in all the territory of
Egypt.
20 But the LORD [a]hardened Pha-
raoh's heart, and he did not let the
children of Israel go.

The Ninth Plague: Darkness

21 Then the LORD said to Moses,
[a]"Stretch out your hand toward
heaven, that there may be dark-
ness over the land of Egypt, [1]dark-
ness *which* may even be felt."
22 So Moses stretched out his
hand toward heaven, and there
was [a]thick darkness in all the land
of Egypt [b]three days.
23 They did not see one another;
nor did anyone rise from his place
for three days. [a]But all the children
of Israel had light in their dwell-
ings.
24 Then Pharaoh called to Moses
and [a]said, "Go, serve the LORD;
only let your flocks and your herds
be kept back. Let your [b]little ones
also go with you."
25 But Moses said, "You must also
give [1]us sacrifices and burnt offer-
ings, that we may sacrifice to the
LORD our God.
26 "Our [a]livestock also shall go
with us; not a hoof shall be left be-
hind. For we must take some of
them to serve the LORD our God,
and even we do not know with
what we must serve the LORD until
we arrive there."
27 But the LORD [a]hardened Pha-
raoh's heart, and he would not let
them go.
28 Then Pharaoh said to him,
[a]"Get away from me! Take heed
to yourself and see my face no

16 [a]Ex. 8:8 [b]Ex. 9:27
17 [a]Ex. 8:8, 28; 9:28; 1 Kin. 13:6 [1]*make supplication to*
18 [a]Ex. 8:30
19 [a]Joel 2:20
20 [a]Ex. 4:21; 10:1; 11:10
21 [a]Ex. 9:22 [1]Lit. *that one may feel the darkness*
22 [a]Ps. 105:28; Rev. 16:10 [b]Ex. 3:18
23 [a]Ex. 8:22, 23
24 [a]Ex. 8:8, 25; 10:8 [b]Ex. 10:10
25 [1]Lit. *into our hands*
26 [a]Ex. 10:9
27 [a]Ex. 4:21; 10:1, 20; 14:4, 8
28 [a]Ex. 10:11
29 [a]Ex. 11:8; Heb. 11:27

CHAPTER 11

1 [a]Ex. 12:31, 33, 39 [b]Ex. 6:1; 12:39
2 [a]Ex. 3:22; 12:35, 36
3 [a]Ex. 3:21; 12:36; Ps. 106:46 [b]Deut. 34:10–12; 2 Sam. 7:9; Esth. 9:4
4 [a]Ex. 12:12, 23, 29
5 [a]Ex. 4:23; 12:12, 29; Ps. 78:51; 105:36; 135:8; 136:10; Amos 4:10
6 [a]Ex. 12:30; Amos 5:17 [b]Ex. 10:14
7 [a]Ex. 8:22 [b]Josh. 10:21 [1]*sharpen*
8 [a]Ex. 12:31–33 [b]Ex. 10:29; Heb. 11:27
9 [a]Ex. 3:19; 7:4; 10:1 [b]Ex. 7:3; 9:16
10 [a]Ex. 7:3; 9:12; 10:1, 20, 27; Josh. 11:20; Is. 63:17; John 12:40; Rom. 2:5

more! For in the day you see my
face you shall die!"
29 So Moses said, "You have spo-
ken well. [a]I will never see your
face again."

Death of the Firstborn Announced

11 And the LORD said to Moses,
"I will bring one more
plague on Pharaoh and on Egypt.
[a]Afterward he will let you go from
here. [b]When he lets *you* go, he will
surely drive you out of here al-
together.
2 "Speak now in the hearing of
the people, and let every man ask
from his neighbor and every
woman from her neighbor, [a]arti-
cles of silver and articles of gold."
3 [a]And the LORD gave the people
favor in the sight of the Egyptians.
Moreover the man [b]Moses *was*
very great in the land of Egypt, in
the sight of Pharaoh's servants
and in the sight of the people.
4 Then Moses said, "Thus says
the LORD: [a]'About midnight I will
go out into the midst of Egypt;
5 'and [a]all the firstborn in the
land of Egypt shall die, from the
firstborn of Pharaoh who sits on
his throne, even to the firstborn of
the female servant who *is* behind
the handmill, and all the firstborn
of the animals.
6 [a]'Then there shall be a great
cry throughout all the land of
Egypt, [b]such as was not like it *be-
fore*, nor shall be like it again.
7 [a]'But against none of the chil-
dren of Israel [b]shall a dog [1]move
its tongue, against man or beast,
that you may know that the LORD
does make a difference between
the Egyptians and Israel.'
8 "And [a]all these your servants
shall come down to me and bow
down to me, saying, 'Get out, and
all the people who follow you!' Af-
ter that I will go out." [b]Then he
went out from Pharaoh in great
anger.
9 But the LORD said to Moses,
[a]"Pharaoh will not heed you, so
that [b]My wonders may be multi-
plied in the land of Egypt."
10 So Moses and Aaron did all
these wonders before Pharaoh;
[a]and the LORD hardened Pharaoh's
heart, and he did not let the chil-
dren of Israel go out of his land.

The Passover Instituted

12 Now the LORD spoke to Mo-
ses and Aaron in the land of
Egypt, saying,
2 [a]"This month *shall be* your be-
ginning of months; it *shall be* the
first month of the year to you.
3 "Speak to all the congregation
of Israel, saying: 'On the [a]tenth of
this month every man shall take
for himself a lamb, according to
the house of *his* father, a lamb for
a household.
4 'And if the household is too
small for the lamb, let him and his
neighbor next to his house take *it*
according to the number of the
persons; according to each man's
need you shall make your count
for the lamb.
5 'Your lamb shall be [a]without[1]
blemish, a male [2]of the first year.
You may take *it* from the sheep
or from the goats.
6 'Now you shall keep it until the
[a]fourteenth day of the same
month. Then the whole assembly
of the congregation of Israel shall
kill it at twilight.
7 'And they shall take *some* of
the blood and put *it* on the two
doorposts and on the lintel of the
houses where they eat it.
8 'Then they shall eat the flesh
on that [a]night; [b]roasted in fire,
with [c]unleavened bread *and* with
bitter *herbs* they shall eat it.
9 'Do not eat it raw, nor boiled
at all with water, but [a]roasted in
fire—its head with its legs and its
entrails.
10 [a]'You shall let none of it remain
until morning, and what remains
of it until morning you shall burn
with fire.
11 'And thus you shall eat it: [1]*with*
a belt on your waist, your sandals
on your feet, and your staff in your
hand. So you shall eat it in haste.
[a]It *is* the LORD's Passover.
12 'For I [a]will pass through the
land of Egypt on that night, and
will strike all the firstborn in the
land of Egypt, both man and beast;
and [b]against all the gods of Egypt
I will execute judgment: [c]I *am* the
LORD.
13 'Now the blood shall be a sign
for you on the houses where you
are. And when I see the blood, I
will pass over you; and the plague
shall not be on you to destroy *you*
when I strike the land of Egypt.
14 'So this day shall be to you [a]a
memorial; and you shall keep it as
a [b]feast to the LORD throughout
your generations. You shall keep
it as a feast [c]by an everlasting ordi-
nance.
15 [a]'Seven days you shall eat un-
leavened bread. On the first day
you shall remove leaven from your
houses. For whoever eats leavened
bread from the first day until the
seventh day, [b]that [1]person shall be
[2]cut off from Israel.
16 'On the first day *there shall be*
[a]a holy convocation, and on the
seventh day there shall be a holy
convocation for you. No manner
of work shall be done on them; but
that which everyone must eat—
that only may be prepared by you.
17 'So you shall observe *the Feast*
of Unleavened Bread, for [a]on this
same day I will have brought your
[1]armies [b]out of the land of Egypt.
Therefore you shall observe this
day throughout your generations
as an everlasting ordinance.
18 [a]'In the first *month*, on the
fourteenth day of the month at
evening, you shall eat unleavened
bread, until the twenty-first day of
the month at evening.
19 'For [a]seven days no leaven
shall be found in your houses,
since whoever eats what is leav-
ened, that same person shall be cut
off from the congregation of Israel,
whether *he is* a stranger or a na-
tive of the land.
20 'You shall eat nothing leav-
ened; in all your dwellings you
shall eat unleavened bread.' "
21 Then [a]Moses called for all the
[b]elders of Israel and said to them,
[c]"Pick out and take lambs for
yourselves according to your fami-
lies, and kill the Passover *lamb*.
22 [a]"And you shall take a bunch
of hyssop, dip *it* in the blood that
is in the basin, and [b]strike the lin-
tel and the two doorposts with the
blood that *is* in the basin. And
none of you shall go out of the
door of his house until morning.
23 [a]"For the LORD will pass
through to strike the Egyptians;
and when He sees the [b]blood on
the [1]lintel and on the two door-

CHAPTER 12
2 [a]Ex. 13:4; 23:15; 34:18; Deut. 16:1
3 [a]Josh. 4:19
5 [a]Lev. 22:18–21; 23:12; Mal. 1:8, 14; [Heb. 9:14; 1 Pet. 1:19] [1]*perfect* or *sound* [2]*a year old*
6 [a]Ex. 12:14, 17; Lev. 23:5; Num. 9:1–3, 11; 28:16; Deut. 16:1, 4, 6
8 [a]Ex. 34:25; Num. 9:12 [b]Deut. 16:7 [c]Deut. 16:3, 4; 1 Cor. 5:8
9 [a]Deut. 16:7
10 [a]Ex. 16:19; 23:18; 34:25
11 [a]Ex. 12:13, 21, 27, 43 [1]Made ready to travel
12 [a]Ex. 11:4, 5 [b]Num. 33:4 [c]Ex. 6:2
14 [a]Ex. 13:9 [b]Lev. 23:4, 5; 2 Kin. 23:21 [c]Ex. 12:17, 24; 13:10
15 [a]Ex. 13:6, 7; 23:15; 34:18; Lev. 23:6; Num. 28:17; Deut. 16:3, 8 [b]Gen. 17:14; Ex. 12:19; Num. 9:13 [1]*soul* [2]Put to death
16 [a]Lev. 23:2, 7, 8; Num. 28:18, 25
17 [a]Ex. 12:14; 13:3, 10 [b]Num. 33:1 [1]*hosts*
18 [a]Ex. 12:2; Lev. 23:5–8; Num. 28:16–25
19 [a]Ex. 12:15; 23:15; 34:18
21 [a][Heb. 11:28] [b]Ex. 3:16 [c]Ex. 12:3; Num. 9:4; Josh. 5:10; 2 Kin. 23:21; Ezra 6:20; Mark 14:12–16
22 [a]Heb. 11:28 [b]Ex. 12:7
23 [a]Ex. 11:4; 12:12, 13 [b]Ex. 24:8 [1]Crosspiece at top of door

posts, the LORD will pass over the
door and [c]not allow [d]the destroyer
to come into your houses to strike
you.
24 "And you shall [a]observe this
thing as an ordinance for you and
your sons forever.
25 "It will come to pass when you
come to the land which the LORD
will give you, [a]just as He promised,
that you shall keep this service.
26 [a]"And it shall be, when your
children say to you, 'What do you
mean by this service?'
27 "that you shall say, [a]'It *is* the
Passover sacrifice of the LORD,
who passed over the houses of the
children of Israel in Egypt when
He struck the Egyptians and deliv-
ered our households.' " So the peo-
ple [b]bowed their heads and wor-
shiped.
28 Then the children of Israel
went away and [a]did *so;* just as the
LORD had commanded Moses and
Aaron, so they did.

The Tenth Plague: Death of the Firstborn

29 [a]And it came to pass at mid-
night that [b]the LORD struck all the
firstborn in the land of Egypt, from
the firstborn of Pharaoh who sat
on his throne to the firstborn of the
captive who *was* [1]in the dungeon,
and all the firstborn of [c]livestock.
30 So Pharaoh rose in the night,
he, all his servants, and all the
Egyptians; and there was a great
cry in Egypt, for *there was* not a
house where *there was* not one
dead.

The Exodus

31 Then he [a]called for Moses and
Aaron by night, and said, "Rise,
go out from among my people,
[b]both you and the children of Is-
rael. And go, serve the LORD as you
have [c]said.
32 [a]"Also take your flocks and
your herds, as you have said, and
be gone; and bless me also."
33 [a]And the Egyptians [b]urged the
people, that they might send them
out of the land in haste. For they
said, "We *shall* all *be* dead."
34 So the people took their dough
before it was leavened, having
their kneading bowls bound up in
their clothes on their shoulders.
35 Now the children of Israel had
done according to the word of Mo-
ses, and they had asked from the
Egyptians [a]articles of silver, arti-
cles of gold, and clothing.
36 [a]And the LORD had given the
people favor in the sight of the
Egyptians, so that they granted
them *what they requested.* Thus
[b]they plundered the Egyptians.
37 Then [a]the children of Israel
journeyed from [b]Rameses to Suc-
coth, about [c]six hundred thousand
men on foot, besides children.
38 A [a]mixed multitude went up
with them also, and flocks and
herds—a great deal of [b]livestock.
39 And they baked unleavened
cakes of the dough which they had
brought out of Egypt; for it was
not leavened, because [a]they were
driven out of Egypt and could not
wait, nor had they prepared provi-
sions for themselves.
40 Now the [1]sojourn of the chil-
dren of Israel who lived in [2]Egypt
was [a]four hundred and thirty
years.
41 And it came to pass at the end
of the four hundred and thirty
years—on that very same day—it
came to pass that [a]all the armies
of the LORD went out from the land
of Egypt.
42 It *is* [a]a [1]night of solemn obser-
vance to the LORD for bringing
them out of the land of Egypt. This
is that night of the LORD, a solemn
observance for all the children of
Israel throughout their genera-
tions.

Passover Regulations

43 And the LORD said to Moses
and Aaron, "This *is* [a]the ordinance
of the Passover: No foreigner shall
eat it.
44 "But every man's servant who
is bought for money, when you
have [a]circumcised him, then he
may eat it.
45 [a]"A sojourner and a hired ser-
vant shall not eat it.
46 "In one house it shall be eaten;
you shall not carry any of the flesh
outside the house, [a]nor shall you
break one of its bones.
47 [a]"All the congregation of Israel
shall keep it.
48 "And [a]when a stranger [1]dwells
with you *and wants* to keep the

23 [c]Ezek. 9:6; Rev. 7:3; 9:4 [d]1 Cor. 10:10; Heb. 11:28
24 [a]Ex. 12:14, 17; 13:5, 10
25 [a]Ex. 3:8, 17
26 [a]Ex. 10:2; 13:8, 14, 15; Deut. 32:7; Josh. 4:6; Ps. 78:6
27 [a]Ex. 12:11 [b]Ex. 4:31
28 [a][Heb. 11:28]
29 [a]Ex. 11:4, 5 [b]Num. 8:17; 33:4; Ps. 135:8; 136:10 [c]Ex. 9:6 [1]*in prison*
31 [a]Ex. 10:28, 29 [b]Ex. 8:25; 11:1 [c]Ex. 10:9
32 [a]Ex. 10:9, 26
33 [a]Ex. 10:7 [b]Ex. 11:8; Ps. 105:38
35 [a]Ex. 3:21, 22; 11:2, 3; Ps. 105:37
36 [a]Ex. 3:21 [b]Gen. 15:14
37 [a]Num. 33:3, 5 [b]Gen. 47:11; Ex. 1:11; Num. 33:3, 4 [c]Gen. 12:2; Ex. 38:26; Num. 1:46; 2:32; 11:21; 26:51
38 [a]Num. 11:4 [b]Ex. 17:3; Num. 20:19; 32:1; Deut. 3:19
39 [a]Ex. 6:1; 11:1; 12:31–33
40 [a]Gen. 15:13, 16; Acts 7:6; Gal. 3:17 [1]Length of the stay [2]Sam., LXX *Egypt and Canaan*
41 [a]Ex. 3:8, 10; 6:6; 7:4
42 [a]Ex. 13:10; 34:18; Deut. 16:1, 6 [1]*night of vigil*
43 [a]Ex. 12:11; Num. 9:14
44 [a]Gen. 17:12, 13; Lev. 22:11
45 [a]Lev. 22:10
46 [a]Num. 9:12; Ps. 34:20; [John 19:33, 36]
47 [a]Ex. 12:6; Num. 9:13, 14
48 [a]Num. 9:14 [1]As a resident alien

Passover to the LORD, let all his
males be circumcised, and then let
him come near and keep it; and
he shall be as a native of the land.
For no uncircumcised person shall
eat it.
49 [a]"One law shall be for the
native-born and for the stranger
who dwells among you."
50 Thus all the children of Israel
did; as the LORD commanded Mo-
ses and Aaron, so they did.
51 [a]And it came to pass, on that
very same day, that the LORD
brought the children of Israel out
of the land of Egypt [b]according to
their armies.

The Firstborn Consecrated

13 Then the LORD spoke to Mo-
ses, saying,
2 [a]"Consecrate[1] to Me all the
firstborn, whatever opens the
womb among the children of Is-
rael, *both* of man and beast; it is
Mine."

The Feast of Unleavened Bread

3 And Moses said to the people:
[a]"Remember this day in which you
went out of Egypt, out of the house
of [1]bondage; for [b]by strength of
hand the LORD brought you out of
this *place*. [c]No leavened bread
shall be eaten.
4 [a]"On this day you are going
out, in the month Abib.
5 "And it shall be, when the LORD
[a]brings you into the [b]land of the
Canaanites and the Hittites and
the Amorites and the Hivites and
the Jebusites, which He [c]swore to
your fathers to give you, a land
flowing with milk and honey, [d]that
you shall keep this service in this
month.
6 [a]"Seven days you shall eat un-
leavened bread, and on the sev-
enth day *there shall be* a feast to
the LORD.
7 "Unleavened bread shall be
eaten seven days. And [a]no leav-
ened bread shall be seen among
you, nor shall leaven be seen
among you in all your quarters.
8 "And you shall [a]tell your son
in that day, saying, '*This is done*
because of what the LORD did for
me when I came up from Egypt.'
9 "It shall be as [a]a sign to you
on your hand and as a memorial
between your eyes, that the LORD's
law may be in your mouth; for
with a strong hand the LORD has
brought you out of Egypt.
10 [a]"You shall therefore keep this
[1]ordinance in its season from year
to year.

The Law of the Firstborn

11 "And it shall be, when the LORD
[a]brings you into the land of the
[b]Canaanites, as He swore to you
and your fathers, and gives it to
you,
12 [a]"that you shall [1]set apart to
the LORD all that open the womb,
that is, every firstborn that comes
from an animal which you have;
the males *shall be* the LORD's.
13 "But [a]every firstborn of a don-
key you shall redeem with a lamb;
and if you will not redeem *it*, then
you shall break its neck. And all
the firstborn of man among your
sons [b]you shall redeem.
14 [a]"So it shall be, when your son
asks you in time to come, saying,
'What *is* this?' that you shall say
to him, [b]'By strength of hand the
LORD brought us out of Egypt, out
of the house of bondage.
15 'And it came to pass, when
Pharaoh was stubborn about let-
ting us go, that [a]the LORD killed all
the firstborn in the land of Egypt,
both the firstborn of man and the
firstborn of beast. Therefore I sac-
rifice to the LORD all males that
open the womb, but all the first-
born of my sons I redeem.'
16 "It shall be as [a]a sign on your
hand and as frontlets between
your eyes, for by strength of hand
the LORD brought us out of Egypt."

The Wilderness Way

17 Then it came to pass, when
Pharaoh had let the people go, that
God did not lead them *by* way of
the land of the Philistines, al-
though that *was* near; for God
said, "Lest perhaps the people
[a]change their minds when they see
war, and [b]return to Egypt."
18 So God [a]led the people around
by way of the wilderness of the
Red Sea. And the children of Israel
went up in orderly ranks out of the
land of Egypt.
19 And Moses took the [a]bones of
[b]Joseph with him, for he had

49 [a]Lev. 24:22; Num. 15:15, 16; [Gal. 3:28]
51 [a]Ex. 12:41; 20:2 [b]Ex. 6:26

CHAPTER 13

2 [a]Ex. 13:12, 13, 15; 22:29; Lev. 27:26; Num. 3:13; 8:16; 18:15; Deut. 15:19; Luke 2:23 [1]*Set apart*
3 [a]Ex. 12:42; Deut. 16:3 [b]Ex. 3:20; 6:1 [c]Ex. 12:8, 19 [1]Lit. *slaves*
4 [a]Ex. 12:2; 23:15; 34:18; Deut. 16:1
5 [a]Ex. 3:8, 17; Josh. 24:11 [b]Gen. 17:8; Deut. 30:5 [c]Ex. 6:8 [d]Ex. 12:25, 26
6 [a]Ex. 12:15–20
7 [a]Ex. 12:19
8 [a]Ex. 10:2; 12:26; 13:14; Ps. 44:1
9 [a]Ex. 12:14; 13:16; 31:13; Deut. 6:8; 11:18; Matt. 23:5
10 [a]Ex. 12:14, 24 [1]*regulation*
11 [a]Ex. 13:5 [b]Num. 21:3
12 [a]Ex. 13:1, 2; 22:29; 34:19; Lev. 27:26; Num. 18:15; Ezek. 44:30; Luke 2:23 [1]Lit. *cause to pass over*
13 [a]Ex. 34:20; Num. 18:15 [b]Num. 3:46, 47; 18:15, 16
14 [a]Ex. 10:2; 12:26, 27; 13:8; Deut. 6:20; Josh. 4:6, 21 [b]Ex. 13:3, 9
15 [a]Ex. 12:29
16 [a]Ex. 13:9; Deut. 6:8
17 [a]Ex. 14:11; Num. 14:1–4 [b]Deut. 17:16
18 [a]Ex. 14:2; Num. 33:6
19 [a]Gen. 50:24, 25; Josh. 24:32 [b]Ex. 1:6; Deut. 33:13–17

placed the children of Israel under
solemn oath, saying, [c]"God will
surely [1]visit you, and you shall
carry up my bones from here with
you."
20 So [a]they took their journey
from [b]Succoth and camped in
Etham at the edge of the wilder-
ness.
21 And [a]the LORD went before
them by day in a pillar of cloud
to lead the way, and by night in a
pillar of fire to give them light, so
as to go by day and night.
22 He did not take away the pil-
lar of cloud by day or the pillar
of fire by night *from* before the
people.

The Red Sea Crossing

14 Now the LORD spoke to Mo-
ses, saying:
2 "Speak to the children of Is-
rael, [a]that they turn and camp be-
fore [b]Pi Hahiroth, between [c]Mig-
dol and the sea, opposite Baal
Zephon; you shall camp before it
by the sea.
3 "For Pharaoh will say of the
children of Israel, [a]'They *are* be-
wildered by the land; the wilder-
ness has closed them in.'
4 "Then [a]I will harden Pharaoh's
heart, so that he will pursue them;
and I [b]will gain honor over Pha-
raoh and over all his army,
[c]that the Egyptians may know
that I *am* the LORD." And they did
so.
5 Now it was told the king of
Egypt that the people had fled, and
[a]the heart of Pharaoh and his ser-
vants was turned against the peo-
ple; and they said, "Why have we
done this, that we have let Israel
go from serving us?"
6 So he [1]made ready his chariot
and took his people with him.
7 Also, he took [a]six hundred
choice chariots, and all the chari-
ots of Egypt with captains over
every one of them.
8 And the LORD [a]hardened the
heart of Pharaoh king of Egypt,
and he pursued the children of Is-
rael; and [b]the children of Israel
went out with boldness.
9 So the [a]Egyptians pursued
them, all the horses *and* chariots
of Pharaoh, his horsemen and his
army, and overtook them camping
by the sea beside Pi Hahiroth, be-
fore Baal Zephon.
10 And when Pharaoh drew near,
the children of Israel lifted their
eyes, and behold, the Egyptians
marched after them. So they were
very afraid, and the children of Is-
rael [a]cried out to the LORD.
11 [a]Then they said to Moses, "Be-
cause *there were* no graves in
Egypt, have you taken us away to
die in the wilderness? Why have
you so dealt with us, to bring us
up out of Egypt?
12 [a]"*Is* this not the word that we
told you in Egypt, saying, 'Let us
alone that we may serve the Egyp-
tians'? For *it would have been* bet-
ter for us to serve the Egyptians
than that we should die in the wil-
derness."
13 And Moses said to the people,
[a]"Do not be afraid. [b]Stand still,
and see the [c]salvation[1] of the LORD,
which He will accomplish for you
today. For the Egyptians whom
you see today, you shall [d]see again
no more forever.
14 [a]"The LORD will fight for you,
and you shall [b]hold[1] your peace."
15 And the LORD said to Moses,
"Why do you cry to Me? Tell
the children of Israel to go for-
ward.
16 "But [a]lift up your rod, and
stretch out your hand over the sea
and divide it. And the children of
Israel shall go on dry *ground*
through the midst of the sea.
17 "And I indeed will [a]harden the
hearts of the Egyptians, and they
shall follow them. So I will [b]gain
honor over Pharaoh and over all
his army, his chariots, and his
horsemen.
18 "Then the Egyptians shall
know that I *am* the LORD, when I
have gained honor for Myself over
Pharaoh, his chariots, and his
horsemen."
19 And the Angel of God, [a]who
went before the camp of Israel,
moved and went behind them; and
the pillar of cloud went from be-
fore them and stood behind
them.
20 So it came between the camp
of the Egyptians and the camp of
Israel. Thus it was a cloud and
darkness *to the one,* and it gave
light by night *to the other,* so that

19 [c]Ex. 4:31 [1]*give attention to*
20 [a]Num. 33:6–8 [b]Ex. 12:37
21 [a]Ex. 14:19, 24; 33:9, 10; Num. 9:15; 14:14; Deut. 1:33; Neh. 9:12; Ps. 78:14; 99:7; 105:39; [Is. 4:5]; 1 Cor. 10:1

CHAPTER 14

2 [a]Ex. 13:18 [b]Num. 33:7 [c]Jer. 44:1
3 [a]Ps. 71:11
4 [a]Ex. 4:21; 7:3; 14:17 [b]Ex. 9:16; 14:17, 18, 23; Rom. 9:17, 22, 23 [c]Ex. 7:5; 14:25
5 [a]Ps. 105:25
6 [1]*harnessed*
7 [a]Ex. 15:4
8 [a]Ex. 14:4 [b]Ex. 6:1; 13:9; Num. 33:3; Acts 13:17
9 [a]Ex. 15:9; Josh. 24:6
10 [a]Josh. 24:7; Neh. 9:9; Ps. 34:17; 107:6
11 [a]Ex. 5:21; 15:24; 16:2; 17:3; Num. 14:2, 3; 20:3; Ps. 106:7, 8
12 [a]Ex. 5:21; 6:9
13 [a]Gen. 15:1; 46:3; Ex. 20:20; 2 Chr. 20:15, 17; Is. 41:10, 13, 14 [b]Ps. 46:10, 11 [c]Ex. 14:30; 15:2 [d]Deut. 28:68 [1]*deliverance*
14 [a]Ex. 14:25; 15:3; Deut. 1:30; 3:22; Josh. 10:14, 42; 23:2; 2 Chr. 20:29; Neh. 4:20; Is. 31:4 [b][Is. 30:15] [1]Lit. *be quiet*
16 [a]Ex. 4:17, 20; 7:19; 14:21, 26; 17:5, 6, 9; Num. 20:8, 9, 11; Is. 10:26
17 [a]Ex. 14:8 [b]Ex. 14:4
19 [a]Ex. 13:21, 22; [Is. 63:9]

the one did not come near the
other all that night.
21 Then Moses stretched out his
hand over the sea; and the LORD
caused the sea to go *back* by a
strong east wind all that night, and
[a]made the sea into dry *land*, and
the waters were [b]divided.
22 So [a]the children of Israel went
into the midst of the sea on the dry
ground, and the waters *were* [b]a
wall to them on their right hand
and on their left.
23 And the Egyptians pursued and
went after them into the midst of
the sea, all Pharaoh's horses, his
chariots, and his horsemen.
24 Now it came to pass, in the
morning [a]watch, that [b]the LORD
looked down upon the army of the
Egyptians through the pillar of fire
and cloud, and He [1]troubled the
army of the Egyptians.
25 And He [1]took off their chariot
wheels, so that they drove them
with difficulty; and the Egyptians
said, "Let us flee from the face of
Israel, for the LORD [a]fights for
them against the Egyptians."
26 Then the LORD said to Moses,
"Stretch out your hand over the
sea, that the waters may come
back upon the Egyptians, on their
chariots, and on their horsemen."
27 And Moses stretched out his
hand over the sea; and when the
morning appeared, the sea [a]re-
turned to its full depth, while the
Egyptians were fleeing into it. So
the LORD [b]overthrew[1] the Egyp-
tians in the midst of the sea.
28 Then [a]the waters returned and
covered the chariots, the horse-
men, *and* all the army of Pharaoh
that came into the sea after them.
Not so much as one of them re-
mained.
29 But [a]the children of Israel had
walked on dry *land* in the midst
of the sea, and the waters *were* a
wall to them on their right hand
and on their left.
30 So the LORD [a]saved[1] Israel that
day out of the hand of the Egyp-
tians, and Israel [b]saw the Egyp-
tians dead on the seashore.
31 Thus Israel saw the great
[1]work which the LORD had done
in Egypt; so the people feared the
LORD, and [a]believed the LORD and
His servant Moses.

21 [a]Ps. 66:6; 106:9; 136:13, 14 [b]Is. 63:12, 13
22 [a]Ex. 15:19 [b]Ex. 14:29; 15:8
24 [a]Judg. 7:19 [b]Ex. 13:21 [1]*confused*
25 [a]Ex. 7:5; 14:4, 14, 18 [1]Sam., LXX, Syr. *bound*
27 [a]Josh. 4:18 [b]Ex. 15:1, 7 [1]Lit. *shook off*
28 [a]Ps. 78:53; 106:11
29 [a]Ps. 66:6; 78:52, 53
30 [a]Ps. 106:8, 10 [b]Ps. 58:10; 59:10 [1]*delivered*
31 [a]John 2:11; 11:45 [1]Lit. *hand with which the LORD* worked

CHAPTER 15

1 [a]Ps. 106:12 [b]Is. 12:1–6
2 [a]Is. 12:2 [b]Gen. 28:21, 22 [c]Ex. 3:6, 15, 16 [d]Is. 25:1
3 [a]Rev. 19:11 [b]Ps. 24:8; 83:18
4 [a]Ex. 14:28 [b]Ex. 14:7
5 [a]Neh. 9:11
6 [a]Ps. 17:7; 118:15
7 [a]Deut. 33:26 [b]Ps. 78:49, 50 [c]Ps. 59:13 [d]Is. 5:24
8 [a]Ex. 14:21, 22, 29 [b]Ps. 78:13 [1]*became firm*
9 [a]Judg. 5:30 [b]Is. 53:12
11 [a]1 Kin. 8:23 [b]Is. 6:3 [c]1 Chr. 16:25 [d]Ps. 77:11, 14 [1]*mighty ones*

The Song of Moses

15 Then [a]Moses and the chil-
dren of Israel sang this
song to the LORD, and spoke, say-
ing:

"I will [b]sing to the LORD,
For He has triumphed gloriously!
The horse and its rider
He has thrown into the sea!
2 The LORD *is* my strength and
[a]song,
And He has become my
salvation;
He *is* my God, and [b]I will praise
Him;
My [c]father's God, and I [d]will exalt
Him.
3 The LORD *is* a man of [a]war;
The LORD *is* His [b]name.
4 [a]Pharaoh's chariots and his army
He has cast into the sea;
[b]His chosen captains also are
drowned in the Red Sea.
5 The depths have covered them;
[a]They sank to the bottom like a
stone.

6 "Your [a]right hand, O LORD, has
become glorious in power;
Your right hand, O LORD, has
dashed the enemy in pieces.
7 And in the greatness of Your
[a]excellence
You have overthrown those who
rose against You;
You sent forth [b]Your wrath;
It [c]consumed them [d]like stubble.
8 And [a]with the blast of Your
nostrils
The waters were gathered
together;
[b]The floods stood upright like a
heap;
The depths [1]congealed in the
heart of the sea.
9 [a]The enemy said, 'I will pursue,
I will overtake,
I will [b]divide the spoil;
My desire shall be satisfied on
them.
I will draw my sword,
My hand shall destroy them.'
10 You blew with Your wind,
The sea covered them;
They sank like lead in the mighty
waters.

11 "Who[a] *is* like You, O LORD, among
the [1]gods?
Who *is* like You, [b]glorious in
holiness,
Fearful in [c]praises, [d]doing
wonders?

12 You stretched out Your right
hand;
The earth swallowed them.
13 You in Your mercy have [a]led
forth
The people whom You have
redeemed;
You have guided *them* in Your
strength
To [b]Your holy habitation.

14 "The [a]people will hear *and* be
afraid;
[b]Sorrow[1] will take hold of the
inhabitants of Philistia.
15 [a]Then [b]the chiefs of Edom will be
dismayed;
[c]The mighty men of Moab,
Trembling will take hold of
them;
[d]All the inhabitants of Canaan will
[e]melt away.
16 [a]Fear and dread will fall on them;
By the greatness of Your arm
They will be [b]*as* still as a stone,
Till Your people pass over,
O LORD,
Till the people pass over
[c]Whom You have purchased.
17 You will bring them in and [a]plant
them
In the [b]mountain of Your
inheritance,
In the place, O LORD, *which* You
have made
For Your own dwelling,
The [c]sanctuary, O LORD, *which*
Your hands have established.

18 "The[a] LORD shall reign forever and
ever."

19 For the [a]horses of Pharaoh
went with his chariots and his
horsemen into the sea, and [b]the
LORD brought back the waters of
the sea upon them. But the chil-
dren of Israel went on dry *land* in
the midst of the sea.

The Song of Miriam

20 Then Miriam [a]the prophetess,
[b]the sister of Aaron, [c]took the tim-
brel in her hand; and all the
women went out after her [d]with
timbrels and with dances.
21 And Miriam [a]answered them:

[b]"Sing to the LORD,
For He has triumphed gloriously!
The horse and its rider
He has thrown into the sea!"

Bitter Waters Made Sweet

22 So Moses brought Israel from
the Red Sea; then they went out

13 [a][Ps. 77:20] [b]Ps. 78:54
14 [a]Josh. 2:9 [b]Ps. 48:6 [1]*Anguish*
15 [a]Gen. 36:15, 40 [b]Deut. 2:4 [c]Num. 22:3, 4 [d]Josh. 5:1 [e]Josh. 2:9–11, 24
16 [a]Josh. 2:9 [b]1 Sam. 25:37 [c]Jer. 31:11
17 [a]Ps. 44:2; 80:8, 15 [b]Ps. 2:6; 78:54, 68 [c]Ps. 68:16; 76:2; 132:13, 14
18 [a]Is. 57:15
19 [a]Ex. 14:23 [b]Ex. 14:28
20 [a]Judg. 4:4 [b]Num. 26:59 [c]1 Sam. 18:6 [d]Judg. 11:34; 21:21
21 [a]1 Sam. 18:7 [b]Ex. 15:1
22 [a]Gen. 16:7; 20:1; 25:18 [b]Num. 20:2
23 [a]Num. 33:8 [1]Lit. *Bitter*
24 [a]Ex. 14:11; 16:2
25 [a]2 Kin. 2:21 [b]Josh. 24:25 [c]Deut. 8:2, 16 [1]*regulation*
26 [a]Deut. 7:12, 15 [b]Deut. 28:27, 58, 60 [c]Ex. 23:25
27 [a]Num. 33:9

CHAPTER 16

1 [a]Num. 33:10, 11 [b]Ex. 12:6, 51; 19:1
2 [a]1 Cor. 10:10
3 [a]Lam. 4:9 [b]Num. 11:4, 5
4 [a][John 6:31–35] [b]Deut. 8:2, 16 [c]Judg. 2:22 [1]Lit. *the portion of a day in its day*

into the Wilderness of [a]Shur. And
they went three days in the wilder-
ness and found no [b]water.
23 Now when they came to
[a]Marah, they could not drink the
waters of Marah, for they *were* bit-
ter. Therefore the name of it was
called [1]Marah.
24 And the people [a]complained
against Moses, saying, "What
shall we drink?"
25 So he cried out to the LORD, and
the LORD showed him a tree.
[a]When he cast *it* into the waters,
the waters were made sweet.
There He [b]made a statute and an
[1]ordinance for them, and there [c]He
tested them,
26 and said, [a]"If you diligently
heed the voice of the LORD your
God and do what is right in His
sight, give ear to His command-
ments and keep all His statutes, I
will put none of the [b]diseases on
you which I have brought on the
Egyptians. For I *am* the LORD [c]who
heals you."
27 [a]Then they came to Elim,
where there *were* twelve wells of
water and seventy palm trees; so
they camped there by the waters.

Bread from Heaven

16 And they [a]journeyed from
Elim, and all the congrega-
tion of the children of Israel came
to the Wilderness of Sin, which is
between Elim and [b]Sinai, on the
fifteenth day of the second month
after they departed from the land
of Egypt.
2 Then the whole congregation
of the children of Israel [a]com-
plained against Moses and Aaron
in the wilderness.
3 And the children of Israel said
to them, [a]"Oh, that we had died
by the hand of the LORD in the land
of Egypt, [b]when we sat by the pots
of meat *and* when we ate bread to
the full! For you have brought us
out into this wilderness to kill this
whole assembly with hunger."
4 Then the LORD said to Moses,
"Behold, I will rain [a]bread from
heaven for you. And the people
shall go out and gather [1]a certain
quota every day, that I may [b]test
them, whether they will [c]walk in
My law or not.
5 "And it shall be on the sixth

day that they shall prepare what they bring in, and [a]it shall be twice as much as they gather daily."
6 Then Moses and Aaron said to all the children of Israel, [a]"At evening you shall know that the LORD has brought you out of the land of Egypt.
7 "And in the morning you shall see [a]the glory of the LORD; for He [b]hears your complaints against the LORD. But [c]what *are* we, that you complain against us?"
8 Also Moses said, "*This shall be seen* when the LORD gives you meat to eat in the evening, and in the morning bread to the full; for the LORD hears your complaints which you make against Him. And what *are* we? Your complaints *are* not against us but [a]against the LORD."
9 Then Moses spoke to Aaron, "Say to all the congregation of the children of Israel, [a]'Come near before the LORD, for He has heard your complaints.' "
10 Now it came to pass, as Aaron spoke to the whole congregation of the children of Israel, that they looked toward the wilderness, and behold, the glory of the LORD [a]appeared in the cloud.
11 And the LORD spoke to Moses, saying,
12 [a]"I have heard the complaints of the children of Israel. Speak to them, saying, [b]'At twilight you shall eat meat, and [c]in the morning you shall be filled with bread. And you shall know that I *am* the LORD your God.' "
13 So it was that [a]quails came up at evening and covered the camp, and in the morning [b]the dew lay all around the camp.
14 And when the layer of dew lifted, there, on the surface of the wilderness, was [a]a small round [b]substance, *as* fine as frost on the ground.
15 So when the children of Israel saw *it,* they said to one another, "What is it?" For they did not know what it *was.* And Moses said to them, [a]"This *is* the bread which the LORD has given you to eat.
16 "This is the thing which the LORD has commanded: 'Let every man gather it [a]according to each one's need, one [b]omer for each person, *according to the* number of persons; let every man take for *those* who *are* in his tent.' "
17 Then the children of Israel did so and gathered, some more, some less.
18 So when they measured *it* by omers, [a]he who gathered much had nothing left over, and he who gathered little had no lack. Every man had gathered according to each one's need.
19 And Moses said, "Let no one [a]leave any of it till morning."
20 Notwithstanding they did not [1]heed Moses. But some of them left part of it until morning, and it bred worms and stank. And Moses was angry with them.
21 So they gathered it every morning, every man according to his need. And when the sun became hot, it melted.
22 And so it was, on the sixth day, *that* they gathered twice as much bread, two omers for each one. And all the rulers of the congregation came and told Moses.
23 Then he said to them, "This *is what* the LORD has said: 'Tomorrow *is* [a]a Sabbath rest, a holy Sabbath to the LORD. Bake what you will bake *today,* and boil what you will boil; and lay up for yourselves all that remains, to be kept until morning.' "
24 So they laid it up till morning, as Moses commanded; and it did not [a]stink, nor were there any worms in it.
25 Then Moses said, "Eat that today, for today *is* a Sabbath to the LORD; today you will not find it in the field.
26 [a]"Six days you shall gather it, but on the seventh day, the Sabbath, there will be none."
27 Now it happened *that some* of the people went out on the seventh day to gather, but they found none.
28 And the LORD said to Moses, "How long [a]do you refuse to keep My commandments and My laws?
29 "See! For the LORD has given you the Sabbath; therefore He gives you on the sixth day bread for two days. Let every man remain in his place; let no man go out of his place on the seventh day."

5 [a]Ex. 16:22, 29; Lev. 25:21
6 [a]Ex. 6:7
7 [a]Ex. 16:10, 12; Is. 35:2; 40:5; John 11:4, 40 [b]Num. 14:27; 17:5 [c]Num. 16:11
8 [a]1 Sam. 8:7; Luke 10:16; [Rom. 13:2]; 1 Thess. 4:8
9 [a]Num. 16:16
10 [a]Ex. 13:21; 16:7; Num. 16:19; 1 Kin. 8:10
12 [a]Ex. 16:8; Num. 14:27 [b]Ex. 16:6 [c]Ex. 16:7; 1 Kin. 20:28; Joel 3:17
13 [a]Num. 11:31; Ps. 78:27–29; 105:40 [b]Num. 11:9
14 [a]Ex. 16:31; Num. 11:7, 8; Deut. 8:3; Neh. 9:15; Ps. 78:24; 105:40 [b]Ps. 147:16
15 [a]Ex. 16:4; Neh. 9:15; Ps. 78:24; [John 6:31, 49, 58]; 1 Cor. 10:3
16 [a]Ex. 12:4 [b]Ex. 16:32, 36
18 [a]2 Cor. 8:15
19 [a]Ex. 12:10; 16:23; 23:18
20 [1]*listen to*
23 [a]Gen. 2:3; Ex. 20:8–11; 23:12; 31:15; 35:2; Lev. 23:3; Neh. 9:13, 14
24 [a]Ex. 16:20
26 [a]Ex. 20:9, 10
28 [a]2 Kin. 17:14; Ps. 78:10; 106:13

30 So the people rested on the sev-
enth day.
31 And the house of Israel called
its name [1]Manna. And [a]it *was* like
white coriander seed, and the taste
of it *was* like wafers *made* with
honey.
32 Then Moses said, "This *is* the
thing which the LORD has com-
manded: 'Fill an omer with it, to
be kept for your generations, that
they may see the bread with which
I fed you in the wilderness, when
I brought you out of the land of
Egypt.' "
33 And Moses said to Aaron,
[a]"Take a pot and put an omer of
manna in it, and lay it up before
the LORD, to be kept for your gen-
erations."
34 As the LORD commanded Mo-
ses, so Aaron laid it up [a]before the
Testimony, to be kept.
35 And the children of Israel [a]ate
manna [b]forty years, [c]until they
came to an inhabited land; they ate
manna until they came to the bor-
der of the land of Canaan.
36 Now an omer *is* one-tenth of an
ephah.

Water from the Rock

17 Then [a]all the congregation
of the children of Israel set
out on their journey from the Wil-
derness of [b]Sin, according to the
commandment of the LORD, and
camped in Rephidim; but *there*
was no water for the people to
[c]drink.
2 [a]Therefore the people con-
tended with Moses, and said,
"Give us water, that we may
drink." So Moses said to them,
"Why do you contend with me?
Why do you [b]tempt the LORD?"
3 And the people thirsted there
for water, and the people [a]com-
plained against Moses, and said,
"Why *is* it you have brought us up
out of Egypt, to kill us and our chil-
dren and our [b]livestock with
thirst?"
4 So Moses [a]cried out to the
LORD, saying, "What shall I do
with this people? They are almost
ready to [b]stone[1] me!"
5 And the LORD said to Moses,
[a]"Go on before the people, and
take with you some of the elders
of Israel. Also take in your hand
your rod with which [b]you struck
the river, and go.
6 [a]"Behold, I will stand before
you there on the rock in Horeb;
and you shall strike the rock, and
water will come out of it, that the
people may drink." And Moses did
so in the sight of the elders of Is-
rael.
7 So he called the name of the
place [a]Massah[1] and [2]Meribah, be-
cause of the contention of the chil-
dren of Israel, and because they
[3]tempted the LORD, saying, "Is the
LORD among us or not?"

Victory over the Amalekites

8 [a]Now Amalek came and fought
with Israel in Rephidim.
9 And Moses said to Joshua,
"Choose us some men and go out,
fight with Amalek. Tomorrow I
will stand on the top of the hill
with [a]the rod of God in my hand."
10 So Joshua did as Moses said to
him, and fought with Amalek. And
Moses, Aaron, and Hur went up to
the top of the hill.
11 And so it was, when Moses
[a]held up his hand, that Israel pre-
vailed; and when he let down his
hand, Amalek prevailed.
12 But Moses' hands *became*
[1]heavy; so they took a stone and
put *it* under him, and he sat on it.
And Aaron and Hur supported his
hands, one on one side, and the
other on the other side; and his
hands were steady until the going
down of the sun.
13 So Joshua defeated Amalek
and his people with the edge of the
sword.
14 Then the LORD said to Moses,
[a]"Write this *for* a memorial in the
book and recount *it* in the hearing
of Joshua, that [b]I will utterly blot
out the remembrance of Amalek
from under heaven."
15 And Moses built an altar and
called its name, [1]The-LORD-Is-My-
Banner;
16 for he said, "Because [1]the LORD
has [a]sworn: the LORD *will have* war
with Amalek from generation to
generation."

Jethro's Advice

18 And [a]Jethro, the priest of
Midian, Moses' father-in-
law, heard of all that [b]God had

31 [a]Num. 11:7–9 [1]Lit. *What?* Ex. 16:15
33 [a]Heb. 9:4
34 [a]Num. 17:10
35 [a]Deut. 8:3, 16 [b]Num. 33:38 [c]Josh. 5:12

CHAPTER 17

1 [a]Ex. 16:1 [b]Num. 33:11–15 [c]Ex. 15:22
2 [a]Num. 20:2, 3, 13 [b][Deut. 6:16]
3 [a]Ex. 16:2, 3 [b]Ex. 12:38
4 [a]Ex. 14:15 [b]John 8:59; 10:31 [1]Put me to death by stoning
5 [a]Ezek. 2:6 [b]Num. 20:8
6 [a]Num. 20:10, 11
7 [a]Num. 20:13, 24; 27:14 [1]Lit. *Tempted* [2]Lit. *Contention* [3]*tested*
8 [a]Gen. 36:12
9 [a]Ex. 4:20
11 [a][James 5:16]
12 [1]Weary of being held up
14 [a]Ex. 24:4; 34:27 [b]1 Sam. 15:3
15 [1]Heb. *YHWH Nissi*
16 [a]Gen. 22:14–16 [1]Lit. *a hand is upon the throne of the LORD*

CHAPTER 18

1 [a]Ex. 2:16, 18; 3:1 [b][Ps. 106:2, 8]

done for Moses and for Israel His
people—that the LORD had brought
Israel out of Egypt.
2 Then Jethro, Moses' father-in-
law, took [a]Zipporah, Moses' wife,
after he had sent her back,
3 with her [a]two sons, of whom
the name of one *was* [1]Gershom
(for he said, [b]"I have been a
[2]stranger in a foreign land")
4 and the name of the other *was*
[1]Eliezer (for *he said,* "The God of
my father *was* my [a]help, and deliv-
ered me from the sword of Pha-
raoh");
5 and Jethro, Moses' father-in-
law, came with his sons and his
wife to Moses in the wilderness,
where he was encamped at [a]the
mountain of God.
6 Now he had said to Moses, "I,
your father-in-law Jethro, am
coming to you with your wife and
her two sons with her."
7 So Moses [a]went out to meet his
father-in-law, bowed down, and
[b]kissed him. And they asked each
other about *their* well-being, and
they went into the tent.
8 And Moses told his father-in-
law all that the LORD had done to
Pharaoh and to the Egyptians for
Israel's sake, all the hardship that
had come upon them on the way,
and *how* the LORD had [a]delivered
them.
9 Then Jethro rejoiced for all the
[a]good which the LORD had done for
Israel, whom He had delivered out
of the hand of the Egyptians.
10 And Jethro said, [a]"Blessed *be*
the LORD, who has delivered you
out of the hand of the Egyptians
and out of the hand of Pharaoh,
and who has delivered the people
from under the hand of the Egyp-
tians.
11 "Now I know that the LORD *is*
[a]greater than all the gods; [b]for in
the very thing in which they [1]be-
haved [c]proudly, *He was* above
them."
12 Then Jethro, Moses' father-in-
law, [1]took a burnt [a]offering and
other sacrifices *to offer* to God.
And Aaron came with all the el-
ders of Israel [b]to eat bread with
Moses' father-in-law before God.
13 And so it was, on the next day,
that Moses [a]sat to judge the peo-
ple; and the people stood before
Moses from morning until eve-
ning.
14 So when Moses' father-in-law
saw all that he did for the people,
he said, "What *is* this thing that
you are doing for the people? Why
do you alone [1]sit, and all the peo-
ple stand before you from morning
until evening?"
15 And Moses said to his father-
in-law, "Because [a]the people come
to me to inquire of God.
16 "When they have [a]a [1]difficulty,
they come to me, and I judge be-
tween one and another; and I
make known the statutes of God
and His laws."
17 So Moses' father-in-law said to
him, "The thing that you do *is* not
good.
18 "Both you and these people
who *are* with you will surely wear
yourselves out. For this thing *is* too
much for you; [a]you are not able
to perform it by yourself.
19 "Listen now to my voice; I will
give you [1]counsel, and God will be
with you: Stand [a]before God for
the people, so that you may [b]bring
the difficulties to God.
20 "And you shall [a]teach them the
statutes and the laws, and show
them the way in which they must
walk and [b]the work they must do.
21 "Moreover you shall select
from all the people [a]able men, such
as [b]fear God, [c]men of truth, [d]hat-
ing covetousness; and place *such*
over them *to be* rulers of thou-
sands, rulers of hundreds, rulers
of fifties, and rulers of tens.
22 "And let them judge the people
at all times. [a]Then it will be *that*
every great matter they shall bring
to you, but every small matter they
themselves shall judge. So it will
be easier for you, for [b]they will
bear *the burden* with you.
23 "If you do this thing, and God
so commands you, then you will
be able to endure, and all this peo-
ple will also go to their [a]place in
peace."
24 So Moses heeded the voice of
his father-in-law and did all that
he had said.
25 And [a]Moses chose able men
out of all Israel, and made them
heads over the people: rulers of
thousands, rulers of hundreds, rul-
ers of fifties, and rulers of tens.

2 [a]Ex. 2:21; 4:20–26
3 [a]Ex. 2:20; 4:20; Acts 7:29 [b]Ex. 2:22 [1]Lit. *Stranger There* [2]*sojourner,* temporary resident
4 [a]Gen. 49:25 [1]Lit. *My God Is Help*
5 [a]Ex. 3:1, 12; 4:27; 24:13
7 [a]Gen. 18:2 [b]Gen. 29:13; Ex. 4:27
8 [a]Ex. 15:6, 16; Ps. 81:7
9 [a][Is. 63:7–14]
10 [a]Gen. 14:20; 2 Sam. 18:28; 1 Kin. 8:56; Ps. 68:19, 20
11 [a]Ex. 12:12; 15:11; 2 Chr. 2:5; Ps. 95:3; 97:9; 135:5 [b]Ex. 1:10, 16, 22; 5:2, 7 [c]Luke 1:51 [1]*acted presumptuously*
12 [a]Ex. 24:5 [b]Gen. 31:54; Deut. 12:7 [1]So with MT, LXX; Syr., Tg., Vg. *offered*
13 [a]Deut. 33:4, 5; Matt. 23:2
14 [1]Sit as judge
15 [a]Lev. 24:12; Num. 9:6, 8; 27:5; Deut. 17:8–13
16 [a]Ex. 24:14; Deut. 19:17 [1]*dispute*
18 [a]Num. 11:14, 17; Deut. 1:12
19 [a]Ex. 4:16; 20:19 [b]Num. 9:8; 27:5 [1]*advice*
20 [a]Deut. 5:1 [b]Deut. 1:18
21 [a]Ex. 18:24, 25; Deut. 1:13, 15; 2 Chr. 19:5–10; Ps. 15:1–5; Acts 6:3 [b]Gen. 42:18; 2 Sam. 23:3 [c]Ezek. 18:8 [d]Deut. 16:19
22 [a]Lev. 24:11; Deut. 1:17 [b]Num. 11:17
23 [a]Ex. 16:29
25 [a]Ex. 18:21; Deut. 1:15

26 So they judged the people at all
times; the [a]hard[1] cases they
brought to Moses, but they judged
every small case themselves.
27 Then Moses let his father-in-
law depart, and [a]he went his way
to his own land.

Israel at Mount Sinai

19 In the third month after the
children of Israel had gone
out of the land of Egypt, on the
same day, [a]they came *to* the Wil-
derness of Sinai.
2 For they had departed from
[a]Rephidim, had come *to* the Wil-
derness of Sinai, and camped in
the wilderness. So Israel camped
there before [b]the mountain.
3 And [a]Moses went up to God,
and the LORD [b]called to him from
the mountain, saying, "Thus you
shall say to the house of Jacob,
and tell the children of Israel:
4 [a]'You have seen what I did to
the Egyptians, and *how* [b]I [1]bore
you on eagles' wings and brought
you to Myself.
5 'Now [a]therefore, if you will in-
deed obey My voice and [b]keep My
covenant, then [c]you shall be a spe-
cial treasure to Me above all peo-
ple; for all the earth *is* [d]Mine.
6 'And you shall be to Me a
[a]kingdom of priests and a [b]holy
nation.' These *are* the words which
you shall speak to the children of
Israel."
7 So Moses came and called for
the [a]elders of the people, and [1]laid
before them all these words which
the LORD commanded him.
8 Then [a]all the people answered
together and said, "All that the
LORD has spoken we will do." So
Moses brought back the words of
the people to the LORD.
9 And the LORD said to Moses,
"Behold, I come to you [a]in the
thick cloud, [b]that the people may
hear when I speak with you, and
believe you forever." So Moses
told the words of the people to the
LORD.
10 Then the LORD said to Moses,
"Go to the people and [a]consecrate
them today and tomorrow, and let
them wash their clothes.
11 "And let them be ready for the
third day. For on the third day the
LORD will come down upon Mount
Sinai in the sight of all the people.
12 "You shall set bounds for the
people all around, saying, 'Take
heed to yourselves *that* you do *not*
go up to the mountain or touch its
base. [a]Whoever touches the moun-
tain shall surely be put to death.
13 'Not a hand shall touch him,
but he shall surely be stoned or
shot *with an arrow;* whether man
or beast, he shall not live.' When
the trumpet sounds long, they
shall come near the mountain."
14 So Moses went down from the
mountain to the people and sancti-
fied the people, and they washed
their clothes.
15 And he said to the people, "Be
ready for the third day; [a]do not
come near *your* wives."
16 Then it came to pass on the
third day, in the morning, that
there were [a]thunderings and light-
nings, and a thick cloud on the
mountain; and the sound of the
trumpet was very loud, so that all
the people who *were* in the camp
[b]trembled.
17 And [a]Moses brought the people
out of the camp to meet with God,
and they stood at the foot of the
mountain.
18 Now [a]Mount Sinai *was* com-
pletely in smoke, because the LORD
descended upon [b]it in fire. [c]Its
smoke ascended like the smoke of
a furnace, and [1]the [d]whole moun-
tain quaked greatly.
19 And when the blast of the trum-
pet sounded long and became
louder and louder, [a]Moses spoke,
and [b]God answered him by voice.
20 Then the LORD came down
upon Mount Sinai, on the top of
the mountain. And the LORD called
Moses to the top of the mountain,
and Moses went up.
21 And the LORD said to Moses,
"Go down and warn the people,
lest they break through [a]to gaze
at the LORD, and many of them per-
ish.
22 "Also let the [a]priests who come
near the LORD [b]consecrate them-
selves, lest the LORD [c]break out
against them."
23 But Moses said to the LORD,
"The people cannot come up to
Mount Sinai; for You warned us,
saying, [a]'Set bounds around the
mountain and consecrate it.'"

26 [a]Job 29:16 [1]*difficult matters*
27 [a]Num. 10:29, 30

CHAPTER 19

1 [a]Num. 33:15
2 [a]Ex. 17:1 [b]Ex. 3:1, 12; 18:5
3 [a]Acts 7:38 [b]Ex. 3:4
4 [a]Deut. 29:2 [b]Is. 63:9 [1]*sustained*
5 [a]Ex. 15:26; 23:22 [b]Deut. 5:2 [c]Ps. 135:4 [d]Ex. 9:29
6 [a][1 Pet. 2:5, 9] [b]Deut. 7:6; 14:21; 26:19
7 [a]Ex. 4:29, 30 [1]*set*
8 [a]Deut. 5:27; 26:17
9 [a]Ex. 19:16; 20:21; 24:15 [b]Deut. 4:12, 36
10 [a]Lev. 11:44, 45
12 [a]Heb. 12:20
15 [a][1 Cor. 7:5]
16 [a]Heb. 12:18, 19 [b]Heb. 12:21
17 [a]Deut. 4:10
18 [a]Deut. 4:11 [b]Ex. 3:2; 24:17 [c]Gen. 15:17; 19:28 [d]Ps. 68:8 [1]LXX *all the people*
19 [a]Heb. 12:21 [b]Ps. 81:7
21 [a]1 Sam. 6:19
22 [a]Ex. 19:24; 24:5 [b]Lev. 10:3; 21:6–8 [c]2 Sam. 6:7, 8
23 [a]Ex. 19:12

24 Then the LORD said to him,
"Away! Get down and then come
up, you and Aaron with you. But
do not let the priests and the peo-
ple break through to come up to
the LORD, lest He break out against
them."
25 So Moses went down to the
people and spoke to them.

The Ten Commandments

20 And God spoke [a]all these
words, saying:
2 [a]"I *am* the LORD your God, who
brought you out of the land
of Egypt, [b]out of the house
of [1]bondage.
3 [a]"You shall have no other gods
before Me.
4 [a]"You shall not make for yourself
a carved image—any like-
ness *of anything* that *is* in
heaven above, or that *is* in
the earth beneath, or that *is*
in the water under the earth;
5 [a]you shall not bow down to
them nor [1]serve them. [b]For I,
the LORD your God, *am* a
jealous God, [c]visiting[2] the
iniquity of the fathers upon
the children to the third and
fourth *generations* of those
who hate Me,
6 but [a]showing mercy to
thousands, to those who love
Me and keep My command-
ments.
7 [a]"You shall not take the name of
the LORD your God in vain,
for the LORD [b]will not hold
him guiltless who takes His
name in vain.
8 [a]"Remember the Sabbath day, to
keep it holy.
9 [a]Six days you shall labor and
do all your work,
10 but the [a]seventh day *is* the
Sabbath of the LORD your
God. *In it* you shall do no
work: you, nor your son, nor
your daughter, nor your male
servant, nor your female
servant, nor your cattle, [b]nor
your stranger who *is* within
your gates.
11 For [a]*in* six days the LORD
made the heavens and the
earth, the sea, and all that *is*
in them, and rested the
seventh day. Therefore the
LORD blessed the Sabbath
day and hallowed it.
12 [a]"Honor your father and your
mother, that your days may
be [b]long upon the land which
the LORD your God is giving
you.
13 [a]"You shall not murder.
14 [a]"You shall not commit [b]adultery.
15 [a]"You shall not steal.
16 [a]"You shall not bear false witness
against your neighbor.
17 [a]"You shall not covet your
neighbor's house; [b]you shall
not covet your neighbor's
wife, nor his male servant,
nor his female servant, nor
his ox, nor his donkey, nor
anything that *is* your neigh-
bor's."

The People Afraid of God's Presence

18 Now [a]all the people [b]witnessed
the thunderings, the lightning
flashes, the sound of the trumpet,
and the mountain [c]smoking; and
when the people saw *it*, they trem-
bled and stood afar off.
19 Then they said to Moses, [a]"You
speak with us, and we will hear;
but [b]let not God speak with us, lest
we die."
20 And Moses said to the people,
[a]"Do not fear; [b]for God has come
to test you, and [c]that His fear may
be before you, so that you may not
sin."
21 So the people stood afar off, but
Moses drew near [a]the thick dark-
ness where God *was*.

The Law of the Altar

22 Then the LORD said to Moses,
"Thus you shall say to the children
of Israel: 'You have seen that I
have talked with you [a]from
heaven.
23 'You shall not make *anything*
to be [a]with Me—gods of silver or
gods of gold you shall not make
for yourselves.
24 'An altar of [a]earth you shall
make for Me, and you shall sacri-
fice on it your burnt offerings and
your peace offerings, [b]your sheep
and your oxen. In every [c]place
where I [1]record My name I will
come to you, and I will [d]bless
you.
25 'And [a]if you make Me an altar
of stone, you shall not build it of
hewn stone; for if you [b]use your
tool on it, you have profaned it.
26 'Nor shall you go up by steps
to My altar, that your [a]nakedness
may not be exposed on it.'

CHAPTER 20
1 [a]Deut. 5:22
2 [a]Hos. 13:4 [b]Ex. 13:3 [1]*slaves*
3 [a]Jer. 25:6; 35:15
4 [a]Deut. 4:15–19; 27:15
5 [a]Is. 44:15, 19 [b]Deut. 4:24 [c]Num. 14:18, 33 [1]*worship* [2]*punishing*
6 [a]Deut. 7:9
7 [a]Lev. 19:12 [b]Mic. 6:11
8 [a]Lev. 26:2
9 [a]Luke 13:14
10 [a]Gen. 2:2, 3 [b]Neh. 13:16–19
11 [a]Ex. 31:17
12 [a]Lev. 19:3 [b]Deut. 5:16, 33; 6:2; 11:8, 9
13 [a]Rom. 13:9
14 [a]Matt. 5:27 [b]Deut. 5:18
15 [a]Lev. 19:11, 13
16 [a]Deut. 5:20
17 [a][Eph. 5:3, 5] [b][Matt. 5:28]
18 [a]Heb. 12:18, 19 [b]Rev. 1:10, 12 [c]Ex. 19:16, 18
19 [a]Heb. 12:19 [b]Deut. 5:5, 23–27
20 [a][Is. 41:10, 13] [b][Deut. 13:3] [c]Is. 8:13
21 [a]Ex. 19:16
22 [a]Deut. 4:36; 5:24, 26
23 [a]Ex. 32:1, 2, 4
24 [a]Ex. 20:25; 27:1–8 [b]Ex. 24:5 [c]2 Chr. 6:6 [d]Gen. 12:2 [1]*cause My name to be remembered*
25 [a]Deut. 27:5 [b]Josh. 8:30, 31
26 [a]Ex. 28:42, 43

The Law Concerning Servants

21 "Now these *are* the [1]judgments which you shall [a]set before them:

2 [a]"If you buy a Hebrew servant, he shall serve six years; and in the seventh he shall go out free and pay nothing.

3 "If he comes in by himself, he shall go out by himself; if he *comes in* married, then his wife shall go out with him.

4 "If his master has given him a wife, and she has borne him sons or daughters, the wife and her children shall be her master's, and he shall go out by himself.

5 [a]"But if the servant plainly says, 'I love my master, my wife, and my children; I will not go out free,'

6 "then his master shall bring him to the [a]judges. He shall also bring him to the door, or to the doorpost, and his master shall pierce his ear with an awl; and he shall serve him forever.

7 "And if a man [a]sells his daughter to be a female slave, she shall not go out as the male slaves do.

8 "If she [1]does not please her master, who has betrothed her to himself, then he shall let her be redeemed. He shall have no right to sell her to a foreign people, since he has dealt deceitfully with her.

9 "And if he has betrothed her to his son, he shall deal with her according to the custom of daughters.

10 "If he takes another *wife*, he shall not diminish her food, her clothing, [a]and her marriage rights.

11 "And if he does not do these three for her, then she shall go out free, without *paying* money.

The Law Concerning Violence

12 [a]"He who strikes a man so that he dies shall surely be put to death.

13 "However, [a]if he did not lie in wait, but God [b]delivered *him* into his hand, then [c]I will appoint for you a place where he may flee.

14 "But if a man acts with [a]premeditation against his neighbor, to kill him by treachery, [b]you shall take him from My altar, that he may die.

15 "And he who strikes his father or his mother shall surely be put to death.

16 [a]"He who kidnaps a man and [b]sells him, or if he is [c]found in his hand, shall surely be put to death.

17 "And [a]he who curses his father or his mother shall surely be put to death.

18 "If men contend with each other, and one strikes the other with a stone or with *his* fist, and he does not die but is confined to *his* bed,

19 "if he rises again and walks about outside [a]with his staff, then he who struck *him* shall be [1]acquitted. He shall only pay *for* the loss of his time, and shall provide *for him* to be thoroughly healed.

20 "And if a man beats his male or female servant with a rod, so that he dies under his hand, he shall surely be punished.

21 "Notwithstanding, if he remains alive a day or two, he shall not be punished; for he *is* his [a]property.

22 "If men [1]fight, and hurt a woman with child, so that [2]she gives birth prematurely, yet no harm follows, he shall surely be punished accordingly as the woman's husband imposes on him; and he shall [a]pay as the judges *determine*.

23 "But if *any* harm follows, then you shall give life for life,

24 [a]"eye for eye, tooth for tooth, hand for hand, foot for foot,

25 "burn for burn, wound for wound, stripe for stripe.

26 "If a man strikes the eye of his male or female servant, and destroys it, he shall let him go free for the sake of his eye.

27 "And if he knocks out the tooth of his male or female servant, he shall let him go free for the sake of his tooth.

Animal Control Laws

28 "If an ox gores a man or a woman to death, then [a]the ox shall surely be stoned, and its flesh shall not be eaten; but the owner of the ox *shall be* [1]acquitted.

29 "But if the ox [1]tended to thrust with its horn in times past, and it has been made known to his owner, and he has not kept it confined, so that it has killed a man

CHAPTER 1

1 [a]Ex. 24:3, 4; Deut. 4:14; 6:1 [1]*ordinances*

2 [a]Lev. 25:39–43; Deut. 15:12–18; Jer. 34:14

5 [a]Deut. 15:16, 17

6 [a]Ex. 12:12; 22:8, 9

7 [a]Neh. 5:5

8 [1]Lit. *is evil in the eyes of*

10 [a][1 Cor. 7:3, 5]

12 [a]Gen. 9:6; Lev. 24:17; Num. 35:30; [Matt. 26:52]

13 [a]Deut. 19:4, 5 [b]1 Sam. 24:4, 10, 18 [c]Num. 35:11; Deut. 19:3; Josh. 20:2

14 [a]Deut. 19:11, 12; [Heb. 10:26] [b]1 Kin. 2:28–34

16 [a]Deut. 24:7 [b]Gen. 37:28 [c]Ex. 22:4

17 [a]Lev. 20:9; Prov. 20:20; Matt. 15:4; Mark 7:10

19 [a]2 Sam. 3:29 [1]*exempt from punishment*

21 [a]Lev. 25:44–46

22 [a]Ex. 18:21, 22; 21:30; Deut. 22:18 [1]*struggle* [2]Lit. *her children come out*

24 [a]Lev. 24:20; Deut. 19:21; [Matt. 5:38–44; 1 Pet. 2:19–21]

28 [a]Gen. 9:5 [1]*exempt from punishment*

29 [1]*was inclined*

or a woman, the ox shall be stoned
and its owner also shall be put to
death.
30 "If there is imposed on him a
sum of money, then he shall pay
[a]to redeem his life, whatever is im-
posed on him.
31 "Whether it has gored a son or
gored a daughter, according to this
judgment it shall be done to him.
32 "If the ox gores a male or fe-
male servant, he shall give to their
master [a]thirty shekels of silver,
and the [b]ox shall be stoned.
33 "And if a man opens a pit, or
if a man digs a pit and does not
cover it, and an ox or a donkey
falls in it,
34 "the owner of the pit shall
make *it* good; he shall give money
to their owner, but the dead *animal*
shall be his.
35 "If one man's ox hurts anoth-
er's, so that it dies, then they shall
sell the live ox and divide the
money from it; and the dead *ox*
they shall also divide.
36 "Or if it was known that the ox
tended to thrust in time past, and
its owner has not kept it confined,
he shall surely pay ox for ox, and
the dead animal shall be his own.

Responsibility for Property

22 "If a man steals an ox or a
sheep, and slaughters it or
sells it, he shall [a]restore five oxen
for an ox and four sheep for a
sheep.
2 "If the thief is found [a]breaking
in, and he is struck so that he dies,
there shall be [b]no guilt for his
bloodshed.
3 "If the sun has risen on him,
there shall be guilt for his blood-
shed. He should make full restitu-
tion; if he has nothing, then he
shall be [a]sold[1] for his theft.
4 "If the theft is certainly [a]found
alive in his hand, whether it is an
ox or donkey or sheep, he shall
[b]restore double.
5 "If a man causes a field or vine-
yard to be grazed, and lets loose
his animal, and it feeds in another
man's field, he shall make restitu-
tion from the best of his own field
and the best of his own vineyard.
6 "If fire breaks out and catches
in thorns, so that stacked grain,
standing grain, or the field is con-
sumed, he who kindled the fire
shall surely make restitution.
7 "If a man [a]delivers to his neigh-
bor money or articles to keep, and
it is stolen out of the man's house,
[b]if the thief is found, he shall pay
double.
8 "If the thief is not found, then
the master of the house shall be
brought to the [a]judges *to see*
whether he has put his hand into
his neighbor's goods.
9 "For any kind of trespass,
whether it concerns an ox, a don-
key, a sheep, or clothing, *or* for
any kind of lost thing which *an-
other* claims to be his, the [a]cause
of both parties shall come before
the judges; *and* whomever the
judges condemn shall pay double
to his neighbor.
10 "If a man delivers to his neigh-
bor a donkey, an ox, a sheep, or
any animal to keep, and it dies, is
hurt, or driven away, no one see-
ing *it*,
11 "*then* an [a]oath of the LORD
shall be between them both, that
he has not put his hand into his
neighbor's goods; and the owner
of it shall accept *that*, and he shall
not make *it* good.
12 "But [a]if, in fact, it is stolen from
him, he shall make restitution to
the owner of it.
13 "If it is [a]torn to pieces *by a
beast, then* he shall bring it as evi-
dence, *and* he shall not make good
what was torn.
14 "And if a man borrows *any-
thing* from his neighbor, and it be-
comes injured or dies, the owner
of it not *being* with it, he shall
surely make *it* good.
15 "If its owner *was* with it, he
shall not make *it* good; if it *was*
hired, it came for its hire.

Moral and Ceremonial Principles

16 [a]"If a man entices a virgin who
is not betrothed, and lies with her,
he shall surely pay the bride-price
for her *to be* his wife.
17 "If her father utterly refuses to
give her to him, he shall pay
money according to the [a]bride-
price of virgins.
18 [a]"You shall not permit a sor-
ceress to live.
19 [a]"Whoever lies with an animal
shall surely be put to death.

30 [a]Ex. 21:22; Num. 35:31
32 [a]Zech. 11:12, 13; Matt. 26:15; 27:3, 9 [b]Ex. 21:28

CHAPTER 22

1 [a]2 Sam. 12:6; Prov. 6:31; Luke 19:8
2 [a]Job 24:16; Matt. 6:19; 24:43; 1 Pet. 4:15 [b]Num. 35:27
3 [a]Ex. 21:2; Matt. 18:25 [1]Sold as a slave
4 [a]Ex. 21:16 [b]Prov. 6:31
7 [a]Lev. 6:1–7 [b]Ex. 22:4
8 [a]Ex. 21:6, 22; 22:28; Deut. 17:8, 9; 19:17
9 [a]Deut. 25:1; 2 Chr. 19:10
11 [a]Heb. 6:16
12 [a]Gen. 31:39
13 [a]Gen. 31:39
16 [a]Deut. 22:28, 29
17 [a]Gen. 34:12; 1 Sam. 18:25
18 [a]Lev. 19:31; 20:6, 27; Deut. 18:10, 11; 1 Sam. 28:3–10; Jer. 27:9, 10
19 [a]Lev. 18:23; 20:15, 16; Deut. 27:21

20 [a]"He who sacrifices to *any* god,
except to the LORD only, he shall
be utterly destroyed.
21 [a]"You shall neither mistreat a
[1]stranger nor oppress him, for you
were strangers in the land of
Egypt.
22 [a]"You shall not afflict any
widow or fatherless child.
23 "If you afflict them in any way,
and they [a]cry at all to Me, I will
surely [b]hear their cry;
24 "and My [a]wrath will become
hot, and I will kill you with the
sword; [b]your wives shall be wid-
ows, and your children fatherless.
25 [a]"If you lend money to *any of*
My people *who are* poor among
you, you shall not be like a money-
lender to him; you shall not charge
him [b]interest.
26 [a]"If you ever take your neigh-
bor's garment as a pledge, you
shall return it to him before the
sun goes down.
27 "For that *is* his only covering,
it *is* his garment for his skin. What
will he sleep in? And it will be that
when he cries to Me, I will hear,
for I *am* [a]gracious.
28 [a]"You shall not revile God, nor
curse a [b]ruler of your people.
29 "You shall not delay *to offer*
[a]the first of your ripe produce and
your juices. [b]The firstborn of your
sons you shall give to Me.
30 [a]"Likewise you shall do with
your oxen *and* your sheep. It shall
be with its mother [b]seven days; on
the eighth day you shall give it to
Me.
31 "And you shall be [a]holy men
to Me: [b]you shall not eat meat torn
by beasts in the field; you shall
throw it to the dogs.

Justice for All

23 "You [a]shall not circulate a
false report. Do not put your
hand with the wicked to be an [b]un-
righteous witness.
2 [a]"You shall not follow a crowd
to do evil; [b]nor shall you testify in
a dispute so as to turn aside after
many to pervert *justice*.
3 "You shall not show partiality
to a [a]poor man in his dispute.
4 [a]"If you meet your enemy's ox
or his donkey going astray, you
shall surely bring it back to him
again.
5 [a]"If you see the donkey of one
who hates you lying under its bur-
den, and you would refrain from
helping it, you shall surely help
him with it.
6 [a]"You shall not pervert the
judgment of your poor in his dis-
pute.
7 [a]"Keep yourself far from a
false matter; [b]do not kill the inno-
cent and righteous. For [c]I will not
justify the wicked.
8 "And [a]you shall take no bribe,
for a bribe blinds the discerning
and perverts the words of the righ-
teous.
9 "Also [a]you shall not oppress a
[1]stranger, for you know the heart
of a stranger, because you were
strangers in the land of Egypt.

The Law of Sabbaths

10 [a]"Six years you shall sow your
land and gather in its produce,
11 "but the seventh *year* you shall
let it rest and lie fallow, that the
poor of your people may eat; and
what they leave, the beasts of the
field may eat. In like manner you
shall do with your vineyard *and*
your [1]olive grove.
12 [a]"Six days you shall do your
work, and on the seventh day you
shall rest, that your ox and your
donkey may rest, and the son of
your female servant and the
stranger may be refreshed.
13 "And in all that I have said to
you, [a]be circumspect and [b]make
no mention of the name of other
gods, nor let it be heard from your
mouth.

Three Annual Feasts

14 [a]"Three times you shall keep a
feast to Me in the year:
15 [a]"You shall keep the Feast of
Unleavened Bread (you shall eat
unleavened bread seven days, as
I commanded you, at the time ap-
pointed in the month of Abib, for
in it you came out of Egypt; [b]none
shall appear before Me empty);
16 [a]"and the Feast of Harvest, the
firstfruits of your labors which you
have sown in the field; and [b]the
Feast of Ingathering at the end of
the year, when you have gathered
in *the fruit of* your labors from the
field.
17 [a]"Three times in the year all

20 [a]Ex. 32:8; 34:15
21 [a]Deut. 10:19 [1]*sojourner*
22 [a][James 1:27]
23 [a][Luke 18:7] [b]Ps. 18:6
24 [a]Ps. 69:24 [b]Ps. 109:9
25 [a]Lev. 25:35–37 [b]Ps. 15:5
26 [a]Deut. 24:6, 10–13
27 [a]Ex. 34:6, 7
28 [a]Eccl. 10:20 [b]Acts 23:5
29 [a]Ex. 23:16, 19 [b]Ex. 13:2, 12, 15
30 [a]Deut. 15:19 [b]Lev. 22:27
31 [a]Lev. 11:44; 19:2 [b]Ezek. 4:14

CHAPTER 23

1 [a]Ps. 101:5 [b]Deut. 19:16–21
2 [a]Gen. 7:1 [b]Lev. 19:15
3 [a]Deut. 1:17; 16:19
4 [a][Rom. 12:20]
5 [a]Deut. 22:4
6 [a]Eccl. 5:8
7 [a]Eph. 4:25 [b]Matt. 27:4 [c]Rom. 1:18
8 [a]Prov. 15:27; 17:8, 23
9 [a]Ex. 22:21 [1]*sojourner*
10 [a]Lev. 25:1–7
11 [1]*olive yards*
12 [a]Luke 13:14
13 [a]1 Tim. 4:16 [b]Josh. 23:7
14 [a]Ex. 23:17; 34:22–24
15 [a]Ex. 12:14–20 [b]Ex. 22:29; 34:20
16 [a]Ex. 34:22 [b]Deut. 16:13
17 [a]Deut. 16:16

your males shall appear before the Lord [1]GOD.
18 [a]"You shall not offer the blood of My sacrifice with leavened [b]bread; nor shall the fat of My [1]sacrifice remain until morning.
19 [a]"The first of the firstfruits of your land you shall bring into the house of the LORD your God. [b]You shall not boil a young goat in its mother's milk.

The Angel and the Promises

20 [a]"Behold, I send an Angel before you to keep you in the way and to bring you into the place which I have prepared.
21 "Beware of Him and obey His voice; [a]do not provoke Him, for He will [b]not pardon your transgressions; for [c]My name *is* in Him.
22 "But if you indeed obey His voice and do all that I speak, then [a]I will be an enemy to your enemies and an adversary to your adversaries.
23 [a]"For My Angel will go before you and [b]bring you in to the Amorites and the Hittites and the Perizzites and the Canaanites and the Hivites and the Jebusites; and I will [1]cut them off.
24 "You shall not [a]bow down to their gods, nor serve them, [b]nor do according to their works; [c]but you shall utterly overthrow them and completely break down their *sacred* pillars.
25 "So you shall [a]serve the LORD your God, and [b]He will bless your bread and your water. And [c]I will take sickness away from the midst of you.
26 [a]"No one shall suffer miscarriage or be barren in your land; I will [b]fulfill the number of your days.
27 "I will send [a]My fear before you, I will [b]cause confusion among all the people to whom you come, and will make all your enemies turn *their* backs to you.
28 "And [a]I will send hornets before you, which shall drive out the Hivite, the Canaanite, and the Hittite from before you.
29 [a]"I will not drive them out from before you in one year, lest the land become desolate and the beasts of the field become too numerous for you.
30 "Little by little I will drive them out from before you, until you have increased, and you inherit the land.
31 "And [a]I will set your [1]bounds from the Red Sea to the sea, Philistia, and from the desert to the [2]River. For I will [b]deliver the inhabitants of the land into your hand, and you shall drive them out before you.
32 [a]"You shall make no [1]covenant with them, nor with their gods.
33 "They shall not dwell in your land, lest they make you sin against Me. For *if* you serve their gods, [a]it will surely be a snare to you."

Israel Affirms the Covenant

24 Now He said to Moses, "Come up to the LORD, you and Aaron, [a]Nadab and Abihu, [b]and seventy of the elders of Israel, and worship from afar.
2 "And Moses alone shall come near the LORD, but they shall not come near; nor shall the people go up with him."
3 So Moses came and told the people all the words of the LORD and all the [1]judgments. And all the people answered with one voice and said, [a]"All the words which the LORD has said we will do."
4 And Moses [a]wrote all the words of the LORD. And he rose early in the morning, and built an altar at the foot of the mountain, and twelve [b]pillars according to the twelve tribes of Israel.
5 Then he sent young men of the children of Israel, who offered [a]burnt offerings and sacrificed peace offerings of oxen to the LORD.
6 And Moses [a]took half the blood and put *it* in basins, and half the blood he sprinkled on the altar.
7 Then he [a]took the Book of the Covenant and read in the hearing of the people. And they said, "All that the LORD has said we will do, and be obedient."
8 And Moses took the blood, sprinkled *it* on the people, and said, "This is [a]the blood of the covenant which the LORD has made with you according to all these words."

17 [1]Heb. *YHWH*, usually translated *LORD*
18 [a]Ex. 34:25 [b]Deut. 16:4 [1]*feast*
19 [a]Deut. 26:2, 10 [b]Deut. 14:21
20 [a]Ex. 3:2; 13:15; 14:19
21 [a]Ps. 78:40, 56 [b]Deut. 18:19 [c]Is. 9:6
22 [a]Deut. 30:7
23 [a]Ex. 23:20 [b]Josh. 24:8, 11 [1]*annihilate them*
24 [a]Ex. 20:5; 23:13, 33 [b]Deut. 12:30, 31 [c]Num. 33:52
25 [a]Deut. 6:13 [b]Deut. 28:5 [c]Ex. 15:26
26 [a]Deut. 7:14; 28:4 [b]1 Chr. 23:1
27 [a]Ex. 15:16 [b]Deut. 7:23
28 [a]Josh. 24:12
29 [a]Deut. 7:22
31 [a]Gen. 15:18 [b]Josh. 21:44 [1]*boundaries* [2]Heb. *Nahar*, the Euphrates
32 [a]Ex. 34:12, 15 [1]*treaty*
33 [a]Ps. 106:36

CHAPTER 24

1 [a]Lev. 10:1, 2 [b]Num. 11:16
3 [a]Ex. 19:8; 24:7 [1]*ordinances*
4 [a]Deut. 31:9 [b]Gen. 28:18
5 [a]Ex. 18:12; 20:24
6 [a]Heb. 9:18
7 [a]Heb. 9:19
8 [a][Luke 22:20]

On the Mountain with God

9 Then Moses went up, also
Aaron, Nadab, and Abihu, and
seventy of the elders of Israel,
10 and they [a]saw the God of Is-
rael. And *there was* under His feet
as it were a paved work of [b]sap-
phire stone, and it was like the
[c]very[1] heavens in *its* clarity.
11 But on the nobles of the chil-
dren of Israel He [a]did not [1]lay His
hand. So [b]they saw God, and they
[c]ate and drank.
12 Then the LORD said to Moses,
[a]"Come up to Me on the mountain
and be there; and I will give you
[b]tablets of stone, and the law and
commandments which I have writ-
ten, that you may teach them."
13 So Moses arose with [a]his assis-
tant Joshua, and Moses went up
to the mountain of God.
14 And he said to the elders,
"Wait here for us until we come
back to you. Indeed, Aaron and
[a]Hur *are* with you. If any man has
a difficulty, let him go to them."
15 Then Moses went up into the
mountain, and [a]a cloud covered
the mountain.
16 Now [a]the glory of the LORD
rested on Mount Sinai, and the
cloud covered it six days. And on
the seventh day He called to Moses
out of the midst of the cloud.
17 The sight of the glory of the
LORD *was* like [a]a consuming fire
on the top of the mountain in the
eyes of the children of Israel.
18 So Moses went into the midst
of the cloud and went up into the
mountain. And [a]Moses was on the
mountain forty days and forty
nights.

Offerings for the Sanctuary

25 Then the LORD spoke to Mo-
ses, saying:
2 "Speak to the children of Is-
rael, that they bring Me an [1]offer-
ing. [a]From everyone who gives it
willingly with his heart you shall
take My offering.
3 "And this *is* the offering which
you shall take from them: gold, sil-
ver, and bronze;
4 "blue, purple, and scarlet
thread, fine linen, and goats' *hair;*
5 "ram skins dyed red, [1]badger
skins, and acacia wood;

10 [a]Ex. 24:11; Num. 12:8; Is. 6:5; [John 1:18; 6:46]; 1 John 4:12 [b]Ezek. 1:26; Rev. 4:3 [c]Matt. 17:2 [1]Lit. *substance of heaven*
11 [a]Ex. 19:21 [b]Gen. 32:30; Judg. 13:22 [c]1 Cor. 10:18 [1]*stretch out His*
12 [a]Ex. 24:2, 15 [b]Ex. 31:18; 32:15; Deut. 5:22
13 [a]Ex. 32:17
14 [a]Ex. 17:10, 12
15 [a]Ex. 19:9; Matt. 17:5
16 [a]Ex. 16:10; 33:18; Num. 14:10
17 [a]Ex. 3:2; Deut. 4:26, 36; 9:3; Heb. 12:18, 29
18 [a]Ex. 34:28; Deut. 9:9; 10:10

CHAPTER 25

2 [a]Ex. 35:4–9, 21; 1 Chr. 29:3, 5, 9; Ezra 2:68; Neh. 11:2; [2 Cor. 8:11–13; 9:7] [1]*heave offering*
5 [1]Or *dolphin*
6 [a]Ex. 27:20 [b]Ex. 30:23
7 [a]Ex. 28:4, 6–14
8 [a]Ex. 36:1, 3, 4; Lev. 4:6; 10:4; 21:12; Heb. 9:1, 2 [b]Ex. 29:45; 1 Kin. 6:13; [2 Cor. 6:16; Heb. 3:6; Rev. 2:13] [1]*sacred place*
10 [a]Ex. 37:1–9; Deut. 10:3; Heb. 9:4
11 [a]Ex. 37:2; Heb. 9:4
15 [a]Num. 4:6; 1 Kin. 8:8
16 [a]Ex. 16:34; 31:18; Deut. 10:2; 31:26; 1 Kin. 8:9; Heb. 9:4
17 [a]Ex. 37:6; Heb. 9:5
20 [a]1 Kin. 8:7; 1 Chr. 28:18; Heb. 9:5

6 [a]"oil for the light, and [b]spices
for the anointing oil and for the
sweet incense;
7 "onyx stones, and stones to be
set in the [a]ephod and in the breast-
plate.
8 "And let them make Me a
[a]sanctuary,[1] that [b]I may dwell
among them.
9 "According to all that I show
you, *that is,* the pattern of the tab-
ernacle and the pattern of all its
furnishings, just so you shall make
it.

The Ark of the Testimony

10 [a]"And they shall make an ark
of acacia wood; two and a half cu-
bits *shall be* its length, a cubit and
a half its width, and a cubit and a
half its height.
11 "And you shall overlay it
with pure gold, inside and out you
shall overlay it, and shall make
on it a molding of [a]gold all
around.
12 "You shall cast four rings of
gold for it, and put *them* in its four
corners; two rings *shall be* on one
side, and two rings on the other
side.
13 "And you shall make poles *of*
acacia wood, and overlay them
with gold.
14 "You shall put the poles into
the rings on the sides of the ark,
that the ark may be carried by
them.
15 [a]"The poles shall be in the
rings of the ark; they shall not be
taken from it.
16 "And you shall put into the ark
[a]the Testimony which I will give
you.
17 [a]"You shall make a mercy seat
of pure gold; two and a half cubits
shall be its length and a cubit and
a half its width.
18 "And you shall make two
cherubim of gold; of hammered
work you shall make them at the
two ends of the mercy seat.
19 "Make one cherub at one end,
and the other cherub at the other
end; you shall make the cherubim
at the two ends of it *of one piece*
with the mercy seat.
20 "And [a]the cherubim shall
stretch out *their* wings above, cov-
ering the mercy seat with their
wings, and they shall face one

another; the faces of the cherubim
shall be toward the mercy seat.
21 [a]"You shall put the mercy seat
on top of the ark, and [b]in the ark
you shall put the Testimony that I
will give you.
22 "And [a]there I will meet with
you, and I will speak with you
from above the mercy seat, from
[b]between the two cherubim which
are on the ark of the Testimony,
about everything which I will give
you in commandment to the chil-
dren of Israel.

The Table for the Showbread

23 [a]"You shall also make a table
of acacia wood; two cubits *shall be*
its length, a cubit its width, and a
cubit and a half its height.
24 "And you shall overlay it with
pure gold, and make a molding of
gold all around.
25 "You shall make for it a frame
of a handbreadth all around, and
you shall make a gold molding for
the frame all around.
26 "And you shall make for it four
rings of gold, and put the rings on
the four corners that *are* at its four
legs.
27 "The rings shall be close to the
frame, as holders for the poles to
bear the table.
28 "And you shall make the poles
of acacia wood, and overlay them
with gold, that the table may be
carried with them.
29 "You shall make [a]its dishes, its
pans, its pitchers, and its bowls for
pouring. You shall make them of
pure gold.
30 "And you shall set the [a]show-
bread on the table before Me al-
ways.

The Gold Lampstand

31 [a]"You shall also make a lamp-
stand of pure gold; the lampstand
shall be of hammered work. Its
shaft, its branches, its bowls, its
ornamental knobs, and flowers
shall be *of one piece.*
32 "And six branches shall come
out of its sides: three branches of
the lampstand out of one side, and
three branches of the lampstand
out of the other side.
33 [a]"Three bowls *shall be* made
like almond *blossoms* on one
branch, *with* an *ornamental* knob
and a flower, and three bowls
made like almond *blossoms* on the
other branch, *with* an *ornamental*
knob and a flower—and so for the
six branches that come out of the
lampstand.
34 [a]"On the lampstand itself four
bowls *shall be* made like almond
blossoms, each with its *orna-
mental* knob and flower.
35 "And *there shall be* a knob un-
der the *first* two branches of the
same, a knob under the *second* two
branches of the same, and a knob
under the *third* two branches of
the same, according to the six
branches that extend from the
lampstand.
36 "Their knobs and their
branches *shall be of one piece;* all
of it *shall be* one hammered piece
of pure gold.
37 "You shall make seven lamps
for it, and [a]they shall arrange its
lamps so that they [b]give light in
front of it.
38 "And its wick-trimmers and
their trays *shall be* of pure gold.
39 "It shall be made of a talent of
pure gold, with all these utensils.
40 "And [a]see to it that you make
them according to the pattern
which was shown you on the
mountain.

The Tabernacle

26 "Moreover [a]you shall make
the tabernacle *with* ten cur-
tains *of* fine woven linen, and blue,
purple, and scarlet *thread;* with ar-
tistic designs of cherubim you
shall weave them.
2 "The length of each curtain
shall be twenty-eight cubits, and
the width of each curtain four cu-
bits. And every one of the curtains
shall have [1]the same measure-
ments.
3 "Five curtains shall be coupled
to one another, and *the other* five
curtains *shall be* coupled to one
another.
4 "And you shall make loops of
blue *yarn* on the edge of the cur-
tain on the selvedge of *one* set, and
likewise you shall do on the outer
edge of *the other* curtain of the
second set.
5 "Fifty loops you shall make in
the one curtain, and fifty loops you
shall make on the edge of the cur-

---

21 [a]Ex. 26:34; 40:20 [b]Ex. 25:16
22 [a]Ex. 29:42, 43; 30:6, 36; Lev. 16:2; Num. 17:4 [b]Num. 7:89; 1 Sam. 4:4; 2 Sam. 6:2; 2 Kin. 19:15; Ps. 80:1; Is. 37:16
23 [a]Ex. 37:10–16; 1 Kin. 7:48; 2 Chr. 4:8; Heb. 9:2
29 [a]Ex. 37:16; Num. 4:7
30 [a]Ex. 39:36; 40:23; Lev. 24:5–9
31 [a]Ex. 37:17–24; 1 Kin. 7:49; Zech. 4:2; Heb. 9:2; Rev. 1:12
33 [a]Ex. 37:19
34 [a]Ex. 37:20–22
37 [a]Ex. 27:21; 30:8; Lev. 24:3, 4; 2 Chr. 13:11 [b]Num. 8:2
40 [a]Ex. 25:9; 26:30; Num. 8:4; 1 Chr. 28:11, 19; Acts 7:44; [Heb. 8:5]

CHAPTER 26

1 [a]Ex. 36:8–19
2 [1]Lit. *one measure*

tain that *is* on the end of the second set, that the loops may be clasped to one another.

6 "And you shall make fifty clasps of gold, and couple the curtains together with the clasps, so that it may be one tabernacle.

7 [a]"You shall also make curtains of goats' *hair*, to be a tent over the tabernacle. You shall make eleven curtains.

8 "The length of each curtain *shall be* thirty cubits, and the width of each curtain four cubits; and the eleven curtains shall all have the same measurements.

9 "And you shall couple five curtains by themselves and six curtains by themselves, and you shall double over the sixth curtain at the forefront of the tent.

10 "You shall make fifty loops on the edge of the curtain that is outermost in *one* set, and fifty loops on the edge of the curtain of the second set.

11 "And you shall make fifty bronze clasps, put the clasps into the loops, and couple the tent together, that it may be one.

12 "The remnant that remains of the curtains of the tent, the half curtain that remains, shall hang over the back of the tabernacle.

13 "And a cubit on one side and a cubit on the other side, of what remains of the length of the curtains of the tent, shall hang over the sides of the tabernacle, on this side and on that side, to cover it.

14 [a]"You shall also make a covering of ram skins dyed red for the tent, and a covering of badger skins above that.

15 "And for the tabernacle you shall [a]make the boards of acacia wood, standing upright.

16 "Ten cubits *shall be* the length of a board, and a cubit and a half *shall be* the width of each board.

17 "Two [1]tenons *shall be* in each board for binding one to another. Thus you shall make for all the boards of the tabernacle.

18 "And you shall make the boards for the tabernacle, twenty boards for the south side.

19 "You shall make forty sockets of silver under the twenty boards: two sockets under each of the boards for its two tenons.

20 "And for the second side of the tabernacle, the north side, *there shall be* twenty boards

21 "and their forty sockets of silver: two sockets under each of the boards.

22 "For the far side of the tabernacle, westward, you shall make six boards.

23 "And you shall also make two boards for the two back corners of the tabernacle.

24 "They shall be [1]coupled together at the bottom and they shall be coupled together at the top by one ring. Thus it shall be for both of them. They shall be for the two corners.

25 "So there shall be eight boards with their sockets of silver—sixteen sockets—two sockets under each of the boards.

26 "And you shall make bars of acacia wood: five for the boards on one side of the tabernacle,

27 "five bars for the boards on the other side of the tabernacle, and five bars for the boards of the side of the tabernacle, for the far side westward.

28 "The [a]middle bar shall pass through the midst of the boards from end to end.

29 "You shall overlay the boards with gold, make their rings of gold *as* holders for the bars, and overlay the bars with gold.

30 "And you shall raise up the tabernacle [a]according to its pattern which you were shown on the mountain.

31 [a]"You shall make a veil woven of blue, purple, and scarlet *thread*, and fine woven linen. It shall be woven with an artistic design of cherubim.

32 "You shall hang it upon the four pillars of acacia *wood* overlaid with gold. Their hooks *shall be* gold, upon four sockets of silver.

33 "And you shall hang the veil from the clasps. Then you shall bring [a]the ark of the Testimony in there, behind the veil. The veil shall be a divider for you between [b]the holy *place* and the Most Holy.

34 [a]"You shall put the mercy seat upon the ark of the Testimony in the Most Holy.

35 [a]"You shall set the table out-

7 [a]Ex. 36:14
14 [a]Ex. 35:7, 23; 36:19
15 [a]Ex. 36:20–34
17 [1]Projections for joining, lit. *hands*
24 [1]Lit. *doubled*
28 [a]Ex. 36:33
30 [a]Ex. 25:9, 40; 27:8; 39:32; Num. 8:4; Acts 7:44; [Heb. 8:2, 5]
31 [a]Ex. 27:21; 36:35–38; Lev. 16:2; 2 Chr. 3:14; Matt. 27:51; Heb. 9:3; 10:20
33 [a]Ex. 25:10–16; 40:21 [b]Lev. 16:2; Heb. 9:2, 3
34 [a]Ex. 25:17–22; 40:20; Heb. 9:5
35 [a]Ex. 40:22; Heb. 9:2

side the veil, and [b]the lampstand across from the table on the side of the tabernacle toward the south; and you shall put the table on the north side.

36 [a]"You shall make a screen for the door of the tabernacle, *woven of* blue, purple, and scarlet *thread,* and fine woven linen, made by a weaver.

37 "And you shall make for the screen [a]five pillars of acacia *wood,* and overlay them with gold; their hooks *shall be* gold, and you shall cast five sockets of bronze for them.

The Altar of Burnt Offering

27 "You shall make [a]an altar of acacia wood, five cubits long and five cubits wide—the altar shall be square—and its height *shall be* three cubits.

2 "You shall make its horns on its four corners; its horns shall be of one piece with it. And you shall overlay it with bronze.

3 "Also you shall make its pans to receive its ashes, and its shovels and its basins and its forks and its firepans; you shall make all its utensils of bronze.

4 "You shall make a grate for it, a network of bronze; and on the network you shall make four bronze rings at its four corners.

5 "You shall put it under the rim of the altar beneath, that the network may be midway up the altar.

6 "And you shall make poles for the altar, poles of acacia wood, and overlay them with bronze.

7 "The poles shall be put in the rings, and the poles shall be on the two sides of the altar to bear it.

8 "You shall make it hollow with boards; [a]as it was shown you on the mountain, so shall they make *it.*

The Court of the Tabernacle

9 [a]"You shall also make the court of the tabernacle. For the south side *there shall be* hangings for the court *made of* fine woven linen, one hundred cubits long for one side.

10 "And its twenty pillars and their twenty sockets *shall be* bronze. The hooks of the pillars and their bands *shall be* silver.

11 "Likewise along the length of the north side *there shall be* hangings one hundred *cubits* long, with its twenty pillars and their twenty sockets of bronze, and the hooks of the pillars and their bands of silver.

12 "And along the width of the court on the west side *shall be* hangings of fifty cubits, with their ten pillars and their ten sockets.

13 "The width of the court on the east side *shall be* fifty cubits.

14 "The hangings on *one* side *of the gate shall be* fifteen cubits, *with* their three pillars and their three sockets.

15 "And on the other side *shall be* hangings of fifteen *cubits, with* their three pillars and their three sockets.

16 "For the gate of the court *there shall be* a screen twenty cubits long, *woven of* blue, purple, and scarlet *thread,* and fine woven linen, made by a weaver. It *shall have* four pillars and four sockets.

17 "All the pillars around the court shall have bands of silver; their [a]hooks *shall be* of silver and their sockets of bronze.

18 "The length of the court *shall be* one hundred cubits, the width fifty throughout, and the height five cubits, *made of* fine woven linen, and its sockets of bronze.

19 "All the utensils of the tabernacle for all its service, all its pegs, and all the pegs of the court, *shall be* of bronze.

The Care of the Lampstand

20 "And [a]you shall command the children of Israel that they bring you pure oil of pressed olives for the light, to cause the lamp to [1]burn continually.

21 "In the tabernacle of meeting, [a]outside the veil which *is* before the Testimony, [b]Aaron and his sons shall tend it from evening until morning before the LORD. [c]*It shall be* a statute forever to their generations on behalf of the children of Israel.

Garments for the Priesthood

28 "Now take [a]Aaron your brother, and his sons with him, from among the children of Israel, that he may minister to Me

35 [b]Ex. 40:24
36 [a]Ex. 36:37
37 [a]Ex. 36:38

CHAPTER 27

1 [a]Ex. 38:1; Ezek. 43:13
8 [a]Ex. 25:40; 26:30; Acts 7:44; [Heb. 8:5]
9 [a]Ex. 38:9–20
17 [a]Ex. 38:19
20 [a]Ex. 35:8, 28; Lev. 24:1–4 [1]Lit. *ascend*
21 [a]Ex. 26:31, 33 [b]Ex. 30:8; 1 Sam. 3:3; 2 Chr. 13:11 [c]Ex. 28:43; 29:9; Lev. 3:17; 16:34; Num. 18:23; 19:21; 1 Sam. 30:25

CHAPTER 28

1 [a]Num. 3:10; 18:7

as [b]priest, Aaron *and* Aaron's
sons: [c]Nadab, Abihu, [d]Eleazar,
and Ithamar.
2 "And [a]you shall make [1]holy
garments for Aaron your brother,
for glory and for beauty.
3 "So [a]you shall speak to all *who*
are gifted artisans, [b]whom I have
filled with the spirit of wisdom,
that they may make Aaron's gar-
ments, to consecrate him, that he
may minister to Me as priest.
4 "And these *are* the garments
which they shall make: [a]a breast-
plate, [b]an [1]ephod, [c]a robe, [d]a skill-
fully woven tunic, a turban, and [e]a
sash. So they shall make holy gar-
ments for Aaron your brother and
his sons, that he may minister to
Me as priest.

The Ephod

5 "They shall take the gold, blue,
purple, and scarlet *thread*, and the
fine linen,
6 [a]"and they shall make the
ephod of gold, blue, purple, *and*
scarlet *thread*, and fine woven
linen, artistically worked.
7 "It shall have two shoulder
straps joined at its two edges, and
so it shall be joined together.
8 "And the [1]intricately woven
band of the ephod, which *is* on it,
shall be of the same workmanship,
made of gold, blue, purple, and
scarlet *thread*, and fine woven
linen.
9 "Then you shall take two onyx
[a]stones and engrave on them the
names of the sons of Israel:
10 "six of their names on one
stone and six names on the other
stone, in order of their [a]birth.
11 "With the work of an [a]engraver
in stone, *like* the engravings of a
signet, you shall engrave the two
stones with the names of the sons
of Israel. You shall set them in set-
tings of gold.
12 "And you shall put the two
stones on the shoulders of the
ephod *as* memorial stones for the
sons of Israel. So [a]Aaron shall
bear their names before the LORD
on his two shoulders [b]as a me-
morial.
13 "You shall also make settings
of gold,
14 "and you shall make two
chains of pure gold like braided
cords, and fasten the braided
chains to the settings.

The Breastplate

15 [a]"You shall make the breast-
plate of judgment. Artistically
woven according to the workman-
ship of the ephod you shall make
it: of gold, blue, purple, and scarlet
thread, and fine woven linen, you
shall make it.
16 "It shall be doubled into a
square: a span *shall be* its length,
and a span *shall be* its width.
17 [a]"And you shall put settings of
stones in it, four rows of stones:
The first row *shall be* a [1]sardius,
a topaz, and an emerald; *this shall*
be the first row;
18 "the second row *shall be* a tur-
quoise, a sapphire, and a diamond;
19 "the third row, a [1]jacinth, an
agate, and an amethyst;
20 "and the fourth row, a [1]beryl,
an [2]onyx, and a jasper. They shall
be set in gold settings.
21 "And the stones shall have the
names of the sons of Israel, twelve
according to their names, *like* the
engravings of a signet, each one
with its own name; they shall be
according to the twelve tribes.
22 "You shall make chains for the
breastplate at the end, like braided
cords of pure gold.
23 "And you shall make two rings
of gold for the breastplate, and put
the two rings on the two ends of
the breastplate.
24 "Then you shall put the two
braided *chains* of gold in the two
rings which are on the ends of the
breastplate;
25 "and the *other* two ends of the
two braided *chains* you shall fas-
ten to the two settings, and put
them on the shoulder straps of the
ephod in the front.
26 "You shall make two rings of
gold, and put them on the two ends
of the breastplate, on the edge of
it, which is on the inner side of the
ephod.
27 "And two *other* rings of gold
you shall make, and put them on
the two shoulder straps, under-
neath the ephod toward its front,
right at the seam above the [1]intri-
cately woven band of the ephod.
28 "They shall bind the breast-
plate by means of its rings to the

1 [b]Ps. 99:6; Heb. 5:4 [c]Ex. 24:1, 9; Lev. 10:1 [d]Ex. 6:23; Lev. 10:6, 16
2 [a]Ex. 29:5, 29; 31:10; 39:1–31; Lev. 8:7–9, 30 [1]*sacred*
3 [a]Ex. 31:6; 36:1 [b]Ex. 31:3; 35:30, 31; Is. 11:2; Eph. 1:17
4 [a]Ex. 28:15 [b]Ex. 28:6 [c]Ex. 28:31 [d]Ex. 28:39 [e]Lev. 8:7 [1]Ornamented vest
6 [a]Ex. 39:2–7; Lev. 8:7
8 [1]*ingenious work of*
9 [a]Ex. 35:27
10 [a]Gen. 29:31—30:24; 35:16–18
11 [a]Ex. 35:35
12 [a]Ex. 28:29, 30; 39:6, 7 [b]Lev. 24:7; Num. 31:54; Josh. 4:7; Zech. 6:14; 1 Cor. 11:24
15 [a]Ex. 39:8–21
17 [a]Ex. 39:10 [1]Or *ruby*
19 [1]Or *amber*
20 [1]Or *yellow jasper* [2]Or *carnelian*
27 [1]*ingenious work of*

rings of the ephod, using a blue cord, so that it is above the intricately woven band of the ephod, and so that the breastplate does not come loose from the ephod.
29 "So Aaron shall [a]bear the names of the sons of Israel on the breastplate of judgment over his heart, when he goes into the holy *place,* as a memorial before the LORD continually.
30 "And [a]you shall put in the breastplate of judgment the [1]Urim and the Thummim, and they shall be over Aaron's heart when he goes in before the LORD. So Aaron shall bear the judgment of the children of Israel over his heart before the LORD continually.

Other Priestly Garments

31 [a]"You shall make the robe of the ephod all of blue.
32 "There shall be an opening for his head in the middle of it; it shall have a woven binding all around its opening, like the opening in a coat of mail, so that it does not tear.
33 "And upon its hem you shall make pomegranates of blue, purple, and scarlet, all around its hem, and bells of gold between them all around:
34 "a golden bell and a pomegranate, a golden bell and a pomegranate, upon the hem of the robe all around.
35 "And it shall be upon Aaron when he ministers, and its sound will be heard when he goes into the holy *place* before the LORD and when he comes out, that he may not die.
36 [a]"You shall also make a plate of pure gold and engrave on it, *like* the engraving of a signet:

HOLINESS TO THE LORD.

37 "And you shall put it on a blue cord, that it may be on the turban; it shall be on the front of the turban.
38 "So it shall be on Aaron's forehead, that Aaron may [a]bear the iniquity of the holy things which the children of Israel hallow in all their [1]holy gifts; and it shall always be on his forehead, that they may be [b]accepted before the LORD.
39 "You shall [a]skillfully weave the tunic of fine linen *thread,* you shall make the turban of fine linen, and you shall make the sash of woven work.
40 [a]"For Aaron's sons you shall make tunics, and you shall make sashes for them. And you shall make [1]hats for them, for glory and [b]beauty.
41 "So you shall put them on Aaron your brother and on his sons with him. You shall [a]anoint them, [b]consecrate them, and [1]sanctify them, that they may minister to Me as priests.
42 "And you shall make [a]for them linen trousers to cover their [1]nakedness; they shall [2]reach from the waist to the thighs.
43 "They shall be on Aaron and on his sons when they come into the tabernacle of meeting, or when they come near [a]the altar to minister in the holy *place,* that they [b]do not incur [1]iniquity and die. [c]*It shall be* a statute forever to him and his descendants after him.

Aaron and His Sons Consecrated

29 "And this is what you shall do to them to hallow them for ministering to Me as priests: [a]Take one young bull and two rams without blemish,
2 "and [a]unleavened bread, unleavened cakes mixed with oil, and unleavened wafers anointed with oil (you shall make them of wheat flour).
3 "You shall put them in one basket and bring them in the basket, with the bull and the two rams.
4 "And Aaron and his sons you shall bring to the door of the tabernacle of meeting, [a]and you shall wash them with water.
5 [a]"Then you shall take the garments, put the tunic on Aaron, and the robe of the ephod, the ephod, and the breastplate, and gird him with [b]the intricately woven band of the ephod.
6 [a]"You shall put the turban on his head, and put the holy crown on the turban.
7 "And you shall take the anointing [a]oil, pour *it* on his head, and anoint him.
8 "Then [a]you shall bring his sons and put tunics on them.
9 "And you shall gird them with

29 [a]Ex. 28:12
30 [a]Lev. 8:8; Num. 27:21; Deut. 33:8; 1 Sam. 28:6; Ezra 2:63; Neh. 7:65 [1]Lit. *Lights and the Perfections*
31 [a]Ex. 39:22–26
36 [a]Ex. 39:30, 31; Lev. 8:9; Zech. 14:20
38 [a]Ex. 28:43; Lev. 10:17; 22:9, 16; Num. 18:1; [Is. 53:11]; Ezek. 4:4–6; [John 1:29; Heb. 9:28; 1 Pet. 2:24] [b]Lev. 1:4; 22:27; 23:11; Is. 56:7 [1]*sacred*
39 [a]Ex. 35:35; 39:27–29
40 [a]Ex. 28:4; 39:27–29, 41; Ezek. 44:17, 18 [b]Ex. 28:2 [1]*headpieces or turbans*
41 [a]Ex. 29:7–9; 30:30; 40:15; Lev. 10:7 [b]Ex. 29:9; Lev. 8; Heb. 7:28 [1]*set them apart*
42 [a]Ex. 39:28; Lev. 6:10; 16:4; Ezek. 44:18 [1]*bare flesh* [2]Lit. *be*
43 [a]Ex. 20:26 [b]Lev. 5:1, 17; 20:19, 20; 22:9; Num. 9:13; 18:22 [c]Ex. 27:21; Lev. 17:7 [1]*guilt*

CHAPTER 29

1 [a]Lev. 8; [Heb. 7:26–28]
2 [a]Lev. 2:4; 6:19–23
4 [a]Ex. 40:12; Lev. 8:6; [Heb. 10:22]
5 [a]Ex. 28:2; Lev. 8:7 [b]Ex. 28:8
6 [a]Ex. 28:36, 37; Lev. 8:9
7 [a]Ex. 25:6; 30:25–31; Lev. 8:12; 10:7; 21:10; Num. 35:25; Ps. 133:2
8 [a]Ex. 28:39, 40; Lev. 8:13

sashes, Aaron and his sons, and
put the hats on them. [a]The priest-
hood shall be theirs for a perpetual
statute. So you shall [b]consecrate
Aaron and his sons.
10 "You shall also have the bull
brought before the tabernacle of
meeting, and [a]Aaron and his sons
shall put their hands on the head
of the bull.
11 "Then you shall kill the bull be-
fore the LORD, *by* the door of the
tabernacle of meeting.
12 "You shall take *some* of the
blood of the bull and put *it* on [a]the
horns of the altar with your finger,
and [b]pour all the blood beside the
base of the altar.
13 "And [a]you shall take all the fat
that covers the entrails, the fatty
lobe *attached* to the liver, and the
two kidneys and the fat that *is* on
them, and burn *them* on the altar.
14 "But [a]the flesh of the bull, with
its skin and its offal, you shall burn
with fire outside the camp. It *is* a
sin offering.
15 [a]"You shall also take one ram,
and Aaron and his sons shall [b]put
their hands on the head of the ram;
16 "and you shall kill the ram, and
you shall take its blood and
[a]sprinkle *it* all around on the altar.
17 "Then you shall cut the ram in
pieces, wash its entrails and its
legs, and put *them* with its pieces
and with its head.
18 "And you shall burn the whole
ram on the altar. It *is* a [a]burnt of-
fering to the LORD; it *is* a sweet
aroma, an offering made by fire to
the LORD.
19 [a]"You shall also take the other
ram, and Aaron and his sons shall
put their hands on the head of the
ram.
20 "Then you shall kill the ram,
and take some of its blood and put
it on the tip of the right ear of
Aaron and on the tip of the right
ear of his sons, on the thumb of
their right hand and on the big toe
of their right foot, and sprinkle the
blood all around on the altar.
21 "And you shall take some of
the blood that is on the altar, and
some of [a]the anointing oil, and
sprinkle *it* on Aaron and on his
garments, on his sons and on the
garments of his sons with him; and
[b]he and his garments shall be hal-
lowed, and his sons and his sons'
garments with him.
22 "Also you shall take the fat of
the ram, the fat tail, the fat that
covers the entrails, the fatty lobe
attached to the liver, the two kid-
neys and the fat on them, the right
thigh (for it *is* a ram of conse-
cration),
23 [a]"one loaf of bread, one cake
made with oil, and one wafer from
the basket of the unleavened bread
that *is* before the LORD;
24 "and you shall put all these in
the hands of Aaron and in the
hands of his sons, and you shall
[a]wave them *as* a wave offering be-
fore the LORD.
25 [a]"You shall receive them back
from their hands and burn *them*
on the altar as a burnt offering, as
a sweet aroma before the LORD. It
is an offering made by fire to the
LORD.
26 "Then you shall take [a]the
breast of the ram of Aaron's con-
secration and wave it *as* a wave
offering before the LORD; and it
shall be your portion.
27 "And from the ram of the con-
secration you shall consecrate [a]the
breast of the wave offering which
is waved, and the thigh of the
heave offering which is raised, of
that which *is* for Aaron and of
that which is for his sons.
28 "It shall be from the children
of Israel *for* Aaron and his sons
[a]by a statute forever. For it is a
heave offering; [b]it shall be a heave
offering from the children of Israel
from the sacrifices of their peace
offerings, *that is*, their heave offer-
ing to the LORD.
29 "And the [a]holy garments of
Aaron [b]shall be his sons' after him,
[c]to be anointed in them and to be
consecrated in them.
30 [a]"That son who becomes priest
in his place shall put them on for
[b]seven days, when he enters the
tabernacle of meeting to minister
in the [1]holy *place*.
31 "And you shall take the ram of
the consecration and [a]boil its flesh
in the holy place.
32 "Then Aaron and his sons shall
eat the flesh of the ram, and the
[a]bread that *is* in the basket, *by* the
door of the tabernacle of meeting.
33 [a]"They shall eat those things

9 [a]Ex. 40:15; Num. 3:10; 18:7; 25:13; Deut. 18:5 [b]Ex. 28:41; Lev. 8
10 [a]Lev. 1:4; 8:14
12 [a]Lev. 8:15 [b]Ex. 27:2; 30:2; Lev. 4:7
13 [a]Lev. 1:8; 3:3, 4
14 [a]Lev. 4:11, 12, 21; Heb. 13:11
15 [a]Lev. 8:18 [b]Lev. 1:4–9
16 [a]Ex. 24:6; Lev. 1:5, 11
18 [a]Ex. 20:24
19 [a]Lev. 8:22
21 [a]Ex. 30:25, 31; Lev. 8:30 [b]Ex. 28:41; 29:1; [Heb. 9:22]
23 [a]Lev. 8:26
24 [a]Lev. 7:30; 10:14
25 [a]Lev. 8:28
26 [a]Lev. 7:31, 34; 8:29
27 [a]Lev. 7:31, 34; Num. 18:11, 18; Deut. 18:3
28 [a]Lev. 10:15 [b]Lev. 3:1; 7:34
29 [a]Ex. 28:2 [b]Num. 20:26, 28 [c]Ex. 28:41; 30:30; Num. 18:8
30 [a]Num. 20:28 [b]Lev. 8:35 [1]*sanctuary*
31 [a]Lev. 8:31
32 [a]Matt. 12:4
33 [a]Lev. 10:14, 15, 17

with which the atonement was
made, to consecrate *and* to sanc-
tify them; [b]but an outsider shall
not eat *them*, because they *are*
holy.
34 "And if any of the flesh of the
consecration offerings, or of the
bread, remains until the morning,
then [a]you shall burn the remainder
with fire. It shall not be eaten, be-
cause it *is* holy.
35 "Thus you shall do to Aaron
and his sons, according to all that
I have commanded you. [a]Seven
days you shall consecrate them.
36 "And you [a]shall offer a bull
every day *as* a sin offering for
atonement. [b]You shall cleanse the
altar when you make atonement
for it, and you shall anoint it to
sanctify it.
37 "Seven days you shall make
atonement for the altar and sanc-
tify it. And the altar shall be most
holy. [a]Whatever touches the altar
must be holy.

The Daily Offerings

38 "Now this *is* what you shall of-
fer on the altar: [a]two lambs of the
first year, [b]day by day continually.
39 "One lamb you shall offer [a]in
the morning, and the other lamb
you shall offer [1]at twilight.
40 "With the one lamb shall be
one-tenth *of an ephah* of flour
mixed with one-fourth of a hin of
pressed oil, and one-fourth of a hin
of wine *as* a drink offering.
41 "And the other lamb you shall
[a]offer [1]at twilight; and you shall
offer with it the grain offering and
the drink offering, as in the morn-
ing, for a sweet aroma, an offering
made by fire to the LORD.
42 "*This shall be* [a]a continual
burnt offering throughout your
generations *at* the door of the tab-
ernacle of meeting before the
LORD, [b]where I will meet you to
speak with you.
43 "And there I will meet with the
children of Israel, and *the taberna-
cle* [a]shall be sanctified by My
glory.
44 "So I will consecrate the taber-
nacle of meeting and the altar. I
will also [a]consecrate both Aaron
and his sons to minister to Me as
priests.
45 [a]"I will dwell among the chil-
dren of Israel and will [b]be their
God.
46 "And they shall know that [a]I
am the LORD their God, who
[b]brought them up out of the land
of Egypt, that I may dwell among
them. I *am* the LORD their God.

The Altar of Incense

30 "You shall make [a]an altar to
burn incense on; you shall
make it of acacia wood.
2 "A cubit *shall be* its length and
a cubit its width—it shall be
square—and two cubits *shall be* its
height. Its horns *shall be* of one
piece with it.
3 "And you shall overlay its top,
its sides all around, and its horns
with pure gold; and you shall
make for it a [1]molding of gold all
around.
4 "Two gold rings you shall
make for it, under the molding on
both its sides. You shall place
them on its two sides, and they will
be holders for the poles with which
to bear it.
5 "You shall make the poles of
acacia wood, and overlay them
with gold.
6 "And you shall put it before the
[a]veil that *is* before the ark of the
Testimony, before the [b]mercy seat
that *is* over the Testimony, where
I will meet with you.
7 "Aaron shall burn on it [a]sweet
incense every morning; when [b]he
tends the lamps, he shall burn in-
cense on it.
8 "And when Aaron lights the
lamps [1]at twilight, he shall burn
incense on it, a perpetual incense
before the LORD throughout your
generations.
9 "You shall not offer [a]strange
incense on it, or a burnt offering,
or a grain offering; nor shall you
pour a drink offering on it.
10 "And [a]Aaron shall make atone-
ment upon its horns once a year
with the blood of the sin offering
of atonement; once a year he shall
make atonement upon it through-
out your generations. It *is* most
holy to the LORD."

The Ransom Money

11 Then the LORD spoke to Moses,
saying:
12 [a]"When you take the census of

33 [b]Ex. 12:43; Lev. 22:10
34 [a]Ex. 12:10; 23:18; 34:25; Lev. 7:18; 8:32
35 [a]Lev. 8:33–35
36 [a]Heb. 10:11 [b]Ex. 30:26–29; 40:10, 11
37 [a]Num. 4:15; Hag. 2:11–13; Matt. 23:19
38 [a]Num. 28:3–31; 29:6–38; 1 Chr. 16:40; Ezra 3:3 [b]Dan. 12:11
39 [a]Ezek. 46:13–15 [1]Lit. *between the two evenings*
41 [a]1 Kin. 18:29, 36; 2 Kin. 16:15; Ezra 9:4, 5; Ps. 141:2 [1]Lit. *between the two evenings*
42 [a]Ex. 30:8 [b]Ex. 25:22; 33:7, 9; Num. 17:4
43 [a]Ex. 40:34; 1 Kin. 8:11; 2 Chr. 5:14; Ezek. 43:5; Hag. 2:7, 9
44 [a]Lev. 21:15
45 [a]Ex. 25:8; Lev. 26:12; Num. 5:3; Deut. 12:11; Zech. 2:10; [John 14:17, 23; Rev. 21:3] [b]Gen. 17:8; Lev. 11:45
46 [a]Ex. 16:12; 20:2; Deut. 4:35 [b]Lev. 11:45

CHAPTER 30

1 [a]Ex. 37:25–29
3 [1]*border*
6 [a]Ex. 26:31–35 [b]Ex. 25:21, 22
7 [a]Ex. 30:34; 1 Sam. 2:28; 1 Chr. 23:13; Luke 1:9 [b]Ex. 27:20, 21
8 [1]Lit. *between the two evenings*
9 [a]Lev. 10:1
10 [a]Lev. 16:3–34
12 [a]Ex. 38:25, 26; Num. 1:2; 26:2; 2 Sam. 24:2

the children of Israel for their number, then every man shall give [b]a [1]ransom for himself to the LORD, when you number them, that there may be no [c]plague among them when *you* number them.
13 [a]"This is what everyone among those who are numbered shall give: half a shekel according to the shekel of the sanctuary [b](a shekel *is* twenty gerahs). [c]The half-shekel *shall be* an offering to the LORD.
14 "Everyone included among those who are numbered, from twenty years old and above, shall give an [1]offering to the LORD.
15 "The [a]rich shall not give more and the poor shall not give less than half a shekel, when *you* give an offering to the LORD, to make atonement for yourselves.
16 "And you shall take the atonement money of the children of Israel, and [a]shall [1]appoint it for the service of the tabernacle of meeting, that it may be [b]a memorial for the children of Israel before the LORD, to make atonement for yourselves."

The Bronze Laver

17 Then the LORD spoke to Moses, saying:
18 [a]"You shall also make a [1]laver of bronze, with its base also of bronze, for washing. You shall [b]put it between the tabernacle of meeting and the altar. And you shall put water in it,
19 "for Aaron and his sons [a]shall wash their hands and their feet in water from it.
20 "When they go into the tabernacle of meeting, or when they come near the altar to minister, to burn an offering made by fire to the LORD, they shall wash with water, lest they die.
21 "So they shall wash their hands and their feet, lest they die. And [a]it shall be a [1]statute forever to them—to him and his descendants throughout their generations."

The Holy Anointing Oil

22 Moreover the LORD spoke to Moses, saying:
23 "Also take for yourself [a]quality spices—five hundred *shekels* of liquid [b]myrrh, half as much sweet-smelling cinnamon (two hundred and fifty *shekels*), two hundred and fifty *shekels* of sweet-smelling [c]cane,
24 "five hundred *shekels* of [a]cassia, according to the shekel of the sanctuary, and a [b]hin of olive oil.
25 "And you shall make from these a holy anointing oil, an ointment compounded according to the art of the perfumer. It shall be [a]a holy anointing oil.
26 [a]"With it you shall anoint the tabernacle of meeting and the ark of the Testimony;
27 "the table and all its utensils, the lampstand and its utensils, and the altar of incense;
28 "the altar of burnt offering with all its utensils, and the laver and its base.
29 "You shall consecrate them, that they may be most holy; [a]whatever touches them must be holy.
30 [a]"And you shall anoint Aaron and his sons, and consecrate them, that *they* may minister to Me as priests.
31 "And you shall speak to the children of Israel, saying: 'This shall be a holy anointing oil to Me throughout your generations.
32 'It shall not be poured on man's flesh; nor shall you make *any other* like it, according to its composition. [a]It *is* holy, *and* it shall be holy to you.
33 [a]'Whoever [1]compounds *any* like it, or whoever puts *any* of it on an outsider, [b]shall be [2]cut off from his people.' "

The Incense

34 And the LORD said to Moses: [a]"Take sweet spices, stacte and onycha and galbanum, and pure frankincense with *these* sweet spices; there shall be equal amounts of each.
35 "You shall make of these an incense, a compound [a]according to the art of the perfumer, salted, pure, *and* holy.
36 "And you shall beat *some* of it very fine, and put some of it before the Testimony in the tabernacle of meeting [a]where I will meet with you. [b]It shall be most holy to you.
37 "But *as for* the incense which you shall make, [a]you shall not

12 [b]Num. 31:50; [Matt. 20:28; 1 Pet. 1:18, 19] [c]2 Sam. 24:15 [1]*the price of a life*
13 [a]Matt. 17:24 [b]Lev. 27:25; Num. 3:47; Ezek. 45:12 [c]Ex. 38:26
14 [1]*contribution*
15 [a]Job 34:19; Prov. 22:2; [Eph. 6:9]
16 [a]Ex. 38:25–31 [b]Num. 16:40 [1]*give*
18 [a]Ex. 38:8; 1 Kin. 7:38 [b]Ex. 40:30 [1]*basin*
19 [a]Ex. 40:31, 32; Ps. 26:6; Is. 52:11; John 13:8, 10; Heb. 10:22
21 [a]Ex. 28:43 [1]*requirement*
23 [a]Song 4:14; Ezek. 27:22 [b]Ps. 45:8; Prov. 7:17 [c]Song 4:14; Jer. 6:20
24 [a]Ps. 45:8 [b]Ex. 29:40
25 [a]Ex. 37:29; 40:9; Lev. 8:10; Num. 35:25; Ps. 89:20; 133:2
26 [a]Ex. 40:9; Lev. 8:10; Num. 7:1
29 [a]Ex. 29:37; Num. 4:15; Hag. 2:11–13
30 [a]Ex. 29:7; Lev. 8:12
32 [a]Ex. 30:25, 37
33 [a]Ex. 30:38 [b]Gen. 17:14; Ex. 12:15; Lev. 7:20, 21 [1]*mixes* [2]Put to death
34 [a]Ex. 25:6; 37:29
35 [a]Ex. 30:25
36 [a]Ex. 29:42; Lev. 16:2 [b][Ex. 29:37; 30:32]; Lev. 2:3
37 [a]Ex. 30:32

make any for yourselves, accord-
ing to its [1]composition. It shall be
to you holy for the LORD.
38 [a]"Whoever makes *any* like it,
to smell it, he shall be cut off from
his people."

Artisans for Building the Tabernacle

31 Then the LORD spoke to Mo-
ses, saying:
2 [a]"See, I have called by name
Bezalel the [b]son of Uri, the son of
Hur, of the tribe of Judah.
3 "And I have [a]filled him with the
Spirit of God, in wisdom, in under-
standing, in knowledge, and in all
manner of workmanship,
4 "to design artistic works, to
work in gold, in silver, in bronze,
5 "in cutting jewels for setting, in
carving wood, and to work in all
manner of workmanship.
6 "And I, indeed I, have ap-
pointed with him [a]Aholiab the son
of Ahisamach, of the tribe of Dan;
and I have put wisdom in the
hearts of all the [b]gifted artisans,
that they may make all that I have
commanded you:
7 [a]"the tabernacle of meeting,
[b]the ark of the Testimony and [c]the
mercy seat that *is* on it, and all the
furniture of the tabernacle—
8 [a]"the table and its utensils, [b]the
pure *gold* lampstand with all its
utensils, the altar of incense,
9 [a]"the altar of burnt offering
with all its utensils, and [b]the laver
and its base—
10 [a]"the [1]garments of ministry,
the holy garments for Aaron the
priest and the garments of his
sons, to minister as priests,
11 [a]"and the anointing oil and
[b]sweet incense for the holy *place*.
According to all that I have com-
manded you they shall do."

The Sabbath Law

12 And the LORD spoke to Moses,
saying,
13 "Speak also to the children of
Israel, saying: [a]'Surely My Sab-
baths you shall keep, for it *is* a sign
between Me and you throughout
your generations, that *you* may
know that I *am* the LORD who
[b]sanctifies[1] you.
14 [a]'You shall keep the Sabbath,
therefore, for *it is* holy to you.
Everyone who [1]profanes it shall
surely be put to death; for [b]who-
ever does *any* work on it, that per-
son shall be cut off from among
his people.
15 'Work shall be done for [a]six
days, but the [b]seventh *is* the Sab-
bath of rest, holy to the LORD.
Whoever does *any* work on the
Sabbath day, he shall surely be put
to death.
16 'Therefore the children of Is-
rael shall keep the Sabbath, to ob-
serve the Sabbath throughout
their generations *as* a perpetual
covenant.
17 'It *is* [a]a sign between Me and
the children of Israel forever; for
[b]*in* six days the LORD made the
heavens and the earth, and on the
seventh day He rested and was re-
freshed.'"
18 And when He had made an end
of speaking with him on Mount Si-
nai, He gave Moses [a]two tablets of
the Testimony, tablets of stone,
written with the finger of God.

The Gold Calf

32 Now when the people saw
that Moses [a]delayed coming
down from the mountain, the peo-
ple [b]gathered together to Aaron,
and said to him, [c]"Come, make us
[1]gods that shall [d]go before us; for
as for this Moses, the man who
[e]brought us up out of the land of
Egypt, we do not know what has
become of him."
2 And Aaron said to them,
"Break off the [a]golden earrings
which *are* in the ears of your
wives, your sons, and your daugh-
ters, and bring *them* to me."
3 So all the people broke off the
golden earrings which *were* in
their ears, and brought *them* to
Aaron.
4 [a]And he received the *gold* from
their hand, and he fashioned it
with an engraving tool, and made
a molded calf. Then they said,
"This *is* your god, O Israel, that
[b]brought you out of the land of
Egypt!"
5 So when Aaron saw it, he built
an altar before it. And Aaron made
a [a]proclamation and said, "Tomor-
row *is* a feast to the LORD."
6 Then they rose early on the
next day, offered burnt offerings,
and brought peace offerings; and

37 [1]Lit. *proportion*
38 [a]Ex. 30:33

CHAPTER 31

2 [a]Ex. 35:30—36:1 [b]1 Chr. 2:20
3 [a]1 Kin. 7:14
6 [a]Ex. 35:34 [b]Ex. 28:3; 35:10, 35; 36:1
7 [a]Ex. 36:8 [b]Ex. 37:1–5 [c]Ex. 37:6–9
8 [a]Ex. 37:10–16 [b]Ex. 37:17–24
9 [a]Ex. 38:1–7 [b]Ex. 38:8
10 [a]Ex. 39:1, 41 [1]Or *woven garments*
11 [a]Ex. 30:23–33 [b]Ex. 30:34–38
13 [a]Ezek. 20:12, 20 [b]Lev. 20:8 [1]*consecrates*
14 [a]Ex. 20:8 [b]Num. 15:32–36 [1]*defiles*
15 [a]Ex. 20:9–11 [b]Gen. 2:2
17 [a]Ex. 31:13 [b]Gen. 1:31; 2:2, 3
18 [a][Ex. 24:12; 32:15, 16]

CHAPTER 32

1 [a]Ex. 24:18; Deut. 9:9–12 [b]Ex. 17:1–3 [c]Acts 7:40 [d]Ex. 13:21 [e]Ex. 32:8 [1]Or *a god*
2 [a]Ex. 11:2; 35:22
4 [a]Ex. 20:3, 4, 23 [b]Ex. 29:45, 46
5 [a]2 Kin. 10:20

the people [a]sat down to eat and
drink, and rose up to play.
7 And the LORD said to Moses,
[a]"Go, get down! For your people
whom you brought out of the land
of Egypt [b]have corrupted *them-
selves.*
8 "They have turned aside
quickly out of the way which [a]I
commanded them. They have
made themselves a molded calf,
and worshiped it and sacrificed to
it, and said, [b]'This *is* your god,
O Israel, that brought you out of
the land of Egypt!' "
9 And the LORD said to Moses, [a]"I
have seen this people, and indeed
it *is* a [1]stiff-necked people!
10 "Now therefore, [a]let Me alone,
that [b]My wrath may burn hot
against them and I may [1]consume
them. And [c]I will make of you a
great nation."
11 [a]Then Moses pleaded with [1]the
LORD his God, and said: "LORD,
why does Your wrath burn hot
against Your people whom You
have brought out of the land of
Egypt with great power and with
a mighty hand?
12 [a]"Why should the Egyptians
speak, and say, 'He brought them
out to harm them, to kill them in
the mountains, and to consume
them from the face of the earth'?
Turn from Your fierce wrath, and
[b]relent from this harm to Your
people.
13 "Remember Abraham, Isaac,
and Israel, Your servants, to whom
You [a]swore by Your own self, and
said to them, [b]'I will multiply your
descendants as the stars of
heaven; and all this land that I
have spoken of I give to your de-
scendants, and they shall inherit
it forever.' "
14 So the LORD [a]relented from the
harm which He said He would do
to His people.
15 And [a]Moses turned and went
down from the mountain, and the
two tablets of the Testimony *were*
in his hand. The tablets *were* writ-
ten on both sides; on the one *side*
and on the other they were writ-
ten.
16 Now the [a]tablets *were* the work
of God, and the writing *was* the
writing of God engraved on the
tablets.

6 [a]Ex. 32:17–19; Num. 25:2; 1 Cor. 10:7
7 [a]Deut. 9:8–21; Dan. 9:14 [b]Gen. 6:11, 12
8 [a]Ex. 20:3, 4, 23; Deut. 32:17 [b]1 Kin. 12:28
9 [a]Ex. 33:3, 5; 34:9; Deut. 9:6; 2 Chr. 30:8; Is. 48:4; [Acts 7:51] [1]*stubborn*
10 [a]Deut. 9:14, 19 [b]Ex. 22:24 [c]Num. 14:12 [1]*destroy*
11 [a]Deut. 9:18, 26–29 [1]Lit. *the face of the LORD*
12 [a]Num. 14:13–19; Deut. 9:28; Josh. 7:9 [b]Ex. 32:14
13 [a]Gen. 22:16–18; [Heb. 6:13] [b]Gen. 12:7; 13:15; 15:7, 18; 22:17; 26:4; 35:11, 12; Ex. 13:5, 11; 33:1
14 [a]2 Sam. 24:16
15 [a]Deut. 9:15
16 [a]Ex. 31:18
19 [a]Deut. 9:16, 17
20 [a]Num. 5:17, 24; Deut. 9:21
21 [a]Gen. 26:10
22 [a]Ex. 14:11; Deut. 9:24
25 [a]Ex. 33:4, 5 [b]2 Chr. 28:19
27 [a]Num. 25:5–13

17 And when Joshua heard the
noise of the people as they
shouted, he said to Moses, "*There
is* a noise of war in the camp."
18 But he said:

"*It is* not the noise of the shout of
victory,
Nor the noise of the cry of defeat,
But the sound of singing I hear."

19 So it was, as soon as he came
near the camp, that [a]he saw the
calf *and* the dancing. So Moses'
anger became hot, and he cast the
tablets out of his hands and broke
them at the foot of the moun-
tain.
20 [a]Then he took the calf which
they had made, burned *it* in the
fire, and ground *it* to powder; and
he scattered *it* on the water and
made the children of Israel drink
it.
21 And Moses said to Aaron,
[a]"What did this people do to you
that you have brought *so* great a
sin upon them?"
22 So Aaron said, "Do not let the
anger of my lord become hot. [a]You
know the people, that they *are set*
on evil.
23 "For they said to me, 'Make us
gods that shall go before us; *as for*
this Moses, the man who brought
us out of the land of Egypt, we do
not know what has become of
him.'
24 "And I said to them, 'Whoever
has any gold, let them break *it* off.'
So they gave *it* to me, and I cast
it into the fire, and this calf came
out."
25 Now when Moses saw that the
people *were* [a]unrestrained (for
Aaron [b]had not restrained them,
to *their* shame among their ene-
mies),
26 then Moses stood in the en-
trance of the camp, and said,
"Whoever *is* on the LORD's side—
come to me!" And all the sons of
Levi gathered themselves together
to him.
27 And he said to them, "Thus
says the LORD God of Israel: 'Let
every man put his sword on his
side, and go in and out from en-
trance to entrance throughout the
camp, and [a]let every man kill his
brother, every man his companion,

and every man his neighbor.' "
28 So the sons of Levi did accord-
ing to the word of Moses. And
about three thousand men of the
people fell that day.
29 [a]Then Moses said, [1]"Conse-
crate yourselves today to the LORD,
that He may bestow on you a
blessing this day, for every man
has opposed his son and his
brother."
30 Now it came to pass on the next
day that Moses said to the people,
[a]"You have committed a great sin.
So now I will go up to the LORD;
[b]perhaps I can [c]make atonement
for your sin."
31 Then Moses [a]returned to the
LORD and said, "Oh, these people
have committed a great sin, and
have [b]made for themselves a god
of gold!
32 "Yet now, if You will forgive
their sin—but if not, I pray, [a]blot
me [b]out of Your book which You
have written."
33 And the LORD said to Moses,
[a]"Whoever has sinned against Me,
I will [b]blot him out of My book.
34 "Now therefore, go, lead the
people to *the place* of which I have
[a]spoken to you. [b]Behold, My Angel
shall go before you. Nevertheless,
[c]in the day when I [d]visit for pun-
ishment, I will visit punishment
upon them for their sin."
35 So the LORD plagued the people
because of [a]what they did with the
calf which Aaron made.

The Command to Leave Sinai

33 Then the LORD said to Mo-
ses, "Depart *and* go up from
here, you [a]and the people whom
you have brought out of the land
of Egypt, to the land of which I
swore to Abraham, Isaac, and Ja-
cob, saying, [b]'To your descendants
I will give it.'
2 [a]"And I will send *My* Angel be-
fore you, [b]and I will drive out the
Canaanite and the Amorite and
the Hittite and the Perizzite and
the Hivite and the Jebusite.
3 "*Go up* [a]to a land flowing with
milk and honey; for I will not go
up in your midst, lest [b]I [1]consume
you on the way, for you *are* a [c]stiff-
necked[2] people."
4 And when the people heard
this bad news, [a]they mourned,

29 [a]Ex. 28:41; 1 Sam. 15:18, 22; Prov. 21:3; Zech. 13:3 [1]Lit. *Fill your hand*
30 [a]1 Sam. 12:20, 23 [b]2 Sam. 16:12 [c]Num. 25:13
31 [a]Deut. 9:18 [b]Ex. 20:23
32 [a]Ps. 69:28; Is. 4:3; Mal. 3:16; Rom. 9:3 [b]Dan. 12:1; Phil. 4:3; Rev. 3:5; 21:27
33 [a]Lev. 23:30; [Ezek. 18:4; 33:2, 14, 15] [b]Ex. 17:14; Deut. 29:20; Ps. 9:5; Rev. 3:5; 21:27
34 [a]Ex. 3:17 [b]Ex. 23:20; Josh. 5:14 [c]Deut. 32:35; Rom. 2:5, 6 [d]Ps. 89:32
35 [a]Neh. 9:18

CHAPTER 33

1 [a]Ex. 32:1, 7, 13; Josh. 3:17 [b]Gen. 12:7
2 [a]Ex. 32:34; Josh. 5:14 [b]Ex. 23:27–31; Josh. 24:11
3 [a]Ex. 3:8 [b]Num. 16:21, 45 [c]Ex. 32:9; 33:5 [1]*destroy* [2]*stubborn*
4 [a]Num. 14:1, 39 [b]Ezra 9:3; Esth. 4:1, 4; Ezek. 24:17, 23
5 [a][Ps. 139:23] [1]*jewelry*
7 [a]Ex. 29:42, 43 [b]Deut. 4:29
8 [a]Num. 16:27
9 [a]Ex. 25:22; 31:18; Ps. 99:7
10 [a]Ex. 4:31
11 [a]Num. 12:8; Deut. 34:10 [b]Ex. 24:13
12 [a]Ex. 3:10; 32:34 [b]Ex. 33:17; John 10:14, 15; 2 Tim. 2:19
13 [a]Ex. 34:9 [b]Ps. 25:4; 27:11; 86:11; 119:33 [c]Ex. 3:7, 10; 5:1; 32:12, 14; Deut. 9:26, 29
14 [a]Ex. 3:12; Deut. 4:37; Is. 63:9

[b]and no one put on his ornaments.
5 For the LORD had said to Moses,
"Say to the children of Israel, 'You
are a stiff-necked people. I could
come up into your midst in one
moment and consume you. Now
therefore, take off your [1]orna-
ments, that I may [a]know what to
do to you.' "
6 So the children of Israel
stripped themselves of their orna-
ments by Mount Horeb.

Moses Meets with the LORD

7 Moses took his tent and pitched
it outside the camp, far from the
camp, and [a]called it the tabernacle
of meeting. And it came to pass
that everyone who [b]sought the
LORD went out to the tabernacle of
meeting which *was* outside the
camp.
8 So it was, whenever Moses
went out to the tabernacle, *that* all
the people rose, and each man
stood [a]*at* his tent door and
watched Moses until he had gone
into the tabernacle.
9 And it came to pass, when Mo-
ses entered the tabernacle, that the
pillar of cloud descended and
stood *at* the door of the tabernacle,
and *the LORD* [a]talked with Moses.
10 All the people saw the pillar of
cloud standing *at* the tabernacle
door, and all the people rose and
[a]worshiped, each man *in* his tent
door.
11 So [a]the LORD spoke to Moses
face to face, as a man speaks to
his friend. And he would return to
the camp, but [b]his servant Joshua
the son of Nun, a young man, did
not depart from the tabernacle.

The Promise of God's Presence

12 Then Moses said to the LORD,
"See, [a]You say to me, 'Bring up
this people.' But You have not let
me know whom You will send
with me. Yet You have said, [b]'I
know you by name, and you have
also found grace in My sight.'
13 "Now therefore, I pray, [a]if I
have found grace in Your sight,
[b]show me now Your way, that I
may know You and that I may find
grace in Your sight. And consider
that this nation *is* [c]Your people."
14 And He said, [a]"My Presence

will go *with you,* and I will give
you [b]rest."
15 Then he said to Him, [a]"If Your
Presence does not go *with us,* do
not bring us up from here.
16 "For how then will it be known
that Your people and I have found
grace in Your sight, [a]except You
go with us? So we [b]shall be sepa-
rate, Your people and I, from all
the people who *are* upon the face
of the earth."
17 So the LORD said to Moses, [a]"I
will also do this thing that you
have spoken; for you have found
grace in My sight, and I know you
by name."
18 And he said, "Please, show me
[a]Your glory."
19 Then He said, "I will make all
My [a]goodness pass before you,
and I will proclaim the name of the
LORD before you. [b]I will be gra-
cious to whom I will be [c]gracious,
and I will have compassion on
whom I will have compassion."
20 But He said, "You cannot see
My face; for [a]no man shall see Me,
and live."
21 And the LORD said, "Here is a
place by Me, and you shall stand
on the rock.
22 "So it shall be, while My glory
passes by, that I will put you [a]in
the cleft of the rock, and will
[b]cover you with My hand while I
pass by.
23 "Then I will take away My
hand, and you shall see My back;
but My face shall [a]not be seen."

Moses Makes New Tablets

34 And the LORD said to Moses,
[a]"Cut two tablets of stone
like the first *ones,* and [b]I will write
on *these* tablets the words that
were on the first tablets which you
broke.
2 "So be ready in the morning,
and come up in the morning to
Mount Sinai, and present yourself
to Me there [a]on the top of the
mountain.
3 "And no man shall [a]come up
with you, and let no man be seen
throughout all the mountain; let
neither flocks nor herds feed be-
fore that mountain."
4 So he cut two tablets of stone
like the first *ones.* Then Moses
rose early in the morning and went
up Mount Sinai, as the LORD had
commanded him; and he took in
his hand the two tablets of stone.
5 Now the LORD descended in the
[a]cloud and stood with him there,
and [b]proclaimed the name of the
LORD.
6 And the LORD passed before
him and proclaimed, "The LORD,
the LORD [a]God, merciful and gra-
cious, longsuffering, and abound-
ing in [b]goodness and [c]truth,
7 [a]"keeping mercy for thou-
sands, [b]forgiving iniquity and
transgression and sin, [c]by no
means clearing *the guilty,* visiting
the iniquity of the fathers upon the
children and the children's chil-
dren to the third and the fourth
generation."
8 So Moses made haste and
[a]bowed his head toward the earth,
and worshiped.
9 Then he said, "If now I have
found grace in Your sight, O Lord,
[a]let my Lord, I pray, go among us,
even though we *are* a [b]stiff-
necked[1] people; and pardon our
iniquity and our sin, and take us
as [c]Your inheritance."

The Covenant Renewed

10 And He said: "Behold, [a]I make
a covenant. Before all your people
I will [b]do [1]marvels such as have
not been done in all the earth, nor
in any nation; and all the people
among whom you *are* shall see the
work of the LORD. For it *is* [c]an awe-
some thing that I will do with you.
11 [a]"Observe what I command
you this day. Behold, [b]I am driving
out from before you the Amorite
and the Canaanite and the Hittite
and the Perizzite and the Hivite
and the Jebusite.
12 [a]"Take heed to yourself, lest
you make a covenant with the in-
habitants of the land where you
are going, lest it be a snare in your
midst.
13 "But you shall [a]destroy their al-
tars, break their *sacred* pillars, and
[b]cut down their wooden images
14 "(for you shall worship [a]no
other god, for the LORD, whose
[b]name *is* Jealous, *is* a [c]jealous
God),
15 "lest you make a covenant with
the inhabitants of the land, and
they [a]play the harlot with their

14 [b]Deut. 12:10; 25:19; Josh. 21:44; 22:4
15 [a]Ex. 33:3
16 [a]Num. 14:14 [b]Ex. 34:10
17 [a][James 5:16]
18 [a][1 Tim. 6:16]
19 [a]Ex. 34:6, 7 [b][Rom. 9:15, 16, 18] [c][Rom. 4:4, 16]
20 [a][Gen. 32:30]
22 [a]Is. 2:21 [b]Ps. 91:1, 4
23 [a][John 1:18]

CHAPTER 34

1 [a][Ex. 24:12; 31:18; 32:15, 16, 19] [b]Deut. 10:2, 4
2 [a]Ex. 19:11, 18, 20
3 [a]Ex. 19:12, 13; 24:9–11
5 [a]Ex. 19:9 [b]Ex. 33:19
6 [a]Neh. 9:17 [b]Rom. 2:4 [c]Ps. 108:4
7 [a]Ex. 20:6 [b]Ps. 103:3, 4 [c]Job 10:14
8 [a]Ex. 4:31
9 [a]Ex. 33:12–16 [b]Ex. 33:3 [c]Ps. 33:12; 94:14 [1]*stubborn*
10 [a]Deut. 5:2 [b]Ps. 77:14 [c]Ps. 145:6 [1]*wonderful acts*
11 [a]Deut. 6:25 [b]Ex. 23:20–33; 33:2
12 [a]Ex. 23:32, 33
13 [a]Deut. 12:3 [b]2 Kin. 18:4
14 [a][Ex. 20:3–5] [b][Is. 9:6; 57:15] [c][Deut. 4:24]
15 [a]Judg. 2:17

gods and make sacrifice to their
gods, and *one of them* [b]invites you
and you [c]eat of his sacrifice,
16 "and you take of [a]his daughters
for your sons, and his daughters
[b]play the harlot with their gods
and make your sons play the har-
lot with their gods.
17 [a]"You shall make no molded
gods for yourselves.
18 "The Feast of [a]Unleavened
Bread you shall keep. Seven days
you shall eat unleavened bread, as
I commanded you, in the ap-
pointed time of the month of Abib;
for in the [b]month of Abib you came
out from Egypt.
19 [a]"All [1]that open the womb *are*
Mine, and every male firstborn
among your livestock, *whether* ox
or sheep.
20 "But [a]the firstborn of a donkey
you shall redeem with a lamb. And
if you will not redeem *him,* then
you shall break his neck. All the
firstborn of your sons you shall re-
deem. And none shall appear be-
fore Me [b]empty-handed.
21 [a]"Six days you shall work, but
on the seventh day you shall rest;
in plowing time and in harvest you
shall rest.
22 "And you shall observe the
Feast of Weeks, of the firstfruits
of wheat harvest, and the Feast of
Ingathering at the year's end.
23 [a]"Three times in the year all
your men shall appear before the
Lord, the LORD God of Israel.
24 "For I will [a]cast out the nations
before you and enlarge your bor-
ders; neither will any man covet
your land when you go up to ap-
pear before the LORD your God
three times in the year.
25 "You shall not offer the blood
of My sacrifice with leaven, [a]nor
shall the sacrifice of the Feast of
the Passover be left until morning.
26 [a]"The first of the firstfruits of
your land you shall bring to the
house of the LORD your God. You
shall not boil a young goat in its
mother's milk."
27 Then the LORD said to Moses,
"Write [a]these words, for according
to the tenor of these words I have
made a covenant with you and
with Israel."
28 [a]So he was there with the LORD
forty days and forty nights; he nei-
ther ate bread nor drank water.
And [b]He wrote on the tablets the
words of the covenant, the [1]Ten
Commandments.

The Shining Face of Moses

29 Now it was so, when Moses
came down from Mount Sinai (and
the [a]two tablets of the Testimony
were in Moses' hand when he
came down from the mountain),
that Moses did not know that [b]the
skin of his face shone while he
talked with Him.
30 So when Aaron and all the
children of Israel saw Moses, be-
hold, the skin of his face shone,
and they were afraid to come near
him.
31 Then Moses called to them, and
Aaron and all the rulers of the con-
gregation returned to him; and
Moses talked with them.
32 Afterward all the children of Is-
rael came near, [a]and he gave them
as commandments all that the
LORD had spoken with him on
Mount Sinai.
33 And when Moses had finished
speaking with them, he put [a]a veil
on his face.
34 But [a]whenever Moses went in
before the LORD to speak with
Him, he would take the veil off un-
til he came out; and he would come
out and speak to the children of
Israel whatever he had been com-
manded.
35 And whenever the children of
Israel saw the face of Moses, that
the skin of Moses' face shone, then
Moses would put the veil on his
face again, until he went in to
speak with Him.

Sabbath Regulations

35 Then Moses gathered all the
congregation of the children
of Israel together, and said to
them, [a]"These *are* the words
which the LORD has commanded
you to do:
2 "Work shall be done for [a]six
days, but the seventh day shall be
a holy day for you, a Sabbath of
rest to the LORD. Whoever does
any work on it shall be put to
[b]death.
3 [a]"You shall kindle no fire
throughout your dwellings on the
Sabbath day."

15 [b]Num. 25:1, 2; Deut. 32:37, 38 [c]1 Cor. 8:4, 7, 10
16 [a]Gen. 28:1; Deut. 7:3; Josh. 23:12, 13; 1 Kin. 11:2; Ezra 9:2; Neh. 13:25 [b]Num. 25:1, 2; 1 Kin. 11:4
17 [a]Ex. 20:4, 23; 32:8; Lev. 19:4; Deut. 5:8
18 [a]Ex. 12:15, 16 [b]Ex. 12:2; 13:4
19 [a]Ex. 13:2; 22:29 [1]*the firstborn*
20 [a]Ex. 13:13 [b]Ex. 22:29; 23:15; Deut. 16:16
21 [a]Ex. 20:9; 23:12; 31:15; 35:2; Lev. 23:3; Deut. 5:13
23 [a]Ex. 23:14–17
24 [a][Ex. 33:2]; Josh. 11:23; 1 Kin. 4:21; 2 Chr. 36:14–16; Ps. 78:55
25 [a]Ex. 12:10
26 [a]Ex. 23:19; Deut. 26:2
27 [a]Ex. 17:14; 24:4; Deut. 31:9
28 [a]Ex. 24:18 [b]Ex. 34:1, 4; Deut. 4:31; 10:2, 4 [1]Lit. *Ten Words*
29 [a]Ex. 32:15 [b]Matt. 17:2; 2 Cor. 3:7
32 [a]Ex. 24:3
33 [a][2 Cor. 3:13, 14]
34 [a][2 Cor. 3:13–16]

CHAPTER 35

1 [a]Ex. 34:32
2 [a]Ex. 20:9, 10; Lev. 23:3; Deut. 5:13 [b]Num. 15:32–36
3 [a]Ex. 12:16; 16:23

Offerings for the Tabernacle

4 And Moses spoke to all the congregation of the children of Israel, saying, [a]"This *is* the thing which the LORD commanded, saying:
5 'Take from among you an offering to the LORD. [a]Whoever *is* of a willing heart, let him bring it as an offering to the LORD: [b]gold, silver, and bronze;
6 [a]'blue, purple, and scarlet *thread*, fine linen, and [b]goats' *hair;*
7 'ram skins dyed red, badger skins, and acacia wood;
8 'oil for the light, [a]and spices for the anointing oil and for the sweet incense;
9 'onyx stones, and stones to be set in the ephod and in the breastplate.

Articles of the Tabernacle

10 [a]'All *who are* gifted artisans among you shall come and make all that the LORD has commanded:
11 [a]'the tabernacle, its tent, its covering, its clasps, its boards, its bars, its pillars, and its sockets;
12 [a]'the ark and its poles, *with* the mercy seat, and the veil of the covering;
13 'the [a]table and its poles, all its utensils, [b]and the showbread;
14 'also [a]the lampstand for the light, its utensils, its lamps, and the oil for the light;
15 [a]'the incense altar, its poles, [b]the anointing oil, [c]the sweet incense, and the screen for the door at the entrance of the tabernacle;
16 [a]'the altar of burnt offering with its bronze grating, its poles, all its utensils, *and* the laver and its base;
17 [a]'the hangings of the court, its pillars, their sockets, and the screen for the gate of the court;
18 'the pegs of the tabernacle, the pegs of the court, and their cords;
19 [a]'the [1]garments of ministry, for ministering in the holy *place*—the holy garments for Aaron the priest and the garments of his sons, to minister as priests.' "

The Tabernacle Offerings Presented

20 And all the congregation of the children of Israel departed from the presence of Moses.

4 [a]Ex. 25:1, 2

5 [a]Ex. 25:2; 1 Chr. 29:14; Mark 12:41–44; 2 Cor. 8:10–12; 9:7 [b]Ex. 38:24

6 [a]Ex. 36:8 [b]Ex. 36:14

8 [a]Ex. 25:6; 30:23–25

10 [a]Ex. 31:2–6; 36:1, 2

11 [a]Ex. 26:1, 2; 36:14

12 [a]Ex. 25:10–22

13 [a]Ex. 25:23 [b]Ex. 25:30; Lev. 24:5, 6

14 [a]Ex. 25:31

15 [a]Ex. 30:1 [b]Ex. 30:25 [c]Ex. 30:34–38

16 [a]Ex. 27:1–8

17 [a]Ex. 27:9–18

19 [a]Ex. 31:10; 39:1, 41 [1]Or *woven garments*

21 [a]Ex. 25:2; 35:5, 22, 26, 29; 36:2 [b]Ex. 35:24 [1]Lit. *lifted him up*

22 [a]Ex. 32:2, 3 [b]Ex. 11:2

23 [a]1 Chr. 29:8 [1]Or *dolphin*

25 [a]Ex. 28:3; 31:6; 36:1

26 [1]Lit. *lifted them up*

27 [a]1 Chr. 29:6; Ezra 2:68

28 [a]Ex. 30:23

29 [a]Ex. 35:5, 21; 36:3; 1 Chr. 29:9

30 [a]Ex. 31:1–6

21 Then everyone came [a]whose heart [1]was stirred, and everyone whose spirit was willing, *and* they [b]brought the LORD's offering for the work of the tabernacle of meeting, for all its service, and for the holy garments.
22 They came, both men and women, as many as had a willing heart, *and* brought [a]earrings and nose rings, rings and necklaces, all [b]jewelry of gold, that is, every man who *made* an offering of gold to the LORD.
23 And [a]every man, with whom was found blue, purple, and scarlet *thread*, fine linen, and goats' *hair*, red skins of rams, and [1]badger skins, brought *them*.
24 Everyone who offered an offering of silver or bronze brought the LORD's offering. And everyone with whom was found acacia wood for any work of the service, brought *it*.
25 All the women *who were* [a]gifted artisans spun yarn with their hands, and brought what they had spun, of blue, purple, *and* scarlet, and fine linen.
26 And all the women whose hearts [1]stirred with wisdom spun yarn of goats' *hair*.
27 [a]The rulers brought onyx stones, and the stones to be set in the ephod and in the breastplate,
28 and [a]spices and oil for the light, for the anointing oil, and for the sweet incense.
29 The children of Israel brought a [a]freewill offering to the LORD, all the men and women whose hearts were willing to bring *material* for all kinds of work which the LORD, by the hand of Moses, had commanded to be done.

The Artisans Called by God

30 And Moses said to the children of Israel, "See, [a]the LORD has called by name Bezalel the son of Uri, the son of Hur, of the tribe of Judah;
31 "and He has filled him with the Spirit of God, in wisdom and understanding, in knowledge and all manner of workmanship,
32 "to design artistic works, to work in gold and silver and bronze,
33 "in cutting jewels for setting, in

carving wood, and to work in all
manner of artistic workmanship.
34 "And He has put in his heart
the ability to teach, *in* him and
[a]Aholiab the son of Ahisamach, of
the tribe of Dan.
35 "He has [a]filled them with skill
to do all manner of work of the
engraver and the designer and the
tapestry maker, in blue, purple,
and scarlet *thread*, and fine linen,
and of the weaver—those who do
every work and those who design
artistic works.
36 "And Bezalel and Aholiab,
and every [a]gifted artisan in
whom the LORD has put wisdom
and understanding, to know how
to do all manner of work for the
service of the [b]sanctuary,[1] shall do
according to all that the LORD has
commanded."

The People Give More than Enough

2 Then Moses called Bezalel and
Aholiab, and every gifted artisan
in whose heart the LORD had put
wisdom, everyone [a]whose heart
[1]was stirred, to come and do the
work.
3 And they received from Moses
all the [a]offering which the children
of Israel [b]had brought for the work
of the service of making the sanc-
tuary. So they continued bringing
to him freewill offerings every
morning.
4 Then all the craftsmen who
were doing all the work of the
sanctuary came, each from the
work he was doing,
5 and they spoke to Moses, say-
ing, [a]"The people bring much
more than enough for the service
of the work which the LORD com-
manded *us* to do."
6 So Moses gave a command-
ment, and they caused it to be pro-
claimed throughout the camp, say-
ing, "Let neither man nor woman
do any more work for the offering
of the sanctuary." And the people
were restrained from bringing,
7 for the material they had was
sufficient for all the work to be
done—indeed too [a]much.

Building the Tabernacle

8 [a]Then all the gifted artisans
among them who worked on the
tabernacle made ten curtains
woven of fine linen, and of blue,
purple, and scarlet *thread; with* ar-
tistic designs of cherubim they
made them.
9 The length of each curtain *was*
twenty-eight cubits, and the width
of each curtain four cubits; the
curtains *were* all the same size.
10 And he coupled five curtains to
one another, and *the other* five
curtains he coupled to one an-
other.
11 He made loops of blue *yarn* on
the edge of the curtain on the sel-
vedge of one set; likewise he did
on the outer edge of *the other* cur-
tain of the second set.
12 [a]Fifty loops he made on one
curtain, and fifty loops he made on
the edge of the curtain on the end
of the second set; the loops held
one *curtain* to another.
13 And he made fifty clasps of
gold, and coupled the curtains to
one another with the clasps, that
it might be one tabernacle.
14 [a]He made curtains of goats'
hair for the tent over the taberna-
cle; he made eleven curtains.
15 The length of each curtain *was*
thirty cubits, and the width of each
curtain four cubits; the eleven cur-
tains *were* the same size.
16 He coupled five curtains by
themselves and six curtains by
themselves.
17 And he made fifty loops on the
edge of the curtain that is outer-
most in one set, and fifty loops he
made on the edge of the curtain
of the second set.
18 He also made fifty bronze
clasps to couple the tent together,
that it might be one.
19 [a]Then he made a covering for
the tent of ram skins dyed red, and
a covering of [1]badger skins above
that.
20 For the tabernacle [a]he made
boards of acacia wood, standing
upright.
21 The length of each board *was*
ten cubits, and the width of each
board a cubit and a half.
22 Each board had two [1]tenons
[a]for binding one to another. Thus
he made for all the boards of the
tabernacle.
23 And he made boards for the
tabernacle, twenty boards for the
south side.

34 [a]Ex. 31:6
35 [a]Ex. 31:3, 6; 35:31; 1 Kin. 7:14; 2 Chr. 2:14; Is. 28:26

CHAPTER 36

1 [a]Ex. 28:3; 31:6; 35:10, 35 [b]Ex. 25:8 [1]*holy place*
2 [a]Ex. 35:21, 26; 1 Chr. 29:5, 9, 17 [1]*lifted him up*
3 [a]Ex. 35:5 [b]Ex. 35:27
5 [a]2 Chr. 24:14; 31:6–10; [2 Cor. 8:2, 3]
7 [a]1 Kin. 8:64
8 [a]Ex. 26:1–14
12 [a]Ex. 26:5
14 [a]Ex. 26:7
19 [a]Ex. 26:14 [1]Or *dolphin*
20 [a]Ex. 26:15–29
22 [a]Ex. 26:17 [1]Projections for joining, lit. *hands*

24 Forty sockets of silver he made
to go under the twenty boards: two
sockets under each of the boards
for its two tenons.
25 And for the other side of the
tabernacle, the north side, he
made twenty boards
26 and their forty sockets of sil-
ver: two sockets under each of the
boards.
27 For the west side of the taber-
nacle he made six boards.
28 He also made two boards for
the two back corners of the taber-
nacle.
29 And they were coupled at the
bottom and [1]coupled together at
the top by one ring. Thus he
made both of them for the two cor-
ners.
30 So there were eight boards and
their sockets—sixteen sockets of
silver—two sockets under each of
the boards.
31 And he made [a]bars of acacia
wood: five for the boards on one
side of the tabernacle,
32 five bars for the boards on the
other side of the tabernacle, and
five bars for the boards of the tab-
ernacle on the far side westward.
33 And he made the middle bar to
pass through the boards from one
end to the other.
34 He overlaid the boards with
gold, made their rings of gold *to
be* holders for the bars, and over-
laid the bars with gold.
35 And he made [a]a veil of blue,
purple, and scarlet *thread,* and
fine woven linen; it was worked
with an artistic design of cher-
ubim.
36 He made for it four pillars of
acacia *wood,* and overlaid them
with gold, with their hooks of gold;
and he cast four sockets of silver
for them.
37 He also made a [a]screen for the
tabernacle door, of blue, purple,
and scarlet *thread,* and fine woven
linen, made by a [1]weaver,
38 and its five pillars with their
hooks. And he overlaid their capi-
tals and their rings with gold, but
their five sockets *were* bronze.

Making the Ark of the Testimony

37 Then [a]Bezalel made [b]the ark
of acacia wood; two and a
half cubits *was* its length, a cubit
and a half its width, and a cubit
and a half its height.
2 He overlaid it with pure gold
inside and outside, and made a
molding of gold all around it.
3 And he cast for it four rings of
gold *to be set* in its four corners:
two rings on one side, and two
rings on the other side of it.
4 He made poles of acacia wood,
and overlaid them with gold.
5 And he put the poles into the
rings at the sides of the ark, to bear
the ark.
6 He also made the [a]mercy seat
of pure gold; two and a half cubits
was its length and a cubit and a
half its width.
7 He made two cherubim of
beaten gold; he made them of one
piece at the two ends of the mercy
seat:
8 one cherub at one end on this
side, and the other cherub at
the *other* end on that side. He
made the cherubim at the two
ends *of one piece* with the mercy
seat.
9 The cherubim spread out *their*
wings above, *and* covered the
[a]mercy seat with their wings. They
faced one another; the faces of the
cherubim were toward the mercy
seat.

Making the Table for the Showbread

10 He made [a]the table of acacia
wood; two cubits *was* its length, a
cubit its width, and a cubit and a
half its height.
11 And he overlaid it with pure
gold, and made a molding of gold
all around it.
12 Also he made a frame of a
handbreadth all around it, and
made a molding of gold for the
frame all around it.
13 And he cast for it four rings of
gold, and put the rings on the four
corners that *were* at its four
legs.
14 The rings were close to the
frame, as holders for the poles to
bear the table.
15 And he made the poles of aca-
cia wood to bear the table, and
overlaid them with gold.
16 He made of pure gold the uten-
sils which were on the table: its
[a]dishes, its cups, its bowls, and its
pitchers for pouring.

29 [1]Lit. *doubled*
31 [a]Ex. 26:26–29
35 [a]Ex. 26:31–37
37 [a]Ex. 26:36 [1]Lit. *variegator,* a weaver in colors

CHAPTER 37

1 [a]Ex. 35:30; 36:1 [b]Ex. 25:10–20
6 [a]Ex. 25:17
9 [a]Ex. 25:20
10 [a]Ex. 25:23–29
16 [a]Ex. 25:29

Making the Gold Lampstand

17 He also made the [a]lampstand
of pure gold; of hammered work
he made the lampstand. Its shaft,
its branches, its bowls, its *orna-*
mental knobs, and its flowers were
of the same piece.
18 And six branches came out of
its sides: three branches of the
lampstand out of one side, and
three branches of the lampstand
out of the other side.
19 There were three bowls made
like almond *blossoms* on one
branch, with an *ornamental* knob
and a flower, and three bowls
made like almond *blossoms* on the
other branch, with an *ornamental*
knob and a flower—and so for the
six branches coming out of the
lampstand.
20 And on the lampstand itself
were four bowls made like almond
blossoms, each with its *orna-*
mental knob and flower.
21 *There was* a knob under the
first two branches of the same,
a knob under the *second* two
branches of the same, and a knob
under the *third* two branches of
the same, according to the six
branches extending from it.
22 Their knobs and their branches
were of one piece; all of it *was* one
hammered piece of pure gold.
23 And he made its seven lamps,
its [a]wick-trimmers, and its trays of
pure gold.
24 Of a talent of pure gold he
made it, with all its utensils.

Making the Altar of Incense

25 [a]He made the incense altar of
acacia wood. Its length *was* a cubit
and its width a cubit—*it was*
square—and two cubits *was* its
height. Its horns were *of one piece*
with it.
26 And he overlaid it with pure
gold: its top, its sides all around,
and its horns. He also made for it
a molding of gold all around it.
27 He made two rings of gold
for it under its molding, by its
two corners on both sides, as
holders for the poles with which
to bear it.
28 And he [a]made the poles of aca-
cia wood, and overlaid them with
gold.

Making the Anointing Oil and the Incense

29 He also made [a]the holy anoint-
ing oil and the pure incense of
sweet spices, according to the
work of the perfumer.

Making the Altar of Burnt Offering

38 He made [a]the altar of burnt
offering of acacia wood; five
cubits *was* its length and five cu-
bits its width—*it was* square—and
its height *was* three cubits.
2 He made its horns on its four
corners; the horns were *of one*
piece with it. And he overlaid it
with bronze.
3 He made all the utensils for the
altar: the pans, the shovels, the ba-
sins, the forks, and the firepans;
all its utensils he made of bronze.
4 And he made a grate of bronze
network for the altar, under its
rim, midway from the bottom.
5 He cast four rings for the four
corners of the bronze grating, *as*
holders for the poles.
6 And he made the poles of aca-
cia wood, and overlaid them with
bronze.
7 Then he put the poles into the
rings on the sides of the altar, with
which to bear it. He made the altar
hollow with boards.

Making the Bronze Laver

8 He made [a]the laver of bronze
and its base of bronze, from the
bronze mirrors of the serving
women who assembled at the door
of the tabernacle of meeting.

Making the Court of the Tabernacle

9 Then he made [a]the court on the
south side; the hangings of the
court *were of* fine woven linen, one
hundred cubits long.
10 There *were* twenty pillars for
them, with twenty bronze sockets.
The hooks of the pillars and their
bands *were* silver.
11 On the north side *the hangings*
were one hundred cubits *long*,
with twenty pillars and their
twenty bronze sockets. The hooks
of the pillars and their bands *were*
silver.
12 And on the west side *there*
were hangings of fifty cubits, with
ten pillars and their ten sockets.

17 [a]Ex. 25:31–39
23 [a]Num. 4:9
25 [a]Ex. 30:1–5
28 [a]Ex. 30:5
29 [a]Ex. 30:23–25

CHAPTER 38
1 [a]Ex. 27:1–8
8 [a]Ex. 30:18
9 [a]Ex. 27:9–19

The hooks of the pillars and their
bands *were* silver.
13 For the east side *the hangings*
were fifty cubits.
14 The hangings of one side *of the*
gate were fifteen cubits *long, with*
their three pillars and their three
sockets,
15 and the same for the other side
of the court gate; on this side and
that *were* hangings of fifteen cu-
bits, *with* their three pillars and
their three sockets.
16 All the hangings of the court
all around *were of* fine woven
linen.
17 The sockets for the pillars *were*
bronze, the hooks of the pillars
and their bands *were* silver, and
the overlay of their capitals *was*
silver; and all the pillars of the
court had bands of silver.
18 The screen for the gate of the
court *was* woven of blue, purple,
and scarlet *thread*, and of fine
woven linen. The length *was*
twenty cubits, and the height
along its width *was* five cubits,
corresponding to the hangings of
the court.
19 And *there were* four pillars
with their four sockets of bronze;
their hooks *were* silver, and the
overlay of their capitals and their
bands *was* silver.
20 All the [a]pegs of the tabernacle,
and of the court all around, *were*
bronze.

Materials of the Tabernacle

21 [1]This is the inventory of the
tabernacle, [a]the tabernacle of the
Testimony, which was counted ac-
cording to the commandment of
Moses, for the service of the Le-
vites, [b]by the hand of [c]Ithamar,
son of Aaron the priest.
22 [a]Bezalel the son of Uri, the son
of Hur, of the tribe of Judah, made
all that the LORD had commanded
Moses.
23 And with him *was* [a]Aholiab the
son of Ahisamach, of the tribe of
Dan, an engraver and [1]designer, a
weaver of blue, purple, and scarlet
thread, and of fine linen.
24 All the gold that was used in
all the work of the holy *place*, that
is, the gold of the [a]offering, was
twenty-nine talents and seven
hundred and thirty shekels, ac-

20 [a]Ex. 27:19

21 [a]Num. 1:50, 53; 9:15; 10:11; 17:7, 8; 2 Chr. 24:6; Acts 7:44 [b]Num. 4:28, 33 [c]Ex. 28:1; Lev. 10:6, 16 [1]Lit. *These are the things appointed for*

22 [a]Ex. 31:2, 6; 1 Chr. 2:18–20

23 [a]Ex. 31:6; 36:1 [1]*skillful workman*

24 [a]Ex. 35:5, 22 [b]Ex. 30:13, 24; Lev. 5:15; 27:3, 25; Num. 3:47; 18:16

25 [a]Ex. 30:11–16; Num. 1:2

26 [a]Ex. 30:13, 15 [b]Ex. 12:37; Num. 1:46; 26:51 [1]Lit. *a head*

27 [a]Ex. 26:19, 21, 25, 32

28 [a]Ex. 27:17

CHAPTER 39

1 [a]Ex. 25:4; 35:23 [b]Ex. 31:10; 35:19 [c]Ex. 28:4 [1]Or *woven garments* [2]*sanctuary*

2 [a]Ex. 28:6–14 [b]Lev. 8:7

cording to [b]the shekel of the sanc-
tuary.
25 And the silver from those who
were [a]numbered of the congrega-
tion *was* one hundred talents and
one thousand seven hundred and
seventy-five shekels, according to
the shekel of the sanctuary:
26 [a]a bekah for [1]each man (*that*
is, half a shekel, according to the
shekel of the sanctuary), for every-
one included in the numbering
from twenty years old and above,
for [b]six hundred and three thou-
sand, five hundred and fifty *men*.
27 And from the hundred talents
of silver were cast [a]the sockets of
the sanctuary and the bases of the
veil: one hundred sockets from the
hundred talents, one talent for
each socket.
28 Then from the one thousand
seven hundred and seventy-five
shekels he made hooks for the pil-
lars, overlaid their capitals, and
[a]made bands for them.
29 The offering of bronze *was* sev-
enty talents and two thousand four
hundred shekels.
30 And with it he made the sock-
ets for the door of the tabernacle
of meeting, the bronze altar, the
bronze grating for it, and all the
utensils for the altar,
31 the sockets for the court all
around, the bases for the court
gate, all the pegs for the taberna-
cle, and all the pegs for the court
all around.

Making the Garments of the Priesthood

39 Of the [a]blue, purple, and
scarlet *thread* they made
[b]garments[1] of ministry, for minis-
tering in the [2]holy *place*, and made
the holy garments for Aaron, [c]as
the LORD had commanded Moses.

Making the Ephod

2 [a]He made the [b]ephod of gold,
blue, purple, and scarlet *thread*,
and of fine woven linen.
3 And they beat the gold into thin
sheets and cut *it into* threads, to
work *it* in *with* the blue, purple,
and scarlet *thread*, and the fine
linen, *into* artistic designs.
4 They made shoulder straps for
it to couple *it* together; it was cou-
pled together at its two edges.

5 And the intricately woven band
of his ephod that *was* on it *was* of
the same workmanship, *woven of*
gold, blue, purple, and scarlet
thread, and *of* fine woven linen, as
the LORD had commanded Moses.
6 [a]And they set onyx stones, en-
closed in [1]settings of gold; they
were engraved, as signets are en-
graved, with the names of the sons
of Israel.
7 He put them on the shoulders
of the ephod *as* [a]memorial stones
for the sons of Israel, as the LORD
had commanded Moses.

Making the Breastplate

8 [a]And he made the breastplate,
artistically woven like the work-
manship of the ephod, of gold,
blue, purple, and scarlet *thread*,
and of fine woven linen.
9 They made the breastplate
square by doubling it; a span *was*
its length and a span its width
when doubled.
10 [a]And they set in it four rows
of stones: a row with a sardius, a
topaz, and an emerald was the first
row;
11 the second row, a turquoise, a
sapphire, and a diamond;
12 the third row, a jacinth, an
agate, and an amethyst;
13 the fourth row, a beryl, an
onyx, and a jasper. *They were* en-
closed in settings of gold in their
mountings.
14 *There were* [a]twelve stones ac-
cording to the names of the sons
of Israel: according to their names,
engraved like a signet, each one
with its own name according to the
twelve tribes.
15 And they made chains for the
breastplate at the ends, like
braided cords of pure gold.
16 They also made two settings of
gold and two gold rings, and put
the two rings on the two ends of
the breastplate.
17 And they put the two braided
chains of gold in the two rings on
the ends of the breastplate.
18 The two ends of the two
braided *chains* they fastened in the
two settings, and put them on the
shoulder straps of the ephod in the
front.
19 And they made two rings of
gold and put *them* on the two ends
of the breastplate, on the edge of
it, which *was* on the inward side
of the ephod.
20 They made two *other* gold
rings and put them on the two
shoulder straps, underneath the
ephod toward its front, right at the
seam above the intricately woven
band of the ephod.
21 And they bound the breastplate
by means of its rings to the rings
of the ephod with a blue cord, so
that it would be above the intri-
cately woven band of the ephod,
and that the breastplate would not
come loose from the ephod, as the
LORD had commanded Moses.

Making the Other Priestly Garments

22 [a]He made the [b]robe of the
ephod of woven work, all of blue.
23 And *there was* an opening in
the middle of the robe, like the
opening in a coat of mail, *with* a
woven binding all around the
opening, so that it would not tear.
24 They made on the hem of the
robe pomegranates of blue, pur-
ple, and scarlet, and of fine woven
linen.
25 And they made [a]bells of pure
gold, and put the bells between the
pomegranates on the hem of the
robe all around between the pome-
granates:
26 a bell and a pomegranate, a
bell and a pomegranate, all around
the hem of the robe to [1]minister
in, as the LORD had commanded
Moses.
27 [a]They made tunics, artistically
woven of fine linen, for Aaron and
his sons,
28 [a]a turban of fine linen, exqui-
site hats of fine linen, [b]short trou-
sers of fine woven linen,
29 [a]and a sash of fine woven linen
with blue, purple, and scarlet
thread, made by a weaver, as the
LORD had commanded Moses.
30 [a]Then they made the plate of
the holy crown of pure gold, and
wrote on it an inscription *like* the
engraving of a signet:

[b]HOLINESS TO THE LORD.

31 And they tied to it a blue cord,
to fasten *it* above on the turban,
as the LORD had commanded Mo-
ses.

6 [a]Ex. 28:9–11 [1]*plaited work*
7 [a]Ex. 28:12, 29; Josh. 4:7
8 [a]Ex. 28:15–30
10 [a]Ex. 28:17
14 [a]Rev. 21:12
22 [a]Ex. 28:31–35 [b]Ex. 29:5; Lev. 8:7
25 [a]Ex. 28:33
26 [1]*serve*
27 [a]Ex. 28:39, 40
28 [a]Ex. 28:4, 39; Lev. 8:9; Ezek. 44:18 [b]Ex. 28:42; Lev. 6:10
29 [a]Ex. 28:39
30 [a]Ex. 28:36, 37 [b]Zech. 14:20

The Work Completed

32 Thus all the work of the taber-
nacle of the tent of meeting was
[a]finished. And the children of Is-
rael did [b]according to all that the
LORD had commanded Moses; so
they did.
33 And they brought the taberna-
cle to Moses, the tent and all its
furnishings: its clasps, its boards,
its bars, its pillars, and its sockets;
34 the covering of ram skins dyed
red, the covering of badger skins,
and the veil of the covering;
35 the ark of the Testimony with
its poles, and the mercy seat;
36 the table, all its utensils, and
the [a]showbread;
37 the pure *gold* lampstand with
its lamps (the lamps set in order),
all its utensils, and the oil for light;
38 the gold altar, the anointing oil,
and the sweet incense; the screen
for the tabernacle door;
39 the bronze altar, its grate of
bronze, its poles, and all its uten-
sils; the laver with its base;
40 the hangings of the court, its
pillars and its sockets, the screen
for the court gate, its cords, and
its pegs; all the utensils for the ser-
vice of the tabernacle, for the tent
of meeting;
41 and the [1]garments of ministry,
to [2]minister in the holy *place:* the
holy garments for Aaron the
priest, and his sons' garments, to
minister as priests.
42 According to all that the LORD
had commanded Moses, so the
children of Israel [a]did all the
work.
43 Then Moses looked over all the
work, and indeed they had done
it; as the LORD had commanded,
just so they had done it. And Mo-
ses [a]blessed them.

The Tabernacle Erected and Arranged

40 Then the LORD [a]spoke to Mo-
ses, saying:
2 "On the first day of the [a]first
month you shall set up [b]the taber-
nacle of the tent of meeting.
3 [a]"You shall put in it the ark of
the Testimony, and [1]partition off
the ark with the veil.
4 [a]"You shall bring in the table
and [b]arrange the things that are
to be set in order on it; [c]and you
shall bring in the lampstand and
[1]light its lamps.
5 [a]"You shall also set the altar
of gold for the incense before the
ark of the Testimony, and put up
the screen for the door of the tab-
ernacle.
6 "Then you shall set the [a]altar
of the burnt offering before the
door of the tabernacle of the tent
of meeting.
7 "And [a]you shall set the laver
between the tabernacle of meeting
and the altar, and put water in it.
8 "You shall set up the court all
around, and hang up the screen at
the court gate.
9 "And you shall take the anoint-
ing oil, and [a]anoint the tabernacle
and all that *is* in it; and you shall
hallow it and all its utensils, and
it shall be holy.
10 "You shall [a]anoint the altar of
the burnt offering and all its uten-
sils, and consecrate the altar. [b]The
altar shall be most holy.
11 "And you shall anoint the laver
and its base, and consecrate it.
12 [a]"Then you shall bring Aaron
and his sons to the door of the tab-
ernacle of meeting and wash them
with water.
13 "You shall put the holy [a]gar-
ments on Aaron, [b]and anoint him
and consecrate him, that he may
minister to Me as priest.
14 "And you shall bring his sons
and clothe them with tunics.
15 "You shall anoint them, as you
anointed their father, that they
may minister to Me as priests; for
their anointing shall surely be [a]an
everlasting priesthood throughout
their generations."
16 Thus Moses did; according to
all that the LORD had commanded
him, so he did.
17 And it came to pass in the first
month of the second year, on the
first *day* of the month, *that* the
[a]tabernacle was [1]raised up.
18 So Moses raised up the taber-
nacle, fastened its sockets, set up
its boards, put in its bars, and
raised up its pillars.
19 And he spread out the tent over
the tabernacle and put the cover-
ing of the tent on top of it, as the
LORD had commanded Moses.
20 He took [a]the Testimony and
put *it* into the ark, inserted the

32 [a]Ex. 40:17 [b]Ex. 25:40; 39:42, 43
36 [a]Ex. 25:23–30
41 [1]Or *woven garments* [2]*serve*
42 [a]Ex. 35:10
43 [a]Lev. 9:22, 23; Num. 6:23–26; Josh. 22:6; 2 Sam. 6:18; 1 Kin. 8:14; 2 Chr. 30:27

CHAPTER 40

1 [a]Ex. 25:1—31:18
2 [a]Ex. 12:2; 13:4 [b]Ex. 26:1, 30; 40:17
3 [a]Ex. 26:33; 40:21; Lev. 16:2; Num. 4:5 [1]*screen*
4 [a]Ex. 26:35; 40:22 [b]Ex. 25:30; 40:23 [c]Ex. 40:24, 25 [1]*set up*
5 [a]Ex. 40:26
6 [a]Ex. 39:39
7 [a]Ex. 30:18; 40:30
9 [a]Ex. 30:26; Lev. 8:10
10 [a]Ex. 30:26–30 [b]Ex. 29:36, 37
12 [a]Ex. 29:4–9; Lev. 8:1–13
13 [a]Ex. 29:5; 39:1, 41 [b][Ex. 28:41]; Lev. 8:12
15 [a]Ex. 29:9; Num. 25:13
17 [a]Ex. 40:2; Num. 7:1 [1]*erected*
20 [a]Ex. 25:16; Deut. 10:5; 1 Kin. 8:9; 2 Chr. 5:10; Heb. 9:4

poles through the rings of the ark,
and put the mercy seat on top of
the ark.
21 And he brought the ark into the
tabernacle, [a]hung up the veil of the
covering, and partitioned off the
ark of the Testimony, as the LORD
had commanded Moses.
22 [a]He put the table in the taber-
nacle of meeting, on the north
side of the tabernacle, outside the
veil;
23 [a]and he set the bread in order
upon it before the LORD, as the
LORD had commanded Moses.
24 [a]He put the lampstand in the
tabernacle of meeting, across from
the table, on the south side of the
tabernacle;
25 and [a]he lit the lamps before the
LORD, as the LORD had commanded
Moses.
26 [a]He put the gold altar in the
tabernacle of meeting in front of
the veil;
27 [a]and he burned sweet incense
on it, as the LORD had commanded
Moses.
28 [a]He hung up the screen *at* the
door of the tabernacle.
29 [a]And he put the altar of burnt
offering *before* the door of the tab-
ernacle of the tent of meeting, and
[b]offered upon it the burnt offering
and the grain offering, as the LORD
had commanded Moses.
30 [a]He set the laver between the
tabernacle of meeting and the al-
tar, and put water there for wash-
ing;
31 and Moses, Aaron, and his sons
would [a]wash their hands and their
feet *with water* from it.
32 Whenever they went into the
tabernacle of meeting, and when
they came near the altar, they
washed, [a]as the LORD had com-
manded Moses.
33 [a]And he raised up the court all
around the tabernacle and the al-
tar, and hung up the screen of the
court gate. So Moses [b]finished the
work.

The Cloud and the Glory

34 [a]Then the [b]cloud covered the
tabernacle of meeting, and the
[c]glory of the LORD filled the tab-
ernacle.
35 And Moses [a]was not able to en-
ter the tabernacle of meeting, be-
cause the cloud rested above it,
and the glory of the LORD filled the
tabernacle.
36 [a]Whenever the cloud was
taken up from above the taberna-
cle, the children of Israel would
[1]go onward in all their journeys.
37 But [a]if the cloud was not taken
up, then they did not journey till
the day that it was taken up.
38 For [a]the cloud of the LORD *was*
above the tabernacle by day, and
fire was over it by night, in the
sight of all the house of Israel,
throughout all their journeys.

21 [a]Ex. 26:33
22 [a]Ex. 26:35
23 [a]Ex. 40:4; Lev. 24:5, 6
24 [a]Ex. 26:35
25 [a]Ex. 25:37; 30:7, 8; 40:4; Lev. 24:3, 4
26 [a]Ex. 30:1, 6; 40:5
27 [a]Ex. 30:7
28 [a]Ex. 26:36; 40:5
29 [a]Ex. 40:6 [b]Ex. 29:38–42
30 [a]Ex. 30:18; 40:7
31 [a]Ex. 30:19, 20; John 13:8
32 [a]Ex. 30:19
33 [a]Ex. 27:9–18; 40:8 [b][Heb. 3:2–5]
34 [a]Ex. 29:43; Lev. 16:2; Num. 9:15; 2 Chr. 5:13; Is. 6:4 [b]1 Kin. 8:10, 11 [c]Lev. 9:6, 23
35 [a][Lev. 16:2]; 1 Kin. 8:11; 2 Chr. 5:13, 14
36 [a]Ex. 13:21, 22; Num. 9:17; Neh. 9:19 [1]*Journey*
37 [a]Num. 9:19–22
38 [a]Ex. 13:21; Num. 9:15; Ps. 78:14; Is. 4:5

The Third Book of Moses Called

Leviticus

LEVITICUS is God's guidebook for His newly redeemed people, showing them how to worship, serve, and obey a holy God. Fellowship with God through sacrifice and obedience show the awesome holiness of the God of Israel. Indeed, " 'you shall be holy, for I the Lord your God *am* holy' " (19:2).

Leviticus focuses on the worship and walk of the nation of God. In Exodus, Israel was redeemed and established as a kingdom of priests and a holy nation. Leviticus shows how God's people are to fulfill their priestly calling.

The Hebrew title is *Wayyiqra*, "And He Called." The Talmud refers to Leviticus as the "Law of the Priests," and the "Law of the Offerings." The Greek title appearing in the Septuagint is *Leuitikon*, "That Which Pertains to the Levites." From this word, the Latin Vulgate derived its name *Leviticus* which was adopted as the English title. This title is slightly misleading because the book does not deal with the Levites as a whole but more with the priests, a segment of the Levites.

The Burnt Offering

NOW the LORD [a]called to Moses,
and spoke to him [b]from the
tabernacle of meeting, say-
ing,
2 "Speak to the children of Is-
rael, and say to them: [a]'When any
one of you brings an offering to
the LORD, you shall bring your of-
fering of the livestock—of the herd
and of the flock.
3 'If his offering *is* a burnt sacri-
fice of the herd, let him offer a
male [a]without blemish; he shall of-
fer it of his own free will at the
door of the tabernacle of meeting
before the LORD.
4 [a]'Then he shall put his hand on
the head of the burnt offering, and
it will be [b]accepted on his behalf
[c]to make atonement for him.
5 'He shall kill the [a]bull before
the LORD; [b]and the priests, Aaron's
sons, shall bring the blood [c]and
sprinkle the blood all around on
the altar that *is by* the door of the
tabernacle of meeting.
6 'And he shall [a]skin the burnt
offering and cut it into its pieces.
7 'The sons of Aaron the priest
shall put [a]fire on the altar, and [b]lay
the wood in order on the fire.
8 'Then the priests, Aaron's sons,
shall lay the parts, the head, and
the fat in order on the wood that
is on the fire upon the altar;
9 'but he shall wash its entrails
and its legs with water. And the
priest shall burn all on the altar
as a burnt sacrifice, an offering
made by fire, a [a]sweet[1] aroma to
the LORD.
10 'If his offering *is* of the flocks—
of the sheep or of the goats—as a
burnt sacrifice, he shall bring a
male [a]without blemish.
11 [a]'He shall kill it on the north
side of the altar before the LORD;
and the priests, Aaron's sons, shall
sprinkle its blood all around on the
altar.
12 'And he shall cut it into its
pieces, with its head and its fat;
and the priest shall lay them in or-
der on the wood that *is* on the fire
upon the altar;
13 'but he shall wash the entrails
and the legs with water. Then the
priest shall bring *it* all and burn
it on the altar; it *is* a burnt sacri-
fice, an [a]offering made by fire, a
sweet aroma to the LORD.
14 'And if the burnt sacrifice of his
offering to the LORD *is* of birds,
then he shall bring his offering

CHAPTER 1

1 [a]Ex. 19:3; 25:22 [b]Ex. 40:34
2 [a]Lev. 22:18, 19
3 [a]Eph. 5:27
4 [a]Lev. 3:2, 8, 13; 4:15 [b][Rom. 12:1] [c]2 Chr. 29:23, 24
5 [a]Mic. 6:6 [b]2 Chr. 35:11 [c][Heb. 12:24]
6 [a]Lev. 7:8
7 [a]Mal. 1:10 [b]Gen. 22:9
9 [a]Gen. 8:21 [1]*soothing* or *pleasing aroma*
10 [a]Lev. 1:3
11 [a]Lev. 1:5
13 [a]Num. 15:4–7; 28:12–14

of [a]turtledoves or young pigeons.
15 'The priest shall bring it to the
altar, [1]wring off its head, and burn
it on the altar; its blood shall be
drained out at the side of the altar.
16 'And he shall remove its crop
with its feathers and cast it [a]beside
the altar on the east side, into the
place for ashes.
17 'Then he shall split it at its
wings, *but* [a]shall not divide *it* com-
pletely; and the priest shall burn
it on the altar, on the wood that
is on the fire. [b]It *is* a burnt sacri-
fice, an offering made by fire, a
[1]sweet aroma to the LORD.

The Grain Offering

2 'When anyone offers [a]a grain
offering to the LORD, his offer-
ing shall be *of* fine flour. And he
shall pour oil on it, and put [b]frank-
incense on it.
2 'He shall bring it to Aaron's
sons, the priests, one of whom
shall take from it his handful of
fine flour and oil with all the frank-
incense. And the priest shall burn
[a]*it as* a memorial on the altar, an
offering made by fire, a sweet
aroma to the LORD.
3 [a]'The rest of the grain offering
shall be Aaron's and his [b]sons'. [c]*It*
is most holy of the offerings to the
LORD made by fire.
4 'And if you bring as an offering
a grain offering baked in the oven,
it shall be unleavened cakes of fine
flour mixed with oil, or unleavened
wafers [a]anointed[1] with oil.
5 'But if your offering *is* a grain
offering *baked* in a [1]pan, *it shall*
be of fine flour, unleavened, mixed
with oil.
6 'You shall break it in pieces
and pour oil on it; it *is* a grain of-
fering.
7 'If your offering *is* a grain offer-
ing *baked* in a [a]covered pan, it
shall be made *of* fine flour with oil.
8 'You shall bring the grain offer-
ing that is made of these things to
the LORD. And when it is presented
to the priest, he shall bring it to
the altar.
9 'Then the priest shall take from
the grain offering [a]a memorial por-
tion, and burn *it* on the altar. *It is*
an [b]offering made by fire, a sweet
aroma to the LORD.
10 'And [a]what is left of the grain
offering *shall be* Aaron's and his
sons'. *It is* most holy of the offer-
ings to the LORD made by fire.
11 'No grain offering which you
bring to the LORD shall be made
with [a]leaven, for you shall burn no
leaven nor any honey in any offer-
ing to the LORD made by fire.
12 [a]'As for the offering of the first-
fruits, you shall offer them to the
LORD, but they shall not be burned
on the altar for a sweet aroma.
13 'And every offering of your
grain offering [a]you shall season
with salt; you shall not allow [b]the
salt of the covenant of your God
to be lacking from your grain of-
fering. [c]With all your offerings you
shall offer salt.
14 'If you offer a grain offering of
your firstfruits to the LORD, [a]you
shall offer for the grain offering of
your firstfruits green heads of
grain roasted on the fire, grain
beaten from [b]full heads.
15 'And [a]you shall put oil on it,
and lay frankincense on it. It *is* a
grain offering.
16 'Then the priest shall burn [a]the
memorial portion: *part* of its
beaten grain and *part* of its oil,
with all the frankincense, as an of-
fering made by fire to the LORD.

The Peace Offering

3 'When his offering *is* a [a]sacri-
fice of a peace offering, if he
offers *it* of the herd, whether male
or female, he shall offer it [b]without
[1]blemish before the LORD.
2 'And [a]he shall lay his hand on
the head of his offering, and kill
it *at* the door of the tabernacle of
meeting; and Aaron's sons, the
priests, shall [b]sprinkle the blood
all around on the altar.
3 'Then he shall offer from the
sacrifice of the peace offering an
offering made by fire to the LORD.
[a]The fat that covers the entrails
and all the fat that is on the en-
trails,
4 'the two kidneys and the fat
that *is* on them by the flanks, and
the fatty lobe *attached* to the liver
above the kidneys, he shall re-
move;
5 'and Aaron's sons [a]shall burn
it on the altar upon the [b]burnt sac-
rifice, which *is* on the wood that
is on the fire, *as* an [c]offering made

14 [a]Lev. 5:7, 11; 12:8
15 [1]Lit. *nip* or *chop off*
16 [a]Lev. 6:10
17 [a]Gen. 15:10 [b]Lev. 1:9, 13 [1]*soothing* or *pleasing aroma*

CHAPTER 2

1 [a]Num. 15:4 [b]Lev. 5:11
2 [a]Lev. 2:9; 5:12; 6:15; 24:7
3 [a]Lev. 7:9 [b]Lev. 6:6; 10:12, 13 [c]Num. 18:9
4 [a]Ex. 29:2 [1]*spread*
5 [1]*flat plate* or *griddle*
7 [a]Lev. 7:9
9 [a]Lev. 2:2, 16; 5:12; 6:15 [b]Ex. 29:18
10 [a]Lev. 2:3; 6:16
11 [a]Lev. 6:16, 17
12 [a]Lev. 23:10, 11, 17, 18
13 [a][Col. 4:6] [b]Num. 18:19 [c]Ezek. 43:24
14 [a]Lev. 23:10, 14 [b]2 Kin. 4:42
15 [a]Lev. 2:1
16 [a]Lev. 2:2

CHAPTER 3

1 [a]Lev. 7:11, 29 [b]Lev. 1:3; 22:20–24 [1]*imperfection* or *defect*
2 [a]Lev. 1:4, 5; 16:21 [b]Lev. 1:5
3 [a]Lev. 1:8; 3:16; 4:8, 9
5 [a]Ex. 29:13 [b]2 Chr. 35:14 [c]Num. 28:3–10

by fire, a [d]sweet aroma to the
LORD.
6 'If his offering as a sacrifice of
a peace offering to the LORD *is* of
the flock, *whether* male or female,
[a]he shall offer it without blemish.
7 'If he offers a [a]lamb as his of-
fering, then he shall [b]offer it [c]be-
fore the LORD.
8 'And he shall lay his hand on
the head of his offering, and kill
it before the tabernacle of meeting;
and Aaron's sons shall sprinkle its
blood all around on the altar.
9 'Then he shall offer from the
sacrifice of the peace offering, as
an offering made by fire to the
LORD, its fat *and* the whole fat tail
which he shall remove close to the
backbone. And the fat that covers
the entrails and all the fat that *is*
on the entrails,
10 'the two kidneys and the fat
that *is* on them by the flanks, and
the fatty lobe *attached* to the liver
above the kidneys, he shall re-
move;
11 'and the priest shall burn *them*
on the altar *as* [a]food, an offering
made by fire to the LORD.
12 'And if his [a]offering *is* a goat,
then [b]he shall offer it before the
LORD.
13 'He shall lay his hand on its
head and kill it before the taberna-
cle of meeting; and the sons of
Aaron shall sprinkle its blood all
around on the altar.
14 'Then he shall offer from it his
offering, as an offering made by
fire to the LORD. The fat that covers
the entrails and all the fat that *is*
on the entrails,
15 'the two kidneys and the fat
that *is* on them by the flanks, and
the fatty lobe *attached* to the liver
above the kidneys, he shall re-
move;
16 'and the priest shall burn them
on the altar *as* food, an offering
made by fire for a sweet aroma;
[a]all the fat *is* the LORD's.
17 '*This shall be* a [a]perpetual[1] stat-
ute throughout your generations in
all your dwellings: you shall eat
neither fat nor [b]blood.' "

The Sin Offering

4 Now the LORD spoke to Moses,
saying,
2 "Speak to the children of Is-
rael, saying: [a]'If a person sins
[1]unintentionally against any of the
commandments of the LORD *in
anything* which ought not to be
done, and does any of them,
3 [a]'if the anointed priest sins,
bringing guilt on the people, then
let him offer to the LORD for his
sin which he has sinned [b]a young
bull without blemish as a [c]sin of-
fering.
4 'He shall bring the bull [a]to the
door of the tabernacle of meeting
before the LORD, lay his hand on
the bull's head, and kill the bull
before the LORD.
5 'Then the anointed priest [a]shall
take some of the bull's blood and
bring it to the tabernacle of meet-
ing.
6 'The priest shall dip his finger
in the blood and sprinkle some of
the blood seven times before the
LORD, in front of the [a]veil of the
sanctuary.
7 'And the priest shall [a]put some
of the blood on the horns of the
altar of sweet incense before the
LORD, which is in the tabernacle
of meeting; and he shall pour [b]the
remaining blood of the bull at the
base of the altar of the burnt offer-
ing, which is at the door of the tab-
ernacle of meeting.
8 'He shall take from it all the fat
of the bull as the sin offering. The
fat that covers the entrails and all
the fat which *is* on the entrails,
9 'the two kidneys and the fat
that *is* on them by the flanks, and
the fatty lobe *attached* to the liver
above the kidneys, he shall re-
move,
10 [a]'as it was taken from the bull
of the sacrifice of the peace of-
fering; and the priest shall burn
them on the altar of the burnt of-
fering.
11 [a]'But the bull's hide and all its
flesh, with its head and legs, its en-
trails and offal—
12 'the whole bull he shall carry
outside the camp to a clean place,
[a]where the ashes are poured out,
and [b]burn it on wood with fire;
where the ashes are poured out it
shall be burned.
13 'Now [a]if the whole congrega-
tion of Israel sins unintentionally,
[b]and the thing is hidden from the
eyes of the assembly, and they

5 [d]Num. 15:8–10
6 [a]Lev. 3:1; 22:20–24
7 [a]Num. 15:4, 5 [b]1 Kin. 8:62 [c]Lev. 17:8, 9
11 [a]Lev. 21:6, 8, 17, 21, 22; 22:25; Num. 28:2; [Ezek. 44:7; Mal. 1:7, 12]
12 [a]Num. 15:6–11 [b]Lev. 3:1, 7
16 [a]Lev. 7:23–25; 1 Sam. 2:15; 2 Chr. 7:7
17 [a]Lev. 6:18; 7:36; 17:7; 23:14 [b]Gen. 9:4; Lev. 7:23, 26; 17:10, 14; 1 Sam. 14:33 [1]*everlasting* or *never-ending*

CHAPTER 4

2 [a]Lev. 5:15–18; Num. 15:22–30; 1 Sam. 14:27; Acts 3:17 [1]*through error*
3 [a]Ex. 40:15; Lev. 8:12 [b]Lev. 3:1; 9:2 [c]Lev. 9:7
4 [a]Lev. 1:3, 4; 4:15; Num. 8:12
5 [a]Lev. 16:14; Num. 19:4
6 [a]Ex. 40:21, 26
7 [a]Lev. 4:18, 25, 30, 34; 8:15; 9:9; 16:18 [b]Ex. 40:5, 6; Lev. 5:9
10 [a]Lev. 3:3–5
11 [a]Ex. 29:14; Lev. 9:11; Num. 19:5
12 [a]Lev. 4:21; 6:10, 11; 16:27 [b][Heb. 13:11, 12]
13 [a]Num. 15:24–26; Josh. 7:11 [b]Lev. 5:2–4, 17

have done *something against* any of the commandments of the LORD *in anything* which should not be done, and are guilty;

14 'when the sin which they have committed becomes known, then the assembly shall offer a young bull for the sin, and bring it before the tabernacle of meeting.

15 'And the elders of the congregation [a]shall lay their hands on the head of the bull before the LORD. Then the bull shall be killed before the LORD.

16 [a]'The anointed priest shall bring some of the bull's blood to the tabernacle of meeting.

17 'Then the priest shall dip his finger in the blood and sprinkle *it* seven times before the LORD, in front of the veil.

18 'And he shall put *some* of the blood on the horns of the altar which *is* before the LORD, which *is* in the tabernacle of meeting; and he shall pour the remaining blood at the base of the altar of burnt offering, which is at the door of the tabernacle of meeting.

19 'He shall take all the fat from it and burn *it* on the altar.

20 'And he shall do [a]with the bull as he did with the bull as a sin offering; thus he shall do with it. [b]So the priest shall make [1]atonement for them, and it shall be forgiven them.

21 'Then he shall carry the bull outside the camp, and burn it as he burned the first bull. It *is* a sin offering for the assembly.

22 'When a [1]ruler has sinned, and [a]done *something* unintentionally *against* any of the commandments of the LORD his God *in anything* which should not be done, and is guilty,

23 'or [a]if his sin which he has committed [1]comes to his knowledge, he shall bring as his offering a kid of the goats, a male without blemish.

24 'And [a]he shall lay his hand on the head of the goat, and kill it at the place where they kill the burnt offering before the LORD. It *is* a sin offering.

25 [a]'The priest shall take some of the blood of the sin offering with his finger, put *it* on the horns of the altar of burnt offering, and pour its blood at the base of the altar of burnt offering.

26 'And he shall burn all its fat on the altar, like [a]the fat of the sacrifice of the peace offering. [b]So the priest shall make [1]atonement for him concerning his sin, and it shall be forgiven him.

27 [a]'If [1]anyone of the [2]common people sins unintentionally by doing *something against* any of the commandments of the LORD *in anything* which ought not to be done, and is guilty,

28 'or [a]if his sin which he has committed comes to his knowledge, then he shall bring as his offering a kid of the goats, a female without blemish, for his sin which he has committed.

29 [a]'And he shall lay his hand on the head of the sin offering, and kill the sin offering at the place of the burnt offering.

30 'Then the priest shall take *some* of its blood with his finger, put *it* on the horns of the altar of burnt offering, and pour all *the remaining* blood at the base of the altar.

31 [a]'He shall remove all its fat, [b]as fat is removed from the sacrifice of the peace offering; and the priest shall burn it on the altar for a [c]sweet aroma to the LORD. [d]So the priest shall make atonement for him, and it shall be forgiven him.

32 'If he brings a lamb as his sin offering, [a]he shall bring a female without blemish.

33 'Then he shall [a]lay his hand on the head of the sin offering, and kill it as a sin offering at the place where they kill the burnt offering.

34 'The priest shall take *some* of the blood of the sin offering with his finger, put *it* on the horns of the altar of burnt offering, and pour all *the remaining* blood at the base of the altar.

35 'He shall remove all its fat, as the fat of the lamb is removed from the sacrifice of the peace offering. Then the priest shall burn it on the altar, [a]according to the offerings made by fire to the LORD. [b]So the priest shall make atonement for his sin that he has committed, and it shall be forgiven him.

15 [a]Lev. 1:3, 4
16 [a]Lev. 4:5; [Heb. 9:12–14]
20 [a]Lev. 4:3 [b]Lev. 1:4; Num. 15:25 [1]Lit. *covering*
22 [a]Lev. 4:2, 13, 27 [1]*leader*
23 [a]Lev. 4:14; 5:4 [1]*is made known to him*
24 [a]Lev. 4:4; [Is. 53:6]
25 [a]Lev. 4:7, 18, 30, 34
26 [a]Lev. 3:3–5 [b]Lev. 4:20; Num. 15:28 [1]Lit. *covering*
27 [a]Lev. 4:2; Num. 15:27 [1]Lit. *any soul* [2]Lit. *people of the land*
28 [a]Lev. 4:23
29 [a]Lev. 1:4; 4:4, 24
31 [a]Lev. 3:14 [b]Lev. 3:3, 4 [c]Gen. 8:21; Ex. 29:18; Lev. 1:9, 13; 2:2, 9, 12 [d]Lev. 4:26
32 [a]Lev. 4:28
33 [a]Lev. 1:4; Num. 8:12
35 [a]Lev. 3:5 [b]Lev. 4:26, 31

The Trespass Offering

5 'If a person sins in [a]hearing the
utterance of an oath, and *is* a
witness, whether he has seen or
known *of the matter*—if he does
not tell *it*, he [b]bears [1]guilt.
2 'Or [a]if a person touches any un-
clean thing, whether *it is* the car-
cass of an unclean beast, or the
carcass of unclean livestock, or the
carcass of unclean creeping
things, and he is unaware of it, he
also shall be unclean and [b]guilty.
3 'Or if he touches [a]human un-
cleanness—whatever uncleanness
with which a man may be defiled,
and he is unaware of it—when
he realizes *it*, then he shall be
guilty.
4 'Or if a person [1]swears, speak-
ing thoughtlessly with *his* lips [a]to
do evil or [b]to do good, whatever
it is that a man may pronounce by
an oath, and he is unaware of it—
when he realizes *it*, then he shall
be guilty in any of these *matters*.
5 'And it shall be, when he is
guilty in any of these *matters*, that
he shall [a]confess that he has
sinned in that *thing*;
6 'and he shall bring his trespass
offering to the LORD for his sin
which he has committed, a female
from the flock, a lamb or a kid of
the goats as a sin offering. So the
priest shall make atonement for
him concerning his sin.
7 [a]'If he is not able to bring a
lamb, then he shall bring to the
LORD, for his trespass which he has
committed, two [b]turtledoves or
two young pigeons: one as a sin
offering and the other as a burnt
offering.
8 'And he shall bring them to the
priest, who shall offer *that* which
is for the sin offering first, and
[a]wring off its head from its neck,
but shall not divide *it* [1]completely.
9 'Then he shall sprinkle *some* of
the blood of the sin offering on the
side of the altar, and the [a]rest of
the blood shall be drained out at
the base of the altar. It *is* a sin of-
fering.
10 'And he shall offer the second
as a burnt offering according to
the [a]prescribed manner. So [b]the
priest shall make atonement on his
behalf for his sin which he has
committed, and it shall be forgiven
him.
11 'But if he is [a]not able to bring
two turtledoves or two young pi-
geons, then he who sinned shall
bring for his offering one-tenth of
an ephah of fine flour as a sin of-
fering. [b]He shall put no oil on it,
nor shall he put frankincense on
it, for it *is* a sin offering.
12 'Then he shall bring it to the
priest, and the priest shall take his
handful of it [a]as a memorial por-
tion, and burn *it* on the altar [b]ac-
cording to the offerings made by
fire to the LORD. It *is* a sin offering.
13 [a]'The priest shall make atone-
ment for him, [1]for his sin that he
has committed in any of these mat-
ters; and it shall be forgiven him.
[b]*The rest* shall be the priest's as a
grain offering.' "

Offerings with Restitution

14 Then the LORD spoke to Moses,
saying:
15 [a]"If a person commits a tres-
pass, and sins unintentionally in
regard to the holy things of the
LORD, then [b]he shall bring to the
LORD as his trespass offering a ram
without blemish from the flocks,
with your valuation in shekels of
silver according to [c]the shekel of
the sanctuary, as a trespass of-
fering.
16 "And he shall make restitution
for the harm that he has done in
regard to the holy thing, [a]and shall
add one-fifth to it and give it to the
priest. [b]So the priest shall make
atonement for him with the ram
of the trespass offering, and it shall
be forgiven him.
17 "If a person sins, and commits
any of these things which are for-
bidden to be done by the com-
mandments of the LORD, [a]though
he does not know *it*, yet he is
[b]guilty and shall bear his [1]iniquity.
18 [a]"And he shall bring to the
priest a ram without blemish from
the flock, with your valuation, as
a trespass offering. So the priest
shall make atonement for him re-
garding his ignorance in which he
erred and did not know *it*, and it
shall be forgiven him.
19 "It is a trespass offering; [a]he
has certainly trespassed against
the LORD."

CHAPTER 5

1 [a]Prov. 29:24; [Jer. 23:10] [b]Lev. 5:17; 7:18; 17:16; 19:8; 20:17; Num. 9:13 [1]*his iniquity*
2 [a]Lev. 11:24, 28, 31, 39; Num. 19:11–16; Deut. 14:8 [b]Lev. 5:17
3 [a]Lev. 5:12, 13, 15
4 [a]1 Sam. 25:22; Acts 23:12 [b][Matt. 5:33–37]; Mark 6:23; [James 5:12] [1]*vows*
5 [a]Lev. 16:21; 26:40; Num. 5:7; Ezra 10:11, 12; Ps. 32:5; Prov. 28:13
7 [a]Lev. 12:6, 8; 14:21 [b]Lev. 1:14
8 [a]Lev. 1:15–17 [1]Lit. *apart*
9 [a]Lev. 4:7, 18, 30, 34
10 [a]Lev. 1:14–17 [b]Lev. 4:20, 26; 5:13, 16
11 [a]Lev. 14:21–32 [b]Lev. 2:1, 2; 6:15; Num. 5:15
12 [a]Lev. 2:2 [b]Lev. 4:35
13 [a]Lev. 4:26 [b]Lev. 2:3; 6:17, 26 [1]*concerning his sin*
15 [a]Lev. 4:2; 22:14; Num. 5:5–8 [b]Ezra 10:19 [c]Ex. 30:13; Lev. 27:25
16 [a]Lev. 6:5; 22:14; 27:13, 15, 27, 31; Num. 5:7 [b]Lev. 4:26
17 [a]Lev. 4:2, 13, 22, 27 [b]Lev. 5:1, 2 [1]*punishment*
18 [a]Lev. 5:15
19 [a]Ezra 10:2

6 And the LORD spoke to Moses, saying:

2 "If a person sins and [a]commits a trespass against the LORD by [b]lying[1] to his neighbor about [c]what was delivered to him for safekeeping, or about [2]a pledge, or about a robbery, or if he has [d]extorted from his neighbor,

3 "or if he [a]has found what was lost and lies concerning it, and [b]swears falsely—in any one of these things that a man may do in which he sins:

4 "then it shall be, because he has sinned and is guilty, that he shall [1]restore [a]what he has stolen, or the thing which he has extorted, or what was delivered to him for safekeeping, or the lost thing which he found,

5 "or all that about which he has sworn falsely. He shall [a]restore its full value, add one-fifth more to it, *and* give it to whomever it belongs, on the day of his trespass offering.

6 "And he shall bring his trespass offering to the LORD, [a]a ram without blemish from the flock, with your [1]valuation, as a trespass offering, to the priest.

7 [a]"So the priest shall make atonement for him before the LORD, and he shall be forgiven for any one of these things that he may have done in which he trespasses."

The Law of the Burnt Offering

8 Then the LORD spoke to Moses, saying,

9 "Command Aaron and his sons, saying, 'This *is* the [a]law of the burnt offering: The burnt offering *shall be* on the hearth upon the altar all night until morning, and the fire of the altar shall be kept burning on it.

10 [a]'And the priest shall put on his linen garment, and his linen trousers he shall put on his body, and take up the ashes of the burnt offering which the fire has consumed on the altar, and he shall put them [b]beside the altar.

11 'Then [a]he shall take off his garments, put on other garments, and carry the ashes outside the camp [b]to a clean place.

12 'And the fire on the altar shall be kept burning on it; it shall not be put out. And the priest shall burn wood on it every morning, and lay the burnt offering in order on it; and he shall burn on it [a]the fat of the peace offerings.

13 'A fire shall always be burning on the [a]altar; it shall never go out.

The Law of the Grain Offering

14 'This *is* the law of the grain offering: The sons of Aaron shall offer it on the altar before the LORD.

15 'He shall take from it his handful of the fine flour of the grain offering, with its oil, and all the frankincense which *is* on the grain offering, and shall burn *it* on the altar *for* a sweet aroma, as a memorial to the LORD.

16 'And the remainder of it Aaron and his sons shall eat; with unleavened bread it shall be eaten in a holy place; in the court of the tabernacle of meeting they shall eat it.

17 'It shall not be baked with leaven. I have given it *as* their [1]portion of My offerings made by fire; it *is* most holy, like the sin offering and the [a]trespass offering.

18 [a]'All the males among the children of Aaron may eat it. [b]*It shall be* a statute forever in your generations concerning the offerings made by fire to the LORD. [c]Everyone who touches them must be holy.' "

19 And the LORD spoke to Moses, saying,

20 [a]"This *is* the offering of Aaron and his sons, which they shall offer to the LORD, *beginning* on the day when he is anointed: one-tenth of an [b]ephah of fine flour as a daily grain offering, half of it in the morning and half of it at night.

21 "It shall be made in a [a]pan with oil. *When it is* mixed, you shall bring it in. The baked pieces of the grain offering you shall offer *for* a [1]sweet aroma to the LORD.

22 "The priest from among his sons, [a]who is anointed in his place, shall offer it. *It is* a statute forever to the LORD. [b]It shall be [1]wholly burned.

23 "For every grain offering for the priest shall be wholly burned. It shall not be eaten."

CHAPTER 6

2 [a]Num. 5:6 [b]Lev. 19:11; Acts 5:4; Col. 3:9 [c]Ex. 22:7, 10 [d]Prov. 24:28 [1]*deceiving his associate* [2]*an entrusted security*

3 [a]Ex. 23:4; Deut. 22:1–4 [b]Ex. 22:11; Lev. 19:12; Jer. 7:9; Zech. 5:4

4 [a]Lev. 24:18, 21 [1]*return*

5 [a]Lev. 5:16; Num. 5:7, 8; 2 Sam. 12:6

6 [a]Lev. 1:3; 5:15 [1]*appraisal*

7 [a]Lev. 4:26

9 [a]Ex. 29:38–42; Num. 28:3–10

10 [a]Ex. 28:39–43; Lev. 16:4; Ezek. 44:17, 18 [b]Lev. 1:16

11 [a]Ezek. 44:19 [b]Lev. 4:12

12 [a]Lev. 3:3, 5, 9, 14

13 [a]Lev. 1:7

17 [a]Lev. 7:7 [1]*share*

18 [a]Lev. 6:29; 7:6; Num. 18:10; 1 Cor. 9:13 [b]Lev. 3:17 [c]Ex. 29:37; Lev. 22:3–7; Num. 4:15; Hag. 2:11–13

20 [a]Ex. 29:2 [b]Ex. 16:36

21 [a]Lev. 2:5; 7:9 [1]*pleasing*

22 [a]Lev. 4:3 [b]Ex. 29:25 [1]*completely*

The Law of the Sin Offering

24 Also the LORD spoke to Moses,
saying,
25 "Speak to Aaron and to his
sons, saying, 'This *is* the law of the
sin offering: [a]In the place where
the burnt offering is killed, the sin
offering shall be killed before the
LORD. It *is* most holy.
26 [a]'The priest who offers it for sin
shall eat it. In a holy place it shall
be eaten, in the court of the taber-
nacle of meeting.
27 [a]'Everyone who touches its
flesh [1]must be holy. And when
its blood is sprinkled on any gar-
ment, you shall wash that on
which it was sprinkled, in a holy
place.
28 'But the earthen vessel in
which it is boiled [a]shall be broken.
And if it is boiled in a bronze pot,
it shall be both scoured and rinsed
in water.
29 'All the males among the
priests may eat it. It *is* most holy.
30 [a]'But no sin offering from
which *any* of the blood is brought
into the tabernacle of meeting, to
make atonement in [1]the holy
[b]*place*, shall be [c]eaten. It shall be
[d]burned in the fire.

The Law of the Trespass Offering

7 'Likewise [a]this *is* the law of the
trespass offering (it *is* most
holy):
2 'In the place where they kill the
burnt offering they shall kill the
trespass offering. And its blood he
shall sprinkle all around on the al-
tar.
3 'And he shall offer from it all
its fat. The fat tail and the fat that
covers the entrails,
4 'the two kidneys and the fat
that *is* on them by the flanks, and
the fatty lobe *attached* to the liver
above the kidneys, he shall re-
move;
5 'and the priest shall burn them
on the altar *as* an offering made
by fire to the LORD. It *is* a trespass
offering.
6 [a]'Every male among the priests
may eat it. It shall be eaten in a
holy place. [b]It *is* most holy.
7 [a]'The trespass offering *is* like
the sin offering; *there is* one law
for them both: the priest who

25 [a]Lev. 1:1, 3, 5, 11

26 [a][Lev. 10:17, 18]; Num. 18:9, 10; [Ezek. 44:28, 29]

27 [a]Ex. 29:37; Num. 4:15; Hag. 2:11–13 [1]Lit. *shall*

28 [a]Lev. 11:33; 15:12

30 [a]Lev. 4:7, 11, 12, 18, 21; 10:18; 16:27; [Heb. 13:11, 12] [b]Ex. 26:33 [c]Lev. 6:16, 23, 26 [d]Lev. 16:27 [1]The Most Holy Place when capitalized

CHAPTER 7

1 [a]Lev. 5:14—6:7

6 [a]Lev. 6:16–18, 29; Num. 18:9 [b]Lev. 2:3

7 [a]Lev. 6:24–30; 14:13

9 [a]Lev. 2:3, 10; Num. 18:9; Ezek. 44:29 [1]*on a griddle*

11 [a]Lev. 3:1; 22:18, 21; Ezek. 45:15

12 [a]Lev. 2:4; Num. 6:15

13 [a]Lev. 2:12; 23:17, 18; Amos 4:5

14 [a]Num. 18:8, 11, 19

15 [a]Lev. 22:29, 30

16 [a]Lev. 19:5–8

18 [a]Num. 18:27 [b]Lev. 11:10, 11, 41; 19:7; [Prov. 15:8] [1]*his iniquity*

makes atonement with it shall
have *it*.
8 'And the priest who offers any-
one's burnt offering, that priest
shall have for himself the skin of
the burnt offering which he has of-
fered.
9 'Also [a]every grain offering that
is baked in the oven and all that
is prepared in the covered pan, or
[1]in a pan, shall be the priest's who
offers it.
10 'Every grain offering, *whether*
mixed with oil or dry, shall belong
to all the sons of Aaron, to one *as*
much as the other.

The Law of Peace Offerings

11 [a]'This *is* the law of the sacrifice
of peace offerings which he shall
offer to the LORD:
12 'If he offers it for a thanksgiv-
ing, then he shall offer, with the
sacrifice of thanksgiving, unleav-
ened cakes mixed with oil, unleav-
ened wafers [a]anointed with oil, or
cakes of blended flour mixed with
oil.
13 'Besides the cakes, *as* his offer-
ing he shall offer [a]leavened bread
with the sacrifice of thanksgiving
of his peace offering.
14 'And from it he shall offer one
cake from each offering *as* a heave
offering to the LORD. [a]It shall be-
long to the priest who sprinkles
the blood of the peace offering.
15 [a]'The flesh of the sacrifice of
his peace offering for thanksgiving
shall be eaten the same day it is
offered. He shall not leave any of
it until morning.
16 'But [a]if the sacrifice of his offer-
ing *is* a vow or a voluntary offer-
ing, it shall be eaten the same day
that he offers his sacrifice; but on
the next day the remainder of it
also may be eaten;
17 'the remainder of the flesh of
the sacrifice on the third day must
be burned with fire.
18 'And if *any* of the flesh of the
sacrifice of his peace offering is
eaten at all on the third day, it shall
not be accepted, nor shall it be
[a]imputed to him; it shall be an
[b]abomination *to* him who offers it,
and the person who eats of it shall
bear [1]guilt.
19 'The flesh that touches any un-
clean thing shall not be eaten. It

shall be burned with fire. And as for the *clean* flesh, all who are [1]clean may eat of it.
20 'But the person who eats the flesh of the sacrifice of the peace offering that *belongs* to the [a]LORD, [b]while he is unclean, that person [c]shall be cut off from his people.
21 'Moreover the person who touches any unclean thing, *such as* [a]human uncleanness, *an* [b]unclean animal, or any [c]abominable[1] unclean thing, and who eats the flesh of the sacrifice of the peace offering that *belongs* to the LORD, that person [d]shall be cut off from his people.' "

Fat and Blood May Not Be Eaten

22 And the LORD spoke to Moses, saying,
23 "Speak to the children of Israel, saying: [a]'You shall not eat any fat, of ox or sheep or goat.
24 'And the fat of an animal that dies *naturally*, and the fat of what is torn by wild beasts, may be used in any other way; but you shall by no means eat it.
25 'For whoever eats the fat of the animal of which men offer an offering made by fire to the LORD, the person who eats *it* shall be cut off from his people.
26 [a]'Moreover you shall not eat any blood in any of your dwellings, *whether* of bird or beast.
27 'Whoever eats any blood, that person shall be cut off from his people.' "

The Portion of Aaron and His Sons

28 Then the LORD spoke to Moses, saying,
29 "Speak to the children of Israel, saying: [a]'He who offers the sacrifice of his peace offering to the LORD shall bring his offering to the LORD from the sacrifice of his peace offering.
30 [a]'His own hands shall bring the offerings made by fire to the LORD. The fat with the breast he shall bring, that the [b]breast may be waved *as* a wave offering before the LORD.
31 [a]'And the priest shall burn the fat on the altar, but the [b]breast shall be Aaron's and his sons'.
32 [a]'Also the right thigh you shall give to the priest *as* a heave offering from the sacrifices of your peace offerings.
33 'He among the sons of Aaron, who offers the blood of the peace offering and the fat, shall have the right thigh for *his* part.
34 'For [a]the breast of the wave offering and the thigh of the heave offering I have taken from the children of Israel, from the sacrifices of their peace offerings, and I have given them to Aaron the priest and to his sons from the children of Israel by a statute forever.' "
35 This *is* the consecrated portion for Aaron and his sons, from the offerings made by fire to the LORD, on the day when *Moses* presented them to [1]minister to the LORD as priests.
36 The LORD commanded this to be given to them by the children of Israel, [a]on the day that He anointed them, *by* a statute forever throughout their generations.
37 This *is* the law [a]of the burnt offering, [b]the grain offering, [c]the sin offering, [d]the trespass offering, [e]the consecrations, and [f]the sacrifice of the peace offering,
38 which the LORD commanded Moses on Mount Sinai, on the day when He commanded the children of Israel [a]to offer their offerings to the LORD in the Wilderness of Sinai.

Aaron and His Sons Consecrated

8 And the LORD spoke to Moses, saying:
2 [a]"Take Aaron and his sons with him, and [b]the garments, [c]the anointing oil, a [d]bull as the sin offering, two [e]rams, and a basket of unleavened bread;
3 "and gather all the congregation together at the door of the tabernacle of meeting."
4 So Moses did as the LORD commanded him. And the congregation was gathered together at the door of the tabernacle of meeting.
5 And Moses said to the congregation, "This *is* what the LORD commanded to be done."
6 Then Moses brought Aaron and his sons and [a]washed them with water.
7 And he [a]put the tunic on him, girded him with the sash, clothed him with the robe, and put the

19 [1]*pure*
20 [a][Heb. 2:17] [b]Lev. 5:3; 15:3; 22:3–7; Num. 19:13; [1 Cor. 11:28] [c]Gen. 17:14; Ex. 31:14
21 [a]Lev. 5:2, 3, 5 [b]Lev. 11:24, 28 [c]Ezek. 4:14 [d]Lev. 7:20 [1]So with MT, LXX, Vg.; Sam., Syr., Tg. *swarming thing* (cf. 5:2)
23 [a]Lev. 3:17; 17:10–15; Deut. 14:21; Ezek. 4:14; 44:31
26 [a]Gen. 9:4; Lev. 3:17; 17:10–16; 19:26; Deut. 12:23; 1 Sam. 14:33; Ezek. 33:25; [John 6:53]; Acts 15:20, 29
29 [a]Lev. 3:1; 22:21; Ezek. 45:15
30 [a]Lev. 3:3, 4, 9, 14 [b]Ex. 29:24, 27; Lev. 8:27; 9:21; Num. 6:20
31 [a]Lev. 3:5, 11, 16 [b]Num. 18:11; Deut. 18:3
32 [a]Ex. 29:27; Lev. 7:34; 9:21; Num. 6:20
34 [a]Ex. 29:28; Lev. 10:14, 15; Num. 18:18, 19; Deut. 18:3
35 [1]*serve*
36 [a]Ex. 40:13–15; Lev. 8:12, 30
37 [a]Lev. 6:9 [b]Lev. 6:14 [c]Lev. 6:25 [d]Lev. 7:1 [e]Ex. 29:1; Lev. 6:20 [f]Lev. 7:11
38 [a]Lev. 1:1, 2; Deut. 4:5

CHAPTER 8

2 [a]Ex. 29:1–3 [b]Ex. 28:2, 4 [c]Ex. 30:24, 25 [d]Ex. 29:10 [e]Ex. 29:15, 19
6 [a]Ex. 30:20; Heb. 10:22
7 [a]Ex. 39:1–31

ephod on him; and he girded him
with the intricately woven band of
the ephod, and with it tied *the
ephod* on him.
8 Then he put the breastplate on
him, and he [a]put the [1]Urim and the
Thummim in the breastplate.
9 [a]And he put the turban on his
head. Also on the turban, on its
front, he put the golden plate, the
holy crown, as the LORD had com-
manded Moses.
10 [a]Also Moses took the anointing
oil, and anointed the tabernacle
and all that *was* in it, and conse-
crated them.
11 He sprinkled some of it on the
altar seven times, anointed the al-
tar and all its utensils, and the
laver and its base, to [1]consecrate
them.
12 And he [a]poured some of the
anointing oil on Aaron's head and
anointed him, to consecrate him.
13 [a]Then Moses brought Aaron's
sons and put tunics on them,
girded them with sashes, and put
[1]hats on them, as the LORD had
commanded Moses.
14 [a]And he brought the bull for
the sin offering. Then Aaron and
his sons [b]laid their hands on the
head of the bull for the sin of-
fering,
15 and Moses killed *it*. [a]Then he
took the blood, and put *some* on
the horns of the altar all around
with his finger, and purified the al-
tar. And he poured the blood at the
base of the altar, and consecrated
it, to make [1]atonement for it.
16 [a]Then he took all the fat that
was on the entrails, the fatty lobe
attached to the liver, and the two
kidneys with their fat, and Moses
burned *them* on the altar.
17 But the bull, its hide, its flesh,
and its offal, he burned with fire
outside the camp, as the LORD [a]had
commanded Moses.
18 [a]Then he brought the ram as
the burnt offering. And Aaron and
his sons laid their hands on the
head of the ram,
19 and Moses killed *it*. Then he
sprinkled the blood all around on
the altar.
20 And he cut the ram into pieces;
and Moses [a]burned the head, the
pieces, and the fat.
21 Then he washed the entrails
and the legs in water. And Moses
burned the whole ram on the altar.
It *was* a burnt sacrifice for a [1]sweet
aroma, an offering made by fire to
the LORD, [a]as the LORD had com-
manded Moses.
22 And [a]he brought the second
ram, the ram of consecration.
Then Aaron and his sons laid their
hands on the head of the ram,
23 and Moses killed *it*. Also he
took *some* of [a]its blood and put it
on the tip of Aaron's right ear, on
the thumb of his right hand, and
on the big toe of his right foot.
24 Then he brought Aaron's sons.
And Moses put *some* of the [a]blood
on the tips of their right ears, on
the thumbs of their right hands,
and on the big toes of their right
feet. And Moses sprinkled the
blood all around on the altar.
25 [a]Then he took the fat and the
fat tail, all the fat that *was* on the
entrails, the fatty lobe *attached to*
the liver, the two kidneys and their
fat, and the right thigh;
26 [a]and from the basket of unleav-
ened bread that was before the
LORD he took one unleavened
cake, a cake of bread *anointed
with* oil, and one wafer, and put
them on the fat and on the right
thigh;
27 and he put all *these* [a]in Aaron's
hands and in his sons' hands, and
waved them *as* a wave offering be-
fore the LORD.
28 [a]Then Moses took them from
their hands and burned *them* on
the altar, on the burnt offering.
They *were* consecration offerings
for a sweet aroma. That *was* an
offering made by fire to the LORD.
29 And [a]Moses took the [b]breast
and waved it *as* a wave offering
before the LORD. It was Moses'
[c]part of the ram of consecration,
as the LORD had commanded Mo-
ses.
30 Then [a]Moses took some of the
anointing oil and some of the
blood which *was* on the altar, and
sprinkled *it* on Aaron, on his gar-
ments, on his sons, and on the gar-
ments of his sons with him; and
he consecrated Aaron, his gar-
ments, his sons, and the garments
of his sons with him.
31 And Moses said to Aaron and
his sons, [a]"Boil the flesh *at* the

8 [a]Ex. 28:30; Num. 27:21; Deut. 33:8; 1 Sam. 28:6; Ezra 2:63; Neh. 7:65 [1]Lit. *Lights and the Perfections*, Ex. 28:30
9 [a]Ex. 28:36, 37; 29:6
10 [a]Ex. 30:26–29; 40:10, 11; Lev. 8:2
11 [1]*set them apart* for the LORD
12 [a]Ex. 29:7; 30:30; Lev. 21:10, 12; Ps. 133:2
13 [a]Ex. 29:8, 9 [1]*headpieces*
14 [a]Ex. 29:10; Ps. 66:15; Ezek. 43:19 [b]Lev. 4:4
15 [a]Ex. 29:12, 36; Lev. 4:7; Ezek. 43:20, 26; [Heb. 9:22] [1]Lit. *covering*
16 [a]Ex. 29:13; Lev. 4:8
17 [a]Ex. 29:14; Lev. 4:11, 12
18 [a]Ex. 29:15
20 [a]Lev. 1:8
21 [a]Ex. 29:18 [1]*pleasing*
22 [a]Ex. 29:19, 31; Lev. 8:2
23 [a]Ex. 29:20, 21; Lev. 14:14
24 [a][Heb. 9:13, 14, 18–23]
25 [a]Ex. 29:22
26 [a]Ex. 29:23
27 [a]Ex. 29:24; Lev. 7:30, 34
28 [a]Ex. 29:25
29 [a]Ps. 99:6 [b]Ex. 29:27 [c]Ex. 29:26
30 [a]Ex. 29:21; 30:30; Num. 3:3
31 [a]Ex. 29:31, 32

door of the tabernacle of meeting,
and eat it there with the bread that
is in the basket of consecration of-
ferings, as I commanded, saying,
'Aaron and his sons shall eat it.'
32 [a]"What remains of the flesh
and of the bread you shall burn
with fire.
33 "And you shall not go outside
the door of the tabernacle of meet-
ing *for* seven days, until the days
of your consecration are ended.
For [a]seven days he shall conse-
crate you.
34 [a]"As he has done this day, *so*
the LORD has commanded to do,
to make atonement for you.
35 "Therefore you shall stay *at*
the door of the tabernacle of meet-
ing day and night for seven days,
and [a]keep the [1]charge of the LORD,
so that you may not die; for so I
have been commanded."
36 So Aaron and his sons did all
the things that the LORD had com-
manded by the hand of Moses.

The Priestly Ministry Begins

9 It came to pass on the [a]eighth
day that Moses called Aaron
and his sons and the elders of Is-
rael.
2 And he said to Aaron, "Take
for yourself a young [a]bull as a sin
offering and a ram as a burnt offer-
ing, without blemish, and offer
them before the LORD.
3 "And to the children of Israel
you shall speak, saying, [a]'Take a
kid of the goats as a sin offering,
and a calf and a lamb, *both* of the
first year, without blemish, as a
burnt offering,
4 'also a bull and a ram as peace
offerings, to sacrifice before the
LORD, and [a]a grain offering mixed
with oil; for [b]today the LORD will
appear to you.'"
5 So they brought what Moses
commanded before the tabernacle
of meeting. And all the congrega-
tion drew near and stood [1]before
the LORD.
6 Then Moses said, "This *is* the
thing which the LORD commanded
you to do, and the glory of the
LORD will appear to you."
7 And Moses said to Aaron, "Go
to the altar, [a]offer your sin offering
and your burnt offering, and make
atonement for yourself and for the
people. [b]Offer the offering of the
people, and make atonement for
them, as the LORD commanded."
8 Aaron therefore went to the al-
tar and killed the calf of the sin
offering, which *was* for himself.
9 Then the sons of Aaron
brought the blood to him. And he
dipped his finger in the blood, put
it on the horns of the altar, and
poured the blood at the base of the
altar.
10 [a]But the fat, the kidneys, and
the fatty lobe from the liver of the
sin offering he burned on the altar,
as the LORD had commanded Mo-
ses.
11 [a]The flesh and the hide he
burned with fire outside the camp.
12 And he killed the burnt offer-
ing; and Aaron's sons presented to
him the blood, [a]which he sprinkled
all around on the altar.
13 [a]Then they presented the burnt
offering to him, with its pieces and
head, and he burned *them* on the
altar.
14 [a]And he washed the entrails
and the legs, and burned *them*
with the burnt offering on the al-
tar.
15 [a]Then he brought the people's
offering, and took the goat, which
was the sin offering for the people,
and killed it and offered it for sin,
like the first one.
16 And he brought the burnt offer-
ing and offered it [a]according to the
[1]prescribed manner.
17 Then he brought the grain of-
fering, took a handful of it, and
burned *it* on the altar, [a]besides the
burnt sacrifice of the morning.
18 He also killed the bull and the
ram *as* [a]sacrifices of peace offer-
ings, which *were* for the people.
And Aaron's sons presented to
him the blood, which he sprinkled
all around on the altar,
19 and the fat from the bull and
the ram—the fatty tail, what cov-
ers *the entrails* and the kidneys,
and the fatty lobe *attached to* the
liver;
20 and they put the fat on the
breasts. [a]Then he burned the fat
on the altar;
21 but the breasts and the right
thigh Aaron waved [a]*as* a wave of-
fering before the LORD, as Moses
had commanded.

32 [a]Ex. 29:34
33 [a]Ex. 29:30, 35; Lev. 10:7; Ezek. 43:25, 26
34 [a][Heb. 7:16]
35 [a]Num. 1:53; 3:7; 9:19; Deut. 11:1; 1 Kin. 2:3; Ezek. 48:11 [1]*office*

CHAPTER 9

1 [a]Ezek. 43:27
2 [a]Ex. 29:21; Lev. 4:1–12
3 [a]Lev. 4:23, 28; Ezra 6:17; 10:19
4 [a]Lev. 2:4 [b]Ex. 29:43; Lev. 9:6, 23
5 [1]*in the presence of*
7 [a]Lev. 4:3; 1 Sam. 3:14; [Heb. 5:3–5; 7:27] [b]Lev. 4:16, 20; Heb. 5:1
10 [a]Ex. 23:18; Lev. 8:16
11 [a]Lev. 4:11, 12; 8:17
12 [a]Lev. 1:5; 8:19
13 [a]Lev. 8:20
14 [a]Lev. 8:21
15 [a][Is. 53:10; Heb. 2:17; 5:3]
16 [a]Lev. 1:1–13 [1]*ordinance*
17 [a]Ex. 29:38, 39
18 [a]Lev. 3:1–11
20 [a]Lev. 3:5, 16
21 [a]Ex. 29:24, 26, 27; Lev. 7:30–34

22 Then Aaron lifted his hand toward the people, [a]blessed them, and came down from offering the sin offering, the burnt offering, and peace offerings.

23 And Moses and Aaron went into the tabernacle of meeting, and came out and blessed the people. Then the glory of the LORD appeared to all the people,

24 and [a]fire came out from before the LORD and consumed the burnt offering and the fat on the altar. When all the people saw *it*, they [b]shouted and fell on their [c]faces.

The Profane Fire of Nadab and Abihu

10 Then [a]Nadab and Abihu, the sons of Aaron, [b]each took his censer and put fire in it, put incense on it, and offered [c]profane fire before the LORD, which He had not commanded them.

2 So [a]fire went out from the LORD and devoured them, and they died before the LORD.

3 And Moses said to Aaron, "This is what the LORD spoke, saying:

'By those [a]who come near Me
I must be regarded as holy;
And before all the people
I must be glorified.'"

So Aaron held his peace.

4 Then Moses called Mishael and Elzaphan, the sons of Uzziel the uncle of Aaron, and said to them, "Come near, [a]carry your brethren from [1]before the sanctuary out of the camp."

5 So they went near and carried them by their tunics out of the camp, as Moses had said.

6 And Moses said to Aaron, and to Eleazar and Ithamar, his sons, "Do not [1]uncover your heads nor tear your clothes, lest you die, and [a]wrath come upon all the people. But let your brethren, the whole house of Israel, [2]bewail the burning which the LORD has kindled.

7 [a]"You shall not go out from the door of the tabernacle of meeting, lest you die, [b]for the anointing oil of the LORD *is* upon you." And they did according to the word of Moses.

Conduct Prescribed for Priests

8 Then the LORD spoke to Aaron, saying:

9 [a]"Do not drink wine or intoxicating drink, you, nor your sons with you, when you go into the tabernacle of meeting, lest you die. *It shall be* a statute forever throughout your generations,

10 "that you may [a]distinguish between holy and unholy, and between unclean and clean,

11 [a]"and that you may teach the children of Israel all the statutes which the LORD has spoken to them by the hand of Moses."

12 And Moses spoke to Aaron, and to Eleazar and Ithamar, his sons who were left: [a]"Take the grain offering that remains of the offerings made by fire to the LORD, and eat it without leaven beside the altar; [b]for it *is* most holy.

13 "You shall eat it in a [a]holy place, because it *is* your [1]due and your sons' due, of the sacrifices made by fire to the LORD; for [b]so I have been commanded.

14 [a]"The breast of the wave offering and the thigh of the heave offering you shall eat in a clean place, you, your sons, and your [b]daughters with you; for *they are* your due and your sons' [c]due, *which* are given from the sacrifices of peace offerings of the children of Israel.

15 [a]"The thigh of the heave offering and the breast of the wave offering they shall bring with the offerings of fat made by fire, to offer *as* a wave offering before the LORD. And it shall be yours and your sons' with you, by a statute forever, as the LORD has commanded."

16 Then Moses made careful inquiry about [a]the goat of the sin offering, and there it was—burned up. And he was angry with Eleazar and Ithamar, the sons of Aaron *who were* left, saying,

17 [a]"Why have you not eaten the sin offering in a holy place, since it *is* most holy, and *God* has given it to you to bear [b]the guilt of the congregation, to make atonement for them before the LORD?

18 "See! [a]Its blood was not brought inside [1]the holy *place*;

---

22 [a]Num. 6:22–26; Deut. 21:5; Luke 24:50
24 [a]Gen. 4:4; Judg. 6:21; 2 Chr. 7:1; Ps. 20:3 [b]Ezra 3:11 [c]1 Kin. 18:38, 39

CHAPTER 10

1 [a]Ex. 24:1, 9; Num. 3:2–4; 1 Chr. 24:2 [b]Lev. 16:12 [c]Ex. 30:9; 1 Sam. 2:17
2 [a]Gen. 19:24; Num. 11:1; 16:35; Rev. 20:9
3 [a]Ex. 19:22; Lev. 21:6; Is. 52:11; Ezek. 20:41
4 [a]Acts 5:6, 10 [1]*in front of*
6 [a]Num. 1:53; 16:22, 46; 18:5; Josh. 7:1; 22:18, 20; 2 Sam. 24:1 [1]An act of mourning [2]*weep bitterly*
7 [a]Lev. 8:33; 21:12 [b]Lev. 8:30
9 [a]Gen. 9:21; [Prov. 20:1; 31:5]; Is. 28:7; Ezek. 44:21; Hos. 4:11; Luke 1:15; [Eph. 5:18]; 1 Tim. 3:3; Titus 1:7
10 [a]Lev. 11:47; 20:25; Ezek. 22:26; 44:23
11 [a]Deut. 24:8; Neh. 8:2, 8; Jer. 18:18; Mal. 2:7
12 [a]Num. 18:9 [b]Lev. 21:22
13 [a]Num. 18:10 [b]Lev. 2:3; 6:16 [1]*portion*
14 [a]Ex. 29:24, 26, 27; Lev. 7:30–34; Num. 18:11 [b]Lev. 22:13 [c]Num. 18:10
15 [a]Lev. 7:29, 30, 34
16 [a]Lev. 9:3, 15
17 [a]Lev. 6:24–30 [b]Ex. 28:38; Lev. 22:16; Num. 18:1
18 [a]Lev. 6:30 [1]The Most Holy Place when capitalized

indeed you should have eaten it in
a holy *place*, [b]as I commanded."
19 And Aaron said to Moses,
"Look, [a]this day they have offered
their sin offering and their burnt
offering before the LORD, and such
things have befallen me! *If* I had
eaten the sin offering today,
[b]would it have been accepted in
the sight of the LORD?"
20 So when Moses heard *that*, he
was content.

Foods Permitted and Forbidden

11 Now the LORD spoke to Moses and Aaron, saying to
them,
2 "Speak to the children of Is-
rael, saying, [a]'These *are* the ani-
mals which you may eat among all
the animals that *are* on the earth:
3 'Among the animals, whatever
divides the hoof, having cloven
hooves *and* chewing the cud—that
you may eat.
4 'Nevertheless these you shall
[a]not eat among those that chew the
cud or those that have cloven
hooves: the camel, because it
chews the cud but does not have
cloven hooves, is [1]unclean to you;
5 'the [1]rock hyrax, because it
chews the cud but does not have
cloven hooves, *is* [2]unclean to
you;
6 'the hare, because it chews the
cud but does not have cloven
hooves, *is* unclean to you;
7 'and the swine, though it di-
vides the hoof, having cloven
hooves, yet does not chew the cud,
[a]*is* unclean to you.
8 'Their flesh you shall not eat,
and their carcasses you shall not
touch. [a]They *are* unclean to you.
9 [a]'These you may eat of all that
are in the water: whatever in the
water has fins and scales, whether
in the seas or in the rivers—that
you may eat.
10 'But all in the seas or in the riv-
ers that do not have fins and
scales, all that move in the water
or any living thing which *is* in the
water, they *are* [1]an [a]abomination
to you.
11 'They shall be an abomination
to you; you shall not eat their flesh,
but you shall regard their car-
casses as an abomination.
12 'Whatever in the water does
not have fins or scales—that *shall
be* an abomination to you.
13 [a]'And these you shall regard as
an abomination among the birds;
they shall not be eaten, they *are*
an abomination: the eagle, the vul-
ture, the buzzard,
14 'the kite, and the falcon after
its kind;
15 'every raven after its kind,
16 'the ostrich, the short-eared
owl, the sea gull, and the hawk af-
ter its kind;
17 'the little owl, the fisher owl,
and the screech owl;
18 'the white owl, the jackdaw,
and the carrion vulture;
19 'the stork, the heron after its
kind, the hoopoe, and the bat.
20 'All flying insects that creep on
all fours *shall be* an abomination
to you.
21 'Yet these you may eat of every
flying insect that creeps on *all*
fours: those which have jointed
legs above their feet with which to
leap on the earth.
22 'These you may eat: [a]the locust
after its kind, the destroying locust
after its kind, the cricket after its
kind, and the grasshopper after its
kind.
23 'But all *other* flying insects
which have four feet *shall be* an
abomination to you.

Unclean Animals

24 'By these you shall become
[1]unclean; whoever touches the
carcass of any of them shall be un-
clean until evening;
25 'whoever carries part of the
carcass of any of them [a]shall wash
his clothes and be unclean until
evening:
26 '*The carcass* of any animal
which divides the foot, but is not
cloven-hoofed or does not chew
the cud, *is* unclean to you. Every-
one who touches it shall be un-
clean.
27 'And whatever goes on its
paws, among all kinds of animals
that go on *all* fours, those *are* un-
clean to you. Whoever touches any
such carcass shall be unclean until
evening.
28 'Whoever carries *any such* car-
cass shall wash his clothes and be
unclean until evening. It *is* unclean
to you.

18 [b]Lev. 6:26, 30
19 [a]Lev. 9:8, 12 [b][Is. 1:11–15]; Jer. 6:20; 14:12; Hos. 9:4; [Mal. 1:10, 13; 3:1–4]

CHAPTER 11
2 [a]Deut. 14:4; Ezek. 4:14; Dan. 1:8; [Matt. 15:11]; Acts 10:12, 14; [Rom. 14:14; Heb. 9:10; 13:9]
4 [a]Acts 10:14 [1]*impure*
5 [1]*rock badger* [2]*impure*
7 [a]Is. 65:4; 66:3, 17; Mark 5:1–17
8 [a]Is. 52:11; [Mark 7:2, 15, 18]; Acts 10:14, 15; 15:29
9 [a]Deut. 14:9
10 [a]Lev. 7:18, 21; Deut. 14:3 [1]*detestable*
13 [a]Deut. 14:12–19; Is. 66:17
22 [a]Matt. 3:4; Mark 1:6
24 [1]*impure*
25 [a]Lev. 14:8; 15:5; Num. 19:10, 21, 22; 31:24; Zech. 13:1; [Heb. 9:10; 10:22; Rev. 7:14]

29 'These also *shall be* unclean to you among the creeping things that creep on the earth: the mole, [a]the mouse, and the large lizard after its kind;

30 'the gecko, the monitor lizard, the sand reptile, the sand lizard, and the chameleon.

31 'These *are* unclean to you among all that creep. Whoever [a]touches them when they are dead shall be unclean until evening.

32 'Anything on which *any* of them falls, when they are dead shall be [1]unclean, whether *it is* any item of wood or clothing or skin or sack, whatever item *it is,* in which *any* work is done, [a]it must be put in water. And it shall be unclean until evening; then it shall be clean.

33 'Any [a]earthen vessel into which *any* of them falls [b]you shall break; and whatever *is* in it shall be unclean:

34 'in such a vessel, any edible food upon which water falls becomes unclean, and any drink that may be drunk from it becomes unclean.

35 'And everything on which *a part* of *any such* carcass falls shall be unclean; *whether it is* an oven or cooking stove, it shall be broken down; *for* they *are* unclean, and shall be unclean to you.

36 'Nevertheless a spring or a cistern, *in which there is* plenty of water, shall be clean, but whatever touches any such carcass becomes unclean.

37 'And if a part of *any such* carcass falls on any planting seed which is to be sown, it *remains* clean.

38 'But if water is put on the seed, and if *a part* of *any such* carcass falls on it, it *becomes* [1]unclean to you.

39 'And if any animal which you may eat dies, he who touches its carcass shall be [a]unclean until evening.

40 [a]'He who eats of its carcass shall wash his clothes and be unclean until evening. He also who carries its carcass shall wash his clothes and be unclean until evening.

41 'And every creeping thing that creeps on the earth *shall be* [1]an abomination. It shall not be eaten.

42 'Whatever crawls on its belly, whatever goes on *all* fours, or whatever has many feet among all creeping things that creep on the earth—these you shall not eat, for they *are* an abomination.

43 [a]'You shall not make [1]yourselves [2]abominable with any creeping thing that creeps; nor shall you make yourselves unclean with them, lest you be defiled by them.

44 'For I *am* the LORD your [a]God. You shall therefore consecrate yourselves, and [b]you shall be holy; for I *am* holy. Neither shall you defile yourselves with any creeping thing that creeps on the earth.

45 [a]'For I *am* the LORD who brings you up out of the land of Egypt, to be your God. [b]You shall therefore be holy, for I *am* holy.

46 'This *is* the law [1]of the animals and the birds and every living creature that moves in the waters, and of every creature that creeps on the earth,

47 [a]'to distinguish between the unclean and the clean, and between the animal that may be eaten and the animal that may not be eaten.' "

The Ritual After Childbirth

12 Then the LORD spoke to Moses, saying,

2 "Speak to the children of Israel, saying: 'If a [a]woman has conceived, and borne a male child, then [b]she shall be [1]unclean seven days; [c]as in the days of her customary impurity she shall be unclean.

3 'And on the [a]eighth day the flesh of his foreskin shall be circumcised.

4 'She shall then continue in the blood of *her* purification thirty-three days. She shall not touch any [1]hallowed thing, nor come into the sanctuary until the days of her purification are fulfilled.

5 'But if she bears a female child, then she shall be unclean two weeks, as in her customary impurity, and she shall continue in the blood of *her* purification sixty-six days.

6 [a]'When the days of her purification are fulfilled, whether for a

29 [a]Is. 66:17
31 [a]Hag. 2:13
32 [a]Lev. 15:12 [1]*impure*
33 [a]Lev. 6:28 [b]Lev. 15:12; Ps. 2:9; Jer. 48:38; [2 Tim. 2:21]; Rev. 2:27
38 [1]*impure*
39 [a]Hag. 2:11–13
40 [a]Ex. 22:31; Lev. 17:15; 22:8; Deut. 14:21; Ezek. 4:14; 44:31
41 [1]*detestable*
43 [a]Lev. 20:25 [1]Lit. *your souls* [2]*impure*
44 [a]Ex. 6:7; Lev. 22:33; 25:38; 26:45 [b]Ex. 19:6; Lev. 19:2; 20:7, 26; [Amos 3:3]; Matt. 5:48; 1 Thess. 4:7; 1 Pet. 1:15, 16; [Rev. 22:11, 14]
45 [a]Ex. 6:7; 20:2; Lev. 22:33; 25:38; 26:45; Ps. 105:43–45; Hos. 11:1 [b]Lev. 11:44
46 [1]*concerning*
47 [a]Lev. 10:10; Ezek. 44:23; Mal. 3:18

CHAPTER 12

2 [a]Lev. 15:19; [Job 14:4; Ps. 51:5] [b]Ex. 22:30; Lev. 8:33; 13:4; Luke 2:22 [c]Lev. 18:19 [1]*impure*
3 [a]Gen. 17:12; Luke 1:59; 2:21; John 7:22, 23; Gal. 5:3
4 [1]*consecrated*
6 [a]Luke 2:22

son or a daughter, she shall bring
to the priest a [b]lamb [1]of the first
year as a burnt offering, and a
young pigeon or a turtledove as a
[c]sin offering, to the door of the tab-
ernacle of meeting.
7 'Then he shall offer it before
the LORD, and make [1]atonement
for her. And she shall be clean
from the flow of her blood. This
is the law for her who has borne
a male or a female.
8 [a]'And if she is not able to bring
a lamb, then she may bring two
turtledoves or two young pi-
geons—one as a burnt offering and
the other as a sin offering. [b]So the
priest shall make atonement for
her, and she will be [1]clean.' "

The Law Concerning Leprosy

13 And the LORD spoke to Mo-
ses and Aaron, saying:
2 "When a man has on the skin
of his body a swelling, [a]a scab, or
a bright spot, and it becomes on
the skin of his body *like* a [1]leprous
sore, [b]then he shall be brought to
Aaron the priest or to one of his
sons the priests.
3 "The priest shall examine the
sore on the skin of the body; and
if the hair on the sore has turned
white, and the sore appears *to be*
deeper than the skin of his body,
it *is* a leprous sore. Then the priest
shall examine him, and pronounce
him [1]unclean.
4 "But if the bright spot *is* white
on the skin of his body, and does
not appear *to be* deeper than the
skin, and its hair has not turned
white, then the priest shall isolate
the one who has the sore [a]seven
days.
5 "And the priest shall examine
him on the seventh day; and in-
deed *if* the sore appears to be as
it was, *and* the sore has not spread
on the skin, then the priest shall
isolate him another seven days.
6 "Then the priest shall examine
him again on the seventh day; and
indeed *if* the sore has faded, *and*
the sore has not spread on the
skin, then the priest shall pro-
nounce him clean; it *is only* a scab,
and he [a]shall wash his clothes and
be clean.
7 "But if the scab should at all
spread over the skin, after he has
been seen by the priest for his
cleansing, he shall be seen by the
priest again.
8 "And *if* the priest sees that the
scab has indeed spread on the
skin, then the priest shall pro-
nounce him [1]unclean. It *is* leprosy.
9 "When the leprous sore is on
a person, then he shall be brought
to the priest.
10 [a]"And the priest shall examine
him; and indeed *if* the swelling on
the skin *is* white, and it has turned
the hair white, and *there is* a spot
of raw flesh in the swelling,
11 "it *is* an old leprosy on the skin
of his body. The priest shall pro-
nounce him [1]unclean, and shall
not isolate him, for he *is* unclean.
12 "And if leprosy breaks out all
over the skin, and the leprosy cov-
ers all the skin of *the one who has*
the sore, from his head to his foot,
wherever the priest looks,
13 "then the priest shall consider;
and indeed *if* the leprosy has cov-
ered all his body, he shall pro-
nounce *him* clean *who has* the
sore. It has all turned [a]white. He
is clean.
14 "But when raw flesh appears
on him, he shall be unclean.
15 "And the priest shall examine
the raw flesh and pronounce him
to be unclean; *for* the raw flesh *is*
unclean. It *is* leprosy.
16 "Or if the raw flesh changes
and turns white again, he shall
come to the priest.
17 "And the priest shall examine
him; and indeed *if* the sore has
turned white, then the priest shall
pronounce *him* clean *who has* the
sore. He *is* clean.
18 "If the body develops a [a]boil in
the skin, and it is healed,
19 "and in the place of the boil
there comes a white swelling or a
bright spot, reddish-white, then it
shall be shown to the priest;
20 "and *if,* when the priest sees it,
it indeed *appears* deeper than the
skin, and its hair has turned white,
the priest shall pronounce him un-
clean. It *is* a leprous sore which
has broken out of the boil.
21 "But if the priest examines it,
and indeed *there are* no white
hairs in it, and it *is* not deeper than
the skin, but has faded, then the
priest shall isolate him seven days;

12:6 [b][John 1:29; 1 Pet. 1:18, 19] [c]Lev. 5:7 [1]Lit. *a son of his year*
7 [1]Lit. *covering*
8 [a]Lev. 5:7; Luke 2:22–24 [b]Lev. 4:26 [1]*pure*

CHAPTER 13

2 [a]Deut. 28:27; Is. 3:17 [b]Deut. 17:8, 9; 24:8; Mal. 2:7; Luke 17:14 [1]Heb. *saraath,* disfiguring skin diseases, including leprosy, and so in vv. 2–46 and 14:1–32
3 [1]*defiled*
4 [a]Lev. 14:8
6 [a]Lev. 11:25; 14:8; [John 13:8, 10]
8 [1]*defiled*
10 [a]Num. 12:10, 12; 2 Kin. 5:27; 2 Chr. 26:19, 20
11 [1]*defiled*
13 [a]Ex. 4:6
18 [a]Ex. 9:9; 15:26

22 "and if it should at all spread
over the skin, then the priest shall
pronounce him unclean. It *is* a
[1]leprous sore.
23 "But if the bright spot stays in
one place, *and* has not spread, it
is the scar of the boil; and the
priest shall pronounce him
clean.
24 "Or if the body receives a [a]burn
on its skin by fire, and the raw
flesh of the burn becomes a bright
spot, reddish-white or white,
25 "then the priest shall examine
it; and indeed *if* the hair of the
bright spot has turned white, and
it appears deeper than the skin, it
is leprosy broken out in the burn.
Therefore the priest shall pro-
nounce him unclean. It *is* a leprous
sore.
26 "But if the priest examines it,
and indeed *there are* no white
hairs in the bright spot, and it *is*
not deeper than the skin, but has
faded, then the priest shall isolate
him seven days.
27 "And the priest shall examine
him on the seventh day. If it has
at all spread over the skin, then
the priest shall pronounce him un-
clean. It *is* a leprous sore.
28 "But if the bright spot stays in
one place, *and* has not spread on
the skin, but has faded, it *is* a
swelling from the burn. The priest
shall pronounce him clean, for it
is the scar from the burn.
29 "If a man or woman has a sore
on the head or the beard,
30 "then the priest shall examine
the sore; and indeed if it appears
deeper than the skin, *and there is*
in it thin yellow hair, then the
priest shall pronounce him un-
clean. It *is* a scaly leprosy of the
head or beard.
31 "But if the priest examines the
scaly sore, and indeed it does not
appear deeper than the skin, and
there is no black hair in it, then
the priest shall isolate *the one who
has* the scale seven days.
32 "And on the seventh day the
priest shall examine the sore; and
indeed *if* the scale has not spread,
and there is no yellow hair in it,
and the scale does not appear
deeper than the skin,
33 "he shall shave himself, but the
scale he shall not shave. And the

22 [1]*infection*

24 [a]Is. 3:24

42 [a]2 Chr. 26:19

44 [a]Is. 1:5 [1]*altogether defiled*

45 [a]Lev. 10:6; 21:10 [b]Ezek. 24:17, 22; Mic. 3:7 [c]Is. 6:5; 64:6; Lam. 4:15; Luke 5:8

priest shall isolate *the one who has*
the scale another seven days.
34 "On the seventh day the priest
shall examine the scale; and in-
deed *if* the scale has not spread
over the skin, and does not appear
deeper than the skin, then the
priest shall pronounce him clean.
He shall wash his clothes and be
clean.
35 "But if the scale should at all
spread over the skin after his
cleansing,
36 "then the priest shall examine
him; and indeed *if* the scale has
spread over the skin, the priest
need not seek for yellow hair. He
is unclean.
37 "But if the scale appears to be
at a standstill, and there is black
hair grown up in it, the scale has
healed. He *is* clean, and the priest
shall pronounce him clean.
38 "If a man or a woman has
bright spots on the skin of the
body, *specifically* white bright
spots,
39 "then the priest shall look; and
indeed *if* the bright spots on the
skin of the body *are* dull white, it
is a white spot *that* grows on the
skin. He *is* clean.
40 "As for the man whose hair has
fallen from his head, he *is* bald,
but he *is* clean.
41 "He whose hair has fallen from
his forehead, he *is* bald on the fore-
head, *but* he *is* clean.
42 "And if there is on the bald
head or bald [a]forehead a reddish-
white sore, it *is* leprosy breaking
out on his bald head or his bald
forehead.
43 "Then the priest shall examine
it; and indeed *if* the swelling of the
sore *is* reddish-white on his bald
head or on his bald forehead, as
the appearance of leprosy on the
skin of the body,
44 "he is a leprous man. He *is* un-
clean. The priest shall surely pro-
nounce him [1]unclean; his sore *is*
on his [a]head.
45 "Now the leper on whom the
sore *is*, his clothes shall be torn
and his head [a]bare; and he shall
[b]cover his mustache, and cry,
[c]'Unclean! Unclean!'
46 "He shall be unclean. All the
days he has the sore he shall be
unclean. He *is* unclean, and he

shall [1]dwell alone; his dwelling
shall be [a]outside the camp.

The Law Concerning Leprous Garments

47 "Also, if a garment has a [1]lep-
rous plague in it, *whether it is* a
woolen garment or a linen gar-
ment,
48 "whether *it is* in the warp or
woof of linen or wool, whether in
leather or in anything made of
leather,
49 "and if the plague is greenish
or reddish in the garment or in the
leather, whether in the warp or in
the woof, or in anything made of
leather, it *is* a leprous [1]plague and
shall be shown to the priest.
50 "The priest shall examine the
plague and isolate *that which has*
the plague seven days.
51 "And he shall examine the
plague on the seventh day. If the
plague has spread in the garment,
either in the warp or in the woof,
in the leather *or* in anything made
of leather, the plague *is* [a]an active
leprosy. It *is* unclean.
52 "He shall therefore burn that
garment in which is the plague,
whether warp or woof, in wool or
in linen, or anything of leather, for
it *is* an active leprosy; *the garment*
shall be burned in the fire.
53 "But if the priest examines *it*,
and indeed the plague has not
spread in the garment, either in the
warp or in the woof, or in anything
made of leather,
54 "then the priest shall command
that they wash *the thing* in which
is the plague; and he shall isolate
it another seven days.
55 "Then the priest shall examine
the plague after it has been
washed; and indeed *if* the plague
has not changed its color, though
the plague has not spread, it *is* un-
clean, and you shall burn it in the
fire; it continues eating away,
whether the damage *is* outside or
inside.
56 "If the priest examines *it*, and
indeed the plague has faded after
washing it, then he shall tear it out
of the garment, whether out of the
warp or out of the woof, or out of
the leather.
57 "But if it appears again in the
garment, either in the warp or in
the woof, or in anything made of
leather, it *is* a spreading *plague;*
you shall burn with fire that in
which is the plague.
58 "And if you wash the garment,
either warp or woof, or whatever
is made of leather, if the plague
has disappeared from it, then it
shall be washed a second time, and
shall be clean.
59 "This *is* the law of the leprous
plague in a garment of wool or
linen, either in the warp or woof,
or in anything made of leather, to
pronounce it clean or to pronounce
it unclean."

The Ritual for Cleansing Healed Lepers

14 Then the LORD spoke to Mo-
ses, saying,
2 "This shall be the law of the
[1]leper for the day of his cleansing:
He [a]shall be brought to the priest.
3 "And the priest shall go out of
the camp, and the priest shall ex-
amine *him;* and indeed, *if* the [1]lep-
rosy is healed in the leper,
4 "then the priest shall command
to take for him who is to be
cleansed two living *and* clean
birds, [a]cedar wood, [b]scarlet, and
[c]hyssop.
5 "And the priest shall command
that one of the birds be killed in
an earthen vessel over running
water.
6 "As for the living bird, he shall
take it, the cedar wood and the
scarlet and the hyssop, and dip
them and the living bird in the
blood of the bird *that was* killed
over the running water.
7 "And he shall [a]sprinkle it
[b]seven times on him who is to be
cleansed from the leprosy, and
shall pronounce him clean, and
shall let the living bird loose in the
open field.
8 "He who is to be cleansed
[a]shall wash his clothes, shave off
all his hair, and [b]wash himself in
water, that he may be clean. After
that he shall come into the camp,
and [c]shall stay outside his tent
seven days.
9 "But on the [a]seventh day he
shall shave all the hair off his head
and his beard and his eyebrows—
all his hair he shall shave off. He
shall wash his clothes and wash

46 [a]Num. 5:1–4; 12:14; 2 Kin. 7:3; 15:5; 2 Chr. 26:21; Ps. 38:11; Luke 17:12 [1]*live alone*
47 [1]A mold, fungus, or similar infestation, and so in vv. 47–59
49 [1]*mark*
51 [a]Lev. 14:44

CHAPTER 14

2 [a]Matt. 8:2, 4; Mark 1:40, 44; Luke 5:12, 14; 17:14 [1]See note at 13:2
3 [1]Heb. *saraath,* disfiguring skin diseases, including leprosy, and so in vv. 1–32
4 [a]Lev. 14:6, 49, 51, 52; Num. 19:6; Heb. 9:19 [b]Ex. 25:4 [c]Ex. 12:22; Ps. 51:7
7 [a]Num. 19:18, 19; [Heb. 9:13, 21; 12:24] [b]2 Kin. 5:10, 14; Ps. 51:2
8 [a]Lev. 11:25; 13:6; Num. 8:7 [b]Lev. 11:25; [Eph. 5:26; Heb. 10:22; Rev. 1:5, 6] [c]Lev. 13:5; Num. 5:2, 3; 12:14, 15; 2 Chr. 26:21
9 [a]Num. 19:19

his body in water, and he shall be clean.

10 "And on the eighth day [a]he shall take two male lambs without blemish, one ewe lamb of the first year without blemish, three-tenths *of an ephah* of fine flour mixed with oil as [b]a grain offering, and one log of oil.

11 "Then the priest who makes *him* clean shall present the man who is to be made clean, and those things, before the LORD, *at* the door of the tabernacle of meeting.

12 "And the priest shall take one male lamb and [a]offer it as a trespass offering, and the log of oil, and [b]wave them *as* a wave offering before the LORD.

13 "Then he shall kill the lamb [a]in the place where he kills the sin offering and the burnt offering, in a holy place; for [b]as the sin offering *is* the priest's, so *is* the trespass offering. [c]It *is* most holy.

14 "The priest shall take *some* of the blood of the trespass offering, and the priest shall put *it* [a]on the tip of the right ear of him who is to be cleansed, on the thumb of his right hand, and on the big toe of his right foot.

15 "And the priest shall take *some* of the log of oil, and pour *it* into the palm of his own left hand.

16 "Then the priest shall dip his right finger in the oil that *is* in his left hand, and shall [a]sprinkle some of the oil with his finger seven times before the LORD.

17 "And of the rest of the oil in his hand, the priest shall put *some* on the tip of the right ear of him who is to be cleansed, on the thumb of his right hand, and on the big toe of his right foot, on the blood of the trespass offering.

18 "The rest of the oil that *is* in the priest's hand he shall put on the head of him who is to be cleansed. [a]So the priest shall make [1]atonement for him before the LORD.

19 "Then the priest shall offer [a]the sin offering, and make atonement for him who is to be cleansed from his uncleanness. Afterward he shall kill the burnt offering.

20 "And the priest shall offer the burnt offering and the grain offering on the altar. So the priest shall make atonement for him, and he shall be [a]clean.

21 "But [a]if he *is* poor and cannot afford it, then he shall take one male lamb *as* a trespass offering to be waved, to make atonement for him, [1]one-tenth *of an ephah* of fine flour mixed with oil as a grain offering, a log of oil,

22 [a]"and two turtledoves or two young pigeons, such as he is able to afford: one shall be a sin offering and the other a burnt offering.

23 [a]"He shall bring them to the priest on the eighth day for his cleansing, to the door of the tabernacle of meeting, before the LORD.

24 [a]"And the priest shall take the lamb of the trespass offering and the log of oil, and the priest shall wave them *as* a wave offering before the LORD.

25 "Then he shall kill the lamb of the trespass offering, [a]and the priest shall take *some* of the blood of the trespass offering and put *it* on the tip of the right ear of him who is to be cleansed, on the thumb of his right hand, and on the big toe of his right foot.

26 "And the priest shall pour some of the oil into the palm of his own left hand.

27 "Then the priest shall sprinkle with his right finger *some* of the oil that *is* in his left hand seven times before the LORD.

28 "And the priest shall put *some* of the oil that *is* in his hand on the tip of the right ear of him who is to be cleansed, on the thumb of the right hand, and on the big toe of his right foot, on the place of the blood of the trespass offering.

29 "The rest of the oil that *is* in the priest's hand he shall put on the head of him who is to be cleansed, to make atonement for him before the LORD.

30 "And he shall offer one of [a]the turtledoves or young pigeons, such as he can afford—

31 "such as he is able to afford, the one *as* a sin offering and the other *as* a burnt offering, with the grain offering. So the priest shall make atonement for him who is to be cleansed before the LORD.

32 "This *is* the law *for one* who had a leprous sore, who cannot afford [a]the usual cleansing."

10 [a]Matt. 8:4; Mark 1:44; Luke 5:14 [b]Lev. 2:1; Num. 15:4
12 [a]Lev. 5:6, 18; 6:6; 14:19 [b]Ex. 29:22–24, 26
13 [a]Ex. 29:11; Lev. 1:5, 11; 4:4, 24 [b]Lev. 6:24–30; 7:7 [c]Lev. 2:3; 7:6; 21:22
14 [a]Ex. 29:20; Lev. 8:23, 24
16 [a]Lev. 4:6
18 [a]Lev. 4:26; 5:6; Num. 15:28; [Heb. 2:17] [1]Lit. *covering*
19 [a]Lev. 5:1, 6; 12:7; [2 Cor. 5:21]
20 [a]Lev. 14:8, 9
21 [a]Lev. 5:7, 11; 12:8; 27:8 [1]Approximately two dry quarts
22 [a]Lev. 12:8; 15:14, 15
23 [a]Lev. 14:10, 11
24 [a]Lev. 14:12
25 [a]Lev. 14:14, 17
30 [a]Lev. 14:22; 15:14, 15
32 [a]Lev. 14:10

The Law Concerning Leprous Houses

33 And the LORD spoke to Moses
and Aaron, saying:
34 [a]"When you have come into
the land of Canaan, which I give
you as a possession, and [b]I put the
[1]leprous plague in a house in the
land of your possession,
35 "and he who owns the house
comes and tells the priest, saying,
'It seems to me that *there is* [a]some
plague in the house,'
36 "then the priest shall command
that they empty the house, before
the priest goes *into it* to examine
the plague, that all that *is* in the
house may not be made unclean;
and afterward the priest shall go
in to examine the house.
37 "And he shall examine the
plague; and indeed *if* the plague
is on the walls of the house with
ingrained streaks, greenish or red-
dish, which appear to be [1]deep in
the wall,
38 "then the priest shall go out of
the house, to the door of the house,
and [1]shut up the house seven
days.
39 "And the priest shall come
again on the seventh day and look;
and indeed *if* the plague has
spread on the walls of the house,
40 "then the priest shall command
that they take away the stones in
which *is* the plague, and they shall
cast them into an unclean place
outside the city.
41 "And he shall cause the house
to be scraped inside, all around,
and the dust that they scrape off
they shall pour out in an unclean
place outside the city.
42 "Then they shall take other
stones and put *them* in the place
of *those* stones, and he shall take
other mortar and plaster the
house.
43 "Now if the plague comes back
and breaks out in the house, after
he has taken away the stones, after
he has scraped the house, and af-
ter it is plastered,
44 "then the priest shall come and
look; and indeed *if* the plague has
spread in the house, it *is* [a]an active
leprosy in the house. It *is* unclean.
45 "And he shall break down the
house, its stones, its timber, and
all the plaster of the house, and he

34 [a]Gen. 12:7; 13:17; 17:8; Num. 32:22; Deut. 7:1; 32:49 [b][Prov. 3:33] [1]Decomposition by mildew, mold, dry rot, etc., and so in vv. 34–53

35 [a][Ps. 91:9, 10; Prov. 3:33; Zech. 5:4]

37 [1]Lit. *lower than the wall*

38 [1]*quarantine*

44 [a]Lev. 13:51; [Zech. 5:4]

46 [a]Lev. 11:24; 15:5 [1]*defiled*

47 [a]Lev. 14:8

49 [a]Lev. 14:4

52 [1]*ceremonially cleanse*

53 [a]Lev. 14:20

54 [a]Lev. 13:30; 26:21

55 [a]Lev. 13:47–52 [b]Lev. 14:34

56 [a]Lev. 13:2

57 [a]Lev. 11:47; 20:25; Deut. 24:8; Ezek. 44:23

CHAPTER 15

2 [a]Lev. 22:4; Num. 5:2; 2 Sam. 3:29

shall carry *them* outside the city
to an unclean place.
46 "Moreover he who goes into
the house at all while it is shut
up shall be [1]unclean [a]until eve-
ning.
47 "And he who lies down in the
house shall [a]wash his clothes, and
he who eats in the house shall
wash his clothes.
48 "But if the priest comes in and
examines *it*, and indeed the plague
has not spread in the house after
the house was plastered, then the
priest shall pronounce the house
clean, because the plague is
healed.
49 "And [a]he shall take, to cleanse
the house, two birds, cedar wood,
scarlet, and hyssop.
50 "Then he shall kill one of the
birds in an earthen vessel over
running water;
51 "and he shall take the cedar
wood, the hyssop, the scarlet, and
the living bird, and dip them in the
blood of the slain bird and in the
running water, and sprinkle the
house seven times.
52 "And he shall [1]cleanse the
house with the blood of the bird
and the running water and the liv-
ing bird, with the cedar wood, the
hyssop, and the scarlet.
53 "Then he shall let the living
bird loose outside the city in the
open field, and [a]make atonement
for the house, and it shall be clean.
54 "This *is* the law for any [a]lep-
rous sore and scale,
55 "for the [a]leprosy of a garment
[b]and of a house,
56 [a]"for a swelling and a scab and
a bright spot,
57 "to [a]teach when *it is* unclean
and when *it is* clean. This *is* the
law of leprosy."

The Law Concerning Bodily Discharges

15 And the LORD spoke to Mo-
ses and Aaron, saying,
2 "Speak to the children of Is-
rael, and say to them: [a]'When any
man has a discharge from his
body, his discharge *is* unclean.
3 'And this shall be his unclean-
ness in regard to his discharge—
whether his body runs with his dis-
charge, or his body is stopped up

by his discharge, it *is* his unclean-
ness.
4 'Every bed is [1]unclean on
which he who has the discharge
lies, and everything on which he
sits shall be unclean.
5 'And whoever [a]touches his bed
shall [b]wash his clothes and [c]bathe
in water, and be unclean until eve-
ning.
6 'He who sits on anything on
which he who has the [a]discharge
sat shall wash his clothes and
bathe in water, and be unclean un-
til evening.
7 'And he who touches the body
of him who has the discharge shall
wash his clothes and bathe in wa-
ter, and be unclean until evening.
8 'If he who has the discharge
[a]spits on him who is clean, then
he shall wash his clothes and
bathe in water, and be unclean un-
til evening.
9 'Any saddle on which he who
has the discharge rides shall be
unclean.
10 'Whoever touches anything
that was under him shall be un-
clean until evening. He who car-
ries *any of* those things shall wash
his clothes and bathe in water, and
be unclean until evening.
11 'And whomever the one who
has the discharge touches, and has
not rinsed his hands in water, he
shall wash his clothes and bathe
in water, and be unclean until eve-
ning.
12 'The [a]vessel of earth that he
who has the discharge touches
shall be broken, and every ves-
sel of wood shall be rinsed in wa-
ter.
13 'And when he who has a dis-
charge is cleansed of his dis-
charge, then [a]he shall count for
himself seven days for his cleans-
ing, wash his clothes, and bathe
his body in running water; then he
shall be clean.
14 'On the eighth day he shall take
for himself [a]two turtledoves or two
young pigeons, and come before
the LORD, to the door of the taber-
nacle of meeting, and give them to
the priest.
15 'Then the priest shall offer
them, [a]the one *as* a sin offering
and the other *as* a burnt offering.
[b]So the priest shall make [1]atone-

4 [1]*defiled*
5 [a]Lev. 5:2; 14:46 [b]Lev. 14:8, 47 [c]Lev. 11:25; 17:15
6 [a]Lev. 15:10; Deut. 23:10
8 [a]Num. 12:14
12 [a]Lev. 6:28; 11:32, 33
13 [a]Lev. 14:8; 15:28; Num. 19:11, 12
14 [a]Lev. 14:22, 23, 30, 31
15 [a]Lev. 14:30, 31 [b]Lev. 14:19, 31 [1]Lit. *covering*
16 [a]Lev. 22:4; Deut. 23:10, 11
18 [a][Ex. 19:15; 1 Sam. 21:4; 1 Cor. 6:18]
19 [a]Lev. 12:2 [1]Lit. *in her impurity*
24 [a]Lev. 18:19; 20:18 [1]*defiled*
25 [a]Matt. 9:20; Mark 5:25; Luke 8:43
28 [a]Lev. 15:13–15

ment for him before the LORD be-
cause of his discharge.
16 [a]'If any man has an emission
of semen, then he shall wash all
his body in water, and be unclean
until evening.
17 'And any garment and any
leather on which there is semen,
it shall be washed with water, and
be unclean until evening.
18 'Also, when a woman lies with
a man, and *there is* an emission
of semen, they shall bathe in wa-
ter, and [a]be unclean until evening.
19 [a]'If a woman has a discharge,
and the discharge from her body
is blood, she shall be [1]set apart
seven days; and whoever touches
her shall be unclean until evening.
20 'Everything that she lies on
during her impurity shall be un-
clean; also everything that she sits
on shall be unclean.
21 'Whoever touches her bed shall
wash his clothes and bathe in wa-
ter, and be unclean until evening.
22 'And whoever touches any-
thing that she sat on shall wash
his clothes and bathe in water, and
be unclean until evening.
23 'If *anything* is on *her* bed or on
anything on which she sits, when
he touches it, he shall be unclean
until evening.
24 'And [a]if any man lies with her
at all, so that her impurity is on
him, he shall be [1]unclean seven
days; and every bed on which he
lies shall be unclean.
25 'If [a]a woman has a discharge
of blood for many days, other than
at the time of her *customary* im-
purity, or if it runs beyond her
usual time of impurity, all the days
of her unclean discharge shall be
as the days of her *customary* im-
purity. She *shall be* unclean.
26 'Every bed on which she lies all
the days of her discharge shall be
to her as the bed of her impurity;
and whatever she sits on shall be
unclean, as the uncleanness of her
impurity.
27 'Whoever touches those things
shall be unclean; he shall wash his
clothes and bathe in water, and be
unclean until evening.
28 'But [a]if she is cleansed of her
discharge, then she shall count for
herself seven days, and after that
she shall be clean.

29 'And on the eighth day she
shall take for herself two turtle-
doves or two young pigeons, and
bring them to the priest, to the
door of the tabernacle of meeting.
30 'Then the priest shall offer the
one *as* a sin offering and the other
as a [a]burnt offering, and the priest
shall make atonement for her be-
fore the LORD for the discharge of
her uncleanness.
31 'Thus you shall [a]separate the
children of Israel from their
uncleanness, lest they die in their
uncleanness when they [b]defile My
tabernacle that *is* among them.
32 [a]'This *is* the law for one who
has a discharge, [b]and *for him* who
emits semen and is unclean
thereby,
33 [a]'and for her who is indisposed
because of her *customary* im-
purity, and for one who has a dis-
charge, either man [b]or woman,
[c]and for him who lies with her who
is unclean.' "

The Day of Atonement

16 Now the LORD spoke to Mo-
ses after [a]the death of the
two sons of Aaron, when they of-
fered *profane fire* before the LORD,
and died;
2 and the LORD said to Moses:
"Tell Aaron your brother [a]not to
come at *just* any time into the Holy
Place inside the veil, before the
mercy seat which *is* on the ark, lest
he die; for [b]I will appear in the
cloud above the mercy seat.
3 [1]"Thus Aaron shall [a]come into
the Holy *Place:* [b]with *the blood of*
a young bull as a sin offering, and
of a ram as a burnt offering.
4 "He shall put the [a]holy linen
tunic and the linen trousers on his
body; he shall be girded with a
linen sash, and with the linen tur-
ban he shall be attired. These *are*
holy garments. Therefore [b]he shall
wash his body in water, and put
them on.
5 "And he shall take from [a]the
congregation of the children of Is-
rael two kids of the goats as a sin
offering, and one ram as a burnt
offering.
6 "Aaron shall offer the bull as
a sin offering, which *is* for himself,
and [a]make atonement for himself
and for his house.

30 [a]Lev. 5:7
31 [a]Deut. 24:8 [b]Num. 5:3; 19:13, 20
32 [a]Lev. 15:2 [b]Lev. 15:16
33 [a]Lev. 15:19 [b]Lev. 15:25 [c]Lev. 15:24

CHAPTER 16

1 [a]Lev. 10:1, 2
2 [a]Ex. 30:10 [b]Ex. 25:21, 22; 40:34
3 [a][Heb. 9:7, 12, 24, 25] [b]Lev. 4:3 [1]Lit. *With this*
4 [a]Ex. 28:39, 42, 43 [b]Ex. 30:20
5 [a]Lev. 4:14
6 [a][Heb. 5:3; 7:27, 28; 9:7]
10 [a][1 John 2:2]
11 [a][Heb. 7:27; 9:7]
12 [a]Lev. 10:1 [b]Ex. 30:34–38
13 [a]Ex. 30:7, 8 [b]Ex. 25:21 [c]Ex. 28:43
14 [a][Heb. 9:25; 10:4] [b]Lev. 4:6, 17
15 [a][Heb. 2:17] [b][Heb. 6:19; 7:27; 9:3, 7, 12]
16 [a]Ex. 29:36; 30:10
17 [a]Luke 1:10

7 "He shall take the two goats
and present them before the LORD
at the door of the tabernacle of
meeting.
8 "Then Aaron shall cast lots for
the two goats: one lot for the LORD
and the other lot for the scapegoat.
9 "And Aaron shall bring the
goat on which the LORD's lot fell,
and offer it *as* a sin offering.
10 "But the goat on which the lot
fell to be the scapegoat shall be
presented alive before the LORD, to
make [a]atonement upon it, *and* to
let it go as the scapegoat into the
wilderness.
11 "And Aaron shall bring the bull
of the sin offering, which is for
[a]himself, and make atonement for
himself and for his house, and
shall kill the bull as the sin offering
which *is* for himself.
12 "Then he shall take [a]a censer
full of burning coals of fire from
the altar before the LORD, with his
hands full of [b]sweet incense
beaten fine, and bring *it* inside the
veil.
13 [a]"And he shall put the incense
on the fire before the LORD, that
the cloud of incense may cover the
[b]mercy seat that *is* on the Testi-
mony, lest he [c]die.
14 [a]"He shall take some of the
blood of the bull and [b]sprinkle *it*
with his finger on the mercy seat
on the east *side;* and before the
mercy seat he shall sprinkle some
of the blood with his finger seven
times.
15 [a]"Then he shall kill the goat of
the sin offering, which *is* for the
people, bring its blood [b]inside the
veil, do with that blood as he did
with the blood of the bull, and
sprinkle it on the mercy seat and
before the mercy seat.
16 "So he shall [a]make atonement
for the Holy *Place,* because of the
uncleanness of the children of Is-
rael, and because of their trans-
gressions, for all their sins; and so
he shall do for the tabernacle of
meeting which remains among
them in the midst of their un-
cleanness.
17 "There shall be [a]no man in the
tabernacle of meeting when he
goes in to make atonement in the
Holy *Place,* until he comes out,
that he may make atonement for

himself, for his household, and for
all the assembly of Israel.
18 "And he shall go out to the al-
tar that *is* before the LORD, and
make atonement for [a]it, and shall
take some of the blood of the bull
and some of the blood of the goat,
and put it on the horns of the altar
all around.
19 "Then he shall sprinkle some
of the blood on it with his finger
seven times, cleanse it, and [a]con-
secrate[1] it from the [2]uncleanness
of the children of Israel.
20 "And when he has made an
end of atoning for the Holy *Place*,
the tabernacle of meeting, and the
altar, he shall bring the live goat.
21 "Aaron shall lay both his hands
on the head of the live goat, [a]con-
fess over it all the iniquities of the
children of Israel, and all their
transgressions, concerning all
their sins, [b]putting them on the
head of the goat, and shall send
it away into the wilderness by the
hand of a suitable man.
22 "The goat [1]shall [a]bear on itself
all their iniquities to an [2]uninhab-
ited land; and he shall [b]release the
goat in the wilderness.
23 "Then Aaron shall come into
the tabernacle of meeting, [a]shall
take off the linen garments which
he put on when he went into the
Holy *Place*, and shall leave them
there.
24 "And he shall wash his body
with water in a holy place, put on
his garments, come out and offer
his burnt offering and the burnt of-
fering of the people, and make
[1]atonement for himself and for the
people.
25 [a]"The fat of the sin offering he
shall burn on the altar.
26 "And he who released the goat
as the scapegoat shall wash his
clothes [a]and bathe his body in wa-
ter, and afterward he may come
into the camp.
27 [a]"The bull *for* the sin offering
and the goat *for* the sin offering,
whose blood was brought in to
make atonement in the Holy *Place*,
shall be carried outside the camp.
And they shall burn in the fire
their skins, their flesh, and their
offal.
28 "Then he who burns them shall
wash his clothes and bathe his

18 [a]Ex. 29:36
19 [a]Lev. 16:14; Ezek. 43:20 [1]*set it apart* [2]*impurity*
21 [a]Lev. 5:5; 26:40 [b][Is. 53:6]
22 [a]Lev. 8:14; [Is. 53:6, 11, 12; John 1:29; Heb. 9:28; 1 Pet. 2:24] [b]Lev. 14:7 [1]*shall carry* [2]*solitary land*
23 [a]Lev. 6:11; 16:4; Ezek. 42:14; 44:19
24 [1]Lit. *covering*
25 [a]Lev. 1:8; 4:10
26 [a]Lev. 15:5
27 [a]Lev. 4:12, 21; 6:30; Heb. 13:11
29 [a]Ex. 30:10; Lev. 23:27–32; Num. 29:7 [1]*humble yourselves* [2]As a resident alien
30 [a]Ps. 51:2; Jer. 33:8; [Eph. 5:26; Heb. 9:13, 14; 1 John 1:7, 9] [1]Lit. *covering*
31 [a]Lev. 23:27, 32; Ezra 8:21; Is. 58:3, 5; Dan. 10:12
32 [a]Lev. 4:3, 5, 16; 21:10 [b]Ex. 29:29, 30; Num. 20:26, 28
33 [1]Lit. *covering* [2]The Most Holy Place
34 [a]Lev. 23:31; Num. 29:7 [b]Ex. 30:10; [Heb. 9:7, 25, 28]

CHAPTER 17

3 [a]Deut. 12:5, 15, 21
4 [a]Rom. 5:13 [1]Put to death
5 [a]Gen. 21:33; 22:2; 31:54; Deut. 12:1–27; Ezek. 20:28

body in water, and afterward he
may come into the camp.
29 "*This* shall be a statute forever
for you: [a]In the seventh month, on
the tenth *day* of the month, you
shall [1]afflict your souls, and do no
work at all, *whether* a native of
your own country or a stranger
who [2]dwells among you.
30 "For on that day *the priest*
shall make [1]atonement for you, to
[a]cleanse you, *that* you may be
clean from all your sins before the
LORD.
31 [a]"It *is* a sabbath of solemn rest
for you, and you shall afflict your
souls. *It is* a statute forever.
32 [a]"And the priest, who is
anointed and [b]consecrated to min-
ister as priest in his father's place,
shall make atonement, and put on
the linen clothes, the holy gar-
ments;
33 "then he shall make [1]atone-
ment for [2]the Holy Sanctuary, and
he shall make atonement for the
tabernacle of meeting and for the
altar, and he shall make atone-
ment for the priests and for all the
people of the assembly.
34 [a]"This shall be an everlasting
statute for you, to make atonement
for the children of Israel, for all
their sins, [b]once a year." And he
did as the LORD commanded Mo-
ses.

The Sanctity of Blood

17 And the LORD spoke to Mo-
ses, saying,
2 "Speak to Aaron, to his sons,
and to all the children of Israel,
and say to them, 'This *is* the thing
which the LORD has commanded,
saying:
3 "Whatever man of the house of
Israel who [a]kills an ox or lamb or
goat in the camp, or who kills *it*
outside the camp,
4 "and does not bring it to the
door of the tabernacle of meeting
to offer an offering to the LORD be-
fore the tabernacle of the LORD, the
guilt of bloodshed shall be [a]im-
puted to that man. He has shed
blood; and that man shall be [1]cut
off from among his people,
5 "to the end that the children of
Israel may bring their sacrifices
[a]which they offer in the open field,
that they may bring them to the

LORD at the door of the tabernacle
of meeting, to the priest, and offer
them *as* peace offerings to the
LORD.
6 "And the priest [a]shall sprinkle
the blood on the altar of the LORD
at the door of the tabernacle of
meeting, and [b]burn the fat for a
sweet aroma to the LORD.
7 "They shall no more offer their
sacrifices [a]to [1]demons, after whom
they [b]have played the harlot. This
shall be a statute forever for them
throughout their generations."'
8 "Also you shall say to them:
'Whatever man of the house of Is-
rael, or of the strangers who dwell
among you, [a]who offers a burnt of-
fering or sacrifice,
9 'and does not [a]bring it to the
door of the tabernacle of meeting,
to offer it to the LORD, that man
shall be [1]cut off from among his
people.
10 [a]'And whatever man of the
house of Israel, or of the strangers
who dwell among you, who eats
any blood, [b]I will set My face
against that person who eats
blood, and will cut him off from
among his people.
11 'For the [a]life of the flesh *is* in
the blood, and I have given it to
you upon the altar [b]to make atone-
ment for your souls; for [c]it *is* the
blood *that* makes atonement for
the soul.'
12 "Therefore I said to the chil-
dren of Israel, 'No one among you
shall eat blood, nor shall any
stranger who dwells among you
eat blood.'
13 "Whatever man of the children
of Israel, or of the strangers who
dwell among you, who [a]hunts and
catches any animal or bird that
may be eaten, he shall [b]pour out
its blood and [c]cover it with dust;
14 [a]"for *it is* the life of all flesh.
Its blood sustains its life. There-
fore I said to the children of Israel,
'You shall not eat the blood of any
flesh, for the life of all flesh is its
blood. Whoever eats it shall be cut
off.'
15 [a]"And every person who eats
what died *naturally* or what was
torn *by beasts, whether he is* a na-
tive of your own country or a
stranger, [b]he shall both wash his
clothes and [c]bathe in water, and

6 [a]Lev. 3:2 [b]Ex. 29:13, 18; Num. 18:17
7 [a]Ex. 22:20; 32:8; 34:15; Deut. 32:17; 2 Chr. 11:15; Ps. 106:37; 1 Cor. 10:20 [b]Ex. 34:15; Deut. 31:16; Ezek. 23:8 [1]Having the form of a goat or satyr
8 [a]Lev. 1:2, 3; 18:26
9 [a]Lev. 14:23 [1]Put to death
10 [a]Gen. 9:4; Lev. 3:17; 7:26, 27; Deut. 12:16, 23–25; 15:23; 1 Sam. 14:33 [b]Lev. 20:3, 5, 6
11 [a]Gen. 9:4; Lev. 17:14 [b][Matt. 26:28; Rom. 3:25; Eph. 1:7; Col. 1:14, 20; 1 Pet. 1:2; 1 John 1:7] [c][Heb. 9:22]
13 [a]Lev. 7:26 [b]Deut. 12:16, 24 [c]Ezek. 24:7
14 [a]Gen. 9:4; Lev. 17:11; Deut. 12:23
15 [a]Ex. 22:31; Lev. 7:24; 22:8; Deut. 14:21; Ezek. 4:14; 44:31 [b]Lev. 11:25 [c]Lev. 15:5
16 [a]Lev. 5:1 [1]*iniquity*

CHAPTER 18

2 [a]Ex. 6:7; Lev. 11:44, 45; 19:3; Ezek. 20:5, 7, 19, 20
3 [a]Josh. 24:14; Ezek. 20:7, 8 [b]Ex. 23:24; Lev. 18:24–30; 20:23; Deut. 12:30, 31 [1]*what is done in* [2]*statutes*
4 [a]Ezek. 20:19
8 [a]Gen. 35:22
9 [a]Lev. 18:11; 20:17; Deut. 27:22
12 [a]Lev. 20:19
14 [a]Lev. 20:20

be unclean until evening. Then he
shall be clean.
16 "But if he does not wash *them*
or bathe his body, then [a]he shall
bear his [1]guilt."

Laws of Sexual Morality

18 Then the LORD spoke to Mo-
ses, saying,
2 "Speak to the children of Is-
rael, and say to them: [a]'I am the
LORD your God.
3 [a]'According to [1]the doings of
the land of Egypt, where you
dwelt, you shall not do; and [b]ac-
cording to the doings of the land
of Canaan, where I am bringing
you, you shall not do; nor shall you
walk in their [2]ordinances.
4 [a]'You shall observe My judg-
ments and keep My ordinances, to
walk in them: I *am* the LORD your
God.
5 'You shall therefore keep My
statutes and My judgments, which
if a man does, he shall live by
them: I *am* the LORD.
6 'None of you shall approach
anyone who is near of kin to him,
to uncover his nakedness: I *am* the
LORD.
7 'The nakedness of your father
or the nakedness of your mother
you shall not uncover. She *is* your
mother; you shall not uncover her
nakedness.
8 'The nakedness of your [a]fa-
ther's wife you shall not uncover;
it *is* your father's nakedness.
9 [a]'The nakedness of your sister,
the daughter of your father, or the
daughter of your mother, *whether*
born at home or elsewhere, their
nakedness you shall not uncover.
10 'The nakedness of your son's
daughter or your daughter's
daughter, their nakedness you
shall not uncover; for theirs *is* your
own nakedness.
11 'The nakedness of your father's
wife's daughter, begotten by your
father—she *is* your sister—you
shall not uncover her nakedness.
12 [a]'You shall not uncover the
nakedness of your father's sister;
she *is* near of kin to your father.
13 'You shall not uncover the
nakedness of your mother's sister,
for she *is* near of kin to your
mother.
14 [a]'You shall not uncover the

nakedness of your father's
brother. You shall not approach
his wife; she *is* your aunt.
15 'You shall not uncover the
nakedness of your daughter-in-
law—she *is* your son's wife—you
shall not uncover her nakedness.
16 'You shall not uncover the
nakedness of your brother's wife;
it *is* your brother's nakedness.
17 'You shall not uncover the
nakedness of a woman and her
[a]daughter, nor shall you take her
son's daughter or her daughter's
daughter, to uncover her naked-
ness. They *are* near of kin to her.
It *is* wickedness.
18 'Nor shall you take a woman
[a]as a rival to her sister, to uncover
her nakedness while the other is
alive.
19 'Also you shall not approach a
woman to uncover her nakedness
as [a]long as she is in her [b]*custom-
ary* impurity.
20 [a]'Moreover you shall not lie
carnally with your [b]neighbor's
wife, to defile yourself with her.
21 'And you shall not let any of
your descendants [a]pass through
[b]*the fire* to [c]Molech, nor shall you
profane the name of your God: I
am the LORD.
22 'You shall not lie with [a]a male
as with a woman. It *is* an abom-
ination.
23 'Nor shall you mate with any
[a]animal, to defile yourself with it.
Nor shall any woman stand before
an animal to mate with it. It *is* per-
version.
24 [a]'Do not defile yourselves with
any of these things; [b]for by all
these the nations are defiled,
which I am casting out before you.
25 'For [a]the land is defiled; there-
fore I [b]visit[1] the punishment of its
iniquity upon it, and the land
[c]vomits out its inhabitants.
26 [a]'You shall therefore [1]keep My
statutes and My judgments, and
shall not commit *any* of these
abominations, *either* any of your
own nation or any stranger who
dwells among you
27 '(for all these abominations the
men of the land have done, who
were before you, and thus the land
is defiled),
28 'lest [a]the land vomit you out
also when you defile it, as it vom-
ited out the nations that *were* be-
fore you.
29 'For whoever commits any of
these abominations, the persons
who commit *them* shall be [1]cut off
from among their people.
30 'Therefore you shall keep My
[1]ordinance, so [a]that *you* do not
commit *any* of these abominable
customs which were committed
before you, and that you do not de-
file yourselves by them: [b]I *am* the
LORD your God.' "

Moral and Ceremonial Laws

19 And the LORD spoke to Mo-
ses, saying,
2 "Speak to all the congregation
of the children of Israel, and say
to them: [a]'You shall be holy, for I
the LORD your God *am* holy.
3 [a]'Every one of you shall revere
his mother and his father, and
[b]keep My Sabbaths: I *am* the LORD
your God.
4 [a]'Do not turn to idols, [b]nor
make for yourselves [1]molded
gods: I *am* the LORD your God.
5 'And [a]if you offer a sacrifice of
a peace offering to the LORD, you
shall offer it of your own free will.
6 'It shall be eaten the same day
you offer *it*, and on the next day.
And if any remains until the third
day, it shall be burned in the fire.
7 'And if it is eaten at all on the
third day, it *is* an abomination. It
shall not be accepted.
8 'Therefore *everyone* who eats
it shall bear his iniquity, because
he has profaned the hallowed *of-
fering* of the LORD; and that person
shall be cut off from his people.
9 [a]'When you reap the harvest of
your land, you shall not wholly
reap the corners of your field, nor
shall you gather the gleanings of
your harvest.
10 'And you shall not glean your
vineyard, nor shall you gather
every grape of your vineyard; you
shall leave them for the poor and
the stranger: I *am* the LORD your
God.
11 [a]'You shall not steal, nor deal
falsely, [b]nor lie to one another.
12 'And you shall not [a]swear by
My name falsely, [b]nor shall you
profane the name of your God: I
am the LORD.
13 [a]'You shall not cheat your

17 [a]Lev. 20:14
18 [a]1 Sam. 1:6, 8
19 [a]Ezek. 18:6 [b]Lev. 15:24; 20:18
20 [a][Prov. 6:25–33] [b]Ex. 20:14; Lev. 20:10; [Matt. 5:27, 28; 1 Cor. 6:9; Heb. 13:4]
21 [a]Lev. 20:2–5; Deut. 12:31 [b]2 Kin. 16:3 [c]1 Kin. 11:7, 33; Acts 7:43
22 [a]Lev. 20:13; Rom. 1:27
23 [a]Ex. 22:19; Lev. 20:15, 16; Deut. 27:21
24 [a]Matt. 15:18–20; 1 Cor. 3:17 [b]Lev. 18:3; 20:23; Deut. 18:12
25 [a]Num. 35:33, 34; Ezek. 36:17 [b]Is. 26:21; Jer. 5:9 [c]Lev. 18:28; 20:22 [1]*bring judgment for*
26 [a]Lev. 18:5, 30 [1]*obey*
28 [a]Jer. 9:19
29 [1]Put to death
30 [a]Lev. 18:3; 22:9 [b]Lev. 18:2 [1]*charge*

CHAPTER 19

2 [a]Ex. 19:6; Lev. 11:44; 20:7, 26; [Eph. 1:4]; 1 Pet. 1:16
3 [a]Ex. 20:12; Deut. 5:16; Matt. 15:4; Eph. 6:2 [b]Ex. 16:23; 20:8; 31:13
4 [a]Ex. 20:4; Ps. 96:5; 115:4–7; 1 Cor. 10:14; [Col. 3:5] [b]Ex. 34:17 [1]*molten*
5 [a]Lev. 7:16
9 [a]Lev. 23:22; Deut. 24:19–22
11 [a]Ex. 20:15, 16 [b]Jer. 9:3–5; Eph. 4:25
12 [a]Ex. 20:7; Deut. 5:11; [Matt. 5:33–37; James 5:12] [b]Lev. 18:21
13 [a]Ex. 22:7–15, 21–27; Mark 10:19

neighbor, nor rob *him*. [b]The wages
of him who is hired shall not re-
main with you all night until morn-
ing.
14 'You shall not curse the deaf,
[a]nor put a stumbling block before
the blind, but shall fear your God:
I *am* the LORD.
15 'You shall do no injustice in
[a]judgment. You shall not [b]be par-
tial to the poor, nor honor the per-
son of the mighty. In righteousness
you shall judge your neighbor.
16 'You shall not go about *as* a
[a]talebearer among your people;
nor shall you [b]take a stand against
the life of your neighbor: I *am* the
LORD.
17 [a]'You shall not hate your
brother in your heart. [b]You shall
surely [1]rebuke your neighbor, and
not bear sin because of him.
18 [a]'You shall not take vengeance,
nor bear any grudge against the
children of your people, [b]but you
shall love your neighbor as your-
self: I *am* the LORD.
19 'You shall keep My statutes.
You shall not let your livestock
breed with another kind. You shall
not sow your field with mixed
seed. Nor shall a garment of mixed
linen and wool come upon you.
20 'Whoever lies carnally with a
woman who *is* [a]betrothed to a man
as a concubine, and who has not
at all been redeemed nor given her
freedom, for this there shall be
[1]scourging; *but* they shall not be
put to death, because she was not
free.
21 'And he shall bring his trespass
offering to the LORD, to the door
of the tabernacle of meeting, a ram
as a trespass offering.
22 'The priest shall make [1]atone-
ment for him with the ram of the
trespass offering before the LORD
for his sin which he has commit-
ted. And the sin which he has com-
mitted shall be forgiven him.
23 'When you come into the land,
and have planted all kinds of trees
for food, then you shall count their
fruit as [1]uncircumcised. Three
years it shall be as uncircumcised
to you. *It* shall not be eaten.
24 'But in the fourth year all its
fruit shall be holy, a praise to the
LORD.
25 'And in the fifth year you may
eat its fruit, that it may yield to you
its increase: I *am* the LORD your
God.
26 'You shall not eat *anything*
with the blood, nor shall you prac-
tice divination or soothsaying.
27 'You shall not shave around the
sides of your head, nor shall you
disfigure the edges of your beard.
28 'You shall not [a]make any cut-
tings in your flesh for the dead, nor
tattoo any marks on you: I *am* the
LORD.
29 [a]'Do not prostitute your daugh-
ter, to cause her to be a harlot, lest
the land fall into harlotry, and the
land become full of wickedness.
30 'You shall [1]keep My Sabbaths
and [a]reverence My sanctuary: I *am*
the LORD.
31 'Give no regard to mediums
and familiar spirits; do not seek af-
ter [a]them, to be defiled by them: I
am the LORD your God.
32 [a]'You shall [1]rise before the
gray headed and honor the pres-
ence of an old man, and [b]fear your
God: I *am* the LORD.
33 'And [a]if a stranger dwells with
you in your land, you shall not
mistreat him.
34 [a]'The stranger who dwells
among you shall be to you as [1]one
born among you, and [b]you shall
love him as yourself; for you were
strangers in the land of Egypt: I
am the LORD your God.
35 'You shall do no injustice in
judgment, in measurement of
length, weight, or volume.
36 'You shall have [a]honest scales,
honest weights, an honest ephah,
and an honest hin: I *am* the LORD
your God, who brought you out of
the land of Egypt.
37 [a]'Therefore you shall observe
all My statutes and all My judg-
ments, and perform them: I *am* the
LORD.' "

Penalties for Breaking the Law

20 Then the LORD spoke to Mo-
ses, saying,
2 [a]"Again, you shall say to the
children of Israel: [b]'Whoever of
the children of Israel, or of the
strangers who [1]dwell in Israel,
who gives *any* of his descendants
to Molech, he shall surely be put
to death. The people of the land
shall [c]stone him with stones.

13 [b]Deut. 24:15; Mal. 3:5; James 5:4
14 [a]Deut. 27:18
15 [a]Deut. 16:19 [b]Ex. 23:3, 6; Deut. 1:17; 10:17; Ps. 82:2
16 [a]Prov. 11:13; 18:8; 20:19 [b]Ex. 23:7; Deut. 27:25; 1 Kin. 21:7–19
17 [a][1 John 2:9, 11; 3:15] [b]Matt. 18:15; [Luke 17:3]; Eph. 5:11 [1]*reprove*
18 [a][Deut. 32:35; 1 Sam. 24:12; Rom. 12:19; Heb. 10:30] [b]Matt. 5:43; 19:19; Mark 12:31; Luke 10:27; [Rom. 13:9; Gal. 5:14]; James 2:8
20 [a]Deut. 22:23–27 [1]*punishment*
22 [1]Lit. *covering*
23 [1]*unclean*
28 [a]1 Kin. 18:28; Jer. 16:6
29 [a]Lev. 21:9; Deut. 22:21; 23:17, 18
30 [a]Lev. 26:2; Eccl. 5:1 [1]*observe*
31 [a]Lev. 20:6, 27; Deut. 18:11; 1 Sam. 28:3; Is. 8:19
32 [a]Prov. 23:22; Lam. 5:12; 1 Tim. 5:1 [b]Lev. 19:14 [1]*rise to give honor*
33 [a]Ex. 22:21; Deut. 24:17, 18
34 [a]Ex. 12:48 [b]Deut. 10:19 [1]*native among you*
36 [a]Deut. 25:13–15; Prov. 20:10
37 [a]Lev. 18:4, 5; Deut. 4:5, 6; 5:1; 6:25

CHAPTER 20

2 [a]Lev. 18:2 [b]Lev. 18:21; 2 Kin. 23:10; 2 Chr. 33:6; Jer. 7:31 [c]Deut. 17:2–5 [1]As resident aliens

3 [a]'I will set My face against that
man, and will [1]cut him off from his
people, because he has given *some*
of his descendants to Molech, to
defile My sanctuary and profane
My holy name.
4 'And if the people of the land
should in any way [1]hide their eyes
from the man, when he gives *some*
of his descendants to Molech, and
they do not kill him,
5 'then I will set My face against
that man and against his family;
and I will cut him off from his peo-
ple, and all who prostitute them-
selves with him to commit harlotry
with Molech.
6 'And [a]the person who turns to
mediums and familiar spirits, to
prostitute himself with them, I will
set My face against that person
and cut him off from his people.
7 [a]'Consecrate[1] yourselves there-
fore, and be holy, for I *am* the LORD
your God.
8 'And you shall keep [a]My stat-
utes, and perform them: [b]I *am* the
LORD who [1]sanctifies you.
9 'For [a]everyone who curses his
father or his mother shall surely
be put to death. He has cursed his
father or his mother. [b]His blood
shall be upon him.
10 [a]'The man who commits adul-
tery with *another* man's wife, *he*
who commits adultery with his
neighbor's wife, the adulterer and
the adulteress, shall surely be put
to death.
11 'The man who lies with his [a]fa-
ther's wife has uncovered his fa-
ther's nakedness; both of them
shall surely be put to death. Their
blood *shall be* upon them.
12 'If a man lies with his
[a]daughter-in-law, both of them
shall surely be put to death. They
have committed perversion. Their
blood *shall be* upon them.
13 [a]'If a man lies with a male as
he lies with a woman, both of
them have committed an abomina-
tion. They shall surely be put to
death. Their blood *shall be* upon
them.
14 'If a man marries a woman and
her [a]mother, it *is* wickedness. They
shall be burned with fire, both he
and they, that there may be no
wickedness among you.
15 'If a man mates with an [a]ani-
mal, he shall surely be put to
death, and you shall kill the ani-
mal.
16 'If a woman approaches any
animal and mates with it, you shall
kill the woman and the animal.
They shall surely be put to death.
Their blood *is* upon them.
17 'If a man takes his [a]sister, his
father's daughter or his mother's
daughter, and sees her nakedness
and she sees his nakedness, it *is*
a wicked thing. And they shall be
[1]cut off in the sight of their people.
He has uncovered his sister's
nakedness. He shall bear his [2]guilt.
18 [a]'If a man lies with a woman
during her [1]sickness and uncovers
her nakedness, he has [2]exposed
her flow, and she has uncovered
the flow of her blood. Both of them
shall be [3]cut off from their people.
19 'You shall not uncover the
nakedness of your [a]mother's sister
nor of your [b]father's sister, for that
would uncover his near of kin.
They shall bear their guilt.
20 'If a man lies with his [a]uncle's
wife, he has uncovered his uncle's
nakedness. They shall bear their
sin; they shall die childless.
21 'If a man takes his [a]brother's
wife, it *is* an [1]unclean thing. He has
uncovered his brother's naked-
ness. They shall be childless.
22 'You shall therefore keep all
My [a]statutes and all My judg-
ments, and perform them, that the
land where I am bringing you to
dwell [b]may not vomit you out.
23 [a]'And you shall not walk in the
statutes of the nation which I am
casting out before you; for they
commit all these things, and
[b]therefore I abhor them.
24 'But [a]I have said to you, "You
shall inherit their land, and I will
give it to you to possess, a land
flowing with milk and honey." I
am the LORD your God, [b]who has
separated you from the peoples.
25 [a]'You shall therefore distin-
guish between clean animals and
unclean, between unclean birds
and clean, [b]and you shall not make
yourselves [1]abominable by beast
or by bird, or by any kind of living
thing that creeps on the ground,
which I have separated from you
as [2]unclean.
26 'And you shall be holy to Me,
[a]for I the LORD *am* holy, and have

3 [a]Lev. 17:10 [1]Put him to death
4 [1]*disregard*
6 [a]Lev. 19:31; 1 Sam. 28:7–25
7 [a]Lev. 19:2; Heb. 12:14 [1]*Set yourselves apart for the* LORD
8 [a]Lev. 19:19, 37 [b]Ex. 31:13; Deut. 14:2; Ezek. 37:28 [1]*sets you apart*
9 [a]Ex. 21:17; Deut. 27:16; Prov. 20:20; Matt. 15:4 [b]2 Sam. 1:16
10 [a]Ex. 20:14; Lev. 18:20; Deut. 5:18; 22:22; John 8:4, 5
11 [a]Lev. 18:7, 8; Deut. 27:20
12 [a]Lev. 18:15
13 [a]Lev. 18:22; Deut. 23:17; Judg. 19:22
14 [a]Lev. 18:17
15 [a]Lev. 18:23; Deut. 27:21
17 [a]Lev. 18:9; Deut. 27:22 [1]Put to death [2]*iniquity*
18 [a]Lev. 15:24; 18:19 [1]Or *customary impurity* [2]Lit. *made bare* [3]Put to death
19 [a]Lev. 18:13 [b]Lev. 18:12
20 [a]Lev. 18:14
21 [a]Lev. 18:16; Matt. 14:3, 4 [1]*indecent, impure*
22 [a]Lev. 18:26; 19:37 [b]Lev. 18:25, 28; 2 Chr. 36:14–16
23 [a]Lev. 18:3, 24 [b]Deut. 9:5
24 [a]Ex. 3:17; 6:8; 13:5; 33:1–3 [b]Ex. 19:5; 33:16; Lev. 20:26; Deut. 7:6; 14:2; 1 Kin. 8:53
25 [a]Lev. 10:10; 11:1–47; Deut. 14:3–21 [b]Lev. 11:43 [1]*detestable* or *loathsome* [2]*defiled*
26 [a]Lev. 19:2; 1 Pet. 1:16

separated you from the peoples,
that you should be Mine.
27 [a]'A man or a woman who is a
medium, or who has familiar spir-
its, shall surely be put to death;
they shall stone them with stones.
Their blood *shall be* upon them.' "

Regulations for Conduct of Priests

21 And the LORD said to Moses,
"Speak to the priests, the
sons of Aaron, and say to them:
[a]'None shall defile himself for the
dead among his people,
2 'except for his relatives who
are nearest to him: his mother, his
father, his son, his daughter, and
his brother;
3 'also his virgin sister who is
near to him, who has had no hus-
band, for her he may defile him-
self.
4 '*Otherwise* he shall not defile
himself, *being* a [1]chief man among
his people, to profane himself.
5 [a]'They shall not make any bald
place on their heads, nor shall they
shave the edges of their beards nor
make any cuttings in their flesh.
6 'They shall be [a]holy to their
God and not profane the name of
their God, for they offer the offer-
ings of the LORD made by fire, *and*
the [b]bread of their God; [c]therefore
they shall be holy.
7 [a]'They shall not take a wife
who is a harlot or a defiled woman,
nor shall they take a woman [b]di-
vorced from her husband; for [1]*the
priest* is holy to his God.
8 'Therefore you shall [1]conse-
crate him, for he offers the bread
of your God. He shall be holy to
you, for [a]I the LORD, who [b]sanctify
you, *am* holy.
9 'The daughter of any priest, if
she profanes herself by playing the
harlot, she profanes her father.
She shall be [a]burned with fire.
10 '*He who is* the high priest
among his brethren, on whose
head the anointing oil was [a]poured
and who is consecrated to wear
the garments, shall not [b]uncover[1]
his head nor tear his clothes;
11 'nor shall he go [a]near any dead
body, nor defile himself for his fa-
ther or his mother;
12 [a]'nor shall he go out of the
sanctuary, nor profane the sanctu-
ary of his God; for the [b]consecra-
tion of the anointing oil of his God
is upon him: I *am* the LORD.
13 'And he shall take a wife in her
virginity.
14 'A widow or a divorced woman
or a defiled woman *or* a harlot—
these he shall not marry; but he
shall take a virgin of his own peo-
ple as wife.
15 'Nor shall he profane his pos-
terity among his people, for I the
LORD sanctify him.' "
16 And the LORD spoke to Moses,
saying,
17 "Speak to Aaron, saying: 'No
man of your descendants in *suc-
ceeding* generations, who has *any*
defect, may approach to offer the
bread of his God.
18 'For any man who has a [a]defect
shall not approach: a man blind or
lame, who has a marred *face* or
any *limb* [b]too long,
19 'a man who has a broken foot
or broken hand,
20 'or is a hunchback or a dwarf,
or *a man* who has a defect in his
eye, or eczema or scab, or is a eu-
nuch.
21 'No man of the descendants of
Aaron the priest, who has a defect,
shall come near to offer the offer-
ings made by fire to the LORD. He
has a defect; he shall not come
near to offer the bread of his God.
22 'He may eat the bread of his
God, *both* the most holy and the
holy;
23 'only he shall not go near the
[a]veil or approach the altar, be-
cause he has a defect, lest [b]he pro-
fane My sanctuaries; for I the LORD
sanctify them.' "
24 And Moses told *it* to Aaron and
his sons, and to all the children of
Israel.

22 Then the LORD spoke to Mo-
ses, saying,
2 "Speak to Aaron and his sons,
that they [a]separate[1] themselves
from the holy things of the chil-
dren of Israel, and that they [b]do
not profane My holy name *by* what
they [c]dedicate to Me: I *am* the
LORD.
3 "Say to them: 'Whoever of all
your descendants throughout your
generations, who goes near the
holy things which the children of
Israel dedicate to the LORD, [a]while
he has [1]uncleanness upon him,

27 [a]Lev. 19:31; 1 Sam. 28:9

CHAPTER 21

1 [a]Lev. 19:28; Ezek. 44:25

4 [1]Lit. *master or husband*

5 [a]Lev. 19:27; Deut. 14:1; Ezek. 44:20

6 [a]Ex. 22:31 [b]Lev. 3:11 [c]Is. 52:11

7 [a]Ezek. 44:22 [b]Deut. 24:1, 2 [1]Lit. *he*

8 [a]Lev. 11:44, 45 [b]Lev. 8:12, 30 [1]*set him apart*

9 [a]Deut. 22:21

10 [a]Lev. 8:12 [b]Lev. 10:6, 7 [1]In mourning

11 [a]Num. 19:14

12 [a]Lev. 10:7 [b]Ex. 29:6, 7

18 [a]Lev. 22:19–25 [b]Lev. 22:23

23 [a]Lev. 16:2 [b]Lev. 21:12

CHAPTER 22

2 [a]Num. 6:3 [b]Lev. 18:21 [c]Ex. 28:38; Lev. 16:19; 25:10; Num. 18:32; Deut. 15:19 [1]*keep themselves apart from*

3 [a]Lev. 7:20, 21; Num. 19:13 [1]*defilement*

that person shall be cut off from My presence: I *am* the LORD.
4 'Whatever man of the descendants of Aaron, who *is* a [a]leper or has [b]a discharge, shall not eat the holy offerings [c]until he is clean. And [d]whoever touches anything made unclean *by* a corpse, or [e]a man who has had an emission of semen,
5 'or [a]whoever touches any creeping thing by which he would be made unclean, or [b]any person by whom he would become unclean, whatever his uncleanness may be—
6 'the person who has touched any such thing shall be unclean until evening, and shall not eat the holy *offerings* unless he [a]washes his body with water.
7 'And when the sun goes down he shall be clean; and afterward he may eat the holy *offerings*, because [a]it *is* his food.
8 [a]'Whatever dies *naturally* or is torn *by beasts* he shall not eat, to defile himself with it: I *am* the LORD.
9 'They shall therefore keep [a]My [1]ordinance, [b]lest they bear sin for it and die thereby, if they profane it: I the LORD sanctify them.
10 [a]'No outsider shall eat the holy *offering*; one who [1]dwells with the priest, or a hired servant, shall not eat the holy thing.
11 'But if the priest [a]buys a person with his money, he may eat it; and one who is born in his house may eat his food.
12 'If the priest's daughter is married to an outsider, she may not eat of the holy offerings.
13 'But if the priest's daughter is a widow or divorced, and has no child, and has returned to her father's house as in her youth, she may eat her father's food; but no outsider shall eat it.
14 'And if a man eats the holy *offering* unintentionally, then he shall restore a holy *offering* to the priest, and add one-fifth to it.
15 'They shall not profane the [a]holy *offerings* of the children of Israel, which they offer to the LORD,
16 'or allow them to bear the guilt of trespass when they eat their holy *offerings*; for I the LORD sanctify them.' "

Offerings Accepted and Not Accepted

17 And the LORD spoke to Moses, saying,
18 "Speak to Aaron and his sons, and to all the children of Israel, and say to them: [a]'Whatever man of the house of Israel, or of the strangers in Israel, who [1]offers his sacrifice for any of his vows or for any of his freewill offerings, which they offer to the LORD as a burnt offering—
19 [a]'*you shall offer* of your own free will a male without blemish from the cattle, from the sheep, or from the goats.
20 [a]'Whatever has a defect, you shall not offer, for it shall not be acceptable on your behalf.
21 'And [a]whoever offers a sacrifice of a peace offering to the LORD, [b]to fulfill *his* vow, or a freewill offering from the cattle or the sheep, it must be perfect to be accepted; there shall be no defect in it.
22 [a]'Those *that are* blind or broken or maimed, or have an [1]ulcer or eczema or scabs, you shall not offer to the LORD, nor make [b]an offering by fire of them on the altar to the LORD.
23 'Either a bull or a lamb that has any limb [a]too long or too short you may offer *as* a freewill offering, but for a vow it shall not be accepted.
24 'You shall not offer to the LORD what is bruised or crushed, or torn or cut; nor shall you make *any offering of them* in your land.
25 'Nor [a]from a foreigner's hand shall you offer any of these as [b]the bread of your God, because their [c]corruption *is* in them, *and* defects *are* in them. They shall not be accepted on your behalf.' "
26 And the LORD spoke to Moses, saying:
27 [a]"When a bull or a sheep or a goat is born, it shall be seven days with its mother; and from the eighth day and thereafter it shall be accepted as an offering made by fire to the LORD.
28 "*Whether it is* a cow or ewe, do not kill both her [a]and her young on the same day.
29 "And when you [a]offer a sacri-

4 [a]Num. 5:2 [b]Lev. 15:2 [c]Lev. 14:2; 15:13 [d]Lev. 11:24–28, 39, 40; Num. 19:11 [e]Lev. 15:16, 17
5 [a]Lev. 11:23–28 [b]Lev. 15:7, 19
6 [a]Lev. 15:5
7 [a]Lev. 21:22; Num. 18:11, 13
8 [a]Ex. 22:31; Lev. 7:24; 11:39, 40; 17:15; Ezek. 44:31
9 [a]Lev. 18:30 [b]Ex. 28:43; Lev. 22:16; Num. 18:22 [1]*charge*
10 [a]Ex. 29:33; Lev. 22:13; Num. 3:10 [1]As a visitor
11 [a]Ex. 12:44
15 [a]Num. 18:32
18 [a]Lev. 1:2, 3, 10 [1]*brings his offering*
19 [a]Lev. 1:3; Deut. 15:21
20 [a]Deut. 15:21; 17:1; Mal. 1:8, 14; [Eph. 5:27; Heb. 9:14; 1 Pet. 1:19]
21 [a]Lev. 3:1, 6 [b]Num. 15:3, 8; Ps. 61:8; 65:1; Eccl. 5:4, 5
22 [a]Lev. 22:20; Mal. 1:8 [b]Lev. 1:9, 13; 3:3, 5 [1]*running sore*
23 [a]Lev. 21:18
25 [a]Num. 15:15, 16 [b]Lev. 21:6, 17 [c]Mal. 1:14
27 [a]Ex. 22:30
28 [a]Deut. 22:6, 7
29 [a]Lev. 7:12; Ps. 107:22; 116:17; Amos 4:5

fice of thanksgiving to the LORD,
offer *it* of your own free will.
30 "On the same day it shall be
eaten; you shall leave [a]none of it
until morning: I *am* the LORD.
31 [a]"Therefore you shall keep My
commandments, and perform
them: I *am* the LORD.
32 [a]"You shall not profane My
holy name, but [b]I will be [1]hallowed
among the children of Israel. I *am*
the LORD who [c]sanctifies you,
33 [a]"who brought you out of the
land of Egypt, to be your God: I
am the LORD."

Feasts of the LORD

23 And the LORD spoke to Mo-
ses, saying,
2 "Speak to the children of Is-
rael, and say to them: 'The feasts
of the LORD, which you shall pro-
claim *to be* [a]holy convocations,
these *are* My feasts.

The Sabbath

3 [a]'Six days shall work be done,
but the seventh day *is* a Sabbath
of solemn rest, a holy convocation.
You shall do no work *on it;* it *is*
the Sabbath of the LORD in all your
dwellings.

The Passover and Unleavened Bread

4 [a]'These *are* the feasts of the
LORD, holy convocations which
you shall proclaim at their ap-
pointed times.
5 [a]'On the fourteenth *day* of the
first month at twilight *is* the LORD'S
Passover.
6 'And on the fifteenth day of the
same month *is* the Feast of Unleav-
ened Bread to the LORD; seven
days you must eat unleavened
bread.
7 [a]'On the first day you shall
have a holy convocation; you shall
do no [1]customary work on it.
8 'But you shall offer an offering
made by fire to the LORD for seven
days. The seventh day *shall be* a
holy convocation; you shall do no
customary work *on it.*' "

The Feast of Firstfruits

9 And the LORD spoke to Moses,
saying,
10 "Speak to the children of Is-
rael, and say to them: [a]'When you
come into the land which I give to
you, and reap its harvest, then you
shall bring a sheaf of [b]the first-
fruits of your harvest to the priest.
11 'He shall [a]wave the sheaf be-
fore the LORD, to be accepted on
your behalf; on the day after the
Sabbath the priest shall wave it.
12 'And you shall offer on that
day, when you wave the sheaf, a
male lamb of the first year, without
blemish, as a burnt offering to the
LORD.
13 'Its grain offering *shall be* two-
tenths *of an ephah* of fine flour
mixed with oil, an offering made
by fire to the LORD, for a [1]sweet
aroma; and its drink offering *shall
be* of wine, one-fourth of a hin.
14 'You shall eat neither bread nor
parched grain nor fresh grain until
the same day that you have
brought an offering to your God;
it shall be a statute forever
throughout your generations in all
your dwellings.

The Feast of Weeks

15 'And you shall count for your-
selves from the day after the Sab-
bath, from the day that you
brought the sheaf of the wave of-
fering: seven Sabbaths shall be
completed.
16 'Count [a]fifty days to the day af-
ter the seventh Sabbath; then you
shall offer [b]a new grain offering to
the LORD.
17 'You shall bring from your
dwellings two wave *loaves* of two-
tenths *of an ephah.* They shall be
of fine flour; they shall be baked
with leaven. *They are* [a]the first-
fruits to the LORD.
18 'And you shall offer with the
bread seven lambs of the first year,
without blemish, one young bull,
and two rams. They shall be *as* a
burnt offering to the LORD, with
their grain offering and their drink
offerings, an offering made by fire
for a sweet aroma to the LORD.
19 'Then you shall sacrifice [a]one
kid of the goats as a sin offering,
and two male lambs of the first
year as a sacrifice of a [b]peace of-
fering.
20 'The priest shall wave them
with the bread of the firstfruits *as*
a wave offering before the LORD,
with the two lambs. [a]They shall be
holy to the LORD for the priest.

30 [a]Lev. 7:15
31 [a]Lev. 19:37; Num. 15:40; Deut. 4:40
32 [a]Lev. 18:21 [b]Lev. 10:3; Matt. 6:9; Luke 11:2 [c]Lev. 20:8 [1]*treated as holy*
33 [a]Lev. 19:36, 37; Num. 15:40; Deut. 4:40
CHAPTER 23
2 [a]Ex. 12:16
3 [a]Ex. 20:9; 23:12; 31:15; Lev. 19:3; Deut. 5:13, 14; Luke 13:14
4 [a]Ex. 23:14–16; Lev. 23:2, 37
5 [a]Ex. 12:1–28; Num. 9:1–5; 28:16–25; Deut. 16:1–8; Josh. 5:10
7 [a]Ex. 12:16; Num. 28:18, 25 [1]*occupational*
10 [a]Ex. 23:19; 34:26 [b][Rom. 11:16]; James 1:18; Rev. 14:4
11 [a]Ex. 29:24
13 [1]*pleasing*
16 [a]Acts 2:1 [b]Num. 28:26
17 [a]Ex. 23:16, 19; Num. 15:17–21
19 [a]Lev. 4:23, 28; Num. 28:30; [2 Cor. 5:21] [b]Lev. 3:1
20 [a]Lev. 14:13; Num. 18:12; Deut. 18:4

21 'And you shall proclaim on the
same day *that* it is a holy convoca-
tion to you. You shall do no cus-
tomary work *on it. It shall be* a
statute forever in all your dwell-
ings throughout your generations.
22 [a]'When you reap the harvest of
your land, you shall not wholly
reap the corners of your field when
you reap, nor shall you gather any
gleaning from your harvest. You
shall leave them for the poor and
for the stranger: I *am* the LORD
your God.'"

The Feast of Trumpets

23 Then the LORD spoke to Moses,
saying,
24 "Speak to the children of Is-
rael, saying: 'In the [a]seventh
month, on the first *day* of the
month, you shall have a sabbath-
rest, [b]a memorial of blowing of
trumpets, a holy convocation.
25 'You shall do no customary
work *on it;* and you shall offer an
offering made by fire to the
LORD.'"

The Day of Atonement

26 And the LORD spoke to Moses,
saying:
27 [a]"Also the tenth *day* of this sev-
enth month *shall be* the Day of
Atonement. It shall be a holy con-
vocation for you; you shall afflict
your souls, and offer an offering
made by fire to the LORD.
28 "And you shall do no work on
that same day, for it *is* the Day of
Atonement, [a]to make atonement
for you before the LORD your
God.
29 "For any person who is not [a]af-
flicted *in soul* on that same day
[b]shall be cut off from his people.
30 "And any person who does any
work on that same day, [a]that per-
son I will destroy from among his
people.
31 "You shall do no manner of
work; *it shall be* a statute forever
throughout your generations in all
your dwellings.
32 "It *shall be* to you a sabbath of
solemn rest, and you shall [1]afflict
your souls; on the ninth *day* of the
month at evening, from evening to
evening, you shall [2]celebrate your
sabbath."

22 [a]Lev. 19:9, 10; Deut. 24:19–22; Ruth 2:2, 15
24 [a]Num. 29:1 [b]Lev. 25:9
27 [a]Lev. 16:1–34; 25:9; Num. 29:7
28 [a]Lev. 16:34
29 [a]Is. 22:12; Jer. 31:9; Ezek. 7:16 [b]Gen. 17:14; Lev. 13:46; Num. 5:2
30 [a]Lev. 20:3–6
32 [1]*humble yourselves* [2]*observe your sabbath*
34 [a]Ex. 23:16; Num. 29:12; Deut. 16:13–16; Ezra 3:4; Neh. 8:14; Zech. 14:16–19; John 7:2
36 [a]Num. 29:12–34 [b]Num. 29:35–38; Neh. 8:18; John 7:37 [c]Deut. 16:8; 2 Chr. 7:8 [1]*solemn*
37 [a]Lev. 23:2, 4
38 [a]Num. 29:39
39 [a]Ex. 23:16; Deut. 16:13
40 [a]Neh. 8:15 [b]Deut. 12:7; 16:14, 15 [1]*foliage*
41 [a]Num. 29:12; Neh. 8:18
42 [a][Is. 4:6] [b]Neh. 8:14–16 [1]*tabernacles;* shelters made of boughs
43 [a]Ex. 13:14; Deut. 31:13; Ps. 78:5 [b]Ex. 10:2 [c]Lev. 22:33
44 [a]Lev. 23:2

The Feast of Tabernacles

33 Then the LORD spoke to Moses,
saying,
34 "Speak to the children of Is-
rael, saying: [a]'The fifteenth day of
this seventh month *shall be* the
Feast of Tabernacles *for* seven
days to the LORD.
35 'On the first day *there shall be*
a holy convocation. You shall do
no customary work *on it.*
36 '*For* seven days you shall offer
an [a]offering made by fire to the
LORD. [b]On the eighth day you shall
have a holy convocation, and you
shall offer an offering made by fire
to the LORD. It *is* a [c]sacred[1] assem-
bly, *and* you shall do no customary
work *on it.*
37 [a]'These *are* the feasts of the
LORD which you shall proclaim *to
be* holy convocations, to offer an
offering made by fire to the LORD,
a burnt offering and a grain offer-
ing, a sacrifice and drink offerings,
everything on its day—
38 [a]besides the Sabbaths of the
LORD, besides your gifts, besides
all your vows, and besides all your
freewill offerings which you give
to the LORD.
39 'Also on the fifteenth day of the
seventh month, when you have
[a]gathered in the fruit of the land,
you shall keep the feast of the
LORD *for* seven days; on the first
day *there shall be* a sabbath-*rest*,
and on the eighth day a sabbath-
rest.
40 'And [a]you shall take for your-
selves on the first day the [1]fruit of
beautiful trees, branches of palm
trees, the boughs of leafy trees,
and willows of the brook; [b]and you
shall rejoice before the LORD your
God for seven days.
41 [a]'You shall keep it as a feast
to the LORD for seven days in the
year. *It shall be* a statute forever
in your generations. You shall cel-
ebrate it in the seventh month.
42 [a]'You shall dwell in [1]booths for
seven days. [b]All who are native Is-
raelites shall dwell in booths,
43 [a]'that your generations may
[b]know that I made the children of
Israel dwell in booths when [c]I
brought them out of the land of
Egypt: I *am* the LORD your God.'"
44 So Moses [a]declared to the

children of Israel the feasts of the LORD.

Care of the Tabernacle Lamps

24 Then the LORD spoke to Moses, saying:
2 [a]"Command the children of Israel that they bring to you pure oil of pressed olives for the light, to make the lamps burn continually.
3 "Outside the veil of the Testimony, in the tabernacle of meeting, Aaron shall be in charge of it from evening until morning before the LORD continually; *it shall be* a statute forever in your generations.
4 "He shall [1]be in charge of the lamps on [a]the pure *gold* lampstand before the LORD continually.

The Bread of the Tabernacle

5 "And you shall take fine flour and bake twelve [a]cakes with it. Two-tenths *of an ephah* shall be in each cake.
6 "You shall set them in two rows, six in a row, [a]on the pure *gold* table before the LORD.
7 "And you shall put pure frankincense on *each* row, that it may be on the bread for a [a]memorial, an offering made by fire to the LORD.
8 [a]"Every Sabbath he shall set it in order before the LORD continually, *being taken* from the children of Israel by an everlasting covenant.
9 "And [a]it shall be for Aaron and his sons, [b]and they shall eat it in a holy place; for it *is* most holy to him from the offerings of the LORD made by fire, by a perpetual statute."

The Penalty for Blasphemy

10 Now the son of an Israelite woman, whose father *was* an Egyptian, went out among the children of Israel; and this Israelite *woman's* son and a man of Israel fought each other in the camp.
11 And the Israelite woman's son [a]blasphemed the name *of the LORD* and [b]cursed; and so they [c]brought him to Moses. (His mother's name *was* Shelomith the daughter of Dibri, of the tribe of Dan.)
12 Then they [a]put him [1]in custody,

CHAPTER 24

2 [a]Ex. 27:20, 21
4 [a]Ex. 25:31; 31:8; 37:17 [1]*arrange* or *set in order*
5 [a]Ex. 25:30; 39:36; 40:23
6 [a]Ex. 25:23, 24; 1 Kin. 7:48; 2 Chr. 4:19; 13:11; Heb. 9:2
7 [a]Lev. 2:2, 9, 16
8 [a]Num. 4:7; 1 Chr. 9:32; 2 Chr. 2:4; Matt. 12:4, 5
9 [a]1 Sam. 21:6; Matt. 12:4; Mark 2:26; Luke 6:4 [b]Ex. 29:33; Lev. 8:31
11 [a]Ex. 22:28 [b]Job 1:5, 11, 22; Is. 8:21 [c]Ex. 18:22, 26
12 [a]Num. 15:34 [b]Num. 27:5 [1]*under guard* [2]Lit. *it might be declared to them from the mouth of the LORD*
14 [a]Deut. 13:9; 17:7
15 [a]Lev. 20:17; Num. 9:13 [1]*be responsible for*
16 [a]Ex. 20:7; 1 Kin. 21:10, 13; [Matt. 12:31; Mark 3:28, 29]
17 [a]Gen. 9:6; Ex. 21:12; Num. 35:30, 31; Deut. 19:11, 12; 27:24
18 [a]Lev. 24:21
19 [a]Ex. 21:24
20 [a]Ex. 21:23; Deut. 19:21 [b][Matt. 5:38, 39]
22 [a]Ex. 12:49; Lev. 19:33–37; Num. 9:14; 15:15, 16, 29 [1]*one standard of judgment*

CHAPTER 25

1 [a]Lev. 26:46
2 [a]Lev. 26:34, 35
4 [a]Deut. 15:1; Neh. 10:31 [b][Heb. 4:9]

[b]that [2]the mind of the LORD might be shown to them.
13 And the LORD spoke to Moses, saying,
14 "Take outside the camp him who has cursed; then let all who heard *him* [a]lay their hands on his head, and let all the congregation stone him.
15 "Then you shall speak to the children of Israel, saying: 'Whoever curses his God [a]shall [1]bear his sin.
16 'And whoever [a]blasphemes the name of the LORD shall surely be put to death. All the congregation shall certainly stone him, the stranger as well as him who is born in the land. When he blasphemes the name *of the LORD*, he shall be put to death.
17 [a]'Whoever kills any man shall surely be put to death.
18 [a]'Whoever kills an animal shall make it good, animal for animal.
19 'If a man causes disfigurement of his neighbor, as [a]he has done, so shall it be done to him—
20 'fracture for [a]fracture, [b]eye for eye, tooth for tooth; as he has caused disfigurement of a man, so shall it be done to him.
21 'And whoever kills an animal shall restore it; but whoever kills a man shall be put to death.
22 'You shall have [a]the[1] same law for the stranger and for one from your own country; for I *am* the LORD your God.'"
23 Then Moses spoke to the children of Israel; and they took outside the camp him who had cursed, and stoned him with stones. So the children of Israel did as the LORD commanded Moses.

The Sabbath of the Seventh Year

25 And the LORD spoke to Moses on Mount [a]Sinai, saying,
2 "Speak to the children of Israel, and say to them: 'When you come into the land which I give you, then the land shall [a]keep a sabbath to the LORD.
3 'Six years you shall sow your field, and six years you shall prune your vineyard, and gather its fruit;
4 'but in the [a]seventh year there shall be a sabbath of solemn [b]rest for the land, a sabbath to the LORD.

You shall neither sow your field
nor prune your vineyard.
5 [a]'What grows of its own accord
of your harvest you shall not reap,
nor gather the grapes of your un-
tended vine, *for* it is a year of rest
for the land.
6 'And the sabbath *produce* of
the land shall be food for you: for
you, your male and female ser-
vants, your hired man, and the
stranger who dwells with you,
7 'for your livestock and the
beasts that *are* in your land—all
its produce shall be for food.

The Year of Jubilee

8 'And you shall count seven sab-
baths of years for yourself, seven
times seven years; and the time of
the seven sabbaths of years shall
be to you forty-nine years.
9 'Then you shall cause the trum-
pet of the Jubilee to sound on the
tenth *day* of the seventh month;
[a]on the Day of Atonement you
shall make the trumpet to sound
throughout all your land.
10 'And you shall consecrate the
fiftieth year, and [a]proclaim liberty
throughout *all* the land to all its
inhabitants. It shall be a Jubilee
for you; [b]and each of you shall
return to his possession, and
each of you shall return to his
family.
11 'That fiftieth year shall be a Ju-
bilee to you; in it [a]you shall neither
sow nor reap what grows of its
own accord, nor gather *the grapes*
of your untended vine.
12 'For it *is* the Jubilee; it shall be
holy to you; [a]you shall eat its pro-
duce from the field.
13 [a]'In this Year of Jubilee, each
of you shall return to his pos-
session.
14 'And if you sell anything to
your neighbor or buy from your
neighbor's hand, you shall not
[a]oppress one another.
15 [a]'According to the number of
years after the Jubilee you shall
buy from your neighbor, and ac-
cording to the number of years of
crops he shall sell to you.
16 'According to the multitude of
years you shall increase its price,
and according to the fewer num-
ber of years you shall diminish its
price; for he sells to you *according*
to the number *of the years* of the
crops.
17 'Therefore [a]you shall not [1]op-
press one another, [b]but you shall
fear your God; for I *am* the LORD
your God.

Provisions for the Seventh Year

18 [a]'So you shall observe My stat-
utes and keep My judgments, and
perform them; [b]and you will dwell
in the land in safety.
19 'Then the land will yield its
fruit, and [a]you will eat your fill,
and dwell there in safety.
20 'And if you say, [a]"What shall
we eat in the seventh year, since
[b]we shall not sow nor gather in our
produce?"
21 'Then I will [a]command My
blessing on you in the [b]sixth year,
and it will bring forth produce
enough for three years.
22 [a]'And you shall sow in the
eighth year, and eat [b]old produce
until the ninth year; until its pro-
duce comes in, you shall eat *of* the
old *harvest*.

Redemption of Property

23 'The land shall not be sold per-
manently, for [a]the land *is* Mine; for
you *are* [b]strangers and sojourners
with Me.
24 'And in all the land of your pos-
session you shall grant redemption
of the land.
25 [a]'If one of your brethren be-
comes poor, and has sold *some* of
his possession, and if [b]his redeem-
ing relative comes to redeem it,
then he may redeem what his
brother sold.
26 'Or if the man has no one to
redeem it, but he himself becomes
able to redeem it,
27 'then [a]let him count the years
since its sale, and restore the re-
mainder to the man to whom he
sold it, that he may return to his
possession.
28 'But if he is not able to have *it*
restored to himself, then what was
sold shall remain in the hand of
him who bought it until the Year
of Jubilee; [a]and in the Jubilee it
shall be released, and he shall re-
turn to his possession.
29 'If a man sells a house in a
walled city, then he may redeem
it within a whole year after it is

5 [a]2 Kin. 19:29
9 [a]Lev. 23:24, 27
10 [a]Is. 61:2; 63:4; Jer. 34:8, 15, 17; [Luke 4:19] [b]Lev. 25:13, 28, 54; Num. 36:4
11 [a]Lev. 25:5
12 [a]Lev. 25:6, 7
13 [a]Lev. 25:10; 27:24; Num. 36:4
14 [a]Lev. 19:13
15 [a]Lev. 27:18, 23
17 [a]Lev. 25:14; Prov. 14:31; 22:22; Jer. 7:5, 6; 1 Thess. 4:6 [b]Lev. 19:14, 32; 25:43 [1]*mistreat*
18 [a]Lev. 19:37 [b]Lev. 26:5; Deut. 12:10; Ps. 4:8; Jer. 23:6
19 [a]Lev. 26:5; Ezek. 34:25
20 [a]Matt. 6:25, 31 [b]Lev. 25:4, 5
21 [a]Deut. 28:8 [b]Ex. 16:29
22 [a]2 Kin. 19:29 [b]Lev. 26:10; Josh. 5:11
23 [a]Ex. 19:5; 2 Chr. 7:20 [b]Gen. 23:4; Ex. 6:4; 1 Chr. 29:15; Ps. 39:12; Heb. 11:13; 1 Pet. 2:11
25 [a]Ruth 2:20; 4:4, 6 [b]Num. 5:8; Ruth 3:2, 9, 12; [Job 19:25]; Jer. 32:7, 8
27 [a]Lev. 25:50–52
28 [a]Lev. 25:10, 13

sold; *within* a full year he may redeem it.

30 'But if it is not redeemed within the space of a full year, then the house in the walled city shall belong permanently to him who bought it, throughout his generations. It shall not be released in the Jubilee.

31 'However the houses of villages which have no wall around them shall be counted as the fields of the country. They may be redeemed, and they shall be released in the Jubilee.

32 'Nevertheless [a]the cities of the Levites, *and* the houses in the cities of their possession, the Levites may redeem at any time.

33 'And if a man purchases a house from the Levites, then the house that was sold in the city of his possession shall be released in the Jubilee; for the houses in the cities of the Levites *are* their possession among the children of Israel.

34 'But [a]the field of the common-land of their cities may not be [b]sold, for it *is* their perpetual possession.

Lending to the Poor

35 'If one of your brethren becomes poor, and [1]falls into poverty among you, then you shall [a]help him, like a stranger or a sojourner, that he may live with you.

36 [a]'Take no usury or interest from him; but [b]fear your God, that your brother may live with you.

37 'You shall not lend him your money for usury, nor lend him your food at a profit.

38 [a]'I *am* the LORD your God, who brought you out of the land of Egypt, to give you the land of Canaan *and* to be your God.

The Law Concerning Slavery

39 'And if *one of* your brethren *who dwells* by you becomes poor, and sells himself to you, you shall not compel him to serve as a slave.

40 'As a hired servant *and* a sojourner he shall be with you, *and* shall serve you until the Year of Jubilee.

41 'And *then* he shall depart from you—he and his children [a]with him—and shall return to his own family. He shall return to the possession of his fathers.

42 'For they *are* [a]My servants, whom I brought out of the land of Egypt; they shall not be sold as slaves.

43 [a]'You shall not rule over him [b]with [1]rigor, but you [c]shall fear your God.

44 'And as for your male and female slaves whom you may have—from the nations that are around you, from them you may buy male and female slaves.

45 'Moreover you may buy [a]the children of the strangers who dwell among you, and their families who are with you, which they beget in your land; and they shall become your property.

46 'And [a]you may take them as an inheritance for your children after you, to inherit *them as* a possession; they shall be your permanent slaves. But regarding your brethren, the children of Israel, you shall not rule over one another with rigor.

47 'Now if a sojourner or stranger close to you becomes rich, and *one of* your brethren *who dwells* by him becomes poor, and sells himself to the stranger *or* sojourner close to you, or to a member of the stranger's family,

48 'after he is sold he may be redeemed again. One of his brothers may redeem him;

49 'or his uncle or his uncle's son may redeem him; or *anyone* who is near of kin to him in his family may redeem him; or if he is able he may redeem himself.

50 'Thus he shall reckon with him who bought him: The price of his release shall be according to the number of years, from the year that he was sold to him until the Year of Jubilee; *it shall be* [a]according to the time of a hired servant for him.

51 'If *there are* still many years *remaining*, according to them he shall repay the price of his redemption from the money with which he was bought.

52 'And if there remain but a few years until the Year of Jubilee, then he shall reckon with him, *and* according to his years he shall re-

32 [a]Num. 35:1–8; Josh. 21:2
34 [a]Num. 35:2–5 [b]Acts 4:36, 37
35 [a]Deut. 15:7–11; 24:14, 15; Luke 6:35; 1 John 3:17 [1]Lit. *his hand fails*
36 [a]Ex. 22:25; Deut. 23:19, 20 [b]Neh. 5:9
38 [a]Lev. 11:45; 22:32, 33
41 [a]Ex. 21:3
42 [a]Lev. 25:55; [Rom. 6:22; 1 Cor. 7:22, 23]
43 [a]Eph. 6:9; Col. 4:1 [b]Ex. 1:13, 14; Lev. 25:46, 53; Ezek. 34:4 [c]Ex. 1:17; Deut. 25:18; Mal. 3:5 [1]*severity*
45 [a][Is. 56:3, 6, 7]
46 [a]Is. 14:2
50 [a]Job 7:1; Is. 16:14

pay him the price of his redemption.
53 'He shall be with him as a yearly hired servant, and he shall not rule with rigor over him in your sight.
54 'And if he is not redeemed in these *years*, then he shall be released in the Year of Jubilee—he and his children with him.
55 'For the children of Israel *are* servants to Me; they *are* My servants whom I brought out of the land of Egypt: I *am* the LORD your God.

Promise of Blessing and Retribution

26 'You shall [a]not make idols for yourselves;
neither a carved image nor a *sacred* pillar shall you rear up for yourselves;
nor shall you set up an engraved stone in your land, to bow down to it;
for I *am* the LORD your God.
2 [a]You shall [1]keep My Sabbaths and reverence My sanctuary:
I *am* the LORD.

3 [a]'If you walk in My statutes and keep My commandments, and perform them,
4 [a]then I will give you rain in its season, [b]the land shall yield its produce, and the trees of the field shall yield their fruit.
5 [a]Your threshing shall last till the time of vintage, and the vintage shall last till the time of sowing;
you shall eat your bread to the full, and [b]dwell in your land safely.
6 [a]I will give peace in the land, and [b]you shall lie down, and none will make *you* afraid;
I will rid the land of [c]evil[1] beasts, and [d]the sword will not go through your land.
7 You will chase your enemies, and they shall fall by the sword before you.
8 [a]Five of you shall chase a hundred, and a hundred of you shall put ten thousand to flight;
your enemies shall fall by the sword before you.

9 'For I will [a]look on you favorably and [b]make you fruitful, multiply you and confirm My [c]covenant with you.
10 You shall eat the [a]old harvest, and clear out the old because of the new.
11 [a]I will set My [1]tabernacle among you, and My soul shall not abhor you.
12 [a]I will walk among you and be your God, and you shall be My people.
13 I *am* the LORD your God, who brought you out of the land of Egypt, that *you* should not be their slaves;
I have broken the bands of your [a]yoke and made you walk [1]upright.

14 'But if you do not obey Me, and do not observe all these commandments,
15 and if you despise My statutes, or if your soul abhors My judgments, so that you do not perform all My commandments, *but* break My covenant,
16 I also will do this to you:
I will even appoint terror over you, [a]wasting disease and fever which shall [b]consume the eyes and [c]cause sorrow of heart.
And [d]you shall sow your seed [1]in vain, for your enemies shall eat it.
17 I will [1]set [a]My face against you, and [b]you shall be defeated by your enemies.
[c]Those who hate you shall reign over you, and you shall [d]flee when no one pursues you.

18 'And after all this, if you do not obey Me, then I will punish you [a]seven times more for your sins.
19 I will [a]break the pride of your power;
I [b]will make your heavens like iron and your earth like bronze.
20 And your [a]strength shall be spent in vain;
for your [b]land shall not yield its produce, nor shall the trees of the land yield their fruit.

21 'Then, if you walk contrary to Me, and are not willing to obey Me,
I will bring on you seven times more plagues, according to your sins.
22 [a]I will also send wild beasts among you, which shall rob you of your children, destroy your livestock, and make you few in number;
and [b]your highways shall be desolate.

CHAPTER 26

1 [a]Ex. 20:4, 5; Deut. 4:15–18; 5:8
2 [a]Lev. 19:30 [1]*observe*
3 [a]Deut. 28:1–14
4 [a]Is. 30:23 [b]Ps. 67:6
5 [a]Deut. 11:15; Joel 2:19, 26; Amos 9:13 [b]Lev. 25:18, 19; Ezek. 34:25
6 [a]Is. 45:7 [b]Job 11:19; Ps. 4:8; Zeph. 3:13 [c]2 Kin. 17:25; Hos. 2:18 [d]Ezek. 14:17 [1]*wild beasts*
8 [a]Deut. 32:30; Judg. 7:7–12
9 [a]Ex. 2:25; 2 Kin. 13:23 [b]Gen. 17:6, 7; Ps. 107:38 [c]Gen. 17:1–7
10 [a]Lev. 25:22
11 [a]Ex. 25:8; 29:45, 46; Josh. 22:19; Ps. 76:2; Ezek. 37:26; Rev. 21:3 [1]*dwelling place*
12 [a]Deut. 23:14; [2 Cor. 6:16]
13 [a]Gen. 27:40 [1]*erect*
16 [a]Deut. 28:22 [b]1 Sam. 2:33 [c]Ezek. 24:23; 33:10 [d]Judg. 6:3–6; Job 31:8; Mic. 6:15 [1]*without profit*
17 [a]Ps. 34:16 [b]Deut. 28:25; 1 Sam. 4:10; 31:1 [c]Ps. 106:41 [d]Prov. 28:1 [1]*oppose you*
18 [a]1 Sam. 2:5
19 [a]Is. 25:11 [b]Deut. 28:23
20 [a]Ps. 127:1; Is. 17:10, 11; 49:4; Jer. 12:13 [b]Gen. 4:12; Deut. 11:17
22 [a]Deut. 32:24; Ezek. 14:21 [b]Judg. 5:6; 2 Chr. 15:5; Zech. 7:14

23 'And if [a]by these things you are not reformed by Me, but walk contrary to Me,
24 [a]then I also will walk contrary to you, and I will punish you yet seven times for your sins.
25 And [a]I will bring a sword against you that will execute the vengeance of the covenant;
when you are gathered together within your cities [b]I will send pestilence among you;
and you shall be delivered into the hand of the enemy.
26 [a]When I have cut off your supply of bread, ten women shall bake your bread in one oven, and they shall bring back your bread by weight, [b]and you shall eat and not be satisfied.

27 'And after all this, if you do not obey Me, but walk contrary to Me,
28 then I also will walk contrary to you in fury;
and I, even I, will chastise you seven times for your sins.
29 [a]You[1] shall eat the flesh of your sons, and you shall eat the flesh of your daughters.
30 [a]I will destroy your high places, cut down your incense altars, and cast your carcasses on the lifeless forms of your idols;
and My soul shall abhor you.
31 I will lay your [a]cities waste and [b]bring your sanctuaries to desolation, and I will not [c]smell the fragrance of your [1]sweet aromas.
32 [a]I will bring the land to desolation, and your enemies who dwell in it shall be astonished at it.
33 [a]I will scatter you among the nations and draw out a sword after you;
your land shall be desolate and your cities waste.
34 [a]Then the land shall enjoy its sabbaths as long as it lies desolate and you *are* in your enemies' land;
then the land shall rest and enjoy its sabbaths.
35 As long as *it* lies desolate it shall rest—
for the time it did not rest on your [a]sabbaths when you dwelt in it.

36 'And as for those of you who are left, I will send [a]faintness[1] into their hearts in the lands of their enemies;
the sound of a shaken leaf shall cause them to flee;
they shall flee as though fleeing from a sword, and they shall fall when no one pursues.
37 [a]They shall stumble over one another, as it were before a sword, when no one pursues;
and [b]you shall have no *power* to stand before your enemies.
38 You shall [a]perish among the nations, and the land of your enemies shall eat you up.
39 And those of you who are left [a]shall [1]waste away in their iniquity in your enemies' lands;
also in their [b]fathers' iniquities, which are with them, they shall waste away.

40 '*But* [a]if they confess their iniquity and the iniquity of their fathers, with their unfaithfulness in which they were unfaithful to Me, and that they also have walked contrary to Me,
41 and *that* I also have walked contrary to them and have brought them into the land of their enemies;
if their [a]uncircumcised hearts are [b]humbled, and they [c]accept their guilt—
42 then I will [a]remember My covenant with Jacob, and My covenant with Isaac and My covenant with Abraham I will remember;
I will [b]remember the land.
43 [a]The land also shall be left empty by them, and will enjoy its sabbaths while it lies desolate without them;
they will accept their guilt, because they [b]despised My judgments and because their soul abhorred My statutes.
44 Yet for all that, when they are in the land of their enemies, [a]I will not cast them away, nor shall I abhor them, to utterly destroy them and break My covenant with them;
for I *am* the LORD their God.
45 But [a]for their sake I will remember the covenant of their ancestors, [b]whom I brought out of the land of Egypt [c]in the sight of the nations, that I might be their God:
I *am* the LORD.' "

46 [a]These *are* the statutes and judgments and laws which the LORD made between Himself and

---

23 [a]Amos 4:6–12
24 [a]Lev. 26:28, 41
25 [a]Ezek. 5:17 [b]Deut. 28:21
26 [a]Ps. 105:16 [b]Mic. 6:14
29 [a]2 Kin. 6:28, 29 [1]In time of famine
30 [a]2 Chr. 34:3
31 [a]2 Kin. 25:4, 10 [b]Ps. 74:7 [c]Is. 1:11–15 [1]*pleasing*
32 [a]Jer. 9:11; 18:16
33 [a]Deut. 4:27
34 [a]2 Chr. 36:21
35 [a]Lev. 25:2
36 [a]Ezek. 21:7, 12, 15 [1]*fear*
37 [a]1 Sam. 14:15, 16 [b]Josh. 7:12, 13
38 [a]Deut. 4:26
39 [a]Ezek. 4:17; 33:10 [b]Ex. 34:7 [1]*rot away*
40 [a]Neh. 9:2
41 [a]Acts 7:51 [b]2 Chr. 12:6, 7, 12 [c]Dan. 9:7
42 [a]Ex. 2:24; 6:5 [b]Ps. 136:23
43 [a]Lev. 26:34, 35 [b]Lev. 26:15
44 [a]Deut. 4:31
45 [a][Rom. 11:28] [b]Lev. 22:33; 25:38 [c]Ps. 98:2
46 [a][John 1:17]

the children of Israel [b]on Mount
Sinai by the hand of Moses.

Redeeming Persons and Property Dedicated to God

27 Now the LORD spoke to Mo-
ses, saying,
2 "Speak to the children of Is-
rael, and say to them: [a]'When a
man [1]consecrates by a vow certain
persons to the LORD, according to
your [2]valuation,
3 'if your valuation is of a male
from twenty years old up to sixty
years old, then your valuation
shall be fifty shekels of silver, [a]ac-
cording to the shekel of the sanctu-
ary.
4 'If it *is* a female, then your valu-
ation shall be thirty shekels;
5 'and if from five years old up
to twenty years old, then your val-
uation for a male shall be twenty
shekels, and for a female ten shek-
els;
6 'and if from a month old up to
five years old, then your valuation
for a male shall be five shekels of
silver, and for a female your valua-
tion shall be three shekels of sil-
ver;
7 'and if from sixty years old and
above, if *it is* a male, then your val-
uation shall be fifteen shekels, and
for a female ten shekels.
8 'But if he is too poor to pay
your valuation, then he shall pre-
sent himself before the priest, and
the priest shall set a value for
[a]him; according to the ability of
him who vowed, the priest shall
value him.
9 'If *it is* an animal that men may
bring as an offering to the LORD,
all that *anyone* gives to the LORD
shall be holy.
10 'He shall not substitute it or ex-
change it, good for bad or bad for
good; and if he at all exchanges
animal for animal, then both it and
the one exchanged for it shall be
[a]holy.
11 'If *it is* an unclean animal
which they do not offer as a sacri-
fice to the LORD, then he shall pre-
sent the animal before the priest;
12 'and the priest shall set a value
for it, whether it is good or bad;
as you, the priest, value it, so it
shall be.
13 [a]'But if he *wants* at all *to* re-
deem it, then he must add one-fifth
to your valuation.
14 'And when a man [1]dedicates
his house *to be* holy to the LORD,
then the priest shall set a value for
it, whether it is good or bad; as the
priest values it, so it shall stand.
15 'If he who dedicated it *wants*
to [1]redeem his house, then he must
add one-fifth of the money of your
valuation to it, and it shall be
his.
16 'If a man [1]dedicates to the LORD
part of a field of his possession,
then your valuation shall be ac-
cording to the seed for it. A homer
of barley seed *shall be valued* at
fifty shekels of silver.
17 'If he dedicates his field from
the Year of Jubilee, according to
your valuation it shall stand.
18 'But if he dedicates his field af-
ter the Jubilee, then the priest shall
[a]reckon to him the money due ac-
cording to the years that remain
till the Year of Jubilee, and it shall
be deducted from your valuation.
19 'And if he who dedicates the
field ever wishes to redeem it, then
he must add one-fifth of the money
of your valuation to it, and it shall
belong to him.
20 'But if he does not want to re-
deem the field, or if he has sold
the field to another man, it shall
not be redeemed anymore;
21 'but the field, [a]when it is re-
leased in the Jubilee, shall be holy
to the LORD, as a [b]devoted field; it
shall be [c]the possession of the
priest.
22 'And if a man dedicates to the
LORD a field which he has bought,
which is not the field of [a]his pos-
session,
23 'then the priest shall reckon to
him the worth of your valuation,
up to the Year of Jubilee, and he
shall give your valuation on that
day *as* a holy *offering* to the LORD.
24 [a]'In the Year of Jubilee the field
shall return to him from whom it
was bought, to the one who *owned*
the land as a possession.
25 'And all your valuations shall
be according to the shekel of the
sanctuary: [a]twenty gerahs to the
shekel.
26 'But the [a]firstborn of the ani-
mals, which should be the LORD's

46 [b]Lev. 25:1

CHAPTER 27

2 [a]Lev. 7:16; Num. 6:2; Deut. 23:21–23; Judg. 11:30, 31, 39 [1]Or *makes a difficult* or *extraordinary vow* [2]*appraisal*

3 [a]Ex. 30:13; Lev. 27:25; Num. 3:47; 18:16

8 [a]Lev. 5:11; 14:21–24

10 [a]Lev. 27:33

13 [a]Lev. 6:5; 22:14; 27:15, 19

14 [1]*sets apart*

15 [1]*buy back*

16 [1]*sets apart*

18 [a]Lev. 25:15, 16, 28

21 [a]Lev. 25:10, 28, 31 [b]Lev. 27:28 [c]Num. 18:14; Ezek. 44:29

22 [a]Lev. 25:10, 25

24 [a]Lev. 25:10–13, 28

25 [a]Ex. 30:13; Lev. 27:3; Num. 3:47; 18:16; Ezek. 45:12

26 [a]Ex. 13:2, 12; 22:30

firstborn, no man shall dedicate;
whether *it is* an ox or sheep, it *is*
the LORD's.
27 'And if *it is* an unclean animal,
then he shall redeem *it* according
to your valuation, and [a]shall add
one-fifth to it; or if it is not re-
deemed, then it shall be sold ac-
cording to your valuation.
28 [a]'Nevertheless no [1]devoted *of-
fering* that a man may devote to
the LORD of all that he has, *both*
man and beast, or the field of his
possession, shall be sold or re-
deemed; every devoted *offering is*
most holy to the LORD.
29 [a]'No person under the ban, who
may become doomed to destruc-
tion among men, shall be re-
deemed, *but* shall surely be put to
death.
30 'And [a]all the tithe of the land,
whether of the seed of the land *or*
of the fruit of the tree, *is* the
LORD's. It *is* holy to the LORD.
31 [a]'If a man wants at all to re-
deem *any* of his tithes, he shall add
one-fifth to it.
32 'And concerning the tithe of the
herd or the flock, of whatever
[a]passes under the rod, the tenth
one shall be holy to the LORD.
33 'He shall not inquire whether
it is good or bad, [a]nor shall he ex-
change it; and if he exchanges it
at all, then both it and the one ex-
changed for it shall be holy; it shall
not be redeemed.' "
34 [a]These *are* the commandments
which the LORD commanded Mo-
ses for the children of Israel on
Mount [b]Sinai.

27 [a]Lev. 27:11, 12
28 [a]Lev. 27:21; Num. 18:14; Josh. 6:17–19 [1]Given exclusively and irrevocably
29 [a]Num. 21:2
30 [a]Gen. 28:22; Num. 18:21, 24; 2 Chr. 31:5, 6, 12; Neh. 13:12; Mal. 3:8
31 [a]Lev. 27:13
32 [a]Jer. 33:13; Ezek. 20:37; Mic. 7:14
33 [a]Lev. 27:10
34 [a]Lev. 26:46; Deut. 4:5; Mal. 4:4 [b]Ex. 19:1–6, 25; [Heb. 12:18–29]

The Fourth Book of Moses Called

Numbers

NUMBERS is the book of wanderings. It takes its name from the two numberings of the Israelites—the first at Mount Sinai and the second on the plains of Moab. Most of the book, however, describes Israel's experiences as they wander in the wilderness. The lesson of Numbers is clear. While it may be necessary to pass through wilderness experiences, one does not have to live there. For Israel, an eleven-day journey became a forty-year agony.

The title of Numbers comes from the first word in the Hebrew text, *Wayyedabber,* "And He Said." Jewish writings, however, usually refer to it by the fifth Hebrew word in 1:1, *Bemidbar,* "In the Wilderness," which more nearly indicates the content of the book. The Greek title in the Septuagint is *Arithmoi,* "Numbers." The Latin Vulgate followed this title and translated it *Liber Numeri,* "Book of Numbers." These titles are based on the two numberings: the generation of Exodus (Num. 1) and the generation that grew up in the wilderness and conquered Canaan (Num. 26). Numbers has also been called the "Book of the Journeyings," the "Book of the Murmurings," and the "Fourth Book of Moses."

The First Census of Israel

NOW the LORD spoke to Moses [a]in the Wilderness of Sinai, [b]in the tabernacle of meeting, on the [c]first *day* of the second month, in the second year after they had come out of the land of Egypt, saying:

2 [a]"Take a census of all the congregation of the children of Israel, by their families, by their fathers' houses, according to the number of names, every male [b]individually,

3 "from [a]twenty years old and above—all who *are able to* go to war in Israel. You and Aaron shall number them by their armies.

4 "And with you there shall be a man from every tribe, each one the head of his father's house.

5 "These are the names of the men who shall stand with you: from Reuben, Elizur the son of Shedeur;

6 "from Simeon, Shelumiel the son of Zurishaddai;

7 "from Judah, Nahshon the son of Amminadab;

8 "from Issachar, Nethanel the son of Zuar;

9 "from Zebulun, Eliab the son of Helon;

10 "from the sons of Joseph: from Ephraim, Elishama the son of Ammihud; from Manasseh, Gamaliel the son of Pedahzur;

11 "from Benjamin, Abidan the son of Gideoni;

12 "from Dan, Ahiezer the son of Ammishaddai;

13 "from Asher, Pagiel the son of Ocran;

14 "from Gad, Eliasaph the son of [a]Deuel;[1]

15 "from Naphtali, Ahira the son of Enan."

16 [a]These *were* [b]chosen[1] from the congregation, leaders of their fathers' tribes, [c]heads of the divisions in Israel.

17 Then Moses and Aaron took these men who had been [1]mentioned [a]by name,

18 and they assembled all the congregation together on the first *day* of the second month; and they recited their [a]ancestry by families, by their fathers' houses, according to the number of names, from twenty years old and above, each one individually.

CHAPTER 1

1 [a]Ex. 19:1; Num. 10:11, 12 [b]Ex. 25:22 [c]Ex. 40:2, 17; Num. 9:1; 10:11

2 [a]Ex. 30:12; Num. 26:2, 63, 64; 2 Sam. 24:2; 1 Chr. 21:2 [b]Ex. 30:12, 13; 38:26

3 [a]Ex. 30:14; 38:26

14 [a]Num. 7:42 [1]*Reuel,* Num. 2:14

16 [a]Ex. 18:21; Num. 7:2; 1 Chr. 27:16–22 [b]Num. 16:2 [c]Ex. 18:21, 25; Jer. 5:5; Mic. 3:1, 9; 5:2 [1]*called*

17 [a]Is. 43:1 [1]*designated*

18 [a]Ezra 2:59; Heb. 7:3

19 As the LORD commanded Mo-
ses, so he numbered them in the
Wilderness of Sinai.
20 Now the [a]children of Reuben,
Israel's oldest son, their genealo-
gies by their families, by their fa-
thers' house, according to the
number of names, every male indi-
vidually, from twenty years old
and above, all who *were able to*
go to war:
21 those who were numbered of
the tribe of Reuben *were* forty-six
thousand five hundred.
22 From the [a]children of Simeon,
their genealogies by their families,
by their fathers' house, of those
who were numbered, according to
the number of names, every male
individually, from twenty years
old and above, all who *were able
to* go to war:
23 those who were numbered of
the tribe of Simeon *were* fifty-nine
thousand three hundred.
24 From the [a]children of Gad,
their genealogies by their families,
by their fathers' house, according
to the number of names, from
twenty years old and above, all
who *were able to* go to war:
25 those who were numbered of
the tribe of Gad *were* forty-five
thousand six hundred and fifty.
26 From the [a]children of Judah,
their genealogies by their families,
by their fathers' house, according
to the number of names, from
twenty years old and above, all
who *were able to* go to war:
27 those who were numbered of
the tribe of Judah *were* [a]seventy-
four thousand six hundred.
28 From the [a]children of Issachar,
their genealogies by their families,
by their fathers' house, according
to the number of names, from
twenty years old and above, all
who *were able to* go to war:
29 those who were numbered of
the tribe of Issachar *were* fifty-four
thousand four hundred.
30 From the [a]children of Zebulun,
their genealogies by their families,
by their fathers' house, according
to the number of names, from
twenty years old and above, all
who *were able to* go to war:
31 those who were numbered of
the tribe of Zebulun *were* fifty-
seven thousand four hundred.
32 From the sons of Joseph, the
[a]children of Ephraim, their geneal-
ogies by their families, by their
fathers' house, according to the
number of names, from twenty
years old and above, all who *were
able to* go to war:
33 those who were numbered of
the tribe of Ephraim *were* forty
thousand five hundred.
34 From the [a]children of Manas-
seh, their genealogies by their
families, by their fathers' house,
according to the number of names,
from twenty years old and above,
all who *were able to* go to war:
35 those who were numbered of
the tribe of Manasseh *were* thirty-
two thousand two hundred.
36 From the [a]children of Benja-
min, their genealogies by their
families, by their fathers' house,
according to the number of names,
from twenty years old and above,
all who *were able to* go to war:
37 those who were numbered of
the tribe of Benjamin *were* thirty-
five thousand four hundred.
38 From the [a]children of Dan,
their genealogies by their families,
by their fathers' house, according
to the number of names, from
twenty years old and above, all
who *were able to* go to war:
39 those who were numbered of
the tribe of Dan *were* sixty-two
thousand seven hundred.
40 From the [a]children of Asher,
their genealogies by their families,
by their fathers' house, according
to the number of names, from
twenty years old and above, all
who *were able to* go to war:
41 those who were numbered of
the tribe of Asher *were* forty-one
thousand five hundred.
42 From the children of Naphtali,
their genealogies by their families,
by their fathers' house, according
to the number of names, from
twenty years old and above, all
who *were able to* go to war:
43 those who were numbered of
the tribe of Naphtali *were* fifty-
three thousand four hundred.
44 [a]These are the ones who were
numbered, whom Moses and
Aaron numbered, with the leaders
of Israel, twelve men, each one
representing his father's house.
45 So all who were numbered of

20 [a]Num. 2:10, 11; 26:5–11; 32:6, 15, 21, 29
22 [a]Num. 2:12, 13; 26:12–14
24 [a]Gen. 30:11; Num. 26:15–18; Josh. 4:12; Jer. 49:1
26 [a]Gen. 29:35; Num. 26:19–22; 2 Sam. 24:9; Ps. 78:68; Matt. 1:2
27 [a]2 Chr. 17:14
28 [a]Num. 2:5, 6
30 [a]Num. 2:7, 8; 26:26, 27
32 [a]Gen. 48:1–22; Num. 26:28–37; Deut. 33:13–17; Jer. 7:15; Obad. 19
34 [a]Num. 2:20, 21; 26:28–34
36 [a]Gen. 49:27; Num. 26:38–41; 2 Chr. 17:17; Rev. 7:8
38 [a]Gen. 30:6; 46:23; Num. 2:25, 26; 26:42, 43
40 [a]Num. 2:27, 28; 26:44–47
44 [a]Num. 26:64

the children of Israel, by their fa-
thers' houses, from twenty years
old and above, all who *were able
to* go to war in Israel—
46 all who were numbered were
[a]six hundred and three thousand
five hundred and fifty.
47 But [a]the Levites were not num-
bered among them by their fa-
thers' tribe;
48 for the LORD had spoken to Mo-
ses, saying:
49 [a]"Only the tribe of Levi you
shall not number, nor take a cen-
sus of them among the children of
Israel;
50 [a]"but you shall appoint the
Levites over the tabernacle of the
Testimony, over all its furnishings,
and over all things that belong to
it; they shall carry the tabernacle
and all its furnishings; they shall
attend to it [b]and camp around the
tabernacle.
51 [a]"And when the tabernacle is
to go forward, the Levites shall
take it down; and when the taber-
nacle is to be set up, the Levites
shall set it [b]up. [c]The outsider
who comes near shall be put to
death.
52 "The children of Israel shall
pitch their tents, [a]everyone by his
own camp, everyone by his own
standard, according to their ar-
mies;
53 [a]"but the Levites shall camp
around the tabernacle of the Testi-
mony, that there may be no [b]wrath
on the congregation of the chil-
dren of Israel; and the Levites
shall [c]keep[1] charge of the taberna-
cle of the Testimony."
54 Thus the children of Israel did;
according to all that the LORD com-
manded Moses, so they did.

The Tribes and Leaders by Armies

2 And the LORD spoke to Moses
and Aaron, saying:
2 [a]"Everyone of the children of
Israel shall camp by his own
[1]standard, beside the emblems of
his father's house; they shall camp
[b]some distance from the taberna-
cle of meeting.
3 "On the [a]east side, toward the
rising of the sun, those of the stan-
dard of the forces with Judah shall
camp according to their armies;
and [b]Nahshon the son of Ammina-

46 [a]Ex. 12:37; 38:26; Num. 2:32; 26:51, 63; Heb. 11:12; Rev. 7:4–8

47 [a]Num. 2:33; 3:14–22; 26:57–62; 1 Chr. 6:1–47; 21:6

49 [a]Num. 2:33; 26:62

50 [a]Ex. 38:21; Num. 3:7, 8; 4:15, 25–27, 33 [b]Num. 3:23, 29, 35, 38

51 [a]Num. 4:5–15; 10:17, 21 [b]Num. 10:21 [c]Num. 3:10, 38; 4:15, 19, 20; 18:22

52 [a]Num. 2:2, 34; 24:2

53 [a]Num. 1:50 [b]Lev. 10:6; Num. 8:19; 16:46; 18:5; 1 Sam. 6:19 [c]Num. 8:24; 18:2–4; 1 Chr. 23:32 [1]*have in their care*

CHAPTER 2

2 [a]Num. 1:52; 24:2 [b]Josh. 3:4 [1]*banner*

3 [a]Num. 10:5 [b]Num. 1:7; 7:12; 10:14; Ruth 4:20; 1 Chr. 2:10; Matt. 1:4; Luke 3:32, 33

9 [a]Num. 10:14 [1]Lit. *set forth*

10 [a]Num. 10:6

14 [1]*Deuel,* Num. 1:14; 7:42

16 [a]Num. 10:18 [1]Lit. *set forth second*

17 [a]Num. 10:17, 21 [b]Num. 1:53 [1]*company* [2]*whole company* [3]*banners*

dab *shall be* the leader of the chil-
dren of Judah."
4 And his army was numbered at
seventy-four thousand six hun-
dred.
5 "Those who camp next to him
shall be the tribe of Issachar, and
Nethanel the son of Zuar *shall be*
the leader of the children of Issa-
char."
6 And his army was numbered at
fifty-four thousand four hundred.
7 "Then *comes* the tribe of Zebu-
lun, and Eliab the son of Helon
shall be the leader of the children
of Zebulun."
8 And his army was numbered at
fifty-seven thousand four hundred.
9 "All who were numbered ac-
cording to their armies of the
forces with Judah, one hundred
and eighty-six thousand four hun-
dred—[a]these shall [1]break camp
first.
10 "On the [a]south side *shall be* the
standard of the forces with Reuben
according to their armies, and the
leader of the children of Reuben
shall be Elizur the son of Shed-
eur."
11 And his army was numbered at
forty-six thousand five hundred.
12 "Those who camp next to him
shall be the tribe of Simeon, and
the leader of the children of
Simeon *shall be* Shelumiel the son
of Zurishaddai."
13 And his army was numbered at
fifty-nine thousand three hundred.
14 "Then *comes* the tribe of Gad,
and the leader of the children of
Gad *shall be* Eliasaph the son of
[1]Reuel."
15 And his army was numbered at
forty-five thousand six hundred
and fifty.
16 "All who were numbered ac-
cording to their armies of the
forces with Reuben, one hundred
and fifty-one thousand four hun-
dred and fifty—[a]they shall [1]be the
second to break camp.
17 [a]"And the tabernacle of meet-
ing shall move out with the [1]camp
of the Levites [b]in the middle of the
[2]camps; as they camp, so they
shall move out, everyone in his
place, by their [3]standards.
18 "On the west side *shall be* the
standard of the forces with
Ephraim according to their armies,

and the leader of the children of
Ephraim *shall be* Elishama the son
of Ammihud."
19 And his army was numbered at
forty thousand five hundred.
20 "Next to him *comes* the tribe
of Manasseh, and the leader of the
children of Manasseh *shall be*
Gamaliel the son of Pedahzur."
21 And his army was numbered at
thirty-two thousand two hundred.
22 "Then *comes* the tribe of Ben-
jamin, and the leader of the chil-
dren of Benjamin *shall be* Abidan
the son of Gideoni."
23 And his army was numbered at
thirty-five thousand four hundred.
24 "All who were numbered ac-
cording to their armies of the
forces with Ephraim, one hundred
and eight thousand one hundred—
[a]they shall [1]be the third to break
camp.
25 "The [1]standard of the forces
with Dan *shall be* on the north side
according to their armies, and the
leader of the children of Dan *shall
be* Ahiezer the son of Ammishad-
dai."
26 And his army was numbered at
sixty-two thousand seven hun-
dred.
27 "Those who camp next to him
shall be the tribe of Asher, and the
leader of the children of Asher
shall be Pagiel the son of Ocran."
28 And his army was numbered at
forty-one thousand five hundred.
29 "Then *comes* the tribe of Naph-
tali, and the leader of the children
of Naphtali *shall be* Ahira the son
of Enan."
30 And his army was numbered at
fifty-three thousand four hundred.
31 "All who were numbered of the
forces with Dan, one hundred and
fifty-seven thousand six hun-
dred—[a]they shall [1]break camp
last, with their [2]standards."
32 These *are* the ones who were
numbered of the children of Israel
by their fathers' houses. [a]All who
were numbered according to their
armies of the forces *were* six hun-
dred and three thousand five hun-
dred and fifty.
33 But [a]the Levites were not num-
bered among the children of Israel,
just as the LORD commanded Mo-
ses.
34 Thus the children of Israel [a]did
according to all that the LORD com-
manded Moses; [b]so they camped
by their [1]standards and so they
broke camp, each one by his fam-
ily, according to their fathers'
houses.

The Sons of Aaron

3 Now these *are* the [a]records[1] of
Aaron and Moses when the
LORD spoke with Moses on Mount
Sinai.
2 And these *are* the names of the
sons of Aaron: Nadab, the [a]first-
born, and [b]Abihu, Eleazar, and
Ithamar.
3 These *are* the names of the
sons of Aaron, [a]the anointed
priests, [1]whom he consecrated to
minister as priests.
4 [a]Nadab and Abihu had died be-
fore the LORD when they offered
profane fire before the LORD in
the Wilderness of Sinai; and they
had no children. So Eleazar and
Ithamar ministered as priests
in the presence of Aaron their fa-
ther.

The Levites Serve in the Tabernacle

5 And the LORD spoke to Moses,
saying:
6 [a]"Bring the tribe of Levi near,
and present them before Aaron the
priest, that they may serve him.
7 "And they shall attend to his
needs and the needs of the whole
congregation before the taberna-
cle of meeting, to do [a]the work of
the tabernacle.
8 "Also they shall attend to all
the furnishings of the tabernacle
of meeting, and to the needs of the
children of Israel, to do the work
of the tabernacle.
9 "And [a]you shall give the Le-
vites to Aaron and his sons; they
are given entirely to [1]him from
among the children of Israel.
10 "So you shall appoint Aaron
and his sons, [a]and they shall at-
tend to their priesthood; [b]but the
outsider who comes near shall be
put to death."
11 Then the LORD spoke to Moses,
saying:
12 "Now behold, [a]I Myself have
taken the Levites from among the
children of Israel instead of every
firstborn who opens the womb
among the children of Israel.

24 [a]Num. 10:22 [1]Lit. *set forth third*
25 [1]*banner*
31 [a]Num. 10:25 [1]Lit. *set forth last* [2]*banners*
32 [a]Ex. 38:26; Num. 1:46; 11:21
33 [a]Num. 1:47; 26:57–62
34 [a]Num. 1:54 [b]Num. 24:2, 5, 6 [1]*banners*

CHAPTER 3

1 [a]Ex. 6:16–27 [1]Lit. *generations*
2 [a]Ex. 6:23 [b]Lev. 10:1, 2; Num. 26:60, 61; 1 Chr. 24:2
3 [a]Ex. 28:41; Lev. 8 [1]Lit. *whose hands he filled*
4 [a]Lev. 10:1, 2; Num. 26:61; 1 Chr. 24:2
6 [a]Num. 8:6–22; 18:1–7; Deut. 10:8; 33:8–11
7 [a]Num. 1:50; 8:11, 15, 24, 26
9 [a]Num. 8:19; 18:6, 7 [1]Sam., LXX *Me*
10 [a]Ex. 29:9; Num. 18:7 [b]Num. 1:51; 3:38; 16:40
12 [a]Num. 3:41; 8:16; 18:6

Therefore the Levites shall be
[b]Mine,
13 "because [a]all the firstborn *are*
Mine. [b]On the day that I struck all
the firstborn in the land of Egypt,
I sanctified to Myself all the first-
born in Israel, both man and beast.
They shall be Mine: I *am* the
LORD."

Census of the Levites Commanded

14 Then the LORD spoke to Moses
in the Wilderness of Sinai, say-
ing:
15 "Number the children of Levi
by their fathers' houses, by their
families; you shall number [a]every
male from a month old and
above."
16 So Moses numbered them ac-
cording to the [1]word of the LORD,
as he was commanded.
17 [a]These were the sons of Levi
by their names: Gershon, Kohath,
and Merari.
18 And these *are* the names of the
sons of [a]Gershon by their families:
[b]Libni and Shimei.
19 And the sons of [a]Kohath by
their families: [b]Amram, Izehar,
Hebron, and Uzziel.
20 [a]And the sons of Merari by
their families: Mahli and Mushi.
These *are* the families of the Le-
vites by their fathers' houses.
21 From Gershon *came* the family
of the Libnites and the family of
the Shimites; these *were* the fami-
lies of the Gershonites.
22 Those who were numbered, ac-
cording to the number of all the
males from a month old and
above—of those who were num-
bered *there were* seven thousand
five hundred.
23 [a]The families of the Gershon-
ites were to camp behind the tab-
ernacle westward.
24 And the leader of the father's
house of the Gershonites *was* Elia-
saph the son of Lael.
25 [a]The duties of the children of
Gershon in the tabernacle of meet-
ing *included* [b]the tabernacle, [c]the
tent with [d]its covering, [e]the screen
for the door of the tabernacle of
meeting,
26 [a]the screen for the door of the
court, [b]the hangings of the court
which *are* around the tabernacle
and the altar, and [c]their cords, ac-
cording to all the work relating to
them.
27 [a]From Kohath *came* the family
of the Amramites, the family of the
Izharites, the family of the He-
bronites, and the family of the Uz-
zielites; these *were* the families of
the Kohathites.
28 According to the number of all
the males, from a month old and
above, *there were* eight thousand
[1]six hundred [2]keeping charge of
the sanctuary.
29 [a]The families of the children of
Kohath were to camp on the south
side of the tabernacle.
30 And the leader of the fathers'
house of the families of the Ko-
hathites *was* Elizaphan the son of
[a]Uzziel.
31 [a]Their duty *included* [b]the ark,
[c]the table, [d]the lampstand, [e]the al-
tars, the utensils of the sanctuary
with which they ministered, [f]the
screen, and all the work relating
to them.
32 And Eleazar the son of Aaron
the priest *was to be* chief over the
leaders of the Levites, *with* over-
sight of those who kept charge of
the sanctuary.
33 From Merari *came* the family
of the Mahlites and the family of
the Mushites; these *were* the fami-
lies of Merari.
34 And those who were num-
bered, according to the number of
all the males from a month old and
above, *were* six thousand two hun-
dred.
35 The leader of the fathers' house
of the families of Merari *was* Zu-
riel the son of Abihail. [a]These *were*
to camp on the north side of the
tabernacle.
36 And [a]the appointed duty of
the children of Merari *included*
the boards of the tabernacle, its
bars, its pillars, its sockets, its
utensils, all the work relating to
them,
37 and the pillars of the court all
around, with their sockets, their
pegs, and their cords.
38 [a]Moreover those who were to
camp before the tabernacle on
the east, before the tabernacle
of meeting, *were* Moses, Aaron,
and his sons, [b]keeping charge of
the sanctuary, [c]to meet the needs
of the children of Israel; but [d]the

12 [b]Ex. 13:2; Num. 3:45; 8:14
13 [a]Ex. 13:2; Lev. 27:26; Num. 8:16, 17; Neh. 10:36; Luke 2:23 [b]Ex. 13:12, 15; Num. 8:17
15 [a]Num. 3:39; 26:62
16 [1]Lit. *mouth*
17 [a]Gen. 46:11; Ex. 6:16–22; Num. 26:57; 1 Chr. 6:1, 16; 23:6
18 [a]Num. 4:38–41 [b]Ex. 6:17
19 [a]Num. 4:34–37 [b]Ex. 6:18
20 [a]Ex. 6:19; Num. 4:42–45
23 [a]Num. 1:53
25 [a]Num. 4:24–26 [b]Ex. 25:9 [c]Ex. 26:1 [d]Ex. 26:7, 14 [e]Ex. 26:36
26 [a]Ex. 27:9, 12, 14, 15 [b]Ex. 27:16 [c]Ex. 35:18
27 [a]1 Chr. 26:23
28 [1]Some LXX mss. *three* [2]*taking care of*
29 [a]Ex. 6:18; Num. 1:53
30 [a]Lev. 10:4
31 [a]Num. 4:15 [b]Ex. 25:10 [c]Ex. 25:23 [d]Ex. 25:31 [e]Ex. 27:1; 30:1 [f]Ex. 26:31–33
35 [a]Num. 1:53; 2:25
36 [a]Num. 4:31, 32
38 [a]Num. 1:53 [b]Num. 18:5 [c]Num. 3:7, 8 [d]Num. 3:10

outsider who came near was to be
put to death.
39 [a]All who were numbered of the
Levites, whom Moses and Aaron
numbered at the commandment of
the LORD, by their families, all the
males from a month old and
above, *were* twenty-two thousand.

Levites Dedicated Instead of the Firstborn

40 Then the LORD said to Moses:
[a]"Number[1] all the firstborn males
of the children of Israel from a
month old and above, and take the
number of their names.
41 [a]"And you shall take the Le-
vites for Me—I *am* the LORD—in-
stead of all the firstborn among the
children of Israel, and the live-
stock of the Levites instead of all
the firstborn among the livestock
of the children of Israel."
42 So Moses numbered all the
firstborn among the children of Is-
rael, as the LORD commanded him.
43 And all the firstborn males, ac-
cording to the number of names
from a month old and above, of
those who were numbered of
them, were twenty-two thousand
two hundred and seventy-three.
44 Then the LORD spoke to Moses,
saying:
45 [a]"Take the Levites instead of
all the firstborn among the chil-
dren of Israel, and the livestock of
the Levites instead of their live-
stock. The Levites shall be Mine:
I *am* the LORD.
46 "And for [a]the redemption of
the two hundred and seventy-three
of the firstborn of the children of
Israel, [b]who are more than the
number of the Levites,
47 "you shall take [a]five shekels
for each one [b]individually; you
shall take *them* in the currency of
the shekel of the sanctuary, [c]the
shekel of twenty gerahs.
48 "And you shall give the money,
with which the excess number of
them is redeemed, to Aaron and
his sons."
49 So Moses took the redemption
money from those who were over
and above those who were re-
deemed by the Levites.
50 From the firstborn of the chil-
dren of Israel he took the money,
[a]one thousand three hundred and

39 [a]Num. 3:43; 4:48; 26:62
40 [a]Num. 3:15 [1]*Take a census of*
41 [a]Num. 3:12, 45
45 [a]Num. 3:12, 41
46 [a]Ex. 13:13, 15; Num. 18:15, 16 [b]Num. 3:39, 43
47 [a]Lev. 27:6; Num. 18:16 [b]Num. 1:2, 18, 20 [c]Ex. 30:13
50 [a]Num. 3:46, 47
51 [a]Num. 3:48

CHAPTER 4
2 [a]Num. 3:27–32
3 [a]Num. 4:23, 30, 35; 8:24; 1 Chr. 23:3, 24, 27; Ezra 3:8
4 [a]Num. 4:15 [b]Num. 4:19
5 [a]Ex. 26:31; Heb. 9:3 [b]Ex. 25:10, 16
6 [a]Ex. 39:1 [b]Ex. 25:13; 1 Kin. 8:7, 8
7 [a]Ex. 25:23, 29, 30 [b]Lev. 24:5–9 [1]*Jars for the drink offering* [2]Lit. *continual bread*
9 [a]Ex. 25:31 [b]Ex. 25:37, 38
11 [a]Ex. 30:1–5
12 [a]Ex. 25:9; 1 Chr. 9:29

sixty-five *shekels*, according to the
shekel of the sanctuary.
51 And Moses [a]gave their redemp-
tion money to Aaron and his sons,
according to the word of the LORD,
as the LORD commanded Moses.

Duties of the Sons of Kohath

4 Then the LORD spoke to Moses
and Aaron, saying:
2 "Take a census of the sons of
[a]Kohath from among the children
of Levi, by their families, by their
fathers' house,
3 [a]"from thirty years old and
above, even to fifty years old, all
who enter the service to do the
work in the tabernacle of meeting.
4 [a]"This *is* the service of the sons
of Kohath in the tabernacle of
meeting, *relating to* [b]the most holy
things:
5 "When the camp prepares to
journey, Aaron and his sons shall
come, and they shall take down
[a]the covering veil and cover the
[b]ark of the Testimony with it.
6 "Then they shall put on it a
covering of badger skins, and
spread over *that* a cloth entirely
of [a]blue; and they shall insert [b]its
poles.
7 "On the [a]table of showbread
they shall spread a blue cloth, and
put on it the dishes, the pans, the
bowls, and the [1]pitchers for pour-
ing; and the [b]showbread[2] shall be
on it.
8 "They shall spread over them
a scarlet cloth, and cover the same
with a covering of badger skins;
and they shall insert its poles.
9 "And they shall take a blue
cloth and cover the [a]lampstand of
the light, [b]with its lamps, its wick-
trimmers, its trays, and all its oil
vessels, with which they service it.
10 "Then they shall put it with all
its utensils in a covering of badger
skins, and put *it* on a carrying
beam.
11 "Over [a]the golden altar they
shall spread a blue cloth, and
cover it with a covering of badger
skins; and they shall insert its
poles.
12 "Then they shall take all the
[a]utensils of service with which
they minister in the sanctuary, put
them in a blue cloth, cover them
with a covering of badger skins,

and put *them* on a carrying beam.
13 "Also they shall take away the
ashes from the altar, and spread
a purple cloth over it.
14 "They shall put on it all its im-
plements with which they minister
there—the firepans, the forks, the
shovels, the [1]basins, and all the
utensils of the altar—and they
shall spread on it a covering of
badger skins, and insert its poles.
15 "And when Aaron and his sons
have finished covering the sanctu-
ary and all the furnishings of the
sanctuary, when the camp is set
to go, then [a]the sons of Kohath
shall come to carry *them;* [b]but
they shall not touch any holy
thing, lest they die. [c]These *are* the
things in the tabernacle of meeting
which the sons of Kohath are to
carry.
16 "The appointed duty of Eleazar
the son of Aaron the priest *is* [a]the
oil for the light, the [b]sweet incense,
[c]the daily grain offering, the
[d]anointing oil, the oversight of all
the tabernacle, of all that *is* in it,
with the sanctuary and its furnish-
ings."
17 Then the LORD spoke to Moses
and Aaron, saying:
18 "Do not cut off the tribe of the
families of the Kohathites from
among the Levites;
19 "but do this in regard to them,
that they may live and not die
when they approach [a]the most
holy things: Aaron and his sons
shall go in and [1]appoint each of
them to his service and his task.
20 [a]"But they shall not go in to
watch while the holy things are be-
ing covered, lest they die."

Duties of the Sons of Gershon

21 Then the LORD spoke to Moses,
saying:
22 "Also take a census of the sons
of [a]Gershon, by their fathers'
house, by their families.
23 [a]"From thirty years old and
above, even to fifty years old, you
shall number them, all who enter
to perform the service, to do the
work in the tabernacle of meet-
ing.
24 "This *is* the [a]service of the fam-
ilies of the Gershonites, in serving
and carrying:
25 [a]"They shall carry the [b]cur-

14 [1]*bowls*
15 [a]Num. 7:9; 10:21; Deut. 31:9; Josh. 4:10; 2 Sam. 6:13; 1 Chr. 15:2, 15 [b]2 Sam. 6:6, 7; 1 Chr. 13:9, 10 [c]Num. 3:31
16 [a]Ex. 25:6; Lev. 24:2 [b]Ex. 30:34 [c]Ex. 29:38 [d]Ex. 30:23–25
19 [a]Num. 4:4 [1]*assign*
20 [a]Ex. 19:21; 1 Sam. 6:19
22 [a]Num. 3:22
23 [a]Num. 4:3; 1 Chr. 23:3, 24, 27
24 [a]Num. 7:7
25 [a]Num. 3:25, 26 [b]Ex. 36:8 [c]Ex. 26:14
27 [1]*command* [2]*assign*
28 [a]Num. 4:33 [1]Lit. *hand*
29 [a]Num. 3:33–37
30 [a]Num. 4:3; 8:24–26
31 [a]Num. 3:36, 37 [b]Num. 7:8 [c]Ex. 26:15
32 [a]Ex. 25:9; 38:21
33 [1]Lit. *hand*
34 [a]Num. 4:2
35 [a]Num. 4:47

tains of the tabernacle and the tab-
ernacle of meeting *with* its cover-
ing, the covering of [c]badger skins
that *is* on it, the screen for the door
of the tabernacle of meeting,
26 "the screen for the door of the
gate of the court, the hangings of
the court which *are* around the
tabernacle and altar, and their
cords, all the furnishings for their
service and all that is made for
these things: so shall they serve.
27 "Aaron and his sons shall [1]as-
sign all the service of the sons of
the Gershonites, all their tasks and
all their service. And you shall
[2]appoint to them all their tasks as
their duty.
28 "This *is* the service of the fami-
lies of the sons of Gershon in the
tabernacle of meeting. And their
duties *shall be* [a]under the [1]author-
ity of Ithamar the son of Aaron the
priest.

Duties of the Sons of Merari

29 "*As for* the sons of [a]Merari, you
shall number them by their fami-
lies and by their fathers' house.
30 [a]"From thirty years old and
above, even to fifty years old, you
shall number them, everyone who
enters the service to do the work
of the tabernacle of meeting.
31 "And [a]this *is* [b]what they must
carry as all their service for the
tabernacle of meeting: [c]the boards
of the tabernacle, its bars, its pil-
lars, its sockets,
32 "and the pillars around the
court with their sockets, pegs, and
cords, with all their furnishings
and all their service; and you shall
[a]assign *to each man* by name the
items he must carry.
33 "This *is* the service of the fami-
lies of the sons of Merari, as all
their service for the tabernacle of
meeting, under the [1]authority of
Ithamar the son of Aaron the
priest."

Census of the Levites

34 [a]And Moses, Aaron, and the
leaders of the congregation num-
bered the sons of the Kohathites
by their families and by their fa-
thers' house,
35 from thirty [a]years old and
above, even to fifty years old,
everyone who entered the service

for work in the tabernacle of meet-
ing;
36 and those who were numbered
by their families were two thou-
sand seven hundred and fifty.
37 These *were* the ones who were
numbered of the families of the
Kohathites, all who might serve in
the tabernacle of meeting, whom
Moses and Aaron numbered ac-
cording to the commandment of
the LORD by the hand of Moses.
38 And those who were numbered
of the sons of Gershon, by their
families and by their fathers'
house,
39 from thirty years old and
above, even to fifty years old,
everyone who entered the service
for work in the tabernacle of meet-
ing—
40 those who were numbered by
their families, by their fathers'
house, were two thousand six hun-
dred and thirty.
41 [a]These *are* the ones who were
numbered of the families of the
sons of Gershon, of all who might
serve in the tabernacle of meeting,
whom Moses and Aaron num-
bered according to the command-
ment of the LORD.
42 Those of the families of the
sons of Merari who were num-
bered, by their families, by their
fathers' [1]house,
43 from thirty years old and
above, even to fifty years old,
everyone who entered the service
for work in the tabernacle of meet-
ing—
44 those who were numbered by
their families were three thousand
two hundred.
45 These *are* the ones who were
numbered of the families of the
sons of Merari, whom Moses and
Aaron numbered [a]according to the
word of the LORD by the hand of
Moses.
46 All who were [a]numbered of the
Levites, whom Moses, Aaron, and
the leaders of Israel numbered, by
their families and by their fathers'
houses,
47 [a]from thirty years old and
above, even to fifty years old,
everyone who came to do the work
of service and the work of bearing
burdens in the tabernacle of meet-
ing—

41 [a]Num. 4:22
42 [1]*household*
45 [a]Num. 4:29
46 [a]Num. 3:39; 26:57–62; 1 Chr. 23:3–23
47 [a]Num. 4:3, 23, 30
49 [a]Num. 4:15, 24, 31 [b]Num. 4:1, 21

CHAPTER 5

2 [a]Lev. 13:3, 8, 46; Num. 12:10, 14, 15 [b]Lev. 15:2 [c]Lev. 21:1; Num. 9:6, 10; 19:11, 13; 31:19 [1]*by contact with*
3 [a]Lev. 26:11, 12; Num. 35:34; [2 Cor. 6:16]
6 [a]Lev. 5:14—6:7
7 [a]Lev. 5:5; 26:40, 41; Josh. 7:19; Ps. 32:5; 1 John 1:9 [b]Lev. 6:4, 5
8 [a]Lev. 5:15; 6:6, 7; 7:7 [1]*redeemer*, Heb. *goel*
9 [a]Ex. 29:28; Lev. 6:17, 18, 26; 7:6–14 [b]Lev. 7:32–34; 10:14, 15 [1]*heave offering*
10 [a]Lev. 10:13 [1]*consecrated*

48 those who were numbered
were eight thousand five hundred
and eighty.
49 According to the command-
ment of the LORD they were num-
bered by the hand of Moses, [a]each
according to his service and ac-
cording to his task; thus were they
numbered by him, [b]as the LORD
commanded Moses.

Ceremonially Unclean Persons Isolated

5 And the LORD spoke to Moses,
saying:
2 "Command the children of Is-
rael that they put out of the camp
every [a]leper, everyone who has a
[b]discharge, and whoever becomes
[c]defiled [1]by a corpse.
3 "You shall put out both male
and female; you shall put them
outside the camp, that they may
not defile their camps [a]in the midst
of which I dwell."
4 And the children of Israel did
so, and put them outside the camp;
as the LORD spoke to Moses, so the
children of Israel did.

Confession and Restitution

5 Then the LORD spoke to Moses,
saying,
6 "Speak to the children of Is-
rael: [a]'When a man or woman
commits any sin that men commit
in unfaithfulness against the LORD,
and that person is guilty,
7 [a]'then he shall confess the sin
which he has committed. He shall
make restitution for his trespass
[b]in full, plus one-fifth of it, and
give *it* to the one he has wronged.
8 'But if the man has no [1]relative
to whom restitution may be made
for the wrong, the restitution for
the wrong *must go* to the LORD for
the priest, in addition to [a]the ram
of the atonement with which
atonement is made for him.
9 'Every [a]offering[1] of all the holy
things of the children of Israel,
which they bring to the priest,
shall be [b]his.
10 'And every man's [1]holy things
shall be his; whatever any man
gives the priest shall be [a]his.' "

Concerning Unfaithful Wives

11 And the LORD spoke to Moses,
saying,

12 "Speak to the children of Is-
rael, and say to them: 'If any man's
wife goes astray and behaves
unfaithfully toward him,
13 'and a man [a]lies with her car-
nally, and it is hidden from the
eyes of her husband, and it is con-
cealed that she has defiled herself,
and *there was* no witness against
her, nor was she [b]caught—
14 'if the spirit of jealousy comes
upon him and he becomes [a]jealous
of his wife, who has defiled her-
self; or if the spirit of jealousy
comes upon him and he becomes
jealous of his wife, although she
has not defiled herself—
15 'then the man shall bring his
wife to the priest. He shall [a]bring
the offering required for her, one-
tenth of an ephah of barley meal;
he shall pour no oil on it and put
no frankincense on it, because
it *is* a grain offering of jealousy,
an offering for remembering,
for [b]bringing iniquity to remem-
brance.
16 'And the priest shall bring her
near, and set her before the LORD.
17 'The priest shall take holy wa-
ter in an earthen vessel, and take
some of the dust that is on the floor
of the tabernacle and put *it* into
the water.
18 'Then the priest shall stand the
woman before the [a]LORD, uncover
the woman's head, and put the of-
fering for remembering in her
hands, which *is* the grain offering
of jealousy. And the priest shall
have in his hand the bitter water
that brings a curse.
19 'And the priest shall put her un-
der oath, and say to the woman,
"If no man has lain with you, and
if you have not gone astray to
uncleanness *while* under your hus-
band's *authority*, be free from this
bitter water that brings a curse.
20 "But if you have gone astray
while under your husband's *au-
thority*, and if you have defiled
yourself and some man other than
your husband has lain with you"—
21 'then the priest shall [a]put the
woman under the oath of the
curse, and he shall say to the
woman—[b]"the LORD make you a
curse and an oath among your
people, when the LORD makes your
thigh [1]rot and your belly swell;
22 "and may this water that
causes the curse [a]go into your
stomach, and make *your* belly
swell and *your* thigh rot." [b]Then
the woman shall say, "Amen, so
be it."
23 'Then the priest shall write
these curses in a book, and he
shall scrape *them* off into the bitter
water.
24 'And he shall make the woman
drink the bitter water that brings
a curse, and the water that brings
the curse shall enter her *to become*
bitter.
25 [a]'Then the priest shall take the
grain offering of jealousy from the
woman's hand, shall [b]wave the of-
fering before the LORD, and bring
it to the altar;
26 'and the priest shall take a
handful of the offering, [a]as its
memorial portion, burn *it* on the
altar, and afterward make the
woman drink the water.
27 'When he has made her drink
the water, then it shall be, if she
has defiled herself and behaved
unfaithfully toward her husband,
that the water that brings a [a]curse
will enter her *and become* bitter,
and her belly will swell, her thigh
will rot, and the woman [b]will be-
come a curse among her people.
28 'But if the woman has not de-
filed herself, and is clean, then she
shall be free and may conceive
children.
29 'This *is* the law of jealousy,
when a wife, *while* under her hus-
band's *authority*, [a]goes astray and
defiles herself,
30 'or when the spirit of jealousy
comes upon a man, and he be-
comes jealous of his wife; then he
shall stand the woman before the
LORD, and the priest shall execute
all this law upon her.
31 'Then the man shall be free
from [1]iniquity, but that woman
[a]shall bear her [2]guilt.' "

The Law of the Nazirite

6 Then the LORD spoke to Moses,
saying,
2 "Speak to the children of Is-
rael, and say to them: 'When either
a man or woman [1]consecrates an
offering to take the vow of a
Nazirite, [a]to separate himself to
the LORD,

13 [a]Lev. 18:20; 20:10 [b]John 8:4
14 [a]Prov. 6:34; Song 8:6
15 [a]Lev. 5:11 [b]1 Kin. 17:18; Ezek. 29:16; Heb. 10:3
18 [a]Heb. 13:4
21 [a]Josh. 6:26; 1 Sam. 14:24; Neh. 10:29 [b]Jer. 29:22 [1]Lit. *fall away*
22 [a]Ps. 109:18 [b]Deut. 27:15–26
25 [a]Lev. 8:27 [b]Lev. 2:2, 9
26 [a]Lev. 2:2, 9
27 [a]Deut. 28:37; Is. 65:15; Jer. 24:9; 29:18, 22; 42:18 [b]Num. 5:21
29 [a]Num. 5:19
31 [a]Lev. 20:17, 19, 20 [1]*guilt* [2]*iniquity*

CHAPTER 6

2 [a]Lev. 27:2; Judg. 13:5; [Lam. 4:7; Amos 2:11, 12]; Acts 21:23; Rom. 1:1 [1]Or *makes a difficult vow*

3 [a]'he shall separate himself
from wine and *similar* drink; he
shall drink neither vinegar made
from wine nor vinegar made from
similar drink; neither shall he
drink any grape juice, nor eat
fresh grapes or raisins.
4 'All the days of his [1]separation
he shall eat nothing that is pro-
duced by the grapevine, from seed
to skin.
5 'All the days of the vow of his
separation no [a]razor shall come
upon his head; until the days are
fulfilled for which he separated
himself to the LORD, he shall be
holy. *Then* he shall let the locks
of the hair of his head grow.
6 'All the days that he separates
himself to the LORD [a]he shall not
go near a dead body.
7 [a]'He shall not [1]make himself
unclean even for his father or his
mother, for his brother or his sis-
ter, when they die, because his
separation to God *is* on his head.
8 [a]'All the days of his separation
he shall be holy to the LORD.
9 'And if anyone dies very sud-
denly beside him, and he defiles
his consecrated head, then he shall
[a]shave his head on the day of his
cleansing; on the seventh day he
shall shave it.
10 'Then [a]on the eighth day he
shall bring two turtledoves or two
young pigeons to the priest, to the
door of the tabernacle of meeting;
11 'and the priest shall offer one
as a sin offering and *the* other as
a burnt offering, and make atone-
ment for him, because he sinned
in regard to the corpse; and he
shall sanctify his head that same
day.
12 'He shall consecrate to the
LORD the days of his separation,
and bring a male lamb in its first
year [a]as a trespass offering; but
the former days shall be [1]lost, be-
cause his separation was defiled.
13 'Now this *is* the law of the
Nazirite: [a]When the days of his
separation are fulfilled, he shall be
brought to the door of the taberna-
cle of meeting.
14 'And he shall present his offer-
ing to the LORD: one male lamb in
its first year without blemish as a
burnt offering, one ewe lamb in its
first year without blemish [a]as a sin
offering, one ram without blemish
[b]as a peace offering,
15 'a basket of unleavened bread,
[a]cakes of fine flour mixed with oil,
unleavened wafers [b]anointed with
oil, and their grain offering with
their [c]drink offerings.
16 'Then the priest shall bring
them before the LORD and offer his
sin offering and his burnt offering;
17 'and he shall offer the ram as
a sacrifice of a peace offering to
the LORD, with the basket of un-
leavened bread; the priest shall
also offer its grain offering and its
drink offering.
18 [a]'Then the Nazirite shall shave
his consecrated head *at* the door
of the tabernacle of meeting, and
shall take the hair from his conse-
crated head and put *it* on the fire
which is under the sacrifice of the
peace offering.
19 'And the priest shall take the
[a]boiled shoulder of the ram, one
[b]unleavened cake from the basket,
and one unleavened wafer, and
[c]put *them* upon the hands of the
Nazirite after he has shaved his
consecrated *hair*,
20 'and the priest shall wave them
as a wave offering before the
LORD; [a]they *are* holy for the priest,
together with the breast of the
wave offering and the thigh of
the heave offering. After that the
Nazirite may drink wine.'
21 "This is the law of the Nazirite
who vows to the LORD the offering
for his separation, and besides
that, whatever else his hand is able
to provide; according to the vow
which he takes, so he must do ac-
cording to the law of his separa-
tion."

The Priestly Blessing

22 And the LORD spoke to Moses,
saying:
23 "Speak to Aaron and his sons,
saying, 'This is the way you shall
bless the children of Israel. Say to
them:

24 "The LORD [a]bless you and [b]keep
you;
25 The LORD [a]make His face shine
upon you,
And [b]be gracious to you;
26 [a]The LORD [1]lift up His
countenance upon you,
And [b]give you peace." '

3 [a]Lev. 10:9; Amos 2:12; Luke 1:15
4 [1]Separation as a Nazirite
5 [a]Judg. 13:5; 16:17; 1 Sam. 1:11
6 [a]Lev. 21:1–3, 11; Num. 19:11–22
7 [a]Lev. 21:1, 2, 11; Num. 9:6 [1]By touching a dead body
8 [a][2 Cor. 6:17, 18]
9 [a]Lev. 14:8, 9; Acts 18:18; 21:24
10 [a]Lev. 5:7; 14:22; 15:14, 29
12 [a]Lev. 5:6 [1]*void*
13 [a]Acts 21:26
14 [a]Lev. 4:2, 27, 32 [b]Lev. 3:6
15 [a]Lev. 2:4 [b]Ex. 29:2 [c]Num. 15:5, 7, 10
18 [a]Num. 6:9; Acts 21:23, 24
19 [a]1 Sam. 2:15 [b]Ex. 29:23, 24 [c]Lev. 7:30
20 [a]Ex. 29:27, 28
24 [a]Deut. 28:3–6 [b]Ps. 121:7; John 7:11
25 [a]Ps. 31:16; 67:1; 80:3, 7, 19; 119:135; Dan. 9:17 [b]Gen. 43:29; Ex. 33:19; Mal. 1:9
26 [a]Ps. 4:6; 89:15 [b]Lev. 26:6; Is. 26:3, 12; John 14:27; Phil. 4:7 [1]Look upon you with favor

27 [a]"So they shall [1]put My name
on the children of Israel, and [b]I
will bless them."

Offerings of the Leaders

7 Now it came to pass, when Mo-
ses had finished [a]setting up the
tabernacle, that he [b]anointed it
and consecrated it and all its fur-
nishings, and the altar and all its
utensils; so he anointed them and
consecrated them.
2 Then [a]the leaders of Israel, the
heads of their fathers' houses, who
were the leaders of the tribes [1]and
over those who were numbered,
made an offering.
3 And they brought their offering
before the LORD, six covered carts
and twelve oxen, a cart for *every*
two of the leaders, and for each
one an ox; and they presented
them before the tabernacle.
4 Then the LORD spoke to Moses,
saying,
5 "Accept *these* from them, that
they may be used in doing the
work of the tabernacle of meeting;
and you shall give them to the Le-
vites, *to* every man according to
his service."
6 So Moses took the carts and the
oxen, and gave them to the Le-
vites.
7 Two carts and four oxen [a]he
gave to the sons of Gershon, ac-
cording to their service;
8 [a]and four carts and eight oxen
he gave to the sons of Merari, ac-
cording to their service, under the
[1]authority of Ithamar the son of
Aaron the priest.
9 But to the sons of Kohath he
gave none, because theirs *was* [a]the
service of the holy things, [b]*which*
they carried on their shoulders.
10 Now the leaders offered [a]the
dedication *offering* for the altar
when it was anointed; so the lead-
ers offered their offering before
the altar.
11 For the LORD said to Moses,
"They shall offer their offering,
one leader each day, for the dedi-
cation of the altar."
12 And the one who offered his of-
fering on the first day *was* [a]Nah-
shon the son of Amminadab, from
the tribe of Judah.
13 His offering *was* one silver
platter, the weight of which *was*
one hundred and thirty *shekels*,
and one silver bowl of seventy
shekels, according to [a]the shekel
of the sanctuary, both of them full
of fine flour mixed with oil as a
[b]grain offering;
14 one gold pan of ten *shekels*, full
of [a]incense;
15 [a]one young bull, one ram, and
one male lamb [b]in its first year, as
a burnt offering;
16 one kid of the goats as a [a]sin
offering;
17 and for [a]the sacrifice of peace
offerings: two oxen, five rams, five
male goats, and five male lambs
in their first year. This *was* the of-
fering of Nahshon the son of Am-
minadab.
18 On the second day Nethanel
the son of Zuar, leader of Issachar,
presented *an offering*.
19 *For* his offering he offered one
silver platter, the weight of which
was one hundred and thirty *shek-
els*, and one silver bowl of seventy
shekels, according to the shekel of
the sanctuary, both of them full of
fine flour mixed with oil as a grain
offering;
20 one gold pan of ten *shekels*, full
of incense;
21 one young bull, one ram, and
one male lamb in its first year, as
a burnt offering;
22 one kid of the goats as a sin
offering;
23 and as the sacrifice of peace of-
ferings: two oxen, five rams, five
male goats, and five male lambs
in their first year. This *was* the of-
fering of Nethanel the son of Zuar.
24 On the third day Eliab the son
of Helon, leader of the children of
Zebulun, *presented an offering*.
25 His offering *was* one silver
platter, the weight of which *was*
one hundred and thirty *shekels*,
and one silver bowl of seventy
shekels, according to the shekel of
the sanctuary, both of them full of
fine flour mixed with oil as a grain
offering;
26 one gold pan of ten *shekels*, full
of incense;
27 one young bull, one ram, and
one male lamb in its first year, as
a burnt offering;
28 one kid of the goats as a sin
offering;
29 and for the sacrifice of peace

27 [a]Deut. 28:10; 2 Sam. 7:23; 2 Chr. 7:14; Is. 43:7; Dan. 9:18, 19 [b]Ex. 20:24; Num. 23:20; Ps. 5:12; 67:7; 115:12, 13; Eph. 1:3 [1]*invoke*

CHAPTER 7

1 [a]Ex. 40:17–33 [b]Lev. 8:10, 11

2 [a]Num. 1:4 [1]Lit. *who stood over*

7 [a]Num. 4:24–28

8 [a]Num. 4:29–33 [1]Lit. *hand*

9 [a]Num. 4:15 [b]Num. 4:6–14

10 [a]Num. 7:1; Deut. 20:5; 1 Kin. 8:63; 2 Chr. 7:5, 9; Ezra 6:16; Neh. 12:27

12 [a]Num. 2:3

13 [a]Ex. 30:13 [b]Lev. 2:1

14 [a]Ex. 30:34, 35

15 [a]Lev. 1:2 [b]Ex. 12:5

16 [a]Lev. 4:23

17 [a]Lev. 3:1

offerings: two oxen, five rams, five
male goats, and five male lambs
in their first year. This *was* the of-
fering of Eliab the son of Helon.
30 On the fourth day [a]Elizur the
son of Shedeur, leader of the chil-
dren of Reuben, *presented an of-
fering.*
31 His offering *was* one silver
platter, the weight of which *was*
one hundred and thirty *shekels,*
and one silver bowl of seventy
shekels, according to the shekel of
the sanctuary, both of them full of
fine flour mixed with oil as a grain
offering;
32 one gold pan of ten *shekels,* full
of incense;
33 one young bull, one ram, and
one male lamb in its first year, as
a burnt offering;
34 one kid of the goats as a sin
offering;
35 and as the sacrifice of peace of-
ferings: two oxen, five rams, five
male goats, and five male lambs
in their first year. This *was* the of-
fering of Elizur the son of Shedeur.
36 On the fifth day [a]Shelumiel the
son of Zurishaddai, leader of the
children of Simeon, *presented an
offering.*
37 His offering *was* one silver
platter, the weight of which *was*
one hundred and thirty *shekels,*
and one silver bowl of seventy
shekels, according to the shekel of
the sanctuary, both of them full of
fine flour mixed with oil as a grain
offering;
38 one gold pan of ten *shekels,* full
of incense;
39 one young bull, one ram, and
one male lamb in its first year, as
a burnt offering;
40 one kid of the goats as a sin
offering;
41 and as the sacrifice of peace of-
ferings: two oxen, five rams, five
male goats, and five male lambs
in their first year. This *was* the of-
fering of Shelumiel the son of Zu-
rishaddai.
42 On the sixth day [a]Eliasaph the
son of [1]Deuel, leader of the chil-
dren of Gad, *presented an offering.*
43 His offering *was* one silver
platter, the weight of which *was*
one hundred and thirty *shekels,*
and one silver bowl of seventy
shekels, according to the shekel of
the sanctuary, both of them full of
fine flour mixed with oil as a grain
offering;
44 one gold pan of ten *shekels,* full
of incense;
45 one young bull, one ram, and
one male lamb in its first year, as
[a]a burnt offering;
46 one kid of the goats as a sin
offering;
47 and as the sacrifice of peace of-
ferings: two oxen, five rams, five
male goats, and five male lambs
in their first year. This *was* the of-
fering of Eliasaph the son of
Deuel.
48 On the seventh day [a]Elishama
the son of Ammihud, leader of the
children of Ephraim, *presented an
offering.*
49 His offering *was* one silver
platter, the weight of which *was*
one hundred and thirty *shekels,*
and one silver bowl of seventy
shekels, according to the shekel of
the sanctuary, both of them full of
fine flour mixed with oil as a grain
offering;
50 one gold pan of ten *shekels,* full
of incense;
51 one young bull, one ram, and
one male lamb in its first year, as
a burnt offering;
52 one kid of the goats as a sin
offering;
53 and as the sacrifice of peace of-
ferings: two oxen, five rams, five
male goats, and five male lambs
in their first year. This *was* the of-
fering of Elishama the son of Am-
mihud.
54 On the eighth day [a]Gamaliel
the son of Pedahzur, leader of the
children of Manasseh, *presented
an offering.*
55 His offering *was* one silver
platter, the weight of which *was*
one hundred and thirty *shekels,*
and one silver bowl of seventy
shekels, according to the shekel of
the sanctuary, both of them full of
fine flour mixed with oil as a grain
offering;
56 one gold pan of ten *shekels,* full
of incense;
57 one young bull, one ram, and
one male lamb in its first year, as
a burnt offering;
58 one kid of the goats as a sin
offering;
59 and as the sacrifice of peace of-

30 [a]Num. 1:5; 2:10
36 [a]Num. 1:6; 2:12; 7:41
42 [a]Num. 1:14; 2:14; 10:20 [1]*Reuel,* Num. 2:14
45 [a]Ps. 40:6
48 [a]Num. 1:10; 2:18; 1 Chr. 7:26
54 [a]Num. 1:10; 2:20

ferings: two oxen, five rams, five
male goats, and five male lambs
in their first year. This *was* the of-
fering of Gamaliel the son of Pe-
dahzur.
60 On the ninth day [a]Abidan the
son of Gideoni, leader of the chil-
dren of Benjamin, *presented an of-*
fering.
61 His offering *was* one silver
platter, the weight of which *was*
one hundred and thirty *shekels,*
and one silver bowl of seventy
shekels, according to the shekel of
the sanctuary, both of them full of
fine flour mixed with oil as a grain
offering;
62 one gold pan of ten *shekels,* full
of incense;
63 one young bull, one ram, and
one male lamb in its first year, as
a burnt offering;
64 one kid of the goats as a sin
offering;
65 and as the sacrifice of peace of-
ferings: two oxen, five rams, five
male goats, and five male lambs
in their first year. This *was* the of-
fering of Abidan the son of Gid-
eoni.
66 On the tenth day [a]Ahiezer the
son of Ammishaddai, leader of the
children of Dan, *presented an of-*
fering.
67 His offering *was* one silver
platter, the weight of which *was*
one hundred and thirty *shekels,*
and one silver bowl of seventy
shekels, according to the shekel of
the sanctuary, both of them full of
fine flour mixed with oil as a grain
offering;
68 one gold pan of ten *shekels,* full
of incense;
69 one young bull, one ram, and
one male lamb in its first year, as
a burnt offering;
70 one kid of the goats as a sin
offering;
71 and as the sacrifice of peace of-
ferings: two oxen, five rams, five
male goats, and five male lambs
in their first year. This *was* the of-
fering of Ahiezer the son of Am-
mishaddai.
72 On the eleventh day [a]Pagiel the
son of Ocran, leader of the chil-
dren of Asher, *presented an offer-*
ing.
73 His offering *was* one silver
platter, the weight of which *was*

60 [a]Num. 1:11; 2:22
66 [a]Num. 1:12; 2:25
72 [a]Num. 1:13; 2:27
78 [a]Num. 1:15; 2:29
84 [a]Num. 7:10

one hundred and thirty *shekels,*
and one silver bowl of seventy
shekels, according to the shekel of
the sanctuary, both of them full of
fine flour mixed with oil as a grain
offering;
74 one gold pan of ten *shekels,* full
of incense;
75 one young bull, one ram, and
one male lamb in its first year, as
a burnt offering;
76 one kid of the goats as a sin
offering;
77 and as the sacrifice of peace of-
ferings: two oxen, five rams, five
male goats, and five male lambs
in their first year. This *was* the of-
fering of Pagiel the son of Ocran.
78 On the twelfth day [a]Ahira the
son of Enan, leader of the children
of Naphtali, *presented an offering.*
79 His offering *was* one silver
platter, the weight of which *was*
one hundred and thirty *shekels,*
and one silver bowl of seventy
shekels, according to the shekel of
the sanctuary, both of them full of
fine flour mixed with oil as a grain
offering;
80 one gold pan of ten *shekels,* full
of incense;
81 one young bull, one ram, and
one male lamb in its first year, as
a burnt offering;
82 one kid of the goats as a sin
offering;
83 and as the sacrifice of peace of-
ferings: two oxen, five rams, five
male goats, and five male lambs
in their first year. This *was* the of-
fering of Ahira the son of Enan.
84 This *was* [a]the dedication *offer-*
ing for the altar from the leaders
of Israel, when it was anointed:
twelve silver platters, twelve silver
bowls, and twelve gold pans.
85 Each silver platter *weighed* one
hundred and thirty *shekels* and
each bowl seventy *shekels.* All the
silver of the vessels *weighed* two
thousand four hundred *shekels,*
according to the shekel of the
sanctuary.
86 The twelve gold pans full of in-
cense *weighed* ten *shekels* apiece,
according to the shekel of the
sanctuary; all the gold of the pans
weighed one hundred and twenty
shekels.
87 All the oxen for the burnt offer-
ing *were* twelve young bulls, the

rams twelve, the male lambs in
their first year twelve, with their
grain offering, and the kids of the
goats as a sin offering twelve.
88 And all the oxen for the sacri-
fice of peace offerings were
twenty-four bulls, the rams sixty,
the male goats sixty, and the lambs
in their first year sixty. This *was*
the dedication *offering* for the altar
after it was [a]anointed.
89 Now when Moses went into the
tabernacle of meeting [a]to speak
with Him, he heard [b]the voice of
One speaking to him from above
the mercy seat that *was* on the ark
of the Testimony, from [c]between
the two cherubim; thus He spoke
to him.

Arrangement of the Lamps

8 And the LORD spoke to Moses,
saying:
2 "Speak to Aaron, and say to
him, 'When you [a]arrange the
lamps, the seven [b]lamps shall
give light in front of the lamp-
stand.'"
3 And Aaron did so; he arranged
the lamps to face toward the front
of the lampstand, as the LORD com-
manded Moses.
4 [a]Now this workmanship of the
lampstand *was* hammered gold;
from its shaft to its flowers it *was*
[b]hammered work. [c]According to
the pattern which the LORD had
shown Moses, so he made the
lampstand.

Cleansing and Dedication of the Levites

5 Then the LORD spoke to Moses,
saying:
6 "Take the Levites from among
the children of Israel and cleanse
them *ceremonially.*
7 "Thus you shall do to them to
cleanse them: Sprinkle [a]water of
purification on them, and [b]let[1]
them shave all their body, and let
them wash their clothes, and so
make themselves clean.
8 "Then let them take a young
bull with [a]its grain offering of fine
flour mixed with oil, and you shall
take another young bull as a sin
offering.
9 [a]"And you shall bring the Le-
vites before the tabernacle of
meeting, [b]and you shall gather to-
gether the whole congregation of
the children of Israel.
10 "So you shall bring the Levites
before the LORD, and the children
of Israel [a]shall lay their hands on
the Levites;
11 "and Aaron shall [1]offer the
Levites before the LORD, *like* a
[a]wave offering from the children
of Israel, that they may perform
the work of the LORD.
12 [a]"Then the Levites shall lay
their hands on the heads of the
young bulls, and you shall offer
one as a sin offering and the other
as a burnt offering to the LORD, to
make atonement for the Levites.
13 "And you shall stand the Le-
vites before Aaron and his sons,
and then offer them *like* a wave
offering to the LORD.
14 "Thus you shall [a]separate the
Levites from among the children
of Israel, and the Levites shall be
[b]Mine.
15 "After that the Levites shall go
in to service the tabernacle of
meeting. So you shall cleanse
them and [a]offer them, *like* a wave
offering.
16 "For they *are* [a]wholly given to
Me from among the children of Is-
rael; I have taken them for Myself
[b]instead of all who open the womb,
the firstborn of all the children of
Israel.
17 [a]"For all the firstborn among
the children of Israel *are* Mine,
both man and beast; on the day
that I struck all the firstborn in the
land of Egypt I [1]sanctified them to
Myself.
18 "I have taken the Levites in-
stead of all the firstborn of the chil-
dren of Israel.
19 "And [a]I have given the Levites
as a gift to Aaron and his sons
from among the children of Israel,
to do the work for the children of
Israel in the tabernacle of meeting,
and to make atonement for the
children of Israel, [b]that there be no
plague among the children of Is-
rael when the children of Israel
come near the sanctuary."
20 Thus Moses and Aaron and all
the congregation of the children of
Israel did to the Levites; according
to all that the LORD commanded
Moses concerning the Levites, so
the children of Israel did to them.

88 [a]Num. 7:1, 10
89 [a][Ex. 33:9, 11]; Num. 12:8 [b]Ex. 25:21, 22 [c]Ps. 80:1; 99:1

CHAPTER 8

2 [a]Lev. 24:2–4 [b]Ex. 25:37; 40:25
4 [a]Ex. 25:31 [b]Ex. 25:18 [c]Ex. 25:40; Acts 7:44
7 [a]Num. 19:9, 13, 17, 20; Ps. 51:2, 7; [Heb. 9:13, 14] [b]Lev. 14:8, 9 [1]Heb. *let them cause a razor to pass over*
8 [a]Lev. 2:1; Num. 15:8–10
9 [a]Ex. 29:4; 40:12 [b]Lev. 8:3
10 [a]Lev. 1:4
11 [a]Num. 18:6 [1]*present*
12 [a]Ex. 29:10
14 [a]Num. 16:9 [b]Num. 3:12, 45; 16:9
15 [a]Num. 8:11, 13
16 [a]Num. 3:9 [b]Ex. 13:2; Num. 3:12, 45
17 [a]Ex. 12:2, 12, 13, 15; Num. 3:13; Luke 2:23 [1]*set them apart*
19 [a]Num. 3:9 [b]Num. 1:53; 16:46; 18:5; 2 Chr. 26:16

21 [a]And the Levites purified them-
selves and washed their clothes;
then Aaron presented them, *like* a
wave offering before the LORD, and
Aaron made atonement for them
to cleanse them.
22 [a]After that the Levites went in
to do their work in the tabernacle
of meeting before Aaron and his
sons; [b]as the LORD commanded
Moses concerning the Levites, so
they did to them.
23 Then the LORD spoke to Moses,
saying,
24 "This *is* what *pertains* to the
Levites: [a]From twenty-five years
old and above one may enter to
perform service in the work of the
tabernacle of meeting;
25 "and at the age of fifty years
they must cease performing this
work, and shall work no more.
26 "They may minister with their
brethren in the tabernacle of meet-
ing, [a]to attend to needs, but they
themselves shall do no work. Thus
you shall do to the Levites regard-
ing their duties."

The Second Passover

9 Now the LORD spoke to Moses
in the Wilderness of Sinai, in
the first month of the second year
after they had come out of the land
of Egypt, saying:
2 "Let the children of Israel keep
[a]the Passover at its appointed
[b]time.
3 "On the fourteenth day of this
month, [1]at twilight, you shall
[2]keep it at its appointed time. Ac-
cording to all its [3]rites and ceremo-
nies you shall keep it."
4 So Moses told the children of
Israel that they should keep the
Passover.
5 And [a]they kept the Passover on
the fourteenth day of the first
month, at twilight, in the Wilder-
ness of Sinai; according to all that
the LORD commanded Moses, so
the children of Israel did.
6 Now there were *certain* men
who were [a]defiled by a human
corpse, so that they could not keep
the Passover on that day; [b]and
they came before Moses and
Aaron that day.
7 And those men said to him,
"We *became* defiled by a human
corpse. Why are we kept from
presenting the offering of the LORD
at its appointed time among the
children of Israel?"
8 And Moses said to them,
"Stand still, that [a]I may hear what
the LORD will command concern-
ing you."
9 Then the LORD spoke to Moses,
saying,
10 "Speak to the children of Is-
rael, saying: 'If anyone of you or
your [1]posterity is unclean because
of a corpse, or *is* far away on a
journey, he may still keep the
LORD's Passover.
11 'On [a]the fourteenth day of the
second month, at twilight, they
may keep it. They shall [b]eat it with
unleavened bread and bitter herbs.
12 [a]'They shall leave none of it un-
til morning, [b]nor break one of its
bones. [c]According to all the [1]ordi-
nances of the Passover they shall
keep it.
13 'But the man who *is* clean and
is not on a journey, and ceases to
keep the Passover, that same per-
son [a]shall be cut off from among
his people, because he [b]did not
bring the offering of the LORD at
its appointed time; that man shall
[c]bear his sin.
14 'And if a stranger [1]dwells
among you, and would keep the
LORD's Passover, he must do so ac-
cording to the rite of the Passover
and according to its ceremony;
[a]you shall have one [2]ordinance,
both for the stranger and the na-
tive of the land.'"

The Cloud and the Fire

15 Now [a]on the day that the taber-
nacle was raised up, the cloud
[b]covered the tabernacle, the tent
of the Testimony; [c]from evening
until morning it was above the tab-
ernacle like the appearance of fire.
16 So it was always: the cloud
covered it *by day*, and the appear-
ance of fire by night.
17 Whenever the cloud [a]was
[1]taken up from above the taberna-
cle, after that the children of Israel
would journey; and in the place
where the cloud settled, there the
children of Israel would pitch their
tents.
18 At the [1]command of the LORD
the children of Israel would jour-
ney, and at the command of the

21 [a]Num. 8:7
22 [a]Num. 8:15 [b]Num. 8:5
24 [a]Num. 4:3; 1 Chr. 23:3, 24, 27
26 [a]Num. 1:53

CHAPTER 9

2 [a]Ex. 12:1–16; Lev. 23:5; Num. 28:16; Deut. 16:1, 2 [b]2 Chr. 30:1–15; Luke 22:7; [1 Cor. 5:7, 8]
3 [1]Lit. *between the evenings* [2]*observe* [3]*statutes*
5 [a]Josh. 5:10
6 [a]Num. 5:2; 19:11–22; John 18:28 [b]Ex. 18:15, 19, 26; Num. 27:2
8 [a]Ex. 18:22; Num. 27:5
10 [1]*descendants*
11 [a]2 Chr. 30:2, 15 [b]Ex. 12:8
12 [a]Ex. 12:10 [b]Ex. 12:46; [John 19:36] [c]Ex. 12:43 [1]*statutes*
13 [a]Gen. 17:14; Ex. 12:15, 47 [b]Num. 9:7 [c]Num. 5:31
14 [a]Ex. 12:49; Lev. 24:22; Num. 15:15, 16, 29 [1]As a resident alien [2]*statute*
15 [a]Ex. 40:33, 34; Neh. 9:12, 19; Ps. 78:14 [b]Is. 4:5 [c]Ex. 13:21, 22; 40:38
17 [a]Ex. 40:36–38; Num. 10:11, 12, 33, 34; Ps. 80:1 [1]*lifted up*
18 [1]Lit. *mouth*

LORD they would camp; [a]as long
as the cloud stayed above the tab-
ernacle they remained encamped.
19 Even when the cloud continued
long, many days above the taber-
nacle, the children of Israel [a]kept
the charge of the LORD and did not
journey.
20 So it was, when the cloud was
above the tabernacle a few days:
according to the command of the
LORD they would remain en-
camped, and according to the com-
mand of the LORD they would jour-
ney.
21 So it was, when the cloud re-
mained only from evening until
morning: when the cloud was
taken up in the morning, then they
would journey; whether by day or
by night, whenever the cloud was
taken up, they would journey.
22 *Whether it was* two days, a
month, or a year that the cloud re-
mained above the tabernacle, the
children of Israel [a]would remain
encamped and not journey; but
when it was taken up, they would
journey.
23 At the command of the LORD
they remained encamped, and at
the command of the LORD they
journeyed; they [a]kept the charge
of the LORD, at the command of the
LORD by the hand of Moses.

Two Silver Trumpets

10 And the LORD spoke to Mo-
ses, saying:
2 "Make two silver trumpets for
yourself; you shall make them of
hammered work; you shall use
them for [a]calling the congregation
and for directing the movement of
the camps.
3 "When [a]they blow both of
them, all the congregation shall
gather before you at the door of
the tabernacle of meeting.
4 "But if they blow *only* one, then
the leaders, the [a]heads of the di-
visions of Israel, shall gather to
you.
5 "When you sound the [a]ad-
vance, [b]the camps that lie on the
east side shall then begin their
journey.
6 "When you sound the advance
the second time, then the camps
that lie [a]on the south side shall be-
gin their journey; they shall sound
the call for them to begin their
journeys.
7 "And when the assembly is to
be gathered together, [a]you shall
blow, but not [b]sound the advance.
8 [a]"The sons of Aaron, the
priests, shall blow the trumpets;
and these shall be to you as an [1]or-
dinance forever throughout your
generations.
9 [a]"When you go to war in your
land against the enemy who [b]op-
presses you, then you shall sound
an alarm with the trumpets, and
you will be [c]remembered before
the LORD your God, and you will
be saved from your enemies.
10 "Also [a]in the day of your glad-
ness, in your appointed feasts, and
at the beginning of your months,
you shall blow the trumpets over
your burnt offerings and over the
sacrifices of your peace offerings;
and they shall be [b]a memorial for
you before your God: I *am* the
LORD your God."

Departure from Sinai

11 Now it came to pass on the
twentieth *day* of the second month,
in the second year, that the cloud
[a]was taken up from above the tab-
ernacle of the Testimony.
12 And the children of Israel set
out from the [a]Wilderness of Sinai
on [b]their journeys; then the cloud
settled down in the [c]Wilderness of
Paran.
13 So they started out for the
first time [a]according to the com-
mand of the LORD by the hand of
Moses.
14 The [1]standard of the camp of
the children of Judah [a]set out first
according to their armies; over
their army was [b]Nahshon the son
of Amminadab.
15 Over the army of the tribe of
the children of Issachar *was* Ne-
thanel the son of Zuar.
16 And over the army of the tribe
of the children of Zebulun *was*
Eliab the son of Helon.
17 Then [a]the tabernacle was taken
down; and the sons of Gershon
and the sons of Merari set out,
[b]carrying the tabernacle.
18 And [a]the standard of the camp
of Reuben set out according to
their armies; over their army *was*
Elizur the son of Shedeur.

18 [a]1 Cor. 10:1
19 [a]Num. 1:53; 3:8
22 [a]Ex. 40:36, 37
23 [a]Num. 9:19

CHAPTER 10
2 [a]Is. 1:13
3 [a]Jer. 4:5; Joel 2:15
4 [a]Ex. 18:21; Num. 1:16; 7:2
5 [a]Joel 2:1 [b]Num. 2:3
6 [a]Num. 2:10
7 [a]Num. 10:3 [b]Joel 2:1
8 [a]Num. 31:6; Josh. 6:4; 1 Chr. 15:24; 2 Chr. 13:12 [1]*statute*
9 [a]Num. 31:6; Josh. 6:5; 2 Chr. 13:14 [b]Judg. 2:18; 4:3; 6:9; 10:8, 12 [c]Gen. 8:1; Ps. 106:4
10 [a]Lev. 23:24; Num. 29:1; 1 Chr. 15:24; 2 Chr. 5:12; Ps. 81:3 [b]Lev. 23:24; Num. 10:9
11 [a]Num. 9:17
12 [a]Ex. 19:1; Num. 1:1; 9:5 [b]Ex. 40:36 [c]Gen. 21:21; Num. 12:16; Deut. 1:1
13 [a]Num. 10:5, 6
14 [a]Num. 2:3–9 [b]Num. 1:7 [1]*banner*
17 [a]Num. 1:51 [b]Num. 4:21–32; 7:7–9
18 [a]Num. 2:10–16

19 Over the army of the tribe of
the children of Simeon *was* Shelu-
miel the son of Zurishaddai.
20 And over the army of the tribe
of the children of Gad *was* Elia-
saph the son of Deuel.
21 Then the Kohathites set out,
carrying the [a]holy things. (The
tabernacle would be [1]prepared for
their arrival.)
22 And [a]the standard of the camp
of the children of Ephraim set out
according to their armies; over
their army *was* Elishama the son
of Ammihud.
23 Over the army of the tribe of
the children of Manasseh *was*
Gamaliel the son of Pedahzur.
24 And over the army of the tribe
of the children of Benjamin *was*
Abidan the son of Gideoni.
25 Then [a]the standard of the camp
of the children of Dan (the rear
guard of all the camps) set out ac-
cording to their armies; over their
army *was* Ahiezer the son of Am-
mishaddai.
26 Over the army of the tribe of
the children of Asher *was* Pagiel
the son of Ocran.
27 And over the army of the tribe
of the children of Naphtali *was*
Ahira the son of Enan.
28 [a]Thus *was* the order of march
of the children of Israel, according
to their armies, when they began
their journey.
29 Now Moses said to [a]Hobab the
son of [b]Reuel[1] the Midianite, Mo-
ses' father-in-law, "We are setting
out for the place of which the LORD
said, [c]'I will give it to you.' Come
with us, and [d]we will treat you
well; for [e]the LORD has promised
good things to Israel."
30 And he said to him, "I will not
go, but I will depart to my *own*
land and to my relatives."
31 So *Moses* said, "Please do not
leave, inasmuch as you know how
we are to camp in the wilderness,
and you can [1]be our [a]eyes.
32 "And it shall be, if you go with
us—indeed it shall be—that [a]what-
ever good the LORD will do to us,
the same we will do to you."
33 So they departed from [a]the
mountain of the LORD on a journey
of three days; and the ark of the
covenant of the LORD [b]went before
them for the three days' journey,
to search out a resting place for
them.
34 And [a]the cloud of the LORD *was*
above them by day when they
went out from the camp.
35 So it was, whenever the ark set
out, that Moses said:

[a]"Rise up, O LORD!
Let Your enemies be scattered,
And let those who hate You flee
before You."

36 And when it rested, he said:

"Return, O LORD,
To the many thousands of Israel."

The People Complain

11 Now [a]*when* the people com-
plained, it displeased the
LORD; [b]for the LORD heard *it,* and
His anger was aroused. So the [c]fire
of the LORD burned among them,
and consumed *some* in the out-
skirts of the camp.
2 Then the people [a]cried out to
Moses, and when Moses [b]prayed
to the LORD, the fire was
[1]quenched.
3 So he called the name of the
place [1]Taberah, because the fire
of the LORD had burned among
them.
4 Now the [a]mixed multitude who
were among them [1]yielded to [b]in-
tense craving; so the children of
Israel also wept again and said:
[c]"Who will give us meat to eat?
5 [a]"We remember the fish which
we ate freely in Egypt, the cucum-
bers, the melons, the leeks, the on-
ions, and the garlic;
6 "but now [a]our whole being *is*
dried up; *there is* nothing at all ex-
cept this manna *before* our eyes!"
7 Now [a]the manna *was* like co-
riander seed, and its color like the
color of bdellium.
8 The people went about and
gathered *it,* ground *it* on mill-
stones or beat *it* in the mortar,
cooked *it* in pans, and made cakes
of it; and [a]its taste was like the
taste of pastry prepared with oil.
9 And [a]when the dew fell on the
camp in the night, the manna fell
on it.
10 Then Moses heard the people
weeping throughout their families,
everyone at the door of his tent;
and [a]the anger of the LORD was

21 [a]Num. 4:4–20; 7:9 [1]Prepared by the Gershonites and the Merarites
22 [a]Num. 2:18–24
25 [a]Num. 2:25–31; Josh. 6:9
28 [a]Num. 2:34
29 [a]Judg. 4:11 [b]Ex. 2:18; 3:1; 18:12 [c]Gen. 12:7; Ex. 6:4–8 [d]Judg. 1:16 [e]Gen. 32:12; Ex. 3:8 [1]*Jethro,* Ex. 3:1; LXX *Raguel*
31 [a]Job 29:15 [1]Act as our guide
32 [a]Ex. 18:9; Lev. 19:34; Judg. 1:16
33 [a]Ex. 3:1; Deut. 1:6 [b]Deut. 1:33; Josh. 3:3–6; Ezek. 20:6
34 [a]Ex. 13:21; Neh. 9:12, 19
35 [a]Ps. 68:1, 2; 132:8; Is. 17:12–14

CHAPTER 11

1 [a]Num. 14:2; 16:11; 17:5; Deut. 9:22 [b]Ps. 78:21 [c]Lev. 10:2; 2 Kin. 1:12
2 [a]Num. 12:11, 13; 21:7 [b][James 5:16] [1]*extinguished*
3 [1]Lit. *Burning*
4 [a]Ex. 12:38 [b]1 Cor. 10:6 [c][Ps. 78:18] [1]Lit. *lusted intensely*
5 [a]Ex. 16:3
6 [a]Num. 21:5
7 [a]Ex. 16:14, 31
8 [a]Ex. 16:31
9 [a]Ex. 16:13, 14
10 [a]Ps. 78:21

greatly aroused; Moses also was displeased.

11 [a]So Moses said to the LORD, "Why have You afflicted Your servant? And why have I not found favor in Your sight, that You have laid the [1]burden of all these people on me?

12 "Did I conceive all these people? Did I beget them, that You should say to me, [a]'Carry them in your bosom, as a [b]guardian carries a nursing child,' to the land which You [c]swore[1] to their fathers?

13 [a]"Where am I to get meat to give to all these people? For they weep all over me, saying, 'Give us meat, that we may eat.'

14 [a]"I am not able to bear all these people alone, because the burden *is* too heavy for me.

15 "If You treat me like this, please kill me here and now—if I have found favor in Your sight—and [a]do not let me see my wretchedness!"

The Seventy Elders

16 So the LORD said to Moses: "Gather to Me [a]seventy men of the elders of Israel, whom you know to be the elders of the people and [b]officers over them; bring them to the tabernacle of meeting, that they may stand there with you.

17 "Then I will come down and talk with you there. [a]I will take of the Spirit that *is* upon you and will put *the same* upon them; and they shall bear the burden of the people with you, that you may not bear *it* yourself alone.

18 "Then you shall say to the people, [1]'Consecrate yourselves for tomorrow, and you shall eat meat; for you have wept [a]in the hearing of the LORD, saying, "Who will give us meat to eat? For *it was* well with us in Egypt." Therefore the LORD will give you meat, and you shall eat.

19 'You shall eat, not one day, nor two days, nor five days, nor ten days, nor twenty days,

20 [a]'but *for* a whole month, until it comes out of your nostrils and becomes loathsome to you, because you have [b]despised the LORD who is among you, and have wept before Him, saying, [c]"Why did we ever come up out of Egypt?" ' "

21 And Moses said, [a]"The people whom I *am* among *are* six hundred thousand men on foot; yet You have said, 'I will give them meat, that they may eat *for* a whole month.'

22 [a]"Shall flocks and herds be slaughtered for them, to provide enough for them? Or shall all the fish of the sea be gathered together for them, to provide enough for them?"

23 And the LORD said to Moses, [a]"Has[1] the LORD's arm been shortened? Now you shall see whether [b]what I say will happen to you or not."

24 So Moses went out and told the people the words of the LORD, and he [a]gathered the seventy men of the elders of the people and placed them around the tabernacle.

25 Then the LORD came down in the cloud, and spoke to him, and took of the Spirit that *was* upon him, and placed *the same* upon the seventy elders; and it happened, [a]when the Spirit rested upon them, that [b]they prophesied, [1]although they never did *so* again.

26 But two men had remained in the camp: the name of one *was* Eldad, and the name of the other Medad. And the Spirit rested upon them. Now they *were* among those listed, but who [a]had not gone out to the tabernacle; yet they prophesied in the camp.

27 And a young man ran and told Moses, and said, "Eldad and Medad are prophesying in the camp."

28 So Joshua the son of Nun, Moses' assistant, *one* of his choice men, answered and said, "Moses my lord, [a]forbid them!"

29 Then Moses said to him, "Are you [1]zealous for my sake? [a]Oh, that all the LORD's people were prophets *and* that the LORD would put His Spirit upon them!"

30 And Moses returned to the camp, *both* he and the elders of Israel.

The LORD Sends Quail

31 Now a [a]wind went out from the LORD, and it brought quail from the sea and left *them* fluttering near the camp, about a day's journey on this side and about a day's journey on the other side, all around

11 [a]Ex. 5:22; Deut. 1:12 [1]*responsibility*
12 [a]Is. 40:11 [b]Is. 49:23; 1 Thess. 2:7 [c]Gen. 26:3 [1]*solemnly promised*
13 [a]Matt. 15:33; Mark 8:4
14 [a]Ex. 18:18; Deut. 1:12
15 [a]Rev. 3:17
16 [a]Ex. 18:25; 24:1, 9 [b]Deut. 16:18
17 [a]1 Sam. 10:6; 2 Kin. 2:15; [Joel 2:28]
18 [a]Ex. 16:7 [1]*Set yourselves apart*
20 [a]Ps. 78:29; 106:15 [b]1 Sam. 10:19 [c]Num. 21:5
21 [a]Gen. 12:2; Ex. 12:37; Num. 1:46; 2:32
22 [a]2 Kin. 7:2
23 [a]Is. 50:2; 59:1 [b]Num. 23:19 [1]Is the LORD's power limited?
24 [a]Num. 11:16
25 [a]2 Kin. 2:15 [b]1 Sam. 10:5, 6, 10; Joel 2:28; Acts 2:17, 18; 1 Cor. 14:1 [1]Tg., Vg. *and they did not cease*
26 [a]Jer. 36:5
28 [a][Mark 9:38–40; Luke 9:49]
29 [a]1 Cor. 14:5 [1]*jealous*
31 [a]Ex. 16:13; Ps. 78:26–28; 105:40

the camp, and about two cubits
above the surface of the ground.
32 And the people stayed up all
that day, all night, and all the next
day, and gathered the quail (he
who gathered least gathered ten
[a]homers); and they spread *them*
out for themselves all around the
camp.
33 But while the [a]meat *was* still
between their teeth, before it was
chewed, the wrath of the LORD was
aroused against the people, and
the LORD struck the people with a
very great plague.
34 So he called the name of that
place [1]Kibroth Hattaavah, because
there they buried the people who
had yielded to craving.
35 [a]From Kibroth Hattaavah the
people moved to Hazeroth, and
camped at Hazeroth.

Dissension of Aaron and Miriam

12 Then [a]Miriam and Aaron
[1]spoke [b]against Moses be-
cause of the [2]Ethiopian woman
whom he had married; for [c]he had
married an Ethiopian woman.
2 So they said, "Has the LORD in-
deed spoken only through [a]Moses?
[b]Has He not spoken through us
also?" And the LORD [c]heard *it*.
3 (Now the man Moses *was* very
humble, more than all men who
were on the face of the earth.)
4 [a]Suddenly the LORD said to Mo-
ses, Aaron, and Miriam, "Come
out, you three, to the tabernacle of
meeting!" So the three came out.
5 [a]Then the LORD came down in
the pillar of cloud and stood *in* the
door of the tabernacle, and called
Aaron and Miriam. And they both
went forward.
6 Then He said,

"Hear now My words:
If there is a prophet among you,
I, the LORD, make Myself known
to him [a]in a vision;
I speak to him [b]in a dream.
7 Not so with [a]My servant Moses;
[b]He *is* faithful in all [c]My house.
8 I speak with him [a]face to face,
Even [b]plainly,[1] and not in [2]dark
sayings;
And he sees [c]the form of the
LORD.
Why then [d]were you not afraid
To speak against My servant
Moses?"

32 [a]Ezek. 45:11
33 [a]Ps. 78:29–31; 106:15
34 [1]Lit. *Graves of Craving*
35 [a]Num. 33:17

CHAPTER 12

1 [a]Num. 20:1 [b]Num. 11:1 [c]Ex. 2:21 [1]*criticized* [2]*Cushite*
2 [a]Num. 16:3 [b]Mic. 6:4 [c]Ezek. 35:12, 13
4 [a][Ps. 76:9]
5 [a]Ex. 19:9; 34:5
6 [a]Gen. 46:2 [b]Gen. 31:10
7 [a]Josh. 1:1 [b]Heb. 3:2, 5 [c]1 Tim. 1:12
8 [a]Deut. 34:10 [b][1 Cor. 13:12] [c]Ex. 33:19–23 [d]2 Pet. 2:10 [1]*appearing* [2]*riddles*
10 [a]Deut. 24:9 [b]2 Kin. 5:27; 15:5
11 [a]2 Sam. 19:19; 24:10 [1]*the penalty for this*
12 [a]Ps. 88:4
13 [a]Ps. 103:3
14 [a]Deut. 25:9 [b]Lev. 13:46 [1]*exiled*
15 [a]Deut. 24:9
16 [a]Num. 11:35; 33:17, 18

CHAPTER 13

2 [a]Deut. 1:22; 9:23
3 [a]Num. 12:16; 32:8
6 [a]Num. 34:19 [b]Josh. 14:6, 7
8 [1]LXX, Vg. *Oshea*

9 So the anger of the LORD was
aroused against them, and He de-
parted.
10 And when the cloud departed
from above the tabernacle, [a]sud-
denly Miriam *became* [b]leprous, as
white as snow. Then Aaron turned
toward Miriam, and there she was,
a leper.
11 So Aaron said to Moses, "Oh,
my lord! Please [a]do not lay [1]*this*
sin on us, in which we have done
foolishly and in which we have
sinned.
12 "Please [a]do not let her be as
one dead, whose flesh is half con-
sumed when he comes out of his
mother's womb!"
13 So Moses cried out to the LORD,
saying, "Please [a]heal her, O God,
I pray!"
14 Then the LORD said to Moses,
"If her father had but [a]spit in her
face, would she not be shamed
seven days? Let her be [b]shut[1] out
of the camp seven days, and after-
ward she may be received *again*."
15 [a]So Miriam was shut out of the
camp seven days, and the people
did not journey till Miriam was
brought in *again*.
16 And afterward the people
moved from [a]Hazeroth and
camped in the Wilderness of
Paran.

Spies Sent into Canaan

13 And the LORD spoke to Mo-
ses, saying,
2 [a]"Send men to spy out the land
of Canaan, which I am giving to
the children of Israel; from each
tribe of their fathers you shall send
a man, every one a leader among
them."
3 So Moses sent them [a]from the
Wilderness of Paran according to
the command of the LORD, all of
them men who *were* heads of the
children of Israel.
4 Now these *were* their names:
from the tribe of Reuben, Sham-
mua the son of Zaccur;
5 from the tribe of Simeon, Sha-
phat the son of Hori;
6 [a]from the tribe of Judah, [b]Ca-
leb the son of Jephunneh;
7 from the tribe of Issachar, Igal
the son of Joseph;
8 from the tribe of Ephraim,
[1]Hoshea the son of Nun;

9 from the tribe of Benjamin,
Palti the son of Raphu;
10 from the tribe of Zebulun, Gad-
diel the son of Sodi;
11 from the tribe of Joseph, *that
is,* from the tribe of Manasseh,
Gaddi the son of Susi;
12 from the tribe of Dan, Ammiel
the son of Gemalli;
13 from the tribe of Asher, Sethur
the son of Michael;
14 from the tribe of Naphtali,
Nahbi the son of Vophsi;
15 from the tribe of Gad, Geuel the
son of Machi.
16 These *are* the names of the men
whom Moses sent to [1]spy out the
land. And Moses called [a]Hoshea[2]
the son of Nun, Joshua.
17 Then Moses sent them to spy
out the land of Canaan, and said
to them, "Go up this *way* into the
South, and go up to [a]the moun-
tains,
18 "and see what the land is like:
whether the people who dwell in
it *are* strong or weak, few or many;
19 "whether the land they dwell
in *is* good or bad; whether the cit-
ies they inhabit *are* like camps or
strongholds;
20 "whether the land *is* [1]rich or
poor; and whether there are for-
ests there or not. [a]Be of good cour-
age. And bring some of the fruit
of the land." Now the time *was* the
season of the first ripe grapes.
21 So they went up and spied out
the land [a]from the Wilderness of
Zin as far as [b]Rehob, near the en-
trance of [c]Hamath.
22 And they went up through the
South and came to [a]Hebron; Ahi-
man, Sheshai, and Talmai, the de-
scendants of [b]Anak, *were* there.
(Now Hebron was built seven
years before Zoan in Egypt.)
23 [a]Then they came to the [1]Valley
of Eshcol, and there cut down a
branch with one cluster of grapes;
they carried it between two of
them on a pole. *They* also *brought*
some of the pomegranates and
figs.
24 The place was called the Valley
of [1]Eshcol, because of the cluster
which the men of Israel cut down
there.
25 And they returned from spying
out the land after forty days.
26 Now they departed and came
back to Moses and Aaron and all
the congregation of the children of
Israel in the Wilderness of Paran,
at [a]Kadesh; they brought back
word to them and to all the congre-
gation, and showed them the fruit
of the land.
27 Then they told him, and said:
"We went to the land where you
sent us. It truly [1]flows with [a]milk
and honey, [b]and this *is* its fruit.
28 "Nevertheless the [a]people who
dwell in the land *are* strong; the
cities *are* fortified *and* very large;
moreover we saw the descendants
of [b]Anak there.
29 [a]"The Amalekites dwell in the
land of the South; the Hittites, the
Jebusites, and the Amorites dwell
in the mountains; and the Canaan-
ites dwell by the sea and along the
banks of the Jordan."
30 Then [a]Caleb quieted the people
before Moses, and said, "Let us go
up at once and take possession, for
we are well able to overcome it."
31 [a]But the men who had gone up
with him said, "We are not able
to go up against the people, for
they *are* stronger than we."
32 And they [a]gave the children of
Israel a bad report of the land
which they had spied out, saying,
"The land through which we have
gone as spies *is* a land that devours
its inhabitants, and [b]all the people
whom we saw in it *are* men of
great stature.
33 "There we saw the [1]giants ([a]the
descendants of Anak came from
the giants); and we were [b]like[2]
grasshoppers in our own sight,
and so we were [c]in their sight."

Israel Refuses to Enter Canaan

14 So all the congregation
lifted up their voices and
cried, and the people [a]wept that
night.
2 [a]And all the children of Israel
complained against Moses and
Aaron, and the whole congrega-
tion said to them, "If only we had
died in the land of Egypt! Or if only
we had died in this wilderness!
3 "Why has the LORD brought us
to this land to [1]fall by the sword,
that our wives and [a]children
should become victims? Would it
not be better for us to return to
Egypt?"

16 [a]Ex. 17:9; Deut. 32:44 [1]*secretly search* [2]LXX, Vg. *Oshea*
17 [a]Judg. 1:9
20 [a]Deut. 31:6, 7, 23 [1]*fertile or barren*
21 [a]Num. 20:1; 27:14; 33:36; Josh. 15:1 [b]Josh. 19:28 [c]Num. 34:8; Josh. 13:5
22 [a]Josh. 15:13, 14; Judg. 1:10 [b]Josh. 11:21, 22
23 [a]Gen. 14:13; Num. 13:24; 32:9; Deut. 1:24, 25 [1]*Wadi*
24 [1]Lit. *Cluster*
26 [a]Num. 20:1, 16; 32:8; 33:36; Deut. 1:19; Josh. 14:6
27 [a]Ex. 3:8, 17; 13:5; 33:3 [b]Deut. 1:25 [1]Has an abundance of food
28 [a]Deut. 1:28; 9:1, 2 [b]Josh. 11:21, 22
29 [a]Ex. 17:8; Judg. 6:3
30 [a]Num. 14:6, 24
31 [a]Num. 32:9; Deut. 1:28; 9:1–3; Josh. 14:8
32 [a]Num. 14:36, 37; Ps. 106:24 [b]Amos 2:9
33 [a]Deut. 1:28; 9:2; Josh. 11:21 [b]Is. 40:22 [c]1 Sam. 17:42 [1]Heb. *nephilim* [2]As mere insects

CHAPTER 14

1 [a]Num. 11:4; Deut. 1:45
2 [a]Ex. 16:2; 17:3; Num. 16:41; Ps. 106:25; 1 Cor. 10:10
3 [a]Num. 14:31; Deut. 1:39 [1]*be killed in battle*

4 So they said to one another,
[a]"Let us select a leader and [b]return
to Egypt."
5 Then Moses and Aaron [1]fell on
their faces before all the assembly
of the congregation of the children
of Israel.
6 But Joshua the son of Nun and
Caleb the son of Jephunneh, *who*
were among those who had spied
out the land, tore their clothes;
7 and they spoke to all the con-
gregation of the children of Israel,
saying: [a]"The land we passed
through to spy out *is* an exceed-
ingly good land.
8 "If the LORD [a]delights in us,
then He will bring us into this land
and give it to us, [b]'a land which
flows with milk and honey.'
9 "Only [a]do not rebel against the
LORD, [b]nor fear the people of the
land, for [c]they[1] *are* our bread; their
protection has departed from
them, [d]and the LORD *is* with us. Do
not fear them."
10 [a]And all the congregation said
to stone them with stones. Now
[b]the glory of the LORD appeared in
the tabernacle of meeting before
all the children of Israel.

Moses Intercedes for the People

11 Then the LORD said to Moses:
"How long will these people [a]re-
ject[1] Me? And how long will they
not [b]believe Me, with all the [2]signs
which I have performed among
them?
12 "I will strike them with the pes-
tilence and disinherit them, and I
will [a]make of you a nation greater
and mightier than they."
13 And [a]Moses said to the LORD:
[b]"Then the Egyptians will hear *it*,
for by Your might You brought
these people up from among them,
14 "and they will tell *it* to the in-
habitants of this land. They have
[a]heard that You, LORD, *are* among
these people; that You, LORD, are
seen face to face and Your cloud
stands above them, and You go be-
fore them in a pillar of cloud by
day and in a pillar of fire by night.
15 "Now *if* You kill these people
as one man, then the nations
which have heard of Your fame
will speak, saying,
16 'Because the LORD was not
[a]able to bring this people to the

4 [a]Neh. 9:17 [b]Acts 7:39
5 [1]*prostrated themselves*
7 [a]Num. 13:27
8 [a]Deut. 10:15 [b]Num. 13:27
9 [a]Deut. 1:26; 9:7, 23, 24 [b]Deut. 7:18 [c]Num. 24:8 [d]Deut. 20:1, 3, 4; 31:6–8 [1]They shall be as food for our consumption.
10 [a]Ex. 17:4 [b]Ex. 16:10
11 [a]Heb. 3:8 [b]Deut. 9:23 [1]*despise* [2]*miraculous signs*
12 [a]Ex. 32:10
13 [a]Ps. 106:23 [b]Ex. 32:12
14 [a]Deut. 2:25
16 [a]Deut. 9:28
18 [a]Ex. 34:6, 7 [b]Ex. 20:5
19 [a]Ex. 32:32; 34:9 [b]Ps. 51:1; 106:45 [c]Ps. 78:38
20 [a]Mic. 7:18–20
21 [a]Ps. 72:19
22 [a]Deut. 1:35 [b]Gen. 31:7
23 [a]Num. 26:65; 32:11 [1]*solemnly promised*
24 [a]Josh. 14:6, 8, 9 [b]Num. 32:12
25 [a]Deut. 1:40
27 [a]Ex. 16:28 [b]Ex. 16:12
28 [a]Heb. 3:16–19
29 [a]Num. 1:45, 46; 26:64

land which He swore to give them,
therefore He killed them in the wil-
derness.'
17 "And now, I pray, let the power
of my Lord be great, just as You
have spoken, saying,
18 [a]'The LORD is longsuffering and
abundant in mercy, forgiving in-
iquity and transgression; but He
by no means clears *the guilty*, [b]vis-
iting the iniquity of the fathers on
the children to the third and fourth
generation.'
19 [a]"Pardon the iniquity of this
people, I pray, [b]according to the
greatness of Your mercy, just [c]as
You have forgiven this people,
from Egypt even until now."
20 Then the LORD said: "I have
pardoned, [a]according to your
word;
21 "but truly, as I live, [a]all the
earth shall be filled with the glory
of the LORD—
22 [a]"because all these men who
have seen My glory and the signs
which I did in Egypt and in the wil-
derness, and have put Me to the
test now [b]these ten times, and have
not heeded My voice,
23 "they certainly shall not [a]see
the land of which I [1]swore to their
fathers, nor shall any of those who
rejected Me see it.
24 "But My servant [a]Caleb, be-
cause he has a different spirit in
him and [b]has followed Me fully, I
will bring into the land where he
went, and his descendants shall in-
herit it.
25 "Now the Amalekites and the
Canaanites dwell in the valley; to-
morrow turn and [a]move out into
the wilderness by the Way of the
Red Sea."

Death Sentence on the Rebels

26 And the LORD spoke to Moses
and Aaron, saying,
27 [a]"How long *shall I bear with*
this evil congregation who com-
plain against Me? [b]I have heard
the complaints which the children
of Israel make against Me.
28 "Say to them, [a]'As I live,' says
the LORD, 'just as you have spoken
in My hearing, so I will do to
you:
29 'The carcasses of you who have
complained against Me shall fall
in this wilderness, [a]all of you who

were numbered, according to your
entire number, from twenty years
old and above.
30 [a]'Except for Caleb the son of
Jephunneh and Joshua the son of
Nun, you shall by no means enter
the land which I [1]swore I would
make you dwell in.
31 [a]'But your little ones, whom
you said would be victims, I will
bring in, and they shall [1]know the
land which [b]you have despised.
32 'But *as for* you, [a]your[1] car-
casses shall fall in this wilder-
ness.
33 'And your sons shall [a]be [1]shep-
herds in the wilderness [b]forty
years, and [c]bear the brunt of your
infidelity, until your carcasses are
consumed in the wilderness.
34 [a]'According to the number of
the days in which you spied out
the land, [b]forty days, for each day
you shall bear your [1]guilt one year,
namely forty years, [c]and you shall
know My [2]rejection.
35 [a]'I the LORD have spoken this.
I will surely do so to all [b]this evil
congregation who are gathered to-
gether against Me. In this wilder-
ness they shall be consumed, and
there they shall die.'"
36 Now the men whom Moses
sent to spy out the land, who re-
turned and made all the congrega-
tion complain against him by
bringing a bad report of the land,
37 those very men who brought
the evil report about the land,
[a]died by the plague before the
LORD.
38 [a]But Joshua the son of Nun and
Caleb the son of Jephunneh re-
mained alive, of the men who went
to spy out the land.

A Futile Invasion Attempt

39 Then Moses told these words
to all the children of Israel, [a]and
the people mourned greatly.
40 And they rose early in the
morning and went up to the top
of the mountain, saying, [a]"Here
we are, and we will go up to the
place which the LORD has prom-
ised, for we have sinned!"
41 And Moses said, "Now why do
you [1]transgress the command of
the LORD? For this will not suc-
ceed.
42 [a]"Do not go up, lest you be de-
feated by your enemies, for the
LORD *is* not among you.
43 "For the Amalekites and the
Canaanites *are* there before you,
and you shall fall by the sword;
[a]because you have turned away
from the LORD, the LORD will not
be with you."
44 [a]But they presumed to go up to
the mountaintop. Nevertheless,
neither the ark of the covenant of
the LORD nor Moses departed from
the camp.
45 Then the Amalekites and the
Canaanites who dwelt in that
mountain came down and at-
tacked them, and drove them back
as far as [a]Hormah.

Laws of Grain and Drink Offerings

15 And the LORD spoke to Mo-
ses, saying,
2 [a]"Speak to the children of Is-
rael, and say to them: 'When you
have come into the land you are
to inhabit, which I am giving to
you,
3 'and you [a]make an offering by
fire to the LORD, a burnt offering
or a sacrifice, [b]to fulfill a vow or
as a freewill offering or [c]in your
appointed feasts, to make a
[d]sweet[1] aroma to the LORD, from
the herd or the flock,
4 'then [a]he who presents his of-
fering to the LORD shall bring [b]a
grain offering of one-tenth *of an
ephah* of fine flour mixed [c]with
one-fourth of a hin of oil;
5 [a]'and one-fourth of a hin of
wine as a drink offering you shall
prepare with the burnt offering or
the sacrifice, for each [b]lamb.
6 [a]'Or for a ram you shall pre-
pare as a grain offering two-tenths
of an ephah of fine flour mixed
with one-third of a hin of oil;
7 'and as a drink offering you
shall offer one-third of a hin of
wine as a sweet aroma to the
LORD.
8 'And when you prepare a
young bull as a burnt offering, or
as a sacrifice to fulfill a vow, or
as a [a]peace offering to the LORD,
9 'then shall be offered [a]with the
young bull a grain offering of
three-tenths *of an ephah* of fine
flour mixed with half a hin of oil;
10 'and you shall bring as the
drink offering half a hin of wine

30 [a]Num. 26:65; 32:12; Deut. 1:36–38; Josh. 14:6–15 [1]*solemnly promised*
31 [a]Num. 14:3; Deut. 1:39 [b]Ps. 106:24 [1]*be acquainted with*
32 [a]Num. 26:64, 65; 32:13; 1 Cor. 10:5 [1]You shall die.
33 [a]Num. 32:13; Ps. 107:40 [b]Deut. 2:14 [c]Ezek. 23:35 [1]Vg. *wanderers*
34 [a]Num. 13:25 [b]Ps. 95:10; Ezek. 4:6 [c]1 Kin. 8:56; [Heb. 4:1] [1]*iniquity* [2]*opposition*
35 [a]Num. 23:19 [b]1 Cor. 10:5
37 [a]Num. 16:49; [1 Cor. 10:10]; Heb. 3:17, 18
38 [a]Josh. 14:6, 10
39 [a]Ex. 33:4
40 [a]Deut. 1:41–44
41 [1]*overstep*
42 [a]Deut. 1:42; 31:17
43 [a]2 Chr. 15:2
44 [a]Deut. 1:43
45 [a]Num. 21:3

CHAPTER 15

2 [a]Lev. 23:10; Num. 15:18; Deut. 7:1
3 [a]Lev. 1:2, 3 [b]Lev. 7:16; 22:18, 21 [c]Lev. 23:2, 8, 12, 38; Num. 28:18, 19, 27; Deut. 16:10 [d]Gen. 8:21; Ex. 29:18; Lev. 1:9 [1]*pleasing*
4 [a]Lev. 2:1; 6:14 [b]Ex. 29:40; Lev. 23:13 [c]Lev. 14:10; Num. 28:5
5 [a]Num. 28:7, 14 [b]Lev. 1:10; 3:6; Num. 15:11; 28:4, 5
6 [a]Num. 28:12, 14
8 [a]Lev. 7:11
9 [a]Num. 28:12, 14

as an offering made by fire, a
sweet aroma to the LORD.
11 [a]'Thus it shall be done for each
young bull, for each ram, or for
each lamb or young goat.
12 'According to the number that
you prepare, so you shall do with
everyone according to their num-
ber.
13 'All who are native-born shall
do these things in this manner, in
presenting an offering made by
fire, a sweet aroma to the LORD.
14 'And if a stranger [1]dwells with
you, or whoever *is* among you
throughout your generations, and
would present an offering made by
fire, a sweet aroma to the LORD,
just as you do, so shall he do.
15 [a]'One [1]ordinance *shall be* for
you of the assembly and for the
stranger who dwells *with you,* an
ordinance forever throughout your
generations; as you are, so shall
the stranger be before the LORD.
16 'One law and one custom shall
be for you and for the stranger
who dwells with you.' "
17 Again the LORD spoke to Mo-
ses, saying,
18 [a]"Speak to the children of Is-
rael, and say to them: 'When you
come into the land to which I bring
you,
19 'then it will be, when you eat
of [a]the bread of the land, that you
shall offer up a heave offering to
the LORD.
20 [a]'You shall offer up a cake of
the first of your ground meal *as* a
heave offering; as [b]a heave offer-
ing of the threshing floor, so shall
you offer it up.
21 'Of the first of your ground
meal you shall give to the LORD a
heave offering throughout your
generations.

Laws Concerning Unintentional Sin

22 [a]'If you sin unintentionally, and
do not observe all these command-
ments which the LORD has spoken
to Moses—
23 'all that the LORD has com-
manded you by the hand of Moses,
from the day the LORD gave com-
mandment and onward through-
out your generations—
24 'then it will be, [a]if it is unin-
tentionally committed, [1]without
the knowledge of the congrega-

11 [a]Num. 28
14 [1]As a resident alien
15 [a]Ex. 12:49; Num. 9:14; 15:29 [1]*statute*
18 [a]Num. 15:2; Deut. 26:1
19 [a]Josh. 5:11, 12
20 [a]Ex. 34:26; Lev. 23:10, 14, 17; Deut. 26:2, 10; Prov. 3:9, 10 [b]Lev. 2:14; 23:10, 16
22 [a]Lev. 4:2
24 [a]Lev. 4:13 [b]Num. 15:8–10 [c]Lev. 4:23 [1]Lit. *away from the eyes*
25 [a]Lev. 4:20; [Heb. 2:17]
27 [a]Lev. 4:27–31
28 [a]Lev. 4:35
29 [a]Num. 15:15
30 [a]Num. 14:40–44; Deut. 1:43; 17:12; Ps. 19:13; Heb. 10:26 [1]*defiantly,* lit. *with a high hand* [2]*blasphemes* [3]Put to death
31 [a]2 Sam. 12:9; Prov. 13:13 [1]*iniquity*
32 [a]Ex. 31:14, 15; 35:2, 3
34 [a]Lev. 24:12

tion, that the whole congregation
shall offer one young bull as a
burnt offering, as a sweet aroma
to the LORD, [b]with its grain offering
and its drink offering, according to
the ordinance, and [c]one kid of the
goats as a sin offering.
25 [a]'So the priest shall make
atonement for the whole congre-
gation of the children of Israel, and
it shall be forgiven them, for it was
unintentional; they shall bring
their offering, an offering made by
fire to the LORD, and their sin offer-
ing before the LORD, for their un-
intended sin.
26 'It shall be forgiven the whole
congregation of the children of Is-
rael and the stranger who dwells
among them, because all the peo-
ple *did it* unintentionally.
27 'And [a]if a person sins un-
intentionally, then he shall bring
a female goat in its first year as a
sin offering.
28 [a]'So the priest shall make
atonement for the person who sins
unintentionally, when he sins
unintentionally before the LORD, to
make atonement for him; and it
shall be forgiven him.
29 [a]'You shall have one law for
him who sins unintentionally, *for*
him who is native-born among
the children of Israel and for the
stranger who dwells among them.

Law Concerning Presumptuous Sin

30 [a]'But the person who does *any-
thing* [1]presumptuously, *whether
he is* native-born or a stranger,
that one [2]brings reproach on the
LORD, and he shall be [3]cut off from
among his people.
31 'Because he has [a]despised the
word of the LORD, and has broken
His commandment, that person
shall be completely cut off; his
[1]guilt *shall be* upon him.' "

Penalty for Violating the Sabbath

32 Now while the children of Is-
rael were in the wilderness, [a]they
found a man gathering sticks on
the Sabbath day.
33 And those who found him gath-
ering sticks brought him to Moses
and Aaron, and to all the congre-
gation.
34 They put him [a]under guard,

because it had not been explained
what should be done to him.
35 Then the LORD said to Moses,
[a]"The man must surely be put to
death; all the congregation shall
[b]stone him with stones outside the
camp."
36 So, as the LORD commanded
Moses, all the congregation
brought him outside the camp and
stoned him with stones, and he
died.

Tassels on Garments

37 Again the LORD spoke to Moses, saying,
38 "Speak to the children of Israel: Tell [a]them to make tassels on
the corners of their garments
throughout their generations, and
to put a blue thread in the tassels
of the corners.
39 "And you shall have the tassel,
that you may look upon it and
[a]remember all the commandments
of the LORD and do them, and that
you [b]*may* not [c]follow the harlotry
to which your own heart and your
own eyes are inclined,
40 "and that you may remember
and do all My commandments,
and be [a]holy for your God.
41 "I *am* the LORD your God, who
brought you out of the land of
Egypt, to be your God: I *am* the
LORD your God."

Rebellion Against Moses and Aaron

16 Now [a]Korah the son of
Izhar, the son of Kohath, the
son of Levi, with [b]Dathan and Abiram the sons of Eliab, and On the
son of Peleth, sons of Reuben, took
men;
2 and they rose up before Moses
with some of the children of Israel,
two hundred and fifty leaders of
the congregation, [a]representatives
of the congregation, men of renown.
3 [a]They gathered together
against Moses and Aaron, and said
to them, "*You* [1]*take* too much
upon yourselves, for [b]all the congregation *is* holy, every one of
them, [c]and the LORD *is* among
them. Why then do you exalt yourselves above the assembly of the
LORD?"
4 So when Moses heard *it*, he
[a]fell on his face;

35 [a]Ex. 31:14, 15 [b]Lev. 24:14; Deut. 21:21; 1 Kin. 21:13; Acts 7:58
38 [a]Deut. 22:12; Matt. 23:5
39 [a]Ps. 103:18 [b]Deut. 29:19 [c]Ps. 73:27; 106:39; James 4:4
40 [a][Lev. 11:44, 45; Rom. 12:1; Col. 1:22; 1 Pet. 1:15, 16]

CHAPTER 16

1 [a]Ex. 6:21 [b]Num. 26:9; Deut. 11:6
2 [a]Num. 1:16; 26:9
3 [a]Num. 12:2; 14:2; Ps. 106:16 [b]Ex. 19:6 [c]Ex. 29:45 [1]*assume too much for*
4 [a]Num. 14:5; 20:6
5 [a][2 Tim. 2:19] [b]Lev. 21:6–8, 12 [c]Ezek. 40:46; 44:15, 16 [1]*set aside* for His use only
9 [a]1 Sam. 18:23; Is. 7:13 [b]Num. 3:41, 45; 8:13–16; Deut. 10:8
11 [a]Ex. 16:7, 8
13 [a]Ex. 16:3; Num. 11:4–6 [b]Ex. 2:14; Acts 7:27, 35
14 [a]Num. 14:1–4 [b]Ex. 3:8; Lev. 20:24
15 [a]Gen. 4:4, 5 [b]1 Sam. 12:3; Acts 20:33 [1]*graciously regard*
16 [a]1 Sam. 12:3, 7

5 and he spoke to Korah and all
his company, saying, "Tomorrow
morning the LORD will show who
is [a]His and *who is* [b]holy,[1] and will
cause *him* to come near to Him.
That one whom He chooses He
will cause to [c]come near to Him.
6 "Do this: Take censers, Korah
and all your company;
7 "put fire in them and put incense in them before the LORD tomorrow, and it shall be *that* the
man whom the LORD chooses *is* the
holy one. *You take* too much upon
yourselves, you sons of Levi!"
8 Then Moses said to Korah,
"Hear now, you sons of Levi:
9 "*Is it* [a]a small thing to you that
the God of Israel has [b]separated
you from the congregation of Israel, to bring you near to Himself,
to do the work of the tabernacle
of the LORD, and to stand before
the congregation to serve them;
10 "and that He has brought you
near *to Himself*, you and all your
brethren, the sons of Levi, with
you? And are you seeking the
priesthood also?
11 "Therefore you and all your
company *are* gathered together
against the LORD. [a]And what *is*
Aaron that you complain against
him?"
12 And Moses sent to call Dathan
and Abiram the sons of Eliab, but
they said, "We will not come up!
13 "*Is it* a small thing that you
have brought us up out of [a]a land
flowing with milk and honey, to
kill us in the wilderness, that you
should [b]keep acting like a prince
over us?
14 "Moreover [a]you have not
brought us into [b]a land flowing
with milk and honey, nor given us
inheritance of fields and vineyards. Will you put out the eyes
of these men? We will not come
up!"
15 Then Moses was very angry,
and said to the LORD, [a]"Do not [1]respect their offering. [b]I have not
taken one donkey from them, nor
have I hurt one of them."
16 And Moses said to Korah, "Tomorrow, you and all your company be present [a]before the
LORD—you and they, as well as
Aaron.
17 "Let each take his censer and

put incense in it, and each of you
bring his censer before the LORD,
two hundred and fifty censers;
both you and Aaron, each *with* his
censer."
18 So every man took his censer,
put fire in it, laid incense on it, and
stood at the door of the tabernacle
of meeting with Moses and Aaron.
19 And Korah gathered all the
congregation against them at the
door of the tabernacle of meeting.
Then [a]the glory of the LORD ap-
peared to all the congregation.
20 And the LORD spoke to Moses
and Aaron, saying,
21 [a]"Separate yourselves from
among this congregation, that I
may [b]consume them in a mo-
ment."
22 Then they [a]fell[1] on their faces,
and said, "O God, [b]the God of the
spirits of all flesh, shall one man
sin, and You be angry with all the
[c]congregation?"
23 So the LORD spoke to Moses,
saying,
24 "Speak to the congregation,
saying, 'Get away from the tents
of Korah, Dathan, and Abiram.' "
25 Then Moses rose and went to
Dathan and Abiram, and the el-
ders of Israel followed him.
26 And he spoke to the congrega-
tion, saying, [a]"Depart now from
the tents of these wicked men!
Touch nothing of theirs, lest you
be consumed in all their sins."
27 So they got away from around
the tents of Korah, Dathan, and
Abiram; and Dathan and Abiram
came out and stood at the door of
their tents, with their wives, their
sons, and their little [a]children.
28 And Moses said: [a]"By this you
shall know that the LORD has sent
me to do all these works, for *I have*
not *done them* [b]of my own will.
29 "If these men die naturally like
all men, or if they are [a]visited by
the common fate of all men, *then*
the LORD has not sent me.
30 "But if the LORD creates [a]a new
thing, and the earth opens its
mouth and swallows them up with
all that belongs to them, and they
[b]go down alive into the pit, then
you will understand that these
men have rejected the LORD."
31 [a]Now it came to pass, as he fin-
ished speaking all these words,
that the ground split apart under
them,
32 and the earth opened its mouth
and swallowed them up, with their
households and [a]all the men with
Korah, with all *their* goods.
33 So they and all those with them
went down alive into the pit; the
earth closed over them, and they
perished from among the assem-
bly.
34 Then all Israel who *were*
around them fled at their cry, for
they said, "Lest the earth swallow
us up *also!*"
35 And [a]a fire came out from the
LORD and consumed the two hun-
dred and fifty men who were offer-
ing incense.
36 Then the LORD spoke to Moses,
saying:
37 "Tell Eleazar, the son of Aaron
the priest, to pick up the censers
out of the blaze, for [a]they are holy,
and scatter the fire some distance
away.
38 "The censers of [a]these men
who sinned [1]against their own
souls, let them be made into ham-
mered plates as a covering for the
altar. Because they presented
them before the LORD, therefore
they are holy; [b]and they shall be
a sign to the children of Israel."
39 So Eleazar the priest took the
bronze censers, which those who
were burned up had presented,
and they were hammered out as
a covering on the altar,
40 *to be* a [1]memorial to the chil-
dren of Israel [a]that no outsider,
who *is* not a descendant of Aaron,
should come near to offer incense
before the LORD, that he might not
become like Korah and his com-
panions, just as the LORD had said
to him through Moses.

Complaints of the People

41 On the next day [a]all the congre-
gation of the children of Israel
complained against Moses and
Aaron, saying, "You have killed
the people of the LORD."
42 Now it happened, when the
congregation had gathered against
Moses and Aaron, that they turned
toward the tabernacle of meeting;
and suddenly [a]the cloud covered
it, and the glory of the LORD ap-
peared.

19 [a]Ex. 16:7, 10; Lev. 9:6, 23; Num. 14:10
21 [a]Gen. 19:17; Jer. 51:6 [b]Ex. 32:10; 33:5
22 [a]Num. 14:5 [b]Num. 27:16; Job 12:10; Eccl. 12:7; Heb. 12:9 [c]Gen. 18:23–32; 20:4 [1]*prostrated themselves*
26 [a]Gen. 19:12, 14, 15, 17
27 [a]Ex. 20:5; Num. 26:11
28 [a]Ex. 3:12; John 5:36 [b]Num. 24:13; John 5:30
29 [a]Ex. 20:5; Job 35:15; Is. 10:3
30 [a]Job 31:3; Is. 28:21 [b][Ps. 55:15]
31 [a]Num. 26:10; Ps. 106:17
32 [a]Num. 26:11; 1 Chr. 6:22, 37
35 [a]Lev. 10:2; Num. 11:1–3; 26:10; Ps. 106:18
37 [a]Lev. 27:28
38 [a]Prov. 20:2; Hab. 2:10 [b]Num. 17:10; Ezek. 14:8 [1]Or *at the cost of their own lives*
40 [a]Num. 3:10; 2 Chr. 26:18 [1]*reminder*
41 [a]Num. 14:2; Ps. 106:25
42 [a]Ex. 40:34

43 Then Moses and Aaron came
before the tabernacle of meeting.
44 And the LORD spoke to Moses,
saying,
45 "Get away from among this
congregation, that I may consume
them in a moment." And they fell
on their faces.
46 So Moses said to Aaron, "Take
a censer and put fire in it from the
altar, put incense *on it*, and take
it quickly to the congregation and
make [1]atonement for them; [a]for
wrath has gone out from the LORD.
The plague has begun."
47 Then Aaron took *it* as Moses
commanded, and ran into the
midst of the assembly; and already
the plague had begun among the
people. So he put in the incense
and made atonement for the peo-
ple.
48 And he stood between the dead
and the living; so [a]the plague was
stopped.
49 Now those who died in the
plague were fourteen thousand
seven hundred, besides those who
died in the Korah incident.
50 So Aaron returned to Moses at
the door of the tabernacle of meet-
ing, for the plague had stopped.

The Budding of Aaron's Rod

17 And the LORD spoke to Mo-
ses, saying:
2 "Speak to the children of Is-
rael, and get from them a rod from
each father's house, all their lead-
ers according to their fathers'
houses—twelve rods. Write each
man's name on his rod.
3 "And you shall write Aaron's
name on the rod of Levi. For there
shall be one rod for the head of
each father's house.
4 "Then you shall place them in
the tabernacle of meeting before
[a]the Testimony, [b]where I meet
with you.
5 "And it shall be *that* the rod
of the man [a]whom I choose will
blossom; thus I will rid Myself of
the complaints of the children of
Israel, [b]which they make against
you."
6 So Moses spoke to the children
of Israel, and each of their leaders
gave him a rod apiece, for each
leader according to their fathers'
houses, twelve rods; and the rod

46 [a]Lev. 10:6; Num. 18:5 [1]Lit. *covering*
48 [a]Num. 25:8; Ps. 106:30

CHAPTER 17

4 [a]Ex. 25:16 [b]Ex. 25:22; 29:42, 43; 30:36; Num. 17:7
5 [a]Num. 16:5 [b]Num. 16:11
7 [a]Ex. 38:21; Num. 1:50, 51; 9:15; 18:2; Acts 7:44
8 [a][Ezek. 17:24]; Heb. 9:4
10 [a]Heb. 9:4 [b]Num. 16:38; Deut. 9:7, 24 [c]Num. 17:5
13 [a]Num. 1:51, 53; 18:4, 7

CHAPTER 18

1 [a]Num. 17:13 [b]Ex. 28:38; Lev. 10:17; 22:16 [1]*guilt*
2 [a]Gen. 29:34; Num. 1:47 [b]Num. 3:5–10 [1]*testimony*
3 [a]Num. 3:25, 31, 36 [b]Num. 16:40 [c]Num. 4:15 [1]*service*
4 [a]Num. 3:10
5 [a]Ex. 27:21; 30:7; Lev. 24:3 [b]Num. 8:19; 16:46

of Aaron *was* among their rods.
7 And Moses placed the rods be-
fore the LORD in [a]the tabernacle of
witness.
8 Now it came to pass on the next
day that Moses went into the tab-
ernacle of witness, and behold, the
[a]rod of Aaron, of the house of Levi,
had sprouted and put forth buds,
had produced blossoms and
yielded ripe almonds.
9 Then Moses brought out all the
rods from before the LORD to all
the children of Israel; and they
looked, and each man took his rod.
10 And the LORD said to Moses,
"Bring [a]Aaron's rod back before
the Testimony, to be kept [b]as a
sign against the rebels, [c]that you
may put their complaints away
from Me, lest they die."
11 Thus did Moses; just as the
LORD had commanded him, so he
did.
12 So the children of Israel spoke
to Moses, saying, "Surely we die,
we perish, we all perish!
13 [a]"Whoever even comes near
the tabernacle of the LORD must
die. Shall we all utterly die?"

Duties of Priests and Levites

18 Then the LORD said to
Aaron: [a]"You and your sons
and your father's house with you
shall [b]bear the [1]iniquity *related to*
the sanctuary, and you and your
sons with you shall bear the in-
iquity *associated with* your priest-
hood.
2 "Also bring with you your
brethren of the [a]tribe of Levi, the
tribe of your father, that they may
be [b]joined with you and serve you
while you and your sons *are* with
you before the tabernacle of [1]wit-
ness.
3 "They shall attend to your
[1]needs and [a]all the needs of the
tabernacle; [b]but they shall not
come near the articles of the sanc-
tuary and the altar, [c]lest they die—
they and you also.
4 "They shall be joined with you
and attend to the needs of the tab-
ernacle of meeting, for all the work
of the tabernacle; [a]but an outsider
shall not come near you.
5 "And you shall attend to [a]the
duties of the sanctuary and the du-
ties of the altar, [b]that there *may*

be no more wrath on the children
of Israel.
6 "Behold, I Myself have [a]taken
your brethren the Levites from
among the children of Israel; [b]*they*
are a gift to you, given by the LORD,
to do the work of the tabernacle
of meeting.
7 "Therefore [a]you and your sons
with you shall attend to your
priesthood for everything at the al-
tar and [b]behind the veil; and you
shall serve. I give your priesthood
to you as a [c]gift for service, but
the outsider who comes near shall
be put to death."

Offerings for Support of the Priests

8 And the LORD spoke to Aaron:
"Here, [a]I Myself have also given
you [1]charge of My heave offerings,
all the holy gifts of the children of
Israel; I have given them [b]as a por-
tion to you and your sons, as an
ordinance forever.
9 "This shall be yours of the most
holy things *reserved* from the fire:
every offering of theirs, every
[a]grain offering and every [b]sin of-
fering and every [c]trespass offering
which they render to Me, *shall be*
most holy for you and your sons.
10 [a]"In a most holy *place* you shall
eat it; every male shall eat it. It
shall be holy to you.
11 "This also *is* yours: [a]the heave
offering of their gift, with all the
wave offerings of the children of
Israel; I have given them to you,
and your sons and daughters with
you, as an ordinance forever.
[b]Everyone who is [1]clean in your
house may eat it.
12 [a]"All the [1]best of the oil, all the
best of the new wine and the grain,
[b]their firstfruits which they offer
to the LORD, I have given them to
you.
13 "Whatever first ripe fruit is in
their land, [a]which they bring to the
LORD, shall be yours. Everyone
who is clean in your house may
eat it.
14 [a]"Every [1]devoted thing in Is-
rael shall be yours.
15 "Everything that first opens
[a]the womb of all flesh, which they
bring to the LORD, whether man or
beast, shall be yours; nevertheless
[b]the firstborn of man you shall
surely redeem, and the firstborn of
unclean animals you shall redeem.
16 "And those redeemed of the de-
voted things you shall redeem
when one month old, [a]according
to your valuation, for five shekels
of silver, according to the shekel
of the sanctuary, which *is* [b]twenty
gerahs.
17 [a]"But the firstborn of a cow, the
firstborn of a sheep, or the first-
born of a goat you shall not re-
deem; they *are* holy. [b]You shall
sprinkle their blood on the altar,
and burn their fat *as* an offering
made by fire for a sweet aroma to
the LORD.
18 "And their flesh shall be yours,
just as the [a]wave[1] breast and the
right thigh are yours.
19 "All the heave offerings of the
holy things, which the children of
Israel offer to the LORD, I have
given to you and your sons and
daughters with you as an ordi-
nance forever; [a]it *is* a covenant of
salt forever before the LORD with
you and your descendants with
you."
20 Then the LORD said to Aaron:
"You shall have [a]no inheritance in
their land, nor shall you have any
portion among them; [b]I *am* your
portion and your inheritance
among the children of Israel.

Tithes for Support of the Levites

21 "Behold, [a]I have given the chil-
dren of Levi all the tithes in Israel
as [1]an inheritance in return for the
work which they perform, [b]the
work of the tabernacle of meeting.
22 [a]"Hereafter the children of Is-
rael shall not come near the taber-
nacle of meeting, [b]lest they bear
sin and die.
23 "But the Levites shall perform
the work of the tabernacle of meet-
ing, and they shall bear their in-
iquity; *it shall be* a statute forever,
throughout your generations, that
among the children of Israel they
shall have no inheritance.
24 "For the tithes of the children
of Israel, which they offer up *as* a
heave offering to the LORD, I have
given to the Levites [1]as an inheri-
tance; therefore I have said to
them, 'Among the children of Is-
rael they shall have no inheri-
tance.' "

6 [a]Num. 3:12, 45 [b]Num. 3:9
7 [a]Num. 3:10; 18:5 [b]Heb. 9:3, 6 [c]Matt. 10:8; 1 Pet. 5:2, 3
8 [a]Lev. 6:16, 18; 7:28–34; Num. 5:9 [b]Ex. 29:29; 40:13, 15 [1]*custody*
9 [a]Lev. 2:2, 3; 10:12, 13 [b]Lev. 6:25, 26 [c]Lev. 7:7; Num. 5:8–10
10 [a]Lev. 6:16, 26
11 [a]Ex. 29:27, 28; Deut. 18:3–5 [b]Lev. 22:1–16 [1]*purified*
12 [a]Ex. 23:19; Neh. 10:35, 36 [b]Ex. 22:29; Lev. 23:20 [1]Lit. *fat*
13 [a]Ex. 22:29; 23:19; 34:26
14 [a]Lev. 27:1–33 [1]*consecrated*
15 [a]Ex. 13:2 [b]Ex. 13:12–15; Num. 3:46; Luke 2:22–24
16 [a]Lev. 27:6 [b]Ex. 30:13
17 [a]Deut. 15:19 [b]Lev. 3:2, 5
18 [a]Ex. 29:26–28; Lev. 7:31–36 [1]*breast of the wave offering*
19 [a]Lev. 2:13; 2 Chr. 13:5; [Mark 9:49, 50]
20 [a]Deut. 10:8, 9; 12:12; 14:27–29; 18:1, 2; Josh. 13:14, 33 [b]Ps. 16:5; Ezek. 44:28
21 [a]Lev. 27:30–33; Deut. 14:22–29; Neh. 10:37; 12:44; Mal. 3:8–10; [Heb. 7:4–10] [b]Num. 3:7, 8 [1]*a possession*
22 [a]Num. 1:51 [b]Lev. 22:9
24 [1]*for a possession*

The Tithe of the Levites

25 Then the LORD spoke to Moses, saying,

26 "Speak thus to the Levites, and say to them: 'When you take from the children of Israel the tithes which I have given you from them as your inheritance, then you shall offer up a heave offering of it to the LORD, [a]a tenth of the tithe.

27 'And your heave offering shall be reckoned to you as though *it were* the grain of the [a]threshing floor and as the fullness of the winepress.

28 'Thus you shall also offer a heave offering to the LORD from all your tithes which you receive from the children of Israel, and you shall give the LORD's heave offering from it to Aaron the priest.

29 'Of all your gifts you shall offer up every heave offering due to the LORD, from all the [1]best of them, the consecrated part of them.'

30 "Therefore you shall say to them: 'When you have lifted up the best of it, then *the rest* shall be accounted to the Levites as the produce of the threshing floor and as the produce of the winepress.

31 'You may eat it in any place, you and your households, for it *is* [a]your [1]reward for your work in the tabernacle of meeting.

32 'And you shall [a]bear no sin because of it, when you have lifted up the best of it. But you shall not [b]profane the holy gifts of the children of Israel, lest you die.' "

Laws of Purification

19 Now the LORD spoke to Moses and Aaron, saying,

2 "This *is* the [1]ordinance of the law which the LORD has commanded, saying: 'Speak to the children of Israel, that they bring you a red heifer without [2]blemish, in which there *is* no [a]defect [b]*and* on which a yoke has never come.

3 'You shall give it to Eleazar the priest, that he may take it [a]outside the camp, and it shall be slaughtered before him;

4 'and Eleazar the priest shall take some of its blood with his finger, and [a]sprinkle some of its blood seven times directly in front of the tabernacle of meeting.

5 'Then the heifer shall be burned in his sight: [a]its hide, its flesh, its blood, and its offal shall be burned.

6 'And the priest shall take [a]cedar wood and [b]hyssop and scarlet, and cast *them* into the midst of the fire burning the heifer.

7 [a]'Then the priest shall wash his clothes, he shall bathe in water, and afterward he shall come into the camp; the priest shall be unclean until evening.

8 'And the one who burns it shall wash his clothes in water, bathe in water, and shall be unclean until evening.

9 'Then a man *who is* clean shall gather up [a]the ashes of the heifer, and store *them* outside the camp in a clean place; and they shall be kept for the congregation of the children of Israel [b]for the water of [1]purification; it *is* for purifying from sin.

10 'And the one who gathers the ashes of the heifer shall wash his clothes, and be unclean until evening. It shall be a statute forever to the children of Israel and to the stranger who dwells among them.

11 [a]'He who touches the dead [1]body of anyone shall be unclean seven days.

12 [a]'He shall purify himself with the water on the third day and on the seventh day; *then* he will be clean. But if he does not purify himself on the third day and on the seventh day, he will not be clean.

13 'Whoever touches the body of anyone who has died, and [a]does not purify himself, [b]defiles the tabernacle of the LORD. That person shall be cut off from Israel. He shall be unclean, because [c]the water of purification was not sprinkled on him; [d]his uncleanness *is* still on him.

14 'This *is* the law when a man dies in a tent: All who come into the tent and all who *are* in the tent shall be unclean seven days;

15 'and every [a]open vessel, which has no cover fastened on it, *is* unclean.

16 [a]'Whoever in the open field touches one who is slain by a sword or who has died, or a bone of a man, or a grave, shall be unclean seven days.

---

26 [a]Neh. 10:38
27 [a]Num. 15:20; [2 Cor. 8:12]
29 [1]Lit. *fat*
31 [a][Matt. 10:10; Luke 10:7]; 1 Cor. 9:13; [1 Tim. 5:18] [1]*wages*
32 [a]Lev. 19:8; 22:16; Ezek. 22:26 [b]Lev. 22:2, 15

CHAPTER 19

2 [a]Lev. 22:20–25 [b]Deut. 21:3; 1 Sam. 6:7 [1]*statute* [2]*defect*
3 [a]Lev. 4:12, 21; Num. 19:9; Heb. 13:11
4 [a]Lev. 4:6; Heb. 9:13
5 [a]Ex. 29:14; Lev. 4:11, 12; 9:11
6 [a]Lev. 14:4, 6, 49 [b]Ex. 12:22; 1 Kin. 4:33
7 [a]Lev. 11:25; 15:5; 16:26, 28
9 [a][Heb. 9:13, 14] [b]Num. 19:13, 20, 21 [1]Lit. *impurity*
11 [a]Lev. 21:1, 11; Num. 5:2; 6:6; 9:6, 10; 31:19; Lam. 4:14; Hag. 2:13 [1]Lit. *soul of man*
12 [a]Num. 19:19; 31:19
13 [a]Lev. 22:3–7 [b]Lev. 15:31 [c]Num. 8:7; 19:9 [d]Lev. 7:20; 22:3
15 [a]Lev. 11:32; Num. 31:20
16 [a]Num. 19:11; 31:19

17 'And for an unclean *person* they shall take some of the [a]ashes of the heifer burnt for purification from sin, and [1]running water shall be put on them in a vessel.

18 'A clean person shall take [a]hyssop and dip *it* in the water, sprinkle *it* on the tent, on all the vessels, on the persons who were there, or on the one who touched a bone, the slain, the dead, or a grave.

19 'The clean *person* shall sprinkle the unclean on the third day and on the seventh day; [a]and on the seventh day he shall purify himself, wash his clothes, and bathe in water; and at evening he shall be clean.

20 'But the man who is unclean and does not purify himself, that person shall be cut off from among the assembly, because he has [a]defiled the sanctuary of the LORD. The water of purification has not been sprinkled on him; he *is* unclean.

21 'It shall be a perpetual statute for them. He who sprinkles the water of purification shall wash his clothes; and he who touches the water of purification shall be unclean until evening.

22 [a]'Whatever the unclean *person* touches shall be unclean; and [b]the person who touches *it* shall be unclean until evening.' "

Moses' Error at Kadesh

20 Then[a] the children of Israel, the whole congregation, came into the Wilderness of Zin in the first month, and the people stayed in [b]Kadesh; and [c]Miriam died there and was buried there.

2 [a]Now there was no water for the congregation; [b]so they gathered together against Moses and Aaron.

3 And the people [a]contended with Moses and spoke, saying: "If only we had died [b]when our brethren died before the LORD!

4 [a]"Why have you brought up the assembly of the LORD into this wilderness, that we and our animals should die here?

5 "And why have you made us come up out of Egypt, to bring us to this evil place? It *is* not a place of grain or figs or vines or pomegranates; nor *is* there any water to drink."

6 So Moses and Aaron went from the presence of the assembly to the door of the tabernacle of meeting, and [a]they [1]fell on their faces. And [b]the glory of the LORD appeared to them.

7 Then the LORD spoke to Moses, saying,

8 [a]"Take the rod; you and your brother Aaron gather the congregation together. Speak to the rock before their eyes, and it will yield its water; thus [b]you shall bring water for them out of the rock, and give drink to the congregation and their animals."

9 So Moses took the rod [a]from before the LORD as He commanded him.

10 And Moses and Aaron gathered the assembly together before the rock; and he said to them, [a]"Hear now, you rebels! Must we bring water for you out of this rock?"

11 Then Moses lifted his hand and struck the rock twice with his rod; [a]and water came out abundantly, and the congregation and their animals drank.

12 Then the LORD spoke to Moses and Aaron, "Because [a]you did not believe Me, to [b]hallow Me in the eyes of the children of Israel, therefore you shall not bring this assembly into the land which I have given them."

13 [a]This *was* the water of [1]Meribah, because the children of Israel contended with the LORD, and He was hallowed among them.

Passage Through Edom Refused

14 [a]Now Moses sent messengers from Kadesh to the king of [b]Edom. [c]"Thus says your brother Israel: 'You know all the hardship that has befallen us,

15 [a]'how our fathers went down to Egypt, [b]and we dwelt in Egypt a long time, [c]and the Egyptians [1]afflicted us and our fathers.

16 [a]'When we cried out to the LORD, He heard our voice and [b]sent the Angel and brought us up out of Egypt; now here we are in Kadesh, a city on the edge of your border.

17 'Please [a]let us pass through

17 [a]Num. 19:9 [1]Lit. *living*
18 [a]Ps. 51:7
19 [a]Lev. 14:9
20 [a]Num. 19:13
22 [a]Hag. 2:11–13 [b]Lev. 15:5

CHAPTER 20

1 [a]Num. 13:21; 33:36 [b]Num. 13:26 [c]Ex. 15:20; Num. 26:59
2 [a]Ex. 17:1 [b]Num. 16:19, 42
3 [a]Ex. 17:2; Num. 14:2 [b]Num. 11:1, 33; 14:37; 16:31–35, 49
4 [a]Ex. 17:3
6 [a]Num. 14:5; 16:4, 22, 45 [b]Num. 14:10 [1]*prostrated themselves*
8 [a]Ex. 4:17, 20; 17:5, 6 [b]Neh. 9:15; Ps. 78:15, 16; 105:41; Is. 43:20; 48:21; [1 Cor. 10:4]
9 [a]Num. 17:10
10 [a]Ps. 106:33
11 [a]Ex. 17:6; Deut. 8:15; Ps. 78:16; Is. 48:21; [1 Cor. 10:4]
12 [a]Num. 20:28; 27:14; Deut. 1:37; 3:26, 27; 34:5 [b]Lev. 10:3; Ezek. 20:41; 36:23; 1 Pet. 3:15
13 [a]Deut. 33:8; Ps. 106:32 [1]Lit. *Contention*
14 [a]Judg. 11:16, 17 [b]Gen. 36:31–39 [c]Deut. 2:4; Obad. 10–12
15 [a]Gen. 46:6; Acts 7:15 [b]Ex. 12:40 [c]Ex. 1:11; Deut. 26:6; Acts 7:19 [1]*did evil to*
16 [a]Ex. 2:23; 3:7 [b]Ex. 3:2; 14:19
17 [a]Num. 21:22

your country. We will not pass
through fields or vineyards, nor
will we drink water from wells; we
will go along the King's Highway;
we will not turn aside to the right
hand or to the left until we have
passed through your territory.' "
18 Then [a]Edom said to him, "You
shall not pass through my *land*,
lest I come out against you with
the sword."
19 So the children of Israel said
to him, "We will go by the High-
way, and if I or my livestock drink
any of your water, [a]then I will pay
for it; let me only pass through on
foot, nothing *more*."
20 Then he said, [a]"You shall not
pass through." So Edom came out
against them with many men and
with a strong hand.
21 Thus Edom [a]refused to give Is-
rael passage through his territory;
so Israel [b]turned away from him.

Death of Aaron

22 Now the children of Israel, the
whole congregation, journeyed
from [a]Kadesh [b]and came to Mount
Hor.
23 And the LORD spoke to Moses
and Aaron in Mount Hor by the
border of the land of Edom, say-
ing:
24 "Aaron shall [1]be [a]gathered to
his people, for he shall not enter
the land which I have given to the
children of Israel, because you re-
belled against My word at the wa-
ter of Meribah.
25 [a]"Take Aaron and Eleazar his
son, and bring them up to Mount
Hor;
26 "and strip Aaron of his gar-
ments and put them on Eleazar his
son; for Aaron shall be gathered
to his people and die there."
27 So Moses did just as the LORD
commanded, and they went up to
Mount Hor in the sight of all the
congregation.
28 [a]Moses stripped Aaron of his
garments and put them on Eleazar
his son; and [b]Aaron died there on
the top of the mountain. Then Mo-
ses and Eleazar came down from
the mountain.
29 Now when all the congregation
saw that Aaron was dead, all the
house of Israel mourned for Aaron
[a]thirty days.

Canaanites Defeated at Hormah

21 The [a]king of Arad, the Ca-
naanite, who dwelt in the
South, heard that Israel was com-
ing on the road to Atharim. Then
he fought against Israel and took
some of them prisoners.
2 [a]So Israel made a vow to the
LORD, and said, "If You will indeed
deliver this people into my hand,
then [b]I will utterly destroy their
cities."
3 And the LORD listened to the
voice of Israel and delivered up the
Canaanites, and they utterly de-
stroyed them and their cities. So
the name of that place was called
[1]Hormah.

The Bronze Serpent

4 Then they journeyed from
Mount Hor by the Way of the Red
Sea, to [a]go around the land of
Edom; and the soul of the people
became very [1]discouraged on the
way.
5 And the people [a]spoke against
God and against Moses: "Why
have you brought us up out of
Egypt to die in the wilderness? For
there is no food and no water, and
our soul [1]loathes this worthless
bread."
6 So [a]the LORD sent [b]fiery ser-
pents among the people, and they
bit the people; and many of the
people of Israel died.
7 [a]Therefore the people came to
Moses, and said, "We have
[b]sinned, for we have spoken
against the LORD and against you;
[c]pray to the LORD that He take
away the serpents from us." So
Moses prayed for the people.
8 Then the LORD said to Moses,
[a]"Make a [b]fiery *serpent*, and set
it on a pole; and it shall be that
everyone who is bitten, when he
looks at it, shall live."
9 So [a]Moses made a bronze ser-
pent, and put it on a pole; and so
it was, if a serpent had bitten any-
one, when he looked at the bronze
serpent, he lived.

From Mount Hor to Moab

10 Now the children of Israel
moved on and [a]camped in Oboth.
11 And they journeyed from
Oboth and camped at [1]Ije Abarim,

18 [a]Num. 24:18; Ps. 137:7; Ezek. 25:12, 13; Obad. 10–15
19 [a]Deut. 2:6, 28
20 [a]Judg. 11:17
21 [a]Deut. 2:27, 30 [b]Deut. 2:8; Judg. 11:18
22 [a]Num. 33:37 [b]Num. 21:4
24 [a]Gen. 25:8; Deut. 32:50 [1]Die and join his ancestors
25 [a]Num. 33:38; Deut. 32:50
28 [a]Ex. 29:29, 30; Deut. 10:6 [b]Num. 33:38
29 [a]Gen. 50:3, 10; Deut. 34:8

CHAPTER 21

1 [a]Num. 33:40; Josh. 12:14; Judg. 1:16
2 [a]Gen. 28:20; Judg. 11:30 [b]Deut. 2:34
3 [1]Lit. *Utter Destruction*
4 [a]Judg. 11:18 [1]*impatient*
5 [a]Num. 20:4, 5 [1]*detests*
6 [a]1 Cor. 10:9 [b]Deut. 8:15
7 [a]Num. 11:2; Ps. 78:34; Is. 26:16; Hos. 5:15 [b]Lev. 26:40 [c]Ex. 8:8; 1 Sam. 12:19; 1 Kin. 13:6; Acts 8:24
8 [a][John 3:14, 15] [b]Is. 14:29; 30:6
9 [a]2 Kin. 18:4; John 3:14, 15
10 [a]Num. 33:43, 44
11 [1]Lit. *The Heaps of Abarim*

in the wilderness which *is* east of
Moab, toward the sunrise.
12 [a]From there they moved and
camped in the Valley of Zered.
13 From there they moved and
camped on the other side of the
Arnon, which *is* in the wilderness
that extends from the border of the
Amorites; for [a]the Arnon *is* the
border of Moab, between Moab
and the Amorites.
14 Therefore it is said in the Book
of the Wars of the LORD:

[1]"Waheb in Suphah,
The brooks of the Arnon,
15 And the slope of the brooks
That reaches to the dwelling of
[a]Ar,
And lies on the border of Moab."

16 From there *they went* [a]to Beer,
which *is* the well where the LORD
said to Moses, "Gather the people
together, and I will give them wa-
ter."
17 [a]Then Israel sang this song:

"Spring up, O well!
All of you sing to it—
18 The well the leaders sank,
Dug by the nation's nobles,
By the [a]lawgiver, with their
staves."

And from the wilderness *they
went* to Mattanah,
19 from Mattanah to Nahaliel,
from Nahaliel to Bamoth,
20 and from Bamoth, *in* the valley
that *is* in the [1]country of Moab, to
the top of Pisgah which looks
[a]down on the [2]wasteland.

King Sihon Defeated

21 Then [a]Israel sent messengers
to Sihon king of the Amorites, say-
ing,
22 [a]"Let me pass through your
land. We will not turn aside into
fields or vineyards; we will not
drink water from wells. We will go
by the King's Highway until we
have passed through your terri-
tory."

12 [a]Deut. 2:13
13 [a]Num. 22:36; Judg. 11:18
14 [1]Ancient unknown places; Vg. *What He did in the Red Sea*
15 [a]Num. 21:28; Deut. 2:9, 18, 29
16 [a]Judg. 9:21
17 [a]Ex. 15:1
18 [a]Is. 33:22
20 [a]Num. 23:28 [1]Lit. *field* [2]Heb. *Jeshimon*
21 [a]Num. 32:33; Deut. 2:26–37; Judg. 11:19
22 [a]Num. 20:16, 17

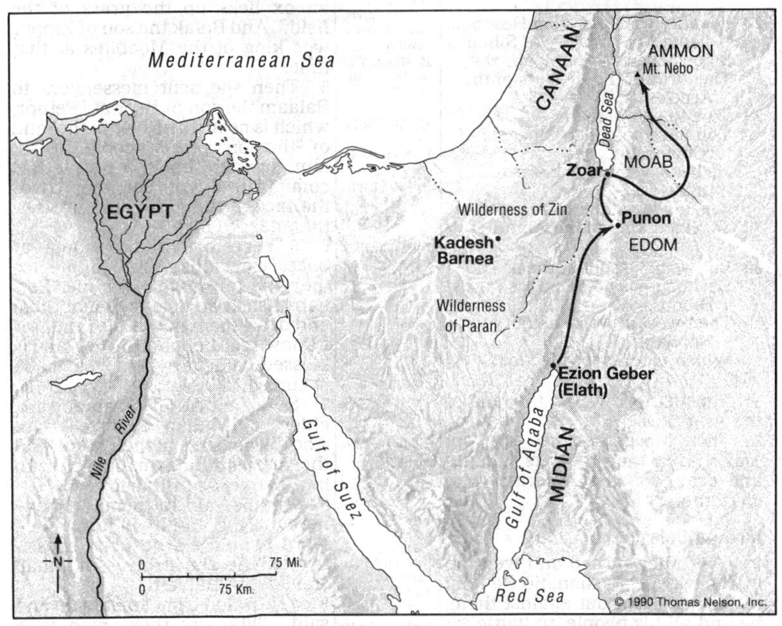

From the Wilderness to Canaan

23 [a]But Sihon would not allow Is-
rael to pass through his territory.
So Sihon gathered all his people
together and [1]went out against Is-
rael in the wilderness, [b]and he
came to Jahaz and fought against
Israel.
24 Then [a]Israel defeated him with
the edge of the sword, and took
possession of his land from the Ar-
non to the Jabbok, as far as the
people of Ammon; for the border
of the people of Ammon *was* forti-
fied.
25 So Israel took all these cities,
and Israel [a]dwelt in all the cities
of the Amorites, in Heshbon and
in all its villages.
26 For Heshbon *was* the city of Si-
hon king of the Amorites, who had
fought against the former king of
Moab, and had taken all his land
from his hand as far as the Arnon.
27 Therefore those who speak in
[1]proverbs say:

"Come to Heshbon, let it be built;
Let the city of Sihon be repaired.

28 "For [a]fire went out from Heshbon,
A flame from the city of Sihon;
It consumed [b]Ar of Moab,
The lords of the [c]heights of the
Arnon.
29 Woe to you, [a]Moab!
You have perished, O people of
[b]Chemosh!
He has given his [c]sons as
fugitives,
And his [d]daughters into captivity,
To Sihon king of the Amorites.

30 "But we have shot at them;
Heshbon has perished [a]as far as
Dibon.
Then we laid waste as far as
Nophah,
Which *reaches* to [b]Medeba."

31 Thus Israel dwelt in the land of
the Amorites.
32 Then Moses sent to [1]spy out
[a]Jazer; and they took its villages
and drove out the Amorites who
were there.

King Og Defeated

33 [a]And they turned and went up
by the way to [b]Bashan. So Og king
of Bashan went out against them,
he and all his people, to battle [c]at
Edrei.
34 Then the LORD said to Moses,
[a]"Do not fear him, for I have [1]de-
livered him into your hand, with
all his people and his land; and
[b]you shall do to him as you did to
Sihon king of the Amorites, who
dwelt at Heshbon."
35 [a]So they defeated him, his
sons, and all his people, until there
was no survivor left him; and they
took possession of his land.

Balak Sends for Balaam

22 Then [a]the children of Israel
moved, and camped in the
plains of Moab on the side of the
Jordan *across from* Jericho.
2 Now [a]Balak the son of Zippor
saw all that Israel had done to the
Amorites.
3 And [a]Moab was exceedingly
afraid of the people because they
were many, and Moab was sick
with dread because of the children
of Israel.
4 So Moab said to [a]the elders of
Midian, "Now this company will
[1]lick up everything around us, as
an ox licks up the grass of the
field." And Balak the son of Zippor
was king of the Moabites at that
time.
5 Then [a]he sent messengers to
Balaam the son of Beor at [b]Pethor,
which *is* near [1]the River in the land
of [2]the sons of his people, to call
him, saying: "Look, a people has
come from Egypt. See, they cover
the face of the earth, and are set-
tling next to me!
6 [a]"Therefore please come at
once, [b]curse this people for me, for
they *are* too mighty for me. Per-
haps I shall be able to defeat them
and drive them out of the land, for
I know that he whom you bless *is*
blessed, and he whom you curse
is cursed."
7 So the elders of Moab and the
elders of Midian departed with
[a]the diviner's fee in their hand, and
they came to Balaam and spoke to
him the words of Balak.
8 And he said to them, [a]"Lodge
here tonight, and I will bring back
word to you, as the LORD speaks
to me." So the princes of Moab
stayed with Balaam.
9 [a]Then God came to Balaam and
said, "Who *are* these men with
you?"

23 [a]Deut. 29:7 [b]Deut. 2:32; Judg. 11:20 [1]*attacked*
24 [a]Deut. 2:33; Josh. 12:1; Neh. 9:22; Ps. 135:10; 136:19; Amos 2:9
25 [a]Amos 2:10
27 [1]*parables*
28 [a]Jer. 48:45, 46 [b]Deut. 2:9, 18; Is. 15:1 [c]Num. 22:41; 33:52
29 [a]Jer. 48:46 [b]Judg. 11:24; 1 Kin. 11:33; 2 Kin. 23:13 [c]Is. 15:2, 5 [d]Is. 16:2
30 [a]Num. 32:3, 34; Jer. 48:18, 22 [b]Is. 15:2
32 [a]Num. 32:1, 3, 35; Jer. 48:32 [1]*secretly search*
33 [a]Deut. 29:7 [b]Deut. 3:1 [c]Josh. 13:12
34 [a]Deut. 3:2 [b]Num. 21:24; Ps. 135:10; 136:20 [1]*given you victory over him*
35 [a]Deut. 3:3, 4; 29:7; Josh. 13:12

CHAPTER 22

1 [a]Num. 33:48, 49
2 [a]Josh. 24:9; Judg. 11:25; Mic. 6:5; Rev. 2:14
3 [a]Ex. 15:15
4 [a]Num. 25:15–18; 31:1–3; Josh. 13:21 [1]*consume*
5 [a]Num. 31:8, 16; Deut. 23:4; Josh. 13:22; 24:9; Neh. 13:1, 2; Mic. 6:5; 2 Pet. 2:15; Jude 11; Rev. 2:14 [b]Deut. 23:4 [1]The Euphrates [2]Or *the people of Amau*
6 [a]Num. 22:17; 23:7, 8 [b]Num. 22:12; 24:9
7 [a]1 Sam. 9:7, 8
8 [a]Num. 22:19
9 [a]Gen. 20:3

10 So Balaam said to God, "Balak
the son of Zippor, king of Moab,
has sent to me, *saying*,
11 'Look, a people has come out
of Egypt, and they cover the face
of the earth. Come now, curse
them for me; perhaps I shall be
able to overpower them and drive
them out.' "
12 And God said to Balaam, "You
shall not go with them; you shall
not curse the people, for [a]they *are*
blessed."
13 So Balaam rose in the morning
and said to the princes of Balak,
"Go back to your land, for the
LORD has refused to give me per-
mission to go with you."
14 And the princes of Moab rose
and went to Balak, and said, "Ba-
laam refuses to come with us."
15 Then Balak again sent princes,
more numerous and more [1]honor-
able than they.
16 And they came to Balaam and
said to him, "Thus says Balak the
son of Zippor: 'Please let nothing
hinder you from coming to me;
17 'for I will certainly [a]honor you
greatly, and I will do whatever you
say to me. [b]Therefore please come,
curse this people for me.' "
18 Then Balaam answered and
said to the servants of Balak,
[a]"Though Balak were to give me
his house full of silver and gold,
[b]I could not go beyond the word
of the LORD my God, to do less or
more.
19 "Now therefore, please, you
also [a]stay here tonight, that I may
know what more the LORD will say
to me."
20 [a]And God came to Balaam at
night and said to him, "If the men
come to call you, rise *and* go with
them; but [b]only the word which I
speak to you—that you shall do."
21 So Balaam rose in the morning,
saddled his donkey, and went with
the princes of Moab.

Balaam, the Donkey, and the Angel

22 Then God's anger was aroused
because he went, [a]and the Angel
of the LORD took His stand in the
way as an adversary against him.
And he was riding on his donkey,
and his two servants *were* with
him.
23 Now [a]the donkey saw the An-
gel of the LORD standing in the way
with His drawn sword in His hand,
and the donkey turned aside out
of the way and went into the field.
So Balaam struck the donkey to
turn her back onto the road.
24 Then the Angel of the LORD
stood in a narrow path between
the vineyards, *with* a wall on this
side and a wall on that side.
25 And when the donkey saw the
Angel of the LORD, she pushed her-
self against the wall and crushed
Balaam's foot against the wall; so
he struck her again.
26 Then the Angel of the LORD
went further, and stood in a nar-
row place where there *was* no way
to turn either to the right hand or
to the left.
27 And when the donkey saw the
Angel of the LORD, she lay down
under Balaam; so Balaam's anger
was aroused, and he struck the
donkey with his staff.
28 Then the LORD [a]opened the
mouth of the donkey, and she said
to Balaam, "What have I done to
you, that you have struck me these
three times?"
29 And Balaam said to the don-
key, "Because you have [1]abused
me. I wish there were a sword in
my hand, [a]for now I would kill
you!"
30 [a]So the donkey said to Balaam,
"*Am* I not your donkey on which
you have ridden, ever since *I be-
came* yours, to this day? Was I
ever [1]disposed to do this to you?"
And he said, "No."
31 Then the LORD [a]opened Ba-
laam's eyes, and he saw the Angel
of the LORD standing in the way
with His drawn sword in His hand;
and he bowed his head and fell flat
on his face.
32 And the Angel of the LORD said
to him, "Why have you struck
your donkey these three times?
Behold, I have come out [1]to stand
against you, because *your* way is
[a]perverse[2] before Me.
33 "The donkey saw Me and
turned aside from Me these three
times. If she had not turned aside
from Me, surely I would also have
killed you by now, and let her
live."
34 And Balaam said to the Angel
of the LORD, [a]"I have sinned, for I

12 [a]Num. 23:20; [Rom. 11:28]
15 [1]*distinguished*
17 [a]Num. 24:11 [b]Num. 22:6
18 [a]Num. 22:38; 24:13 [b]1 Kin. 22:14; 2 Chr. 18:13
19 [a]Num. 22:8
20 [a]Num. 22:9 [b]Num. 22:35; 23:5, 12, 16, 26; 24:13
22 [a]Ex. 4:24
23 [a]Josh. 5:13; 2 Kin. 6:17; Dan. 10:7; Acts 22:9
28 [a]2 Pet. 2:16
29 [a][Prov. 12:10; Matt. 15:19] [1]*mocked*
30 [a]2 Pet. 2:16 [1]*accustomed*
31 [a]Gen. 21:19; 2 Kin. 6:17; Luke 24:16, 31
32 [a][2 Pet. 2:14, 15] [1]*as an adversary* [2]*contrary*
34 [a]1 Sam. 15:24, 30; 26:21; 2 Sam. 12:13

did not know You stood in the way
against me. Now therefore, if it
[1]displeases You, I will turn back."
35 Then the Angel of the LORD
said to Balaam, "Go with the men,
[a]but only the word that I speak to
you, that you shall speak." So Ba-
laam went with the princes of Ba-
lak.
36 Now when Balak heard that
Balaam was coming, [a]he went out
to meet him at the city of Moab,
[b]which *is* on the border at the Ar-
non, the boundary of the territory.
37 Then Balak said to Balaam,
"Did I not earnestly send to you,
calling for you? Why did you not
come to me? Am I not able [a]to
honor you?"
38 And Balaam said to Balak,
"Look, I have come to you! Now,
have I any power at all to say any-
thing? [a]The word that God puts in
my mouth, that I must speak."
39 So Balaam went with Balak,
and they came to Kirjath Huzoth.
40 Then Balak offered oxen and
sheep, and he sent *some* to Balaam
and to the princes who *were* with
him.

Balaam's First Prophecy

41 So it was, the next day, that Ba-
lak took Balaam and brought him
up to the [a]high places of Baal, that
from there he might observe [1]the
extent of the people.

23 Then Balaam said to Balak,
[a]"Build seven altars for me
here, and prepare for me here
seven bulls and seven rams."
2 And Balak did just as Balaam
had spoken, and Balak and Ba-
laam [a]offered a bull and a ram on
each altar.
3 Then Balaam said to Balak,
[a]"Stand by your burnt offering,
and I will go; perhaps the LORD
will come [b]to meet me, and what-
ever He shows me I will tell you."
So he went to a desolate height.
4 [a]And God met Balaam, and he
said to Him, "I have prepared the
seven altars, and I have offered on
each altar a bull and a ram."
5 Then the LORD [a]put a word in
Balaam's mouth, and said, "Re-
turn to Balak, and thus you shall
speak."
6 So he returned to him, and
there he was, standing by his burnt
offering, he and all the princes of
Moab.
7 And he [a]took up his [1]oracle and
said:

"Balak the king of Moab has
brought me from Aram,
From the mountains of the east.
[b]'Come, curse Jacob for me,
And come, [c]denounce Israel!'
8 "How[a] shall I curse whom God has
not cursed?
And how shall I denounce *whom*
the LORD has not denounced?
9 For from the top of the rocks I
see him,
And from the hills I behold him;
There! [a]A people dwelling alone,
[b]Not reckoning itself among the
nations.
10 "Who[a] can count the [1]dust of
Jacob,
Or number one-fourth of Israel?
Let me die [b]the death of the
righteous,
And let my end be like his!"

11 Then Balak said to Balaam,
"What have you done to me? [a]I
took you to curse my enemies, and
look, you have blessed *them* boun-
tifully!"
12 So he answered and said,
[a]"Must I not take heed to speak
what the LORD has put in my
mouth?"

Balaam's Second Prophecy

13 Then Balak said to him,
"Please come with me to another
place from which you may see
them; you shall see only the outer
part of them, and shall not see
them all; curse them for me from
there."
14 So he brought him to the field
of Zophim, to the top of Pisgah,
[a]and built seven altars, and offered
a bull and a ram on *each* altar.
15 And he said to Balak, "Stand
here by your burnt offering while
I [1]meet *the LORD* over there."
16 Then the LORD met Balaam,
and [a]put a word in his mouth, and
said, "Go back to Balak, and thus
you shall speak."
17 So he came to him, and there
he was, standing by his burnt of-
fering, and the princes of Moab
were with him. And Balak said to
him, "What has the LORD spoken?"

34 [1]Lit. *is evil in your eyes*
35 [a]Num. 22:20
36 [a]Gen. 14:17 [b]Num. 21:13
37 [a]Num. 22:17; 24:11
38 [a]Num. 23:26; 24:13; 1 Kin. 22:14; 2 Chr. 18:13
41 [a]Num. 21:28; Deut. 12:2 [1]*the farthest extent*

CHAPTER 23

1 [a]Num. 23:29
2 [a]Num. 23:14, 30
3 [a]Num. 23:15 [b]Num. 23:4, 16
4 [a]Num. 23:16
5 [a]Num. 22:20, 35, 38; 23:16; Deut. 18:18; Jer. 1:9
7 [a]Deut. 23:4; Job 27:1; 29:1; Ps. 78:2 [b]Num. 22:6, 11, 17 [c]1 Sam. 17:10 [1]*prophetic discourse*
8 [a]Num. 22:12
9 [a]Deut. 32:8; 33:28; Josh. 11:23 [b]Ex. 33:16; Ezra 9:2; [Eph. 2:14]
10 [a]Gen. 13:16; 22:17; 28:14; 2 Chr. 1:9 [b]Ps.116:15 [1]Or *dust cloud*
11 [a]Num. 22:11
12 [a]Num. 22:38
14 [a]Num. 23:1, 2
15 [1]So with MT, Tg., Vg.; Syr. *call;* LXX *go and ask God*
16 [a]Num. 22:35; 23:5

18 Then he took up his oracle and
said:

[a]"Rise up, Balak, and hear!
Listen to me, son of Zippor!

19"God[a] *is* not a man, that He should
lie,
Nor a son of man, that He should
repent.
Has He [b]said, and will He not do?
Or has He spoken, and will He
not make it good?
20 Behold, I have received *a
command* to bless;
[a]He has blessed, and I cannot
reverse it.

21"He[a] has not observed iniquity in
Jacob,
Nor has He seen [1]wickedness in
Israel.
The LORD his God *is* with him,
[b]And the shout of a King *is* among
them.
22 [a]God brings them out of Egypt;
He has [b]strength like a wild ox.

23"For *there is* no [1]sorcery against
Jacob,
Nor any [2]divination against
Israel.
It now must be said of Jacob
And of Israel, 'Oh, [a]what God has
done!'
24 Look, a people rises [a]like a
lioness,
And lifts itself up like a lion;
[b]It shall not lie down until it
devours the prey,
And drinks the blood of the
slain."

25 Then Balak said to Balaam,
"Neither curse them at all, nor
bless them at all!"
26 So Balaam answered and said
to Balak, "Did I not tell you, say-
ing, [a]'All that the LORD speaks,
that I must do'?"

Balaam's Third Prophecy

27 Then Balak said to Balaam,
"Please come, I will take you to
another place; perhaps it will
please God that you may curse
them for me from there."
28 So Balak took Balaam to the
top of Peor, that [a]overlooks [1]the
wasteland.
29 Then Balaam said to Balak,
"Build for me here seven altars,
and prepare for me here seven
bulls and seven rams."

18 [a]Judg. 3:20
19 [a]1 Sam. 15:29; Mal. 3:6; James 1:17 [b]Num. 11:23; 1 Kin. 8:56
20 [a]Gen. 12:2; 22:17; Num. 22:12
21 [a]Ps. 32:2; [Rom. 4:7, 8] [b]Ps. 89:15–18 [1]*trouble*
22 [a]Num. 24:8 [b]Deut. 33:17; Job 39:10
23 [a]Ps. 31:19; 44:1 [1]*enchantment* [2]*fortunetelling*
24 [a]Gen. 49:9 [b]Gen. 49:27; Josh. 11:23
26 [a]Num. 22:38
28 [a]Num. 21:20 [1]Heb. *Jeshimon*
CHAPTER 24
1 [a]Num. 23:3, 15 [1]*enchantments*
2 [a]Num. 2:2, 34 [b]Num. 11:25; 1 Sam. 10:10; 19:20, 23; 2 Chr. 15:1
3 [a]Num. 23:7, 18
4 [a]Ezek. 1:28
6 [a]Ps. 1:3; Jer. 17:8 [b]Ps. 104:16
7 [a]Jer. 51:13; Rev. 17:1, 15 [b]1 Sam. 15:8, 9 [c]2 Sam. 5:12; 1 Chr. 14:2
8 [a]Num. 23:22 [b]Num. 14:9; 23:24 [c]Ps. 2:9; Jer. 50:17 [d]Ps. 45:5
9 [a]Gen. 49:9; Num. 23:24 [b]Gen. 12:3; 27:29
10 [a]Ezek. 21:14, 17 [b]Num. 23:11; Neh. 13:2

30 And Balak did as Balaam had
said, and offered a bull and a ram
on *every* altar.

24 Now when Balaam saw that
it pleased the LORD to bless
Israel, he did not go as at [a]other
times, to seek to use [1]sorcery, but
he set his face toward the wilder-
ness.
2 And Balaam raised his eyes,
and saw Israel [a]encamped accord-
ing to their tribes; and [b]the Spirit
of God came upon him.
3 [a]Then he took up his oracle and
said:

"The utterance of Balaam the son
of Beor,
The utterance of the man whose
eyes are opened,
4 The utterance of him who hears
the words of God,
Who sees the vision of the
Almighty,
Who [a]falls down, with eyes wide
open:

5 "How lovely are your tents,
O Jacob!
Your dwellings, O Israel!
6 Like valleys that stretch out,
Like gardens by the riverside,
[a]Like aloes [b]planted by the LORD,
Like cedars beside the waters.
7 He shall pour water from his
buckets,
And his seed *shall be* [a]in many
waters.

"His king shall be higher than
[b]Agag,
And his [c]kingdom shall be
exalted.

8 "God[a] brings him out of Egypt;
He has strength like a wild ox;
He shall [b]consume the nations,
his enemies;
He shall [c]break their bones
And [d]pierce *them* with his
arrows.
9 'He[a] bows down, he lies down as
a lion;
And as a lion, who shall rouse
him?'

[b]"Blessed *is* he who blesses you,
And cursed *is* he who curses
you."

10 Then Balak's anger was
aroused against Balaam, and he
[a]struck his hands together; and
Balak said to Balaam, [b]"I called

you to curse my enemies, and look,
you have bountifully blessed *them*
these three times!
11 "Now therefore, flee to your
place. [a]I said I would greatly honor
you, but in fact, the LORD has kept
you back from honor."
12 So Balaam said to Balak, "Did
I not also speak to your messen-
gers whom you sent to me, say-
ing,
13 'If Balak were to give me his
house full of silver and gold, I
could not go beyond the word of
the LORD, to do good or bad of my
own will. What the LORD says, that
I must speak'?
14 "And now, indeed, I am going
to my people. Come, [a]I will advise
you what this people will do to
your people in the [b]latter days."

Balaam's Fourth Prophecy

15 So he took up his oracle and
said:

"The utterance of Balaam the son
of Beor,
And the utterance of the man
whose eyes are opened;
16 The utterance of him who hears
the words of God,
And has the knowledge of the
Most High,
Who sees the vision of the
Almighty,
Who falls down, with eyes wide
open:

17 "I[a] see Him, but not now;
I behold Him, but not near;
[b]A Star shall come out of Jacob;
[c]A Scepter shall rise out of Israel,
And [1]batter the brow of Moab,
And destroy all the sons of
[2]tumult.

18 "And [a]Edom shall be a possession;
Seir also, his enemies, shall be a
possession,
While Israel does [1]valiantly.
19 [a]Out of Jacob One [1]shall have
dominion,
And destroy the remains of the
city."

20 Then he looked on Amalek,
and he took up his oracle and said:

"Amalek *was* first among the
nations,
But *shall be* last until he
perishes."

21 Then he looked on the Kenites,
and he took up his oracle and said:

"Firm is your dwelling place,
And your nest is set in the rock;
22 Nevertheless Kain shall be
burned.
How long until Asshur carries
you away captive?"

23 Then he took up his oracle and
said:

"Alas! Who shall live when God
does this?
24 But ships *shall come* from the
coasts of [a]Cyprus,[1]
And they shall afflict Asshur and
afflict [b]Eber,
And so shall [2]*Amalek,* until he
perishes."

25 So Balaam rose and departed
and [a]returned to his place; Balak
also went his way.

Israel's Harlotry in Moab

25 Now Israel remained in
[a]Acacia Grove,[1] and the
[b]people began to commit harlotry
with the women of Moab.
2 [a]They invited the people to [b]the
sacrifices of their gods, and the
people ate and [c]bowed down to
their gods.
3 So Israel was joined to Baal of
Peor, and [a]the anger of the LORD
was aroused against Israel.
4 Then the LORD said to Moses,
[a]"Take all the leaders of the people
and hang the offenders before the
LORD, out in the sun, [b]that the
fierce anger of the LORD may turn
away from Israel."
5 So Moses said to [a]the judges of
Israel, [b]"Every one of you kill his
men who were joined to Baal of
Peor."
6 And indeed, one of the children
of Israel came and presented to his
brethren a Midianite woman in the
sight of Moses and in the sight of
all the congregation of the chil-
dren of Israel, [a]who *were* weeping
at the door of the tabernacle of
meeting.
7 Now [a]when Phinehas [b]the son
of Eleazar, the son of Aaron the
priest, saw *it,* he rose from among
the congregation and took a jave-
lin in his hand;
8 and he went after the man of

11 [a]Num. 22:17, 37
14 [a][Mic. 6:5] [b]Gen. 49:1; Deut. 4:30; Dan. 2:28
17 [a]Rev. 1:7; Matt. 1:2; Luke 3:34 [b]Matt. 2:2 [c]Gen. 49:10 [1]*shatter the forehead* [2]Heb. *Sheth,* Jer. 48:45
18 [a]2 Sam. 8:14 [1]*mightily*
19 [a]Gen. 49:10; Amos 9:11, 12 [1]*shall rule*
24 [a]Gen. 10:4; Ezek. 27:6; Dan. 11:30 [b]Gen. 10:21, 25 [1]Heb. *Kittim* [2]Lit. *he* or *that one*
25 [a]Num. 22:5; 31:8

CHAPTER 25

1 [a]Num. 33:49; Josh. 2:1 [b]Rev. 2:14 [1]Heb. *Shittim*
2 [a]Josh. 22:17; Hos. 9:10 [b]Ex. 34:15; Deut. 32:38; 1 Cor. 10:20 [c]Ex. 20:5
3 [a]Ps. 106:28, 29
4 [a]Deut. 4:3 [b]Num. 25:11; Deut. 13:17
5 [a]Ex. 18:21 [b]Deut. 13:6, 9
6 [a]Joel 2:17
7 [a]Ps. 106:30 [b]Ex. 6:25

Israel into the tent and thrust both
of them through, the man of Israel,
and the woman through her body.
So [a]the plague was [b]stopped
among the children of Israel.
9 And [a]those who died in the
plague were twenty-four thou-
sand.
10 Then the LORD spoke to Moses,
saying:
11 [a]"Phinehas the son of Eleazar,
the son of Aaron the priest, has
turned back My wrath from the
children of Israel, because he was
zealous with My zeal among them,
so that I did not consume the chil-
dren of Israel in [b]My zeal.
12 "Therefore say, [a]'Behold, I give
to him My [b]covenant of peace;
13 'and it shall be to him and [a]his
descendants after him a covenant
of [b]an everlasting priesthood, be-
cause he was [c]zealous for his God,
and [d]made [1]atonement for the chil-
dren of Israel.' "
14 Now the name of the Israelite
who was killed, who was killed
with the Midianite woman, *was*
Zimri the son of Salu, a leader of
a father's house among the Sim-
eonites.
15 And the name of the Midianite
woman who was killed *was* Cozbi
the daughter of [a]Zur; he *was* head
of the people of a father's house
in Midian.
16 Then the LORD spoke to Moses,
saying:
17 [a]"Harass the Midianites, and
[1]attack them;
18 "for they harassed you with
their [a]schemes[1] by which they se-
duced you in the matter of Peor
and in the matter of Cozbi, the
daughter of a leader of Midian,
their sister, who was killed in the
day of the plague because of
Peor."

The Second Census of Israel

26 And it came to pass, after
the [a]plague, that the LORD
spoke to Moses and Eleazar the
son of Aaron the priest, saying:
2 [a]"Take a census of all the con-
gregation of the children of Israel
[b]from twenty years old and above,
by their fathers' houses, all who
are able to go to war in Israel."
3 So Moses and Eleazar the
priest spoke with them [a]in the

8 [a]Ps. 106:30 [b]Num. 16:46–48
9 [a]Deut. 4:3
11 [a]Ps. 106:30 [b][Ex. 20:5]; Deut. 32:16, 21; 1 Kin. 14:22; Ps. 78:58; Ezek. 16:38
12 [a][Mal. 2:4, 5; 3:1] [b]Is. 54:10; Ezek. 34:25; 37:26; Mal. 2:5
13 [a]1 Chr. 6:4–15 [b]Ex. 40:15 [c]Acts 22:3; Rom. 10:2 [d][Heb. 2:17] [1]Lit. *covering*
15 [a]Num. 31:8; Josh. 13:21
17 [a]Num. 31:1–3 [1]*be hostile toward*
18 [a]Num. 31:16; Rev. 2:14 [1]*tricks*

CHAPTER 26

1 [a]Num. 25:9
2 [a]Ex. 30:12; 38:25, 26; Num. 1:2; 14:29 [b]Num. 1:3
3 [a]Num. 22:1; 31:12; 33:48; 35:1
4 [a]Num. 1:1
5 [a]Gen. 46:8; Ex. 6:14; 1 Chr. 5:1–3
9 [a]Num. 1:16; 16:1, 2
10 [a]Num. 16:32–35 [b]Num. 16:38–40; 1 Cor. 10:6; 2 Pet. 2:6
11 [a]Ex. 6:24; 1 Chr. 6:22, 23
12 [1]*Jemuel,* Gen. 46:10; Ex. 6:15 [2]*Jarib,* 1 Chr. 4:24
13 [1]*Zohar,* Gen. 46:10
15 [1]*Ziphion,* Gen. 46:16
16 [1]*Ezbon,* Gen. 46:16
17 [1]Sam., Syr. *Arodi* and Gen. 46:16

plains of Moab by the Jordan,
across from Jericho, saying:
4 "*Take a census of the people*
from twenty years old and above,
just as the LORD [a]commanded Mo-
ses and the children of Israel who
came out of the land of Egypt."
5 [a]Reuben *was* the firstborn of Is-
rael. The children of Reuben *were:*
of Hanoch, the family of the Ha-
nochites; *of* Pallu, the family of the
Palluites;
6 *of* Hezron, the family of the
Hezronites; *of* Carmi, the family of
the Carmites.
7 These *are* the families of the
Reubenites: those who were num-
bered of them were forty-three
thousand seven hundred and
thirty.
8 And the son of Pallu *was* Eliab.
9 The sons of Eliab *were* Nemuel,
Dathan, and Abiram. These *are*
the Dathan and Abiram, [a]repre-
sentatives of the congregation,
who contended against Moses and
Aaron in the company of Korah,
when they contended against the
LORD;
10 [a]and the earth opened its
mouth and swallowed them up to-
gether with Korah when that com-
pany died, when the fire devoured
two hundred and fifty men; [b]and
they became a sign.
11 Nevertheless [a]the children of
Korah did not die.
12 The sons of Simeon according
to their families *were: of* [1]Nemuel,
the family of the Nemuelites; *of* Ja-
min, the family of the Jaminites;
of [2]Jachin, the family of the Ja-
chinites;
13 *of* [1]Zerah, the family of the
Zarhites; *of* Shaul, the family of
the Shaulites.
14 These *are* the families of the
Simeonites: twenty-two thousand
two hundred.
15 The sons of Gad according to
their families *were: of* [1]Zephon,
the family of the Zephonites; *of*
Haggi, the family of the Haggites;
of Shuni, the family of the Shu-
nites;
16 *of* [1]Ozni, the family of the Oz-
nites; *of* Eri, the family of the
Erites;
17 *of* [1]Arod, the family of the
Arodites; *of* Areli, the family of the
Arelites.

18 These *are* the families of the
sons of Gad according to those
who were numbered of them: forty
thousand five hundred.
19 [a]The sons of Judah *were* Er and
Onan; and Er and Onan died in the
land of Canaan.
20 And [a]the sons of Judah accord-
ing to their families were: *of* She-
lah, the family of the Shelanites;
of Perez, the family of the Parzites;
of Zerah, the family of the Zar-
hites.
21 And the sons of Perez were: *of*
Hezron, the family of the Hezron-
ites; *of* Hamul, the family of the
Hamulites.
22 These *are* the families of Judah
according to those who were num-
bered of them: seventy-six thou-
sand five hundred.
23 The sons of Issachar according
to their families *were: of* Tola, the
family of the Tolaites; of [1]Puah,
the family of the [2]Punites;
24 of [1]Jashub, the family of the Ja-
shubites; of Shimron, the family of
the Shimronites.
25 These *are* the families of Issa-
char according to those who were
numbered of them: sixty-four
thousand three hundred.
26 [a]The sons of Zebulun accord-
ing to their families *were:* of Sered,
the family of the Sardites; of Elon,
the family of the Elonites; of Jah-
leel, the family of the Jahleelites.
27 These *are* the families of the
Zebulunites according to those
who were numbered of them: sixty
thousand five hundred.
28 [a]The sons of Joseph according
to their families, by Manasseh and
Ephraim, *were:*
29 The sons of [a]Manasseh: of
[b]Machir, the family of the Machir-
ites; and Machir begot Gilead; of
Gilead, the family of the Gilead-
ites.
30 These *are* the sons of Gilead:
of [1]Jeezer, the family of the Jeezer-
ites; of Helek, the family of the He-
lekites;
31 *of* Asriel, the family of the As-
rielites; *of* Shechem, the family of
the Shechemites;
32 *of* Shemida, the family of the
Shemidaites; *of* Hepher, the family
of the Hepherites.
33 Now [a]Zelophehad the son of
Hepher had no sons, but daugh-
ters; and the names of the daugh-
ters of Zelophehad *were* Mahlah,
Noah, Hoglah, Milcah, and Tirzah.
34 These *are* the families of Ma-
nasseh; and those who were num-
bered of them *were* fifty-two thou-
sand seven hundred.
35 These *are* the sons of Ephraim
according to their families: of Shu-
thelah, the family of the Shuthal-
hites; of [1]Becher, the family of the
Bachrites; of Tahan, the family of
the Tahanites.
36 And these *are* the sons of Shu-
thelah: of Eran, the family of the
Eranites.
37 These *are* the families of the
sons of Ephraim according to
those who were numbered of
them: thirty-two thousand five
hundred. These *are* the sons of
Joseph according to their fami-
lies.
38 [a]The sons of Benjamin accord-
ing to their families were: of Bela,
the family of the Belaites; of Ash-
bel, the family of the Ashbelites;
of [b]Ahiram, the family of the Ahi-
ramites;
39 of [a]Shupham,[1] the family of the
Shuphamites; of [2]Hupham, the
family of the Huphamites.
40 And the sons of Bela were [1]Ard
and Naaman: [a]*of Ard,* the family
of the Ardites; of Naaman, the
family of the Naamites.
41 These *are* the sons of Benjamin
according to their families; and
those who were numbered of them
were forty-five thousand six hun-
dred.
42 These *are* the sons of Dan ac-
cording to their families: of
[1]Shuham, the family of the Shu-
hamites. These *are* the families of
Dan according to their families.
43 All the families of the Shuham-
ites, according to those who were
numbered of them, *were* sixty-four
thousand four hundred.
44 [a]The sons of Asher according
to their families *were:* of Jimna,
the family of the Jimnites; of Jesui,
the family of the Jesuites; of Be-
riah, the family of the Beriites.
45 Of the sons of Beriah: of Heber,
the family of the Heberites; of Mal-
chiel, the family of the Malchiel-
ites.
46 And the name of the daughter
of Asher *was* Serah.

19 [a]Gen. 38:2; 46:12
20 [a]1 Chr. 2:3
23 [1]So with Sam., LXX, Syr., Vg.; Heb. *Puvah,* Gen. 46:13; 1 Chr. 7:1 [2]Sam., LXX, Syr., Vg. *Puaites*
24 [1]*Job,* Gen. 46:13
26 [a]Gen. 46:14
28 [a]Gen. 46:20; Deut. 33:16
29 [a]Josh. 17:1 [b]1 Chr. 7:14, 15
30 [1]*Abiezer,* Josh. 17:2
33 [a]Num. 27:1; 36:11
35 [1]*Bered,* 1 Chr. 7:20
38 [a]Gen. 46:21; 1 Chr. 7:6 [b]Gen. 46:21; 1 Chr. 8:1, 2
39 [a]1 Chr. 7:12 [1]MT *Shephupham; Shephuphan,* 1 Chr. 8:5 [2]*Huppim,* Gen. 46:21
40 [a]1 Chr. 8:3 [1]*Addar,* 1 Chr. 8:3
42 [1]*Hushim,* Gen. 46:23
44 [a]Gen. 46:17; 1 Chr. 7:30

47 These *are* the families of the
sons of Asher according to those
who were numbered of them: fifty-
three thousand four hundred.
48 [a]The sons of Naphtali accord-
ing to their families *were:* of
[1]Jahzeel, the family of the Jahzeel-
ites; of Guni, the family of the
Gunites;
49 of Jezer, the family of the Je-
zerites; of [a]Shillem, the family of
the Shillemites.
50 These *are* the families of Naph-
tali according to their families; and
those who were numbered of them
were forty-five thousand four hun-
dred.
51 [a]These *are* those who were
numbered of the children of Israel:
six hundred and one thousand
seven hundred and thirty.
52 Then the LORD spoke to Moses,
saying:
53 [a]"To these the land shall be
[b]divided as an inheritance, accord-
ing to the number of names.
54 [a]"To a large *tribe* you shall
give a larger inheritance, and to a
small *tribe* you shall give a smaller
inheritance. Each shall be given its
inheritance according to those
who were numbered of them.
55 "But the land shall be [a]divided
by lot; they shall inherit according
to the names of the tribes of their
fathers.
56 "According to the lot their in-
heritance shall be divided between
the larger and the smaller."
57 [a]And these *are* those who were
numbered of the Levites according
to their families: of Gershon, the
family of the Gershonites; of Ko-
hath, the family of the Kohathites;
of Merari, the family of the Mera-
rites.
58 These *are* the families of the
Levites: the family of the Libnites,
the family of the Hebronites, the
family of the Mahlites, the family
of the Mushites, and the family of
the Korathites. And Kohath begot
Amram.
59 The name of Amram's wife *was*
[a]Jochebed the daughter of Levi,
who was born to Levi in Egypt;
and to Amram she bore Aaron and
Moses and their sister Miriam.
60 [a]To Aaron were born Nadab
and Abihu, Eleazar and Ithamar.
61 And [a]Nadab and Abihu died
when they offered profane fire be-
fore the LORD.
62 [a]Now those who were num-
bered of them were twenty-three
thousand, every male from a
month old and above; [b]for they
were not numbered among the
other children of Israel, because
there was [c]no inheritance given to
them among the children of Israel.
63 These *are* those who were
numbered by Moses and Eleazar
the priest, who numbered the chil-
dren of Israel [a]in the plains of
Moab by the Jordan, *across from*
Jericho.
64 [a]But among these there was not
a man of those who were num-
bered by Moses and Aaron the
priest when they numbered the
children of Israel in the [b]Wilder-
ness of Sinai.
65 For the LORD had said of them,
"They [a]shall surely die in the wil-
derness." So there was not left a
man of them, [b]except Caleb the
son of Jephunneh and Joshua the
son of Nun.

Inheritance Laws

27 Then came the daughters of
[a]Zelophehad the son of He-
pher, the son of Gilead, the son of
Machir, the son of Manasseh, from
the families of Manasseh the son
of Joseph; and these *were* the
names of his daughters: Mahlah,
Noah, Hoglah, Milcah, and Tirzah.
2 And they stood before Moses,
before Eleazar the priest, and be-
fore the leaders and all the congre-
gation, *by* the doorway of the tab-
ernacle of meeting, saying:
3 "Our father [a]died in the wilder-
ness; but he was not in the com-
pany of those who gathered to-
gether against the LORD, [b]in
company with Korah, but he died
in his own sin; and he had no sons.
4 "Why should the name of our
father be [a]removed[1] from among
his family because he had no son?
[b]Give us a [2]possession among our
father's brothers."
5 So Moses [a]brought their case
before the LORD.
6 And the LORD spoke to Moses,
saying:
7 "The daughters of Zelophehad
speak *what is* right; [a]you shall
surely give them a possession of

48 [a]Gen. 46:24; 1 Chr. 7:13 [1]*Jahziel,* 1 Chr. 7:13
49 [a]1 Chr. 7:13
51 [a]Ex. 12:37; 38:26; Num. 1:46; 11:21
53 [a]Josh. 11:23; 14:1 [b]Num. 33:54
54 [a]Num. 33:54
55 [a]Num. 33:54; 34:13; Josh. 11:23; 14:2
57 [a]Gen. 46:11; Ex. 6:16–19; Num. 3:15; 1 Chr. 6:1, 16
59 [a]Ex. 2:1, 2; 6:20
60 [a]Num. 3:2
61 [a]Lev. 10:1, 2; Num. 3:3, 4; 1 Chr. 24:2
62 [a]Num. 3:39 [b]Num. 1:49 [c]Num. 18:20, 23, 24
63 [a]Num. 26:3
64 [a]Num. 14:29–35; Deut. 2:14–16; Heb. 3:17 [b]Num. 1:1–46
65 [a]Num. 14:26–35; [1 Cor. 10:5, 6] [b]Num. 14:30

CHAPTER 27

1 [a]Num. 26:33; 36:1, 11; Josh. 17:3
3 [a]Num. 14:35; 26:64, 65 [b]Num. 16:1, 2
4 [a]Deut. 25:6 [b]Josh. 17:4 [1]*withdrawn* [2]*inheritance*
5 [a]Ex. 18:13–26
7 [a]Num. 36:2; Josh. 17:4

inheritance among their father's
brothers, and cause the inheri-
tance of their father to pass to
them.
8 "And you shall speak to the
children of Israel, saying: 'If a man
dies and has no son, then you shall
cause his inheritance to pass to his
daughter.
9 'If he has no daughter, then you
shall give his inheritance to his
brothers.
10 'If he has no brothers, then you
shall give his inheritance to his fa-
ther's brothers.
11 'And if his father has no broth-
ers, then you shall give his inheri-
tance to the relative closest to him
in his family, and he shall possess
it.'" And it shall be to the children
of Israel [a]a statute of judgment,
just as the LORD commanded Mo-
ses.

Joshua the Next Leader of Israel

12 Now the LORD said to Moses:
[a]"Go up into this Mount Abarim,
and see the land which I have
given to the children of Israel.
13 "And when you have seen it,
you also [a]shall [1]be gathered to
your people, as Aaron your
brother was gathered.
14 "For in the Wilderness of Zin,
during the strife of the congrega-
tion, you [a]rebelled against My
command to hallow Me at the wa-
ters before their eyes." (These *are*
the [b]waters of Meribah, at Kadesh
in the Wilderness of Zin.)
15 Then Moses spoke to the LORD,
saying:
16 "Let the LORD, [a]the God of the
spirits of all flesh, set a man over
the congregation,
17 [a]"who may go out before them
and go in before them, who may
lead them out and bring them in,
that the congregation of the LORD
may not be [b]like sheep which have
no shepherd."
18 And the LORD said to Moses:
"Take Joshua the son of Nun with
you, a man [a]in whom *is* the Spirit,
and [b]lay your hand on him;
19 "set him before Eleazar the
priest and before all the congrega-
tion, and [a]inaugurate[1] him in their
sight.
20 "And [a]you shall give *some* of
your authority to him, that all the
congregation of the children of Is-
rael [b]may be obedient.
21 [a]"He shall stand before Eleazar
the priest, who shall inquire before
the LORD for him [b]by the judgment
of the Urim. [c]At his word they
shall go out, and at his word they
shall come in, he and all the chil-
dren of Israel with him—all the
congregation."
22 So Moses did as the LORD com-
manded him. He took Joshua and
set him before Eleazar the priest
and before all the congregation.
23 And he laid his hands on him
[a]and [1]inaugurated him, just as the
LORD commanded by the hand of
Moses.

Daily Offerings

28 Now the LORD spoke to Mo-
ses, saying,
2 "Command the children of Is-
rael, and say to them, 'My offering,
[a]My food for My offerings made
by fire as a sweet aroma to Me,
you shall be careful to offer to Me
at their appointed time.'
3 "And you shall say to them,
[a]'This *is* the offering made by fire
which you shall offer to the LORD:
two male lambs in their first year
without blemish, day by day, as a
regular burnt offering.
4 'The one lamb you shall offer
in the morning, the other lamb you
shall offer in the evening,
5 'and [a]one-tenth of an ephah of
fine flour as a [b]grain offering
mixed with one-fourth of a hin of
pressed oil.
6 '*It is* [a]a regular burnt offering
which was ordained at Mount Si-
nai for a sweet aroma, an offering
made by fire to the LORD.
7 'And its drink offering *shall be*
one-fourth of a hin for each lamb;
[a]in a holy *place* you shall pour out
the drink to the LORD as an offer-
ing.
8 'The other lamb you shall offer
in the evening; as the morning
grain offering and its drink offer-
ing, you shall offer *it* as an offering
made by fire, a [1]sweet aroma to
the LORD.

Sabbath Offerings

9 'And on the Sabbath day two
lambs in their first year, without
blemish, and two-tenths *of an*

11 [a]Num. 35:29
12 [a]Num. 33:47; Deut. 3:23–27; 32:48–52; 34:1–4
13 [a]Num. 20:12, 24, 28; 31:2; Deut. 10:6; 34:5, 6 [1]Die and join your ancestors
14 [a]Num. 20:12, 24; Deut. 1:37; 32:51; Ps. 106:32, 33 [b]Ex. 17:7
16 [a]Num. 16:22; Heb. 12:9
17 [a]Deut. 31:2; 1 Sam. 8:20; 18:13; 2 Chr. 1:10 [b]1 Kin. 22:17; Zech. 10:2; Matt. 9:36; Mark 6:34
18 [a]Gen. 41:38; Judg. 3:10; 1 Sam. 16:13, 18 [b]Deut. 34:9
19 [a]Deut. 3:28; 31:3, 7, 8, 23 [1]*commission*
20 [a]Num. 11:17 [b]Josh. 1:16–18
21 [a]Judg. 20:18, 23, 26; 1 Sam. 23:9; 30:7 [b]Ex. 28:30; 1 Sam. 28:6 [c]Josh. 9:14; 1 Sam. 22:10
23 [a]Deut. 3:28; 31:7, 8 [1]*commissioned*

CHAPTER 28
2 [a]Lev. 3:11; 21:6, 8; [Mal. 1:7, 12]
3 [a]Ex. 29:38–42
5 [a]Ex. 16:36; Num. 15:4 [b]Lev. 2:1
6 [a]Ex. 29:42; Amos 5:25
7 [a]Ex. 29:42
8 [1]*pleasing*

ephah of fine flour as a grain offer-
ing, mixed with oil, with its drink
offering—
10 '*this is* [a]the burnt offering for
every Sabbath, besides the regular
burnt offering with its drink offer-
ing.

Monthly Offerings

11 [a]'At the beginnings of your
months you shall present a burnt
offering to the LORD: two young
bulls, one ram, and seven lambs
in their first year, without blem-
ish;
12 [a]'three-tenths *of an ephah* of
fine flour as a grain offering,
mixed with oil, for each bull; two-
tenths *of an ephah* of fine flour as
a grain offering, mixed with oil, for
the one ram;
13 'and one-tenth *of an ephah* of
fine flour, mixed with oil, as a
grain offering for each lamb, as a
burnt offering of sweet aroma, an
offering made by fire to the LORD.
14 'Their drink offering shall be
half a hin of wine for a bull, one-
third of a hin for a ram, and one-
fourth of a hin for a lamb; this *is*
the burnt offering for each month
throughout the months of the year.
15 'Also [a]one kid of the goats as
a sin offering to the LORD shall be
offered, besides the regular burnt
offering and its drink offering.

Offerings at Passover

16 [a]'On the fourteenth day of the
first month *is* the Passover of the
LORD.
17 [a]'And on the fifteenth day of
this month *is* the feast; unleavened
bread shall be eaten for seven
days.
18 'On the [a]first day *you shall have*
a holy [1]convocation. You shall do
no [2]customary work.
19 'And you shall present an offer-
ing made by fire as a burnt offer-
ing to the LORD: two young bulls,
one ram, and seven lambs in their
first year. [a]Be sure they are with-
out blemish.
20 'Their grain offering shall be of
fine flour mixed with oil: three-
tenths *of an ephah* you shall offer
for a bull, and two-tenths for a
ram;
21 'you shall offer one-tenth *of an*
ephah for each of the seven lambs;
22 'also [a]one goat *as* a sin offering,
to make [1]atonement for you.
23 'You shall offer these besides
the burnt offering of the morning,
which *is* for a regular burnt offer-
ing.
24 'In this manner you shall offer
the food of the offering made by
fire daily for seven days, as a
sweet aroma to the LORD; it shall
be offered besides the regular
burnt offering and its drink offer-
ing.
25 'And [a]on the seventh day you
shall have a holy convocation. You
shall do no customary work.

Offerings at the Feast of Weeks

26 'Also [a]on the day of the first-
fruits, when you bring a new grain
offering to the LORD at your *Feast*
of Weeks, you shall have a holy
convocation. You shall do no cus-
tomary work.
27 'You shall present a burnt of-
fering as a sweet aroma to the
LORD: [a]two young bulls, one ram,
and seven lambs in their first year,
28 'with their grain offering of fine
flour mixed with oil: three-tenths
of an ephah for each bull, two-
tenths for the one ram,
29 'and one-tenth for each of the
seven lambs;
30 '*also* one kid of the goats, to
make [1]atonement for you.
31 [a]'Be sure they are without
[1]blemish. You shall present *them*
with their drink offerings, besides
the regular burnt offering with its
grain offering.

Offerings at the Feast of Trumpets

29 'And in the seventh month,
on the first *day* of the month,
you shall have a holy convocation.
You shall do no customary work.
For you [a]it is a day of blowing the
trumpets.
2 'You shall offer a burnt offering
as a sweet aroma to the LORD: one
young bull, one ram, *and* seven
lambs in their first year, without
blemish.
3 'Their grain offering *shall be*
fine flour mixed with oil: three-
tenths *of an ephah* for the bull,
two-tenths for the ram,
4 'and one-tenth for each of the
seven lambs;
5 'also one kid of the goats *as* a

10 [a]Ezek. 46:4

11 [a]Num. 10:10; 1 Sam. 20:5; 1 Chr. 23:31; 2 Chr. 2:4; Ezra 3:5; Neh. 10:33; Is. 1:13, 14; Ezek. 45:17; 46:6, 7; Hos. 2:11; Col. 2:16

12 [a]Num. 15:4–12

15 [a]Num. 15:24; 28:3, 22

16 [a]Ex. 12:1–20; Lev. 23:5–8; Num. 9:2–5; Deut. 16:1–8; Ezek. 45:21

17 [a]Lev. 23:6

18 [a]Ex. 12:16; Lev. 23:7 [1]*assembly* or *gathering* [2]*occupational*

19 [a]Lev. 22:20; Num. 28:31; 29:8; Deut. 15:21

22 [a]Num. 28:15 [1]Lit. *covering*

25 [a]Ex. 12:16; 13:6; Lev. 23:8

26 [a]Ex. 23:16; 34:22; Lev. 23:10–21; Deut. 16:9–12; Acts 2:1

27 [a]Lev. 23:18, 19

30 [1]Lit. *covering*

31 [a]Num. 28:3, 19 [1]*defect*

CHAPTER 29

1 [a]Ex. 23:16; 34:22; Lev. 23:23–25

sin offering, to make atonement for you;

6 'besides [a]the burnt offering with its grain offering for the New Moon, [b]the regular burnt offering with its grain offering, and their drink offerings, [c]according to their ordinance, as a sweet aroma, an offering made by fire to the LORD.

Offerings on the Day of Atonement

7 [a]'On the tenth *day* of this seventh month you shall have a holy convocation. You shall [b]afflict your souls; you shall not do any work.

8 'You shall present a burnt offering to the LORD *as* a sweet aroma: one young bull, one ram, *and* seven lambs in their first year. [a]Be sure they are without blemish.

9 'Their grain offering *shall be of* fine flour mixed with oil: three-tenths *of an ephah* for the bull, two-tenths for the one ram,

10 'and one-tenth for each of the seven lambs;

11 'also one kid of the goats *as* a sin offering, besides [a]the sin offering for atonement, the regular burnt offering with its grain offering, and their drink offerings.

Offerings at the Feast of Tabernacles

12 [a]'On the fifteenth day of the seventh month you shall have a holy convocation. You shall do no customary work, and you shall keep a feast to the LORD seven days.

13 [a]'You shall present a burnt offering, an offering made by fire as a sweet aroma to the LORD: thirteen young bulls, two rams, *and* fourteen lambs in their first year. They shall be without blemish.

14 'Their grain offering *shall be of* fine flour mixed with oil: three-tenths *of an ephah* for each of the thirteen bulls, two-tenths for each of the two rams,

15 'and one-tenth for each of the fourteen lambs;

16 'also one kid of the goats *as* a sin offering, besides the regular burnt offering, its grain offering, and its drink offering.

17 'On the [a]second day *present* twelve young bulls, two rams, fourteen lambs in their first year without blemish,

18 'and their grain offering and their drink offerings for the bulls, for the rams, and for the lambs, by their number, [a]according to the ordinance;

19 'also one kid of the goats *as* a sin offering, besides the regular burnt offering with its grain offering, and their drink offerings.

20 'On the third day *present* eleven bulls, two rams, fourteen lambs in their first year without blemish,

21 'and their grain offering and their drink offerings for the bulls, for the rams, and for the lambs, by their number, [a]according to the ordinance;

22 'also one goat *as* a sin offering, besides the regular burnt offering, its grain offering, and its drink offering.

23 'On the fourth day *present* ten bulls, two rams, *and* fourteen lambs in their first year, without blemish,

24 'and their grain offering and their drink offerings for the bulls, for the rams, and for the lambs, by their number, according to the ordinance;

25 'also one kid of the goats *as* a sin offering, besides the regular burnt offering, its grain offering, and its drink offering.

26 'On the fifth day *present* nine bulls, two rams, *and* fourteen lambs in their first year without blemish,

27 'and their grain offering and their drink offerings for the bulls, for the rams, and for the lambs, by their number, according to the ordinance;

28 'also one goat *as* a sin offering, besides the regular burnt offering, its grain offering, and its drink offering.

29 'On the sixth day *present* eight bulls, two rams, *and* fourteen lambs in their first year without blemish,

30 'and their grain offering and their drink offerings for the bulls, for the rams, and for the lambs, by their number, according to the ordinance;

31 'also one goat *as* a sin offering, besides the regular burnt offering, its grain offering, and its drink offering.

6 [a]Num. 28:11–15 [b]Num. 28:3 [c]Num. 15:11, 12
7 [a]Lev. 16:29–34; 23:26–32 [b]Ps. 35:13; Is. 58:5
8 [a]Num. 28:19
11 [a]Lev. 16:3, 5
12 [a]Lev. 23:33–35; Deut. 16:13–15; Ezek. 45:25
13 [a]Ezra 3:4
17 [a]Lev. 23:36
18 [a]Num. 15:12; 28:7, 14; 29:3, 4, 9, 10
21 [a]Num. 29:18

32 'On the seventh day *present*
seven bulls, two rams, *and* four-
teen lambs in their first year with-
out blemish,
33 'and their grain offering and
their drink offerings for the bulls,
for the rams, and for the lambs,
by their number, according to the
ordinance;
34 'also one goat *as* a sin offering,
besides the regular burnt offering,
its grain offering, and its drink of-
fering.
35 'On the eighth day you shall
have a [a]sacred[1] assembly. You
shall do no customary work.
36 'You shall present a burnt of-
fering, an offering made by fire as
a sweet aroma to the LORD: one
bull, one ram, seven lambs in their
first year without blemish,
37 'and their grain offering and
their drink offerings for the bull,
for the ram, and for the lambs, by
their number, according to the or-
dinance;
38 'also one goat *as* a sin offering,
besides the regular burnt offering,
its grain offering, and its drink of-
fering.
39 'These you shall present to the
LORD at your [a]appointed feasts (be-
sides your [b]vowed offerings and
your freewill offerings) as your
burnt offerings and your grain of-
ferings, as your drink offerings
and your peace offerings.' "
40 So Moses told the children of
Israel everything, just as the LORD
commanded Moses.

The Law Concerning Vows

30 Then Moses spoke to [a]the
heads of the tribes concern-
ing the children of Israel, saying,
"This *is* the thing which the LORD
has commanded:
2 [a]"If a man makes a vow to the
LORD, or [b]swears an oath to bind
himself by some agreement, he
shall not break his word; he shall
[c]do according to all that proceeds
out of his mouth.
3 "Or if a woman makes a vow
to the LORD, and binds *herself* by
some agreement while in her fa-
ther's house in her youth,
4 "and her father hears her vow
and the agreement by which she
has bound herself, and her father
[1]holds his peace, then all her vows
shall stand, and every agreement
with which she has bound herself
shall stand.
5 "But if her father overrules her
on the day that he hears, then none
of her vows nor her agreements by
which she has bound herself shall
stand; and the LORD will release
her, because her father overruled
her.
6 "If indeed she takes a husband,
while bound by her vows or by a
rash utterance from her lips by
which she bound herself,
7 "and her husband hears *it*, and
makes no response to her on the
day that he hears, then her vows
shall stand, and her agreements by
which she bound herself shall
stand.
8 "But if her husband [a]overrules
her on the day that he hears *it*, he
shall make void her vow which she
took and what she uttered with her
lips, by which she bound herself,
and the LORD will release her.
9 "Also any vow of a widow or
a divorced woman, by which she
has bound herself, shall stand
against her.
10 "If she vowed in her husband's
house, or bound herself by an
agreement with an oath,
11 "and her husband heard *it*, and
made no response to her *and* did
not overrule her, then all her vows
shall stand, and every agreement
by which she bound herself shall
stand.
12 "But if her husband truly made
them void on the day he heard
them, then whatever proceeded
from her lips concerning her vows
or concerning the agreement bind-
ing her, it shall not stand; her hus-
band has made them [1]void, and the
LORD will release her.
13 "Every vow and every binding
oath to afflict her soul, her hus-
band may confirm it, or her hus-
band may make it void.
14 "Now if her husband makes no
response whatever to her from day
to day, then he confirms all her
vows or all the agreements that
bind her; he confirms them, be-
cause he made no response to her
on the day that he heard *them*.
15 "But if he does make them void
after he has heard *them*, then he
shall bear her guilt."

35 [a]Lev. 23:36 [1]*solemn*
39 [a]Lev. 23:1–44; 1 Chr. 23:31; 2 Chr. 31:3; Ezra 3:5; Neh. 10:33; Is. 1:14 [b]Lev. 7:16; 22:18, 21, 23; 23:38

CHAPTER 30

1 [a]Num. 1:4, 16; 7:2
2 [a]Lev. 27:2; Deut. 23:21–23; Judg. 11:30, 31, 35; Eccl. 5:4 [b]Lev. 5:4; Matt. 14:9; Acts 23:14 [c]Job 22:27; Ps. 22:25; 50:14; 66:13, 14; Nah. 1:15
4 [1]*says nothing* to interfere
8 [a][Gen. 3:16]
12 [1]*annulled* or *invalidated*

16 These *are* the statutes which
the LORD commanded Moses, be-
tween a man and his wife, and be-
tween a father and his daughter in
her youth in her father's house.

Vengeance on the Midianites

31 And the LORD spoke to Mo-
ses, saying:
2 [a]"Take vengeance on the Midi-
anites for the children of Israel. Af-
terward you shall [b]be gathered to
your people."
3 So Moses spoke to the people,
saying, "Arm some of yourselves
for war, and let them go against
the Midianites to take vengeance
for the LORD on [a]Midian.
4 "A thousand from each tribe of
all the tribes of Israel you shall
send to the war."
5 So there were recruited from
the divisions of Israel one thou-
sand from *each* tribe, twelve thou-
sand armed for war.
6 Then Moses sent them to the
war, one thousand from *each*
tribe; he sent them to the war with
Phinehas the son of Eleazar the
priest, with the holy articles and
[a]the signal trumpets in his hand.
7 And they warred against the
Midianites, just as the LORD com-
manded Moses, and [a]they killed all
the [b]males.
8 They killed the kings of Midian
with *the rest of* those who were
killed—[a]Evi, Rekem, [b]Zur, Hur,
and Reba, the five kings of Midian.
[c]Balaam the son of Beor they also
killed with the sword.
9 And the children of Israel took
the women of Midian captive, with
their little ones, and took as spoil
all their cattle, all their flocks, and
all their goods.
10 They also burned with fire all
the cities where they dwelt, and all
their forts.
11 And [a]they took all the spoil and
all the booty—of man and beast.

Return from the War

12 Then they brought the cap-
tives, the booty, and the spoil to
Moses, to Eleazar the priest, and
to the congregation of the children
of Israel, to the camp in the plains
of Moab by the Jordan, *across
from* Jericho.
13 And Moses, Eleazar the priest,
and all the leaders of the congre-
gation, went to meet them outside
the camp.
14 But Moses was angry with the
officers of the army, *with* the cap-
tains over thousands and captains
over hundreds, who had come
from the battle.
15 And Moses said to them: "Have
you kept [a]all the women alive?
16 "Look, [a]these *women* caused
the children of Israel, through the
[b]counsel of Balaam, to trespass
against the LORD in the incident of
Peor, and [c]there was a plague
among the congregation of the
LORD.
17 "Now therefore, [a]kill every
male among the little ones, and kill
every woman who has known a
man intimately.
18 "But keep alive [a]for yourselves
all the young girls who have not
known a man intimately.
19 "And as for you, [a]remain out-
side the camp seven days; who-
ever has killed any person, and
[b]whoever has touched any slain,
purify yourselves and your cap-
tives on the third day and on the
seventh day.
20 "Purify every garment, every-
thing made of leather, everything
woven of goats' *hair*, and every-
thing made of wood."
21 Then Eleazar the priest said to
the men of war who had gone to
the battle, "This *is* the [1]ordinance
of the law which the LORD com-
manded Moses:
22 "Only the gold, the silver, the
bronze, the iron, the tin, and the
lead,
23 "everything that can endure
fire, you shall put through the fire,
and it shall be clean; and it shall
be purified [a]with the water of puri-
fication. But all that cannot endure
fire you shall put through water.
24 [a]"And you shall wash your
clothes on the seventh day and be
clean, and afterward you may
come into the camp."

Division of the Plunder

25 Now the LORD spoke to Moses,
saying:
26 "Count up the plunder that was
[1]taken—of man and beast—you
and Eleazar the priest and the
chief fathers of the congregation;

CHAPTER 31

2 [a]Num. 25:17 [b]Num. 27:12, 13

3 [a]Josh. 13:21

6 [a]Num. 10:9

7 [a]Deut. 20:13; Judg. 21:11; 1 Sam. 27:9; 1 Kin. 11:15, 16 [b]Gen. 34:25

8 [a]Josh. 13:21 [b]Num. 25:15 [c]Num. 31:16; Josh. 13:22

11 [a]Deut. 20:14

15 [a]Deut. 20:14

16 [a]Num. 25:2 [b]Num. 24:14; 2 Pet. 2:15; Rev. 2:14 [c]Num. 25:9

17 [a]Deut. 7:2; 20:16–18; Judg. 21:11

18 [a]Deut. 21:10–14

19 [a]Num. 5:2 [b]Num. 19:11–22

21 [1]*statute*

23 [a]Num. 19:9, 17

24 [a]Lev. 11:25

26 [1]*captured*

27 "and [a]divide the plunder into two parts, between those who took part in the war, who went out to battle, and all the congregation.

28 "And levy a [1]tribute for the LORD on the men of war who went out to battle: [a]one of every five hundred of the persons, the cattle, the donkeys, and the sheep;

29 "take *it* from their half, and [a]give *it* to Eleazar the priest as a heave offering to the LORD.

30 "And from the children of Israel's half you shall take [a]one of every fifty, drawn from the persons, the cattle, the donkeys, and the sheep, from all the livestock, and give them to the Levites [b]who [1]keep charge of the tabernacle of the LORD."

31 So Moses and Eleazar the priest did as the LORD commanded Moses.

32 The booty remaining from the plunder, which the men of war had taken, was six hundred and seventy-five thousand sheep,

33 seventy-two thousand cattle,

34 sixty-one thousand donkeys,

35 and thirty-two thousand persons in all, of women who had not known a man intimately.

36 And the half, the portion for those who had gone out to war, was in number three hundred and thirty-seven thousand five hundred sheep;

37 and the LORD's [1]tribute of the sheep was six hundred and seventy-five.

38 The cattle *were* thirty-six thousand, of which the LORD's tribute *was* seventy-two.

39 The donkeys *were* thirty thousand five hundred, of which the LORD's tribute *was* sixty-one.

40 The persons *were* sixteen thousand, of which the LORD's tribute *was* thirty-two persons.

41 So Moses gave the tribute *which was* the LORD's heave offering to Eleazar the priest, [a]as the LORD commanded Moses.

42 And from the children of Israel's half, which Moses separated from the men who fought—

43 now the half belonging to the congregation was three hundred and thirty-seven thousand five hundred sheep,

44 thirty-six thousand cattle,

45 thirty thousand five hundred donkeys,

46 and sixteen thousand persons—

47 and [a]from the children of Israel's half Moses took one of every fifty, drawn from man and beast, and gave them to the Levites, who kept charge of the tabernacle of the LORD, as the LORD commanded Moses.

48 Then the officers who *were* over thousands of the army, the captains of thousands and captains of hundreds, came near to Moses;

49 and they said to Moses, "Your servants have taken a count of the men of war who *are* under our command, and not a man of us is missing.

50 "Therefore we have brought an offering for the LORD, what every man found of ornaments of gold: armlets and bracelets and signet rings and earrings and necklaces, [a]to make [1]atonement for ourselves before the LORD."

51 So Moses and Eleazar the priest received the gold from them, all the fashioned ornaments.

52 And all the gold of the offering that they offered to the LORD, from the captains of thousands and captains of hundreds, was sixteen thousand seven hundred and fifty shekels.

53 [a](The men of war had taken spoil, every man for himself.)

54 And Moses and Eleazar the priest received the gold from the captains of thousands and of hundreds, and brought it into the tabernacle of meeting [a]as a memorial for the children of Israel before the LORD.

The Tribes Settling East of the Jordan

32 Now the children of Reuben and the children of Gad had a very great multitude of livestock; and when they saw the land of [a]Jazer and the land of [b]Gilead, that indeed the region *was* a place for livestock,

2 the children of Gad and the children of Reuben came and spoke to Moses, to Eleazar the priest, and to the leaders of the congregation, saying,

27 [a]Josh. 22:8; 1 Sam. 30:24
28 [a]Num. 31:30, 47 [1]*tax*
29 [a]Deut. 18:1–5
30 [a]Num. 31:42–47 [b]Num. 3:7, 8, 25, 31, 36; 18:3, 4 [1]*perform the service*
37 [1]*tax*
41 [a]Num. 5:9, 10; 18:8, 19
47 [a]Num. 31:30
50 [a]Ex. 30:12–16 [1]Lit. *covering*
53 [a]Num. 31:32; Deut. 20:14
54 [a]Ex. 30:16

CHAPTER 32

1 [a]Num. 21:32; Josh. 13:25; 2 Sam. 24:5 [b]Deut. 3:13

3 "Ataroth, Dibon, Jazer, [a]Nimrah, [b]Heshbon, Elealeh, [c]Shebam, Nebo, and [d]Beon,

4 "the country [a]which the LORD defeated before the congregation of Israel, *is* a land for livestock, and your servants have livestock."

5 Therefore they said, "If we have found favor in your sight, let this land be given to your servants as a possession. Do not take us over the Jordan."

6 And Moses said to the children of Gad and to the children of Reuben: "Shall your brethren go to war while you sit here?

7 "Now why will you [a]discourage the heart of the children of Israel from going over into the land which the LORD has given them?

8 "Thus your fathers did [a]when I sent them away from Kadesh Barnea [b]to see the land.

9 "For [a]when they went up to the Valley of Eshcol and saw the land, they discouraged the heart of the children of Israel, so that they did not go into the land which the LORD had given them.

10 [a]"So the LORD's anger was aroused on that day, and He swore an oath, saying,

11 'Surely none of the men who came up from Egypt, [a]from twenty years old and above, shall see the land of which I swore to Abraham, Isaac, and Jacob, because [b]they have not wholly followed Me,

12 'except Caleb the son of Jephunneh, the Kenizzite, and Joshua the son of Nun, [a]for they have wholly followed the LORD.'

13 "So the LORD's anger was aroused against Israel, and He made them [a]wander in the wilderness forty years, until [b]all the generation that had done evil in the sight of the LORD was gone.

14 "And look! You have risen in your fathers' place, a brood of sinful men, to increase still more the [a]fierce anger of the LORD against Israel.

15 "For if you [a]turn away from following Him, He will once again leave them in the wilderness, and you will destroy all these people."

16 Then they came near to him and said: "We will build sheepfolds here for our livestock, and cities for our little ones,

17 "but [a]we ourselves will be armed, ready *to go* before the children of Israel until we have brought them to their place; and our little ones will dwell in the fortified cities because of the inhabitants of the land.

18 [a]"We will not return to our homes until every one of the children of Israel has [1]received his inheritance.

19 "For we will not inherit with them on the other side of the Jordan and beyond, [a]because our inheritance has fallen to us on this eastern side of the Jordan."

20 Then [a]Moses said to them: "If you do this thing, if you arm yourselves before the LORD for the war,

21 "and all your armed men cross over the Jordan before the LORD until He has driven out His enemies from before Him,

22 "and [a]the land is subdued before the LORD, then afterward [b]you may return and be blameless before the LORD and before Israel; and [c]this land shall be your possession before the LORD.

23 "But if you do not do so, then take note, you have sinned against the LORD; and be sure [a]your sin will find you out.

24 [a]"Build cities for your little ones and folds for your sheep, and do [1]what has proceeded out of your mouth."

25 And the children of Gad and the children of Reuben spoke to Moses, saying: "Your servants will do as my lord commands.

26 [a]"Our little ones, our wives, our flocks, and all our livestock will be there in the cities of Gilead;

27 [a]"but your servants will cross over, every man armed for war, before the LORD to battle, just as my lord says."

28 So Moses gave command [a]concerning them to Eleazar the priest, to Joshua the son of Nun, and to the chief fathers of the tribes of the children of Israel.

29 And Moses said to them: "If the children of Gad and the children of Reuben cross over the Jordan with you, every man armed for battle before the LORD, and the land is subdued before you, then you shall give them the land of Gilead as a possession.

3 [a]Num. 32:36 [b]Josh. 13:17, 26 [c]Num. 32:38 [d]Num. 32:38
4 [a]Num. 21:24, 34, 35
7 [a]Num. 13:27—14:4
8 [a]Num. 13:3, 26 [b]Deut. 1:19–25
9 [a]Num. 13:24, 31; Deut. 1:24, 28
10 [a]Num. 14:11; Deut. 1:34–36
11 [a]Num. 14:28, 29; 26:63–65; Deut. 1:35 [b]Num. 14:24, 30
12 [a]Num. 14:6–9, 24, 30; Deut. 1:36; Josh. 14:8, 9
13 [a]Num. 14:33–35 [b]Num. 26:64, 65
14 [a]Num. 11:1; Deut. 1:34
15 [a]Deut. 30:17, 18; Josh. 22:16–18; 2 Chr. 7:19; 15:2
17 [a]Josh. 4:12, 13
18 [a]Josh. 22:1–4 [1]*possessed*
19 [a]Josh. 12:1; 13:8
20 [a]Deut. 3:18; Josh. 1:14
22 [a]Deut. 3:20; Josh. 11:23 [b]Josh. 22:4 [c]Deut. 3:12, 15, 16, 18; Josh. 1:15; 13:8, 32; 22:4, 9
23 [a]Gen. 4:7; 44:16; Josh. 7:1–26; Is. 59:12; [Gal. 6:7]
24 [a]Num. 32:16 [1]*what you said you would do*
26 [a]Josh. 1:14
27 [a]Josh. 4:12
28 [a]Josh. 1:13

rael, and say to them: 'When you
come into [a]the land of Canaan, this
is the land that shall fall to you as
an inheritance—the land of Canaan
to its boundaries.
3 [a]'Your southern border shall be
from the Wilderness of Zin along
the border of Edom; then your
southern border shall extend eastward
to the end of [b]the Salt Sea;
4 'your border shall turn from
the southern side of [a]the Ascent of
Akrabbim, continue to Zin, and be
on the south of [b]Kadesh Barnea;
then it shall go on to [c]Hazar Addar,
and continue to Azmon;
5 'the border shall turn from Azmon
[a]to the Brook of Egypt, and
it shall end at the Sea.
6 'As for the [a]western border,
you shall have the Great Sea for
a border; this shall be your western
border.
7 'And this shall be your northern
border: From the Great Sea
you shall mark out your *border*
line to [a]Mount Hor;
8 'from Mount Hor you shall
mark out *your border* [a]to the entrance
of Hamath; then the direction
of the border shall be toward
[b]Zedad;
9 'the border shall proceed to
Ziphron, and it shall end at [a]Hazar
Enan. This shall be your northern
border.
10 'You shall mark out your eastern
border from Hazar Enan to
Shepham;
11 'the border shall go down from
Shepham [a]to Riblah on the east
side of Ain; the border shall go
down and reach to the eastern
[1]side of the Sea [b]of Chinnereth;
12 'the border shall go down along
the Jordan, and it shall end at
[a]the Salt Sea. This shall be your
land with its surrounding boundaries.'"
13 Then Moses commanded the
children of Israel, saying: [a]"This
is the land which you shall inherit
by lot, which the LORD has commanded
to give to the nine tribes
and to the half-tribe.
14 [a]"For the tribe of the children
of Reuben according to the house
of their fathers, and the tribe of the
children of Gad according to the
house of their fathers, have received
their inheritance; and the
half-tribe of Manasseh has received
its inheritance.
15 "The two tribes and the half-tribe
have received their inheritance
on this side of the Jordan,
across from Jericho eastward, toward
the sunrise."

The Leaders Appointed to Divide the Land

16 And the LORD spoke to Moses,
saying,
17 "These *are* the names of the
men who shall divide the land
among you as an inheritance:
[a]Eleazar the priest and Joshua the
son of Nun.
18 "And you shall take one
[a]leader of every tribe to divide the
land for the inheritance.
19 "These *are* the names of the
men: from the tribe of Judah, Caleb
the son of Jephunneh;
20 "from the tribe of the children
of Simeon, Shemuel the son of
Ammihud;
21 "from the tribe of Benjamin,
Elidad the son of Chislon;
22 "a leader from the tribe of the
children of Dan, Bukki the son of
Jogli;
23 "from the sons of Joseph: a
leader from the tribe of the children
of Manasseh, Hanniel the son
of Ephod,
24 "and a leader from the tribe of
the children of Ephraim, Kemuel
the son of Shiphtan;
25 "a leader from the tribe of the
children of Zebulun, Elizaphan the
son of Parnach;
26 "a leader from the tribe of the
children of Issachar, Paltiel the
son of Azzan;
27 "a leader from the tribe of the
children of Asher, Ahihud the son
of Shelomi;
28 "and a leader from the tribe of
the children of Naphtali, Pedahel
the son of Ammihud."
29 These *are* the ones the LORD
commanded to [1]divide the inheritance
among the children of Israel
in the land of Canaan.

Cities for the Levites

35 And the LORD spoke to Moses
in [a]the plains of Moab by
the Jordan *across from* Jericho,
saying:
2 [a]"Command the children of

CHAPTER 34

2 [a]Gen. 17:8; Deut. 1:7, 8; Ps. 78:54, 55; 105:11

3 [a]Josh. 15:1–3; Ezek. 47:13, 19 [b]Gen. 14:3; Josh. 15:2

4 [a]Josh. 15:3 [b]Num. 13:26; 32:8 [c]Josh. 15:3, 4

5 [a]Gen. 15:18; Josh. 15:4, 47; 1 Kin. 8:65; Is. 27:12

6 [a]Ex. 23:31; Josh. 15:12; Ezek. 47:20

7 [a]Num. 33:37

8 [a]Num. 13:21; Josh. 13:5; 2 Kin. 14:25 [b]Ezek. 47:15

9 [a]Ezek. 47:17

11 [a]2 Kin. 23:33; Jer. 39:5, 6 [b]Deut. 3:17; Josh. 11:2; 12:3; 13:27; 19:35; Matt. 14:34; Luke 5:1 [1]Lit. *shoulder*

12 [a]Num. 34:3

13 [a]Gen. 15:18; Num. 26:52–56; Deut. 11:24; Josh. 14:1–5

14 [a]Num. 32:33

17 [a]Josh. 14:1, 2; 19:51

18 [a]Num. 1:4, 16

29 [1]*apportion*

CHAPTER 35

1 [a]Num. 33:50

2 [a]Josh. 14:3, 4; 21:2, 3; Ezek. 45:1; 48:10–20

Israel that they give the Levites
cities to dwell in from the inheritance of their possession, and
you shall *also* give the Levites
[b]common-land around the cities.
3 "They shall have the cities to
dwell in; and their common-land
shall be for their cattle, for their
herds, and for all their animals.
4 "The common-land of the cities
which you will give the Levites
shall extend from the wall of the
city outward a thousand cubits all
around.
5 "And you shall measure outside the city on the east side two
thousand cubits, on the south side
two thousand cubits, on the west
side two thousand cubits, and on
the north side two thousand cubits.
The city *shall be* in the middle.
This shall belong to them as
common-land for the cities.
6 "Now among the cities which
you will give to the Levites *you
shall appoint* [a]six cities of refuge,
to which a manslayer may flee.
And to these you shall add forty-two cities.
7 "So all the cities you will give
to the Levites *shall be* [a]forty-eight;
these *you shall give* with their
common-land.
8 "And the cities which you will
give *shall be* [a]from the possession
of the children of Israel; [b]from the
larger *tribe* you shall give many,
from the smaller you shall give
few. Each shall give some of its cities to the Levites, in proportion
to the inheritance that each receives."

Cities of Refuge

9 Then the LORD spoke to Moses,
saying,
10 "Speak to the children of Israel, and say to them: [a]'When you
cross the Jordan into the land of
Canaan,
11 'then [a]you shall appoint cities
to be cities of refuge for you,
that the manslayer who kills any
person accidentally may flee
there.
12 [a]'They shall be cities of refuge
for you from the avenger, that the
manslayer may not die until he
stands before the congregation in
judgment.
13 'And of the cities which you
give, you shall have [a]six cities of
refuge.
14 [a]'You shall appoint three cities
on this side of the Jordan, and
three cities you shall appoint in the
land of Canaan, *which* will be cities of refuge.
15 'These six cities shall be for refuge for the children of Israel, [a]for
the stranger, and for the sojourner
among them, that anyone who
kills a person accidentally may
flee there.
16 [a]'But if he strikes him with an
iron implement, so that he dies, he
is a murderer; the murderer shall
surely be put to death.
17 'And if he strikes him with a
stone in the hand, by which one
could die, and he does die, he *is* a
murderer; the murderer shall
surely be put to death.
18 'Or *if* he strikes him with a
wooden hand weapon, by which
one could die, and he does die, he
is a murderer; the murderer shall
surely be put to death.
19 [a]'The[1] avenger of blood himself
shall put the murderer to death;
when he meets him, he shall put
him to death.
20 [a]'If he pushes him out of hatred
or, [b]while lying in wait, hurls
something at him so that he dies,
21 'or in enmity he strikes him
with his hand so that he dies, the
one who struck *him* shall surely
be put to death. He *is* a murderer.
The avenger of blood shall put the
murderer to death when he meets
him.
22 'However, if he pushes him
suddenly [a]without enmity, or
throws anything at him without lying in wait,
23 'or uses a stone, by which a
man could die, throwing *it* at him
without seeing *him,* so that he dies,
while he was not his enemy or
seeking his harm,
24 'then [a]the congregation shall
judge between the manslayer and
the avenger of blood according to
these judgments.
25 'So the congregation shall deliver the manslayer from the hand
of the avenger of blood, and the
congregation shall return him to
the city of refuge where he had
fled, and [a]he shall remain there
until the death of the high priest

2 [b]Lev. 25:32–34
6 [a]Deut. 4:41; Josh. 20:2, 7, 8; 21:3, 13
7 [a]Josh. 21:41
8 [a]Josh. 21:3 [b]Num. 26:54; 33:54
10 [a]Deut. 19:2; Josh. 20:1–9
11 [a]Ex. 21:13; Num. 35:22–25; Deut. 19:1–13
12 [a]Deut. 19:6; Josh. 20:3, 5, 6
13 [a]Num. 35:6
14 [a]Deut. 4:41; Josh. 20:8
15 [a]Num. 15:16
16 [a]Ex. 21:12, 14; Lev. 24:17; Deut. 19:11, 12
19 [a]Num. 35:21, 24, 27; Deut. 19:6, 12 [1]A family member who is to avenge the victim
20 [a]Gen. 4:8; 2 Sam. 3:27; 20:10; 1 Kin. 2:31, 32 [b]Ex. 21:14; Deut. 19:11, 12
22 [a]Ex. 21:13
24 [a]Num. 35:12; Josh. 20:6
25 [a]Josh. 20:6

[b]who was anointed with the holy
oil.
26 'But if the manslayer at any
time goes outside the limits of the
city of refuge where he fled,
27 'and the avenger of blood finds
him outside the limits of his city
of refuge, and the avenger of blood
kills the manslayer, he shall not be
guilty of [1]blood,
28 'because he should have re-
mained in his city of refuge until
the death of the high priest. But
after the death of the high priest
the manslayer may return to the
land of his possession.
29 'And these *things* shall be [a]a
statute of judgment to you
throughout your generations in all
your dwellings.
30 'Whoever kills a person, the
murderer shall be put to death on
the [a]testimony of witnesses; but
one witness is not *sufficient* testi-
mony against a person for the
death *penalty*.
31 'Moreover you shall take no
ransom for the life of a murderer
who *is* guilty of death, but he shall
surely be put to death.
32 'And you shall take no ransom
for him who has fled to his city of
refuge, that he may return to dwell
in the land before the death of the
priest.
33 'So you shall not pollute the
land where you *are;* for blood
[a]defiles the land, and no [1]atone-
ment can be made for the land,
for the blood that is shed on it, ex-
cept [b]by the blood of him who
shed it.
34 'Therefore [a]do not defile the
land which you inhabit, in the
midst of which I dwell; for [b]I the
LORD dwell among the children of
Israel.' "

Marriage of Female Heirs

36 Now the chief fathers of the
families of the [a]children of
Gilead the son of Machir, the son
of Manasseh, of the families of the
sons of Joseph, came near and
[b]spoke before Moses and before
the leaders, the chief fathers of the
children of Israel.
2 And they said: [a]"The LORD
commanded my lord *Moses* to give
the land as an inheritance by lot
to the children of Israel, and [b]my
lord was commanded by the LORD
to give the inheritance of our
brother Zelophehad to his daugh-
ters.
3 "Now if they are married to
any of the sons of the *other* tribes
of the children of Israel, then their
inheritance will be [a]taken from the
inheritance of our fathers, and it
will be added to the inheritance of
the tribe into which they marry;
so it will be taken from the lot of
our inheritance.
4 "And when [a]the Jubilee of the
children of Israel comes, then their
inheritance will be added to the in-
heritance of the tribe into which
they marry; so their inheritance
will be taken away from the in-
heritance of the tribe of our fa-
thers."
5 Then Moses commanded the
children of Israel according to the
word of the LORD, saying: [a]"What
the tribe of the sons of Joseph
speaks is right.
6 "This *is* what the LORD com-
mands concerning the daugh-
ters of Zelophehad, saying, 'Let
them [1]marry whom they think
best, [a]but they may marry only
within the family of their father's
tribe.'
7 "So the inheritance of the chil-
dren of Israel shall not change
hands from tribe to tribe, for every
one of the children of Israel shall
[a]keep the inheritance of the tribe
of his fathers.
8 "And [a]every daughter who
possesses an inheritance in any
tribe of the children of Israel shall
be the wife of one of the family
of her father's tribe, so that the
children of Israel each may pos-
sess the inheritance of his fa-
thers.
9 "Thus no inheritance shall
change hands from *one* tribe to an-
other, but every tribe of the chil-
dren of Israel shall keep its own
inheritance."
10 Just as the LORD commanded
Moses, so did the daughters of Ze-
lophehad;
11 [a]for Mahlah, Tirzah, Hoglah,
Milcah, and Noah, the daughters
of Zelophehad, were married to
the sons of their father's broth-
ers.
12 They were married into the

25 [b]Ex. 29:7; Lev. 4:3; 21:10
27 [1]Murder
29 [a]Num. 27:11
30 [a]Deut. 17:6; 19:15; Matt. 18:16; John 7:51; 8:17, 18; 2 Cor. 13:1; Heb. 10:28
33 [a]Deut. 21:7, 8; Ps. 106:38 [b]Gen. 9:6 [1]Lit. *covering*
34 [a]Lev. 18:24, 25; Deut. 21:23 [b]Ex. 29:45, 46

CHAPTER 36

1 [a]Num. 26:29 [b]Num. 27:1–11
2 [a]Num. 26:55; 33:54; Josh. 17:4 [b]Num. 27:1, 5–7
3 [a]Num. 27:4
4 [a]Lev. 25:10
5 [a]Num. 27:7
6 [a]Num. 36:11, 12 [1]Lit. *be wives to*
7 [a]1 Kin. 21:3
8 [a]1 Chr. 23:22
11 [a]Num. 26:33; 27:1

families of the children of Manasseh the son of Joseph, and their inheritance remained in the tribe of their father's family.
13 These *are* the commandments and the judgments which the LORD commanded the children of Israel by the hand of Moses [a]in the plains of Moab by the Jordan, *across from* Jericho.

13 [a]Num. 26:3; 33:50

The Fifth Book of Moses Called

Deuteronomy

DEUTERONOMY, Moses' "Upper Desert Discourse," consists of a series of farewell messages by Israel's 120-year-old leader. It is addressed to the new generation destined to possess the Land of Promise—those who survived the forty years of wilderness wandering. Like Leviticus, Deuteronomy contains a vast amount of legal detail, but its emphasis is on the laymen rather than the priests. Moses reminds the new generation of the importance of obedience if they are to learn from the sad example of their parents.

The Hebrew title of Deuteronomy is *Haddebharim,* "The Words," taken from the opening phrase in 1:1, "These *are* the words." The parting words of Moses to the new generation are given in oral and written form so that they will endure to all generations. Deuteronomy has been called "five-fifths of the Law" since it completes the five books of Moses. The Jewish people have also called it *Mishneh Hattorah,* "Repetition of the Law," which is translated in the Septuagint as *To Deuteronomion Touto,* "This Second Law." Deuteronomy, however, is not a second law but an adaptation and expansion of much of the original law given on Mount Sinai. The English title comes from the Greek title *Deuteronomion,* "Second Law." Deuteronomy has also been appropriately called the "Book of Remembrance."

The Previous Command to Enter Canaan

THESE *are* the words which Moses spoke to all Israel [a]on this
side of the Jordan in the wilderness, in the [1]plain opposite [2]Suph,
between Paran, Tophel, Laban,
Hazeroth, and Dizahab.
2 *It is* eleven days' *journey* from
Horeb by way of Mount Seir [a]to
Kadesh Barnea.
3 Now it came to pass [a]in the fortieth year, in the eleventh month,
on the first *day* of the month, *that*
Moses spoke to the children of Israel according to all that the LORD
had given him as commandments
to them,
4 [a]after he had killed Sihon king
of the Amorites, who dwelt in
Heshbon, and Og king of Bashan,
who dwelt at Ashtaroth [b]in[1] Edrei.
5 On this side of the Jordan in
the land of Moab, Moses began to
explain this law, saying,
6 "The LORD our God spoke to us
[a]in Horeb, saying: 'You have dwelt
long [b]enough at this mountain.
7 'Turn and take your journey,
and go to the mountains of the
Amorites, to all the neighboring
places in the [1]plain, in the mountains and in the lowland, in the
South and on the seacoast, to the
land of the Canaanites and to Lebanon, as far as the great river, the
River Euphrates.
8 'See, I have set the land before
you; go in and possess the land
which the LORD [1]swore to your fathers—to [a]Abraham, Isaac, and Jacob—to give to them and their descendants after them.'

Tribal Leaders Appointed

9 "And [a]I spoke to you at that
time, saying: 'I [1]alone am not able
to bear you.
10 'The LORD your God has multiplied you, [a]and here you *are* today,
as the stars of heaven in multitude.
11 [a]'May the LORD God of your
fathers make you a thousand times
more numerous than you are, and

CHAPTER 1

1 [a]Deut. 4:44–46 [1]Heb. *arabah* [2]One LXX ms., Tg., Vg. *Red Sea*
2 [a]Num. 13:26; 32:8
3 [a]Num. 33:38
4 [a]Num. 21:23, 24, 33–35 [b]Josh. 13:12 [1]LXX, Syr., Vg. *and;* cf. Josh. 12:4
6 [a]Ex. 3:1, 12 [b]Ex. 19:1, 2
7 [1]Heb. *arabah*
8 [a]Gen. 12:7; 15:5; 22:17; 26:3; 28:13 [1]*promised*
9 [a]Ex. 18:18, 24 [1]*am not able to bear you by myself*
10 [a]Gen. 15:5; 22:17
11 [a]2 Sam. 24:3

bless you [b]as He has promised
you!
12 [a]'How can I alone bear your
problems and your burdens and
your complaints?
13 'Choose wise, understanding,
and knowledgeable men from
among your tribes, and I will make
them [1]heads over you.'
14 "And you answered me and
said, 'The thing which you have
told *us* to do *is* good.'
15 "So I took [a]the heads of your
tribes, wise and knowledgeable
men, and [1]made them heads over
you, leaders of thousands, leaders
of hundreds, leaders of fifties,
leaders of tens, and officers for
your tribes.
16 "Then I commanded your
judges at that time, saying, 'Hear
the cases between your brethren,
and [a]judge righteously between a
man and his [b]brother or the
stranger who is with him.
17 [a]'You shall not show partiality
in judgment; you shall hear the
small as well as the great; you
shall not be afraid in any man's
presence, for [b]the judgment *is*
God's. The case that is too hard
for you, [c]bring to me, and I will
hear it.'
18 "And I commanded you at that
time all the things which you
should do.

Israel's Refusal to Enter the Land

19 "So we departed from Horeb,
[a]and went through all that great
and terrible wilderness which you
saw on the way to the mountains
of the Amorites, as the LORD our
God had commanded us. Then [b]we
came to Kadesh Barnea.
20 "And I said to you, 'You have
come to the mountains of the Amo-
rites, which the LORD our God is
giving us.
21 'Look, the LORD your God has
set the land before you; go up *and*
possess *it*, as the LORD God of your
fathers has spoken to you; [a]do not
fear or be discouraged.'
22 "And every one of you came
near to me and said, 'Let us send
men before us, and let them search
out the land for us, and bring
back word to us of the way by
which we should go up, and of the
cities into which we shall come.'
23 "The plan pleased me well; so
[a]I took twelve of your men, one
man from *each* tribe.
24 [a]"And they departed and went
up into the mountains, and came
to the Valley of Eshcol, and spied
it out.
25 "They also took *some* of the
fruit of the land in their hands and
brought *it* down to us; and they
brought back word to us, saying,
'*It is* a [a]good land which the LORD
our God is giving us.'
26 [a]"Nevertheless you would not
go up, but rebelled against the
command of the LORD your God;
27 "and you [a]complained in your
tents, and said, 'Because the LORD
[b]hates us, He has brought us out
of the land of Egypt to deliver us
into the hand of the Amorites, to
destroy us.
28 'Where can we go up? Our
brethren have [1]discouraged our
hearts, saying, [a]"The people *are*
greater and taller than we; the cit-
ies *are* great and fortified up to
heaven; moreover we have seen
the sons of the [b]Anakim there." '
29 "Then I said to you, 'Do not be
terrified, [a]or afraid of them.
30 [a]'The LORD your God, who goes
before you, He will fight for you,
according to all He did for you in
Egypt before your eyes,
31 'and in the wilderness where
you saw how the LORD your God
carried you, as a [a]man carries his
son, in all the way that you went
until you came to this place.'
32 "Yet, for all that, [a]you did not
believe the LORD your God,
33 [a]"who went in the way before
you [b]to search out a place for you
to pitch your tents, to show you
the way you should go, in the fire
by night and in the cloud by day.

The Penalty for Israel's Rebellion

34 "And the LORD heard the sound
of your words, and was angry,
[a]and took an oath, saying,
35 [a]'Surely not one of these men
of this evil generation shall see
that good land of which I [1]swore
to give to your fathers,
36 [a]'except Caleb the son of Je-
phunneh; he shall see it, and to
him and his children I am giving

11 [b]Gen. 15:5
12 [a]1 Kin. 3:8, 9
13 [1]*rulers*
15 [a]Ex. 18:25 [1]*appointed*
16 [a]Deut. 16:18; John 7:24 [b]Lev. 24:22
17 [a]Lev. 19:15; Deut. 10:17; 16:19; 24:17; 1 Sam. 16:7; Prov. 24:23–26; Acts 10:34; James 2:1, 9 [b]2 Chr. 19:6 [c]Ex. 18:22, 26
19 [a]Num. 10:12; Deut. 2:7; 8:15; 32:10; Jer. 2:6 [b]Num. 13:26
21 [a]Josh. 1:6, 9
23 [a]Num. 13:2, 3
24 [a]Num. 13:21–25
25 [a]Num. 13:27
26 [a]Num. 14:1–4; Ps. 106:24
27 [a]Ps. 106:25 [b]Deut. 9:28
28 [a]Num. 13:28, 31–33; Deut. 9:1, 2 [b]Num. 13:28 [1]Lit. *melted*
29 [a]Num. 14:9; Deut. 7:18
30 [a]Ex. 14:14; Deut. 3:22; 20:4; Neh. 4:20
31 [a]Deut. 32:10–12; Is. 46:3, 4; 63:9; Hos. 11:3
32 [a]Num. 14:11; 20:12; Ps. 106:24; Heb. 3:9, 10, 16–19; 4:1, 2; Jude 5
33 [a]Ex. 13:21; Num. 9:15–23; Neh. 9:12; Ps. 78:14 [b]Num. 10:33; Ezek. 20:6
34 [a]Deut. 2:14, 15
35 [a]Num. 14:22, 23; Ps. 95:10, 11 [1]*promised*
36 [a]Num. 14:24; [Josh. 14:9]

the land on which he walked, be-
cause [b]he [1]wholly followed the
LORD.'
37 [a]"The LORD was also angry
with me for your sakes, saying,
'Even you shall not go in there.
38 [a]'Joshua the son of Nun, [b]who
stands before you, he shall go in
there. [c]Encourage him, for he shall
cause Israel to inherit it.
39 [a]'Moreover your little ones and
your children, who [b]you say will
be victims, who today [c]have no
knowledge of good and evil, they
shall go in there; to them I will give
it, and they shall possess it.
40 [a]'But *as for* you, turn and take
your journey into the wilderness
by the Way of the Red Sea.'
41 "Then you answered and said
to me, [a]'We have sinned against
the LORD; we will go up and fight,
just as the LORD our God com-
manded us.' And when everyone
of you had girded on his weapons
of war, you were ready to go up
into the mountain.
42 "And the LORD said to me, 'Tell
them, [a]"Do not go up nor fight, for
I *am* not among you; lest you be
defeated before your enemies." '
43 "So I spoke to you; yet you
would not listen, but [a]rebelled
against the command of the LORD,
and [b]presumptuously[1] went up
into the mountain.
44 "And the Amorites who dwelt
in that mountain came out against
you and chased you [a]as bees do,
and drove you back from Seir to
Hormah.
45 "Then you returned and wept
before the LORD, but the LORD
would not listen to your voice nor
give ear to you.
46 [a]"So you remained in Kadesh
many days, according to the days
that you spent *there*.

The Desert Years

2 "Then we turned and [a]jour-
neyed into the wilderness of the
Way of the Red Sea, [b]as the LORD
spoke to me, and we [1]skirted
Mount Seir for many days.
2 "And the LORD spoke to me,
saying:
3 'You have skirted this moun-
tain [a]long enough; turn northward.
4 'And command the people, say-
ing, [a]"You *are about to* pass

36 [b]Num. 32:11, 12 [1]*fully*
37 [a]Num. 20:12; 27:14; Deut. 3:26; 4:21; 34:4; Ps. 106:32
38 [a]Num. 14:30 [b]Ex. 24:13; 33:11; 1 Sam. 16:22 [c]Num. 27:18, 19; Deut. 31:7, 23; Josh. 11:23
39 [a]Num. 14:31 [b]Num. 14:3 [c]Is. 7:15, 16
40 [a]Num. 14:25
41 [a]Num. 14:40
42 [a]Num. 14:41–43
43 [a]Num. 14:44 [b]Deut. 17:12, 13 [1]*willfully*
44 [a]Num. 14:45; Ps. 118:12
46 [a]Num. 13:25; 20:1, 22; Deut. 2:7, 14

CHAPTER 2

1 [a]Deut. 1:40 [b]Num. 14:25 [1]*circled around*
3 [a]Deut. 2:7, 14
4 [a]Num. 20:14–21 [b]Deut. 23:7
5 [a]Gen. 36:8; Josh. 24:4
7 [a]Deut. 8:2–4; [Matt. 6:8, 32] [1]Lit. *goings*
8 [a]Judg. 11:18; 1 Kin. 9:26 [b]Num. 21:4
9 [a]Num. 21:15, 28; Deut. 2:18, 29 [b]Gen. 19:36–38
10 [a]Gen. 14:5 [b]Num. 13:22, 33; Deut. 9:2
11 [1]Heb. *rephaim*
12 [a]Gen. 14:6; 36:20; Deut. 2:22 [1]*stead*
13 [a]Num. 21:12 [1]*Wadi* or *Brook*
14 [a]Num. 13:26 [b]Num. 14:33; 26:64; Deut. 1:34, 35 [c]Num. 14:35; Ezek. 20:15 [1]*perished*

through the territory of [b]your
brethren, the descendants of Esau,
who live in Seir; and they will be
afraid of you. Therefore watch
yourselves carefully.
5 "Do not meddle with them, for
I will not give you *any* of their
land, no, not so much as one foot-
step, [a]because I have given Mount
Seir to Esau *as* a possession.
6 "You shall buy food from them
with money, that you may eat; and
you shall also buy water from
them with money, that you may
drink.
7 "For the LORD your God has
blessed you in all the work of your
hand. He knows your [1]trudging
through this great wilderness.
[a]These forty years the LORD your
God *has been* with you; you have
lacked nothing." '
8 "And when we passed beyond
our brethren, the descendants of
Esau who dwell in Seir, away from
the road of the plain, away from
[a]Elath and Ezion Geber, we
[b]turned and passed by way of the
Wilderness of Moab.
9 "Then the LORD said to me, 'Do
not harass Moab, nor contend with
them in battle, for I will not give
you *any* of their land *as* a posses-
sion, because I have given [a]Ar to
[b]the descendants of Lot *as* a pos-
session.' "
10 [a](The Emim had dwelt there in
times past, a people as great and
numerous and tall as [b]the Anakim.
11 They were also regarded as
[1]giants, like the Anakim, but the
Moabites call them Emim.
12 [a]The Horites formerly dwelt in
Seir, but the descendants of Esau
dispossessed them and destroyed
them from before them, and dwelt
in their [1]place, just as Israel did
to the land of their possession
which the LORD gave them.)
13 " 'Now rise and cross over [a]the
[1]Valley of the Zered.' So we
crossed over the Valley of the
Zered.
14 "And the time we took to come
[a]from Kadesh Barnea until we
crossed over the Valley of the
Zered *was* thirty-eight years, [b]un-
til all the generation of the men
of war [1]was consumed from the
midst of the camp, [c]just as the
LORD had sworn to them.

15 "For indeed the hand of the
LORD was against them, to destroy
them from the midst of the camp
until they [1]were consumed.
16 "So it was, when all the men
of war had finally perished from
among the people,
17 "that the LORD spoke to me,
saying:
18 'This day you are to cross over
at Ar, the boundary of Moab.
19 'And *when* you come near the
people of Ammon, do not harass
them or meddle with them, for I
will not give you *any* of the land
of the people of Ammon *as* a pos-
session, because I have given it to
[a]the descendants of Lot *as* a pos-
session.' "
20 (That was also regarded as a
land of [1]giants; giants formerly
dwelt there. But the Ammonites
call them [a]Zamzummim,
21 [a]a people as great and numer-
ous and tall as the Anakim. But the
LORD destroyed them before them,
and they dispossessed them and
dwelt in their place,
22 just as He had done for the de-
scendants of Esau, [a]who dwelt in
Seir, when He destroyed [b]the Ho-
rites from before them. They
dispossessed them and dwelt in
their place, even to this day.
23 And [a]the Avim, who dwelt in
villages as far as Gaza—[b]the
Caphtorim, who came from Caph-
tor, destroyed them and dwelt in
their place.)
24 " 'Rise, take your journey, and
[a]cross over the River Arnon. Look,
I have given into your hand [b]Sihon
the Amorite, king of Heshbon, and
his land. Begin [1]to possess *it*, and
engage him in battle.
25 [a]'This day I will begin to put
the dread and fear of you upon the
nations [1]under the whole heaven,
who shall hear the report of you,
and shall [b]tremble and be in an-
guish because of you.'

King Sihon Defeated

26 "And I [a]sent messengers from
the Wilderness of Kedemoth to Si-
hon king of Heshbon, [b]with words
of peace, saying,
27 [a]'Let me pass through your
land; I will keep strictly to the
road, and I will turn neither to the
right nor to the left.
28 'You shall sell me food for
money, that I may eat, and give
me water for money, that I may
drink; [a]only let me pass through
on foot,
29 [a]'just as the descendants of
Esau who dwell in Seir and the
Moabites who dwell in Ar did for
me, until I cross the Jordan to the
land which the LORD our God is
giving us.'
30 [a]"But Sihon king of Heshbon
would not let us pass through, for
[b]the LORD your God [c]hardened his
spirit and made his heart obsti-
nate, that He might deliver him
into your hand, as *it is* this day.
31 "And the LORD said to me, 'See,
I have begun to [a]give Sihon and
his land over to you. Begin to pos-
sess *it*, that you may inherit his
land.'
32 [a]"Then Sihon and all his people
came out against us to fight at Ja-
haz.
33 "And [a]the LORD our God deliv-
ered him [1]over to us; so [b]we de-
feated him, his sons, and all his
people.
34 "We took all his cities at that
time, and we [a]utterly destroyed the
men, women, and little ones of
every city; we left none remaining.
35 "We took only the livestock as
plunder for ourselves, with the
spoil of the cities which we took.
36 [a]"From Aroer, which *is* on the
bank of the River Arnon, and *from*
[b]the city that *is* in the ravine, as
far as Gilead, there was not one
city too strong for us; [c]the LORD
our God delivered all to us.
37 "Only you did not go near the
land of the people of Ammon—
anywhere along the River [a]Jab-
bok, or to the cities of the moun-
tains, or [b]wherever the LORD our
God had forbidden us.

King Og Defeated

3 "Then we turned and went up
the road to Bashan; and [a]Og
king of Bashan came out against
us, he and all his people, to battle
[b]at Edrei.
2 "And the LORD said to me, 'Do
not fear him, for I have delivered
him and all his people and his land
into your hand; you shall do to him
as you did to [a]Sihon king of the
Amorites, who dwelt at Heshbon.'

15 [1]*perished*
19 [a]Gen. 19:38; Num. 21:24
20 [a]Gen. 14:5 [1]Heb. *rephaim*
21 [a]Deut. 2:10
22 [a]Gen. 36:8; Deut. 2:5 [b]Gen. 14:6; 36:20–30
23 [a]Josh. 13:3 [b]Gen. 10:14; 1 Chr. 1:12; Jer. 47:4; Amos 9:7
24 [a]Num. 21:13, 14; Judg. 11:18 [b]Deut. 1:4 [1]*to take possession*
25 [a]Ex. 23:27; Deut. 11:25; Josh. 2:9 [b]Ex. 15:14–16 [1]*everywhere under the heavens*
26 [a]Num. 21:21–32; Deut. 1:4; Judg. 11:19–21 [b]Deut. 20:10
27 [a]Num. 21:21, 22; Judg. 11:19
28 [a]Num. 20:19
29 [a]Num. 20:18; Deut. 23:3, 4; Judg. 11:17
30 [a]Num. 21:23 [b]Josh. 11:20 [c]Ex. 4:21
31 [a]Deut. 1:3, 8
32 [a]Num. 21:23
33 [a]Ex. 23:31; Deut. 7:2 [b]Num. 21:24 [1]Lit. *before us*
34 [a]Lev. 27:28
36 [a]Deut. 3:12; 4:48; Josh. 13:9 [b]Josh. 13:9, 16 [c]Ps. 44:3
37 [a]Gen. 32:22; Num. 21:24; Deut. 3:16 [b]Deut. 2:5, 9, 19

CHAPTER 3

1 [a]Num. 21:33–35; Deut. 29:7 [b]Deut. 1:4
2 [a]Num. 21:34; Josh. 13:21

3 "So the LORD our God also de-
livered into our hands Og king of
Bashan, with all his people, and
we [1]attacked him until he had no
survivors remaining.
4 "And we took all his cities at
that time; there was not a city
which we did not take from them:
sixty cities, [a]all the region of Ar-
gob, the kingdom of Og in Bashan.
5 "All these cities *were* fortified
with high walls, gates, and bars,
besides a great many rural towns.
6 "And we utterly destroyed
them, as we did to Sihon king [a]of
Heshbon, utterly destroying the
men, women, and children of
every city.
7 "But all the livestock and the
spoil of the cities we took as booty
for ourselves.
8 "And at that time we took the
[a]land from the hand of the two
kings of the Amorites who *were*
on this side of the Jordan, from the
River Arnon to Mount [b]Hermon
9 "(the Sidonians call [a]Hermon
Sirion, and the Amorites call it
Senir),
10 [a]"all the cities of the plain, all
Gilead, and [b]all Bashan, as far as
Salcah and Edrei, cities of the
kingdom of Og in Bashan.
11 [a]"For only Og king of Bashan
remained of the remnant of [b]the
[1]giants. Indeed his bedstead *was*
an iron bedstead. (*Is* it not in [c]Rab-
bah of the people of Ammon?) Nine
cubits *is* its length and four cubits
its width, according to the stan-
dard cubit.

The Land East of the Jordan Divided

12 "And this [a]land, *which* we pos-
sessed at that time, [b]from Aroer,
which *is* by the River Arnon, and
half the mountains of Gilead and
[c]its cities, I gave to the Reubenites
and the Gadites.
13 [a]"The rest of Gilead, and all
Bashan, the kingdom of Og, I gave
to half the tribe of Manasseh. (All
the region of Argob, with all
Bashan, was called the land of the
[1]giants.
14 [a]"Jair the son of Manasseh
took all the region of Argob, [b]as
far as the border of the Geshurites
and the Maachathites, and [c]called
Bashan after his own name,
[1]Havoth Jair, to this day.)
15 "Also I gave [a]Gilead to Machir.
16 "And to the Reubenites [a]and
the Gadites I gave from Gilead as
far as the River Arnon, the middle
of the river as *the* border, as far
as the River Jabbok, [b]the border
of the people of Ammon;
17 "the plain also, with the Jordan
as *the* border, from Chinnereth [a]as
far as the east side of the Sea of
the Arabah [b](the Salt Sea), below
the slopes of Pisgah.
18 "Then I commanded you at
that time, saying: 'The LORD your
God has given you this land to pos-
sess. [a]All you men of valor shall
cross over armed before your
brethren, the children of Israel.
19 'But your wives, your little
ones, and your livestock (I know
that you have much livestock)
shall stay in your cities which I
have given you,
20 'until the LORD has given [a]rest
to your brethren as to you, and
they also possess the land which
the LORD your God is giving them
beyond the Jordan. Then each of
you may [b]return to his possession
which I have given you.'
21 "And [a]I commanded Joshua at
that time, saying, 'Your eyes have
seen all that the LORD your God
has done to these two kings; so
will the LORD do to all the king-
doms through which you pass.
22 'You must not fear them, for
[a]the LORD your God Himself fights
for you.'

Moses Forbidden to Enter the Land

23 "Then [a]I pleaded with the LORD
at that time, saying:
24 'O Lord GOD, You have begun
to show Your servant [a]Your great-
ness and Your [1]mighty hand, for
[b]what god *is there* in heaven or on
earth who can do *anything* like
Your works and Your mighty
deeds?
25 'I pray, let me cross over and
see [a]the good land beyond the Jor-
dan, those pleasant mountains,
and Lebanon.'
26 "But the LORD [a]was angry with
me on your account, and would
not listen to me. So the LORD said
to me: 'Enough of that! Speak no
more to Me of this matter.
27 [a]'Go up to the top of Pisgah,
and lift your eyes toward the west,

3 [1]*struck*
4 [a]Deut. 3:13, 14
6 [a]Deut. 2:24, 34, 35
8 [a]Num. 32:33; Josh. 12:6; 13:8–12 [b]Deut. 4:48; 1 Chr. 5:23
9 [a]1 Chr. 5:23
10 [a]Deut. 4:49 [b]Josh. 12:5; 13:11
11 [a]Amos 2:9 [b]Gen. 14:5; Deut. 2:11, 20 [c]2 Sam. 12:26; Jer. 49:2; Ezek. 21:20 [1]Heb. *rephaim*
12 [a]Num. 32:33; Josh. 12:6; 13:8–12 [b]Deut. 2:36; Josh. 12:2 [c]Num. 34:14
13 [a]Josh. 13:29–31; 17:1 [1]Heb. *rephaim*
14 [a]1 Chr. 2:22 [b]Josh. 13:13; 2 Sam. 3:3; 10:6 [c]Num. 32:41 [1]Lit. *Towns of Jair*
15 [a]Num. 32:39, 40
16 [a]2 Sam. 24:5 [b]Num. 21:24; Deut. 2:37; Josh. 12:2
17 [a]Num. 34:11, 12; Deut. 4:49; Josh. 12:3 [b]Gen. 14:3; Josh. 3:16
18 [a]Num. 32:20; Josh. 4:12, 13
20 [a]Deut. 12:9, 10 [b]Josh. 22:4
21 [a][Num. 27:22, 23]; Josh. 11:23
22 [a]Ex. 14:14; Deut. 1:30; 20:4; Neh. 4:20
23 [a][2 Cor. 12:8, 9]
24 [a]Deut. 5:24; 11:2 [b]Ex. 8:10; 15:11; 2 Sam. 7:22; Ps. 71:19; 86:8 [1]*strong*
25 [a]Ex. 3:8; Deut. 4:22
26 [a]Num. 20:12; 27:14; Deut. 1:37; 31:2; 32:51, 52; 34:4
27 [a]Num. 23:14; 27:12

the north, the south, and the east;
behold *it* with your eyes, for you
shall not cross over this Jordan.
28 'But [a]command[1] Joshua, and
encourage him and strengthen
him; for he shall go over before
this people, and he shall cause
them to inherit the land which you
will see.'
29 "So we stayed in [a]the valley op-
posite Beth Peor.

Moses Commands Obedience

4 "Now, O Israel, listen to [a]the
statutes and the judgments
which I teach you to observe, that
you may live, and go in and [1]pos-
sess the land which the LORD God
of your fathers is giving you.
2 [a]"You shall not add to the word
which I command you, nor take
from it, that you may keep the
commandments of the LORD your
God which I command you.
3 "Your eyes have seen what the
LORD did at [a]Baal Peor; for the
LORD your God has destroyed from
among you all the men who fol-
lowed Baal of Peor.
4 "But you who held fast to the
LORD your God *are* alive today,
every one of you.
5 "Surely I have taught you stat-
utes and judgments, just as the
LORD my God commanded me,
that you should act according *to*
them in the land which you go to
possess.
6 "Therefore be careful to ob-
serve *them;* for this *is* [a]your wis-
dom and your understanding in
the sight of the peoples who will
hear all these statutes, and say,
'Surely this great nation *is* a wise
and understanding people.'
7 "For [a]what great nation *is*
there that has [b]God[1] *so* near to it,
as the LORD our God *is* to us, for
whatever *reason* we may call upon
Him?
8 "And what great nation *is there*
that has *such* statutes and righ-
teous judgments as are in all this
law which I set before you this
day?
9 "Only take heed to yourself,
and diligently [a]keep yourself, lest
you [b]forget the things your eyes
have seen, and lest they depart
from your heart all the days of
your life. And [c]teach them to your

28 [a]Num. 27:18, 23; Deut. 31:3, 7, 8, 23 [1]*charge*
29 [a]Deut. 4:46; 34:6

CHAPTER 4

1 [a]Lev. 19:37; 20:8; 22:31; Deut. 5:1; 8:1; Ezek. 20:11; [Rom. 10:5] [1]*take possession of*
2 [a]Deut. 12:32; [Josh. 1:7]; Prov. 30:6; [Rev. 22:18, 19]
3 [a]Num. 25:1–9; Josh. 22:17; Ps. 106:28
6 [a]Deut. 30:19, 20; 32:46, 47; Job 28:28; Ps. 19:7; 111:10; Prov. 1:7; [2 Tim. 3:15]
7 [a][Deut. 4:32–34; 2 Sam. 7:23] [b][Ps. 46:1; Is. 55:6] [1]Or *a god*
9 [a]Prov. 4:23 [b]Deut. 29:2–8 [c]Gen. 18:19; Deut. 4:10; 6:7, 20–25; Ps. 78:5, 6; Prov. 22:6; Eph. 6:4
10 [a]Ex. 19:9, 16, 17
12 [a]Deut. 5:4, 22 [b]Ex. 19:17–19; 20:22; 1 Kin. 19:11–18 [1]*similitude*
13 [a]Deut. 9:9, 11 [b]Ex. 34:28; Deut. 10:4 [c]Ex. 24:12
14 [a]Ex. 21:1 [1]*do or perform*
15 [a]Josh. 23:11 [b]Is. 40:18
16 [a]Ex. 32:7; Deut. 9:12; 31:29 [b]Ex. 20:4, 5 [c]Rom. 1:23 [1]*similitude*
19 [a]Deut. 17:3; Job 31:26–28 [b]2 Kin. 21:3 [c][Rom. 1:25] [1]*divided*
20 [a]1 Kin. 8:51; Jer. 11:4 [b]Deut. 7:6; 27:9; [Titus 2:14]

children and your grandchildren,
10 "*especially concerning* [a]the day
you stood before the LORD your
God in Horeb, when the LORD said
to me, 'Gather the people to Me,
and I will let them hear My words,
that they may learn to fear Me all
the days they live on the earth, and
that they may teach their chil-
dren.'
11 "Then you came near and
stood at the foot of the mountain,
and the mountain burned with
fire to the midst of heaven, with
darkness, cloud, and thick dark-
ness.
12 [a]"And the LORD spoke to you
out of the midst of the fire. You
heard the sound of the words, but
saw no [1]form; [b]*you* only *heard* a
voice.
13 [a]"So He declared to you His
covenant which He commanded
you to perform, [b]the Ten Com-
mandments; and [c]He wrote them
on two tablets of stone.
14 "And [a]the LORD commanded
me at that time to teach you stat-
utes and judgments, that you
might [1]observe them in the land
which you cross over to possess.

Beware of Idolatry

15 [a]"Take careful heed to your-
selves, for you saw no [b]form when
the LORD spoke to you at Horeb
out of the midst of the fire,
16 "lest you [a]act corruptly and
[b]make for yourselves a carved im-
age in the [1]form of any figure: [c]the
likeness of male or female,
17 "the likeness of any animal
that *is* on the earth or the likeness
of any winged bird that flies in the
air,
18 "the likeness of anything that
creeps on the ground or the like-
ness of any fish that *is* in the water
beneath the earth.
19 "And *take heed,* lest you [a]lift
your eyes to heaven, and *when* you
see the sun, the moon, and the
stars, [b]all the host of heaven, you
feel driven to [c]worship them and
serve them, which the LORD your
God has [1]given to all the peoples
under the whole heaven as a heri-
tage.
20 "But the LORD has taken you
and [a]brought you out of the iron
furnace, out of Egypt, to be [b]His

people, an inheritance, as you are
this day.
21 "Furthermore [a]the LORD was
angry with me for your sakes, and
swore that [b]I would not cross over
the Jordan, and that I would not
enter the good land which the
LORD your God is giving you as an
inheritance.
22 "But [a]I must die in this land,
[b]I must not cross over the Jordan;
but you shall cross over and [1]pos-
sess [c]that good land.
23 "Take heed to yourselves, lest
you forget the covenant of the
LORD your God which He made
with you, [a]and make for your-
selves a carved image in the form
of anything which the LORD your
God has forbidden you.
24 "For [a]the LORD your God *is* a
consuming fire, [b]a jealous God.
25 "When you beget children and
grandchildren and have grown old
in the land, and act corruptly and
make a carved image in the form
of anything, and [a]do evil in the
sight of the LORD your God to pro-
voke Him to anger,
26 [a]"I call heaven and earth to wit-
ness against you this day, that you
will soon utterly perish from the
land which you cross over the Jor-
dan to possess; you will not [1]pro-
long *your* days in it, but will be
utterly destroyed.
27 "And the LORD [a]will scatter you
among the peoples, and you will
be left few in number among the
nations where the LORD will drive
you.
28 "And [a]there you will serve
gods, the work of men's hands,
wood and stone, [b]which neither
see nor hear nor eat nor smell.
29 [a]"But from there you will seek
the LORD your God, and you will
find *Him* if you seek Him with all
your heart and with all your soul.
30 "When you are in [1]distress, and
all these things come upon you in
the [a]latter days, when you [b]turn to
the LORD your God and obey His
voice
31 "(for the LORD your God *is* a
merciful God), He will not forsake
you nor [a]destroy you, nor forget
the covenant of your fathers which
He swore to them.
32 "For [a]ask now concerning the
days that are past, which were be-

21 [a]Num. 20:12 [b]Num. 27:13, 14
22 [a]2 Pet. 1:13–15 [b]Deut. 3:27 [c]Deut. 3:25 [1]*take possession of*
23 [a]Deut. 4:16
24 [a]Deut. 9:3 [b]Ex. 20:5; 34:14
25 [a]2 Kin. 17:17
26 [a]Deut. 30:18, 19 [1]*live long on it*
27 [a]Deut. 28:62
28 [a]Jer. 16:13 [b]Ps. 115:4–7; 135:15–17
29 [a][2 Chr. 15:4]
30 [a]Hos. 3:5 [b]Joel 2:12 [1]*tribulation*
31 [a]Jer. 30:11
32 [a]Job 8:8 [b]Matt. 24:31
33 [a]Deut. 5:24–26
34 [a]Deut. 7:19 [b]Ex. 7:3 [c]Ex. 13:3 [d]Ex. 6:6 [e]Deut. 26:8 [1]*calamities*
35 [a]Mark 12:32
36 [a]Heb. 12:19, 25
37 [a]Deut. 7:7, 8; 10:15; 33:3 [b]Ex. 13:3, 9, 14 [1]Lit. *seed*
38 [a]Deut. 7:1
39 [a]Josh. 2:11
40 [a]Lev. 22:31 [1]*you may prosper* [2]*live long*
41 [a]Num. 35:6
42 [a]Deut. 19:4

fore you, since the day that God
created man on the earth, and *ask*
[b]from one end of heaven to the
other, whether *any* great *thing* like
this has happened, or *anything*
like it has been heard.
33 [a]"Did *any* people *ever* hear the
voice of God speaking out of the
midst of the fire, as you have
heard, and live?
34 "Or did God *ever* try to go *and*
take for Himself a nation from the
midst of *another* nation, [a]by trials,
[b]by signs, by wonders, by war, [c]by
a mighty hand and [d]an out-
stretched arm, [e]and by great [1]ter-
rors, according to all that the LORD
your God did for you in Egypt be-
fore your eyes?
35 "To you it was shown, that you
might know that the LORD Himself
is God; [a]*there is* none other be-
sides Him.
36 [a]"Out of heaven He let you
hear His voice, that He might in-
struct you; on earth He showed
you His great fire, and you heard
His words out of the midst of the
fire.
37 "And because [a]He loved your
fathers, therefore He chose their
[1]descendants after them; and [b]He
brought you out of Egypt with His
Presence, with His mighty power,
38 [a]"driving out from before you
nations greater and mightier than
you, to bring you in, to give you
their land *as* an inheritance, as *it*
is this day.
39 "Therefore know this day, and
consider *it* in your heart, that [a]the
LORD Himself *is* God in heaven
above and on the earth beneath;
there is no other.
40 [a]"You shall therefore keep His
statutes and His commandments
which I command you today, that
[1]it may go well with you and with
your children after you, and that
you may [2]prolong *your* days in the
land which the LORD your God is
giving you for all time."

Cities of Refuge East of the Jordan

41 Then Moses [a]set apart three cit-
ies on this side of the Jordan, to-
ward the rising of the sun,
42 [a]that the manslayer might flee
there, who kills his neighbor un-
intentionally, without having hated
him in time past, and that by

fleeing to one of these cities he
might live:
43 [a]Bezer in the wilderness on the
plateau for the Reubenites, Ra-
moth in Gilead for the Gadites, and
Golan in Bashan for the Manas-
sites.

Introduction to God's Law

44 Now this *is* the law which Mo-
ses set before the children of Is-
rael.
45 These *are* the testimonies, the
statutes, and the judgments which
Moses spoke to the children of Is-
rael after they came out of Egypt,
46 on this side of the Jordan, [a]in
the valley opposite Beth Peor, in
the land of Sihon king of the Amo-
rites, who dwelt at Heshbon,
whom Moses and the children of
Israel [b]defeated[1] after they came
out of Egypt.
47 And they took possession of his
land and the land [a]of Og king of
Bashan, two kings of the Amorites,
who *were* on this side of the Jor-
dan, toward the [1]rising of the
sun,
48 [a]from Aroer, which *is* on the
bank of the River Arnon, even to
Mount [1]Sion (that is, [b]Hermon),
49 and all the plain on the east
side of the Jordan as far as the Sea
of the Arabah, below the [a]slopes
of Pisgah.

The Ten Commandments Reviewed

5 And Moses called all Israel,
and said to them: "Hear, O Is-
rael, the statutes and judgments
which I speak in your hearing to-
day, that you may learn them and
be careful to observe them.
2 [a]"The LORD our God made a
covenant with us in Horeb.
3 "The LORD [a]did not make this
covenant with our fathers, but
with us, those who *are* here today,
all of us who *are* alive.
4 [a]"The LORD talked with you
face to face on the mountain from
the midst of the fire.
5 [a]"I stood between the LORD and
you at that time, to declare to you
the word of the LORD; for [b]you
were afraid because of the fire,
and you did not go up the moun-
tain. *He* said:
6 [a]'I *am* the LORD your God who
brought you out of the land
of Egypt, out of the house of
[1]bondage.
7 [a]'You shall have no other gods
[1]before Me.
8 [a]'You shall not make for yourself
a carved image—any like-
ness *of anything* that *is* in
heaven above, or that *is* in
the earth beneath, or that *is*
in the water under the earth;
9 you shall not [a]bow[1] down to
them nor serve them. For I,
the LORD your God, *am* a
jealous God, [2]visiting the
iniquity of the fathers upon
the children to the third and
fourth *generations* of those
who hate Me,
10 [a]but showing mercy to
thousands, to those who love
Me and [1]keep My command-
ments.
11 [a]'You shall not take the name of
the LORD your God in vain,
for the LORD will not hold
him [1]guiltless who takes His
name in vain.
12 [a]'Observe the Sabbath day, to
[1]keep it holy, as the LORD
your God commanded you.
13 [a]Six days you shall labor and
do all your work,
14 but the seventh day *is* the
[a]Sabbath of the LORD your
God. *In it* you shall do no
work: you, nor your son, nor
your daughter, nor your male
servant, nor your female
servant, nor your ox, nor
your donkey, nor any of your
cattle, nor your stranger who
is within your gates, that
your male servant and your
female servant may rest as
well as you.
15 [a]And remember that you
were a slave in the land of
Egypt, and the LORD your
God brought you out from
there [b]by a mighty hand and
by an outstretched arm;
therefore the LORD your God
commanded you to keep the
Sabbath day.
16 [a]'Honor your father and your
mother, as the LORD your
God has commanded you,
[b]that your days may be long,
and that it may be well with
[c]you in the land which the
LORD your God is giving
you.
17 [a]'You shall not murder.
18 [a]'You shall not commit adultery.
19 [a]'You shall not steal.

43 [a]Josh. 20:8
46 [a]Deut. 3:29 [b]Num. 21:24; Deut. 1:4 [1]*struck*
47 [a]Num. 21:33–35 [1]*east*
48 [a]Deut. 2:36; 3:12 [b]Deut. 3:9; Ps. 133:3 [1]Syr. *Sirion*
49 [a]Deut. 3:17

CHAPTER 5

2 [a]Ex. 19:5; Deut. 4:23; Mal. 4:4
3 [a]Jer. 31:32; Matt. 13:17; Heb. 8:9
4 [a]Ex. 19:9
5 [a]Ex. 20:21; Gal. 3:19 [b]Ex. 19:16
6 [a]Ex. 20:2–17; Lev. 26:1; Deut. 6:4; Ps. 81:10 [1]*slavery*
7 [a]Ex. 20:2, 3; 23:13; Hos. 13:4 [1]*besides*
8 [a]Ex. 20:4
9 [a]Ex. 34:7, 14–16; Num. 14:18; Deut. 7:10 [1]*worship them* [2]*punishing*
10 [a]Num. 14:18; Deut. 7:9; Jer. 32:18; Dan. 9:4 [1]*observe*
11 [a]Ex. 20:7; Lev. 19:12; Deut. 6:13; 10:20; Matt. 5:33 [1]*innocent*
12 [a]Ex. 20:8; Ezek. 20:12; Mark 2:27 [1]*sanctify it*
13 [a]Ex. 23:12; 35:2
14 [a][Gen. 2:2]; Ex. 16:29; [Heb. 4:4]
15 [a]Deut. 15:15 [b]Deut. 4:34, 37
16 [a]Ex. 20:12; Lev. 19:3; Matt. 15:4; Eph. 6:2, 3; Col. 3:20 [b]Deut. 6:2 [c]Deut. 4:40
17 [a]Ex. 20:13; Matt. 5:21
18 [a]Ex. 20:14; Mark 10:19; Luke 18:20; [Rom. 13:9]; James 2:11
19 [a]Ex. 20:15; Lev. 19:11; [Rom. 13:9]

20 [a]'You shall not bear false witness
against your neighbor.
21 [a]'You shall not covet your
neighbor's wife; and you
shall not desire your
neighbor's house, his field,
his male servant, his female
servant, his ox, his donkey,
or anything that *is* your
neighbor's.'
22 "These words the LORD spoke
to all your assembly, in the moun-
tain from the midst of the fire, the
cloud, and the thick darkness, with
a loud voice; and He added no
more. And [a]He wrote them on two
tablets of stone and gave them to
me.

The People Afraid of God's Presence

23 [a]"So it was, when you heard
the voice from the midst of the
darkness, while the mountain was
burning with fire, that you came
near to me, all the heads of your
tribes and your elders.
24 "And you said: 'Surely the
LORD our God has shown us His
glory and His greatness, and [a]we
have heard His voice from the
midst of the fire. We have seen this
day that God speaks with man; yet
he [b]*still* lives.
25 'Now therefore, why should we
die? For this great fire will con-
sume us; [a]if we hear the voice of
the LORD our God anymore, then
we shall die.
26 [a]'For who *is there* of all flesh
who has heard the voice of the
living God speaking from the
midst of the fire, as we *have*, and
lived?
27 'You go near and hear all that
the LORD our God may say, and
[a]tell us all that the LORD our God
says to you, and we will hear and
do *it*.'
28 "Then the LORD heard the voice
of your words when you spoke to
me, and the LORD said to me: 'I
have heard the voice of the words
of this people which they have
spoken to you. [a]They are right *in*
all that they have spoken.
29 [a]'Oh, that they had such a heart
in them that they would fear Me
and [b]always keep all My com-
mandments, [c]that it might be well
with them and with their children
forever!

20 [a]Ex. 20:16; 23:1; Matt. 19:18
21 [a]Ex. 20:17; [Rom. 7:7; 13:9]
22 [a]Ex. 24:12; 31:18; Deut. 4:13
23 [a]Ex. 20:18, 19
24 [a]Ex. 19:19 [b]Deut. 4:33; Judg. 13:22
25 [a]Ex. 20:18, 19; Deut. 18:16
26 [a]Deut. 4:33
27 [a]Ex. 20:19; Heb. 12:19
28 [a]Deut. 18:17
29 [a]Deut. 32:29; Ps. 81:13; Is. 48:18 [b]Deut. 11:1 [c]Deut. 4:40
31 [a][Gal. 3:19]
32 [a]Deut. 17:20; 28:14; Josh. 1:7; 23:6; Prov. 4:27 [1]*observe*
33 [a]Deut. 10:12; Ps. 119:3; Jer. 7:23; Luke 1:6 [b]Deut. 4:40; Eph. 6:3

CHAPTER 6

1 [a]Deut. 12:1
2 [a]Ex. 20:20; Deut. 10:12, 13; [Ps. 111:10; 128:1; Eccl. 12:13] [b]Deut. 4:40
3 [a]Deut. 7:13 [b]Gen. 22:17 [c]Ex. 3:8, 17 [1]Lit. *observe to do*
4 [a]Deut. 4:35; Mark 12:29; John 17:3; [1 Cor. 8:4, 6] [1]Or *The LORD is our God, the LORD alone,* i.e., the only one
5 [a]Matt. 22:37; Mark 12:30; Luke 10:27 [b]2 Kin. 23:25
6 [a]Deut. 11:18–20; Ps. 119:11, 98
7 [a]Deut. 4:9; 11:19; [Eph. 6:4]
8 [a]Ex. 12:14; 13:9, 16; Deut. 11:18; Prov. 3:3; 6:21; 7:3

30 'Go and say to them, "Return
to your tents."
31 'But as for you, stand here by
Me, [a]and I will speak to you all the
commandments, the statutes, and
the judgments which you shall
teach them, that they may observe
them in the land which I am giving
them to possess.'
32 "Therefore you shall [1]be care-
ful to do as the LORD your God has
commanded you; [a]you shall not
turn aside to the right hand or to
the left.
33 "You shall walk in [a]all the
ways which the LORD your God
has commanded you, that you may
live [b]and *that it may be* well with
you, and *that* you may prolong
your days in the land which you
shall possess.

The Greatest Commandment

6 "Now this *is* [a]the command-
ment, *and these are* the stat-
utes and judgments which the
LORD your God has commanded to
teach you, that you may observe
them in the land which you are
crossing over to possess,
2 [a]"that you may fear the LORD
your God, to keep all His statutes
and His commandments which I
command you, you and your son
and your grandson, all the days of
your life, [b]and that your days may
be prolonged.
3 "Therefore hear, O Israel, and
[1]be careful to observe *it*, that it
may be well with you, and that you
may [a]multiply greatly [b]as the LORD
God of your fathers has promised
you—[c]'a land flowing with milk
and honey.'
4 [a]"Hear, O Israel: [1]The LORD our
God, the LORD *is* one!
5 [a]"You shall love the LORD your
God with all your heart, [b]with all
your soul, and with all your
strength.
6 "And [a]these words which I
command you today shall be in
your heart.
7 [a]"You shall teach them dili-
gently to your children, and shall
talk of them when you sit in your
house, when you walk by the way,
when you lie down, and when you
rise up.
8 [a]"You shall bind them as a sign

on your hand, and they shall be
as frontlets between your eyes.
9 [a]"You shall write them on the
doorposts of your house and on
your gates.

Caution Against Disobedience

10 "So it shall be, when the LORD
your God brings you into the land
of which He [1]swore to your fa-
thers, to Abraham, Isaac, and Ja-
cob, to give you large and beau-
tiful cities [a]which you did not
build,
11 "houses full of all good things,
which you did not fill, hewn-out
wells which you did not dig, vine-
yards and olive trees which you
did not plant—[a]when you have
eaten and are full—
12 "*then* beware, lest you forget
the [a]LORD who brought you out of
the land of Egypt, from the house
of bondage.
13 "You shall [a]fear the LORD your
God and serve Him, and [b]shall
take oaths in His name.
14 "You shall not go after other
gods, [a]the gods of the peoples who
are all around you
15 "(for [a]the LORD your God *is* a
jealous God [b]among you), lest the
anger of the LORD your God be
aroused against you and destroy
you from the face of the earth.
16 [a]"You shall not [1]tempt the
LORD your God [b]as you [2]tempted
Him in Massah.
17 "You shall [a]diligently keep the
commandments of the LORD your
God, His testimonies, and His stat-
utes which He has commanded
you.
18 "And you [a]shall do *what is*
right and good in the sight of the
LORD, that it may be well with you,
and that you may go in and pos-
sess the good land of which the
LORD swore to your fathers,
19 [a]"to cast out all your enemies
from before you, as the LORD has
spoken.
20 [a]"When your son asks you in
time to come, saying, 'What *is the*
meaning of the testimonies, the
statutes, and the judgments which
the LORD our God has commanded
you?'
21 "then you shall say to your son:
'We were slaves of Pharaoh in
Egypt, and the LORD brought us
out of Egypt [a]with a mighty hand;
22 'and the LORD showed signs
and wonders before our eyes,
great and severe, against Egypt,
Pharaoh, and all his household.
23 'Then He brought us out from
there, that He might bring us in,
to give us the land of which He
[1]swore to our fathers.
24 'And the LORD commanded us
to [1]observe all these [2]statutes, [a]to
fear the LORD our God, [b]for our
good always, that [c]He might pre-
serve us alive, as *it is* [3]this day.
25 'Then [a]it will be righteousness
for us, if we are careful to observe
all these commandments before
the LORD our God, as He has com-
manded us.'

A Chosen People

7 "When the LORD your God
brings you into the land which
you go to [a]possess, and has cast
out many [b]nations before you, [c]the
Hittites and the Girgashites and
the Amorites and the Canaanites
and the Perizzites and the Hivites
and the Jebusites, seven nations
greater and mightier than you,
2 "and when the LORD your God
delivers [a]them over to you, you
shall conquer them *and* utterly de-
stroy them. [b]You shall make no
covenant with them nor show
mercy to them.
3 [a]"Nor shall you make mar-
riages with them. You shall not
give your daughter to their son,
nor take their daughter for your
son.
4 "For they will turn your sons
away from following Me, to serve
other gods; [a]so the anger of the
LORD will be aroused against you
and destroy you suddenly.
5 "But thus you shall deal with
them: you shall [a]destroy their al-
tars, and break down their *sacred*
pillars, and cut down their
[1]wooden images, and burn their
carved images with fire.
6 "For you *are* a [1]holy people to
the LORD your God; [a]the LORD your
God has chosen you to be a people
for Himself, a special treasure
above all the peoples on the face
of the earth.
7 "The LORD did not set His [a]love
on you nor choose you because
you were more in number than

9 [a]Deut. 11:20; Is. 57:8
10 [a]Deut. 9:1; 19:1; Josh. 24:13; Ps. 105:44 [1]*promised*
11 [a]Deut. 8:10; 11:15; 14:29
12 [a]Deut. 8:11–18
13 [a]Deut. 13:4; Matt. 4:10; Luke 4:8 [b]Deut. 5:11; [Is. 45:23; Jer. 4:2]
14 [a]Deut. 13:7
15 [a]Ex. 20:5; Deut. 4:24 [b]Ex. 33:3
16 [a]Matt. 4:7; Luke 4:12 [b][1 Cor. 10:9] [1]*test* [2]*tested*
17 [a]Deut. 11:22; Ps. 119:4
18 [a]Ex. 15:26; Deut. 8:7–10
19 [a]Num. 33:52, 53
20 [a]Ex. 13:8, 14
21 [a]Ex. 13:3
23 [1]*promised*
24 [a]Deut. 6:2 [b]Deut. 10:12, 13; Job 35:7, 8; Jer. 32:39 [c]Deut. 4:1 [1]*do* [2]*ordinances* [3]*today*
25 [a]Deut. 24:13; [Rom. 10:3, 5]

CHAPTER 7

1 [a]Deut. 6:10 [b]Gen. 15:19–21 [c]Ex. 33:2
2 [a]Num. 31:17; Deut. 20:16–18 [b]Ex. 23:32, 33; Josh. 2:14
3 [a]Ex. 34:15, 16; Josh. 23:12; 1 Kin. 11:2; Ezra 9:2
4 [a]Deut. 6:15
5 [a]Ex. 23:24; 34:13; Deut. 12:3 [1]Heb. *Asherim*, Canaanite deities
6 [a]Ex. 19:5, 6; Amos 3:2; 1 Pet. 2:9 [1]*set-apart*
7 [a]Deut. 4:37

any other people, for you were
[b]the least of all peoples;
8 "but [a]because the LORD loves
you, and because He would keep
[b]the oath which He swore to your
fathers, [c]the LORD has brought you
out with a mighty hand, and re-
deemed you from the house of
[1]bondage, from the hand of Pha-
raoh king of Egypt.
9 "Therefore know that the LORD
your God, He *is* God, [a]the faithful
God [b]who keeps covenant and
mercy for a thousand generations
with those who love Him and keep
His commandments;
10 "and He repays those who hate
Him to their face, to destroy them.
He will not [1]be [a]slack with him
who hates Him; He will repay him
to his face.
11 "Therefore you shall keep the
commandment, the statutes, and
the judgments which I command
you today, to observe them.

Blessings of Obedience

12 "Then it shall come to pass, be-
cause you listen to these judg-
ments, and keep and do them, that
the LORD your God will keep with
you the covenant and the mercy
which He swore to your fa-
thers.
13 "And He will [a]love you and
bless you and [1]multiply you; [b]He
will also bless the fruit of your
womb and the fruit of your land,
your grain and your new wine and
your oil, the increase of your cattle
and the offspring of your flock, in
the land of which He [2]swore to
your fathers to give you.
14 "You shall be blessed above all
peoples; there shall not be a male
or female [a]barren among you or
among your livestock.
15 "And the LORD will take away
from you all sickness, and will af-
flict you with none of the [a]terrible
diseases of Egypt which you have
known, but will lay *them* on all
those who hate you.
16 "Also you shall [1]destroy all the
peoples whom the LORD your God
delivers over to you; your eye shall
have no pity on them; nor shall
you serve their gods, for that *will*
[a]*be* a snare to you.
17 "If you should say in your
heart, 'These nations are greater
than I; how can I dispossess
them?'—
18 "you shall not be afraid of
them, *but* you shall [a]remember
well what the LORD your God did
to Pharaoh and to all Egypt:
19 [a]"the great trials which your
eyes saw, the signs and the won-
ders, the mighty hand and the out-
stretched arm, by which the LORD
your God brought you out. So shall
the LORD your God do to all the
peoples of whom you are afraid.
20 [a]"Moreover the LORD your God
will send the hornet among them
until those who are left, who hide
themselves from you, are de-
stroyed.
21 "You shall not be terrified of
them; for the LORD your God, the
great and awesome God, *is* among
you.
22 "And the LORD your God will
drive out those nations before you
[a]little by little; you will be unable
to [1]destroy them at once, lest the
beasts of the field become *too* nu-
merous for you.
23 "But the LORD your God will
deliver them over to you, and will
inflict defeat upon them until they
are destroyed.
24 "And [a]He will deliver their
kings into your hand, and you will
destroy their name from under
heaven; [b]no one shall be able to
stand [1]against you until you have
destroyed them.
25 "You shall burn the carved im-
ages of their gods with fire; you
shall not [a]covet[1] the silver or gold
that is on them, nor take *it* for
yourselves, lest you be snared by
it; for it *is* an abomination to the
LORD your God.
26 "Nor shall you bring an
abomination into your house, lest
you be doomed to destruction like
it. You shall utterly detest it and
utterly abhor it, [a]for it *is* an [1]ac-
cursed thing.

Remember the LORD Your God

8 "Every commandment which I
command you today [a]you must
[1]be careful to observe, that you
may live and [b]multiply,[2] and go in
and possess the land of which the
LORD [3]swore to your fathers.
2 "And you shall remember that
the LORD your God [a]led you all the

7 [b]Deut. 10:22
8 [a]Deut. 10:15 [b]Luke 1:55, 72, 73 [c]Ex. 13:3, 14 [1]*slavery*
9 [a]1 Cor. 1:9; 2 Thess. 3:3; 2 Tim. 2:13 [b]Ex. 20:6; Deut. 5:10; Neh. 1:5; Dan. 9:4
10 [a][2 Pet. 3:9, 10] [1]*delay*
13 [a]Ps. 146:8; Prov. 15:9; John 14:21 [b]Deut. 28:4 [1]*cause you to increase* [2]*promised*
14 [a]Ex. 23:26
15 [a]Ex. 9:14; 15:26; Deut. 28:27, 60
16 [a]Ex. 23:33; Judg. 8:27; Ps. 106:36 [1]*consume*
18 [a]Ps. 105:5
19 [a]Deut. 4:34; 29:3
20 [a]Ex. 23:28; Josh. 24:12
22 [a]Ex. 23:29, 30 [1]*consume*
24 [a]Josh. 10:24, 42; 12:1–24 [b]Josh. 23:9 [1]*before*
25 [a]Prov. 23:6 [1]*desire*
26 [a]Deut. 13:17 [1]*devoted* or *banned*

CHAPTER 8
1 [a]Deut. 4:1; 6:24 [b]Deut. 30:16 [1]*observe to do* [2]*increase in number* [3]*promised*
2 [a]Deut. 1:3; 2:7; 29:5; Ps. 136:16; Amos 2:10

way these forty years in the wil-
derness, to humble you *and* [b]test
you, [c]to know what *was* in your
heart, whether you would keep His
commandments or not.
3 "So He humbled you, [a]allowed
you to hunger, and [b]fed you with
manna which you did not know
nor did your fathers know, that He
might make you know that man
shall [c]not live by bread alone; but
man lives by every *word* that pro-
ceeds from the mouth of the LORD.
4 [a]"Your garments did not wear
out on you, nor did your foot swell
these forty years.
5 [a]"You should [1]know in your
heart that as a man chastens his
son, *so* the LORD your God chas-
tens you.
6 "Therefore you shall keep the
commandments of the LORD your
God, [a]to walk in His ways and to
fear Him.
7 "For the LORD your God is
bringing you into a good land, [a]a
land of brooks of water, of foun-
tains and springs, that flow out of
valleys and hills;
8 "a land of wheat and barley, of
vines and fig trees and pomegran-
ates, a land of olive oil and honey;
9 "a land in which you will eat
bread without scarcity, in which
you will lack nothing; a land
whose stones *are* iron and out of
whose hills you can dig copper.
10 [a]"When you have eaten and
are full, then you shall bless the
LORD your God for the good land
which He has given you.
11 "Beware that you do not forget
the LORD your God by not keeping
His commandments, His judg-
ments, and His statutes which I
command you today,
12 [a]"lest—*when* you have eaten
and are [1]full, and have built beau-
tiful houses and dwell *in them;*
13 "and *when* your herds and
your flocks multiply, and your sil-
ver and your gold are [1]multiplied,
and all that you have is multiplied;
14 [a]"when your heart [1]is lifted up,
and you [b]forget the LORD your God
who brought you out of the land
of Egypt, from the house of bond-
age;
15 "who [a]led you through that
great and terrible wilderness, [b]*in
which were* fiery serpents and
scorpions and thirsty land where
there was no water; [c]who brought
water for you out of the flinty rock;
16 "who fed you in the wilderness
with [a]manna, which your fathers
did not know, that He might hum-
ble you and that He might test you,
[b]to do you good in the end—
17 "then you say in your heart,
'My power and the might of my
hand have gained me this wealth.'
18 "And you shall remember the
LORD your God, [a]for *it is* He who
gives you power to get wealth,
[b]that He may [1]establish His cov-
enant which He swore to your
fathers, as *it is* this day.
19 "Then it shall be, if you by any
means forget the LORD your God,
and follow other gods, and serve
them and worship them, [a]I testify
against you this day that you shall
surely perish.
20 "As the nations which the LORD
destroys before you, [a]so you shall
perish, because you would not be
obedient to the voice of the LORD
your God.

Israel's Rebellions Reviewed

9 "Hear, O Israel: You *are* to
cross over the Jordan today,
and go in to dispossess nations
greater and mightier than your-
self, cities great and fortified up to
heaven,
2 "a people great and tall, the
[a]descendants of the Anakim,
whom you know, and *of whom* you
heard *it said,* 'Who can stand be-
fore the descendants of Anak?'
3 "Therefore understand today
that the LORD your God *is* He who
[a]goes over before you *as* a [b]con-
suming fire. [c]He will destroy them
and bring them down before you;
[d]so you shall drive them out and
destroy them quickly, as the LORD
has said to you.
4 [a]"Do not think in your heart,
after the LORD your God has cast
them out before you, saying, 'Be-
cause of my righteousness the
LORD has brought me in to possess
this land'; but *it is* [b]because of the
wickedness of these nations that
the LORD is driving them out from
before you.
5 [a]"*It is* not because of your righ-
teousness or the uprightness of
your heart *that* you go in to pos-

2 [b]Ex. 16:4 [c][John 2:25]
3 [a]Ex. 16:2, 3 [b]Ex. 16:12, 14, 35 [c]Matt. 4:4; Luke 4:4
4 [a]Deut. 29:5; Neh. 9:21
5 [a]2 Sam. 7:14; Ps. 89:30–33; Prov. 3:11, 12; Heb. 12:5–11; Rev. 3:19 [1]*consider*
6 [a][Deut. 5:33]
7 [a]Deut. 11:9–12; Jer. 2:7
10 [a]Deut. 6:11, 12
12 [a]Deut. 28:47; Prov. 30:9; Hos. 13:6 [1]*satisfied*
13 [1]*increased*
14 [a]1 Cor. 4:7 [b]Deut. 8:11; Ps. 106:21 [1]*becomes proud*
15 [a]Is. 63:12–14 [b]Num. 21:6 [c]Ex. 17:6; Num. 20:11
16 [a]Ex. 16:15 [b]Jer. 24:5, 6; [Heb. 12:11]
18 [a]Prov. 10:22; Hos. 2:8 [b]Deut. 7:8, 12 [1]*confirm*
19 [a]Deut. 4:26; 30:18
20 [a][Dan. 9:11, 12]

CHAPTER 9

2 [a]Num. 13:22, 28, 33; Josh. 11:21, 22
3 [a]Deut. 1:33; 31:3; Josh. 3:11; 5:14; John 10:4 [b]Deut. 4:24; Heb. 12:29 [c]Deut. 7:24 [d]Ex. 23:31
4 [a]Deut. 8:17; [Rom. 11:6, 20; 1 Cor. 4:4, 7] [b]Gen. 15:16; Lev. 18:3, 24–30; Deut. 12:31; 18:9–14
5 [a][Titus 3:5]

sess their land, but because of the wickedness of these nations *that* the LORD your God drives them out from before you, and that He may [1]fulfill the [b]word which the LORD swore to your fathers, to Abraham, Isaac, and Jacob.

6 "Therefore understand that the LORD your God is not giving you this good land to possess because of your righteousness, for you *are* a [a]stiff-necked[1] people.

7 "Remember! Do not forget how you [a]provoked the LORD your God to wrath in the wilderness. [b]From the day that you departed from the land of Egypt until you came to this place, you have been rebellious against the LORD.

8 "Also [a]in Horeb you provoked the LORD to wrath, so that the LORD was angry *enough* with you to have destroyed you.

9 [a]"When I went up into the mountain to receive the tablets of stone, the tablets of the covenant which the LORD made with you, then I stayed on the mountain forty days and [b]forty nights. I neither ate bread nor drank water.

10 [a]"Then the LORD delivered to me two tablets of stone written with the finger of God, and on them *were* all the words which the LORD had spoken to you on the mountain from the midst of the fire [b]in[1] the day of the assembly.

11 "And it came to pass, at the end of forty days and forty nights, *that* the LORD gave me the two tablets of stone, the tablets of the covenant.

12 "Then the LORD said to me, [a]'Arise, go down quickly from here, for your people whom you brought out of Egypt have acted corruptly; they have [b]quickly turned aside from the way which I commanded them; they have made themselves a molded image.'

13 "Furthermore [a]the LORD spoke to me, saying, 'I have seen this people, and indeed [b]they are a [1]stiff-necked people.

14 [a]'Let Me alone, that I may destroy them and [b]blot out their name from under heaven; [c]and I will make of you a nation mightier and greater than they.'

15 [a]"So I turned and came down from the mountain, and [b]the mountain burned with fire; and the two tablets of the covenant *were* in my two hands.

16 "And [a]I looked, and behold, you had sinned against the LORD your God—had made for yourselves a molded calf! You had turned aside quickly from the way which the LORD had commanded you.

17 "Then I took the two tablets and threw them out of my two hands and [a]broke them before your eyes.

18 "And I [a]fell[1] down before the LORD, as at the first, forty days and forty nights; I neither ate bread nor drank water, because of all your sin which you committed in doing wickedly in the sight of the LORD, to provoke Him to anger.

19 [a]"For I was afraid of the anger and hot displeasure with which the LORD was angry with you, to destroy you. [b]But the LORD listened to me at that time also.

20 "And the LORD was very angry with Aaron *and* would have destroyed him; so I prayed for Aaron also at the same time.

21 "Then I took your sin, the calf which you had made, and burned it with fire and crushed it *and* ground *it* very small, until it was as fine as dust; and I [a]threw its dust into the brook that descended from the mountain.

22 "Also at [a]Taberah and [b]Massah and [c]Kibroth Hattaavah you [1]provoked the LORD to wrath.

23 "Likewise, [a]when the LORD sent you from Kadesh Barnea, saying, 'Go up and possess the land which I have given you,' then you rebelled against the commandment of the LORD your God, and [b]you did not believe Him nor obey His voice.

24 [a]"You have been rebellious against the LORD from the day that I knew you.

25 [a]"Thus I [1]prostrated myself before the LORD; forty days and forty nights I kept prostrating myself, because the LORD had said He would destroy you.

26 "Therefore I prayed to the LORD, and said: 'O Lord GOD, do not destroy Your people and [a]Your inheritance whom You have redeemed through Your greatness,

5 [b]Gen. 50:24 [1]*perform*
6 [a]Ex. 34:9; Deut. 31:27 [1]*stubborn* or *rebellious*
7 [a]Num. 14:22 [b]Ex. 14:11
8 [a]Ex. 32:1–8; Ps. 106:19
9 [a]Ex. 24:12, 15; Deut. 5:2–22 [b]Ex. 24:18
10 [a]Ex. 31:18; Deut. 4:13 [b]Ex. 19:17 [1]*when you were all gathered together*
12 [a]Ex. 32:7, 8 [b]Deut. 31:29
13 [a]Ex. 32:9 [b]Deut. 9:6 [1]*stubborn* or *rebellious*
14 [a]Ex. 32:10 [b]Deut. 29:20 [c]Num. 14:12
15 [a]Ex. 32:15–19 [b]Ex. 19:18
16 [a]Ex. 32:19
17 [a]Ex. 32:19
18 [a]Ex. 34:28; Ps. 106:23 [1]*prostrated myself*
19 [a]Ex. 32:10, 11; Heb. 12:21 [b]Ex. 32:14
21 [a]Ex. 32:20
22 [a]Num. 11:1, 3 [b]Ex. 17:7 [c]Num. 11:4, 34 [1]*caused the LORD to be angry*
23 [a]Num. 13:3 [b]Ps. 106:24, 25
24 [a]Deut. 9:7; 31:27
25 [a]Deut. 9:18 [1]*fell down*
26 [a]Deut. 32:9

whom You have brought out of
Egypt with a mighty hand.
27 'Remember Your servants,
Abraham, Isaac, and Jacob; do not
look on the stubbornness of this
people, or on their wickedness or
their sin,
28 'lest the land from which You
brought us should say, "Because
the LORD was not able to bring
them to the land which He prom-
ised them, and because He hated
them, He has brought them out to
kill them in the wilderness."
29 'Yet they *are* Your people and
Your inheritance, whom You
brought out by Your mighty power
and by Your outstretched arm.'

The Second Pair of Tablets

10 "At that time the LORD said
to me, [1]'Hew for yourself
two tablets of stone like the first,
and come up to Me on the moun-
tain and make yourself an [a]ark of
wood.
2 'And I will write on the tablets
the words that were on the first
tablets, which you broke; and [a]you
shall put them in the ark.'
3 "So I made an ark of acacia
wood, hewed two tablets of stone
like the first, and went up the
mountain, having the two tablets
in my hand.
4 "And He wrote on the tablets
according to the first writing, the
Ten [1]Commandments, [a]which the
LORD had spoken to you in the
mountain from the midst of the fire
in the day of the assembly; and the
LORD gave them to me.
5 "Then I turned and [a]came
down from the mountain, and [b]put
the tablets in the ark which I had
made; [c]and there they are, just as
the LORD commanded me."
6 (Now the children of Israel
journeyed from the wells of Bene
Jaakan to Moserah, where Aaron
[a]died, and where he was buried;
and Eleazar his son ministered as
priest in his [1]stead.
7 [a]From there they journeyed to
Gudgodah, and from Gudgodah to
Jotbathah, a land of [1]rivers of wa-
ter.
8 At that time [a]the LORD [1]sepa-
rated the tribe of Levi [b]to bear the
ark of the covenant of the LORD,
[c]to stand before the LORD to minis-
ter to Him and [d]to bless in His
name, to this day.
9 [a]Therefore Levi has no portion
nor inheritance with his brethren;
the LORD *is* his inheritance, just as
the LORD your God promised him.)
10 "As at the first time, [a]I stayed
in the mountain forty days and
forty nights; [b]the LORD also heard
me at that time, *and* the LORD
chose not to destroy you.
11 [a]"Then the LORD said to me,
'Arise, begin *your* journey before
the people, that they may go in and
possess the land which I swore to
their fathers to give them.'

The Essence of the Law

12 "And now, Israel, [a]what does
the LORD your God require of you,
but to fear the LORD your God, to
walk in all His ways and to [b]love
Him, to serve the LORD your God
with all your heart and with all
your soul,
13 "*and* to keep the command-
ments of the LORD and His statutes
which I command you today [a]for
your [1]good?
14 "Indeed heaven and the high-
est heavens belong to the [a]LORD
your God, *also* the earth with all
that *is* in it.
15 "The LORD delighted only in
your fathers, to love them; and He
chose their [1]descendants after
them, you above all peoples, as *it*
is this day.
16 "Therefore circumcise the fore-
skin of your [a]heart, and be [b]stiff-
necked[1] no longer.
17 "For the LORD your God *is* [a]God
of gods and [b]Lord of lords, the
great God, [c]mighty and awesome,
who [d]shows no partiality nor takes
a bribe.
18 [a]"He administers justice for the
fatherless and the widow, and
loves the stranger, giving him food
and clothing.
19 "Therefore love the stranger,
for you were strangers in the land
of Egypt.
20 [a]"You shall fear the LORD your
God; you shall serve Him, and to
Him you shall hold fast, and take
oaths in His name.
21 "He *is* your praise, and He *is*
your God, who has done for you
these great and awesome things
which your eyes have seen.

CHAPTER 10

1 [a]Ex. 25:10 [1]*Cut out*

2 [a]Ex. 25:16, 21

4 [a]Ex. 20:1; 34:28 [1]Lit. *Words*

5 [a]Ex. 34:29 [b]Ex. 40:20 [c]1 Kin. 8:9

6 [a]Num. 20:25–28; 33:38 [1]*place*

7 [a]Num. 33:32–34 [1]*brooks*

8 [a]Num. 3:6 [b]Num. 4:5, 15; 10:21 [c]Deut. 18:5 [d]Num. 6:23 [1]*set apart*

9 [a]Num. 18:20, 24; Deut. 18:1, 2; Ezek. 44:28

10 [a]Ex. 34:28; Deut. 9:18 [b]Ex. 32:14

11 [a]Ex. 33:1

12 [a]Mic. 6:8 [b]Deut. 6:5; Matt. 22:37; 1 Tim. 1:5

13 [a]Deut. 6:24 [1]*benefit* or *welfare*

14 [a][Neh. 9:6; Ps. 68:33; 115:16]

15 [1]Lit. *seed*

16 [a]Lev. 26:41; Deut. 30:6; Jer. 4:4; Rom. 2:28, 29 [b]Deut. 9:6, 13 [1]*rebellious*

17 [a]Deut. 4:35, 39; Is. 44:8; 46:9; Dan. 2:47; 1 Cor. 8:5, 6 [b]Rev. 19:16 [c]Deut. 7:21 [d]Acts 10:34

18 [a]Ex. 22:22–24; Ps. 68:5; 146:9

20 [a]Matt. 4:10

22 "Your fathers went down to
Egypt with seventy persons, and
now the LORD your God has made
you as the stars of heaven in multi-
tude.

Love and Obedience Rewarded

11 "Therefore you shall love
the LORD your God, and
keep His charge, His statutes, His
judgments, and His command-
ments always.
2 "Know today that *I do* not
speak with your children, who
have not known and who have not
seen the [1]chastening of the LORD
your God, His greatness and His
mighty hand and His outstretched
arm—
3 "His signs and His acts which
He did in the midst of Egypt, to
Pharaoh king of Egypt, and to all
his land;
4 "what He did to the army of
Egypt, to their horses and their
chariots: [a]how He made the waters
of the Red Sea overflow them as
they pursued you, and *how* the
LORD has destroyed them to this
day;
5 "what He did for you in the wil-
derness until you came to this
place;
6 "and [a]what He did to Dathan
and Abiram the sons of Eliab, the
son of Reuben: how the earth
opened its mouth and swallowed
them up, their households, their
tents, and all the substance that
was [1]in their possession, in the
midst of all Israel—
7 "but your eyes have [a]seen
every great [1]act of the LORD which
He did.
8 "Therefore you shall keep
every commandment which I com-
mand you today, that you may [a]be
strong, and go in and possess the
land which you cross over to pos-
sess,
9 "and [a]that you may prolong
your days in the land [b]which the
LORD [1]swore to give your fathers,
to them and their descendants, [c]'a
land flowing with milk and honey.'
10 "For the land which you go to
possess *is* not like the land of
Egypt from which you have come,
where you sowed your seed and
watered *it* by foot, as a vegetable
garden;
11 [a]"but the land which you cross
over to possess *is* a land of hills
and valleys, which drinks water
from the rain of heaven,
12 "a land for which the LORD
your God cares; [a]the eyes of the
LORD your God *are* always on it,
from the beginning of the year to
the very end of the year.
13 'And it shall be that if you ear-
nestly [1]obey My commandments
which I command you today, to
love the LORD your God and serve
Him with all your heart and with
all your soul,
14 'then [a]I[1] will give *you* the rain
for your land in its season, [b]the
early rain and the latter rain, that
you may gather in your grain, your
new wine, and your oil.
15 [a]'And I will send grass in your
fields for your livestock, that you
may [b]eat and be [1]filled.'
16 "Take heed to yourselves, [a]lest
your heart be deceived, and you
turn aside and [b]serve other gods
and worship them,
17 "lest [a]the LORD's anger be
aroused against you, and He [b]shut
up the heavens so that there be no
rain, and the land yield no pro-
duce, and [c]you perish quickly from
the good land which the LORD is
giving you.
18 "Therefore [a]you shall [1]lay up
these words of mine in your heart
and in your [b]soul, and [c]bind them
as a sign on your hand, and they
shall be as frontlets between your
eyes.
19 [a]"You shall teach them to your
children, speaking of them when
you sit in your house, when you
walk by the way, when you lie
down, and when you rise up.
20 [a]"And you shall write them on
the doorposts of your house and
on your gates,
21 "that [a]your days and the days
of your children may be multiplied
in the land of which the LORD
swore to your fathers to give them,
like [b]the days of the heavens
above the earth.
22 "For if [a]you carefully keep all
these commandments which I
command you to do—to love the
LORD your God, to walk in all His
ways, and [b]to hold fast to Him—
23 "then the LORD will [a]drive out
all these nations from before you,

CHAPTER 11

2 [1]*discipline*

4 [a]Ex. 14:28; Ps. 106:11

6 [a]Num. 16:1–35; Ps. 106:16–18 [1]*at their feet*

7 [a]Deut. 10:21; 29:2 [1]*work*

8 [a]Deut. 31:6, 7, 23; Josh. 1:6, 7

9 [a]Deut. 4:40; 5:16, 33; 6:2; Prov. 10:27 [b]Deut. 9:5 [c]Ex. 3:8 [1]*promised*

11 [a]Deut. 8:7

12 [a]1 Kin. 9:3

13 [1]Lit. *listen to*

14 [a]Lev. 26:4; Deut. 28:12 [b]Joel 2:23; James 5:7 [1]So with MT, Tg.; Sam., LXX, Vg. *He*

15 [a]Ps. 104:14 [b]Deut. 6:11; Joel 2:19 [1]*satisfied*

16 [a]Deut. 29:18; Job 31:27 [b]Deut. 8:19

17 [a]Deut. 6:15; 9:19 [b]Deut. 28:24; 1 Kin. 8:35; 2 Chr. 6:26; 7:13 [c]Deut. 4:26; 2 Chr. 36:14–20

18 [a]Deut. 6:6–9 [b]Ps. 119:2, 34 [c]Deut. 6:8 [1]Lit. *put*

19 [a]Deut. 4:9, 10; 6:7; Prov. 22:6

20 [a]Deut. 6:9

21 [a]Deut. 4:40 [b]Ps. 72:5; 89:29; Prov. 3:2; 4:10; 9:11

22 [a]Deut. 11:1 [b]Deut. 10:20

23 [a]Deut. 4:38

and you will [b]dispossess greater and mightier nations than yourselves.

24 [a]"Every place on which the sole of your foot treads shall be yours: [b]from the wilderness and Lebanon, from the river, the River Euphrates, even to the [1]Western Sea, shall be your territory.

25 "No man shall be able to [a]stand [1]against you; the LORD your God will put the [b]dread of you and the fear of you upon all the land where you tread, just as He has said to you.

26 [a]"Behold, I set before you today a blessing and a curse:

27 [a]"the blessing, if you obey the commandments of the LORD your God which I command you today;

28 "and the [a]curse, if you do not obey the commandments of the LORD your God, but turn aside from the way which I command you today, to go after other gods which you have not known.

29 "Now it shall be, when the LORD your God has brought you into the land which you go to possess, that you shall put the [a]blessing on Mount Gerizim and the [b]curse on Mount Ebal.

30 "*Are* they not on the other side of the Jordan, toward the setting sun, in the land of the Canaanites who dwell in the plain opposite Gilgal, [a]beside the terebinth trees of Moreh?

31 "For you will cross over the Jordan and go in to possess the land which the LORD your God is giving you, and you will possess it and dwell in it.

32 "And you shall be careful to observe all the statutes and judgments which I set before you today.

A Prescribed Place of Worship

12 "These [a]*are* the statutes and judgments which you shall be careful to observe in the land which the LORD God of your fathers is giving you to possess, [b]all[1] the days that you live on the earth.

2 [a]"You shall utterly destroy all the places where the nations which you shall dispossess served their gods, [b]on the high mountains and on the hills and under every green tree.

3 "And [a]you shall destroy their altars, break their *sacred* pillars, and burn their [1]wooden images with fire; you shall cut down the carved images of their gods and destroy their names from that place.

4 "You shall not [a]worship the LORD your God *with* such *things.*

5 "But you shall seek the [a]place where the LORD your God chooses, out of all your tribes, to put His name for His [b]dwelling[1] place; and there you shall go.

6 [a]"There you shall take your burnt offerings, your sacrifices, your tithes, the heave offerings of your hand, your vowed offerings, your freewill offerings, and the [b]firstborn of your herds and flocks.

7 "And [a]there you shall eat before the LORD your God, and [b]you shall rejoice in [1]all to which you have put your hand, you and your households, in which the LORD your God has blessed you.

8 "You shall not at all do as we are doing here today—[a]every man doing whatever *is* right in his own eyes—

9 "for as yet you have not come to the [a]rest[1] and the inheritance which the LORD your God is giving you.

10 "But *when* you cross over the Jordan and dwell in the land which the LORD your God is giving you to inherit, and He gives you [a]rest from all your enemies round about, so that you dwell in safety,

11 "then there will be the place where the LORD your God chooses to make His name abide. There you shall bring all that I command you: your burnt offerings, your sacrifices, your tithes, the heave offerings of your hand, and all your choice offerings which you vow to the LORD.

12 "And [a]you shall rejoice before the LORD your God, you and your sons and your daughters, your male and female servants, and the [b]Levite who *is* within your gates, since he has no portion nor inheritance with you.

13 "Take heed to yourself that you do not offer your burnt offerings in every place that you see;

14 "but in the place which the LORD chooses, in one of your

23 [b]Deut. 9:1
24 [a]Josh. 1:3; 14:9 [b]Gen. 15:18; Ex. 23:31; Deut. 1:7, 8 [1]Mediterranean
25 [a]Deut. 7:24 [b]Ex. 23:27; Deut. 2:25; Josh. 2:9–11 [1]*before*
26 [a]Deut. 30:1, 15, 19
27 [a]Deut. 28:1–14
28 [a]Deut. 28:15–68
29 [a]Deut. 27:12, 13; Josh. 8:33 [b]Deut. 27:13–26
30 [a]Gen. 12:6

CHAPTER 12

1 [a]Deut. 6:1 [b]Deut. 4:9, 10; 1 Kin. 8:40 [1]As long as
2 [a]Ex. 34:13 [b]2 Kin. 16:4; 17:10, 11
3 [a]Num. 33:52; Deut. 7:5; Judg. 2:2 [1]Heb. *Asherim*
4 [a]Deut. 12:31
5 [a]Ex. 20:24 [b]Ex. 15:13; 1 Sam. 2:29 [1]*home*
6 [a]Lev. 17:3, 4 [b]Deut. 14:23
7 [a]Deut. 14:26 [b]Deut. 12:12, 18 [1]*all that you undertake*
8 [a]Judg. 17:6; 21:25
9 [a]Deut. 3:20; 25:19; Ps. 95:11 [1]Or *place of rest*
10 [a]Josh. 11:23
12 [a]Deut. 12:18; 26:11 [b]Deut. 10:9; 14:29

tribes, there you shall offer your
burnt offerings, and there you
shall do all that I command you.
15 "However, [a]you may slaughter
and eat meat within all your gates,
whatever your heart desires, ac-
cording to the blessing of the LORD
your God which He has given you;
[b]the unclean and the clean may eat
of it, [c]of the gazelle and the deer
alike.
16 [a]"Only you shall not eat the
blood; you shall pour it on the
earth like water.
17 "You may not eat within your
gates the tithe of your grain or
your new wine or your oil, of the
firstborn of your herd or your
flock, of any of your offerings
which you vow, of your freewill of-
ferings, or of the [1]heave offering
of your hand.
18 "But you must eat them before
the LORD your God in the place
which the LORD your God chooses,
you and your son and your daugh-
ter, your male servant and your fe-
male servant, and the Levite who
is within your gates; and you shall
rejoice before the LORD your God
in [1]all to which you put your
hands.
19 [1]"Take heed to yourself that
you do not forsake the Levite as
long as you live in your land.
20 "When the LORD your God [a]en-
larges your border as He has
promised you, and you say, 'Let
me eat meat,' because you long to
eat meat, you may eat as much
meat as your heart desires.
21 "If the place where the LORD
your God chooses to put His name
is too far from [a]you, then you may
slaughter from your herd and from
your flock which the LORD has
given you, just as I have com-
manded you, and you may eat
within your gates as much as your
heart desires.
22 "Just as the gazelle and the
deer are eaten, so you may eat
them; the unclean and the clean
alike may eat them.
23 "Only be sure that you do not
eat the blood, [a]for the blood *is* the
life; you may not eat the life with
the meat.
24 "You shall not eat it; you shall
pour it on the earth like water.
25 "You shall not eat it, [a]that it
may go well with you and your
children after you, [b]when you do
what is right in the sight of the
LORD.
26 "Only the [a]holy things which
you have, and your vowed offer-
ings, you shall take and go to the
place which the LORD chooses.
27 "And [a]you shall offer your
burnt offerings, the meat and the
blood, on the altar of the LORD
your God; and the blood of your
sacrifices shall be poured out on
the altar of the LORD your God, and
you shall eat the meat.
28 "Observe and obey all these
words which I command you, [a]that
it may go well with you and your
children after you forever, when
you do *what is* good and right in
the sight of the LORD your God.

Beware of False Gods

29 "When [a]the LORD your God
cuts off from before you the na-
tions which you go to dispossess,
and you displace them and dwell
in their land,
30 "take heed to yourself that you
are not ensnared to follow them,
after they are destroyed from be-
fore you, and that you do not in-
quire after their gods, saying,
'How did these nations serve their
gods? I also will do likewise.'
31 [a]"You shall not worship the
LORD your God in that way; for
every [1]abomination to the LORD
which He hates they have done to
their gods; for [b]they burn even
their sons and daughters in the fire
to their gods.
32 "Whatever I command you, be
careful to observe it; [a]you shall not
add to it nor take away from it.

Punishment of Apostates

13 "If there arises among you
a prophet or a [a]dreamer of
dreams, [b]and he gives you a sign
or a wonder,
2 "and [a]the sign or the wonder
comes to pass, of which he spoke
to you, saying, 'Let us go after
other gods'—which you have not
known—'and let us serve them,'
3 "you shall not listen to the
words of that prophet or that
dreamer of dreams, for the LORD
your God [a]is testing you to know
whether you love the LORD your

15 [a]Deut. 12:21 [b]Deut. 12:22 [c]Deut. 14:5
16 [a]Gen. 9:4; Lev. 7:26; 17:10–12; 1 Sam. 14:33; Acts 15:20, 29
17 [1]*contribution*
18 [1]*all your undertakings*
19 [1]*Be careful*
20 [a]Gen. 15:18; Ex. 34:24; Deut. 11:24; 19:8
21 [a]Deut. 14:24
23 [a]Gen. 9:4; Lev. 17:10–14; Deut. 12:16
25 [a]Deut. 4:40; 6:18; Is. 3:10 [b]Ex. 15:26; 1 Kin. 11:38
26 [a]Num. 5:9, 10; 18:19
27 [a]Lev. 1:5, 9, 13, 17
28 [a]Deut. 12:25
29 [a]Ex. 23:23; Deut. 19:1; Josh. 23:4
31 [a]Lev. 18:3, 26, 30; 20:1, 2 [b]Deut. 18:10; Ps. 106:37; Jer. 32:35 [1]*detestable action*
32 [a]Deut. 4:2; 13:18; Josh. 1:7; Prov. 30:6; Rev. 22:18, 19

CHAPTER 13

1 [a]Num. 12:6; Jer. 23:28; Zech. 10:2 [b]Matt. 24:24; Mark 13:22; 2 Thess. 2:9
2 [a]Deut. 18:22
3 [a]Ex. 20:20; Deut. 8:2, 16

God with all your heart and with
all your soul.
4 "You shall [a]walk[1] after the
LORD your God and fear Him, and
keep His commandments and
obey His voice; you shall serve
Him and [b]hold fast to Him.
5 "But [a]that prophet or that
dreamer of dreams shall be put to
death, because he has spoken in
order to turn *you* away from the
LORD your God, who brought you
out of the land of Egypt and re-
deemed you from the house of
bondage, to entice you from the
way in which the LORD your God
commanded you to walk. [b]So you
shall [1]put away the evil from your
midst.
6 [a]"If your brother, the son of
your mother, your son or your
daughter, [b]the wife [1]of your bo-
som, or your friend [c]who is as your
own soul, secretly entices you,
saying, 'Let us go and serve other
gods,' which you have not known,
neither you nor your fathers,
7 "of the gods of the people
which *are* all around you, near to
you or far off from you, from *one*
end of the earth to the *other* end
of the earth,
8 "you shall [a]not [1]consent to him
or listen to him, nor shall your eye
pity him, nor shall you spare him
or conceal him;
9 "but you shall surely kill him;
your hand shall be first against
him to put him to [a]death, and after-
ward the hand of all the people.
10 "And you shall stone him with
stones until he dies, because he
sought to entice you away from the
LORD your God, who brought you
out of the land of Egypt, from the
house of bondage.
11 "So all Israel shall hear and
[a]fear, and not again do such wick-
edness as this among you.
12 [a]"If you hear someone in one
of your cities, which the LORD your
God gives you to dwell in, saying,
13 [1]'Corrupt men have gone out
from among you and enticed the
inhabitants of their city, say-
ing, "Let us go and serve other
gods" '—which you have not
known—
14 "then you shall inquire, search
out, and ask diligently. And *if it
is* indeed true *and* certain *that*

4 [a]Deut. 10:12, 20; 2 Kin. 23:3 [b]Deut. 30:20 [1]*follow the LORD*

5 [a]Deut. 18:20; Jer. 14:15 [b]Deut. 17:5, 7; 1 Cor. 5:13 [1]*exterminate*

6 [a]Deut. 17:2 [b]Gen. 16:5 [c]1 Sam. 18:1, 3 [1]Whom you cherish

8 [a]Deut. 7:16; Prov. 1:10 [1]*yield*

9 [a]Lev. 24:14; Deut. 17:7

11 [a]Deut. 17:13

12 [a]Judg. 20:1–48

13 [1]Lit. *Sons of Belial*

14 [1]*detestable action*

16 [a]Josh. 6:24 [b]Josh. 8:28; Is. 17:1; 25:2; Jer. 49:2 [1]Or *as a whole-offering* [2]Lit. *mound* or *ruin*

17 [a]Josh. 6:18 [b]Josh. 7:26 [1]*increase*

18 [a]Deut. 12:25, 28, 32

CHAPTER 14

1 [a][Rom. 8:16; Gal. 3:26] [b]Lev. 19:28; 21:1–5 [1]*make any baldness between your eyes*

2 [a]Lev. 20:26; Deut. 7:6; [Rom. 12:1]

3 [a]Ezek. 4:14 [1]*abominable*

4 [a]Lev. 11:2–45

5 [1]Or *addax*

such an [1]abomination was com-
mitted among you,
15 "you shall surely strike the in-
habitants of that city with the edge
of the sword, utterly destroying it,
all that is in it and its livestock—
with the edge of the sword.
16 "And you shall gather all its
plunder into the middle of the
street, and [1]completely [a]burn with
fire the city and all its plunder, for
the LORD your God. It shall be [b]a
[2]heap forever; it shall not be built
again.
17 [a]"So none of the accursed
things shall remain in your hand,
that the LORD may [b]turn from the
fierceness of His anger and show
you mercy, have compassion on
you and [1]multiply you, just as He
swore to your fathers,
18 "because you have listened to
the voice of the LORD your God,
[a]to keep all His commandments
which I command you today, to do
what is right in the eyes of the
LORD your God.

Improper Mourning

14 "You *are* [a]the children of the
LORD your God; [b]you shall
not cut yourselves nor [1]shave
the front of your head for the
dead.
2 [a]"For you *are* a holy people to
the LORD your God, and the LORD
has chosen you to be a people for
Himself, a special treasure above
all the peoples who *are* on the face
of the earth.

Clean and Unclean Meat

3 [a]"You shall not eat any [1]detest-
able thing.
4 [a]"These *are* the animals which
you may eat: the ox, the sheep, the
goat,
5 "the deer, the gazelle, the roe
deer, the wild goat, the [1]mountain
goat, the antelope, and the moun-
tain sheep.
6 "And you may eat every ani-
mal with cloven hooves, having
the hoof split into two parts, *and
that* chews the cud, among the an-
imals.
7 "Nevertheless, of those that
chew the cud or have cloven
hooves, you shall not eat, *such as*
these: the camel, the hare, and the
rock hyrax; for they chew the cud

but do not have cloven hooves;
they *are* unclean for you.
8 "Also the swine is unclean for
you, because it has cloven hooves,
yet *does* not *chew* the cud; you
shall not eat their flesh [a]or touch
their dead carcasses.
9 [a]"These you may eat of all that
are in the waters: you may eat all
that have fins and scales.
10 "And whatever does not have
fins and scales you shall not eat;
it *is* unclean for you.
11 "All clean birds you may eat.
12 [a]"But these you shall not eat:
the eagle, the vulture, the buzzard,
13 "the red kite, the falcon, and
the kite after their kinds;
14 "every raven after its kind;
15 "the ostrich, the short-eared
owl, the sea gull, and the hawk af-
ter their kinds;
16 "the little owl, the screech owl,
the white owl,
17 "the jackdaw, the carrion vul-
ture, the fisher owl,
18 "the stork, the heron after its
kind, and the hoopoe and the bat.
19 "Also [a]every [1]creeping thing
that flies is unclean for you; [b]they
shall not be eaten.
20 "You may eat all clean birds.
21 [a]"You shall not eat anything
that dies *of itself;* you may give it
to the alien who *is* within your
gates, that he may eat it, or you
may sell it to a foreigner; [b]for you
are a holy people to the LORD your
God. [c]You shall not boil a young
goat in its mother's milk.

Tithing Principles

22 [a]"You shall truly tithe all the
increase of your grain that the
field produces year by year.
23 [a]"And you shall eat before the
LORD your God, in the place where
He chooses to make His name
abide, the tithe of your grain and
your new wine and your oil, of [b]the
firstborn of your herds and your
flocks, that you may learn to fear
the LORD your God always.
24 "But if the journey is too long
for you, so that you are not able
to carry *the tithe, or* [a]if the place
where the LORD your God chooses
to put His name is too far from
you, when the LORD your God has
blessed you,
25 "then you shall exchange *it* for
money, take the money in your
hand, and go to the place which
the LORD your God chooses.
26 "And you shall spend that
money for whatever your heart de-
sires: for oxen or sheep, for wine
or similar drink, for whatever your
heart desires; you shall eat there
before the LORD your God, and you
shall [a]rejoice, you and your house-
hold.
27 "You shall not [1]forsake the
[a]Levite who *is* within your gates,
for he has no part nor inheritance
with you.
28 [a]"At the end of *every* third year
you shall bring out the [b]tithe of
your produce of that year and
store *it* up within your gates.
29 "And the Levite, because he
has no portion nor inheritance
with you, and the stranger and the
fatherless and the widow who *are*
within your gates, may come and
eat and be satisfied, that the LORD
your God may bless you in all
the work of your hand which
you do.

Debts Canceled Every Seven Years

15 "At the end of [a]*every* seven
years you shall grant a [1]re-
lease *of debts.*
2 "And this *is* the form of the re-
lease: Every creditor who has lent
anything to his neighbor shall [1]re-
lease *it;* he shall not [2]require *it* of
his neighbor or his brother, be-
cause it is called the LORD's re-
lease.
3 "Of a foreigner you may re-
quire *it;* but you shall give up your
claim to what is owed by your
brother,
4 "except when there may be no
poor among you; for the LORD will
greatly [a]bless you in the land
which the LORD your God is giv-
ing you to possess *as* an inheri-
tance—
5 "only if you carefully obey the
voice of the LORD your God, to ob-
serve with care all these com-
mandments which I command you
today.
6 "For the LORD your God will
bless you just as He promised you;
[a]you shall lend to many nations,
but you shall not borrow; you shall
reign over many nations, but they
shall not reign over you.

8 [a]Lev. 11:26, 27
9 [a]Lev. 11:9
12 [a]Lev. 11:13
19 [a]Lev. 11:20 [b]Lev. 11:23 [1]*swarming*
21 [a]Lev. 17:15; 22:8; Ezek. 4:14; 44:31 [b]Deut. 14:2 [c]Ex. 23:19; 34:26
22 [a]Lev. 27:30; Deut. 12:6, 17; Neh. 10:37
23 [a]Deut. 12:5–7 [b]Deut. 15:19, 20
24 [a]Deut. 12:5, 21
26 [a]Deut. 12:7
27 [a]Deut. 12:12 [1]*neglect*
28 [a]Deut. 26:12; Amos 4:4 [b]Num. 18:21–24

CHAPTER 15

1 [a]Ex. 21:2; 23:10, 11; Lev. 25:4; Jer. 34:14 [1]*remission*
2 [1]*cancel the debt* [2]*exact it*
4 [a]Deut. 7:13
6 [a]Deut. 28:12, 44

Generosity to the Poor

7 "If there is among you a poor
man of your brethren, within any
of the [1]gates in your land which
the LORD your God is giving you,
[a]you shall not harden your heart
nor shut your hand from your poor
brother,
8 "but [a]you shall [1]open your
hand wide to him and willingly
lend him sufficient for his need,
whatever he needs.
9 "Beware lest there be a wicked
thought in your heart, saying, 'The
seventh year, the year of release,
is at hand,' and your [a]eye be evil
against your poor brother and you
give him nothing, and [b]he cry out
to the LORD against you, and [c]it be-
come sin among you.
10 "You shall surely give to him,
and [a]your heart should not be
grieved when you give to him, be-
cause [b]for this thing the LORD your
God will bless you in all your
works and in all to which you put
your hand.
11 "For [a]the poor will never cease
from the land; therefore I com-
mand you, saying, 'You shall
[1]open your hand wide to your
brother, to your poor and your
needy, in your land.'

The Law Concerning Bondservants

12 [a]"If your brother, a Hebrew
man, or a Hebrew woman, is [b]sold
to you and serves you six years,
then in the seventh year you shall
let him go free from you.
13 "And when you [1]send him
away free from you, you shall not
let him go away empty-handed;
14 "you shall supply him liberally
from your flock, from your thresh-
ing floor, and from your wine-
press. *From what* the LORD has
[a]blessed you with, you shall give
to him.
15 [a]"You shall remember that you
were a slave in the land of Egypt,
and the LORD your God redeemed
you; therefore I command you this
thing today.
16 "And [a]if it happens that he says
to you, 'I will not go away from
you,' because he loves you and
your house, since he prospers with
you,
17 "then you shall take an awl and

7 [a]Ex. 23:6; Lev. 25:35–37; Deut. 24:12–14; [1 John 3:17] [1]*towns*
8 [a]Matt. 5:42; Gal. 2:10 [1]*freely open*
9 [a]Deut. 28:54, 56 [b]Ex. 22:23; Deut. 24:15; Job 34:28; Ps. 12:5; James 5:4 [c][Matt. 25:41, 42]
10 [a]2 Cor. 9:5, 7 [b]Deut. 14:29; Ps. 41:1; Prov. 22:9
11 [a]Matt. 26:11; Mark 14:7; John 12:8 [1]*freely open*
12 [a]Ex. 21:2–6; Jer. 34:14 [b]Lev. 25:39–46
13 [1]*set him free*
14 [a]Prov. 10:22
15 [a]Deut. 5:15
16 [a]Ex. 21:5, 6
18 [a]Is. 16:14
19 [a]Ex. 13:2, 12 [1]*set apart* or *consecrate*
20 [a]Lev. 7:15–18; Deut. 12:5; 14:23
21 [a]Lev. 22:19–25; Deut. 17:1
22 [a]Deut. 12:15, 16, 22

CHAPTER 16

1 [a]Ex. 12:2 [b]Ex. 13:4
2 [a]Num. 28:19 [b]Deut. 12:5, 26; 15:20
3 [a]Num. 29:12 [b]Ex. 13:3; Deut. 4:9
4 [a]Ex. 13:7

thrust *it* through his ear to the
door, and he shall be your servant
forever. Also to your female ser-
vant you shall do likewise.
18 "It shall not seem hard to you
when you send him away free
from you; for he has been worth
[a]a double hired servant in serving
you six years. Then the LORD your
God will bless you in all that you
do.

The Law Concerning Firstborn Animals

19 [a]"All the firstborn males that
come from your herd and your
flock you shall [1]sanctify to the
LORD your God; you shall do no
work with the firstborn of your
herd, nor shear the firstborn of
your flock.
20 [a]"You and your household
shall eat *it* before the LORD your
God year by year in the place
which the LORD chooses.
21 [a]"But if there is a defect in it,
if it is lame or blind *or has* any
serious defect, you shall not sacri-
fice it to the LORD your God.
22 "You may eat it within your
gates; [a]the unclean and the clean
person alike *may eat it,* as *if it
were* a gazelle or a deer.
23 "Only you shall not eat its
blood; you shall pour it on the
ground like water.

The Passover Reviewed

16 "Observe the [a]month of
Abib, and keep the Passover
to the LORD your God, for [b]in the
month of Abib the LORD your God
brought you out of Egypt by night.
2 "Therefore you shall sacrifice
the Passover to the LORD your God,
from the flock and [a]the herd, in the
[b]place where the LORD chooses to
put His name.
3 "You shall eat no leavened
bread with it; [a]seven days you
shall eat unleavened bread with it,
that is, the bread of affliction (for
you came out of the land of Egypt
in haste), that you may [b]remember
the day in which you came out of
the land of Egypt all the days of
your life.
4 [a]"And no leaven shall be seen
among you in all your territory for
seven days, nor shall any of the

meat which you sacrifice the first
day at twilight remain overnight
until [b]morning.
5 "You may not sacrifice the
Passover within any of your gates
which the LORD your God gives
you;
6 "but at the place where the
LORD your God chooses to make
His name abide, there you shall
sacrifice the Passover [a]at twilight,
at the going down of the sun, at
the time you came out of Egypt.
7 "And you shall roast and eat
it [a]in the place which the LORD
your God chooses, and in the
morning you shall turn and go to
your tents.
8 "Six days you shall eat unleav-
ened bread, and [a]on the seventh
day there *shall be* a [1]sacred assem-
bly to the LORD your God. You
shall do no work *on it*.

The Feast of Weeks Reviewed

9 "You shall count seven weeks
for yourself; begin to count the
seven weeks from *the time* you be-
gin *to put* the sickle to the grain.
10 "Then you shall keep the
[a]Feast of Weeks to the LORD your
God with the tribute of a freewill
offering from your hand, which
you shall give [b]as the LORD your
God blesses you.
11 [a]"You shall rejoice before the
LORD your God, you and your son
and your daughter, your male ser-
vant and your female servant, the
Levite who *is* within your gates,
the stranger and the fatherless and
the widow who *are* among you, at
the place where the LORD your
God chooses to make His name
abide.
12 [a]"And you shall remember that
you were a slave in Egypt, and you
shall be careful to observe these
statutes.

The Feast of Tabernacles Reviewed

13 [a]"You shall observe the Feast
of Tabernacles seven days, when
you have gathered from your
threshing floor and from your
winepress.
14 "And [a]you shall rejoice in your
feast, you and your son and your
daughter, your male servant and
your female servant and the Le-
vite, the stranger and the father-

4 [b]Num. 9:12
6 [a]Ex. 12:7–10
7 [a]2 Kin. 23:23
8 [a]Ex. 12:16; 13:6; Lev. 23:8, 36 [1]Lit. *restraint*
10 [a]Ex. 34:22; Lev. 23:15, 16; Num. 28:26 [b]1 Cor. 16:2
11 [a]Deut. 16:14
12 [a]Deut. 15:15
13 [a]Ex. 23:16
14 [a]Neh. 8:9 [1]*towns*
15 [a]Lev. 23:39–41
16 [a]Ex. 23:14–17; 34:22–24 [b]Ex. 23:15
17 [a]Lev. 14:30, 31; Deut. 16:10
18 [a]Ex. 23:1–8; Deut. 1:16, 17; John 7:24 [1]*towns*
19 [a]Ex. 23:2, 6 [b]Deut. 1:17 [c]Ex. 23:8 [1]Lit. *regard faces* [2]*perverts*
20 [a]Ezek. 18:5–9
21 [a]Ex. 34:13 [1]Or *Asherah*
22 [a]Lev. 26:1

CHAPTER 17

1 [a]Deut. 15:21; Mal. 1:8, 13 [1]Lit. *evil thing* [2]*detestable thing*
2 [a]Deut. 13:6 [b]Josh. 7:11 [1]*towns*
3 [a]Deut. 4:19 [b]Jer. 7:22

less and the widow, who *are*
within your [1]gates.
15 [a]"Seven days you shall keep a
sacred feast to the LORD your God
in the place which the LORD
chooses, because the LORD your
God will bless you in all your pro-
duce and in all the work of your
hands, so that you surely re-
joice.
16 [a]"Three times a year all your
males shall appear before the
LORD your God in the place which
He chooses: at the Feast of Unleav-
ened Bread, at the Feast of Weeks,
and at the Feast of Tabernacles;
and [b]they shall not appear before
the LORD empty-handed.
17 "Every man *shall give* as he is
able, [a]according to the blessing of
the LORD your God which He has
given you.

Justice Must Be Administered

18 "You shall appoint [a]judges and
officers in all your [1]gates, which
the LORD your God gives you, ac-
cording to your tribes, and they
shall judge the people with just
judgment.
19 [a]"You shall not pervert justice;
[b]you shall not [1]show partiality,
[c]nor take a bribe, for a bribe blinds
the eyes of the wise and [2]twists the
words of the righteous.
20 "You shall follow what is al-
together just, that you may [a]live
and inherit the land which the
LORD your God is giving you.
21 [a]"You shall not plant for your-
self any tree, as a [1]wooden image,
near the altar which you build for
yourself to the LORD your God.
22 [a]"You shall not set up a sacred
pillar, which the LORD your God
hates.

17

"You [a]shall not sacrifice to
the LORD your God a bull or
sheep which has any [1]blemish *or*
defect, for that *is* an [2]abomination
to the LORD your God.
2 [a]"If there is found among you,
within any of your [1]gates which
the LORD your God gives you, a
man or a woman who has been
wicked in the sight of the LORD
your God, [b]in transgressing His
covenant,
3 "who has gone and served
other gods and worshiped them,
either [a]the sun or moon or any of

the host of heaven, [b]which I have
not commanded,
4 [a]"and it is told you, and you
hear *of it,* then you shall inquire
diligently. And if *it is* indeed true
and certain that such an [1]abomina-
tion has been committed in Israel,
5 "then you shall bring out to
your gates that man or woman
who has committed that wicked
thing, and [a]shall stone [b]to death
that man or woman with stones.
6 "Whoever is deserving of death
shall be put to death on the testi-
mony of two or three [a]witnesses;
he shall not be put to death on the
testimony of one witness.
7 "The hands of the witnesses
shall be the first against him to put
him to death, and afterward the
hands of all the people. So you
shall put away the evil from
among [a]you.
8 [a]"If a matter arises which is too
hard for you to judge, between de-
grees of guilt for bloodshed, be-
tween one judgment or another, or
between one punishment or an-
other, matters of controversy
within your gates, then you shall
arise and go up to the [b]place which
the LORD your God chooses.
9 "And [a]you shall come to the
priests, the Levites, and [b]to the
judge *there* in those days, and in-
quire *of them;* [c]they shall pro-
nounce upon you the sentence of
judgment.
10 "You shall do according to the
sentence which they pronounce
upon you in that place which the
LORD chooses. And you shall be
careful to do according to all that
they order you.
11 "According to the sentence of
the law in which they instruct you,
according to the judgment which
they tell you, you shall do; you
shall not turn aside *to* the right
hand or *to* the left from the sen-
tence which they pronounce upon
you.
12 "Now [a]the man who acts pre-
sumptuously and will not heed the
priest who stands to minister there
before the LORD your God, or the
judge, that man shall die. So you
shall put away the evil from Israel.
13 [a]"And all the people shall hear
and fear, and no longer act pre-
sumptuously.

4 [a]Deut. 13:12, 14 [1]*detestable thing*
5 [a]Lev. 24:14–16; Josh. 7:25 [b]Deut. 13:6–18
6 [a]Num. 35:30; Deut. 19:15; Matt. 18:16; John 8:17; 2 Cor. 13:1; 1 Tim. 5:19; Heb. 10:28
7 [a]Deut. 13:5; 19:19; 1 Cor. 5:13
8 [a]Deut. 1:17; 2 Chr. 19:10 [b]Deut. 12:5; 16:2
9 [a]Jer. 18:18 [b]Deut. 19:17–19 [c]Ezek. 44:24
12 [a]Num. 15:30; Deut. 1:43
13 [a]Deut. 13:11
14 [a]1 Sam. 8:5, 19, 20; 10:19
15 [a]1 Sam. 9:15, 16; 10:24; 16:12, 13; 1 Chr. 22:8–10; Hos. 8:4 [b]Jer. 30:21
16 [a]1 Kin. 4:26; 10:26–29; Ps. 20:7 [b]Is. 31:1; Ezek. 17:15 [c]Ex. 13:17, 18; Hos. 11:5 [d]Deut. 28:68
17 [a]1 Kin. 10:14
18 [a]Deut. 31:24–26
19 [a]Ps. 119:97, 98
20 [a]Deut. 5:32; 1 Kin. 15:5 [1]*become proud* [2]*continue long in his kingdom*

CHAPTER 18

1 [a]Deut. 10:9; 1 Cor. 9:13 [1]*no portion*
3 [a]Lev. 7:32–34; Num. 18:11, 12; 1 Sam. 2:13–16, 29 [1]*right*

Principles Governing Kings

14 "When you come to the land
which the LORD your God is giving
you, and possess it and dwell in
it, and say, [a]'I will set a king over
me like all the nations that *are*
around me,'
15 "you shall surely set a king
over you [a]whom the LORD your
God chooses; *one* [b]from among
your brethren you shall set as king
over you; you may not set a for-
eigner over you, who *is* not your
brother.
16 "But he shall not multiply
[a]horses for himself, nor cause the
people [b]to return to Egypt to multi-
ply horses, for [c]the LORD has said
to you, [d]'You shall not return that
way again.'
17 "Neither shall he multiply
wives for himself, lest his heart
turn away; nor shall he greatly
multiply silver and [a]gold for him-
self.
18 "Also it shall be, when he sits
on the throne of his kingdom, that
he shall write for himself a copy
of this law in a book, from *the one*
[a]before the priests, the Levites.
19 "And [a]it shall be with him, and
he shall read it all the days of his
life, that he may learn to fear the
LORD his God and be careful to ob-
serve all the words of this law and
these statutes,
20 "that his heart may not [1]be
lifted above his brethren, that he
[a]may not turn aside from the com-
mandment *to* the right hand or
to the left, and that he may [2]pro-
long *his* days in his kingdom, he
and his children in the midst of
Israel.

The Portion of the Priests and Levites

18 "The priests, the Levites—
all the tribe of Levi—shall
have [1]no part nor [a]inheritance
with Israel; they shall eat the offer-
ings of the LORD made by fire, and
His portion.
2 "Therefore they shall have no
inheritance among their brethren;
the LORD is their inheritance, as He
said to them.
3 "And this shall be the priest's
[a]due[1] from the people, from those
who offer a sacrifice, whether *it is*

bull or sheep: they shall give to the
priest the shoulder, the cheeks,
and the stomach.
4 [a]"The firstfruits of your grain
and your new wine and your oil,
and the first of the fleece of your
sheep, you shall give him.
5 "For [a]the LORD your God has
chosen him out of all your tribes
[b]to stand to minister in the name
of the LORD, him and his sons for-
ever.
6 "So if a Levite comes from any
of your [1]gates, from where he
[a]dwells among all Israel, and
comes with all the desire of his
mind [b]to the place which the LORD
chooses,
7 "then he may serve in the name
of the LORD his God [a]as all his
brethren the Levites *do*, who stand
there before the LORD.
8 "They shall have equal [a]por-
tions to eat, besides what comes
from the sale of his inheritance.

Avoid Wicked Customs

9 "When you come into the land
which the LORD your God is giving
you, [a]you shall not learn to follow
the [1]abominations of those na-
tions.
10 "There shall not be found
among you *anyone* who makes his
son or his daughter [a]pass[1] through
the fire, [b]*or one* who practices
witchcraft, *or* a soothsayer, or one
who interprets omens, or a sor-
cerer,
11 [a]"or one who conjures spells,
or a medium, or a spiritist, or [b]one
who calls up the dead.
12 "For all who do these things
are [1]an abomination to the LORD,
and [a]because of these abomina-
tions the LORD your God drives
them out from before you.
13 "You shall be [1]blameless be-
fore the LORD your God.
14 "For these nations which you
will dispossess listened to sooth-
sayers and diviners; but as for you,
the LORD your God has not [1]ap-
pointed such for you.

A New Prophet Like Moses

15 [a]"The LORD your God will raise
up for you a Prophet like me from
your midst, from your brethren.
Him you shall hear,
16 "according to all you desired of

4 [a]Ex. 22:29
5 [a]Ex. 28:1 [b]Deut. 10:8
6 [a]Num. 35:2 [b]Deut. 12:5; 14:23 [1]*towns*
7 [a]Num. 1:50; 2 Chr. 31:2
8 [a]Lev. 27:30–33; Num. 18:21–24; 2 Chr. 31:4; Neh. 12:44
9 [a]Lev. 18:26, 27, 30; Deut. 12:29, 30; 20:16–18 [1]*detestable acts*
10 [a]Lev. 18:21; Deut. 12:31 [b]Ex. 22:18; Lev. 19:26, 31; 20:6, 27; Is. 8:19 [1]Be burned as an offering to an idol
11 [a]Lev. 20:27 [b]1 Sam. 28:7
12 [a]Lev. 18:24; Deut. 9:4 [1]*detestable*
13 [1]Lit. *perfect*
14 [1]*allowed you to do so*
15 [a]Matt. 21:11; Luke 1:76; 2:25–34; 7:16; 24:19; Acts 3:22
16 [a]Deut. 5:23–27 [b]Ex. 20:18, 19; Heb. 12:19
17 [a]Deut. 5:28
18 [a]Deut. 34:10; John 1:45; Acts 3:22 [b]Num. 23:5; Is. 49:2; 51:16; John 17:8 [c][John 4:25; 8:28]
19 [a]Acts 3:23; [Heb. 12:25]
20 [a]Deut. 13:5; Jer. 14:14, 15; Zech. 13:2–5 [b]Deut. 13:1–3; Jer. 2:8
22 [a]Jer. 28:9 [b]Deut. 13:2 [c]Deut. 18:20

CHAPTER 19

1 [a]Deut. 12:29
2 [a]Ex. 21:13; Num. 35:10–15; Deut. 4:41; Josh. 20:2
4 [a]Num. 35:9–34; Deut. 4:42 [1]*ignorantly*, lit. *without knowledge*

the LORD your God in Horeb [a]in
the day of the assembly, saying,
[b]'Let me not hear again the voice
of the LORD my God, nor let me
see this great fire anymore, lest I
die.'
17 "And the LORD said to me:
[a]'What they have spoken is good.
18 [a]'I will raise up for them a
Prophet like you from among their
brethren, and [b]will put My words
in His mouth, [c]and He shall speak
to them all that I command Him.
19 [a]'And it shall be *that* whoever
will not hear My words, which He
speaks in My name, I will require
it of him.
20 'But [a]the prophet who pre-
sumes to speak a word in My
name, which I have not com-
manded him to speak, or [b]who
speaks in the name of other gods,
that prophet shall die.'
21 "And if you say in your heart,
'How shall we know the word
which the LORD has not spoken?'—
22 [a]"when a prophet speaks in the
name of the LORD, [b]if the thing
does not happen or come to pass,
that *is* the thing which the LORD
has not spoken; the prophet has
spoken it [c]presumptuously; you
shall not be afraid of him.

Three Cities of Refuge

19 "When the LORD your God
[a]has cut off the nations
whose land the LORD your God is
giving you, and you dispossess
them and dwell in their cities and
in their houses,
2 [a]"you shall separate three cit-
ies for yourself in the midst of your
land which the LORD your God is
giving you to possess.
3 "You shall prepare roads for
yourself, and divide into three
parts the territory of your land
which the LORD your God is giving
you to inherit, that any manslayer
may flee there.
4 "And [a]this *is* the case of the
manslayer who flees there, that he
may live: Whoever kills his neigh-
bor [1]unintentionally, not having
hated him in time past—
5 "as when *a man* goes to the
woods with his neighbor to cut
timber, and his hand swings a
stroke with the ax to cut down the
tree, and the head slips from the

handle and strikes his neighbor so
that he dies—he shall flee to one
of these cities and live;
6 [a]"lest the avenger of blood,
while his anger is hot, pursue the
manslayer and overtake him, be-
cause the way is long, and kill him,
though he *was* not deserving of
death, since he had not hated the
victim in time past.
7 "Therefore I command you,
saying, 'You shall separate three
cities for yourself.'
8 "Now if the LORD your God [a]en-
larges your territory, as He swore
to [b]your fathers, and gives you the
land which He promised to give to
your fathers,
9 "and if you keep all these com-
mandments and do them, which I
command you today, to love the
LORD your God and to walk always
in His ways, [a]then you shall add
three more cities for yourself be-
sides these three,
10 [a]"lest innocent blood be shed
in the midst of your land which the
LORD your God is giving you *as* an
inheritance, and *thus* guilt of
bloodshed be upon you.
11 "But [a]if anyone hates his
neighbor, lies in wait for him, rises
against him and strikes him mor-
tally, so that he dies, and he flees
to one of these cities,
12 "then the elders of his city shall
send and bring him from there,
and deliver him over to the hand
of the avenger of blood, that he
may die.
13 [a]"Your eye shall not pity him,
[b]but you shall [1]put away *the guilt
of* innocent blood from Israel, that
it may go well with you.

Property Boundaries

14 [a]"You shall not remove your
neighbor's landmark, which the
men of old have set, in your inheri-
tance which you will inherit in the
land that the LORD your God is giv-
ing you to possess.

The Law Concerning Witnesses

15 [a]"One witness shall not rise
against a man concerning any in-
iquity or any sin that he commits;
by the mouth of two or three wit-
nesses the matter shall be estab-
lished.
16 "If a false witness [a]rises
against any man to testify against
him of wrongdoing,
17 "then both men in the contro-
versy shall stand before the LORD,
[a]before the priests and the judges
who serve in those days.
18 "And the judges shall make
careful inquiry, and indeed, *if* the
witness *is* a false witness, who
has testified falsely against his
brother,
19 [a]"then you shall do to him as
he thought to have done to his
brother; so [b]you shall put away the
evil from among you.
20 [a]"And those who remain shall
hear and fear, and hereafter they
shall not again commit such evil
among you.
21 [a]"Your eye shall not pity: [b]life
shall be for life, eye for eye, tooth
for tooth, hand for hand, foot for
foot.

Principles Governing Warfare

20 "When you go out to battle
against your enemies, and
see [a]horses and chariots *and* peo-
ple more numerous than you, do
not be [b]afraid of them; for the
LORD your God *is* [c]with you, who
brought you up from the land of
Egypt.
2 "So it shall be, when you are
on the verge of battle, that the
priest shall approach and speak to
the people.
3 "And he shall say to them,
'Hear, O Israel: Today you are on
the verge of battle with your ene-
mies. Do not let your heart faint,
do not be afraid, and do not trem-
ble or be terrified because of
them;
4 'for the LORD your God *is* He
who goes with you, [a]to fight for
you against your enemies, to save
you.'
5 "Then the officers shall speak
to the people, saying: 'What man
is there who has built a new house
and has not [a]dedicated it? Let him
go and return to his house, lest he
die in the battle and another man
dedicate it.
6 'Also what man *is there* who
has planted a vineyard and has not
eaten of it? Let him go and return
to his house, lest he die in the bat-
tle and another man eat of it.
7 [a]'And what man *is there* who

6 [a]Num. 35:12
8 [a]Deut. 12:20 [b]Gen. 15:18–21
9 [a]Josh. 20:7–9
10 [a]Num. 35:33; Deut. 21:1–9
11 [a]Num. 35:16, 24; Deut. 27:24; [1 John 3:15]
13 [a]Deut. 13:8 [b]Num. 35:33, 34; 1 Kin. 2:31 [1]*purge the blood of the innocent*
14 [a]Deut. 27:17; Job 24:2; Prov. 22:28; Hos. 5:10
15 [a]Num. 35:30; Deut. 17:6; Matt. 18:16; John 8:17; 2 Cor. 13:1; 1 Tim. 5:19; Heb. 10:28
16 [a]Ex. 23:1; Ps. 27:12; 35:11
17 [a]Deut. 17:8–11; 21:5
19 [a]Prov. 19:5; Dan. 6:24 [b]Deut. 13:5; 17:7; 21:21; 22:21
20 [a]Deut. 17:13; 21:21
21 [a]Deut. 19:13 [b]Ex. 21:23, 24; Lev. 24:20; Matt. 5:38, 39

CHAPTER 20

1 [a]Ps. 20:7; Is. 31:1 [b]Deut. 7:18 [c]Num. 23:21; Deut. 5:6; 31:6, 8; 2 Chr. 13:12; 32:7, 8; Ps. 23:4; Is. 41:10
4 [a]Deut. 1:30; 3:22; Josh. 23:10
5 [a]Neh. 12:27
7 [a]Deut. 24:5

is betrothed to a woman and has
not married her? Let him go and
return to his house, lest he die in
the battle and another man marry
her.'
8 "The officers shall speak fur-
ther to the people, and say, [a]'What
man *is there who is* fearful and
fainthearted? Let him go and re-
turn to his house, [1]lest the heart
of his brethren faint like his heart.'
9 "And so it shall be, when the
officers have finished speaking to
the people, that they shall make
captains of the armies to lead the
people.
10 "When you go near a city to
fight against it, [a]then proclaim an
offer of peace to it.
11 "And it shall be that if they ac-
cept your offer of peace, and open
to you, then all the people *who
are* found in it shall be placed
under tribute to you, and serve
you.
12 "Now if *the city* will not make
peace with you, but makes war
against you, then you shall besiege
it.
13 "And when the LORD your God
delivers it into your hands, [a]you
shall strike every male in it with
the edge of the sword.
14 "But the women, the little ones,
[a]the livestock, and all that is in the
city, all its spoil, you shall plunder
for yourself; and [b]you shall eat the
enemies' plunder which the LORD
your God gives you.
15 "Thus you shall do to all the
cities *which are* very far from you,
which *are* not of the cities of these
nations.
16 "But [a]of the cities of these peo-
ples which the LORD your God
gives you *as* an inheritance, you
shall let nothing that breathes re-
main alive,
17 "but you shall utterly destroy
them: the Hittite and the Amorite
and the Canaanite and the Periz-
zite and the Hivite and the Jebu-
site, just as the LORD your God has
commanded you,
18 "lest [a]they teach you to do ac-
cording to all their [1]abominations
which they have done for their
gods, and you [b]sin against the
LORD your God.
19 "When you besiege a city for
a long time, while making war
against it to take it, you shall not
destroy its trees by wielding an ax
against them; if you can eat of
them, do not cut them down to use
in the siege, for the tree of the field
is man's *food*.
20 "Only the trees which you
know *are* not trees for food you
may destroy and cut down, to
build siegeworks against the city
that makes war with you, until it
is subdued.

The Law Concerning Unsolved Murder

21 "If *anyone* is found slain, ly-
ing in the field in the land
which the LORD your God is giving
you to possess, *and* it is not known
who killed him,
2 "then your elders and your
judges shall go out and measure
the distance from the slain man to
the surrounding cities.
3 "And it shall be *that* the elders
of the city nearest to the slain man
will take a heifer which has not
been worked *and* which has not
pulled with a [a]yoke.
4 "The elders of that city shall
bring the heifer down to a valley
with flowing water, which is nei-
ther plowed nor sown, and they
shall break the heifer's neck there
in the valley.
5 "Then the priests, the sons of
Levi, shall come near, for [a]the
LORD your God has chosen them
to minister to Him and to bless in
the name of the LORD; [b]by their
word every controversy and every
[1]assault shall be *settled*.
6 "And all the elders of that city
nearest to the slain *man* [a]shall
wash their hands over the heifer
whose neck was broken in the val-
ley.
7 "Then they shall answer and
say, 'Our hands have not shed
this blood, nor have our eyes
seen *it*.
8 'Provide atonement, O LORD,
for Your people Israel, whom You
have redeemed, [a]and do not lay in-
nocent blood to the charge of Your
people Israel.' And atonement
shall be provided on their behalf
for the blood.
9 "So [a]you shall put away the
guilt of innocent blood from
among you when you do *what is*
right in the sight of the LORD.

8 [a]Judg. 7:3 [1]So with MT, Tg.; Sam., LXX, Syr., Vg. *lest he make his brother's heart faint*
10 [a]2 Sam. 10:19
13 [a]Num. 31:7
14 [a]Josh. 8:2 [b]1 Sam. 14:30
16 [a]Ex. 23:31–33; Num. 21:2, 3; Deut. 7:1–5; Josh. 11:14
18 [a]Ex. 34:12–16; Deut. 7:4; 12:30; 18:9 [b]Ex. 23:33; 2 Kin. 21:3–15; Ps. 106:34–41 [1]*detestable things*

CHAPTER 21

3 [a]Num. 19:2
5 [a]Deut. 10:8; 1 Chr. 23:13 [b]Deut. 17:8, 9 [1]Lit. *stroke*
6 [a]Ps. 19:12; 26:6; Matt. 27:24
8 [a]Deut. 19:10, 13; Jon. 1:14
9 [a]Deut. 19:13

Female Captives

10 "When you go out to war against your enemies, and the LORD your God delivers them into your hand, and you take them captive,

11 "and you see among the captives a beautiful woman, and desire her and would take her for your [a]wife,

12 "then you shall bring her home to your house, and she shall [a]shave her head and trim her nails.

13 "She shall put off the clothes of her captivity, remain in your house, and [a]mourn her father and her mother a full month; after that you may go in to her and be her husband, and she shall be your wife.

14 "And it shall be, if you have no delight in her, then you shall set her free, but you certainly shall not sell her for money; you shall not treat her brutally, because you have [a]humbled her.

Firstborn Inheritance Rights

15 "If a man has two wives, one loved [a]and the other unloved, and they have borne him children, *both* the loved and the unloved, and *if* the firstborn son is of her who is unloved,

16 "then it shall be, [a]on the day he bequeaths his possessions to his sons, *that* he must not bestow firstborn status on the son of the loved wife in preference to the son of the unloved, the *true* firstborn.

17 "But he shall acknowledge the son of the unloved wife *as* the firstborn [a]by giving him a double portion of all that he has, for he [b]*is* the beginning of his strength; [c]the right of the firstborn *is* his.

The Rebellious Son

18 "If a man has a stubborn and rebellious son who will not obey the voice of his father or the voice of his mother, and *who*, when they have chastened him, will not heed them,

19 "then his father and his mother shall take hold of him and bring him out to the elders of his city, to the gate of his city.

20 "And they shall say to the elders of his city, 'This son of ours is stubborn and rebellious; he will not obey our voice; he is a glutton and a drunkard.'

21 "Then all the men of his city shall stone him to death with stones; [a]so you shall put away the evil from among you, [b]and all Israel shall hear and fear.

Miscellaneous Laws

22 "If a man has committed a sin [a]deserving of death, and he is put to death, and you hang him on a tree,

23 [a]"his body shall not remain overnight on the tree, but you shall surely bury him that day, so that [b]you do not defile the land which the LORD your God is giving you *as* an inheritance; for [c]he who is hanged *is* accursed of God.

22 "You [a]shall not see your brother's ox or his sheep going astray, and [1]hide yourself from them; you shall certainly bring them back to your brother.

2 "And if your brother *is* not near you, or if you do not know him, then you shall bring it to your own house, and it shall remain with you until your brother seeks it; then you shall restore it to him.

3 "You shall do the same with his donkey, and so shall you do with his garment; with any lost thing of your brother's, which he has lost and you have found, you shall do likewise; you [1]must not hide yourself.

4 [a]"You shall not see your brother's donkey or his ox fall down along the road, and hide yourself from them; you shall surely help him lift *them* up again.

5 "A woman shall not wear anything that pertains to a man, nor shall a man put on a woman's garment, for all who do so *are* [1]an abomination to the LORD your God.

6 "If a bird's nest happens to be before you along the way, in any tree or on the ground, with young ones or eggs, with the mother sitting on the young or on the eggs, [a]you shall not take the mother with the young;

7 "you shall surely let the mother go, and take the young for yourself, [a]that it may be well with you

11 [a]Num. 31:18
12 [a]Lev. 14:8, 9; Num. 6:9
13 [a]Ps. 45:10
14 [a]Gen. 34:2; Deut. 22:29; Judg. 19:24
15 [a]Gen. 29:33
16 [a]1 Chr. 5:2; 26:10
17 [a]2 Kin. 2:9 [b]Gen. 49:3 [c]Gen. 25:31, 33
21 [a]Deut. 13:5; 19:19, 20; 22:21, 24 [b]Deut. 13:11
22 [a]Deut. 22:26; Matt. 26:66; Mark 14:64; Acts 23:29
23 [a]Josh. 8:29; 10:26, 27; John 19:31 [b]Lev. 18:25; Num. 35:34 [c]Gal. 3:13

CHAPTER 22

1 [a]Ex. 23:4 [1]*ignore them*
3 [1]*may not avoid responsibility*
4 [a]Ex. 23:5
5 [1]*detestable*
6 [a]Lev. 22:28
7 [a]Deut. 4:40

and *that* you may prolong *your*
days.
8 "When you build a new house,
then you shall make a parapet for
your roof, that you may not bring
guilt of bloodshed on your house-
hold if anyone falls from it.
9 [a]"You shall not sow your vine-
yard with different kinds of seed,
lest the yield of the seed which you
have sown and the fruit of your
vineyard be defiled.
10 [a]"You shall not plow with an
ox and a donkey together.
11 [a]"You shall not wear a garment
of different sorts, *such as* wool and
linen mixed together.
12 "You shall make [a]tassels on the
four corners of the clothing with
which you cover *yourself*.

Laws of Sexual Morality

13 "If any man takes a wife, and
goes in to her, and [a]detests her,
14 "and charges her with shame-
ful conduct, and brings a bad name
on her, and says, 'I took this
woman, and when I came to her I
found she *was* not a virgin,'
15 "then the father and mother of
the young woman shall take and
bring out *the evidence of* the
young woman's virginity to the
elders of the city at the gate.
16 "And the young woman's fa-
ther shall say to the elders, 'I gave
my daughter to this man as wife,
and he detests her.
17 'Now he has charged her with
shameful conduct, saying, "I found
your daughter *was* not a virgin,"
and yet these *are the evidences of*
my daughter's virginity.' And they
shall spread the cloth before the
elders of the city.
18 "Then the elders of that city
shall take that man and punish
him;
19 "and they shall fine him one
hundred *shekels* of silver and give
them to the father of the young
woman, because he has brought a
bad name on a virgin of Israel.
And she shall be his wife; he can-
not divorce her all his days.
20 "But if the thing is true, *and ev-
idences of* virginity are not found
for the young woman,
21 "then they shall bring out the
young woman to the door of her
father's house, and the men of her
city shall stone her to death with
[a]stones, because she has [b]done a
disgraceful thing in Israel, to play
the harlot in her father's house.
[c]So you shall [1]put away the evil
from among you.
22 [a]"If a man is found lying with
a woman married to a husband,
then both of them shall die—the
man that lay with the woman, and
the woman; so you shall put away
the evil from Israel.
23 "If a young woman *who is* a
virgin is [a]betrothed to a husband,
and a man finds her in the city and
lies with her,
24 "then you shall bring them
both out to the gate of that city,
and you shall stone them to death
with stones, the young woman be-
cause she did not cry out in the
city, and the man because he
[a]humbled his neighbor's wife; [b]so
you shall put away the evil from
among you.
25 "But if a man finds a betrothed
young woman in the countryside,
and the man forces her and lies
with her, then only the man who
lay with her shall die.
26 "But you shall do nothing to
the young woman; *there is* in the
young woman no sin *deserving* of
death, for just as when a man rises
against his neighbor and kills him,
even so *is* this matter.
27 "For he found her in the coun-
tryside, *and* the betrothed young
woman cried out, but *there was* no
one to save her.
28 [a]"If a man finds a young
woman *who is* a virgin, who is not
betrothed, and he seizes her and
lies with her, and they are found
out,
29 "then the man who lay with her
shall give to the young woman's
father [a]fifty *shekels* of silver, and
she shall be his wife [b]because he
has humbled her; he shall not be
permitted to divorce her all his
days.
30 [a]"A man shall not take his fa-
ther's wife, nor [b]uncover his fa-
ther's bed.

Those Excluded from the Congregation

23 "He who is emasculated by
crushing or mutilation shall
[a]not enter the assembly of the
LORD.

9 [a]Lev. 19:19
10 [a][2 Cor. 6:14–16]
11 [a]Lev. 19:19
12 [a]Num. 15:37–41; Matt. 23:5
13 [a]Deut. 21:15; 24:3
21 [a]Deut. 21:21 [b]Gen. 34:7; Judg. 20:5–10; 2 Sam. 13:12, 13 [c]Deut. 13:5 [1]*purge the evil person*
22 [a]Lev. 20:10; Num. 5:22–27; Ezek. 16:38; [Matt. 5:27, 28]; John 8:5; [1 Cor. 6:9; Heb. 13:4]
23 [a]Lev. 19:20–22; Matt. 1:18, 19
24 [a]Deut. 21:14 [b]Deut. 22:21, 22; 1 Cor. 5:2, 13
28 [a]Ex. 22:16, 17
29 [a]Ex. 22:16, 17 [b]Deut. 22:24
30 [a]Lev. 18:8; 20:11; Deut. 27:20; 1 Cor. 5:1 [b]Ruth 3:9; Ezek. 16:8
CHAPTER 23
1 [a]Lev. 21:20; 22:24

2 "One of illegitimate birth shall not enter the assembly of the LORD; even to the tenth generation none of his *descendants* shall enter the assembly of the LORD.
3 [a]"An Ammonite or Moabite shall not enter the assembly of the LORD; even to the tenth generation none of his *descendants* shall enter the assembly of the LORD forever,
4 [a]"because they did not meet you with bread and water on the road when you came out of Egypt, and [b]because they hired against you Balaam the son of Beor from Pethor of [1]Mesopotamia, to curse you.
5 "Nevertheless the LORD your God would not listen to Balaam, but the LORD your God turned the curse into a blessing for you, because the LORD your God [a]loves you.
6 [a]"You shall not seek their peace nor their prosperity all your days forever.
7 "You shall not abhor an Edomite, [a]for he *is* your brother. You shall not abhor an Egyptian, because [b]you were an alien in his land.
8 "The children of the third generation born to them may enter the assembly of the LORD.

Cleanliness of the Camp Site

9 "When the army goes out against your enemies, then keep yourself from every wicked thing.
10 [a]"If there is any man among you who becomes unclean by some occurrence in the night, then he shall go outside the camp; he shall not come inside the camp.
11 "But it shall be, when evening comes, that [a]he shall wash with water; and when the sun sets, he may come into the camp.
12 "Also you shall have a place outside the camp, where you may go out;
13 "and you shall have an implement among your equipment, and when you sit down outside, you shall dig with it and turn and cover your refuse.
14 "For the LORD your God [a]walks in the midst of your camp, to deliver you and give your enemies over to you; therefore your camp shall be holy, that He may see no unclean thing among you, and turn away from you.

Miscellaneous Laws

15 [a]"You shall not give back to his master the slave who has escaped from his master to you.
16 "He may dwell with you in your midst, in the place which he chooses within one of your gates, where it [1]seems best to him; [a]you shall not oppress him.
17 "There shall be no *ritual* [1]harlot [a]of the daughters of Israel, or a [b]perverted[2] one of the sons of Israel.
18 "You shall not bring the wages of a harlot or the price of a dog to the house of the LORD your God for any vowed offering, for both of these *are* [1]an abomination to the LORD your God.
19 [a]"You shall not charge interest to your brother—interest on money *or* food *or* anything that is lent out at interest.
20 [a]"To a foreigner you may charge interest, but to your brother you shall not charge interest, [b]that the LORD your God may bless you in all to which you set your hand in the land which you are entering to possess.
21 [a]"When you make a vow to the LORD your God, you shall not delay to pay it; for the LORD your God will surely require it of you, and it would be sin to you.
22 "But if you abstain from vowing, it shall not be sin to you.
23 [a]"That which has gone from your lips you shall keep and perform, for you voluntarily vowed to the LORD your God what you have promised with your mouth.
24 "When you come into your neighbor's vineyard, you may eat your fill of grapes at your pleasure, but you shall not put *any* in your container.
25 "When you come into your neighbor's standing grain, [a]you may pluck the heads with your hand, but you shall not use a sickle on your neighbor's standing grain.

Law Concerning Divorce

24 "When a [a]man takes a wife and marries her, and it happens that she finds no favor in his

3 [a]Neh. 13:1, 2
4 [a]Deut. 2:27–30 [b]Num. 22:5, 6; 23:7; Josh. 24:9; 2 Pet. 2:15; Jude 11 [1]Heb. *Aram Naharaim*
5 [a]Deut. 4:37
6 [a]Ezra 9:12
7 [a]Gen. 25:24–26; Deut. 2:4, 8; Amos 1:11; Obad. 10, 12 [b]Ex. 22:21; 23:9; Lev. 19:34; Deut. 10:19
10 [a]Lev. 15:16
11 [a]Lev. 15:5
14 [a]Lev. 26:12; Deut. 7:21
15 [a]1 Sam. 30:15
16 [a]Ex. 22:21; Prov. 22:22 [1]*pleases him best*
17 [a]Lev. 19:29; Deut. 22:21 [b]Gen. 19:5; 2 Kin. 23:7 [1]Heb. *qedeshah*, fem. of *qadesh* (note 2) [2]Heb. *qadesh*, one practicing sodomy and prostitution in religious rituals
18 [1]*detestable*
19 [a]Ex. 22:25; Lev. 25:35–37; Neh. 5:2–7; Ps. 15:5
20 [a]Deut. 15:3 [b]Deut. 15:10
21 [a]Num. 30:1, 2; Job 22:27; Ps. 61:8; Eccl. 5:4, 5; Matt. 5:33
23 [a]Num. 30:2; Ps. 66:13, 14
25 [a]Matt. 12:1; Mark 2:23; Luke 6:1

CHAPTER 24
1 [a][Matt. 5:31; 19:7; Mark 10:4]

eyes because he has found some
[1]uncleanness in her, and he writes
her a [b]certificate of divorce, puts
it in her hand, and sends her out
of his house,
2 "when she has departed from
his house, and goes and becomes
another man's *wife,*
3 "*if* the latter husband detests
her and writes her a certificate of
divorce, puts *it* in her hand, and
sends her out of his house, or if
the latter husband dies who took
her as his wife,
4 [a]"*then* her former husband
who divorced her must not take
her back to be his wife after she
has been defiled; for that *is* [1]an
abomination before the LORD, and
you shall not bring sin on the land
which the LORD your God is giving
you *as* an inheritance.

Miscellaneous Laws

5 [a]"When a man has taken a new
wife, he shall not go out to war or
be charged with any business; he
shall be free at home one year, and
[b]bring happiness to his wife whom
he has taken.
6 "No man shall take the lower
or the upper millstone in pledge,
for he takes [1]*one's* living in pledge.
7 "If a man is [a]found [1]kidnapping
any of his brethren of the children
of Israel, and mistreats him or sells
him, then that kidnapper shall die;
[b]and you shall put away the evil
from among you.
8 "Take heed in [a]an outbreak of
leprosy, that you carefully observe
and do according to all that the
priests, the Levites, shall teach
you; just as I commanded them, *so*
you shall be careful to do.
9 [a]"Remember what the LORD
your God did [b]to Miriam on the
way when you came out of Egypt!
10 "When you [a]lend your brother
anything, you shall not go into his
house to get his pledge.
11 "You shall stand outside, and
the man to whom you lend shall
bring the pledge out to you.
12 "And if the man *is* poor, you
shall not [1]keep his pledge over-
night.
13 [a]"You shall in any case return
the pledge to him again when the
sun goes down, that he may sleep
in his own garment and [b]bless you;

1 [b][Jer. 3:8] [1]*indecency,* lit. *nakedness of a thing*
4 [a][Jer. 3:1] [1]*a detestable thing*
5 [a]Deut. 20:7 [b]Prov. 5:18
6 [1]*life*
7 [a]Ex. 21:16 [b]Deut. 19:19 [1]Lit. *stealing*
8 [a]Lev. 13:2; 14:2
9 [a][1 Cor. 10:6] [b]Num. 12:10
10 [a]Matt. 5:42
12 [1]Lit. *sleep with his pledge*
13 [a]Ex. 22:26; Ezek. 18:7 [b]Job 29:11; 2 Tim. 1:18 [c]Deut. 6:25; Ps. 106:31; Dan. 4:27
14 [a]Lev. 19:13; Deut. 15:7–18; [Prov. 14:31]; Amos 4:1; [Mal. 3:5; 1 Tim. 5:18]
15 [a]Lev. 19:13; Jer. 22:13 [b]Ex. 22:23; Deut. 15:9; Job 35:9; James 5:4
16 [a]2 Kin. 14:6; 2 Chr. 25:4; Jer. 31:29, 30; Ezek. 18:20
17 [a]Ex. 23:6 [b]Ex. 22:26
18 [a]Deut. 24:22
19 [a]Lev. 19:9, 10 [b]Deut. 15:10; Ps. 41:1; Prov. 19:17

CHAPTER 25

1 [a]Deut. 17:8–13; 19:17; Ezek. 44:24 [b]Prov. 17:15 [1]Lit. *the judgment*
2 [a]Prov. 19:29; Luke 12:48 [b]Matt. 10:17
3 [a]2 Cor. 11:24

and [c]it shall be righteousness to
you before the LORD your God.
14 "You shall not [a]oppress a hired
servant *who is* poor and needy,
whether one of your brethren or
one of the aliens who *is* in your
land within your gates.
15 "Each day [a]you shall give *him*
his wages, and not let the sun go
down on it, for he *is* poor and has
set his heart on it; [b]lest he cry out
against you to the LORD, and it be
sin to you.
16 [a]"Fathers shall not be put to
death for *their* children, nor shall
children be put to death for *their*
fathers; a person shall be put to
death for his own sin.
17 [a]"You shall not pervert justice
due the stranger or the fatherless,
[b]nor take a widow's garment as a
pledge.
18 "But [a]you shall remember that
you were a slave in Egypt, and the
LORD your God redeemed you
from there; therefore I command
you to do this thing.
19 [a]"When you reap your harvest
in your field, and forget a sheaf in
the field, you shall not go back to
get it; it shall be for the stranger,
the fatherless, and the widow, that
the LORD your God may [b]bless you
in all the work of your hands.
20 "When you beat your olive
trees, you shall not go over the
boughs again; it shall be for
the stranger, the fatherless, and
the widow.
21 "When you gather the grapes
of your vineyard, you shall not
glean *it* afterward; it shall be for
the stranger, the fatherless, and
the widow.
22 "And you shall remember that
you were a slave in the land of
Egypt; therefore I command you
to do this thing.

25 "If there is a [a]dispute be-
tween men, and they come
to [1]court, that *the judges* may
judge them, and they [b]justify the
righteous and condemn the
wicked,
2 "then it shall be, if the wicked
man [a]deserves to be beaten, that
the judge will cause him to lie
down [b]and be beaten in his pres-
ence, according to his guilt, with
a certain number of blows.
3 [a]"Forty blows he may give him

and no more, lest he should exceed
this and beat him with many blows
above these, and your brother [b]be
humiliated in your sight.
4 [a]"You shall not muzzle an ox
while it [1]treads out *the grain*.

Marriage Duty of the Surviving Brother

5 [a]"If brothers dwell together,
and one of them dies and has no
son, the widow of the dead man
shall not be *married* to a stranger
outside *the family;* her husband's
brother shall go in to her, take her
as his wife, and perform the duty
of a husband's brother to her.
6 "And it shall be *that* the first-
born son which she bears [a]will
succeed to the name of his dead
brother, that [b]his name may not be
blotted out of Israel.
7 "But if the man does not want
to take his brother's wife, then let
his brother's wife go up to the
[a]gate to the elders, and say, 'My
husband's brother refuses to raise
up a name to his brother in Israel;
he will not perform the duty of my
husband's brother.'
8 "Then the elders of his city
shall call him and speak to him.
But *if* he stands firm and says, [a]'I
do not want to take her,'
9 "then his brother's wife shall
come to him in the presence of the
elders, [a]remove his sandal from
his foot, spit in his face, and an-
swer and say, 'So shall it be done
to the man who will not [b]build up
his brother's house.'
10 "And his name shall be called
in Israel, 'The house of him who
had his sandal removed.'

Miscellaneous Laws

11 "If *two* men fight together, and
the wife of one draws near to res-
cue her husband from the hand of
the one attacking him, and puts
out her hand and seizes him by the
genitals,
12 "then you shall cut off her
hand; [a]your eye shall not pity *her*.
13 [a]"You shall not have in your
bag differing weights, a heavy and
a light.
14 "You shall not have in your
house differing measures, a large
and a small.
15 "You shall have a perfect and
just weight, a perfect and just mea-
sure, [a]that your days may be
lengthened in the land which the
LORD your God is giving you.
16 "For [a]all who do such things,
all who behave unrighteously, *are*
[1]an abomination to the LORD your
God.

Destroy the Amalekites

17 [a]"Remember what Amalek did
to you on the way as you were
coming out of Egypt,
18 "how he met you on the way
and attacked your rear ranks, all
the stragglers at your rear, when
you *were* tired and weary; and he
[a]did not fear God.
19 "Therefore it shall be, [a]when
the LORD your God has given you
rest from your enemies all around,
in the land which the LORD your
God is giving you to possess *as* an
inheritance, *that* you will [b]blot out
the remembrance of Amalek from
under heaven. You shall not for-
get.

Offerings of Firstfruits and Tithes

26 "And it shall be, when you
come into the land which the
LORD your God is giving you *as* an
inheritance, and you possess it and
dwell in it,
2 [a]"that you shall take some of
the first of all the produce of the
ground, which you shall bring
from your land that the LORD your
God is giving you, and put *it* in a
basket and [b]go to the place where
the LORD your God chooses to
make His name abide.
3 "And you shall go to the one
who is priest in those days, and
say to him, 'I declare today to the
LORD [1]your God that I have come
to the country which the LORD
swore to our fathers to give us.'
4 "Then the priest shall take the
basket out of your hand and set it
down before the altar of the LORD
your God.
5 "And you shall answer and say
before the LORD your God: 'My fa-
ther *was* [a]a [1]Syrian, [b]about to per-
ish, and [c]he went down to Egypt
and [2]dwelt there, [d]few in number;
and there he became a nation,
[e]great, mighty, and populous.
6 'But the [a]Egyptians mistreated
us, afflicted us, and laid hard
bondage on us.

3 [b]Job 18:3
4 [a][Prov. 12:10; 1 Cor. 9:9; 1 Tim. 5:18] [1]*threshes*
5 [a]Matt. 22:24; Mark 12:19; Luke 20:28
6 [a]Gen. 38:9 [b]Ruth 4:5, 10
7 [a]Ruth 4:1, 2
8 [a]Ruth 4:6
9 [a]Ruth 4:7, 8 [b]Ruth 4:11
12 [a]Deut. 7:2; 19:13
13 [a]Lev. 19:35–37; Prov. 11:1; 20:23; Ezek. 45:10; Mic. 6:11
15 [a]Ex. 20:12
16 [a]Prov. 11:1; [1 Thess. 4:6] [1]*detestable*
17 [a]Ex. 17:8–16; 1 Sam. 15:1–3
18 [a][Ps. 36:1]; Rom. 3:18
19 [a]1 Sam. 15:3 [b]Ex. 17:14

CHAPTER 26

2 [a]Ex. 22:29; 23:16, 19; Num. 18:13; Deut. 16:10; Prov. 3:9 [b]Deut. 12:5
3 [1]LXX *my*
5 [a]Gen. 25:20; Hos. 12:12 [b]Gen. 43:1, 2; 45:7, 11 [c]Gen. 46:1, 6; Acts 7:15 [d]Gen. 46:27; Deut. 10:22 [e]Deut. 1:10 [1]Or *Aramean* [2]As a resident alien
6 [a]Ex. 1:8–11, 14

7 [a]'Then we cried out to the LORD God of our fathers, and the LORD heard our voice and looked on our affliction and our labor and our oppression.

8 'So [a]the LORD brought us out of Egypt with a mighty hand and with an outstretched arm, [b]with great terror and with signs and wonders.

9 'He has brought us to this place and has given us this land, [a]"a land flowing with milk and honey";

10 'and now, behold, I have brought the firstfruits of the land which you, O LORD, have given me.' Then you shall set it before the LORD your God, and worship before the LORD your God.

11 "So [a]you shall rejoice in every good *thing* which the LORD your God has given to you and your house, you and the Levite and the stranger who *is* among you.

12 "When you have finished laying aside all the [a]tithe of your increase in the third year—[b]the year of tithing—and have given *it* to the Levite, the stranger, the fatherless, and the widow, so that they may eat within your gates and be filled,

13 "then you shall say before the LORD your God: 'I have removed the [1]holy *tithe* from *my* house, and also have given them to the Levite, the stranger, the fatherless, and the widow, according to all Your commandments which You have commanded me; I have not transgressed Your commandments, [a]nor have I forgotten *them.*

14 [a]'I have not eaten any of it [1]when in mourning, nor have I removed *any* of it [2]for an unclean *use,* nor given *any* of it for the dead. I have obeyed the voice of the LORD my God, and have done according to all that You have commanded me.

15 [a]'Look down from Your holy [1]habitation, from heaven, and bless Your people Israel and the land which You have given us, just as You swore to our fathers, [b]"a land flowing with milk and honey." '

A Special People of God

16 "This day the LORD your God commands you to observe these statutes and judgments; therefore you shall be careful to observe them with all your heart and with all your soul.

17 "Today you have [a]proclaimed the LORD to be your God, and that you will walk in His ways and keep His statutes, His commandments, and His judgments, and that you will [b]obey His voice.

18 "Also today [a]the LORD has proclaimed you to be His special people, just as He promised you, that *you* should keep all His commandments,

19 "and that He will set you [a]high above all nations which He has made, in praise, in name, and in honor, and that you may be [b]a [1]holy people to the LORD your God, just as He has spoken."

The Law Inscribed on Stones

27 Now Moses, with the elders of Israel, commanded the people, saying: "Keep all the commandments which I command you today.

2 "And it shall be, on the day [a]when you cross over the Jordan to the land which the LORD your God is giving you, that [b]you shall set up for yourselves large stones, and whitewash them with lime.

3 "You shall write on them all the words of this law, when you have crossed over, that you may enter the land which the LORD your God is giving you, [a]'a land flowing with milk and honey,' just as the LORD God of your fathers promised you.

4 "Therefore it shall be, when you have crossed over the Jordan, *that* [a]on Mount Ebal you shall set up these stones, which I command you today, and you shall whitewash them with lime.

5 "And there you shall build an altar to the LORD your God, an altar of stones; [a]you shall not use an iron *tool* on them.

6 "You shall build with [1]whole stones the altar of the LORD your God, and offer burnt offerings on it to the LORD your God.

7 "You shall offer peace offerings, and shall eat there, and [a]rejoice before the LORD your God.

8 "And you shall [a]write very plainly on the stones all the words of this law."

7 [a]Ex. 2:23–25; 3:9; 4:31
8 [a]Ex. 12:37, 51; 13:3, 14, 16; Deut. 5:15 [b]Deut. 4:34; 34:11, 12
9 [a]Ex. 3:8, 17
11 [a]Deut. 12:7; 16:11; Eccl. 3:12, 13; 5:18–20
12 [a]Lev. 27:30; Num. 18:24 [b]Deut. 14:28, 29
13 [a]Ps. 119:141, 153, 176 [1]*hallowed things*
14 [a]Lev. 7:20; Jer. 16:7; Hos. 9:4 [1]Lit. *in my mourning* [2]Or *while I was unclean*
15 [a]Ps. 80:14; Is. 63:15; Zech. 2:13 [b]Ex. 3:8 [1]*home*
17 [a]Ex. 20:19 [b]Deut. 15:5
18 [a]Ex. 6:7; 19:5; Deut. 7:6; 14:2; 28:9; [Titus 2:14; 1 Pet. 2:9]
19 [a]Deut. 4:7, 8; 28:1 [b]Ex. 19:6; Deut. 7:6; 28:9; Is. 62:12; [1 Pet. 2:9] [1]*consecrated*

CHAPTER 27

2 [a]Josh. 4:1 [b]Josh. 8:32
3 [a]Ex. 3:8
4 [a]Deut. 11:29; Josh. 8:30, 31
5 [a]Ex. 20:25; Josh. 8:31
6 [1]*uncut*
7 [a]Deut. 26:11
8 [a]Josh. 8:32

9 Then Moses and the priests, the
Levites, spoke to all Israel, saying,
"Take heed and listen, O Israel:
[a]This day you have become the
people of the LORD your God.
10 "Therefore you shall obey the
voice of the LORD your God, and
observe His commandments and
His statutes which I command you
today."

Curses Pronounced from Mount Ebal

11 And Moses commanded the
people on the same day, saying,
12 "These shall stand [a]on Mount
Gerizim to bless the people, when
you have crossed over the Jordan:
Simeon, Levi, Judah, Issachar, Jo-
seph, and Benjamin;
13 "and [a]these shall stand on
Mount Ebal to curse: Reuben, Gad,
Asher, Zebulun, Dan, and Naph-
tali.
14 "And [a]the Levites shall speak
with a loud voice and say to all
the men of Israel:
15 [a]'Cursed *is* the one who makes
a carved or molded image, [1]an
abomination to the LORD, the work
of the hands of the craftsman, and
sets *it* up in secret.'
[b]"And all the people shall an-
swer and say, 'Amen!'
16 [a]'Cursed *is* the one who treats
his father or his mother with con-
tempt.'
"And all the people shall say,
'Amen!'
17 [a]'Cursed *is* the one who moves
his neighbor's landmark.'
"And all the people shall say,
'Amen!'
18 [a]'Cursed *is* the one who makes
the blind to wander off the road.'
"And all the people shall say,
'Amen!'
19 [a]'Cursed *is* the one who per-
verts the justice due the stranger,
the fatherless, and widow.'
"And all the people shall say,
'Amen!'
20 [a]'Cursed *is* the one who lies
with his father's wife, because he
has uncovered his father's bed.'
"And all the people shall say,
'Amen!'
21 [a]'Cursed *is* the one who lies
with any kind of animal.'
"And all the people shall say,
'Amen!'
22 [a]'Cursed *is* the one who lies
with his sister, the daughter of his
father or the daughter of his
mother.'
"And all the people shall say,
'Amen!'
23 [a]'Cursed *is* the one who lies
with his mother-in-law.'
"And all the people shall say,
'Amen!'
24 [a]'Cursed *is* the one who attacks
his neighbor secretly.'
"And all the people shall say,
'Amen!'
25 [a]'Cursed *is* the one who takes
a bribe to slay an innocent person.'
"And all the people shall say,
'Amen!'
26 [a]'Cursed *is* the one who does
not confirm *all* the words of this
law.'
"And all the people shall say,
'Amen!'

Blessings on Obedience

28 "Now it shall come to pass,
[a]if you diligently obey the
voice of the LORD your God, to ob-
serve carefully all His command-
ments which I command you to-
day, that the LORD your God [b]will
set you high above all nations of
the earth.
2 "And all these blessings shall
come upon you and [a]overtake you,
because you obey the voice of the
LORD your God:
3 [a]"Blessed *shall* you *be* in the
city, and blessed *shall* you *be* [b]in
the country.
4 "Blessed *shall be* [a]the [1]fruit of
your body, the produce of your
ground and the increase of your
herds, the increase of your cattle
and the offspring of your flocks.
5 "Blessed *shall be* your basket
and your kneading bowl.
6 [a]"Blessed *shall* you *be* when
you come in, and blessed *shall* you
be when you go out.
7 "The LORD [a]will cause your en-
emies who rise against you to be
defeated before your face; they
shall come out against you one
way and flee before you seven
ways.
8 "The LORD will [a]command the
blessing on you in your store-
houses and in all to which you [b]set
your hand, and He will bless you
in the land which the LORD your
God is giving you.

9 [a]Deut. 26:18
12 [a]Deut. 11:29; Josh. 8:33; Judg. 9:7
13 [a]Deut. 11:29; Josh. 8:33
14 [a]Deut. 33:10; Josh. 8:33; Dan. 9:11
15 [a]Ex. 20:4, 23; 34:17; Lev. 19:4; 26:1; Deut. 4:16, 23; Is. 44:9; Hos. 13:2 [b]Num. 5:22; Jer. 11:5; 1 Cor. 14:16 [1]*a detestable thing*
16 [a]Ex. 20:12; Lev. 19:3; 20:9; Deut. 5:16; 21:18–21; Ezek. 22:7
17 [a]Deut. 19:14; Prov. 22:28
18 [a]Lev. 19:14
19 [a]Ex. 22:21, 22; 23:9; Lev. 19:33; Deut. 10:18; 24:17
20 [a]Lev. 18:8; 20:11; Deut. 22:30; 1 Cor. 5:1
21 [a]Ex. 22:19; Lev. 18:23; 20:15, 16
22 [a]Lev. 18:9
23 [a]Lev. 18:17; 20:14
24 [a]Ex. 20:13; 21:12; Lev. 24:17; Num. 35:30, 31
25 [a]Ex. 23:7; Ps. 15:5; Ezek. 22:12
26 [a]Ps. 119:21; Jer. 11:3; Gal. 3:10

CHAPTER 28

1 [a]Ex. 15:26; Lev. 26:3–13; Deut. 7:12–26; 11:13 [b]Deut. 26:19; 1 Chr. 14:2
2 [a]Deut. 28:15
3 [a]Ps. 128:1, 4 [b]Gen. 39:5
4 [a]Gen. 22:17 [1]*offspring*
6 [a]Ps. 121:8
7 [a]Lev. 26:7, 8
8 [a]Lev. 25:21 [b]Deut. 15:10

9 [a]"The LORD will establish you
as a holy people to Himself, just
as He has sworn to you, if you
keep the commandments of the
LORD your God and walk in His
ways.
10 "Then all peoples of the earth
shall see that you are [a]called by
the name of the LORD, and they
shall be [b]afraid of you.
11 "And [a]the LORD will grant you
plenty of goods, in the fruit of your
body, in the increase of your live-
stock, and in the produce of your
ground, in the land of which the
LORD [1]swore to your fathers to give
you.
12 "The LORD will open to you His
good [1]treasure, the heavens, [a]to
give the rain to your land in its sea-
son, and [b]to bless all the work of
your hand. [c]You shall lend to
many nations, but you shall not
borrow.
13 "And the LORD will make [a]you
the head and not the tail; you shall
be above only, and not be beneath,
if you [1]heed the commandments of
the LORD your God, which I com-
mand you today, and are careful
to observe *them.*
14 [a]"So you shall not turn aside
from any of the words which I
command you this day, *to* the right
or the left, to go after other gods
to serve them.

Curses on Disobedience

15 "But it shall come to pass, [a]if
you do not obey the voice of the
LORD your God, to observe care-
fully all His commandments and
His statutes which I command you
today, that all these curses will
come upon you and overtake you:
16 "Cursed *shall* you *be* in the
city, and cursed *shall* you *be* in the
country.
17 "Cursed *shall be* your basket
and your kneading bowl.
18 "Cursed *shall be* the [1]fruit of
your body and the produce of your
land, the increase of your cattle
and the offspring of your flocks.
19 "Cursed *shall* you *be* when you
come in, and cursed *shall* you *be*
when you go out.
20 "The LORD will send on you
[a]cursing, [b]confusion, and [c]rebuke
in all that you set your hand to do,
until you are destroyed and until
you perish quickly, because of the
wickedness of your doings in
which you have forsaken Me.
21 "The LORD will make the
[1]plague cling to you until He has
consumed you from the land
which you are going to possess.
22 [a]"The LORD will strike you with
consumption, with fever, with in-
flammation, with severe burning
fever, with the sword, with
[b]scorching,[1] and with mildew;
they shall pursue you until you
perish.
23 "And [a]your heavens which *are*
over your head shall be bronze,
and the earth which is under you
shall be iron.
24 "The LORD will change the rain
of your land to powder and dust;
from the heaven it shall come
down on you until you are de-
stroyed.
25 [a]"The LORD will cause you to
be defeated before your enemies;
you shall go out one way against
them and flee seven ways before
them; and you shall become [1]trou-
blesome to all the kingdoms of the
earth.
26 [a]"Your carcasses shall be food
for all the birds of the air and the
beasts of the earth, and no one
shall frighten *them* away.
27 "The LORD will strike you with
[a]the boils of Egypt, with [b]tumors,
with the scab, and with the itch,
from which you cannot be healed.
28 "The LORD will strike you with
madness and blindness and [a]con-
fusion of heart.
29 "And you shall [a]grope at noon-
day, as a blind man gropes in
darkness; you shall not prosper in
your ways; you shall be only op-
pressed and plundered continu-
ally, and no one shall save *you.*
30 [a]"You shall betroth a wife, but
another man shall lie with her;
[b]you shall build a house, but you
shall not dwell in it; [c]you shall
plant a vineyard, but shall not
gather its grapes.
31 "Your ox *shall be* slaughtered
before your eyes, but you shall not
eat of it; your donkey *shall be* vio-
lently taken away from before you,
and shall not be restored to you;
your sheep *shall be* given to your
enemies, and you shall have no
one to rescue *them.*

9 [a]Ex. 19:5, 6
10 [a]Num. 6:27; 2 Chr. 7:14; Is. 63:19; Dan. 9:18, 19 [b]Deut. 11:25
11 [a]Deut. 30:9 [1]*promised*
12 [a]Lev. 26:4; Deut. 11:14 [b]Deut. 14:29 [c]Deut. 15:6 [1]*storehouse*
13 [a][Is. 9:14, 15] [1]*listen to*
14 [a]Deut. 5:32; Josh. 1:7
15 [a]Lev. 26:14–39; Josh. 23:15; Dan. 9:10–14; Mal. 2:2
18 [1]*offspring*
20 [a]Mal. 2:2 [b]Is. 65:14 [c]Ps. 80:16; Is. 30:17
21 [1]*pestilence*
22 [a]Lev. 26:16 [b]Amos 4:9 [1]*blight*
23 [a]Lev. 26:19
25 [a]Deut. 32:30 [1]*a terror*
26 [a]1 Sam. 17:44; Ps. 79:2
27 [a]Ex. 15:26 [b]1 Sam. 5:6
28 [a]Jer. 4:9
29 [a]Job 5:14
30 [a]2 Sam. 12:11; Job 31:10; Jer. 8:10 [b]Amos 5:11; Zeph. 1:13 [c]Deut. 20:6; Job 31:8; Jer. 12:13; Mic. 6:15

32 "Your sons and your daughters
shall be given to [a]another people,
and your eyes shall look and [b]fail
with longing for them all day long;
and *there shall be* [1]no strength in
your [c]hand.
33 "A nation whom you have not
known shall eat [a]the fruit of your
land and the produce of your la-
bor, and you shall be only op-
pressed and crushed continually.
34 "So you shall be driven mad
because of the sight which your
eyes see.
35 "The LORD will strike you in the
knees and on the legs with severe
boils which cannot be healed, and
from the sole of your foot to the
top of your head.
36 "The LORD will [a]bring you and
the king whom you set over you
to a nation which neither you nor
your fathers have known, and
[b]there you shall serve other gods—
wood and stone.
37 "And you shall become [a]an[1] as-
tonishment, a proverb, [b]and a by-
word among all nations where the
LORD will drive you.
38 [a]"You shall carry much seed
out to the field but gather little in,
for [b]the locust shall [1]consume it.
39 "You shall plant vineyards and
tend *them*, but you shall neither
drink *of* the [a]wine nor gather the
grapes; for the worms shall eat
them.
40 "You shall have olive trees
throughout all your territory, but
you shall not anoint *yourself* with
the oil; for your olives shall drop
off.
41 "You shall beget sons and
daughters, but they shall not be
yours; for [a]they shall go into cap-
tivity.
42 "Locusts shall [1]consume all
your trees and the produce of your
land.
43 "The alien who *is* among you
shall rise higher and higher above
you, and you shall come down
lower and lower.
44 "He shall lend to you, but you
shall not lend to him; he shall be
the head, and you shall be the tail.
45 "Moreover all these curses
shall come upon you and pursue
and overtake you, until you are de-
stroyed, because you [1]did not obey
the voice of the LORD your God,

32 [a]2 Chr. 29:9 [b]Ps. 119:82 [c]Neh. 5:5 [1]*nothing you can do*

33 [a]Lev. 26:16; Jer. 5:15, 17

36 [a]2 Kin. 17:4, 6; 24:12, 14; 25:7, 11; 2 Chr. 36:1–21; Jer. 39:1–9 [b]Deut. 4:28; Jer. 16:13

37 [a]1 Kin. 9:7, 8; Jer. 24:9; 25:9 [b]Ps. 44:14 [1]*a thing of horror*

38 [a]Mic. 6:15; Hag. 1:6 [b]Ex. 10:4; Joel 1:4 [1]*devour*

39 [a]Zeph. 1:13

41 [a]Lam. 1:5

42 [1]*possess*

45 [1]*did not listen to*

46 [a]Num. 26:10; Is. 8:18; Ezek. 14:8

47 [a]Deut. 12:7; Neh. 9:35–37 [b]Deut. 32:15

48 [a]Lam. 4:4–6 [b]Jer. 28:13, 14

49 [a]Is. 5:26–30; 7:18–20; Jer. 5:15 [b]Jer. 48:40; 49:22; Lam. 4:19; Hos. 8:1

50 [a]2 Chr. 36:17

52 [a]2 Kin. 25:1, 2, 4

53 [a]Lev. 26:29; 2 Kin. 6:28, 29; Jer. 19:9; Lam. 2:20; 4:10 [1]*offspring*

54 [a]Deut. 15:9 [b]Deut. 13:6 [1]Lit. *tender* [2]Lit. *his eye shall be evil toward*

to keep His commandments and
His statutes which He commanded
you.
46 "And they shall be upon [a]you
for a sign and a wonder, and on
your descendants forever.
47 [a]"Because you did not serve
the LORD your God with joy and
gladness of heart, [b]for the abun-
dance of everything,
48 "therefore you shall serve your
enemies, whom the LORD will send
against you, in [a]hunger, in thirst,
in nakedness, and in need of
everything; and He [b]will put a
yoke of iron on your neck until He
has destroyed you.
49 [a]"The LORD will bring a nation
against you from afar, from the
end of the earth, [b]*as swift* as the
eagle flies, a nation whose lan-
guage you will not understand,
50 "a nation of fierce counte-
nance, [a]which does not respect the
elderly nor show favor to the
young.
51 "And they shall eat the in-
crease of your livestock and the
produce of your land, until you are
destroyed; they shall not leave you
grain or new wine or oil, *or* the
increase of your cattle or the off-
spring of your flocks, until they
have destroyed you.
52 "They shall [a]besiege you at all
your gates until your high and for-
tified walls, in which you trust,
come down throughout all your
land; and they shall besiege you
at all your gates throughout all
your land which the LORD your
God has given you.
53 [a]"You shall eat the [1]fruit of
your own body, the flesh of your
sons and your daughters whom
the LORD your God has given you,
in the siege and desperate straits
in which your enemy shall distress
you.
54 "The [1]sensitive and very re-
fined man among you [a]will[2] be
hostile toward his brother, toward
[b]the wife of his bosom, and toward
the rest of his children whom he
leaves behind,
55 "so that he will not give any of
them the flesh of his children
whom he will eat, because he has
nothing left in the siege and des-
perate straits in which your enemy
shall distress you at all your gates.

56 "The [1]tender and [2]delicate
woman among you, who would
not venture to set the sole of her
foot on the ground because of her
delicateness and sensitivity, [3]will
refuse to the husband of her bo-
som, and to her son and her
daughter,
57 "her [1]placenta which comes
out [a]from between her feet and her
children whom she bears; for she
will eat them secretly for lack of
everything in the siege and desper-
ate straits in which your enemy
shall distress you at all your gates.
58 "If you do not carefully observe
all the words of this law that are
written in this book, that you may
fear [a]this glorious and awesome
name, THE LORD YOUR GOD,
59 "then the LORD will bring upon
you and your descendants [a]ex-
traordinary plagues—great and
prolonged plagues—and serious
and prolonged sicknesses.
60 "Moreover He will bring back
on you all [a]the diseases of Egypt,
of which you were afraid, and they
shall cling to you.
61 "Also every sickness and every
plague, which *is* not written in this
Book of the Law, will the LORD
bring upon you until you are de-
stroyed.
62 "You [a]shall be left few in num-
ber, whereas you were [b]as the
stars of heaven in multitude, be-
cause you would not obey the
voice of the LORD your God.
63 "And it shall be, *that* just as
the LORD [a]rejoiced over you to do
you good and multiply you, so the
LORD [b]will rejoice over you to de-
stroy you and bring you to noth-
ing; and you shall be [c]plucked[1]
from off the land which you go to
possess.
64 "Then the LORD [a]will scatter
you among all peoples, from one
end of the earth to the other, and
[b]there you shall serve other gods,
which neither you nor your fathers
have known—wood and stone.
65 "And [a]among those nations
you shall find no rest, nor shall the
sole of your foot have a resting
place; [b]but there the LORD will give
you a [1]trembling heart, failing
eyes, and [c]anguish of soul.
66 "Your life shall hang in doubt
before you; you shall fear day and

56 [1]*sensitive* [2]*refined* [3]Lit. *her eye shall be evil toward*
57 [a]Gen. 49:10 [1]*afterbirth*
58 [a]Ex. 6:3
59 [a]Dan. 9:12
60 [a]Deut. 7:15
62 [a]Deut. 4:27 [b]Deut. 10:22; Neh. 9:23
63 [a]Deut. 30:9; Jer. 32:41 [b]Prov. 1:26; [Is. 1:24] [c]Jer. 12:14; 45:4 [1]*torn*
64 [a]Lev. 26:33; Deut. 4:27, 28; Neh. 1:8; Jer. 16:13; Amos 9:9 [b]Deut. 28:36
65 [a]Lam. 1:3; Amos 9:4 [b]Lev. 26:36 [c]Lev. 26:16 [1]*anxious*
67 [a]Job 7:4 [b]Deut. 28:34
68 [a]Jer. 43:7; Hos. 8:13 [b]Deut. 17:16

CHAPTER 29

1 [a]Lev. 26:46; Deut. 5:2, 3
2 [a]Ex. 19:4; Deut. 11:7
3 [a]Deut. 4:34; 7:19
4 [a][Is. 6:9, 10; Ezek. 12:2]; Matt. 13:14; [Acts 28:26, 27]; Rom. 11:8; [Eph. 4:18] [1]*understand* or *know*
5 [a]Deut. 1:3; 8:2 [b]Deut. 8:4
6 [a]Ex. 16:12; Deut. 8:3
7 [a]Num. 21:23, 24; Deut. 2:26—3:3
8 [a]Num. 32:33; Deut. 3:12, 13
9 [a]Deut. 4:6; 1 Kin. 2:3 [b]Josh. 1:7

night, and have no assurance of
life.
67 [a]"In the morning you shall say,
'Oh, that it were evening!' And at
evening you shall say, 'Oh, that it
were morning!' because of the fear
which terrifies your heart, and
[b]because of the sight which your
eyes see.
68 "And the LORD [a]will take you
back to Egypt in ships, by the way
of which I said to you, [b]'You shall
never see it again.' And there you
shall be offered for sale to your en-
emies as male and female slaves,
but no one will buy *you.*"

The Covenant Renewed in Moab

29 These *are* the words of the
covenant which the LORD
commanded Moses to make with
the children of Israel in the land
of Moab, besides the [a]covenant
which He made with them in
Horeb.
2 Now Moses called all Israel
and said to them: [a]"You have seen
all that the LORD did before your
eyes in the land of Egypt, to Pha-
raoh and to all his servants and
to all his land—
3 [a]"the great trials which your
eyes have seen, the signs, and
those great wonders.
4 "Yet [a]the LORD has not given
you a heart to [1]perceive and eyes
to see and ears to hear, to this *very*
day.
5 [a]"And I have led you forty
years in the wilderness. [b]Your
clothes have not worn out on you,
and your sandals have not worn
out on your feet.
6 [a]"You have not eaten bread,
nor have you drunk wine or *simi-
lar* drink, that you may know that
I *am* the LORD your God.
7 "And when you came to this
place, [a]Sihon king of Heshbon and
Og king of Bashan came out
against us to battle, and we con-
quered them.
8 "We took their land and [a]gave
it as an inheritance to the Reuben-
ites, to the Gadites, and to half the
tribe of Manasseh.
9 "Therefore [a]keep the words of
this covenant, and do them, that
you may [b]prosper in all that you
do.
10 "All of you stand today before

the LORD your God: your leaders
and your tribes and your elders
and your officers, all the men of
Israel,
11 "your little ones and your
wives—also the stranger who *is* in
your camp, from [a]the one who cuts
your wood to the one who draws
your water—
12 "that you may enter into cov-
enant with the LORD your God, and
[a]into His oath, which the LORD
your God makes with you today,
13 "that He may [a]establish you to-
day as a people for Himself, and
that He may be God to you, [b]just
as He has spoken to you, and [c]just
as He has sworn to your fathers,
to Abraham, Isaac, and Jacob.
14 "I make this covenant and this
oath, [a]not with you alone,
15 "but with *him* who stands here
with us today before the LORD our
God, [a]as well as with *him* who *is*
not here with us today
16 (for you know that we dwelt in
the land of Egypt and that we
came through the nations which
you passed by,
17 and you saw their [1]abomina-
tions and their idols which *were*
among them—wood and stone and
silver and gold);
18 "so that there may not be
among you man or woman or fam-
ily or tribe, [a]whose heart turns
away today from the LORD our
God, to go *and* serve the gods of
these nations, [b]and that there may
not be among you a root bearing
[c]bitterness or wormwood;
19 "and so it may not happen,
when he hears the words of this
curse, that he blesses himself in his
heart, saying, 'I shall have peace,
even though I [1]follow the [a]dictates
of my heart'—[b]as though the
drunkard could be included with
the sober.
20 [a]"The LORD would not spare
him; for then [b]the anger of the
LORD and [c]His jealousy would
burn against that man, and every
curse that is written in this book
would settle on him, and the LORD
[d]would blot out his name from un-
der heaven.
21 "And the LORD [a]would separate
him from all the tribes of Israel for
adversity, according to all the
curses of the covenant that are
written in this Book of the [b]Law,
22 "so that the coming generation
of your children who rise up after
you, and the foreigner who comes
from a far land, would say, when
they [a]see the plagues of that land
and the sicknesses which the LORD
has laid on it:
23 'The whole land *is* brimstone,
[a]salt, and burning; it is not sown,
nor does it bear, nor does any
grass grow there, [b]like the over-
throw of Sodom and Gomorrah,
Admah, and Zeboiim, which the
LORD overthrew in His anger and
His wrath.'
24 "All nations would say, [a]'Why
has the LORD done so to this land?
What does the heat of this great
anger mean?'
25 "Then *people* would say: 'Be-
cause they have forsaken the cov-
enant of the LORD God of their fa-
thers, which He made with them
when He brought them out of the
land of Egypt;
26 'for they went and served other
gods and worshiped them, gods
that they did not know and that
He had not given to them.
27 'Then the anger of the LORD
was aroused against this land, [a]to
bring on it every curse that is writ-
ten in this book.
28 'And the LORD [a]uprooted them
from their land in anger, in wrath,
and in great indignation, and cast
them into another land, as *it is* this
day.'
29 "The secret *things belong* to
the LORD our God, but those *things*
which are revealed *belong* to us
and to our children forever, that
we may do all the words of this
law.

The Blessing of Returning to God

30 "Now [a]it shall come to pass,
when [b]all these things come
upon you, the blessing and the
[c]curse which I have set before you,
and [d]you [1]call *them* to mind
among all the nations where the
LORD your God drives you,
2 "and you [a]return to the LORD
your God and obey His voice, ac-
cording to all that I command you
today, you and your children, with
all your heart and with all your
soul,
3 [a]"that the LORD your God will

11 [a]Josh. 9:21, 23, 27
12 [a]Neh. 10:29
13 [a]Deut. 28:9 [b]Ex. 6:7 [c]Gen. 17:7, 8
14 [a][Jer. 31:31; Heb. 8:7, 8]
15 [a]Acts 2:39
17 [1]*detestable things*
18 [a]Deut. 11:16 [b]Heb. 12:15 [c]Deut. 32:32; Acts 8:23
19 [a]Jer. 3:17; 7:24 [b]Is. 30:1 [1]*walk in the stubbornness* or *imagination*
20 [a]Ezek. 14:7 [b]Ps. 74:1 [c]Ps. 79:5; Ezek. 23:25 [d]Ex. 32:33; Deut. 9:14; 2 Kin. 14:27
21 [a][Matt. 24:51] [b]Deut. 30:10
22 [a]Jer. 19:8; 49:17; 50:13
23 [a]Jer. 17:6; Zeph. 2:9 [b]Gen. 19:24, 25; Is. 1:9; Jer. 20:16; Hos. 11:8
24 [a]1 Kin. 9:8; Jer. 22:8
27 [a]Dan. 9:11
28 [a]1 Kin. 14:15; 2 Chr. 7:20; Ps. 52:5; Prov. 2:22

CHAPTER 30

1 [a]Lev. 26:40 [b]Deut. 28:2 [c]Deut. 28:15–45 [d]Deut. 4:29, 30 [1]Lit. *cause them to return to your heart*
2 [a]Deut. 4:29, 30; Neh. 1:9; Is. 55:7; Lam. 3:40; Joel 2:12
3 [a]Ps. 106:45; Jer. 29:14; Lam. 3:22, 32

bring you back from captivity, and
have compassion on you, and
[b]gather you again from all the na-
tions where the LORD your God has
scattered you.
4 [a]"If *any* of you are driven out
to the farthest *parts* under heaven,
from there the LORD your God will
gather you, and from there He will
bring you.
5 "Then the LORD your God will
bring you to the land which your
fathers possessed, and you shall
possess it. He will prosper you and
multiply you more than your fa-
thers.
6 "And [a]the LORD your God will
circumcise your heart and the
heart of your descendants, to love
the LORD your God with all your
heart and with all your soul, that
you may live.
7 "Also the LORD your God will
put all these [a]curses on your ene-
mies and on those who hate you,
who persecuted you.
8 "And you will [a]again obey the
voice of the LORD and do all His
commandments which I command
you today.
9 [a]"The LORD your God will
make you abound in all the work
of your hand, in the [1]fruit of your
body, in the increase of your live-
stock, and in the produce of your
land for good. For the LORD will
again [b]rejoice over you for good
as He rejoiced over your fathers,
10 "if you obey the voice of the
LORD your God, to keep His com-
mandments and His statutes
which are written in this Book of
the Law, *and* if you turn to the
LORD your God with all your heart
and with all your soul.

The Choice of Life or Death

11 "For this commandment which
I command you today [a]*is* [1]not *too*
mysterious for you, nor *is* it far off.
12 [a]"It *is* not in heaven, that you
should say, 'Who will ascend into
heaven for us and bring it to us,
that we may hear it and do it?'
13 "Nor *is* it beyond the sea, that
you should say, 'Who will go over
the sea for us and bring it to us,
that we may hear it and do it?'
14 "But the word *is* very near you,
[a]in your mouth and in your heart,
that you may do it.

3 [b]Ps. 147:2; Jer. 32:37; Ezek. 34:13
4 [a]Deut. 28:64; Neh. 1:9; Is. 62:11
6 [a]Deut. 10:16; Jer. 32:39; Ezek. 11:19
7 [a]Is. 54:15–17; Jer. 30:16, 20
8 [a]Zeph. 3:20
9 [a]Deut. 28:11 [b]Deut. 28:63; Jer. 32:41 [1]*offspring*
11 [a]Is. 45:19 [1]*not hidden from*
12 [a]Prov. 30:4; Rom. 10:6–8
14 [a]Rom. 10:8
15 [a]Deut. 30:1, 19
18 [a]Deut. 4:26; 8:19
19 [a]Deut. 4:26 [b]Deut. 30:15
20 [a]Ps. 27:1; [John 11:25; 14:6; Col. 3:4]

CHAPTER 31

2 [a]Ex. 7:7; Deut. 34:7 [b]Num. 27:17; 1 Kin. 3:7 [c]Num. 20:12
3 [a]Deut. 9:3; Josh. 11:23 [b]Num. 27:18 [c]Num. 27:21
4 [a]Deut. 3:21 [b]Num. 21:24, 33
5 [a]Deut. 7:2; 20:10–20
6 [a]Josh. 10:25; 1 Chr. 22:13 [b]Deut. 1:29

15 "See, [a]I have set before you to-
day life and good, death and evil,
16 "in that I command you today
to love the LORD your God, to walk
in His ways, and to keep His com-
mandments, His statutes, and His
judgments, that you may live and
multiply; and the LORD your God
will bless you in the land which
you go to possess.
17 "But if your heart turns away
so that you do not hear, and are
drawn away, and worship other
gods and serve them,
18 [a]"I announce to you today that
you shall surely perish; you shall
not prolong *your* days in the land
which you cross over the Jordan
to go in and possess.
19 [a]"I call heaven and earth as
witnesses today against you, *that*
[b]I have set before you life and
death, blessing and cursing; there-
fore choose life, that both you and
your descendants may live;
20 "that you may love the LORD
your God, that you may obey His
voice, and that you may cling to
Him, for He *is* your [a]life and the
length of your days; and that you
may dwell in the land which the
LORD swore to your fathers, to
Abraham, Isaac, and Jacob, to give
them."

Joshua the New Leader of Israel

31 Then Moses went and spoke
these words to all Israel.
2 And he said to them: "I [a]*am*
one hundred and twenty years old
today. I can no longer [b]go out and
come in. Also the LORD has said
to me, [c]'You shall not cross over
this Jordan.'
3 "The LORD your God [a]Himself
crosses over before you; He will
destroy these nations from before
you, and you shall dispossess
them. [b]Joshua himself crosses
over before you, just [c]as the LORD
has said.
4 [a]"And the LORD will do to them
[b]as He did to Sihon and Og, the
kings of the Amorites and their
land, when He destroyed them.
5 [a]"The LORD will give them over
to you, that you may do to them
according to every commandment
which I have commanded you.
6 [a]"Be strong and of good cour-
age, [b]do not fear nor be afraid of

them; for the LORD your God, [c]He
is the One who goes with you. [d]He
will not leave you nor forsake
you."
7 Then Moses called Joshua and
said to him in the sight of all Israel,
[a]"Be strong and of good courage,
for you must go with this peo-
ple to the land which the LORD
has sworn to their fathers to give
them, and you shall cause them to
inherit it.
8 "And the LORD, [a]He *is* the One
who goes before you. [b]He will be
with you, He will not leave you nor
forsake you; do not fear nor be dis-
mayed."

The Law to Be Read Every Seven Years

9 So Moses wrote this law [a]and
delivered it to the priests, the sons
of Levi, [b]who bore the ark of the
covenant of the LORD, and to all
the elders of Israel.
10 And Moses commanded them,
saying: "At the end of *every* seven
years, at the appointed time in the
[a]year of release, [b]at the Feast of
Tabernacles,
11 "when all Israel comes to [a]ap-
pear before the LORD your God in
the [b]place which He chooses, [c]you
shall read this law before all Israel
in their hearing.
12 [a]"Gather the people together,
men and women and little ones,
and the stranger who *is* within
your gates, that they may hear and
that they may learn to fear the
LORD your God and carefully ob-
serve all the words of this law,
13 "and *that* their children, [a]who
have not known it, [b]may hear and
learn to fear the LORD your God
as long as you live in the land
which you cross the Jordan to pos-
sess."

Prediction of Israel's Rebellion

14 Then the LORD said to Moses,
[a]"Behold, the days approach when
you must die; call Joshua, and
present yourselves in the taberna-
cle of meeting, that [b]I may [1]inau-
gurate him." So Moses and Joshua
went and presented themselves in
the tabernacle of meeting.
15 Now [a]the LORD appeared at the
tabernacle in a pillar of cloud, and
the pillar of cloud stood above the
door of the tabernacle.
16 And the LORD said to Moses:
"Behold, you will [1]rest with your
fathers; and this people will [a]rise
and [b]play the harlot with the gods
of the foreigners of the land, where
they go *to be* among them, and
they will [c]forsake Me and [d]break
My covenant which I have made
with them.
17 "Then My anger shall be
[a]aroused against them in that day,
and [b]I will forsake them, and I will
[c]hide My face from them, and they
shall be [1]devoured. And many
evils and troubles shall befall
them, so that they will say in that
day, [d]'Have not these evils come
upon us because our God *is* [e]not
among us?'
18 "And [a]I will surely hide My
face in that day because of all the
evil which they have done, in that
they have turned to other gods.
19 "Now therefore, write down
this song for yourselves, and teach
it to the children of Israel; put it
in their mouths, that this song may
be [a]a witness for Me against the
children of Israel.
20 "When I have brought them to
the land flowing with milk and
honey, of which I swore to their
fathers, and they have eaten and
filled themselves [a]and grown fat,
[b]then they will turn to other gods
and serve them; and they will
provoke Me and break My cov-
enant.
21 "Then it shall be, [a]when many
evils and troubles have come upon
them, that this song will testify
against them as a witness; for it
will not be forgotten in the mouths
of their descendants, for [b]I know
the inclination [c]of their behavior
today, even before I have brought
them to the land of which I swore
to give them."
22 Therefore Moses wrote this
song the same day, and taught it
to the children of Israel.
23 [a]Then He inaugurated Joshua
the son of Nun, and said, [b]"Be
strong and of good courage; for
you shall bring the children of Is-
rael into the land of which I swore
to them, and I will be with you."
24 So it was, when Moses had
completed writing the words of

6 [c]Deut. 20:4 [d]Josh. 1:5; Heb. 13:5
7 [a]Num. 27:19; Deut. 31:23; Josh. 1:6
8 [a]Ex. 13:21 [b]Deut. 31:6; Josh. 1:5; 1 Chr. 28:20; Heb. 13:5
9 [a]Deut. 17:18; 31:25, 26 [b]Num. 4:5, 6, 15; Deut. 10:8; 31:25, 26; Josh. 3:3
10 [a]Deut. 15:1, 2 [b]Lev. 23:34; Deut. 16:13
11 [a]Deut. 16:16 [b]Deut. 12:5 [c]Josh. 8:34; 2 Kin. 23:2
12 [a]Deut. 4:10
13 [a]Deut. 11:2 [b]Ps. 78:6, 7
14 [a]Num. 27:13 [b]Num. 27:19; Deut. 3:28 [1]*commission*
15 [a]Ex. 33:9
16 [a]Deut. 29:22 [b]Ex. 34:15; Deut. 4:25–28; Judg. 2:11, 12, 17 [c]Deut. 32:15 [d]Judg. 2:20 [1]Die and join your ancestors
17 [a]Judg. 2:14; 6:13 [b]2 Chr. 15:2 [c]Deut. 32:20 [d]Judg. 6:13 [e]Num. 14:42 [1]*consumed*
18 [a]Deut. 31:17; [Is. 1:15, 16]
19 [a]Deut. 31:22, 26
20 [a]Deut. 32:15–17 [b]Deut. 31:16
21 [a]Deut. 31:17 [b]Hos. 5:3 [c]Amos 5:25, 26
23 [a]Num. 27:23; Deut. 31:14 [b]Deut. 31:7

this law in a book, when they were
finished,
25 that Moses commanded the
Levites, who bore the ark of the
covenant of the LORD, saying:
26 "Take this Book of the Law,
[a]and put it beside the ark of the
covenant of the LORD your God,
that it may be there [b]as a witness
against you;
27 [a]"for I know your rebellion and
your [b]stiff neck. *If* today, while I
am yet alive with you, you have
been rebellious against the LORD,
then how much more after my
death?
28 "Gather to me all the elders of
your tribes, and your officers, that
I may speak these words in their
hearing [a]and call heaven and earth
to witness against them.
29 "For I know that after my death
you will [a]become utterly corrupt,
and turn aside from the way which
I have commanded you. And [b]evil
will befall you [c]in the latter days,
because you will do evil in the
sight of the LORD, to provoke Him
to anger through the work of your
hands."

The Song of Moses

30 Then Moses spoke in the hear-
ing of all the assembly of Israel the
words of this song until they were
ended:

32 "Give [a]ear, O heavens, and
I will speak;
And hear, O [b]earth, the words of
my mouth.
2 Let [a]my [1]teaching drop as the
rain,
My speech distill as the dew,
[b]As raindrops on the tender herb,
And as showers on the grass.
3 For I proclaim the [a]name of the
LORD:
[b]Ascribe greatness to our God.
4 *He is* [a]the Rock, [b]His work *is*
perfect;
For all His ways *are* justice,
[c]A God of truth and [d]without
injustice;
Righteous and upright *is* He.

5 "They[a] have corrupted
themselves;
They are not His children,
Because of their blemish:
A [b]perverse and crooked
generation.

26 [a]2 Kin. 22:8 [b]Deut. 31:19
27 [a]Deut. 9:7, 24 [b]Ex. 32:9; Deut. 9:6, 13
28 [a]Deut. 30:19
29 [a]Deut. 32:5; Judg. 2:19; [Acts 20:29, 30] [b]Deut. 28:15 [c]Gen. 49:1; Deut. 4:30

CHAPTER 32

1 [a]Deut. 4:26; Ps. 50:4; Is. 1:2 [b]Jer. 6:19
2 [a]Is. 55:10, 11 [b]Ps. 72:6 [1]*doctrine*
3 [a]Deut. 28:58 [b]1 Chr. 29:11
4 [a]Deut. 32:15, 18, 30; Ps. 18:2 [b]2 Sam. 22:31 [c]Deut. 7:9; Is. 65:16; Jer. 10:10 [d]Job 34:10
5 [a]Deut. 4:25; 31:29 [b]Phil. 2:15
6 [a]Ps. 116:12 [b]Ex. 4:22; Deut. 1:31; Is. 63:16 [c]Ps. 74:2 [d]Deut. 32:15 [1]*repay the*
7 [a]Ps. 44:1 [b]Ex. 12:26; 13:14; Ps. 78:5–8
8 [a]Acts 17:26 [b]Gen. 11:8 [1]LXX, DSS *angels of God;* Symmachus, Lat. *sons of God*
9 [a]Ex. 19:5
10 [a]Jer. 2:6; Hos. 13:5 [b]Ps. 17:8; Prov. 7:2; Zech. 2:8 [1]*pupil*
11 [a]Is. 31:5
13 [a]Is. 58:14
14 [a]Ps. 81:16 [b]Gen. 49:11
15 [a]Deut. 31:20 [b]Is. 1:4 [c]Is. 51:13

6 Do you thus [a]deal[1] with the LORD,
O foolish and unwise people?
Is He not [b]your Father, *who*
[c]bought you?
Has He not [d]made you and
established you?

7 "Remember[a] the days of old,
Consider the years of many
generations.
[b]Ask your father, and he will show
you;
Your elders, and they will tell
you:
8 When the Most High [a]divided
their inheritance to the
nations,
When He [b]separated the sons of
Adam,
He set the boundaries of the
peoples
According to the number of the
[1]children of Israel.
9 For [a]the LORD's portion *is* His
people;
Jacob *is* the place of His
inheritance.

10 "He found him [a]in a desert land
And in the wasteland, a howling
wilderness;
He encircled him, He instructed
him,
He [b]kept him as the [1]apple of His
eye.
11 [a]As an eagle stirs up its nest,
Hovers over its young,
Spreading out its wings, taking
them up,
Carrying them on its wings,
12 *So* the LORD alone led him,
And *there was* no foreign god
with him.

13 "He[a] made him ride in the heights
of the earth,
That he might eat the produce of
the fields;
He made him draw honey from
the rock,
And oil from the flinty rock;
14 Curds from the cattle, and milk
of the flock,
[a]With fat of lambs;
And rams of the breed of Bashan,
and goats,
With the choicest wheat;
And you drank wine, the [b]blood
of the grapes.

15 "But Jeshurun grew fat and
kicked;
[a]You grew fat, you grew thick,
You are obese!
Then he [b]forsook God *who* [c]made
him,

And scornfully esteemed the
[d]Rock of his salvation.
16 [a]They provoked Him to jealousy
with foreign *gods;*
With [1]abominations they
provoked Him to anger.
17 [a]They sacrificed to demons, not to
God,
To gods they did not know,
To new *gods*, new arrivals
That your fathers did not fear.
18 [a]Of the Rock *who* begot you, you
are unmindful,
And have [b]forgotten the God who
fathered you.

19 "And[a] when the LORD saw *it*, He
spurned *them*,
Because of the provocation of His
sons and His daughters.
20 And He said: 'I will hide My face
from them,
I will see what their end *will be*,
For they *are* a perverse
generation,
[a]Children in whom *is* no faith.
21 [a]They have provoked Me to
jealousy by *what* is not God;
They have moved Me to anger
[b]by their [1]foolish idols.
But [c]I will provoke them to
jealousy by *those who are* not
a nation;
I will move them to anger by a
foolish nation.
22 For [a]a fire is kindled in My
anger,
And shall burn to the [1]lowest
[2]hell;
It shall consume the earth with
her increase,
And set on fire the foundations
of the mountains.

23 'I will [a]heap disasters on them;
[b]I will spend My arrows on them.
24 *They shall be* wasted with
hunger,
Devoured by pestilence and bitter
destruction;
I will also send against them the
[a]teeth of beasts,
With the poison of serpents of the
dust.
25 The sword shall destroy outside;
There shall be terror within
For the young man and virgin,
The nursing child with the man
of gray hairs.
26 [a]I would have said, "I will dash
them in pieces,
I will make the memory of them
to cease from among men,"
27 Had I not feared the wrath of the
enemy,

15 [d]Ps. 95:1
16 [a]Ps. 78:58; 1 Cor. 10:22 [1]*detestable acts*
17 [a]Rev. 9:20
18 [a]Is. 17:10 [b]Jer. 2:32
19 [a]Judg. 2:14
20 [a]Matt. 17:17
21 [a]Ps. 78:58 [b]Ps. 31:6 [c]Rom. 10:19 [1]*foolishness*, lit. *vanities*
22 [a]Num. 16:33–35; Ps. 18:7, 8; Lam. 4:11 [1]*lowest part of* [2]Or *Sheol*
23 [a]Ex. 32:12; Deut. 29:21, 24 [b]Ps. 7:12, 13
24 [a]Lev. 26:22
26 [a]Ezek. 20:23
27 [a]Is. 10:12–15
29 [a]Ps. 81:13; [Luke 19:42] [b]Deut. 31:29
30 [a]Judg. 2:14; Ps. 44:12
31 [a][1 Sam. 4:7, 8; Jer. 40:2, 3]
32 [a]Is. 1:8–10
33 [a]Ps. 58:4 [b]Rom. 3:13
34 [a][Jer. 2:22]
35 [a]Ps. 94:1; Rom. 12:19; Heb. 10:30 [b]2 Pet. 2:3
36 [a]Ps. 135:14; Heb. 10:30 [b]Ps. 106:45; Jer. 31:20 [c]2 Kin. 14:26
37 [a]Judg. 10:14; Jer. 2:28
39 [a]Is. 41:4; 43:10 [b]Deut. 32:12; Is. 45:5

Lest their adversaries should
misunderstand,
Lest they should say, [a]"Our hand
is high;
And it is not the LORD who has
done all this." '

28 "For they *are* a nation void of
counsel,
Nor *is there any* understanding
in them.
29 [a]Oh, that they were wise, *that* they
understood this,
That they would consider their
[b]latter end!
30 How could one chase a thousand,
And two put ten thousand to
flight,
Unless their Rock [a]had sold them,
And the LORD had surrendered
them?
31 For their rock *is* not like our
Rock,
[a]Even our enemies themselves
being judges.
32 For [a]their vine *is* of the vine of
Sodom
And of the fields of Gomorrah;
Their grapes *are* grapes of gall,
Their clusters *are* bitter.
33 Their wine *is* [a]the poison of
serpents,
And the cruel [b]venom of cobras.

34 '*Is* this not [a]laid up in store with
Me,
Sealed up among My treasures?
35 [a]Vengeance is Mine, and
recompense;
Their foot shall slip in *due* time;
[b]For the day of their calamity *is*
at hand,
And the things to come hasten
upon them.'

36 "For[a] the LORD will judge His
people
[b]And have compassion on His
servants,
When He sees that *their* power
is gone,
And [c]*there is* no one *remaining*,
bond or free.
37 He will say: [a]'Where *are* their
gods,
The rock in which they sought
refuge?
38 Who ate the fat of their sacrifices,
And drank the wine of their drink
offering?
Let them rise and help you,
And be your refuge.
39 'Now see that [a]I, *even* I, *am* He,
And [b]*there is* no God besides Me;

[c]I kill and I make alive;
I wound and I heal;
Nor *is there any* who can deliver
from My hand.
40 For I raise My hand to heaven,
And say, "*As* I live forever,
41 [a]If I [1]whet My glittering sword,
And My hand takes hold on
judgment,
I will render vengeance to My
enemies,
And repay those who hate Me.
42 I will make My arrows drunk
with blood,
And My sword shall devour flesh,
With the blood of the slain and
the captives,
From the heads of the leaders of
the enemy."'

43 "Rejoice,[a] O Gentiles, *with* His
[1]people;
For He will [b]avenge the blood of
His servants,
And render vengeance to His
adversaries;
He [c]will provide atonement for
His land *and* His people."

44 So Moses came with [1]Joshua
the son of Nun and spoke all the
words of this song in the hearing
of the people.
45 Moses finished speaking all
these words to all Israel,
46 and he said to them: [a]"Set your
hearts on all the words which I tes-
tify among you today, which you
shall command your [b]children to
be careful to observe—all the
words of this law.
47 "For it *is* not a [1]futile thing for
you, because it *is* your [a]life, and
by this word you shall prolong
your days in the land which you
cross over the Jordan to possess."

Moses to Die on Mount Nebo

48 Then the LORD spoke to Moses
that very same day, saying:
49 [a]"Go up this mountain of the
Abarim, Mount Nebo, which *is* in
the land of Moab, across from Jeri-
cho; view the land of Canaan,
which I give to the children of Is-
rael as a possession;
50 "and die on the mountain
which you ascend, and be [1]gath-
ered to your people, just as [a]Aaron
your brother died on Mount Hor
and was gathered to his people;
51 "because [a]you trespassed
against Me among the children of

39 [c]1 Sam. 2:6
41 [a]Is. 1:24; 66:16 [1]*sharpen*
43 [a]Rom. 15:10 [b]Rev. 6:10; 19:2 [c]Ps. 65:3; 79:9; 85:1 [1]DSS fragment adds *And let all the gods (angels) worship Him;* cf. LXX and Heb. 1:6
44 [1]Heb. *Hoshea,* Num. 13:8, 16
46 [a]Ezek. 40:4; 44:5 [b]Deut. 11:19
47 [a]Deut. 8:3; 30:15–20 [1]*vain*
49 [a]Num. 27:12–14
50 [a]Num. 20:25, 28; 33:38 [1]*Join your ancestors*
51 [a]Num. 20:11–13 [b]Lev. 10:3 [1]Lit. *Contention at Kadesh*
52 [a]Deut. 34:1–5

CHAPTER 33

1 [a]Gen. 49:28 [b]Ps. 90
2 [a]Ps. 68:8, 17 [b]Deut. 2:1, 4 [c]Num. 10:12 [d]Dan. 7:10
3 [a]Hos. 11:1 [b]1 Sam. 2:9 [c][Luke 10:39] [d]Prov. 2:1
4 [a]John 1:17; 7:19 [b]Ps. 119:111 [1]*charged us with*
5 [a]Ex. 15:18 [b]Deut. 32:15
6 [a]Gen. 49:3, 4
7 [a]Gen. 49:8–12 [b]Gen. 49:8 [c]Ps. 146:5
8 [a]Gen. 49:5 [b]Ex. 28:30 [c]Ps. 81:7 [1]Lit. *Perfections and Your Lights*
9 [a][Num. 25:5–8] [b][Gen. 29:32] [c]Ex. 32:26–28 [d]Mal. 2:5, 6

Israel at the waters of [1]Meribah
Kadesh, in the Wilderness of Zin,
because you [b]did not hallow Me
in the midst of the children of Is-
rael.
52 [a]"Yet you shall see the land be-
fore *you,* though you shall not go
there, into the land which I am giv-
ing to the children of Israel."

Moses' Final Blessing on Israel

33 Now this *is* [a]the blessing
with which Moses [b]the man
of God blessed the children of Is-
rael before his death.
2 And he said:

[a]"The LORD came from Sinai,
And dawned on them from [b]Seir;
He shone forth from [c]Mount
Paran,
And He came with [d]ten
thousands of saints;
From His right hand
Came a fiery law for them.
3 Yes, [a]He loves the people;
[b]All His saints *are* in Your hand;
They [c]sit down at Your feet;
Everyone [d]receives Your words.
4 [a]Moses [1]commanded a law for us,
[b]A heritage of the congregation of
Jacob.
5 And He was [a]King in [b]Jeshurun,
When the leaders of the people
were gathered,
All the tribes of Israel together.

6 "Let [a]Reuben live, and not die,
Nor let his men be few."

7 And this he said of [a]Judah:

"Hear, LORD, the voice of Judah,
And bring him to his people;
[b]Let his hands be sufficient for
him,
And may You be [c]a help against
his enemies."

8 And of [a]Levi he said:

[b]"*Let* Your [1]Thummim and Your
Urim *be* with Your holy one,
[c]Whom You tested at Massah,
And with whom You contended
at the waters of Meribah,
9 [a]Who says of his father and
mother,
'I have not [b]seen them';
[c]Nor did he acknowledge his
brothers,
Or know his own children;
For [d]they have observed Your
word

And kept Your covenant.
10 [a]They shall teach Jacob Your judgments,
And Israel Your law.
They shall put incense before You,
[b]And a whole burnt sacrifice on Your altar.
11 Bless his substance, LORD,
And [a]accept the work of his hands;
Strike the loins of those who rise against him,
And of those who hate him, that they rise not again."

12 Of Benjamin he said:

"The beloved of the LORD shall dwell in safety by Him,
Who shelters him all the day long;
And he shall dwell between His shoulders."

13 And of Joseph he said:

[a]"Blessed of the LORD *is* his land,
With the precious things of heaven, with the [b]dew,
And the deep lying beneath,
14 With the precious fruits of the sun,
With the precious produce of the months,
15 With the best things of [a]the ancient mountains,
With the precious things [b]of the everlasting hills,
16 With the precious things of the earth and its fullness,
And the favor of [a]Him who dwelt in the bush.
Let *the blessing* come [b]'on the head of Joseph,
And on the crown of the head of him *who was* separate from his brothers.'
17 His glory *is like* a [a]firstborn bull,
And his horns *like* the [b]horns of the wild ox;
Together with them
[c]He shall push the peoples
To the ends of the earth;
[d]They *are* the ten thousands of Ephraim,
And they *are* the thousands of Manasseh."

18 And of Zebulun he said:

[a]"Rejoice, Zebulun, in your going out,
And Issachar in your tents!

10 [a]Lev. 10:11; Deut. 31:9–13; Mal. 2:7 [b]Lev. 1:9; Ps. 51:19
11 [a]2 Sam. 24:23; Ezek. 20:40
13 [a]Gen. 49:22–26 [b]Gen. 27:28
15 [a]Gen. 49:26 [b]Hab. 3:6
16 [a]Ex. 3:2–4; Acts 7:30–35 [b]Gen. 49:26
17 [a]1 Chr. 5:1 [b]Num. 23:22 [c]1 Kin. 22:11; Ps. 44:5 [d]Gen. 48:19
18 [a]Gen. 49:13–15
19 [a]Ex. 15:17; Ps. 2:6; Is. 2:3 [b]Ps. 4:5; 51:19
20 [a]1 Chr. 12:8
21 [a]Num. 32:16, 17 [b]Josh. 4:12
22 [a]Gen. 49:16, 17; Josh. 19:47
23 [a]Gen. 49:21 [b]Josh. 19:32
24 [a]Gen. 49:20 [b]Job 29:6
25 [a]Deut. 8:9
26 [a]Ex. 15:11; Deut. 4:35; Ps. 86:8; Jer. 10:6 [b]Deut. 32:15 [c]Deut. 10:14; Ps. 68:3, 33, 34; 104:3
27 [a][Ps. 90:1; 91:2, 9] [b]Deut. 9:3–5
28 [a]Deut. 33:12; Jer. 23:6; 33:16 [b]Deut. 8:7, 8 [c]Num. 23:9

19 They shall [a]call the peoples *to* the mountain;
There [b]they shall offer sacrifices of righteousness;
For they shall partake *of* the abundance of the seas
And *of* treasures hidden in the sand."

20 And of Gad he said:

"Blessed *is* he who [a]enlarges Gad;
He dwells as a lion,
And tears the arm and the crown of his head.
21 [a]He provided the first *part* for himself,
Because a lawgiver's portion was reserved there.
[b]He came *with* the heads of the people;
He administered the justice of the LORD,
And His judgments with Israel."

22 And of Dan he said:

"Dan *is* a lion's whelp;
[a]He shall leap from Bashan."

23 And of Naphtali he said:

"O Naphtali, [a]satisfied with favor,
And full of the blessing of the LORD,
[b]Possess the west and the south."

24 And of Asher he said:

[a]"Asher *is* most blessed of sons;
Let him be favored by his brothers,
And let him [b]dip his foot in oil.
25 Your sandals *shall be* [a]iron and bronze;
As your days, *so shall* your strength *be*.

26 "*There is* [a]no one like the God of [b]Jeshurun,
[c]*Who* rides the heavens to help you,
And in His excellency on the clouds.
27 The eternal God *is your* [a]refuge,
And underneath *are* the everlasting arms;
[b]He will thrust out the enemy from before you,
And will say, 'Destroy!'
28 Then [a]Israel shall dwell in safety,
[b]The fountain of Jacob [c]alone,
In a land of grain and new wine;

His [d]heavens shall also drop dew.
29 [a]Happy *are* you, O Israel!
[b]Who *is* like you, a people saved
by the LORD,
[c]The shield of your help
And the sword of your majesty!
Your enemies [d]shall submit to
you,
And [e]you shall tread down their
[1]high places."

Moses Dies on Mount Nebo

34 Then Moses went up from
the plains of Moab [a]to
Mount Nebo, to the top of Pisgah,
which is across from Jericho. And
the LORD showed him all the land
of Gilead as far as Dan,
2 all Naphtali and the land of
Ephraim and Manasseh, all the
land of Judah as far as the [1]Western Sea,
3 the South, and the plain of the
Valley of Jericho, [a]the city of palm
trees, as far as Zoar.
4 Then the LORD said to him,
[a]"This *is* the land of which I swore
to give Abraham, Isaac, and Jacob,
saying, 'I will give it to your descendants.' [b]I have caused you to
see *it* with your eyes, but you shall
not cross over there."
5 [a]So Moses the servant of the
LORD died there in the land of
Moab, according to the word of the
LORD.
6 And He buried him in a valley
in the land of Moab, opposite Beth
Peor; but [a]no one knows his grave
to this day.
7 [a]Moses *was* one hundred and
twenty years old when he died.
[b]His [1]eyes were not dim nor his
natural vigor [2]diminished.
8 And the children of Israel wept
for Moses in the plains of Moab
[a]thirty days. So the days of weeping *and* mourning for Moses
ended.
9 Now Joshua the son of Nun
was full of the [a]spirit of wisdom,
for [b]Moses had laid his hands on
him; so the children of Israel
heeded him, and did as the LORD
had commanded Moses.
10 But since then there [a]has not
arisen in Israel a prophet like Moses, [b]whom the LORD knew face to
face,
11 in all [a]the signs and wonders
which the LORD sent him to do in
the land of Egypt, before Pharaoh,
before all his servants, and in all
his land,
12 and by all that mighty power
and all the great terror which Moses performed in the sight of all
Israel.

28 [d]Gen. 27:28
29 [a]Ps. 144:15 [b]Deut. 4:32–34; 2 Sam. 7:23 [c]Gen. 15:1; Ps. 115:9 [d]Ps. 18:44; 66:3 [e]Num. 33:52 [1]Places for pagan worship

CHAPTER 34

1 [a]Num. 27:12; Deut. 32:49
2 [1]Mediterranean
3 [a]2 Chr. 28:15
4 [a]Gen. 12:7 [b]Deut. 3:27
5 [a]Num. 20:12; Deut. 32:50; Josh. 1:1, 2
6 [a]Jude 9
7 [a]Deut. 31:2 [b]Gen. 27:1; 48:10 [1]*eyesight was not weakened* [2]*reduced*
8 [a]Gen. 50:3, 10
9 [a]Is. 11:2 [b]Num. 27:18, 23
10 [a]Deut. 18:15, 18 [b]Ex. 33:11; Num. 12:8; Deut. 5:4
11 [a]Deut. 7:19

The Book of

Joshua

JOSHUA, the first of the twelve historical books (Joshua–Esther), forges a link between the Pentateuch and the remainder of Israel's history. Through three major military campaigns involving more than thirty enemy armies, the people of Israel learn a crucial lesson under Joshua's capable leadership: victory comes through faith in God and obedience to His word, rather than through military might or numerical superiority.

The title of this book is appropriately named after its central figure, Joshua. His original name is *Hoshea,* "Salvation" (Num. 13:8); but Moses evidently changes it to *Yehoshua,* "Yahweh Is Salvation" (Num. 13:16). He is also called *Yeshua,* a shortened form of *Yehoshua.* This is the Hebrew equivalent of the Greek name *Iesous* (Jesus). Thus, the Greek title given to the book in the Septuagint is *Iesous Naus,* "Joshua the Son of Nun." The Latin title is *Liber Josue,* the "Book of Joshua."

His name is symbolic of the fact that although he is the leader of the Israelite nation during the conquest, the Lord is the Conqueror.

God's Commission to Joshua

AFTER the death of Moses the
servant of the LORD, it came
to pass that the LORD spoke
to Joshua the son of Nun, Moses'
[a]assistant, saying:
2 [a]"Moses My servant is dead.
Now therefore, arise, go over this
Jordan, you and all this people, to
the land which I am giving to
them—the children of Israel.
3 [a]"Every place that the sole of
your foot will tread upon I have
given you, as I said to Moses.
4 [a]"From the wilderness and this
Lebanon as far as the great river,
the River Euphrates, all the land
of the Hittites, and to the Great Sea
toward the going down of the sun,
shall be your territory.
5 [a]"No man shall *be able to* stand
before you all the days of your life;
[b]as I was with Moses, *so* [c]I will be
with you. [d]I will not leave you nor
forsake you.
6 [a]"Be strong and of good courage, for to this people you shall
[1]divide as an inheritance the land
which I swore to their fathers to
give them.
7 "Only be strong and very courageous, that you may observe to
do according to all the law [a]which
Moses My servant commanded
you; [b]do not turn from it to the
right hand or to the left, that you
may [1]prosper wherever you go.
8 [a]"This Book of the Law shall
not depart from your mouth, but
[b]you[1] shall meditate in it day and
night, that you may observe to do
according to all that is written in
it. For then you will make your
way prosperous, and then you will
have good success.
9 [a]"Have I not commanded you?
Be strong and of good courage;
[b]do not be afraid, nor be dismayed,
for the LORD your God *is* with you
wherever you go."

The Order to Cross the Jordan

10 Then Joshua commanded the
officers of the people, saying,
11 "Pass through the camp and
command the people, saying, 'Prepare provisions for yourselves, for
[a]within three days you will cross
over this Jordan, to go in to possess the land which the LORD
your God is giving you to possess.' "
12 And to the Reubenites, the
Gadites, and half the tribe of Manasseh Joshua spoke, saying,
13 "Remember [a]the word which
Moses the servant of the LORD
commanded you, saying, 'The

CHAPTER 1

1 [a]Ex. 24:13; Num. 13:16; 14:6, 29, 30, 37, 38; Deut. 1:38; Acts 7:45

2 [a]Num. 12:7; Deut. 34:5

3 [a]Deut. 11:24; Josh. 11:23

4 [a]Gen. 15:18; Ex. 23:31; Num. 34:3–12

5 [a]Deut. 7:24 [b]Ex. 3:12 [c]Deut. 31:8, 23 [d]Deut. 31:6, 7; Heb. 13:5

6 [a]Deut. 31:7, 23 [1]*give as a possession*

7 [a]Num. 27:23; Deut. 31:7; Josh. 11:15 [b]Deut. 5:32 [1]*have success* or *act wisely*

8 [a]Deut. 17:18, 19; 31:24, 26; Josh. 8:34 [b]Deut. 29:9; Ps. 1:1–3 [1]*you shall be constantly in*

9 [a]Deut. 31:7 [b]Ps. 27:1

11 [a]Deut. 9:1; Josh. 3:17

13 [a]Num. 32:20–28

LORD your God is giving you rest
and is giving you this land.'
14 "Your wives, your little ones,
and your livestock shall remain in
the land which Moses gave you on
this side of the Jordan. But you
shall [1]pass before your brethren
armed, all your mighty men of
valor, and help them,
15 "until the LORD has given your
brethren rest, as He *gave* you, and
they also have taken possession of
the land which the LORD your God
is giving them. [a]Then you shall re-
turn to the land of your possession
and enjoy it, which Moses the
LORD's servant gave you on this
side of the Jordan toward the sun-
rise."
16 So they answered Joshua, say-
ing, "All that you command us we
will do, and wherever you send us
we will go.
17 "Just as we heeded Moses in
all things, so we will heed you.
Only the LORD your God [a]be with
you, as He was with Moses.
18 "Whoever rebels against your
command and does not heed your
words, in all that you command
him, shall be put to death. Only be
strong and of good courage."

Rahab Hides the Spies

2 Now Joshua the son of Nun
sent out two men [a]from [1]Aca-
cia Grove to spy secretly, saying,
"Go, view the land, especially Jeri-
cho." So they went, and [b]came to
the house of a harlot named [c]Ra-
hab, and [2]lodged there.
2 And [a]it was told the king of Jer-
icho, saying, "Behold, men have
come here tonight from the chil-
dren of Israel to search out the
country."
3 So the king of Jericho sent to
Rahab, saying, "Bring out the men
who have come to you, who have
entered your house, for they have
come to search out all the coun-
try."
4 [a]Then the woman took the two
men and hid them. So she said,
"Yes, the men came to me, but I
did not know where they *were*
from.
5 "And it happened as the gate
was being shut, when it was dark,
that the men went out. Where the
men went I do not know; pursue
them quickly, for you may over-
take them."
6 (But [a]she had brought them up
to the roof and hidden them with
the stalks of flax, which she had
laid in order on the roof.)
7 Then the men pursued them by
the road to the Jordan, to the fords.
And as soon as those who pursued
them had gone out, they shut the
gate.
8 Now before they lay down, she
came up to them on the roof,
9 and said to the men: [a]"I know
that the LORD has given you the
land, that [b]the terror of you has
fallen on us, and that all the inhab-
itants of the land [c]are fainthearted
because of you.
10 "For we have heard how the
LORD [a]dried up the water of the
Red Sea for you when you came
out of Egypt, and [b]what you did
to the two kings of the Amorites
who *were* on the other side of the
Jordan, Sihon and Og, whom you
[c]utterly destroyed.
11 "And as soon as we [a]heard
these things, [b]our hearts melted;
neither did there remain any more
courage in anyone because of you,
for [c]the LORD your God, He *is* God
in heaven above and on earth be-
neath.
12 "Now therefore, I beg you,
[a]swear to me by the LORD, since I
have shown you kindness, that
you also will show kindness to [b]my
father's house, and [c]give me [1]a
true token,
13 "and [a]spare my father, my
mother, my brothers, my sisters,
and all that they have, and deliver
our lives from death."
14 So the men answered her, "Our
lives for yours, if none of you tell
this business of ours. And it shall
be, when the LORD has given us the
land, that [a]we will deal kindly and
truly with you."
15 Then she [a]let them down by a
rope through the window, for her
house *was* on the city wall; she
dwelt on the wall.
16 And she said to them, "Get to
the mountain, lest the pursuers
meet you. Hide there three days,
until the pursuers have returned.
Afterward you may go your way."
17 So the men said to her: "We
will be [a]blameless[1] of this oath of

---

14 [1]*cross over ahead of*
15 [a]Josh. 22:1–4
17 [a]1 Sam. 20:13; 1 Kin. 1:37

CHAPTER 2

1 [a]Num. 25:1; Josh. 3:1 [b]Heb. 11:31; James 2:25 [c]Matt. 1:5 [1]Heb. *Shittim* [2]Lit. *lay down*
2 [a]Josh. 2:22
4 [a]2 Sam. 17:19, 20
6 [a]Ex. 1:17; 2 Sam. 17:19
9 [a]Deut. 1:8 [b]Gen. 35:5; Ex. 23:27; Deut. 2:25; 11:25; Josh. 9:9, 10 [c]Ex. 15:15; Josh. 5:1
10 [a]Ex. 14:21; Josh. 4:23 [b]Num. 21:21–35 [c]Deut. 20:17; Josh. 6:21
11 [a]Ex. 15:14, 15 [b]Josh. 5:1; 7:5; Ps. 22:14; Is. 13:7 [c]Deut. 4:39
12 [a]1 Sam. 20:14, 15, 17 [b]1 Tim. 5:8 [c]Ex. 12:13; Josh. 2:18 [1]*a pledge of truth*
13 [a]Josh. 6:23–25
14 [a]Gen. 47:29; Judg. 1:24; [Matt. 5:7]
15 [a]Acts 9:25
17 [a]Ex. 20:7 [1]*free from obligation to this oath*

yours which you have made us
swear,
18 [a]"unless, *when* we come into
the land, you bind this line of scar-
let cord in the window through
which you let us down, [b]and unless
you [1]bring your father, your
mother, your brothers, and all
your father's household to your
own home.
19 "So it shall be *that* whoever
goes outside the doors of your
house into the street, his blood
shall be on his own head, and we
will be [1]guiltless. And whoever is
with you in the house, [a]his [2]blood
shall be on our head if a hand is
laid on him.
20 "And if you tell this business
of ours, then we will be [1]free from
your oath which you made us
swear."
21 Then she said, "According to
your words, so *be* it." And she sent
them away, and they departed.
And she bound the scarlet cord in
the window.
22 They departed and went to the
mountain, and stayed there three
days until the pursuers returned.
The pursuers sought *them* all along
the way, but did not find *them*.
23 So the two men returned, de-
scended from the mountain, and
crossed over; and they came to
Joshua the son of Nun, and told
him all that had befallen them.
24 And they said to Joshua,
"Truly [a]the LORD has delivered all
the land into our hands, for indeed
all the inhabitants of the country
are fainthearted because of us."

Israel Crosses the Jordan

3 Then Joshua rose early in the
morning; and they set out
[a]from [1]Acacia Grove and came to
the Jordan, he and all the children
of Israel, and lodged there before
they crossed over.
2 So it was, [a]after three days,
that the officers went through the
camp;
3 and they commanded the peo-
ple, saying, [a]"When you see the
ark of the covenant of the LORD
your God, [b]and the priests, the
Levites, [1]bearing it, then you shall
set out from your place and go af-
ter it.
4 [a]"Yet there shall be a space be-
tween you and it, about two thou-
sand cubits by measure. Do not
come near it, that you may know
the way by which you must go, for
you have not passed *this* way be-
fore."
5 And Joshua said to the people,
[a]"Sanctify[1] yourselves, for tomor-
row the LORD will do wonders
among you."
6 Then Joshua spoke to the
priests, saying, [a]"Take up the ark
of the covenant and cross over be-
fore the people." So they took up
the ark of the covenant and went
before the people.
7 And the LORD said to Joshua,
"This day I will begin to [a]exalt[1]
you in the sight of all Israel, that
they may know that, [b]as I was with
Moses, *so* I will be with you.
8 "You shall command [a]the
priests who bear the ark of the
covenant, saying, 'When you have
come to the edge of the water of
the Jordan, [b]you shall stand in the
Jordan.' "
9 So Joshua said to the children
of Israel, "Come here, and hear the
words of the LORD your God."
10 And Joshua said, "By this you
shall know that [a]the living God *is*
among you, and *that* He will with-
out fail [b]drive out from before you
the [c]Canaanites and the Hittites
and the Hivites and the Perizzites
and the Girgashites and the Amo-
rites and the Jebusites:
11 "Behold, the ark of the cov-
enant of [a]the Lord of all the earth
is crossing over before you into the
Jordan.
12 "Now therefore, [a]take for your-
selves twelve men from the tribes
of Israel, one man from every
tribe.
13 "And it shall come to pass, [a]as
soon as the soles of the feet of the
priests who bear the ark of the
LORD, [b]the Lord of all the earth,
shall rest in the waters of the Jor-
dan, *that* the waters of the Jordan
shall be cut off, the waters that
come down from upstream, and
they [c]shall stand as a heap."
14 So it was, when the people set
out from their camp to cross over
the Jordan, with the priests bear-
ing the [a]ark of the covenant before
the people,
15 and as those who bore the ark

18 [a]Josh. 2:12 [b]Josh. 6:23 [1]Lit. *gather*
19 [a]1 Kin. 2:32; Matt. 27:25 [1]*free from obligation* [2]*guilt of bloodshed*
20 [1]*free from obligation to*
24 [a]Ex. 23:31; Josh. 6:2; 21:44

CHAPTER 3

1 [a]Josh. 2:1 [1]Heb. *Shittim*
2 [a]Josh. 1:10, 11
3 [a]Num. 10:33 [b]Deut. 31:9, 25 [1]*carrying*
4 [a]Ex. 19:12
5 [a]Ex. 19:10, 14, 15; Lev. 20:7; Num. 11:18; Josh. 7:13; 1 Sam. 16:5; Job 1:5; Joel 2:16 [1]*Consecrate*
6 [a]Num. 4:15
7 [a]Josh. 4:14; 1 Chr. 29:25; 2 Chr. 1:1 [b]Josh. 1:5, 9 [1]*make you great*
8 [a]Josh. 3:3 [b]Josh. 3:17
10 [a]Deut. 5:26; Josh. 11:23; 1 Sam. 17:26; 2 Kin. 19:4; Hos. 1:10; Matt. 16:16; 1 Thess. 1:9 [b]Ex. 33:2; Deut. 7:1; 18:12; Ps. 44:2 [c]Acts 13:19
11 [a]Josh. 3:13; Job 41:11; Ps. 24:1; Mic. 4:13; Zech. 4:14; 6:5
12 [a]Josh. 4:2, 4
13 [a]Josh. 3:15, 16 [b]Josh. 3:11 [c]Ps. 78:13; 114:3
14 [a]Ps. 132:8; Acts 7:44, 45

came to the Jordan, and [a]the feet
of the priests who bore the ark
dipped in the edge of the water (for
the [b]Jordan overflows all its banks
[c]during the whole time of harvest),
16 that the waters which came
down from upstream stood *still*,
and rose in a heap very far away
[1]at Adam, the city that *is* beside
[a]Zaretan. So the waters that went
down [b]into the Sea of the Arabah,
[c]the Salt Sea, failed, *and* were cut
off; and the people crossed over
opposite Jericho.
17 Then the priests who bore the
ark of the covenant of the LORD
stood firm on dry ground in the
midst of the Jordan; [a]and all Israel
crossed over on dry ground, until
all the people had crossed com-
pletely over the Jordan.

The Memorial Stones

4 And it came to pass, when all
the people had completely
crossed [a]over the Jordan, that the
LORD spoke to Joshua, saying:
2 [a]"Take for yourselves twelve
men from the people, one man
from every tribe,
3 "and command them, saying,
'Take for yourselves twelve stones
from here, out of the midst of the
Jordan, from the place where [a]the
priests' feet stood firm. You shall
carry them over with you and
leave them in [b]the lodging place
where you lodge tonight.' "
4 Then Joshua called the twelve
men whom he had appointed from
the children of Israel, one man
from every tribe;
5 and Joshua said to them:
"Cross over before the ark of the
LORD your God into the midst of
the Jordan, and each one of you
take up a stone on his shoulder,
according to the number of the
tribes of the children of Israel,
6 "that this may be [a]a sign
among you [b]when your children
ask in time to come, saying, 'What
do these stones *mean* to you?'
7 "Then you shall answer them
that [a]the waters of the Jordan were
cut off before the ark of the cov-
enant of the LORD; when it crossed
over the Jordan, the waters of the
Jordan were cut off. And these
stones shall be for [b]a memorial to
the children of Israel forever."

15 [a]Josh. 3:13 [b]1 Chr. 12:15; Jer. 12:5; 49:19 [c]Josh. 4:18; 5:10, 12
16 [a]1 Kin. 4:12; 7:46 [b]Deut. 3:17 [c]Gen. 14:3; Num. 34:3 [1]Qr., many mss. and vss. *from Adam*
17 [a]Gen. 50:24; Ex. 3:8; 6:1–8; 14:21, 22, 29; 33:1; Deut. 6:10; Heb. 11:29

CHAPTER 4

1 [a]Deut. 27:2; Josh. 3:17
2 [a]Josh. 3:12
3 [a]Josh. 3:13 [b]Josh. 4:19, 20
6 [a]Deut. 27:2; Ps. 103:2 [b]Ex. 12:26; 13:14; Deut. 6:20
7 [a]Josh. 3:13, 16 [b]Ex. 12:14; Num. 16:40
11 [a]Josh. 3:11; 6:11
12 [a]Num. 32:17, 20, 27, 28; Josh. 1:14
13 [1]*equipped*
14 [a]Josh. 3:7; 1 Chr. 29:25 [1]*made Joshua great*
16 [a]Ex. 25:16, 22
18 [a]Josh. 3:15; 1 Chr. 12:15

8 And the children of Israel did
so, just as Joshua commanded,
and took up twelve stones from the
midst of the Jordan, as the LORD
had spoken to Joshua, according
to the number of the tribes of the
children of Israel, and carried
them over with them to the place
where they lodged, and laid them
down there.
9 Then Joshua set up twelve
stones in the midst of the Jordan,
in the place where the feet of the
priests who bore the ark of the
covenant stood; and they are there
to this day.
10 So the priests who bore the ark
stood in the midst of the Jordan
until everything was finished that
the LORD had commanded Joshua
to speak to the people, according
to all that Moses had commanded
Joshua; and the people hurried
and crossed over.
11 Then it came to pass, when all
the people had completely crossed
over, that the [a]ark of the LORD and
the priests crossed over in the
presence of the people.
12 And [a]the men of Reuben, the
men of Gad, and half the tribe of
Manasseh crossed over armed be-
fore the children of Israel, as Mo-
ses had spoken to them.
13 About forty thousand [1]pre-
pared for war crossed over before
the LORD for battle, to the plains
of Jericho.
14 On that day the LORD [a]exalted[1]
Joshua in the sight of all Israel;
and they feared him, as they had
feared Moses, all the days of his
life.
15 Then the LORD spoke to Joshua,
saying,
16 "Command the priests who
bear [a]the ark of the Testimony to
come up from the Jordan."
17 Joshua therefore commanded
the priests, saying, "Come up from
the Jordan."
18 And it came to pass, when the
priests who bore the ark of the
covenant of the LORD had come
from the midst of the Jordan, *and*
the soles of the priests' feet
touched the dry land, that the wa-
ters of the Jordan returned to their
place [a]and overflowed all its banks
as before.

19 Now the people came up from
the Jordan on the tenth *day* of the
first month, and they camped [a]in
Gilgal on the east border of Jeri-
cho.
20 And [a]those twelve stones
which they took out of the Jordan,
Joshua set up in Gilgal.
21 Then he spoke to the children
of Israel, saying: [a]"When your
children ask their fathers in time
to come, saying, 'What *are* these
stones?'
22 "then you shall let your chil-
dren know, saying, [a]'Israel crossed
over this Jordan on [b]dry land';
23 "for the LORD your God dried
up the waters of the Jordan before
you until you had crossed over, as
the LORD your God did to the Red
Sea, [a]which He dried up before us
until we had crossed over,
24 [a]"that all the peoples of the
earth may know the hand of the
LORD, that it *is* [b]mighty, that you
may [c]fear the LORD your God [1]for-
ever."

The Second Generation Circumcised

5 So it was, when all the kings
of the Amorites who *were* on
the west side of the Jordan, and
all the kings of the Canaanites
[a]who *were* by the sea, [b]heard that
the LORD had dried up the waters
of the Jordan from before the chil-
dren of Israel until [1]we had
crossed over, that [2]their heart
melted; [c]and there was no spirit in
them any longer because of the
children of Israel.
2 At that time the LORD said to
Joshua, "Make [a]flint knives for
yourself, and circumcise the sons
of Israel again the second time."
3 So Joshua made flint knives for
himself, and circumcised the sons
of Israel at [1]the hill of the fore-
skins.
4 And this *is* the reason why
Joshua circumcised them: [a]All the
people who came out of Egypt *who*
were males, all the men of war,
had died in the wilderness on the
way, after they had come out of
Egypt.
5 For all the people who came
out had been circumcised, but all
the people born in the wilderness,
on the way as they came out of
Egypt, had not been circumcised.
6 For the children of Israel
walked [a]forty years in the wilder-
ness, till all the people *who were*
men of war, who came out of
Egypt, were [1]consumed, because
they did not obey the voice of the
LORD—to whom the LORD swore
that [b]He would not show them the
land which the LORD had sworn to
their fathers that He would give us,
[c]"a land flowing with milk and
honey."
7 Then Joshua circumcised [a]their
sons *whom* He raised up in their
place; for they were uncircum-
cised, because they had not been
circumcised on the way.
8 So it was, when they had fin-
ished circumcising all the people,
that they stayed in their places in
the camp [a]till they were healed.
9 Then the LORD said to Joshua,
"This day I have rolled away [a]the
reproach of Egypt from you."
Therefore the name of the place
is called [b]Gilgal[1] to this day.
10 Now the children of Israel
camped in Gilgal, and kept the
Passover [a]on the fourteenth day of
the month at twilight on the plains
of Jericho.
11 And they ate of the produce of
the land on the day after the Pass-
over, unleavened bread and
[1]parched grain, on the very same
day.
12 Then [a]the manna ceased on the
day after they had eaten the pro-
duce of the land; and the children
of Israel no longer had manna, but
they ate the food of the land of Ca-
naan that year.

The Commander of the Army of the LORD

13 And it came to pass, when
Joshua was by Jericho, that he
lifted his eyes and looked, and be-
hold, [a]a Man stood opposite him
[b]with His sword drawn in His
hand. And Joshua went to Him
and said to Him, "*Are* You for us
or for our adversaries?"
14 So He said, "No, but *as* Com-
mander of the army of the LORD I
have now come." And Joshua [a]fell
on his face to the earth and [b]wor-
shiped, and said to Him, "What
does my Lord say to His servant?"
15 Then the Commander of the

---

19 [a]Josh. 5:9
20 [a]Deut. 11:30; Josh. 4:3; 5:9, 10
21 [a]Josh. 4:6
22 [a]Ex. 12:26, 27; 13:8–14; Deut. 26:5–9 [b]Josh. 3:17
23 [a]Ex. 14:21
24 [a]1 Kin. 8:42; 2 Kin. 19:19; Ps. 106:8 [b]Ex. 15:16; 1 Chr. 29:12; Ps. 89:13 [c]Ex. 14:31; Deut. 6:2; Ps. 76:7; Jer. 10:7 [1]Lit. *all days*

CHAPTER 5

1 [a]Num. 13:29 [b]Ex. 15:14, 15 [c]Josh. 2:10, 11; 9:9; 1 Kin. 10:5 [1]So with Kt.; Qr., some Heb. mss. and editions, LXX, Syr., Tg., Vg. *they* [2]*their courage failed*
2 [a]Ex. 4:25
3 [1]Heb. *Gibeath Haaraloth*
4 [a]Num. 14:29; 26:64, 65; Deut. 2:14–16
6 [a]Num. 14:33; Deut. 1:3; 29:5 [b]Num. 14:23, 29–35; 26:23–65; Heb. 3:11 [c]Ex. 3:8 [1]*destroyed*
7 [a]Num. 14:31; Deut. 1:39
8 [a]Gen. 34:25
9 [a]Gen. 34:14 [b]Josh. 4:19 [1]Lit. *Rolling*
10 [a]Ex. 12:6; Num. 9:5
11 [1]*roasted*
12 [a]Ex. 16:35
13 [a]Gen. 18:1, 2; 32:24, 30; Ex. 23:23; Num. 22:31; Zech. 1:8; Acts 1:10 [b]Num. 22:23; 1 Chr. 21:16
14 [a]Gen. 17:3; Num. 20:6 [b]Ex. 34:8

LORD's army said to Joshua,
[a]"Take your sandal off your foot,
for the place where you stand *is*
holy." And Joshua did so.

The Destruction of Jericho

6 Now [a]Jericho was securely
shut up because of the children
of Israel; none went out, and none
came in.
2 And the LORD said to Joshua:
"See! [a]I have given Jericho into
your hand, its [b]king, *and* the
mighty men of valor.
3 "You shall march around the
city, all *you* men of war; you shall
go all around the city once. This
you shall do six days.
4 "And seven priests shall bear
seven [a]trumpets of rams' horns be-
fore the ark. But the seventh day
you shall march around the city
[b]seven times, and [c]the priests shall
blow the trumpets.
5 "It shall come to pass, when
they make a long *blast* with the
ram's horn, *and* when you hear the
sound of the trumpet, that all the
people shall shout with a great
shout; then the wall of the city will
fall down flat. And the people shall
go up every man straight before
him."
6 Then Joshua the son of Nun
called the priests and said to them,
"Take up the ark of the covenant,
and let seven priests bear seven
trumpets of rams' horns before the
ark of the LORD."
7 And he said to the people,
"Proceed, and march around the
city, and let him who is armed
advance before the ark of the
LORD."
8 So it was, when Joshua had
spoken to the people, that the
seven priests bearing the seven
trumpets of rams' horns before the
LORD advanced and blew the trum-
pets, and the ark of the covenant
of the LORD followed them.
9 The armed men went before
the priests who blew the trumpets,
[a]and the rear guard came after the
ark, while *the priests* continued
blowing the trumpets.
10 Now Joshua had commanded
the people, saying, "You shall not
shout or make any noise with your
voice, nor shall a word proceed out
of your mouth, until the day I say
to you, 'Shout!' Then you shall
shout."
11 So he had [a]the ark of the LORD
circle the city, going around *it*
once. Then they came into the
camp and [1]lodged in the camp.
12 And Joshua rose early in the
morning, [a]and the priests took up
the ark of the LORD.
13 Then seven priests bearing
seven trumpets of rams' horns be-
fore the ark of the LORD went on
continually and blew with the
trumpets. And the armed men
went before them. But the rear
guard came after the ark of the
LORD, while *the priests* continued
blowing the trumpets.
14 And the second day they
marched around the city once and
returned to the camp. So they did
six days.
15 But it came to pass on the sev-
enth day that they rose early,
about the dawning of the day, and
marched around the city seven
times in the same manner. On that
day only they marched around the
city seven times.
16 And the seventh time it hap-
pened, when the priests blew the
trumpets, that Joshua said to the
people: "Shout, for the LORD has
given you the city!
17 "Now the city shall be [a]doomed
by the LORD to destruction, it and
all who *are* in it. Only [b]Rahab the
harlot shall live, she and all who
are with her in the house, because
[c]she hid the messengers that we
sent.
18 "And you, [a]by all means ab-
stain from the accursed things, lest
you become accursed when you
take of the accursed things, and
make the camp of Israel a curse,
[b]and trouble it.
19 "But all the silver and gold, and
vessels of bronze and iron, *are*
[1]consecrated to the LORD; they
[2]shall come into the treasury of the
LORD."
20 So the people shouted when
the priests blew the trumpets. And
it happened when the people
heard the sound of the trumpet,
and the people shouted with a
great shout, that [a]the wall fell
down flat. Then the people went
up into the city, every man straight
before him, and they took the city.

15 [a]Ex. 3:5; Acts 7:33

CHAPTER 6

1 [a]Josh. 2:1

2 [a]Josh. 2:9, 24; 8:1 [b]Deut. 7:24

4 [a]Lev. 25:9; Judg. 7:16, 22 [b]1 Kin. 18:43; 2 Kin. 4:35; 5:10 [c]Num. 10:8

9 [a]Num. 10:25

11 [a]Josh. 4:11 [1]*spent the night*

12 [a]Deut. 31:25

17 [a]Deut. 13:17; Josh. 7:1 [b]Josh. 2:1; Matt. 1:5 [c]Josh. 2:4, 6

18 [a]Deut. 7:26 [b]Josh. 7:1, 12, 25; 1 Kin. 18:17, 18; [Jon. 1:12]

19 [1]*set apart* [2]*shall go*

20 [a]Heb. 11:30

21 And they [a]utterly destroyed all
that *was* in the city, both man and
woman, young and old, ox and
sheep and donkey, with the edge
of the sword.
22 But Joshua had said to the two
men who had spied out the coun-
try, "Go into the harlot's house,
and from there bring out the
woman and all that she has, [a]as
you swore to her."
23 And the young men who had
been spies went in and brought out
Rahab, [a]her father, her mother,
her brothers, and all that she had.
So they brought out all her rela-
tives and left them outside the
camp of Israel.
24 But they burned the city and all
that *was* in it with fire. Only the
silver and gold, and the vessels of
bronze and iron, they put into the
treasury of the house of the LORD.
25 And Joshua spared Rahab the
harlot, her father's household, and
all that she had. So [a]she dwells in
Israel to this day, because she hid
the messengers whom Joshua sent
to spy out Jericho.
26 Then Joshua [1]charged *them* at
that time, saying, [a]"Cursed *be* the
man before the LORD who rises up
and builds this city Jericho; he
shall lay its foundation with his
firstborn, and with his youngest he
shall set up its gates."
27 So the LORD was with Joshua,
and his fame spread throughout all
the country.

Defeat at Ai

7 But the children of Israel
[1]committed a [a]trespass regard-
ing the [b]accursed[2] things, for
[c]Achan the son of Carmi, the son
of [3]Zabdi, the son of Zerah, of the
tribe of Judah, took of the ac-
cursed things; so the anger of the
LORD burned against the children
of Israel.
2 Now Joshua sent men from
Jericho to Ai, which *is* beside Beth
Aven, on the east side of Bethel,
and spoke to them, saying, "Go up
and spy out the country." So the
men went up and spied out Ai.
3 And they returned to Joshua
and said to him, "Do not let all the
people go up, but let about two or
three thousand men go up and at-
tack Ai. Do not weary all the peo-
ple there, for *the people of Ai are*
few."
4 So about three thousand men
went up there from the people,
[a]but they fled before the men of
Ai.
5 And the men of Ai struck down
about thirty-six men, for they
chased them *from* before the gate
as far as Shebarim, and struck
them down on the descent; there-
fore [a]the[1] hearts of the people
melted and became like water.
6 Then Joshua [a]tore his clothes,
and fell to the earth on his face
before the ark of the LORD until
evening, he and the elders of Is-
rael; and they [b]put dust on their
heads.
7 And Joshua said, "Alas, Lord
[1]GOD, [a]why have You brought this
people over the Jordan at all—to
deliver us into the hand of the Am-
orites, to destroy us? Oh, that we
had been content, and dwelt on the
other side of the Jordan!
8 "O Lord, what shall I say when
Israel turns its [1]back before its en-
emies?
9 "For the Canaanites and all the
inhabitants of the land will hear
it, and surround us, and [a]cut off
our name from the earth. Then
[b]what will You do for Your great
name?"

The Sin of Achan

10 So the LORD said to Joshua:
"Get up! Why do you lie thus on
your face?
11 "Israel has sinned, and they
have also transgressed My cov-
enant which I commanded them.
[a]For they have even taken some
of the [1]accursed things, and have
both stolen and [b]deceived; and
they have also put *it* among their
own stuff.
12 [a]"Therefore the children of Is-
rael could not stand before their
enemies, *but* turned *their* backs
before their enemies, because
[b]they have become doomed to de-
struction. Neither will I be with
you anymore, unless you destroy
the accursed from among you.
13 "Get up, [a]sanctify[1] the people,
and say, [b]'Sanctify yourselves for
tomorrow, because thus says the
LORD God of Israel: "*There is* an
accursed thing in your midst, O Is-

21 [a]Deut. 7:2; 20:16, 17
22 [a]Josh. 2:12–19; Heb. 11:31
23 [a]Josh. 2:13
25 [a][Matt. 1:5]
26 [a]1 Kin. 16:34 [1]*warned*

CHAPTER 7
1 [a]Josh. 7:20, 21 [b]Josh. 6:17–19 [c]Josh. 22:20 [1]*acted unfaithfully* [2]*devoted* [3]*Zimri*, 1 Chr. 2:6
4 [a]Lev. 26:17; Deut. 28:25
5 [a]Lev. 26:36; Josh. 2:9, 11 [1]*the people's courage failed*
6 [a]Gen. 37:29, 34 [b]1 Sam. 4:12
7 [a]Ex. 17:3; Num. 21:5 [1]Heb. *YHWH*, LORD
8 [1]Lit. *neck*
9 [a]Deut. 32:26 [b]Ex. 32:12; Num. 14:13
11 [a]Josh. 6:17–19 [b]Acts 5:1, 2 [1]*devoted*
12 [a]Judg. 2:14 [b]Deut. 7:26; [Hag. 2:13, 14]
13 [a]Ex. 19:10 [b]Josh. 3:5 [1]*set apart*

rael; you cannot stand before your
enemies until you take away the
accursed thing from among you."
14 'In the morning therefore you
shall be brought according to your
tribes. And it shall be *that* the tribe
which [a]the LORD takes shall come
according to families; and the fam-
ily which the LORD takes shall
come by households; and the
household which the LORD takes
shall come man by man.
15 [a]'Then it shall be *that* he who
is taken with the accursed thing
shall be burned with fire, he and
all that he has, because he has
[b]transgressed[1] the covenant of the
LORD, and because he [c]has done a
disgraceful thing in Israel.' "
16 So Joshua rose early in the
morning and brought Israel by
their tribes, and the tribe of Judah
was taken.
17 He brought the clan of Judah,
and he took the family of the
Zarhites; and he brought the fam-
ily of the Zarhites man by man,
and Zabdi was taken.
18 Then he brought his household
man by man, and Achan the son
of Carmi, the son of Zabdi, the son
of Zerah, of the tribe of Judah,
[a]was taken.
19 Now Joshua said to Achan,
"My son, I beg you, [a]give glory to
the LORD God of Israel, [b]and make
confession to Him, and [c]tell me
now what you have done; do not
hide *it* from me."
20 And Achan answered Joshua
and said, "Indeed [a]I have sinned
against the LORD God of Israel, and
this is what I have done:
21 "When I saw among the spoils
a beautiful Babylonian garment,
two hundred shekels of silver, and
a wedge of gold weighing fifty
shekels, I [1]coveted them and took
them. And there they are, hidden
in the earth in the midst of my tent,
with the silver under it."
22 So Joshua sent messengers,
and they ran to the tent; and there
it was, hidden in his tent, with the
silver under it.
23 And they took them from the
midst of the tent, brought them to
Joshua and to all the children of
Israel, and laid them out before the
LORD.
24 Then Joshua, and all Israel

14 [a][Prov. 16:33]
15 [a]1 Sam. 14:38, 39 [b]Josh. 7:11 [c]Gen. 34:7; Judg. 20:6 [1]*overstepped*
18 [a]1 Sam. 14:42
19 [a]1 Sam. 6:5; Jer. 13:16; John 9:24 [b]Num. 5:6, 7; 2 Chr. 30:22; Ezra 10:10, 11; Ps. 32:5; Prov. 28:13; Jer. 3:12, 13; Dan. 9:4 [c]1 Sam. 14:43
20 [a]Num. 22:34; 1 Sam. 15:24
21 [1]*desired*
24 [a]Num. 16:32, 33; Dan. 6:24 [b]Josh. 7:26; 15:7
25 [a]Josh. 6:18; 1 Chr. 2:7; [Gal. 5:12] [b]Deut. 17:5
26 [a]Josh. 8:29; 2 Sam. 18:17; Lam. 3:53 [b]Deut. 13:17 [c]Josh. 7:24; Is. 65:10; Hos. 2:15 [1]Lit. *Trouble*

CHAPTER 8

1 [a]Deut. 1:21; 7:18; 31:8; Josh. 1:9; 10:8 [b]Josh. 6:2
2 [a]Josh. 6:21 [b]Deut. 20:14; Josh. 8:27
4 [a]Judg. 20:29
5 [a]Josh. 7:5; Judg. 20:32

with him, took Achan the son of
Zerah, the silver, the garment, the
wedge of gold, his sons, his daugh-
ters, his oxen, his donkeys, his
sheep, his tent, and [a]all that he
had, and they brought them to [b]the
Valley of Achor.
25 And Joshua said, [a]"Why have
you troubled us? The LORD will
trouble you this day." [b]So all Israel
stoned him with stones; and they
burned them with fire after they
had stoned them with stones.
26 Then they [a]raised over him a
great heap of stones, still there to
this day. So [b]the LORD turned from
the fierceness of His anger. There-
fore the name of that place has
been called [c]the Valley of [1]Achor
to this day.

The Fall of Ai

8 Now the LORD said to Joshua:
[a]"Do not be afraid, nor be dis-
mayed; take all the people of war
with you, and arise, go up to Ai.
See, [b]I have given into your hand
the king of Ai, his people, his city,
and his land.
2 "And you shall do to Ai and its
king as you did to [a]Jericho and its
king. Only [b]its spoil and its cattle
you shall take as booty for your-
selves. Lay an ambush for the city
behind it."
3 So Joshua arose, and all the
people of war, to go up against Ai;
and Joshua chose thirty thousand
mighty men of valor and sent them
away by night.
4 And he commanded them, say-
ing: "Behold, [a]you shall lie in am-
bush against the city, behind the
city. Do not go very far from the
city, but all of you be ready.
5 "Then I and all the people who
are with me will approach the city;
and it will come about, when they
come out against us as at the first,
that [a]we shall flee before them.
6 "For they will come out after
us till we have drawn them from
the city, for they will say, '*They
are* fleeing before us as at the first.'
Therefore we will flee before them.
7 "Then you shall rise from the
ambush and seize the city, for the
LORD your God will deliver it into
your hand.
8 "And it will be, when you have
taken the city, *that* you shall set

the city on fire. According to the
commandment of the LORD you
shall do. [a]See, I have commanded
you."
9 Joshua therefore sent them out;
and they went to lie in ambush,
and stayed between Bethel and Ai,
on the west side of Ai; but Joshua
lodged that night among the peo-
ple.
10 Then Joshua rose up early in
the morning and mustered the
people, and went up, he and the
elders of Israel, before the people
to Ai.
11 [a]And all the people of war who
were with him went up and drew
near; and they came before the
city and camped on the north side
of Ai. Now a valley *lay* between
them and Ai.
12 So he took about five thousand
men and set them in ambush be-
tween Bethel and Ai, on the west
side of [1]the city.
13 And when they had set the peo-
ple, all the army that *was* on the
north of the city, and its rear guard
on the west of the city, Joshua
went that night into the midst of
the valley.
14 Now it happened, when the
king of Ai saw *it*, that the men of
the city hurried and rose early and
went out against Israel to battle,
he and all his people, at an ap-
pointed place before the plain. But
he [a]did not know that *there was*
an ambush against him behind the
city.
15 And Joshua and all Israel
[a]made as if they were beaten be-
fore them, and fled by the way of
the wilderness.
16 So all the people who *were* in
Ai were called together to pursue
them. And they pursued Joshua
and were drawn away from the
city.
17 There was not a man left in Ai
or Bethel who did not go out after
Israel. So they left the city open
and pursued Israel.
18 Then the LORD said to Joshua,
"Stretch out the spear that *is* in
your hand toward Ai, for I will give
it into your hand." And Joshua
stretched out the spear that *was*
in his hand toward the city.
19 So *those in* ambush arose
quickly out of their place; they ran

8 [a]2 Sam. 13:28
11 [a]Josh. 8:5
12 [1]Ai
14 [a]Judg. 20:34; Eccl. 9:12
15 [a]Judg. 20:36
22 [a]Deut. 7:2
26 [a]Josh. 6:21
27 [a]Num. 31:22, 26 [b]Josh. 8:2
28 [a]Deut. 13:16
29 [a]Josh. 10:26 [b]Deut. 21:22, 23; Josh. 10:27 [c]Josh. 7:26; 10:27

as soon as he had stretched out his
hand, and they entered the city
and took it, and hurried to set the
city on fire.
20 And when the men of Ai looked
behind them, they saw, and be-
hold, the smoke of the city as-
cended to heaven. So they had no
power to flee this way or that way,
and the people who had fled to the
wilderness turned back on the pur-
suers.
21 Now when Joshua and all Is-
rael saw that the ambush had
taken the city and that the smoke
of the city ascended, they turned
back and struck down the men of
Ai.
22 Then the others came out of the
city against them; so they were
caught in the midst of Israel, some
on this side and some on that side.
And they struck them down, so
that they [a]let none of them remain
or escape.
23 But the king of Ai they took
alive, and brought him to Joshua.
24 And it came to pass when Is-
rael had made an end of slaying
all the inhabitants of Ai in the
field, in the wilderness where they
pursued them, and when they all
had fallen by the edge of the sword
until they were consumed, that all
the Israelites returned to Ai and
struck it with the edge of the
sword.
25 So it was *that* all who fell that
day, both men and women, *were*
twelve thousand—all the people of
Ai.
26 For Joshua did not draw back
his hand, with which he stretched
out the spear, until he had [a]utterly
destroyed all the inhabitants of Ai.
27 [a]Only the livestock and the
spoil of that city Israel took as
booty for themselves, according to
the word of the LORD which He had
[b]commanded Joshua.
28 So Joshua burned Ai and made
it [a]a heap forever, a desolation to
this day.
29 [a]And the king of Ai he hanged
on a tree until evening. [b]And as
soon as the sun was down, Joshua
commanded that they should take
his corpse down from the tree, cast
it at the entrance of the gate of the
city, and [c]raise over it a great heap
of stones *that remains* to this day.

Joshua Renews the Covenant

30 Now Joshua built an altar to
the LORD God of Israel [a]in Mount
Ebal,
31 as Moses the servant of the
LORD had commanded the children
of Israel, as it is written in the
Book of the Law of Moses: [a]"an
altar of whole stones over which
no man has wielded an iron *tool*."
And [b]they offered on it burnt offer-
ings to the LORD, and sacrificed
peace offerings.
32 And there, in the presence of
the children of Israel, [a]he wrote on
the stones a copy of the law of Mo-
ses, which he had written.
33 Then all Israel, with their el-
ders and officers and judges, stood
on either side of the ark before the
priests, the Levites, [a]who bore the
ark of the covenant of the LORD,
[b]the stranger as well as he who
was born among them. Half of
them *were* in front of Mount Ger-
izim and half of them in front of
Mount Ebal, [c]as Moses the servant
of the LORD had commanded be-
fore, that they should bless the
people of Israel.
34 And afterward [a]he read all the
words of the law, [b]the blessings
and the cursings, according to all
that is written in the [c]Book of the
Law.
35 There was not a word of all that
Moses had commanded which
Joshua did not read before all the
assembly of Israel, [a]with the
women, the little ones, [b]and the
strangers who were living among
them.

The Treaty with the Gibeonites

9 And it came to pass when [a]all
the kings who *were* on this side
of the Jordan, in the hills and in
the lowland and in all the coasts
of [b]the Great Sea toward Leba-
non—[c]the Hittite, the Amorite, the
Canaanite, the Perizzite, the Hi-
vite, and the Jebusite—heard
about it,
2 that they [a]gathered together to
fight with Joshua and Israel with
one [1]accord.
3 But when the inhabitants of
[a]Gibeon [b]heard what Joshua had
done to Jericho and Ai,
4 they worked craftily, and went
and [1]pretended to be ambassa-
dors. And they took old sacks on
their donkeys, old wineskins torn
and [2]mended,
5 old and patched sandals on
their feet, and old garments on
themselves; and all the bread of
their provision was dry *and* moldy.
6 And they went to Joshua, [a]to
the camp at Gilgal, and said to him
and to the men of Israel, "We have
come from a far country; now
therefore, make a [1]covenant with
us."
7 Then the men of Israel said to
the [a]Hivites, "Perhaps you dwell
among us; so [b]how can we make
a covenant with you?"
8 But they said to Joshua, [a]"We
are your servants." And Joshua
said to them, "Who *are* you, and
where do you come from?"
9 So they said to him: [a]"From a
very far country your servants
have come, because of the name
of the LORD your God; for we have
[b]heard of His fame, and all that He
did in Egypt,
10 "and [a]all that He did to the two
kings of the Amorites who *were*
beyond the Jordan—to Sihon king
of Heshbon, and Og king of
Bashan, who was at Ashtaroth.
11 "Therefore our elders and all
the inhabitants of our country
spoke to us, saying, 'Take provi-
sions with you for the journey,
and go to meet them, and say to
them, "We *are* your servants; now
therefore, make a covenant with
us." '
12 "This bread of ours we took hot
for our provision from our houses
on the day we departed to come
to you. But now look, it is dry and
moldy.
13 "And these wineskins which
we filled *were* new, and see, they
are torn; and these our garments
and our sandals have become old
because of the very long journey."
14 Then the men of Israel took
some of their provisions; [a]but they
[1]did not ask counsel of the LORD.
15 So Joshua [a]made peace with
them, and made a covenant with
them to let them live; and the rul-
ers of the congregation swore to
them.
16 And it happened at the end of
three days, after they had made a

30 [a]Deut. 27:4–8
31 [a]Ex. 20:25; Deut. 27:5, 6 [b]Ex. 20:24
32 [a]Deut. 27:2, 3, 8
33 [a]Deut. 31:9, 25 [b]Deut. 31:12 [c]Deut. 11:29; 27:12
34 [a]Deut. 31:11; Neh. 8:3 [b]Deut. 28:2, 15, 45; 29:20, 21; 30:19 [c]Josh. 1:8
35 [a]Ex. 12:38; Deut. 31:12 [b]Josh. 8:33

CHAPTER 9

1 [a]Num. 13:29; Josh. 3:10 [b]Num. 34:6 [c]Ex. 3:17; 23:23
2 [a]Josh. 10:5; Ps. 83:3, 5 [1]Lit. *mouth*
3 [a]Josh. 9:17, 22; 10:2; 21:17; 2 Sam. 21:1, 2 [b]Josh. 6:27
4 [1]*acted as envoys* [2]Lit. *tied up*
6 [a]Josh. 5:10 [1]*treaty*
7 [a]Josh. 9:1; 11:19 [b]Ex. 23:32; Deut. 7:2
8 [a]Deut. 20:11; 2 Kin. 10:5
9 [a]Deut. 20:15 [b]Ex. 15:14; Josh. 2:9, 10; 5:1
10 [a]Num. 21:24, 33
14 [a]Num. 27:21; Is. 30:1 [1]Lit. *did not inquire at the mouth of*
15 [a]2 Sam. 21:2

covenant with them, that they
heard that they *were* their neigh-
bors who dwelt near them.
17 Then the children of Israel
journeyed and came to their cities
on the third day. Now their cities
were [a]Gibeon, Chephirah, Beer-
oth, and Kirjath Jearim.
18 But the children of Israel did
not [1]attack them, [a]because the rul-
ers of the congregation had sworn
to them by the LORD God of Israel.
And all the congregation com-
plained against the rulers.
19 Then all the rulers said to all
the congregation, "We have sworn
to them by the LORD God of Israel;
now therefore, we may not touch
them.
20 "This we will do to them: We
will let them live, lest [a]wrath be
upon us because of the oath which
we swore to them."
21 And the rulers said to them,
"Let them live, but let them be
[a]woodcutters and water carriers
for all the congregation, as the rul-
ers had [b]promised them."
22 Then Joshua called for them,
and he spoke to them, saying,
"Why have you deceived us, say-
ing, [a]'We *are* very far from you,'
when [b]you dwell near us?
23 "Now therefore, you *are*
[a]cursed, and none of you shall be
freed from being slaves—wood-
cutters and water carriers for the
house of my God."
24 So they answered Joshua and
said, "Because your servants were
clearly told that the LORD your God
[a]commanded His servant Moses to
give you all the land, and to de-
stroy all the inhabitants of the land
from before you; therefore [b]we
were very much afraid for our
lives because of you, and have
done this thing.
25 "And now, here we are, [a]in
your hands; do with us as it seems
good and right to do to us."
26 So he did to them, and deliv-
ered them out of the hand of the
children of Israel, so that they did
not kill them.
27 And that day Joshua made
them [a]woodcutters and water car-
riers for the congregation and for
the altar of the LORD, [b]in the place
which He would choose, even to
this day.

17 [a]Josh. 18:25
18 [a]Ps. 15:4 [1]*strike*
20 [a]2 Sam. 21:1, 2, 6; Ezek. 17:13, 15
21 [a]Deut. 29:11 [b]Josh. 9:15
22 [a]Josh. 9:6, 9 [b]Josh. 9:16
23 [a]Gen. 9:25
24 [a]Ex. 23:31–33; Deut. 7:1, 2 [b]Ex. 15:14
25 [a]Gen. 16:6
27 [a]Josh. 9:21, 23 [b]Deut. 12:5

CHAPTER 10

1 [a]Josh. 9:1 [b]Josh. 8:1 [c]Josh. 6:21 [d]Josh. 8:22, 26, 28 [e]Josh. 9:15
2 [a]Ex. 15:14–16; Deut. 11:25; 1 Chr. 14:17
4 [a]Josh. 9:15; 10:1
5 [a]Num. 13:29 [b]Josh. 9:2
6 [a]Josh. 5:10; 9:6
7 [a]Josh. 8:1
8 [a]Josh. 11:6; Judg. 4:14 [b]Josh. 1:5, 9 [c]Josh. 21:44
10 [a]Judg. 4:15; 1 Sam. 7:10, 12; Is. 28:21 [b]Josh. 16:3, 5 [c]Josh. 15:35

The Sun Stands Still

10 Now it came to pass when
Adoni-Zedek king of Jerusa-
lem [a]heard how Joshua had taken
[b]Ai and had utterly destroyed it—
[c]as he had done to Jericho and its
king, so he had done to [d]Ai and
its king—and [e]how the inhabitants
of Gibeon had made peace with Is-
rael and were among them,
2 that they [a]feared greatly, be-
cause Gibeon *was* a great city, like
one of the royal cities, and because
it *was* greater than Ai, and all its
men *were* mighty.
3 Therefore Adoni-Zedek king of
Jerusalem sent to Hoham king of
Hebron, Piram king of Jarmuth,
Japhia king of Lachish, and Debir
king of Eglon, saying,
4 "Come up to me and help me,
that we may attack Gibeon, for [a]it
has made peace with Joshua and
with the children of Israel."
5 Therefore the five kings of the
[a]Amorites, the king of Jerusalem,
the king of Hebron, the king of
Jarmuth, the king of Lachish, *and*
the king of Eglon, [b]gathered to-
gether and went up, they and all
their armies, and camped before
Gibeon and made war against it.
6 And the men of Gibeon sent to
Joshua at the camp [a]at Gilgal, say-
ing, "Do not forsake your ser-
vants; come up to us quickly, save
us and help us, for all the kings
of the Amorites who dwell in the
mountains have gathered together
against us."
7 So Joshua ascended from Gil-
gal, he and [a]all the people of war
with him, and all the mighty men
of valor.
8 And the LORD said to Joshua,
[a]"Do not fear them, for I have de-
livered them into your hand; [b]not
a man of them shall [c]stand before
you."
9 Joshua therefore came upon
them suddenly, having marched
all night from Gilgal.
10 So the LORD [a]routed them be-
fore Israel, killed them with a great
slaughter at Gibeon, chased them
along the road that goes [b]to Beth
Horon, and struck them down as
far as [c]Azekah and Makkedah.
11 And it happened, as they fled
before Israel *and* were on the de-

scent of Beth Horon, [a]that the
LORD cast down large hailstones
from heaven on them as far as
Azekah, and they died. *There were*
more who died from the hailstones
than the children of Israel killed
with the sword.
12 Then Joshua spoke to the LORD
in the day when the LORD deliv-
ered up the Amorites before the
children of Israel, and he said in
the sight of Israel:

[a]"Sun, stand still over Gibeon;
And Moon, in the Valley of
[b]Aijalon."
13 So the sun stood still,
And the moon stopped,
Till the people had revenge
Upon their enemies.

[a]*Is* this not written in the Book of
Jasher? So the sun stood still in
the midst of heaven, and did not
hasten to go *down* for about a
whole day.
14 And there has been [a]no day
like that, before it or after it, that
the LORD heeded the voice of a
man; for [b]the LORD fought for Is-
rael.
15 [a]Then Joshua returned, and all
Israel with him, to the camp at Gil-
gal.

The Amorite Kings Executed

16 But these five kings had fled
and hidden themselves in a cave
at Makkedah.
17 And it was told Joshua, saying,
"The five kings have been found
hidden in the cave at Makkedah."
18 So Joshua said, "Roll large
stones against the mouth of the
cave, and set men by it to guard
them.
19 "And do not stay *there* your-
selves, *but* pursue your enemies,
and attack their rear *guard*. Do not
allow them to enter their cities, for
the LORD your God has delivered
them into your hand."
20 Then it happened, while
Joshua and the children of Israel
made an end of slaying them with
a very great slaughter, till they had
finished, that those who escaped
entered fortified cities.
21 And all the people returned to
the camp, to Joshua at Makkedah,
in peace. [a]No one [1]moved his
tongue against any of the children
of Israel.
22 Then Joshua said, "Open the
mouth of the cave, and bring out
those five kings to me from the
cave."
23 And they did so, and brought
out those five kings to him from
the cave: the king of Jerusalem,
the king of Hebron, the king of
Jarmuth, the king of Lachish, *and*
the king of Eglon.
24 So it was, when they brought
out those kings to Joshua, that
Joshua called for all the men of Is-
rael, and said to the captains of the
men of war who went with him,
"Come near, put your feet on the
necks of these kings." And they
drew near and [a]put their feet on
their necks.
25 Then Joshua said to [1]them,
[a]"Do not be afraid, nor be dis-
mayed; be strong and of good
courage, for [b]thus the LORD will do
to all your enemies against whom
you fight."
26 And afterward Joshua struck
[1]them and killed them, and hanged
them on five trees; and they [a]were
hanging on the trees until evening.
27 So it was at the time of the go-
ing down of the sun *that* Joshua
commanded, and they [a]took them
down from the trees, cast them
into the cave where they had been
hidden, and laid large stones
against the cave's mouth, *which*
remain until this very day.

Conquest of the Southland

28 On that day Joshua took Mak-
kedah, and struck it and its king
with the edge of the sword. He ut-
terly [a]destroyed [1]them—all the
people who *were* in it. He let none
remain. He also did to the king of
Makkedah [b]as he had done to the
king of Jericho.
29 Then Joshua passed from Mak-
kedah, and all Israel with him, to
[a]Libnah; and they fought against
Libnah.
30 And the LORD also delivered it
and its king into the hand of Israel;
he struck it and all the people who
were in it with the edge of the
sword. He let none remain in it,
but did to its king as he had done
to the king of Jericho.
31 Then Joshua passed from

11 [a]Is. 30:30; Rev. 16:21
12 [a]Is. 28:21; Hab. 3:11 [b]Judg. 12:12
13 [a]2 Sam. 1:18
14 [a]Is. 38:7, 8 [b]Ex. 14:14; Deut. 1:30; 20:4; Josh. 10:42; 23:3
15 [a]Josh. 10:43
21 [a]Ex. 11:7 [1]*criticized,* lit. *sharpened his tongue*
24 [a]Ps. 107:40; Is. 26:5, 6; Mal. 4:3
25 [a]Deut. 31:6–8; Josh. 1:9 [b]Deut. 3:21; 7:19 [1]The captains
26 [a]Josh. 8:29; 2 Sam. 21:9 [1]The kings
27 [a]Deut. 21:22, 23; Josh. 8:29
28 [a]Deut. 7:2, 16 [b]Josh. 6:21 [1]So with MT and most authorities; many Heb. mss., some LXX mss., and some Tg. mss. *it*
29 [a]Josh. 15:42; 21:13; 2 Kin. 8:22; 19:8

Libnah, and all Israel with him,
to Lachish; and they encamped
against it and fought against it.
32 And the LORD delivered La-
chish into the hand of Israel, who
took it on the second day, and
struck it and all the people who
were in it with the edge of the
sword, according to all that he had
done to Libnah.
33 Then Horam king of Gezer
came up to help Lachish; and
Joshua struck him and his peo-
ple, until he left him none remain-
ing.
34 From Lachish Joshua passed to
Eglon, and all Israel with him; and
they encamped against it and
fought against it.
35 They took it on that day and
struck it with the edge of the
sword; all the people who *were* in
it he utterly destroyed that day, ac-
cording to all that he had done to
Lachish.
36 So Joshua went up from Eglon,
and all Israel with him, to [a]He-
bron; and they fought against it.
37 And they took it and struck it
with the edge of the sword—its
king, all its cities, and all the peo-
ple who *were* in it; he left none re-
maining, according to all that he
had done to Eglon, but utterly de-
stroyed it and all the people who
were in it.
38 Then Joshua returned, and all
Israel with him, to [a]Debir; and
they fought against it.
39 And he took it and its king and
all its cities; they struck them with
the edge of the sword and utterly
destroyed all the people who *were*
in it. He left none remaining; as
he had done to Hebron, so he did
to Debir and its king, as he had
done also to Libnah and its king.
40 So Joshua conquered all the
land: the [a]mountain country and
the [1]South and the lowland and the
wilderness slopes, and [b]all their
kings; he left none remaining,
but [c]utterly destroyed all that
breathed, as the LORD God of Israel
had commanded.
41 And Joshua conquered them
from [a]Kadesh Barnea as far as
[b]Gaza, [c]and all the country of
Goshen, even as far as Gibeon.
42 All these kings and their land
Joshua took at one time, [a]because
the LORD God of Israel fought for
Israel.
43 Then Joshua returned, and all
Israel with him, to the camp at Gil-
gal.

The Northern Conquest

11 And it came to pass, when
Jabin king of Hazor heard
these things, that he [a]sent to Jobab
king of Madon, to the king [b]of
Shimron, to the king of Achshaph,
2 and to the kings who *were* from
the north, in the mountains, in the
plain south of [a]Chinneroth, in the
lowland, and in the heights [b]of Dor
on the west,
3 to the Canaanites in the east
and in the west, the [a]Amorite, the
Hittite, the Perizzite, the Jebusite
in the mountains, [b]and the Hivite
below [c]Hermon [d]in the land of
Mizpah.
4 So they went out, they and all
their armies with them, *as* many
people [a]*as* the sand that *is* on the
seashore in multitude, with very
many horses and chariots.
5 And when all these kings had
[1]met together, they came and
camped together at the waters of
Merom to fight against Israel.
6 But the LORD said to Joshua,
[a]"Do not be afraid because of
them, for tomorrow about this
time I will deliver all of them slain
before Israel. You shall [b]ham-
string their horses and burn their
chariots with fire."
7 So Joshua and all the people
of war with him came against
them suddenly by the waters of
Merom, and they attacked them.
8 And the LORD delivered them
into the hand of Israel, who de-
feated them and chased them to
[1]Greater [a]Sidon, to the [2]Brook
[b]Misrephoth, and to the Valley of
Mizpah eastward; they attacked
them until they left none of them
remaining.
9 So Joshua did to them as the
LORD had told him: he hamstrung
their horses and burned their char-
iots with fire.
10 Joshua turned back at that time
and took Hazor, and struck its
king with the sword; for Hazor
was formerly the head of all those
kingdoms.

36 [a]Num. 13:22; Josh. 14:13–15; 15:13; Judg. 1:10, 20; 2 Sam. 5:1, 3, 5, 13; 2 Chr. 11:10

38 [a]Josh. 15:15; Judg. 1:11; 1 Chr. 6:58

40 [a]Deut. 1:7 [b]Deut. 7:24 [c]Deut. 20:16, 17 [1]Heb. *Negev*, and so throughout the book

41 [a]Num. 13:26; Deut. 9:23 [b]Gen. 10:19; Josh. 11:22 [c]Josh. 11:16; 15:51

42 [a]Josh. 10:14

CHAPTER 11

1 [a]Josh. 10:3 [b]Josh. 19:15

2 [a]Num. 34:11 [b]Josh. 17:11; Judg. 1:27; 1 Kin. 4:11

3 [a]Josh. 9:1 [b]Deut. 7:1; Judg. 3:3, 5; 1 Kin. 9:20 [c]Josh. 11:17; 13:5, 11 [d]Gen. 31:49

4 [a]Gen. 22:17; 32:12; Judg. 7:12; 1 Sam. 13:5

5 [1]Lit. *assembled by appointment*

6 [a]Josh. 10:8 [b]2 Sam. 8:4

8 [a]Gen. 49:13 [b]Josh. 13:6 [1]Heb. *Sidon Rabbah* [2]Heb. *Misrephoth Maim*, lit. *Burnings of Water*

11 And they struck all the people
who *were* in it with the edge of the
sword, [a]utterly destroying *them.*
There was none left [b]breathing.
Then he burned Hazor with fire.
12 So all the cities of those kings,
and all their kings, Joshua took
and struck with the edge of the
sword. He utterly destroyed them,
[a]as Moses the servant of the LORD
had commanded.
13 But *as for* the cities that stood
on their [1]mounds, Israel burned
none of them, except Hazor only,
which Joshua burned.
14 And all the [a]spoil of these cities
and the livestock, the children of
Israel took as booty for them-
selves; but they struck every man
with the edge of the sword until
they had destroyed them, and they
left none breathing.
15 [a]As the LORD had commanded
Moses his servant, so [b]Moses com-
manded Joshua, and [c]so Joshua
did. [1]He left nothing undone of all
that the LORD had commanded Mo-
ses.

Summary of Joshua's Conquests

16 Thus Joshua took all this land:
[a]the mountain country, all the
South, [b]all the land of Goshen, the
lowland, and the Jordan [1]plain—
the mountains of Israel and its
lowlands,
17 [a]from [1]Mount Halak and the
ascent to Seir, even as far as Baal
Gad in the Valley of Lebanon be-
low Mount Hermon. He captured
[b]all their kings, and struck them
down and killed them.
18 Joshua made war a long time
with all those kings.
19 There was not a city that made
peace with the children of Israel,
except [a]the Hivites, the inhabitants
of Gibeon. All *the others* they took
in battle.
20 For [a]it was of the LORD [1]to
harden their hearts, that they
should come against Israel in bat-
tle, that He might utterly destroy
them, *and* that they might receive
no mercy, but that He might de-
stroy them, [b]as the LORD had com-
manded Moses.
21 And at that time Joshua came
and cut off [a]the Anakim from the
mountains: from Hebron, from De-
bir, from Anab, from all the moun-
tains of Judah, and from all the
mountains of Israel; Joshua utterly
destroyed them with their cities.
22 None of the Anakim were left
in the land of the children of Israel;
they remained only [a]in Gaza, in
Gath, [b]and in Ashdod.
23 So Joshua took the whole land,
[a]according to all that the LORD had
said to Moses; and Joshua gave it
as an inheritance to Israel [b]accord-
ing to their divisions by their
tribes. Then the land [c]rested from
war.

The Kings Conquered by Moses

12 These *are* the kings of the
land whom the children of
Israel defeated, and whose land
they possessed on the other side
of the Jordan toward the rising of
the sun, [a]from the River Arnon [b]to
Mount Hermon, and all the eastern
Jordan plain:
2 *One king was* [a]Sihon king of
the Amorites, who dwelt in Hesh-
bon *and* ruled half of Gilead, from
Aroer, which is on the bank of the
River Arnon, from the middle of
that river, even as far as the River
Jabbok, *which is* the border of the
Ammonites,
3 and [a]the eastern Jordan plain
from the [1]Sea of Chinneroth as far
as the [2]Sea of the Arabah (the Salt
Sea), [b]the road to Beth Jeshimoth,
and [3]southward below [c]the[4] slopes
of Pisgah.
4 *The other king was* [a]Og king
of Bashan and his territory, *who*
was of [b]the remnant of the giants,
[c]who dwelt at Ashtaroth and at
Edrei,
5 and reigned over [a]Mount Her-
mon, [b]over Salcah, over all Ba-
shan, [c]as far as the border of the
Geshurites and the Maachathites,
and over half of Gilead *to* the bor-
der of Sihon king of Heshbon.
6 [a]These Moses the servant of
the LORD and the children of Israel
had conquered; and [b]Moses the
servant of the LORD had given it
as a possession to the Reubenites,
the Gadites, and half the tribe of
Manasseh.

The Kings Conquered by Joshua

7 And these *are* the kings of the
country [a]which Joshua and the
children of Israel conquered on

11 [a]Deut. 20:16 [b]Josh. 10:40
12 [a]Num. 33:50–56
13 [1]Heb. *tel,* a heap of successive city ruins
14 [a]Deut. 20:14–18
15 [a]Ex. 34:10–17 [b]Deut. 31:7, 8 [c]Josh. 1:7 [1]Lit. *He turned aside from nothing*
16 [a]Josh. 12:8 [b]Josh. 10:40, 41 [1]Heb. *arabah*
17 [a]Josh. 12:7 [b]Deut. 7:24 [1]Lit. *The Smooth* or *Bald Mountain*
19 [a]Josh. 9:3–7
20 [a]Deut. 2:30 [b]Deut. 20:16, 17 [1]Lit. *to make strong*
21 [a]Num. 13:22, 33
22 [a]1 Sam. 17:4 [b]Josh. 15:46
23 [a]Num. 34:2–15 [b]Num. 26:53 [c]Deut. 12:9, 10; 25:19

CHAPTER 12

1 [a]Num. 21:24 [b]Deut. 3:8
2 [a]Deut. 2:24–27
3 [a]Deut. 3:17 [b]Josh. 13:20 [c]Deut. 3:17; 4:49 [1]Sea of Galilee [2]Lit. *Sea of the Plain,* the Dead Sea [3]Or *Teman* [4]Or *Ashdoth Pisgah*
4 [a]Num. 21:33 [b]Deut. 3:11 [c]Deut. 1:4
5 [a]Deut. 3:8 [b]Deut. 3:10 [c]Deut. 3:14
6 [a]Num. 21:24, 35 [b]Num. 32:29–33
7 [a]Josh. 11:17

this side of the Jordan, on the west,
from Baal Gad in the Valley of
Lebanon as far as [1]Mount Halak
and the ascent to [b]Seir, which
Joshua [c]gave to the tribes of Israel
as a possession according to their
divisions,
8 [a]in the mountain country, in
the lowlands, in the *Jordan* plain,
in the slopes, in the wilderness,
and in the South—[b]the Hittites, the
Amorites, the Canaanites, the Per-
izzites, the Hivites, and the Jebu-
sites:
9 [a]the king of Jericho, one; [b]the
king of Ai, which *is* beside Bethel,
one;
10 [a]the king of Jerusalem, one; the
king of Hebron, one;
11 the king of Jarmuth, one; the
king of Lachish, one;
12 the king of Eglon, one; [a]the
king of Gezer, one;
13 [a]the king of Debir, one; the
king of Geder, one;
14 the king of Hormah, one; the
king of Arad, one;
15 [a]the king of Libnah, one; the
king of Adullam, one;
16 [a]the king of Makkedah, one;
[b]the king of Bethel, one;
17 the king of Tappuah, one; [a]the
king of Hepher, one;
18 the king of Aphek, one; the
king of [1]Lasharon, one;
19 the king of Madon, one; [a]the
king of Hazor, one;
20 the king of [a]Shimron Meron,
one; the king of Achshaph, one;
21 the king of Taanach, one; the
king of Megiddo, one;
22 [a]the king of Kedesh, one; the
king of Jokneam in Carmel, one;
23 the king of Dor in the [a]heights
of Dor, one; the king of [b]the people
of Gilgal, one;
24 the king of Tirzah, one—[a]all
the kings, thirty-one.

Remaining Land to Be Conquered

13 Now Joshua [a]was old, ad-
vanced in years. And the
LORD said to him: "You are old, ad-
vanced in years, and there remains
very much land yet to be pos-
sessed.
2 [a]"This is the land that yet re-
mains: [b]all the territory of the Phi-
listines and all [c]*that of* the Geshu-
rites,

7 [b]Gen. 14:6; 32:3 [c]Josh. 11:23 [1]Lit. *The Bald Mountain*
8 [a]Josh. 10:40; 11:16 [b]Ex. 3:8; 23:23
9 [a]Josh. 6:2 [b]Josh. 8:29
10 [a]Josh. 10:23
12 [a]Josh. 10:33
13 [a]Josh. 10:38, 39
15 [a]Josh. 10:29, 30
16 [a]Josh. 10:28 [b]Judg. 1:22
17 [a]1 Kin. 4:10
18 [1]Or *Sharon*
19 [a]Josh. 11:10
20 [a]Josh. 11:1; 19:15
22 [a]Josh. 19:37; 20:7; 21:32
23 [a]Josh. 11:2 [b]Is. 9:1
24 [a]Deut. 7:24

CHAPTER 13

1 [a]Josh. 14:10; 23:1, 2
2 [a]Judg. 3:1–3 [b]Joel 3:4 [c]2 Sam. 3:3
3 [a]Jer. 2:18 [b]Judg. 3:3 [c]Deut. 2:23
4 [a]Josh. 12:18; 19:30 [b]Judg. 1:34
5 [a]1 Kin. 5:18; Ezek. 27:9 [b]Josh. 12:7 [1]Or *Giblites*
6 [a]Josh. 11:8 [b]Josh. 23:13 [c]Josh. 14:1, 2 [1]Heb. *Misrephoth Maim,* lit. *Burnings of Water* [2]*apportion*
8 [a]Num. 32:33 [b]Josh. 12:1–6
9 [a]Num. 21:30
10 [a]Num. 21:24, 25
11 [a]Josh. 12:5
12 [a]Deut. 3:11 [b]Num. 21:24, 34, 35 [1]Lit. *struck* [2]*dispossessed*
13 [a]Josh. 13:11

3 [a]"from Sihor, which *is* east of
Egypt, as far as the border of Ek-
ron northward (*which* is counted
as Canaanite); the [b]five lords of the
Philistines—the Gazites, the Ash-
dodites, the Ashkelonites, the Git-
tites, and the Ekronites; also [c]the
Avites;
4 "from the south, all the land of
the Canaanites, and Mearah that
belongs to the Sidonians [a]as far as
Aphek, to the border of [b]the Amo-
rites;
5 "the land of [a]the [1]Gebalites,
and all Lebanon, toward the sun-
rise, [b]from Baal Gad below Mount
Hermon as far as the entrance to
Hamath;
6 "all the inhabitants of the
mountains from Lebanon as far as
[a]the [1]Brook Misrephoth, *and* all
the Sidonians—them [b]I will drive
out from before the children of Is-
rael; only [c]divide[2] it by lot to Israel
as an inheritance, as I have com-
manded you.
7 "Now therefore, divide this
land as an inheritance to the nine
tribes and half the tribe of Manas-
seh."

The Land Divided East of the Jordan

8 With the other half-tribe the
Reubenites and the Gadites re-
ceived their inheritance, [a]which
Moses had given them, [b]beyond
the Jordan eastward, as Moses the
servant of the LORD had given
them:
9 from Aroer which *is* on the
bank of the River Arnon, and the
town that *is* in the midst of the ra-
vine, [a]and all the plain of Medeba
as far as Dibon;
10 [a]all the cities of Sihon king of
the Amorites, who reigned in
Heshbon, as far as the border of
the children of Ammon;
11 [a]Gilead, and the border of the
Geshurites and Maachathites, all
Mount Hermon, and all Bashan as
far as Salcah;
12 all the kingdom of Og in
Bashan, who reigned in Ashtaroth
and Edrei, who remained of [a]the
remnant of the giants; [b]for Moses
had [1]defeated and [2]cast out
these.
13 Nevertheless the children of Is-
rael [a]did not drive out the Geshu-

Division of Land Among the Twelve Tribes

rites or the Maachathites, but the
Geshurites and the Maachathites
dwell among the Israelites until
this day.
14 [a]Only to the tribe of Levi
he had given [1]no inheritance;
the sacrifices of the LORD
God of Israel made by fire *are*
their inheritance, [b]as He said to
them.

14 [a]Num. 18:20, 23, 24; Deut. 18:1; Josh. 14:3, 4 [b]Josh. 13:33 [1]*no land as a possession*

The Land of Reuben

15 [a]And Moses had given to the
tribe of the children of Reuben *an*
inheritance according to their fam-
ilies.
16 Their territory was [a]from
Aroer, which *is* on the bank of the
River Arnon, [b]and the city that *is*
in the midst of the ravine, [c]and all
the plain by Medeba;
17 [a]Heshbon and all its cities that
are in the plain: Dibon, Bamoth
Baal, Beth Baal Meon,
18 [a]Jahaza, Kedemoth, Mephaath,
19 [a]Kirjathaim, [b]Sibmah, Zereth
Shahar on the mountain of the val-
ley,
20 Beth Peor, [a]the slopes of Pis-
gah, and Beth Jeshimoth—
21 [a]all the cities of the plain and
all the kingdom of Sihon king of
the Amorites, who reigned in
Heshbon, [b]whom Moses had
struck [c]with the princes of Midian:
Evi, Rekem, Zur, Hur, and Reba,
who *were* princes of Sihon dwell-
ing in the country.
22 The children of Israel also
killed with the sword [a]Balaam the
son of Beor, the [1]soothsayer,
among those who were killed by
them.
23 And the border of the children
of Reuben was the bank of the Jor-
dan. This *was* the inheritance of
the children of Reuben according
to their families, the cities and
their villages.

The Land of Gad

24 [a]Moses also had given *an in-*
heritance to the tribe of Gad, to
the children of Gad according to
their families.
25 [a]Their territory was Jazer, and
all the cities of Gilead, [b]and half
the land of the Ammonites as far
as Aroer, which *is* before [c]Rabbah,
26 and from Heshbon to Ramath
Mizpah and Betonim, and from
Mahanaim to the border of Debir,
27 and in the valley [a]Beth Haram,
Beth Nimrah, [b]Succoth, and Za-
phon, the rest of the kingdom of
Sihon king of Heshbon, with the
Jordan as *its* border, as far as the
edge [c]of the [1]Sea of Chinnereth,
on the other side of the Jordan
eastward.
28 This *is* the inheritance of the
children of Gad according to their
families, the cities and their vil-
lages.

Half the Tribe of Manasseh (East)

29 [a]Moses also had given *an in-*
heritance to half the tribe of Ma-
nasseh; it was for half the tribe of
the children of Manasseh accord-
ing to their families:
30 Their territory was from Maha-
naim, all Bashan, all the kingdom
of Og king of Bashan, and [a]all the
towns of Jair which are in Bashan,
sixty cities;
31 half of Gilead, and [a]Ashtaroth
and Edrei, cities of the kingdom
of Og in Bashan, *were* for the
[b]children of Machir the son of Ma-
nasseh, for half of the children of
Machir according to their fami-
lies.
32 These *are the areas* which Mo-
ses had [1]distributed as an inheri-
tance in the plains of Moab on the
other side of the Jordan, by Jeri-
cho eastward.
33 [a]But to the tribe of Levi Moses
had given no inheritance; the LORD
God of Israel *was* their inheri-
tance, [b]as He had said to them.

The Land Divided West of the Jordan

14 These *are the areas* which
the children of Israel inher-
ited in the land of Canaan, [a]which
Eleazar the priest, Joshua the son
of Nun, and the heads of the fa-
thers of the tribes of the children
of Israel distributed as an inheri-
tance to them.
2 Their inheritance *was* [a]by lot,
as the LORD had commanded by
the hand of Moses, for the nine
tribes and the half-tribe.
3 [a]For Moses had given the in-
heritance of the two tribes and
the half-tribe on the other side of
the Jordan; but to the Levites he
had given no inheritance among
them.
4 For [a]the children of Joseph
were two tribes: Manasseh and
Ephraim. And they gave no part
to the Levites in the land, except
[b]cities to dwell *in*, with their
common-lands for their livestock
and their property.
5 [a]As the LORD had commanded
Moses, so the children of Israel
did; and they divided the land.

15 [a]Num. 34:14; Josh. 13:15–23
16 [a]Josh. 12:2 [b]Num. 21:28 [c]Num. 21:30; Josh. 13:9
17 [a]Num. 21:28, 30
18 [a]Num. 21:23; Judg. 11:20; Is. 15:4; Jer. 48:34
19 [a]Num. 32:37; Jer. 48:1, 23; Ezek. 25:9 [b]Num. 32:38
20 [a]Deut. 3:17; Josh. 12:3
21 [a]Deut. 3:10 [b]Num. 21:24 [c]Num. 31:8
22 [a]Num. 22:5; 31:8 [1]*diviner*
24 [a]Num. 34:14; 1 Chr. 5:11
25 [a]Num. 32:1, 35 [b]Judg. 11:13, 15 [c]Deut. 3:11; 2 Sam. 11:1; 12:26
27 [a]Num. 32:36 [b]Gen. 33:17; 1 Kin. 7:46 [c]Num. 34:11; Deut. 3:17 [1]Sea of Galilee
29 [a]Num. 34:14; 1 Chr. 5:23
30 [a]Num. 32:41; 1 Chr. 2:23
31 [a]Josh. 9:10; 12:4; 13:12; 1 Chr. 6:71 [b]Num. 32:39, 40; Josh. 17:1
32 [1]*apportioned*
33 [a]Deut. 18:1; Josh. 13:14; 18:7 [b]Num. 18:20; Deut. 10:9; 18:1, 2

CHAPTER 14

1 [a]Num. 34:16–29
2 [a]Num. 26:55; 33:54; 34:13; Ps. 16:5
3 [a]Num. 32:33; Josh. 13:8, 32, 33
4 [a]Gen. 41:51; 46:20; 48:1, 5; Num. 26:28; 2 Chr. 30:1 [b]Num. 35:2–8; Josh. 21:1–42
5 [a]Num. 35:2; Josh. 21:2

Caleb Inherits Hebron

6 Then the children of Judah
came to Joshua in Gilgal. And Ca-
leb the son of Jephunneh the [a]Ken-
izzite said to him: "You know [b]the
word which the LORD said to Mo-
ses the man of God concern-
ing [c]you and me in Kadesh Bar-
nea.
7 "I *was* forty years old when
Moses the servant of the LORD
[a]sent me from Kadesh Barnea to
spy out the land, and I brought
back word to him as *it was* in my
heart.
8 "Nevertheless [a]my brethren
who went up with me made the
[1]heart of the people melt, but I
wholly [b]followed the LORD my
God.
9 "So Moses swore on that day,
saying, [a]'Surely the land [b]where
your foot has trodden shall be your
inheritance and your children's
forever, because you have wholly
followed the LORD my God.'
10 "And now, behold, the LORD
has kept me [a]alive, [b]as He said,
these forty-five years, ever since
the LORD spoke this word to Moses
while Israel [1]wandered in the wil-
derness; and now, here I am this
day, eighty-five years old.
11 [a]"As yet I *am as* strong this day
as on the day that Moses sent me;
just as my strength *was* then, so
now *is* my strength for war, both
[b]for going out and for coming in.
12 "Now therefore, give me this
mountain of which the LORD spoke
in that day; for you heard in that
day how [a]the Anakim *were* there,
and *that* the cities *were* great *and*
fortified. [b]It may be that the LORD
will be with me, and [c]I shall be able
to drive them out as the LORD
said."
13 And Joshua [a]blessed him, [b]and
gave Hebron to Caleb the son of
Jephunneh as an inheritance.
14 [a]Hebron therefore became the
inheritance of Caleb the son of Je-
phunneh the Kenizzite to this day,
because he [b]wholly followed the
LORD God of Israel.
15 And [a]the name of Hebron for-
merly was Kirjath Arba (*Arba was*
the greatest man among the
Anakim). [b]Then the land had rest
from war.

The Land of Judah

15 So *this* was the [1]lot of the
tribe of the children of Ju-
dah according to their families:
[a]The border of Edom at the [b]Wil-
derness of Zin southward *was* the
extreme southern boundary.
2 And their [a]southern border be-
gan at the shore of the Salt Sea,
from the bay that faces southward.
3 Then it went out to the south-
ern side of [a]the Ascent of Akrab-
bim, passed along to Zin, ascended
on the south side of Kadesh Bar-
nea, passed along to Hezron, went
up to Adar, and went around to
Karkaa.
4 *From there* it passed [a]toward
Azmon and went out to the Brook
of Egypt; and the border ended at
the sea. This shall be your south-
ern border.
5 The east border *was* the Salt
Sea as far as the mouth of the Jor-
dan. And the [a]border on the north-
ern quarter *began* at the bay of the
sea at the mouth of the Jordan.
6 The border went up to [a]Beth
Hoglah and passed north of Beth
Arabah; and the border went up
[b]to the stone of Bohan the son of
Reuben.
7 Then the border went up to-
ward [a]Debir from [b]the Valley of
Achor, and it turned northward to-
ward Gilgal, which *is* before the
Ascent of Adummim, which *is* on
the south side of the valley. The
border continued toward the wa-
ters of En Shemesh and ended at
[c]En Rogel.
8 And the border went up [a]by the
Valley of the Son of Hinnom to the
southern slope of the [b]Jebusite *city*
(which *is* Jerusalem). The border
went up to the top of the mountain
that *lies* before the Valley of Hin-
nom westward, which *is* at the end
of the Valley [c]of [1]Rephaim north-
ward.
9 Then the border went around
from the top of the hill to [a]the
fountain of the water of Nephtoah,
and extended to the cities of
Mount Ephron. And the border
went around [b]to Baalah (which *is*
[c]Kirjath Jearim).
10 Then the border [1]turned west-
ward from Baalah to Mount Seir,
passed along to the side of Mount

6 [a]Num. 32:11, 12 [b]Num. 14:24, 30 [c]Num. 13:26
7 [a]Num. 13:6, 17; 14:6
8 [a]Num. 13:31, 32; Deut. 1:28 [b]Num. 14:24; Deut. 1:36 [1]*courage of the people fail*
9 [a]Num. 14:23, 24 [b]Num. 13:22; Deut. 1:36
10 [a]Num. 14:24, 30, 38 [b]Josh. 5:6; Neh. 9:21 [1]Lit. *walked*
11 [a]Deut. 34:7 [b]Deut. 31:2
12 [a]Num. 13:28, 33 [b]Rom. 8:31 [c]Josh. 15:14; Judg. 1:20
13 [a]Josh. 22:6 [b]Josh. 10:37; 15:13
14 [a]Josh. 21:12 [b]Josh. 14:8, 9
15 [a]Gen. 23:2; Josh. 15:13 [b]Josh. 11:23

CHAPTER 15

1 [a]Num. 34:3 [b]Num. 33:36 [1]*allotment*
2 [a]Num. 34:3, 4
3 [a]Num. 34:4
4 [a]Num. 34:5
5 [a]Josh. 18:15–19
6 [a]Josh. 18:19, 21 [b]Josh. 18:17
7 [a]Josh. 13:26 [b]Josh. 7:26 [c]2 Sam. 17:17; 1 Kin. 1:9
8 [a]Josh. 18:16; 2 Kin. 23:10; Jer. 19:2, 6 [b]Josh. 15:63; 18:28; Judg. 1:21; 19:10 [c]Josh. 18:16 [1]Lit. *Giants*
9 [a]Josh. 18:15 [b]1 Chr. 13:6 [c]Judg. 18:12
10 [a]Gen. 38:13; Judg. 14:1 [1]*turned around*

Jearim on the north (which *is*
Chesalon), went down to Beth
Shemesh, and passed on to [a]Tim-
nah.
11 And the border went out to the
side of [a]Ekron northward. Then
the border went around to Shic-
ron, passed along to Mount
Baalah, and extended to Jabneel;
and the border ended at the sea.
12 The west border *was* [a]the
coastline of the Great Sea. This *is*
the boundary of the children of Ju-
dah all around according to their
families.

Caleb Occupies Hebron and Debir

13 [a]Now to Caleb the son of Je-
phunneh he gave a share among
the children of [b]Judah, according
to the commandment of the LORD
to Joshua, *namely*, [c]Kirjath Arba,
which *is* Hebron (*Arba was* the fa-
ther of Anak).
14 Caleb drove out [a]the three sons
of Anak from there: [b]Sheshai, Ahi-
man, and Talmai, the children of
Anak.
15 Then [a]he went up from there
to the inhabitants of Debir (for-
merly the name of Debir *was* Kir-
jath Sepher).
16 [a]And Caleb said, "He who [1]at-
tacks Kirjath Sepher and takes it,
to him I will give Achsah my
daughter as wife."
17 So [a]Othniel the [b]son of Kenaz,
the brother of Caleb, took it; and
he gave him [c]Achsah his daughter
as wife.
18 [a]Now it was so, when she came
to him, that she persuaded him to
ask her father for a field. So [b]she
dismounted from *her* donkey, and
Caleb said to her, "What do you
wish?"
19 She answered, "Give me a
[a]blessing; since you have given me
land in the South, give me also
springs of water." So he gave her
the upper springs and the lower
springs.

The Cities of Judah

20 This *was* the inheritance of the
tribe of the children of Judah ac-
cording to their families:
21 The cities at the limits of the
tribe of the children of Judah, to-
ward the border of Edom in the
South, were Kabzeel, [a]Eder, Jagur,
22 Kinah, Dimonah, Adadah,
23 Kedesh, Hazor, Ithnan,
24 [a]Ziph, Telem, Bealoth,
25 Hazor, Hadattah, Kerioth,
Hezron (which *is* Hazor),
26 Amam, Shema, Moladah,
27 Hazar Gaddah, Heshmon, Beth
Pelet,
28 Hazar Shual, [a]Beersheba, Biz-
jothjah,
29 Baalah, Ijim, Ezem,
30 Eltolad, Chesil, [a]Hormah,
31 [a]Ziklag, Madmannah, Sansan-
nah,
32 Lebaoth, Shilhim, Ain, and
[a]Rimmon: all the cities *are* twenty-
nine, with their villages.
33 In the lowland: [a]Eshtaol, Zorah,
Ashnah,
34 Zanoah, En Gannim, Tappuah,
Enam,
35 Jarmuth, [a]Adullam, Socoh,
Azekah,
36 Sharaim, Adithaim, Gederah,
and Gederothaim: fourteen cities
with their villages;
37 Zenan, Hadashah, Migdal Gad,
38 Dilean, Mizpah, [a]Joktheel,
39 [a]Lachish, Bozkath, [b]Eglon,
40 Cabbon, [1]Lahmas, Kithlish,
41 Gederoth, Beth Dagon, Naa-
mah, and Makkedah: sixteen cities
with their villages;
42 [a]Libnah, Ether, Ashan,
43 Jiphtah, Ashnah, Nezib,
44 Keilah, Achzib, and Mareshah:
nine cities with their villages;
45 Ekron, with its towns and vil-
lages;
46 from Ekron to the sea, all that
lay near [a]Ashdod, with their vil-
lages;
47 Ashdod with its towns and vil-
lages, Gaza with its towns and vil-
lages—as far as [a]the Brook of
Egypt and [b]the Great Sea with *its*
coastline.
48 And in the mountain country:
Shamir, Jattir, Sochoh,
49 Dannah, Kirjath Sannah
(which *is* Debir),
50 Anab, Eshtemoh, Anim,
51 [a]Goshen, Holon, and Giloh:
eleven cities with their villages;
52 Arab, Dumah, Eshean,
53 Janum, Beth Tappuah, Aphe-
kah,
54 Humtah, [a]Kirjath Arba (which
is Hebron), and Zior: nine cities
with their villages;
55 [a]Maon, Carmel, Ziph, Juttah,

11 [a]Josh. 19:43
12 [a]Num. 34:6, 7; Josh. 15:47
13 [a]Josh. 14:13 [b]Num. 13:6 [c]Josh. 14:15
14 [a]Judg. 1:10, 20 [b]Num. 13:22
15 [a]Josh. 10:38; Judg. 1:11
16 [a]Judg. 1:12 [1]Lit. *strikes*
17 [a]Judg. 1:13; 3:9 [b]Num. 32:12; Josh. 14:6 [c]Judg. 1:12
18 [a]Judg. 1:14 [b]Gen. 24:64; 1 Sam. 25:23
19 [a]Gen. 33:11
21 [a]Gen. 35:21
24 [a]1 Sam. 23:14
28 [a]Gen. 21:31; Josh. 19:2
30 [a]Josh. 19:4
31 [a]Josh. 19:5; 1 Sam. 27:6; 30:1
32 [a]Judg. 20:45, 47
33 [a]Judg. 13:25; 16:31
35 [a]1 Sam. 22:1
38 [a]2 Kin. 14:7
39 [a]2 Kin. 14:19 [b]Josh. 10:3
40 [1]Or *Lahmam*
42 [a]Josh. 21:13
46 [a]Josh. 11:22
47 [a]Josh. 15:4 [b]Num. 34:6
51 [a]Josh. 10:41; 11:16
54 [a]Josh. 14:15

56 Jezreel, Jokdeam, Zanoah,
57 Kain, Gibeah, and Timnah: ten cities with their villages;
58 Halhul, Beth Zur, Gedor,
59 Maarath, Beth Anoth, and Eltekon: six cities with their villages;
60 [a]Kirjath Baal (which *is* Kirjath Jearim) and Rabbah: two cities with their villages.
61 In the wilderness: Beth Arabah, Middin, Secacah,
62 Nibshan, the City of Salt, and [a]En Gedi: six cities with their villages.
63 As for the Jebusites, the inhabitants of Jerusalem, [a]the children of Judah could not drive them out; [b]but the Jebusites dwell with the children of Judah at Jerusalem to this day.

Ephraim and West Manasseh

16 The lot [1]fell to the children of Joseph from the Jordan, by Jericho, to the waters of Jericho on the east, to the [a]wilderness that goes up from Jericho through the mountains to [2]Bethel,
2 then went out [1]from [a]Bethel to Luz, passed along to the border of the Archites at Ataroth,
3 and went down westward to the boundary of the Japhletites, [a]as far as the boundary of Lower Beth Horon to [b]Gezer; and [1]it ended at the sea.
4 [a]So the children of Joseph, Manasseh and Ephraim, took their [1]inheritance.

The Land of Ephraim

5 [a]The border of the children of Ephraim, according to their families, was *thus:* The border of their inheritance on the east side was [b]Ataroth Addar [c]as far as Upper Beth Horon.
6 And the border went out toward the sea on the north side of [a]Michmethath; then the border went around eastward to Taanath Shiloh, and passed by it on the east of Janohah.
7 Then it went down from Janohah to Ataroth and [1]Naarah, reached to Jericho, and came out at the Jordan.
8 The border went out from [a]Tappuah westward to the [b]Brook Kanah, and [1]it ended at the sea. This *was* the inheritance of the tribe of the children of Ephraim according to their families.
9 [a]The separate cities for the children of Ephraim *were* among the inheritance of the children of Manasseh, all the cities with their villages.
10 [a]And they did not drive out the Canaanites who dwelt in Gezer; but the Canaanites dwell among the Ephraimites to this day and have become forced laborers.

The Other Half-Tribe of Manasseh (West)

17 There was also a lot for the tribe of Manasseh, for he *was* the [a]firstborn of Joseph: *namely* for [b]Machir the firstborn of Manasseh, the father of Gilead, because he was a man of war; therefore he was given [c]Gilead and Bashan.
2 And there was *a lot* for [a]the rest of the children of Manasseh according to their families: [b]for the children of [1]Abiezer, the children of Helek, [c]the children of Asriel, the children of Shechem, [d]the children of Hepher, and the children of Shemida; these *were* the male children of Manasseh the son of Joseph according to their families.
3 But [a]Zelophehad the son of Hepher, the son of Gilead, the son of Machir, the son of Manasseh, had no sons, but only daughters. And these *are* the names of his daughters: Mahlah, Noah, Hoglah, Milcah, and Tirzah.
4 And they came near before [a]Eleazar the priest, before Joshua the son of Nun, and before the rulers, saying, [b]"The LORD commanded Moses to give us an [1]inheritance among our brothers." Therefore, according to the commandment of the LORD, he gave them an inheritance among their father's brothers.
5 Ten shares fell to [a]Manasseh, besides the land of Gilead and Bashan, which *were* on the other side of the Jordan,
6 because the daughters of Manasseh received an inheritance among his sons; and the rest of Manasseh's sons had the land of Gilead.

55 [a]1 Sam. 23:24, 25
60 [a]Josh. 18:14; 1 Sam. 7:1, 2
62 [a]1 Sam. 23:29; Ezek. 47:10
63 [a]Judg. 1:8, 21; 2 Sam. 5:6; 1 Chr. 11:4 [b]Judg. 1:21

CHAPTER 16

1 [a]Josh. 8:15; 18:12 [1]Lit. *went out* [2]LXX *Bethel Luz*
2 [a]Josh. 18:13; Judg. 1:26 [1]LXX *to Bethel,*
3 [a]Josh. 18:13; 1 Kin. 9:17; 2 Chr. 8:5 [b]Josh. 21:21; 1 Kin. 9:15; 1 Chr. 7:28 [1]Lit. *the goings out of it were at the sea*
4 [a]Josh. 17:14 [1]*possession*
5 [a]Judg. 1:29; 1 Chr. 7:28, 29 [b]Josh. 18:13 [c]2 Chr. 8:5
6 [a]Josh. 17:7
7 [1]*Naaran,* 1 Chr. 7:28
8 [a]Josh. 17:8 [b]Josh. 17:9 [1]Lit. *the goings out of it were at the sea*
9 [a]Josh. 17:9
10 [a]Josh. 15:63; 17:12, 13; Judg. 1:29; 1 Kin. 9:16

CHAPTER 17

1 [a]Gen. 41:51; 46:20; 48:18 [b]Gen. 50:23; Judg. 5:14 [c]Deut. 3:15
2 [a]Num. 26:29–33 [b]1 Chr. 7:18 [c]Num. 26:31 [d]Num. 26:32 [1]*Jeezer,* Num. 26:30
3 [a]Num. 26:33; 27:1; 36:2
4 [a]Josh. 14:1 [b]Num. 27:2–11 [1]*possession*
5 [a]Josh. 22:7

7 And the territory of Manasseh
was from Asher to [a]Michmethath,
that *lies* east of Shechem; and the
border went along south to the in-
habitants of En Tappuah.
8 Manasseh had the land of Tap-
puah, but [a]Tappuah on the border
of Manasseh *belonged* to the chil-
dren of Ephraim.
9 And the [1]border descended to
the [2]Brook Kanah, southward to
the brook. [a]These cities of
Ephraim *are* among the cities of
Manasseh. The border of Manas-
seh *was* on the north side of the
brook; and it ended at the sea.
10 Southward *it was* Ephraim's,
northward *it was* Manasseh's, and
the sea was its border. Manasseh's
territory was adjoining Asher on
the north and Issachar on the east.
11 And in Issachar and in Asher,
[a]Manasseh had [b]Beth Shean and
its towns, Ibleam and its towns, the
inhabitants of Dor and its towns,
the inhabitants of En Dor and its
towns, the inhabitants of Taanach
and its towns, and the inhabitants
of Megiddo and its towns—three
hilly regions.
12 Yet [a]the children of Manasseh
could not drive out *the inhabitants
of* those cities, but the Canaanites
were determined to dwell in that
land.
13 And it happened, when the
children of Israel grew strong, that
they put the Canaanites to [a]forced
labor, but did not utterly drive
them out.

More Land for Ephraim and Manasseh

14 [a]Then the children of Joseph
spoke to Joshua, saying, "Why
have you given us *only* [b]one [1]lot
and one share to inherit, since we
are [c]a great people, inasmuch as
the LORD has blessed us until
now?"
15 So Joshua answered them, "If
you *are* a great people, *then* go up
to the forest *country* and clear a
place for yourself there in the land
of the Perizzites and the giants,
since the mountains of Ephraim
are too confined for you."
16 But the children of Joseph said,
"The mountain country is not
enough for us; and all the Canaan-
ites who dwell in the land of the
valley have [a]chariots of iron, *both*
those who *are* of Beth Shean and
its towns and *those* who *are* [b]of
the Valley of Jezreel."
17 And Joshua spoke to the house
of Joseph—to Ephraim and Ma-
nasseh—saying, "You *are* a great
people and have great power; you
shall not have *only* one [1]lot,
18 "but the mountain country
shall be yours. Although it *is*
wooded, you shall cut it down, and
its [1]farthest extent shall be yours;
for you shall drive out the Canaan-
ites, [a]though they have iron chari-
ots *and* are strong."

The Remainder of the Land Divided

18 Now the whole congrega-
tion of the children of Israel
assembled together [a]at Shiloh, and
[b]set up the tabernacle of meeting
there. And the land was subdued
before them.
2 But there remained among the
children of Israel seven tribes
which had not yet received their
inheritance.
3 Then Joshua said to the chil-
dren of Israel: [a]"How long will you
neglect to go and possess the land
which the LORD God of your fa-
thers has given you?
4 "Pick out from among you
three men for *each* tribe, and I will
send them; they shall rise and go
through the land, survey it accord-
ing to their inheritance, and come
back to me.
5 "And they shall divide it into
seven parts. [a]Judah shall remain
in their territory on the south, and
the [b]house of Joseph shall remain
in their territory on the north.
6 "You shall therefore [1]survey
the land in seven parts and bring
the survey here to me, [a]that I may
cast lots for you here before the
LORD our God.
7 [a]"But the Levites have no part
among you, for the priesthood of
the LORD *is* their inheritance. [b]And
Gad, Reuben, and half the tribe of
Manasseh have received their in-
heritance beyond the Jordan on
the east, which Moses the servant
of the LORD gave them."
8 Then the men arose to go
away; and Joshua charged those
who went to [1]survey the land, say-
ing, "Go, walk [a]through the land,
survey it, and come back to me,

---

7 [a]Josh. 16:6
8 [a]Josh. 16:8
9 [a]Josh. 16:9 [1]*boundary* [2]*Wadi*
11 [a]1 Chr. 7:29 [b]Judg. 1:27; 1 Sam. 31:10; 1 Kin. 4:12
12 [a]Judg. 1:19, 27, 28
13 [a]Josh. 16:10
14 [a]Josh. 16:4 [b]Gen. 48:22 [c]Gen. 48:19; Num. 26:34, 37 [1]*allotment*
16 [a]Josh. 17:18; Judg. 1:19; 4:3 [b]Josh. 19:18; 1 Kin. 4:12
17 [1]*allotment*
18 [a]Deut. 20:1 [1]Lit. *goings out*
CHAPTER 18
1 [a]Josh. 19:51; 21:2; 22:9; Jer. 7:12 [b]Judg. 18:31; 1 Sam. 1:3, 24; 4:3, 4
3 [a]Judg. 18:9
5 [a]Josh. 15:1 [b]Josh. 16:1—17:18
6 [a]Josh. 14:2; 18:10 [1]*describe in writing*
7 [a]Num. 18:7, 20; Josh. 13:33 [b]Josh. 13:8
8 [a]Gen. 13:17 [1]*describe in writing*

that I may cast lots for you here
before the LORD in Shiloh."
9 So the men went, passed
through the land, and [1]wrote the
survey in a book in seven parts by
cities; and they came to Joshua at
the camp in Shiloh.
10 Then Joshua cast [a]lots for them
in Shiloh before the LORD, and
there [b]Joshua divided the land to
the children of Israel according to
their [1]divisions.

The Land of Benjamin

11 [a]Now the lot of the tribe of the
children of Benjamin came up ac-
cording to their families, and the
territory of their lot came out be-
tween the children of Judah and
the children of Joseph.
12 [a]Their border on the north side
began at the Jordan, and the bor-
der went up to the side of Jericho
on the north, and went up through
the mountains westward; it ended
at the Wilderness of Beth Aven.
13 The border went over from
there toward Luz, to the side of
Luz [a](which *is* Bethel) southward;
and the border descended to Ata-
roth Addar, near the hill that *lies*
on the south side [b]of Lower Beth
Horon.
14 Then the border extended
around the west side to the south,
from the hill that *lies* before Beth
Horon southward; and [1]it ended at
[a]Kirjath Baal (which *is* Kirjath
Jearim), a city of the children of
Judah. This *was* the west side.
15 The south side *began* at the end
of Kirjath Jearim, and the border
extended on the west and went out
to [a]the spring of the waters of
Nephtoah.
16 Then the border came down to
the end of the mountain that *lies*
before [a]the Valley of the Son of
Hinnom, which *is* in the Valley of
the [1]Rephaim on the north, de-
scended to the Valley of Hinnom,
to the side of the Jebusite *city* on
the south, and descended to [b]En
Rogel.
17 And it went around from the
north, went out to En Shemesh,
and extended toward Geliloth,
which is before the Ascent of
Adummim, and descended to [a]the
stone of Bohan the son of Reuben.
18 Then it passed along toward
the north side of [1]Arabah, and
went down to Arabah.
19 And the border passed along to
the north side of Beth Hoglah; then
[1]the border ended at the north bay
at the [a]Salt Sea, at the south end
of the Jordan. This *was* the south-
ern boundary.
20 The Jordan was its border on
the east side. This *was* the inheri-
tance of the children of Benjamin,
according to its boundaries all
around, according to their fami-
lies.
21 Now the cities of the tribe of
the children of Benjamin, accord-
ing to their families, were Jericho,
Beth Hoglah, Emek Keziz,
22 Beth Arabah, Zemaraim,
Bethel,
23 Avim, Parah, Ophrah,
24 Chephar Haammoni, Ophni,
and Gaba: twelve cities with their
villages;
25 [a]Gibeon, [b]Ramah, Beeroth,
26 Mizpah, Chephirah, Mozah,
27 Rekem, Irpeel, Taralah,
28 Zelah, Eleph, [a]Jebus (which *is*
Jerusalem), Gibeath, *and* Kirjath:
fourteen cities with their villages.
This was the inheritance of the
children of Benjamin according to
their families.

Simeon's Inheritance with Judah

19 The [a]second lot came out for
Simeon, for the tribe of the
children of Simeon according to
their families. [b]And their inheri-
tance was within the inheritance
of the children of Judah.
2 [a]They had in their inheritance
Beersheba (Sheba), Moladah,
3 Hazar Shual, Balah, Ezem,
4 Eltolad, Bethul, Hormah,
5 Ziklag, Beth Marcaboth, Hazar
Susah,
6 Beth Lebaoth, and Sharuhen:
thirteen cities and their villages;
7 Ain, Rimmon, Ether, and
Ashan: four cities and their vil-
lages;
8 and all the villages that *were*
all around these cities as far as
Baalath Beer, [a]Ramah of the
South. This *was* the inheritance of
the tribe of the children of Simeon
according to their families.
9 The inheritance of the children
of Simeon *was included* in the
share of the children of Judah, for

9 [1]*described it in writing*
10 [a]Acts 13:19 [b]Num. 34:16–29; Josh. 19:51 [1]*portions*
11 [a]Judg. 1:21
12 [a]Josh. 16:1
13 [a]Gen. 28:19; Josh. 16:2; Judg. 1:23 [b]Josh. 16:3
14 [a]Josh. 15:9 [1]Lit. *its goings out were*
15 [a]Josh. 15:9
16 [a]Josh. 15:8 [b]Josh. 15:7 [1]Lit. *Giants*
17 [a]Josh. 15:6
18 [1]*Beth Arabah*, Josh. 15:6; 18:22
19 [a]Josh. 15:2, 5 [1]Lit. *the goings out of the border were*
25 [a]Josh. 11:19; 21:17; 1 Kin. 3:4, 5 [b]Jer. 31:15
28 [a]Josh. 15:8, 63

CHAPTER 19

1 [a]Judg. 1:3 [b]Josh. 19:9
2 [a]1 Chr. 4:28
8 [a]1 Sam. 30:27

the share of the children of Judah
was [1]too much for them. [a]There-
fore the children of Simeon had
their inheritance within the inheri-
tance of [2]that people.

The Land of Zebulun

10 The third lot came out for the
children of Zebulun according to
their families, and the border of
their inheritance was as far as
Sarid.
11 [a]Their border went toward the
west and to Maralah, went to
Dabbasheth, and extended along
the brook that is [b]east of Jok-
neam.
12 Then from Sarid it went east-
ward toward the sunrise along the
border of Chisloth Tabor, and
went out toward [a]Daberath, by-
passing Japhia.
13 And from there it passed along
on the east of [a]Gath Hepher, to-
ward Eth Kazin, and extended
to Rimmon, which borders on
Neah.
14 Then the border went around
it on the north side of Hannathon,
and [1]it ended in the Valley of
Jiphthah El.
15 Included were Kattath, Nahal-
lal, Shimron, Idalah, and Bethle-
hem: twelve cities with their vil-
lages.
16 This *was* the inheritance of the
children of Zebulun according to
their families, these cities with
their villages.

The Land of Issachar

17 The fourth lot came out to Is-
sachar, for the children of Issachar
according to their families.
18 And their territory went to
Jezreel, and *included* Chesulloth,
Shunem,
19 Haphraim, Shion, Anaharath,
20 Rabbith, Kishion, Abez,
21 Remeth, En Gannim, En Had-
dah, and Beth Pazzez.
22 And the border reached to Ta-
bor, Shahazimah, and [a]Beth
Shemesh; their border ended at
the Jordan: sixteen cities with
their villages.
23 This *was* the inheritance of the
tribe of the children of Issachar ac-
cording to their families, the cities
and their villages.

9 [a]Josh. 19:1 [1]*too large* [2]Lit. *them*
11 [a]Gen. 49:13 [b]Josh. 12:22
12 [a]1 Chr. 6:72
13 [a]2 Kin. 14:25
14 [1]Lit. *the goings out of it were*
22 [a]Josh. 15:10; Judg. 1:33
24 [a]Judg. 1:31, 32
26 [a]1 Sam. 15:12; 1 Kin. 18:20; Is. 33:9; 35:2; Jer. 46:18
27 [a]1 Kin. 9:13
28 [a]Gen. 10:19; Josh. 11:8; Judg. 1:31; Acts 27:3 [1]So with MT, Tg., Vg.; a few Heb. mss. *Abdon* (cf. 21:30 and 1 Chr. 6:74)
29 [a]Judg. 1:31
32 [a]Josh. 19:32–39; Judg. 1:33
33 [1]Lit. *its goings out were*
34 [a]Deut. 33:23
37 [a]Josh. 20:7

The Land of Asher

24 [a]The fifth lot came out for the
tribe of the children of Asher ac-
cording to their families.
25 And their territory included
Helkath, Hali, Beten, Achshaph,
26 Alammelech, Amad, and
Mishal; it reached to [a]Mount Car-
mel westward, along *the Brook*
Shihor Libnath.
27 It turned toward the sunrise to
Beth Dagon; and it reached to
Zebulun and to the Valley of
Jiphthah El, then northward be-
yond Beth Emek and Neiel,
bypassing [a]Cabul *which was* on
the left,
28 including [1]Ebron, Rehob, Ham-
mon, and Kanah, [a]as far as
Greater Sidon.
29 And the border turned to Ra-
mah and to the fortified city of
Tyre; then the border turned to
Hosah, and ended at the sea by the
region of [a]Achzib.
30 Also Ummah, Aphek, and Re-
hob *were included:* twenty-two cit-
ies with their villages.
31 This *was* the inheritance of the
tribe of the children of Asher ac-
cording to their families, these cit-
ies with their villages.

The Land of Naphtali

32 [a]The sixth lot came out to the
children of Naphtali, for the chil-
dren of Naphtali according to their
families.
33 And their border began at He-
leph, enclosing the territory from
the terebinth tree in Zaanannim,
Adami Nekeb, and Jabneel, as far
as Lakkum; [1]it ended at the Jor-
dan.
34 [a]From Heleph the border ex-
tended westward to Aznoth Tabor,
and went out from there toward
Hukkok; it adjoined Zebulun on
the south side and Asher on the
west side, and ended at Judah by
the Jordan toward the sunrise.
35 And the fortified cities *are* Zid-
dim, Zer, Hammath, Rakkath,
Chinnereth,
36 Adamah, Ramah, Hazor,
37 [a]Kedesh, Edrei, En Hazor,
38 Iron, Migdal El, Horem, Beth
Anath, and Beth Shemesh: nine-
teen cities with their villages.
39 This *was* the inheritance of the

tribe of the children of Naphtali
according to their families, the cit-
ies and their villages.

The Land of Dan

40 [a]The seventh lot came out for
the tribe of the children of Dan ac-
cording to their families.
41 And the territory of their inher-
itance was Zorah, [a]Eshtaol, Ir
Shemesh,
42 [a]Shaalabbin, [b]Aijalon, Jethlah,
43 Elon, Timnah, [a]Ekron,
44 Eltekeh, Gibbethon, Baalath,
45 Jehud, Bene Berak, Gath Rim-
mon,
46 Me Jarkon, and Rakkon, with
the region [1]near [2]Joppa.
47 And the [a]border of the children
of Dan went beyond these, be-
cause the children of Dan went up
to fight against Leshem and took
it; and they struck it with the edge
of the sword, took possession of
it, and dwelt in it. They called
Leshem, [b]Dan, after the name of
Dan their father.
48 This *is* the inheritance of the
tribe of the children of Dan ac-
cording to their families, these cit-
ies with their villages.

Joshua's Inheritance

49 When they had [1]made an end
of dividing the land as an inheri-
tance according to their borders,
the children of Israel gave an in-
heritance among them to Joshua
the son of Nun.
50 According to the word of the
LORD they gave him the city which
he asked for, [a]Timnath [b]Serah in
the mountains of Ephraim; and he
built the city and dwelt in it.
51 [a]These *were* the inheritances
which Eleazar the priest, Joshua
the son of Nun, and the heads of
the fathers of the tribes of the chil-
dren of Israel divided as an inheri-
tance by lot [b]in Shiloh before the
LORD, at the door of the tabernacle
of meeting. So they made an end
of dividing the country.

The Cities of Refuge

20 The LORD also spoke to
Joshua, saying,
2 "Speak to the children of Is-
rael, saying: [a]'Appoint[1] for your-
selves cities of refuge, of which I
spoke to you through Moses,
3 'that the slayer who kills a per-
son accidentally *or* unintentionally
may flee there; and they shall be
your refuge from the avenger of
blood.
4 'And when he flees to one of
those cities, and stands at the en-
trance of the gate of the city, and
[1]declares his case in the hearing
of the elders of that city, they shall
take him into the city as one of
them, and give him a place, that
he may dwell among them.
5 [a]'Then if the avenger of blood
pursues him, they shall not deliver
the slayer into his hand, because
he struck his neighbor unin-
tentionally, but did not hate him
beforehand.
6 'And he shall dwell in that city
[a]until he stands before the congre-
gation for judgment, *and* until the
death of the one who is high priest
in those days. Then the slayer may
return and come to his own city
and his own house, to the city from
which he fled.' "
7 So they appointed [a]Kedesh in
Galilee, in the mountains of Naph-
tali, [b]Shechem in the mountains of
Ephraim, and [c]Kirjath Arba
(which *is* Hebron) in [d]the moun-
tains of Judah.
8 And on the other side of the
Jordan, by Jericho eastward, they
assigned [a]Bezer in the wilderness
on the plain, from the tribe of Reu-
ben, [b]Ramoth in Gilead, from the
tribe of Gad, and [c]Golan in
Bashan, from the tribe of Manas-
seh.
9 [a]These were the cities ap-
pointed for all the children of Is-
rael and for the stranger who
[1]dwelt among them, that whoever
killed a person accidentally might
flee there, and not die by the hand
of the avenger of blood [b]until he
stood before the congregation.

Cities of the Levites

21 Then the heads of the fa-
thers' *houses* of the [a]Levites
came near to [b]Eleazar the priest,
to Joshua the son of Nun, and to
the heads of the fathers' *houses* of
the tribes of the children of Israel.
2 And they spoke to them at [a]Shi-
loh in the land of Canaan, saying,
[b]"The LORD commanded through
Moses to give us cities to dwell in,

40 [a]Josh. 19:40–48; Judg. 1:34–36
41 [a]Josh. 15:33
42 [a]Judg. 1:35; 1 Kin. 4:9 [b]Josh. 10:12; 21:24
43 [a]Josh. 15:11; Judg. 1:18
46 [1]*over against* [2]Heb. *Japho*
47 [a]Judg. 18 [b]Judg. 18:29
49 [1]*finished*
50 [a]Josh. 24:30 [b]1 Chr. 7:24
51 [a]Num. 34:17; Josh. 14:1 [b]Josh. 18:1, 10

CHAPTER 20

2 [a]Ex. 21:13; Num. 35:6–34; Deut. 19:2, 9 [1]*Designate*
4 [1]*states*
5 [a]Num. 35:12
6 [a]Num. 35:12, 24, 25
7 [a]Josh. 21:32; 1 Chr. 6:76 [b]Josh. 21:21; 2 Chr. 10:1 [c]Josh. 14:15; 21:11, 13 [d]Luke 1:39
8 [a]Deut. 4:43; Josh. 21:36; 1 Chr. 6:78 [b]Josh. 21:38; 1 Kin. 22:3 [c]Josh. 21:27
9 [a]Num. 35:15 [b]Josh. 20:6 [1]*As a resident alien*

CHAPTER 21

1 [a]Num. 35:1–8 [b]Num. 34:16–29; Josh. 14:1; 17:4
2 [a]Josh. 18:1 [b]Num. 35:2

with their common-lands for our
livestock."
3 So the children of Israel gave
to the Levites from their inheri-
tance, at the commandment of
the LORD, these cities and their
common-lands:
4 Now the lot came out for the
families of the Kohathites. And
[a]the children of Aaron the priest,
who were of the Levites, [b]had thir-
teen cities by lot from the tribe of
Judah, from the tribe of Simeon,
and from the tribe of Benjamin.
5 [a]The rest of the children of Ko-
hath had ten cities by lot from the
families of the tribe of Ephraim,
from the tribe of Dan, and from
the half-tribe of Manasseh.
6 And [a]the children of Gershon
had thirteen cities by lot from the
families of the tribe of Issachar,
from the tribe of Asher, from the
tribe of Naphtali, and from the
half-tribe of Manasseh in Bashan.
7 [a]The children of Merari accord-
ing to their families had twelve cit-
ies from the tribe of Reuben, from
the tribe of Gad, and from the tribe
of Zebulun.
8 [a]And the children of Israel
gave these cities with their
common-lands by lot to the Le-
vites, [b]as the LORD had com-
manded by the hand of Moses.
9 So they gave from the tribe of
the children of Judah and from the
tribe of the children of Simeon
these cities which are [1]designated
by name,
10 which were for the children of
Aaron, one of the families of the
Kohathites, *who were* of the chil-
dren of Levi; for the lot was theirs
first.
11 [a]And they gave them [1]Kirjath
Arba (*Arba was* the father of
[b]Anak), [c]which *is* Hebron, in the
mountains of Judah, with the
common-land surrounding it.
12 But [a]the fields of the city and
its villages they gave to Caleb the
son of Jephunneh as his posses-
sion.
13 Thus [a]to the children of Aaron
the priest they gave [b]Hebron with
its common-land (a city of refuge
for the slayer), [c]Libnah with its
common-land,
14 [a]Jattir with its common-land,
[b]Eshtemoa with its common-land,
15 [a]Holon with its common-land,
[b]Debir with its common-land,
16 [a]Ain with its common-land,
[b]Juttah with its common-land, and
[c]Beth Shemesh with its common-
land: nine cities from those two
tribes;
17 and from the tribe of Benjamin,
[a]Gibeon with its common-land,
[b]Geba with its common-land,
18 Anathoth with its common-
land, and [a]Almon with its common-
land: four cities.
19 All the cities of the children of
Aaron, the priests, *were* thirteen
cities with their common-lands.
20 [a]And the families of the chil-
dren of Kohath, the Levites, the
rest of the children of Kohath,
even they had the cities of their
[1]lot from the tribe of Ephraim.
21 For they gave them [a]Shechem
with its common-land in the moun-
tains of Ephraim (a city of refuge
for the slayer), [b]Gezer with its
common-land,
22 Kibzaim with its common-land,
and Beth Horon with its common-
land: four cities;
23 and from the tribe of Dan, Elte-
keh with its common-land, Gibbe-
thon with its common-land,
24 [a]Aijalon with its common-land,
and Gath Rimmon with its common-
land: four cities;
25 and from the half-tribe of Ma-
nasseh, Tanach with its common-
land and Gath Rimmon with its
common-land: two cities.
26 All the ten cities with their
common-lands were for the rest of
the families of the children of Ko-
hath.
27 [a]Also to the children of Ger-
shon, of the families of the Levites,
from the *other* half-tribe of Manas-
seh, *they gave* [b]Golan in Bashan
with its common-land (a city of
refuge for the slayer), and Be Esh-
terah with its common-land: two
cities;
28 and from the tribe of Issachar,
Kishion with its common-land, Dab-
erath with its common-land,
29 Jarmuth with its common-land,
and En Gannim with its common-
land: four cities;
30 and from the tribe of Asher,
Mishal with its common-land, Ab-
don with its common-land,
31 Helkath with its common-land,

4 [a]Josh. 21:8, 19 [b]Josh. 19:51
5 [a]Josh. 21:20
6 [a]Josh. 21:27
7 [a]Josh. 21:34
8 [a]Josh. 21:3 [b]Num. 35:2
9 [1]Lit. *called*
11 [a]Josh. 20:7; 1 Chr. 6:55 [b]Josh. 14:15; 15:13, 14 [c]Josh. 20:7; Luke 1:39 [1]Lit. *City of Arba*
12 [a]Josh. 14:14; 1 Chr. 6:56
13 [a]1 Chr. 6:57 [b]Josh. 15:54; 20:2, 7 [c]Josh. 15:42; 2 Kin. 8:22
14 [a]Josh. 15:48 [b]Josh. 15:50
15 [a]1 Chr. 6:58 [b]Josh. 15:49
16 [a]1 Chr. 6:59 [b]Josh. 15:55 [c]Josh. 15:10
17 [a]Josh. 18:25 [b]Josh. 18:24
18 [a]1 Chr. 6:60
20 [a]1 Chr. 6:66 [1]*allotment*
21 [a]Josh. 20:7 [b]Judg. 1:29
24 [a]Josh. 10:12
27 [a]Josh. 21:6; 1 Chr. 6:71 [b]Josh. 20:8

and Rehob with its common-land:
four cities;
32 and from the tribe of Naphtali,
[a]Kedesh in Galilee with its com-
mon-land (a city of refuge for the
slayer), Hammoth Dor with its
common-land, and Kartan with its
common-land: three cities.
33 All the cities of the Gershonites
according to their families *were*
thirteen cities with their common-
lands.
34 [a]And to the families of the chil-
dren of Merari, the rest of the Le-
vites, from the tribe of Zebulun,
Jokneam with its common-land,
Kartah with its common-land,
35 Dimnah with its common-land,
and Nahalal with its common-
land: four cities;
36 [1]and from the tribe of Reuben,
[a]Bezer with its common-land, Ja-
haz with its common-land,
37 Kedemoth with its common-
land, and Mephaath with its
common-land: four cities;
38 and from the tribe of Gad,
[a]Ramoth in Gilead with its
common-land (a city of refuge for
the slayer), Mahanaim with its
common-land,
39 Heshbon with its common-
land, *and* Jazer with its common-
land: four cities in all.
40 So all the cities for the children
of Merari according to their fami-
lies, the rest of the families of the
Levites, were *by* their lot twelve
cities.
41 [a]All the cities of the Levites
within the possession of the chil-
dren of Israel *were* forty-eight cit-
ies with their common-lands.
42 Every one of these cities had
its common-land surrounding it;
thus *were* all these cities.

The Promise Fulfilled

43 So the LORD gave to Israel [a]all
the land of which He had sworn to
give to their fathers, and they [b]took
possession of it and dwelt in it.
44 [a]The LORD gave them [b]rest all
around, according to all that He
had sworn to their fathers. And
[c]not a man of all their enemies
stood against them; the LORD de-
livered all their enemies into their
hand.
45 [a]Not a word failed of any good
thing which the LORD had spoken
to the house of Israel. All came to
pass.

Eastern Tribes Return to Their Lands

22 Then Joshua called the Reu-
benites, the Gadites, and
half the tribe of Manasseh,
2 and said to them: "You have
kept [a]all that Moses the servant of
the LORD commanded you, [b]and
have obeyed my voice in all that I
commanded you.
3 "You have not [1]left your breth-
ren these many days, up to this
day, but have kept the charge of
the commandment of the LORD
your God.
4 "And now the LORD your God
has given [a]rest to your brethren,
as He promised them; now there-
fore, return and go to your tents
and to the land of your possession,
[b]which Moses the servant of the
LORD gave you on the other side
of the Jordan.
5 "But [a]take[1] careful heed to do
the commandment and the law
which Moses the servant of the
LORD commanded you, [b]to love the
LORD your God, to walk in all His
ways, to keep His commandments,
to hold fast to Him, and to serve
Him with all your heart and with
all your soul."
6 So Joshua [a]blessed them and
sent them away, and they went to
their tents.
7 Now to half the tribe of Manas-
seh Moses had given a possession
in Bashan, [a]but to the *other* half
of it Joshua gave *a possession*
among their brethren on this side
of the Jordan, westward. And in-
deed, when Joshua sent them
away to their tents, he blessed
them,
8 and spoke to them, saying,
"Return with much riches to your
tents, with very much livestock,
with silver, with gold, with bronze,
with iron, and with very much
clothing. [a]Divide the [1]spoil of your
enemies with your brethren."
9 So the children of Reuben, the
children of Gad, and half the tribe
of Manasseh returned, and de-
parted from the children of Israel
at Shiloh, which *is* in the land of
Canaan, to go to [a]the country of
Gilead, to the land of their posses-
sion, which they had obtained

32 [a]Josh. 20:7
34 [a]Josh. 21:7; 1 Chr. 6:77–81
36 [a]Deut. 4:43; Josh. 20:8 [1]So with LXX, Vg. (cf. 1 Chr. 6:78, 79); MT, Bg., Tg. omit vv. 36, 37
38 [a]Josh. 20:8
41 [a]Num. 35:7
43 [a]Gen. 12:7; 26:3, 4; 28:4, 13, 14 [b]Num. 33:53; Josh. 1:11
44 [a]Deut. 7:23, 24; Josh. 11:23; 22:4 [b]Josh. 1:13, 15; 11:23 [c]Deut. 7:24
45 [a][Num. 23:19]; Josh. 23:14; 1 Kin. 8:56

CHAPTER 22

2 [a]Num. 32:20–22; Deut. 3:18 [b]Josh. 1:12–18
3 [1]*forsaken*
4 [a]Josh. 21:44 [b]Num. 32:33
5 [a]Deut. 6:6, 17; 11:22; Jer. 12:16 [b]Deut. 10:12; 11:13, 22 [1]*be very careful to do*
6 [a]Gen. 47:7; Ex. 39:43; Josh. 14:13; 2 Sam. 6:18; Luke 24:50
7 [a]Josh. 17:1–13
8 [a]Num. 31:27; 1 Sam. 30:24 [1]*plunder*
9 [a]Num. 32:1, 26, 29

cording to the word of the LORD by the hand of Moses.

An Altar by the Jordan

10 And when they came to the region of the Jordan which *is* in the land of Canaan, the children of Reuben, the children of Gad, and half the tribe of Manasseh built an altar there by the Jordan—a great, impressive altar.
11 Now the children of Israel [a]heard *someone* say, "Behold, the children of Reuben, the children of Gad, and half the tribe of Manasseh have built an altar on the [1]frontier of the land of Canaan, in the region of the Jordan—on the children of Israel's side."
12 And when the children of Israel heard *of it,* [a]the whole congregation of the children of Israel gathered together at Shiloh to go to war against them.
13 Then the children of Israel [a]sent [b]Phinehas the son of Eleazar the priest to the children of Reuben, to the children of Gad, and to half the tribe of Manasseh, into the land of Gilead,
14 and with him ten rulers, one ruler each from the chief house of every tribe of Israel; and [a]each one *was* the head of the house of his father among the [1]divisions of Israel.
15 Then they came to the children of Reuben, to the children of Gad, and to half the tribe of Manasseh, to the land of Gilead, and they spoke with them, saying,
16 "Thus says the whole congregation of the LORD: 'What [a]treachery[1] *is* this that you have committed against the God of Israel, to turn away this day from following the LORD, in that you have built for yourselves an altar, [b]that you might rebel this day against the LORD?
17 '*Is* the iniquity [a]of Peor not enough for us, from which we are not cleansed till this day, although there was a plague in the congregation of the LORD,
18 'but that you must turn away this day from following the LORD? And it shall be, if you rebel today against the LORD, that tomorrow [a]He will be angry with the whole congregation of Israel.

11 [a]Deut. 13:12–18; Judg. 20:12, 13 [1]Lit. *front*
12 [a]Josh. 18:1; Judg. 20:1
13 [a]Deut. 13:14; Judg. 20:12 [b]Ex. 6:25; Num. 25:7, 11–13
14 [a]Num. 1:4 [1]Lit. *thousands*
16 [a]Deut. 12:5–14 [b]Lev. 17:8, 9 [1]*unfaithful act*
17 [a]Num. 25:1–9; Deut. 4:3
18 [a]Num. 16:22
19 [a]Josh. 18:1 [1]*However*
20 [a]Josh. 7:1–26 [1]*act unfaithfully* [2]*devoted thing*
21 [1]Lit. *thousands*
22 [a]Deut. 4:35; 10:17; Is. 44:8; 45:5; 46:9; [1 Cor. 8:5, 6] [b][Job 10:7; 23:10; Jer. 12:3; 2 Cor. 11:11, 31]
23 [a]Deut. 18:19; 1 Sam. 20:16
24 [1]Lit. *from fear*
27 [a]Gen. 31:48; Josh. 22:34; 24:27 [b]Deut. 12:5, 14 [1]*testimony*

19 [1]'Nevertheless, if the land of your possession *is* unclean, *then* cross over to the land of the possession of the LORD, [a]where the LORD's tabernacle stands, and take possession among us; but do not rebel against the LORD, nor rebel against us, by building yourselves an altar besides the altar of the LORD our God.
20 [a]'Did not Achan the son of Zerah [1]commit a trespass in the [2]accursed thing, and wrath fell on all the congregation of Israel? And that man did not perish alone in his iniquity.'"
21 Then the children of Reuben, the children of Gad, and half the tribe of Manasseh answered and said to the heads of the [1]divisions of Israel:
22 "The LORD [a]God of gods, the LORD God of gods, He [b]knows, and let Israel itself know—if *it is* in rebellion, or if in treachery against the LORD, do not save us this day.
23 "If we have built ourselves an altar to turn from following the LORD, or if to offer on it burnt offerings or grain offerings, or if to offer peace offerings on it, let the LORD Himself [a]require *an account.*
24 "But in fact we have done it [1]for fear, for a reason, saying, 'In time to come your descendants may speak to our descendants, saying, "What have you to do with the LORD God of Israel?
25 "For the LORD has made the Jordan a border between you and us, *you* children of Reuben and children of Gad. You have no part in the LORD." So your descendants would make our descendants cease fearing the LORD.'
26 "Therefore we said, 'Let us now prepare to build ourselves an altar, not for burnt offering nor for sacrifice,
27 'but *that* it *may be* [a]a [1]witness between you and us and our generations after us, that we may [b]perform the service of the LORD before Him with our burnt offerings, with our sacrifices, and with our peace offerings; that your descendants may not say to our descendants in time to come, "You have no part in the LORD."'

28 "Therefore we said that it will be, when they say *this* to us or to our generations in time to come, that we may say, 'Here is the replica of the altar of the LORD which our fathers made, though not for burnt offerings nor for sacrifices; but it *is* a witness between you and us.'

29 "Far be it from us that we should rebel against the LORD, and turn from following the LORD this day, [a]to build an altar for burnt offerings, for grain offerings, or for sacrifices, besides the altar of the LORD our God which *is* before His tabernacle."

30 Now when Phinehas the priest and the rulers of the congregation, the heads of the [1]divisions of Israel who *were* with him, heard the words that the children of Reuben, the children of Gad, and the children of Manasseh spoke, it pleased them.

31 Then Phinehas the son of Eleazar the priest said to the children of Reuben, the children of Gad, and the children of Manasseh, "This day we perceive that the LORD *is* [a]among us, because you have not committed this treachery against the LORD. Now you have delivered the children of Israel out of the hand of the LORD."

32 And Phinehas the son of Eleazar the priest, and the rulers, returned from the children of Reuben and the children of Gad, from the land of Gilead to the land of Canaan, to the children of Israel, and brought back word to them.

33 So the thing pleased the children of Israel, and the children of Israel [a]blessed God; they spoke no more of going against them in battle, to destroy the land where the children of Reuben and Gad dwelt.

34 The children of Reuben and the children of [1]Gad called the altar, *Witness,* "For *it is* a witness between us that the LORD *is* God."

Joshua's Farewell Address

23 Now it came to pass, a long time after the LORD [a]had given rest to Israel from all their enemies round about, that Joshua [b]was old, advanced in age.

2 And Joshua [a]called for all Israel, for their elders, for their heads, for their judges, and for their officers, and said to them: "I am old, advanced in age.

3 "You have seen all that the [a]LORD your God has done to all these nations because of you, for the [b]LORD your God *is* He who has fought for you.

4 "See, [a]I have divided to you by lot these nations that remain, to be an inheritance for your tribes, from the Jordan, with all the nations that I have cut off, as far as the Great Sea westward.

5 "And the LORD your God [a]will expel them from before you and drive them out of your sight. So you shall possess their land, [b]as the LORD your God promised you.

6 [a]"Therefore be very courageous to keep and to do all that is written in the Book of the Law of Moses, [b]lest you turn aside from it to the right hand or to the left,

7 "*and* lest you [a]go[1] among these nations, these who remain among you. You shall not [b]make mention of the name of their gods, nor cause *anyone* to [c]swear *by them;* you shall not [d]serve them nor bow down to them,

8 "but you shall [a]hold fast to the LORD your God, as you have done to this day.

9 [a]"For the LORD has [1]driven out from before you great and strong nations; but *as for* you, no one has been able to stand against you to this day.

10 [a]"One man of you shall chase a thousand, for the LORD your God *is* He who fights for you, [b]as He promised you.

11 [a]"Therefore take careful heed to yourselves, that you love the LORD your God.

12 "Or else, if indeed you do [a]go back, and cling to the remnant of these nations—these that remain among you—and [b]make marriages with them, and go in to them and they to you,

13 "know for certain that [a]the LORD your God will no longer drive out these nations from before you. [b]But they shall be snares and traps to you, and scourges on your sides and thorns in your eyes, until you perish from this good land which the LORD your God has given you.

14 "Behold, this day [a]I[1] *am* going

---

29 [a]Deut. 12:13, 14
30 [1]Lit. *thousands*
31 [a]Ex. 25:8; Lev. 26:11, 12; 2 Chr. 15:2; Zech. 8:23
33 [a]1 Chr. 29:20; Neh. 8:6; Dan. 2:19; Luke 2:28
34 [1]LXX adds *and half the tribe of Manasseh*

CHAPTER 23

1 [a]Josh. 21:44; 22:4 [b]Josh. 13:1; 24:29
2 [a]Deut. 31:28
3 [a]Ps. 44:3 [b]Ex. 14:14; Deut. 1:30; Josh. 10:14, 42
4 [a]Josh. 13:2, 6; 18:10
5 [a]Ex. 23:30; 33:2 [b]Num. 33:53
6 [a]Josh. 1:7 [b]Deut. 5:32
7 [a]Ex. 23:33; Deut. 7:2, 3; [Prov. 4:14; Eph. 5:11] [b]Ex. 23:13; Ps. 16:4; Jer. 5:7; Hos. 2:17 [c]Deut. 6:13; 10:20 [d]Ex. 20:5 [1]*associate with*
8 [a]Deut. 10:20
9 [a]Deut. 7:24; 11:23; Josh. 1:5 [1]*dispossessed*
10 [a]Lev. 26:8; Deut. 28:7; Is. 30:17 [b]Ex. 14:14
11 [a]Josh. 22:5
12 [a][2 Pet. 2:20, 21] [b]Deut. 7:3, 4; Ezra 9:2; Neh. 13:25
13 [a]Judg. 2:3 [b]Ex. 23:33; 34:12; Deut. 7:16
14 [a]1 Kin. 2:2 [1]I am going to die.

the way of all the earth. And you
know in all your hearts and in all
your souls that [b]not one thing has
failed of all the good things which
the LORD your God spoke concern-
ing you. All have come to pass for
you; not one word of them has
failed.
15 [a]"Therefore it shall come to
pass, that as all the good things
have come upon you which the
LORD your God promised you, so
the LORD will bring upon you [b]all
harmful things, until He has de-
stroyed you from this good land
which the LORD your God has
given you.
16 [1]"When you have transgressed
the covenant of the LORD your
God, which He commanded you,
and have gone and served other
gods, and bowed down to them,
then the [a]anger of the LORD will
burn against you, and you shall
perish quickly from the good land
which He has given you."

The Covenant at Shechem

24 Then Joshua gathered all
the tribes of Israel to [a]She-
chem and [b]called for the elders of
Israel, for their heads, for their
judges, and for their officers; and
they [c]presented themselves before
God.
2 And Joshua said to all the peo-
ple, "Thus says the LORD God of
Israel: [a]'Your fathers, *including*
Terah, the father of Abraham and
the father of Nahor, dwelt on the
other side of [1]the River in old
times; and [b]they served other
gods.
3 [a]'Then I took your father Abra-
ham from the other side of [1]the
River, led him throughout all the
land of Canaan, and multiplied his
[2]descendants and [b]gave him Isaac.
4 'To Isaac I gave [a]Jacob and
Esau. To [b]Esau I gave the moun-
tains of Seir to possess, [c]but Jacob
and his children went down to
Egypt.
5 [a]'Also I sent Moses and Aaron,
and [b]I plagued Egypt, according to
what I did among them. Afterward
I brought you out.
6 'Then I [a]brought your fathers
out of Egypt, and you came to the
sea; and the Egyptians pursued
your fathers with chariots and
horsemen to the Red Sea.
7 'So they cried out to the LORD;
and He put [a]darkness between you
and the Egyptians, brought the sea
upon them, and covered them.
And [b]your eyes saw what I did in
Egypt. Then you dwelt in the wil-
derness [c]a long time.
8 'And I brought you into the
land of the Amorites, who dwelt
on the other side of the Jordan,
[a]and they fought with you. But I
gave them into your hand, that you
might possess their land, and I de-
stroyed them from before you.
9 'Then [a]Balak the son of Zippor,
king of Moab, arose to make war
against Israel, and [b]sent and called
Balaam the son of Beor to curse
you.
10 [a]'But I would not listen to Ba-
laam; [b]therefore he continued to
bless you. So I delivered you out
of his hand.
11 'Then [a]you went over the Jor-
dan and came to Jericho. And [b]the
men of Jericho fought against
you—*also* the Amorites, the Periz-
zites, the Canaanites, the Hittites,
the Girgashites, the Hivites, and
the Jebusites. But I delivered them
into your hand.
12 [a]'I sent the hornet before you
which drove them out from before
you, *also* the two kings of the Am-
orites, *but* [b]not with your sword
or with your bow.
13 'I have given you a land for
which you did not labor, and [a]cit-
ies which you did not build, and
you dwell in them; you eat of the
vineyards and olive groves which
you did not plant.'
14 [a]"Now therefore, fear the LORD,
serve Him in [b]sincerity and in
truth, and [c]put away the gods
which your fathers served on the
other side of [1]the River and [d]in
Egypt. Serve the LORD!
15 "And if it seems evil to you to
serve the LORD, [a]choose for your-
selves this day whom you will
serve, whether [b]the gods which
your fathers served that *were* on
the other side of [1]the River, or [c]the
gods of the Amorites, in whose
land you dwell. [d]But as for me and
my house, we will serve the LORD."
16 So the people answered and
said: "Far be it from us that we

14 [b]Josh. 21:45; [Luke 21:33]
15 [a]Deut. 28:63 [b]Lev. 26:14–39; Deut. 28:15–68
16 [a]Deut. 4:24–28 [1]Or *if ever*

CHAPTER 24

1 [a]Gen. 35:4 [b]Josh. 23:2 [c]1 Sam. 10:19
2 [a]Gen. 11:7–32 [b]Josh. 24:14 [1]The Euphrates
3 [a]Gen. 12:1; Acts 7:2, 3 [b]Gen. 21:1–8; [Ps. 127:3] [1]The Euphrates [2]Lit. *seed*
4 [a]Gen. 25:24–26 [b]Gen. 36:8; Deut. 2:5 [c]Gen. 46:1, 3, 6
5 [a]Ex. 3:10 [b]Ex. 7—10
6 [a]Ex. 12:37, 51; 14:2–31
7 [a]Ex. 14:20 [b]Deut. 4:34 [c]Josh. 5:6
8 [a]Num. 21:21–35
9 [a]Judg. 11:25 [b]Num. 22:2–14
10 [a]Deut. 23:5 [b]Num. 23:11, 20; 24:10
11 [a]Josh. 3:14, 17 [b]Josh. 6:1; 10:1
12 [a]Ex. 23:28; Deut. 7:20 [b]Ps. 44:3
13 [a]Deut. 6:10, 11
14 [a]Deut. 10:12, 13; 1 Sam. 12:24 [b]2 Cor. 1:12 [c]Josh. 24:2, 23; Ezek. 20:18 [d]Ezek. 20:7, 8 [1]The Euphrates
15 [a]Ruth 1:15; 1 Kin. 18:21 [b]Josh. 24:2; Ezek. 20:39 [c]Ex. 23:24, 32 [d]Gen. 18:19; Ps. 101:2; [1 Tim. 3:4, 5] [1]The Euphrates

should forsake the LORD to serve
other gods;
17 "for the LORD our God *is* He
who brought us and our fathers up
out of the land of Egypt, from the
house of bondage, who did those
great signs in our sight, and pre-
served us in all the way that we
went and among all the people
through whom we passed.
18 "And the LORD drove out from
before us all the people, including
the Amorites who dwelt in the
land. [a]We also will serve the LORD,
for He *is* our God."
19 But Joshua said to the people,
[a]"You cannot serve the LORD, for
He *is* a [b]holy God. He *is* [c]a jealous
God; [d]He will not forgive your
transgressions nor your sins.
20 [a]"If you forsake the LORD and
serve foreign gods, [b]then He will
turn and do you harm and con-
sume you, after He has done you
good."
21 And the people said to Joshua,
"No, but we will serve the LORD!"
22 So Joshua said to the people,
"You *are* witnesses against your-
selves that [a]you have chosen the
LORD for yourselves, to serve
Him." And they said, "*We are* wit-
nesses!"
23 "Now therefore," *he said,* [a]"put
away the foreign gods which *are*
among you, and [b]incline your
heart to the LORD God of Israel."
24 And the people [a]said to Joshua,
"The LORD our God we will serve,
and His voice we will obey!"
25 So Joshua [a]made[1] a covenant
with the people that day, and made
for them a statute and an ordi-
nance [b]in Shechem.
26 Then Joshua [a]wrote these
words in the Book of the Law of

18 [a]Ps. 116:16
19 [a]Matt. 6:24 [b]Lev. 11:44, 45; 1 Sam. 6:20 [c]Ex. 20:5 [d]Ex. 23:21
20 [a]1 Chr. 28:9; Ezra 8:22; Is. 1:28; 63:10; 65:11, 12; Jer. 17:13 [b]Deut. 4:24–26; Josh. 23:15
22 [a]Ps. 119:173
23 [a]Gen. 35:2; Josh. 24:14; Judg. 10:15, 16; 1 Sam. 7:3 [b]1 Kin. 8:57, 58; Ps. 119:36; 141:4
24 [a]Ex. 19:8; 24:3, 7; Deut. 5:24–27
25 [a]Ex. 15:25 [b]Josh. 24:1 [1]Lit. *cut a covenant*
26 [a]Deut. 31:24 [b]Judg. 9:6 [c]Gen. 28:18 [d]Gen. 35:4
27 [a]Gen. 31:48 [b]Deut. 32:1
28 [a]Judg. 2:6, 7
29 [a]Judg. 2:8
30 [a]Josh. 19:50; Judg. 2:9
31 [a]Judg. 2:7 [b]Deut. 11:2
32 [a]Gen. 50:25; Ex. 13:19; Heb. 11:22 [b]Gen. 33:19; John 4:5 [1]Heb. *qesitah,* an unknown ancient measure of weight
33 [a]Ex. 28:1; Num. 20:28; Josh. 14:1 [b]Ex. 6:25

God. And he took [b]a large stone,
and [c]set it up there [d]under the oak
that *was* by the sanctuary of the
LORD.
27 And Joshua said to all the peo-
ple, "Behold, this stone shall be [a]a
witness to us, for [b]it has heard all
the words of the LORD which He
spoke to us. It shall therefore be
a witness to you, lest you deny
your God."
28 So [a]Joshua let the people de-
part, each to his own inheritance.

Death of Joshua and Eleazar

29 [a]Now it came to pass after
these things that Joshua the son
of Nun, the servant of the LORD,
died, *being* one hundred and ten
years old.
30 And they buried him within the
border of his inheritance at [a]Tim-
nath Serah, which *is* in the moun-
tains of Ephraim, on the north side
of Mount Gaash.
31 [a]Israel served the LORD all the
days of Joshua, and all the days
of the elders who outlived Joshua,
who had [b]known all the works of
the LORD which He had done for
Israel.
32 [a]The bones of Joseph, which
the children of Israel had brought
up out of Egypt, they buried at
Shechem, in the plot of ground
[b]which Jacob had bought from the
sons of Hamor the father of She-
chem for one hundred [1]pieces of
silver, and which had become an
inheritance of the children of Jo-
seph.
33 And [a]Eleazar the son of Aaron
died. They buried him in a hill *be-
longing to* [b]Phinehas his son,
which was given to him in the
mountains of Ephraim.

The Book of

Judges

THE Book of Judges stands in stark contrast to Joshua. In Joshua an obedient people conquered the land through trust in the power of God. In Judges, however, a disobedient and idolatrous people are defeated time and time again because of their rebellion against God.

In seven distinct cycles of sin to salvation, Judges shows how Israel had set aside God's law and in its place substituted *"what was* right in his own eyes" (21:25). The recurring result of abandonment from God's law is corruption from within and oppression from without. During the nearly four centuries spanned by this book, God raises up military champions to throw off the yoke of bondage and to restore the nation to pure worship. But all too soon the "sin cycle" begins again as the nation's spiritual temperature grows steadily colder.

The Hebrew title is *Shophetim,* meaning "judges," "rulers," "deliverers," or "saviors." *Shophet* not only carries the idea of maintaining justice and settling disputes, but it is also used to mean "liberating" and "delivering." First the judges deliver the people; then they rule and administer justice. The Septuagint used the Greek equivalent of this word, *Kritai* ("Judges"). The Latin Vulgate called it *Liber Judicum,* the "Book of Judges." This book could also appropriately be titled the "Book of Failure."

The Continuing Conquest of Canaan

NOW after the [a]death of Joshua
it came to pass that the
children of Israel [b]asked
the LORD, saying, "Who shall
be first to go up for us against
the [c]Canaanites to fight against
them?"
2 And the LORD said, [a]"Judah
shall go up. Indeed I have deliv-
ered the land into his hand."
3 So Judah said to [a]Simeon his
brother, "Come up with me to my
allotted territory, that we may
fight against the Canaanites; and
[b]I will likewise go with you to your
allotted territory." And Simeon
went with him.
4 Then Judah went up, and the
LORD delivered the Canaanites and
the Perizzites into their hand; and
they killed ten thousand men at
[a]Bezek.
5 And they found Adoni-Bezek
in Bezek, and fought against him;
and they defeated the Canaanites
and the Perizzites.
6 Then Adoni-Bezek fled, and
they pursued him and caught him
and cut off his thumbs and big
toes.

CHAPTER 1

1 [a]Josh. 24:29 [b]Num. 27:21; Judg. 20:18 [c]Josh. 17:12, 13

2 [a]Gen. 49:8, 9; Rev. 5:5

3 [a]Josh. 19:1 [b]Judg. 1:17

4 [a]1 Sam. 11:8

7 [a]Lev. 24:19; 1 Sam. 15:33; [James 2:13]

8 [a]Josh. 15:63; Judg. 1:21

9 [a]Josh. 10:36; 11:21; 15:13 [1]Heb. *Negev,* and so throughout the book

10 [a]Josh. 15:13–19 [b]Josh. 14:15 [1]*attacked*

11 [a]Josh. 15:15

12 [a]Josh. 15:16, 17

13 [a]Judg. 3:9

7 And Adoni-Bezek said, "Sev-
enty kings with their thumbs and
big toes cut off used to gather
scraps under my table; [a]as I have
done, so God has repaid me." Then
they brought him to Jerusalem,
and there he died.
8 Now [a]the children of Judah
fought against Jerusalem and took
it; they struck it with the edge of
the sword and set the city on fire.
9 [a]And afterward the children of
Judah went down to fight against
the Canaanites who dwelt in the
mountains, in the [1]South, and in
the lowland.
10 Then Judah [1]went against the
Canaanites who dwelt in [a]Hebron.
(Now the name of Hebron *was* for-
merly [b]Kirjath Arba.) And they
killed Sheshai, Ahiman, and Tal-
mai.
11 [a]From there they went against
the inhabitants of Debir. (The
name of Debir *was* formerly Kir-
jath Sepher.)
12 [a]Then Caleb said, "Whoever
attacks Kirjath Sepher and takes
it, to him I will give my daughter
Achsah as wife."
13 And Othniel the son of Kenaz,
[a]Caleb's younger brother, took it;

so he gave him his daughter Achsah as wife.

14 [a]Now it happened, when she came *to him*, that [1]she urged him to ask her father for a field. And she dismounted from *her* donkey, and Caleb said to her, "What do you wish?"

15 So she said to him, [a]"Give me a blessing; since you have given me land in the South, give me also springs of water." And Caleb gave her the upper springs and the lower springs.

16 [a]Now the children of the Kenite, Moses' father-in-law, went up [b]from the City of Palms with the children of Judah into the Wilderness of Judah, which *lies* in the South *near* [c]Arad; [d]and they went and dwelt among the people.

17 [a]And Judah went with his brother Simeon, and they attacked the Canaanites who inhabited Zephath, and utterly destroyed it. So the name of the city was called [b]Hormah.

18 Also Judah took [a]Gaza with its territory, Ashkelon with its territory, and Ekron with its territory.

19 So the LORD was with Judah. And they drove out the mountaineers, but they could not drive out the inhabitants of the lowland, because they had [a]chariots of iron.

20 [a]And they gave Hebron to Caleb, as Moses had said. Then he [1]expelled from there the [b]three sons of Anak.

21 [a]But the children of Benjamin did not drive out the Jebusites who inhabited Jerusalem; so the Jebusites dwell with the children of Benjamin in Jerusalem to this day.

22 And the [1]house of Joseph also went up against Bethel, [a]and the LORD *was* with them.

23 So the [1]house of Joseph [a]sent men to spy out Bethel. (The name of the city *was* formerly [b]Luz.)

24 And when the spies saw a man coming out of the city, they said to him, "Please show us the entrance to the city, and [a]we will show you mercy."

25 So he showed them the entrance to the city, and they struck the city with the edge of the sword; but they let the man and all his family go.

26 And the man went to the land of the Hittites, built a city, and called its name Luz, which *is* its name to this day.

Incomplete Conquest of the Land

27 [a]However, Manasseh did not drive out *the inhabitants of* Beth Shean and its villages, or [b]Taanach and its villages, or the inhabitants of [c]Dor and its villages, or the inhabitants of Ibleam and its villages, or the inhabitants of Megiddo and its villages; for the Canaanites were determined to dwell in that land.

28 And it came to pass, when Israel was strong, that they put the Canaanites [1]under tribute, but did not completely drive them out.

29 [a]Nor did Ephraim drive out the Canaanites who dwelt in Gezer; so the Canaanites dwelt in Gezer among them.

30 Nor did [a]Zebulun drive out the inhabitants of Kitron or the inhabitants of Nahalol; so the Canaanites dwelt among them, and [1]were put under tribute.

31 [a]Nor did Asher drive out the inhabitants of Acco or the inhabitants of Sidon, or of Ahlab, Achzib, Helbah, Aphik, or Rehob.

32 So the Asherites [a]dwelt among the Canaanites, the inhabitants of the land; for they did not drive them out.

33 [a]Nor did Naphtali drive out the inhabitants of Beth Shemesh or the inhabitants of Beth Anath; but they dwelt among the Canaanites, the inhabitants of the land. Nevertheless the inhabitants of Beth Shemesh and Beth Anath were put under tribute to them.

34 And the Amorites forced the children of Dan into the mountains, for they would not allow them to come down to the valley;

35 and the Amorites were determined to dwell in Mount Heres, [a]in Aijalon, and in [1]Shaalbim; yet when the strength of the house of Joseph became greater, they [2]were put under tribute.

36 Now the boundary of the Amorites *was* [a]from the Ascent of Akrabbim, from Sela, and upward.

Israel's Disobedience

2 Then the Angel of the LORD came up from Gilgal to

14 [a]Josh. 15:18, 19 [1]LXX, Vg. *he urged her*
15 [a]Gen. 33:11
16 [a]Num. 10:29–32; Judg. 4:11, 17; 1 Sam. 15:6; 1 Chr. 2:55 [b]Deut. 34:3; Judg. 3:13 [c]Josh. 12:14 [d]1 Sam. 15:6
17 [a]Judg. 1:3 [b]Num. 21:3; Josh. 19:4
18 [a]Josh. 11:22
19 [a]Josh. 17:16, 18; Judg. 4:3, 13
20 [a]Num. 14:24; Josh. 14:9, 14 [b]Josh. 15:14; Judg. 1:10 [1]*drove out from there*
21 [a]Josh. 15:63; Judg. 1:8
22 [a]Judg. 1:19 [1]*family*
23 [a]Josh. 2:1; 7:2 [b]Gen. 28:19 [1]*family*
24 [a]Josh. 2:12, 14
27 [a]Josh. 17:11–13 [b]Josh. 21:25 [c]Josh. 17:11
28 [1]*to forced labor*
29 [a]Josh. 16:10; 1 Kin. 9:16
30 [a]Josh. 19:10–16 [1]*became forced laborers*
31 [a]Josh. 19:24–31
32 [a]Ps. 106:34, 35
33 [a]Josh. 19:32–39
35 [a]Josh. 19:42 [1]*Shaalabbin,* Josh. 19:42 [2]*became forced laborers*
36 [a]Num. 34:4; Josh. 15:3

Bochim, and said: [a]"I led you up
from Egypt and [b]brought you to
the land of which I swore to your
fathers; and [c]I said, 'I will never
break My covenant with you.
2 'And [a]you shall make no
[1]covenant with the inhabitants of
this land; [b]you shall tear down
their altars.' [c]But you have not
obeyed My voice. Why have you
done this?
3 "Therefore I also said, 'I will
not drive them out before you; but
they shall be [a]*thorns*[1] in your side,
and [b]their gods shall [2]be a [c]snare
to you.'"
4 So it was, when the Angel of
the LORD spoke these words to all
the children of Israel, that the peo-
ple lifted up their voices and wept.
5 Then they called the name of
that place [1]Bochim; and they sacri-
ficed there to the LORD.
6 And when [a]Joshua had dis-
missed the people, the children of
Israel went each to his own inheri-
tance to possess the land.

Death of Joshua

7 [a]So the people served the LORD
all the days of Joshua, and all the
days of the elders who outlived
Joshua, who had seen all the great
works of the LORD which He had
done for Israel.
8 Now [a]Joshua the son of Nun,
the servant of the LORD, died *when
he was* one hundred and ten years
old.
9 [a]And they buried him within
the border of his inheritance at
[b]Timnath Heres, in the mountains
of Ephraim, on the north side of
Mount Gaash.
10 When all that generation had
[1]been gathered to their fathers, an-
other generation arose after them
who [a]did not know the LORD nor
the work which He had done for
Israel.

Israel's Unfaithfulness

11 Then the children of Israel did
[a]evil in the sight of the LORD, and
served the Baals;
12 and they [a]forsook the LORD
God of their fathers, who had
brought them out of the land of
Egypt; and they followed [b]other
gods from *among* the gods of the
people who *were* all around them,
and they [c]bowed down to them;
and they provoked the LORD to an-
ger.
13 They forsook the LORD [a]and
served [1]Baal and the [2]Ashtoreths.
14 [a]And the anger of the LORD was
hot against Israel. So He [b]deliv-
ered them into the hands of plun-
derers who despoiled them; and
[c]He sold them into the hands of
their enemies all around, so that
they [d]could no longer stand before
their enemies.
15 Wherever they went out, the
hand of the LORD was against them
for calamity, as the LORD had said,
and as the LORD had [a]sworn to
them. And they were greatly dis-
tressed.
16 Nevertheless, [a]the LORD raised
up judges who delivered them out
of the hand of those who plun-
dered them.
17 Yet they would not listen to
their judges, but they [a]played the
harlot with other gods, and bowed
down to them. They turned
quickly from the way in which
their fathers walked, in obeying
the commandments of the LORD;
they did not do so.
18 And when the LORD raised up
judges for them, [a]the LORD was
with the judge and delivered them
out of the hand of their enemies
all the days of the judge; [b]for the
LORD was moved to pity by their
groaning because of those who
oppressed them and harassed
them.
19 And it came to pass, [a]when the
judge was dead, that they reverted
and behaved more corruptly than
their fathers, by following other
gods, to serve them and bow down
to them. They did not cease from
their own doings nor from their
stubborn way.
20 Then the anger of the LORD was
hot against Israel; and He said,
"Because this nation has [a]trans-
gressed My covenant which I com-
manded their fathers, and has not
heeded My voice,
21 "I also will no longer drive
out before them any of the na-
tions which Joshua [a]left when he
died,
22 "so [a]that through them I may
[b]test Israel, whether they will keep
the ways of the LORD, to walk in

CHAPTER 2

1 [a]Ex. 20:2; Judg. 6:8, 9 [b]Deut. 1:8 [c]Gen. 17:7, 8; Lev. 26:42, 44; Deut. 7:9; Ps. 89:34
2 [a]Ex. 23:32; Deut. 7:2 [b]Ex. 34:12, 13; Deut. 12:3 [c]Ps. 106:34 [1]*treaty*
3 [a]Num. 33:55; Josh. 23:13 [b]Judg. 3:6 [c]Ex. 23:33; Deut. 7:16; Ps. 106:36 [1]LXX, Tg., Vg. *enemies to you* [2]*entrap you*
5 [1]Lit. *Weeping*
6 [a]Josh. 22:6; 24:28–31
7 [a]Josh. 24:31
8 [a]Josh. 24:29
9 [a]Josh. 24:30 [b]Josh. 19:49, 50
10 [a]Ex. 5:2; 1 Sam. 2:12; Gal. 4:8; [Titus 1:16] [1]Died and joined their ancestors
11 [a]Judg. 3:7, 12; 4:1; 6:1
12 [a]Deut. 31:16; Judg. 8:33; 10:6 [b]Deut. 6:14 [c]Ex. 20:5
13 [a]Judg. 10:6; Ps. 106:36 [1]A Canaanite god [2]Canaanite goddesses
14 [a]Deut. 31:17; Judg. 3:8; Ps. 106:40–42 [b]2 Kin. 17:20 [c]Is. 50:1 [d]Lev. 26:37; Josh. 7:12, 13
15 [a]Lev. 26:14–26; Deut. 28:15–68
16 [a]Judg. 3:9, 10, 15; Ps. 106:43–45
17 [a]Ex. 34:15
18 [a]Josh. 1:5 [b]Gen. 6:6
19 [a]Judg. 3:12
20 [a][Josh. 23:16]
21 [a]Josh. 23:4, 5, 13
22 [a]Judg. 3:1, 4 [b]Deut. 8:2, 16; 13:3

them as their fathers kept *them*, or not."
23 Therefore the LORD left those nations, without driving them out immediately; nor did He deliver them into the hand of Joshua.

The Nations Remaining in the Land

3 Now these *are* [a]the nations which the LORD left, that He might test Israel by them, *that is*, all who had not [1]known any of the wars in Canaan
2 (*this was* only so that the generations of the children of Israel might be taught to know war, at least those who had not formerly known it),
3 *namely*, [a]five lords of the Philistines, all the Canaanites, the Sidonians, and the Hivites who dwelt in Mount Lebanon, from Mount Baal Hermon to the entrance of Hamath.
4 And they were *left*, *that He might* test Israel by them, to [1]know whether they would obey the commandments of the LORD, which He had commanded their fathers by the hand of Moses.
5 [a]Thus the children of Israel dwelt among the Canaanites, the Hittites, the Amorites, the Perizzites, the Hivites, and the Jebusites.
6 And [a]they took their daughters to be their wives, and gave their daughters to their sons; and they served their gods.

Othniel

7 So the children of Israel did [a]evil in the sight of the LORD. They [b]forgot the LORD their God, and served the Baals and [1]Asherahs.
8 Therefore the anger of the LORD was hot against Israel, and He [a]sold them into the hand of [b]Cushan-Rishathaim king of Mesopotamia; and the children of Israel served Cushan-Rishathaim eight years.
9 When the children of Israel [a]cried out to the LORD, the LORD [b]raised up a deliverer for the children of Israel, who delivered them: [c]Othniel the son of Kenaz, Caleb's younger brother.
10 [a]The Spirit of the LORD came upon him, and he judged Israel. He went out to war, and the LORD delivered Cushan-Rishathaim king of Mesopotamia into his hand; and his hand prevailed over Cushan-Rishathaim.
11 So the land had rest for forty years. Then Othniel the son of Kenaz died.

Ehud

12 [a]And the children of Israel again did evil in the sight of the LORD. So the LORD strengthened [b]Eglon king of Moab against Israel, because they had done evil in the sight of the LORD.
13 Then he gathered to himself the people of Ammon and [a]Amalek, went and [1]defeated Israel, and took possession of [b]the City of Palms.
14 So the children of Israel [a]served Eglon king of Moab eighteen years.
15 But when the children of Israel [a]cried out to the LORD, the LORD raised up a deliverer for them: Ehud the son of Gera, the Benjamite, a [b]left-handed man. By him the children of Israel sent tribute to Eglon king of Moab.
16 Now Ehud made himself a dagger (it was double-edged and a cubit in length) and fastened it under his clothes on his right thigh.
17 So he brought the tribute to Eglon king of Moab. (Now Eglon *was* a very fat man.)
18 And when he had finished presenting the tribute, he sent away the people who had carried the tribute.
19 But he himself turned back [a]from the [1]stone images that *were* at Gilgal, and said, "I have a secret message for you, O king." He said, "Keep silence!" And all who attended him went out from him.
20 So Ehud came to him (now he was sitting upstairs in his cool private chamber). Then Ehud said, "I have a message from God for you." So he arose from *his* seat.
21 Then Ehud reached with his left hand, took the dagger from his right thigh, and thrust it into his belly.
22 Even the [1]hilt went in after the blade, and the fat closed over the blade, for he did not draw the

CHAPTER 3
1 [a]Judg. 1:1; 2:21, 22 [1]*experienced*
3 [a]Josh. 13:3
4 [1]*find out*
5 [a]Ps. 106:35
6 [a]Ex. 34:15, 16; Deut. 7:3, 4; Josh. 23:12
7 [a]Judg. 2:11 [b]Deut. 32:18 [1]Name or symbol for Canaanite goddesses
8 [a]Deut. 32:30; Judg. 2:14 [b]Hab. 3:7
9 [a]Judg. 3:15 [b]Judg. 2:16 [c]Judg. 1:13
10 [a]Num. 27:18; 1 Sam. 11:6; 2 Chr. 15:1
12 [a]Judg. 2:19 [b]1 Sam. 12:9
13 [a]Judg. 5:14 [b]Deut. 34:3; Judg. 1:16; 2 Chr. 28:15 [1]*struck*
14 [a]Deut. 28:48
15 [a]Ps. 78:34 [b]Judg. 20:16
19 [a]Josh. 4:20 [1]Tg. *quarries*
22 [1]*handle*

dagger out of his belly; and his en-
trails came out.
23 Then Ehud went out through
the porch and shut the doors of the
upper room behind him and
locked them.
24 When he had gone out,
[1]*Eglon's* servants came to look,
and *to their* surprise, the doors of
the upper room were locked. So
they said, "He is probably [a]attend-
ing[2] to his needs in the cool cham-
ber."
25 So they waited till they were
[a]embarrassed, and still he had not
opened the doors of the upper
room. Therefore they took the key
and opened *them.* And there was
their master, fallen dead on the
floor.
26 But Ehud had escaped while
they delayed, and passed beyond
the [1]stone images and escaped to
Seirah.
27 And it happened, when he ar-
rived, that [a]he blew the trumpet in
the [b]mountains of Ephraim, and
the children of Israel went down
with him from the mountains; and
[1]he led them.
28 Then he said to them, "Follow
me, for [a]the LORD has delivered
your enemies the Moabites into
your hand." So they went down
after him, seized the [b]fords of
the Jordan leading to Moab, and
did not allow anyone to cross
over.
29 And at that time they killed
about ten thousand men of Moab,
all stout men of valor; not a man
escaped.
30 So Moab was subdued that day
under the hand of Israel. And [a]the
land had rest for eighty years.

Shamgar

31 After him was [a]Shamgar the
son of Anath, who killed six hun-
dred men of the Philistines [b]with
an ox goad; [c]and he also delivered
[d]Israel.

Deborah

4 When Ehud was dead, [a]the
children of Israel again did
[b]evil in the sight of the LORD.
2 So the LORD [a]sold them into
the hand of Jabin king of Canaan,
who reigned in [b]Hazor. The
commander of his army *was* [c]Sis-

24 [a]1 Sam. 24:3 [1]Lit. *his* [2]Lit. *covering his feet*

25 [a]2 Kin. 2:17; 8:11

26 [1]Tg. *quarries*

27 [a]Judg. 6:34; 1 Sam. 13:3 [b]Josh. 17:15 [1]Lit. *he went before them*

28 [a]Judg. 7:9, 15; 1 Sam. 17:47 [b]Josh. 2:7; Judg. 12:5

30 [a]Judg. 3:11

31 [a]Judg. 5:6 [b]1 Sam. 17:47 [c]Judg. 2:16 [d]1 Sam. 4:1

CHAPTER 4

1 [a]Judg. 2:19 [b]Judg. 2:11

2 [a]Judg. 2:14 [b]Josh. 11:1, 10 [c]1 Sam. 12:9; Ps. 83:9 [d]Judg. 4:13, 16

3 [a]Deut. 20:1; Judg. 1:19 [b]Ps. 106:42

5 [a]Gen. 35:8

6 [a]Heb. 11:32 [b]Josh. 19:37; 21:32 [c]Judg. 8:18 [1]*march*

7 [a]Ex. 14:4 [b]Judg. 5:21; 1 Kin. 18:40; Ps. 83:9, 10 [1]Lit. *draw*

9 [a]Judg. 2:14

10 [a]Judg. 5:18 [b]Ex. 11:8; 1 Kin. 20:10 [1]Lit. *at his feet*

11 [a]Judg. 1:16 [b]Num. 10:29 [c]Judg. 4:6

era, who dwelt in [d]Harosheth Ha-
goyim.
3 And the children of Israel cried
out to the LORD; for Jabin had nine
hundred [a]chariots of iron, and for
twenty years [b]he had harshly op-
pressed the children of Israel.
4 Now Deborah, a prophetess,
the wife of Lapidoth, was judging
Israel at that time.
5 [a]And she would sit under the
palm tree of Deborah between Ra-
mah and Bethel in the mountains
of Ephraim. And the children of Is-
rael came up to her for judgment.
6 Then she sent and called for
[a]Barak the son of Abinoam from
[b]Kedesh in Naphtali, and said to
him, "Has not the LORD God of Is-
rael commanded, 'Go and [1]deploy
troops at Mount [c]Tabor; take with
you ten thousand men of the sons
of Naphtali and of the sons of Zeb-
ulun;
7 'and against you [a]I will deploy
Sisera, the commander of Jabin's
army, with his chariots and his
multitude at the [b]River Kishon;
and I will [1]deliver him into your
hand'?"
8 And Barak said to her, "If you
will go with me, then I will go; but
if you will not go with me, I will
not go!"
9 So she said, "I will surely go
with you; nevertheless there will
be no glory for you in the journey
you are taking, for the LORD will
[a]sell Sisera into the hand of a
woman." Then Deborah arose and
went with Barak to Kedesh.
10 And Barak called [a]Zebulun and
Naphtali to Kedesh; he went up
with ten thousand men [b]under[1] his
command, and Deborah went up
with him.
11 Now Heber [a]the Kenite, of the
children of [b]Hobab the father-in-
law of Moses, had separated him-
self from the Kenites and pitched
his tent near the terebinth tree at
Zaanaim, [c]which *is* beside Kedesh.
12 And they reported to Sisera
that Barak the son of Abinoam had
gone up to Mount Tabor.
13 So Sisera gathered together all
his chariots, nine hundred chariots
of iron, and all the people who
were with him, from Harosheth
Hagoyim to the River Kishon.
14 Then Deborah said to Barak,

[1]“Up! For this *is* the day in which
the LORD has delivered Sisera into
your hand. [a]Has not the LORD gone
out before you?” So Barak went
down from Mount Tabor with ten
thousand men following him.
15 And the LORD routed Sisera
and all *his* chariots and all *his*
army with the edge of the sword
before Barak; and Sisera alighted
from *his* chariot and fled away on
foot.
16 But Barak pursued the chariots
and the army as far as Harosheth
Hagoyim, and all the army of Sis-
era fell by the edge of the sword;
not a man was [a]left.
17 However, Sisera had fled away
on foot to the tent of [a]Jael, the wife
of Heber the Kenite; for *there was*
peace between Jabin king of Ha-
zor and the house of Heber the
Kenite.
18 And Jael went out to meet Sis-
era, and said to him, “Turn aside,
my lord, turn aside to me; do not
fear.” And when he had turned
aside with her into the tent, she
covered him with a [1]blanket.
19 Then he said to her, “Please
give me a little water to drink, for
I am thirsty.” So she opened [a]a jug
of milk, gave him a drink, and cov-
ered him.
20 And he said to her, “Stand at
the door of the tent, and if any man
comes and inquires of you, and
says, ‘Is there any man here?’ you
shall say, ‘No.’ ”
21 Then Jael, Heber’s wife, [a]took
a tent peg and took a hammer in
her hand, and went softly to him
and drove the peg into his temple,
and it went down into the ground;
for he was fast asleep and weary.
So he died.
22 And then, as Barak pursued
Sisera, Jael came out to meet him,
and said to him, “Come, I will
show you the man whom you
seek.” And when he went into her
tent, there lay Sisera, dead with
the peg in his temple.
23 So on that day God subdued Ja-
bin king of Canaan in the presence
of the children of Israel.
24 And the hand of the children
of Israel grew stronger and stron-
ger against Jabin king of Canaan,
until they had destroyed Jabin
king of Canaan.

The Song of Deborah

5 Then Deborah and Barak the
son of Abinoam [a]sang on that
day, saying:

2 “When[1] leaders [a]lead in Israel,
[b]When the people [2]willingly offer
themselves,
Bless the LORD!

3 “Hear,[a] O kings! Give ear,
O princes!
I, *even* [b]I, will sing to the LORD;
I will sing praise to the LORD God
of Israel.

4 “LORD, [a]when You went out from
Seir,
When You marched from [b]the
field of Edom,
The earth trembled and the
heavens poured,
The clouds also poured water;
5 [a]The mountains [1]gushed before
the LORD,
[b]This Sinai, before the LORD God
of Israel.

6 “In the days of [a]Shamgar, son of
Anath,
In the days of [b]Jael,
[c]The highways were deserted,
And the travelers walked along
the byways.
7 Village life ceased, it ceased in
Israel,
Until I, Deborah, arose,
Arose a mother in Israel.
8 They chose [a]new gods;
Then *there was* war in the
gates;
Not a shield or spear was seen
among forty thousand in Israel.
9 My heart *is* with the rulers of
Israel
Who offered themselves willingly
with the people.
Bless the LORD!

10 “Speak, you who ride on white
[a]donkeys,
Who sit in judges’ attire,
And who walk along the road.
11 Far from the noise of the archers,
among the watering places,
There they shall recount the
righteous acts of the LORD,
The righteous acts *for* His
villagers in Israel;
Then the people of the LORD shall
go down to the gates.

12 “Awake,[a] awake, Deborah!
Awake, awake, sing a song!

14 [a]Deut. 9:3; 31:3; 2 Sam. 5:24; Ps. 68:7; Is. 52:12 [1]*Arise!*
16 [a]Ex. 14:28; Ps. 83:9
17 [a]Judg. 5:6
18 [1]*rug*
19 [a]Judg. 5:24–27
21 [a]Judg. 5:24–27

CHAPTER 5

1 [a]Ex. 15:1; Judg. 4:4
2 [a]Ps. 18:47 [b]2 Chr. 17:16 [1]Or *When locks are loosed* [2]*volunteer*
3 [a]Deut. 32:1, 3 [b]Ps. 27:6
4 [a]Deut. 33:2; Ps. 68:7 [b]Ps. 68:8
5 [a]Ps. 97:5 [b]Ex. 19:18 [1]*flowed*
6 [a]Judg. 3:31 [b]Judg. 4:17 [c]Is. 33:8
8 [a]Deut. 32:17
10 [a]Judg. 10:4; 12:14
12 [a]Ps. 57:8

Arise, Barak, and lead your
captives away,
O son of Abinoam!

13 "Then the survivors came down,
the people against the nobles;
The LORD came down for me
against the mighty.
14 From Ephraim *were* those whose
roots were in [a]Amalek.
After you, Benjamin, with your
peoples,
From Machir rulers came down,
And from Zebulun those who
bear the recruiter's staff.
15 And [1]the princes of Issachar *were*
with Deborah;
As Issachar, so *was* Barak
Sent into the valley [2]under his
command;
Among the divisions of Reuben
There were great resolves of
heart.
16 Why did you sit among the
sheepfolds,
To hear the pipings for the
flocks?
The divisions of Reuben have
great searchings of heart.
17 [a]Gilead stayed beyond the Jordan,
And why did Dan remain [1]on
ships?
[b]Asher continued at the seashore,
And stayed by his inlets.
18 [a]Zebulun *is* a people *who*
jeopardized their lives to the
point of death,
Naphtali also, on the heights of
the battlefield.

19 "The kings came *and* fought,
Then the kings of Canaan fought
In [a]Taanach, by the waters of
Megiddo;
They took no spoils of silver.
20 They fought from the heavens;
The stars from their courses
fought against Sisera.
21 [a]The torrent of Kishon swept them
away,
That ancient torrent, the torrent
of Kishon.
O my soul, march on in strength!
22 Then the horses' hooves
pounded,
The galloping, galloping of his
steeds.
23 'Curse Meroz,' said the [1]angel of
the LORD,
'Curse its inhabitants bitterly,
Because they did not come to the
help of the LORD,
To the help of the LORD against
the mighty.'

14 [a]Judg. 3:13
15 [1]So with LXX, Syr., Tg., Vg.; MT *And my princes in Issachar* [2]Lit. *at his feet*
17 [a]Josh. 22:9 [b]Josh. 19:29, 31 [1]Or *at ease*
18 [a]Judg. 4:6, 10
19 [a]Judg. 1:27
21 [a]Judg. 4:7
23 [1]Or *Angel*
24 [a][Luke 1:28]
27 [a]Judg. 4:18–21
29 [1]*princesses* [2]Lit. *repeats her words to herself*
31 [a]Ps. 92:9 [b]2 Sam. 23:4 [c]Ps. 37:6; 89:36, 37 [d]Ps. 19:5

CHAPTER 6

1 [a]Judg. 2:11 [b]Num. 22:4; 31:1–3
2 [a]1 Sam. 13:6; Heb. 11:38

24 "Most blessed among women is
Jael,
The wife of Heber the Kenite;
[a]Blessed is she among women in
tents.
25 He asked for water, she gave
milk;
She brought out cream in a lordly
bowl.
26 She stretched her hand to the tent
peg,
Her right hand to the workmen's
hammer;
She pounded Sisera, she pierced
his head,
She split and struck through his
temple.
27 At her feet he sank, he fell, he
lay still;
At her feet he sank, he fell;
Where he sank, there he fell
[a]dead.

28 "The mother of Sisera looked
through the window,
And cried out through the lattice,
'Why is his chariot *so* long in
coming?
Why tarries the clatter of his
chariots?'
29 Her wisest [1]ladies answered her,
Yes, she [2]answered herself,
30 'Are they not finding and dividing
the spoil:
To every man a girl *or* two;
For Sisera, plunder of dyed
garments,
Plunder of garments
embroidered and dyed,
Two pieces of dyed embroidery
for the neck of the looter?'

31 "Thus let all Your enemies [a]perish,
O LORD!
But *let* those who love Him *be*
[b]like the [c]sun
When it comes out in full
[d]strength."

So the land had rest for forty
years.

Midianites Oppress Israel

6 Then the children of Israel did
[a]evil in the sight of the LORD.
So the LORD delivered them into
the hand of [b]Midian for seven
years,
2 and the hand of Midian pre-
vailed against Israel. Because of
the Midianites, the children of Is-
rael made for themselves the dens,
[a]the caves, and the strongholds
which *are* in the mountains.

3 So it was, whenever Israel had
sown, Midianites would come up;
also Amalekites and the [a]people of
the East would come up against
them.
4 Then they would encamp
against them and [a]destroy the pro-
duce of the earth as far as Gaza,
and leave no sustenance for Israel,
neither sheep nor ox nor [b]donkey.
5 For they would come up with
their livestock and their tents,
coming in as numerous as locusts;
both they and their camels were
[1]without number; and they would
enter the land to destroy it.
6 So Israel was greatly impover-
ished because of the Midianites,
and the children of Israel [a]cried
out to the LORD.
7 And it came to pass, when the
children of Israel cried out to the
LORD because of the Midianites,
8 that the LORD sent a prophet to
the children of Israel, who said to
them, "Thus says the LORD God of
Israel: 'I brought you up from
Egypt and brought you out of the
[a]house of [1]bondage;
9 'and I delivered you out of the
hand of the Egyptians and out of
the hand of all who oppressed you,
and [a]drove them out before you
and gave you their land.
10 'Also I said to you, "I *am* the
LORD your God; [a]do not fear the
gods of the Amorites, in whose
land you dwell." But you have not
obeyed My [b]voice.' "

Gideon

11 Now the Angel of the LORD
came and sat under the terebinth
tree which *was* in Ophrah, which
belonged to Joash [a]the Abiezrite,
while his son [b]Gideon threshed
wheat in the winepress, in order
to hide *it* from the Midianites.
12 And the [a]Angel of the LORD ap-
peared to him, and said to him,
"The LORD *is* [b]with you, you
mighty man of valor!"
13 Gideon said to Him, "O [1]my
lord, if the LORD is with us, why
then has all this happened to us?
And [a]where *are* all His miracles
[b]which our fathers told us about,
saying, 'Did not the LORD bring us
up from Egypt?' But now the LORD
has [c]forsaken us and delivered us
into the hands of the Midianites."
14 Then the LORD turned to him
and said, [a]"Go in this might of
yours, and you shall save Israel
from the hand of the Midianites.
[b]Have I not sent you?"
15 So he said to Him, "O [1]my
Lord, how can I save Israel? In-
deed [a]my clan *is* the weakest in
Manasseh, and I *am* the least in
my father's house."
16 And the LORD said to him,
[a]"Surely I will be with you, and
you shall [1]defeat the Midianites as
one man."
17 Then he said to Him, "If now I
have found favor in Your sight,
then [a]show me a sign that it is You
who talk with me.
18 [a]"Do not depart from here, I
pray, until I come to You and bring
out my offering and set *it* before
You." And He said, "I will wait un-
til you come back."
19 [a]So Gideon went in and pre-
pared a young goat, and unleav-
ened bread from an ephah of flour.
The meat he put in a basket, and
he put the broth in a pot; and he
brought *them* out to Him under
the terebinth tree and presented
them.
20 The Angel of God said to him,
"Take the meat and the unleav-
ened bread and [a]lay *them* on this
rock, and [b]pour out the broth."
And he did so.
21 Then the Angel of the LORD put
out the end of the staff that *was*
in His hand, and touched the meat
and the unleavened bread; and
[a]fire rose out of the rock and con-
sumed the meat and the unleav-
ened bread. And the Angel of the
LORD departed out of his sight.
22 Now Gideon [a]perceived that He
was the Angel of the LORD. So Gid-
eon said, "Alas, O Lord GOD! [b]For
I have seen the Angel of the LORD
face to face."
23 Then the LORD said to him,
[a]"Peace *be* with you; do not fear,
you shall not die."
24 So Gideon built an altar there
to the LORD, and called it [1]The-
LORD-*Is*-Peace. To this day it *is* still
[a]in Ophrah of the Abiezrites.
25 Now it came to pass the same
night that the LORD said to him,
"Take your father's young bull, the
second bull of seven years old, and
[a]tear down the altar of [b]Baal that

3 [a]Judg. 7:12
4 [a]Lev. 26:16 [b]Deut. 28:31
5 [1]*innumerable*
6 [a]Ps. 50:15; Hos. 5:15
8 [a]Josh. 24:17 [1]*slavery*
9 [a]Ps. 44:2, 3
10 [a]2 Kin. 17:35, 37, 38; Jer. 10:2 [b]Judg. 2:1, 2
11 [a]Josh. 17:2; Judg. 6:15 [b]Judg. 7:1; Heb. 11:32
12 [a]Judg. 13:3; Luke 1:11, 28 [b]Josh. 1:5
13 [a][Is. 59:1] [b]Josh. 4:6, 21; Ps. 44:1 [c]Deut. 31:17; 2 Chr. 15:2; Ps. 44:9–16 [1]Heb. *adoni,* used of man
14 [a]1 Sam. 12:11 [b]Josh. 1:9
15 [a]1 Sam. 9:21 [1]Heb. *Adonai,* used of God
16 [a]Ex. 3:12; Josh. 1:5 [1]Lit. *strike*
17 [a]Judg. 6:36, 37; 2 Kin. 20:8; Ps. 86:17; Is. 7:11; 38:7, 8
18 [a]Gen. 18:3, 5
19 [a]Gen. 18:6–8
20 [a]Judg. 13:19 [b]1 Kin. 18:33, 34
21 [a]Lev. 9:24
22 [a]Gen. 32:30; Ex. 33:20; Judg. 13:21, 22 [b]Gen. 16:13
23 [a]Dan. 10:19
24 [a]Judg. 8:32 [1]Heb. *YHWH Shalom*
25 [a]Judg. 2:2 [b]Judg. 3:7

your father has, and [c]cut down the
[1]wooden image that *is* beside it;
26 "and build an altar to the LORD
your God on top of this [1]rock in
the proper arrangement, and take
the second bull and offer a burnt
sacrifice with the wood of the im-
age which you shall cut down."
27 So Gideon took ten men from
among his servants and did as the
LORD had said to him. But because
he feared his father's household
and the men of the city too much
to do *it* by day, he did *it* by night.

Gideon Destroys the Altar of Baal

28 And when the men of the city
arose early in the morning, there
was the altar of Baal, torn down;
and the wooden image that *was*
beside it was cut down, and the
second bull was being offered on
the altar *which had been* built.
29 So they said to one another,
"Who has done this thing?" And
when they had inquired and
asked, they said, "Gideon the son
of Joash has done this thing."
30 Then the men of the city said
to Joash, "Bring out your son, that
he may die, because he has torn
down the altar of Baal, and be-
cause he has cut down the wooden
image that *was* beside it."
31 But Joash said to all who stood
against him, "Would you [1]plead
for Baal? Would you save him? Let
the one who would plead for him
be put to death by morning! If he
is a god, let him plead for himself,
because his altar has been torn
down!"
32 Therefore on that day he called
him [a]Jerubbaal,[1] saying, "Let Baal
plead against him, because he has
torn down his altar."
33 Then all [a]the Midianites and
Amalekites, the people of the East,
gathered together; and they
crossed over and encamped in [b]the
Valley of Jezreel.
34 But [a]the Spirit of the LORD
came upon Gideon; then he [b]blew
the trumpet, and the Abiezrites
gathered behind him.
35 And he sent messengers
throughout all Manasseh, who
also gathered behind him. He also
sent messengers to [a]Asher, [b]Zebu-
lun, and Naphtali; and they came
up to meet them.

25 [c]Ex. 34:13; Deut. 7:5 [1]Heb. *Asherah*, a Canaanite goddess
26 [1]*stronghold*
31 [1]*contend*
32 [a]Judg. 7:1; 1 Sam. 12:11; 2 Sam. 11:21 [1]Lit. *Let Baal Plead*
33 [a]Judg. 6:3 [b]Josh. 17:16; Hos. 1:5
34 [a]Judg. 3:10; 1 Chr. 12:18; 2 Chr. 24:20 [b]Num. 10:3; Judg. 3:27
35 [a]Judg. 5:17; 7:23 [b]Judg. 4:6, 10; 5:18
37 [a][Ex. 4:3–7]
39 [a]Gen. 18:32

CHAPTER 7

1 [a]Judg. 6:32
2 [a]Deut. 8:17; Is. 10:13
3 [a]Deut. 20:8

The Sign of the Fleece

36 So Gideon said to God, "If You
will save Israel by my hand as You
have said—
37 [a]"look, I shall put a fleece of
wool on the threshing floor; if
there is dew on the fleece only, and
it is dry on all the ground, then I
shall know that You will save Is-
rael by my hand, as You have
said."
38 And it was so. When he rose
early the next morning and
squeezed the fleece together, he
wrung the dew out of the fleece,
a bowlful of water.
39 Then Gideon said to God, [a]"Do
not be angry with me, but let me
speak just once more: Let me test,
I pray, just once more with the
fleece; let it now be dry only on
the fleece, but on all the ground
let there be dew."
40 And God did so that night. It
was dry on the fleece only, but
there was dew on all the ground.

Gideon's Valiant Three Hundred

7 Then [a]Jerubbaal (that *is*, Gid-
eon) and all the people who
were with him rose early and en-
camped beside the well of Harod,
so that the camp of the Midianites
was on the north side of them by
the hill of Moreh in the valley.
2 And the LORD said to Gideon,
"The people who *are* with you *are*
too many for Me to give the Midi-
anites into their hands, lest Israel
[a]claim glory for itself against Me,
saying, 'My own hand has saved
me.'
3 "Now therefore, proclaim in
the hearing of the people, saying,
[a]'Whoever *is* fearful and afraid, let
him turn and depart at once from
Mount Gilead.'" And twenty-two
thousand of the people returned,
and ten thousand remained.
4 But the LORD said to Gideon,
"The people *are* still *too* many;
bring them down to the water, and
I will test them for you there. Then
it will be, *that* of whom I say to
you, 'This one shall go with you,'
the same shall go with you; and
of whomever I say to you, 'This
one shall not go with you,' the
same shall not go."
5 So he brought the people down

to the water. And the LORD said
to Gideon, "Everyone who laps
from the water with his tongue, as
a dog laps, you shall set apart by
himself; likewise everyone who
gets down on his knees to drink."
6 And the number of those who
lapped, *putting* their hand to their
mouth, was three hundred men;
but all the rest of the people got
down on their knees to drink wa-
ter.
7 Then the LORD said to Gideon,
[a]"By the three hundred men who
lapped I will save you, and deliver
the Midianites into your hand. Let
all the *other* people go, every man
to his [1]place."
8 So the people took provisions
and their trumpets in their hands.
And he sent away all *the rest of*
Israel, every man to his tent, and
retained those three hundred men.
Now the camp of Midian was be-
low him in the valley.
9 It happened on the same [a]night
that the LORD said to him, "Arise,
go down against the camp, for I
have delivered it into your hand.
10 "But if you are afraid to go
down, go down to the camp with
Purah your servant,
11 "and you shall [a]hear what they
say; and afterward [1]your hands
shall be strengthened to go down
against the camp." Then he went
down with Purah his servant to the
outpost of the armed men who
were in the camp.
12 Now the Midianites and Ama-
lekites, [a]all the people of the East,
were lying in the valley [b]as numer-
ous as locusts; and their camels
were [1]without number, as the sand
by the seashore in multitude.
13 And when Gideon had come,
there was a man telling a dream
to his companion. He said, "I have
had a dream: *To my* surprise, a
loaf of barley bread tumbled into
the camp of Midian; it came to a
tent and struck it so that it fell and
overturned, and the tent col-
lapsed."
14 Then his companion answered
and said, "This *is* nothing else but
the sword of Gideon the son of
Joash, a man of Israel! Into his
hand [a]God has delivered Midian
and the whole camp."
15 And so it was, when Gideon
heard the telling of the dream and
its interpretation, that he wor-
shiped. He returned to the camp
of Israel, and said, "Arise, for the
LORD has delivered the camp of
Midian into your hand."
16 Then he divided the three hun-
dred men *into* three companies,
and he put a trumpet into every
man's hand, with empty pitchers,
and torches inside the pitchers.
17 And he said to them, "Look at
me and do likewise; watch, and
when I come to the edge of the
camp you shall do as I do:
18 "When I blow the trumpet, I
and all who *are* with me, then you
also blow the trumpets on every
side of the whole camp, and say,
'*The sword of* the LORD and of Gid-
eon!' "
19 So Gideon and the hundred
men who *were* with him came to
the outpost of the camp at the be-
ginning of the middle watch, just
as they had posted the watch; and
they blew the trumpets and broke
the pitchers that *were* in their
hands.
20 Then the three companies blew
the trumpets and broke the pitch-
ers—they held the torches in their
left hands and the trumpets in
their right hands for blowing—and
they cried, "The sword of the LORD
and of Gideon!"
21 And [a]every man stood in his
place all around the camp; [b]and
the whole army ran and cried out
and fled.
22 When the three hundred [a]blew
the trumpets, [b]the LORD set [c]every
man's sword against his compan-
ion throughout the whole camp;
and the army fled to [1]Beth Acacia,
toward Zererah, as far as the bor-
der of [d]Abel Meholah, by Tabbath.
23 And the men of Israel gathered
together from [a]Naphtali, Asher,
and all Manasseh, and pursued the
Midianites.
24 Then Gideon sent messengers
throughout all the [a]mountains of
Ephraim, saying, "Come down
against the Midianites, and seize
from them the watering places as
far as Beth Barah and the Jordan."
Then all the men of Ephraim gath-
ered together and [b]seized the wa-
tering places as far as [c]Beth Barah
and the Jordan.

7 [a]1 Sam. 14:6 [1]*home*

9 [a]Gen. 46:2, 3; Judg. 6:25

11 [a]Gen. 24:14; 1 Sam. 14:9, 10 [1]*you shall be encouraged*

12 [a]Judg. 6:3, 33; 8:10 [b]Judg. 6:5 [1]*innumerable*

14 [a]Judg. 6:14, 16

21 [a]Ex. 14:13, 14; 2 Chr. 20:17 [b]2 Kin. 7:7

22 [a]Josh. 6:4, 16, 20 [b]Ps. 83:9; Is. 9:4 [c]1 Sam. 14:20; 2 Chr. 20:23 [d]1 Kin. 4:12 [1]Heb. *Beth Shittah*

23 [a]Judg. 6:35

24 [a]Judg. 3:27 [b]Judg. 3:28 [c]John 1:28

25 And they captured [a]two
princes of the Midianites, [b]Oreb
and Zeeb. They killed Oreb at the
rock of Oreb, and Zeeb they killed
at the winepress of Zeeb. They
pursued Midian and brought the
heads of Oreb and Zeeb to Gideon
on the [c]other side of the Jordan.

Gideon Subdues the Midianites

8 Now [a]the men of Ephraim said
to him, "Why have you done
this to us by not calling us when
you went to fight with the Midian-
ites?" And they reprimanded him
sharply.
2 So he said to them, "What have
I done now in comparison with
you? *Is* not the [1]gleaning *of the*
grapes of Ephraim better than [2]the
vintage of [a]Abiezer?
3 [a]"God has delivered into your
hands the princes of Midian, Oreb
and Zeeb. And what was I able to
do in comparison with you?" Then
their [b]anger toward him subsided
when he said that.
4 When Gideon came [a]to the Jor-
dan, he and [b]the three hundred
men who *were* with him crossed
over, exhausted but still in pursuit.
5 Then he said to the men of
[a]Succoth, "Please give loaves of
bread to the people who follow me,
for they are exhausted, and I am
pursuing Zebah and Zalmunna,
kings of Midian."
6 And the leaders of Succoth
said, [a]"*Are*[1] the hands of Zebah
and Zalmunna now in your hand,
that [b]we should give bread to your
army?"
7 So Gideon said, "For this
cause, when the LORD has deliv-
ered Zebah and Zalmunna into my
hand, [a]then I will tear your flesh
with the thorns of the wilderness
and with briers!"
8 Then he went up from there [a]to
Penuel and spoke to them in the
same way. And the men of Penuel
answered him as the men of Suc-
coth had answered.
9 So he also spoke to the men of
Penuel, saying, "When I [a]come
back in peace, [b]I will tear down
this tower!"
10 Now Zebah and Zalmunna
were at Karkor, and their armies
with them, about fifteen thousand,
all who were left of [a]all the army

25 [a]Judg. 8:3 [b]Ps. 83:11; Is. 10:26 [c]Judg. 8:4

CHAPTER 8

1 [a]Judg. 12:1; 2 Sam. 19:41

2 [a]Judg. 6:11 [1]Few grapes left after the harvest [2]The whole harvest

3 [a]Judg. 7:24, 25 [b]Prov. 15:1

4 [a]Judg. 7:25 [b]Judg. 7:6

5 [a]Gen. 33:17; Ps. 60:6

6 [a]1 Kin. 20:11; Judg. 8:15 [b]1 Sam. 25:11 [1]Lit. *Is the palm*

7 [a]Judg. 8:16

8 [a]Gen. 32:30, 31; 1 Kin. 12:25

9 [a]1 Kin. 22:27 [b]Judg. 8:17

10 [a]Judg. 7:12 [b]Judg. 6:5

11 [a]Num. 32:35, 42 [b]Judg. 18:27; [1 Thess. 5:3] [1]Lit. *struck*

12 [a]Ps. 83:11

15 [a]Judg. 8:6

16 [a]Judg. 8:7 [1]*disciplined*

17 [a]Judg. 8:9 [b]1 Kin. 12:25

18 [a]Judg. 4:6; Ps. 89:12

21 [a]Ps. 83:11

22 [a][Judg. 9:8]

of the people of the East; for [b]one
hundred and twenty thousand men
who drew the sword had fallen.
11 Then Gideon went up by the
road of those who dwell in tents
on the east of [a]Nobah and Jogbe-
hah; and he [1]attacked the army
while the camp felt [b]secure.
12 When Zebah and Zalmunna
fled, he pursued them; and he
[a]took the two kings of Midian, Ze-
bah and Zalmunna, and routed the
whole army.
13 Then Gideon the son of Joash
returned from battle, from the As-
cent of Heres.
14 And he caught a young man of
the men of Succoth and interro-
gated him; and he wrote down for
him the leaders of Succoth and its
elders, seventy-seven men.
15 Then he came to the men of
Succoth and said, "Here are Zebah
and Zalmunna, about whom you
[a]ridiculed me, saying, '*Are* the
hands of Zebah and Zalmunna
now in your hand, that we should
give bread to your weary men?' "
16 [a]And he took the elders of the
city, and thorns of the wilderness
and briers, and with them he
[1]taught the men of Succoth.
17 [a]Then he tore down the tower
of [b]Penuel and killed the men of
the city.
18 And he said to Zebah and Zal-
munna, "What kind of men *were*
they whom you killed at [a]Tabor?"
So they answered, "As you *are*, so
were they; each one resembled the
son of a king."
19 Then he said, "They *were* my
brothers, the sons of my mother.
As the LORD lives, if you had let
them live, I would not kill you."
20 And he said to Jether his first-
born, "Rise, kill them!" But the
youth would not draw his sword;
for he was afraid, because he *was*
still a youth.
21 So Zebah and Zalmunna said,
"Rise yourself, and kill us; for as
a man *is, so is* his strength." So
Gideon arose and [a]killed Zebah
and Zalmunna, and took the cres-
cent ornaments that *were* on their
camels' necks.

Gideon's Ephod

22 Then the men of Israel said to
Gideon, [a]"Rule over us, both you

and your son, and your grandson also; for you have [b]delivered us from the hand of Midian."
23 But Gideon said to them, "I will not rule over you, nor shall my son rule over you; [a]the LORD shall rule over you."
24 Then Gideon said to them, "I would like to [1]make a request of you, that each of you would give me the earrings from his plunder." For they had golden earrings, [a]because they *were* Ishmaelites.
25 So they answered, "We will gladly give *them*." And they spread out a garment, and each man threw into it the earrings from his plunder.
26 Now the weight of the gold earrings that he requested was one thousand seven hundred *shekels* of gold, besides the crescent ornaments, pendants, and purple robes which *were* on the kings of Midian, and besides the chains that *were* around their camels' necks.
27 Then Gideon [a]made it into an ephod and set it up in his city, [b]Ophrah. And all Israel [c]played the harlot with it there. It became [d]a snare to Gideon and to his house.
28 Thus Midian was subdued before the children of Israel, so that they lifted their heads no more. [a]And the country was quiet for forty years in the days of Gideon.

Death of Gideon

29 Then [a]Jerubbaal the son of Joash went and dwelt in his own house.
30 Gideon had [a]seventy sons who were his own offspring, for he had many wives.
31 [a]And his concubine who *was* in Shechem also bore him a son, whose name he called Abimelech.
32 Now Gideon the son of Joash died [a]at a good old age, and was buried in the tomb of Joash his father, [b]in Ophrah of the Abiezrites.
33 So it was, [a]as soon as Gideon was dead, that the children of Israel again [b]played the harlot with the Baals, [c]and made Baal-Berith their god.
34 Thus the children of Israel [a]did not remember the LORD their God, who had delivered them from the hands of all their enemies on every side;

22 [b]Judg. 3:9; 9:17
23 [a]1 Sam. 8:7; 10:19; 12:12; Ps. 10:16
24 [a]Gen. 37:25, 28 [1]Lit. *request a request*
27 [a]Judg. 17:5 [b]Judg. 6:11, 24 [c][Ps. 106:39] [d]Deut. 7:16
28 [a]Judg. 5:31
29 [a]Judg. 6:32; 7:1
30 [a]Judg. 9:2, 5
31 [a]Judg. 9:1
32 [a]Gen. 25:8; Job 5:26 [b]Judg. 6:24; 8:27
33 [a]Judg. 2:19 [b]Judg. 2:17 [c]Judg. 9:4, 46
34 [a]Deut. 4:9; Judg. 3:7; Ps. 78:11, 42; 106:13, 21
35 [a]Judg. 9:16–18
CHAPTER 9
1 [a]Judg. 8:31, 35
2 [a]Judg. 8:30; 9:5, 18 [b]Gen. 29:14
3 [a]Gen. 29:15
4 [a]Judg. 8:33 [b]Judg. 11:3; 2 Chr. 13:7; Acts 17:5
5 [a]Judg. 6:24 [b]Judg. 8:30; 9:2, 18; 2 Kin. 11:1, 2
7 [a]Deut. 11:29; 27:12; Josh. 8:33; John 4:20
8 [a]2 Kin. 14:9 [b]Judg. 8:22, 23
9 [a][John 5:23]

35 [a]nor did they show kindness to the house of Jerubbaal (Gideon) in accordance with the good he had done for Israel.

Abimelech's Conspiracy

9 Then Abimelech the son of Jerubbaal went to Shechem, to [a]his mother's brothers, and spoke with them and with all the family of the house of his mother's father, saying,
2 "Please speak in the hearing of all the men of Shechem: 'Which is better for you, that all [a]seventy of the sons of Jerubbaal reign over you, or that one reign over you?' Remember that I *am* your own flesh and [b]bone."
3 And his mother's brothers spoke all these words concerning him in the hearing of all the men of Shechem; and their heart was inclined to follow Abimelech, for they said, "He is our [a]brother."
4 So they gave him seventy *shekels* of silver from the temple of [a]Baal-Berith, with which Abimelech hired [b]worthless and reckless men; and they followed him.
5 Then he went to his father's house [a]at Ophrah and [b]killed his brothers, the seventy sons of Jerubbaal, on one stone. But Jotham the youngest son of Jerubbaal was left, because he hid himself.
6 And all the men of Shechem gathered together, all of Beth Millo, and they went and made Abimelech king beside the terebinth tree at the pillar that *was* in Shechem.

The Parable of the Trees

7 Now when they told Jotham, he went and stood on top of [a]Mount Gerizim, and lifted his voice and cried out. And he said to them:

"Listen to me, you men of
Shechem,
That God may listen to you!

8 "The[a] trees once went forth to
anoint a king over them.
And they said to the olive tree,
[b]'Reign over us!'
9 But the olive tree said to them,
'Should I cease giving my oil,
[a]With which they honor God and
men,
And go to sway over trees?'

10 "Then the trees said to the fig tree,
'You come *and* reign over us!'
11 But the fig tree said to them,
'Should I cease my sweetness and
my good fruit,
And go to sway over trees?'

12 "Then the trees said to the vine,
'You come *and* reign over us!'
13 But the vine said to them,
'Should I cease my new wine,
[a]Which cheers *both* God and men,
And go to sway over trees?'

14 "Then all the trees said to the
bramble,
'You come *and* reign over us!'
15 And the bramble said to the trees,
'If in truth you anoint me as king
over you,
Then come *and* take shelter in my
[a]shade;
But if not, [b]let fire come out of
the bramble
And devour the [c]cedars of
Lebanon!'

16 "Now therefore, if you have
acted in truth and sincerity in
making Abimelech king, and if
you have dealt well with Jerubbaal
and his house, and have done to
him [a]as[1] he deserves—
17 "for my [a]father fought for you,
risked his life, and [b]delivered you
out of the hand of Midian;
18 [a]"but you have risen up against
my father's house this day, and
killed his seventy sons on one
stone, and made Abimelech, the
son of his [b]female servant, king
over the men of Shechem, because
he is your brother—
19 "if then you have acted in truth
and sincerity with Jerubbaal and
with his house this day, *then* [a]re-
joice in Abimelech, and let him
also rejoice in you.
20 "But if not, [a]let fire come from
Abimelech and devour the men of
Shechem and Beth Millo; and let
fire come from the men of She-
chem and from Beth Millo and de-
vour Abimelech!"
21 And Jotham ran away and fled;
and he went to [a]Beer and dwelt
there, for fear of Abimelech his
brother.

Downfall of Abimelech

22 After Abimelech had reigned
over Israel three years,
23 [a]God sent a [b]spirit of ill will be-
tween Abimelech and the men of
Shechem; and the men of She-
chem [c]dealt treacherously with
Abimelech,
24 [a]that the crime *done* to the sev-
enty sons of Jerubbaal might be
settled and their [b]blood be laid on
Abimelech their brother, who
killed them, and on the men of
Shechem, who aided him in the
killing of his brothers.
25 And the men of Shechem set
[1]men in ambush against him on
the tops of the mountains, and
they robbed all who passed by
them along that way; and it was
told Abimelech.
26 Now Gaal the son of Ebed
came with his brothers and went
over to Shechem; and the men of
Shechem put their confidence in
him.
27 So they went out into the fields,
and gathered *grapes* from their
vineyards and trod *them*, and
[1]made merry. And they went into
[a]the house of their god, and ate
and drank, and cursed Abime-
lech.
28 Then Gaal the son of Ebed said,
[a]"Who *is* Abimelech, and who *is*
Shechem, that we should serve
him? *Is he* not the son of Jerub-
baal, and *is not* Zebul his officer?
Serve the men of [b]Hamor the fa-
ther of Shechem; but why should
we serve him?
29 [a]"If only this people were un-
der my [1]authority! Then I would
remove Abimelech." So [2]he said to
Abimelech, "Increase your army
and come out!"
30 When Zebul, the ruler of the
city, heard the words of Gaal the
son of Ebed, his anger was
aroused.
31 And he sent messengers to
Abimelech secretly, saying, "Take
note! Gaal the son of Ebed and his
brothers have come to Shechem;
and here they are, fortifying the
city against you.
32 "Now therefore, get up by
night, you and the people who *are*
with you, and [1]lie in wait in the
field.
33 "And it shall be, as soon as the
sun is up in the morning, *that* you
shall rise early and rush upon the
city; and *when* he and the people
who are with him come out against

13 [a]Ps. 104:15
15 [a]Is. 30:2; Dan. 4:12; Hos. 14:7 [b]Num. 21:28; Judg. 9:20; Ezek. 19:14 [c]2 Kin. 14:9; Is. 2:13; Ezek. 31:3
16 [a]Judg. 8:35 [1]Lit. *according to the doing of his hands*
17 [a]Judg. 7 [b]Judg. 8:22
18 [a]Judg. 8:30, 35; 9:2, 5, 6 [b]Judg. 8:31
19 [a]Is. 8:6; [Phil. 3:3]
20 [a]Judg. 9:15, 45, 56, 57
21 [a]Num. 21:16
23 [a]1 Kin. 12:15; Is. 19:14 [b]1 Sam. 16:14; 18:9, 10; 1 Kin. 22:22; 2 Chr. 18:22 [c]Is. 33:1
24 [a]1 Kin. 2:32; Esth. 9:25; Matt. 23:35, 36 [b]Num. 35:33
25 [1]Lit. *liers-in-wait for*
27 [a]Judg. 9:4 [1]*rejoiced*
28 [a]1 Sam. 25:10; 1 Kin. 12:16 [b]Gen. 34:2, 6; Josh. 24:32
29 [a]2 Sam. 15:4 [1]Lit. *hand* [2]So with MT, Tg.; DSS *they;* LXX *I*
32 [1]Set up an ambush

you, you may then do to them [1]as you find opportunity."

34 So Abimelech and all the people who *were* with him rose by night, and [1]lay in wait against Shechem in four companies.

35 When Gaal the son of Ebed went out and stood in the entrance to the city gate, Abimelech and the people who *were* with him rose from lying in wait.

36 And when Gaal saw the people, he said to Zebul, "Look, people are coming down from the tops of the mountains!" But Zebul said to him, "You see the shadows of the mountains as *if they were* men."

37 So Gaal spoke again and said, "See, people are coming down from the center of the land, and another company is coming from the [1]Diviners' Terebinth Tree."

38 Then Zebul said to him, "Where indeed *is* your mouth now, with which you [a]said, 'Who is Abimelech, that we should serve him?' *Are* not these the people whom you despised? Go out, if you will, and fight with them now."

39 So Gaal went out, leading the men of Shechem, and fought with Abimelech.

40 And Abimelech chased him, and he fled from him; and many fell wounded, to the *very* entrance of the gate.

41 Then Abimelech dwelt at Arumah, and Zebul [1]drove out Gaal and his brothers, so that they would not dwell in Shechem.

42 And it came about on the next day that the people went out into the field, and they told Abimelech.

43 So he took his people, divided them into three companies, and lay in wait in the field. And he looked, and there were the people, coming out of the city; and he rose against them and [1]attacked them.

44 Then Abimelech and the company that *was* with him rushed forward and stood at the entrance of the gate of the city; and the *other* two companies rushed upon all who *were* in the fields and killed them.

45 So Abimelech fought against the city all that day; [a]he took the city and killed the people who *were* in it; and he [b]demolished the city and sowed it with salt.

46 Now when all the men of the tower of Shechem had heard *that*, they entered the [1]stronghold of the temple [a]of the god Berith.

47 And it was told Abimelech that all the men of the tower of Shechem were gathered together.

48 Then Abimelech went up to Mount [a]Zalmon, he and all the people who *were* with him. And Abimelech took an ax in his hand and cut down a bough from the trees, and took it and laid *it* on his shoulder; then he said to the people who were with him, "What you have seen me do, make haste *and* do as I *have done*."

49 So each of the people likewise cut down his own bough and followed Abimelech, put *them* against the [1]stronghold, and set the stronghold on fire above them, so that all the people of the tower of Shechem died, about a thousand men and women.

50 Then Abimelech went to Thebez, and he [1]encamped against Thebez and took it.

51 But there was a strong tower in the city, and all the men and women—all the people of the city—fled there and shut themselves in; then they went up to the top of the tower.

52 So Abimelech came as far as the tower and fought against it; and he drew near the door of the tower to burn it with fire.

53 But a certain woman [a]dropped an upper millstone on Abimelech's head and crushed his skull.

54 Then [a]he called quickly to the young man, his armorbearer, and said to him, "Draw your sword and kill me, lest men say of me, 'A woman killed him.'" So his young man thrust him through, and he died.

55 And when the men of Israel saw that Abimelech was dead, they departed, every man to his [1]place.

56 [a]Thus God repaid the wickedness of Abimelech, which he had done to his father by killing his seventy brothers.

57 And all the evil of the men of Shechem God returned on their own heads, and on them came [a]the curse of Jotham the son of Jerubbaal.

33 [1]Lit. *as your hand can find*
34 [1]Set up an ambush
37 [1]Heb. *Meonenim*
38 [a]Judg. 9:28, 29
41 [1]*exiled*
43 [1]Lit. *struck*
45 [a]Judg. 9:20 [b]Deut. 29:23; 2 Kin. 3:25
46 [a]Judg. 8:33 [1]*fortified room*
48 [a]Ps. 68:14
49 [1]*fortified room*
50 [1]*besieged*
53 [a]2 Sam. 11:21
54 [a]1 Sam. 31:4
55 [1]*home*
56 [a]Judg. 9:24; Job 31:3; Prov. 5:22
57 [a]Judg. 9:20

Tola

10 After Abimelech there
[a]arose to save Israel Tola the
son of Puah, the son of Dodo, a
man of Issachar; and he dwelt in
Shamir in the mountains of
Ephraim.
2 He judged Israel twenty-three
years; and he died and was buried
in Shamir.

Jair

3 After him arose Jair, a Gilead-
ite; and he judged Israel twenty-
two years.
4 Now he had thirty sons who
[a]rode on thirty donkeys; they also
had thirty towns, [b]which are called
[1]"Havoth Jair" to this day, which
are in the land of Gilead.
5 And Jair died and was buried
in Camon.

Israel Oppressed Again

6 Then [a]the children of Israel
again did evil in the sight of the
LORD, and [b]served the Baals and
the Ashtoreths, [c]the gods of Syria,
the gods of [d]Sidon, the gods of
Moab, the gods of the people of
Ammon, and the gods of the Phi-
listines; and they forsook the LORD
and did not serve Him.
7 So the anger of the LORD was
hot against Israel; and He [a]sold
them into the hands of the [b]Philis-
tines and into the hands of the
people of [c]Ammon.
8 From that year they [1]harassed
and oppressed the children of Is-
rael for eighteen years—all the
children of Israel who *were* on the
other side of the Jordan in the
[a]land of the Amorites, in Gilead.
9 Moreover the people of Am-
mon crossed over the Jordan to
fight against Judah also, against
Benjamin, and against the house
of Ephraim, so that Israel was se-
verely distressed.
10 [a]And the children of Israel
cried out to the LORD, saying, "We
have [b]sinned against You, because
we have both forsaken our God
and served the Baals!"
11 So the LORD said to the children
of Israel, "*Did I* not *deliver you*
[a]from the Egyptians and [b]from the
Amorites and [c]from the people of
Ammon and [d]from the Philistines?

CHAPTER 10

1 [a]Judg. 2:16

4 [a]Judg. 5:10; 12:14 [b]Deut. 3:14 [1]Lit. *Towns of Jair,* Num. 32:41; Deut. 3:14

6 [a]Judg. 2:11; 3:7; 6:1; 13:1 [b]Judg. 2:13 [c]Judg. 2:12 [d]1 Kin. 11:33; Ps. 106:36

7 [a]Judg. 2:14; 4:2; 1 Sam. 12:9 [b]Judg. 13:1 [c]Judg. 3:13

8 [a]Num. 32:33 [1]Lit. *shattered*

10 [a]Judg. 6:6; 1 Sam. 12:10 [b]Deut. 1:41

11 [a]Ex. 14:30 [b]Num. 21:21, 24, 25 [c]Judg. 3:12, 13 [d]Judg. 3:31

12 [a]Judg. 1:31; 5:19 [b]Judg. 6:3; 7:12 [c]Ps. 106:42, 43 [1]LXX mss. *Midianites*

13 [a][Deut. 32:15; Judg. 2:12; Jer. 2:13]

14 [a]Deut. 32:37, 38

15 [a]1 Sam. 3:18; 2 Sam. 15:26

16 [a]2 Chr. 7:14; Jer. 18:7, 8 [b]Ps. 106:44, 45; Is. 63:9

17 [a]Gen. 31:49; Judg. 11:11, 29

18 [a]Judg. 11:8, 11

CHAPTER 11

1 [a]Heb. 11:32 [b]Judg. 6:12; 2 Kin. 5:1

2 [a]Gen. 21:10; Deut. 23:2

3 [a]2 Sam. 10:6, 8 [b]1 Sam. 22:2

4 [a]Judg. 10:9, 17

7 [a]Gen. 26:27

12 "Also [a]the Sidonians [b]and Am-
alekites and [1]Maonites [c]oppressed
you; and you cried out to Me, and
I delivered you from their hand.
13 [a]"Yet you have forsaken Me
and served other gods. Therefore
I will deliver you no more.
14 "Go and [a]cry out to the gods
which you have chosen; let them
deliver you in your time of dis-
tress."
15 And the children of Israel said
to the LORD, "We have sinned! [a]Do
to us whatever seems best to You;
only deliver us this day, we pray."
16 [a]So they put away the foreign
gods from among them and served
the LORD. And [b]His soul could no
longer endure the misery of Israel.
17 Then the people of Ammon
gathered together and encamped
in Gilead. And the children of Is-
rael assembled together and en-
camped in [a]Mizpah.
18 And the people, the leaders of
Gilead, said to one another, "Who
is the man who will begin the fight
against the people of Ammon? He
shall [a]be head over all the inhabit-
ants of Gilead."

Jephthah

11 Now [a]Jephthah the Gilead-
ite was [b]a mighty man of
valor, but he *was* the son of a har-
lot; and Gilead begot Jephthah.
2 Gilead's wife bore sons; and
when his wife's sons grew up, they
drove Jephthah out, and said to
him, "You shall have [a]no inheri-
tance in our father's house, for you
are the son of another woman."
3 Then Jephthah fled from his
brothers and dwelt in the land of
[a]Tob; and [b]worthless men banded
together with Jephthah and went
out *raiding* with him.
4 It came to pass after a time that
the [a]people of Ammon made war
against Israel.
5 And so it was, when the people
of Ammon made war against Is-
rael, that the elders of Gilead went
to get Jephthah from the land of
Tob.
6 Then they said to Jephthah,
"Come and be our commander,
that we may fight against the peo-
ple of Ammon."
7 So Jephthah said to the elders
of Gilead, [a]"Did you not hate me,

and expel me from my father's
house? Why have you come to me
now when you are in [1]distress?"
8 [a]And the elders of Gilead said
to Jephthah, "That is why we have
[b]turned[1] again to you now, that
you may go with us and fight
against the people of Ammon, and
be [c]our head over all the inhabit-
ants of Gilead."

7 [1]*trouble*
8 [a]Judg. 10:18
[b][Luke 17:4]
[c]Judg. 10:18
[1]*returned*

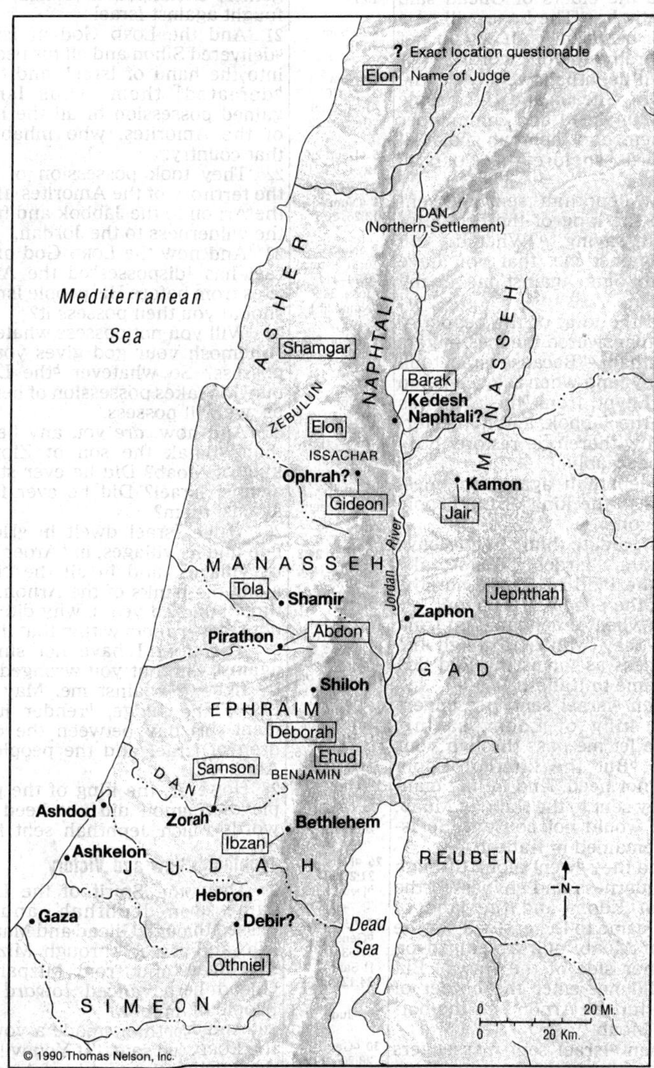

The Judges of Israel

9 So Jephthah said to the elders of Gilead, "If you take me back home to fight against the people of Ammon, and the LORD delivers them to me, shall I be your head?"

10 And the elders of Gilead said to Jephthah, [a]"The LORD will be a witness between us, if we do not do according to your words."

11 Then Jephthah went with the elders of Gilead, and the people made him [a]head and commander over them; and Jephthah spoke all his words [b]before the LORD in Mizpah.

12 Now Jephthah sent messengers to the king of the people of Ammon, saying, [a]"What do you have against me, that you have come to fight against me in my land?"

13 And the king of the people of Ammon answered the messengers of Jephthah, [a]"Because Israel took away my land when they came up out of Egypt, from [b]the Arnon as far as [c]the Jabbok, and to the Jordan. Now therefore, restore those *lands* peaceably."

14 So Jephthah again sent messengers to the king of the people of Ammon,

15 and said to him, "Thus says Jephthah: [a]'Israel did not take away the land of Moab, nor the land of the people of Ammon;

16 'for when Israel came up from Egypt, they walked through the wilderness as far as the Red Sea and [a]came to Kadesh.

17 'Then [a]Israel sent messengers to the king of Edom, saying, "Please let me pass through your land." [b]But the king of Edom would not heed. And in like manner they sent to the [c]king of Moab, but he would not *consent*. So Israel [d]remained in Kadesh.

18 'And they [a]went along through the wilderness and [b]bypassed the land of Edom and the land of Moab, came to the east side of the land of Moab, and encamped on the other side of the Arnon. But they did not enter the border of Moab, for the Arnon *was* the border of Moab.

19 'Then [a]Israel sent messengers to Sihon king of the Amorites, king of Heshbon; and Israel said to him, "Please [b]let us pass through your land into our place."

20 [a]'But Sihon did not trust Israel to pass through his territory. So Sihon gathered all his people together, encamped in Jahaz, and fought against Israel.

21 'And the LORD God of Israel [a]delivered Sihon and all his people into the hand of Israel, and they [b]defeated[1] them. Thus Israel gained possession of all the land of the Amorites, who inhabited that country.

22 'They took possession of [a]all the territory of the Amorites, from the Arnon to the Jabbok and from the wilderness to the Jordan.

23 'And now the LORD God of Israel has [1]dispossessed the Amorites from before His people Israel; should you then possess it?

24 'Will you not possess whatever [a]Chemosh your god gives you to possess? So whatever [b]the LORD our God takes possession of before us, we will possess.

25 'And now, *are* you any better than [a]Balak the son of Zippor, king of Moab? Did he ever strive against Israel? Did he ever fight against them?

26 'While Israel dwelt in [a]Heshbon and its villages, in [b]Aroer and its villages, and in all the cities along the banks of the Arnon, for three hundred years, why did you not recover *them* within that time?

27 'Therefore I have not sinned against you, but you wronged me by fighting against me. May the LORD, [a]the Judge, [b]render judgment this day between the children of Israel and the people of Ammon.'"

28 However, the king of the people of Ammon did not heed the words which Jephthah sent him.

Jephthah's Vow and Victory

29 Then [a]the Spirit of the LORD came upon Jephthah, and he passed through Gilead and Manasseh, and passed through Mizpah of Gilead; and from Mizpah of Gilead he advanced *toward* the people of Ammon.

30 And Jephthah [a]made a vow to the LORD, and said, "If You will indeed deliver the people of Ammon into my hands,

10 [a]Gen. 31:49, 50; Jer. 29:23; 42:5
11 [a]Judg. 11:8 [b]Judg. 10:17; 20:1; 1 Sam. 10:17
12 [a]2 Sam. 16:10
13 [a]Num. 21:24–26 [b]Josh. 13:9 [c]Gen. 32:22
15 [a]Deut. 2:9, 19
16 [a]Num. 13:26; 20:1
17 [a]Num. 20:14 [b]Num. 20:14–21 [c]Josh. 24:9 [d]Num. 20:1
18 [a]Deut. 2:9, 18, 19 [b]Num. 21:4
19 [a]Num. 21:21; Deut. 2:26–36 [b]Num. 21:22; Deut. 2:27
20 [a]Num. 21:23; Deut. 2:27
21 [a]Josh. 24:8 [b]Num. 21:24, 25 [1]Lit. *struck*
22 [a]Deut. 2:36, 37
23 [1]*driven out*
24 [a]Num. 21:29; 1 Kin. 11:7; Jer. 48:7 [b][Deut. 9:4, 5; Josh. 3:10]
25 [a]Num. 22:2; Josh. 24:9; Mic. 6:5
26 [a]Num. 21:25, 26 [b]Deut. 2:36
27 [a]Gen. 18:25 [b]Gen. 16:5; 31:53; [1 Sam. 24:12, 15]
29 [a]Judg. 3:10
30 [a]Gen. 28:20; Num. 30:2; 1 Sam. 1:11

31 "then it will be that whatever
comes out of the doors of my
house to meet me, when I return
in peace from the people of Am-
mon, [a]shall surely be the LORD's,
[b]and I will offer it up as a burnt
offering."
32 So Jephthah advanced toward
the people of Ammon to fight
against them, and the LORD deliv-
ered them into his hands.
33 And he [1]defeated them from
Aroer as far as [a]Minnith—twenty
cities—and to [2]Abel Keramim,
with a very great slaughter. Thus
the people of Ammon were sub-
dued before the children of Israel.

Jephthah's Daughter

34 When Jephthah came to his
house at [a]Mizpah, there was [b]his
daughter, coming out to meet him
with timbrels and dancing; and
she *was his* only child. Besides her
he had neither son nor daughter.
35 And it came to pass, when he
saw her, that he [a]tore his clothes,
and said, "Alas, my daughter! You
have brought me very low! You
are among those who trouble me!
For I [b]have [1]given my word to the
LORD, and [c]I cannot [2]go back on
it."
36 So she said to him, "My father,
if you have given your word to the
LORD, [a]do to me according to what
has gone out of your mouth, be-
cause [b]the LORD has avenged you
of your enemies, the people of Am-
mon."
37 Then she said to her father,
"Let this thing be done for me: let
me alone for two months, that I
may go and wander on the moun-
tains and [1]bewail my virginity, my
[2]friends and I."
38 So he said, "Go." And he sent
her away *for* two months; and she
went with her friends, and be-
wailed her virginity on the moun-
tains.
39 And it was so at the end of two
months that she returned to her fa-
ther, and he [a]carried out his vow
with her which he had vowed. She
[1]knew no man. And it became a
custom in Israel
40 *that* the daughters of Israel
went four days each year to [1]la-
ment the daughter of Jephthah the
Gileadite.

Jephthah's Conflict with Ephraim

12 Then [a]the men of Ephraim
[1]gathered together, crossed
over toward Zaphon, and said to
Jephthah, "Why did you cross
over to fight against the people of
Ammon, and did not call us to go
with you? We will burn your house
down on you with fire!"
2 And Jephthah said to them,
"My people and I were in a great
struggle with the people of Am-
mon; and when I called you, you
did not deliver me out of their
hands.
3 "So when I saw that you would
not deliver *me,* I [a]took my life in
my hands and crossed over
against the people of Ammon; and
the LORD delivered them into my
hand. Why then have you come
up to me this day to fight against
me?"
4 Now Jephthah gathered to-
gether all the men of Gilead and
fought against Ephraim. And the
men of Gilead defeated Ephraim,
because they said, "You Gileadites
[a]*are* fugitives of Ephraim among
the Ephraimites *and* among the
Manassites."
5 The Gileadites seized the [a]fords
of the Jordan before the Ephra-
imites *arrived.* And when *any*
Ephraimite who escaped said,
"Let me cross over," the men of
Gilead would say to him, "*Are*
you an Ephraimite?" If he said,
"No,"
6 then they would say to him,
"Then say, [a]'Shibboleth'!"[1] And he
would say, "Sibboleth," for he
could not [2]pronounce *it* right.
Then they would take him and kill
him at the fords of the Jordan.
There fell at that time forty-two
thousand Ephraimites.
7 And Jephthah judged Israel six
years. Then Jephthah the Gileadite
died and was buried in among the
cities of Gilead.

Ibzan, Elon, and Abdon

8 After him, Ibzan of Bethlehem
judged Israel.
9 He had thirty sons. And he
gave away thirty daughters in
marriage, and brought in thirty
daughters from elsewhere for his
sons. He judged Israel seven years.

31 [a]Lev. 27:2, 3, 28; 1 Sam. 1:11 [b]Ps. 66:13
33 [a]Ezek. 27:17 [1]Lit. *struck* [2]Lit. *Plain of Vineyards*
34 [a]Judg. 10:17; 11:11 [b]Ex. 15:20; 1 Sam. 18:6; Ps. 68:25; Jer. 31:4
35 [a]Gen. 37:29, 34 [b]Eccl. 5:2, 4, 5 [c]Num. 30:2 [1]Lit. *opened my mouth* [2]Lit. *take it back*
36 [a]Num. 30:2 [b]2 Sam. 18:19, 31
37 [1]*lament* [2]*companions*
39 [a]Judg. 11:31 [1]Remained a virgin
40 [1]*commemorate*

CHAPTER 12

1 [a]Judg. 8:1 [1]*were summoned*
3 [a]1 Sam. 19:5; 28:21; Job 13:14
4 [a]1 Sam. 25:10
5 [a]Josh. 22:11
6 [a]Ps. 69:2, 15 [1]Lit. *a flowing stream;* used as a test of dialect [2]Lit. *speak so*

10 Then Ibzan died and was bur-
ied at Bethlehem.
11 After him, Elon the Zebulunite
judged Israel. He judged Israel ten
years.
12 And Elon the Zebulunite died
and was buried at Aijalon in the
country of Zebulun.
13 After him, Abdon the son of
Hillel the Pirathonite judged Is-
rael.
14 He had forty sons and thirty
grandsons, who [a]rode on seventy
young donkeys. He judged Israel
eight years.
15 Then Abdon the son of Hillel
the Pirathonite died and was bur-
ied in Pirathon in the land of
Ephraim, [a]in the mountains of the
Amalekites.

The Birth of Samson

13 Again the children of Israel
[a]did evil in the sight of the
LORD, and the LORD delivered them
[b]into the hand of the Philistines for
forty years.
2 Now there was a certain man
from [a]Zorah, of the family of the
Danites, whose name *was* Ma-
noah; and his wife *was* barren and
had no children.
3 And the [a]Angel of the LORD ap-
peared to the woman and said to
her, "Indeed now, you are barren
and have borne no children, but
you shall conceive and bear a son.
4 "Now therefore, please be
careful [a]not to drink wine or *simi-
lar* drink, and not to eat anything
unclean.
5 "For behold, you shall conceive
and bear a son. And no [a]razor
shall come upon his head, for the
child shall be [b]a Nazirite to God
from the womb; and he shall [c]be-
gin to deliver Israel out of the hand
of the Philistines."
6 So the woman came and told
her husband, saying, [a]"A Man of
God came to me, and His [b]counte-
nance[1] *was* like the countenance of
the Angel of God, very awesome;
but I [c]did not ask Him where He
was from, and He did not tell me
His name.
7 "And He said to me, 'Behold,
you shall conceive and bear a son.
Now drink no wine or *similar*
drink, nor eat anything unclean,
for the child shall be a Nazirite to
God from the womb to the day of
his death.' "
8 Then Manoah prayed to the
LORD, and said, "O my Lord,
please let the Man of God whom
You sent come to us again and
teach us what we shall do for the
child who will be born."
9 And God listened to the voice
of Manoah, and the Angel of God
came to the woman again as she
was sitting in the field; but Ma-
noah her husband *was* not with
her.
10 Then the woman ran in haste
and told her husband, and said to
him, "Look, the Man who came to
me the *other* day has just now ap-
peared to me!"
11 So Manoah arose and followed
his wife. When he came to the
Man, he said to Him, "Are You the
Man who spoke to this woman?"
And He said, "I *am.*"
12 Manoah said, "Now let Your
words come *to pass!* What will be
the boy's rule of life, and his
work?"
13 So the Angel of the LORD said
to Manoah, "Of all that I said to
the woman let her be careful.
14 "She may not eat anything that
comes from the vine, [a]nor may she
drink wine or *similar* drink, nor
eat anything unclean. All that I
commanded her let her observe."
15 Then Manoah said to the Angel
of the LORD, "Please [a]let us detain
You, and we will prepare a young
goat for You."
16 And the Angel of the LORD said
to Manoah, "Though you detain
Me, I will not eat your food. But
if you offer a burnt offering, you
must offer it to the LORD." (For Ma-
noah did not know He *was* the An-
gel of the LORD.)
17 Then Manoah said to the Angel
of the LORD, "What *is* Your name,
that when Your words come *to
pass* we may honor You?"
18 And the Angel of the LORD said
to him, [a]"Why do you ask My
name, seeing it *is* wonderful?"
19 So Manoah took the young
goat with the grain offering, [a]and
offered it upon the rock to the
LORD. And He did a wondrous
thing while Manoah and his wife
looked on—
20 it happened as the flame went

14 [a]Judg. 5:10; 10:4
15 [a]Judg. 3:13, 27; 5:14

CHAPTER 13

1 [a]Judg. 2:11 [b]Judg. 10:7; 1 Sam. 12:9
2 [a]Josh. 19:41; Judg. 16:31
3 [a]Judg. 6:12
4 [a]Num. 6:2, 3, 20; Judg. 13:4; Luke 1:15
5 [a]Num. 6:5; 1 Sam. 1:11 [b]Num. 6:2 [c]1 Sam. 7:13; 2 Sam. 8:1; 1 Chr. 18:1
6 [a]Gen. 32:24–30 [b]Matt. 28:3; Luke 9:29; Acts 6:15 [c]Judg. 13:17, 18 [1]*appearance*
14 [a]Num. 6:3, 4; Judg. 13:4
15 [a]Gen. 18:5; Judg. 6:18
18 [a]Gen. 32:29
19 [a]Judg. 6:19–21

up toward heaven from the altar—
the Angel of the LORD ascended in
the flame of the altar! When Ma-
noah and his wife saw *this,* they
[a]fell on their faces to the ground.
21 When the Angel of the LORD
appeared no more to Manoah and
his wife, [a]then Manoah knew that
He *was* the Angel of the LORD.
22 And Manoah said to his wife,
[a]"We shall surely die, because we
have seen God!"
23 But his wife said to him, "If the
LORD had desired to kill us, He
would not have accepted a burnt
offering and a grain offering from
our hands, nor would He have
shown us all these *things,* nor
would He have told us *such things*
as these at this time."
24 So the woman bore a son and
called his name [a]Samson; and [b]the
child grew, and the LORD blessed
him.
25 [a]And the Spirit of the LORD
began to move upon him at
[1]Mahaneh Dan [b]between Zorah
and [c]Eshtaol.

Samson's Philistine Wife

14 Now Samson went down [a]to
Timnah, and [b]saw a woman
in Timnah of the daughters of the
Philistines.
2 So he went up and told his fa-
ther and mother, saying, "I have
seen a woman in Timnah of the
daughters of the Philistines; now
therefore, [a]get her for me as a
wife."
3 Then his father and mother
said to him, "*Is there* no woman
among the daughters of [a]your
brethren, or among all my people,
that you must go and get a wife
from the [b]uncircumcised Philis-
tines?" And Samson said to his fa-
ther, "Get her for me, for [1]she
pleases me well."
4 But his father and mother did
not know that it was [a]of the
LORD—that He was seeking an oc-
casion to move against the Philis-
tines. For at that time [b]the Philis-
tines had dominion over Israel.
5 So Samson went down to Tim-
nah with his father and mother,
and came to the vineyards of Tim-
nah.
Now *to his* surprise, a young
lion *came* roaring against him.

20 [a]Lev. 9:24; 1 Chr. 21:16; Ezek. 1:28; Matt. 17:6
21 [a]Judg. 6:22
22 [a]Gen. 32:30; Ex. 33:20; Deut. 5:26; Judg. 6:22, 23
24 [a]Heb. 11:32 [b]1 Sam. 3:19; Luke 1:80
25 [a]Judg. 3:10; 1 Sam. 11:6; Matt. 4:1 [b]Josh. 15:33; Judg. 18:11 [c]Judg. 16:31 [1]Lit. *Camp of Dan,* Judg. 18:12

CHAPTER 14

1 [a]Gen. 38:13; Josh. 15:10, 57 [b]Gen. 34:2
2 [a]Gen. 21:21
3 [a]Gen. 24:3, 4 [b]Gen. 34:14; Ex. 34:16; Deut. 7:3 [1]Lit. *she is right in my eyes*
4 [a]Josh. 11:20; 1 Kin. 12:15; 2 Kin. 6:33; 2 Chr. 10:15 [b]Deut. 28:48; Judg. 13:1
6 [a]Judg. 3:10
9 [a]Lev. 11:27
12 [a]1 Kin. 10:1; Ezek. 17:2 [b]Gen. 29:27 [c]Gen. 45:22; 2 Kin. 5:22
13 [a]Ezek. 17:2
15 [a]Judg. 16:5 [b]Judg. 15:6 [1]So with MT, Tg., Vg.; LXX, Syr. *fourth*

6 And [a]the Spirit of the LORD
came mightily upon him, and he
tore the lion apart as one would
have torn apart a young goat,
though *he had* nothing in his hand.
But he did not tell his father or his
mother what he had done.
7 Then he went down and talked
with the woman; and she pleased
Samson well.
8 After some time, when he re-
turned to get her, he turned aside
to see the carcass of the lion. And
behold, a swarm of bees and
honey *were* in the carcass of the
lion.
9 He took some of it in his hands
and went along, eating. When he
came to his father and mother, he
gave *some* to them, and they also
ate. But he did not tell them that
he had taken the honey out of the
[a]carcass of the lion.
10 So his father went down to the
woman. And Samson gave a feast
there, for young men used to do
so.
11 And it happened, when they
saw him, that they brought thirty
companions to be with him.
12 Then Samson said to them,
"Let me [a]pose a riddle to you. If
you can correctly solve and ex-
plain it to me [b]within the seven
days of the feast, then I will give
you thirty linen garments and
thirty [c]changes of clothing.
13 "But if you cannot explain *it* to
me, then you shall give me thirty
linen garments and thirty changes
of clothing." And they said to him,
[a]"Pose your riddle, that we may
hear it."
14 So he said to them:

"Out of the eater came something
to eat,
And out of the strong came
something sweet."

Now for three days they could not
explain the riddle.
15 But it came to pass on the [1]sev-
enth day that they said to Sam-
son's wife, [a]"Entice your husband,
that he may explain the riddle to
us, [b]or else we will burn you and
your father's house with fire. Have
you invited us in order to take
what is ours? *Is that* not *so?*"
16 Then Samson's wife wept on

him, and said, [a]"You only hate me!
You do not love me! You have
posed a riddle to the sons of my
people, but you have not explained
it to me." And he said to her,
"Look, I have not explained *it* to
my father or my mother; so should
I explain *it* to you?"
17 Now she had wept on him the
seven days while their feast lasted.
And it happened on the seventh
day that he told her, because she
pressed him so much. Then she ex-
plained the riddle to the sons of
her people.
18 So the men of the city said to
him on the seventh day before the
sun went down:

"What *is* sweeter than honey?
And what *is* stronger than a
lion?"

And he said to them:

"If you had not plowed with my
heifer,
You would not have solved my
riddle!"

19 Then [a]the Spirit of the LORD
came upon him mightily, and he
went down to Ashkelon and killed
thirty of their men, took their ap-
parel, and gave the changes *of
clothing* to those who had ex-
plained the riddle. So his anger
was aroused, and he went back up
to his father's house.
20 And Samson's wife [a]was *given*
to his companion, who had been
[b]his best man.

Samson Defeats the Philistines

15 After a while, in the time of
wheat harvest, it happened
that Samson visited his wife with
a [a]young goat. And he said, "Let
me go in to my wife, into *her*
room." But her father would not
permit him to go in.
2 Her father said, "I really
thought that you thoroughly
[a]hated her; therefore I gave her to
your companion. *Is* not her youn-
ger sister better than she? Please,
take her instead."
3 And Samson said to them,
"This time I shall be blameless re-
garding the Philistines if I harm
them!"
4 Then Samson went and caught
three hundred foxes; and he took
torches, turned *the foxes* tail to
tail, and put a torch between each
pair of tails.
5 When he had set the torches on
fire, he let *the foxes* go into the
standing grain of the Philistines,
and burned up both the shocks and
the standing grain, as well as the
vineyards *and* olive groves.
6 Then the Philistines said, "Who
has done this?" And they an-
swered, "Samson, the son-in-law
of the Timnite, because he has
taken his wife and given her to his
companion." [a]So the Philistines
came up and burned her and her
father with fire.
7 Samson said to them, "Since
you would do a thing like this, I
will surely take revenge on you,
and after that I will cease."
8 So he attacked them hip and
thigh with a great slaughter; then
he went down and dwelt in the
cleft of the rock of [a]Etam.
9 Now the Philistines went up,
encamped in Judah, and deployed
themselves [a]against Lehi.
10 And the men of Judah said,
"Why have you come up against
us?" So they answered, "We have
come up to [1]arrest Samson, to do
to him as he has done to us."
11 Then three thousand men of
Judah went down to the cleft of
the rock of Etam, and said to Sam-
son, "Do you not know that the
Philistines [a]rule over us? What *is*
this you have done to us?" And he
said to them, "As they did to me,
so I have done to them."
12 But they said to him, "We have
come down to arrest you, that we
may deliver you into the hand of
the Philistines." Then Samson said
to them, "Swear to me that you
will not kill me yourselves."
13 So they spoke to him, saying,
"No, but we will tie you securely
and deliver you into their hand;
but we will surely not kill you."
And they bound him with two
[a]new ropes and brought him up
from the rock.
14 When he came to Lehi, the
Philistines came shouting against
him. Then [a]the Spirit of the LORD
came mightily upon him; and the
ropes that *were* on his arms be-
came like flax that is burned with

16 [a]Judg. 16:15
19 [a]Judg. 3:10; 13:25
20 [a]Judg. 15:2 [b]John 3:29

CHAPTER 15

1 [a]Gen. 38:17
2 [a]Judg. 14:20
6 [a]Judg. 14:15
8 [a]2 Chr. 11:6
9 [a]Judg. 15:19
10 [1]Lit. *bind*
11 [a]Lev. 26:25; Deut. 28:43; Judg. 13:1; 14:4; Ps. 106:40–42
13 [a]Judg. 16:11, 12
14 [a]Judg. 3:10; 14:6

fire, and his bonds [1]broke loose
from his hands.
15 He found a fresh jawbone of a
donkey, reached out his hand and
took it, and [a]killed a thousand men
with it.
16 Then Samson said:

"With the jawbone of a donkey,
Heaps upon heaps,
With the jawbone of a donkey
I have slain a thousand men!"

17 And so it was, when he had fin-
ished speaking, that he threw the
jawbone from his hand, and called
that place [1]Ramath Lehi.
18 Then he became very thirsty;
so he cried out to the LORD and
said, [a]"You have given this great
deliverance by the hand of Your
servant; and now shall I die of
thirst and fall into the hand of the
uncircumcised?"
19 So God split the hollow place
that *is* in [1]Lehi, and water came
out, and he drank; and [a]his spirit
returned, and he revived. There-
fore he called its name [2]En Hak-
kore, which is in Lehi to this day.
20 And [a]he judged Israel [b]twenty
years [c]in the days of the Phi-
listines.

Samson and Delilah

16 Now Samson went to [a]Gaza
and saw a harlot there, and
went in to her.
2 *When* the Gazites *were told*,
"Samson has come here!" they
[a]surrounded *the place* and lay in
wait for him all night at the gate
of the city. They were quiet all
night, saying, "In the morning,
when it is daylight, we will kill
him."
3 And Samson lay *low* till mid-
night; then he arose at midnight,
took hold of the doors of the gate
of the city and the two gateposts,
pulled them up, bar and all, put
them on his shoulders, and carried
them to the top of the hill that
faces Hebron.
4 Afterward it happened that he
loved a woman in the Valley of So-
rek, whose name *was* Delilah.
5 And the [a]lords of the Philis-
tines came up to her and said to
her, [b]"Entice him, and find out
where his great strength *lies*, and
by what *means* we may overpower
him, that we may bind him to af-
flict him; and every one of us will
give you eleven hundred *pieces* of
silver."
6 So Delilah said to Samson,
"Please tell me where your great
strength *lies*, and with what you
may be bound to afflict you."
7 And Samson said to her, "If
they bind me with seven fresh
bowstrings, not yet dried, then I
shall become weak, and be like
any *other* man."
8 So the lords of the Philistines
brought up to her seven fresh
bowstrings, not yet dried, and she
bound him with them.
9 Now *men were* lying in wait,
staying with her in the room. And
she said to him, "The Philistines
are upon you, Samson!" But he
broke the bowstrings as a strand
of yarn breaks when it touches
fire. So the secret of his strength
was not known.
10 Then Delilah said to Samson,
"Look, you have mocked me and
told me lies. Now, please tell me
what you may be bound with."
11 So he said to her, "If they bind
me securely with [a]new ropes [1]that
have never been used, then I shall
become weak, and be like any
other man."
12 Therefore Delilah took new
ropes and bound him with them,
and said to him, "The Philistines
are upon you, Samson!" And *men
were* lying in wait, staying in the
room. But he broke them off his
arms like a thread.
13 Delilah said to Samson, "Until
now you have mocked me and told
me lies. Tell me what you may be
bound with." And he said to her,
"If you weave the seven locks of
my head into the web of the
loom"—
14 So she wove *it* tightly with the
batten of the loom, and said to
him, "The Philistines *are* upon
you, Samson!" But he awoke from
his sleep, and pulled out the batten
and the web from the loom.
15 Then she said to him, [a]"How
can you say, 'I love you,' when
your heart *is* not with me? You
have mocked me these three times,
and have not told me where your
great strength *lies*."

14 [1]Lit. *were melted*
15 [a]Lev. 26:8; Josh. 23:10; Judg. 3:31
17 [1]Lit. *Jawbone Height*
18 [a]Ps. 3:7
19 [a]Gen. 45:27; Is. 40:29 [1]Lit. *Jawbone*, Judg. 15:14 [2]Lit. *Spring of the Caller*
20 [a]Judg. 10:2; 12:7–14 [b]Judg. 16:31 [c]Judg. 13:1

CHAPTER 16
1 [a]Josh. 15:47
2 [a]1 Sam. 23:26; Ps. 118:10–12
5 [a]Josh. 13:3 [b]Judg. 14:15
11 [a]Judg. 15:13 [1]Lit. *with which work has never been done*
15 [a]Judg. 14:16

16 And it came to pass, when she
pestered him daily with her words
and pressed him, *so* that his soul
was [1]vexed to death,
17 that he [a]told her all his heart,
and said to her, [b]"No razor has
ever come upon my head, for I
have been a Nazirite to God from
my mother's womb. If I am shaven,
then my strength will leave me,
and I shall become weak, and be
like any *other* man."
18 When Delilah saw that he had
told her all his heart, she sent and
called for the lords of the Philis-
tines, saying, "Come up once
more, for he has told me all his
heart." So the lords of the Philis-
tines came up to her and brought
the money in their hand.
19 [a]Then she lulled him to sleep
on her knees, and called for a man
and had him shave off the seven
locks of his head. Then [1]she began
to torment him, and his strength
left him.
20 And she said, "The Philistines
are upon you, Samson!" So he
awoke from his sleep, and said, "I
will go out as before, at other
times, and shake myself free!" But
he did not know that the LORD [a]had
departed from him.
21 Then the Philistines took him
and [1]put out his [a]eyes, and brought
him down to Gaza. They bound
him with bronze fetters, and he be-
came a grinder in the prison.
22 However, the hair of his head
began to grow again after it had
been shaven.

Samson Dies with the Philistines

23 Now the lords of the Philistines
gathered together to offer a great
sacrifice to [a]Dagon their god, and
to rejoice. And they said:

"Our god has delivered into our
hands
Samson our enemy!"

24 When the people saw him, they
[a]praised their god; for they said:

"Our god has delivered into our
hands our enemy,
The destroyer of our land,
And the one who multiplied our
dead."

16 [1]Lit. *impatient to the point of*
17 [a][Mic. 7:5] [b]Num. 6:5; Judg. 13:5
19 [a]Prov. 7:26, 27 [1]So with MT, Tg., Vg.; LXX *he began to be weak,*
20 [a]Num. 14:9, 42, 43; [Josh. 7:12]; 1 Sam. 16:14; 18:12; 28:15, 16; 2 Chr. 15:2
21 [a]2 Kin. 25:7 [1]Lit. *bored out*
23 [a]1 Sam. 5:2
24 [a]Dan. 5:4
25 [a]Judg. 9:27
27 [a]Deut. 22:8
28 [a]Jer. 15:15
31 [a]Judg. 13:25 [b]Judg. 15:20
CHAPTER 17
1 [a]Judg. 18:2
2 [a]Lev. 5:1 [b]Gen. 14:19

25 So it happened, when their
hearts were [a]merry, that they said,
"Call for Samson, that he may per-
form for us." So they called for
Samson from the prison, and he
performed for them. And they sta-
tioned him between the pillars.
26 Then Samson said to the lad
who held him by the hand, "Let
me feel the pillars which support
the temple, so that I can lean on
them."
27 Now the temple was full of men
and women. All the lords of the
Philistines *were* there—about
three thousand men and women
on the [a]roof watching while Sam-
son performed.
28 Then Samson called to the
LORD, saying, "O Lord GOD, [a]re-
member me, I pray! Strengthen me,
I pray, just this once, O God, that
I may with one *blow* take ven-
geance on the Philistines for my
two eyes!"
29 And Samson took hold of the
two middle pillars which sup-
ported the temple, and he braced
himself against them, one on his
right and the other on his left.
30 Then Samson said, "Let me die
with the Philistines!" And he
pushed with *all his* might, and the
temple fell on the lords and all the
people who *were* in it. So the dead
that he killed at his death were
more than he had killed in his life.
31 And his brothers and all his
father's household came down
and took him, and brought *him*
up and [a]buried him between Zorah
and Eshtaol in the tomb of his fa-
ther Manoah. He had judged Israel
[b]twenty years.

Micah's Idolatry

17 Now there was a man from
the mountains of Ephraim,
whose name *was* [a]Micah.
2 And he said to his mother,
"The eleven hundred *shekels* of
silver that were taken from you,
and on which you [a]put a curse,
even saying it in my ears—here *is*
the silver with me; I took it." And
his mother said, [b]"*May you be*
blessed by the LORD, my son!"
3 So when he had returned the
eleven hundred *shekels* of silver to
his mother, his mother said, "I had
wholly dedicated the silver from

my hand to the LORD for my son,
to [a]make a carved image and a
molded image; now therefore, I
will return it to you."
4 Thus he returned the silver to
his mother. Then his mother [a]took
two hundred *shekels* of silver and
gave them to the silversmith, and
he made it into a carved image
and a molded image; and they
were in the house of Micah.
5 The man Micah had a [a]shrine,
and made an [b]ephod and [c]house-
hold[1] idols; and he consecrated one
of his sons, who became his priest.
6 [a]In those days *there was* no
king in Israel; [b]everyone did *what*
was right in his own eyes.
7 Now there was a young man
from [a]Bethlehem in Judah, of the
family of Judah; he *was* a Levite,
and [b]was staying there.
8 The man departed from the city
of Bethlehem in Judah to stay
wherever he could find *a place*.
Then he came to the mountains of
Ephraim, to the house of Micah,
as he journeyed.
9 And Micah said to him, "Where
do you come from?" So he said to
him, "I *am* a Levite from Bethle-
hem in Judah, and I am on my way
to find *a place* to stay."
10 Micah said to him, "Dwell with
me, [a]and be a [b]father and a priest
to me, and I will give you ten *shek-*
els of silver per year, a suit of
clothes, and your sustenance." So
the Levite went in.
11 Then the Levite was content to
dwell with the man; and the young
man became like one of his sons
to him.
12 So Micah [a]consecrated[1] the
Levite, and the young man [b]be-
came his priest, and lived in the
house of Micah.
13 Then Micah said, "Now I know
that the LORD will be good to me,
since I have a Levite as [a]priest!"

The Danites Adopt Micah's Idolatry

18 In [a]those days *there was* no
king in Israel. And in those
days [b]the tribe of the Danites was
seeking an inheritance for itself to
dwell in; for until that day *their*
inheritance among the tribes of Is-
rael had not fallen to them.
2 So the children of Dan sent five
men of their family from their ter-
ritory, men of valor from [a]Zorah
and Eshtaol, [b]to spy out the land
and search it. They said to them,
"Go, search the land." So they
went to the mountains of Ephraim,
to the [c]house of Micah, and lodged
there.
3 While they *were* at the house
of Micah, they recognized the
voice of the young Levite. They
turned aside and said to him,
"Who brought you here? What are
you doing in this *place*? What do
you have here?"
4 He said to them, "Thus and so
Micah did for me. He has [a]hired
me, and I have become his priest."
5 So they said to him, "Please
[a]inquire [b]of God, that we may
know whether the journey on
which we go will be prosperous."
6 And the priest said to them,
[a]"Go in peace. [1]The presence of
the LORD *be* with you on your
way."
7 So the five men departed and
went to [a]Laish. They saw the peo-
ple who *were* there, [b]how they
dwelt safely, in the manner of the
Sidonians, quiet and secure. *There*
were no rulers in the land who
might put *them* to shame for any-
thing. They *were* far from the [c]Si-
donians, and they had no ties [1]with
anyone.
8 Then *the spies* came back to
their brethren at [a]Zorah and Esh-
taol, and their brethren said to
them, "What *is* your *report?*"
9 So they said, [a]"Arise, let us go
up against them. For we have seen
the land, and indeed it *is* very
good. *Would* you [b]*do* nothing? Do
not hesitate to go, *and* enter to pos-
sess the land.
10 "When you go, you will come
to a [a]secure people and a large
land. For God has given it into
your hands, [b]a place where *there*
is no lack of anything that *is* on
the earth."
11 And six hundred men of the
family of the Danites went from
there, from Zorah and Eshtaol,
armed with weapons of war.
12 Then they went up and en-
camped in [a]Kirjath Jearim in Ju-
dah. (Therefore they call that place
[b]Mahaneh Dan[1] to this day. There
it is, west of Kirjath Jearim.)
13 And they passed from there to

3 [a]Ex. 20:4, 23; 34:17; Lev. 19:4
4 [a]Is. 46:6
5 [a]Judg. 18:24 [b]Judg. 8:27; 18:14 [c]Gen. 31:19, 30; Hos. 3:4 [1]Heb. *teraphim*
6 [a]Judg. 18:1; 19:1 [b]Deut. 12:8; Judg. 21:25
7 [a]Josh. 19:15; Judg. 19:1; Ruth 1:1, 2; Mic. 5:2; Matt. 2:1, 5, 6 [b]Deut. 18:6
10 [a]Judg. 18:19 [b]Gen. 45:8; Job 29:16
12 [a]Judg. 17:5 [b]Judg. 18:30 [1]Lit. *filled the hand of*
13 [a]Judg. 18:4

CHAPTER 18

1 [a]Judg. 17:6; 19:1; 21:25 [b]Josh. 19:40–48
2 [a]Judg. 13:25 [b]Num. 13:17; Josh. 2:1 [c]Judg. 17:1
4 [a]Judg. 17:10, 12
5 [a]1 Kin. 22:5; [Is. 30:1]; Hos. 4:12 [b]Judg. 1:1; 17:5; 18:14
6 [a]1 Kin. 22:6 [1]Lit. *The LORD is before the way in which you go*
7 [a]Josh. 19:47 [b]Judg. 18:27–29 [c]Judg. 10:12 [1]So with MT, Tg., Vg.; LXX *with Syria*
8 [a]Judg. 18:2
9 [a]Num. 13:30; Josh. 2:23, 24 [b]1 Kin. 22:3
10 [a]Judg. 18:7, 27 [b]Deut. 8:9
12 [a]Josh. 15:60 [b]Judg. 13:25 [1]Lit. *Camp of Dan*

the mountains of Ephraim, and came to [a]the house of Micah.

14 [a]Then the five men who had gone to spy out the country of Laish answered and said to their brethren, "Do you know that [b]there are in these houses an ephod, household idols, a carved image, and a molded image? Now therefore, consider what you should do."

15 So they turned aside there, and came to the house of the young Levite man—to the house of Micah—and greeted him.

16 The [a]six hundred men armed with their weapons of war, who *were* of the children of Dan, stood by the entrance of the gate.

17 Then [a]the five men who had gone to spy out the land went up. Entering there, they took [b]the carved image, the ephod, the household idols, and the molded image. The priest stood at the entrance of the gate with the six hundred men *who were* armed with weapons of war.

18 When these went into Micah's house and took the carved image, the ephod, the household idols, and the molded image, the priest said to them, "What are you doing?"

19 And they said to him, "Be quiet, [a]put your hand over your mouth, and come with us; [b]be a father and a priest to us. *Is it* better for you to be a priest to the household of one man, or that you be a priest to a tribe and a family in Israel?"

20 So the priest's heart was glad; and he took the ephod, the household idols, and the carved image, and took his place among the people.

21 Then they turned and departed, and put the little ones, the livestock, and the goods in front of them.

22 When they were a good way from the house of Micah, the men who *were* in the houses near Micah's house gathered together and overtook the children of Dan.

23 And they called out to the children of Dan. So they turned around and said to Micah, [a]"What ails you, that you have gathered such a company?"

13 [a]Judg. 18:2
14 [a]1 Sam. 14:28 [b]Judg. 17:5
16 [a]Judg. 18:11
17 [a]Judg. 18:2, 14 [b]Judg. 17:4, 5
19 [a]Job 21:5; 29:9; 40:4; Mic. 7:16 [b]Judg. 17:10
23 [a]2 Kin. 6:28
24 [a]Gen. 31:30; Judg. 17:5 [1]*idols*
25 [1]Lit. *bitter of soul*
27 [a]Josh. 19:47
28 [a]Judg. 18:7 [b]Num. 13:21; 2 Sam. 10:6
29 [a]Josh. 19:47 [b]Judg. 20:1; 1 Kin. 12:29, 30; 15:20
30 [a]2 Kin. 15:29 [1]LXX, Vg. *Moses*
31 [a]Deut. 12:1–32; Josh. 18:1, 8; Judg. 19:18; 21:12

CHAPTER 19

1 [a]Judg. 17:6; 18:1; 21:25 [b]Judg. 17:7; Ruth 1:1

24 So he said, "You have [a]taken away my [1]gods which I made, and the priest, and you have gone away. Now what more do I have? How can you say to me, 'What ails you?' "

25 And the children of Dan said to him, "Do not let your voice be heard among us, lest [1]angry men fall upon you, and you lose your life, with the lives of your household!"

26 Then the children of Dan went their way. And when Micah saw that they *were* too strong for him, he turned and went back to his house.

Danites Settle in Laish

27 So they took *the things* Micah had made, and the priest who had belonged to him, and went to Laish, to a people quiet and secure; [a]and they struck them with the edge of the sword and burned the city with fire.

28 *There was* no deliverer, because it *was* [a]far from Sidon, and they had no ties with anyone. It was in the valley that belongs [b]to Beth Rehob. So they rebuilt the city and dwelt there.

29 And [a]they called the name of the city [b]Dan, after the name of Dan their father, who was born to Israel. However, the name of the city formerly *was* Laish.

30 Then the children of Dan set up for themselves the carved image; and Jonathan the son of Gershom, the son of [1]Manasseh, and his sons were priests to the tribe of Dan [a]until the day of the captivity of the land.

31 So they set up for themselves Micah's carved image which he made, [a]all the time that the house of God was in Shiloh.

The Levite's Concubine

19 And it came to pass in those days, [a]when *there was* no king in Israel, that there was a certain Levite staying in the remote mountains of Ephraim. He took for himself a concubine from [b]Bethlehem in Judah.

2 But his concubine played the harlot against him, and went away from him to her father's house at

Bethlehem in Judah, and was
there four whole months.
3 Then her husband arose and
went after her, to [a]speak [1]kindly
to her *and* bring her back, having
his servant and a couple of don-
keys with him. So she brought him
into her father's house; and when
the father of the young woman
saw him, he was glad to meet him.
4 Now his father-in-law, the
young woman's father, detained
him; and he stayed with him three
days. So they ate and drank and
lodged there.
5 Then it came to pass on the
fourth day that they arose early in
the morning, and he stood to de-
part; but the young woman's fa-
ther said to his son-in-law, [a]"Re-
fresh your heart with a morsel of
bread, and afterward go your
way."
6 So they sat down, and the two
of them ate and drank together.
Then the young woman's father
said to the man, "Please be content
to stay all night, and let your heart
be merry."
7 And when the man stood to de-
part, his father-in-law urged him;
so he lodged there again.
8 Then he arose early in the
morning on the fifth day to depart,
but the young woman's father
said, "Please refresh your heart."
So they delayed until afternoon;
and both of them ate.
9 And when the man stood to de-
part—he and his concubine and
his servant—his father-in-law, the
young woman's father, said to
him, "Look, the day is now draw-
ing toward evening; please spend
the night. See, the day is coming
to an end; lodge here, that your
heart may be merry. Tomorrow go
your way early, so that you may
get [1]home."
10 However, the man was not will-
ing to spend that night; so he rose
and departed, and came to oppo-
site [a]Jebus (that *is*, Jerusalem).
With him were the two saddled
donkeys; his concubine *was* also
with him.
11 They *were* near Jebus, and the
day was far spent; and the servant
said to his master, "Come, please,
and let us turn aside into this city
[a]of the Jebusites and lodge in it."
12 But his master said to him, "We
will not turn aside here into a city
of foreigners, who *are* not of the
children of Israel; we will go on
[a]to Gibeah."
13 So he said to his servant,
"Come, let us draw near to one of
these places, and spend the night
in Gibeah or in [a]Ramah."
14 And they passed by and went
their way; and the sun went down
on them near Gibeah, which be-
longs to Benjamin.
15 They turned aside there to go
in to lodge in Gibeah. And when
he went in, he sat down in the open
square of the city, for no one
would [a]take them into *his* house
to spend the night.
16 Just then an old man came in
from [a]his work in the field at eve-
ning, who also *was* from the
mountains of Ephraim; he was
staying in Gibeah, whereas the
men of the place *were* Benjamites.
17 And when he raised his eyes,
he saw the traveler in the open
square of the city; and the old man
said, "Where are you going, and
where do you come from?"
18 So he said to him, "We *are*
passing from Bethlehem in Judah
toward the remote mountains of
Ephraim; I *am* from there. I went
to Bethlehem in Judah; *now* I am
going to [a]the house of the LORD.
But there *is* no one who will take
me into his house,
19 "although we have both straw
and fodder for our donkeys, and
bread and wine for myself, for
your female servant, and for the
young man *who is* with your ser-
vant; *there is* no lack of anything."
20 And the old man said, [a]"Peace
be with you! However, *let* all your
needs *be* my responsibility; [b]only
do not spend the night in the open
square."
21 [a]So he brought him into his
house, and gave fodder to the don-
keys. [b]And they washed their feet,
and ate and drank.

Gibeah's Crime

22 As they were [a]enjoying them-
selves, suddenly [b]certain men of
the city, [c]perverted[1] men, sur-
rounded the house *and* beat on the
door. They spoke to the master of
the house, the old man, saying,

3 [a]Gen. 34:3; 50:21 [1]Lit. *to her heart*
5 [a]Gen. 18:5; Judg. 19:8; Ps. 104:15
9 [1]Lit. *to your tent*
10 [a]Josh. 18:28; 1 Chr. 11:4, 5
11 [a]Josh. 15:8, 63; Judg. 1:21; 2 Sam. 5:6
12 [a]Josh. 18:28
13 [a]Josh. 18:25
15 [a]Matt. 25:43
16 [a]Ps. 104:23
18 [a]Josh. 18:1; Judg. 18:31; 20:18; 1 Sam. 1:3, 7
20 [a]Gen. 43:23; Judg. 6:23; 1 Sam. 25:6 [b]Gen. 19:2
21 [a]Gen. 24:32; 43:24 [b]Gen. 18:4; John 13:5
22 [a]Judg. 16:25; 19:6, 9 [b]Gen. 19:4, 5; Judg. 20:5; Hos. 9:9; 10:9 [c]Deut. 13:13; 1 Sam. 2:12; 1 Kin. 21:10; [2 Cor. 6:15] [1]Lit. *sons of Belial*

[d]"Bring out the man who came to
your house, that we may know him
carnally!"
23 But [a]the man, the master of the
house, went out to them and said
to them, "No, my brethren! I beg
you, do not act *so* wickedly! See-
ing this man has come into my
house, [b]do not commit this out-
rage.
24 [a]"Look, *here is* my virgin
daughter and [1]*the man's* concu-
bine; let me bring them out now.
[b]Humble them, and do with them
as you please; but to this man do
not do such a vile thing!"
25 But the men would not heed
him. So the man took his concu-
bine and brought *her* out to them.
And they [a]knew her and abused
her all night until morning; and
when the day began to break, they
let her go.
26 Then the woman came as the
day was dawning, and fell down
at the door of the man's house
where her master *was*, till it was
light.
27 When her master arose in the
morning, and opened the doors of
the house and went out to go his
way, there was his concubine,
fallen *at* the door of the house with
her hands on the threshold.
28 And he said to her, "Get up and
let us be going." But [a]there was
no answer. So the man lifted her
onto the donkey; and the man got
up and went to his place.
29 When he entered his house he
took a knife, laid hold of his concu-
bine, and [a]divided her into twelve
pieces, [1]limb by limb, and sent her
throughout all the territory of Is-
rael.
30 And so it was that all who saw
it said, "No such deed has been
done or seen from the day that the
children of Israel came up from the
land of Egypt until this day. Con-
sider it, [a]confer, and speak up!"

Israel's War with the Benjamites

20 So [a]all the children of Israel
came out, from [b]Dan to
[c]Beersheba, as well as from the
land of Gilead, and the congrega-
tion gathered together as one man
before the LORD [d]at Mizpah.
2 And the leaders of all the peo-
ple, all the tribes of Israel, pre-
sented themselves in the assembly
of the people of God, four hundred
thousand foot soldiers [a]who drew
the sword.
3 (Now the children of Benjamin
heard that the children of Israel
had gone up to Mizpah.) Then the
children of Israel said, "Tell *us*,
how did this wicked deed hap-
pen?"
4 So the Levite, the husband of
the woman who was murdered,
answered and said, "My concu-
bine and [a]I went into Gibeah,
which belongs to Benjamin, to
spend the night.
5 [a]"And the men of Gibeah rose
against me, and surrounded the
house at night because of me. They
intended to kill me, [b]but instead
they ravished my concubine so
that she died.
6 "So [a]I took hold of my concu-
bine, cut her in pieces, and sent
her throughout all the territory of
the inheritance of Israel, because
they [b]committed lewdness and
outrage in Israel.
7 "Look! All of you *are* children
of Israel; [a]give your advice and
counsel here and now!"
8 So all the people arose as one
man, saying, "None *of us* will go
to his tent, nor will any turn back
to his house;
9 "but now this *is* the thing
which we will do to Gibeah: *We
will go up* [a]against it by lot.
10 "We will take ten men out of
every hundred throughout all the
tribes of Israel, a hundred out of
every thousand, and a thousand
out of *every* ten thousand, to make
provisions for the people, that
when they come to Gibeah in Ben-
jamin, they may repay all the vile-
ness that they have done in Israel."
11 So all the men of Israel were
gathered against the city, united
together as one man.
12 [a]Then the tribes of Israel sent
men through all the tribe of Benja-
min, saying, "What *is* this wicked-
ness that has occurred among
you?
13 "Now therefore, deliver up the
men, [a]the [1]perverted men who *are*
in Gibeah, that we may put them
to death and [b]remove the evil from
Israel!" But the children of Benja-
min would not listen to the voice

22 [d]Gen. 19:5; [Rom. 1:26, 27]
23 [a]Gen. 19:6, 7 [b]Gen. 34:7; Deut. 22:21; Judg. 20:6, 10; 2 Sam. 13:12
24 [a]Gen. 19:8 [b]Gen. 34:2; Deut. 21:14 [1]Lit. *his*
25 [a]Gen. 4:1
28 [a]Judg. 20:5
29 [a]Judg. 20:6; 1 Sam. 11:7 [1]Lit. *with her bones*
30 [a]Judg. 20:7; Prov. 13:10

CHAPTER 20

1 [a]Josh. 22:12; Judg. 20:11; 21:5 [b]Judg. 18:29; 1 Sam. 3:20; 2 Sam. 3:10; 24:2 [c]Josh. 19:2 [d]Judg. 10:17; 1 Sam. 7:5
2 [a]Judg. 8:10
4 [a]Judg. 19:15
5 [a]Judg. 19:22 [b]Judg. 19:25, 26
6 [a]Judg. 19:29 [b]Josh. 7:15
7 [a]Judg. 19:30
9 [a]Judg. 1:3
12 [a]Deut. 13:14; Josh. 22:13, 16
13 [a]Deut. 13:13; Judg. 19:22 [b]Deut. 17:12; 1 Cor. 5:13 [1]Lit. *sons of Belial*

of their brethren, the children of
Israel.
14 Instead, the children of Benja-
min gathered together from their
cities to Gibeah, to go to battle
against the children of Israel.
15 And from their cities at that
time [a]the children of Benjamin
numbered twenty-six thousand
men who drew the sword, besides
the inhabitants of Gibeah, who
numbered seven hundred select
men.
16 Among all this people *were*
seven hundred select men *who*
were [a]left-handed; every one could
sling a stone at a hair's *breadth*
and not miss.
17 Now besides Benjamin, the
men of Israel numbered four hun-
dred thousand men who drew the
sword; all of these *were* men of
war.
18 Then the children of Israel
arose and [a]went up to [1]the house
of God to [b]inquire of God. They
said, "Which of us shall go up first
to battle against the children of
Benjamin?" The LORD said, [c]"Ju-
dah first!"
19 So the children of Israel rose
in the morning and encamped
against Gibeah.
20 And the men of Israel went out
to battle against Benjamin, and the
men of Israel put themselves in
battle array to fight against them
at Gibeah.
21 Then [a]the children of Benjamin
came out of Gibeah, and on that
day cut down to the ground
twenty-two thousand men of the
Israelites.
22 And the people, that is, the men
of Israel, encouraged themselves
and again formed the battle line
at the place where they had put
themselves in array on the first
day.
23 [a]Then the children of Israel
went up and wept before the LORD
until evening, and asked counsel
of the LORD, saying, "Shall I again
draw near for battle against the
children of my brother Benjamin?"
And the LORD said, "Go up against
him."
24 So the children of Israel ap-
proached the children of Benjamin
on the second day.
25 And [a]Benjamin went out
against them from Gibeah on the
second day, and cut down to the
ground eighteen thousand more of
the children of Israel; all these
drew the sword.
26 Then all the children of Israel,
that is, all the people, [a]went up and
came to [1]the house of God and
wept. They sat there before the
LORD and fasted that day until eve-
ning; and they offered burnt offer-
ings and peace offerings before the
LORD.
27 So the children of Israel in-
quired of the LORD ([a]the ark of the
covenant of God *was* there in
those days,
28 [a]and Phinehas the son of Elea-
zar, the son of Aaron, [b]stood be-
fore it in those days), saying,
"Shall I yet again go out to battle
against the children of my brother
Benjamin, or shall I cease?" And
the LORD said, "Go up, for tomor-
row I will deliver them into your
hand."
29 Then Israel [a]set men in ambush
all around Gibeah.
30 And the children of Israel went
up against the children of Benja-
min on the third day, and put
themselves in battle array against
Gibeah as at the other times.
31 So the children of Benjamin
went out against the people, *and*
were drawn away from the city.
They began to strike down *and* kill
some of the people, as at the other
times, in the highways [a](one of
which goes up to Bethel and the
other to Gibeah) and in the field,
about thirty men of Israel.
32 And the children of Benjamin
said, "They *are* defeated before us,
as at first." But the children of Is-
rael said, "Let us flee and draw
them away from the city to the
highways."
33 So all the men of Israel rose
from their place and put them-
selves in battle array at Baal Ta-
mar. Then Israel's men in ambush
burst forth from their position in
the plain of Geba.
34 And ten thousand select men
from all Israel came against
Gibeah, and the battle was
fierce. [a]But [1]*the Benjamites* did
not know that disaster *was* upon
them.
35 The LORD [1]defeated Benjamin
before Israel. And the children of

15 [a]Num. 1:36, 37; 2:23; 26:41
16 [a]Judg. 3:15; 1 Chr. 12:2
18 [a]Judg. 20:23, 26 [b]Num. 27:21 [c]Judg. 1:1, 2 [1]Or *Bethel*
21 [a][Gen. 49:27]
23 [a]Judg. 20:26, 27
25 [a]Judg. 20:21
26 [a]Judg. 20:18, 23; 21:2 [1]Or *Bethel*
27 [a]Josh. 18:1; 1 Sam. 1:3; 3:3; 4:3, 4
28 [a]Num. 25:7, 13; Josh. 24:33 [b]Deut. 10:8; 18:5
29 [a]Josh. 8:4
31 [a]Judg. 21:19
34 [a]Josh. 8:14; Job 21:13; Is. 47:11 [1]Lit. *they*
35 [1]Lit. *struck*

Israel destroyed that day twenty-
five thousand one hundred Ben-
jamites; all these drew the sword.
36 So the children of Benjamin
saw that they were defeated. [a]The
men of Israel had given ground to
the Benjamites, because they re-
lied on the men in ambush whom
they had set against Gibeah.
37 [a]And the men in ambush
quickly rushed upon Gibeah; the
men in ambush spread out and
struck the whole city with the edge
of the sword.
38 Now the appointed signal be-
tween the men of Israel and the
men in ambush was that they
would make a great cloud of
[a]smoke rise up from the city,
39 whereupon the men of Israel
would turn in battle. Now Benja-
min had begun [1]to strike *and* kill
about thirty of the men of Israel.
For they said, "Surely they are de-
feated before us, as *in* the first bat-
tle."
40 But when the cloud began to
rise from the city in a column of
smoke, the Benjamites [a]looked be-
hind them, and there was the
whole city going up *in smoke* to
heaven.
41 And when the men of Israel
turned back, the men of Benjamin
panicked, for they saw that dis-
aster had come upon them.
42 Therefore they [1]turned *their
backs* before the men of Israel in
the direction of the wilderness; but
the battle overtook them, and
whoever *came* out of the cities
they destroyed in their midst.
43 They surrounded the Benjam-
ites, chased them, *and* easily tram-
pled them down as far as the front
of Gibeah toward the east.
44 And eighteen thousand men of
Benjamin fell; all these *were* men
of valor.
45 Then [1]they turned and fled to-
ward the wilderness to the rock of
[a]Rimmon; and they cut down five
thousand of them on the high-
ways. Then they pursued them re-
lentlessly up to Gidom, and killed
two thousand of them.
46 So all who fell of Benjamin that
day were twenty-five thousand
men who drew the sword; all these
were [1]men of valor.
47 [a]But six hundred men turned
and fled toward the wilderness to
the rock of Rimmon, and they
stayed at the rock of Rimmon for
four months.
48 And the men of Israel turned
back against the children of Benja-
min, and struck them down with
the edge of the sword—from *every*
city, men and beasts, all who were
found. They also set fire to all the
cities they came to.

Wives Provided for the Benjamites

21 Now [a]the men of Israel had
sworn an oath at Mizpah,
saying, "None of us shall give his
daughter to Benjamin as a wife."
2 Then the people came [a]to [1]the
house of God, and remained there
before God till evening. They lifted
up their voices and wept bitterly,
3 and said, "O LORD God of Is-
rael, why has this come to pass in
Israel, that today there should be
one tribe *missing* in Israel?"
4 So it was, on the next morning,
that the people rose early and
[a]built an altar there, and offered
burnt offerings and peace offer-
ings.
5 The children of Israel said,
"Who *is there* among all the tribes
of Israel who did not come up with
the assembly to the LORD?" [a]For
they had made a great oath con-
cerning anyone who had not come
up to the LORD at Mizpah, saying,
"He shall surely be put to death."
6 And the children of Israel
grieved for Benjamin their
brother, and said, "One tribe is cut
off from Israel today.
7 "What shall we do for wives for
those who remain, seeing we have
sworn by the LORD that we will not
give them our daughters as
wives?"
8 And they said, "What one *is
there* from the tribes of Israel who
did not come up to Mizpah to the
LORD?" And, in fact, no one had
come to the camp from [a]Jabesh
Gilead to the assembly.
9 For when the people were
counted, indeed, not one of the in-
habitants of Jabesh Gilead *was*
there.
10 So the congregation sent out
there twelve thousand of their
most valiant men, and com-
manded them, saying, [a]"Go and

36 [a]Josh. 8:15
37 [a]Josh. 8:19
38 [a]Josh. 8:20
39 [1]Lit. *to strike the slain ones*
40 [a]Josh. 8:20
42 [1]*fled*
45 [a]Josh. 15:32; 1 Chr. 6:77; Zech. 14:10 [1]LXX *the rest*
46 [1]*valiant warriors*
47 [a]Judg. 21:13

CHAPTER 21

1 [a]Judg. 20:1
2 [a]Judg. 20:18, 26 [1]Or *Bethel*
4 [a]Deut. 12:5; 2 Sam. 24:25
5 [a]Judg. 20:1–3
8 [a]1 Sam. 11:1; 31:11
10 [a]Num. 31:17; Judg. 5:23; 1 Sam. 11:7

strike the inhabitants of Jabesh
Gilead with the edge of the sword,
including the women and children.
11 "And this *is* the thing that you
shall do: [a]You shall utterly destroy
every male, and every woman who
has known a man intimately."
12 So they found among the in-
habitants of Jabesh Gilead four
hundred young virgins who had
not known a man intimately; and
they brought them to the camp at
[a]Shiloh, which is in the land of Ca-
naan.
13 Then the whole congregation
sent *word* to the children of Benja-
min [a]who *were* at the rock of Rim-
mon, and announced peace to
them.
14 So Benjamin came back at that
time, and they gave them the
women whom they had saved alive
of the women of Jabesh Gilead;
and yet they had not found enough
for them.
15 And the people [a]grieved for
Benjamin, because the LORD had
made a void in the tribes of Israel.
16 Then the elders of the congre-
gation said, "What shall we do for
wives for those who remain, since
the women of Benjamin have been
destroyed?"
17 And they said, "*There must be*
an inheritance for the survivors of
Benjamin, that a tribe may not be
destroyed from Israel.
18 "However, we cannot give
them wives from our daughters,
[a]for the children of Israel have
sworn an oath, saying, 'Cursed *be*
the one who gives a wife to Benja-
min.' "
19 Then they said, "In fact, *there
is* a yearly [a]feast of the LORD
in [b]Shiloh, which *is* north of
Bethel, on the east side of the
[c]highway that goes up from
Bethel to Shechem, and south of
Lebonah."
20 Therefore they instructed the
children of Benjamin, saying, "Go,
lie in wait in the vineyards,
21 "and watch; and just when
the daughters of Shiloh come
out [a]to perform their dances,
then come out from the vine-
yards, and every man catch a wife
for himself from the daughters of
Shiloh; then go to the land of Ben-
jamin.
22 "Then it shall be, when their fa-
thers or their brothers come to us
to complain, that we will say to
them, 'Be kind to them for our
sakes, because we did not take a
wife for any of them in the war;
for *it is* not *as though* you have
given the *women* to them at this
time, making yourselves guilty of
your oath.' "
23 And the children of Benjamin
did so; they took enough wives for
their number from those who
danced, whom they caught. Then
they went and returned to their in-
heritance, and they [a]rebuilt the cit-
ies and dwelt in them.
24 So the children of Israel de-
parted from there at that time,
every man to his tribe and family;
they went out from there, every
man to his inheritance.
25 [a]In those days *there was* no
king in Israel; [b]everyone did *what
was* right in his own eyes.

11 [a]Num. 31:17; Deut. 20:13, 14
12 [a]Josh. 18:1; Judg. 18:31
13 [a]Judg. 20:47
15 [a]Judg. 21:6
18 [a]Judg. 11:35; 21:1
19 [a]Lev. 23:2 [b]Deut. 12:5; Josh. 18:1; Judg. 18:31; 1 Sam. 1:3 [c]Judg. 20:31
21 [a]Ex. 15:20; Judg. 11:34; 1 Sam. 18:6
23 [a]Judg. 20:48
25 [a]Judg. 17:6; 18:1; 19:1 [b]Deut. 12:8; Judg. 17:6

The Book of

Ruth

RUTH is a cameo story of love, devotion, and redemption set in the black context of the days of the judges. It is the story of a Moabite woman who forsakes her pagan heritage in order to cling to the people of Israel and to the God of Israel. Because of her *faithfulness* in a time of national *faithlessness,* God rewards her by giving her a new husband (Boaz), a son (Obed), and a privileged position in the lineage of David and Christ (she is the great-grandmother of David).

Ruth is the Hebrew title of this book. This name may be a Moabite modification of the Hebrew word *reuit,* meaning "friendship" or "association." The Septuagint entitles the book *Routh,* the Greek equivalent of the Hebrew name. The Latin title is *Ruth,* a transliteration of *Routh*.

Elimelech's Family Goes to Moab

NOW it came to pass, in the
days when [a]the judges [1]ruled,
that there was [b]a famine in
the land. And a certain man of
[c]Bethlehem, Judah, went to [2]dwell
in the country of [d]Moab, he and
his wife and his two sons.
2 The name of the man *was*
Elimelech, the name of his wife
was Naomi, and the names of his
two sons *were* Mahlon and Chil-
ion—[a]Ephrathites of Bethlehem,
Judah. And they went [b]to the
country of Moab and remained
there.
3 Then Elimelech, Naomi's hus-
band, died; and she was left, and
her two sons.
4 Now they took wives of the
women of Moab: the name of the
one *was* Orpah, and the name of
the other Ruth. And they [1]dwelt
there about ten years.
5 Then both Mahlon and Chilion
also died; so the woman survived
her two sons and her husband.

Naomi Returns with Ruth

6 Then she arose with her daugh-
ters-in-law that she might return
from the country of Moab, for she
had heard in the country of Moab
that the LORD had [a]visited[1] His
people by [b]giving them bread.
7 Therefore she went out from
the place where she was, and her
two daughters-in-law with her;
and they went on the way to return
to the land of Judah.

CHAPTER 1

1 [a]Judg. 2:16–18 [b]Gen. 12:10; 26:1; 2 Kin. 8:1 [c]Judg. 17:8; Mic. 5:2 [d]Gen. 19:37 [1]Lit. *judged* [2]As a resident alien

2 [a]Gen. 35:19; 1 Sam. 1:1; 1 Kin. 11:26 [b]Judg. 3:30

4 [1]*lived*

6 [a]Ex. 3:16; 4:31; Jer. 29:10; Zeph. 2:7; Luke 1:68 [b]Ps. 132:15; Matt. 6:11 [1]*attended to*

8 [a]Josh. 24:15 [b]2 Tim. 1:16–18 [c]Ruth 2:20

9 [a]Ruth 3:1

11 [a]Gen. 38:11; Deut. 25:5

13 [a]Judg. 2:15; Job 19:21; Ps. 32:4; 38:2

14 [a][Prov. 17:17]

15 [a]Judg. 11:24 [b]Josh. 1:15

8 And Naomi said to her two
daughters-in-law, [a]"Go, return
each to her mother's house. [b]The
LORD deal kindly with you, as you
have dealt [c]with the dead and with
me.
9 "The LORD grant that you may
find [a]rest, each in the house of her
husband." So she kissed them, and
they lifted up their voices and
wept.
10 And they said to her, "Surely
we will return with you to your
people."
11 But Naomi said, "Turn back,
my daughters; why will you go
with me? *Are* there still sons in my
womb, [a]that they may be your hus-
bands?
12 "Turn back, my daughters,
go—for I am too old to have a hus-
band. If I should say I have hope,
if I should have a husband tonight
and should also bear sons,
13 "would you wait for them
till they were grown? Would
you restrain yourselves from
having husbands? No, my daugh-
ters; for it grieves me very much
for your sakes that [a]the hand of
the LORD has gone out against
me!"
14 Then they lifted up their voices
and wept again; and Orpah kissed
her mother-in-law, but Ruth [a]clung
to her.
15 And she said, "Look, your
sister-in-law has gone back to [a]her
people and to her gods; [b]return af-
ter your sister-in-law."

16 But Ruth said:

[a]"Entreat[1] me not to leave you,
Or *to* turn back from following
after you;
For wherever you go, I will go;
And wherever you lodge, I will
lodge;
[b]Your people *shall be* my people,
And your God, my God.
17 Where you die, I will die,
And there will I be buried.
[a]The LORD do so to me, and more
also,
If *anything but* death parts you
and me."

18 [a]When she saw that she [1]was
determined to go with her, she
stopped speaking to her.
19 Now the two of them went until
they came to Bethlehem. And it
happened, when they had come to
Bethlehem, that [a]all the city was
excited because of them; and the
women said, [b]"*Is* this Naomi?"
20 But she said to them, "Do not
call me [1]Naomi; call me [2]Mara, for
the Almighty has dealt very bit-
terly with me.
21 "I went out full, [a]and the LORD
has brought me home again
empty. Why do you call me Naomi,
since the LORD has testified against
me, and [1]the Almighty has af-
flicted me?"
22 So Naomi returned, and Ruth
the Moabitess her daughter-in-law
with her, who returned from the
country of Moab. Now they came
to Bethlehem [a]at the beginning of
barley harvest.

Ruth Meets Boaz

2 There was a [a]relative of
Naomi's husband, a man of
great wealth, of the family of
[b]Elimelech. His name *was* [c]Boaz.
2 So Ruth the Moabitess said to
Naomi, "Please let me go to the
[a]field, and glean heads of grain af-
ter *him* in whose sight I may find
favor." And she said to her, "Go,
my daughter."
3 Then she left, and went and
gleaned in the field after the reap-
ers. And she happened to come to
the part of the field *belonging* to
Boaz, who *was* of the family of
Elimelech.
4 Now behold, Boaz came from
[a]Bethlehem, and said to the reap-

16 [a]2 Kin. 2:2, 4, 6 [b]Ruth 2:11, 12 [1]*Urge me not*

17 [a]1 Sam. 3:17; 2 Sam. 19:13; 2 Kin. 6:31

18 [a]Acts 21:14 [1]Lit. *made herself strong to go*

19 [a]Matt. 21:10 [b]Is. 23:7; Lam. 2:15

20 [1]Lit. *Pleasant* [2]Lit. *Bitter*

21 [a]Job 1:21 [1]Heb. *Shaddai*

22 [a]Ruth 2:23; 2 Sam. 21:9

CHAPTER 2

1 [a]Ruth 3:2, 12 [b]Ruth 1:2 [c]Ruth 4:21

2 [a]Lev. 19:9, 10; 23:22; Deut. 24:19

4 [a]Ruth 1:1 [b]Ps. 129:7, 8; Luke 1:28; 2 Thess. 3:16

6 [a]Ruth 1:22

10 [a]1 Sam. 25:23 [b]1 Sam. 1:18

11 [a]Ruth 1:14–18

12 [a]1 Sam. 24:19; Ps. 58:11 [b]Ruth 1:16; Ps. 17:8; 36:7; 57:1; 61:4; 63:7; 91:4

13 [a]Gen. 33:15; 1 Sam. 1:18 [b]1 Sam. 25:41 [1]Lit. *to the heart of*

ers, [b]"The LORD *be* with you!" And
they answered him, "The LORD
bless you!"
5 Then Boaz said to his servant
who was in charge of the reapers,
"Whose young woman *is* this?"
6 So the servant who was in
charge of the reapers answered
and said, "It *is* the young Moab-
ite woman [a]who came back
with Naomi from the country of
Moab.
7 "And she said, 'Please let me
glean and gather after the reapers
among the sheaves.' So she came
and has continued from morning
until now, though she rested a lit-
tle in the house."
8 Then Boaz said to Ruth, "You
will listen, my daughter, will you
not? Do not go to glean in another
field, nor go from here, but stay
close by my young women.
9 "*Let* your eyes *be* on the field
which they reap, and go after
them. Have I not commanded the
young men not to touch you? And
when you are thirsty, go to the ves-
sels and drink from what the
young men have drawn."
10 So she [a]fell on her face, bowed
down to the ground, and said to
him, "Why have I found [b]favor in
your eyes, that you should take no-
tice of me, since I *am* a foreigner?"
11 And Boaz answered and said
to her, "It has been fully reported
to me, [a]all that you have done for
your mother-in-law since the
death of your husband, and *how*
you have left your father and your
mother and the land of your birth,
and have come to a people whom
you did not know before.
12 [a]"The LORD repay your work,
and a full reward be given you by
the LORD God of Israel, [b]under
whose wings you have come for
refuge."
13 Then she said, [a]"Let me find fa-
vor in your sight, my lord; for you
have comforted me, and have spo-
ken [1]kindly to your maidservant,
[b]though I am not like one of your
maidservants."
14 Now Boaz said to her at meal-
time, "Come here, and eat of the
bread, and dip your piece of bread
in the vinegar." So she sat beside
the reapers, and he passed
parched *grain* to her; and she ate

and [a]was satisfied, and kept some
back.
15 And when she rose up to
[1]glean, Boaz commanded his
young men, saying, "Let her glean
even among the sheaves, and do
not [2]reproach her.
16 "Also let *grain* from the bun-
dles fall purposely for her; leave
it that she may glean, and do not
rebuke her."
17 So she gleaned in the field until
evening, and beat out what she
had gleaned, and it was about an
ephah of [a]barley.
18 Then she took *it* up and went
into the city, and her mother-in-
law saw what she had gleaned. So
she brought out and gave to her
[a]what she had kept back after she
had been satisfied.
19 And her mother-in-law said to
her, "Where have you gleaned to-
day? And where did you work?
Blessed be the one who [a]took no-
tice of you." So she told her
mother-in-law with whom she had
worked, and said, "The man's
name with whom I worked today
is Boaz."
20 Then Naomi said to her daugh-
ter-in-law, [a]"Blessed *be* he of the
LORD, who [b]has not forsaken His
kindness to the living and the
dead!" And Naomi said to her,
"This man *is* a relation of ours,
[c]one of [1]our close relatives."
21 Ruth the Moabitess said, "He
also said to me, 'You shall stay
close by my young men until they
have finished all my harvest.' "
22 And Naomi said to Ruth her
daughter-in-law, "*It is* good, my
daughter, that you go out with
his young women, and that peo-
ple do not [1]meet you in any other
field."
23 So she stayed close by the
young women of Boaz, to glean
until the end of barley harvest and
wheat harvest; and she dwelt with
her mother-in-law.

Ruth's Redemption Assured

3 Then Naomi her mother-in-law
said to her, "My daughter,
[a]shall I not seek [b]security[1] for you,
that it may be well with you?
2 "Now Boaz, [a]whose young
women you were with, *is he* not
our relative? In fact, he is winnow-

14 [a]Ruth 2:18

15 [1]Gather after the reapers [2]*rebuke*

17 [a]Ruth 1:22

18 [a]Ruth 2:14

19 [a]Ruth 2:10; [Ps. 41:1]

20 [a]Ruth 3:10; 2 Sam. 2:5 [b]Prov. 17:17 [c]Ruth 3:9; 4:4, 6 [1]*our redeemers,* Heb. *goalenu*

22 [1]*encounter*

CHAPTER 3

1 [a]1 Cor. 7:36; 1 Tim. 5:8 [b]Ruth 1:9 [1]Lit. *rest*

2 [a]Ruth 2:3, 8

3 [a]2 Sam. 14:2

7 [a]Judg. 19:6, 9, 22; 2 Sam. 13:28; Esth. 1:10

9 [a]Ezek. 16:8 [b]Ruth 2:20; 3:12 [1]Or *Spread the corner of your garment over your maidservant* [2]*redeemer,* Heb. *goel*

10 [a]Ruth 2:20 [b]Ruth 1:8

11 [a]Prov. 12:4; 31:10–31

12 [a]Ruth 3:9 [b]Ruth 4:1

13 [a]Deut. 25:5–10; Ruth 4:5, 10; Matt. 22:24 [b]Judg. 8:19; Jer. 4:2; 12:16

ing barley tonight at the threshing
floor.
3 "Therefore wash yourself and
[a]anoint yourself, put on your *best*
garment and go down to the
threshing floor; *but* do not make
yourself known to the man until
he has finished eating and drink-
ing.
4 "Then it shall be, when he lies
down, that you shall notice the
place where he lies; and you shall
go in, uncover his feet, and lie
down; and he will tell you what
you should do."
5 And she said to her, "All that
you say to me I will do."
6 So she went down to the
threshing floor and did according
to all that her mother-in-law in-
structed her.
7 And after Boaz had eaten and
drunk, and [a]his heart was cheerful,
he went to lie down at the end of
the heap of grain; and she came
softly, uncovered his feet, and lay
down.
8 Now it happened at midnight
that the man was startled, and
turned himself; and there, a
woman was lying at his feet.
9 And he said, "Who *are* you?"
So she answered, "I *am* Ruth, your
maidservant. [a]Take[1] your maid-
servant under your wing, for you
are [b]a [2]close relative."
10 Then he said, [a]"Blessed *are* you
of the LORD, my daughter! For you
have shown more kindness at the
end than [b]at the beginning, in that
you did not go after young men,
whether poor or rich.
11 "And now, my daughter, do not
fear. I will do for you all that you
request, for all the people of my
town know that you *are* [a]a virtu-
ous woman.
12 "Now it is true that I *am* a
[a]close relative; however, [b]there is
a relative closer than I.
13 "Stay this night, and in the
morning it shall be *that* if he will
[a]perform the duty of a close rela-
tive for you—good; let him do it.
But if he does not want to perform
the duty for you, then I will per-
form the duty for you, [b]*as* the LORD
lives! Lie down until morning."
14 So she lay at his feet until
morning, and she arose before one
could recognize another. Then he

The First Book of

Samuel

THE Book of First Samuel describes the transition of leadership in Israel from judges to kings. Three characters are prominent in the book: Samuel, the last judge and first prophet; Saul, the first king of Israel; and David, the king-elect, anointed but not yet recognized as Saul's successor.

The books of First and Second Samuel were originally one book in the Hebrew Bible, known as the "Book of Samuel" or simply "Samuel." This name has been variously translated "The Name of God," "His Name Is God," "Heard of God," and "Asked of God." The Septuagint divides Samuel into two books even though it is one continuous account. This division artificially breaks up the history of David. The Greek (Septuagint) title is *Bibloi Basileion,* "Books of Kingdoms," referring to the later kingdoms of Israel and Judah. First Samuel is called *Basileion Alpha,* "First Kingdoms." Second Samuel and First and Second Kings are called "Second, Third, and Fourth Kingdoms." The Latin Vulgate originally called the books of Samuel and Kings *Libri Regum,* "Books of the Kings." Later the Latin Bible combined the Hebrew and Greek titles for the first of these books, calling it *Liber I Samuelis,* the "First Book of Samuel," or simply "First Samuel."

The Family of Elkanah

NOW there was a certain man of Ramathaim Zophim, of the [a]mountains of Ephraim, and his name *was* [b]Elkanah the son of Jeroham, the son of [1]Elihu, the son of [2]Tohu, the son of Zuph, [c]an Ephraimite.

2 And he had [a]two wives: the name of one *was* Hannah, and the name of the other Peninnah. Peninnah had children, but Hannah had no children.

3 This man went up from his city [a]yearly [b]to worship and sacrifice to the LORD of hosts in [c]Shiloh. Also the two sons of Eli, Hophni and Phinehas, the priests of the LORD, *were* there.

4 And whenever the time came for Elkanah to make an [a]offering, he would give portions to Peninnah his wife and to all her sons and daughters.

5 But to Hannah he would give a double portion, for he loved Hannah, [a]although the LORD had closed her womb.

6 And her rival also [a]provoked her severely, to make her miserable, because the LORD had closed her womb.

CHAPTER 1

1 [a]Josh. 17:17, 18; 24:33 [b]1 Chr. 6:27, 33–38 [c]Ruth 1:2 [1]*Eliel,* 1 Chr. 6:34 [2]*Toah,* 1 Chr. 6:34
2 [a]Deut. 21:15–17
3 [a]Ex. 34:14, 23; Judg. 21:19; 1 Sam. 1:21; Luke 2:41 [b]Deut. 12:5–7; 16:16 [c]Josh. 18:1
4 [a]Deut. 12:17, 18
5 [a]Gen. 16:1; 30:1, 2
6 [a]Job 24:21
8 [a]Ruth 4:15
9 [a]1 Sam. 3:3 [1]*palace* or *temple,* Heb. *heykal*
10 [a]Job 7:11 [1]Lit. *wept greatly*
11 [a]Gen. 28:20; Num. 30:6–11 [b]Ps. 25:18 [c]Gen. 8:1 [d]Num. 6:5; Judg. 13:5

7 So it was, year by year, when she went up to the house of the LORD, that she provoked her; therefore she wept and did not eat.

Hannah's Vow

8 Then Elkanah her husband said to her, "Hannah, why do you weep? Why do you not eat? And why is your heart grieved? *Am* I not [a]better to you than ten sons?"

9 So Hannah arose after they had finished eating and drinking in Shiloh. Now Eli the priest was sitting on the seat by the doorpost of [a]the [1]tabernacle of the LORD.

10 [a]And she *was* in bitterness of soul, and prayed to the LORD and [1]wept in anguish.

11 Then she [a]made a vow and said, "O LORD of hosts, if You will indeed [b]look on the affliction of Your maidservant and [c]remember me, and not forget Your maidservant, but will give Your maidservant a male child, then I will give him to the LORD all the days of his life, and [d]no razor shall come upon his head."

12 And it happened, as she continued praying before the LORD, that Eli watched her mouth.

13 Now Hannah spoke in her
heart; only her lips moved, but her
voice was not heard. Therefore Eli
thought she was drunk.
14 So Eli said to her, "How long
will you be drunk? Put your wine
away from you!"
15 But Hannah answered and
said, "No, my lord, I *am* a woman
of sorrowful spirit. I have drunk
neither wine nor intoxicating
drink, but have [a]poured out my
soul before the LORD.
16 "Do not consider your maid-
servant a [a]wicked[1] woman, for out
of the abundance of my complaint
and grief I have spoken until
now."
17 Then Eli answered and said,
[a]"Go in peace, and [b]the God of Is-
rael grant your petition which you
have asked of Him."
18 And she said, [a]"Let your
maidservant find favor in your
sight." So the woman [b]went her
way and ate, and her face was no
longer *sad*.

Samuel Is Born and Dedicated

19 Then they rose early in the
morning and worshiped before the
LORD, and returned and came to
their house at Ramah. And Elka-
nah [a]knew Hannah his wife, and
the LORD [b]remembered her.
20 So it came to pass in the pro-
cess of time that Hannah con-
ceived and bore a son, and called
his name [1]Samuel, *saying*, "Be-
cause I have asked for him from
the LORD."
21 Now the man Elkanah and all
his house [a]went up to offer to the
LORD the yearly sacrifice and his
vow.
22 But Hannah did not go up, for
she said to her husband, "*Not* until
the child is weaned; then I will
[a]take him, that he may appear be-
fore the LORD and [b]remain there
[c]forever."
23 So [a]Elkanah her husband said
to her, "Do what seems best to
you; wait until you have weaned
him. Only let the LORD [1]establish
[2]His word." Then the woman
stayed and nursed her son until
she had weaned him.
24 Now when she had weaned
him, she [a]took him up with her,
with [1]three bulls, one ephah of
flour, and a skin of wine, and
brought him to [b]the house of the
LORD in Shiloh. And the child *was*
young.
25 Then they slaughtered a bull,
and [a]brought the child to Eli.
26 And she said, "O my lord! [a]As
your soul lives, my lord, I *am* the
woman who stood by you here,
praying to the LORD.
27 [a]"For this child I prayed, and
the LORD has granted me my peti-
tion which I asked of Him.
28 "Therefore I also have lent him
to the LORD; as long as he lives he
shall be [1]lent to the LORD." So they
[a]worshiped the LORD there.

Hannah's Prayer

2 And Hannah [a]prayed and said:

[b]"My heart rejoices in the LORD;
[c]My [1]horn is exalted in the LORD.
[2]I smile at my enemies,
Because I [d]rejoice in Your
salvation.

2 "No[a] one is holy like the LORD,
For *there is* [b]none besides You,
Nor *is there* any [c]rock like our
God.

3 "Talk no more so very proudly;
[a]Let no arrogance come from your
mouth,
For the LORD *is* the God of
[b]knowledge;
And by Him actions are weighed.

4 "The[a] bows of the mighty men *are*
broken,
And those who stumbled are
girded with strength.
5 *Those who were* full have hired
themselves out for bread,
And the hungry have ceased *to
hunger*.
Even [a]the barren has borne
seven,
And [b]she who has many children
has become feeble.

6 "The[a] LORD kills and makes alive;
He brings down to the grave and
brings up.
7 The LORD [a]makes poor and
makes rich;
[b]He brings low and lifts up.
8 [a]He raises the poor from the dust
And lifts the beggar from the ash
heap,
[b]To set *them* among princes
And make them inherit the
throne of glory.

15 [a]Ps. 42:4; 62:8
16 [a]Deut. 13:13 [1]Lit. *daughter of Belial*
17 [a]Mark 5:34 [b]Ps. 20:3–5
18 [a]Ruth 2:13 [b]Rom. 15:13
19 [a]Gen. 4:1 [b]Gen. 21:1; 30:22
20 [1]Lit. *Heard by God*
21 [a]1 Sam. 1:3
22 [a]Luke 2:22 [b]1 Sam. 1:11, 28 [c]Ex. 21:6
23 [a]Num. 30:7, 10, 11 [1]*confirm* [2]So with MT, Tg., Vg.; DSS, LXX, Syr. *your*
24 [a]Num. 15:9, 10 [b]Josh. 18:1 [1]DSS, LXX, Syr. *a three-year-old bull*
25 [a]Luke 2:22
26 [a]2 Kin. 2:2, 4, 6; 4:30
27 [a][Matt. 7:7]
28 [a]Gen. 24:26, 52 [1]*granted*

CHAPTER 2

1 [a]Phil. 4:6 [b]Luke 1:46–55 [c]Ps. 75:10; 89:17, 24; 92:10; 112:9 [d]Ps. 9:14; 13:5; 35:9 [1]Strength [2]Lit. *My mouth is enlarged*
2 [a]Ex. 15:11 [b]Deut. 4:35 [c]Deut. 32:4, 30, 31
3 [a]Ps. 94:4 [b]1 Sam. 16:7
4 [a]Ps. 37:15; 46:9
5 [a]Ps. 113:9 [b]Is. 54:1
6 [a]Deut. 32:39
7 [a]Deut. 8:17, 18 [b]Ps. 75:7
8 [a]Luke 1:52 [b]Job 36:7

[c]"For the pillars of the earth *are* the LORD's,
And He has set the world upon them.
9 [a]He will guard the feet of His saints,
But the [b]wicked shall be silent in darkness.

"For by strength no man shall prevail.
10 The adversaries of the LORD shall be [a]broken in pieces;
[b]From heaven He will thunder against them.
[c]The LORD will judge the ends of the earth.

[d]"He will give [e]strength to His king,
And [f]exalt the [1]horn of His anointed."

11 Then Elkanah went to his
house at Ramah. But the child
[1]ministered to the LORD before Eli
the priest.

The Wicked Sons of Eli

12 Now the sons of Eli *were* [a]cor-
rupt;[1] [b]they did not know the LORD.
13 And the priests' custom with
the people *was that* when any man
offered a sacrifice, the priest's ser-
vant would come with a three-
pronged fleshhook in his hand
while the meat was boiling.
14 Then he would thrust *it* into the
pan, or kettle, or caldron, or pot;
and the priest would take for
himself all that the fleshhook
brought up. So they did in [a]Shiloh
to all the Israelites who came
there.
15 Also, before they [a]burned the
fat, the priest's servant would
come and say to the man who sac-
rificed, "Give meat for roasting
to the priest, for he will not
take boiled meat from you, but
raw."
16 And *if* the man said to him,
"They should really burn the fat
first; *then* you may take *as much*
as your heart desires," he would
then answer him, "*No,* but you
must give *it* now; and if not, I will
take *it* by force."
17 Therefore the sin of the young
men was very great [a]before the
LORD, for men [b]abhorred[1] the of-
fering of the LORD.

8 [c]Job 38:4–6; Ps. 75:3; 104:5
9 [a]Ps. 37:23, 24; 91:11, 12; 94:18; 121:3; Prov. 3:26; [1 Pet. 1:5] [b][Rom. 3:19]
10 [a]Ex. 15:6; Ps. 2:9 [b]1 Sam. 7:10; 2 Sam. 22:14, 15; Ps. 18:13, 14 [c]Ps. 96:13; 98:9; [Matt. 25:31, 32] [d][Matt. 28:18] [e]Ps. 21:1, 7 [f]Ps. 89:24 [1]Strength
11 [1]*served*
12 [a]Deut. 13:13 [b]Judg. 2:10; [Rom. 1:28] [1]Lit. *sons of Belial*
14 [a]1 Sam. 1:3
15 [a]Lev. 3:3–5, 16
17 [a]Gen. 6:11 [b][Mal. 2:7–9] [1]*despised*
18 [a]1 Sam. 2:11; 3:1 [b]Ex. 28:4
19 [a]1 Sam. 1:3, 21
20 [a]Gen. 14:19 [b]1 Sam. 1:11, 27, 28 [1]*gift*
21 [a]Gen. 21:1 [b]Judg. 13:24; 1 Sam. 2:26; 3:19–21; Luke 1:80; 2:40 [1]*attended to*
22 [a]Ex. 38:8 [1]So with MT, Tg., Vg.; DSS, LXX omit rest of verse
25 [a]Deut. 1:17; 25:1, 2 [b]Num. 15:30 [c]Josh. 11:20 [1]Tg. *the Judge*
26 [a]1 Sam. 2:21 [b]Prov. 3:4
27 [a]Deut. 33:1; Judg. 13:6; 1 Sam. 9:6; 1 Kin. 13:1 [b]Ex. 4:14–16; 12:1
28 [a]Ex. 28:1, 4; Num. 16:5 [b]Lev. 2:3, 10; 6:16; 7:7, 8, 34, 35; Num. 5:9
29 [a]Deut. 32:15

Samuel's Childhood Ministry

18 [a]But Samuel ministered before
the LORD, *even as* a child, [b]wearing
a linen ephod.
19 Moreover his mother used to
make him a little robe, and bring
it to him year by year when she
[a]came up with her husband to offer
the yearly sacrifice.
20 And Eli [a]would bless Elkanah
and his wife, and say, "The LORD
give you descendants from this
woman for the [1]loan that was
[b]given to the LORD." Then they
would go to their own home.
21 And the LORD [a]visited[1] Han-
nah, so that she conceived and
bore three sons and two daugh-
ters. Meanwhile the child Samuel
[b]grew before the LORD.

Prophecy Against Eli's Household

22 Now Eli was very old; and he
heard everything his sons did to
all Israel, [1]and how they lay with
[a]the women who assembled at the
door of the tabernacle of meeting.
23 So he said to them, "Why do
you do such things? For I hear of
your evil dealings from all the peo-
ple.
24 "No, my sons! For *it is* not a
good report that I hear. You make
the LORD's people transgress.
25 "If one man sins against an-
other, [a]God[1] will judge him. But if
a man [b]sins against the LORD, who
will intercede for him?" Neverthe-
less they did not heed the voice of
their father, [c]because the LORD de-
sired to kill them.
26 And the child Samuel [a]grew in
stature, and [b]in favor both with the
LORD and men.
27 Then a [a]man of God came to
Eli and said to him, "Thus says the
LORD: [b]'Did I not clearly reveal
Myself to the house of your father
when they were in Egypt in Pha-
raoh's house?
28 'Did I not [a]choose him out of
all the tribes of Israel *to be* My
priest, to offer upon My altar, to
burn incense, and to wear an
ephod before Me? And [b]did I not
give to the house of your father all
the offerings of the children of Is-
rael made by fire?
29 'Why do you [a]kick at My sacri-
fice and My offering which I have

commanded *in My* [b]dwelling
place, and honor your sons more
than [c]Me, to make yourselves fat
with the best of all the offerings
of Israel My people?'
30 "Therefore the LORD God of Is-
rael says: [a]'I said indeed *that* your
house and the house of your father
would walk before Me forever.'
But now the LORD says: [b]'Far be
it from Me; for those who honor
Me I will honor, and [c]those who
despise Me shall be lightly es-
teemed.
31 'Behold, [a]the days are coming
that I will cut off your [1]arm and
the arm of your father's house, so
that there will not be an old man
in your house.
32 'And you will see an enemy *in*
My dwelling place, *despite* all the
good which God does for Israel.
And there shall not be [a]an old man
in your house forever.
33 'But any of your men *whom* I
do not cut off from My altar shall
consume your eyes and grieve
your heart. And all the descen-
dants of your house shall die in the
flower of their age.
34 'Now this *shall be* [a]a sign to
you that will come upon your two
sons, on Hophni and Phinehas: [b]in
one day they shall die, both of
them.
35 'Then [a]I will raise up for Myself
a faithful priest *who* shall do ac-
cording to what *is* in My heart and
in My mind. [b]I will build him a sure
house, and he shall walk before
[c]My anointed forever.
36 [a]'And it shall come to pass that
everyone who is left in your house
will come *and* bow down to him
for a piece of silver and a morsel
of bread, and say, "Please, [1]put me
in one of the priestly positions,
that I may eat a piece of bread." ' "

Samuel's First Prophecy

3 Now [a]the boy Samuel minis-
tered to the LORD before Eli.
And [b]the word of the LORD was
rare in those days; *there was* no
widespread revelation.
2 And it came to pass at that
time, while Eli *was* lying down in
his place, and when his eyes had
begun to grow [a]so dim that he
could not see,
3 and before [a]the lamp of God
went out in the [1]tabernacle of the
LORD where the ark of God *was*,
and while Samuel was lying down,
4 that the LORD called Samuel.
And he answered, "Here I am!"
5 So he ran to Eli and said, "Here
I am, for you called me." And he
said, "I did not call; lie down
again." And he went and lay
down.
6 Then the LORD called yet again,
"Samuel!" So Samuel arose and
went to Eli, and said, "Here I am,
for you called me." He answered,
"I did not call, my son; lie down
again."
7 (Now Samuel [a]did not yet
know the LORD, nor was the word
of the LORD yet revealed to him.)
8 And the LORD called Samuel
again the third time. So he arose
and went to Eli, and said, "Here I
am, for you did call me." Then Eli
perceived that the LORD had called
the boy.
9 Therefore Eli said to Samuel,
"Go, lie down; and it shall be, if
He calls you, that you must say,
[a]'Speak, LORD, for Your servant
hears.' " So Samuel went and lay
down in his place.
10 Now the LORD came and stood
and called as at other times, "Sam-
uel! Samuel!" And Samuel an-
swered, "Speak, for Your servant
hears."
11 Then the LORD said to Samuel:
"Behold, I will do something in Is-
rael [a]at which both ears of every-
one who hears it will tingle.
12 "In that day I will perform
against Eli [a]all that I have spoken
concerning his house, from begin-
ning to end.
13 [a]"For I have told him that I will
[b]judge his house forever for the in-
iquity which he knows, because
[c]his sons made themselves vile,
and he [d]did not [1]restrain them.
14 "And therefore I have sworn to
the house of Eli that the iniquity
of Eli's house [a]shall not be atoned
for by sacrifice or offering for-
ever."
15 So Samuel lay down until
[1]morning, and opened the doors of
the house of the LORD. And Samuel
was afraid to tell Eli the vision.
16 Then Eli called Samuel and
said, "Samuel, my son!" He an-
swered, "Here I am."

29 [b]Deut. 12:5; Ps. 26:8 [c]Matt. 10:37
30 [a]Ex. 29:9; Num. 25:13 [b]Jer. 18:9, 10 [c]Ps. 91:14; Mal. 2:9–12
31 [a]1 Sam. 4:11–18; 22:18, 19; 1 Kin. 2:27, 35 [1]*strength*
32 [a]Zech. 8:4
34 [a]1 Sam. 10:7–9; 1 Kin. 13:3 [b]1 Sam. 4:11, 17
35 [a]1 Kin. 2:35; Ezek. 44:15; [Heb. 2:17; 7:26–28] [b]2 Sam. 7:11, 27; 1 Kin. 11:38 [c]Ps. 18:50
36 [a]1 Kin. 2:27 [1]*assign*

CHAPTER 3
1 [a]1 Sam. 2:11, 18 [b]Ps. 74:9; Ezek. 7:26; Amos 8:11, 12
2 [a]Gen. 27:1; 48:10; 1 Sam. 4:15
3 [a]Ex. 27:20, 21 [1]*palace* or *temple*
7 [a]1 Sam. 2:12; Acts 19:2; 1 Cor. 13:11
9 [a]1 Kin. 2:17
11 [a]2 Kin. 21:12; Jer. 19:3
12 [a]1 Sam. 2:27–36; Ezek. 12:25; Luke 21:33
13 [a]1 Sam. 2:29–31 [b]1 Sam. 2:22; Ezek. 7:3; 18:30 [c]1 Sam. 2:12, 17, 22 [d]1 Sam. 2:23, 25 [1]Lit. *rebuke*
14 [a]Num. 15:30, 31; Is. 22:14; Heb. 10:4, 26–31
15 [1]So with MT, Tg., Vg.; LXX adds *and he arose in the morning*

17 And he said, "What *is* the word
that *the* LORD spoke to you? Please
do not hide *it* from me. [a]God do
so to you, and more also, if you
hide anything from me of all the
things that He said to you."
18 Then Samuel told him every-
thing, and hid nothing from him.
And he said, [a]"It *is* the LORD. Let
Him do what seems good to Him."
19 So Samuel [a]grew, and [b]the
LORD was with him [c]and let none
of his words [1]fall to the ground.
20 And all Israel [a]from Dan to
Beersheba knew that Samuel *had
been* [1]established as a prophet of
the LORD.
21 Then the LORD appeared again
in Shiloh. For the LORD revealed
Himself to Samuel in Shiloh by
[a]the word of the LORD.

4 And the word of Samuel came
to all [1]Israel.

The Ark of God Captured

Now Israel went out to battle
against the Philistines, and en-
camped beside [a]Ebenezer; and the
Philistines encamped in Aphek.
2 Then the [a]Philistines put them-
selves in battle array against Is-
rael. And when they joined battle,
Israel was [1]defeated by the Philis-
tines, who killed about four thou-
sand men of the army in the field.
3 And when the people had come
into the camp, the elders of Israel
said, "Why has the LORD defeated
us today before the Philistines?
[a]Let us bring the ark of the cov-
enant of the LORD from Shiloh to
us, that when it comes among us
it may save us from the hand of
our enemies."
4 So the people sent to Shiloh,
that they might bring from there
the ark of the covenant of the LORD
of hosts, [a]who dwells *between* [b]the
cherubim. And the [c]two sons of
Eli, Hophni and Phinehas, *were*
there with the ark of the covenant
of God.
5 And when the ark of the cov-
enant of the LORD came into the
camp, all Israel shouted so loudly
that the earth shook.
6 Now when the Philistines
heard the noise of the shout, they
said, "What *does* the sound of this
great shout in the camp of the He-
brews *mean?*" Then they under-
stood that the ark of the LORD had
come into the camp.
7 So the Philistines were afraid,
for they said, "God has come into
the camp!" And they said, [a]"Woe
to us! For such a thing has never
happened before.
8 "Woe to us! Who will deliver
us from the hand of these mighty
gods? These *are* the gods who
struck the Egyptians with all the
plagues in the wilderness.
9 [a]"Be strong and conduct your-
selves like men, you Philistines,
that you do not become servants
of the Hebrews, [b]as they have been
to you. [1]Conduct yourselves like
men, and fight!"
10 So the Philistines fought, and
[a]Israel was [1]defeated, and every
man fled to his tent. There was a
very great slaughter, and there fell
of Israel thirty thousand foot sol-
diers.
11 Also [a]the ark of God was cap-
tured; and [b]the two sons of Eli,
Hophni and Phinehas, died.

Death of Eli

12 Then a man of Benjamin ran
from the battle line the same day,
and [a]came to Shiloh with his
clothes torn and [b]dirt on his head.
13 Now when he came, there was
Eli, sitting on [a]a seat [1]by the way-
side watching, for his heart [2]trem-
bled for the ark of God. And when
the man came into the city and told
it, all the city cried out.
14 When Eli heard the noise of the
outcry, he said, "What *does* the
sound of this tumult *mean?*" And
the man came quickly and told Eli.
15 Eli was ninety-eight years old,
and [a]his eyes were so [1]dim that he
could not see.
16 Then the man said to Eli, "I *am*
he who came from the battle. And
I fled today from the battle line."
And he said, [a]"What happened,
my son?"
17 So the messenger answered
and said, "Israel has fled before
the Philistines, and there has been
a great slaughter among the peo-
ple. Also your two sons, Hophni
and Phinehas, are dead; and the
ark of God has been captured."
18 Then it happened, when he
made mention of the ark of God,
that Eli fell off the seat backward

17 [a]Ruth 1:17
18 [a]Gen. 24:50; Ex. 34:5–7; Lev. 10:3; Is. 39:8; Acts 5:39
19 [a]1 Sam. 2:21 [b]Gen. 21:22; 28:15; 39:2, 21, 23 [c]1 Sam. 9:6 [1]*fail*
20 [a]Judg. 20:1 [1]*confirmed*
21 [a]1 Sam. 3:1, 4

CHAPTER 4

1 [a]1 Sam. 7:12 [1]So with MT, Tg.; LXX, Vg. add *And it came to pass in those days that the Philistines gathered themselves together to fight;* LXX adds further *against Israel*
2 [a]1 Sam. 12:9 [1]Lit. *struck*
3 [a]Num. 10:35; Josh. 6:6–21
4 [a]Ex. 25:18–21; 1 Sam. 6:2; Ps. 80:1 [b]Num. 7:89 [c]1 Sam. 2:12
7 [a]Ex. 15:14
9 [a]1 Cor. 16:13 [b]Judg. 13:1; 1 Sam. 14:21 [1]Lit. *Be men*
10 [a]Lev. 26:17; Deut. 28:15, 25; 1 Sam. 4:2; 2 Sam. 18:17; 19:8; 2 Kin. 14:12; 2 Chr. 25:22 [1]Lit. *struck down*
11 [a]1 Sam. 2:32; Ps. 78:60, 61 [b]1 Sam. 2:34; Ps. 78:64
12 [a]2 Sam. 1:2 [b]Josh. 7:6; 2 Sam. 13:19; 15:32; Neh. 9:1; Job 2:12
13 [a]1 Sam. 1:9; 4:18 [1]So with MT, Vg.; LXX *beside the gate watching the road* [2]*trembled with anxiety*
15 [a]1 Sam. 3:2; 1 Kin. 14:4 [1]*fixed*
16 [a]2 Sam. 1:4

by the side of the gate; and his
neck was broken and he died, for
the man was old and heavy. And
he had judged Israel forty years.

Ichabod

19 Now his daughter-in-law, Phin-
ehas' wife, was with child, *due* to
be delivered; and when she heard
the news that the ark of God was
captured, and that her father-in-
law and her husband were dead,
she bowed herself and gave birth,
for her labor pains came upon her.
20 And about the time of her death
[a]the women who stood by her said
to her, "Do not fear, for you have
borne a son." But she did not an-
swer, nor did she [1]regard *it*.
21 Then she named the child
[a]Ichabod,[1] saying, [b]"The glory has
departed from Israel!" because the
ark of God had been captured and
because of her father-in-law and
her husband.
22 And she said, "The glory has
departed from Israel, for the ark
of God has been captured."

The Philistines and the Ark

5 Then the Philistines took the
ark of God and brought it
[a]from Ebenezer to Ashdod.
2 When the Philistines took the
ark of God, they brought it into the
house of [a]Dagon[1] and set it by Da-
gon.
3 And when the people of Ash-
dod arose early in the morning,
there was Dagon, [a]fallen on its
face to the earth before the ark of
the LORD. So they took Dagon and
[b]set it in its place again.
4 And when they arose early the
next morning, there was Dagon,
fallen on its face to the ground be-
fore the ark of the LORD. [a]The head
of Dagon and both the palms of
its hands *were* broken off on the
threshold; only [1]Dagon's torso
was left of it.
5 Therefore neither the priests of
Dagon nor any who come into Da-
gon's house [a]tread on the thresh-
old of Dagon in Ashdod to this
day.
6 But the [a]hand of the LORD was
heavy on the people of Ashdod,
and He [b]ravaged them and struck
them with [c]tumors,[1] *both* Ashdod
and its [d]territory.
7 And when the men of Ashdod
saw how *it was*, they said, "The
ark of the [a]God of Israel must not
remain with us, for His hand is
harsh toward us and Dagon our
god."
8 Therefore they sent and gath-
ered to themselves all the [a]lords
of the Philistines, and said, "What
shall we do with the ark of the God
of Israel?" And they answered,
"Let the ark of the God of Israel
be carried away to [b]Gath." So they
carried the ark of the God of Israel
away.
9 So it was, after they had car-
ried it away, that [a]the hand of the
LORD was against the city with a
very great destruction; and He
struck the men of the city, both
small and great, [1]and tumors
broke out on them.
10 Therefore they sent the ark of
God to Ekron. So it was, as the ark
of God came to Ekron, that the Ek-
ronites cried out, saying, "They
have brought the ark of the God
of Israel to us, to kill us and our
people!"
11 So they sent and gathered to-
gether all the lords of the Philis-
tines, and said, "Send away the
ark of the God of Israel, and let it
go back to its own place, so that
it does not kill us and our people."
For there was a deadly destruction
throughout all the city; the hand
of God was very heavy there.
12 And the men who did not die
were stricken with the tumors, and
the [a]cry of the city went up to
heaven.

The Ark Returned to Israel

6 Now the ark of the LORD was
in the country of the Philistines
seven months.
2 And the Philistines [a]called for
the priests and the diviners, say-
ing, "What shall we do with the
ark of the LORD? Tell us how we
should send it to its place."
3 So they said, "If you send away
the ark of the God of Israel, do not
send it [a]empty; but by all means
return *it* to Him *with* [b]a trespass
offering. Then you will be healed,
and it will be known to you why
His hand is not removed from
you."
4 Then they said, "What *is* the

---

20 [a]Gen. 35:16–19 [1]*pay any attention to*
21 [a]1 Sam. 14:3 [b]Ps. 26:8; 78:61; [Jer. 2:11] [1]Lit. *Inglorious*

CHAPTER 5

1 [a]1 Sam. 4:1; 7:12
2 [a]Judg. 16:23–30; 1 Chr. 10:8–10 [1]A Philistine idol
3 [a]Is. 19:1; 46:1, 2 [b]Is. 46:7
4 [a]Jer. 50:2; Ezek. 6:4, 6; Mic. 1:7 [1]So with LXX, Syr., Tg., Vg.; MT *Dagon*
5 [a]Zeph. 1:9
6 [a]Ex. 9:3; Deut. 2:15; 1 Sam. 5:7; 7:13; Ps. 32:4; 145:20; 147:6 [b]1 Sam. 6:5 [c]Deut. 28:27; Ps. 78:66 [d]Josh. 15:46, 47 [1]Probably bubonic plague. LXX, Vg. add *And in the midst of their land rats sprang up, and there was a great death panic in the city.*
7 [a]1 Sam. 6:5
8 [a]1 Sam. 6:4 [b]Josh. 11:22
9 [a]Deut. 2:15; 1 Sam. 5:11; 7:13; 12:15 [1]Vg. *and they had tumors in their secret parts*
12 [a]1 Sam. 9:16; Jer. 14:2

CHAPTER 6

2 [a]Gen. 41:8; Ex. 7:11; Is. 2:6; 47:13; Dan. 2:2; 5:7
3 [a]Ex. 23:15; Deut. 16:16 [b]Lev. 5:15, 16

trespass offering which we shall
return to Him?" They answered,
[a]"Five golden tumors and five
golden rats, *according to* the num-
ber of the lords of the Philistines.
For the same plague *was* on all of
[1]you and on your lords.
5 "Therefore you shall make im-
ages of your tumors and images
of your rats that [a]ravage the land,
and you shall [b]give glory to the
God of Israel; perhaps He will
[c]lighten[1] His hand from you, from
[d]your gods, and from your land.
6 "Why then do you harden your
hearts [a]as the Egyptians and Pha-
raoh hardened their hearts? When
He did mighty things among them,
[b]did they not let the people go, that
they might depart?
7 "Now therefore, make [a]a new
cart, take two milk cows [b]which
have never been yoked, and hitch
the cows to the cart; and take their
calves home, away from them.
8 "Then take the ark of the LORD
and set it on the cart; and put [a]the
articles of gold which you are re-
turning to Him *as* a trespass offer-
ing in a chest by its side. Then send
it away, and let it go.
9 "And watch: if it goes up the
road to its own territory, to [a]Beth
Shemesh, *then* He has done [1]us
this great evil. But if not, then [b]we
shall know that *it is* not His hand
that struck us—it happened to us
by chance."
10 Then the men did so; they took
two milk cows and hitched them
to the cart, and shut up their calves
at home.
11 And they set the ark of the
LORD on the cart, and the chest
with the gold rats and the images
of their tumors.
12 Then the cows headed straight
for the road to Beth Shemesh, *and*
went along the [a]highway, lowing
as they went, and did not turn
aside to the right hand or the left.
And the lords of the Philistines
went after them to the border of
Beth Shemesh.
13 Now *the people of* Beth She-
mesh *were* reaping their [a]wheat
harvest in the valley; and they
lifted their eyes and saw the ark,
and rejoiced to see *it*.
14 Then the cart came into the
field of Joshua of Beth Shemesh,

4 [a]1 Sam. 5:6, 9, 12; 6:17 [1]Lit. *them*
5 [a]1 Sam. 5:6 [b]Josh. 7:19; 1 Chr. 16:28, 29; Is. 42:12; Jer. 13:16; Mal. 2:2; Rev. 14:7 [c]1 Sam. 5:6, 11; Ps. 39:10 [d]1 Sam. 5:3, 4, 7 [1]*ease*
6 [a]Ex. 7:13; 8:15; 9:34; 14:17 [b]Ex. 12:31
7 [a]2 Sam. 6:3 [b]Num. 19:2; Deut. 21:3, 4
8 [a]1 Sam. 6:4, 5
9 [a]Josh. 15:10; 21:16 [b]1 Sam. 6:3 [1]*this calamity to us*
12 [a]Num. 20:19
13 [a]1 Sam. 12:17
16 [a]Josh. 13:3; Judg. 3:3
17 [a]1 Sam. 6:4 [b]1 Sam. 5:8
19 [a]Ex. 19:21; Num. 4:5, 15, 16, 20 [b]2 Sam. 6:7 [1]Or *He struck seventy men of the people and fifty oxen of a man*
20 [a]Lev. 11:44, 45; Ps. 24:3, 4; Mal. 3:2; Rev. 6:17
21 [a]Josh. 9:17; 15:9, 60; 18:14; Judg. 18:12; 1 Chr. 13:5, 6

CHAPTER 7

1 [a]1 Sam. 6:21; Ps. 132:6 [b]2 Sam. 6:3, 4 [c]Lev. 21:8

and stood there; a large stone *was*
there. So they split the wood of the
cart and offered the cows as a
burnt offering to the LORD.
15 The Levites took down the ark
of the LORD and the chest that *was*
with it, in which *were* the articles
of gold, and put *them* on the large
stone. Then the men of Beth She-
mesh offered burnt offerings and
made sacrifices the same day to
the LORD.
16 So when [a]the five lords of the
Philistines had seen *it*, they re-
turned to Ekron the same day.
17 [a]These *are* the golden tumors
which the Philistines returned *as*
a trespass offering to the LORD:
one for Ashdod, one for Gaza, one
for Ashkelon, one for [b]Gath, one
for Ekron;
18 and the golden rats, *according
to* the number of all the cities of
the Philistines *belonging* to the five
lords, *both* fortified cities and
country villages, even as far as the
large *stone of* Abel on which they
set the ark of the LORD, *which
stone remains* to this day in the
field of Joshua of Beth Shemesh.
19 Then [a]He struck the men of
Beth Shemesh, because they had
looked into the ark of the LORD.
[1]He [b]struck fifty thousand and sev-
enty men of the people, and the
people lamented because the LORD
had struck the people with a great
slaughter.

The Ark at Kirjath Jearim

20 And the men of Beth Shemesh
said, [a]"Who is able to stand before
this holy LORD God? And to whom
shall it go up from us?"
21 So they sent messengers to the
inhabitants of [a]Kirjath Jearim,
saying, "The Philistines have
brought back the ark of the LORD;
come down *and* take it up with
you."

7 Then the men of [a]Kirjath
Jearim came and took the ark
of the LORD, and brought it into the
house of [b]Abinadab on the hill,
and [c]consecrated Eleazar his son
to keep the ark of the LORD.

Samuel Judges Israel

2 So it was that the ark remained
in Kirjath Jearim a long time; it
was there twenty years. And all

the house of Israel lamented after
the LORD.
3 Then Samuel spoke to all the
house of Israel, saying, "If you [a]re-
turn to the LORD with all your
hearts, *then* [b]put away the foreign
gods and the [c]Ashtoreths[1] from
among you, and [d]prepare your
hearts for the LORD, and [e]serve
Him only; and He will deliver you
from the hand of the Philistines."
4 So the children of Israel put
away the [a]Baals and the [1]Ash-
toreths, and served the LORD only.
5 And Samuel said, [a]"Gather all
Israel to Mizpah, and [b]I will pray
to the LORD for you."
6 So they gathered together at
Mizpah, [a]drew water, and poured
it out before the LORD. And they
[b]fasted that day, and said there,
[c]"We have sinned against the
LORD." And Samuel judged the
children of Israel at Mizpah.
7 Now when the Philistines
heard that the children of Israel
had gathered together at Mizpah,
the lords of the Philistines went up
against Israel. And when the chil-
dren of Israel heard *of it,* they
were afraid of the Philistines.
8 So the children of Israel said
to Samuel, [a]"Do not cease to cry
out to the LORD our God for us, that
He may save us from the hand of
the Philistines."
9 And Samuel took a [a]suckling
lamb and offered *it as* a whole
burnt offering to the LORD. Then
[b]Samuel cried out to the LORD for
Israel, and the LORD answered
him.
10 Now as Samuel was offering up
the burnt offering, the Philistines
drew near to battle against Israel.
[a]But the LORD thundered with a
loud thunder upon the Philistines
that day, and so confused them
that they were overcome before Is-
rael.
11 And the men of Israel went out
of Mizpah and pursued the Philis-
tines, and [1]drove them back as far
as below Beth Car.
12 Then Samuel [a]took a stone and
set *it* up between Mizpah and
Shen, and called its name [1]Eben-
ezer, saying, "Thus far the LORD
has helped us."
13 [a]So the Philistines were sub-
dued, and they [b]did not come any-

3 [a]Deut. 30:2–10 [b]Gen. 35:2 [c]Judg. 2:13 [d]Job 11:13 [e]Luke 4:8 [1]Images of Canaanite goddesses
4 [a]Judg. 2:11; 10:16 [1]Images of Canaanite goddesses
5 [a]Judg. 10:17; 20:1 [b]1 Sam. 12:17–19
6 [a]2 Sam. 14:14 [b]Neh. 9:1, 2 [c]1 Sam. 12:10
8 [a]Is. 37:4
9 [a]Lev. 22:27 [b]1 Sam. 12:18
10 [a]2 Sam. 22:14, 15
11 [1]*struck them down*
12 [a]Josh. 4:9; 24:26 [1]Lit. *Stone of Help*
13 [a]Judg. 13:1 [b]1 Sam. 13:5
15 [a]1 Sam. 12:11
17 [a]1 Sam. 8:4 [b]Judg. 21:4

CHAPTER 8

1 [a]1 Sam. 12:2 [b]Deut. 16:18, 19 [c]Judg. 10:4
3 [a]Jer. 22:15–17 [b]Ex. 18:21 [c]Ex. 23:6–8
5 [a]Deut. 17:14, 15
6 [a]1 Sam. 12:17 [b]1 Sam. 7:9
7 [a]Ex. 16:8 [b]1 Sam. 10:19
9 [a]1 Sam. 8:11–18

more into the territory of Israel.
And the hand of the LORD was
against the Philistines all the days
of Samuel.
14 Then the cities which the Phi-
listines had taken from Israel were
restored to Israel, from Ekron to
Gath; and Israel recovered its ter-
ritory from the hands of the Philis-
tines. Also there was peace be-
tween Israel and the Amorites.
15 And Samuel [a]judged Israel all
the days of his life.
16 He went from year to year on
a circuit to Bethel, Gilgal, and
Mizpah, and judged Israel in all
those places.
17 But [a]he always returned to Ra-
mah, for his home *was* there.
There he judged Israel, and there
he [b]built an altar to the LORD.

Israel Demands a King

8 Now it came to pass when
Samuel was [a]old that he [b]made
his [c]sons judges over Israel.
2 The name of his firstborn was
Joel, and the name of his second,
Abijah; *they were* judges in Beer-
sheba.
3 But his sons [a]did not walk in
his ways; they turned aside [b]after
dishonest gain, [c]took bribes, and
perverted justice.
4 Then all the elders of Israel
gathered together and came to
Samuel at Ramah,
5 and said to him, "Look, you are
old, and your sons do not walk in
your ways. Now [a]make us a king
to judge us like all the nations."
6 But the thing [a]displeased Sam-
uel when they said, "Give us a king
to judge us." So Samuel [b]prayed
to the LORD.
7 And the LORD said to Samuel,
"Heed the voice of the people in
all that they say to you; for [a]they
have not rejected you, but [b]they
have rejected Me, that I should not
reign over them.
8 "According to all the works
which they have done since the
day that I brought them up out of
Egypt, even to this day—with
which they have forsaken Me and
served other gods—so they are do-
ing to you also.
9 "Now therefore, heed their
voice. However, you shall sol-
emnly forewarn them, and [a]show

them the behavior of the king who
will reign over them."
10 So Samuel told all the words
of the LORD to the people who
asked him for a king.
11 And he said, [a]"This will be the
behavior of the king who will reign
over you: He will take your [b]sons
and appoint *them* for his own
[c]chariots and *to be* his horsemen,
and *some* will run before his chari-
ots.
12 "He will [a]appoint captains over
his thousands and captains over
his fifties, *will set some* to plow his
ground and reap his harvest, and
some to make his weapons of war
and equipment for his chariots.
13 "He will take your daughters *to*
be perfumers, cooks, and bakers.
14 "And [a]he will take the best of
your fields, your vineyards, and
your olive groves, and give *them*
to his servants.
15 "He will take a tenth of your
grain and your vintage, and give
it to his officers and servants.
16 "And he will take your male
servants, your female servants,
your finest [1]young men, and your
donkeys, and put *them* to his
work.
17 "He will take a tenth of your
sheep. And you will be his ser-
vants.
18 "And you will cry out in that
day because of your king whom
you have chosen for yourselves,
and the LORD [a]will not hear you
in that day."
19 Nevertheless the people [a]re-
fused to obey the voice of Samuel;
and they said, "No, but we will
have a king over us,
20 "that we also may be [a]like all
the nations, and that our king may
judge us and go out before us and
fight our battles."
21 And Samuel heard all the
words of the people, and he re-
peated them in the hearing of the
LORD.
22 So the LORD said to Samuel,
[a]"Heed their voice, and make them
a king." And Samuel said to the
men of Israel, "Every man go to
his city."

Saul Chosen to Be King

9 There was a man of Benjamin
whose name *was* [a]Kish the son
of Abiel, the son of Zeror, the son
of Bechorath, the son of Aphiah,
a Benjamite, a mighty man of
[1]power.
2 And he had a choice and hand-
some son whose name *was* Saul.
There was not a more handsome
person than he among the children
of Israel. [a]From his shoulders up-
ward *he was* taller than any of the
people.
3 Now the donkeys of Kish,
Saul's father, were lost. And Kish
said to his son Saul, "Please take
one of the servants with you, and
arise, go and look for the don-
keys."
4 So he passed through the
mountains of Ephraim and
through the land of [a]Shalisha, but
they did not find *them*. Then they
passed through the land of
Shaalim, and *they were* not *there*.
Then he passed through the land
of the Benjamites, but they did not
find *them*.
5 When they had come to the
land of [a]Zuph, Saul said to his ser-
vant who *was* with him, "Come,
let [b]us return, lest my father cease
caring about the donkeys and be-
come worried about us."
6 And he said to him, "Look now,
there is in this city [a]a man of God,
and *he is* an honorable man; [b]all
that he says surely comes to pass.
So let us go there; perhaps he can
show us the way that we should
go."
7 Then Saul said to his servant,
"But look, *if* we go, [a]what shall we
bring the man? For the bread in
our vessels is all gone, and *there*
is no present to bring to the man
of God. What do we have?"
8 And the servant answered Saul
again and said, "Look, I have here
at hand one-fourth of a shekel of
silver. I will give *that* to the man
of God, to tell us our way."
9 (Formerly in Israel, when a
man [a]went [1]to inquire of God, he
spoke thus: "Come, let us go to the
seer"; for *he who is* now *called* a
prophet was formerly called [b]a
seer.)
10 Then Saul said to his servant,
[1]"Well said; come, let us go." So
they went to the city where the
man of God *was*.
11 As they went up the hill to the

---

11 [a]Deut. 17:14–20 [b]1 Sam. 14:52 [c]2 Sam. 15:1
12 [a]1 Sam. 22:7
14 [a]1 Kin. 21:7; [Ezek. 46:18]
16 [1]LXX *cattle*
18 [a]Prov. 1:25–28; Is. 1:15; Mic. 3:4
19 [a]Is. 66:4; Jer. 44:16
20 [a]1 Sam. 8:5
22 [a]1 Sam. 8:7; Hos. 13:11

CHAPTER 9

1 [a]1 Sam. 14:51; 1 Chr. 8:33; 9:36–39 [1]*wealth*
2 [a]1 Sam. 10:23
4 [a]2 Kin. 4:42
5 [a]1 Sam. 1:1 [b]1 Sam. 10:2
6 [a]Deut. 33:1; 1 Kin. 13:1; 2 Kin. 5:8 [b]1 Sam. 3:19
7 [a]Judg. 6:18; 13:17; 1 Kin. 14:3; 2 Kin. 4:42; 8:8
9 [a]Gen. 25:22 [b]2 Sam. 24:11; 2 Kin. 17:13; 1 Chr. 26:28; 29:29; 2 Chr. 16:7, 10; Is. 30:10; Amos 7:12 [1]Lit. *to seek God*
10 [1]Lit. *Your word is good*

city, [a]they met some young women
going out to draw water, and said
to them, "Is the seer here?"
12 And they answered them and
said, "Yes, there he is, just ahead
of you. Hurry now; for today he
came to this city, because [a]there
is a sacrifice of the people today
[b]on the high place.
13 "As soon as you come into the
city, you will surely find him be-
fore he goes up to the high place
to eat. For the people will not eat
until he comes, because he must
bless the sacrifice; afterward those
who are invited will eat. Now
therefore, go up, for about this
time you will find him."
14 So they went up to the city. As
they were coming into the city,
there was Samuel, coming out to-
ward them on his way up to the
high place.
15 [a]Now the LORD had told Sam-
uel in his ear the day before Saul
came, saying,
16 "Tomorrow about this time [a]I
will send you a man from the land
of Benjamin, [b]and you shall anoint
him [1]commander over My people
Israel, that he may save My people
from the hand of the Philistines;
for I have [c]looked upon My people,
because their cry has come to
Me."
17 So when Samuel saw Saul, the
LORD said to him, [a]"There he is,
the man of whom I spoke to you.
This one shall reign over My peo-
ple."
18 Then Saul drew near to Samuel
in the gate, and said, "Please tell
me, where *is* the seer's house?"
19 Samuel answered Saul and
said, "I *am* the seer. Go up before
me to the high place, for you shall
eat with me today; and tomorrow
I will let you go and will tell you
all that *is* in your heart.
20 "But as for [a]your donkeys that
were lost three days ago, do not
be anxious about them, for they
have been found. And [1]on whom
[b]*is* all the desire of Israel? *Is it* not
on you and on all your father's
house?"
21 And Saul answered and said,
[a]"*Am* I not a Benjamite, of the
[b]smallest of the tribes of Israel,
and [c]my family the least of all the
families of the [1]tribe of Benjamin?
Why then do you speak like this
to me?"
22 Now Samuel took Saul and his
servant and brought them into the
hall, and had them sit in the place
of honor among those who were
invited; there *were* about thirty
persons.
23 And Samuel said to the cook,
"Bring the portion which I gave
you, of which I said to you, 'Set it
apart.'"
24 So the cook took up [a]the thigh
with its upper part and set *it* before
Saul. And *Samuel* said, "Here it is,
what was kept back. *It* was set
apart for you. Eat; for until this
time it has been kept for you, since
I said I invited the people." So Saul
ate with Samuel that day.
25 When they had come down
from the high place into the city,
[1]*Samuel* spoke with Saul on [a]the
top of the house.
26 They arose early; and it was
about the dawning of the day that
Samuel called to Saul on the top
of the house, saying, "Get up, that
I may send you on your way." And
Saul arose, and both of them went
outside, he and Samuel.

Saul Anointed King

27 As they were going down to the
outskirts of the city, Samuel said
to Saul, "Tell the servant to go on
ahead of us." And he went on.
"But you stand here [1]awhile, that
I may announce to you the word
of God."

10 Then [a]Samuel took a flask
of oil and poured *it* on his
head, [b]and kissed him and said: "*Is*
it not because [c]the LORD has
anointed you commander over
[d]His [1]inheritance?
2 "When you have departed from
me today, you will find two men
by [a]Rachel's tomb in the territory
of Benjamin [b]at Zelzah; and they
will say to you, 'The donkeys
which you went to look for have
been found. And now your father
has ceased caring about the don-
keys and is worrying about [c]you,
saying, "What shall I do about my
son?"'
3 "Then you shall go on forward
from there and come to the tere-
binth tree of Tabor. There three

11 [a]Ex. 2:16
12 [a]Gen. 31:54 [b]1 Kin. 3:2
15 [a]1 Sam. 15:1
16 [a]Deut. 17:15 [b]1 Sam. 10:1 [c]Ex. 2:23–25; 3:7, 9 [1]*prince* or *ruler*
17 [a]1 Sam. 16:12
20 [a]1 Sam. 9:3 [b]1 Sam. 8:5, 19; 12:13 [1]*for whom*
21 [a]1 Sam. 15:17 [b]Judg. 20:46–48 [c]Judg. 6:15 [1]Lit. *tribes*
24 [a]Lev. 7:32, 33
25 [a]Deut. 22:8 [1]So with MT, Tg.; LXX omits *He spoke with Saul on the top of the house;* LXX, Vg. afterward add *And he prepared a bed for Saul on the top of the house, and he slept.*
27 [1]*now*

CHAPTER 10

1 [a]2 Kin. 9:3, 6 [b]Ps. 2:12 [c]Acts 13:21 [d]Deut. 32:9 [1]So with MT, Tg., Vg.; LXX *people Israel; and you shall rule the people of the Lord;* LXX, Vg. add *And you shall deliver His people from the hands of their enemies all around them. And this shall be a sign to you, that God has anointed you to be a prince.*
2 [a]Gen. 35:16–20; 48:7 [b]Josh. 18:28 [c]1 Sam. 9:3–5

men going up [a]to God at Bethel
will meet you, one carrying three
young goats, another carrying
three loaves of bread, and another
carrying a skin of wine.
4 "And they will [1]greet you and
give you two *loaves* of bread,
which you shall receive from their
hands.
5 "After that you shall come to
the hill of God [a]where the Philis-
tine garrison *is*. And it will hap-
pen, when you have come there to
the city, that you will meet a group
of prophets coming down [b]from
the high place with a stringed in-
strument, a tambourine, a flute,
and a harp before them; [c]and they
will be prophesying.
6 "Then [a]the Spirit of the LORD
will come upon you, and [b]you will
prophesy with them and be turned
into another man.
7 "And let it be, when these
[a]signs come to you, *that* you do
as the occasion demands; for [b]God
is with you.
8 "You shall go down before me
[a]to Gilgal; and surely I will come
down to you to offer burnt offer-
ings *and* make sacrifices of peace
offerings. [b]Seven days you shall
wait, till I come to you and show
you what you should do."
9 So it was, when he had turned
his back to go from Samuel, that
God [1]gave him another heart; and
all those signs came to pass that
day.
10 [a]When they came there to the
hill, there was [b]a group of proph-
ets to meet him; then the Spirit of
God came upon him, and he
prophesied among them.
11 And it happened, when all who
knew him formerly saw that he in-
deed prophesied among the proph-
ets, that the people said to one
another, "What *is* this *that* has
come upon the son of Kish? [a]*Is*
Saul also among the prophets?"
12 Then a man from there an-
swered and said, "But [a]who *is* their
father?" Therefore it became a
proverb: "*Is* Saul also among the
prophets?"
13 And when he had finished
prophesying, he went to the high
place.
14 Then Saul's [a]uncle said to him
and his servant, "Where did you
go?" So he said, "To look for the
donkeys. When we saw that *they
were* nowhere *to be found*, we
went to Samuel."
15 And Saul's uncle said, "Tell
me, please, what Samuel said to
you."
16 So Saul said to his uncle, "He
told us plainly that the donkeys
had been [a]found." But about the
matter of the kingdom, he did not
tell him what Samuel had said.

Saul Proclaimed King

17 Then Samuel called the people
together [a]to the LORD [b]at Miz-
pah,
18 and said to the children of Is-
rael, [a]"Thus says the LORD God of
Israel: 'I brought up Israel out of
Egypt, and delivered you from the
hand of the Egyptians *and* from
the hand of all kingdoms and from
those who oppressed you.'
19 [a]"But you have today rejected
your God, who Himself saved you
from all your adversities and your
tribulations; and you have said to
Him, 'No, set a king over us!' Now
therefore, present yourselves be-
fore the LORD by your tribes and
by your [1]clans."
20 And when Samuel had [a]caused
all the tribes of Israel to come
near, the tribe of Benjamin was
chosen.
21 When he had caused the
tribe of Benjamin to come near
by their families, the family of
Matri was chosen. And Saul the
son of Kish was chosen. But when
they sought him, he could not be
found.
22 Therefore they [a]inquired of the
LORD further, "Has the man come
here yet?" And the LORD an-
swered, "There he is, hidden
among the equipment."
23 So they ran and brought him
from there; and when he stood
among the people, [a]he was taller
than any of the people from his
shoulders upward.
24 And Samuel said to all the peo-
ple, "Do you see him [a]whom the
LORD has chosen, that *there is* no
one like him among all the peo-
ple?" So all the people shouted and
said, [b]"Long[1] live the king!"
25 Then Samuel explained to the

3 [a]Gen. 28:22; 35:1, 3, 7
4 [1]*ask you about your welfare*
5 [a]1 Sam. 13:2, 3 [b]1 Sam. 19:12, 20; 2 Kin. 2:3, 5, 15 [c]Ex. 15:20, 21; 2 Kin. 3:15; 1 Chr. 25:1–6; 1 Cor. 14:1
6 [a]Num. 11:25, 29; Judg. 14:6; 1 Sam. 16:13 [b]1 Sam. 10:10; 19:23, 24
7 [a]Ex. 4:8; Luke 2:12 [b]Josh. 1:5; Judg. 6:12; 1 Sam. 3:19; [Heb. 13:5]
8 [a]1 Sam. 11:14, 15; 13:8 [b]1 Sam. 13:8–10
9 [1]*changed his heart*
10 [a]1 Sam. 10:5 [b]1 Sam. 19:20
11 [a]1 Sam. 19:24; Amos 7:14, 15; Matt. 13:54–57; John 7:15; Acts 4:13
12 [a]John 5:30, 36
14 [a]1 Sam. 14:50
16 [a]1 Sam. 9:20
17 [a]Judg. 20:1 [b]1 Sam. 7:5, 6
18 [a]Judg. 6:8, 9; 1 Sam. 8:8; 12:6, 8
19 [a]1 Sam. 8:7, 19; 12:12 [1]Lit. *thousands*
20 [a]Acts 1:24, 26
22 [a]1 Sam. 23:2, 4, 10, 11
23 [a]1 Sam. 9:2
24 [a]Deut. 17:15; 1 Sam. 9:16; 2 Sam. 21:6 [b]1 Kin. 1:25, 39 [1]Lit. *May the king live*

people [a]the behavior of royalty,
and wrote *it* in a book and laid *it*
up before the LORD. And Samuel
sent all the people away, every
man to his house.
26 And Saul also went home [a]to
Gibeah; and valiant *men* went with
him, whose hearts God had
touched.
27 [a]But some [b]rebels said, "How
can this man save us?" So they
despised him, [c]and brought him no
presents. But he [1]held his peace.

Saul Saves Jabesh Gilead

11 Then [a]Nahash the Ammon-
ite came up and [1]encamped
against [b]Jabesh Gilead; and all the
men of Jabesh said to Nahash,
[c]"Make a covenant with us, and
we will serve you."
2 And Nahash the Ammonite an-
swered them, "On this *condition* I
will make *a covenant* with you,
that I may put out all your right
eyes, and bring [a]reproach on all
Israel."
3 Then the elders of Jabesh said
to him, "Hold off for seven days,
that we may send messengers to
all the territory of Israel. And then,
if *there is* no one to [1]save us, we
will come out to you."
4 So the messengers came [a]to
Gibeah of Saul and told the news
in the hearing of the people. And
[b]all the people lifted up their voices
and wept.
5 Now there was Saul, coming
behind the herd from the field; and
Saul said, "What *troubles* the peo-
ple, that they weep?" And they
told him the words of the men of
Jabesh.
6 [a]Then the Spirit of God came
upon Saul when he heard this
news, and his anger was greatly
aroused.
7 So he took a yoke of oxen and
[a]cut them in pieces, and sent *them*
throughout all the territory of Is-
rael by the hands of messengers,
saying, [b]"Whoever does not go out
with Saul and Samuel to battle, so
it shall be done to his oxen." And
the fear of the LORD fell on the peo-
ple, and they came out [1]with one
consent.
8 When he numbered them in
[a]Bezek, the children [b]of Israel
were three hundred thousand,
and the men of Judah thirty thou-
sand.
9 And they said to the messen-
gers who came, "Thus you shall
say to the men of Jabesh Gilead:
'Tomorrow, by *the time* the sun is
hot, you shall have help.'" Then
the messengers came and reported
it to the men of Jabesh, and they
were glad.
10 Therefore the men of Jabesh
said, "Tomorrow we will come out
to you, and you may do with us
whatever seems good to you."
11 So it was, on the next day,
that [a]Saul put the people [b]in three
companies; and they came into
the midst of the camp in the morn-
ing watch, and killed Ammon-
ites until the heat of the day. And
it happened that those who sur-
vived were scattered, so that no
two of them were left together.
12 Then the people said to Sam-
uel, [a]"Who *is* he who said, 'Shall
Saul reign over us?' [b]Bring the
men, that we may put them to
death."
13 But Saul said, [a]"Not a man
shall be put to death this day, for
today [b]the LORD has accomplished
salvation in Israel."
14 Then Samuel said to the peo-
ple, "Come, let us go [a]to Gilgal and
renew the kingdom there."
15 So all the people went to Gilgal,
and there they made Saul king [a]be-
fore the LORD in Gilgal. [b]There
they made sacrifices of peace of-
ferings before the LORD, and there
Saul and all the men of Israel re-
joiced greatly.

Samuel's Address at Saul's Coronation

12 Now Samuel said to all Is-
rael: "Indeed I have [1]heeded
[a]your voice in all that you said to
me, and [b]have made a king over
you.
2 "And now here is the king,
[a]walking before you; [b]and I am old
and grayheaded, and look, my
sons *are* with you. I have walked
before you from my childhood to
this day.
3 "Here I am. Witness against me
before the LORD and before [a]His
anointed: [b]Whose ox have I taken,
or whose donkey have I taken, or
whom have I cheated? Whom have

25 [a]1 Sam. 8:11–18
26 [a]Judg. 20:14
27 [a]1 Sam. 11:12 [b]Deut. 13:13 [c]1 Kin. 4:21; 10:25 [1]*kept silent*

CHAPTER 11

1 [a]1 Sam. 12:12 [b]Judg. 21:8 [c]Gen. 26:28 [1]*besieged*
2 [a]Gen. 34:14
3 [1]*deliver*
4 [a]1 Sam. 10:26; 15:34 [b]Judg. 2:4; 20:23, 26; 21:2
6 [a]Judg. 3:10; 6:34; 11:29; 13:25; 14:6
7 [a]Judg. 19:29 [b]Judg. 21:5, 8, 10 [1]Lit. *as one man*
8 [a]Judg. 1:5 [b]2 Sam. 24:9
11 [a]1 Sam. 31:11 [b]Judg. 7:16, 20
12 [a]1 Sam. 10:27 [b]Luke 19:27
13 [a]2 Sam. 19:22 [b]Ex. 14:13, 30
14 [a]1 Sam. 7:16; 10:8
15 [a]1 Sam. 10:17 [b]1 Sam. 10:8

CHAPTER 12

1 [a]1 Sam. 8:5, 7, 9, 20, 22 [b]1 Sam. 10:24; 11:14, 15 [1]*listened to*
2 [a]Num. 27:17 [b]1 Sam. 8:1, 5
3 [a]1 Sam. 10:1; 24:6 [b]Num. 16:15

I oppressed, or from whose hand
have I received *any* [c]bribe with
which to [d]blind my eyes? I will re-
store *it* to you."
4 And they said, [a]"You have not
cheated us or oppressed us, nor
have you taken anything from any
man's hand."
5 Then he said to them, "The
LORD *is* witness against you, and
His anointed *is* witness this day,
[a]that you have not found anything
[b]in my hand." And they answered,
"*He is* witness."
6 Then Samuel said to the peo-
ple, [a]"*It is* the LORD who raised up
Moses and Aaron, and who
brought your fathers up from the
land of Egypt.
7 "Now therefore, stand still, that
I may [a]reason with you before the
LORD concerning all the [b]righteous
acts of the LORD which He did to
you and your fathers:
8 [a]"When Jacob had gone in-
to [1]Egypt, and your fathers
[b]cried out to the LORD, then the
LORD [c]sent Moses and Aaron, who
brought your fathers out of Egypt
and made them dwell in this place.
9 "And when they [a]forgot the
LORD their God, He sold them into
the hand of [b]Sisera, commander of
the army of Hazor, into the hand
of the [c]Philistines, and into the
hand of the king of [d]Moab; and
they fought against them.
10 "Then they cried out to the
LORD, and said, [a]'We have sinned,
because we have forsaken the
LORD [b]and served the Baals and
[1]Ashtoreths; but now deliver us
from the hand of our enemies, and
we will serve You.'
11 "And the LORD sent [1]Jerubbaal,
[2]Bedan, [a]Jephthah, and [b]Samuel,[3]
and delivered you out of the hand
of your enemies on every side; and
you dwelt in safety.
12 "And when you saw that [a]Na-
hash king of the Ammonites came
against you, [b]you said to me, 'No,
but a king shall reign over us,'
when [c]the LORD your God *was*
your king.
13 "Now therefore, [a]here is the
king [b]whom you have chosen *and*
whom you have desired. And take
note, [c]the LORD has set a king over
you.

3 [c]Ex. 23:8 [d]Deut. 16:19
4 [a]Lev. 19:13
5 [a]Acts 23:9; 24:20 [b]Ex. 22:4
6 [a]Mic. 6:4
7 [a]Is. 1:18 [b]Judg. 5:11
8 [a]Gen. 46:5, 6 [b]Ex. 2:23–25 [c]Ex. 3:10; 4:14–16 [1]So with MT, Tg., Vg.; LXX adds *and the Egyptians afflicted them*
9 [a]Judg. 3:7 [b]Judg. 4:2 [c]Judg. 3:31; 10:7; 13:1 [d]Judg. 3:12–30
10 [a]Judg. 10:10 [b]Judg. 2:13; 3:7 [1]Images of Canaanite goddesses
11 [a]Judg. 11:1 [b]1 Sam. 7:13 [1]Gideon, cf. Judg. 6:25–32; Syr. *Deborah;* Tg. *Gideon* [2]LXX, Syr. *Barak;* Tg. *Simson* [3]Syr. *Simson*
12 [a]1 Sam. 11:1, 2 [b]1 Sam. 8:5, 19, 20 [c]Judg. 8:23
13 [a]1 Sam. 10:24 [b]1 Sam. 8:5; 12:17, 19 [c]Hos. 13:11
14 [a]Josh. 24:14
15 [a]Deut. 28:15 [b]Is. 1:20
16 [a]Ex. 14:13, 31
17 [a]Gen. 30:14 [b][James 5:16–18] [c]Ezra 10:9 [d]1 Sam. 8:7
18 [a]Ex. 14:31
19 [a]Ex. 9:28
20 [a]Deut. 11:16
21 [a]2 Chr. 25:15 [b]Is. 41:29
22 [a]Deut. 31:6 [b]Is. 43:21 [c]Jer. 14:21 [d]Deut. 7:6–11
23 [a]Rom. 1:9 [b]Ps. 34:11 [c]1 Kin. 8:36
24 [a]Eccl. 12:13 [b]Is. 5:12 [c]Deut. 10:21
25 [a]Josh. 24:20 [b]Deut. 28:36

14 "If you [a]fear the LORD and
serve Him and obey His voice, and
do not rebel against the command-
ment of the LORD, then both you
and the king who reigns over you
will continue following the LORD
your God.
15 "However, if you do [a]not obey
the voice of the LORD, but [b]rebel
against the commandment of the
LORD, then the hand of the LORD
will be against you, as *it was*
against your fathers.
16 "Now therefore, [a]stand and see
this great thing which the LORD
will do before your eyes:
17 "*Is* today not the [a]wheat har-
vest? [b]I will call to the LORD, and
He will send thunder and [c]rain,
that you may perceive and see that
[d]your wickedness *is* great, which
you have done in the sight of the
LORD, in asking a king for your-
selves."
18 So Samuel called to the LORD,
and the LORD sent thunder and
rain that day; and [a]all the people
greatly feared the LORD and Sam-
uel.
19 And all the people said to Sam-
uel, [a]"Pray for your servants to the
LORD your God, that we may not
die; for we have added to all our
sins the evil of asking a king for
ourselves."
20 Then Samuel said to the peo-
ple, "Do not fear. You have done
all this wickedness; [a]yet do not
turn aside from following the
LORD, but serve the LORD with all
your heart.
21 "And [a]do not turn aside; [b]for
then you would go after empty
things which cannot profit or de-
liver, for they *are* nothing.
22 "For [a]the LORD will not forsake
[b]His people, [c]for His great name's
sake, because [d]it has pleased the
LORD to make you His people.
23 "Moreover, as for me, far be it
from me that I should sin against
the LORD [a]in ceasing to pray for
you; but [b]I will teach you the [c]good
and the right way.
24 [a]"Only fear the LORD, and serve
Him in truth with all your heart;
for [b]consider what [c]great things
He has done for you.
25 "But if you still do wickedly,
[a]you shall be swept away, [b]both
you and your king."

Saul's Unlawful Sacrifice

13 Saul [1]reigned one year; and
when he had reigned two
years over Israel,
2 Saul chose for himself three
thousand *men* of Israel. Two thou-
sand were with Saul in [a]Michmash
and in the mountains of Bethel,
and a thousand were with [b]Jona-
than in [c]Gibeah of Benjamin. The
rest of the people he sent away,
every man to his tent.
3 And Jonathan attacked [a]the
garrison of the Philistines that *was*
in [b]Geba, and the Philistines heard
of it. Then Saul blew the trumpet
throughout all the land, saying,
"Let the Hebrews hear!"
4 Now all Israel heard it said
that Saul had attacked a garrison
of the Philistines, and *that* Israel
had also become [1]an abomination
to the Philistines. And the people
were called together to Saul at Gil-
gal.
5 Then the Philistines gathered
together to fight with Israel, [1]thirty
thousand chariots and six thou-
sand horsemen, and people [a]as the
sand which *is* on the seashore in
multitude. And they came up and
encamped in Michmash, to the
east of [b]Beth Aven.
6 When the men of Israel saw
that they were in danger (for the
people were distressed), then the
people [a]hid in caves, in thickets,
in rocks, in holes, and in pits.
7 And *some of* the Hebrews
crossed over the Jordan to the
[a]land of Gad and Gilead. As for
Saul, he *was* still in Gilgal, and all
the people followed him trembling.
8 [a]Then he waited seven days,
according to the time set by Sam-
uel. But Samuel did not come to
Gilgal; and the people were scat-
tered from him.
9 So Saul said, "Bring a burnt of-
fering and peace offerings here to
me." And he offered the burnt of-
fering.
10 Now it happened, as soon as he
had finished presenting the burnt
offering, that Samuel came; and
Saul went out to meet him, that he
might [1]greet him.
11 And Samuel said, "What have
you done?" Saul said, "When I
saw that the people were scattered
from me, and *that* you did not
come within the days appointed,
and *that* the Philistines gathered
together at Michmash,
12 "then I said, 'The Philistines
will now come down on me at Gil-
gal, and I have not made supplica-
tion to the LORD.' Therefore I felt
compelled, and offered a burnt of-
fering."
13 And Samuel said to Saul,
[a]"You have done foolishly. [b]You
have not kept the commandment
of the LORD your God, which He
commanded you. For now the
LORD would have established your
kingdom over Israel forever.
14 [a]"But now your kingdom shall
not continue. [b]The LORD has
sought for Himself a man [c]after
His own heart, and the LORD has
commanded him *to be* commander
over His people, because you have
[d]not kept what the LORD com-
manded you."
15 Then Samuel arose and went
up from Gilgal to Gibeah of [1]Ben-
jamin. And Saul numbered the
people present with him, [a]about
six hundred men.

No Weapons for the Army

16 Saul, Jonathan his son, and the
people present with them re-
mained in [1]Gibeah of Benjamin.
But the Philistines encamped in
Michmash.
17 Then raiders came out of the
camp of the Philistines in three
companies. One company turned
onto the road to [a]Ophrah, to the
land of Shual,
18 another company turned to the
road *to* [a]Beth Horon, and another
company turned to the road of the
border that overlooks the Valley
of [b]Zeboim toward the wilderness.
19 Now [a]there was no blacksmith
to be found throughout all the land
of Israel, for the Philistines said,
"Lest the Hebrews make swords
or spears."
20 But all the Israelites would go
down to the Philistines to sharpen
each man's plowshare, his mat-
tock, his ax, and his sickle;
21 and the charge for a sharpen-
ing was a [1]pim for the plowshares,
the mattocks, the forks, and the
axes, and to set the points of the
goads.

CHAPTER 13
1 [1]Heb. is difficult; cf. 2 Sam. 5:4; 2 Kin. 14:2; see also 2 Sam. 2:10; Acts 13:21
2 [a]1 Sam. 14:5, 31 [b]1 Sam. 14:1 [c]1 Sam. 10:26
3 [a]1 Sam. 10:5 [b]2 Sam. 5:25
4 [1]*odious*
5 [a]Judg. 7:12 [b]Josh. 7:2; 1 Sam. 14:23 [1]So with MT, LXX, Tg., Vg.; Syr. and some mss. of LXX *three thousand*
6 [a]Judg. 6:2; 1 Sam. 14:11
7 [a]Num. 32:1–42
8 [a]1 Sam. 10:8
10 [1]Lit. *bless him*
13 [a]2 Chr. 16:9 [b]1 Sam. 15:11, 22, 28
14 [a]1 Sam. 15:28; 31:6 [b]1 Sam. 16:1 [c]Ps. 89:20; Acts 7:46; 13:22 [d]1 Sam. 15:11, 19
15 [a]1 Sam. 13:2, 6, 7; 14:2 [1]So with MT, Tg.; LXX, Vg. add *And the rest of the people went up after Saul to meet the people who fought against them, going from Gilgal to Gibeah in the hill of Benjamin.*
16 [1]Heb. *Geba*
17 [a]Josh. 18:23
18 [a]Josh. 16:3; 18:13, 14 [b]Gen. 14:2; Neh. 11:34
19 [a]Judg. 5:8; 2 Kin. 24:14; Jer. 24:1; 29:2
21 [1]About two-thirds shekel weight

22 So it came about, on the day
of battle, that [a]there was neither
sword nor spear found in the hand
of any of the people who *were* with
Saul and Jonathan. But they were
found with Saul and Jonathan his
son.
23 [a]And the garrison of the Philis-
tines went out to the pass of Mich-
mash.

Jonathan Defeats the Philistines

14 Now it happened one day
that Jonathan the son of
Saul said to the young man who
[1]bore his armor, "Come, let us go
over to the Philistines' garrison
that *is* on the other side." But he
did not tell his father.
2 And Saul was sitting in the out-
skirts of [a]Gibeah under a pome-
granate tree which *is* in Migron.
The people who *were* with him
were about six hundred men.
3 [a]Ahijah the son of Ahitub, [b]Ich-
abod's brother, the son of Phin-
ehas, the son of Eli, the LORD's
priest in Shiloh, was [c]wearing an
ephod. But the people did not
know that Jonathan had gone.
4 Between the passes, by which
Jonathan sought to go over [a]to the
Philistines' garrison, *there was* a
sharp rock on one side and a sharp
rock on the other side. And the
name of one *was* Bozez, and the
name of the other Seneh.
5 The front of one faced north-
ward opposite Michmash, and the
other southward opposite Gibeah.
6 Then Jonathan said to the
young man who bore his armor,
"Come, let us go over to the garri-
son of these [a]uncircumcised; it
may be that the LORD will work for
us. For nothing restrains the LORD
[b]from saving by many or by few."
7 So his armorbearer said to him,
"Do all that is in your heart. Go
then; here I am with you, accord-
ing to your heart."
8 Then Jonathan said, "Very
well, let us cross over to *these*
men, and we will show ourselves
to them.
9 "If they say thus to us, 'Wait
until we come to you,' then we will
stand still in our place and not go
up to them.
10 "But if they say thus, 'Come up
to us,' then we will go up. For the
LORD has delivered them into our
hand, and [a]this *will be* a sign to
us."
11 So both of them showed them-
selves to the garrison of the Philis-
tines. And the Philistines said,
"Look, the Hebrews are coming
out of the holes where they have
[a]hidden."
12 Then the men of the garrison
called to Jonathan and his armor-
bearer, and said, "Come up to us,
and we will [1]show you some-
thing." Jonathan said to his armor-
bearer, "Come up after me, for the
LORD has delivered them into the
hand of Israel."
13 And Jonathan climbed up on
his hands and knees with his
armorbearer after him; and they
[a]fell before Jonathan. And as he
came after him, his armorbearer
killed them.
14 That first slaughter which Jon-
athan and his armorbearer made
was about twenty men within
about [1]half an acre of land.
15 And [a]there was [1]trembling in
the camp, in the field, and among
all the people. The garrison and
[b]the raiders also trembled; and the
earth quaked, so that it was [c]a very
great trembling.
16 Now the watchmen of Saul in
Gibeah of Benjamin looked, and
there was the multitude, melting
away; and they [a]went here and
there.
17 Then Saul said to the people
who *were* with him, "Now call the
roll and see who has gone from
us." And when they had called the
roll, surprisingly, Jonathan and
his armorbearer *were* not *there*.
18 And Saul said to Ahijah,
"Bring the [1]ark of God here" (for
at that time the [1]ark of God was
with the children of Israel).
19 Now it happened, while Saul
[a]talked to the priest, that the noise
which *was* in the camp of the Phi-
listines continued to increase; so
Saul said to the priest, "Withdraw
your hand."
20 Then Saul and all the people
who *were* with him assembled,
and they went to the battle; and
indeed [a]every man's sword was
against his neighbor, *and there
was* very great confusion.
21 Moreover the Hebrews *who*

22 [a]Judg. 5:8
23 [a]1 Sam. 14:1, 4

CHAPTER 14

1 [1]*carried*
2 [a]1 Sam. 13:15, 16
3 [a]1 Sam. 22:9, 11, 20 [b]1 Sam. 4:21 [c]1 Sam. 2:28
4 [a]1 Sam. 13:23
6 [a]1 Sam. 17:26, 36; Jer. 9:25, 26 [b]Judg. 7:4, 7; 1 Sam. 17:46, 47; 2 Chr. 14:11; [Ps. 115:3; 135:6; Zech. 4:6; Matt. 19:26; Rom. 8:31]
10 [a]Gen. 24:14; Judg. 6:36–40
11 [a]1 Sam. 13:6; 14:22
12 [1]*teach*
13 [a]Lev. 26:8; Josh. 23:10
14 [1]Lit. *half the area plowed by a yoke* of oxen in a day
15 [a]Deut. 28:7; 2 Kin. 7:6, 7; Job 18:11 [b]1 Sam. 13:17 [c]Gen. 35:5 [1]*terror*
16 [a]1 Sam. 14:20
18 [1]So with MT, Tg., Vg.; LXX *ephod*
19 [a]Num. 27:21
20 [a]Judg. 7:22; 2 Chr. 20:23

were with the Philistines before that time, who went up with them into the camp *from the* surrounding *country,* they also joined the Israelites who *were* with Saul and Jonathan.

22 Likewise all the men of Israel who [a]had hidden in the mountains of Ephraim, *when* they heard that the Philistines fled, they also followed hard after them in the battle.

23 [a]So the LORD saved Israel that day, and the battle shifted [b]to Beth Aven.

Saul's Rash Oath

24 And the men of Israel were distressed that day, for Saul had [a]placed the people under oath, saying, "Cursed *is* the man who eats *any* food until evening, before I have taken vengeance on my enemies." So none of the people tasted food.

25 [a]Now all *the people* of the land came to a forest; and there was [b]honey on the ground.

26 And when the people had come into the woods, there was the honey, dripping; but no one put his hand to his mouth, for the people feared the oath.

27 But Jonathan had not heard his father charge the people with the oath; therefore he stretched out the end of the rod that *was* in his hand and dipped it in a honeycomb, and put his hand to his mouth; and his [1]countenance brightened.

28 Then one of the people said, "Your father strictly charged the people with an oath, saying, 'Cursed *is* the man who eats food this day.'" And the people were faint.

29 But Jonathan said, "My father has troubled the land. Look now, how my countenance has brightened because I tasted a little of this honey.

30 "How much better if the people had eaten freely today of the spoil of their enemies which they found! For now would there not have been a much greater slaughter among the Philistines?"

31 Now they had [1]driven back the Philistines that day from Michmash to Aijalon. So the people were very faint.

32 And the people rushed on the [1]spoil, and took sheep, oxen, and calves, and slaughtered *them* on the ground; and the people ate *them* [a]with the blood.

33 Then they told Saul, saying, "Look, the people are sinning against the LORD by eating with the blood!" So he said, "You have dealt treacherously; roll a large stone to me this day."

34 Then Saul said, "Disperse yourselves among the people, and say to them, 'Bring me here every man's ox and every man's sheep, slaughter *them* here, and eat; and do not sin against the LORD by eating with the blood.'" So every one of the people brought his ox with him that night, and slaughtered *it* there.

35 Then Saul [a]built an altar to the LORD. This was the first altar that he built to the LORD.

36 Now Saul said, "Let us go down after the Philistines by night, and plunder them until the morning light; and let us not leave a man of them." And they said, "Do whatever seems good to you." Then the priest said, "Let us draw near to God here."

37 So Saul [a]asked counsel of God, "Shall I go down after the Philistines? Will You deliver them into the hand of Israel?" But [b]He did not answer him that day.

38 And Saul said, [a]"Come over here, all you chiefs of the people, and know and see what this sin was today.

39 "For [a]*as* the LORD lives, who saves Israel, though it be in Jonathan my son, he shall surely die." But not a man among all the people answered him.

40 Then he said to all Israel, "You be on one side, and my son Jonathan and I will be on the other side." And the people said to Saul, "Do what seems good to you."

41 Therefore Saul said to the LORD God of Israel, [a]"Give[1] a perfect *lot.*" [b]So Saul and Jonathan were taken, but the people escaped.

42 And Saul said, "Cast *lots* between my son Jonathan and me." So Jonathan was taken.

43 Then Saul said to Jonathan,

22 [a]1 Sam. 13:6
23 [a]Ex. 14:30; 2 Chr. 32:22; Hos. 1:7 [b]1 Sam. 13:5
24 [a]Josh. 6:26
25 [a]Deut. 9:28; Matt. 3:5 [b]Ex. 3:8; Num. 13:27; Matt. 3:4
27 [1]Lit. *eyes*
31 [1]Lit. *struck*
32 [a]Gen. 9:4; Lev. 3:17; 17:10–14; 19:26; Deut. 12:16, 23, 24; Acts 15:20 [1]*plunder*
35 [a]1 Sam. 7:12, 17; 2 Sam. 24:25
37 [a]Judg. 20:18 [b]1 Sam. 28:6
38 [a]Josh. 7:14; 1 Sam. 10:19
39 [a]1 Sam. 14:24, 44; 2 Sam. 12:5
41 [a]Prov. 16:33; Acts 1:24–26 [b]Josh. 7:16; 1 Sam. 10:20, 21 [1]So with MT, Tg.; LXX, Vg. *Why do You not answer Your servant today? If the injustice is with me or Jonathan my son, O LORD God of Israel, give proof; and if You say it is with Your people Israel, give holiness.*

[a]"Tell me what you have done."
And Jonathan told him, and said,
[b]"I only tasted a little honey with
the end of the rod that *was* in my
hand. So now I must die!"
44 Saul answered, [a]"God do so
and more also; [b]for you shall
surely die, Jonathan."
45 But the people said to Saul,
"Shall Jonathan die, who has ac-
complished this great deliverance
in Israel? Certainly not! [a]*As* the
LORD lives, not one hair of his head
shall fall to the ground, for he has
worked [b]with God this day." So
the people rescued Jonathan, and
he did not die.
46 Then Saul returned from pur-
suing the Philistines, and the Phi-
listines went to their own place.

Saul's Continuing Wars

47 So Saul established his sover-
eignty over Israel, and fought
against all his enemies on every
side, against Moab, against the
people of [a]Ammon, against Edom,
against the kings of [b]Zobah, and
against the Philistines. Wherever
he turned, he [1]harassed *them.*
48 And he gathered an army and
[a]attacked[1] the Amalekites, and de-
livered Israel from the hands of
those who plundered them.
49 [a]The sons of Saul were Jona-
than, [1]Jishui, and Malchishua.
And the names of his two daugh-
ters *were these:* the name of the
firstborn Merab, and the name of
the younger [b]Michal.
50 The name of Saul's wife *was*
Ahinoam the daughter of Ahim-
aaz. And the name of the com-
mander of his army *was* Abner the
son of Ner, Saul's [a]uncle.
51 [a]Kish *was* the father of Saul,
and Ner the father of Abner *was*
the son of Abiel.
52 Now there was fierce war with
the Philistines all the days of Saul.
And when Saul saw any strong
man or any valiant man, [a]he took
him for himself.

Saul Spares King Agag

15 Samuel also said to Saul,
[a]"The LORD sent me to
anoint you king over His people,
over Israel. Now therefore, heed
the voice of the words of the LORD.
2 "Thus says the LORD of hosts:
'I will punish Amalek *for* what he
did to Israel, [a]how he ambushed
him on the way when he came up
from Egypt.
3 'Now go and [a]attack[1] Amalek,
and [b]utterly destroy all that they
have, and do not spare them. But
kill both man and woman, infant
and nursing child, ox and sheep,
camel and donkey.'"
4 So Saul gathered the people to-
gether and numbered them in Te-
laim, two hundred thousand foot
soldiers and ten thousand men of
Judah.
5 And Saul came to a city of Am-
alek, and lay in wait in the valley.
6 Then Saul said to [a]the Kenites,
[b]"Go, depart, get down from
among the Amalekites, lest I de-
stroy you with them. For [c]you
showed kindness to all the chil-
dren of Israel when they came up
out of Egypt." So the Kenites de-
parted from among the Amalek-
ites.
7 [a]And Saul attacked the Ama-
lekites, from [b]Havilah all the way
to [c]Shur, which is east of Egypt.
8 [a]He also took Agag king of the
Amalekites alive, and [b]utterly de-
stroyed all the people with the
edge of the sword.
9 But Saul and the people
[a]spared Agag and the best of the
sheep, the oxen, the fatlings, the
lambs, and all *that was* good, and
were unwilling to utterly destroy
them. But everything despised and
worthless, that they utterly de-
stroyed.

Saul Rejected as King

10 Now the word of the LORD
came to Samuel, saying,
11 [a]"I greatly regret that I have set
up Saul *as* king, for he has [b]turned
back from following Me, [c]and has
not performed My command-
ments." And it [d]grieved Samuel,
and he cried out to the LORD all
night.
12 So when Samuel rose early in
the morning to meet Saul, it was
told Samuel, saying, "Saul went to
[a]Carmel, and indeed, he set up a
monument for himself; and he has
gone on around, passed by, and
gone down to Gilgal."
13 Then Samuel went to Saul, and
Saul said to him, [a]"Blessed *are* you

43 [a]Josh. 7:19 [b]1 Sam. 14:27
44 [a]Ruth 1:17 [b]1 Sam. 14:39
45 [a]1 Kin. 1:52 [b][2 Cor. 6:1]
47 [a]1 Sam. 11:1–13 [b]2 Sam. 10:6 [1]LXX, Vg. *prospered*
48 [a]1 Sam. 15:3–7 [1]Lit. *struck*
49 [a]1 Sam. 31:2 [b]1 Sam. 18:17–20, 27; 19:12 [1]*Abinadab,* 1 Chr. 8:33; 9:39
50 [a]1 Sam. 10:14
51 [a]1 Sam. 9:1, 21
52 [a]1 Sam. 8:11

CHAPTER 15

1 [a]1 Sam. 9:16; 10:1
2 [a]Deut. 25:17–19
3 [a]Deut. 25:19 [b]Num. 24:20 [1]Lit. *strike*
6 [a]Num. 24:21 [b]Gen. 18:25; 19:12, 14 [c]Ex. 18:10, 19
7 [a]1 Sam. 14:48 [b]Gen. 2:11; 25:17, 18 [c]Gen. 16:7
8 [a]1 Sam. 15:32, 33 [b]1 Sam. 27:8, 9
9 [a]1 Sam. 15:3, 15, 19
11 [a]Gen. 6:6, 7 [b]1 Kin. 9:6 [c]1 Sam. 13:13; 15:3, 9 [d]1 Sam. 15:35; 16:1
12 [a]Josh. 15:55
13 [a]Judg. 17:2

of the LORD! I have performed the
commandment of the LORD."
14 But Samuel said, "What then
is this bleating of the sheep in my
ears, and the lowing of the oxen
which I hear?"
15 And Saul said, "They have
brought them from the Amalek-
ites; [a]for the people spared the best
of the sheep and the oxen, to sacri-
fice to the LORD your God; and the
rest we have utterly destroyed."
16 Then Samuel said to Saul, "Be
quiet! And I will tell you what the
LORD said to me last night." And
he said to him, "Speak on."
17 So Samuel said, [a]"When you
were little in your own eyes, *were*
you not head of the tribes of Israel?
And did not the LORD anoint you
king over Israel?
18 "Now the LORD sent you on a
mission, and said, 'Go, and utterly
destroy the sinners, the Amalek-
ites, and fight against them until
they are [1]consumed.'
19 "Why then did you not obey
the voice of the LORD? Why did
you swoop down on the [1]spoil, and
do evil in the sight of the LORD?"
20 And Saul said to Samuel, [a]"But
I have obeyed the voice of the
LORD, and gone on the mission on
which the LORD sent me, and
brought back Agag king of Ama-
lek; I have utterly destroyed the
Amalekites.
21 [a]"But the people took of the
plunder, sheep and oxen, the best
of the things which should have
been utterly destroyed, to sacrifice
to the LORD your God in Gilgal."
22 So Samuel said:

[a]"Has the LORD *as great* delight in
  burnt offerings and sacrifices,
As in obeying the voice of the
  LORD?
Behold, [b]to obey is better than
  sacrifice,
And to heed than the fat of rams.
23 For rebellion *is as* the sin of
  [1]witchcraft,
And stubbornness *is as* iniquity
  and idolatry.
Because you have rejected the
  word of the LORD,
[a]He also has rejected you from
  being king."

24 [a]Then Saul said to Samuel, "I
have sinned, for I have trans-
gressed the commandment of the
LORD and your words, because I
[b]feared the people and obeyed
their voice.
25 "Now therefore, please pardon
my sin, and return with me, that I
may worship the LORD."
26 But Samuel said to Saul, "I will
not return with you, [a]for you have
rejected the word of the LORD, and
the LORD has rejected you from be-
ing king over Israel."
27 And as Samuel turned around
to go away, [a]*Saul* seized the edge
of his robe, and it tore.
28 So Samuel said to him, [a]"The
LORD has torn the kingdom of Is-
rael from you today, and has given
it to a neighbor of yours, *who is*
better than you.
29 "And also the Strength of Is-
rael [a]will not lie nor relent. For He
is not a man, that He should re-
lent."
30 Then he said, "I have sinned;
yet [a]honor me now, please, before
the elders of my people and before
Israel, and return with me, that I
may worship the LORD your God."
31 So Samuel turned back after
Saul, and Saul worshiped the
LORD.
32 Then Samuel said, "Bring
Agag king of the Amalekites here
to me." So Agag came to him cau-
tiously. And Agag said, "Surely
the bitterness of death is past."
33 But Samuel said, [a]"As your
sword has made women childless,
so shall your mother be childless
among women." And Samuel
hacked Agag in pieces before the
LORD in Gilgal.
34 Then Samuel went to [a]Ramah,
and Saul went up to his house at
[b]Gibeah of Saul.
35 And [a]Samuel went no more to
see Saul until the day of his death.
Nevertheless Samuel mourned for
Saul, and the LORD regretted
that He had made Saul king over
Israel.

David Anointed King

16 Now the LORD said to Sam-
uel, [a]"How long will you
mourn for Saul, seeing I have re-
jected him from reigning over Is-
rael? [b]Fill your horn with oil, and
go; I am sending you to [c]Jesse the
Bethlehemite. For [d]I have [1]pro-

15 [a][Gen. 3:12, 13; Ex. 32:22, 23]; 1 Sam. 15:9, 21; [Prov. 28:13]
17 [a]1 Sam. 9:21; 10:22
18 [1]*exterminated*
19 [1]*plunder*
20 [a]1 Sam. 15:13; [Prov. 28:13]
21 [a]1 Sam. 15:15
22 [a]Ps. 50:8, 9; 51:16, 17; [Prov. 21:3; Is. 1:11–17; Jer. 7:22, 23; Mic. 6:6–8; Heb. 10:4–10] [b][Eccl. 5:1; Hos. 6:6; Matt. 5:24; 9:13; 12:7; Mark 12:33]
23 [a]1 Sam. 13:14; 16:1 [1]*divination*
24 [a]Num. 22:34; Josh. 7:20; 1 Sam. 26:21; 2 Sam. 12:13; Ps. 51:4 [b][Ex. 23:2; Prov. 29:25; Is. 51:12, 13]
26 [a]1 Sam. 2:30
27 [a]1 Kin. 11:30, 31
28 [a]1 Sam. 28:17, 18; 1 Kin. 11:31
29 [a]Num. 23:19; Ezek. 24:14; 2 Tim. 2:13; Titus 1:2
30 [a][John 5:44; 12:43]
33 [a][Gen. 9:6]; Num. 14:45; Judg. 1:7; [Matt. 7:2]
34 [a]1 Sam. 7:17 [b]1 Sam. 11:4
35 [a]1 Sam. 19:24

CHAPTER 16

1 [a]1 Sam. 15:23, 35 [b]1 Sam. 9:16; 10:1; 2 Kin. 9:1 [c]Ruth 4:18–22 [d]Ps. 78:70, 71; Acts 13:22 [1]Lit. *seen*

vided Myself a king among his
sons."
2 And Samuel said, "How can I
go? If Saul hears *it*, he will kill
me." But the LORD said, "Take a
heifer with you, and say, [a]'I have
come to sacrifice to the LORD.'
3 "Then invite Jesse to the sacri-
fice, and I will show you what you
shall do; you shall anoint for Me
the one I name to you."
4 So Samuel did what the LORD
said, and went to Bethlehem. And
the elders of the town [a]trembled
at his coming, and said, [b]"Do you
come peaceably?"
5 And he said, "Peaceably; I
have come to sacrifice to the LORD.
[a]Sanctify[1] yourselves, and come
with me to the sacrifice." Then he
consecrated Jesse and his sons,
and invited them to the sacrifice.
6 So it was, when they came, that
he looked at [a]Eliab and [b]said,
"Surely the LORD's anointed *is* be-
fore Him!"
7 But the LORD said to Samuel,
[a]"Do not look at his appearance
or at his physical stature, because
I have [1]refused him. [b]For[2] *the* LORD
does not *see* as man sees; for man
[c]looks at the outward appearance,
but the LORD looks at the [d]heart."
8 So Jesse called Abinadab, and
made him pass before Samuel.
And he said, "Neither has the
LORD chosen this one."
9 Then Jesse made Shammah
pass by. And he said, "Neither has
the LORD chosen this one."
10 Thus Jesse made seven of his
sons pass before Samuel. And
Samuel said to Jesse, "The LORD
has not chosen these."
11 And Samuel said to Jesse, "Are
all the young men here?" Then he
said, "There remains yet the
youngest, and there he is, keeping
the [a]sheep." And Samuel said to
Jesse, "Send and bring him. For
we will not [1]sit down till he comes
here."
12 So he sent and brought him in.
Now he *was* [a]ruddy, [b]with [1]bright
eyes, and good-looking. [c]And the
LORD said, "Arise, anoint him; for
this *is* the one!"
13 Then Samuel took the horn of
oil and anointed him in the midst
of his brothers; and [a]the Spirit of
the LORD came upon David from
that day forward. So Samuel arose
and went to Ramah.

A Distressing Spirit Troubles Saul

14 [a]But the Spirit of the LORD de-
parted from Saul, and [b]a distress-
ing spirit from the LORD troubled
him.
15 And Saul's servants said to
him, "Surely, a distressing spirit
from God is troubling you.
16 "Let our master now command
your servants, *who are* before you,
to seek out a man *who is* a skillful
player on the harp. And it shall be
that he will [a]play it with his hand
when the [1]distressing spirit from
God is upon you, and you shall be
well."
17 So Saul said to his servants,
[1]"Provide me now a man who can
play well, and bring *him* to me."
18 Then one of the servants an-
swered and said, "Look, I have
seen a son of Jesse the Bethlehem-
ite, *who is* skillful in playing, a
mighty man of valor, a man of war,
prudent in speech, and a hand-
some person; and [a]the LORD *is* with
him."
19 Therefore Saul sent messen-
gers to Jesse, and said, "Send me
your son David, who *is* with the
sheep."
20 And Jesse [a]took a donkey
loaded with bread, a skin of wine,
and a young goat, and sent *them*
by his son David to Saul.
21 So David came to Saul and
[a]stood before him. And he loved
him greatly, and he became his
armorbearer.
22 Then Saul sent to Jesse, saying,
"Please let David stand before me,
for he has found favor in my
sight."
23 And so it was, whenever the
spirit from God was upon Saul,
that David would take a harp and
play *it* with his hand. Then Saul
would become refreshed and well,
and the distressing spirit would
depart from him.

David and Goliath

17 Now the Philistines gath-
ered their armies together to
battle, and were gathered at [a]So-
choh, which *belongs* to Judah; they
encamped between Sochoh and
Azekah, in Ephes Dammim.

---

2 [a]1 Sam. 9:12
4 [a]1 Sam. 21:1 [b]1 Kin. 2:13; 2 Kin. 9:22
5 [a]Gen. 35:2; Ex. 19:10 [1]*Consecrate*
6 [a]1 Sam. 17:13, 28 [b]1 Kin. 12:26
7 [a]Ps. 147:10 [b]Is. 55:8, 9 [c]2 Cor. 10:7 [d]1 Kin. 8:39 [1]*rejected* [2]LXX *For God does not see as man sees;* Tg. *It is not by the appearance of a man;* Vg. *Nor do I judge according to the looks of a man*
11 [a]2 Sam. 7:8; Ps. 78:70–72 [1]So with LXX, Vg.; MT *turn around;* Tg., Syr. *turn away*
12 [a]1 Sam. 17:42 [b]Gen. 39:6; Ex. 2:2; Acts 7:20 [c]1 Sam. 9:17 [1]Lit. *beautiful*
13 [a]Num. 27:18; 1 Sam. 10:6, 9, 10
14 [a]Judg. 16:20; 1 Sam. 11:6; 18:12; 28:15 [b]Judg. 9:23; 1 Sam. 16:15, 16; 18:10; 19:9; 1 Kin. 22:19–22
16 [a]1 Sam. 18:10; 19:9; 2 Kin. 3:15 [1]Lit. *evil*
17 [1]Lit. *Look now for a man for me*
18 [a]1 Sam. 3:19; 18:12, 14
20 [a]1 Sam. 10:4, 27; Prov. 18:16
21 [a]Gen. 41:46; Prov. 22:29

CHAPTER 17

1 [a]Josh. 15:35; 2 Chr. 28:18

2 And Saul and the men of Israel were gathered together, and they encamped in the Valley of Elah, and drew up in battle array against the Philistines.
3 The Philistines stood on a mountain on one side, and Israel stood on a mountain on the other side, with a valley between them.
4 And a champion went out from the camp of the Philistines, named [a]Goliath, from [b]Gath, whose height *was* six cubits and a span.
5 *He had* a bronze helmet on his head, and he *was* [1]armed with a coat of mail, and the weight of the coat *was* five thousand shekels of bronze.
6 And *he had* bronze armor on his legs and a bronze javelin between his shoulders.
7 Now the staff of his spear *was* like a weaver's beam, and his iron spearhead *weighed* six hundred shekels; and a shield-bearer went before him.
8 Then he stood and cried out to the armies of Israel, and said to them, "Why have you come out to line up for battle? *Am* I not a Philistine, and you the [a]servants of Saul? Choose a man for yourselves, and let him come down to me.
9 "If he is able to fight with me and kill me, then we will be your servants. But if I prevail against him and kill him, then you shall be our servants and [a]serve us."
10 And the Philistine said, "I [a]defy the armies of Israel this day; give me a man, that we may fight together."
11 When Saul and all Israel heard these words of the Philistine, they were dismayed and greatly afraid.
12 Now David *was* [a]the son of that [b]Ephrathite of Bethlehem Judah, whose name *was* Jesse, and who had [c]eight sons. And the man was old, advanced *in years*, in the days of Saul.
13 The three oldest sons of Jesse had gone to follow Saul to the battle. The [a]names of his three sons who went to the battle *were* Eliab the firstborn, next to him Abinadab, and the third Shammah.
14 David *was* the youngest. And the three oldest followed Saul.
15 But David occasionally went and returned from Saul [a]to feed his father's sheep at Bethlehem.
16 And the Philistine drew near and presented himself forty days, morning and evening.
17 Then Jesse said to his son David, "Take now for your brothers an ephah of this dried *grain* and these ten loaves, and run to your brothers at the camp.
18 "And carry these ten cheeses to the captain of *their* thousand, and [a]see how your brothers fare, and bring back news of them."
19 Now Saul and they and all the men of Israel *were* in the Valley of Elah, fighting with the Philistines.
20 So David rose early in the morning, left the sheep with a keeper, and took *the things* and went as Jesse had commanded him. And he came to the camp as the army was going out to the fight and shouting for the battle.
21 For Israel and the Philistines had drawn up in battle array, army against army.
22 And David left his supplies in the hand of the supply keeper, ran to the army, and came and greeted his brothers.
23 Then as he talked with them, there was the champion, the Philistine of Gath, Goliath by name, coming up from the armies of the Philistines; and he spoke [a]according to the same words. So David heard *them*.
24 And all the men of Israel, when they saw the man, fled from him and were dreadfully afraid.
25 So the men of Israel said, "Have you seen this man who has come up? Surely he has come up to defy Israel; and it shall be *that* the man who kills him the king will enrich with great riches, [a]will give him his daughter, and give his father's house exemption *from taxes* in Israel."
26 Then David spoke to the men who stood by him, saying, "What shall be done for the man who kills this Philistine and takes away [a]the reproach from Israel? For who *is* this [b]uncircumcised Philistine, that he should [c]defy the armies of [d]the living God?"
27 And the people answered him in this manner, saying, [a]"So shall

4 [a]2 Sam. 21:19 [b]Josh. 11:21, 22
5 [1]*clothed with scaled body armor*
8 [a]1 Sam. 8:17
9 [a]1 Sam. 11:1
10 [a]1 Sam. 17:26, 36, 45; 2 Sam. 21:21
12 [a]Ruth 4:22; 1 Sam. 16:1, 18; 17:58 [b]Gen. 35:19 [c]1 Sam. 16:10, 11; 1 Chr. 2:13–15
13 [a]1 Sam. 16:6, 8, 9; 1 Chr. 2:13
15 [a]1 Sam. 16:11, 19; 2 Sam. 7:8
18 [a]Gen. 37:13, 14
23 [a]1 Sam. 17:8–10
25 [a]Josh. 15:16
26 [a]1 Sam. 11:2 [b]1 Sam. 14:6; 17:36; Jer. 9:25, 26 [c]1 Sam. 17:10 [d]Deut. 5:26; 2 Kin. 19:4; Jer. 10:10
27 [a]1 Sam. 17:25

it be done for the man who kills
him."
28 Now Eliab his oldest brother
heard when he spoke to the men;
and Eliab's [a]anger was aroused
against David, and he said, "Why
did you come down here? And
with whom have you left those few
sheep in the wilderness? I know
your pride and the insolence of
your heart, for you have come
down to see the battle."
29 And David said, "What have I
done now? [a]*Is*[1] *there* not a cause?"
30 Then he turned from him to-
ward another and [a]said the same
thing; and these people answered
him as the first ones *did*.
31 Now when the words which
David spoke were heard, they re-
ported *them* to Saul; and he sent
for him.
32 Then David said to Saul, [a]"Let
no man's heart fail because of him;
[b]your servant will go and fight
with this Philistine."
33 And Saul said to David, [a]"You
are not able to go against this Phi-
listine to fight with him; for you
are a youth, and he a man of war
from his youth."
34 But David said to Saul, "Your
servant used to keep his father's
sheep, and when a [a]lion or a bear
came and took a lamb out of the
flock,
35 "I went out after it and struck
it, and delivered *the lamb* from its
mouth; and when it arose against
me, I caught *it* by its beard, and
struck and killed it.
36 "Your servant has killed both
lion and bear; and this uncircum-
cised Philistine will be like one of
them, seeing he has defied the ar-
mies of the living God."
37 Moreover David said, [a]"The
LORD, who delivered me from the
paw of the lion and from the paw
of the bear, He will deliver me
from the hand of this Philistine."
And Saul said to David, [b]"Go, and
the LORD be with you!"
38 So Saul clothed David with his
[1]armor, and he put a bronze hel-
met on his head; he also clothed
him with a coat of mail.
39 David fastened his sword to his
armor and tried to walk, for he had
not tested *them*. And David said
to Saul, "I cannot walk with these,
for I have not tested *them*." So Da-
vid took them off.
40 Then he took his staff in his
hand; and he chose for himself five
smooth stones from the brook, and
put them in a shepherd's bag, in
a pouch which he had, and his
sling was in his hand. And he drew
near to the Philistine.
41 So the Philistine came, and be-
gan drawing near to David, and
the man who bore the shield *went*
before him.
42 And when the Philistine looked
about and saw David, he [a]dis-
dained[1] him; for he was *only* a
youth, [b]ruddy and good-looking.
43 So the Philistine [a]said to David,
"*Am* I a dog, that you come to me
with sticks?" And the Philistine
cursed David by his gods.
44 And the Philistine [a]said to
David, "Come to me, and I will
give your flesh to the birds of
the air and the beasts of the
field!"
45 Then David said to the Philis-
tine, "You come to me with a
sword, with a spear, and with a
javelin. [a]But I come to you in the
name of the LORD of hosts, the God
of the armies of Israel, whom you
have [b]defied.
46 "This day the LORD will deliver
you into my hand, and I will strike
you and take your head from you.
And this day I will give [a]the car-
casses of the camp of the Philis-
tines to the birds of the air and the
wild beasts of the earth, [b]that all
the earth may know that there is
a God in Israel.
47 "Then all this assembly shall
know that the LORD [a]does not save
with sword and spear; for [b]the bat-
tle *is* the LORD's, and He will give
you into our hands."
48 So it was, when the Philistine
arose and came and drew near to
meet David, that David hurried
and [a]ran toward the army to meet
the Philistine.
49 Then David put his hand in his
bag and took out a stone; and he
slung *it* and struck the Philistine
in his forehead, so that the stone
sank into his forehead, and he fell
on his face to the earth.
50 So David prevailed over the
Philistine with a [a]sling and a stone,
and struck the Philistine and killed

28 [a]Gen. 37:4, 8–36; [Prov. 18:19; Matt. 10:36]
29 [a]1 Sam. 17:17 [1]Lit. *Is it not a word?* or *matter?*
30 [a]1 Sam. 17:26, 27
32 [a]Deut. 20:1–4 [b]1 Sam. 16:18
33 [a]Num. 13:31; Deut. 9:2
34 [a]Judg. 14:5
37 [a][2 Cor. 1:10; 2 Tim. 4:17, 18] [b]1 Sam. 20:13; 1 Chr. 22:11, 16
38 [1]Lit. *clothes*
42 [a][Ps. 123:4; Prov. 16:18; 1 Cor. 1:27, 28] [b]1 Sam. 16:12 [1]*belittled*
43 [a]1 Sam. 24:14; 2 Sam. 3:8; 9:8; 16:9; 2 Kin. 8:13
44 [a]1 Sam. 17:46; 1 Kin. 20:10, 11
45 [a]2 Sam. 22:33, 35; 2 Chr. 32:8; Ps. 124:8; [2 Cor. 10:4]; Heb. 11:33, 34 [b]1 Sam. 17:10
46 [a]Deut. 28:26 [b]Josh. 4:24; 1 Kin. 8:43; 18:36; 2 Kin. 19:19; Is. 52:10
47 [a]1 Sam. 14:6; 2 Chr. 14:11; 20:15; Ps. 44:6; Hos. 1:7; Zech. 4:6 [b]2 Chr. 20:15
48 [a]Ps. 27:3
50 [a]Judg. 3:31; 15:15; 20:16

him. But *there was* no sword in the
hand of David.
51 Therefore David ran and stood
over the Philistine, took his [a]sword
and drew it out of its sheath and
killed him, and cut off his head
with it. And when the Philistines
saw that their champion was dead,
[b]they fled.
52 Now the men of Israel and Ju-
dah arose and shouted, and pur-
sued the Philistines as far as the
entrance of [1]the valley and to the
gates of Ekron. And the wounded
of the Philistines fell along the
road to [a]Shaaraim, even as far as
Gath and Ekron.
53 Then the children of Israel re-
turned from chasing the Philis-
tines, and they plundered their
tents.
54 And David took the head of the
Philistine and brought it to Jerusa-
lem, but he put his armor in his
tent.
55 When Saul saw David going
out against the Philistine, he said
to [a]Abner, the commander of the
army, "Abner, [b]whose son *is* this
youth?" And Abner said, "As your
soul lives, O king, I do not know."
56 So the king said, "Inquire
whose son this young man *is*."
57 Then, as David returned from
the slaughter of the Philistine, Ab-
ner took him and brought him be-
fore Saul [a]with the head of the
Philistine in his hand.
58 And Saul said to him, "Whose
son *are* you, young man?" So
David answered, [a]"*I am* the son of
your servant Jesse the Beth-
lehemite."

Saul Resents David

18 Now when he had finished
speaking to Saul, [a]the [1]soul
of Jonathan was knit to the soul
of David, [b]and Jonathan loved him
as his own soul.
2 Saul took him that day, [a]and
would not let him go home to his
father's house anymore.
3 Then Jonathan and David
made a [a]covenant, because he
loved him as his own soul.
4 And Jonathan took off the robe
that *was* on him and gave it to Da-
vid, with his armor, even to his
sword and his bow and his belt.
5 So David went out wherever
Saul sent him, *and* [1]behaved
wisely. And Saul set him over the
men of war, and he was accepted
in the sight of all the people and
also in the sight of Saul's servants.
6 Now it had happened as they
were coming *home,* when David
was returning from the slaughter
of the [1]Philistine, that [a]the women
had come out of all the cities of
Israel, singing and dancing, to
meet King Saul, with tambourines,
with joy, and with musical instru-
ments.
7 So the women [a]sang as they
danced, and said:

> [b]"Saul has slain his thousands,
> And David his ten thousands."

8 Then Saul was very angry, and
the saying [a]displeased him; and he
said, "They have ascribed to David
ten thousands, and to me they
have ascribed *only* thousands.
Now *what* more can he have but
[b]the kingdom?"
9 So Saul [1]eyed David from that
day forward.
10 And it happened on the next
day that [a]the distressing spirit
from God came upon Saul, [b]and
he prophesied inside the house. So
David [c]played *music* with his
hand, as at other times; [d]but *there*
was a spear in Saul's hand.
11 And Saul [a]cast the spear, for
he said, "I will pin David to the
wall!" But David escaped his pres-
ence twice.
12 Now Saul was [a]afraid of David,
because [b]the LORD was with him,
but had [c]departed from Saul.
13 Therefore Saul removed him
from [1]his presence, and made him
his captain over a thousand; and
[a]he went out and came in before
the people.
14 And David behaved wisely in
all his ways, and [a]the LORD *was*
with him.
15 Therefore, when Saul saw that
he behaved very wisely, he was
afraid of him.
16 But [a]all Israel and Judah loved
David, because he went out and
came in before them.

David Marries Michal

17 Then Saul said to David, "Here
is my older daughter Merab; [a]I will

51 [a]1 Sam. 21:9; 2 Sam. 23:21 [b]Heb. 11:34
52 [a]Josh. 15:36 [1]So with MT, Syr., Tg., Vg.; LXX *Gath*
55 [a]1 Sam. 14:50 [b]1 Sam. 16:21, 22
57 [a]1 Sam. 17:54
58 [a]1 Sam. 17:12

CHAPTER 18

1 [a]Gen. 44:30 [b]Deut. 13:6; 1 Sam. 20:17; 2 Sam. 1:26 [1]*life of Jonathan was bound up with the life of*
2 [a]1 Sam. 17:15
3 [a]1 Sam. 20:8–17
5 [1]Or *prospered*
6 [a]Ex. 15:20, 21; Judg. 11:34; Ps. 68:25; 149:3 [1]*Philistines*
7 [a]Ex. 15:21 [b]1 Sam. 21:11; 29:5
8 [a]Eccl. 4:4 [b]1 Sam. 15:28
9 [1]Viewed with suspicion
10 [a]1 Sam. 16:14 [b]1 Sam. 19:24; 1 Kin. 18:29; Acts 16:16 [c]1 Sam. 16:23 [d]1 Sam. 19:9, 10
11 [a]1 Sam. 19:10; 20:33
12 [a]1 Sam. 18:15, 29 [b]1 Sam. 16:13, 18 [c]1 Sam. 16:14; 28:15
13 [a]Num. 27:17; 1 Sam. 18:16; 29:6; 2 Sam. 5:2 [1]Lit. *himself*
14 [a]Gen. 39:2, 3, 23; Josh. 6:27; 1 Sam. 16:18
16 [a]Num. 27:16, 17; 1 Sam. 18:5; 2 Sam. 5:2; 1 Kin. 3:7
17 [a]1 Sam. 14:49; 17:25

give her to you as a wife. Only be
valiant for me, and fight [b]the
LORD's battles." For Saul thought,
[c]"Let my hand not be against him,
but let the hand of the Philistines
be against him."
18 So David said to Saul, [a]"Who
am I, and what *is* my life *or* my
father's family in Israel, that I
should be son-in-law to the king?"
19 But it happened at the time
when Merab, Saul's daughter,
should have been given to David,
that she was given to [a]Adriel the
[b]Meholathite as a wife.
20 [a]Now Michal, Saul's daughter,
loved David. And they told Saul,
and the thing pleased him.
21 So Saul said, "I will give her
to him, that she may [1]be a snare
to him, and that [a]the hand of the
Philistines may be against him."
Therefore Saul said to David a sec-
ond time, [b]"You shall be my son-
in-law today."
22 And Saul commanded his ser-
vants, "Communicate with David
secretly, and say, 'Look, the king
has delight in you, and all his ser-
vants love you. Now therefore, be-
come the king's son-in-law.'"
23 So Saul's servants spoke those
words in the hearing of David.
And David said, "Does it seem to
you *a* light *thing* to be a king's son-
in-law, seeing I *am* a poor and
lightly esteemed man?"
24 And the servants of Saul told
him, saying, [1]"In this manner Da-
vid spoke."
25 Then Saul said, "Thus you
shall say to David: 'The king does
not desire any [a]dowry but one
hundred foreskins of the Philis-
tines, to take [b]vengeance on the
king's enemies.'" But Saul
[c]thought to make David fall by the
hand of the Philistines.
26 So when his servants told Da-
vid these words, it pleased David
well to become the king's son-in-
law. Now [a]the days had not ex-
pired;
27 therefore David arose and
went, he and [a]his men, and killed
two hundred men of the Philis-
tines. And [b]David brought their
foreskins, and they gave them in
full count to the king, that he might
become the king's son-in-law.
Then Saul gave him Michal his
daughter as a wife.
28 Thus Saul saw and knew that
the LORD *was* with David, and *that*
Michal, Saul's daughter, loved
him;
29 and Saul was still more afraid
of David. So Saul became David's
enemy [1]continually.
30 Then the princes of the Philis-
tines [a]went out *to war*. And so it
was, whenever they went out, *that*
David [b]behaved more wisely than
all the servants of Saul, so that his
name became highly esteemed.

Saul Persecutes David

19 Now Saul spoke to Jonathan
his son and to all his ser-
vants, that they should kill [a]David;
but Jonathan, Saul's son, [b]de-
lighted greatly in David.
2 So Jonathan told David, say-
ing, "My father Saul seeks to kill
you. Therefore please be on your
guard until morning, and stay in
a secret *place* and hide.
3 "And I will go out and stand
beside my father in the field where
you *are*, and I will speak with my
father about you. Then what I ob-
serve, I will tell [a]you."
4 Thus Jonathan [a]spoke well of
David to Saul his father, and said
to him, "Let not the king [b]sin
against his servant, against David,
because he has not sinned against
you, and because his works *have
been* very good toward you.
5 "For he took his [a]life in his
hands and [b]killed the Philistine,
and [c]the LORD brought about a
great deliverance for all Israel.
You saw *it* and rejoiced. [d]Why
then will you [e]sin against innocent
blood, to kill David without a
cause?"
6 So Saul heeded the voice of
Jonathan, and Saul swore, "*As* the
LORD lives, he shall not be killed."
7 Then Jonathan called David,
and Jonathan told him all these
things. So Jonathan brought David
to Saul, and he was in his presence
[a]as in times past.
8 And there was war again; and
David went out and fought with
the Philistines, [a]and struck them
with a mighty blow, and they fled
from him.

17 [b]Num. 32:20, 27, 29; 1 Sam. 25:28 [c]1 Sam. 18:21, 25; 2 Sam. 12:9
18 [a]1 Sam. 9:21; 18:23; 2 Sam. 7:18
19 [a]2 Sam. 21:8 [b]Judg. 7:22; 2 Sam. 21:8; 1 Kin. 19:16
20 [a]1 Sam. 18:28
21 [a]1 Sam. 18:17 [b]1 Sam. 18:26 [1]*be bait for*
24 [1]Lit. *According to these words*
25 [a]Gen. 34:12; Ex. 22:17 [b]1 Sam. 14:24 [c]1 Sam. 18:17
26 [a]1 Sam. 18:21
27 [a]1 Sam. 18:13 [b]2 Sam. 3:14
29 [1]*all the days*
30 [a]2 Sam. 11:1 [b]1 Sam. 18:5

CHAPTER 19

1 [a]1 Sam. 8:8, 9 [b]1 Sam. 18:1
3 [a]1 Sam. 20:8–13
4 [a]1 Sam. 20:32; [Prov. 31:8, 9] [b]Gen. 42:22; [Prov. 17:13]; Jer. 18:20
5 [a]Judg. 9:17; 12:3 [b]1 Sam. 17:49, 50 [c]1 Sam. 11:13; 1 Chr. 11:14 [d]1 Sam. 20:32 [e][Deut. 19:10–13]
7 [a]1 Sam. 16:21; 18:2, 10, 13
8 [a]1 Sam. 18:27; 23:5

9 Now [a]the distressing spirit
from the LORD came upon Saul as
he sat in his house with his spear
in his hand. And David was play-
ing *music* with *his* hand.
10 Then Saul sought to pin David
to the wall with the spear, but he
slipped away from Saul's pres-
ence; and he drove the spear into
the wall. So David fled and es-
caped that night.
11 [a]Saul also sent messengers to
David's house to watch him and
to kill him in the morning. And Mi-
chal, David's wife, told him, say-
ing, "If you do not save your life
tonight, tomorrow you will be
killed."
12 So Michal [a]let David down
through a window. And he went
and fled and escaped.
13 And Michal took [1]an image and
laid *it* in the bed, put a cover of
goats' *hair* for his head, and cov-
ered *it* with clothes.
14 So when Saul sent messengers
to take David, she said, "He *is*
sick."
15 Then Saul sent the messengers
back to see David, saying, "Bring
him up to me in the bed, that I may
kill him."
16 And when the messengers had
come in, there was the image in
the bed, with a cover of goats' *hair*
for his head.
17 Then Saul said to Michal,
"Why have you deceived me like
this, and sent my enemy away, so
that he has escaped?" And Michal
answered Saul, "He said to me,
'Let me go! [a]Why should I kill
you?' "
18 So David fled and escaped, and
went to [a]Samuel at [b]Ramah, and
told him all that Saul had done to
him. And he and Samuel went and
stayed in Naioth.
19 Now it was told Saul, saying,
"Take note, David *is* at Naioth in
Ramah!"
20 Then [a]Saul sent messengers to
take David. [b]And when they saw
the group of prophets prophesy-
ing, and Samuel standing *as* leader
over them, the Spirit of God came
upon the messengers of Saul, and
they also [c]prophesied.
21 And when Saul was told, he
sent other messengers, and they
prophesied likewise. Then Saul

9 [a]1 Sam. 16:14; 18:10, 11
11 [a]Judg. 16:2; Ps. 59:title
12 [a]Josh. 2:15; Acts 9:25; 2 Cor. 11:33
13 [1]*household idols,* Heb. *teraphim*
17 [a]2 Sam. 2:22
18 [a]1 Sam. 16:13 [b]1 Sam. 7:17
20 [a]1 Sam. 19:11, 14; John 7:32 [b]1 Sam. 10:5, 6, 10; [1 Cor. 14:3, 24, 25] [c]Num. 11:25; Joel 2:28
23 [a]1 Sam. 10:10
24 [a]Is. 20:2 [b]Mic. 1:8 [c]1 Sam. 10:10–12

CHAPTER 20

3 [a]1 Sam. 27:1; 2 Kin. 2:6
5 [a]Num. 10:10; 28:11–15 [b]1 Sam. 19:2, 3
6 [a]1 Sam. 16:4; 17:12; John 7:42
7 [a]Deut. 1:23; 2 Sam. 17:4

sent messengers again the third
time, and they prophesied also.
22 Then he also went to Ramah,
and came to the great well that *is*
at Sechu. So he asked, and said,
"Where *are* Samuel and David?"
And *someone* said, "Indeed *they*
are at Naioth in Ramah."
23 So he went there to Naioth in
Ramah. Then [a]the Spirit of God
was upon him also, and he went
on and prophesied until he came
to Naioth in Ramah.
24 [a]And he also stripped off
his clothes and prophesied be-
fore Samuel in like manner,
and lay down [b]naked all that day
and all that night. Therefore they
say, [c]"*Is* Saul also among the
prophets?"

Jonathan's Loyalty to David

20 Then David fled from Naioth
in Ramah, and went and
said to Jonathan, "What have I
done? What *is* my iniquity, and
what *is* my sin before your father,
that he seeks my life?"
2 So Jonathan said to him, "By
no means! You shall not die! In-
deed, my father will do nothing ei-
ther great or small without first
telling me. And why should my fa-
ther hide this thing from me? It *is*
not *so!*"
3 Then David took an oath again,
and said, "Your father certainly
knows that I have found favor in
your eyes, and he has said, 'Do not
let Jonathan know this, lest he be
grieved.' But [a]truly, *as* the LORD
lives and *as* your soul lives, *there*
is but a step between me and
death."
4 So Jonathan said to David,
"Whatever you yourself desire, I
will do *it* for you."
5 And David said to Jonathan,
"Indeed tomorrow *is* the [a]New
Moon, and I should not fail to sit
with the king to eat. But let me go,
that I may [b]hide in the field until
the third *day* at evening.
6 "If your father misses me at all,
then say, 'David earnestly asked
permission of me that he might run
over [a]to Bethlehem, his city, for
there is a yearly sacrifice there for
all the family.'
7 [a]"If he says thus: '*It is* well,'
your servant will be safe. But if he

is very angry, be sure that [b]evil is
determined by him.
8 "Therefore you shall [a]deal
kindly with your servant, for [b]you
have brought your servant into a
covenant of the LORD with you.
Nevertheless, [c]if there is iniquity
in me, kill me yourself, for why
should you bring me to your fa-
ther?"
9 But Jonathan said, "Far be it
from you! For if I knew certainly
that evil was determined by my fa-
ther to come upon you, then would
I not tell you?"
10 Then David said to Jonathan,
"Who will tell me, or what *if* your
father answers you roughly?"
11 And Jonathan said to David,
"Come, let us go out into the field."
So both of them went out into the
field.
12 Then Jonathan said to David:
"The LORD God of Israel *is wit-*
ness! When I have [1]sounded out
my father sometime tomorrow, *or*
the third *day*, and indeed *there is*
good toward David, and I do not
send to you and tell you,
13 "may [a]the LORD do so and
much more to Jonathan. But if it
pleases my father *to do* you evil,
then I will report it to you and send
you away, that you may go in
safety. And [b]the LORD be with you
as He has [c]been with my father.
14 "And you shall not only show
me the kindness of the LORD while
I still live, that I may not die;
15 "but [a]you shall not [1]cut off your
kindness from my [2]house forever,
no, not when the LORD has cut off
every one of the enemies of David
from the face of the earth."
16 So Jonathan made *a covenant*
with the [1]house of David, *saying,*
[a]"Let the LORD require *it* at the
hand of David's enemies."
17 Now Jonathan again caused
David to vow, because he loved
him; [a]for he loved him as he loved
his own soul.
18 Then Jonathan said to David,
[a]"Tomorrow *is* the New Moon; and
you will be missed, because your
seat will be empty.
19 "And *when* you have stayed
three days, go down quickly and
come to [a]the place where you hid
on the day of the deed; and remain
by the stone Ezel.

7 [b]1 Sam. 25:17; Esth. 7:7
8 [a]Josh. 2:14 [b]1 Sam. 18:3; 20:16; 23:18 [c]2 Sam. 14:32
12 [1]*searched out*
13 [a]Ruth 1:17; 1 Sam. 3:17 [b]Josh. 1:5; 1 Sam. 17:37; 18:12; 1 Chr. 22:11, 16 [c]1 Sam. 10:7
15 [a]1 Sam. 24:21; 2 Sam. 9:1, 3, 7; 21:7 [1]*stop being kind* [2]*family*
16 [a]Deut. 23:21; 1 Sam. 25:22; 31:2; 2 Sam. 4:7; 21:8 [1]*family*
17 [a]1 Sam. 18:1
18 [a]1 Sam. 20:5, 24
19 [a]1 Sam. 19:2
21 [a]Jer. 4:2
23 [a]1 Sam. 20:14, 15
25 [1]So with MT, Syr., Tg., Vg.; LXX *he sat across from Jonathan*
26 [a]Lev. 7:20, 21; 15:5
28 [a]1 Sam. 20:6

20 "Then I will shoot three arrows
to the side, as though I shot at a
target;
21 "and there I will send a lad,
saying, 'Go, find the arrows.' If I
expressly say to the lad, 'Look, the
arrows *are* on this side of you; get
them and come'—then, [a]as the
LORD lives, *there is* safety for you
and no harm.
22 "But if I say thus to the young
man, 'Look, the arrows *are* beyond
you'—go your way, for the LORD
has sent you away.
23 "And as for [a]the matter which
you and I have spoken of, indeed
the LORD *be* between you and me
forever."
24 Then David hid in the field.
And when the New Moon had
come, the king sat down to eat the
feast.
25 Now the king sat on his seat,
as at other times, on a seat by the
wall. And [1]Jonathan arose, and
Abner sat by Saul's side, but Da-
vid's place was empty.
26 Nevertheless Saul did not say
anything that day, for he thought,
"Something has happened to him;
he *is* unclean, surely he *is* [a]un-
clean."
27 And it happened the next day,
the second *day* of the month, that
David's place was empty. And
Saul said to Jonathan his son,
"Why has the son of Jesse not
come to eat, either yesterday or to-
day?"
28 So Jonathan [a]answered Saul,
"David earnestly asked *permis-*
sion of me *to go* to Bethlehem.
29 "And he said, 'Please let me go,
for our family has a sacrifice in the
city, and my brother has com-
manded me *to be there.* And now,
if I have found favor in your eyes,
please let me get away and see my
brothers.' Therefore he has not
come to the king's table."
30 Then Saul's anger was aroused
against Jonathan, and he said to
him, "You son of a perverse, re-
bellious *woman!* Do I not know
that you have chosen the son of
Jesse to your own shame and to
the shame of your mother's naked-
ness?
31 "For as long as the son of Jesse
lives on the earth, you shall not be
established, nor your kingdom.

Now therefore, send and bring him
to me, for he [1]shall surely die."
32 And Jonathan answered Saul
his father, and said to him, [a]"Why
should he be killed? What has he
done?"
33 Then Saul [a]cast a spear at him
to [1]kill him, [b]by which Jonathan
knew that it was determined by his
father to kill David.
34 So Jonathan arose from the ta-
ble in fierce anger, and ate no food
the second day of the month, for
he was grieved for David, because
his father had treated him shame-
fully.
35 And so it was, in the morning,
that Jonathan went out into the
field at the time appointed with
David, and a little lad *was* with
him.
36 Then he said to his lad, "Now
run, find the arrows which I
shoot." As the lad ran, he shot an
arrow beyond him.
37 When the lad had come to the
place where the arrow was which
Jonathan had shot, Jonathan cried
out after the lad and said, "*Is* not
the arrow beyond you?"
38 And Jonathan cried out after
the lad, "Make haste, hurry, do not
delay!" So Jonathan's lad gath-
ered up the arrows and came back
to his master.
39 But the lad did not know any-
thing. Only Jonathan and David
knew of the matter.
40 Then Jonathan gave his
[1]weapons to his lad, and said to
him, "Go, carry *them* to the city."
41 As soon as the lad had gone,
David arose from *a place* toward
the south, fell on his face to the
ground, and bowed down three
times. And they kissed one an-
other; and they wept together, but
David more so.
42 Then Jonathan said to David,
[a]"Go in peace, since we have both
sworn in the name of the LORD,
saying, 'May the LORD be between
you and me, and between your
descendants and my descendants,
forever.'" So he arose and de-
parted, and Jonathan went into the
city.

David and the Holy Bread

21 Now David came to Nob, to
Ahimelech the priest. And
[a]Ahimelech was [b]afraid when he
met David, and said to him, "Why
are you alone, and no one is with
you?"
2 So David said to Ahimelech the
priest, "The king has ordered me
on some business, and said to me,
'Do not let anyone know anything
about the business on which I send
you, or what I have commanded
you.' And I have directed *my*
young men to such and such a
place.
3 "Now therefore, what have you
on hand? Give *me* five *loaves of*
bread in my hand, or whatever can
be found."
4 And the priest answered David
and said, "*There is* no [1]common
bread on hand; but there is [a]holy[2]
bread, [b]if the young men have
at least kept themselves from
women."
5 Then David answered the
priest, and said to him, "Truly,
women *have been* kept from us
about three days since I came out.
And [1]the [a]vessels of the young
men are holy, and *the bread is* in
effect common, even though it was
consecrated [b]in the vessel this
day."
6 So the priest [a]gave him holy
bread; for there was no bread
there but the showbread [b]which
had been taken from before the
LORD, in order to put hot bread *in
its place* on the day when it was
taken away.
7 Now a certain man of the ser-
vants of Saul *was* there that day,
detained before the LORD. And his
name *was* [a]Doeg, an Edomite, the
chief of the herdsmen who *be-
longed* to Saul.
8 And David said to Ahimelech,
"Is there not here on hand a
spear or a sword? For I have
brought neither my sword nor
my weapons with me, because
the king's business required
haste."
9 So the priest said, "The sword
of Goliath the Philistine, whom
you killed in [a]the Valley of Elah,
[b]there it is, wrapped in a cloth be-
hind the ephod. If you will take
that, take *it*. For *there is* no other
except that one here." And David
said, "*There is* none like it; give it
to me."

31 [1]Lit. *is a son of death*
32 [a]Gen. 31:36; 1 Sam. 19:5; [Prov. 31:9]; Matt. 27:23; Luke 23:22
33 [a]1 Sam. 18:11; 19:10 [b]1 Sam. 20:7 [1]*strike him down*
40 [1]*equipment*
42 [a]1 Sam. 1:17

CHAPTER 21

1 [a]1 Sam. 14:3; Mark 2:26 [b]1 Sam. 16:4
4 [a]Ex. 25:30; Lev. 24:5–9; Matt. 12:4 [b]Ex. 19:15 [1]*ordinary* [2]*consecrated*
5 [a]Ex. 19:14, 15; 1 Thess. 4:4 [b]Lev. 8:26 [1]The young men are ceremonially undefiled
6 [a]Matt. 12:3, 4; Mark 2:25, 26; Luke 6:3, 4 [b]Lev. 24:8, 9
7 [a]1 Sam. 14:47; 22:9; Ps. 52:title
9 [a]1 Sam. 17:2, 50 [b]1 Sam. 31:10

David Flees to Gath

10 Then David arose and fled that day from before Saul, and went to Achish the king of Gath.

11 And [a]the servants of Achish said to him, "*Is* this not David the king of the land? Did they not sing of him to one another in dances, saying:

[b]'Saul has slain his thousands,
And David his ten thousands'?"

12 Now David [a]took these words [1]to heart, and was very much afraid of Achish the king of Gath.

13 So [a]he changed his behavior before them, pretended [1]madness in their hands, [2]scratched on the doors of the gate, and let his saliva fall down on his beard.

14 Then Achish said to his servants, "Look, you see the man is insane. Why have you brought him to me?

15 "Have I need of madmen, that you have brought this *fellow* to play the madman in my presence? Shall this *fellow* come into my house?"

David's Four Hundred Men

22 David therefore departed from there and [a]escaped [b]to the cave of Adullam. So when his brothers and all his father's house heard *it*, they went down there to him.

2 [a]And everyone *who was* in distress, everyone who *was* in debt, and everyone *who was* [1]discontented gathered to him. So he became captain over them. And there were about [b]four hundred men with him.

3 Then David went from there to Mizpah of [a]Moab; and he said to the king of Moab, "Please let my father and mother come here with you, till I know what God will do for me."

4 So he brought them before the king of Moab, and they dwelt with him all the time that David was in the stronghold.

5 Now the prophet [a]Gad said to David, "Do not stay in the stronghold; depart, and go to the land of Judah." So David departed and went into the forest of Hereth.

11 [a]Ps. 56:title [b]1 Sam. 18:6–8; 29:5
12 [a]Luke 2:19 [1]Lit. *in his heart*
13 [a]Ps. 34:title [1]*insanity* [2]*scribbled*

CHAPTER 22

1 [a]Ps. 57:title; 142:title [b]Josh. 12:15; 15:35; 2 Sam. 23:13
2 [a]Judg. 11:3 [b]1 Sam. 25:13 [1]Lit. *bitter of soul*
3 [a]2 Sam. 8:2
5 [a]2 Sam. 24:11; 1 Chr. 21:9; 29:29; 2 Chr. 29:25
6 [a]1 Sam. 15:34
7 [a]1 Sam. 8:14
8 [a]1 Sam. 18:3; 20:16, 30
9 [a]1 Sam. 21:7; 22:22; Ps. 52:title [b]1 Sam. 21:1 [c]1 Sam. 14:3
10 [a]Num. 27:21; 1 Sam. 10:22 [b]1 Sam. 21:6, 9
14 [a]1 Sam. 19:4, 5; 20:32; 24:11

Saul Murders the Priests

6 When Saul heard that David and the men who *were* with him had been discovered—now Saul was staying in [a]Gibeah under a tamarisk tree in Ramah, with his spear in his hand, and all his servants standing about him—

7 then Saul said to his servants who stood about him, "Hear now, you Benjamites! Will the son of Jesse [a]give every one of you fields and vineyards, *and* make you all captains of thousands and captains of hundreds?

8 "All of you have conspired against me, and *there is* no one who reveals to me that [a]my son has made a covenant with the son of Jesse; and *there is* not one of you who is sorry for me or reveals to me that my son has stirred up my servant against me, to lie in wait, as *it is* this day."

9 Then answered [a]Doeg the Edomite, who was set over the servants of Saul, and said, "I saw the son of Jesse going to Nob, to [b]Ahimelech the son of [c]Ahitub.

10 [a]"And he inquired of the LORD for him, [b]gave him provisions, and gave him the sword of Goliath the Philistine."

11 So the king sent to call Ahimelech the priest, the son of Ahitub, and all his father's house, the priests who *were* in Nob. And they all came to the king.

12 And Saul said, "Hear now, son of Ahitub!" He answered, "Here I am, my lord."

13 Then Saul said to him, "Why have you conspired against me, you and the son of Jesse, in that you have given him bread and a sword, and have inquired of God for him, that he should rise against me, to lie in wait, as it is this day?"

14 So Ahimelech answered the king and said, "And who among all your servants *is as* [a]faithful as David, who is the king's son-in-law, who goes at your bidding, and is honorable in your house?

15 "Did I then begin to inquire of God for him? Far be it from me! Let not the king impute anything to his servant, *or* to any in the house of my father. For your

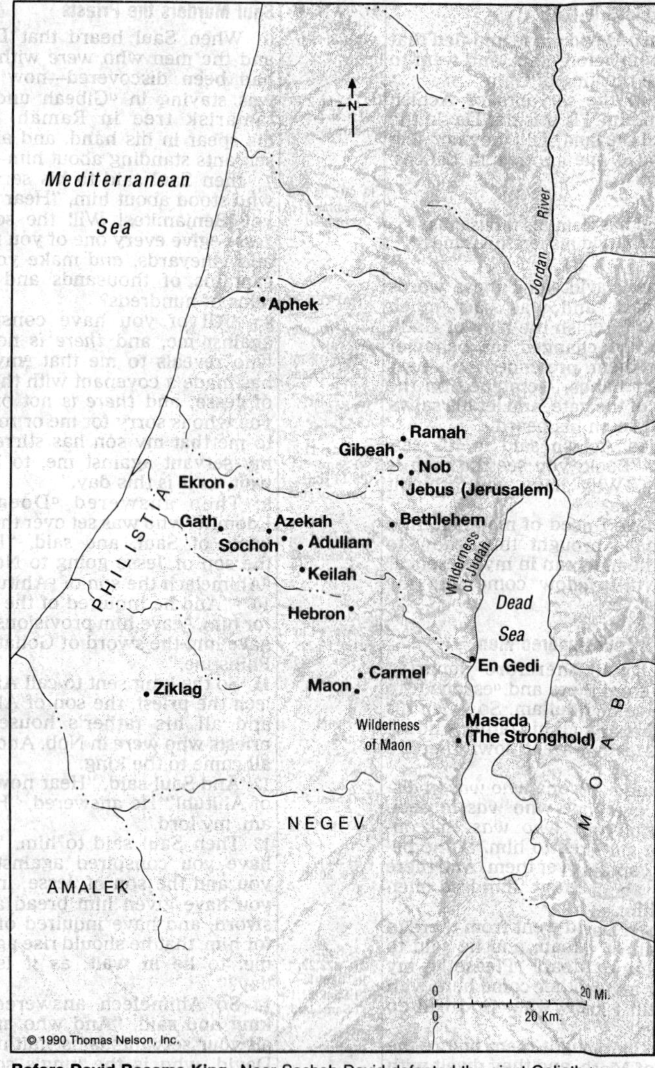

Before David Became King. Near Sochoh David defeated the giant Goliath (1 Sam. 17). Once Saul's wrath was kindled against the shepherd soldier, David fled Saul's presence and journeyed to Adullam. Taking his family to the safety of Moab, he established camp at the stronghold (1 Sam. 22:4), now known as Masada. From there his activity took him north to Aphek and south to Amalek.

servant knew nothing of all this,
little or much."
16 And the king said, "You shall
surely die, Ahimelech, you and all
[a]your father's house!"
17 Then the king said to the
guards who stood about him,
"Turn and kill the priests of the
LORD, because their hand also *is*
with David, and because they
knew when he fled and did not tell
it to me." But the servants of the
king [a]would not lift their hands to
strike the priests of the LORD.
18 And the king said to Doeg,
"You turn and kill the priests!" So
Doeg the Edomite turned and
[1]struck the priests, and [a]killed on
that day eighty-five men who wore
a linen ephod.
19 [a]Also Nob, the city of the
priests, he struck with the edge of
the sword, both men and women,
children and nursing infants, oxen
and donkeys and sheep—with the
edge of the sword.
20 [a]Now one of the sons of Ahime-
lech the son of Ahitub, named Abi-
athar, [b]escaped and fled after Da-
vid.
21 And Abiathar told David that
Saul had killed the LORD's priests.
22 So David said to Abiathar, "I
knew that day, when Doeg the
Edomite *was* there, that he would
surely tell Saul. I have caused *the*
death of all the persons of your fa-
ther's [1]house.
23 "Stay with me; do not fear. [a]For
he who seeks my life seeks your
life, but with me you *shall be* safe."

David Saves the City of Keilah

23 Then they told David, say-
ing, "Look, the Philistines
are fighting against [a]Keilah, and
they are robbing the threshing
floors."
2 Therefore David [a]inquired of
the LORD, saying, "Shall I go and
[1]attack these Philistines?" And the
LORD said to David, "Go and at-
tack the Philistines, and save
Keilah."
3 But David's men said to him,
"Look, we are afraid here in Ju-
dah. How much more then if we
go to Keilah against the armies of
the Philistines?"
4 Then David inquired of the
LORD once again. And the LORD an-
swered him and said, "Arise, go
down to Keilah. For I will deliver
the Philistines into your hand."
5 And David and his men went
to Keilah and [a]fought with the
Philistines, struck them with a
mighty blow, and took away their
livestock. So David saved the in-
habitants of Keilah.
6 Now it happened, when Abia-
thar the son of Ahimelech [a]fled to
David at Keilah, *that* he went
down *with* an ephod in his hand.
7 And Saul was told that David
had gone to Keilah. So Saul said,
"God has delivered him into my
hand, for he has shut himself in
by entering a town that has gates
and bars."
8 Then Saul called all the people
together for war, to go down to
Keilah to besiege David and his
men.
9 When David knew that Saul
plotted evil against him, [a]he said
to Abiathar the priest, "Bring the
ephod here."
10 Then David said, "O LORD God
of Israel, Your servant has cer-
tainly heard that Saul seeks to
come to Keilah [a]to destroy the city
for my sake.
11 "Will the men of Keilah deliver
me into his hand? Will Saul come
down, as Your servant has heard?
O LORD God of Israel, I pray, tell
Your servant." And the LORD said,
"He will come down."
12 Then David said, "Will the men
of Keilah [1]deliver me and my men
into the hand of Saul?" And the
LORD said, "They will deliver *you*."
13 So David and his men, [a]about
six hundred, arose and departed
from Keilah and went wherever
they could go. Then it was told
Saul that David had escaped from
Keilah; so he halted the expe-
dition.

David in Wilderness Strongholds

14 And David stayed in strong-
holds in the wilderness, and re-
mained in [a]the mountains in the
Wilderness of [b]Ziph. Saul [c]sought
him every day, but God did not de-
liver him into his hand.
15 So David saw that Saul had
come out to seek his life. And Da-
vid *was* in the Wilderness of Ziph
[1]in a forest.

16 [a]Deut. 24:16
17 [a]Ex. 1:17
18 [a]1 Sam. 2:31 [1]*attacked*
19 [a]Josh. 21:1–45; 1 Sam. 22:9, 11
20 [a]1 Sam. 23:6, 9; 30:7; 1 Kin. 2:26, 27 [b]1 Sam. 2:33
22 [1]*family*
23 [a]1 Kin. 2:26

CHAPTER 23

1 [a]Josh. 15:44; Neh. 3:17, 18
2 [a]1 Sam. 22:10; 23:4, 6, 9; 28:6; 30:8; 2 Sam. 5:19, 23 [1]Lit. *strike*
5 [a]1 Sam. 19:8; 2 Sam. 5:20
6 [a]1 Sam. 22:20
9 [a]Num. 27:21; 1 Sam. 23:6; 30:7
10 [a]1 Sam. 22:19
12 [1]Lit. *shut up*
13 [a]1 Sam. 22:2; 25:13
14 [a]Ps. 11:1 [b]Josh. 15:55; 2 Chr. 11:8 [c]Ps. 32:7; 54:3, 4
15 [1]Or *in Horesh*

16 Then Jonathan, Saul's son,
arose and went to David in the
woods and [1]strengthened his hand
in God.
17 And he said to him, [a]"Do not
fear, for the hand of Saul my fa-
ther shall not find you. You shall
be king over Israel, and I shall be
next to you. [b]Even my father Saul
knows that."
18 So the two of them [a]made a
covenant before the LORD. And
David stayed in the woods, and
Jonathan went to his own house.
19 Then the Ziphites [a]came up to
Saul at Gibeah, saying, "Is David
not hiding with us in strongholds
in the woods, in the hill of Hachi-
lah, which *is* on the south of Jeshi-
mon?
20 "Now therefore, O king, come
down according to all the desire
of your soul to come down; and
[a]our part *shall be* to deliver him
into the king's hand."
21 And Saul said, "Blessed *are*
you of the LORD, for you have com-
passion on me.
22 "Please go and find out for
sure, and see the place where his
hideout is, *and* who has seen him
there. For I am told he is very
crafty.
23 "See therefore, and take
knowledge of all the lurking places
where he hides; and come back to
me with certainty, and I will go
with you. And it shall be, if he is
in the land, that I will search for
him throughout all the [1]clans of
Judah."
24 So they arose and went to Ziph
before Saul. But David and his
men *were* in the Wilderness [a]of
Maon, in the plain on the south of
Jeshimon.
25 When Saul and his men went
to seek *him*, they told David.
Therefore he went down [1]to the
rock, and stayed in the Wilderness
of Maon. And when Saul heard
that, he pursued David in the Wil-
derness of Maon.
26 Then Saul went on one side of
the mountain, and David and his
men on the other side of the moun-
tain. [a]So David made haste to get
away from Saul, for Saul and his
men [b]were encircling David and
his men to take them.
27 [a]But a messenger came to Saul,
saying, "Hurry and come, for the
Philistines have invaded the land!"
28 Therefore Saul returned from
pursuing David, and went against
the Philistines; so they called that
place [1]the Rock of Escape.
29 Then David went up from there
and dwelt in strongholds at [a]En
Gedi.

David Spares Saul

24 Now it happened, [a]when
Saul had returned from fol-
lowing the Philistines, that it was
told him, saying, "Take note! Da-
vid *is* in the Wilderness of En
Gedi."
2 Then Saul took three thousand
chosen men from all Israel, and
[a]went to seek David and his men
on the Rocks of the Wild Goats.
3 So he came to the sheepfolds
by the road, where there *was* a
cave; and [a]Saul went in to [b]attend
to his needs. ([c]David and his men
were staying in the recesses of the
cave.)
4 [a]Then the men of David said to
him, "This is the day of which the
LORD said to you, 'Behold, I will
deliver your enemy into your
hand, that you may do to him as
it seems good to you.' " And David
arose and secretly cut off a corner
of Saul's robe.
5 Now it happened afterward
that [a]David's heart troubled him
because he had cut Saul's *robe*.
6 And he said to his men, [a]"The
LORD forbid that I should do this
thing to my master, the LORD's
anointed, to stretch out my hand
against him, seeing he *is* the
anointed of the LORD."
7 So David [a]restrained his ser-
vants with *these* words, and did
not allow them to rise against
Saul. And Saul got up from the
cave and went on *his* way.
8 David also arose afterward,
went out of the cave, and called
out to Saul, saying, "My lord the
king!" And when Saul looked be-
hind him, David stooped with his
face to the earth, and bowed down.
9 And David said to Saul: [a]"Why
do you listen to the words of men
who say, 'Indeed David seeks your
harm'?
10 "Look, this day your eyes have
seen that the LORD delivered you

16 [1]*encouraged him*
17 [a][Ps. 27:1–3; Heb. 13:6] [b]1 Sam. 20:31; 24:20
18 [a]1 Sam. 18:3; 20:12–17, 42; 2 Sam. 9:1; 21:7
19 [a]1 Sam. 26:1; Ps. 54:title
20 [a]Ps. 54:3
23 [1]Lit. *thousands*
24 [a]Josh. 15:55; 1 Sam. 25:2
25 [1]Or *from the rock*
26 [a]Ps. 31:22 [b]Ps. 17:9
27 [a]2 Kin. 19:9
28 [1]Heb. *Sela Hammahlekoth*
29 [a]Josh. 15:62; 2 Chr. 20:2

CHAPTER 24

1 [a]1 Sam. 23:19, 28, 29
2 [a]1 Sam. 26:2; Ps. 38:12
3 [a]1 Sam. 24:10 [b]Judg. 3:24 [c]Ps. 57:title; 142:title
4 [a]1 Sam. 26:8–11
5 [a]2 Sam. 24:10
6 [a]1 Sam. 26:11
7 [a]Ps. 7:4; [Matt. 5:44; Rom. 12:17, 19]
9 [a]Ps. 141:6; [Prov. 16:28; 17:9]

today into my hand in the cave,
and *someone* urged *me* to kill you.
But *my eye* spared you, and I said,
'I will not stretch out my hand
against my lord, for he *is* the
LORD's anointed.'
11 "Moreover, my father, see!
Yes, see the corner of your robe
in my hand! For in that I cut off
the corner of your robe, and did
not kill you, know and see that
there is [a]neither evil nor rebellion
in my hand, and I have not sinned
against you. Yet you [b]hunt my life
to take it.
12 [a]"Let the LORD judge between
you and me, and let the LORD
avenge me on you. But my hand
shall not be against you.
13 "As the proverb of the ancients
says, [a]'Wickedness proceeds from
the wicked.' But my hand shall not
be against you.
14 "After whom has the king of
Israel come out? Whom do you
pursue? [a]A dead dog? [b]A flea?
15 [a]"Therefore let the LORD be
judge, and judge between you and
me, and [b]see and [c]plead my case,
and deliver me out of your hand."
16 So it was, when David had fin-
ished speaking these words to
Saul, that Saul said, [a]"*Is* this your
voice, my son David?" And Saul
lifted up his voice and wept.
17 [a]Then he said to David: "You
are [b]more righteous than I; for
[c]you have rewarded me with good,
whereas I have rewarded you with
evil.
18 "And you have shown this day
how you have dealt well with me;
for when [a]the LORD delivered me
into your hand, you did not kill me.
19 "For if a man finds his enemy,
will he let him get away safely?
Therefore may the LORD reward
you with good for what you have
done to me this day.
20 "And now [a]I know indeed that
you shall surely be king, and that
the kingdom of Israel shall be es-
tablished in your hand.
21 [a]"Therefore swear now to me
by the LORD [b]that you will not cut
off my descendants after me, and
that you will not destroy my name
from my father's house."
22 So David swore to Saul. And
Saul went home, but David and his
men went up to [a]the stronghold.

11 [a]Judg. 11:27; Ps. 7:3; 35:7 [b]1 Sam. 26:20
12 [a]Gen. 16:5; Judg. 11:27; 1 Sam. 26:10–23; Job 5:8
13 [a][Matt. 7:16–20]
14 [a]1 Sam. 17:43; 2 Sam. 9:8 [b]1 Sam. 26:20
15 [a]1 Sam. 24:12 [b]2 Chr. 24:22 [c]Ps. 35:1; 43:1; 119:154; Mic. 7:9
16 [a]1 Sam. 26:17
17 [a]1 Sam. 26:21 [b]Gen. 38:26 [c][Matt. 5:44]
18 [a]1 Sam. 26:23
20 [a]1 Sam. 23:17
21 [a]Gen. 21:23; 1 Sam. 20:14–17 [b]2 Sam. 21:6–8
22 [a]1 Sam. 23:29

CHAPTER 25

1 [a]1 Sam. 28:3 [b]Num. 20:29; Deut. 34:8 [c]Gen. 21:21; Num. 10:12; 13:3 [1]So with MT, Syr., Tg., Vg.; LXX *Maon*
2 [a]1 Sam. 23:24 [b]Josh. 15:55
3 [a]Josh. 15:13; 1 Sam. 30:14
4 [a]Gen. 38:13; 2 Sam. 13:23
6 [a]Judg. 19:20; 1 Chr. 12:18; Ps. 122:7; Luke 10:5
7 [a]1 Sam. 25:15, 21
8 [a]Neh. 8:10–12; Esth. 8:17; 9:19, 22 [1]*be gracious to the young men*
10 [a]Judg. 9:28
11 [a]Judg. 8:6, 15 [1]Lit. *slaughter*

Death of Samuel

25 Then [a]Samuel died; and the
Israelites gathered together
and [b]lamented for him, and buried
him at his home in Ramah. And
David arose and went down [c]to the
Wilderness of [1]Paran.

David and the Wife of Nabal

2 Now *there was* a man [a]in Maon
whose business *was* in [b]Carmel,
and the man *was* very rich. He had
three thousand sheep and a thou-
sand goats. And he was shearing
his sheep in Carmel.
3 The name of the man *was* Na-
bal, and the name of his wife Abi-
gail. And *she was* a woman of
good understanding and beautiful
appearance; but the man *was*
harsh and evil in *his* doings. He
was of the house of [a]Caleb.
4 When David heard in the wil-
derness that Nabal was [a]shearing
his sheep,
5 David sent ten young men; and
David said to the young men, "Go
up to Carmel, go to Nabal, and
greet him in my name.
6 "And thus you shall say to him
who lives *in prosperity:* [a]'Peace *be*
to you, peace to your house, and
peace to all that you have!
7 'Now I have heard that you
have shearers. Your shepherds
were with us, and we did not hurt
them, [a]nor was there anything
missing from them all the while
they were in Carmel.
8 'Ask your young men, and they
will tell you. Therefore [1]let *my*
young men find favor in your eyes,
for we come on [a]a feast day. Please
give whatever comes to your hand
to your servants and to your son
David.' "
9 So when David's young men
came, they spoke to Nabal accord-
ing to all these words in the name
of David, and waited.
10 Then Nabal answered David's
servants, and said, [a]"Who *is* Da-
vid, and who *is* the son of Jesse?
There are many servants now-
adays who break away each one
from his master.
11 [a]"Shall I then take my bread
and my water and my [1]meat that
I have killed for my shearers, and

give *it* to men when I do not know
where they *are* from?"
12 So David's young men turned
on their heels and went back; and
they came and told him all these
words.
13 Then David said to his men,
"Every man gird on his sword." So
every man girded on his sword,
and David also girded on his
sword. And about four hundred
men went with David, and two
hundred [a]stayed with the supplies.
14 Now one of the young men told
Abigail, Nabal's wife, saying,
"Look, David sent messengers
from the wilderness to greet our
master; and he [1]reviled them.
15 "But the men *were* very good
to us, and [a]we were not hurt, nor
did we miss anything as long as
we accompanied them, when we
were in the fields.
16 "They were [a]a wall to us both
by night and day, all the time we
were with them keeping the sheep.
17 "Now therefore, know and con-
sider what you will do, for [a]harm
is determined against our master
and against all his household. For
he *is such* a [b]scoundrel[1] that *one*
cannot speak to him."
18 Then Abigail made haste and
[a]took two hundred *loaves* of bread,
two skins of wine, five sheep al-
ready dressed, five seahs of
roasted *grain*, one hundred clus-
ters of raisins, and two hundred
cakes of figs, and loaded *them* on
donkeys.
19 And she said to her servants,
[a]"Go on before me; see, I am com-
ing after you." But she did not tell
her husband Nabal.
20 So it was, *as* she rode on the
donkey, that she went down under
cover of the hill; and there were
David and his men, coming down
toward her, and she met them.
21 Now David had said, "Surely
in vain I have protected all that
this *fellow* has in the wilderness,
so that nothing was missed of all
that *belongs* to him. And he has
[a]repaid me evil for good.
22 [a]"May God do so, and more
also, to the enemies of David, if I
[b]leave [c]one male of all who *belong*
to him by morning light."
23 Now when Abigail saw David,
she [a]dismounted quickly from the
donkey, fell on her face before Da-
vid, and bowed down to the
ground.
24 So she fell at his feet and said:
"On me, my lord, *on* me *let* this
iniquity *be!* And please let your
maidservant [1]speak in your ears,
and hear the words of your
maidservant.
25 "Please, let not my lord [1]regard
this scoundrel Nabal. For as his
name *is*, so *is* he: [2]Nabal *is* his
name, and folly *is* with him! But
I, your maidservant, did not see
the young men of my lord whom
you sent.
26 "Now therefore, my lord, [a]*as*
the LORD lives and *as* your soul
lives, since the LORD has [b]held you
back from coming to bloodshed
and from [c]avenging[1] yourself with
your own hand, now then, [d]let
your enemies and those who seek
harm for my lord be as Nabal.
27 "And now [a]this present which
your maidservant has brought to
my lord, let it be given to the
young men who follow my lord.
28 "Please forgive the trespass of
your maidservant. For [a]the LORD
will certainly make for my lord an
enduring house, because my lord
[b]fights the battles of the LORD, [c]and
evil is not found in you throughout
your days.
29 "Yet a man has risen to pursue
you and seek your life, but the life
of my lord shall be [a]bound in the
bundle of the living with the LORD
your God; and the lives of your en-
emies He shall [b]sling out, *as from*
the pocket of a sling.
30 "And it shall come to pass,
when the LORD has done for my
lord according to all the good that
He has spoken concerning you,
and has appointed you [a]ruler over
Israel,
31 "that this will be no grief to
you, nor offense of heart to my
lord, either that you have shed
blood without cause, or that my
lord has avenged himself. But
when the LORD has dealt well with
my lord, then remember your
maidservant."
32 Then David said to Abigail:
[a]"Blessed *is* the LORD God of Is-
rael, who sent you this day to meet
me!
33 "And blessed *is* your advice

13 [a]1 Sam. 30:24
14 [1]*scolded* or *scorned at*
15 [a]1 Sam. 25:7, 21
16 [a]Ex. 14:22; Job 1:10
17 [a]1 Sam. 20:7 [b]Deut. 13:13; Judg. 19:22 [1]Lit. *son of Belial*
18 [a]Gen. 32:13; [Prov. 18:16; 21:14]
19 [a]Gen. 32:16, 20
21 [a]1 Sam. 24:17; Ps. 109:5; [Prov. 17:13]
22 [a]Ruth 1:17; 1 Sam. 3:17; 20:13, 16 [b]1 Sam. 25:34 [c]1 Kin. 14:10; 21:21; 2 Kin. 9:8
23 [a]Josh. 15:18; Judg. 1:14
24 [1]*speak to you*
25 [1]*pay attention to* [2]Lit. *Fool*
26 [a]2 Kin. 2:2 [b]Gen. 20:6; 1 Sam. 25:33 [c][Rom. 12:19] [d]2 Sam. 18:32 [1]Lit. *saving yourself*
27 [a]Gen. 33:11; 1 Sam. 30:26; 2 Kin. 5:15
28 [a]2 Sam. 7:11–16, 27; 1 Kin. 9:5; 1 Chr. 17:10, 25 [b]1 Sam. 18:17 [c]1 Sam. 24:11; Ps. 7:3
29 [a][Ps. 66:9; Col. 3:3] [b]Jer. 10:18
30 [a]1 Sam. 13:14; 15:28
32 [a]Gen. 24:27; Ex. 18:10; 1 Kin. 1:48; Ps. 41:13; 72:18; 106:48; Luke 1:68

and blessed *are* you, because you
have [a]kept me this day from com-
ing to bloodshed and from aveng-
ing myself with my own hand.
34 "For indeed, *as* the LORD God
of Israel lives, who has [a]kept me
back from hurting you, unless you
had hurried and come to meet me,
surely [b]by morning light no males
would have been left to Nabal!"
35 So David received from her
hand what she had brought him,
and said to her, [a]"Go up in peace
to your house. See, I have heeded
your voice and [b]respected your
person."
36 Now Abigail went to Nabal,
and there he was, [a]holding a feast
in his house, like the feast of a
king. And Nabal's heart *was*
merry within him, for he *was* very
drunk; therefore she told him
nothing, little or much, until morn-
ing light.
37 So it was, in the morning, when
the wine had gone from Nabal,
and his wife had told him these
things, that his heart died within
him, and he became *like* a stone.
38 Then it happened, *after* about
ten days, that the LORD [a]struck Na-
bal, and he died.
39 So when David heard that Na-
bal was dead, he said, [a]"Blessed
be the LORD, who has [b]pleaded the
cause of my reproach from the
hand of Nabal, and has [c]kept His
servant from evil! For the LORD has
[d]returned the wickedness of Nabal
on his own head." And David sent
and proposed to Abigail, to take
her as his wife.
40 When the servants of David
had come to Abigail at Carmel,
they spoke to her saying, "David
sent us to you, to ask you to be-
come his wife."
41 Then she arose, bowed her face
to the earth, and said, "Here is
your maidservant, a servant to
[a]wash the feet of the servants of
my lord."
42 So Abigail rose in haste and
rode on a donkey, [1]attended by
five of her maidens; and she fol-
lowed the messengers of David,
and became his wife.
43 David also took Ahinoam [a]of
Jezreel, [b]and so both of them were
his wives.
44 But Saul had given [a]Michal his
daughter, David's wife, to [1]Palti
the son of Laish, who *was* from
[b]Gallim.

David Spares Saul a Second Time

26 Now the Ziphites came to
Saul at Gibeah, saying, [a]"Is
David not hiding in the hill of Ha-
chilah, opposite Jeshimon?"
2 Then Saul arose and went
down to the Wilderness of Ziph,
having [a]three thousand chosen
men of Israel with him, to seek Da-
vid in the Wilderness of Ziph.
3 And Saul encamped in the hill
of Hachilah, which *is* opposite
Jeshimon, by the road. But David
stayed in the wilderness, and he
saw that Saul came after him into
the wilderness.
4 David therefore sent out spies,
and understood that Saul had in-
deed come.
5 So David arose and came to the
place where Saul had encamped.
And David saw the place where
Saul lay, and [a]Abner the son of
Ner, the commander of his army.
Now Saul lay within the camp,
with the people encamped all
around him.
6 Then David answered, and said
to Ahimelech the Hittite and to
Abishai [a]the son of Zeruiah,
brother of [b]Joab, saying, "Who
will [c]go down with me to Saul in
the camp?" And [d]Abishai said, "I
will go down with you."
7 So David and Abishai came to
the people by night; and there Saul
lay sleeping within the camp, with
his spear stuck in the ground by
his head. And Abner and the peo-
ple lay all around him.
8 Then Abishai said to David,
[a]"God has delivered your enemy
into your hand this day. Now
therefore, please, let me strike him
[1]at once with the spear, right to the
earth; and I will not *have to strike*
him a second time!"
9 But David said to Abishai, "Do
not destroy him; [a]for who can
stretch out his hand against the
LORD's anointed, and be guiltless?"
10 David said furthermore, "*As*
the LORD lives, [a]the LORD shall
strike him, or [b]his day shall come
to die, or he shall [c]go out to battle
and perish.
11 [a]"The LORD forbid that I should

33 [a]1 Sam. 25:26
34 [a]1 Sam. 25:26 [b]1 Sam. 25:22
35 [a]1 Sam. 20:42; 2 Sam. 15:9; 2 Kin. 5:19; Luke 7:50; 8:48 [b]Gen. 19:21
36 [a]2 Sam. 13:28; Prov. 20:1; Is. 5:11; Dan. 5:1; [Hos. 4:11]
38 [a]1 Sam. 26:10; 2 Sam. 6:7; Ps. 104:29
39 [a]1 Sam. 25:32 [b]1 Sam. 24:15; Prov. 22:23 [c]1 Sam. 25:26, 34 [d]1 Kin. 2:44
41 [a][Prov. 15:33]; Luke 7:38, 44
42 [1]Lit. *with five of her maidens at her feet*
43 [a]Josh. 15:56 [b]1 Sam. 27:3; 30:5
44 [a]1 Sam. 18:20; 2 Sam. 3:14 [b]Is. 10:30 [1]*Paltiel,* 2 Sam. 3:15

CHAPTER 26

1 [a]1 Sam. 23:19; Ps. 54:title
2 [a]1 Sam. 13:2; 24:2
5 [a]1 Sam. 14:50, 51; 17:55
6 [a]1 Chr. 2:16 [b]2 Sam. 2:13 [c]Judg. 7:10, 11 [d]2 Sam. 2:18, 24
8 [a]1 Sam. 24:4 [1]Or *one time*
9 [a]1 Sam. 24:6, 7; 2 Sam. 1:14, 16
10 [a][Deut. 32:35]; 1 Sam. 25:26, 38; [Luke 18:7; Rom. 12:19; Heb. 10:30] [b]Gen. 47:29; Deut. 31:14; [Job 7:1; 14:5]; Ps. 37:13 [c]1 Sam. 31:6
11 [a]1 Sam. 24:6–12; [Rom. 12:17, 19]

stretch out my hand against the
LORD's anointed. But please, take
now the spear and the jug of water
that *are* by his head, and let us go."
12 So David took the spear and
the jug of water *by* Saul's head,
and they got away; and no man
saw or knew *it* or awoke. For they
were all asleep, because [a]a deep
sleep from the LORD had fallen on
them.
13 Now David went over to the
other side, and stood on the top
of a hill afar off, a great distance
being between them.
14 And David called out to the
people and to Abner the son of
Ner, saying, "Do you not answer,
Abner?" Then Abner answered
and said, "Who *are* you, calling
out to the king?"
15 So David said to Abner, "*Are*
you not a man? And who *is* like
you in Israel? Why then have you
not guarded your lord the king?
For one of the people came in to
destroy your lord the king.
16 "This thing that you have done
is not good. *As* the LORD lives, you
deserve to die, because you have
not guarded your master, the
LORD's anointed. And now see
where the king's spear *is*, and the
jug of water that *was* by his head."
17 Then Saul knew David's voice,
and said, [a]"*Is* that your voice, my
son David?" David said, "*It is* my
voice, my lord, O king."
18 And he said, [a]"Why does my
lord thus pursue his servant? For
what have I done, or what evil *is*
in my hand?
19 "Now therefore, please, let my
lord the king hear the words of his
servant: If the LORD has [a]stirred
you up against me, let Him accept
an offering. But if *it is* the children
of men, *may* they *be* cursed before
the LORD, [b]for they have driven me
out this day from sharing in the
[c]inheritance of the LORD, saying,
'Go, serve other gods.'
20 "So now, do not let my blood
fall to the earth before the face of
the LORD. For the king of Israel has
come out to seek [a]a flea, as when
one hunts a partridge in the moun-
tains."
21 Then Saul said, [a]"I have
sinned. Return, my son David. For
I will harm you no more, because
my life was precious in your eyes
this day. Indeed I have played the
fool and erred exceedingly."
22 And David answered and said,
"Here is the king's spear. Let one
of the young men come over and
get it.
23 [a]"May the LORD [b]repay every
man *for* his righteousness and his
faithfulness; for the LORD deliv-
ered you into *my* hand today, but
I would not stretch out my hand
against the LORD's anointed.
24 "And indeed, as your life was
valued much this day in my eyes,
so let my life be valued much in
the eyes of the LORD, and let Him
deliver me out of all tribulation."
25 Then Saul said to David, "*May*
you *be* blessed, my son David! You
shall both do great things and also
still [a]prevail." So David went on
his way, and Saul returned to his
place.

David Allied with the Philistines

27 And David said in his heart,
"Now I shall perish some-
day by the hand of Saul. *There is*
nothing better for me than that I
should speedily escape to the land
of the Philistines; and Saul will
[1]despair of me, to seek me any-
more in any part of Israel. So I
shall escape out of his hand."
2 Then David arose [a]and went
over with the six hundred men
who *were* with him [b]to Achish the
son of Maoch, king of Gath.
3 So David dwelt with Achish at
Gath, he and his men, each man
with his household, *and* David
[a]with his two wives, Ahinoam the
Jezreelitess, and Abigail the Car-
melitess, Nabal's widow.
4 And it was told Saul that David
had fled to Gath; so he sought him
no more.
5 Then David said to Achish, "If
I have now found favor in your
eyes, let them give me a place in
some town in the country, that I
may dwell there. For why should
your servant dwell in the royal city
with you?"
6 So Achish gave him Ziklag that
day. Therefore [a]Ziklag has be-
longed to the kings of Judah to this
day.
7 Now [1]the time that David
[a]dwelt in the country of the Philis-

12 [a]Gen. 2:21; 15:12; Is. 29:10
17 [a]1 Sam. 24:16
18 [a]1 Sam. 24:9, 11–14
19 [a]2 Sam. 16:11; 24:1 [b]Deut. 4:27, 28 [c]2 Sam. 14:16; 20:19
20 [a]1 Sam. 24:14
21 [a]Ex. 9:27; 1 Sam. 15:24, 30; 24:17; 2 Sam. 12:13
23 [a]1 Sam. 24:19; Ps. 7:8; 18:20; 62:12 [b]2 Sam. 22:21
25 [a]Gen. 32:28; 1 Sam. 24:20

CHAPTER 27

1 [1]*despair of searching for*
2 [a]1 Sam. 25:13 [b]1 Sam. 21:10; 1 Kin. 2:39
3 [a]1 Sam. 25:42, 43
6 [a]Josh. 15:31; 19:5; 1 Chr. 12:1; Neh. 11:28
7 [a]1 Sam. 29:3 [1]Lit. *the number of days*

tines was one full year and four
months.
8 And David and his men went
up and raided [a]the Geshurites, [b]the
[1]Girzites, and the [c]Amalekites. For
those nations were the inhabitants
of the land from [2]of old, [d]as you
go to Shur, even as far as the land
of Egypt.
9 Whenever David [1]attacked the
land, he left neither man nor
woman alive, but took away the
sheep, the oxen, the donkeys, the
camels, and the apparel, and re-
turned and came to Achish.
10 Then Achish would say,
"Where have you made a raid to-
day?" And David would say,
"Against the southern *area* of Ju-
dah, or against the southern *area*
of [a]the Jerahmeelites, or against
the southern *area* of [b]the Kenites."
11 David would save neither man
nor woman alive, to bring *news* to
Gath, saying, "Lest they should in-
form on us, saying, 'Thus David
did.'" And thus *was* his behavior
all the time he dwelt in the country
of the Philistines.
12 So Achish believed David, say-
ing, "He has made his people Is-
rael utterly abhor him; therefore
he will be my servant forever."

28 Now [a]it happened in those
days that the Philistines
gathered their armies together for
war, to fight with Israel. And
Achish said to David, "You as-
suredly know that you will go out
with me to battle, you and your
men."
2 So David said to Achish,
"Surely you know what your ser-
vant can do." And Achish said to
David, "Therefore I will make you
one of my chief guardians for-
ever."

Saul Consults a Medium

3 Now [a]Samuel had died, and all
Israel had lamented for him and
buried him in [b]Ramah, in his own
city. And Saul had put [c]the medi-
ums and the spiritists out of the
land.
4 Then the Philistines gathered
together, and came and encamped
at [a]Shunem. So Saul gathered all
Israel together, and they en-
camped at [b]Gilboa.
5 When Saul saw the army of the
Philistines, he was [a]afraid, and his
heart trembled greatly.
6 And when Saul inquired of the
LORD, [a]the LORD did not answer
him, either by [b]dreams or [c]by Urim
or by the prophets.
7 Then Saul said to his servants,
"Find me a woman who is a me-
dium, [a]that I may go to her and
inquire of her." And his servants
said to him, "In fact, *there is* a
woman who is a medium at En
Dor."
8 So Saul disguised himself and
put on other clothes, and he went,
and two men with him; and they
came to the woman by night. And
[a]he said, "Please conduct a séance
for me, and bring up for me the
one I shall name to you."
9 Then the woman said to him,
"Look, you know what Saul has
done, how he has [a]cut off the medi-
ums and the spiritists from the
land. Why then do you lay a snare
for my life, to cause me to die?"
10 And Saul swore to her by the
LORD, saying, "*As* the LORD lives,
no punishment shall come upon
you for this thing."
11 Then the woman said, "Whom
shall I bring up for you?" And he
said, "Bring up Samuel for me."
12 When the woman saw Samuel,
she cried out with a loud voice.
And the woman spoke to Saul,
saying, "Why have you deceived
me? For you *are* Saul!"
13 And the king said to her, "Do
not be afraid. What did you see?"
And the woman said to Saul, "I
saw [a]a[1] spirit ascending out of the
earth."
14 So he said to her, "What *is* his
form?" And she said, "An old man
is coming up, and he *is* covered
with [a]a mantle." And Saul per-
ceived that it *was* Samuel, and he
stooped with *his* face to the ground
and bowed down.
15 Now Samuel said to Saul,
"Why have you [a]disturbed me by
bringing me up?" And Saul an-
swered, "I am deeply distressed;
for the Philistines make war
against me, and [b]God has departed
from me and [c]does not answer me
anymore, neither by prophets nor
by dreams. Therefore I have called
you, that you may reveal to me
what I should do."

8 [a]Josh. 13:2, 13 [b]Josh. 16:10; Judg. 1:29 [c]Ex. 17:8, 16; 1 Sam. 15:7, 8 [d]Gen. 25:18; Ex. 15:22 [1]Or *Gezrites* [2]*ancient times*
9 [1]Lit. *struck*
10 [a]1 Chr. 2:9, 25 [b]Judg. 1:16

CHAPTER 28

1 [a]1 Sam. 29:1, 2
3 [a]1 Sam. 25:1 [b]1 Sam. 1:19 [c]Ex. 22:18; Lev. 19:31; 20:27; Deut. 18:10, 11; 1 Sam. 15:23; 28:9
4 [a]Josh. 19:18; 1 Sam. 28:4; 1 Kin. 1:3; 2 Kin. 4:8 [b]1 Sam. 31:1
5 [a]Job 18:11; [Is. 57:20]
6 [a]1 Sam. 14:37; Prov. 1:28; Lam. 2:9 [b]Num. 12:6; Joel 2:28 [c]Ex. 28:30; Num. 27:21; Deut. 33:8
7 [a]1 Chr. 10:13
8 [a]Deut. 18:10, 11; 1 Chr. 10:13; Is. 8:19
9 [a]1 Sam. 28:3
13 [a]Ex. 22:28; Ps. 138:1 [1]Heb. *elohim*
14 [a]1 Sam. 15:27; 2 Kin. 2:8, 13
15 [a]Is. 14:9 [b]1 Sam. 16:14; 18:12 [c]1 Sam. 28:6

16 Then Samuel said: "So why do
you ask me, seeing the LORD has
departed from you and has be-
come your enemy?
17 "And the LORD has done for
[1]Himself [a]as He spoke by me. For
the LORD has torn the kingdom out
of your hand and given it to your
neighbor, David.
18 [a]"Because you did not obey the
voice of the LORD nor execute His
fierce wrath upon [b]Amalek, there-
fore the LORD has done this thing
to you this day.
19 "Moreover the LORD will also
deliver Israel with you into the
hand of the Philistines. And to-
morrow you and your sons *will be*
with [a]me. The LORD will also de-
liver the army of Israel into the
hand of the Philistines."
20 Immediately Saul fell full
length on the ground, and was
dreadfully afraid because of the
words of Samuel. And there
was no strength in him, for he
had eaten no food all day or all
night.
21 And the woman came to Saul
and saw that he was severely trou-
bled, and said to him, "Look, your
maidservant has obeyed your
voice, and I have [a]put my life in
my hands and heeded the words
which you spoke to me.
22 "Now therefore, please, heed
also the voice of your maidservant,
and let me set a piece of bread be-
fore you; and eat, that you may
have strength when you go on
your way."
23 But he refused and said, "I will
not eat." So his servants, together
with the woman, urged him; and
he heeded their voice. Then he
arose from the ground and sat on
the bed.
24 Now the woman had a fatted
calf in the house, and she hastened
to kill it. And she took flour and
kneaded *it*, and baked unleavened
bread from it.
25 So she brought *it* before Saul
and his servants, and they ate.
Then they rose and went away that
night.

The Philistines Reject David

29 Then [a]the Philistines gath-
ered together all their ar-
mies [b]at Aphek, and the Israelites
encamped by a fountain which *is*
in Jezreel.
2 And the [a]lords of the Philis-
tines [1]passed in review by hun-
dreds and by thousands, but [b]Da-
vid and his men passed in review
at the rear with Achish.
3 Then the princes of the Philis-
tines said, "What *are* these He-
brews *doing here?*" And Achish
said to the princes of the Philis-
tines, "*Is* this not David, the ser-
vant of Saul king of Israel, who
has been with me [a]these days, or
these years? And to this day I have
[b]found no fault in him since he de-
fected *to me.*"
4 But the princes of the Philis-
tines were angry with him; so the
princes of the Philistines said to
him, [a]"Make this fellow return,
that he may go back to the place
which you have appointed for him,
and do not let him go down with
us to [b]battle, lest [c]in the battle he
become our adversary. For with
what could he reconcile himself to
his master, if not with the heads
of these [d]men?
5 "*Is* this not David, [a]of whom
they sang to one another in
dances, saying:

[b]'Saul has slain his thousands,
And David his ten thousands'?"

6 Then Achish called David and
said to him, "Surely, *as* the LORD
lives, you have been upright, and
[a]your going out and your coming
in with me in the army *is* good in
my sight. For to this day [b]I have
not found evil in you since the day
of your coming to me. Neverthe-
less the lords do not favor you.
7 "Therefore return now, and go
in peace, that you may not dis-
please the lords of the Philistines."
8 So David said to Achish, "But
what have I done? And to this day
what have you found in your ser-
vant as long as I have been with
you, that I may not go and fight
against the enemies of my lord the
king?"
9 Then Achish answered and
said to David, "I know that you *are*
as good in my sight [a]as an angel of
God; nevertheless [b]the princes of
the Philistines have said, 'He shall
not go up with us to the battle.'
10 "Now therefore, rise early in

---

17 [a]1 Sam. 15:28 [1]Or *him,* i.e., David
18 [a]1 Sam. 13:9–13; 15:1–26; 1 Kin. 20:42; 1 Chr. 10:13; Jer. 48:10 [b]1 Sam. 15:3–9
19 [a]1 Sam. 31:1–6; Job 3:17–19
21 [a]Judg. 12:3; 1 Sam. 19:5; Job 13:14

CHAPTER 29

1 [a]1 Sam. 28:1 [b]Josh. 12:18; 19:30; 1 Sam. 4:1; 1 Kin. 20:30
2 [a]1 Sam. 6:4; 7:7 [b]1 Sam. 28:1, 2 [1]*passed on in the rear*
3 [a]1 Sam. 27:7 [b]1 Sam. 27:1–6; 1 Chr. 12:19, 20; Dan. 6:5
4 [a]1 Sam. 27:6 [b]1 Sam. 14:21 [c]1 Sam. 29:9 [d]1 Chr. 12:19, 20
5 [a]1 Sam. 21:11 [b]1 Sam. 18:7
6 [a]2 Sam. 3:25; 2 Kin. 19:27 [b]1 Sam. 29:3
9 [a]2 Sam. 14:17, 20; 19:27 [b]1 Sam. 29:4

the morning with your master's
servants [a]who have come with
[1]you. And as soon as you are up
early in the morning and have
light, depart."
11 So David and his men rose
early to depart in the morning, to
return to the land of the Philis-
tines. [a]And the Philistines went up
to Jezreel.

David's Conflict with the Amalekites

30 Now it happened, when Da-
vid and his men came to
[a]Ziklag, on the third day, that the
[b]Amalekites had invaded the
South and Ziklag, attacked Ziklag
and burned it with fire,
2 and had taken captive the
[a]women and those who *were*
there, from small to great; they did
not kill anyone, but carried *them*
away and went their way.
3 So David and his men came to
the city, and there it was, burned
with fire; and their wives, their
sons, and their daughters had been
taken captive.
4 Then David and the people
who *were* with him lifted up their
voices and wept, until they had no
more power to weep.
5 And David's two [a]wives, Ahin-
oam the Jezreelitess, and Abigail
the widow of Nabal the Carmelite,
had been taken captive.
6 Now David was greatly dis-
tressed, for [a]the people spoke of
stoning him, because the soul of
all the people was [1]grieved, every
man for his sons and his daugh-
ters. [b]But David strengthened him-
self in the LORD his God.
7 [a]Then David said to Abiathar
the priest, Ahimelech's son,
"Please bring the ephod here to
me." And [b]Abiathar brought the
ephod to David.
8 [a]So David inquired of the LORD,
saying, "Shall I pursue this troop?
Shall I overtake them?" And He
answered him, "Pursue, for you
shall surely overtake *them* and
without fail recover *all*."
9 So David went, he and the six
hundred men who *were* with him,
and came to the Brook Besor,
where those stayed who were left
behind.
10 But David pursued, he and four
hundred men; [a]for two hundred

10 [a]1 Chr. 12:19, 22 [1]So with MT, Tg., Vg.; LXX adds *and go to the place which I have selected for you there; and set no bothersome word in your heart, for you are good before me. And rise on your way*
11 [a]2 Sam. 4:4

CHAPTER 30

1 [a]1 Sam. 27:6 [b]1 Sam. 15:7; 27:8
2 [a]1 Sam. 27:2, 3
5 [a]1 Sam. 25:42, 43
6 [a]Ex. 17:4; John 8:59 [b]1 Sam. 23:16; Is. 25:4; Hab. 3:17–19 [1]Lit. *bitter*
7 [a]1 Sam. 23:2–9 [b]1 Sam. 23:6
8 [a]1 Sam. 23:2, 4; Ps. 50:15; 91:15
10 [a]1 Sam. 30:9, 21
12 [a]1 Sam. 25:18; 1 Kin. 20:7 [b]Judg. 15:19; 1 Sam. 14:27
14 [a]2 Sam. 8:18; 1 Kin. 1:38, 44; Ezek. 25:16; Zeph. 2:5 [b]Josh. 14:13; 15:13
15 [a]Deut. 23:15
16 [a]1 Thess. 5:3
19 [a]1 Sam. 30:8
21 [a]1 Sam. 30:10

stayed *behind*, who were so weary
that they could not cross the Brook
Besor.
11 Then they found an Egyptian
in the field, and brought him to Da-
vid; and they gave him bread and
he ate, and they let him drink
water.
12 And they gave him a piece of
[a]a cake of figs and two clusters of
raisins. So [b]when he had eaten, his
strength came back to him; for he
had eaten no bread nor drunk
water for three days and three
nights.
13 Then David said to him, "To
whom do you *belong*, and where
are you from?" And he said, "I *am*
a young man from Egypt, servant
of an Amalekite; and my master
left me behind, because three days
ago I fell sick.
14 "We made an invasion of the
southern *area* of [a]the Cherethites,
in the *territory* which *belongs* to
Judah, and of the southern *area*
[b]of Caleb; and we burned Ziklag
with fire."
15 And David said to him, "Can
you take me down to this troop?"
So he said, "Swear to me by God
that you will neither kill me nor
deliver me into the hands of my
[a]master, and I will take you down
to this troop."
16 And when he had brought him
down, there they were, spread out
over all the land, [a]eating and
drinking and dancing, because of
all the great spoil which they had
taken from the land of the Philis-
tines and from the land of Judah.
17 Then David attacked them
from twilight until the evening of
the next day. Not a man of them
escaped, except four hundred
young men who rode on camels
and fled.
18 So David recovered all that the
Amalekites had carried away, and
David rescued his two wives.
19 And nothing of theirs was lack-
ing, either small or great, sons or
daughters, spoil or anything which
they had taken from them; [a]David
recovered all.
20 Then David took all the flocks
and herds they had driven before
those *other* livestock, and said,
"This *is* David's spoil."
21 Now David came to the [a]two

hundred men who had been so weary that they could not follow David, whom they also had made to stay at the Brook Besor. So they went out to meet David and to meet the people who *were* with him. And when David came near the people, he [1]greeted them.

22 Then all the wicked and [a]worthless[1] men of those who went with David answered and said, "Because they did not go with us, we will not give them *any* of the spoil that we have recovered, except for every man's wife and children, that they may lead *them* away and depart."

23 But David said, "My brethren, you shall not do so with what the LORD has given us, who has preserved us and delivered into our hand the troop that came against us.

24 "For who will heed you in this matter? But [a]as his part *is* who goes down to the battle, so *shall* his part *be* who stays by the supplies; they shall share alike."

25 So it was, from that day forward; he made it a statute and an ordinance for Israel to this day.

26 Now when David came to Ziklag, he sent *some* of the [1]spoil to the elders of Judah, to his friends, saying, "Here is a present for you from the spoil of the enemies of the LORD"—

27 to *those* who *were* in Bethel, *those* who *were* in [a]Ramoth of the South, *those* who *were* in [b]Jattir,

28 *those* who *were* in [a]Aroer, *those* who *were* in [b]Siphmoth, *those* who *were* in [c]Eshtemoa,

29 *those* who *were* in Rachal, *those* who *were* in the cities of [a]the Jerahmeelites, *those* who *were* in the cities of the [b]Kenites,

30 *those* who *were* in [a]Hormah, *those* who *were* in [1]Chorashan, *those* who *were* in Athach,

31 *those* who *were* in [a]Hebron, and to all the places where David himself and his men were accustomed to [b]rove.

The Tragic End of Saul and His Sons

31 Now [a]the Philistines fought against Israel; and the men of Israel fled from before the Philistines, and fell slain on Mount [b]Gilboa.

2 Then the Philistines followed hard after Saul and his sons. And the Philistines killed [a]Jonathan, Abinadab, and Malchishua, Saul's sons.

3 [a]The battle became fierce against Saul. The archers [1]hit him, and he was severely wounded by the archers.

4 [a]Then Saul said to his armorbearer, "Draw your sword, and thrust me through with it, lest [b]these uncircumcised men come and thrust me through and [1]abuse me." But his armorbearer would not, [c]for he was greatly afraid. Therefore Saul took a sword and [d]fell on it.

5 And when his armorbearer saw that Saul was dead, he also fell on his sword, and died with him.

6 So Saul, his three sons, his armorbearer, and all his men died together that same day.

7 And when the men of Israel who *were* on the other side of the valley, and *those* who *were* on the other side of the Jordan, saw that the men of Israel had fled and that Saul and his sons were dead, they forsook the cities and fled; and the Philistines came and dwelt in them.

8 So it happened the next day, when the Philistines came to strip the slain, that they found Saul and his three sons fallen on Mount Gilboa.

9 And they cut off his head and stripped off his armor, and sent *word* throughout the land of the Philistines, to [a]proclaim *it in* the temple of their idols and among the people.

10 [a]Then they put his armor in the temple of the [b]Ashtoreths, and [c]they fastened his body to the wall of [d]Beth[1] Shan.

11 [a]Now when the inhabitants of Jabesh Gilead heard what the Philistines had done to Saul,

12 [a]all the valiant men arose and traveled all night, and took the body of Saul and the bodies of his sons from the wall of Beth Shan; and they came to Jabesh and [b]burned them there.

13 Then they took their bones and [a]buried *them* under the tamarisk tree at Jabesh, [b]and fasted seven days.

21 [1]*asked them concerning their welfare*
22 [a]Deut. 13:13; Judg. 19:22 [1]Lit. *men of Belial*
24 [a]Num. 31:27; Josh. 22:8
26 [1]*booty*
27 [a]Josh. 19:8 [b]Josh. 15:48; 21:14
28 [a]Josh. 13:16 [b]1 Chr. 27:27 [c]Josh. 15:50
29 [a]1 Sam. 27:10 [b]Judg. 1:16; 1 Sam. 15:6; 27:10
30 [a]Num. 14:45; 21:3; Josh. 12:14; 15:30; 19:4; Judg. 1:17 [1]Or *Borashan*
31 [a]Num. 13:22; Josh. 14:13–15; 21:11–13; 2 Sam. 2:1 [b]1 Sam. 23:22

CHAPTER 31

1 [a]1 Chr. 10:1–12 [b]1 Sam. 28:4
2 [a]1 Sam. 14:49; 1 Chr. 8:33
3 [a]2 Sam. 1:6 [1]Lit. *found him*
4 [a]Judg. 9:54; 1 Chr. 10:4 [b]Judg. 14:3; 1 Sam. 14:6; 17:26, 36 [c]2 Sam. 1:14 [d]2 Sam. 1:6, 10 [1]*torture*
9 [a]Judg. 16:23, 24; 2 Sam. 1:20
10 [a]1 Sam. 21:9 [b]Judg. 2:13; 1 Sam. 7:3 [c]2 Sam. 21:12 [d]Judg. 1:27 [1]*Beth Shean*, Josh. 17:11
11 [a]1 Sam. 11:1–13
12 [a]1 Sam. 11:1–11; 2 Sam. 2:4–7 [b]2 Chr. 16:14; Jer. 34:5; Amos 6:10
13 [a]2 Sam. 2:4, 5; 21:12–14 [b]Gen. 50:10

The Second Book of

Samuel

THE Book of Second Samuel records the highlights of David's reign, first over the territory of Judah, and finally over the entire nation of Israel. It traces the ascension of David to the throne, his climactic sins of adultery and murder, and the shattering consequences of those sins upon his family and the nation.

See First Samuel for details on the titles of the books of Samuel. The Hebrew title for both books (originally one) is "Samuel." The Greek title for Second Samuel is *Basileion Beta,* "Second Kingdoms." The Latin title is *Liber II Samuelis,* the "Second Book of Samuel," or simply "Second Samuel."

The Report of Saul's Death

NOW it came to pass after the
[a]death of Saul, when David
had returned from [b]the
slaughter of the Amalekites, and
David had stayed two days in Zik-
lag,
2 on the third day, behold, it hap-
pened that [a]a man came from
Saul's camp [b]with his clothes [1]torn
and dust on his head. So it was,
when he came to David, that he
[c]fell to the ground and prostrated
himself.
3 And David said to him, "Where
have you come from?" So he said
to him, "I have escaped from the
camp of Israel."
4 Then David said to him, [a]"How
did the matter go? Please tell me."
And he answered, "The people
have fled from the battle, many of
the people are fallen and dead, and
Saul and [b]Jonathan his son are
dead also."
5 So David said to the young
man who told him, "How do you
know that Saul and Jonathan his
son are dead?"
6 Then the young man who told
him said, "As I happened by
chance *to be* on [a]Mount Gilboa,
there was [b]Saul, leaning on his
spear; and indeed the chariots and
horsemen followed hard after him.
7 "Now when he looked behind
him, he saw me and called to me.
And I answered, 'Here I am.'
8 "And he said to me, 'Who *are*
you?' So I answered him, 'I *am* an
Amalekite.'
9 "He said to me again, 'Please
stand over me and kill me, for [1]an-
guish has come upon me, but my
life still *remains* in me.'
10 "So I stood over him and
[a]killed him, because I was sure
that he could not live after he had
fallen. And I took the crown that
was on his head and the bracelet
that *was* on his arm, and have
brought them here to my lord."
11 Therefore David took hold of
his own clothes and [a]tore them,
and *so did* all the men who *were*
with him.
12 And they [a]mourned and wept
and [b]fasted until evening for Saul
and for Jonathan his son, for the
[c]people of the LORD and for the
house of Israel, because they had
fallen by the sword.
13 Then David said to the young
man who told him, "Where *are*
you from?" And he answered, "I
am the son of an alien, an Amalek-
ite."
14 So David said to him, "How
[a]was it you were not [b]afraid to [c]put
forth your hand to destroy the
LORD's anointed?"
15 Then [a]David called one of the
young men and said, "Go near,
and execute him!" And he struck
him so that he died.
16 So David said to him, [a]"Your
blood *is* on your own head, for
[b]your own mouth has testified
against you, saying, 'I have killed
the LORD's anointed.' "

The Song of the Bow

17 Then David lamented with this
lamentation over Saul and over
Jonathan his son,
18 [a]and he told *them* to teach the

CHAPTER 1

1 [a]1 Sam. 31:6 [b]1 Sam. 30:1, 17, 26

2 [a]2 Sam. 4:10 [b]1 Sam. 4:12 [c]1 Sam. 25:23 [1]To show grief

4 [a]1 Sam. 4:16; 31:3 [b]1 Sam. 31:2

6 [a]1 Sam. 31:1 [b]1 Sam. 31:2–4

9 [1]*agony*

10 [a]Judg. 9:54; 2 Kin. 11:12

11 [a]2 Sam. 3:31; 13:31

12 [a]2 Sam. 3:31 [b]1 Sam. 31:13 [c]2 Sam. 6:21

14 [a]Num. 12:8 [b]1 Sam. 31:4 [c]1 Sam. 24:6; 26:9

15 [a]2 Sam. 4:10, 12

16 [a]1 Sam. 26:9; 2 Sam. 3:28; 1 Kin. 2:32–37 [b]2 Sam. 1:10; Luke 19:22

18 [a]1 Sam. 31:3

children of Judah *the Song of*
the Bow; indeed *it is* written [b]in
the Book [1]of Jasher:

19 "The beauty of Israel is slain on
your high places!
[a]How the mighty have fallen!
20 [a]Tell *it* not in Gath,
Proclaim *it* not in the streets of
[b]Ashkelon—
Lest [c]the daughters of the
Philistines rejoice,
Lest the daughters of [d]the
uncircumcised triumph.

21 "O [a]mountains of Gilboa,
[b]*Let there be* no dew nor rain
upon you,
Nor fields of offerings.
For the shield of the mighty is
[1]cast away there!
The shield of Saul, not [c]anointed
with oil.
22 From the blood of the slain,
From the fat of the mighty,
[a]The bow of Jonathan did not turn
back,
And the sword of Saul did not
return empty.

23 "Saul and Jonathan *were* beloved
and pleasant in their lives,
And in their [a]death they were not
divided;
They were swifter than eagles,
They were [b]stronger than lions.

24 "O daughters of Israel, weep over
Saul,
Who clothed you in scarlet, with
luxury;
Who put ornaments of gold on
your apparel.

25 "How the mighty have fallen in the
midst of the battle!
Jonathan *was* slain in your high
places.
26 I am distressed for you, my
brother Jonathan;
You have been very pleasant to
me;
[a]Your love to me was wonderful,
Surpassing the love of women.

27 "How[a] the mighty have fallen,
And the weapons of war
perished!"

David Anointed King of Judah

2 It happened after this that Da-
vid [a]inquired of the LORD, say-
ing, "Shall I go up to any of the
cities of Judah?" And the LORD
said to him, "Go up." David said,
"Where shall I go up?" And He
said, "To [b]Hebron."
2 So David went up there, and
his [a]two wives also, Ahinoam the
Jezreelitess, and Abigail the
widow of Nabal the Carmelite.
3 And David brought up [a]the
men who *were* with him, every
man with his household. So they
dwelt in the cities of Hebron.
4 [a]Then the men of Judah came,
and there they [b]anointed David
king over the house of Judah. And
they told David, saying, [c]"The men
of Jabesh Gilead *were the ones*
who buried Saul."
5 So David sent messengers to
the men of Jabesh Gilead, and said
to them, [a]"You *are* blessed of the
LORD, for you have shown this
kindness to your lord, to Saul, and
have buried him.
6 "And now may [a]the LORD show
kindness and truth to you. I also
will repay you this kindness, be-
cause you have done this thing.
7 "Now therefore, let your hands
be strengthened, and be valiant;
for your master Saul is dead, and
also the house of Judah has
anointed me king over them."

Ishbosheth Made King of Israel

8 But [a]Abner the son of Ner,
commander of Saul's army, took
[1]Ishbosheth the son of Saul and
brought him over to [b]Mahanaim;
9 and he made him king over
[a]Gilead, over the [b]Ashurites, over
[c]Jezreel, over Ephraim, over Ben-
jamin, and over all Israel.
10 Ishbosheth, Saul's son, *was*
forty years old when he began to
reign over Israel, and he reigned
two years. Only the house of Judah
followed David.
11 And [a]the [1]time that David was
king in Hebron over the house of
Judah was seven years and six
months.

Israel and Judah at War

12 Now Abner the son of Ner, and
the servants of Ishbosheth the son
of Saul, went out from Mahanaim
to [a]Gibeon.
13 And [a]Joab the son of Zeruiah,
and the servants of David, went
out and met them by [b]the pool of
Gibeon. So they sat down, one on

18 [b]Josh. 10:13 [1]Lit. *of the Upright*
19 [a]2 Sam. 1:27
20 [a]1 Sam. 27:2; 31:8–13; Mic. 1:10 [b]1 Sam. 6:17; Jer. 25:20 [c]Ex. 15:20; Judg. 11:34; 1 Sam. 18:6 [d]1 Sam. 31:4
21 [a]1 Sam. 31:1 [b]Ezek. 31:15 [c]1 Sam. 10:1 [1]Lit. *defiled*
22 [a]Deut. 32:42; 1 Sam. 18:4
23 [a]1 Sam. 31:2–4 [b]Judg. 14:18
26 [a]1 Sam. 18:1–4; 19:2; 20:17
27 [a]2 Sam. 1:19, 25

CHAPTER 2

1 [a]Judg. 1:1; 1 Sam. 23:2, 4, 9; 30:7, 8 [b]1 Sam. 30:31; 2 Sam. 2:11; 5:1–3; 1 Kin. 2:11
2 [a]1 Sam. 25:42, 43; 30:5
3 [a]1 Sam. 27:2, 3; 30:1; 1 Chr. 12:1
4 [a]1 Sam. 30:26; 2 Sam. 2:11; 5:5; 19:14, 41–43 [b]1 Sam. 16:13; 2 Sam. 5:3 [c]1 Sam. 31:11–13
5 [a]Ruth 2:20; 3:10
6 [a]Ex. 34:6; 2 Tim. 1:16, 18
8 [a]1 Sam. 14:50; 2 Sam. 3:6 [b]Gen. 32:2; Josh. 21:38; 2 Sam. 17:24 [1]*Esh-Baal,* 1 Chr. 8:33; 9:39
9 [a]Josh. 22:9 [b]Judg. 1:32 [c]1 Sam. 29:1
11 [a]2 Sam. 5:5; 1 Kin. 2:11 [1]Lit. *number of days*
12 [a]Josh. 10:2–12; 18:25
13 [a]1 Sam. 26:6; 2 Sam. 8:16; 1 Chr. 2:16; 11:6 [b]Jer. 41:12

one side of the pool and the other
on the other side of the pool.
14 Then Abner said to Joab, "Let
the young men now arise and com-
pete before us." And Joab said,
"Let them arise."
15 So they arose and went over by
number, twelve from Benjamin,
followers of Ishbosheth the son of
Saul, and twelve from the servants
of David.
16 And each one grasped his op-
ponent by the head and *thrust* his
sword in his opponent's side; so
they fell down together. Therefore
that place was called [1]the Field
of Sharp Swords, which *is* in Gib-
eon.
17 So there was a very fierce bat-
tle that day, and Abner and the
men of Israel were beaten before
the servants of David.
18 Now the [a]three sons of Zeruiah
were there: Joab and Abishai and
Asahel. And Asahel *was* [b]*as* fleet
of foot [c]as a wild gazelle.
19 So Asahel pursued Abner, and
in going he did not turn to the right
hand or to the left from following
Abner.
20 Then Abner looked behind him
and said, "*Are* you Asahel?" He
answered, "I *am*."
21 And Abner said to him, "Turn
aside to your right hand or to your
left, and lay hold on one of the
young men and take his armor for
yourself." But Asahel would not
turn aside from following him.
22 So Abner said again to Asahel,
"Turn aside from following me.
Why should I strike you to the
ground? How then could I face
your brother Joab?"
23 However, he refused to turn
aside. Therefore Abner struck him
[a]in the stomach with the blunt end
of the spear, so that the spear came
out of his back; and he fell down
there and died on the spot. So it
was *that* as many as came to the
place where Asahel fell down and
died, stood [b]still.
24 Joab and Abishai also pursued
Abner. And the sun was going
down when they came to the hill
of Ammah, which *is* before Giah
by the road to the Wilderness of
Gibeon.
25 Now the children of Benjamin
gathered together behind Abner
and became [1]a unit, and took their
stand on top of a hill.
26 Then Abner called to Joab and
said, "Shall the sword devour for-
ever? Do you not know that it will
be bitter in the latter end? How
long will it be then until you tell
the people to return from pursuing
their brethren?"
27 And Joab said, "*As* God lives,
[1]unless [a]you had spoken, surely
then by morning all the people
would have given up pursuing
their brethren."
28 So Joab blew a trumpet; and
all the people stood still and did
not pursue Israel anymore, nor did
they fight anymore.
29 Then Abner and his men went
on all that night through the plain,
crossed over the Jordan, and went
through all Bithron; and they came
to Mahanaim.
30 So Joab returned from pursu-
ing Abner. And when he had gath-
ered all the people together,
there were missing of David's
servants nineteen men and As-
ahel.
31 But the servants of David had
struck down, of Benjamin and Ab-
ner's men, three hundred and sixty
men who died.
32 Then they took up Asahel and
buried him in his father's tomb,
which *was in* [a]Bethlehem. And
Joab and his men went all night,
and they came to Hebron at day-
break.
3 Now there was a long [a]war be-
tween the house of Saul and
the house of David. But David
grew stronger and stronger, and
the house of Saul grew weaker and
weaker.

Sons of David

2 Sons were born [a]to David in
Hebron: His firstborn was Amnon
[b]by Ahinoam the Jezreelitess;
3 his second, [1]Chileab, by Abi-
gail the widow of Nabal the Car-
melite; the third, [a]Absalom the son
of Maacah, the daughter of Tal-
mai, king [b]of Geshur;
4 the fourth, [a]Adonijah the son
of Haggith; the fifth, Shephatiah
the son of Abital;
5 and the sixth, Ithream, by Da-
vid's wife Eglah. These were born
to David in Hebron.

16 [1]Heb. *Helkath Hazzurim*
18 [a]1 Chr. 2:16 [b]1 Chr. 12:8; Hab. 3:19 [c]Ps. 18:33
23 [a]2 Sam. 3:27; 4:6; 20:10 [b]2 Sam. 20:12
25 [1]*one band*
27 [a]2 Sam. 2:14 [1]*if you had not spoken*
32 [a]1 Sam. 20:6
CHAPTER 3
1 [a]1 Kin. 14:30; [Ps. 46:9]
2 [a]1 Chr. 3:1–4 [b]1 Sam. 25:42, 43
3 [a]2 Sam. 15:1–10 [b]Josh. 13:13; 1 Sam. 27:8; 2 Sam. 13:37; 14:32; 15:8 [1]*Daniel*, 1 Chr. 3:1
4 [a]1 Kin. 1:5

Abner Joins Forces with David

6 Now it was so, while there was
war between the house of Saul and
the house of David, that Abner
was strengthening *his hold* on the
house of Saul.
7 And Saul had a concubine,
whose name *was* [a]Rizpah, the
daughter of Aiah. So *Ishbosheth*
said to Abner, "Why have you
[b]gone in to my father's con-
cubine?"
8 Then Abner became very an-
gry at the words of Ishbosheth,
and said, "*Am* I [a]a dog's head that
belongs to Judah? Today I show
loyalty to the house of Saul your
father, to his brothers, and to his
friends, and have not delivered
you into the hand of David; and
you charge me today with a fault
concerning this woman?
9 [a]"May God do so to Abner, and
more also, if I do not do for Da-
vid [b]as the LORD has sworn to
him—
10 "to transfer the kingdom from
the [1]house of Saul, and set up the
throne of David over Israel and
over Judah, [a]from Dan to Beer-
sheba."
11 And he could not answer Ab-
ner another word, because he
feared him.
12 Then Abner sent messengers
on his behalf to David, saying,
"Whose *is* the land?" saying *also*,
"Make your covenant with me,
and indeed my hand *shall be* with
you to bring all Israel to you."
13 And *David* said, "Good, I will
make a covenant with you. But one
thing I require of you: [a]you shall
not see my face unless you first
bring [b]Michal, Saul's daughter,
when you come to see my face."
14 So David sent messengers to
[a]Ishbosheth, Saul's son, saying,
"Give *me* my wife Michal, whom
I betrothed to myself [b]for a hun-
dred foreskins of the Philistines."
15 And Ishbosheth sent and took
her from *her* husband, from
[1]Paltiel the son of Laish.
16 Then her husband went along
with her to [a]Bahurim, [1]weeping
behind her. So Abner said to him,
"Go, return!" And he returned.
17 Now Abner had communicated
with the elders of Israel, saying,
"In time past you were seeking for
David *to be* king over you.
18 "Now then, do *it!* [a]For the LORD
has spoken of David, saying, 'By
the hand of My servant David, [1]I
will save My people Israel from the
hand of the Philistines and the
hand of all their enemies.'"
19 And Abner also spoke in the
hearing of [a]Benjamin. Then Abner
also went to speak in the hearing
of David in Hebron all that seemed
good to Israel and the whole house
of Benjamin.
20 So Abner and twenty men with
him came to David at Hebron. And
David made a feast for Abner and
the men who *were* with him.
21 Then Abner said to David, "I
will arise and go, and [a]gather all
Israel to my lord the king, that
they may make a covenant with
you, and that you may [b]reign over
all that your heart desires." So Da-
vid sent Abner away, and he went
in peace.

Joab Murders Abner

22 At that moment the servants of
David and Joab came from a raid
and brought much [1]spoil with
them. But Abner *was* not with Da-
vid in Hebron, for he had sent him
away, and he had gone in peace.
23 When Joab and all the troops
that *were* with him had come, they
told Joab, saying, "Abner the son
of Ner came to the king, and he
sent him away, and he has gone
in peace."
24 Then Joab came to the king
and said, "What have you done?
Look, Abner came to you; why *is*
it *that* you sent him away, and he
has already gone?
25 "Surely you realize that Abner
the son of Ner came to deceive
you, to know [a]your going out and
your coming in, and to know all
that you are doing."
26 And when Joab had gone from
David's presence, he sent messen-
gers after Abner, who brought him
back from the well of Sirah. But
David did not know *it.*
27 Now when Abner had returned
to Hebron, Joab [a]took him aside
in the gate to speak with him pri-
vately, and there [1]stabbed him [b]in
the stomach, so that he died for
the blood of [c]Asahel his brother.

7 [a]2 Sam. 21:8–11 [b]2 Sam. 16:21
8 [a]Deut. 23:18; 1 Sam. 24:14; 2 Sam. 9:8; 16:9
9 [a]Ruth 1:17; 1 Kin. 19:2 [b]1 Sam. 15:28; 16:1, 12; 28:17; 1 Chr. 12:23
10 [a]Judg. 20:1; 1 Sam. 3:20; 2 Sam. 17:11; 1 Kin. 4:25 [1]*family*
13 [a]Gen. 43:3 [b]1 Sam. 18:20; 19:11; 25:44; 2 Sam. 6:16
14 [a]2 Sam. 2:10 [b]1 Sam. 18:25–27
15 [1]*Palti*, 1 Sam. 25:44
16 [a]2 Sam. 16:5; 19:16 [1]Lit. *going and weeping*
18 [a]2 Sam. 3:9 [1]So with many Heb. mss., LXX, Syr., Tg.; MT *he*
19 [a]1 Sam. 10:20, 21; 1 Chr. 12:29
21 [a]2 Sam. 3:10, 12 [b]1 Kin. 11:37
22 [1]*booty*
25 [a]Deut. 28:6; 1 Sam. 29:6; Is. 37:28
27 [a]2 Sam. 20:9, 10; 1 Kin. 2:5 [b]2 Sam. 4:6 [c]2 Sam. 2:23 [1]Lit. *struck*

28 Afterward, when David heard
it, he said, "My kingdom and I *are*
[1]guiltless before the LORD forever
of the blood of Abner the son of
Ner.
29 [a]"Let it rest on the head of Joab
and on all his father's house; and
let there never fail to be in the
[1]house of Joab one [b]who has a dis-
charge or is a leper, who leans on
a staff or falls by the sword, or who
lacks bread."
30 So Joab and Abishai his
brother killed Abner, because he
had killed their brother [a]Asahel at
Gibeon in the battle.

David's Mourning for Abner

31 Then David said to Joab and
to all the people who were with
him, [a]"Tear your clothes, [b]gird
yourselves with sackcloth, and
mourn for Abner." And King Da-
vid followed the coffin.
32 So they buried Abner in He-
bron; and the king lifted up his
voice and wept at the grave of Ab-
ner, and all the people wept.
33 And the king sang *a lament*
over Abner and said:

"Should Abner die as a [a]fool dies?
34 Your hands were not bound
Nor your feet put into fetters;
As a man falls before wicked
men, *so* you fell."

Then all the people wept over him
again.
35 And when all the people came
[a]to persuade David to eat food
while it was still day, David took
an oath, saying, [b]"God do so to me,
and more also, if I taste bread or
anything else [c]till the sun goes
down!"
36 Now all the people took note
of it, and it pleased them, since
whatever the king did pleased all
the people.
37 For all the people and all Israel
understood that day that it had not
been the king's *intent* to kill Abner
the son of Ner.
38 Then the king said to his ser-
vants, "Do you not know that a
prince and a great man has fallen
this day in Israel?
39 "And I *am* weak today, though
anointed king; and these men, the
sons of Zeruiah, [a]*are* too harsh for
me. [b]The LORD shall repay the evil-
doer according to his wickedness."

Ishbosheth Is Murdered

4 When Saul's [1]son heard that
Abner had died in Hebron, [a]he[2]
lost heart, and all Israel was [b]trou-
bled.
2 Now Saul's son *had* two men
who were captains of troops. The
name of one *was* Baanah and the
name of the other Rechab, the sons
of Rimmon the Beerothite, of the
children of Benjamin. (For [a]Bee-
roth also was [1]*part* of Benjamin,
3 because the Beerothites fled to
[a]Gittaim and have been sojourners
there until this day.)
4 [a]Jonathan, Saul's son, had a
son *who was* lame in *his* feet. He
was five years old when the news
about Saul and Jonathan came
[b]from Jezreel; and his nurse took
him up and fled. And it happened,
as she made haste to flee, that he
fell and became lame. His name
was [c]Mephibosheth.[1]
5 Then the sons of Rimmon the
Beerothite, Rechab and Baanah,
set out and came at about the heat
of the day to the [a]house of Ish-
bosheth, who was lying on his bed
at noon.
6 And they came there, all the
way into the house, *as though* to
get wheat, and they [1]stabbed him
[a]in the stomach. Then Rechab and
Baanah his brother escaped.
7 For when they came into the
house, he was lying on his bed in
his bedroom; then they struck him
and killed him, beheaded him and
took his head, and were all night
escaping through the plain.
8 And they brought the head of
Ishbosheth to David at Hebron,
and said to the king, "Here is the
head of Ishbosheth, the son of Saul
your enemy, [a]who sought your
life; and the LORD has avenged my
lord the king this day of Saul and
his descendants."
9 But David answered Rechab
and Baanah his brother, the sons
of Rimmon the Beerothite, and
said to them, "*As* the LORD lives,
[a]who has redeemed my life from
all adversity,
10 "when [a]someone told me, say-
ing, 'Look, Saul is dead,' thinking
to have brought good news, I

28 [1]*innocent*

29 [a]Deut. 21:6–9; 1 Kin. 2:32, 33 [b]Lev. 15:2 [1]*family*

30 [a]2 Sam. 2:23

31 [a]Josh. 7:6; 2 Sam. 1:2, 11 [b]Gen. 37:34

33 [a]2 Sam. 13:12, 13

35 [a]2 Sam. 12:17; Jer. 16:7, 8 [b]Ruth 1:17 [c]Judg. 20:26; 2 Sam. 1:12

39 [a]2 Sam. 19:5–7 [b]1 Kin. 2:5, 6, 32–34; 2 Tim. 4:14

CHAPTER 4

1 [a]Ezra 4:4; Is. 13:7 [b]Matt. 2:3 [1]Ishbosheth [2]Lit. *his hands dropped*

2 [a]Josh. 18:25 [1]*considered part of*

3 [a]Neh. 11:33

4 [a]2 Sam. 9:3 [b]1 Sam. 29:1, 11 [c]2 Sam. 9:6 [1]*Merib-Baal,* 1 Chr. 8:34; 9:40

5 [a]2 Sam. 2:8, 9

6 [a]2 Sam. 2:23; 20:10 [1]Lit. *struck*

8 [a]1 Sam. 19:2, 10, 11; 23:15; 25:29

9 [a]Gen. 48:16; 1 Kin. 1:29; Ps. 31:7

10 [a]2 Sam. 1:2–16

arrested him and had him exe-
cuted in Ziklag—the one who
thought I would give him a reward
for *his* news.
11 "How much more, when
wicked men have killed a righ-
teous person in his own house on
his bed? Therefore, shall I not now
[a]require his [1]blood at your hand
and [2]remove you from the earth?"
12 So David [a]commanded his
young men, and they executed
them, cut off their hands and feet,
and hanged *them* by the pool in
Hebron. But they took the head of
Ishbosheth and buried *it* in the
[b]tomb of Abner in Hebron.

David Reigns over All Israel

5 Then all the tribes of Israel
[a]came to David at Hebron and
spoke, saying, "Indeed [b]we *are*
your bone and your flesh.
2 "Also, in time past, when Saul
was king over us, [a]you were the
one who led Israel out and brought
them in; and the LORD said to you,
[b]'You shall shepherd My people Is-
rael, and be ruler over Israel.' "
3 [a]Therefore all the elders of Is-
rael came to the king at Hebron,
[b]and King David made a covenant
with them at Hebron [c]before the
LORD. And they anointed David
king over Israel.
4 David *was* [a]thirty years old
when he began to reign, *and* [b]he
reigned forty years.
5 In Hebron he reigned over Ju-
dah [a]seven years and six months,
and in Jerusalem he reigned
thirty-three years over all Israel
and Judah.

The Conquest of Jerusalem

6 [a]And the king and his men
went to Jerusalem against [b]the
Jebusites, the inhabitants of the
land, who spoke to David, saying,
"You shall not come in here; but
the blind and the lame will repel
you," thinking, "David cannot
come in here."
7 Nevertheless David took the
stronghold of Zion [a](that *is,* the
City of David).
8 Now David said on that day,
"Whoever climbs up by way of the
water shaft and defeats the Jebu-
sites (the lame and the blind, *who
are* hated by David's soul), [a]*he*
shall be chief and captain." There-
fore they say, "The blind and the
lame shall not come into the
house."
9 Then David dwelt in the
stronghold, and called it [a]the City
of David. And David built all
around from [1]the Millo and in-
ward.
10 So David went on and became
great, and [a]the LORD God of hosts
was with [b]him.
11 Then [a]Hiram [b]king of Tyre sent
messengers to David, and cedar
trees, and carpenters and masons.
And they built David a house.
12 So David knew that the LORD
had established him as king over
Israel, and that He had [a]exalted
His kingdom [b]for the sake of His
people Israel.
13 And [a]David took more concu-
bines and wives from Jerusalem,
after he had come from Hebron.
Also more sons and daughters
were born to David.
14 Now [a]these *are* the names of
those who were born to him in Je-
rusalem: [1]Shammua, Shobab, Na-
than, [b]Solomon,
15 Ibhar, [1]Elishua, Nepheg, Ja-
phia,
16 Elishama, Eliada, and Eliph-
elet.

The Philistines Defeated

17 [a]Now when the Philistines
heard that they had anointed Da-
vid king over Israel, all the Philis-
tines went up to search for David.
And David heard *of it* [b]and went
down to the stronghold.
18 The Philistines also went and
deployed themselves in [a]the Valley
of Rephaim.
19 So David [a]inquired of the LORD,
saying, "Shall I go up against the
Philistines? Will You deliver them
into my hand?" And the LORD said
to David, "Go up, for I will doubt-
less deliver the Philistines into
your hand."
20 So David went to [a]Baal Pera-
zim, and David defeated them
there; and he said, "The LORD
has broken through my enemies
before me, like a breakthrough
of water." Therefore he called
the name of that place [1]Baal Pera-
zim.
21 And they left their [1]images

11 [a][Gen. 9:5, 6; Ps. 9:12] [1]Or *blood-shed* [2]Lit. *consume you*
12 [a]2 Sam. 1:15 [b]2 Sam. 3:32

CHAPTER 5

1 [a]1 Chr. 11:1–3 [b]Gen. 29:14; Judg. 9:2; 2 Sam. 19:12, 13
2 [a]1 Sam. 18:5, 13, 16 [b]1 Sam. 16:1
3 [a]2 Sam. 3:17; 1 Chr. 11:3 [b]2 Sam. 2:4; 3:21; 2 Kin. 11:17 [c]Judg. 11:11; 1 Sam. 23:18
4 [a]Gen. 41:46; Num. 4:3; Luke 3:23 [b]1 Kin. 2:11; 1 Chr. 26:31; 29:27
5 [a]2 Sam. 2:11; 1 Chr. 3:4; 29:27
6 [a]Judg. 1:21 [b]Josh. 15:63; Judg. 1:8; 19:11, 12
7 [a]2 Sam. 6:12, 16; 1 Kin. 2:10; 8:1; 9:24
8 [a]1 Chr. 11:6–9
9 [a]2 Sam. 5:7; 1 Kin. 9:15, 24 [1]Lit. *The Landfill*
10 [a]1 Sam. 17:45 [b]1 Sam. 18:12, 28
11 [a]1 Kin. 5:1–18 [b]1 Chr. 14:1
12 [a]Num. 24:7 [b]Is. 45:4
13 [a][Deut. 17:17]; 1 Chr. 3:9
14 [a]1 Chr. 3:5–8 [b]2 Sam. 12:24 [1]*Shimea,* 1 Chr. 3:5
15 [1]*Elishama,* 1 Chr. 3:6
17 [a]1 Chr. 11:16 [b]2 Sam. 23:14
18 [a]Gen. 14:5; Josh. 15:8; 1 Chr. 11:15; Is. 17:5
19 [a]1 Sam. 23:2; 2 Sam. 2:1
20 [a]1 Chr. 14:11; Is. 28:21 [1]Lit. *Master of Break-throughs*
21 [1]*idols*

there, and David and his men [a]car-
ried them away.
22 [a]Then the Philistines went up
once again and deployed them-
selves in the Valley of Rephaim.
23 Therefore [a]David inquired of
the LORD, and He said, "You shall
not go up; circle around behind
them, and come upon them in front
of the mulberry trees.
24 "And it shall be, when you
[a]hear the sound of marching in the
tops of the mulberry trees, then
you shall advance quickly. For
then [b]the LORD will go out before
you to strike the camp of the Phi-
listines."
25 And David did so, as the LORD
commanded him; and he drove
back the Philistines from [a]Geba[1]
as far as [b]Gezer.

The Ark Brought to Jerusalem

6 Again David gathered all *the*
choice *men* of Israel, thirty
thousand.
2 And [a]David arose and went
with all the people who *were* with
him from [1]Baale Judah to bring up
from there the ark of God, whose
name is called [2]by the Name, the
LORD of Hosts, [b]who dwells *be-*
tween the cherubim.
3 So they set the ark of God on
a new cart, and brought it out of
the house of Abinadab, which *was*
on [a]the hill; and Uzzah and Ahio,
the sons of Abinadab, drove the
new [1]cart.
4 And they brought it out of [a]the
house of Abinadab, which *was* on
the hill, accompanying the ark of
God; and Ahio went before the
ark.
5 Then David and all the house
of Israel [a]played *music* before the
LORD on all kinds of *instruments*
of fir wood, on harps, on stringed
instruments, on tambourines, on
sistrums, and on cymbals.
6 And when they came to [a]Na-
chon's threshing floor, Uzzah put
out *his* [b]*hand* to the ark of God and
[1]took hold of it, for the oxen stum-
bled.
7 Then the anger of the LORD was
aroused against Uzzah, and God
struck him there for *his* [1]error; and
he died there by the ark of God.
8 And David became angry be-
cause of the LORD's outbreak

21 [a]Deut. 7:5, 25
22 [a]1 Chr. 14:13
23 [a]2 Sam. 5:19
24 [a]2 Kin. 7:6; 1 Chr. 14:15 [b]Judg. 4:14
25 [a]1 Chr. 14:16 [b]Josh. 16:10 [1]So with MT, Tg., Vg.; LXX *Gibeon*

CHAPTER 6

2 [a]1 Chr. 13:5, 6 [b]Ex. 25:22; 1 Sam. 4:4; Ps. 80:1 [1]*Baalah, Kirjath Jearim,* Josh. 15:9; 1 Chr. 13:6 [2]LXX, Tg., Vg. omit *by the Name;* many Heb. mss., Syr. *there*
3 [a]1 Sam. 26:1 [1]LXX adds *with the ark*
4 [a]1 Sam. 7:1; 1 Chr. 13:7
5 [a]1 Sam. 18:6, 7
6 [a]1 Chr. 13:9 [b]Num. 4:15, 19, 20 [1]*held it*
7 [1]Or *irreverence*
8 [1]Lit. *Outburst Against Uzzah*
9 [a]Deut. 9:19; Ps. 119:120; Luke 5:8
10 [a]2 Sam. 5:7 [b]1 Chr. 13:13; 26:4–8
11 [a]1 Chr. 13:14 [b]Gen. 30:27; 39:5
12 [a]1 Chr. 15:25—16:3
13 [a]Num. 4:15; Josh. 3:3; 1 Sam. 6:15; 2 Sam. 15:24; 1 Chr. 15:2, 15 [b]1 Kin. 8:5
14 [a]Ps. 30:11; 149:3 [b]1 Sam. 2:18, 28 [1]*whirled about*
15 [a]1 Chr. 15:28
16 [a]2 Sam. 3:14
17 [a]1 Chr. 16:1 [b]1 Chr. 15:1; 2 Chr. 1:4 [c]1 Kin. 8:5, 62, 63
18 [a]1 Kin. 8:14, 15, 55
19 [a]1 Chr. 16:3
20 [a]Ps. 30:title

against Uzzah; and he called the
name of the place [1]Perez Uzzah to
this day.
9 [a]David was afraid of the LORD
that day; and he said, "How can
the ark of the LORD come to me?"
10 So David would not move the
ark of the LORD with him into the
[a]City of David; but David took it
aside into the house of Obed-Edom
the [b]Gittite.
11 [a]The ark of the LORD remained
in the house of Obed-Edom the
Gittite three months. And the LORD
[b]blessed Obed-Edom and all his
household.
12 Now it was told King David,
saying, "The LORD has blessed the
house of Obed-Edom and all that
belongs to him, because of the ark
of God." [a]So David went and
brought up the ark of God from
the house of Obed-Edom to the
City of David with gladness.
13 And so it was, when [a]those
bearing the ark of the LORD had
gone six paces, that he sacrificed
[b]oxen and fatted sheep.
14 Then David [a]danced[1] before
the LORD with all *his* might; and
David *was* wearing [b]a linen ephod.
15 [a]So David and all the house of
Israel brought up the ark of the
LORD with shouting and with the
sound of the trumpet.
16 Now as the ark of the LORD
came into the City of David, [a]Mi-
chal, Saul's daughter, looked
through a window and saw King
David leaping and whirling before
the LORD; and she despised him in
her heart.
17 So [a]they brought the ark of the
LORD, and set it in [b]its place in the
midst of the tabernacle that David
had erected for it. Then David [c]of-
fered burnt offerings and peace of-
ferings before the LORD.
18 And when David had finished
offering burnt offerings and peace
offerings, [a]he blessed the people in
the name of the LORD of hosts.
19 [a]Then he distributed among all
the people, among the whole mul-
titude of Israel, both the women
and the men, to everyone a loaf
of bread, a piece *of meat,* and a
cake of raisins. So all the people
departed, everyone to his house.
20 [a]Then David returned to bless
his household. And Michal the

daughter of Saul came out to meet
David, and said, "How glorious
was the king of Israel today,
[b]uncovering himself today in the
eyes of the maids of his servants,
as one of the [c]base fellows [1]shame-
lessly uncovers himself!"
21 So David said to Michal, "*It*
was before the LORD, [a]who chose
me instead of your father and all
his house, to appoint me ruler over
the [b]people of the LORD, over Is-
rael. Therefore I will play *music*
before the LORD.
22 "And I will be even more un-
dignified than this, and will be
humble in my own sight. But as
for the maidservants of whom you
have spoken, by them I will be
held in honor."
23 Therefore Michal the daughter
of Saul had no children [a]to the day
of her death.

God's Covenant with David

7 Now it came to pass [a]when the
king was dwelling in his house,
and the LORD had given him rest
from all his enemies all around,
2 that the king said to Nathan the
prophet, "See now, I dwell in [a]a
house of cedar, [b]but the ark of God
dwells inside tent [c]curtains."
3 Then Nathan said to the king,
"Go, do all that *is* in your [a]heart,
for the LORD *is* with you."
4 But it happened that night that
the word of the LORD came to Na-
than, saying,
5 "Go and tell My servant David,
'Thus says the LORD: [a]"Would you
build a house for Me to dwell in?
6 "For I have not dwelt in a house
[a]since the time that I brought the
children of Israel up from Egypt,
even to this day, but have moved
about in [b]a tent and in a taber-
nacle.
7 "Wherever I have [a]moved
about with all the children of Is-
rael, have I ever spoken a word to
anyone from the tribes of Israel,
whom I commanded [b]to shepherd
My people Israel, saying, 'Why
have you not built Me a house of
cedar?' " '
8 "Now therefore, thus shall you
say to My servant David, 'Thus
says the LORD of hosts: [a]"I took
you from the sheepfold, from fol-
lowing the sheep, to be ruler over
My people, over Israel.
9 "And [a]I have been with you
wherever you have gone, [b]and
have [1]cut off all your enemies from
before you, and have made you a
great name, like the name of the
great men who *are* on the earth.
10 "Moreover I will appoint a
place for My people Israel, and
will [a]plant them, that they may
dwell in a place of their own and
move no more; [b]nor shall the sons
of wickedness oppress them any-
more, as previously,
11 [a]"since the time that I com-
manded judges *to be* over My peo-
ple Israel, and have caused you to
rest from all your enemies. Also
the LORD [1]tells you [b]that He will
make you a [2]house.
12 [a]"When your days are fulfilled
and you [b]rest with your fathers, [c]I
will set up your seed after you,
who will come from your body,
and I will establish his kingdom.
13 [a]"He shall build a house for My
name, and I will [b]establish the
throne of his kingdom forever.
14 [a]"I will be his Father, and he
shall be [b]My son. If he commits in-
iquity, I will chasten him with the
rod of men and with the [1]blows of
the sons of men.
15 "But My mercy shall not depart
from him, [a]as I took *it* from Saul,
whom I removed from before you.
16 "And [a]your house and your
kingdom shall be established for-
ever before [1]you. Your throne
shall be established forever." ' "
17 According to all these words
and according to all this vision, so
Nathan spoke to David.

David's Thanksgiving to God

18 Then King David went in and
sat before the LORD; and he said:
[a]"Who *am* I, O Lord GOD? And
what is my house, that You have
brought me this far?
19 "And yet this was a small thing
in Your sight, O Lord GOD; and
You have also spoken of Your ser-
vant's house for a great while to
come. [a]*Is* this the manner of man,
O Lord GOD?
20 "Now what more can David
say to You? For You, Lord GOD,
[a]know Your servant.
21 "For Your word's sake, and ac-

20 [b]2 Sam. 6:14, 16 [c]Judg. 9:4 [1]*openly*
21 [a]1 Sam. 13:14; 15:28 [b]2 Kin. 11:17
23 [a]Is. 22:14

CHAPTER 7

1 [a]1 Chr. 17:1–27
2 [a]2 Sam. 5:11 [b]Acts 7:46 [c]Ex. 26:1
3 [a]1 Kin. 8:17, 18
5 [a]1 Kin. 5:3, 4; 8:19
6 [a]1 Kin. 8:16 [b]Ex. 40:18, 34
7 [a]Lev. 26:11, 12 [b]2 Sam. 5:2
8 [a]1 Sam. 16:11, 12
9 [a]2 Sam. 5:10 [b]1 Sam. 31:6 [1]*destroyed*
10 [a]Ps. 44:2; 80:8 [b]Ps. 89:22, 23
11 [a]Judg. 2:14–16 [b]2 Sam. 7:27 [1]*declares to you* [2]Royal dynasty
12 [a]1 Kin. 2:1 [b]Deut. 31:16 [c]Ps. 132:11
13 [a]1 Kin. 5:5; 8:19 [b][Is. 9:7; 49:8]
14 [a][Heb. 1:5] [b][Ps. 2:7; 89:26, 27, 30] [1]*strokes*
15 [a]1 Sam. 15:23, 28; 16:14
16 [a]2 Sam. 7:13 [1]LXX *Me*
18 [a]Ex. 3:11
19 [a][Is. 55:8, 9]
20 [a]John 21:17

cording to Your own heart, You
have done all these great things,
to make Your servant know *them*.
22 "Therefore [a]You are great, [1]O
Lord GOD. For [b]*there is* none like
You, nor *is there any* God besides
You, according to all that we have
heard with our [c]ears.
23 "And who *is* like Your people,
like Israel, [a]the one nation on the
earth whom God went to redeem
for Himself as a people, to make
for Himself a name—and to do for
Yourself great and awesome deeds
for Your land—before [b]Your peo-
ple whom You redeemed for Your-
self from Egypt, the nations, and
their gods?
24 "For [a]You have made Your
people Israel Your very own peo-
ple forever; [b]and You, LORD, have
become their God.
25 "Now, O LORD God, the word
which You have spoken concern-
ing Your servant and concerning
his house, establish *it* forever and
do as You have said.
26 "So let Your name be magni-
fied forever, saying, 'The LORD of
hosts *is* the God over Israel.' And
let the house of Your servant Da-
vid be established before You.
27 "For You, O LORD of hosts, God
of Israel, have revealed *this* to
Your servant, saying, 'I will build
you a house.' Therefore Your ser-
vant has found it in his heart to
pray this prayer to You.
28 "And now, O Lord GOD, You
are God, and [a]Your words are true,
and You have promised this good-
ness to Your servant.
29 "Now therefore, let it please
You to bless the house of Your ser-
vant, that it may continue before
You forever; for You, O Lord GOD,
have spoken *it*, and with Your
blessing let the house of Your ser-
vant be blessed [a]forever."

David's Further Conquests

8 After this it came to pass that
David [1]attacked the Philistines
and subdued them. And David
took [2]Metheg Ammah from the
hand of the Philistines.
2 Then [a]he defeated Moab. Forc-
ing them down to the ground, he
measured them off with a line.
With two lines he measured off
those to be put to death, and with
one full line those to be kept alive.
So the Moabites became David's
[b]servants, *and* [c]brought tribute.
3 David also defeated Hadadezer
the son of Rehob, king of [a]Zobah,
as he went to recover [b]his territory
at the River Euphrates.
4 David took from him one thou-
sand *chariots*, [1]seven hundred
horsemen, and twenty thousand
foot soldiers. Also David [a]ham-
strung all the chariot horses, ex-
cept that he spared *enough* of them
for one hundred chariots.
5 [a]When the Syrians of Damas-
cus came to help Hadadezer king
of Zobah, David killed twenty-two
thousand of the Syrians.
6 Then David put garrisons in
Syria of Damascus; and the Syr-
ians became David's servants, *and*
brought tribute. So [a]the LORD
preserved David wherever he
went.
7 And David took [a]the shields of
gold that had belonged to the ser-
vants of Hadadezer, and brought
them to Jerusalem.
8 Also from [1]Betah and from
[a]Berothai,[2] cities of Hadadezer,
King David took a large amount
of bronze.
9 When [1]Toi king of [a]Hamath
heard that David had defeated all
the army of Hadadezer,
10 then Toi sent [1]Joram his son to
King David, to [2]greet him and
bless him, because he had fought
against Hadadezer and defeated
him (for Hadadezer had been at
war with Toi); and *Joram* brought
with him articles of silver, articles
of gold, and articles of bronze.
11 King David also [a]dedicated
these to the LORD, along with the
silver and gold that he had dedi-
cated from all the nations which
he had subdued—
12 from [1]Syria, from Moab, from
the people of Ammon, from the
[a]Philistines, from Amalek, and
from the spoil of Hadadezer the
son of Rehob, king of Zobah.
13 And David made *himself* a
[a]name when he returned from kill-
ing [b]eighteen thousand [1]Syrians in
[c]the Valley of Salt.
14 He also put garrisons in Edom;
throughout all Edom he put garri-
sons, and [a]all the Edomites be-
came David's servants. And the

22 [a]Deut. 10:17 [b]Ex. 15:11 [c]Ex. 10:2 [1]Tg., Syr. *O LORD God*
23 [a]Ps. 147:20 [b]Deut. 9:26; 33:29
24 [a][Deut. 26:18] [b]Ps. 48:14
28 [a]John 17:17
29 [a]2 Sam. 22:51

CHAPTER 8

1 [1]Lit. *struck* [2]Lit. *The Bridle of the Mother City*
2 [a]Num. 24:17 [b]2 Sam. 12:31 [c]1 Kin. 4:21
3 [a]1 Sam. 14:47 [b]2 Sam. 10:15–19
4 [a]Josh. 11:6, 9 [1]*seven thousand*, 1 Chr. 18:4
5 [a]1 Kin. 11:23–25
6 [a]2 Sam. 7:9; 8:14
7 [a]1 Kin. 10:16
8 [a]Ezek. 47:16 [1]*Tibhath*, 1 Chr. 18:8 [2]*Chun*, 1 Chr. 18:8
9 [a]1 Kin. 8:65 [1]*Tou*, 1 Chr. 18:9
10 [1]*Hadoram*, 1 Chr. 18:10 [2]Lit. *ask him of his welfare*
11 [a]1 Kin. 7:51
12 [a]2 Sam. 5:17–25 [1]LXX, Syr., Heb. mss. *Edom*
13 [a]2 Sam. 7:9 [b]2 Kin. 14:7 [c]1 Chr. 18:12 [1]LXX, Syr., Heb. mss. *Edomites* and 1 Chr. 18:12
14 [a]Gen. 27:29, 37–40

LORD preserved David wherever
he went.

David's Administration

15 So David reigned over all Is-
rael; and David administered judg-
ment and justice to all his people.
16 [a]Joab the son of Zeruiah *was*
over the army; [b]Jehoshaphat the
son of Ahilud *was* recorder;
17 [a]Zadok the son of Ahitub and
Ahimelech the son of Abiathar
were the priests; [1]Seraiah *was* the
[2]scribe;
18 [a]Benaiah the son of Jehoiada
was over both the [b]Cherethites
and the Pelethites; and David's
sons were [1]chief ministers.

David's Kindness to Mephibosheth

9 Now David said, "Is there still
anyone who is left of the house
of Saul, that I may [a]show him
[1]kindness for Jonathan's sake?"
2 And *there was* a servant of the
house of Saul whose name *was*
[a]Ziba. So when they had called
him to David, the king said to him,
"*Are* you Ziba?" He said, "At your
service!"
3 Then the king said, "*Is* there
not still someone of the house of
Saul, to whom I may show [a]the
kindness of God?" And Ziba said
to the king, "There is still a son
of Jonathan *who is* [b]lame in *his*
feet."
4 So the king said to him,
"Where *is* he?" And Ziba said to
the king, "Indeed he *is* in the house
of [a]Machir the son of Ammiel, in
Lo Debar."
5 Then King David sent and
brought him out of the house of
Machir the son of Ammiel, from
Lo Debar.
6 Now when [a]Mephibosheth[1] the
son of Jonathan, the son of Saul,
had come to David, he fell on his
face and prostrated himself. Then
David said, "Mephibosheth?" And
he answered, "Here is your ser-
vant!"
7 So David said to him, "Do not
fear, for I will surely show you
kindness for Jonathan your fa-
ther's sake, and will restore to you
all the land of Saul your grand-
father; and you shall eat bread at
my table continually."
8 Then he bowed himself, and
said, "What *is* your servant, that
you should look upon such [a]a dead
dog as I?"
9 And the king called to Ziba,
Saul's servant, and said to him, [a]"I
have given to your master's son all
that belonged to Saul and to all his
house.
10 "You therefore, and your sons
and your servants, shall work the
land for him, and you shall bring
in *the harvest*, that your master's
son may have food to eat. But
Mephibosheth your master's son
[a]shall eat bread at my table al-
ways." Now Ziba had [b]fifteen sons
and twenty servants.
11 Then Ziba said to the king,
"According to all that my lord the
king has commanded his servant,
so will your servant do." "As for
Mephibosheth," *said the king*, "he
shall eat at [1]my table like one of
the king's sons."
12 Mephibosheth had a young son
[a]whose name *was* Micha. And all
who dwelt in the house of Ziba
were servants of Mephibosheth.
13 So Mephibosheth dwelt in Je-
rusalem, [a]for he ate continually at
the king's table. And he [b]was lame
in both his feet.

The Ammonites and Syrians Defeated

10 It happened after this that
the [a]king of the people of
Ammon died, and Hanun his son
reigned in his place.
2 Then David said, "I will show
[a]kindness to Hanun the son of
[b]Nahash, as his father showed
kindness to me." So David sent by
the hand of his servants to comfort
him concerning his father. And
David's servants came into the
land of the people of Ammon.
3 And the princes of the people
of Ammon said to Hanun their
lord, "Do you think that David re-
ally honors your father because he
has sent comforters to you? Has
David not *rather* sent his servants
to you to search the city, to spy it
out, and to overthrow it?"
4 Therefore Hanun took David's
servants, shaved off half of their
beards, cut off their garments in
the middle, [a]at their buttocks, and
sent them away.
5 When they told David, he sent
to meet them, because the men

16 [a]2 Sam. 19:13; 20:23; 1 Chr. 11:6 [b]1 Kin. 4:3
17 [a]1 Chr. 6:4–8; 24:3 [1]*Shavsha*, 1 Chr. 18:16 [2]*secretary*
18 [a]1 Kin. 1:8; 1 Chr. 18:17 [b]1 Sam. 30:14; 1 Kin. 1:38 [1]Lit. *priests*

CHAPTER 9

1 [a]1 Sam. 18:3; 20:14–16; 2 Sam. 21:7; [Prov. 27:10] [1]*covenant faithfulness*
2 [a]2 Sam. 16:1–4; 19:17, 29
3 [a]1 Sam. 20:14 [b]2 Sam. 4:4
4 [a]2 Sam. 17:27–29
6 [a]2 Sam. 16:4; 19:24–30 [1]Or *Merib-Baal*
8 [a]2 Sam. 16:9
9 [a]2 Sam. 16:4; 19:29
10 [a]2 Sam. 9:7, 11, 13; 19:28 [b]2 Sam. 19:17
11 [1]LXX *David's table*
12 [a]1 Chr. 8:34
13 [a]2 Sam. 9:7, 10, 11; 1 Kin. 2:7; 2 Kin. 25:29 [b]2 Sam. 9:3

CHAPTER 10

1 [a]2 Sam. 11:1; 1 Chr. 19:1
2 [a]2 Sam. 9:1; 1 Kin. 2:7 [b]1 Sam. 11:1
4 [a]Is. 20:4; 47:2

were greatly [1]ashamed. And the
king said, "Wait at Jericho until
your beards have grown, and *then*
return."
6 When the people of Ammon
saw that they [a]had made them-
selves repulsive to David, the peo-
ple of Ammon sent and hired [b]the
Syrians of [c]Beth Rehob and the
Syrians of Zoba, twenty thousand
foot soldiers; and from the king of
[d]Maacah one thousand men, and
from [e]Ish-Tob twelve thousand
men.
7 Now when David heard *of it,*
he sent Joab and all the army of
[a]the mighty men.
8 Then the people of Ammon
came out and put themselves in
battle array at the entrance of the
gate. And [a]the Syrians of Zoba,
Beth Rehob, Ish-Tob, and Maacah
were by themselves in the field.
9 When Joab saw that the battle
line was against him before and
behind, he chose some of Israel's
best and put *them* in battle array
against the Syrians.
10 And the rest of the people he
put under the command of
[a]Abishai his brother, that he might
set *them* in battle array against the
people of Ammon.
11 Then he said, "If the Syrians
are too strong for me, then you
shall help me; but if the people of
Ammon are too strong for you,
then I will come and help you.
12 [a]"Be of good courage, and let
us [b]be strong for our people and
for the cities of our God. And may
[c]the LORD do *what is* good in His
sight."
13 So Joab and the people who
were with him drew near for the
battle against the Syrians, and
they fled before him.
14 When the people of Ammon
saw that the Syrians were fleeing,
they also fled before Abishai, and
entered the city. So Joab returned
from the people of Ammon and
went to [a]Jerusalem.
15 When the Syrians saw that
they had been defeated by Israel,
they gathered together.
16 Then [1]Hadadezer sent and
brought out the Syrians who *were*
beyond [2]the River, and they came
to Helam. And [3]Shobach the com-
mander of Hadadezer's army *went*
before them.
17 When it was told David, he
gathered all Israel, crossed over
the Jordan, and came to Helam.
And the Syrians set themselves in
battle array against David and
fought with him.
18 Then the Syrians fled before Is-
rael; and David killed seven hun-
dred charioteers and forty thou-
sand [a]horsemen of the Syrians,
and struck Shobach the com-
mander of their army, who died
there.
19 And when all the kings *who*
were servants to [1]Hadadezer saw
that they were defeated by Israel,
they made peace with Israel and
[a]served them. So the Syrians were
afraid to help the people of Am-
mon anymore.

David, Bathsheba, and Uriah

11 It happened in the spring of
the year, at the [a]time when
kings go out *to battle,* that [b]David
sent Joab and his servants with
him, and all Israel; and they de-
stroyed the people of Ammon and
besieged [c]Rabbah. But David re-
mained at Jerusalem.
2 Then it happened one evening
that David arose from his bed [a]and
walked on the roof of the king's
house. And from the roof he [b]saw
a woman bathing, and the woman
was very beautiful to behold.
3 So David sent and inquired
about the woman. And *someone*
said, "*Is* this not [1]Bathsheba, the
daughter of [2]Eliam, the wife [a]of
Uriah the [b]Hittite?"
4 Then David sent messengers,
and took her; and she came to him,
and [a]he lay with her, for she was
[b]cleansed from her impurity; and
she returned to her house.
5 And the woman conceived; so
she sent and told David, and said,
"I *am* with child."
6 Then David sent to Joab, *say-*
ing, "Send me Uriah the Hittite."
And Joab sent Uriah to David.
7 When Uriah had come to him,
David asked how Joab was doing,
and how the people were doing,
and how the war prospered.
8 And David said to Uriah, "Go
down to your house and [a]wash
your feet." So Uriah departed from

5 [1]*humiliated*
6 [a]Gen. 34:30; Ex. 5:21 [b]2 Sam. 8:3, 5 [c]Judg. 18:28 [d]Deut. 3:14; Josh. 13:11, 13 [e]Judg. 11:3, 5
7 [a]2 Sam. 23:8
8 [a]2 Sam. 10:6
10 [a]1 Sam. 26:6; 2 Sam. 3:30
12 [a]Deut. 31:6; Josh. 1:6, 7, 9; Neh. 4:14 [b]1 Sam. 4:9; 1 Cor. 16:13 [c]1 Sam. 3:18
14 [a]2 Sam. 11:1
16 [1]Heb. *Hadarezer* [2]The Euphrates [3]*Shophach,* 1 Chr. 19:16
18 [a]1 Chr. 19:18
19 [a]2 Sam. 8:6 [1]Heb. *Hadarezer*

CHAPTER 11

1 [a]1 Kin. 20:22–26 [b]1 Chr. 20:1 [c]2 Sam. 12:26; Jer. 49:2, 3; Amos 1:14
2 [a]Deut. 22:8; 1 Sam. 9:25; Matt. 24:17; Acts 10:9 [b]Gen. 34:2; [Ex. 20:17]; Job 31:1; [Matt. 5:28]
3 [a]2 Sam. 23:39 [b]1 Sam. 26:6 [1]*Bathshua,* 1 Chr. 3:5 [2]*Ammiel,* 1 Chr. 3:5
4 [a][Lev. 20:10; Deut. 22:22]; Ps. 51:title; [James 1:14, 15] [b]Lev. 15:19, 28
8 [a]Gen. 18:4; 19:2

the king's house, and a gift *of food*
from the king followed him.
9 But Uriah slept at the [a]door of
the king's house with all the ser-
vants of his lord, and did not go
down to his house.
10 So when they told David, say-
ing, "Uriah did not go down to his
house," David said to Uriah, "Did
you not come from a journey?
Why did you not go down to your
house?"
11 And Uriah said to David, [a]"The
ark and Israel and Judah are
dwelling in tents, and [b]my lord
Joab and the servants of my lord
are encamped in the open fields.
Shall I then go to my house to eat
and drink, and to lie with my wife?
As you live, and *as* your soul lives,
I will not do this thing."
12 Then David said to Uriah,
"Wait here today also, and tomor-
row I will let you depart." So Uriah
remained in Jerusalem that day
and the next.
13 Now when David called him,
he ate and drank before him; and
he made him [a]drunk. And at eve-
ning he went out to lie on his bed
[b]with the servants of his lord, but
he did not go down to his house.
14 In the morning it happened
that David [a]wrote a letter to Joab
and sent *it* by the hand of Uriah.
15 And he wrote in the letter, say-
ing, "Set Uriah in the forefront of
the [1]hottest battle, and retreat
from him, that he may [a]be struck
down and die."
16 So it was, while Joab besieged
the city, that he assigned Uriah to
a place where he knew there *were*
valiant men.
17 Then the men of the city came
out and fought with Joab. And
some of the people of the servants
of David fell; and Uriah the Hittite
died also.
18 Then Joab sent and told David
all the things concerning the war,
19 and charged the messenger,
saying, "When you have finished
telling the matters of the war to
the king,
20 "if it happens that the king's
wrath rises, and he says to you:
'Why did you approach so near to
the city when you fought? Did you
not know that they would shoot
from the wall?
21 'Who struck [a]Abimelech the
son of [1]Jerubbesheth? Was it not
a woman who cast a piece of a
millstone on him from the wall, so
that he died in Thebez? Why did
you go near the wall?'—then you
shall say, 'Your servant Uriah the
Hittite is dead also.' "
22 So the messenger went, and
came and told David all that Joab
had sent by him.
23 And the messenger said to Da-
vid, "Surely the men prevailed
against us and came out to us in
the field; then we drove them back
as far as the entrance of the gate.
24 "The archers shot from the
wall at your servants; and *some* of
the king's servants are dead, and
your servant Uriah the Hittite is
dead also."
25 Then David said to the messen-
ger, "Thus you shall say to Joab:
'Do not let this thing [1]displease
you, for the sword devours one as
well as another. Strengthen your
attack against the city, and over-
throw it.' So encourage him."
26 When the wife of Uriah heard
that Uriah her husband was dead,
she mourned for her husband.
27 And when her mourning was
over, David sent and brought her
to his house, and she [a]became his
wife and bore him a son. But the
thing that David had done [b]dis-
pleased[1] the LORD.

Nathan's Parable and David's Confession

12 Then the LORD sent Nathan
to David. And [a]he came to
him, and [b]said to him: "There were
two men in one city, one rich and
the other poor.
2 "The rich *man* had exceedingly
many flocks and herds.
3 "But the poor *man* had noth-
ing, except one little ewe lamb
which he had bought and nour-
ished; and it grew up together with
him and with his children. It ate
of his own food and drank from
his own cup and lay in his bosom;
and it was like a daughter to him.
4 "And a traveler came to the
rich man, who refused to take
from his own flock and from his
own herd to prepare one for the
wayfaring man who had come to
him; but he took the poor man's

9 [a]1 Kin. 14:27, 28
11 [a]2 Sam. 7:2, 6 [b]2 Sam. 20:6–22
13 [a]Gen. 19:33, 35 [b]2 Sam. 11:9
14 [a]1 Kin. 21:8, 9
15 [a]2 Sam. 12:9 [1]*fiercest*
21 [a]Judg. 9:50–54 [1]*Jerubbaal* (Gideon), Judg. 6:32ff.
25 [1]Lit. *be evil in your sight*
27 [a]2 Sam. 12:9 [b]1 Chr. 21:7; [Heb. 13:4] [1]Lit. *was evil in the eyes of*

CHAPTER 12

1 [a]Ps. 51:title [b]1 Kin. 20:35–41

lamb and prepared it for the man
who had come to him."
5 So David's anger was greatly
aroused against the man, and he
said to Nathan, "*As* the LORD lives,
the man who has done this [1]shall
surely die!
6 "And he shall restore [a]fourfold
for the lamb, because he did this
thing and because he had no pity."
7 Then Nathan said to David,
"You *are* the man! Thus says the
LORD God of Israel: 'I [a]anointed
you king over Israel, and I deliv-
ered you from the hand of Saul.
8 'I gave you your master's house
and your master's wives into your
keeping, and gave you the house
of Israel and Judah. And if *that
had been* too little, I also would
have given you much more!
9 [a]'Why have you [b]despised the
commandment of the LORD, to do
evil in His sight? [c]You have killed
Uriah the Hittite with the sword;
you have taken his wife *to be* your
wife, and have killed him with the
sword of the people of Ammon.
10 'Now therefore, [a]the sword
shall never depart from your
house, because you have despised
Me, and have taken the wife of
Uriah the Hittite to be your wife.'
11 "Thus says the LORD: 'Behold,
I will raise up adversity against
you from your own house; and I
will [a]take your wives before your
eyes and give *them* to your neigh-
bor, and he shall lie with your
wives in the sight of this sun.
12 'For you did *it* secretly, [a]but I
will do this thing before all Israel,
before the sun.' "
13 [a]So David said to Nathan, [b]"I
have sinned against the LORD."
And Nathan said to David, "The
LORD also has [c]put away your sin;
you shall not die.
14 "However, because by this
deed you have given great occa-
sion to the enemies of the LORD [a]to
blaspheme, the child also *who is*
born to you shall surely die."
15 Then Nathan departed to his
house.

The Death of David's Son

And the [a]LORD struck the child
that Uriah's wife bore to David,
and it became ill.
16 David therefore pleaded with
God for the child, and David fasted
and went in and [a]lay all night on
the ground.
17 So the elders of his house arose
and went to him, to raise him
up from the ground. But he would
not, nor did he eat food with
them.
18 Then on the seventh day it
came to pass that the child died.
And the servants of David were
afraid to tell him that the child was
dead. For they said, "Indeed, while
the child was alive, we spoke to
him, and he would not heed our
voice. How can we tell him that
the child is dead? He may do some
harm!"
19 When David saw that his ser-
vants were whispering, David per-
ceived that the child was dead.
Therefore David said to his ser-
vants, "Is the child dead?" And
they said, "He is dead."
20 So David arose from the
ground, washed and [a]anointed
himself, and changed his clothes;
and he went into the house of the
LORD and [b]worshiped. Then he
went to his own house; and when
he requested, they set food before
him, and he ate.
21 Then his servants said to him,
"What *is* this that you have done?
You fasted and wept for the child
while he was alive, but when the
child died, you arose and ate
food."
22 And he said, "While the child
was alive, I fasted and wept; [a]for
I said, 'Who can tell *whether* [1]the
LORD will be gracious to me, that
the child may live?'
23 "But now he is dead; why
should I fast? Can I bring him back
again? I shall go [a]to him, but [b]he
shall not return to me."

Solomon Is Born

24 Then David comforted Bath-
sheba his wife, and went in to her
and lay with her. So [a]she bore a
son, and [b]he[1] called his name
Solomon. Now the LORD loved
him,
25 and He sent *word* by the hand
of Nathan the prophet: So [1]he
called his name [2]Jedidiah, because
of the LORD.

5 [1]*deserves to die*, lit. *is a son of death*
6 [a][Ex. 22:1]; Luke 19:8
7 [a]1 Sam. 16:13; 2 Sam. 5:3
9 [a]1 Sam. 15:19 [b]Num. 15:31 [c]2 Sam. 11:14–17, 27
10 [a]2 Sam. 13:28; 18:14; 1 Kin. 2:25; [Amos 7:9]
11 [a]Deut. 28:30; 2 Sam. 16:21, 22
12 [a]2 Sam. 16:22
13 [a]1 Sam. 15:24 [b]2 Sam. 24:10; Job 7:20; Ps. 51; Luke 18:13 [c]2 Sam. 24:10; Job 7:21; [Ps. 32:1–5; Prov. 28:13; Mic. 7:18]; Zech. 3:4
14 [a]Is. 52:5; [Ezek. 36:20, 23]; Rom. 2:24
15 [a]1 Sam. 25:38
16 [a]2 Sam. 13:31
20 [a]Ruth 3:3; Matt. 6:17 [b]Job 1:20
22 [a]Is. 38:1–5; Joel 2:14; Jon. 3:9 [1]Heb. mss., Syr. *God*
23 [a]Gen. 37:35 [b]Job 7:8–10
24 [a]Matt. 1:6 [b]1 Chr. 22:9 [1]So with Kt., LXX, Vg.; Qr., a few Heb. mss., Syr., Tg. *she*
25 [1]Qr., some Heb. mss., Syr., Tg. *she* [2]Lit. *Beloved of the LORD*

Rabbah Is Captured

26 Now [a]Joab fought against [b]Rabbah of the people of Ammon, and took the royal city.

27 And Joab sent messengers to David, and said, "I have fought against Rabbah, and I have taken the city's water *supply*.

28 "Now therefore, gather the rest of the people together and encamp against the city and take it, lest I take the city and it be called after my name."

29 So David gathered all the people together and went to Rabbah, fought against it, and took it.

30 [a]Then he took their king's crown from his head. Its weight *was* a talent of gold, with precious stones. And it was *set* on David's head. Also he brought out the [1]spoil of the city in great abundance.

31 And he brought out the people who *were* in it, and put *them to work* with saws and iron picks and iron axes, and made them cross over to the brick works. So he did to all the cities of the people of Ammon. Then David and all the people returned to Jerusalem.

Amnon and Tamar

13 After this [a]Absalom the son of David had a lovely sister, whose name *was* [b]Tamar; and [c]Amnon the son of David loved her.

2 Amnon was so distressed over his sister Tamar that he became sick; for she *was* a virgin. And it was improper for Amnon to do anything to her.

3 But Amnon had a friend whose name *was* Jonadab [a]the son of Shimeah, David's brother. Now Jonadab *was* a very crafty man.

4 And he said to him, "Why *are* you, the king's son, becoming thinner day after day? Will you not tell me?" Amnon said to him, "I love Tamar, my brother Absalom's sister."

5 So Jonadab said to him, "Lie down on your bed and pretend to be ill. And when your father comes to see you, say to him, 'Please let my sister Tamar come and give me food, and prepare the food in my sight, that I may see *it* and eat *it* from her hand.' "

6 Then Amnon lay down and pretended to be ill; and when the king came to see him, Amnon said to the king, "Please let Tamar my sister come and [a]make a couple of cakes for me in my sight, that I may eat from her hand."

7 And David sent home to Tamar, saying, "Now go to your brother Amnon's house, and prepare food for him."

8 So Tamar went to her brother Amnon's house; and he was lying down. Then she took flour and kneaded *it*, made cakes in his sight, and baked the cakes.

9 And she took the pan and placed *them* out before him, but he refused to eat. Then Amnon said, [a]"Have everyone go out from me." And they all went out from him.

10 Then Amnon said to Tamar, "Bring the food into the bedroom, that I may eat from your hand." And Tamar took the cakes which she had made, and brought *them* to Amnon her brother in the bedroom.

11 Now when she had brought *them* to him to eat, [a]he took hold of her and said to her, "Come, lie with me, my sister."

12 But she answered him, "No, my brother, do not [1]force me, for [a]no such thing should be done in Israel. Do not do this [b]disgraceful thing!

13 "And I, where could I take my shame? And as for you, you would be like one of the fools in Israel. Now therefore, please speak to the king; [a]for he will not withhold me from you."

14 However, he would not heed her voice; and being stronger than she, he [a]forced her and lay with her.

15 Then Amnon hated her [1]exceedingly, so that the hatred with which he hated her *was* greater than the love with which he had loved her. And Amnon said to her, "Arise, be gone!"

16 So she said to him, "No, indeed! This evil of sending me away *is* worse than the other that you did to me." But he would not listen to her.

12:26 [a]1 Chr. 20:1 [b]Deut. 3:11; 2 Sam. 11:1
30 [a]1 Chr. 20:2 [1]*plunder*

CHAPTER 13

1 [a]2 Sam. 3:2, 3; 1 Chr. 3:2 [b]1 Chr. 3:9 [c]2 Sam. 3:2
3 [a]1 Sam. 16:9
6 [a]Gen. 18:6
9 [a]Gen. 45:1
11 [a]Gen. 39:12; [Deut. 27:22]; Ezek. 22:11
12 [a][Lev. 18:9–11; 20:17] [b]Gen. 34:7; Judg. 19:23; 20:6 [1]Lit. *humble me*
13 [a]Gen. 20:12
14 [a]Lev. 18:9; [Deut. 22:25; 27:22]; 2 Sam. 12:11
15 [1]*with a very great hatred*

17 Then he called his servant
who attended him, and said,
"Here! Put this *woman* out, away
from me, and bolt the door behind
her."
18 Now she had on [a]a robe of
many colors, for the king's virgin
daughters wore such apparel. And
his servant put her out and bolted
the door behind her.
19 Then Tamar put [a]ashes on her
head, and tore her robe of many
colors that *was* on her, and [b]laid
her hand on her head and went
away crying bitterly.
20 And Absalom her brother said
to her, "Has Amnon your brother
been with you? But now hold your
peace, my sister. He *is* your
brother; do not take this thing to
heart." So Tamar remained deso-
late in her brother Absalom's
house.
21 But when King David heard of
all these things, he was very an-
gry.
22 And Absalom spoke to his
brother Amnon [a]neither good nor
bad. For Absalom [b]hated Amnon,
because he had forced his sister
Tamar.

Absalom Murders Amnon

23 And it came to pass, after two
full years, that Absalom [a]had
sheepshearers in Baal Hazor,
which *is* near Ephraim; so Absa-
lom invited all the king's sons.
24 Then Absalom came to the
king and said, "Kindly note, your
servant has sheepshearers; please,
let the king and his servants go
with your servant."
25 But the king said to Absalom,
"No, my son, let us not all go now,
lest we be a burden to you." Then
he urged him, but he would not go;
and he blessed him.
26 Then Absalom said, "If not,
please let my brother Amnon go
with us." And the king said to him,
"Why should he go with you?"
27 But Absalom urged him; so he
let Amnon and all the king's sons
go with him.
28 Now Absalom had commanded
his servants, saying, "Watch now,
when Amnon's [a]heart is merry
with wine, and when I say to you,
'Strike Amnon!' then kill him. Do
not be afraid. Have I not com-
manded you? Be courageous and
[1]valiant."
29 So the servants of Absalom
[a]did to Amnon as Absalom had
commanded. Then all the king's
sons arose, and each one got on
[b]his mule and fled.
30 And it came to pass, while they
were on the way, that news came
to David, saying, "Absalom has
killed all the king's sons, and not
one of them is left!"
31 So the king arose and [a]tore his
garments and [b]lay on the ground,
and all his servants stood by with
their clothes torn.
32 Then [a]Jonadab the son of
Shimeah, David's brother, an-
swered and said, "Let not my
lord suppose they have killed
all the young men, the king's
sons, for only Amnon is dead.
For by the command of Absalom
this has been determined from
the day that he forced his sister Ta-
mar.
33 "Now therefore, [a]let not my
lord the king take the thing to his
heart, to think that all the king's
sons are dead. For only Amnon is
dead."

Absalom Flees to Geshur

34 [a]Then Absalom fled. And the
young man who was keeping
watch lifted his eyes and looked,
and there, many people were com-
ing from the road on the hillside
behind [1]him.
35 And Jonadab said to the
king, "Look, the king's sons are
coming; as your servant said, so
it is."
36 So it was, as soon as he had
finished speaking, that the king's
sons indeed came, and they lifted
up their voice and wept. Also the
king and all his servants wept very
bitterly.
37 But Absalom fled and went to
[a]Talmai the son of Ammihud, king
of Geshur. And *David* mourned for
his son every day.
38 So Absalom fled and went to
[a]Geshur, and was there three
years.
39 And [1]King David [2]longed to go
to Absalom. For he had been [a]com-
forted concerning Amnon, be-
cause he was dead.

18 [a]Gen. 37:3; Judg. 5:30; Ps. 45:13, 14

19 [a]Josh. 7:6; 2 Sam. 1:2; Job 2:12; 42:6 [b]Jer. 2:37

22 [a]Gen. 24:50; 31:24 [b][Lev. 19:17, 18; 1 John 2:9, 11; 3:10, 12, 15]

23 [a]Gen. 38:12, 13; 1 Sam. 25:4

28 [a]Judg. 19:6, 9, 22; Ruth 3:7; 1 Sam. 25:36; Esth. 1:10 [1]Lit. *sons of valor*

29 [a]2 Sam. 12:10 [b]2 Sam. 18:9; 1 Kin. 1:33, 38

31 [a]2 Sam. 1:11 [b]2 Sam. 12:16

32 [a]2 Sam. 13:3–5

33 [a]2 Sam. 19:19

34 [a]2 Sam. 13:37, 38 [1]LXX adds *And the watchman went and told the king, and said, "I see men from the way of Horonaim, from the regions of the mountains."*

37 [a]2 Sam. 3:3; 1 Chr. 3:2

38 [a]2 Sam. 14:23, 32; 15:8

39 [a]Gen. 38:12; 2 Sam. 12:19, 23 [1]So with MT, Syr., Vg.; LXX *the spirit of the king;* Tg. *the soul of King David* [2]So with MT, Tg.; LXX, Vg. *ceased to pursue after*

Absalom Returns to Jerusalem

14 So Joab the son of Zeruiah
perceived that the king's
heart *was* concerned [a]about Absa-
lom.
2 And Joab sent to [a]Tekoa and
brought from there a wise woman,
and said to her, "Please pretend
to be a mourner, [b]and put on
mourning apparel; do not anoint
yourself with oil, but act like a
woman who has been mourning a
long time for the dead.
3 "Go to the king and speak to
him in this manner." So Joab [a]put
the words in her mouth.
4 And when the woman of Tekoa
[1]spoke to the king, she [a]fell on her
face to the ground and prostrated
herself, and said, [b]"Help, O king!"
5 Then the king said to her,
"What troubles you?" And she an-
swered, [a]"Indeed I *am* a widow,
my husband is dead.
6 "Now your maidservant had
two sons; and the two fought with
each other in the field, and *there
was* no one to part them, but the
one struck the other and killed
him.
7 "And now the whole family has
risen up against your maidservant,
and they said, 'Deliver him who
struck his brother, that we may ex-
ecute him [a]for the life of his
brother whom he killed; and we
will destroy the heir also.' So they
would extinguish my ember that
is left, and leave to my husband
neither name nor remnant on the
earth."
8 Then the king said to the
woman, "Go to your house, and
I will give orders concerning
you."
9 And the woman of Tekoa said
to the king, "My lord, O king, *let*
[a]the [1]iniquity *be* on me and on my
father's house, [b]and the king and
his throne *be* guiltless."
10 So the king said, "Whoever
says *anything* to you, bring him to
me, and he shall not touch you
anymore."
11 Then she said, "Please let the
king remember the LORD your
God, and do not permit [a]the aven-
ger of blood to destroy anymore,
lest they destroy my son." And he
said, [b]"*As* the LORD lives, not one
hair of your son shall fall to the
ground."
12 Therefore the woman said,
"Please, let your maidservant
speak *another* word to my lord the
king." And he said, "Say on."
13 So the woman said: "Why then
have you schemed such a thing
against [a]the people of God? For the
king speaks this thing as one who
is guilty, *in that* the king does not
bring [b]his banished one home
again.
14 "For we [a]will surely die and *be-
come* like water spilled on the
ground, which cannot be gathered
up again. Yet God does not [b]take
away a life; but He [c]devises means,
so that His banished ones are not
[1]expelled from Him.
15 "Now therefore, I have come to
speak of this thing to my lord the
king because the people have
made me afraid. And your
maidservant said, 'I will now
speak to the king; it may be that
the king will perform the request
of his maidservant.
16 'For the king will hear and de-
liver his maidservant from the
hand of the man *who would* de-
stroy me and my son together from
the [a]inheritance of God.'
17 "Your maidservant said, 'The
word of my lord the king will now
be comforting; for [a]as the angel of
God, so *is* my lord the king in [b]dis-
cerning good and evil. And may
the LORD your God be with you.' "
18 Then the king answered and
said to the woman, "Please do not
hide from me anything that I ask
you." And the woman said,
"Please, let my lord the king
speak."
19 So the king said, "*Is* the hand
of Joab with you in all this?" And
the woman answered and said,
"*As* you live, my lord the king, no
one can turn to the right hand or
to the left from anything that my
lord the king has spoken. For your
servant Joab commanded me, and
[a]he put all these words in the
mouth of your maidservant.
20 "To bring about this change of
affairs your servant Joab has done
this thing; but my lord *is* wise, [a]ac-
cording to the wisdom of the angel
of God, to know everything that
is in the earth."

CHAPTER 14
1 [a]2 Sam. 13:39
2 [a]2 Sam. 23:26; 2 Chr. 11:6; Amos 1:1 [b]Ruth 3:3
3 [a]Ex. 4:15; 2 Sam. 14:19
4 [a]1 Sam. 20:41; 25:23; 2 Sam. 1:2 [b]2 Kin. 6:26, 28 [1]Many Heb. mss., LXX, Syr., Vg. *came*
5 [a][Zech. 7:10]
7 [a]Num. 35:19; Deut. 19:12, 13
9 [a]Gen. 27:13; 43:9; 1 Sam. 25:24; Matt. 27:25 [b]2 Sam. 3:28, 29; 1 Kin. 2:33 [1]*guilt*
11 [a]Num. 35:19, 21; [Deut. 19:4–10] [b]1 Sam. 14:45; 1 Kin. 1:52; Matt. 10:30; Acts 27:34
13 [a]Judg. 20:2 [b]2 Sam. 13:37, 38
14 [a]Job 30:23; 34:15; [Heb. 9:27] [b]Job 34:19; Matt. 22:16; Acts 10:34; Rom. 2:11 [c]Num. 35:15 [1]*cast out*
16 [a]Deut. 32:9; 1 Sam. 26:19; 2 Sam. 20:19
17 [a]1 Sam. 29:9; 2 Sam. 19:27 [b]1 Kin. 3:9
19 [a]2 Sam. 14:3
20 [a]2 Sam. 14:17; 19:27

21 And the king said to Joab, "All
right, I have granted this thing. Go
therefore, bring back the young
man Absalom."
22 Then Joab fell to the ground on
his face and bowed himself, and
[1]thanked the king. And Joab said,
"Today your servant knows that I
have found favor in your sight, my
lord, O king, in that the king has
fulfilled the request of his ser-
vant."
23 So Joab arose [a]and went to
Geshur, and brought Absalom to
Jerusalem.
24 And the king said, "Let him re-
turn to his own house, but [a]do not
let him see my face." So Absalom
returned to his own house, but did
not see the king's face.

David Forgives Absalom

25 Now in all Israel there was no
one who was praised as much as
Absalom for his good looks. [a]From
the sole of his foot to the crown
of his head there was no blemish
in him.
26 And when he cut the hair of his
head—at the end of every year he
cut *it* because it was heavy on
him—when he cut it, he weighed
the hair of his head at two hundred
shekels according to the king's
standard.
27 [a]To Absalom were born three
sons, and one daughter whose
name *was* Tamar. She was a
woman of beautiful appearance.
28 And Absalom dwelt two full
years in Jerusalem, [a]but did not
see the king's face.
29 Therefore Absalom sent for
Joab, to send him to the king, but
he would not come to him. And
when he sent again the second
time, he would not come.
30 So he said to his servants, "See,
Joab's field is near mine, and he
has barley there; go and set it on
fire." And Absalom's servants set
the field on fire.
31 Then Joab arose and came to
Absalom's house, and said to him,
"Why have your servants set my
field on fire?"
32 And Absalom answered Joab,
"Look, I sent to you, saying, 'Come
here, so that I may send you to the
king, to say, "Why have I come
from Geshur? *It would be* better
for me *to be* there still."' Now
therefore, let me see the king's
face; but [a]if there is iniquity in me,
let him execute me."
33 So Joab went to the king and
told him. And when he had called
for Absalom, he came to the king
and bowed himself on his face to
the ground before the king. Then
the king [a]kissed Absalom.

Absalom's Treason

15 After this [a]it happened that
Absalom [b]provided himself
with chariots and horses, and fifty
men to run before him.
2 Now Absalom would rise early
and stand beside the way to the
gate. *So* it was, whenever anyone
who had a [a]lawsuit[1] came to the
king for a decision, that Absalom
would call to him and say, "What
city *are* you from?" And he would
say, "Your servant *is* from such
and such a tribe of Israel."
3 Then Absalom would say to
him, "Look, your [1]case *is* good and
right; but *there is* no [2]deputy of the
king to hear you."
4 Moreover Absalom would say,
[a]"Oh, that I were made judge in
the land, and everyone who has
any suit or cause would come to
me; then I would give him justice."
5 And *so* it was, whenever any-
one came near to bow down to
him, that he would put out his
hand and take him and [a]kiss him.
6 In this manner Absalom acted
toward all Israel who came to the
king for judgment. [a]So Absalom
stole the hearts of the men of Is-
rael.
7 Now it came to pass [a]after
[1]forty years that Absalom said to
the king, "Please, let me go to [b]He-
bron and pay the vow which I
made to the LORD.
8 [a]"For your servant [b]took a vow
[c]while I dwelt at Geshur in Syria,
saying, 'If the LORD indeed brings
me back to Jerusalem, then I will
serve the LORD.'"
9 And the king said to him, "Go
in peace." So he arose and went
to Hebron.
10 Then Absalom sent spies
throughout all the tribes of Israel,
saying, "As soon as you hear the
sound of the trumpet, then you

22 [1]Lit. *blessed*
23 [a]2 Sam. 13:37, 38
24 [a]Gen. 43:3; 2 Sam. 3:13
25 [a]Deut. 28:35; Job 2:7; Is. 1:6
27 [a]2 Sam. 13:1; 18:18
28 [a]2 Sam. 14:24
32 [a]1 Sam. 20:8; [Prov. 28:13]
33 [a]Gen. 33:4; 45:15; Luke 15:20

CHAPTER 15

1 [a]2 Sam. 12:11 [b]1 Kin. 1:5
2 [a]Deut. 19:17 [1]Lit. *controversy*
3 [1]Lit. *words* [2]Lit. *listener*
4 [a]Judg. 9:29
5 [a]2 Sam. 14:33; 20:9
6 [a][Rom. 16:18]
7 [a][Deut. 23:21] [b]2 Sam. 3:2, 3 [1]LXX mss., Syr., Josephus *four*
8 [a]1 Sam. 16:2 [b]Gen. 28:20, 21 [c]2 Sam. 13:38

shall say, 'Absalom [a]reigns in He-
bron!' "
11 And with Absalom went two
hundred men [a]invited from Jeru-
salem, and they [b]went along inno-
cently and did not know any-
thing.
12 Then Absalom sent for Ahitho-
phel the Gilonite, [a]David's coun-
selor, from his city—from [b]Giloh—
while he offered sacrifices. And
the conspiracy grew strong, for the
people with Absalom [c]continually
increased in number.

David Escapes from Jerusalem

13 Now a messenger came to Da-
vid, saying, [a]"The hearts of the
men of Israel are [1]with Absalom."
14 So David said to all his ser-
vants who *were* with him at Jeru-
salem, "Arise, and let us [a]flee, or
we shall not escape from Absalom.
Make haste to depart, lest he over-
take us suddenly and bring disas-
ter upon us, and strike the city
with the edge of the sword."
15 And the king's servants said to
the king, "We *are* your servants,
ready to do whatever my lord the
king commands."
16 Then [a]the king went out with
all his household after him. But the
king left [b]ten women, concubines,
to keep the house.
17 And the king went out with all
the people after him, and stopped
at the outskirts.
18 Then all his servants passed
[1]before him; [a]and all the Chereth-
ites, all the Pelethites, and all the
Gittites, [b]six hundred men who
had followed him from Gath,
passed before the king.
19 Then the king said to [a]Ittai the
Gittite, "Why are you also going
with us? Return and remain with
the king. For you *are* a foreigner
and also an exile from your own
place.
20 "In fact, you came *only* yester-
day. Should I make you wander up
and down with us today, since I
go [a]I know not where? Return, and
take your brethren back. Mercy
and truth *be* with you."
21 But Ittai answered the king and
said, [a]"*As* the LORD lives, and *as*
my lord the king lives, surely in
whatever place my lord the king
shall be, whether in death or life,
even there also your servant will
be."
22 So David said to Ittai, "Go, and
cross over." Then Ittai the Gittite
and all his men and all the little
ones who *were* with him crossed
over.
23 And all the country wept with
a loud voice, and all the people
crossed over. The king himself
also crossed over the Brook Kid-
ron, and all the people crossed
over toward the way of the [a]wil-
derness.
24 There was [a]Zadok also, and all
the Levites with him, bearing the
[b]ark of the covenant of God. And
they set down the ark of God, and
[c]Abiathar went up until all the peo-
ple had finished crossing over
from the city.
25 Then the king said to Zadok,
"Carry the ark of God back into
the city. If I find favor in the eyes
of the LORD, He [a]will bring me
back and show me *both* it and [b]His
dwelling place.
26 "But if He says thus: 'I have no
[a]delight in you,' here I am, [b]let Him
do to me as seems good to
Him."
27 The king also said to Zadok the
priest, "*Are* you *not* a [a]seer?[1] Re-
turn to the city in peace, and [b]your
two sons with you, Ahimaaz your
son, and Jonathan the son of Abi-
athar.
28 "See, [a]I will wait in the plains
of the wilderness until word comes
from you to inform me."
29 Therefore Zadok and Abiathar
carried the ark of God back to
Jerusalem. And they remained
there.
30 So David went up by the As-
cent of the *Mount* of Olives, and
wept as he went up; and he [a]had
his head covered and went [b]bare-
foot. And all the people who *were*
with him [c]covered their heads and
went up, [d]weeping as they went
up.
31 Then *someone* told David, say-
ing, [a]"Ahithophel is among the
conspirators with Absalom." And
David said, "O LORD, I pray, [b]turn
the counsel of Ahithophel into
foolishness!"
32 Now it happened when David
had come to the top *of the moun-
tain*, where he worshiped God—

10 [a]1 Kin. 1:34; 2 Kin. 9:13
11 [a]1 Sam. 16:3, 5 [b]Gen. 20:5
12 [a]2 Sam. 16:15; 1 Chr. 27:33; Ps. 41:9; 55:12–14 [b]Josh. 15:51 [c]Ps. 3:1
13 [a]Judg. 9:3; 2 Sam. 15:6 [1]Lit. *after*
14 [a]2 Sam. 12:11; Ps. 3:title
16 [a]Ps. 3:title [b]2 Sam. 12:11; 16:21, 22
18 [a]2 Sam. 8:18 [b]1 Sam. 23:13; 25:13; 30:1, 9 [1]Lit. *by his hand*
19 [a]2 Sam. 18:2
20 [a]1 Sam. 23:13
21 [a]Ruth 1:16, 17; [Prov. 17:17]
23 [a]2 Sam. 15:28; 16:2
24 [a]2 Sam. 8:17 [b]Num. 4:15; 1 Sam. 4:4 [c]1 Sam. 22:20
25 [a][Ps. 43:3] [b]Ex. 15:13; Jer. 25:30
26 [a]Num. 14:8; 2 Sam. 22:20; 1 Kin. 10:9; 2 Chr. 9:8; Is. 62:4 [b]1 Sam. 3:18
27 [a]1 Sam. 9:6–9 [b]2 Sam. 17:17–20 [1]*prophet*
28 [a]Josh. 5:10; 2 Sam. 17:16
30 [a]2 Sam. 19:4; Esth. 6:12; Ezek. 24:17, 23 [b]Is. 20:2–4 [c]Jer. 14:3, 4 [d][Ps. 126:6]
31 [a]Ps. 3:1, 2; 55:12 [b]2 Sam. 16:23; 17:14, 23

there was Hushai the [a]Archite
coming to meet him [b]with his robe
torn and dust on his head.
33 David said to him, "If you go
on with me, then you will become
[a]a burden to me.
34 "But if you return to the city,
and say to Absalom, [a]'I will be
your servant, O king; *as* I *was* your
father's servant previously, so I
will now also *be* your servant,'
then you may defeat the counsel
of Ahithophel for me.
35 "And *do* you not *have* Zadok
and Abiathar the priests with you
there? Therefore it will be *that*
whatever you hear from the king's
house, you shall tell to [a]Zadok and
Abiathar the priests.
36 "Indeed *they have* there [a]with
them their two sons, Ahimaaz,
Zadok's *son*, and Jonathan, Abia-
thar's *son;* and by them you
shall send me everything you
hear."
37 So Hushai, [a]David's friend,
went into the city. [b]And Absalom
came into Jerusalem.

Mephibosheth's Servant

16 When[a] David was a little
past the top *of the mountain*,
there was [b]Ziba the servant of Me-
phibosheth, who met him with a
couple of saddled donkeys, and on
them two hundred *loaves* of bread,
one hundred clusters of raisins,
one hundred summer fruits, and a
skin of wine.
2 And the king said to Ziba,
"What do you mean to do with
these?" So Ziba said, "The don-
keys *are* for the king's house-
hold to ride on, the bread and
summer fruit for the young men
to eat, and the wine for [a]those
who are faint in the wilderness to
drink."
3 Then the king said, "And
where *is* your [a]master's son?"
[b]And Ziba said to the king, "In-
deed he is staying in Jerusalem,
for he said, 'Today the house of
Israel will restore the kingdom of
my father to me.'"
4 So the king said to Ziba, "Here,
all that *belongs* to Mephibosheth
is yours." And Ziba said, "I hum-
bly bow before you, *that* I may
find favor in your sight, my lord,
O king!"

32 [a]Josh. 16:2 [b]2 Sam. 1:2
33 [a]2 Sam. 19:35
34 [a]2 Sam. 16:19
35 [a]2 Sam. 17:15, 16
36 [a]2 Sam. 15:27
37 [a]2 Sam. 16:16; 1 Chr. 27:33 [b]2 Sam. 16:15

CHAPTER 16

1 [a]2 Sam. 15:30, 32 [b]2 Sam. 9:2; 19:17, 29
2 [a]2 Sam. 15:23; 17:29
3 [a]2 Sam. 9:9, 10 [b]2 Sam. 19:27
5 [a]2 Sam. 3:16 [b]2 Sam. 19:21; 1 Kin. 2:8, 9, 44–46
7 [a]Deut. 13:13 [1]Lit. *man of bloodshed* [2]*worthless man*
8 [a]Judg. 9:24, 56, 57; 1 Kin. 2:32, 33 [b]2 Sam. 1:16; 3:28, 29; 4:11, 12 [1]Lit. *man of bloodshed*
9 [a]1 Sam. 24:14; 2 Sam. 9:8 [b]Ex. 22:28
10 [a]2 Sam. 3:39; 19:22; [1 Pet. 2:23] [b]2 Kin. 18:25; [Lam. 3:38] [c][Rom. 9:20]
11 [a]2 Sam. 12:11 [b]Gen. 15:4
12 [a]Deut. 23:5; Neh. 13:2; Prov. 20:22 [b]Deut. 23:5; [Rom. 8:28; Heb. 12:10, 11] [1]So with Kt., LXX, Syr., Vg.; Qr. *my eyes;* Tg. *tears of my eyes*
13 [1]Lit. *dusted him with dust*
15 [a]2 Sam. 15:12, 37

Shimei Curses David

5 Now when King David came to
[a]Bahurim, there was a man from
the family of the house of Saul,
whose name *was* [b]Shimei the son
of Gera, coming from there. He
came out, cursing continuously as
he came.
6 And he threw stones at David
and at all the servants of King Da-
vid. And all the people and all the
mighty men *were* on his right hand
and on his left.
7 Also Shimei said thus when he
cursed: "Come out! Come out! You
[1]bloodthirsty man, [a]you [2]rogue!
8 "The LORD has [a]brought upon
you all [b]the blood of the house of
Saul, in whose place you have
reigned; and the LORD has deliv-
ered the kingdom into the hand
of Absalom your son. So now
you *are caught* in your own evil,
because you are a [1]bloodthirsty
man!"
9 Then Abishai the son of Zeru-
iah said to the king, "Why should
this [a]dead dog [b]curse my lord the
king? Please, let me go over and
take off his head!"
10 But the king said, [a]"What have
I to do with you, you sons of
Zeruiah? So let him curse, because
[b]the LORD has said to him, 'Curse
David.' [c]Who then shall say, 'Why
have you done so?'"
11 And David said to Abishai and
all his servants, "See how [a]my son
who [b]came from my own body
seeks my life. How much more
now *may this* Benjamite? Let him
alone, and let him curse; for so the
LORD has ordered him.
12 "It may be that the LORD will
look on [1]my affliction, and that the
LORD will [a]repay me with [b]good for
his cursing this day."
13 And as David and his men went
along the road, Shimei went along
the hillside opposite him and
cursed as he went, threw stones at
him and [1]kicked up dust.
14 Now the king and all the people
who *were* with him became weary;
so they refreshed themselves
there.

The Advice of Ahithophel

15 Meanwhile [a]Absalom and all
the people, the men of Israel, came

to Jerusalem; and Ahithophel *was*
with him.
16 And so it was, when Hushai the
Archite, [a]David's friend, came to
Absalom, that [b]Hushai said to Ab-
salom, "*Long* live the king! *Long*
live the king!"
17 So Absalom said to Hushai, "*Is*
this your loyalty to your friend?
[a]Why did you not go with your
friend?"
18 And Hushai said to Absalom,
"No, but whom the LORD and this
people and all the men of Israel
choose, his I will be, and with him
I will remain.
19 "Furthermore, [a]whom should I
serve? *Should I* not *serve* in the
presence of his son? As I have
served in your father's presence,
so will I be in your presence."
20 Then Absalom said to [a]Ahitho-
phel, "Give advice as to what we
should do."
21 And Ahithophel said to Absa-
lom, "Go in to your father's [a]con-
cubines, whom he has left to keep
the house; and all Israel will hear
that you [b]are abhorred by your fa-
ther. Then [c]the hands of all who
are with you will be strong."
22 So they pitched a tent for Absa-
lom on the top of the house, and
Absalom went in to his father's
concubines [a]in the sight of all Is-
rael.
23 Now the advice of Ahithophel,
which he gave in those days, *was*
as if one had inquired at the oracle
of God. So *was* all the advice of
Ahithophel [a]both with David and
with Absalom.

17 Moreover Ahithophel said to
Absalom, "Now let me
choose twelve thousand men, and
I will arise and pursue David to-
night.
2 "I will come upon him while he
is [a]weary and weak, and make him
[1]afraid. And all the people who *are*
with him will flee, and I will [b]strike
only the king.
3 "Then I will bring back all the
people to you. When all return ex-
cept the man whom you seek, all
the people will be at peace."
4 And the saying pleased Absa-
lom and all the [a]elders of Israel.

The Advice of Hushai

5 Then Absalom said, "Now call
Hushai the Archite also, and let us
hear what he [a]says too."
6 And when Hushai came to Ab-
salom, Absalom spoke to him, say-
ing, "Ahithophel has spoken in
this manner. Shall we do as he
says? If not, speak up."
7 So Hushai said to Absalom:
"The advice that Ahithophel has
given *is* not good at this time.
8 "For," said Hushai, "you know
your father and his men, that they
are mighty men, and they *are* en-
raged in their minds, like [a]a bear
robbed of her cubs in the field; and
your father *is* a man of war, and
will not camp with the people.
9 "Surely by now he is hidden in
some pit, or in some *other* place.
And it will be, when some of them
are overthrown at the first, that
whoever hears *it* will say, 'There
is a slaughter among the people
who follow Absalom.'
10 "And even he *who is* valiant,
whose heart *is* like the heart of a
lion, will [a]melt completely. For all
Israel knows that your father *is* a
mighty man, and *those* who *are*
with him *are* valiant men.
11 "Therefore I advise that all Is-
rael be fully gathered to you, [a]from
Dan to Beersheba, [b]like the sand
that *is* by the sea for multitude,
and that you go to battle in person.
12 "So we will come upon him in
some place where he may be
found, and we will fall on him as
the dew falls on the ground. And
of him and all the men who *are*
with him there shall not be left so
much as one.
13 "Moreover, if he has with-
drawn into a city, then all Israel
shall bring ropes to that city; and
we will [a]pull it into the river, until
there is not one small stone found
there."
14 So Absalom and all the men of
Israel said, "The advice of Hushai
the Archite *is* better than the ad-
vice of Ahithophel." For [a]the LORD
had purposed to defeat the good
advice of Ahithophel, to the intent
that the LORD might bring disaster
on Absalom.

16 [a]2 Sam. 15:37 [b]2 Sam. 15:34
17 [a]2 Sam. 19:25; [Prov. 17:17]
19 [a]2 Sam. 15:34
20 [a]2 Sam. 15:12
21 [a]2 Sam. 15:16; 20:3 [b]Gen. 34:30; 1 Sam. 13:4 [c]2 Sam. 2:7; Zech. 8:13
22 [a]2 Sam. 12:11, 12
23 [a]2 Sam. 15:12

CHAPTER 17

2 [a]Deut. 25:18; 2 Sam. 16:14 [b]Zech. 13:7 [1]*tremble with fear*
4 [a]2 Sam. 5:3; 19:11
5 [a]2 Sam. 15:32–34
8 [a]Hos. 13:8
10 [a]Josh. 2:11
11 [a]Judg. 20:1; 2 Sam. 3:10 [b]Gen. 22:17; Josh. 11:4; 1 Kin. 20:10
13 [a]Mic. 1:6
14 [a]2 Sam. 15:31, 34

Hushai Warns David to Escape

15 [a]Then Hushai said to Zadok
and Abiathar the priests, "Thus
and so Ahithophel advised Absa-
lom and the elders of Israel, and
thus and so I have advised.
16 "Now therefore, send quickly
and tell David, saying, 'Do not
spend this night [a]in the plains of
the wilderness, but speedily cross
over, lest the king and all the peo-
ple who *are* with him be swal-
lowed up.' "
17 [a]Now Jonathan and Ahimaaz
[b]stayed at [c]En Rogel, for they
dared not be seen coming into the
city; so a female servant would
come and tell them, and they
would go and tell King David.
18 Nevertheless a lad saw them,
and told Absalom. But both of
them went away quickly and came
to a man's house [a]in Bahurim, who
had a well in his court; and they
went down into it.
19 [a]Then the woman took and
spread a covering over the well's
mouth, and spread ground grain
on it; and the thing was not
known.
20 And when Absalom's servants
came to the woman at the house,
they said, "Where *are* Ahimaaz
and Jonathan?" So [a]the woman
said to them, "They have gone
over the water brook." And when
they had searched and could not
find *them*, they returned to Jerusa-
lem.
21 Now it came to pass, after they
had departed, that they came up
out of the well and went and told
King David, and said to David,
[a]"Arise and cross over the water
quickly. For thus has Ahithophel
advised against you."
22 So David and all the people
who *were* with him arose and
crossed over the Jordan. By morn-
ing light not one of them was left
who had not gone over the Jordan.
23 Now when Ahithophel saw that
his advice was not followed, he
saddled a donkey, and arose and
went home to [a]his house, to his
city. Then he [1]put his [b]household
in order, and [c]changed himself, and
died; and he was buried in his fa-
ther's tomb.
24 Then David went to [a]Maha-
naim. And Absalom crossed over
the Jordan, he and all the men of
Israel with him.
25 And Absalom made [a]Amasa
captain of the army instead of
Joab. This Amasa *was* the son of
a man whose name *was* [1]Jithra, an
[2]Israelite, who had gone in to
[b]Abigail the daughter of Nahash,
sister of Zeruiah, Joab's mother.
26 So Israel and Absalom en-
camped in the land of Gilead.
27 Now it happened, when David
had come to Mahanaim, that
[a]Shobi the son of Nahash from
Rabbah of the people of Ammon,
[b]Machir the son of Ammiel from
Lo Debar, and [c]Barzillai the Gil-
eadite from Rogelim,
28 brought beds and basins,
earthen vessels and wheat, barley
and flour, parched *grain* and
beans, lentils and parched *seeds*,
29 honey and curds, sheep and
cheese of the herd, for David and
the people who *were* with him to
eat. For they said, "The people are
hungry and weary and thirsty [a]in
the wilderness."

Absalom's Defeat and Death

18 And David [1]numbered the
people who *were* with him,
and [a]set captains of thousands and
captains of hundreds over them.
2 Then David sent out one third
of the people under the hand of
Joab, [a]one third under the hand of
Abishai the son of Zeruiah, Joab's
brother, and one third under the
hand of [b]Ittai the Gittite. And the
king said to the people, "I also will
surely go out with you myself."
3 [a]But the people answered,
"You shall not go out! For if we
flee away, they will not care about
us; nor if half of us die, will they
care about us. But *you are* worth
ten thousand of us now. For you
are now more help to us in the
city."
4 Then the king said to them,
"Whatever seems best to you I will
do." So the king stood beside the
gate, and all the people went out
by hundreds and by thousands.
5 Now the king had commanded
Joab, Abishai, and Ittai, saying,
"*Deal* gently for my sake with the
young man Absalom." [a]And all the
people heard when the king gave

15 [a]2 Sam. 15:35, 36
16 [a]2 Sam. 15:28
17 [a]2 Sam. 15:27, 36; 1 Kin. 1:42, 43 [b]Josh. 2:4–6 [c]Josh. 15:7; 18:16
18 [a]2 Sam. 3:16; 16:5
19 [a]Josh. 2:4–6
20 [a]Ex. 1:19; [Lev. 19:11]; Josh. 2:3–5
21 [a]2 Sam. 17:15, 16
23 [a]2 Sam. 15:12 [b]2 Kin. 20:1 [c]Matt. 27:5 [1]Lit. *gave charge concerning his house*
24 [a]Gen. 32:2; Josh. 13:26; 2 Sam. 2:8; 19:32
25 [a]2 Sam. 19:13; 20:9–12; 1 Kin. 2:5, 32 [b]1 Chr. 2:16 [1]*Jether*, 1 Chr. 2:17 [2]So with MT, some LXX mss., Tg.; some LXX mss. *Ishmaelite* (cf. 1 Chr. 2:17); Vg. *of Jezrael*
27 [a]1 Sam. 11:1; 2 Sam. 10:1; 12:29 [b]2 Sam. 9:4 [c]2 Sam. 19:31, 32; 1 Kin. 2:7
29 [a]2 Sam. 16:2, 14

CHAPTER 18

1 [a]Ex. 18:25; Num. 31:14; 1 Sam. 22:7 [1]Lit. *attended to*
2 [a]Judg. 7:16; 1 Sam. 11:11 [b]2 Sam. 15:19–22
3 [a]2 Sam. 21:17
5 [a]2 Sam. 18:12

all the captains orders concerning
Absalom.
6 So the people went out into the
field of battle against Israel. And
the battle was in the [a]woods of
Ephraim.
7 The people of Israel were over-
thrown there before the servants
of David, and a great slaughter of
twenty thousand took place there
that day.
8 For the battle there was scat-
tered over the face of the whole
countryside, and the woods de-
voured more people that day than
the sword devoured.
9 Then Absalom met the ser-
vants of David. Absalom rode on
a mule. The mule went under the
thick boughs of a great terebinth
tree, and [a]his head caught in the
terebinth; so he was left hanging
between heaven and earth. And
the mule which *was* under him
went on.
10 Now a certain man saw *it* and
told Joab, and said, "I just saw Ab-
salom hanging in a terebinth tree!"
11 So Joab said to the man who
told him, "You just saw *him!* And
why did you not strike him there
to the ground? I would have given
you ten *shekels* of silver and a
belt."
12 But the man said to Joab,
"Though I were to receive a thou-
sand *shekels* of silver in my hand,
I would not raise my hand against
the king's son. [a]For in our hearing
the king commanded you and
Abishai and Ittai, saying, [1]'Beware
lest anyone *touch* the young man
Absalom!'
13 "Otherwise I would have dealt
falsely against my own life. For
there is nothing hidden from the
king, and you yourself would have
set yourself against *me.*"
14 Then Joab said, "I cannot lin-
ger with you." And he took three
spears in his hand and thrust them
through Absalom's heart, while he
was *still* alive in the midst of the
terebinth tree.
15 And ten young men who bore
Joab's armor surrounded Absa-
lom, and struck and killed him.
16 So Joab blew the trumpet, and
the people returned from pursuing
Israel. For Joab held back the peo-
ple.

6 [a]Josh. 17:15, 18; 2 Sam. 17:26

9 [a]2 Sam. 14:26

12 [a]2 Sam. 18:5 [1]Vss. *'Protect the young man Absalom for me!'*

17 [a]Deut. 21:20, 21; Josh. 7:26; 8:29 [b]2 Sam. 19:8; 20:1, 22

18 [a]Gen. 14:17 [b]2 Sam. 14:27 [1]*monument*

19 [a]2 Sam. 15:36; 17:17 [1]*vindicated*

22 [1]Lit. *be what may*

24 [a]Judg. 5:11; 2 Sam. 13:34; 2 Kin. 9:17

27 [1]Lit. *I see the running*

17 And they took Absalom and
cast him into a large pit in the
woods, and [a]laid a very large heap
of stones over him. Then all Israel
[b]fled, everyone to his tent.
18 Now Absalom in his lifetime
had taken and set up a [1]pillar for
himself, which *is* in [a]the King's
Valley. For he said, [b]"I have no son
to keep my name in remem-
brance." He called the pillar after
his own name. And to this day it
is called Absalom's Monument.

David Hears of Absalom's Death

19 Then [a]Ahimaaz the son of Za-
dok said, "Let me run now and
take the news to the king, how the
LORD has [1]avenged him of his ene-
mies."
20 And Joab said to him, "You
shall not take the news this day,
for you shall take the news an-
other day. But today you shall take
no news, because the king's son
is dead."
21 Then Joab said to the Cushite,
"Go, tell the king what you have
seen." So the Cushite bowed him-
self to Joab and ran.
22 And Ahimaaz the son of Zadok
said again to Joab, "But [1]whatever
happens, please let me also run af-
ter the Cushite." So Joab said,
"Why will you run, my son, since
you have no news ready?"
23 "But whatever happens," *he
said,* "let me run." So he said to
him, "Run." Then Ahimaaz ran by
way of the plain, and outran the
Cushite.
24 Now David was sitting be-
tween the [a]two gates. And the
watchman went up to the roof over
the gate, to the wall, lifted his eyes
and looked, and there was a man,
running alone.
25 Then the watchman cried out
and told the king. And the king
said, "If he *is* alone, *there is* news
in his mouth." And he came rap-
idly and drew near.
26 Then the watchman saw *an-
other* man running, and the watch-
man called to the gatekeeper and
said, "There is *another* man, run-
ning alone!" And the king said,
"He also brings news."
27 So the watchman said, [1]"I
think the running of the first is like
the running of Ahimaaz the son of

Zadok." And the king said, "He *is*
a good man, and comes with [a]good
news."
28 So Ahimaaz called out and said
to the king, [1]"All is well!" Then he
bowed down with his face to the
earth before the king, and said,
[a]"Blessed *be* the LORD your God,
who has delivered up the men who
raised their hand against my lord
the king!"
29 The king said, "Is the young
man Absalom safe?" Ahimaaz answered,
"When Joab sent the
king's servant and *me* your servant,
I saw a great tumult, but I
did not know what *it was about.*"
30 And the king said, "Turn aside
and stand here." So he turned
aside and stood still.
31 Just then the Cushite came,
and the Cushite said, "There is
good news, my lord the king! For
the LORD has avenged you this day
of all those who rose against you."
32 And the king said to the Cushite,
"Is the young man Absalom
safe?" So the Cushite answered,
"May the enemies of my lord the
king, and all who rise against you
to do harm, be like *that* young
man!"

David's Mourning for Absalom

33 Then the king was deeply
moved, and went up to the chamber
over the gate, and wept. And
as he went, he said thus: [a]"O my
son Absalom—my son, my son Absalom—if
only I had died in your
place! O Absalom my son, [b]my
son!"

19 And Joab was told, "Behold,
the king is weeping and
[a]mourning for Absalom."
2 So the victory that day was
turned into [a]mourning for all the
people. For the people heard it said
that day, "The king is grieved for
his son."
3 And the people [1]stole back
[a]into the city that day, as people
who are ashamed steal away when
they flee in battle.
4 But the king [a]covered his face,
and the king cried out with a loud
voice, [b]"O my son Absalom! O Absalom,
my son, my son!"
5 Then [a]Joab came into the
house to the king, and said, "Today
you have disgraced all your
servants who today have saved
your life, the lives of your sons and
daughters, the lives of your wives
and the lives of your concubines,
6 "in that you love your enemies
and hate your friends. For you
have declared today that you [1]regard
neither princes nor servants;
for today I perceive that if Absalom
had lived and all of us had
died today, then it would have
pleased you well.
7 "Now therefore, arise, go out
and speak [1]comfort to your servants.
For I swear by the LORD, if
you do not go out, not one will stay
with you this night. And that will
be worse for you than all the evil
that has befallen you from your
youth until now."
8 Then the king arose and sat in
the [a]gate. And they told all the
people, saying, "There is the king,
sitting in the gate." So all the people
came before the king. For
everyone of Israel had [b]fled to his
tent.

David Returns to Jerusalem

9 Now all the people were in a
dispute throughout all the tribes of
Israel, saying, "The king saved us
from the hand of our [a]enemies, he
delivered us from the hand of the
[b]Philistines, and now he has [c]fled
from the land because of Absalom.
10 "But Absalom, whom we
anointed over us, has died in battle.
Now therefore, why do you say
nothing about bringing back the
king?"
11 So King David sent to [a]Zadok
and Abiathar the priests, saying,
"Speak to the elders of Judah, saying,
'Why are you the last to bring
the king back to his house, since
the words of all Israel have come
to the king, to his *very* house?
12 'You *are* my brethren, you *are*
[a]my bone and my flesh. Why then
are you the last to bring back the
king?'
13 [a]"And say to Amasa, '*Are* you
not my bone and my flesh? [b]God
do so to me, and more also, if you
are not commander of the army
before me [1]continually in place of
Joab.'"
14 So he swayed the hearts of all
the men of Judah, [a]just as *the*

---

27 [a]1 Kin. 1:42
28 [a]2 Sam. 16:12 [1]*Peace be to you*
33 [a]2 Sam. 12:10 [b]2 Sam. 19:4

CHAPTER 19

1 [a]Jer. 14:2
2 [a]Esth. 4:3
3 [a]2 Sam. 17:24, 27; 19:32 [1]*went by stealth*
4 [a]2 Sam. 15:30 [b]2 Sam. 18:33
5 [a]2 Sam. 18:14
6 [1]*have no respect for*
7 [1]Lit. *to the heart of*
8 [a]2 Sam. 15:2; 18:24 [b]2 Sam. 18:17
9 [a]2 Sam. 8:1–14 [b]2 Sam. 3:18 [c]2 Sam. 15:14
11 [a]2 Sam. 15:24
12 [a]2 Sam. 5:1; 1 Chr. 11:1
13 [a]2 Sam. 17:25; 1 Chr. 2:17 [b]Ruth 1:17 [1]*permanently*
14 [a]Judg. 20:1

heart of one man, so that they sent
this word to the king: "Return, you
and all your servants!"
15 Then the king returned and
came to the Jordan. And Judah
came to [a]Gilgal, to go to meet the
king, to escort the king [b]across the
Jordan.
16 And [a]Shimei the son of Gera,
a Benjamite, who *was* from Ba-
hurim, hurried and came down
with the men of Judah to meet
King David.
17 *There were* a thousand men of
[a]Benjamin with him, and [b]Ziba the
servant of the house of Saul, and
his fifteen sons and his twenty ser-
vants with him; and they went
over the Jordan before the king.
18 Then a ferryboat went across
to carry over the king's household,
and to do what he thought good.

David's Mercy to Shimei

Now Shimei the son of Gera
fell down before the king when he
had crossed the Jordan.
19 Then he said to the king, [a]"Do
not let my lord [1]impute iniquity to
me, or remember what [b]wrong
your servant did on the day that
my lord the king left Jerusalem,
that the king should [c]take *it* to
heart.
20 "For I, your servant, know that
I have sinned. Therefore here I am,
the first to come today of all [a]the
house of Joseph to go down to
meet my lord the king."
21 But Abishai the son of Zeruiah
answered and said, "Shall not
Shimei be put to death for this,
[a]because he [b]cursed the LORD's
anointed?"
22 And David said, [a]"What have
I to do with you, you sons of Zer-
uiah, that you should be adversar-
ies to me today? [b]Shall any man
be put to death today in Israel? For
do I not know that today I *am* king
over Israel?"
23 Therefore [a]the king said to
Shimei, "You shall not die." And
the king swore to him.

David and Mephibosheth Meet

24 Now [a]Mephibosheth the son of
Saul came down to meet the king.
And he had not cared for his feet,
nor trimmed his mustache, nor
washed his clothes, from the day

15 [a]Josh. 5:9; 1 Sam. 11:14, 15 [b]2 Sam. 17:22
16 [a]2 Sam. 16:5; 1 Kin. 2:8
17 [a]2 Sam. 3:19; 1 Kin. 12:21 [b]2 Sam. 9:2, 10; 16:1, 2
19 [a]1 Sam. 22:15 [b]2 Sam. 16:5, 6 [c]2 Sam. 13:33 [1]*charge me with iniquity*
20 [a]Judg. 1:22; 1 Kin. 11:28
21 [a][Ex. 22:28] [b][1 Sam. 26:9]
22 [a]2 Sam. 3:39; 16:10 [b]1 Sam. 11:13
23 [a]1 Kin. 2:8, 9, 37, 46
24 [a]2 Sam. 9:6; 21:7
25 [a]2 Sam. 16:17
27 [a]2 Sam. 16:3, 4 [b]2 Sam. 14:17, 20
28 [a]2 Sam. 9:7–13 [1]*complain*
31 [a]2 Sam. 17:27–29; 1 Kin. 2:7
32 [a]2 Sam. 17:27–29
35 [a]Ps. 90:10

the king departed until the day he
returned in peace.
25 So it was, when he had come
to Jerusalem to meet the king, that
the king said to him, [a]"Why did
you not go with me, Mephib-
osheth?"
26 And he answered, "My lord, O
king, my servant deceived me. For
your servant said, 'I will saddle a
donkey for myself, that I may ride
on it and go to the king,' because
your servant *is* lame.
27 "And [a]he has slandered your
servant to my lord the king, [b]but
my lord the king *is* like the angel
of God. Therefore do *what is* good
in your eyes.
28 "For all my father's house were
but dead men before my lord the
king. [a]Yet you set your servant
among those who eat at your own
table. Therefore what right have I
still to [1]cry out anymore to the
king?"
29 So the king said to him, "Why
do you speak anymore of your
matters? I have said, 'You and
Ziba divide the land.'"
30 Then Mephibosheth said to the
king, "Rather, let him take it all,
inasmuch as my lord the king has
come back in peace to his own
house."

David's Kindness to Barzillai

31 And [a]Barzillai the Gileadite
came down from Rogelim and
went across the Jordan with the
king, to escort him across the Jor-
dan.
32 Now Barzillai was a very aged
man, eighty years old. And [a]he had
provided the king with supplies
while he stayed at Mahanaim, for
he *was* a very rich man.
33 And the king said to Barzillai,
"Come across with me, and I will
provide for you while you are with
me in Jerusalem."
34 But Barzillai said to the king,
"How long have I to live, that I
should go up with the king to Jeru-
salem?
35 "I *am* today [a]eighty years old.
Can I discern between the good
and bad? Can your servant taste
what I eat or what I drink? Can I
hear any longer the voice of sing-
ing men and singing women?
Why then should your servant be

7 But the king spared [a]Mephib-
osheth the son of Jonathan, the
son of Saul, because of [b]the LORD's
oath that *was* between them, be-
tween David and Jonathan the son
of Saul.
8 So the king took Armoni and
Mephibosheth, the two sons of
[a]Rizpah the daughter of Aiah,
whom she bore to Saul, and the
five sons of [1]Michal the daughter
of Saul, whom she [2]brought up for
Adriel the son of Barzillai the
Meholathite;
9 and he delivered them into the
hands of the Gibeonites, and they
hanged them on the hill [a]before
the LORD. So they fell, *all* seven to-
gether, and were put to death in
the days of harvest, in the first
days, in the beginning of barley
harvest.
10 Now [a]Rizpah the daughter of
Aiah took sackcloth and spread it
for herself on the rock, [b]from the
beginning of harvest until the late
rains poured on them from
heaven. And she did not allow the
birds of the air to rest on them by
day nor the beasts of the field by
night.
11 And David was told what
Rizpah the daughter of Aiah, the
concubine of Saul, had done.
12 Then David went and took the
bones of Saul, and the bones of
Jonathan his son, from the men of
[a]Jabesh Gilead who had stolen
them from the street of [1]Beth
Shan, where the [b]Philistines had
hung them up, after the Philistines
had struck down Saul in Gilboa.
13 So he brought up the bones of
Saul and the bones of Jonathan his
son from there; and they gathered
the bones of those who had been
hanged.
14 They buried the bones of Saul
and Jonathan his son in the coun-
try of Benjamin in [a]Zelah, in the
tomb of Kish his father. So they
performed all that the king com-
manded. And after that [b]God
heeded the prayer for the land.

Philistine Giants Destroyed

15 When the Philistines were at
war again with Israel, David and
his servants with him went down
and fought against the Philistines;
and David grew faint.
16 Then Ishbi-Benob, who *was*
one of the sons of [1]the [a]giant, the
weight of whose bronze spear *was*
three hundred *shekels,* who was
bearing a new *sword,* thought he
could kill David.
17 But [a]Abishai the son of Zeruiah
came to his aid, and struck the
Philistine and killed him. Then the
men of David swore to him, say-
ing, [b]"You shall go out no more
with us to battle, lest you quench
the [c]lamp of Israel."
18 [a]Now it happened afterward
that there was again a battle with
the Philistines at Gob. Then [b]Sib-
bechai the Hushathite killed [1]Saph,
who *was* one of the sons of [2]the
giant.
19 Again there was war at Gob
with the Philistines, where [a]El-
hanan the son of [1]Jaare-Oregim
the Bethlehemite killed [b]*the
brother of* Goliath the Gittite, the
shaft of whose spear *was* like a
weaver's beam.
20 Yet again [a]there was war at
Gath, where there was a man of
great stature, who had six fingers
on each hand and six toes on each
foot, twenty-four in number; and
he also was born to [1]the giant.
21 So when he [a]defied Israel, Jon-
athan the son of [1]Shimea, David's
brother, killed him.
22 [a]These four were born to [1]the
giant in Gath, and fell by the hand
of David and by the hand of his
servants.

Praise for God's Deliverance

22 Then David [a]spoke to the
LORD the words of this song,
on the day when the LORD had [b]de-
livered him from the hand of all
his enemies, and from the hand of
Saul.
2 And he [a]said:

[b]"The LORD *is* my rock and my
[c]fortress and my deliverer;
3 The God of my strength, [a]in
whom I will trust;
My [b]shield and the [c]horn[1] of my
salvation,
My [d]stronghold and my [e]refuge;
My Savior, You save me from
violence.
4 I will call upon the LORD, *who is
worthy* to be praised;
So shall I be saved from my
enemies.

7 [a]2 Sam. 4:4; 9:10 [b]1 Sam. 18:3; 20:12–17; 23:18; 2 Sam. 9:1–7
8 [a]2 Sam. 3:7 [1]*Merab,* 1 Sam. 18:19; 25:44; 2 Sam. 3:14; 6:23 [2]Lit. *bore to Adriel*
9 [a]2 Sam. 6:17
10 [a]2 Sam. 3:7; 21:8 [b]Deut. 21:23
12 [a]1 Sam. 31:11–13 [b]1 Sam. 31:8 [1]*Beth Shean,* Josh. 17:11
14 [a]Josh. 18:28 [b]Josh. 7:26; 2 Sam. 24:25
16 [a]Num. 13:22, 28; Josh. 15:14; 2 Sam. 21:18–22 [1]Or *Rapha*
17 [a]2 Sam. 20:6–10 [b]2 Sam. 18:3 [c]2 Sam. 22:29; 1 Kin. 11:36
18 [a]1 Chr. 20:4–8 [b]1 Chr. 11:29; 27:11 [1]*Sippai,* 1 Chr. 20:4 [2]Or *Rapha*
19 [a]2 Sam. 23:24 [b]1 Sam. 17:4; 1 Chr. 20:5 [1]*Jair,* 1 Chr. 20:5
20 [a]1 Chr. 20:6 [1]Or *Rapha*
21 [a]1 Sam. 17:10 [1]*Shammah,* 1 Sam. 16:9 and elsewhere
22 [a]1 Chr. 20:8 [1]Or *Rapha*

CHAPTER 22

1 [a]Ex. 15:1; Deut. 31:30; Judg. 5:1 [b]Ps. 18:title; 34:19
2 [a]Ps. 18 [b]Deut. 32:4; 1 Sam. 2:2 [c]Ps. 91:2
3 [a]Ps. 7:1; Heb. 2:13 [b]Gen. 15:1; Deut. 33:29; Ps. 84:11 [c]Luke 1:69 [d]Prov. 18:10 [e]Ps. 9:9; 46:1, 7, 11; Jer. 16:19 [1]Strength

5 "When the waves of death surrounded me,
The floods of ungodliness [1]made me afraid.
6 The [a]sorrows of Sheol surrounded me;
The snares of death confronted me.
7 In my distress [a]I called upon the LORD,
And cried out to my God;
He [b]heard my voice from His temple,
And my cry *entered* His ears.

8 "Then [a]the earth shook and trembled;
[b]The foundations of [1]heaven quaked and were shaken,
Because He was angry.
9 Smoke went up from His nostrils,
And devouring [a]fire from His mouth;
Coals were kindled by it.
10 He [a]bowed the heavens also, and came down
With [b]darkness under His feet.
11 He rode upon a cherub, and flew;
And He [1]was seen [a]upon the wings of the wind.
12 He made [a]darkness canopies around Him,
Dark waters *and* thick clouds of the skies.
13 From the brightness before Him
Coals of fire were kindled.

14 "The LORD [a]thundered from heaven,
And the Most High uttered His voice.
15 He sent out [a]arrows and scattered them;
Lightning bolts, and He vanquished them.
16 Then the channels of the sea [a]were seen,
The foundations of the world were uncovered,
At the [b]rebuke of the LORD,
At the blast of the breath of His nostrils.

17 "He[a] sent from above, He took me,
He drew me out of many waters.
18 He delivered me from my strong enemy,
From those who hated me;
For they were too strong for me.
19 They confronted me in the day of my calamity,
But the LORD was my [a]support.
20 [a]He also brought me out into a broad place;
He delivered me because He [b]delighted in me.

21 "The[a] LORD rewarded me according to my righteousness;
According to the [b]cleanness of my hands
He has recompensed me.
22 For I have [a]kept the ways of the LORD,
And have not wickedly departed from my God.
23 For all His [a]judgments *were* before me;
And *as for* His statutes, I did not depart from them.
24 I was also [a]blameless before Him,
And I kept myself from my iniquity.
25 Therefore [a]the LORD has [1]recompensed me according to my righteousness,
According to [2]my cleanness in His eyes.

26 "With [a]the merciful You will show Yourself merciful;
With a blameless man You will show Yourself blameless;
27 With the pure You will show Yourself pure;
And [a]with the devious You will show Yourself shrewd.
28 You will save the [a]humble[1] people;
But Your eyes *are* on [b]the haughty, *that* You may bring *them* down.

29 "For You *are* my [a]lamp, O LORD;
The LORD shall enlighten my darkness.
30 For by You I can run against a troop;
By my God I can leap over a [a]wall.
31 *As for* God, [a]His way *is* perfect;
[b]The word of the LORD *is* proven;
He *is* a shield to all who trust in Him.

32 "For [a]who *is* God, except the LORD?
And who *is* a rock, except our God?
33 [1]God *is* my [a]strength *and* power,
And He [b]makes [2]my way [c]perfect.

5 [1]Or *overwhelmed*
6 [a]Ps. 116:3
7 [a]Ps. 116:4; 120:1 [b]Ex. 3:7
8 [a]Judg. 5:4 [b]Job 26:11 [1]So with MT, LXX, Tg.; Syr., Vg. *hills* (cf. Ps. 18:7)
9 [a]Heb. 12:29
10 [a]Is. 64:1 [b]Ex. 20:21
11 [a]Ps. 104:3 [1]So with MT, LXX; many Heb. mss., Syr., Vg. *flew* (cf. Ps. 18:10); Tg. *spoke with power*
12 [a]Job 36:29
14 [a]Job 37:2–5
15 [a]Deut. 32:23
16 [a]Nah. 1:4 [b]Ex. 15:8
17 [a]Ps. 144:7
19 [a]Is. 10:20
20 [a]Ps. 31:8; 118:5 [b]2 Sam. 15:26
21 [a]1 Sam. 26:23 [b]Ps. 24:4
22 [a]Ps. 119:3
23 [a][Deut. 6:6–9; 7:12]
24 [a][Eph. 1:4]
25 [a]2 Sam. 22:21 [1]*rewarded* [2]LXX, Syr., Vg. *the cleanness of my hands in His sight* (cf. Ps. 18:24); Tg. *my cleanness before His word*
26 [a][Matt. 5:7]
27 [a][Lev. 26:23, 24]
28 [a]Ps. 72:12 [b]Job 40:11 [1]*afflicted*
29 [a]Ps. 119:105; 132:17
30 [a]2 Sam. 5:6–8
31 [a][Matt. 5:48] [b]Ps. 12:6
32 [a]Is. 45:5, 6
33 [a]Ps. 27:1 [b][Heb. 13:21] [c]Ps. 101:2, 6 [1]DSS, LXX, Syr., Vg. *It is God who arms me with strength* (cf. Ps. 18:32); Tg. *It is God who sustains me with strength* [2]So with Qr., LXX, Syr., Tg., Vg. (cf. Ps. 18:32); Kt. *His*

34 He makes [1]my feet [a]like the *feet*
of deer,
And [b]sets me on my high places.
35 He teaches my hands [1]to make
war,
So that my arms can bend a bow
of bronze.
36 "You have also given me the shield
of Your salvation;
Your gentleness has made me
great.
37 You [a]enlarged my path under me;
So my feet did not slip.
38 "I have pursued my enemies and
destroyed them;
Neither did I turn back again till
they were destroyed.
39 And I have destroyed them and
wounded them,
So that they could not rise;
They have fallen [a]under my feet.
40 For You have [a]armed me with
strength for the battle;
You have [1]subdued under me
[b]those who rose against me.
41 You have also [1]given me the
[a]necks of my enemies,
So that I destroyed those who
hated me.
42 They looked, but *there was* none
to save;
Even [a]to the LORD, but He did not
answer them.
43 Then I beat them as fine [a]as the
dust of the earth;
I trod them [b]like dirt in the
streets,
And I [1]spread them out.
44 "You[a] have also delivered me from
the [1]strivings of my people;
You have kept me as the [b]head
of the nations.
[c]A people I have not known shall
serve me.
45 The foreigners submit to me;
As soon as they hear, they obey
me.
46 The foreigners fade away,
And [1]come frightened [a]from their
hideouts.
47 "The LORD lives!
Blessed *be* my Rock!
Let God be exalted,
The [a]Rock of my salvation!
48 *It is* God who avenges me,
And [a]subdues the peoples under
me;
49 He delivers me from my enemies.
You also lift me up above those
who rise against me;
You have delivered me from the
[a]violent man.

34 [a]2 Sam. 2:18; Hab. 3:19 [b]Is. 33:16 [1]So with Qr., LXX, Syr., Tg., Vg. (cf. Ps. 18:33); Kt. *His*
35 [1]Lit. *for the war*
37 [a]2 Sam. 22:20; Prov. 4:12
39 [a]Mal. 4:3
40 [a][Ps. 18:32] [b][Ps. 44:5] [1]Lit. *caused to bow down*
41 [a]Gen. 49:8; Josh. 10:24 [1]*given me victory over*
42 [a]1 Sam. 28:6; Prov. 1:28; Is. 1:15
43 [a]2 Kin. 13:7; Ps. 18:42 [b]Is. 10:6 [1]*scattered*
44 [a]2 Sam. 3:1 [b]Deut. 28:13 [c][Is. 55:5] [1]*contentions*
46 [a]1 Sam. 14:11; [Mic. 7:17] [1]So with LXX, Tg., Vg. (cf. Ps. 18:45); MT *gird themselves*
47 [a][2 Sam. 22:3]; Ps. 89:26
48 [a]1 Sam. 24:12; Ps. 144:2
49 [a]Ps. 140:1, 4, 11
50 [a]2 Sam. 8:1–14 [b]Ps. 57:7; Rom. 15:9
51 [a]Ps. 144:10 [b]Ps. 89:20 [c]2 Sam. 7:12–16; Ps. 89:29

CHAPTER 23

1 [a]2 Sam. 7:8, 9; Ps. 78:70, 71 [b]1 Sam. 16:12, 13; Ps. 89:20
2 [a]Matt. 22:43; [2 Pet. 1:21]
3 [a][Deut. 32:4] [b]Ex. 18:21; [Is. 11:1–5]
4 [a]Ps. 89:36; Is. 60:1
5 [a]2 Sam. 7:12; Ps. 89:29; Is. 55:3
7 [1]Lit. *filled*
8 [1]Lit. *One Who Sits in the Seat* (1 Chr. 11:11) [2]So with MT, Tg.; LXX, Vg. *the three*

50 Therefore I will give thanks to
You, O LORD, among [a]the
Gentiles,
And sing praises to Your [b]name.
51 "He[a] *is* the tower of salvation to
His king,
And shows mercy to His
[b]anointed,
To David and [c]his descendants
forevermore."

David's Last Words

23 Now these *are* the last words
of David.

Thus says David the son of Jesse;
Thus says [a]the man raised up on
high,
[b]The anointed of the God of Jacob,
And the sweet psalmist of Israel:

2 "The[a] Spirit of the LORD spoke by
me,
And His word *was* on my tongue.
3 The God of Israel said,
[a]The Rock of Israel spoke to me:
'He who rules over men *must be*
just,
Ruling [b]in the fear of God.
4 And [a]*he shall be* like the light of
the morning *when* the sun
rises,
A morning without clouds,
Like the tender grass *springing*
out of the earth,
By clear shining after rain.'

5 "Although my house *is* not so with
God,
[a]Yet He has made with me an
everlasting covenant,
Ordered in all *things* and secure.
For *this is* all my salvation and
all *my* desire;
Will He not make *it* increase?
6 But *the sons* of rebellion *shall* all
be as thorns thrust away,
Because they cannot be taken
with hands.
7 But the man *who* touches them
Must be [1]armed with iron and the
shaft of a spear,
And they shall be utterly burned
with fire in *their* place."

David's Mighty Men

8 These *are* the names of the
mighty men whom David had:
[1]Josheb-Basshebeth the Tachmo-
nite, chief among [2]the captains.
He was called Adino the Eznite,
because he had killed eight hun-
dred men at one time.

9 And after him *was* [a]Eleazar the
son of [1]Dodo, the Ahohite, *one* of
the three mighty men with David
when they defied the Philistines
who were gathered there for bat-
tle, and the men of Israel had re-
treated.
10 He arose and attacked the Phi-
listines until his hand was [a]weary,
and his hand stuck to the sword.
The LORD brought about a great
victory that day; and the people re-
turned after him only to [b]plunder.
11 And after him *was* [a]Shammah
the son of Agee the Hararite. [b]The
Philistines had gathered together
into a troop where there was a
piece of ground full of lentils. So
the people fled from the Phi-
listines.
12 But he stationed himself in the
middle of the field, defended it,
and killed the Philistines. So the
LORD brought about a great vic-
tory.
13 Then [a]three of the thirty chief
men went down at harvest time
and came to David at [b]the cave of
Adullam. And the troop of Philis-
tines encamped in [c]the Valley of
Rephaim.
14 David *was* then in [a]the strong-
hold, and the garrison of the Phi-
listines *was* then *in* Bethlehem.
15 And David said with longing,
"Oh, that someone would give me
a drink of the water from the well
of Bethlehem, which *is* by the
gate!"
16 So the three mighty men broke
through the camp of the Philis-
tines, drew water from the well of
Bethlehem that *was* by the gate,
and took it and brought *it* to Da-
vid. Nevertheless he would not
drink it, but poured it out to the
LORD.
17 And he said, "Far be it from
me, O LORD, that I should do this!
Is *this not* [a]the blood of the men
who went in *jeopardy of* their
lives?" Therefore he would not
drink it. These things were done
by the three mighty men.
18 Now [a]Abishai the brother of
Joab, the son of Zeruiah, was chief
of [1]*another* three. He lifted his
spear against three hundred *men*,
killed *them*, and won a name
among *these* three.
19 Was he not the most honored
of three? Therefore he became
their captain. However, he did not
attain to the *first* three.
20 Benaiah *was* the son of Jehoi-
ada, the son of a valiant man from
[a]Kabzeel, [1]who had done many
deeds. [b]He had killed two lion-like
heroes of Moab. He also had gone
down and killed a lion in the midst
of a pit on a snowy day.
21 And he killed an Egyptian, [1]a
spectacular man. The Egyptian
had a spear in his hand; so he went
down to him with a staff, wrested
the spear out of the Egyptian's
hand, and killed him with his own
spear.
22 These *things* Benaiah the son
of Jehoiada did, and won a name
among three mighty men.
23 He was more honored than the
thirty, but he did not attain to the
first three. And David appointed
him [a]over his guard.
24 [a]Asahel the brother of Joab
was one of the thirty; Elhanan the
son of Dodo of Bethlehem,
25 [a]Shammah the Harodite, Elika
the Harodite,
26 Helez the Paltite, Ira the son of
Ikkesh the Tekoite,
27 Abiezer the Anathothite, Me-
bunnai the Hushathite,
28 Zalmon the Ahohite, Maharai
the Netophathite,
29 Heleb the son of Baanah (the
Netophathite), Ittai the son of Ri-
bai from Gibeah of the children of
Benjamin,
30 Benaiah a Pirathonite, Hiddai
from the brooks of [a]Gaash,
31 Abi-Albon the Arbathite, Az-
maveth the Barhumite,
32 Eliahba the Shaalbonite (of the
sons of Jashen), Jonathan,
33 [a]Shammah the [1]Hararite,
Ahiam the son of Sharar the Ha-
rarite,
34 Eliphelet the son of Ahasbai,
the son of the Maachathite, Eliam
the son of [a]Ahithophel the Gi-
lonite,
35 [1]Hezrai the Carmelite, Paarai
the Arbite,
36 Igal the son of Nathan of [a]Zo-
bah, Bani the Gadite,
37 Zelek the Ammonite, Naharai
the Beerothite (armorbearer of
Joab the son of Zeruiah),
38 [a]Ira the Ithrite, Gareb the Ith-
rite,

9 [a]1 Chr. 11:12; 27:4 [1]*Dodai,* 1 Chr. 27:4
10 [a]Judg. 8:4 [b]1 Sam. 30:24, 25
11 [a]1 Chr. 11:27 [b]1 Chr. 11:13, 14
13 [a]1 Chr. 11:15 [b]1 Sam. 22:1 [c]2 Sam. 5:18
14 [a]1 Sam. 22:4, 5
17 [a][Lev. 17:10]
18 [a]2 Sam. 21:17; 1 Chr. 11:20 [1]So with MT, LXX, Vg.; some Heb. mss., Syr. *thirty;* Tg. *the mighty men*
20 [a]Josh. 15:21 [b]Ex. 15:15 [1]Lit. *great of acts*
21 [1]Lit. *a man of appearance*
23 [a]2 Sam. 8:18; 20:23
24 [a]2 Sam. 2:18; 1 Chr. 27:7
25 [a]1 Chr. 11:27
30 [a]Judg. 2:9
33 [a]2 Sam. 23:11 [1]Or *Ararite*
34 [a]2 Sam. 15:12
35 [1]*Hezro,* 1 Chr. 11:37
36 [a]2 Sam. 8:3
38 [a]1 Chr. 2:53

39 *and* [a]Uriah the Hittite: thirty-
seven in all.

David's Census of Israel and Judah

24 Again [a]the anger of the LORD
was aroused against Israel,
and He moved David against them
to say, [b]"Go, [1]number Israel and
Judah."
2 So the king said to Joab the
commander of the army who *was*
with him, "Now go throughout all
the tribes of Israel, [a]from Dan to
Beersheba, and count the people,
that [b]I may know the number of
the people."
3 And Joab said to the king,
"Now may the LORD your God
[a]add to the people a hundred times
more than there are, and may the
eyes of my lord the king see *it*. But
why does my lord the king desire
this thing?"
4 Nevertheless the king's word
[1]prevailed against Joab and
against the captains of the army.
Therefore Joab and the captains of
the army went out from the pres-
ence of the king to count the peo-
ple of Israel.
5 And they crossed over the Jor-
dan and camped in [a]Aroer, on the
right side of the town which *is* in
the midst of the ravine of Gad, and
toward [b]Jazer.
6 Then they came to Gilead and
to the land of Tahtim Hodshi; they
came to [a]Dan Jaan and around to
[b]Sidon;
7 and they came to the strong-
hold of [a]Tyre and to all the cities
of the [b]Hivites and the Canaanites.
Then they went out to South Judah
as far as Beersheba.
8 So when they had gone
through all the land, they came to
Jerusalem at the end of nine
months and twenty days.
9 Then Joab gave the sum of the
number of the people to the king.
[a]And there were in Israel eight
hundred thousand valiant men
who drew the sword, and the men
of Judah were five hundred thou-
sand men.

The Judgment on David's Sin

10 And [a]David's heart condemned
him after he had numbered the
people. So [b]David said to the LORD,
[c]"I have sinned greatly in what
I have done; but now, I pray, O
LORD, take away the iniquity of
Your servant, for I have [d]done
very foolishly."
11 Now when David arose in the
morning, the word of the LORD
came to the prophet [a]Gad, David's
[b]seer, saying,
12 "Go and tell David, 'Thus says
the LORD: "I offer you three *things;*
choose one of them for yourself,
that I may do *it* to you." ' "
13 So Gad came to David and told
him; and he said to him, "Shall
[a]seven[1] years of famine come to
you in your land? Or shall you flee
three months before your enemies,
while they pursue you? Or shall
there be three days' plague in your
land? Now consider and see what
answer I should take back to Him
who sent me."
14 And David said to Gad, "I am
in great distress. Please let us fall
into the hand of the LORD, [a]for His
mercies *are* great; but [b]do not let
me fall into the hand of man."
15 So [a]the LORD sent a plague
upon Israel from the morning till
the appointed time. From Dan to
Beersheba seventy thousand men
of the people died.
16 [a]And when the [1]angel stretched
out His hand over Jerusalem to de-
stroy it, [b]the LORD relented from
the destruction, and said to the
[1]angel who was destroying the
people, "It is enough; now restrain
your hand." And the [1]angel of the
LORD was by the threshing floor of
[2]Araunah the Jebusite.
17 Then David spoke to the LORD
when he saw the angel who was
striking the people, and said,
"Surely [a]I have sinned, and I have
done wickedly; but these sheep,
what have they done? Let Your
hand, I pray, be against me and
against my father's house."

The Altar on the Threshing Floor

18 And Gad came that day to Da-
vid and said to him, [a]"Go up, erect
an altar to the LORD on the thresh-
ing floor of Araunah the Jebusite."
19 So David, according to the
word of Gad, went up as the LORD
commanded.
20 Now Araunah looked, and saw
the king and his servants coming
toward him. So Araunah went out

39 [a]2 Sam. 11:3, 6

CHAPTER 24

1 [a]2 Sam. 21:1, 2 [b]Num. 26:2; 1 Chr. 27:23, 24 [1]*take a census of*

2 [a]Judg. 20:1; 2 Sam. 3:10 [b][Jer. 17:5]

3 [a]Deut. 1:11

4 [1]*overruled*

5 [a]Deut. 2:36; Josh. 13:9, 16 [b]Num. 32:1, 3

6 [a]Josh. 19:47; Judg. 18:29 [b]Josh. 19:28; Judg. 18:28

7 [a]Josh. 19:29 [b]Josh. 11:3; Judg. 3:3

9 [a]1 Chr. 21:5

10 [a]1 Sam. 24:5 [b]2 Sam. 23:1 [c]2 Sam. 12:13 [d]1 Sam. 13:13; [2 Chr. 16:9]

11 [a]1 Sam. 22:5 [b]1 Sam. 9:9; 1 Chr. 29:29

13 [a]Ezek. 14:21 [1]So with MT, Syr., Tg., Vg.; LXX *three* (cf. 1 Chr. 21:12)

14 [a][Ps. 51:1; 103:8, 13, 14; 119:156; 130:4, 7] [b][Is. 47:6; Zech. 1:15]

15 [a]1 Chr. 21:14

16 [a]Ex. 12:23; 2 Kin. 19:35; Acts 12:23 [b]Gen. 6:6; 1 Sam. 15:11 [1]Or *Angel* [2]*Ornan,* 1 Chr. 21:15

17 [a]2 Sam. 7:8; 1 Chr. 21:17; Ps. 74:1

18 [a]1 Chr. 21:18

The Davidic Kingdom. David's military exploits successfully incorporated into the Israelite kingdom the powers of Edom, Moab, Ammon, and Zobah.

and bowed before the king with
his face to the ground.
21 Then Araunah said, "Why has
my lord the king come to his ser-
vant?" [a]And David said, "To buy
the threshing floor from you, to
build an altar to the LORD, that [b]the
plague may be withdrawn from
the people."
22 Now Araunah said to David,
"Let my lord the king take and of-
fer up whatever *seems* good to
him. [a]Look, *here are* oxen for
burnt sacrifice, and threshing im-
plements and the yokes of the
oxen for wood.
23 "All these, O king, Araunah
has given to the king." And Arau-
nah said to the king, "May the
LORD your God [a]accept you."
24 Then the king said to Araunah,
"No, but I will surely buy *it* from
you for a price; nor will I offer
burnt offerings to the LORD my
God with that which costs me
nothing." So [a]David bought the
threshing floor and the oxen for
fifty shekels of silver.
25 And David built there an altar
to the LORD, and offered burnt of-
ferings and peace offerings. [a]So
the LORD heeded the prayers for
the land, and [b]the plague was
withdrawn from Israel.

21 [a]Gen. 23:8–16 [b]Num. 16:48, 50
22 [a]1 Sam. 6:14; 1 Kin. 19:21
23 [a][Ezek. 20:40, 41]
24 [a]1 Chr. 21:24, 25
25 [a]2 Sam. 21:14 [b]2 Sam. 24:21

The First Book of the

Kings

THE first half of First Kings traces the life of Solomon. Under his leadership Israel rises to the peak of her size and glory. Solomon's great accomplishments, including the unsurpassed splendor of the temple which he constructs in Jerusalem, bring him worldwide fame and respect. However, Solomon's zeal for God diminishes in his later years, as pagan wives turn his heart away from worship in the temple of God. As a result, the king with the divided heart leaves behind a divided kingdom. For the next century, the Book of First Kings traces the twin histories of two sets of kings and two nations of disobedient people who are growing indifferent to God's prophets and precepts.

Like the two books of Samuel, the two books of Kings were originally one in the Hebrew Bible. The original title was *Melechim,* "Kings," taken from the first word in 1:1, *Vehamelech,* "Now King." The Septuagint artificially divided the book of Kings in the middle of the story of Ahaziah into two books. It called the books of Samuel "First and Second Kingdoms" and the books of Kings "Third and Fourth Kingdoms." The Septuagint may have divided Samuel, Kings, and Chronicles into two books each because the Greek required a greater amount of scroll space than did the Hebrew. The Latin title for these books is *Liber Regum Tertius et Quartus,* "Third and Fourth Books of Kings."

NOW King David was [a]old, [1]advanced in years; and they put
covers on him, but he could
not get warm.
2 Therefore his servants said to
him, "Let a young woman, a virgin, be sought for our lord the
king, and let her [1]stand before the
king, and let her care for him; and
let her lie in your bosom, that our
lord the king may be warm."
3 So they sought for a lovely
young woman throughout all the
territory of Israel, and found [a]Abishag the [b]Shunammite, and
brought her to the king.
4 The young woman *was* very
lovely; and she cared for the king,
and served him; but the king did
not know her.
5 Then [a]Adonijah the [1]son of
Haggith exalted himself, saying, "I
will [2]be king"; and [b]he prepared
for himself chariots and horsemen,
and fifty men to run before him.
6 (And his father had not [1]rebuked him at any time by saying,
"Why have you done so?" He *was*
also very good-looking. [a]*His*
mother had borne him after Absalom.)
7 Then he conferred with [a]Joab
the son of Zeruiah and with [b]Abiathar the priest, and [c]they followed
and helped Adonijah.
8 But [a]Zadok the priest, [b]Benaiah the son of Jehoiada, [c]Nathan
the prophet, [d]Shimei, Rei, and [e]the
mighty men who *belonged* to David were not with Adonijah.
9 And Adonijah sacrificed sheep
and oxen and fattened cattle by the
stone of [1]Zoheleth, which *is* by [a]En
Rogel;[2] he also invited all his
brothers, the king's sons, and all
the men of Judah, the king's servants.
10 But he did not invite Nathan
the prophet, Benaiah, the mighty
men, or [a]Solomon his brother.
11 So Nathan spoke to Bathsheba
the mother of Solomon, saying,
"Have you not heard that Adonijah the son of [a]Haggith has become king, and David our lord
does not know *it?*
12 "Come, please, let me now give
you advice, that you may save

CHAPTER 1

1 [a]1 Chr. 23:1 [1]Seventy years
2 [1]Or *serve*
3 [a]1 Kin. 2:17 [b]Josh. 19:18; 1 Sam. 28:4
5 [a]2 Sam. 3:4 [b]2 Sam. 15:1 [1]The fourth son [2]Lit. *reign*
6 [a]2 Sam. 3:3, 4; 1 Chr. 3:2 [1]Lit. *pained*
7 [a]1 Chr. 11:6 [b]2 Sam. 20:25 [c]1 Kin. 2:22, 28
8 [a]1 Kin. 2:35 [b]1 Kin. 2:25; 2 Sam. 8:18 [c]2 Sam. 12:1 [d]1 Kin. 4:18 [e]2 Sam. 23:8
9 [a]Josh. 15:7; 18:16; 2 Sam. 17:17 [1]Lit. *Serpent* [2]A spring south of Jerusalem in the Kidron Valley
10 [a]2 Sam. 12:24
11 [a]2 Sam. 3:4

your own life and the life of your
son Solomon.
13 "Go immediately to King David
and say to him, 'Did you not, my
lord, O king, swear to your
maidservant, saying, [a]"Assuredly
your son Solomon shall reign after
me, and he shall sit on my
throne"? Why then has Adonijah
become king?'
14 "Then, while you are still talk-
ing there with the king, I also will
come in after you and confirm
your words."
15 So Bathsheba went into the
chamber to the king. (Now the
king was very old, and Abishag
the Shunammite was serving the
king.)
16 And Bathsheba bowed and did
homage to the king. Then the king
said, "What is your wish?"
17 Then she said to him, "My lord,
[a]you swore by the LORD your God
to your maidservant, *saying*, 'As-
suredly Solomon your son shall
reign after me, and he shall sit on
my throne.'
18 "So now, look! Adonijah has
become king; and now, my lord
the king, you do not know about
it.
19 [a]"He has sacrificed oxen and
fattened cattle and sheep in abun-
dance, and has invited all the sons
of the king, Abiathar the priest,
and Joab the commander of the
army; but Solomon your servant
he has not invited.
20 "And as for you, my lord, O
king, the eyes of all Israel *are* on
you, that you should tell them who
will sit on the throne of my lord
the king after him.
21 "Otherwise it will happen,
when my lord the king [a]rests with
his fathers, that I and my son Sol-
omon will be counted as offend-
ers."
22 And just then, while she was
still talking with the king, Nathan
the prophet also came in.
23 So they told the king, saying,
"Here is Nathan the prophet." And
when he came in before the king,
he bowed down before the king
with his face to the ground.
24 And Nathan said, "My lord, O
king, have you said, 'Adonijah
shall reign after me, and he shall
sit on my throne'?
25 [a]"For he has gone down today,
and has sacrificed oxen and fat-
tened cattle and sheep in abun-
dance, and has invited all the
king's sons, and the commanders
of the army, and Abiathar the
priest; and look! They are eating
and drinking before him; and they
say, [b]'*Long*[1] live King Adonijah!'
26 "But he has not invited me—me
your servant—nor Zadok the
priest, nor Benaiah the son of Je-
hoiada, nor your servant Solomon.
27 "Has this thing been done by
my lord the king, and you have not
told your servant who should sit
on the throne of my lord the king
after him?"

David Proclaims Solomon King

28 Then King David answered
and said, "Call Bathsheba to me."
So she came into the king's pres-
ence and stood before the king.
29 And the king took an oath and
said, [a]"*As* the LORD lives, who has
redeemed my life from every dis-
tress,
30 [a]"just as I swore to you by the
LORD God of Israel, saying, 'As-
suredly Solomon your son shall be
king after me, and he shall sit on
my throne in my place,' so I cer-
tainly will do this day."
31 Then Bathsheba bowed with
her face to the earth, and paid
homage to the king, and said,
[a]"Let my lord King David live for-
ever!"
32 And King David said, "Call to
me Zadok the priest, Nathan the
prophet, and Benaiah the son of
Jehoiada." So they came before
the king.
33 The king also said to them,
[a]"Take with you the servants of
your lord, and have Solomon my
son ride on my own [b]mule, and
take him down to [c]Gihon.[1]
34 "There let Zadok the priest and
Nathan the prophet [a]anoint him
king over Israel; and [b]blow the
horn, and say, [1]'*Long* live King
Solomon!'
35 "Then you shall come up after
him, and he shall come and sit on
my throne, and he shall be king
in my place. For I have appointed
him to be ruler over Israel and Ju-
dah."
36 Benaiah the son of Jehoiada

13 [a]1 Kin. 1:30; 1 Chr. 22:9–13
17 [a]1 Kin. 1:13, 30
19 [a]1 Kin. 1:7–9, 25
21 [a]Deut. 31:16; 2 Sam. 7:12; 1 Kin. 2:10
25 [a]1 Kin. 1:9, 19 [b]1 Sam. 10:24 [1]Lit. *Let King Adonijah live*
29 [a]2 Sam. 4:9; 12:5
30 [a]1 Kin. 1:13, 17
31 [a]Neh. 2:3; Dan. 2:4; 3:9
33 [a]2 Sam. 20:6 [b]Esth. 6:8 [c]2 Chr. 32:30; 33:14 [1]A spring east of Jerusalem in the Kidron Valley
34 [a]1 Sam. 10:1; 16:3, 12; 2 Sam. 2:4; 5:3; 1 Kin. 19:16; 2 Kin. 9:3; 11:12; 1 Chr. 29:22 [b]2 Sam. 15:10; 2 Kin. 9:13; 11:14 [1]Lit. *Let King Solomon live*

answered the king and said,
[a]"Amen! May the LORD God of my
lord the king say so *too*.
37 [a]"As the LORD has been with
my lord the king, even so may He
be with Solomon, and [b]make his
throne greater than the throne of
my lord King David."
38 So Zadok the priest, Nathan
the prophet, [a]Benaiah the son of
Jehoiada, the [b]Cherethites, and the
Pelethites went down and had Sol-
omon ride on King David's mule,
and took him to Gihon.
39 Then Zadok the priest took a
horn of [a]oil from the tabernacle
and [b]anointed Solomon. And they
blew the horn, [c]and all the people
said, [1]"*Long* live King Solomon!"
40 And all the people went up af-
ter him; and the people played the
flutes and rejoiced with great joy,
so that the earth *seemed to* split
with their sound.
41 Now Adonijah and all the
guests who *were* with him heard
it as they finished eating. And
when Joab heard the sound of the
horn, he said, "Why *is* the city in
such a noisy uproar?"
42 While he was still speaking,
there came [a]Jonathan, the son of
Abiathar the priest. And Adonijah
said to him, "Come in, for [b]you *are*
a prominent man, and bring good
news."
43 Then Jonathan answered and
said to Adonijah, "No! Our lord
King David has made Solomon
king.
44 "The king has sent with him
Zadok the priest, Nathan the
prophet, Benaiah the son of Jehoi-
ada, the Cherethites, and the Pel-
ethites; and they have made him
ride on the king's mule.
45 "So Zadok the priest and Na-
than the prophet have anointed
him king at Gihon; and they have
gone up from there rejoicing,
so that the city is in an uproar.
This *is* the noise that you have
heard.
46 "Also Solomon [a]sits on the
throne of the kingdom.
47 "And moreover the king's ser-
vants have gone to bless our lord
King David, saying, [a]'May God
make the name of Solomon better
than your name, and may He make
his throne greater than your
throne.' [b]Then the king bowed
himself on the bed.
48 "Also the king said thus,
'Blessed *be* the LORD God of Israel,
who has [a]given *one* to sit on my
throne this day, while my eyes see
[b]*it!*'"
49 So all the guests who were with
Adonijah were afraid, and arose,
and each one went his way.
50 Now Adonijah was afraid of
Solomon; so he arose, and went
and [a]took hold of the horns of the
altar.
51 And it was told Solomon, say-
ing, "Indeed Adonijah is afraid of
King Solomon; for look, he has
taken hold of the horns of the al-
tar, saying, 'Let King Solomon
swear to me today that he will not
put his servant to death with the
sword.'"
52 Then Solomon said, "If he
proves himself a worthy man, [a]not
one hair of him shall fall to the
earth; but if wickedness is found
in him, he shall die."
53 So King Solomon sent them to
bring him down from the altar.
And he came and fell down before
King Solomon; and Solomon said
to him, "Go to your house."

David's Instructions to Solomon

2 Now [a]the days of David drew
near that he should die, and he
[1]charged Solomon his son, saying:
2 [a]"I go the way of all the earth;
[b]be strong, therefore, and prove
yourself a man.
3 "And keep the charge of the
LORD your God: to walk in His
ways, to keep His statutes, His
commandments, His judgments,
and His testimonies, as it is written
in the Law of Moses, that you may
[a]prosper in all that you do and
wherever you turn;
4 "that the LORD may [a]fulfill His
word which He spoke concerning
me, saying, [b]'If your sons take
heed to their way, to [c]walk before
Me in truth with all their heart and
with all their soul,' He said, [d]'you
shall not lack a man on the throne
of Israel.'
5 "Moreover you know also what
Joab the son of Zeruiah [a]did to me,
and what he did to the two com-
manders of the armies of Israel, to
[b]Abner the son of Ner and [c]Amasa

36 [a]Jer. 28:6

37 [a]Josh. 1:5, 17; 1 Sam. 20:13 [b]1 Kin. 1:47

38 [a]2 Sam. 8:18; 23:20–23 [b]2 Sam. 20:7; 1 Chr. 18:17

39 [a]Ex. 30:23, 25, 32; Ps. 89:20 [b]1 Chr. 29:22 [c]1 Sam. 10:24 [1]Lit. *Let King Solomon live*

42 [a]2 Sam. 17:17, 20 [b]2 Sam. 18:27

46 [a]1 Kin. 2:12; 1 Chr. 29:23

47 [a]1 Kin. 1:37 [b]Gen. 47:31

48 [a]1 Kin. 3:6; [Ps. 132:11, 12] [b]2 Sam. 7:12

50 [a]Ex. 27:2; 30:10; 1 Kin. 2:28

52 [a]1 Sam. 14:45; 2 Sam. 14:11; Acts 27:34

CHAPTER 2

1 [a]Gen. 47:29; Deut. 31:14 [1]*commanded*

2 [a]Josh. 23:14 [b]Deut. 31:7, 23; 1 Chr. 22:13

3 [a][Deut. 29:9; Josh. 1:7]; 1 Chr. 22:12, 13

4 [a]2 Sam. 7:25 [b][Ps. 132:12] [c]2 Kin. 20:3 [d]2 Sam. 7:12, 13; 1 Kin. 8:25

5 [a]2 Sam. 3:39; 18:5, 12, 14 [b]2 Sam. 3:27; 1 Kin. 2:32 [c]2 Sam. 20:10

the son of Jether, whom he killed.
And he shed the blood of war in
peacetime, and put the blood of
war on his belt that *was* around
his waist, and on his sandals that
were on his feet.
6 "Therefore do [a]according to
your wisdom, and do not let his
gray hair go down to the grave in
peace.
7 "But show kindness to the sons
of [a]Barzillai the Gileadite, and let
them be among those who [b]eat at
your table, for so [c]they came to me
when I fled from Absalom your
brother.
8 "And see, *you have* with you
[a]Shimei the son of Gera, a Benja-
mite from Bahurim, who cursed
me with a malicious curse in the
day when I went to Mahanaim. But
[b]he came down to meet me at the
Jordan, and [c]I swore to him by the
LORD, saying, 'I will not put you
to death with the sword.'
9 "Now therefore, [a]do not hold
him guiltless, for you *are* a wise
man and know what you ought to
do to him; but [b]bring his gray hair
down to the grave with blood."

Death of David

10 So [a]David [1]rested with his fa-
thers, and was buried in [b]the City
of David.
11 The period that David [a]reigned
over Israel *was* forty years; seven
years he reigned in Hebron, and
in Jerusalem he reigned thirty-
three years.
12 [a]Then Solomon sat on the
throne of his father David; and his
kingdom was [b]firmly established.

Solomon Executes Adonijah

13 Now Adonijah the son of Hag-
gith came to Bathsheba the mother
of Solomon. So she said, [a]"Do you
come peaceably?" And he said,
"Peaceably."
14 Moreover he said, "I have
something *to say* to you." And she
said, "Say it."
15 Then he said, "You know that
the kingdom was [a]mine, and all Is-
rael had set their expectations on
me, that I should reign. However,
the kingdom has been turned over,
and has become my brother's; for
[b]it was his from the LORD.
16 "Now I ask one petition of you;
do not [1]deny me." And she said
to him, "Say it."
17 Then he said, "Please speak to
King Solomon, for he will not re-
fuse you, that he may give me [a]Ab-
ishag the Shunammite as wife."
18 So Bathsheba said, "Very well,
I will speak for you to the king."
19 Bathsheba therefore went to
King Solomon, to speak to him for
Adonijah. And the king rose up to
meet her and [a]bowed down to her,
and sat down on his throne and
had a throne set for the king's
mother; [b]so she sat at his right
hand.
20 Then she said, "I desire one
small petition of you; do not [1]re-
fuse me." And the king said to her,
"Ask it, my mother, for I will not
refuse you."
21 So she said, "Let Abishag the
Shunammite be given to Adonijah
your brother as wife."
22 And King Solomon answered
and said to his mother, "Now why
do you ask Abishag the Shunam-
mite for Adonijah? Ask for him the
kingdom also—for he *is* my [a]older
brother—for him, and for [b]Abia-
thar the priest, and for Joab the
son of Zeruiah."
23 Then King Solomon swore by
the LORD, saying, [a]"May God do
so to me, and more also, if Adoni-
jah has not spoken this word
against his own life!
24 "Now therefore, *as* the LORD
lives, who has confirmed me and
set me on the throne of David my
father, and who has established a
[1]house for me, as He [a]promised,
Adonijah shall be put to death to-
day!"
25 So King Solomon sent by the
hand of [a]Benaiah the son of Jehoi-
ada; and he struck him down, and
he died.

Abiathar Exiled, Joab Executed

26 And to Abiathar the priest the
king said, "Go to [a]Anathoth, to
your own fields, for [1]you *are* de-
serving of death; but I will not put
you to death at this time, [b]because
you carried the ark of the Lord
GOD before my father David, and
because you were afflicted every
time my father was afflicted."
27 So Solomon removed Abiathar
from being priest to the LORD, that

6 [a]1 Kin. 2:9; Prov. 20:26
7 [a]2 Sam. 19:31–39 [b]2 Sam. 9:7, 10; 19:28 [c]2 Sam. 17:17–29
8 [a]2 Sam. 16:5–13 [b]2 Sam. 19:18 [c]2 Sam. 19:23
9 [a]Ex. 20:7; Job 9:28 [b]Gen. 42:38; 44:31
10 [a]1 Kin. 1:21; Acts 2:29; 13:36 [b]2 Sam. 5:7; 1 Kin. 3:1 [1]Died and joined his ancestors
11 [a]2 Sam. 5:4, 5; 1 Chr. 3:4; 29:26, 27
12 [a]1 Kin. 1:46; 1 Chr. 29:23 [b]1 Kin. 2:46; 2 Chr. 1:1
13 [a]1 Sam. 16:4, 5
15 [a]1 Kin. 1:11, 18 [b]1 Chr. 22:9, 10; 28:5–7; [Dan. 2:21]
16 [1]Lit. *turn away the face*
17 [a]1 Kin. 1:3, 4
19 [a][Ex. 20:12] [b]Ps. 45:9
20 [1]Lit. *turn away the face*
22 [a]1 Kin. 1:6; 2:15; 1 Chr. 3:2, 5 [b]1 Kin. 1:7
23 [a]Ruth 1:17
24 [a]2 Sam. 7:11, 13; 1 Chr. 22:10 [1]Royal dynasty
25 [a]2 Sam. 8:18; 1 Kin. 4:4
26 [a]Josh. 21:18; Jer. 1:1 [b]1 Sam. 22:23; 23:6; 2 Sam. 15:14, 29 [1]Lit. *you are a man of death*

he might [a]fulfill the word of the LORD which He spoke concerning the house of Eli at Shiloh.

28 Then news came to Joab, for Joab [a]had defected to Adonijah, though he had not defected to Absalom. So Joab fled to the tabernacle of the LORD, and [b]took hold of the horns of the altar.

29 And King Solomon was told, "Joab has fled to the tabernacle of the LORD; there *he is,* by the altar." Then Solomon sent Benaiah the son of Jehoiada, saying, "Go, [a]strike him down."

30 So Benaiah went to the tabernacle of the LORD, and said to him, "Thus says the king, [a]'Come out!' " And he said, "No, but I will die here." And Benaiah brought back word to the king, saying, "Thus said Joab, and thus he answered me."

31 Then the king said to him, [a]"Do as he has said, and strike him down and bury him, [b]that you may take away from me and from the house of my father the innocent blood which Joab shed.

32 "So the LORD [a]will return his [1]blood on his head, because he struck down two men more righteous [b]and better than he, and killed them with the sword—[c]Abner the son of Ner, the commander of the army of Israel, and [d]Amasa the son of Jether, the commander of the army of Judah—though my father David did not know *it.*

33 "Their blood shall therefore return upon the head of Joab and [a]upon the head of his descendants forever. [b]But upon David and his descendants, upon his house and his throne, there shall be peace forever from the LORD."

34 So Benaiah the son of Jehoiada went up and struck and killed him; and he was buried in his own house in the wilderness.

35 The king put Benaiah the son of Jehoiada in his place over the army, and the king put [a]Zadok the priest in the place of [b]Abiathar.

Shimei Executed

36 Then the king sent and called for [a]Shimei, and said to him, "Build yourself a house in Jerusalem and dwell there, and do not go out from there anywhere.

37 "For it shall be, on the day you go out and cross [a]the Brook Kidron, know for certain you shall surely die; [b]your [1]blood shall be on your own head."

38 And Shimei said to the king, "The saying *is* good. As my lord the king has said, so your servant will do." So Shimei dwelt in Jerusalem many days.

39 Now it happened at the end of three years, that two slaves of Shimei ran away to [a]Achish the son of Maachah, king of Gath. And they told Shimei, saying, "Look, your slaves *are* in Gath!"

40 So Shimei arose, saddled his donkey, and went to Achish at Gath to seek his slaves. And Shimei went and brought his slaves from Gath.

41 And Solomon was told that Shimei had gone from Jerusalem to Gath and had come back.

42 Then the king sent and called for Shimei, and said to him, "Did I not make you swear by the LORD, and warn you, saying, 'Know for certain that on the day you go out and travel anywhere, you shall surely die'? And you said to me, 'The word I have heard *is* good.'

43 "Why then have you not kept the oath of the LORD and the commandment that I gave you?"

44 The king said moreover to Shimei, "You know, as your heart acknowledges, [a]all the wickedness that you did to my father David; therefore the LORD will [b]return your wickedness on your own head.

45 "But King Solomon *shall be* blessed, and [a]the throne of David shall be established before the LORD forever."

46 So the king commanded Benaiah the son of Jehoiada; and he went out and struck him down, and he died. Thus the [a]kingdom was established in the hand of Solomon.

Solomon Requests Wisdom

3 Now [a]Solomon made [1]a treaty with Pharaoh king of Egypt, and married Pharaoh's daughter; then he brought her [b]to the City of David until he had finished building his [c]own house, and [d]the

27 [a]1 Sam. 2:31–35
28 [a]1 Kin. 1:7 [b]1 Kin. 1:50
29 [a]1 Kin. 2:5, 6
30 [a][Ex. 21:14]
31 [a][Ex. 21:14] [b][Num. 35:33; Deut. 19:13; 21:8, 9]
32 [a][Gen. 9:6]; Judg. 9:24, 57 [b]2 Chr. 21:13, 14 [c]2 Sam. 3:27 [d]2 Sam. 20:9, 10 [1]Or *bloodshed*
33 [a]2 Sam. 3:29 [b][Prov. 25:5]
35 [a]1 Sam. 2:35; 1 Kin. 4:4; 1 Chr. 6:53; 24:3; 29:22 [b]1 Kin. 2:27
36 [a]2 Sam. 16:5–13; 1 Kin. 2:8
37 [a]2 Sam. 15:23; 2 Kin. 23:6; John 18:1 [b]Lev. 20:9; Josh. 2:19; 2 Sam. 1:16; Ezek. 18:13 [1]Or *bloodshed*
39 [a]1 Sam. 27:2
44 [a]2 Sam. 16:5–13 [b]1 Sam. 25:39; 2 Kin. 11:1, 12–16; Ps. 7:16; Ezek. 17:19
45 [a]2 Sam. 7:13; [Prov. 25:5]
46 [a]1 Kin. 2:12; 2 Chr. 1:1

CHAPTER 3

1 [a]1 Kin. 7:8; 9:24 [b]2 Sam. 5:7 [c]1 Kin. 7:1 [d]1 Kin. 6 [1]an *alliance*

house of the LORD, and [e]the wall
all around Jerusalem.
2 [a]Meanwhile the people sacri-
ficed at the high places, because
there was no house built for the
name of the LORD until those days.
3 And Solomon [a]loved the LORD,
[b]walking in the statutes of his fa-
ther David, except that he sacri-
ficed and burned incense at the
high places.
4 Now [a]the king went to Gibeon
to sacrifice there, [b]for that *was* the
great high place: Solomon offered
a thousand burnt offerings on that
altar.
5 [a]At Gibeon the LORD appeared
to Solomon [b]in a dream by night;
and God said, "Ask! What shall I
give you?"
6 [a]And Solomon said: "You have
shown great mercy to Your ser-
vant David my father, because he
[b]walked before You in truth, in
righteousness, and in uprightness
of heart with You; You have con-
tinued this great kindness for him,
and You [c]have given him a son
to sit on his throne, as *it is* this
day.
7 "Now, O LORD my God, You
have made Your servant king in-
stead of my father David, but I *am*
a [a]little child; I do not know *how*
[b]to go out or come in.
8 "And Your servant *is* in the
midst of Your people whom You
[a]have chosen, a great people, [b]too
numerous to be numbered or
counted.
9 [a]"Therefore give to Your ser-
vant an [1]understanding heart [b]to
judge Your people, that I may [c]dis-
cern between good and evil. For
who is able to judge this great peo-
ple of Yours?"
10 The speech pleased the LORD,
that Solomon had asked this thing.
11 Then God said to him: "Be-
cause you have asked this thing,
and have [a]not asked long life for
yourself, nor have asked riches for
yourself, nor have asked the life
of your enemies, but have asked
for yourself understanding to dis-
cern justice,
12 [a]"behold, I have done accord-
ing to your words; [b]see, I have
given you a wise and understand-
ing heart, so that there has not
been anyone like you before you,
nor shall any like you arise after
you.
13 "And I have also [a]given you
what you have not asked: both
[b]riches and honor, so that there
shall not be anyone like you
among the kings all your days.
14 "So [a]if you walk in My ways,
to keep My statutes and My com-
mandments, [b]as your father David
walked, then I will [c]lengthen[1] your
days."
15 Then Solomon [a]awoke; and in-
deed it had been a dream. And he
came to Jerusalem and stood be-
fore the ark of the covenant of the
LORD, offered up burnt offerings,
offered peace offerings, and [b]made
a feast for all his servants.

Solomon's Wise Judgment

16 Now two women *who were*
harlots came to the king, and
[a]stood before him.
17 And one woman said, "O my
lord, this woman and I dwell in the
same house; and I gave birth while
she *was* in the house.
18 "Then it happened, the third
day after I had given birth, that
this woman also gave birth. And
we *were* together; [1]no one *was*
with us in the house, except the
two of us in the house.
19 "And this woman's son died in
the night, because she lay on him.
20 "So she arose in the middle of
the night and took my son from
my side, while your maidservant
slept, and laid him in her bosom,
and laid her dead child in my bo-
som.
21 "And when I rose in the morn-
ing to nurse my son, there he was,
dead. But when I had examined
him in the morning, indeed, he was
not my son whom I had borne."
22 Then the other woman said,
"No! But the living one *is* my son,
and the dead one *is* your son." And
the first woman said, "No! But the
dead one *is* your son, and the liv-
ing one *is* my son." Thus they
spoke before the king.
23 And the king said, "The one
says, 'This *is* my son, who lives,
and your son *is* the dead one'; and
the other says, 'No! But your son
is the dead one, and my son *is* the
living one.' "
24 Then the king said, "Bring me

1 [e]1 Kin. 9:15, 19
2 [a][Deut. 12:2–5, 13, 14]; 1 Kin. 11:7; 22:43
3 [a][Rom. 8:28] [b][1 Kin. 3:6, 14]
4 [a]1 Kin. 9:2; 2 Chr. 1:3 [b]1 Chr. 16:39; 21:29
5 [a]1 Kin. 9:2; 11:9; 2 Chr. 1:7 [b]Num. 12:6; Matt. 1:20; 2:13
6 [a]2 Chr. 1:8 [b]1 Kin. 2:4; 9:4; 2 Kin. 20:3 [c]2 Sam. 7:8–17; 1 Kin. 1:48
7 [a]1 Chr. 22:5; Jer. 1:6, 7 [b]Num. 27:17; 2 Sam. 5:2
8 [a][Ex. 19:6; Deut. 7:6] [b]Gen. 13:6; 15:5; 22:17
9 [a]2 Chr. 1:10; [James 1:5] [b]Ps. 72:1, 2 [c]2 Sam. 14:17; Is. 7:15; [Heb. 5:14] [1]Lit. *hearing*
11 [a][James 4:3]
12 [a][1 John 5:14, 15] [b]1 Kin. 4:29–31; 5:12; 10:24; Eccl. 1:16
13 [a][Matt. 6:33; Eph. 3:20] [b]1 Kin. 4:21, 24; 10:23; 1 Chr. 29:12
14 [a][1 Kin. 6:12] [b]1 Kin. 15:5 [c]Ps. 91:16; Prov. 3:2 [1]*prolong*
15 [a]Gen. 41:7 [b]Gen. 40:20; 1 Kin. 8:65; Esth. 1:3; Dan. 5:1; Mark 6:21
16 [a]Num. 27:2
18 [1]Lit. *no stranger*

a sword." So they brought a sword
before the king.
25 And the king said, "Divide the
living child in two, and give half
to one, and half to the other."
26 Then the woman whose son
was living spoke to the king, for
[a]she yearned with compassion for
her son; and she said, "O my lord,
give her the living child, and by
no means kill him!" But the other
said, "Let him be neither mine nor
yours, *but* divide *him*."
27 So the king answered and said,
"Give the first woman the living
child, and by no means kill him;
she *is* his mother."
28 And all Israel heard of the
judgment which the king had ren-
dered; and they feared the king,
for they saw that the [a]wisdom of
God *was* in him to administer jus-
tice.

Solomon's Administration

4 So King Solomon was king
over all Israel.
2 And these *were* his officials:
Azariah the son of Zadok, the
priest;
3 Elihoreph and Ahijah, the sons
of Shisha, [1]scribes; [a]Jehoshaphat
the son of Ahilud, the recorder;
4 [a]Benaiah the son of Jehoiada,
over the army; Zadok and [b]Abia-
thar, the priests;
5 Azariah the son of Nathan,
over [a]the officers; Zabud the son
of Nathan, [b]a priest *and* [c]the king's
friend;
6 Ahishar, over the household;
and [a]Adoniram the son of Abda,
over the labor force.
7 And Solomon had twelve gov-
ernors over all Israel, who pro-
vided food for the king and his
household; each one made provi-
sion for one month of the year.
8 These *are* their names: [1]Ben-
Hur, in the mountains of Ephraim;
9 [1]Ben-Deker, in Makaz, Shaal-
bim, Beth Shemesh, and Elon Beth
Hanan;
10 [1]Ben-Hesed, in Arubboth; to
him *belonged* Sochoh and all the
land of Hepher;
11 [1]Ben-Abinadab, *in* all the re-
gions of Dor; he had Taphath the
daughter of Solomon as wife;
12 Baana the son of Ahilud, *in*
Taanach, Megiddo, and all Beth

26 [a]Gen. 43:30; Is. 49:15; Jer. 31:20; Hos. 11:8
28 [a]1 Kin. 3:9, 11, 12; 2 Chr. 1:12; Dan. 1:17; [Col. 2:2, 3]

CHAPTER 4

3 [a]2 Sam. 8:16; 20:24 [1]*secretaries*
4 [a]1 Kin. 2:35 [b]1 Kin. 2:27
5 [a]1 Kin. 4:7 [b]2 Sam. 8:18; 20:26 [c]2 Sam. 15:37; 16:16; 1 Chr. 27:33
6 [a]1 Kin. 5:14
8 [1]Lit. *Son of Hur*
9 [1]Lit. *Son of Deker*
10 [1]Lit. *Son of Hesed*
11 [1]Lit. *Son of Abinadab*
13 [a]Num. 32:41; 1 Chr. 2:22 [b]Deut. 3:4 [1]Lit. *Son of Geber*
15 [a]2 Sam. 15:27
16 [a]2 Sam. 15:32; 1 Chr. 27:33
18 [a]1 Kin. 1:8
19 [a]Deut. 3:8–10
20 [a]Gen. 22:17; 32:12; 1 Kin. 3:8; [Prov. 14:28] [b]Ps. 72:3, 7; Mic. 4:4
21 [a]Ex. 34:24; 2 Chr. 9:26; Ps. 72:8 [b]Gen. 15:18; Josh. 1:4 [c]Ps. 68:29 [1]The Euphrates
22 [a]Neh. 5:18 [1]Lit. *bread* [2]Each about 5 bushels
24 [a]Ps. 72:11 [b]1 Kin. 5:4; 1 Chr. 22:9 [1]The Euphrates
25 [a][Jer. 23:6] [b][Mic. 4:4; Zech. 3:10] [c]Judg. 20:1 [1]*lived in safety*

Shean, which *is* beside Zaretan be-
low Jezreel, from Beth Shean to
Abel Meholah, as far as the other
side of Jokneam;
13 [1]Ben-Geber, in Ramoth Gilead;
to him *belonged* [a]the towns of Jair
the son of Manasseh, in Gilead; to
him *also belonged* [b]the region of
Argob in Bashan—sixty large cit-
ies with walls and bronze gate-
bars;
14 Ahinadab the son of Iddo, *in*
Mahanaim;
15 [a]Ahimaaz, in Naphtali; he also
took Basemath the daughter of
Solomon as wife;
16 Baanah the son of [a]Hushai, in
Asher and Aloth;
17 Jehoshaphat the son of Paruah,
in Issachar;
18 [a]Shimei the son of Elah, in Ben-
jamin;
19 Geber the son of Uri, in the
land of Gilead, *in* [a]the country of
Sihon king of the Amorites, and
of Og king of Bashan. *He was* the
only governor who *was* in the
land.

Prosperity and Wisdom of Solomon's Reign

20 Judah and Israel *were* as nu-
merous [a]as the sand by the sea in
multitude, [b]eating and drinking
and rejoicing.
21 So [a]Solomon reigned over all
kingdoms from [b]the[1] River *to* the
land of the Philistines, as far as the
border of Egypt. [c]*They* brought
tribute and served Solomon all the
days of his life.
22 [a]Now Solomon's [1]provision for
one day was thirty [2]kors of fine
flour, sixty kors of meal,
23 ten fatted oxen, twenty oxen
from the pastures, and one hun-
dred sheep, besides deer, gazelles,
roebucks, and fatted fowl.
24 For he had dominion over all
the region on this side of [1]the River
from Tiphsah even to Gaza,
namely over [a]all the kings on this
side of the River; and [b]he had
peace on every side all around
him.
25 And Judah and Israel [a]dwelt[1]
safely, [b]each man under his vine
and his fig tree, [c]from Dan as far
as Beersheba, all the days of Sol-
omon.

26 [a]Solomon had [1]forty thousand
stalls of [b]horses for his chariots,
and twelve thousand horsemen.
27 And [a]these governors, each
man in his month, provided food
for King Solomon and for all who
came to King Solomon's table.
There was no lack in their supply.
28 They also brought barley and
straw to the proper place, for the
horses and steeds, each man ac-
cording to his charge.
29 And [a]God gave Solomon wis-
dom and exceedingly great under-
standing, and largeness of heart
like the sand on the seashore.
30 Thus Solomon's wisdom ex-
celled the wisdom of all the men
[a]of the East and all [b]the wisdom
of Egypt.
31 For he was [a]wiser than all
men—[b]than Ethan the Ezrahite,
[c]and Heman, Chalcol, and Darda,
the sons of Mahol; and his fame
was in all the surrounding nations.
32 [a]He spoke three thousand
proverbs, and his [b]songs were one
thousand and five.
33 Also he spoke of trees, from the
cedar tree of Lebanon even to the
hyssop that springs out of the wall;
he spoke also of animals, of birds,
of creeping things, and of fish.
34 And men of all nations, from
all the kings of the earth who had
heard of his wisdom, [a]came to
hear the wisdom of Solomon.

Solomon Prepares to Build the Temple

5 Now [a]Hiram king of Tyre sent
his servants to Solomon, be-
cause he heard that they had
anointed him king in place of his
father, [b]for Hiram had always
loved David.
2 Then [a]Solomon sent to Hiram,
saying:

3 [a]You know how my father
David could not build a house
for the name of the LORD his
God [b]because of the wars
which were fought against him
on every side, until the LORD
put [1]*his foes* under the soles of
his feet.
4 But now the LORD my God has
given me [a]rest[1] on every side;
there is neither adversary nor
[2]evil occurrence.
5 [a]And behold, [1]I propose to

26 [a]1 Kin. 10:26; 2 Chr. 1:14 [b][Deut. 17:16] [1]So with MT, most other authorities; some LXX mss. *four thousand;* cf. 2 Chr. 9:25
27 [a]1 Kin. 4:7
29 [a]1 Kin. 3:12
30 [a]Gen. 25:6 [b]Is. 19:11, 12; Acts 7:22
31 [a]1 Kin. 3:12 [b]1 Chr. 15:19; Ps. 89:title [c]1 Chr. 2:6; Ps. 88:title
32 [a]Prov. 1:1; 10:1; 25:1; Eccl. 12:9 [b]Song 1:1
34 [a]1 Kin. 10:1; 2 Chr. 9:1, 23

CHAPTER 5

1 [a]1 Kin. 5:10, 18; 2 Chr. 2:3 [b]2 Sam. 5:11; 1 Chr. 14:1
2 [a]2 Chr. 2:3
3 [a]1 Chr. 28:2, 3 [b]1 Chr. 22:8; 28:3 [1]Lit. *them*
4 [a]1 Kin. 4:24; 1 Chr. 22:9 [1]*peace* [2]*misfortune*
5 [a]2 Chr. 2:4 [b]2 Sam. 7:12, 13; 1 Kin. 6:38; 1 Chr. 17:12; 22:10; 28:6; 2 Chr. 6:2 [1]Lit. *I am saying*
6 [a]2 Chr. 2:8, 10
9 [a]Ezra 3:7 [b]Ezek. 27:17; Acts 12:20
11 [a]2 Chr. 2:10 [1]Each about 5 bushels [2]So with MT, Tg., Vg.; LXX, Syr. *twenty thousand kors*
12 [a]1 Kin. 3:12

build a house for the name of
the LORD my God, [b]as the LORD
spoke to my father David,
saying, "Your son, whom I will
set on your throne in your
place, he shall build the house
for My name."
6 Now therefore, command that
they cut down [a]cedars for me
from Lebanon; and my
servants will be with your
servants, and I will pay you
wages for your servants
according to whatever you say.
For you know *there is* none
among us who has skill to cut
timber like the Sidonians.

7 So it was, when Hiram heard
the words of Solomon, that he re-
joiced greatly and said,

Blessed *be* the LORD this day,
for He has given David a wise
son over this great people!

8 Then Hiram sent to Solomon,
saying:

I have considered *the message*
which you sent me, *and* I will
do all you desire concerning
the cedar and cypress logs.
9 My servants shall bring *them*
down [a]from Lebanon to the
sea; I will float them in rafts by
sea to the place you indicate to
me, and will have them broken
apart there; then you can take
them away. And you shall
fulfill my desire [b]by giving food
for my household.

10 Then Hiram gave Solomon ce-
dar and cypress logs *according to*
all his desire.
11 [a]And Solomon gave Hiram
twenty thousand [1]kors of wheat *as*
food for his household, and
[2]twenty kors of pressed oil. Thus
Solomon gave to Hiram year by
year.
12 So the LORD gave Solomon wis-
dom, [a]as He had promised him;
and there was peace between
Hiram and Solomon, and the two
of them made a treaty together.
13 Then King Solomon raised up
a labor force out of all Israel; and
the labor force was thirty thou-
sand men.

14 And he sent them to Lebanon, ten thousand a month in shifts: they were one month in Lebanon *and* two months at home; [a]Adoniram *was* in charge of the labor force.

15 [a]Solomon had seventy thousand who carried burdens, and eighty thousand who quarried *stone* in the mountains,

16 besides three thousand [1]three hundred from the [a]chiefs of Solomon's deputies, who supervised the people who labored in the work.

17 And the king commanded them to quarry large stones, costly stones, *and* [a]hewn stones, to lay the foundation of the [1]temple.

18 So Solomon's builders, Hiram's builders, and the Gebalites quarried *them;* and they prepared timber and stones to build the [1]temple.

Solomon Builds the Temple

6 And [a]it came to pass in the four hundred and [1]eightieth year after the children of Israel had come out of the land of Egypt, in the fourth year of Solomon's reign over Israel, in the month of [2]Ziv, which *is* the second month, [b]that he began to build the house of the LORD.

2 Now [a]the house which King Solomon built for the LORD, its length *was* sixty cubits, its width twenty, and its height thirty cubits.

3 The vestibule in front of the [1]sanctuary of the house *was* [2]twenty cubits long across the width of the house, *and* the width of [3]*the vestibule extended* [4]ten cubits from the front of the house.

4 And he made for the house [a]windows with beveled frames.

5 Against the wall of the [1]temple he built [a]chambers all around, *against* the walls of the temple, all around the sanctuary [b]and the [2]inner sanctuary. Thus he made side chambers all around it.

6 The lowest chamber *was* five cubits wide, the middle *was* six cubits wide, and the third *was* seven cubits wide; for he made narrow ledges around the outside of the temple, so that *the support beams* would not be fastened into the walls of the [1]temple.

7 And [a]the temple, when it was being built, was built with stone finished at the quarry, so that no hammer or chisel *or* any iron tool was heard in the temple while it was being built.

8 The doorway for the [1]middle story *was* on the right side of the temple. They went up by stairs to the middle *story,* and from the middle to the third.

9 [a]So he built the [1]temple and finished it, and he paneled the temple with beams and boards of cedar.

10 And he built side chambers against the entire temple, each five cubits high; they were attached to the temple with cedar beams.

11 Then the word of the LORD came to Solomon, saying:

12 "*Concerning* this [1]temple which you are building, [a]if you walk in My statutes, execute My judgments, keep all My commandments, and walk in them, then I will perform My [2]word with you, [b]which I spoke to your father David.

13 "And [a]I will dwell among the children of Israel, and will not [b]forsake My people Israel."

14 So Solomon built the temple and finished it.

15 And he built the inside walls of the temple with cedar boards; from the floor of the temple to the ceiling he paneled the inside with wood; and he covered the floor of the temple with planks of cypress.

16 Then he built the twenty-cubit room at the rear of the temple, from floor to ceiling, with cedar boards; he built *it* inside as the inner sanctuary, as the [a]Most Holy *Place.*

17 And in front of it the temple sanctuary was forty cubits *long.*

18 The inside of the temple was cedar, carved with ornamental buds and open flowers. All *was* cedar; there was no stone *to be* seen.

19 And he prepared the [1]inner sanctuary inside the temple, to set the ark of the covenant of the LORD there.

20 The inner sanctuary *was* twenty cubits long, twenty cubits wide, and twenty cubits high. He

14 [a]1 Kin. 12:18
15 [a]1 Kin. 9:20–22; 2 Chr. 2:17, 18
16 [a]1 Kin. 9:23 [1]So with MT, Tg., Vg.; LXX *six hundred*
17 [a]1 Kin. 6:7; 1 Chr. 22:2 [1]Lit. *house*
18 [1]Lit. *house*

CHAPTER 6

1 [a]2 Chr. 3:1, 2 [b]Acts 7:47 [1]So with MT, Tg., Vg.; LXX *fortieth* [2]Or *Ayyar,* April or May
2 [a]Ezek. 41:1
3 [1]Heb. *heykal;* here the main room of the temple; elsewhere called the holy place, Ex. 26:33; Ezek. 41:1 [2]About 30 feet [3]Lit. *it* [4]About 15 feet
4 [a]Ezek. 40:16; 41:16
5 [a]Ezek. 41:6 [b]1 Kin. 6:16, 19–21, 31 [1]Lit. *house* [2]Heb. *debir;* here the inner room of the temple; elsewhere called the Most Holy Place, v. 16
6 [1]Lit. *house*
7 [a]Ex. 20:25; Deut. 27:5, 6
8 [1]So with MT, Vg.; LXX *upper story;* Tg. *ground story*
9 [a]1 Kin. 6:14, 38 [1]Lit. *house*
12 [a]1 Kin. 2:4; 9:4 [b][2 Sam. 7:13; 1 Chr. 22:10] [1]Lit. *house* [2]*promise*
13 [a]Ex. 25:8; Lev. 26:11; [2 Cor. 6:16; Rev. 21:3] [b][Deut. 31:6]
16 [a]Ex. 26:33; Lev. 16:2; 1 Kin. 8:6; 2 Chr. 3:8; Ezek. 45:3; Heb. 9:3
19 [1]The Most Holy Place

overlaid it with pure gold, and
overlaid the altar of cedar.
21 So Solomon overlaid the inside
of the temple with pure gold. He
stretched gold chains across the
front of the inner sanctuary, and
overlaid it with gold.
22 The whole temple he overlaid
with gold, until he had finished all
the temple; also he overlaid with
gold [a]the entire altar that *was* by
the inner sanctuary.
23 Inside the inner sanctuary [a]he
made two cherubim *of* olive wood,
each ten cubits high.
24 One wing of the cherub *was*
five cubits, and the other wing of
the cherub five cubits: ten cubits
from the tip of one wing to the tip
of the other.
25 And the other cherub *was* ten
cubits; both cherubim *were* of the
same size and shape.
26 The height of one cherub *was*
ten cubits, and so *was* the other
cherub.
27 Then he set the cherubim in-
side the inner [1]room; and [a]they
stretched out the wings of the
cherubim so that the wing of
the one touched *one* wall, and the
wing of the other cherub touched
the other wall. And their wings
touched each other in the middle
of the room.
28 Also he overlaid the cherubim
with gold.
29 Then he carved all the walls of
the temple all around, both the in-
ner and outer *sanctuaries,* with
carved [a]figures of cherubim, palm
trees, and open flowers.
30 And the floor of the temple he
overlaid with gold, both the inner
and outer *sanctuaries.*
31 For the entrance of the inner
sanctuary he made doors *of* olive
wood; the lintel *and* doorposts
were [1]one-fifth *of the wall.*
32 The two doors *were of* olive
wood; and he carved on them fig-
ures of cherubim, palm trees, and
open flowers, and overlaid *them*
with gold; and he spread gold on
the cherubim and on the palm
trees.
33 So for the door of the [1]sanctu-
ary he also made doorposts *of* olive
wood, [2]one-fourth *of the wall.*
34 And the two doors *were of* cy-
press wood; [a]two panels *com-
prised* one folding door, and two
panels *comprised* the other folding
door.
35 Then he carved cherubim,
palm trees, and open flowers *on
them,* and overlaid *them* with gold
applied evenly on the carved work.
36 And he built the [a]inner court
with three rows of hewn stone and
a row of cedar beams.
37 [a]In the fourth year the founda-
tion of the house of the LORD was
laid, in the month of [1]Ziv.
38 And in the eleventh year, in the
month of [1]Bul, which is the eighth
month, the house was finished in
all its details and according to all
its plans. So he was [a]seven years
in building it.

Solomon's Other Buildings

7 But Solomon took [a]thirteen
years to build his own house;
so he finished all his house.
2 He also built the [a]House of the
Forest of Lebanon; its length *was*
[1]one hundred cubits, its width
[2]fifty cubits, and its height thirty
cubits, with four rows of cedar pil-
lars, and cedar beams on the pil-
lars.
3 And *it was* paneled with cedar
above the beams that *were* on
forty-five pillars, fifteen *to* a row.
4 *There were* windows *with bev-
eled frames in* three rows, and win-
dow *was* opposite window *in* three
tiers.
5 And all the doorways and door-
posts *had* rectangular frames; and
window *was* opposite window *in*
three tiers.
6 He also made the Hall of Pil-
lars: its length *was* fifty cubits, and
its width thirty cubits; and in front
of them *was* a portico with pillars,
and a canopy *was* in front of them.
7 Then he made a hall for the
throne, the Hall of Judgment,
where he might judge; and *it was*
paneled with cedar from floor to
[1]ceiling.
8 And the house where he dwelt
had another court inside the hall,
of like workmanship. Solomon
also made a house like this hall for
Pharaoh's daughter, [a]whom he
had taken *as wife.*
9 All these *were of* costly stones
cut to size, trimmed with saws, in-
side and out, from the foundation

22 [a]Ex. 30:1, 3, 6
23 [a]Ex. 37:7–9; 2 Chr. 3:10–12
27 [a]Ex. 25:20; 37:9; 1 Kin. 8:7; 2 Chr. 5:8 [1]Lit. *house*
29 [a]Ex. 36:8, 35
31 [1]Or *five-sided*
33 [1]*temple* [2]Or *four-sided*
34 [a]Ezek. 41:23–25
36 [a]1 Kin. 7:12; Jer. 36:10
37 [a]1 Kin. 6:1 [1]Or *Ayyar,* April or May
38 [a]2 Sam. 7:13; 1 Kin. 5:5; 6:1; 8:19 [1]Or *Heshvan,* October or November

CHAPTER 7

1 [a]1 Kin. 3:1; 9:10; 2 Chr. 8:1
2 [a]1 Kin. 10:17, 21; 2 Chr. 9:16 [1]About 150 feet [2]About 75 feet
7 [1]Lit. *floor* of the upper level
8 [a]1 Kin. 3:1; 9:24; 11:1; 2 Chr. 8:11

to the eaves, and also on the out-
side to the great court.
10 The foundation *was of* costly
stones, large stones, some ten cu-
bits and some eight cubits.
11 And above *were* costly stones,
hewn to size, and cedar wood.
12 The great court *was* enclosed
with three rows of hewn stones
and a row of cedar beams. So were
the [a]inner court of the house of the
LORD [b]and the vestibule of the tem-
ple.

Hiram the Craftsman

13 Now King Solomon sent and
brought [1]Huram from Tyre.
14 [a]He *was* the son of a widow
from the tribe of Naphtali, and [b]his
father *was* a man of Tyre, a bronze
worker; [c]he was filled with wis-
dom and understanding and skill
in working with all kinds of bronze
work. So he came to King Sol-
omon and did all his work.

The Bronze Pillars for the Temple

15 And he [1]cast [a]two pillars of
bronze, each one eighteen cubits
high, and a line of twelve cubits
measured the circumference of
each.
16 Then he made two capitals *of*
cast bronze, to set on the tops of
the pillars. The height of one capi-
tal *was* five cubits, and the height
of the other capital *was* five cubits.
17 *He made* a lattice network,
with wreaths of chainwork, for the
capitals which *were* on top of the
pillars: seven chains for one capi-
tal and seven for the other capital.
18 So he made the pillars, and two
rows of pomegranates above the
network all around to cover the
capitals that *were* on top; and thus
he did for the other capital.
19 The capitals which *were* on top
of the pillars in the hall *were* in
the shape of lilies, four cubits.
20 The capitals on the two pillars
also *had pomegranates* above, by
the convex surface which *was* next
to the network; and there *were*
[a]two hundred such pomegranates
in rows on each of the capitals all
around.
21 [a]Then he set up the pillars by
the vestibule of the temple; he set
up the pillar on the right and called
its name [1]Jachin, and he set up the
pillar on the left and called its
name [2]Boaz.
22 The tops of the pillars were in
the shape of lilies. So the work of
the pillars was finished.

The Sea and the Oxen

23 And he made [a]the Sea of cast
bronze, ten cubits from one brim
to the other; *it was* completely
round. Its height *was* five cubits,
and a line of thirty cubits mea-
sured its circumference.
24 Below its brim *were* ornamen-
tal buds encircling it all around,
ten to a cubit, [a]all the way around
the Sea. The ornamental buds
were cast in two rows when it was
cast.
25 It stood on [a]twelve oxen: three
looking toward the north, three
looking toward the west, three
looking toward the south, and
three looking toward the east; the
Sea *was set* upon them, and all
their back parts *pointed* inward.
26 It *was* a handbreadth thick;
and its brim was shaped like the
brim of a cup, *like* a lily blossom.
It contained [1]two thousand baths.

The Carts and the Lavers

27 He also made ten [1]carts of
bronze; four cubits *was* the length
of each cart, four cubits its width,
and three cubits its height.
28 And this *was* the design of the
carts: They had panels, and the
panels *were* between frames;
29 on the panels that *were* be-
tween the frames *were* lions, oxen,
and cherubim. And on the frames
was a pedestal on top. Below the
lions and oxen *were* wreaths of
plaited work.
30 Every cart had four bronze
wheels and axles of bronze, and
its four feet had supports. Under
the laver *were* supports of cast
bronze beside each wreath.
31 Its opening inside the crown at
the top *was* one cubit in diameter;
and the opening *was* round,
shaped *like* a pedestal, one and a
half cubits in outside diameter;
and also on the opening *were* en-
gravings, but the panels were
square, not round.
32 Under the panels *were* the four
wheels, and the axles of the wheels
were joined to the cart. The height

12 [a]1 Kin. 6:36 [b]John 10:23; Acts 3:11
13 [1]Heb. *Hiram;* cf. 2 Chr. 2:13, 14
14 [a]2 Chr. 2:14 [b]2 Chr. 4:16 [c]Ex. 31:3; 36:1
15 [a]2 Kin. 25:17; 2 Chr. 3:15; 4:12; Jer. 52:21 [1]*fashioned*
20 [a]2 Chr. 3:16; 4:13; Jer. 52:23
21 [a]2 Chr. 3:17 [1]Lit. *He Shall Establish* [2]Lit. *In It Is Strength*
23 [a]2 Kin. 25:13; 2 Chr. 4:2; Jer. 52:17
24 [a]2 Chr. 4:3
25 [a]2 Chr. 4:4, 5; Jer. 52:20
26 [1]About 12,000 gallons; *three thousand,* 2 Chr. 4:5
27 [1]Or *stands*

of a wheel *was* one and a half cu-
bits.
33 The workmanship of the
wheels *was* like the workmanship
of a chariot wheel; their axle pins,
their rims, their spokes, and their
hubs *were* all of cast *bronze.*
34 And *there were* four supports
at the four corners of each cart;
its supports *were* part of the cart
itself.
35 On the top of the cart, at the
height of half a cubit, *it was* per-
fectly round. And on the top of the
cart, its flanges and its panels *were*
of the same casting.
36 On the plates of its flanges and
on its panels he engraved cheru-
bim, lions, and palm trees, wher-
ever there was a clear space on
each, with wreaths all around.
37 Thus he made the ten carts. All
of them were of [1]the same mold,
one measure, *and* one shape.
38 Then [a]he made ten lavers of
bronze; each laver contained
[1]forty baths, *and* each laver *was*
four cubits. On each of the ten
carts *was* a laver.
39 And he put five carts on the
right side of the house, and five on
the left side of the house. He set
the Sea on the right side of the
house, toward the southeast.

Furnishings of the Temple

40 [a]Huram[1] made the lavers and
the shovels and the bowls. So Hu-
ram finished doing all the work
that he was to do for King Sol-
omon *for* the house of the LORD:
41 the two pillars, the *two* bowl-
shaped capitals that *were* on top
of the two pillars; the two [a]net-
works covering the two bowl-
shaped capitals which *were* on top
of the pillars;
42 [a]four hundred pomegranates
for the two networks (two rows of
pomegranates for each network, to
cover the two bowl-shaped capi-
tals that *were* on top of the pillars);
43 the ten carts, and ten lavers on
the carts;
44 one Sea, and twelve oxen un-
der the Sea;
45 [a]the pots, the shovels, and the
bowls. All these articles which
[1]Huram made for King Solomon
for the house of the LORD *were of*
burnished bronze.

37 [1]*one*

38 [a]Ex. 30:18; 2 Chr. 4:6 [1]About 240 gallons

40 [a]2 Chr. 4:11—5:1 [1]Heb. *Hiram;* cf. 2 Chr. 2:13, 14

41 [a]1 Kin. 7:17, 18

42 [a]1 Kin. 7:20

45 [a]Ex. 27:3; 2 Chr. 4:16 [1]Heb. *Hiram;* cf. 2 Chr. 2:13, 14

46 [a]2 Chr. 4:17 [b]Gen. 33:17; Josh. 13:27 [c]Josh. 3:16

47 [a]1 Chr. 22:3, 14

48 [a]Ex. 37:25, 26; 2 Chr. 4:8 [b]Ex. 37:10, 11 [c]Lev. 24:5–8

50 [1]*firepans*

51 [a]2 Sam. 8:11; 1 Chr. 18:11; 2 Chr. 5:1

CHAPTER 8

1 [a]Num. 1:4; 7:2; 2 Chr. 5:2–14 [b]2 Sam. 6:12–17; 1 Chr. 15:25–29 [c]2 Sam. 5:7; 6:12, 16

2 [a]Lev. 23:34; 1 Kin. 8:65; 2 Chr. 7:8–10 [1]Or *Tishri.* September or October

3 [a]Num. 4:15; 7:9; Deut. 31:9; Josh. 3:3, 6

4 [a]1 Kin. 3:4; 2 Chr. 1:3 [1]*tent*

5 [a]2 Sam. 6:13; 2 Chr. 1:6

46 [a]In the plain of Jordan the king
had them cast in clay molds, be-
tween [b]Succoth and [c]Zaretan.
47 And Solomon did not weigh all
the articles, because *there were* so
many; the weight of the bronze
was not [a]determined.
48 Thus Solomon had all the fur-
nishings made for the house of
the LORD: [a]the altar of gold, and
[b]the table of gold on which *was*
[c]the showbread;
49 the lampstands of pure gold,
five on the right *side* and five on
the left in front of the inner sanctu-
ary, with the flowers and the
lamps and the wick-trimmers of
gold;
50 the basins, the trimmers, the
bowls, the ladles, and the [1]censers
of pure gold; and the hinges of
gold, *both* for the doors of the in-
ner room (the Most Holy *Place*)
and for the doors of the main hall
of the temple.
51 So all the work that King Sol-
omon had done for the house of
the LORD was finished; and Sol-
omon brought in the things [a]which
his father David had dedicated: the
silver and the gold and the furnish-
ings. He put them in the treasuries
of the house of the LORD.

The Ark Brought into the Temple

8 Now [a]Solomon assembled the
elders of Israel and all the
heads of the tribes, the chief fa-
thers of the children of Israel, to
King Solomon in Jerusalem, [b]that
they might bring [c]up the ark of the
covenant of the LORD from the City
of David, which *is* Zion.
2 Therefore all the men of Israel
assembled with King Solomon
at the [a]feast in the month of
[1]Ethanim, which *is* the seventh
month.
3 So all the elders of Israel came,
[a]and the priests took up the ark.
4 Then they brought up the ark
of the LORD, [a]the [1]tabernacle of
meeting, and all the holy furnish-
ings that *were* in the tabernacle.
The priests and the Levites
brought them up.
5 Also King Solomon, and all the
congregation of Israel who were
assembled with him, *were* with
him before the ark, [a]sacrificing
sheep and oxen that could not be

counted or numbered for multi-
tude.
6 Then the priests [a]brought in the
ark of the covenant of the LORD to
[b]its place, into the inner sanctuary
of the temple, to the Most Holy
Place, [c]under the wings of the che-
rubim.
7 For the cherubim spread *their*
two wings over the place of the
ark, and the cherubim oversha-
dowed the ark and its poles.
8 The poles [a]extended so that the
[1]ends of the poles could be seen
from the holy *place*, in front of the
inner sanctuary; but they could not
be seen from outside. And they are
there to this day.
9 [a]Nothing *was* in the ark [b]ex-
cept the two tablets of stone which
Moses [c]put there at Horeb, [d]when
the LORD made *a covenant* with
the children of Israel, when they
came out of the land of Egypt.
10 And it came to pass, when the
priests came out of the holy *place*,
that the cloud [a]filled the house of
the LORD,
11 so that the priests could not
continue ministering because of
the cloud; for the [a]glory of the
LORD filled the house of the LORD.
12 [a]Then Solomon spoke:

"The LORD said He would dwell [b]in
the dark cloud.
13 [a]I have surely built You an exalted
house,
[b]And a place for You to dwell in
forever."

Solomon's Speech at Completion of the Work

14 Then the king turned around
and [a]blessed the whole assembly
of Israel, while all the assembly of
Israel was standing.
15 And he said: [a]"Blessed *be* the
LORD God of Israel, who [b]spoke
with His mouth to my father Da-
vid, and with His hand has fulfilled
it, saying,
16 'Since the day that I brought
My people Israel out of Egypt, I
have chosen no city from any tribe
of Israel *in which* to build a house,
that [a]My name might be there; but
I chose [b]David to be over My peo-
ple Israel.'
17 "Now [a]it was in the heart of my
father David to build a [1]temple for
the name of the LORD God of Israel.
18 [a]"But the LORD said to my fa-
ther David, 'Whereas it was in
your heart to build a temple for My
name, you did well that it was in
your heart.
19 'Nevertheless [a]you shall not
build the temple, but your son who
will come from your body, he shall
build the temple for My name.'
20 "So the LORD has fulfilled His
word which He spoke; and I have
[1]filled the position of my father
David, and sit on the throne of Is-
rael, [a]as the LORD promised; and I
have built a temple for the name
of the LORD God of Israel.
21 "And there I have made a place
for the ark, in which *is* [a]the cov-
enant of the LORD which He made
with our fathers, when He brought
them out of the land of Egypt."

Solomon's Prayer of Dedication

22 Then Solomon stood before
[a]the altar of the LORD in the pres-
ence of all the assembly of Israel,
and [b]spread out his hands toward
heaven;
23 and he said: "LORD God of Is-
rael, [a]*there is* no God in heaven
above or on earth below like You,
[b]who keep *Your* covenant and
mercy with Your servants who
[c]walk before You with all their
hearts.
24 "You have kept what You
promised Your servant David my
father; You have both spoken with
Your mouth and fulfilled *it* with
Your hand, as *it is* this day.
25 "Therefore, LORD God of Israel,
now keep what You promised
Your servant David my father,
saying, [a]'You shall not fail to have
a man sit before Me on the throne
of Israel, only if your sons take
heed to their way, that they walk
before Me as you have walked be-
fore Me.'
26 [a]"And now I pray, O God of Is-
rael, let Your word come true,
which You have spoken to Your
servant David my father.
27 "But [a]will God indeed dwell on
the earth? Behold, heaven and the
[b]heaven of heavens cannot contain
You. How much less this temple
which I have built!
28 "Yet regard the prayer of Your
servant and his supplication, O

6 [a]2 Sam. 6:17 [b]1 Kin. 6:19 [c]1 Kin. 6:27
8 [a]Ex. 25:13–15; 37:4, 5 [1]*heads*
9 [a]Ex. 25:21 [b]Deut. 10:5 [c]Ex. 24:7, 8; 40:20 [d]Ex. 34:27, 28
10 [a]Ex. 40:34, 35
11 [a]2 Chr. 7:1, 2
12 [a]2 Chr. 6:1 [b]Ps. 18:11; 97:2
13 [a]2 Sam. 7:13 [b]Ps. 132:14
14 [a]2 Sam. 6:18
15 [a]Luke 1:68 [b]2 Sam. 7:2, 12, 13, 25
16 [a]1 Kin. 8:29 [b]2 Sam. 7:8
17 [a]2 Sam. 7:2, 3 [1]Lit. *house*, and so in vv. 18–20
18 [a]2 Chr. 6:8, 9
19 [a]2 Sam. 7:5, 12, 13
20 [a]1 Chr. 28:5, 6 [1]*risen in the place of*
21 [a]Deut. 31:26
22 [a]2 Chr. 6:12 [b]Ezra 9:5
23 [a]Ex. 15:11 [b][Neh. 1:5] [c][Gen. 17:1]
25 [a]1 Kin. 2:4; 9:5
26 [a]2 Sam. 7:25
27 [a][Acts 7:49; 17:24] [b]2 Cor. 12:2

LORD my God, and listen to the cry and the prayer which Your servant is praying before You today:

29 "that Your eyes may be open toward this [1]temple night and day, toward the place of which You said, [a]'My name shall be [b]there,' that You may hear the prayer which Your servant makes [c]toward this place.

30 [a]"And may You hear the supplication of Your servant and of Your people Israel, when they pray toward this place. Hear in heaven Your dwelling place; and when You hear, forgive.

31 "When anyone sins against his neighbor, and is forced to take [a]an oath, and comes *and* takes an oath before Your altar in this temple,

32 "then hear in heaven, and act, and judge Your servants, [a]condemning the wicked, bringing his way on his head, and justifying the righteous by giving him according to his righteousness.

33 [a]"When Your people Israel are defeated before an enemy because they have sinned against You, and [b]when they turn back to You and confess Your name, and pray and make supplication to You in this temple,

34 "then hear in heaven, and forgive the sin of Your people Israel, and bring them back to the land which You gave to their [a]fathers.

35 [a]"When the heavens are shut up and there is no rain because they have sinned against You, when they pray toward this place and confess Your name, and turn from their sin because You afflict them,

36 "then hear in heaven, and forgive the sin of Your servants, Your people Israel, that You may [a]teach them [b]the good way in which they should walk; and send rain on Your land which You have given to Your people as an inheritance.

37 [a]"When there is famine in the land, pestilence *or* blight *or* mildew, locusts *or* grasshoppers; when their enemy besieges them in the land of their [1]cities; whatever plague or whatever sickness *there is;*

38 "whatever prayer, whatever supplication is made by anyone, *or* by all Your people Israel, when each one knows the plague of his own heart, and spreads out his hands toward this temple:

39 "then hear in heaven Your dwelling place, and forgive, and act, and give to everyone according to all his ways, whose heart You know (for You alone [a]know the hearts of all the sons of men),

40 [a]"that they may fear You all the days that they live in the land which You gave to our fathers.

41 "Moreover, concerning a foreigner, who *is* not of Your people Israel, but has come from a far country for Your name's sake

42 "(for they will hear of Your great name and Your [a]strong hand and Your outstretched arm), when he comes and prays toward this temple,

43 "hear in heaven Your dwelling place, and do according to all for which the foreigner calls to You, [a]that all peoples of the earth may know Your name and [b]fear You, as *do* Your people Israel, and that they may know that this temple which I have built is called by Your name.

44 "When Your people go out to battle against their enemy, wherever You send them, and when they pray to the LORD toward the city which You have chosen and the temple which I have built for Your name,

45 "then hear in heaven their prayer and their supplication, and maintain their [1]cause.

46 "When they sin against You [a](for *there is* no one who does not sin), and You become angry with them and deliver them to the enemy, and they take them captive [b]to the land of the enemy, far or near;

47 [a]"*yet* when they [1]come to themselves in the land where they were carried captive, and repent, and make supplication to You in the land of those who took them captive, [b]saying, 'We have sinned and done wrong, we have committed wickedness';

48 "and *when* they [a]return to You with all their heart and with all their soul in the land of their enemies who led them away captive, and [b]pray to You toward their land which You gave to their fathers,

29 [a]Deut. 12:11 [b]1 Kin. 9:3; 2 Chr. 7:15 [c]Dan. 6:10 [1]Lit. *house*
30 [a]Neh. 1:6
31 [a]Ex. 22:8–11
32 [a]Deut. 25:1
33 [a]Lev. 26:17; Deut. 28:25 [b]Lev. 26:39, 40
34 [a][Lev. 26:40–42; Deut. 30:1–3]
35 [a]Lev. 26:19; Deut. 28:23
36 [a]Ps. 25:4; 27:11; 94:12 [b]1 Sam. 12:23
37 [a]Lev. 26:16, 25, 26; Deut. 28:21, 22, 27, 38, 42, 52 [1]Lit. *gates*
39 [a][1 Sam. 16:7; 1 Chr. 28:9; Jer. 17:10]; Acts 1:24
40 [a][Ps. 130:4]
42 [a]Ex. 13:3; Deut. 3:24
43 [a][Ex. 9:16; 1 Sam. 17:46; 2 Kin. 19:19] [b]Ps. 102:15
45 [1]*justice*
46 [a]2 Chr. 6:36; Ps. 130:3; Prov. 20:9; Eccl. 7:20; [Rom. 3:23; 1 John 1:8, 10] [b]Lev. 26:34, 44; Deut. 28:36, 64; 2 Kin. 17:6, 18; 25:21
47 [a][Lev. 26:40–42]; Neh. 9:2 [b]Ezra 9:6, 7; Neh. 1:6; Ps. 106:6; Dan. 9:5 [1]Lit. *bring back to their heart*
48 [a]Jer. 29:12–14 [b]Dan. 6:10; Jon. 2:4

the city which You have chosen
and the temple which I have built
for Your name:
49 "then hear in heaven Your
dwelling place their prayer and
their supplication, and maintain
their [1]cause,
50 "and forgive Your people who
have sinned against You, and all
their transgressions which they
have transgressed against You;
and [a]grant them compassion be-
fore those who took them captive,
that they may have compassion on
them
51 "(for [a]they *are* Your people and
Your inheritance, whom You
brought out of Egypt, [b]out of the
iron furnace),
52 [a]"that Your eyes may be open
to the supplication of Your servant
and the supplication of Your peo-
ple Israel, to listen to them when-
ever they call to You.
53 "For You separated them from
among all the peoples of the earth
to be Your inheritance, [a]as You
spoke by Your servant Moses,
when You brought our fathers out
of Egypt, O Lord GOD."

Solomon Blesses the Assembly

54 [a]And so it was, when Solomon
had finished praying all this
prayer and supplication to the
LORD, that he arose from before
the altar of the LORD, from kneel-
ing on his knees with his hands
spread up to heaven.
55 Then he stood [a]and blessed all
the assembly of Israel with a loud
voice, saying:
56 "Blessed *be* the LORD, who has
given [a]rest[1] to His people Israel,
according to all that He promised.
[b]There has not failed one word of
all His good promise, which He
promised through His servant Mo-
ses.
57 "May the LORD our God be with
us, as He was with our fathers.
[a]May He not leave us nor forsake
us,
58 "that He may [a]incline our
hearts to Himself, to walk in all His
ways, and to keep His command-
ments and His statutes and His
judgments, which He commanded
our fathers.
59 "And may these words of mine,
with which I have made supplica-

49 [1]*justice*
50 [a][2 Chr. 30:9]; Ezra 7:6; Ps. 106:46; Acts 7:10
51 [a]Ex. 32:11, 12; Deut. 9:26–29; Neh. 1:10; [Rom. 11:28, 29] [b]Deut. 4:20; Jer. 11:4
52 [a]1 Kin. 8:29
53 [a]Ex. 19:5, 6
54 [a]2 Chr. 7:1
55 [a]Num. 6:23–26; 2 Sam. 6:18; 1 Kin. 8:14
56 [a]1 Chr. 22:18 [b]Deut. 12:10; Josh. 21:45; 23:14 [1]*peace*
57 [a]Deut. 31:6; Josh. 1:5; 1 Sam. 12:22; [Rom. 8:31–37]; Heb. 13:5
58 [a]Ps. 119:36; Jer. 31:33
60 [a]Josh. 4:24; 1 Sam. 17:46; 1 Kin. 8:43; 2 Kin. 19:19 [b]Deut. 4:35, 39; 1 Kin. 18:39; [Jer. 10:10–12]
61 [a]Deut. 18:13; 1 Kin. 11:4; 15:3, 14; 2 Kin. 20:3 [1]Lit. *at peace with*
62 [a]2 Chr. 7:4–10
64 [a]2 Chr. 7:7 [b]2 Chr. 4:1
65 [a]Lev. 23:34; 1 Kin. 8:2 [b]Num. 34:8; Josh. 13:5; Judg. 3:3; 2 Kin. 14:25 [c]Gen. 15:18; Ex. 23:31; Num. 34:5 [d]2 Chr. 7:8
66 [a]2 Chr. 7:9 [1]*thanked*

CHAPTER 9

1 [a]2 Chr. 7:11 [b]1 Kin. 7:1 [c]2 Chr. 8:6
2 [a]1 Kin. 3:5; 11:9; 2 Chr. 1:7
3 [a]2 Kin. 20:5; Ps. 10:17

tion before the LORD, be near the
LORD our God day and night, that
He may maintain the cause of His
servant and the cause of His peo-
ple Israel, as each day may re-
quire,
60 [a]"that all the peoples of the
earth may know that [b]the LORD *is*
God; *there is* no other.
61 "Let your [a]heart therefore be
[1]loyal to the LORD our God, to walk
in His statutes and keep His com-
mandments, as at this day."

Solomon Dedicates the Temple

62 Then [a]the king and all Israel
with him offered sacrifices before
the LORD.
63 And Solomon offered a sacri-
fice of peace offerings, which he
offered to the LORD, twenty-two
thousand bulls and one hundred
and twenty thousand sheep. So the
king and all the children of Israel
dedicated the house of the LORD.
64 On [a]the same day the king con-
secrated the middle of the court
that *was* in front of the house of
the LORD; for there he offered
burnt offerings, grain offerings,
and the fat of the peace offerings,
because the [b]bronze altar that *was*
before the LORD *was* too small to
receive the burnt offerings, the
grain offerings, and the fat of the
peace offerings.
65 At that time Solomon held [a]a
feast, and all Israel with him, a
great assembly from [b]the entrance
of Hamath to [c]the Brook of Egypt,
before the LORD our God, [d]seven
days and seven *more* days—four-
teen days.
66 [a]On the eighth day he sent the
people away; and they [1]blessed the
king, and went to their tents joyful
and glad of heart for all the good
that the LORD had done for His ser-
vant David, and for Israel His peo-
ple.

God's Second Appearance to Solomon

9 And [a]it came to pass, when
Solomon had finished building
the house of the LORD [b]and the
king's house, and [c]all Solomon's
desire which he wanted to do,
2 that the LORD appeared to Sol-
omon the second time, [a]as He had
appeared to him at Gibeon.
3 And the LORD said to him: [a]"I

have heard your prayer and your
supplication that you have made
before Me; I have consecrated this
house which you have built [b]to put
My name there forever, [c]and My
eyes and My heart will be there
perpetually.
4 "Now if you [a]walk before Me
[b]as your father David walked, in
integrity of heart and in upright-
ness, to do according to all that I
have commanded you, *and* if you
[c]keep My statutes and My judg-
ments,
5 "then I will establish the throne
of your kingdom over Israel for-
ever, [a]as I promised David your fa-
ther, saying, 'You shall not fail to
have a man on the throne of Is-
rael.'
6 [a]"*But* if you or your sons at all
[1]turn from following Me, and do
not keep My commandments *and*
My statutes which I have set be-
fore you, but go and serve other
gods and worship them,
7 [a]"then I will [1]cut off Israel from
the land which I have given them;
and this house which I have con-
secrated [b]for My name I will cast
out of My sight. [c]Israel will be a
proverb and a byword among all
peoples.
8 "And *as for* [a]this house, *which*
is exalted, everyone who passes
by it will be astonished and will
hiss, and say, [b]'Why has the LORD
done thus to this land and to this
house?'
9 "Then they will answer, 'Be-
cause they forsook the LORD their
God, who brought their fathers out
of the land of Egypt, and have em-
braced other gods, and worshiped
them and served them; therefore
the LORD has brought all this [a]ca-
lamity on them.' "

Solomon and Hiram Exchange Gifts

10 Now [a]it happened at the end of
twenty years, when Solomon had
built the two houses, the house of
the LORD and the king's house
11 [a](Hiram the king of Tyre had
supplied Solomon with cedar and
cypress and gold, as much as he
desired), *that* King Solomon then
gave Hiram twenty cities in the
land of Galilee.
12 Then Hiram went from Tyre to
see the cities which Solomon had
given him, but they did not please
him.
13 So he said, "What *kind of* cities
are these which you have given
me, my brother?" [a]And he called
them the land of [1]Cabul, as they
are to this day.
14 Then Hiram sent the king one
hundred and twenty talents of
gold.

Solomon's Additional Achievements

15 And this *is* the reason for [a]the
labor force which King Solomon
raised: to build the house of the
LORD, his own house, [1]the [b]Millo,
the wall of Jerusalem, [c]Hazor,
[d]Megiddo, and [e]Gezer.
16 (Pharaoh king of Egypt had
gone up and taken Gezer and
burned it with fire, [a]had killed the
Canaanites who dwelt in the city,
and had given it *as* a dowry to his
daughter, Solomon's wife.)
17 And Solomon built Gezer,
Lower [a]Beth Horon,
18 [a]Baalath, and Tadmor in the
wilderness, in the land *of Judah,*
19 all the storage cities that Sol-
omon had, cities for [a]his chariots
and cities for his [b]cavalry, and
whatever Solomon [c]desired to
build in Jerusalem, in Lebanon,
and in all the land of his domin-
ion.
20 [a]All the people *who were* left
of the Amorites, Hittites, Periz-
zites, Hivites, and Jebusites, who
were not of the children of Israel—
21 that is, their descendants [a]who
were left in the land after them,
[b]whom the children of Israel had
not been able to destroy com-
pletely—[c]from these Solomon
raised [d]forced labor, as it is to this
day.
22 But of the children of Israel
Solomon [a]made no forced labor-
ers, because they *were* men of war
and his servants: his officers, his
captains, commanders of his char-
iots, and his cavalry.
23 Others *were* chiefs of the offi-
cials who *were* over Solomon's
work: [a]five hundred and fifty, who
ruled over the people who did the
work.
24 But [a]Pharaoh's daughter came
up from the City of David to [b]her
house which [1]*Solomon* had built
for her. [c]Then he built the Millo.

3 [b]1 Kin. 8:29 [c]Deut. 11:12
4 [a]Gen. 17:1 [b]1 Kin. 11:4, 6; 15:5 [c]1 Kin. 8:61
5 [a]2 Sam. 7:12, 16
6 [a]2 Sam. 7:14–16 [1]*turn back*
7 [a][Lev. 18:24–29] [b][Jer. 7:4–14] [c]Ps. 44:14 [1]*destroy*
8 [a]2 Chr. 7:21 [b][Deut. 29:24–26]
9 [a][Deut. 29:25–28]
10 [a]2 Chr. 8:1
11 [a]1 Kin. 5:1
13 [a]Josh. 19:27 [1]Lit. *Good for Nothing*
15 [a]1 Kin. 5:13 [b]2 Sam. 5:9 [c]Josh. 11:1; 19:36 [d]Josh. 17:11 [e]Josh. 16:10 [1]Lit. *The Landfill*
16 [a]Josh. 16:10
17 [a]2 Chr. 8:5
18 [a]Josh. 19:44
19 [a]1 Kin. 10:26 [b]1 Kin. 4:26 [c]1 Kin. 9:1
20 [a]2 Chr. 8:7
21 [a]Judg. 1:21–36; 3:1 [b]Josh. 15:63; 17:12, 13 [c]Judg. 1:28, 35 [d]Ezra 2:55, 58
22 [a][Lev. 25:39]
23 [a]2 Chr. 8:10
24 [a]1 Kin. 3:1 [b]1 Kin. 7:8 [c]2 Sam. 5:9 [1]Lit. *he;* cf. 2 Chr. 8:11

25 [a]Now three times a year Sol-
omon offered burnt offerings and
peace offerings on the altar which
he had built for the LORD, and he
burned incense with them *on the*
altar that *was* before the LORD. So
he finished the temple.
26 [a]King Solomon also built a fleet
of ships at [b]Ezion Geber, which *is*
near [1]Elath on the shore of the Red
Sea, in the land of Edom.
27 [a]Then Hiram sent his servants
with the fleet, seamen who knew
the sea, to work with the servants
of Solomon.
28 And they went to [a]Ophir, and
acquired four hundred and twenty
talents of gold from there, and
brought *it* to King Solomon.

The Queen of Sheba's Praise of Solomon

10 Now when the [a]queen of
Sheba heard of the fame of
Solomon concerning the name
of the LORD, she came [b]to test him
with hard questions.
2 She came to Jerusalem with a
very great [1]retinue, with camels
that bore spices, very much gold,
and precious stones; and when she
came to Solomon, she spoke with
him about all that was in her heart.
3 So Solomon answered all her
questions; there was nothing [1]so
difficult for the king that he could
not explain *it* to her.
4 And when the queen of Sheba
had seen all the wisdom of Sol-
omon, the house that he had built,
5 the food on his table, the seat-
ing of his servants, the service of
his waiters and their apparel, his
cupbearers, [a]and his entryway by
which he went up to the house of
the LORD, there was no more spirit
in her.
6 Then she said to the king: "It
was a true report which I heard
in my own land about your words
and your wisdom.
7 "However I did not believe the
words until I came and saw with
my own eyes; and indeed the half
was not told me. Your wisdom and
prosperity exceed the fame of
which I heard.
8 [a]"Happy *are* your men and
happy *are* these your servants,
who stand continually before you
and hear your wisdom!
9 [a]"Blessed be the LORD your
God, who [b]delighted in you, set-
ting you on the throne of Israel!
Because the LORD has loved Israel
forever, therefore He made you
king, [c]to do justice and righteous-
ness."
10 Then she [a]gave the king one
hundred and twenty talents of
gold, spices in great quantity, and
precious stones. There never again
came such abundance of spices as
the queen of Sheba gave to King
Solomon.
11 [a]Also, the ships of Hiram,
which brought gold from Ophir,
brought great *quantities* of [1]almug
wood and precious stones from
Ophir.
12 [a]And the king made [1]steps of
the almug wood for the house of
the LORD and for the king's house,
also harps and stringed instru-
ments for singers. There never
again came such [b]almug wood, nor
has the like been seen to this day.
13 Now King Solomon gave the
queen of Sheba all she desired,
whatever she asked, besides what
Solomon had given her according
to the royal generosity. So she
turned and went to her own coun-
try, she and her servants.

Solomon's Great Wealth

14 The weight of gold that came
to Solomon yearly was six hun-
dred and sixty-six talents of gold,
15 besides *that* from the [a]travel-
ing merchants, from the income of
traders, [b]from all the kings of Ara-
bia, and from the governors of the
country.
16 And King Solomon made two
hundred large shields *of* ham-
mered gold; six hundred *shekels*
of gold went into each shield.
17 He also *made* [a]three hundred
shields *of* hammered gold; three
minas of gold went into each
shield. The king put them in the
[b]House of the Forest of Lebanon.
18 [a]Moreover the king made a
great throne of ivory, and overlaid
it with pure gold.
19 The throne had six steps, and
the top of the throne *was* round
at the back; *there were* armrests
on either side of the place of the
seat, and two lions stood beside
the armrests.

25 [a]Ex. 23:14–17; Deut. 16:16; 2 Chr. 8:12, 13
26 [a]2 Chr. 8:17, 18 [b]Num. 33:35; Deut. 2:8; 1 Kin. 22:48 [1]Heb. *Eloth*
27 [a]1 Kin. 5:6, 9; 10:11
28 [a]Job 22:24

CHAPTER 10

1 [a]2 Chr. 9:1; Matt. 12:42; Luke 11:31 [b]Judg. 14:12; Ps. 49:4; Prov. 1:6
2 [1]*company*
3 [1]*too*
5 [a]1 Chr. 26:16; 2 Chr. 9:4
8 [a]Prov. 8:34
9 [a]1 Kin. 5:7 [b]2 Sam. 22:20 [c]2 Sam. 8:15; Ps. 72:2; [Prov. 8:15]
10 [a]Ps. 72:10, 15
11 [a]1 Kin. 9:27, 28; Job 22:24 [1]*algum*, 2 Chr. 9:10, 11
12 [a]2 Chr. 9:11 [b]2 Chr. 9:10 [1]Or *supports*
15 [a]2 Chr. 1:16 [b]2 Chr. 9:24; Ps. 72:10
17 [a]1 Kin. 14:26 [b]1 Kin. 7:2
18 [a]1 Kin. 10:22; 2 Chr. 9:17; Ps. 45:8

20 Twelve lions stood there, one
on each side of the six steps; noth-
ing like *this* had been made for
any *other* kingdom.
21 [a]All King Solomon's drinking
vessels *were* gold, and all the ves-
sels of the House of the Forest of
Lebanon *were* pure gold. Not *one*
was silver, for this was accounted
as nothing in the days of Sol-
omon.
22 For the king had [a]merchant[1]
ships at sea with the fleet of
Hiram. Once every three years the
merchant [b]ships came bringing
gold, silver, ivory, apes, and
[2]monkeys.
23 So [a]King Solomon surpassed
all the kings of the earth in riches
and wisdom.
24 Now all the earth sought the
presence of Solomon to hear his
wisdom, which God had put in his
heart.
25 Each man brought his pres-
ent: articles of silver and gold,
garments, armor, spices, horses,
and mules, at a set rate year by
year.
26 [a]And Solomon [b]gathered chari-
ots and horsemen; he had one
thousand four hundred chariots
and twelve thousand horsemen,
whom he [1]stationed in the chariot
cities and with the king at Jerusa-
lem.
27 [a]The king made silver *as com-*
mon in Jerusalem as stones, and
he made cedar trees as abundant
as the sycamores which *are* in the
lowland.
28 [a]Also Solomon had horses im-
ported from Egypt and Keveh; the
king's merchants bought them in
Keveh at the *current* price.
29 Now a chariot that was im-
ported from Egypt cost six hun-
dred *shekels* of silver, and a horse
one hundred and fifty; [a]and [1]thus,
through their agents, they ex-
ported *them* to all the kings of the
Hittites and the kings of Syria.

Solomon's Heart Turns from the LORD

11 But [a]King Solomon loved
[b]many foreign women, as
well as the daughter of Pharaoh:
women of the Moabites, Ammon-
ites, Edomites, Sidonians, *and* Hit-
tites—
2 from the nations of whom the
LORD had said to the children of
Israel, [a]"You shall not intermarry
with them, nor they with you.
Surely they will turn away your
hearts after their gods." Solomon
clung to these in love.
3 And he had seven hundred
wives, princesses, and three hun-
dred concubines; and his wives
turned away his heart.
4 For it was so, when Solomon
was old, [a]that his wives turned his
heart after other gods; and his
[b]heart was not [1]loyal to the LORD
his God, [c]as *was* the heart of his
father David.
5 For Solomon went after [a]Ash-
toreth the goddess of the Sidoni-
ans, and after [b]Milcom[1] the
abomination of the [c]Ammonites.
6 Solomon did evil in the sight
of the LORD, and did not fully fol-
low the LORD, as *did* his father Da-
vid.
7 [a]Then Solomon built a [1]high
place for [b]Chemosh the abomina-
tion of Moab, on [c]the hill that *is*
east of Jerusalem, and for Molech
the abomination of the people of
Ammon.
8 And he did likewise for all his
foreign wives, who burned incense
and sacrificed to their gods.
9 So the LORD became angry with
Solomon, because his heart had
turned from the LORD God of Is-
rael, [a]who had appeared to him
twice,
10 and [a]had commanded him con-
cerning this thing, that he should
not go after other gods; but he did
not keep what the LORD had com-
manded.
11 Therefore the LORD said to Sol-
omon, "Because you have done
this, and have not kept My cov-
enant and My statutes, which I
have commanded you, [a]I will
surely tear the kingdom away
from you and give it to your [b]ser-
vant.
12 "Nevertheless I will not do it
in your days, for the sake of your
father David; I will tear it out of
the hand of your son.
13 [a]"However I will not tear away
the whole kingdom; I will give
[b]one tribe to your son [c]for the sake
of my servant David, and for the
sake of Jerusalem [d]which I have
chosen."

21 [a]2 Chr. 9:20
22 [a]Gen. 10:4; 2 Chr. 20:36 [b]1 Kin. 9:26–28; 22:48; Ps. 72:10 [1]Lit. *ships of Tarshish*, deep-sea vessels [2]Or *peacocks*
23 [a]1 Kin. 3:12, 13; 4:30; 2 Chr. 1:12
26 [a]1 Kin. 4:26; 2 Chr. 1:14; 9:25 [b][Deut. 17:16]; 1 Kin. 9:19 [1]So with LXX, Syr., Tg., Vg. (cf. 2 Chr. 9:25); MT *led*
27 [a][Deut. 17:17]; 2 Chr. 1:15–17
28 [a][Deut. 17:16]; 2 Chr. 1:16; 9:28
29 [a]Josh. 1:4; 2 Kin. 7:6, 7 [1]Lit. *by their hands*

CHAPTER 11

1 [a][Neh. 13:26] [b][Deut. 17:17]; 1 Kin. 3:1
2 [a]Ex. 34:16; [Deut. 7:3, 4]
4 [a][Deut. 17:17; Neh. 13:26] [b]1 Kin. 8:61 [c]1 Kin. 9:4 [1]Lit. *at peace with*
5 [a]Judg. 2:13; 1 Kin. 11:33 [b][Lev. 20:2–5] [c]2 Kin. 23:13 [1]Or *Molech*
7 [a]Num. 33:52 [b]Num. 21:29; Judg. 11:24 [c]2 Kin. 23:13 [1]A place for pagan worship
9 [a]1 Kin. 3:5; 9:2
10 [a]1 Kin. 6:12; 9:6, 7
11 [a]1 Kin. 11:31; 12:15, 16 [b]1 Kin. 11:31, 37
13 [a]2 Sam. 7:15; 1 Chr. 17:13; Ps. 89:33 [b]1 Kin. 12:20 [c]2 Sam. 7:15, 16 [d]Deut. 12:11; 1 Kin. 9:3; 14:21

Adversaries of Solomon

14 Now the LORD [a]raised up an adversary against Solomon, Hadad the Edomite; he *was* a descendant of the king in Edom.
15 [a]For it happened, when David was in Edom, and Joab the commander of the army had gone up to bury the slain, [b]after he had killed every male in Edom
16 (because for six months Joab remained there with all Israel, until he had cut down every male in Edom),
17 that Hadad fled to go to Egypt, he and certain Edomites of his father's servants with him. Hadad *was* still a little child.
18 Then they arose from Midian and came to Paran; and they took men with them from Paran and came to Egypt, to Pharaoh king of Egypt, who gave him a house, apportioned food for him, and gave him land.
19 And Hadad found great favor in the sight of Pharaoh, so that he gave him as wife the sister of his own wife, that is, the sister of Queen Tahpenes.
20 Then the sister of Tahpenes bore him Genubath his son, whom Tahpenes weaned in Pharaoh's house. And Genubath was in Pharaoh's household among the sons of Pharaoh.
21 [a]So when Hadad heard in Egypt that David [1]rested with his fathers, and that Joab the commander of the army was dead, Hadad said to Pharaoh, [2]"Let me depart, that I may go to my own country."
22 Then Pharaoh said to him, "But what have you lacked with me, that suddenly you seek to go to your own country?" So he answered, "Nothing, but do let me go anyway."
23 And God raised up *another* adversary against him, Rezon the son of Eliadah, who had fled from his lord, [a]Hadadezer king of Zobah.
24 So he gathered men to him and became captain over a band *of raiders*, [a]when David killed those *of Zobah*. And they went to Damascus and dwelt there, and reigned in Damascus.

14 [a]1 Chr. 5:26
15 [a]2 Sam. 8:14; 1 Chr. 18:12, 13 [b]Num. 24:18, 19; [Deut. 20:13]
21 [a]1 Kin. 2:10, 34 [1]Died and joined his ancestors [2]Lit. *Send me away*
23 [a]2 Sam. 8:3; 10:16
24 [a]2 Sam. 8:3; 10:8, 18
26 [a]1 Kin. 12:2 [b]1 Kin. 11:11; 2 Chr. 13:6 [c]2 Sam. 20:21
27 [a]1 Kin. 9:15, 24 [1]Lit. *closed up the breaches*
28 [a][Prov. 22:29]
29 [a]1 Kin. 12:15; 14:2; 2 Chr. 9:29
30 [a]1 Sam. 15:27, 28; 24:5
31 [a]1 Kin. 11:11, 13
33 [a]1 Sam. 7:3; 1 Kin. 11:5–8 [1]So with MT, Tg.; LXX, Syr., Vg. *he has*
35 [a]1 Kin. 12:16, 17

25 He was an adversary of Israel all the days of Solomon (besides the trouble that Hadad *caused*); and he abhorred Israel, and reigned over Syria.

Jeroboam's Rebellion

26 Then Solomon's servant, [a]Jeroboam the son of Nebat, an Ephraimite from Zereda, whose mother's name *was* Zeruah, a widow, [b]also [c]rebelled against the king.
27 And this *is* what caused him to rebel against the king: [a]Solomon had built the Millo *and* [1]repaired the damages to the City of David his father.
28 The man Jeroboam *was* a mighty man of valor; and Solomon, seeing that the young man was [a]industrious, made him the officer over all the labor force of the house of Joseph.
29 Now it happened at that time, when Jeroboam went out of Jerusalem, that the prophet [a]Ahijah the Shilonite met him on the way; and he had clothed himself with a new garment, and the two *were* alone in the field.
30 Then Ahijah took hold of the new garment that *was* on him, and [a]tore it *into* twelve pieces.
31 And he said to Jeroboam, "Take for yourself ten pieces, for [a]thus says the LORD, the God of Israel: 'Behold, I will tear the kingdom out of the hand of Solomon and will give ten tribes to you
32 '(but he shall have one tribe for the sake of My servant David, and for the sake of Jerusalem, the city which I have chosen out of all the tribes of Israel),
33 [a]'because [1]they have forsaken Me, and worshiped Ashtoreth the goddess of the Sidonians, Chemosh the god of the Moabites, and Milcom the god of the people of Ammon, and have not walked in My ways to do *what is* right in My eyes and *keep* My statutes and My judgments, as *did* his father David.
34 'However I will not take the whole kingdom out of his hand, because I have made him ruler all the days of his life for the sake of My servant David, whom I chose because he kept My commandments and My statutes.
35 'But [a]I will take the kingdom

out of his son's hand and give it
to you—ten tribes.
36 'And to his son I will give one
tribe, that [a]My servant David may
always have a lamp before Me in
Jerusalem, the city which I have
chosen for Myself, to put My name
there.
37 'So I will take you, and you
shall reign over all your heart desires,
and you shall be king over
Israel.
38 'Then it shall be, if you heed
all that I command you, walk in
My ways, and do *what is* right in
My sight, to keep My statutes and
My commandments, as My servant
David did, then [a]I will be with you
and [b]build for you an enduring
house, as I built for David, and will
give Israel to you.
39 'And I will afflict the descendants
of David because of this, but
not forever.' "
40 Solomon therefore sought to
kill Jeroboam. But Jeroboam arose
and fled to Egypt, to [a]Shishak king
of Egypt, and was in Egypt until
the death of Solomon.

Death of Solomon

41 Now [a]the rest of the acts of Solomon,
all that he did, and his wisdom,
are they not written in the
book of the acts of Solomon?
42 [a]And the period that Solomon
reigned in Jerusalem over all Israel
was forty years.
43 [a]Then Solomon [1]rested with his
fathers, and was buried in the City
of David his father. And Rehoboam
his son reigned in his [b]place.

The Revolt Against Rehoboam

12 And [a]Rehoboam went to
[b]Shechem, for all Israel had
gone to Shechem to make him
king.
2 So it happened, when [a]Jeroboam
the son of Nebat heard *it* (he
was still in [b]Egypt, for he had fled
from the presence of King Solomon
and had been dwelling in
Egypt),
3 that they sent and called him.
Then Jeroboam and the whole assembly
of Israel came and spoke
to Rehoboam, saying,
4 "Your father made our [a]yoke
[1]heavy; now therefore, lighten the
burdensome service of your father,

36 [a][1 Kin. 15:4; 2 Kin. 8:19]
38 [a]Deut. 31:8; Josh. 1:5 [b]2 Sam. 7:11, 27
40 [a]1 Kin. 11:17; 14:25; 2 Chr. 12:2–9
41 [a]2 Chr. 9:29
42 [a]2 Chr. 9:30
43 [a]1 Kin. 2:10; 2 Chr. 9:31 [b]1 Kin. 14:21; 2 Chr. 10:1 [1]Died and joined his ancestors

CHAPTER 12

1 [a]2 Chr. 10:1 [b]Judg. 9:6
2 [a]1 Kin. 11:26 [b]1 Kin. 11:40
4 [a]1 Sam. 8:11–18; 1 Kin. 4:7; 5:13–15 [1]*hard*
7 [a]2 Chr. 10:7; [Prov. 15:1]
11 [1]Scourges with points or barbs, lit. *scorpions*
13 [1]*harshly*
14 [1]Lit. *scorpions*
15 [a]Deut. 2:30; Judg. 14:4; 1 Kin. 12:24; 2 Chr. 10:15

and his heavy yoke which he put
on us, and we will serve you."
5 So he said to them, "Depart *for*
three days, then come back to me."
And the people departed.
6 Then King Rehoboam consulted
the elders who stood before
his father Solomon while he still
lived, and he said, "How do you
advise *me* to answer these people?"
7 And they spoke to him, saying,
[a]"If you will be a servant to these
people today, and serve them, and
answer them, and speak good
words to them, then they will be
your servants forever."
8 But he rejected the advice
which the elders had given him,
and consulted the young men who
had grown up with him, who stood
before him.
9 And he said to them, "What advice
do you give? How should we
answer this people who have spoken
to me, saying, 'Lighten the
yoke which your father put on
us'?"
10 Then the young men who had
grown up with him spoke to him,
saying, "Thus you should speak to
this people who have spoken to
you, saying, 'Your father made
our yoke heavy, but you make *it*
lighter on us'—thus you shall say
to them: 'My little *finger* shall be
thicker than my father's waist!
11 'And now, whereas my father
put a heavy yoke on you, I will add
to your yoke; my father chastised
you with whips, but I will chastise
you with [1]scourges!' "
12 So Jeroboam and all the people
came to Rehoboam the third
day, as the king had directed, saying,
"Come back to me the third
day."
13 Then the king answered the
people [1]roughly, and rejected the
advice which the elders had given
him;
14 and he spoke to them according
to the advice of the young men,
saying, "My father made your
yoke heavy, but I will add to your
yoke; my father chastised you with
whips, but I will chastise you with
[1]scourges!"
15 So the king did not listen to the
people; for [a]the turn *of events* was
from the LORD, that He might fulfill

His word, which the LORD had [b]spoken by Ahijah the Shilonite to Jeroboam the son of Nebat.
16 Now when all Israel saw that the king did not listen to them, the people answered the king, saying:

[a]"What share have we in David?
We have no inheritance in the
son of Jesse.
To your tents, O Israel!
Now, see to your own house,
O David!"

So Israel departed to their tents.
17 But Rehoboam reigned over [a]the children of Israel who dwelt in the cities of Judah.
18 Then King Rehoboam [a]sent Adoram, who *was* in charge of the revenue; but all Israel stoned him with stones, and he died. Therefore King Rehoboam mounted his chariot in haste to flee to Jerusalem.
19 So [a]Israel has been in rebellion against the house of David to this day.
20 Now it came to pass when all Israel heard that Jeroboam had come back, they sent for him and called him to the congregation, and made him king over all [a]Israel. There was none who followed the house of David, but the tribe of Judah [b]only.
21 And when [a]Rehoboam came to Jerusalem, he assembled all the house of Judah with the tribe of [b]Benjamin, one hundred and eighty thousand chosen *men* who were warriors, to fight against the house of Israel, that he might restore the kingdom to Rehoboam the son of Solomon.
22 But [a]the word of God came to Shemaiah the man of God, saying,
23 "Speak to Rehoboam the son of Solomon, king of Judah, to all the house of Judah and Benjamin, and to the rest of the people, saying,
24 'Thus says the LORD: "You shall not go up nor fight against your brethren the children of Israel. Let every man return to his house, [a]for this thing is from Me." ' " Therefore they obeyed the word of the LORD, and turned back, according to the word of the LORD.

Jeroboam's Gold Calves

25 Then Jeroboam [a]built[1] Shechem in the mountains of Ephraim, and dwelt there. Also he went out from there and built [b]Penuel.
26 And Jeroboam said in his heart, "Now the kingdom may return to the house of David:
27 "If these people [a]go up to offer sacrifices in the house of the LORD at Jerusalem, then the heart of this people will turn back to their lord, Rehoboam king of Judah, and they will kill me and go back to Rehoboam king of Judah."
28 Therefore the king asked advice, [a]made two calves of gold, and said to the people, "It is too much for you to go up to Jerusalem. [b]Here are your gods, O Israel, which brought you up from the land of Egypt!"
29 And he set up one in [a]Bethel, and the other he put in [b]Dan.
30 Now this thing became [a]a sin, for the people went *to worship* before the one as far as Dan.
31 He made [1]shrines on the high places, [a]and made priests from every class of people, who were not of the sons of Levi.
32 Jeroboam [1]ordained a feast on the fifteenth day of the eighth month, like [a]the feast that *was* in Judah, and offered sacrifices on the altar. So he did at Bethel, sacrificing to the calves that he had made. [b]And at Bethel he installed the priests of the high places which he had made.
33 So he made offerings on the altar which he had made at Bethel on the fifteenth day of the eighth month, in the month which he had [a]devised in his own heart. And he [1]ordained a feast for the children of Israel, and offered sacrifices on the altar and [b]burned incense.

The Message of the Man of God

13 And behold, [a]a man of God went from Judah to Bethel [1]by the word of the LORD, [b]and Jeroboam stood by the altar to burn incense.
2 Then he cried out against the altar [1]by the word of the LORD, and said, "O altar, altar! Thus says the LORD: 'Behold, a child, [a]Josiah by

15 [b]1 Kin. 11:11, 29, 31
16 [a]2 Sam. 20:1
17 [a]1 Kin. 11:13, 36; 2 Chr. 11:14–17
18 [a]1 Kin. 4:6; 5:14
19 [a]2 Kin. 17:21
20 [a]2 Kin. 17:21 [b]1 Kin. 11:13, 32, 36
21 [a]2 Chr. 11:1–4 [b]2 Sam. 19:17
22 [a]2 Chr. 11:2; 12:5–7
24 [a]1 Kin. 12:15
25 [a]Gen. 12:6; Judg. 9:45–49; 1 Kin. 12:1 [b]Gen. 32:30, 31; Judg. 8:8, 17 [1]*fortified*
27 [a][Deut. 12:5–7, 14]
28 [a]2 Kin. 10:29; 17:16; [Hos. 8:4–7] [b]Ex. 32:4, 8
29 [a]Gen. 28:19 [b]Judg. 18:26–31
30 [a]1 Kin. 13:34; 2 Kin. 17:21
31 [a][Num. 3:10; 17:1–11]; Judg. 17:5; 1 Kin. 13:33; 2 Kin. 17:32; 2 Chr. 11:14, 15 [1]Lit. *a house;* cf. 1 Kin. 13:32, lit. *houses*
32 [a]Lev. 23:33, 34; Num. 29:12; 1 Kin. 8:2, 5 [b]Amos 7:10–13 [1]*instituted*
33 [a]Num. 15:39 [b]1 Kin. 13:1 [1]*instituted*

CHAPTER 13

1 [a]2 Kin. 23:17 [b]1 Kin. 12:32, 33 [1]*at the LORD's command*
2 [a]2 Kin. 23:15, 16 [1]*at the LORD's command*

name, shall be born to the house
of David; and on you he shall sac-
rifice the priests of the high places
who burn incense on you, and
men's bones shall be [b]burned on
you.' "
3 And he gave [a]a sign the same
day, saying, "This *is* the sign
which the LORD has spoken:
Surely the altar shall split apart,
and the ashes on it shall be poured
out."
4 So it came to pass when King
Jeroboam heard the saying of the
man of God, who cried out against
the altar in Bethel, that he
stretched out his hand from the al-
tar, saying, "Arrest him!" Then his
hand, which he stretched out to-
ward him, withered, so that he
could not pull it back to himself.
5 The altar also was split apart,
and the ashes poured out from the
altar, according to the sign which
the man of God had given by the
word of the LORD.
6 Then the king answered and
said to the man of God, "Please
[a]entreat the favor of the LORD your
God, and pray for me, that my
hand may be restored to me." So
the man of God entreated the
LORD, and the king's hand was re-
stored to him, and became as be-
fore.
7 Then the king said to the man
of God, "Come home with me and
refresh yourself, and [a]I will give
you a reward."
8 But the man of God said to the
king, [a]"If you were to give me half
your house, I would not go in with
you; nor would I eat bread nor
drink water in this place.
9 "For so it was commanded me
by the word of the LORD, saying,
[a]'You shall not eat bread, nor
drink water, nor return by the
same way you came.' "
10 So he went another way and
did not return by the way he came
to Bethel.

Death of the Man of God

11 Now an [a]old prophet dwelt in
Bethel, and his [1]sons came and
told him all the works that the man
of God had done that day in
Bethel; they also told their father
the words which he had spoken to
the king.
12 And their father said to them,
"Which way did he go?" For his
sons [1]had seen which way the man
of God went who came from Ju-
dah.
13 Then he said to his sons, "Sad-
dle the donkey for me." So they
saddled the donkey for him; and
he rode on it,
14 and went after the man of God,
and found him sitting under an
oak. Then he said to him, "*Are* you
the man of God who came from
Judah?" And he said, "I *am*."
15 Then he said to him, "Come
home with me and eat bread."
16 And he said, [a]"I cannot return
with you nor go in with you; nei-
ther can I eat bread nor drink wa-
ter with you in this place.
17 "For [1]I have been told [a]by the
word of the LORD, 'You shall not
eat bread nor drink water there,
nor return by going the way you
came.' "
18 He said to him, "I too *am* a
prophet as you *are*, and an angel
spoke to me by the word of the
LORD, saying, 'Bring him back with
you to your house, that he may eat
bread and drink water.' " (He was
lying to him.)
19 So he went back with him, and
ate bread in his house, and drank
water.
20 Now it happened, as they sat
at the table, that the word of the
LORD came to the prophet who had
brought him back;
21 and he cried out to the man of
God who came from Judah, say-
ing, "Thus says the LORD: 'Because
you have disobeyed the word of
the LORD, and have not kept the
commandment which the LORD
your God commanded you,
22 'but you came back, ate bread,
and drank water in the [a]place of
which *the LORD* said to you, "Eat
no bread and drink no water,"
your corpse shall not come to the
tomb of your fathers.' "
23 So it was, after he had eaten
bread and after he had drunk, that
he saddled the donkey for him, the
prophet whom he had brought
back.
24 When he was gone, [a]a lion met
him on the road and killed him.
And his corpse was thrown on the
road, and the donkey stood by it.

2 [b][Lev. 26:30]
3 [a]Ex. 4:1–5; Judg. 6:17; Is. 7:14; 38:7; John 2:18; 1 Cor. 1:22
6 [a]Ex. 8:8; 9:28; 10:17; Num. 21:7; Jer. 37:3; Acts 8:24; [James 5:16]
7 [a]1 Sam. 9:7; 2 Kin. 5:15
8 [a]Num. 22:18; 24:13; 1 Kin. 13:16, 17
9 [a][1 Cor. 5:11]
11 [a]1 Kin. 13:25 [1]Lit. *son*
12 [1]LXX, Syr., Tg., Vg. *showed him*
16 [a]1 Kin. 13:8, 9
17 [a]1 Kin. 20:35; 1 Thess. 4:15 [1]Lit. *a command came to me by*
22 [a]1 Kin. 13:9
24 [a]1 Kin. 20:36

The lion also stood by the corpse.
25 And there, men passed by and
saw the corpse thrown on the
road, and the lion standing by the
corpse. Then they went and told
it in the city where the old prophet
dwelt.
26 Now when the prophet who
had brought him back from the
way heard *it*, he said, "It *is* the
man of God who was disobedient
to the word of the LORD. Therefore
the LORD has delivered him to the
lion, which has torn him and killed
him, according to the word of the
LORD which He spoke to him."
27 And he spoke to his sons, say-
ing, "Saddle the donkey for me."
So they saddled *it*.
28 Then he went and found his
corpse thrown on the road, and the
donkey and the lion standing by
the corpse. The lion had not eaten
the corpse nor torn the donkey.
29 And the prophet took up the
corpse of the man of God, laid it
on the donkey, and brought it
back. So the old prophet came to
the city to mourn, and to bury him.
30 Then he laid the corpse in his
own tomb; and they mourned over
him, *saying*, [a]"Alas, my brother!"
31 So it was, after he had buried
him, that he spoke to his sons, say-
ing, "When I am dead, then bury
me in the tomb where the man of
God *is* buried; [a]lay my bones be-
side his bones.
32 [a]"For the [1]saying which he
cried out by the word of the LORD
against the altar in Bethel, and
against all the [2]shrines on the high
places which *are* in the cities of
[b]Samaria, will surely come to
pass."
33 [a]After this event Jeroboam did
not turn from his evil way, but
again he made priests from every
class of people for the high places;
whoever wished, he consecrated
him, and he became *one* of the
priests of the high places.
34 [a]And this thing was the sin of
the house of Jeroboam, so as [b]to
exterminate and destroy *it* from
the face of the earth.

Judgment on the House of Jeroboam

14 At that time Abijah the son
of Jeroboam became sick.
2 And Jeroboam said to his wife,
"Please arise, and disguise your-
self, that they may not recognize
you as the wife of Jeroboam, and
go to Shiloh. Indeed, Ahijah the
prophet *is* there, who told me that
[a]*I would be* king over this people.
3 [a]"Also take [1]with you ten
loaves, *some* cakes, and a jar of
honey, and go to him; he will tell
you what will become of the
child."
4 And Jeroboam's wife did so;
she arose [a]and went to Shiloh, and
came to the house of Ahijah. But
Ahijah could not see, for his eyes
were [1]glazed by reason of his
age.
5 Now the LORD had said to Ahi-
jah, "Here is the wife of Jeroboam,
coming to ask you something
about her son, for he *is* sick. Thus
and thus you shall say to her; for
it will be, when she comes in, that
she will pretend *to be* another
woman."
6 And so it was, when Ahijah
heard the sound of her footsteps
as she came through the door, he
said, "Come in, wife of Jeroboam.
Why do you pretend *to be* another
person? For I *have been* sent to you
with bad *news*.
7 "Go, tell Jeroboam, 'Thus says
the LORD God of Israel: [a]"Because
I exalted you from among the peo-
ple, and made you ruler over My
people Israel,
8 "and [a]tore the kingdom away
from the house of David, and gave
it to you; and *yet* you have not
been as My servant David, [b]who
kept My commandments and who
followed Me with all his heart, to
do only *what was* right in My
eyes;
9 "but you have done more evil
than all who were before you, [a]for
you have gone and made for your-
self other gods and molded images
to provoke Me to anger, and [b]have
cast Me behind your back—
10 "therefore behold! [a]I will bring
disaster on the house of Jeroboam,
and [b]will cut off from Jeroboam
every male in Israel, [c]bond and
free; I will take away the remnant
of the house of Jeroboam, as one
takes away refuse until it is all
gone.
11 "The dogs shall eat [a]whoever
belongs to Jeroboam and dies in

30 [a]Jer. 22:18
31 [a]Ruth 1:17; 2 Kin. 23:17, 18
32 [a]1 Kin. 13:2; 2 Kin. 23:16, 19 [b]1 Kin. 16:24; John 4:5; Acts 8:14 [1]Lit. *word* [2]Lit. *houses*
33 [a]1 Kin. 12:31, 32; 2 Chr. 11:15; 13:9
34 [a]1 Kin. 12:30; 2 Kin. 17:21 [b][1 Kin. 14:10; 15:29, 30]

CHAPTER 14

2 [a]1 Kin. 11:29–31
3 [a]1 Sam. 9:7, 8; 1 Kin. 13:7; 2 Kin. 4:42 [1]Lit. *in your hand*
4 [a]1 Kin. 11:29 [1]Lit. *set*
7 [a]2 Sam. 12:7, 8; 1 Kin. 16:2
8 [a]1 Kin. 11:31 [b]1 Kin. 11:33, 38; 15:5
9 [a]1 Kin. 12:28; 2 Chr. 11:15 [b]2 Chr. 29:6; Neh. 9:26; Ps. 50:17
10 [a]1 Kin. 15:29 [b]1 Kin. 21:21; 2 Kin. 9:8 [c]Deut. 32:36; 2 Kin. 14:26
11 [a]1 Kin. 16:4; 21:24

the city, and the birds of the air
shall eat whoever dies in the field;
for the LORD has spoken!"'
12 "Arise therefore, go to your
own house. [a]When your feet enter
the city, the child shall die.
13 "And all Israel shall mourn for
him and bury him, for he is the
only one of Jeroboam who shall
[1]come to the grave, because in him
[a]there is found something good to-
ward the LORD God of Israel in the
house of Jeroboam.
14 [a]"Moreover the LORD will raise
up for Himself a king over Israel
who shall cut off the house of Jero-
boam; [1]this is the day. What? Even
now!
15 "For the LORD will strike Israel,
as a reed is shaken in the water.
He will [a]uproot Israel from this
[b]good land which He gave to their
fathers, and will scatter them [c]be-
yond [1]the River, [d]because they
have made their [2]wooden images,
provoking the LORD to anger.
16 "And He will give Israel up be-
cause of the sins of Jeroboam,
[a]who sinned and who made Israel
sin."
17 Then Jeroboam's wife arose
and departed, and came to [a]Tir-
zah. [b]When she came to the thresh-
old of the house, the child died.
18 And they buried him; and all
Israel mourned for him, [a]accord-
ing to the word of the LORD which
He spoke through His servant Ahi-
jah the prophet.

Death of Jeroboam

19 Now the rest of the acts of Jero-
boam, how he [a]made war and how
he reigned, indeed they *are* written
in the book of the chronicles of the
kings of Israel.
20 The period that Jeroboam
reigned *was* twenty-two years. So
he rested with his fathers. Then
[a]Nadab his son reigned in his
place.

Rehoboam Reigns in Judah

21 And Rehoboam the son of Sol-
omon reigned in Judah. [a]Reho-
boam *was* forty-one years old
when he became king. He reigned
seventeen years in Jerusalem, the
city [b]which the LORD had chosen
out of all the tribes of Israel, to put
His name there. [c]His mother's
name *was* Naamah, an Ammon-
itess.
22 [a]Now Judah did evil in the
sight of the LORD, and they [b]pro-
voked Him to jealousy with their
sins which they committed, more
than all that their fathers had
done.
23 For they also built for them-
selves [a]high[1] places, [b]*sacred* pil-
lars, and [c]wooden images on every
high hill and [d]under every green
tree.
24 [a]And there were also [1]per-
verted persons in the land. They
did according to all the [b]abomina-
tions of the nations which the
LORD had cast out before the chil-
dren of [c]Israel.
25 [a]It happened in the fifth year
of King Rehoboam *that* Shishak
king of Egypt came up against Je-
rusalem.
26 [a]And he took away the trea-
sures of the house of the LORD and
the treasures of the king's house;
he took away everything. He also
took away all the gold shields
[b]which Solomon had made.
27 Then King Rehoboam made
bronze shields in their place, and
[1]committed *them* to the hands of
the captains of the [2]guard, who
guarded the doorway of the king's
house.
28 And whenever the king entered
the house of the LORD, the guards
carried them, then brought them
back into the guardroom.
29 [a]Now the rest of the acts of Re-
hoboam, and all that he did, *are*
they not written in the book of the
chronicles of the kings of Ju-
dah?
30 And there was [a]war between
Rehoboam and Jeroboam all *their*
days.
31 [a]So Rehoboam [1]rested with his
fathers, and was buried with his
fathers in the City of David.
[b]His mother's name *was* Naamah,
an Ammonitess. Then [c]Abijam[2]
his son reigned in his place.

Abijam Reigns in Judah

15 [a]In the eighteenth year of
King Jeroboam the son of
Nebat, Abijam became king over
Judah.
2 He reigned three years in Jeru-
salem. [a]His mother's name *was*

12 [a]1 Kin. 14:17
13 [a]2 Chr. 12:12; 19:3 [1]Be buried
14 [a]1 Kin. 15:27–29 [1]Or *this day and from now on*
15 [a]2 Kin. 17:6 [b][Josh. 23:15, 16] [c]2 Kin. 15:29 [d][Ex. 34:13, 14] [1]The Euphrates [2]Heb. *Asherim*, Canaanite deities
16 [a]1 Kin. 12:30; 13:34; 15:30, 34; 16:2
17 [a]Song 6:4 [b]1 Kin. 14:12
18 [a]1 Kin. 14:13
19 [a]2 Chr. 13:2–20
20 [a]1 Kin. 15:25
21 [a]2 Chr. 12:13 [b]1 Kin. 11:32, 36 [c]1 Kin. 14:31
22 [a]2 Chr. 12:1, 14 [b]Deut. 32:21
23 [a]Deut. 12:2 [b][Deut. 16:22] [c][2 Kin. 17:9, 10] [d]Is. 57:5 [1]Places for pagan worship
24 [a]Deut. 23:17 [b]Deut. 20:18 [c][Deut. 9:4, 5] [1]Heb. *qadesh*, one practicing sodomy and prostitution in religious rituals
25 [a]1 Kin. 11:40
26 [a]2 Chr. 12:9–11 [b]1 Kin. 10:17
27 [1]*entrusted* [2]Lit. *runners*
29 [a]2 Chr. 12:15, 16
30 [a]1 Kin. 12:21–24; 15:6
31 [a]2 Chr. 12:16 [b]1 Kin. 14:21 [c]2 Chr. 12:16 [1]Died and joined his ancestors [2]*Abijah*, 2 Chr. 12:16

CHAPTER 15

1 [a]2 Chr. 13:1
2 [a]2 Chr. 11:20–22

[b]Maachah the granddaughter of
[c]Abishalom.
3 And he walked in all the sins
of his father, which he had done
before him; [a]his heart was not
[1]loyal to the LORD his God, as was
the heart of his father David.
4 Nevertheless [a]for David's sake
the LORD his God gave him a lamp
in Jerusalem, by setting up his son
after him and by establishing Jeru-
salem;
5 because David [a]did *what was*
right in the eyes of the LORD, and
had not turned aside from any-
thing that He commanded him all
the days of his life, [b]except in the
matter of Uriah the Hittite.
6 [a]And there was war between
[1]Rehoboam and Jeroboam all the
days of his life.
7 [a]Now the rest of the acts of Abi-
jam, and all that he did, *are* they
not written in the book of the
chronicles of the kings of Judah?
And there was war between Abi-
jam and Jeroboam.
8 [a]So Abijam [1]rested with his fa-
thers, and they buried him in the
City of David. Then Asa his son
reigned in his place.

Asa Reigns in Judah

9 In the twentieth year of Jero-
boam king of Israel, Asa became
king over Judah.
10 And he reigned forty-one years
in Jerusalem. His grandmother's
name *was* Maachah the grand-
daughter of Abishalom.
11 [a]Asa did *what was* right in the
eyes of the LORD, as *did* his father
David.
12 [a]And he banished the [1]per-
verted persons from the land, and
removed all the idols that his fa-
thers had made.
13 Also he removed [a]Maachah his
grandmother from *being* queen
mother, because she had made an
obscene image of [1]Asherah. And
Asa cut down her obscene image
and [b]burned *it* by the Brook Kid-
ron.
14 [a]But the [1]high places were not
removed. Nevertheless Asa's
[b]heart was loyal to the LORD all his
days.
15 He also brought into the house
of the LORD the things which his
father [a]had dedicated, and the

2 [b]2 Chr. 13:2 [c]2 Chr. 11:21
3 [a]Ps. 119:80 [1]Lit. *at peace with*
4 [a]2 Sam. 21:17
5 [a]1 Kin. 9:4; 14:8 [b]2 Sam. 11:3, 15–17; 12:9, 10
6 [a]1 Kin. 14:30 [1]So with MT, LXX, Tg., Vg.; some Heb. mss., Syr. *Abijam*
7 [a]2 Chr. 13:2–22
8 [a]2 Chr. 14:1 [1]Died and joined his ancestors
11 [a]2 Chr. 14:2
12 [a]1 Kin. 14:24; 22:46 [1]Heb. *qedeshim,* those practicing sodomy and prostitution in religious rituals
13 [a]2 Chr. 15:16–18 [b]Ex. 32:20 [1]A Canaanite goddess
14 [a]1 Kin. 3:2; 22:43 [b]1 Kin. 8:61; 15:3 [1]Places for pagan worship
15 [a]1 Kin. 7:51
17 [a]2 Chr. 16:1–6 [b]Josh. 18:25 [c]1 Kin. 12:26–29
18 [a]2 Chr. 16:2 [b]1 Kin. 11:23, 24
20 [a]1 Kin. 20:1 [b]2 Kin. 15:29 [c]Judg. 18:29 [d]2 Sam. 20:14, 15
21 [a]1 Kin. 14:17; 16:15–18
22 [a]2 Chr. 16:6 [b]Josh. 21:17 [c]Josh. 18:26
23 [a]2 Chr. 16:11–14
24 [a]2 Chr. 17:1 [b]Matt. 1:8 [1]Died and joined his ancestors
25 [a]1 Kin. 14:20

things which he himself had dedi-
cated: silver and gold and uten-
sils.
16 Now there was war between
Asa and Baasha king of Israel all
their days.
17 And [a]Baasha king of Israel
came up against Judah, and built
[b]Ramah, [c]that he might let none
go out or come in to Asa king of
Judah.
18 Then Asa took all the silver and
gold *that was* left in the treasuries
of the house of the LORD and the
treasuries of the king's house, and
delivered them into the hand of his
servants. And King Asa sent them
to [a]Ben-Hadad the son of Tabrim-
mon, the son of Hezion, king of
Syria, who dwelt in [b]Damascus,
saying,
19 "*Let there be* a treaty between
you and me, as there was between
my father and your father. See, I
have sent you a present of silver
and gold. Come and break your
treaty with Baasha king of Israel,
so that he will withdraw from me."
20 So Ben-Hadad heeded King
Asa, and [a]sent the captains of his
armies against the cities of Israel.
He attacked [b]Ijon, [c]Dan, [d]Abel
Beth Maachah, and all Chinne-
roth, with all the land of Naphtali.
21 Now it happened, when Baasha
heard *it,* that he stopped building
Ramah, and remained in [a]Tirzah.
22 [a]Then King Asa made a procla-
mation throughout all Judah; none
was exempted. And they took
away the stones and timber of Ra-
mah, which Baasha had used for
building; and with them King Asa
built [b]Geba of Benjamin, and
[c]Mizpah.
23 The rest of all the acts of Asa,
all his might, all that he did, and
the cities which he built, *are* they
not written in the book of the
chronicles of the kings of Judah?
But [a]in the time of his old age he
was diseased in his feet.
24 So Asa [1]rested with his fathers,
and was buried with his fathers in
the City of David his father. [a]Then
[b]Jehoshaphat his son reigned in
his place.

Nadab Reigns in Israel

25 Now [a]Nadab the son of Jero-
boam became king over Israel in

the second year of Asa king of Judah, and he reigned over Israel two years.
26 And he did evil in the sight of the LORD, and walked in the way of his father, and in [a]his sin by which he had made Israel sin.
27 [a]Then Baasha the son of Ahijah, of the house of Issachar, conspired against him. And Baasha killed him at [b]Gibbethon, which *belonged* to the Philistines, while Nadab and all Israel laid siege to Gibbethon.
28 Baasha killed him in the third year of Asa king of Judah, and reigned in his place.
29 And it was so, when he became king, *that* he killed all the house of Jeroboam. He did not leave to Jeroboam anyone that breathed, until he had destroyed him, according to [a]the word of the LORD which He had spoken by His servant Ahijah the Shilonite,
30 [a]because of the sins of Jeroboam, which he had sinned and by which he had made Israel sin, because of his provocation with which he had provoked the LORD God of Israel to anger.
31 Now the rest of the acts of Nadab, and all that he did, *are* they not written in the book of the chronicles of the kings of Israel?
32 [a]And there was war between Asa and Baasha king of Israel all their days.

Baasha Reigns in Israel

33 In the third year of Asa king of Judah, Baasha the son of Ahijah became king over all Israel in Tirzah, and *reigned* twenty-four years.
34 He did evil in the sight of the LORD, and walked in [a]the way of Jeroboam, and in his sin by which he had made Israel sin.

16 Then the word of the LORD came to [a]Jehu the son of [b]Hanani, against [c]Baasha, saying:
2 [a]"Inasmuch as I lifted you out of the dust and made you ruler over My people Israel, and [b]you have walked in the way of Jeroboam, and have made My people Israel sin, to provoke Me to anger with their sins,
3 "surely I will [a]take[1] away the posterity of Baasha and the posterity of his house, and I will make your house like [b]the house of Jeroboam the son of Nebat.
4 "The dogs shall eat [a]whoever belongs to Baasha and dies in the city, and the birds of the air shall eat whoever dies in the fields."
5 Now the rest of the acts of Baasha, what he did, and his might, [a]*are* they not written in the book of the chronicles of the kings of Israel?
6 So Baasha [1]rested with his fathers and was buried in [a]Tirzah. Then Elah his son reigned in his place.
7 And also the word of the LORD came by the prophet [a]Jehu the son of Hanani against Baasha and his house, because of all the evil that he did in the sight of the LORD in provoking Him to anger with the work of his hands, in being like the house of Jeroboam, and because [b]he killed them.

Elah Reigns in Israel

8 In the twenty-sixth year of Asa king of Judah, Elah the son of Baasha became king over Israel, *and reigned* two years in Tirzah.
9 [a]Now his servant Zimri, commander of half *his* chariots, conspired against him as he was in Tirzah drinking himself drunk in the house of Arza, [b]steward[1] of *his* house in Tirzah.
10 And Zimri went in and struck him and killed him in the twenty-seventh year of Asa king of Judah, and reigned in his place.
11 Then it came to pass, when he began to reign, as soon as he was seated on his throne, *that* he killed all the household of Baasha; he [a]did not leave him one male, neither of his relatives nor of his friends.
12 Thus Zimri destroyed all the household of Baasha, [a]according to the word of the LORD, which He spoke against Baasha by Jehu the prophet,
13 for all the sins of Baasha and the sins of Elah his son, by which they had sinned and by which they had made Israel sin, in provoking the LORD God of Israel to anger [a]with their [1]idols.
14 Now the rest of the acts of Elah, and all that he did, *are* they not

---

26 [a]1 Kin. 12:28–33; 14:16
27 [a]1 Kin. 14:14 [b]Josh. 19:44; 21:23; 1 Kin. 16:15
29 [a]1 Kin. 14:10–14
30 [a]1 Kin. 14:9, 16
32 [a]1 Kin. 15:16
34 [a]1 Kin. 13:33; 14:16

CHAPTER 16

1 [a]1 Kin. 16:7; 2 Chr. 19:2; 20:34 [b]2 Chr. 16:7–10 [c]1 Kin. 15:27
2 [a]1 Sam. 2:8; 1 Kin. 14:7 [b]1 Kin. 12:25–33; 15:34
3 [a]1 Kin. 16:11; 21:21 [b]1 Kin. 14:10; 15:29 [1]*consume*
4 [a]1 Kin. 14:11; 21:24
5 [a]2 Chr. 16:11
6 [a]1 Kin. 14:17; 15:21 [1]Died and joined his ancestors
7 [a]1 Kin. 16:1 [b]1 Kin. 15:27, 29
9 [a]2 Kin. 9:30–33 [b]Gen. 24:2; 39:4; 1 Kin. 18:3 [1]Lit. *who was over the house*
11 [a]1 Sam. 25:22
12 [a]1 Kin. 16:3
13 [a]Deut. 32:21; 1 Sam. 12:21; [Is. 41:29; Jon. 2:8; 1 Cor. 8:4; 10:19] [1]Lit. *vanities*

written in the book of the chroni-
cles of the kings of Israel?

Zimri Reigns in Israel

15 In the twenty-seventh year of
Asa king of Judah, Zimri had
reigned in Tirzah seven days. And
the people *were* encamped
[a]against Gibbethon, which *be-
longed* to the Philistines.
16 Now the people *who were* en-
camped heard it said, "Zimri has
conspired and also has killed the
king." So all Israel made Omri, the
commander of the army, king over
Israel that day in the camp.
17 Then Omri and all Israel with
him went up from Gibbethon, and
they besieged Tirzah.
18 And it happened, when Zimri
saw that the city was [1]taken, that
he went into the citadel of the
king's house and burned the king's
house [2]down upon himself with
fire, and died,
19 because of the sins which he
had committed in doing evil in the
sight of the LORD, [a]in walking in
the [b]way of Jeroboam, and in his
sin which he had committed to
make Israel sin.
20 Now the rest of the acts of
Zimri, and the treason he commit-
ted, *are* they not written in the
book of the chronicles of the kings
of Israel?

Omri Reigns in Israel

21 Then the people of Israel were
divided into two parts: half of the
people followed Tibni the son of
Ginath, to make him king, and half
followed Omri.
22 But the people who followed
Omri prevailed over the people
who followed Tibni the son of Gi-
nath. So Tibni died and Omri
reigned.
23 In the thirty-first year of Asa
king of Judah, Omri became king
over Israel, *and reigned* twelve
years. Six years he reigned in [a]Tir-
zah.
24 And he bought the hill of Sa-
maria from Shemer for two talents
of silver; then he built on the hill,
and called the name of the city
which he built, [a]Samaria,[1] after
the name of Shemer, owner of the
hill.
25 [a]Omri did evil in the eyes of the
LORD, and did worse than all who
were before him.
26 For he [a]walked in all the ways
of Jeroboam the son of Nebat, and
in his sin by which he had made
Israel sin, provoking the LORD God
of Israel to anger with their [b]idols.[1]
27 Now the rest of the acts of Omri
which he did, and the might that
he showed, *are* they not written in
the book of the chronicles of the
kings of Israel?
28 So Omri rested with his fathers
and was buried in Samaria. Then
Ahab his son reigned in his place.

Ahab Reigns in Israel

29 In the thirty-eighth year of Asa
king of Judah, Ahab the son of
Omri became king over Israel; and
Ahab the son of Omri reigned over
Israel in Samaria twenty-two
years.
30 Now Ahab the son of Omri did
evil in the sight of the LORD, more
than all who *were* before him.
31 And it came to pass, as though
it had been a trivial thing for him
to walk in the sins of Jeroboam the
son of Nebat, [a]that he took as wife
Jezebel the daughter of Ethbaal,
king of the [b]Sidonians; [c]and he
went and served Baal and wor-
shiped him.
32 Then he set up an altar for Baal
in [a]the temple of Baal, which he
had built in Samaria.
33 [a]And Ahab made a [1]wooden
image. Ahab [b]did more to provoke
the LORD God of Israel to anger
than all the kings of Israel who
were before him.
34 In his days Hiel of Bethel built
Jericho. He laid its foundation
[1]with Abiram his firstborn, and
with his youngest *son* Segub he set
up its gates, [a]according to the
word of the LORD, which He had
spoken through Joshua the son of
Nun.

Elijah Proclaims a Drought

17 And Elijah the Tishbite, of
the [a]inhabitants of Gilead,
said to Ahab, [b]"*As* the LORD God
of Israel lives, [c]before whom I
stand, [d]there shall not be dew nor
rain [e]these years, except at my
word."
2 Then the word of the LORD
came to him, saying,

15 [a]1 Kin. 15:27
18 [1]*captured* [2]Lit. *over him*
19 [a]1 Kin. 15:26, 34 [b]1 Kin. 12:25–33
23 [a]1 Kin. 15:21; 2 Kin. 15:14
24 [a]1 Kin. 13:32; 2 Kin. 17:24; John 4:4 [1]Heb. *Shomeron*
25 [a]Mic. 6:16
26 [a]1 Kin. 16:19 [b]1 Kin. 16:13 [1]Lit. *vanities*
31 [a]Deut. 7:3 [b]Judg. 18:7; 1 Kin. 11:1–5 [c]1 Kin. 21:25, 26; 2 Kin. 10:18; 17:16
32 [a]2 Kin. 10:21, 26, 27
33 [a]2 Kin. 13:6 [b]1 Kin. 14:9; 16:29, 30; 21:25 [1]Heb. *Asherah*, a Canaanite goddess
34 [a]Josh. 6:26 [1]At the cost of the life of

CHAPTER 17

1 [a]Judg. 12:4 [b]1 Kin. 18:10; 22:14; 2 Kin. 3:14; 5:20 [c]Deut. 10:8 [d]1 Kin. 18:1; James 5:17 [e]Luke 4:25

3 "Get away from here and turn
eastward, and hide by the Brook
Cherith, which flows into the Jordan.
4 "And it will be *that* you shall
drink from the brook, and I have
commanded the [a]ravens to feed
you there."
5 So he went and did according
to the word of the LORD, for he
went and stayed by the Brook
Cherith, which flows into the Jordan.
6 The ravens brought him bread
and meat in the morning, and
bread and meat in the evening;
and he drank from the brook.
7 And it happened after a while
that the brook dried up, because
there had been no rain in the land.

Elijah and the Widow

8 Then the word of the LORD
came to him, saying,
9 "Arise, go to [a]Zarephath,
which *belongs* to [b]Sidon, and
dwell there. See, I have commanded
a widow there to provide
for you."
10 So he arose and went to Zarephath.
And when he came to the
gate of the city, indeed a widow
was there gathering sticks. And he
called to her and said, "Please
bring me a little water in a cup,
that I may drink."
11 And as she was going to get *it*,
he called to her and said, "Please
bring me a morsel of bread in your
hand."
12 So she said, "As the LORD your
God lives, I do not have bread,
only a handful of flour in a bin,
and a little oil in a [1]jar; and see, I
am gathering a couple of sticks
that I may go in and prepare it for
myself and my son, that we may
eat it, and [a]die."
13 And Elijah said to her, "Do not
fear; go *and* do as you have said,
but make me a small cake from it
first, and bring *it* to me; and afterward
make *some* for yourself and
your son.
14 "For thus says the LORD God of
Israel: 'The bin of flour shall not
be used up, nor shall the jar of oil
run dry, until the day the LORD
sends rain on the earth.'"
15 So she went away and did according
to the word of Elijah; and
she and he and her household ate
for *many* days.
16 The bin of flour was not used
up, nor did the jar of oil run dry,
according to the word of the LORD
which He spoke by Elijah.

Elijah Revives the Widow's Son

17 Now it happened after these
things *that* the son of the woman
who owned the house became
sick. And his sickness was so [1]serious
that [2]there was no breath left
in him.
18 So she said to Elijah, [a]"What
have I to do with you, O man of
God? Have you come to me to
bring my sin to remembrance, and
to kill my son?"
19 And he said to her, "Give me
your son." So he took him out of
her arms and carried him to the
upper room where he was staying,
and laid him on his own bed.
20 Then he cried out to the LORD
and said, "O LORD my God, have
You also brought tragedy on the
widow with whom I lodge, by killing
her son?"
21 [a]And he stretched himself out
on the child three times, and cried
out to the LORD and said, "O LORD
my God, I pray, let this child's soul
come back to him."
22 Then the LORD heard the voice
of Elijah; and the soul of the child
came back to him, and he [a]revived.
23 And Elijah took the child and
brought him down from the upper
room into the house, and gave him
to his mother. And Elijah said,
"See, your son lives!"
24 Then the woman said to Elijah,
"Now by this [a]I know that you *are*
a man of God, *and* that the word
of the LORD in your mouth *is* the
truth."

Elijah's Message to Ahab

18 And it came to pass *after*
[a]many days that the word of
the LORD came to Elijah, in the
third year, saying, "Go, present
yourself to Ahab, and [b]I will send
rain on the earth."
2 So Elijah went to present himself
to Ahab; and *there was* a severe
famine in Samaria.
3 And Ahab had called Obadiah,
who *was* [1]in charge of *his* house.

4 [a]Job 38:41
9 [a]Obad. 20; Luke 4:25, 26 [b]2 Sam. 24:6
12 [a]Deut. 28:23, 24 [1]Lit. *pitcher* or *water jar*
17 [1]*severe* [2]He died.
18 [a]Luke 5:8
21 [a]2 Kin. 4:34, 35; Acts 20:10
22 [a]Luke 7:14, 15; Heb. 11:35
24 [a]John 2:11; 3:2; 16:30
CHAPTER 18
1 [a]1 Kin. 17:1; Luke 4:25; James 5:17 [b]Deut. 28:12
3 [1]Lit. *over the house*

(Now Obadiah feared the LORD
greatly.
4 For so it was, while Jezebel
[1]massacred the prophets of the
LORD, that Obadiah had taken one
hundred prophets and hidden
them, fifty to a cave, and had fed
them with bread and water.)
5 And Ahab had said to Obadiah,
"Go into the land to all the springs
of water and to all the brooks; per-
haps we may find grass to keep
the horses and mules alive, so that
we will not have to kill any live-
stock."
6 So they divided the land be-
tween them to explore it; Ahab
went one way by himself, and
Obadiah went another way by
himself.
7 Now as Obadiah was on his
way, suddenly Elijah met him; and
he [a]recognized him, and fell on his
face, and said, "*Is* that you, my
lord Elijah?"
8 And he answered him, "*It is* I.
Go, tell your master, 'Elijah *is
here.*' "
9 So he said, "How have I sinned,
that you are delivering your ser-
vant into the hand of Ahab, to kill
me?
10 "*As* the LORD your God lives,
there is no nation or kingdom
where my master has not sent
someone to hunt for you; and
when they said, '*He is* not *here,*'
he took an oath from the kingdom
or nation that they could not find
you.
11 "And now you say, 'Go, tell
your master, "Elijah *is here*" '!
12 "And it shall come to pass, *as
soon as* I am gone from you, that
[a]the Spirit of the LORD will carry
you to a place I do not know; so
when I go and tell Ahab, and he
cannot find you, he will kill me.
But I your servant have feared the
LORD from my youth.
13 "Was it not reported to my lord
what I did when Jezebel killed the
prophets of the LORD, how I hid
one hundred men of the LORD's
prophets, fifty to a cave, and fed
them with bread and water?
14 "And now you say, 'Go, tell
your master, "Elijah *is here.*" ' He
will kill me!"
15 Then Elijah said, "*As* the LORD
of hosts lives, before whom I
stand, I will surely present myself
to him today."
16 So Obadiah went to meet
Ahab, and told him; and Ahab
went to meet Elijah.
17 Then it happened, when Ahab
saw Elijah, that Ahab said to him,
[a]"*Is that* you, O [b]troubler of Is-
rael?"
18 And he answered, "I have not
troubled Israel, but you and your
father's house *have,* [a]in that you
have forsaken the commandments
of the LORD and have followed the
Baals.
19 "Now therefore, send *and*
gather all Israel to me on [a]Mount
Carmel, the four hundred and fifty
prophets of Baal, [b]and the four
hundred prophets of [1]Asherah,
who [2]eat at Jezebel's table."

Elijah's Mount Carmel Victory

20 So Ahab sent for all the chil-
dren of Israel, and [a]gathered the
prophets together on Mount Car-
mel.
21 And Elijah came to all the peo-
ple, and said, [a]"How long will you
falter between two opinions? If the
LORD *is* God, follow Him; but if
Baal, [b]follow him." But the people
answered him not a word.
22 Then Elijah said to the people,
[a]"I alone am left a prophet of the
LORD; [b]but Baal's prophets *are*
four hundred and fifty men.
23 "Therefore let them give us two
bulls; and let them choose one bull
for themselves, cut it in pieces, and
lay *it* on the wood, but put no fire
under it; and I will prepare the
other bull, and lay *it* on the wood,
but put no fire *under it.*
24 "Then you call on the name of
your gods, and I will call on the
name of the LORD; and the God
who [a]answers by fire, He is God."
So all the people answered and
said, [1]"It is well spoken."
25 Now Elijah said to the prophets
of Baal, "Choose one bull for your-
selves and prepare *it* first, for you
are many; and call on the name
of your god, but put no fire *under
it.*"
26 So they took the bull which
was given them, and they pre-
pared *it,* and called on the name
of Baal from morning even till
noon, saying, "O Baal, [1]hear us!"

4 [1]Lit. *cut off*
7 [a]2 Kin. 1:6–8
12 [a]2 Kin. 2:16; Ezek. 3:12, 14; Matt. 4:1; Acts 8:39
17 [a]1 Kin. 21:20 [b]Josh. 7:25; Acts 16:20
18 [a]1 Kin. 16:30–33; [2 Chr. 15:2]
19 [a]Josh. 19:26; 2 Kin. 2:25 [b]1 Kin. 16:33 [1]A Canaanite goddess [2]Are provided for by Jezebel
20 [a]1 Kin. 22:6
21 [a]2 Kin. 17:41; [Matt. 6:24] [b]Josh. 24:15
22 [a]1 Kin. 19:10, 14 [b]1 Kin. 18:19
24 [a]1 Kin. 18:38; 1 Chr. 21:26 [1]Lit. *The word is good*
26 [a]Ps. 115:5; Jer. 10:5; [1 Cor. 8:4] [1]*answer*

But *there was* [a]no voice; no one
answered. Then they [2]leaped
about the altar which they had
made.
27 And so it was, at noon, that Eli-
jah mocked them and said, "Cry
[1]aloud, for he *is* a god; either he
is meditating, or he is busy, or he
is on a journey, *or* perhaps he is
sleeping and must be awakened."
28 So they cried aloud, and [a]cut
themselves, as was their custom,
with [1]knives and lances, until the
blood gushed out on them.
29 And when midday was past,
[a]they prophesied until the *time* of
the offering of the *evening* sacri-
fice. But *there was* [b]no voice; no
one answered, no one paid atten-
tion.
30 Then Elijah said to all the peo-
ple, "Come near to me." So all the
people came near to him. [a]And he
repaired the altar of the LORD *that*
was broken down.
31 And Elijah took twelve stones,
according to the number of the
tribes of the sons of Jacob, to
whom the word of the LORD had
come, saying, [a]"Israel shall be
your name."
32 Then with the stones he built
an altar [a]in the name of the LORD;
and he made a trench around the
altar large enough to hold two
seahs of seed.
33 And he [a]put the wood in order,
cut the bull in pieces, and laid *it*
on the wood, and said, "Fill four
waterpots with water, and [b]pour *it*
on the burnt sacrifice and on the
wood."
34 Then he said, "Do *it* a second
time," and they did *it* a second
time; and he said, "Do *it* a third
time," and they did *it* a third time.
35 So the water ran all around the
altar; and he also filled [a]the trench
with water.
36 And it came to pass, at *the time*
of the offering of the *evening* sacri-
fice, that Elijah the prophet came
near and said, "LORD [a]God of
Abraham, Isaac, and Israel, [b]let it
be known this day that You *are*
God in Israel and I *am* Your ser-
vant, and *that* [c]I have done all
these things at Your word.
37 "Hear me, O LORD, hear me,
that this people may know that
You *are* the LORD God, and *that*
You have turned their hearts back
to *You* again."
38 Then [a]the fire of the LORD fell
and consumed the burnt sacrifice,
and the wood and the stones and
the dust, and it licked up the water
that *was* in the trench.
39 Now when all the people saw
it, they fell on their faces; and they
said, [a]"The LORD, He *is* God! The
LORD, He *is* God!"
40 And Elijah said to them,
[a]"Seize the prophets of Baal! Do
not let one of them escape!" So
they seized them; and Elijah
brought them down to the Brook
[b]Kishon and [c]executed them there.

The Drought Ends

41 Then Elijah said to Ahab, "Go
up, eat and drink; for *there is* the
sound of abundance of rain."
42 So Ahab went up to eat and
drink. And Elijah went up to the
top of Carmel; [a]then he bowed
down on the ground, and put his
face between his knees,
43 and said to his servant, "Go up
now, look toward the sea." So he
went up and looked, and said,
"*There is* nothing." And seven
times he said, "Go again."
44 Then it came to pass the sev-
enth *time*, that he said, "There is
a cloud, as small as a man's hand,
rising out of the sea!" So he said,
"Go up, say to Ahab, '[1]Prepare
your chariot, and go down before
the rain stops you.' "
45 Now it happened in the mean-
time that the sky became black
with clouds and wind, and there
was a heavy rain. So Ahab rode
away and went to Jezreel.
46 Then the [a]hand of the LORD
came upon Elijah; and he [b]girded[1]
up his loins and ran ahead of Ahab
to the entrance of Jezreel.

Elijah Escapes from Jezebel

19 And Ahab told Jezebel all
that Elijah had done, also
how he had [a]executed all the
prophets with the sword.
2 Then Jezebel sent a messenger
to Elijah, saying, [a]"So let the gods
do *to me*, and more also, if I do
not make your life as the life of
one of them by tomorrow about
this time."
3 And when he saw *that*, he

26 [2]Lit. *limped about, leaped in dancing around*
27 [1]*with a loud voice*
28 [a][Lev. 19:28; Deut. 14:1] [1]*swords*
29 [a]Ex. 29:39, 41 [b]1 Kin. 18:26
30 [a]1 Kin. 19:10, 14; 2 Chr. 33:16
31 [a]Gen. 32:28; 35:10; 2 Kin. 17:34
32 [a][Ex. 20:25; Col. 3:17]
33 [a]Gen. 22:9; Lev. 1:6–8 [b]Judg. 6:20
35 [a]1 Kin. 18:32, 38
36 [a]Gen. 28:13; Ex. 3:6; 4:5; [Matt. 22:32] [b]1 Kin. 8:43; 2 Kin. 19:19 [c]Num. 16:28
38 [a]Gen. 15:17; Lev. 9:24; 10:1, 2; Judg. 6:21; 2 Kin. 1:12; 1 Chr. 21:26; 2 Chr. 7:1; Job 1:16
39 [a]1 Kin. 18:21, 24
40 [a]2 Kin. 10:25 [b]Judg. 4:7; 5:21 [c][Deut. 13:5; 18:20]
42 [a]James 5:17, 18
44 [1]Lit. *Bind* or *Harness*
46 [a]2 Kin. 3:15; Is. 8:11; Ezek. 3:14 [b]2 Kin. 4:29; 9:1; Jer. 1:17; 1 Pet. 1:13 [1]Tucked the skirts of his robe in his belt in preparation for quick travel

CHAPTER 19

1 [a]1 Kin. 18:40
2 [a]Ruth 1:17; 1 Kin. 20:10; 2 Kin. 6:31

arose and ran for his life, and went
to Beersheba, which *belongs* to Ju-
dah, and left his servant there.
4 But he himself went a day's
journey into the wilderness, and
came and sat down under a
[1]broom tree. And he [a]prayed that
he might die, and said, "It is
enough! Now, LORD, take my life,
for I *am* no better than my fa-
thers!"
5 Then as he lay and slept under
a broom tree, suddenly an [1]angel
touched him, and said to him,
"Arise *and* eat."
6 Then he looked, and there by
his head *was* a cake baked on
[1]coals, and a jar of water. So he
ate and drank, and lay down
again.
7 And the [1]angel of the LORD
came back the second time, and
touched him, and said, "Arise *and*
eat, because the journey *is* too
great for you."
8 So he arose, and ate and drank;
and he went in the strength of that
food forty days and [a]forty nights
as far as [b]Horeb, the mountain of
God.
9 And there he went into a cave,
and spent the night in that place;
and behold, the word of the LORD
came to him, and He said to him,
"What are you doing here, Eli-
jah?"
10 So he said, [a]"I have been very
[b]zealous for the LORD God of hosts;
for the children of Israel have for-
saken Your covenant, torn down
Your altars, and [c]killed Your
prophets with the sword. [d]I alone
am left; and they seek to take my
life."

God's Revelation to Elijah

11 Then He said, "Go out, and
stand [a]on the mountain before the
LORD." And behold, the LORD
[b]passed by, and [c]a great and
strong wind tore into the moun-
tains and broke the rocks in pieces
before the LORD, *but* the LORD *was*
not in the wind; and after the wind
an earthquake, *but* the LORD *was*
not in the earthquake;
12 and after the earthquake a fire,
but the LORD *was* not in the fire;
and after the fire [1]a still small
voice.
13 So it was, when Elijah heard
it, that [a]he wrapped his face in his
mantle and went out and stood in
the entrance of the cave. [b]Sud-
denly a voice *came* to him, and
said, "What are you doing here,
Elijah?"
14 [a]And he said, "I have been very
zealous for the LORD God of hosts;
because the children of Israel have
forsaken Your covenant, torn
down Your altars, and killed Your
prophets with the sword. I alone
am left; and they seek to take my
life."
15 Then the LORD said to him:
"Go, return on your way to the
Wilderness of Damascus; [a]and
when you arrive, anoint Hazael *as*
king over Syria.
16 "Also you shall anoint [a]Jehu
the son of Nimshi *as* king over Is-
rael. And [b]Elisha the son of Sha-
phat of Abel Meholah you shall
anoint *as* prophet in your place.
17 [a]"It shall be *that* whoever es-
capes the sword of Hazael, Jehu
will [b]kill; and whoever escapes the
sword of Jehu, [c]Elisha will kill.
18 [a]"Yet I have reserved seven
thousand in Israel, all whose knees
have not bowed to Baal, [b]and ev-
ery mouth that has not kissed
him."

Elisha Follows Elijah

19 So he departed from there, and
found Elisha the son of Shaphat,
who *was* plowing *with* twelve
yoke *of oxen* before him, and he
was with the twelfth. Then Elijah
passed by him and threw his [a]man-
tle on him.
20 And he left the oxen and ran
after Elijah, and said, [a]"Please let
me kiss my father and my mother,
and *then* I will follow you." And
he said to him, "Go back again,
for what have I done to you?"
21 So *Elisha* turned back from
him, and took a yoke of oxen and
slaughtered them and [a]boiled their
flesh, using the oxen's equipment,
and gave it to the people, and they
ate. Then he arose and followed
Elijah, and became his servant.

Ahab Defeats the Syrians

20 Now [a]Ben-Hadad the king of
Syria gathered all his forces
together; thirty-two kings *were*
with him, with horses and chari-

4 [a]Num. 11:15; Jer. 20:14–18; Jon. 4:3, 8 [1]*juniper*
5 [1]Or *Angel*
6 [1]*hot stones*
7 [1]Or *Angel*
8 [a]Ex. 24:18; 34:28; Deut. 9:9–11, 18; Matt. 4:2 [b]Ex. 3:1; 4:27
10 [a]Rom. 11:3 [b]Num. 25:11, 13; Ps. 69:9 [c]1 Kin. 18:4 [d]1 Kin. 18:22; Rom. 11:3
11 [a]Ex. 19:20; 24:12, 18 [b]Ex. 33:21, 22 [c]Ezek. 1:4; 37:7
12 [1]*a delicate whispering voice*
13 [a]Ex. 3:6; Is. 6:2 [b]1 Kin. 19:9
14 [a]1 Kin. 19:10
15 [a]2 Kin. 8:8–15
16 [a]2 Kin. 9:1–10 [b]1 Kin. 19:19–21; 2 Kin. 2:9–15
17 [a]2 Kin. 8:12; 13:3, 22 [b]2 Kin. 9:14—10:28 [c][Hos. 6:5]
18 [a]Rom. 11:4 [b]Hos. 13:2
19 [a]1 Sam. 28:14; 2 Kin. 2:8, 13, 14
20 [a][Matt. 8:21, 22; Luke 9:61, 62]; Acts 20:37
21 [a]2 Sam. 24:22

CHAPTER 20

1 [a]1 Kin. 15:18, 20; 2 Kin. 6:24

ots. And he went up and besieged
[b]Samaria, and made war against
it.
2 Then he sent messengers into
the city to Ahab king of Israel, and
said to him, "Thus says Ben-
Hadad:
3 'Your silver and your gold *are*
mine; your loveliest wives and
children are mine.' "
4 And the king of Israel an-
swered and said, "My lord, O king,
just as you say, I and all that I have
are yours."
5 Then the messengers came
back and said, "Thus speaks Ben-
Hadad, saying, 'Indeed I have sent
to you, saying, "You shall deliver
to me your silver and your gold,
your wives and your children";
6 'but I will send my servants to
you tomorrow about this time, and
they shall search your house and
the houses of your servants. And
it shall be, *that* whatever is [1]pleas-
ant in your eyes, they will put in
their hands and take *it*.' "
7 So the king of Israel called all
the elders of the land, and said,
"Notice, please, and see how this
man seeks trouble, for he sent to
me for my wives, my children, my
silver, and my gold; and I did not
deny him."
8 And all the elders and all the
people said to him, "Do not listen
or consent."
9 Therefore he said to the mes-
sengers of Ben-Hadad, "Tell my
lord the king, 'All that you sent for
to your servant the first time I will
do, but this thing I cannot do.' "
And the messengers departed and
brought back word to him.
10 Then Ben-Hadad sent to him
and said, [a]"The gods do *so* to me,
and more also, if enough dust is
left of Samaria for a handful for
each of the people [1]who follow
me."
11 So the king of Israel answered
and said, "Tell *him*, 'Let not the
one who puts on *his armor* [a]boast
like the one who takes *it off*.' "
12 And it happened when *Ben-
Hadad* heard this message, as he
and the kings *were* [a]drinking at
the [1]command post, that he said
to his servants, "Get ready." And
they got ready to attack the city.
13 Suddenly a prophet ap-
proached Ahab king of Israel, say-
ing, "Thus says the LORD: 'Have
you seen all this great multitude?
Behold, [a]I will deliver it into your
hand today, and you shall know
that I *am* the LORD.' "
14 So Ahab said, "By whom?"
And he said, "Thus says the LORD:
'By the young leaders of the prov-
inces.' " Then he said, "Who will
set the battle in order?" And he an-
swered, "You."
15 Then he mustered the young
leaders of the provinces, and there
were two hundred and thirty-two;
and after them he mustered all the
people, all the children of Israel—
seven thousand.
16 So they went out at noon.
Meanwhile Ben-Hadad and the
thirty-two kings helping him were
[a]getting drunk at the command
post.
17 The young leaders of the prov-
inces went out first. And Ben-
Hadad sent out *a patrol*, and they
told him, saying, "Men are coming
out of Samaria!"
18 So he said, "If they have come
out for peace, take them alive; and
if they have come out for war, take
them alive."
19 Then these young leaders of
the provinces went out of the city
with the army which followed
them.
20 And each one killed his man;
so the Syrians fled, and Israel pur-
sued them; and Ben-Hadad the
king of Syria escaped on a horse
with the cavalry.
21 Then the king of Israel went
out and attacked the horses and
chariots, and killed the Syrians
with a great slaughter.
22 And the prophet came to the
king of Israel and said to him, "Go,
strengthen yourself; take note, and
see what you should do, [a]for [1]in
the spring of the year the king of
Syria will come up against you."

The Syrians Again Defeated

23 Then the servants of the king
of Syria said to him, "Their gods
are gods of the hills. Therefore
they were stronger than we; but
if we fight against them in the
plain, surely we will be stronger
than they.
24 "So do this thing: Dismiss the

1 [b]1 Kin. 16:24; 2 Kin. 6:24
6 [1]*pleasing*
10 [a]1 Kin. 19:2; 2 Kin. 6:31 [1]Lit. *at my feet*
11 [a]Prov. 27:1; [Eccl. 7:8]
12 [a]1 Kin. 20:16 [1]Lit. *booths* or *shelters*
13 [a]1 Kin. 20:28
16 [a]1 Kin. 16:9; 20:12; [Prov. 20:1]
22 [a]2 Sam. 11:1; 1 Kin. 20:26 [1]Lit. *at the return*

kings, each from his position, and
put captains in their [1]places;
25 "and you shall muster an army
like the army [1]that you have lost,
horse for horse and chariot for
chariot. Then we will fight against
them in the plain; surely we will
be stronger than they." And he lis-
tened to their voice and did so.
26 So it was, in the spring of the
year, that Ben-Hadad mustered
the Syrians and went up to [a]Aphek
to fight against Israel.
27 And the children of Israel were
mustered and given provisions,
and they went against them. Now
the children of Israel encamped
before them like two little flocks
of goats, while the Syrians filled
the [a]countryside.
28 Then a [a]man of God came and
spoke to the king of Israel, and
said, "Thus says the LORD: 'Be-
cause the Syrians have said, "The
LORD *is* God of the hills, but He *is*
not God of the valleys," therefore
[b]I will deliver all this great multi-
tude into your hand, and you shall
know that I *am* the LORD.' "
29 And they encamped opposite
each other for seven days. So it
was that on the seventh day the
battle was joined; and the children
of Israel killed one hundred thou-
sand foot soldiers *of* the Syrians
in one day.
30 But the rest fled to Aphek, into
the city; then a wall fell on twenty-
seven thousand of the men *who*
were left. And Ben-Hadad fled and
went into the city, into an inner
chamber.

Ahab's Treaty with Ben-Hadad

31 Then his servants said to him,
"Look now, we have heard that the
kings of the house of Israel *are*
merciful kings. Please, let us [a]put
sackcloth around our waists and
ropes around our heads, and go
out to the king of Israel; perhaps
he will spare your life."
32 So they wore sackcloth around
their waists and *put* ropes around
their heads, and came to the king
of Israel and said, "Your servant
Ben-Hadad says, 'Please let me
live.' " And he said, "*Is* he still
alive? He *is* my brother."
33 Now the men were watching
closely to see whether *any sign of*
mercy would come from him; and
they quickly grasped *at this word*
and said, "Your brother Ben-
Hadad." So he said, "Go, bring
him." Then Ben-Hadad came out
to him; and he had him come up
into the chariot.
34 So *Ben-Hadad* said to him,
[a]"The cities which my father took
from your father I will restore; and
you may set up marketplaces for
yourself in Damascus, as my fa-
ther did in Samaria." Then *Ahab*
said, "I will send you away with
this treaty." So he made a treaty
with him and sent him away.

Ahab Condemned

35 Now a certain man of [a]the sons
of the prophets said to his neigh-
bor [b]by the word of the LORD,
"Strike me, please." And the man
refused to strike him.
36 Then he said to him, "Because
you have not obeyed the voice of
the LORD, surely, as soon as you
depart from me, a lion shall kill
you." And as soon as he left him,
[a]a lion found him and killed him.
37 And he found another man,
and said, "Strike me, please." So
the man struck him, inflicting a
wound.
38 Then the prophet departed and
waited for the king by the road,
and disguised himself with a ban-
dage over his eyes.
39 Now [a]as the king passed by, he
cried out to the king and said,
"Your servant went out into the
midst of the battle; and there, a
man came over and brought a man
to me, and said, 'Guard this man;
if by any means he is missing,
[b]your life shall be for his life, or
else you shall [1]pay a talent of sil-
ver.'
40 "While your servant was busy
here and there, he was gone."
Then the king of Israel said to him,
"So *shall* your judgment *be;* you
yourself have decided *it.*"
41 And he hastened to take the
bandage away from his eyes; and
the king of Israel recognized him
as one of the prophets.
42 Then he said to him, "Thus
says the LORD: [a]'Because you have
let slip out of *your* hand a man
whom I appointed to utter destruc-
tion, therefore your life shall go for

24 [1]*positions*
25 [1]Lit. *that fell from you*
26 [a]Josh. 13:4; 2 Kin. 13:17
27 [a]Judg. 6:3–5; 1 Sam. 13:5–8
28 [a]1 Kin. 17:18 [b]1 Kin. 20:13
31 [a]Gen. 37:34; 2 Sam. 3:31
34 [a]1 Kin. 15:20
35 [a]2 Kin. 2:3, 5, 7, 15 [b]1 Kin. 13:17, 18
36 [a]1 Kin. 13:24
39 [a]2 Sam. 12:1 [b]2 Kin. 10:24 [1]Lit. *weigh*
42 [a]1 Kin. 22:31–37

his life, and your people for his
people.' "
43 So the king of Israel [a]went to
his house sullen and displeased,
and came to Samaria.

Naboth Is Murdered for His Vineyard

21 And it came to pass after
these things *that* Naboth the
Jezreelite had a vineyard which
was in [a]Jezreel, next to the palace
of Ahab king of Samaria.
2 So Ahab spoke to Naboth, say-
ing, "Give me your [a]vineyard, that
I may have it for a vegetable gar-
den, because it *is* near, next to my
house; and for it I will give you a
vineyard better than it. *Or,* if it
seems good to you, I will give you
its worth in money."
3 But Naboth said to Ahab, "The
LORD forbid [a]that I should give the
inheritance of my fathers to you!"
4 So Ahab went into his house
sullen and displeased because of
the word which Naboth the
Jezreelite had spoken to him; for
he had said, "I will not give you
the inheritance of my fathers."
And he lay down on his bed, and
turned away his face, and would
eat no food.
5 But [a]Jezebel his wife came to
him, and said to him, "Why is your
spirit so sullen that you eat no
food?"
6 He said to her, "Because I
spoke to Naboth the Jezreelite,
and said to him, 'Give me your
vineyard for money; or else, if it
pleases you, I will give you *an-
other* vineyard for it.' And he an-
swered, 'I will not give you my
vineyard.' "
7 Then Jezebel his wife said to
him, "You now exercise authority
over Israel! Arise, eat food, and let
your heart be cheerful; I will give
you the vineyard of Naboth the
Jezreelite."
8 And she wrote letters in Ahab's
name, sealed *them* with his seal,
and sent the letters to the elders
and the nobles who *were* dwelling
in the city with Naboth.
9 She wrote in the letters, saying,

Proclaim a fast, and seat
Naboth [1]with high honor
among the people;
10 and seat two men, scoundrels,
before him to bear witness
against him, saying, "You have
[a]blasphemed God and the
king." *Then* take him out, and
[b]stone him, that he may die.

11 So the men of his city, the el-
ders and nobles who were inhab-
itants of his city, did as Jezebel
had sent to them, as it *was* written
in the letters which she had sent
to them.
12 [a]They proclaimed a fast, and
seated Naboth with high honor
among the people.
13 And two men, scoundrels,
came in and sat before him; and
the scoundrels [a]witnessed against
him, against Naboth, in the pres-
ence of the people, saying, "Na-
both has blasphemed God and the
king!" [b]Then they took him out-
side the city and stoned him with
stones, so that he died.
14 Then they sent to Jezebel, say-
ing, "Naboth has been stoned and
is dead."
15 And it came to pass, when Jez-
ebel heard that Naboth had been
stoned and was dead, that Jezebel
said to Ahab, "Arise, take posses-
sion of the vineyard of Naboth the
Jezreelite, which he refused to
give you for money; for Naboth is
not alive, but dead."
16 So it was, when Ahab heard
that Naboth was dead, that Ahab
got up and went down to take pos-
session of the vineyard of Naboth
the Jezreelite.

The LORD Condemns Ahab

17 [a]Then the word of the LORD
came to [b]Elijah the Tishbite, say-
ing,
18 "Arise, go down to meet Ahab
king of Israel, [a]who *lives* in Sa-
maria. There *he is,* in the vineyard
of Naboth, where he has gone
down to take possession of it.
19 "You shall speak to him, say-
ing, 'Thus says the LORD: "Have
you murdered and also taken pos-
session?" ' And you shall speak to
him, saying, 'Thus says the LORD:
[a]"In the place where dogs licked
the blood of Naboth, dogs shall
lick your blood, even yours." ' "
20 So Ahab said to Elijah, [a]"Have
you found me, O my enemy?" And
he answered, "I have found *you,*

43 [a]1 Kin. 21:4
CHAPTER 21
1 [a]Judg. 6:33; 1 Kin. 18:45, 46
2 [a]1 Sam. 8:14
3 [a][Lev. 25:23; Num. 36:7; Ezek. 46:18]
5 [a]1 Kin. 19:1, 2
9 [1]Lit. *at the head*
10 [a][Ex. 22:28; Lev. 24:15, 16]; Acts 6:11 [b][Lev. 24:14]
12 [a]Is. 58:4
13 [a][Ex. 20:16; 23:1, 7] [b]2 Kin. 9:26; 2 Chr. 24:21; Acts 7:58, 59; Heb. 11:37
17 [a][Ps. 9:12] [b]1 Kin. 19:1
18 [a]1 Kin. 13:32; 2 Chr. 22:9
19 [a]1 Kin. 22:38; 2 Kin. 9:26
20 [a]1 Kin. 18:17

because [b]you have sold yourself to
do evil in the sight of the LORD:
21 'Behold, [a]I will bring calamity
on you. I will take away your [b]pos-
terity, and will cut off from Ahab
[c]every male in Israel, both [d]bond
and free.
22 'I will make your house like the
house of [a]Jeroboam the son of Ne-
bat, and like the house of [b]Baasha
the son of Ahijah, because of the
provocation with which you have
provoked *Me* to anger, and made
Israel sin.'
23 "And [a]concerning Jezebel the
LORD also spoke, saying, 'The dogs
shall eat Jezebel by the [1]wall of
Jezreel.'
24 "The dogs shall eat [a]whoever
belongs to Ahab and dies in the
city, and the birds of the air shall
eat whoever dies in the field."
25 But [a]there was no one like
Ahab who sold himself to do wick-
edness in the sight of the LORD,
[b]because Jezebel his wife [1]stirred
him up.
26 And he behaved very abomin-
ably in following idols, according
to all [a]*that* the Amorites had done,
whom the LORD had cast out be-
fore the children of Israel.
27 So it was, when Ahab heard
those words, that he tore his
clothes and [a]put sackcloth on his
body, and fasted and lay in sack-
cloth, and went about mourning.
28 And the word of the LORD came
to Elijah the Tishbite, saying,
29 "See how Ahab has humbled
himself before Me? Because he
[a]has humbled himself before Me,
I will not bring the calamity in his
days. [b]In the days of his son I will
bring the calamity on his house."

Micaiah Warns Ahab

22 Now three years passed
without war between Syria
and Israel.
2 Then it came to pass, in the
third year, that [a]Jehoshaphat the
king of Judah went down to *visit*
the king of Israel.
3 And the king of Israel said to
his servants, "Do you know that
[a]Ramoth in Gilead *is* ours, but we
hesitate to take it out of the hand
of the king of Syria?"
4 So he said to Jehoshaphat,
"Will you go with me to fight at

20 [b]1 Kin. 21:25; 2 Kin. 17:17; [Rom. 7:14]
21 [a]1 Kin. 14:10; 2 Kin. 9:8 [b]2 Kin. 10:10 [c]1 Sam. 25:22 [d]1 Kin. 14:10
22 [a]1 Kin. 15:29 [b]1 Kin. 16:3, 11
23 [a]2 Kin. 9:10, 30–37 [1]So with MT, LXX; some Heb. mss., Syr., Tg., Vg. *plot of ground* instead of *wall* (cf. 2 Kin. 9:36)
24 [a]1 Kin. 14:11; 16:4
25 [a]1 Kin. 16:30–33; 21:20 [b]1 Kin. 16:31 [1]*incited him*
26 [a]Gen. 15:16; [Lev. 18:25–30]; 2 Kin. 21:11
27 [a]Gen. 37:34; 2 Sam. 3:31; 2 Kin. 6:30
29 [a][2 Kin. 22:19] [b]2 Kin. 9:25; 10:11, 17

CHAPTER 22

2 [a]1 Kin. 15:24; 2 Chr. 18:2
3 [a]Deut. 4:43; Josh. 21:38; 1 Kin. 4:13
4 [a]2 Kin. 3:7
5 [a]2 Kin. 3:11
6 [a]1 Kin. 18:19 [1]The false prophets
7 [a]2 Kin. 3:11 [1]Or *him*
11 [a]Zech. 1:18–21 [b]Deut. 33:17
14 [a]Num. 22:38; 24:13

Ramoth Gilead?" Jehoshaphat
said to the king of Israel, [a]"I *am*
as you *are*, my people as your peo-
ple, my horses as your horses."
5 Also Jehoshaphat said to the
king of Israel, [a]"Please inquire for
the word of the LORD today."
6 Then the king of Israel [a]gath-
ered [1]the prophets together, about
four hundred men, and said to
them, "Shall I go against Ramoth
Gilead to fight, or shall I refrain?"
So they said, "Go up, for the Lord
will deliver *it* into the hand of the
king."
7 And [a]Jehoshaphat said, "*Is*
there not still a prophet of the
LORD here, that we may inquire of
[1]Him?"
8 So the king of Israel said to Je-
hoshaphat, "*There is* still one man,
Micaiah the son of Imlah, by
whom we may inquire of the LORD;
but I hate him, because he does not
prophesy good concerning me, but
evil." And Jehoshaphat said, "Let
not the king say such things!"
9 Then the king of Israel called
an officer and said, "Bring Micaiah
the son of Imlah quickly!"
10 The king of Israel and Jehosh-
aphat the king of Judah, having
put on *their* robes, sat each on his
throne, at a threshing floor at the
entrance of the gate of Samaria;
and all the prophets prophesied
before them.
11 Now Zedekiah the son of Che-
naanah had made [a]horns of iron
for himself; and he said, "Thus
says the LORD: 'With these you
shall [b]gore the Syrians until they
are destroyed.'"
12 And all the prophets prophe-
sied so, saying, "Go up to Ramoth
Gilead and prosper, for the LORD
will deliver *it* into the king's
hand."
13 Then the messenger who had
gone to call Micaiah spoke to him,
saying, "Now listen, the words of
the prophets with one accord en-
courage the king. Please, let your
word be like the word of one of
them, and speak encouragement."
14 And Micaiah said, "*As* the
LORD lives, [a]whatever the LORD
says to me, that I will speak."
15 Then he came to the king; and
the king said to him, "Micaiah,
shall we go to war against Ramoth

Gilead, or shall we refrain?" And
he answered him, "Go and pros-
per, for the LORD will deliver *it* into
the hand of the king!"
16 So the king said to him, "How
many times shall I make you
swear that you tell me nothing
but the truth in the name of the
LORD?"
17 Then he said, "I saw all Israel
[a]scattered on the mountains, as
sheep that have no shepherd. And
the LORD said, 'These have no mas-
ter. Let each return to his house
in peace.'"
18 And the king of Israel said to
Jehoshaphat, "Did I not tell you he
would not prophesy good concern-
ing me, but evil?"
19 Then *Micaiah* said, "Therefore
hear the word of the LORD: [a]I saw
the LORD sitting on His throne,
[b]and all the host of heaven stand-
ing by, on His right hand and on
His left.
20 "And the LORD said, 'Who will
persuade Ahab to go up, that he
may fall at Ramoth Gilead?' So
one spoke in this manner, and an-
other spoke in that manner.
21 "Then a spirit came forward
and stood before the LORD, and
said, 'I will persuade him.'
22 "The LORD said to him, 'In what
way?' So he said, 'I will go out
and be a lying spirit in the mouth
of all his prophets.' And the LORD
said, [a]'You shall persuade *him*,
and also prevail. Go out and do so.'
23 [a]"Therefore look! The LORD
has put a lying spirit in the mouth
of all these prophets of yours, and
the LORD has declared disaster
against you."
24 Now Zedekiah the son of Che-
naanah went near and [a]struck
Micaiah on the cheek, and said,
[b]"Which way did the spirit from
the LORD go from me to speak to
you?"
25 And Micaiah said, "Indeed,
you shall see on that day when
you go into an [a]inner chamber to
hide!"
26 So the king of Israel said,
"Take Micaiah, and return him to
Amon the governor of the city and
to Joash the king's son;
27 "and say, 'Thus says the king:
"Put this *fellow* in [a]prison, and
feed him with bread of affliction
and water of affliction, until I come
in peace."'"
28 But Micaiah said, "If you ever
return in peace, [a]the LORD has not
spoken by me." And he said,
"Take heed, all you people!"

Ahab Dies in Battle

29 So the king of Israel and Je-
hoshaphat the king of Judah went
up to Ramoth Gilead.
30 And the king of Israel said to
Jehoshaphat, "I will disguise my-
self and go into battle; but you put
on your robes." So the king of Is-
rael [a]disguised himself and went
into battle.
31 Now the [a]king of Syria had
commanded the thirty-two [b]cap-
tains of his chariots, saying, "Fight
with no one small or great, but
only with the king of Israel."
32 So it was, when the captains of
the chariots saw Jehoshaphat, that
they said, "Surely it *is* the king of
Israel!" Therefore they turned
aside to fight against him, and Je-
hoshaphat [a]cried out.
33 And it happened, when the
captains of the chariots saw that
it *was* not the king of Israel, that
they turned back from pursuing
him.
34 Now a *certain* man drew a bow
at random, and struck the king of
Israel between the joints of his ar-
mor. So he said to the driver of
his chariot, "Turn around and take
me out of the battle, for I am
wounded."
35 The battle increased that day;
and the king was propped up in
his chariot, facing the Syrians, and
died at evening. The blood ran out
from the wound onto the floor of
the chariot.
36 Then, as the sun was going
down, a shout went throughout the
army, saying, "Every man to his
city, and every man to his own
country!"
37 So the king died, and was
brought to Samaria. And they bur-
ied the king in Samaria.
38 Then *someone* washed the
chariot at a pool in Samaria, and
the dogs licked up his blood while
[1]the harlots bathed, according [a]to
the word of the LORD which He had
spoken.
39 Now the rest of the acts of

17 [a]Num. 27:17; 1 Kin. 22:34–36; 2 Chr. 18:16; Matt. 9:36; Mark 6:34
19 [a]Is. 6:1; Ezek. 1:26–28; Dan. 7:9 [b]Job 1:6; 2:1; Ps. 103:20; Dan. 7:10; Zech. 1:10; [Matt. 18:10; Heb. 1:7, 14]
22 [a]Judg. 9:23; 1 Sam. 16:14; 18:10; 19:9; Job 12:16; [Ezek. 14:9; 2 Thess. 2:11]
23 [a][Ezek. 14:9]
24 [a]Jer. 20:2 [b]2 Chr. 18:23
25 [a]1 Kin. 20:30
27 [a]2 Chr. 16:10; 18:25–27
28 [a]Num. 16:29; Deut. 18:20–22
30 [a]2 Chr. 35:22
31 [a]1 Kin. 20:1 [b]1 Kin. 20:24; 2 Chr. 18:30
32 [a]2 Chr. 18:31
38 [a]1 Kin. 21:19 [1]Tg., Syr. *they washed his armor*

Ahab, and all that he did, [a]the
ivory house which he built and all
the cities that he built, *are* they not
written in the book of the chroni-
cles of the kings of Israel?
40 So Ahab [1]rested with his fa-
thers. Then [a]Ahaziah his son
reigned in his place.

Jehoshaphat Reigns in Judah

41 [a]Jehoshaphat the son of Asa
had become king over Judah in
the fourth year of Ahab king of
Israel.
42 Jehoshaphat *was* thirty-five
years old when he became king,
and he reigned twenty-five years
in Jerusalem. His mother's name
was Azubah the daughter of
Shilhi.
43 And [a]he walked in all the ways
of his father Asa. He did not turn
aside from them, doing *what was*
right in the eyes of the LORD. Nev-
ertheless [b]the high places were not
taken away, *for* the people offered
sacrifices and burned incense on
the high places.
44 Also [a]Jehoshaphat made
[b]peace with the king of Israel.
45 Now the rest of the acts of Je-
hoshaphat, the might that he
showed, and how he made war,
are they not written [a]in the book
of the chronicles of the kings of
Judah?
46 [a]And the rest of the [1]perverted
persons, who remained in the days

39 [a]Ps. 45:8; Amos 3:15
40 [a]2 Kin. 1:2, 18 [1]Died and joined his ancestors
41 [a]2 Chr. 20:31
43 [a]2 Chr. 17:3; 20:32, 33 [b]1 Kin. 14:23; 15:14; 2 Kin. 12:3
44 [a]2 Chr. 19:2 [b]2 Chr. 18:1
45 [a]2 Chr. 20:34
46 [a]Gen. 19:5; Deut. 23:17; 1 Kin. 14:24; 15:12; 2 Kin. 23:7; Jude 7 [1]Heb. *qadesh*, one practicing sodomy and prostitution in religious rituals
47 [a]2 Sam. 8:14; 2 Kin. 3:9; 8:20
48 [a]2 Chr. 20:35–37 [b]1 Kin. 10:22 [c]1 Kin. 9:28 [d]2 Chr. 20:37 [e]1 Kin. 9:26 [1]Or *ships of Tarshish*
50 [a]2 Chr. 21:1 [1]Died and joined his ancestors
51 [a]1 Kin. 22:40
52 [a]1 Kin. 15:26; 21:25
53 [a]Judg. 2:11 [b]1 Kin. 16:30–32 [1]In the same way that

of his father Asa, he banished from
the land.
47 [a]*There was* then no king in
Edom, only a deputy of the
king.
48 [a]Jehoshaphat [b]made [1]mer-
chant ships to go to [c]Ophir for
gold; [d]but they never sailed, for the
ships were wrecked at [e]Ezion Ge-
ber.
49 Then Ahaziah the son of Ahab
said to Jehoshaphat, "Let my ser-
vants go with your servants in the
ships." But Jehoshaphat would
not.
50 And [a]Jehoshaphat [1]rested with
his fathers, and was buried with
his fathers in the City of David his
father. Then Jehoram his son
reigned in his place.

Ahaziah Reigns in Israel

51 [a]Ahaziah the son of Ahab be-
came king over Israel in Samaria
in the seventeenth year of Je-
hoshaphat king of Judah, and
reigned two years over Israel.
52 He did evil in the sight of the
LORD, and [a]walked in the way of
his father and in the way of his
mother and in the way of Jero-
boam the son of Nebat, who had
made Israel sin;
53 for [a]he served Baal and wor-
shiped him, and provoked the
LORD God of Israel to anger, [b]ac-
cording[1] to all that his father had
done.

The Second Book of the

Kings

THE Book of Second Kings continues the drama begun in First Kings—the tragic history of two nations on a collision course with captivity. The author systematically traces the reigning monarchs of Israel and Judah, first by carrying one nation's history forward, then retracing the same period for the other nation.

Nineteen consecutive evil kings rule in Israel, leading to the captivity by Assyria. The picture is somewhat brighter in Judah, where godly kings occasionally emerge to reform the evils of their predecessors. In the end, however, sin outweighs righteousness and Judah is marched off to Babylon.

God Judges Ahaziah

MOAB [a]rebelled against Israel [b]after the death of Ahab.
2 Now [a]Ahaziah fell through the
lattice of his upper room in Samaria, and was injured; so he sent messengers and said to them, "Go, inquire of [b]Baal-Zebub,[1] the god of [c]Ekron, whether I shall recover from this injury."
3 But the [1]angel of the LORD said
to Elijah the Tishbite, "Arise, go up to meet the messengers of the king of Samaria, and say to them, '*Is it* because *there is* no God in Israel *that* you are going to inquire of Baal-Zebub, the god of Ekron?'
4 "Now therefore, thus says the
LORD: 'You shall not come down from the bed to which you have gone up, but you shall surely die.'" So Elijah departed.
5 And when the messengers re-
turned to [1]him, he said to them, "Why have you come back?"
6 So they said to him, "A man
came up to meet us, and said to us, 'Go, return to the king who sent you, and say to him, "Thus says the LORD: '*Is it* because *there is* no God in Israel *that* you are sending to inquire of Baal-Zebub, the god of Ekron? Therefore you shall not come down from the bed to which you have gone up, but you shall surely die.'"'"
7 Then he said to them, "What
kind of man *was it* who came up to meet you and told you these words?"
8 So they answered him, [a]"A
hairy man wearing a leather belt around his waist." And he said, [b]"It *is* Elijah the Tishbite."
9 Then the king sent to him a
captain of fifty with his fifty men. So he went up to him; and there he was, sitting on the top of a hill. And he spoke to him: "Man of God, the king has said, 'Come down!'"
10 So Elijah answered and said to
the captain of fifty, "If I *am* a man of God, then [a]let fire come down from heaven and consume you and your fifty men." And fire came down from heaven and consumed him and his fifty.
11 Then he sent to him another
captain of fifty with his fifty men. And he answered and said to him: "Man of God, thus has the king said, 'Come down quickly!'"
12 So Elijah answered and said to
them, "If I *am* a man of God, let fire come down from heaven and consume you and your fifty men." And the fire of God came down from heaven and consumed him and his fifty.
13 Again, he sent a third captain
of fifty with his fifty men. And the third captain of fifty went up, and came and [1]fell on his knees before Elijah, and pleaded with him, and said to him: "Man of God, please let my life and the life of these fifty servants of yours [a]be precious in your sight.
14 "Look, fire has come down
from heaven and burned up the first two captains of fifties with their fifties. But let my life now be precious in your sight."
15 And the [1]angel of the LORD said

CHAPTER 1
1 [a]2 Sam. 8:2 [b]2 Kin. 3:5
2 [a]1 Kin. 22:40 [b]2 Kin. 1:3, 6, 16; Matt. 10:25; Mark 3:22 [c]1 Sam. 5:10 [1]Lit. *Lord of Flies*
3 [1]Or *Angel*
5 [1]Ahaziah
8 [a]Zech. 13:4; Matt. 3:4; Mark 1:6 [b]1 Kin. 18:7
10 [a]1 Kin. 18:36–38; Luke 9:54
13 [a]1 Sam. 26:21; Ps. 72:14 [1]Lit. *bowed down*
15 [1]Or *Angel*

to Elijah, "Go down with him; do
not be afraid of him." So he arose
and went down with him to the
king.
16 Then he said to him, "Thus
says the LORD: 'Because you have
sent messengers to inquire of Baal-
Zebub, the god of Ekron, *is it* be-
cause *there is* no God in Israel to
inquire of His word? Therefore
you shall not come down from the
bed to which you have gone up,
but you shall surely die.' "
17 So *Ahaziah* died according to
the word of the LORD which Elijah
had spoken. Because he had no
son, [a]Jehoram[1] became king in his
place, in the second year of Jeho-
ram the son of Jehoshaphat, king
of Judah.
18 Now the rest of the acts of Aha-
ziah which he did, *are* they not
written in the book of the chroni-
cles of the kings of Israel?

Elijah Ascends to Heaven

2 And it came to pass, when the
LORD was about to [a]take up Eli-
jah into heaven by a whirlwind,
that Elijah went with [b]Elisha from
Gilgal.
2 Then Elijah said to Elisha,
[a]"Stay here, please, for the LORD
has sent me on to Bethel." But Eli-
sha said, "*As* the LORD lives, and
[b]*as* your soul lives, I will not leave
you!" So they went down to
Bethel.
3 Now [a]the sons of the prophets
who *were* at Bethel came out to
Elisha, and said to him, "Do you
know that the LORD will take away
your master [1]from over you to-
day?" And he said, "Yes, I know;
keep silent!"
4 Then Elijah said to him, "Eli-
sha, stay here, please, for the LORD
has sent me on to Jericho." But he
said, "*As* the LORD lives, and *as*
your soul lives, I will not leave
you!" So they came to Jericho.
5 Now the sons of the prophets
who *were* at Jericho came to Eli-
sha and said to him, "Do you know
that the LORD will take away your
master from over you today?" So
he answered, "Yes, I know; keep
silent!"
6 Then Elijah said to him, "Stay
here, please, for the LORD has sent
me on to the Jordan." But he said,

17 [a]1 Kin. 22:50; 2 Kin. 8:16; Matt. 1:8 [1]The son of Ahab king of Israel, 2 Kin. 3:1

CHAPTER 2

1 [a]Gen. 5:24; [Heb. 11:5] [b]1 Kin. 19:16–21

2 [a]Ruth 1:15, 16 [b]1 Sam. 1:26; 2 Kin. 2:4, 6; 4:30

3 [a]1 Kin. 20:35; 2 Kin. 2:5, 7, 15; 4:1, 38; 9:1 [1]Lit. *from your head*

8 [a]Ex. 14:21, 22; Josh. 3:16; 2 Kin. 2:14 [b]Josh. 3:17

11 [a]2 Kin. 6:17; Ps. 104:4 [b]Gen. 5:24; Heb. 11:5

12 [a]2 Kin. 13:14

14 [a]2 Kin. 2:8

15 [a]2 Kin. 2:7 [1]Or *at Jericho opposite him saw*

16 [a]1 Kin. 18:12; Ezek. 8:3; Acts 8:39

"*As* the LORD lives, and *as* your
soul lives, I will not leave you!" So
the two of them went on.
7 And fifty men of the sons of the
prophets went and stood facing
them at a distance, while the two
of them stood by the Jordan.
8 Now Elijah took his mantle,
rolled *it* up, and struck the water;
and [a]it was divided this way and
that, so that the two of them
crossed over on dry [b]ground.
9 And so it was, when they had
crossed over, that Elijah said to
Elisha, "Ask! What may I do for
you, before I am taken away from
you?" Elisha said, "Please let a
double portion of your spirit be
upon me."
10 So he said, "You have asked a
hard thing. *Nevertheless,* if you
see me *when I am* taken from you,
it shall be so for you; but if not, it
shall not be *so.*"
11 Then it happened, as they con-
tinued on and talked, that sud-
denly [a]a chariot of fire *appeared*
with horses of fire, and separated
the two of them; and Elijah [b]went
up by a whirlwind into heaven.
12 And Elisha saw *it,* and he cried
out, [a]"My father, my father, the
chariot of Israel and its horse-
men!" So he saw him no more.
And he took hold of his own
clothes and tore them into two
pieces.
13 He also took up the mantle of
Elijah that had fallen from him,
and went back and stood by the
bank of the Jordan.
14 Then he took the mantle of Eli-
jah that had fallen from him, and
struck the water, and said, "Where
is the LORD God of Elijah?" And
when he also had struck the water,
[a]it was divided this way and that;
and Elisha crossed over.
15 Now when the sons of the
prophets who *were* [a]from[1] Jericho
saw him, they said, "The spirit of
Elijah rests on Elisha." And they
came to meet him, and bowed to
the ground before him.
16 Then they said to him, "Look
now, there are fifty strong men
with your servants. Please let them
go and search for your master,
[a]lest perhaps the Spirit of the LORD
has taken him up and cast him
upon some mountain or into some

valley." And he said, "You shall
not send anyone."
17 But when they urged him till
he was [a]ashamed, he said, "Send
them!" Therefore they sent fifty
men, and they searched for three
days but did not find him.
18 And when they came back to
him, for he had stayed in Jericho,
he said to them, "Did I not say to
you, 'Do not go'?"

Elisha Performs Miracles

19 Then the men of the city said
to Elisha, "Please notice, the situa-
tion of this city *is* pleasant, as my
lord sees; but the water *is* bad, and
the ground barren."
20 And he said, "Bring me a new
bowl, and put salt in it." So they
brought *it* to him.
21 Then he went out to the source
of the water, and [a]cast in the salt
there, and said, "Thus says the
LORD: 'I have [1]healed this water;
from it there shall be no more
death or barrenness.' "
22 So the water remains [a]healed
to this day, according to the word
of Elisha which he spoke.
23 Then he went up from there to
Bethel; and as he was going up the
road, some youths came from the
city and mocked him, and said to
him, "Go up, you baldhead! Go up,
you baldhead!"
24 So he turned around and
looked at them, and [a]pronounced
a curse on them in the name of the
LORD. And two female bears came
out of the woods and mauled forty-
two of the youths.
25 Then he went from there to
[a]Mount Carmel, and from there he
returned to Samaria.

Moab Rebels Against Israel

3 Now [a]Jehoram the son of Ahab
became king over Israel at Sa-
maria in the eighteenth year of Je-
hoshaphat king of Judah, and
reigned twelve years.
2 And he did evil in the sight of
the LORD, but not like his father
and mother; for he put away the
sacred pillar of Baal [a]that his fa-
ther had made.
3 Nevertheless he persisted in
[a]the sins of Jeroboam the son of
Nebat, who had made Israel sin;
he did not depart from them.
4 Now Mesha king of Moab was
a sheepbreeder, and he [a]regularly
paid the king of Israel one hun-
dred thousand [b]lambs and the
wool of one hundred thousand
rams.
5 But it happened, when [a]Ahab
died, that the king of Moab re-
belled against the king of Israel.
6 So King Jehoram went out of
Samaria at that time and mustered
all Israel.
7 Then he went and sent to Je-
hoshaphat king of Judah, saying,
"The king of Moab has rebelled
against me. Will you go with me
to fight against Moab?" And he
said, "I will go up; [a]I *am* as you
are, my people as your people, my
horses as your horses."
8 Then he said, "Which way
shall we go up?" And he answered,
"By way of the Wilderness of
Edom."
9 So the king of Israel went with
the king of Judah and the king of
Edom, and they marched on that
roundabout route seven days; and
there was no water for the army,
nor for the animals that followed
them.
10 And the king of Israel said,
"Alas! For the LORD has called
these three kings together to de-
liver them into the hand of Moab."
11 But [a]Jehoshaphat said, "*Is
there* no prophet of the LORD here,
that we may inquire of the LORD
by him?" So one of the servants
of the king of Israel answered and
said, "Elisha the son of Shaphat
is here, who [b]poured[1] water on the
hands of Elijah."
12 And Jehoshaphat said, "The
word of the LORD is with him." So
the king of Israel and Jehoshaphat
and the king of Edom [a]went down
to him.
13 Then Elisha said to the king of
Israel, [a]"What have I to do with
you? [b]Go to [c]the prophets of your
father and the [d]prophets of your
mother." But the king of Israel
said to him, "No, for the LORD has
called these three kings *together*
to deliver them into the hand of
Moab."
14 And Elisha said, [a]"*As* the LORD
of hosts lives, before whom I
stand, surely were it not that I re-
gard the presence of Jehoshaphat

17 [a]2 Kin. 8:11
21 [a]Ex. 15:25, 26; 2 Kin. 4:41; 6:6; John 9:6 [1]*purified*
22 [a]Ezek. 47:8, 9
24 [a]Deut. 27:13–26
25 [a]1 Kin. 18:19, 20; 2 Kin. 4:25

CHAPTER 3
1 [a]2 Kin. 1:17
2 [a]1 Kin. 16:31, 32
3 [a]1 Kin. 12:28–32
4 [a]2 Sam. 8:2 [b]Is. 16:1, 2
5 [a]2 Kin. 1:1
7 [a]1 Kin. 22:4
11 [a]1 Kin. 22:7 [b]1 Kin. 19:21; [John 13:4, 5, 13, 14] [1]Was the personal servant of
12 [a]2 Kin. 2:25
13 [a][Ezek. 14:3] [b]Judg. 10:14; Ruth 1:15 [c]1 Kin. 22:6–11 [d]1 Kin. 18:19
14 [a]1 Kin. 17:1; 2 Kin. 5:16

king of Judah, I would not look at
you, nor see you.
15 "But now bring me [a]a musi-
cian." Then it happened, when the
musician [b]played, that [c]the hand
of the LORD came upon him.
16 And he said, "Thus says the
LORD: [a]'Make this valley full of
[1]ditches.'
17 "For thus says the LORD: 'You
shall not see wind, nor shall you
see rain; yet that valley shall be
filled with water, so that you, your
cattle, and your animals may
drink.'
18 "And this is a simple matter in
the sight of the LORD; He will also
deliver the Moabites into your
hand.
19 "Also you shall attack every
fortified city and every choice city,
and shall cut down every good
tree, and stop up every spring of
water, and ruin every good piece
of land with stones."
20 Now it happened in the morn-
ing, when [a]the grain offering was
offered, that suddenly water came
by way of Edom, and the land was
filled with water.
21 And when all the Moabites
heard that the kings had come up
to fight against them, all who were
able to bear arms and older were
[1]gathered; and they stood at the
border.
22 Then they rose up early in the
morning, and the sun was shining
on the water; and the Moabites
saw the water on the other side *as*
red as blood.
23 And they said, "This is blood;
the kings have surely struck
swords and have killed one an-
other; now therefore, Moab, to the
spoil!"
24 So when they came to the camp
of Israel, Israel rose up and at-
tacked the Moabites, so that they
fled before them; and they entered
their land, killing the Moabites.
25 Then they destroyed the cities,
and each man threw a stone on ev-
ery good piece of land and filled
it; and they stopped up all the
springs of water and cut down all
the good trees. But they left the
stones of [a]Kir Haraseth *intact*.
However the slingers surrounded
and attacked it.
26 And when the king of Moab

15 [a]1 Sam. 10:5 [b]1 Sam. 16:16, 23; 1 Chr. 25:1 [c]Ezek. 1:3; 3:14, 22; 8:1
16 [a]Jer. 14:3 [1]*water canals*
20 [a]Ex. 29:39, 40
21 [1]*summoned*
25 [a]Is. 16:7, 11; Jer. 48:31, 36
27 [a][Deut. 18:10; Amos 2:1; Mic. 6:7] [b]2 Kin. 8:20 [1]*wrath*

CHAPTER 4

1 [a]1 Kin. 20:35; 2 Kin. 2:3 [b][Lev. 25:39–41, 48]; 1 Sam. 22:2; Neh. 5:2–5; Matt. 18:25
3 [a]2 Kin. 3:16
8 [a]Josh. 19:18 [1]Lit. *great* [2]Lit. *laid hold on him*

saw that the battle was too fierce
for him, he took with him seven
hundred men who drew swords, to
break through to the king of
Edom, but they could not.
27 Then [a]he took his eldest son
who would have reigned in his
place, and offered him *as* a burnt
offering upon the wall; and there
was great [1]indignation against Is-
rael. [b]So they departed from him
and returned to *their own* land.

Elisha and the Widow's Oil

4 A certain woman of the wives
of [a]the sons of the prophets
cried out to Elisha, saying, "Your
servant my husband is dead, and
you know that your servant feared
the LORD. And the creditor is com-
ing [b]to take my two sons to be his
slaves."
2 So Elisha said to her, "What
shall I do for you? Tell me, what
do you have in the house?" And
she said, "Your maidservant has
nothing in the house but a jar of
oil."
3 Then he said, "Go, borrow ves-
sels from everywhere, from all
your neighbors—empty vessels;
[a]do not gather just a few.
4 "And when you have come in,
you shall shut the door behind you
and your sons; then pour it into
all those vessels, and set aside the
full ones."
5 So she went from him and shut
the door behind her and her sons,
who brought *the vessels* to her;
and she poured *it* out.
6 Now it came to pass, when the
vessels were full, that she said to
her son, "Bring me another ves-
sel." And he said to her, "*There*
is not another vessel." So the oil
ceased.
7 Then she came and told the
man of God. And he said, "Go, sell
the oil and pay your debt; and you
and your sons live on the rest."

Elisha Raises the Shunammite's Son

8 Now it happened one day that
Elisha went to [a]Shunem, where
there *was* a [1]notable woman, and
she [2]persuaded him to eat some
food. So it was, as often as he
passed by, he would turn in there
to eat some food.
9 And she said to her husband,

"Look now, I know that this *is* a
holy man of God, who passes by
us regularly.
10 "Please, let us make [1]a small
upper room on the wall; and let
us put a bed for him there, and a
table and a chair and a lampstand;
so it will be, whenever he comes
to us, he can turn in there."
11 And it happened one day that
he came there, and he turned in
to the upper room and lay down
there.
12 Then he said to [a]Gehazi his ser-
vant, "Call this Shunammite
woman." When he had called her,
she stood before him.
13 And he said to him, "Say now
to her, 'Look, you have been con-
cerned for us with all this care.
What *can I* do for you? Do you
want me to speak on your behalf
to the king or to the commander
of the army?' " She answered, "I
dwell among my own people."
14 So he said, "What then *is* to be
done for her?" And Gehazi an-
swered, "Actually, she has no son,
and her husband is old."
15 So he said, "Call her." When
he had called her, she stood in the
doorway.
16 Then he said, [1]"About this time
next year you shall embrace a
son." And she said, "No, my lord.
Man of God, [a]do not lie to your
maidservant!"
17 But the woman conceived, and
bore a son when the appointed
time had come, of which Elisha
had told her.
18 And the child grew. Now it
happened one day that he went out
to his father, to the reapers.
19 And he said to his father, "My
head, my head!" So he said to
a servant, "Carry him to his
mother."
20 When he had taken him and
brought him to his mother, he sat
on her knees till noon, and *then*
died.
21 And she went up and laid him
on the bed of the man of God,
shut *the door* upon him, and went
out.
22 Then she called to her hus-
band, and said, "Please send me
one of the young men and one of
the donkeys, that I may run to the
man of God and come back."
23 So he said, "Why are you going
to him today? *It is* neither the
[a]New Moon nor the Sabbath." And
she said, [1]"*It is* well."
24 Then she saddled a donkey,
and said to her servant, "Drive,
and go forward; do not slacken the
pace for me unless I tell you."
25 And so she departed, and went
to the man of God [a]at Mount Car-
mel.
So it was, when the man of God
saw her afar off, that he said to
his servant Gehazi, "Look, the
Shunammite woman!
26 "Please run now to meet her,
and say to her, '*Is it* well with you?
Is it well with your husband? *Is it*
well with the child?' " And she an-
swered, "*It is* well."
27 Now when she came to the man
of God at the hill, she caught him
by the feet, but Gehazi came near
to push her away. But the man of
God said, "Let her alone; for her
soul *is* in deep distress, and the
LORD has hidden *it* from me, and
has not told me."
28 So she said, "Did I ask a son
of my lord? [a]Did I not say, 'Do not
deceive me'?"
29 Then he said to Gehazi, [a]"Get[1]
yourself ready, and take my staff
in your hand, and be on your way.
If you meet anyone, [b]do not greet
him; and if anyone greets you, do
not answer him; but [c]lay my staff
on the face of the child."
30 And the mother of the child
said, [a]"*As* the LORD lives, and *as*
your soul lives, I will not [b]leave
you." So he arose and followed
her.
31 Now Gehazi went on ahead of
them, and laid the staff on the face
of the child; but *there was* neither
voice nor hearing. Therefore he
went back to meet him, and told
him, saying, "The child has [a]not
awakened."
32 When Elisha came into the
house, there was the child, lying
dead on his bed.
33 He [a]went in therefore, shut the
door behind the two of them, [b]and
prayed to the LORD.
34 And he went up and lay on the
child, and put his mouth on his
mouth, his eyes on his eyes, and
his hands on his hands; and [a]he
stretched himself out on the child,

10 [1]Or *a small walled upper chamber*
12 [a]2 Kin. 4:29–31; 5:20–27; 8:4, 5
16 [a]2 Kin. 4:28 [1]Lit. *About this season, as the time of life*
23 [a]Num. 10:10; 28:11; 1 Chr. 23:31 [1]Or *It will be well*
25 [a]2 Kin. 2:25
28 [a]2 Kin. 4:16
29 [a]1 Kin. 18:46; 2 Kin. 9:1 [b]Luke 10:4 [c]Ex. 7:19; 14:16; 2 Kin. 2:8, 14; Acts 19:12 [1]Lit. *Gird up your loins.* The skirt of the robe was wrapped around the legs and tucked in the belt to gain freedom of movement.
30 [a]2 Kin. 2:2 [b]2 Kin. 2:4
31 [a]John 11:11
33 [a]2 Kin. 4:4; [Matt. 6:6]; Luke 8:51 [b]1 Kin. 17:20
34 [a]1 Kin. 17:21–23; Acts 20:10

and the flesh of the child became
warm.
35 He returned and walked back
and forth in the house, and again
went up [a]and stretched himself out
on him; then [b]the child sneezed
seven times, and the child opened
his eyes.
36 And he called Gehazi and said,
"Call this Shunammite woman."
So he called her. And when she
came in to him, he said, "Pick up
your son."
37 So she went in, fell at his feet,
and bowed to the ground; then she
[a]picked up her son and went out.

Elisha Purifies the Pot of Stew

38 And Elisha returned to [a]Gilgal,
and *there was* a [b]famine in the
land. Now the sons of the prophets
were [c]sitting before him; and he
said to his servant, "Put on the
large pot, and boil stew for the
sons of the prophets."
39 So one went out into the field
to gather herbs, and found a wild
vine, and gathered from it a lapful
of wild gourds, and came and
sliced *them* into the pot of stew,
though they did not know *what
they were.*
40 Then they served it to the men
to eat. Now it happened, as they
were eating the stew, that they
cried out and said, "Man of God,
there is [a]death in the pot!" And
they could not eat *it*.
41 So he said, "Then bring some
flour." And [a]he put *it* into the pot,
and said, "Serve *it* to the people,
that they may eat." And there was
nothing harmful in the pot.

Elisha Feeds One Hundred Men

42 Then a man came from [a]Baal
Shalisha, [b]and brought the man of
God bread of the firstfruits, twenty
loaves of barley bread, and newly
ripened grain in his knapsack.
And he said, "Give *it* to the people,
that they may eat."
43 But his servant said, [a]"What?
Shall I set this before one hundred
men?" He said again, "Give it to
the people, that they may eat; for
thus says the LORD: [b]'They shall
eat and have *some* left over.' "
44 So he set *it* before them; and
they ate [a]and had *some* left over,
according to the word of the LORD.

35 [a]1 Kin. 17:21 [b]2 Kin. 8:1, 5
37 [a]1 Kin. 17:23; [Heb. 11:35]
38 [a]2 Kin. 2:1 [b]2 Kin. 8:1 [c]Luke 10:39; Acts 22:3
40 [a]Ex. 10:17
41 [a]Ex. 15:25; 2 Kin. 2:21
42 [a]1 Sam. 9:4 [b]1 Sam. 9:7; [1 Cor. 9:11; Gal. 6:6]
43 [a]Luke 9:13; John 6:9 [b]Luke 9:17; John 6:11
44 [a]Matt. 14:20; 15:37; John 6:13

CHAPTER 5

1 [a]Luke 4:27 [b]Ex. 11:3
2 [a]2 Kin. 6:23; 13:20 [1]Or *in bands* [2]Served, lit. *was before*
5 [a]1 Sam. 9:8; 2 Kin. 8:8, 9
7 [a][Gen. 30:2; Deut. 32:39; 1 Sam. 2:6]
10 [a]2 Kin. 4:41; John 9:7

Naaman's Leprosy Healed

5 Now [a]Naaman, commander of
the army of the king of Syria,
was [b]a great and honorable man
in the eyes of his master, because
by him the LORD had given victory
to Syria. He was also a mighty
man of valor, *but* a leper.
2 And the Syrians had gone out
[a]on[1] raids, and had brought back
captive a young girl from the land
of Israel. She [2]waited on Naaman's
wife.
3 Then she said to her mistress,
"If only my master *were* with
the prophet who *is* in Samaria!
For he would heal him of his lep-
rosy."
4 And *Naaman* went in and told
his master, saying, "Thus and thus
said the girl who *is* from the land
of Israel."
5 Then the king of Syria said,
"Go now, and I will send a letter
to the king of Israel." So he de-
parted and [a]took with him ten tal-
ents of silver, six thousand *shek-
els* of gold, and ten changes of
clothing.
6 Then he brought the letter to
the king of Israel, which said,

> Now be advised, when this
> letter comes to you, that I have
> sent Naaman my servant to
> you, that you may heal him of
> his leprosy.

7 And it happened, when the
king of Israel read the letter, that
he tore his clothes and said, *"Am*
I [a]God, to kill and make alive, that
this man sends a man to me to heal
him of his leprosy? Therefore
please consider, and see how he
seeks a quarrel with me."
8 So it was, when Elisha the man
of God heard that the king of Israel
had torn his clothes, that he sent
to the king, saying, "Why have
you torn your clothes? Please let
him come to me, and he shall
know that there is a prophet in Is-
rael."
9 Then Naaman went with his
horses and chariot, and he stood
at the door of Elisha's house.
10 And Elisha sent a messenger to
him, saying, "Go and [a]wash in the
Jordan seven times, and your flesh

shall be restored to you, and *you*
shall be clean."
11 But Naaman became furious,
and went away and said, "Indeed,
I said to myself, 'He will surely
come out *to me,* and stand and call
on the name of the LORD his God,
and wave his hand over the place,
and heal the leprosy.'
12 "*Are* not the [1]Abanah and the
Pharpar, the rivers of Damascus,
better than all the waters of Israel?
Could I not wash in them and be
clean?" So he turned and went
away in a rage.
13 And his [a]servants came near
and spoke to him, and said, "My
father, *if* the prophet had told you
to do something great, would you
not have done *it?* How much more
then, when he says to you, 'Wash,
and be clean'?"
14 So he went down and dipped
seven times in the Jordan, accord-
ing to the saying of the man of
God; and his [a]flesh was restored
like the flesh of a little child, and
[b]he was clean.
15 And he returned to the man of
God, he and all his aides, and came
and stood before him; and he said,
"Indeed, now I know that *there is*
[a]no God in all the earth, except in
Israel; now therefore, please take
[b]a gift from your servant."
16 But he said, [a]"As the LORD
lives, before whom I stand, [b]I will
receive nothing." And he urged
him to take *it,* but he refused.
17 So Naaman said, "Then, if not,
please let your servant be given
two mule-loads of earth; for your
servant will no longer offer either
burnt offering or sacrifice to other
gods, but to the LORD.
18 "Yet in this thing may the LORD
pardon your servant: when my
master goes into the temple of
Rimmon to worship there, and [a]he
leans on my hand, and I bow down
in the temple of Rimmon—when I
bow down in the temple of Rim-
mon, may the LORD please pardon
your servant in this thing."
19 Then he said to him, "Go in
peace." So he departed from him
a short distance.

Gehazi's Greed

20 But [a]Gehazi, the servant of Eli-
sha the man of God, said, "Look,
my master has spared Naaman
this Syrian, while not receiving
from his hands what he brought;
but *as* the LORD lives, I will run af-
ter him and take something from
him."
21 So Gehazi pursued Naaman.
When Naaman saw *him* running
after him, he got down from the
chariot to meet him, and said, "*Is*
all well?"
22 And he said, "All *is* [a]well. My
master has sent me, saying, 'In-
deed, just now two young men of
the sons of the prophets have come
to me from the mountains of
Ephraim. Please give them a talent
of silver and two changes of gar-
ments.'"
23 So Naaman said, "Please, take
two talents." And he urged him,
and bound two talents of silver in
two bags, with two changes of gar-
ments, and handed *them* to two of
his servants; and they carried
them on ahead of him.
24 When he came to [1]the citadel,
he took *them* from their hand, and
stored *them* away in the house;
then he let the men go, and they
departed.
25 Now he went in and stood be-
fore his master. Elisha said to him,
"Where *did you go,* Gehazi?" And
he said, "Your servant did not go
anywhere."
26 Then he said to him, "Did not
my heart go *with you* when the
man turned back from his chariot
to meet you? *Is it* [a]time to receive
money and to receive clothing,
olive groves and vineyards, sheep
and oxen, male and female ser-
vants?
27 "Therefore the leprosy of Naa-
man [a]shall cling to you and your
descendants forever." And he
went out from his presence [b]lep-
rous, *as white* as snow.

The Floating Ax Head

6 And [a]the sons of the prophets
said to Elisha, "See now, the
place where we dwell with you is
too small for us.
2 "Please, let us go to the Jordan,
and let every man take a beam
from there, and let us make there
a place where we may dwell." So
he answered, "Go."
3 Then one said, [a]"Please con-

12 [1]So with Kt., LXX, Vg.; Qr., Syr., Tg. *Amanah*
13 [a]1 Sam. 28:23
14 [a]2 Kin. 5:10; Job 33:25 [b]Luke 4:27; 5:13
15 [a]Dan. 2:47; 3:29; 6:26, 27 [b]Gen. 33:11
16 [a]2 Kin. 3:14 [b]Gen. 14:22, 23; 2 Kin. 5:20, 26; [Matt. 10:8]; Acts 8:18, 20
18 [a]2 Kin. 7:2, 17
20 [a]2 Kin. 4:12; 8:4, 5
22 [a]2 Kin. 4:26
24 [1]Lit. *the hill*
26 [a][Eccl. 3:1, 6]
27 [a][1 Tim. 6:10] [b]Ex. 4:6; Num. 12:10; 2 Kin. 15:5

CHAPTER 6

1 [a]2 Kin. 4:38
3 [a]2 Kin. 5:23

sent to go with your servants."
And he answered, "I will go."
4 So he went with them. And
when they came to the Jordan,
they cut down trees.
5 But as one was cutting down a
tree, the iron *ax head* fell into the
water; and he cried out and said,
"Alas, master! For it was [a]bor-
rowed."
6 So the man of God said,
"Where did it fall?" And he
showed him the place. So [a]he cut
off a stick, and threw *it* in there;
and he made the iron float.
7 Therefore he said, "Pick *it* up
for yourself." So he reached out
his hand and took it.

The Blinded Syrians Captured

8 Now the [a]king of Syria was
making war against Israel; and he
consulted with his servants, say-
ing, "My camp *will be* in such and
such a place."
9 And the man of God sent to the
king of Israel, saying, "Beware
that you do not pass this place, for
the Syrians are coming down
there."
10 Then the king of Israel sent
someone to the place of which the
man of God had told him. Thus he
warned him, and he was watchful
there, not just once or twice.
11 Therefore the heart of the king
of Syria was greatly troubled by
this thing; and he called his ser-
vants and said to them, "Will you
not show me which of us *is* for the
king of Israel?"
12 And one of his servants said,
"None, my lord, O king; but Eli-
sha, the prophet who *is* in Israel,
tells the king of Israel the words
that you speak in your bedroom."
13 So he said, "Go and see where
he *is*, that I may send and get him."
And it was told him, saying,
"Surely *he is* in [a]Dothan."
14 Therefore he sent horses and
chariots and a great army there,
and they came by night and sur-
rounded the city.
15 And when the servant of the
man of God arose early and went
out, there was an army, surround-
ing the city with horses and chari-
ots. And his servant said to him,
"Alas, my master! What shall we
do?"

5 [a][Ex. 22:14]
6 [a]Ex. 15:25; 2 Kin. 2:21; 4:41
8 [a]2 Kin. 8:28, 29
13 [a]Gen. 37:17
16 [a]Ex. 14:13; 1 Kin. 17:13 [b]2 Chr. 32:7; Ps. 55:18; [Rom. 8:31]
17 [a]Num. 22:31; Luke 24:31 [b]2 Kin. 2:11; Ps. 34:7; 68:17; Zech. 1:8; 6:1–7
18 [a]Gen. 19:11; Acts 13:11
21 [a]2 Kin. 2:12; 5:13; 8:9
22 [a][Rom. 12:20]
23 [a]2 Kin. 5:2; 6:8, 9
24 [a]1 Kin. 20:1
25 [a]2 Kin. 4:38; 8:1 [1]Approximately 1 pint

16 So he answered, [a]"Do not fear,
for [b]those who *are* with us *are*
more than those who *are* with
them."
17 And Elisha prayed, and said,
"LORD, I pray, open his eyes that
he may see." Then the LORD
[a]opened the eyes of the young
man, and he saw. And behold, the
mountain *was* full of [b]horses and
chariots of fire all around Elisha.
18 So when *the Syrians* came
down to him, Elisha prayed to the
LORD, and said, "Strike this peo-
ple, I pray, with blindness." And
[a]He struck them with blindness ac-
cording to the word of Elisha.
19 Now Elisha said to them, "This
is not the way, nor *is* this the city.
Follow me, and I will bring you to
the man whom you seek." But he
led them to Samaria.
20 So it was, when they had come
to Samaria, that Elisha said,
"LORD, open the eyes of these *men*,
that they may see." And the LORD
opened their eyes, and they saw;
and there *they were*, inside Sa-
maria!
21 Now when the king of Israel
saw them, he said to Elisha, "My
[a]father, shall I kill *them*? Shall I
kill *them*?"
22 But he answered, "You shall
not kill *them*. Would you kill those
whom you have taken captive with
your sword and your bow? [a]Set
food and water before them, that
they may eat and drink and go to
their master."
23 Then he prepared a great feast
for them; and after they ate and
drank, he sent them away and they
went to their master. So [a]the bands
of Syrian *raiders* came no more
into the land of Israel.

Syria Besieges Samaria in Famine

24 And it happened after this that
[a]Ben-Hadad king of Syria gath-
ered all his army, and went up and
besieged Samaria.
25 And there was a great [a]famine
in Samaria; and indeed they be-
sieged it until a donkey's head was
sold for eighty *shekels* of silver,
and one-fourth of a [1]kab of dove
droppings for five *shekels* of sil-
ver.
26 Then, as the king of Israel was
passing by on the wall, a woman

cried out to him, saying, "Help, my
lord, O king!"
27 And he said, "If the LORD does
not help you, where can I find help
for you? From the threshing floor
or from the winepress?"
28 Then the king said to her,
"What is troubling you?" And she
answered, "This woman said to
me, 'Give your son, that we may
eat him today, and we will eat my
son tomorrow.'
29 "So [a]we boiled my son, and ate
him. And I said to her on the next
day, 'Give your son, that we may
eat him'; but she has hidden her
son."
30 Now it happened, when the
king heard the words of the
woman, that he [a]tore his clothes;
and as he passed by on the wall,
the people looked, and there un-
derneath *he had* sackcloth on his
body.
31 Then he said, [a]"God do so to
me and more also, if the head of
Elisha the son of Shaphat remains
on him today!"
32 But Elisha was sitting in his
house, and [a]the elders were sitting
with him. And *the king* sent a man
ahead of him, but before the mes-
senger came to him, he said to the
elders, [b]"Do you see how this son
of [c]a murderer has sent someone
to take away my head? Look,
when the messenger comes, shut
the door, and hold him fast at the
door. *Is* not the sound of his mas-
ter's feet behind him?"
33 And while he was still talking
with them, there was the messen-
ger, coming down to him; and then
the king said, "Surely this calam-
ity *is* from the LORD; [a]why should
I wait for the LORD any longer?"
7 Then Elisha said, "Hear the
word of the LORD. Thus says
the LORD: [a]'Tomorrow about this
time a [1]seah of fine flour *shall be*
sold for a shekel, and two seahs
of barley for a shekel, at the gate
of Samaria.' "
2 [a]So an officer on whose hand
the king leaned answered the man
of God and said, "Look, [b]*if* the
LORD would make windows in
heaven, could this thing be?" And
he said, "In fact, you shall see *it*
with your eyes, but you shall not
eat of it."

The Syrians Flee

3 Now there were four leprous
men [a]at the entrance of the gate;
and they said to one another,
"Why are we sitting here until we
die?
4 "If we say, 'We will enter the
city,' the famine *is* in the city, and
we shall die there. And if we sit
here, we die also. Now therefore,
come, let us surrender to the [a]army
of the Syrians. If they keep us
alive, we shall live; and if they kill
us, we shall only die."
5 And they rose at twilight to go
to the camp of the Syrians; and
when they had come to the out-
skirts of the Syrian camp, to their
surprise no one *was* there.
6 For the LORD had caused the
army of the Syrians [a]to hear the
noise of chariots and the noise of
horses—the noise of a great army;
so they said to one another, "Look,
the king of Israel has hired against
us [b]the kings of the Hittites and
the kings of the Egyptians to at-
tack us!"
7 Therefore they [a]arose and fled
at twilight, and left the camp in-
tact—their tents, their horses, and
their donkeys—and they fled for
their lives.
8 And when these lepers came to
the outskirts of the camp, they
went into one tent and ate and
drank, and carried from it silver
and gold and clothing, and went
and hid *them;* then they came
back and entered another tent, and
carried *some* from there *also,* and
went and hid *it.*
9 Then they said to one another,
"We are not doing right. This day
is a day of good news, and we re-
main silent. If we wait until morn-
ing light, some [1]punishment will
come upon us. Now therefore,
come, let us go and tell the king's
household."
10 So they went and called to the
gatekeepers of the city, and told
them, saying, "We went to the Syr-
ian camp, and surprisingly no one
was there, not a human sound—
only horses and donkeys tied, and
the tents intact."
11 And the gatekeepers called out,
and they told *it* to the king's
household inside.

29 [a]Lev. 26:27–29; Deut. 28:52–57; Lam. 4:10
30 [a]1 Kin. 21:27
31 [a]Ruth 1:17; 1 Kin. 19:2
32 [a]Ezek. 8:1; 14:1; 20:1 [b]Luke 13:32 [c]1 Kin. 18:4, 13, 14; 21:10, 13
33 [a]Job 2:9

CHAPTER 7

1 [a]2 Kin. 7:18, 19 [1]A third of an ephah, or about 8 gallons
2 [a]2 Kin. 5:18; 7:17, 19, 20 [b]Gen. 7:11; Mal. 3:10
3 [a][Lev. 13:45, 46; Num. 5:2–4; 12:10–14]
4 [a]2 Kin. 6:24
6 [a]2 Sam. 5:24; 2 Kin. 19:7; Job 15:21 [b]1 Kin. 10:29
7 [a]Ps. 48:4–6; [Prov. 28:1]
9 [1]Calamity

12 So the king arose in the night
and said to his servants, "Let me
now tell you what the Syrians have
done to us. They know that we *are*
[a]hungry; therefore they have gone
out of the camp to [l]hide them-
selves in the field, saying, 'When
they come out of the city, we shall
catch them alive, and get into the
city.'"
13 And one of his servants an-
swered and said, "Please, let sev-
eral *men* take five of the remaining
horses which are left in the city.
Look, they *may either become* like
all the multitude of Israel that are
left in it; or indeed, *I say*, they *may
become* like all the multitude of Is-
rael left from those who are con-
sumed; so let us send them and
see."
14 Therefore they took two chari-
ots with horses; and the king sent
them in the direction of the Syrian
army, saying, "Go and see."
15 And they went after them to the
Jordan; and indeed all the road
was full of garments and weapons
which the Syrians had thrown
away in their haste. So the mes-
sengers returned and told the king.
16 Then the people went out and
plundered the tents of the Syrians.
So a seah of fine flour was *sold*
for a shekel, and two seahs of bar-
ley for a shekel, [a]according to the
word of the LORD.
17 Now the king had appointed
the officer on whose hand he
leaned to have charge of the gate.
But the people trampled him in the
gate, and he died, just [a]as the man
of God had said, who spoke when
the king came down to him.
18 So it happened just as the man
of God had spoken to the king,
saying, [a]"Two seahs of barley for
a shekel, and a seah of fine flour
for a shekel, shall be *sold* tomor-
row about this time in the gate of
Samaria."
19 Then that officer had answered
the man of God, and said, "Now
look, *if* the LORD would make win-
dows in heaven, could such a thing
be?" And he had said, "In fact, you
shall see *it* with your eyes, but you
shall not eat of it."
20 And so it happened to him, for
the people trampled him in the
gate, and he died.

12 [a]2 Kin. 6:24–29 [l]Hide themselves in ambush
16 [a]2 Kin. 7:1
17 [a]2 Kin. 6:32; 7:2
18 [a]2 Kin. 7:1

CHAPTER 8

1 [a]2 Kin. 4:18, 31–35 [b]Ps. 105:16; Hag. 1:11 [c]2 Sam. 21:1; 1 Kin. 18:2; 2 Kin. 4:38; 6:25
4 [a]2 Kin. 4:12; 5:20–27
5 [a]2 Kin. 4:35
7 [a]2 Kin. 6:24
8 [a]1 Kin. 19:15 [b]1 Sam. 9:7; 1 Kin. 14:3; 2 Kin. 5:5 [c]2 Kin. 1:2
9 [a]1 Kin. 19:15

The King Restores the Shunammite's Land

8 Then Elisha spoke to the
woman [a]whose son he had re-
stored to life, saying, "Arise and
go, you and your household, and
stay wherever you can; for the
LORD [b]has called for a [c]famine, and
furthermore, it will come upon the
land for seven years."
2 So the woman arose and did
according to the saying of the man
of God, and she went with her
household and dwelt in the land
of the Philistines seven years.
3 It came to pass, at the end of
seven years, that the woman re-
turned from the land of the Philis-
tines; and she went to make an ap-
peal to the king for her house and
for her land.
4 Then the king talked with [a]Ge-
hazi, the servant of the man of God,
saying, "Tell me, please, all the
great things Elisha has done."
5 Now it happened, as he was
telling the king how he had re-
stored the dead to life, that there
was the woman whose son he had
[a]restored to life, appealing to the
king for her house and for her
land. And Gehazi said, "My lord,
O king, this *is* the woman, and this
is her son whom Elisha restored
to life."
6 And when the king asked the
woman, she told him. So the king
appointed a certain officer for her,
saying, "Restore all that *was* hers,
and all the proceeds of the field
from the day that she left the land
until now."

Death of Ben-Hadad

7 Then Elisha went to Damascus,
and [a]Ben-Hadad king of Syria was
sick; and it was told him, saying,
"The man of God has come here."
8 And the king said to [a]Hazael,
[b]"Take a present in your hand, and
go to meet the man of God, and
[c]inquire of the LORD by him, say-
ing, 'Shall I recover from this dis-
ease?'"
9 So [a]Hazael went to meet him
and took a present with him, of ev-
ery good thing of Damascus, forty
camel-loads; and he came and
stood before him, and said, "Your
son Ben-Hadad king of Syria has

sent me to you, saying, 'Shall I re-
cover from this disease?' "
10 And Elisha said to him, "Go,
say to him, 'You shall certainly re-
cover.' However the LORD has
shown me that [a]he will really die."
11 Then he [1]set his countenance
in a stare until he was ashamed;
and the man of God [a]wept.
12 And Hazael said, "Why is my
lord weeping?" He answered, "Be-
cause I know [a]the evil that you will
do to the children of Israel: Their
strongholds you will set on fire,
and their young men you will kill
with the sword; and you [b]will dash
their children, and rip open their
women with child."
13 So Hazael said, "But what [a]*is*
your servant—a dog, that he
should do this gross thing?" And
Elisha answered, [b]"The LORD has
shown me that you *will become*
king over Syria."
14 Then he departed from Elisha,
and came to his master, who said
to him, "What did Elisha say to
you?" And he answered, "He told
me you would surely recover."
15 But it happened on the next
day that he took a thick cloth and
dipped *it* in water, and spread *it*
over his face so that he died; and
Hazael reigned in his place.

Jehoram Reigns in Judah

16 Now [a]in the fifth year of Joram
the son of Ahab, king of Israel, Je-
hoshaphat *having been* king of Ju-
dah, [b]Jehoram the son of Je-
hoshaphat began to reign as [1]king
of Judah.
17 He was [a]thirty-two years old
when he became king, and he
reigned eight years in Jerusalem.
18 And he walked in the way of
the kings of Israel, just as the
house of Ahab had done, for [a]the
daughter of Ahab was his wife;
and he did evil in the sight of the
LORD.
19 Yet the LORD would not destroy
Judah, for the sake of his servant
David, [a]as He promised him to
give a lamp to him *and* his sons
forever.
20 In his days [a]Edom revolted
against Judah's authority, [b]and
made a king over themselves.
21 So [1]Joram went to Zair, and all
his chariots with him. Then he rose
by night and attacked the Edom-
ites who had surrounded him and
the captains of the chariots; and
the troops fled to their tents.
22 Thus Edom has been in revolt
against Judah's authority to this
day. [a]And Libnah revolted at that
time.
23 Now the rest of the acts of
Joram, and all that he did, *are* they
not written in the book of the
chronicles of the kings of Judah?
24 So Joram [1]rested with his fa-
thers, and was buried with his fa-
thers in the City of David. Then
[a]Ahaziah[2] his son reigned in his
place.

Ahaziah Reigns in Judah

25 In the twelfth year of Joram the
son of Ahab, king of Israel, Aha-
ziah the son of Jehoram, king of
Judah, began to reign.
26 Ahaziah *was* [a]twenty-two
years old when he became king,
and he reigned one year in Jerusa-
lem. His mother's name *was* Atha-
liah the granddaughter of Omri,
king of Israel.
27 [a]And he walked in the way of
the house of Ahab, and did evil in
the sight of the LORD, like the
house of Ahab, for he *was* the son-
in-law of the house of Ahab.
28 Now he went [a]with Joram the
son of Ahab to war against Hazael
king of Syria at [b]Ramoth Gilead;
and the Syrians wounded Joram.
29 Then [a]King Joram went back
to Jezreel to recover from the
wounds which the Syrians had in-
flicted on him at [1]Ramah, when he
fought against Hazael king of
Syria. [b]And Ahaziah the son of Je-
horam, king of Judah, went down
to see Joram the son of Ahab in
Jezreel, because he was sick.

Jehu Anointed King of Israel

9 And Elisha the prophet called
one of [a]the sons of the proph-
ets, and said to him, [b]"Get[1] your-
self ready, take this flask of oil in
your hand, [c]and go to Ramoth Gil-
ead.
2 "Now when you arrive at that
place, look there for Jehu the son
of Jehoshaphat, the son of Nimshi,
and go in and make him rise up
from among [a]his associates, and
take him to an inner room.

10 [a]2 Kin. 8:15
11 [a]Luke 19:41 [1]*fixed his gaze*
12 [a]2 Kin. 10:32; 12:17; 13:3, 7; Amos 1:3, 4 [b]2 Kin. 15:16; Hos. 13:16; Amos 1:13; Nah. 3:10
13 [a]1 Sam. 17:43; 2 Sam. 9:8 [b]1 Kin. 19:15
16 [a]2 Kin. 1:17; 3:1 [b]2 Chr. 21:3 [1]Co-regent with his father
17 [a]2 Chr. 21:5–10
18 [a]2 Kin. 8:26, 27
19 [a]2 Sam. 7:13; 1 Kin. 11:36; 15:4; 2 Chr. 21:7
20 [a]Gen. 27:40; 2 Chr. 21:8–10 [b]1 Kin. 22:47
21 [1]*Jehoram,* v. 16
22 [a]Josh. 21:13; 2 Kin. 19:8; 2 Chr. 21:10
24 [a]2 Chr. 22:1, 7 [1]Died and joined his ancestors [2]Or *Azariah* or *Jehoahaz*
26 [a]2 Chr. 22:2
27 [a]2 Chr. 22:3, 4
28 [a]2 Chr. 22:5 [b]1 Kin. 22:3, 29
29 [a]2 Kin. 9:15 [b]2 Kin. 9:16; 2 Chr. 22:6, 7 [1]*Ramoth,* v. 28

CHAPTER 9

1 [a]1 Kin. 20:35 [b]2 Kin. 4:29; Jer. 1:17 [c]2 Kin. 8:28, 29 [1]Lit. *Gird up your loins*
2 [a]2 Kin. 9:5, 11

3 "Then [a]take the flask of oil, and
pour *it* on his head, and say, 'Thus
says the LORD: "I have anointed
you king over Israel." ' Then open
the door and flee, and do not de-
lay."
4 So the young man, the servant
of the prophet, went to Ramoth Gil-
ead.
5 And when he arrived, there
were the captains of the army sit-
ting; and he said, "I have a mes-
sage for you, Commander." Jehu
said, "For which *one* of us?" And
he said, "For you, Commander."
6 Then he arose and went into
the house. And he poured the oil
on his head, and said to him,
[a]"Thus says the LORD God of Is-
rael: 'I have anointed you king
over the people of the LORD, over
Israel.
7 'You shall strike down the
house of Ahab your master, that I
may [a]avenge the blood of My ser-
vants the prophets, and the blood
of all the servants of the LORD, [b]at
the hand of Jezebel.
8 'For the whole house of Ahab
shall perish; and [a]I will cut off
from Ahab all [b]the males in Israel,
both [c]bond and free.
9 'So I will make the house of
Ahab like the house of [a]Jeroboam
the son of Nebat, and like the
house of [b]Baasha the son of Ahi-
jah.
10 [a]'The dogs shall eat Jezebel on
the plot *of ground* at Jezreel, and
there shall be none to bury *her.*' "
And he opened the door and fled.
11 Then Jehu came out to the ser-
vants of his master, and *one* said
to him, "*Is* all well? Why did [a]this
madman come to you?" And he
said to them, "You know the man
and his babble."
12 And they said, "A lie! Tell us
now." So he said, "Thus and thus
he spoke to me, saying, 'Thus says
the LORD: "I have anointed you
king over Israel." ' "
13 Then each man hastened [a]to
take his garment and put *it* [1]under
him on the top of the steps; and
they blew trumpets, saying, "Jehu
is king!"

Joram of Israel Killed

14 So Jehu the son of Jehosha-
phat, the son of Nimshi, conspired
against [a]Joram. (Now Joram had
been defending Ramoth Gilead, he
and all Israel, against Hazael king
of Syria.
15 But [a]King [1]Joram had returned
to Jezreel to recover from the
wounds which the Syrians had in-
flicted on him when he fought with
Hazael king of Syria.) And Jehu
said, "If you are so minded, let no
one leave *or* escape from the city
to go and tell *it* in Jezreel."
16 So Jehu rode in a chariot and
went to Jezreel, for Joram was laid
up there; [a]and Ahaziah king of Ju-
dah had come down to see Joram.
17 Now a watchman stood on the
tower in Jezreel, and he saw the
company of Jehu as he came, and
said, "I see a company of men."
And Joram said, "Get a horseman
and send him to meet them, and
let him say, [1]'*Is it* peace?' "
18 So the horseman went to meet
him, and said, "Thus says the king:
'*Is it* peace?' " And Jehu said,
"What have you to do with peace?
[1]Turn around and follow me." So
the watchman reported, saying,
"The messenger went to them, but
is not coming back."
19 Then he sent out a second
horseman who came to them, and
said, "Thus says the king: '*Is it*
peace?' " And Jehu answered,
"What have you to do with peace?
Turn around and follow me."
20 So the watchman reported,
saying, "He went up to them and
is not coming back; and the driv-
ing *is* like the driving of Jehu the
son of Nimshi, for he drives furi-
ously!"
21 Then Joram said, [1]"Make
ready." And his chariot was made
ready. Then [a]Joram king of Israel
and Ahaziah king of Judah went
out, each in his chariot; and they
went out to meet Jehu, and [2]met
him [b]on the property of Naboth the
Jezreelite.
22 Now it happened, when Joram
saw Jehu, that he said, "*Is it* peace,
Jehu?" So he answered, "What
peace, as long as the harlotries of
your mother Jezebel and her
witchcraft *are so* many?"
23 Then Joram turned around and
fled, and said to Ahaziah, "Treach-
ery, Ahaziah!"
24 Now Jehu [1]drew his bow with

3 [a]1 Kin. 19:16
6 [a]1 Sam. 2:7, 8; 1 Kin. 19:16; 2 Kin. 9:3; 2 Chr. 22:7
7 [a][Deut. 32:35, 41] [b]1 Kin. 18:4; 21:15
8 [a]1 Kin. 14:10; 21:21; 2 Kin. 10:17 [b]1 Sam. 25:22 [c]Deut. 32:36; 2 Kin. 14:26
9 [a]1 Kin. 14:10; 15:29; 21:22 [b]1 Kin. 16:3, 11
10 [a]1 Kin. 21:23; 2 Kin. 9:35, 36
11 [a]Jer. 29:26; Hos. 9:7; Mark 3:21; John 10:20; Acts 26:24; [1 Cor. 4:10]
13 [a]Matt. 21:7, 8; Mark 11:7, 8 [1]Lit. *under his feet*
14 [a]2 Kin. 8:28
15 [a]2 Kin. 8:29 [1]*Jehoram*, v. 24
16 [a]2 Kin. 8:29
17 [1]Are you peaceful?
18 [1]Lit. *Turn behind me*
21 [a]1 Kin. 19:17; 2 Chr. 22:7 [b]1 Kin. 21:1–14 [1]*Harness up* [2]Lit. *found*
24 [1]Lit. *filled his hand*

full strength and shot Jehoram be-
tween his arms; and the arrow
came out at his heart, and he sank
down in his chariot.
25 Then *Jehu* said to Bidkar his
captain, "Pick *him* up, *and* throw
him into the tract of the field of
Naboth the Jezreelite; for remem-
ber, when you and I were riding
together behind Ahab his father,
that [a]the LORD laid this [b]burden
upon him:
26 'Surely I saw yesterday the
blood of Naboth and the blood of
his sons,' says the LORD, [a]'and I
will repay you [1]in this plot,' says
the LORD. Now therefore, take *and*
throw him on the plot *of ground,*
according to the word of the
LORD."

Ahaziah of Judah Killed

27 But when Ahaziah king of Ju-
dah saw *this,* he fled by the road
to [1]Beth Haggan. So Jehu pursued
him, and said, [2]"Shoot him also in
the chariot." *And they shot him* at
the Ascent of Gur, which is by Ib-
leam. Then he fled to [a]Megiddo,
and died there.
28 And his servants carried him in
the chariot to Jerusalem, and bur-
ied him in his tomb with his fa-
thers in the City of David.
29 In the eleventh year of Joram
the son of Ahab, Ahaziah had be-
come king over Judah.

Jezebel's Violent Death

30 Now when Jehu had come to
Jezreel, Jezebel heard *of it;* [a]and
she put paint on her eyes and
adorned her head, and looked
through a window.
31 Then, as Jehu entered at the
gate, she said, [a]"*Is it* peace, Zimri,
murderer of your master?"
32 And he looked up at the win-
dow, and said, "Who *is* on my
side? Who?" So two *or* three eu-
nuchs looked out at him.
33 Then he said, "Throw her
down." So they threw her down,
and *some* of her blood spattered
on the wall and on the horses; and
he trampled her underfoot.
34 And when he had gone in, he
ate and drank. Then he said, "Go
now, see to this accursed *woman,*
and bury her, for [a]she was a king's
daughter."
35 So they went to bury her, but
they found no more of her than the
skull and the feet and the palms
of *her* hands.
36 Therefore they came back and
told him. And he said, "This *is* the
word of the LORD, which He spoke
by His servant Elijah the Tishbite,
saying, [a]'On the plot *of ground* at
Jezreel dogs shall eat the flesh of
Jezebel;
37 'and the corpse of Jezebel shall
be [a]as refuse on the surface of the
field, in the plot at Jezreel, so that
they shall not say, "Here *lies* Jeze-
bel." ' "

Ahab's Seventy Sons Killed

10 Now Ahab had seventy sons
in Samaria. And Jehu wrote
and sent letters to Samaria, to the
rulers of [1]Jezreel, to the elders,
and to [2]those who reared Ahab's
sons, saying:

2 Now as soon as this letter
comes to you, since your
master's sons *are* with you, and
you have chariots and horses,
a fortified city also, and
weapons,
3 choose the [1]best qualified of
your master's sons, set *him* on
his father's throne, and fight
for your master's house.

4 But they were exceedingly
afraid, and said, "Look, [a]two kings
could not [1]stand up to him; how
then can we stand?"
5 And he who *was* in charge of
the house, and he who *was* in
charge of the city, the elders also,
and those who reared *the sons,*
sent to Jehu, saying, "We *are* your
servants, we will do all you tell us;
but we will not make anyone king.
Do *what is* good in your sight."
6 Then he wrote a second letter
to them, saying:

If you *are* for me and will obey
my voice, take the heads of the
men, your master's sons, and
come to me at Jezreel by this
time tomorrow.

Now the king's sons, seventy per-
sons, *were* with the great men of
the city, *who* were rearing them.
7 So it was, when the letter came
to them, that they took the king's

25 [a]1 Kin. 21:19, 24–29 [b]Is. 13:1
26 [a]1 Kin. 21:13, 19 [1]*on this property*
27 [a]2 Chr. 22:7, 9 [1]Lit. *The Garden House* [2]Lit. *Strike*
30 [a][Jer. 4:30]; Ezek. 23:40
31 [a]1 Kin. 16:9–20; 2 Kin. 9:18–22
34 [a][Ex. 22:28]; 1 Kin. 16:31
36 [a]1 Kin. 21:23
37 [a]Ps. 83:10

CHAPTER 10
1 [1]So with MT, Syr., Tg.; LXX *Samaria;* Vg. *city* [2]*the guardians of*
3 [1]*most upright*
4 [a]2 Kin. 9:24, 27 [1]Lit. *stand before*

sons and [a]slaughtered seventy per-
sons, put their heads in baskets
and sent *them* to him at Jezreel.
8 Then a messenger came and
told him, saying, "They have
brought the heads of the king's
sons." And he said, "Lay them in
two heaps at the entrance of the
gate until morning."
9 So it was, in the morning, that
he went out and stood, and said
to all the people, "You *are* righ-
teous. Indeed [a]I conspired against
my master and killed him; but who
killed all these?
10 "Know now that nothing shall
[a]fall to the earth of the word of the
LORD which the LORD spoke con-
cerning the house of Ahab; for the
LORD has done what He spoke [b]by
His servant Elijah."
11 So Jehu killed all who re-
mained of the house of Ahab in
Jezreel, and all his great men and
his close acquaintances and his
priests, until he left him none re-
maining.

Ahaziah's Forty-two Brothers Killed

12 And he arose and departed and
went to Samaria. On the way, at
[1]Beth Eked of the Shepherds,
13 [a]Jehu met with the brothers of
Ahaziah king of Judah, and said,
"Who *are* you?" So they an-
swered, "We *are* the brothers of
Ahaziah; we have come down to
greet the sons of the king and the
sons of the queen mother."
14 And he said, "Take them
alive!" So they took them alive,
and [a]killed them at the well of
[1]Beth Eked, forty-two men; and he
left none of them.

The Rest of Ahab's Family Killed

15 Now when he departed from
there, he [1]met [a]Jehonadab the son
of [b]Rechab, *coming* to meet him;
and he greeted him and said to
him, "Is your heart right, as my
heart *is* toward your heart?" And
Jehonadab answered, "It is." *Jehu*
said, "If it is, [c]give *me* your hand."
So he gave *him* his hand, and he
took him up to him into the char-
iot.
16 Then he said, "Come with me,
and see my [a]zeal for the LORD." So
they had him ride in his chariot.
17 And when he came to Samaria,
[a]he killed all who remained to
Ahab in Samaria, till he had de-
stroyed them, according to the
word of the LORD [b]which He spoke
to Elijah.

Worshipers of Baal Killed

18 Then Jehu gathered all the peo-
ple together, and said to them,
[a]"Ahab served Baal a little, Jehu
will serve him much.
19 "Now therefore, call to me all
the [a]prophets of Baal, all his ser-
vants, and all his priests. Let no
one be missing, for I have a great
sacrifice for Baal. Whoever is
missing shall not live." But Jehu
acted deceptively, with the intent
of destroying the worshipers of
Baal.
20 And Jehu said, [1]"Proclaim a
solemn assembly for Baal." So
they proclaimed *it*.
21 Then Jehu sent throughout all
Israel; and all the worshipers of
Baal came, so that there was not
a man left who did not come. So
they came into the [1]temple of Baal,
and the [a]temple of Baal was full
from one end to the other.
22 And he said to the one in
charge of the wardrobe, "Bring out
vestments for all the worshipers of
Baal." So he brought out vest-
ments for them.
23 Then Jehu and Jehonadab the
son of Rechab went into the tem-
ple of Baal, and said to the wor-
shipers of Baal, "Search and see
that no servants of the LORD are
here with you, but only the wor-
shipers of Baal."
24 So they went in to offer sacri-
fices and burnt offerings. Now
Jehu had appointed for himself
eighty men on the outside, and had
said, "*If* any of the men whom I
have brought into your hands es-
capes, *whoever lets him escape, it*
shall be [a]his life for the life of the
other."
25 Now it happened, as soon as he
had made an end of offering the
burnt offering, that Jehu said to
the guard and to the captains, "Go
in *and* kill them; let no one come
out!" And they killed them with
the edge of the sword; then the
guards and the officers threw *them*
out, and went into the [1]inner room
of the temple of Baal.

7 [a]Judg. 9:5; 1 Kin. 21:21; 2 Kin. 11:1
9 [a]2 Kin. 9:14–24
10 [a]1 Sam. 3:19; 1 Kin. 8:56; Jer. 44:28 [b]1 Kin. 21:17–24, 29
12 [1]Or *The Shearing House*
13 [a]2 Chr. 22:8
14 [a]2 Chr. 22:8 [1]Or *The Shearing House*
15 [a]Jer. 35:6 [b]1 Chr. 2:55 [c]Ezra 10:19; Ezek. 17:18 [1]Lit. *found*
16 [a]1 Kin. 19:10
17 [a]2 Kin. 9:8; 2 Chr. 22:8 [b]1 Kin. 21:21, 29
18 [a]1 Kin. 16:31, 32
19 [a]1 Kin. 18:19; 22:6
20 [1]*Consecrate*
21 [a]1 Kin. 16:32; 2 Kin. 11:18 [1]Lit. *house*
24 [a]1 Kin. 20:39
25 [1]Lit. *city*

26 And they brought the [a]sacred
pillars out of the temple of Baal
and burned them.
27 Then they broke down the *sa-
cred* pillar of Baal, and tore down
the [1]temple of Baal and [a]made it
a refuse dump to this day.
28 Thus Jehu destroyed Baal from
Israel.
29 However Jehu did not turn
away from the sins of Jeroboam
the son of Nebat, who had made
Israel sin, *that is,* from [a]the golden
calves that *were* at Bethel and
Dan.
30 And the LORD [a]said to Jehu,
"Because you have done well in
doing *what is* right in My sight,
and have done to the house of
Ahab all that *was* in My heart,
[b]your sons shall sit on the throne
of Israel to the fourth *generation.*"
31 But Jehu [1]took no heed to walk
in the law of the LORD God of Israel
with all his heart; for he did not
depart from [a]the sins of Jeroboam,
who had made Israel sin.

Death of Jehu

32 In those days the LORD began
to cut off *parts* of Israel; and
[a]Hazael conquered them in all the
territory of Israel
33 from the Jordan eastward: all
the land of Gilead—Gad, Reuben,
and Manasseh—from [a]Aroer,
which *is* by the River Arnon, in-
cluding [b]Gilead and Bashan.
34 Now the rest of the acts of
Jehu, all that he did, and all his
might, *are* they not written in the
book of the chronicles of the kings
of Israel?
35 So Jehu [1]rested with his fa-
thers, and they buried him in Sa-
maria. Then [a]Jehoahaz his son
reigned in his place.
36 And the period that Jehu
reigned over Israel in Samaria *was*
twenty-eight years.

Athaliah Reigns in Judah

11 When [a]Athaliah [b]the mother
of Ahaziah saw that her son
was [c]dead, she arose and de-
stroyed all the royal heirs.
2 But [1]Jehosheba, the daughter
of King Joram, sister of [a]Ahaziah,
took [2]Joash the son of Ahaziah,
and stole him away from among
the king's sons *who were* being
murdered; and they hid him and
his nurse in the bedroom, from
Athaliah, so that he was not killed.
3 So he was hidden with her in
the house of the LORD for six years,
while Athaliah reigned over the
land.

Joash Crowned King of Judah

4 In [a]the seventh year Jehoiada
sent and brought the captains of
hundreds—of the bodyguards and
the [1]escorts—and brought them
into the house of the LORD to him.
And he made a covenant with
them and took an oath from them
in the house of the LORD, and
showed them the king's son.
5 Then he commanded them,
saying, "This *is* what you shall do:
One-third of you who [1]come on
duty [a]on the Sabbath shall be
keeping watch over the king's
house,
6 "one-third *shall be* at the gate
of Sur, and one-third at the gate
behind the escorts. You shall keep
the watch of the house, lest it be
broken down.
7 "The two [1]contingents of you
who go off duty on the Sabbath
shall keep the watch of the house
of the LORD for the king.
8 "But you shall surround the
king on all sides, every man with
his weapons in his hand; and
whoever comes within range, let
him be put to death. You are to
be with the king as he goes out and
as he comes in."
9 [a]So the captains of the hun-
dreds did according to all that Je-
hoiada the priest commanded.
Each of them took his men who
were to be on duty on the Sabbath,
with those who were going off
duty on the Sabbath, and came to
Jehoiada the priest.
10 And the priest gave the cap-
tains of hundreds the spears and
shields which *had belonged* to
King David, [a]that were in the tem-
ple of the LORD.
11 Then the escorts stood, every
man with his weapons in his hand,
all around the king, from the right
[1]side of the temple to the left side
of the temple, by the altar and the
house.
12 And he brought out the king's
son, put the crown on him, and

---

26 [a][Deut. 7:5, 25]; 1 Kin. 14:23; 2 Kin. 3:2
27 [a]Ezra 6:11; Dan. 2:5; 3:29 [1]Lit. *house*
29 [a]1 Kin. 12:28–30; 13:33, 34
30 [a]2 Kin. 9:6, 7 [b]2 Kin. 13:1, 10; 14:23; 15:8, 12
31 [a]1 Kin. 14:16 [1]*was not careful*
32 [a]1 Kin. 19:17; 2 Kin. 8:12; 13:22
33 [a]Deut. 2:36 [b]Amos 1:3–5
35 [a]2 Kin. 13:1 [1]Died and joined his ancestors

CHAPTER 11

1 [a]2 Chr. 22:10 [b]2 Kin. 8:26 [c]2 Kin. 9:27
2 [a]2 Kin. 8:25 [1]*Jehoshabeath,* 2 Chr. 22:11 [2]Or *Jehoash*
4 [a]2 Kin. 12:2; 2 Chr. 23:1 [1]*guards*
5 [a]1 Chr. 9:25 [1]Lit. *enter in*
7 [1]*companies*
9 [a]2 Chr. 23:8
10 [a]2 Sam. 8:7; 1 Chr. 18:7
11 [1]Lit. *shoulder*

gave him the [a]Testimony;[1] they
made him king and anointed him,
and they clapped their hands and
said, [b]"Long live the king!"

Death of Athaliah

13 [a]Now when Athaliah heard the
noise of the escorts *and* the people,
she came to the people *in* the tem-
ple of the LORD.
14 When she looked, there was
the king standing by [a]a pillar ac-
cording to custom; and the leaders
and the trumpeters were by the
king. All the people of the land
were rejoicing and blowing trum-
pets. So Athaliah tore her clothes
and cried out, "Treason! Treason!"
15 And Jehoiada the priest com-
manded the captains of the hun-
dreds, the officers of the army, and
said to them, "Take her outside
[1]under guard, and slay with the
sword whoever follows her." For
the priest had said, "Do not let her
be killed in the house of the LORD."
16 So they seized her; and she
went by way of the horses' en-
trance *into* the king's house, and
there she was killed.
17 [a]Then Jehoiada [b]made a cov-
enant between the LORD, the king,
and the people, that they should
be the LORD's people, and *also* [c]be-
tween the king and the people.
18 And all the people of the land
went to the [a]temple of Baal, and
tore it down. They thoroughly
[b]broke in pieces its altars and [1]im-
ages, and [c]killed Mattan the priest
of Baal before the altars. And [d]the
priest appointed [2]officers over the
house of the LORD.
19 Then he took the captains of
hundreds, the bodyguards, the es-
corts, and all the people of the
land; and they brought the king
down from the house of the LORD,
and went by way of the gate of the
escorts to the king's house. Then
he sat on the throne of the kings.
20 So all the people of the land re-
joiced; and the city was quiet, for
they had slain Athaliah with the
sword *in* the king's house.
21 Jehoash *was* [a]seven years old
when he became king.

Jehoash Repairs the Temple

12 In the seventh year of Jehu,
[a]Jehoash[1] became king, and
he reigned forty years in Jerusa-
lem. His mother's name *was* Zib-
iah of Beersheba.
2 Jehoash did *what was* right in
the sight of the LORD all the days
in which [a]Jehoiada the priest in-
structed him.
3 But [a]the [1]high places were not
taken away; the people still sacri-
ficed and burned incense on the
high places.
4 And Jehoash said to the
priests, [a]"All the money of the ded-
icated gifts that are brought into
the house of the LORD—each man's
[b]census[1] money, each man's [c]as-
sessment money—*and* all the
money that [2]a man [d]purposes in
his heart to bring into the house
of the LORD,
5 "let the priests take *it* them-
selves, each from his constituency;
and let them repair the [1]damages
of the temple, wherever any dilapi-
dation is found."
6 Now it was so, by the twenty-
third year of King Jehoash, [a]*that*
the priests had not repaired the
damages of the temple.
7 [a]So King Jehoash called Jehoi-
ada the priest and the *other*
priests, and said to them, "Why
have you not repaired the dam-
ages of the temple? Now therefore,
do not take *more* money from your
constituency, but deliver it for re-
pairing the damages of the tem-
ple."
8 And the priests agreed that
they would neither receive *more*
money from the people, nor repair
the damages of the temple.
9 Then Jehoiada the priest took
[a]a chest, bored a hole in its lid, and
set it beside the altar, on the right
side as one comes into the house
of the LORD; and the priests who
[1]kept the door put [b]there all the
money brought into the house of
the LORD.
10 So it was, whenever they saw
that *there was* much money in the
chest, that the king's [a]scribe[1] and
the high priest came up and [2]put
it in bags, and counted the money
that was found in the house of the
LORD.
11 Then they gave the money,
which had been apportioned, into
the hands of those who did the
work, who had the oversight of the

12 [a]Ex. 25:16; 31:18 [b]1 Sam. 10:24 [1]Law, Ex. 25:16, 21; Deut. 31:9
13 [a]2 Kin. 8:26; 2 Chr. 23:12
14 [a]2 Kin. 23:3; 2 Chr. 34:31
15 [1]Lit. *between ranks*
17 [a]2 Chr. 23:16 [b]Josh. 24:24, 25; 2 Chr. 15:12–15 [c]2 Sam. 5:3
18 [a]2 Kin. 10:26, 27 [b][Deut. 12:3] [c]1 Kin. 18:40; 2 Kin. 10:11 [d]2 Chr. 23:18 [1]Idols [2]Lit. *offices*
21 [a]2 Chr. 24:1–14

CHAPTER 12

1 [a]2 Chr. 24:1 [1]*Joash,* 2 Kin. 11:2ff.
2 [a]2 Kin. 11:4
3 [a]1 Kin. 15:14; 22:43; 2 Kin. 14:4; 15:35 [1]Places for pagan worship
4 [a]2 Kin. 22:4 [b]Ex. 30:13–16 [c]Lev. 27:2–28 [d]Ex. 35:5; 1 Chr. 29:3–9 [1]Lit. *the money coming over* [2]*any man's heart prompts him to bring*
5 [1]Lit. *breaches*
6 [a]2 Chr. 24:5
7 [a]2 Chr. 24:6
9 [a]2 Chr. 23:1; 24:8 [b]Mark 12:41; Luke 21:1 [1]*guarded at the door*
10 [a]2 Sam. 8:17; 2 Kin. 19:2; 22:3, 4, 12 [1]*secretary* [2]*tied it up*

house of the LORD; and they [1]paid
it out to the carpenters and build-
ers who worked on the house of
the LORD,
12 and to masons and stone-
cutters, and for buying timber and
hewn stone, to [a]repair the damage
of the house of the LORD, and for
all that was paid out to repair the
temple.
13 However [a]there were not made
for the house of the LORD basins
of silver, trimmers, sprinkling-
bowls, trumpets, any articles of
gold or articles of silver, from the
money brought into the house of
the LORD.
14 But they gave that to the work-
men, and they repaired the house
of the LORD with it.
15 Moreover [a]they did not require
an account from the men into
whose hand they delivered the
money to be paid to workmen, for
they dealt faithfully.
16 [a]The money from the trespass
offerings and the money from the
sin offerings was not brought into
the house of the LORD. [b]It belonged
to the priests.

Hazael Threatens Jerusalem

17 [a]Hazael king of Syria went up
and fought against Gath, and took
it; then [b]Hazael set his face to [1]go
up to Jerusalem.
18 And Jehoash king of Judah
[a]took all the sacred things that his
fathers, Jehoshaphat and Jehoram
and Ahaziah, kings of Judah, had
dedicated, and his own sacred
things, and all the gold found in
the treasuries of the house of the
LORD and in the king's house, and
sent *them* to Hazael king of Syria.
Then he went away from Jerusa-
lem.

Death of Joash

19 Now the rest of the acts of
[1]Joash, and all that he did, *are* they
not written in the book of the
chronicles of the kings of Judah?
20 And [a]his servants arose and
formed a conspiracy, and killed
Joash in the house of [1]the Millo,
which goes down to Silla.
21 For [1]Jozachar the son of Shim-
eath and Jehozabad the son of
[2]Shomer, his servants, struck him.
So he died, and they buried him

11 [1]Lit. *weighed*
12 [a]2 Kin. 22:5, 6
13 [a]2 Chr. 24:14
15 [a]2 Kin. 22:7; [1 Cor. 4:2]; 2 Cor. 8:20
16 [a][Lev. 5:15, 18] [b][Lev. 7:7; Num. 18:9]
17 [a]2 Kin. 8:12 [b]2 Chr. 24:23 [1]Advance upon
18 [a]1 Kin. 15:18; 2 Kin. 16:8; 18:15, 16
19 [1]*Jehoash,* vv. 1–18
20 [a]2 Kin. 14:5; 2 Chr. 24:25 [1]Lit. *The Landfill*
21 [a]2 Chr. 24:27 [1]*Zabad,* 2 Chr. 24:26 [2]*Shimrith,* 2 Chr. 24:26

CHAPTER 13

1 [a]2 Kin. 12:1 [b]2 Kin. 10:35 [1]*Jehoash,* 2 Kin. 12:1–18
2 [a]1 Kin. 12:26–33 [1]Lit. *turn*
3 [a]Judg. 2:14 [b]2 Kin. 8:12 [c]Amos 1:4
4 [a][Ps. 78:34] [b][Ex. 3:7, 9; Judg. 2:18]; 2 Kin. 14:26
5 [a]2 Kin. 13:25; 14:25, 27; Neh. 9:27
6 [a]1 Kin. 16:33 [1]Heb. *Asherah,* a Canaanite goddess
7 [a]2 Kin. 10:32 [b][Amos 1:3]
9 [1]Died and joined his ancestors [2]Or *Jehoash*
10 [1]*Joash,* v. 9

with his fathers in the City of Da-
vid. Then [a]Amaziah his son
reigned in his place.

Jehoahaz Reigns in Israel

13 In the twenty-third year of
[a]Joash[1] the son of Ahaziah,
king of Judah, [b]Jehoahaz the son
of Jehu became king over Israel
in Samaria, *and reigned* seventeen
years.
2 And he did evil in the sight of
the LORD, and followed the [a]sins
of Jeroboam the son of Nebat, who
had made Israel sin. He did not
[1]depart from them.
3 Then [a]the anger of the LORD
was aroused against Israel, and He
delivered them into the hand of
[b]Hazael king of Syria, and into the
hand of [c]Ben-Hadad the son of
Hazael, all *their* days.
4 So Jehoahaz [a]pleaded with the
LORD, and the LORD listened to
him; for [b]He saw the oppression
of Israel, because the king of Syria
oppressed them.
5 [a]Then the LORD gave Israel a
deliverer, so that they escaped
from under the hand of the Syr-
ians; and the children of Israel
dwelt in their tents as before.
6 Nevertheless they did not de-
part from the sins of the house of
Jeroboam, who had made Israel
sin, *but* walked in them; [a]and the
[1]wooden image also remained in
Samaria.
7 For He left of the army of Je-
hoahaz only fifty horsemen, ten
chariots, and ten thousand foot
soldiers; for the king of Syria had
destroyed them [a]and made them
[b]like the dust at threshing.
8 Now the rest of the acts of Je-
hoahaz, all that he did, and his
might, *are* they not written in the
book of the chronicles of the kings
of Israel?
9 So Jehoahaz [1]rested with his
fathers, and they buried him in Sa-
maria. Then [2]Joash his son
reigned in his place.

Jehoash Reigns in Israel

10 In the thirty-seventh year of
Joash king of Judah, [1]Jehoash the
son of Jehoahaz became king over
Israel in Samaria, *and reigned* six-
teen years.
11 And he did evil in the sight of

the LORD. He did not depart from
all the sins of Jeroboam the son
of Nebat, who made Israel sin, *but*
walked in them.
12 [a]Now the rest of the acts of
Joash, [b]all that he did, and [c]his
might with which he fought
against Amaziah king of Judah,
are they not written in the book
of the chronicles of the kings of
Israel?
13 So Joash [a]rested[1] with his fa-
thers. Then Jeroboam sat on his
throne. And Joash was buried in
Samaria with the kings of Israel.

Death of Elisha

14 Elisha had become sick with
the illness of which he would die.
Then Joash the king of Israel came
down to him, and wept over his
face, and said, "O my father, my
father, [a]the chariots of Israel and
their horsemen!"
15 And Elisha said to him, "Take
a bow and some arrows." So he
took himself a bow and some ar-
rows.
16 Then he said to the king of Is-
rael, "Put your hand on the bow."
So he put his hand *on it*, and Eli-
sha put his hands on the king's
hands.
17 And he said, "Open the east
window"; and he opened *it*. Then
Elisha said, "Shoot"; and he shot.
And he said, "The arrow of the
LORD's deliverance and the arrow
of deliverance from Syria; for you
must strike the Syrians at [a]Aphek
till you have destroyed *them*."
18 Then he said, "Take the ar-
rows"; so he took *them*. And he
said to the king of Israel, "Strike
the ground"; so he struck three
times, and stopped.
19 And the man of God was angry
with him, and said, "You should
have struck five or six times; then
you would have struck Syria till
you had destroyed *it!* [a]But now
you will strike Syria *only* three
times."
20 Then Elisha [1]died, and they
buried him. And the [a]*raiding*
bands from Moab invaded the land
in the spring of the year.
21 So it was, as they were burying
a man, that suddenly they spied a
band *of raiders;* and they put the
man in the tomb of Elisha; and
when the man was let down and
touched the bones of Elisha, he re-
vived and stood on his feet.

Israel Recaptures Cities from Syria

22 And [a]Hazael king of Syria op-
pressed Israel all the days of Je-
hoahaz.
23 But the LORD was [a]gracious to
them, had compassion on them,
and [b]regarded them, [c]because of
His covenant with Abraham,
Isaac, and Jacob, and would not
yet destroy them or cast them from
His presence.
24 Now Hazael king of Syria died.
Then Ben-Hadad his son reigned
in his place.
25 And [1]Jehoash the son of Jehoa-
haz recaptured from the hand of
Ben-Hadad, the son of Hazael, the
cities which he had taken out of
the hand of Jehoahaz his father by
war. [a]Three times Joash defeated
him and recaptured the cities of Is-
rael.

Amaziah Reigns in Judah

14 In [a]the second year of Joash
the son of Jehoahaz, king of
Israel, [b]Amaziah the son of Joash,
king of Judah, became king.
2 He was twenty-five years old
when he became king, and he
reigned twenty-nine years in Jeru-
salem. His mother's name was Je-
hoaddan of Jerusalem.
3 And he did *what was* right in
the sight of the LORD, yet not like
his father David; he did everything
[a]as his father Joash had done.
4 [a]However the [1]high places
were not taken away, and the peo-
ple still sacrificed and burned in-
cense on the high places.
5 Now it happened, as soon as
the kingdom was established in his
hand, that he executed his ser-
vants [a]who had murdered his fa-
ther the king.
6 But the children of the murder-
ers he did not execute, according
to what is written in the Book of
the Law of Moses, in which the
LORD commanded, saying, [a]"Fa-
thers shall not be put to death for
their children, nor shall children
be put to death for their fathers;
but a person shall be put to death
for his own sin."
7 [a]He killed ten thousand Edom-

---

12 [a]2 Kin. 14:8–15 [b]2 Kin. 13:14–19, 25 [c]2 Kin. 14:9; 2 Chr. 25:17–25
13 [a]2 Kin. 14:16 [1]Died and joined his ancestors
14 [a]2 Kin. 2:12
17 [a]1 Kin. 20:26
19 [a]2 Kin. 13:25
20 [a]2 Kin. 3:5; 24:2 [1]Having prophesied at least 55 years
22 [a]2 Kin. 8:12, 13
23 [a]2 Kin. 14:27 [b][Ex. 2:24, 25] [c]Gen. 13:16, 17; 17:2–7; Ex. 32:13
25 [a]2 Kin. 13:18, 19 [1]*Joash*, vv. 12–14, 25

CHAPTER 14

1 [a]2 Kin. 13:10 [b]2 Chr. 25:1, 2
3 [a]2 Kin. 12:2
4 [a]2 Kin. 12:3 [1]Places for pagan worship
5 [a]2 Kin. 12:20
6 [a]Deut. 24:16; [Jer. 31:30; Ezek. 18:4, 20]
7 [a]2 Chr. 25:5–16

ites in [b]the Valley of Salt, and took
[1]Sela by war, [c]and called its name
Joktheel to this day.
8 [a]Then Amaziah sent messen-
gers to [1]Jehoash the son of Jehoa-
haz, the son of Jehu, king of Israel,
saying, "Come, let us face one an-
other *in battle.*"
9 And Jehoash king of Israel sent
to Amaziah king of Judah, saying,
[a]"The thistle that *was* in Lebanon
sent to the [b]cedar that *was* in Leb-
anon, saying, 'Give your daughter
to my son as wife'; and a wild
beast that *was* in Lebanon passed
by and trampled the thistle.
10 "You have indeed defeated
Edom, and [a]your heart has [1]lifted
you up. Glory *in that,* and stay at
home; for why should you meddle
with trouble so that you fall—you
and Judah with you?"
11 But Amaziah would not heed.
Therefore Jehoash king of Israel
went out; so he and Amaziah king
of Judah faced one another at
[a]Beth Shemesh, which *belongs* to
Judah.
12 And Judah was defeated by Is-
rael, and every man fled to his
tent.
13 Then Jehoash king of Israel
captured Amaziah king of Judah,
the son of Jehoash, the son of Aha-
ziah, at Beth Shemesh; and he
went to Jerusalem, and broke
down the wall of Jerusalem from
[a]the Gate of Ephraim to [b]the
Corner Gate—[1]four hundred cu-
bits.
14 And he took all [a]the gold and
silver, all the articles that were
found in the house of the LORD and
in the treasuries of the king's
house, and hostages, and returned
to Samaria.
15 [a]Now the rest of the acts of Je-
hoash which he did—his might,
and how he fought with Amaziah
king of Judah—*are* they not writ-
ten in the book of the chronicles
of the kings of Israel?
16 So Jehoash [1]rested with his fa-
thers, and was buried in Samaria
with the kings of Israel. Then Jero-
boam his son reigned in his place.
17 [a]Amaziah the son of Joash,
king of Judah, lived fifteen years
after the death of Jehoash the son
of Jehoahaz, king of Israel.
18 Now the rest of the acts of
Amaziah, *are* they not written in
the book of the chronicles of the
kings of Judah?
19 And [a]they formed a conspiracy
against him in Jerusalem, and he
fled to [b]Lachish; but they sent after
him to Lachish and killed him
there.
20 Then they brought him on
horses, and he was buried at Jeru-
salem with his fathers in the City
of David.
21 And all the people of Judah
took [a]Azariah,[1] who *was* sixteen
years old, and made him king in-
stead of his father Amaziah.
22 He built [a]Elath[1] and restored it
to Judah, after [2]the king rested
with his fathers.

Jeroboam II Reigns in Israel

23 In the fifteenth year of Ama-
ziah the son of Joash, king of Ju-
dah, Jeroboam the son of Joash,
king of Israel, became king in Sa-
maria, *and reigned* forty-one
years.
24 And he did evil in the sight of
the LORD; he did not depart from
all the [a]sins of Jeroboam the son
of Nebat, who had made Israel
sin.
25 He [a]restored the [1]territory of
Israel [b]from the entrance of Ha-
math to [c]the[2] Sea of the Arabah,
according to the word of the LORD
God of Israel, which He had spo-
ken through His servant [d]Jonah
the son of Amittai, the prophet
who *was* from [e]Gath Hepher.
26 For the LORD [a]saw *that* the af-
fliction of Israel *was* very bitter;
and whether bond or free, [b]there
was no helper for Israel.
27 [a]And the LORD did not say that
He would blot out the name of Is-
rael from under heaven; but He
saved them by the hand of Jero-
boam the son of Joash.
28 Now the rest of the acts of Jero-
boam, and all that he did—his
might, how he made war, and how
he recaptured for Israel, from
[a]Damascus and Hamath, [b]*what
had belonged* to Judah—*are* they
not written in the book of the
chronicles of the kings of Israel?
29 So Jeroboam [1]rested with his
fathers, the kings of Israel. Then
[a]Zechariah his son reigned in his
place.

7 [b]2 Sam. 8:13 [c]Josh. 15:38 [1]Lit. *The Rock;* the city of Petra
8 [a]2 Chr. 25:17, 18 [1]*Joash,* 2 Kin. 13:9, 12–14, 25; 2 Chr. 25:17ff.
9 [a]Judg. 9:8–15 [b]1 Kin. 4:33
10 [a]Deut. 8:14 [1]Made you proud
11 [a]Josh. 19:38; 21:16
13 [a]Neh. 8:16; 12:39 [b]Jer. 31:38 [1]About 600 feet
14 [a]1 Kin. 7:51
15 [a]2 Kin. 13:12, 13
16 [1]Died and joined his ancestors
17 [a]2 Chr. 25:25–28
19 [a]2 Chr. 25:27 [b]Josh. 10:31
21 [a]2 Kin. 15:13 [1]*Uzziah,* 2 Chr. 26:1ff.; Is. 6:1; etc.
22 [a]2 Kin. 16:6 [1]Heb. *Eloth* [2]Amaziah died and joined his ancestors.
24 [a]1 Kin. 12:26–33
25 [a]2 Kin. 10:32; 13:5, 25 [b]1 Kin. 8:65 [c]Deut. 3:17 [d]Jon. 1:1 [e]Josh. 19:13 [1]*border* [2]The Dead Sea
26 [a]2 Kin. 13:4 [b]Deut. 32:36
27 [a][2 Kin. 13:5, 23]
28 [a]1 Kin. 11:24 [b]2 Chr. 8:3
29 [a]2 Kin. 15:8 [1]Died and joined his ancestors

Azariah Reigns in Judah

15 In the twenty-seventh year of Jeroboam king of Israel, [a]Azariah the son of Amaziah, king of Judah, [b]became king.

2 He was sixteen years old when he became king, and he reigned fifty-two years in Jerusalem. His mother's name *was* Jecholiah of Jerusalem.

3 And he did *what was* right in the sight of the LORD, according to all that his father Amaziah had done,

4 [a]except that the [1]high places were not removed; the people still sacrificed and burned incense on the high places.

5 Then the LORD [a]struck the king, so that he was a leper until the day of his [b]death; so he [c]dwelt in an isolated house. And Jotham the king's son *was* over the *royal* house, judging the people of the land.

6 Now the rest of the acts of Azariah, and all that he did, *are* they not written in the book of the chronicles of the kings of Judah?

7 So Azariah [1]rested with his fathers, and [a]they buried him with his fathers in the City of David. Then Jotham his son reigned in his place.

Zechariah Reigns in Israel

8 In the thirty-eighth year of Azariah king of Judah, [a]Zechariah the son of Jeroboam reigned over Israel in Samaria six months.

9 And he did evil in the sight of the LORD, [a]as his fathers had done; he did not depart from the sins of Jeroboam the son of Nebat, who had made Israel sin.

10 Then Shallum the son of Jabesh conspired against him, and [a]struck and killed him in front of the people; and he reigned in his place.

11 Now the rest of the acts of Zechariah, indeed they *are* written in the book of the chronicles of the kings of Israel.

12 This *was* the word of the LORD which He spoke to Jehu, saying, [a]"Your sons shall sit on the throne of Israel to the fourth *generation*." And so it was.

Shallum Reigns in Israel

13 Shallum the son of Jabesh became king in the thirty-ninth year of [1]Uzziah king of Judah; and he reigned a full month in Samaria.

14 For Menahem the son of Gadi went up from [a]Tirzah, came to Samaria, and struck Shallum the son of Jabesh in Samaria and killed him; and he reigned in his place.

15 Now the rest of the acts of Shallum, and the conspiracy which he [1]led, indeed they *are* written in the book of the chronicles of the kings of Israel.

16 Then from Tirzah, Menahem attacked [a]Tiphsah, all who *were* there, and its territory. Because they did not surrender, therefore he attacked *it*. All [b]the women there who were with child he ripped open.

Menahem Reigns in Israel

17 In the thirty-ninth year of Azariah king of Judah, Menahem the son of Gadi became king over Israel, *and reigned* ten years in Samaria.

18 And he did evil in the sight of the LORD; he did not depart all his days from the sins of Jeroboam the son of Nebat, who had made Israel sin.

19 [a]Pul[1] king of Assyria came against the land; and Menahem gave Pul a thousand talents of silver, that his [2]hand might be with him to [b]strengthen the kingdom under his control.

20 And Menahem [a]exacted[1] the money from Israel, from all the very wealthy, from each man fifty shekels of silver, to give to the king of Assyria. So the king of Assyria turned back, and did not stay there in the land.

21 Now the rest of the acts of Menahem, and all that he did, *are* they not written in the book of the chronicles of the kings of Israel?

22 So Menahem [1]rested with his fathers. Then Pekahiah his son reigned in his place.

Pekahiah Reigns in Israel

23 In the fiftieth year of Azariah king of Judah, Pekahiah the son

CHAPTER 15

1 [a]2 Kin. 15:13, 30 [b]2 Kin. 14:21; 2 Chr. 26:1, 3, 4
4 [a]2 Kin. 12:3; 14:4; 15:35 [1]Places for pagan worship
5 [a]2 Chr. 26:19–23; Ps. 78:31 [b]Is. 6:1 [c][Lev. 13:46]; Num. 12:14
7 [a]2 Chr. 26:23 [1]Died and joined his ancestors
8 [a]2 Kin. 14:29
9 [a]2 Kin. 14:24
10 [a]Amos 7:9
12 [a]2 Kin. 10:30
13 [1]*Azariah*, 2 Kin. 14:21ff.; 15:1ff.
14 [a]1 Kin. 14:17; Song 6:4
15 [1]Lit. *conspired*
16 [a]1 Kin. 4:24 [b]2 Kin. 8:12; Hos. 13:16
19 [a]1 Chr. 5:26; Is. 66:19; Hos. 8:9 [b]2 Kin. 14:5 [1]Tiglath-Pileser III, v. 29 [2]Support
20 [a]2 Kin. 23:35 [1]*took*
22 [1]Died and joined his ancestors

of Menahem became king over Is-
rael in Samaria, *and reigned* two
years.
24 And he did evil in the sight of
the LORD; he did not depart from
the sins of Jeroboam the son of Ne-
bat, who had made Israel sin.
25 Then Pekah the son of Rema-
liah, an officer of his, conspired
against him and [1]killed him in Sa-
maria, in the [a]citadel of the king's
house, along with Argob and
Arieh; and with him were fifty men
of Gilead. He killed him and
reigned in his place.
26 Now the rest of the acts of
Pekahiah, and all that he did, in-
deed they *are* written in the book
of the chronicles of the kings of
Israel.

Pekah Reigns in Israel

27 In the fifty-second year of Aza-
riah king of Judah, [a]Pekah the son
of Remaliah became king over Is-
rael in Samaria, *and reigned*
twenty years.
28 And he did evil in the sight of
the LORD; he did not depart from
the sins of Jeroboam the son of Ne-
bat, who had made Israel sin.
29 In the days of Pekah king of
Israel, [1]Tiglath-Pileser king of As-
syria [a]came and took [b]Ijon, Abel
Beth Maachah, Janoah, Kedesh,
Hazor, Gilead, and Galilee, all the
land of Naphtali; and he [c]carried
them captive to Assyria.
30 Then Hoshea the son of Elah
led a conspiracy against Pekah the
son of Remaliah, and struck and
killed him; so he [a]reigned in his
place in the twentieth year of Jo-
tham the son of Uzziah.
31 Now the rest of the acts of
Pekah, and all that he did, indeed
they *are* written in the book of the
chronicles of the kings of Israel.

Jotham Reigns in Judah

32 In the second year of Pekah the
son of Remaliah, king of Israel,
[a]Jotham the son of Uzziah, king
of Judah, began to reign.
33 He was twenty-five years old
when he became king, and he
reigned sixteen years in Jerusa-
lem. His mother's name *was*
[1]Jerusha the daughter of Zadok.
34 And he did *what was* right in
the sight of the LORD; he did [a]ac-
cording to all that his father Uz-
ziah had done.
35 [a]However the [1]high places
were not removed; the people still
sacrificed and burned incense on
the high places. [b]He built the Up-
per Gate of the house of the LORD.
36 Now the rest of the acts of Jo-
tham, and all that he did, *are* they
not written in the book of the
chronicles of the kings of Judah?
37 In those days the LORD began
to send [a]Rezin king of Syria and
[b]Pekah the son of Remaliah
against Judah.
38 So Jotham [1]rested with his
fathers, and was buried with his
fathers in the City of David his fa-
ther. Then Ahaz his son reigned
in his place.

Ahaz Reigns in Judah

16 In the seventeenth year of
Pekah the son of Remaliah,
Ahaz the son of Jotham, king of
Judah, began to reign.
2 Ahaz *was* twenty years old
when he became king, and he
reigned sixteen years in Jerusa-
lem; and he did not do *what was*
right in the sight of the LORD his
God, as his father David *had done.*
3 But he walked in the way of the
kings of Israel; indeed [a]he made
his son pass through the fire, ac-
cording to the [b]abominations of
the nations whom the LORD had
cast out from before the children
of Israel.
4 And he sacrificed and burned
incense on the [a]high places, [b]on
the hills, and under every green
tree.
5 [a]Then Rezin king of Syria and
Pekah the son of Remaliah, king
of Israel, came up to Jerusalem to
make war; and they besieged Ahaz
but could not overcome *him.*
6 At that time Rezin king of Syria
[a]captured [1]Elath for Syria, and
drove the men of Judah from
Elath. Then the [2]Edomites went to
Elath, and dwell there to this day.
7 So Ahaz sent messengers to
[a]Tiglath-Pileser[1] king of Assyria,
saying, "I *am* your servant and
your son. Come up and save me
from the hand of the king of Syria
and from the hand of the king of
Israel, who rise up against me."
8 And Ahaz [a]took the silver and

25 [a]1 Kin. 16:18 [1]Lit. *struck*
27 [a]2 Chr. 28:6; Is. 7:1
29 [a]2 Kin. 16:7, 10; 1 Chr. 5:26 [b]1 Kin. 15:20 [c]2 Kin. 17:6 [1]A later name of *Pul,* v. 19
30 [a]2 Kin. 17:1; [Hos. 10:3, 7, 15]
32 [a]2 Chr. 27:1
33 [1]*Jerushah,* 2 Chr. 27:1
34 [a]2 Kin. 15:3, 4; 2 Chr. 26:4, 5
35 [a]2 Kin. 15:4 [b]2 Chr. 23:20; 27:3 [1]Places for pagan worship
37 [a]2 Kin. 16:5–9; Is. 7:1–17 [b]2 Kin. 15:26, 27
38 [1]Died and joined his ancestors

CHAPTER 16

3 [a][Lev. 18:21]; 2 Kin. 17:17; 2 Chr. 28:3; Ps. 106:37, 38; Is. 1:1 [b][Deut. 12:31]; 2 Kin. 21:2, 11
4 [a]2 Kin. 15:34, 35 [b][Deut. 12:2]; 1 Kin. 14:23
5 [a]2 Kin. 15:37; Is. 7:1, 4
6 [a]2 Kin. 14:22; 2 Chr. 26:2 [1]Lit. *Large Tree;* sing. of *Eloth* [2]A few ancient mss. *Syrians*
7 [a]2 Kin. 15:29; 1 Chr. 5:26; 2 Chr. 28:20 [1]A later name of *Pul,* 2 Kin. 15:19
8 [a]2 Kin. 12:17, 18; 2 Chr. 28:21

gold that was found in the house
of the LORD, and in the treasuries
of the king's house, and sent *it as*
a present to the king of Assyria.
9 So the king of Assyria heeded
him; for the king of Assyria went
up against [a]Damascus and [b]took
it, carried *its people* captive to
[c]Kir, and killed Rezin.
10 Now King Ahaz went to Da-
mascus to meet Tiglath-Pileser
king of Assyria, and saw an altar
that *was* at Damascus; and King
Ahaz sent to Urijah the priest the
design of the altar and its pattern,
according to all its workmanship.
11 Then [a]Urijah the priest built an
altar according to all that King
Ahaz had sent from Damascus. So
Urijah the priest made *it* before
King Ahaz came back from Da-
mascus.
12 And when the king came back
from Damascus, the king saw the
altar; and [a]the king approached
the altar and made offerings on it.
13 So he burned his burnt offering
and his grain offering; and he
poured his drink offering and
sprinkled the blood of his peace of-
ferings on the altar.
14 He also brought [a]the bronze al-
tar which *was* before the LORD,
from the front of the [1]temple—
from between the *new* altar and
the house of the LORD—and put it
on the north side of the *new* altar.
15 Then King Ahaz commanded
Urijah the priest, saying, "On the
great *new* altar burn [a]the morning
burnt offering, the evening grain
offering, the king's burnt sacrifice,
and his grain offering, with the
burnt offering of all the people of
the land, their grain offering, and
their drink offerings; and sprinkle
on it all the blood of the burnt of-
fering and all the blood of the sac-
rifice. And the bronze altar shall
be for me to inquire *by*."
16 Thus did Urijah the priest, ac-
cording to all that King Ahaz com-
manded.
17 [a]And King Ahaz cut off [b]the
panels of the carts, and removed
the lavers from them; and he took
down [c]the Sea from the bronze
oxen that *were* under it, and put
it on a pavement of stones.
18 Also he removed the Sabbath
pavilion which they had built in
the temple, and he removed the
king's outer entrance from the
house of the LORD, on account of
the king of Assyria.
19 Now the rest of the acts of
Ahaz which he did, *are* they not
written in the book of the chroni-
cles of the kings of Judah?
20 So Ahaz rested with his fa-
thers, and [a]was buried with his fa-
thers in the City of David. Then
Hezekiah his son reigned in his
place.

Hoshea Reigns in Israel

17 In the twelfth year of Ahaz
king of Judah, [a]Hoshea the
son of Elah became king of Israel
in Samaria, *and he reigned* nine
years.
2 And he did evil in the sight of
the LORD, but not as the kings of
Israel who were before him.
3 [a]Shalmaneser king of Assyria
came up against him; and Hoshea
[b]became his vassal, and paid him
tribute money.
4 And the king of Assyria uncov-
ered a conspiracy by Hoshea; for
he had sent messengers to So, king
of Egypt, and brought no tribute
to the king of Assyria, as *he had
done* year by year. Therefore the
king of Assyria shut him up, and
bound him in prison.

Israel Carried Captive to Assyria

5 Now [a]the king of Assyria went
throughout all the land, and went
up to Samaria and besieged it for
three years.
6 [a]In the ninth year of Hoshea,
the king of Assyria took Samaria
and [b]carried Israel away to As-
syria, [c]and placed them in Halah
and by the Habor, the River of Go-
zan, and in the cities of the Medes.
7 For [a]so it was that the children
of Israel had sinned against the
LORD their God, who had brought
them up out of the land of Egypt,
from under the hand of Pharaoh
king of Egypt; and they had
[b]feared other gods,
8 and [a]had walked in the statutes
of the nations whom the LORD had
cast out from before the children
of Israel, and of the kings of Israel,
which they had made.
9 Also the children of Israel se-
cretly did against the LORD their

---

9 [a]2 Kin. 14:28 [b]Amos 1:5 [c]Is. 22:6; Amos 9:7
11 [a]Is. 8:2
12 [a]2 Chr. 26:16, 19
14 [a]Ex. 27:1, 2; 40:6, 29; 2 Chr. 4:1 [1]Lit. *house*
15 [a]Ex. 29:39–41
17 [a]2 Chr. 28:24 [b]1 Kin. 7:27–29 [c]1 Kin. 7:23–25
20 [a]2 Chr. 28:27

CHAPTER 17

1 [a]2 Kin. 15:30
3 [a]2 Kin. 18:9–12 [b]2 Kin. 24:1
5 [a]2 Kin. 18:9; Hos. 13:16
6 [a]2 Kin. 18:10, 11; Is. 7:7–9; Hos. 1:4; 13:16; Amos 4:2 [b]Lev. 26:32, 33; [Deut. 28:36, 64; 29:27, 28] [c]1 Chr. 5:26
7 [a][Josh. 23:16] [b]Judg. 6:10
8 [a][Lev. 18:3; Deut. 18:9]; 2 Kin. 16:3

God things that *were* not right, and
they built for themselves [1]high
places in all their cities, [a]from
watchtower to fortified city.
10 [a]They set up for themselves *sa-
cred* pillars and [b]wooden images[1]
[c]on every high hill and under ev-
ery green tree.
11 There they burned incense on
all the high places, like the nations
whom the LORD had carried away
before them; and they did wicked
things to provoke the LORD to an-
ger,
12 for they served idols, [a]of which
the LORD had said to them, [b]"You
shall not do this thing."
13 Yet the LORD testified against
Israel and against Judah, by all of
His [a]prophets, [b]every seer, saying,
[c]"Turn from your evil ways, and
keep My commandments *and* My
statutes, according to all the law
which I commanded your fathers,
and which I sent to you by My ser-
vants the prophets."
14 Nevertheless they would not
hear, but [a]stiffened their necks,
like the necks of their fathers, who
[b]did not believe in the LORD their
God.
15 And they [a]rejected His statutes
[b]and His covenant that He had
made with their fathers, and His
testimonies which He had testified
against them; they followed [c]idols,
[d]became idolaters, and *went* after
the nations who *were* all around
them, *concerning* whom the LORD
had charged them that they should
[e]not do like them.
16 So they left all the command-
ments of the LORD their God,
[a]made for themselves a molded
image *and* two calves, [b]made a
wooden image and worshiped all
the [c]host of heaven, [d]and served
Baal.
17 [a]And they caused their sons
and daughters to pass through the
fire, [b]practiced witchcraft and
soothsaying, and [c]sold themselves
to do evil in the sight of the LORD,
to provoke Him to anger.
18 Therefore the LORD was very
angry with Israel, and removed
them from His sight; there was
none left [a]but the tribe of Judah
alone.
19 Also [a]Judah did not keep the
commandments of the LORD their

9 [a]2 Kin. 18:8 [1]Places for pagan worship
10 [a]1 Kin. 14:23; Is. 57:5 [b][Ex. 34:12–14; Deut. 16:21]; Mic. 5:14 [c][Deut. 12:2]; 2 Kin. 16:4 [1]Heb. *Asherim*, Canaanite deities
12 [a][Ex. 20:3–5; Lev. 26:1; Deut. 5:7, 8] [b][Deut. 4:19]
13 [a]Neh. 9:29, 30 [b]1 Sam. 9:9 [c][Jer. 18:11; 25:5; 35:15; Ezek. 18:31]
14 [a]Ex. 32:9; 33:3; Deut. 31:27; [Prov. 29:1; Acts 7:51] [b]Deut. 9:23; Ps. 78:22
15 [a]Jer. 44:3 [b]Ex. 24:6–8; Deut. 29:25 [c]Deut. 32:21; 1 Kin. 16:31; [1 Cor. 8:4] [d]2 Chr. 13:7; Jer. 2:5; [Rom. 1:21–23] [e][Deut. 12:30, 31]
16 [a]Ex. 32:8; 1 Kin. 12:28 [b][1 Kin. 14:15] [c][Deut. 4:19] [d]1 Kin. 16:31; 22:53
17 [a][Lev. 18:21]; 2 Kin. 16:3; Ezek. 23:37 [b][Lev. 19:26; Deut. 18:10–12] [c]1 Kin. 21:20
18 [a]1 Kin. 11:13, 32
19 [a]Jer. 3:8
20 [a]Judg. 2:14; 2 Kin. 13:3; 15:29 [b]2 Kin. 24:20
21 [a]1 Kin. 11:11, 31 [b]1 Kin. 12:20, 28
23 [a]1 Kin. 14:16; Is. 8:4 [b]2 Kin. 17:6
24 [a]Ezra 4:2, 10 [b]2 Kin. 18:34
29 [a]1 Kin. 12:31; 13:32

God, but walked in the statutes of
Israel which they made.
20 And the LORD rejected all the
descendants of Israel, afflicted
them, and [a]delivered them into the
hand of plunderers, until He had
cast them from His [b]sight.
21 For [a]He tore Israel from the
house of David, and [b]they made
Jeroboam the son of Nebat king.
Then Jeroboam drove Israel from
following the LORD, and made
them commit a great sin.
22 For the children of Israel
walked in all the sins of Jeroboam
which he did; they did not depart
from them,
23 until the LORD removed Israel
out of His sight, [a]as He had said
by all His servants the prophets.
[b]So Israel was carried away from
their own land to Assyria, *as it is*
to this day.

Assyria Resettles Samaria

24 [a]Then the king of Assyria
brought *people* from Babylon, Cu-
thah, [b]Ava, Hamath, and from
Sepharvaim, and placed *them* in
the cities of Samaria instead of the
children of Israel; and they took
possession of Samaria and dwelt
in its cities.
25 And it was so, at the beginning
of their dwelling there, *that* they
did not fear the LORD; therefore the
LORD sent lions among them,
which killed *some* of them.
26 So they spoke to the king of As-
syria, saying, "The nations whom
you have removed and placed in
the cities of Samaria do not know
the rituals of the God of the land;
therefore He has sent lions among
them, and indeed, they are killing
them because they do not know
the rituals of the God of the land."
27 Then the king of Assyria com-
manded, saying, "Send there one
of the priests whom you brought
from there; let him go and dwell
there, and let him teach them the
rituals of the God of the land."
28 Then one of the priests whom
they had carried away from Sa-
maria came and dwelt in Bethel,
and taught them how they should
fear the LORD.
29 However every nation contin-
ued to make gods of its own, and
put *them* [a]in the shrines on the

high places which the Samaritans
had made, *every* nation in the cit-
ies where they dwelt.
30 The men of [a]Babylon made
Succoth Benoth, the men of Cuth
made Nergal, the men of Hamath
made Ashima,
31 [a]and the Avites made Nibhaz
and Tartak; and the Sepharvites
[b]burned their children in fire to
Adrammelech and Anammelech,
the gods of Sepharvaim.
32 So they feared the LORD, [a]and
from every class they appointed
for themselves priests of the [1]high
places, who sacrificed for them in
the shrines of the high places.
33 [a]They feared the LORD, yet
served their own gods—according
to the rituals of the nations from
among whom they were carried
away.
34 To this day they continue prac-
ticing the former rituals; they do
not fear the LORD, nor do they
follow their statutes or their ordi-
nances, or the law and command-
ment which the LORD had com-
manded the children of Jacob,
[a]whom He named Israel,
35 with whom the LORD had made
a covenant and charged them, say-
ing: [a]"You shall not fear other
gods, nor [b]bow down to them nor
serve them nor sacrifice to them;
36 "but the LORD, who [a]brought
you up from the land of Egypt with
great power and [b]an outstretched
arm, [c]Him you shall fear, Him you
shall worship, and to Him you
shall offer sacrifice.
37 "And the statutes, the ordi-
nances, the law, and the com-
mandment which He wrote for
you, [a]you shall be careful to ob-
serve forever; you shall not fear
other gods.
38 "And the covenant that I have
made with you, [a]you shall not for-
get, nor shall you fear other gods.
39 "But the LORD your God you
shall fear; and He will deliver you
from the hand of all your ene-
mies."
40 However they did not obey, but
they followed their former rituals.
41 [a]So these nations feared the
LORD, yet served their carved im-
ages; also their children and their
children's children have continued

30 [a]2 Kin. 17:24
31 [a]Ezra 4:9 [b][Lev. 18:21; Deut. 12:31]
32 [a]1 Kin. 12:31; 13:33 [1]Places for pagan worship
33 [a]Zeph. 1:5
34 [a]Gen. 32:28; 35:10
35 [a]Judg. 6:10 [b][Ex. 20:5]
36 [a]Ex. 14:15–30 [b]Ex. 6:6; 9:15 [c][Deut. 10:20]
37 [a]Deut. 5:32
38 [a]Deut. 4:23; 6:12
41 [a]2 Kin. 17:32, 33

CHAPTER 18

1 [a]2 Kin. 17:1 [b]2 Chr. 28:27; 29:1
2 [a]Is. 38:5 [1]*Abijah*, 2 Chr. 29:1ff.
4 [a]2 Chr. 31:1 [b]Num. 21:5–9 [1]Places for pagan worship [2]Heb. *Asherah*, a Canaanite goddess [3]Lit. *Bronze Thing*, also similar to Heb. *nahash*, *serpent*
5 [a]2 Kin. 19:10; [Job 13:15; Ps. 13:5] [b]2 Kin. 23:25
6 [a]Deut. 10:20; Josh. 23:8
7 [a][2 Chr. 15:2] [b]Gen. 39:2, 3; 1 Sam. 18:5, 14; Ps. 60:12 [c]2 Kin. 16:7
8 [a]1 Chr. 4:41; 2 Chr. 28:18; Is. 14:29 [b]2 Kin. 17:9 [1]Lit. *struck*
9 [a]2 Kin. 17:3
10 [a]2 Kin. 17:6
11 [a]2 Kin. 17:6; Hos. 1:4; Amos 4:2 [b]1 Chr. 5:26
12 [a]2 Kin. 17:7–18

doing as their fathers did, even to
this day.

Hezekiah Reigns in Judah

18 Now it came to pass in the
third year of [a]Hoshea the
son of Elah, king of Israel, *that*
[b]Hezekiah the son of Ahaz, king
of Judah, began to reign.
2 He was twenty-five years old
when he became king, and he
reigned twenty-nine years in Jeru-
salem. His mother's name *was*
[a]Abi[1] the daughter of Zechariah.
3 And he did *what was* right in
the sight of the LORD, according to
all that his father David had done.
4 [a]He removed the [1]high places
and broke the *sacred* pillars, cut
down the [2]wooden image and
broke in pieces the [b]bronze ser-
pent that Moses had made; for un-
til those days the children of Israel
burned incense to it, and called it
[3]Nehushtan.
5 He [a]trusted in the LORD God of
Israel, [b]so that after him was none
like him among all the kings of Ju-
dah, nor who were before him.
6 For he [a]held fast to the LORD;
he did not depart from following
Him, but kept His commandments,
which the LORD had commanded
Moses.
7 The LORD [a]was with him; he
[b]prospered wherever he went. And
he [c]rebelled against the king of As-
syria and did not serve him.
8 [a]He [1]subdued the Philistines, as
far as Gaza and its territory, [b]from
watchtower to fortified city.
9 Now [a]it came to pass in the
fourth year of King Hezekiah,
which *was* the seventh year of
Hoshea the son of Elah, king of Is-
rael, *that* Shalmaneser king of As-
syria came up against Samaria
and besieged it.
10 And at the end of three years
they took it. In the sixth year of
Hezekiah, that *is*, [a]the ninth year
of Hoshea king of Israel, Samaria
was taken.
11 [a]Then the king of Assyria car-
ried Israel away captive to As-
syria, and put them [b]in Halah and
by the Habor, the River of Gozan,
and in the cities of the Medes,
12 because they [a]did not obey the
voice of the LORD their God, but
transgressed His covenant *and* all

that Moses the servant of the LORD had commanded; and they would neither hear nor do *them.*

13 And [a]in the fourteenth year of King Hezekiah, Sennacherib king of Assyria came up against all the fortified cities of Judah and took them.

14 Then Hezekiah king of Judah sent to the king of Assyria at Lachish, saying, "I have done wrong; turn away from me; whatever you impose on me I will pay." And the king of Assyria assessed Hezekiah king of Judah three hundred talents of silver and thirty talents of gold.

15 So Hezekiah [a]gave *him* all the silver that was found in the house of the LORD and in the treasuries of the king's house.

16 At that time Hezekiah stripped *the gold from* the doors of the temple of the LORD, and *from* the pillars which Hezekiah king of Judah had overlaid, and gave [1]it to the king of Assyria.

Sennacherib Boasts Against the LORD

17 Then the king of Assyria sent *the* [1]Tartan, *the* [2]Rabsaris, *and the* [3]Rabshakeh from Lachish, with a great army against Jerusalem, to King Hezekiah. And they went up and came to Jerusalem. When they had come up, they went and stood by the [a]aqueduct from the upper pool, [b]which *was* on the highway to the Fuller's Field.

18 And when they had called to the king, [a]Eliakim the son of Hilkiah, who *was* over the household, Shebna the [1]scribe, and Joah the son of Asaph, the recorder, came out to them.

19 Then *the* Rabshakeh said to them, "Say now to Hezekiah, 'Thus says the great king, the king of Assyria: [a]"What confidence *is* this in which you trust?

20 "You speak of *having* plans and power for war; but *they are* [1]mere words. And in whom do you trust, that you rebel against me?

21 [a]"Now look! You are trusting in the staff of this broken reed, Egypt, on which if a man leans, it will go into his hand and pierce it. So *is* Pharaoh king of Egypt to all who trust in him.

22 "But if you say to me, 'We trust in the LORD our God,' *is* it not He [a]whose [1]high places and whose altars Hezekiah has taken away, and said to Judah and Jerusalem, 'You shall worship before this altar in Jerusalem'?" '

23 "Now therefore, I urge you, give a pledge to my master the king of Assyria, and I will give you two thousand horses—if you are able on your part to put riders on them!

24 "How then will you repel one captain of the least of my master's servants, and put your trust in Egypt for chariots and horsemen?

25 "Have I now come up without the LORD against this place to destroy it? The LORD said to me, 'Go up against this land, and destroy it.' "

26 [a]Then Eliakim the son of Hilkiah, Shebna, and Joah said to *the* Rabshakeh, "Please speak to your servants in [b]Aramaic, for we understand *it;* and do not speak to us in [1]Hebrew in the hearing of the people who *are* on the wall."

27 But *the* Rabshakeh said to them, "Has my master sent me to your master and to you to speak these words, and not to the men who sit on the wall, who will eat and drink their own waste with you?"

28 Then *the* Rabshakeh stood and called out with a loud voice in [1]Hebrew, and spoke, saying, "Hear the word of the great king, the king of Assyria!

29 "Thus says the king: [a]'Do not let Hezekiah deceive you, for he shall not be able to deliver you from his hand;

30 'nor let Hezekiah make you trust in the LORD, saying, "The LORD will surely deliver us; this city shall not be given into the hand of the king of Assyria." '

31 "Do not listen to Hezekiah; for thus says the king of Assyria: 'Make *peace* with me [1]by a present and come out to me; and every one of you eat from his own [a]vine and every one from his own fig tree, and every one of you drink the waters of his own cistern;

32 'until I come and take you away to a land like your own land, [a]a land of grain and new wine, a land of bread and vineyards, a

---

13 [a]2 Chr. 32:1; Is. 36:1—39:8

15 [a]1 Kin. 15:18, 19; 2 Kin. 12:18; 16:8

16 [1]Lit. *them*

17 [a]2 Kin. 20:20 [b]Is. 7:3 [1]A title, probably *Commander in Chief* [2]A title, probably *Chief Officer* [3]A title, probably *Chief of Staff* or *Governor*

18 [a]2 Kin. 19:2; Is. 22:20 [1]*secretary*

19 [a]2 Chr. 32:10; [Ps. 118:8, 9]

20 [1]Lit. *a word of the lips*

21 [a]Is. 30:2–7; Ezek. 29:6, 7

22 [a]2 Kin. 18:4; 2 Chr. 31:1; 32:12 [1]Places for pagan worship

26 [a]Is. 36:11—39:8 [b]Ezra 4:7; Dan. 2:4 [1]Lit. *Judean*

28 [1]Lit. *Judean*

29 [a]2 Chr. 32:15

31 [a]1 Kin. 4:20, 25 [1]By paying tribute

32 [a]Deut. 8:7–9; 11:12

land of olive groves and honey,
that you may live and not die. But
do not listen to Hezekiah, lest he
persuade you, saying, "The LORD
will deliver us."
33 [a]'Has any of the gods of the na-
tions at all delivered its land from
the hand of the king of Assyria?
34 'Where *are* the gods of [a]Ha-
math and Arpad? Where *are* the
gods of Sepharvaim and Hena and
[b]Ivah? Indeed, have they delivered
Samaria from my hand?
35 'Who among all the gods of the
lands have delivered their coun-
tries from my hand, [a]that the LORD
should deliver Jerusalem from my
hand?' "
36 But the people held their peace
and answered him not a word; for
the king's commandment was,
"Do not answer him."
37 Then Eliakim the son of Hil-
kiah, who *was* over the household,
Shebna the scribe, and Joah the
son of Asaph, the recorder, came
to Hezekiah [a]with *their* clothes
torn, and told him the words of *the*
Rabshakeh.

Isaiah Assures Deliverance

19 And [a]so it was, when King
Hezekiah heard *it*, that he
tore his clothes, covered himself
with [b]sackcloth, and went into the
house of the LORD.
2 Then he sent Eliakim, who *was*
over the household, Shebna the
scribe, and the elders of the
priests, covered with sackcloth, to
Isaiah the prophet, the son of
Amoz.
3 And they said to him, "Thus
says Hezekiah: 'This day *is* a day
of trouble, and rebuke, and blas-
phemy; for the children have come
to birth, but *there is* no strength
to [1]bring them forth.
4 [a]'It may be that the LORD your
God will hear all the words of *the*
Rabshakeh, whom his master the
king of Assyria has sent to [b]re-
proach the living God, and will [c]re-
buke the words which the LORD
your God has heard. Therefore lift
up *your* prayer for the remnant
that is left.' "
5 So the servants of King Heze-
kiah came to Isaiah.
6 [a]And Isaiah said to them,
"Thus you shall say to your mas-
ter, 'Thus says the LORD: "Do not
be [b]afraid of the words which you
have heard, with which the [c]ser-
vants of the king of Assyria have
blasphemed Me.
7 "Surely I will send [a]a spirit
upon him, and he shall hear a ru-
mor and return to his own land;
and I will cause him to fall by the
sword in his own land." ' "

Sennacherib's Threat and Hezekiah's Prayer

8 Then *the* Rabshakeh returned
and found the king of Assyria war-
ring against Libnah, for he heard
that he had departed [a]from La-
chish.
9 And [a]the king heard concern-
ing Tirhakah king of Ethiopia,
"Look, he has come out to make
war with you." So he again sent
messengers to Hezekiah, saying,
10 "Thus you shall speak to Heze-
kiah king of Judah, saying: 'Do not
let your God [a]in whom you trust
deceive you, saying, "Jerusalem
shall not be given into the hand
of the king of Assyria."
11 'Look! You have heard what
the kings of Assyria have done to
all lands by utterly destroying
them; and shall you be delivered?
12 [a]'Have the gods of the nations
delivered those whom my fathers
have destroyed, Gozan and Haran
and Rezeph, and the people of
[b]Eden who *were* in Telassar?
13 [a]'Where *is* the king of Hamath,
the king of Arpad, and the king of
the city of Sepharvaim, Hena, and
Ivah?' "
14 [a]And Hezekiah received the
letter from the hand of the messen-
gers, and read it; and Hezekiah
went up to the house of the LORD,
and spread it before the LORD.
15 Then Hezekiah prayed before
the LORD, and said: "O LORD God
of Israel, *the One* [a]who dwells *be-
tween* the cherubim, [b]You are
God, You alone, of all the king-
doms of the earth. You have made
heaven and earth.
16 [a]"Incline Your ear, O LORD, and
hear; [b]open Your eyes, O LORD,
and see; and hear the words of
Sennacherib, [c]which he has sent
to reproach the living God.
17 "Truly, LORD, the kings of As-

33 [a]2 Kin. 19:12; Is. 10:10, 11
34 [a]2 Kin. 19:13 [b]2 Kin. 17:24
35 [a]Dan. 3:15
37 [a]Is. 33:7

CHAPTER 19

1 [a]2 Kin. 18:13; 2 Chr. 32:20–22; Is. 37:1 [b]Ps. 69:11
3 [1]*give birth*
4 [a]2 Sam. 16:12 [b]2 Kin. 18:35 [c]Ps. 50:21
6 [a]Is. 37:6 [b][Ps. 112:7] [c]2 Kin. 18:17
7 [a]2 Kin. 19:35–37; Jer. 51:1
8 [a]2 Kin. 18:14, 17
9 [a]1 Sam. 23:27; Is. 37:9
10 [a]2 Kin. 18:5
12 [a]2 Kin. 18:33, 34 [b]Ezek. 27:23
13 [a]2 Kin. 18:34
14 [a]Is. 37:14
15 [a]Ex. 25:22; Ps. 80:1; Is. 37:16 [b][Is. 44:6]
16 [a]Ps. 31:2; Is. 37:17 [b]1 Kin. 8:29; 2 Chr. 6:40 [c]2 Kin. 19:4

syria have laid waste the nations
and their lands,
18 "and have cast their gods into
the fire; for they *were* [a]not gods,
but [b]the work of men's hands—
wood and stone. Therefore they
destroyed them.
19 "Now therefore, O LORD our
God, I pray, save us from his hand,
[a]that all the kingdoms of the earth
may [b]know that You *are* the LORD
God, You alone."

The Word of the LORD Concerning Sennacherib

20 Then Isaiah the son of Amoz
sent to Hezekiah, saying, "Thus
says the LORD God of Israel: [a]'Be-
cause you have prayed to Me
against Sennacherib king of As-
syria, [b]I have heard.'
21 "This *is* the word which the
LORD has spoken concerning him:

'The virgin, [a]the daughter of Zion,
Has despised you, laughed you to scorn;
The daughter of Jerusalem
[b]Has shaken *her* head behind your back!

22 'Whom have you reproached and blasphemed?
Against whom have you raised *your* voice,
And lifted up your eyes on high?
Against [a]the Holy *One* of Israel.
23 [a]By your messengers you have reproached the Lord,
And said: [b]"By the multitude of my chariots
I have come up to the height of the mountains,
To the limits of Lebanon;
I will cut down its tall cedars
And its choice cypress trees;
I will enter the extremity of its borders,
To its fruitful forest.
24 I have dug and drunk strange water,
And with the soles of my feet I have [a]dried up
All the brooks of defense."

25 'Did you not hear long ago
How [a]I made it,
From ancient times that I formed it?
Now I have brought it to pass,
That [b]you should be
For crushing fortified cities *into* heaps of ruins.
26 Therefore their inhabitants had little power;
They were dismayed and confounded;
They were *as* the grass of the field
And the green herb,
As [a]the grass on the housetops
And *grain* blighted before it is grown.

27 'But [a]I know your dwelling place,
Your going out and your coming in,
And your rage against Me.
28 Because your rage against Me and your tumult
Have come up to My ears,
Therefore [a]I will put My hook in your nose
And My bridle in your lips,
And I will turn you back
[b]By the way which you came.

29 'This *shall be* a [a]sign to you:

You shall eat this year such as grows [1]of itself,
And in the second year what springs from the same;
Also in the third year sow and reap,
Plant vineyards and eat the fruit of them.
30 [a]And the remnant who have escaped of the house of Judah
Shall again take root downward,
And bear fruit upward.
31 For out of Jerusalem shall go a remnant,
And those who escape from Mount Zion.
[a]The zeal of the LORD [1]of hosts will do this.'

32 "Therefore thus says the LORD
concerning the king of Assyria:

'He shall [a]not come into this city,
Nor shoot an arrow there,
Nor come before it with shield,
Nor build a siege mound against it.
33 By the way that he came,
By the same shall he return;
And he shall not come into this city,'
Says the LORD.
34 'For [a]I will [b]defend this city, to save it
For My own sake and [c]for My servant David's sake.'"

Sennacherib's Defeat and Death

35 And [a]it came to pass on a cer-
tain night that the [1]angel of the

18 [a][Is. 44:9–20; Jer. 10:3–5] [b]Ps. 115:4; Jer. 10:3; [Acts 17:29]
19 [a]Ps. 83:18 [b]1 Kin. 8:42, 43
20 [a]Is. 37:21 [b]2 Kin. 20:5; Ps. 65:2
21 [a]Jer. 14:17; Lam. 2:13 [b]Ps. 22:7, 8
22 [a]Jer. 51:5
23 [a]2 Kin. 18:17 [b]Ps. 20:7
24 [a]Is. 19:6
25 [a][Is. 45:7] [b]Is. 10:5, 6
26 [a]Ps. 129:6
27 [a]Ps. 139:1–3; Is. 37:28
28 [a]Job 41:2; Ezek. 29:4; 38:4; Amos 4:2 [b]2 Kin. 19:33, 36
29 [a]Ex. 3:12; 1 Sam. 2:34; 2 Kin. 20:8, 9; Is. 7:11–14; Luke 2:12 [1]Without cultivation
30 [a]2 Kin. 19:4; 2 Chr. 32:22, 23
31 [a]2 Kin. 25:26; Is. 9:7 [1]So with many Heb. mss. and ancient vss. (cf. Is. 37:32); MT omits *of hosts*
32 [a]Is. 8:7–10
34 [a]2 Kin. 20:6; 2 Chr. 32:21 [b]Is. 31:5 [c]1 Kin. 11:12, 13
35 [a]Ex. 12:29; Is. 10:12–19; 37:36; Hos. 1:7 [1]Or *Angel*

LORD went out, and killed in the
camp of the Assyrians one hun-
dred and eighty-five thousand; and
when *people* arose early in the
morning, there were the corpses—
all dead.
36 So Sennacherib king of As-
syria departed and went away, re-
turned *home,* and remained at
[a]Nineveh.
37 Now it came to pass, as he
was worshiping in the temple of
Nisroch his god, that his sons
[a]Adrammelech and Sharezer
[b]struck him down with the sword;
and they escaped into the land of
Ararat. Then [c]Esarhaddon his son
reigned in his place.

Hezekiah's Life Extended

20 In [a]those days Hezekiah was
sick and near death. And
Isaiah the prophet, the son of
Amoz, went to him and said to
him, "Thus says the LORD: 'Set
your house in order, for you shall
die, and not live.' "
2 Then he turned his face toward
the wall, and prayed to the LORD,
saying,
3 [a]"Remember now, O LORD, I
pray, how I have walked before
You in truth and with a loyal heart,
and have done *what was* good in
Your sight." And Hezekiah wept
bitterly.
4 And it happened, before Isaiah
had gone out into the middle court,
that the word of the LORD came to
him, saying,
5 "Return and tell Hezekiah [a]the
leader of My people, 'Thus says
the LORD, the God of David your
father: [b]"I have heard your prayer,
I have seen [c]your tears; surely I
will heal you. On the third day you
shall go up to the house of the
LORD.
6 "And I will add to your days
fifteen years. I will deliver you and
this city from the hand of the king
of Assyria; and [a]I will defend this
city for My own sake, and for the
sake of My servant David." ' "
7 Then [a]Isaiah said, "Take a
lump of figs." So they took and
laid *it* on the boil, and he recov-
ered.
8 And Hezekiah said to Isaiah,
[a]"What *is* the sign that the LORD
will heal me, and that I shall go
up to the house of the LORD the
third day?"
9 Then Isaiah said, [a]"This is the
sign to you from the LORD, that the
LORD will do the thing which He
has spoken: *shall* the shadow go
forward ten degrees or go back-
ward ten degrees?"
10 And Hezekiah answered, "It is
an easy thing for the shadow to
go down ten [1]degrees; no, but let
the shadow go backward ten de-
grees."
11 So Isaiah the prophet cried out
to the LORD, and [a]He brought the
shadow ten [1]degrees backward, by
which it had gone down on the
sundial of Ahaz.

The Babylonian Envoys

12 [a]At that time [1]Berodach-
Baladan the son of Baladan, king
of Babylon, sent letters and a pres-
ent to Hezekiah, for he heard that
Hezekiah had been sick.
13 And [a]Hezekiah was attentive to
them, and showed them all the
house of his treasures—the silver
and gold, the spices and precious
ointment, and [1]all [2]his armory—all
that was found among his trea-
sures. There was nothing in his
house or in all his dominion that
Hezekiah did not show them.
14 Then Isaiah the prophet went
to King Hezekiah, and said to him,
"What did these men say, and
from where did they come to you?"
So Hezekiah said, "They came
from a far country, from Babylon."
15 And he said, "What have they
seen in your house?" So Hezekiah
answered, [a]"They have seen all
that *is* in my house; there is noth-
ing among my treasures that I
have not shown them."
16 Then Isaiah said to Hezekiah,
"Hear the word of the LORD:
17 'Behold, the days are coming
when all that *is* in your house, and
what your fathers have accumu-
lated until this day, [a]shall be car-
ried to Babylon; nothing shall be
left,' says the LORD.
18 'And [a]they shall take away
some of your sons who will [1]de-
scend from you, whom you will be-
get; [b]and they shall be [c]eunuchs
in the palace of the king of Bab-
ylon.' "
19 So Hezekiah said to Isaiah,

36 [a]Gen. 10:11
37 [a]2 Kin. 17:31 [b]2 Kin. 19:7; 2 Chr. 32:21 [c]Ezra 4:2

CHAPTER 20

1 [a]2 Kin. 18:13; 2 Chr. 32:24; Is. 38:1–22
3 [a]2 Kin. 18:3–6; Neh. 13:22
5 [a]1 Sam. 9:16; 10:1 [b]2 Kin. 19:20; Ps. 65:2 [c]Ps. 39:12; 56:8
6 [a]2 Kin. 19:34; 2 Chr. 32:21
7 [a]Is. 38:21
8 [a]Judg. 6:17, 37, 39; Is. 7:11, 14; 38:22
9 [a]Num. 23:19; Is. 38:7, 8
10 [1]Lit. *steps*
11 [a]Josh. 10:12–14; Is. 38:8 [1]Lit. *steps*
12 [a]2 Kin. 8:8, 9; 2 Chr. 32:31; Is. 39:1–8 [1]*Merodach-Baladan,* Is. 39:1
13 [a]2 Kin. 16:9; 2 Chr. 32:27, 31 [1]So with many Heb. mss., Syr., Tg.; MT omits *all* [2]Lit. *the house of his armor*
15 [a]2 Kin. 20:13
17 [a]2 Kin. 24:13; 25:13–15; 2 Chr. 36:10; Jer. 27:21, 22; 52:17
18 [a]2 Kin. 24:12; 2 Chr. 33:11 [b]Dan. 1:3–7 [c]Dan. 1:11, 18 [1]*be born from*

[a]"The word of the LORD which you have spoken *is* good!" For he said, "Will there not be peace and truth at least in my days?"

Death of Hezekiah

20 [a]Now the rest of the acts of Hezekiah—all his might, and how he [b]made a [c]pool and a [1]tunnel and [d]brought water into the city—*are* they not written in the book of the chronicles of the kings of Judah?
21 So [a]Hezekiah [1]rested with his fathers. Then Manasseh his son reigned in his place.

Manasseh Reigns in Judah

21 Manasseh [a]*was* twelve years old when he became king, and he reigned fifty-five years in Jerusalem. His mother's name *was* Hephzibah.
2 And he did evil in the sight of the LORD, [a]according to the abominations of the nations whom the LORD had cast out before the children of Israel.
3 For he rebuilt the [1]high places [a]which Hezekiah his father had destroyed; he raised up altars for Baal, and made a [2]wooden image, [b]as Ahab king of Israel had done; and he [c]worshiped all [3]the host of heaven and served them.
4 [a]He also built altars in the house of the LORD, of which the LORD had said, [b]"In Jerusalem I will put My name."
5 And he built altars for all the host of heaven in the [a]two courts of the house of the LORD.
6 [a]Also he made his son pass through the fire, practiced [b]soothsaying, used witchcraft, and consulted spiritists and mediums. He did much evil in the sight of the LORD, to provoke *Him* to anger.
7 He even set a carved image of [1]Asherah that he had made, in the [2]house of which the LORD had said to David and to Solomon his son, [a]"In this house and in Jerusalem, which I have chosen out of all the tribes of Israel, I will put My name forever;
8 [a]"and I will not make the feet of Israel wander anymore from the land which I gave their fathers—only if they are careful to do according to all that I have commanded them, and according to all the law that My servant Moses commanded them."
9 But they paid no attention, and Manasseh [a]seduced them to do more evil than the nations whom the LORD had destroyed before the children of Israel.
10 And the LORD spoke [a]by His servants the prophets, saying,
11 [a]"Because Manasseh king of Judah has done these abominations ([b]he has acted more wickedly than all the [c]Amorites who *were* before him, and [d]has also made Judah sin with his idols),
12 "therefore thus says the LORD God of Israel: 'Behold, *I* am bringing *such* calamity upon Jerusalem and Judah, that whoever hears of it, both [a]his ears will tingle.
13 'And I will stretch over Jerusalem [a]the measuring line of Samaria and the plummet of the house of Ahab; [b]I will wipe Jerusalem as *one* wipes a dish, wiping *it* and turning *it* upside down.
14 'So I will forsake the [a]remnant of My inheritance and deliver them into the hand of their enemies; and they shall become victims of plunder to all their enemies,
15 'because they have done evil in My sight, and have provoked Me to anger since the day their fathers came out of Egypt, even to this day.' "
16 [a]Moreover Manasseh shed very much innocent blood, till he had filled Jerusalem from one end to another, besides his sin by which he made Judah sin, in doing evil in the sight of the LORD.
17 Now [a]the rest of the acts of [b]Manasseh—all that he did, and the sin that he committed—*are* they not written in the book of the chronicles of the kings of Judah?
18 So [a]Manasseh [1]rested with his fathers, and was buried in the garden of his own house, in the garden of Uzza. Then his son Amon reigned in his place.

Amon's Reign and Death

19 [a]Amon *was* twenty-two years old when he became king, and he reigned two years in Jerusalem. His mother's name *was* Meshullemeth the daughter of Haruz of Jotbah.

---

19 [a]1 Sam. 3:18
19 [a]1 Sam. 3:18
20 [a]2 Chr. 32:32 [b]Neh. 3:16 [c]Is. 7:3 [d]2 Chr. 32:3, 30 [1]*aqueduct*
21 [a]2 Chr. 32:33 [1]Died and joined his ancestors

CHAPTER 21

1 [a]2 Chr. 33:1–9
2 [a]2 Kin. 16:3
3 [a]2 Kin. 18:4, 22 [b]1 Kin. 16:31–33 [c][Deut. 4:19; 17:2–5] [1]Places for pagan worship [2]Heb. *Asherah,* a Canaanite goddess [3]The gods of the Assyrians
4 [a]Jer. 7:30; 32:34 [b]1 Kin. 11:13
5 [a]1 Kin. 6:36; 7:12
6 [a][Lev. 18:21; 20:2] [b][Deut. 18:10–14]
7 [a]1 Kin. 8:29; 9:3 [1]A Canaanite goddess [2]Temple
8 [a]2 Sam. 7:10
9 [a][Prov. 29:12]
10 [a]2 Kin. 17:13
11 [a]2 Kin. 23:26, 27; 24:3, 4 [b]1 Kin. 21:26 [c]Gen. 15:16 [d]2 Kin. 21:9
12 [a]Jer. 19:3
13 [a]Amos 7:7, 8 [b]2 Kin. 22:16–19; 25:4–11
14 [a]Jer. 6:9
16 [a]2 Kin. 24:4
17 [a]2 Chr. 33:11–19 [b]2 Kin. 20:21
18 [a]2 Chr. 33:20 [1]Died and joined his ancestors
19 [a]2 Chr. 33:21–23

20 And he did evil in the sight of
the LORD, [a]as his father Manasseh
had done.
21 So he walked in all the ways
that his father had walked; and he
served the idols that his father had
served, and worshiped them.
22 He [a]forsook the LORD God of
his fathers, and did not walk in the
way of the LORD.
23 [a]Then the servants of Amon
[b]conspired against him, and killed
the king in his own house.
24 But the people of the land [a]exe-
cuted all those who had conspired
against King Amon. Then the peo-
ple of the land made his son Josiah
king in his place.
25 Now the rest of the acts of
Amon which he did, *are* they not
written in the book of the chroni-
cles of the kings of Judah?
26 And he was buried in his tomb
in the garden of Uzza. Then Josiah
his son reigned in his place.

Josiah Reigns in Judah

22 Josiah [a]*was* eight years old
when he became king, and
he reigned thirty-one years in Je-
rusalem. His mother's name *was*
Jedidah the daughter of Adaiah of
[b]Bozkath.
2 And he did *what was* right in
the sight of the LORD, and walked
in all the ways of his father David;
he [a]did not turn aside to the right
hand or to the left.

Hilkiah Finds the Book of the Law

3 [a]Now it came to pass, in the
eighteenth year of King Josiah,
that the king sent Shaphan the
scribe, the son of Azaliah, the son
of Meshullam, to the house of the
LORD, saying:
4 "Go up to Hilkiah the high
priest, that he may count the
money which has been [a]brought
into the house of the LORD, which
[b]the doorkeepers have gathered
from the people.
5 "And let them [a]deliver it into
the hand of those doing the work,
who are the overseers in the house
of the LORD; let them give it to
those who *are* in the house of the
LORD doing the work, to repair the
damages of the house—
6 "to carpenters and builders
and masons—and to buy timber
and hewn stone to repair the
house.
7 "However [a]there need be no
accounting made with them of the
money delivered into their hand,
because they deal faithfully."
8 Then Hilkiah the high priest
said to Shaphan the scribe, [a]"I
have found the Book of the Law
in the house of the LORD." And Hil-
kiah gave the book to Shaphan,
and he read it.
9 So Shaphan the scribe went to
the king, bringing the king word,
saying, "Your servants have
[1]gathered the money that was
found in the house, and have deliv-
ered it into the hand of those who
do the work, who oversee the
house of the LORD."
10 Then Shaphan the scribe
showed the king, saying, "Hilkiah
the priest has given me a book."
And Shaphan read it before the
king.
11 Now it happened, when the
king heard the words of the Book
of the Law, that he tore his clothes.
12 Then the king commanded Hil-
kiah the priest, [a]Ahikam the son
of Shaphan, [1]Achbor the son of
Michaiah, Shaphan the scribe, and
Asaiah a servant of the king, say-
ing,
13 "Go, inquire of the LORD for
me, for the people and for all Ju-
dah, concerning the words of this
book that has been found; for
great *is* [a]the wrath of the LORD that
is aroused against us, because our
fathers have not obeyed the words
of this book, to do according to all
that is written concerning us."
14 So Hilkiah the priest, Ahikam,
Achbor, Shaphan, and Asaiah
went to Huldah the prophetess, the
wife of Shallum the son of
[a]Tikvah, the son of Harhas, keeper
of the wardrobe. (She dwelt in Je-
rusalem in the Second Quarter.)
And they spoke with her.
15 Then she said to them, "Thus
says the LORD God of Israel, 'Tell
the man who sent you to Me,
16 "Thus says the LORD: 'Behold,
[a]I will bring calamity on this place
and on its inhabitants—all the
words of the book which the king
of Judah has read—
17 [a]'because they have forsaken
Me and burned incense to other

20 [a]2 Kin. 21:2–6, 11, 16
22 [a]Judg. 2:12, 13; 1 Kin. 11:33; 1 Chr. 28:9
23 [a]1 Chr. 3:14; 2 Chr. 33:24, 25; Matt. 1:10 [b]2 Kin. 12:20; 14:19
24 [a]2 Kin. 14:5

CHAPTER 22

1 [a]1 Kin. 13:2; 2 Chr. 34:1 [b]Josh. 15:39
2 [a]Deut. 5:32; Josh. 1:7
3 [a]2 Chr. 34:8
4 [a]2 Kin. 12:4 [b]2 Kin. 12:9, 10
5 [a]2 Kin. 12:11–14
7 [a]2 Kin. 12:15; [1 Cor. 4:2]
8 [a]Deut. 31:24–26; 2 Chr. 34:14
9 [1]Lit. *poured out*
12 [a]2 Kin. 25:22; Jer. 26:24 [1]*Abdon the son of Micah,* 2 Chr. 34:20
13 [a][Deut. 29:23–28; 31:17, 18]
14 [a]2 Chr. 34:22
16 [a]Deut. 29:27; [Dan. 9:11–14]
17 [a]Deut. 29:25–27; 2 Kin. 21:22

gods, that they might provoke Me to anger with all the works of their hands. Therefore My wrath shall be aroused against this place and shall not be quenched.’ ” ’

18 “But as for [a]the king of Judah, who sent you to inquire of the LORD, in this manner you shall speak to him, ‘Thus says the LORD God of Israel: “*Concerning* the words which you have heard—

19 “because your [a]heart was tender, and you [b]humbled yourself before the LORD when you heard what I spoke against this place and against its inhabitants, that they would become [c]a desolation and [d]a curse, and you tore your clothes and wept before Me, I also have heard *you*,” says the LORD.

20 “Surely, therefore, I will [1]gather you to your fathers, and you [a]shall [2]be gathered to your grave in peace; and your eyes shall not see all the calamity which I will bring on this place.” ’ ” So they brought back word to the king.

Josiah Restores True Worship

23 Now [a]the king sent them to gather all the elders of Judah and Jerusalem to him.

2 The king went up to the house of the LORD with all the men of Judah, and with him all the inhabitants of Jerusalem—the priests and the prophets and all the people, both small and great. And he [a]read in their hearing all the words of the Book of the Covenant [b]which had been found in the house of the LORD.

3 Then the king [a]stood by a pillar and made a [b]covenant before the LORD, to follow the LORD and to keep His commandments and His testimonies and His statutes, with all *his* heart and all *his* soul, to perform the words of this covenant that were written in this book. And all the people took a stand for the covenant.

4 And the king commanded Hilkiah the high priest, the [a]priests of the second order, and the doorkeepers, to bring [b]out of the temple of the LORD all the articles that were made for Baal, for [1]Asherah, and for all [2]the host of heaven; and he burned them outside Jerusalem in the fields of Kidron, and carried their ashes to Bethel.

5 Then he removed the idolatrous priests whom the kings of Judah had ordained to burn incense on the high places in the cities of Judah and in the places all around Jerusalem, and those who burned incense to Baal, to the sun, to the moon, to the [1]constellations, and to [a]all the host of heaven.

6 And he brought out the [a]wooden[1] image from the house of the LORD, to the Brook Kidron outside Jerusalem, burned it at the Brook Kidron and ground *it* to [b]ashes, and threw its ashes on [c]the graves of the common people.

7 Then he tore down the *ritual* [1]booths [a]of the [2]perverted persons that *were* in the house of the LORD, [b]where the [c]women wove hangings for the wooden image.

8 And he brought all the priests from the cities of Judah, and defiled the high places where the priests had burned incense, from [a]Geba to Beersheba; also he broke down the high places at the gates which *were* at the entrance of the Gate of Joshua the governor of the city, which *were* to the left of the city gate.

9 [a]Nevertheless the priests of the high places did not come up to the altar of the LORD in Jerusalem, [b]but they ate unleavened bread among their brethren.

10 And he defiled [a]Topheth, which *is* in [b]the Valley of the [1]Son of Hinnom, [c]that no man might make his son or his daughter [d]pass through the fire to Molech.

11 Then he removed the horses that the kings of Judah had [1]dedicated to the sun, at the entrance to the house of the LORD, by the chamber of Nathan-Melech, the officer who *was* in the court; and he burned the chariots of the sun with fire.

12 The altars that *were* [a]on the roof, the upper chamber of Ahaz, which the kings of Judah had made, and the altars which [b]Manasseh had made in the two courts of the house of the LORD, the king broke down and pulverized there, and threw their dust into the Brook Kidron.

13 Then the king defiled the [1]high

---

18 [a]2 Chr. 34:26

19 [a][Ps. 51:17] [b]1 Kin. 21:29 [c]Lev. 26:31, 32 [d]Jer. 26:6; 44:22

20 [a][Is. 57:1, 2] [1]Cause you to join your ancestors in death [2]Die a natural death

CHAPTER 23

1 [a]2 Chr. 34:29, 30

2 [a]Deut. 31:10–13 [b]2 Kin. 22:8

3 [a]2 Kin. 11:14 [b]2 Kin. 11:17

4 [a]2 Kin. 25:18 [b]2 Kin. 21:3–7 [1]A Canaanite goddess [2]The gods of the Assyrians

5 [a]2 Kin. 21:3 [1]Of the Zodiac

6 [a]2 Kin. 21:7 [b]Ex. 32:20 [c]2 Chr. 34:4 [1]Heb. *Asherah*, a Canaanite goddess

7 [a]1 Kin. 14:24; 15:12 [b]Ezek. 16:16 [c]Ex. 38:8 [1]Lit. *houses* [2]Heb. *qedeshim*, those practicing sodomy and prostitution in religious rituals

8 [a]Josh. 21:17

9 [a][Ezek. 44:10–14] [b]1 Sam. 2:36

10 [a]Is. 30:33 [b]Josh. 15:8 [c][Lev. 18:21] [d]2 Kin. 21:6 [1]Kt. *Sons*

11 [1]*given*

12 [a]Jer. 19:13 [b]2 Kin. 21:5

13 [1]Places for pagan worship

places that *were* east of Jerusalem,
which *were* on the [2]south of [3]the
Mount of Corruption, which [a]Sol-
omon king of Israel had built for
Ashtoreth the abomination of the
Sidonians, for Chemosh the
abomination of the Moabites, and
for Milcom the abomination of the
people of Ammon.
14 And he [a]broke in pieces the *sa-
cred* pillars and cut down the
wooden images, and filled their
places with the bones of men.
15 Moreover the altar that *was* at
Bethel, *and* the [1]high place [a]which
Jeroboam the son of Nebat, who
made Israel sin, had made, both
that altar and the high place he
broke down; and he burned the
high place *and* crushed *it* to pow-
der, and burned the wooden im-
age.
16 As Josiah turned, he saw the
tombs that *were* there on the
mountain. And he sent and took
the bones out of the tombs and
burned *them* on the altar, and de-
filed it according to the [a]word of
the LORD which the man of God
proclaimed, who proclaimed these
words.
17 Then he said, "What grave-
stone *is* this that I see?" So the men
of the city told him, "*It is* [a]the tomb
of the man of God who came from
Judah and proclaimed these things
which you have done against the
altar of Bethel."
18 And he said, "Let him alone;
let no one move his bones." So
they let his bones alone, with the
bones of [a]the prophet who came
from Samaria.
19 Now Josiah also took away all
the [1]shrines of the [2]high places
that *were* [a]in the cities of Samaria,
which the kings of Israel had made
to provoke [3]the LORD to anger; and
he did to them according to all the
deeds he had done in Bethel.
20 [a]He [b]executed all the priests of
the [1]high places who *were* there,
on the altars, and [c]burned men's
bones on them; and he returned to
Jerusalem.
21 Then the king commanded all
the people, saying, [a]"Keep the
Passover to the LORD your God, [b]as
it is written in this Book of the
Covenant."
22 [a]Such a Passover surely had
never been held since the days of
the judges who judged Israel, nor
in all the days of the kings of Israel
and the kings of Judah.
23 But in the eighteenth year of
King Josiah this Passover was
held before the LORD in Jerusalem.
24 Moreover Josiah put away
those who consulted mediums and
spiritists, the household gods and
idols, all the abominations that
were seen in the land of Judah and
in Jerusalem, that he might per-
form the words of [a]the law which
were written in the book [b]that Hil-
kiah the priest found in the house
of the LORD.
25 [a]Now before him there was no
king like him, who turned to the
LORD with all his heart, with all his
soul, and with all his might, ac-
cording to all the Law of Moses;
nor after him did *any* arise like
him.

Impending Judgment on Judah

26 Nevertheless the LORD did not
turn from the fierceness of His
great wrath, with which His anger
was aroused against Judah, [a]be-
cause of all the provocations with
which Manasseh had provoked
Him.
27 And the LORD said, "I will also
remove Judah from My sight, as
[a]I have removed Israel, and will
cast off this city Jerusalem which
I have chosen, and the house of
which I said, [b]'My name shall be
there.' "

Josiah Dies in Battle

28 Now the rest of the acts of Jo-
siah, and all that he did, *are* they
not written in the book of the
chronicles of the kings of Judah?
29 [a]In his days Pharaoh Necho
king of Egypt went [1]to the aid of
the king of Assyria, to the River
Euphrates; and King Josiah went
against him. And *Pharaoh Necho*
killed him at [b]Megiddo when he
[c]confronted him.
30 [a]Then his servants moved his
body in a chariot from Megiddo,
brought him to Jerusalem, and
buried him in his own tomb. And
[b]the people of the land took Jehoa-
haz the son of Josiah, anointed
him, and made him king in his fa-
ther's place.

13 [a]1 Kin. 11:5–7 [2]Lit. *right of* [3]The Mount of Olives
14 [a][Ex. 23:24; Deut. 7:5–25]
15 [a]1 Kin. 12:28–33 [1]A place for pagan worship
16 [a]1 Kin. 13:2
17 [a]1 Kin. 13:1, 30, 31
18 [a]1 Kin. 13:11, 31
19 [a]2 Chr. 34:6, 7 [1]Lit. *houses* [2]Places for pagan worship [3]So with LXX, Syr., Vg.; MT, Tg. omit *the LORD*
20 [a]1 Kin. 13:2 [b][Ex. 22:20]; 1 Kin. 18:40; 2 Kin. 10:25; 11:18 [c]2 Chr. 34:5 [1]Places for pagan worship
21 [a]Num. 9:5; Josh. 5:10; 2 Chr. 35:1 [b]Ex. 12:3; Lev. 23:5; Num. 9:2; Deut. 16:2–8
22 [a]2 Chr. 35:18, 19
24 [a][Lev. 19:31; 20:27]; Deut. 18:11 [b]2 Kin. 22:8
25 [a]2 Kin. 18:5
26 [a]2 Kin. 21:11, 12; 24:3, 4; Jer. 15:4
27 [a]2 Kin. 17:18, 20; 18:11; 21:13 [b]1 Kin. 8:29; 9:3; 2 Kin. 21:4, 7
29 [a]2 Chr. 35:20; Jer. 2:16; 46:2 [b]Judg. 5:19; Zech. 12:11 [c]2 Kin. 14:8 [1]Or *to attack*, Heb. *al* can mean *together with* or *against*
30 [a]2 Chr. 35:24; 2 Kin. 22:20 [b]2 Chr. 36:1–4

The Reign and Captivity of Jehoahaz

31 [a]Jehoahaz *was* twenty-three
years old when he became king,
and he reigned three months in Je-
rusalem. His mother's name *was*
[b]Hamutal the daughter of Jere-
miah of Libnah.
32 And he did evil in the sight of
the LORD, according to all that his
fathers had done.
33 Now Pharaoh Necho put him
in prison [a]at Riblah in the land of
Hamath, that he might not reign
in Jerusalem; and he imposed on
the land a tribute of one hundred
talents of silver and a talent of
gold.
34 Then [a]Pharaoh Necho made
Eliakim the son of Josiah king in
place of his father Josiah, and
[b]changed his name to [c]Jehoiakim.
And *Pharaoh* took Jehoahaz [d]and
went to Egypt, and [1]he died there.

Jehoiakim Reigns in Judah

35 So Jehoiakim gave [a]the silver
and gold to Pharaoh; but he taxed
the land to give money according
to the command of Pharaoh; he ex-
acted the silver and gold from the
people of the land, from every one
according to his assessment, to
give *it* to Pharaoh Necho.
36 [a]Jehoiakim *was* twenty-five
years old when he became king,
and he reigned eleven years in Je-
rusalem. His mother's name *was*
Zebudah the daughter of Pedaiah
of Rumah.
37 And he did evil in the sight of
the LORD, according to all that his
fathers had done.

Judah Overrun by Enemies

24 In [a]his days Nebuchadnez-
zar king of [b]Babylon came
up, and Jehoiakim became his vas-
sal *for* three years. Then he turned
and rebelled against him.
2 [a]And the LORD sent against him
raiding [1]bands of Chaldeans,
bands of Syrians, bands of Moab-
ites, and bands of the people of
Ammon; He sent them against Ju-
dah to destroy it, [b]according to the
word of the LORD which He had
spoken by His servants the proph-
ets.
3 Surely at the commandment of
the LORD *this* came upon Judah,
to remove *them* from His sight
[a]because of the sins of Manasseh,
according to all that he had done,
4 [a]and also because of the inno-
cent blood that he had shed; for
he had filled Jerusalem with inno-
cent blood, which the LORD would
not pardon.
5 Now the rest of the acts of Je-
hoiakim, and all that he did, *are*
they not written in the book of the
chronicles of the kings of Judah?
6 [a]So Jehoiakim rested with his
fathers. Then Jehoiachin his son
reigned in his place.
7 And [a]the king of Egypt did not
come out of his land anymore, for
[b]the king of Babylon had taken all
that belonged to the king of Egypt
from the Brook of Egypt to the
River Euphrates.

The Reign and Captivity of Jehoiachin

8 [a]Jehoiachin[1] *was* eighteen
years old when he became king,
and he reigned in Jerusalem three
months. His mother's name *was*
Nehushta the daughter of El-
nathan of Jerusalem.
9 And he did evil in the sight of
the LORD, according to all that his
father had done.
10 [a]At that time the servants of
Nebuchadnezzar king of Babylon
came up against Jerusalem, and
the city [1]was besieged.
11 And Nebuchadnezzar king of
Babylon came against the city, as
his servants were besieging it.
12 [a]Then Jehoiachin king of Ju-
dah, his mother, his servants, his
princes, and his officers went out
to the king of Babylon; and the
king of Babylon, [b]in the eighth
year of his reign, took him pris-
oner.

The Captivity of Jerusalem

13 [a]And he carried out from there
all the treasures of the house of the
LORD and the treasures of the
king's house, and he [b]cut in pieces
all the articles of gold which Sol-
omon king of Israel had made in
the temple of the LORD, [c]as the
LORD had said.
14 Also [a]he carried into captiv-
ity all Jerusalem: all the captains
and all the mighty men of valor,
[b]ten thousand captives, and [c]all
the craftsmen and smiths. None

---

31 [a]1 Chr. 3:15; Jer. 22:11 [b]2 Kin. 24:18
33 [a]2 Kin. 25:6; Jer. 52:27
34 [a]2 Chr. 36:4 [b]2 Kin. 24:17; Dan. 1:7 [c]Matt. 1:11 [d]Jer. 22:11, 12; Ezek. 19:3, 4 [1]Jehoahaz
35 [a]2 Kin. 23:33
36 [a]2 Chr. 36:5; Jer. 22:18, 19; 26:1

CHAPTER 24

1 [a]2 Chr. 36:6; Jer. 25:1, 9; Dan. 1:1 [b]2 Kin. 20:14
2 [a]Jer. 25:9; 32:28; 35:11; Ezek. 19:8 [b]2 Kin. 20:17; 21:12–14; 23:27 [1]*troops*
3 [a]2 Kin. 21:2, 11; 23:26
4 [a]2 Kin. 21:16
6 [a]2 Chr. 36:6, 8; Jer. 22:18, 19
7 [a]Jer. 37:5–7 [b]Jer. 46:2
8 [a]1 Chr. 3:16; 2 Chr. 36:9 [1]*Jeconiah*, 1 Chr. 3:16; Jer. 24:1; or *Coniah*, Jer. 22:24, 28
10 [a]Dan. 1:1 [1]Lit. *came into siege*
12 [a]Jer. 22:24–30; 24:1; 29:1, 2; Ezek. 17:12 [b]2 Chr. 36:10
13 [a]2 Kin. 20:17; Is. 39:6 [b]Dan. 5:2, 3 [c]Jer. 20:5
14 [a]Is. 3:2, 3; Jer. 24:1 [b]2 Kin. 24:16; Jer. 52:28 [c]1 Sam. 13:19

remained except [d]the poorest people of the land.
15 And [a]he carried Jehoiachin captive to Babylon. The king's mother, the king's wives, his officers, and the mighty of the land he carried into captivity from Jerusalem to Babylon.
16 [a]All the valiant men, seven thousand, and craftsmen and smiths, one thousand, all *who were* strong *and* fit for war, these the king of Babylon brought captive to Babylon.

Zedekiah Reigns in Judah

17 Then [a]the king of Babylon made Mattaniah, [b]*Jehoiachin's*[1] uncle, king in his place, and [c]changed his name to Zedekiah.
18 [a]Zedekiah *was* twenty-one years old when he became king, and he reigned eleven years in Jerusalem. His mother's name *was* [b]Hamutal the daughter of Jeremiah of Libnah.
19 [a]He also did evil in the sight of the LORD, according to all that Jehoiakim had done.
20 For because of the anger of the LORD *this* happened in Jerusalem and Judah, that He finally cast them out from His presence. [a]Then Zedekiah rebelled against the king of Babylon.

The Fall and Captivity of Judah

25 Now it came to pass [a]in the ninth year of his reign, in the tenth month, on the tenth *day* of the month, *that* Nebuchadnezzar king of Babylon and all his army came against Jerusalem and encamped against it; and they built a siege wall against it all around.
2 So the city was besieged until the eleventh year of King Zedekiah.
3 By the ninth *day* of the [a]*fourth* month the famine had become so severe in the city that there was no food for the people of the land.
4 Then [a]the city wall was broken through, and all the men of war *fled* at night by way of the gate between two walls, which was by the king's garden, even though the Chaldeans *were* still encamped all around against the city. And [b]*the king*[1] went by way of the [2]plain.
5 But the army of the Chaldeans pursued the king, and they overtook him in the plains of Jericho. All his army was scattered from him.
6 So they took the king and brought him up to the king of Babylon [a]at Riblah, and they pronounced judgment on him.
7 Then they killed the sons of Zedekiah before his eyes, [a]put[1] out the eyes of Zedekiah, bound him with bronze fetters, and took him to Babylon.
8 And in the fifth month, [a]on the seventh *day* of the month (which *was* [b]the nineteenth year of King Nebuchadnezzar king of Babylon), [c]Nebuzaradan the captain of the guard, a servant of the king of Babylon, came to Jerusalem.
9 [a]He burned the house of the LORD [b]and the king's house; all the houses of Jerusalem, that is, all the houses of the great, [c]he burned with fire.
10 And all the army of the Chaldeans who *were with* the captain of the guard [a]broke down the walls of Jerusalem all around.
11 Then Nebuzaradan the captain of the guard carried away captive [a]the rest of the people *who* remained in the city and the defectors who had deserted to the king of Babylon, with the rest of the multitude.
12 But the captain of the guard [a]left *some* of the poor of the land as vinedressers and farmers.
13 [a]The bronze [b]pillars that *were* in the house of the LORD, and [c]the carts and [d]the bronze Sea that *were* in the house of the LORD, the Chaldeans broke in pieces, and [e]carried their bronze to Babylon.
14 They also took away [a]the pots, the shovels, the trimmers, the spoons, and all the bronze utensils with which the priests ministered.
15 The firepans and the basins, the things of solid gold and solid silver, the captain of the guard took away.
16 The two pillars, one Sea, and the carts, which Solomon had made for the house of the LORD, [a]the bronze of all these articles was beyond measure.
17 [a]The height of one pillar *was* [1]eighteen cubits, and the capital on it *was* of bronze. The height of the

14 [d]2 Kin. 25:12
15 [a]2 Chr. 36:10; Esth. 2:6; Jer. 22:24–28; Ezek. 17:12
16 [a]Jer. 52:28
17 [a]Jer. 37:1 [b]1 Chr. 3:15; 2 Chr. 36:10 [c]2 Chr. 36:4 [1]Lit. *his*
18 [a]2 Chr. 36:11; Jer. 52:1 [b]2 Kin. 23:31
19 [a]2 Chr. 36:12
20 [a]2 Chr. 36:13; Ezek. 17:15

CHAPTER 25

1 [a]2 Chr. 36:17; Jer. 6:6; 34:2; Ezek. 4:2; 24:1, 2; Hab. 1:6
3 [a]2 Kin. 6:24, 25; Is. 3:1; Jer. 39:2; Lam. 4:9, 10
4 [a]Jer. 39:2 [b]Jer. 39:4–7; Ezek. 12:12 [1]Lit. *he* [2]Or *Arabah*, the Jordan Valley
6 [a]2 Kin. 23:33; Jer. 52:9
7 [a]Jer. 39:7; Ezek. 17:16 [1]*blinded*
8 [a]Jer. 52:12 [b]2 Kin. 24:12 [c]Jer. 39:9
9 [a]2 Kin. 25:13; 2 Chr. 36:19; Ps. 79:1; Jer. 7:14 [b]Jer. 39:8 [c]Jer. 17:27
10 [a]2 Kin. 14:13; Neh. 1:3
11 [a]Is. 1:9; Jer. 5:19; 39:9
12 [a]2 Kin. 24:14; Jer. 39:10; 40:7; 52:16
13 [a]Jer. 52:17 [b]1 Kin. 7:15 [c]1 Kin. 7:27 [d]1 Kin. 7:23 [e]2 Kin. 20:17; Jer. 27:19–22
14 [a]Ex. 27:3; 1 Kin. 7:45
16 [a]1 Kin. 7:47
17 [a]1 Kin. 7:15–22; Jer. 52:21 [1]About 27 feet

capital was three cubits, and the
network and pomegranates all
around the capital were all of
bronze. The second pillar was the
same, with a network.
18 [a]And the captain of the guard
took [b]Seraiah the chief priest,
[c]Zephaniah the second priest, and
the three doorkeepers.
19 He also took out of the city an
officer who had charge of the men
of war, [a]five men of [1]the king's
close associates who were found
in the city, the chief recruiting offi-
cer of the army, who mustered the
people of the land, and sixty men
of the people of the land *who were*
found in the city.
20 So Nebuzaradan, captain of the
guard, took these and brought
them to the king of Babylon at Rib-
lah.
21 Then the king of Babylon
struck them and put them to death
at Riblah in the land of Hamath.
[a]Thus Judah was carried away
captive from its own land.

Gedaliah Made Governor of Judah

22 Then he made Gedaliah the son
of [a]Ahikam, the son of Shaphan,
governor over [b]the people who re-
mained in the land of Judah,
whom Nebuchadnezzar king of
Babylon had left.
23 Now when all the [a]captains of
the armies, they and *their* men,
heard that the king of Babylon had
made Gedaliah governor, they
came to Gedaliah at Mizpah—Ish-
mael the son of Nethaniah, Jo-
hanan the son of Careah, Seraiah
the son of Tanhumeth the Netoph-
athite, and [1]Jaazaniah the son of
a Maachathite, they and their
men.
24 And Gedaliah took an oath be-
fore them and their men, and said
to them, "Do not be afraid of the
servants of the Chaldeans. Dwell
in the land and serve the king of
Babylon, and it shall be well with
you."
25 But [a]it happened in the seventh
month that Ishmael the son of
Nethaniah, the son of Elishama, of
the royal family, came with ten
men and struck and killed Geda-
liah, the Jews, as well as the Chal-
deans who were with him at
Mizpah.
26 And all the people, small and
great, and the captains of the ar-
mies, arose [a]and went to Egypt; for
they were afraid of the Chaldeans.

Jehoiachin Released from Prison

27 [a]Now it came to pass in the
thirty-seventh year of the captivity
of Jehoiachin king of Judah, in the
twelfth month, on the twenty-
seventh *day* of the month, *that*
[1]Evil-Merodach king of Babylon,
in the year that he began to reign,
[b]released Jehoiachin king of Ju-
dah from prison.
28 He spoke kindly to him, and
gave him a more prominent seat
than those of the kings who *were*
with him in Babylon.
29 So Jehoiachin changed from
his prison garments, and he [a]ate
[1]bread regularly before the king
all the days of his life.
30 And as for his [1]provisions,
there was a [2]regular ration given
him by the king, a portion for each
day, all the days of his life.

18 [a]Jer. 39:9–13; 52:12–16, 24 [b]1 Chr. 6:14; Ezra 7:1 [c]Jer. 21:1; 29:25, 29
19 [a]Esth. 1:14; Jer. 52:25 [1]Lit. *those seeing the king's face*
21 [a]Lev. 26:33; Deut. 28:36, 64; 2 Kin. 23:27
22 [a]2 Kin. 22:12 [b]Is. 1:9; Jer. 40:5
23 [a]Jer. 40:7–9 [1]*Jezaniah*, Jer. 40:8
25 [a]Jer. 41:1–3
26 [a]2 Kin. 19:31; Jer. 43:4–7
27 [a]2 Kin. 24:12, 15; Jer. 52:31–34 [b]Gen. 40:13, 20 [1]Lit. *Man of Marduk*
29 [a]2 Sam. 9:7 [1]Food
30 [1]Lit. *allowance* [2]Lit. *allowance*

The First Book of the

Chronicles

THE books of First and Second Chronicles cover the same period of Jewish history described in Second Samuel through Second Kings, but the perspective is different. These books are no mere repetition of the same material, but rather form a divine editorial on the history of God's people. While Second Samuel and First and Second Kings give a political history of Israel and Judah, First and Second Chronicles present a religious history of the Davidic dynasty of Judah. The former are written from a prophetic and moral viewpoint, and the latter from a priestly and spiritual perspective. The Book of First Chronicles begins with the royal line of David and then traces the spiritual significance of David's righteous reign.

The books of First and Second Chronicles were originally one continuous work in the Hebrew. The title was *Dibere Hayyamim,* meaning "The Words [accounts, events] of the Days." The equivalent meaning today would be "The Events of the Times." Chronicles was divided into two parts in the third-century B.C. Greek translation of the Hebrew Bible (the Septuagint). At that time it was given the name *Paraleipomenon,* "Of Things Omitted," referring to the things omitted from Samuel and Kings. Some copies add the phrase, *Basileon Iouda,* "Concerning the Kings of Judah." The first book of Chronicles was called *Paraleipomenon Primus,* "The First Book of Things Omitted." The name "Chronicles" comes from Jerome in his Latin Vulgate Bible (A.D. 385–405): *Chronicorum Liber.* He meant his title in the sense of the "Chronicles of the Whole of Sacred History."

The Family of Adam—Seth to Abraham

CHAPTER 1

ADAM,[a] [b]Seth, Enosh,
2 Cainan, Mahalalel, Jared,
3 Enoch, Methuselah, Lamech,
4 [a]Noah,[1] Shem, Ham, and Japheth.
5 [a]The sons of Japheth *were* Gomer, Magog, Madai, Javan, Tubal, Meshech, and Tiras.
6 The sons of Gomer *were* Ashkenaz, [1]Diphath, and Togarmah.
7 The sons of Javan *were* Elishah, [1]Tarshishah, Kittim, and [2]Rodanim.
8 [a]The sons of Ham *were* Cush, Mizraim, Put, and Canaan.
9 The sons of Cush *were* Seba, Havilah, [1]Sabta, [2]Raama, and Sabtecha. The sons of Raama *were* Sheba and Dedan.
10 Cush [a]begot Nimrod; he began to be a mighty one on the earth.
11 Mizraim begot Ludim, Anamim, Lehabim, Naphtuhim,
12 Pathrusim, Casluhim (from whom came the Philistines and the [a]Caphtorim).
13 [a]Canaan begot Sidon, his firstborn, and Heth;
14 the Jebusite, the Amorite, and the Girgashite;
15 the Hivite, the Arkite, and the Sinite;
16 the Arvadite, the Zemarite, and the Hamathite.
17 The sons of [a]Shem *were* Elam, Asshur, [b]Arphaxad, Lud, Aram, Uz, Hul, Gether, and [1]Meshech.
18 Arphaxad begot Shelah, and Shelah begot Eber.
19 To Eber were born two sons: the name of one *was* [1]Peleg, for in his days the [2]earth was divided; and his brother's name *was* Joktan.

1 [a]Gen. 1:27; 2:7; 5:1, 2, 5 [b]Gen. 4:25, 26; 5:3–9
4 [a]Gen. 5:28–10:1 [1]So with MT, Vg.; LXX adds *the sons of Noah*
5 [a]Gen. 10:2–4
6 [1]*Riphath,* Gen. 10:3
7 [1]*Tarshish,* Gen. 10:4 [2]*Dodanim,* Gen. 10:4
8 [a]Gen. 10:6
9 [1]*Sabtah,* Gen. 10:7 [2]*Raamah,* Gen. 10:7
10 [a]Gen. 10:8–10, 13
12 [a]Deut. 2:23
13 [a]Gen. 9:18, 25–27; 10:15
17 [a]Gen. 10:22–29; 11:10 [b]Luke 3:36 [1]*Mash,* Gen. 10:23

19 [1]Lit. *Division,* Gen. 10:25 [2]Or land

20 [a]Joktan begot Almodad, She-
leph, Hazarmaveth, Jerah,
21 Hadoram, Uzal, Diklah,
22 [1]Ebal, Abimael, Sheba,
23 Ophir, Havilah, and Jobab. All
these *were* the sons of Joktan.
24 [a]Shem, Arphaxad, Shelah,
25 [a]Eber, Peleg, Reu,
26 Serug, Nahor, Terah,
27 and [a]Abram, who *is* Abraham.
28 [a]The sons of Abraham *were*
[b]Isaac and [c]Ishmael.

The Family of Ishmael

29 These *are* their genealogies:
The [a]firstborn of Ishmael *was*
Nebajoth; then Kedar, Adbeel,
Mibsam,
30 Mishma, Dumah, Massa,
[1]Hadad, Tema,
31 Jetur, Naphish, and Kedemah.
These *were* the sons of Ishmael.

The Family of Keturah

32 Now [a]the sons born to Keturah,
Abraham's concubine, *were* Zim-
ran, Jokshan, Medan, Midian, Ish-
bak, and Shuah. The sons of Jok-
shan *were* Sheba and Dedan.
33 The sons of Midian *were*
Ephah, Epher, Hanoch, Abida, and
Eldaah. All these were the children
of Keturah.

The Family of Isaac

34 And [a]Abraham begot Isaac.
[b]The sons of Isaac *were* Esau and
Israel.
35 The sons of [a]Esau *were* Eli-
phaz, Reuel, Jeush, Jaalam, and
Korah.
36 And the sons of Eliphaz *were*
Teman, Omar, [1]Zephi, Gatam, *and*
Kenaz; and *by* [a]Timna, Amalek.
37 The sons of Reuel *were* Na-
hath, Zerah, Shammah, and Miz-
zah.

The Family of Seir

38 [a]The sons of Seir *were* Lotan,
Shobal, Zibeon, Anah, Dishon,
Ezer, and Dishan.
39 And the sons of Lotan *were*
Hori and [1]Homam; Lotan's sister
was Timna.
40 The sons of Shobal *were*
[1]Alian, Manahath, Ebal, [2]Shephi,
and Onam. The sons of Zibeon
were Ajah and Anah.
41 The son of Anah *was* [a]Dishon.
The sons of Dishon *were* [1]Hamran,
Eshban, Ithran, and Cheran.
42 The sons of Ezer *were* Bilhan,
Zaavan, *and* [1]Jaakan. The sons of
Dishan *were* Uz and Aran.

The Kings of Edom

43 Now these *were* the [a]kings who
reigned in the land of Edom before
a king reigned over the children
of Israel: Bela the son of Beor, and
the name of his city was Dinhabah.
44 And when Bela died, Jobab the
son of Zerah of Bozrah reigned in
his place.
45 When Jobab died, Husham of
the land of the Temanites reigned
in his place.
46 And when Husham died, Ha-
dad the son of Bedad, who [1]at-
tacked Midian in the field of Moab,
reigned in his place. The name of
his city *was* Avith.
47 When Hadad died, Samlah of
Masrekah reigned in his place.
48 [a]And when Samlah died, Saul
of Rehoboth-by-the-River reigned
in his place.
49 When Saul died, Baal-Hanan
the son of Achbor reigned in his
place.
50 And when Baal-Hanan died,
[1]Hadad reigned in his place; and
the name of his city was [2]Pai. His
wife's name was Mehetabel the
daughter of Matred, the daughter
of Mezahab.
51 Hadad died also. And the chiefs
of Edom were Chief Timnah, Chief
[1]Aliah, Chief Jetheth,
52 Chief Aholibamah, Chief Elah,
Chief Pinon,
53 Chief Kenaz, Chief Teman,
Chief Mibzar,
54 Chief Magdiel, and Chief Iram.
These *were* the chiefs of Edom.

The Family of Israel

2 These *were* the [a]sons of [1]Israel:
[b]Reuben, Simeon, Levi, Judah,
Issachar, Zebulun,
2 Dan, Joseph, Benjamin, Naph-
tali, Gad, and Asher.

From Judah to David

3 The sons of [a]Judah *were* Er,
Onan, and Shelah. *These* three
were born to him by the daughter
of [b]Shua, the Canaanitess. [c]Er, the
firstborn of Judah, was wicked in

20 [a]Gen. 10:26
22 [1]*Obal*, Gen. 10:28
24 [a]Gen. 11:10–26; Luke 3:34–36
25 [a]Gen. 11:15
27 [a]Gen. 17:5
28 [a]Gen. 21:2, 3 [b]Gen. 21:2 [c]Gen. 16:11, 15
29 [a]Gen. 25:13–16
30 [1]*Hadar*, Gen. 25:15
32 [a]Gen. 25:1–4
34 [a]Gen. 21:2 [b]Gen. 25:9, 25, 26, 29; 32:28
35 [a]Gen. 36:10–19
36 [a]Gen. 36:12 [1]*Zepho*, Gen. 36:11
38 [a]Gen. 36:20–28
39 [1]*Hemam* or *Heman*, Gen. 36:22
40 [1]*Alvan*, Gen. 36:23 [2]*Shepho*, Gen. 36:23
41 [a]Gen. 36:25 [1]*Hemdan*, Gen. 36:26
42 [1]*Akan*, Gen. 36:27
43 [a]Gen. 36:31–43
46 [1]Lit. *struck*
48 [a]Gen. 36:37
50 [1]*Hadar*, Gen. 36:39 [2]*Pau*, Gen. 36:39
51 [1]*Alvah*, Gen. 36:40

CHAPTER 2

1 [a]Gen. 29:32–35; 35:23, 26; 46:8–27 [b]Gen. 29:32; 35:22 [1]*Jacob*, Gen. 32:28
3 [a]Gen. 38:3–5; 46:12; Num. 26:19 [b]Gen. 38:2 [c]Gen. 38:7

the sight of the LORD; so He killed
him.
4 And [a]Tamar, his daughter-
in-law, [b]bore him Perez and
Zerah. All the sons of Judah *were*
five.
5 The sons of [a]Perez *were* Hez-
ron and Hamul.
6 The sons of Zerah *were* [1]Zimri,
[a]Ethan, Heman, Calcol, and
[2]Dara—five of them in all.
7 The son of [a]Carmi *was* [1]Achar,
the troubler of Israel, who trans-
gressed in the [b]accursed[2] thing.
8 The son of Ethan *was* Azariah.
9 Also the sons of Hezron who
were born to him *were* Jerahmeel,
[1]Ram, and [2]Chelubai.
10 Ram [a]begot Amminadab, and
Amminadab begot Nahshon,
[b]leader of the children of Judah;
11 Nahshon begot [1]Salma, and
Salma begot Boaz;
12 Boaz begot Obed, and Obed be-
got Jesse;
13 [a]Jesse begot Eliab his firstborn,
Abinadab the second, [1]Shimea the
third,
14 Nethanel the fourth, Raddai the
fifth,
15 Ozem the sixth, *and* David the
[a]seventh.
16 Now their sisters *were* Zeruiah
and Abigail. [a]And the sons of Zer-
uiah *were* Abishai, Joab, and Asa-
hel—three.
17 Abigail bore Amasa; and the
father of Amasa *was* [1]Jether the
Ishmaelite.

The Family of Hezron

18 Caleb the son of Hezron had
children by Azubah, *his* wife, and
by Jerioth. Now these were her
sons: Jesher, Shobab, and Ardon.
19 When Azubah died, Caleb
[1]took [a]Ephrath[2] as his wife, who
bore him Hur.
20 And Hur begot Uri, and Uri be-
got [a]Bezalel.
21 Now afterward Hezron went in
to the daughter of [a]Machir the fa-
ther of Gilead, whom he married
when he *was* sixty years old; and
she bore him Segub.
22 Segub begot [a]Jair,[1] who had
twenty-three cities in the land of
Gilead.
23 [a](Geshur and Syria took from
them the towns of Jair, with Ke-
nath and its towns—sixty towns.)
All these *belonged to* the sons of
Machir the father of Gilead.
24 After Hezron died in Caleb
Ephrathah, Hezron's wife Abijah
bore him [a]Ashhur the father of
Tekoa.

The Family of Jerahmeel

25 The sons of Jerahmeel, the
firstborn of Hezron, *were* Ram, the
firstborn, and Bunah, Oren, Ozem,
and Ahijah.
26 Jerahmeel had another wife,
whose name was Atarah; she was
the mother of Onam.
27 The sons of Ram, the firstborn
of Jerahmeel, were Maaz, Jamin,
and Eker.
28 The sons of Onam were Sham-
mai and Jada. The sons of Sham-
mai *were* Nadab and Abishur.
29 And the name of the wife of
Abishur *was* Abihail, and she bore
him Ahban and Molid.
30 The sons of Nadab *were* Seled
and Appaim; Seled died without
children.
31 The son of Appaim *was* Ishi,
the son of Ishi *was* Sheshan, and
[a]Sheshan's son *was* Ahlai.
32 The sons of Jada, the brother
of Shammai, *were* Jether and
Jonathan; Jether died without
children.
33 The sons of Jonathan *were* Pe-
leth and Zaza. These were the sons
of Jerahmeel.
34 Now Sheshan had no sons,
only daughters. And Sheshan had
an Egyptian servant whose name
was Jarha.
35 Sheshan gave his daughter to
Jarha his servant as wife, and she
bore him Attai.
36 Attai begot Nathan, and Na-
than begot [a]Zabad;
37 Zabad begot Ephlal, and Ephlal
begot [a]Obed;
38 Obed begot Jehu, and Jehu be-
got Azariah;
39 Azariah begot Helez, and He-
lez begot Eleasah;
40 Eleasah begot Sismai, and Sis-
mai begot Shallum;
41 Shallum begot Jekamiah, and
Jekamiah begot Elishama.

The Family of Caleb

42 The descendants of Caleb the
brother of Jerahmeel *were* Mesha,
his firstborn, who was the father

4 [a]Gen. 38:6 [b]Matt. 1:3
5 [a]Gen. 46:12; Ruth 4:18
6 [a]1 Kin. 4:31 [1]*Zabdi*, Josh. 7:1 [2]*Darda*, 1 Kin. 4:31
7 [a]1 Chr. 4:1 [b]Josh. 6:18 [1]*Achan*, Josh. 7:1 [2]*banned* or *devoted*
9 [1]*Aram*, Matt. 1:3, 4 [2]*Caleb*, vv. 18, 42
10 [a]Ruth 4:19–22; Matt. 1:4 [b]Num. 1:7; 2:3
11 [1]*Salmon*, Ruth 4:21; Luke 3:32
13 [a]1 Sam. 16:6 [1]*Shammah*, 1 Sam. 16:9
15 [a]1 Sam. 16:10, 11; 17:12
16 [a]2 Sam. 2:18
17 [1]*Jithra the Israelite*, 2 Sam. 17:25
19 [a]1 Chr. 2:50 [1]Lit. *took to himself* [2]Or *Ephrathah*
20 [a]Ex. 31:2; 38:22
21 [a]Num. 27:1; Judg. 5:14; 1 Chr. 7:14
22 [a]Judg. 10:3 [1]Reckoned to Manasseh through the daughter of Machir, Num. 32:41; Deut. 3:14; 25:5, 6; 1 Kin. 4:13; 1 Chr. 7:14
23 [a]Num. 32:41; Deut. 3:14; Josh. 13:30
24 [a]1 Chr. 4:5
31 [a]1 Chr. 2:34, 35
36 [a]1 Chr. 11:41
37 [a]2 Chr. 23:1

of Ziph, and the sons of Mareshah
the father of Hebron.
43 The sons of Hebron *were* Ko-
rah, Tappuah, Rekem, and Shema.
44 Shema begot Raham the father
of Jorkoam, and Rekem begot
Shammai.
45 And the son of Shammai *was*
Maon, and Maon *was* the father
of Beth Zur.
46 Ephah, Caleb's concubine,
bore Haran, Moza, and Gazez; and
Haran begot Gazez.
47 And the sons of Jahdai *were*
Regem, Jotham, Geshan, Pelet,
Ephah, and Shaaph.
48 Maachah, Caleb's concubine,
bore Sheber and Tirhanah.
49 She also bore Shaaph the fa-
ther of Madmannah, Sheva the fa-
ther of Machbenah and the father
of Gibea. And the daughter of Ca-
leb *was* [a]Achsah.[1]
50 These were the descendants of
Caleb: The sons of [a]Hur, the first-
born of [1]Ephrathah, *were* Shobal
the father of [b]Kirjath Jearim,
51 Salma the father of Bethlehem,
and Hareph the father of Beth
Gader.
52 And Shobal the father of Kir-
jath Jearim had descendants:
[1]Haroeh, *and* half of the [2]*families*
of Manuhoth.
53 The families of Kirjath Jearim
were the Ithrites, the Puthites, the
Shumathites, and the Mishraites.
From these came the Zorathites
and the Eshtaolites.
54 The sons of Salma *were* Beth-
lehem, the Netophathites, [1]Atroth
Beth Joab, half of the Manaheth-
ites, and the Zorites.
55 And the families of the scribes
who dwelt at Jabez *were* the Ti-
rathites, the Shimeathites, *and* the
Suchathites. These *were* the [a]Ke-
nites who came from Hammath,
the father of the house of [b]Rechab.

The Family of David

3 Now these were the sons of
David who were born to him
in Hebron: The firstborn *was*
[a]Amnon, by [b]Ahinoam the
[c]Jezreelitess; the second, [1]Daniel,
by [d]Abigail the Carmelitess;
2 the third, [a]Absalom the son of
Maacah, the daughter of Talmai,
king of Geshur; the fourth, [b]Adoni-
jah the son of Haggith;

49 [a]Josh. 15:17 [1]Or *Achsa*
50 [a]1 Chr. 4:4 [b]Josh. 9:17; 18:14 [1]*Ephrath,* v. 19
52 [1]*Reaiah,* 1 Chr. 4:2 [2]Or *Manuhoth-ites,* same as *Manaheth-ites,* v. 54
54 [1]Or *Ataroth of the house of Joab*
55 [a]Judg. 1:16 [b]Jer. 35:2

CHAPTER 3

1 [a]2 Sam. 3:2–5 [b]1 Sam. 25:43 [c]Josh. 15:56 [d]1 Sam. 25:39–42 [1]*Chileab,* 2 Sam. 3:3
2 [a]2 Sam. 13:37; 15:1 [b]1 Kin. 1:5
3 [a]2 Sam. 3:5
4 [a]2 Sam. 2:11 [b]2 Sam. 5:5
5 [a]1 Chr. 14:4–7 [b]2 Sam. 12:24, 25 [1]*Shammua,* 1 Chr. 14:4; 2 Sam. 5:14 [2]*Bathsheba,* 2 Sam. 11:3 [3]*Eliam,* 2 Sam. 11:3
6 [1]*Elishua,* 1 Chr. 14:5; 2 Sam. 5:15 [2]*Elpelet,* 1 Chr. 14:5
8 [a]2 Sam. 5:14–16 [1]*Beeliada,* 1 Chr. 14:7
9 [a]2 Sam. 13:1
10 [a]1 Kin. 11:43 [1]*Abijam,* 1 Kin. 15:1
11 [1]*Jehoram,* 2 Kin. 1:17; 8:16 [2]Or *Azariah* or *Jehoahaz* [3]*Jehoash,* 2 Kin. 12:1
12 [1]*Uzziah,* Is. 6:1
15 [1]*Eliakim,* 2 Kin. 23:34 [2]*Jehoahaz,* 2 Kin. 23:31
16 [a]Matt. 1:11 [1]*Jehoiachin,* 2 Kin. 24:8, or *Coniah,* Jer. 22:24 [2]*Mattaniah,* 2 Kin. 24:17

3 the fifth, Shephatiah, by Abital;
the sixth, Ithream, by his wife
[a]Eglah.
4 *These* six were born to him in
Hebron. [a]There he reigned seven
years and six months, and [b]in Je-
rusalem he reigned thirty-three
years.
5 [a]And these were born to him
in Jerusalem: [1]Shimea, Shobab,
Nathan, and [b]Solomon—four by
[2]Bathshua the daughter of [3]Am-
miel.
6 Also *there* were Ibhar, [1]Elish-
ama, [2]Eliphelet,
7 Nogah, Nepheg, Japhia,
8 Elishama, [1]Eliada, and Eliphe-
let—[a]nine *in all.*
9 *These were* all the sons of Da-
vid, besides the sons of the concu-
bines, and [a]Tamar their sister.

The Family of Solomon

10 Solomon's son *was* [a]Reho-
boam; [1]Abijah *was* his son, Asa his
son, Jehoshaphat his son,
11 [1]Joram his son, [2]Ahaziah his
son, [3]Joash his son,
12 Amaziah his son, [1]Azariah his
son, Jotham his son,
13 Ahaz his son, Hezekiah his
son, Manasseh his son,
14 Amon his son, *and* Josiah his
son.
15 The sons of Josiah *were* Jo-
hanan the firstborn, the second
[1]Jehoiakim, the third Zedekiah,
and the fourth [2]Shallum.
16 The sons of [a]Jehoiakim *were*
[1]Jeconiah his son *and* [2]Zedekiah
his son.

The Family of Jeconiah

17 And the sons of [1]Jeconiah
[2]*were* Assir, Shealtiel [a]his son,
18 *and* Malchiram, Pedaiah, She-
nazzar, Jecamiah, Hoshama, and
Nedabiah.
19 The sons of Pedaiah *were* Ze-
rubbabel and Shimei. The sons of
Zerubbabel *were* Meshullam, Han-
aniah, Shelomith their sister,
20 and Hashubah, Ohel, Bere-
chiah, Hasadiah, and Jushab-
Hesed—five *in all.*
21 The sons of Hananiah *were* Pel-
atiah and Jeshaiah, the sons of
Rephaiah, the sons of Arnan, the

17 [a]Matt. 1:12 [1]*Jehoiachin,* 2 Kin. 24:8, or *Coniah,* Jer. 22:24 [2]Or *the captive were Shealtiel*

sons of Obadiah, and the sons of
Shechaniah.
22 The son of Shechaniah was
Shemaiah. The sons of Shemaiah
were [a]Hattush, Igal, Bariah, Nea-
riah, and Shaphat—six *in all.*
23 The sons of Neariah *were* Eli-
oenai, Hezekiah, and Azrikam—
three *in all.*
24 The sons of Elioenai *were*
Hodaviah, Eliashib, Pelaiah, Ak-
kub, Johanan, Delaiah, and
Anani—seven *in all.*

The Family of Judah

4 The sons of Judah *were* [a]Perez,
Hezron, [1]Carmi, Hur, and Sho-
bal.
2 And [1]Reaiah the son of Shobal
begot Jahath, and Jahath begot
Ahumai and Lahad. These *were*
the families of the Zorathites.
3 These *were* the sons *of the fa-
ther* of Etam: Jezreel, Ishma, and
Idbash; and the name of their sis-
ter *was* Hazelelponi;
4 and Penuel *was* the father of
Gedor, and Ezer *was the* father
of Hushah. These *were* the sons of
[a]Hur, the firstborn of Ephrathah
the father of Bethlehem.
5 And [a]Ashhur the father of
Tekoa had two wives, Helah and
Naarah.
6 Naarah bore him Ahuzzam,
Hepher, Temeni, and Haahashtari.
These *were* the sons of Naarah.
7 The sons of Helah *were* Zereth,
Zohar, and Ethnan;
8 and Koz begot Anub, Zobebah,
and the families of Aharhel the son
of Harum.
9 Now Jabez was [a]more honor-
able than his brothers, and his
mother called his name [1]Jabez,
saying, "Because I bore *him* in
pain."
10 And Jabez called on the God
of Israel saying, "Oh, that You
would bless me indeed, and en-
large my [1]territory, that Your
hand would be with me, and that
You would keep *me* from evil,
that I may not cause pain!"
So God granted him what he re-
quested.
11 Chelub the brother of [a]Shuhah
begot Mehir, who *was* the father
of Eshton.
12 And Eshton begot Beth-Rapha,
Paseah, and Tehinnah the father
of [1]Ir-Nahash. These *were* the men
of Rechah.
13 The sons of Kenaz *were* [a]Oth-
niel and Seraiah. The sons of
Othniel *were* [1]Hathath,
14 and Meonothai *who* begot
Ophrah. Seraiah begot Joab the fa-
ther of [a]Ge Harashim,[1] for they
were craftsmen.
15 The sons of [a]Caleb the son of
Jephunneh *were* Iru, Elah, and
Naam. The son of Elah *was*
[1]Kenaz.
16 The sons of Jehallelel *were*
Ziph, Ziphah, Tiria, and Asarel.
17 The sons of Ezrah *were* Jether,
Mered, Epher, and Jalon. And
[1]*Mered's wife bore* Miriam, Sham-
mai, and Ishbah the father of Esh-
temoa.
18 ([1]His wife Jehudijah bore Jered
the father of Gedor, Heber the fa-
ther of Sochoh, and Jekuthiel the
father of Zanoah.) And these were
the sons of Bithiah the daughter
of Pharaoh, whom Mered took.
19 The sons of Hodiah's wife, the
sister of Naham, *were* the fathers
of Keilah the Garmite and of Esh-
temoa the [a]Maachathite.
20 And the sons of Shimon *were*
Amnon, Rinnah, Ben-Hanan, and
Tilon. And the sons of Ishi *were*
Zoheth and Ben-Zoheth.
21 The sons of [a]Shelah [b]the son
of Judah *were* Er the father of Le-
cah, Laadah the father of Mare-
shah, and the families of the
house of the linen workers of the
house of Ashbea;
22 also Jokim, the men of Cho-
zeba, and Joash; Saraph, who
ruled in Moab, and Jashubi-
Lehem. Now the [1]records are
ancient.
23 These *were* the potters and
those who dwell at [1]Netaim and
[2]Gederah; there they dwelt with
the king for his work.

The Family of Simeon

24 The [a]sons of Simeon *were*
[1]Nemuel, Jamin, [2]Jarib, [3]Zerah,
and Shaul,
25 Shallum his son, Mibsam his
son, and Mishma his son.
26 And the sons of Mishma *were*
Hamuel his son, Zacchur his son,
and Shimei his son.
27 Shimei had sixteen sons and
six daughters; but his brothers did

22 [a]Ezra 8:2

CHAPTER 4

1 [a]Gen. 38:29; 46:12 [1]*Chelubai,* 1 Chr. 2:9 or *Caleb,* 1 Chr. 2:18

2 [1]*Haroeh,* 1 Chr. 2:52

4 [a]Ex. 31:2; 1 Chr. 2:50

5 [a]1 Chr. 2:24

9 [a]Gen. 34:19 [1]Lit. *He Will Cause Pain*

10 [1]*border*

11 [a]Job 8:1

12 [1]Lit. *City of Nahash*

13 [a]Josh. 15:17; Judg. 3:9, 11 [1]LXX, Vg. add *and Meonothai*

14 [a]Neh. 11:35 [1]Lit. *Valley of Craftsmen*

15 [a]Josh. 14:6, 14; 15:13, 17; 1 Chr. 6:56 [1]Or *Uknaz*

17 [1]Lit. *she*

18 [1]Or *His Judean wife*

19 [a]2 Kin. 25:23

21 [a]Gen. 38:11, 14 [b]Gen. 38:1–5; 46:12

22 [1]Lit. *words*

23 [1]Lit. *Plants* [2]Lit. *Hedges*

24 [a]Num. 26:12–14 [1]*Jemuel,* Gen. 46:10; Ex. 6:15; Num. 26:12 [2]*Jachin,* Gen. 46:10; Num. 26:12 [3]*Zohar,* Gen. 46:10; Ex. 6:15

not have many children, [a]nor did
any of their families multiply as
much as the children of Judah.
28 They dwelt at Beersheba, Mol-
adah, Hazar Shual,
29 [1]Bilhah, Ezem, [2]Tolad,
30 Bethuel, Hormah, Ziklag,
31 Beth Marcaboth, [1]Hazar Su-
sim, Beth Biri, and at Shaaraim.
These *were* their cities until the
reign of David.
32 And their villages *were* [1]Etam,
Ain, Rimmon, Tochen, and
Ashan—five cities—
33 and all the villages that *were*
around these cities as far as [1]Baal.
These *were* their dwelling places,
and they maintained their ge-
nealogy:
34 Meshobab, Jamlech, and Jo-
shah the son of Amaziah;
35 Joel, and Jehu the son of Joshi-
biah, the son of Seraiah, the son
of Asiel;
36 Elioenai, Jaakobah, Jeshoha-
iah, Asaiah, Adiel, Jesimiel, and
Benaiah;
37 Ziza the son of Shiphi, the son
of Allon, the son of Jedaiah, the
son of Shimri, the son of Shema-
iah—
38 these mentioned by name *were*
leaders in their families, and
their father's house increased
greatly.
39 So they went to the entrance
of Gedor, as far as the east side
of the valley, to seek pasture for
their flocks.
40 And they found rich, good pas-
ture, and the land *was* broad,
quiet, and peaceful; for some Ham-
ites formerly lived there.
41 These recorded by name came
in the days of Hezekiah king of Ju-
dah; and they [a]attacked[1] their
tents and the Meunites who were
found there, and [b]utterly de-
stroyed them, as *it* is to this day.
So they dwelt in their place, be-
cause *there was* pasture for their
flocks there.
42 Now *some* of them, five hun-
dred men of the sons of Simeon,
went to Mount Seir, having as
their captains Pelatiah, Neariah,
Rephaiah, and Uzziel, the sons of
Ishi.
43 And they [1]defeated [a]the rest of
the Amalekites who had escaped.
They have dwelt there to this day.

The Family of Reuben

5 Now the sons of Reuben the
firstborn of Israel—[a]he *was* in-
deed the firstborn, but because he
[b]defiled his father's bed, [c]his birth-
right was given to the sons of Jo-
seph, the son of Israel, so that the
genealogy is not listed according
to the birthright;
2 yet [a]Judah prevailed over his
brothers, and from him *came* a
[b]ruler, although [1]the birthright
was Joseph's—
3 the sons of [a]Reuben the first-
born of Israel were Hanoch, Pallu,
Hezron, and Carmi.
4 The sons of Joel *were* Shema-
iah his son, Gog his son, Shimei
his son,
5 Micah his son, Reaiah his son,
Baal his son,
6 and Beerah his son, whom
[1]Tiglath-Pileser king of Assyria
[a]carried into captivity. He *was*
leader of the Reubenites.
7 And his brethren by their fami-
lies, [a]when the genealogy of their
generations was registered: the
chief, Jeiel, and Zechariah,
8 and Bela the son of Azaz, the
son of Shema, the son of Joel, who
dwelt in [a]Aroer, as far as Nebo and
Baal Meon.
9 Eastward they settled as far as
the [1]entrance of the wilderness
this side of the River Euphrates,
because their cattle had [2]multi-
plied [a]in the land of Gilead.
10 Now in the days of Saul they
made war [a]with the Hagrites, who
fell by their hand; and they dwelt
in their tents throughout the entire
area east of Gilead.

The Family of Gad

11 And the [a]children of Gad dwelt
next to them in the land of
[b]Bashan as far as [c]Salcah:
12 Joel *was* the chief, Shapham
the next, then Jaanai and Shaphat
in Bashan,
13 and their brethren of their fa-
ther's house: Michael, Meshullam,
Sheba, Jorai, Jachan, Zia, and
Eber—seven *in all.*
14 These *were* the children of Abi-
hail the son of Huri, the son of Ja-
roah, the son of Gilead, the son of
Michael, the son of Jeshishai, the
son of Jahdo, the son of Buz;

27 [a]Num. 2:9
29 [1]*Balah,* Josh. 19:3 [2]*Eltolad,* Josh. 19:4
31 [1]*Hazar Susah,* Josh. 19:5
32 [1]*Ether,* Josh. 19:7
33 [1]*Baalath Beer,* Josh. 19:8
41 [a]2 Kin. 18:8 [b]2 Kin. 19:11 [1]Lit. *struck*
43 [a]Ex. 17:14; 1 Sam. 15:8; 30:17 [1]Lit. *struck*

CHAPTER 5

1 [a]Gen. 29:32; 49:3 [b]Gen. 35:22; 49:4 [c]Gen. 48:15, 22
2 [a]Gen. 49:8, 10; Ps. 60:7; 108:8 [b]Mic. 5:2; Matt. 2:6 [1]*the right of the firstborn*
3 [a]Gen. 46:9; Ex. 6:14; Num. 26:5
6 [a]2 Kin. 18:11 [1]Heb. *Tilgath-Pilneser*
7 [a]1 Chr. 5:17
8 [a]Num. 32:34; Josh. 12:2; 13:15, 16
9 [a]Josh. 22:8, 9 [1]*beginning* [2]*increased*
10 [a]Gen. 25:12
11 [a]Num. 26:15–18 [b]Josh. 13:11, 24–28 [c]Deut. 3:10

15 Ahi the son of Abdiel, the son
of Guni, *was* chief of their father's
house.
16 And *the Gadites* dwelt in Gil-
ead, in Bashan and in its villages,
and in all the [1]common-lands of
[a]Sharon within their borders.
17 All these were registered by
genealogies in the days of [a]Jotham
king of Judah, and in the days of
[b]Jeroboam king of Israel.
18 The sons of Reuben, the Gad-
ites, and half the tribe of Manasseh
had forty-four thousand seven
hundred and sixty valiant men,
men able to bear shield and sword,
to shoot with the bow, and skillful
in war, who went to war.
19 They made war with the Hag-
rites, [a]Jetur, Naphish, and Nodab.
20 And [a]they were helped against
them, and the Hagrites were deliv-
ered into their hand, and all who
were with them, for they [b]cried out
to God in the battle. He [1]heeded
their prayer, because they [c]put
their trust in Him.
21 Then they took away their live-
stock—fifty thousand of their cam-
els, two hundred and fifty thou-
sand of their sheep, and two
thousand of their donkeys—also
one hundred thousand of their
men;
22 for many fell dead, because the
war [a]*was* God's. And they dwelt
in their place until [b]the captivity.

The Family of Manasseh (East)

23 So the children of the half-tribe
of Manasseh dwelt in the land.
Their *numbers* increased from
Bashan to Baal Hermon, that is, to
[a]Senir, or Mount Hermon.
24 These *were* the heads of their
fathers' houses: Epher, Ishi, Eliel,
Azriel, Jeremiah, Hodaviah, and
Jahdiel. They were mighty men of
valor, famous men, *and* heads of
their fathers' houses.
25 And they were unfaithful to the
God of their fathers, and [a]played
the harlot after the gods of the peo-
ples of the land, whom God had
destroyed before them.
26 So the God of Israel stirred up
the spirit of [a]Pul king of Assyria,
that is, [b]Tiglath-Pileser[1] king of
Assyria. He carried the Reuben-
ites, the Gadites, and the half-tribe
of Manasseh into captivity. He
took them to [c]Halah, Habor, Hara,
and the river of Gozan to this day.

16 [a]1 Chr. 27:29; Song 2:1; Is. 35:2; 65:10 [1]*open lands*
17 [a]2 Kin. 15:5, 32 [b]2 Kin. 14:16, 28
19 [a]Gen. 25:15; 1 Chr. 1:31
20 [a][1 Chr. 5:22] [b]2 Chr. 14:11–13 [c]Ps. 9:10; 20:7, 8; 22:4, 5 [1]Lit. *was entreated for them*
22 [a][Josh. 23:10; 2 Chr. 32:8; Rom. 8:31] [b]2 Kin. 15:29; 17:6
23 [a]Deut. 3:9
25 [a]2 Kin. 17:7
26 [a]2 Kin. 15:19 [b]2 Kin. 15:29 [c]2 Kin. 17:6; 18:11 [1]Heb. *Tilgath-Pilneser*

CHAPTER 6

1 [a]Gen. 46:11; Ex. 6:16; Num. 26:57; 1 Chr. 23:6 [1]Or *Gershom*, v. 16
2 [a]1 Chr. 6:18, 22
3 [a]Lev. 10:1, 2
8 [a]2 Sam. 8:17 [b]2 Sam. 15:27
10 [a]2 Chr. 26:17, 18 [b]1 Kin. 6:1; 2 Chr. 3:1 [1]Lit. *house*
11 [a]Ezra 7:3 [b]2 Chr. 19:11
12 [1]*Meshullam*, 1 Chr. 9:11
14 [a]2 Kin. 25:18–21; Neh. 11:11
15 [a]2 Kin. 25:21
16 [a]Gen. 46:11; Ex. 6:16 [1]Heb. *Gershom*, an alternate spelling for *Gershon*, vv. 1, 17, 20, 43, 62, 71
20 [a]1 Chr. 6:42
21 [1]*Ethan*, v. 42 [2]*Adaiah*, v. 41 [3]*Ethni*, v. 41
22 [a]Num. 16:1 [1]*Izhar*, vv. 2, 18

The Family of Levi

6 The sons of Levi *were* [a]Ger-
shon,[1] Kohath, and Merari.
2 The sons of Kohath *were* Am-
ram, [a]Izhar, Hebron, and Uzziel.
3 The children of Amram *were*
Aaron, Moses, and Miriam. And
the sons of Aaron *were* [a]Nadab,
Abihu, Eleazar, and Ithamar.
4 Eleazar begot Phinehas, *and*
Phinehas begot Abishua;
5 Abishua begot Bukki, and
Bukki begot Uzzi;
6 Uzzi begot Zerahiah, and Zera-
hiah begot Meraioth;
7 Meraioth begot Amariah, and
Amariah begot Ahitub;
8 [a]Ahitub begot [b]Zadok, and Za-
dok begot Ahimaaz;
9 Ahimaaz begot Azariah, and
Azariah begot Johanan;
10 Johanan begot Azariah (it was
he [a]who ministered as priest in the
[b]temple[1] that Solomon built in Je-
rusalem);
11 [a]Azariah begot [b]Amariah, and
Amariah begot Ahitub;
12 Ahitub begot Zadok, and Za-
dok begot [1]Shallum;
13 Shallum begot Hilkiah, and
Hilkiah begot Azariah;
14 Azariah begot [a]Seraiah, and
Seraiah begot Jehozadak.
15 Jehozadak went *into captivity*
[a]when the LORD carried Judah and
Jerusalem into captivity by the
hand of Nebuchadnezzar.
16 The sons of Levi *were* [a]Ger-
shon,[1] Kohath, and Merari.
17 These are the names of the
sons of Gershon: Libni and
Shimei.
18 The sons of Kohath *were* Am-
ram, Izhar, Hebron, and Uzziel.
19 The sons of Merari *were* Mahli
and Mushi. Now these *are* the fam-
ilies of the Levites according to
their fathers:
20 Of Gershon *were* Libni his son,
Jahath his son, [a]Zimmah his son,
21 [1]Joah his son, [2]Iddo his son,
Zerah his son, *and* [3]Jeatherai his
son.
22 The sons of Kohath *were*
[1]Amminadab his son, [a]Korah his
son, Assir his son,
23 Elkanah his son, Ebiasaph his
son, Assir his son,

24 Tahath his son, Uriel his son,
Uzziah his son, and Shaul his
son.
25 The sons of Elkanah *were*
[a]Amasai and Ahimoth.
26 *As for* Elkanah, the sons of El-
kanah *were* [1]Zophai his son,
[2]Nahath his son,
27 [1]Eliab his son, Jeroham his son,
and Elkanah his son.
28 The sons of Samuel *were* [1]*Joel*
the firstborn, and Abijah [2]the sec-
ond.
29 The sons of Merari *were* Mahli,
Libni his son, Shimei his son, Uz-
zah his son,
30 Shimea his son, Haggiah his
son, *and* Asaiah his son.

Musicians in the House of the LORD

31 Now these are [a]the men whom
David appointed over the service
of song in the house of the LORD,
after the [b]ark came to rest.
32 They were ministering with
music before the dwelling place of
the tabernacle of meeting, until
Solomon had built the house of the
LORD in Jerusalem, and they
served in their office according to
their order.
33 And these *are* the ones who
[1]ministered with their sons: Of the
sons of the [a]Kohathites *were* He-
man the singer, the son of Joel, the
son of Samuel,
34 the son of Elkanah, the son of
Jeroham, the son of [1]Eliel, the son
of [2]Toah,
35 the son of Zuph, the son of El-
kanah, the son of Mahath, the son
of Amasai,
36 the son of Elkanah, the son of
Joel, the son of Azariah, the son
of Zephaniah,
37 the son of Tahath, the son of
Assir, the son of [a]Ebiasaph, the
son of Korah,
38 the son of Izhar, the son of Ko-
hath, the son of Levi, the son of
Israel.
39 And his brother [a]Asaph, who
stood at his right hand, *was* Asaph
the son of Berachiah, the son of
Shimea,
40 the son of Michael, the son of
Baaseiah, the son of Malchijah,
41 the son of [a]Ethni, the son of
Zerah, the son of Adaiah,
42 the son of Ethan, the son of
Zimmah, the son of Shimei,

25 [a]1 Chr. 6:35, 36
26 [1]*Zuph*, v. 35; 1 Sam. 1:1 [2]*Toah*, v. 34
27 [1]*Eliel*, v. 34
28 [1]So with LXX, Syr., Arab.; cf. v. 33 and 1 Sam. 8:2 [2]Heb. *Vasheni*
31 [a]1 Chr. 15:16–22, 27; 16:4–6 [b]2 Sam. 6:17; 1 Kin. 8:4; 1 Chr. 15:25—16:1
33 [a]Num. 26:57 [1]Lit. *stood with*
34 [1]*Elihu*, 1 Sam. 1:1 [2]*Tohu*, 1 Sam. 1:1
37 [a]Ex. 6:24
39 [a]2 Chr. 5:12
41 [a]1 Chr. 6:21
44 [1]*Jeduthun*, 1 Chr. 9:16; 25:1, 3, 6; 2 Chr. 35:15; Ps. 62:title [2]Or *Kushaiah*
48 [a]1 Chr. 9:14–34
49 [a]Ex. 28:1; [Num. 18:1–8] [b]Lev. 1:8, 9 [c]Ex. 30:7
50 [a]1 Chr. 6:4–8; Ezra 7:5
54 [a]Josh. 21
55 [a]Josh. 14:13; 21:11, 12 [1]*open lands*
56 [a]Josh. 14:13; 15:13
57 [a]Josh. 21:13, 19
58 [1]*Holon*, Josh. 21:15
59 [1]*Ain*, Josh. 21:16

43 the son of Jahath, the son of
Gershon, the son of Levi.
44 Their brethren, the sons of
Merari, on the left hand, *were*
[1]Ethan the son of [2]Kishi, the son
of Abdi, the son of Malluch,
45 the son of Hashabiah, the son
of Amaziah, the son of Hilkiah,
46 the son of Amzi, the son of
Bani, the son of Shamer,
47 the son of Mahli, the son of Mu-
shi, the son of Merari, the son of
Levi.
48 And their brethren, the Levites,
were appointed to every [a]kind of
service of the tabernacle of the
house of God.

The Family of Aaron

49 [a]But Aaron and his sons of-
fered sacrifices [b]on the altar of
burnt offering and [c]on the altar
of incense, for all the work of the
Most Holy *Place*, and to make
atonement for Israel, according to
all that Moses the servant of God
had commanded.
50 Now these *are* the [a]sons of
Aaron: Eleazar his son, Phinehas
his son, Abishua his son,
51 Bukki his son, Uzzi his son,
Zerahiah his son,
52 Meraioth his son, Amariah his
son, Ahitub his son,
53 Zadok his son, *and* Ahimaaz
his son.

Dwelling Places of the Levites

54 [a]Now these *are* their dwelling
places throughout their settle-
ments in their territory, for they
were *given* by lot to the sons of
Aaron, of the family of the Ko-
hathites:
55 [a]They gave them Hebron in the
land of Judah, with its surround-
ing [1]common-lands.
56 [a]But the fields of the city and
its villages they gave to Caleb the
son of Jephunneh.
57 And [a]to the sons of Aaron they
gave *one of* the cities of refuge,
Hebron; also Libnah with its
common-lands, Jattir, Eshtemoa
with its common-lands,
58 [1]Hilen with its common-lands,
Debir with its common-lands,
59 [1]Ashan with its common-lands,
and Beth Shemesh with its
common-lands.
60 And from the tribe of Benja-

min: Geba with its common-lands,
[1]Alemeth with its common-lands,
and Anathoth with its common-
lands. All their cities among their
families *were* thirteen.
61 [a]To the rest of the family of the
tribe of the Kohathites *they gave*
[b]by lot ten cities from half the tribe
of Manasseh.
62 And to the sons of Gershon,
throughout their families, *they*
gave thirteen cities from the tribe
of Issachar, from the tribe of
Asher, from the tribe of Naphtali,
and from the tribe of Manasseh in
Bashan.
63 To the sons of Merari, through-
out their families, *they gave*
[a]twelve cities from the tribe of
Reuben, from the tribe of Gad,
and from the tribe of Zebulun.
64 So the children of Israel gave
these cities with their [1]common-
lands to the Levites.
65 And they gave by lot from the
tribe of the children of Judah, from
the tribe of the children of Simeon,
and from the tribe of the children
of Benjamin these cities which are
called by *their* names.
66 Now [a]some of the families of
the sons of Kohath *were given* cit-
ies as their territory from the tribe
of Ephraim.
67 [a]And they gave them *one of* the
cities of refuge, Shechem with its
common-lands, in the mountains
of Ephraim, also Gezer with its
common-lands,
68 [a]Jokmeam with its common-
lands, Beth Horon with its
common-lands,
69 Aijalon with its common-lands,
and Gath Rimmon with its
common-lands.
70 And from the half-tribe of Ma-
nasseh: Aner with its common-
lands and Bileam with its
common-lands, for the rest of the
family of the sons of Kohath.
71 From the family of the half-
tribe of Manasseh the sons of Ger-
shon *were given* Golan in Bashan
with its common-lands and
[1]Ashtaroth with its common-lands.
72 And from the tribe of Issachar:
[1]Kedesh with its common-lands,
Daberath with its common-lands,
73 Ramoth with its common-
lands, and Anem with its common-
lands.

60 [1]*Almon.* Josh. 21:18

61 [a]1 Chr. 6:66–70 [b]Josh. 21:5

63 [a]Josh. 21:7, 34–40

64 [1]*open lands*

66 [a]1 Chr. 6:61

67 [a]Josh. 21:21

68 [a]Josh. 21:22

71 [1]*Beeshterah.* Josh. 21:27

72 [1]*Kishon.* Josh. 21:28

77 [1]Heb. *Rimmono,* an alternate spelling of *Rimmon,* 1 Chr. 4:32

CHAPTER 7

1 [a]Num. 26:23–25 [1]*Puvah,* Gen. 46:13 [2]*Job.* Gen. 46:13

2 [a]2 Sam. 24:1–9; 1 Chr. 27:1

74 And from the tribe of Asher:
Mashal with its common-lands,
Abdon with its common-lands,
75 Hukok with its common-lands,
and Rehob with its common-
lands.
76 And from the tribe of Naphtali:
Kedesh in Galilee with its
common-lands, Hammon with its
common-lands, and Kirjathaim
with its common-lands.
77 From the tribe of Zebulun the
rest of the children of Merari *were*
given [1]Rimmon with its common-
lands and Tabor with its common-
lands.
78 And on the other side of the
Jordan, across from Jericho, on
the east side of the Jordan, *they*
were given from the tribe of Reu-
ben: Bezer in the wilderness with
its common-lands, Jahzah with its
common-lands,
79 Kedemoth with its common-
lands, and Mephaath with its
common-lands.
80 And from the tribe of Gad: Ra-
moth in Gilead with its common-
lands, Mahanaim with its
common-lands,
81 Heshbon with its common-
lands, and Jazer with its common-
lands.

The Family of Issachar

7 The sons of Issachar *were*
[a]Tola, [1]Puah, [2]Jashub, and
Shimron—four *in all.*
2 The sons of Tola were Uzzi,
Rephaiah, Jeriel, Jahmai, Jibsam,
and Shemuel, heads of their fa-
ther's house. *The sons* of Tola
were mighty men of valor in their
generations; [a]their number in the
days of David *was* twenty-two
thousand six hundred.
3 The son of Uzzi *was* Izrahiah,
and the sons of Izrahiah were
Michael, Obadiah, Joel, and
Ishiah. All five of them *were* chief
men.
4 And with them, by their gen-
erations, according to their fa-
thers' houses, *were* thirty-six thou-
sand troops ready for war; for they
had many wives and sons.
5 Now their brethren among all
the families of Issachar *were*
mighty men of valor, listed by their
genealogies, eighty-seven thou-
sand in all.

The Family of Benjamin

6 *The sons* of [a]Benjamin *were* Bela, Becher, and Jediael—three *in all.*

7 The sons of Bela were Ezbon, Uzzi, Uzziel, Jerimoth, and Iri—five *in all.* They *were* heads of *their* fathers' houses, and they were listed by their genealogies, twenty-two thousand and thirty-four mighty men of valor.

8 The sons of Becher *were* Zemirah, Joash, Eliezer, Elioenai, Omri, Jerimoth, Abijah, Anathoth, and Alemeth. All these *are* the sons of Becher.

9 And they were recorded by genealogy according to their generations, heads of their fathers' houses, twenty thousand two hundred mighty men of valor.

10 The son of Jediael *was* Bilhan, and the sons of Bilhan *were* Jeush, Benjamin, Ehud, Chenaanah, Zethan, Tharshish, and Ahishahar.

11 All these sons of Jediael *were* heads of their fathers' houses; *there were* seventeen thousand two hundred mighty men of valor fit to go out for war *and* battle.

12 [1]Shuppim and [2]Huppim *were* the sons of [3]Ir, *and* Hushim *was* the son of [4]Aher.

The Family of Naphtali

13 The [a]sons of Naphtali *were* [1]Jahziel, Guni, Jezer, and [2]Shallum, the sons of Bilhah.

The Family of Manasseh (West)

14 The [a]descendants of Manasseh: his Syrian concubine bore him [b]Machir the father of Gilead, the father of Asriel.

15 Machir took as his wife *the sister* of [1]Huppim and [2]Shuppim, whose name *was* Maachah. The name of Gilead's [3]grandson *was* [a]Zelophehad, but Zelophehad begot only daughters.

16 (Maachah the wife of Machir bore a son, and she called his name Peresh. The name of his brother *was* Sheresh, and his sons *were* Ulam and Rakem.

17 The son of Ulam *was* [a]Bedan.) These *were* the descendants of Gilead the son of Machir, the son of Manasseh.

18 His sister Hammoleketh bore Ishhod, [1]Abiezer, and Mahlah.

19 And the sons of Shemida were Ahian, Shechem, Likhi, and Aniam.

The Family of Ephraim

20 [a]The sons of Ephraim *were* Shuthelah, Bered his son, Tahath his son, Eladah his son, Tahath his son,

21 Zabad his son, Shuthelah his son, and Ezer and Elead. The men of Gath who were born in *that* land killed *them* because they came down to take away their cattle.

22 Then Ephraim their father mourned many days, and his brethren came to comfort him.

23 And when he went in to his wife, she conceived and bore a son; and he called his name [1]Beriah, because tragedy had come upon his house.

24 Now his daughter *was* Sheerah, who built Lower and Upper [a]Beth Horon and Uzzen Sheerah;

25 and Rephah *was* his son, *as well* as Resheph, and Telah his son, Tahan his son,

26 Laadan his son, Ammihud his son, [a]Elishama his son,

27 [1]Nun his son, and [a]Joshua his son.

28 Now their [a]possessions and dwelling places *were* Bethel and its towns: to the east [1]Naaran, to the west Gezer and its towns, and Shechem and its towns, as far as [2]Ayyah and its towns;

29 and by the borders of the children of [a]Manasseh *were* Beth Shean and its towns, Taanach and its towns, [b]Megiddo and its towns, Dor and its towns. In these dwelt the children of Joseph, the son of Israel.

The Family of Asher

30 [a]The sons of Asher *were* Imnah, Ishvah, Ishvi, Beriah, and their sister Serah.

31 The sons of Beriah *were* Heber and Malchiel, who was the father of [1]Birzaith.

32 And Heber begot Japhlet, [1]Shomer, [2]Hotham, and their sister Shua.

33 The sons of Japhlet *were*

---

6 [a]Gen. 46:21; Num. 26:38–41; 1 Chr. 8:1
12 [1]*Shupham,* Num. 26:39 [2]*Hupham,* Num. 26:39 [3]*Iri,* v. 7 [4]*Ahiram,* Num. 26:38
13 [a]Num. 26:48–50 [1]*Jahzeel,* Gen. 46:24 [2]*Shillem,* Gen. 46:24
14 [a]Num. 26:29–34 [b]1 Chr. 2:21
15 [a]Num. 26:30–33; 27:1 [1]*Hupham,* v. 12; Num. 26:39 [2]*Shupham,* v. 12; Num. 26:39 [3]Lit. *the second*
17 [a]1 Sam. 12:11
18 [1]*Jeezer,* Num. 26:30
20 [a]Num. 26:35–37
23 [1]Lit. *In Tragedy*
24 [a]Josh. 16:3, 5; 2 Chr. 8:5
26 [a]Num. 10:22
27 [a]Ex. 17:9, 14; 24:13; 33:11 [1]Heb. *Non*
28 [a]Josh. 16:1–10 [1]*Naarath,* Josh. 16:7 [2]Many Heb. mss., Bg., LXX, Tg., Vg. *Gazza*
29 [a]Gen. 41:51; Josh. 17:7 [b]Josh. 17:11
30 [a]Gen. 46:17; Num. 26:44–47
31 [1]Or *Birzavith* or *Birzoth*
32 [1]*Shemer,* 1 Chr. 7:34 [2]*Helem,* 1 Chr. 7:35

Pasach, Bimhal, and Ashvath. These *were* the children of Japhlet.
34 The sons of [a]Shemer *were* Ahi, Rohgah, Jehubbah, and Aram.
35 And the sons of his brother Helem *were* Zophah, Imna, Shelesh, and Amal.
36 The sons of Zophah *were* Suah, Harnepher, Shual, Beri, Imrah,
37 Bezer, Hod, Shamma, Shilshah, [1]Jithran, and Beera.
38 The sons of Jether *were* Jephunneh, Pispah, and Ara.
39 The sons of Ulla *were* Arah, Haniel, and Rizia.
40 All these *were* the children of Asher, heads of *their* fathers' houses, choice men, mighty men of valor, chief leaders. And they were recorded by genealogies among the army fit for battle; their number *was* twenty-six thousand.

The Family Tree of King Saul of Benjamin

8 Now Benjamin begot [a]Bela his firstborn, Ashbel the second,
[1]Aharah the third,
2 Nohah the fourth, and Rapha the fifth.
3 The sons of Bela *were* [1]Addar, Gera, Abihud,
4 Abishua, Naaman, Ahoah,
5 Gera, [1]Shephuphan, and Huram.
6 These *are* the sons of Ehud, who were the heads of the fathers' *houses* of the inhabitants of [a]Geba, and who forced them to move to [b]Manahath:
7 Naaman, Ahijah, and Gera who forced them to move. He begot Uzza and Ahihud.
8 Also Shaharaim had children in the country of Moab, after he had sent away Hushim and Baara his wives.
9 By Hodesh his wife he begot Jobab, Zibia, Mesha, Malcam,
10 Jeuz, Sachiah, and Mirmah. These *were* his sons, heads of their fathers' *houses*.
11 And by Hushim he begot Abitub and Elpaal.
12 The sons of Elpaal *were* Eber, Misham, and Shemed, who built Ono and Lod with its towns;
13 and Beriah and [a]Shema, who *were* heads of their fathers' *houses* of the inhabitants of Aijalon, who drove out the inhabitants of Gath.
14 Ahio, Shashak, Jeremoth,
15 Zebadiah, Arad, Eder,
16 Michael, Ispah, and Joha *were* the sons of Beriah.
17 Zebadiah, Meshullam, Hizki, Heber,
18 Ishmerai, Jizliah, and Jobab *were* the sons of Elpaal.
19 Jakim, Zichri, Zabdi,
20 Elienai, Zillethai, Eliel,
21 Adaiah, Beraiah, and Shimrath *were* the sons of [1]Shimei.
22 Ishpan, Eber, Eliel,
23 Abdon, Zichri, Hanan,
24 Hananiah, Elam, Antothijah,
25 Iphdeiah, and Penuel *were* the sons of Shashak.
26 Shamsherai, Shehariah, Athaliah,
27 Jaareshiah, Elijah, and Zichri *were* the sons of Jeroham.
28 These *were* heads of the fathers' *houses* by their generations, chief men. These dwelt in Jerusalem.
29 Now [1]the father of Gibeon, whose [a]wife's name *was* Maacah, dwelt at Gibeon.
30 And his firstborn son *was* Abdon, then Zur, Kish, Baal, Nadab,
31 Gedor, Ahio, [1]Zecher,
32 and Mikloth, who begot [1]Shimeah. They also dwelt [2]alongside their [3]relatives in Jerusalem, with their brethren.
33 [a]Ner[1] begot Kish, Kish begot Saul, and Saul begot Jonathan, Malchishua, [2]Abinadab, and [3]Esh-Baal.
34 The son of Jonathan *was* [1]Merib-Baal, and Merib-Baal begot [a]Micah.
35 The sons of Micah *were* Pithon, Melech, [1]Tarea, and Ahaz.
36 And Ahaz begot [1]Jehoaddah; Jehoaddah begot Alemeth, Azmaveth, and Zimri; and Zimri begot Moza.
37 Moza begot Binea, [1]Raphah his son, Eleasah his son, *and* Azel his son.
38 Azel had six sons whose names *were* these: Azrikam, Bocheru, Ishmael, Sheariah, Obadiah, and Hanan. All these *were* the sons of Azel.
39 And the sons of Eshek his brother *were* Ulam his firstborn, Jeush the second, and Eliphelet the third.

---

34 [a]1 Chr. 7:32
37 [1]*Jether*, v. 38

CHAPTER 8

1 [a]Gen. 46:21; Num. 26:38; 1 Chr. 7:6 [1]*Ahiram*, Num. 26:38
3 [1]*Ard*, Num. 26:40
5 [1]*Shupham*, Num. 26:39, or *Shuppim*, 1 Chr. 7:12
6 [a]1 Chr. 6:60 [b]1 Chr. 2:52
13 [a]1 Chr. 8:21
21 [1]*Shema*, 1 Chr. 7:13
29 [a]1 Chr. 9:35–38 [1]Jeiel, 1 Chr. 9:35
31 [1]*Zechariah*, 1 Chr. 9:37
32 [1]*Shimeam*, 1 Chr. 9:38 [2]Lit. *opposite* [3]*brethren*
33 [a]1 Sam. 14:51 [1]Also the son of Gibeon, 1 Chr. 9:36, 39 [2]*Jishui*, 1 Sam. 14:49 [3]*Ishbosheth*, 2 Sam. 2:8
34 [a]2 Sam. 9:12 [1]*Mephibosheth*, 2 Sam. 4:4
35 [1]*Tahrea*, 1 Chr. 9:41
36 [1]*Jarah*, 1 Chr. 9:42
37 [1]*Raphaiah*, 1 Chr. 9:43

40 The sons of Ulam were mighty
men of valor—archers. *They* had
many sons and grandsons, one
hundred and fifty *in all.* These
were all sons of Benjamin.
9 So [a]all Israel was [1]recorded by
genealogies, and indeed, they
were inscribed in the book of the
kings of Israel. But Judah was car-
ried away captive to Babylon be-
cause of their unfaithfulness.
2 [a]And the first inhabitants who
dwelt in their possessions in their
cities *were* Israelites, priests, Le-
vites, and [b]the Nethinim.

Dwellers in Jerusalem

3 Now in [a]Jerusalem the children
of Judah dwelt, and some of the
children of Benjamin, and of the
children of Ephraim and Ma-
nasseh:
4 Uthai the son of Ammihud, the
son of Omri, the son of Imri, the
son of Bani, of the descendants of
Perez, the son of Judah.
5 Of the Shilonites: Asaiah the
firstborn and his sons.
6 Of the sons of Zerah: Jeuel, and
their brethren—six hundred and
ninety.
7 Of the sons of Benjamin: Sallu
the son of Meshullam, the son of
Hodaviah, the son of Hassenuah;
8 Ibneiah the son of Jeroham;
Elah the son of Uzzi, the son of
Michri; Meshullam the son of
Shephatiah, the son of Reuel, the
son of Ibnijah;
9 and their brethren, according
to their generations—nine hun-
dred and fifty-six. All these men
were heads of a father's *house* in
their fathers' houses.

The Priests at Jerusalem

10 [a]Of the priests: Jedaiah, Je-
hoiarib, and Jachin;
11 [1]Azariah the son of Hilkiah, the
son of Meshullam, the son of Za-
dok, the son of Meraioth, the son
of Ahitub, the [a]officer over the
house of God;
12 Adaiah the son of Jeroham, the
son of Pashur, the son of Malchi-
jah; Maasai the son of Adiel, the
son of Jahzerah, the son of Me-
shullam, the son of Meshillemith,
the son of Immer;
13 and their brethren, heads of
their fathers' *houses*—one thou-
sand seven hundred and sixty.
They were [1]very able men for the
work of the service of the house
of God.

The Levites at Jerusalem

14 Of the Levites: Shemaiah the
son of Hasshub, the son of Azri-
kam, the son of Hashabiah, of the
sons of Merari;
15 Bakbakkar, Heresh, Galal, and
Mattaniah the son of Micah, the
son of [a]Zichri, the son of Asaph;
16 [a]Obadiah the son of [b]Shema-
iah, the son of Galal, the son of
Jeduthun; and Berechiah the son
of Asa, the son of Elkanah, who
lived in the villages of the Ne-
tophathites.

The Levite Gatekeepers

17 And the gatekeepers *were*
Shallum, Akkub, Talmon, Ahi-
man, and their brethren. Shallum
was the chief.
18 Until then *they had been* gate-
keepers for the camps of the chil-
dren of Levi at the King's Gate on
the east.
19 Shallum the son of Kore, the
son of Ebiasaph, the son of Korah,
and his brethren, from his father's
house, the Korahites, *were* in
charge of the work of the service,
[1]gatekeepers of the tabernacle.
Their fathers had been keepers of
the entrance to the camp of the
LORD.
20 And [a]Phinehas the son of Elea-
zar had been the officer over them
in time past; the LORD *was* with
him.
21 [a]Zechariah the son of Meshele-
miah *was* [1]keeper of the door of
the tabernacle of meeting.
22 All those chosen as gatekeep-
ers *were* two hundred and twelve.
[a]They were recorded by their
genealogy, in their villages. Da-
vid and Samuel [b]the seer had ap-
pointed them to their trusted office.
23 So they and their children *were*
in charge of the gates of the house
of the LORD, the house of the taber-
nacle, by assignment.
24 The gatekeepers were assigned
to the four directions: the east,
west, north, and south.
25 And their brethren in their vil-
lages *had* to come with them from
time to time [a]for seven days.

CHAPTER 9

1 [a]Ezra 2:59 [1]*enrolled*

2 [a]Ezra 2:70; Neh. 7:73 [b]Ezra 2:43; 8:20

3 [a]Neh. 11:1, 2

10 [a]Neh. 11:10–14

11 [a]2 Chr. 31:13; Jer. 20:1 [1]*Seraiah,* Neh. 11:11

13 [1]Lit. *mighty men of strength*

15 [a]Neh. 11:17

16 [a]Neh. 11:17 [b]Neh. 11:17

19 [1]Lit. *thresholds*

20 [a]Num. 25:6–13; 31:6

21 [a]1 Chr. 26:2, 14 [1]*gatekeeper*

22 [a]1 Chr. 26:1, 2 [b]1 Sam. 9:9

25 [a]2 Kin. 11:4–7; 2 Chr. 23:8

26 For in this trusted office *were*
four chief gatekeepers; they were
Levites. And they had charge over
the chambers and treasuries of the
house of God.
27 And they lodged *all* around the
house of God because [1]they *had*
the [a]responsibility, and they *were*
in charge of opening *it* every
morning.

Other Levite Responsibilities

28 Now *some* of them were in
charge of the serving vessels, for
they brought them in and took
them out by count.
29 *Some* of them *were* appointed
over the furnishings and over all
the implements of the sanctuary,
and over the [a]fine flour and the
wine and the oil and the incense
and the spices.
30 And *some* of the sons of the
priests made [a]the ointment of the
spices.
31 Mattithiah of the Levites, the
firstborn of Shallum the Korahite,
had the trusted office [a]over the
things that were baked in the pans.
32 And some of their brethren of
the sons of the Kohathites [a]*were*
in charge of preparing the show-
bread for every Sabbath.
33 These are [a]the singers, heads
of the fathers' *houses* of the Le-
vites, *who lodged* in the chambers,
and were free *from other duties;*
for they were employed in *that*
work day and night.
34 These heads of the fathers'
houses of the Levites *were* heads
throughout their generations.
They dwelt at Jerusalem.

The Family of King Saul

35 Jeiel the father of Gibeon,
whose wife's name *was* [a]Maacah,
dwelt at Gibeon.
36 His firstborn son *was* Abdon,
then Zur, Kish, Baal, Ner, Nadab,
37 Gedor, Ahio, [1]Zechariah, and
Mikloth.
38 And Mikloth begot [1]Shimeam.
They also dwelt alongside their
relatives in Jerusalem, with their
brethren.
39 [a]Ner begot Kish, Kish begot
Saul, and Saul begot Jonathan,
Malchishua, Abinadab, and Esh-
Baal.
40 The son of Jonathan *was*
Merib-Baal, and Merib-Baal begot
Micah.
41 The sons of Micah *were* Pithon,
Melech, [1]Tahrea, [a]*and*[2] *Ahaz.*
42 And Ahaz begot [1]Jarah; Jarah
begot Alemeth, Azmaveth, and
Zimri; and Zimri begot Moza;
43 Moza begot Binea, [1]Rephaiah
his son, Eleasah his son, and Azel
his son.
44 And Azel had six sons whose
names *were* these: Azrikam, Bo-
cheru, Ishmael, Sheariah, Oba-
diah, and Hanan; these *were* the
sons of Azel.

Tragic End of Saul and His Sons

10 Now [a]the Philistines fought
against Israel; and the men
of Israel fled from before the Phi-
listines, and fell slain on Mount
Gilboa.
2 Then the Philistines followed
hard after Saul and his sons. And
the Philistines killed Jonathan,
[1]Abinadab, and Malchishua,
Saul's sons.
3 The battle became fierce
against Saul. The archers hit him,
and he was wounded by the arch-
ers.
4 Then Saul said to his armor-
bearer, "Draw your sword, and
thrust me through with it, lest
these uncircumcised men come
and abuse me." But his armor-
bearer would not, for he was
greatly afraid. Therefore Saul took
a sword and fell on it.
5 And when his armorbearer saw
that Saul was dead, he also fell on
his sword and died.
6 So Saul and his three sons died,
and all his house died together.
7 And when all the men of Israel
who *were* in the valley saw that
they had fled and that Saul and his
sons were dead, they forsook their
cities and fled; then the Philistines
came and dwelt in them.
8 So it happened the next day,
when the Philistines came to [1]strip
the slain, that they found Saul and
his sons fallen on Mount Gilboa.
9 And they stripped him and
took his head and his armor, and
sent word *throughout* the land of
the Philistines to proclaim the
news *in the temple* of their idols
and among the people.
10 [a]Then they put his armor in the

27 [a]1 Chr. 23:30–32 [1]*the watch was committed to them*
29 [a]1 Chr. 23:29
30 [a]Ex. 30:22–25
31 [a]Lev. 2:5; 6:21
32 [a]Lev. 24:5–8
33 [a]1 Chr. 6:31; 25:1
35 [a]1 Chr. 8:29–32
37 [1]*Zecher,* 1 Chr. 8:31
38 [1]*Shimeah,* 1 Chr. 8:32
39 [a]1 Chr. 8:33–38
41 [a]1 Chr. 8:35 [1]*Tarea,* 1 Chr. 8:35 [2]So with Arab., Syr., Tg., Vg. (cf. 8:35); MT, LXX omit *and Ahaz*
42 [1]*Jehoaddah,* 1 Chr. 8:36
43 [1]*Raphah,* 1 Chr. 8:37

CHAPTER 10
1 [a]1 Sam. 31:1, 2
2 [1]*Jishui,* 1 Sam. 14:49
8 [1]*plunder*
10 [a]1 Sam. 31:10

[1]temple of their gods, and fastened
his head in the temple of Dagon.
11 And when all Jabesh Gilead
heard all that the Philistines had
done to Saul,
12 all the [a]valiant men arose and
took the body of Saul and the bod-
ies of his sons; and they brought
them to [b]Jabesh, and buried their
bones under the tamarisk tree at
Jabesh, and fasted seven days.
13 So Saul died for his unfaithful-
ness which he had [1]committed
against the LORD, [a]because he did
not keep the word of the LORD, and
also because [b]he consulted a me-
dium for guidance.
14 But *he* did not inquire of the
LORD; therefore He killed him, and
[a]turned the kingdom over to David
the son of Jesse.

David Made King over All Israel

11 Then [a]all Israel came to-
gether to David at Hebron,
saying, "Indeed we *are* your bone
and your flesh.
2 "Also, in time past, even when
Saul was king, you *were* the one
who led Israel out and brought
them in; and the LORD your [a]God
said to you, 'You shall [b]shepherd
My people Israel, and be ruler over
My people Israel.' "
3 Therefore all the elders of Is-
rael came to the king at Hebron,
and David made a covenant with
them at Hebron before the LORD.
And [a]they anointed David king
over Israel, according to the word
of the LORD [1]by [b]Samuel.

The City of David

4 And David and all Israel [a]went
to Jerusalem, which is Jebus,
[b]where the Jebusites *were*, the in-
habitants of the land.
5 But the inhabitants of Jebus
said to David, "You shall not come
in here!" Nevertheless David took
the stronghold of Zion (that is, the
City of David).
6 Now David said, "Whoever at-
tacks the Jebusites first shall be
[1]chief and captain." And Joab the
son of Zeruiah went up first, and
became chief.
7 Then David dwelt in the
stronghold; therefore they called it
[1]the City of David.
8 And he built the city around it,

10 [1]Lit. *house*

12 [a]1 Sam. 14:52 [b]2 Sam. 21:12

13 [a]1 Sam. 13:13, 14; 15:22–26 [b][Lev. 19:31; 20:6]; 1 Sam. 28:7 [1]Lit. *transgressed*

14 [a]1 Sam. 15:28; 2 Sam. 3:9, 10; 5:3; 1 Chr. 12:23

CHAPTER 11

1 [a]2 Sam. 5:1

2 [a]1 Sam. 16:1–3; Ps. 78:70–72 [b]2 Sam. 7:7

3 [a]2 Sam. 5:3 [b]1 Sam. 16:1, 4, 12, 13 [1]Lit. *by the hand of Samuel*

4 [a]2 Sam. 5:6 [b]Josh. 15:8, 63; Judg. 1:21; 19:10, 11

6 [1]Lit. *head*

7 [1]*Zion*, 2 Sam. 5:7

8 [1]Lit. *The Landfill* [2]Lit. *revived*

9 [a]2 Sam. 3:1 [b]1 Sam. 16:18

10 [a]2 Sam. 23:8 [b]1 Sam. 16:1, 12

11 [a]1 Chr. 27:2 [b]1 Chr. 12:18 [1]So with Qr.; Kt., LXX, Vg. *the thirty* (cf. 2 Sam. 23:8)

12 [a]1 Chr. 27:4

13 [1]*Ephes Dammim*, 1 Sam. 17:1

14 [1]Lit. *took their stand*

15 [a]2 Sam. 23:13 [b]2 Sam. 5:18; 1 Chr. 14:9 [1]Lit. *Giants*

from [1]the Millo to the surrounding
area. Joab [2]repaired the rest of the
city.
9 So David [a]went on and became
great, and the LORD of hosts *was*
with [b]him.

The Mighty Men of David

10 Now [a]these *were* the heads of
the mighty men whom David had,
who strengthened themselves with
him in his kingdom, with all Israel,
to make him king, according to
[b]the word of the LORD concerning
Israel.
11 And this *is* the number of the
mighty men whom David had:
[a]Jashobeam the son of a Hach-
monite, [b]chief of [1]the captains; he
had lifted up his spear against
three hundred, killed *by him* at one
time.
12 After him *was* Eleazar the son
of [a]Dodo, the Ahohite, who *was*
one of the three mighty men.
13 He was with David at [1]Pas-
dammim. Now there the Philis-
tines were gathered for battle,
and there was a piece of ground
full of barley. So the people fled
from the Philistines.
14 But they [1]stationed themselves
in the middle of *that* field, de-
fended it, and killed the Philis-
tines. So the LORD brought about
a great victory.
15 Now three of the thirty chief
men [a]went down to the rock to
David, into the cave of Adullam;
and the army of the Philistines
encamped [b]in the Valley of [1]Reph-
aim.
16 David *was* then in the strong-
hold, and the garrison of the Phi-
listines *was* then in Bethlehem.
17 And David said with longing,
"Oh, that someone would give me
a drink of water from the well of
Bethlehem, which is by the gate!"
18 So the three broke through the
camp of the Philistines, drew wa-
ter from the well of Bethlehem that
was by the gate, and took *it* and
brought *it* to David. Nevertheless
David would not drink it, but
poured it out to the LORD.
19 And he said, "Far be it from
me, O my God, that I should do
this! Shall I drink the blood of
these men *who have put* their lives
in jeopardy? For at the risk of their

lives they brought it." Therefore he would not drink it. These things were done by the three mighty men.

20 [a]Abishai the brother of Joab was chief of *another* [1]three. He had lifted up his spear against three hundred *men*, killed *them*, and won a name among *these* three.

21 [a]Of the three he was more honored than the other two men. Therefore he became their captain. However he did not attain to the *first* three.

22 Benaiah was the son of Jehoiada, the son of a valiant man from Kabzeel, who [1]had done many deeds. [a]He had killed two lion-like heroes of Moab. He also had gone down and killed a lion in the midst of a pit on a snowy day.

23 And he killed an Egyptian, a man of *great* height, [1]five cubits tall. In the Egyptian's hand *there was* a spear like a weaver's beam; and he went down to him with a staff, wrested the spear out of the Egyptian's hand, and killed him with his own spear.

24 These *things* Benaiah the son of Jehoiada did, and won a name among three mighty men.

25 Indeed he was more honored than the thirty, but he did not attain to the *first* three. And David appointed him over his guard.

26 Also the mighty warriors *were* [a]Asahel the brother of Joab, Elhanan the son of Dodo of Bethlehem,

27 [1]Shammoth the Harorite, [a]Helez the [2]Pelonite,

28 [a]Ira the son of Ikkesh the Tekoite, [b]Abiezer the Anathothite,

29 [1]Sibbechai the Hushathite, [2]Ilai the Ahohite,

30 [a]Maharai the Netophathite, [1]Heled the son of Baanah the Netophathite,

31 [1]Ithai the son of Ribai of Gibeah, of the sons of Benjamin, [a]Benaiah the Pirathonite,

32 [1]Hurai of the brooks of Gaash, [2]Abiel the Arbathite,

33 Azmaveth the [1]Baharumite, Eliahba the Shaalbonite,

34 the sons of [1]Hashem the Gizonite, Jonathan the son of Shageh the Hararite,

35 Ahiam the son of [1]Sacar the Hararite, [2]Eliphal the son of [3]Ur,

36 Hepher the Mecherathite, Ahijah the Pelonite,

37 [1]Hezro the Carmelite, [2]Naarai the son of Ezbai,

38 Joel the brother of Nathan, Mibhar the son of Hagri,

39 Zelek the Ammonite, Naharai the [1]Berothite (the armorbearer of Joab the son of Zeruiah),

40 Ira the Ithrite, Gareb the Ithrite,

41 [a]Uriah the Hittite, [1]Zabad the son of Ahlai,

42 Adina the son of Shiza the Reubenite (a chief of the Reubenites) and thirty with him,

43 Hanan the son of Maachah, Joshaphat the Mithnite,

44 Uzzia the Ashterathite, Shama and Jeiel the sons of Hotham the Aroerite,

45 Jediael the son of Shimri, and Joha his brother, the Tizite,

46 Eliel the Mahavite, Jeribai and Joshaviah the sons of Elnaam, Ithmah the Moabite,

47 Eliel, Obed, and Jaasiel the Mezobaite.

The Growth of David's Army

12 Now [a]these *were* the men who came to David at [b]Ziklag while he was still a fugitive from Saul the son of Kish; and they *were* among the mighty men, helpers in the war,

2 armed with bows, using both the right hand and [a]the left in *hurling* stones and *shooting* arrows with the bow. *They were* of Benjamin, Saul's brethren.

3 The chief *was* Ahiezer, then Joash, the sons of [1]Shemaah the Gibeathite; Jeziel and Pelet the sons of Azmaveth; Berachah, and Jehu the Anathothite;

4 Ishmaiah the Gibeonite, a mighty man among the thirty, and over the thirty; Jeremiah, Jahaziel, Johanan, and Jozabad the Gederathite;

5 Eluzai, Jerimoth, Bealiah, Shemariah, and Shephatiah the Haruphite;

6 Elkanah, Jisshiah, Azarel, Joezer, and Jashobeam, the Korahites;

7 and Joelah and Zebadiah the sons of Jeroham of Gedor.

8 *Some* Gadites [1]joined David at

---

20 [a]2 Sam. 23:18; 1 Chr. 18:12 [1]So with MT, LXX, Vg.; Syr. *thirty*
21 [a]2 Sam. 23:19
22 [a]2 Sam. 23:20 [1]*was great in deeds*
23 [1]About 7½ feet
26 [a]2 Sam. 23:24
27 [a]2 Sam. 23:26; 1 Chr. 27:10 [1]*Shammah the Harodite*, 2 Sam. 23:25 [2]*Paltite*, 2 Sam. 23:26
28 [a]1 Chr. 27:9 [b]1 Chr. 27:12
29 [1]*Mebunnai*, 2 Sam. 23:27 [2]*Zalmon*, 2 Sam. 23:28
30 [a]1 Chr. 27:13 [1]*Heleb*, 2 Sam. 23:29, or *Heldai*, 1 Chr. 27:15
31 [a]1 Chr. 27:14 [1]*Ittai*, 2 Sam. 23:29
32 [1]*Hiddai*, 2 Sam. 23:30 [2]*Abi-Albon*, 2 Sam. 23:31
33 [1]*Barhumite*, 2 Sam. 23:31
34 [1]*Jashen*, 2 Sam. 23:32
35 [1]*Sharar*, 2 Sam. 23:33 [2]*Eliphelet*, 2 Sam. 23:34 [3]*Ahasbai*, 2 Sam. 23:34
37 [1]*Hezrai*, 2 Sam. 23:38 [2]*Paarai the Arbite*, 2 Sam. 23:35
39 [1]*Beerothite*, 2 Sam. 23:37
41 [a]2 Sam. 11 [1]The last sixteen are not added in 2 Sam. 23.

CHAPTER 12

1 [a]1 Sam. 27:2 [b]1 Sam. 27:6
2 [a]Judg. 3:15; 20:16
3 [1]Or *Hasmaah*
8 [a]2 Sam. 2:18 [1]Lit. *separated themselves to*

the stronghold in the wilderness,
mighty men of valor, men trained
for battle, who could handle shield
and spear, whose faces *were like*
the faces of lions, and *were* [a]as
swift as gazelles on the mountains:
9 Ezer the first, Obadiah the sec-
ond, Eliab the third,
10 Mishmannah the fourth, Jere-
miah the fifth,
11 Attai the sixth, Eliel the sev-
enth,
12 Johanan the eighth, Elzabad
the ninth,
13 Jeremiah the tenth, and Mach-
banai the eleventh.
14 These *were* from the sons of
Gad, captains of the army; the
least was over a hundred, and the
greatest was over a [a]thousand.
15 These *are* the ones who crossed
the Jordan in the first month,
when it had overflowed all its
[a]banks; and they put to flight all
those in the valleys, to the east and
to the west.
16 Then some of the sons of Ben-
jamin and Judah came to David at
the stronghold.
17 And David went out [1]to meet
them, and answered and said to
them, "If you have come peace-
ably to me to help me, my heart
will be united with you; but if to
betray me to my enemies, since
there is no [2]wrong in my hands,
may the God of our fathers look
and bring judgment."
18 Then the Spirit [1]came upon
[a]Amasai, chief of the captains, *and*
he said:

"*We are* yours, O David;
We are on your side, O son of
Jesse!
Peace, peace to you,
And peace to your helpers!
For your God helps you."

So David received them, and made
them captains of the troop.
19 And *some* from Manasseh de-
fected to David [a]when he was go-
ing with the Philistines to battle
against Saul; but they did not help
them, *for* the lords of the Philis-
tines sent him away by agreement,
saying, [b]"He may defect to his
master Saul *and endanger* our
heads."
20 When he went to Ziklag, those
of Manasseh who defected to him
were Adnah, Jozabad, Jediael, Mi-
chael, Jozabad, Elihu, and Zille-
thai, captains of the thousands
who *were* from Manasseh.
21 And they helped David against
[a]the bands *of raiders*, for they *were*
all mighty men of valor, and they
were captains in the army.
22 For at *that* time they came to
David day by day to help him, until
it was a great army, [a]like the army
of God.

David's Army at Hebron

23 Now these *were* the num-
bers of the [1]divisions *that were*
equipped for war, *and* [a]came to
David at [b]Hebron to [c]turn *over*
the kingdom of Saul to him, [d]ac-
cording to the word of the LORD:
24 of the sons of Judah bearing
shield and spear, six thousand
eight hundred [1]armed for war;
25 of the sons of Simeon, mighty
men of valor fit for war, seven
thousand one hundred;
26 of the sons of Levi four thou-
sand six hundred;
27 Jehoiada, the leader of the Aar-
onites, and with him three thou-
sand seven hundred;
28 [a]Zadok, a young man, a valiant
warrior, and from his father's
house twenty-two captains;
29 of the sons of Benjamin, rela-
tives of Saul, three thousand (until
then [a]the greatest part of them had
remained loyal to the house of
Saul);
30 of the sons of Ephraim twenty
thousand eight hundred, mighty
men of valor, [1]famous men
throughout their father's house;
31 of the half-tribe of Manasseh
eighteen thousand, who were des-
ignated by name to come and
make David king;
32 of the sons of Issachar [a]who
had understanding of the times, to
know what Israel ought to do, their
chiefs were two hundred; and all
their brethren were at their com-
mand;
33 of Zebulun there were fifty
thousand who went out to battle,
expert in war with all weapons of
war, [a]stouthearted men who could
keep ranks;
34 of Naphtali one thousand cap-
tains, and with them thirty-seven

14 [a]1 Sam. 18:13
15 [a]Josh. 3:15; 4:18, 19
17 [1]Lit. *before them* [2]Lit. *violence*
18 [a]2 Sam. 17:25 [1]Lit. *clothed*
19 [a]1 Sam. 29:2 [b]1 Sam. 29:4
21 [a]1 Sam. 30:1, 9, 10
22 [a]Gen. 32:2; Josh. 5:13–15
23 [a]2 Sam. 2:1–4 [b]1 Chr. 11:1 [c]1 Chr. 10:14 [d]1 Sam. 16:1–4 [1]Lit. *heads of those*
24 [1]*equipped*
28 [a]2 Sam. 8:17; 1 Chr. 6:8, 53
29 [a]2 Sam. 2:8, 9
30 [1]Lit. *men of names*
32 [a]Esth. 1:13
33 [a]Ps. 12:2; [James 1:8]

thousand with shield and spear;
35 of the Danites who could keep
battle formation, twenty-eight
thousand six hundred;
36 of Asher, those who could go
out to war, able to keep battle for-
mation, forty thousand;
37 of the Reubenites and the Gad-
ites and the half-tribe of Manas-
seh, from the other side of the Jor-
dan, one hundred and twenty
thousand armed for battle with
every *kind* of weapon of war.
38 All these men of war, who
could keep ranks, came to Hebron
with a loyal heart, to make David
king over all Israel; and all the rest
of Israel *were* of [a]one mind to
make David king.
39 And they were there with Da-
vid three days, eating and drink-
ing, for their brethren had pre-
pared for them.
40 Moreover those who were near
to them, from as far away as Issa-
char and Zebulun and Naphtali,
were bringing food on donkeys
and camels, on mules and oxen—
provisions of flour and cakes of
figs and cakes of raisins, wine and
oil and oxen and sheep abun-
dantly, for *there was* joy in Israel.

The Ark Brought from Kirjath Jearim

13 Then David consulted with
the [a]captains of thousands
and hundreds, *and* with every
leader.
2 And David said to all the as-
sembly of Israel, "If *it seems* good
to you, and if it is of the LORD our
God, let us send out to our breth-
ren everywhere *who are* [a]left in all
the land of Israel, and with them
to the priests and Levites *who are*
in their cities *and* their common-
lands, that they may gather to-
gether to us;
3 "and let us bring the ark of our
God back to us, [a]for we have not
inquired at it since the days of
Saul."
4 Then all the assembly said that
they would do so, for the thing was
right in the eyes of all the people.
5 So [a]David gathered all Israel
together, from [b]Shihor in Egypt to
as far as the entrance of Hamath,
to bring the ark of God [c]from Kir-
jath Jearim.
6 And David and all Israel went
up to [a]Baalah,[1] to Kirjath Jearim,
which belonged to Judah, to bring
up from there the ark of God the
LORD, [b]who dwells *between* the
cherubim, where *His* name is pro-
claimed.
7 So they [1]carried the ark of God
[a]on a new cart [b]from the house of
Abinadab, and Uzza and Ahio
drove the cart.
8 Then [a]David and all Israel
played *music* before God with all
their might, with [1]singing, on
harps, on stringed instruments, on
tambourines, on cymbals, and
with trumpets.
9 And when they came to [1]Chi-
don's threshing floor, Uzza put
out his hand to hold the ark, for
the oxen [2]stumbled.
10 Then the anger of the LORD was
aroused against Uzza, and He
struck him [a]because he put his
hand to the ark; and he [b]died there
before God.
11 And David became angry be-
cause of the LORD's outbreak
against Uzza; therefore that place
is called [1]Perez Uzza to this day.
12 David was afraid of God that
day, saying, "How can I bring the
ark of God to me?"
13 So David would not move the
ark with him into the City of Da-
vid, but took it aside into the house
of Obed-Edom the Gittite.
14 [a]The ark of God remained with
the family of Obed-Edom in his
house three months. And the LORD
blessed [b]the house of Obed-Edom
and all that he had.

David Established at Jerusalem

14 Now [a]Hiram king of Tyre
sent messengers to David,
and cedar trees, with masons and
carpenters, to build him a house.
2 So David knew that the LORD
had established him as king over
Israel, for his kingdom was [a]highly
exalted for the sake of His people
Israel.
3 Then David took more wives in
Jerusalem, and David begot more
sons and daughters.
4 And [a]these are the names of his
children whom he had in Jerusa-
lem: [1]Shammua, Shobab, Nathan,
Solomon,
5 Ibhar, [1]Elishua, [2]Elpelet,
6 Nogah, Nepheg, Japhia,

38 [a]2 Chr. 30:12

CHAPTER 13

1 [a]1 Chr. 11:15; 12:34

2 [a]1 Sam. 31:1; Is. 37:4

3 [a]1 Sam. 7:1, 2

5 [a]1 Sam. 7:5 [b]Josh. 13:3 [c]1 Sam. 6:21; 7:1, 2

6 [a]Josh. 15:9, 60 [b]Ex. 25:22; 1 Sam. 4:4; 2 Kin. 19:15 [1]*Baale Judah,* 2 Sam. 6:2

7 [a]Num. 4:15; 1 Sam. 6:7 [b]1 Sam. 7:1 [1]Lit. *caused the ark of God to ride*

8 [a]2 Sam. 6:5 [1]*songs*

9 [1]*Nachon,* 2 Sam. 6:6 [2]Or *let it go off*

10 [a][Num. 4:15]; 1 Chr. 15:13, 15 [b]Lev. 10:2

11 [1]Lit. *Outburst Against Uzza*

14 [a]2 Sam. 6:11 [b][Gen. 30:27]; 1 Chr. 26:4–8

CHAPTER 14

1 [a]2 Sam. 5:11; 1 Kin. 5:1

2 [a]Num. 24:7

4 [a]1 Chr. 3:5–8 [1]*Shimea,* 1 Chr. 3:5

5 [1]*Elishama,* 1 Chr. 3:6 [2]*Eliphelet,* 1 Chr. 3:6

7 Elishama, [1]Beeliada, and Eliph-
elet.

The Philistines Defeated

8 Now when the Philistines
heard that [a]David had been
anointed king over all Israel, all
the Philistines went up to search
for David. And David heard *of it*
and went out against them.
9 Then the Philistines went and
made a raid [a]on the Valley of
[1]Rephaim.
10 And David [a]inquired of God,
saying, "Shall I go up against the
Philistines? Will You deliver them
into my hand?" The LORD said to
him, "Go up, for I will deliver them
into your hand."
11 So they went up to Baal Pera-
zim, and David defeated them
there. Then David said, "God has
broken through my enemies by my
hand like a breakthrough of wa-
ter." Therefore they called the
name of that place [1]Baal Perazim.
12 And when they left their gods
there, David gave a command-
ment, and they were burned with
fire.
13 [a]Then the Philistines once
again made a raid on the valley.
14 Therefore David inquired
again of God, and God said to him,
"You shall not go up after them;
circle around them, [a]and come
upon them in front of the mulberry
trees.
15 "And it shall be, when you hear
a sound of marching in the tops
of the mulberry trees, then you
shall go out to battle, for God has
gone out before you to strike the
camp of the Philistines."
16 So David did as God com-
manded him, and they drove back
the army of the Philistines from
[1]Gibeon as far as Gezer.
17 Then [a]the fame of David went
out into all lands, and the LORD
[b]brought the fear of him upon all
nations.

The Ark Brought to Jerusalem

15 *David* built houses for him-
self in the City of David; and
he prepared a place for the ark of
God, [a]and pitched a tent for it.
2 Then David said, "No one may
carry the [a]ark of God but the Le-
vites, for [b]the LORD has chosen
them to carry the ark of God
and to minister before Him for-
ever."
3 And David [a]gathered all Israel
together at Jerusalem, to bring up
the ark of the LORD to its place,
which he had prepared for it.
4 Then David assembled the chil-
dren of Aaron and the Levites:
5 of the sons of Kohath, Uriel the
chief, and one hundred and twenty
of his [1]brethren;
6 of the sons of Merari, Asaiah
the chief, and two hundred and
twenty of his brethren;
7 of the sons of Gershom, Joel
the chief, and one hundred and
thirty of his brethren;
8 of the sons of [a]Elizaphan,
Shemaiah the chief, and two hun-
dred of his brethren;
9 of the sons of [a]Hebron, Eliel the
chief, and eighty of his brethren;
10 of the sons of Uzziel, Ammina-
dab the chief, and one hundred
and twelve of his brethren.
11 And David called for [a]Zadok
and [b]Abiathar the priests, and for
the Levites: for Uriel, Asaiah, Joel,
Shemaiah, Eliel, and Amminadab.
12 He said to them, "You *are* the
heads of the fathers' *houses* of the
Levites; [1]sanctify yourselves, you
and your brethren, that you may
bring up the ark of the LORD God
of Israel to *the place* I have pre-
pared for it.
13 "For [a]because you *did* not *do
it* the first *time,* [b]the LORD our God
broke out against us, because we
did not consult Him [1]about the
proper order."
14 So the priests and the Levites
[1]sanctified themselves to bring up
the ark of the LORD God of Israel.
15 And the children of the Levites
bore the ark of God on their shoul-
ders, by its poles, as [a]Moses had
commanded according to the word
of the LORD.
16 Then David spoke to the lead-
ers of the Levites to appoint their
brethren *to be* the singers accom-
panied by instruments of music,
stringed instruments, harps, and
cymbals, by raising the voice with
resounding joy.
17 So the Levites appointed [a]He-
man the son of Joel; and of his
brethren, [b]Asaph the son of Bere-
chiah; and of their brethren, the

7 [1]*Eliada,* 2 Sam. 5:6; 1 Chr. 3:8
8 [a]2 Sam. 5:17–21
9 [a]Josh. 17:15; 18:16; 1 Chr. 11:15; 14:13 [1]Lit. *Giants*
10 [a]1 Sam. 23:2, 4; 30:8; 2 Sam. 2:1; 5:19, 23; 21:1
11 [1]Lit. *Master of Breakthroughs*
13 [a]2 Sam. 5:22–25
14 [a]2 Sam. 5:23
16 [1]*Geba,* 2 Sam. 5:25
17 [a]Josh. 6:27; 2 Chr. 26:8 [b][Ex. 15:14–16; Deut. 2:25; 11:25]; 2 Chr. 20:29

CHAPTER 15

1 [a]1 Chr. 16:1
2 [a][Num. 4:15]; 2 Sam. 6:1–11 [b]Num. 4:2–15; Deut. 10:8; 31:9
3 [a]Ex. 40:20, 21; 2 Sam. 6:12; 1 Kin. 8:1; 1 Chr. 13:5
5 [1]*kinsmen*
8 [a]Ex. 6:22
9 [a]Ex. 6:18
11 [a]2 Sam. 8:17; 15:24–29, 35, 36; 18:19, 22, 27; 19:11; 20:25; 1 Chr. 12:28 [b]1 Sam. 22:20–23; 23:6; 30:7; 1 Kin. 2:22, 26, 27; Mark 2:6
12 [1]*consecrate*
13 [a]2 Sam. 6:3 [b]1 Chr. 13:7–11 [1]*regarding the ordinance*
14 [1]*consecrated*
15 [a]Ex. 25:14; Num. 4:15; 7:9
17 [a]1 Chr. 6:33; 25:1 [b]1 Chr. 6:39

sons of Merari, [c]Ethan the son of
Kushaiah;
18 and with them their brethren of
the second *rank:* Zechariah, [1]Ben,
Jaaziel, Shemiramoth, Jehiel,
Unni, Eliab, Benaiah, Maaseiah,
Mattithiah, Elipheleh, Mikneiah,
Obed-Edom, and Jeiel, the gate-
keepers;
19 the singers, Heman, Asaph,
and Ethan, *were* to sound the cym-
bals of bronze;
20 Zechariah, [1]Aziel, Shemira-
moth, Jehiel, Unni, Eliab, Maase-
iah, and Benaiah, with strings ac-
cording to [a]Alamoth;
21 Mattithiah, Elipheleh, Mik-
neiah, Obed-Edom, Jeiel, and Aza-
ziah, to direct with harps on the
[a]Sheminith;
22 Chenaniah, leader of the Le-
vites, was instructor *in charge of*
the music, because he *was* skill-
ful;
23 Berechiah and Elkanah *were*
doorkeepers for the ark;
24 Shebaniah, Joshaphat, Ne-
thanel, Amasai, Zechariah, Bena-
iah, and Eliezer, the priests, [a]were
to blow the trumpets before the
ark of God; and [b]Obed-Edom and
Jehiah, doorkeepers for the ark.
25 So [a]David, the elders of Israel,
and the captains over thousands
went to bring up the ark of the cov-
enant of the LORD from the house
of Obed-Edom with joy.
26 And so it was, when God
helped the Levites who bore the
ark of the covenant of the LORD,
that they offered seven bulls and
seven rams.
27 David was clothed with a robe
of fine [a]linen, as were all the Le-
vites who bore the ark, the sing-
ers, and Chenaniah the music mas-
ter *with* the singers. David also
wore a linen ephod.
28 [a]Thus all Israel brought up the
ark of the covenant of the LORD
with shouting and with the sound
of the horn, with trumpets and
with cymbals, making music with
stringed instruments and harps.
29 And it happened, [a]as the ark
of the covenant of the LORD came
to the City of David, that Michal,
Saul's daughter, looked through a
window and saw King David
whirling and playing music; and
she despised him in her heart.

17 [c]1 Chr. 6:44
18 [1]So with MT, Vg.; LXX omits *Ben*
20 [a]Ps. 46:title [1]*Jaaziel,* v. 18
21 [a]Ps. 6:title
24 [a][Num. 10:8]; Ps. 81:3 [b]1 Chr. 13:13, 14
25 [a]2 Sam. 6:12, 13; 1 Kin. 8:1
27 [a]1 Sam. 2:18, 28
28 [a]Num. 23:21; Josh. 6:20; 1 Chr. 13:8; Zech. 4:7; 1 Thess. 4:16
29 [a]1 Sam. 18:20, 27; 19:11–17; 2 Sam. 3:13, 14; 6:16, 20–23

CHAPTER 16
1 [a]2 Sam. 6:17; 1 Chr. 15:1
2 [a]1 Kin. 8:14
4 [a]Ps. 38:title; 70:title
5 [a]1 Chr. 15:18
7 [a]2 Sam. 22:1; 23:1 [b]Ps. 105:1–15
8 [a]1 Chr. 17:19, 20; Ps. 105:1–15
14 [a]Ps. 48:10; [Is. 26:9]

The Ark Placed in the Tabernacle

16 So [a]they brought the ark of
God, and set it in the midst
of the tabernacle that David had
erected for it. Then they offered
burnt offerings and peace offer-
ings before God.
2 And when David had finished
offering the burnt offerings and
the peace offerings, [a]he blessed the
people in the name of the LORD.
3 Then he distributed to every-
one of Israel, both man and
woman, to everyone a loaf of
bread, a piece *of meat,* and a cake
of raisins.
4 And he appointed some of the
Levites to minister before the ark
of the LORD, to [a]commemorate, to
thank, and to praise the LORD God
of Israel:
5 Asaph the chief, and next to
him Zechariah, *then* [a]Jeiel,
Shemiramoth, Jehiel, Mattithiah,
Eliab, Benaiah, and Obed-Edom:
Jeiel with stringed instruments
and harps, but Asaph made music
with cymbals;
6 Benaiah and Jahaziel the
priests regularly *blew* the trumpets
before the ark of the covenant of
God.

David's Song of Thanksgiving

7 On that day [a]David [b]first deliv-
ered *this psalm* into the hand of
Asaph and his brethren, to thank
the LORD:

8 [a]Oh, give thanks to the LORD!
Call upon His name;
Make known His deeds among
the peoples!
9 Sing to Him, sing psalms to Him;
Talk of all His wondrous works!
10 Glory in His holy name;
Let the hearts of those rejoice
who seek the LORD!
11 Seek the LORD and His strength;
Seek His face evermore!
12 Remember His marvelous works
which He has done,
His wonders, and the judgments
of His mouth,
13 O seed of Israel His servant,
You children of Jacob, His
chosen ones!

14 He *is* the LORD our God;
His [a]judgments *are* in all the
earth.
15 Remember His covenant forever,

The word which He commanded,
for a thousand generations,
16 *The* [a]*covenant which* He made
with Abraham,
And His oath to Isaac,
17 And [a]confirmed it to [b]Jacob for
a statute,
To Israel *for* an everlasting
covenant,
18 Saying, "To you I will give the
land of Canaan
As the allotment of your
inheritance,"
19 When you were [a]few in number,
Indeed very few, and strangers in
it.

20 When they went from one nation
to another,
And from *one* kingdom to
another people,
21 He permitted no man to do them
wrong;
Yes, He [a]rebuked kings for their
sakes,
22 *Saying,* [a]"Do not touch My
anointed ones,
And do My prophets no harm."

23 [a]Sing to the LORD, all the
earth;
Proclaim the good news of His
salvation from day to day.
24 Declare His glory among the
nations,
His wonders among all peoples.

25 For the LORD *is* great and greatly
to be praised;
He *is* also to be feared above all
gods.
26 For all the gods [a]of the peoples
are [1]idols,
But the LORD made the heavens.
27 Honor and majesty *are* before
Him;
Strength and gladness are in His
place.

28 Give to the LORD, O families of
the peoples,
Give to the LORD glory and
strength.
29 Give to the LORD the glory *due*
His name;
Bring an offering, and come
before Him.
Oh, worship the LORD in the
beauty of holiness!
30 Tremble before Him, all the
earth.
The world also is firmly
established,
It shall not be moved.

16 [a]Gen. 17:2; 26:3; 28:13; 35:11
17 [a]Gen. 35:11, 12 [b]Gen. 28:10–15
19 [a]Gen. 34:30; Deut. 7:7
21 [a]Gen. 12:17; 20:3; Ex. 7:15–18
22 [a]Gen. 20:7; Ps. 105:15
23 [a]Ps. 96:1–13
26 [a]Lev. 19:4; [1 Cor. 8:5, 6] [1]*worthless things*
33 [a]Is. 55:12, 13 [b][Joel 3:1–14]; Zech. 14:1–14; [Matt. 25:31–46]
34 [a]2 Chr. 5:13; 7:3; Ezra 3:11; Ps. 106:1; 107:1; 118:1; 136:1; Jer. 33:11
35 [a]Ps. 106:47, 48
36 [a]1 Kin. 8:15, 56; Ps. 72:18 [b]Deut. 27:15; Neh. 8:6
37 [a]1 Chr. 16:4, 5 [b]2 Chr. 8:14; Ezra 3:4
38 [a]1 Chr. 13:14
39 [a]1 Chr. 21:29; 2 Chr. 1:3 [b]1 Kin. 3:4 [1]Place for pagan worship
40 [a][Ex. 29:38–42; Num. 28:3, 4]
41 [a]1 Chr. 25:1–6; 2 Chr. 5:13; 7:3; Ezra 3:11; Jer. 33:11
43 [a]2 Sam. 6:18–20

31 Let the heavens rejoice, and let
the earth be glad;
And let them say among the
nations, "The LORD reigns."
32 Let the sea roar, and all its
fullness;
Let the field rejoice, and all that
is in it.
33 Then the [a]trees of the woods shall
rejoice before the LORD,
For He is [b]coming to judge the
earth.

34 [a]Oh, give thanks to the LORD, for
He is good!
For His mercy *endures* forever.
35 [a]And say, "Save us, O God of our
salvation;
Gather us together, and deliver us
from the Gentiles,
To give thanks to Your holy
name,
To triumph in Your praise."

36 [a]Blessed *be* the LORD God of Israel
From everlasting to everlasting!

And all [b]the people said, "Amen!"
and praised the LORD.

Regular Worship Maintained

37 So he left [a]Asaph and his
brothers there before the ark of the
covenant of the LORD to minister
before the ark regularly, as every
day's work [b]required;
38 and [a]Obed-Edom with his
sixty-eight brethren, including
Obed-Edom the son of Jeduthun,
and Hosah, *to be* gatekeepers;
39 and Zadok the priest and his
brethren the priests, [a]before the
tabernacle of the LORD [b]at the
[1]high place that *was* at Gibeon,
40 to offer burnt offerings to the
LORD on the altar of burnt offering
regularly [a]morning and evening,
and *to do* according to all that is
written in the Law of the LORD
which He commanded Israel;
41 and with them Heman and Jeduthun and the rest who were chosen, who were designated by
name, to give thanks to the LORD,
[a]because His mercy *endures* forever;
42 and with them Heman and Jeduthun, to sound aloud with trumpets and cymbals and the musical
instruments of God. Now the sons
of Jeduthun *were* gatekeepers.
43 [a]Then all the people departed,

every man to his house; and David
returned to bless his house.

God's Covenant with David

17 Now [a]it came to pass, when
David was dwelling in his
house, that David said to Nathan
the prophet, "See now, I dwell in
a house of cedar, but the ark of
the covenant of the LORD *is* under
tent curtains."
2 Then Nathan said to David,
"Do all that *is* in your heart, for
God *is* with you."
3 But it happened that night that
the word of God came to Nathan,
saying,
4 "Go and tell My servant David,
'Thus says the LORD: "You shall
[a]not build Me a house to dwell in.
5 "For I have not dwelt in a house
since the time that I brought up Is-
rael, even to this day, but have
gone from tent to tent, and from
one tabernacle *to another.*
6 "Wherever I have moved about
with all Israel, have I ever spoken
a word to any of the judges of Is-
rael, whom I commanded to shep-
herd My people, saying, 'Why
have you not built Me a house of
cedar?' " '
7 "Now therefore, thus shall you
say to My servant David, 'Thus
says the LORD of hosts: "I took you
[a]from the sheepfold, from follow-
ing the sheep, to be [1]ruler over My
people Israel.
8 "And I have been with you
wherever you have gone, and have
cut off all your enemies from be-
fore you, and have [1]made you a
name like the name of the great
men who *are* on the earth.
9 "Moreover I will appoint a
place for My people Israel, and
will [a]plant them, that they may
dwell in a place of their own and
move no more; nor shall the sons
of wickedness oppress them any-
more, as previously,
10 "since the time that I com-
manded judges *to be* over My peo-
ple Israel. Also I will subdue all
your enemies. Furthermore I tell
you that the LORD will build you a
[1]house.
11 "And it shall be, when your
days are [a]fulfilled, when you must
[1]go *to be* with your fathers, that I
will set up your [b]seed after you,
who will be of your sons; and I will
establish his kingdom.
12 [a]"He shall build Me a house,
and I will establish his throne for-
ever.
13 [a]"I will be his Father, and he
shall be My son; and I will not take
My mercy away from him, [b]as I
took *it* from *him* who was before
you.
14 "And [a]I will establish him in
My house and in My kingdom for-
ever; and his throne shall be estab-
lished forever." ' "
15 According to all these words
and according to all this vision, so
Nathan spoke to David.
16 [a]Then King David went in and
sat before the LORD; and he said:
"Who *am* I, O LORD God? And
what is my house, that You have
brought me this far?
17 "And *yet* this was a small thing
in Your sight, O God; and You
have *also* spoken of Your servant's
house for a great while to come,
and have regarded me according
to the rank of a man of high de-
gree, O LORD God.
18 "What more can David *say* to
You for the honor of Your servant?
For You know Your servant.
19 "O LORD, for Your servant's
sake, and according to Your own
heart, You have done all this
greatness, in making known all
these great things.
20 "O LORD, *there is* none like
You, nor *is there any* God besides
You, according to all that we have
heard with our ears.
21 [a]"And who *is* like Your people
Israel, the one nation on the earth
whom God went to redeem for
Himself *as* a people—to make for
Yourself a name by great and awe-
some deeds, by driving out nations
from before Your people whom
You redeemed from Egypt?
22 "For You have made Your peo-
ple Israel Your very own people
forever; and You, LORD, have be-
come their God.
23 "And now, O LORD, the word
which You have spoken concern-
ing Your servant and concerning
his house, *let it* be established for-
ever, and do as You have said.
24 "So let it be established, that
Your name may be magnified for-
ever, saying, 'The LORD of hosts,

CHAPTER 17
1 [a]2 Sam. 7:1; 1 Chr. 14:1
4 [a][1 Chr. 28:2, 3]
7 [a]1 Sam. 16:11–13 [1]*leader*
8 [1]*given you prestige*
9 [a][Deut. 30:1–9; Jer. 16:14–16; 23:5–8; 24:6; Ezek. 37:21–27]; Amos 9:14
10 [1]Royal dynasty
11 [a]1 Kin. 2:10; 1 Chr. 29:28 [b]1 Kin. 5:5; 6:12; 8:19–21; [1 Chr. 22:9–13; 28:20]; Matt. 1:6; Luke 3:31 [1]Die and join your ancestors
12 [a]1 Kin. 6:38; 2 Chr. 6:2; [Ps. 89:20–37]
13 [a]2 Sam. 7:14, 15; Matt. 3:17; Mark 1:11; Luke 3:22; 2 Cor. 6:18; Heb. 1:5 [b][1 Sam. 15:23–28]; 1 Chr. 10:14
14 [a]Ps. 89:3, 4; Matt. 19:28; 25:31; [Luke 1:31–33]
16 [a]2 Sam. 7:18
21 [a][Deut. 4:6–8, 33–38]; Ps. 147:20

the God of Israel, *is* Israel's God.'
And let the house of Your servant
David be established before You.
25 "For You, O my God, [1]have re-
vealed to Your servant that You
will build him a house. Therefore
Your servant has found it *in his*
heart to pray before You.
26 "And now, LORD, [1]You are God,
and have promised this goodness
to Your servant.
27 "Now You have been pleased
to bless the house of Your servant,
that it may continue before You
forever; for You have blessed it,
O LORD, and *it shall be* blessed for-
ever."

David's Further Conquests

18 After this [a]it came to pass
that David [1]attacked the
Philistines, subdued them, and
took Gath and its towns from the
hand of the Philistines.
2 Then he [1]defeated [a]Moab, and
the Moabites became David's [b]ser-
vants, *and* brought tribute.
3 And [a]David [1]defeated [2]Had-
adezer king of Zobah *as far as*
Hamath, as he went to establish his
power by the River Euphrates.
4 David took from him one thou-
sand chariots, [1]seven thousand
horsemen, and twenty thousand
foot soldiers. Also David [2]ham-
strung all the chariot *horses*, ex-
cept that he spared enough of
them for one hundred chariots.
5 When the [a]Syrians of Damas-
cus came to help Hadadezer king
of Zobah, David killed twenty-two
thousand of the Syrians.
6 Then David put *garrisons* in
Syria of Damascus; and the Syr-
ians became David's servants, *and*
brought tribute. So the LORD pre-
served David wherever he went.
7 And David took the shields of
gold that were on the servants of
Hadadezer, and brought them to
Jerusalem.
8 Also from [1]Tibhath and from
[2]Chun, cities of [3]Hadadezer, David
brought a large amount of
[a]bronze, with which [b]Solomon
made the bronze [4]Sea, the pillars,
and the articles of bronze.
9 Now when [1]Tou king of Ha-
math heard that David had [2]de-
feated all the army of Hadadezer
king of Zobah,
10 he sent [1]Hadoram his son to
King David, to greet him and bless
him, because he had fought
against Hadadezer and [2]defeated
him (for Hadadezer had been at
war with Tou); and *Hadoram*
brought with him all kinds of [a]arti-
cles of gold, silver, and bronze.
11 King David also dedicated
these to the LORD, along with the
silver and gold that he had brought
from all *these* nations—from
Edom, from Moab, from the [a]peo-
ple of Ammon, from the [b]Philis-
tines, and from [c]Amalek.
12 Moreover [a]Abishai the son of
Zeruiah killed [b]eighteen thousand
[1]Edomites in the Valley of Salt.
13 [a]He also put garrisons in Edom,
and all the Edomites became Da-
vid's servants. And the LORD pre-
served David wherever he went.

David's Administration

14 So David reigned over all Is-
rael, and administered judgment
and justice to all his people.
15 Joab the son of Zeruiah *was*
over the army; Jehoshaphat the
son of Ahilud *was* recorder;
16 Zadok the son of Ahitub and
[1]Abimelech the son of Abiathar
were the priests; [2]Shavsha *was* the
scribe;
17 [a]Benaiah the son of Jehoiada
was over the Cherethites and the
Pelethites; and David's sons *were*
[1]chief ministers at the king's side.

The Ammonites and Syrians Defeated

19 It[a] happened after this that
Nahash the king of the peo-
ple of Ammon died, and his son
reigned in his place.
2 Then David said, "I will show
kindness to Hanun the son of Na-
hash, because his father showed
kindness to me." So David sent
messengers to comfort him con-
cerning his father. And David's
servants came to Hanun in the
land of the people of Ammon to
comfort him.
3 And the princes of the people
of Ammon said to Hanun, [1]"Do
you think that David really honors
your father because he has sent
comforters to you? Did his ser-
vants not come to you to search
and to overthrow and to spy out
the land?"

25 [1]Lit. *have uncovered the ear of*
26 [1]Or *You alone are*

CHAPTER 18

1 [a]2 Sam. 8:1–18 [1]Lit. *struck*
2 [a]2 Sam. 8:2; Zeph. 2:9 [b]Ps. 60:8 [1]Lit. *struck*
3 [a]2 Sam. 8:3 [1]Lit. *struck* [2]Heb. *Hadarezer*
4 [1]*seven hundred,* 2 Sam. 8:4 [2]*crippled*
5 [a]2 Sam. 8:5, 6; 1 Kin. 11:23–25
8 [a]2 Sam. 8:8 [b]1 Kin. 7:15, 23; 2 Chr. 4:12, 15, 16 [1]*Betah,* 2 Sam. 8:8 [2]*Berothai,* 2 Sam. 8:8 [3]Heb. *Hadarezer* [4]Great laver or basin
9 [1]*Toi,* 2 Sam. 8:9, 10 [2]Lit. *struck*
10 [a]2 Sam. 8:10–12 [1]*Joram,* 2 Sam. 8:10 [2]Lit. *struck*
11 [a]2 Sam. 10:14 [b]2 Sam. 5:17–25 [c]2 Sam. 1:1
12 [a]2 Sam. 23:18; 1 Chr. 2:16 [b]2 Sam. 8:13 [1]*Syrians,* 2 Sam. 8:13
13 [a]Gen. 27:29–40; Num. 24:18; 2 Sam. 8:14
16 [1]*Ahimelech,* 2 Sam. 8:17 [2]*Seraiah,* 2 Sam. 8:17, or *Shisha,* 1 Kin. 4:3
17 [a]2 Sam. 8:18 [1]Lit. *at the hand of the king*

CHAPTER 19

1 [a]1 Sam. 11:1; 2 Sam. 10:1–19
3 [1]Lit. *In your eyes is David honoring your father because*

4 Therefore Hanun took David's servants, shaved them, and cut off their garments [1]in the middle, at their [a]buttocks, and sent them away.

5 Then *some* went and told David about the men; and he sent to meet them, because the men were greatly ashamed. And the king said, "Wait at Jericho until your beards have grown, and *then* return."

6 When the people of Ammon saw that they had made themselves repulsive to David, Hanun and the people of Ammon sent a thousand talents of silver to hire for themselves chariots and horsemen from [1]Mesopotamia, from Syrian Maacah, [a]and from [2]Zobah.

7 So they hired for themselves thirty-two thousand chariots, with the king of Maacah and his people, who came and encamped before Medeba. Also the people of Ammon gathered together from their cities, and came to battle.

8 Now when David heard *of it,* he sent Joab and all the army of the mighty men.

9 Then the people of Ammon came out and put themselves in battle array before the gate of the city, and the kings who had come *were* by themselves in the field.

10 When Joab saw that the battle line was against him before and behind, he chose some of Israel's best and put *them* in battle array against the Syrians.

11 And the rest of the people he put under the command of Abishai his brother, and they set *themselves* in battle array against the people of Ammon.

12 Then he said, "If the Syrians are too strong for me, then you shall help me; but if the people of Ammon are too strong for you, then I will help you.

13 "Be of good courage, and let us be strong for our people and for the cities of our God. And may the LORD do *what is* good in His sight."

14 So Joab and the people who *were* with him drew near for the battle against the Syrians, and they fled before him.

15 When the people of Ammon saw that the Syrians were fleeing, they also fled before Abishai his brother, and entered the city. So Joab went to Jerusalem.

16 Now when the Syrians saw that they had been defeated by Israel, they sent messengers and brought the Syrians who were beyond [1]the River, and [2]Shophach the commander of Hadadezer's army *went* before them.

17 When it was told David, he gathered all Israel, crossed over the Jordan and came upon them, and set up in battle array against them. So when David had set up in *battle* array against the Syrians, they fought with him.

18 Then the Syrians fled before Israel; and David killed [1]seven thousand charioteers and forty thousand [2]foot soldiers of the Syrians, and killed Shophach the commander of the army.

19 And when the servants of Hadadezer saw that they were defeated by Israel, they made peace with David and became his servants. So the Syrians were not willing to help the people of Ammon anymore.

Rabbah Is Conquered

20 It[a] happened [1]in the spring of the year, at the time kings go out *to battle,* that Joab led out the armed forces and ravaged the country of the people of Ammon, and came and besieged Rabbah. But [b]David stayed at Jerusalem. And [c]Joab defeated Rabbah and overthrew it.

2 Then David [a]took their king's crown from his head, and found it to weigh a talent of gold, and *there were* precious stones in it. And it was set on David's head. Also he brought out the [1]spoil of the city in great abundance.

3 And he brought out the people who *were* in it, and [1]put *them* to work with saws, with iron picks, and with axes. So David did to all the cities of the people of Ammon. Then David and all the people returned *to* Jerusalem.

Philistine Giants Destroyed

4 Now it happened afterward [a]that war broke out at [1]Gezer with the Philistines, at which time [b]Sibbechai the Hushathite killed [2]Sippai, *who was one* of the sons

4 [a]Is. 20:4 [1]*in half*

6 [a]1 Chr. 18:5, 9 [1]Heb. *Aram Naharaim* [2]*Zoba,* 2 Sam. 10:6

16 [1]The Euphrates [2]*Zoba,* 2 Sam. 10:6, or *Shobach,* 2 Sam. 10:16

18 [1]*seven hundred,* 2 Sam. 10:18 [2]*horsemen,* 2 Sam. 10:18

CHAPTER 20

1 [a]2 Sam. 11:1 [b]2 Sam. 11:2—12:25 [c]2 Sam. 12:26 [1]Lit. *at the return of the year*

2 [a]2 Sam. 12:30, 31 [1]*plunder*

3 [1]LXX *cut them with*

4 [a]2 Sam. 21:18 [b]1 Chr. 11:29 [1]*Gob,* 2 Sam. 21:18 [2]*Saph,* 2 Sam. 21:18

of [3]the giant. And they were sub-
dued.
5 Again there was war with the
Philistines, and Elhanan the son
of [1]Jair killed Lahmi the brother
of Goliath the Gittite, the shaft of
whose spear *was* like a weaver's
[a]beam.
6 Yet again [a]there was war at
Gath, where there was a man of
great stature, with twenty-four fin-
gers and toes, six *on each hand*
and six *on each foot;* and he also
was born to [1]the giant.
7 So when he defied Israel, Jona-
than the son of [1]Shimea, David's
brother, killed him.
8 These were born to the giant
in Gath, and they fell by the hand
of David and by the hand of his
servants.

The Census of Israel and Judah

21 Now [a]Satan stood up
against Israel, and moved
David to [1]number Israel.
2 So David said to Joab and to
the leaders of the people, "Go,
number Israel from Beersheba to
Dan, [a]and bring the number of
them to me that I may know *it.*"
3 And Joab answered, "May the
LORD make His people a hundred
times more than they are. But, my
lord the king, *are* they not all my
lord's servants? Why then does
my lord require this thing? Why
should he be a cause of guilt in Is-
rael?"
4 Nevertheless the king's word
prevailed against Joab. Therefore
Joab departed and went through-
out all Israel and came to Jeru-
salem.
5 Then Joab gave the sum of the
number of the people to David. All
Israel *had* one million one hundred
thousand *men* who drew the
sword, and Judah *had* four hun-
dred and seventy thousand men
who drew the sword.
6 [a]But he did not count Levi and
Benjamin among them, for the
king's [1]word was abominable to
Joab.
7 And [1]God was displeased with
this thing; therefore He struck Is-
rael.
8 So David said to God, [a]"I have
sinned greatly, because I have
done this thing; [b]but now, I pray,
take away the iniquity of Your
servant, for I have done very
foolishly."
9 Then the LORD spoke to Gad,
David's [a]seer, saying,
10 "Go and tell David, [a]saying,
'Thus says the LORD: "I offer you
three *things;* choose one of them
for yourself, that I may do *it* to
you." ' "
11 So Gad came to David and said
to him, "Thus says the LORD:
'Choose for yourself,
12 [a]'either [1]three years of famine,
or three months to be defeated by
your foes with the sword of your
enemies overtaking *you,* or else for
three days the sword of the LORD—
the plague in the land, with the
[2]angel of the LORD destroying
throughout all the territory of Is-
rael.' Now consider what answer
I should take back to Him who
sent me."
13 And David said to Gad, "I am
in great distress. Please let me fall
into the hand of the LORD, for His
[a]mercies *are* very great; but do not
let me fall into the hand of man."
14 So the LORD sent a [a]plague
upon Israel, and seventy thousand
men of Israel fell.
15 And God sent [1]an [a]angel to Je-
rusalem to destroy it. As [2]he was
destroying, the LORD looked and
[b]relented of the disaster, and said
to the angel who was destroying,
"It is enough; now restrain [3]your
hand." And the angel of the LORD
stood by the [c]threshing floor of
[4]Ornan the Jebusite.
16 Then David lifted his eyes and
[a]saw the angel of the LORD stand-
ing between earth and heaven,
having in his hand a drawn sword
stretched out over Jerusalem. So
David and the elders, clothed in
sackcloth, fell on their faces.
17 And David said to God, "Was
it not I who commanded the people
to be numbered? I am the one who
has sinned and done evil indeed;
but these [a]sheep, what have they
done? Let Your hand, I pray, O
LORD my God, be against me and
my father's house, but not against
Your people that they should be
plagued."
18 Therefore, the [a]angel of the
LORD commanded Gad to say to
David that David should go and

4 [3]Or *Raphah*

5 [a]1 Sam. 17:7; 1 Chr. 11:23 [1]*Jaare-Oregim,* 2 Sam. 21:19

6 [a]1 Sam. 5:8; 2 Sam. 21:20 [1]Or *Raphah*

7 [1]*Shammah,* 1 Sam. 16:9 or *Shimeah,* 2 Sam. 21:21

CHAPTER 21

1 [a]2 Sam. 24:1–25; Job 1:6 [1]*take a census of*

2 [a]1 Chr. 27:23, 24

6 [a]1 Chr. 27:24 [1]*command*

7 [1]Lit. *it was evil in the eyes of God*

8 [a]2 Sam. 24:10 [b]2 Sam. 12:13

9 [a]1 Sam. 9:9; 2 Kin. 17:13; 1 Chr. 29:29; 2 Chr. 16:7, 10; Is. 30:9, 10; Amos 7:12, 13

10 [a]2 Sam. 24:12–14

12 [a]2 Sam. 24:13 [1]*seven,* 2 Sam. 24:13 [2]Or *Angel,* and so throughout the chapter

13 [a]Ps. 51:1; 130:4, 7

14 [a]1 Chr. 27:24

15 [a]2 Sam. 24:16 [b]Gen. 6:6 [c]2 Chr. 3:1 [1]Or *the Angel* [2]Or *He* [3]Or *Your* [4]*Araunah,* 2 Sam. 24:16, 18–24

16 [a]Josh. 5:13; 2 Chr. 3:1

17 [a]2 Sam. 7:8; Ps. 74:1

18 [a]1 Chr. 21:11, 12; 2 Chr. 3:1

erect an altar to the LORD on the
threshing floor of Ornan the Jebu-
site.
19 So David went up at the word
of Gad, which he had spoken in
the name of the LORD.
20 Now Ornan turned and saw the
angel; and his four sons *who were*
with him hid themselves, but Or-
nan continued threshing wheat.
21 So David came to Ornan, and
Ornan looked and saw David. And
he went out from the threshing
floor, and bowed before David
with *his* face to the ground.
22 Then David said to Ornan,
[1]"Grant me the place of *this*
threshing floor, that I may build
an altar on it to the LORD. You shall
grant it to me at the full price, that
the plague may be withdrawn
from the people."
23 But Ornan said to David, "Take
it to yourself, and let my lord the
king do *what is* good in his eyes.
Look, I *also* give *you* the oxen for
burnt offerings, the threshing im-
plements for wood, and the wheat
for the grain offering; I give *it*
all."
24 Then King David said to Or-
nan, "No, but I will surely buy *it*
for the full price, for I will not take
what is yours for the LORD, nor of-
fer burnt offerings with *that which*
costs *me* nothing."
25 So [a]David gave Ornan six hun-
dred shekels of gold by weight for
the place.
26 And David built there an altar
to the LORD, and offered burnt of-
ferings and peace offerings, and
called on the LORD; and [a]He an-
swered him from heaven by fire
on the altar of burnt offering.
27 So the LORD commanded the
angel, and he returned his sword
to its sheath.
28 At that time, when David saw
that the LORD had answered him
on the threshing floor of Ornan the
Jebusite, he sacrificed there.
29 [a]For the tabernacle of the LORD
and the altar of the burnt offering,
which Moses had made in the wil-
derness, *were* at that time at the
high place in [b]Gibeon.
30 But David could not go before
it to inquire of God, for he was
afraid of the sword of the angel of
the LORD.

David Prepares to Build the Temple

22 Then David said, [a]"This *is*
the house of the LORD God,
and this *is* the altar of burnt offer-
ing for Israel."
2 So David commanded to gather
the [a]aliens who *were* in the land
of Israel; and he appointed masons
to [b]cut hewn stones to build the
house of God.
3 And David prepared iron in
abundance for the nails of the
doors of the gates and for the
joints, and bronze in abundance
[a]beyond measure,
4 and cedar trees in abundance;
for the [a]Sidonians and those from
Tyre brought much cedar wood to
David.
5 Now David said, [a]"Solomon
my son *is* young and inexperi-
enced, and the house to be built
for the LORD *must be* exceedingly
magnificent, famous and glorious
throughout all countries. I will
now make preparation for it." So
David made abundant prepara-
tions before his death.
6 Then he called for his son Sol-
omon, and [1]charged him to build
a house for the LORD God of Israel.
7 And David said to Solomon:
"My son, as for me, [a]it was in my
mind to build a house [b]to the name
of the LORD my God;
8 "but the word of the LORD came
to me, saying, [a]'You have shed
much blood and have made great
wars; you shall not build a house
for My name, because you have
shed much blood on the earth in
My sight.
9 [a]'Behold, a son shall be born
to you, who shall be a man of rest;
and I will give him [b]rest from all
his enemies all around. His name
shall be [1]Solomon, for I will give
peace and quietness to Israel in his
days.
10 [a]'He shall build a house for My
name, and [b]he shall be My son,
and I *will be* his Father; and I will
establish the throne of his king-
dom over Israel forever.'
11 "Now, my son, may [a]the LORD
be with you; and may you prosper,
and build the house of the LORD
your God, as He has said to you.
12 "Only may the LORD [a]give you
wisdom and understanding, and

22 [1]Lit. *Give*

25 [a]2 Sam. 24:24

26 [a]Lev. 9:24; Judg. 6:21; 1 Kin. 18:36–38; 2 Chr. 3:1; 7:1

29 [a]1 Kin. 3:4; 2 Chr. 1:3 [b]1 Chr. 16:39

CHAPTER 22

1 [a]Deut. 12:5; 2 Sam. 24:18; 1 Chr. 21:18, 19, 26, 28; 2 Chr. 3:1

2 [a]1 Kin. 9:20, 21; 2 Chr. 2:17, 18 [b]1 Kin. 5:17, 18

3 [a]1 Kin. 7:47; 1 Chr. 22:14

4 [a]1 Kin. 5:6–10

5 [a]1 Kin. 3:7; 1 Chr. 29:1, 2

6 [1]*commanded*

7 [a]2 Sam. 7:1, 2; 1 Kin. 8:17; 1 Chr. 17:1; 28:2 [b]Deut. 12:5, 11

8 [a]2 Sam. 7:5–13; 1 Kin. 5:3; 1 Chr. 28:3

9 [a]1 Chr. 28:5 [b]1 Kin. 4:20, 25; 5:4 [1]Lit. *Peaceful*

10 [a]2 Sam. 7:13; 1 Kin. 5:5; 6:38; 1 Chr. 17:12, 13; 28:6; 2 Chr. 6:2 [b]Heb. 1:5

11 [a]1 Chr. 22:16

12 [a]1 Kin. 3:9–12; 2 Chr. 1:10

give you charge concerning Israel,
that you may keep the law of the
LORD your God.
13 [a]"Then you will prosper, if you
take care to fulfill the statutes
and judgments with which the
LORD [1]charged Moses concerning
Israel. [b]Be strong and of good
courage; do not fear nor be dis-
mayed.
14 "Indeed I have taken much
trouble to prepare for the house of
the LORD one hundred thousand
talents of gold and one million tal-
ents of silver, and bronze and iron
[a]beyond measure, for it is so abun-
dant. I have prepared timber and
stone also, and you may add to
them.
15 "Moreover *there are* workmen
with you in abundance: woodsmen
and stonecutters, and all types of
skillful men for every kind of
work.
16 "Of gold and silver and bronze
and iron *there is* no limit. Arise
and begin working, and [a]the LORD
be with you."
17 David also commanded all the
[a]leaders of Israel to help Solomon
his son, *saying,*
18 "*Is* not the LORD your God with
you? [a]And has He *not* given you
rest on every side? For He has
given the inhabitants of the land
into my hand, and the land is sub-
dued before the LORD and before
His people.
19 "Now set your heart and your
soul to seek the LORD your God.
Therefore arise and build the sanc-
tuary of the LORD God, to [a]bring
the ark of the covenant of the LORD
and the holy articles of God into
the house that *is* to be built [b]for
the name of the LORD."

The Divisions of the Levites

23 So when David was old and
full of days, he made his son
[a]Solomon king over Israel.
2 And he gathered together all
the leaders of Israel, with the
priests and the Levites.
3 Now the Levites were num-
bered from the age of [a]thirty years
and above; and the number of indi-
vidual males was thirty-eight thou-
sand.
4 Of these, twenty-four thousand
were to [a]look after the work of the
house of the LORD, six thousand
were [b]officers and judges,
5 four thousand *were* gatekeep-
ers, and four thousand [a]praised
the LORD with *musical* instru-
ments, [b]"which I made," *said Da-
vid,* "for giving praise."
6 Also [a]David separated them
into [1]divisions among the sons of
Levi: Gershon, Kohath, and Me-
rari.
7 Of the [a]Gershonites: [1]Laadan
and Shimei.
8 The sons of Laadan: the first
Jehiel, then Zetham and Joel—
three *in all.*
9 The sons of Shimei: Shelomith,
Haziel, and Haran—three *in all.*
These were the heads of the fa-
thers' *houses* of Laadan.
10 And the sons of Shimei: Ja-
hath, [1]Zina, Jeush, and Beriah.
These *were* the four sons of
Shimei.
11 Jahath was the first and Zizah
the second. But Jeush and Beriah
did not have many sons; therefore
they were assigned as one father's
house.
12 [a]The sons of Kohath: Amram,
Izhar, Hebron, and Uzziel—four *in
all.*
13 The sons of [a]Amram: Aaron
and Moses; and [b]Aaron was set
apart, he and his sons forever, that
he should [1]sanctify the most holy
things, [c]to burn incense before the
LORD, [d]to minister to Him, and [e]to
give the blessing in His name for-
ever.
14 Now [a]the sons of Moses the
man of God were reckoned to the
tribe of Levi.
15 [a]The sons of Moses *were* [1]Ger-
shon and Eliezer.
16 Of the sons of Gershon, [a]She-
buel[1] *was* the first.
17 Of the descendants of Eliezer,
[a]Rehabiah was the first. And El-
iezer had no other sons, but the
sons of Rehabiah were very many.
18 Of the sons of Izhar, [a]Shelo-
mith *was* the first.
19 [a]Of the sons of Hebron, Jeriah
was the first, Amariah the second,
Jahaziel the third, and Jekameam
the fourth.
20 Of the sons of Uzziel, Michah
was the first and Jesshiah the sec-
ond.
21 [a]The sons of Merari *were* Mahli

13 [a][Josh. 1:7, 8]; 1 Chr. 28:7 [b][Deut. 31:7, 8; Josh. 1:6, 7, 9; 1 Chr. 28:20] [1]*commanded*
14 [a]1 Chr. 22:3
16 [a]1 Chr. 22:11
17 [a]1 Chr. 28:1–6
18 [a]Deut. 12:10; Josh. 22:4; 2 Sam. 7:1; [1 Kin. 5:4; 8:56]
19 [a]1 Kin. 8:1–11; 2 Chr. 5:2–14 [b]1 Kin. 5:3

CHAPTER 23

1 [a]1 Kin. 1:33–40; 1 Chr. 28:4, 5
3 [a]Num. 4:1–3
4 [a]2 Chr. 2:2, 18; Ezra 3:8, 9 [b]Deut. 16:18–20
5 [a]1 Chr. 15:16 [b]2 Chr. 29:25–27
6 [a]Ex. 6:16; Num. 26:57; 2 Chr. 8:14 [1]*groups*
7 [a]1 Chr. 26:21 [1]*Libni,* Ex. 6:17
10 [1]LXX, Vg. *Zizah* and v. 11
12 [a]Ex. 6:18
13 [a]Ex. 6:20 [b]Ex. 28:1; Heb. 5:4 [c]Ex. 30:7; 1 Sam. 2:28 [d][Deut. 21:5] [e]Num. 6:23 [1]*consecrate*
14 [a]1 Chr. 26:20–24
15 [a]Ex. 18:3, 4 [1]Heb. *Gershom,* 1 Chr. 6:16
16 [a]1 Chr. 26:24 [1]*Shubael,* 1 Chr. 24:20
17 [a]1 Chr. 26:25
18 [a]1 Chr. 24:22
19 [a]1 Chr. 24:23
21 [a]1 Chr. 24:26

and Mushi. The sons of Mahli *were*
Eleazar and [b]Kish.
22 And Eleazar died, and [a]had no
sons, but only daughters; and their
[1]brethren, the sons of Kish, [b]took
them *as wives*.
23 [a]The sons of Mushi *were* Mahli,
Eder, and Jeremoth—three *in*
all.
24 These *were* the sons of [a]Levi
by their fathers' houses—the
heads of the fathers' *houses* as
they were counted individually by
the number of their names, who
did the work for the service of the
house of the LORD, from the age
of [b]twenty years and above.
25 For David said, "The LORD God
of Israel [a]has given rest to His peo-
ple, that they may dwell in Jerusa-
lem forever";
26 and also to the Levites, "They
shall no longer [a]carry the taberna-
cle, or any of the articles for its
service."
27 For by the [a]last words of David
the Levites *were* numbered from
twenty years old and above;
28 because their duty *was* to help
the sons of Aaron in the service
of the house of the LORD, in the
courts and in the chambers, in the
purifying of all holy things and
the work of the service of the
house of God,
29 both with [a]the showbread and
[b]the fine flour for the grain offer-
ing, with [c]the unleavened cakes
and [d]*what is baked in* the pan,
with what is mixed and with all
kinds of [e]measures and sizes;
30 to stand every morning to
thank and praise the LORD, and
likewise at evening;
31 and at every presentation of a
burnt offering to the LORD [a]on the
Sabbaths and on the New Moons
and on the [b]set[1] feasts, by number
according to the ordinance gov-
erning them, regularly before the
LORD;
32 and that they should [a]attend to
the [b]needs of the tabernacle of
meeting, the needs of the holy
place, and the [c]needs of the sons
of Aaron their brethren in the
work of the house of the LORD.

The Divisions of the Priests

24 Now *these are* the divisions
of the sons of Aaron. [a]The
sons of Aaron *were* Nadab, Abihu,
Eleazar, and Ithamar.
2 And [a]Nadab and Abihu died
before their father, and had no
children; therefore Eleazar and
Ithamar ministered as priests.
3 Then David with Zadok of the
sons of Eleazar, and [a]Ahimelech
of the sons of Ithamar, divided
them according to the schedule of
their service.
4 There were more leaders found
of the sons of Eleazar than of the
sons of Ithamar, and *thus* they
were divided. Among the sons of
Eleazar *were* sixteen heads of
their fathers' houses, and eight
heads of their fathers' houses
among the sons of Ithamar.
5 Thus they were divided by lot,
one group as another, for there
were officials of the sanctuary and
officials *of the house* of God, from
the sons of Eleazar and from the
sons of Ithamar.
6 And the scribe, Shemaiah the
son of Nethanel, *one of* the Levites,
wrote them down before the king,
the leaders, Zadok the priest,
Ahimelech the son of Abiathar,
and the heads of the fathers'
houses of the priests and Levites,
one father's house taken for Elea-
zar and *one* for Ithamar.
7 Now the first lot fell to Je-
hoiarib, the second to Jedaiah,
8 the third to Harim, the fourth
to Seorim,
9 the fifth to Malchijah, the sixth
to Mijamin,
10 the seventh to Hakkoz, the
eighth to [a]Abijah,
11 the ninth to Jeshua, the tenth
to Shecaniah,
12 the eleventh to Eliashib, the
twelfth to Jakim,
13 the thirteenth to Huppah, the
fourteenth to Jeshebeab,
14 the fifteenth to Bilgah, the six-
teenth to Immer,
15 the seventeenth to Hezir, the
eighteenth to [1]Happizzez,
16 the nineteenth to Pethahiah,
the twentieth to [1]Jehezekel,
17 the twenty-first to Jachin, the
twenty-second to Gamul,
18 the twenty-third to Delaiah, the
twenty-fourth to Maaziah.
19 This *was* the schedule of their
service [a]for coming into the house
of the LORD according to their ordi-

21 [b]1 Chr. 24:29
22 [a]1 Chr. 24:28 [b]Num. 36:6 [1]*kinsmen*
23 [a]1 Chr. 24:30
24 [a]Num. 10:17, 21 [b]Num. 1:3; Ezra 3:8
25 [a]1 Chr. 22:18
26 [a]Num. 4:5, 15; 7:9; Deut. 10:8
27 [a]2 Sam. 23:1
29 [a]Ex. 25:30 [b]Lev. 6:20 [c]Lev. 2:1, 4 [d]Lev. 2:5, 7 [e]Lev. 19:35
31 [a]Num. 10:10 [b]Lev. 23:2–4 [1]*appointed feasts*
32 [a]2 Chr. 13:10, 11 [b][Num. 1:53]; 1 Chr. 9:27 [c]Num. 3:6–9, 38

CHAPTER 24
1 [a]Lev. 10:1–6; Num. 26:60, 61; 1 Chr. 6:3
2 [a]Num. 3:1–4; 26:61
3 [a]1 Chr. 18:16
10 [a]Neh. 12:4, 17; Luke 1:5
15 [1]LXX, Vg. *Aphses*
16 [1]MT *Jehezkel*
19 [a]1 Chr. 9:25

nance by the hand of Aaron their
father, as the LORD God of Israel
had commanded him.

Other Levites

20 And the rest of the sons of Levi:
of the sons of Amram, [1]Shubael;
of the sons of Shubael, Jehdeiah.
21 Concerning [a]Rehabiah, of the
sons of Rehabiah, the first *was* Is-
shiah.
22 Of the Izharites, [1]Shelomoth; of
the sons of Shelomoth, Jahath.
23 Of the sons [1]*of* [a]*Hebron*, Jeriah
[1]*was the first*, Amariah the sec-
ond, Jahaziel the third, *and* Jeka-
meam the fourth.
24 *Of* the sons of Uzziel, Michah;
of the sons of Michah, Shamir.
25 The brother of Michah, Isshiah;
of the sons of Isshiah, Zechariah.
26 [a]The sons of Merari *were* Mahli
and Mushi; the son of Jaaziah,
Beno.
27 The sons of Merari by Jaaziah
were Beno, Shoham, Zaccur, and
Ibri.
28 Of Mahli: Eleazar, [a]who had no
sons.
29 Of Kish: the son of Kish, Jerah-
meel.
30 Also [a]the sons of Mushi *were*
Mahli, Eder, and Jerimoth. These
were the sons of the Levites ac-
cording to their fathers' houses.
31 These also cast lots just as their
brothers the sons of Aaron did, in
the presence of King David, Za-
dok, Ahimelech, and the heads of
the fathers' *houses* of the priests
and Levites. The chief fathers *did*
just as their younger brethren.

The Musicians

25 Moreover David and the
captains of the army sepa-
rated for the service *some* of the
sons of [a]Asaph, of Heman, and of
Jeduthun, who *should* prophesy
with harps, stringed instruments,
and cymbals. And the number of
the skilled men performing their
service was:
2 Of the sons of Asaph: Zaccur,
Joseph, Nethaniah, and [1]Ash-
arelah; the sons of Asaph *were*
[2]under the direction of Asaph,
who prophesied according to the
order of the king.
3 Of [a]Jeduthun, the sons of Jedu-
thun: Gedaliah, [1]Zeri, Jeshaiah,

20 [1]*Shebuel.* 1 Chr. 23:16

21 [a]1 Chr. 23:17

22 [1]*Shelomith.* 1 Chr. 23:18

23 [a]1 Chr. 23:19; 26:31 [1]Supplied from 23:19 (following some Heb. mss. and LXX mss.)

26 [a]Ex. 6:19; 1 Chr. 23:21

28 [a]1 Chr. 23:22

30 [a]1 Chr. 23:23

CHAPTER 25

1 [a]1 Chr. 6:30, 33, 39, 44; 2 Chr. 5:12

2 [1]*Jesharelah,* v. 14 [2]Lit. *at the hands of*

3 [a]1 Chr. 16:41, 42 [1]*Jizri,* v. 11 [2]So with one Heb. ms., LXX mss. [3]Shimei is the sixth, v. 17

4 [1]*Azarel,* v. 18 [2]*Shubael,* v. 20 [3]*Jeremoth,* v. 22

5 [a]1 Chr. 16:42 [1]Increase his power or influence

6 [a]1 Chr. 15:16 [b]1 Chr. 15:19; 25:2

7 [a]1 Chr. 23:5

8 [a]2 Chr. 23:13

11 [1]*Zeri,* v. 3

14 [1]*Asharelah,* v. 2

18 [1]*Uzziel,* v. 4

20 [1]*Shebuel,* v. 4

[2]Shimei, Hashabiah, and Matti-
thiah, [3]six, under the direction of
their father Jeduthun, who proph-
esied with a harp to give thanks
and to praise the LORD.
4 Of Heman, the sons of Heman:
Bukkiah, Mattaniah, [1]Uzziel,
[2]Shebuel, [3]Jerimoth, Hananiah,
Hanani, Eliathah, Giddalti,
Romamti-Ezer, Joshbekashah,
Mallothi, Hothir, *and* Mahazioth.
5 All these *were* the sons of He-
man the king's seer in the words
of God, to [1]exalt his [a]horn. For God
gave Heman fourteen sons and
three daughters.
6 All these *were* under the direc-
tion of their father for the music
in the house of the LORD, with cym-
bals, stringed instruments, and
[a]harps, for the service of the house
of God. Asaph, Jeduthun, and He-
man *were* [b]under the authority of
the king.
7 So the [a]number of them, with
their brethren who were instructed
in the songs of the LORD, all who
were skillful, *was* two hundred
and eighty-eight.
8 And they cast lots for their
duty, the small as well as the
great, [a]the teacher with the stu-
dent.
9 Now the first lot for Asaph
came out for Joseph; the second
for Gedaliah, him with his breth-
ren and sons, twelve;
10 the third for Zaccur, his sons
and his brethren, twelve;
11 the fourth for [1]Jizri, his sons
and his brethren, twelve;
12 the fifth for Nethaniah, his sons
and his brethren, twelve;
13 the sixth for Bukkiah, his sons
and his brethren, twelve;
14 the seventh for [1]Jesharelah, his
sons and his brethren, twelve;
15 the eighth for Jeshaiah, his
sons and his brethren, twelve;
16 the ninth for Mattaniah, his
sons and his brethren, twelve;
17 the tenth for Shimei, his sons
and his brethren, twelve;
18 the eleventh for [1]Azarel, his
sons and his brethren, twelve;
19 the twelfth for Hashabiah, his
sons and his brethren, twelve;
20 the thirteenth for [1]Shubael, his
sons and his brethren, twelve;
21 the fourteenth for Mattithiah,
his sons and his brethren, twelve;

22 the fifteenth for [1]Jeremoth, his
sons and his brethren, twelve;
23 the sixteenth for Hananiah, his
sons and his brethren, twelve;
24 the seventeenth for Joshbe-
kashah, his sons and his brethren,
twelve;
25 the eighteenth for Hanani, his
sons and his brethren, twelve;
26 the nineteenth for Mallothi, his
sons and his brethren, twelve;
27 the twentieth for Eliathah, his
sons and his brethren, twelve;
28 the twenty-first for Hothir, his
sons and his brethren, twelve;
29 the twenty-second for Giddalti,
his sons and his brethren, twelve;
30 the twenty-third for Maha-
zioth, his sons and his brethren,
twelve;
31 the twenty-fourth for Romamti-
Ezer, his sons and his brethren,
twelve.

The Gatekeepers

26 Concerning the divisions of
the gatekeepers: of the Ko-
rahites, [1]Meshelemiah the son of
[a]Kore, of the sons of [2]Asaph.
2 And the sons of Meshelemiah
were [a]Zechariah the firstborn, Je-
diael the second, Zebadiah the
third, Jathniel the fourth,
3 Elam the fifth, Jehohanan the
sixth, Eliehoenai the seventh.
4 Moreover the sons of [a]Obed-
Edom *were* Shemaiah the first-
born, Jehozabad the second, Joah
the third, Sacar the fourth, Ne-
thanel the fifth,
5 Ammiel the sixth, Issachar the
seventh, Peulthai the eighth; for
God blessed him.
6 Also to Shemaiah his son were
sons born who governed their fa-
thers' houses, because they *were*
men of great ability.
7 The sons of Shemaiah *were*
Othni, Rephael, Obed, and El-
zabad, whose brothers Elihu and
Semachiah *were* able men.
8 All these *were* of the sons of
Obed-Edom, they and their sons
and their brethren, [a]able men with
strength for the work: sixty-two of
Obed-Edom.
9 And Meshelemiah had sons
and brethren, eighteen able men.
10 Also [a]Hosah, of the children of
Merari, had sons: Shimri the first
(for *though* he was not the first-
born, his father made him the
first),
11 Hilkiah the second, Tebaliah
the third, Zechariah the fourth; all
the sons and brethren of Hosah
were thirteen.
12 Among these *were* the divi-
sions of the gatekeepers, among
the chief men, *having* duties just
like their brethren, to serve in the
house of the LORD.
13 And they [a]cast lots for each
gate, the small as well as the great,
according to their father's house.
14 The lot for the East *Gate* fell
to [1]Shelemiah. Then they cast lots
for his son Zechariah, a wise coun-
selor, and his lot came out for the
North Gate;
15 to Obed-Edom the South Gate,
and to his sons the [1]storehouse.
16 To Shuppim and Hosah *the lot
came out* for the West Gate, with
the Shallecheth Gate on the [a]as-
cending highway—watchman op-
posite watchman.
17 On the east were *six* Levites,
on the north four each day, on the
south four each day, and for the
[1]storehouse two by two.
18 As for the [1]Parbar on the west,
there were four on the highway
and two at the Parbar.
19 These were the divisions of the
gatekeepers among the sons of
Korah and among the sons of Me-
rari.

The Treasuries and Other Duties

20 Of the Levites, Ahijah *was*
[a]over the treasuries of the house
of God and over the treasuries of
the [b]dedicated[1] things.
21 The sons of [1]Laadan, the de-
scendants of the Gershonites of
Laadan, heads of their fathers'
houses, of Laadan the Gershonite:
[2]Jehieli.
22 The sons of Jehieli, Zetham
and Joel his brother, *were* over the
treasuries of the house of the LORD.
23 Of the [a]Amramites, the Izhar-
ites, the Hebronites, and the Uz-
zielites:
24 [a]Shebuel the son of Gershom,
the son of Moses, *was* overseer of
the treasuries.
25 And his brethren by Eliezer
were Rehabiah his son, Jeshaiah
his son, Joram his son, Zichri his
son, and [a]Shelomith his son.

22 [1]*Jerimoth.* v. 4

CHAPTER 26

1 [a]Ps. 42:title [1]*Shelemiah.* v. 14 [2]*Ebiasaph.* 1 Chr. 6:37; 9:19

2 [a]1 Chr. 9:21

4 [a]1 Chr. 15:18, 21

8 [a]1 Chr. 9:13

10 [a]1 Chr. 16:38

13 [a]1 Chr. 24:5, 31; 25:8

14 [1]*Meshelemiah.* v. 1

15 [1]Heb. *asuppim*

16 [a]1 Kin. 10:5; 2 Chr. 9:4

17 [1]Heb. *asuppim*

18 [1]Probably a court or colonnade extending west of the temple

20 [a]1 Chr. 9:26 [b]2 Sam. 8:11; 1 Chr. 26:22, 24, 26; 28:12; Ezra 2:69 [1]*holy things*

21 [1]*Libni.* 1 Chr. 6:17 [2]*Jehiel.* 1 Chr. 23:8; 29:8

23 [a]Ex. 6:18; Num. 3:19

24 [a]1 Chr. 23:16

25 [a]1 Chr. 23:18

26 This Shelomith and his breth-
ren *were* over all the treasuries of
the dedicated things [a]which King
David and the heads of fathers'
houses, the captains over thou-
sands and hundreds, and the cap-
tains of the army, had dedicated.
27 Some of the [1]spoils won in bat-
tles they dedicated to maintain the
house of the LORD.
28 And all that Samuel [a]the seer,
Saul the son of Kish, Abner the son
of Ner, and Joab the son of Zer-
uiah had dedicated, every dedi-
cated *thing*, was under the hand
of Shelomith and his brethren.
29 Of the Izharites, Chenaniah
and his sons [a]*performed* duties as
[b]officials and judges over Israel
outside Jerusalem.
30 Of the Hebronites, [a]Hashabiah
and his brethren, one thousand
seven hundred able men, had the
oversight of Israel on the west side
of the Jordan for all the business
of the LORD, and in the service of
the king.
31 Among the Hebronites, [a]Jeri-
jah *was* head of the Hebronites ac-
cording to his genealogy of the fa-
thers. In the fortieth year of the
reign of David they were sought,
and there were found among
them capable men [b]at Jazer of
Gilead.
32 And his brethren *were* two
thousand seven hundred able men,
heads of fathers' *houses*, whom
King David made officials over the
Reubenites, the Gadites, and the
half-tribe of Manasseh, for every
matter pertaining to God and the
[a]affairs of the king.

The Military Divisions

27 And the children of Israel,
according to their number,
the heads of fathers' *houses*, the
captains of thousands and hun-
dreds and their officers, served the
king in every matter of the *military*
divisions. *These divisions* came in
and went out month by month
throughout all the months of the
year, each division *having* twenty-
four thousand.
2 Over the first division for the
first month *was* [a]Jashobeam the
son of Zabdiel, and in his division
were twenty-four thousand;
3 *he was* of the children of Perez,
and the chief of all the captains of
the army for the first month.
4 Over the division of the second
month *was* [1]Dodai an Ahohite, and
of his division Mikloth also *was*
the leader; in his division *were*
twenty-four thousand.
5 The third captain of the army
for the third month *was* [a]Benaiah,
the son of Jehoiada the priest, who
was chief; in his division *were*
twenty-four thousand.
6 This was the Benaiah *who was*
[a]mighty *among* the thirty, and was
over the thirty; in his division *was*
Ammizabad his son.
7 The fourth *captain* for the
fourth month *was* [a]Asahel the
brother of Joab, and Zebadiah his
son after him; in his division *were*
twenty-four thousand.
8 The fifth *captain* for the fifth
month *was* [1]Shamhuth the Izra-
hite; in his division were twenty-
four thousand.
9 The sixth *captain* for the sixth
month *was* [a]Ira the son of Ikkesh
the Tekoite; in his division *were*
twenty-four thousand.
10 The seventh *captain* for the
seventh month *was* [a]Helez the Pel-
onite, of the children of Ephraim;
in his division *were* twenty-four
thousand.
11 The eighth *captain* for the
eighth month *was* [a]Sibbechai the
Hushathite, of the Zarhites; in his
division *were* twenty-four thou-
sand.
12 The ninth *captain* for the ninth
month *was* [a]Abiezer the Anathoth-
ite, of the Benjamites; in his divi-
sion *were* twenty-four thousand.
13 The tenth *captain* for the tenth
month *was* [a]Maharai the Ne-
tophathite, of the Zarhites; in his
division *were* twenty-four thou-
sand.
14 The eleventh *captain* for the
eleventh month *was* [a]Benaiah the
Pirathonite, of the children of
Ephraim; in his division *were*
twenty-four thousand.
15 The twelfth *captain* for the
twelfth month *was* [1]Heldai the Ne-
tophathite, of Othniel; in his divi-
sion *were* twenty-four thousand.

Leaders of Tribes

16 Furthermore, over the tribes of
Israel: the officer over the Reuben-

---

26 [a]2 Sam. 8:11
27 [1]*plunder*
28 [a]1 Sam. 9:9
29 [a]Neh. 11:16 [b]1 Chr. 23:4
30 [a]1 Chr. 27:17
31 [a]1 Chr. 23:19 [b]Josh. 21:39
32 [a]2 Chr. 19:11

CHAPTER 27
2 [a]1 Chr. 11:11
4 [1]Heb. *Dodai*, usually spelled *Dodo*, 2 Sam. 23:9
5 [a]1 Chr. 18:17
6 [a]2 Sam. 23:20–23
7 [a]2 Sam. 23:24; 1 Chr. 11:26
8 [1]*Shammah*, 2 Sam. 23:11, or *Shammoth*, 1 Chr. 11:27
9 [a]1 Chr. 11:28
10 [a]1 Chr. 11:27
11 [a]2 Sam. 21:18; 1 Chr. 11:29; 20:4
12 [a]1 Chr. 11:28
13 [a]2 Sam. 23:28; 1 Chr. 11:30
14 [a]1 Chr. 11:31
15 [1]*Heleb*, 2 Sam. 23:29, or *Heled*, 1 Chr. 11:30

ites *was* Eliezer the son of Zichri;
over the Simeonites, Shephatiah
the son of Maachah;
17 *over* the Levites, [a]Hashabiah
the son of Kemuel; over the Aaron-
ites, Zadok;
18 *over* Judah, [a]Elihu, *one* of Da-
vid's brothers; *over* Issachar, Omri
the son of Michael;
19 *over* Zebulun, Ishmaiah the son
of Obadiah; *over* Naphtali, Jeri-
moth the son of Azriel;
20 *over* the children of Ephraim,
Hoshea the son of Azaziah; *over*
the half-tribe of Manasseh, Joel
the son of Pedaiah;
21 *over* the half-*tribe* of Manasseh
in Gilead, Iddo the son of Zecha-
riah; *over* Benjamin, Jaasiel the
son of Abner;
22 *over* Dan, Azarel the son of Je-
roham. These *were* the leaders of
the tribes of Israel.
23 But David did not take the
number of those twenty years old
and under, because [a]the LORD had
said He would multiply Israel like
the [b]stars of the heavens.
24 Joab the son of Zeruiah began
a census, but he did not finish, for
[a]wrath came upon Israel because
of this census; nor was the number
recorded in the account of the
chronicles of King David.

Other State Officials

25 And Azmaveth the son of Adiel
was over the king's treasuries; and
Jehonathan the son of Uzziah was
over the storehouses in the field,
in the cities, in the villages, and
in the fortresses.
26 Ezri the son of Chelub was over
those who did the work of the field
for tilling the ground.
27 And Shimei the Ramathite *was*
over the vineyards, and Zabdi the
Shiphmite was over the produce of
the vineyards for the supply of
wine.
28 Baal-Hanan the Gederite was
over the olive trees and the syca-
more trees that *were* in the low-
lands, and Joash *was* over the
store of oil.
29 And Shitrai the Sharonite *was*
over the herds that fed in Sharon,
and Shaphat the son of Adlai was
over the herds *that were* in the val-
leys.
30 Obil the Ishmaelite *was* over
the camels, Jehdeiah the Meron-
othite *was* over the donkeys,
31 and Jaziz the [a]Hagrite *was*
over the flocks. All these *were*
the officials over King David's
property.
32 Also Jehonathan, David's un-
cle, *was* a counselor, a wise man,
and a [1]scribe; and Jehiel the [2]son
of Hachmoni *was* with the king's
sons.
33 [a]Ahithophel *was* the king's
counselor, and [b]Hushai the Ar-
chite *was* the king's companion.
34 After Ahithophel *was* Jehoi-
ada the son of Benaiah, then
[a]Abiathar. And the general of the
king's army *was* [b]Joab.

Solomon Instructed to Build the Temple

28 Now David assembled at Je-
rusalem all [a]the leaders of
Israel: the officers of the tribes and
[b]the captains of the divisions who
served the king, the captains over
thousands and captains over hun-
dreds, and [c]the stewards over all
the substance and [1]possessions of
the king and of his sons, with the
officials, the valiant men, and all
[d]the mighty men of valor.
2 Then King David rose to his
feet and said, "Hear me, my breth-
ren and my people: [a]I *had* it in my
heart to build a house of rest for
the ark of the covenant of the
LORD, and for [b]the footstool of our
God, and had made preparations
to build it.
3 "But God said to me, [a]'You
shall not build a house for My
name, because you *have been*
a man of war and have shed
[b]blood.'
4 "However the LORD God of Is-
rael [a]chose me above all the house
of my father to be king over Israel
forever, for He has chosen [b]Judah
to be the ruler. And of the house
of Judah, [c]the house of my father,
and [d]among the sons of my father,
He was pleased with me to make
me king over all Israel.
5 [a]"And of all my sons (for the
LORD has given me many sons) [b]He
has chosen my son Solomon to sit
on the throne of the kingdom of
the LORD over Israel.
6 "Now He said to me, 'It is [a]your
son Solomon *who* shall build My

17 [a]1 Chr. 26:30
18 [a]1 Sam. 16:6
23 [a][Deut. 6:3] [b]Gen. 15:5; 22:17; 26:4; Ex. 32:13; Deut. 1:10
24 [a]2 Sam. 24:12–15; 1 Chr. 21:1–7
31 [a]1 Chr. 5:10
32 [1]*secretary* [2]Or *Hachmonite*
33 [a]2 Sam. 15:12 [b]2 Sam. 15:32–37
34 [a]1 Kin. 1:7 [b]1 Chr. 11:6

CHAPTER 28

1 [a]1 Chr. 27:16 [b]1 Chr. 27:1, 2 [c]1 Chr. 27:25 [d]2 Sam. 23:8–39; 1 Chr. 11:10–47 [1]Or *livestock*
2 [a]2 Sam. 7:2 [b]Ps. 99:5; 132:7; [Is. 66:1]
3 [a]2 Sam. 7:5, 13; 1 Kin. 5:3 [b][1 Chr. 17:4; 22:8]
4 [a]1 Sam. 16:6–13 [b]Gen. 49:8–10; 1 Chr. 5:2; Ps. 60:7 [c]1 Sam. 16:1 [d]1 Sam. 13:14; 16:12, 13; Acts 13:22
5 [a]1 Chr. 3:1–9; 14:3–7; 23:1 [b]1 Chr. 22:9; 29:1
6 [a]2 Sam. 7:13, 14; 1 Kin. 6:38; 1 Chr. 22:9, 10; 2 Chr. 1:9; 6:2

house and My courts; for I have
chosen him *to be* My son, and I
will be his Father.
7 'Moreover I will establish his
kingdom forever, [a]if he is steadfast
to observe My commandments
and My judgments, as it is this
day.'
8 "Now therefore, in the sight of
all Israel, the assembly of the
LORD, and in the hearing of our
God, be careful to seek out all the
commandments of the LORD your
God, that you may possess this
good land, and leave *it* as an inher-
itance for your children after you
forever.
9 "As for you, my son Solomon,
[a]know the God of your father, and
serve Him [b]with a loyal heart and
with a willing mind; for [c]the LORD
searches all hearts and under-
stands all the intent of the
thoughts. [d]If you seek Him, He will
be found by you; but if you forsake
Him, He will [e]cast you off forever.
10 "Consider now, [a]for the LORD
has chosen you to build a house
for the sanctuary; be strong, and
do it."
11 Then David gave his son Sol-
omon [a]the plans for the vestibule,
its houses, its treasuries, its upper
chambers, its inner chambers, and
the place of the mercy seat;
12 and the [a]plans for all that he
had by the Spirit, of the courts of
the house of the LORD, of all the
chambers all around, [b]of the trea-
suries of the house of God, and of
the treasuries for the dedicated
things;
13 also for the division of the
priests and the [a]Levites, for all the
work of the service of the house
of the LORD, and for all the articles
of service in the house of the LORD.
14 *He gave* gold by weight for
things of gold, for all articles used
in every kind of service; also *silver*
for all articles of silver by weight,
for all articles used in every kind
of service;
15 the weight *for* the [a]lampstands
of gold, and their lamps of gold,
by weight for each lampstand and
its lamps; for the lampstands of sil-
ver by weight, for the lampstand
and its lamps, according to the use
of each lampstand.
16 And by weight *he gave* gold for

7 [a]1 Chr. 22:13

9 [a][1 Sam. 12:24]; Jer. 9:24; Hos. 4:1; [John 17:3] [b]2 Kin. 20:3 [c][1 Sam. 16:7; 1 Kin. 8:39; 1 Chr. 29:17]; Jer. 11:20; 17:10; 20:12; Rev. 2:23 [d]2 Chr. 15:2; [Jer. 29:13] [e]Deut. 31:17

10 [a]1 Chr. 22:13; 28:6

11 [a]1 Kin. 6:3; 1 Chr. 28:19

12 [a]Ex. 25:40; Heb. 8:5 [b]1 Chr. 26:20, 28

13 [a]1 Chr. 23:6

15 [a]Ex. 25:31–39; 1 Kin. 7:49

16 [a]1 Kin. 7:48

18 [a]Ex. 30:1–10 [b]Ex. 25:18–22; 1 Sam. 4:4; 1 Kin. 6:23

19 [a]Ex. 25:40; 1 Chr. 28:11, 12 [1]*details*

20 [a]Deut. 31:6, 7; [Josh. 1:6–9]; 1 Chr. 22:13 [b]Josh. 1:5; Heb. 13:5

21 [a]1 Chr. 24—26 [b]Ex. 35:25–35; 36:1, 2; 2 Chr. 2:13, 14

CHAPTER 29

1 [a]1 Chr. 28:5 [b]1 Kin. 3:7; 1 Chr. 22:5; Prov. 4:3 [1]Lit. *palace*

2 [a]Is. 54:11, 12; Rev. 21:18

the tables of the showbread, for
each [a]table, and silver for the ta-
bles of silver;
17 also pure gold for the forks, the
basins, the pitchers of pure gold,
and the golden bowls—*he gave*
gold by weight for every bowl; and
for the silver bowls, *silver* by
weight for every bowl;
18 and refined gold by weight for
the [a]altar of incense, and for the
construction of the chariot, that is,
the gold [b]cherubim that spread
their wings and overshadowed the
ark of the covenant of the LORD.
19 "All *this*," *said David*, [a]"the
LORD made me understand in writ-
ing, by *His* hand upon me, all the
[1]works of these plans."
20 And David said to his son Sol-
omon, [a]"Be strong and of good
courage, and do *it;* do not fear nor
be dismayed, for the LORD God—
my God—*will be* with you. [b]He will
not leave you nor forsake you, un-
til you have finished all the work
for the service of the house of the
LORD.
21 "*Here are* [a]the divisions of the
priests and the Levites for all the
service of the house of God; and
[b]every willing craftsman *will be*
with you for all manner of work-
manship, for every kind of service;
also the leaders and all the peo-
ple *will be* completely at your
command."

Offerings for Building the Temple

29 Furthermore King David
said to all the assembly: "My
son Solomon, whom alone God
has [a]chosen, *is* [b]young and inexpe-
rienced; and the work *is* great, be-
cause the [1]temple *is* not for man
but for the LORD God.
2 "Now for the house of my God
I have prepared with all my might:
gold for *things to be made of* gold,
silver for *things of* silver, bronze
for *things of* bronze, iron for
things of iron, wood for *things of*
wood, [a]onyx stones, *stones* to be
set, glistening stones of various
colors, all kinds of precious stones,
and marble slabs in abundance.
3 "Moreover, because I have set
my affection on the house of my
God, I have given to the house of
my God, over and above all that I
have prepared for the holy house,

my own special treasure of gold
and silver:
4 "three thousand talents of
gold, of the gold of [a]Ophir, and
seven thousand talents of refined
silver, to overlay the walls of the
houses;
5 "the gold for *things of* gold and
the silver for *things of* silver, and
for all kinds of work *to be done*
by the hands of craftsmen. Who
then is [a]willing to [1]consecrate him-
self this day to the LORD?"
6 Then [a]the leaders of the fa-
thers' *houses*, leaders of the tribes
of Israel, the captains of thousands
and of hundreds, with [b]the officers
over the king's work, [c]offered will-
ingly.
7 They gave for the work of the
house of God five thousand tal-
ents and ten thousand darics of
gold, ten thousand talents of sil-
ver, eighteen thousand talents of
bronze, and one hundred thousand
talents of iron.
8 And whoever had *precious*
stones gave *them* to the treasury
of the house of the LORD, into the
hand of [a]Jehiel[1] the Gershonite.
9 Then the people rejoiced, for
they had offered willingly, because
with a loyal heart they had [a]of-
fered willingly to the LORD; and
King David also rejoiced greatly.

David's Praise to God

10 Therefore David blessed the
LORD before all the assembly; and
David said:

"Blessed are You, LORD God of
Israel, our Father, forever and
ever.
11 [a]Yours, O LORD, *is* the greatness,
The power and the glory,
The victory and the majesty;
For all *that is* in heaven and in
earth *is Yours;*
Yours *is* the kingdom, O LORD,
And You are exalted as head over
all.
12 [a]Both riches and honor *come* from
You,
And You reign over all.
In Your hand *is* power and might;
In Your hand *it is* to make great
And to give strength to all.

13 "Now therefore, our God,
We thank You
And praise Your glorious name.

4 [a]1 Kin. 9:28

5 [a]2 Chr. 29:31; [2 Cor. 8:5, 12] [1]Lit. *fill his hand*

6 [a]1 Chr. 27:1; 28:1 [b]1 Chr. 27:25–31 [c]Ex. 35:21–35

8 [a]1 Chr. 23:8 [1]Possibly the same as *Jehieli*, 1 Chr. 26:21, 22

9 [a]Ex. 25:2; 1 Kin. 8:61; 2 Cor. 9:7

11 [a]Matt. 6:13; 1 Tim. 1:17; Rev. 5:13

12 [a]Rom. 11:36

14 [1]Lit. *of Your hand*

15 [a]Lev. 25:23; Ps. 39:12; Heb. 11:13, 14; 1 Pet. 2:11 [b]Job 14:2; Ps. 90:9 [1]*sojourners*, temporary residents [2]*transients*, temporary residents in an even more temporary sense

17 [a][1 Sam. 16:7; 1 Chr. 28:9] [b]Prov. 11:20

19 [a][1 Chr. 28:9]; Ps. 72:1 [b]1 Chr. 29:1, 2 [1]Lit. *palace*

21 [a]1 Kin. 8:62, 63

22 [a]1 Kin. 1:32–35, 39; 1 Chr. 23:1

14 But who *am* I, and who *are* my
people,
That we should be able to offer
so willingly as this?
For all things *come* from You,
And [1]of Your own we have given
You.
15 For [a]we *are* [1]aliens and [2]pilgrims
before You,
As *were* all our fathers;
[b]Our days on earth *are* as a
shadow,
And without hope.

16 "O LORD our God, all this abun-
dance that we have prepared to
build You a house for Your holy
name is from Your hand, and *is*
all Your own.
17 "I know also, my God, that You
[a]test the heart and [b]have pleasure
in uprightness. As for me, in the
uprightness of my heart I have
willingly offered all these *things;*
and now with joy I have seen Your
people, who are present here to of-
fer willingly to You.
18 "O LORD God of Abraham,
Isaac, and Israel, our fathers, keep
this forever in the intent of the
thoughts of the heart of Your peo-
ple, and fix their heart toward
You.
19 "And [a]give my son Solomon a
loyal heart to keep Your com-
mandments and Your testimonies
and Your statutes, to do all *these*
things, and to build the [1]temple for
which [b]I have made provision."
20 Then David said to all the as-
sembly, "Now bless the LORD your
God." So all the assembly blessed
the LORD God of their fathers, and
bowed their heads and prostrated
themselves before the LORD and
the king.

Solomon Anointed King

21 And they made sacrifices to the
LORD and offered burnt offerings
to the LORD on the next day: a
thousand bulls, a thousand rams,
a thousand lambs, with their drink
offerings, and [a]sacrifices in abun-
dance for all Israel.
22 So they ate and drank before
the LORD with great gladness on
that day. And they made Solomon
the son of David king the second
time, and [a]anointed *him* before the
LORD *to be* the leader, and Zadok
to be priest.

23 Then Solomon sat on the
throne of the LORD as king instead
of David his father, and prospered;
and all Israel obeyed him.
24 All the leaders and the mighty
men, and also all the sons of King
David, [a]submitted[1] themselves to
King Solomon.
25 So the LORD exalted Solomon
exceedingly in the sight of all Is-
rael, and [a]bestowed on him *such*
royal majesty as had not been on
any king before him in Israel.

The Close of David's Reign

26 Thus David the son of Jesse
reigned over all Israel.
27 [a]And the period that he reigned
over Israel *was* forty years; [b]seven
years he reigned in Hebron, and
thirty-three *years* he reigned in Je-
rusalem.
28 So he [a]died in a good old age,
[b]full of days and riches and honor;
and Solomon his son reigned in his
place.
29 Now the acts of King David,
first and last, indeed they *are* writ-
ten in the [1]book of Samuel the
seer, in the book of Nathan the
prophet, and in the book of Gad
the seer,
30 with all his reign and his might,
[a]and the events that happened to
him, to Israel, and to all the king-
doms of the lands.

24 [a]Eccl. 8:2 [1]Lit. *gave the hand*

25 [a]1 Kin. 3:13; 2 Chr. 1:12; Eccl. 2:9

27 [a]2 Sam. 5:4; 1 Kin. 2:11 [b]2 Sam. 5:5

28 [a]Gen. 25:8 [b]1 Chr. 23:1

29 [1]Lit. *words*

30 [a]Dan. 2:21; 4:23, 25

The Second Book of the

Chronicles

THE Book of Second Chronicles parallels First and Second Kings but virtually ignores the northern kingdom of Israel because of its false worship and refusal to acknowledge the temple in Jerusalem. Chronicles focuses on those kings who pattern their lives and reigns after the life and reign of godly King David. It gives extended treatment to such zealous reformers as Asa, Jehoshaphat, Joash, Hezekiah, and Josiah.

The temple and temple worship, central throughout the book, befit a nation whose worship of God is central to its very survival. The book begins with Solomon's glorious temple and concludes with Cyrus's edict to rebuild the temple more than four hundred years later.

Solomon Requests Wisdom

NOW [a]Solomon the son of David was strengthened in his kingdom, and [b]the LORD his God *was* with him and [c]exalted him exceedingly.

2 And Solomon spoke to all Israel, to [a]the captains of thousands and of hundreds, to the judges, and to every leader in all Israel, the heads of the fathers' *houses.*

3 Then Solomon, and all the assembly with him, went to [1]the high place that *was* at [a]Gibeon; for the tabernacle of meeting with God was there, which Moses the servant of the LORD had [b]made in the wilderness.

4 [a]But David had brought up the ark of God from Kirjath Jearim to *the place* David had prepared for it, for he had pitched a tent for it at Jerusalem.

5 Now [a]the bronze altar that [b]Bezalel the son of Uri, the son of Hur, had made, [1]he put before the tabernacle of the LORD; Solomon and the assembly sought Him *there.*

6 And Solomon went up there to the bronze altar before the LORD, which *was* at the tabernacle of meeting, and [a]offered a thousand burnt offerings on it.

7 [a]On that night God appeared to Solomon, and said to him, "Ask! What shall I give you?"

8 And Solomon said to God: "You have shown great [a]mercy to David my father, and have made me [b]king in his place.

9 "Now, O LORD God, let Your promise to David my father be established, [a]for You have made me king over a people like the [b]dust of the earth in multitude.

10 [a]"Now give me wisdom and knowledge, that I may [b]go out and come in before this people; for who can judge this great people of Yours?"

11 [a]Then God said to Solomon: "Because this was in your heart, and you have not asked riches or wealth or honor or the life of your enemies, nor have you asked long life—but have asked wisdom and knowledge for yourself, that you may judge My people over whom I have made you king—

12 "wisdom and knowledge *are* granted to you; and I will give you riches and wealth and honor, such as [a]none of the kings have had who *were* before you, nor shall any after you have the like."

Solomon's Military and Economic Power

13 So Solomon came to Jerusalem from [1]the high place that was at Gibeon, from before the tabernacle of meeting, and reigned over Israel.

14 [a]And Solomon gathered chariots and horsemen; he had one thousand four hundred chariots and twelve thousand horsemen, whom he stationed in the chariot cities and with the king in Jerusalem.

CHAPTER 1

1 [a]1 Kin. 2:46 [b]Gen. 39:2 [c]1 Chr. 29:25
2 [a]1 Chr. 27:1–34
3 [a]1 Kin. 3:4; 1 Chr. 16:39; 21:29 [b]Ex. 25—27; 35:4—36:38 [1]Place for worship
4 [a]Ex. 25:10–22; 2 Sam. 6:2–17; 1 Chr. 15:25—16:1
5 [a]Ex. 27:1, 2; 38:1, 2 [b]Ex. 31:2 [1]Some authorities *it was there*
6 [a]1 Kin. 3:4
7 [a]1 Kin. 3:5–14; 9:2
8 [a]Ps. 18:50 [b]1 Chr. 28:5
9 [a]2 Sam. 7:8–16; 1 Kin. 3:7, 8 [b]Gen. 13:16; Num. 23:10
10 [a]1 Kin. 3:9 [b]Num. 27:17; Deut. 31:2
11 [a]1 Kin. 3:11–13
12 [a]1 Kin. 10:23; 1 Chr. 29:25; 2 Chr. 9:22; Eccl. 2:9
13 [1]Place for worship
14 [a]1 Kin. 10:26; 2 Chr. 9:25

15 [a]Also the king made silver and
gold as common in Jerusalem as
stones, and he made cedars as
abundant as the sycamores which
are in the lowland.
16 [a]And Solomon had horses imported from Egypt and Keveh; the
king's merchants bought them in
Keveh at the *current* price.
17 They also acquired and imported from Egypt a chariot for six
hundred *shekels* of silver, and a
horse for one hundred and fifty;
thus, [1]through their agents, they
exported them to all the kings of
the Hittites and the kings of Syria.

Solomon Prepares to Build the Temple

2 Then Solomon [a]determined to
build a temple for the name of
the LORD, and a royal house for
himself.
2 [a]Solomon selected seventy
thousand men to bear burdens,
eighty thousand to quarry *stone* in
the mountains, and three thousand
six hundred to oversee them.
3 Then Solomon sent to [1]Hiram
king of Tyre, saying:

[a]As you have dealt with David
my father, and sent him cedars
to build himself a house to
dwell in, *so deal with me.*
4 Behold, [a]I am building a temple
for the name of the LORD my
God, to dedicate *it* to Him, [b]to
burn before Him [1]sweet
incense, for [c]the continual
showbread, for [d]the burnt
offerings morning and evening,
on the [e]Sabbaths, on the New
Moons, and on the [2]set feasts
of the LORD our God. This *is an*
ordinance forever *to* Israel.
5 And the temple which I build
will be great, for [a]our God is
greater than all gods.
6 [a]But who is able to build Him
a temple, since heaven and the
heaven of heavens cannot
contain Him? Who *am* I then,
that I should build Him a
temple, except to burn sacrifice
before Him?
7 Therefore send me at once a
man skillful to work in gold
and silver, in bronze and iron,
in purple and crimson and
blue, who has skill to engrave
with the skillful men who are
with me in Judah and
Jerusalem, [a]whom David my
father provided.
8 [a]Also send me cedar and
cypress and algum logs from
Lebanon, for I know that your
servants have skill to cut
timber in Lebanon; and indeed
my servants *will be* with your
servants,
9 to prepare timber for me in
abundance, for the [1]temple
which I am about to build *shall*
be great and wonderful.
10 [a]And indeed I will give to your
servants, the woodsmen who
cut timber, twenty thousand
kors of ground wheat, twenty
thousand kors of barley,
twenty thousand baths of wine,
and twenty thousand baths of
oil.

11 Then Hiram king of Tyre answered in writing, which he sent
to Solomon:

[a]Because the LORD loves His
people, He has made you king
over them.

12 [1]Hiram also said:

[a]Blessed *be* the LORD God of
Israel, [b]who made heaven and
earth, for He has given King
David a wise son, endowed
with prudence and
understanding, who will build
a temple for the LORD and a
royal house for himself!
13 And now I have sent a skillful
man, endowed with
understanding, [1]Huram my
[2]master *craftsman*
14 [a](the son of a woman of the
daughters of Dan, and his
father was a man of Tyre),
skilled to work in gold and
silver, bronze and iron, stone
and wood, purple and blue, fine
linen and crimson, and to make
any engraving and to
accomplish any plan which
may be given to him, with your
skillful men and with the
skillful men of my lord David
your father.
15 Now therefore, the wheat, the
barley, the oil, and the wine

---

15 [a]1 Kin. 10:27; 2 Chr. 9:27; Job 22:24
16 [a]1 Kin. 10:28; 22:36; 2 Chr. 9:28
17 [1]Lit. *by their hands*

CHAPTER 2
1 [a]1 Kin. 5:5
2 [a]1 Kin. 5:15, 16; 2 Chr. 2:18
3 [a]1 Chr. 14:1 [1]Heb. *Huram;* cf. 1 Kin. 5:1
4 [a]2 Chr. 2:1 [b]Ex. 30:7 [c]Ex. 25:30; Lev. 24:8 [d]Ex. 29:38–42 [e]Num. 28:3, 9–11 [1]Lit. *incense of spices* [2]*appointed*
5 [a]Ps. 135:5; [1 Cor. 8:5, 6]
6 [a]1 Kin. 8:27; 2 Chr. 6:18; Is. 66:1
7 [a]1 Chr. 22:15
8 [a]1 Kin. 5:6
9 [1]Lit. *house*
10 [a]1 Kin. 5:11
11 [a]1 Kin. 10:9; 2 Chr. 9:8
12 [a]1 Kin. 5:7 [b]Gen. 1; 2; Acts 4:24; 14:15; Rev. 10:6 [1]Heb. *Huram;* cf. 1 Kin. 5:1
13 [1]*Hiram.* 1 Kin. 7:13 [2]Lit. *father.* 1 Kin. 7:13, 14
14 [a]1 Kin. 7:13, 14

which [a]my lord has spoken of,
let him send to his servants.
16 [a]And we will cut wood from
Lebanon, as much as you need;
we will bring it to you in rafts
by sea to [1]Joppa, and you will
carry it up to Jerusalem.

17 [a]Then Solomon numbered all
the aliens who *were* in the land of
Israel, after the census in which
[b]David his father had numbered
them; and there were found to be
one hundred and fifty-three thou-
sand six hundred.
18 And he made [a]seventy thou-
sand of them bearers of burdens,
eighty thousand stonecutters in
the mountain, and three thousand
six hundred overseers to make the
people work.

Solomon Builds the Temple

3 Now [a]Solomon began to build
the house of the LORD at [b]Jeru-
salem on Mount Moriah, where
[1]*the* LORD had appeared to his fa-
ther David, at the place that David
had prepared on the threshing
floor of [c]Ornan[2] the Jebusite.
2 And he began to build on the
second *day* of the second month
in the fourth year of his reign.
3 This is the foundation [a]which
Solomon laid for building the
house of God: The length *was* sixty
cubits (by cubits according to the
former measure) and the width
twenty cubits.
4 And the [a]vestibule that *was* in
front *of* [1]*the sanctuary* was twenty
cubits long across the width of the
house, and the height *was* [2]one
hundred and twenty. He overlaid
the inside with pure gold.
5 [a]The larger [1]room he [b]paneled
with cypress which he overlaid
with fine gold, and he carved palm
trees and chainwork on it.
6 And he decorated the house
with precious stones for beauty,
and the gold *was* gold from Par-
vaim.
7 He also overlaid the house—
the beams and doorposts, its walls
and doors—with gold; and he
carved cherubim on the walls.
8 And he made the [a]Most Holy
Place. Its length was according to
the width of the house, twenty cu-
bits, and its width twenty cubits.

15 [a]2 Chr. 2:10
16 [a]1 Kin. 5:8, 9 [1]Heb. *Japho*
17 [a]1 Kin. 5:13; 2 Chr. 8:7, 8 [b]1 Chr. 22:2
18 [a]2 Chr. 2:2

CHAPTER 3

1 [a]1 Kin. 6:1 [b]Gen. 22:2–14 [c]1 Chr. 21:18; 22:1 [1]Lit. *He*, following MT, Vg.; LXX *the* LORD; Tg. *the Angel of the* LORD [2]*Araunah*, 2 Sam. 24:16
3 [a]1 Kin. 6:2; 1 Chr. 28:11–19
4 [a]1 Kin. 6:3; 1 Chr. 28:11 [1]The holy place, the main room of the temple, 1 Kin. 6:3 [2]So with MT, LXX, Vg.; Arab., some LXX mss., Syr. *twenty*
5 [a]1 Kin. 6:17 [b]1 Kin. 6:15; Jer. 22:14 [1]Lit. *house*
8 [a]Ex. 26:33; 1 Kin. 6:16
9 [a]1 Chr. 28:11
10 [a]Ex. 25:18–20; 1 Kin. 6:23–28
14 [a]Ex. 26:31; Matt. 27:51; Heb. 9:3
15 [a]1 Kin. 7:15–20; Jer. 52:21 [1]Lit. *house* [2]*eighteen*, 1 Kin. 7:15; 2 Kin. 25:17; Jer. 52:21 [3]Lit. *long*
16 [a]1 Kin. 7:20
17 [a]1 Kin. 7:21 [1]Lit. *He Shall Establish* [2]Lit. *In It Is Strength*

CHAPTER 4

1 [a]Ex. 27:1, 2; 2 Kin. 16:14; Ezek. 43:13, 16
2 [a]Ex. 30:17–21; 1 Kin. 7:23–26 [1]Great laver or basin
3 [a]1 Kin. 7:24–26

He overlaid it with six hundred tal-
ents of fine gold.
9 The weight of the nails *was*
fifty shekels of gold; and he over-
laid the upper [a]area with gold.
10 [a]In the Most Holy Place he
made two cherubim, fashioned by
carving, and overlaid them with
gold.
11 The wings of the cherubim
were twenty cubits in *overall*
length: one wing *of the one cherub*
was five cubits, touching the wall
of the room, and the other wing
was five cubits, touching the wing
of the other cherub;
12 *one* wing of the other cherub
was five cubits, touching the wall
of the room, and the other wing
also was five cubits, touching the
wing of the other cherub.
13 The wings of these cherubim
spanned twenty cubits overall.
They stood on their feet, and they
faced inward.
14 And he made the [a]veil of blue,
purple, crimson, and fine linen,
and wove cherubim into it.
15 Also he made in front of the
[1]temple [a]two pillars [2]thirty-five cu-
bits [3]high, and the capital that *was*
on the top of each of *them* was five
cubits.
16 He made wreaths of chain-
work, as in the inner sanctuary,
and put *them* on top of the pillars;
and he made [a]one hundred pome-
granates, and put *them* on the
wreaths of chainwork.
17 Then he [a]set up the pillars be-
fore the temple, one on the right
hand and the other on the left; he
called the name of the one on the
right hand [1]Jachin, and the name
of the one on the left [2]Boaz.

Furnishings of the Temple

4 Moreover he made [a]a bronze
altar: twenty cubits was its
length, twenty cubits its width, and
ten cubits its height.
2 [a]Then he made the [1]Sea of cast
bronze, ten cubits from one brim
to the other; *it was* completely
round. Its height *was* five cubits,
and a line of thirty cubits mea-
sured its circumference.
3 [a]And under it *was* the likeness
of oxen encircling it all around, ten
to a cubit, all the way around the

Sea. The oxen *were* cast in two
rows, when it was cast.
4 It stood on twelve [a]oxen: three
looking toward the north, three
looking toward the west, three
looking toward the south, and
three looking toward the east; the
Sea *was set* upon them, and all
their back parts *pointed* inward.
5 It *was* a handbreadth thick;
and its brim was shaped like the
brim of a cup, *like* a lily blos-
som. It contained [1]three thousand
baths.
6 He also made [a]ten lavers, and
put five on the right side and five
on the left, to wash in them; such
things as they offered for the burnt
offering they would wash in them,
but the [1]Sea *was* for the [b]priests
to wash in.
7 [a]And he made ten lampstands
of gold [b]according to their design,
and set *them* in the temple, five
on the right side and five on the
left.
8 [a]He also made ten tables, and
placed *them* in the temple, five on
the right side and five on the left.
And he made one hundred [b]bowls
of gold.
9 Furthermore [a]he made the
court of the priests, and the [b]great
court and doors for the court; and
he overlaid these doors with
bronze.
10 [a]He set the Sea on the right
side, toward the southeast.
11 Then [a]Huram made the pots
and the shovels and the bowls. So
Huram finished doing the work
that he was to do for King Sol-
omon for the house of God:
12 the two pillars and [a]the bowl-
shaped capitals *that were* on top
of the two pillars; the two net-
works covering the two bowl-
shaped capitals which *were* on top
of the pillars;
13 [a]four hundred pomegranates
for the two networks (two rows of
pomegranates for each network, to
cover the two bowl-shaped capi-
tals that *were* on the pillars);
14 he also made [a]carts and the la-
vers on the carts;
15 one Sea and twelve oxen under
it;
16 also the pots, the shovels, the
forks—and all their articles [a]Hu-
ram his [1]master *craftsman* made
of burnished bronze for King Sol-
omon for the house of the LORD.
17 In the plain of Jordan the king
had them cast in clay molds, be-
tween Succoth and [1]Zeredah.
18 [a]And Solomon had all these ar-
ticles made in such great abun-
dance that the weight of the
bronze was not determined.
19 Thus [a]Solomon had all the fur-
nishings made for the house of
God: the altar of gold and the ta-
bles on which *was* [b]the show-
bread;
20 the lampstands with their
lamps of pure gold, to burn [a]in the
prescribed manner in front of the
inner sanctuary,
21 with [a]the flowers and the lamps
and the wick-trimmers of gold, of
purest gold;
22 the trimmers, the bowls, the la-
dles, and the censers of pure gold.
As for the entry of the [1]sanctuary,
its inner doors to the Most Holy
Place, and the doors of the main
hall of the temple, *were* gold.

5 So [a]all the work that Solomon
had done for the house of the
LORD was finished; and Solomon
brought in the things which his fa-
ther David had dedicated: the sil-
ver and the gold and all the fur-
nishings. And he put *them* in the
treasuries of the house of God.

The Ark Brought into the Temple

2 [a]Now Solomon assembled the
elders of Israel and all the heads
of the tribes, the chief fathers of
the children of Israel, in Jerusa-
lem, that they might bring the ark
of the covenant of the LORD up
[b]from the City of David, which *is*
Zion.
3 [a]Therefore all the men of Israel
assembled with the king [b]at the
feast, which *was* in the seventh
month.
4 So all the elders of Israel came,
and the [a]Levites took up the ark.
5 Then they brought up the ark,
the tabernacle of meeting, and all
the holy furnishings that *were* in
the tabernacle. The priests and the
Levites brought them up.
6 Also King Solomon, and all the
congregation of Israel who were
assembled with him before the
ark, were sacrificing sheep and
oxen that could not be counted or
numbered for multitude.

4 [a]1 Kin. 7:25
5 [1]About 8,000 gallons; *two thousand*, 1 Kin. 7:26
6 [a]1 Kin. 7:38, 40 [b]Ex. 30:19–21 [1]Great basin
7 [a]1 Kin. 7:49 [b]Ex. 25:31; 1 Chr. 28:12, 19
8 [a]1 Kin. 7:48 [b]1 Chr. 28:17
9 [a]1 Kin. 6:36 [b]2 Kin. 21:5
10 [a]1 Kin. 7:39
11 [a]1 Kin. 7:40–51
12 [a]1 Kin. 7:41
13 [a]1 Kin. 7:20
14 [a]1 Kin. 7:27, 43
16 [a]1 Kin. 7:45; 2 Chr. 2:13 [1]Lit. *father*
17 [1]*Zaretan*, 1 Kin. 7:46
18 [a]1 Kin. 7:47
19 [a]1 Kin. 7:48–50 [b]Ex. 25:30
20 [a]Ex. 27:20, 21
21 [a]Ex. 25:31
22 [1]Lit. *house*

CHAPTER 5
1 [a]1 Kin. 7:51
2 [a]1 Kin. 8:1–9; Ps. 47:9 [b]2 Sam. 6:12
3 [a]1 Kin. 8:2 [b]Lev. 23:34; 2 Chr. 7:8–10
4 [a]1 Chr. 15:2, 15

7 Then the priests brought in the ark of the covenant of the LORD to its place, into the [a]inner sanctuary of the [1]temple, to the Most Holy *Place*, under the wings of the cherubim.

8 For the cherubim spread *their* wings over the place of the ark, and the cherubim overshadowed the ark and its poles.

9 The poles extended so that the ends of the [a]poles of the ark could be seen from *the holy place*, in front of the inner sanctuary; but they could not be seen from outside. And [1]they are there to this day.

10 Nothing was in the ark except the two tablets which Moses [a]put *there* at Horeb, [1]when the LORD made *a covenant* with the children of Israel, when they had come out of Egypt.

11 And it came to pass when the priests came out of the *Most* Holy *Place* (for all the priests who *were* present had [1]sanctified themselves, without keeping to their [a]divisions),

12 [a]and the Levites *who were* the singers, all those of Asaph and Heman and Jeduthun, with their sons and their brethren, stood at the east end of the altar, clothed in white linen, having cymbals, stringed instruments and harps, [b]and with them one hundred and twenty priests sounding with trumpets—

13 indeed it came to pass, when the trumpeters and singers *were* as one, to make one sound to be heard in praising and thanking the LORD, and when they lifted up their voice with the trumpets and cymbals and instruments of music, and praised the LORD, *saying:*

[a]"*For He is* good,
For His mercy *endures* forever,"

that the house, the house of the LORD, was filled with a cloud,

14 so that the priests could not [1]continue ministering because of the cloud; [a]for the glory of the LORD filled the house of God.

6 Then [a]Solomon spoke:

"The LORD said He would dwell in
the [b]dark cloud.

2 I have surely built You an exalted
house,
And [a]a place for You to dwell in
forever."

Solomon's Speech upon Completion of the Work

3 Then the king turned around and [a]blessed the whole assembly of Israel, while all the assembly of Israel was standing.

4 And he said: "Blessed *be* the LORD God of Israel, who has fulfilled with His hands *what* He spoke with His mouth to my father David, [a]saying,

5 'Since the day that I brought My people out of the land of Egypt, I have chosen no city from any tribe of Israel *in which* to build a house, that My name might be there, nor did I choose any man to be a ruler over My people Israel.

6 [a]Yet I have chosen Jerusalem, that My name may be there, and I [b]have chosen David to be over My people Israel.'

7 "Now [a]it was in the heart of my father David to build a [1]temple for the name of the LORD God of Israel.

8 "But the LORD said to my father David, 'Whereas it was in your heart to build a temple for My name, you did well in that it was in your heart.

9 'Nevertheless you shall not build the temple, but your son who will come from your body, he shall build the temple for My [a]name.'

10 "So the LORD has fulfilled His word which He spoke, and I have filled the position of my father David, and [a]sit on the throne of Israel, as the LORD promised; and I have built the temple for the name of the LORD God of Israel.

11 "And there I have put the ark, [a]in which *is* the covenant of the LORD which He made with the children of Israel."

Solomon's Prayer of Dedication

12 [a]Then [1]*Solomon* stood before the altar of the LORD in the presence of all the assembly of Israel, and spread out his hands

13 (for Solomon had made a bronze platform five cubits long, five cubits wide, and three cubits high, and had set it in the midst of the court; and he stood on it,

7 [a]2 Chr. 4:20 [1]Lit. *house*
9 [a]Ex. 25:13–15 [1]Lit. *it is*
10 [a]Ex. 25:16; Deut. 10:2, 5; 2 Chr. 6:11; Heb. 9:4 [1]Or *where*
11 [a]1 Chr. 24:1–5 [1]*consecrated*
12 [a]Ex. 32:26; 1 Chr. 25:1–7 [b]1 Chr. 13:8; 15:16, 24
13 [a]1 Chr. 16:34, 41; 2 Chr. 7:3; Ezra 3:11; Ps. 100:5; 106:1; 136; Jer. 33:11
14 [a]Ex. 40:35; 1 Kin. 8:11; 2 Chr. 7:2; Ezek. 43:5 [1]Lit. *stand to minister*

CHAPTER 6

1 [a]Ex. 19:9; 20:21; 1 Kin. 8:12–21 [b][Lev. 16:2]; Ps. 97:2
2 [a]2 Sam. 7:13; 1 Chr. 17:12; 2 Chr. 7:12
3 [a]2 Sam. 6:18
4 [a]1 Chr. 17:5
6 [a]Deut. 12:5–7; 2 Chr. 12:13; Zech. 2:12 [b]1 Sam. 16:7–13; 1 Chr. 28:4
7 [a]2 Sam. 7:2; 1 Chr. 17:1; 28:2; Ps. 132:1–5 [1]Lit. *house*, and so in vv. 8–10
9 [a]1 Chr. 28:3–6
10 [a]1 Kin. 2:12; 10:9
11 [a]2 Chr. 5:7–10
12 [a]1 Kin. 8:22; 2 Chr. 7:7–9 [1]Lit. *he*

knelt down on his knees before all
the assembly of Israel, and spread
out his hands toward heaven);
14 and he said: "LORD God of Is-
rael, [a]*there is* no God in heaven
or on earth like You, who keep
Your [b]covenant and mercy with
Your servants who walk before
You with all their hearts.
15 [a]"You have kept what You
promised Your servant David my
father; You have both spoken with
Your mouth and fulfilled *it* with
Your hand, as *it is* this day.
16 "Therefore, LORD God of Israel,
now keep what You promised
Your servant David my father,
saying, [a]'You shall not fail to have
a man sit before Me on the throne
of Israel, [b]only if your sons take
heed to their way, that they walk
in My law as you have walked be-
fore Me.'
17 "And now, O LORD God of Is-
rael, let Your word come true,
which You have spoken to Your
servant David.
18 "But will God indeed dwell
with men on the earth? [a]Behold,
heaven and the heaven of heavens
cannot contain You. How much
less this [1]temple which I have
built!
19 "Yet regard the prayer of Your
servant and his supplication, O
LORD my God, and listen to the cry
and the prayer which Your servant
is praying before You:
20 "that Your eyes may be [a]open
toward this temple day and night,
toward the place where *You* said
You would put Your name, that
You may hear the prayer which
Your servant makes [b]toward this
place.
21 "And may You hear the suppli-
cations of Your servant and of
Your people Israel, when they
pray toward this place. Hear from
heaven Your dwelling place, and
when You hear, [a]forgive.
22 "If anyone sins against his
neighbor, and is forced to take an
[a]oath, and comes *and* takes an
oath before Your altar in this tem-
ple,
23 "then hear from heaven, and
act, and judge Your servants,
bringing retribution on the wicked
by bringing his way on his own
head, and justifying the righteous

14 [a][Ex. 15:11; Deut. 4:39] [b][Deut. 7:9]
15 [a]1 Chr. 22:9, 10
16 [a]2 Sam. 7:12, 16; 1 Kin. 2:4; 6:12; 2 Chr. 7:18 [b]Ps. 132:12
18 [a][2 Chr. 2:6; Is. 66:1; Acts 7:49] [1]Lit. *house*
20 [a]2 Chr. 7:15 [b]Ps. 5:7; Dan. 6:10
21 [a][Is. 43:25; 44:22; Mic. 7:18]
22 [a]Ex. 22:8–11
23 [a][Job 34:11]
24 [a]2 Kin. 21:14, 15
26 [a]Deut. 28:23, 24; 1 Kin. 17:1
28 [a]2 Chr. 20:9 [b][Mic. 6:13]
30 [a][1 Chr. 28:9; Prov. 21:2; 24:12] [b][1 Sam. 16:7]
32 [a]John 12:20; Acts 8:27

by giving him according to his
[a]righteousness.
24 "Or if Your people Israel are
defeated before an [a]enemy be-
cause they have sinned against
You, and return and confess Your
name, and pray and make suppli-
cation before You in this temple,
25 "then hear from heaven and
forgive the sin of Your people Is-
rael, and bring them back to the
land which You gave to them and
their fathers.
26 "When the [a]heavens are shut
up and there is no rain because
they have sinned against You,
when they pray toward this place
and confess Your name, and turn
from their sin because You afflict
them,
27 "then hear *in* heaven, and for-
give the sin of Your servants, Your
people Israel, that You may teach
them the good way in which they
should walk; and send rain on
Your land which You have given
to Your people as an inheritance.
28 "When there [a]is famine in the
land, pestilence or blight or mil-
dew, locusts or grasshoppers;
when their enemies besiege them
in the land of their cities; whatever
plague or whatever [b]sickness
there is;
29 "whatever prayer, whatever
supplication is *made* by anyone, or
by all Your people Israel, when
each one knows his own burden
and his own grief, and spreads out
his hands to this temple:
30 "then hear from heaven Your
dwelling place, and forgive, and
give to everyone according to all
his ways, whose heart You know
(for You alone [a]know the [b]hearts
of the sons of men),
31 "that they may fear You, to
walk in Your ways as long as they
live in the land which You gave
to our fathers.
32 "Moreover, concerning a for-
eigner, [a]who is not of Your people
Israel, but has come from a far
country for the sake of Your great
name and Your mighty hand and
Your outstretched arm, when they
come and pray in this temple;
33 "then hear from heaven Your
dwelling place, and do according
to all for which the foreigner calls
to You, that all peoples of the earth

may know Your name and fear
You, as *do* Your people Israel, and
that they may know that [1]this tem-
ple which I have built is called by
Your name.
34 "When Your people go out to
battle against their enemies, wher-
ever You send them, and when
they pray to You toward this city
which You have chosen and the
temple which I have built for Your
name,
35 "then hear from heaven their
prayer and their supplication, and
maintain their cause.
36 "When they sin against You
(for *there is* [a]no one who does not
sin), and You become angry with
them and deliver them to the en-
emy, and they take them [b]captive
to a land far or near;
37 "*yet* when they [1]come to them-
selves in the land where they were
carried captive, and repent, and
make supplication to You in the
land of their captivity, saying, 'We
have sinned, we have done
wrong, and have committed wick-
edness';
38 "and *when* they return to You
with all their heart and with all
their soul in the land of their cap-
tivity, where they have been car-
ried captive, and pray toward their
land which You gave to their fa-
thers, the [a]city which You have
chosen, and toward the temple
which I have built for Your name:
39 "then hear from heaven Your
dwelling place their prayer and
their supplications, and maintain
their cause, and forgive Your
people who have sinned against
You.
40 "Now, my God, I pray, let Your
eyes be [a]open and *let* Your ears
be attentive to the prayer *made* in
this place.

41 "Now[a] therefore,
Arise, O LORD God, to Your
[b]resting place,
You and the ark of Your strength.
Let Your priests, O LORD God, be
clothed with salvation,
And let Your saints [c]rejoice in
goodness.

42 "O LORD God, do not turn away
the face of Your Anointed;
[a]Remember the mercies of Your
servant David."

33 [1]Lit. *Your name is called upon this house*

36 [a]Prov. 20:9; Eccl. 7:20; [Rom. 3:9, 19; 5:12; Gal. 3:10]; James 3:2; 1 John 1:8 [b]Deut. 28:63–68

37 [1]Lit. *bring back to their hearts*

38 [a]Dan. 6:10

40 [a]2 Chr. 6:20

41 [a]Ps. 132:8–10, 16 [b]1 Chr. 28:2 [c]Neh. 9:25

42 [a]2 Sam. 7:15; Ps. 89:49; 132:1, 8–10; Is. 55:3

CHAPTER 7

1 [a]1 Kin. 8:54 [b]Lev. 9:24; Judg. 6:21; 1 Kin. 18:38; 1 Chr. 21:26 [c]1 Kin. 8:10, 11 [1]Lit. *house*

2 [a]2 Chr. 5:14

3 [a]2 Chr. 5:13; Ps. 106:1; 136:1 [b]1 Chr. 16:41; 2 Chr. 20:21

4 [a]1 Kin. 8:62, 63

6 [a]1 Chr. 15:16 [b]2 Chr. 5:12 [1]Lit. *hand*

7 [a]1 Kin. 8:64–66; 9:3

8 [a]1 Kin. 8:65 [b]1 Kin. 4:21, 24; 2 Kin. 14:25 [c]Josh. 13:3 [1]The Shihor, 1 Chr. 13:5

9 [a]Lev. 23:36

10 [a]1 Kin. 8:66

Solomon Dedicates the Temple

7 When [a]Solomon had finished
praying, [b]fire came down from
heaven and consumed the burnt
offering and the sacrifices; and
[c]the glory of the LORD filled the
[1]temple.
2 [a]And the priests could not enter
the house of the LORD, because the
glory of the LORD had filled the
LORD's house.
3 When all the children of Israel
saw how the fire came down, and
the glory of the LORD on the tem-
ple, they bowed their faces to the
ground on the pavement, and wor-
shiped and praised the LORD, *say-
ing:*

[a]"For *He is* good,
[b]For His mercy *endures* forever."

4 [a]Then the king and all the peo-
ple offered sacrifices before the
LORD.
5 King Solomon offered a sacri-
fice of twenty-two thousand bulls
and one hundred and twenty thou-
sand sheep. So the king and all the
people dedicated the house of God.
6 [a]And the priests attended to
their services; the Levites also
with instruments of the music of
the LORD, which King David had
made to praise the LORD, saying,
"For His mercy *endures* forever,"
whenever David offered praise
by their [1]ministry. [b]The priests
sounded trumpets opposite them,
while all Israel stood.
7 Furthermore [a]Solomon conse-
crated the middle of the court that
was in front of the house of the
LORD; for there he offered burnt of-
ferings and the fat of the peace of-
ferings, because the bronze altar
which Solomon had made was not
able to receive the burnt offerings,
the grain offerings, and the fat.
8 [a]At that time Solomon kept the
feast seven days, and all Israel
with him, a very great assembly
[b]from the entrance of Hamath to
[c]the[1] Brook of Egypt.
9 And on the eighth day they
held a [a]sacred assembly, for they
observed the dedication of the al-
tar seven days, and the feast seven
days.
10 [a]On the twenty-third day of the

seventh month he sent the people
away to their tents, joyful and glad
of heart for the good that the LORD
had done for David, for Solomon,
and for His people Israel.
11 Thus [a]Solomon finished the
house of the LORD and the king's
house; and Solomon successfully
accomplished all that came into
his heart to make in the house of
the LORD and in his own house.

God's Second Appearance to Solomon

12 Then the LORD [a]appeared to
Solomon by night, and said to him:
"I have heard your prayer, [b]and
have chosen this [c]place for Myself
as a house of sacrifice.
13 [a]"When I shut up heaven and
there is no rain, or command the
locusts to devour the land, or send
pestilence among My people,
14 "if My people who are [a]called
by My name will [b]humble them-
selves, and pray and seek My face,
and turn from their wicked ways,
[c]then I will hear from heaven, and
will forgive their sin and heal their
land.
15 "Now [a]My eyes will be open
and My ears attentive to prayer
made in this place.
16 "For now [a]I have chosen and
[1]sanctified this house, that My
name may be there forever; and
[2]My eyes and [3]My heart will be
there perpetually.
17 [a]"As for you, if you walk before
Me as your father David walked,
and do according to all that I have
commanded you, and if you keep
My statutes and My judgments,
18 "then I will establish the throne
of your kingdom, as I covenanted
with David your father, saying,
[a]'You shall not fail *to have* a man
as ruler in Israel.'
19 [a]"But if you turn away and for-
sake My statutes and My com-
mandments which I have set be-
fore you, and go and serve other
gods, and worship them,
20 [a]"then I will uproot them from
My land which I have given them;
and this house which I have [1]sancti-
fied for My name I will cast out
of My sight, and will make it a
proverb and a [b]byword among all
peoples.
21 "And *as for* [a]this [1]house, which
[2]is exalted, everyone who passes

11 [a]1 Kin. 9:1
12 [a]1 Kin. 3:5; 11:9 [b]Deut. 12:5, 11 [c]2 Chr. 6:20
13 [a]Deut. 28:23, 24; 1 Kin. 17:1; 2 Chr. 6:26–28
14 [a]Deut. 28:10; [Is. 43:7] [b]2 Chr. 12:6, 7; [James 4:10] [c]2 Chr. 6:27, 30
15 [a]2 Chr. 6:20, 40
16 [a]1 Kin. 9:3; 2 Chr. 6:6 [1]*set apart* [2]My attention [3]My concern
17 [a]1 Kin. 9:4
18 [a]2 Sam. 7:12–16; 1 Kin. 2:4; 2 Chr. 6:16
19 [a]Lev. 26:14, 33; [Deut. 28:15, 36]
20 [a]Deut. 28:63–68; 2 Kin. 25:1–7 [b]Ps. 44:14 [1]*set apart*
21 [a]2 Kin. 25:9 [b]2 Chr. 29:8 [c][Deut. 29:24, 25; Jer. 22:8, 9] [1]Temple [2]Or *was*

CHAPTER 8

1 [a]1 Kin. 9:10–14 [b]1 Kin. 6:38—7:1
2 [1]Heb. *Huram.* 2 Chr. 2:3
4 [a]1 Kin. 9:17, 18 [b]1 Chr. 18:3, 9
5 [a]1 Chr. 7:24
6 [a]2 Chr. 7:11
7 [a]Gen. 15:18–21; 1 Kin. 9:20
9 [1]*slaves*
10 [a]1 Kin. 9:23
11 [a]1 Kin. 3:1; 7:8; 9:24; 11:1

by it will be [b]astonished and say,
[c]'Why has the LORD done thus to
this land and this house?'
22 "Then they will answer, 'Be-
cause they forsook the LORD God
of their fathers, who brought them
out of the land of Egypt, and em-
braced other gods, and worshiped
them and served them; therefore
He has brought all this calamity
on them.' "

Solomon's Additional Achievements

8 It [a]came to pass at the end of
[b]twenty years, when Solomon
had built the house of the LORD
and his own house,
2 that the cities which [1]Hiram
had given to Solomon, Solomon
built them; and he settled the chil-
dren of Israel there.
3 And Solomon went to Hamath
Zobah and seized it.
4 [a]He also built Tadmor in the
wilderness, and all the storage cit-
ies which he built in [b]Hamath.
5 He built Upper Beth Horon and
[a]Lower Beth Horon, fortified cities
with walls, gates, and bars,
6 also Baalath and all the storage
cities that Solomon had, and all
the chariot cities and the cities of
the cavalry, and all that Solomon
[a]desired to build in Jerusalem, in
Lebanon, and in all the land of his
dominion.
7 [a]All the people *who were* left
of the Hittites, Amorites, Periz-
zites, Hivites, and Jebusites, who
were not of Israel—
8 that is, their descendants who
were left in the land after them,
whom the children of Israel did not
destroy—from these Solomon
raised forced labor, as it is to this
day.
9 But Solomon did not make the
children of Israel [1]servants for his
work. Some *were* men of war, cap-
tains of his officers, captains of his
chariots, and his cavalry.
10 And others *were* chiefs of the
officials of King Solomon: [a]two
hundred and fifty, who ruled over
the people.
11 Now Solomon [a]brought the
daughter of Pharaoh up from the
City of David to the house he had
built for her, for he said, "My wife
shall not dwell in the house of Da-
vid king of Israel, because *the*

places to which the ark of the LORD
has come are holy."
12 Then Solomon offered burnt
offerings to the LORD on the altar
of the LORD which he had built be-
fore the vestibule,
13 according to the [a]daily rate, of-
fering according to the command-
ment of Moses, for the Sabbaths,
the New Moons, and the [b]three ap-
pointed yearly [c]feasts—the Feast
of Unleavened Bread, the Feast of
Weeks, and the Feast of Taber-
nacles.
14 And, according to the [1]order of
David his father, he appointed the
[a]divisions of the priests for their
service, [b]the Levites for their du-
ties (to praise and serve before the
priests) as the duty of each day re-
quired, and the [c]gatekeepers by
their divisions at each gate; for so
David the man of God had com-
manded.
15 They did not depart from the
command of the king to the priests
and Levites concerning any matter
or concerning the [a]treasuries.
16 Now all the work of Solomon
was well-ordered [1]from the day of
the foundation of the house of the
LORD until it was finished. So the
house of the LORD was completed.
17 Then Solomon went to [a]Ezion
Geber and [1]Elath on the seacoast,
in the land of Edom.
18 [a]And Hiram sent him ships by
the hand of his servants, and ser-
vants who knew the sea. They
went with the servants of Solomon
to [b]Ophir, and acquired four hun-
dred and fifty talents of gold from
there, and brought it to King Sol-
omon.

The Queen of Sheba's Praise of Solomon

9 Now [a]when the queen of Sheba
heard of the fame of Solomon,
she came to Jerusalem to test Sol-
omon with hard questions, *having*
a very great retinue, camels that
bore spices, gold in abundance,
and precious stones; and when she
came to Solomon, she spoke with
him about all that was in her heart.
2 So Solomon answered all her
questions; there was nothing so
difficult for Solomon that he could
not explain it to her.
3 And when the queen of Sheba
had seen the wisdom of Solomon,
the house that he had built,
4 the food on his table, the seat-
ing of his servants, the service of
his waiters and their apparel, his
[a]cupbearers and their apparel, and
his entryway by which he went up
to the house of the LORD, there was
no more spirit in her.
5 Then she said to the king: "*It
was* a true report which I heard
in my own land about your words
and your wisdom.
6 "However I did not believe
their words until I came and saw
with my own eyes; and indeed the
half of the greatness of your wis-
dom was not told me. You exceed
the fame of which I heard.
7 "Happy *are* your men and
happy *are* these your servants,
who stand continually before you
and hear your wisdom!
8 "Blessed be the LORD your God,
who delighted in you, setting you
on His throne *to be* king for the
LORD your God! Because your God
has [a]loved Israel, to establish them
forever, therefore He made you
king over them, to do justice and
righteousness."
9 And she gave the king one hun-
dred and twenty talents of gold,
spices in great abundance, and
precious stones; there never were
any spices such as those the queen
of Sheba gave to King Solomon.
10 Also, the servants of Hiram and
the servants of Solomon, [a]who
brought gold from Ophir, brought
[1]algum wood and precious stones.
11 And the king made walkways
of the [1]algum wood for the house
of the LORD and for the king's
house, also harps and stringed in-
struments for singers; and there
were none such *as these* seen be-
fore in the land of Judah.
12 Now King Solomon gave to the
queen of Sheba all she desired,
whatever she asked, *much more*
than she had brought to the king.
So she turned and went to her own
country, she and her servants.

Solomon's Great Wealth

13 [a]The weight of gold that came
to Solomon yearly was six hun-
dred and sixty-six talents of gold,
14 besides *what* the traveling
merchants and traders brought.

13 [a]Ex. 29:38–42; Num. 28:3, 9, 11, 26; 29:1 [b]Ex. 23:14–17; 34:22, 23; Deut. 16:16 [c]Lev. 23:1–44
14 [a]1 Chr. 24:3 [b]1 Chr. 25:1 [c]1 Chr. 9:17; 26:1 [1]*ordinance*
15 [a]1 Chr. 26:20–28
16 [1]So with LXX, Syr., Vg.; MT *as far as*
17 [a]1 Kin. 9:26; 2 Chr. 20:36 [1]Heb. *Eloth*, 2 Kin. 14:22
18 [a]1 Kin. 9:27; 2 Chr. 9:10, 13 [b]1 Chr. 29:4

CHAPTER 9

1 [a]1 Kin. 10:1; Ps. 72:10; [Matt. 12:42; Luke 11:31]
4 [a]Neh. 1:11
8 [a]Deut. 7:8; 2 Chr. 2:11; [Ps. 44:3]
10 [a]2 Chr. 8:18 [1]*almug*, 1 Kin. 10:11, 12
11 [1]*almug*, 1 Kin. 10:11, 12
13 [a]1 Kin. 10:14–29

And all the kings of Arabia and
governors of the country brought
gold and silver to Solomon.
15 And King Solomon made two
hundred large shields of ham-
mered gold; six hundred *shekels*
of hammered gold went into each
shield.
16 *He* also *made* three hundred
shields of hammered gold; [1]three
hundred *shekels* of gold went into
each shield. The king put them in
the [a]House of the Forest of Leba-
non.
17 Moreover the king made a
great throne of ivory, and overlaid
it with pure gold.
18 The throne *had* six steps, with
a footstool of gold, *which were* fas-
tened to the throne; there were
[1]armrests on either side of the
place of the seat, and two lions
stood beside the armrests.
19 Twelve lions stood there, one
on each side of the six steps; noth-
ing like *this* had been made for
any *other* kingdom.
20 All King Solomon's drinking
vessels *were* gold, and all the ves-
sels of the House of the Forest of
Lebanon *were* pure gold. Not *one*
was silver, for this was accounted
as nothing in the days of Solomon.
21 For the king's ships went to
[a]Tarshish with the servants of
[1]Hiram. Once every three years
the [2]merchant ships came, bring-
ing gold, silver, ivory, apes, and
[3]monkeys.
22 So King Solomon surpassed all
the kings of the earth in riches and
wisdom.
23 And all the kings of the earth
sought the presence of Solomon to
hear his wisdom, which God had
put in his heart.
24 Each man brought his present:
articles of silver and gold, gar-
ments, [a]armor, spices, horses, and
mules, at a set rate year by year.
25 Solomon [a]had four thousand
stalls for horses and chariots, and
twelve thousand horsemen whom
he stationed in the chariot cities
and with the king at Jerusalem.
26 [a]So he reigned over all the
kings [b]from [1]the River to the land
of the Philistines, as far as the bor-
der of Egypt.
27 [a]The king made silver *as com-*
mon in Jerusalem as stones, and
he made cedar trees [b]as abundant
as the sycamores which *are* in the
lowland.
28 [a]And they brought horses to
Solomon from Egypt and from all
lands.

Death of Solomon

29 [a]Now the rest of the acts of Sol-
omon, first and last, *are* they not
written in the book of Nathan the
prophet, in the prophecy of [b]Ahi-
jah the Shilonite, and in the vi-
sions of [c]Iddo the seer concerning
Jeroboam the son of Nebat?
30 [a]Solomon reigned in Jerusalem
over all Israel forty years.
31 Then Solomon [1]rested with his
fathers, and was buried in the City
of David his father. And Reho-
boam his son reigned in his place.

The Revolt Against Rehoboam

10 And [a]Rehoboam went to
Shechem, for all Israel had
gone to Shechem to make him
king.
2 So it happened, when Jero-
boam the son of Nebat heard *it* (he
was in Egypt, [a]where he had fled
from the presence of King Sol-
omon), that Jeroboam returned
from Egypt.
3 Then they sent for him and
called him. And Jeroboam and all
Israel came and spoke to Reho-
boam, saying,
4 "Your father made our yoke
heavy; now therefore, lighten the
burdensome service of your father
and his heavy yoke which he put
on us, and we will serve you."
5 So he said to them, "Come
back to me after three days." And
the people departed.
6 Then King Rehoboam con-
sulted the elders who stood before
his father Solomon while he still
lived, saying, "How do you advise
me to answer these people?"
7 And they spoke to him, saying,
"If you are kind to these people,
and please them, and speak good
words to them, they will be your
servants forever."
8 [a]But he rejected the advice
which the elders had given him,
and consulted the young men who
had grown up with him, who stood
before him.
9 And he said to them, "What

16 [a]1 Kin. 7:2 [1]*three minas.* 1 Kin. 10:17
18 [1]Lit. *hands*
21 [a]2 Chr. 20:36, 37; Ps. 72:10 [1]Heb. *Huram;* cf. 1 Kin. 10:22 [2]Lit. *ships of Tarshish,* deep-sea vessels [3]Or *peacocks*
24 [a]1 Kin. 20:11
25 [a]Deut. 17:16; 1 Kin. 4:26; 10:26; 2 Chr. 1:14; Is. 2:7
26 [a]1 Kin. 4:21 [b]Gen. 15:18; Ps. 72:8 [1]The Euphrates
27 [a]1 Kin. 10:27 [b]2 Chr. 1:15–17
28 [a]1 Kin. 10:28; 2 Chr. 1:16
29 [a]1 Kin. 11:41 [b]1 Kin. 11:29 [c]2 Chr. 12:15; 13:22
30 [a]1 Kin. 4:21; 11:42, 43; 1 Chr. 29:28
31 [1]Died and joined his ancestors

CHAPTER 10

1 [a]1 Kin. 12:1–20
2 [a]1 Kin. 11:40
8 [a]1 Kin. 12:8–11

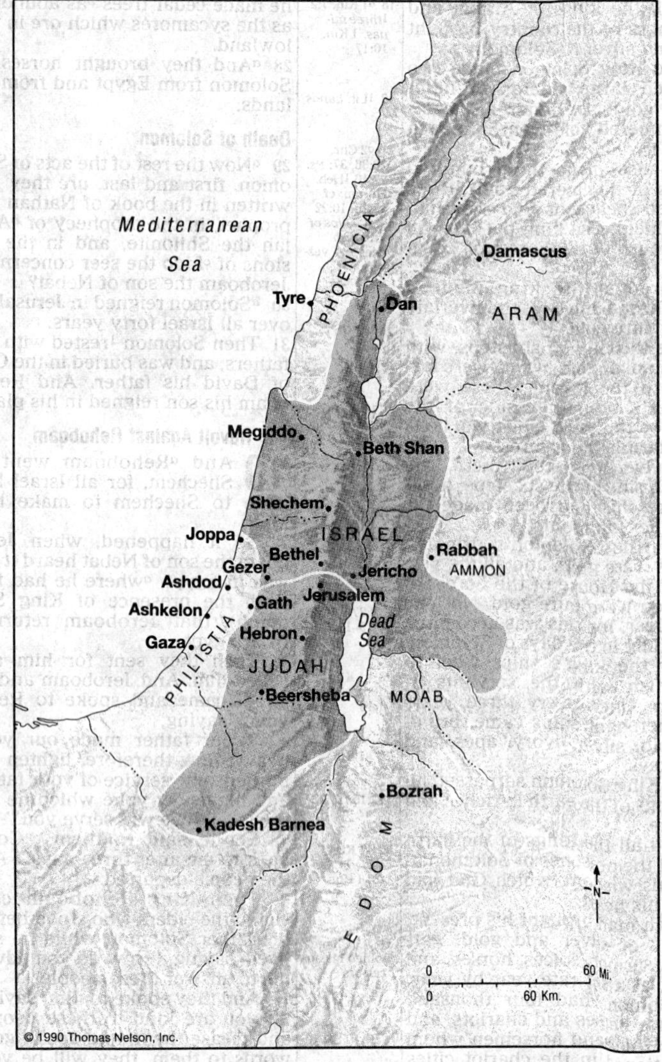

A Kingdom Divided. The glory of the united kingdom began to fade at the death of Solomon when his son Rehoboam spoke harshly to Jeroboam and those following him. Their response: "Every man to your tents, O Israel! Now, see to your own house, O David!" Rehoboam reigned over Judah to the south, and Jeroboam became king of Israel to the north.

advice do you give? How should
we answer this people who have
spoken to me, saying, 'Lighten the
yoke which your father put on
us'?"
10 Then the young men who had
grown up with him spoke to him,
saying, "Thus you should speak to
the people who have spoken to
you, saying, 'Your father made our
yoke heavy, but you make *it*
lighter on us'—thus you shall say
to them: 'My little *finger* shall be
thicker than my father's waist!
11 'And now, whereas my father
put a heavy yoke on you, I will add
to your yoke; my father chastised
you with whips, but I *will chastise*
you with [1]scourges!' "
12 So [a]Jeroboam and all the peo-
ple came to Rehoboam on the third
day, as the king had directed, say-
ing, "Come back to me the third
day."
13 Then the king answered them
roughly. King Rehoboam rejected
the advice of the elders,
14 and he spoke to them accord-
ing to the advice of the young men,
saying, [1]"My father made your
yoke heavy, but I will add to it;
my father chastised you with
whips, but I *will chastise you* with
[2]scourges!"
15 So the king did not listen to the
people; [a]for the turn *of events* was
from God, that the LORD might ful-
fill His [b]word, which He had spo-
ken by the hand of Ahijah the Shi-
lonite to Jeroboam the son of
Nebat.
16 Now when all Israel *saw* that
the king did not listen to them, the
people answered the king, saying:

"What share have we in David?
We have no inheritance in the
son of Jesse.
Every man to your tents, O Israel!
Now see to your own house,
O David!"

So all Israel departed to their tents.
17 But Rehoboam reigned over
the children of Israel who dwelt in
the cities of Judah.
18 Then King Rehoboam sent Ha-
doram, who *was* in charge of reve-
nue; but the children of Israel
stoned him with stones, and he
died. Therefore King Rehoboam
mounted *his* chariot in haste to flee
to Jerusalem.
19 [a]So Israel has been in rebellion
against the house of David to this
day.

11 Now [a]when Rehoboam
came to Jerusalem, he as-
sembled from the house of Judah
and Benjamin one hundred and
eighty thousand chosen *men* who
were warriors, to fight against Is-
rael, that he might restore the
kingdom to Rehoboam.
2 But the word of the LORD came
[a]to Shemaiah the man of God, say-
ing,
3 "Speak to Rehoboam the son
of Solomon, king of Judah, and to
all Israel in Judah and Benjamin,
saying,
4 'Thus says the LORD: "You
shall not go up or fight against
your brethren! Let every man re-
turn to his house, for this thing is
from Me." ' " Therefore they
obeyed the words of the LORD,
and turned back from attacking
Jeroboam.

Rehoboam Fortifies the Cities

5 So Rehoboam dwelt in Jerusa-
lem, and built cities for defense in
Judah.
6 And he built Bethlehem, Etam,
Tekoa,
7 Beth Zur, Sochoh, Adullam,
8 Gath, Mareshah, Ziph,
9 Adoraim, Lachish, Azekah,
10 Zorah, Aijalon, and Hebron,
which are in Judah and Benjamin,
fortified cities.
11 And he fortified the strong-
holds, and put captains in them,
and stores of food, oil, and wine.
12 Also in every city *he put*
shields and spears, and made them
very strong, having Judah and
Benjamin on his side.

Priests and Levites Move to Judah

13 And from all their territories
the priests and the Levites who
were in all Israel took their stand
with him.
14 For the Levites left [a]their
common-lands and their posses-
sions and came to Judah and Jeru-
salem, for [b]Jeroboam and his sons
had rejected them from serving as
priests to the LORD.
15 [a]Then he appointed for himself

11 [1]Scourges with points or barbs, lit. *scorpions*
12 [a]1 Kin. 12:12–14
14 [1]So with many Heb. mss., LXX, Syr., Vg. (cf. v. 10; 1 Kin. 12:14); MT *I* [2]Lit. *scorpions*
15 [a]Judg. 14:4; 1 Chr. 5:22; 2 Chr. 11:4; 22:7 [b]1 Kin. 11:29–39
19 [a]1 Kin. 12:19

CHAPTER 11
1 [a]1 Kin. 12:21–24
2 [a]1 Chr. 12:5; 2 Chr. 12:15
14 [a]Num. 35:2–5 [b]1 Kin. 12:28–33; 2 Chr. 13:9
15 [a]1 Kin. 12:31; 13:33; 14:9; [Hos. 13:2]

priests for the [1]high places, for
[b]the demons, and [c]the calf idols
which he had made.
16 [a]And [1]after *the Levites left,*
those from all the tribes of Israel,
such as set their heart to seek the
LORD God of Israel, [b]came to Jeru-
salem to sacrifice to the LORD God
of their fathers.
17 So they [a]strengthened the king-
dom of Judah, and made Reho-
boam the son of Solomon strong
for three years, because they
walked in the way of David and
Solomon for three years.

The Family of Rehoboam

18 Then Rehoboam took for him-
self as wife Mahalath the daughter
of Jerimoth the son of David, *and*
of Abihail the daughter of [a]Eliah
the son of Jesse.
19 And she bore him children:
Jeush, Shamariah, and Zaham.
20 After her he took [a]Maachah the
[1]granddaughter of [b]Absalom; and
she bore him [c]Abijah, Attai, Ziza,
and Shelomith.
21 Now Rehoboam loved Maa-
chah the granddaughter of Absa-
lom more than all his [a]wives and
his concubines; for he took eigh-
teen wives and sixty concubines,
and begot twenty-eight sons and
sixty daughters.
22 And Rehoboam [a]appointed
[b]Abijah the son of Maachah as
chief, *to be* leader among his
brothers; for he *intended* to make
him king.
23 He dealt wisely, and [1]dispersed
some of his sons throughout all the
territories of Judah and Benjamin,
to every [a]fortified city; and he gave
them provisions in abundance. He
also sought many wives *for them.*

Egypt Attacks Judah

12 Now [a]it came to pass, when
Rehoboam had established
the kingdom and had strengthened
himself, that [b]he forsook the law
of the LORD, and all Israel along
with him.
2 [a]And it happened in the fifth
year of King Rehoboam *that* Shi-
shak king of Egypt came up against
Jerusalem, because they had
transgressed against the LORD,
3 with twelve hundred chariots,
sixty thousand horsemen, and
people without number who came
with him out of Egypt—[a]the Lubim
and the Sukkiim and the Ethi-
opians.
4 And he took the fortified cities
of Judah and came to Jerusalem.
5 Then [a]Shemaiah the prophet
came to Rehoboam and the leaders
of Judah, who were gathered to-
gether in Jerusalem because of
Shishak, and said to them, "Thus
says the LORD: 'You have forsaken
Me, and therefore I also have left
you in the hand of Shishak.' "
6 So the leaders of Israel and the
king [a]humbled themselves; and
they said, [b]"The LORD *is* righ-
teous."
7 Now when the LORD saw that
they humbled themselves, [a]the
word of the LORD came to Shema-
iah, saying, "They have humbled
themselves; *therefore* I will not de-
stroy them, but I will grant them
some deliverance. My wrath shall
not be poured out on Jerusalem by
the hand of Shishak.
8 "Nevertheless [a]they will be his
servants, that they may distin-
guish [b]My service from the service
of the kingdoms of the nations."
9 [a]So Shishak king of Egypt
came up against Jerusalem, and
took away the treasures of the
house of the LORD and the trea-
sures of the king's house; he took
everything. He also carried away
the gold shields which Solomon
had [b]made.
10 Then King Rehoboam made
bronze shields in their place, and
committed *them* [a]to the hands of
the captains of the guard, who
guarded the doorway of the king's
house.
11 And whenever the king entered
the house of the LORD, the guard
would go and bring them out; then
they would take them back into
the guardroom.
12 When he humbled himself, the
wrath of the LORD turned from
him, so as not to destroy *him* com-
pletely; and things also went well
in Judah.

The End of Rehoboam's Reign

13 Thus King Rehoboam strength-
ened himself in Jerusalem and
reigned. Now [a]Rehoboam *was*

15 [b][Lev. 17:7; 1 Cor. 10:20] [c]1 Kin. 12:28 [1]Places for pagan worship
16 [a]2 Chr. 14:7 [b]2 Chr. 15:9, 10; 30:11, 18 [1]Lit. *after them*
17 [a]2 Chr. 12:1, 13
18 [a]1 Sam. 16:6
20 [a]2 Chr. 13:2 [b]1 Kin. 15:2 [c]1 Kin. 14:31 [1]Lit. *daughter,* but in the broader sense of granddaughter
21 [a]Deut. 17:17
22 [a]Deut. 21:15–17 [b]2 Chr. 13:1
23 [a]2 Chr. 11:5 [1]*distributed*

CHAPTER 12

1 [a]2 Chr. 11:17 [b]1 Kin. 14:22–24
2 [a]1 Kin. 11:40; 14:25
3 [a]2 Chr. 16:8; Nah. 3:9
5 [a]2 Chr. 11:2
6 [a][James 4:10] [b]Ex. 9:27; [Dan. 9:14]
7 [a]1 Kin. 21:28, 29
8 [a]Is. 26:13 [b][Deut. 28:47, 48]
9 [a]1 Kin. 14:25, 26 [b]1 Kin. 10:16, 17; 2 Chr. 9:15, 16
10 [a]1 Kin. 14:27
13 [a]1 Kin. 14:21

forty-one years old when he be-
came king; and he reigned seven-
teen years in Jerusalem, [b]the city
which the LORD had chosen out of
all the tribes of Israel, to put His
name there. His mother's name
was Naamah, an [c]Ammonitess.
14 And he did evil, because he did
not prepare his heart to seek the
LORD.
15 The acts of Rehoboam, first
and last, *are* they not written in the
book of Shemaiah the prophet,
[a]and of Iddo the seer concerning
genealogies? [b]And *there were*
wars between Rehoboam and Jer-
oboam all their days.
16 So Rehoboam [1]rested with his
fathers, and was buried in the City
of David. Then [a]Abijah[2] his son
reigned in his place.

Abijah Reigns in Judah

13 In [a]the eighteenth year of
King Jeroboam, Abijah be-
came king over [b]Judah.
2 He reigned three years in Jeru-
salem. His mother's name *was*
[1]Michaiah the daughter of Uriel of
Gibeah. And there was war be-
tween Abijah and Jeroboam.
3 Abijah set the battle in order
with an army of valiant warriors,
four hundred thousand choice
men. Jeroboam also drew up in
battle formation against him with
eight hundred thousand choice
men, mighty men of valor.
4 Then Abijah stood on Mount
[a]Zemaraim, which *is* in the moun-
tains of Ephraim, and said, "Hear
me, Jeroboam and all Israel:
5 "Should you not know that the
LORD God of Israel [a]gave the do-
minion over Israel to David for-
ever, to him and his sons, [b]by a
covenant of salt?
6 "Yet Jeroboam the son of Ne-
bat, the servant of Solomon the
son of David, rose up and [a]rebelled
against his lord.
7 "Then [a]worthless rogues gath-
ered to him, and strengthened
themselves against Rehoboam the
son of Solomon, when Rehoboam
was [b]young and inexperienced
and could not withstand them.
8 "And now you think to with-
stand the kingdom of the LORD,
which is in the hand of the sons
of David; and you *are* a great mul-
titude, and with you are the gold
calves which Jeroboam [a]made for
you as gods.
9 [a]"Have you not cast out the
priests of the LORD, the sons of
Aaron, and the Levites, and made
for yourselves priests, like the peo-
ples of *other* lands, [b]so that who-
ever comes to consecrate himself
with a young bull and seven rams
may be a priest of [c]*things that are*
not gods?
10 "But as for us, the LORD *is* our
[a]God, and we have not forsaken
Him; and the priests who minister
to the LORD *are* the sons of Aaron,
and the Levites *attend* to *their* du-
ties.
11 [a]"And they burn to the LORD
every morning and every evening
burnt sacrifices and sweet incense;
they also *set* the [b]showbread *in or-
der on* the pure *gold* table, and the
lampstand of gold with its lamps
[c]to burn every evening; for we
keep the command of the LORD our
God, but you have forsaken Him.
12 "Now look, God Himself is
with us as *our* [a]head, [b]and His
priests with sounding trumpets to
sound the alarm against you. O
children of Israel, do not fight
against the LORD God of your fa-
thers, for you shall not prosper!"
13 But Jeroboam caused an am-
bush to go around behind them;
so they were in front of Judah, and
the ambush *was* behind them.
14 And when Judah looked
around, to their surprise the battle
line *was* at both front and rear;
and they [a]cried out to the LORD,
and the priests sounded the trum-
pets.
15 Then the men of Judah gave a
shout; and as the men of Judah
shouted, it happened that God
[a]struck Jeroboam and all Israel
before Abijah and Judah.
16 And the children of Israel fled
before Judah, and God delivered
them into their hand.
17 Then Abijah and his people
struck them with a great slaughter;
so five hundred thousand choice
men of Israel fell slain.
18 Thus the children of Israel
were subdued at that time; and the
children of Judah prevailed, [a]be-
cause they relied on the LORD God
of their fathers.

13 [b]2 Chr. 6:6 [c]1 Kin. 11:1, 5
15 [a]2 Chr. 9:29; 13:22 [b]1 Kin. 14:30
16 [a]2 Chr. 11:20–22 [1]Died and joined his ancestors [2]*Abijam*, 1 Kin. 14:31

CHAPTER 13

1 [a]1 Kin. 15:1 [b]1 Kin. 12:17
2 [1]*Maachah*, 1 Kin. 15:2; 2 Chr. 11:20, 21
4 [a]Josh. 18:22
5 [a]2 Sam. 7:8–16 [b]Lev. 2:13; Num. 18:19
6 [a]1 Kin. 11:28; 12:20
7 [a]Judg. 9:4 [b]2 Chr. 12:13
8 [a]1 Kin. 12:28; 14:9; 2 Chr. 11:15; [Hos. 8:4–6]
9 [a]2 Chr. 11:13–15 [b]Ex. 29:29–33 [c]Jer. 2:11; 5:7
10 [a]Josh. 24:15
11 [a]Ex. 29:38; 2 Chr. 2:4 [b]Ex. 25:30; Lev. 24:5–9 [c]Ex. 27:20, 21; Lev. 24:2, 3
12 [a]Josh. 5:13–15; [Heb. 2:10] [b][Num. 10:8–10]
14 [a]Josh. 24:7; 2 Chr. 6:34, 35; 14:11
15 [a]1 Kin. 14:14; 2 Chr. 14:12
18 [a]1 Chr. 5:20; 2 Chr. 14:11; [Ps. 22:5]

19 And Abijah pursued Jeroboam and took cities from him: Bethel with its villages, Jeshanah with its villages, and [a]Ephrain[1] with its villages.

20 So Jeroboam did not recover strength again in the days of Abijah; and the LORD [a]struck him, and [b]he died.

21 But Abijah grew mighty, married fourteen wives, and begot twenty-two sons and sixteen daughters.

22 Now the rest of the acts of Abijah, his ways, and his sayings *are* written in [a]the [1]annals of the prophet Iddo.

14 So Abijah rested with his fathers, and they buried him in the City of David. Then [a]Asa his son reigned in his place. In his days the land was quiet for ten years.

Asa Reigns in Judah

2 Asa did *what was* good and right in the eyes of the LORD his God,

3 for he removed the altars of the foreign *gods* and [a]the [1]high places, and [b]broke down the *sacred* pillars [c]and cut down the wooden images.

4 He commanded Judah to [a]seek the LORD God of their fathers, and to observe the law and the commandment.

5 He also removed the [1]high places and the incense altars from all the cities of Judah, and the kingdom was quiet under him.

6 And he built fortified cities in Judah, for the land had rest; he had no war in those years, because the LORD had given him [a]rest.

7 Therefore he said to Judah, "Let us build these cities and make walls around *them,* and towers, gates, and bars, *while* the land *is* yet before us, because we have sought the LORD our God; we have sought *Him,* and He has given us rest on every side." So they built and prospered.

8 And Asa had an army of three hundred thousand from Judah who carried [1]shields and spears, and from Benjamin two hundred and eighty thousand men who carried shields and drew [a]bows; all these *were* mighty men of [b]valor.

9 [a]Then Zerah the Ethiopian

19 [a]Josh. 15:9 [1]Or *Ephron*

20 [a]1 Sam. 2:6; 25:38; Acts 12:23 [b]1 Kin. 14:20

22 [a]2 Chr. 9:29 [1]Or *commentary,* Heb. *midrash*

CHAPTER 14

1 [a]1 Kin. 15:8

3 [a]1 Kin. 15:14; 2 Chr. 15:17 [b][Ex. 34:13] [c]1 Kin. 11:7 [1]Places for pagan worship

4 [a][2 Chr. 7:14]

5 [1]Places for pagan worship

6 [a]2 Chr. 15:15

8 [a]1 Chr. 12:2 [b]2 Chr. 13:3 [1]*large shields*

9 [a]2 Chr. 12:2, 3; 16:8 [b]Josh. 15:44

11 [a]Ex. 14:10; 2 Chr. 13:14; [Ps. 22:5] [b][1 Sam. 14:6] [c]1 Sam. 17:45; [Prov. 18:10]

12 [a]2 Chr. 13:15

13 [a]Gen. 10:19; 20:1 [1]*plunder*

14 [a]Gen. 35:5; Deut. 11:25; Josh. 2:9; 2 Chr. 17:10 [1]*plunder*

15 [1]Lit. *struck*

CHAPTER 15

1 [a]Num. 24:2; Judg. 3:10; 2 Chr. 20:14; 24:20

2 [a][James 4:8] [b][1 Chr. 28:9]; 2 Chr. 14:4; 33:12, 13; [Jer. 29:13; Matt. 7:7] [c]2 Chr. 24:20 [1]Lit. *before*

3 [a]Hos. 3:4 [b]2 Kin. 12:2 [c]Lev. 10:11; 2 Chr. 17:8, 9

4 [a][Deut. 4:29]

came out against them with an army of a million men and three hundred chariots, and he came to [b]Mareshah.

10 So Asa went out against him, and they set the troops in battle array in the Valley of Zephathah at Mareshah.

11 And Asa [a]cried out to the LORD his God, and said, "LORD, *it is* [b]nothing for You to help, whether with many or with those who have no power; help us, O LORD our God, for we rest on You, and [c]in Your name we go against this multitude. O LORD, You *are* our God; do not let man prevail against You!"

12 So the LORD [a]struck the Ethiopians before Asa and Judah, and the Ethiopians fled.

13 And Asa and the people who *were* with him pursued them to [a]Gerar. So the Ethiopians were overthrown, and they could not recover, for they were broken before the LORD and His army. And they carried away very much [1]spoil.

14 Then they defeated all the cities around Gerar, for [a]the fear of the LORD came upon them; and they plundered all the cities, for there was exceedingly much [1]spoil in them.

15 They also [1]attacked the livestock enclosures, and carried off sheep and camels in abundance, and returned to Jerusalem.

The Reforms of Asa

15 Now [a]the Spirit of God came upon Azariah the son of Oded.

2 And he went out [1]to meet Asa, and said to him: "Hear me, Asa, and all Judah and Benjamin. [a]The LORD *is* with you while you are with Him. [b]If you seek Him, He will be found by you; but [c]if you forsake Him, He will forsake you.

3 [a]"For a long time Israel *has been* without the true God, without a [b]teaching priest, and without [c]law;

4 "but [a]when in their trouble they turned to the LORD God of Israel, and sought Him, He was found by them.

5 "And in those times *there was* no peace to the one who went out, nor to the one who came in, but

great turmoil *was* on all the inhabitants of the lands.

6 [a]"So nation was [1]destroyed by nation, and city by city, for God troubled them with every adversity.

7 "But you, be strong and do not let your hands be weak, for your work shall be rewarded!"

8 And when Asa heard these words and the prophecy of [1]Oded the prophet, he took courage, and removed the abominable idols from all the land of Judah and Benjamin and from the cities [a]which he had taken in the mountains of Ephraim; and he restored the altar of the LORD that *was* before the vestibule of the LORD.

9 Then he gathered all Judah and Benjamin, and [a]those who dwelt with them from Ephraim, Manasseh, and Simeon, for they came over to him in great numbers from Israel when they saw that the LORD his God was with him.

10 So they gathered together at Jerusalem in the third month, in the fifteenth year of the reign of Asa.

11 [a]And they offered to the LORD [1]at that time seven hundred bulls and seven thousand sheep from the [2]spoil they had brought.

12 Then they [a]entered into a covenant to seek the LORD God of their fathers with all their heart and with all their soul;

13 [a]and whoever would not seek the LORD God of Israel [b]was to be put to death, whether small or great, whether man or woman.

14 Then they took an oath before the LORD with a loud voice, with shouting and trumpets and rams' horns.

15 And all Judah rejoiced at the oath, for they had sworn with all their heart and [a]sought Him with all their soul; and He was found by them, and the LORD gave them [b]rest all around.

16 Also he removed [a]Maachah, the [1]mother of Asa the king, from *being* queen mother, because she had made an obscene image of [2]Asherah; and Asa cut down her obscene image, then crushed and burned *it* by the Brook Kidron.

17 But [a]the [1]high places were not removed from Israel. Nevertheless the heart of Asa was loyal all his days.

18 He also brought into the house of God the things that his father had dedicated and that he himself had dedicated: silver and gold and utensils.

19 And there was no war until the thirty-fifth year of the reign of Asa.

Asa's Treaty with Syria

16 In the thirty-sixth year of the reign of Asa, [a]Baasha king of Israel came up against Judah and built Ramah, [b]that he might let none go out or come in to Asa king of Judah.

2 Then Asa brought silver and gold from the treasuries of the house of the LORD and of the king's house, and sent to Ben-Hadad king of Syria, who dwelt in Damascus, saying,

3 "*Let there be* a treaty between you and me, as there was between my father and your father. See, I have sent you silver and gold; come, break your treaty with Baasha king of Israel, so that he will withdraw from me."

4 So Ben-Hadad heeded King Asa, and sent the captains of his armies against the cities of Israel. They attacked Ijon, Dan, Abel Maim, and all the storage cities of Naphtali.

5 Now it happened, when Baasha heard *it*, that he stopped building Ramah and ceased his work.

6 Then King Asa took all Judah, and they carried away the stones and timber of Ramah, which Baasha had used for building; and with them he built Geba and Mizpah.

Hanani's Message to Asa

7 And at that time [a]Hanani the seer came to Asa king of Judah, and said to him: [b]"Because you have relied on the king of Syria, and have not relied on the LORD your God, therefore the army of the king of Syria has escaped from your hand.

8 "Were [a]the Ethiopians and [b]the Lubim not a huge army with very many chariots and horsemen? Yet, because you relied on the LORD, He delivered them into your [c]hand.

9 [a]"For the eyes of the LORD run

6 [a]Matt. 24:7 [1]Lit. *beaten in pieces*
8 [a]2 Chr. 13:19 [1]So with MT, LXX; Syr., Vg. *Azariah the son of Oded* (cf. v. 1)
9 [a]2 Chr. 11:16
11 [a]2 Chr. 14:13–15 [1]Lit. *in that day* [2]*plunder*
12 [a]2 Kin. 23:3; 2 Chr. 23:16; 34:31; Neh. 10:29
13 [a]Ex. 22:20 [b]Deut. 13:5–15
15 [a]2 Chr. 15:2 [b]2 Chr. 14:7
16 [a]1 Kin. 15:2, 10, 13 [1]Or *grandmother* [2]A Canaanite deity
17 [a]1 Kin. 15:14; 2 Chr. 14:3, 5 [1]Places for pagan worship

CHAPTER 16

1 [a]1 Kin. 15:17–22 [b]2 Chr. 15:9
7 [a]1 Kin. 16:1; 2 Chr. 19:2 [b]2 Chr. 32:8–10; Ps. 118:9; [Is. 31:1; Jer. 17:5]
8 [a]2 Chr. 14:9 [b]2 Chr. 12:3 [c]2 Chr. 13:16, 18
9 [a]Job 34:21; [Prov. 5:21; 15:3; Jer. 16:17; 32:19]; Zech. 4:10

to and fro throughout the whole
earth, to show Himself strong on
behalf of *those* whose heart *is*
loyal to Him. In this [b]you have
done foolishly; therefore from now
on [c]you shall have wars."
10 Then Asa was angry with the
seer, and [a]put him in prison, for
he was enraged at him because of
this. And Asa oppressed *some* of
the people at that time.

Illness and Death of Asa

11 [a]Note that the acts of Asa, first
and last, are indeed written in the
book of the kings of Judah and Is-
rael.
12 And in the thirty-ninth year of
his reign, Asa became diseased in
his feet, and his malady was se-
vere; yet in his disease he [a]did not
seek the LORD, but the physicians.
13 [a]So Asa [1]rested with his fa-
thers; he died in the forty-first year
of his reign.
14 They buried him in his own
tomb, which he had [1]made for
himself in the City of David; and
they laid him in the bed which was
filled [a]with spices and various in-
gredients prepared in a mixture of
ointments. They made [b]a very
great burning for him.

Jehoshaphat Reigns in Judah

17 Then [a]Jehoshaphat his son
reigned in his place, and
strengthened himself against Is-
rael.
2 And he placed troops in all the
fortified cities of Judah, and set
garrisons in the land of [a]Judah and
in the cities of Ephraim [b]which
Asa his father had taken.
3 Now the LORD was with Jehosh-
aphat, because he walked in the
former ways of his father David;
he did not seek the Baals,
4 but sought [1]the God of his fa-
ther, and walked in His command-
ments and not according to [a]the
acts of Israel.
5 Therefore the LORD established
the kingdom in his hand; and all
Judah [a]gave presents to Jehosha-
phat, [b]and he had riches and honor
in abundance.
6 And his heart took delight in
the ways of the LORD; moreover
[a]he removed the [1]high places and
wooden images from Judah.
7 Also in the third year of his
reign he sent his leaders, Ben-Hail,
Obadiah, Zechariah, Nethanel,
and Michaiah, [a]to teach in the cit-
ies of Judah.
8 And with them *he sent* Levites:
Shemaiah, Nethaniah, Zebadiah,
Asahel, Shemiramoth, Jehona-
than, Adonijah, Tobijah, and Tob-
adonijah—the Levites; and with
them Elishama and Jehoram, the
priests.
9 [a]So they taught in Judah, and
had the Book of the Law of the
LORD with them; they went
throughout all the cities of Judah
and taught the people.
10 And [a]the fear of the LORD fell
on all the kingdoms of the lands
that *were* around Judah, so that
they did not make war against Je-
hoshaphat.
11 Also *some* of the Philistines
[a]brought Jehoshaphat presents
and silver as tribute; and the Ara-
bians brought him flocks, seven
thousand seven hundred rams and
seven thousand seven hundred
male goats.
12 So Jehoshaphat became in-
creasingly powerful, and he built
fortresses and storage cities in Ju-
dah.
13 He had much property in the
cities of Judah; and the men of
war, mighty men of valor, *were* in
Jerusalem.
14 These *are* their numbers, ac-
cording to their fathers' houses. Of
Judah, the captains of thousands:
Adnah the captain, and with him
three hundred thousand mighty
men of valor;
15 and next to him *was* Jeho-
hanan the captain, and with
him two hundred and eighty thou-
sand;
16 and next to him *was* Amasiah
the son of Zichri, [a]who willingly
offered himself to the LORD, and
with him two hundred thousand
mighty men of valor.
17 Of Benjamin: Eliada a mighty
man of valor, and with him two
hundred thousand men armed
with bow and shield;
18 and next to him *was* Jehoza-
bad, and with him one hundred
and eighty thousand prepared for
war.
19 These served the king, besides

9 [b]1 Sam. 13:13 [c]1 Kin. 15:32
10 [a]2 Chr. 18:26; Jer. 20:2; Matt. 14:3
11 [a]1 Kin. 15:23, 24; 2 Chr. 14:2
12 [a][Jer. 17:5]
13 [a]1 Kin. 15:24 [1]Died and joined his ancestors
14 [a]Gen. 50:2; Mark 16:1; John 19:39, 40 [b]2 Chr. 21:19; Jer. 34:5 [1]Lit. *dug*

CHAPTER 17

1 [a]1 Kin. 15:24; 2 Chr. 20:31
2 [a]2 Chr. 11:5 [b]2 Chr. 15:8
4 [a]1 Kin. 12:28 [1]LXX *the* LORD *God*
5 [a]1 Sam. 10:27; 1 Kin. 10:25 [b]2 Chr. 18:1
6 [a]1 Kin. 22:43; 2 Chr. 15:17; 19:3; 20:33 [1]Places for pagan worship
7 [a]2 Chr. 15:3; 35:3
9 [a]Deut. 6:4–9; 2 Chr. 35:3; Neh. 8:3, 7
10 [a]Gen. 35:5; 2 Chr. 14:14
11 [a]2 Sam. 8:2; 2 Chr. 9:14; 26:8
16 [a]Judg. 5:2, 9; 1 Chr. 29:9

[a]those the king put in the fortified
cities throughout all Judah.

Micaiah Warns Ahab

18 Jehoshaphat [a]had riches
and honor in abundance;
and by marriage he [b]allied himself
with [c]Ahab.
2 [a]After some years he went
down to *visit* Ahab in Samaria;
and Ahab killed sheep and oxen
in abundance for him and the peo-
ple who were with him, and per-
suaded him to go up *with him* to
Ramoth Gilead.
3 So Ahab king of Israel said to
Jehoshaphat king of Judah, "Will
you go with me *against* Ramoth
Gilead?" And he answered him, "I
am as you *are*, and my people as
your people; *we will be* with you
in the war."
4 Also Jehoshaphat said to the
king of Israel, [a]"Please inquire for
the word of the LORD today."
5 Then the king of Israel gath-
ered the prophets together, four
hundred men, and said to them,
"Shall we go to war against Ra-
moth Gilead, or shall I refrain?"
So they said, "Go up, for God will
deliver it into the king's hand."
6 But Jehoshaphat said, "*Is there*
not still a prophet of the LORD here,
that we may inquire of [a]Him?"[1]
7 So the king of Israel said to Je-
hoshaphat, "*There is* still one man
by whom we may inquire of the
LORD; but I hate him, because he
never prophesies good concerning
me, but always evil. He *is* Micaiah
the son of Imla." And Jehoshaphat
said, "Let not the king say such
things!"
8 Then the king of Israel called
one *of his* officers and said, "Bring
Micaiah the son of Imla quickly!"
9 The king of Israel and Jehosh-
aphat king of Judah, clothed in
their robes, sat each on his throne;
and they sat at a threshing floor
at the entrance of the gate of Sa-
maria; and all the prophets proph-
esied before them.
10 Now Zedekiah the son of Che-
naanah had made [a]horns of iron
for himself; and he said, "Thus
says the LORD: 'With these you
shall gore the Syrians until they
are destroyed.'"
11 And all the prophets prophe-
sied so, saying, "Go up to Ramoth
Gilead and prosper, for the LORD
will deliver *it* into the king's
hand."
12 Then the messenger who had
gone to call Micaiah spoke to him,
saying, "Now listen, the words of
the prophets with one accord en-
courage the king. Therefore please
let your word be like *the word
of* one of them, and speak en-
couragement."
13 And Micaiah said, "*As* the
LORD lives, [a]whatever my God
says, that I will speak."
14 Then he came to the king; and
the king said to him, "Micaiah,
shall we go to war against Ramoth
Gilead, or shall I refrain?" And he
said, "Go and prosper, and they
shall be delivered into your hand!"
15 So the king said to him, "How
many times shall I make you
swear that you tell me nothing but
the truth in the name of the LORD?"
16 Then he said, "I saw all Israel
[a]scattered on the mountains, as
sheep that have no [b]shepherd. And
the LORD said, 'These have no mas-
ter. Let each return to his house
in peace.'"
17 And the king of Israel said to
Jehoshaphat, "Did I not tell you he
would not prophesy good concern-
ing me, but evil?"
18 Then *Micaiah* said, "Therefore
hear the word of the LORD: I saw
the LORD sitting on His [a]throne,
and all the host of heaven standing
on His right hand and His left.
19 "And the LORD said, 'Who will
persuade Ahab king of Israel to go
up, that he may fall at Ramoth
Gilead?' So one spoke in this
manner, and another spoke in
that manner.
20 "Then a [a]spirit came forward
and stood before the LORD, and
said, 'I will persuade him.' The
LORD said to him, 'In what way?'
21 "So he said, 'I will go out and
be a lying spirit in the mouth of
all his prophets.' And *the* LORD
said, 'You shall persuade *him* and
also prevail; go out and do so.'
22 "Therefore look! [a]The LORD
has put a lying spirit in the mouth
of these prophets of yours, and the
LORD has declared disaster against
you."
23 Then Zedekiah the son of

19 [a]2 Chr. 17:2

CHAPTER 18

1 [a]2 Chr. 17:5 [b]1 Kin. 22:44; 2 Kin. 8:18 [c]1 Kin. 22:40

2 [a][Ex. 23:2]; 1 Kin. 22:2

4 [a]1 Sam. 23:2, 4, 9; 2 Sam. 2:1

6 [a]2 Kin. 3:11 [1]Or *him*

10 [a]Zech. 1:18–21

13 [a]Num. 22:18–20, 35; 23:12, 26; 1 Kin. 22:14

16 [a][Jer. 23:1–8; 31:10] [b]Num. 27:17; 1 Kin. 22:17; [Ezek. 34:5–8]; Matt. 9:36; Mark 6:34

18 [a]Is. 6:1–5; Dan. 7:9, 10

20 [a]Job 1:6; 2 Thess. 2:9

22 [a]Job 12:16, 17; Is. 19:12–14; Ezek. 14:9

Chenaanah went near and [a]struck
Micaiah on the cheek, and said,
"Which way did the spirit from the
LORD go from me to speak to you?"
24 And Micaiah said, "Indeed you
shall see on that day when you go
into an inner chamber to hide!"
25 Then the king of Israel said,
"Take Micaiah, and return him to
Amon the governor of the city and
to Joash the king's son;
26 "and say, 'Thus says the king:
[a]"Put this *fellow* in prison, and
feed him with bread of affliction
and water of affliction, until I re-
turn in peace." ' "
27 But Micaiah said, "If you ever
return in peace, the LORD has not
spoken by [a]me." And he said,
"Take heed, all you people!"

Ahab Dies in Battle

28 So the king of Israel and Je-
hoshaphat the king of Judah went
up to Ramoth Gilead.
29 And the king of Israel said to
Jehoshaphat, "I will [a]disguise my-
self and go into battle; but you put
on your robes." So the king of Is-
rael disguised himself, and they
went into battle.
30 Now the king of Syria had com-
manded the captains of the chari-
ots who *were* with him, saying,
"Fight with no one small or great,
but only with the king of Israel."
31 So it was, when the captains of
the chariots saw Jehoshaphat, that
they said, "It *is* the king of Israel!"
Therefore they surrounded him to
attack; but Jehoshaphat [a]cried out,
and the LORD helped him, and God
diverted them from him.
32 For so it was, when the cap-
tains of the chariots saw that it
was not the king of Israel, that
they turned back from pursuing
him.
33 Now a certain man drew a bow
at random, and struck the king of
Israel between the [1]joints of his ar-
mor. So he said to the driver of
his chariot, "Turn around and take
me out of the battle, for I am
wounded."
34 The battle increased that day,
and the king of Israel propped
himself up in *his* chariot facing the
Syrians until evening; and about
the time of sunset he died.

23 [a]Jer. 20:2; Mark 14:65; Acts 23:2
26 [a]2 Chr. 16:10
27 [a]Deut. 18:22
29 [a]2 Chr. 35:22
31 [a]2 Chr. 13:14, 15
33 [1]Or *scale armor and the breastplate*

CHAPTER 19

2 [a]1 Sam. 9:9; 1 Kin. 16:1; 2 Chr. 20:34 [b]Ps. 139:21 [c]2 Chr. 32:25
3 [a]2 Chr. 17:4, 6 [b]2 Chr. 30:19 [1]Or *Asherim*, Heb. *Asheroth*
4 [a]2 Chr. 15:8–13
5 [a][Deut. 16:18–20]
6 [a][Lev. 19:15; Deut. 1:17]; Ps. 58:1 [b]Ps. 82:1; [Eccl. 5:8] [1]Lit. *in the matter of the judgment*
7 [a][Gen. 18:25; Deut. 32:4]; Rom. 9:17 [b][Deut. 10:17, 18; Job 34:19]; Acts 10:34; Rom. 2:11; Gal. 2:6; [Eph. 6:9; Col. 3:25]
8 [a]Deut. 16:18; 2 Chr. 17:8 [1]LXX, Vg. *for the inhabitants of Jerusalem*
9 [a][2 Sam. 23:3]
10 [a]Deut. 17:8 [b]Num. 16:46 [c][Ezek. 3:18]
11 [a]Ezra 7:3 [b]1 Chr. 26:30

19 Then Jehoshaphat the king
of Judah returned safely to
his house in Jerusalem.
2 And Jehu the son of Hanani
[a]the seer went out to meet him,
and said to King Jehoshaphat,
"Should you help the wicked and
[b]love those who hate the LORD?
Therefore the [c]wrath of the LORD
is upon you.
3 "Nevertheless [a]good things are
found in you, in that you have re-
moved the [1]wooden images from
the land, and have [b]prepared your
heart to seek God."

The Reforms of Jehoshaphat

4 So Jehoshaphat dwelt at Jeru-
salem; and he went out again
among the people from Beersheba
to the mountains of Ephraim, and
brought them back to the LORD
God of their [a]fathers.
5 Then he set [a]judges in the land
throughout all the fortified cities
of Judah, city by city,
6 and said to the judges, "Take
heed to what you are doing, for
[a]you do not judge for man but for
the LORD, [b]who *is* with you [1]in the
judgment.
7 "Now therefore, let the fear of
the LORD be upon you; take care
and do *it*, for [a]*there is* no iniquity
with the LORD our God, no [b]partial-
ity, nor taking of bribes."
8 Moreover in Jerusalem, for the
judgment of the LORD and for con-
troversies, Jehoshaphat [a]ap-
pointed some of the Levites and
priests, and some of the chief fa-
thers of Israel, [1]when they re-
turned to Jerusalem.
9 And he commanded them, say-
ing, "Thus you shall act [a]in the
fear of the LORD, faithfully and
with a loyal heart:
10 [a]"Whatever case comes to you
from your brethren who dwell in
their cities, whether of bloodshed
or offenses against law or com-
mandment, against statutes or or-
dinances, you shall warn them,
lest they trespass against the LORD
and [b]wrath come upon [c]you and
your brethren. Do this, and you
will not be guilty.
11 "And take notice: [a]Amariah
the chief priest *is* over you [b]in all
matters of the LORD; and Zebadiah
the son of Ishmael, the ruler of the

house of Judah, for all the king's
matters; also the Levites *will be* of-
ficials before you. Behave coura-
geously, and the LORD will be [c]with
the good."

Ammon, Moab, and Mount Seir Defeated

20 It happened after this *that*
the people of [a]Moab with the
people of [b]Ammon, and *others*
with them besides the [c]Ammon-
ites,[1] came to battle against Je-
hoshaphat.
2 Then some came and told Je-
hoshaphat, saying, "A great multi-
tude is coming against you from
beyond the sea, from [1]Syria; and
they are [a]in Hazazon Tamar"
(which *is* [b]En Gedi).
3 And Jehoshaphat feared, and
set [1]himself to [a]seek the LORD, and
[b]proclaimed a fast throughout all
Judah.
4 So Judah gathered together to
ask [a]*help* from the LORD; and from
all the cities of Judah they came
to seek the LORD.
5 Then Jehoshaphat stood in the
assembly of Judah and Jerusalem,
in the house of the LORD, before
the new court,
6 and said: "O LORD God of our
fathers, *are* You not [a]God in
heaven, and [b]do You *not* rule over
all the kingdoms of the nations,
and [c]in Your hand *is there not*
power and might, so that no one
is able to withstand You?
7 "*Are* You not [a]our God, *who*
[b]drove out the inhabitants of this
land before Your people Israel,
and gave it to the descendants of
Abraham [c]Your friend forever?
8 "And they dwell in it, and have
built You a sanctuary in it for Your
name, saying,
9 [a]'If disaster comes upon us—
sword, judgment, pestilence, or
famine—we will stand before this
temple and in Your presence (for
Your [b]name *is* in this temple), and
cry out to You in our affliction, and
You will hear and save.'
10 "And now, here are the people
of Ammon, Moab, and Mount
Seir—whom You [a]would not let Is-
rael invade when they came out of
the land of Egypt, but [b]they turned
from them and did not destroy
them—
11 "here they are, rewarding us
[a]by coming to throw us out of Your
possession which You have given
us to inherit.
12 "O our God, will You not
[a]judge them? For we have no
power against this great multitude
that is coming against us; nor do
we know what to do, but [b]our eyes
are upon You."
13 Now all Judah, with their little
ones, their wives, and their chil-
dren, stood before the LORD.
14 Then [a]the Spirit of the LORD
came upon Jahaziel the son of
Zechariah, the son of Benaiah, the
son of Jeiel, the son of Mattaniah,
a Levite of the sons of Asaph, in
the midst of the assembly.
15 And he said, "Listen, all you of
Judah and you inhabitants of Jeru-
salem, and you, King Jehosha-
phat! Thus says the LORD to you:
[a]'Do not be afraid nor dismayed
because of this great multitude,
[b]for the battle *is* not yours, but
God's.
16 'Tomorrow go down against
them. They will surely come up by
the Ascent of Ziz, and you will find
them at the end of the [1]brook be-
fore the Wilderness of Jeruel.
17 [a]'You will not *need* to fight in
this *battle.* Position yourselves,
stand still and see the salvation of
the LORD, who is with you, O Judah
and Jerusalem!' Do not fear or
be dismayed; tomorrow go out
against them, [b]for the LORD *is* with
you."
18 And Jehoshaphat [a]bowed his
head with *his* face to the ground,
and all Judah and the inhabitants
of Jerusalem bowed before the
LORD, worshiping the LORD.
19 Then the Levites of the chil-
dren of the Kohathites and of the
children of the Korahites stood up
to praise the LORD God of Israel
with voices loud and high.
20 So they rose early in the morn-
ing and went out into the Wilder-
ness of Tekoa; and as they went
out, Jehoshaphat stood and said,
"Hear me, O Judah and you inhab-
itants of Jerusalem: [a]Believe in the
LORD your God, and you shall be
established; believe His prophets,
and you shall prosper."
21 And when he had consulted
with the people, he appointed

11 [c][2 Chr. 15:2; 20:17]

CHAPTER 20

1 [a]1 Chr. 18:2 [b]1 Chr. 19:15 [c]2 Chr. 26:7 [1]So with MT, Vg.; LXX *Meunites* (cf. 2 Chr. 26:7)
2 [a]Gen. 14:7 [b]Josh. 15:62 [1]So with MT, LXX, Vg.; Heb. mss., Old Lat. *Edom*
3 [a]2 Chr. 19:3 [b]1 Sam. 7:6; Ezra 8:21; Jer. 36:9; Jon. 3:5 [1]Lit. *his face*
4 [a]2 Chr. 14:11
6 [a]Deut. 4:39; Josh. 2:11; [1 Kin. 8:23]; Matt. 6:9 [b]Ps. 22:28; 47:2, 8; Dan. 4:17, 25, 32 [c]1 Chr. 29:12; 2 Chr. 25:8; Ps. 62:11; Matt. 6:13
7 [a]Gen. 13:14–17; 17:7; Ex. 6:7 [b]Ps. 44:2 [c]Is. 41:8; James 2:23
9 [a]1 Kin. 8:33, 37; 2 Chr. 6:28–30 [b]2 Chr. 6:20
10 [a]Deut. 2:4, 9, 19 [b]Num. 20:21
11 [a]Ps. 83:1–18
12 [a]Judg. 11:27; [1 Sam. 3:13] [b]Ps. 25:15; 121:1, 2; 123:1, 2; 141:8
14 [a]Num. 11:25, 26; 24:2; 2 Chr. 15:1; 24:20
15 [a]Ex. 14:13, 14; [Deut. 1:29, 30; 31:6, 8]; 2 Chr. 32:7 [b]1 Sam. 17:47; Zech. 14:3
16 [1]*streambed* or *wadi*
17 [a]Ex. 14:13, 14 [b]Num. 14:9; [2 Chr. 15:2; 32:8]
18 [a]Ex. 4:31; 2 Chr. 7:3; 29:28
20 [a]Is. 7:9

those who should sing to the LORD,
[a]and who should praise the beauty
of holiness, as they went out be-
fore the army and were saying:

[b]"Praise the LORD,
[c]For His mercy *endures* forever."

22 Now when they began to sing
and to praise, [a]the LORD set am-
bushes against the people of Am-
mon, Moab, and Mount Seir, who
had come against Judah; and they
were defeated.
23 For the people of Ammon and
Moab stood up against the inhabit-
ants of Mount Seir to utterly kill
and destroy *them*. And when they
[1]had made an end of the inhabit-
ants of Seir, [a]they helped to de-
stroy one another.
24 So when Judah came to a place
overlooking the wilderness, they
looked toward the multitude; and
there *were* their dead bodies,
fallen on the earth. No one had es-
caped.
25 When Jehoshaphat and his
people came to take away their
spoil, they found among them an
abundance of valuables on the
[1]dead bodies, and precious jew-
elry, which they stripped off for
themselves, more than they could
carry away; and they were three
days gathering the spoil because
there was so much.
26 And on the fourth day they as-
sembled in the Valley of [1]Bera-
chah, for there they blessed the
LORD; therefore the name of that
place was called The Valley of
Berachah until this day.
27 Then they returned, every man
of Judah and Jerusalem, with Je-
hoshaphat in front of them, to go
back to Jerusalem with joy, for the
LORD had [a]made them rejoice over
their enemies.
28 So they came to Jerusalem,
with stringed instruments and
harps and trumpets, to the house
of the LORD.
29 And [a]the fear of God was on
all the kingdoms of *those* coun-
tries when they heard that the
LORD had fought against the ene-
mies of Israel.
30 Then the realm of Jehoshaphat
was quiet, for his [a]God gave him
rest all around.

The End of Jehoshaphat's Reign

31 [a]So Jehoshaphat was king over
Judah. *He was* thirty-five years old
when he became king, and he
reigned twenty-five years in Jeru-
salem. His mother's name *was*
Azubah the daughter of Shilhi.
32 And he walked in the way of
his father [a]Asa, and did not turn
aside from it, doing *what was* right
in the sight of the LORD.
33 Nevertheless [a]the [1]high places
were not taken away, for as yet the
people had not [b]directed their
hearts to the God of their fathers.
34 Now the rest of the acts of Je-
hoshaphat, first and last, indeed
they *are* written in the book of
Jehu the son of Hanani, [a]which *is*
mentioned in the book of the kings
of Israel.
35 After this [a]Jehoshaphat king of
Judah allied himself with Ahaziah
king of Israel, [b]who acted very
[c]wickedly.
36 And he allied himself with him
[a]to make ships to go to Tarshish,
and they made the ships in Ezion
Geber.
37 But Eliezer the son of Dodavah
of Mareshah prophesied against
Jehoshaphat, saying, "Because
you have allied yourself with Aha-
ziah, the LORD has destroyed your
works." [a]Then the ships were
wrecked, so that they were not
able to go [b]to Tarshish.

Jehoram Reigns in Judah

21 And [a]Jehoshaphat [1]rested
with his fathers, and was
buried with his fathers in the City
of David. Then Jehoram his son
reigned in his place.
2 He had brothers, the sons of Je-
hoshaphat: Azariah, Jehiel, Zech-
ariah, Azaryahu, Michael, and
Shephatiah; all these *were* the
sons of Jehoshaphat king of Is-
rael.
3 Their father gave them great
gifts of silver and gold and pre-
cious things, with fortified cities in
Judah; but he gave the kingdom
to Jehoram, because he *was* the
firstborn.
4 Now when Jehoram [1]was es-
tablished over the kingdom of his
father, he strengthened himself
and killed all his brothers with the

21 [a]1 Chr. 16:29; Ps. 29:2; 90:17; 96:9; 110:3 [b]1 Chr. 16:34; Ps. 106:1; 136:1 [c]1 Chr. 16:41; 2 Chr. 5:13
22 [a]Judg. 7:22; 1 Sam. 14:20
23 [a]Judg. 7:22; 1 Sam. 14:20 [1]*had finished*
25 [1]A few Heb. mss., Old Lat., Vg. *garments*; LXX *armor*
26 [1]Lit. *Blessing*
27 [a]Neh. 12:43
29 [a]2 Chr. 14:14; 17:10
30 [a]1 Kin. 22:41–43; 2 Chr. 14:6, 7; 15:15; Job 34:29
31 [a][1 Kin. 22:41–43]
32 [a]2 Chr. 14:2
33 [a]2 Chr. 15:17; 17:6 [b]2 Chr. 12:14; 19:3 [1]Places for pagan worship
34 [a]1 Kin. 16:1, 7
35 [a]2 Chr. 18:1 [b]1 Kin. 22:48–53 [c][2 Chr. 19:2]
36 [a]1 Kin. 9:26; 10:22
37 [a]1 Kin. 22:48 [b]2 Chr. 9:21

CHAPTER 21

1 [a]1 Kin. 22:50 [1]Died and joined his ancestors
4 [1]Lit. *arose*

sword, and also *others* of the
princes of Israel.
5 [a]Jehoram *was* thirty-two years
old when he became king, and he
reigned eight years in Jerusalem.
6 And he walked in the way of
the kings of Israel, just as the
house of Ahab had done, for he
had the daughter of [a]Ahab as a
wife; and he did evil in the sight
of the LORD.
7 Yet the LORD would not destroy
the house of David, because of the
[a]covenant that He had made with
David, and since He had promised
to give a lamp to him and to his
[b]sons forever.
8 [a]In his days Edom revolted
against Judah's authority, and
made a king over themselves.
9 So Jehoram went out with his
officers, and all his chariots with
him. And he rose by night and at-
tacked the Edomites who had sur-
rounded him and the captains of
the chariots.
10 Thus Edom has been in revolt
against Judah's authority to this
day. At that time Libnah revolted
against his rule, because he had
forsaken the LORD God of his fa-
thers.
11 Moreover he made [1]high places
in the mountains of Judah, and
caused the inhabitants of Jerusa-
lem to [a]commit harlotry, and led
Judah astray.
12 And a letter came to him from
Elijah the prophet, saying,

Thus says the LORD God of your
father David:
Because you have not walked
in the ways of Jehoshaphat
your father, or in the ways of
Asa king of Judah,
13 but have walked in the way of
the kings of Israel, and have
[a]made Judah and the
inhabitants of Jerusalem to
[b]play the harlot like the
[c]harlotry of the house of Ahab,
and also have [d]killed your
brothers, those of your father's
household, *who were* better
than yourself,
14 behold, the LORD will strike
your people with a serious
affliction—your children, your
wives, and all your
possessions;
15 and you *will become* very sick
with a [a]disease of your
intestines, until your intestines
come out by reason of the
sickness, day by day.

16 Moreover the [a]LORD [b]stirred up
against Jehoram the spirit of the
Philistines and the [c]Arabians who
were near the Ethiopians.
17 And they came up into Judah
and invaded it, and carried away
all the possessions that were found
in the king's house, and also [a]his
sons and his wives, so that there
was not a son left to him except
[1]Jehoahaz, the youngest of his
sons.
18 After all this the LORD struck
him [a]in his intestines with an in-
curable disease.
19 Then it happened in the course
of time, after the end of two years,
that his intestines came out be-
cause of his sickness; so he died
in severe pain. And his people
made no [1]burning for him, like
[a]the burning for his fathers.
20 He was thirty-two years old
when he became king. He reigned
in Jerusalem eight years and, to no
one's sorrow, departed. However
they buried him in the City of Da-
vid, but not in the tombs of the
kings.

Ahaziah Reigns in Judah

22 Then the inhabitants of Je-
rusalem made [a]Ahaziah his
youngest son king in his place, for
the raiders who came with the
[b]Arabians into the camp had killed
all the [c]older *sons*. So Ahaziah the
son of Jehoram, king of Judah,
reigned.
2 Ahaziah *was* [1]forty-two years
old when he became king, and he
reigned one year in Jerusalem. His
mother's name *was* [a]Athaliah the
[2]granddaughter of Omri.
3 He also walked in the ways of
the house of Ahab, for his mother
advised him to do wickedly.
4 Therefore he did evil in the
sight of the LORD, like the house
of Ahab; for they were his counsel-
ors after the death of his father,
to his destruction.
5 He also followed their advice,
and went with [1]Jehoram the son
of Ahab king of Israel to war

5 [a]2 Kin. 8:17–22
6 [a]2 Chr. 18:1
7 [a]2 Sam. 7:8–17 [b]1 Kin. 11:36; 2 Kin. 8:19; Ps. 132:11
8 [a]2 Kin. 8:20; 14:7, 10; 2 Chr. 25:14, 19
11 [a][Lev. 20:5] [1]Places for pagan worship
13 [a]2 Chr. 21:11 [b][Ex. 34:15]; Deut. 31:16 [c]1 Kin. 16:31–33; 2 Kin. 9:22 [d]1 Kin. 2:32; 2 Chr. 21:4
15 [a]2 Chr. 21:18, 19
16 [a]2 Chr. 33:11; [Jer. 51:11] [b]1 Kin. 11:14, 23 [c]2 Chr. 17:11
17 [a]2 Chr. 24:7 [1]*Ahaziah* or *Azariah,* 2 Chr. 22:1
18 [a]2 Chr. 13:20; 21:15; Acts 12:23
19 [a]2 Chr. 16:14 [1]Burning of spices

CHAPTER 22

1 [a]2 Chr. 21:17; 22:6 [b]2 Chr. 21:16 [c]2 Chr. 21:17
2 [a]2 Chr. 21:6 [1]*twenty-two,* 2 Kin. 8:26 [2]Lit. *daughter*
5 [1]*Joram,* v. 7; 2 Kin. 8:28

against Hazael king of Syria at Ra-
moth Gilead; and the Syrians
wounded Joram.
6 [a]Then he returned to Jezreel to
recover from the wounds which he
had received at Ramah, when he
fought against Hazael king of
Syria. And [1]Azariah the son of Je-
horam, king of Judah, went down
to see Jehoram the son of Ahab
in Jezreel, because he was sick.
7 His going to Joram [a]was God's
occasion for Ahaziah's [1]downfall;
for when he arrived, [b]he went out
with [2]Jehoram against Jehu the
son of Nimshi, [c]whom the LORD
had anointed to [3]cut off the house
of Ahab.
8 And it happened, when Jehu
was [a]executing judgment on the
house of Ahab, and [b]found the
princes of Judah and the sons of
Ahaziah's brothers who served
Ahaziah, that he killed them.
9 [a]Then he searched for Aha-
ziah; and they caught him (he was
hiding in Samaria), and brought
him to Jehu. When they had killed
him, they buried him, "because,"
they said, "he is the son of [b]Je-
hoshaphat, who [c]sought the LORD
with all his heart." So the house
of Ahaziah had no one to assume
power over the kingdom.

Athaliah Reigns in Judah

10 [a]Now when Athaliah the
mother of Ahaziah saw that her
son was dead, she arose and de-
stroyed all the royal heirs of the
house of Judah.
11 But [1]Jehoshabeath, the daugh-
ter of the king, took [a]Joash the son
of Ahaziah, and stole him away
from among the king's sons who
were being murdered, and put him
and his nurse in a bedroom. So Je-
hoshabeath, the daughter of King
Jehoram, the wife of Jehoiada the
priest (for she was the sister of
Ahaziah), hid him from Athaliah
so that she did not kill him.
12 And he was hidden with them
in the house of God for six years,
while Athaliah reigned over the
land.

Joash Crowned King of Judah

23 In [a]the seventh year [b]Jehoi-
ada strengthened himself,
and made a covenant with the cap-
tains of hundreds: Azariah the son
of Jeroham, Ishmael the son of Je-
hohanan, Azariah the son of
[c]Obed, Maaseiah the son of Ada-
iah, and Elishaphat the son of
Zichri.
2 And they went throughout Ju-
dah and gathered the Levites from
all the cities of Judah, and the
[a]chief fathers of Israel, and they
came to Jerusalem.
3 Then all the assembly made a
covenant with the king in the
house of God. And he said to them,
"Behold, the king's son shall reign,
as the LORD has [a]said of the sons
of David.
4 "This *is* what you shall do:
One-third of you [a]entering on the
Sabbath, of the priests and the
Levites, *shall be* keeping watch
over the doors;
5 "one-third *shall be* at the king's
house; and one-third at the Gate
of the Foundation. All the people
shall be in the courts of the house
of the LORD.
6 "But let no one come into the
house of the LORD except the
priests and [a]those of the Levites
who serve. They may go in, for
they *are* holy; but all the people
shall keep the watch of the LORD.
7 "And the Levites shall sur-
round the king on all sides, every
man with his weapons in his hand;
and whoever comes into the
house, let him be put to death. You
are to be with the king when he
comes in and when he goes out."
8 So the Levites and all Judah
did according to all that Jehoiada
the priest commanded. And each
man took his men who were to be
on duty on the Sabbath, with those
who were going *off duty* on the
Sabbath; for Jehoiada the priest
had not dismissed [a]the divisions.
9 And Jehoiada the priest gave
to the captains of hundreds the
spears and the large and small
[a]shields which *had belonged* to
King David, that *were* in the tem-
ple of God.
10 Then he set all the people,
every man with his weapon in his
hand, from the right side of the
temple to the left side of the tem-
ple, along by the altar and by the
temple, all around the king.
11 And they brought out the

6 [a]2 Kin. 9:15 [1]Heb. mss., LXX, Syr., Vg. *Ahaziah* and 2 Kin. 8:29
7 [a]Judg. 14:4; 1 Kin. 12:15; 2 Chr. 10:15 [b]2 Kin. 9:21–24 [c]2 Kin. 9:6, 7 [1]Lit. *crushing* [2]*Joram,* vv. 5, 7; 2 Kin. 8:28 [3]*destroy*
8 [a]2 Kin. 9:22–24 [b]2 Kin. 10:10–14; Hos. 1:4
9 [a][2 Kin. 9:27] [b]1 Kin. 15:24 [c]2 Chr. 17:4; 20:3, 4
10 [a]2 Kin. 11:1–3
11 [a]2 Kin. 12:18 [1]*Jehosheba,* 2 Kin. 11:2
CHAPTER 23
1 [a]2 Kin. 11:4 [b]2 Kin. 12:2 [c]1 Chr. 2:37, 38
2 [a]Ezra 1:5
3 [a]2 Sam. 7:12; 1 Kin. 2:4; 9:5; 2 Chr. 6:16; 7:18; 21:7
4 [a]1 Chr. 9:25
6 [a]1 Chr. 23:28–32
8 [a]1 Chr. 24:1–31
9 [a]2 Sam. 8:7

king's son, put the crown on him,
[a]*gave him* the [1]Testimony, and
made him king. Then Jehoiada
and his sons anointed him, and
said, "*Long* live the king!"

Death of Athaliah

12 Now when [a]Athaliah heard the
noise of the people running and
praising the king, she came to the
people *in* the temple of the LORD.
13 When she looked, there was
the king standing by his pillar at
the entrance; and the leaders and
the trumpeters *were* by the king.
All the people of the land were
rejoicing and blowing trumpets,
also the singers with musical in-
struments, and [a]those who led
in praise. So Athaliah tore her
clothes and said, [b]"Treason! Trea-
son!"
14 And Jehoiada the priest
brought out the captains of hun-
dreds who were set over the army,
and said to them, "Take her out-
side under guard, and slay with the
sword whoever follows her." For
the priest had said, "Do not kill her
in the house of the LORD."
15 So they seized her; and she
went by way of the entrance [a]of
the Horse Gate *into* the king's
house, and they killed her there.
16 Then Jehoiada made a [a]cov-
enant between himself, the people,
and the king, that they should be
the LORD's people.
17 And all the people went to the
[1]temple of Baal, and tore it down.
They broke in pieces its altars and
images, and [a]killed Mattan the
priest of Baal before the altars.
18 Also Jehoiada appointed the
oversight of the house of the LORD
to the hand of the priests, the Le-
vites, whom David had [a]assigned
in the house of the LORD, to offer
the burnt offerings of the LORD, as
it is written in the [b]Law of Moses,
with rejoicing and with singing, *as
it was established* by David.
19 And he set the [a]gatekeepers at
the gates of the house of the LORD,
so that no one *who was* in any way
unclean should enter.
20 [a]Then he took the captains of
hundreds, the nobles, the gover-
nors of the people, and all the peo-
ple of the land, and brought the
king down from the house of

11 [a]Deut. 17:18 [1]Law, Ex. 25:16, 21; 31:18
12 [a]2 Chr. 22:10
13 [a]1 Chr. 25:6–8 [b]2 Kin. 9:23
15 [a]Neh. 3:28; Jer. 31:40
16 [a]Josh. 24:24, 25; 2 Chr. 15:12–15
17 [a]Deut. 13:6–9; 1 Kin. 18:40 [1]Lit. *house*
18 [a]1 Chr. 23:6, 30, 31; 24:1 [b]Num. 28:2
19 [a]1 Chr. 26:1–19
20 [a]1 Kin. 9:22; 2 Kin. 11:19
CHAPTER 24
1 [a]2 Kin. 11:21; 12:1–15
2 [a]2 Chr. 26:4, 5
5 [a]2 Kin. 12:4
6 [a]2 Kin. 12:7 [b]Ex. 30:12–16 [c]Num. 1:50; Acts 7:44
7 [a]2 Chr. 21:17 [b]2 Kin. 12:4
8 [a]2 Kin. 12:9
9 [a]2 Chr. 24:6

the LORD; and they went through
the Upper Gate to the king's
house, and set the king on the
throne of the kingdom.
21 So all the people of the land re-
joiced; and the city was quiet, for
they had slain Athaliah with the
sword.

Joash Repairs the Temple

24 Joash [a]*was* seven years old
when he became king, and
he reigned forty years in Jerusa-
lem. His mother's name *was* Zib-
iah of Beersheba.
2 Joash [a]did *what was* right in
the sight of the LORD all the days
of Jehoiada the priest.
3 And Jehoiada took two wives
for him, and he had sons and
daughters.
4 Now it happened after this *that*
Joash set his heart on repairing the
house of the LORD.
5 Then he gathered the priests
and the Levites, and said to them,
"Go out to the cities of Judah, and
[a]gather from all Israel money to
repair the house of your God from
year to year, and see that you do
it quickly." However the Levites
did not do it quickly.
6 [a]So the king called Jehoiada
the chief *priest*, and said to him,
"Why have you not required the
Levites to bring in from Judah and
from Jerusalem the collection, *ac-
cording to the commandment* of
[b]Moses the servant of the LORD
and of the assembly of Israel, for
the [c]tabernacle of witness?"
7 For [a]the sons of Athaliah, that
wicked woman, had broken into
the house of God, and had also
presented all the [b]dedicated things
of the house of the LORD to the
Baals.
8 Then at the king's command
[a]they made a chest, and set it out-
side at the gate of the house of the
LORD.
9 And they made a proclamation
throughout Judah and Jerusalem
to bring to the LORD [a]the collection
that Moses the servant of God *had
imposed* on Israel in the wilder-
ness.
10 Then all the leaders and all the
people rejoiced, brought their con-
tributions, and put *them* into the
chest until all had given.

11 So it was, at that time, when
the chest was brought to the king's
official by the hand of the Levites,
and [a]when they saw that *there was*
much money, that the king's scribe
and the high priest's officer came
and emptied the chest, and took
it and returned it to its place. Thus
they did day by day, and gathered
money in abundance.
12 The king and Jehoiada gave it
to those who did the work of the
service of the house of the LORD;
and they hired masons and
carpenters to [a]repair the house of
the LORD, and also those who
worked in iron and bronze to re-
store the house of the LORD.
13 So the workmen labored, and
the work was completed by them;
they restored the house of God
to its original condition and re-
inforced it.
14 When they had finished, they
brought the rest of the money be-
fore the king and Jehoiada; [a]they
made from it articles for the house
of the LORD, articles for serving
and offering, spoons and vessels
of gold and silver. And they of-
fered burnt offerings in the house
of the LORD continually all the
days of Jehoiada.

Apostasy of Joash

15 But Jehoiada grew old and was
full of days, and he died; *he was*
one hundred and thirty years old
when he died.
16 And they buried him in the City
of David among the kings, because
he had done good in Israel, both
toward God and His house.
17 Now after the death of Jehoi-
ada the leaders of Judah came and
bowed down to the king. And the
king listened to them.
18 Therefore they left the house of
the LORD God of their fathers, and
served [a]wooden images and idols;
and [b]wrath came upon Judah and
Jerusalem because of their tres-
pass.
19 Yet He [a]sent prophets to them,
to bring them back to the LORD;
and they testified against them,
but they would not listen.
20 Then the Spirit of God [1]came
upon [a]Zechariah the son of Jehoi-
ada the priest, who stood above
the people, and said to them,

11 [a]2 Kin. 12:10

12 [a]2 Chr. 30:12

14 [a]2 Kin. 12:13

18 [a]1 Kin. 14:23 [b][Ex. 34:12–14]; Judg. 5:8; 2 Chr. 19:2; 28:13; 29:8; 32:25

19 [a]2 Kin. 17:13; 21:10–15; 2 Chr. 36:15, 16; Jer. 7:25, 26; 25:4

20 [a]Judg. 6:34; Matt. 23:35 [b]Num. 14:41; [Prov. 28:13] [c][2 Chr. 15:2] [1]Lit. *clothed*

21 [a][Neh. 9:26]; Matt. 23:35; Acts 7:58, 59

22 [a][Gen. 9:5] [1]Foster father

23 [a]2 Kin. 12:17; Is. 7:2 [1]*plunder*

24 [a]Lev. 26:8; [Deut. 32:30]; Is. 30:17 [b]Lev. 26:25; [Deut. 28:25] [c]2 Chr. 22:8; Is. 10:5

25 [a]2 Kin. 12:20, 21; 2 Chr. 25:3 [1]LXX, Vg. *son* and vv. 20–22

26 [1]*Jozachar,* 2 Kin. 12:21 [2]*Shomer,* 2 Kin. 12:21

27 [a]2 Kin. 12:18 [b]2 Kin. 12:21 [1]Or *commentary,* Heb. *midrash*

CHAPTER 25

1 [a]2 Kin. 14:1–6

"Thus says God: [b]'Why do you
transgress the commandments of
the LORD, so that you cannot pros-
per? [c]Because you have forsaken
the LORD, He also has forsaken
you.' "
21 So they conspired against him,
and at the command of the king
they [a]stoned him with stones in the
court of the house of the LORD.
22 Thus Joash the king did not re-
member the kindness which Jehoi-
ada his [1]father had done to him,
but killed his son; and as he died,
he said, "The LORD look on *it,* and
[a]repay!"

Death of Joash

23 So it happened in the spring of
the year *that* [a]the army of Syria
came up against him; and they
came to Judah and Jerusalem, and
destroyed all the leaders of the
people from among the people,
and sent all their [1]spoil to the king
of Damascus.
24 For the army of the Syrians
[a]came with a small company of
men; but the LORD [b]delivered a
very great army into their hand,
because they had forsaken the
LORD God of their fathers. So they
[c]executed judgment against Joash.
25 And when they had withdrawn
from him (for they left him se-
verely wounded), [a]his own ser-
vants conspired against him be-
cause of the blood of the [1]sons of
Jehoiada the priest, and killed him
on his bed. So he died. And they
buried him in the City of David,
but they did not bury him in the
tombs of the kings.
26 These are the ones who con-
spired against him: [1]Zabad the son
of Shimeath the Ammonitess, and
Jehozabad the son of [2]Shimrith
the Moabitess.
27 Now *concerning* his sons, and
[a]the many oracles about him, and
the repairing of the house of God,
indeed they *are* written in the [1]an-
nals of the book of the kings. [b]Then
Amaziah his son reigned in his
place.

Amaziah Reigns in Judah

25 Amaziah [a]*was* twenty-five
years old *when* he became
king, and he reigned twenty-nine
years in Jerusalem. His mother's

name *was* Jehoaddan of Jeru-
salem.
2 And he did *what was* right in
the sight of the LORD, [a]but not with
a loyal heart.
3 [a]Now it happened, as soon as
the kingdom was established for
him, that he executed his servants
who had murdered his father the
king.
4 However he did not execute
their children, but *did* as *it is* writ-
ten in the Law in the Book of Mo-
ses, where the LORD commanded,
saying, [a]"The fathers shall not be
put to death for their children, nor
shall the children be put to death
for their fathers; but a person shall
die for his own sin."

The War Against Edom

5 Moreover Amaziah gathered
Judah together and set over them
captains of thousands and cap-
tains of hundreds, according to
their fathers' houses, throughout
all Judah and Benjamin; and he
numbered them [a]from twenty
years old and above, and found
them to be three hundred thou-
sand choice *men, able* to go to war,
who could handle spear and
shield.
6 He also hired one hundred
thousand mighty men of valor
from Israel for one hundred talents
of silver.
7 But a [a]man of God came to him,
saying, "O king, do not let the
army of Israel go with you, for the
LORD *is* not with Israel—*not with*
any of the children of Ephraim.
8 "But if you go, be gone! Be
strong in battle! *Even so,* God shall
make you fall before the enemy;
for God has [a]power to help and to
overthrow."
9 Then Amaziah said to the man
of God, "But what *shall we* do
about the hundred talents which I
have given to the troops of Israel?"
And the man of God answered,
[a]"The LORD is able to give you
much more than this."
10 So Amaziah discharged the
troops that had come to him from
Ephraim, to go back home. There-
fore their anger was greatly
aroused against Judah, and they
returned home in great anger.
11 Then Amaziah strengthened
himself, and leading his people, he
went to [a]the Valley of Salt and
killed ten thousand of the people
of Seir.
12 Also the children of Judah took
captive ten thousand alive,
brought them to the top of the
rock, and cast them down from the
top of the rock, so that they all
were dashed in pieces.
13 But as for the soldiers of the
army which Amaziah had dis-
charged, so that they would not go
with him to battle, they raided the
cities of Judah from Samaria to
Beth Horon, killed three thousand
in them, and took much [1]spoil.
14 Now it was so, after Amaziah
came from the slaughter of the
Edomites, that [a]he brought the
gods of the people of Seir, set them
up *to be* [b]his gods, and bowed
down before them and burned in-
cense to them.
15 Therefore the anger of the
LORD was aroused against Ama-
ziah, and He sent him a prophet
who said to him, "Why have you
sought [a]the gods of the people,
which [b]could not rescue their own
people from your hand?"
16 So it was, as he talked with
him, that *the king* said to him,
"Have we made you the king's
counselor? Cease! Why should you
be killed?" Then the prophet
ceased, and said, "I know that God
has [a]determined to destroy you,
because you have done this and
have not heeded my advice."

Israel Defeats Judah

17 Now [a]Amaziah king of Judah
asked advice and sent to [1]Joash
the son of Jehoahaz, the son of
Jehu, king of Israel, saying,
"Come, let us face one another *in
battle.*"
18 And Joash king of Israel sent
to Amaziah king of Judah, saying,
"The thistle that *was* in Lebanon
sent to the cedar that was in Leba-
non, saying, 'Give your daughter
to my son as wife'; and a wild
beast that *was* in Lebanon passed
by and trampled the thistle.
19 "Indeed you say that you have
defeated the Edomites, and your
heart is lifted up to [a]boast. Stay
at home now; why should you
meddle with trouble, that you

2 [a]2 Kin. 14:4; 2 Chr. 25:14
3 [a]2 Kin. 14:5; 2 Chr. 24:25
4 [a]Deut. 24:16; 2 Kin. 14:6; Jer. 31:30; [Ezek. 18:20]
5 [a]Num. 1:3
7 [a]2 Chr. 11:2
8 [a]2 Chr. 14:11; 20:6
9 [a][Deut. 8:18]; Prov. 10:22
11 [a]2 Kin. 14:7
13 [1]*plunder*
14 [a]2 Chr. 28:23 [b][Ex. 20:3, 5]
15 [a][Ps. 96:5] [b]2 Chr. 25:11
16 [a][1 Sam. 2:25]
17 [a]2 Kin. 14:8–14 [1]*Jehoash,* 2 Kin. 14:8ff.
19 [a]2 Chr. 26:16; 32:25; [Prov. 16:18]

should fall—you and Judah with
you?"
20 But Amaziah would not heed,
for [a]it *came* from God, that He
might give them into the hand *of*
their enemies, because they
[b]sought the gods of Edom.
21 So Joash king of Israel went
out; and he and Amaziah king of
Judah faced one another at [a]Beth
Shemesh, which *belongs* to Judah.
22 And Judah was defeated by Is-
rael, and every man fled to his tent.
23 Then Joash the king of Israel
captured Amaziah king of Judah,
the son of Joash, the son of [a]Je-
hoahaz, at Beth Shemesh; and he
brought him to Jerusalem, and
broke down the wall of Jerusalem
from the Gate of Ephraim to the
Corner Gate—four hundred cubits.
24 And *he took* all the gold and
silver, all the articles that were
found in the house of God with
[a]Obed-Edom, the treasures of the
king's house, and hostages, and re-
turned to Samaria.

Death of Amaziah

25 [a]Amaziah the son of Joash,
king of Judah, lived fifteen years
after the death of Joash the son of
Jehoahaz, king of Israel.
26 Now the rest of the acts of
Amaziah, from first to last, indeed
are they not written in the book
of the kings of Judah and Israel?
27 After the time that Amaziah
turned away from following the
LORD, they made a conspiracy
against him in Jerusalem, and he
fled to Lachish; but they sent after
him to Lachish and killed him
there.
28 Then they brought him on
horses and buried him with his fa-
thers in [1]the City of Judah.

Uzziah Reigns in Judah

26 Now all the people of Judah
took [1]Uzziah, who *was* six-
teen years old, and made him king
instead of his father Amaziah.
2 He built [1]Elath and restored it
to Judah, after the king rested with
his fathers.
3 Uzziah *was* sixteen years old
when he became king, and he
reigned fifty-two years in Jerusa-
lem. His mother's name was Jech-
oliah of Jerusalem.
4 And he did *what was* [a]right in
the sight of the LORD, according to
all that his father Amaziah had
done.
5 [a]He sought God in the days of
Zechariah, who [b]had understand-
ing in the [1]visions of God; and as
long as he sought the LORD, God
made him [c]prosper.
6 Now he went out and [a]made
war against the Philistines, and
broke down the wall of Gath, the
wall of Jabneh, and the wall of
Ashdod; and he built cities *around*
Ashdod and among the Philistines.
7 God helped him against [a]the
Philistines, against the Arabians
who lived in Gur Baal, and against
the Meunites.
8 Also the Ammonites [a]brought
tribute to Uzziah. His fame spread
as far as the entrance of Egypt, for
he became exceedingly strong.
9 And Uzziah built towers in Je-
rusalem at the [a]Corner Gate, at the
Valley Gate, and at the corner but-
tress of the wall; then he fortified
them.
10 Also he built towers in the des-
ert. He dug many wells, for he
had much livestock, both in the
lowlands and in the plains; *he also*
had farmers and vinedressers in
the mountains and in [1]Carmel, for
he loved the soil.
11 Moreover Uzziah had an army
of fighting men who went out to
war by companies, according to
the number on their roll as pre-
pared by Jeiel the scribe and
Maaseiah the officer, under the
hand of Hananiah, *one* of the
king's captains.
12 The total number of [1]chief
officers of the mighty men of
valor *was* two thousand six hun-
dred.
13 And under their authority *was*
an army of three hundred and
seven thousand five hundred, that
made war with mighty power, to
help the king against the enemy.
14 Then Uzziah prepared for
them, for the entire army, shields,
spears, helmets, body armor,
bows, and slings *to cast* stones.
15 And he made devices in Jerusa-
lem, invented by [a]skillful men, to
be on the towers and the corners,
to shoot arrows and large stones.
So his fame spread far and wide,

20 [a]1 Kin. 12:15; 2 Chr. 22:7 [b]2 Chr. 25:14
21 [a]Josh. 19:38
23 [a]2 Chr. 21:17; 22:1, 6
24 [a]1 Chr. 26:15
25 [a]2 Kin. 14:17–22
28 [1]The City of David

CHAPTER 26

1 [1]*Azariah*, 2 Kin. 14:21ff.
2 [1]Heb. *Eloth*
4 [a]2 Chr. 24:2
5 [a]2 Chr. 24:2 [b]Gen. 41:15; Dan. 1:17; 10:1 [c][2 Chr. 15:2; 20:20; 31:21] [1]Heb. mss., LXX, Syr., Tg., Arab. *fear*
6 [a]Is. 14:29
7 [a]2 Chr. 21:16
8 [a]2 Sam. 8:2; 2 Chr. 17:11
9 [a]2 Kin. 14:13; 2 Chr. 25:23; Neh. 3:13, 19, 32; Zech. 14:10
10 [1]Or *the fertile fields*
12 [1]Lit. *chief fathers*
15 [a]Ex. 39:3, 8

for he was marvelously helped till
he became strong.

The Penalty for Uzziah's Pride

16 But [a]when he was strong his
heart was [b]lifted up, to *his* destruc-
tion, for he transgressed against
the LORD his God [c]by entering the
temple of the LORD to burn incense
on the altar of incense.
17 So [a]Azariah the priest went in
after him, and with him were
eighty priests of the LORD—valiant
men.
18 And they withstood King Uz-
ziah, and said to him, "*It* [a]*is* not
for you, Uzziah, to burn incense
to the LORD, but for the [b]priests,
the sons of Aaron, who are conse-
crated to burn incense. Get out of
the sanctuary, for you have tres-
passed! You *shall have* no honor
from the LORD God."
19 Then Uzziah became furious;
and he *had* a censer in his hand
to burn incense. And while he was
angry with the priests, [a]leprosy
broke out on his forehead, before
the priests in the house of the
LORD, beside the incense altar.
20 And Azariah the chief priest
and all the priests looked at him,
and there, on his forehead, he *was*
leprous; so they thrust him out of
that place. Indeed he also [a]hurried
to get out, because the LORD had
struck him.
21 [a]King Uzziah was a leper until
the day of his death. He dwelt in
an [b]isolated house, because he was
a leper; for he was cut off from the
house of the LORD. Then Jotham
his son *was* over the king's house,
judging the people of the land.
22 Now the rest of the acts of Uz-
ziah, from first to last, the prophet
[a]Isaiah the son of Amoz wrote.
23 [a]So Uzziah [1]rested with his fa-
thers, and they buried him with his
fathers in the field of burial which
belonged to the kings, for they
said, "He is a leper." Then Jotham
his son reigned in his place.

Jotham Reigns in Judah

27 Jotham [a]*was* twenty-five
years old when he became
king, and he reigned sixteen years
in Jerusalem. His mother's name
was [1]Jerushah the daughter of Za-
dok.
2 And he did *what was* right in
the sight of the LORD, according to
all that his father Uzziah had done
(although he did not enter the tem-
ple of the LORD). But still [a]the peo-
ple acted corruptly.
3 He built the Upper Gate of
the house of the LORD, and he
built extensively on the wall of
[a]Ophel.
4 Moreover he built cities in the
mountains of Judah, and in the
forests he built fortresses and tow-
ers.
5 He also fought with the king of
the [a]Ammonites and defeated
them. And the people of Ammon
gave him in that year one hundred
talents of silver, ten thousand kors
of wheat, and ten thousand of bar-
ley. The people of Ammon paid
this to him in the second and third
years also.
6 So Jotham became mighty,
[a]because he prepared his ways be-
fore the LORD his God.
7 Now the rest of the acts of Jo-
tham, and all his wars and his
ways, indeed they *are* written in
the book of the kings of Israel and
Judah.
8 He was twenty-five years old
when he became king, and he
reigned sixteen years in Jeru-
salem.
9 [a]So Jotham [1]rested with his fa-
thers, and they buried him in the
City of David. Then [b]Ahaz his son
reigned in his place.

Ahaz Reigns in Judah

28 Ahaz [a]*was* twenty years old
when he became king, and
he reigned sixteen years in Jerusa-
lem; and he did not do *what was*
right in the sight of the LORD, as
his father David *had done*.
2 For he walked in the ways of
the kings of Israel, and made
[a]molded images for [b]the Baals.
3 He burned incense in [a]the Val-
ley of the Son of Hinnom, and
burned [b]his children in the [c]fire,
according to the abominations of
the nations whom the LORD had
[d]cast out before the children of Is-
rael.
4 And he sacrificed and burned
incense on the [1]high places, on
the hills, and under every green
tree.

---

16 [a][Deut. 32:15] [b]Deut. 8:14; 2 Chr. 25:19 [c]1 Kin. 13:1–4; 2 Kin. 16:12, 13
17 [a]1 Chr. 6:10
18 [a][Num. 3:10; 16:39, 40; 18:7] [b]Ex. 30:7, 8; Heb. 7:14
19 [a]Lev. 13:42; Num. 12:10; 2 Kin. 5:25–27
20 [a]Esth. 6:12
21 [a]2 Kin. 15:5 [b][Lev. 13:46; Num. 5:2]
22 [a]2 Kin. 20:1; 2 Chr. 32:20, 32; Is. 1:1
23 [a]2 Kin. 15:7; 2 Chr. 21:20; 28:27; Is. 6:1 [1]Died and joined his ancestors

CHAPTER 27

1 [a]2 Kin. 15:32–35 [1]*Jerusha*, 2 Kin. 15:33
2 [a]2 Kin. 15:35; Ezek. 20:44; 30:13
3 [a]2 Chr. 33:14; Neh. 3:26
5 [a]2 Chr. 26:8
6 [a]2 Chr. 26:5
9 [a]2 Kin. 15:38 [b]Is. 1:1; Hos. 1:1; Mic. 1:1 [1]Died and joined his ancestors

CHAPTER 28

1 [a]2 Kin. 16:2–4
2 [a]Ex. 34:17; Lev. 19:4 [b]Judg. 2:11
3 [a]Josh. 15:8 [b]2 Kin. 23:10 [c][Lev. 18:21]; 2 Kin. 16:3; 2 Chr. 33:6 [d][Lev. 18:24–30]
4 [1]Places for pagan worship

Syria and Israel Defeat Judah

5 Therefore [a]the LORD his God
delivered him into the hand of the
king of Syria. They [b]defeated him,
and carried away a great multitude
of them as captives, and brought
them to Damascus. Then he was
also delivered into the hand of the
king of Israel, who defeated him
with a great slaughter.
6 For [a]Pekah the son of Remaliah
killed one hundred and twenty
thousand in Judah in one day, all
valiant men, [b]because they had
forsaken the LORD God of their fa-
thers.
7 Zichri, a mighty man of
Ephraim, killed Maaseiah the
king's son, Azrikam the officer
over the house, and Elkanah *who*
was second to the king.
8 And the children of Israel car-
ried away captive of their [a]breth-
ren two hundred thousand women,
sons, and daughters; and they also
took away much [1]spoil from them,
and brought the spoil to Samaria.

Israel Returns the Captives

9 But a [a]prophet of the LORD was
there, whose name *was* Oded; and
he went out before the army that
came to Samaria, and said to
them: "Look, [b]because the LORD
God of your fathers was angry
with Judah, He has delivered them
into your hand; but you have killed
them in a rage *that* [c]reaches up
to heaven.
10 "And now you propose to force
the children of Judah and Jerusa-
lem to be your [a]male and female
slaves; *but are* you not also guilty
before the LORD your God?
11 "Now hear me, therefore, and
return the captives, whom you
have taken captive from your
brethren, [a]for the fierce wrath of
the LORD *is* upon you."
12 Then some of the heads of the
children of Ephraim, Azariah the
son of Johanan, Berechiah the son
of Meshillemoth, Jehizkiah the son
of Shallum, and Amasa the son of
Hadlai, stood up against those who
came from the war,
13 and said to them, "You shall
not bring the captives here, for we
already have offended the LORD.
You intend to add to our sins and
to our guilt; for our guilt is great,
and *there is* fierce wrath against
Israel."
14 So the armed men left the cap-
tives and the [1]spoil before the lead-
ers and all the assembly.
15 Then the men [a]who were desig-
nated by name rose up and took
the captives, and from the [1]spoil
they clothed all who were naked
among them, dressed them and
gave them sandals, [b]gave them
food and drink, and anointed
them; and they let all the feeble
ones ride on donkeys. So they
brought them to their brethren at
Jericho, [c]the city of palm trees.
Then they returned to Samaria.

Assyria Refuses to Help Judah

16 [a]At the same time King Ahaz
sent to the [1]kings of Assyria to
help him.
17 For again the [a]Edomites had
come, attacked Judah, and carried
away captives.
18 [a]The Philistines also had in-
vaded the cities of the lowland and
of the South of Judah, and had
taken Beth Shemesh, Aijalon,
Gederoth, Sochoh with its villages,
Timnah with its villages, and
Gimzo with its villages; and they
dwelt there.
19 For the LORD [1]brought Judah
low because of Ahaz king of [a]Is-
rael, for he had [b]encouraged
moral decline in Judah and had
been continually unfaithful to the
LORD.
20 Also [a]Tiglath-Pileser[1] king of
Assyria came to him and dis-
tressed him, and did not assist
him.
21 For Ahaz took part *of the trea-*
sures from the house of the LORD,
from the house of the king, and
from the leaders, and he gave *it*
to the king of Assyria; but he did
not help him.

Apostasy and Death of Ahaz

22 Now in the time of his distress
King Ahaz became increasingly
unfaithful to the LORD. This *is that*
King Ahaz.
23 For [a]he sacrificed to the gods
of Damascus which had defeated
him, saying, "Because the gods of
the kings of Syria help them, I will
sacrifice to them [b]that they may

5 [a][Is. 10:5] [b]2 Kin. 16:5, 6; [2 Chr. 24:24]; Is. 7:1, 17
6 [a]2 Kin. 15:27 [b][2 Chr. 29:8]
8 [a]Deut. 28:25, 41; 2 Chr. 11:4 [1]*plunder*
9 [a]2 Chr. 25:15 [b]Ps. 69:26; [Is. 10:5; 47:6]; Ezek. 25:12, 15; 26:2; Obad. 10; [Zech. 1:15] [c]Ezra 9:6; Rev. 18:5
10 [a][Lev. 25:39, 42, 43, 46]
11 [a]Ps. 78:49; James 2:13
14 [1]*plunder*
15 [a]2 Chr. 28:12 [b][Prov. 25:21, 22; Luke 6:27; Rom. 12:20] [c]Deut. 34:3; Judg. 1:16 [1]*plunder*
16 [a]2 Kin. 16:7 [1]LXX, Syr., Vg. *king* (cf. v. 20)
17 [a]2 Chr. 21:10; Obad. 10–14
18 [a]2 Chr. 21:16, 17; Ezek. 16:27, 57
19 [a]2 Kin. 16:2; 2 Chr. 21:2 [b]Ex. 32:25 [1]*humbled Judah*
20 [a]2 Kin. 15:29; 16:7–9; 1 Chr. 5:26 [1]Heb. *Tilgath-Pilneser*
23 [a]2 Chr. 25:14 [b]Jer. 44:17, 18

help me." But they were the ruin
of him and of all Israel.
24 So Ahaz gathered the articles
of the house of God, cut in pieces
the articles of the house of God,
[a]shut up the doors of the house of
the LORD, and made for himself al-
tars in every corner of Jerusalem.
25 And in every single city of Ju-
dah he made [1]high places to burn
incense to other gods, and pro-
voked to anger the LORD God of
his fathers.
26 [a]Now the rest of his acts and
all his ways, from first to last, in-
deed they *are* written in the book
of the kings of Judah and Israel.
27 So Ahaz [1]rested with his fa-
thers, and they buried him in the
city, in Jerusalem; but they [a]did
not bring him into the tombs of the
kings of Israel. Then Hezekiah his
son reigned in his place.

Hezekiah Reigns in Judah

29 Hezekiah [a]became king
when he was twenty-five
years old, and he reigned twenty-
nine years in Jerusalem. His moth-
er's name *was* [1]Abijah the daugh-
ter of Zechariah.
2 And he did *what was* right in
the sight of the LORD, according to
all that his father David had done.

Hezekiah Cleanses the Temple

3 In the first year of his reign, in
the first month, he [a]opened the
doors of the house of the LORD and
repaired them.
4 Then he brought in the priests
and the Levites, and gathered
them in the East Square,
5 and said to them: "Hear me,
Levites! Now [1]sanctify yourselves,
[a]sanctify the house of the LORD
God of your fathers, and carry out
the rubbish from the holy *place*.
6 "For our fathers have tres-
passed and done evil in the eyes
of the LORD our God; they have for-
saken Him, have [a]turned their
faces away from the [1]dwelling
place of the LORD, and turned *their*
backs *on Him*.
7 [a]"They have also shut up the
doors of the vestibule, put out the
lamps, and have not burned in-
cense or offered burnt offerings in
the holy *place* to the God of Israel.
8 "Therefore the [a]wrath of the
LORD fell upon Judah and Jerusa-
lem, and He has [b]given them up
to trouble, to desolation, and to
[c]jeering, as you see with your
[d]eyes.
9 "For indeed, because of this
[a]our fathers have fallen by the
sword; and our sons, our daugh-
ters, and our wives *are* in captivity.
10 "Now *it is* in my heart to make
[a]a covenant with the LORD God of
Israel, that His fierce wrath may
turn away from us.
11 "My sons, do not be negligent
now, for the LORD has [a]chosen you
to stand before Him, to serve Him,
and that you should minister to
Him and burn incense."
12 Then these Levites arose: [a]Ma-
hath the son of Amasai and Joel
the son of Azariah, of the sons of
the [b]Kohathites; of the sons of
Merari, Kish the son of Abdi and
Azariah the son of Jehallelel; of
the Gershonites, Joah the son of
Zimmah and Eden the son of Joah;
13 of the sons of Elizaphan,
Shimri and Jeiel; of the sons of
Asaph, Zechariah and Mattaniah;
14 of the sons of Heman, Jehiel
and Shimei; and of the sons of Je-
duthun, Shemaiah and Uzziel.
15 And they gathered their breth-
ren, [a]sanctified[1] themselves, and
went according to the command-
ment of the king, at the words of
the LORD, [b]to cleanse the house of
the LORD.
16 Then the priests went into the
inner part of the house of the LORD
to cleanse *it*, and brought out all
the debris that they found in the
temple of the LORD to the court of
the house of the LORD. And the
Levites took *it* out and carried *it*
to the Brook [a]Kidron.
17 Now they began to [1]sanctify on
the first *day* of the first month, and
on the eighth day of the month
they came to the vestibule of the
LORD. So they sanctified the house
of the LORD in eight days, and on
the sixteenth day of the first month
they finished.
18 Then they went in to King
Hezekiah and said, "We have
cleansed all the house of the LORD,
the altar of burnt offerings with all
its articles, and the table of the
showbread with all its articles.
19 "Moreover all the articles

24 [a]2 Chr. 29:3, 7
25 [1]Places for pagan worship
26 [a]2 Kin. 16:19, 20
27 [a]2 Chr. 21:20; 24:25 [1]Died and joined his ancestors

CHAPTER 29

1 [a]2 Kin. 18:1; 2 Chr. 32:22, 33 [1]*Abi*, 2 Kin. 18:2
3 [a]2 Chr. 28:24; 29:7
5 [a]1 Chr. 15:12; 2 Chr. 29:15, 34; 35:6 [1]*consecrate*
6 [a][Is. 1:4]; Jer. 2:27; Ezek. 8:16 [1]Temple
7 [a]2 Chr. 28:24
8 [a]2 Chr. 24:18 [b]2 Chr. 28:5 [c]1 Kin. 9:8; Jer. 18:16; 19:8; 25:9, 18; 29:18 [d]Deut. 28:32
9 [a]Deut. 28:25; 2 Chr. 28:5–8, 17
10 [a]2 Chr. 15:12; 23:16
11 [a]Num. 3:6; 8:14; 18:2, 6; 2 Chr. 30:16, 17
12 [a]2 Chr. 31:13 [b]Num. 3:19, 20
15 [a]2 Chr. 29:5 [b]1 Chr. 23:28 [1]*consecrated*
16 [a]2 Chr. 15:16; 30:14
17 [1]*consecrate*

which King Ahaz in his reign had
[a]cast aside in his transgression we
have prepared and [1]sanctified; and
there they *are*, before the altar of
the LORD."

Hezekiah Restores Temple Worship

20 Then King Hezekiah rose
early, gathered the rulers of the
city, and went up to the house of
the LORD.
21 And they brought seven bulls,
seven rams, seven lambs, and
seven male goats for a [a]sin offer-
ing for the kingdom, for the sanc-
tuary, and for Judah. Then he
commanded the priests, the sons
of Aaron, to offer *them* on the altar
of the LORD.
22 So they killed the bulls, and the
priests received the blood and
[a]sprinkled *it* on the altar. Likewise
they killed the rams and sprinkled
the blood on the altar. They also
killed the lambs and sprinkled the
blood on the altar.
23 Then they brought out the male
goats *for* the sin offering before the
king and the assembly, and they
laid their [a]hands on them.
24 And the priests killed them;
and they presented their blood on
the altar as a sin offering [a]to make
an atonement for all Israel, for the
king commanded *that* the burnt
offering and the sin offering *be*
made for all Israel.
25 [a]And he stationed the Levites
in the house of the LORD with cym-
bals, with stringed instruments,
and with harps, [b]according to the
commandment of David, of [c]Gad
the king's seer, and of Nathan the
prophet; [d]for thus *was* the com-
mandment of the LORD by his
prophets.
26 The Levites stood with the in-
struments [a]of David, and the
priests with [b]the trumpets.
27 Then Hezekiah commanded
them to offer the burnt offering on
the altar. And when the burnt of-
fering began, [a]the song of the LORD
also began, with the trumpets and
with the instruments of David king
of Israel.
28 So all the assembly worshiped,
the singers sang, and the trumpet-
ers sounded; all *this continued* un-
til the burnt offering was finished.
29 And when they had finished of-
fering, [a]the king and all who were
present with him bowed and wor-
shiped.
30 Moreover King Hezekiah and
the leaders commanded the Le-
vites to sing praise to the LORD
with the words of David and of
Asaph the seer. So they sang
praises with gladness, and they
bowed their heads and worshiped.
31 Then Hezekiah answered and
said, "Now *that* you have conse-
crated yourselves to the LORD,
come near, and bring sacrifices
and [a]thank offerings into the
house of the LORD." So the as-
sembly brought in sacrifices and
thank offerings, and as many as
were of a [b]willing heart *brought*
burnt offerings.
32 And the number of the burnt
offerings which the assembly
brought was seventy bulls, one
hundred rams, *and* two hundred
lambs; all these *were* for a burnt
offering to the LORD.
33 The consecrated things *were*
six hundred bulls and three thou-
sand sheep.
34 But the priests were too few, so
that they could not skin all the
burnt offerings; therefore [a]their
brethren the Levites helped them
until the work was ended and until
the *other* priests had [1]sanctified
themselves, [b]for the Levites were
[c]more diligent in [d]sanctifying
themselves than the priests.
35 Also the burnt offerings *were*
in abundance, with [a]the fat of the
peace offerings and *with* [b]the
drink offerings for *every* burnt of-
fering. So the service of the house
of the LORD was set in order.
36 Then Hezekiah and all the peo-
ple rejoiced that God had prepared
the people, since the events took
place so suddenly.

Hezekiah Keeps the Passover

30 And Hezekiah sent to all Is-
rael and Judah, and also
wrote letters to Ephraim and Ma-
nasseh, that they should come to
the house of the LORD at Jerusa-
lem, to keep the Passover to the
LORD God of Israel.
2 For the king and his leaders
and all the assembly in Jerusalem
had agreed to keep the Passover
in the second [a]month.

19 [a]2 Chr. 28:24 [1]*consecrated*
21 [a]Lev. 4:3–14
22 [a]Lev. 8:14, 15, 19, 24; Heb. 9:21
23 [a]Lev. 4:15, 24; 8:14
24 [a]Lev. 14:20
25 [a]1 Chr. 16:4; 25:6 [b]1 Chr. 23:5; 25:1; 2 Chr. 8:14 [c]2 Sam. 24:11 [d]2 Chr. 30:12
26 [a]1 Chr. 23:5; Amos 6:5 [b]Num. 10:8, 10; 1 Chr. 15:24; 16:6; 2 Chr. 5:12
27 [a]2 Chr. 23:18
29 [a]2 Chr. 20:18
31 [a]Lev. 7:12 [b]Ex. 35:5, 22
34 [a]2 Chr. 35:11 [b]2 Chr. 30:3 [c]Ps. 7:10 [d]2 Chr. 29:5 [1]*consecrated*
35 [a]Lev. 3:15, 16 [b]Num. 15:5–10

CHAPTER 30

2 [a]Num. 9:10, 11; 2 Chr. 30:13, 15

3 For they could not keep it [a]at [1]the regular time, [b]because a sufficient number of priests had not consecrated themselves, nor had the people gathered together at Jerusalem.

4 And the matter pleased the king and all the assembly.

5 So they [1]resolved to make a proclamation throughout all Israel, from Beersheba to Dan, that they should come to keep the Passover to the LORD God of Israel at Jerusalem, since they had not done *it* for a long *time* in the *prescribed* manner.

6 Then the [a]runners went throughout all Israel and Judah with the letters from the king and his leaders, and spoke according to the command of the king: "Children of Israel, [b]return to the LORD God of Abraham, Isaac, and Israel; then He will return to the remnant of you who have escaped from the hand of [c]the kings of [d]Assyria.

7 "And do not be [a]like your fathers and your brethren, who trespassed against the LORD God of their fathers, so that He [b]gave them up to [c]desolation, as you see.

8 "Now do not be [a]stiff-necked,[1] as your fathers *were, but* yield yourselves to the LORD; and enter His sanctuary, which He has sanctified forever, and serve the LORD your God, [b]that the fierceness of His wrath may turn away from you.

9 "For if you return to the LORD, your brethren and your children *will be treated* with [a]compassion by those who lead them captive, so that they may come back to this land; for the LORD your God *is* [b]gracious and merciful, and will not turn *His* face from you if you [c]return to Him."

10 So the runners passed from city to city through the country of Ephraim and Manasseh, as far as Zebulun; but [a]they laughed at them and mocked them.

11 Nevertheless [a]some from Asher, Manasseh, and Zebulun humbled themselves and came to Jerusalem.

12 Also [a]the hand of God was on Judah to give them singleness of heart to obey the command of the king and the leaders, [b]at the word of the LORD.

13 Now many people, a very great assembly, gathered at Jerusalem to keep the Feast of [a]Unleavened Bread in the second month.

14 They arose and took away the [a]altars that *were* in Jerusalem, and they took away all the incense altars and cast *them* into the Brook [b]Kidron.

15 Then they slaughtered the Passover *lambs* on the fourteenth *day* of the second month. The priests and the Levites [1]were [a]ashamed, and [2]sanctified themselves, and brought the burnt offerings to the house of the LORD.

16 They stood in their [a]place [1]according to their custom, according to the Law of Moses the man of God; the priests sprinkled the blood *received* from the hand of the Levites.

17 For *there were* many in the assembly who had not [1]sanctified themselves; [a]therefore the Levites had charge of the slaughter of the Passover *lambs* for everyone *who was* not clean, to sanctify *them* to the LORD.

18 For a multitude of the people, [a]many from Ephraim, Manasseh, Issachar, and Zebulun, had not cleansed themselves, [b]yet they ate the Passover contrary to what was written. But Hezekiah prayed for them, saying, "May the good LORD provide atonement for everyone

19 "*who* [a]prepares his heart to seek God, the LORD God of his fathers, though *he is* not *cleansed* according to the purification of the sanctuary."

20 And the LORD listened to Hezekiah and healed the people.

21 So the children of Israel who were present at Jerusalem kept [a]the Feast of Unleavened Bread seven days with great gladness; and the Levites and the priests praised the LORD day by day, *singing* to the LORD, accompanied by loud instruments.

22 And Hezekiah gave encouragement to all the Levites [a]who taught the good knowledge of the LORD; and they ate throughout the feast seven days, offering peace offerings

3 [a]Ex. 12:6, 18 [b]2 Chr. 29:17, 34 [1]The first month, Lev. 23:5; lit. *that time*
5 [1]*established a decree to*
6 [a]Esth. 8:14; Job 9:25; Jer. 51:31 [b][Jer. 4:1; Joel 2:13] [c]2 Kin. 15:19, 29 [d]2 Chr. 28:20
7 [a]Ezek. 20:18 [b]Is. 1:9 [c]2 Chr. 29:8
8 [a]Ex. 32:9; Deut. 10:16; Acts 7:51 [b]2 Chr. 29:10 [1]Rebellious
9 [a]Ps. 106:46 [b][Ex. 34:6; Mic. 7:18] [c][Is. 55:7]
10 [a]2 Chr. 36:16
11 [a]2 Chr. 11:16; 30:18, 21
12 [a][2 Cor. 3:5; Phil. 2:13; Heb. 13:20, 21] [b]2 Chr. 29:25
13 [a]Lev. 23:6; Num. 9:11
14 [a]2 Chr. 28:24 [b]2 Chr. 29:16
15 [a]2 Chr. 29:34 [1]*humbled themselves* [2]*set themselves apart*
16 [a]2 Chr. 35:10, 15 [1]Or *in their proper order*
17 [a]2 Chr. 29:34 [1]*consecrated*
18 [a]2 Chr. 30:1, 11, 25 [b]Ex. 12:43–49; [Num. 9:10]
19 [a]2 Chr. 19:3
21 [a]Ex. 12:15; 13:6; 1 Kin. 8:65
22 [a][Deut. 33:10]; 2 Chr. 17:9; 35:3

and [b]making confession to the
LORD God of their fathers.
23 Then the whole assembly
agreed to keep *the feast* [a]another
seven days, and they kept it *an-
other* seven days with gladness.
24 For Hezekiah king of Judah
[a]gave to the assembly a thousand
bulls and seven thousand sheep,
and the leaders gave to the assem-
bly a thousand bulls and ten thou-
sand sheep; and a great number
of priests [b]sanctified[1] themselves.
25 The whole assembly of Judah
rejoiced, also the priests and Le-
vites, all the assembly that came
from Israel, the sojourners [a]who
came from the land of Israel, and
those who dwelt in Judah.
26 So there was great joy in Jeru-
salem, for since the time of [a]Sol-
omon the son of David, king of Is-
rael, *there had* been nothing like
this in Jerusalem.
27 Then the priests, the Levites,
arose and [a]blessed the people, and
their voice was heard; and their
prayer came *up* to [b]His holy dwell-
ing place, to heaven.

The Reforms of Hezekiah

31 Now when all this was fin-
ished, all Israel who were
present went out to the cities of Ju-
dah and [a]broke the sacred pillars
in pieces, cut down the wooden im-
ages, and threw down the [1]high
places and the altars—from all Ju-
dah, Benjamin, Ephraim, and Ma-
nasseh—until they had utterly de-
stroyed them all. Then all the
children of Israel returned to their
own cities, every man to his pos-
session.
2 And Hezekiah appointed [a]the
divisions of the priests and the
Levites according to their divi-
sions, each man according to his
service, the priests and Levites
[b]for burnt offerings and peace of-
ferings, to serve, to give thanks,
and to praise in the gates of the
[1]camp of the LORD.
3 The king also *appointed* a [1]por-
tion of his [a]possessions[2] for the
burnt offerings: for the morning
and evening burnt offerings, the
burnt offerings for the Sabbaths
and the New Moons and the set
feasts, as *it is* written in the [b]Law
of the LORD.

22 [b]Ezra 10:11
23 [a]1 Kin. 8:65; 2 Chr. 35:17, 18
24 [a]2 Chr. 35:7, 8 [b]2 Chr. 29:34 [1]*consecrated*
25 [a]2 Chr. 30:11, 18
26 [a]2 Chr. 7:8–10
27 [a]Num. 6:23 [b]Deut. 26:15; Ps. 68:5

CHAPTER 31

1 [a]2 Kin. 18:4 [1]Places for pagan worship
2 [a]1 Chr. 23:6; 24:1 [b]1 Chr. 23:30, 31 [1]Temple
3 [a]2 Chr. 35:7 [b]Num. 28:1—29:40 [1]*share* [2]*property*
4 [a]Num. 18:8; 2 Kin. 12:16; Neh. 13:10; Ezek. 44:29 [b]Mal. 2:7 [1]*the portion due*
5 [a]Ex. 22:29; Neh. 13:12 [b][Lev. 27:30]; Deut. 14:28; 26:12, 13
6 [a][Lev. 27:30]; Deut. 14:28
10 [a]1 Chr. 6:8, 9 [b][Mal. 3:10] [c]Ex. 36:5
11 [a]1 Kin. 6:5–8 [1]*storerooms*
12 [a]2 Chr. 35:9; Neh. 13:13
13 [a]1 Chr. 9:11; Jer. 20:1
14 [a]Deut. 23:23; 2 Chr. 35:8

4 Moreover he commanded the
people who dwelt in Jerusalem to
contribute [a]support[1] for the priests
and the Levites, that they might
devote themselves to [b]the Law of
the LORD.
5 As soon as the commandment
was circulated, the children of Is-
rael brought in abundance [a]the
firstfruits of grain and wine, oil
and honey, and of all the produce
of the field; and they brought in
abundantly the [b]tithe of every-
thing.
6 And the children of Israel and
Judah, who dwelt in the cities of
Judah, brought the tithe of oxen
and sheep; also the [a]tithe of holy
things which were consecrated to
the LORD their God they laid in
heaps.
7 In the third month they began
laying them in heaps, and they fin-
ished in the seventh month.
8 And when Hezekiah and the
leaders came and saw the heaps,
they blessed the LORD and His peo-
ple Israel.
9 Then Hezekiah questioned the
priests and the Levites concerning
the heaps.
10 And Azariah the chief priest,
from the [a]house of Zadok, an-
swered him and said, [b]"Since *the
people* began to bring the offerings
into the house of the LORD, we
have had enough to eat and have
plenty left, for the LORD has
blessed His people; and what is left
is this great [c]abundance."
11 Now Hezekiah commanded
them to prepare [a]rooms[1] in the
house of the LORD, and they pre-
pared them.
12 Then they faithfully brought in
the offerings, the tithes, and the
dedicated things; [a]Cononiah the
Levite had charge of them, and
Shimei his brother *was* the next.
13 Jehiel, Azaziah, Nahath, Asa-
hel, Jerimoth, Jozabad, Eliel, Is-
machiah, Mahath, and Benaiah
were overseers under the hand of
Cononiah and Shimei his brother,
at the commandment of Hezekiah
the king and Azariah the [a]ruler of
the house of God.
14 Kore the son of Imnah the Le-
vite, the keeper of the East Gate,
was over the [a]freewill offerings to
God, to distribute the offerings of

the LORD and the most holy things.

15 And under him *were* [a]Eden, Miniamin, Jeshua, Shemaiah, Amariah, and Shecaniah, *his* faithful assistants in [b]the cities of the priests, to distribute [c]allotments to their brethren by divisions, to the great as well as the small.

16 Besides those males from three years old and up who were written in the genealogy, they distributed to everyone who entered the house of the LORD his daily portion for the work of his service, by his division,

17 and to the priests who were written in the genealogy according to their father's house, and to the Levites [a]from twenty years old and up according to their work, by their divisions,

18 and to all who were written in the genealogy—their little ones and their wives, their sons and daughters, the whole company of them—for in their faithfulness they [1]sanctified themselves in holiness.

19 Also for the sons of Aaron the priests, *who were* in [a]the fields of the common-lands of their cities, in every single city, *there were* men who were [b]designated by name to distribute portions to all the males among the priests and to all who were listed by genealogies among the Levites.

20 Thus Hezekiah did throughout all Judah, and he [a]did what *was* good and right and true before the LORD his God.

21 And in every work that he began in the service of the house of God, in the law and in the commandment, to seek his God, he did *it* with all his heart. So he [a]prospered.

Sennacherib Boasts Against the LORD

32 After [a]these deeds of faithfulness, Sennacherib king of Assyria came and entered Judah; he encamped against the fortified cities, thinking to win them over to himself.

2 And when Hezekiah saw that Sennacherib had come, and that his purpose was to make war against Jerusalem,

3 he consulted with his leaders and [1]commanders to stop the water from the springs which *were* outside the city; and they helped him.

4 Thus many people gathered together who stopped all the [a]springs and the brook that ran through the land, saying, "Why should the [1]kings of Assyria come and find much water?"

5 And [a]he strengthened himself, [b]built up all the wall that was broken, raised *it* up to the towers, and *built* another wall outside; also he repaired [1]the [c]Millo *in* the City of David, and made [2]weapons and shields in abundance.

6 Then he set military captains over the people, gathered them together to him in the open square of the city gate, and [a]gave them encouragement, saying,

7 [a]"Be strong and courageous; [b]do not be afraid nor dismayed before the king of Assyria, nor before all the multitude that *is* with him; for [c]*there are* more with us than with him.

8 "With him *is* an [a]arm of flesh; but [b]with us *is* the LORD our God, to help us and to fight our battles." And the people were strengthened by the words of Hezekiah king of Judah.

9 [a]After this Sennacherib king of Assyria sent his servants to Jerusalem (but he and all the forces with him *laid siege* against Lachish), to Hezekiah king of Judah, and to all Judah who *were* in Jerusalem, saying,

10 [a]"Thus says Sennacherib king of Assyria: 'In what do you trust, that you remain under siege in Jerusalem?

11 'Does not Hezekiah persuade you to give yourselves over to die by famine and by thirst, saying, [a]"The LORD our God will deliver us from the hand of the king of Assyria"?

12 [a]'Has not the same Hezekiah taken away His high places and His altars, and commanded Judah and Jerusalem, saying, "You shall worship before one altar and burn incense on [b]it"?

13 'Do you not know what I and my fathers have done to all the peoples of *other* lands? [a]Were the gods of the nations of those lands

15 [a]2 Chr. 29:12 [b]Josh. 21:1–3, 9 [c]1 Chr. 9:26
17 [a]1 Chr. 23:24, 27
18 [1]*consecrated*
19 [a]Lev. 25:34; Num. 35:1–4 [b]2 Chr. 31:12–15
20 [a]2 Kin. 20:3; 22:2
21 [a]2 Chr. 26:5; 32:30; Ps. 1:3

CHAPTER 32

1 [a]2 Kin. 18:13—19:37; Is. 36:1—37:38
3 [1]Lit. *mighty men*
4 [a]2 Kin. 20:20 [1]So with MT, Vg.; Arab., LXX, Syr. *king*
5 [a]Is. 22:9, 10 [b]2 Kin. 25:4; 2 Chr. 25:23 [c]2 Sam. 5:9; 1 Kin. 9:15, 24; 11:27; 2 Kin. 12:20; 1 Chr. 11:8 [1]Lit. *The Landfill* [2]*javelins*
6 [a]2 Chr. 30:22; Is. 40:2
7 [a][Deut. 31:6] [b]2 Chr. 20:15 [c]2 Kin. 6:16; [Rom. 8:31]
8 [a][Jer. 17:5; 1 John 4:4] [b]Ex. 14:13; [1 Sam. 17:45–47]; 2 Chr. 13:12; 20:17; [Rom. 8:31]
9 [a]2 Kin. 18:17
10 [a]2 Kin. 18:19
11 [a]2 Kin. 18:30
12 [a]2 Kin. 18:22 [b]2 Chr. 31:1, 2
13 [a]2 Kin. 18:33–35

in any way able to deliver their
lands out of my hand?
14 'Who *was there* among all the
gods of those nations that my fa-
thers utterly destroyed that could
deliver his people from my hand,
that your God should be able to
deliver you from my [a]hand?
15 'Now therefore, [a]do not let
Hezekiah deceive you or persuade
you like this, and do not believe
him; for no god of any nation or
kingdom was able to deliver his
people from my hand or the hand
of my fathers. How much less will
your God deliver you from my
hand?' "
16 Furthermore, his servants
spoke against the LORD God and
against His servant Hezekiah.
17 He also wrote letters to revile
the LORD God of Israel, and to
speak against Him, saying, [a]"As
the gods of the nations of *other*
lands have not delivered their peo-
ple from my hand, so the God of
Hezekiah will not deliver His peo-
ple from my [b]hand."
18 [a]Then they called out with a
loud voice in [1]Hebrew to the peo-
ple of Jerusalem who *were* on the
wall, to frighten them and trouble
them, that they might take the city.
19 And they spoke against the
God of Jerusalem, as against the
gods of the people of the earth—
[a]the work of men's hands.

Sennacherib's Defeat and Death

20 [a]Now because of this King
Hezekiah and [b]the prophet Isaiah,
the son of Amoz, prayed and cried
out to heaven.
21 [a]Then the LORD sent an angel
who cut down every mighty man
of valor, leader, and captain in the
camp of the king of Assyria. So he
returned [b]shamefaced to his own
land. And when he had gone into
the temple of his god, some of his
own offspring struck him down
with the sword there.
22 Thus the LORD saved Hezekiah
and the inhabitants of Jerusalem
from the hand of Sennacherib the
king of Assyria, and from the hand
of all *others*, and [1]guided them on
every side.
23 And many brought gifts to the
LORD at Jerusalem, and [a]presents[1]
to Hezekiah king of Judah, so that
he was [b]exalted in the sight of all
nations thereafter.

Hezekiah Humbles Himself

24 [a]In those days Hezekiah was
sick and near death, and he prayed
to the LORD; and He spoke to him
and gave him a sign.
25 But Hezekiah [a]did not repay
according to the favor *shown*
him, for [b]his heart was lifted up;
[c]therefore wrath was looming
over him and over Judah and Jeru-
salem.
26 [a]Then Hezekiah humbled him-
self for the pride of his heart, he
and the inhabitants of Jerusalem,
so that the wrath of the LORD did
not come upon them [b]in the days
of Hezekiah.

Hezekiah's Wealth and Honor

27 Hezekiah had very great riches
and honor. And he made himself
treasuries for silver, for gold, for
precious stones, for spices, for
shields, and for all kinds of desir-
able items;
28 storehouses for the harvest of
grain, wine, and oil; and stalls for
all kinds of livestock, and [1]folds
for flocks.
29 Moreover he provided cities for
himself, and possessions of flocks
and herds in abundance; for [a]God
had given him very much prop-
erty.
30 [a]This same Hezekiah also
stopped the water outlet of Upper
Gihon, and [1]brought the water
by tunnel to the west side of the
City of David. Hezekiah [b]pros-
pered in all his works.
31 However, *regarding* the ambas-
sadors of the princes of Babylon,
whom they [a]sent to him to inquire
about the wonder that was *done*
in the land, God withdrew from
him, in order to [b]test him, that He
might know all *that was* in his
heart.

Death of Hezekiah

32 Now the rest of the acts of
Hezekiah, and his goodness, in-
deed they *are* written in [a]the vision
of Isaiah the prophet, the son of
Amoz, *and* in the [b]book of the
kings of Judah and Israel.
33 [a]So Hezekiah [1]rested with his

14 [a][Is. 10:5–12]
15 [a]2 Kin. 18:29
17 [a]2 Kin. 19:9; [1 Cor. 8:5, 6] [b]2 Kin. 19:12; Dan. 3:15
18 [a]2 Kin. 18:28; Ps. 59:6 [1]Lit. *Judean*
19 [a]2 Kin. 19:18; [Ps. 96:5; 115:4–8]
20 [a]2 Kin. 19:15 [b]2 Kin. 19:2
21 [a]2 Kin. 19:35; Is. 10:12–19; Zech. 14:3 [b]Ps. 44:7
22 [1]LXX *gave them rest;* Vg. *gave them treasures*
23 [a]2 Sam. 8:10; 2 Chr. 17:5; 26:8; Ps. 45:12 [b]2 Chr. 1:1 [1]Lit. *precious things*
24 [a]2 Kin. 20:1–11; Is. 38:1–8
25 [a]Ps. 116:12 [b]2 Chr. 26:16; [Hab. 2:4] [c]2 Chr. 24:18
26 [a]Jer. 26:18, 19 [b]2 Kin. 20:19
28 [1]So with LXX, Vg.; Arab., Syr. omit *folds for flocks;* MT *flocks for sheepfolds*
29 [a]1 Chr. 29:12
30 [a]Is. 22:9–11 [b]2 Chr. 31:21 [1]Lit. *brought it straight to* (cf. 2 Kin. 20:20)
31 [a]2 Kin. 20:12; Is. 39:1 [b][Deut. 8:2, 16]
32 [a]Is. 36—39 [b]2 Kin. 18—20
33 [a]1 Kin. 1:21; 2 Kin. 20:21 [1]Died and joined his ancestors

fathers, and they buried him in the upper tombs of the sons of David; and all Judah and the inhabitants of Jerusalem [b]honored him at his death. Then Manasseh his son reigned in his place.

Manasseh Reigns in Judah

33 Manasseh [a]*was* twelve years old when he became king, and he reigned fifty-five years in Jerusalem.
2 But he did evil in the sight of the LORD, according to the [a]abominations of the nations whom the LORD had cast out before the children of Israel.
3 For he rebuilt the [1]high places which Hezekiah his father had [a]broken down; he raised up altars for the Baals, and [b]made wooden images; and he worshiped [c]all [2]the host of heaven and served them.
4 He also built altars in the house of the LORD, of which the LORD had said, [a]"In Jerusalem shall My name be forever."
5 And he built altars for all the host of heaven [a]in the two courts of the house of the LORD.
6 [a]Also he caused his sons to pass through the fire in the Valley of the Son of Hinnom; he practiced [b]soothsaying, used witchcraft and sorcery, and [c]consulted mediums and spiritists. He did much evil in the sight of the LORD, to provoke Him to anger.
7 [a]He even set a carved image, the idol which he had made, in the [1]house of God, of which God had said to David and to Solomon his son, [b]"In this house and in Jerusalem, which I have chosen out of all the tribes of Israel, I will put My name forever;
8 [a]"and I will not again remove the foot of Israel from the land which I have appointed for your fathers—only if they are careful to do all that I have commanded them, according to the whole law and the statutes and the ordinances by the hand of Moses."
9 So Manasseh seduced Judah and the inhabitants of Jerusalem to do more evil than the nations whom the LORD had destroyed before the children of Israel.

Manasseh Restored After Repentance

10 And the LORD spoke to Manasseh and his people, but they would not [1]listen.
11 [a]Therefore the LORD brought upon them the captains of the army of the king of Assyria, who took Manasseh with [1]hooks, [b]bound him with [2]bronze *fetters,* and carried him off to Babylon.
12 Now when he was in affliction, he implored the LORD his God, and [a]humbled himself greatly before the God of his fathers,
13 and prayed to Him; and He [a]received his entreaty, heard his supplication, and brought him back to Jerusalem into his kingdom. Then Manasseh [b]knew that the LORD *was* God.
14 After this he built a wall outside the City of David on the west side of [a]Gihon, in the valley, as far as the entrance of the Fish Gate; and *it* [b]enclosed Ophel, and he raised it to a very great height. Then he put military captains in all the fortified cities of Judah.
15 He took away [a]the foreign gods and the idol from the house of the LORD, and all the altars that he had built in the mount of the house of the LORD and in Jerusalem; and he cast *them* out of the city.
16 He also repaired the altar of the LORD, sacrificed peace offerings and [a]thank offerings on it, and commanded Judah to serve the LORD God of Israel.
17 [a]Nevertheless the people still sacrificed on the [1]high places, *but* only to the LORD their God.

Death of Manasseh

18 Now the rest of the acts of Manasseh, his prayer to his God, and the words of [a]the seers who spoke to him in the name of the LORD God of Israel, indeed they *are written* in the [1]book of the kings of Israel.
19 Also his prayer and *how God* received his entreaty, and all his sin and trespass, and the sites where he built [1]high places and set up wooden images and carved images, before he was humbled, indeed they *are* written among the sayings of [2]Hozai.
20 [a]So Manasseh rested with his

33 [b]Ps. 112:6; Prov. 10:7

CHAPTER 33

1 [a]2 Kin. 21:1–9
2 [a][Deut. 18:9–12]; 2 Chr. 28:3; [Jer. 15:4]
3 [a]2 Kin. 18:4; 2 Chr. 30:14; 31:1 [b]Deut. 16:21; 2 Kin. 23:5, 6 [c]Deut. 17:3 [1]Places for pagan worship [2]The gods of the Assyrians
4 [a]Deut. 12:11; 1 Kin. 8:29; 9:3; 2 Chr. 6:6; 7:16
5 [a]2 Chr. 4:9
6 [a][Lev. 18:21]; Deut. 18:10; 2 Kin. 23:10; 2 Chr. 28:3; Ezek. 23:37, 39 [b]Deut. 18:11; 2 Kin. 17:17 [c][Lev. 19:31; 20:27]; 2 Kin. 21:6
7 [a]2 Kin. 21:7; 2 Chr. 25:14 [b]Ps. 132:14 [1]Temple
8 [a]2 Sam. 7:10
10 [1]*obey*
11 [a]Deut. 28:36 [b]2 Chr. 36:6; Job 36:8; Ps. 107:10, 11 [1]Nose hooks, 2 Kin. 19:28 [2]*chains*
12 [a]2 Chr. 7:14; 32:26; [1 Pet. 5:6]
13 [a]1 Chr. 5:20; Ezra 8:23 [b]1 Kin. 20:13; Ps. 9:16; Dan. 4:25
14 [a]1 Kin. 1:33 [b]2 Chr. 27:3
15 [a]2 Chr. 33:3, 5, 7
16 [a]Lev. 7:12
17 [a]2 Chr. 32:12 [1]Places for pagan worship
18 [a]1 Sam. 9:9 [1]Lit. *words*
19 [1]Places for pagan worship [2]LXX *the seers*
20 [a]1 Kin. 1:21; 2 Kin. 21:18

fathers, and they buried him in his
own house. Then his son Amon
reigned in his place.

Amon's Reign and Death

21 [a]Amon *was* twenty-two years
old when he became king, and he
reigned two years in Jerusalem.
22 But he did evil in the sight of
the LORD, as his father Manasseh
had done; for Amon sacrificed to
all the carved images which his fa-
ther Manasseh had made, and
served them.
23 And he did not humble himself
before the LORD, [a]as his father Ma-
nasseh had humbled himself; but
Amon trespassed more and more.
24 [a]Then his servants conspired
against him, and [b]killed him in his
own house.
25 But the people of the land exe-
cuted all those who had conspired
against King Amon. Then the peo-
ple of the land made his son Josiah
king in his place.

Josiah Reigns in Judah

34 Josiah [a]*was* eight years old
when he became king, and
he reigned thirty-one years in Je-
rusalem.
2 And he did *what was* right in
the sight of the LORD, and walked
in the ways of his father David; *he*
did *not* turn aside to the right hand
or to the left.
3 For in the eighth year of his
reign, while he was still [a]young,
he began to [b]seek the God of his
father David; and in the twelfth
year he began [c]to purge Judah and
Jerusalem [d]of the [1]high places, the
wooden images, the carved im-
ages, and the molded images.
4 [a]They broke down the altars of
the Baals in his presence, and the
incense altars which *were* above
them he cut down; and the wooden
images, the carved images, and the
molded images he broke in pieces,
and made dust of them [b]and scat-
tered *it* on the graves of those who
had sacrificed to them.
5 He also [a]burned the bones of
the priests on their [b]altars, and
cleansed Judah and Jerusalem.
6 And *so he did* in the cities of
Manasseh, Ephraim, and Simeon,
as far as Naphtali and all around,
with [1]axes.
7 When he had broken down the
altars and the wooden images, had
[a]beaten the carved images into
powder, and cut down all the in-
cense altars throughout all the
land of Israel, he returned to Jeru-
salem.

Hilkiah Finds the Book of the Law

8 [a]In the eighteenth year of his
reign, when he had purged the
land and the [1]temple, he sent
[b]Shaphan the son of Azaliah,
Maaseiah the [c]governor of the city,
and Joah the son of Joahaz the re-
corder, to repair the house of the
LORD his God.
9 When they came to Hilkiah
the high priest, they delivered [a]the
money that was brought into the
house of God, which the Levites
who kept the doors had gathered
from the hand of Manasseh and
Ephraim, from all the [b]remnant of
Israel, from all Judah and Benja-
min, and *which* they had brought
back to Jerusalem.
10 Then they put *it* in the hand of
the foremen who had the oversight
of the house of the LORD; and they
gave it to the workmen who
worked in the house of the LORD,
to repair and restore the house.
11 They gave *it* to the craftsmen
and builders to buy hewn stone
and timber for beams, and to floor
the houses which the kings of Ju-
dah had destroyed.
12 And the men did the work
faithfully. Their overseers *were* Ja-
hath and Obadiah the Levites, of
the sons of Merari, and Zechariah
and Meshullam, of the sons of the
Kohathites, to supervise. *Others of*
the Levites, all of whom were skill-
ful with instruments of music,
13 *were* [a]over the burden bearers
and *were* overseers of all who did
work in any kind of service. [b]And
some of the Levites *were* scribes,
officers, and gatekeepers.
14 Now when they brought out
the money that was brought into
the house of the LORD, Hilkiah the
priest [a]found the Book of the Law
of the LORD *given* by Moses.
15 Then Hilkiah answered and
said to Shaphan the scribe, "I have
found the Book of the Law in the
house of the LORD." And Hilkiah
gave the [a]book to Shaphan.

21 [a]2 Kin. 21:19–24; 1 Chr. 3:14
23 [a]2 Chr. 33:12, 19
24 [a]2 Kin. 21:23, 24; 2 Chr. 24:25 [b]2 Chr. 25:27

CHAPTER 34

1 [a]2 Kin. 22:1, 2; Jer. 1:2; 3:6
3 [a]Eccl. 12:1 [b]2 Chr. 15:2; [Prov. 8:17] [c]1 Kin. 13:2 [d]2 Chr. 33:17–19, 22 [1]Places for pagan worship
4 [a]Lev. 26:30; 2 Kin. 23:4 [b]2 Kin. 23:6
5 [a]1 Kin. 13:2 [b]2 Kin. 23:20
6 [1]Lit. *swords*
7 [a]Deut. 9:21
8 [a]2 Kin. 22:3–20 [b]2 Kin. 25:22 [c]2 Chr. 18:25 [1]Lit. *house*
9 [a]2 Kin. 12:4 [b]2 Chr. 30:6
13 [a]2 Chr. 8:10 [b]1 Chr. 23:4, 5
14 [a]2 Kin. 22:8
15 [a]Deut. 31:24, 26

16 So Shaphan carried the book
to the king, bringing the king
word, saying, "All that was com-
mitted to your servants they are
doing.
17 "And they have [1]gathered the
money that was found in the house
of the LORD, and have delivered it
into the hand of the overseers and
the workmen."
18 Then Shaphan the scribe told
the king, saying, "Hilkiah the
priest has given me a book." And
Shaphan read it before the king.
19 Thus it happened, when the
king heard the words of the Law,
that he tore his clothes.
20 Then the king commanded Hil-
kiah, [a]Ahikam the son of Shaphan,
[1]Abdon the son of Micah, Shaphan
the scribe, and Asaiah a servant
of the king, saying,
21 "Go, inquire of the LORD for
me, and for those who are left in
Israel and Judah, concerning the
words of the book that is found;
for great *is* the wrath of the LORD
that is poured out on us, because
our fathers have not [a]kept the
word of the LORD, to do according
to all that is written in this book."
22 So Hilkiah and those the king
had appointed went to Huldah the
prophetess, the wife of Shallum
the son of [1]Tokhath, the son of
[2]Hasrah, keeper of the wardrobe.
(She dwelt in Jerusalem in the Sec-
ond Quarter.) And they spoke to
her to that *effect*.
23 Then she answered them,
"Thus says the LORD God of Israel,
'Tell the man who sent you to Me,
24 "Thus says the LORD: 'Behold,
I will [a]bring calamity on this place
and on its inhabitants, all the
curses that are written in the
[b]book which they have read before
the king of Judah,
25 'because they have forsaken
Me and burned incense to other
gods, that they might provoke Me
to anger with all the works of their
hands. Therefore My wrath will be
poured out on this place, and not
be quenched.' " '
26 "But as for the king of Judah,
who sent you to inquire of the
LORD, in this manner you shall
speak to him, 'Thus says the LORD
God of Israel: "*Concerning* the
words which you have heard—

17 [1]Lit. *poured out*
20 [a]Jer. 26:24 [1]*Achbor the son of Michaiah,* 2 Kin. 22:12
21 [a]2 Kin. 17:15–19
22 [1]*Tikvah,* 2 Kin. 22:14 [2]*Harhas,* 2 Kin. 22:14
24 [a]2 Chr. 36:14–20 [b]Deut. 28:15–68
27 [a]2 Kin. 22:19; 2 Chr. 12:7; 30:6; 33:12, 13
29 [a]2 Kin. 23:1–3
30 [a]Neh. 8:1–3
31 [a]2 Chr. 6:13 [b]2 Kin. 11:14; 23:3; 2 Chr. 30:16 [c]2 Chr. 23:16; 29:10
33 [a]1 Kin. 11:5; 2 Chr. 33:2 [b]Jer. 3:10 [1]Lit. *serve to serve*

CHAPTER 35

1 [a]2 Kin. 23:21, 22 [b]Ex. 12:6; Num. 9:3; Ezra 6:19

27 "because your heart was ten-
der, and you humbled yourself be-
fore God when you heard His
words against this place and
against its inhabitants, and you
humbled yourself before Me, and
you tore your clothes and wept be-
fore Me, I also have heard *you*,"
says the [a]LORD.
28 "Surely I will gather you to
your fathers, and you shall be
gathered to your grave in peace;
and your eyes shall not see all the
calamity which I will bring on this
place and its inhabitants." ' " So
they brought back word to the
king.

Josiah Restores True Worship

29 [a]Then the king sent and gath-
ered all the elders of Judah and
Jerusalem.
30 The king went up to the house
of the LORD, with all the men of
Judah and the inhabitants of Jeru-
salem—the priests and the Levites,
and all the people, great and small.
And he [a]read in their hearing all
the words of the Book of the Cov-
enant which had been found in
the house of the LORD.
31 Then the king [a]stood in [b]his
place and made a [c]covenant before
the LORD, to follow the LORD, and
to keep His commandments and
His testimonies and His statutes
with all his heart and all his soul,
to perform the words of the cov-
enant that were written in this
book.
32 And he made all who were
present in Jerusalem and Benja-
min take a stand. So the inhabit-
ants of Jerusalem did according to
the covenant of God, the God of
their fathers.
33 Thus Josiah removed all the
[a]abominations from all the coun-
try that *belonged* to the children
of Israel, and made all who were
present in Israel [1]diligently serve
the LORD their God. [b]All his days
they did not depart from following
the LORD God of their fathers.

Josiah Keeps the Passover

35 Now [a]Josiah kept a Pass-
over to the LORD in Jerusa-
lem, and they slaughtered the
Passover *lambs* on the [b]fourteenth
day of the first month.

2 And he set the priests in their
[a]duties and [b]encouraged them for
the service of the house of the
LORD.
3 Then he said to the Levites
[a]who taught all Israel, who were
holy to the LORD: [b]"Put the holy
ark [c]in the house which Solomon
the son of David, king of Israel,
built. [d]*It shall* no longer *be* a bur-
den on *your* shoulders. Now serve
the LORD your God and His people
Israel.
4 "Prepare *yourselves* [a]accord-
ing to your fathers' [1]houses, ac-
cording to your divisions, follow-
ing the [b]written instruction of
David king of Israel and the [c]writ-
ten instruction of Solomon his son.
5 "And [a]stand in the holy *place*
according to the divisions of the
fathers' houses of your brethren
the *lay* people, and *according to*
the division of the father's house
of the Levites.
6 "So slaughter the Passover *of-
ferings*, [a]consecrate yourselves,
and prepare *them* for your breth-
ren, that *they* may do according
to the word of the LORD by the
hand of Moses."
7 Then Josiah [a]gave the *lay* peo-
ple lambs and young goats from
the flock, all for Passover *offerings*
for all who were present, to the
number of thirty thousand, as well
as three thousand cattle; these
were from the king's [b]possessions.
8 And his [a]leaders gave willingly
to the people, to the priests, and
to the Levites. Hilkiah, Zechariah,
and Jehiel, rulers of the house of
God, gave to the priests for the
Passover *offerings* two thousand
six hundred *from the flock*, and
three hundred cattle.
9 Also [a]Conaniah, his brothers
Shemaiah and Nethanel, and
Hashabiah and Jeiel and Jozabad,
chief of the Levites, gave to the
Levites for Passover *offerings* five
thousand *from the flock* and five
hundred cattle.
10 So the service was prepared,
and the priests [a]stood in their
places, and the [b]Levites in their
divisions, according to the king's
command.
11 And they slaughtered the Pass-
over *offerings*; and the priests
[a]sprinkled *the blood* with their

2 [a]2 Chr. 23:18; Ezra 6:18 [b]2 Chr. 29:5–15
3 [a]Deut. 33:10; 2 Chr. 17:8, 9; Neh. 8:7 [b]2 Chr. 34:14 [c]Ex. 40:21; 2 Chr. 5:7 [d]1 Chr. 23:26
4 [a]1 Chr. 9:10–13 [b]1 Chr. 23—26 [c]2 Chr. 8:14 [1]*households*
5 [a]Ps. 134:1
6 [a]2 Chr. 29:5, 15
7 [a]2 Chr. 30:24 [b]2 Chr. 31:3
8 [a]Num. 7:2
9 [a]2 Chr. 31:12
10 [a]Ezra 6:18; Heb. 9:6 [b]2 Chr. 5:12; 7:6; 8:14, 15; 13:10; 29:25–34
11 [a]Ex. 12:22; 2 Chr. 29:22 [b]2 Chr. 29:34
12 [a]Lev. 3:3; Ezra 6:18
13 [a]Ex. 12:8, 9; Deut. 16:7 [b]1 Sam. 2:13–15
15 [a]1 Chr. 25:1–6 [b]1 Chr. 9:17, 18
17 [a]Ex. 12:15; 13:6; 2 Chr. 30:21
18 [a]2 Kin. 23:22, 23
20 [a]2 Kin. 23:29 [b]Is. 10:9; Jer. 46:2

hands, while the Levites [b]skinned
the animals.
12 Then they removed the burnt
offerings that *they* might give
them to the divisions of the fa-
thers' houses of the *lay* people, to
offer to the LORD, as *it is* written
[a]in the Book of Moses. And so *they
did* with the cattle.
13 Also they [a]roasted the Pass-
over *offerings* with fire according
to the ordinance; but the *other*
holy *offerings* they [b]boiled in pots,
in caldrons, and in pans, and di-
vided *them* quickly among all the
lay people.
14 Then afterward they prepared
portions for themselves and for the
priests, because the priests, the
sons of Aaron, *were busy* in offer-
ing burnt offerings and fat until
night; therefore the Levites pre-
pared portions for themselves and
for the priests, the sons of Aaron.
15 And the singers, the sons of
Asaph, *were* in their places, ac-
cording to the [a]command of David,
Asaph, Heman, and Jeduthun the
king's seer. Also the gatekeepers
[b]were at each gate; they did not
have to leave their position, be-
cause their brethren the Levites
prepared portions for them.
16 So all the service of the LORD
was prepared the same day, to
keep the Passover and to offer
burnt offerings on the altar of the
LORD, according to the command
of King Josiah.
17 And the children of Israel who
were present kept the Passover at
that time, and the Feast of [a]Un-
leavened Bread for seven days.
18 [a]There had been no Passover
kept in Israel like that since the
days of Samuel the prophet; and
none of the kings of Israel had
kept such a Passover as Josiah
kept, with the priests and the Le-
vites, all Judah and Israel who
were present, and the inhabitants
of Jerusalem.
19 In the eighteenth year of the
reign of Josiah this Passover was
kept.

Josiah Dies in Battle

20 [a]After all this, when Josiah had
prepared the temple, Necho king
of Egypt came up to fight against
[b]Carchemish by the Euphrates;

and Josiah went out against him.
21 But he sent messengers to him,
saying, "What have I to do with
you, king of Judah? *I have* not
come against you this day, but
against the house with which I
have war; for God commanded me
to make haste. Refrain *from med-*
dling with God, who *is* with me,
lest He destroy you."
22 Nevertheless Josiah would not
turn his face from him, but [a]dis-
guised himself so that he might
fight with him, and did not heed
the words of Necho from the
mouth of God. So he came to fight
in the Valley of Megiddo.
23 And the archers shot King Jo-
siah; and the king said to his ser-
vants, "Take me away, for I am se-
verely wounded."
24 [a]His servants therefore took
him out of that chariot and put him
in the second chariot that he had,
and they brought him to Jerusa-
lem. So he died, and was buried
in *one of* the tombs of his fathers.
And [b]all Judah and Jerusalem
mourned for Josiah.
25 Jeremiah also [a]lamented for
[b]Josiah. And to this day [c]all the
singing men and the singing
women speak of Josiah in their
lamentations. [d]They made it a
custom in Israel; and indeed they
are written in the Laments.
26 Now the rest of the acts of Jo-
siah and his goodness, according
to *what was* written in the Law of
the LORD,
27 and his deeds from first to last,
indeed they *are* written in the book
of the kings of Israel and Judah.

The Reign and Captivity of Jehoahaz

36 Then [a]the people of the land
took Jehoahaz the son of Jo-
siah, and made him king in his fa-
ther's place in Jerusalem.
2 [1]Jehoahaz *was* twenty-three
years old when he became king,
and he reigned three months in Je-
rusalem.
3 Now the king of Egypt deposed
him at Jerusalem; and he imposed
on the land a tribute of one hun-
dred talents of silver and a talent
of gold.
4 Then the king of Egypt made
[1]*Jehoahaz's* brother Eliakim king
over Judah and Jerusalem, and
changed his name to Jehoiakim.
And Necho took [2]Jehoahaz his
brother and carried him off to
Egypt.

The Reign and Captivity of Jehoiakim

5 [a]Jehoiakim *was* twenty-five
years old when he became king,
and he reigned eleven years in Je-
rusalem. And he did [b]evil in the
sight of the LORD his God.
6 [a]Nebuchadnezzar king of Bab-
ylon came up against him, and
bound him in [1]bronze *fetters* to
[b]carry him off to Babylon.
7 [a]Nebuchadnezzar also carried
off *some* of the articles from the
house of the LORD to Babylon, and
put them in his temple at Babylon.
8 Now the rest of the acts of Je-
hoiakim, the abominations which
he did, and what was found
against him, indeed they *are* writ-
ten in the book of the kings of Is-
rael and Judah. Then [1]Jehoiachin
his son reigned in his place.

The Reign and Captivity of Jehoiachin

9 [a]Jehoiachin *was* [1]eight years
old when he became king, and he
reigned in Jerusalem three months
and ten days. And he did evil in
the sight of the LORD.
10 At the turn of the year [a]King
Nebuchadnezzar summoned *him*
and took him to Babylon, [b]with the
costly articles from the house of
the LORD, and made [c]Zedekiah,[1]
[2]*Jehoiakim's* brother, king over Ju-
dah and Jerusalem.

Zedekiah Reigns in Judah

11 [a]Zedekiah *was* twenty-one
years old when he became king,
and he reigned eleven years in Je-
rusalem.
12 He did evil in the sight of the
LORD his God, *and* [a]did not humble
himself before Jeremiah the
prophet, *who spoke* from the
mouth of the LORD.
13 And he also [a]rebelled against
King Nebuchadnezzar, who had
made him swear *an oath* by God;
but he [b]stiffened his neck and
hardened his heart against turning
to the LORD God of Israel.
14 Moreover all the leaders of the
priests and the people trans-
gressed more and more, *according*
to all the abominations of the

---

22 [a]1 Kin. 22:30; 2 Chr. 18:29
24 [a]2 Kin. 23:30 [b]1 Kin. 14:18; Zech. 12:11
25 [a]Lam. 4:20 [b]Jer. 22:10, 11 [c]Matt. 9:23 [d]Jer. 22:20

CHAPTER 36

1 [a]2 Kin. 23:30–34
2 [1]MT *Joahaz*
4 [1]Lit. *his* [2]MT *Joahaz*
5 [a]2 Kin. 23:36, 37; 1 Chr. 3:15 [b][Jer. 22:13–19]
6 [a]2 Kin. 24:1; Hab. 1:6 [b][Deut. 29:22–29]; 2 Chr. 33:11; Jer. 36:30 [1]*chains*
7 [a]2 Kin. 24:13; Dan. 1:1, 2
8 [1]Or *Jeconiah*
9 [a]2 Kin. 24:8–17 [1]Heb. mss., LXX, Syr. *eighteen* and 2 Kin. 24:8
10 [a]2 Kin. 24:10–17 [b]Dan. 1:1, 2 [c]Jer. 37:1 [1]Or *Mattaniah* [2]Lit. *his brother*, 2 Kin. 24:17
11 [a]2 Kin. 24:18–20; Jer. 52:1
12 [a]Jer. 21:3–7; 44:10
13 [a]Jer. 52:3; Ezek. 17:15 [b]2 Kin. 17:14; [2 Chr. 30:8]

nations, and defiled the house of
the LORD which He had conse-
crated in Jerusalem.

The Fall of Jerusalem

15 [a]And the LORD God of their fa-
thers sent *warnings* to them by His
messengers, rising up early and
sending *them*, because He had
compassion on His people and on
His dwelling place.
16 But [a]they mocked the messen-
gers of God, [b]despised His words,
and [c]scoffed at His prophets, until
the [d]wrath of the LORD arose
against His people, till *there was*
no remedy.
17 [a]Therefore He brought against
them the king of the Chaldeans,
who [b]killed their young men with
the sword in the house of their
sanctuary, and had no compassion
on young man or virgin, on the
aged or the weak; He gave *them*
all into his hand.
18 [a]And all the articles from the
house of God, great and small, the
treasures of the house of the LORD,
and the treasures of the king and
of his leaders, all *these* he took to
Babylon.
19 [a]Then they burned the house of
God, broke down the wall of Jeru-
salem, burned all its palaces with
fire, and destroyed all its precious
possessions.
20 And [a]those who escaped from
the sword he carried away to Bab-
bylon, [b]where they became ser-
vants to him and his sons until the
rule of the kingdom of Persia,
21 to fulfill the word of the LORD
by the mouth of [a]Jeremiah, until
the land [b]had enjoyed her Sab-
baths. As long as she lay desolate
[c]she kept Sabbath, to fulfill sev-
enty years.

The Proclamation of Cyrus

22 [a]Now in the first year of Cyrus
king of Persia, that the word of the
LORD by the mouth of [b]Jeremiah
might be fulfilled, the LORD stirred
up the spirit of [c]Cyrus king of Per-
sia, so that he made a proclama-
tion throughout all his kingdom,
and also *put it* in writing, saying,

23 [a]Thus says Cyrus king of
Persia: All the kingdoms of the
earth the LORD God of heaven
has given me. And He has
commanded me to build Him a
[1]house at Jerusalem which is in
Judah. Who *is* among you of all
His people? May the LORD his
God *be* with him, and let him
go up!

15 [a]Jer. 7:13; 25:3, 4
16 [a]2 Chr. 30:10; Jer. 5:12, 13 [b][Prov. 1:24–32] [c]Jer. 38:6; Matt. 23:34 [d]2 Chr. 34:25; Ps. 79:5
17 [a]Num. 33:56; Deut. 4:26; 28:49; 2 Kin. 25:1; Ezra 9:7; Is. 3:8 [b]Ps. 74:20
18 [a]2 Kin. 25:13–15; 2 Chr. 36:7, 10
19 [a]2 Kin. 25:9; Ps. 79:1, 7; Is. 1:7, 8; Jer. 52:13
20 [a]2 Kin. 25:11; Jer. 5:19; Mic. 4:10 [b]Jer. 17:4; 27:7
21 [a]Jer. 25:9–12; 27:6–8; 29:10 [b]Lev. 26:34–43; Dan. 9:2 [c]Lev. 25:4, 5
22 [a]Ezra 1:1–3 [b]Jer. 29:10 [c]Is. 44:28; 45:1
23 [a]Ezra 1:2, 3 [1]Temple

The Book of

Ezra

EZRA continues the Old Testament narrative of Second Chronicles by showing how God fulfills His promise to return His people to the Land of Promise after seventy years of exile. Israel's "second exodus," this one from Babylon, is less impressive than the return from Egypt because only a remnant chooses to leave Babylon.

Ezra relates the story of two returns from Babylon—the first led by Zerubbabel to rebuild the temple (1—6), and the second under the leadership of Ezra to rebuild the spiritual condition of the people (7—10). Sandwiched between these two accounts is a gap of nearly six decades, during which Esther lives and rules as queen in Persia.

Ezra is the Aramaic form of the Hebrew word *ezer,* "help," and perhaps means "Yahweh helps." Ezra and Nehemiah were originally bound together as one book because Chronicles, Ezra, and Nehemiah were viewed as one continuous history. The Septuagint, a Greek-language version of the Old Testament translated in the third century B.C., calls Ezra–Nehemiah, *Esdras Deuteron,* "Second Esdras." First Esdras is the name of the apocryphal book of Esdras. The Latin title is *Liber Primus Esdrae,* "First Book of Ezra." In the Latin Bible, Ezra is called First Ezra and Nehemiah is called Second Ezra.

End of The Babylonian Captivity

CHAPTER 1

NOW in the first year of Cyrus
king of Persia, that the word
of the LORD [a]by the mouth of
Jeremiah might be fulfilled, the
LORD stirred up the spirit of Cyrus
king of Persia, [b]so that he made a
proclamation throughout all his
kingdom, and also *put it* in writ-
ing, saying,

2 Thus says Cyrus king of Persia:
All the kingdoms of the earth
the LORD God of heaven has
given me. And He has
[a]commanded me to build Him
a [1]house at Jerusalem which *is*
in Judah.
3 Who *is* among you of all His
people? May his God be
with him, and let him go
up to Jerusalem which *is*
in Judah, and build the house
of the LORD God of Israel
[a](He *is* God), which *is* in
Jerusalem.
4 And whoever is left in any
place where he dwells, let the
men of his place help him with
silver and gold, with goods and
livestock, besides the freewill
offerings for the house of God
which *is* in Jerusalem.

5 Then the heads of the fathers'
houses of Judah and Benjamin,
and the priests and the Levites,
with all whose spirits [a]God [1]had
moved, arose to go up and build
the house of the LORD which *is* in
Jerusalem.
6 And all those who *were* around
them [1]encouraged them with arti-
cles of silver and gold, with goods
and livestock, and with precious
things, besides all *that* was [a]will-
ingly offered.
7 [a]King Cyrus also brought out
the articles of the house of the
LORD, [b]which Nebuchadnezzar
had taken from Jerusalem and put
in the [1]temple of his gods;
8 and Cyrus king of Persia
brought them out by the hand of
Mithredath the treasurer, and
counted them out to [a]Sheshbazzar
the prince of Judah.
9 This *is* the number of them:
thirty gold platters, one thou-
sand silver platters, twenty-nine
knives,
10 thirty gold basins, four

1 [a]2 Chr. 36:22, 23; Jer. 25:12; 29:10 [b]Ezra 5:13, 14; Is. 44:28—45:13
2 [a]Is. 44:28; 45:1, 13 [1]Temple
3 [a]1 Kin. 8:23; 18:39; Is. 37:16; Dan. 6:26
5 [a][Phil. 2:13] [1]*stirred up*
6 [a]Ezra 2:68 [1]Lit. *strengthened their hands*
7 [a]Ezra 5:14; 6:5; Dan. 1:2; 5:2, 3 [b]2 Kin. 24:13; 2 Chr. 36:7, 18 [1]Lit. *house*
8 [a]Ezra 5:14, 16

hundred and ten silver basins of a
similar *kind, and* one thousand
other articles.
11 All the articles of gold and sil-
ver *were* five thousand four hun-
dred. All *these* Sheshbazzar took
with the captives who were
brought from Babylon to Jeru-
salem.

The Captives Who Returned to Jerusalem

2 Now [a]these *are* the people of
the province who came back
from the captivity, of those who
had been carried away, [b]whom
Nebuchadnezzar the king of Bab-
ylon had carried away to Babylon,
and who returned to Jerusalem
and Judah, everyone to his *own*
city.
2 *Those* who came with Zerubba-
bel *were* Jeshua, Nehemiah,
[1]Seraiah, [2]Reelaiah, Mordecai, Bil-
shan, [3]Mispar, Bigvai, [4]Rehum,
and Baanah. The number of the
men of the people of Israel:
3 the people of Parosh, two thou-
sand one hundred and seventy-
two;
4 the people of Shephatiah, three
hundred and seventy-two;
5 the people of Arah, [a]seven hun-
dred and seventy-five;
6 the people of [a]Pahath-Moab, of
the people of Jeshua *and* Joab, two
thousand eight hundred and
twelve;
7 the people of Elam, one thou-
sand two hundred and fifty-four;
8 the people of Zattu, nine hun-
dred and forty-five;
9 the people of Zaccai, seven
hundred and sixty;
10 the people of [1]Bani, six hun-
dred and forty-two;
11 the people of Bebai, six hun-
dred and twenty-three;

CHAPTER 2
1 [a]Neh. 7:6–73; Jer. 32:15; 50:5; Ezek. 14:22 [b]2 Kin. 24:14–16; 25:11; 2 Chr. 36:20
2 [1]*Azariah,* Neh. 7:7 [2]*Raamiah,* Neh. 7:7 [3]*Mispereth,* Neh. 7:7 [4]*Nehum,* Neh. 7:7
5 [a]Neh. 7:10
6 [a]Neh. 7:11
10 [1]*Binnui,* Neh. 7:15

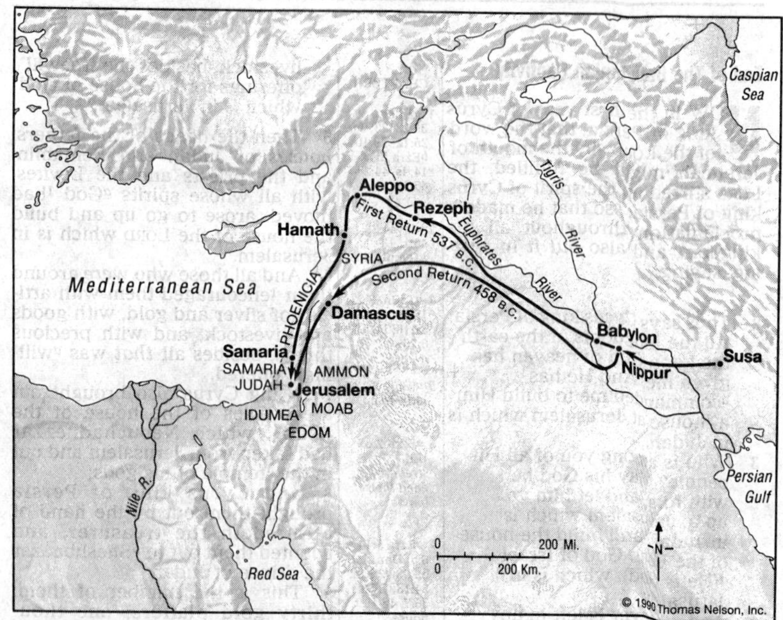

The Return from Exile. When Cyrus the Persian captured Babylon in 539 B.C., the way was opened for captive Judah to begin the return to her homeland. Two major expeditions made the journey, one in 537 B.C. and another in 458 B.C.

12 the people of Azgad, one thou-
sand two hundred and twenty-two;
13 the people of Adonikam, six
hundred and sixty-six;
14 the people of Bigvai, two thou-
sand and fifty-six;
15 the people of Adin, four hun-
dred and fifty-four;
16 the people of Ater of Hezekiah,
ninety-eight;
17 the people of Bezai, three hun-
dred and twenty-three;
18 the people of [1]Jorah, one hun-
dred and twelve;
19 the people of Hashum, two
hundred and twenty-three;
20 the people of [1]Gibbar, ninety-
five;
21 the people of Bethlehem, one
hundred and twenty-three;
22 the men of Netophah, fifty-six;
23 the men of Anathoth, one hun-
dred and twenty-eight;
24 the people of [1]Azmaveth, forty-
two;
25 the people of [1]Kirjath Arim,
Chephirah, and Beeroth, seven
hundred and forty-three;
26 the people of Ramah and Geba,
six hundred and twenty-one;
27 the men of Michmas, one hun-
dred and twenty-two;
28 the men of Bethel and Ai, two
hundred and twenty-three;
29 the people of Nebo, fifty-two;
30 the people of Magbish, one
hundred and fifty-six;
31 the people of the other [a]Elam,
one thousand two hundred and
fifty-four;
32 the people of Harim, three hun-
dred and twenty;
33 the people of Lod, Hadid, and
Ono, seven hundred and twenty-
five;
34 the people of Jericho, three
hundred and forty-five;
35 the people of Senaah, three
thousand six hundred and thirty.
36 The priests: the sons of [a]Je-
daiah, of the house of Jeshua, nine
hundred and seventy-three;
37 the sons of [a]Immer, one thou-
sand and fifty-two;
38 the sons of [a]Pashhur, one thou-
sand two hundred and forty-seven;
39 the sons of [a]Harim, one thou-
sand and seventeen.
40 The Levites: the sons of Jeshua
and Kadmiel, of the sons of
[1]Hodaviah, seventy-four.
41 The singers: the sons of Asaph,
one hundred and twenty-eight.
42 The sons of the gatekeepers:
the sons of Shallum, the sons of
Ater, the sons of Talmon, the sons
of Akkub, the sons of Hatita, and
the sons of Shobai, one hundred
and thirty-nine *in* all.
43 [a]The Nethinim: the sons of
Ziha, the sons of Hasupha, the
sons of Tabbaoth,
44 the sons of Keros, the sons of
[1]Siaha, the sons of Padon,
45 the sons of Lebanah, the sons
of Hagabah, the sons of Akkub,
46 the sons of Hagab, the sons of
Shalmai, the sons of Hanan,
47 the sons of Giddel, the sons of
Gahar, the sons of Reaiah,
48 the sons of Rezin, the sons of
Nekoda, the sons of Gazzam,
49 the sons of Uzza, the sons of
Paseah, the sons of Besai,
50 the sons of Asnah, the sons of
Meunim, the sons of [1]Nephusim,
51 the sons of Bakbuk, the sons
of Hakupha, the sons of Harhur,
52 the sons of [1]Bazluth, the sons
of Mehida, the sons of Harsha,
53 the sons of Barkos, the sons of
Sisera, the sons of Tamah,
54 the sons of Neziah, and the
sons of Hatipha.
55 The sons of [a]Solomon's ser-
vants: the sons of Sotai, the sons
of [b]Sophereth, the sons of [1]Peruda,
56 the sons of Jaala, the sons of
Darkon, the sons of Giddel,
57 the sons of Shephatiah, the
sons of Hattil, the sons of Poche-
reth of Zebaim, and the sons of
[1]Ami.
58 All the [a]Nethinim and the chil-
dren of [b]Solomon's servants were
three hundred and ninety-two.
59 And these *were* the ones who
came up from Tel Melah, Tel Har-
sha, Cherub, [1]Addan, and Immer;
but they could not [2]identify their
father's house or their [3]genealogy,
whether they *were* of Israel:
60 the sons of Delaiah, the sons
of Tobiah, and the sons of Nekoda,
six hundred and fifty-two;
61 and of the sons of the priests:
the sons of [a]Habaiah, the sons of
[1]Koz, and the sons of [b]Barzillai,
who took a wife of the daughters
of Barzillai the Gileadite, and was
called by their name.
62 These sought their listing

18 [1]*Hariph,* Neh. 7:24
20 [1]*Gibeon,* Neh. 7:25
24 [1]*Beth Azmaveth,* Neh. 7:28
25 [1]*Kirjath Jearim,* Neh. 7:29
31 [a]Ezra 2:7
36 [a]1 Chr. 24:7–18
37 [a]1 Chr. 24:14
38 [a]1 Chr. 9:12
39 [a]1 Chr. 24:8
40 [1]*Judah,* Ezra 3:9, or *Hodevah,* Neh. 7:43
43 [a]1 Chr. 9:2; Ezra 7:7
44 [1]*Sia,* Neh. 7:47
50 [1]*Nephishesim,* Neh. 7:52
52 [1]*Bazlith,* Neh. 7:54
55 [a]1 Kin. 9:21 [b]Neh. 7:57–60 [1]*Perida,* Neh. 7:57
57 [1]*Amon,* Neh. 7:59
58 [a]Josh. 9:21, 27; 1 Chr. 9:2 [b]1 Kin. 9:21
59 [1]Or *Addon,* Neh. 7:61 [2]Lit. *tell* [3]Lit. *seed*
61 [a]Neh. 7:63 [b]2 Sam. 17:27; 1 Kin. 2:7 [1]Or *Hakkoz*

among those who were registered
by genealogy, but they were not
found; [a]therefore they *were ex-*
cluded from the priesthood as de-
filed.
63 And the [1]governor said to them
that they [a]should not eat of the
most holy things till a priest could
consult with the [b]Urim and Thum-
mim.
64 [a]The whole assembly together
was forty-two thousand three hun-
dred *and* sixty,
65 besides their male and female
servants, of whom *there were*
seven thousand three hundred and
thirty-seven; and they had two
hundred men and women singers.
66 Their horses *were* seven hun-
dred and thirty-six, their mules
two hundred and forty-five,
67 their camels four hundred and
thirty-five, and *their* donkeys six
thousand seven hundred and
twenty.
68 [a]*Some* of the heads of the fa-
thers' *houses*, when they came to
the house of the LORD which *is* in
Jerusalem, offered freely for the
house of God, to erect it in its
place:
69 According to their ability, they
gave to the [a]treasury for the work
sixty-one thousand gold drach-
mas, five thousand minas of silver,
and one hundred priestly gar-
ments.
70 [a]So the priests and the Levites,
some of the people, the singers, the
gatekeepers, and the Nethinim,
dwelt in their cities, and all Israel
in their cities.

Worship Restored at Jerusalem

3 And when the [a]seventh month
had come, and the children of
Israel *were* in the cities, the people
gathered together as one man to
Jerusalem.
2 Then [1]Jeshua the son of [a]Joza-
dak[2] and his brethren the priests,
[b]and Zerubbabel the son of [c]Sheal-
tiel and his brethren, arose and
built the altar of the God of Israel,
to offer burnt offerings on it, as *it*
is [d]written in the Law of Moses the
man of God.
3 Though fear *had come* upon
them because of the people of
those countries, they set the altar
on its [1]bases; and they offered
[a]burnt offerings on it to the LORD,
both the morning and evening
burnt offerings.
4 [a]They also kept the Feast of
Tabernacles, [b]as *it is* written, and
[c]*offered* the daily burnt offerings
in the number required by ordi-
nance for each day.
5 Afterwards *they offered* the
[a]regular burnt offering, and *those*
for New Moons and for all the ap-
pointed feasts of the LORD that
were consecrated, and *those* of
everyone who willingly offered a
freewill offering to the LORD.
6 From the first day of the sev-
enth month they began to offer
burnt offerings to the LORD, al-
though the foundation of the tem-
ple of the LORD had not been laid.
7 They also gave money to the
masons and the carpenters, and
[a]food, drink, and oil to the people
of Sidon and Tyre to bring cedar
logs from Lebanon to the sea, to
[b]Joppa, [c]according to the permis-
sion which they had from Cyrus
king of Persia.

Restoration of the Temple Begins

8 Now in the second month of the
second year of their coming to the
house of God at Jerusalem, [a]Ze-
rubbabel the son of Shealtiel,
Jeshua the son of [1]Jozadak, and
the rest of their brethren the
priests and the Levites, and all
those who had come out of the
captivity to Jerusalem, began
work [b]and appointed the Levites
from twenty years old and above
to oversee the work of the house
of the LORD.
9 Then Jeshua *with* his sons and
brothers, Kadmiel *with* his sons,
and the sons of [1]Judah, arose as
one to oversee those working on
the house of God: the sons of
Henadad *with* their sons and their
brethren the Levites.
10 When the builders laid the
foundation of the temple of the
LORD, [a]the[1] priests stood in their
apparel with trumpets, and the
Levites, the sons of Asaph, with
cymbals, to praise the LORD, ac-
cording to the [b]ordinance[2] of Da-
vid king of Israel.
11 [a]And they sang responsively,
praising and giving thanks to the
LORD:

62 [a]Num. 3:10
63 [a]Lev. 22:2, 10, 15, 16 [b]Ex. 28:30; Num. 27:21 [1]Heb. *Tirshatha*
64 [a]Neh. 7:66; Is. 10:22
68 [a]Ezra 1:6; 3:5; Neh. 7:70
69 [a]1 Chr. 26:20; Ezra 8:25–35
70 [a]Ezra 6:16, 17; Neh. 7:73

CHAPTER 3

1 [a]Neh. 7:73; 8:1, 2
2 [a]1 Chr. 6:14, 15; Ezra 4:3; Neh. 12:1, 8; Hag. 1:1; 2:2 [b]Ezra 2:2; 4:2, 3; 5:2 [c]1 Chr. 3:17 [d]Deut. 12:5, 6 [1]Or *Joshua* [2]*Jehozadak,* 1 Chr. 6:14
3 [a]Num. 28:3 [1]*foundations*
4 [a]Lev. 23:33–43; Neh. 8:14–18; Zech. 14:16 [b]Ex. 23:16 [c]Num. 29:12, 13
5 [a]Ex. 29:38; Num. 28:3, 11, 19, 26; Ezra 1:4; 2:68; 7:15, 16; 8:28
7 [a]1 Kin. 5:6, 9; 2 Chr. 2:10; Acts 12:20 [b]2 Chr. 2:16; Acts 9:36 [c]Ezra 1:2; 6:3
8 [a]Ezra 3:2; 4:3 [b]1 Chr. 23:4, 24 [1]*Jehozadak,* 1 Chr. 6:14
9 [1]*Hodaviah,* Ezra 2:40
10 [a]1 Chr. 16:5, 6 [b]1 Chr. 6:31; 16:4; 25:1 [1]So with LXX, Syr., Vg.; MT *they stationed the priests* [2]Lit. *hands*
11 [a]Ex. 15:21; 2 Chr. 7:3; Neh. 12:24

[b]"For *He is* good,
[c]For His mercy *endures* forever
toward Israel."

Then all the people shouted with
a great shout, when they praised
the LORD, because the foundation
of the house of the LORD was laid.
12 But many of the priests and
Levites and [a]heads of the fathers'
houses, old men who had seen the
first temple, wept with a loud voice
when the foundation of this temple
was laid before their eyes. Yet
many shouted aloud for joy,
13 so that the people could not dis-
cern the noise of the shout of joy
from the noise of the weeping of
the people, for the people shouted
with a loud shout, and the sound
was heard afar off.

Resistance to Rebuilding the Temple

4 Now when [a]the [1]adversaries of
Judah and Benjamin heard
that the descendants of the captiv-
ity were building the temple of the
LORD God of Israel,
2 they came to Zerubbabel and
the heads of the fathers' *houses*,
and said to them, "Let us build
with you, for we seek your God as
you *do;* and we have sacrificed to
Him [a]since the days of Esarhad-
don king of Assyria, who brought
us here."
3 But Zerubbabel and Jeshua
and the rest of the heads of the fa-
thers' *houses* of Israel said to
them, [a]"You may do nothing with
us to build a [1]house for our God;
but we alone will build to the LORD
God of Israel, as [b]King Cyrus the
king of Persia has commanded
us."
4 Then [a]the people of the land
tried to discourage the people of
Judah. They troubled them in
building,
5 and hired counselors against
them to frustrate their purpose all
the days of Cyrus king of Persia,
even until the reign of [a]Darius
king of Persia.

Rebuilding of Jerusalem Opposed

6 In the reign of Ahasuerus, in
the beginning of his reign, they
wrote an accusation against the in-
habitants of Judah and Jerusalem.
7 In the days of [a]Artaxerxes also,
[1]Bishlam, Mithredath, Tabel, and
the rest of their companions wrote
to Artaxerxes king of Persia; and
the letter *was* written in [b]Aramaic
script, and translated into the Ara-
maic language.
8 [1]Rehum the commander and
Shimshai the scribe wrote a letter
against Jerusalem to King Artax-
erxes in this fashion:

9 [1]From Rehum the commander,
Shimshai the scribe, and the
rest of their companions—
representatives of [a]the
Dinaites, the Apharsathchites,
the Tarpelites, the people of
Persia and Erech and Babylon
and [2]Shushan, the Dehavites,
the Elamites,
10 [a]and the rest of the nations
whom the great and noble
Osnapper took captive and
settled in the cities of Samaria
and the remainder beyond [1]the
River—[b]and[2] so forth.

11 (This *is* a copy of the letter that
they sent him)

To King Artaxerxes from your
servants, the men *of the region*
beyond the River, [1]and so
forth:

12 Let it be known to the king that
the Jews who came up from
you have come to us at
Jerusalem, and are building the
[a]rebellious and evil city, and
are finishing *its* [b]walls and
repairing the foundations.
13 Let it now be known to the king
that, if this city is built and the
walls completed, they will not
pay [a]tax, tribute, or custom,
and the king's treasury will be
diminished.
14 Now because we receive
support from the palace, it was
not proper for us to see the
king's dishonor; therefore we
have sent and informed the
king,
15 that search may be made in the
book of the records of your
fathers. And you will find in the
book of the records and know
that this city *is* a rebellious city,
harmful to kings and
provinces, and that they have

---

11 [b]1 Chr. 16:34; Ps. 136:1 [c]1 Chr. 16:41; Jer. 33:11

12 [a]Ezra 2:68

CHAPTER 4

1 [a]Ezra 4:7–9 [1]*enemies*

2 [a]2 Kin. 17:24; 19:37; Ezra 4:10

3 [a]Neh. 2:20 [b]Ezra 1:1–4 [1]Temple

4 [a]Ezra 3:3

5 [a]Ezra 5:5; 6:1

7 [a]Ezra 7:1, 7, 21 [b]2 Kin. 18:26 [1]Or *in peace*

8 [1]The original language of Ezra 4:8 through 6:18 is Aramaic.

9 [a]2 Kin. 17:30, 31 [1]Lit. *Then* [2]Or *Susa*

10 [a]2 Kin. 17:24; Ezra 4:1 [b]Ezra 4:11, 17; 7:12 [1]The Euphrates [2]Lit. *and now*

11 [1]Lit. *and now*

12 [a]2 Chr. 36:13 [b]Ezra 5:3, 9

13 [a]Ezra 4:20; 7:24

incited sedition within the city
in former times, for which
cause this city was destroyed.
16 We inform the king that if this
city is rebuilt and its walls are
completed, the result will be
that you will have no dominion
beyond the River.

17 The king sent an answer:

To Rehum the commander, *to*
Shimshai the scribe, *to* the rest
of their companions who dwell
in Samaria, and *to* the
remainder beyond the River:

Peace, [1]and so forth.

18 The letter which you sent to us
has been clearly read before
me.
19 And [1]I gave the command, and
a search has been made, and
it was found that this city in
former times has revolted
against kings, and rebellion
and sedition have been
fostered in it.
20 There have also been mighty
kings over Jerusalem, who
have [a]ruled over all *the region*
[b]beyond the River; and tax,
tribute, and custom were paid
to them.
21 Now [1]give the command to
make these men cease, that this
city may not be built until the
command is given by me.
22 Take heed now that you do not
fail to do this. Why should
damage increase to the hurt of
the kings?

23 Now when the copy of King Ar-
taxerxes' letter *was* read before
Rehum, Shimshai the scribe, and
their companions, they went up in
haste to Jerusalem against the
Jews, and by force of arms made
them cease.
24 Thus the work of the house of
God which *is* at Jerusalem ceased,
and it was discontinued until the
second year of the reign of Darius
king of Persia.

Restoration of the Temple Resumed

5 Then the prophet [a]Haggai and
[b]Zechariah the son of Iddo,
prophets, prophesied to the Jews
who *were* in Judah and Jerusalem,
in the name of the God of Israel,
who was over them.
2 So [a]Zerubbabel the son of
Shealtiel and Jeshua the son of
[1]Jozadak rose up and began to
build the house of God which *is*
in Jerusalem; and [b]the prophets of
God *were* with them, helping
them.
3 At the same time [a]Tattenai the
governor of *the region* beyond [1]the
River and Shethar-Boznai and
their companions came to them
and spoke thus *to* them: [b]"Who
has commanded you to build this
[2]temple and finish this wall?"
4 [a]Then, accordingly, we told
them the names of the men who
were constructing this building.
5 But [a]the eye of their God was
upon the elders of the Jews, so that
they could not make them cease
till a report could go to Darius.
Then a [b]written answer was re-
turned concerning this *matter*.
6 This is a copy of the letter that
Tattenai sent:

The governor of *the region*
beyond the River, and Shethar-
Boznai, [a]and his companions,
the Persians who *were in the
region* beyond the River, to
Darius the king.

7 (They sent a letter to him, in
which was written thus)

To Darius the king:

All peace.

8 Let it be known to the king that
we went into the province of
Judea, to the [1]temple of the
great God, which is being built
with [2]heavy stones, and timber
is being laid in the walls; and
this work goes on diligently
and prospers in their hands.
9 Then we asked those elders,
and spoke thus to them: [a]"Who
commanded you to build this
temple and to finish these
walls?"
10 We also asked them their
names to inform you, that we
might write the names of the
men who *were* chief among
them.

---

17 [1]Lit. *and now*
19 [1]Lit. *by me a decree has been put forth*
20 [a]1 Kin. 4:21; 1 Chr. 18:3; Ps. 72:8 [b]Gen. 15:18; Josh. 1:4
21 [1]*put forth a decree*

CHAPTER 5

1 [a]Hag. 1:1 [b]Zech. 1:1
2 [a]Ezra 3:2; Hag. 1:12 [b]Ezra 6:14; Hag. 2:4 [1]*Jehozadak*, 1 Chr. 6:14
3 [a]Ezra 5:6; 6:6 [b]Ezra 1:3; 5:9 [1]The Euphrates [2]Lit. *house*
4 [a]Ezra 5:10
5 [a]2 Chr. 16:9; Ezra 7:6, 28; Ps. 33:18 [b]Ezra 6:6
6 [a]Ezra 4:7–10
8 [1]Lit. *house* [2]Lit. *stones of rolling*, stones too heavy to be carried
9 [a]Ezra 5:3, 4

11 And thus they returned us an
answer, saying: "We are the
servants of the God of heaven
and earth, and we are
rebuilding the [1]temple that was
built many years ago, which a
great king of Israel built [a]and
completed.
12 "But [a]because our fathers
provoked the God of heaven to
wrath, He gave them into the
hand of [b]Nebuchadnezzar king
of Babylon, the Chaldean, *who*
destroyed this temple and
[c]carried the people away to
Babylon.
13 "However, in the first year of
[a]Cyrus king of Babylon, King
Cyrus issued a decree to build
this [1]house of God.
14 "Also, [a]the gold and silver
articles of the house of God,
which Nebuchadnezzar had
taken from the temple that *was*
in Jerusalem and carried into
the temple of Babylon—those
King Cyrus took from the
temple of Babylon, and they
were given to [b]one named
Sheshbazzar, whom he had
made governor.
15 "And he said to him, 'Take
these articles; go, carry them to
the temple *site* that *is* in
Jerusalem, and let the house of
God be rebuilt on its former
site.'
16 "Then the same Sheshbazzar
came *and* [a]laid the foundation
of the house of God which *is*
in Jerusalem; but from that
time even until now it has been
under construction, and [b]it is
not finished."
17 Now therefore, if *it seems* good
to the king, [a]let a search be
made in the king's treasure
house, which *is* there in
Babylon, whether it is *so* that
a decree was issued by King
Cyrus to build this house of
God at Jerusalem, and let the
king send us his pleasure
concerning this *matter*.

The Decree of Darius

6 Then King Darius issued a de-
cree, [a]and a search was made
in the [1]archives, where the trea-
sures were stored in Babylon.
2 And at [1]Achmetha, in the pal-
ace that *is* in the province of [a]Me-
dia, a scroll was found, and in it a
record *was* written thus:

3 In the first year of King Cyrus,
King Cyrus issued a [a]decree
concerning the house of God at
Jerusalem: "Let the house be
rebuilt, the place where they
offered sacrifices; and let the
foundations of it be firmly laid,
its height sixty cubits *and* its
width sixty cubits,
4 [a]*with* three rows of heavy
stones and one row of new
timber. Let the [b]expenses be
paid from the king's treasury.
5 Also let [a]the gold and silver
articles of the house of God,
which Nebuchadnezzar took
from the temple which *is* in
Jerusalem and brought to
Babylon, be restored and taken
back to the temple which *is* in
Jerusalem, *each* to its place;
and deposit *them* in the house
of God"—
6 [a]Now *therefore*, Tattenai,
governor of *the region* beyond
the River, and Shethar-Boznai,
and your companions the
Persians who *are* beyond the
River, keep yourselves far from
there.
7 Let the work of this house of
God alone; let the governor of
the Jews and the elders of the
Jews build this house of God
on its site.
8 Moreover I issue a decree *as to*
what you shall do for the elders
of these Jews, for the building
of this [1]house of God: Let the
cost be paid at the king's
expense from taxes *on the*
region beyond the River; this is
to be given immediately to
these men, so that they are not
hindered.
9 And whatever they need—
young bulls, rams, and lambs
for the burnt offerings of the
God of heaven, wheat, salt,
wine, and oil, according to the
request of the priests who *are*
in Jerusalem—let it be given
them day by day without fail,
10 [a]that they may offer sacrifices
of sweet aroma to the God of
heaven, and pray for the life of
the king and his sons.

11 [a]1 Kin. 6:1, 38 [1]Lit. *house*
12 [a]2 Chr. 34:25; 36:16, 17 [b]2 Kin. 24:2; 25:8–11; 2 Chr. 36:17; Jer. 52:12–15 [c]Jer. 13:19
13 [a]Ezra 1:1 [1]Temple
14 [a]Ezra 1:7, 8; 6:5; Dan. 5:2 [b]Hag. 1:14; 2:2, 21
16 [a]Ezra 3:8–10; Hag. 2:18 [b]Ezra 6:15
17 [a]Ezra 6:1, 2

CHAPTER 6

1 [a]Ezra 5:17 [1]Lit. *house of the scrolls*
2 [a]2 Kin. 17:6 [1]Probably *Ecbatana*, the ancient capital of Media
3 [a]Ezra 1:1; 5:13
4 [a]1 Kin. 6:36 [b]Ezra 3:7
5 [a]Ezra 1:7, 8; 5:14
6 [a]Ezra 5:3, 6
8 [1]Temple
10 [a]Ezra 7:23; [Jer. 29:7; 1 Tim. 2:1, 2]

11 Also I issue a decree that whoever alters this edict, let a timber be pulled from his house and erected, and let him be hanged on it; [a]and let his house be made a refuse heap because of this.

12 And may the God who causes His [a]name to dwell there destroy any king or people who put their hand to alter it, or to destroy this [1]house of God which is in Jerusalem. I Darius issue a decree; let it be done diligently.

The Temple Completed and Dedicated

13 Then Tattenai, governor of *the region* beyond the River, Shethar-Boznai, and their companions diligently did according to what King Darius had sent.

14 [a]So the elders of the Jews built, and they prospered through the prophesying of Haggai the prophet and Zechariah the son of Iddo. And they built and finished *it*, according to the commandment of the God of Israel, and according to the [1]command of [b]Cyrus, [c]Darius, and [d]Artaxerxes king of Persia.

15 Now the temple was finished on the third day of the month of Adar, which was in the sixth year of the reign of King Darius.

16 Then the children of Israel, the priests and the Levites and the rest of the descendants of the captivity, celebrated [a]the dedication of this [1]house of God with joy.

17 And they [a]offered sacrifices at the dedication of this house of God, one hundred bulls, two hundred rams, four hundred lambs, and as a sin offering for all Israel twelve male goats, according to the number of the tribes of Israel.

18 They assigned the priests to their [a]divisions and the Levites to their [b]divisions, over the service of God in Jerusalem, [c]as it is written in the Book of Moses.

The Passover Celebrated

19 [1]And the descendants of the captivity kept the Passover [a]on the fourteenth *day* of the first month.

20 For the priests and the Levites had [a]purified themselves; all of them *were ritually* clean. And they [b]slaughtered the Passover *lambs* for all the descendants of the captivity, for their brethren the priests, and for themselves.

21 Then the children of Israel who had returned from the captivity ate together with all who had separated themselves from the [a]filth[1] of the nations of the land in order to seek the LORD God of Israel.

22 And they kept the [a]Feast of Unleavened Bread seven days with joy; for the LORD made them joyful, and [b]turned the heart [c]of the king of Assyria toward them, to strengthen their hands in the work of the house of God, the God of Israel.

The Arrival of Ezra

7 Now after these things, in the reign of [a]Artaxerxes king of Persia, Ezra the [b]son of Seraiah, [c]the son of Azariah, the son of [d]Hilkiah,

2 the son of Shallum, the son of Zadok, the son of Ahitub,

3 the son of Amariah, the son of Azariah, the son of Meraioth,

4 the son of Zerahiah, the son of Uzzi, the son of Bukki,

5 the son of Abishua, the son of Phinehas, the son of Eleazar, the son of Aaron the chief priest—

6 this Ezra came up from Babylon; and he *was* [a]a skilled scribe in the Law of Moses, which the LORD God of Israel had given. The king granted him all his request, [b]according to the hand of the LORD his God upon him.

7 [a]*Some* of the children of Israel, the priests, [b]the Levites, the singers, the gatekeepers, and [c]the Nethinim came up to Jerusalem in the seventh year of King Artaxerxes.

8 And Ezra came to Jerusalem in the fifth month, which *was* in the seventh year of the king.

9 On the first *day* of the first month he began *his* journey from Babylon, and on the first *day* of the fifth month he came to Jerusalem, [a]according to the good hand of his God upon him.

10 For Ezra had prepared his heart to [a]seek[1] the Law of the LORD, and to do *it*, and to [b]teach statutes and ordinances in Israel.

11 [a]Dan. 2:5; 3:29

12 [a]Deut. 12:5, 11; 1 Kin. 9:3 [1]Temple

14 [a]Ezra 5:1, 2 [b]Ezra 1:1; 5:13; 6:3 [c]Ezra 4:24; 6:12 [d]Ezra 7:1, 11; Neh. 2:1 [1]*decree*

16 [a]1 Kin. 8:63; 2 Chr. 7:5 [1]Temple

17 [a]Ezra 8:35

18 [a]1 Chr. 24:1; 2 Chr. 35:5 [b]1 Chr. 23:6 [c]Num. 3:6; 8:9

19 [a]Ex. 12:6 [1]The Hebrew language resumes in Ezra 6:19 and continues through 7:11.

20 [a]2 Chr. 29:34; 30:15 [b]2 Chr. 35:11

21 [a]Ezra 9:11 [1]*uncleanness*

22 [a]Ex. 12:15; 13:6, 7; 2 Chr. 30:21; 35:17 [b]Ezra 7:27; [Prov. 21:1] [c]2 Kin. 23:29; 2 Chr. 33:11; Ezra 1:1; 6:1

CHAPTER 7

1 [a]Neh. 2:1 [b]1 Chr. 6:14 [c]Jer. 52:24 [d]2 Chr. 35:8

6 [a]Ezra 7:11, 12, 21 [b]Ezra 7:9, 28; 8:22

7 [a]Ezra 8:1–14 [b]Ezra 8:15 [c]Ezra 2:43; 8:20

9 [a]Ezra 7:6; Neh. 2:8, 18

10 [a]Ps. 119:45 [b]Deut. 33:10; Ezra 7:6, 25; Neh. 8:1–8; [Mal. 2:7] [1]Study

The Letter of Artaxerxes to Ezra

11 This *is* a copy of the letter that
King Artaxerxes gave Ezra the
priest, the scribe, expert in the
words of the commandments of
the LORD, and of His statutes to
Israel:

12 [1]Artaxerxes, [a]king of kings,

To Ezra the priest, a scribe of
the Law of the God of heaven:

Perfect *peace,* [b]and so forth.[2]

13 I issue a decree that all those
of the people of Israel and the
priests and Levites in my
realm, who volunteer to go up
to Jerusalem, may go with
you.
14 And whereas you are being
sent [1]by the king and his [a]seven
counselors to inquire
concerning Judah and
Jerusalem, with regard to the
Law of your God which *is* in
your hand;
15 and *whereas you are* to carry
the silver and gold which the
king and his counselors have
freely offered to the God of
Israel, [a]whose dwelling *is* in
Jerusalem;
16 [a]and *whereas* all the silver and
gold that you may find in all
the province of Babylon, along
with the freewill offering of the
people and the priests, *are to
be* [b]freely offered for the
[1]house of their God in
Jerusalem—
17 now therefore, be careful to
buy with this money bulls,
rams, and lambs, with their
[a]grain offerings and their drink
offerings, and [b]offer them on
the altar of the house of your
God in Jerusalem.
18 And whatever seems good to
you and your brethren to do
with the rest of the silver and
the gold, do it according to the
will of your God.
19 Also the articles that are given
to you for the service of the
house of your God, deliver in
full before the God of
Jerusalem.
20 And whatever more may be
needed for the house of your
God, which you may have
occasion to provide, pay *for it*
from the king's treasury.
21 And I, *even* I, Artaxerxes the
king, issue a decree to all the
treasurers who *are in the
region* beyond the River, that
whatever Ezra the priest, the
scribe of the Law of the God
of heaven, may require of you,
let it be done diligently,
22 up to one hundred talents of
silver, one hundred kors of
wheat, one hundred baths of
wine, one hundred baths of oil,
and salt without prescribed
limit.
23 Whatever [1]is commanded by
the God of heaven, let it
diligently be done for the
[2]house of the God of heaven.
For why should there be wrath
against the realm of the king
and his sons?
24 Also we inform you that it shall
not be lawful to impose tax,
tribute, or custom *on* any of the
priests, Levites, singers,
gatekeepers, Nethinim, or
servants of this house of
God.
25 And you, Ezra, according to
your God-given wisdom, [a]set
magistrates and judges who
may judge all the people who
are in the region beyond the
River, all such as know the
laws of your God; and [b]teach
those who do not know
them.
26 Whoever will not observe the
law of your God and the law
of the king, let judgment be
executed speedily on him,
whether *it be* death, or
[1]banishment, or confiscation of
goods, or imprisonment.

27 [a]Blessed[1] *be* the LORD God of
our fathers, [b]who has put *such a
thing* as this in the king's heart,
to beautify the house of the LORD
which *is* in Jerusalem,
28 and [a]has extended mercy to me
before the king and his counselors,
and before all the king's mighty
princes.
So I was encouraged, as [b]the
hand of the LORD my God *was*
upon me; and I gathered leading
men of Israel to go up with me.

12 [a]Ezek. 26:7; Dan. 2:37 [b]Ezra 4:10 [1]The original language of Ezra 7:12–26 is Aramaic. [2]Lit. *and now*

14 [a]Esth. 1:14 [1]*from before*

15 [a]2 Chr. 6:2; Ezra 6:12; Ps. 135:21

16 [a]Ezra 8:25 [b]1 Chr. 29:6, 9 [1]Temple

17 [a]Num. 15:4–13 [b]Deut. 12:5–11

23 [1]Lit. *is from the decree* [2]Temple

25 [a]Ex. 18:21, 22; Deut. 16:18 [b]2 Chr. 17:7; Ezra 7:10; [Mal. 2:7; Col. 1:28]

26 [1]Lit. *rooting out*

27 [a]1 Chr. 29:10 [b]Ezra 6:22; [Prov. 21:1] [1]The Hebrew language resumes in Ezra 7:27.

28 [a]Ezra 9:9 [b]Ezra 5:5; 7:6, 9; 8:18

Heads of Families Who Returned with Ezra

8 These *are* the heads of their fa-
thers' *houses*, and *this is* the
genealogy of those who went up
with me from Babylon, in the reign
of King Artaxerxes:
2 of the sons of Phinehas, Ger-
shom; of the sons of Ithamar, Dan-
iel; of the sons of David, [a]Hattush;
3 of the sons of Shecaniah, of the
sons of [a]Parosh, Zechariah; and
registered with him *were* one hun-
dred and fifty males;
4 of the sons of [a]Pahath-Moab,
Eliehoenai the son of Zerahiah,
and with him two hundred males;
5 of [1]the sons of Shechaniah,
Ben-Jahaziel, and with him three
hundred males;
6 of the sons of Adin, Ebed the
son of Jonathan, and with him fifty
males;
7 of the sons of Elam, Jeshaiah
the son of Athaliah, and with him
seventy males;
8 of the sons of Shephatiah,
Zebadiah the son of Michael, and
with him eighty males;
9 of the sons of Joab, Obadiah
the son of Jehiel, and with him two
hundred and eighteen males;
10 of [1]the sons of Shelomith, Ben-
Josiphiah, and with him one hun-
dred and sixty males;
11 of the sons of [a]Bebai, Zecha-
riah the son of Bebai, and with him
twenty-eight males;
12 of the sons of Azgad, Johanan
[1]the son of Hakkatan, and with
him one hundred and ten males;
13 of the last sons of Adonikam,
whose names *are* these—Eliphelet,
Jeiel, and Shemaiah—and with
them sixty males;
14 also of the sons of Bigvai, Uthai
and [1]Zabbud, and with them sev-
enty males.

Servants for the Temple

15 Now I gathered them by the
river that flows to Ahava, and we
camped there three days. And I
looked among the people and the
priests, and found none of the
[a]sons of Levi there.
16 Then I sent for Eliezer, Ariel,
Shemaiah, Elnathan, Jarib, El-
nathan, Nathan, Zechariah, and
[a]Meshullam, leaders; also for Joia-
rib and Elnathan, men of under-
standing.
17 And I gave them a command
for Iddo the chief man at the place
Casiphia, and [1]I told them what
they should say to [2]Iddo *and* his
brethren the Nethinim at the place
Casiphia—that they should bring
us servants for the house of our
God.
18 Then, by the good hand of our
God upon us, they [a]brought us a
man of understanding, of the sons
of Mahli the son of Levi, the son
of Israel, namely Sherebiah, with
his sons and brothers, eighteen
men;
19 and [a]Hashabiah, and with him
Jeshaiah of the sons of Merari, his
brothers and their sons, twenty
men;
20 [a]also of the Nethinim, whom
David and the leaders had ap-
pointed for the service of the Le-
vites, two hundred and twenty
Nethinim. All of them were desig-
nated by name.

Fasting and Prayer for Protection

21 Then I [a]proclaimed a fast there
at the river of Ahava, that we
might [b]humble ourselves before
our God, to seek from Him the
[c]right way for us and our little
ones and all our possessions.
22 For [a]I was ashamed to request
of the king an escort of soldiers
and horsemen to help us against
the enemy on the road, because we
had spoken to the king, saying,
[b]"The hand of our God *is* upon all
those for [c]good who seek Him, but
His power and His wrath *are*
[d]against all those who [e]forsake
Him."
23 So we fasted and entreated our
God for this, and He [a]answered
our prayer.

Gifts for the Temple

24 And I separated twelve of the
leaders of the priests—Sherebiah,
Hashabiah, and ten of their breth-
ren with them—
25 and weighed out to them [a]the
silver, the gold, and the articles,
the offering for the house of our
God which the king and his coun-
selors and his princes, and all Is-
rael *who were* present, had of-
fered.

CHAPTER 8

2 [a]1 Chr. 3:22; Ezra 2:68

3 [a]Ezra 2:3

4 [a]Ezra 10:30

5 [1]So with MT, Vg.; LXX *the sons of Zatho, Shechaniah*

10 [1]So with MT, Vg.; LXX *the sons of Banni, Shelomith*

11 [a]Ezra 10:28

12 [1]Or *the youngest son,*

14 [1]Or *Zakkur*

15 [a]Ezra 7:7; 8:2

16 [a]Ezra 10:15

17 [1]Lit. *I put words in their mouths to say* [2]So with Vg.; MT *to Iddo his brother;* LXX *to their brethren*

18 [a]2 Chr. 30:22; Neh. 8:7

19 [a]Neh. 12:24

20 [a]Ezra 2:43; 7:7

21 [a]1 Sam. 7:6; 2 Chr. 20:3 [b]Lev. 16:29; 23:29; Is. 58:3, 5 [c]Ps. 5:8

22 [a]1 Cor. 9:15 [b]Ezra 7:6, 9, 28 [c][Ps. 33:18, 19; 34:15, 22; Rom. 8:28] [d][Ps. 34:16] [e][2 Chr. 15:2]

23 [a][1 Chr. 5:20]; 2 Chr. 33:13; Is. 19:22

25 [a]Ezra 7:15, 16

26 I weighed into their hand six
hundred and fifty talents of silver,
silver articles *weighing* one hun-
dred talents, one hundred talents
of gold,
27 twenty gold basins *worth* a
thousand drachmas, and two ves-
sels of fine polished bronze, pre-
cious as gold.
28 And I said to them, "You *are*
[a]holy[1] to the LORD; the articles *are*
[b]holy also; and the silver and the
gold *are* a freewill offering to the
LORD God of your fathers.
29 "Watch and keep *them* until
you weigh *them* before the leaders
of the priests and the Levites and
[a]heads of the fathers' *houses* of Is-
rael in Jerusalem, *in* the chambers
of the house of the LORD."
30 So the priests and the Levites
received the silver and the gold
and the articles by weight, to bring
them to Jerusalem to the house of
our God.

The Return to Jerusalem

31 Then we departed from the
river of Ahava on the twelfth *day*
of the first month, to go to Jerusa-
lem. And [a]the hand of our God was
upon us, and He delivered us from
the hand of the enemy and from
ambush along the road.
32 So we [a]came to Jerusalem, and
stayed there three days.
33 Now on the fourth day the sil-
ver and the gold and the articles
were [a]weighed in the house of our
God by the hand of Meremoth the
son of Uriah the priest, and with
him *was* Eleazar the son of Phin-
ehas; with them *were* the Levites,
[b]Jozabad the son of Jeshua and
Noadiah the son of Binnui,
34 with the number *and* weight of
everything. All the weight was
written down at that time.
35 The children of those who had
been [a]carried away captive, who
had come from the captivity, [b]of-
fered burnt offerings to the God of
Israel: twelve bulls for all Israel,
ninety-six rams, seventy-seven
lambs, and twelve male goats *as*
a sin offering. All *this was* a burnt
offering to the LORD.
36 And they delivered the king's
[a]orders to the king's satraps and
the governors *in the region* beyond
[1]the River. So they gave support
to the people and the [2]house of
God.

Intermarriage with Pagans

9 When these things were done,
the leaders came to me, saying,
"The people of Israel and the
priests and the Levites have not
[a]separated themselves from the
peoples of the lands, [b]with respect
to the abominations of the Ca-
naanites, the Hittites, the Periz-
zites, the Jebusites, the Ammon-
ites, the Moabites, the Egyptians,
and the Amorites.
2 "For they have [a]taken some of
their daughters *as wives* for them-
selves and their sons, so that the
[b]holy seed is [c]mixed with the peo-
ples of *those* lands. Indeed, the
hand of the leaders and rulers has
been foremost in this [1]trespass."
3 So when I heard this thing, [a]I
tore my garment and my robe, and
plucked out some of the hair of my
head and beard, and sat down [b]as-
tonished.
4 Then everyone who [a]trembled
at the words of the God of Israel
assembled to me, because of the
transgression of those who had
been carried away captive, and I
sat astonished until the [b]evening
sacrifice.
5 At the evening sacrifice I arose
from my fasting; and having torn
my garment and my robe, I fell on
my knees and [a]spread out my
hands to the LORD my God.
6 And I said: "O my God, I am
too [a]ashamed and humiliated to
lift up my face to You, my God;
for [b]our iniquities have risen
higher than *our* heads, and our
guilt has [c]grown up to the heavens.
7 "Since the days of our fathers
to this day [a]we *have been* very
guilty, and for our iniquities [b]we,
our kings, *and* our priests have
been delivered into the hand of the
kings of the lands, to the [c]sword,
to captivity, to plunder, and to
[d]humiliation,[1] as *it is* this day.
8 "And now for a little while
grace has been *shown* from the
LORD our God, to leave us a rem-
nant to escape, and to give us a
peg in His holy place, that our God
may [a]enlighten our eyes and give
us a measure of revival in our
bondage.

28 [a]Lev. 21:6–9; Deut. 33:8 [b]Lev. 22:2, 3; Num. 4:4, 15, 19, 20 [1]*consecrated*
29 [a]Ezra 4:3
31 [a]Ezra 7:6, 9, 28
32 [a]Neh. 2:11
33 [a]Ezra 8:26, 30 [b]Neh. 11:16
35 [a]Ezra 2:1 [b]Ezra 6:17
36 [a]Ezra 7:21–24 [1]The Euphrates [2]Temple

CHAPTER 9

1 [a]Ezra 6:21; Neh. 9:2 [b]Deut. 12:30, 31
2 [a]Ex. 34:16; [Deut. 7:3]; Ezra 10:2; Neh. 13:23 [b]Ex. 22:31; [Deut. 7:6] [c][2 Cor. 6:14] [1]*unfaithfulness*
3 [a]Job 1:20 [b]Ps. 143:4
4 [a]Ezra 10:3; Is. 66:2 [b]Ex. 29:39
5 [a]Ex. 9:29
6 [a]Dan. 9:7, 8 [b]Ps. 38:4 [c]2 Chr. 28:9; [Ezra 9:13, 15]; Rev. 18:5
7 [a]2 Chr. 36:14–17; Ps. 106:6; Dan. 9:5, 6 [b]Deut. 28:36; Neh. 9:30 [c]Deut. 32:25 [d]Dan. 9:7, 8 [1]Lit. *shame of faces*
8 [a]Ps. 34:5

9 [a]"For we *were* slaves. [b]Yet our
God did not forsake us in our
bondage; but [c]He extended mercy
to us in the sight of the kings of
Persia, to revive us, to repair the
house of our God, to rebuild its
ruins, and to give us [d]a wall in Ju-
dah and Jerusalem.
10 "And now, O our God, what
shall we say after this? For we
have forsaken Your command-
ments,
11 "which You commanded by
Your servants the prophets, say-
ing, 'The land which you are enter-
ing to possess is an unclean land,
with the [a]uncleanness of the peo-
ples of the lands, with their
abominations which have filled it
from one end to another with their
impurity.
12 'Now therefore, [a]do not give
your daughters as wives for their
sons, nor take their daughters to
your sons; and [b]never seek their
peace or prosperity, that you may
be strong and eat the good of the
land, and [c]leave *it* as an inheri-
tance to your children forever.'
13 "And after all that has come
upon us for our evil deeds and for
our great guilt, since You our God
[a]have punished us less than our in-
iquities *deserve*, and have given us
such deliverance as this,
14 "should we [a]again break Your
commandments, and [b]join in mar-
riage with the people *committing*
these abominations? Would You
not be [c]angry with us until You
had [1]consumed *us*, so that *there
would be* no remnant or survivor?
15 "O LORD God of Israel, [a]You
are righteous, for we are left as a
remnant, as *it is* this day. [b]Here
we *are* before You, [c]in our guilt,
though no one can stand before
You because of this!"

Confession of Improper Marriages

10 Now [a]while Ezra was pray-
ing, and while he was con-
fessing, weeping, and bowing
down [b]before the house of God, a
very large assembly of men,
women, and children gathered to
him from Israel; for the people
wept very [c]bitterly.
2 And Shechaniah the son of
Jehiel, *one* of the sons of Elam,
spoke up and said to Ezra, "We

9 [a]Neh. 9:36; Esth. 7:4 [b]Neh. 9:17; Ps. 136:23 [c]Ezra 7:28 [d]Is. 5:2
11 [a]Ezra 6:21
12 [a][Ex. 23:32; 34:15, 16; Deut. 7:3, 4]; Ezra 9:2 [b]Deut. 23:6 [c][Prov. 13:22; 20:7]
13 [a][Ps. 103:10]
14 [a][John 5:14; 2 Pet. 2:20] [b]Neh. 13:23 [c]Deut. 9:8 [1]*destroyed*
15 [a]Neh. 9:33; Dan. 9:14 [b][Rom. 3:19] [c]1 Cor. 15:17

CHAPTER 10

1 [a]Dan. 9:4, 20 [b]2 Chr. 20:9 [c]Neh. 8:1–9
2 [a]Ezra 10:10, 13, 14, 17, 18; Neh. 13:23–27 [1]*been unfaithful to*
3 [a]2 Chr. 34:31 [b]Ezra 9:4 [c]Deut. 7:2, 3 [d]Deut. 24:1, 2
4 [a]1 Chr. 28:10
5 [a]Ezra 10:12, 19; Neh. 5:12; 13:25
6 [a]Deut. 9:18
9 [a]1 Sam. 12:18; Ezra 9:4; 10:3
10 [1]*acted unfaithfully* [2]Heb. *have caused to dwell* or *have brought back*
11 [a][Lev. 26:40–42]; Josh. 7:19; [Prov. 28:13] [b]Ezra 10:3

have [a]trespassed[1] against our God,
and have taken pagan wives from
the peoples of the land; yet now
there is hope in Israel in spite of
this.
3 "Now therefore, let us make [a]a
covenant with our God to put away
all these wives and those who have
been born to them, according to
the advice of my master and of
those who [b]tremble at [c]the com-
mandment of our God; and let it
be done according to the [d]law.
4 "Arise, for *this* matter *is* your
responsibility. We also *are* with
you. [a]Be of good courage, and do
it."
5 Then Ezra arose, and made the
leaders of the priests, the Levites,
and all Israel [a]swear an oath that
they would do according to this
word. So they swore an oath.
6 Then Ezra rose up from before
the house of God, and went into
the chamber of Jehohanan the son
of Eliashib; and *when* he came
there, he [a]ate no bread and drank
no water, for he mourned because
of the guilt of those from the cap-
tivity.
7 And they issued a proclama-
tion throughout Judah and Jerusa-
lem to all the descendants of the
captivity, that they must gather at
Jerusalem,
8 and that whoever would not
come within three days, according
to the instructions of the leaders
and elders, all his property would
be confiscated, and he himself
would be separated from the as-
sembly of those from the captivity.
9 So all the men of Judah and
Benjamin gathered at Jerusalem
within three days. It *was* the ninth
month, on the twentieth of the
month; and [a]all the people sat in
the open square of the house of
God, trembling because of *this*
matter and because of heavy rain.
10 Then Ezra the priest stood up
and said to them, "You have
[1]transgressed and [2]have taken pa-
gan wives, adding to the guilt of
Israel.
11 "Now therefore, [a]make confes-
sion to the LORD God of your fa-
thers, and do His will; [b]separate
yourselves from the peoples of the
land, and from the pagan wives."
12 Then all the assembly an-

swered and said with a loud voice,
"Yes! As you have said, so we
must do.
13 "But *there are* many people; *it*
is the season for heavy rain, and
we are not able to stand outside.
Nor *is this* the work of one or two
days, for *there are* many of us
who have transgressed in this mat-
ter.
14 "Please, let the leaders of our
entire assembly stand; and let all
those in our cities who have taken
pagan wives come at appointed
times, together with the elders and
judges of their cities, until [a]the
fierce wrath of our God is turned
away from us in this matter."
15 Only Jonathan the son of Asa-
hel and Jahaziah the son of Tikvah
opposed this, and [a]Meshullam and
Shabbethai the Levite gave them
support.
16 Then the descendants of the
captivity did so. And Ezra the
priest, *with* certain [a]heads of
the fathers' *households*, were set
apart by the fathers' *households*,
each of them by name; and they
sat down on the first day of the
tenth month to examine the mat-
ter.
17 By the first day of the first
month they finished *questioning*
all the men who had taken pagan
wives.

Pagan Wives Put Away

18 And among the sons of the
priests who had taken pagan
wives *the following* were found of
the sons of [a]Jeshua the son of
[1]Jozadak, and his brothers: Maa-
seiah, Eliezer, Jarib, and Gedaliah.
19 And they [a]gave their promise
that they would put away their
wives; and *being* [b]guilty, *they pre-*
sented a ram of the flock as their
[c]trespass offering.
20 Also of the sons of Immer:
Hanani and Zebadiah;
21 of the sons of Harim: Maa-
seiah, Elijah, Shemaiah, Jehiel,
and Uzziah;
22 of the sons of Pashhur: Elio-
enai, Maaseiah, Ishmael, Nethanel,
Jozabad, and Elasah.
23 Also of the Levites: Jozabad,
Shimei, Kelaiah (the same *is* Kel-
ita), Pethahiah, Judah, and Elie-
zer.
24 Also of the singers: Eliashib;
and of the gatekeepers: Shallum,
Telem, and Uri.
25 And others of Israel: of the
[a]sons of Parosh: Ramiah, Jeziah,
Malchiah, Mijamin, Eleazar, Mal-
chijah, and Benaiah;
26 of the sons of Elam: Mattaniah,
Zechariah, Jehiel, Abdi, Jeremoth,
and Eliah;
27 of the sons of Zattu: Elioenai,
Eliashib, Mattaniah, Jeremoth, Za-
bad, and Aziza;
28 of the [a]sons of Bebai: Jeho-
hanan, Hananiah, Zabbai, *and*
Athlai;
29 of the sons of Bani: Meshullam,
Malluch, Adaiah, Jashub, Sheal,
and [1]Ramoth;
30 of the [a]sons of Pahath-Moab:
Adna, Chelal, Benaiah, Maaseiah,
Mattaniah, Bezalel, Binnui, and
Manasseh;
31 *of* the sons of Harim: Eliezer,
Ishijah, Malchijah, Shemaiah,
Shimeon,
32 Benjamin, Malluch, *and* Shem-
ariah;
33 of the sons of Hashum: Matte-
nai, Mattattah, Zabad, Eliphelet,
Jeremai, Manasseh, *and* Shimei;
34 of the sons of Bani: Maadai,
Amram, Uel,
35 Benaiah, Bedeiah, [1]Cheluh,
36 Vaniah, Meremoth, Eliashib,
37 Mattaniah, Mattenai, [1]Jaasai,
38 Bani, Binnui, Shimei,
39 Shelemiah, Nathan, Adaiah,
40 Machnadebai, Shashai, Sharai,
41 Azarel, Shelemiah, Shemariah,
42 Shallum, Amariah, *and* Joseph;
43 of the sons of Nebo: Jeiel, Mat-
tithiah, Zabad, Zebina, [1]Jaddai,
Joel, *and* Benaiah.
44 All these had taken pagan
wives, and *some* of them had
wives *by whom* they had chil-
dren.

14 [a]2 Kin. 23:26; 2 Chr. 28:11–13; 29:10; 30:8
15 [a]Ezra 8:16; Neh. 3:4
16 [a]Ezra 4:3
18 [a]Ezra 5:2; Hag. 1:1, 12; 2:4; Zech. 3:1; 6:11 [1]*Jehozadak*, 1 Chr. 6:14
19 [a]2 Kin. 10:15 [b]Lev. 6:4, 6 [c]Lev. 5:6, 15
25 [a]Ezra 2:3; 8:3; Neh. 7:8
28 [a]Ezra 8:11
29 [1]Or *Jeremoth*
30 [a]Ezra 8:4
35 [1]Or *Cheluhi* or *Cheluhu*
37 [1]Or *Jaasu*
43 [1]Or *Jaddu*

The Book of

Nehemiah

NEHEMIAH, contemporary of Ezra and cupbearer to the king in the Persian palace, leads the third and last return to Jerusalem after the Babylonian exile. His concern for the welfare of Jerusalem and its inhabitants prompts him to take bold action. Granted permission to return to his homeland, Nehemiah challenges his countrymen to arise and rebuild the shattered wall of Jerusalem. In spite of opposition from without and abuse from within, the task is completed in only fifty-two days, a feat even the enemies of Israel must attribute to God's enabling. By contrast, the task of reviving and reforming the people of God within the rebuilt wall demands years of Nehemiah's godly life and leadership.

The Hebrew for Nehemiah is *Nehemyah,* "Comfort of Yahweh." The book is named after its chief character, whose name appears in the opening verse. The combined book of Ezra–Nehemiah is given the Greek title *Esdras Deuteron,* "Second Esdras" in the Septuagint, a third-century B.C. Greek-language translation of the Hebrew Old Testament. The Latin title of Nehemiah is *Liber Secundus Esdrae,* "Second Book of Ezra" (Ezra was the first). At this point, it is considered a separate book from Ezra, and is later called *Liber Nehemiae,* "Book of Nehemiah."

Nehemiah Prays for His People

1 THE words of [a]Nehemiah the
son of Hachaliah.
It came to pass in the month
of Chislev, *in* the [b]twentieth year,
as I was in [c]Shushan[1] the [2]citadel,
2 that [a]Hanani one of my brethren
came with men from Judah;
and I asked them concerning the
Jews who had escaped, who had
survived the captivity, and concerning
Jerusalem.
3 And they said to me, "The survivors
who are left from the captivity
in the [a]province *are* there in
great distress and [b]reproach. [c]The
wall of Jerusalem [d]*is* also broken
down, and its gates *are* burned
with fire."
4 So it was, when I heard these
words, that I sat down and wept,
and mourned *for many* days; I was
fasting and praying before the God
of heaven.
5 And I said: "I pray, [a]LORD God
of heaven, O great and [b]awesome
God, [c]*You* who keep *Your* covenant
and mercy with those who
love [1]You and observe [2]Your commandments,
6 "please let Your ear be attentive
and [a]Your eyes open, that You
may hear the prayer of Your servant
which I pray before You now,
day and night, for the children of
Israel Your servants, and [b]confess
the sins of the children of Israel
which we have sinned against
You. Both my father's house and
I have sinned.
7 [a]"We have acted very corruptly
against You, and have [b]not kept
the commandments, the statutes,
nor the ordinances which
You commanded Your servant
Moses.
8 "Remember, I pray, the word
that You commanded Your servant
Moses, saying, [a]'*If* you [1]are
unfaithful, I will scatter you
among the nations;
9 [a]'but *if* you return to Me, and
keep My commandments and do
them, [b]though some of you were
cast out to the farthest part of the
heavens, *yet* I will gather them
from there, and bring them to the
place which I have chosen as a
dwelling for My name.'
10 [a]"Now these *are* Your servants
and Your people, whom You have

CHAPTER 1

1 [a]Neh. 10:1 [b]Neh. 2:1 [c]Esth. 1:1, 2, 5 [1]Or *Susa* [2]Or *fortified palace,* and so elsewhere in the book

2 [a]Neh. 7:2

3 [a]Neh. 7:6 [b]Neh. 2:17 [c]Neh. 2:17 [d]2 Kin. 25:10

5 [a]Dan. 9:4 [b]Neh. 4:14 [c][Ex. 20:6; 34:6, 7] [1]Lit. *Him* [2]Lit. *His*

6 [a]2 Chr. 6:40 [b]Dan. 9:20

7 [a]Dan. 9:5 [b]Deut. 28:15

8 [a]Lev. 26:33 [1]*act treacherously*

9 [a][Deut. 4:29–31; 30:2–5] [b]Deut. 30:4

10 [a]Deut. 9:29

redeemed by Your great power,
and by Your strong hand.
11 "O Lord, I pray, please [a]let
Your ear be attentive to the prayer
of Your servant, and to the prayer
of Your servants who [b]desire to
fear Your name; and let Your ser-
vant prosper this day, I pray, and
grant him mercy in the sight of this
man." For I was the king's [c]cup-
bearer.

Nehemiah Sent to Judah

2 And it came to pass in the
month of Nisan, in the twenti-
eth year of [a]King [1]Artaxerxes,
when wine *was* before him, that
[b]I took the wine and gave it to the
king. Now I had never been sad
in his presence before.
2 Therefore the king said to me,
"Why *is* your face sad, since you
are not sick? This *is* nothing but
[a]sorrow of heart." So I became
[1]dreadfully afraid,
3 and said to the king, [a]"May the
king live forever! Why should my
face not be sad, when [b]the city, the
place of my fathers' tombs, *lies*
waste, and its gates are burned
with [c]fire?"
4 Then the king said to me,
"What do you request?" So I
[a]prayed to the God of heaven.
5 And I said to the king, "If it
pleases the king, and if your ser-
vant has found favor in your sight,
I ask that you send me to Judah,
to the city of my fathers' tombs,
that I may rebuild it."
6 Then the king said to me (the
queen also sitting beside him),
"How long will your journey be?
And when will you return?" So it
pleased the king to send me; and
I set him [a]a time.
7 Furthermore I said to the king,
"If it pleases the king, let letters
be given to me for the [a]governors
of the region beyond [1]the River,
that they must permit me to pass
through till I come to Judah,
8 "and a letter to Asaph the
keeper of the king's forest, that he
must give me timber to make
beams for the gates of the [1]citadel
which *pertains* [a]to the [2]temple, for
the city wall, and for the house
that I will occupy." And the king
granted *them* to me [b]according to
the good hand of my God upon me.
9 Then I went to the governors
in the region beyond the River,
and gave them the king's letters.
Now the king had sent captains of
the army and horsemen with me.
10 When [a]Sanballat the Horonite
and Tobiah the Ammonite [1]official
heard *of it*, they were deeply dis-
turbed that a man had come to
seek the well-being of the children
of Israel.

Nehemiah Views the Wall of Jerusalem

11 So I [a]came to Jerusalem and
was there three days.
12 Then I arose in the night, I and
a few men with me; I told no one
what my God had put in my heart
to do at Jerusalem; nor was there
any animal with me, except the
one on which I rode.
13 And I went out by night
[a]through the Valley Gate to the
Serpent Well and the [1]Refuse
Gate, and [2]viewed the walls of
Jerusalem which were [b]broken
down and its gates which were
burned with fire.
14 Then I went on to the [a]Fountain
Gate and to the [b]King's Pool, but
there was no room for the animal
under me to pass.
15 So I went up in the night by
the [a]valley,[1] and [2]viewed the wall;
then I turned back and entered by
the Valley Gate, and so returned.
16 And the officials did not know
where I had gone or what I had
done; I had not yet told the Jews,
the priests, the nobles, the offi-
cials, or the others who did the
work.
17 Then I said to them, "You see
the distress that we *are* in, how Je-
rusalem *lies* [1]waste, and its gates
are burned with fire. Come and let
us build the wall of Jerusalem, that
we may no longer be [a]a reproach."
18 And I told them of [a]the hand
of my God which had been good
upon me, and also of the king's
words that he had spoken to me.
So they said, "Let us rise up and
build." Then they [b]set[1] their hands
to *this* good *work*.
19 But when Sanballat the Horo-
nite, Tobiah the Ammonite official,
and Geshem the Arab heard *of it*,
they laughed at us and despised
us, and said, "What *is* this thing

11 [a]Neh. 1:6 [b]Is. 26:8; [Heb. 13:18] [c]Gen. 40:21; Neh. 2:1

CHAPTER 2

1 [a]Ezra 7:1 [b]Neh. 1:11 [1]Artaxerxes Longimanus

2 [a]Prov. 15:13 [1]Lit. *very much*

3 [a]1 Kin. 1:31; Dan. 2:4; 5:10; 6:6, 21 [b]2 Kin. 25:8–10; 2 Chr. 36:19; Jer. 52:12–14 [c]2 Kin. 24:10; Neh. 1:3

4 [a]Neh. 1:4

6 [a]Neh. 5:14; 13:6

7 [a]Ezra 7:21; 8:36 [1]The Euphrates

8 [a]Neh. 3:7 [b]Ezra 5:5; 7:6, 9, 28; Neh. 2:18 [1]*palace* [2]Lit. *house*

10 [a]Neh. 2:19; 4:1 [1]Lit. *servant*

11 [a]Ezra 8:32

13 [a]2 Chr. 26:9; Neh. 3:13 [b]Neh. 1:3; 2:17 [1]*Dung* [2]*examined*

14 [a]Neh. 3:15 [b]2 Kin. 20:20

15 [a]2 Sam. 15:23; Jer. 31:40 [1]*torrent valley, wadi* [2]*examined*

17 [a]Neh. 1:3; Ps. 44:13; 79:4; Jer. 24:9; Ezek. 5:14, 15; 22:4 [1]*desolate*

18 [a]Neh. 2:8 [b]2 Sam. 2:7 [1]Lit. *strengthened*

that you are doing? [a]Will you rebel
against the king?"
20 So I answered them, and said
to them, "The God of heaven Him-
self will prosper us; therefore we
His servants will arise and build,
[a]but you have no heritage or right
or memorial in Jerusalem."

Rebuilding the Wall

3 Then [a]Eliashib the high priest
rose up with his brethren the
priests [b]and built the Sheep Gate;
they consecrated it and hung its
doors. They built [c]as far as the
Tower of [1]the Hundred, *and* con-
secrated it, then as far as the
Tower of [d]Hananel.
2 [1]Next to *Eliashib* [a]the men of
Jericho built. And next to them
Zaccur the son of Imri built.
3 Also the sons of Hassenaah
built [a]the Fish Gate; they laid its
beams and [b]hung its doors with its
bolts and bars.
4 And next to them [a]Meremoth
the son of Urijah, the son of [1]Koz,
made repairs. Next to them
[b]Meshullam the son of Berechiah,
the son of Meshezabel, made re-
pairs. Next to them Zadok the son
of Baana made repairs.
5 Next to them the Tekoites
made repairs; but their nobles did
not put their [1]shoulders to [a]the
work of their Lord.
6 Moreover Jehoiada the son of
Paseah and Meshullam the son of
Besodeiah repaired [a]the Old Gate;
they laid its beams and hung its
doors, with its bolts and bars.
7 And next to them Melatiah the
Gibeonite, Jadon the Meronothite,
the [a]men of Gibeon and Mizpah,
repaired the [b]residence[1] of the
governor *of the region* [2]beyond the
River.
8 Next to him Uzziel the son of
Harhaiah, one of the goldsmiths,
made repairs. Also next to him
Hananiah, [1]one of the perfumers,
made repairs; and they [2]fortified
Jerusalem as far as the [a]Broad
Wall.
9 And next to them Rephaiah the
son of Hur, leader of half the dis-
trict of Jerusalem, made repairs.
10 Next to them Jedaiah the son
of Harumaph made repairs in front
of his house. And next to him Hat-
tush the son of Hashabniah made
repairs.
11 Malchijah the son of Harim and
Hashub the son of Pahath-Moab
repaired another section, [a]as well
as the Tower of the Ovens.
12 And next to him was Shallum
the son of Hallohesh, leader of half
the district of Jerusalem; he and
his daughters made repairs.
13 Hanun and the inhabitants of
Zanoah repaired [a]the Valley Gate.
They built it, hung its doors with
its bolts and bars, and *repaired* a
thousand cubits of the wall as far
as [b]the Refuse Gate.
14 Malchijah the son of Rechab,
leader of the district of [a]Beth Hac-
cerem, repaired the Refuse Gate;
he built it and hung its doors with
its bolts and bars.
15 Shallun the son of Col-Hozeh,
leader of the district of Mizpah, re-
paired [a]the Fountain Gate; he built
it, covered it, hung its doors with
its bolts and bars, and repaired the
wall of the Pool of [b]Shelah[1] by the
[c]King's Garden, as far as the stairs
that go down from the City of Da-
vid.
16 After him Nehemiah the son of
Azbuk, leader of half the district
of Beth Zur, made repairs as far
as *the place* in front of the [1]tombs
of David, to the [a]man-made pool,
and as far as the House of the
Mighty.
17 After him the Levites, *under*
Rehum the son of Bani, made re-
pairs. Next to him Hashabiah,
leader of half the district of Keilah,
made repairs for his district.
18 After him their brethren, *under*
[1]Bavai the son of Henadad, leader
of the *other* half of the district of
Keilah, made repairs.
19 And next to him Ezer the son
of Jeshua, the leader of Mizpah,
repaired another section in front
of the Ascent to the Armory at the
[a]buttress.[1]
20 After him Baruch the son of
[1]Zabbai carefully repaired the
other section, from the [2]buttress to
the door of the house of Eliashib
the high priest.
21 After him Meremoth the son of
Urijah, the son of [1]Koz, repaired
another section, from the door of
the house of Eliashib to the end
of the house of Eliashib.

19 [a]Neh. 6:6
20 [a]Ezra 4:3; Neh. 6:16

CHAPTER 3

1 [a]Neh. 3:20; 12:10; 13:4, 7, 28 [b]John 5:2 [c]Neh. 12:39 [d]Jer. 31:38; Zech. 14:10 [1]Heb. *Hammeah*
2 [a]Ezra 2:34; Neh. 7:36 [1]Lit. *On his hand*
3 [a]2 Chr. 33:14; Neh. 12:39; Zeph. 1:10 [b]Neh. 6:1; 7:1
4 [a]Ezra 8:33 [b]Ezra 10:15 [1]Or *Hakkoz*
5 [a][Judg. 5:23] [1]Lit. *necks*
6 [a]Neh. 12:39
7 [a]Neh. 7:25 [b]Ezra 8:36; Neh. 2:7–9 [1]Lit. *throne* [2]West of the Euphrates
8 [a]Neh. 12:38 [1]Lit. *the son* [2]*restored*
11 [a]Neh. 12:38
13 [a]Neh. 2:13, 15 [b]Neh. 2:13
14 [a]Jer. 6:1
15 [a]Neh. 2:14 [b]Is. 8:6; John 9:7 [c]2 Kin. 25:4 [1]Or *Shiloah*
16 [a]2 Kin. 20:20; Is. 7:3; 22:11 [1]LXX, Syr., Vg. *tomb*
18 [1]So with MT, Vg.; some Heb. mss., LXX, Syr. *Binnui* (cf. v. 24)
19 [a]2 Chr. 26:9 [1]Lit. *turning*
20 [1]A few Heb. mss., Syr., Vg. *Zaccai* [2]Lit. *turning*
21 [1]Or *Hakkoz*

22 And after him the priests, the
men of the plain, made repairs.
23 After him Benjamin and Has-
shub made repairs opposite their
house. After them Azariah the son
of Maaseiah, the son of Ananiah,
made repairs by his house.
24 After him [a]Binnui the son of
Henadad repaired another section,
from the house of Azariah to [b]the
[1]buttress, even as far as the corner.
25 Palal the son of Uzai *made re-
pairs* opposite the [1]buttress, and
on the tower which projects from
the king's upper house that *was* by
the [a]court of the prison. After him
Pedaiah the son of Parosh *made
repairs.*
26 Moreover [a]the Nethinim who
dwelt in [b]Ophel *made repairs* as
far as *the place* in front of [c]the Wa-
ter Gate toward the east, and on
the projecting tower.
27 After them the Tekoites re-
paired another section, next to the
great projecting tower, and as far
as the wall of Ophel.
28 Beyond the [a]Horse Gate the
priests made repairs, each in front
of his *own* house.
29 After them Zadok the son of
Immer made repairs in front of his
own house. After him Shemaiah
the son of Shechaniah, the keeper
of the East Gate, made repairs.
30 After him Hananiah the son of
Shelemiah, and Hanun, the sixth
son of Zalaph, repaired another
section. After him Meshullam the
son of Berechiah made repairs in
front of his [1]dwelling.
31 After him Malchijah, [1]one of
the goldsmiths, made repairs as
far as the house of the Nethinim
and of the merchants, in front of
the [2]Miphkad Gate, and as far as
the upper room at the corner.
32 And between the upper room
at the corner, as far as the [a]Sheep
Gate, the goldsmiths and the mer-
chants made repairs.

The Wall Defended Against Enemies

4 But it so happened, [a]when San-
ballat heard that we were
rebuilding the wall, that he was fu-
rious and very indignant, and
mocked the Jews.
2 And he spoke before his breth-
ren and the army of Samaria, and
said, "What are these feeble Jews
doing? Will they fortify them-
selves? Will they offer sacrifices?
Will they complete it in a day? Will
they revive the stones from the
heaps of rubbish—*stones* that are
burned?"
3 Now [a]Tobiah the Ammonite
was beside him, and he said,
"Whatever they build, if even a fox
goes up *on it,* he will break down
their stone wall."
4 [a]Hear, O our God, for we are
despised; [b]turn their reproach on
their own heads, and give them as
plunder to a land of captivity!
5 [a]Do not cover their iniquity,
and do not let their sin be blotted
out from before You; for they have
provoked *You* to anger before the
builders.
6 So we built the wall, and the
entire wall was joined together up
to half its *height,* for the people
had a mind to work.
7 Now it happened, [a]when San-
ballat, Tobiah, [b]the Arabs, the Am-
monites, and the Ashdodites heard
that the walls of Jerusalem were
being restored and the [1]gaps were
beginning to be closed, that they
became very angry,
8 and all of them [a]conspired to-
gether to come *and* attack Jerusa-
lem and create confusion.
9 Nevertheless [a]we made our
prayer to our God, and because of
them we set a watch against them
day and night.
10 Then Judah said, "The strength
of the laborers is failing, and *there
is* so much rubbish that we are not
able to build the wall."
11 And our adversaries said,
"They will neither know nor see
anything, till we come into their
midst and kill them and cause the
work to cease."
12 So it was, when the Jews who
dwelt near them came, that they
told us ten times, "From whatever
place you turn, *they will be* upon
us."
13 Therefore I positioned *men* be-
hind the lower parts of the wall,
at the openings; and I set the peo-
ple according to their families,
with their swords, their spears,
and their bows.
14 And I looked, and arose and
said to the nobles, to the leaders,
and to the rest of the people, [a]"Do

24 [a]Ezra 8:33 [b]Neh. 3:19 [1]Lit. *turning*
25 [a]Jer. 32:2; 33:1; 37:21 [1]Lit. *turning*
26 [a]Ezra 2:43; Neh. 11:21 [b]2 Chr. 27:3 [c]Neh. 8:1, 3; 12:37
28 [a]2 Kin. 11:16; 2 Chr. 23:15; Jer. 31:40
30 [1]Lit. *room*
31 [1]Lit. *a son of the goldsmiths* [2]Lit. *Inspection* or *Recruiting*
32 [a]Neh. 3:1; 12:39

CHAPTER 4

1 [a]Neh. 2:10, 19
3 [a]Neh. 2:10, 19
4 [a]Ps. 123:3, 4 [b]Ps. 79:12; Prov. 3:34
5 [a]Ps. 69:27, 28; 109:14, 15; Jer. 18:23
7 [a]Neh. 4:1 [b]Neh. 2:19 [1]Lit. *breaks*
8 [a]Ps. 83:3–5
9 [a][Ps. 50:15]
14 [a][Num. 14:9]; Deut. 1:29

not be afraid of them. Remember
the Lord, [b]great and awesome, and
[c]fight for your brethren, your sons,
your daughters, your wives, and
your houses."
15 And it happened, when our en-
emies heard that it was known to
us, and [a]*that* God had brought
their plot to nothing, that all of us
returned to the wall, everyone to
his work.
16 So it was, from that time on,
that half of my servants worked
at construction, while the other
half held the spears, the shields,
the bows, and *wore* armor; and the
leaders [1]*were* behind all the house
of Judah.
17 Those who built on the wall,
and those who carried burdens,
loaded themselves so that with one
hand they worked at construction,
and with the other held a weapon.
18 Every one of the builders had
his sword girded at his side as he
built. And the one who sounded
the trumpet *was* beside me.
19 Then I said to the nobles, the
rulers, and the rest of the people,
"The work *is* great and extensive,
and we are separated far from one
another on the wall.
20 "Wherever you hear the sound
of the trumpet, rally to us there.
[a]Our God will fight for us."
21 So we labored in the work, and
half of [1]*the men* held the spears
from daybreak until the stars ap-
peared.
22 At the same time I also said to
the people, "Let each man and his
servant stay at night in Jerusalem,
that they may be our guard by
night and a working party by
day."
23 So neither I, my brethren, my
servants, nor the men of the guard
who followed me took off our
clothes, *except* that everyone took
them off for washing.

Nehemiah Deals with Oppression

5 And there was a great [a]outcry
of the people and their wives
against their [b]Jewish brethren.
2 For there were those who said,
"We, our sons, and our daughters
are many; therefore let us get
grain, that we may eat and live."
3 There were also *some* who
said, "We have mortgaged our
lands and vineyards and houses,
that we might buy grain because
of the famine."
4 There were also those who
said, "We have borrowed money
for the king's tax *on* our lands and
vineyards.
5 "Yet now [a]our flesh *is* as the
flesh of our brethren, our children
as their children; and indeed we
[b]are forcing our sons and our
daughters to be slaves, and *some*
of our daughters have been
brought into slavery. *It is* not in
our power *to redeem them,* for
other men have our lands and
vineyards."
6 And I became very angry when
I heard their outcry and these
words.
7 After serious thought, I re-
buked the nobles and rulers, and
said to them, [a]"Each of you is [1]ex-
acting usury from his brother." So
I [2]called a great assembly against
them.
8 And I said to them, "According
to our ability we have [a]redeemed
our Jewish brethren who were
sold to the nations. Now indeed,
will you even sell your brethren?
Or should they be sold to us?"
Then they were silenced and found
nothing *to say.*
9 Then I said, "What you are do-
ing *is* not good. Should you not
walk [a]in the fear of our God [b]be-
cause of the reproach of the na-
tions, our enemies?
10 "I also, *with* my brethren and
my servants, am lending them
money and grain. Please, let us
stop this [1]usury!
11 "Restore now to them, even
this day, their lands, their vine-
yards, their olive groves, and their
houses, also a hundredth of the
money and the grain, the new wine
and the oil, that you have charged
them."
12 So they said, "We will restore
it, and will require nothing from
them; we will do as you say." Then
I called the priests, [a]and required
an oath from them that they would
do according to this promise.
13 Then [a]I shook out [1]the fold of
my garment and said, "So may
God shake out each man from his
house, and from his property, who
does not perform this promise.

14 [b][Deut. 10:17] [c]2 Sam. 10:12
15 [a]Job 5:12
16 [1]Supported
20 [a]Ex. 14:14, 25; Deut. 1:30; 3:22; 20:4; Josh. 23:10; 2 Chr. 20:29
21 [1]Lit. *them*

CHAPTER 5

1 [a]Lev. 25:35–37; Neh. 5:7, 8 [b]Deut. 15:7
5 [a]Is. 58:7 [b]Ex. 21:7; [Lev. 25:39]
7 [a][Ex. 22:25; Lev. 25:36; Deut. 23:19, 20]; Ezek. 22:12 [1]*charging interest* [2]Lit. *held*
8 [a]Lev. 25:48
9 [a]Lev. 25:36 [b]2 Sam. 12:14; Rom. 2:24; [1 Pet. 2:12]
10 [1]*interest*
12 [a]Ezra 10:5; Jer. 34:8, 9
13 [a]Matt. 10:14; Acts 13:51; 18:6 [1]Lit. *my lap*

Even thus may he be shaken out
and emptied." And all the assem-
bly said, "Amen!" and praised the
LORD. [b]Then the people did accord-
ing to this promise.

The Generosity of Nehemiah

14 Moreover, from the time that I
was appointed to be their governor
in the land of Judah, from the
twentieth year [a]until the thirty-
second year of King Artaxerxes,
twelve years, neither I nor my
brothers [b]ate the governor's provi-
sions.
15 But the former governors who
were before me laid burdens on
the people, and took from them
bread and wine, besides forty
shekels of silver. Yes, even their
servants bore rule over the people,
but [a]I did not do so, because of the
[b]fear of God.
16 Indeed, I also continued the
[a]work on this wall, and [1]we did not
buy any land. All my servants
were gathered there for the
work.
17 And [a]at my table *were* one hun-
dred and fifty Jews and rulers, be-
sides those who came to us from
the nations around us.
18 Now *that* [a]which was prepared
daily *was* one ox *and* six choice
sheep. Also fowl were prepared for
me, and once every ten days an
abundance of all kinds of wine.
Yet in spite of this [b]I did not de-
mand the governor's provisions,
because the bondage was heavy
on this people.
19 [a]Remember me, my God, for
good, *according to* all that I have
done for this people.

Conspiracy Against Nehemiah

6 Now it happened [a]when San-
ballat, Tobiah, [1]Geshem the
Arab, and the rest of our enemies
heard that I had rebuilt the wall,
and *that* there were no breaks left
in it [b](though at that time I had not
hung the doors in the gates),
2 that Sanballat and [1]Geshem
[a]sent to me, saying, "Come, let us
meet together [2]among the villages
in the plain of [b]Ono." But they
[c]thought to do me harm.
3 So I sent messengers to them,
saying, "I *am* doing a great work,
so that I cannot come down. Why
should the work cease while I
leave it and go down to you?"
4 But they sent me this message
four times, and I answered them
in the same manner.
5 Then Sanballat sent his servant
to me as before, the fifth time, with
an open letter in his hand.
6 In it *was* written:

It is reported among the
nations, and [1]Geshem says,
that you and the Jews plan to
rebel; therefore, according to
these rumors, you are
rebuilding the wall, [a]that you
may be their king.
7 And you have also appointed
prophets to proclaim
concerning you at Jerusalem,
saying, "*There is* a king in
Judah!" Now these matters will
be reported to the king. So
come, therefore, and let us
consult together.

8 Then I sent to him, saying, "No
such things as you say are being
done, but you invent them in your
own heart."
9 For they all *were trying to*
make us afraid, saying, "Their
hands will be weakened in the
work, and it will not be done."
Now therefore, *O God*,
strengthen my hands.
10 Afterward I came to the house
of Shemaiah the son of Delaiah,
the son of Mehetabel, who *was* a
secret informer; and he said, "Let
us meet together in the house of
God, within the [1]temple, and let us
close the doors of the temple, for
they are coming to kill you; in-
deed, at night they will come to kill
you."
11 And I said, "Should such a man
as I flee? And who *is there* such
as I who would go into the temple
to save his life? I will not go in!"
12 Then I perceived that God had
not sent him at all, but that [a]he
pronounced *this* prophecy against
me because Tobiah and Sanballat
had hired him.
13 For this reason he *was* hired,
that I should be afraid and act that
way and sin, so *that* they might
have *cause* for an evil report, that
they might reproach me.
14 [a]My God, remember Tobiah

13 [b]2 Kin. 23:3
14 [a]Neh. 2:1; 13:6 [b][1 Cor. 9:4–15]
15 [a]2 Cor. 11:9; 12:13 [b]Neh. 5:9
16 [a]Neh. 4:1; 6:1 [1]So with MT; LXX, Syr., Vg. *I*
17 [a]2 Sam. 9:7; 1 Kin. 18:19
18 [a]1 Kin. 4:22 [b]Neh. 5:14, 15
19 [a]2 Kin. 20:3; Neh. 13:14, 22, 31

CHAPTER 6

1 [a]Neh. 2:10, 19; 4:1, 7; 13:28 [b]Neh. 3:1, 3 [1]Or *Gashmu*
2 [a]Prov. 26:24, 25 [b]1 Chr. 8:12; Neh. 11:35 [c]Ps. 37:12, 32 [1]Or *Gashmu* [2]Or *in Kephirim*, exact location unknown
6 [a]Neh. 2:19 [1]Heb. *Gashmu*
10 [1]Lit. *house*
12 [a]Ezek. 13:22
14 [a]Neh. 13:29

and Sanballat, according to these
their works, and the [b]prophetess
Noadiah and the rest of the proph-
ets who would have made me
afraid.

The Wall Completed

15 So the wall was finished on the
twenty-fifth *day* of Elul, in fifty-
two days.
16 And it happened, [a]when all our
enemies heard *of it,* and all the na-
tions around us saw *these things,*
that they were very disheartened
in their own eyes; for [b]they per-
ceived that this work was done by
our God.
17 Also in those days the nobles
of Judah sent many letters to To-
biah, and *the letters of* Tobiah
came to them.
18 For many in Judah were
pledged to him, because he was
the [a]son-in-law of Shechaniah the
son of Arah, and his son Jeho-
hanan had married the daughter
of [b]Meshullam the son of Bere-
chiah.
19 Also they reported his good
deeds before me, and reported my
[1]words to him. Tobiah sent letters
to frighten me.

7 Then it was, when the wall was
built and I had [a]hung the
doors, when the gatekeepers, the
singers, and the Levites had been
appointed,
2 that I gave the charge of Jeru-
salem to my brother [a]Hanani, and
Hananiah the leader [b]of the [1]cita-
del, for he *was* a faithful man and
[c]feared God more than many.
3 And I said to them, "Do not let
the gates of Jerusalem be opened
until the sun is hot; and while they
stand *guard,* let them shut and bar
the doors; and appoint guards
from among the inhabitants of Je-
rusalem, one at his watch station
and another in front of his own
house."

The Captives Who Returned to Jerusalem

4 Now the city *was* large and
spacious, but the people in it *were*
[a]few, and the houses *were* not re-
built.
5 Then my God put it into my
heart to gather the nobles, the rul-
ers, and the people, that they
might be registered by genealogy.
And I found a register of the ge-
nealogy of those who had come
up in the first *return,* and found
written in it:

6 [a]These *are* the people of the
province who came back from
the captivity, of those who had
been carried away, whom
Nebuchadnezzar the king of
Babylon had carried away, and
who returned to Jerusalem and
Judah, everyone to his city.
7 Those who came with
[a]Zerubbabel *were* Jeshua,
Nehemiah, [1]Azariah, Raamiah,
Nahamani, Mordecai, Bilshan,
[2]Mispereth, Bigvai, Nehum,
and Baanah.
The number of the men of
the people of Israel:
8 the sons of Parosh, two
thousand one hundred and
seventy-two;
9 the sons of Shephatiah, three
hundred and seventy-two;
10 the sons of Arah, six hundred
and fifty-two;
11 the sons of Pahath-Moab, of
the sons of Jeshua and Joab,
two thousand eight hundred
and eighteen;
12 the sons of Elam, one thousand
two hundred and fifty-four;
13 the sons of Zattu, eight
hundred and forty-five;
14 the sons of Zaccai, seven
hundred and sixty;
15 the sons of [1]Binnui, six
hundred and forty-eight;
16 the sons of Bebai, six hundred
and twenty-eight;
17 the sons of Azgad, two
thousand three hundred and
twenty-two;
18 the sons of Adonikam, six
hundred and sixty-seven;
19 the sons of Bigvai, two
thousand and sixty-seven;
20 the sons of Adin, six hundred
and fifty-five;
21 the sons of Ater of Hezekiah,
ninety-eight;
22 the sons of Hashum, three
hundred and twenty-eight;
23 the sons of Bezai, three
hundred and twenty-four;
24 the sons of [1]Hariph, one
hundred and twelve;

14 [b]Ezek. 13:17
16 [a]Neh. 2:10, 20; 4:1, 7; 6:1 [b]Ps. 126:2
18 [a]Neh. 13:4, 28 [b]Ezra 10:15; Neh. 3:4
19 [1]Or *affairs*

CHAPTER 7
1 [a]Neh. 6:1, 15
2 [a]Neh. 1:2 [b]Neh. 2:8; 10:23 [c]Ex. 18:21 [1]*palace*
4 [a]Deut. 4:27
6 [a]Ezra 2:1–70
7 [a]Ezra 5:2; Neh. 12:1, 47; Matt. 1:12, 13 [1]*Seraiah,* Ezra 2:2 [2]*Mispar,* Ezra 2:2
15 [1]*Bani,* Ezra 2:10
24 [1]*Jorah,* Ezra 2:18

25 the sons of [1]Gibeon, ninety-
five;
26 the men of Bethlehem and
Netophah, one hundred and
eighty-eight;
27 the men of Anathoth, one
hundred and twenty-eight;
28 the men of [1]Beth Azmaveth,
forty-two;
29 the men of [1]Kirjath Jearim,
Chephirah, and Beeroth, seven
hundred and forty-three;
30 the men of Ramah and Geba,
six hundred and twenty-one;
31 the men of Michmas, one
hundred and twenty-two;
32 the men of Bethel and Ai, one
hundred and twenty-three;
33 the men of the other Nebo,
fifty-two;
34 the sons of the other [a]Elam, one
thousand two hundred and
fifty-four;
35 the sons of Harim, three
hundred and twenty;
36 the sons of Jericho, three
hundred and forty-five;
37 the sons of Lod, Hadid, and
Ono, seven hundred and
twenty-one;
38 the sons of Senaah, three
thousand nine hundred and
thirty.
39 The priests: the sons of
[a]Jedaiah, of the house of
Jeshua, nine hundred and
seventy-three;
40 the sons of [a]Immer, one
thousand and fifty-two;
41 the sons of [a]Pashhur, one
thousand two hundred and
forty-seven;
42 the sons of [a]Harim, one
thousand and seventeen.
43 The Levites: the sons of Jeshua,
of Kadmiel, *and* of the sons of
[1]Hodevah, seventy-four.
44 The singers: the sons of Asaph,
one hundred and forty-eight.
45 The gatekeepers: the sons of
Shallum, the sons of Ater, the
sons of Talmon, the sons of
Akkub, the sons of Hatita, the
sons of Shobai, one hundred
and thirty-eight.
46 The Nethinim: the sons of Ziha,
the sons of Hasupha, the sons
of Tabbaoth,
47 the sons of Keros, the sons of
[1]Sia, the sons of Padon,
48 the sons of [1]Lebana, the sons
of [2]Hagaba, the sons of
[3]Salmai,
49 the sons of Hanan, the sons of
Giddel, the sons of Gahar,
50 the sons of Reaiah, the sons of
Rezin, the sons of Nekoda,
51 the sons of Gazzam, the sons
of Uzza, the sons of Paseah,
52 the sons of Besai, the sons of
Meunim, the sons of
[1]Nephishesim,
53 the sons of Bakbuk, the sons
of Hakupha, the sons of
Harhur,
54 the sons of [1]Bazlith, the sons
of Mehida, the sons of Harsha,
55 the sons of Barkos, the sons of
Sisera, the sons of Tamah,
56 the sons of Neziah, and the
sons of Hatipha.
57 The sons of Solomon's
servants: the sons of Sotai, the
sons of Sophereth, the sons of
[1]Perida,
58 the sons of Jaala, the sons of
Darkon, the sons of Giddel,
59 the sons of Shephatiah, the
sons of Hattil, the sons of
Pochereth of Zebaim, and the
sons of [1]Amon.
60 All the Nethinim, and the sons
of Solomon's servants, *were*
three hundred and ninety-two.
61 And these *were* the ones who
came up from Tel Melah, Tel
Harsha, Cherub, [1]Addon, and
Immer, but they could not
identify their father's house
nor their lineage, whether they
were of Israel:
62 the sons of Delaiah, the sons
of Tobiah, the sons of Nekoda,
six hundred and forty-two;
63 and of the priests: the sons of
Habaiah, the sons of [1]Koz, the
sons of Barzillai, who took a
wife of the daughters of
Barzillai the Gileadite, and was
called by their name.
64 These sought their listing
among those who were
registered by genealogy, but it
was not found; therefore they
were excluded from the
priesthood as defiled.
65 And the [1]governor said to them
that they should not eat of the
most holy things till a priest
could consult with the Urim
and Thummim.
66 Altogether the whole assembly

25 [1]*Gibbar*, Ezra 2:20
28 [1]*Azmaveth*, Ezra 2:24
29 [1]*Kirjath Arim*, Ezra 2:25
34 [a]Neh. 7:12
39 [a]1 Chr. 24:7
40 [a]1 Chr. 9:12
41 [a]Ezra 2:38; 10:22
42 [a]1 Chr. 24:8
43 [1]*Hodaviah*, Ezra 2:40; or *Judah*, Ezra 3:9
47 [1]*Siaha*, Ezra 2:44
48 [1]MT *Lebanah* [2]MT *Hogabah* [3]*Shalmai*, Ezra 2:46; or *Shamlai*
52 [1]*Nephusim*, Ezra 2:50
54 [1]*Bazluth*, Ezra 2:52
57 [1]*Peruda*, Ezra 2:55
59 [1]*Ami*, Ezra 2:57
61 [1]*Addan*, Ezra 2:59
63 [1]Or *Hakkoz*
65 [1]Heb. *Tirshatha*

was forty-two thousand three
hundred and sixty,
67 besides their male and female
servants, of whom *there*
were seven thousand three
hundred and thirty-seven; and
they had two hundred and
forty-five men and women
singers.
68 Their horses were seven
hundred and thirty-six, their
mules two hundred and forty-
five,
69 *their* camels four hundred and
thirty-five, *and* donkeys six
thousand seven hundred and
twenty.
70 And some of the heads of the
fathers' houses gave to the
work. [a]The [1]governor gave to
the treasury one thousand gold
drachmas, fifty basins, and five
hundred and thirty priestly
garments.
71 Some of the heads of the
fathers' *houses* gave to the
treasury of the work [a]twenty
thousand gold drachmas, and
two thousand two hundred
silver minas.
72 And that which the rest of the
people gave *was* twenty
thousand gold drachmas, two
thousand silver minas, and
sixty-seven priestly garments.

73 So the priests, the Levites, the
gatekeepers, the singers, *some* of
the people, the Nethinim, and all
Israel dwelt in their cities.

Ezra Reads the Law

[a]When the seventh month
came, the children of Israel *were*
in their cities.

8 Now all [a]the people gathered
together as one man in the
open square that *was* [b]in front of
the Water Gate; and they told Ezra
the [c]scribe to bring the Book of the
Law of Moses, which the LORD had
commanded Israel.
2 So Ezra the priest brought [a]the
Law before the assembly of men
and women and all who *could* hear
with understanding [b]on the first
day of the seventh month.
3 Then he [a]read from it in the
open square that *was* in front of
the Water Gate [1]from morning un-
til midday, before the men and
women and those who could un-
derstand; and the ears of all the
people *were attentive* to the Book
of the Law.
4 So Ezra the scribe stood on a
platform of wood which they had
made for the purpose; and beside
him, at his right hand, stood Mat-
tithiah, Shema, Anaiah, Urijah,
Hilkiah, and Maaseiah; and at his
left hand Pedaiah, Mishael, Mal-
chijah, Hashum, Hashbadana,
Zechariah, *and* Meshullam.
5 And Ezra opened the book in
the sight of all the people, for he
was *standing* above all the people;
and when he opened it, all the peo-
ple [a]stood up.
6 And Ezra blessed the LORD, the
great God. Then all the people [a]an-
swered, "Amen, Amen!" while
[b]lifting up their hands. And they
[c]bowed their heads and worshiped
the LORD with *their* faces to the
ground.
7 Also Jeshua, Bani, Sherebiah,
Jamin, Akkub, Shabbethai, Hodi-
jah, Maaseiah, Kelita, Azariah,
Jozabad, Hanan, Pelaiah, and the
Levites, [a]helped the people to un-
derstand the Law; and the people
[b]*stood* in their place.
8 So they read distinctly from the
book, in the Law of God; and they
gave the sense, and helped *them*
to understand the reading.
9 [a]And Nehemiah, who *was*
the [1]governor, Ezra the priest
and scribe, and the Levites who
taught the people said to all the
people, [b]"This day *is* holy to the
LORD your God; [c]do not mourn nor
weep." For all the people wept,
when they heard the words of the
Law.
10 Then he said to them, "Go your
way, eat the fat, drink the sweet,
[a]and send portions to those for
whom nothing is prepared; for *this*
day *is* holy to our Lord. Do not sor-
row, for the joy of the LORD is your
strength."
11 So the Levites quieted all the
people, saying, "Be still, for the
day *is* holy; do not be grieved."
12 And all the people went their
way to eat and drink, to [a]send por-
tions and rejoice greatly, because
they [b]understood the words that
were declared to them.

70 [a]Neh. 8:9 [1]Heb. *Tirshatha*
71 [a]Ezra 2:69
73 [a]Ezra 3:1

CHAPTER 8

1 [a]Ezra 3:1 [b]Neh. 3:26 [c]Ezra 7:6
2 [a][Deut. 31:11, 12]; Neh. 8:9 [b]Lev. 23:24; Num. 29:1–6
3 [a]Deut. 31:9–11; 2 Kin. 23:2 [1]Lit. *from the light*
5 [a]Judg. 3:20; 1 Kin. 8:12–14
6 [a]Neh. 5:13; [1 Cor. 14:16] [b]Ps. 28:2; Lam. 3:41; 1 Tim. 2:8 [c]Ex. 4:31; 12:27; 2 Chr. 20:18
7 [a]Lev. 10:11; Deut. 33:10; 2 Chr. 17:7; [Mal. 2:7] [b]Neh. 9:3
9 [a]Ezra 2:63; Neh. 7:65, 70; 10:1 [b]Lev. 23:24; Num. 29:1 [c]Deut. 16:14; Eccl. 3:4 [1]Heb. *Tirshatha*
10 [a][Deut. 26:11–13]; Esth. 9:19, 22; Rev. 11:10
12 [a]Neh. 8:10 [b]Neh. 8:7, 8

The Feast of Tabernacles

13 Now on the second day the
heads of the fathers' *houses* of all
the people, with the priests and
Levites, were gathered to Ezra the
scribe, in order to understand the
words of the Law.
14 And they found written in the
Law, which the LORD had com-
manded by Moses, that the chil-
dren of Israel should dwell in
[a]booths[1] during the feast of the
seventh month,
15 and [a]that they should an-
nounce and proclaim in all their
cities and [b]in Jerusalem, saying,
"Go out to the mountain, and
[c]bring olive branches, branches of
oil trees, myrtle branches, palm
branches, and branches of leafy
trees, to make booths, as *it is* writ-
ten."
16 Then the people went out and
brought *them* and made them-
selves booths, each one on the
[a]roof of his house, or in their court-
yards or the courts of the house
of God, and in the open square of
the [b]Water Gate [c]and in the open
square of the Gate of Ephraim.
17 So the whole assembly of those
who had returned from the captiv-
ity made [1]booths and sat under the
booths; for since the days of
Joshua the son of Nun until that
day the children of Israel had not
done so. And there was very [a]great
gladness.
18 Also [a]day by day, from the first
day until the last day, he read from
the Book of the Law of God. And
they kept the feast [b]seven days;
and on the [c]eighth day *there was*
a sacred assembly, according to
the *prescribed* manner.

The People Confess Their Sins

9 Now on the twenty-fourth day
of [a]this month the children of
Israel were assembled with fast-
ing, in sackcloth, [b]and with [1]dust
on their heads.
2 Then [a]those of Israelite lineage
separated themselves from all for-
eigners; and they stood and [b]con-
fessed their sins and the iniquities
of their fathers.
3 And they stood up in their
place and [a]read from the Book of
the Law of the LORD their God *for*
one-fourth of the day; and *for an-*
other fourth they confessed and
worshiped the LORD their God.
4 Then Jeshua, Bani, Kadmiel,
Shebaniah, Bunni, Sherebiah,
Bani, *and* Chenani stood on the
[1]stairs of the Levites and cried out
with a loud voice to the LORD their
God.
5 And the Levites, Jeshua, Kad-
miel, Bani, Hashabniah, Shere-
biah, Hodijah, Shebaniah, *and*
Pethahiah, said:

"Stand up *and* bless the LORD your
God
Forever and ever!

"Blessed be [a]Your glorious name,
Which is exalted above all
blessing and praise!
6 [a]You alone *are* the LORD;
[b]You have made heaven,
[c]The heaven of heavens, with [d]all
their host,
The earth and everything on it,
The seas and all that is in them,
And You [e]preserve them all.
The host of heaven worships
You.

7 "You *are* the LORD God,
Who chose [a]Abram,
And brought him out of Ur of the
Chaldeans,
And gave him the name
[b]Abraham;
8 You found his heart [a]faithful
before You,
And made a [b]covenant with him
To give the land of the
Canaanites,
The Hittites, the Amorites,
The Perizzites, the Jebusites,
And the Girgashites—
To give *it* to his descendants.
You [c]have performed Your
words,
For You *are* righteous.

9 "You[a] saw the affliction of our
fathers in Egypt,
And [b]heard their cry by the Red
Sea.
10 You [a]showed signs and wonders
against Pharaoh,
Against all his servants,
And against all the people of his
land.
For You knew that they [b]acted
[1]proudly against them.
So You [c]made a name for
Yourself, as *it is* this day.

---

14 [a]Lev. 23:34, 40, 42; Deut. 16:13 [1]Temporary shelters
15 [a]Lev. 23:4 [b]Deut. 16:16 [c]Lev. 23:40
16 [a]Deut. 22:8 [b]Neh. 12:37 [c]2 Kin. 14:13; Neh. 12:39
17 [a]2 Chr. 30:21 [1]Temporary shelters
18 [a]Deut. 31:11 [b]Lev. 23:36 [c]Num. 29:35

CHAPTER 9

1 [a]Neh. 8:2 [b]Josh. 7:6; 1 Sam. 4:12; 2 Sam. 1:2; Job 2:12 [1]Lit. *earth on them*
2 [a]Ezra 10:11; Neh. 13:3, 30 [b]Neh. 1:6
3 [a]Neh. 8:7, 8
4 [1]Lit. *ascent*
5 [a]1 Chr. 29:13
6 [a]Deut. 6:4; 2 Kin. 19:15, 19; [Ps. 86:10]; Is. 37:16, 20 [b]Gen. 1:1; Ex. 20:11; Rev. 14:7 [c][Deut. 10:14]; 1 Kin. 8:27 [d]Gen. 2:1 [e][Ps. 36:6]
7 [a]Gen. 11:31 [b]Gen. 17:5
8 [a]Gen. 15:6; 22:1–3; [James 2:21–23] [b]Gen. 15:18 [c]Josh. 23:14
9 [a]Ex. 2:25; 3:7 [b]Ex. 14:10
10 [a]Ex. 7—14 [b]Ex. 18:11 [c]Jer. 32:20 [1]*presumptuously* or *insolently*

11 [a]And You divided the sea before
them,
So that they went through the
midst of the sea on the dry
land;
And their persecutors You threw
into the deep,
[b]As a stone into the mighty waters.
12 Moreover You [a]led them by day
with a cloudy pillar,
And by night with a pillar of fire,
To give them light on the road
Which they should travel.

13 "You[a] came down also on Mount
Sinai,
And spoke with them from
heaven,
And gave them [b]just ordinances
and true laws,
Good statutes and
commandments.
14 You made known to them Your
[a]holy Sabbath,
And commanded them precepts,
statutes and laws,
By the hand of Moses Your
servant.
15 You [a]gave them bread from
heaven for their hunger,
And [b]brought them water out of
the rock for their thirst,
And told them to [c]go in to possess
the land
Which You had [1]sworn to give
them.

16 "But[a] they and our fathers acted
[1]proudly,
[b]Hardened[2] their necks,
And did not heed Your
commandments.
17 They refused to obey,
And [a]they were not mindful of
Your wonders
That You did among them.
But they hardened their necks,
And [1]in their rebellion
They appointed [b]a leader
To return to their bondage.
But You *are* God,
Ready to pardon,
[c]Gracious and merciful,
Slow to anger,
Abundant in kindness,
And did not forsake them.

18 "Even [a]when they made a molded
calf for themselves,
And said, 'This *is* your god
That brought you up out of
Egypt,'
And worked great provocations,
19 Yet in Your [a]manifold mercies
You did not forsake them in the
wilderness.
The [b]pillar of the cloud did not
depart from them by day,
To lead them on the road;
Nor the pillar of fire by night,
To show them light,
And the way they should go.
20 You also gave Your [a]good Spirit
to instruct them,
And did not withhold Your
[b]manna from their mouth,
And gave them [c]water for their
thirst.
21 [a]Forty years You sustained them
in the wilderness;
They lacked nothing;
Their [b]clothes did not wear out
And their feet did not swell.

22 "Moreover You gave them
kingdoms and nations,
And divided them into [1]districts.
So they took possession of the
land of [a]Sihon,
[2]The land of the king of Heshbon,
And the land of Og king of
Bashan.
23 You also multiplied [a]their
children as the stars of heaven,
And brought them into the land
Which You had told their fathers
To go in and possess.
24 So [a]the [1]people went in
And possessed the land;
[b]You subdued before them the
inhabitants of the land,
The Canaanites,
And gave them into their hands,
With their kings
And the people of the land,
That they might do with them as
they wished.
25 And they took strong cities and
a [a]rich land,
And possessed [b]houses full of all
goods,
Cisterns *already* dug, vineyards,
olive groves,
And [1]fruit trees in abundance.
So they ate and were filled and
[c]grew fat,
And delighted themselves in
Your great [d]goodness.

26 "Nevertheless they [a]were
disobedient
And rebelled against You,
[b]Cast Your law behind their backs
And killed Your [c]prophets, who
[1]testified against them
To turn them to Yourself;
And they worked great
provocations.
27 [a]Therefore You delivered them

---

11 [a]Ex. 14:20–28 [b]Ex. 15:1, 5
12 [a]Ex. 13:21, 22
13 [a]Ex. 20:1–18 [b][Rom. 7:12]
14 [a]Gen. 2:3; Ex. 16:23; 20:8; 23:12
15 [a]Ex. 16:14–17; John 6:31 [b]Ex. 17:6; Num. 20:8; [1 Cor. 10:4] [c]Deut. 1:8 [1]Lit. *raised Your hand to*
16 [a]Ps. 106:6 [b]Deut. 1:26–33; 31:27; Neh. 9:29 [1]*presumptuously* [2]*Stiffened their necks,* became stubborn
17 [a]Ps. 78:11, 42–45 [b]Num. 14:4; Acts 7:39 [c]Joel 2:13 [1]So with MT, Vg.; LXX *in Egypt*
18 [a]Ex. 32:4–8, 31
19 [a]Ps. 106:45 [b]Ex. 13:20–22; 1 Cor. 10:1
20 [a]Num. 11:17 [b]Ex. 16:14–16 [c]Ex. 17:6
21 [a]Deut. 2:7 [b]Deut. 8:4; 29:5
22 [a]Num. 21:21–35 [1]Lit. *corners* [2]So with MT, Vg.; LXX omits *The land of*
23 [a]Gen. 15:5; 22:17; Heb. 11:12
24 [a]Josh. 1:2–4 [b]Josh. 18:1; [Ps. 44:2, 3] [1]Lit. *sons*
25 [a]Num. 13:27 [b]Deut. 6:11; Josh. 24:13 [c][Deut. 32:15] [d]Hos. 3:5 [1]Lit. *trees for eating*
26 [a]Judg. 2:11 [b]1 Kin. 14:9; Ps. 50:17 [c]1 Kin. 18:4; 19:10; Matt. 23:37; Acts 7:52 [1]*admonished* or *warned them*
27 [a]Judg. 2:14; Ps. 106:41

into the hand of their enemies,
Who oppressed them;
And in the time of their trouble,
When they cried to You,
You [b]heard from heaven;
And according to Your abundant
mercies
[c]You gave them deliverers who
saved them
From the hand of their enemies.

28 "But after they had rest,
[a]They again did evil before You.
Therefore You left them in the
hand of their enemies,
So that they had dominion over
them;
Yet when they returned and cried
out to You,
You heard from heaven;
And [b]many times You delivered
them according to Your
mercies,
29 And [1]testified against them,
That You might bring them back
to Your law.
Yet they acted [2]proudly,
And did not heed Your
commandments,
But sinned against Your
judgments,
[a]'Which if a man does, he shall live
by them.'
And they shrugged their
shoulders,
[3]Stiffened their necks,
And would not hear.
30 Yet for many years You had
patience with them,
And [1]testified [a]against them by
Your Spirit [b]in Your prophets.
Yet they would not listen;
[c]Therefore You gave them into the
hand of the peoples of the
lands.
31 Nevertheless in Your great mercy
[a]You did not utterly consume
them nor forsake them;
For You *are* God, gracious and
merciful.

32 "Now therefore, our God,
The great, the [a]mighty, and
awesome God,
Who keeps covenant and
mercy:
Do not let all the [1]trouble seem
small before You
That has come upon us,
Our kings and our princes,
Our priests and our prophets,
Our fathers and on all Your
people,
[b]From the days of the kings of
Assyria until this day.

27 [b]Ps. 106:44 [c]Judg. 2:18

28 [a]Judg. 3:12 [b]Ps. 106:43

29 [a]Lev. 18:5; Rom. 10:5; [Gal. 3:12] [1]*admonished them* [2]*presumptuously* [3]Became stubborn

30 [a]2 Kin. 17:13–18; 2 Chr. 36:11–20; Jer. 7:25 [b][Acts 7:51]; 1 Pet. 1:11 [c]Is. 5:5 [1]*admonished or warned them*

31 [a]Jer. 4:27; [Rom. 11:2–5]

32 [a][Ex. 34:6, 7] [b]2 Kin. 15:19; 17:3–6; Ezra 4:2, 10 [1]*hardship*

33 [a]Ps. 119:137; [Dan. 9:14] [b]Ps. 106:6; [Dan. 9:5, 6, 8]

35 [a]Deut. 28:47

36 [a]Deut. 28:48; Ezra 9:9

37 [a]Deut. 28:33, 51 [b]Deut. 28:48

38 [a]2 Kin. 23:3; 2 Chr. 29:10; Ezra 10:3 [b]Neh. 10:1

CHAPTER 10

1 [a]Neh. 1:1 [1]Heb. *Tirshatha*

2 [a]Neh. 12:1–21

33 However [a]You *are* just in all that
has befallen us;
For You have dealt faithfully,
But [b]we have done wickedly.
34 Neither our kings nor our
princes,
Our priests nor our fathers,
Have kept Your law,
Nor heeded Your
commandments and Your
testimonies,
With which You testified against
them.
35 For they have [a]not served You in
their kingdom,
Or in the many good *things* that
You gave them,
Or in the large and rich land
which You set before them;
Nor did they turn from their
wicked works.

36 "Here [a]we *are*, servants today!
And the land that You gave to our
fathers,
To eat its fruit and its bounty,
Here we *are*, servants in it!
37 And [a]it yields much increase to
the kings
You have set over us,
Because of our sins;
Also they have [b]dominion over
our bodies and our cattle
At their pleasure;
And we *are* in great distress.

38 "And because of all this,
We [a]make a sure *covenant* and
write *it;*
Our leaders, our Levites, *and* our
priests [b]seal *it.*"

The People Who Sealed the Covenant

10 Now those who placed *their*
seal on *the document were:*
Nehemiah the [1]governor, [a]the
son of Hacaliah, and Zedekiah,
2 [a]Seraiah, Azariah, Jeremiah,
3 Pashhur, Amariah, Malchijah,
4 Hattush, Shebaniah, Malluch,
5 Harim, Meremoth, Obadiah,
6 Daniel, Ginnethon, Baruch,
7 Meshullam, Abijah, Mijamin,
8 Maaziah, Bilgai, *and* Shemaiah.
These *were* the priests.
9 The Levites: Jeshua the son of
Azaniah, Binnui of the sons of Hen-
adad, *and* Kadmiel.
10 Their brethren: Shebaniah, Ho-
dijah, Kelita, Pelaiah, Hanan,
11 Micha, Rehob, Hashabiah,
12 Zaccur, Sherebiah, Shebaniah,

13 Hodijah, Bani, *and* Beninu.

14 The leaders of the people: [a]Parosh, Pahath-Moab, Elam, Zattu, Bani,

15 Bunni, Azgad, Bebai,

16 Adonijah, Bigvai, Adin,

17 Ater, Hezekiah, Azzur,

18 Hodijah, Hashum, Bezai,

19 Hariph, Anathoth, Nebai,

20 Magpiash, Meshullam, Hezir,

21 Meshezabel, Zadok, Jaddua,

22 Pelatiah, Hanan, Anaiah,

23 Hoshea, Hananiah, Hasshub,

24 Hallohesh, Pilha, Shobek,

25 Rehum, Hashabnah, Maaseiah,

26 Ahijah, Hanan, Anan,

27 Malluch, Harim, *and* Baanah.

The Covenant That Was Sealed

28 [a]Now the rest of the people—the priests, the Levites, the gatekeepers, the singers, the Nethinim, [b]and all those who had separated themselves from the peoples of the lands to the Law of God, their wives, their sons, and their daughters, everyone who had knowledge and understanding—

29 these joined with their brethren, their nobles, [a]and entered into a curse and an oath [b]to walk in God's Law, which was given by Moses the servant of God, and to observe and do all the commandments of the LORD our Lord, and His ordinances and His statutes:

30 We would not give [a]our daughters as wives to the peoples of the land, nor take their daughters for our sons;

31 [a]*if* the peoples of the land brought [1]wares or any grain to sell on the Sabbath day, we would not buy it from them on the Sabbath, or on a holy day; and we would forego the [b]seventh year's *produce* and the [c]exacting[2] of every debt.

32 Also we made ordinances for ourselves, to exact from ourselves yearly [a]one-third of a shekel for the service of the house of our God:

33 for [a]the showbread, for the regular grain offering, for the [b]regular burnt offering of the Sabbaths, the New Moons, and the set feasts; for the holy things, for the sin offerings to make atonement for Israel, and all the work of the house of our God.

34 We cast lots among the priests, the Levites, and the people, [a]for *bringing* the wood offering into the house of our God, according to our fathers' houses, at the appointed times year by year, to burn on the altar of the LORD our God [b]as *it is* written in the Law.

35 And *we made ordinances* [a]to bring the firstfruits of our ground and the firstfruits of all fruit of all trees, year by year, to the house of the LORD;

36 to bring the [a]firstborn of our sons and our cattle, as *it is* written in the Law, and the firstborn of our herds and our flocks, to the house of our God, to the priests who minister in the house of our God;

37 [a]to bring the firstfruits of our dough, our offerings, the fruit from all kinds of trees, *the* new wine and oil, to the priests, to the storerooms of the [1]house of our God; and to bring [b]the tithes of our land to the Levites, for the Levites should receive the tithes in all our farming communities.

38 And the priest, the descendant of Aaron, shall be with the Levites [a]when the Levites receive tithes; and the Levites shall bring up a tenth of the tithes to the house of our God, to [b]the rooms of the storehouse.

39 For the children of Israel and the children of Levi [a]shall bring the offering of the grain, of the new wine and the oil, to the storerooms where the articles of the sanctuary *are, where* the priests who minister and the gatekeepers [b]and the singers *are;* and we will not [c]neglect the house of our God.

The People Dwelling in Jerusalem

11 Now the leaders of the people dwelt at Jerusalem; the rest of the people cast lots to bring one out of ten to dwell in Jerusalem, [a]the holy city, and nine-tenths *were to dwell* in other cities.

2 And the people blessed all the men who [a]willingly offered themselves to dwell at Jerusalem.

3 [a]These *are* the heads of the province who dwelt in Jerusalem. (But in the cities of Judah everyone dwelt in his own possession in their cities—Israelites, priests, Levites, [b]Nethinim, and [c]descendants of Solomon's servants.)

---

14 [a]Ezra 2:3
28 [a]Ezra 2:36–43 [b]Ezra 9:1; Neh. 13:3
29 [a]Deut. 29:12; Neh. 5:12; Ps. 119:106 [b]2 Kin. 23:3; 2 Chr. 34:31
30 [a]Ex. 34:16; Deut. 7:3; [Ezra 9:12]
31 [a]Ex. 20:10; Lev. 23:3; Deut. 5:12 [b]Ex. 23:10, 11; Lev. 25:4; Jer. 34:14 [c][Deut. 15:1, 2]; Neh. 5:12 [1]*merchandise* [2]*collection*
32 [a]Ex. 30:11–16; 38:25, 26; 2 Chr. 24:6, 9; Matt. 17:24
33 [a]Lev. 24:5; 2 Chr. 2:4 [b]Num. 28; 29
34 [a]Neh. 13:31; [Is. 40:16] [b]Lev. 6:12
35 [a]Ex. 23:19; 34:26; Lev. 19:23; Num. 18:12; Deut. 26:1, 2
36 [a]Ex. 13:2, 12, 13; Lev. 27:26, 27; Num. 18:15, 16
37 [a]Lev. 23:17; Num. 15:19; 18:12; Deut. 18:4; 26:2 [b]Lev. 27:30; Num. 18:21; Mal. 3:10 [1]Temple
38 [a]Num. 18:26 [b]1 Chr. 9:26; 2 Chr. 31:11
39 [a]Deut. 12:6 11; 2 Chr. 31:12; Neh. 13:12 [b]Neh. 13:10, 11 [c][Heb. 10:25]

CHAPTER 11

1 [a]Neh. 10:18; Matt. 4:5; 5:35; 27:53
2 [a]Judg. 5:9; 2 Chr. 17:16
3 [a]1 Chr. 9:2, 3 [b]Ezra 2:43 [c]Ezra 2:55

4 Also [a]in Jerusalem dwelt *some*
of the children of Judah and of the
children of Benjamin.
The children of Judah: Athaiah
the son of Uzziah, the son of Zech-
ariah, the son of Amariah, the son
of Shephatiah, the son of Mahala-
lel, of the children of [b]Perez;
5 and Maaseiah the son of Bar-
uch, the son of Col-Hozeh, the son
of Hazaiah, the son of Adaiah, the
son of Joiarib, the son of Zecha-
riah, the son of Shiloni.
6 All the sons of Perez who dwelt
at Jerusalem *were* four hundred
and sixty-eight valiant men.
7 And these are the sons of Ben-
jamin: Sallu the son of Meshullam,
the son of Joed, the son of Pedaiah,
the son of Kolaiah, the son of
Maaseiah, the son of Ithiel, the son
of Jeshaiah;
8 and after him Gabbai *and* Sal-
lai, nine hundred and twenty-
eight.
9 Joel the son of Zichri *was* their
overseer, and Judah the son of
[1]Senuah *was* second over the city.
10 [a]Of the priests: Jedaiah the son
of Joiarib, and Jachin;
11 Seraiah the son of Hilkiah, the
son of Meshullam, the son of Za-
dok, the son of Meraioth, the son
of Ahitub, *was* the leader of the
house of God.
12 Their brethren who did the
work of the house *were* eight hun-
dred and twenty-two; and Adaiah
the son of Jeroham, the son of
Pelaliah, the son of Amzi, the son of
Zechariah, the son of Pashhur, the
son of Malchijah,
13 and his brethren, heads of the
fathers' *houses, were* two hundred
and forty-two; and Amashai the
son of Azarel, the son of Ahzai,
the son of Meshillemoth, the son
of Immer,
14 and their brethren, mighty men
of valor, *were* one hundred and
twenty-eight. Their overseer *was*
Zabdiel [1]the son of *one of* the great
men.
15 Also of the Levites: Shemaiah
the son of Hasshub, the son of
Azrikam, the son of Hashabiah,
the son of Bunni;
16 [a]Shabbethai and [b]Jozabad, of
the heads of the Levites, *had* the
oversight of [c]the business outside
of the [1]house of God;
17 Mattaniah the son of [1]Micha,

4 [a]1 Chr. 9:3 [b]Gen. 38:29
4 [a]Gen. 38:29
9 [1]Or *Hassenuah*
10 [a]1 Chr. 9:10
14 [1]Or *the son of Haggedolim*
16 [a]Ezra 10:15 [b]Ezra 8:33 [c]1 Chr. 26:29 [1]Temple
17 [1]Or *Michah*
18 [a]Neh. 11:1
21 [a]2 Chr. 27:3; Neh. 3:26
22 [1]*work* [2]Temple
23 [a]Ezra 6:8, 9; 7:20 [1]*fixed share*
24 [a]Gen. 38:30 [b]1 Chr. 18:17 [1]Lit. *at the king's hand*
25 [a]Josh. 14:15

the son of Zabdi, the son of Asaph,
the leader *who* began the
thanksgiving with prayer; Bakbu-
kiah, the second among his breth-
ren; and Abda the son of Sham-
mua, the son of Galal, the son of
Jeduthun.
18 All the Levites in [a]the holy city
were two hundred and eighty-four.
19 Moreover the gatekeepers, Ak-
kub, Talmon, and their brethren
who kept the gates, *were* one hun-
dred and seventy-two.
20 And the rest of Israel, of the
priests *and* Levites, *were* in all the
cities of Judah, everyone in his in-
heritance.
21 [a]But the Nethinim dwelt in
Ophel. And Ziha and Gishpa *were*
over the Nethinim.
22 Also the overseer of the Levites
at Jerusalem *was* Uzzi the son of
Bani, the son of Hashabiah, the
son of Mattaniah, the son of Mi-
cha, of the sons of Asaph, the sing-
ers in charge of the [1]service of the
[2]house of God.
23 For [a]*it was* the king's com-
mand concerning them that a [1]cer-
tain portion should be for the sing-
ers, a quota day by day.
24 Pethahiah the son of Mesheza-
bel, of the children of [a]Zerah the
son of Judah, *was* [b]the[1] king's dep-
uty in all matters concerning the
people.

The People Dwelling Outside Jerusalem

25 And as for the villages with
their fields, *some* of the children
of Judah dwelt in [a]Kirjath Arba
and its villages, Dibon and its vil-
lages, Jekabzeel and its villages;
26 in Jeshua, Moladah, Beth Pelet,
27 Hazar Shual, and Beersheba
and its villages;
28 in Ziklag and Meconah and its
villages;
29 in En Rimmon, Zorah, Jar-
muth,
30 Zanoah, Adullam, and their vil-
lages; in Lachish and its fields; in
Azekah and its villages. They
dwelt from Beersheba to the Val-
ley of Hinnom.
31 Also the children of Benjamin
from Geba *dwelt* in Michmash,
Aija, and Bethel, and their vil-
lages;

32 in Anathoth, Nob, Ananiah;
33 in Hazor, Ramah, Gittaim;
34 in Hadid, Zeboim, Neballat;
35 in Lod, Ono, *and* [a]the Valley of
Craftsmen.
36 Some of the Judean divisions
of Levites *were* in Benjamin.

The Priests and Levites

12 Now these *are* the [a]priests
and the Levites who came
up with [b]Zerubbabel the son of
Shealtiel, and Jeshua: [c]Seraiah,
Jeremiah, Ezra,
2 Amariah, [1]Malluch, Hattush,
3 [1]Shechaniah, [2]Rehum, [3]Mere-
moth,
4 Iddo, [1]Ginnethoi, [a]Abijah,
5 [1]Mijamin, [2]Maadiah, Bilgah,
6 Shemaiah, Joiarib, Jedaiah,
7 [1]Sallu, Amok, Hilkiah, *and* Je-
daiah.
These *were* the heads of the
priests and their brethren in the
days of [a]Jeshua.
8 Moreover the Levites *were*
Jeshua, Binnui, Kadmiel, Shere-
biah, Judah, *and* Mattaniah [a]*who
led* the thanksgiving *psalms*, he
and his brethren.
9 Also Bakbukiah and Unni,
their brethren, *stood* across from
them in *their* duties.
10 Jeshua begot Joiakim, Joiakim
begot Eliashib, Eliashib begot Joi-
ada,
11 Joiada begot Jonathan, and
Jonathan begot Jaddua.
12 Now in the days of Joiakim, the
priests, the [a]heads of the fathers'
houses were: of Seraiah, Meraiah;
of Jeremiah, Hananiah;
13 of Ezra, Meshullam; of Ama-
riah, Jehohanan;
14 of [1]Melichu, Jonathan; of
[2]Shebaniah, Joseph;
15 of [1]Harim, Adna; of [2]Meraioth,
Helkai;
16 of Iddo, Zechariah; of Ginne-
thon, Meshullam;
17 of Abijah, Zichri; *the son* of
[1]Minjamin; of [2]Moadiah, Piltai;
18 of Bilgah, Shammua; of She-
maiah, Jehonathan;
19 of Joiarib, Mattenai; of Je-
daiah, Uzzi;
20 of [1]Sallai, Kallai; of Amok,
Eber;
21 of Hilkiah, Hashabiah; *and* of
Jedaiah, Nethanel.
22 During the reign of Darius the
Persian, a record *was also kept* of
the Levites and priests *who had
been* [a]heads of their fathers'
houses in the days of Eliashib, Joi-
ada, Johanan, and Jaddua.
23 The sons of Levi, the heads of
the fathers' *houses* until the days
of Johanan the son of Eliashib,
were written in the book of the
[a]chronicles.
24 And the heads of the Levites
were Hashabiah, Sherebiah, and
Jeshua the son of Kadmiel, with
their brothers across from them,
to [a]praise *and* give thanks, [b]group[1]
alternating with group, [c]according
to the command of David the man
of God.
25 Mattaniah, Bakbukiah, Oba-
diah, Meshullam, Talmon, and Ak-
kub *were* gatekeepers keeping the
watch at the storerooms of the
gates.
26 These *lived* in the days of
Joiakim the son of Jeshua, the son
of [1]Jozadak, and in the days of
Nehemiah [a]the governor, and of
Ezra the priest, [b]the scribe.

Nehemiah Dedicates the Wall

27 Now at [a]the dedication of the
wall of Jerusalem they sought out
the Levites in all their places, to
bring them to Jerusalem to cele-
brate the dedication with gladness,
[b]both with thanksgivings and sing-
ing, *with* cymbals and stringed in-
struments and harps.
28 And the sons of the singers
gathered together from the coun-
tryside around Jerusalem, from
the [a]villages of the Netoph-
athites,
29 from the house of Gilgal, and
from the fields of Geba and Azma-
veth; for the singers had built
themselves villages all around Je-
rusalem.
30 Then the priests and Levites
[a]purified themselves, and purified
the people, the gates, and the wall.
31 So I brought the leaders of Ju-
dah up on the wall, and appointed
two large thanksgiving choirs.
[a]*One* went to the right hand on the
wall [b]toward the Refuse Gate.
32 After them went Hoshaiah and
half of the leaders of Judah,
33 and Azariah, Ezra, Meshullam,
34 Judah, Benjamin, Shemaiah,
Jeremiah,

35 [a]1 Chr. 4:14

CHAPTER 12

1 [a]Ezra 2:1, 2; 7:7 [b]Neh. 7:7; Matt. 1:12, 13 [c]Neh. 10:2–8

2 [1]*Melichu*, v. 14

3 [1]*Shebaniah*, v. 14 [2]*Harim*, v. 15 [3]*Meraioth*, v. 15

4 [a]Luke 1:5 [1]*Ginnethon*, v. 16

5 [1]*Minjamin*, v. 17 [2]*Moadiah*, v. 17

7 [a]Ezra 3:2; Hag. 1:1; Zech. 3:1 [1]*Sallai*, v. 20

8 [a]Neh. 11:17

12 [a]Neh. 7:70, 71; 8:13; 11:13

14 [1]*Malluch*, v. 2 [2]*Shechaniah*, v. 3

15 [1]*Rehum*, v. 3 [2]*Meremoth*, v. 3

17 [1]*Mijamin*, v. 5 [2]*Maadiah*, v. 5

20 [1]*Sallu*, v. 7

22 [a]1 Chr. 24:6

23 [a]1 Chr. 9:14–22

24 [a]Neh. 11:17 [b]Ezra 3:11 [c]1 Chr. 23—26 [1]Lit. *watch by watch*

26 [a]Neh. 8:9 [b]Ezra 7:6, 11 [1]*Jehozadak*, 1 Chr. 6:14

27 [a]Deut. 20:5; Neh. 7:1; Ps. 30:title [b]1 Chr. 25:6; 2 Chr. 5:13; 7:6

28 [a]1 Chr. 9:16

30 [a]Ezra 6:20; Neh. 13:22, 30

31 [a]Neh. 12:38 [b]Neh. 2:13; 3:13

35 and some of the priests' sons
[a]with trumpets—Zechariah the
son of Jonathan, the son of She-
maiah, the son of Mattaniah, the
son of Michaiah, the son of Zac-
cur, the son of Asaph,
36 and his brethren, Shemaiah,
Azarel, Milalai, Gilalai, Maai,
Nethanel, Judah, *and* Hanani, with
[a]the musical [b]instruments of David
the man of God. Ezra the scribe
went before them.
37 [a]By the Fountain Gate, in front
of them, they went up [b]the stairs
of the [c]City of David, on the stair-
way of the wall, beyond the house
of David, as far as [d]the Water Gate
eastward.
38 [a]The other thanksgiving choir
went the opposite *way*, and I *was*
behind them with half of the peo-
ple on the wall, going past the
[b]Tower of the Ovens as far as [c]the
Broad Wall,
39 [a]and above the Gate of
Ephraim, above [b]the Old Gate,
above [c]the Fish Gate, [d]the Tower
of Hananel, the Tower of [1]the Hun-
dred, as far as [e]the Sheep Gate;
and they stopped by [f]the Gate of
the Prison.
40 So the two thanksgiving choirs
stood in the house of God, likewise
I and the half of the rulers with me;
41 and the priests, Eliakim, Maa-
seiah, [1]Minjamin, Michaiah, Elio-
enai, Zechariah, *and* Hananiah,
with trumpets;
42 also Maaseiah, Shemaiah,
Eleazar, Uzzi, Jehohanan, Malchi-
jah, Elam, and Ezer. The singers
[1]sang loudly with Jezrahiah the di-
rector.
43 Also that day they offered great
sacrifices, and rejoiced, for God
had made them rejoice with great
joy; the women and the children
also rejoiced, so that the joy of Je-
rusalem was heard [a]afar off.

Temple Responsibilities

44 [a]And at the same time some
were appointed over the rooms of
the storehouse for the offerings,
the firstfruits, and the [b]tithes, to
gather into them from the fields of
the cities the portions specified by
the Law for the priests and Le-
vites; for Judah rejoiced over the
priests and Levites who [1]min-
istered.

35 [a]Num. 10:2, 8
36 [a]1 Chr. 23:5 [b]2 Chr. 29:26, 27
37 [a]Neh. 2:14; 3:15 [b]Neh. 3:15 [c]2 Sam. 5:7–9 [d]Neh. 3:26; 8:1, 3, 16
38 [a]Neh. 12:31 [b]Neh. 3:11 [c]Neh. 3:8
39 [a]2 Kin. 14:13; Neh. 8:16 [b]Neh. 3:6 [c]Neh. 3:3 [d]Neh. 3:1 [e]Neh. 3:32 [f]Jer. 32:2 [1]Heb. *Hammeah*
41 [1]Or *Mijamin*, v. 5
42 [1]Lit. *made their voice to be heard*
43 [a]Ezra 3:13
44 [a]2 Chr. 31:11, 12; Neh. 13:5, 12, 13 [b]Neh. 10:37–39 [1]Lit. *stood*
45 [a]1 Chr. 25; 26
46 [a]1 Chr. 25:1; 2 Chr. 29:30
47 [a]Neh. 11:23 [b]Num. 18:21, 24 [c]Num. 18:26 [1]*set apart*

CHAPTER 13

1 [a][Deut. 31:11, 12]; 2 Kin. 23:2; Neh. 8:3, 8; 9:3; Is. 34:16 [b]Deut. 23:3, 4
2 [a]Num. 22:5; Josh. 24:9, 10 [b]Num. 23:1; 24:10; Deut. 23:5
3 [a]Neh. 9:2; 10:28
4 [a]Neh. 12:10 [b]Neh. 2:10; 4:3; 6:1
5 [a]Neh. 12:44 [b]Num. 18:21, 24
6 [a]Neh. 5:14–16
7 [a]Neh. 13:1, 5 [1]Temple

45 Both the singers and the gate-
keepers kept the charge of their
God and the charge of the purifica-
tion, [a]according to the command
of David *and* Solomon his son.
46 For in the days of David [a]and
Asaph of old *there were* chiefs of
the singers, and songs of praise
and thanksgiving to God.
47 In the days of Zerubbabel and
in the days of Nehemiah all Israel
gave the portions for the singers
and the gatekeepers, a portion for
[a]each day. [b]They also [1]conse-
crated *holy things* for the Levites,
[c]and the Levites consecrated *them*
for the children of Aaron.

Principles of Separation

13 On that day [a]they read from
the Book of Moses in the
hearing of the people, and in it was
found written [b]that no Ammonite
or Moabite should ever come into
the assembly of God,
2 because they had not met the
children of Israel with bread and
water, but [a]hired Balaam against
them to curse them. [b]However, our
God turned the curse into a bless-
ing.
3 So it was, when they had heard
the Law, [a]that they separated all
the mixed multitude from Israel.

The Reforms of Nehemiah

4 Now before this, [a]Eliashib the
priest, having authority over the
storerooms of the house of our
God, *was* allied with [b]Tobiah.
5 And he had prepared for him
a large room, [a]where previously
they had stored the grain offer-
ings, the frankincense, the articles,
the tithes of grain, the new wine
and oil, [b]which were commanded
to be given to the Levites and sing-
ers and gatekeepers, and the offer-
ings for the priests.
6 But during all this I was not in
Jerusalem, [a]for in the thirty-
second year of Artaxerxes king of
Babylon I had returned to the
king. Then after certain days I ob-
tained leave from the king,
7 and I came to Jerusalem and
discovered the evil that Eliashib
had done for Tobiah, in [a]preparing
a room for him in the courts of the
[1]house of God.
8 And it grieved me bitterly;

therefore I threw all the house-
hold goods of Tobiah out of the
room.
9 Then I commanded them to
[a]cleanse the rooms; and I brought
back into them the articles of the
house of God, with the grain offer-
ing and the frankincense.
10 I also realized that the portions
for the Levites had [a]not been given
them; for each of the Levites and
the singers who did the work had
gone back to [b]his field.
11 So [a]I contended with the rulers,
and said, [b]"Why is the house of
God forsaken?" And I gathered
them together and set them in their
place.
12 [a]Then all Judah brought the
tithe of the grain and the new wine
and the oil to the storehouse.
13 [a]And I appointed as treasurers
over the storehouse Shelemiah the
priest and Zadok the scribe, and
of the Levites, Pedaiah; and next
to them *was* Hanan the son of Zac-
cur, the son of Mattaniah; for they
were considered [b]faithful, and
their task *was* to distribute to their
brethren.
14 [a]Remember me, O my God,
concerning this, and do not wipe
out my good deeds that I have
done for the house of my God, and
for its services!
15 In those days I saw *people* in
Judah treading wine presses [a]on
the Sabbath, and bringing in
sheaves, and loading donkeys with
wine, grapes, figs, and all *kinds of*
burdens, [b]which they brought into
Jerusalem on the Sabbath day.
And I warned *them* about the day
on which they were selling pro-
visions.
16 Men of Tyre dwelt there also,
who brought in fish and all kinds
of goods, and sold *them* on the
Sabbath to the children of Judah,
and in Jerusalem.
17 Then I contended with the no-
bles of Judah, and said to them,
"What evil thing *is* this that you
do, by which you profane the Sab-
bath day?
18 [a]"Did not your fathers do thus,
and did not our God bring all this
disaster on us and on this city? Yet
you bring added wrath on Israel
by profaning the Sabbath."
19 So it was, at the gates of Jeru-
salem, as it [a]began to be dark be-
fore the Sabbath, that I com-
manded the gates to be shut, and
charged that they must not be
opened till after the Sabbath.
[b]Then I posted *some* of my ser-
vants at the gates, *so that* no bur-
dens would be brought in on the
Sabbath day.
20 Now the merchants and sellers
of all kinds of [1]wares [2]lodged
outside Jerusalem once or twice.
21 Then I warned them, and said
to them, "Why do you spend the
night [1]around the wall? If you do
so again, I will lay hands on you!"
From that time on they came no
more on the Sabbath.
22 And I commanded the Levites
that [a]they should cleanse them-
selves, and that they should go and
guard the gates, to sanctify the
Sabbath day.
Remember me, O my God, *con-
cerning* this also, and spare me ac-
cording to the greatness of Your
mercy!
23 In those days I also saw Jews
who [a]had married women of [b]Ash-
dod, Ammon, *and* Moab.
24 And half of their children
spoke the language of Ashdod,
and could not speak the language
of Judah, but spoke according to
the language of one or the other
people.
25 So I [a]contended with them and
[1]cursed them, struck some of them
and pulled out their hair, and
made them [b]swear by God, *saying,*
"You shall not give your daughters
as wives to their sons, nor take
their daughters for your sons or
yourselves.
26 [a]"Did not Solomon king of Is-
rael sin by these things? Yet
among many nations there was no
king like him, [b]who was beloved
of his God; and God made him
king over all Israel. [c]Nevertheless
pagan women caused even him to
sin.
27 "Should we then hear of your
doing all this great evil, [a]trans-
gressing against our God by mar-
rying pagan women?"
28 And *one* of the sons [a]of Joiada,
the son of Eliashib the high priest,
was a son-in-law of [b]Sanballat the
Horonite; therefore I drove him
from me.

9 [a]2 Chr. 29:5, 15, 16
10 [a]Neh. 10:37; Mal. 3:8 [b]Num. 35:2
11 [a]Neh. 13:17, 25 [b]Neh. 10:39
12 [a]Neh. 10:38; 12:44
13 [a]2 Chr. 31:12 [b]1 Cor. 4:2
14 [a]Neh. 5:19; 13:22, 31
15 [a][Ex. 20:10] [b]Neh. 10:31; [Jer. 17:21]
18 [a]Ezra 9:13; [Jer. 17:21]
19 [a]Lev. 23:32 [b]Jer. 17:21, 22
20 [1]*merchandise* [2]*spent the night*
21 [1]Lit. *before*
22 [a]1 Chr. 15:12; Neh. 12:30
23 [a][Ex. 34:16; Deut. 7:3, 4]; Ezra 9:2; Neh. 10:30 [b]Neh. 4:7
25 [a]Prov. 28:4 [b]Ezra 10:5; Neh. 10:29, 30 [1]*pronounced them cursed*
26 [a]1 Kin. 11:1, 2 [b]2 Sam. 12:24, 25 [c]1 Kin. 11:4–8
27 [a][Ezra 10:2]; Neh. 13:23
28 [a]Neh. 12:10, 12 [b]Neh. 4:1, 7; 6:1, 2

29 [a]Remember them, O my
God, because they have defiled
the priesthood and [b]the cov-
enant of the priesthood and the
Levites.
30 [a]Thus I cleansed them of every-
thing pagan. I also [b]assigned du-
ties to the priests and the Levites,
each to his service,
31 and *to bringing* [a]the wood of-
fering and the firstfruits at ap-
pointed times.
[b]Remember me, O my God, for
good!

29 [a]Neh. 6:14 [b]Mal. 2:4, 11, 12
30 [a]Neh. 10:30 [b]Neh. 12:1
31 [a]Neh. 10:34 [b]Neh. 13:14, 22

The Book of

Esther

GOD'S hand of providence and protection on behalf of His people is evident throughout the Book of Esther, though His name does not appear once. Haman's plot brings grave danger to the Jews and is countered by the courage of beautiful Esther and the counsel of her wise cousin Mordecai, resulting in a great deliverance. The Feast of Purim becomes an annual reminder of God's faithfulness on behalf of His people.

Esther's Hebrew name was *Hadassah,* "Myrtle" (2:7), but her Persian name *Ester* was derived from the Persian word for "Star" (*Stara*). The Greek title for this book is *Esther,* and the Latin title is *Hester.*

The King Dethrones Queen Vashti

CHAPTER 1

NOW it came to pass in the days of [a]Ahasuerus[1] (this *was* the Ahasuerus who reigned [b]over one hundred and twenty-seven provinces, [c]from India to Ethiopia),

2 in those days when King Ahasuerus [a]sat on the throne of his kingdom, which *was* in [b]Shushan[1] the [2]citadel,

3 *that* in the third year of his reign he [a]made a feast for all his officials and servants—the powers of Persia and Media, the nobles, and the princes of the provinces *being* before him—

4 when he showed the riches of his glorious kingdom and the splendor of his excellent majesty for many days, one hundred and eighty days *in all.*

5 And when these days were completed, the king made a feast lasting seven days for all the people who were present in [1]Shushan the [2]citadel, from great to small, in the court of the garden of the king's palace.

6 *There were* white and blue linen *curtains* fastened with cords of fine linen and purple on silver rods and marble pillars; *and the* [a]couches *were* of gold and silver on a *mosaic* pavement of alabaster, turquoise, and white and black marble.

7 And they served drinks in golden vessels, each vessel being different from the other, with royal wine in abundance, [a]according to the [1]generosity of the king.

8 In accordance with the law, the drinking was not compulsory; for so the king had ordered all the officers of his household, that they should do according to each man's pleasure.

9 Queen Vashti also made a feast for the women *in* the royal palace which *belonged* to King Ahasuerus.

10 On the seventh day, when the heart of the king was merry with wine, he commanded Mehuman, Biztha, [a]Harbona, Bigtha, Abagtha, Zethar, and Carcas, seven eunuchs who served in the presence of King Ahasuerus,

11 to bring Queen Vashti before the king, *wearing* her royal crown, in order to show her beauty to the people and the officials, for she *was* beautiful to behold.

12 But Queen Vashti refused to come at the king's command *brought* by *his* eunuchs; therefore the king was furious, and his anger burned within him.

13 Then the king said to the [a]wise men [b]who understood the times (for this *was* the king's manner toward all who knew law and justice,

14 those closest to him *being* Carshena, Shethar, Admatha, Tarshish, Meres, Marsena, and Memucan, the [a]seven princes of Persia and Media, [b]who had access to the king's presence, *and* who [1]ranked highest in the kingdom):

15 "What *shall we* do to Queen Vashti, according to law, because she did not obey the command of

1 [a]Ezra 4:6; Dan. 9:1 [b]Esth. 8:9 [c]Dan. 6:1 [1]Generally identified with Xerxes I (485–464 B.C.)
2 [a]1 Kin. 1:46 [b]Neh. 1:1; Dan. 8:2 [1]Or *Susa* [2]Or *fortified palace,* and so elsewhere in the book
3 [a]Gen. 40:20; Esth. 2:18
5 [1]Or *Susa* [2]*palace*
6 [a]Esth. 7:8; Ezek. 23:41; Amos 2:8; 6:4
7 [a]Esth. 2:18 [1]Lit. *hand*
10 [a]Esth. 7:9
13 [a]Jer. 10:7; Dan. 2:12; Matt. 2:1 [b]1 Chr. 12:32
14 [a]Ezra 7:14 [b]2 Kin. 25:19; [Matt. 18:10] [1]Lit. *sat in first place*

King Ahasuerus *brought to her* by
the eunuchs?"
16 And Memucan answered be-
fore the king and the princes:
"Queen Vashti has not only
wronged the king, but also all the
princes, and all the people who *are*
in all the provinces of King Aha-
suerus.
17 "For the queen's behavior will
become known to all women, so
that they will [a]despise their hus-
bands in their eyes, when they re-
port, 'King Ahasuerus commanded
Queen Vashti to be brought in be-
fore him, but she did not come.'
18 "This very day the *noble* ladies
of Persia and Media will say to all
the king's officials that they have
heard of the behavior of the queen.
Thus *there will be* excessive con-
tempt and wrath.
19 "If it pleases the king, let a
royal [1]decree go out from him, and
let it be recorded in the laws of the
Persians and the Medes, so that it
will [a]not [2]be altered, that Vashti
shall come no more before King
Ahasuerus; and let the king give
her royal position to another who
is better than she.
20 "When the king's decree which
he will make is proclaimed
throughout all his empire (for it is
great), all wives will [a]honor their
husbands, both great and small."
21 And the reply pleased the king
and the princes, and the king did
according to the word of Me-
mucan.
22 Then he sent letters to all the
king's provinces, [a]to each province
in its own script, and to every peo-
ple in their own language, that
each man should [b]be master in his
own house, and speak in the lan-
guage of his own people.

Esther Becomes Queen

2 After these things, when the
wrath of King Ahasuerus sub-
sided, he remembered Vashti,
[a]what she had done, and what had
been decreed against her.
2 Then the king's servants who
attended him said: "Let beautiful
young virgins be sought for the
king;
3 "and let the king appoint offi-
cers in all the provinces of his
kingdom, that they may gather all
the beautiful young virgins to
[1]Shushan the [2]citadel, into the
women's quarters, under the cus-
tody of [3]Hegai the king's eunuch,
custodian of the women. And let
beauty preparations be given
them.
4 "Then let the young woman
who pleases the king be queen in-
stead of Vashti." This thing
pleased the king, and he did so.
5 In [1]Shushan the [2]citadel there
was a certain Jew whose name
was Mordecai the son of Jair, the
son of Shimei, the son of [a]Kish, a
Benjamite.
6 [a]*Kish*[1] had been carried away
from Jerusalem with the captives
who had been captured with
[2]Jeconiah king of Judah, whom
Nebuchadnezzar the king of Bab-
ylon had carried away.
7 And *Mordecai* had brought up
Hadassah, that *is*, Esther, [a]his un-
cle's daughter, for she had neither
father nor mother. The young
woman *was* lovely and beautiful.
When her father and mother died,
Mordecai took her as his own
daughter.
8 So it was, when the king's com-
mand and decree were heard, and
when many young women were
[a]gathered at [1]Shushan the [2]citadel,
under the custody of Hegai, that
Esther also was taken to the king's
palace, into the care of Hegai the
custodian of the women.
9 Now the young woman pleased
him, and she obtained his favor;
so he readily gave [a]beauty prepa-
rations to her, besides [1]her allow-
ance. Then seven choice maid-
servants were provided for her
from the king's palace, and he
moved her and her maidservants
to the best *place* in the house
of the women.
10 [a]Esther had not [1]revealed her
people or family, for Mordecai had
charged her not to reveal *it*.
11 And every day Mordecai paced
in front of the court of the women's
quarters, to learn of Esther's wel-
fare and what was happening to
her.
12 Each young woman's turn
came to go in to King Ahasuerus
after she had completed twelve
months' preparation, according to
the regulations for the women, for

17 [a][Eph. 5:33]
19 [a]Esth. 8:8; Dan. 6:8 [1]Lit. *word* [2]*pass away*
20 [a][Eph. 5:33; Col. 3:18; 1 Pet. 3:1]
22 [a]Esth. 3:12; 8:9 [b][Eph. 5:22–24; 1 Tim. 2:12]

CHAPTER 2

1 [a]Esth. 1:19, 20
3 [1]Or *Susa* [2]*palace* [3]Heb. *Hege*
5 [a]1 Sam. 9:1 [1]Or *Susa* [2]*palace*
6 [a]2 Kin. 24:14, 15; 2 Chr. 36:10, 20; Jer. 24:1 [1]Lit. *Who* [2]*Jehoiachin*, 2 Kin. 24:6
7 [a]Esth. 2:15
8 [a]Esth. 2:3 [1]Or *Susa* [2]*palace*
9 [a]Esth. 2:3, 12 [1]Lit. *her portions*
10 [a]Esth. 2:20 [1]Revealed the identity of

thus were the days of their prepa-
ration apportioned: six months
with oil of myrrh, and six months
with perfumes and preparations
for beautifying women.
13 Thus *prepared, each* young
woman went to the king, and she
was given whatever she desired to
take with her from the women's
quarters to the king's palace.
14 In the evening she went, and
in the morning she returned to the
second house of the women, to the
custody of Shaashgaz, the king's
eunuch who kept the concubines.
She would not go in to the king
again unless the king delighted in
her and called for her by name.
15 Now when the turn came for
Esther [a]the daughter of Abihail
the uncle of Mordecai, who had
taken her as his daughter, to go
in to the king, she requested
nothing but what Hegai the
king's eunuch, the custodian of the
women, advised. And Esther [b]ob-
tained favor in the sight of all who
saw her.
16 So Esther was taken to King
Ahasuerus, into his royal palace,
in the tenth month, which *is* the
month of Tebeth, in the seventh
year of his reign.
17 The king loved Esther more
than all the *other* women, and she
obtained grace and favor in his
sight more than all the virgins; so
he set the royal [a]crown upon her
head and made her queen instead
of Vashti.
18 Then the king [a]made a great
feast, the Feast of Esther, for all
his officials and servants; and he
proclaimed a holiday in the prov-
inces and gave gifts according to
the [1]generosity of a king.

Mordecai Discovers a Plot

19 When virgins were gathered
together a second time, Mordecai
sat within the king's gate.
20 [a]*Now* Esther had not revealed
her family and her people, just as
Mordecai had charged her, for Es-
ther obeyed the command of Mor-
decai as when she was brought up
by him.
21 In those days, while Mordecai
sat within the king's gate, two of
the king's eunuchs, [1]Bigthan and
Teresh, doorkeepers, became furi-
ous and sought to lay hands on
King Ahasuerus.
22 So the matter became known
to Mordecai, [a]who told Queen Es-
ther, and Esther informed the king
in Mordecai's name.
23 And when an inquiry was
made into the matter, it was con-
firmed, and both were hanged on
a gallows; and it was written in
[a]the book of the chronicles in the
presence of the king.

Haman's Conspiracy Against the Jews

3 After these things King Ahas-
uerus promoted Haman, the
son of Hammedatha the [a]Agagite,
and [b]advanced him and set his seat
above all the princes who *were*
with him.
2 And all the king's servants who
were [a]within the king's gate
bowed and paid homage to Ha-
man, for so the king had com-
manded concerning him. But Mor-
decai [b]would not bow or pay
homage.
3 Then the king's servants who
were within the king's gate said to
Mordecai, "Why do you transgress
the [a]king's command?"
4 Now it happened, when they
spoke to him daily and he would
not listen to them, that they told
it to Haman, to see whether Mor-
decai's words would stand; for
Mordecai had told them that he
was a Jew.
5 When Haman saw that Morde-
cai [a]did not bow or pay him hom-
age, Haman was [b]filled with
wrath.
6 But he disdained to lay hands
on Mordecai alone, for they had
told him of the people of Mordecai.
Instead, Haman [a]sought to destroy
all the Jews who *were* throughout
the whole kingdom of Ahasue-
rus—the people of Mordecai.
7 In the first month, which is the
month of Nisan, in the twelfth year
of King Ahasuerus, [a]they cast Pur
(that *is*, the lot), before Haman [1]to
determine the day and the [2]month,
[3]until *it fell on the* twelfth *month*,
which *is* the month of Adar.
8 Then Haman said to King
Ahasuerus, "There is a certain
people scattered and dispersed
among the people in all the prov-
inces of your kingdom; [a]their laws

15 [a]Esth. 2:7; 9:29 [b]Esth. 5:2, 8
17 [a]Esth. 1:11
18 [a]Esth. 1:3 [1]Lit. *hand*
20 [a]Esth. 2:10; [Prov. 22:6]
21 [1]*Bigthana*, Esth. 6:2
22 [a]Esth. 6:1, 2
23 [a]Esth. 6:1

CHAPTER 3

1 [a]Num. 24:7; 1 Sam. 15:8 [b]Esth. 5:11
2 [a]Esth. 2:19, 21; 5:9 [b]Esth. 3:5; Ps. 15:4
3 [a]Esth. 3:2
5 [a]Esth. 3:2; 5:9 [b]Dan. 3:19
6 [a]Ps. 83:4; [Rev. 12:1–17]
7 [a]Esth. 9:24–26 [1]Lit. *from day to day and month to month* [2]LXX adds *to destroy the people of Mordecai in one day*; Vg. adds *the nation of the Jews should be destroyed* [3]So with MT, Vg.; LXX *and the lot fell on the fourteenth of the month*
8 [a]Ezra 4:12–15; Acts 16:20, 21

are different from all other
people's, and they do not keep the
king's laws. Therefore it *is* not fit-
ting for the king to let them re-
main.
9 "If it pleases the king, let *a de-*
cree be written that they be de-
stroyed, and I will pay ten thou-
sand talents of silver into the
hands of those who do the work,
to bring *it* into the king's treasur-
ies."
10 So the king [a]took [b]his signet
ring from his hand and gave it to
Haman, the son of Hammedatha
the Agagite, the [c]enemy of the
Jews.
11 And the king said to Haman,
"The money and the people *are*
given to you, to do with them as
seems good to you."
12 [a]Then the king's scribes were
called on the thirteenth day of the
first month, and *a decree* was writ-
ten according to all that Haman
commanded—to the king's sa-
traps, to the governors who *were*
over each province, to the officials
of all people, to every province
[b]according to its script, and to
every people in their language.
[c]In the name of King Ahasuerus
it was written, and sealed with
the king's signet ring.
13 And the letters were [a]sent by
couriers into all the king's prov-
inces, to destroy, to kill, and to an-
nihilate all the Jews, both young
and old, little children and women,
[b]in one day, on the thirteenth *day*
of the twelfth *month*, which *is* the
month of Adar, and [c]to plunder
their [1]possessions.
14 [a]A copy of the document was
to be issued as law in every prov-
ince, being published for all peo-
ple, that they should be ready for
that day.
15 The couriers went out, has-
tened by the king's command; and
the decree was proclaimed in
[1]Shushan the [2]citadel. So the king
and Haman sat down to drink, but
[a]the city of Shushan was [3]per-
plexed.

Esther Agrees to Help the Jews

4 When Mordecai learned all
that had happened, [1]he [a]tore
his clothes and put on sackcloth
[b]and ashes, and went out into the
midst of the city. He [c]cried out with
a loud and bitter cry.
2 He went as far as the front of
the king's gate, for no one *might*
enter the king's gate clothed with
sackcloth.
3 And in every province where
the king's command and decree
arrived, *there was* great mourning
among the Jews, with fasting,
weeping, and wailing; and many
lay in sackcloth and ashes.
4 So Esther's maids and eunuchs
came and told her, and the queen
was deeply distressed. Then she
sent garments to clothe Mordecai
and take his sackcloth away from
him, but he would not accept
them.
5 Then Esther called Hathach,
one of the king's eunuchs whom
he had appointed to attend her,
and she gave him a command con-
cerning Mordecai, to learn what
and why this *was.*
6 So Hathach went out to Morde-
cai in the city square that *was* in
front of the king's gate.
7 And Mordecai told him all that
had happened to him, and [a]the
sum of money that Haman had
promised to pay into the king's
treasuries to destroy the Jews.
8 He also gave him [a]a copy of the
written decree for their destruc-
tion, which was given at [1]Shushan,
that he might show it to Esther and
explain it to her, and that he might
command her to go in to the king
to make supplication to him and
plead before him for her people.
9 So Hathach returned and told
Esther the words of Mordecai.
10 Then Esther spoke to Hathach,
and gave him a command for Mor-
decai:
11 "All the king's servants and the
people of the king's provinces
know that any man or woman who
goes into [a]the inner court to the
king, who has not been called, [b]*he*
has but one law: put *all* to death,
except the one [c]to whom the king
holds out the golden scepter, that
he may live. Yet I myself have not
been [d]called to go in to the king
these thirty days."
12 So they told Mordecai Esther's
words.
13 And Mordecai told *them* to an-
swer Esther: "Do not think in your

---

10 [a]Gen. 41:42 [b]Esth. 8:2, 8 [c]Esth. 7:6
12 [a]Esth. 8:9 [b]Esth. 1:22 [c]1 Kin. 21:8; Esth. 8:8–10
13 [a]2 Chr. 30:6; Esth. 8:10, 14 [b]Esth. 8:12 [c]Esth. 8:11; 9:10 [1]LXX adds the text of the letter here
14 [a]Esth. 8:13, 14
15 [a]Esth. 8:15; [Prov. 29:2] [1]Or *Susa* [2]*palace* [3]*in confusion*

CHAPTER 4

1 [a]2 Sam. 1:11; Esth. 3:8–10; Jon. 3:5, 6 [b]Josh. 7:6; Ezek. 27:30 [c]Gen. 27:34 [1]Lit. *Mordecai*
7 [a]Esth. 3:9
8 [a]Esth. 3:14, 15 [1]Or *Susa*
11 [a]Esth. 5:1; 6:4 [b]Dan. 2:9 [c]Esth. 5:2; 8:4 [d]Esth. 2:14

heart that you will escape in the
king's palace any more than all the
other Jews.
14 "For if you remain completely
silent at this time, relief and deliv-
erance will arise for the Jews from
another place, but you and your
father's house will perish. Yet who
knows whether you have come to
the kingdom for *such* a time as
this?"
15 Then Esther told *them* to reply
to Mordecai:
16 "Go, gather all the Jews who
are present in [1]Shushan, and fast
for me; neither eat nor drink for
[a]three days, night or day. My
maids and I will fast likewise. And
so I will go to the king, which *is*
against the law; [b]and if I perish, I
perish!"
17 So Mordecai went his way and
did according to all that Esther
commanded [1]him.

Esther's Banquet

5 Now it happened [a]on the third
day that Esther put on *her*
royal *robes* and stood in [b]the inner
court of the king's palace, across
from the king's house, while the
king sat on his royal throne in the
royal house, facing the entrance of
the [1]house.
2 So it was, when the king saw
Queen Esther standing in the
court, *that* [a]she found favor in his
sight, and [b]the king held out to Es-
ther the golden scepter that *was*
in his hand. Then Esther went near
and touched the top of the scepter.
3 And the king said to her,
"What do you wish, Queen Esther?
What *is* your request? [a]It shall be
given to you—up to half the king-
dom!"
4 So Esther answered, "If it
pleases the king, let the king and
Haman come today to the banquet
that I have prepared for him."
5 Then the king said, "Bring Ha-
man quickly, that he may do as Es-
ther has said." So the king and Ha-
man went to the banquet that
Esther had prepared.
6 At the banquet of wine [a]the
king said to Esther, [b]"What *is* your
petition? It shall be granted you.
What *is* your request, up to half
the kingdom? It shall be done!"
7 Then Esther answered and
said, "My petition and request *is*
this:
8 "If I have found favor in the
sight of the king, and if it pleases
the king to grant my petition and
[1]fulfill my request, then let the
king and Haman come to the
[a]banquet which I will prepare for
them, and tomorrow I will do as
the king has said."

Haman's Plot Against Mordecai

9 So Haman went out that day
[a]joyful and with a glad heart; but
when Haman saw Mordecai in the
king's gate, and [b]that he did not
stand or tremble before him, he
was filled with indignation against
Mordecai.
10 Nevertheless Haman [a]re-
strained himself and went home,
and he sent and called for his
friends and his wife Zeresh.
11 Then Haman told them of his
great riches, [a]the multitude of his
children, everything in which the
king had promoted him, and how
he had [b]advanced him above the
officials and servants of the king.
12 Moreover Haman said, "Be-
sides, Queen Esther invited no one
but me to come in with the king
to the banquet that she prepared;
and tomorrow I am again invited
by her, along with the king.
13 "Yet all this avails me nothing,
so long as I see Mordecai the Jew
sitting at the king's gate."
14 Then his wife Zeresh and all
his friends said to him, "Let a [a]gal-
lows[1] be made, [2]fifty cubits high,
and in the morning [b]suggest to the
king that Mordecai be hanged on
it; then go merrily with the king
to the banquet." And the thing
pleased Haman; so he had [c]the gal-
lows made.

The King Honors Mordecai

6 That night [1]the king could not
sleep. So one was commanded
to bring [a]the book of the records
of the chronicles; and they were
read before the king.
2 And it was found written that
Mordecai had told of [1]Bigthana
and Teresh, two of the king's eu-
nuchs, the doorkeepers who had
sought to lay hands on King Ahas-
uerus.
3 Then the king said, "What

16 [a]Esth. 5:1 [b]Gen. 43:14 [1]Or *Susa*

17 [1]LXX adds a prayer of Mordecai here

CHAPTER 5

1 [a]Esth. 4:16 [b]Esth. 4:11; 6:4 [1]LXX adds many extra details in vv. 1, 2

2 [a][Prov. 21:1] [b]Esth. 4:11; 8:4

3 [a]Esth. 7:2; Mark 6:23

6 [a]Esth. 7:2 [b]Esth. 9:12

8 [a]Esth. 6:14 [1]Lit. *to do*

9 [a][Job 20:5; Luke 6:25] [b]Esth. 3:5

10 [a]2 Sam. 13:22

11 [a]Esth. 9:7–10 [b]Esth. 3:1

14 [a]Esth. 7:9 [b]Esth. 6:4 [c]Esth. 7:10 [1]Lit. *tree* or *wood* [2]About 75 feet

CHAPTER 6

1 [a]Esth. 2:23; 10:2 [1]Lit. *the king's sleep fled away*

2 [1]*Bigthan,* Esth. 2:21

honor or dignity has been be-
stowed on Mordecai for this?" And
the king's servants who attended
him said, "Nothing has been done
for him."
4 So the king said, "Who *is* in the
court?" Now Haman had *just* en-
tered [a]the outer court of the king's
palace [b]to suggest that the king
hang Mordecai on the gallows that
he had prepared for him.
5 The king's servants said to him,
"Haman is there, standing in the
court." And the king said, "Let
him come in."
6 So Haman came in, and the
king asked him, "What shall be
done for the man whom the king
delights to honor?" Now Haman
thought in his heart, "Whom
would the king delight to honor
more than [a]me?"
7 And Haman answered the
king, "*For* the man whom the king
delights to honor,
8 "let a royal robe be brought
which the king has worn, and [a]a
horse on which the king has rid-
den, which has a royal [1]crest
placed on its head.
9 "Then let this robe and horse
be delivered to the hand of one of
the king's most noble princes, that
he may array the man whom the
king delights to honor. Then [1]pa-
rade him on horseback through
the city square, [a]and proclaim be-
fore him: 'Thus shall it be done to
the man whom the king delights
to honor!' "
10 Then the king said to Haman,
"Hurry, take the robe and the
horse, as you have suggested, and
do so for Mordecai the Jew who
sits within the king's gate! Leave
nothing undone of all that you
have spoken."
11 So Haman took the robe and
the horse, arrayed Mordecai and
led him on horseback through the
city square, and proclaimed before
him, "Thus shall it be done to the
man whom the king delights to
honor!"
12 Afterward Mordecai went back
to the king's gate. But Haman
[a]hurried to his house, mourning
[b]and with his head covered.
13 When Haman told his wife Ze-
resh and all his friends everything
that had happened to him, his wise

4 [a]Esth. 5:1 [b]Esth. 5:14
6 [a][Prov. 16:18; 18:12]
8 [a]1 Kin. 1:33 [1]*crown*
9 [a]Gen. 41:43 [1]Lit. *cause him to ride*
12 [a]2 Chr. 26:20 [b]2 Sam. 15:30; Jer. 14:3, 4
13 [a][Gen. 12:3]; Zech. 2:8
14 [a]Esth. 5:8

CHAPTER 7

2 [a]Esth. 5:6
4 [a]Esth. 3:9; 4:7 [b]Deut. 28:68
6 [a]Esth. 3:10
8 [a]Esth. 1:6 [b]Job 9:24

men and his wife Zeresh said to
him, "If Mordecai, before whom
you have begun to fall, is of Jewish
descent, you will not prevail
against [a]him but will surely fall be-
fore him."
14 While they *were* still talking
with him, the king's eunuchs
came, and hastened to bring Ha-
man to [a]the banquet which Esther
had prepared.

Haman Hanged Instead of Mordecai

7 So the king and Haman went
to dine with Queen Esther.
2 And on the second day, [a]at the
banquet of wine, the king again
said to Esther, "What *is* your peti-
tion, Queen Esther? It shall be
granted you. And what *is* your re-
quest, up to half the kingdom? It
shall be done!"
3 Then Queen Esther answered
and said, "If I have found favor in
your sight, O king, and if it pleases
the king, let my life be given me
at my petition, and my people at
my request.
4 "For we have been [a]sold, my
people and I, to be destroyed, to
be killed, and to be annihilated.
Had we been sold as [b]male and fe-
male slaves, I would have held my
tongue, although the enemy could
never compensate for the king's
loss."
5 So King Ahasuerus answered
and said to Queen Esther, "Who
is he, and where is he, who would
dare presume in his heart to do
such a thing?"
6 And Esther said, "The adver-
sary and [a]enemy *is* this wicked
Haman!" So Haman was terrified
before the king and queen.
7 Then the king arose in his
wrath from the banquet of wine
and went into the palace garden;
but Haman stood before Queen Es-
ther, pleading for his life, for he
saw that evil was determined
against him by the king.
8 When the king returned from
the palace garden to the place of
the banquet of wine, Haman had
fallen across [a]the couch where Es-
ther *was*. Then the king said, "Will
he also assault the queen while I
am in the house?" As the word left
the king's mouth, they [b]covered
Haman's face.

9 Now [a]Harbonah, one of the eu-
nuchs, said to the king, "Look!
[b]The [1]gallows, fifty cubits high,
which Haman made for Mordecai,
who spoke [c]good on the king's be-
half, is standing at the house of
Haman." Then the king said,
"Hang him on it!"
10 So [a]they [b]hanged Haman on
the gallows that he had prepared
for Mordecai. Then the king's
wrath subsided.

Esther Saves the Jews

8 On that day King Ahasuerus
gave Queen Esther the house
of Haman, the [a]enemy of the Jews.
And Mordecai came before the
king, for Esther had told [b]how he
was related to her.
2 So the king took off [a]his signet
ring, which he had taken from Ha-
man, and gave it to Mordecai; and
Esther appointed Mordecai over
the house of Haman.
3 Now Esther spoke again to the
king, fell down at his feet, and
implored him with tears to coun-
teract the evil of Haman the Agag-
ite, and the scheme which he had
devised against the Jews.
4 And [a]the king held out the
golden scepter toward Esther. So
Esther arose and stood before the
king,
5 and said, "If it pleases the king,
and if I have found favor in his
sight and the thing *seems* right to
the king and I am pleasing in his
eyes, let it be written to revoke the
[a]letters devised by Haman, the son
of Hammedatha the Agagite,
which he wrote to annihilate the
Jews who *are* in all the king's
provinces.
6 "For how can I endure to see
[a]the evil that will come to my peo-
ple? Or how can I endure to see
the destruction of my country-
men?"
7 Then King Ahasuerus said to
Queen Esther and Mordecai the
Jew, "Indeed, [a]I have given Esther
the house of Haman, and they
have hanged him on the gallows
because he *tried to* lay his hand
on the Jews.
8 "You yourselves write *a decree*
concerning the Jews, [1]as you
please, in the king's name, and
seal *it* with the king's signet ring;
for whatever is written in the
king's name and sealed with the
king's signet ring [a]no one can re-
voke."
9 [a]So the king's scribes were
called at that time, in the third
month, which *is* the month of Si-
van, on the twenty-third *day;* and
it was written, according to all that
Mordecai commanded, to the
Jews, the satraps, the governors,
and the princes of the provinces
[b]from India to Ethiopia, one hun-
dred and twenty-seven provinces
in all, to every province [c]in its own
script, to every people in their own
language, and to the Jews in their
own script and language.
10 [a]And he wrote in the name of
King Ahasuerus, sealed *it* with the
king's signet ring, and sent letters
by couriers on horseback, riding
on royal horses [1]bred from swift
steeds.
11 By these letters the king per-
mitted the Jews who *were* in every
city to [a]gather together and protect
their lives—to [b]destroy, kill, and
annihilate all the forces of any
people or province that would as-
sault them, *both* little children and
women, and to plunder their pos-
sessions,
12 [a]on one day in all the provinces
of King Ahasuerus, on the thir-
teenth *day* of the twelfth month,
which *is* the month of [1]Adar.
13 [a]A copy of the document was
to be issued as a decree in every
province and published for all peo-
ple, so that the Jews would be
ready on that day to avenge them-
selves on their enemies.
14 The couriers who rode on royal
horses went out, hastened and
pressed on by the king's com-
mand. And the decree was issued
in [1]Shushan the [2]citadel.
15 So Mordecai went out from the
presence of the king in royal ap-
parel of [1]blue and white, with a
great crown of gold and a garment
of fine linen and purple; and [a]the
city of [2]Shushan rejoiced and was
glad.
16 The Jews had [a]light and glad-
ness, joy and honor.
17 And in every province and city,
wherever the king's command and
decree came, the Jews had joy and
gladness, a feast [a]and a holiday.

9 [a]Esth. 1:10 [b]Esth. 5:14; [Ps. 7:16; Prov. 11:5, 6] [c]Esth. 6:2 [1]Lit. *tree* or *wood*
10 [a][Ps. 7:16; 94:23; Prov. 11:5, 6] [b]Ps. 37:35, 36; Dan. 6:24

CHAPTER 8

1 [a]Esth. 7:6 [b]Esth. 2:7, 15
2 [a]Esth. 3:10
4 [a]Esth. 4:11; 5:2
5 [a]Esth. 3:13
6 [a]Neh. 2:3; Esth. 7:4; 9:1
7 [a]Esth. 8:1; Prov. 13:22
8 [a]Esth. 1:19; Dan. 6:8, 12, 15 [1]Lit. *as is good in your eyes*
9 [a]Esth. 3:12 [b]Esth. 1:1 [c]Esth. 1:22; 3:12
10 [a]1 Kin. 21:8; Esth. 3:12, 13 [1]Lit. *sons of the swift horses*
11 [a]Esth. 9:2 [b]Esth. 9:10, 15, 16
12 [a]Esth. 3:13; 9:1 [1]LXX adds the text of the letter here
13 [a]Esth. 3:14, 15
14 [1]Or *Susa* [2]*palace*
15 [a]Esth. 3:15; Prov. 29:2 [1]*violet* [2]Or *Susa*
16 [a]Ps. 97:11; 112:4
17 [a]1 Sam. 25:8; Esth. 9:19

Then many of the people of the
land [b]became Jews, because [c]fear
of the Jews fell upon them.

The Jews Destroy Their Tormentors

9 Now [a]in the twelfth month,
that *is*, the month of Adar, on
the thirteenth day, [b]*the time* came
for the king's command and his
decree to be executed. On the day
that the enemies of the Jews had
hoped to overpower them, the op-
posite occurred, in that the Jews
themselves [c]overpowered those
who hated them.
2 The Jews [a]gathered together in
their cities throughout all the prov-
inces of King Ahasuerus to lay
hands on those who [b]sought their
harm. And no one could withstand
them, [c]because fear of them fell
upon all people.
3 And all the officials of the prov-
inces, the satraps, the governors,
and all those doing the king's
work, helped the Jews, because
the fear of Mordecai fell upon
them.
4 For Mordecai *was* great in the
king's palace, and his fame spread
throughout all the provinces; for
this man Mordecai [a]became in-
creasingly prominent.
5 Thus the Jews defeated all their
enemies with the stroke of the
sword, with slaughter and destruc-
tion, and did what they pleased
with those who hated them.
6 And in [a]Shushan[1] the [2]citadel
the Jews killed and destroyed five
hundred men.
7 Also Parshandatha, Dalphon,
Aspatha,
8 Poratha, Adalia, Aridatha,
9 Parmashta, Arisai, Aridai, and
Vajezatha—
10 [a]the ten sons of Haman the son
of Hammedatha, the enemy of the
Jews—they killed; [b]but they did
not lay a hand on the [1]plunder.
11 On that day the number of
those who were killed in [1]Shushan
the [2]citadel [3]was brought to the
king.
12 And the king said to Queen Es-
ther, "The Jews have killed and
destroyed five hundred men in
Shushan the citadel, and the ten
sons of Haman. What have they
done in the rest of the king's prov-
inces? Now [a]what *is* your petition?
It shall be granted to you. Or what
is your further request? It shall be
done."
13 Then Esther said, "If it pleases
the king, let it be granted to the
Jews who *are* in Shushan to do
again tomorrow [a]according to to-
day's decree, and let Haman's ten
sons [b]be hanged on the gallows."
14 So the king commanded this to
be done; the decree was issued in
Shushan, and they hanged Ha-
man's ten sons.
15 And the Jews who *were* in
[1]Shushan [a]gathered together
again on the fourteenth day of the
month of Adar and killed three
hundred men at Shushan; [b]but
they did not lay a hand on the
plunder.
16 The remainder of the Jews in
the king's provinces [a]gathered to-
gether and protected their lives,
had rest from their enemies, and
killed seventy-five thousand of
their enemies; [b]but they did not lay
a hand on the plunder.
17 *This was* on the thirteenth day
of the month of Adar. And on the
fourteenth of [1]*the month* they
rested and made it a day of feast-
ing and gladness.

The Feast of Purim

18 But the Jews who *were* at
[1]Shushan assembled together [a]on
the thirteenth *day*, as well as on
the fourteenth; and on the fifteenth
of [2]*the month* they rested, and
made it a day of feasting and glad-
ness.
19 Therefore the Jews of the vil-
lages who dwelt in the unwalled
towns celebrated the fourteenth
day of the month of Adar [a]*with*
gladness and feasting, [b]as a holi-
day, and for [c]sending presents to
one another.
20 And Mordecai wrote these
things and sent letters to all the
Jews, near and far, who *were* in
all the provinces of King Ahas-
uerus,
21 to establish among them that
they should celebrate yearly the
fourteenth and fifteenth days of
the month of Adar,
22 as the days on which the Jews
had rest from their enemies, as the
month which was turned from sor-
row to joy for them, and from

---

17 [b]Ps. 18:43 [c]Gen. 35:5; Ex. 15:16; Deut. 2:25; 11:25; 1 Chr. 14:17; Esth. 9:2

CHAPTER 9

1 [a]Esth. 8:12 [b]Esth. 3:13 [c]2 Sam. 22:41

2 [a]Esth. 8:11; 9:15–18 [b]Ps. 71:13, 14 [c]Esth. 8:17

4 [a]2 Sam. 3:1; 1 Chr. 11:9; [Prov. 4:18]

6 [a]Esth. 1:2; 3:15; 4:16 [1]Or *Susa* [2]*palace*

10 [a]Esth. 5:11; 9:7–10; Job 18:19; 27:13–15; Ps. 21:10 [b]Esth. 8:11 [1]*spoil*

11 [1]Or *Susa* [2]*palace* [3]Lit. *came*

12 [a]Esth. 5:6; 7:2

13 [a]Esth. 8:11; 9:15 [b]2 Sam. 21:6, 9

15 [a]Esth. 8:11; 9:2 [b]Esth. 9:10 [1]Or *Susa*

16 [a]Esth. 9:2 [b]Esth. 8:11

17 [1]Lit. *it*

18 [a]Esth. 9:11, 15 [1]Or *Susa* [2]Lit. *it*

19 [a]Deut. 16:11, 14 [b]Esth. 8:16, 17 [c]Neh. 8:10, 12; Esth. 9:22

mourning to a holiday; that they
should make them days of feasting
and joy, of [a]sending presents to
one another and gifts to the [b]poor.
23 So the Jews accepted the cus-
tom which they had begun, as
Mordecai had written to them,
24 because Haman, the son of
Hammedatha the Agagite, the en-
emy of all the Jews, [a]had plotted
against the Jews to annihilate
them, and had cast Pur (that *is*, the
lot), to consume them and destroy
them;
25 but [a]when [1]*Esther* came before
the king, he commanded by letter
that [2]this wicked plot which *Ha-
man* had devised against the Jews
should [b]return on his own head,
and that he and his sons should
be hanged on the gallows.
26 So they called these days
Purim, after the name [1]Pur. There-
fore, because of all the words of
[a]this letter, what they had seen
concerning this matter, and what
had happened to them,
27 the Jews established and im-
posed it upon themselves and their
descendants and all who would
[a]join them, that without fail they
should celebrate these two days
every year, according to the writ-
ten *instructions* and according to
the *prescribed* time,
28 *that* these days *should be* re-
membered and kept throughout
every generation, every family,
every province, and every city,
that these days of Purim should
not fail *to be observed* among the
Jews, and *that* the memory of
them should not perish among
their descendants.
29 Then Queen Esther, [a]the daugh-
ter of Abihail, with Mordecai the
Jew, wrote with full authority to
confirm this [b]second letter about
Purim.
30 And *Mordecai* sent letters to all
the Jews, to [a]the one hundred and
twenty-seven provinces of the
kingdom of Ahasuerus, *with*
words of peace and truth,
31 to confirm these days of Purim
at their *appointed* time, as Morde-
cai the Jew and Queen Esther had
prescribed for them, and as they
had decreed for themselves and
their descendants concerning mat-
ters of their [a]fasting and lament-
ing.
32 So the decree of Esther con-
firmed these matters of Purim, and
it was written in the book.

Mordecai's Advancement

10 And King Ahasuerus im-
posed tribute on the land
and *on* [a]the islands of the sea.
2 Now all the acts of his power
and his might, and the account of
the greatness of Mordecai, [a]to
which the king [1]advanced him, *are*
they not written in the book of the
[b]chronicles of the kings of Media
and Persia?
3 For Mordecai the Jew *was*
[a]second to King Ahasuerus, and
was great among the Jews and
well received by the multitude of
his brethren, [b]seeking the good of
his people and speaking peace to
all his [1]countrymen.

22 [a]Neh. 8:10; Esth. 9:19 [b][Deut. 15:7–11]; Job 29:16
24 [a]Esth. 3:6, 7; 9:26
25 [a]Esth. 7:4–10; 8:3; 9:13, 14 [b]Esth. 7:10 [1]Lit. *she* or *it* [2]Lit. *his*
26 [a]Esth. 9:20 [1]Lit. *Lot*
27 [a]Esth. 8:17; [Is. 56:3, 6]; Zech. 2:11
29 [a]Esth. 2:15 [b]Esth. 8:10; 9:20, 21
30 [a]Esth. 1:1
31 [a]Esth. 4:3, 16

CHAPTER 10

1 [a]Gen. 10:5; Ps. 72:10; Is. 11:11; 24:15
2 [a]Esth. 8:15; 9:4 [b]Esth. 6:1 [1]Lit. *made him great*
3 [a]Gen. 41:40, 43, 44; 2 Chr. 28:7 [b]Neh. 2:10; Ps. 122:8, 9 [1]Lit. *seed.* LXX, Vg. add a dream of Mordecai here; Vg. adds six more chapters

The Book of

Job

JOB is perhaps the earliest book of the Bible. Set in the period of the patriarchs (Abraham, Isaac, Jacob, and Joseph), it tells the story of a man who loses everything—his wealth, his family, his health—and wrestles with the question, Why?

The book begins with a heavenly debate between God and Satan, moves through three cycles of earthly debates between Job and his friends, and concludes with a dramatic "divine diagnosis" of Job's problem. In the end, Job acknowledges the sovereignty of God in his life and receives back more than he had before his trials.

Iyyōb is the Hebrew title for this book, and the name has two possible meanings. If derived from the Hebrew word for "Persecution," it means "Persecuted One." It is more likely that it comes from the Arabic word meaning "To Come Back" or "Repent." If so, it may be defined "Repentant One." Both meanings apply to the book. The Greek title is *Iob*, and the Latin title is *Iob*.

Job and His Family in Uz

THERE was a man [a]in the land of Uz, whose name *was* [b]Job; and that man was [c]blameless and upright, and one who [d]feared God and [1]shunned evil.

2 And seven sons and three daughters were born to him.

3 Also, his possessions were seven thousand sheep, three thousand camels, five hundred yoke of oxen, five hundred female donkeys, and a very large household, so that this man was the greatest of all the [1]people of the East.

4 And his sons would go and feast *in their* houses, each on his *appointed* day, and would send and invite their three sisters to eat and drink with them.

5 So it was, when the days of feasting had run their course, that Job would send and [1]sanctify them, and he would rise early in the morning [a]and offer burnt offerings *according to* the number of them all. For Job said, "It may be that my sons have sinned and [b]cursed[2] God in their hearts." Thus Job did regularly.

Satan Attacks Job's Character

6 Now [a]there was a day when the sons of God came to present themselves before the LORD, and [1]Satan also came among them.

7 And the LORD said to [1]Satan, "From where do you come?" So Satan answered the LORD and said, "From [a]going to and fro on the earth, and from walking back and forth on it."

8 Then the LORD said to Satan, "Have you [1]considered My servant Job, that *there is* none like him on the earth, a blameless and upright man, one who fears God and [2]shuns evil?"

9 So Satan answered the LORD and said, "Does Job fear God for nothing?

10 [a]"Have You not [1]made a hedge around him, around his household, and around all that he has on every side? [b]You have blessed the work of his hands, and his possessions have increased in the land.

11 [a]"But now, stretch out Your hand and touch all that he has, and he will surely [b]curse[1] You to Your face!"

12 And the LORD said to Satan, "Behold, all that he has *is* in your [1]power; only do not lay a hand on his *person*." So Satan went out from the presence of the LORD.

Job Loses His Property and Children

13 Now there was a day [a]when his sons and daughters *were* eating and drinking wine in their oldest brother's house;

14 and a messenger came to Job and said, "The oxen were plowing

CHAPTER 1

1 [a]1 Chr. 1:17 [b]Ezek. 14:14, 20; James 5:11 [c]Gen. 6:9; 17:1; [Deut. 18:13] [d][Prov. 16:6] [1]Lit. *turned away from*

3 [1]Lit. *sons*

5 [a]Gen. 8:20; [Job 42:8] [b]1 Kin. 21:10, 13 [1]*consecrate* [2]Lit. *blessed,* but in an evil sense; cf. Job 1:11; 2:5, 9

6 [a]Job 2:1 [1]Lit. *the Adversary*

7 [a][1 Pet. 5:8] [1]Lit. *the Adversary*

8 [1]Lit. *set your heart on* [2]Lit. *turns away from*

10 [a]Job 29:2–6; Ps. 34:7; Is. 5:2 [b][Ps. 128:1, 2; Prov. 10:22] [1]Protected him

11 [a]Job 2:5; 19:21 [b]Is. 8:21; Mal. 3:13, 14 [1]Lit. *bless,* but in an evil sense; cf. Job 1:5

12 [1]Lit. *hand*

13 [a][Eccl. 9:12]

and the donkeys feeding beside
them,
15 "when the [1]Sabeans [2]raided
them and took them away—indeed
they have killed the servants with
the edge of the sword; and I alone
have escaped to tell you!"
16 While he *was* still speaking,
another also came and said, "The
fire of God fell from heaven and
burned up the sheep and the
servants, and [1]consumed them;
and I alone have escaped to tell
you!"
17 While he *was* still speaking,
another also came and said, "The
Chaldeans formed three bands,
raided the camels and took them
away, yes, and killed the servants
with the edge of the sword; and I
alone have escaped to tell you!"
18 While he *was* still speaking,
another also came and said,
[a]"Your sons and daughters *were*
eating and drinking wine in their
oldest brother's house,
19 "and suddenly a great wind
came from [1]across the wilderness
and struck the four corners of the
house, and it fell on the young peo-
ple, and they are dead; and I alone
have escaped to tell you!"
20 Then Job arose, [a]tore his robe,
and shaved his head; and he [b]fell
to the ground and worshiped.
21 And he said:

[a]"Naked I came from my mother's
womb,
And naked shall I return there.
The LORD [b]gave, and the LORD
has [c]taken away;
[d]Blessed be the name of the
LORD."

22 [a]In all this Job did not sin nor
charge God with wrong.

Satan Attacks Job's Health

2 Again [a]there was a day when
the sons of God came to pre-
sent themselves before the LORD,
and Satan came also among them
to present himself before the
LORD.
2 And the LORD said to Satan,
"From where do you come?" So
[a]Satan answered the LORD and
said, "From going to and fro on
the earth, and from walking back
and forth on it."
3 Then the LORD said to Satan,
"Have you considered My servant
Job, that *there is* none like him on
the earth, [a]a blameless and upright
man, one who fears God and shuns
evil? And still he [b]holds fast to his
integrity, although you incited Me
against him, [c]to [1]destroy him with-
out cause."
4 So Satan answered the LORD
and said, "Skin for skin! Yes, all
that a man has he will give for his
life.
5 [a]"But stretch out Your hand
now, and touch his [b]bone and his
flesh, and he will surely [1]curse
You to Your face!"
6 [a]And the LORD said to Satan,
"Behold, he *is* in your hand, but
spare his life."
7 So Satan went out from the
presence of the LORD, and struck
Job with painful boils [a]from the
sole of his foot to the crown of his
head.
8 And he took for himself a
potsherd with which to scrape
himself [a]while he sat in the midst
of the ashes.
9 Then his wife said to him, "Do
you still hold fast to your integrity?
[1]Curse God and die!"
10 But he said to her, "You
speak as one of the foolish
women speaks. [a]Shall we indeed
accept good from God, and shall
we not accept adversity?" [b]In
all this Job did not [c]sin with his
lips.

Job's Three Friends

11 Now when Job's three friends
heard of all this adversity that had
come upon him, each one came
from his own place—Eliphaz the
[a]Temanite, Bildad the [b]Shuhite,
and Zophar the Naamathite. For
they had made an appointment to-
gether to come [c]and mourn with
him, and to comfort him.
12 And when they raised their
eyes from afar, and did not recog-
nize him, they lifted their voices
and wept; and each one tore his
robe and [a]sprinkled dust on his
head toward heaven.
13 So they sat down with him on
the ground [a]seven days and seven
nights, and no one spoke a word
to him, for they saw that *his* grief
was very great.

15 [1]Lit. *Sheba;* cf. Job 6:19 [2]Lit. *fell upon*
16 [1]*destroyed*
18 [a]Job 1:4, 13
19 [1]LXX omits *across*
20 [a]Gen. 37:29, 34; Josh. 7:6; Ezra 9:3 [b][1 Pet. 5:6]
21 [a][Ps. 49:17; Eccl. 5:15]; 1 Tim. 6:7 [b]Eccl. 5:19; [James 1:17] [c]Gen. 31:16; [1 Sam. 2:6] [d]Eph. 5:20; [1 Thess. 5:18]
22 [a]Job 2:10

CHAPTER 2

1 [a]Job 1:6–8
2 [a]Job 1:7
3 [a]Job 1:1, 8 [b]Job 27:5, 6 [c]Job 9:17 [1]Lit. *consume*
5 [a]Job 1:11 [b]Job 19:20 [1]Lit. *bless,* but in an evil sense; cf. Job 1:5
6 [a]Job 1:12
7 [a]Is. 1:6
8 [a]Job 42:6; Jer. 6:26; Ezek. 27:30; Jon. 3:6; Matt. 11:21
9 [1]Lit. *Bless,* but in an evil sense; cf. Job 1:5
10 [a]Job 1:21, 22; [Heb. 12:6; James 5:10, 11] [b]Job 1:22; [James 1:12] [c]Ps. 39:1
11 [a]Gen. 36:11; 1 Chr. 1:36; Job 6:19; Jer. 49:7; Obad. 9 [b]Gen. 25:2; 1 Chr. 1:32 [c]Job 42:11; Rom. 12:15
12 [a]Josh. 7:6; Neh. 9:1; Lam. 2:10; Ezek. 27:30
13 [a]Gen. 50:10; Ezek. 3:15

Job Deplores His Birth

3 After this Job opened his mouth and cursed the day of his *birth*.

2 And Job [1]spoke, and said:

3 "May[a] the day perish on which I was born,
And the night *in which* it was said,
'A male child is conceived.'
4 May that day be darkness;
May God above not seek it,
Nor the light shine upon it.
5 May darkness and [a]the shadow of death claim it;
May a cloud settle on it;
May the blackness of the day terrify it.
6 *As for* that night, may darkness seize it;
May it not [1]rejoice among the days of the year,
May it not come into the number of the months.
7 Oh, may that night be barren!
May no joyful shout come into it!
8 May those curse it who curse the day,
Those [a]who are ready to arouse Leviathan.
9 May the stars of its morning be dark;
May it look for light, but *have* none,
And not see the [1]dawning of the day;
10 Because it did not shut up the doors of my *mother's* womb,
Nor hide sorrow from my eyes.

11 "Why[a] did I not die at birth?
Why did I *not* [1]perish when I came from the womb?
12 [a]Why did the knees receive me?
Or why the breasts, that I should nurse?
13 For now I would have lain still and been quiet,
I would have been asleep;
Then I would have been at rest
14 With kings and counselors of the earth,
Who [a]built ruins for themselves,
15 Or with princes who had gold,
Who filled their houses *with* silver;
16 Or *why* was I not hidden [a]like a stillborn child,
Like infants who never saw light?
17 There the wicked cease *from* troubling,
And there the [1]weary are at [a]rest.
18 *There* the prisoners [1]rest together;
[a]They do not hear the voice of the oppressor.
19 The small and great are there,
And the servant *is* free from his master.

20 "Why[a] is light given to him who is in misery,
And life to the [b]bitter of soul,
21 Who [a]long[1] for death, but it does not *come,*
And search for it more than [b]hidden treasures;
22 Who rejoice exceedingly,
And are glad when they can find the [a]grave?
23 *Why is light given* to a man whose way is hidden,
[a]And whom God has hedged in?
24 For my sighing comes before [1]I eat,
And my groanings pour out like water.
25 For the thing I greatly [a]feared has come upon me,
And what I dreaded has happened to me.
26 I am not at ease, nor am I quiet;
I have no rest, for trouble comes."

Eliphaz: Job Has Sinned

4 Then Eliphaz the Temanite answered and said:

2 "*If* one attempts a word with you, will you become weary?
But who can withhold himself from speaking?
3 Surely you have instructed many,
And you [a]have strengthened weak hands.
4 Your words have upheld him who was stumbling,
And you [a]have strengthened the [1]feeble knees;
5 But now it comes upon you, and you are weary;
It touches you, and you are troubled.
6 *Is* not [a]your reverence [b]your confidence?
And the integrity of your ways your hope?

7 "Remember now, [a]who *ever* perished being innocent?
Or where were the upright *ever* cut off?
8 Even as I have seen,
[a]Those who plow iniquity
And sow trouble reap the same.
9 By the blast of God they perish,

CHAPTER 3

2 [1]Lit. *answered*
3 [a]Job 10:18, 19; Jer. 20:14–18
5 [a]Job 10:21, 22; Jer. 13:16; Amos 5:8
6 [1]LXX, Syr., Tg., Vg. *be joined*
8 [a]Jer. 9:17
9 [1]*eyelids of the dawn*
11 [a]Job 10:18, 19 [1]*expire*
12 [a]Gen. 30:3
14 [a]Job 15:28; Is. 58:12
16 [a]Ps. 58:8
17 [a]Job 17:16 [1]Lit. *weary of strength*
18 [a]Job 39:7 [1]*are at ease*
20 [a]Jer. 20:18 [b]2 Kin. 4:27
21 [a]Rev. 9:6 [b]Prov. 2:4 [1]Lit. *wait*
22 [a]Job 7:15, 16
23 [a]Job 19:8; Ps. 88:8; Lam. 3:7
24 [1]Lit. *my bread*
25 [a][Job 9:28; 30:15]

CHAPTER 4

3 [a]Is. 35:3
4 [a]Is. 35:3 [1]Lit. *bending*
6 [a]Job 1:1 [b]Prov. 3:26
7 [a][Job 8:20; 36:6, 7; Ps. 37:25]
8 [a][Job 15:31, 35; Prov. 22:8; Hos. 10:13; Gal. 6:7]

And by the breath of His anger
they are consumed.
10 The roaring of the lion,
The voice of the fierce lion,
And [a]the teeth of the young lions
are broken.
11 [a]The old lion perishes for lack of
prey,
And the cubs of the lioness are
scattered.

12 "Now a word was secretly brought
to me,
And my ear received a whisper
of it.
13 [a]In disquieting thoughts from the
visions of the night,
When deep sleep falls on men,
14 Fear came upon me, and
[a]trembling,
Which made all my bones shake.
15 Then a spirit passed before my
face;
The hair on my body stood up.
16 It stood still,
But I could not discern its
appearance.
A form *was* before my eyes;
There was silence;
Then I heard a voice *saying:*
17 'Can a mortal be more righteous
than God?
Can a man be more pure than his
Maker?
18 If He [a]puts no trust in His
servants,
If He charges His angels with
error,
19 How much more those who dwell
in houses of clay,
Whose foundation is in the dust,
Who are crushed before a moth?
20 [a]They are broken in pieces from
morning till evening;
They perish forever, with no one
regarding.
21 Does not their own excellence go
away?
They die, even without wisdom.'

Eliphaz: Job Is Chastened by God

5 "Call out now;
Is there anyone who will answer
you?
And to which of the holy ones
will you turn?
2 For wrath kills a foolish man,
And envy slays a simple one.
3 [a]I have seen the foolish taking
root,
But suddenly I cursed his
dwelling place.
4 His sons are [a]far from safety,
They are crushed in the gate,
And [b]*there is* no deliverer.

10 [a]Job 5:15; Ps. 58:6
11 [a]Job 29:17; Ps. 34:10
13 [a]Job 33:15
14 [a]Hab. 3:16
18 [a]Job 15:15
20 [a]Ps. 90:5, 6

CHAPTER 5

3 [a][Ps. 37:35, 36]; Jer. 12:1–3
4 [a]Ps. 119:155 [b]Ps. 109:12
5 [1]LXX *They shall not be taken from evil men;* Vg. *And the armed man shall take him by violence* [2]LXX *The might shall draw them off;* Vg. *And the thirsty shall drink up their riches* [3]*wealth*
7 [a]Job 14:1 [1]*labor*
10 [a][Job 36:27–29; 37:6–11; 38:26]
11 [a]Ps. 113:7
12 [a]Neh. 4:15
13 [a][Job 37:24; 1 Cor. 3:19]
15 [a]Job 4:10, 11; Ps. 35:10
16 [a]1 Sam. 2:8; Ps. 107:41, 42
17 [a]Ps. 94:12; [Prov. 3:11, 12; Heb. 12:5, 6; Rev. 3:19]
18 [a][Deut. 32:39; 1 Sam. 2:6, 7]; Is. 30:26; Hos. 6:1
19 [a]Ps. 34:19; 91:3; [1 Cor. 10:13] [b]Ps. 91:10; [Prov. 24:16]
20 [a]Ps. 33:19, 20; 37:19 [1]Lit. *hand*
21 [a]Job 5:15; Ps. 31:20

5 Because the hungry eat up his
harvest,
[1]Taking it even from the thorns,
[2]And a snare snatches their
[3]substance.
6 For affliction does not come from
the dust,
Nor does trouble spring from the
ground;
7 Yet man is [a]born to [1]trouble,
As the sparks fly upward.

8 "But as for me, I would seek God,
And to God I would commit my
cause—
9 Who does great things, and
unsearchable,
Marvelous things without
number.
10 [a]He gives rain on the earth,
And sends waters on the fields.
11 [a]He sets on high those who are
lowly,
And those who mourn are lifted
to safety.
12 [a]He frustrates the devices of the
crafty,
So that their hands cannot carry
out their plans.
13 He catches the [a]wise in their own
craftiness,
And the counsel of the cunning
comes quickly upon them.
14 They meet with darkness in the
daytime,
And grope at noontime as in the
night.
15 But [a]He saves the needy from the
sword,
From the mouth of the mighty,
And from their hand.
16 [a]So the poor have hope,
And injustice shuts her mouth.

17 "Behold,[a] happy *is* the man whom
God corrects;
Therefore do not despise the
chastening of the Almighty.
18 [a]For He bruises, but He binds up;
He wounds, but His hands make
whole.
19 [a]He shall deliver you in six
troubles,
Yes, in seven [b]no evil shall touch
you.
20 [a]In famine He shall redeem you
from death,
And in war from the [1]power of
the sword.
21 [a]You shall be hidden from the
scourge of the tongue,
And you shall not be afraid of
destruction when it comes.
22 You shall laugh at destruction
and famine,

And [a]you shall not be afraid of
the [b]beasts of the earth.
23 [a]For you shall have a covenant
with the stones of the field,
And the beasts of the field shall
be at peace with you.
24 You shall know that your tent *is*
in peace;
You shall visit your dwelling and
find nothing amiss.
25 You shall also know that [a]your
descendants *shall be* many,
And your offspring [b]like the grass
of the earth.
26 [a]You shall come to the grave at a
full age,
As a sheaf of grain ripens in its
season.
27 Behold, this we have [a]searched
out;
It *is* true.
Hear it, and know for yourself."

Job: My Complaint Is Just

6 Then Job answered and said:
2 "Oh, that my grief were fully
weighed,
And my calamity laid with it on
the scales!
3 For then it would be heavier than
the sand of the sea—
Therefore my words have been
rash.
4 [a]For the arrows of the Almighty
are within me;
My spirit drinks in their poison;
[b]The terrors of God are arrayed
[c]against me.
5 Does the [a]wild donkey bray when
it has grass,
Or does the ox low over its
fodder?
6 Can flavorless food be eaten
without salt?
Or is there *any* taste in the white
of an egg?
7 My soul refuses to touch
them;
They *are* as loathsome food to
me.

8 "Oh, that I might have my request,
That God would grant *me* the
thing that I long for!
9 That it would please God to crush
me,
That He would loose His hand
and [a]cut me off!
10 Then I would still have comfort;
Though in anguish I would exult,
He will not spare;
For [a]I have not concealed the
words of [b]the Holy One.

22 [a]Ps. 91:13; Is. 11:9; 35:9; 65:25; Ezek. 34:25 [b]Hos. 2:18
23 [a]Ps. 91:12
25 [a]Ps. 112:2 [b]Ps. 72:16
26 [a][Prov. 9:11; 10:27]
27 [a]Ps. 111:2

CHAPTER 6

4 [a]Job 16:13; Ps. 38:2 [b]Ps. 88:15, 16 [c]Job 30:15
5 [a]Job 39:5–8
9 [a]Num. 11:15; 1 Kin. 19:4; Job 7:16; 9:21; 10:1
10 [a]Acts 20:20 [b][Lev. 19:2; Is. 57:15]
14 [a][Prov. 17:17] [1]Or *despairing*
15 [a]Ps. 38:11 [b]Jer. 15:18
19 [a]Gen. 25:15; Is. 21:14; Jer. 25:23 [b]1 Kin. 10:1; Ps. 72:10; Ezek. 27:22, 23
20 [a]Jer. 14:3 [1]Lit. *ashamed*
21 [a]Job 13:4 [b]Ps. 38:11
27 [a]Ps. 57:6

11 "What strength do I have, that I
should hope?
And what *is* my end, that I should
prolong my life?
12 *Is* my strength the strength of
stones?
Or is my flesh bronze?
13 *Is* my help not within me?
And is success driven from me?

14 "To[a] him who is [1]afflicted,
kindness *should be shown* by
his friend,
Even though he forsakes the fear
of the Almighty.
15 [a]My brothers have dealt
deceitfully like a brook,
[b]Like the streams of the brooks
that pass away,
16 Which are dark because of the
ice,
And into which the snow
vanishes.
17 When it is warm, they cease to
flow;
When it is hot, they vanish from
their place.
18 The paths of their way turn
aside,
They go nowhere and perish.
19 The caravans of [a]Tema look,
The travelers of [b]Sheba hope for
them.
20 They are [a]disappointed[1] because
they were confident;
They come there and are
confused.
21 For now [a]you are nothing,
You see terror and [b]are afraid.
22 Did I ever say, 'Bring *something*
to me'?
Or, 'Offer a bribe for me from
your wealth'?
23 Or, 'Deliver me from the enemy's
hand'?
Or, 'Redeem me from the hand
of oppressors'?

24 "Teach me, and I will hold my
tongue;
Cause me to understand wherein
I have erred.
25 How forceful are right words!
But what does your arguing
prove?
26 Do you intend to rebuke *my*
words,
And the speeches of a desperate
one, *which are* as wind?
27 Yes, you overwhelm the
fatherless,
And you [a]undermine your friend.
28 Now therefore, be pleased to look
at me;
For I would never lie to your face.

29 [a]Yield now, let there be no
injustice!
Yes, concede, my [b]righteousness
[1]still stands!
30 Is there injustice on my tongue?
Cannot my [1]taste discern the
unsavory?

Job: My Suffering Is Comfortless

7 "*Is there* not [a]a time of hard
service for man on earth?
Are not his days also like the
days of a hired man?
2 Like a servant who [1]earnestly
desires the shade,
And like a hired man who eagerly
looks for his wages,
3 So I have been allotted [a]months
of futility,
And wearisome nights have been
appointed to me.
4 [a]When I lie down, I say, 'When
shall I arise,
And the night be ended?'
For I have had my fill of tossing
till dawn.
5 My flesh is [a]caked with worms
and dust,
My skin is cracked and breaks
out afresh.

6 "My[a] days are swifter than a
weaver's shuttle,
And are spent without hope.
7 Oh, remember that [a]my life *is* a
breath!
My eye will never again see
good.
8 [a]The eye of him who sees me will
see me no *more;*
While your *eyes* are upon me, I
shall no longer *be.*
9 *As* the cloud disappears and
vanishes away,
So [a]he who goes down to the
grave does not come up.
10 He shall never return to his
house,
[a]Nor shall his place know him
anymore.

11 "Therefore I will [a]not restrain my
mouth;
I will speak in the anguish of my
spirit;
I will [b]complain in the bitterness
of my soul.
12 *Am* I a sea, or a sea serpent,
That You set a guard over me?
13 [a]When I say, 'My bed will comfort
me,
My couch will ease my
complaint,'
14 Then You scare me with dreams
And terrify me with visions,

29 [a]Job 17:10 [b]Job 27:5, 6; 34:5 [1]Lit. *is in it*
30 [1]*palate*

CHAPTER 7
1 [a][Job 14:5, 13, 14]; Ps. 39:4
2 [1]Lit. *pants for*
3 [a][Job 15:31]
4 [a]Deut. 28:67; Job 7:13, 14
5 [a]Is. 14:11
6 [a]Job 9:25; 16:22; 17:11; Is. 38:12; [James 4:14]
7 [a]Job 7:16; Ps. 78:39; 89:47
8 [a]Job 8:18; 20:9
9 [a]2 Sam. 12:23
10 [a]Ps. 103:16
11 [a]Ps. 39:1, 9 [b]1 Sam. 1:10
13 [a]Job 9:27
15 [1]Lit. *my bones*
16 [a]Job 10:1 [b]Job 14:6 [c]Ps. 62:9 [1]Without substance, futile
17 [a]Job 22:2; Ps. 8:4; 144:3; Heb. 2:6
18 [1]*attend to*
20 [a]Ps. 36:6 [b]Ps. 21:12 [1]So with MT, Tg., Vg.; LXX, Jewish tradition *to You*

CHAPTER 8
3 [a]Gen. 18:25; [Deut. 32:4; 2 Chr. 19:7; Job 34:10, 12; 36:23; 37:23]; Rom. 3:5
4 [a]Job 1:5, 18, 19 [1]Lit. *into the hand of their transgression*
5 [a][Job 5:17–27; 11:13]
6 [1]*arise*
7 [a]Job 42:12
8 [a]Deut. 4:32; 32:7; Job 15:18; 20:4

15 So that my soul chooses
strangling
And death rather than [1]my body.
16 [a]I loathe *my life;*
I would not live forever.
[b]Let me alone,
For [c]my days *are but* [1]a breath.

17 "What[a] *is* man, that You should
exalt him,
That You should set Your heart
on him,
18 That You should [1]visit him every
morning,
And test him every moment?
19 How long?
Will You not look away from me,
And let me alone till I swallow
my saliva?
20 Have I sinned?
What have I done to You,
[a]O watcher of men?
Why [b]have You set me as Your
target,
So that I am a burden [1]to myself?
21 Why then do You not pardon my
transgression,
And take away my iniquity?
For now I will lie down in the
dust,
And You will seek me diligently,
But I *will* no longer *be.*"

Bildad: Job Should Repent

8 Then Bildad the Shuhite an-
swered and said:

2 "How long will you speak these
things,
And the words of your mouth *be
like* a strong wind?
3 [a]Does God subvert judgment?
Or does the Almighty pervert
justice?
4 If [a]your sons have sinned against
Him,
He has cast them away [1]for their
transgression.
5 [a]If you would earnestly seek God
And make your supplication to
the Almighty,
6 If you *were* pure and upright,
Surely now He would [1]awake for
you,
And prosper your rightful
dwelling place.
7 Though your beginning was
small,
Yet your latter end would
[a]increase abundantly.

8 "For[a] inquire, please, of the former
age,
And consider the things
discovered by their fathers;

9 For [a]we *were born* yesterday, and
know [1]nothing,
Because our days on earth *are* a
shadow.
10 Will they not teach you and tell
you,
And utter words from their heart?

11 "Can the papyrus grow up without
a marsh?
Can the reeds flourish without
water?
12 [a]While it *is* yet green *and* not cut
down,
It withers before any *other* plant.
13 So *are* the paths of all who [a]forget
God;
And the hope of the [b]hypocrite
shall perish,
14 Whose confidence shall be cut
off,
And whose trust *is* [1]a spider's
web.
15 [a]He leans on his house, but it does
not stand.
He holds it fast, but it does not
endure.
16 He grows green in the sun,
And his branches spread out in
his garden.
17 His roots wrap around the rock
heap,
And look for a place in the stones.
18 [a]If he is destroyed from his place,
Then *it* will deny him, *saying*, 'I
have not seen you.'

19 "Behold, this is the joy of His way,
And [a]out of the earth others will
grow.
20 Behold, [a]God will not [1]cast away
the blameless,
Nor will He uphold the evildoers.
21 He will yet fill your mouth with
laughing,
And your lips with [1]rejoicing.
22 Those who hate you will be
[a]clothed with shame,
And the dwelling place of the
wicked [1]will come to nothing."

Job: There Is No Mediator

9 Then Job answered and said:

2 "Truly I know *it is* so,
But how can a [a]man be [b]righteous
before God?
3 If one wished to [1]contend with
Him,
He could not answer Him one
time out of a thousand.
4 [a]*God is* wise in heart and mighty
in strength.
Who has hardened *himself*
against Him and prospered?
5 He removes the mountains, and
they do not know
When He overturns them in His
anger;
6 He [a]shakes the earth out of its
place,
And its [b]pillars tremble;
7 He commands the sun, and it
does not rise;
He seals off the stars;
8 [a]He alone spreads out the
heavens,
And [1]treads on the [2]waves of the
sea;
9 [a]He made [1]the Bear, Orion, and
the Pleiades,
And the chambers of the south;
10 [a]He does great things past finding
out,
Yes, wonders without number.
11 [a]If He goes by me, I do not see
Him;
If He moves past, I do not
perceive Him;
12 [a]If He takes away, [1]who can
hinder Him?
Who can say to Him, 'What are
You doing?'
13 God will not withdraw His anger,
[a]The allies of [1]the proud lie
prostrate beneath Him.

14 "How then can I answer Him,
And choose my words *to reason*
with Him?
15 [a]For though I were righteous, I
could not answer Him;
I would beg mercy of my Judge.
16 If I called and He answered
me,
I would not believe that He was
listening to my voice.
17 For He crushes me with a
tempest,
And multiplies my wounds
[a]without cause.
18 He will not allow me to catch my
breath,
But fills me with bitterness.
19 If *it is a matter* of strength,
indeed *He is* strong;
And if of justice, who will appoint
my day *in court?*
20 Though I were righteous, my own
mouth would condemn me;
Though I *were* blameless, it
would prove me perverse.

21 "I am blameless, yet I do not know
myself;
I despise my life.
22 It *is* all one *thing;*
Therefore I say, [a]'He destroys the
blameless and the wicked.'
23 If the scourge slays suddenly,

9 [a]Gen. 47:9; [1 Chr. 29:15]; Job 7:6; [Ps. 39:5; 102:11; 144:4] [1]Lit. *not*
12 [a]Ps. 129:6
13 [a]Ps. 9:17 [b]Job 11:20; 18:14; 27:8; Ps. 112:10; [Prov. 10:28]
14 [1]Lit. *a spider's house*
15 [a]Job 8:22; 27:18; Ps. 49:11
18 [a]Job 7:10
19 [a]Ps. 113:7
20 [a]Job 4:7 [1]*reject*
21 [1]Lit. *shouts of joy*
22 [a]Ps. 35:26; 109:29 [1]Lit. *will not be*

CHAPTER 9

2 [a][Job 4:17; 15:14–16; Ps. 143:2; Rom. 3:20] [b][Hab. 2:4; Rom. 1:17; Gal. 3:11; Heb. 10:38]
3 [1]*argue*
4 [a]Job 36:5
6 [a]Is. 2:19, 21; Hag. 2:6; Heb. 12:26 [b]Job 26:11
8 [a]Gen. 1:6; Job 37:18; Ps. 104:2, 3; Is. 40:22 [1]*walks* [2]Lit. *heights*
9 [a]Gen. 1:16; Job 38:31; Amos 5:8 [1]Heb. *Ash, Kesil,* and *Kimah*
10 [a]Job 5:9
11 [a][Job 23:8, 9; 35:14]
12 [a][Is. 45:9; Dan. 4:35; Rom. 9:20] [1]Lit. *who can turn Him back?*
13 [a]Job 26:12 [1]Heb. *rahab*
15 [a]Job 10:15; 23:1–7
17 [a]Job 2:3
22 [a][Eccl. 9:2, 3]; Ezek. 21:3

He laughs at the plight of the
innocent.
24 The earth is given into the hand
of the wicked.
He covers the faces of its
judges.
If it is not *He*, who else could it
be?

25 "Now [a]my days are swifter than
a runner;
They flee away, they see no good.
26 They pass by like [1]swift ships,
[a]Like an eagle swooping on its
prey.
27 [a]If I say, 'I will forget my
complaint,
I will put off my sad face and
wear a smile,'
28 [a]I am afraid of all my sufferings;
I know that You [b]will not hold me
innocent.
29 *If* I am condemned,
Why then do I labor in vain?
30 [a]If I wash myself with snow water,
And cleanse my hands with
[1]soap,
31 Yet You will plunge me into the
pit,
And my own clothes will [1]abhor
me.

32 "For [a]*He is* not a man, as I *am*,
That I may answer Him,
And that we should go to court
together.
33 [a]Nor is there any mediator
between us,
Who may lay his hand on us both.
34 [a]Let Him take His rod away from
me,
And do not let dread of Him
terrify me.
35 *Then* I would speak and not fear
Him,
But it is not so with me.

Job: I Would Plead with God

10 "My [a]soul loathes my life;
I will [1]give free course to my
complaint,
[b]I will speak in the bitterness of
my soul.
2 I will say to God, 'Do not
condemn me;
Show me why You contend with
me.
3 *Does it* seem good to You that
You should oppress,
That You should despise the
work of Your hands,
And smile on the counsel of the
wicked?
4 Do You have eyes of flesh?
Or [a]do You see as man sees?
5 *Are* Your days like the days of a
mortal man?
Are Your years like the days of
a mighty man,
6 That You should seek for my
iniquity
And search out my sin,
7 Although You know that I am not
wicked,
And *there is* no one who can
deliver from Your hand?

8 'Your[a] hands have made me and
fashioned me,
An intricate unity;
Yet You would [b]destroy me.
9 Remember, I pray, [a]that You
have made me like clay.
And will You turn me into dust
again?
10 [a]Did You not pour me out like
milk,
And curdle me like cheese,
11 Clothe me with skin and flesh,
And knit me together with bones
and sinews?
12 You have granted me life and
favor,
And Your care has preserved my
spirit.

13 'And these *things* You have
hidden in Your heart;
I know that this *was* with You:
14 If I sin, then [a]You mark me,
And will not acquit me of my
iniquity.
15 If I am wicked, [a]woe to me;
[b]Even *if* I am righteous, I [1]cannot
lift up my head.
I am full of disgrace;
[c]See my misery!
16 If *my head* is exalted,
[a]You hunt me like a fierce lion,
And again You show Yourself
awesome against me.
17 You renew Your witnesses
against me,
And increase Your indignation
toward me;
Changes and war are *ever* with
me.

18 'Why[a] then have You brought me
out of the womb?
Oh, that I had perished and no
eye had seen me!
19 I would have been as though I
had not been.
I would have been carried from
the womb to the grave.
20 [a]Are not my days few?
Cease! [b]Leave me alone, that I
may take a little comfort,

25 [a]Job 7:6, 7
26 [a]Job 39:29; Hab. 1:8 [1]Lit. *ships of reeds*
27 [a]Job 7:13
28 [a]Ps. 119:120 [b]Ex. 20:7
30 [a][Jer. 2:22] [1]*lye*
31 [1]*loathe*
32 [a]Eccl. 6:10; [Is. 45:9; Jer. 49:19; Rom. 9:20]
33 [a][1 Sam. 2:25]; Job 9:19; Is. 1:18
34 [a]Job 13:20, 21; Ps. 39:10

CHAPTER 10

1 [a]1 Kin. 19:4; Job 7:16; Jon. 4:3 [b]Job 7:11 [1]Lit. *leave on myself*
4 [a][1 Sam. 16:7; Job 28:24; 34:21]
8 [a]Job 10:3; Ps. 119:73 [b][Job 9:22]
9 [a]Gen. 2:7; Job 33:6
10 [a][Ps. 139:14–16]
14 [a]Job 7:20; Ps. 139:1
15 [a]Job 10:7; Is. 3:11 [b][Job 9:12, 15] [c]Ps. 25:18 [1]Lit. *will not*
16 [a]Is. 38:13; Lam. 3:10; Hos. 13:7
18 [a]Job 3:11–13
20 [a]Ps. 39:5 [b]Job 7:16, 19

21 Before I go *to the place from which* I shall not return,
[a]To the land of darkness [b]and the shadow of death,
22 A land as dark as darkness *itself*,
As the shadow of death, without any order,
Where even the light *is* like darkness.' "

Zophar Urges Job to Repent

11 Then Zophar the Naamathite answered and said:

2 "Should not the multitude of words be answered?
And should [1]a man full of talk be vindicated?
3 Should your empty talk make men [1]hold their peace?
And when you mock, should no one rebuke you?
4 For you have said,
[a]'My doctrine *is* pure,
And I am clean in your eyes.'
5 But oh, that God would speak,
And open His lips against you,
6 That He would show you the secrets of wisdom!
For *they would* double *your* prudence.
Know therefore that [a]God [1]exacts from you
Less than your iniquity *deserves*.

7 "Can[a] you search out the deep things of God?
Can you find out the limits of the Almighty?
8 *They are* higher than heaven—what can you do?
Deeper than [1]Sheol—what can you know?
9 Their measure *is* longer than the earth
And broader than the sea.

10 "If[a] He passes by, imprisons, and gathers *to judgment*,
Then who can [1]hinder Him?
11 For [a]He knows deceitful men;
He sees wickedness also.
Will He not then consider *it*?
12 For an [a]empty-headed man will be wise,
When a wild donkey's colt is born a man.

13 "If you would [a]prepare your heart,
And [b]stretch out your hands toward Him;
14 If iniquity *were* in your hand, *and you* put it far away,
And [a]would not let wickedness dwell in your tents;
15 [a]Then surely you could lift up your face without spot;
Yes, you could be steadfast, and not fear;
16 Because you would [a]forget *your* misery,
And remember *it* as waters *that have* passed away,
17 And *your* life [a]would be brighter than noonday.
Though you were dark, you would be like the morning.
18 And you would be secure, because there is hope;
Yes, you would dig *around you*, *and* [a]take your rest in safety.
19 You would also lie down, and no one would make *you* afraid;
Yes, many would court your favor.
20 But [a]the eyes of the wicked will fail,
And they shall not escape,
And [b]their hope—[1]loss of life!"

Job Answers His Critics

12 Then Job answered and said:

2 "No doubt you *are* the people,
And wisdom will die with you!
3 But I have [1]understanding as well as you;
I *am* not [a]inferior to you.
Indeed, who does not *know* such things as these?

4 "I[a] am one mocked by his friends,
Who [b]called on God, and He answered him,
The just and blameless *who is* ridiculed.
5 A [1]lamp is despised in the thought of one who is at ease;
It is made ready for [a]those whose feet slip.
6 [a]The tents of robbers prosper,
And those who provoke God are secure—
In what God provides by His hand.

7 "But now ask the beasts, and they will teach you;
And the birds of the air, and they will tell you;
8 Or speak to the earth, and it will teach you;
And the fish of the sea will explain to you.
9 Who among all these does not know
That the hand of the LORD has done this,

---

21 [a]Ps. 88:12 [b]Ps. 23:4

CHAPTER 11

2 [1]Lit. *a man of lips*
3 [1]*be silent*
4 [a]Job 6:30
6 [a][Ezra 9:13] [1]Lit. *forgets some of your iniquity for you*
7 [a]Job 33:12, 13; 36:26; [Eccl. 3:11; Rom. 11:33]
8 [1]The abode of the dead
10 [a]Job 9:12; [Rev. 3:7] [1]*restrain*
11 [a][Ps. 10:14]
12 [a][Ps. 39:5]; Rom. 1:22
13 [a][1 Sam. 7:3] [b]Ps. 88:9
14 [a]Ps. 101:3
15 [a]Job 22:26; Ps. 119:6; [1 John 3:21]
16 [a]Is. 65:16
17 [a]Ps. 37:6; Prov. 4:18; Is. 58:8, 10
18 [a]Lev. 26:5, 6; Ps. 3:5; Prov. 3:24
20 [a]Lev. 26:16; Deut. 28:65; Job 17:5 [b]Job 18:14; [Prov. 11:7] [1]Lit. *the breathing out of life*

CHAPTER 12

3 [a]Job 13:2 [1]Lit. *a heart*
4 [a]Job 21:3 [b]Ps. 91:15
5 [a]Prov. 14:2 [1]Or *disaster*
6 [a][Job 9:24; 21:6–16; Ps. 73:12; Jer. 12:1; Mal. 3:15]

10 [a]In whose hand *is* the [1]life of every
living thing,
And the [b]breath of [2]all mankind?
11 Does not the ear test words
And the [1]mouth taste its food?
12 Wisdom *is* with aged men,
And with [1]length of days,
understanding.

13 "With Him *are* [a]wisdom and
strength,
He has counsel and
understanding.
14 If [a]He breaks *a thing* down, it
cannot be rebuilt;
If He imprisons a man, there can
be no release.
15 If He [a]withholds the waters, they
dry up;
If He [b]sends them out, they
overwhelm the earth.
16 With Him *are* strength and
prudence.
The deceived and the deceiver
are His.
17 He leads counselors away
plundered,
And makes fools of the judges.
18 He loosens the bonds of kings,
And binds their waist with a belt.
19 He leads [1]princes away
plundered,
And overthrows the mighty.
20 [a]He deprives the trusted ones of
speech,
And takes away the discernment
of the elders.
21 [a]He pours contempt on princes,
And [1]disarms the mighty.
22 He [a]uncovers deep things out of
darkness,
And brings the shadow of death
to light.
23 [a]He makes nations great, and
destroys them;
He [1]enlarges nations, and guides
them.
24 He takes away the
[1]understanding of the chiefs of
the people of the earth,
And [a]makes them wander in a
pathless wilderness.
25 [a]They grope in the dark without
light,
And He makes them [b]stagger like
a drunken *man*.

13 "Behold, my eye has seen all
this,
My ear has heard and
understood it.
2 [a]What you know, I also know;
I *am* not inferior to you.
3 [a]But I would speak to the
Almighty,
And I desire to reason with God.
4 But you forgers of lies,
[a]You *are* all worthless
physicians.
5 Oh, that you would be silent,
And [a]it would be your wisdom!
6 Now hear my reasoning,
And heed the pleadings of my
lips.
7 [a]Will you speak [1]wickedly for
God,
And talk deceitfully for Him?
8 Will you show partiality for Him?
Will you contend for God?
9 Will it be well when He searches
you out?
Or can you mock Him as one
mocks a man?
10 He will surely rebuke you
If you secretly show partiality.
11 Will not His [1]excellence make
you afraid,
And the dread of Him fall upon
you?
12 Your platitudes *are* proverbs of
ashes,
Your defenses are defenses of
clay.

13 "Hold[1] your peace with me, and let
me speak,
Then let come on me what *may!*
14 Why [a]do I take my flesh in my
teeth,
And put my life in my hands?
15 [a]Though He slay me, yet will I
trust Him.
[b]Even so, I will defend my own
ways before Him.
16 He also *shall* be my salvation,
For a [a]hypocrite could not come
before Him.
17 Listen carefully to my speech,
And to my declaration with your
ears.
18 See now, I have prepared *my*
case,
I know that I shall be [a]vindicated.
19 [a]Who *is* he *who* will contend with
me?
If now I hold my tongue, I perish.

Job's Despondent Prayer

20 "Only[a] two *things* do not do to me,
Then I will not hide myself from
You:
21 [a]Withdraw Your hand far from
me,
And let not the dread of You
make me afraid.
22 Then call, and I will [a]answer;
Or let me speak, then You
respond to me.
23 How many *are* my iniquities and
sins?

12:10 [a][Acts 17:28] [b]Job 27:3; 33:4 [1]Or *soul* [2]Lit. *all flesh of men*
11 [1]*palate*
12 [1]Long life
13 [a]Job 9:4; 36:5
14 [a]Job 11:10; Is. 25:2
15 [a]Deut. 11:17; [1 Kin. 8:35, 36] [b]Gen. 7:11–24
19 [1]Lit. *priests,* but not in a technical sense
20 [a]Job 32:9
21 [a][Job 34:19]; Ps. 107:40; [Dan. 2:21] [1]*loosens the belt of*
22 [a]Dan. 2:22; [1 Cor. 4:5]
23 [a]Is. 9:3; 26:15 [1]Lit. *spreads out*
24 [a]Ps. 107:4 [1]Lit. *heart*
25 [a]Job 5:14; 15:30; 18:18 [b]Ps. 107:27

CHAPTER 13

2 [a]Job 12:3
3 [a]Job 23:3; 31:35
4 [a]Job 6:21; [Jer. 23:32]
5 [a]Job 13:13; 21:5; Prov. 17:28
7 [a]Job 27:4; 36:4 [1]*unrighteously*
11 [1]Lit. *exaltation*
13 [1]*Be silent*
14 [a]Job 18:4
15 [a]Ps. 23:4; [Prov. 14:32] [b]Job 27:5
16 [a]Job 8:13
18 [a][Rom. 8:34]
19 [a]Job 7:21; 10:8; Is. 50:8
20 [a]Job 9:34
21 [a]Job 9:34; Ps. 39:10
22 [a]Job 9:16; 14:15

Make me know my transgression
and my sin.
24 [a]Why do You hide Your face,
And [b]regard me as Your enemy?
25 [a]Will You frighten a leaf driven to
and fro?
And will You pursue dry stubble?
26 For You write bitter things
against me,
And [a]make me inherit the
iniquities of my youth.
27 [a]You put my feet in the stocks,
And watch closely all my paths.
You [1]set a limit for the [2]soles of
my feet.

28 "*Man*[1] decays like a rotten thing,
Like a garment that is moth-
eaten.

14 "Man *who is* born of woman
Is of few days and [a]full of
[1]trouble.
2 [a]He comes forth like a flower and
fades away;
He flees like a shadow and does
not continue.
3 And [a]do You open Your eyes on
such a one,
And [b]bring [1]me to judgment with
Yourself?
4 Who [a]can bring a clean *thing* out
of an unclean?
No one!
5 [a]Since his days *are* determined,
The number of his months *is* with
You;
You have appointed his limits, so
that he cannot pass.
6 [a]Look away from him that he may
[1]rest,
Till [b]like a hired man he finishes
his day.

7 "For there is hope for a tree,
If it is cut down, that it will sprout
again,
And that its tender shoots will not
cease.
8 Though its root may grow old in
the earth,
And its stump may die in the
ground,
9 *Yet* at the scent of water it will
bud
And bring forth branches like a
plant.
10 But man dies and [1]is laid away;
Indeed he [2]breathes his last
And where *is* [a]he?
11 *As* water disappears from the sea,
And a river becomes parched and
dries up,
12 So man lies down and does not
rise.
[a]Till the heavens *are* no more,
They will not awake
Nor be roused from their sleep.

13 "Oh, that You would hide me in
the grave,
That You would conceal me until
Your wrath is past,
That You would appoint me a set
time, and remember me!
14 If a man dies, shall he live *again*?
All the days of my hard service
[a]I will wait,
Till my change comes.
15 [a]You shall call, and I will answer
You;
You shall desire the work of Your
hands.
16 For now [a]You number my steps,
But do not watch over my sin.
17 [a]My transgression *is* sealed up in
a bag,
And You [1]cover my iniquity.

18 "But *as* a mountain falls *and*
crumbles away,
And *as* a rock is moved from its
place;
19 *As* water wears away stones,
And as torrents wash away the
soil of the earth;
So You destroy the hope of man.
20 You prevail forever against him,
and he passes on;
You change his countenance and
send him away.
21 His sons come to honor, and [a]he
does not know *it;*
They are brought low, and he
does not perceive *it*.
22 But his flesh will be in pain
over it,
And his soul will mourn over it."

Eliphaz Accuses Job of Folly

15 Then [a]Eliphaz the Temanite
answered and said:

2 "Should a wise man answer with
empty knowledge,
And fill [1]himself with the east
wind?
3 Should he reason with
unprofitable talk,
Or by speeches with which he can
do no good?
4 Yes, you cast off fear,
And restrain [1]prayer before God.
5 For your iniquity teaches your
mouth,
And you choose the tongue of the
crafty.
6 [a]Your own mouth condemns you,
and not I;

---

24 [a][Deut. 32:20]; Ps. 13:1 [b]Lam. 2:5
25 [a]Is. 42:3
26 [a]Job 20:11
27 [a]Job 33:11 [1]Lit. *inscribe a print* [2]Lit. *roots*
28 [1]Lit. *He*

CHAPTER 14

1 [a]Job 5:7; Eccl. 2:23 [1]*turmoil*
2 [a]Job 8:9; Ps. 90:5, 6, 9; 102:11; 103:15; 144:4; Is. 40:6; James 1:10, 11; 1 Pet. 1:24
3 [a]Ps. 8:4; 144:3 [b][Ps. 143:2] [1]LXX, Syr., Vg. *him*
4 [a][Job 15:14; 25:4; Ps. 51:2, 5, 10; John 3:6; Rom. 5:12; Eph. 2:3]
5 [a]Job 7:1; 21:21; Heb. 9:27
6 [a]Job 7:16, 19; Ps. 39:13 [b]Job 7:1 [1]Lit. *cease*
10 [a]Job 10:21, 22 [1]*lies prostrate* [2]*expires*
12 [a]Ps. 102:25, 26; [Is. 51:6; 65:17; 66:22]; Acts 3:21; [2 Pet. 3:7, 10, 11; Rev. 20:11; 21:1]
14 [a]Job 13:15
15 [a]Job 13:22
16 [a]Job 10:6, 14; 13:27; 31:4; 34:21; Ps. 56:8; 139:1–3; Prov. 5:21; [Jer. 32:19]
17 [a]Deut. 32:32–34 [1]Lit. *plaster over*
21 [a]Eccl. 9:5; Is. 63:16

CHAPTER 15

1 [a]Job 4:1
2 [1]Lit. *his belly*
4 [1]*meditation* or *complaint*
6 [a]Job 9:20; [Luke 19:22]

Yes, your own lips testify against
you.
7 "*Are* you the first man *who* was
born?
[a]Or were you made before the
hills?
8 [a]Have you heard the counsel of
God?
Do you limit wisdom to yourself?
9 [a]What do you know that we do not
know?
What do you understand that *is*
not in us?
10 [a]Both the gray-haired and the
aged *are* among us,
Much older than your father.
11 *Are* the consolations of God too
small for you,
And the word *spoken* [1]gently
with you?
12 Why does your heart carry you
away,
And [1]what do your eyes wink at,
13 That you turn your spirit against
God,
And let *such* words go out of your
mouth?

14 "What[a] *is* man, that he could be
pure?
And *he who is* born of a woman,
that he could be righteous?
15 [a]If *God* puts no trust in His saints,
And the heavens are not pure in
His sight,
16 [a]How much less man, *who is*
abominable and filthy,
[b]Who drinks iniquity like water!

17 "I will tell you, hear me;
What I have seen I will declare,
18 What wise men have told,
Not hiding *anything received*
[a]from their fathers,
19 To whom alone the [1]land was
given,
And [a]no alien passed among
them:
20 The wicked man writhes with
pain all *his* days,
[a]And the number of years is
hidden from the oppressor.
21 [1]Dreadful sounds *are* in his ears;
[a]In prosperity the destroyer comes
upon him.
22 He does not believe that he will
[a]return from darkness,
For a sword is waiting for him.
23 He [a]wanders about for bread,
saying, 'Where *is it?*'
He knows [b]that a day of darkness
is ready at his hand.
24 Trouble and anguish make him
afraid;

7 [a]Job 38:4, 21; Ps. 90:2; Prov. 8:25
8 [a]Job 29:4; Rom. 11:34; [1 Cor. 2:11]
9 [a]Job 12:3; 13:2
10 [a]Job 8:8–10; 12:12; 32:6, 7
11 [1]Or *a secret thing*
12 [1]Or *why do your eyes flash*
14 [a]Job 14:4; Prov. 20:9; [Eccl. 7:20; 1 John 1:8, 10]
15 [a]Job 4:18; 25:5
16 [a]Job 4:19; Ps. 14:3; 53:3 [b]Job 34:7; Prov. 19:28
18 [a]Job 8:8; 20:4
19 [a]Joel 3:17 [1]Or *earth*
20 [a]Ps. 90:12
21 [a]Job 20:21; 1 Thess. 5:3 [1]*Terrifying*
22 [a]Job 14:10–12
23 [a]Ps. 59:15; 109:10 [b]Job 18:12
24 [1]*attack*
27 [a]Ps. 17:10; 73:7; 119:70
29 [a]Job 20:28; 27:16, 17
30 [a]Job 4:9
31 [a]Job 35:13; Is. 59:4
32 [a]Job 22:16; Ps. 55:23; Eccl. 7:17
35 [a]Ps. 7:14; Is. 59:4; [Hos. 10:13]

CHAPTER 16

2 [a]Job 13:4; 21:34 [1]*Troublesome*
3 [1]Empty words
4 [a]Ps. 22:7; 109:25; Lam. 2:15; Zeph. 2:15; Matt. 27:39

They overpower him, like a king
ready for [1]battle.
25 For he stretches out his hand
against God,
And acts defiantly against the
Almighty,
26 Running stubbornly against Him
With his strong, embossed shield.

27 "Though[a] he has covered his face
with his fatness,
And made *his* waist heavy with
fat,
28 He dwells in desolate cities,
In houses which no one inhabits,
Which are destined to become
ruins.
29 He will not be rich,
Nor will his wealth [a]continue,
Nor will his possessions
overspread the earth.
30 He will not depart from darkness;
The flame will dry out his
branches,
And [a]by the breath of His mouth
he will go away.
31 Let him not [a]trust in futile *things*,
deceiving himself,
For futility will be his reward.
32 It will be accomplished [a]before
his time,
And his branch will not be green.
33 He will shake off his unripe grape
like a vine,
And cast off his blossom like an
olive tree.
34 For the company of hypocrites
will be barren,
And fire will consume the tents
of bribery.
35 [a]They conceive trouble and bring
forth futility;
Their womb prepares deceit."

Job Reproaches His Pitiless Friends

16 Then Job answered and
said:
2 "I have heard many such things;
[a]Miserable[1] comforters *are* you
all!
3 Shall [1]words of wind have an
end?
Or what provokes you that you
answer?
4 I also could speak as you *do*,
If your soul were in my soul's
place.
I could heap up words against
you,
And [a]shake my head at you;
5 *But* I would strengthen you with
my mouth,
And the comfort of my lips would
relieve *your grief*.

6 "Though I speak, my grief is not
relieved;
And *if* I remain silent, how am I
eased?
7 But now He has [a]worn me out;
You [b]have made desolate all my
company.
8 You have shriveled me up,
And it is a [a]witness *against me;*
My leanness rises up against me
And bears witness to my face.
9 [a]He tears *me* in His wrath, and
hates me;
He gnashes at me with His teeth;
[b]My adversary sharpens His gaze
on me.
10 They [a]gape at me with their
mouth,
They [b]strike me reproachfully on
the cheek,
They gather together against me.
11 God [a]has delivered me to the
ungodly,
And turned me over to the hands
of the wicked.
12 I was at ease, but He has
[a]shattered me;
He also has taken *me* by my neck,
and shaken me to pieces;
He has [b]set me up for His target,
13 His archers surround me.
He pierces my [1]heart and does
not pity;
He pours out my gall on the
ground.
14 He breaks me with wound upon
wound;
He runs at me like a [1]warrior.

15 "I have sewn sackcloth over my
skin,
And [a]laid my [1]head in the dust.
16 My face is [1]flushed from
weeping,
And on my eyelids *is* the shadow
of death;
17 Although no violence *is* in my
hands,
And my prayer *is* pure.

18 "O earth, do not cover my blood,
And [a]let my cry have no *resting*
place!
19 Surely even now [a]my witness *is*
in heaven,
And my evidence *is* on high.
20 My friends scorn me;
My eyes pour out *tears* to God.
21 [a]Oh, that one might plead for a
man with God,
As a man *pleads* for his
[1]neighbor!
22 For when a few years are
finished,
I shall [a]go the way of no return.

7 [a]Job 7:3 [b]Job 16:20; 19:13–15
8 [a]Job 10:17
9 [a]Job 10:16, 17; 19:11; Hos. 6:1 [b]Job 13:24; 33:10
10 [a]Ps. 22:13; 35:21 [b]Is. 50:6; Lam. 3:30; Mic. 5:1; Matt. 26:67; Mark 14:65; Luke 22:63; Acts 23:2
11 [a]Job 1:15, 17
12 [a]Job 9:17 [b]Job 7:20; Lam. 3:12
13 [1]Lit. *kidneys*
14 [1]Vg. *giant*
15 [a]Job 30:19; Ps. 7:5 [1]Lit. *horn*
16 [1]Lit. *red*
18 [a]Job 27:9; [Ps. 66:18]
19 [a]Gen. 31:50; Rom. 1:9; Phil. 1:8; 1 Thess. 2:5
21 [a]Job 31:35; Eccl. 6:10; [Is. 45:9; Rom. 9:20] [1]*friend*
22 [a]Job 10:21; Eccl. 12:5

CHAPTER 17

1 [a]Ps. 88:3, 4
2 [a]1 Sam. 1:6; Job 12:4; 17:6; 30:1, 9; 34:7 [1]Lit. *lodge*
3 [a]Prov. 6:1; 17:18; 22:26
4 [a]Job 12:20; 32:9
5 [a]Job 11:20
6 [a]Job 30:9
7 [a]Ps. 6:7; 31:9
9 [a]Prov. 4:18 [b]Ps. 24:4
10 [a]Job 6:29 [1]So with some Heb. mss., LXX, Syr., Vg.; MT, Tg. *all of them*
11 [a]Job 7:6 [1]*desires*
15 [a]Job 7:6; 13:15; 14:19; 19:10
16 [a]Jon. 2:6 [b]Job 3:17–19; 21:33 [1]The abode of the dead

CHAPTER 18

1 [a]Job 8:1

Job Prays for Relief

17 "My spirit is broken,
My days are extinguished,
[a]The grave *is ready* for me.
2 *Are* not mockers with me?
And does not my eye [1]dwell on
their [a]provocation?

3 "Now put down a pledge for me
with Yourself.
Who *is* he *who* [a]will shake hands
with me?
4 For You have hidden their heart
from [a]understanding;
Therefore You will not exalt
them.
5 He who speaks flattery to *his*
friends,
Even the eyes of his children will
[a]fail.

6 "But He has made me [a]a byword
of the people,
And I have become one in whose
face men spit.
7 [a]My eye has also grown dim
because of sorrow,
And all my members *are* like
shadows.
8 Upright *men* are astonished at
this,
And the innocent stirs himself up
against the hypocrite.
9 Yet the righteous will hold to his
[a]way,
And he who has [b]clean hands will
be stronger and stronger.

10 "But please, [a]come back again, [1]all
of you,
For I shall not find *one* wise *man*
among you.
11 [a]My days are past,
My purposes are broken off,
Even the [1]thoughts of my heart.
12 They change the night into day;
'The light *is* near,' *they say,* in the
face of darkness.
13 If I wait *for* the grave *as* my
house,
If I make my bed in the darkness,
14 If I say to corruption, 'You *are* my
father,'
And to the worm, '*You are* my
mother and my sister,'
15 Where then *is* my [a]hope?
As for my hope, who can see it?
16 *Will* they go down [a]to the gates
of [1]Sheol?
Shall *we have* [b]rest together in
the dust?"

Bildad: The Wicked Are Punished

18 Then [a]Bildad the Shuhite
answered and said:

2 "How long *till* you put an end to
words?
Gain understanding, and
afterward we will speak.
3 Why are we counted [a]as
beasts,
And regarded as stupid in your
sight?
4 [a]You[1] who tear yourself in anger,
Shall the earth be forsaken for
you?
Or shall the rock be removed
from its place?

5 "The[a] light of the wicked indeed
goes out,
And the flame of his fire does not
shine.
6 The light is dark in his tent,
[a]And his lamp beside him is put
out.
7 The steps of his strength are
shortened,
And [a]his own counsel casts him
down.
8 For [a]he is cast into a net by his
own feet,
And he walks into a snare.
9 The net takes *him* by the heel,
And [a]a snare lays hold of him.
10 A noose *is* hidden for him on the
ground,
And a trap for him in the road.
11 [a]Terrors frighten him on every
side,
And drive him to his feet.
12 His strength is starved,
And [a]destruction *is* ready at his
side.
13 It devours patches of his skin;
The firstborn of death devours his
[1]limbs.
14 He is uprooted from [a]the shelter
of his tent,
And they parade him before the
king of terrors.
15 They dwell in his tent *who are*
none of his;
Brimstone is scattered on his
dwelling.
16 [a]His roots are dried out below,
And his branch withers above.
17 [a]The memory of him perishes
from the earth,
And he has no name [1]among the
renowned.
18 [1]He is driven from light into
darkness,
And chased out of the world.
19 [a]He has neither son nor posterity
among his people,
Nor any remaining in his
dwellings.
20 Those [1]in the west are astonished
[a]at his day,
As those [2]in the east are
frightened.
21 Surely such *are* the dwellings of
the wicked,
And this *is* the place *of him who*
[a]does not know God."

3 [a]Ps. 73:22
4 [a]Job 13:14 [1]Lit. *one who tears his soul*
5 [a]Job 21:17; Prov. 13:9; 20:20; 24:20
6 [a]Job 21:17; Ps. 18:28
7 [a]Job 5:12, 13; 15:6
8 [a]Job 22:10; Ps. 9:15; 35:8; Is. 24:17, 18
9 [a]Job 5:5
11 [a]Job 20:25; Jer. 6:25
12 [a]Job 15:23
13 [1]*parts*
14 [a]Job 11:20
16 [a]Job 29:19
17 [a]Job 24:20; [Ps. 34:16]; Prov. 10:7 [1]Lit. *before the outside,* i.e., the distinguished or famous
18 [1]Or *They drive him*
19 [a]Job 27:14, 15; Is. 14:22
20 [a]Ps. 37:13; Jer. 50:27; Obad. 12 [1]Lit. *who came after* [2]Lit. *who have gone before*
21 [a]Jer. 9:3; 1 Thess. 4:5

CHAPTER 19

3 [1]*shamed* or *disgraced* [2]A Jewish tradition *make yourselves strange to me*
5 [a]Ps. 35:26; 38:16; 55:12, 13
6 [a]Job 16:11
7 [1]*violence*
8 [a]Job 3:23; Ps. 88:8; Lam. 3:7, 9 [1]*walled off my way*
9 [a]Job 12:17, 19; Ps. 89:44
10 [a]Job 17:14–16
11 [a]Job 13:24; 33:10
13 [a]Job 16:20; Ps. 31:11; 38:11; 69:8; 88:8, 18

Job Trusts in His Redeemer

19 Then Job answered and
said:

2 "How long will you torment my
soul,
And break me in pieces with
words?
3 These ten times you have
[1]reproached me;
You are not ashamed *that* you
[2]have wronged me.
4 And if indeed I have erred,
My error remains with me.
5 If indeed you [a]exalt *yourselves*
against me,
And plead my disgrace against
me,
6 Know then that [a]God has
wronged me,
And has surrounded me with His
net.

7 "If I cry out concerning [1]wrong, I
am not heard.
If I cry aloud, *there is* no justice.
8 [a]He has [1]fenced up my way, so
that I cannot pass;
And He has set darkness in my
paths.
9 [a]He has stripped me of my glory,
And taken the crown *from* my
head.
10 He breaks me down on every
side,
And I am gone;
My [a]hope He has uprooted like
a tree.
11 He has also kindled His wrath
against me,
And [a]He counts me as *one of* His
enemies.
12 His troops come together
And build up their road against
me;
They encamp all around my tent.

13 "He[a] has removed my brothers far
from me,
And my acquaintances are
completely estranged from me.
14 My relatives have failed,
And my close friends have
forgotten me.
15 Those who dwell in my house,
and my maidservants,
Count me as a stranger;
I am an alien in their sight.

16 I call my servant, but he gives no
answer;
I beg him with my mouth.
17 My breath is offensive to my wife,
And I am [1]repulsive to the
children of my own body.
18 Even [a]young children despise
me;
I arise, and they speak against
me.
19 [a]All my close friends abhor me,
And those whom I love have
turned against me.
20 [a]My bone clings to my skin and
to my flesh,
And I have escaped by the skin
of my teeth.

21 "Have pity on me, have pity on me,
O you my friends,
For the hand of God has struck
me!
22 Why do you [a]persecute me as
God *does*,
And are not satisfied with my
flesh?

23 "Oh, that my words were written!
Oh, that they were inscribed in a
book!
24 That they were engraved on a
rock
With an iron pen and lead,
forever!
25 For I know *that* my Redeemer
lives,
And He shall stand at last on the
earth;
26 And after my skin is [1]destroyed,
this *I know*,
That [a]in my flesh I shall see God,
27 Whom I shall see for myself,
And my eyes shall behold, and
not another.
How my [1]heart yearns within me!
28 If you should say, 'How shall we
persecute him?'—
Since the root of the matter is
found in me,
29 Be afraid of the sword for
yourselves;
For wrath *brings* the punishment
of the sword,
That you may know *there is* a
judgment."

Zophar's Sermon on the Wicked Man

20

Then [a]Zophar the Naama-
thite answered and said:

2 "Therefore my anxious thoughts
make me answer,
Because of the turmoil within me.
3 I have heard the rebuke [1]that
reproaches me,
And the spirit of my
understanding causes me to
answer.

4 "Do you *not* know this of [a]old,
Since man was placed on earth,
5 [a]That the triumphing of the
wicked is short,
And the joy of the hypocrite is
but for a [b]moment?
6 [a]Though his haughtiness mounts
up to the heavens,
And his head reaches to the
clouds,
7 *Yet* he will perish forever like his
own refuse;
Those who have seen him will
say, 'Where is he?'
8 He will fly away [a]like a dream,
and not be found;
Yes, he [b]will be chased away like
a vision of the night.
9 The eye *that* saw him will *see him*
no more,
Nor will his place behold him
anymore.
10 His children will seek the favor
of the poor,
And his hands will restore his
wealth.
11 His bones are full of [a]his youthful
vigor,
[b]But it will lie down with him in
the dust.

12 "Though evil is sweet in his
mouth,
And he hides it under his tongue,
13 *Though* he spares it and does not
forsake it,
But still keeps it in his [1]mouth,
14 *Yet* his food in his stomach turns
sour;
It becomes cobra venom within
him.
15 He swallows down riches
And vomits them up again;
God casts them out of his belly.
16 He will suck the poison of cobras;
The viper's tongue will slay him.
17 He will not see [a]the streams,
The rivers flowing with honey
and cream.
18 He will restore that for which he
labored,
And will not swallow *it* down;
From the proceeds of business
He will get no enjoyment.
19 For he has [1]oppressed *and*
forsaken the poor,
He has violently seized a house
which he did not build.

20 "Because[a] he knows no quietness
in his [1]heart,

---

17 [1]Lit. *strange*
18 [a]2 Kin. 2:23; Job 17:6
19 [a]Ps. 38:11; 55:12, 13
20 [a]Job 16:8; 33:21; Ps. 102:5; Lam. 4:8
22 [a]Job 13:24, 25; 16:11; 19:6; Ps. 69:26
26 [a][Ps. 17:15]; Matt. 5:8; 1 Cor. 13:12; [1 John 3:2] [1]Lit. *struck off*
27 [1]Lit. *kidneys*

CHAPTER 20

1 [a]Job 11:1
3 [1]Lit. *of my insulting correction*
4 [a]Job 8:8; 15:10
5 [a]Ps. 37:35, 36 [b][Job 8:13; 13:16; 15:34; 27:8]
6 [a]Is. 14:13, 14
8 [a]Ps. 73:20; 90:5 [b]Job 18:18; 27:21–23
11 [a]Job 13:26 [b]Job 21:26
13 [1]Lit. *palate*
17 [a]Ps. 36:8; Jer. 17:8
19 [1]*crushed*
20 [a]Eccl. 5:13–15 [1]Lit. *belly*

He will not save anything he
desires.
21 Nothing is left for him to eat;
Therefore his well-being will not
last.
22 In his self-sufficiency he will be
in distress;
Every hand of [1]misery will come
against him.
23 *When* he is about to fill his
stomach,
God will cast on him the fury of
His wrath,
And will rain *it* on him while he
is eating.
24 [a]He will flee from the iron
weapon;
A bronze bow will pierce him
through.
25 It is drawn, and comes out of the
body;
Yes, [a]the glittering *point comes*
out of his [1]gall.
[b]Terrors *come* upon him;
26 Total darkness *is* reserved for his
treasures.
[a]An unfanned fire will consume
him;
It shall go ill with him who is left
in his tent.
27 The heavens will reveal his
iniquity,
And the earth will rise up against
him.
28 The increase of his house will
depart,
And his goods will flow away in
the day of His [a]wrath.
29 [a]This *is* the portion from God for
a wicked man,
The heritage appointed to him by
God."

Job's Discourse on the Wicked

21 Then Job answered and
said:

2 "Listen carefully to my speech,
And let this be your [1]consolation.
3 Bear with me that I may speak,
And after I have spoken, keep
[a]mocking.

4 "As for me, *is* my complaint
against man?
And if *it were,* why should I not
be impatient?
5 Look at me and be astonished;
[a]Put *your* hand over *your* mouth.
6 Even when I remember I am
terrified,
And trembling takes hold of my
flesh.
7 [a]Why do the wicked live *and*
become old,
Yes, become mighty in power?
8 Their descendants are
established with them in their
sight,
And their offspring before their
eyes.
9 Their houses *are* safe from fear,
[a]Neither *is* [1]the rod of God upon
them.
10 Their bull breeds without failure;
Their cow calves [a]without
miscarriage.
11 They send forth their little ones
like a flock,
And their children dance.
12 They sing to the tambourine and
harp,
And rejoice to the sound of the
flute.
13 They [a]spend their days in wealth,
And [1]in a moment go down to the
[2]grave.
14 [a]Yet they say to God, 'Depart from
us,
For we do not desire the
knowledge of Your ways.
15 [a]Who *is* the Almighty, that we
should serve Him?
And [b]what profit do we have if
we pray to Him?'
16 Indeed [1]their prosperity *is* not in
their hand;
[a]The counsel of the wicked is far
from me.

17 "How often is the lamp of the
wicked put out?
How often does their destruction
come upon them,
The sorrows *God* [a]distributes in
His anger?
18 [a]They are like straw before the
wind,
And like chaff that a storm
[1]carries away.
19 *They say,* 'God [1]lays up [2]one's
iniquity [a]for his children';
Let Him recompense him, that he
may know *it.*
20 Let his eyes see his destruction,
And [a]let him drink of the wrath
of the Almighty.
21 For what does he care about his
household after him,
When the number of his months
is cut in half?

22 "Can[a] *anyone* teach God
knowledge,
Since He judges those on high?
23 One dies in his full strength,
Being wholly at ease and secure;
24 His [1]pails are full of milk,
And the marrow of his bones is
moist.

22 [1]Or *the wretched* or *sufferer*
24 [a]Is. 24:18; Amos 5:19
25 [a]Job 16:13 [b]Job 18:11, 14 [1]Gallbladder
26 [a]Ps. 21:9
28 [a]Job 20:15; 21:30
29 [a]Job 27:13; 31:2, 3

CHAPTER 21

2 [1]*comfort*
3 [a]Job 16:10
5 [a]Judg. 18:19; Job 13:5; 29:9; 40:4
7 [a]Job 12:6; Ps. 17:10, 14; 73:3, 12; [Jer. 12:1]; Hab. 1:13, 16
9 [a]Ps. 73:5 [1]The rod of God's chastisement
10 [a]Ex. 23:26
13 [a]Job 21:23; 36:11 [1]Without lingering [2]Or *Sheol*
14 [a]Job 22:17
15 [a]Ex. 5:2; Job 22:17; 34:9 [b]Job 35:3; Mal. 3:14
16 [a]Job 22:18; Ps. 1:1; Prov. 1:10 [1]Lit. *their goal*
17 [a][Job 31:2, 3; Luke 12:46]
18 [a]Ps. 1:4; 35:5; Is. 17:13; Hos. 13:3 [1]*steals away*
19 [a][Ex. 20:5]; Jer. 31:29; Ezek. 18:2 [1]*stores up* [2]Lit. *his*
20 [a]Ps. 75:8; Is. 51:17; Jer. 25:15; Rev. 14:10; 19:15
22 [a]Job 35:11; 36:22; [Is. 40:13; 45:9; Rom. 11:34; 1 Cor. 2:16]
24 [1]LXX, Vg. *bowels;* Syr. *sides;* Tg. *breasts*

25 Another man dies in the
bitterness of his soul,
Never having eaten with
pleasure.
26 They [a]lie down alike in the dust,
And worms cover them.

27 "Look, I know your thoughts,
And the schemes *with which* you
would wrong me.
28 For you say,
'Where *is* the house of the prince?
And where *is* [1]the tent,
The dwelling place of the
wicked?'
29 Have you not asked those who
travel the road?
And do you not know their signs?
30 [a]For the wicked are reserved for
the day of doom;
They shall be brought out on the
day of wrath.
31 Who condemns his way to his
face?
And who repays him *for what* he
has done?
32 Yet he shall be brought to the
grave,
And a vigil kept over the tomb.
33 The clods of the valley shall be
sweet to him;
[a]Everyone shall follow him,
As countless *have gone* before
him.
34 How then can you comfort me
with empty words,
Since [1]falsehood remains in your
answers?"

Eliphaz Accuses Job of Wickedness

22 Then [a]Eliphaz the Temanite
answered and said:

2 "Can[a] a man be profitable to God,
Though he who is wise may be
profitable to himself?
3 *Is it* any pleasure to the Almighty
that you are righteous?
Or *is it* gain *to Him* that you make
your ways blameless?

4 "Is it because of your fear of Him
that He corrects you,
And enters into judgment with
you?
5 *Is* not your wickedness great,
And your iniquity without end?
6 For you have [a]taken pledges from
your brother for no reason,
And stripped the naked of their
clothing.
7 You have not given the weary
water to drink,
And you [a]have withheld bread
from the hungry.

26 [a]Job 3:13; 20:11; Eccl. 9:2
28 [1]Vg. omits *the tent*
30 [a]Job 20:29; [Prov. 16:4; 2 Pet. 2:9]
33 [a]Heb. 9:27
34 [1]*faithlessness*

CHAPTER 22

1 [a]Job 4:1; 15:1; 42:9
2 [a]Job 35:7; [Ps. 16:2; Luke 17:10]
6 [a][Ex. 22:26, 27]; Deut. 24:6, 10, 17; Job 24:3, 9; Ezek. 18:16
7 [a]Deut. 15:7; Job 31:17; Is. 58:7; Ezek. 18:7; Matt. 25:42
8 [1]Lit. *man of arm*
9 [1]Lit. *arms*
11 [a]Job 38:34; Ps. 69:1, 2; 124:5; Lam. 3:54
13 [a]Ps. 73:11
14 [a]Ps. 139:11, 12
16 [a]Job 14:19; 15:32; Ps. 90:5; Is. 28:2; Matt. 7:26, 27
17 [a]Job 21:14, 15 [1]LXX, Syr. *us*
19 [a]Ps. 52:6; 58:10; 107:42
20 [1]LXX *substance is*
21 [a][Ps. 34:10]; Is. 27:5
22 [a]Job 6:10; 23:12; Prov. 2:6 [b][Ps. 119:11]
24 [a]2 Chr. 1:15

8 But the [1]mighty man possessed
the land,
And the honorable man dwelt
in it.
9 You have sent widows away
empty,
And the [1]strength of the
fatherless was crushed.
10 Therefore snares *are* all around
you,
And sudden fear troubles you,
11 Or darkness *so that* you cannot
see;
And an abundance of [a]water
covers you.

12 "Is not God in the height of
heaven?
And see the highest stars, how
lofty they are!
13 And you say, [a]'What does God
know?
Can He judge through the deep
darkness?
14 [a]Thick clouds cover Him, so that
He cannot see,
And He walks above the circle of
heaven.'
15 Will you keep to the old way
Which wicked men have trod,
16 Who [a]were cut down before their
time,
Whose foundations were swept
away by a flood?
17 [a]They said to God, 'Depart from
us!
What can the Almighty do to
[1]them?'
18 Yet He filled their houses with
good *things;*
But the counsel of the wicked is
far from me.

19 "The[a] righteous see *it* and are
glad,
And the innocent laugh at them:
20 'Surely our [1]adversaries are cut
down,
And the fire consumes their
remnant.'

21 "Now acquaint yourself with Him,
and [a]be at peace;
Thereby good will come to you.
22 Receive, please, [a]instruction from
His mouth,
And [b]lay up His words in your
heart.
23 If you return to the Almighty, you
will be built up;
You will remove iniquity far from
your tents.
24 Then you will [a]lay your gold in
the dust,

And the *gold* of Ophir among the stones of the brooks.
25 Yes, the Almighty will be your [1]gold
And your precious silver;
26 For then you will have your [a]delight in the Almighty,
And lift up your face to God.
27 [a]You will make your prayer to Him,
He will hear you,
And you will pay your vows.
28 You will also declare a thing,
And it will be established for you;
So light will shine on your ways.
29 When they cast *you* down, and you say, 'Exaltation *will come!*'
Then [a]He will save the humble *person.*
30 He will *even* deliver one who is not innocent;
Yes, he will be delivered by the purity of your hands."

Job Proclaims God's Righteous Judgments

23 Then Job answered and said:

2 "Even today my [a]complaint is bitter;
[1]My hand is listless because of my groaning.
3 [a]Oh, that I knew where I might find Him,
That I might come to His seat!
4 I would present *my* case before Him,
And fill my mouth with arguments.
5 I would know the words *which* He would answer me,
And understand what He would say to me.
6 [a]Would He contend with me in His great power?
No! But He would take *note* of me.
7 There the upright could reason with Him,
And I would be delivered forever from my Judge.

8 "Look,[a] I go forward, but He is not *there,*
And backward, but I cannot perceive Him;
9 When He works on the left hand, I cannot behold *Him;*
When He turns to the right hand, I cannot see *Him.*
10 But [a]He knows the way that I take;

25 [1]Ancient vss. suggest *defense;* MT *gold,* as in v. 24
26 [a]Job 27:10; Ps. 37:4; Is. 58:14
27 [a]Job 11:13; 33:26; [Is. 58:9–11]
29 [a]Job 5:11; [Matt. 23:12; James 4:6; 1 Pet. 5:5]

CHAPTER 23

2 [a]Job 7:11 [1]So with MT, Tg., Vg.; LXX, Syr. *His*
3 [a]Job 13:3, 18; 16:21; 31:35
6 [a]Is. 57:16
8 [a]Job 9:11; 35:14
10 [a][Ps. 1:6; 139:1–3] [b][Ps. 17:3; 66:10; James 1:12]
11 [a]Job 31:7; Ps. 17:5
12 [a]Job 6:10; 22:22 [b]Ps. 44:18 [1]Lit. *appointed portion*
13 [a][Ps. 115:3]
14 [a][1 Thess. 3:2–4]
16 [a]Ps. 22:14
17 [a]Job 10:18, 19 [1]Or *by* or *before*

CHAPTER 24

1 [a][Acts 1:7] [b][Is. 2:12]; Jer. 46:10; [Obad. 15]; Zeph. 1:7
2 [a][Deut. 19:14; 27:17]; Prov. 22:28; 23:10; Hos. 5:10
3 [a][Deut. 24:6, 10, 12, 17]; Job 22:6, 9
4 [a]Job 29:16; Prov. 28:28
7 [a]Ex. 22:26, 27; [Deut. 24:12, 13]; Job 22:6; [James 2:15, 16]
8 [a]Lam. 4:5

When [b]He has tested me, I shall come forth as gold.
11 [a]My foot has held fast to His steps;
I have kept His way and not turned aside.
12 I have not departed from the [a]commandment of His lips;
[b]I have treasured the words of His mouth
More than my [1]necessary *food.*

13 "But He *is* unique, and who can make Him change?
And *whatever* [a]His soul desires, *that* He does.
14 For He performs *what is* [a]appointed for me,
And many such *things are* with Him.
15 Therefore I am terrified at His presence;
When I consider *this,* I am afraid of Him.
16 For God [a]made my heart weak,
And the Almighty terrifies me;
17 Because I was not [a]cut off [1]from the presence of darkness,
And He did *not* hide deep darkness from my face.

Job Complains of Violence on the Earth

24 "*Since* [a]times are not hidden from the Almighty,
Why do those who know Him see not His [b]days?

2 "*Some* remove [a]landmarks;
They seize flocks violently and feed *on them;*
3 They drive away the donkey of the fatherless;
They [a]take the widow's ox as a pledge.
4 They push the needy off the road;
All the [a]poor of the land are forced to hide.
5 Indeed, *like* wild donkeys in the desert,
They go out to their work, searching for food.
The wilderness *yields* food for them *and* for *their* children.
6 They gather their fodder in the field
And glean in the vineyard of the wicked.
7 They [a]spend the night naked, without clothing,
And have no covering in the cold.
8 They are wet with the showers of the mountains,
And [a]huddle around the rock for want of shelter.

9 "*Some* snatch the fatherless from
the breast,
And take a pledge from the
poor.
10 They cause *the poor* to go naked,
without [a]clothing;
And they take away the sheaves
from the hungry.
11 They press out oil within their
walls,
And tread winepresses, yet suffer
thirst.
12 The dying groan in the city,
And the souls of the wounded cry
out;
Yet God does not charge *them*
with wrong.

13 "There are those who rebel against
the light;
They do not know its ways
Nor abide in its paths.
14 [a]The murderer rises with the light;
He kills the poor and needy;
And in the night he is like a thief.
15 [a]The eye of the adulterer waits for
the twilight,
[b]Saying, 'No eye will see me';
And he [1]disguises *his* face.
16 In the dark they break into
houses
Which they marked for
themselves in the daytime;
[a]They do not know the light.
17 For the morning is the same to
them as the shadow of death;
If *someone* recognizes *them*,
They are in the terrors of the
shadow of death.

18 "They *should be* swift on the face
of the waters,
Their portion *should be* cursed in
the earth,
So that no *one would* turn into
the way of their vineyards.
19 As drought and heat [1]consume
the snow waters,
So [2]the grave *consumes those
who* have sinned.
20 The womb *should* forget him,
The worm *should* feed sweetly on
him;
[a]He *should* be remembered no
more,
And wickedness *should* be
broken like a tree.
21 For he [1]preys on the barren *who*
do not bear,
And does no good for the widow.

22 "But *God* draws the mighty away
with His power;
He rises up, but no *man* is sure
of life.
23 He gives them security, and they
rely *on it;*
Yet [a]His eyes *are* on their ways.
24 They are exalted for a little while,
Then they are gone.
They are brought low;
They are [1]taken out of the way
like all *others;*
They dry out like the heads of
grain.

25 "Now if *it is* not so, who will prove
me a liar,
And make my speech worth
nothing?"

Bildad: How Can Man Be Righteous?

25 Then [a]Bildad the Shuhite
answered and said:

2 "Dominion and fear *belong* to
Him;
He makes peace in His high
places.
3 [1]Is there any number to His
armies?
Upon whom does [a]His light not
rise?
4 [a]How then can man be righteous
before God?
Or how can he be [b]pure *who is*
born of a woman?
5 If even the moon does not shine,
And the stars are not pure in His
[a]sight,
6 How much less man, *who is* [a]a
maggot,
And a son of man, *who is* a
worm?"

Job: Man's Frailty and God's Majesty

26 But Job answered and said:

2 "How have you helped *him who
is* without power?
How have you saved the arm *that
has* no strength?
3 How have you counseled *one who
has* no wisdom?
And *how* have you declared
sound advice to many?
4 To whom have you uttered
words?
And whose spirit came from you?

5 "The dead tremble,
Those under the waters and those
inhabiting them.
6 [a]Sheol *is* naked before Him,
And Destruction has no covering.
7 [a]He stretches out the north over
empty space;
He hangs the earth on nothing.
8 [a]He binds up the water in His thick
clouds,

10 [a]Job 31:19
14 [a]Ps. 10:8
15 [a]Prov. 7:7–10 [b]Ps. 10:11 [1]Lit. *puts a covering on his face*
16 [a][John 3:20]
19 [1]Lit. *seize* [2]Or *Sheol*
20 [a]Job 18:17; Ps. 34:16; Prov. 10:7
21 [1]Lit. *feeds on*
23 [a]Ps. 11:4; [Prov. 15:3]
24 [1]Lit. *gathered up*

CHAPTER 25

1 [a]Job 8:1; 18:1
3 [a]James 1:17 [1]Can His armies be counted?
4 [a]Job 4:17; 15:14; Ps. 130:3; 143:2 [b][Job 14:4]
5 [a]Job 15:15
6 [a]Ps. 22:6

CHAPTER 26

6 [a][Ps. 139:8]; Prov. 15:11; [Heb. 4:13]
7 [a]Job 9:8; Ps. 24:2; 104:2
8 [a]Job 37:11; Prov. 30:4

Yet the clouds [1]are not broken
under it.
9 He covers the face of *His* throne,
And spreads His cloud over it.
10 [a]He drew a circular horizon on the
face of the waters,
At the boundary of light and
darkness.
11 The pillars of heaven tremble,
And are [1]astonished at His
rebuke.
12 [a]He stirs up the sea with His
power,
And by His understanding He
breaks up [1]the storm.
13 [a]By His Spirit He adorned the
heavens;
His hand pierced [b]the fleeing
serpent.
14 Indeed these *are* the mere edges
of His ways,
And how small a whisper we hear
of Him!
But the thunder of His power who
can understand?"

Job Maintains His Integrity

27 Moreover Job continued his
discourse, and said:

2 "*As* God lives, [a]*who* has taken
away my justice,
And the Almighty, *who* has made
my soul bitter,
3 As long as my breath *is* in me,
And the breath of God in my
nostrils,
4 My lips will not speak
wickedness,
Nor my tongue utter deceit.
5 Far be it from me
That I should say you are right;
Till I die [a]I will not put away my
integrity from me.
6 My righteousness I [a]hold fast,
and will not let it go;
[b]My heart shall not [1]reproach *me*
as long as I live.

7 "May my enemy be like the
wicked,
And he who rises up against me
like the unrighteous.
8 [a]For what is the hope of the
hypocrite,
Though he may gain *much,*
If God takes away his life?
9 [a]Will God hear his cry
When trouble comes upon him?
10 [a]Will he delight himself in the
Almighty?
Will he always call on God?

11 "I will teach you [1]about the hand
of God;
What *is* with the Almighty I will
not conceal.
12 Surely all of you have seen *it;*
Why then do you behave with
complete nonsense?

13 "This[a] is the portion of a wicked
man with God,
And the heritage of oppressors,
received from the Almighty:
14 [a]If his children are multiplied, *it*
is for the sword;
And his offspring shall not be
satisfied with bread.
15 Those who survive him shall be
buried in death,
And [a]their[1] widows shall not
weep,
16 Though he heaps up silver like
dust,
And piles up clothing like clay—
17 He may pile *it* up, but [a]the just
will wear *it,*
And the innocent will divide the
silver.
18 He builds his house like a [1]moth,
[a]Like a [2]booth *which* a watchman
makes.
19 The rich man will lie down,
[1]But not be gathered *up;*
He opens his eyes,
And he *is* [a]no more.
20 [a]Terrors overtake him like a flood;
A tempest steals him away in the
night.
21 The east wind carries him away,
and he is gone;
It sweeps him out of his place.
22 It hurls against him and does not
[a]spare;
He flees desperately from its
[1]power.
23 *Men* shall clap their hands at him,
And shall hiss him out of his
place.

Job's Discourse on Wisdom

28 "Surely there is a mine for
silver,
And a place *where* gold is refined.
2 Iron is taken from the [1]earth,
And copper *is* smelted *from* ore.
3 *Man* puts an end to darkness,
And searches every recess
For ore in the darkness and the
shadow of death.
4 He breaks open a shaft away
from people;
In places forgotten by feet
They hang far away from men;
They swing to and fro.
5 *As for* the earth, from it comes
bread,
But underneath it is turned up as
by fire;

8 [1]*do not break*
10 [a][Job 38:1–11]; Ps. 33:7; 104:9; Prov. 8:29; Jer. 5:22
11 [1]*amazed*
12 [a]Ex. 14:21; Job 9:13; Is. 51:15; [Jer. 31:35] [1]Heb. *rahab*
13 [a][Job 9:8]; Ps. 33:6 [b]Is. 27:1

CHAPTER 27

2 [a]Job 34:5
5 [a]Job 2:9; 13:15
6 [a]Job 2:3; 33:9 [b]Acts 24:16 [1]*reprove*
8 [a]Matt. 16:26; Luke 12:20
9 [a]Job 35:12, 13; Ps. 18:41; Prov. 1:28; 28:9; [Is. 1:15]; Jer. 14:12; Ezek. 8:18; [Mic. 3:4; John 9:31; James 4:3]
10 [a]Job 22:26, 27; [Ps. 37:4; Is. 58:14]
11 [1]Or *by*
13 [a]Job 20:29
14 [a]Deut. 28:41; Esth. 9:10; Hos. 9:13
15 [a]Ps. 78:64 [1]Lit. *his*
17 [a]Prov. 28:8; [Eccl. 2:26]
18 [a]Is. 1:8; Lam. 2:6 [1]So with MT, Vg.; LXX, Syr. *spider* (cf. 8:14); Tg. *decay* [2]Temporary shelter
19 [a]Job 7:8, 21; 20:7 [1]So with MT, Tg.; LXX, Syr. *But shall not add* (i.e., do it again); Vg. *But take away nothing*
20 [a]Job 18:11
22 [a]Jer. 13:14; Ezek. 5:11; 24:14 [1]Lit. *hand*

CHAPTER 28

2 [1]Lit. *dust*

6 Its stones *are* the source of
sapphires,
And it contains gold dust.
7 *That* path no bird knows,
Nor has the falcon's eye seen it.
8 The [1]proud lions have not
trodden it,
Nor has the fierce lion passed
over it.
9 He puts his hand on the flint;
He overturns the mountains [1]at
the roots.
10 He cuts out channels in the
rocks,
And his eye sees every precious
thing.
11 He dams up the streams from
trickling;
What is hidden he brings forth
to light.

12 "But[a] where can wisdom be
found?
And where *is* the place of
understanding?
13 Man does not know its [a]value,
Nor is it found in the land of the
living.
14 [a]The deep says, *'It is* not in me';
And the sea says, *'It is* not with
me.'
15 It [a]cannot be purchased for gold,
Nor can silver be weighed *for* its
price.
16 It cannot be valued in the gold of
Ophir,
In precious onyx or sapphire.
17 Neither [a]gold nor crystal can
equal it,
Nor can it be exchanged for
[1]jewelry of fine gold.
18 No mention shall be made of
[1]coral or quartz,
For the price of wisdom *is* above
[a]rubies.
19 The topaz of Ethiopia cannot
equal it,
Nor can it be valued in pure
[a]gold.

20 "From[a] where then does wisdom
come?
And where *is* the place of
understanding?
21 It is hidden from the eyes of all
living,
And concealed from the birds of
the [1]air.
22 [a]Destruction[1] and Death say,
'We have heard a report about it
with our ears.'
23 God understands its way,
And He knows its place.
24 For He looks to the ends of the
earth,

8 [1]Lit. *sons of pride*, figurative of the great lions
9 [1]At the base
12 [a]Eccl. 7:24
13 [a]Prov. 3:15
14 [a]Job 28:22
15 [a]Prov. 3:13–15; 8:10, 11, 19
17 [a]Prov. 8:10; 16:16 [1]*vessels*
18 [a]Prov. 3:15; 8:11 [1]Heb. *ramoth*
19 [a]Prov. 8:19
20 [a]Job 28:12; [Ps. 111:10; Prov. 1:7; 9:10]
21 [1]*heaven*
22 [a]Job 28:14 [1]Heb. *Abaddon*
24 [a][Ps. 11:4; 33:13, 14; 66:7; Prov. 15:3]
25 [a]Ps. 135:7
26 [a]Job 37:3; 38:25
27 [1]Lit. *it*
28 [a][Deut. 4:6; Ps. 111:10; Prov. 1:7; 9:10; Eccl. 12:13]

CHAPTER 29

2 [a]Job 1:1–5 [b]Job 1:10
3 [a]Job 18:6
4 [a]Job 15:8; [Ps. 25:14; Prov. 3:32]
6 [a]Gen. 49:11; Deut. 32:14; Job 20:17 [b]Deut. 32:13; Ps. 81:16 [1]So with ancient vss. and a few Heb. mss. (cf. Job 20:17); MT *wrath*
9 [a]Job 21:5
10 [a]Ps. 137:6
12 [a]Job 31:16–23; [Ps. 72:12; Prov. 21:13; 24:11]

And [a]sees under the whole
heavens,
25 [a]To establish a weight for the
wind,
And apportion the waters by
measure.
26 When He [a]made a law for the
rain,
And a path for the thunderbolt,
27 Then He saw [1]*wisdom* and
declared it;
He prepared it, indeed, He
searched it out.
28 And to man He said,
'Behold, [a]the fear of the Lord, that
is wisdom,
And to depart from evil *is*
understanding.' "

Job's Summary Defense

29 Job further continued his discourse, and said:

2 "Oh, that I were as *in* months
[a]past,
As *in* the days *when* God
[b]watched over me;
3 [a]When His lamp shone upon my
head,
And when by His light I walked
through darkness;
4 Just as I was in the days of my
prime,
When [a]the friendly counsel of
God *was* over my tent;
5 When the Almighty *was* yet with
me,
When my children *were* around
me;
6 When [a]my steps were bathed
with [1]cream,
And [b]the rock poured out rivers
of oil for me!

7 "When I went out to the gate by
the city,
When I took my seat in the open
square,
8 The young men saw me and hid,
And the aged arose *and* stood;
9 The princes refrained from
talking,
And [a]put *their* hand on their
mouth;
10 The voice of nobles was hushed,
And their [a]tongue stuck to the
roof of their mouth.
11 When the ear heard, then it
blessed me,
And when the eye saw, then it
approved me;
12 Because [a]I delivered the poor
who cried out,
The fatherless and *the one who*
had no helper.

13 The blessing of a perishing *man*
came upon me,
And I caused the widow's heart
to sing for joy.
14 [a]I put on righteousness, and it
clothed me;
My justice *was* like a robe and a
turban.
15 I *was* [a]eyes to the blind,
And I *was* feet to the lame.
16 I *was* a father to the poor,
And [a]I searched out the case *that*
I did not know.
17 I broke [a]the fangs of the wicked,
And plucked the victim from his
teeth.

18 "Then I said, [a]'I shall die in my
nest,
And multiply *my* days as the
sand.
19 [a]My root *is* spread out [b]to the
waters,
And the dew lies all night on my
branch.
20 My glory *is* fresh within me,
And my [a]bow is renewed in my
hand.'

21 "*Men* listened to me and waited,
And kept silence for my counsel.
22 After my words they did not
speak again,
And my speech settled on them
as dew.
23 They waited for me *as* for the
rain,
And they opened their mouth
wide *as* for [a]the spring rain.
24 *If* I mocked at them, they did not
believe *it*,
And the light of my countenance
they did not cast down.
25 I chose the way for them, and sat
as chief;
So I dwelt as a king in the army,
As one *who* comforts mourners.

30

"But now they mock at me,
men [1]younger than I,
Whose fathers I disdained to put
with the dogs of my flock.
2 Indeed, what *profit* is the strength
of their hands to me?
Their vigor has perished.
3 *They are* gaunt from want and
famine,
Fleeing late to the wilderness,
desolate and waste,
4 Who pluck [1]mallow by the
bushes,
And broom tree roots *for* their
food.
5 They were driven out from
among *men*,
They shouted at them as *at* a
thief.
6 *They had* to live in the clefts of
the [1]valleys,
In [2]caves of the earth and the
rocks.
7 Among the bushes they
brayed,
Under the nettles they nestled.
8 *They were* sons of fools,
Yes, sons of vile men;
They were scourged from the
land.

9 "And[a] now I am their taunting
song;
Yes, I am their byword.
10 They abhor me, they keep far
from me;
They do not hesitate [a]to spit in
my face.
11 Because [a]He has loosed [1]my
bowstring and afflicted me,
They have cast off restraint
before me.
12 At *my* right *hand* the rabble
arises;
They push away my feet,
And [a]they raise against me their
ways of destruction.
13 They break up my path,
They promote my calamity;
They have no helper.
14 They come as broad breakers;
Under the ruinous storm they roll
along.
15 Terrors are turned upon me;
They pursue my honor as the
wind,
And my prosperity has passed
like a cloud.

16 "And[a] now my soul is [b]poured out
because of my *plight;*
The days of affliction take hold
of me.
17 My bones are pierced in me at
night,
And my gnawing pains take no
rest.
18 By great force my garment is
disfigured;
It binds me about as the collar of
my coat.
19 He has cast me into the mire,
And I have become like dust and
ashes.

20 "I [a]cry out to You, but You do not
answer me;
I stand up, and You regard me.
21 *But* You have become cruel to
me;
With the strength of Your hand
You [a]oppose me.

14 [a]Deut. 24:13; Job 27:5, 6; Ps. 132:9; [Is. 59:17; 61:10; Eph. 6:14]
15 [a]Num. 10:31
16 [a]Prov. 29:7
17 [a]Ps. 58:6; Prov. 30:14
18 [a]Ps. 30:6
19 [a]Job 18:16 [b]Ps. 1:3; [Jer. 17:7, 8]
20 [a]Gen. 49:24; Ps. 18:34
23 [a][Zech. 10:1]

CHAPTER 30

1 [1]Lit. *of fewer days*
4 [1]A plant of the salty marshes
6 [1]*wadis* [2]Lit. *holes*
9 [a]Job 17:6; Ps. 69:12; Lam. 3:14, 63
10 [a]Num. 12:14; Deut. 25:9; Job 17:6; Is. 50:6; Matt. 26:67; 27:30
11 [a]Job 12:18 [1]So with MT, Syr., Tg.; LXX, Vg. *His*
12 [a]Job 19:12
16 [a]Ps. 42:4 [b]Ps. 22:14; Is. 53:12
20 [a]Job 19:7
21 [a]Job 10:3; 16:9, 14; 19:6, 22

22 You lift me up to the wind and
cause me to ride *on it;*
You spoil my success.
23 For I know *that* You will bring
me *to* death,
And *to* the house [a]appointed for
all living.

24 "Surely He would not stretch out
His hand against a heap of
ruins,
If they cry out when He destroys
it.
25 [a]Have I not wept for him who was
in trouble?
Has *not* my soul grieved for the
poor?
26 [a]But when I looked for good, evil
came *to me;*
And when I waited for light, then
came darkness.
27 [1]My heart is in turmoil and cannot
rest;
Days of affliction confront me.
28 [a]I go about mourning, but not in
the sun;
I stand up in the assembly *and*
cry out for help.
29 [a]I am a brother of jackals,
And a companion of ostriches.
30 [a]My skin grows black and falls
from me;
[b]My bones burn with fever.
31 My harp is *turned* to mourning,
And my flute to the voice of those
who weep.

31

1 "I have made a covenant with
my eyes;
Why then should I [1]look upon a
[a]young woman?
2 For what *is* the [a]allotment of God
from above,
And the inheritance of the
Almighty from on high?
3 *Is* it not destruction for the
wicked,
And disaster for the workers of
iniquity?
4 [a]Does He not see my ways,
And count all my steps?

5 "If I have walked with falsehood,
Or if my foot has hastened to
deceit,
6 [1]Let me be weighed on honest
scales,
That God may know my
[a]integrity.
7 If my step has turned from the
way,
Or [a]my heart walked after my
eyes,
Or if any spot adheres to my
hands,
8 *Then* [a]let me sow, and another
eat;
Yes, let my harvest be [1]rooted
out.

9 "If my heart has been enticed by
a woman,
Or *if* I have lurked at my
neighbor's door,
10 *Then* let my wife grind for
[a]another,
And let others bow down over
her.
11 For that *would be* wickedness;
Yes, [a]it *would be* iniquity
deserving of judgment.
12 For that *would be* a fire *that*
consumes to destruction,
And would root out all my
increase.

13 "If I have [a]despised the cause of
my male or female servant
When they complained against
me,
14 What then shall I do when [a]God
rises up?
When He punishes, how shall I
answer Him?
15 [a]Did not He who made me in the
womb make them?
Did not the same One fashion us
in the womb?

16 "If I have kept the poor from *their*
desire,
Or caused the eyes of the widow
to [a]fail,
17 Or eaten my morsel by myself,
So that the fatherless could not
eat of it
18 (But from my youth I reared him
as a father,
And from my mother's womb I
guided [1]*the widow*);
19 If I have seen anyone perish for
lack of clothing,
Or any poor *man* without
covering;
20 If his [1]heart has not [a]blessed
me,
And *if* he was *not* warmed with
the fleece of my sheep;
21 If I have raised my hand [a]against
the fatherless,
When I saw I had help in the gate;
22 *Then* let my arm fall from my
shoulder,
Let my arm be torn from the
socket.
23 For [a]destruction *from* God *is* a
terror to me,
And because of His magnificence
I cannot endure.

---

23 [a][Heb. 9:27]
25 [a]Ps. 35:13, 14; Rom. 12:15
26 [a]Job 3:25, 26; Jer. 8:15
27 [1]*I seethe inside*
28 [a]Job 30:31; Ps. 38:6; 42:9; 43:2
29 [a]Ps. 44:19; 102:6; Mic. 1:8
30 [a]Ps. 119:83; Lam. 4:8; 5:10 [b]Ps. 102:3

CHAPTER 31

1 [a][Matt. 5:28] [1]*look intently* or *gaze*
2 [a]Job 20:29
4 [a][2 Chr. 16:9]; Job 24:23; 28:24; 34:21; 36:7; [Prov. 5:21; 15:3; Jer. 32:19]
6 [a]Job 23:10; 27:5, 6 [1]Lit. *Let Him weigh me*
7 [a]Num. 15:39; [Eccl. 11:9]; Ezek. 6:9; [Matt. 5:29]
8 [a]Lev. 26:16; Deut. 28:30, 38; Job 20:18; Mic. 6:15 [1]*uprooted*
10 [a]Deut. 28:30; 2 Sam. 12:11; Jer. 8:10
11 [a]Gen. 38:24; [Lev. 20:10; Deut. 22:22]; Job 31:28
13 [a][Deut. 24:14, 15]
14 [a][Ps. 44:21]
15 [a]Job 34:19; Prov. 14:31; 22:2; [Mal. 2:10]
16 [a]Job 29:12
18 [1]Lit. *her*
20 [a][Deut. 24:13] [1]Lit. *loins*
21 [a]Job 22:9
23 [a]Is. 13:6

24"If[a] I have made gold my hope,
Or said to fine gold, '*You are* my confidence';
25 [a]If I have rejoiced because my wealth *was* great,
And because my hand had gained much;
26 [a]If I have observed the [1]sun when it shines,
Or the moon moving *in* brightness,
27 So that my heart has been secretly enticed,
And my mouth has kissed my hand;
28 This also *would be* an iniquity *deserving of* judgment,
For I would have denied God *who is* above.

29"If[a] I have rejoiced at the destruction of him who hated me,
Or lifted myself up when evil found him
30 [a](Indeed I have not allowed my mouth to sin
By asking for a curse on his [1]soul);
31 If the men of my tent have not said,
'Who is there that has not been satisfied with his meat?'
32 [a](*But* no sojourner had to lodge in the street,
For I have opened my doors to the [1]traveler);
33 If I have covered my transgressions [a]as[1] Adam,
By hiding my iniquity in my bosom,
34 Because I feared the great [a]multitude,
And dreaded the contempt of families,
So that I kept silence
And did not go out of the door—
35 [a]Oh, that I had one to hear me!
Here is my mark.
Oh, [b]*that* the Almighty would answer me,
That my [1]Prosecutor had written a book!
36 Surely I would carry it on my shoulder,
And bind it on me *like* a crown;
37 I would declare to Him the number of my steps;
Like a prince I would approach Him.

38"If my land cries out against me,
And its furrows weep together;
39 If [a]I have eaten its [1]fruit without money,
Or [b]caused its owners to lose their lives;
40 *Then* let [a]thistles grow instead of wheat,
And weeds instead of barley."

The words of Job are ended.

Elihu Contradicts Job's Friends

32 So these three men ceased
answering Job, because he
was [a]righteous in his own eyes.
2 Then the wrath of Elihu, the
son of Barachel the [a]Buzite, of
the family of Ram, was aroused
against Job; his wrath was
aroused because he [b]justified him-
self rather than God.
3 Also against his three friends
his wrath was aroused, because
they had found no answer, and *yet*
had condemned Job.
4 Now because they *were* years
older than he, Elihu had waited [1]to
speak to Job.
5 When Elihu saw that *there was*
no answer in the mouth of these
three men, his wrath was aroused.
6 So Elihu, the son of Barachel
the Buzite, answered and said:

"I *am* [a]young in years, and you *are* very old;
Therefore I was afraid,
And dared not declare my opinion to you.
7 I said, [1]'Age should speak,
And multitude of years should teach wisdom.'
8 But *there is* a spirit in man,
And [a]the breath of the Almighty gives him understanding.
9 [a]Great[1] men are not *always* wise,
Nor do the aged *always* understand justice.

10"Therefore I say, 'Listen to me,
I also will declare my opinion.'
11 Indeed I waited for your words,
I listened to your reasonings,
while you searched out what to say.
12 I paid close attention to you;
And surely not one of you convinced Job,
Or answered his words—
13 [a]Lest you say,
'We have found wisdom';
God will vanquish him, not man.
14 Now he has not [1]directed *his* words against me;
So I will not answer him with your words.

---

24 [a][Matt. 6:19, 20; Mark 10:23–25]
25 [a]Job 1:3, 10; Ps. 62:10
26 [a][Deut. 4:19; 17:3]; Ezek. 8:16 [1]Lit. *light*
29 [a][Prov. 17:5; 24:17]; Obad. 12
30 [a][Matt. 5:44] [1]Or *life*
32 [a]Gen. 19:2, 3 [1]So with LXX, Syr., Tg., Vg.; MT *road*
33 [a]Gen. 3:10; [Prov. 28:13] [1]Or *as men do*
34 [a]Ex. 23:2
35 [a]Job 19:7; 30:20, 24, 28 [b]Job 13:22, 24; 33:10 [1]Lit. *Accuser*
39 [a]Job 24:6, 10–12; [James 5:4] [b]1 Kin. 21:19 [1]Lit. *strength*
40 [a]Gen. 3:18

CHAPTER 32
1 [a]Job 6:29; 31:6; 33:9
2 [a]Gen. 22:21 [b]Job 27:5, 6
4 [1]Vg. *till Job had spoken*
6 [a]Lev. 19:32
7 [1]Lit. *Days,* i.e., years
8 [a]1 Kin. 3:12; 4:29; [Job 35:11; 38:36; Prov. 2:6; Eccl. 2:26; Dan. 1:17; 2:21; Matt. 11:25; James 1:5]
9 [a][1 Cor. 1:26] [1]Or *Men of many years*
13 [a][Jer. 9:23; 1 Cor. 1:29]
14 [1]*ordered*

15 "They are dismayed and answer
no more;
Words escape them.
16 And I have waited, because they
did not speak,
Because they stood still *and*
answered no more.
17 I also will answer my part,
I too will declare my opinion.
18 For I am full of words;
The spirit within me compels me.
19 Indeed my [1]belly *is* like wine *that*
has no [2]vent;
It is ready to burst like new
wineskins.
20 I will speak, that I may find relief;
I must open my lips and answer.
21 Let me not, I pray, show partiality
to anyone;
Nor let me flatter any man.
22 For I do not know how to flatter,
Else my Maker would soon take
me [a]away.

Elihu Contradicts Job

33 "But please, Job, hear my
speech,
And listen to all my words.
2 Now, I open my mouth;
My tongue speaks in my mouth.
3 My words *come* from my upright
heart;
My lips utter pure knowledge.
4 [a]The Spirit of God has made me,
And the breath of the Almighty
gives me life.
5 If you can answer me,
Set *your words* in order before
me;
Take your stand.
6 [a]Truly I *am* [1]as your spokesman
before God;
I also have been formed out of
clay.
7 [a]Surely no fear of me will terrify
you,
Nor will my hand be heavy on
you.

8 "Surely you have spoken [1]in my
hearing,
And I have heard the sound of
your words, *saying,*
9 'I[a] *am* pure, without
transgression;
I *am* innocent, and *there is* no
iniquity in me.
10 Yet He finds occasions against
me,
[a]He counts me as His enemy;
11 [a]He puts my feet in the stocks,
He watches all my paths.'

12 "Look, *in* this you are not
righteous.

19 [1]*bosom* [2]*opening*
22 [a]Job 27:8
CHAPTER 33
4 [a][Gen. 2:7]; Job 32:8
6 [a]Job 4:19 [1]Lit. *as your mouth*
7 [a]Job 9:34
8 [1]Lit. *in my ears*
9 [a]Job 10:7
10 [a]Job 13:24; 16:9
11 [a]Job 13:27; 19:8
13 [a]Job 40:2; [Is. 45:9]
14 [a]Job 33:29; 40:5; Ps. 62:11
15 [a][Num. 12:6]
16 [a][Job 36:10, 15]
18 [1]Lit. *passing*
19 [a]Job 30:17
20 [a]Ps. 107:18 [b]Job 3:24; 6:7 [1]*desirable*
24 [1]*an atonement*
27 [a][2 Sam. 12:13; Prov. 28:13; Luke 15:21; 1 John 1:9] [b][Rom. 6:21]
28 [a]Is. 38:17 [1]Kt. *my*

I will answer you,
For God is greater than man.
13 Why do you [a]contend with Him?
For He does not give an
accounting of any of His words.
14 [a]For God may speak in one way,
or in another,
Yet man does not perceive it.
15 [a]In a dream, in a vision of the
night,
When deep sleep falls upon men,
While slumbering on their beds,
16 [a]Then He opens the ears of men,
And seals their instruction.
17 In order to turn man *from his*
deed,
And conceal pride from man,
18 He keeps back his soul from the
Pit,
And his life from [1]perishing by
the sword.

19 "*Man* is also chastened with pain
on his [a]bed,
And with strong *pain* in many of
his bones,
20 [a]So that his life abhors [b]bread,
And his soul [1]succulent food.
21 His flesh wastes away from
sight,
And his bones stick out *which
once* were not seen.
22 Yes, his soul draws near the Pit,
And his life to the executioners.

23 "If there is a messenger for him,
A mediator, one among a
thousand,
To show man His uprightness,
24 Then He is gracious to him, and
says,
'Deliver him from going down to
the Pit;
I have found [1]a ransom';
25 His flesh shall be young like a
child's,
He shall return to the days of his
youth.
26 He shall pray to God, and He will
delight in him,
He shall see His face with joy,
For He restores to man His
righteousness.
27 Then he looks at men and [a]says,
'I have sinned, and perverted
what was right,
And it [b]did not profit me.'
28 He will [a]redeem [1]his soul from
going down to the Pit,
And [1]his life shall see the light.

29 "Behold, God works all these
things,
Twice, *in fact,* three *times* with
a man,

30 [a]To bring back his soul from the
Pit,
That he may be enlightened with
the light of life.
31 "Give ear, Job, listen to me;
Hold your peace, and I will speak.
32 If you have anything to say,
answer me;
Speak, for I desire to justify you.
33 If not, [a]listen to me;
[1]Hold your peace, and I will teach
you wisdom."

Elihu Proclaims God's Justice

34 Elihu further answered and
said:

2 "Hear my words, you wise *men;*
Give ear to me, you who have
knowledge.
3 [a]For the ear tests words
As the palate tastes food.
4 Let us choose justice for
ourselves;
Let us know among ourselves
what *is* good.

5 "For Job has said, [a]'I am righteous,
But [b]God has taken away my
justice;
6 [a]Should I lie concerning my
right?
My [1]wound *is* incurable, *though
I am* without transgression.'
7 What man *is* like Job,
[a]*Who* drinks [1]scorn like water,
8 Who goes in company with the
workers of iniquity,
And walks with wicked men?
9 For [a]he has said, 'It profits a man
nothing
That he should delight in God.'

10 "Therefore listen to me, you [1]men
of understanding:
[a]Far be it from God *to do*
wickedness,
And *from* the Almighty *to
commit* iniquity.
11 [a]For He repays man *according to*
his work,
And makes man to find a reward
according to *his* way.
12 Surely God will never do
wickedly,
Nor will the Almighty [a]pervert
justice.
13 Who gave Him charge over the
earth?
Or who appointed *Him over* the
whole world?
14 If He should set His heart on it,
If He should [a]gather to Himself
His Spirit and His breath,

30 [a]Ps. 56:13
33 [a]Ps. 34:11 [1]*Keep silent*
CHAPTER 34
3 [a]Job 6:30; 12:11
5 [a]Job 13:18; 33:9 [b]Job 27:2
6 [a]Job 6:4; 9:17 [1]Lit. *arrow*
7 [a]Job 15:16 [1]*derision*
9 [a]Mal. 3:14
10 [a][Gen. 18:25; Deut. 32:4; 2 Chr. 19:7]; Job 8:3; 36:23; Ps. 92:15; Rom. 9:14 [1]*men of heart*
11 [a]Job 34:25; Ps. 62:12; [Prov. 24:12; Jer. 32:19]; Ezek. 33:20; [Matt. 16:27]; Rom. 2:6; [2 Cor. 5:10; Rev. 22:12]
12 [a]Job 8:3
14 [a]Job 12:10; Ps. 104:29; [Eccl. 12:7]
15 [a][Gen. 3:19]; Job 10:9; [Eccl. 12:7]
17 [a]2 Sam. 23:3; Job 34:30 [b]Job 40:8
18 [a]Ex. 22:28
19 [a][Deut. 10:17; Acts 10:34; Rom. 2:11, 12] [b]Job 31:15
20 [a]Ex. 12:29; Job 34:25; 36:20
21 [a][2 Chr. 16:9]; Job 31:4; Ps. 34:15; [Prov. 5:21; 15:3; Jer. 16:17; 32:19]
22 [a][Ps. 139:11, 12; Amos 9:2, 3]
24 [a]Job 12:19; [Dan. 2:21]
27 [a]1 Sam. 15:11 [b]Ps. 28:5; Is. 5:12
28 [a]Job 35:9; James 5:4 [b][Ex. 22:23]; Job 22:27

15 [a]All flesh would perish together,
And man would return to dust.

16 "If *you have* understanding, hear
this;
Listen to the sound of my words:
17 [a]Should one who hates justice
govern?
Will you [b]condemn *Him who is*
most just?
18 [a]*Is it fitting* to say to a king, *'You
are* worthless,'
And to nobles, *'You are* wicked'?
19 Yet He [a]is not partial to princes,
Nor does He regard the rich more
than the poor;
For [b]they *are* all the work of His
hands.
20 In a moment they die, [a]in the
middle of the night;
The people are shaken and pass
away;
The mighty are taken away
without a hand.

21 "For[a] His eyes *are* on the ways of
man,
And He sees all his steps.
22 [a]There is no darkness nor shadow
of death
Where the workers of iniquity
may hide themselves.
23 For He need not further consider
a man,
That he should go before God in
judgment.
24 [a]He breaks in pieces mighty men
without inquiry,
And sets others in their place.
25 Therefore He knows their works;
He overthrows *them* in the night,
And they are crushed.
26 He strikes them as wicked *men*
In the open sight of others,
27 Because they [a]turned back from
Him,
And [b]would not consider any of
His ways,
28 So that they [a]caused the cry of
the poor to come to Him;
For He [b]hears the cry of the
afflicted.
29 When He gives quietness, who
then can make trouble?
And when He hides *His* face, who
then can see Him,
Whether *it is* against a nation or
a man alone?—
30 That the hypocrite should not
reign,
Lest the people be ensnared.

31 "For has *anyone* said to God,
'I have borne *chastening;*
I will offend no more;

32 Teach me *what* I do not see;
If I have done iniquity, I will do
no more'?
33 Should He repay *it* according to
your *terms,*
Just because you disavow it?
You must choose, and not I;
Therefore speak what you know.

34 "Men of understanding say to me,
Wise men who listen to me:
35 'Job[a] speaks without knowledge,
His words *are* without wisdom.'
36 Oh, that Job were tried to the
utmost,
Because *his* answers *are like*
those of wicked men!
37 For he adds [a]rebellion to his sin;
He claps *his hands* among us,
And multiplies his words against
God."

Elihu Condemns Self-Righteousness

35 Moreover Elihu answered
and said:

2 "Do you think this is right?
Do you say,
'My righteousness is more than
God's'?
3 For [a]you say,
'What advantage will it be to You?
What profit shall I have, more
than *if* I had sinned?'

4 "I will answer you,
And [a]your companions with you.
5 [a]Look to the heavens and see;
And behold the clouds—
They are higher than you.
6 If you sin, what do you
accomplish [a]against Him?
Or, *if* your transgressions are
multiplied, what do you do to
Him?
7 [a]If you are righteous, what do you
give Him?
Or what does He receive from
your hand?
8 Your wickedness affects a man
such as you,
And your righteousness a son of
man.

9 "Because[a] of the multitude of
oppressions they cry out;
They cry out for help because of
the arm of the mighty.
10 But no one says, [a]'Where *is* God
my Maker,
[b]Who gives songs in the night,
11 Who [a]teaches us more than the
beasts of the earth,
And makes us wiser than the
birds of heaven?'

12 [a]There they cry out, but He does
not answer,
Because of the pride of evil men.
13 [a]Surely God will not listen to
empty *talk,*
Nor will the Almighty regard it.
14 [a]Although you say you do not see
Him,
Yet justice *is* before Him, and
[b]you must wait for Him.
15 And now, because He has not
[a]punished in His anger,
Nor taken much notice of folly,
16 [a]Therefore Job opens his mouth in
vain;
He multiplies words without
knowledge."

Elihu Proclaims God's Goodness

36 Elihu also proceeded and
said:

2 "Bear with me a little, and I will
show you
That *there are* yet words to speak
on God's behalf.
3 I will fetch my knowledge from
afar;
I will ascribe righteousness to my
Maker.
4 For truly my words *are* not false;
One who is perfect in knowledge
is with you.

5 "Behold, God *is* mighty, but
despises *no one;*
[a]*He is* mighty in strength [1]of
understanding.
6 He does not preserve the life of
the wicked,
But gives justice to the
[a]oppressed.
7 [a]He does not withdraw His eyes
from the righteous;
But [b]*they are* on the throne with
kings,
For He has seated them forever,
And they are exalted.
8 And [a]if *they are* bound in [1]fetters,
Held in the cords of affliction,
9 Then He tells them their work
and their transgressions—
That they have acted [1]defiantly.
10 [a]He also opens their ear to
[1]instruction,
And commands that they turn
from iniquity.
11 If they obey and serve *Him,*
They shall [a]spend their days in
prosperity,
And their years in pleasures.
12 But if they do not obey,
They shall perish by the sword,
And they shall die [1]without
[a]knowledge.

35 [a]Job 35:16; 38:2
37 [a]Job 7:11; 10:1

CHAPTER 35

3 [a]Job 21:15; 34:9
4 [a]Job 34:8
5 [a]Gen. 15:5; [Job 22:12; Ps. 8:3]
6 [a]Job 7:20; [Prov. 8:36; Jer. 7:19]
7 [a]Job 22:2; Ps. 16:2; Prov. 9:12; [Luke 17:10]; Rom. 11:35
9 [a]Job 34:28
10 [a]Is. 51:13 [b]Job 8:21; Ps. 42:8; 77:6; 149:5; Acts 16:25
11 [a]Job 36:22; Ps. 94:12; [Is. 48:17]; Jer. 32:33; [1 Cor. 2:13]
12 [a]Prov. 1:28
13 [a]Job 27:9; [Prov. 15:29; Is. 1:15]; Jer. 11:11; [Mic. 3:4]
14 [a]Job 9:11 [b][Ps. 37:5, 6]
15 [a]Ps. 89:32
16 [a]Job 34:35; 38:2

CHAPTER 36

5 [a]Job 12:13, 16; 37:23; [Ps. 99:2–5] [1]*of heart*
6 [a]Job 5:15
7 [a][Ps. 33:18; 34:15] [b]Job 5:11; Ps. 113:8
8 [a]Ps. 107:10 [1]*chains*
9 [1]*proudly*
10 [a]Job 33:16; 36:15 [1]*discipline*
11 [a]Job 21:13; [Is. 1:19, 20]
12 [a]Job 4:21 [1]MT *as one without knowledge*

13 "But the hypocrites in heart [a]store
up wrath;
They do not cry for help when He
binds them.
14 [a]They[1] die in youth,
And their life *ends* among the
[2]perverted persons.
15 He delivers the poor in their
affliction,
And opens their ears in
oppression.

16 "Indeed He would have brought
you out of dire distress,
[a]*Into* a broad place where *there*
is no restraint;
And [b]what is set on your table
would be full of [c]richness.
17 But you are filled with the
judgment due the [a]wicked;
Judgment and justice take hold *of*
you.
18 Because *there is* wrath, *beware*
lest He take you away with *one*
blow;
For [a]a large ransom would not
help you avoid *it.*
19 [a]Will your riches,
Or all the mighty forces,
Keep you from distress?
20 Do not desire the night,
When people are cut off in their
place.
21 Take heed, [a]do not turn to
iniquity,
For [b]you have chosen this rather
than affliction.

22 "Behold, God is exalted by His
power;
Who teaches like Him?
23 [a]Who has assigned Him His way,
Or who has said, 'You have done
[b]wrong'?

Elihu Proclaims God's Majesty

24 "Remember to [a]magnify His work,
Of which men have sung.
25 Everyone has seen it;
Man looks on *it* from afar.

26 "Behold, God *is* great, and we [a]do
not know *Him;*
[b]Nor can the number of His years
be discovered.
27 For He [a]draws up drops of water,
Which distill as rain from the
mist,
28 [a]Which the clouds drop down
And pour abundantly on man.
29 Indeed, can *anyone* understand
the spreading of clouds,
The thunder from His canopy?
30 Look, He [a]scatters His light
upon it,

13 [a][Rom. 2:5]
14 [a]Ps. 55:23 [1]Lit. *Their soul dies* [2]Heb. *qedeshim,* those practicing sodomy or prostitution in religious rituals
16 [a]Ps. 18:19; 31:8; 118:5 [b]Ps. 23:5 [c]Ps. 36:8
17 [a]Job 22:5, 10, 11
18 [a]Ps. 49:7
19 [a][Prov. 11:4]
21 [a][Ps. 31:6; 66:18] [b][Heb. 11:25]
23 [a]Job 34:13; [Is. 40:13, 14] [b]Job 8:3
24 [a][Rev. 15:3]
26 [a][1 Cor. 13:12] [b]Heb. 1:12
27 [a]Ps. 147:8
28 [a][Prov. 3:20]
30 [a]Job 37:3
31 [a][Acts 14:17] [b]Ps. 104:14, 15
32 [a]Ps. 147:8 [1]*strike the mark*
33 [a]1 Kin. 18:41 [1]Lit. *what is rising*

CHAPTER 37

3 [1]Or *light*
4 [a]Ps. 29:3
5 [a]Job 5:9; 9:10; 36:26
6 [a]Ps. 147:16, 17 [1]Lit. *shower of rain*
7 [a]Ps. 109:27 [b]Ps. 19:3, 4
8 [a]Ps. 104:21, 22
10 [a]Ps. 147:17, 18
11 [1]*clouds of light*
12 [a]Job 36:32 [1]Lit. *the world of the earth*
13 [a]Ex. 9:18, 23 [b]Job 38:26, 27 [c]1 Kin. 18:41–46 [1]Lit. *a rod*
14 [a]Ps. 111:2
15 [1]*places them*

And covers the depths of the sea.
31 For [a]by these He judges the
peoples;
He [b]gives food in abundance.
32 [a]He covers *His* hands with
lightning,
And commands it to [1]strike.
33 [a]His thunder declares it,
The cattle also, concerning [1]the
rising *storm.*

37 "At this also my heart
trembles,
And leaps from its place.
2 Hear attentively the thunder of
His voice,
And the rumbling *that* comes
from His mouth.
3 He sends it forth under the whole
heaven,
His [1]lightning to the ends of the
earth.
4 After it [a]a voice roars;
He thunders with His majestic
voice,
And He does not restrain them
when His voice is heard.
5 God thunders marvelously with
His voice;
[a]He does great things which we
cannot comprehend.
6 For [a]He says to the snow, 'Fall *on*
the earth';
Likewise to the [1]gentle rain and
the heavy rain of His strength.
7 He seals the hand of every man,
[a]That [b]all men may know His
work.
8 The beasts [a]go into dens,
And remain in their lairs.
9 From the chamber *of the south*
comes the whirlwind,
And cold from the scattering
winds *of the north.*
10 [a]By the breath of God ice is given,
And the broad waters are
frozen.
11 Also with moisture He saturates
the thick clouds;
He scatters His [1]bright clouds.
12 And they swirl about, being
turned by His guidance,
That they may [a]do whatever He
commands them
On the face of [1]the whole earth.
13 [a]He causes it to come,
Whether for [1]correction,
Or [b]for His land,
Or [c]for mercy.

14 "Listen to this, O Job;
Stand still and [a]consider the
wondrous works of God.
15 Do you know when God
[1]dispatches them,

And causes the light of His cloud to shine?
16 [a]Do you know how the clouds are balanced,
Those wondrous works of [b]Him who is perfect in knowledge?
17 Why *are* your garments hot,
When He quiets the earth by the south *wind?*
18 With Him, have you [a]spread out the [b]skies,
Strong as a cast metal mirror?

19 "Teach us what we should say to Him,
For we can prepare nothing because of the darkness.
20 Should He be told that I *wish to* speak?
If a man were to speak, surely he would be swallowed up.
21 Even now *men* cannot look at the light *when it is* bright in the skies,
When the wind has passed and cleared them.
22 He comes from the north *as* golden *splendor;*
With God *is* awesome majesty.
23 *As for* the Almighty, [a]we cannot find Him;
[b]*He is* excellent in power,
In judgment and abundant justice;
He does not oppress.
24 Therefore men [a]fear Him;
He shows no partiality to any *who are* [b]wise of heart."

The LORD Reveals His Omnipotence to Job

38 Then the LORD answered Job [a]out of the whirlwind, and said:

2 "Who[a] *is* this who darkens counsel
By [b]words without knowledge?
3 [a]Now [1]prepare yourself like a man;
I will question you, and you shall answer Me.

4 "Where[a] were you when I laid the foundations of the earth?
Tell *Me,* if you have understanding.
5 Who determined its measurements?
Surely you know!
Or who stretched the [1]line upon it?
6 To what were its foundations fastened?
Or who laid its cornerstone,
7 When the morning stars sang together,
And all [a]the sons of God shouted for joy?

8 "Or[a] *who* shut in the sea with doors,
When it burst forth *and* issued from the womb;
9 When I made the clouds its garment,
And thick darkness its swaddling band;
10 When [a]I fixed My limit for it,
And set bars and doors;
11 When I said,
'This far you may come, but no farther,
And here your proud waves [a]must stop!'

12 "Have you [a]commanded the morning since your days *began,*
And caused the dawn to know its place,
13 That it might take hold of the ends of the earth,
And [a]the wicked be shaken out of it?
14 It takes on form like clay *under* a seal,
And stands out like a garment.
15 From the wicked their [a]light is withheld,
And [b]the [1]upraised arm is broken.

16 "Have you [a]entered the springs of the sea?
Or have you walked in search of the depths?
17 Have [a]the gates of death been [1]revealed to you?
Or have you seen the doors of the shadow of death?
18 Have you comprehended the breadth of the earth?
Tell *Me,* if you know all this.

19 "Where *is* the way *to* the dwelling of light?
And darkness, where *is* its place,
20 That you may take it to its territory,
That you may know the paths *to* its home?
21 Do you know *it,* because you were born then,
Or *because* the number of your days *is* great?

22 "Have you entered [a]the treasury of snow,

16 [a]Job 36:29 [b]Job 36:4
18 [a]Gen. 1:6; [Is. 44:24] [b]Job 9:8; Ps. 104:2; [Is. 45:12; Jer. 10:12; Zech. 12:1]
23 [a][Job 11:7, 8; Rom. 11:33, 34; 1 Tim. 6:16] [b][Job 9:4; 36:5]
24 [a][Matt. 10:28] [b][Job 5:13; Matt. 11:25]; 1 Cor. 1:26

CHAPTER 38

1 [a]Ex. 19:16; Job 40:6
2 [a]Job 34:35; 42:3 [b]1 Tim. 1:7
3 [a]Job 40:7 [1]Lit. *gird up your loins like*
4 [a]Job 15:7; Ps. 104:5
5 [1]*measuring line*
7 [a]Job 1:6
8 [a]Gen. 1:9; Ps. 33:7; 104:9; Prov. 8:29; [Jer. 5:22]
10 [a]Job 26:10
11 [a][Ps. 89:9; 93:4]
12 [a][Ps. 74:16; 148:5]
13 [a]Job 34:25; Ps. 104:35
15 [a]Job 18:5; [Prov. 13:9] [b][Num. 15:30]; Ps. 10:15; 37:17 [1]Lit. *high*
16 [a][Ps. 77:19]; Prov. 8:24
17 [a]Ps. 9:13 [1]Lit. *opened*
22 [a]Ps. 135:7

Or have you seen the treasury of
hail,
23 [a]Which I have reserved for the
time of trouble,
For the day of battle and war?
24 By what way is light [1]diffused,
Or the east wind scattered over
the earth?

25 "Who [a]has divided a channel for
the overflowing *water,*
Or a path for the thunderbolt,
26 To cause it to rain on a land
where there is no one,
A wilderness in which *there is* no
man;
27 [a]To satisfy the desolate waste,
And cause to spring forth the
growth of tender grass?
28 [a]Has the rain a father?
Or who has begotten the drops
of dew?
29 From whose womb comes the
ice?
And the [a]frost of heaven, who
gives it birth?
30 The waters harden like stone,
And the surface of the deep is
[a]frozen.[1]

31 "Can you bind the cluster of the
[a]Pleiades,[1]
Or loose the belt of Orion?
32 Can you bring out [1]Mazzaroth in
its season?
Or can you guide [2]the Great Bear
with its cubs?
33 Do you know [a]the ordinances of
the heavens?
Can you set their dominion over
the earth?

34 "Can you lift up your voice to the
clouds,
That an abundance of water may
cover you?
35 Can you send out lightnings, that
they may go,
And say to you, 'Here we *are!*'?
36 [a]Who has put wisdom in [1]the
mind?
Or who has given understanding
to the heart?
37 Who can number the clouds by
wisdom?
Or who can pour out the bottles
of heaven,
38 When the dust hardens in
clumps,
And the clods cling together?

39 "Can[a] you hunt the prey for the
lion,
Or satisfy the appetite of the
young lions,

23 [a]Ex. 9:18; Josh. 10:11; Is. 30:30; Ezek. 13:11, 13; Rev. 16:21
24 [1]Lit. *divided*
25 [a]Job 28:26
27 [a]Ps. 104:13, 14; 107:35
28 [a]Job 36:27, 28; [Ps. 147:8; Jer. 14:22]
29 [a][Job 37:10]; Ps. 147:16, 17
30 [a][Job 37:10] [1]Lit. *imprisoned*
31 [a]Job 9:9; Amos 5:8 [1]Or *the Seven Stars*
32 [1]Lit. *Constellations* [2]Or *Arcturus*
33 [a][Ps. 148:6]; Jer. 31:35, 36
36 [a][Job 9:4; 32:8; Ps. 51:6; Eccl. 2:26; James 1:5] [1]Lit. *the inward parts*
39 [a]Ps. 104:21
41 [a]Ps. 147:9; [Matt. 6:26; Luke 12:24]

CHAPTER 39

1 [a]Deut. 14:5; 1 Sam. 24:2; Ps. 104:18 [b]Ps. 29:9
3 [1]Lit. *pangs*
5 [1]A species of wild donkey
6 [a]Job 24:5; Jer. 2:24; Hos. 8:9 [1]Lit. *salt land*
8 [a]Gen. 1:29
9 [a]Num. 23:22; Deut. 33:17; Ps. 22:21; 29:6; 92:10; Is. 34:7
12 [1]Lit. *seed*

40 When they crouch in *their* dens,
Or lurk in their lairs to lie in wait?
41 [a]Who provides food for the
raven,
When its young ones cry to God,
And wander about for lack of
food?

39

"Do you know the time when
the wild [a]mountain goats
bear young?
Or can you mark when [b]the deer
gives birth?
2 Can you number the months *that*
they fulfill?
Or do you know the time when
they bear young?
3 They bow down,
They bring forth their young,
They deliver their [1]offspring.
4 Their young ones are healthy,
They grow strong with grain;
They depart and do not return to
them.

5 "Who set the wild donkey free?
Who loosed the bonds of the
[1]onager,
6 [a]Whose home I have made the
wilderness,
And the [1]barren land his
dwelling?
7 He scorns the tumult of the city;
He does not heed the shouts of
the driver.
8 The range of the mountains *is* his
pasture,
And he searches after [a]every
green thing.

9 "Will the [a]wild ox be willing to
serve you?
Will he bed by your manger?
10 Can you bind the wild ox in the
furrow with ropes?
Or will he plow the valleys
behind you?
11 Will you trust him because his
strength *is* great?
Or will you leave your labor to
him?
12 Will you trust him to bring home
your [1]grain,
And gather it to your threshing
floor?

13 "The wings of the ostrich wave
proudly,
But are her wings and pinions
like the kindly stork's?
14 For she leaves her eggs on the
ground,
And warms them in the dust;
15 She forgets that a foot may crush
them,

Or that a wild beast may break
them.
16 She [a]treats her young harshly, as
though *they were* not hers;
Her labor is in vain, without
[1]concern,
17 Because God deprived her of
wisdom,
And did not [a]endow her with
understanding.
18 When she lifts herself on high,
She scorns the horse and its rider.

19 "Have you given the horse
strength?
Have you clothed his neck with
[1]thunder?
20 Can you [1]frighten him like a
locust?
His majestic snorting strikes
terror.
21 He paws in the valley, and
rejoices in *his* strength;
[a]He gallops into the clash of arms.
22 He mocks at fear, and is not
frightened;
Nor does he turn back from the
sword.
23 The quiver rattles against him,
The glittering spear and
javelin.
24 He devours the distance with
fierceness and rage;
Nor does he come to a halt
because the trumpet *has*
sounded.
25 At *the blast of* the trumpet he
says, 'Aha!'
He smells the battle from afar,
The thunder of captains and
shouting.

26 "Does the hawk fly by your
wisdom,
And spread its wings toward the
south?
27 Does the [a]eagle mount up at your
command,
And [b]make its nest on high?
28 On the rock it dwells and resides,
On the crag of the rock and the
stronghold.
29 From there it spies out the prey;
Its eyes observe from afar.
30 Its young ones suck up blood;
And [a]where the slain *are*, there
it *is*."

40 Moreover the LORD [a]answered Job, and said:

2 "Shall [a]the one who contends with
the Almighty correct *Him*?
He who [b]rebukes God, let him
answer it."

Job's Response to God

3 Then Job answered the LORD
and said:

4 "Behold,[a] I am vile;
What shall I answer You?
[b]I lay my hand over my mouth.
5 Once I have spoken, but I will not
answer;
Yes, twice, but I will proceed no
further."

God's Challenge to Job

6 [a]Then the LORD answered Job
out of the whirlwind, and said:

7 "Now[a] [1]prepare yourself like a
man;
[b]I will question you, and you shall
answer Me:

8 "Would[a] you indeed [1]annul My
judgment?
Would you condemn Me that you
may be justified?
9 Have you an arm like God?
Or can you thunder with [a]a voice
like His?
10 [a]Then adorn yourself *with*
majesty and splendor,
And array yourself with glory
and beauty.
11 Disperse the rage of your wrath;
Look on everyone *who is* proud,
and humble him.
12 Look on everyone *who is* [a]proud,
and bring him low;
Tread down the wicked in their
place.
13 Hide them in the dust together,
Bind their faces in hidden
darkness.
14 Then I will also confess to you
That your own right hand can
save you.

15 "Look now at the [1]behemoth,
which I made *along* with you;
He eats grass like an ox.
16 See now, his strength *is* in his
hips,
And his power *is* in his stomach
muscles.
17 He moves his tail like a cedar;
The sinews of his thighs are
tightly knit.
18 His bones *are like* beams of
bronze,
His ribs like bars of iron.
19 He *is* the first of the [a]ways of God;
Only He who made him can bring
near His sword.
20 Surely the mountains [a]yield food
for him,

---

16 [a]Lam. 4:3 [1]Lit. *fear*
17 [a]Job 35:11
19 [1]Or *a mane*
20 [1]*make him spring*
21 [a]Jer. 8:6
27 [a]Prov. 30:18, 19 [b]Jer. 49:16; Obad. 4
30 [a]Matt. 24:28; Luke 17:37

CHAPTER 40

1 [a]Job 38:1
2 [a]Job 9:3; 10:2; 33:13 [b]Job 13:3; 23:4
4 [a]Ezra 9:6; Job 42:6 [b]Job 29:9; Ps. 39:9
6 [a]Job 38:1
7 [a]Job 38:3 [b]Job 42:4 [1]Lit. *gird up your loins*
8 [a]Job 16:11; 19:6; [Ps. 51:4; Rom. 3:4] [1]*nullify*
9 [a]Job 37:4; [Ps. 29:3, 4]
10 [a]Ps. 93:1; 104:1
12 [a]1 Sam. 2:7; [Is. 2:12; 13:11]; Dan. 4:37
15 [1]A large animal, exact identity unknown
19 [a]Job 26:14
20 [a]Ps. 104:14

And all the beasts of the field play there.
21 He lies under the lotus trees,
In a covert of reeds and marsh.
22 The lotus trees cover him *with* their shade;
The willows by the brook surround him.
23 Indeed the river may rage,
Yet he is not disturbed;
He is confident, though the Jordan gushes into his mouth,
24 *Though* he takes it in his eyes,
Or one pierces *his* nose with a snare.

41 "Can you draw out [a]Leviathan[1] with a hook,
Or *snare* his tongue with a line *which* you lower?
2 Can you [a]put a reed through his nose,
Or pierce his jaw with a [1]hook?
3 Will he make many supplications to you?
Will he speak softly to you?
4 Will he make a covenant with you?
Will you take him as a servant forever?
5 Will you play with him as *with* a bird,
Or will you leash him for your maidens?
6 Will *your* companions [1]make a banquet of him?
Will they apportion him among the merchants?
7 Can you fill his skin with harpoons,
Or his head with fishing spears?
8 Lay your hand on him;
Remember the battle—
Never do it again!
9 Indeed, *any* hope of *overcoming* him is false;
Shall *one not* be overwhelmed at the sight of him?
10 No one *is so* fierce that he would dare stir him up.
Who then is able to stand against Me?
11 [a]Who has preceded Me, that I should pay *him*?
[b]Everything under heaven is Mine.

12 "I will not [1]conceal his limbs,
His mighty power, or his graceful proportions.
13 Who can [1]remove his outer coat?
Who can approach *him* with a double bridle?
14 Who can open the doors of his face,
With his terrible teeth all around?
15 *His* rows of [1]scales are *his* pride,
Shut up tightly *as with* a seal;
16 One is so near another
That no air can come between them;
17 They are joined one to another,
They stick together and cannot be parted.
18 His sneezings flash forth light,
And his eyes *are* like the eyelids of the morning.
19 Out of his mouth go burning lights;
Sparks of fire shoot out.
20 Smoke goes out of his nostrils,
As *from* a boiling pot and burning rushes.
21 His breath kindles coals,
And a flame goes out of his mouth.
22 Strength dwells in his neck,
And [1]sorrow dances before him.
23 The folds of his flesh are joined together;
They are firm on him and cannot be moved.
24 His heart is as hard as stone,
Even as hard as the lower *millstone*.
25 When he raises himself up, the mighty are afraid;
Because of his crashings they [1]are beside themselves.
26 *Though* the sword reaches him, it cannot avail;
Nor does spear, dart, or javelin.
27 He regards iron as straw,
And bronze as rotten wood.
28 The arrow cannot make him flee;
Slingstones become like stubble to him.
29 Darts are regarded as straw;
He laughs at the threat of javelins.
30 His undersides *are* like sharp potsherds;
He spreads pointed *marks* in the mire.
31 He makes the deep boil like a pot;
He makes the sea like a pot of ointment.
32 He leaves a shining wake behind him;
One would think the deep had white hair.
33 On earth there is nothing like him,
Which is made without fear.
34 He beholds every high *thing*;
He *is* king over all the children of pride."

CHAPTER 41
1 [a]Ps. 74:14; 104:26; Is. 27:1 [1]A large sea creature, exact identity unknown
2 [a]2 Kin. 19:38; Is. 37:29 [1]thorn
6 [1]Or *bargain over him*
11 [a][Rom. 11:35] [b]Ex. 19:5; [Deut. 10:14; Job 9:5–10; 26:6–14]; Ps. 24:1; 50:12; 1 Cor. 10:26, 28
12 [1]Lit. *keep silent about*
13 [1]Lit. *take off the face of his garment*
15 [1]Lit. *shields*
22 [1]*despair*
25 [1]Or *purify themselves*

Job's Repentance and Restoration

42 Then Job answered the LORD and said:

2 "I know that You [a]can do everything,
And that no purpose *of Yours* can be withheld from You.
3 *You asked,* [a]'Who *is* this who hides counsel without knowledge?'
Therefore I have uttered what I did not understand,
[b]Things too wonderful for me, which I did not know.
4 Listen, please, and let me speak;
You said, [a]'I will question you, and you shall answer Me.'
5 "I have [a]heard of You by the hearing of the ear,
But now my eye sees You.
6 Therefore I [a]abhor[1] *myself,*
And repent in dust and ashes."

7 And so it was, after the LORD
had spoken these words to Job,
that the LORD said to Eliphaz the
Temanite, "My wrath is aroused
against you and your two friends,
for you have not spoken of Me
what is right, as My servant Job
has.
8 "Now therefore, take for your-
selves [a]seven bulls and seven
rams, [b]go to My servant Job, and
offer up for yourselves a burnt of-
fering; and My servant Job shall
[c]pray for you. For I will accept
[1]him, lest I deal with you *accord-*
ing to your folly; because you have
not spoken of Me *what is* right, as
My servant Job *has.*"

CHAPTER 42
2 [a]Gen. 18:14; [Matt. 19:26; Mark 10:27; 14:36; Luke 18:27]
3 [a]Job 38:2 [b]Ps. 40:5; 131:1; 139:6
4 [a]Job 38:3; 40:7
5 [a]Job 26:14; [Rom. 10:17]
6 [a]Ezra 9:6; Job 40:4 [1]*despise*
8 [a]Num. 23:1 [b][Matt. 5:24] [c]Gen. 20:17; [James 5:15, 16; 1 John 5:16] [1]Lit. *his face*
9 [1]Lit. *lifted up the face of Job*
10 [a]Deut. 30:3; Ps. 14:7; 85:1–3; 126:1 [b]Is. 40:2 [1]Lit. *turned the captivity of Job,* what was captured from Job
11 [a]Job 19:13
12 [a]Job 1:10; 8:7; James 5:11 [b]Job 1:3
13 [a]Job 1:2
14 [1]Lit. *Handsome as the Day* [2]*Cassia,* a fragrance [3]Lit. *The Horn of Color* or *The Colorful Ray*
16 [a]Job 5:26; Prov. 3:16
17 [a]Gen. 15:15; 25:8; Job 5:26

9 So Eliphaz the Temanite and
Bildad the Shuhite *and* Zophar
the Naamathite went and did as the
LORD commanded them; for the
LORD had [1]accepted Job.
10 [a]And the LORD [1]restored Job's
losses when he prayed for his
friends. Indeed the LORD gave Job
[b]twice as much as he had be-
fore.
11 Then [a]all his brothers, all his
sisters, and all those who had been
his acquaintances before, came to
him and ate food with him in his
house; and they consoled him and
comforted him for all the adversity
that the LORD had brought upon
him. Each one gave him a piece
of silver and each a ring of gold.
12 Now the LORD blessed [a]the lat-
ter *days* of Job more than his be-
ginning; for he had [b]fourteen thou-
sand sheep, six thousand camels,
one thousand yoke of oxen, and
one thousand female donkeys.
13 [a]He also had seven sons and
three daughters.
14 And he called the name of the
first [1]Jemimah, the name of the
second [2]Keziah, and the name of
the third [3]Keren-Happuch.
15 In all the land were found no
women *so* beautiful as the daugh-
ters of Job; and their father gave
them an inheritance among their
brothers.
16 After this Job [a]lived one hun-
dred and forty years, and saw his
children and grandchildren *for*
four generations.
17 So Job died, old and [a]full of
days.

The Book of

Psalms

THE Book of Psalms is the largest and perhaps most widely used book in the Bible. It explores the full range of human experience in a very personal and practical way. Its 150 "songs" run from the Creation through the patriarchal, theocratic, monarchical, exilic, and postexilic periods. The tremendous breadth of subject matter in the Psalms includes diverse topics, such as jubilation, war, peace, worship, judgment, messianic prophecy, praise, and lament. The Psalms were set to the accompaniment of stringed instruments and served as the temple hymnbook and devotional guide for the Jewish people.

The Book of Psalms was gradually collected and originally unnamed, perhaps due to the great variety of material. It came to be known as *Sepher Tehillim*—"Book of Praises"—because almost every psalm contains some note of praise to God. The Septuagint uses the Greek word *Psalmoi* as its title for this book, meaning "Poems Sung to the Accompaniment of Musical Instruments." It also calls it the *Psalterium* ("A Collection of Songs"), and this word is the basis for the term *Psalter*. The Latin title is *Liber Psalmorum,* "Book of Psalms."

BOOK ONE

Psalms 1—41

PSALM 1

The Way of the Righteous and the End of the Ungodly

BLESSED [a]*is* the man
Who walks not in the counsel of the [1]ungodly,
Nor stands in the path of sinners,
[b]Nor sits in the seat of the scornful;
2 But [a]his delight *is* in the law of the LORD,
[b]And in His law he [1]meditates day and night.
3 He shall be like a tree
[a]Planted by the [1]rivers of water,
That brings forth its fruit in its season,
Whose leaf also shall not wither;
And whatever he does shall [b]prosper.

4 The ungodly *are* not so,
But *are* [a]like the chaff which the wind drives away.
5 Therefore the ungodly shall not stand in the judgment,
Nor sinners in the congregation of the righteous.
6 For [a]the LORD knows the way of the righteous,
But the way of the ungodly shall perish.

PSALM 2

The Messiah's Triumph and Kingdom

WHY [a]do the [1]nations [2]rage,
And the people plot a [3]vain thing?
2 The kings of the earth set themselves,
And the [a]rulers take counsel together,
Against the LORD and against His [b]Anointed,[1] *saying,*
3 "Let [a]us break Their bonds in pieces
And cast away Their cords from us."

4 He who sits in the heavens [a]shall laugh;
The LORD shall hold them in derision.
5 Then He shall speak to them in His wrath,
And distress them in His deep displeasure:
6 "Yet I have [1]set My King
[2]On My holy hill of Zion."

CHAPTER 1

1 [a]Prov. 4:14 [b]Jer. 15:17 [1]*wicked*
2 [a]Ps. 119:14, 16, 35 [b][Josh. 1:8] [1]*ponders* by talking to himself
3 [a]Jer. 17:8 [b]Gen. 39:2, 3, 23 [1]*channels*
4 [a]Job 21:18
6 [a]Ps. 37:18

PSALM 2

1 [a]Acts 4:25, 26 [1]*Gentiles* [2]*throng tumultuously* [3]*worthless* or *empty*
2 [a][Mark 3:6; 11:18] [b][John 1:41] [1]Christ, Commissioned One, Heb. *Messiah*
3 [a]Luke 19:14
4 [a]Ps. 37:13
6 [1]Lit. *installed* [2]Lit. *Upon Zion, the hill of My holiness*

7 "I will declare the [1]decree:
The LORD has said to Me,
[a]'You *are* My Son,
Today I have begotten You.
8 Ask of Me, and I will give *You*
The nations *for* Your inheritance,
And the ends of the earth *for* Your possession.
9 [a]You shall [1]break them with a rod of iron;
You shall dash them to pieces like a potter's vessel.'"

10 Now therefore, be wise, O kings;
Be instructed, you judges of the earth.
11 Serve the LORD with fear,
And rejoice with trembling.
12 [1]Kiss the Son, lest [2]He be angry,
And you perish *in* the way,
When [a]His wrath is kindled but a little.
[b]Blessed *are* all those who put their trust in Him.

PSALM 3

The LORD Helps His Troubled People

A Psalm of David [a]when he fled from Absalom his son.

LORD, how they have increased who trouble me!
Many *are* they who rise up against me.
2 Many *are* they who say of me,
"*There is* no help for him in God." Selah

3 But You, O LORD, *are* [a]a shield [1]for me,
My glory and [b]the One who lifts up my head.
4 I cried to the LORD with my voice,
And [a]He heard me from His [b]holy hill. Selah

5 [a]I lay down and slept;
I awoke, for the LORD sustained me.
6 [a]I will not be afraid of ten thousands of people
Who have set *themselves* against me all around.

7 Arise, O LORD;
Save me, O my God!
[a]For You have struck all my enemies on the cheekbone;
You have broken the teeth of the ungodly.
8 [a]Salvation *belongs* to the LORD.
Your blessing *is* upon Your people. Selah

7 [a][Heb. 1:5; 5:5] [1]Or *decree of the LORD: He said to Me*
9 [a]Ps. 89:23; 110:5, 6 [1]So with MT, Tg.; LXX, Syr., Vg. *rule* (cf. Rev. 2:27)
12 [a][Rev. 6:16, 17] [b][Ps. 5:11; 34:22] [1]LXX, Vg. *Embrace discipline;* Tg. *Receive instruction* [2]LXX *the LORD*

PSALM 3

title [a]2 Sam. 15:13–17
3 [a]Ps. 5:12; 28:7 [b]Ps. 9:13; 27:6 [1]Lit. *around*
4 [a]Ps. 4:3; 34:4 [b]Ps. 2:6; 15:1; 43:3
5 [a]Lev. 26:6
6 [a]Ps. 23:4; 27:3
7 [a]Job 16:10
8 [a][Is. 43:11]

PSALM 4

title [1]*Choir Director*
1 [1]*Be gracious to me*
3 [a][2 Tim. 2:19] [1]Many Heb. mss., LXX, Tg., Vg. *made wonderful*
4 [a][Eph. 4:26] [b]Ps. 77:6 [1]Lit. *Tremble* or *Be agitated*
5 [a]Deut. 33:19 [b]Ps. 37:3, 5; 62:8
6 [a]Num. 6:26
7 [a]Is. 9:3
8 [a]Ps. 3:5 [b][Lev. 25:18]

PSALM 5

title [1]Heb. *nehiloth*
1 [a]Ps. 4:1 [1]Lit. *groaning*
3 [a]Ps. 55:17; 88:13
4 [1]Lit. *sojourn*
5 [a][Hab. 1:13] [b]Ps. 1:5

PSALM 4

The Safety of the Faithful

To the [1]Chief Musician. With stringed instruments. A Psalm of David.

HEAR me when I call, O God of my righteousness!
You have relieved me in *my* distress;
[1]Have mercy on me, and hear my prayer.

2 How long, O you sons of men,
Will you turn my glory to shame?
How long will you love worthlessness
And seek falsehood? Selah
3 But know that [a]the LORD has [1]set apart for Himself him who is godly;
The LORD will hear when I call to Him.
4 [a]Be[1] angry, and do not sin.
[b]Meditate within your heart on your bed, and be still. Selah
5 Offer [a]the sacrifices of righteousness,
And [b]put your trust in the LORD.

6 *There are* many who say,
"Who will show us *any* good?"
[a]LORD, lift up the light of Your countenance upon us.
7 You have put [a]gladness in my heart,
More than in the season that their grain and wine increased.
8 [a]I will both lie down in peace, and sleep;
[b]For You alone, O LORD, make me dwell in safety.

PSALM 5

A Prayer for Guidance

To the Chief Musician. With [1]flutes. A Psalm of David.

GIVE [a]ear to my words, O LORD,
Consider my [1]meditation.
2 Give heed to the voice of my cry,
My King and my God,
For to You I will pray.
3 My voice You shall hear in the morning, O LORD;
[a]In the morning I will direct *it* to You,
And I will look up.

4 For You *are* not a God who takes pleasure in wickedness,
Nor shall evil [1]dwell with You.
5 The [a]boastful shall not [b]stand in Your sight;
You hate all workers of iniquity.

6 You shall destroy those who
speak falsehood;
The LORD abhors the
[a]bloodthirsty and deceitful
man.

7 But as for me, I will come into
Your house in the multitude of
Your mercy;
In fear of You I will worship
toward [1]Your holy temple.
8 [a]Lead me, O LORD, in Your
righteousness because of my
enemies;
Make Your way straight before
my face.

9 For *there is* no [1]faithfulness in
their mouth;
Their inward part *is* destruction;
[a]Their throat *is* an open tomb;
They flatter with their tongue.
10 Pronounce them guilty, O God!
Let them fall by their own
counsels;
Cast them out in the multitude of
their transgressions,
For they have rebelled against
You.

11 But let all those rejoice who put
their trust in You;
Let them ever shout for joy,
because You [1]defend them;
Let those also who love Your
name
Be joyful in You.
12 For You, O LORD, will bless the
righteous;
With favor You will surround
him as *with* a shield.

PSALM 6

A Prayer of Faith in Time of Distress

To the Chief Musician. With stringed instruments. [a]On [1]an eight-stringed harp. A Psalm of David.

O LORD, [a]do not rebuke me in
Your anger,
Nor chasten me in Your hot
displeasure.
2 Have mercy on me, O LORD, for
I *am* weak;
O LORD, [a]heal me, for my bones
are troubled.
3 My soul also is greatly [a]troubled;
But You, O LORD—how long?

4 Return, O LORD, deliver me!
Oh, save me for Your mercies'
sake!
5 [a]For in death *there is* no
remembrance of You;
In the grave who will give You
thanks?

6 I am weary with my groaning;
[1]All night I make my bed swim;
I drench my couch with my tears.
7 [a]My eye wastes away because of
grief;
It grows old because of all my
enemies.

8 [a]Depart from me, all you workers
of iniquity;
For the LORD has [b]heard the voice
of my weeping.
9 The LORD has heard my
supplication;
The LORD will receive my prayer.
10 Let all my enemies be ashamed
and greatly troubled;
Let them turn back *and* be
ashamed suddenly.

PSALM 7

Prayer and Praise for Deliverance from Enemies

A [a]Meditation[1] of David, which he sang to the LORD [b]concerning the words of Cush, a Benjamite.

O LORD my God, in You I put my
trust;
[a]Save me from all those who
persecute me;
And deliver me,
2 [a]Lest they tear me like a lion,
[b]Rending *me* in pieces, while *there*
is none to deliver.

3 O LORD my God, [a]if I have done
this:
If there is [b]iniquity in my hands,
4 If I have repaid evil to him who
was at peace with me,
Or [a]have plundered my enemy
without cause,
5 Let the enemy pursue me and
overtake *me*;
Yes, let him trample my life to the
earth,
And lay my honor in the dust.
Selah

6 Arise, O LORD, in Your anger;
[a]Lift Yourself up because of the
rage of my enemies;
[b]Rise up [1]for me *to* the judgment
You have commanded!
7 So the congregation of the
peoples shall surround You;
For their sakes, therefore, return
on high.
8 The LORD shall judge the peoples;
[a]Judge me, O LORD, [b]according to
my righteousness,

---

6 [a]Ps. 55:23
7 [1]Lit. *the temple of Your holiness*
8 [a]Ps. 25:4, 5; 27:11; 31:3
9 [a]Rom. 3:13 [1]*uprightness*
11 [1]*protect*, lit. *cover*

PSALM 6

title [a]Ps. 12:title [1]Heb. *sheminith*
1 [a]Ps. 38:1; 118:18; [Jer. 10:24]
2 [a]Ps. 41:4; 147:3; [Hos. 6:1]
3 [a]Ps. 88:3; John 12:27
5 [a]Ps. 30:9; 88:10–12; 115:17; [Eccl. 9:10]; Is. 38:18
6 [1]Or *Every night*
7 [a]Job 17:7; Ps. 31:9
8 [a][Matt. 25:41] [b]Ps. 3:4; 28:6

PSALM 7

title [a]Hab. 3:1 [b]2 Sam. 16 [1]Heb. *Shiggaion*
1 [a]Ps. 31:15
2 [a]Ps. 57:4; Is. 38:13 [b]Ps. 50:22
3 [a]2 Sam. 16:7 [b]1 Sam. 24:11
4 [a]1 Sam. 24:7; 26:9
6 [a]Ps. 94:2 [b]Ps. 35:23; 44:23 [1]So with MT, Tg., Vg.; LXX *O LORD my God*
8 [a]Ps. 26:1; 35:24; 43:1 [b]Ps. 18:20; 35:24

And according to my integrity
within me.

9 Oh, let the wickedness of the
wicked come to an end,
But establish the just;
[a]For the righteous God tests the
hearts and [1]minds.
10 [1]My defense *is* of God,
Who saves the [a]upright in heart.

11 God *is* a just judge,
And God is angry *with the wicked* every day.
12 If he does not turn back,
He will [a]sharpen His sword;
He bends His bow and makes it
ready.
13 He also prepares for Himself
instruments of death;
He makes His arrows into fiery
shafts.

14 [a]Behold, *the wicked* brings forth
iniquity;
Yes, he conceives trouble and
brings forth falsehood.
15 He made a pit and dug it out,
[a]And has fallen into the ditch
which he made.
16 [a]His trouble shall return upon his
own head,
And his violent dealing shall
come down on [1]his own crown.

17 I will praise the LORD according
to His righteousness,
And will sing praise to the name
of the LORD Most High.

PSALM 8

The Glory of the LORD in Creation

To the Chief Musician. [1]On the instrument of Gath. A Psalm of David.

O LORD, our Lord,
How [a]excellent *is* Your name in
all the earth,
Who have [b]set Your glory above
the heavens!

2 [a]Out of the mouth of babes and
nursing infants
You have [1]ordained strength,
Because of Your enemies,
That You may silence [b]the enemy
and the avenger.

3 When I [a]consider Your heavens,
the work of Your fingers,
The moon and the stars, which
You have ordained,
4 [a]What is man that You are
mindful of him,
And the son of man that You
[b]visit[1] him?
5 For You have made him a little
lower than [1]the angels,
And You have crowned him with
glory and honor.

6 [a]You have made him to have
dominion over the works of
Your hands;
[b]You have put all *things* under his
feet,
7 All sheep and oxen—
Even the beasts of the field,
8 The birds of the air,
And the fish of the sea
That pass through the paths of
the seas.

9 [a]O LORD, our Lord,
How excellent *is* Your name in all
the earth!

PSALM 9

Prayer and Thanksgiving for the LORD's Righteous Judgments

To the Chief Musician. To *the tune of* [1]"Death of the Son." A Psalm of David.

I WILL praise *You,* O LORD, with
my whole heart;
I will tell of all Your marvelous
works.
2 I will be glad and [a]rejoice in You;
I will sing praise to Your name,
[b]O Most High.

3 When my enemies turn back,
They shall fall and perish at Your
presence.
4 For You have maintained my
right and my cause;
You sat on the throne judging in
righteousness.
5 You have rebuked the [1]nations,
You have destroyed the wicked;
You have [a]blotted out their name
forever and ever.

6 O enemy, destructions are
finished forever!
And you have destroyed cities;
Even their memory has
[a]perished.
7 [a]But the LORD shall endure
forever;
He has prepared His throne for
judgment.
8 [a]He shall judge the world in
righteousness,
And He shall administer
judgment for the peoples in
uprightness.

---

9 [a][1 Sam. 16:7] [1]Lit. *kidneys,* the most secret part of man
10 [a]Ps. 97:10, 11; 125:4 [1]Lit. *My shield is upon God*
12 [a]Deut. 32:41
14 [a]Job 15:35; Is. 59:4; [James 1:15]
15 [a][Job 4:8]; Ps. 57:6
16 [a]Esth. 9:25; Ps. 140:9 [1]The crown of his own head

PSALM 8

title [1]Heb. *Al Gittith*
1 [a]Ps. 148:13 [b]Ps. 113:4
2 [a]Matt. 21:16; [1 Cor. 1:27] [b]Ps. 44:16 [1]*established*
3 [a]Ps. 111:2
4 [a]Job 7:17, 18; [Heb. 2:6–8] [b][Job 10:12] [1]*give attention to* or *care for*
5 [1]Heb. *Elohim, God;* LXX, Syr., Tg., Jewish tradition *angels*
6 [a][Gen. 1:26, 28] [b][1 Cor. 15:27; Eph. 1:22; Heb. 2:8]
9 [a]Ps. 8:1

PSALM 9

title [1]Heb. *Muth Labben*
2 [a]Ps. 5:11; 104:34 [b][Ps. 83:18; 92:1]
5 [a]Prov. 10:7 [1]*Gentiles*
6 [a][Ps. 34:16]
7 [a]Ps. 102:12, 26; Heb. 1:11
8 [a][Ps. 96:13; 98:9; Acts 17:31]

9 The LORD also will be a [a]refuge[1]
for the oppressed,
A refuge in times of trouble.
10 And those who [a]know Your name
will put their trust in You;
For You, LORD, have not forsaken
those who seek You.

11 Sing praises to the LORD, who
dwells in Zion!
[a]Declare His deeds among the
people.
12 [a]When He avenges blood, He
remembers them;
He does not forget the cry of the
[1]humble.

13 Have mercy on me, O LORD!
Consider my trouble from those
who hate me,
You who lift me up from the gates
of death,
14 That I may tell of all Your praise
In the gates of [1]the daughter of
Zion.
I will [a]rejoice in Your salvation.
15 [a]The [1]nations have sunk down in
the pit *which* they made;
In the net which they hid, their
own foot is caught.
16 The LORD is [a]known *by* the
judgment He executes;
The wicked is snared in the work
of his own hands.
[b]Meditation.[1] Selah
17 The wicked shall be turned into
hell,
And all the [1]nations [a]that forget
God.
18 [a]For the needy shall not always be
forgotten;
[b]The expectation of the poor shall
not perish forever.

19 Arise, O LORD,
Do not let man prevail;
Let the [1]nations be judged in
Your sight.
20 Put them in fear, O LORD,
That the [1]nations may know
themselves *to be but* men.
Selah

PSALM 10

A Song of Confidence in God's Triumph over Evil

WHY do You stand afar off,
O LORD?
Why do You hide in times of
trouble?
2 The wicked in *his* pride
[1]persecutes the poor;
[a]Let them be caught in the plots
which they have devised.

3 For the wicked [a]boasts of his
heart's desire;
[1]He [b]blesses the greedy *and*
renounces the LORD.
4 The wicked in his proud
countenance does not seek
God;
[1]God *is* in none of his [a]thoughts.

5 His ways [1]are always prospering;
Your judgments *are* far above,
out of his sight;
As for all his enemies, he sneers
at them.
6 [a]He has said in his heart,
"I shall not be moved;
[b]I shall never be in adversity."
7 [a]His mouth is full of cursing and
[b]deceit and oppression;
Under his tongue *is* trouble and
iniquity.

8 He sits in the lurking places of
the villages;
In the secret places he murders
the innocent;
His eyes are secretly fixed on the
helpless.
9 He lies in wait secretly, as a lion
in his den;
He lies in wait to catch the poor;
He catches the poor when he
draws him into his net.
10 So [1]he crouches, he lies low,
That the helpless may fall by his
[2]strength.
11 He has said in his heart,
"God has forgotten;
He hides His face;
He will never see."

12 Arise, O LORD!
O God, [a]lift up Your hand!
Do not forget the [b]humble.
13 Why do the wicked renounce
God?
He has said in his heart,
"You will not require *an account.*"

14 But You have [a]seen, for You
observe trouble and grief,
To repay *it* by Your hand.
The helpless [b]commits[1] himself to
You;
[c]You are the helper of the
fatherless.
15 Break the arm of the wicked and
the evil *man;*
Seek out his wickedness *until*
You find none.

16 [a]The LORD *is* King forever and
ever;

---

9 [a]Ps. 32:7; 46:1; 91:2 [1]Lit. *secure height*
10 [a]Ps. 91:14
11 [a]Ps. 66:16; 107:22
12 [a][Gen. 9:5; Ps. 72:14] [1]*afflicted*
14 [a]Ps. 13:5; 20:5; 35:9 [1]Jerusalem
15 [a]Ps. 7:15, 16 [1]*Gentiles*
16 [a]Ex. 7:5 [b]Ps. 92:3 [1]Heb. *Higgaion*
17 [a]Job 8:13; Ps. 50:22 [1]*Gentiles*
18 [a]Ps. 9:12; 12:5 [b][Ps. 62:5; 71:5]; Prov. 23:18
19 [1]*Gentiles*
20 [1]*Gentiles*

PSALM 10

2 [a]Ps. 7:16; 9:16 [1]*hotly pursues*
3 [a]Ps. 49:6; 94:3, 4 [b]Prov. 28:4 [1]Or *The greedy man curses and spurns the LORD*
4 [a]Ps. 14:1; 36:1 [1]Or *All his thoughts are, "There is no God"*
5 [1]Lit. *are strong*
6 [a]Ps. 49:11; [Eccl. 8:11] [b]Rev. 18:7
7 [a][Rom. 3:14] [b]Ps. 55:10, 11
10 [1]Or *he is crushed, is bowed* [2]Or *mighty ones*
12 [a]Ps. 17:7; 94:2; Mic. 5:9 [b]Ps. 9:12
14 [a][Ps. 11:4] [b][2 Tim. 1:12] [c]Ps. 68:5; Hos. 14:3 [1]Lit. *leaves,* entrusts
16 [a]Ps. 29:10

The nations have perished out of
His land.
17 LORD, You have heard the desire
of the humble;
You will prepare their heart;
You will cause Your ear to hear,
18 To [1]do justice to the fatherless
and the oppressed,
That the man of the earth may
[2]oppress no more.

PSALM 11

Faith in the LORD's Righteousness

To the Chief Musician. A Psalm of David.

IN [a]the LORD I put my trust;
How can you say to my soul,
"Flee *as* a bird to your mountain"?
2 For look! [a]The wicked bend *their*
bow,
They make ready their arrow on
the string,
That they may shoot [1]secretly at
the upright in heart.
3 [a]If the foundations are destroyed,
What can the righteous do?

4 The LORD *is* in His holy temple,
The LORD's [a]throne *is* in heaven;
[b]His eyes behold,
His eyelids test the sons of men.
5 The LORD [a]tests the righteous,
But the wicked and the one who
loves violence His soul hates.
6 Upon the wicked He will rain
coals;
Fire and brimstone and a burning
wind
[a]*Shall be* [1]the portion of their cup.

7 For the LORD *is* righteous,
He [a]loves righteousness;
[1]His countenance beholds the
upright.

PSALM 12

Man's Treachery and God's Constancy

To the Chief Musician. [a]On [1]an eight-stringed harp. A Psalm of David.

HELP,[1] LORD, for the godly man
[a]ceases!
For the faithful disappear from
among the sons of men.
2 [a]They speak idly everyone with
his neighbor;
With flattering lips *and* [1]a double
heart they speak.

3 May the LORD [1]cut off all
flattering lips,
And the tongue that speaks
[2]proud things,

18 [1]*vindicate* [2]*terrify*

PSALM 11

1 [a]Ps. 56:11

2 [a]Ps. 64:3, 4 [1]Lit. *in darkness*

3 [a]Ps. 82:5; 87:1; 119:152

4 [a]Ps. 2:4; [Is. 66:1]; Matt. 5:34; 23:22; [Acts 7:49]; Rev. 4:2 [b][Ps. 33:18; 34:15, 16]

5 [a]Gen. 22:1; [James 1:12]

6 [a]1 Sam. 1:4; Ps. 75:8; Ezek. 38:22 [1]Their allotted portion or serving

7 [a]Ps. 33:5; 45:7 [1]Or *The upright beholds His countenance*

PSALM 12

title [a]Ps. 6:title [1]Heb. *sheminith*

1 [a][Is. 57:1]; Mic. 7:2 [1]*Save*

2 [a]Ps. 10:7; 41:6 [1]An inconsistent mind

3 [1]*destroy* [2]*great*

6 [a]2 Sam. 22:31; Ps. 18:30; 119:140; Prov. 30:5

PSALM 13

1 [a]Job 13:24; Ps. 89:46

3 [a]1 Sam. 14:29; Ezra 9:8; Job 33:30; Ps. 18:28 [b]Jer. 51:39

PSALM 14

1 [a]Ps. 10:4; 53:1

4 Who have said,
"With our tongue we will prevail;
Our lips *are* our own;
Who *is* lord over us?"

5 "For the oppression of the poor,
for the sighing of the needy,
Now I will arise," says the LORD;
"I will set *him* in the safety for
which he yearns."

6 The words of the LORD *are* [a]pure
words,
Like silver tried in a furnace of
earth,
Purified seven times.
7 You shall keep them, O LORD,
You shall preserve them from
this generation forever.

8 The wicked prowl on every side,
When vileness is exalted among
the sons of men.

PSALM 13

Trust in the Salvation of the LORD

To the Chief Musician. A Psalm of David.

HOW long, O LORD? Will You
forget me forever?
[a]How long will You hide Your face
from me?
2 How long shall I take counsel in
my soul,
Having sorrow in my heart daily?
How long will my enemy be
exalted over me?

3 Consider *and* hear me, O LORD
my God;
[a]Enlighten my eyes,
[b]Lest I sleep the *sleep of* death;
4 Lest my enemy say,
"I have prevailed against him";
Lest those who trouble me rejoice
when I am moved.

5 But I have trusted in Your mercy;
My heart shall rejoice in Your
salvation.
6 I will sing to the LORD,
Because He has dealt bountifully
with me.

PSALM 14

Folly of the Godless, and God's Final Triumph

To the Chief Musician. A Psalm of David.

THE [a]fool has said in his heart,
"*There is* no God."
They are corrupt,

They have done abominable
works,
There is none who does good.

2 [a]The LORD looks down from
heaven upon the children of
men,
To see if there are any who
understand, who seek God.
3 [a]They have all turned aside,
They have together become
corrupt;
There is none who does good,
No, not one.

4 Have all the workers of iniquity
no knowledge,
Who eat up my people *as* they eat
bread,
And [a]do not call on the LORD?
5 There they are in great fear,
For God *is* with the generation of
the righteous.
6 You shame the counsel of the
poor,
But the LORD *is* his [a]refuge.

7 [a]Oh,[1] that the salvation of Israel
would come out of Zion!
[b]When the LORD brings back [2]the
captivity of His people,
Let Jacob rejoice *and* Israel be
glad.

PSALM 15

The Character of Those Who May Dwell with the LORD

A Psalm of David.

LORD, [a]who may [1]abide in Your
tabernacle?
Who may dwell in Your holy hill?

2 He who walks uprightly,
And works righteousness,
And speaks the [a]truth in his
heart;
3 He *who* [a]does not backbite with
his tongue,
Nor does evil to his neighbor,
[b]Nor does he [1]take up a
reproach against his friend;
4 [a]In whose eyes a vile person is
despised,
But he honors those who fear
the LORD;
He *who* [b]swears to his own hurt
and does not change;
5 He *who* does not put out his
money at usury,
Nor does he take a bribe
against the innocent.

He who does these *things* [a]shall
never be moved.

2 [a]Ps. 33:13, 14; 102:19; Rom. 3:11
3 [a]Rom. 3:12
4 [a]Ps. 79:6; Is. 64:7; Jer. 10:25; Amos 8:4; Mic. 3:3
6 [a]Ps. 9:9; 40:17; 46:1; 142:5
7 [a]Ps. 53:6; [Rom. 11:25–27] [b]Deut. 30:3; Job 42:10 [1]Lit. *Who will give out of Zion the salvation of Israel?* [2]Or *His captive people*

PSALM 15

1 [a]Ps. 24:3–5 [1]*sojourn*
2 [a]Zech. 8:16; [Eph. 4:25]
3 [a][Lev. 19:16–18] [b]Ex. 23:1 [1]*receive*
4 [a]Esth. 3:2 [b]Lev. 5:4
5 [a]2 Pet. 1:10

PSALM 16

title [a]Ps. 56—60
1 [1]*Watch over*
2 [a]Job 35:7
3 [a]Ps. 119:63
4 [a]Ps. 106:37, 38 [b][Ex. 23:13]; Josh. 23:7
5 [1]Lit. *uphold*
7 [1]Mind, lit. *kidneys*
8 [a][Acts 2:25–28]
9 [1]Or *dwell securely*
10 [a]Ps. 49:15; 86:13; Acts 2:31, 32; Heb. 13:20 [1]The abode of the dead [2]*undergo*
11 [a]Ps. 139:24; [Matt. 7:14]

PSALM 16

The Hope of the Faithful, and the Messiah's Victory

A [a]Michtam of David.

PRESERVE[1] me, O God, for in You
I put my trust.

2 *O my soul,* you have said to the
LORD,
"You *are* my Lord,
[a]My goodness is nothing apart
from You."
3 As for the saints who *are* on the
earth,
"They are the excellent ones, in
[a]whom is all my delight."

4 Their sorrows shall be multiplied
who hasten *after* another *god;*
Their drink offerings of [a]blood I
will not offer,
[b]Nor take up their names on my
lips.

5 O LORD, *You are* the portion of
my inheritance and my cup;
You [1]maintain my lot.
6 The lines have fallen to me in
pleasant *places;*
Yes, I have a good inheritance.

7 I will bless the LORD who has
given me counsel;
My [1]heart also instructs me in the
night seasons.
8 [a]I have set the LORD always before
me;
Because *He is* at my right hand I
shall not be moved.

9 Therefore my heart is glad, and
my glory rejoices;
My flesh also will [1]rest in hope.
10 [a]For You will not leave my soul
in [1]Sheol,
Nor will You allow Your Holy
One to [2]see corruption.
11 You will show me the [a]path of
life;
In Your presence *is* fullness of
joy;
At Your right hand *are* pleasures
forevermore.

PSALM 17

Prayer with Confidence in Final Salvation

A Prayer of David.

HEAR a just cause, O LORD,
Attend to my cry;
Give ear to my prayer *which is*
not from deceitful lips.

2 Let my vindication come from
Your presence;
Let Your eyes look on the things
that are upright.

3 You have tested my heart;
You have visited *me* in the night;
[a]You have [1]tried me and have
found [2]nothing;
I have purposed that my mouth
shall not [b]transgress.
4 Concerning the works of men,
By the word of Your lips,
I have kept away from the paths
of the destroyer.
5 [a]Uphold my steps in Your paths,
That my footsteps may not slip.

6 [a]I have called upon You, for You
will hear me, O God;
Incline Your ear to me, *and* hear
my speech.
7 Show Your marvelous
lovingkindness by Your right
hand,
O You who [1]save those who trust
in You
From those who rise up *against
them.*
8 Keep me as the [1]apple of Your
eye;
Hide me under the shadow of
Your wings,
9 From the wicked who oppress
me,
From my deadly enemies who
surround me.

10 They have closed up their [a]fat
hearts;
With their mouths they [b]speak
proudly.
11 They have now surrounded us in
our steps;
They have set their eyes,
crouching down to the earth,
12 As a lion is eager to tear his prey,
And like a young lion lurking in
secret places.

13 Arise, O LORD,
Confront him, cast him down;
Deliver my life from the wicked
with Your sword,
14 With Your hand from men,
O LORD,
From men of the world *who have*
their portion in *this* life,
And whose belly You fill with
Your hidden treasure.
They are satisfied with children,
And leave the rest of their
possession for their babes.

15 As for me, [a]I will see Your face
in righteousness;
[b]I shall be satisfied when I [c]awake
in Your likeness.

PSALM 17

3 [a]Job 23:10; Ps. 66:10; Zech. 13:9; [1 Pet. 1:7] [b]Ps. 39:1 [1]*examined* [2]Nothing evil

5 [a]Job 23:11; Ps. 44:18; 119:133

6 [a]Ps. 86:7; 116:2

7 [1]*deliver*

8 [1]*pupil*

10 [a]Ezek. 16:49 [b][1 Sam. 2:3]

15 [a][1 John 3:2] [b]Ps. 4:6, 7; 16:11 [c][Is. 26:19]

PSALM 18

title [a]Ps. 36:title [b]2 Sam. 22

1 [a]Ps. 144:1

2 [a]Heb. 2:13 [1]Lit. *rock* [2]Strength

3 [a]Ps. 76:4; Rev. 5:12

4 [a]Ps. 116:3 [1]Lit. *Belial*

7 [a]Acts 4:31

9 [a]Ps. 144:5

10 [a]Ps. 80:1; 99:1 [b][Ps. 104:3]

11 [a]Ps. 97:2

12 [a]Ps. 97:3; 140:10; Hab. 3:11

PSALM 18

God the Sovereign Savior

To the Chief Musician. A Psalm of David [a]the servant of the LORD, who spoke to the LORD the words of [b]this song on the day that the LORD delivered him from the hand of all his enemies and from the hand of Saul. And he said:

I [a]WILL love You, O LORD, my
strength.
2 The LORD is my rock and my
fortress and my deliverer;
My God, my [1]strength, [a]in whom
I will trust;
My shield and the [2]horn of my
salvation, my stronghold.
3 I will call upon the LORD, [a]*who
is worthy* to be praised;
So shall I be saved from my
enemies.

4 [a]The pangs of death surrounded
me,
And the floods of [1]ungodliness
made me afraid.
5 The sorrows of Sheol surrounded
me;
The snares of death confronted
me.
6 In my distress I called upon the
LORD,
And cried out to my God;
He heard my voice from His
temple,
And my cry came before Him,
even to His ears.

7 [a]Then the earth shook and
trembled;
The foundations of the hills also
quaked and were shaken,
Because He was angry.
8 Smoke went up from His nostrils,
And devouring fire from His
mouth;
Coals were kindled by it.
9 [a]He bowed the heavens also, and
came down
With darkness under His feet.
10 [a]And He rode upon a cherub, and
flew;
[b]He flew upon the wings of the
wind.
11 He made darkness His secret
place;
[a]His canopy around Him *was* dark
waters
And thick clouds of the skies.
12 [a]From the brightness before Him,
His thick clouds passed with
hailstones and coals of fire.

13 The LORD thundered from
heaven,
And the Most High uttered [a]His
voice,
[1]Hailstones and coals of fire.
14 [a]He sent out His arrows and
scattered [1]the foe,
Lightnings in abundance, and He
vanquished them.
15 Then the channels of the sea were
seen,
The foundations of the world
were uncovered
At Your rebuke, O LORD,
At the blast of the breath of Your
nostrils.

16 [a]He sent from above, He took me;
He drew me out of many waters.
17 He delivered me from my strong
enemy,
From those who hated me,
For they were too strong for me.
18 They confronted me in the day of
my calamity,
But the LORD was my support.
19 [a]He also brought me out into a
broad place;
He delivered me because He
delighted in me.

20 [a]The LORD rewarded me
according to my righteousness;
According to the cleanness of my
hands
He has recompensed me.
21 For I have kept the ways of the
LORD,
And have not wickedly departed
from my God.
22 For all His judgments *were* before
me,
And I did not put away His
statutes from me.
23 I was also blameless [1]before Him,
And I kept myself from my
iniquity.
24 [a]Therefore the LORD has
recompensed me according to
my righteousness,
According to the cleanness of my
hands in His sight.

25 [a]With the merciful You will show
Yourself merciful;
With a blameless man You will
show Yourself blameless;
26 With the pure You will show
Yourself pure;
And [a]with the devious You will
show Yourself shrewd.
27 For You will save the humble
people,
But will bring down [a]haughty
looks.
28 [a]For You will light my lamp;
The LORD my God will enlighten
my darkness.
29 For by You I can [1]run against a
troop,
By my God I can leap over a wall.
30 *As for* God, [a]His way *is* perfect;
[b]The word of the LORD is [1]proven;
He *is* a shield [c]to all who trust in
Him.

31 [a]For who *is* God, except the LORD?
And who *is* a rock, except our
God?
32 *It is* God who [a]arms me with
strength,
And makes my way perfect.
33 [a]He makes my feet like the *feet
of* deer,
And [b]sets me on my high places.
34 [a]He teaches my hands to make
war,
So that my arms can bend a bow
of bronze.

35 You have also given me the shield
of Your salvation;
Your right hand has held me up,
Your gentleness has made me
great.
36 You enlarged my path under me,
[a]So my feet did not slip.

37 I have pursued my enemies and
overtaken them;
Neither did I turn back again till
they were destroyed.
38 I have wounded them,
So that they could not rise;
They have fallen under my feet.
39 For You have armed me with
strength for the battle;
You have [1]subdued under me
those who rose up against me.
40 You have also given me the necks
of my enemies,
So that I destroyed those who
hated me.
41 They cried out, but *there was*
none to save;
[a]*Even* to the LORD, but He did not
answer them.
42 Then I beat them as fine as the
dust before the wind;
I [a]cast them out like dirt in the
streets.

43 You have delivered me from the
strivings of the people;
[a]You have made me the head of
the [1]nations;
[b]A people I have not known shall
serve me.
44 As soon as they hear of me they
obey me;

13 [a][Ps. 29:3–9; 104:7] [1]So with MT, Tg., Vg.; a few Heb. mss., LXX omit *Hailstones and coals of fire*
14 [a]Josh. 10:10; Ps. 144:6; Is. 30:30; Hab. 3:11 [1]Lit. *them*
16 [a]Ps. 144:7
19 [a]Ps. 4:1; 31:8; 118:5
20 [a]1 Sam. 24:19; [Job 33:26]; Ps. 7:8
23 [1]*with*
24 [a]1 Sam. 26:23; Ps. 18:20
25 [a][1 Kin. 8:32; Ps. 62:12]; Matt. 5:7
26 [a][Lev. 26:23–28]; Prov. 3:34
27 [a][Ps. 101:5]; Prov. 6:17
28 [a]1 Kin. 15:4; Job 18:6; [Ps. 119:105]
29 [1]Or *run through*
30 [a][Deut. 32:4]; Rev. 15:3 [b]Ps. 12:6; 119:140; [Prov. 30:5] [c][Ps. 17:7] [1]Lit. *refined*
31 [a][Deut. 32:31, 39; 1 Sam. 2:2; Ps. 86:8–10; Is. 45:5]
32 [a][Ps. 91:2]
33 [a]2 Sam. 2:18; Hab. 3:19 [b]Deut. 32:13; 33:29
34 [a]Ps. 144:1
36 [a]Ps. 66:9; Prov. 4:12
39 [1]Lit. *caused to bow*
41 [a]Job 27:9; Prov. 1:28; Is. 1:15; Ezek. 8:18; Zech. 7:13
42 [a]Zech. 10:5
43 [a]2 Sam. 8; Ps. 89:27 [b]Is. 52:15 [1]*Gentiles*

The foreigners [1]submit to me.
45 [a]The foreigners fade away,
And come frightened from their hideouts.

46 The LORD lives!
Blessed *be* my Rock!
Let the God of my salvation be exalted.
47 *It is* God who avenges me,
[a]And subdues the peoples under me;
48 He delivers me from my enemies.
[a]You also lift me up above those who rise against me;
You have delivered me from the violent man.
49 [a]Therefore I will give thanks to You, O LORD, among the [1]Gentiles,
And sing praises to Your name.

50 [a]Great deliverance He gives to His king,
And shows mercy to His anointed,
To David and his [1]descendants forevermore.

44 [1]*feign submission*
45 [a]Mic. 7:17
47 [a]Ps. 47:3
48 [a]Ps. 27:6; 59:1
49 [a]2 Sam. 22:50; Rom. 15:9 [1]*nations*
50 [a]2 Sam. 7:12; Ps. 21:1; 144:10 [1]Lit. *seed*

PSALM 19

The Perfect Revelation of the LORD

To the Chief Musician. A Psalm of David.

THE [a]heavens declare the glory of God;
And the [b]firmament[1] shows [2]His handiwork.
2 Day unto day utters speech,
And night unto night reveals knowledge.
3 *There is* no speech nor language
Where their voice is not heard.
4 [a]Their [1]line has gone out through all the earth,
And their words to the end of the world.

In them He has set a [2]tabernacle for the sun,
5 Which *is* like a bridegroom coming out of his chamber,
[a]*And* rejoices like a strong man to run its race.
6 Its rising *is* from one end of heaven,
And its circuit to the other end;
And there is nothing hidden from its heat.

7 [a]The law of the LORD *is* perfect, [1]converting the soul;
The testimony of the LORD *is* sure, making [b]wise the simple;
8 The statutes of the LORD *are* right, rejoicing the heart;
The commandment of the LORD *is* pure, enlightening the eyes;
9 The fear of the LORD *is* clean, enduring forever;
The judgments of the LORD *are* true *and* righteous altogether.
10 More to be desired *are they* than [a]gold,
Yea, than much fine gold;
Sweeter also than honey and the [1]honeycomb.
11 Moreover by them Your servant is warned,
And in keeping them *there is* great reward.

12 Who can understand *his* errors?
[a]Cleanse me from secret *faults*.
13 Keep back Your servant also from [a]presumptuous *sins;*
Let them not have [b]dominion over me.
Then I shall be blameless,
And I shall be innocent of [1]great transgression.

14 [a]Let the words of my mouth and the meditation of my heart
Be acceptable in Your sight,
O LORD, my [1]strength and my [b]Redeemer.

PSALM 19

1 [a]Is. 40:22; [Rom. 1:19, 20] [b]Gen. 1:6, 7 [1]*expanse of heaven* [2]*the work of His hands*
4 [a]Rom. 10:18 [1]LXX, Syr., Vg. *sound;* Tg. *business* [2]*tent*
5 [a]Eccl. 1:5
7 [a]Ps. 111:7; [Rom. 7:12] [b]Ps. 119:130 [1]*restoring*
10 [a]Ps. 119:72, 127; Prov. 8:10, 11, 19 [1]*honey in the combs*
12 [a][Ps. 51:1, 2]
13 [a]Num. 15:30 [b]Ps. 119:133; [Rom. 6:12–14] [1]Or *much*
14 [a]Ps. 51:15 [b]Ps. 31:5; Is. 47:4 [1]Lit. *rock*

PSALM 20

The Assurance of God's Saving Work

To the Chief Musician. A Psalm of David.

MAY the LORD answer you in the day of trouble;
May the name of the God of Jacob [1]defend you;
2 May He send you help from the sanctuary,
And strengthen you out of Zion;
3 May He remember all your offerings,
And accept your burnt sacrifice. Selah

4 May He grant you according to your heart's *desire,*
And [a]fulfill all your [1]purpose.
5 We will rejoice in your salvation,
And in the name of our God we will set up *our* banners!
May the LORD fulfill all your petitions.

6 Now I know that the LORD saves His [1]anointed;
He will answer him from His holy heaven
With the saving strength of His right hand.

PSALM 20

1 [1]Lit. *set you on high*
4 [a]Ps. 21:2 [1]*counsel*
6 [1]Commissioned one, Heb. *messiah*

7 Some *trust* in chariots, and some in [a]horses;
But we will remember the name of the LORD our God.
8 They have bowed down and fallen;
But we have risen and stand upright.

9 Save, LORD!
May the King answer us when we call.

PSALM 21

Joy in the Salvation of the LORD

To the Chief Musician. A Psalm of David.

THE king shall have joy in Your strength, O LORD;
And in Your salvation how greatly shall he rejoice!
2 You have given him his heart's desire,
And have not withheld the [a]request of his lips. Selah

3 For You meet him with the blessings of goodness;
You set a crown of pure gold upon his head.
4 [a]He asked life from You, *and* You gave *it* to him—
Length of days forever and ever.
5 His glory *is* great in Your salvation;
Honor and majesty You have placed upon him.
6 For You have made him most blessed forever;
[a]You have made him [1]exceedingly glad with Your presence.
7 For the king trusts in the LORD,
And through the mercy of the Most High he shall not be [1]moved.

8 Your hand will find all Your enemies;
Your right hand will find those who hate You.
9 You shall make them as a fiery oven in the time of Your anger;
The LORD shall swallow them up in His wrath,
And the fire shall devour them.
10 Their offspring You shall destroy from the earth,
And their [1]descendants from among the sons of men.
11 For they intended evil against You;
They devised a plot *which* they are not able *to* [a]*perform*.

7 [a]Deut. 20:1; Ps. 33:16, 17; Prov. 21:31; Is. 31:1

PSALM 21

2 [a]2 Sam. 7:26–29

4 [a]Ps. 61:5, 6; 133:3

6 [a]Ps. 16:11; 45:7 [1]Lit. *joyful with gladness*

7 [1]*shaken*

10 [1]Lit. *seed*

11 [a]Ps. 2:1–4

PSALM 22

title [1]Heb. *Aijeleth Hashahar*

1 [a][Matt. 27:46; Mark 15:34]

3 [a]Deut. 10:21; Ps. 148:14

5 [a]Is. 49:23

6 [a]Job 25:6; Is. 41:14 [b]Ps. 109:25; [Is. 53:3]; Matt. 27:39–44

7 [a]Matt. 27:39; Mark 15:29 [1]*Show contempt with their mouth*

8 [a]Matt. 27:43; Luke 23:35 [b]Ps. 91:14 [1]LXX, Syr., Vg. *hoped;* Tg. *praised*

9 [a][Ps. 71:5, 6]

10 [a][Is. 46:3; 49:1]; Luke 1:35

12 [a]Ps. 22:21; 68:30 [b]Deut. 32:14

12 Therefore You will make them turn their back;
You will make ready *Your arrows* on Your string toward their faces.

13 Be exalted, O LORD, in Your own strength!
We will sing and praise Your power.

PSALM 22

The Suffering, Praise, and Posterity of the Messiah

To the Chief Musician. Set to [1]"The Deer of the Dawn." A Psalm of David.

MY [a]God, My God, why have You forsaken Me?
Why are You so far from helping Me,
And from the words of My groaning?
2 O My God, I cry in the daytime, but You do not hear;
And in the night season, and am not silent.

3 But You *are* holy,
Enthroned in the [a]praises of Israel.
4 Our fathers trusted in You;
They trusted, and You delivered them.
5 They cried to You, and were delivered;
[a]They trusted in You, and were not ashamed.

6 But I *am* [a]a worm, and no man;
[b]A reproach of men, and despised by the people.
7 [a]All those who see Me ridicule Me;
They [1]shoot out the lip, they shake the head, *saying,*
8 "He[a] [1]trusted in the LORD, let Him rescue Him;
[b]Let Him deliver Him, since He delights in Him!"

9 [a]But You *are* He who took Me out of the womb;
You made Me trust *while* on My mother's breasts.
10 I was cast upon You from birth.
From My mother's womb
[a]You *have been* My God.
11 Be not far from Me,
For trouble *is* near;
For *there is* none to help.

12 [a]Many bulls have surrounded Me;
Strong *bulls* of [b]Bashan have encircled Me.

13 [a]They [1]gape at Me *with* their
mouths,
Like a raging and roaring lion.

14 I am poured out like water,
[a]And all My bones are out of joint;
My heart is like wax;
It has melted [1]within Me.
15 [a]My strength is dried up like a
potsherd,
And [b]My tongue clings to My
jaws;
You have brought Me to the dust
of death.

16 For dogs have surrounded Me;
The congregation of the wicked
has enclosed Me.
[a]They[1] pierced My hands and My
feet;
17 I can count all My bones.
[a]They look *and* stare at Me.
18 [a]They divide My garments among
them,
And for My clothing they cast
lots.

19 But You, O LORD, do not be far
from Me;
O My Strength, hasten to help
Me!
20 Deliver Me from the sword,
[a]My[1] precious *life* from the power
of the dog.
21 [a]Save Me from the lion's mouth
And from the horns of the wild
oxen!

[b]You have answered Me.

22 [a]I will declare Your name to [b]My
brethren;
In the midst of the assembly I will
praise You.
23 [a]You who fear the LORD, praise
Him!
All you [1]descendants of Jacob,
glorify Him,
And fear Him, all you offspring
of Israel!
24 For He has not despised nor
abhorred the affliction of the
afflicted;
Nor has He hidden His face from
Him;
But [a]when He cried to Him, He
heard.

25 [a]My praise *shall be* of You in the
great assembly;
[b]I will pay My vows before those
who fear Him.
26 The poor shall eat and be
satisfied;
Those who seek Him will praise
the LORD.
Let your heart live forever!

27 All the ends of the world
Shall remember and turn to the
LORD,
And all the families of the
[1]nations
Shall worship before [2]You.
28 [a]For the kingdom *is* the LORD's,
And He rules over the nations.

29 [a]All the prosperous of the earth
Shall eat and worship;
[b]All those who go down to [1]the
dust
Shall bow before Him,
Even he who cannot keep himself
alive.

30 A posterity shall serve Him.
It will be recounted of the Lord
to the *next* generation,
31 They will come and declare His
righteousness to a people who
will be born,
That He has done *this*.

PSALM 23

The LORD the Shepherd of His People

A Psalm of David.

THE LORD *is* [a]my shepherd;
[b]I shall not [1]want.
2 [a]He makes me to lie down in
[1]green pastures;
[b]He leads me beside the [2]still
waters.
3 He restores my soul;
[a]He leads me in the paths of
righteousness
For His name's sake.

4 Yea, though I walk through the
valley of [a]the shadow of
death,
[b]I will fear no evil;
[c]For You *are* with me;
Your rod and Your staff, they
comfort me.

5 You [a]prepare a table before me
in the presence of my
enemies;
You [b]anoint my head with oil;
My cup runs over.
6 Surely goodness and mercy shall
follow me
All the days of my life;
And I will [1]dwell in the house of
the LORD
[2]Forever.

13 [a]Job 16:10 [1]Lit. *have opened their mouths at Me*
14 [a]Dan. 5:6 [1]Lit. *in the midst of My bowels*
15 [a]Prov. 17:22 [b]John 19:28
16 [a]Matt. 27:35 [1]So with some Heb. mss., LXX, Syr., Vg.; MT *Like a lion* instead of *They pierced*
17 [a]Luke 23:27, 35
18 [a]Matt. 27:35
20 [a]Ps. 35:17 [1]Lit. *My only one*
21 [a]2 Tim. 4:17 [b]Is. 34:7
22 [a]Heb. 2:12 [b][Rom. 8:29]
23 [a]Ps. 135:19, 20 [1]Lit. *seed*
24 [a]Heb. 5:7
25 [a]Ps. 35:18; 40:9, 10 [b]Eccl. 5:4
27 [1]*Gentiles* [2]So with MT, LXX, Tg.; Arab., Syr., Vg. *Him*
28 [a]Matt. 6:13
29 [a]Ps. 17:10; 45:12 [b][Is. 26:19] [1]Death

PSALM 23

1 [a][Is. 40:11] [b][Phil. 4:19] [1]*lack*
2 [a]Ezek. 34:14 [b][Rev. 7:17] [1]Lit. *pastures of tender grass* [2]Lit. *waters of rest*
3 [a]Ps. 5:8; 31:3
4 [a]Job 3:5; 10:21, 22; 24:17 [b][Ps. 3:6; 27:1] [c][Is. 43:2]
5 [a]Ps. 104:15 [b]Ps. 92:10
6 [1]So with LXX, Syr., Tg., Vg.; MT *return* [2]Or *To the end of my days*, lit. *For length of days*

PSALM 24

The King of Glory and His Kingdom

A Psalm of David.

THE [a]earth *is* the LORD's, and all
its fullness,
The world and those who dwell
therein.
2 For He has [a]founded it upon the
seas,
And established it upon the
[1]waters.

3 [a]Who may ascend into the hill of
the LORD?
Or who may stand in His holy
place?
4 He who has [a]clean hands and [b]a
pure heart,
Who has not lifted up his soul to
an idol,
Nor [c]sworn deceitfully.
5 He shall receive blessing from the
LORD,
And righteousness from the God
of his salvation.
6 This *is* Jacob, the generation of
those who [a]seek Him,
Who seek Your face. Selah

7 [a]Lift up your heads, O you gates!
And be lifted up, you everlasting
doors!
[b]And the King of glory shall come
in.
8 Who *is* this King of glory?
The LORD strong and mighty,
The LORD mighty in [a]battle.
9 Lift up your heads, O you gates!
Lift up, you everlasting doors!
And the King of glory shall come
in.
10 Who is this King of glory?
The LORD of hosts,
He *is* the King of glory. Selah

PSALM 25

A Plea for Deliverance and Forgiveness

A Psalm of David.

TO [a]You, O LORD, I lift up
my soul.
2 O my God, I [a]trust in You;
Let me not be ashamed;
[b]Let not my enemies triumph over
me.
3 Indeed, let no one who [1]waits on
You be ashamed;
Let those be ashamed who deal
treacherously without cause.

4 [a]Show me Your ways, O LORD;
Teach me Your paths.
5 Lead me in Your truth and teach
me,
For You *are* the God of my
salvation;
On You I wait all the day.

6 Remember, O LORD, [a]Your tender
mercies and Your
lovingkindnesses,
For they *are* from of old.
7 Do not remember [a]the sins of my
youth, nor my transgressions;
[b]According to Your mercy
remember me,
For Your goodness' sake,
O LORD.

8 Good and upright *is* the LORD;
Therefore He teaches sinners in
the way.
9 The humble He guides in justice,
And the humble He teaches His
way.
10 All the paths of the LORD *are*
mercy and truth,
To such as keep His covenant and
His testimonies.
11 [a]For Your name's sake, O LORD,
Pardon my iniquity, for it *is* great.

12 Who *is* the man that fears the
LORD?
[a]Him shall [1]He teach in the way
[1]He chooses.
13 [a]He himself shall dwell in
[1]prosperity,
And [b]his descendants shall
inherit the earth.
14 [a]The secret of the LORD *is* with
those who fear Him,
And He will show them His
covenant.
15 [a]My eyes *are* ever toward the
LORD,
For He shall [1]pluck my feet out
of the net.

16 [a]Turn Yourself to me, and have
mercy on me,
For I *am* [1]desolate and afflicted.
17 The troubles of my heart have
enlarged;
Bring me out of my distresses!
18 [a]Look on my affliction and my
pain,
And forgive all my sins.
19 Consider my enemies, for they
are many;
And they hate me with [1]cruel
hatred.
20 Keep my soul, and deliver me;
Let me not be ashamed, for I put
my trust in You.
21 Let integrity and uprightness
preserve me,
For I wait for You.

CHAPTER 1

1 [a]1 Cor. 10:26, 28
2 [a]Ps. 89:11 [1]Lit. *rivers*
3 [a]Ps. 15:1–5
4 [a][Job 17:9]; Ps. 26:6 [b]Ps. 51:10; 73:1; [Matt. 5:8] [c]Ps. 15:4
6 [a]Ps. 27:4, 8
7 [a]Ps. 118:20; Is. 26:2 [b]Ps. 29:2, 9; 97:6; Hag. 2:7; Acts 7:2; [1 Cor. 2:8]
8 [a]Rev. 19:13–16

PSALM 25

1 [a]Ps. 86:4; 143:8
2 [a]Ps. 34:8 [b]Ps. 13:4; 41:11
3 [1]Waits for You in faith
4 [a]Ex. 33:13; Ps. 5:8; 27:11; 86:11; 119:27; 143:8
6 [a]Ps. 103:17; 106:1
7 [a]Job 13:26; [Jer. 3:25] [b]Ps. 51:1
11 [a]Ps. 31:3; 79:9; 109:21; 143:11
12 [a][Ps. 25:8; 37:23] [1]Or *he*
13 [a][Prov. 19:23] [b]Ps. 37:11; 69:36; Matt. 5:5 [1]Lit. *goodness*
14 [a][Prov. 3:32; John 7:17]
15 [a][Ps. 123:2; 141:8] [1]Lit. *bring out*
16 [a]Ps. 69:16 [1]*lonely*
18 [a]2 Sam. 16:12; Ps. 31:7
19 [1]*violent hatred*

22 [a]Redeem Israel, O God,
Out of all their troubles!

PSALM 26

A Prayer for Divine Scrutiny and Redemption

A Psalm of David.

VINDICATE [a]me, O LORD,
For I have [b]walked in my integrity.
[c]I have also trusted in the LORD;
I shall not slip.
2 [a]Examine me, O LORD, and [1]prove me;
Try my mind and my heart.
3 For Your lovingkindness *is* before my eyes,
And [a]I have walked in Your truth.
4 I have not [a]sat with idolatrous mortals,
Nor will I go in with hypocrites.
5 I have [a]hated the assembly of evildoers,
And will not sit with the wicked.

6 I will wash my hands in innocence;
So I will go about Your altar, O LORD,
7 That I may proclaim with the voice of thanksgiving,
And tell of all Your wondrous works.
8 LORD, [a]I have loved the habitation of Your house,
And the place [1]where Your glory dwells.

9 [a]Do[1] not gather my soul with sinners,
Nor my life with bloodthirsty men,
10 In whose hands *is* a sinister scheme,
And whose right hand is full of [a]bribes.

11 But as for me, I will walk in my integrity;
Redeem me and be merciful to me.
12 [a]My foot stands in an even place;
In the congregations I will bless the LORD.

PSALM 27

An Exuberant Declaration of Faith

A Psalm of David.

THE LORD *is* my [a]light and my salvation;
Whom shall I fear?
The [b]LORD *is* the strength of my life;
Of whom shall I be afraid?
2 When the wicked came against me
To [a]eat[1] up my flesh,
My enemies and foes,
They stumbled and fell.
3 [a]Though an army may encamp against me,
My heart shall not fear;
Though war may rise against me,
In this I *will be* confident.

4 [a]One *thing* I have desired of the LORD,
That will I seek:
That I may [b]dwell in the house of the LORD
All the days of my life,
To behold the [1]beauty of the LORD,
And to inquire in His temple.
5 For [a]in the time of trouble
He shall hide me in His pavilion;
In the secret place of His tabernacle
He shall hide me;
He shall [b]set me high upon a rock.

6 And now [a]my head shall be [1]lifted up above my enemies all around me;
Therefore I will offer sacrifices of [2]joy in His tabernacle;
I will sing, yes, I will sing praises to the LORD.

7 Hear, O LORD, *when* I cry with my voice!
Have mercy also upon me, and answer me.
8 *When You said,* "Seek My face,"
My heart said to You, "Your face, LORD, I will seek."
9 [a]Do not hide Your face from me;
Do not turn Your servant away in anger;
You have been my help;
Do not leave me nor forsake me,
O God of my salvation.
10 [a]When my father and my mother forsake me,
Then the LORD will take care of me.

11 [a]Teach me Your way, O LORD,
And lead me in a smooth path, because of my enemies.
12 Do not deliver me to the will of my adversaries;
For [a]false witnesses have risen against me,
And such as breathe out violence.

---

22 [a][Ps. 130:8]

PSALM 26

1 [a]Ps. 7:8 [b]2 Kin. 20:3; [Prov. 20:7] [c][Ps. 13:5; 28:7]
2 [a]Ps. 17:3; 139:23 [1]*test me*
3 [a]2 Kin. 20:3; Ps. 86:11
4 [a]Ps. 1:1; Jer. 15:17
5 [a]Ps. 31:6; 139:21
8 [a]Ps. 27:4; 84:1–4, 10 [1]Lit. *of the tabernacle of Your glory*
9 [a]Ps. 28:3 [1]*Do not take away*
10 [a]1 Sam. 8:3
12 [a]Ps. 40:2

PSALM 27

1 [a]Ps. 18:28; 84:11; [Is. 60:19, 20; Mic. 7:8] [b]Ex. 15:2; Ps. 62:7; 118:14; Is. 12:2; 33:2
2 [a]Ps. 14:4 [1]*devour*
3 [a]Ps. 3:6
4 [a]Ps. 26:8; 65:4 [b]Luke 2:37 [1]*delightfulness*
5 [a]Ps. 31:20; 91:1 [b]Ps. 40:2
6 [a]Ps. 3:3 [1]Lifted up in honor [2]*joyous shouts*
9 [a]Ps. 69:17; 143:7
10 [a]Is. 49:15
11 [a]Ps. 25:4; 86:11; 119:33
12 [a]Deut. 19:18; Ps. 35:11; Matt. 26:60; Mark 14:56; John 19:33

13 *I would have lost heart,* unless I
had believed
That I would see the goodness of
the LORD
[a]In the land of the living.

14 [a]Wait[1] on the LORD;
Be of good courage,
And He shall strengthen your
heart;
Wait, I say, on the LORD!

PSALM 28

Rejoicing in Answered Prayer

A Psalm of David.

TO You I will cry, O LORD my
Rock:
[a]Do not be silent to me,
[b]Lest, if You *are* silent to me,
I become like those who go down
to the pit.
2 Hear the voice of my
supplications
When I cry to You,
[a]When I lift up my hands [b]toward
Your holy sanctuary.

3 Do not [1]take me away with the
wicked
And with the workers of iniquity,
[a]Who speak peace to their
neighbors,
But evil *is* in their hearts.
4 [a]Give them according to their
deeds,
And according to the wickedness
of their endeavors;
Give them according to the work
of their hands;
Render to them what they
deserve.
5 Because [a]they do not regard the
works of the LORD,
Nor the operation of His hands,
He shall destroy them
And not build them up.

6 Blessed *be* the LORD,
Because He has heard the voice
of my supplications!
7 The LORD *is* [a]my strength and my
shield;
My heart [b]trusted in Him, and I
am helped;
Therefore my heart greatly
rejoices,
And with my song I will praise
Him.

8 The LORD *is* [1]their strength,
And He *is* the [a]saving refuge of
His [2]anointed.
9 Save Your people,
And bless [a]Your inheritance;
Shepherd them also,
[b]And bear them up forever.

PSALM 29

Praise to God in His Holiness and Majesty

A Psalm of David.

GIVE[1] [a]unto the LORD, O you
mighty ones,
Give unto the LORD glory and
strength.
2 [1]Give unto the LORD the glory [2]due
to His name;
Worship the LORD in [a]the [3]beauty
of holiness.

3 The voice of the LORD *is* over the
waters;
[a]The God of glory thunders;
The LORD *is* over many waters.
4 The voice of the LORD *is*
powerful;
The voice of the LORD *is* full of
majesty.

5 The voice of the LORD breaks [a]the
cedars,
Yes, the LORD splinters the
cedars of Lebanon.
6 [a]He makes them also skip like a
calf,
Lebanon and [b]Sirion like a young
wild ox.
7 The voice of the LORD [1]divides
the flames of fire.

8 The voice of the LORD shakes the
wilderness;
The LORD shakes the Wilderness
of [a]Kadesh.
9 The voice of the LORD makes the
[a]deer give birth,
And strips the forests bare;
And in His temple everyone says,
"Glory!"

10 The [a]LORD sat *enthroned* at the
Flood,
And [b]the LORD sits as King
forever.
11 [a]The LORD will give strength to
His people;
The LORD will bless His people
with peace.

PSALM 30

The Blessedness of Answered Prayer

A Psalm. A Song [a]at the dedication of the
house of David.

I WILL extol You, O LORD, for You
have [a]lifted me up,

---

13 [a]Ezek. 26:20
14 [a]Is. 25:9 [1]Wait in faith

PSALM 28

1 [a]Ps. 35:22; 39:12; 83:1 [b]Ps. 88:4; 143:7
2 [a]Ps. 5:7 [b]Ps. 138:2
3 [a]Ps. 12:2; 55:21; 62:4 [1]*drag*
4 [a][Rev. 18:6; 22:12]
5 [a]Is. 5:12
7 [a]Ps. 18:2; 59:17 [b]Ps. 13:5; 112:7
8 [a]Ps. 20:6 [1]So with MT, Tg.; LXX, Syr., Vg. *the strength of His people* [2]Commissioned one, Heb. *messiah*
9 [a][Deut. 9:29; 32:9] [b]Deut. 1:31

PSALM 29

1 [a]1 Chr. 16:28, 29 [1]*Ascribe*
2 [a]2 Chr. 20:21 [1]*Ascribe* [2]Lit. *of His name* [3]*majesty*
3 [a][Job 37:4, 5]
5 [a]Is. 2:13; 14:8
6 [a]Ps. 114:4 [b]Deut. 3:9
7 [1]*stirs up*, lit. *hews out*
8 [a]Num. 13:26
9 [a]Job 39:1
10 [a]Gen. 6:17 [b]Ps. 10:16
11 [a]Ps. 28:8; 68:35

PSALM 30

title [a]Deut. 20:5
1 [a]Ps. 28:9

And have not let my foes [b]rejoice
over me.
2 O LORD my God, I cried out to
You,
And You [a]healed me.
3 O LORD, [a]You brought my soul up
from the grave;
You have kept me alive, [1]that I
should not go down to the pit.

4 [a]Sing praise to the LORD, you
saints of His,
And give thanks at the
remembrance of [1]His holy
name.
5 For [a]His anger *is but for* a
moment,
[b]His favor *is for* life;
Weeping may endure for a night,
But [1]joy *comes* in the morning.

6 Now in my prosperity I said,
"I shall never be [1]moved."
7 LORD, by Your favor You have
made my mountain stand
strong;
[a]You hid Your face, *and* I was
troubled.

8 I cried out to You, O LORD;
And to the LORD I made
supplication:
9 "What profit *is there* in my blood,
When I go down to the pit?
[a]Will the dust praise You?
Will it declare Your truth?
10 Hear, O LORD, and have mercy
on me;
LORD, be my helper!"

11 [a]You have turned for me my
mourning into dancing;
You have put off [1]my sackcloth
and clothed me with gladness,
12 To the end that *my* [1]glory may
sing praise to You and not be
silent.
O LORD my God, I will give
thanks to You forever.

PSALM 31

The LORD a Fortress in Adversity

To the Chief Musician. A Psalm of David.

IN [a]You, O LORD, I [1]put my trust;
Let me never be ashamed;
Deliver me in Your
righteousness.
2 [a]Bow down Your ear to me,
Deliver me speedily;
Be my rock of [1]refuge,
A [2]fortress of defense to save me.

3 [a]For You *are* my rock and my
fortress;

1 [b]Ps. 25:2
2 [a]Ps. 6:2; 103:3; [Is. 53:5]
3 [a]Ps. 86:13 [1]So with Qr., Tg.; Kt., LXX, Syr., Vg. *from those who descend to the pit*
4 [a]Ps. 97:12 [1]Or *His holiness*
5 [a]Ps. 103:9; Is. 26:20; 54:7, 8 [b]Ps. 63:3 [1]*a shout of joy*
6 [1]*shaken*
7 [a][Deut. 31:17; Ps. 104:29; 143:7]
9 [a][Ps. 6:5]
11 [a]Eccl. 3:4; Is. 61:3; Jer. 31:4 [1]The sackcloth of my mourning
12 [1]*soul*

PSALM 31

1 [a]Ps. 22:5 [1]*have taken refuge*
2 [a]Ps. 17:6; 71:2; 86:1; 102:2 [1]*strength* [2]Lit. *house of fortresses*
3 [a][Ps. 18:2] [b]Ps. 23:3; 25:11
5 [a]Luke 23:46 [b][Deut. 32:4]; Ps. 71:22
6 [a]Jon. 2:8
7 [a][John 10:27] [1]*troubles*
8 [a][Deut. 32:30]; Ps. 37:33 [b][Ps. 4:1; 18:19] [1]*given me over*
9 [a]Ps. 6:7 [1]Lit. *belly*
11 [a][Is. 53:4] [b]Job 19:13; Ps. 38:11; 88:8, 18 [c]Ps. 64:8 [1]*despised thing*
12 [a]Ps. 88:4, 5 [1]Lit. *perishing*
13 [a]Ps. 50:20; Jer. 20:10 [b]Lam. 2:22 [c]Ps. 62:4; Matt. 27:1
15 [a][Job 14:5; 24:1]
16 [a]Ps. 4:6; 80:3
17 [a]Ps. 25:2, 20

Therefore, [b]for Your name's
sake,
Lead me and guide me.
4 Pull me out of the net which they
have secretly laid for me,
For You *are* my strength.
5 [a]Into Your hand I commit my
spirit;
You have redeemed me, O LORD
God of [b]truth.

6 I have hated those [a]who regard
useless idols;
But I trust in the LORD.
7 I will be glad and rejoice in Your
mercy,
For You have considered my
trouble;
You have [a]known my soul in
[1]adversities,
8 And have not [a]shut[1] me up into
the hand of the enemy;
[b]You have set my feet in a wide
place.

9 Have mercy on me, O LORD, for
I am in trouble;
[a]My eye wastes away with grief,
Yes, my soul and my [1]body!
10 For my life is spent with grief,
And my years with sighing;
My strength fails because of my
iniquity,
And my bones waste away.
11 [a]I am a [1]reproach among all my
enemies,
But [b]especially among my
neighbors,
And *am* repulsive to my
acquaintances;
[c]Those who see me outside flee
from me.
12 [a]I am forgotten like a dead man,
out of mind;
I am like a [1]broken vessel.
13 [a]For I hear the slander of many;
[b]Fear *is* on every side;
While they [c]take counsel together
against me,
They scheme to take away my
life.

14 But as for me, I trust in You,
O LORD;
I say, "You *are* my God."
15 My times *are* in Your [a]hand;
Deliver me from the hand of my
enemies,
And from those who persecute
me.
16 [a]Make Your face shine upon Your
servant;
Save me for Your mercies' sake.
17 [a]Do not let me be ashamed,

O LORD, for I have called upon
You;
Let the wicked be ashamed;
[b]Let them be silent in the grave.
18 [a]Let the lying lips be put to silence,
Which [b]speak insolent things
proudly and contemptuously
against the righteous.

19 [a]Oh, how great *is* Your goodness,
Which You have laid up for those
who fear You,
Which You have prepared for
those who trust in You
In the presence of the sons of
men!
20 [a]You shall hide them in the secret
place of Your presence
From the plots of man;
[b]You shall keep them secretly in
a [1]pavilion
From the strife of tongues.

21 Blessed *be* the LORD,
For [a]He has shown me His
marvelous kindness in a
[1]strong city!
22 For I said in my haste,
"I am cut off from before Your
eyes";
Nevertheless You heard the voice
of my supplications
When I cried out to You.

23 Oh, love the LORD, all you His
saints!
For the LORD preserves the
faithful,
And fully repays the proud
person.
24 [a]Be of good courage,
And He shall strengthen your
heart,
All you who hope in the LORD.

PSALM 32

The Joy of Forgiveness

A Psalm of David. A [1]Contemplation.

BLESSED *is he whose*
[a]transgression *is* forgiven,
Whose sin *is* covered.
2 Blessed *is* the man to whom the
LORD [a]does not [1]impute
iniquity,
And [b]in whose spirit *there is* no
deceit.

3 When I kept silent, my bones
grew old
Through my groaning all the day
long.
4 For day and night Your [a]hand
was heavy upon me;
My vitality was turned into the
drought of summer. Selah
5 I acknowledged my sin to You,
And my iniquity I have not
hidden.
[a]I said, "I will confess my
transgressions to the LORD,"
And You forgave the iniquity of
my sin. Selah

6 [a]For this cause everyone who is
godly shall [b]pray to You
In a time when You may be
found;
Surely in a flood of great waters
They shall not come near him.
7 [a]You *are* my hiding place;
You shall preserve me from
trouble;
You shall surround me with
[b]songs of deliverance. Selah

8 I will instruct you and teach you
in the way you should go;
I will guide you with My eye.
9 Do not be like the [a]horse *or* like
the mule,
Which have no understanding,
Which must be harnessed with
bit and bridle,
Else they will not come near
you.

10 [a]Many sorrows *shall be* to the
wicked;
But [b]he who trusts in the LORD,
mercy shall surround him.
11 [a]Be glad in the LORD and rejoice,
you righteous;
And shout for joy, all *you* upright
in heart!

PSALM 33

The Sovereignty of the LORD in Creation and History

REJOICE [a]in the LORD, O you
righteous!
For praise from the upright is
beautiful.
2 Praise the LORD with the harp;
[1]Make melody to Him with an
instrument of ten strings.
3 Sing to Him a new song;
Play skillfully with a shout of
joy.

4 For the word of the LORD *is* right,
And all His work *is done* in truth.
5 He loves righteousness and
justice;
The earth is full of the goodness
of the LORD.

---

17 [b][1 Sam. 2:9]; Ps. 94:17; 115:17
18 [a]Ps. 109:2; 120:2 [b][1 Sam. 2:3]; Ps. 94:4; [Jude 15]
19 [a]Ps. 145:7; [Rom. 2:4; 11:22]
20 [a][Ps. 27:5; 32:7] [b]Job 5:21 [1]*shelter*
21 [a][Ps. 17:7] [1]*fortified*
24 [a][Ps. 27:14]

PSALM 32
title [1]Heb. *Maschil*
1 [a][Ps. 85:2; 103:3]; Rom. 4:7, 8
2 [a][2 Cor. 5:19] [b]John 1:47 [1]*charge his account with*
4 [a]1 Sam. 5:6; Ps. 38:2; 39:10
5 [a]2 Sam. 12:13; Ps. 38:18; [Prov. 28:13; 1 John 1:9]
6 [a][1 Tim. 1:16] [b]Ps. 69:13; Is. 55:6
7 [a]Ps. 9:9 [b]Ex. 15:1; Judg. 5:1; [Ps. 40:3]
9 [a]Prov. 26:3
10 [a]Ps. 16:4; [Prov. 13:21; Rom. 2:9] [b][Ps. 5:11, 12]; Prov. 16:20
11 [a]Ps. 64:10; 68:3; 97:12

PSALM 33
1 [a]Ps. 32:11; 97:12; Phil. 3:1; 4:4
2 [1]Lit. *Sing to Him*

6 [a]By the word of the LORD the
heavens were made,
And all the [b]host of them [c]by the
breath of His mouth.
7 [a]He gathers the waters of the sea
together [1]as a heap;
He lays up the deep in
storehouses.

8 Let all the earth fear the LORD;
Let all the inhabitants of the
world stand in awe of Him.
9 For [a]He spoke, and it was *done;*
He commanded, and it stood fast.

10 [a]The LORD brings the counsel of
the nations to nothing;
He makes the plans of the
peoples of no effect.
11 [a]The counsel of the LORD stands
forever,
The plans of His heart to all
generations.
12 Blessed *is* the nation whose God
is the LORD,
The people He has [a]chosen as His
own inheritance.

13 [a]The LORD looks from heaven;
He sees all the sons of men.
14 From the place of His dwelling He
looks
On all the inhabitants of the
earth;
15 He fashions their hearts
individually;
[a]He [1]considers all their works.

16 [a]No king *is* saved by the multitude
of an army;
A mighty man is not delivered by
great strength.
17 [a]A horse *is* a [1]vain hope for
safety;
Neither shall it deliver *any* by its
great strength.

18 [a]Behold, the eye of the LORD *is* on
those who fear Him,
On those who hope in His mercy,
19 To deliver their soul from death,
And [a]to keep them alive in
famine.

20 Our soul waits for the LORD;
He *is* our help and our shield.
21 For our heart shall rejoice in
Him,
Because we have trusted in His
holy name.
22 Let Your mercy, O LORD, be upon
us,
Just as we hope in You.

6 [a]Gen. 1:6, 7; Ps. 148:5; [Heb. 11:3; 2 Pet. 3:5] [b]Gen. 2:1 [c][Job 26:13]
7 [a]Gen. 1:9; Job 26:10; 38:8 [1]LXX, Tg., Vg. *in a vessel*
9 [a]Gen. 1:3; Ps. 148:5
10 [a][Ps. 2:1–3]; Is. 8:10; 19:3
11 [a][Job 23:13; Prov. 19:21]
12 [a][Ex. 19:5; Deut. 7:6]; Ps. 28:9
13 [a]Job 28:24; [Ps. 14:2]
15 [a][2 Chr. 16:9]; Job 34:21; [Jer. 32:19] [1]*understands*
16 [a]Ps. 44:6; 60:11; [Jer. 9:23, 24]
17 [a][Ps. 20:7; 147:10; Prov. 21:31] [1]*false*
18 [a][Job 36:7]; Ps. 32:8; 34:15; [1 Pet. 3:12]
19 [a]Job 5:20; Ps. 37:19

PSALM 34

title [a]1 Sam. 21:10–15
1 [a][Eph. 5:20; 1 Thess. 5:18]
4 [a][2 Chr. 15:2; Ps. 9:10; Matt. 7:7; Luke 11:9]
7 [a][Ps. 91:11]; Dan. 6:22 [b]2 Kin. 6:17 [1]Or *Angel*
8 [a]Ps. 119:103; [Heb. 6:5]; 1 Pet. 2:3 [b]Ps. 2:12
9 [1]*lack*
10 [a][Ps. 84:11]
11 [a]Ps. 32:8
12 [a][1 Pet. 3:10–12]
13 [a][Eph. 4:25]
14 [a]Ps. 37:27; Is. 1:16, 17 [b][Rom. 14:19; Heb. 12:14]
15 [a]Job 36:7; [Ps. 33:18]
16 [a]Lev. 17:10; Jer. 44:11; Amos 9:4

PSALM 34

The Happiness of Those Who Trust in God

A Psalm of David [a]when he pretended madness before Abimelech, who drove him away, and he departed.

I WILL [a]bless the LORD at all times;
His praise *shall* continually *be* in
my mouth.
2 My soul shall make its boast in
the LORD;
The humble shall hear *of it* and
be glad.
3 Oh, magnify the LORD with me,
And let us exalt His name
together.

4 I [a]sought the LORD, and He heard
me,
And delivered me from all my
fears.
5 They looked to Him and were
radiant,
And their faces were not
ashamed.
6 This poor man cried out, and the
LORD heard *him,*
And saved him out of all his
troubles.
7 [a]The [1]angel of the LORD [b]encamps
all around those who fear Him,
And delivers them.

8 Oh, [a]taste and see that the LORD
is good;
[b]Blessed *is* the man *who* trusts in
Him!
9 Oh, fear the LORD, you His saints!
There is no [1]want to those who
fear Him.
10 The young lions lack and suffer
hunger;
[a]But those who seek the LORD
shall not lack any good *thing.*

11 Come, you children, listen to me;
[a]I will teach you the fear of the
LORD.
12 [a]Who *is* the man *who* desires life,
And loves *many* days, that he
may see good?
13 Keep your tongue from evil,
And your lips from speaking
[a]deceit.
14 [a]Depart from evil and do good;
[b]Seek peace and pursue it.

15 [a]The eyes of the LORD *are* on the
righteous,
And His ears *are open* to their
cry.
16 [a]The face of the LORD *is* against
those who do evil,

[b]To [1]cut off the remembrance of
them from the earth.
17 *The righteous* cry out, and [a]the
LORD hears,
And delivers them out of all their
troubles.
18 [a]The LORD *is* near [b]to those who
have a broken heart,
And saves such as [1]have a
contrite spirit.

19 [a]Many *are* the afflictions of the
righteous,
[b]But the LORD delivers him out of
them all.
20 He guards all his bones;
[a]Not one of them is broken.
21 [a]Evil shall slay the wicked,
And those who hate the righteous
shall be [1]condemned.
22 The LORD [a]redeems the soul of
His servants,
And none of those who trust in
Him shall be condemned.

PSALM 35

The LORD the Avenger of His People

A Psalm of David.

PLEAD[1] *my cause,* O LORD, with
those who strive with me;
Fight against those who fight
against me.
2 Take hold of shield and [1]buckler,
And stand up for my help.
3 Also draw out the spear,
And stop those who pursue me.
Say to my soul,
"I *am* your salvation."

4 [a]Let those be put to shame and
brought to dishonor
Who seek after my life;
Let those be [b]turned back and
brought to confusion
Who plot my hurt.
5 [a]Let them be like chaff before the
wind,
And let the [1]angel of the LORD
chase *them.*
6 Let their way be [a]dark and
slippery,
And let the angel of the LORD
pursue them.
7 For without cause they have
[a]hidden their net for me *in* a pit,
Which they have dug without
cause for my life.
8 [1]Let [a]destruction come upon him
unexpectedly,
And let his net that he has hidden
catch himself;
Into that very destruction let him
fall.

9 And my soul shall be joyful in the
LORD;
It shall rejoice in His salvation.
10 [a]All my bones shall say,
"LORD, [b]who *is* like You,
Delivering the poor from him
who is too strong for him,
Yes, the poor and the needy from
him who plunders him?"

11 Fierce witnesses rise up;
They ask me *things* that I do not
know.
12 [a]They reward me evil for good,
To the sorrow of my soul.
13 But as for me, [a]when they were
sick,
My clothing *was* sackcloth;
I humbled myself with fasting;
And my prayer would return to
my own [1]heart.
14 I paced about as though *he were*
my friend *or* brother;
I bowed down [1]heavily, as one
who mourns *for his* mother.

15 But in my [1]adversity they rejoiced
And gathered together;
Attackers gathered against me,
And I did not know *it;*
They tore *at me* and did not
cease;
16 With ungodly mockers at feasts
They gnashed at me with their
teeth.

17 Lord, how long will You [a]look
on?
Rescue me from their
destructions,
My precious *life* from the lions.
18 I will give You thanks in the great
assembly;
I will praise You among [1]many
people.

19 [a]Let them not rejoice over me who
are wrongfully my enemies;
Nor let them wink with the eye
who hate me without a cause.
20 For they do not speak peace,
But they devise deceitful matters
Against *the* quiet ones in the
land.
21 They also opened their mouth
wide against me,
And said, "Aha, aha!
Our eyes have seen *it.*"

22 *This* You have seen, O LORD;
Do not keep silence.
O Lord, do not be far from me.
23 Stir up Yourself, and awake to
my vindication,
To my cause, my God and my
Lord.

16 [b]Job 18:17; Ps. 9:6; 109:15; [Prov. 10:7] [1]*destroy*
17 [a]Ps. 34:6; 145:19
18 [a][Ps. 145:18] [b]Ps. 51:17; [Is. 57:15] [1]*are crushed in spirit*
19 [a]Prov. 24:16 [b]Ps. 34:4, 6, 17
20 [a]John 19:33, 36
21 [a]Ps. 94:23; 140:11; Prov. 24:16 [1]*held guilty*
22 [a]1 Kin. 1:29

PSALM 35

1 [1]*Contend for me*
2 [1]A small shield
4 [a]Ps. 40:14, 15; 70:2, 3 [b]Ps. 129:5
5 [a]Job 21:18; Ps. 83:13; Is. 29:5 [1]Or *Angel*
6 [a]Ps. 73:18; Jer. 23:12
7 [a]Ps. 9:15
8 [a][Ps. 55:23]; Is. 47:11; [1 Thess. 5:3] [1]Lit. *Let destruction he does not know come upon him.*
10 [a]Ps. 51:8 [b][Ex. 15:11]; Ps. 71:19; 86:8; [Mic. 7:18]
12 [a]Ps. 38:20; 109:5; Jer. 18:20; John 10:32
13 [a]Job 30:25 [1]Lit. *bosom*
14 [1]*in mourning*
15 [1]*limping, stumbling*
17 [a]Ps. 13:1; [Hab. 1:13]
18 [1]*a mighty*
19 [a]Ps. 69:4; 109:3; Lam. 3:52; [John 15:25]

24 Vindicate me, O LORD my God,
according to Your
righteousness;
And let them not rejoice over me.
25 Let them not say in their hearts,
"Ah, so we would have it!"
Let them not say, "We have
swallowed him up."

26 Let them be ashamed and
brought to mutual confusion
Who rejoice at my hurt;
Let them be [a]clothed with shame
and dishonor
Who exalt themselves against
me.

27 [a]Let them shout for joy and be
glad,
Who favor my righteous cause;
And let them say continually,
"Let the LORD be magnified,
Who has pleasure in the
prosperity of His servant."
28 And my tongue shall speak of
Your righteousness
And of Your praise all the day
long.

PSALM 36

Man's Wickedness and God's Perfections

To the Chief Musician. A Psalm of David the servant of the LORD.

AN oracle within my heart
concerning the transgression of
the wicked:
[a]*There is* no fear of God before his
eyes.
2 For he flatters himself in his own
eyes,
When he finds out his iniquity
and when he hates.
3 The words of his mouth *are*
wickedness and deceit;
[a]He has ceased to be wise *and* to
do good.
4 [a]He devises wickedness on his
bed;
He sets himself [b]in a way *that is*
not good;
He does not [1]abhor [c]evil.

5 Your mercy, O LORD, *is* in the
heavens;
Your faithfulness *reaches* to the
clouds.
6 Your righteousness *is* like the
[1]great mountains;
[a]Your judgments *are* a great deep;
O LORD, You preserve man and
beast.

26 [a]Ps. 109:29

27 [a]Rom. 12:15

PSALM 36

1 [a]Rom. 3:18

3 [a]Ps. 94:8; Jer. 4:22

4 [a]Prov. 4:16; [Mic. 2:1] [b]Is. 65:2 [c][Ps. 52:3; Rom. 12:9] [1]*reject, loathe*

6 [a]Job 11:8; Ps. 77:19; [Rom. 11:33] [1]Lit. *mountains of God*

7 [a]Ruth 2:12; Ps. 17:8; 57:1; 91:4

8 [a]Ps. 63:5; 65:4; Is. 25:6; Jer. 31:12–14 [b]Ps. 46:4; Rev. 22:1

9 [a][Jer. 2:13; John 4:10, 14] [b][1 Pet. 2:9]

PSALM 37

1 [a]Ps. 73:3; [Prov. 23:17; 24:19]

2 [a]Job 14:2; Ps. 90:5, 6; 92:7; James 1:11

4 [a]Job 22:26; Ps. 94:19; Is. 58:14 [b]Ps. 21:2; 145:19; [Matt. 7:7, 8]

5 [a][Ps. 55:22; Prov. 16:3; 1 Pet. 5:7] [1]Lit. *Roll off onto*

6 [a]Job 11:17; [Is. 58:8, 10]

7 [a]Ps. 40:1; 62:5; [Lam. 3:26] [b][Ps. 73:3–12]

8 [a][Eph. 4:26] [b]Ps. 73:3

9 [1]*destroyed*

7 How precious *is* Your
lovingkindness, O God!
Therefore the children of men
[a]put their trust under the
shadow of Your wings.
8 [a]They are abundantly satisfied
with the fullness of Your house,
And You give them drink from
[b]the river of Your pleasures.
9 [a]For with You *is* the fountain of
life;
[b]In Your light we see light.
10 Oh, continue Your
lovingkindness to those who
know You,
And Your righteousness to the
upright in heart.
11 Let not the foot of pride come
against me,
And let not the hand of the
wicked drive me away.
12 There the workers of iniquity
have fallen;
They have been cast down and
are not able to rise.

PSALM 37

The Heritage of the Righteous and the Calamity of the Wicked

A Psalm of David.

DO[a] not fret because of evildoers,
Nor be envious of the workers
of iniquity.
2 For they shall soon be cut down
[a]like the grass,
And wither as the green herb.

3 Trust in the LORD, and do good;
Dwell in the land, and feed on His
faithfulness.
4 [a]Delight yourself also in the LORD,
And He shall give you the desires
of your [b]heart.

5 [a]Commit[1] your way to the LORD,
Trust also in Him,
And He shall bring *it* to pass.
6 [a]He shall bring forth your
righteousness as the light,
And your justice as the noonday.

7 Rest in the LORD, [a]and wait
patiently for Him;
Do not fret because of him who
[b]prospers in his way,
Because of the man who brings
wicked schemes to pass.
8 [a]Cease from anger, and forsake
wrath;
[b]Do not fret—*it* only *causes* harm.

9 For evildoers shall be [1]cut off;
But those who wait on the LORD,

They shall [a]inherit the earth.
10 For [a]yet a little while and the
wicked *shall be* no *more;*
Indeed, [b]you will look carefully
for his place,
But it *shall be* no *more.*
11 [a]But the meek shall inherit the
earth,
And shall delight themselves in
the abundance of peace.

12 The wicked plots against the just,
[a]And gnashes at him with his
teeth.
13 [a]The Lord laughs at him,
For He sees that [b]his day is
coming.
14 The wicked have drawn the
sword
And have bent their bow,
To cast down the poor and needy,
To slay those who are of upright
conduct.
15 Their sword shall enter their own
heart,
And their bows shall be broken.

16 [a]A little that a righteous man has
Is better than the riches of many
wicked.
17 For the arms of the wicked shall
be broken,
But the LORD upholds the
righteous.
18 The LORD knows the days of the
upright,
And their inheritance shall be
forever.
19 They shall not be ashamed in the
evil time,
And in the days of famine they
shall be satisfied.
20 But the wicked shall perish;
And the enemies of the LORD,
Like the splendor of the
meadows, shall vanish.
Into smoke they shall vanish
away.

21 The wicked borrows and does not
repay,
But [a]the righteous shows mercy
and gives.
22 [a]For *those* blessed by Him shall
inherit the earth,
But *those* cursed by Him shall be
[1]cut off.

23 [a]The steps of a *good* man are
[1]ordered by the LORD,
And He delights in his way.
24 [a]Though he fall, he shall not be
utterly cast down;
For the LORD upholds *him with*
His hand.

9 [a]Ps. 25:13; Prov. 2:21; [Is. 57:13; 60:21; Matt. 5:5]
10 [a][Heb. 10:37] [b]Job 7:10; Ps. 37:35, 36
11 [a][Matt. 5:5]
12 [a]Ps. 35:16
13 [a]Ps. 2:4; 59:8 [b]1 Sam. 26:10; Job 18:20
16 [a]Prov. 15:16; 16:8; [1 Tim. 6:6]
21 [a]Ps. 112:5, 9
22 [a][Prov. 3:33] [1]*destroyed*
23 [a][1 Sam. 2:9]; Ps. 40:2; 66:9; 119:5 [1]*established*
24 [a]Prov. 24:16
26 [a][Deut. 15:8]; Ps. 37:21 [1]Lit. *all the day*
29 [a]Ps. 37:9; Prov. 2:21
30 [a][Matt. 12:35]
31 [1]*slip*
32 [a]Ps. 10:8; 17:11
33 [a]Ps. 31:8; [2 Pet. 2:9]
34 [a]Ps. 27:14; 37:9
36 [1]So with MT, LXX, Tg.; Syr., Vg. *I passed by*
38 [a][Ps. 1:4–6; 37:20, 28]
39 [a]Ps. 9:9; 37:19
40 [a]Ps. 22:4; Is. 31:5; Dan. 3:17; 6:23

25 I have been young, and *now* am
old;
Yet I have not seen the righteous
forsaken,
Nor his descendants begging
bread.
26 [a]*He is* [1]ever merciful, and lends;
And his descendants *are* blessed.

27 Depart from evil, and do good;
And dwell forevermore.
28 For the LORD loves justice,
And does not forsake His saints;
They are preserved forever,
But the descendants of the
wicked shall be cut off.
29 [a]The righteous shall inherit the
land,
And dwell in it forever.

30 [a]The mouth of the righteous
speaks wisdom,
And his tongue talks of justice.
31 The law of his God *is* in his heart;
None of his steps shall [1]slide.

32 The wicked [a]watches the
righteous,
And seeks to slay him.
33 The LORD [a]will not leave him in
his hand,
Nor condemn him when he is
judged.

34 [a]Wait on the LORD,
And keep His way,
And He shall exalt you to inherit
the land;
When the wicked are cut off, you
shall see *it*.
35 I have seen the wicked in great
power,
And spreading himself like a
native green tree.
36 Yet [1]he passed away, and behold,
he *was* no *more;*
Indeed I sought him, but he could
not be found.

37 Mark the blameless *man*, and
observe the upright;
For the future of *that* man *is*
peace.
38 [a]But the transgressors shall be
destroyed together;
The future of the wicked shall be
cut off.

39 But the salvation of the righteous
is from the LORD;
He is their strength [a]in the time
of trouble.
40 And [a]the LORD shall help them
and deliver them;
He shall deliver them from the
wicked,

And save them,
[b]Because they trust in Him.

PSALM 38

Prayer in Time of Chastening

A Psalm of David. [a]To bring to remembrance.

O LORD, do not [a]rebuke me in
Your wrath,
Nor chasten me in Your hot
displeasure!
2 For Your arrows pierce me
deeply,
And Your hand presses me down.

3 *There is* no soundness in my flesh
Because of Your anger,
Nor *any* health in my bones
Because of my sin.
4 For my iniquities have gone over
my head;
Like a heavy burden they are too
heavy for me.
5 My wounds are foul *and* festering
Because of my foolishness.

6 I am [1]troubled, I am bowed down
greatly;
I go mourning all the day long.
7 For my loins are full of
inflammation,
And *there is* no soundness in my
flesh.
8 I am feeble and severely broken;
I groan because of the turmoil of
my heart.

9 Lord, all my desire *is* before You;
And my sighing is not hidden
from You.
10 My heart pants, my strength fails
me;
As for the light of my eyes, it also
has gone from me.

11 My loved ones and my friends
[a]stand aloof from my plague,
And my relatives stand afar off.
12 Those also who seek my life lay
snares *for me;*
Those who seek my hurt speak
of destruction,
And plan deception all the day
long.

13 But I, like a deaf *man,* do not
hear;
And *I am* like a mute *who* does
not open his mouth.
14 Thus I am like a man who does
not hear,
And in whose mouth *is* no
response.

40 [b]1 Chr. 5:20; Ps. 34:22

PSALM 38

title [a]Ps. 70:title

1 [a]Ps. 6:1

6 [1]Lit. *bent down*

11 [a]Ps. 31:11; 88:18

15 [a][Ps. 39:7] [1]*I wait for You, O LORD* [2]*answer*

17 [a]Ps. 51:3

18 [a]Ps. 32:5 [b][2 Cor. 7:9, 10] [1]*anxiety*

20 [a]Ps. 35:12

21 [a]Ps. 22:19; 35:22

PSALM 39

1 [a]Job 2:10; Ps. 34:13; [James 3:5–12]

2 [a]Ps. 38:13

3 [1]*meditating*

4 [a]Ps. 90:12; 119:84

5 [a]Ps. 62:9; [Eccl. 6:12]

6 [1]*make an uproar for nothing*

7 [a]Ps. 38:15

15 For [1]in You, O LORD, [a]I hope;
You will [2]hear, O Lord my God.
16 For I said, "*Hear me,* lest they
rejoice over me,
Lest, when my foot slips, they
exalt *themselves* against me."

17 [a]For I *am* ready to fall,
And my sorrow *is* continually
before me.
18 For I will [a]declare my iniquity;
I will be [b]in [1]anguish over my sin.
19 But my enemies *are* vigorous, *and*
they are strong;
And those who hate me
wrongfully have multiplied.
20 Those also [a]who render evil for
good,
They are my adversaries, because
I follow *what is* good.

21 Do not forsake me, O LORD;
O my God, [a]be not far from me!
22 Make haste to help me,
O Lord, my salvation!

PSALM 39

Prayer for Wisdom and Forgiveness

To the Chief Musician. To Jeduthun. A Psalm of David.

I SAID, "I will guard my ways,
Lest I sin with my [a]tongue;
I will restrain my mouth with a
muzzle,
While the wicked are before me."
2 [a]I was mute with silence,
I held my peace *even* from good;
And my sorrow was stirred up.
3 My heart was hot within me;
While I was [1]musing, the fire
burned.
Then I spoke with my tongue:

4 "LORD, [a]make me to know my end,
And what *is* the measure of my
days,
That I may know how frail I *am.*
5 Indeed, You have made my days
as handbreadths,
And my age *is* as nothing before
You;
Certainly every man at his best
state *is* but [a]vapor. Selah
6 Surely every man walks about
like a shadow;
Surely they [1]busy themselves in
vain;
He heaps up *riches,*
And does not know who will
gather them.

7 "And now, Lord, what do I wait
for?
My [a]hope *is* in You.

8 Deliver me from all my
transgressions;
Do not make me [a]the reproach of
the foolish.
9 [a]I was mute, I did not open my
mouth,
Because it was [b]You who did *it*.
10 [a]Remove Your plague from me;
I am consumed by the blow of
Your hand.
11 When with rebukes You correct
man for iniquity,
You make his beauty [a]melt away
like a moth;
Surely every man *is* vapor.
Selah
12 "Hear my prayer, O LORD,
And give ear to my cry;
Do not be silent at my tears;
For I *am* a stranger with You,
A sojourner, [a]as all my fathers
were.
13 [a]Remove Your gaze from me, that
I may regain strength,
Before I go away and [b]am no
more."

PSALM 40

Faith Persevering in Trial

To the Chief Musician. A Psalm of David.

I [a]WAITED patiently for the LORD;
And He inclined to me,
And heard my cry.
2 He also brought me up out of a
horrible pit,
Out of [a]the miry clay,
And [b]set my feet upon a rock,
And established my steps.
3 [a]He has put a new song in my
mouth—
Praise to our God;
Many will see *it* and fear,
And will trust in the LORD.
4 [a]Blessed *is* that man who makes
the LORD his trust,
And does not respect the proud,
nor such as turn aside to lies.
5 [a]Many, O LORD my God, *are* Your
wonderful works
Which You have done;
[b]And Your thoughts toward us
Cannot be recounted to You in
order;
If I would declare and speak *of
them*,
They are more than can be
numbered.
6 [a]Sacrifice and offering You did not
desire;
My ears You have opened.
Burnt offering and sin offering
You did not require.

8 [a]Ps. 44:13; 79:4; 119:22 **9** [a]Ps. 39:2 [b]2 Sam. 16:10; Job 2:10 **10** [a]Job 9:34; 13:21 **11** [a]Job 13:28; [Ps. 90:7]; Is. 50:9 **12** [a]Gen. 47:9; Lev. 25:23; 1 Chr. 29:15; Ps. 119:19; Heb. 11:13; 1 Pet. 2:11 **13** [a]Job 7:19; 10:20, 21; 14:6; Ps. 102:24 [b][Job 14:10]

PSALM 40

1 [a]Ps. 25:5; 27:14; 37:7 **2** [a]Ps. 69:2, 14; Jer. 38:6 [b]Ps. 27:5 **3** [a]Ps. 32:7; 33:3 **4** [a]Ps. 34:8; 84:12 **5** [a]Job 9:10 [b]Ps. 139:17; [Is. 55:8] **6** [a][1 Sam. 15:22]; Ps. 51:16; Is. 1:11; [Jer. 6:20; 7:22, 23]; Amos 5:22; [Mic. 6:6–8; Heb. 10:5–9] **8** [a][Matt. 26:39; John 4:34; 6:38]; Heb. 10:7 [b][Ps. 37:31; Jer. 31:33; 2 Cor. 3:3] **9** [a]Ps. 22:22, 25 [b]Ps. 119:13 **10** [a]Acts 20:20, 27 **11** [a]Ps. 61:7; Prov. 20:28 **12** [a]Ps. 38:4; 65:3 **13** [a]Ps. 70:1 **14** [a]Ps. 35:4, 26; 70:2; 71:13 [1]Lit. *soul* **15** [a]Ps. 73:19 **16** [a]Ps. 70:4 [b]Ps. 35:27 **17** [a]Ps. 70:5; 86:1; 109:22 [b]Ps. 40:5; 1 Pet. 5:7

PSALM 41

1 [1]*helpless* or *powerless*

7 Then I said, "Behold, I come;
In the scroll of the book *it is*
written of me.
8 [a]I delight to do Your will, O my
God,
And Your law *is* [b]within my
heart."
9 [a]I have proclaimed the good news
of righteousness
In the great assembly;
Indeed, [b]I do not restrain my lips,
O LORD, You Yourself know.
10 [a]I have not hidden Your
righteousness within my heart;
I have declared Your faithfulness
and Your salvation;
I have not concealed Your
lovingkindness and Your truth
From the great assembly.
11 Do not withhold Your tender
mercies from me, O LORD;
[a]Let Your lovingkindness and
Your truth continually preserve
me.
12 For innumerable evils have
surrounded me;
[a]My iniquities have overtaken me,
so that I am not able to look
up;
They are more than the hairs of
my head;
Therefore my heart fails me.
13 [a]Be pleased, O LORD, to deliver
me;
O LORD, make haste to help me!
14 [a]Let them be ashamed and
brought to mutual confusion
Who seek to destroy my [1]life;
Let them be driven backward and
brought to dishonor
Who wish me evil.
15 Let them be [a]confounded because
of their shame,
Who say to me, "Aha, aha!"
16 [a]Let all those who seek You
rejoice and be glad in You;
Let such as love Your salvation
[b]say continually,
"The LORD be magnified!"
17 [a]But I *am* poor and needy;
[b]*Yet* the LORD thinks upon me.
You *are* my help and my
deliverer;
Do not delay, O my God.

PSALM 41

The Blessing and Suffering of the Godly

To the Chief Musician. A Psalm of David.

BLESSED *is* he who considers the
[1]poor;

The LORD will deliver him in time
of trouble.
2 The LORD will preserve him and
keep him alive,
And he will be blessed on the
earth;
[a]You will not deliver him to the
will of his enemies.
3 The LORD will strengthen him on
his bed of illness;
You will [1]sustain him on his
sickbed.

4 I said, "LORD, be merciful to me;
[a]Heal my soul, for I have sinned
against You."
5 My enemies speak evil of me:
"When will he die, and his name
perish?"
6 And if he comes to see *me,* he
speaks [1]lies;
His heart gathers iniquity to
itself;
When he goes out, he tells *it.*

7 All who hate me whisper together
against me;
Against me they [1]devise my hurt.
8 "An[1] evil disease," *they say,*
"clings to him.
And *now* that he lies down, he
will rise up no more."
9 [a]Even my own familiar friend in
whom I trusted,
[b]Who ate my bread,
Has [1]lifted up *his* heel against me.

10 But You, O LORD, be merciful to
me, and raise me up,
That I may repay them.
11 By this I know that You are well
pleased with me,
Because my enemy does not
triumph over me.
12 As for me, You uphold me in my
integrity,
And [a]set me before Your face
forever.

13 [a]Blessed *be* the LORD God of Israel
From everlasting to everlasting!
Amen and Amen.

BOOK TWO
Psalms 42—72

PSALM 42

Yearning for God in the Midst of Distresses

To the Chief Musician. A [1]Contemplation of the sons of Korah.

AS the deer [1]pants for the water
brooks,
So pants my soul for You,
O God.
2 [a]My soul thirsts for God, for the
[b]living God.
When shall I come and [1]appear
before God?
3 [a]My tears have been my food day
and night,
While they continually say to
me,
[b]"Where *is* your God?"

4 When I remember these *things,*
[a]I pour out my soul within me.
For I used to go with the
multitude;
[b]I went with them to the house of
God,
With the voice of joy and praise,
With a multitude that kept a
pilgrim feast.

5 [a]Why are you [1]cast down, O my
soul?
And *why* are you disquieted
within me?
[b]Hope in God, for I shall yet praise
Him
[2]*For* the help of His countenance.

6 [1]O my God, my soul is cast down
within me;
Therefore I will remember You
from the land of the Jordan,
And from the heights of Hermon,
From [2]the Hill Mizar.
7 Deep calls unto deep at the noise
of Your waterfalls;
[a]All Your waves and billows have
gone over me.
8 The LORD will [a]command His
lovingkindness in the
daytime,
And [b]in the night His song *shall*
be with me—
A prayer to the God of my life.

9 I will say to God my Rock,
[a]"Why have You forgotten me?
Why do I go mourning because
of the oppression of the
enemy?"
10 *As* with a [1]breaking of my bones,
My enemies [2]reproach me,
[a]While they say to me all day long,
"Where *is* your God?"

11 [a]Why are you cast down, O my
soul?
And why are you disquieted
within me?
Hope in God;
For I shall yet praise Him,
The [1]help of my countenance and
my God.

2 [a]Ps. 27:12
3 [1]*restore*
4 [a]Ps. 6:2; 103:3; 147:3
6 [1]*empty words*
7 [1]*plot*
8 [1]Lit. *A thing of Belial*
9 [a]2 Sam. 15:12 [b]John 13:18, 21–30 [1]Acted as a traitor
12 [a][Job 36:7]
13 [a]Ps. 72:18, 19; 89:52; 106:48; 150:6

PSALM 42

title [1]Heb. *Maschil*
1 [1]Lit. *longs for*
2 [a]Ps. 63:1; 84:2; 143:6 [b]1 Thess. 1:9 [1]So with MT, Vg.; some Heb. mss., LXX, Syr., Tg. *I see the face of God*
3 [a]Ps. 80:5; 102:9 [b]Ps. 79:10; 115:2
4 [a]Job 30:16 [b]Is. 30:29
5 [a]Ps. 42:11; 43:5 [b]Lam. 3:24 [1]Lit. *bowed down* [2]So with MT, Tg.; a few Heb. mss., LXX, Syr., Vg. *The help of my countenance, my God*
6 [1]So with MT, Tg.; a few Heb. mss., LXX, Syr., Vg. put *my God* at the end of v. 5 [2]Or *Mount*
7 [a]Ps. 69:1, 2; 88:7
8 [a]Deut. 28:8 [b]Job 35:10
9 [a]Ps. 38:6
10 [a]Joel 2:17 [1]Lit. *shattering* [2]*revile*
11 [a]Ps. 43:5 [1]Lit. *salvation*

PSALM 43

Prayer to God in Time of Trouble

VINDICATE [a]me, O God,
And [b]plead my cause against an ungodly nation;
Oh, deliver me from the deceitful and unjust man!
2 For You *are* the God of my strength;
Why do You cast me off?
[a]Why do I go mourning because of the oppression of the enemy?

3 [a]Oh, send out Your light and Your truth!
Let them lead me;
Let them bring me to [b]Your holy hill
And to Your [1]tabernacle.
4 Then I will go to the altar of God,
To God my exceeding joy;
And on the harp I will praise You,
O God, my God.

5 [a]Why are you cast down, O my soul?
And why are you disquieted within me?
Hope in God;
For I shall yet praise Him,
The [1]help of my countenance and my God.

PSALM 44

Redemption Remembered in Present Dishonor

To the Chief Musician. A [a]Contemplation[1] of the sons of Korah.

WE have heard with our ears, O God,
[a]Our fathers have told us,
The deeds You did in their days,
In days of old:
2 [a]You drove out the [1]nations with Your hand,
But them You planted;
You afflicted the peoples, and cast them out.
3 For [a]they did not gain possession of the land by their own sword,
Nor did their own arm save them;
But it was Your right hand, Your arm, and the light of Your countenance,
[b]Because You favored them.

4 [a]You are my King, [1]O God;
[2]Command victories for Jacob.
5 Through You [a]we will push down our enemies;
Through Your name we will trample those who rise up against us.
6 For [a]I will not trust in my bow,
Nor shall my sword save me.
7 But You have saved us from our enemies,
And have put to shame those who hated us.
8 [a]In God we boast all day long,
And praise Your name forever. Selah

9 But [a]You have cast *us* off and put us to shame,
And You do not go out with our armies.
10 9.5You make us [a]turn back from the enemy,
And those who hate us have taken [1]spoil for themselves.
11 [a]You have given us up like sheep *intended* for food,
And have [b]scattered us among the nations.
12 [a]You sell Your people for *next to* nothing,
And are not enriched by selling them.

13 [a]You make us a reproach to our neighbors,
A scorn and a derision to those all around us.
14 [a]You make us a byword among the nations,
[b]A shaking of the head among the peoples.
15 My dishonor *is* continually before me,
And the shame of my face has covered me,
16 Because of the voice of him who reproaches and reviles,
[a]Because of the enemy and the avenger.

17 [a]All this has come upon us;
But we have not forgotten You,
Nor have we dealt falsely with Your covenant.
18 Our heart has not turned back,
[a]Nor have our steps departed from Your way;
19 But You have severely broken us in [a]the place of jackals,
And covered us [b]with the shadow of death.

20 If we had forgotten the name of our God,
Or [a]stretched[1] out our hands to a foreign god,
21 [a]Would not God search this out?
For He knows the secrets of the heart.

PSALM 43

1 [a][Ps. 26:1; 35:24] [b]1 Sam. 24:15; Ps. 35:1
2 [a]Ps. 42:9
3 [a][Ps. 40:11] [b]Ps. 3:4 [1]*dwelling places*
5 [a]Ps. 42:5, 11 [1]Lit. *salvation*

PSALM 44

title [a]Ps. 42:title [1]Heb. *Maschil*
1 [a][Ex. 12:26, 27; Deut. 6:20]; Judg. 6:13; Ps. 78:3
2 [a]Ex. 15:17; 2 Sam. 7:10; Jer. 24:6; Amos 9:15 [1]*Gentiles, heathen*
3 [a][Deut. 8:17, 18]; Josh. 24:12 [b][Deut. 4:37; 7:7, 8]
4 [a][Ps. 74:12] [1]So with MT, Tg.; LXX, Vg. *and my God* [2]So with MT, Tg.; LXX, Syr., Vg. *Who commands*
5 [a]Deut. 33:17; [Dan. 8:4]
6 [a][1 Sam. 17:47]; Ps. 33:16; [Hos. 1:7]
8 [a]Ps. 34:2; [Jer. 9:24]
9 [a]Ps. 60:1
10 [a]Lev. 26:17; Josh. 7:8, 12; Ps. 89:43 [1]*plunder*
11 [a]Ps. 44:22; Rom. 8:36 [b]Lev. 26:33; Deut. 4:27; 28:64; Ps. 106:27; Ezek. 20:23
12 [a]Is. 52:3, 4; Jer. 15:13
13 [a]Ps. 79:4; 80:6; Jer. 24:9
14 [a]Deut. 28:37 [b]Job 16:4
16 [a]Ps. 8:2
17 [a]Dan. 9:13
18 [a]Job 23:11
19 [a]Is. 34:13 [b][Ps. 23:4]
20 [a][Deut. 6:14] [1]Worshiped
21 [a]Job 31:14; [Ps. 139:1, 2; Jer. 17:10]

22 [a]Yet for Your sake we are killed
all day long;
We are accounted as sheep for
the slaughter.

23 [a]Awake! Why do You sleep,
O Lord?
Arise! Do not cast *us* off forever.
24 [a]Why do You hide Your face,
And forget our affliction and our
oppression?
25 For [a]our soul is bowed down to
the [1]dust;
Our body clings to the ground.
26 Arise for our help,
And redeem us for Your mercies'
sake.

PSALM 45

The Glories of the Messiah and His Bride

To the Chief Musician. [a]Set to [1]"The Lilies." A [2]Contemplation of the sons of Korah. A Song of Love.

MY heart is overflowing with a
good theme;
I recite my composition
concerning the King;
My tongue *is* the pen of a [1]ready
writer.

2 You are fairer than the sons of
men;
[a]Grace is poured upon Your lips;
Therefore God has blessed You
forever.
3 [1]Gird Your [a]sword upon *Your*
thigh, [b]O Mighty One,
With Your [c]glory and Your
majesty.
4 [a]And in Your majesty ride
prosperously because of truth,
humility, *and* righteousness;
And Your right hand shall teach
You awesome things.
5 Your arrows *are* sharp in the
heart of the King's enemies;
The peoples fall under You.

6 [a]Your throne, O God, *is* forever
and ever;
A [b]scepter of righteousness *is* the
scepter of Your kingdom.
7 You love righteousness and hate
wickedness;
Therefore God, Your God, has
[a]anointed You
With the oil of [b]gladness more
than Your companions.
8 All Your garments *are* [a]scented
with myrrh and aloes *and*
cassia,
Out of the ivory palaces, by
which they have made You
glad.
9 [a]Kings' daughters *are* among Your
honorable women;
[b]At Your right hand stands the
queen in gold from Ophir.

10 Listen, O daughter,
Consider and incline your ear;
[a]Forget your own people also, and
your father's house;
11 So the King will greatly desire
your beauty;
[a]Because He *is* your Lord, worship
Him.
12 And the daughter of Tyre *will
come* with a gift;
[a]The rich among the people will
seek your favor.

13 The royal daughter *is* all glorious
within *the palace;*
Her clothing *is* woven with gold.
14 [a]She shall be brought to the King
in robes of many colors;
The virgins, her companions who
follow her, shall be brought to
You.
15 With gladness and rejoicing they
shall be brought;
They shall enter the King's
palace.

16 Instead of Your fathers shall be
Your sons,
[a]Whom You shall make princes in
all the earth.
17 [a]I will make Your name to be
remembered in all generations;
Therefore the people shall praise
You forever and ever.

PSALM 46

God the Refuge of His People and Conqueror of the Nations

To the Chief Musician. A Psalm of the sons of Korah. A Song [a]for Alamoth.

GOD *is* our [a]refuge and
strength,
[b]A[1] very present help in trouble.
2 Therefore we will not fear,
Even though the earth be
removed,
And though the mountains be
carried into the [1]midst of the
sea;
3 [a]*Though* its waters roar *and* be
troubled,
Though the mountains shake
with its swelling. Selah

4 *There is* a [a]river whose streams
shall make glad the [b]city of
God,

---

22 [a]Rom. 8:36
23 [a]Ps. 7:6
24 [a]Job 13:24
25 [a]Ps. 119:25 [1]Ground, in humiliation

PSALM 45

title [a]Ps. 69:title [1]Heb. *Shoshannim* [2]Heb. *Maschil*
1 [1]*skillful*
2 [a]Luke 4:22
3 [a][Is. 49:2; Heb. 4:12]; Rev. 1:16 [b][Is. 9:6] [c]Jude 25 [1]*Belt on*
4 [a]Rev. 6:2
6 [a][Ps. 93:2]; Heb. 1:8, 9 [b][Num. 24:17]
7 [a]Ps. 2:2 [b]Ps. 21:6; Heb. 1:8, 9
8 [a]Song 1:12, 13
9 [a]Song 6:8 [b]1 Kin. 2:19
10 [a]Deut. 21:13; Ruth 1:16, 17
11 [a]Ps. 95:6; [Is. 54:5]
12 [a]Is. 49:23
14 [a]Song 1:4
16 [a][1 Pet. 2:9; Rev. 1:6; 20:6]
17 [a]Mal. 1:11

PSALM 46

title [a]1 Chr. 15:20
1 [a]Ps. 62:7, 8 [b][Deut. 4:7; Ps. 145:18] [1]*An abundantly available help*
2 [1]Lit. *heart*
3 [a][Ps. 93:3, 4]
4 [a][Ezek. 47:1–12] [b]Ps. 48:1, 8; Is. 60:14

The holy *place* of the [1]tabernacle
of the Most High.
5 God *is* [a]in the midst of her, she
shall not be [1]moved;
God shall help her, just [2]at the
break of dawn.
6 [a]The nations raged, the kingdoms
were moved;
He uttered His voice, the earth
melted.

7 The [a]LORD of hosts *is* with us;
The God of Jacob *is* our refuge.
Selah

8 Come, behold the works of the
LORD,
Who has made desolations in the
earth.
9 [a]He makes wars cease to the end
of the earth;
[b]He breaks the bow and cuts the
spear in two;
[c]He burns the chariot in the fire.

10 Be still, and know that I *am* God;
[a]I will be exalted among the
nations,
I will be exalted in the earth!

11 The LORD of hosts *is* with us;
The God of Jacob *is* our refuge.
Selah

PSALM 47

Praise to God, the Ruler of the Earth

To the Chief Musician. A Psalm of the sons of Korah.

OH, clap your hands, all you
peoples!
Shout to God with the voice of
triumph!
2 For the LORD Most High *is*
awesome;
He is a great [a]King over all the
earth.
3 [a]He will subdue the peoples under
us,
And the nations under our feet.
4 He will choose our [a]inheritance
for us,
The excellence of Jacob whom
He loves. Selah

5 [a]God has gone up with a shout,
The LORD with the sound of a
trumpet.
6 Sing praises to God, sing praises!
Sing praises to our King, sing
praises!
7 [a]For God *is* the King of all the
earth;
[b]Sing praises with understanding.

4 [1]*dwelling places*
5 [a][Deut. 23:14; Is. 12:6]; Ezek. 43:7; Hos. 11:9; [Joel 2:27; Zeph. 3:15; Zech. 2:5, 10, 11; 8:3] [1]*shaken* [2]Lit. *at the turning of the morning*
6 [a]Ps. 2:1, 2
7 [a]Num. 14:9; 2 Chr. 13:12
9 [a]Is. 2:4 [b]Ps. 76:3 [c]Ezek. 39:9
10 [a][Is. 2:11, 17]

PSALM 47
2 [a]Deut. 7:21; Neh. 1:5; Ps. 76:12
3 [a]Ps. 18:47
4 [a][1 Pet. 1:4]
5 [a]Ps. 68:24, 25
7 [a]Zech. 14:9 [b]1 Cor. 14:15
8 [a]1 Chr. 16:31 [b]Ps. 97:2 [c]Ps. 48:1
9 [a][Rom. 4:11, 12] [b][Ps. 89:18]

PSALM 48
1 [a]Ps. 46:4; 87:3; Matt. 5:35
2 [a]Ps. 50:2 [1]*height*
4 [a]2 Sam. 10:6, 14
6 [a]Ex. 15:15
7 [a]1 Kin. 10:22; Ezek. 27:25
8 [a][Ps. 87:5; Is. 2:2]; Mic. 4:1
9 [a]Ps. 26:3
10 [a][Deut. 28:58]; Josh. 7:9; Mal. 1:11

8 [a]God reigns over the nations;
God [b]sits on His [c]holy throne.
9 The princes of the people have
gathered together,
[a]The people of the God of
Abraham.
[b]For the shields of the earth *belong*
to God;
He is greatly exalted.

PSALM 48

The Glory of God in Zion

A Song. A Psalm of the sons of Korah.

GREAT *is* the LORD, and greatly
to be praised
In the [a]city of our God,
In His holy mountain.
2 [a]Beautiful in [1]elevation,
The joy of the whole earth,
Is Mount Zion *on* the sides of the
north,
The city of the great King.
3 God *is* in her palaces;
He is known as her refuge.

4 For behold, [a]the kings assembled,
They passed by together.
5 They saw *it, and* so they
marveled;
They were troubled, they
hastened away.
6 Fear [a]took hold of them there,
And pain, as of a woman in birth
pangs,
7 *As when* You break the [a]ships of
Tarshish
With an east wind.

8 As we have heard,
So we have seen
In the city of the LORD of hosts,
In the city of our God:
God will [a]establish it forever.
Selah

9 We have thought, O God, on
[a]Your lovingkindness,
In the midst of Your temple.
10 According to [a]Your name, O God,
So *is* Your praise to the ends of
the earth;
Your right hand is full of
righteousness.
11 Let Mount Zion rejoice,
Let the daughters of Judah be
glad,
Because of Your judgments.

12 Walk about Zion,
And go all around her.
Count her towers;
13 Mark well her bulwarks;
Consider her palaces;

That you may [a]tell *it* to the
generation following.
14 For this *is* God,
Our God forever and ever;
[a]He will be our guide
[1]*Even* to death.

PSALM 49

The Confidence of the Foolish

To the Chief Musician. A Psalm of the sons of Korah.

HEAR this, all peoples;
Give ear, all inhabitants of the
world,
2 Both low and high,
Rich and poor together.
3 My mouth shall speak wisdom,
And the meditation of my heart
shall give understanding.
4 I will incline my ear to a proverb;
I will disclose my [1]dark saying on
the harp.

5 Why should I fear in the days of
evil,
When the iniquity at my heels
surrounds me?
6 Those who [a]trust in their wealth
And boast in the multitude of
their riches,
7 None *of them* can by any means
redeem *his* brother,
Nor [a]give to God a ransom for
him—
8 For [a]the redemption of their souls
is costly,
And it shall cease forever—
9 That he should continue to live
eternally,
And [a]not [1]see the Pit.

10 For he sees wise men die;
Likewise the fool and the
senseless person perish,
And leave their wealth to others.
11 [1]Their inner thought *is that* their
houses *will last* forever,
Their dwelling places to all
generations;
They [a]call *their* lands after their
own names.
12 Nevertheless man, *though* in
honor, does not [1]remain;
He is like the beasts *that* perish.

13 This is the way of those who *are*
[a]foolish,
And of their posterity who
approve their sayings. Selah
14 Like sheep they are laid in the
grave;
Death shall feed on them;
[a]The upright shall have dominion
over them in the morning;
[b]And their beauty shall be
consumed in [1]the grave, far
from their dwelling.
15 But God [a]will redeem my soul
from the power of [1]the grave,
For He shall [b]receive me. Selah

16 Do not be afraid when one
becomes rich,
When the glory of his house is
increased;
17 For when he dies he shall carry
nothing away;
His glory shall not descend after
him.
18 Though while he lives [a]he blesses
himself
(For *men* will praise you when
you do well for yourself),
19 He shall go to the generation of
his fathers;
They shall never see [a]light.[1]
20 A man *who is* in honor, yet does
not understand,
[a]Is like the beasts *that* perish.

PSALM 50

God the Righteous Judge

A Psalm of Asaph.

THE [a]Mighty One, God the LORD,
Has spoken and called the earth
From the rising of the sun to its
going down.
2 Out of Zion, the perfection of
beauty,
[a]God will shine forth.
3 Our God shall come, and shall not
keep silent;
[a]A fire shall devour before Him,
And it shall be very tempestuous
all around Him.

4 [a]He shall call to the heavens from
above,
And to the earth, that He may
judge His people:
5 "Gather [a]My saints together to Me,
[b]Those who have [1]made a
covenant with Me by sacrifice."
6 Let the [a]heavens declare His
righteousness,
For [b]God Himself *is* Judge.
Selah

7 "Hear, O My people, and I will
speak,
O Israel, and I will testify against
you;
[a]I *am* God, your God!
8 [a]I will not [1]rebuke you [b]for your
sacrifices
Or your burnt offerings,
Which are continually before Me.

---

13 [a][Ps. 78:5–7]
14 [a]Is. 58:11 [1]So with MT, Syr.; LXX, Vg. *Forever*

PSALM 49

4 [1]*riddle*
6 [a]Job 31:24; Ps. 52:7; [Prov. 11:28; Mark 10:23, 24]
7 [a]Job 36:18, 19
8 [a][Matt. 16:26]
9 [a]Ps. 89:48 [1]*experience corruption*
11 [a]Gen. 4:17; Deut. 3:14 [1]LXX, Syr., Tg., Vg. *Their graves shall be their houses forever*
12 [1]So with MT, Tg.; LXX, Syr., Vg. *understand* (cf. v. 20)
13 [a][Luke 12:20]
14 [a]Ps. 47:3; [Dan. 7:18; 1 Cor. 6:2; Rev. 2:26] [b]Job 4:21 [1]Or *Sheol*
15 [a][Hos. 13:4]; Mark 16:6, 7; Acts 2:31, 32 [b]Ps. 73:24 [1]Or *Sheol*
18 [a]Deut. 29:19; Luke 12:19
19 [a]Job 33:30 [1]The light of life
20 [a]Eccl. 3:19

PSALM 50

1 [a]Is. 9:6
2 [a]Deut. 33:2; Ps. 80:1
3 [a]Lev. 10:2; Num. 16:35; [Ps. 97:3]
4 [a]Deut. 4:26; 31:28; 32:1; Is. 1:2
5 [a]Deut. 33:3 [b]Ex. 24:7 [1]Lit. *cut*
6 [a][Ps. 97:6] [b]Ps. 75:7
7 [a]Ex. 20:2
8 [a]Jer. 7:22 [b]Is. 1:11; [Hos. 6:6] [1]*reprove*

9 [a]I will not take a bull from your
house,
Nor goats out of your folds.
10 For every beast of the forest *is*
Mine,
And the cattle on a thousand
hills.
11 I know all the birds of the
mountains,
And the wild beasts of the field
are Mine.

12 "If I were hungry, I would not tell
you;
[a]For the world *is* Mine, and all its
fullness.
13 [a]Will I eat the flesh of bulls,
Or drink the blood of goats?
14 [a]Offer to God thanksgiving,
And [b]pay your vows to the Most
High.
15 [a]Call upon Me in the day of
trouble;
I will deliver you, and you shall
glorify Me."

16 But to the wicked God says:
"What *right* have you to declare
My statutes,
Or take My covenant in your
mouth,
17 [a]Seeing you hate instruction
And cast My words behind
you?
18 When you saw a thief, you
[a]consented[1] with him,
And have been a [b]partaker with
adulterers.
19 You give your mouth to evil,
And [a]your tongue frames
deceit.
20 You sit *and* speak against your
brother;
You slander your own mother's
son.
21 These *things* you have done, and
I kept silent;
[a]You thought that I was altogether
like you;
But I will rebuke you,
And [b]set *them* in order before
your eyes.

22 "Now consider this, you who
[a]forget God,
Lest I tear *you* in pieces,
And *there be* none to deliver:
23 Whoever offers praise glorifies
Me;
And [a]to him who orders *his*
conduct *aright*
I will show the salvation of
God."

9 [a]Ps. 69:31
12 [a]Ex. 19:5; [Deut. 10:14; Job 41:11]; 1 Cor. 10:26
13 [a][Ps. 51:15–17]
14 [a]Hos. 14:2; Heb. 13:15 [b]Num. 30:2; Deut. 23:21
15 [a]Job 22:27; [Zech. 13:9]
17 [a]Neh. 9:26; Rom. 2:21
18 [a][Rom. 1:32] [b]1 Tim. 5:22 [1]LXX, Syr., Tg., Vg. *ran*
19 [a]Ps. 52:2
21 [a][Rom. 2:4] [b][Ps. 90:8]
22 [a][Job 8:13]
23 [a]Gal. 6:16

PSALM 51

title [a]2 Sam. 12:1
1 [a][Is. 43:25; 44:22; Acts 3:19; Col. 2:14]
2 [a]Jer. 33:8; Ezek. 36:33; [Heb. 9:14; 1 John 1:7, 9]
4 [a]2 Sam. 12:13 [b][Luke 5:21] [c]Rom. 3:4 [1]LXX, Tg., Vg. *in Your words*
5 [a][Job 14:4; Ps. 58:3; John 3:6; Rom. 5:12]
7 [a]Ex. 12:22; Lev. 14:4; Num. 19:18; Heb. 9:19 [b][Is. 1:18]
8 [a][Matt. 5:4]
10 [a][Ezek. 18:31; Eph. 2:10]
11 [a][Luke 11:13]
12 [a][2 Cor. 3:17]

PSALM 51

A Prayer of Repentance

To the Chief Musician. A Psalm of David [a]when Nathan the prophet went to him, after he had gone in to Bathsheba.

HAVE mercy upon me, O God,
According to Your
lovingkindness;
According to the multitude of
Your tender mercies,
[a]Blot out my transgressions.
2 [a]Wash me thoroughly from my
iniquity,
And cleanse me from my sin.

3 For I acknowledge my
transgressions,
And my sin *is* always before me.
4 [a]Against You, You only, have I
sinned,
And done *this* evil [b]in Your
sight—
[c]That You may be found just
[1]when You speak,
And blameless when You judge.

5 [a]Behold, I was brought forth in
iniquity,
And in sin my mother conceived
me.
6 Behold, You desire truth in the
inward parts,
And in the hidden *part* You will
make me to know wisdom.

7 [a]Purge me with hyssop, and I shall
be clean;
Wash me, and I shall be [b]whiter
than snow.
8 Make me hear joy and gladness,
That the bones You have broken
[a]may rejoice.
9 Hide Your face from my sins,
And blot out all my iniquities.

10 [a]Create in me a clean heart,
O God,
And renew a steadfast spirit
within me.
11 Do not cast me away from Your
presence,
And do not take Your [a]Holy
Spirit from me.

12 Restore to me the joy of Your
salvation,
And uphold me *by Your*
[a]generous Spirit.
13 *Then* I will teach transgressors
Your ways,
And sinners shall be converted to
You.

14 Deliver me from the guilt of bloodshed, O God,
The God of my salvation,
And my tongue shall sing aloud of Your righteousness.
15 O Lord, open my lips,
And my mouth shall show forth Your praise.
16 For [a]You do not desire sacrifice, or else I would give *it;*
You do not delight in burnt offering.
17 [a]The sacrifices of God *are* a broken spirit,
A broken and a contrite heart—
These, O God, You will not despise.

18 Do good in Your good pleasure to Zion;
Build the walls of Jerusalem.
19 Then You shall be pleased with [a]the sacrifices of righteousness,
With burnt offering and whole burnt offering;
Then they shall offer bulls on Your altar.

PSALM 52

The End of the Wicked and the Peace of the Godly

To the Chief Musician. A [1]Contemplation of David [a]when Doeg the Edomite went and [b]told Saul, and said to him, "David has gone to the house of Ahimelech."

WHY do you boast in evil, O mighty man?
The goodness of God *endures* continually.
2 Your tongue devises destruction,
Like a sharp razor, working deceitfully.
3 You love evil more than good,
Lying rather than speaking righteousness. Selah
4 You love all devouring words,
You deceitful tongue.

5 God shall likewise destroy you forever;
He shall take you away, and pluck you out of *your* dwelling place,
And uproot you from the land of the living. Selah
6 The righteous also shall see and fear,
And shall laugh at him, *saying,*
7 "Here is the man *who* did not make God his strength,
But trusted in the abundance of his riches,
And strengthened himself in his [1]wickedness."

8 But I *am* [a]like a green olive tree in the house of God;
I trust in the mercy of God forever and ever.
9 I will praise You forever,
Because You have done *it;*
And in the presence of Your saints
I will wait on Your name, for *it* [1]*is* good.

PSALM 53

Folly of the Godless, and the Restoration of Israel

To the Chief Musician. Set to "Mahalath." A [1]Contemplation of David.

THE [a]fool has said in his heart,
"*There is* no God."
They are corrupt, and have done abominable iniquity;
[b]*There is* none who does good.

2 God looks down from heaven upon the children of men,
To see if there are *any* who understand, who [a]seek God.
3 Every one of them has turned aside;
They have together become corrupt;
There is none who does good,
No, not one.

4 Have the workers of iniquity [a]no knowledge,
Who eat up my people *as* they eat bread,
And do not call upon God?
5 [a]There they are in great fear
Where no fear was,
For God has scattered the bones of him who encamps against you;
You have put *them* to shame,
Because God has despised them.

6 [a]Oh, that the salvation of Israel would come out of Zion!
When God brings back [1]the captivity of His people,
Let Jacob rejoice *and* Israel be glad.

PSALM 54

Answered Prayer for Deliverance from Adversaries

To the Chief Musician. With [1]stringed instruments. A [2]Contemplation of David [a]when the Ziphites went and said to Saul, "Is David not hiding with us?"

SAVE me, O God, by Your name,
And vindicate me by Your strength.

---

16 [a][1 Sam. 15:22]; Ps. 50:8–14; [Mic. 6:6–8]
17 [a]Ps. 34:18; [Is. 57:15]; 66:2
19 [a]Ps. 4:5

PSALM 52

title [a]1 Sam. 22:9 [b]Ezek. 22:9 [1]Heb. *Maschil*
7 [1]Lit. *desire,* in evil sense
8 [a]Jer. 11:16
9 [1]Or *has a good reputation*

PSALM 53

title [1]Heb. *Maschil*
1 [a]Ps. 10:4 [b]Rom. 3:10–12
2 [a][2 Chr. 15:2]
4 [a]Jer. 4:22
5 [a]Lev. 26:17, 36; Prov. 28:1
6 [a]Ps. 14:7 [1]Or *His captive people*

PSALM 54

title [a]1 Sam. 23:19 [1]Heb. *neginoth* [2]Heb. *Maschil*

2 Hear my prayer, O God;
Give ear to the words of my mouth.
3 For strangers have risen up against me,
And oppressors have sought after my life;
They have not set God before them. Selah

4 Behold, God *is* my helper;
The Lord *is* with those who [1]uphold my life.
5 He will repay my enemies for their evil.
[1]Cut them off in Your [2]truth.

6 I will freely sacrifice to You;
I will praise Your name, O LORD, for *it is* good.
7 For He has delivered me out of all trouble;
[a]And my eye has seen *its desire* upon my enemies.

PSALM 55

Trust in God Concerning the Treachery of Friends

To the Chief Musician. With [1]stringed instruments. A [2]Contemplation of David.

GIVE ear to my prayer, O God,
And do not hide Yourself from my supplication.
2 Attend to me, and hear me;
I [a]am[1] restless in my complaint, and moan noisily,
3 Because of the voice of the enemy,
Because of the oppression of the wicked;
[a]For they bring down trouble upon me,
And in wrath they hate me.

4 [a]My heart is severely pained within me,
And the terrors of death have fallen upon me.
5 Fearfulness and trembling have come upon me,
And horror has overwhelmed me.
6 So I said, "Oh, that I had wings like a dove!
I would fly away and be at rest.
7 Indeed, I would wander far off,
And remain in the wilderness. Selah
8 I would hasten my escape
From the windy storm *and* tempest."

9 Destroy, O Lord, *and* divide their [1]tongues,
For I have seen [a]violence and strife in the city.
10 Day and night they go around it on its walls;
[a]Iniquity and trouble *are* also in the midst of it.
11 Destruction *is* in its midst;
[a]Oppression and deceit do not depart from its streets.

12 [a]For *it is* not an enemy *who* reproaches me;
Then I could bear *it*.
Nor *is it* one *who* hates me who has [b]exalted *himself* against me;
Then I could hide from him.
13 But *it was* you, a man my equal,
[a]My companion and my acquaintance.
14 We took sweet counsel together,
And [a]walked to the house of God in the throng.
15 Let death seize them;
Let them [a]go down alive into [1]hell,
For wickedness *is* in their dwellings *and* among them.

16 As for me, I will call upon God,
And the LORD shall save me.
17 [a]Evening and morning and at noon
I will pray, and cry aloud,
And He shall hear my voice.
18 He has redeemed my soul in peace from the battle *that was* against me,
For [a]there were many against me.
19 God will hear, and afflict them,
[a]Even He who abides from of old. Selah
Because they do not change,
Therefore they do not fear God.

20 He has [a]put forth his hands against those who [b]were at peace with him;
He has broken his [1]covenant.
21 [a]*The words* of his mouth were smoother than butter,
But war *was* in his heart;
His words were softer than oil,
Yet they *were* drawn swords.

22 [a]Cast your burden on the LORD,
And [b]He shall sustain you;
He shall never permit the righteous to be [1]moved.

23 But You, O God, shall bring them down to the pit of destruction;
[a]Bloodthirsty and deceitful men [b]shall not live out half their days;
But I will trust in You.

---

4 [1]*sustain my soul*
5 [1]*Destroy them* [2]Or *faithfulness*
7 [a]Ps. 59:10

PSALM 55
title [1]Heb. *neginoth* [2]Heb. *Maschil*
2 [a]Is. 38:14; 59:11; Ezek. 7:16 [1]*wander*
3 [a]2 Sam. 16:7, 8
4 [a]Ps. 116:3
9 [a]Jer. 6:7 [1]*speech, their counsel*
10 [a]Ps. 10:7
11 [a]Ps. 10:7
12 [a]Ps. 41:9 [b]Ps. 35:26; 38:16
13 [a]2 Sam. 15:12
14 [a]Ps. 42:4
15 [a]Num. 16:30, 33 [1]Or *Sheol*
17 [a]Dan. 6:10; Luke 18:1; Acts 3:1; 10:3, 30
18 [a]2 Chr. 32:7, 8
19 [a][Deut. 33:27]
20 [a]Acts 12:1 [b]Ps. 7:4 [1]*treaty*
21 [a]Ps. 28:3; 57:4; [Prov. 5:3, 4; 12:18]
22 [a][Ps. 37:5; Matt. 6:25–34; Luke 12:22–31; 1 Pet. 5:7] [b]Ps. 37:24 [1]*shaken*
23 [a]Ps. 5:6 [b]Prov. 10:27

PSALM 56

Prayer for Relief from Tormentors

To the Chief Musician. Set to [1]"The Silent Dove in Distant Lands." A Michtam of David when the [a]Philistines captured him in Gath.

BE [a]merciful to me, O God, for
man would swallow me up;
Fighting all day he oppresses me.
2 My enemies would [a]hound *me* all
day,
For *there are* many who fight
against me, O Most High.

3 Whenever I am afraid,
I will trust in You.
4 In God (I will praise His word),
In God I have put my trust;
[a]I will not fear.
What can flesh do to me?

5 All day they twist my words;
All their thoughts *are* against me
for evil.
6 They gather together,
They hide, they mark my steps,
When they lie in wait for my life.
7 Shall they escape by iniquity?
In anger cast down the peoples,
O God!

8 You number my wanderings;
Put my tears into Your bottle;
[a]*Are they* not in Your book?
9 When I cry out *to You,*
Then my enemies will turn back;
This I know, because [a]God *is* for
me.
10 In God (I will praise *His* word),
In the LORD (I will praise *His*
word),
11 In God I have put my trust;
I will not be afraid.
What can man do to me?

12 Vows *made* to You *are binding*
upon me, O God;
I will render praises to You,
13 [a]For You have delivered my soul
from death.
Have You not *kept* my feet from
falling,
That I may walk before God
In the [b]light of the living?

PSALM 57

Prayer for Safety from Enemies

To the Chief Musician. Set to [1]"Do Not Destroy." A Michtam of David [a]when he fled from Saul into the cave.

BE merciful to me, O God, be
merciful to me!
For my soul trusts in You;
[a]And in the shadow of Your wings
I will make my refuge,
[b]Until *these* calamities have
passed by.

2 I will cry out to God Most High,
To God [a]who performs *all things*
for me.
3 [a]He shall send from heaven and
save me;
He reproaches the one who
[1]would swallow me up. Selah
God [b]shall send forth His mercy
and His truth.

4 My soul *is* among lions;
I lie *among* the sons of men
Who are set on fire,
[a]Whose teeth *are* spears and
arrows,
And their tongue a sharp sword.
5 [a]Be exalted, O God, above the
heavens;
Let Your glory *be* above all the
earth.

6 [a]They have prepared a net for my
steps;
My soul is bowed down;
They have dug a pit before me;
Into the midst of it they
themselves have fallen. Selah

7 [a]My heart is steadfast, O God, my
heart is steadfast;
I will sing and give praise.
8 Awake, [a]my glory!
Awake, lute and harp!
I will awaken the dawn.

9 [a]I will praise You, O Lord, among
the peoples;
I will sing to You among the
[1]nations.
10 [a]For Your mercy reaches unto the
heavens,
And Your truth unto the clouds.

11 [a]Be exalted, O God, above the
heavens;
Let Your glory *be* above all the
earth.

PSALM 58

The Just Judgment of the Wicked

To the Chief Musician. Set to [1]"Do Not Destroy." A Michtam of David.

DO you indeed speak
righteousness, you silent
ones?
Do you judge uprightly, you sons
of men?
2 No, in heart you work
wickedness;

PSALM 56

title [a]1 Sam. 21:11 [1]Heb. *Jonath Elem Rechokim*
1 [a]Ps. 57:1
2 [a]Ps. 57:3
4 [a]Ps. 118:6; Is. 31:3; [Heb. 13:6]
8 [a][Mal. 3:16]
9 [a][Ps. 118:6; Rom. 8:31]
13 [a]Ps. 116:8, 9 [b]Job 33:30

PSALM 57

title [a]1 Sam. 22:1 [1]Heb. *Al Tashcheth*
1 [a]Ruth 2:12; Ps. 17:8; 63:7 [b]Is. 26:20
2 [a][Ps. 138:8]
3 [a]Ps. 144:5, 7 [b]Ps. 43:3 [1]*snaps at* or *hounds me,* or *crushes me*
4 [a]Prov. 30:14
5 [a]Ps. 108:5
6 [a]Ps. 9:15
7 [a]Ps. 108:1–5
8 [a]Ps. 16:9
9 [a]Ps. 108:3 [1]*Gentiles*
10 [a]Ps. 103:11
11 [a]Ps. 57:5

PSALM 58

title [1]Heb. *Al Tashcheth*

You weigh out the violence of
your hands in the earth.

3 [a]The wicked are estranged from
the womb;
They go astray as soon as they
are born, speaking lies.
4 [a]Their poison *is* like the poison of
a serpent;
They are like the deaf cobra *that*
stops its ear,
5 Which will not [a]heed the voice of
charmers,
Charming ever so skillfully.

6 [a]Break[1] their teeth in their mouth,
O God!
Break out the fangs of the young
lions, O LORD!
7 [a]Let them flow away as waters
which run continually;
When he bends *his bow*,
Let his arrows be as if cut in
pieces.
8 *Let them be* like a snail which
melts away as it goes,
[a]*Like* a stillborn child of a woman,
that they may not see the sun.

9 Before your [a]pots can feel *the*
burning thorns,
He shall take them away [b]as with
a whirlwind,
As in His living and burning
wrath.
10 The righteous shall rejoice when
he sees the [a]vengeance;
[b]He shall wash his feet in the
blood of the wicked,
11 [a]So that men will say,
"Surely *there is* a reward for the
righteous;
Surely He is God who [b]judges in
the earth."

PSALM 59

The Assured Judgment of the Wicked

To the Chief Musician. Set to [1]"Do Not Destroy." A Michtam of David [a]when Saul sent men, and they watched the house in order to kill him.

DELIVER me from my enemies,
O my God;
[1]Defend me from those who rise
up against me.
2 Deliver me from the workers of
iniquity,
And save me from bloodthirsty
men.

3 For look, they lie in wait for my
life;
[a]The mighty gather against me,
Not *for* my transgression nor *for*
my sin, O LORD.
4 They run and prepare themselves
through no fault *of mine*.

[a]Awake to help me, and behold!
5 You therefore, O LORD God of
hosts, the God of Israel,
Awake to punish all the [1]nations;
Do not be merciful to any wicked
transgressors. Selah

6 [a]At evening they return,
They growl like a dog,
And go all around the city.
7 Indeed, they belch with their
mouth;
[a]Swords *are* in their lips;
For *they say*, [b]"Who hears?"

8 But [a]You, O LORD, shall laugh at
them;
You shall have all the [1]nations in
derision.
9 I will wait for You, O You [1]his
Strength;
[a]For God *is* my [2]defense.
10 [1]My God of mercy shall [a]come to
meet me;
God shall let [b]me see *my desire*
on my enemies.

11 Do not slay them, lest my people
forget;
Scatter them by Your power,
And bring them down,
O Lord our shield.
12 [a]*For* the sin of their mouth *and* the
words of their lips,
Let them even be taken in their
pride,
And for the cursing and lying
which they speak.
13 [a]Consume *them* in wrath,
consume *them*,
That they *may* not *be*;
And [b]let them know that God
rules in Jacob
To the ends of the earth. Selah

14 And [a]at evening they return,
They growl like a dog,
And go all around the city.
15 They [a]wander up and down for
food,
And [1]howl if they are not
satisfied.

16 But I will sing of Your power;
Yes, I will sing aloud of Your
mercy in the morning;
For You have been my defense
And refuge in the day of my
trouble.
17 To You, [a]O my Strength, I will
sing praises;

---

3 [a][Ps. 53:3; Is. 48:8]
4 [a]Eccl. 10:11
5 [a]Jer. 8:17
6 [a]Job 4:10 [1]*Break away*
7 [a]Josh. 2:11; 7:5; Ps. 112:10; Is. 13:7; Ezek. 21:7
8 [a]Job 3:16
9 [a]Ps. 118:12; Eccl. 7:6 [b]Job 27:21; Prov. 10:25
10 [a][Deut. 32:43]; Jer. 11:20 [b]Ps. 68:23
11 [a]Ps. 92:15; Prov. 11:18; [2 Cor. 5:10] [b]Ps. 50:6; 75:7

PSALM 59

title [a]1 Sam. 19:11 [1]Heb. *Al Tashcheth*
1 [1]Lit. *Set me on high*
3 [a]Ps. 56:6
4 [a]Ps. 35:23
5 [1]*Gentiles*
6 [a]Ps. 59:14
7 [a]Ps. 57:4; Prov. 12:18 [b]Job 22:13; Ps. 10:11
8 [a]Prov. 1:26 [1]*Gentiles*
9 [a][Ps. 62:2] [1]So with MT, Syr.; some Heb. mss., LXX, Tg., Vg. *my Strength* [2]Lit. *fortress*
10 [a]Ps. 21:3 [b]Ps. 54:7 [1]So with Qr.; some Heb. mss., LXX, Vg. *My God, His mercy;* Kt., some Heb. mss., Tg. *O God, my mercy;* Syr. *O God, Your mercy*
12 [a]Prov. 12:13
13 [a]Ps. 104:35 [b]Ps. 83:18
14 [a]Ps. 59:6
15 [a]Job 15:23 [1]So with LXX, Vg.; MT, Syr., Tg. *spend the night*
17 [a]Ps. 18:1

For God *is* my defense,
My God of mercy.

PSALM 60

Urgent Prayer for the Restored Favor of God

To the Chief Musician. [a]Set to [1]"Lily of the Testimony." A Michtam of David. For teaching. [b]When he fought against Mesopotamia and Syria of Zobah, and Joab returned and killed twelve thousand Edomites in the Valley of Salt.

O GOD, [a]You have cast us off;
You have broken us down;
You have been displeased;
Oh, restore us again!
2 You have made the earth tremble;
You have broken it;
[a]Heal its breaches, for it is shaking.
3 [a]You have shown Your people hard things;
[b]You have made us drink the wine of [1]confusion.

4 [a]You have given a banner to those who fear You,
That it may be displayed because of the truth. Selah
5 [a]That Your beloved may be delivered,
Save *with* Your right hand, and hear me.

6 God has [a]spoken in His holiness:
"I will rejoice;
I will [b]divide [c]Shechem
And measure out [d]the Valley of Succoth.
7 Gilead *is* Mine, and Manasseh *is* Mine;
[a]Ephraim also *is* the [1]helmet for My head;
[b]Judah *is* My lawgiver.
8 [a]Moab *is* My washpot;
[b]Over Edom I will cast My shoe;
[c]Philistia, shout in triumph because of Me."

9 Who will bring me *to* the strong city?
Who will lead me to Edom?
10 *Is it* not You, O God, [a]*who* cast us off?
And You, O God, *who* did [b]not go out with our armies?
11 Give us help from trouble,
[a]For the help of man *is* useless.
12 Through God [a]we will do valiantly,
For *it is* He *who* shall tread down our enemies.

PSALM 60

title [a]Ps. 80 [b]2 Sam. 8:3, 13; 1 Chr. 18:3 [1]Heb. *Shushan Eduth*
1 [a]Ps. 44:9
2 [a][2 Chr. 7:14]; Is. 30:26
3 [a]Ps. 71:20 [b]Is. 51:17, 22; Jer. 25:15 [1]*staggering*
4 [a]Ps. 20:5; Is. 5:26; 11:12; 13:2
5 [a]Ps. 108:6–13
6 [a]Ps. 89:35 [b]Josh. 1:6 [c]Gen. 12:6 [d]Josh. 13:27
7 [a]Deut. 33:17 [b][Gen. 49:10] [1]Lit. *protection*
8 [a]2 Sam. 8:2 [b]2 Sam. 8:14; Ps. 108:9 [c]2 Sam. 8:1
10 [a]Ps. 108:11 [b]Josh. 7:12
11 [a]Ps. 118:8; 146:3
12 [a]Num. 24:18

PSALM 61

title [1]Heb. *neginah*
3 [a]Prov. 18:10
4 [a]Ps. 91:4 [1]*tent*
7 [a]Ps. 40:11 [1]Lit. *guard* or *keep*

PSALM 62

title [a]1 Chr. 25:1
1 [a]Ps. 33:20
2 [a]Ps. 55:22 [1]*strong tower* [2]*shaken*
3 [a]Is. 30:13
4 [a]Ps. 28:3
5 [1]*hope*

PSALM 61

Assurance of God's Eternal Protection

To the Chief Musician. On [1]a stringed instrument. A Psalm of David.

HEAR my cry, O God;
Attend to my prayer.
2 From the end of the earth I will cry to You,
When my heart is overwhelmed;
Lead me to the rock that is higher than I.

3 For You have been a shelter for me,
[a]A strong tower from the enemy.
4 I will abide in Your [1]tabernacle forever;
[a]I will trust in the shelter of Your wings. Selah

5 For You, O God, have heard my vows;
You have given *me* the heritage of those who fear Your name.
6 You will prolong the king's life,
His years as many generations.
7 He shall abide before God forever.
Oh, prepare mercy [a]and truth, *which* may [1]preserve him!

8 So I will sing praise to Your name forever,
That I may daily perform my vows.

PSALM 62

A Calm Resolve to Wait for the Salvation of God

To the Chief Musician. To [a]Jeduthun. A Psalm of David.

TRULY [a]my soul silently *waits* for God;
From Him *comes* my salvation.
2 He only *is* my rock and my salvation;
He is my [1]defense;
I shall not be greatly [a]moved.[2]

3 How long will you attack a man?
You shall be slain, all of you,
[a]Like a leaning wall and a tottering fence.
4 They only consult to cast *him* down from his high position;
They [a]delight in lies;
They bless with their mouth,
But they curse inwardly. Selah

5 My soul, wait silently for God alone,
For my [1]expectation *is* from Him.

6 He only *is* my rock and my
salvation;
He is my defense;
I shall not be [1]moved.
7 [a]In God *is* my salvation and my
glory;
The rock of my strength,
And my refuge, *is* in God.

8 Trust in Him at all times, you
people;
[a]Pour out your heart before Him;
God *is* a refuge for us. Selah

9 [a]Surely men of low degree *are* [1]a
vapor,
Men of high degree *are* a lie;
If they are weighed on the scales,
They *are* altogether *lighter* than
vapor.
10 Do not trust in oppression,
Nor vainly hope in robbery;
[a]If riches increase,
Do not set *your* heart *on them.*

11 God has spoken once,
Twice I have heard this:
That power *belongs* to God.
12 Also to You, O Lord, *belongs*
mercy;
For [a]You [1]render to each one
according to his work.

PSALM 63

Joy in the Fellowship of God

A Psalm of David [a]when he was in the wilderness of Judah.

O GOD, You *are* my God;
Early will I seek You;
[a]My soul thirsts for You;
My flesh longs for You
In a dry and thirsty land
Where there is no water.
2 So I have looked for You in the
sanctuary,
To see [a]Your power and Your
glory.

3 [a]Because Your lovingkindness *is*
better than life,
My lips shall praise You.
4 Thus I will bless You while I live;
I will [a]lift up my hands in Your
name.
5 My soul shall be satisfied as with
[1]marrow and [2]fatness,
And my mouth shall praise You
with joyful lips.

6 When [a]I remember You on my
bed,
I meditate on You in the *night*
watches.
7 Because You have been my help,

6 [1]*shaken*
7 [a][Jer. 3:23]
8 [a]1 Sam. 1:15; Ps. 42:4; Lam. 2:19
9 [a]Job 7:16; Ps. 39:5; Is. 40:17 [1]*vanity*
10 [a]Job 31:25; [Mark 10:24; Luke 12:15; 1 Tim. 6:10]
12 [a][Matt. 16:27]; Rom. 2:6; 1 Cor. 3:8 [1]*reward*

PSALM 63

title [a]1 Sam. 22:5
1 [a]Ps. 42:2; [Matt. 5:6]
2 [a]Ps. 27:4
3 [a]Ps. 138:2
4 [a]Ps. 28:2; 143:6
5 [1]Lit. *fat* [2]Abundance
6 [a]Ps. 42:8
10 [1]Lit. *pour him out by the hand of the sword* [2]Prey
11 [a]Deut. 6:13; [Is. 45:23; 65:16]

PSALM 64

1 [1]*complaint*
3 [a]Ps. 58:7
5 [a]Ps. 10:11; 59:7
8 [a]Ps. 31:11
9 [a]Jer. 50:28; 51:10

Therefore in the shadow of Your
wings I will rejoice.
8 My soul follows close behind
You;
Your right hand upholds me.
9 But those *who* seek my life, to
destroy *it*,
Shall go into the lower parts of
the earth.
10 They shall [1]fall by the sword;
They shall be [2]a portion for
jackals.

11 But the king shall rejoice in God;
[a]Everyone who swears by Him
shall glory;
But the mouth of those who speak
lies shall be stopped.

PSALM 64

Oppressed by the Wicked but Rejoicing in the LORD

To the Chief Musician. A Psalm of David.

HEAR my voice, O God, in my
[1]meditation;
Preserve my life from fear of the
enemy.
2 Hide me from the secret plots of
the wicked,
From the rebellion of the workers
of iniquity,
3 Who sharpen their tongue like a
sword,
[a]And bend *their bows to shoot*
their arrows—bitter words,
4 That they may shoot in secret at
the blameless;
Suddenly they shoot at him and
do not fear.

5 They encourage themselves *in* an
evil matter;
They talk of laying snares
secretly;
[a]They say, "Who will see them?"
6 They devise iniquities:
"We have perfected a shrewd
scheme."
Both the inward thought and the
heart of man are deep.

7 But God shall shoot at them *with*
an arrow;
Suddenly they shall be wounded.
8 So He will make them stumble
over their own tongue;
[a]All who see them shall flee away.
9 All men shall fear,
And shall [a]declare the work of
God;
For they shall wisely consider His
doing.

10 [a]The righteous shall be glad in the
LORD, and trust in Him.
And all the upright in heart shall
glory.

PSALM 65

Praise to God for His Salvation and Providence

To the Chief Musician. A Psalm of David. A Song.

PRAISE is awaiting You, O God,
in Zion;
And to You the [1]vow shall be
performed.
2 O You who hear prayer,
[a]To You all flesh will come.
3 Iniquities prevail against me;
As for our transgressions,
You will [a]provide atonement for
them.

4 [a]Blessed *is the man* You [b]choose,
And cause to approach *You,*
That he may dwell in Your
courts.
[c]We shall be satisfied with the
goodness of Your house,
Of Your holy temple.

5 *By* awesome deeds in
righteousness You will answer
us,
O God of our salvation,
You who are the confidence of all
the ends of the earth,
And of the far-off seas;
6 Who established the mountains
by His strength,
[a]*Being* clothed with power;
7 [a]You who still the noise of the
seas,
The noise of their waves,
[b]And the tumult of the peoples.
8 They also who dwell in the
farthest parts are afraid of
Your signs;
You make the outgoings of
the morning and evening
[1]rejoice.

9 You [1]visit the earth and [a]water
it,
You greatly enrich it;
[b]The river of God is full of water;
You provide their grain,
For so You have prepared it.
10 You water its ridges abundantly,
You settle its furrows;
You make it soft with showers,
You bless its growth.

11 You crown the year with Your
goodness,
And Your paths drip *with*
abundance.
12 They drop *on* the pastures of the
wilderness,
And the little hills rejoice on
every side.
13 The pastures are clothed with
flocks;
[a]The valleys also are covered with
grain;
They shout for joy, they also
sing.

PSALM 66

Praise to God for His Awesome Works

To the Chief Musician. A Song. A Psalm.

MAKE [a]a joyful shout to God, all
the earth!
2 Sing out the honor of His name;
Make His praise glorious.
3 Say to God,
"How [a]awesome are Your works!
[b]Through the greatness of Your
power
Your enemies shall submit
themselves to You.
4 [a]All the earth shall worship You
And sing praises to You;
They shall sing praises *to* Your
name." Selah

5 Come and see the works of God;
He is awesome *in His* doing
toward the sons of men.
6 [a]He turned the sea into dry
land;
[b]They went through the river on
foot.
There we will rejoice in Him.
7 He rules by His power forever;
His eyes observe the nations;
Do not let the rebellious exalt
themselves. Selah

8 Oh, bless our God, you peoples!
And make the voice of His praise
to be heard,
9 Who keeps our soul among the
living,
And does not allow our feet to [1]be
moved.
10 For [a]You, O God, have tested us;
[b]You have refined us as silver is
refined.
11 [a]You brought us into the net;
You laid affliction on our backs.
12 [a]You have caused men to ride over
our heads;
[b]We went through fire and
through water;
But You brought us out to [1]rich
fulfillment.

---

10 [a]Job 22:19; Ps. 32:11

PSALM 65

1 [1]A promised deed
2 [a][Is. 66:23]
3 [a]Ps. 51:2; 79:9; Is. 6:7; [Heb. 9:14; 1 John 1:7, 9]
4 [a]Ps. 33:12 [b]Ps. 4:3 [c]Ps. 36:8
6 [a]Ps. 93:1
7 [a]Matt. 8:26 [b]Is. 17:12, 13
8 [1]*shout for joy*
9 [a][Deut. 11:12]; Jer. 5:24 [b]Ps. 46:4; 104:13; 147:8 [1]*give attention to*
13 [a]Is. 44:23; 55:12

PSALM 66

1 [a]Ps. 100:1
3 [a]Ps. 65:5 [b]Ps. 18:44
4 [a]Ps. 117:1; Zech. 14:16
6 [a]Ex. 14:21 [b]Josh. 3:14–16
9 [1]*slip*
10 [a]Job 23:10; Ps. 17:3 [b][Is. 48:10; Zech. 13:9; Mal. 3:3; 1 Pet. 1:7]
11 [a]Lam. 1:13; Ezek. 12:13
12 [a]Is. 51:23 [b]Is. 43:2 [1]*abundance*

13 [a]I will go into Your house with
burnt offerings;
[b]I will pay You my [1]vows,
14 Which my lips have uttered
And my mouth has spoken when
I was in trouble.
15 I will offer You burnt sacrifices
of fat animals,
With the sweet aroma of rams;
I will offer bulls with goats.
Selah

16 Come *and* hear, all you who fear
God,
And I will declare what He has
done for my soul.
17 I cried to Him with my mouth,
And He was [1]extolled with my
tongue.
18 [a]If I regard iniquity in my heart,
The Lord will not hear.
19 *But* certainly God [a]has heard
me;
He has attended to the voice of
my prayer.

20 Blessed *be* God,
Who has not turned away my
prayer,
Nor His mercy from me!

PSALM 67

An Invocation and a Doxology

To the Chief Musician. On [1]stringed instruments. A Psalm. A Song.

GOD be merciful to us and bless
us,
And [a]cause His face to shine upon
us,
Selah
2 That [a]Your way may be known
on earth,
[b]Your salvation among all nations.

3 Let the peoples praise You,
O God;
Let all the peoples praise You.
4 Oh, let the nations be glad and
sing for joy!
For [a]You shall judge the people
righteously,
And govern the nations on earth.
Selah

5 Let the peoples praise You,
O God;
Let all the peoples praise You.
6 [a]*Then* the earth shall [1]yield her
increase;
God, our own God, shall bless us.
7 God shall bless us,
And all the ends of the earth shall
fear Him.

PSALM 68

The Glory of God in His Goodness to Israel

To the Chief Musician. A Psalm of David. A Song.

LET [a]God arise,
Let His enemies be scattered;
Let those also who hate Him flee
before Him.
2 [a]As smoke is driven away,
So drive *them* away;
[b]As wax melts before the fire,
So let the wicked perish at the
presence of God.
3 But [a]let the righteous be glad;
Let them rejoice before God;
Yes, let them rejoice exceedingly.

4 Sing to God, sing praises to His
name;
[a]Extol[1] Him who rides on the
[2]clouds,
[b]By His name [3]YAH,
And rejoice before Him.

5 [a]A father of the fatherless, a
defender of widows,
Is God in His holy habitation.
6 [a]God sets the solitary in families;
[b]He brings out those who are
bound into prosperity;
But [c]the rebellious dwell in a dry
land.

7 O God, [a]when You went out
before Your people,
When You marched through the
wilderness,
Selah
8 The earth shook;
The heavens also dropped *rain* at
the presence of God;
Sinai itself *was moved* at the
presence of God, the God of
Israel.
9 [a]You, O God, sent a plentiful rain,
Whereby You confirmed Your
inheritance,
When it was weary.
10 Your congregation dwelt in it;
[a]You, O God, provided from Your
goodness for the poor.

11 The Lord gave the word;
Great *was* the [1]company of those
who proclaimed it:
12 "Kings[a] of armies flee, they flee,
And she who remains at home
divides the [1]spoil.
13 [a]Though you lie down among the
[1]sheepfolds,
[b]*You will be* like the wings of a
dove covered with silver,

---

13 [a]Ps. 100:4; 116:14, 17–19 [b][Eccl. 5:4] [1]Promised deeds
17 [1]*praised*
18 [a]Job 27:9; [Prov. 15:29; 28:9]; Is. 1:15; [John 9:31; James 4:3]
19 [a]Ps. 116:1, 2

PSALM 67

title [1]Heb. *neginoth*
1 [a]Num. 6:25
2 [a]Acts 18:25 [b]Is. 52:10; Titus 2:11
4 [a][Ps. 96:10, 13; 98:9]
6 [a]Lev. 26:4; Ps. 85:12; [Ezek. 34:27]; Zech. 8:12 [1]*give her produce*

PSALM 68

1 [a]Num. 10:35
2 [a][Is. 9:18]; Hos. 13:3 [b]Ps. 97:5; Mic. 1:4
3 [a]Ps. 32:11
4 [a]Deut. 33:26 [b][Ex. 6:3] [1]*Praise* [2]MT *deserts;* Tg. *heavens* (cf. v. 34 and Is. 19:1) [3]Lit. LORD, a shortened Heb. form
5 [a][Ps. 10:14, 18; 146:9]
6 [a]Ps. 107:4–7 [b]Acts 12:6–11 [c]Ps. 107:34
7 [a]Ex. 13:21; [Hab. 3:13]
9 [a]Lev. 26:4; Deut. 11:11; Job 5:10; Ezek. 34:26
10 [a]Deut. 26:5; Ps. 74:19
11 [1]*host*
12 [a]Num. 31:8; Josh. 10:16; Judg. 5:19 [1]*plunder*
13 [a]Ps. 81:6 [b]Ps. 105:37 [1]Or *saddlebags*

And her feathers with yellow gold."
14 [a]When the Almighty scattered kings in it,
It was *white* as snow in Zalmon.

15 A mountain of God *is* the mountain of Bashan;
A mountain *of many* peaks *is* the mountain of Bashan.
16 Why do you [1]fume with envy, you mountains of *many* peaks?
[a]*This is* the mountain *which* God desires to dwell in;
Yes, the LORD will dwell *in it* forever.

17 [a]The chariots of God *are* twenty thousand,
Even thousands of thousands;
The Lord is among them *as in* Sinai, in the Holy *Place*.
18 [a]You have ascended on high,
[b]You have led captivity captive;
[c]You have received gifts among men,
Even *from* [d]the rebellious,
[e]That the LORD God might dwell *there*.

19 Blessed *be* the Lord,
Who daily loads us *with benefits*,
The God of our salvation! Selah
20 Our God *is* the God of salvation;
And [a]to GOD the Lord *belong* escapes from death.

21 But [a]God will wound the head of His enemies,
[b]The hairy scalp of the one who still goes on in his trespasses.
22 The Lord said, "I will bring [a]back from Bashan,
I will bring *them* back [b]from the depths of the sea,
23 [a]That [1]your foot may crush *them* in blood,
[b]And the tongues of your dogs *may have* their portion from *your* enemies."

24 They have seen Your [1]procession, O God,
The procession of my God, my King, into the sanctuary.
25 [a]The singers went before, the players on instruments *followed* after;
Among *them were* the maidens playing timbrels.
26 Bless God in the congregations,
The Lord, from [a]the fountain of Israel.
27 [a]There *is* little Benjamin, their leader,

14 [a]Josh. 10:10
16 [a][Deut. 12:5]; 1 Kin. 9:3 [1]Lit. *stare*
17 [a]Deut. 33:2; Dan. 7:10
18 [a]Mark 16:19; Acts 1:9; Eph. 4:8; Phil. 2:9; Col. 3:1; Heb. 1:3 [b]Judg. 5:12 [c]Acts 2:4, 33; 10:44–46; [1 Cor. 12:4–11; Eph. 4:7–12] [d][1 Tim. 1:13] [e]Ps. 78:60
20 [a][Deut. 32:39]
21 [a]Hab. 3:13 [b]Ps. 55:23
22 [a]Num. 21:33; Deut. 30:1–9; Amos 9:1–3 [b]Ex. 14:22
23 [a]Ps. 58:10 [b]1 Kin. 21:19; Jer. 15:3 [1]LXX, Syr., Tg., Vg. *you may dip your foot*
24 [1]Lit. *goings*
25 [a]1 Chr. 13:8
26 [a]Deut. 33:28; Is. 48:1
27 [a]Judg. 5:14; 1 Sam. 9:21 [1]*throng*
28 [a]Ps. 42:8; Is. 26:12 [1]LXX, Syr., Tg., Vg. *Command, O God*
29 [a]1 Kin. 10:10, 25; 2 Chr. 32:23; Ps. 45:12; 72:10; Is. 18:7
30 [a]Ps. 22:12 [b]2 Sam. 8:2
31 [a]Is. 19:19–23 [b]Is. 45:14; Zeph. 3:10 [c]Ps. 44:20
32 [a][Ps. 67:3, 4]
33 [a]Deut. 33:26; Ps. 18:10 [b]Ps. 46:6; Is. 30:30
34 [a]Ps. 29:1
35 [a]Ps. 76:12

PSALM 69

title [1]Heb. *Shoshannim*
1 [a]Job 22:11; Jon. 2:5 [1]Lit. *soul*
2 [a]Ps. 40:2
3 [a]Ps. 6:6 [b]Deut. 28:32; Ps. 119:82, 123; Is. 38:14
4 [a]Ps. 35:19; John 15:25

The princes of Judah *and* their [1]company,
The princes of Zebulun *and* the princes of Naphtali.

28 [1]Your God has [a]commanded your strength;
Strengthen, O God, what You have done for us.
29 Because of Your temple at Jerusalem,
[a]Kings will bring presents to You.
30 Rebuke the beasts of the reeds,
[a]The herd of bulls with the calves of the peoples,
Till everyone [b]submits himself with pieces of silver.
Scatter the peoples *who* delight in war.
31 [a]Envoys will come out of Egypt;
[b]Ethiopia will quickly [c]stretch out her hands to God.

32 Sing to God, you [a]kingdoms of the earth;
Oh, sing praises to the Lord, Selah
33 To Him [a]who rides on the heaven of heavens, *which were* of old!
Indeed, He sends out His voice, a [b]mighty voice.
34 [a]Ascribe strength to God;
His excellence *is* over Israel,
And His strength *is* in the clouds.
35 O God, [a]*You are* more awesome than Your holy places.
The God of Israel *is* He who gives strength and power to *His* people.

Blessed *be* God!

PSALM 69

An Urgent Plea for Help in Trouble

To the Chief Musician. Set to [1]"The Lilies." A Psalm of David.

SAVE me, O God!
For [a]the waters have come up to *my* [1]neck.
2 [a]I sink in deep mire,
Where *there is* no standing;
I have come into deep waters,
Where the floods overflow me.
3 [a]I am weary with my crying;
My throat is dry;
[b]My eyes fail while I wait for my God.

4 Those who [a]hate me without a cause
Are more than the hairs of my head;
They are mighty who would destroy me,

Being my enemies wrongfully;
Though I have stolen nothing,
I *still* must restore *it.*

5 O God, You know my foolishness;
And my sins are not hidden from You.
6 Let not those who [1]wait for You, O Lord GOD of hosts, be ashamed because of me;
Let not those who seek You be [2]confounded because of me, O God of Israel.
7 Because for Your sake I have borne reproach;
Shame has covered my face.
8 [a]I have become a stranger to my brothers,
And an alien to my mother's children;
9 [a]Because zeal for Your house has eaten me up,
[b]And the reproaches of those who reproach You have fallen on me.
10 When I wept *and chastened* my soul with fasting,
That became my reproach.
11 I also [1]made sackcloth my garment;
I became a byword to them.
12 Those who [1]sit in the gate speak against me,
And I *am* the song of the [a]drunkards.

13 But as for me, my prayer *is* to You,
O LORD, *in* the acceptable time;
O God, in the multitude of Your mercy,
Hear me in the truth of Your salvation.
14 Deliver me out of the mire,
And let me not sink;
Let me be delivered from those who hate me,
And out of the deep waters.
15 Let not the floodwater overflow me,
Nor let the deep swallow me up;
And let not the pit shut its mouth on me.

16 Hear me, O LORD, for Your lovingkindness *is* good;
Turn to me according to the multitude of Your tender mercies.
17 And do not hide Your face from Your servant,
For I am in trouble;
Hear me speedily.

6 [1]Wait in faith [2]*dishonored*
8 [a]Is. 53:3; Mark 3:21; Luke 8:19; John 7:3–5
9 [a]John 2:17 [b]Rom. 15:3
11 [1]Symbolic of sorrow
12 [a]Job 30:9 [1]Sit as judges
19 [a]Ps. 22:6, 7; Heb. 12:2
20 [a]Is. 63:5 [b]Job 16:2 [1]Lit. *sickness*
21 [a]Matt. 27:34, 48; Mark 15:23, 36; Luke 23:36; John 19:28–30
22 [a]Rom. 11:9, 10
23 [a]Is. 6:9, 10
24 [a][Jer. 10:25; 1 Thess. 2:16]
25 [a]Matt. 23:38; Luke 13:35; Acts 1:20
26 [a][Is. 53:4; 1 Pet. 2:24]
27 [a]Neh. 4:5; [Rom. 1:28] [b][Is. 26:10]
28 [a][Ex. 32:32]; Phil. 4:3; [Rev. 3:5; 13:8] [b]Ezek. 13:9; Luke 10:20; Heb. 12:23
30 [a][Ps. 28:7]
31 [a]Ps. 50:13, 14, 23; 51:16
32 [a]Ps. 34:2 [b]Ps. 22:26
33 [a][Ps. 68:6]; Eph. 3:1

18 Draw near to my soul, *and* redeem it;
Deliver me because of my enemies.

19 You know [a]my reproach, my shame, and my dishonor;
My adversaries *are* all before You.
20 Reproach has broken my heart,
And I am full of [1]heaviness;
[a]I looked *for someone* to take pity, but *there was* none;
And for [b]comforters, but I found none.
21 They also gave me gall for my food,
[a]And for my thirst they gave me vinegar to drink.

22 [a]Let their table become a snare before them,
And their well-being a trap.
23 [a]Let their eyes be darkened, so that they do not see;
And make their loins shake continually.
24 [a]Pour out Your indignation upon them,
And let Your wrathful anger take hold of them.
25 [a]Let their dwelling place be desolate;
Let no one live in their tents.
26 For they persecute the *ones* [a]You have struck,
And talk of the grief of those You have wounded.
27 [a]Add iniquity to their iniquity,
[b]And let them not come into Your righteousness.
28 Let them [a]be blotted out of the book of the living,
[b]And not be written with the righteous.

29 But I *am* poor and sorrowful;
Let Your salvation, O God, set me up on high.
30 [a]I will praise the name of God with a song,
And will magnify Him with thanksgiving.
31 [a]*This* also shall please the LORD better than an ox *or* bull,
Which has horns and hooves.
32 [a]The humble shall see *this and* be glad;
And you who seek God, [b]your hearts shall live.
33 For the LORD hears the poor,
And does not despise [a]His prisoners.

34 [a]Let heaven and earth praise Him,
The seas [b]and everything that moves in them.
35 [a]For God will save Zion
And build the cities of Judah,
That they may dwell there and possess it.
36 Also, [a]the [1]descendants of His servants shall inherit it,
And those who love His name shall dwell in it.

PSALM 70

Prayer for Relief from Adversaries

To the Chief Musician. *A Psalm* of David. [a]To bring to remembrance.

MAKE *haste,* [a]O God, to deliver me!
Make haste to help me, O LORD!
2 [a]Let them be ashamed and confounded
Who seek my life;
Let them be [1]turned back and confused
Who desire my hurt.
3 [a]Let them be turned back because of their shame,
Who say, [1]"Aha, aha!"

4 Let all those who seek You rejoice and be glad in You;
And let those who love Your salvation say continually,
"Let God be magnified!"

5 [a]But I *am* poor and needy;
[b]Make haste to me, O God!
You *are* my help and my deliverer;
O LORD, do not delay.

PSALM 71

God the Rock of Salvation

IN [a]You, O LORD, I put my trust;
Let me never be put to shame.
2 [a]Deliver me in Your righteousness, and cause me to escape;
[b]Incline Your ear to me, and save me.
3 [a]Be my [1]strong refuge,
To which I may resort continually;
You have given the [b]commandment to save me,
For You *are* my rock and my fortress.

4 [a]Deliver me, O my God, out of the hand of the wicked,
Out of the hand of the unrighteous and cruel man.

34 [a]Ps. 96:11; Is. 44:23; 49:13 [b]Is. 55:12
35 [a]Ps. 51:18; Is. 44:26
36 [a]Ps. 102:28 [1]Lit. *seed*

PSALM 70

title [a]Ps. 38:title
1 [a]Ps. 40:13–17
2 [a]Ps. 35:4, 26 [1]So with MT, LXX, Tg., Vg.; some Heb. mss., Syr. *appalled* (cf. 40:15)
3 [a]Ps. 40:15 [1]An expression of scorn
5 [a]Ps. 72:12, 13 [b]Ps. 141:1

PSALM 71

1 [a]Ps. 25:2, 3
2 [a]Ps. 31:1 [b]Ps. 17:6
3 [a]Ps. 31:2, 3 [b]Ps. 44:4 [1]Lit. *rock of refuge* or *rock of habitation*
4 [a]Ps. 140:1, 3
5 [a]Jer. 14:8; 17:7, 13, 17; 50:7
6 [a]Ps. 22:9, 10; Is. 46:3 [1]*sustained from the womb*
7 [a]Is. 8:18; Zech. 3:8; 1 Cor. 4:9
8 [a]Ps. 35:28
10 [a]2 Sam. 17:1
12 [a]Ps. 35:22 [b]Ps. 70:1
13 [1]*ashamed*
17 [a]Deut. 4:5; 6:7
18 [a][Is. 46:4]
19 [a]Deut. 3:24; Ps. 57:10 [1]*great,* lit. *to the height* of heaven

5 For You are [a]my hope, O Lord GOD;
You are my trust from my youth.
6 [a]By You I have been [1]upheld from birth;
You are He who took me out of my mother's womb.
My praise *shall be* continually of You.

7 [a]I have become as a wonder to many,
But You *are* my strong refuge.
8 Let [a]my mouth be filled *with* Your praise
And with Your glory all the day.

9 Do not cast me off in the time of old age;
Do not forsake me when my strength fails.
10 For my enemies speak against me;
And those who lie in wait for my life [a]take counsel together,
11 Saying, "God has forsaken him;
Pursue and take him, for *there is* none to deliver *him.*"

12 [a]O God, do not be far from me;
O my God, [b]make haste to help me!
13 Let them be [1]confounded *and* consumed
Who are adversaries of my life;
Let them be covered *with* reproach and dishonor
Who seek my hurt.

14 But I will hope continually,
And will praise You yet more and more.
15 My mouth shall tell of Your righteousness
And Your salvation all the day,
For I do not know *their* limits.
16 I will go in the strength of the Lord GOD;
I will make mention of Your righteousness, of Yours only.

17 O God, You have taught me from my [a]youth;
And to this *day* I declare Your wondrous works.
18 Now also [a]when *I am* old and grayheaded,
O God, do not forsake me,
Until I declare Your strength to *this* generation,
Your power to everyone *who* is to come.

19 Also [a]Your righteousness, O God, *is* [1]very high,

You who have done great
things;
[b]O God, who *is* like You?
20 [a]*You,* who have shown me great
and severe troubles,
[b]Shall revive me again,
And bring me up again from the
depths of the earth.
21 You shall increase my
greatness,
And comfort me on every side.

22 Also [a]with the lute I will praise
You—
And Your faithfulness, O my
God!
To You I will sing with the harp,
O [b]Holy One of Israel.
23 My lips shall greatly rejoice when
I sing to You,
And [a]my soul, which You have
redeemed.
24 My tongue also shall talk of Your
righteousness all the day long;
For they are confounded,
For they are brought to shame
Who seek my hurt.

PSALM 72

Glory and Universality of the Messiah's Reign

A Psalm [a]of Solomon.

GIVE the king Your judgments,
O God,
And Your righteousness to the
king's Son.
2 [a]He will judge Your people with
righteousness,
And Your poor with justice.
3 [a]The mountains will bring peace
to the people,
And the little hills, by
righteousness.
4 [a]He will bring justice to the poor
of the people;
He will save the children of the
needy,
And will [1]break in pieces the
oppressor.

5 [1]They shall fear You
[a]As long as the sun and moon
endure,
Throughout all generations.
6 [a]He shall come down like rain
upon the grass before mowing,
Like showers *that* water the
earth.
7 In His days the righteous shall
flourish,
[a]And abundance of peace,
Until the moon is no more.

19 [b]Ps. 35:10
20 [a]Ps. 60:3 [b]Hos. 6:1, 2
22 [a]Ps. 92:1–3 [b]2 Kin. 19:22; Is. 1:4
23 [a]Ps. 103:4

PSALM 72

title [a]Ps. 127:title
2 [a][Is. 9:7; 11:2–5; 32:1]
3 [a]Ps. 85:10
4 [a]Is. 11:4 [1]*crush*
5 [a]Ps. 72:7, 17; 89:36 [1]So with MT, Tg.; LXX, Vg. *They shall continue*
6 [a]Deut. 32:2; 2 Sam. 23:4; Hos. 6:3
7 [a]Is. 2:4
8 [a]Ex. 23:31; [Is. 9:6; Zech. 9:10]
9 [a]Ps. 74:14; Is. 23:13 [b]Is. 49:23; Mic. 7:17
10 [a]1 Kin. 10:2; 2 Chr. 9:21
11 [a]Is. 49:23
12 [a]Job 29:12
14 [a]1 Sam. 26:21; [Ps. 116:15]
15 [a]Is. 60:6
16 [a]1 Kin. 4:20
17 [a][Ps. 89:36] [b][Gen. 12:3] [c]Luke 1:48
18 [a]1 Chr. 29:10 [b]Ex. 15:11; Job 5:9
19 [a][Neh. 9:5] [b]Num. 14:21; Hab. 2:14

8 [a]He shall have dominion also from
sea to sea,
And from the River to the ends
of the earth.
9 [a]Those who dwell in the
wilderness will bow before
Him,
[b]And His enemies will lick the
dust.
10 [a]The kings of Tarshish and of the
isles
Will bring presents;
The kings of Sheba and Seba
Will offer gifts.
11 [a]Yes, all kings shall fall down
before Him;
All nations shall serve Him.

12 For He [a]will deliver the needy
when he cries,
The poor also, and *him* who has
no helper.
13 He will spare the poor and
needy,
And will save the souls of the
needy.
14 He will redeem their life from
oppression and violence;
And [a]precious shall be their
blood in His sight.

15 And He shall live;
And the gold of [a]Sheba will be
given to Him;
Prayer also will be made for Him
continually,
And daily He shall be praised.

16 There will be an abundance of
grain in the earth,
On the top of the mountains;
Its fruit shall wave like
Lebanon;
[a]And *those* of the city shall
flourish like grass of the earth.

17 [a]His name shall endure forever;
His name shall continue as long
as the sun.
And [b]*men* shall be blessed in
Him;
[c]All nations shall call Him blessed.

18 [a]Blessed *be* the LORD God, the God
of Israel,
[b]Who only does wondrous things!
19 And [a]blessed *be* His glorious
name forever!
[b]And let the whole earth be filled
with His glory.
Amen and Amen.

20 The prayers of David the son of
Jesse are ended.

BOOK THREE
Psalms 73—89

PSALM 73

The Tragedy of the Wicked, and the Blessedness of Trust in God

A Psalm of [a]Asaph.

TRULY God *is* good to Israel,
To such as are pure in heart.
2 But as for me, my feet had almost stumbled;
My steps had nearly [a]slipped.
3 [a]For I *was* envious of the boastful,
When I saw the prosperity of the [b]wicked.

4 For *there are* no [1]pangs in their death,
But their strength *is* firm.
5 [a]They *are* not in trouble *as other* men,
Nor are they plagued like *other* men.
6 Therefore pride serves as their necklace;
Violence covers them [a]*like* a garment.
7 [a]Their [1]eyes bulge with abundance;
They have more than heart could wish.
8 [a]They scoff and speak wickedly *concerning* oppression;
They [b]speak [1]loftily.
9 They set their mouth [a]against the heavens,
And their tongue walks through the earth.

10 Therefore his people return here,
[a]And waters of a full *cup* are drained by them.
11 And they say, [a]"How does God know?
And is there knowledge in the Most High?"
12 Behold, these *are* the ungodly,
Who are always at ease;
They increase *in* riches.
13 Surely I have [1]cleansed my heart *in* [a]vain,
And washed my hands in innocence.
14 For all day long I have been plagued,
And chastened every morning.

15 If I had said, "I will speak thus,"
Behold, I would have been untrue to the generation of Your children.

PSALM 73
title [a]Ps. 50:title
2 [a]Job 12:5
3 [a]Ps. 37:1, 7; [Prov. 23:17] [b]Job 21:5–16; Jer. 12:1
4 [1]*pains*
5 [a]Job 21:9
6 [a]Ps. 109:18
7 [a]Job 15:27; Jer. 5:28 [1]Tg. *face bulges;* LXX, Syr., Vg. *iniquity bulges*
8 [a]Ps. 53:1 [b]2 Pet. 2:18; Jude 16 [1]Proudly
9 [a]Rev. 13:6
10 [a][Ps. 75:8]
11 [a]Job 22:13
13 [a]Job 21:15; 35:3; Mal. 3:14 [1]*kept my heart pure in vain*
16 [1]*trouble-some in my eyes*
17 [a][Ps. 37:38; 55:23]
18 [a]Ps. 35:6
21 [1]Lit. *pierced in my kidneys*
22 [a]Ps. 92:6
24 [a]Ps. 32:8; 48:14; Is. 58:11
25 [a][Phil. 3:8]
26 [a]Ps. 84:2 [b]Ps. 16:5 [1]Lit. *rock*
27 [a][Ps. 119:155] [1]Are unfaithful to You
28 [a][Heb. 10:22; James 4:8] [b]Ps. 116:10; 2 Cor. 4:13

PSALM 74
title [1]Heb. *Maschil*

16 When I thought *how* to understand this,
It *was* [1]too painful for me—
17 Until I went into the sanctuary of God;
Then I understood their [a]end.

18 Surely [a]You set them in slippery places;
You cast them down to destruction.
19 Oh, how they are *brought* to desolation, as in a moment!
They are utterly consumed with terrors.
20 As a dream when *one* awakes,
So, Lord, when You awake,
You shall despise their image.

21 Thus my heart was grieved,
And I was [1]vexed in my mind.
22 [a]I *was* so foolish and ignorant;
I was *like* a beast before You.
23 Nevertheless I *am* continually with You;
You hold *me* by my right hand.
24 [a]You will guide me with Your counsel,
And afterward receive me *to* glory.

25 [a]Whom have I in heaven *but You?*
And *there is* none upon earth *that* I desire besides You.
26 [a]My flesh and my heart fail;
But God *is* the [1]strength of my heart and my [b]portion forever.

27 For indeed, [a]those who are far from You shall perish;
You have destroyed all those who [1]desert You for harlotry.
28 But *it is* good for me to [a]draw near to God;
I have put my trust in the Lord GOD,
That I may [b]declare all Your works.

PSALM 74

A Plea for Relief from Oppressors

A [1]Contemplation of Asaph.

O GOD, why have You cast *us* off forever?
Why does Your anger smoke against the sheep of Your pasture?
2 Remember Your congregation, *which* You have purchased of old,
The tribe of Your inheritance, *which* You have redeemed—
This Mount Zion where You have dwelt.

3 Lift up Your feet to the perpetual desolations.
The enemy has damaged everything in the sanctuary.
4 [a]Your enemies roar in the midst of Your meeting place;
[b]They set up their banners *for* signs.
5 They seem like men who lift up
Axes among the thick trees.
6 And now they break down its carved work, all at once,
With axes and hammers.
7 They have set fire to Your sanctuary;
They have defiled the dwelling place of Your name to the ground.
8 [a]They said in their hearts,
"Let us [1]destroy them altogether."
They have burned up all the meeting places of God in the land.

9 We do not see our signs;
[a]*There is* no longer any prophet;
Nor *is there* any among us who knows how long.
10 O God, how long will the adversary [1]reproach?
Will the enemy blaspheme Your name forever?
11 [a]Why do You withdraw Your hand, even Your right hand?
Take it out of Your bosom and destroy *them*.
12 For [a]God *is* my King from of old,
Working salvation in the midst of the earth.
13 [a]You divided the sea by Your strength;
You broke the heads of the [1]sea serpents in the waters.
14 You broke the heads of [1]Leviathan in pieces,
And gave him *as* food to the people inhabiting the wilderness.
15 [a]You broke open the fountain and the flood;
[b]You dried up mighty rivers.
16 The day *is* Yours, the night also *is* [a]Yours;
[b]You have prepared the light and the sun.
17 You have [a]set all the borders of the earth;
[b]You have made summer and winter.

18 Remember this, *that* the enemy has reproached, O LORD,
And *that* a foolish people has blasphemed Your name.
19 Oh, do not deliver the life of Your turtledove to the wild beast!
Do not forget the life of Your poor forever.
20 [a]Have respect to the covenant;
For the [1]dark places of the earth are full of the [2]haunts of [3]cruelty.
21 Oh, do not let the oppressed return ashamed!
Let the poor and needy praise Your name.

22 Arise, O God, plead Your own cause;
Remember how the foolish man [1]reproaches You daily.
23 Do not forget the voice of Your enemies;
The tumult of those who rise up against You increases continually.

PSALM 75

Thanksgiving for God's Righteous Judgment

To the Chief Musician. Set to [a]"Do[1] Not Destroy." A Psalm of Asaph. A Song.

WE give thanks to You, O God, we give thanks!
For Your wondrous works declare *that* Your name is near.

2 "When I choose the [1]proper time,
I will judge uprightly.
3 The earth and all its inhabitants are dissolved;
I set up its pillars firmly. Selah

4 "I said to the boastful, 'Do not deal boastfully,'
And to the wicked, [a]'Do not [1]lift up the horn.
5 Do not lift up your horn on high;
Do *not* speak with [1]a stiff neck.' "
6 For exaltation *comes* neither from the east
Nor from the west nor from the south.
7 But [a]God *is* the Judge:
[b]He puts down one,
And exalts another.
8 For [a]in the hand of the LORD *there is* a cup,
And the wine is red;
It is fully mixed, and He pours it out;
Surely its dregs shall all the wicked of the earth
Drain *and* drink down.
9 But I will declare forever,
I will sing praises to the God of Jacob.

4 [a]Lam. 2:7 [b]Num. 2:2
8 [a]Ps. 83:4 [1]*oppress*
9 [a]1 Sam. 3:1; Lam. 2:9; Ezek. 7:26; Amos 8:11
10 [1]*revile*
11 [a]Lam. 2:3
12 [a]Ps. 44:4
13 [a]Ex. 14:21 [1]*sea monsters*
14 [1]A large sea creature of unknown identity
15 [a]Ex. 17:5, 6; Num. 20:11; Ps. 105:41; Is. 48:21 [b]Ex. 14:21, 22; Josh. 2:10; 3:13
16 [a]Job 38:12 [b]Gen. 1:14–18
17 [a]Deut. 32:8; Acts 17:26 [b]Gen. 8:22
20 [a]Gen. 17:7, 8; Lev. 26:44, 45 [1]*hiding places* [2]*homes* [3]*violence*
22 [1]*reviles* or *taunts*

PSALM 75
title [a]Ps. 57:title [1]Heb. *Al Taschheth*
2 [1]*appointed*
4 [a][1 Sam. 2:3]; Ps. 94:4 [1]Raise the head proudly like a horned animal
5 [1]Insolent pride
7 [a]Ps. 50:6 [b]1 Sam. 2:7; Ps. 147:6; Dan. 2:21
8 [a]Job 21:20; Ps. 60:3; Jer. 25:15; Rev. 14:10; 16:19

10 "All[a] the [1]horns of the wicked I
will also cut off,
But [b]the horns of the righteous
shall be [c]exalted."

PSALM 76

The Majesty of God in Judgment

To the Chief Musician. On [1]stringed instruments. A Psalm of Asaph. A Song.

IN [a]Judah God *is* known;
His name *is* great in Israel.
2 In [1]Salem also is His tabernacle,
And His dwelling place in Zion.
3 There He broke the arrows of the
bow,
The shield and sword of battle.
Selah

4 You *are* more glorious and
excellent
[a]*Than* the mountains of prey.
5 [a]The stouthearted were
plundered;
[b]They [1]have sunk into their sleep;
And none of the mighty men have
found the use of their hands.
6 [a]At Your rebuke, O God of Jacob,
Both the chariot and horse were
cast into a dead sleep.

7 You, Yourself, *are* to be feared;
And [a]who may stand in Your
presence
When once You are angry?
8 [a]You caused judgment to be heard
from heaven;
[b]The earth feared and was still,
9 When God [a]arose to judgment,
To deliver all the oppressed of the
earth. Selah

10 [a]Surely the wrath of man shall
praise You;
With the remainder of wrath You
shall gird Yourself.

11 [a]Make vows to the LORD your God,
and pay *them;*
[b]Let all who are around Him bring
presents to Him who ought to
be feared.
12 He shall cut off the spirit of
princes;
[a]*He is* awesome to the kings of the
earth.

PSALM 77

The Consoling Memory of God's Redemptive Works

To the Chief Musician. [a]To Jeduthun. A Psalm of Asaph.

I CRIED out to God with my voice—
To God with my voice;

10 [a]Ps. 101:8; Jer. 48:25 [b]Ps. 89:17; 148:14 [c]1 Sam. 2:1 [1]Strength

PSALM 76

title [1]Heb. *neginoth*

1 [a]Ps. 48:1, 3

2 [1]Jerusalem

4 [a]Ezek. 38:12

5 [a]Is. 10:12; 46:12 [b]Ps. 13:3 [1]Lit. *have slumbered their sleep*

6 [a]Ex. 15:1–21; Ezek. 39:20; Nah. 2:13; Zech. 12:4

7 [a][Ezra 9:15; Nah. 1:6; Mal. 3:2; Rev. 6:17]

8 [a]Ex. 19:9 [b]1 Chr. 16:30; 2 Chr. 20:29

9 [a][Ps. 9:7–9]

10 [a]Ex. 9:16; Rom. 9:17

11 [a][Eccl. 5:4–6] [b]2 Chr. 32:22, 23

12 [a]Ps. 68:35

PSALM 77

title [a]Ps. 39:title

6 [1]*ponders diligently*

8 [a][2 Pet. 3:8, 9] [1]Lit. *unto generation and generation*

10 [1]Lit. *infirmity*

13 [a]Ps. 73:17 [1]Or *holiness*

16 [a]Ex. 14:21; Hab. 3:8, 10

And He gave ear to me.
2 In the day of my trouble I sought
the Lord;
My hand was stretched out in the
night without ceasing;
My soul refused to be comforted.
3 I remembered God, and was
troubled;
I complained, and my spirit was
overwhelmed. Selah

4 You hold my eyelids *open;*
I am so troubled that I cannot
speak.
5 I have considered the days of old,
The years of ancient times.
6 I call to remembrance my song
in the night;
I meditate within my heart,
And my spirit [1]makes diligent
search.

7 Will the Lord cast off forever?
And will He be favorable no
more?
8 Has His mercy ceased forever?
Has *His* [a]promise failed
[1]forevermore?
9 Has God forgotten to be
gracious?
Has He in anger shut up His
tender mercies? Selah

10 And I said, "This *is* my [1]anguish;
But I will remember the years of
the right hand of the Most
High."
11 I will remember the works of the
LORD;
Surely I will remember Your
wonders of old.
12 I will also meditate on all Your
work,
And talk of Your deeds.
13 Your way, O God, *is* in [1]the
[a]sanctuary;
Who *is* so great a God as *our*
God?
14 You *are* the God who does
wonders;
You have declared Your strength
among the peoples.
15 You have with *Your* arm
redeemed Your people,
The sons of Jacob and Joseph.
Selah

16 The waters saw You, O God;
The waters saw You, they were
[a]afraid;
The depths also trembled.
17 The clouds poured out water;
The skies sent out a sound;
Your arrows also flashed about.

18 The voice of Your thunder *was* in the whirlwind;
The lightnings lit up the world;
The earth trembled and shook.
19 Your way *was* in the sea,
Your path in the great waters,
And Your footsteps were not known.
20 You led Your people like a flock
By the hand of Moses and Aaron.

PSALM 78

God's Kindness to Rebellious Israel

A [a]Contemplation[1] of Asaph.

GIVE ear, O my people, *to* my law;
Incline your ears to the words of my mouth.
2 I will open my mouth in a [a]parable;
I will utter [1]dark sayings of old,
3 Which we have heard and known,
And our fathers have told us.
4 [a]We will not hide *them* from their children,
[b]Telling to the generation to come the praises of the LORD,
And His strength and His wonderful works that He has done.

5 For [a]He established a testimony in Jacob,
And appointed a law in Israel,
Which He commanded our fathers,
That [b]they should make them known to their children;
6 [a]That the generation to come might know *them*,
The children *who* would be born,
That they may arise and declare *them* to their children,
7 That they may set their hope in God,
And not forget the works of God,
But keep His commandments;
8 And [a]may not be like their fathers,
[b]A stubborn and rebellious generation,
A generation [c]*that* did not [1]set its heart aright,
And whose spirit was not faithful to God.

9 The children of Ephraim, *being* armed *and* [1]carrying bows,
Turned back in the day of battle.
10 [a]They did not keep the covenant of God;
They refused to walk in His law,
11 And [a]forgot His works

PSALM 78

title [a]Ps. 74:title [1]Heb. *Maschil*
2 [a]Matt. 13:34, 35 [1]*obscure sayings* or *riddles*
4 [a]Ex. 12:26, 27; Deut. 4:9; 6:7; Job 15:18; Is. 38:19; Joel 1:3 [b]Ex. 13:8, 14
5 [a]Ps. 147:19 [b]Deut. 4:9; 11:19
6 [a]Ps. 102:18
8 [a]2 Kin. 17:14; 2 Chr. 30:7; Ezek. 20:18 [b]Ex. 32:9; Deut. 9:7, 24; 31:27; Judg. 2:19; Is. 30:9 [c]Job 11:13; Ps. 78:37 [1]Lit. *prepare its heart*
9 [1]Lit. *bow shooters*
10 [a]2 Kin. 17:15
11 [a]Ps. 106:13
12 [a]Ex. 7—12 [b]Num. 13:22; Is. 19:11; 30:4; Ezek. 30:14
13 [a]Ex. 14:21 [b]Ex. 15:8
14 [a]Ex. 13:21
15 [a]Ex. 17:6; Num. 20:11; Is. 48:21; [1 Cor. 10:4]
16 [a]Num. 20:8, 10, 11
17 [a]Deut. 9:22; Is. 63:10; Heb. 3:16
18 [a]Ex. 16:2
19 [a]Ex. 16:3; Num. 11:4; 20:3; 21:5
20 [a]Num. 20:11
21 [a]Num. 11:1
22 [a]Deut. 1:32; 9:23; [Heb. 3:18]
23 [a]Gen. 7:11; [Mal. 3:10]
24 [a]Ex. 16:4 [b]John 6:31 [1]Lit. *grain*
25 [1]*satiation*
26 [a]Num. 11:31

And His wonders that He had shown them.
12 [a]Marvelous things He did in the sight of their fathers,
In the land of Egypt, [b]*in* the field of Zoan.
13 [a]He divided the sea and caused them to pass through;
And [b]He made the waters stand up like a heap.
14 [a]In the daytime also He led them with the cloud,
And all the night with a light of fire.
15 [a]He split the rocks in the wilderness,
And gave *them* drink in abundance like the depths.
16 He also brought [a]streams out of the rock,
And caused waters to run down like rivers.

17 But they sinned even more against Him
By [a]rebelling against the Most High in the wilderness.
18 And [a]they tested God in their heart
By asking for the food of their fancy.
19 [a]Yes, they spoke against God:
They said, "Can God prepare a table in the wilderness?
20 [a]Behold, He struck the rock,
So that the waters gushed out,
And the streams overflowed.
Can He give bread also?
Can He provide meat for His people?"

21 Therefore the LORD heard *this* and [a]was furious;
So a fire was kindled against Jacob,
And anger also came up against Israel,
22 Because they [a]did not believe in God,
And did not trust in His salvation.
23 Yet He had commanded the clouds above,
[a]And opened the doors of heaven,
24 [a]Had rained down manna on them to eat,
And given them of the [1]bread of [b]heaven.
25 Men ate angels' food;
He sent them food to [1]the full.

26 [a]He caused an east wind to blow in the heavens;
And by His power He brought in the south wind.

27 He also rained meat on them like
the dust,
Feathered fowl like the sand of
the seas;
28 And He let *them* fall in the midst
of their camp,
All around their dwellings.
29 [a]So they ate and were well filled,
For He gave them their own
desire.
30 They were not [1]deprived of their
craving;
But [a]while their food *was* still in
their mouths,
31 The wrath of God came against
them,
And slew the stoutest of them,
And struck down the choice *men*
of Israel.

32 In spite of this [a]they still sinned,
And [b]did not believe in His
wondrous works.
33 [a]Therefore their days He
consumed in futility,
And their years in fear.

34 [a]When He slew them, then they
sought Him;
And they returned and sought
earnestly for God.
35 Then they remembered that [a]God
was their rock,
And the Most High God [b]their
Redeemer.
36 Nevertheless they [a]flattered Him
with their mouth,
And they lied to Him with their
tongue;
37 For their heart was not steadfast
with Him,
Nor were they faithful in His
covenant.
38 [a]But He, *being* full of [b]compassion,
forgave *their* iniquity,
And did not destroy *them*.
Yes, many a time [c]He turned His
anger away,
And [d]did not stir up all His wrath;
39 For [a]He remembered [b]that they
were but flesh,
[c]A breath that passes away and
does not come again.

40 How often they [a]provoked[1] Him
in the wilderness,
And grieved Him in the desert!
41 Yes, [a]again and again they
tempted God,
And limited the Holy One of
Israel.
42 They did not remember His
[1]power:
The day when He redeemed them
from the enemy,

29 [a]Num. 11:19, 20
30 [a]Num. 11:33 [1]Lit. *separated*
32 [a]Num. 14:16, 17 [b]Num. 14:11; Ps. 78:11, 22
33 [a]Num. 14:29, 35
34 [a]Num. 21:7; [Hos. 5:15]
35 [a][Deut. 32:4, 15] [b][Ex. 15:13]; Deut. 7:8; Is. 41:14; 44:6; 63:9
36 [a]Ex. 24:7, 8; Ezek. 33:31
38 [a][Num. 14:18–20] [b]Ex. 34:6 [c][Is. 48:9] [d]1 Kin. 21:29
39 [a]Job 10:9; Ps. 103:14–16 [b]John 3:6 [c][Job 7:7, 16; James 4:14]
40 [a]Ps. 95:8–10; [Eph. 4:30]; Heb. 3:16 [1]*rebelled against Him*
41 [a]Num. 14:22; Deut. 6:16
42 [1]Lit. *hand*
44 [a]Ex. 7:20
45 [a]Ex. 8:24 [b]Ex. 8:6
46 [a]Ex. 10:14
47 [a]Ex. 9:23–25
48 [a]Ex. 9:19 [1]*lightning bolts*
50 [1]Or *their beasts*
51 [a]Ex. 12:29, 30
52 [a]Ps. 77:20
53 [a]Ex. 14:19, 20 [b]Ex. 14:27, 28
54 [a]Ex. 15:17 [b]Ps. 44:3
55 [a]Josh. 11:16–23; Ps. 44:2 [b]Josh. 13:7; 19:51; 23:4 [1]*surveyed measurement*, lit. *measuring cord*
56 [a]Judg. 2:11–13
57 [a]Ezek. 20:27, 28 [b]Hos. 7:16
58 [a]Deut. 32:16, 21; Judg. 2:12; 1 Kin. 14:9; Is. 65:3 [b]Deut. 12:2

43 When He worked His signs in
Egypt,
And His wonders in the field of
Zoan;
44 [a]Turned their rivers into blood,
And their streams, that they
could not drink.
45 [a]He sent swarms of flies among
them, which devoured them,
And [b]frogs, which destroyed
them.
46 He also gave their crops to the
caterpillar,
And their labor to the [a]locust.
47 [a]He destroyed their vines with
hail,
And their sycamore trees with
frost.
48 He also gave up their [a]cattle to
the hail,
And their flocks to fiery
[1]lightning.
49 He cast on them the fierceness of
His anger,
Wrath, indignation, and trouble,
By sending angels of destruction
among them.
50 He made a path for His anger;
He did not spare their soul from
death,
But gave [1]their life over to the
plague,
51 And destroyed all the [a]firstborn
in Egypt,
The first of *their* strength in the
tents of Ham.
52 But He [a]made His own people go
forth like sheep,
And guided them in the
wilderness like a flock;
53 And He [a]led them on safely, so
that they did not fear;
But the sea [b]overwhelmed their
enemies.
54 And He brought them to His
[a]holy border,
This mountain [b]*which* His right
hand had acquired.
55 [a]He also drove out the nations
before them,
[b]Allotted them an inheritance by
[1]survey,
And made the tribes of Israel
dwell in their tents.

56 [a]Yet they tested and provoked the
Most High God,
And did not keep His
testimonies,
57 But [a]turned back and acted
unfaithfully like their fathers;
They were turned aside [b]like a
deceitful bow.
58 [a]For they provoked Him to anger
with their [b]high places,

And moved Him to jealousy with
their carved images.
59 When God heard *this,* He was
furious,
And greatly abhorred Israel,
60 [a]So that He forsook the tabernacle
of Shiloh,
The tent He had placed among
men,
61 [a]And delivered His strength into
captivity,
And His glory into the enemy's
hand.
62 [a]He also gave His people over to
the sword,
And was furious with His
inheritance.
63 The fire consumed their young
men,
And [a]their maidens were not
given in marriage.
64 [a]Their priests fell by the sword,
And [b]their widows made no
lamentation.
65 Then the Lord awoke as *from*
sleep,
[a]Like a mighty man who shouts
because of wine.
66 And [a]He beat back His enemies;
He put them to a perpetual
reproach.
67 Moreover He rejected the tent of
Joseph,
And did not choose the tribe of
Ephraim,
68 But chose the tribe of Judah,
Mount Zion [a]which He loved.
69 And He built His [a]sanctuary like
the heights,
Like the earth which He has
established forever.
70 [a]He also chose David His servant,
And took him from the
sheepfolds;
71 From following [a]the ewes that
had young He brought him,
[b]To shepherd Jacob His people,
And Israel His inheritance.
72 So he shepherded them
according to the [a]integrity of
his heart,
And guided them by the
skillfulness of his hands.

PSALM 79

A Dirge and a Prayer for Israel, Destroyed by Enemies

A Psalm of Asaph.

O GOD, the [1]nations have come
into [a]Your inheritance;
Your holy temple they have
defiled;
[b]They have laid Jerusalem [2]in
heaps.
2 [a]The dead bodies of Your servants
They have given *as* food for the
birds of the heavens,
The flesh of Your saints to the
beasts of the earth.
3 Their blood they have shed like
water all around Jerusalem,
And *there was* no one to bury
them.
4 We have become a reproach to
our [a]neighbors,
A scorn and derision to those
who are around us.

5 [a]How long, LORD?
Will You be angry forever?
Will Your [b]jealousy burn like
fire?
6 [a]Pour out Your wrath on the
[1]nations that [b]do not know
You,
And on the kingdoms that [c]do not
call on Your name.
7 For they have devoured Jacob,
And laid waste his dwelling
place.

8 [a]Oh, do not remember [1]former
iniquities against us!
Let Your tender mercies come
speedily to meet us,
For we have been brought very
low.
9 Help us, O God of our salvation,
For the glory of Your name;
And deliver us, and provide
atonement for our sins,
[a]For Your name's sake!
10 [a]Why should the [1]nations say,
"Where *is* their God?"
Let there be known among the
nations in our sight
The avenging of the blood of
Your servants *which has been*
shed.

11 Let [a]the groaning of the prisoner
come before You;
According to the greatness of
Your [1]power
Preserve those who are
appointed to die;
12 And return to our neighbors
[a]sevenfold into their bosom
[b]Their reproach with which they
have reproached You, O Lord.

13 So [a]we, Your people and sheep
of Your pasture,
Will give You thanks forever;
[b]We will show forth Your praise
to all generations.

---

60 [a]1 Sam. 4:11; Jer. 7:12–14; 26:6–9
61 [a]Judg. 18:30
62 [a]Judg. 20:21; 1 Sam. 4:10
63 [a]Jer. 7:34; 16:9; 25:10
64 [a]1 Sam. 4:17; 22:18 [b]Job 27:15; Ezek. 24:23
65 [a]Is. 42:13
66 [a]1 Sam. 5:6
68 [a][Ps. 87:2]
69 [a]1 Kin. 6:1–38
70 [a]1 Sam. 16:11, 12; 2 Sam. 7:8
71 [a]2 Sam. 7:8; [Is. 40:11] [b]2 Sam. 5:2; 1 Chr. 11:2
72 [a]1 Kin. 9:4

PSALM 79

1 [a]Ps. 74:2 [b]2 Kin. 25:9, 10; 2 Chr. 36:17–19; Jer. 26:18; 52:12–14; Mic. 3:12 [1]*Gentiles* [2]*in ruins*
2 [a]Deut. 28:26; Jer. 7:33; 19:7; 34:20
4 [a]Ps. 44:13; [Dan. 9:16]
5 [a]Ps. 74:1, 9 [b][Zeph. 3:8]
6 [a]Jer. 10:25; [Zeph. 3:8] [b]Is. 45:4, 5; 1 Thess. 4:5; [2 Thess. 1:8] [c]Ps. 53:4 [1]*Gentiles*
8 [a]Is. 64:9 [1]Or *against us the iniquities of those who were before us*
9 [a]Jer. 14:7, 21
10 [a]Ps. 42:10 [1]*Gentiles*
11 [a]Ps. 102:20 [1]Lit. *arm*
12 [a]Gen. 4:15; Lev. 26:21; Prov. 6:31; Is. 30:26 [b]Ps. 74:10, 18, 22
13 [a]Ps. 74:1; 95:7 [b]Is. 43:21

PSALM 80

Prayer for Israel's Restoration

To the Chief Musician. [a]Set to [1]"The Lilies." A [2]Testimony of Asaph. A Psalm.

GIVE ear, O Shepherd of Israel,
[a]You who lead Joseph [b]like a flock;
You who dwell *between* the cherubim, [c]shine forth!
2 Before [a]Ephraim, Benjamin, and Manasseh,
Stir up Your strength,
And come *and* save us!

3 [a]Restore us, O God;
[b]Cause Your face to shine,
And we shall be saved!

4 O LORD God of hosts,
[a]How long will You be angry
Against the prayer of Your people?
5 [a]You have fed them with the bread of tears,
And given them tears to drink in great measure.
6 You have made us a strife to our neighbors,
And our enemies laugh among themselves.

7 Restore us, O God of hosts;
Cause Your face to shine,
And we shall be saved!

8 You have brought [a]a vine out of Egypt;
[b]You have cast out the [1]nations, and planted it.
9 You prepared *room* for it,
And caused it to take deep root,
And it filled the land.
10 The hills were covered with its shadow,
And the [1]mighty cedars with its [a]boughs.
11 She sent out her boughs to [1]the Sea,
And her branches to [2]the River.

12 Why have You [a]broken down her [1]hedges,
So that all who pass by the way pluck her *fruit*?
13 The boar out of the woods uproots it,
And the wild beast of the field devours it.

14 Return, we beseech You, O God of hosts;
[a]Look down from heaven and see,
And visit this vine
15 And the vineyard which Your right hand has planted,
And the branch *that* You made strong [a]for Yourself.
16 *It is* burned with fire, *it is* cut down;
[a]They perish at the rebuke of Your countenance.
17 [a]Let Your hand be upon the man of Your right hand,
Upon the son of man *whom* You made strong for Yourself.
18 Then we will not turn back from You;
Revive us, and we will call upon Your name.

19 Restore us, O LORD God of hosts;
Cause Your face to shine,
And we shall be saved!

PSALM 81

An Appeal for Israel's Repentance

To the Chief Musician. [a]On[1] an instrument of Gath. A Psalm of Asaph.

SING aloud to God our strength;
Make a joyful shout to the God of Jacob.
2 Raise a song and strike the timbrel,
The pleasant harp with the lute.

3 Blow the trumpet at the time of the New Moon,
At the full moon, on our solemn feast day.
4 For [a]this *is* a statute for Israel,
A law of the God of Jacob.
5 This He established in Joseph *as* a testimony,
When He went throughout the land of Egypt,
[a]*Where* I heard a language I did not understand.

6 "I removed his shoulder from the burden;
His hands were freed from the baskets.
7 [a]You called in trouble, and I delivered you;
[b]I answered you in the secret place of thunder;
I [c]tested you at the waters of [1]Meribah. Selah

8 "Hear,[a] O My people, and I will admonish you!
O Israel, if you will listen to Me!
9 There shall be no [a]foreign god among you;
Nor shall you worship any foreign god.
10 [a]I *am* the LORD your God,

PSALM 80

title [a]Ps. 45:title [1]Heb. *Shoshannim* [2]Heb. *Eduth*
1 [a][Ex. 25:20–22]; 1 Sam. 4:4; 2 Sam. 6:2 [b]Ps. 77:20 [c]Deut. 33:2
2 [a]Ps. 78:9, 67
3 [a]Lam. 5:21 [b]Num. 6:25; Ps. 4:6
4 [a]Ps. 79:5
5 [a]Ps. 42:3; Is. 30:20
8 [a][Is. 5:1, 7]; Jer. 2:21; Ezek. 15:6; 17:6; 19:10 [b]Ps. 44:2; Acts 7:45 [1]*Gentiles*
10 [a]Lev. 23:40 [1]Lit. *cedars of God*
11 [1]The Mediterranean [2]The Euphrates
12 [a]Is. 5:5; Nah. 2:2 [1]*walls* or *fences*
14 [a]Is. 63:15
15 [a][Is. 49:5]
16 [a][Ps. 39:11]
17 [a]Ps. 89:21

PSALM 81

title [a]Ps. 8:title [1]Heb. *Al Gittith*
4 [a]Lev. 23:24; Num. 10:10
5 [a]Deut. 28:49; Ps. 114:1; Jer. 5:15
7 [a]Ex. 2:23; 14:10; Ps. 50:15 [b]Ex. 19:19; 20:18 [c]Ex. 17:6, 7; Num. 20:13 [1]Lit. *Strife* or *Contention*
8 [a][Ps. 50:7]
9 [a][Ex. 20:3; Deut. 5:7; 32:12]; Ps. 44:20; [Is. 43:12]
10 [a]Ex. 20:2; Deut. 5:6

Who brought you out of the land
of Egypt;
[b]Open your mouth wide, and I will
fill it.

11 "But My people would not heed
My voice,
And Israel would *have* [a]none of
Me.
12 [a]So I gave them over to [1]their own
stubborn heart,
To walk in their own counsels.

13 "Oh,[a] that My people would listen
to Me,
That Israel would walk in My
ways!
14 I would soon subdue their
enemies,
And turn My hand against their
adversaries.
15 [a]The haters of the LORD would
pretend submission to Him,
But their [1]fate would endure
forever.
16 He would [a]have fed them also
with [1]the finest of wheat;
And with honey [b]from the rock I
would have satisfied you."

PSALM 82

A Plea for Justice

A Psalm of Asaph.

GOD [a]stands in the congregation
of [1]the mighty;
He judges among [b]the [2]gods.
2 How long will you judge unjustly,
And [a]show partiality to the
wicked? Selah
3 [1]Defend the poor and fatherless;
Do justice to the afflicted and
[a]needy.
4 Deliver the poor and needy;
Free *them* from the hand of the
wicked.

5 They do not know, nor do they
understand;
They walk about in darkness;
All the [a]foundations of the earth
are [1]unstable.

6 I said, [a]"You *are* [1]gods,
And all of you *are* children of the
Most High.
7 But you shall die like men,
And fall like one of the
princes."

8 Arise, O God, judge the earth;
[a]For You shall inherit all
nations.

10 [b]Ps. 103:5
11 [a]Ex. 32:1; Deut. 32:15
12 [a][Job 8:4; Acts 7:42; Rom. 1:24, 26] [1]*the dictates of their heart*
13 [a][Deut. 5:29; Is. 48:18]
15 [a]Rom. 1:30 [1]Lit. *time*
16 [a]Deut. 32:14 [b]Job 29:6 [1]Lit. *fat of wheat*

PSALM 82

1 [a][2 Chr. 19:6; Eccl. 5:8] [b]Ps. 82:6 [1]Heb. *El,* lit. *God* [2]Judges; Heb. *elohim,* lit. *mighty ones* or *gods*
2 [a][Deut. 1:17]; Prov. 18:5
3 [a][Deut. 24:17; Is. 11:4; Jer. 22:16] [1]*Vindicate*
5 [a]Ps. 11:3 [1]*moved*
6 [a]John 10:34 [1]Judges; Heb. *elohim,* lit. *mighty ones* or *gods*
8 [a]Ps. 2:8; [Rev. 11:15]

PSALM 83

1 [a]Ps. 28:1
2 [a]Ps. 81:15; Is. 17:12; Acts 4:25 [1]*uproar* [2]Exalted themselves
3 [a][Ps. 27:5]
4 [a]Esth. 3:6, 9; Jer. 11:19; 31:36
5 [1]Lit. *heart* [2]Lit. *cut a covenant*
6 [a]2 Chr. 20:1, 10, 11
9 [a]Num. 31:7; Judg. 7:22 [b]Judg. 4:15–24; 5:20, 21
10 [a]Zeph. 1:17
11 [a]Judg. 7:25 [b]Judg. 8:12–21
13 [a]Is. 17:13 [b]Job 21:18; Ps. 35:5; Is. 40:24; Jer. 13:24
14 [a]Ex. 19:18; Deut. 32:22

PSALM 83

Prayer to Frustrate Conspiracy Against Israel

A Song. A Psalm of Asaph.

DO[a] not keep silent, O God!
Do not hold Your peace,
And do not be still, O God!
2 For behold, [a]Your enemies make
a [1]tumult;
And those who hate You have
[2]lifted up their head.
3 They have taken crafty counsel
against Your people,
And consulted together [a]against
Your sheltered ones.
4 They have said, "Come, and [a]let
us cut them off from *being* a
nation,
That the name of Israel may be
remembered no more."

5 For they have consulted together
with one [1]consent;
They [2]form a confederacy against
You:
6 [a]The tents of Edom and the
Ishmaelites;
Moab and the Hagrites;
7 Gebal, Ammon, and Amalek;
Philistia with the inhabitants of
Tyre;
8 Assyria also has joined with
them;
They have helped the children of
Lot. Selah

9 Deal with them as *with* [a]Midian,
As *with* [b]Sisera,
As *with* Jabin at the Brook
Kishon,
10 Who perished at En Dor,
[a]*Who* became *as* refuse on the
earth.
11 Make their nobles like [a]Oreb and
like Zeeb,
Yes, all their princes like [b]Zebah
and Zalmunna,
12 Who said, "Let us take for
ourselves
The pastures of God for a
possession."

13 [a]O my God, make them like the
whirling dust,
[b]Like the chaff before the wind!
14 As the fire burns the woods,
And as the flame [a]sets the
mountains on fire,
15 So pursue them with Your
tempest,
And frighten them with Your
storm.
16 Fill their faces with shame,

That they may seek Your name,
O LORD.
17 Let them be [1]confounded and
dismayed forever;
Yes, let them be put to shame and
perish,
18 [a]That they may know that You,
whose [b]name alone *is* the LORD,
Are [c]the Most High over all the
earth.

PSALM 84

The Blessedness of Dwelling in the House of God

To the Chief Musician. [a]On[1] an instrument of Gath. A Psalm of the sons of Korah.

HOW [a]lovely [1]*is* Your tabernacle,
O LORD of hosts!
2 [a]My soul longs, yes, even faints
For the courts of the LORD;
My heart and my flesh cry out for
the living God.

3 Even the sparrow has found a
home,
And the swallow a nest for
herself,
Where she may lay her young—
Even Your altars, O LORD of
hosts,
My King and my God.
4 Blessed *are* those who dwell in
Your [a]house;
They will still be praising You.
Selah

5 Blessed *is* the man whose
strength *is* in You,
Whose heart *is* set on pilgrimage.
6 *As they* pass through the Valley
[a]of [1]Baca,
They make it a spring;
The rain also covers it with
[2]pools.
7 They go [a]from strength to
strength;
[1]*Each one* [b]appears before God in
Zion.

8 O LORD God of hosts, hear my
prayer;
Give ear, O God of Jacob! Selah
9 [a]O God, behold our shield,
And look upon the face of Your
[1]anointed.

10 For a day in Your courts *is* better
than a thousand.
I would rather [1]be a doorkeeper
in the house of my God
Than dwell in the tents of
wickedness.
11 For the LORD God *is* [a]a sun and
[b]shield;
The LORD will give grace and
glory;
[c]No good *thing* will He withhold
From those who walk uprightly.

12 O LORD of hosts,
[a]Blessed *is* the man who trusts in
You!

PSALM 85

Prayer that the LORD Will Restore Favor to the Land

To the Chief Musician. A Psalm [a]of the sons of Korah.

LORD, You have been favorable to
Your land;
You have [a]brought back the
captivity of Jacob.
2 You have forgiven the iniquity of
Your people;
You have covered all their sin.
Selah
3 You have taken away all Your
wrath;
You have turned from the
fierceness of Your anger.

4 [a]Restore us, O God of our
salvation,
And cause Your anger toward us
to cease.
5 [a]Will You be angry with us
forever?
Will You prolong Your anger to
all generations?
6 Will You not [a]revive us again,
That Your people may rejoice in
You?
7 Show us Your mercy, LORD,
And grant us Your salvation.

8 I will hear what God the LORD
will speak,
For He will speak peace
To His people and to His saints;
But let them not turn back to
[1]folly.
9 Surely [a]His salvation *is* near to
those who fear Him,
[b]That glory may dwell in our land.

10 Mercy and truth have met
together;
[a]Righteousness and peace have
kissed.
11 Truth shall spring out of the
earth,
And righteousness shall look
down from heaven.
12 [a]Yes, the LORD will give *what is*
good;
And our land will yield its
increase.

83:17 [1]*ashamed*
18 [a]Ps. 59:13 [b]Ex. 6:3 [c][Ps. 92:8]

PSALM 84

title [a]Ps. 8:title [1]Heb. *Al Gittith*
1 [a]Ps. 27:4; 46:4, 5 [1]*are Your dwellings*
2 [a]Ps. 42:1, 2
4 [a][Ps. 65:4]
6 [a]2 Sam. 5:22–25 [1]Lit. *Weeping* [2]Or *blessings*
7 [a]Prov. 4:18; Is. 40:31; John 1:16; 2 Cor. 3:18 [b]Ex. 34:23; Deut. 16:16 [1]LXX, Syr., Vg. *The God of gods shall be seen*
9 [a]Gen. 15:1 [1]Commissioned one, Heb. *messiah*
10 [1]*stand at the threshold*
11 [a]Is. 60:19, 20; Mal. 4:2; Rev. 21:23 [b]Gen. 15:1 [c]Ps. 34:9, 10
12 [a][Ps. 2:12; 40:4]

PSALM 85

title [a]Ps. 42:title
1 [a]Ezra 1:11—2:1; Ps. 14:7; Jer. 30:18; 31:23; Ezek. 39:25; Hos. 6:11; Joel 3:1
4 [a]Ps. 80:3, 7
5 [a]Ps. 79:5
6 [a]Hab. 3:2
8 [1]*foolishness*
9 [a]Is. 46:13 [b]Hag. 2:7; Zech. 2:5; [John 1:14]
10 [a]Ps. 72:3; [Is. 32:17]; Luke 2:14
12 [a][Ps. 84:11; James 1:17]

13 Righteousness will go before
Him,
And shall make His footsteps *our*
pathway.

PSALM 86

Prayer for Mercy, with Meditation on the Excellencies of the LORD

A Prayer of David.

BOW down Your ear, O LORD,
hear me;
For I *am* poor and needy.
2 Preserve my [1]life, for I *am* holy;
You are my God;
Save Your servant who trusts in
You!
3 Be merciful to me, O Lord,
For I cry to You all day long.
4 [1]Rejoice the soul of Your servant,
[a]For to You, O Lord, I lift up my
soul.
5 For [a]You, Lord, *are* good, and
ready to forgive,
And abundant in mercy to all
those who call upon You.

6 Give ear, O LORD, to my prayer;
And attend to the voice of my
supplications.
7 In the day of my trouble I will call
upon You,
For You will answer me.

8 [a]Among the gods *there is* none
like You, O Lord;
Nor *are there any works* like
Your works.
9 All nations whom You have made
Shall come and worship before
You, O Lord,
And shall glorify Your name.
10 For You *are* great, and [a]do
wondrous things;
[b]You alone *are* God.

11 [a]Teach me Your way, O LORD;
I will walk in Your truth;
[1]Unite my heart to fear Your
name.
12 I will praise You, O Lord my God,
with all my heart,
And I will glorify Your name
forevermore.
13 For great *is* Your mercy toward
me,
And You have delivered my soul
from the depths of [1]Sheol.

14 O God, the proud have risen
against me,
And a mob of violent *men* have
sought my life,
And have not set You before
them.
15 But [a]You, O Lord, *are* a God full
of compassion, and gracious,
Longsuffering and abundant in
mercy and truth.

16 Oh, turn to me, and have mercy
on me!
Give Your strength to Your
servant,
And save the son of Your
maidservant.
17 Show me a sign for good,
That those who hate me may see
it and be ashamed,
Because You, LORD, have helped
me and comforted me.

PSALM 87

The Glories of the City of God

A Psalm of the sons of Korah. A Song.

HIS foundation *is* in the holy
mountains.
2 [a]The LORD loves the gates of Zion
More than all the dwellings of
Jacob.
3 [a]Glorious things are spoken of
you,
O city of God! Selah

4 "I will make mention of [1]Rahab
and Babylon to those who
know Me;
Behold, O Philistia and Tyre, with
Ethiopia:
'This *one* was born there.' "

5 And of Zion it will be said,
"This *one* and that *one* were born
in her;
And the Most High Himself shall
establish her."
6 The LORD will record,
When He [a]registers the peoples:
"This *one* was born there." Selah

7 Both the singers and the players
on instruments *say*,
"All my springs *are* in you."

PSALM 88

A Prayer for Help in Despondency

A Song. A Psalm of the sons of Korah. To the Chief Musician. Set to "Mahalath Leannoth." A [1]Contemplation of [a]Heman the Ezrahite.

O LORD, [a]God of my salvation,
I have cried out day and night
before You.
2 Let my prayer come before You;
[1]Incline Your ear to my cry.

PSALM 86

2 [1]Lit. *soul*

4 [a]Ps. 25:1; 143:8 [1]*Make glad*

5 [a]Ps. 130:7; 145:9; [Joel 2:13]

8 [a][Ex. 15:11]; 2 Sam. 7:22; 1 Kin. 8:23; Ps. 89:6; Jer. 10:6

10 [a][Ex. 15:11] [b]Deut. 6:4; Is. 37:16; Mark 12:29; 1 Cor. 8:4

11 [a]Ps. 27:11; 143:8 [1]Give me singleness of heart

13 [1]The abode of the dead

15 [a]Ex. 34:6; [Ps. 86:5]

PSALM 87

2 [a]Ps. 78:67, 68

3 [a]Is. 60:1

4 [1]Egypt

6 [a]Is. 4:3

PSALM 88

title [a]1 Kin. 4:31; 1 Chr. 2:6 [1]Heb. *Maschil*

1 [a]Ps. 27:9; [Luke 18:7]

2 [1]Listen to

3 For my soul is full of troubles,
And my life [a]draws near to the grave.
4 I am counted with those who [a]go[1] down to the pit;
[b]I am like a man *who has* no strength,
5 [1]Adrift among the dead,
Like the slain who lie in the grave,
Whom You remember no more,
And who are cut off from Your hand.

6 You have laid me in the lowest pit,
In darkness, in the depths.
7 Your wrath lies heavy upon me,
And You have afflicted *me* with all [a]Your waves. Selah
8 [a]You have [1]put away my acquaintances far from me;
You have made me an abomination to them;
[b]*I am* shut up, and I cannot get out;
9 My eye wastes away because of affliction.

[a]LORD, I have called daily upon You;
I have stretched out my hands to You.
10 Will You work wonders for the dead?
Shall [1]the dead arise *and* praise You? Selah
11 Shall Your lovingkindness be declared in the grave?
Or Your faithfulness in the place of destruction?
12 Shall Your wonders be known in the dark?
And Your righteousness in the land of forgetfulness?

13 But to You I have cried out, O LORD,
And in the morning my prayer comes before You.
14 LORD, why do You cast off my soul?
Why do You hide Your face from me?
15 I *have been* afflicted and ready to die from *my* youth;
I suffer Your terrors;
I am distraught.
16 Your fierce wrath has gone over me;
Your terrors have [1]cut me off.
17 They came around me all day long like water;
They engulfed me altogether.
18 [a]Loved one and friend You have put far from me,
And my acquaintances into darkness.

3 [a]Ps. 107:18
4 [a][Ps. 28:1] [b]Ps. 31:12 [1]Die
5 [1]Lit. *Free*
7 [a]Ps. 42:7
8 [a]Job 19:13, 19; Ps. 31:11; 142:4 [b]Lam. 3:7 [1]*taken away my friends*
9 [a]Ps. 86:3
10 [1]*shades, ghosts*
16 [1]*destroyed me*
18 [a]Job 19:13; Ps. 31:11; 38:11

PSALM 89

Remembering the Covenant with David, and Sorrow for Lost Blessings

A [1]Contemplation of [a]Ethan the Ezrahite.

I WILL sing of the mercies of the LORD forever;
With my mouth will I make known Your faithfulness to all generations.
2 For I have said, "Mercy shall be built up forever;
[a]Your faithfulness You shall establish in the very heavens."

3 "I[a] have made a covenant with My chosen,
I have [b]sworn to My servant David:
4 'Your seed I will establish forever,
And build up your throne [a]to all generations.'" Selah

5 And [a]the heavens will praise Your wonders, O LORD;
Your faithfulness also in the assembly of the saints.
6 [a]For who in the heavens can be compared to the LORD?
Who among the sons of the mighty can be likened to the LORD?
7 [a]God is greatly to be feared in the assembly of the saints,
And to be held in reverence by all *those* around Him.
8 O LORD God of hosts,
Who *is* mighty like You, O LORD?
Your faithfulness also surrounds You.
9 [a]You rule the raging of the sea;
When its waves rise, You still them.
10 [a]You have broken [1]Rahab in pieces, as one who is slain;
You have scattered Your enemies with Your mighty arm.

11 [a]The heavens *are* Yours, the earth also *is* Yours;
The world and all its fullness, You have founded them.
12 The north and the south, You have created them;
[a]Tabor and [b]Hermon rejoice in Your name.
13 You have a mighty arm;
Strong is Your hand, *and* high is Your right hand.
14 Righteousness and justice *are* the foundation of Your throne;

PSALM 89

title [a]1 Kin. 4:31 [1]Heb. *Maschil*
2 [a][Ps. 119:89, 90]
3 [a]1 Kin. 8:16 [b]2 Sam. 7:11; 1 Chr. 17:10–12
4 [a][2 Sam. 7:13; Is. 9:7; Luke 1:33]
5 [a][Ps. 19:1]
6 [a]Ps. 86:8; 113:5
7 [a]Ps. 76:7, 11
9 [a]Ps. 65:7; 93:3, 4; 107:29
10 [a]Ex. 14:26–28; Ps. 87:4; Is. 30:7; 51:9 [1]Egypt
11 [a][Gen. 1:1; 1 Chr. 29:11]
12 [a]Josh. 19:22; Judg. 4:6; Jer. 46:18 [b]Deut. 3:8; Josh. 11:17; 12:1; Song 4:8

Mercy and truth go before Your
face.
15 Blessed *are* the people who know
the [a]joyful sound!
They walk, O LORD, in the light
of Your countenance.
16 In Your name they rejoice all day
long,
And in Your righteousness they
are exalted.
17 For You *are* the glory of their
strength,
And in Your favor our [1]horn is
[a]exalted.
18 For our shield *belongs* to the
LORD,
And our king to the Holy One of
Israel.

19 Then You spoke in a vision to
Your [1]holy one,
And said: "I have given help to
one who is mighty;
I have exalted one [a]chosen from
the people.
20 [a]I have found My servant David;
With My holy oil I have anointed
him,
21 [a]With whom My hand shall be
established;
Also My arm shall strengthen
him.
22 The enemy shall not [1]outwit
him,
Nor the son of wickedness afflict
him.
23 I will beat down his foes before
his face,
And plague those who hate
him.

24 "But My faithfulness and My
mercy *shall be* with him,
And in My name his horn shall
be exalted.
25 Also I will [a]set his hand over the
sea,
And his right hand over the
rivers.
26 He shall cry to Me, 'You *are* [a]my
Father,
My God, and [b]the rock of my
salvation.'
27 Also I will make him [a]*My*
firstborn,
[b]The highest of the kings of the
earth.
28 [a]My mercy I will keep for him
forever,
And My covenant shall stand
firm with him.
29 His seed also I will make to
endure forever,
[a]And his throne [b]as the days of
heaven.

30 "If[a] his sons [b]forsake My law
And do not walk in My
judgments,
31 If they [1]break My statutes
And do not keep My
commandments,
32 Then I will punish their
transgression with the rod,
And their iniquity with stripes.
33 [a]Nevertheless My lovingkindness
I will not [1]utterly take from
him,
Nor [2]allow My faithfulness to fail.
34 My covenant I will not break,
Nor [a]alter the word that has gone
out of My lips.
35 Once I have sworn [a]by My
holiness;
I will not lie to David:
36 [a]His seed shall endure forever,
And his throne [b]as the sun before
Me;
37 It shall be established forever like
the moon,
Even *like* the faithful witness in
the sky." Selah

38 But You have [a]cast off and
[b]abhorred,[1]
You have been furious with Your
[2]anointed.
39 You have renounced the
covenant of Your servant;
[a]You have [1]profaned his crown *by
casting it* to the ground.
40 You have broken down all his
hedges;
You have brought his
[1]strongholds to ruin.
41 All who pass by the way [a]plunder
him;
He is a reproach to his neighbors.
42 You have exalted the right hand
of his adversaries;
You have made all his enemies
rejoice.
43 You have also turned back the
edge of his sword,
And have not sustained him in
the battle.
44 You have made his [1]glory cease,
And cast his throne down to the
ground.
45 The days of his youth You have
shortened;
You have covered him with
shame. Selah

46 How long, LORD?
Will You hide Yourself forever?
Will Your wrath burn like fire?
47 Remember how short my time
[a]is;
For what [b]futility have You
created all the children of men?

15 [a]Lev. 23:24; Num. 10:10; Ps. 98:6
17 [a]Ps. 75:10; 92:10; 132:17 [1]Strength
19 [a]1 Kin. 11:34 [1]So with many Heb. mss.; MT, LXX, Tg., Vg. *holy ones*
20 [a]1 Sam. 13:14; 16:1–12; Acts 13:22
21 [a]Ps. 80:17
22 [1]Or *exact usury from him*
25 [a]Ps. 72:8
26 [a]2 Sam. 7:14; [1 Chr. 22:10]; Jer. 3:19 [b]2 Sam. 22:47
27 [a]Ex. 4:22; Ps. 2:7; Jer. 31:9; [Col. 1:15, 18] [b]Num. 24:7; [Ps. 72:11]; Rev. 19:16
28 [a]Is. 55:3
29 [a][1 Kin. 2:4; Is. 9:7]; Jer. 33:17 [b]Deut. 11:21
30 [a][2 Sam. 7:14] [b]Ps. 119:53
31 [1]*profane*
33 [a]2 Sam. 7:14, 15 [1]Lit. *break off* [2]Lit. *deal falsely with My faithfulness*
34 [a][Num. 23:19]; Jer. 33:20–22
35 [a][1 Sam. 15:29]; Amos 4:2; [Titus 1:2]
36 [a][Luke 1:33] [b]Ps. 72:17
38 [a][1 Chr. 28:9] [b]Deut. 32:19 [1]*rejected* [2]Commissioned one, Heb. *messiah*
39 [a]Ps. 74:7; Lam. 5:16 [1]*defiled*
40 [1]*fortresses*
41 [a]Ps. 80:12
44 [1]*splendor* or *brightness*
47 [a]Ps. 90:9 [b]Ps. 62:9

48 What man can live and not [1]see [a]death?
Can he deliver his life from the power of [2]the grave? Selah

49 Lord, where *are* Your former lovingkindnesses,
Which You [a]swore to David [b]in Your truth?
50 Remember, Lord, the reproach of Your servants—
[a]*How* I bear in my bosom *the reproach of* all the many peoples,
51 [a]With which Your enemies have reproached, O LORD,
With which they have reproached the footsteps of Your [1]anointed.

52 [a]Blessed *be* the LORD forevermore!
Amen and Amen.

BOOK FOUR

Psalms 90—106

PSALM 90

The Eternity of God, and Man's Frailty

A Prayer [a]of Moses the man of God.

LORD, [a]You have been our [1]dwelling place in all generations.
2 [a]Before the mountains were brought forth,
Or ever You [1]had formed the earth and the world,
Even from everlasting to everlasting, You *are* God.

3 You turn man to destruction,
And say, [a]"Return, O children of men."
4 [a]For a thousand years in Your sight
Are like yesterday when it is past,
And *like* a watch in the night.
5 You carry them away *like* a flood;
[a]*They are* like a sleep.
In the morning [b]they are like grass *which* grows up:
6 In the morning it flourishes and grows up;
In the evening it is cut down and withers.

7 For we have been consumed by Your anger,
And by Your wrath we are terrified.
8 [a]You have set our iniquities before You,
Our [b]secret *sins* in the light of Your countenance.
9 For all our days have passed away in Your wrath;
We finish our years like a sigh.
10 The days of our lives *are* seventy years;
And if by reason of strength *they are* eighty years,
Yet their boast *is* only labor and sorrow;
For it is soon cut off, and we fly away.
11 Who knows the power of Your anger?
For as the fear of You, *so is* Your wrath.
12 [a]So teach *us* to number our days,
That we may gain a heart of wisdom.

13 Return, O LORD!
How long?
And [a]have compassion on Your servants.
14 Oh, satisfy us early with Your mercy,
[a]That we may rejoice and be glad all our days!
15 Make us glad according to the days *in which* You have afflicted us,
The years *in which* we have seen evil.
16 Let [a]Your work appear to Your servants,
And Your glory to their children.
17 [a]And let the beauty of the LORD our God be upon us,
And [b]establish the work of our hands for us;
Yes, establish the work of our hands.

PSALM 91

Safety of Abiding in the Presence of God

HE [a]who dwells in the secret place of the Most High
Shall abide [b]under the shadow of the Almighty.
2 [a]I will say of the LORD, *"He is* my refuge and my fortress;
My God, in Him I will trust."

3 Surely [a]He shall deliver you from the snare of the [1]fowler
And from the perilous pestilence.
4 [a]He shall cover you with His feathers,
And under His wings you shall take refuge;
His truth *shall be your* shield and [1]buckler.

---

48 [a][Eccl. 3:19] [1]*experience death* [2]Or *Sheol*
49 [a][2 Sam. 7:15]; Jer. 30:9; Ezek. 34:23 [b]Ps. 54:5
50 [a]Ps. 69:9, 19
51 [a]Ps. 74:10, 18, 22 [1]Commissioned one, Heb. *messiah*
52 [a]Ps. 41:13

PSALM 90

title [a]Deut. 33:1
1 [a][Deut. 33:27; Ezek. 11:16] [1]LXX, Tg., Vg. *refuge*
2 [a]Job 15:7; [Prov. 8:25, 26] [1]Lit. *gave birth to*
3 [a]Gen. 3:19; Job 34:14, 15
4 [a]2 Pet. 3:8
5 [a]Ps. 73:20 [b]Is. 40:6
8 [a]Ps. 50:21; [Jer. 16:17] [b]Ps. 19:12; [Eccl. 12:14]
12 [a]Deut. 32:29; Ps. 39:4
13 [a]Ex. 32:12; Deut. 32:36
14 [a]Ps. 85:6
16 [a][Deut. 32:4]; Hab. 3:2
17 [a]Ps. 27:4 [b]Is. 26:12

PSALM 91

1 [a]Ps. 27:5; 31:20; 32:7 [b]Ps. 17:8; Is. 25:4; 32:2
2 [a]Ps. 142:5
3 [a]Ps. 124:7; Prov. 6:5 [1]One who catches birds in a trap or snare
4 [a]Ps. 17:8 [1]A small shield

5 [a]You shall not be afraid of the
terror by night,
Nor of the arrow *that* flies by
day,
6 *Nor* of the pestilence *that* walks
in darkness,
Nor of the destruction *that* lays
waste at noonday.

7 A thousand may fall at your side,
And ten thousand at your right
hand;
But it shall not come near you.
8 Only [a]with your eyes shall you
look,
And see the reward of the
wicked.

9 Because you have made the
LORD, *who is* [a]my refuge,
Even the Most High, [b]your
dwelling place,
10 [a]No evil shall befall you,
Nor shall any plague come near
your dwelling;
11 [a]For He shall give His angels
charge over you,
To keep you in all your ways.
12 In *their* hands they shall [1]bear
you up,
[a]Lest you [2]dash your foot against
a stone.
13 You shall tread upon the lion and
the cobra,
The young lion and the serpent
you shall trample underfoot.

14 "Because he has set his love upon
Me, therefore I will deliver him;
I will [1]set him on high, because
he has [a]known My name.
15 He shall [a]call upon Me, and I will
answer him;
I *will be* [b]with him in trouble;
I will deliver him and honor him.
16 With [1]long life I will satisfy him,
And show him My salvation."

PSALM 92

Praise to the LORD for His Love and Faithfulness

A Psalm. A Song for the Sabbath day.

IT *is* [a]good to give thanks to the
LORD,
And to sing praises to Your name,
O Most High;
2 To [a]declare Your lovingkindness
in the morning,
And Your faithfulness every
night,
3 [a]On an instrument of ten strings,
On the lute,
And on the harp,

5 [a][Job 5:19; Ps. 112:7; Is. 43:2]
8 [a]Ps. 37:34; Mal. 1:5
9 [a]Ps. 91:2 [b]Ps. 90:1
10 [a][Prov. 12:21]
11 [a]Ps. 34:7; Matt. 4:6; Luke 4:10; [Heb. 1:14]
12 [a]Matt. 4:6; Luke 4:11 [1]*lift* [2]*strike*
14 [a][Ps. 9:10] [1]*exalt him*
15 [a]Job 12:4; Ps. 50:15 [b]Is. 43:2
16 [1]Lit. *length of days*

PSALM 92
1 [a]Ps. 147:1
2 [a]Ps. 89:1
3 [a]1 Chr. 23:5
5 [a]Ps. 40:5; [Rev. 15:3] [b]Ps. 139:17, 18; [Is. 28:29; Rom. 11:33, 34]
6 [a]Ps. 73:22
7 [a]Job 12:6; Ps. 37:1, 2; Jer. 12:1, 2; [Mal. 3:15] [1]*sprout*
8 [a][Ps. 83:18]
9 [a]Ps. 68:1
10 [a]Ps. 89:17 [b]Ps. 23:5 [1]Strength
11 [a]Ps. 54:7
12 [a]Num. 24:6; Ps. 52:8; Jer. 17:8; Hos. 14:5, 6
14 [1]Full of oil or sap, lit. *fat* [2]*green*
15 [a][Deut. 32:4] [b][Rom. 9:14]

PSALM 93
1 [a]Ps. 96:10 [b]Ps. 65:6 [1]*shaken*

With harmonious sound.
4 For You, LORD, have made me
glad through Your work;
I will triumph in the works of
Your hands.

5 [a]O LORD, how great are Your
works!
[b]Your thoughts are very deep.
6 [a]A senseless man does not know,
Nor does a fool understand this.
7 When [a]the wicked [1]spring up like
grass,
And when all the workers of
iniquity flourish,
It is that they may be destroyed
forever.

8 [a]But You, LORD, *are* on high
forevermore.
9 For behold, Your enemies,
O LORD,
For behold, Your enemies shall
perish;
All the workers of iniquity shall
[a]be scattered.

10 But [a]my [1]horn You have exalted
like a wild ox;
I have been [b]anointed with fresh
oil.
11 [a]My eye also has seen *my desire*
on my enemies;
My ears hear *my desire* on the
wicked
Who rise up against me.

12 [a]The righteous shall flourish like
a palm tree,
He shall grow like a cedar in
Lebanon.
13 Those who are planted in the
house of the LORD
Shall flourish in the courts of our
God.
14 They shall still bear fruit in old
age;
They shall be [1]fresh and
[2]flourishing,
15 To declare that the LORD is
upright;
[a]*He is* my rock, and [b]*there is* no
unrighteousness in Him.

PSALM 93

The Eternal Reign of the LORD

THE [a]LORD reigns, He is clothed
with majesty;
The LORD is clothed,
[b]He has girded Himself with
strength.
Surely the world is established,
so that it cannot be [1]moved.

2 [a]Your throne *is* established from
of old;
You *are* from everlasting.

3 The floods have [1]lifted up,
O LORD,
The floods have lifted up their
voice;
The floods lift up their waves.
4 [a]The LORD on high *is* mightier
Than the noise of many waters,
Than the mighty waves of the
sea.

5 Your testimonies are very sure;
Holiness adorns Your house,
O LORD, [1]forever.

PSALM 94

God the Refuge of the Righteous

O LORD God, [a]to whom
vengeance belongs—
O God, to whom vengeance
belongs, shine forth!
2 Rise up, O [a]Judge of the earth;
[1]Render punishment to the proud.
3 LORD, [a]how long will the wicked,
How long will the wicked
triumph?

4 They [a]utter speech, *and* speak
insolent things;
All the workers of iniquity boast
in themselves.
5 They break in pieces Your
people, O LORD,
And afflict Your heritage.
6 They slay the widow and the
stranger,
And murder the fatherless.
7 [a]Yet they say, "The LORD does not
see,
Nor does the God of Jacob
[1]understand."

8 Understand, you senseless
among the people;
And *you* fools, when will you be
wise?
9 [a]He who planted the ear, shall He
not hear?
He who formed the eye, shall He
not see?
10 He who [1]instructs the [2]nations,
shall He not correct,
He who teaches man knowledge?
11 The LORD [a]knows the thoughts of
man,
That they *are* futile.

12 Blessed *is* the man whom You
[a]instruct, O LORD,
And teach out of Your law,

2 [a]Ps. 45:6; [Lam. 5:19]
3 [1]*raised up*
4 [a]Ps. 65:7
5 [1]Lit. *for length of days*

PSALM 94

1 [a]Deut. 32:35; [Is. 35:4; Nah. 1:2; Rom. 12:19]
2 [a][Gen. 18:25] [1]*Repay with*
3 [a][Job 20:5]
4 [a]Ps. 31:18; Jude 15
7 [a]Job 22:13; Ps. 10:11 [1]*pay attention*
9 [a][Ex. 4:11; Prov. 20:12]
10 [1]*disciplines* [2]*Gentiles*
11 [a]Job 11:11; 1 Cor. 3:20
12 [a][Deut. 8:5; Job 5:17; Ps. 119:71; Prov. 3:11, 12; Heb. 12:5, 6]
13 [1]*relief*
14 [1]*abandon*
20 [a]Amos 6:3
21 [a][Ex. 23:7]; Ps. 106:38; [Prov. 17:15]; Matt. 27:4
23 [1]*destroy them*

PSALM 95

2 [a]Eph. 5:19; James 5:13
3 [a][Ps. 96:4; 1 Cor. 8:5, 6]
4 [1]*In His possession*
5 [a]Gen. 1:9, 10; Jon. 1:9

13 That You may give him [1]rest from
the days of adversity,
Until the pit is dug for the wicked.
14 For the LORD will not [1]cast off His
people,
Nor will He forsake His
inheritance.
15 But judgment will return to
righteousness,
And all the upright in heart will
follow it.

16 Who will rise up for me against
the evildoers?
Who will stand up for me against
the workers of iniquity?
17 Unless the LORD *had been* my
help,
My soul would soon have settled
in silence.
18 If I say, "My foot slips,"
Your mercy, O LORD, will hold
me up.
19 In the multitude of my anxieties
within me,
Your comforts delight my soul.

20 Shall [a]the throne of iniquity,
which devises evil by law,
Have fellowship with You?
21 They gather together against the
life of the righteous,
And condemn [a]innocent blood.
22 But the LORD has been my
defense,
And my God the rock of my
refuge.
23 He has brought on them their
own iniquity,
And shall [1]cut them off in their
own wickedness;
The LORD our God shall cut them
off.

PSALM 95

A Call to Worship and Obedience

OH come, let us sing to the LORD!
Let us shout joyfully to the
Rock of our salvation.
2 Let us come before His presence
with thanksgiving;
Let us shout joyfully to Him with
[a]psalms.
3 For [a]the LORD *is* the great God,
And the great King above all
gods.
4 [1]In His hand *are* the deep places
of the earth;
The heights of the hills *are* His
also.
5 [a]The sea *is* His, for He made it;
And His hands formed the dry
land.

6 Oh come, let us worship and bow down;
Let [a]us kneel before the LORD our Maker.
7 For He *is* our God,
And [a]we *are* the people of His pasture,
And the sheep [1]of His hand.

[b]Today, if you will hear His voice:
8 "Do not harden your hearts, as in the [1]rebellion,
[a]As *in* the day of [2]trial in the wilderness,
9 When [a]your fathers tested Me;
They tried Me, though they [b]saw My work.
10 For [a]forty years I was [1]grieved with *that* generation,
And said, 'It *is* a people who go astray in their hearts,
And they do not know My ways.'
11 So [a]I swore in My wrath,
'They shall not enter My rest.' "

PSALM 96

A Song of Praise to God Coming in Judgment

OH, [a]sing to the LORD a new song!
Sing to the LORD, all the earth.
2 Sing to the LORD, bless His name;
Proclaim the good news of His salvation from day to day.
3 Declare His glory among the [1]nations,
His wonders among all peoples.

4 For [a]the LORD *is* great and [b]greatly to be praised;
[c]He *is* to be feared above all gods.
5 For [a]all the gods of the peoples *are* idols,
[b]But the LORD made the heavens.
6 Honor and majesty *are* before Him;
Strength and [a]beauty *are* in His sanctuary.

7 [a]Give[1] to the LORD, O families of the peoples,
Give to the LORD glory and strength.
8 [1]Give to the LORD the glory *due* His name;
Bring an offering, and come into His courts.
9 Oh, worship the LORD [a]in the beauty of holiness!
Tremble before Him, all the earth.

10 Say among the [1]nations, [a]"The LORD reigns;

6 [a][Phil. 2:10]
7 [a]Ps. 79:13 [b]Heb. 3:7–11, 15; 4:7 [1]Under His care
8 [a]Ex. 17:2–7 [1]Or *Meribah*, lit. *Strife, Contention* [2]Or *Massah*, lit. *Trial, Testing*
9 [a]Ps. 78:18 [b]Num. 14:22
10 [a]Heb. 3:10, 17 [1]*disgusted*
11 [a]Heb. 4:3, 5

PSALM 96
1 [a]1 Chr. 16:23–33
3 [1]*Gentiles*
4 [a]Ps. 145:3 [b]Ps. 18:3 [c]Ps. 95:3
5 [a][Jer. 10:11] [b]Is. 42:5
6 [a]Ps. 29:2
7 [a]Ps. 29:1, 2 [1]*Ascribe*
8 [1]*Ascribe*
9 [a]Ps. 29:2
10 [a]Ps. 93:1; 97:1 [b]Ps. 67:4 [1]*Gentiles* [2]*shaken*
11 [a]Ps. 69:34 [b]Ps. 98:7 [1]*all that is in it*
13 [a][Rev. 19:11]

PSALM 97
1 [a][Ps. 96:10] [1]Or *coastlands*
2 [a]Ps. 18:11 [b][Ps. 89:14]
3 [a]Ps. 18:8
4 [a]Ex. 19:18
5 [a]Mic. 1:4
6 [a]Ps. 19:1
7 [a][Ex. 20:4] [b][Heb. 1:6]
9 [a]Ps. 83:18 [b]Ex. 18:11
10 [a][Ps. 34:14] [b]Prov. 2:8 [c]Ps. 37:40
11 [a]Job 22:28

The world also is firmly established,
It shall not be [2]moved;
[b]He shall judge the peoples righteously."

11 [a]Let the heavens rejoice, and let the earth be glad;
[b]Let the sea roar, and [1]all its fullness;
12 Let the field be joyful, and all that *is* in it.
Then all the trees of the woods will rejoice before the LORD.
13 For He is coming, for He is coming to judge the earth.
[a]He shall judge the world with righteousness,
And the peoples with His truth.

PSALM 97

A Song of Praise to the Sovereign LORD

THE LORD [a]reigns;
Let the earth rejoice;
Let the multitude of [1]isles be glad!

2 [a]Clouds and darkness surround Him;
[b]Righteousness and justice *are* the foundation of His throne.
3 [a]A fire goes before Him,
And burns up His enemies round about.
4 [a]His lightnings light the world;
The earth sees and trembles.
5 [a]The mountains melt like wax at the presence of the LORD,
At the presence of the Lord of the whole earth.
6 [a]The heavens declare His righteousness,
And all the peoples see His glory.

7 [a]Let all be put to shame who serve carved images,
Who boast of idols.
[b]Worship Him, all *you* gods.
8 Zion hears and is glad,
And the daughters of Judah rejoice
Because of Your judgments, O LORD.
9 For You, LORD, *are* [a]most high above all the earth;
[b]You are exalted far above all gods.

10 You who love the LORD, [a]hate evil!
[b]He preserves the souls of His saints;
[c]He delivers them out of the hand of the wicked.
11 [a]Light is sown for the righteous,

And gladness for the upright in
heart.
12 [a]Rejoice in the LORD, you
righteous,
[b]And give thanks [1]at the
remembrance of [2]His holy
name.

PSALM 98

A Song of Praise to the LORD for His Salvation and Judgment

A Psalm.

OH, [a]sing to the LORD a new song!
For He has [b]done marvelous
things;
His right hand and His holy arm
have gained Him the victory.
2 [a]The LORD has made known His
salvation;
[b]His righteousness He has
revealed in the sight of the
[1]nations.
3 He has remembered His mercy
and His faithfulness to the
house of Israel;
[a]All the ends of the earth have
seen the salvation of our God.

4 Shout joyfully to the LORD, all the
earth;
Break forth in song, rejoice, and
sing praises.
5 Sing to the LORD with the harp,
With the harp and the sound of
a psalm,
6 With trumpets and the sound of
a horn;
Shout joyfully before the LORD,
the King.

7 Let the sea roar, and all its
fullness,
The world and those who dwell
in it;
8 Let the rivers clap *their* hands;
Let the hills be joyful together
before the LORD,
9 [a]For He is coming to judge the
earth.
With righteousness He shall
judge the world,
And the peoples with [1]equity.

PSALM 99

Praise to the LORD for His Holiness

THE LORD reigns;
Let the peoples tremble!
[a]He dwells *between* the cherubim;
Let the earth be [1]moved!
2 The LORD *is* great in Zion,
And He *is* high above all the
peoples.
3 Let them praise Your great and
awesome name—
[1]He *is* holy.
4 The King's strength also loves
justice;
You have established equity;
You have executed justice and
righteousness in Jacob.
5 Exalt the LORD our God,
And worship at His footstool—
He *is* holy.

6 Moses and Aaron were among
His priests,
And Samuel was among those
who [a]called upon His name;
They called upon the LORD, and
He answered them.
7 He spoke to them in the cloudy
pillar;
They kept His testimonies and
the [1]ordinance He gave them.

8 You answered them, O LORD our
God;
You were to them God-Who-
Forgives,
Though You took vengeance on
their deeds.
9 Exalt the LORD our God,
And worship at His holy hill;
For the LORD our God *is* holy.

PSALM 100

A Song of Praise for the LORD's Faithfulness to His People

[a]A Psalm of Thanksgiving.

MAKE [a]a joyful shout to the
LORD, [1]all you lands!
2 Serve the LORD with gladness;
Come before His presence with
singing.
3 Know that the LORD, He *is* God;
[a]*It is* He *who* has made us, and
[1]not we ourselves;
[b]*We are* His people and the sheep
of His pasture.

4 [a]Enter into His gates with
thanksgiving,
And into His courts with praise.
Be thankful to Him, *and* bless His
name.
5 For the LORD *is* good;
[a]His mercy *is* everlasting,
And His truth *endures* to all
generations.

PSALM 101

Promised Faithfulness to the LORD

A Psalm of David.

I WILL sing of mercy and justice;
To You, O LORD, I will sing
praises.

---

12 [a]Ps. 33:1 [b]Ps. 30:4 [1]Or *for the memory* [2]Or *His holiness*

PSALM 98

1 [a]Ps. 33:3; Is. 42:10 [b]Ex. 15:11; Ps. 77:14

2 [a]Is. 52:10; [Luke 1:77; 2:30, 31] [b]Is. 62:2; Rom. 3:25 [1]*Gentiles*

3 [a][Is. 49:6]; Luke 3:6; [Acts 13:47; 28:28]

9 [a][Ps. 96:10, 13] [1]*uprightness*

PSALM 99

1 [a]Ex. 25:22; 1 Sam. 4:4; Ps. 80:1 [1]*shaken*

3 [1]Or *It*

6 [a]1 Sam. 7:9; 12:18

7 [1]*statute*

PSALM 100

title [a]Ps. 145:title

1 [a]Ps. 95:1 [1]Lit. *all the earth*

3 [a]Job 10:3, 8; Ps. 119:73; 139:13, 14; [Eph. 2:10] [b]Ps. 95:7; [Is. 40:11]; Ezek. 34:30, 31 [1]So with Kt., LXX, Vg.; Qr., many Heb. mss., Tg. *we are His*

4 [a]Ps. 66:13; 116:17–19

5 [a]Ps. 136:1

2 I will behave wisely in a [1]perfect way.
Oh, when will You come to me?
I will [a]walk within my house with a perfect heart.

3 I will set nothing [1]wicked before my eyes;
[a]I hate the work of those [b]who fall away;
It shall not cling to me.
4 A perverse heart shall depart from me;
I will not [a]know wickedness.

5 Whoever secretly slanders his neighbor,
Him I will destroy;
[a]The one who has a haughty look and a proud heart,
Him I will not endure.

6 My eyes *shall be* on the faithful of the land,
That they may dwell with me;
He who walks in a [1]perfect way,
He shall serve me.
7 He who works deceit shall not dwell within my house;
He who tells lies shall not [1]continue in my presence.
8 [a]Early I will destroy all the wicked of the land,
That I may cut off all the evildoers [b]from the city of the LORD.

PSALM 102

The LORD's Eternal Love

A Prayer of the afflicted, [a]when he is overwhelmed and pours out his complaint before the LORD.

HEAR my prayer, O LORD,
And let my cry come to You.
2 [a]Do not hide Your face from me in the day of my trouble;
Incline Your ear to me;
In the day that I call, answer me speedily.

3 For my days [1]are [a]consumed like smoke,
And my bones are burned like a hearth.
4 My heart is stricken and withered like grass,
So that I forget to eat my bread.
5 Because of the sound of my groaning
My bones cling to my [1]skin.
6 I am like a pelican of the wilderness;
I am like an owl of the desert.
7 I lie awake,
And am like a sparrow alone on the housetop.

8 My enemies reproach me all day long;
Those who deride me swear an oath against me.
9 For I have eaten ashes like bread,
And mingled my drink with weeping,
10 Because of Your indignation and Your wrath;
For You have lifted me up and cast me away.
11 My days *are* like a shadow that lengthens,
And I wither away like grass.

12 But You, O LORD, shall endure forever,
And the remembrance of Your name to all generations.
13 You will arise *and* have mercy on Zion;
For the time to favor her,
Yes, the set time, has come.
14 For Your servants take pleasure in her stones,
And show favor to her dust.
15 So the [1]nations shall [a]fear the name of the LORD,
And all the kings of the earth Your glory.
16 For the LORD shall build up Zion;
[a]He shall appear in His glory.
17 [a]He shall regard the prayer of the destitute,
And shall not despise their prayer.

18 This will be [a]written for the generation to come,
That [b]a people yet to be created may praise the LORD.
19 For He [a]looked down from the height of His sanctuary;
From heaven the LORD viewed the earth,
20 [a]To hear the groaning of the prisoner,
To release those appointed to death,
21 To [a]declare the name of the LORD in Zion,
And His praise in Jerusalem,
22 [a]When the peoples are gathered together,
And the kingdoms, to serve the LORD.

23 He weakened my strength in the way;
He [a]shortened my days.
24 [a]I said, "O my God,

PSALM 101
2 [a]1 Kin. 11:4 [1]*blameless*
3 [a]Ps. 97:10 [b]Josh. 23:6 [1]*worthless*
4 [a][Ps. 119:115]
5 [a]Prov. 6:17
6 [1]*blameless*
7 [1]Lit. *be established*
8 [a][Ps. 75:10]; Jer. 21:12 [b]Ps. 48:2, 8

PSALM 102
title [a]Ps. 61:2
2 [a]Ps. 27:9; 69:17
3 [a]James 4:14 [1]Lit. *end in*
5 [1]*flesh*
15 [a]1 Kin. 8:43 [1]*Gentiles*
16 [a][Is. 60:1, 2]
17 [a]Neh. 1:6; Ps. 22:24
18 [a]Deut. 31:19; [Rom. 15:4; 1 Cor. 10:11] [b]Ps. 22:31
19 [a]Deut. 26:15; Ps. 14:2
20 [a]Ps. 79:11
21 [a]Ps. 22:22
22 [a][Is. 2:2, 3; 49:22, 23; 60:3]; Zech. 8:20–23
23 [a]Job 21:21
24 [a][Ps. 39:13]; Is. 38:10

Do not take me away in the midst
of my days;
[b]Your years *are* throughout all
generations.
25 [a]Of old You laid the foundation of
the earth,
And the heavens *are* the work of
Your hands.
26 [a]They will perish, but You will
[1]endure;
Yes, they will all grow old like a
garment;
Like a cloak You will change
them,
And they will be changed.
27 But [a]You *are* the same,
And Your years will have no end.
28 [a]The children of Your servants
will continue,
And their descendants will be
established before You."

PSALM 103

Praise for the LORD's Mercies

A Psalm of David.

BLESS [a]the LORD, O my soul;
And all that is within me, *bless*
His holy name!
2 Bless the LORD, O my soul,
And forget not all His benefits:
3 [a]Who forgives all your iniquities,
Who [b]heals all your diseases,
4 Who redeems your life from
destruction,
[a]Who crowns you with
lovingkindness and tender
mercies,
5 Who satisfies your mouth with
good *things*,
So that [a]your youth is renewed
like the eagle's.

6 The LORD executes righteousness
And justice for all who are
oppressed.
7 [a]He made known His ways to
Moses,
His acts to the children of Israel.
8 [a]The LORD *is* merciful and
gracious,
Slow to anger, and abounding in
mercy.
9 [a]He will not always strive *with us*,
Nor will He keep *His anger*
forever.
10 [a]He has not dealt with us
according to our sins,
Nor punished us according to our
iniquities.

11 For as the heavens are high above
the earth,
So great is His mercy toward
those who fear Him;
12 As far as the east is from the west,
So far has He [a]removed our
transgressions from us.
13 [a]As a father pities *his* children,
So the LORD pities those who fear
Him.
14 For He [1]knows our frame;
He remembers that we *are* dust.

15 *As for* man, [a]his days *are* like
grass;
As a flower of the field, so he
flourishes.
16 [a]For the wind passes over it, and
it is [1]gone,
And [b]its place remembers it no
more.
17 But the mercy of the LORD *is* from
everlasting to everlasting
On those who fear Him,
And His righteousness to
children's children,
18 [a]To such as keep His covenant,
And to those who remember His
commandments to do them.

19 The LORD has established His
throne in heaven,
And [a]His kingdom rules over all.

20 [a]Bless the LORD, you His angels,
Who excel in strength, who [b]do
His word,
Heeding the voice of His word.
21 Bless the LORD, all *you* His hosts,
[a]*You* [1]ministers of His, who do His
pleasure.
22 Bless the LORD, all His works,
In all places of His dominion.

Bless the LORD, O my soul!

PSALM 104

Praise to the Sovereign LORD for His Creation and Providence

BLESS [a]the LORD, O my soul!

O LORD my God, You are very
great:
You are clothed with honor and
majesty,
2 Who cover *Yourself* with light as
with a garment,
Who stretch out the heavens like
a curtain.

3 [a]He lays the beams of His upper
chambers in the waters,
Who makes the clouds His
chariot,
Who walks on the wings of the
wind,
4 Who makes His angels spirits,
His [1]ministers a flame of fire.

---

24 [b]Job 36:26; [Ps. 90:2]; Hab. 1:12
25 [a][Gen. 1:1; Neh. 9:6; Heb. 1:10–12]
26 [a]Is. 34:4; 51:6; Matt. 24:35; [2 Pet. 3:7, 10–12]; Rev. 20:11 [1]*continue*
27 [a][Is. 41:4; 43:10; Mal. 3:6; Heb. 13:8]; James 1:17
28 [a]Ps. 69:36

PSALM 103

1 [a]Ps. 104:1, 35
3 [a]Ps. 130:8; Is. 33:24 [b][Ex. 15:26]; Ps. 147:3; [Is. 53:5]; Jer. 17:14
4 [a][Ps. 5:12]
5 [a][Is. 40:31]
7 [a]Ex. 33:12–17; Ps. 147:19
8 [a][Ex. 34:6, 7; Num. 14:18]; Deut. 5:10; Neh. 9:17; Ps. 86:15; Jer. 32:18; Jon. 4:2; James 5:11
9 [a][Ps. 30:5; Is. 57:16]; Jer. 3:5; [Mic. 7:18]
10 [a][Ezra 9:13; Lam. 3:22]
12 [a][2 Sam. 12:13; Is. 38:17; 43:25; Zech. 3:9; Heb. 9:26]
13 [a]Mal. 3:17
14 [1]Understands our constitution
15 [a]Is. 40:6–8; James 1:10, 11; 1 Pet. 1:24
16 [a][Is. 40:7] [b]Job 7:10 [1]*not*
18 [a][Deut. 7:9]; Ps. 25:10
19 [a][Ps. 47:2; Dan. 4:17, 25]
20 [a]Ps. 148:2 [b][Matt. 6:10]
21 [a][Heb. 1:14] [1]*servants*

PSALM 104

1 [a]Ps. 103:1
3 [a][Amos 9:6]
4 [1]*servants*

5 *You who* [1]laid the foundations of
the earth,
So *that* it should not be moved
forever,
6 You [a]covered it with the deep as
with a garment;
The waters stood above the
mountains.
7 At Your rebuke they fled;
At the voice of Your thunder they
hastened away.
8 [1]They went up over the
mountains;
They went down into the
valleys,
To the place which You founded
for them.
9 You have [a]set a boundary that
they may not pass over,
[b]That they may not return to cover
the earth.

10 He sends the springs into the
valleys;
They flow among the hills.
11 They give drink to every beast of
the field;
The wild donkeys quench their
thirst.
12 By them the birds of the heavens
have their home;
They sing among the branches.
13 [a]He waters the hills from His
upper chambers;
The earth is satisfied with [b]the
fruit of Your works.

14 [a]He causes the grass to grow for
the cattle,
And vegetation for the service of
man,
That he may bring forth [b]food
from the earth,
15 And [a]wine *that* makes glad the
heart of man,
Oil to make *his* face shine,
And bread *which* strengthens
man's heart.
16 The trees of the LORD are full *of
sap*,
The cedars of Lebanon which He
planted,
17 Where the birds make their nests;
The stork has her home in the fir
trees.
18 The high hills *are* for the wild
goats;
The cliffs are a refuge for the
[a]rock[1] badgers.

19 [a]He appointed the moon for
seasons;
The [b]sun knows its going down.
20 [a]You make darkness, and it is
night,
In which all the beasts of the
forest creep about.
21 [a]The young lions roar after their
prey,
And seek their food from God.
22 *When* the sun rises, they gather
together
And lie down in their dens.
23 Man goes out to [a]his work
And to his labor until the evening.

24 [a]O LORD, how manifold are Your
works!
In wisdom You have made them
all.
The earth is full of Your
[b]possessions—
25 This great and wide sea,
In which *are* innumerable
teeming things,
Living things both small and
great.
26 There the ships sail about;
There is that [a]Leviathan[1]
Which You have [2]made to play
there.

27 [a]These all wait for You,
That You may give *them* their
food in due season.
28 *What* You give them they gather
in;
You open Your hand, they are
filled with good.
29 You hide Your face, they are
troubled;
[a]You take away their breath, they
die and return to their dust.
30 [a]You send forth Your Spirit, they
are created;
And You renew the face of the
earth.

31 May the glory of the LORD endure
forever;
May the LORD [a]rejoice in His
works.
32 He looks on the earth, and it
[a]trembles;
[b]He touches the hills, and they
smoke.

33 [a]I will sing to the LORD as long as
I live;
I will sing praise to my God while
I have my being.
34 May my [a]meditation be sweet to
Him;
I will be glad in the LORD.
35 May [a]sinners be consumed from
the earth,
And the wicked be no more.

Bless the LORD, O my soul!
[1]Praise the LORD!

5 [1]Lit. *founded the earth upon her bases*
6 [a]Gen. 1:6
8 [1]Or *The mountains rose up; The valleys sank down*
9 [a]Job 26:10; Ps. 33:7; [Jer. 5:22] [b]Gen. 9:11–15
13 [a]Ps. 147:8 [b]Jer. 10:13
14 [a]Gen. 1:29 [b]Job 28:5
15 [a]Judg. 9:13; Ps. 23:5; Prov. 31:6; Eccl. 10:19
18 [a]Lev. 11:5 [1]*rock hyraxes*
19 [a]Gen. 1:14 [b]Job 38:12; Ps. 19:6
20 [a][Ps. 74:16; Is. 45:7]
21 [a]Job 38:39
23 [a]Gen. 3:19
24 [a]Ps. 40:5; Prov. 3:19; [Jer. 10:12]; 51:15 [b]Ps. 65:9
26 [a]Job 41:1; Is. 27:1 [1]A large sea creature of unknown identity [2]Lit. *formed*
27 [a]Job 36:31; Ps. 136:25
29 [a]Job 34:15; [Eccl. 12:7]
30 [a]Is. 32:15
31 [a]Gen. 1:31; Prov. 8:31
32 [a]Hab. 3:10 [b]Ex. 19:18; Ps. 144:5
33 [a]Ps. 63:4
34 [a]Ps. 19:14
35 [a]Ps. 37:38 [1]Heb. *Hallelujah*

PSALM 105

The Eternal Faithfulness of the LORD

OH, [a]give thanks to the LORD!
Call upon His name;
[b]Make known His deeds among the peoples!
2 Sing to Him, sing psalms to Him;
[a]Talk of all His wondrous works!
3 Glory in His holy name;
Let the hearts of those rejoice who seek the LORD!
4 Seek the LORD and His strength;
[a]Seek His face evermore!
5 [a]Remember His marvelous works which He has done,
His wonders, and the judgments of His mouth,
6 O seed of Abraham His servant,
You children of Jacob, His chosen ones!

7 He *is* the LORD our God;
[a]His judgments *are* in all the earth.
8 He [a]remembers His covenant forever,
The word *which* He commanded, for a thousand generations,
9 [a]*The covenant* which He made with Abraham,
And His oath to Isaac,
10 And confirmed it to Jacob for a statute,
To Israel *as* an everlasting covenant,
11 Saying, [a]"To you I will give the land of Canaan
As the allotment of your inheritance,"
12 [a]When they were few in number,
Indeed very few, [b]and strangers in it.

13 When they went from one nation to another,
From *one* kingdom to another people,
14 [a]He permitted no one to do them wrong;
Yes, [b]He rebuked kings for their sakes,
15 *Saying*, "Do not touch My anointed ones,
And do My prophets no harm."

16 Moreover [a]He called for a famine in the land;
He destroyed all the [b]provision of bread.
17 [a]He sent a man before them—
Joseph—*who* [b]was sold as a slave.
18 [a]They hurt his feet with fetters,
[1]He was laid in irons.

PSALM 105

1 [a]1 Chr. 16:8–22, 34; Ps. 106:1; Is. 12:4 [b]Ps. 145:12
2 [a]Ps. 119:27
4 [a]Ps. 27:8
5 [a]Ps. 77:11
7 [a][Is. 26:9]
8 [a]Luke 1:72
9 [a]Gen. 17:2; Luke 1:73; [Gal. 3:17]; Heb. 6:17
11 [a]Gen. 13:15; 15:18
12 [a]Gen. 34:30; [Deut. 7:7] [b]Gen. 23:4; Heb. 11:9
14 [a]Gen. 35:5 [b]Gen. 12:17
16 [a]Gen. 41:54 [b]Lev. 26:26; Is. 3:1; Ezek. 4:16
17 [a][Gen. 45:5] [b]Gen. 37:28, 36; Acts 7:9
18 [a]Gen. 40:15 [1]*His soul came into iron*
19 [a]Gen. 39:11–21; 41:25, 42, 43
20 [a]Gen. 41:14
21 [a]Gen. 41:40–44
22 [1]Bind as prisoners
23 [a]Gen. 46:6; Acts 7:15 [b]Ps. 78:51
24 [a]Ex. 1:7, 9
25 [a]Ex. 1:8–10; 4:21
26 [a]Ex. 3:10; 4:12–15
27 [a]Ex. 7—12; Ps. 78:43
29 [a]Ex. 7:20, 21; Ps. 78:44
30 [a]Ex. 8:6
31 [a]Ex. 8:16, 17
32 [a]Ex. 9:23–25
33 [a]Ps. 78:47
34 [a]Ex. 10:4
36 [a]Ex. 12:29; 13:15; Ps. 135:8; 136:10 [b]Gen. 49:3 [1]Lit. *struck down*
37 [a]Ex. 12:35, 36
38 [a]Ex. 12:33
39 [a]Ex. 13:21; Neh. 9:12; Ps. 78:14; Is. 4:5

19 Until the time that his word came to pass,
[a]The word of the LORD tested him.
20 [a]The king sent and released him,
The ruler of the people let him go free.
21 [a]He made him lord of his house,
And ruler of all his possessions,
22 To [1]bind his princes at his pleasure,
And teach his elders wisdom.

23 [a]Israel also came into Egypt,
And Jacob dwelt [b]in the land of Ham.
24 [a]He increased His people greatly,
And made them stronger than their enemies.
25 [a]He turned their heart to hate His people,
To deal craftily with His servants.

26 [a]He sent Moses His servant,
And Aaron whom He had chosen.
27 They [a]performed His signs among them,
And wonders in the land of Ham.
28 He sent darkness, and made *it* dark;
And they did not rebel against His word.
29 [a]He turned their waters into blood,
And killed their fish.
30 [a]Their land abounded with frogs,
Even in the chambers of their kings.
31 [a]He spoke, and there came swarms of flies,
And lice in all their territory.
32 [a]He gave them hail for rain,
And flaming fire in their land.
33 [a]He struck their vines also, and their fig trees,
And splintered the trees of their territory.
34 [a]He spoke, and locusts came,
Young locusts without number,
35 And ate up all the vegetation in their land,
And devoured the fruit of their ground.
36 [a]He also [1]destroyed all the firstborn in their land,
[b]The first of all their strength.

37 [a]He also brought them out with silver and gold,
And *there was* none feeble among His tribes.
38 [a]Egypt was glad when they departed,
For the fear of them had fallen upon them.
39 [a]He spread a cloud for a covering,
And fire to give light in the night.

40 [a]*The people* asked, and He
brought quail,
And [b]satisfied them with the
bread of heaven.
41 [a]He opened the rock, and water
gushed out;
It ran in the dry places *like* a
river.
42 For He remembered [a]His holy
promise,
And Abraham His servant.
43 He brought out His people with
joy,
His chosen ones with [1]gladness.
44 [a]He gave them the lands of the
[1]Gentiles,
And they inherited the labor of
the nations,
45 [a]That they might observe His
statutes
And keep His laws.

[1]Praise the LORD!

PSALM 106

Joy in Forgiveness of Israel's Sins

PRAISE[1] the LORD!
[a]Oh, give thanks to the LORD, for
He is good!
For His mercy *endures* forever.
2 Who can [1]utter the mighty acts
of the LORD?
Who can declare all His praise?
3 Blessed *are* those who keep
justice,
And [1]he who [a]does righteousness
at [b]all times!
4 [a]Remember me, O LORD, with the
favor *You have toward* Your
people.
Oh, visit me with Your salvation,
5 That I may see the benefit of Your
chosen ones,
That I may rejoice in the gladness
of Your nation,
That I may glory with [1]Your
inheritance.
6 [a]We have sinned with our fathers,
We have committed iniquity,
We have done wickedly.
7 Our fathers in Egypt did not
understand Your wonders;
They did not remember the
multitude of Your mercies,
[a]But rebelled by the sea—the Red
Sea.
8 Nevertheless He saved them for
His name's sake,
[a]That He might make His mighty
power known.
9 [a]He rebuked the Red Sea also, and
it dried up;
So [b]He led them through the
depths,
As through the wilderness.
10 He [a]saved them from the hand of
him who hated *them*,
And redeemed them from the
hand of the enemy.
11 [a]The waters covered their
enemies;
There was not one of them left.
12 [a]Then they believed His words;
They sang His praise.
13 [a]They soon forgot His works;
They did not wait for His counsel,
14 [a]But lusted exceedingly in the
wilderness,
And tested God in the desert.
15 [a]And He gave them their request,
But [b]sent leanness into their soul.
16 When [a]they envied Moses in the
camp,
And Aaron the saint of the LORD,
17 [a]The earth opened up and
swallowed Dathan,
And covered the faction of
Abiram.
18 [a]A fire was kindled in their
company;
The flame burned up the wicked.
19 [a]They made a calf in Horeb,
And worshiped the molded
image.
20 Thus [a]they changed their glory
Into the image of an ox that eats
grass.
21 They forgot God their Savior,
Who had done great things in
Egypt,
22 Wondrous works in the land of
Ham,
Awesome things by the Red Sea.
23 [a]Therefore He said that He would
destroy them,
Had not Moses His chosen one
[b]stood before Him in the
breach,
To turn away His wrath, lest He
destroy *them*.
24 Then they despised [a]the pleasant
land;
They [b]did not believe His word,
25 [a]But complained in their tents,
And did not heed the voice of the
LORD.
26 [a]Therefore He raised up His hand
in an oath against them,
[b]To [1]overthrow them in the
wilderness,

40 [a]Ex. 16:12 [b]Ps. 78:24
41 [a]Ex. 17:6
42 [a]Gen. 15:13, 14
43 [1]*a joyful shout*
44 [a]Josh. 11:16–23; 13:7 [1]*nations*
45 [a][Deut. 4:1, 40] [1]Heb. *Hallelujah*

PSALM 106

1 [a]1 Chr. 16:34, 41 [1]Heb. *Hallelujah*
2 [1]*express*
3 [a]Ps. 15:2 [b][Gal. 6:9] [1]LXX, Syr., Tg., Vg. *those who do*
4 [a]Ps. 119:132
5 [1]The people of Your inheritance
6 [a][Dan. 9:5]
7 [a]Ex. 14:11, 12
8 [a]Ex. 9:16
9 [a]Ex. 14:21 [b]Is. 63:11–13
10 [a]Ex. 14:30
11 [a]Ex. 14:27, 28; 15:5
12 [a]Ex. 15:1–21
13 [a]Ex. 15:24; 16:2; 17:2
14 [a]1 Cor. 10:6
15 [a]Num. 11:31 [b]Is. 10:16
16 [a]Num. 16:1–3
17 [a]Deut. 11:6
18 [a]Num. 16:35, 46
19 [a]Ex. 32:1–4
20 [a]Rom. 1:23
23 [a]Ex. 32:10 [b]Ezek. 22:30
24 [a]Deut. 8:7 [b][Heb. 3:18, 19]
25 [a]Num. 14:2, 27
26 [a]Ezek. 20:15, 16 [b]Num. 14:28–30 [1]*make them fall*

27 [a]To [1]overthrow their descendants among the [2]nations,
And to scatter them in the lands.

28 [a]They joined themselves also to Baal of Peor,
And ate sacrifices [1]made to the dead.
29 Thus they provoked *Him* to anger with their deeds,
And the plague broke out among them.
30 [a]Then Phinehas stood up and intervened,
And the plague was stopped.
31 And that was accounted to him [a]for righteousness
To all generations forevermore.

32 [a]They angered *Him* also at the waters of [1]strife,
[b]So that it went ill with Moses on account of them;
33 [a]Because they rebelled against His Spirit,
So that he spoke rashly with his lips.

34 [a]They did not destroy the peoples,
[b]Concerning whom the LORD had commanded them,
35 [a]But they mingled with the Gentiles
And learned their works;
36 [a]They served their idols,
[b]Which became a snare to them.
37 [a]They even sacrificed their sons
And their daughters to [b]demons,
38 And shed innocent blood,
The blood of their sons and daughters,
Whom they sacrificed to the idols of Canaan;
And [a]the land was polluted with blood.
39 Thus they [1]were [a]defiled by their own works,
And [b]played[2] the harlot by their own deeds.

40 Therefore [a]the wrath of the LORD was kindled against His people,
So that He abhorred [b]His own inheritance.
41 And [a]He gave them into the hand of the Gentiles,
And those who hated them ruled over them.
42 Their enemies also oppressed them,
And they were brought into subjection under their hand.
43 [a]Many times He delivered them;
But they rebelled in their counsel,

27 [a]Lev. 26:33 [1]*make their descendants fall also* [2]*Gentiles*
28 [a]Hos. 9:10 [1]*offered*
30 [a]Num. 25:7, 8
31 [a]Num. 25:11–13
32 [a]Num. 20:3–13 [b]Deut. 1:37; 3:26 [1]Or *Meribah*
33 [a]Num. 20:3, 10
34 [a]Judg. 1:21 [b][Deut. 7:2, 16]
35 [a]Judg. 3:5, 6
36 [a]Judg. 2:12 [b]Deut. 7:16
37 [a]2 Kin. 16:3; 17:17 [b][Lev. 17:7]
38 [a][Num. 35:33]
39 [a]Ezek. 20:18 [b][Lev. 17:7] [1]*became unclean* [2]Were unfaithful
40 [a]Judg. 2:14 [b][Deut. 9:29; 32:9]
41 [a]Judg. 2:14
43 [a]Judg. 2:16
44 [a]Judg. 3:9; 6:7; 10:10
45 [a][Lev. 26:41, 42] [b]Judg. 2:18 [c]Ps. 69:16
46 [a]Ezra 9:9
47 [a]1 Chr. 16:35, 36
48 [a]Ps. 41:13 [1]Heb. *Hallelujah*

PSALM 107
1 [a]Ps. 106:1 [1]Heb. same as *goodness*, vv. 8, 15, 21, 31, and *lovingkindness*, v. 43
3 [a]Is. 43:5, 6
4 [a][Deut. 2:7; 32:10]
6 [a]Ps. 50:15
7 [a]Ezra 8:21
8 [a]Ps. 107:15, 21

And were brought low for their iniquity.
44 Nevertheless He regarded their affliction,
When [a]He heard their cry;
45 [a]And for their sake He remembered His covenant,
And [b]relented [c]according to the multitude of His mercies.
46 [a]He also made them to be pitied
By all those who carried them away captive.

47 [a]Save us, O LORD our God,
And gather us from among the Gentiles,
To give thanks to Your holy name,
To triumph in Your praise.

48 [a]Blessed *be* the LORD God of Israel
From everlasting to everlasting!
And let all the people say, "Amen!"

[1]Praise the LORD!

BOOK FIVE

Psalms 107—150

PSALM 107

Thanksgiving to the LORD for His Great Works of Deliverance

OH, [a]give thanks to the LORD, for *He is* good!
For His [1]mercy *endures* forever.
2 Let the redeemed of the LORD say *so*,
Whom He has redeemed from the hand of the enemy,
3 And [a]gathered out of the lands,
From the east and from the west,
From the north and from the south.

4 They wandered in [a]the wilderness in a desolate way;
They found no city to dwell in.
5 Hungry and thirsty,
Their soul fainted in them.
6 [a]Then they cried out to the LORD in their trouble,
And He delivered them out of their distresses.
7 And He led them forth by the [a]right way,
That they might go to a city for a dwelling place.
8 [a]Oh, that *men* would give thanks to the LORD *for* His goodness,

And *for* His wonderful works to
the children of men!
9 For [a]He satisfies the longing
soul,
And fills the hungry soul with
goodness.

10 Those who [a]sat in darkness and
in the shadow of death,
[b]Bound[1] in affliction and irons—
11 Because they [a]rebelled against
the words of God,
And [1]despised [b]the counsel of the
Most High,
12 Therefore He brought down their
heart with labor;
They fell down, and *there was*
[a]none to help.
13 Then they cried out to the LORD
in their trouble,
And He saved them out of their
distresses.
14 [a]He brought them out of darkness
and the shadow of death,
And broke their chains in pieces.
15 Oh, that *men* would give thanks
to the LORD *for* His goodness,
And *for* His wonderful works to
the children of men!
16 For He has [a]broken the gates of
bronze,
And cut the bars of iron in two.

17 Fools, [a]because of their
transgression,
And because of their iniquities,
were afflicted.
18 [a]Their soul abhorred all manner
of food,
And they [b]drew near to the gates
of death.
19 Then they cried out to the LORD
in their trouble,
And He saved them out of their
distresses.
20 [a]He sent His word and [b]healed
them,
And [c]delivered *them* from their
destructions.
21 Oh, that *men* would give thanks
to the LORD *for* His goodness,
And *for* His wonderful works to
the children of men!
22 [a]Let them sacrifice the sacrifices
of thanksgiving,
And [b]declare His works with
[1]rejoicing.

23 Those who go down to the sea in
ships,
Who do business on great waters,
24 They see the works of the LORD,
And His wonders in the deep.
25 For He commands and [a]raises the
stormy wind,
Which lifts up the waves of the
sea.
26 They mount up to the heavens,
They go down again to the
depths;
[a]Their soul melts because of
trouble.
27 They reel to and fro, and stagger
like a drunken man,
And [1]are at their wits' end.
28 Then they cry out to the LORD in
their trouble,
And He brings them out of their
distresses.
29 [a]He calms the storm,
So that its waves are still.
30 Then they are glad because they
are quiet;
So He guides them to their
desired haven.
31 [a]Oh, that *men* would give thanks
to the LORD *for* His goodness,
And *for* His wonderful works to
the children of men!
32 Let them exalt Him also [a]in the
assembly of the people,
And praise Him in the company
of the elders.

33 He [a]turns rivers into a
wilderness,
And the watersprings into dry
ground;
34 A [a]fruitful land into [1]barrenness,
For the wickedness of those who
dwell in it.
35 [a]He turns a wilderness into pools
of water,
And dry land into watersprings.
36 There He makes the hungry
dwell,
That they may establish a city for
a dwelling place,
37 And sow fields and plant
vineyards,
That they may yield a fruitful
harvest.
38 [a]He also blesses them, and they
multiply greatly;
And He does not let their cattle
[b]decrease.

39 When they are [a]diminished and
brought low
Through oppression, affliction
and sorrow,
40 [a]He pours contempt on princes,
And causes them to wander in the
wilderness *where there is* no
way;
41 [a]Yet He sets the poor on high, far
from affliction,
And [b]makes *their* families like a
flock.

9 [a][Ps. 34:10; Luke 1:53]
10 [a][Is. 42:7; Mic. 7:8; Luke 1:79] [b]Job 36:8 [1]*Prisoners*
11 [a]Lam. 3:42 [b][Ps. 73:24] [1]*scorned*
12 [a]Ps. 22:11
14 [a]Ps. 68:6
16 [a]Is. 45:1, 2
17 [a][Is. 65:6, 7; Jer. 30:14, 15]; Lam. 3:39; Ezek. 24:23
18 [a]Job 33:20 [b]Job 33:22
20 [a]Matt. 8:8 [b]2 Kin. 20:5; Ps. 30:2 [c]Job 33:28, 30
22 [a]Lev. 7:12; Ps. 50:14; Heb. 13:15 [b]Ps. 9:11 [1]*joyful singing*
25 [a]Jon. 1:4
26 [a]Ps. 22:14
27 [1]Lit. *all their wisdom is swallowed up*
29 [a]Ps. 89:9; Matt. 8:26; Luke 8:24
31 [a]Ps. 107:8, 15, 21
32 [a]Ps. 22:22, 25
33 [a]1 Kin. 17:1, 7; Is. 50:2
34 [a]Gen. 13:10; Deut. 29:23 [1]Lit. *a salty waste*
35 [a]Ps. 114:8; [Is. 41:17, 18]
38 [a]Gen. 12:2; 17:16, 20 [b]Ex. 1:7; [Deut. 7:14]
39 [a]2 Kin. 10:32
40 [a]Job 12:21, 24
41 [a]1 Sam. 2:8; [Ps. 113:7, 8] [b]Ps. 78:52

42 [a]The righteous see *it* and rejoice,
And all [b]iniquity stops its mouth.

43 [a]Whoever *is* wise will observe
these *things*,
And they will understand the
lovingkindness of the LORD.

PSALM 108

Assurance of God's Victory over Enemies

A Song. A Psalm of David.

O [a]GOD, my heart is steadfast;
I will sing and give praise, even
with my glory.
2 [a]Awake, lute and harp!
I will awaken the dawn.
3 I will praise You, O LORD, among
the peoples,
And I will sing praises to You
among the nations.
4 For Your mercy *is* great above the
[1]heavens,
And Your truth *reaches* to the
clouds.

5 [a]Be exalted, O God, above the
heavens,
And Your glory above all the
earth;
6 [a]That Your beloved may be
delivered,
Save *with* Your right hand, and
[1]hear me.

7 God has spoken in His holiness:
"I will rejoice;
I will divide Shechem
And measure out the Valley of
Succoth.
8 Gilead *is* Mine; Manasseh *is*
Mine;
Ephraim also *is* the [1]helmet for
My head;
[a]Judah *is* My lawgiver.
9 Moab *is* My washpot;
Over Edom I will cast My shoe;
Over Philistia I will triumph."

10 [a]Who will bring me *into* the strong
city?
Who will lead me to Edom?
11 *Is it* not *You*, O God, *who* cast
us off?
And *You*, O God, *who* did not go
out with our armies?
12 Give us help from trouble,
For the help of man is useless.
13 [a]Through God we will do
valiantly,
For *it is* He *who* shall tread down
our enemies.

42 [a]Job 5:15, 16 [b]Job 5:16; Ps. 63:11; [Rom. 3:19]
43 [a]Ps. 64:9; Jer. 9:12; [Hos. 14:9]

PSALM 108
1 [a]Ps. 57:7–11
2 [a]Ps. 57:8–11
4 [1]*skies*
5 [a]Ps. 57:5, 11
6 [a]Ps. 60:5–12 [1]Lit. *answer*
8 [a][Gen. 49:10] [1]Lit. *protection*
10 [a]Ps. 60:9
13 [a]Ps. 60:12

PSALM 109
1 [a]Ps. 83:1
2 [a]Ps. 27:12
3 [a]Ps. 35:7; 69:4; John 15:25
5 [a]Ps. 35:7, 12; 38:20; Prov. 17:13
6 [a]Zech. 3:1 [1]Heb. *satan*
7 [a][Prov. 28:9]
8 [a][Ps. 55:23]; John 17:12 [b]Ps. 69:25; Acts 1:20
9 [a]Ex. 22:24
10 [1]*wander continuously* [2]So with MT, Tg.; LXX, Vg. *be cast out*
11 [a]Neh. 5:7; Job 5:5; 18:9
13 [a]Job 18:19; Ps. 37:28 [b]Prov. 10:7 [1]*descendants be destroyed*
14 [a][Ex. 20:5; Num. 14:18]; Is. 65:6; [Jer. 32:18] [b]Neh. 4:5; Jer. 18:23
15 [a]Job 18:17; [Ps. 34:16]
16 [a][Ps. 34:18]

PSALM 109

Plea for Judgment of False Accusers

To the Chief Musician. A Psalm of David.

DO[a] not keep silent,
O God of my praise!
2 For the mouth of the wicked and
the mouth of the deceitful
Have opened against me;
They have spoken against me
with a [a]lying tongue.
3 They have also surrounded me
with words of hatred,
And fought against me [a]without
a cause.
4 In return for my love they are my
accusers,
But I *give myself to* prayer.
5 Thus [a]they have rewarded me
evil for good,
And hatred for my love.

6 Set a wicked man over him,
And let [a]an [1]accuser stand at his
right hand.
7 When he is judged, let him be
found guilty,
And [a]let his prayer become sin.
8 Let his days be [a]few,
And [b]let another take his office.
9 [a]Let his children be fatherless,
And his wife a widow.
10 Let his children [1]continually be
vagabonds, and beg;
Let them [2]seek *their bread* also
from their desolate places.
11 [a]Let the creditor seize all that he
has,
And let strangers plunder his
labor.
12 Let there be none to extend
mercy to him,
Nor let there be any to favor his
fatherless children.
13 [a]Let his [1]posterity be cut off,
And in the generation
following let their [b]name be
blotted out.

14 [a]Let the iniquity of his fathers be
remembered before the LORD,
And let not the sin of his mother
[b]be blotted out.
15 Let them be continually before
the LORD,
That He may [a]cut off the memory
of them from the earth;
16 Because he did not remember to
show mercy,
But persecuted the poor and
needy man,
That he might even slay the
[a]broken in heart.

17 [a]As he loved cursing, so let it come
to him;
As he did not delight in
blessing, so let it be far from
him.
18 As he clothed himself with
cursing as with his garment,
So let it [a]enter his body like
water,
And like oil into his bones.
19 Let it be to him like the garment
which covers him,
And for a belt with which he girds
himself continually.
20 *Let* this *be* the LORD's reward to
my accusers,
And to those who speak evil
against my person.

21 But You, O GOD the Lord,
Deal with me for Your name's
sake;
Because Your mercy *is* good,
deliver me.
22 For I *am* poor and needy,
And my heart is wounded within
me.
23 I am gone [a]like a shadow when
it lengthens;
I am shaken off like a locust.
24 My [a]knees are weak through
fasting,
And my flesh is feeble from lack
of fatness.
25 I also have become [a]a reproach
to them;
When they look at me, [b]they
shake their heads.

26 Help me, O LORD my God!
Oh, save me according to Your
mercy,
27 [a]That they may know that this *is*
Your hand—
That You, LORD, have done it!
28 [a]Let them curse, but You
bless;
When they arise, let them be
ashamed,
But let [b]Your servant rejoice.
29 [a]Let my accusers be clothed with
shame,
And let them cover themselves
with their own disgrace as with
a mantle.

30 I will greatly praise the LORD with
my mouth;
Yes, [a]I will praise Him among the
multitude.
31 For [a]He shall stand at the right
hand of the poor,
To save *him* from those [1]who
condemn him.

PSALM 110

Announcement of the Messiah's Reign

A Psalm of David.

THE [a]LORD said to my Lord,
"Sit at My right hand,
Till I make Your enemies Your
[b]footstool."
2 The LORD shall send the rod of
Your strength [a]out of Zion.
[b]Rule in the midst of Your
enemies!

3 [a]Your people *shall be* volunteers
In the day of Your power;
[b]In the beauties of holiness, from
the womb of the morning,
You have the dew of Your youth.
4 The LORD has sworn
And [a]will not relent,
"You *are* a [b]priest forever
According to the order of
[c]Melchizedek."

5 The Lord *is* [a]at Your right hand;
He shall [1]execute kings [b]in the
day of His wrath.
6 He shall judge among the
nations,
He shall fill *the places* with dead
bodies,
[a]He shall [1]execute the heads of
many countries.
7 He shall drink of the brook by the
wayside;
[a]Therefore He shall lift up the
head.

PSALM 111

Praise to God for His Faithfulness and Justice

PRAISE[1] the LORD!
[a]I will praise the LORD with *my*
whole heart,
In the assembly of the upright
and *in* the congregation.

2 [a]The works of the LORD *are* great,
[b]Studied by all who have pleasure
in them.
3 His work *is* [a]honorable and
glorious,
And His righteousness endures
forever.
4 He has made His wonderful
works to be remembered;
[a]The LORD *is* gracious and full of
compassion.
5 He has given food to those who
fear Him;
He will ever be mindful of His
covenant.

---

17 [a]Prov. 14:14; [Matt. 7:2]
18 [a]Num. 5:22
23 [a]Ps. 102:11
24 [a]Heb. 12:12
25 [a]Ps. 22:7; Jer. 18:16; Lam. 2:15 [b]Matt. 27:39; Mark 15:29
27 [a]Job 37:7
28 [a]2 Sam. 6:11, 12 [b]Is. 65:14
29 [a]Job 8:22; Ps. 35:26
30 [a]Ps. 35:18; 111:1
31 [a][Ps. 16:8] [1]Lit. *judging his soul*

PSALM 110

1 [a]Matt. 22:44; Mark 12:36; 16:19; Luke 20:42, 43; Acts 2:34, 35; Col. 3:1; Heb. 1:13 [b][1 Cor. 15:25; Eph. 1:22]
2 [a][Rom. 11:26, 27] [b][Ps. 2:9; Dan. 7:13, 14]
3 [a]Judg. 5:2; Neh. 11:2 [b]1 Chr. 16:29; Ps. 96:9
4 [a][Num. 23:19] [b][Zech. 6:13] [c][Heb. 5:6, 10; 6:20]
5 [a][Ps. 16:8] [b]Ps. 2:5, 12; [Rom. 2:5; Rev. 6:17] [1]Lit. *break kings in pieces*
6 [a]Ps. 68:21 [1]Lit. *break in pieces*
7 [a][Is. 53:12]

PSALM 111

1 [a]Ps. 35:18 [1]Heb. *Hallelujah*
2 [a]Ps. 92:5 [b]Ps. 143:5
3 [a]Ps. 145:4, 5
4 [a][Ps. 86:5]

6 He has declared to His people the
power of His works,
In giving them the [1]heritage of
the nations.

7 The works of His hands *are*
[a]verity[1] and justice;
All His precepts *are* sure.
8 [a]They stand fast forever and ever,
And are [b]done in truth and
uprightness.
9 [a]He has sent redemption to His
people;
He has commanded His covenant
forever:
[b]Holy and awesome *is* His name.

10 [a]The fear of the LORD *is* the
beginning of wisdom;
A good understanding have all
those who do *His*
commandments.
His praise endures forever.

PSALM 112

The Blessed State of the Righteous

PRAISE[1] the LORD!

Blessed *is* the man *who* fears the
LORD,
Who [a]delights greatly in His
commandments.

2 [a]His descendants will be mighty
on earth;
The generation of the upright will
be blessed.
3 [a]Wealth and riches *will be* in his
house,
And his righteousness [1]endures
forever.
4 [a]Unto the upright there arises light
in the darkness;
He is gracious, and full of
compassion, and righteous.
5 [a]A good man deals graciously and
lends;
He will guide his affairs [b]with
discretion.
6 Surely he will never be shaken;
[a]The righteous will be in
everlasting remembrance.
7 [a]He will not be afraid of evil
tidings;
His heart is steadfast, trusting in
the LORD.
8 His [a]heart *is* established;
[b]He will not be afraid,
Until he [c]sees *his desire* upon his
enemies.

9 He has dispersed abroad,
He has given to the poor;

6 [1]*inheritance*
7 [a][Rev. 15:3] [1]*truth*
8 [a]Is. 40:8; Matt. 5:18 [b][Rev. 15:3]
9 [a]Luke 1:68 [b]Luke 1:49
10 [a]Job 28:28; [Prov. 1:7; 9:10]; Eccl. 12:13

PSALM 112

1 [a]Ps. 128:1 [1]Heb. *Hallelujah*
2 [a][Ps. 102:28]
3 [a]Prov. 3:16; 8:18; [Matt. 6:33] [1]*stands*
4 [a]Job 11:17; Ps. 97:11
5 [a]Ps. 37:26; [Luke 6:35] [b][Eph. 5:15; Col. 4:5]
6 [a]Prov. 10:7
7 [a][Prov. 1:33]
8 [a]Heb. 13:9 [b][Ps. 27:1; 56:11]; Prov. 1:33; 3:24; [Is. 12:2] [c]Ps. 59:10
9 [1]Strength

PSALM 113

1 [a]Ps. 135:1 [1]Heb. *Hallelujah*
2 [a][Dan. 2:20]
3 [a]Is. 59:19; Mal. 1:11
4 [a]Ps. 97:9; 99:2 [b][Ps. 8:1]
5 [a]Ps. 89:6; [Is. 57:15]
6 [a][Ps. 11:4; Is. 57:15]
7 [a]1 Sam. 2:8; Ps. 107:41 [b]Ps. 72:12
8 [a][Job 36:7]
9 [a]1 Sam. 2:5; Is. 54:1 [1]*childless*

PSALM 114

1 [a]Ex. 12:51; 13:3 [b]Ps. 81:5 [1]*who spoke unintelligibly*
2 [a]Ex. 6:7; 19:6; 25:8; 29:45, 46; Deut. 27:9
3 [a]Ex. 14:21; Ps. 77:16 [b]Josh. 3:13–16
4 [a]Ex. 19:18; Judg. 5:5; Ps. 29:6; Hab. 3:6
5 [a]Hab. 3:8

His righteousness endures
forever;
His [1]horn will be exalted with
honor.
10 The wicked will see *it* and be
grieved;
He will gnash his teeth and melt
away;
The desire of the wicked shall
perish.

PSALM 113

The Majesty and Condescension of God

PRAISE[1] the LORD!

[a]Praise, O servants of the LORD,
Praise the name of the LORD!
2 [a]Blessed be the name of the LORD
From this time forth and
forevermore!
3 [a]From the rising of the sun to its
going down
The LORD's name *is* to be praised.

4 The LORD *is* [a]high above all
nations,
[b]His glory above the heavens.
5 [a]Who *is* like the LORD our God,
Who dwells on high,
6 [a]Who humbles Himself to behold
The things that are in the
heavens and in the earth?

7 [a]He raises the poor out of the dust,
And lifts the [b]needy out of the ash
heap,
8 That He may [a]seat *him* with
princes—
With the princes of His people.
9 [a]He grants the [1]barren woman a
home,
Like a joyful mother of children.

Praise the LORD!

PSALM 114

The Power of God in His Deliverance of Israel

WHEN [a]Israel went out of Egypt,
The house of Jacob [b]from a
people [1]of strange language,
2 [a]Judah became His sanctuary,
And Israel His dominion.

3 [a]The sea saw *it* and fled;
[b]Jordan turned back.
4 [a]The mountains skipped like
rams,
The little hills like lambs.
5 [a]What ails you, O sea, that you
fled?

O Jordan, *that* you turned
back?
6 O mountains, *that* you skipped
like rams?
O little hills, like lambs?

7 Tremble, O earth, at the presence
of the Lord,
At the presence of the God of
Jacob,
8 [a]Who turned the rock *into* a pool
of water,
The flint into a fountain of
waters.

PSALM 115

The Futility of Idols and the Trustworthiness of God

NOT [a]unto us, O LORD, not unto
us,
But to Your name give glory,
Because of Your mercy,
Because of Your truth.
2 Why should the [1]Gentiles say,
[a]"So where *is* their God?"

3 [a]But our God *is* in heaven;
He does whatever He pleases.
4 [a]Their idols *are* silver and gold,
The work of men's hands.
5 They have mouths, but they do
not speak;
Eyes they have, but they do not
see;
6 They have ears, but they do not
hear;
Noses they have, but they do not
smell;
7 They have hands, but they do not
handle;
Feet they have, but they do not
walk;
Nor do they mutter through their
throat.
8 [a]Those who make them are like
them;
So is everyone who trusts in
them.

9 [a]O Israel, trust in the LORD;
[b]He *is* their help and their shield.
10 O house of Aaron, trust in the
LORD;
He *is* their help and their shield.
11 You who fear the LORD, trust in
the LORD;
He *is* their help and their shield.

12 The LORD [1]has been mindful of
us;
He will bless us;
He will bless the house of Israel;
He will bless the house of Aaron.
13 [a]He will bless those who fear the
LORD,
Both small and great.
14 May the LORD give you increase
more and more,
You and your children.
15 *May* you *be* [a]blessed by the LORD,
[b]Who made heaven and earth.

16 The heaven, *even* the heavens,
are the LORD's;
But the earth He has given to the
children of men.
17 [a]The dead do not praise the LORD,
Nor any who go down into
silence.
18 [a]But we will bless the LORD
From this time forth and
forevermore.

Praise the LORD!

PSALM 116

Thanksgiving for Deliverance from Death

I [a]LOVE the LORD, because He has
heard
My voice *and* my supplications.
2 Because He has inclined His ear
to me,
Therefore I will call *upon Him* as
long as I live.

3 [a]The [1]pains of death surrounded
me,
And the [2]pangs of Sheol [3]laid
hold of me;
I found trouble and sorrow.
4 Then I called upon the name of
the LORD:
"O LORD, I implore You, deliver
my soul!"

5 [a]Gracious *is* the LORD, and
[b]righteous;
Yes, our God *is* merciful.
6 The LORD preserves the simple;
I was brought low, and He saved
me.
7 Return to your [a]rest, O my soul,
For [b]the LORD has dealt
bountifully with you.

8 [a]For You have delivered my soul
from death,
My eyes from tears,
And my feet from falling.
9 I will walk before the LORD
[a]In the land of the living.
10 [a]I believed, therefore I spoke,
"I am greatly afflicted."
11 [a]I said in my haste,
[b]"All men *are* liars."

---

8 [a]Ex. 17:6; Num. 20:11; Ps. 107:35

PSALM 115

1 [a][Is. 48:11]; Ezek. 36:32
2 [a]Ps. 42:3, 10 [1]*nations*
3 [a][1 Chr. 16:26]
4 [a]Deut. 4:28; 2 Kin. 19:18; Is. 37:19; 44:10, 20; Jer. 10:3
8 [a]Ps. 135:18; Is. 44:9–11
9 [a]Ps. 118:2, 3 [b]Ps. 33:20
12 [1]*has remembered us*
13 [a]Ps. 128:1, 4
15 [a][Gen. 14:19] [b]Gen. 1:1; Acts 14:15; Rev. 14:7
17 [a]Ps. 6:5; 88:10–12; [Is. 38:18]
18 [a]Ps. 113:2; Dan. 2:20

PSALM 116

1 [a]Ps. 18:1
3 [a]Ps. 18:4–6 [1]Lit. *cords* [2]*distresses* [3]Lit. *found me*
5 [a][Ps. 103:8] [b][Ezra 9:15]; Neh. 9:8; [Ps. 119:137; 145:17; Jer. 12:1; Dan. 9:14]
7 [a][Jer. 6:16; Matt. 11:29] [b]Ps. 13:6
8 [a]Ps. 56:13
9 [a]Ps. 27:13
10 [a]2 Cor. 4:13
11 [a]Ps. 31:22 [b]Rom. 3:4

12 What shall I render to the LORD
For all His benefits toward me?
13 I will take up the cup of salvation,
And call upon the name of the LORD.
14 [a]I will pay my vows to the LORD
Now in the presence of all His people.

15 [a]Precious in the sight of the LORD
Is the death of His saints.

16 O LORD, truly [a]I *am* Your servant;
I *am* Your servant, [b]the son of Your maidservant;
You have loosed my bonds.
17 I will offer to You [a]the sacrifice of thanksgiving,
And will call upon the name of the LORD.

18 I will pay my vows to the LORD
Now in the presence of all His people,
19 In the [a]courts of the LORD's house,
In the midst of you, O Jerusalem.

[1]Praise the LORD!

PSALM 117

Let All Peoples Praise the LORD

PRAISE [a]the LORD, all you Gentiles!
[1]Laud Him, all you peoples!
2 For His merciful kindness is great toward us,
And [a]the truth of the LORD *endures* forever.

Praise the LORD!

PSALM 118

Praise to God for His Everlasting Mercy

OH, [a]give thanks to the LORD, for *He is* good!
[b]For His mercy *endures* forever.

2 [a]Let Israel now say,
"His mercy *endures* forever."
3 Let the house of Aaron now say,
"His mercy *endures* forever."
4 Let those who fear the LORD now say,
"His mercy *endures* forever."

5 [a]I called on the LORD in distress;
The LORD answered me *and* [b]set *me* in a broad place.
6 [a]The LORD *is* on my side;
I will not fear.
What can man do to me?
7 [a]The LORD is for me among those who help me;
Therefore [b]I shall see *my desire* on those who hate me.
8 [a]*It is* better to trust in the LORD
Than to put confidence in man.
9 [a]*It is* better to trust in the LORD
Than to put confidence in princes.

10 All nations surrounded me,
But in the name of the LORD I will destroy them.
11 They [a]surrounded me,
Yes, they surrounded me;
But in the name of the LORD I will destroy them.
12 They surrounded me [a]like bees;
They were quenched [b]like a fire of thorns;
For in the name of the LORD I will [1]destroy them.
13 You pushed me violently, that I might fall,
But the LORD helped me.
14 [a]The LORD *is* my strength and song,
And He has become my salvation.

15 The voice of rejoicing and salvation
Is in the tents of the righteous;
The right hand of the LORD does valiantly.
16 [a]The right hand of the LORD is exalted;
The right hand of the LORD does valiantly.
17 [a]I shall not die, but live,
And [b]declare the works of the LORD.
18 The LORD has [a]chastened[1] me severely,
But He has not given me over to death.

19 [a]Open to me the gates of righteousness;
I will go through them,
And I will praise the LORD.
20 [a]This is the gate of the LORD,
[b]Through which the righteous shall enter.

21 I will praise You,
For You have [a]answered me,
And have become my salvation.

22 [a]The stone *which* the builders rejected
Has become the chief cornerstone.

---

14 [a]Ps. 116:18
15 [a]Ps. 72:14; [Rev. 14:13]
16 [a]Ps. 119:125; 143:12 [b]Ps. 86:16
17 [a]Lev. 7:12; Ps. 50:14; 107:22
19 [a]Ps. 96:8 [1]Heb. *Hallelujah*

PSALM 117

1 [a]Rom. 15:11 [1]*Praise*
2 [a][Ps. 100:5]

PSALM 118

1 [a]1 Chr. 16:8, 34; Jer. 33:11 [b]2 Chr. 5:13; 7:3; Ezra 3:11; [Ps. 136:1–26]
2 [a][Ps. 115:9]
5 [a]Ps. 120:1 [b]Ps. 18:19
6 [a]Ps. 27:1; 56:9; [Rom. 8:31; Heb. 13:6]
7 [a]Ps. 54:4 [b]Ps. 59:10
8 [a]2 Chr. 32:7, 8; Ps. 40:4; Is. 31:1, 3; 57:13; Jer. 17:5
9 [a]Ps. 146:3
11 [a]Ps. 88:17
12 [a]Deut. 1:44 [b]Eccl. 7:6; Nah. 1:10 [1]*cut them off*
14 [a]Ex. 15:2; Is. 12:2
16 [a]Ex. 15:6
17 [a][Ps. 6:5]; Hab. 1:12 [b]Ps. 73:28
18 [a]Ps. 73:14; Jer. 31:18; [1 Cor. 11:32]; 2 Cor. 6:9 [1]*disciplined*
19 [a]Is. 26:2
20 [a]Ps. 24:7 [b]Is. 35:8; [Rev. 21:27; 22:14, 15]
21 [a]Ps. 116:1
22 [a]Matt. 21:42; Mark 12:10, 11; Luke 20:17; Acts 4:11; [Eph. 2:20; 1 Pet. 2:7, 8]

23 [1]This was the LORD's doing;
It *is* marvelous in our eyes.
24 This *is* the day the LORD has made;
We will rejoice and be glad in it.
25 Save now, I pray, O LORD;
O LORD, I pray, send now prosperity.
26 [a]Blessed *is* he who comes in the name of the LORD!
We have blessed you from the house of the LORD.
27 God *is* the LORD,
And He has given us [a]light;
Bind the sacrifice with cords to the horns of the altar.
28 You *are* my God, and I will praise You;
[a]*You are* my God, I will exalt You.
29 Oh, give thanks to the LORD, for *He is* good!
For His mercy *endures* forever.

PSALM 119

Meditations on the Excellencies of the Word of God

א ALEPH

BLESSED *are* the [1]undefiled in the way,
[a]Who walk in the law of the LORD!
2 Blessed *are* those who keep His testimonies,
Who seek Him with the [a]whole heart!
3 [a]They also do no iniquity;
They walk in His ways.
4 You have commanded *us*
To keep Your precepts diligently.
5 Oh, that my ways were directed
To keep Your statutes!
6 [a]Then I would not be ashamed,
When I look into all Your commandments.
7 I will praise You with uprightness of heart,
When I learn Your righteous judgments.
8 I will keep Your statutes;
Oh, do not forsake me utterly!

ב BETH

9 How can a young man cleanse his way?
By taking heed according to Your word.
10 With my whole heart I have [a]sought You;
Oh, let me not wander from Your commandments!
11 [a]Your word I have hidden in my heart,
That I might not sin against You.
12 Blessed *are* You, O LORD!
Teach me Your statutes.
13 With my lips I have [a]declared
All the judgments of Your mouth.
14 I have rejoiced in the way of Your testimonies,
As *much as* in all riches.
15 I will meditate on Your precepts,
And [1]contemplate Your ways.
16 I will [a]delight myself in Your statutes;
I will not forget Your word.

ג GIMEL

17 [a]Deal bountifully with Your servant,
That I may live and keep Your word.
18 Open my eyes, that I may see
Wondrous things from Your law.
19 [a]I *am* a stranger in the earth;
Do not hide Your commandments from me.
20 [a]My soul [1]breaks with longing
For Your judgments at all times.
21 You rebuke the proud—the cursed,
Who stray from Your commandments.
22 [a]Remove from me reproach and contempt,
For I have kept Your testimonies.
23 Princes also sit *and* speak against me,
But Your servant meditates on Your statutes.
24 Your testimonies also *are* my delight
And my counselors.

ד DALETH

25 [a]My soul clings to the dust;
[b]Revive me according to Your word.
26 I have declared my ways, and You answered me;
[a]Teach me Your statutes.
27 Make me understand the way of Your precepts;
So [a]shall I meditate on Your wonderful works.
28 [a]My soul [1]melts from [2]heaviness;
Strengthen me according to Your word.
29 Remove from me the way of lying,
And grant me Your law graciously.
30 I have chosen the way of truth;

---

23 [1]Lit. *This is from the LORD*
26 [a]Matt. 21:9; 23:39; Mark 11:9; Luke 13:35; 19:38
27 [a]Esth. 8:16; [1 Pet. 2:9]
28 [a]Ex. 15:2; Is. 25:1

PSALM 119
1 [a]Ps. 128:1; [Ezek. 11:20; 18:17]; Mic. 4:2 [1]*blameless*
2 [a]Deut. 6:5; 10:12; 11:13; 13:3
3 [a][1 John 3:9; 5:18]
6 [a]Job 22:26
10 [a]2 Chr. 15:15
11 [a]Ps. 37:31; Luke 2:19
13 [a]Ps. 34:11
15 [1]*look into*
16 [a]Ps. 1:2
17 [a]Ps. 116:7
19 [a]Gen. 47:9; Lev. 25:23; 1 Chr. 29:15; Ps. 39:12; Heb. 11:13
20 [a]Ps. 42:1, 2; 63:1; 84:2 [1]*is crushed*
22 [a]Ps. 39:8
25 [a]Ps. 44:25 [b]Ps. 143:11
26 [a]Ps. 25:4; 27:11; 86:11
27 [a]Ps. 145:5, 6
28 [a]Ps. 107:26 [1]Lit. *drops* [2]*grief*

Your judgments I have laid
before me.
31 I cling to Your testimonies;
O LORD, do not put me to shame!
32 I will run the course of Your
commandments,
For You shall [a]enlarge my heart.

ה HE

33 [a]Teach me, O LORD, the way of
Your statutes,
And I shall keep it *to* the end.
34 [a]Give me understanding, and I
shall keep Your law;
Indeed, I shall observe it with *my*
whole heart.
35 Make me walk in the path of
Your commandments,
For I delight in it.
36 [1]Incline my heart to Your
testimonies,
And not to [a]covetousness.
37 [a]Turn[1] away my eyes from
[b]looking at worthless things,
And revive me in [2]Your way.
38 [a]Establish Your word to Your
servant,
Who *is devoted* to fearing You.
39 Turn away my reproach which I
dread,
For Your judgments *are* good.
40 Behold, I long for Your precepts;
Revive me in Your righteousness.

ו WAW

41 Let Your mercies come also to
me, O LORD—
Your salvation according to Your
word.
42 So shall I have an answer for him
who [1]reproaches me,
For I trust in Your word.
43 And take not the word of truth
utterly out of my mouth,
For I have hoped in Your
ordinances.
44 So shall I keep Your law
continually,
Forever and ever.
45 And I will walk [1]at [a]liberty,
For I seek Your precepts.
46 [a]I will speak of Your testimonies
also before kings,
And will not be ashamed.
47 And I will delight myself in Your
commandments,
Which I love.
48 My hands also I will lift up to
Your commandments,
Which I love,
And I will meditate on Your
statutes.

32 [a]1 Kin. 4:29; Is. 60:5; 2 Cor. 6:11, 13
33 [a][Matt. 10:22; Rev. 2:26]
34 [a][Prov. 2:6; James 1:5]
36 [a]Ezek. 33:31; [Mark 7:20–23]; Luke 12:15; [Heb. 13:5] [1]Cause me to long for
37 [a]Is. 33:15 [b]Prov. 23:5 [1]Lit. *Cause my eyes to pass away from* [2]So with MT, LXX, Vg.; Tg. *Your words*
38 [a]2 Sam. 7:25
42 [1]*taunts*
45 [a]Prov. 4:12 [1]Lit. *in a wide place*
46 [a]Ps. 138:1; Matt. 10:18; Acts 26
50 [a]Job 6:10; [Rom. 15:4]
53 [a]Ex. 32:19; Ezra 9:3; Neh. 13:25
55 [a]Ps. 63:6
57 [a]Num. 18:20; Ps. 16:5; Jer. 10:16; Lam. 3:24
59 [a]Mark 14:72; Luke 15:17
62 [a]Acts 16:25
64 [a]Ps. 33:5
66 [a]Phil. 1:9

ז ZAYIN

49 Remember the word to Your
servant,
Upon which You have caused me
to hope.
50 This *is* my [a]comfort in my
affliction,
For Your word has given me life.
51 The proud have me in great
derision,
Yet I do not turn aside from Your
law.
52 I remembered Your judgments of
old, O LORD,
And have comforted myself.
53 [a]Indignation has taken hold of me
Because of the wicked, who
forsake Your law.
54 Your statutes have been my
songs
In the house of my pilgrimage.
55 [a]I remember Your name in the
night, O LORD,
And I keep Your law.
56 This has become mine,
Because I kept Your precepts.

ח HETH

57 [a]*You are* my portion, O LORD;
I have said that I would keep
Your words.
58 I entreated Your favor with *my*
whole heart;
Be merciful to me according to
Your word.
59 I [a]thought about my ways,
And turned my feet to Your
testimonies.
60 I made haste, and did not delay
To keep Your commandments.
61 The cords of the wicked have
bound me,
But I have not forgotten Your
law.
62 [a]At midnight I will rise to give
thanks to You,
Because of Your righteous
judgments.
63 I *am* a companion of all who fear
You,
And of those who keep Your
precepts.
64 [a]The earth, O LORD, is full of Your
mercy;
Teach me Your statutes.

ט TETH

65 You have dealt well with Your
servant,
O LORD, according to Your word.
66 Teach me good judgment and
[a]knowledge,

For I believe Your
commandments.
67 Before I was [a]afflicted I went
astray,
But now I keep Your word.
68 You *are* [a]good, and do good;
Teach me Your statutes.
69 The proud have [a]forged[1] a lie
against me,
But I will keep Your precepts
with *my* whole heart.
70 [a]Their heart is [1]as fat as grease,
But I delight in Your law.
71 *It is* good for me that I have been
afflicted,
That I may learn Your statutes.
72 [a]The law of Your mouth *is* better
to me
Than thousands of *coins of* gold
and silver.

י YOD

73 [a]Your hands have made me and
fashioned me;
Give me understanding, that I
may learn Your
commandments.
74 [a]Those who fear You will be glad
when they see me,
Because I have hoped in Your
word.
75 I know, O LORD, [a]that Your
judgments *are* [1]right,
And *that* in faithfulness You
have afflicted me.
76 Let, I pray, Your merciful
kindness be for my comfort,
According to Your word to Your
servant.
77 Let Your tender mercies come to
me, that I may live;
For Your law *is* my delight.
78 Let the proud [a]be ashamed,
For they treated me wrongfully
with falsehood;
But I will meditate on Your
precepts.
79 Let those who fear You turn to
me,
Those who know Your
testimonies.
80 Let my heart be blameless
regarding Your statutes,
That I may not be ashamed.

כ KAPH

81 [a]My soul faints for Your salvation,
But I hope in Your word.
82 My eyes fail *from searching* Your
word,
Saying, "When will You comfort
me?"

67 [a]Prov. 3:11; Jer. 31:18, 19; [Heb. 12:5–11]
68 [a]Ps. 106:1; 107:1; [Matt. 19:17]
69 [a]Job 13:4; Ps. 109:2 [1]Lit. *smeared me with a lie*
70 [a]Deut. 32:15; Job 15:27; Ps. 17:10; Is. 6:10; Jer. 5:28; Acts 28:27 [1]Insensible
72 [a]Ps. 19:10; Prov. 8:10, 11, 19
73 [a]Job 10:8; 31:15; [Ps. 139:15, 16]
74 [a]Ps. 34:2
75 [a][Heb. 12:10] [1]Lit. *righteous*
78 [a]Ps. 25:3
81 [a]Ps. 73:26; 84:2
83 [a]Job 30:30
84 [a]Ps. 39:4 [b]Rev. 6:10
85 [a]Ps. 35:7; Prov. 16:27; Jer. 18:22
86 [a]Ps. 35:19
89 [a]Ps. 89:2; Is. 40:8; Matt. 24:35; [1 Pet. 1:25] [1]Lit. *stands firm*
90 [1]Lit. *stands*
91 [a]Jer. 33:25
95 [1]*give attention to*
96 [a]Matt. 5:18
97 [a]Ps. 1:2
98 [a]Deut. 4:6
99 [a][2 Tim. 3:15]

83 For [a]I have become like a
wineskin in smoke,
Yet I do not forget Your statutes.
84 [a]How many *are* the days of Your
servant?
[b]When will You execute judgment
on those who persecute me?
85 [a]The proud have dug pits for me,
Which *is* not according to Your
law.
86 All Your commandments *are*
faithful;
They persecute me [a]wrongfully;
Help me!
87 They almost made an end of me
on earth,
But I did not forsake Your
precepts.
88 Revive me according to Your
lovingkindness,
So that I may keep the testimony
of Your mouth.

ל LAMED

89 [a]Forever, O LORD,
Your word [1]is settled in heaven.
90 Your faithfulness *endures* to all
generations;
You established the earth, and it
[1]abides.
91 They continue this day according
to [a]Your ordinances,
For all *are* Your servants.
92 Unless Your law *had been* my
delight,
I would then have perished in my
affliction.
93 I will never forget Your precepts,
For by them You have given me
life.
94 I *am* Yours, save me;
For I have sought Your precepts.
95 The wicked wait for me to
destroy me,
But I will [1]consider Your
testimonies.
96 [a]I have seen the consummation of
all perfection,
But Your commandment *is*
exceedingly broad.

מ MEM

97 Oh, how I love Your law!
[a]It *is* my meditation all the day.
98 You, through Your
commandments, make me
[a]wiser than my enemies;
For they *are* ever with me.
99 I have more understanding than
all my teachers,
[a]For Your testimonies *are* my
meditation.

100 [a]I understand more than the [1]ancients,
Because I keep Your precepts.
101 I have restrained my feet from every evil way,
That I may keep Your word.
102 I have not departed from Your judgments,
For You Yourself have taught me.
103 [a]How sweet are Your words to my taste,
Sweeter than honey to my mouth!
104 Through Your precepts I get understanding;
Therefore I hate every false way.

נ NUN

105 [a]Your word *is* a lamp to my feet
And a light to my path.
106 [a]I have sworn and confirmed
That I will keep Your righteous judgments.
107 I am afflicted very much;
Revive me, O LORD, according to Your word.
108 Accept, I pray, [a]the freewill offerings of my mouth, O LORD,
And teach me Your judgments.
109 [a]My life *is* continually [1]in my hand,
Yet I do not forget Your law.
110 [a]The wicked have laid a snare for me,
Yet I have not strayed from Your precepts.
111 [a]Your testimonies I have taken as a [1]heritage forever,
For they *are* the rejoicing of my heart.
112 I have inclined my heart to perform Your statutes
Forever, to the very end.

ס SAMEK

113 I hate the [1]double-minded,
But I love Your law.
114 [a]You *are* my hiding place and my shield;
I hope in Your word.
115 [a]Depart from me, you evildoers,
For I will keep the commandments of my God!
116 Uphold me according to Your word, that I may live;
And do not let me [a]be ashamed of my hope.

100 [a][Job 32:7–9] [1]*aged*
103 [a]Ps. 19:10; Prov. 8:11
105 [a]Prov. 6:23
106 [a]Neh. 10:29
108 [a]Hos. 14:2; Heb. 13:15
109 [a]Judg. 12:3; Job 13:14 [1]In danger
110 [a]Ps. 140:5
111 [a]Deut. 33:4 [1]*inheritance*
113 [1]Lit. *divided* in heart or mind
114 [a][Ps. 32:7]
115 [a]Ps. 6:8; Matt. 7:23
116 [a]Ps. 25:2; [Rom. 5:5; 9:33; 10:11; Phil. 1:20]
117 [1]*Uphold me*
119 [a]Is. 1:22, 25; Ezek. 22:18, 19 [1]*destroy*, lit. *cause to cease* [2]*slag* or *refuse*
120 [a]Job 4:14; Hab. 3:16
122 [a]Job 17:3; Heb. 7:22 [1]*guaranty*
125 [a]Ps. 116:16
126 [1]*broken Your law*
127 [a]Ps. 19:10
130 [a]Prov. 6:23 [b][Ps. 19:7]; Prov. 1:4
131 [a]Ps. 42:1
132 [a]Ps. 106:4

117 [1]Hold me up, and I shall be safe,
And I shall observe Your statutes continually.
118 You reject all those who stray from Your statutes,
For their deceit *is* falsehood.
119 You [1]put away all the wicked of the earth [a]*like* [2]dross;
Therefore I love Your testimonies.
120 [a]My flesh trembles for fear of You,
And I am afraid of Your judgments.

ע AYIN

121 I have done justice and righteousness;
Do not leave me to my oppressors.
122 Be [a]surety[1] for Your servant for good;
Do not let the proud oppress me.
123 My eyes fail *from seeking* Your salvation
And Your righteous word.
124 Deal with Your servant according to Your mercy,
And teach me Your statutes.
125 [a]I *am* Your servant;
Give me understanding,
That I may know Your testimonies.
126 *It is* time for *You* to act, O LORD,
For they have [1]regarded Your law as void.
127 [a]Therefore I love Your commandments
More than gold, yes, than fine gold!
128 Therefore all *Your* precepts *concerning* all *things*
I consider *to be* right;
I hate every false way.

פ PE

129 Your testimonies are wonderful;
Therefore my soul keeps them.
130 The entrance of Your words gives light;
[a]It gives understanding to the [b]simple.
131 I opened my mouth and [a]panted,
For I longed for Your commandments.
132 [a]Look upon me and be merciful to me,

[b]As Your custom *is* toward
those who love Your name.
133 [a]Direct my steps by Your word,
And [b]let no iniquity have
dominion over me.
134 [a]Redeem me from the
oppression of man,
That I may keep Your
precepts.
135 [a]Make Your face shine upon
Your servant,
And teach me Your statutes.
136 [a]Rivers of water run down
from my eyes,
Because *men* do not keep
Your law.

צ TSADDE

137 [a]Righteous *are* You, O LORD,
And upright *are* Your
judgments.
138 [a]Your testimonies, *which* You
have commanded,
Are righteous and very
faithful.
139 [a]My zeal has [1]consumed me,
Because my enemies have
forgotten Your words.
140 [a]Your word *is* very [1]pure;
Therefore Your servant loves
it.
141 I *am* small and despised,
Yet I do not forget Your
precepts.
142 Your righteousness *is* an
everlasting righteousness,
And Your law *is* [a]truth.
143 Trouble and anguish have
[1]overtaken me,
Yet Your commandments *are*
my delights.
144 The righteousness of Your
testimonies *is* everlasting;
Give me understanding, and I
shall live.

ק QOPH

145 I cry out with *my* whole heart;
Hear me, O LORD!
I will keep Your statutes.
146 I cry out to You;
Save me, and I will keep Your
testimonies.
147 [a]I rise before the dawning of
the morning,
And cry for help;
I hope in Your word.
148 [a]My eyes are awake through
the *night* watches,
That I may meditate on Your
word.
149 Hear my voice according to
Your lovingkindness;
O LORD, revive me according
to Your justice.
150 They draw near who follow
after wickedness;
They are far from Your law.
151 You *are* [a]near, O LORD,
And all Your commandments
are truth.
152 Concerning Your testimonies,
I have known of old that You
have founded them
[a]forever.

ר RESH

153 [a]Consider my affliction and
deliver me,
For I do not forget Your law.
154 [a]Plead my cause and redeem
me;
Revive me according to Your
word.
155 Salvation *is* far from the
wicked,
For they do not seek Your
statutes.
156 [1]Great *are* Your tender
mercies, O LORD;
Revive me according to Your
judgments.
157 Many *are* my persecutors and
my enemies,
Yet I do not [a]turn from Your
testimonies.
158 I see the treacherous, and [a]am
disgusted,
Because they do not keep
Your word.
159 Consider how I love Your
precepts;
Revive me, O LORD, according
to Your lovingkindness.
160 The entirety of Your word *is*
truth,
And every one of Your
righteous judgments
endures forever.

ש SHIN

161 [a]Princes persecute me without
a cause,
But my heart stands in awe of
Your word.
162 I rejoice at Your word
As one who finds great
treasure.
163 I hate and abhor lying,
But I love Your law.
164 Seven times a day I praise
You,
Because of Your righteous
judgments.
165 [a]Great peace have those who
love Your law,

132 [b]Ps. 51:1; [2 Thess. 1:6]
133 [a]Ps. 17:5 [b][Ps. 19:13; Rom. 6:12]
134 [a]Luke 1:74
135 [a]Num. 6:25; Ps. 4:6
136 [a]Jer. 9:1, 18; 14:17; Lam. 3:48; Ezek. 9:4
137 [a]Ezra 9:15; Neh. 9:33; Jer. 12:1; Lam. 1:18; Dan. 9:7, 14
138 [a][Ps. 19:7–9]
139 [a]Ps. 69:9; John 2:17 [1]*put an end to*
140 [a]Ps. 12:6 [1]Lit. *refined* or *tried*
142 [a][Ps. 19:9; John 17:17]
143 [1]Lit. *found*
147 [a]Ps. 5:3
148 [a]Ps. 63:1, 6
151 [a][Ps. 145:18]; Is. 50:8
152 [a]Luke 21:33
153 [a]Lam. 5:1
154 [a]1 Sam. 24:15; Mic. 7:9
156 [1]Or *Many*
157 [a]Ps. 44:18
158 [a]Ezek. 9:4
161 [a]1 Sam. 24:11; 26:18
165 [a]Prov. 3:2; [Is. 26:3; 32:17]

And [1]nothing causes them to stumble.
166 [a]LORD, I hope for Your salvation,
And I do Your commandments.
167 My soul keeps Your testimonies,
And I love them exceedingly.
168 I keep Your precepts and Your testimonies,
[a]For all my ways *are* before You.

ת TAU

169 Let my cry come before You, O LORD;
[a]Give me understanding according to Your word.
170 Let my [1]supplication come before You;
Deliver me according to Your word.
171 [a]My lips shall utter praise,
For You teach me Your statutes.
172 My tongue shall speak of Your word,
For all Your commandments *are* righteousness.
173 Let Your hand become my help,
For [a]I have chosen Your precepts.
174 [a]I long for Your salvation, O LORD,
And [b]Your law *is* my delight.
175 Let my soul live, and it shall praise You;
And let Your judgments help me.
176 [a]I have gone astray like a lost sheep;
Seek Your servant,
For I do not forget Your commandments.

PSALM 120

Plea for Relief from Bitter Foes

A Song of Ascents.

IN [a]my distress I cried to the LORD,
And He heard me.
2 Deliver my soul, O LORD, from lying lips
And from a deceitful tongue.

3 What shall be given to you,
Or what shall be done to you,
You false tongue?
4 Sharp arrows of the [1]warrior,
With coals of the broom tree!
5 Woe is me, that I dwell in [a]Meshech,
[b]*That* I dwell among the tents of Kedar!
6 My soul has dwelt too long
With one who hates peace.
7 I *am for* peace;
But when I speak, they *are* for war.

PSALM 121

God the Help of Those Who Seek Him

A Song of Ascents.

I [a]WILL lift up my eyes to the hills—
From whence comes my help?
2 [a]My help *comes* from the LORD,
Who made heaven and earth.

3 [a]He will not allow your foot to [1]be moved;
[b]He who keeps you will not slumber.
4 Behold, He who keeps Israel
Shall neither slumber nor sleep.

5 The LORD *is* your [1]keeper;
The LORD *is* [a]your shade [b]at your right hand.
6 [a]The sun shall not strike you by day,
Nor the moon by night.

7 The LORD shall [1]preserve you from all evil;
He shall [a]preserve your soul.
8 The LORD shall [a]preserve[1] your going out and your coming in
From this time forth, and even forevermore.

PSALM 122

The Joy of Going to the House of the LORD

A Song of Ascents. Of David.

I WAS glad when they said to me,
[a]"Let us go into the house of the LORD."
2 Our feet have been standing
Within your gates, O Jerusalem!

3 Jerusalem is built
As a city that is [a]compact together,
4 [a]Where the tribes go up,
The tribes of the LORD,
[1]To [b]the Testimony of Israel,
To give thanks to the name of the LORD.
5 [a]For thrones are set there for judgment,

---

165 [1]Lit. *they have no stumbling block*
166 [a]Gen. 49:18
168 [a]Job 24:23; Prov. 5:21
169 [a]Ps. 119:27, 144
170 [1]Prayer of supplication
171 [a]Ps. 119:7
173 [a]Josh. 24:22; Luke 10:42
174 [a]Ps. 119:166 [b]Ps. 119:16, 24
176 [a][Is. 53:6]; Jer. 50:6; Matt. 18:12; Luke 15:4; [1 Pet. 2:25]

PSALM 120

1 [a]Jon. 2:2
4 [1]*mighty one*
5 [a]Gen. 10:2; 1 Chr. 1:5; Ezek. 27:13; 38:2, 3; 39:1 [b]Gen. 25:13; Is. 21:16; 60:7; Jer. 2:10; 49:28; Ezek. 27:21

PSALM 121

1 [a][Jer. 3:23]
2 [a][Ps. 124:8]
3 [a]1 Sam. 2:9; Prov. 3:23, 26 [b][Ps. 127:1; Prov. 24:12]; Is. 27:3 [1]*slip*
5 [a]Is. 25:4 [b]Ps. 16:8 [1]*protector*
6 [a]Ps. 91:5; Is. 49:10; Jon. 4:8; Rev. 7:16
7 [a]Ps. 41:2 [1]*keep*
8 [a]Deut. 28:6; [Prov. 2:8; 3:6] [1]*keep*

PSALM 122

1 [a][Is. 2:3; Mic. 4:2]; Zech. 8:21
3 [a]2 Sam. 5:9
4 [a]Ex. 23:17; Deut. 16:16 [b]Ex. 16:34 [1]Or *As a testimony to*
5 [a]Deut. 17:8; 2 Chr. 19:8

The thrones of the house of
David.
6 [a]Pray for the peace of Jerusalem:
"May they prosper who love you.
7 Peace be within your walls,
Prosperity within your palaces."
8 For the sake of my brethren and
companions,
I will now say, "Peace *be* within
you."
9 Because of the house of the LORD
our God
I will [a]seek your good.

PSALM 123

Prayer for Relief from Contempt

A Song of Ascents.

UNTO You [a]I lift up my eyes,
O You [b]who dwell in the
heavens.
2 Behold, as the eyes of servants
look to the hand of their
masters,
As the eyes of a maid to the hand
of her mistress,
[a]So our eyes *look* to the LORD our
God,
Until He has mercy on us.

3 Have mercy on us, O LORD, have
mercy on us!
For we are exceedingly filled with
contempt.
4 Our soul is exceedingly filled
With the scorn of those who are
at ease,
With the contempt of the proud.

PSALM 124

The LORD the Defense of His People

A Song of Ascents. Of David.

"IF it had not been the LORD who
was on our [a]side,"
[b]Let Israel now say—
2 "If it had not been the LORD who
was on our side,
When men rose up against us,
3 Then they would have
[a]swallowed us alive,
When their wrath was kindled
against us;
4 Then the waters would have
overwhelmed us,
The stream would have [1]gone
over our soul;
5 Then the swollen waters
Would have [1]gone over our soul."
6 Blessed *be* the LORD,
Who has not given us *as* prey to
their teeth.
7 [a]Our soul has escaped [b]as a bird
from the snare of the [1]fowlers;
The snare is broken, and we have
escaped.
8 [a]Our help *is* in the name of the
LORD,
[b]Who made heaven and earth.

PSALM 125

The LORD the Strength of His People

A Song of Ascents.

THOSE who trust in the LORD
Are like Mount Zion,
Which cannot be moved, *but*
abides forever.
2 As the mountains surround
Jerusalem,
So the LORD surrounds His
people
From this time forth and forever.
3 For [a]the scepter of wickedness
shall not rest
On the land allotted to the
righteous,
Lest the righteous reach out their
hands to iniquity.
4 Do good, O LORD, to *those who*
are good,
And to *those who are* upright in
their hearts.
5 As for such as turn aside to their
[a]crooked ways,
The LORD shall lead them away
With the workers of iniquity.

[b]Peace *be* upon Israel!

PSALM 126

A Joyful Return to Zion

A Song of Ascents.

WHEN [a]the LORD brought back
[1]the captivity of Zion,
[b]We were like those who dream.
2 Then [a]our mouth was filled with
laughter,
And our tongue with singing.
Then they said among the
[1]nations,
"The LORD has done great things
for them."
3 The LORD has done great things
for us,
And we are glad.
4 Bring back our captivity, O LORD,
As the streams in the South.
5 [a]Those who sow in tears
Shall reap in joy.

---

6 [a]Ps. 51:18
9 [a]Neh. 2:10; Esth. 10:3

PSALM 123
1 [a]Ps. 121:1; 141:8 [b]Ps. 2:4; 11:4; 115:3
2 [a]Ps. 25:15

PSALM 124
1 [a]Ps. 118:6; [Rom. 8:31] [b]Ps. 129:1
3 [a]Num. 16:30; Ps. 56:1, 2; 57:3; Prov. 1:12
4 [1]*swept over*
5 [1]*swept over*
7 [a]Ps. 91:3 [b]Prov. 6:5; Hos. 9:8 [1]Persons who catch birds in a trap or snare
8 [a][Ps. 121:2] [b]Gen. 1:1; Ps. 134:3

PSALM 125
3 [a]Prov. 22:8; Is. 14:5
5 [a]Prov. 2:15; Is. 59:8 [b]Ps. 128:6; [Gal. 6:16]

PSALM 126
1 [a]Ps. 85:1; Jer. 29:14; Hos. 6:11; Joel 3:1 [b]Acts 12:9 [1]Those of the captivity
2 [a]Job 8:21 [1]*Gentiles*
5 [a]Is. 35:10; 51:11; 61:7; Jer. 31:9; [Gal. 6:9]

6 He who continually goes [1]forth
weeping,
Bearing [2]seed for sowing,
Shall doubtless come again [3]with
[a]rejoicing,
Bringing his sheaves *with him.*

PSALM 127

Laboring and Prospering with the LORD

A Song of Ascents. Of Solomon.

UNLESS the LORD builds the
house,
They labor in vain who build it;
Unless [a]the LORD guards the city,
The watchman stays awake in
vain.
2 *It is* vain for you to rise up early,
To sit up late,
To [a]eat the bread of sorrows;
For so He gives His beloved sleep.

3 Behold, [a]children *are* a heritage
from the LORD,
[b]The fruit of the womb *is* a
[c]reward.
4 Like arrows in the hand of a
warrior,
So *are* the children of one's
youth.
5 [a]Happy *is* the man who has his
quiver full of them;
[b]They shall not be ashamed,
But shall speak with their
enemies in the gate.

PSALM 128

Blessings of Those Who Fear the LORD

A Song of Ascents.

BLESSED [a]*is* every one who fears
the LORD,
Who walks in His ways.

2 [a]When you eat the [1]labor of your
hands,
You *shall be* happy, and *it shall*
be [b]well with you.
3 Your wife *shall be* [a]like a fruitful
vine
In the very heart of your house,
Your [b]children [c]like olive plants
All around your table.
4 Behold, thus shall the man be
blessed
Who fears the LORD.

5 [a]The LORD bless you out of Zion,
And may you see the good of
Jerusalem
All the days of your life.
6 Yes, may you [a]see your children's
children.
[b]Peace *be* upon Israel!

6 [a]Is. 61:3 [1]*to and fro* [2]Lit. *a bag of seed for sowing* [3]*with shouts of joy*

PSALM 127

1 [a][Ps. 121:3–5]
2 [a][Gen. 3:17, 19]
3 [a][Gen. 33:5; Josh. 24:3, 4; Ps. 113:9] [b]Deut. 7:13; 28:4; Is. 13:18 [c][Ps. 113:9]
5 [a]Ps. 128:2, 3 [b]Job 5:4; Prov. 27:11

PSALM 128

1 [a]Ps. 119:1
2 [a]Is. 3:10 [b]Deut. 4:40 [1]Fruit of the labor
3 [a]Ezek. 19:10 [b]Ps. 127:3–5 [c]Ps. 52:8; 144:12
5 [a]Ps. 134:3
6 [a]Gen. 48:11; 50:23; Job 42:16; Ps. 103:17; [Prov. 17:6] [b]Ps. 125:5

PSALM 129

1 [a][Jer. 1:19; 15:20]; Matt. 16:18; 2 Cor. 4:8, 9 [b]Ezek. 23:3; Hos. 2:15 [c]Ps. 124:1 [1]*persecuted*
6 [a]Ps. 37:2
7 [1]*arms full,* lit. *bosom*
8 [a]Ruth 2:4

PSALM 130

1 [a]Lam. 3:55
3 [a][Ps. 143:2] [b][Nah. 1:6; Mal. 3:2]; Rev. 6:17 [1]*take note of*
4 [a][Ex. 34:7; Neh. 9:17; Ps. 86:5; Is. 55:7; Dan. 9:9] [b][1 Kin. 8:39, 40; Jer. 33:8, 9]
5 [a][Ps. 27:14] [b]Ps. 119:81
6 [a]Ps. 119:147
7 [a]Ps. 131:3 [b][Ps. 86:5, 15; Is. 55:7]

PSALM 129

Song of Victory over Zion's Enemies

A Song of Ascents.

"MANY a time they have
[a]afflicted[1] me from [b]my
youth,"
[c]Let Israel now say—
2 "Many a time they have afflicted
me from my youth;
Yet they have not prevailed
against me.
3 The plowers plowed on my back;
They made their furrows long."
4 The LORD *is* righteous;
He has cut in pieces the cords of
the wicked.

5 Let all those who hate Zion
Be put to shame and turned back.
6 Let them be as the [a]grass *on* the
housetops,
Which withers before it grows up,
7 With which the reaper does not
fill his hand,
Nor he who binds sheaves, his
[1]arms.
8 Neither let those who pass by
them say,
[a]"The blessing of the LORD *be* upon
you;
We bless you in the name of the
LORD!"

PSALM 130

Waiting for the Redemption of the LORD

A Song of Ascents.

OUT [a]of the depths I have cried
to You, O LORD;
2 Lord, hear my voice!
Let Your ears be attentive
To the voice of my supplications.

3 [a]If You, LORD, should [1]mark
iniquities,
O Lord, who could [b]stand?
4 But *there is* [a]forgiveness with
You,
That [b]You may be feared.

5 [a]I wait for the LORD, my soul
waits,
And [b]in His word I do hope.
6 [a]My soul *waits* for the Lord
More than those who watch for
the morning—
Yes, more than those who watch
for the morning.

7 [a]O Israel, hope in the LORD;
For [b]with the LORD *there is*
mercy,

And with Him *is* abundant
redemption.
8 And [a]He shall redeem Israel
From all his iniquities.

PSALM 131

Simple Trust in the LORD

A Song of Ascents. Of David.

LORD, my heart is not [1]haughty,
Nor my eyes [2]lofty.
[a]Neither do I [3]concern myself with
great matters,
Nor with things too [4]profound for
me.

2 Surely I have calmed and quieted
my soul,
[a]Like a weaned child with his
mother;
Like a weaned child *is* my soul
within me.

3 [a]O Israel, hope in the LORD
From this time forth and forever.

PSALM 132

The Eternal Dwelling of God in Zion

A Song of Ascents.

LORD, remember David
And all his afflictions;
2 How he swore to the LORD,
[a]*And* vowed to [b]the Mighty One
of Jacob:
3 "Surely I will not go into the
chamber of my house,
Or go up to the comfort of my
bed;
4 I will [a]not give sleep to my eyes
Or slumber to my eyelids,
5 Until I [a]find a place for the LORD,
A dwelling place for the Mighty
One of Jacob."

6 Behold, we heard of it [a]in
Ephrathah;
[b]We found it [c]in the fields of [1]the
woods.
7 Let us go into His tabernacle;
[a]Let us worship at His footstool.
8 [a]Arise, O LORD, to Your resting
place,
You and [b]the ark of Your
strength.
9 Let Your priests [a]be clothed with
righteousness,
And let Your saints shout for joy.

10 For Your servant David's sake,
Do not turn away the face of Your
[1]Anointed.

11 [a]The LORD has sworn *in* truth to
David;
He will not turn from it:
"I will set upon your throne [b]the
[1]fruit of your body.
12 If your sons will keep My
covenant
And My testimony which I shall
teach them,
Their sons also shall sit upon
your throne forevermore."

13 [a]For the LORD has chosen Zion;
He has desired *it* for His
[1]dwelling place:
14 "This[a] *is* My resting place forever;
Here I will dwell, for I have
desired it.
15 [a]I will abundantly bless her
[1]provision;
I will satisfy her poor with bread.
16 [a]I will also clothe her priests with
salvation,
[b]And her saints shall shout aloud
for joy.
17 [a]There I will make the [1]horn of
David grow;
[b]I will prepare a lamp for My
[2]Anointed.
18 His enemies I will [a]clothe with
shame,
But upon Himself His crown shall
flourish."

PSALM 133

Blessed Unity of the People of God

A Song of Ascents. Of David.

BEHOLD, how good and how
pleasant *it is*
For [a]brethren to dwell together in
unity!

2 *It is* like the precious oil upon the
head,
Running down on the beard,
The beard of Aaron,
Running down on the edge of his
garments.
3 *It is* like the dew of [a]Hermon,
Descending upon the mountains
of Zion;
For [b]there the LORD commanded
the blessing—
Life forevermore.

PSALM 134

Praising the LORD in His House at Night

A Song of Ascents.

BEHOLD, bless the LORD,
All you servants of the LORD,
Who by night stand in the house
of the LORD!

---

8 [a][Ps. 103:3, 4]; Luke 1:68; Titus 2:14

PSALM 131

1 [a]Jer. 45:5; [Rom. 12:16] [1]Proud [2]Arrogant [3]Lit. *walk in* [4]*difficult*
2 [a][Matt. 18:3; 1 Cor. 14:20]
3 [a][Ps. 130:7]

PSALM 132

2 [a]Ps. 65:1 [b]Gen. 49:24; Is. 49:26; 60:16
4 [a]Prov. 6:4
5 [a]1 Kin. 8:17; 1 Chr. 22:7; Ps. 26:8; Acts 7:46
6 [a]1 Sam. 17:12 [b]1 Sam. 7:1 [c]1 Chr. 13:5 [1]Heb. *Jaar,* lit. *Woods*
7 [a]Ps. 5:7; 99:5
8 [a]Num. 10:35 [b]Ps. 78:61
9 [a]Job 29:14
10 [1]Commissioned One, Heb. *Messiah*
11 [a][Ps. 89:3, 4, 33; 110:4] [b]2 Sam. 7:12; [1 Kin. 8:25; 2 Chr. 6:16; Luke 1:69; Acts 2:30] [1]*offspring*
13 [a][Ps. 48:1, 2] [1]*home*
14 [a]Ps. 68:16; Matt. 23:21
15 [a]Ps. 147:14 [1]*supply of food*
16 [a]2 Chr. 6:41; Ps. 132:9; 149:4 [b]1 Sam. 4:5; Hos. 11:12
17 [a]Ezek. 29:21; Luke 1:69 [b]1 Kin. 11:36; 15:4; 2 Kin. 8:19; 2 Chr. 21:7; Ps. 18:28 [1]Government [2]Heb. *Messiah*
18 [a]Job 8:22; Ps. 35:26

PSALM 133

1 [a]Gen. 13:8; Heb. 13:1
3 [a]Deut. 4:48 [b]Lev. 25:21; Deut. 28:8; Ps. 42:8

2 [a]Lift up your hands *in* the
sanctuary,
And bless the LORD.

3 The LORD who made heaven and
earth
Bless you from Zion!

PSALM 135

Praise to God in Creation and Redemption

PRAISE the LORD!

Praise the name of the LORD;
[a]Praise *Him*, O you servants of the
LORD!
2 [a]You who stand in the house of
the LORD,
In [b]the courts of the house of our
God,
3 Praise the LORD, for [a]the LORD *is*
good;
Sing praises to His name, [b]for *it*
is pleasant.
4 For [a]the LORD has chosen Jacob
for Himself,
Israel for His [1]special treasure.

5 For I know that [a]the LORD *is*
great,
And our Lord *is* above all gods.
6 [a]Whatever the LORD pleases He
does,
In heaven and in earth,
In the seas and in all deep places.
7 [a]He causes the [1]vapors to ascend
from the ends of the earth;
[b]He makes lightning for the rain;
He brings the wind out of His
[c]treasuries.

8 [a]He [1]destroyed the firstborn of
Egypt,
[2]Both of man and beast.
9 [a]He sent signs and wonders into
the midst of you, O Egypt,
[b]Upon Pharaoh and all his
servants.
10 [a]He defeated many nations
And slew mighty kings—
11 Sihon king of the Amorites,
Og king of Bashan,
And [a]all the kingdoms of
Canaan—
12 [a]And gave their land *as* a
[1]heritage,
A heritage to Israel His people.

13 [a]Your name, O LORD, *endures*
forever,
Your fame, O LORD, throughout
all generations.
14 [a]For the LORD will judge His
people,

PSALM 134
2 [a][1 Tim. 2:8]

PSALM 135
1 [a]Ps. 113:1
2 [a]Luke 2:37 [b]Ps. 116:19
3 [a][Ps. 119:68] [b]Ps. 147:1
4 [a][Ex. 19:5]; Mal. 3:17; [Titus 2:14; 1 Pet. 2:9] [1]*precious possession*
5 [a]Ps. 95:3; 97:9
6 [a]Ps. 115:3
7 [a]Jer. 10:13 [b]Job 28:25, 26; 38:24–28 [c]Jer. 51:16 [1]Water vapor
8 [a]Ex. 12:12; Ps. 78:51 [1]Lit. *struck down* [2]Lit. *From man to beast*
9 [a]Ex. 7:10; Deut. 6:22; Ps. 78:43 [b]Ps. 136:15
10 [a]Num. 21:24; Ps. 136:17
11 [a]Josh. 12:7–24
12 [a]Ps. 78:55; 136:21, 22 [1]*inheritance*
13 [a][Ex. 3:15; Ps. 102:12]
14 [a]Deut. 32:36
15 [a][Ps. 115:4–8]
19 [a][Ps. 115:9]
21 [a]Ps. 134:3

PSALM 136
1 [a]Ps. 106:1 [b]1 Chr. 16:34; Jer. 33:11
2 [a][Deut. 10:17]
4 [a]Deut. 6:22; Job 9:10; Ps. 72:18
5 [a]Gen. 1:1, 6–8; Prov. 3:19; Jer. 51:15
6 [a]Gen. 1:9; Ps. 24:2; [Is. 42:5]; Jer. 10:12
7 [a]Gen. 1:14–18
8 [a]Gen. 1:16
10 [a]Ex. 12:29; Ps. 135:8

And He will have compassion on
His servants.
15 [a]The idols of the nations *are* silver
and gold,
The work of men's hands.
16 They have mouths, but they do
not speak;
Eyes they have, but they do not
see;
17 They have ears, but they do not
hear;
Nor is there *any* breath in their
mouths.
18 Those who make them are like
them;
So is everyone who trusts in
them.

19 [a]Bless the LORD, O house of Israel!
Bless the LORD, O house of
Aaron!
20 Bless the LORD, O house of Levi!
You who fear the LORD, bless the
LORD!
21 Blessed be the LORD [a]out of Zion,
Who dwells in Jerusalem!

Praise the LORD!

PSALM 136

Thanksgiving to God for His Enduring Mercy

OH, [a]give thanks to the LORD, for
He is good!
[b]For His mercy *endures* forever.
2 Oh, give thanks to [a]the God of
gods!
For His mercy *endures* forever.
3 Oh, give thanks to the Lord of
lords!
For His mercy *endures* forever:

4 To Him [a]who alone does great
wonders,
For His mercy *endures* forever;
5 [a]To Him who by wisdom made the
heavens,
For His mercy *endures* forever;
6 [a]To Him who laid out the earth
above the waters,
For His mercy *endures* forever;
7 [a]To Him who made great lights,
For His mercy *endures*
forever—
8 [a]The sun to rule by day,
For His mercy *endures* forever;
9 The moon and stars to rule by
night,
For His mercy *endures* forever.

10 [a]To Him who struck Egypt in their
firstborn,
For His mercy *endures* forever;

11 [a]And brought out Israel from among them,
For His mercy *endures* forever;
12 [a]With a strong hand, and with [1]an outstretched arm,
For His mercy *endures* forever;
13 [a]To Him who divided the Red Sea in two,
For His mercy *endures* forever;
14 And made Israel pass through the midst of it,
For His mercy *endures* forever;
15 [a]But overthrew Pharaoh and his army in the Red Sea,
For His mercy *endures* forever;
16 [a]To Him who led His people through the wilderness,
For His mercy *endures* forever;
17 [a]To Him who struck down great kings,
For His mercy *endures* forever;
18 [a]And slew famous kings,
For His mercy *endures* forever—
19 [a]Sihon king of the Amorites,
For His mercy *endures* forever;
20 [a]And Og king of Bashan,
For His mercy *endures* forever—
21 [a]And gave their land as a [1]heritage,
For His mercy *endures* forever;
22 A heritage to Israel His servant,
For His mercy *endures* forever.

23 Who [a]remembered us in our lowly state,
For His mercy *endures* forever;
24 And [a]rescued us from our enemies,
For His mercy *endures* forever;
25 [a]Who gives food to all flesh,
For His mercy *endures* forever.

26 Oh, give thanks to the God of heaven!
For His mercy *endures* forever.

PSALM 137

Longing for Zion in a Foreign Land

BY the rivers of Babylon,
There we sat down, yea, we wept
When we remembered Zion.
2 We hung our harps
Upon the willows in the midst of it.
3 For there those who carried us away captive asked of us a song,
And those who [a]plundered us *requested* mirth,
Saying, "Sing us *one* of the songs of Zion!"

4 How shall we sing the LORD's song
In a foreign land?
5 If I forget you, O Jerusalem,
Let my right hand forget *its skill!*
6 If I do not remember you,
Let my [a]tongue cling to the roof of my mouth—
If I do not exalt Jerusalem
Above my chief joy.

7 Remember, O LORD, against [a]the sons of Edom
The day of Jerusalem,
Who said, [1]"Raze *it,* raze *it,*
To its very foundation!"

8 O daughter of Babylon, [a]who are to be destroyed,
Happy the one [b]who repays you as you have served us!
9 Happy the one who takes and [a]dashes
Your little ones against the rock!

PSALM 138

The LORD's Goodness to the Faithful

A Psalm of David.

I WILL praise You with my whole heart;
[a]Before the gods I will sing praises to You.
2 [a]I will worship [b]toward Your holy temple,
And praise Your name
For Your lovingkindness and Your truth;
For You have [c]magnified Your word above all Your name.
3 In the day when I cried out, You answered me,
And made me bold *with* strength in my soul.

4 [a]All the kings of the earth shall praise You, O LORD,
When they hear the words of Your mouth.
5 Yes, they shall sing of the ways of the LORD,
For great *is* the glory of the LORD.
6 [a]Though the LORD *is* on high,
Yet [b]He regards the lowly;
But the proud He knows from afar.

7 [a]Though I walk in the midst of trouble, You will revive me;
You will stretch out Your hand
Against the wrath of my enemies,
And Your right hand will save me.
8 [a]The LORD will [1]perfect *that which* concerns me;

---

11 [a]Ex. 12:51; 13:3, 16
12 [a]Ex. 6:6; Deut. 4:34; 5:15; 7:19; 9:29; 11:2; 2 Kin. 17:36; 2 Chr. 6:32; Jer. 32:17 [1]Mighty power
13 [a]Ex. 14:21
15 [a]Ex. 14:27
16 [a]Ex. 13:18; 15:22; Deut. 8:15
17 [a]Ps. 135:10–12
18 [a]Deut. 29:7
19 [a]Num. 21:21
20 [a]Num. 21:33
21 [a]Josh. 12:1 [1]*inheritance*
23 [a]Gen. 8:1; Deut. 32:36; Ps. 113:7
24 [a]Ps. 44:7
25 [a]Ps. 104:27; 145:15

PSALM 137

3 [a]Ps. 79:1
6 [a]Job 29:10; Ps. 22:15; Ezek. 3:26
7 [a]Jer. 49:7–22; Lam. 4:21; Ezek. 25:12–14; 35:2; Amos 1:11; Obad. 10–14 [1]Lit. *Make bare*
8 [a]Is. 13:1–6; 47:1 [b]Jer. 50:15; Rev. 18:6
9 [a]2 Kin. 8:12; Is. 13:16; Hos. 13:16; Nah. 3:10

PSALM 138

1 [a]Ps. 119:46
2 [a]Ps. 28:2 [b]1 Kin. 8:29 [c]Is. 42:21
4 [a]Ps. 102:15
6 [a][Ps. 113:4–7] [b]Prov. 3:34; [Is. 57:15]; Luke 1:48; [James 4:6; 1 Pet. 5:5]
7 [a][Ps. 23:3, 4]
8 [a]Ps. 57:2; [Phil. 1:6] [1]*complete*

Your mercy, O LORD, *endures*
forever;
[b]Do not forsake the works of Your
hands.

PSALM 139

God's Perfect Knowledge of Man

For the Chief Musician. A Psalm of David.

O LORD, [a]You have searched me
and known *me*.
2 [a]You know my sitting down and
my rising up;
You [b]understand my thought afar
off.
3 [a]You [1]comprehend my path and
my lying down,
And are acquainted with all my
ways.
4 For *there is* not a word on my
tongue,
But behold, O LORD, [a]You know
it altogether.
5 You have [1]hedged me behind and
before,
And laid Your hand upon me.
6 [a]*Such* knowledge *is* too wonderful
for me;
It is high, I cannot *attain* it.

7 [a]Where can I go from Your Spirit?
Or where can I flee from Your
presence?
8 [a]If I ascend into heaven, You *are*
there;
[b]If I make my bed in [1]hell, behold,
You *are there*.
9 *If* I take the wings of the morning,
And dwell in the uttermost parts
of the sea,
10 Even there Your hand shall lead
me,
And Your right hand shall hold
me.
11 If I say, "Surely the darkness
shall [1]fall on me,"
Even the night shall be light
about me;
12 Indeed, [a]the darkness [1]shall not
hide from You,
But the night shines as the day;
The darkness and the light *are*
both alike *to You*.

13 For You formed my inward parts;
You [1]covered me in my mother's
womb.
14 I will praise You, for [1]I am
fearfully *and* wonderfully
made;
Marvelous are Your works,
And *that* my soul knows very
well.

8 [b]Job 10:3, 8

PSALM 139

1 [a]Ps. 17:3; Jer. 12:3
2 [a]2 Kin. 19:27 [b]Is. 66:18; Matt. 9:4
3 [a]Job 14:16; 31:4 [1]Lit. *winnow*
4 [a][Heb. 4:13]
5 [1]*enclosed*
6 [a]Job 42:3; Ps. 40:5
7 [a][Jer. 23:24; Amos 9:2–4]
8 [a][Amos 9:2–4] [b][Job 26:6; Prov. 15:11] [1]Or *Sheol*
11 [1]Vg., Symmachus *cover*
12 [a]Job 26:6; 34:22; [Dan. 2:22; Heb. 4:13] [1]Lit. *is not dark*
13 [1]*wove*
14 [1]So with MT, Tg.; LXX, Syr., Vg. *You are fearfully wonderful*
15 [a]Job 10:8, 9; Eccl. 11:5 [1]Lit. *bones were*
17 [a][Ps. 40:5; Rom. 11:33]
19 [a][Is. 11:4] [b]Ps. 119:115 [1]Lit. *men of bloodshed*
20 [a]Jude 15 [1]LXX, Vg. *They take your cities in vain*
21 [a]2 Chr. 19:2
22 [1]*complete*
23 [a]Job 31:6; Ps. 26:2
24 [a]Ps. 5:8; 143:10

PSALM 140

2 [a]Ps. 56:6
3 [a]Ps. 58:4; Rom. 3:13; James 3:8
4 [a]Ps. 71:4

15 [a]My [1]frame was not hidden from
You,
When I was made in secret,
And skillfully wrought in the
lowest parts of the earth.
16 Your eyes saw my substance,
being yet unformed.
And in Your book they all were
written,
The days fashioned for me,
When *as yet there were* none of
them.

17 [a]How precious also are Your
thoughts to me, O God!
How great is the sum of them!
18 *If* I should count them, they
would be more in number than
the sand;
When I awake, I am still with
You.

19 Oh, that You would [a]slay the
wicked, O God!
[b]Depart from me, therefore, you
[1]bloodthirsty men.
20 For they [a]speak against You
wickedly;
[1]Your enemies take *Your name* in
vain.
21 [a]Do I not hate them, O LORD, who
hate You?
And do I not loathe those who
rise up against You?
22 I hate them with [1]perfect hatred;
I count them my enemies.

23 [a]Search me, O God, and know my
heart;
Try me, and know my anxieties;
24 And see if *there is any* wicked
way in me,
And [a]lead me in the way
everlasting.

PSALM 140

Prayer for Deliverance from Evil Men

To the Chief Musician. A Psalm of David.

DELIVER me, O LORD, from evil
men;
Preserve me from violent men,
2 Who plan evil things in *their*
hearts;
[a]They continually gather together
for war.
3 They sharpen their tongues like
a serpent;
The [a]poison of asps *is* under their
lips. Selah
4 [a]Keep me, O LORD, from the hands
of the wicked;
Preserve me from violent men,

Who have purposed to make my
steps stumble.
5 The proud have hidden a [a]snare
for me, and cords;
They have spread a net by the
wayside;
They have set traps for me.
Selah

6 I said to the LORD: "You *are* my
God;
Hear the voice of my
supplications, O LORD.
7 O GOD the Lord, the strength of
my salvation,
You have [1]covered my head in
the day of battle.
8 Do not grant, O LORD, the desires
of the wicked;
Do not further his *wicked*
scheme,
[a]*Lest* they be exalted. Selah

9 "*As for* the head of those who
surround me,
Let the evil of their lips cover
them;
10 [a]Let burning coals fall upon them;
Let them be cast into the fire,
Into deep pits, that they rise not
up again.
11 Let not a slanderer be established
in the earth;
Let evil hunt the violent man to
overthrow *him*."

12 I know that the LORD will
[a]maintain
The cause of the afflicted,
And justice for the poor.
13 Surely the righteous shall give
thanks to Your name;
The upright shall dwell in Your
presence.

PSALM 141

Prayer for Safekeeping from Wickedness

A Psalm of David.

LORD, I cry out to You;
Make haste to me!
Give ear to my voice when I cry
out to You.
2 Let my prayer be set before You
[a]*as* incense,
[b]The lifting up of my hands *as* [c]the
evening sacrifice.

3 Set a guard, O LORD, over my
[a]mouth;
Keep watch over the door of my
lips.

5 [a]Ps. 35:7; Jer. 18:22
7 [1]*sheltered*
8 [a]Deut. 32:27
10 [a]Ps. 11:6
12 [a]1 Kin. 8:45; Ps. 9:4

PSALM 141
2 [a][Ex. 30:8]; Luke 1:10; [Rev. 5:8; 8:3, 4] [b]Ps. 134:2; [1 Tim. 2:8] [c]Ex. 29:39, 41; 1 Kin. 18:29, 36; Dan. 9:21
3 [a][Prov. 13:3; 21:23]
4 [a]Prov. 23:6
5 [a][Prov. 9:8; Eccl. 7:5; Gal. 6:1]
6 [1]*rock*
8 [a]2 Chr. 20:12; Ps. 25:15 [1]Lit. *Do not make my soul bare*
9 [a]Ps. 119:110
10 [a]Ps. 35:8

PSALM 142
title [a]Ps. 32:title [b]1 Sam. 22:1; Ps. 57:title [1]Heb. *Maschil*
3 [a]Ps. 77:3 [b]Ps. 141:9 [1]Lit. *fainted*

4 Do not incline my heart to any
evil thing,
To practice wicked works
With men who work iniquity;
[a]And do not let me eat of their
delicacies.

5 [a]Let the righteous strike me;
It shall be a kindness.
And let him rebuke me;
It shall be as excellent oil;
Let my head not refuse it.

For still my prayer *is* against the
deeds of the wicked.
6 Their judges are overthrown by
the sides of the [1]cliff,
And they hear my words, for they
are sweet.
7 Our bones are scattered at the
mouth of the grave,
As when one plows and breaks
up the earth.

8 But [a]my eyes *are* upon You,
O GOD the Lord;
In You I take refuge;
[1]Do not leave my soul destitute.
9 Keep me from [a]the snares they
have laid for me,
And from the traps of the
workers of iniquity.
10 [a]Let the wicked fall into their own
nets,
While I escape safely.

PSALM 142

A Plea for Relief from Persecutors

A [a]Contemplation[1] of David. A Prayer [b]when he was in the cave.

I CRY out to the LORD with my
voice;
With my voice to the LORD I make
my supplication.
2 I pour out my complaint before
Him;
I declare before Him my trouble.

3 When my spirit [1]was
[a]overwhelmed within me,
Then You knew my path.
In the way in which I walk
They have secretly [b]set a snare
for me.
4 Look on *my* right hand and see,
For *there is* no one who
acknowledges me;
Refuge has failed me;
No one cares for my soul.

5 I cried out to You, O LORD:
I said, "You *are* my refuge,
My portion in the land of the
living.

6 [1]Attend to my cry,
For I am brought very low;
Deliver me from my persecutors,
For they are stronger than I.
7 Bring my soul out of prison,
That I may [a]praise Your name;
The righteous shall surround me,
For You shall deal bountifully
with me."

PSALM 143

An Earnest Appeal for Guidance and Deliverance

A Psalm of David.

HEAR my prayer, O LORD,
Give ear to my supplications!
In Your faithfulness answer me,
And in Your righteousness.
2 Do not enter into judgment with
Your servant,
[a]For in Your sight no one living
is righteous.

3 For the enemy has persecuted my
soul;
He has crushed my life to the
ground;
He has made me dwell in
[1]darkness,
Like those who have long been
dead.
4 [a]Therefore my spirit is
overwhelmed within me;
My heart within me is distressed.

5 [a]I remember the days of old;
I meditate on all Your works;
I [1]muse on the work of Your
hands.
6 I spread out my hands to You;
[a]My soul *longs* for You like a
thirsty land. Selah

7 Answer me speedily, O LORD;
My spirit fails!
Do not hide Your face from me,
[a]Lest I [1]be like those who [2]go
down into the pit.
8 Cause me to hear Your
lovingkindness [a]in the
morning,
For in You do I trust;
[b]Cause me to know the way in
which I should walk,
For [c]I lift up my soul to You.

9 Deliver me, O LORD, from my
enemies;
[1]In You I take shelter.
10 [a]Teach me to do Your will,
For You *are* my God;
[b]Your Spirit *is* good.

6 [1]*Give heed*
7 [a]Ps. 34:1, 2

PSALM 143

2 [a][Ex. 34:7]; Job 4:17; 9:2; 25:4; Ps. 130:3; Eccl. 7:20; [Rom. 3:20–23; Gal. 2:16]
3 [1]*dark places*
4 [a]Ps. 77:3
5 [a]Ps. 77:5, 10, 11 [1]*ponder*
6 [a]Ps. 63:1
7 [a]Ps. 28:1 [1]*become* [2]Die
8 [a]Ps. 46:5 [b]Ps. 5:8 [c]Ps. 25:1
9 [1]LXX, Vg. *To You I flee*
10 [a]Ps. 25:4, 5 [b]Neh. 9:20 [c]Is. 26:10
11 [a]Ps. 119:25
12 [a]Ps. 54:5 [1]*put an end to*

PSALM 144

1 [a]2 Sam. 22:35; Ps. 18:34
2 [1]So with MT, LXX, Vg.; Syr., Tg. *the peoples* (cf. 18:47)
3 [a]Job 7:17; Ps. 8:4; Heb. 2:6
4 [a]Ps. 39:11 [b]Job 8:9; 14:2; Ps. 102:11
5 [a]Ps. 18:9; Is. 64:1 [b]Ps. 104:32
6 [a]Ps. 18:13, 14
8 [a]Ps. 12:2 [1]*empty* or *worthless*
9 [a]Ps. 33:2, 3; 40:3
10 [a]Ps. 18:50 [1]*deliverance*

Lead me in [c]the land of
uprightness.

11 [a]Revive me, O LORD, for Your
name's sake!
For Your righteousness' sake
bring my soul out of trouble.
12 In Your mercy [a]cut[1] off my
enemies,
And destroy all those who afflict
my soul;
For I *am* Your servant.

PSALM 144

A Song to the LORD Who Preserves and Prospers His People

A Psalm of David.

BLESSED *be* the LORD my Rock,
[a]Who trains my hands for war,
And my fingers for battle—
2 My lovingkindness and my
fortress;
My high tower and my deliverer,
My shield and *the One* in whom
I take refuge,
Who subdues [1]my people under
me.

3 [a]LORD, what *is* man, that You take
knowledge of him?
Or the son of man, that You are
mindful of him?
4 [a]Man is like a breath;
[b]His days *are* like a passing
shadow.

5 [a]Bow down Your heavens,
O LORD, and come down;
[b]Touch the mountains, and they
shall smoke.
6 [a]Flash forth lightning and scatter
them;
Shoot out Your arrows and
destroy them.
7 Stretch out Your hand from
above;
Rescue me and deliver me out of
great waters,
From the hand of foreigners,
8 Whose mouth [a]speaks [1]lying
words,
And whose right hand *is* a right
hand of falsehood.

9 I will [a]sing a new song to You,
O God;
On a harp of ten strings I will sing
praises to You,
10 *The One* who gives [1]salvation to
kings,
[a]Who delivers David His servant
From the deadly sword.

11 Rescue me and deliver me from
the hand of foreigners,
Whose mouth speaks lying
words,
And whose right hand *is* a right
hand of falsehood—
12 That our sons *may be* [a]as plants
grown up in their youth;
That our daughters *may be* as
[1]pillars,
Sculptured in palace style;
13 *That* our barns *may be* full,
Supplying all kinds of produce;
That our sheep may bring forth
thousands
And ten thousands in our fields;
14 *That* our oxen *may be* well laden;
That there be no [1]breaking in or
going out;
That there be no outcry in our
streets.
15 [a]Happy *are* the people who are in
such a state;
Happy *are* the people whose God
is the LORD!

PSALM 145

A Song of God's Majesty and Love

[a]A Praise of David.

I WILL [1]extol You, my God, O King;
And I will bless Your name
forever and ever.
2 Every day I will bless You,
And I will praise Your name
forever and ever.
3 [a]Great *is* the LORD, and greatly to
be praised;
And [b]His greatness *is*
[1]unsearchable.

4 [a]One generation shall praise Your
works to another,
And shall declare Your mighty
acts.
5 [1]I will meditate on the glorious
splendor of Your majesty,
And [2]on Your wondrous works.
6 *Men* shall speak of the might of
Your awesome acts,
And I will declare Your
greatness.
7 They shall [1]utter the memory of
Your great goodness,
And shall sing of Your
righteousness.

8 [a]The LORD *is* gracious and full of
compassion,
Slow to anger and great in mercy.
9 [a]The LORD *is* good to all,
And His tender mercies *are* over
all His works.

12 [a]Ps. 128:3 [1]*corner pillars*
14 [1]Lit. *breach*
15 [a]Deut. 33:29; [Ps. 33:12; Jer. 17:7]

PSALM 145

title [a]Ps. 100:title
1 [1]*praise*
3 [a][Ps. 147:5] [b]Job 5:9; 9:10; 11:7; Is. 40:28; [Rom. 11:33] [1]Beyond our understanding
4 [a]Is. 38:19
5 [1]So with MT, Tg.; DSS, LXX, Syr., Vg. *They* [2]Lit. *on the words of Your wondrous works*
7 [1]*eagerly utter*, lit. *bubble forth*
8 [a][Ex. 34:6, 7; Num. 14:18]; Ps. 86:5, 15
9 [a][Ps. 100:5]; Jer. 33:11; Nah. 1:7; [Matt. 19:17; Mark 10:18]
10 [a]Ps. 19:1
13 [a]Dan. 2:44; 4:3; [1 Tim. 1:17; 2 Pet. 1:11] [1]So with MT, Tg.; DSS, LXX, Syr., Vg. add *The LORD is faithful in all His words, And holy in all His works*
14 [a]Ps. 146:8
15 [a]Ps. 104:27 [b]Ps. 136:25
16 [a]Ps. 104:21, 28
18 [a][Deut. 4:7] [b][John 4:24]
20 [a][Ps. 31:23]

PSALM 146

1 [a]Ps. 103:1 [1]Heb. *Hallelujah*
2 [a]Ps. 104:33
3 [a][Is. 2:22] [1]A human being [2]*salvation*
4 [a][Eccl. 12:7] [b][Ps. 33:10; 1 Cor. 2:6]

10 [a]All Your works shall praise You,
O LORD,
And Your saints shall bless You.
11 They shall speak of the glory of
Your kingdom,
And talk of Your power,
12 To make known to the sons of
men His mighty acts,
And the glorious majesty of His
kingdom.
13 [a]Your kingdom *is* an everlasting
kingdom,
And Your dominion *endures*
throughout all [1]generations.

14 The LORD upholds all who fall,
And [a]raises up all *who are* bowed
down.
15 [a]The eyes of all look expectantly
to You,
And [b]You give them their food in
due season.
16 You open Your hand
[a]And satisfy the desire of every
living thing.

17 The LORD *is* righteous in all His
ways,
Gracious in all His works.
18 [a]The LORD *is* near to all who call
upon Him,
To all who call upon Him [b]in
truth.
19 He will fulfill the desire of those
who fear Him;
He also will hear their cry and
save them.
20 [a]The LORD preserves all who love
Him,
But all the wicked He will
destroy.
21 My mouth shall speak the praise
of the LORD,
And all flesh shall bless His holy
name
Forever and ever.

PSALM 146

The Happiness of Those Whose Help Is the LORD

PRAISE[1] the LORD!

[a]Praise the LORD, O my soul!
2 [a]While I live I will praise the LORD;
I will sing praises to my God
while I have my being.

3 [a]Do not put your trust in princes,
Nor in [1]a son of man, in whom
there is no [2]help.
4 [a]His spirit departs, he returns to
his earth;
In that very day [b]his plans perish.

5 [a]Happy *is he* who *has* the God of
Jacob for his help,
Whose hope *is* in the LORD his
God,
6 [a]Who made heaven and earth,
The sea, and all that *is* in them;
Who keeps truth forever,
7 [a]Who executes justice for the
oppressed,
[b]Who gives food to the hungry.
[c]The LORD gives freedom to the
prisoners.

8 [a]The LORD opens *the eyes of* the
blind;
[b]The LORD raises those who are
bowed down;
The LORD loves the righteous.
9 [a]The LORD watches over the
strangers;
He relieves the fatherless and
widow;
[b]But the way of the wicked He
[1]turns upside down.

10 [a]The LORD shall reign forever—
Your God, O Zion, to all
generations.

Praise the LORD!

PSALM 147

Praise to God for His Word and Providence

PRAISE[1] the LORD!
For [a]*it is* good to sing praises to
our God;
[b]For *it is* pleasant, *and* [c]praise is
beautiful.

2 The LORD [a]builds up Jerusalem;
[b]He gathers together the outcasts
of Israel.
3 [a]He heals the brokenhearted
And binds up their [1]wounds.
4 [a]He counts the number of the
stars;
He calls them all by name.
5 [a]Great *is* our Lord, and [b]mighty in
power;
[c]His understanding *is* infinite.
6 [a]The LORD lifts up the humble;
He casts the wicked down to the
ground.

7 Sing to the LORD with
thanksgiving;
Sing praises on the harp to our
God,
8 [a]Who covers the heavens with
clouds,
Who prepares rain for the earth,
Who makes grass to grow on the
mountains.
9 [a]He gives to the beast its food,
And [b]to the young ravens that
cry.

10 [a]He does not delight in the
strength of the horse;
He takes no pleasure in the legs
of a man.
11 The LORD takes pleasure in those
who fear Him,
In those who hope in His mercy.

12 Praise the LORD, O Jerusalem!
Praise your God, O Zion!
13 For He has strengthened the bars
of your gates;
He has blessed your children
within you.
14 [a]He makes peace *in* your borders,
And [b]fills you with [1]the finest
wheat.

15 [a]He sends out His command *to the*
earth;
His word runs very swiftly.
16 [a]He gives snow like wool;
He scatters the frost like ashes;
17 He casts out His hail like
[1]morsels;
Who can stand before His cold?
18 [a]He sends out His word and melts
them;
He causes His wind to blow, *and*
the waters flow.

19 [a]He declares His word to Jacob,
[b]His statutes and His judgments to
Israel.
20 [a]He has not dealt thus with any
nation;
And *as for His* judgments, they
have not known them.

[1]Praise the LORD!

PSALM 148

Praise to the LORD from Creation

PRAISE[1] the LORD!

Praise the LORD from the
heavens;
Praise Him in the heights!
2 Praise Him, all His angels;
Praise Him, all His hosts!
3 Praise Him, sun and moon;
Praise Him, all you stars of light!
4 Praise Him, [a]you heavens of
heavens,
And [b]you waters above the
heavens!

5 Let them praise the name of the
LORD,

---

5 [a]Jer. 17:7
6 [a]Gen. 1:1; Ex. 20:11; Acts 4:24; Rev. 14:7
7 [a]Ps. 103:6 [b]Ps. 107:9 [c]Ps. 107:10; Is. 61:1
8 [a]Matt. 9:30; [John 9:7, 32, 33] [b]Luke 13:13
9 [a]Deut. 10:18; Ps. 68:5 [b]Ps. 147:6 [1]Lit. *makes crooked*
10 [a]Ex. 15:18; Ps. 10:16; [Rev. 11:15]

PSALM 147

1 [a]Ps. 92:1 [b]Ps. 135:3 [c]Ps. 33:1 [1]Heb. *Hallelujah*
2 [a]Ps. 102:16 [b]Deut. 30:3; Is. 11:12; 56:8; Ezek. 39:28
3 [a][Ps. 51:17]; Is. 61:1; Luke 4:18 [1]Lit. *sorrows*
4 [a]Is. 40:26
5 [a]Ps. 48:1 [b]Nah. 1:3 [c]Is. 40:28
6 [a]Ps. 146:8, 9
8 [a]Job 38:26; Ps. 104:13
9 [a]Job 38:41 [b][Matt. 6:26]
10 [a]Ps. 33:16, 17
14 [a]Is. 54:13; 60:17, 18 [b]Ps. 132:15 [1]Lit. *fat of wheat*
15 [a][Ps. 107:20]
16 [a]Job 37:6
17 [1]*fragments* of food
18 [a]Job 37:10
19 [a]Deut. 33:4; Ps. 103:7 [b]Mal. 4:4
20 [a]Deut. 4:32–34; [Rom. 3:1, 2] [1]Heb. *Hallelujah*

PSALM 148

1 [1]Heb. *Hallelujah*
4 [a]Deut. 10:14; 1 Kin. 8:27; [Neh. 9:6] [b]Gen. 1:7

For [a]He commanded and they were created.
6 [a]He also established them forever and ever;
He made a decree which shall not pass away.

7 Praise the LORD from the earth,
[a]You great sea creatures and all the depths;
8 Fire and hail, snow and clouds;
Stormy wind, fulfilling His word;
9 [a]Mountains and all hills;
Fruitful trees and all cedars;
10 Beasts and all cattle;
Creeping things and flying fowl;
11 Kings of the earth and all peoples;
Princes and all judges of the earth;
12 Both young men and maidens;
Old men and children.

13 Let them praise the name of the LORD,
For His [a]name alone is exalted;
His glory *is* above the earth and heaven.
14 And He [a]has exalted the [1]horn of His people,
The praise of [b]all His saints—
Of the children of Israel,
[c]A people near to Him.

[2]Praise the LORD!

PSALM 149

Praise to God for His Salvation and Judgment

PRAISE[1] the LORD!

[a]Sing to the LORD a new song,
And His praise in the assembly of saints.

2 Let Israel rejoice in their Maker;
Let the children of Zion be joyful in their [a]King.
3 [a]Let them praise His name with the dance;
Let them sing praises to Him with the timbrel and harp.
4 For [a]the LORD takes pleasure in His people;
[b]He will beautify the [1]humble with salvation.

5 Let the saints be joyful in glory;
Let them [a]sing aloud on their beds.
6 *Let* the high praises of God *be* in their mouth,
And [a]a two-edged sword in their hand,
7 To execute vengeance on the nations,
And punishments on the peoples;
8 To bind their kings with chains,
And their nobles with fetters of iron;
9 [a]To execute on them the written judgment—
[b]This honor have all His saints.

[1]Praise the LORD!

PSALM 150

Let All Things Praise the LORD

PRAISE[a1] the LORD!

Praise God in His sanctuary;
Praise Him in His mighty [2]firmament!

2 Praise Him for His mighty acts;
Praise Him according to His excellent [a]greatness!

3 Praise Him with the sound of the [1]trumpet;
Praise Him with the lute and harp!
4 Praise Him with the timbrel and dance;
Praise Him with stringed instruments and flutes!
5 Praise Him with loud cymbals;
Praise Him with clashing cymbals!

6 Let everything that has breath praise the LORD.

[1]Praise the LORD!

---

5 [a]Gen. 1:1, 6
6 [a]Ps. 89:37; [Jer. 31:35, 36; 33:20, 25]
7 [a]Is. 43:20
9 [a]Is. 44:23; 49:13
13 [a]Ps. 8:1
14 [a]1 Sam. 2:1; Ps. 75:10 [b]Ps. 149:9 [c]Lev. 10:3; Eph. 2:17 [1]Strength or dominion [2]Heb. *Hallelujah*

PSALM 149

1 [a]Ps. 33:3 [1]Heb. *Hallelujah*
2 [a]Judg. 8:23; Zech. 9:9; Matt. 21:5
3 [a]Ex. 15:20; Ps. 81:2
4 [a]Ps. 35:27 [b]Ps. 132:16; Is. 61:3 [1]*meek*
5 [a]Job 35:10
6 [a]Heb. 4:12; Rev. 1:16
9 [a]Deut. 7:1, 2; Ezek. 28:26 [b]Ps. 148:14; 1 Cor. 6:2 [1]Heb. *Hallelujah*

PSALM 150

1 [a]Ps. 145:5, 6 [1]Heb. *Hallelujah* [2]*expanse* of heaven
2 [a]Deut. 3:24
3 [1]*cornet*
6 [1]Heb. *Hallelujah*

The Book of Proverbs

THE key word in Proverbs is *wisdom,* "the ability to live life skillfully." A godly life in an ungodly world, however, is no simple assignment. Proverbs provides God's detailed instructions for His people to deal successfully with the practical affairs of everyday life: how to relate to God, parents, children, neighbors, and government. Solomon, the principal author, uses a combination of poetry, parables, pithy questions, short stories, and wise maxims to give in strikingly memorable form the common sense and divine perspective necessary to handle life's issues.

Because Solomon, the pinnacle of Israel's wise men, was the principal contributor, the Hebrew title of this book is *Mishle Shelomoh,* "Proverbs of Solomon" (1:1). The Greek title is *Paroimiai Salomontos,* "Proverbs of Solomon." The Latin title *Liber Proverbiorum,* "Book of Proverbs," combines the words *pro* "for" and *verba* "words" to describe the way the proverbs concentrate many words into a few. The rabbinical writings called Proverbs *Sepher Hokhmah,* "Book of Wisdom."

The Beginning of Knowledge

THE [a]proverbs of Solomon the son of David, king of Israel:

2 To know wisdom and instruction,
To [1]perceive the words of understanding,
3 To receive the instruction of wisdom,
Justice, judgment, and equity;
4 To give prudence to the [a]simple,
To the young man knowledge and discretion—
5 [a]A wise *man* will hear and increase learning,
And a man of understanding will [1]attain wise counsel,
6 To understand a proverb and an enigma,
The words of the wise and their [a]riddles.

7 [a]The fear of the LORD *is* the beginning of knowledge,
But fools despise wisdom and instruction.

Shun Evil Counsel

8 [a]My son, hear the instruction of your father,
And do not forsake the law of your mother;
9 For they *will be* a [a]graceful ornament on your head,
And chains about your neck.

10 My son, if sinners entice you,
[a]Do not consent.
11 If they say, "Come with us,
Let us [a]lie in wait to *shed* blood;
Let us lurk secretly for the innocent without cause;
12 Let us swallow them alive like [1]Sheol,
And whole, [a]like those who go down to the Pit;
13 We shall find all *kinds* of precious [1]possessions,
We shall fill our houses with [2]spoil;
14 Cast in your lot among us,
Let us all have one purse"—
15 My son, [a]do not walk in the way with them,
[b]Keep your foot from their path;
16 [a]For their feet run to evil,
And they make haste to shed blood.
17 Surely, in [1]vain the net is spread
In the sight of any [2]bird;
18 But they lie in wait for their *own* blood,
They lurk secretly for their *own* lives.
19 [a]So *are* the ways of everyone who is greedy for gain;
It takes away the life of its owners.

The Call of Wisdom

20 [a]Wisdom calls aloud [1]outside;
She raises her voice in the open squares.

CHAPTER 1

1 [a]1 Kin. 4:32
2 [1]*understand* or *discern*
4 [a]Prov. 9:4
5 [a]Prov. 9:9 [1]*acquire*
6 [a]Ps. 78:2
7 [a]Job 28:28
8 [a]Prov. 4:1
9 [a]Prov. 3:22
10 [a]Gen. 39:7–10
11 [a]Jer. 5:26
12 [a]Ps. 28:1 [1]Or *the grave*
13 [1]Lit. *wealth* [2]*plunder*
15 [a]Ps. 1:1 [b]Ps. 119:101
16 [a][Is. 59:7]
17 [1]*futility* [2]Lit. *lord of the wing*
19 [a][1 Tim. 6:10]
20 [a][John 7:37] [1]*in the street*

21 She cries out in the [1]chief
concourses,
At the openings of the gates in
the city
She speaks her words:
22 "How long, you [1]simple ones, will
you love [2]simplicity?
For scorners delight in their
scorning,
And fools hate knowledge.
23 Turn at my rebuke;
Surely [a]I will pour out my spirit
on you;
I will make my words known to
you.
24 [a]Because I have called and you
refused,
I have stretched out my hand and
no one regarded,
25 Because you [a]disdained all my
counsel,
And would have none of my
rebuke,
26 [a]I also will laugh at your
calamity;
I will mock when your terror
comes,
27 When [a]your terror comes like a
storm,
And your destruction comes like
a whirlwind,
When distress and anguish come
upon you.
28 "Then[a] they will call on me, but I
will not answer;
They will seek me diligently, but
they will not find me.
29 Because they [a]hated knowledge
And did not [b]choose the fear of
the LORD,
30 [a]They would have none of my
counsel
And despised my every rebuke.
31 Therefore [a]they shall eat the fruit
of their own way,
And be filled to the full with their
own fancies.
32 For the [1]turning away of the
simple will slay them,
And the complacency of fools will
destroy them;
33 But whoever listens to me will
dwell [a]safely,
And [b]will be [1]secure, without fear
of evil."

The Value of Wisdom

2 My son, if you receive my words,
And [a]treasure my commands
within you,
2 So that you incline your ear to
wisdom,
And apply your heart to
understanding;
3 Yes, if you cry out for
discernment,
And lift up your voice for
understanding,
4 [a]If you seek her as silver,
And search for her as *for* hidden
treasures;
5 [a]Then you will understand the fear
of the LORD,
And find the knowledge of God.
6 [a]For the LORD gives wisdom;
From His mouth *come* knowledge
and understanding;
7 He stores up sound wisdom for
the upright;
[a]*He is* a shield to those who walk
uprightly;
8 He guards the paths of justice,
And [a]preserves the way of His
saints.
9 Then you will understand
righteousness and justice,
Equity *and* every good path.

10 When wisdom enters your
heart,
And knowledge is pleasant to
your soul,
11 Discretion will preserve you;
[a]Understanding will keep you,
12 To deliver you from the way of
evil,
From the man who speaks
perverse things,
13 From those who leave the paths
of uprightness
To [a]walk in the ways of darkness;
14 [a]Who rejoice in doing evil,
And delight in the perversity of
the wicked;
15 [a]Whose ways *are* crooked,
And *who are* devious in their
paths;
16 To deliver you from [a]the immoral
woman,
[b]From the seductress *who* flatters
with her words,
17 Who forsakes the companion of
her youth,
And forgets the covenant of her
God.
18 For [a]her house [1]leads down to
death,
And her paths to the dead;
19 None who go to her return,
Nor do they [1]regain the paths of
life—
20 So you may walk in the way of
goodness,
And keep *to* the paths of
righteousness.
21 For the upright will dwell in the
[a]land,
And the blameless will remain
in it;

21 [1]LXX, Syr., Tg. *top of the walls;* Vg. *the head of multitudes*
22 [1]*naive* [2]*naivete*
23 [a]Is. 32:15; Joel 2:28; [John 7:39]
24 [a]Is. 65:12; 66:4; Jer. 7:13; Zech. 7:11
25 [a]Ps. 107:11; Luke 7:30
26 [a]Ps. 2:4
27 [a][Prov. 10:24, 25]
28 [a]1 Sam. 8:18; Job 27:9; 35:12; Ps. 18:41; Is. 1:15; Jer. 11:11; 14:12; Ezek. 8:18; Mic. 3:4; Zech. 7:13; [James 4:3]
29 [a]Job 21:14; Prov. 1:22 [b]Ps. 119:173
30 [a]Ps. 81:11; Prov. 1:25
31 [a]Job 4:8; Prov. 5:22, 23; 22:8; Is. 3:11; Jer. 6:19
32 [1]*waywardness*
33 [a]Prov. 3:24–26 [b]Ps. 112:7 [1]*at ease*

CHAPTER 2

1 [a][Prov. 4:21]
4 [a][Prov. 3:14]
5 [a][James 1:5, 6]
6 [a]1 Kin. 3:9, 12; [Job 32:8; James 1:5]
7 [a][Ps. 84:11]; Prov. 30:5
8 [a][1 Sam. 2:9]; Ps. 66:9
11 [a]Prov. 4:6; 6:22
13 [a]Ps. 82:5; Prov. 4:19; [John 3:19, 20]
14 [a]Prov. 10:23; Jer. 11:15; [Rom. 1:32]
15 [a]Ps. 125:5; [Prov. 21:8]
16 [a]Prov. 5:20; 6:24; 7:5 [b]Prov. 5:3
18 [a]Prov. 7:27 [1]*sinks*
19 [1]Lit. *reach*
21 [a]Ps. 37:3

22 But the wicked will be [1]cut off
from the [2]earth,
And the unfaithful will be
uprooted from it.

Guidance for the Young

3 My son, do not forget my law,
[a]But let your heart keep my
commands;
2 For length of days and long life
And [a]peace they will add to you.

3 Let not mercy and truth forsake
you;
[a]Bind them around your neck,
[b]Write them on the tablet of your
heart,
4 [a]*And* so find favor and [1]high
esteem
In the sight of God and man.

5 [a]Trust in the LORD with all your
heart,
[b]And lean not on your own
understanding;
6 [a]In all your ways acknowledge
Him,
And He shall [1]direct your paths.

7 Do not be wise in your own [a]eyes;
Fear the LORD and depart from
evil.
8 It will be health to your [1]flesh,
And [a]strength[2] to your bones.

9 [a]Honor the LORD with your
possessions,
And with the firstfruits of all your
increase;
10 [a]So your barns will be filled with
plenty,
And your vats will overflow with
new wine.

11 [a]My son, do not despise the
chastening of the LORD,
Nor detest His correction;
12 For whom the LORD loves He
corrects,
[a]Just as a father the son *in whom*
he delights.

13 [a]Happy *is* the man *who* finds
wisdom,
And the man *who* gains
understanding;
14 [a]For her proceeds *are* better than
the profits of silver,
And her gain than fine gold.
15 She *is* more precious than rubies,
And [a]all the things you may
desire cannot compare with
her.
16 [a]Length of days *is* in her right
hand,
In her left hand riches and honor.
17 [a]Her ways *are* ways of
pleasantness,
And all her paths *are* peace.
18 She *is* [a]a tree of life to those who
take hold of her,
And happy *are all* who [1]retain
her.

19 [a]The LORD by wisdom founded the
earth;
By understanding He established
the heavens;
20 By His knowledge the depths
were [a]broken up,
And clouds drop down the dew.

21 My son, let them not depart from
your eyes—
Keep sound wisdom and
discretion;
22 So they will be life to your soul
And grace to your neck.
23 [a]Then you will walk safely in your
way,
And your foot will not stumble.
24 When you lie down, you will not
be afraid;
Yes, you will lie down and your
sleep will be sweet.
25 [a]Do not be afraid of sudden
terror,
Nor of trouble from the wicked
when it comes;
26 For the LORD will be your
confidence,
And will keep your foot from
being caught.

27 [a]Do not withhold good from [1]those
to whom it is due,
When it is in the power of your
hand to do *so*.
28 [a]Do not say to your neighbor,
"Go, and come back,
And tomorrow I will give *it*,"
When *you have* it with you.
29 Do not devise evil against your
neighbor,
For he dwells by you for safety's
sake.
30 [a]Do not strive with a man without
cause,
If he has done you no harm.

31 [a]Do not envy the oppressor,
And choose none of his ways;
32 For the perverse *person is* an
abomination to the LORD,
[a]But His secret counsel *is* with the
upright.
33 [a]The curse of the LORD *is* on the
house of the wicked,
But [b]He blesses the home of the
just.

22 [1]*destroyed* [2]*land*

CHAPTER 3

1 [a]Deut. 8:1
2 [a]Ps. 119:165
3 [a]Prov. 6:21 [b][2 Cor. 3:3]
4 [a]Rom. 14:18 [1]Lit. *good understanding*
5 [a][Ps. 37:3, 5] [b][Jer. 9:23, 24]
6 [a][1 Chr. 28:9] [1]Or *make smooth* or *straight*
7 [a]Rom. 12:16
8 [a]Job 21:24 [1]Body, lit. *navel* [2]Lit. *drink*
9 [a]Ex. 22:29
10 [a]Deut. 28:8
11 [a]Job 5:17
12 [a]Deut. 8:5
13 [a]Prov. 8:32, 34, 35
14 [a]Job 28:13
15 [a]Matt. 13:44
16 [a][1 Tim. 4:8]
17 [a][Matt. 11:29]
18 [a]Gen. 2:9 [1]*hold her fast*
19 [a]Ps. 104:24
20 [a]Gen. 7:11
23 [a]Prov. 10:9
25 [a]Ps. 91:5
27 [a]Rom. 13:7 [1]Lit. *its owners*
28 [a]Lev. 19:13
30 [a][Rom. 12:18]
31 [a]Ps. 37:1
32 [a]Ps. 25:14
33 [a]Zech. 5:3, 4 [b]Ps. 1:3

34 [a]Surely He scorns the scornful,
But gives grace to the humble.
35 The wise shall inherit glory,
But shame shall be the legacy of fools.

Security in Wisdom

4 Hear, [a]my children, the instruction of a father,
And give attention to know understanding;
2 For I give you good doctrine:
Do not forsake my law.
3 When I was my father's son,
[a]Tender and the only one in the sight of my mother,
4 [a]He also taught me, and said to me:
"Let your heart retain my words;
[b]Keep my commands, and live.
5 [a]Get wisdom! Get understanding!
Do not forget, nor turn away from the words of my mouth.
6 Do not forsake her, and she will preserve you;
[a]Love her, and she will keep you.
7 [a]Wisdom *is* the principal thing;
Therefore get wisdom.
And in all your getting, get understanding.
8 [a]Exalt her, and she will promote you;
She will bring you honor, when you embrace her.
9 She will place on your head [a]an ornament of grace;
A crown of glory she will deliver to you."

10 Hear, my son, and receive my sayings,
[a]And the years of your life will be many.
11 I have [a]taught you in the way of wisdom;
I have led you in right paths.
12 When you walk, [a]your steps will not be hindered,
[b]And when you run, you will not stumble.
13 Take firm hold of instruction, do not let go;
Keep her, for she *is* your life.

14 [a]Do not enter the path of the wicked,
And do not walk in the way of evil.
15 Avoid it, do not travel on it;
Turn away from it and pass on.
16 [a]For they do not sleep unless they have done evil;
And their sleep is [1]taken away unless they make *someone* fall.
17 For they eat the bread of wickedness,
And drink the wine of violence.

18 [a]But the path of the just [b]*is* like the shining [1]sun,
That shines ever brighter unto the perfect day.
19 [a]The way of the wicked *is* like darkness;
They do not know what makes them stumble.

20 My son, give attention to my words;
Incline your ear to my sayings.
21 Do not let them depart from your eyes;
Keep them in the midst of your heart;
22 For they *are* life to those who find them,
And health to all their flesh.
23 Keep your heart with all diligence,
For out of it *spring* the issues of [a]life.
24 Put away from you a [1]deceitful mouth,
And put perverse lips far from you.
25 Let your eyes look straight ahead,
And your eyelids look right before you.
26 Ponder the path of your [a]feet,
And let all your ways be established.
27 Do not turn to the right or the left;
Remove your foot from evil.

The Peril of Adultery

5 My son, pay attention to my wisdom;
[1]Lend your ear to my understanding,
2 That you may [1]preserve discretion,
And your lips [a]may keep knowledge.
3 [a]For the lips of [1]an immoral woman drip honey,
And her mouth *is* [b]smoother than oil;
4 But in the end she is bitter as wormwood,
Sharp as a two-edged sword.
5 Her feet go down to death,
[a]Her steps lay hold of [1]hell.
6 Lest you ponder *her* path of life—
Her ways are unstable;
You do not know *them.*
7 Therefore hear me now, *my* children,

34 [a]James 4:6; 1 Pet. 5:5

CHAPTER 4

1 [a]Ps. 34:11; Prov. 1:8
3 [a]1 Chr. 29:1
4 [a]1 Chr. 28:9; Eph. 6:4 [b]Prov. 7:2
5 [a]Prov. 2:2, 3
6 [a]2 Thess. 2:10
7 [a]Prov. 3:13, 14; Matt. 13:44
8 [a]1 Sam. 2:30
9 [a]Prov. 3:22
10 [a]Prov. 3:2
11 [a]1 Sam. 12:23
12 [a]Job 18:7; Ps. 18:36 [b][Ps. 91:11]; Prov. 3:23
14 [a]Ps. 1:1; Prov. 1:15
16 [a]Ps. 36:4; Mic. 2:1 [1]Lit. *robbed*
18 [a]Is. 26:7; Matt. 5:14, 45; Phil. 2:15 [b]2 Sam. 23:4 [1]Lit. *light*
19 [a]1 Sam. 2:9; [Job 18:5, 6]; Prov. 2:13; [Is. 59:9, 10; Jer. 23:12]; John 12:35
23 [a][Matt. 12:34; 15:18, 19; Mark 7:21; Luke 6:45]
24 [1]*devious*
26 [a]Prov. 5:21; Heb. 12:13

CHAPTER 5

1 [1]Lit. *Bow*
2 [a]Mal. 2:7 [1]*appreciate good judgment*
3 [a]Prov. 2:16 [b]Ps. 55:21 [1]Lit. *a strange*
5 [a]Prov. 7:27 [1]Or *Sheol*

And do not depart from the words
of my mouth.
8 Remove your way far from her,
And do not go near the door of
her house,
9 Lest you give your [1]honor to
others,
And your years to the cruel *one;*
10 Lest aliens be filled with your
[1]wealth,
And your labors *go* to the house
of a foreigner;
11 And you mourn at last,
When your flesh and your body
are consumed,
12 And say:
"How I have hated instruction,
And my heart despised
correction!
13 I have not obeyed the voice of my
teachers,
Nor inclined my ear to those who
instructed me!
14 I was on the verge of total ruin,
In the midst of the assembly and
congregation."

15 Drink water from your own
cistern,
And running water from your
own well.
16 Should your fountains be
dispersed abroad,
[1]Streams of water in the streets?
17 Let them be only your own,
And not for strangers with you.
18 Let your fountain be blessed,
And rejoice with [a]the wife of your
youth.
19 [a]*As a* loving deer and a graceful
doe,
Let her breasts satisfy you at all
times;
And always be [1]enraptured with
her love.
20 For why should you, my son, be
enraptured by [a]an immoral
woman,
And be embraced in the arms of
a seductress?

21 [a]For the ways of man *are* before
the eyes of the LORD,
And He [1]ponders all his paths.
22 [a]His own iniquities entrap the
wicked *man,*
And he is caught in the cords of
his sin.
23 [a]He shall die for lack of
instruction,
And in the greatness of his folly
he shall go astray.

Dangerous Promises

6 My son, [a]if you become [1]surety
for your friend,

9 [1]*vigor*
10 [1]Lit. *strength*
16 [1]*Channels*
18 [a]Deut. 24:5; Eccl. 9:9; Mal. 2:14
19 [a]Song 2:9 [1]Lit. *intoxicated*
20 [a]Prov. 2:16
21 [a]2 Chr. 16:9; Job 31:4; 34:21; Prov. 15:3; Jer. 16:17; 32:19; Hos. 7:2; Heb. 4:13 [1]*observes,* lit. *weighs*
22 [a]Num. 32:23; Ps. 9:5; Prov. 1:31; Is. 3:11
23 [a]Job 4:21

CHAPTER 6

1 [a]Prov. 11:15 [1]*guaranty* or *collateral* [2]Lit. *struck*
4 [a]Ps. 132:4
5 [1]One who catches birds in a trap or snare
6 [a]Job 12:7
7 [1]Lit. *leader*
8 [1]Lit. *bread*
9 [a]Prov. 24:33, 34 [1]Lit. *lie down*
11 [a]Prov. 10:4
13 [a]Job 15:12; Ps. 35:19; Prov. 10:10 [1]*gives signals,* lit. *scrapes*
14 [a]Prov. 3:29; Mic. 2:1 [b]Prov. 6:19
15 [a]Prov. 24:22; Is. 30:13; 1 Thess. 5:3 [b]Jer. 19:11 [c]2 Chr. 36:16
16 [1]Lit. *His soul*
17 [a]Ps. 101:5; Prov. 21:4 [b]Ps. 120:2; Prov. 12:22 [c]Deut. 19:10; Prov. 28:17; Is. 1:15 [1]Lit. *Haughty eyes*
18 [a]Gen. 6:5; Ps. 36:4; Prov. 24:2; Jer. 18:18; Mark 14:1, 43–46

If you have [2]shaken hands in
pledge for a stranger,
2 You are snared by the words of
your mouth;
You are taken by the words of
your mouth.
3 So do this, my son, and deliver
yourself;
For you have come into the hand
of your friend:
Go and humble yourself;
Plead with your friend.
4 [a]Give no sleep to your eyes,
Nor slumber to your eyelids.
5 Deliver yourself like a gazelle
from the hand *of the hunter,*
And like a bird from the hand of
the [1]fowler.

The Folly of Indolence

6 [a]Go to the ant, you sluggard!
Consider her ways and be
wise,
7 Which, having no [1]captain,
Overseer or ruler,
8 Provides her [1]supplies in the
summer,
And gathers her food in the
harvest.
9 [a]How long will you [1]slumber,
O sluggard?
When will you rise from your
sleep?
10 A little sleep, a little slumber,
A little folding of the hands to
sleep—
11 [a]So shall your poverty come on
you like a prowler,
And your need like an armed
man.

The Wicked Man

12 A worthless person, a wicked
man,
Walks with a perverse mouth;
13 [a]He winks with his eyes,
He [1]shuffles his feet,
He points with his fingers;
14 Perversity *is* in his heart,
[a]He devises evil continually,
[b]He sows discord.
15 Therefore his calamity shall
come [a]suddenly;
Suddenly he shall [b]be broken
[c]without remedy.

16 These six *things* the LORD
hates,
Yes, seven *are* an abomination to
[1]Him:
17 [a]A[1] proud look,
[b]A lying tongue,
[c]Hands that shed innocent blood,
18 [a]A heart that devises wicked
plans,

[b]Feet that are swift in running to
evil,
19 [a]A false witness *who* speaks lies,
And one who [b]sows discord
among brethren.

Beware of Adultery

20 [a]My son, keep your father's
command,
And do not forsake the law of
your mother.
21 [a]Bind them continually upon your
heart;
Tie them around your neck.
22 [a]When you roam, [1]they will lead
you;
When you sleep, [b]they will keep
you;
And *when* you awake, they will
speak with you.
23 [a]For the commandment *is* a lamp,
And the law a light;
Reproofs of instruction *are* the
way of life,
24 [a]To keep you from the evil
woman,
From the flattering tongue of a
seductress.
25 [a]Do not lust after her beauty in
your heart,
Nor let her allure you with her
eyelids.
26 For [a]by means of a harlot
A man is reduced to a crust of
bread;
[b]And [1]an adulteress will [c]prey
upon his precious life.
27 Can a man take fire to his bosom,
And his clothes not be burned?
28 Can one walk on hot coals,
And his feet not be seared?
29 So *is* he who goes in to his
neighbor's wife;
Whoever touches her shall not be
innocent.

30 *People* do not despise a thief
If he steals to satisfy himself
when he is starving.
31 Yet *when* he is found, [a]he must
restore sevenfold;
He may have to give up all the
substance of his house.
32 Whoever commits adultery with
a woman [a]lacks understanding;
He *who* does so destroys his own
soul.
33 Wounds and dishonor he will
get,
And his reproach will not be
wiped away.
34 For [a]jealousy *is* a husband's fury;
Therefore he will not spare in the
day of vengeance.
35 He will [1]accept no recompense,

18 [b]2 Kin. 5:20–27; Is. 59:7; Rom. 3:15
19 [a]Ps. 27:12; Prov. 19:5, 9; Matt. 26:59–66 [b]Prov. 6:14; 1 Cor. 1:11–13; [Jude 3, 4, 16–19]
20 [a]Eph. 6:1
21 [a]Prov. 3:3
22 [a][Prov. 3:23] [b]Prov. 2:11 [1]Lit. *it*
23 [a]Ps. 19:8; 2 Pet. 1:19
24 [a]Prov. 2:16
25 [a]Matt. 5:28
26 [a]Prov. 29:3 [b]Gen. 39:14 [c]Ezek. 13:18 [1]Wife of another, lit. *a man's wife*
31 [a]Ex. 22:1–4
32 [a]Prov. 7:7
34 [a]Prov. 27:4; Song 8:6
35 [1]Lit. *lift up the face of any*

CHAPTER 7

1 [a]Prov. 2:1
2 [a]Lev. 18:5; Prov. 4:4; [Is. 55:3] [b]Deut. 32:10; Ps. 17:8; Zech. 2:8
3 [a]Deut. 6:8; Prov. 6:21
5 [a]Prov. 2:16; 5:3
7 [a][Prov. 6:32; 9:4, 16] [1]Lit. *sons* [2]*lacking*
9 [a]Job 24:15
11 [a]Prov. 9:13; 1 Tim. 5:13 [b]Titus 2:5
13 [1]*shameless*
16 [a]Is. 19:9; Ezek. 27:7
19 [1]Lit. *the man*

Nor will he be appeased though
you give many gifts.

7 My son, keep my words,
And [a]treasure my commands
within you.
2 [a]Keep my commands and live,
[b]And my law as the apple of your
eye.
3 [a]Bind them on your fingers;
Write them on the tablet of your
heart.
4 Say to wisdom, "You *are* my
sister,"
And call understanding *your*
nearest kin,
5 [a]That they may keep you from the
immoral woman,
From the seductress *who* flatters
with her words.

The Crafty Harlot

6 For at the window of my house
I looked through my lattice,
7 And saw among the simple,
I perceived among the [1]youths,
A young man [a]devoid[2] of
understanding,
8 Passing along the street near her
corner;
And he took the path to her
house
9 [a]In the twilight, in the evening,
In the black and dark night.
10 And there a woman met him,
With the attire of a harlot, and a
crafty heart.
11 [a]She *was* loud and rebellious,
[b]Her feet would not stay at home.
12 At times *she was* outside, at times
in the open square,
Lurking at every corner.
13 So she caught him and kissed
him;
With an [1]impudent face she said
to him:
14 "*I have* peace offerings with me;
Today I have paid my vows.
15 So I came out to meet you,
Diligently to seek your face,
And I have found you.
16 I have spread my bed with
tapestry,
Colored coverings of [a]Egyptian
linen.
17 I have perfumed my bed
With myrrh, aloes, and
cinnamon.
18 Come, let us take our fill of love
until morning;
Let us delight ourselves with
love.
19 For [1]my husband *is* not at home;
He has gone on a long journey;

20 He has taken a bag of money
[1]with him,
And will come home [2]on the
appointed day."

21 [1]With [a]her enticing speech she
caused him to yield,
[b]With her flattering lips she
[2]seduced him.
22 Immediately he went after her, as
an ox goes to the slaughter,
Or [1]as a fool to the correction of
the [2]stocks,
23 Till an arrow struck his liver.
[a]As a bird hastens to the snare,
He did not know it [1]*would cost*
his life.

24 Now therefore, listen to me, *my*
children;
Pay attention to the words of my
mouth:
25 Do not let your heart turn aside
to her ways,
Do not stray into her paths;
26 For she has cast down many
wounded,
And [a]all who were slain by her
were strong *men*.
27 [a]Her house *is* the way to [1]hell,
Descending to the chambers of
death.

The Excellence of Wisdom

8 Does not [a]wisdom cry out,
And understanding lift up her
voice?
2 She takes her stand on the top of
the [1]high hill,
Beside the way, where the paths
meet.
3 She cries out by the gates, at the
entry of the city,
At the entrance of the doors:
4 "To you, O men, I call,
And my voice *is* to the sons of
men.
5 O you [1]simple ones, understand
prudence,
And you fools, be of an
understanding heart.
6 Listen, for I will speak of
[a]excellent things,
And from the opening of my lips
will come right things;
7 For my mouth will speak truth;
Wickedness *is* an abomination to
my lips.
8 All the words of my mouth *are*
with righteousness;
Nothing crooked or perverse *is* in
them.
9 They *are* all plain to him who
understands,

20 [1]Lit. *in his hand* [2]*at the full moon*
21 [a]Prov. 5:3 [b]Ps. 12:2 [1]*By the greatness of her words* [2]*compelled*
22 [1]LXX, Syr., Tg. *as a dog to bonds;* Vg. *as a lamb . . . to bonds* [2]*shackles*
23 [a]Eccl. 9:12 [1]Lit. *is for*
26 [a]Neh. 13:26
27 [a]Prov. 2:18; 5:5; 9:18; [1 Cor. 6:9, 10; Rev. 22:15] [1]Or *Sheol*

CHAPTER 8

1 [a]Prov. 1:20, 21; 9:3; [1 Cor. 1:24]
2 [1]Lit. *heights*
5 [1]*naive*
6 [a]Prov. 22:20
11 [a]Job 28:15; Ps. 19:10; 119:127; Prov. 3:14, 15; 4:5, 7; 16:16
13 [a]Prov. 3:7; 16:6 [b]1 Sam. 2:3; [Prov. 16:17, 18; Is. 13:11] [c]Prov. 4:24
14 [a]Eccl. 7:19; 9:16
15 [a]2 Chr. 1:10; Prov. 29:4; Dan. 2:21; [Matt. 28:18]; Rom. 13:1
16 [1]MT, Syr., Tg., Vg. *righteousness;* LXX, Bg., some mss. and editions *earth*
17 [a]1 Sam. 2:30; [Ps. 91:14]; Prov. 4:6; [John 14:21] [b]Prov. 2:4, 5; John 7:37; James 1:5
18 [a]Prov. 3:16; [Matt. 6:33]
20 [1]*walk about on*
22 [a]Job 28:26–28; Ps. 104:24; Prov. 3:19; [John 1:1]
23 [a][Ps. 2:6]
25 [a]Job 15:7, 8
26 [1]*outer places* [2]Lit. *beginning of the dust*

And right to those who find
knowledge.
10 Receive my instruction, and not
silver,
And knowledge rather than
choice gold;
11 [a]For wisdom *is* better than rubies,
And all the things one may
desire cannot be compared
with her.

12 "I, wisdom, dwell with prudence,
And find out knowledge *and*
discretion.
13 [a]The fear of the LORD *is* to hate
evil;
[b]Pride and arrogance and the evil
way
And [c]the perverse mouth I hate.
14 Counsel *is* mine, and sound
wisdom;
I *am* understanding, [a]I have
strength.
15 [a]By me kings reign,
And rulers decree justice.
16 By me princes rule, and nobles,
All the judges of [1]the earth.
17 [a]I love those who love me,
And [b]those who seek me
diligently will find me.
18 [a]Riches and honor *are* with me,
Enduring riches and
righteousness.
19 My fruit *is* better than gold, yes,
than fine gold,
And my revenue than choice
silver.
20 I [1]traverse the way of
righteousness,
In the midst of the paths of
justice,
21 That I may cause those who love
me to inherit wealth,
That I may fill their treasuries.

22 "The[a] LORD possessed me at the
beginning of His way,
Before His works of old.
23 [a]I have been established from
everlasting,
From the beginning, before there
was ever an earth.
24 When *there were* no depths I was
brought forth,
When *there were* no fountains
abounding with water.
25 [a]Before the mountains were
settled,
Before the hills, I was brought
forth;
26 While as yet He had not made the
earth or the [1]fields,
Or the [2]primal dust of the world.
27 When He prepared the heavens,
I *was* there,

When He drew a circle on the
face of the deep,
28 When He established the clouds
above,
When He strengthened the
fountains of the deep,
29 [a]When He assigned to the sea its
limit,
So that the waters would not
transgress His command,
When [b]He marked out the
foundations of the earth,
30 [a]Then I was beside Him *as* [1]a
master craftsman;
[b]And I was daily *His* delight,
Rejoicing always before Him,
31 Rejoicing in His inhabited world,
And [a]my delight *was* with the
sons of men.

32 "Now therefore, listen to me, *my*
children,
For [a]blessed *are those who* keep
my ways.
33 Hear instruction and be wise,
And do not disdain *it*.
34 [a]Blessed is the man who listens
to me,
Watching daily at my gates,
Waiting at the posts of my doors.
35 For whoever finds me finds life,
And [a]obtains favor from the
LORD;
36 But he who sins against me
[a]wrongs his own soul;
All those who hate me love
death."

The Way of Wisdom

9 Wisdom has [a]built her house,
She has hewn out her seven
pillars;
2 [a]She has slaughtered her meat,
[b]She has mixed her wine,
She has also [1]furnished her table.
3 She has sent out her maidens,
She cries out from the highest
places of the city,
4 "Whoever[a] *is* simple, let him turn
in here!"
As for him who lacks
understanding, she says to him,
5 "Come,[a] eat of my bread
And drink of the wine I have
mixed.
6 Forsake foolishness and live,
And go in the way of
understanding.

7 "He who corrects a scoffer gets
shame for himself,
And he who rebukes a wicked
man only harms himself.
8 [a]Do not correct a scoffer, lest he
hate you;
[b]Rebuke a wise *man*, and he will
love you.
9 Give *instruction* to a wise *man*,
and he will be still wiser;
Teach a just *man*, [a]and he will
increase in learning.

10 "The[a] fear of the LORD *is* the
beginning of wisdom,
And the knowledge of the Holy
One *is* understanding.
11 [a]For by me your days will be
multiplied,
And years of life will be added
to you.
12 [a]If you are wise, you are wise for
yourself,
And *if* you scoff, you will bear *it*
alone."

The Way of Folly

13 [a]A foolish woman is [1]clamorous;
She is simple, and knows
nothing.
14 For she sits at the door of her
house,
On a seat [a]*by* the highest places
of the city,
15 To call to those who pass by,
Who go straight on their way:
16 "Whoever[a] *is* [1]simple, let him turn
in here";
And *as for* him who lacks
understanding, she says to him,
17 "Stolen[a] water is sweet,
And bread *eaten* in secret is
pleasant."
18 But he does not know that [a]the
dead *are* there,
That her guests *are* in the depths
of [1]hell.

Wise Sayings of Solomon

10 The proverbs of [a]Solomon:

[b]A wise son makes a glad father,
But a foolish son *is* the grief of
his mother.

2 [a]Treasures of wickedness profit
nothing,
[b]But righteousness delivers from
death.
3 [a]The LORD will not allow the
righteous soul to famish,
But He casts away the desire of
the wicked.

4 [a]He who has a slack hand
becomes poor,
But [b]the hand of the diligent
makes rich.
5 He who gathers in [a]summer *is* a
wise son;

29 [a]Gen. 1:9, 10 [b]Job 28:4, 6
30 [a][John 1:1–3, 18] [b][Matt. 3:17] [1]A Jewish tradition *one brought up*
31 [a]Ps. 16:3
32 [a]Luke 11:28
34 [a]Prov. 3:13, 18
35 [a][John 17:3]
36 [a]Prov. 20:2

CHAPTER 9
1 [a][Matt. 16:18]
2 [a]Matt. 22:4 [b]Prov. 23:30 [1]*arranged*
4 [a]Ps. 19:7
5 [a]Is. 55:1
8 [a]Matt. 7:6 [b]Ps. 141:5
9 [a][Matt. 13:12]
10 [a]Job 28:28
11 [a]Prov. 3:2, 16
12 [a]Job 35:6, 7
13 [a]Prov. 7:11 [1]*boisterous*
14 [a]Prov. 9:3
16 [a]Prov. 7:7, 8 [1]*naive*
17 [a]Prov. 20:17
18 [a]Prov. 2:18; 7:27 [1]Or *Sheol*

CHAPTER 10
1 [a]Prov. 1:1; 25:1 [b]Prov. 15:20; 17:21, 25; 19:13; 29:3, 15
2 [a][Luke 12:19, 20] [b]Dan. 4:27
3 [a]Ps. 34:9, 10; 37:25
4 [a]Prov. 19:15 [b]Prov. 12:24; 13:4; 21:5
5 [a]Prov. 6:8

He who sleeps in harvest *is* [b]a son
who causes shame.

6 Blessings *are* on the head of the
righteous,
But violence covers the mouth of
the wicked.
7 [a]The memory of the righteous *is*
blessed,
But the name of the wicked will
rot.

8 The wise in heart will receive
commands,
[a]But [1]a prating fool will [2]fall.

9 [a]He who walks with integrity
walks securely,
But he who perverts his ways will
become known.

10 He who winks with the eye
causes trouble,
But a prating fool will fall.

11 The mouth of the righteous *is* a
well of life,
But violence covers the mouth of
the wicked.

12 Hatred stirs up strife,
But [a]love covers all sins.

13 Wisdom is found on the lips of
him who has understanding,
But [a]a rod *is* for the back of him
who [1]is devoid of
understanding.

14 Wise *people* store up knowledge,
But [a]the mouth of the foolish *is*
near destruction.

15 The [a]rich man's wealth *is* his
strong city;
The destruction of the poor *is*
their poverty.

16 The labor of the righteous *leads*
to [a]life,
The wages of the wicked to sin.

17 He who keeps instruction *is in* the
way of life,
But he who refuses correction
[1]goes astray.

18 Whoever [a]hides hatred *has* lying
lips,
And [b]whoever spreads slander *is*
a fool.

19 [a]In the multitude of words sin is
not lacking,
But [b]he who restrains his lips *is*
wise.

20 The tongue of the righteous *is*
choice silver;
The heart of the wicked *is worth*
little.
21 The lips of the righteous feed
many,
But fools die for lack of [1]wisdom.

22 [a]The blessing of the LORD makes
one rich,
And He adds no sorrow with it.

23 [a]To do evil *is* like sport to a fool,
But a man of understanding has
wisdom.
24 [a]The fear of the wicked will come
upon him,
And [b]the desire of the righteous
will be granted.
25 When the whirlwind passes by,
[a]the wicked *is* no *more*,
But [b]the righteous *has* an
everlasting foundation.

26 As vinegar to the teeth and
smoke to the eyes,
So *is* the lazy *man* to those who
send him.

27 [a]The fear of the LORD prolongs
days,
But [b]the years of the wicked will
be shortened.
28 The hope of the righteous *will be*
gladness,
But the [a]expectation of the
wicked will perish.
29 The way of the LORD *is* strength
for the upright,
But [a]destruction *will come* to the
workers of iniquity.

30 [a]The righteous will never be
removed,
But the wicked will not inhabit
the [1]earth.
31 [a]The mouth of the righteous
brings forth wisdom,
But the perverse tongue will be
cut out.
32 The lips of the righteous know
what is acceptable,
But the mouth of the wicked *what
is* perverse.

11 [a]Dishonest[1] scales *are* an
abomination to the LORD,
But a [2]just weight *is* His delight.

2 When pride comes, then comes
[a]shame;
But with the humble *is* wisdom.

3 The integrity of the upright will
guide [a]them,

5 [b]Prov. 19:26
7 [a]Ps. 112:6; Eccl. 8:10
8 [a]Prov. 10:10 [1]Lit. *the foolish of lips* [2]*be thrust down* or *ruined*
9 [a][Ps. 23:4; Prov. 3:23; 28:18; Is. 33:15, 16]
12 [a]Prov. 17:9; [1 Cor. 13:4–7; James 5:20]; 1 Pet. 4:8
13 [a]Prov. 26:3 [1]Lit. *lacks heart*
14 [a]Prov. 18:7
15 [a]Job 31:24; Ps. 52:7; Prov. 18:11; [1 Tim. 6:17]
16 [a]Prov. 6:23
17 [1]*leads*
18 [a]Prov. 26:24 [b]Ps. 15:3; 101:5
19 [a]Job 11:2; [Prov. 18:21]; Eccl. 5:3 [b]Prov. 17:27; [James 1:19; 3:2]
21 [1]Lit. *heart*
22 [a]Gen. 24:35; 26:12; Deut. 8:18; Ps. 37:22; Prov. 8:21
23 [a]Prov. 2:14; 15:21
24 [a]Job 15:21; Prov. 1:27; Is. 66:4 [b]Ps. 145:19; Prov. 15:8; Matt. 5:6; [1 John 5:14, 15]
25 [a]Ps. 37:9, 10 [b]Ps. 15:5; Prov. 12:3; Matt. 7:24, 25
27 [a]Prov. 9:11 [b]Job 15:32
28 [a]Job 8:13
29 [a]Ps. 1:6
30 [a]Ps. 37:22; Prov. 2:21 [1]*land*
31 [a]Ps. 37:30; Prov. 10:13

CHAPTER 11

1 [a]Lev. 19:35, 36; Deut. 25:13–16; Prov. 20:10, 23; Mic. 6:11 [1]*deceptive* [2]Lit. *perfect stone*
2 [a]Prov. 16:18; 18:12; 29:23
3 [a]Prov. 13:6

But the perversity of the
unfaithful will destroy them.
4 [a]Riches do not profit in the day of
wrath,
But [b]righteousness delivers from
death.
5 The righteousness of the
blameless will [1]direct his way
aright,
But the wicked will fall by his
own [a]wickedness.
6 The righteousness of the upright
will deliver them,
But the unfaithful will be caught
by *their* lust.

7 When a wicked man dies, *his*
expectation will [a]perish,
And the hope of the unjust
perishes.
8 [a]The righteous is delivered from
trouble,
And it comes to the wicked
instead.
9 The hypocrite with *his* mouth
destroys his neighbor,
But through knowledge the
righteous will be delivered.
10 [a]When it goes well with the
righteous, the city rejoices;
And when the wicked perish,
there is jubilation.
11 By the blessing of the upright the
city is [a]exalted,
But it is overthrown by the mouth
of the wicked.

12 He who [1]is devoid of wisdom
despises his neighbor,
But a man of understanding holds
his peace.

13 [a]A talebearer reveals secrets,
But he who is of a faithful spirit
[b]conceals a matter.

14 [a]Where *there is* no counsel, the
people fall;
But in the multitude of counselors
there is safety.

15 He who is [a]surety[1] for a stranger
will suffer,
But one who hates [2]being surety
is secure.

16 A gracious woman retains honor,
But ruthless *men* retain riches.
17 [a]The merciful man does good for
his own soul,
But *he who is* cruel troubles his
own flesh.
18 The wicked *man* does deceptive
work,
But [a]he who sows righteousness
will have a sure reward.
19 As righteousness *leads* to [a]life,
So he who pursues evil *pursues*
it to his own [b]death.
20 Those who are of a perverse heart
are an abomination to the
LORD,
But *the* blameless in their ways
are His delight.
21 [a]*Though they join* [1]forces, the
wicked will not go unpunished;
But [b]the posterity of the righteous
will be delivered.

22 *As* a ring of gold in a swine's
snout,
So is a lovely woman who lacks
[1]discretion.

23 The desire of the righteous *is* only
good,
But the expectation of the wicked
[a]*is* wrath.

24 There is *one* who [a]scatters, yet
increases more;
And there is *one* who withholds
more than is right,
But it *leads* to poverty.
25 [a]The generous soul will be made
rich,
[b]And he who waters will also be
watered himself.
26 The people will curse [a]him who
withholds grain,
But [b]blessing *will be* on the head
of him who sells *it*.

27 He who earnestly seeks good
[1]finds favor,
[a]But trouble will come to him who
seeks *evil*.
28 [a]He who trusts in his riches will
fall,
But [b]the righteous will flourish
like foliage.

29 He who troubles his own house
[a]will inherit the wind,
And the fool *will be* [b]servant to
the wise of heart.

30 The fruit of the righteous *is a* tree
of life,
And [a]he who [1]wins souls *is* wise.

31 [a]If the righteous will be
[1]recompensed on the earth,
How much more the ungodly and
the sinner.

12 Whoever loves instruction
loves knowledge,
But he who hates correction *is*
stupid.

4 [a]Prov. 10:2; Ezek. 7:19; Zeph. 1:18 [b]Gen. 7:1
5 [a]Prov. 5:22 [1]Or *make smooth* or *straight*
7 [a]Prov. 10:28
8 [a]Prov. 21:18
10 [a]Prov. 28:12
11 [a]Prov. 14:34
12 [1]Lit. *lacks heart*
13 [a]Lev. 19:16; Prov. 20:19; 1 Tim. 5:13 [b]Prov. 19:11
14 [a]1 Kin. 12:1
15 [a]Prov. 6:1, 2 [1]*guaranty* [2]*those pledging guaranty*, lit. *those who strike hands*
17 [a][Matt. 5:7; 25:34–36]
18 [a]Hos. 10:12; [Gal. 6:8, 9]; James 3:18
19 [a]Prov. 10:16; 12:28 [b]Prov. 21:16; [Rom. 6:23; James 1:15]
21 [a]Prov. 16:5 [b]Ps. 112:2; Prov. 14:26 [1]Lit. *hand to hand*
22 [1]*taste*
23 [a]Prov. 10:28; Rom. 2:8, 9
24 [a]Ps. 112:9; Prov. 13:7; 19:17
25 [a]Prov. 3:9, 10; [2 Cor. 9:6, 7] [b][Matt. 5:7]
26 [a]Amos 8:5, 6 [b]Job 29:13
27 [a]Esth. 7:10; Ps. 7:15, 16; 57:6 [1]Lit. *seeks*
28 [a]Job 31:24 [b]Ps. 1:3; Jer. 17:8
29 [a]Eccl. 5:16 [b]Prov. 14:19
30 [a]Prov. 14:25; [Dan. 12:3; 1 Cor. 9:19–22; James 5:20] [1]Lit. *takes*, in the sense of *brings*, cf. 1 Sam. 16:11
31 [a]Jer. 25:29 [1]*rewarded*

2 A good *man* obtains favor from
the LORD,
But a man of wicked intentions
He will condemn.

3 A man is not established by
wickedness,
But the [a]root of the righteous
cannot be moved.

4 [a]An[1] excellent wife *is* the crown
of her husband,
But she who causes shame *is* [b]like
rottenness in his bones.

5 The thoughts of the righteous *are*
right,
But the counsels of the wicked
are deceitful.
6 [a]The words of the wicked *are*, "Lie
in wait for blood,"
[b]But the mouth of the upright will
deliver them.

7 [a]The wicked are overthrown and
are no more,
But the house of the righteous
will stand.

8 A man will be commended
according to his wisdom,
[a]But he who is of a perverse heart
will be despised.

9 [a]Better *is the one* who is [1]slighted
but has a servant,
Than he who honors himself but
lacks bread.

10 [a]A righteous *man* regards the life
of his animal,
But the tender mercies of the
wicked *are* cruel.

11 [a]He who [1]tills his land will be
satisfied with [b]bread,
But he who follows [2]frivolity [c]*is*
devoid of [3]understanding.

12 The wicked covet the catch of evil
men,
But the root of the righteous
yields *fruit*.
13 [a]The wicked is ensnared by the
transgression of *his* lips,
[b]But the righteous will come
through trouble.
14 [a]A man will be satisfied with good
by the fruit of *his* mouth,
[b]And the recompense of a man's
hands will be rendered to him.

15 [a]The way of a fool *is* right in his
own eyes,
But he who heeds counsel *is* wise.

CHAPTER 12

3 [a][Prov. 10:25]
4 [a]Prov. 31:23; 1 Cor. 11:7 [b]Prov. 14:30; Hab. 3:16 [1]Lit. *A wife of valor*
6 [a]Prov. 1:11, 18 [b]Prov. 14:3
7 [a]Ps. 37:35–37; Prov. 11:21; Matt. 7:24–27
8 [a]1 Sam. 25:17; Prov. 18:3
9 [a]Prov. 13:7 [1]*lightly esteemed*
10 [a]Deut. 25:4
11 [a]Gen. 3:19 [b]Prov. 28:19 [c]Prov. 6:32 [1]*works* or *cultivates* [2]Lit. *vain things* [3]Lit. *heart*
13 [a]Prov. 18:7 [b][2 Pet. 2:9]
14 [a]Prov. 13:2; 15:23; 18:20 [b]Job 34:11; Prov. 1:31; 24:12; [Is. 3:10, 11]; Hos. 4:9
15 [a]Prov. 3:7; Luke 18:11
16 [a]Prov. 11:13; 29:11
17 [a]Prov. 14:5
18 [a]Ps. 57:4; Prov. 4:22; 15:4
19 [a][Ps. 52:4, 5]; Prov. 19:9
21 [a]Ps. 91:10; Prov. 1:33; 1 Pet. 3:13 [1]*harm*
22 [a]Prov. 6:17; 11:20; Rev. 22:15
23 [a]Prov. 13:16
24 [a]Prov. 10:4
25 [a]Prov. 15:13 [b]Is. 50:4

CHAPTER 13

1 [a]Is. 28:14, 15
2 [a]Prov. 12:14
3 [a]Ps. 39:1; Prov. 21:23; [James 3:2]

16 [a]A fool's wrath is known at once,
But a prudent *man* covers shame.

17 [a]He *who* speaks truth declares
righteousness,
But a false witness, deceit.
18 [a]There is one who speaks like the
piercings of a sword,
But the tongue of the wise
promotes health.
19 The truthful lip shall be
established forever,
[a]But a lying tongue *is* but for a
moment.
20 Deceit is in the heart of those who
devise evil,
But counselors of peace have joy.
21 [a]No grave [1]trouble will overtake
the righteous,
But the wicked shall be filled with
evil.
22 [a]Lying lips *are* an abomination to
the LORD,
But those who deal truthfully *are*
His delight.

23 [a]A prudent man conceals
knowledge,
But the heart of fools proclaims
foolishness.

24 [a]The hand of the diligent will rule,
But the lazy *man* will be put to
forced labor.

25 [a]Anxiety in the heart of man
causes depression,
But [b]a good word makes it glad.

26 The righteous should choose his
friends carefully,
For the way of the wicked leads
them astray.

27 The lazy *man* does not roast what
he took in hunting,
But diligence *is* man's precious
possession.

28 In the way of righteousness *is* life,
And in *its* pathway *there is* no
death.

13 A wise son *heeds* his father's
instruction,
[a]But a scoffer does not listen to
rebuke.

2 [a]A man shall eat well by the fruit
of *his* mouth,
But the soul of the unfaithful
feeds on violence.
3 [a]He who guards his mouth
preserves his life,

But he who opens wide his lips
shall have destruction.

4 [a]The soul of a lazy *man* desires,
and *has* nothing;
But the soul of the diligent shall
be made rich.

5 A righteous *man* hates lying,
But a wicked *man* is loathsome
and comes to shame.
6 [a]Righteousness guards *him whose*
way is blameless,
But wickedness overthrows the
sinner.

7 [a]There is one who makes himself
rich, yet *has* nothing;
And one who makes himself
poor, yet *has* great riches.

8 The ransom of a man's life *is* his
riches,
But the poor does not hear
rebuke.

9 The light of the righteous
rejoices,
[a]But the lamp of the wicked will
be put out.

10 By pride comes nothing but
[a]strife,
But with the well-advised *is*
wisdom.

11 [a]Wealth *gained by* dishonesty will
be diminished,
But he who gathers by labor will
increase.

12 Hope deferred makes the heart
sick,
But [a]*when* the desire comes, *it is*
a tree of life.

13 He who [a]despises the word will
be destroyed,
But he who fears the
commandment will be
rewarded.
14 [a]The law of the wise *is* a fountain
of life,
To turn *one* away from [b]the
snares of death.

15 Good understanding [1]gains
[a]favor,
But the way of the unfaithful *is*
hard.
16 [a]Every prudent *man* acts with
knowledge,
But a fool lays open *his* folly.

4 [a]Prov. 10:4
6 [a]Prov. 11:3, 5, 6
7 [a][Prov. 11:24; 12:9; Luke 12:20, 21]
9 [a]Job 18:5, 6; 21:17; Prov. 24:20
10 [a]Prov. 10:12
11 [a]Prov. 10:2; 20:21
12 [a]Prov. 13:19
13 [a]Num. 15:31; 2 Chr. 36:16; Is. 5:24
14 [a]Prov. 6:22; 10:11; 14:27 [b]2 Sam. 22:6
15 [a]Ps. 111:10; Prov. 3:4 [1]*gives*
16 [a]Prov. 12:23
17 [a]Prov. 25:13
18 [a]Prov. 15:5, 31, 32 [1]Lit. *ignores*
21 [a]Ps. 32:10; Is. 47:11
22 [a]Job 27:16, 17; Prov. 28:8; [Eccl. 2:26]
23 [a]Prov. 12:11 [1]*uncultivated* [2]Lit. *what is swept away*
24 [a]Prov. 19:18 [1]*early*
25 [a]Ps. 34:10; Prov. 10:3
CHAPTER 14
2 [a][Rom. 2:4]
3 [a]Prov. 12:6
4 [1]*manger* or *feed trough*

17 A wicked messenger falls into
trouble,
But [a]a faithful ambassador *brings*
health.

18 Poverty and shame *will come* to
him who [1]disdains correction,
But [a]he who regards a rebuke will
be honored.

19 A desire accomplished is sweet to
the soul,
But *it is* an abomination to fools
to depart from evil.

20 He who walks with wise *men* will
be wise,
But the companion of fools will
be destroyed.

21 [a]Evil pursues sinners,
But to the righteous, good shall
be repaid.

22 A good *man* leaves an
inheritance to his children's
children,
But [a]the wealth of the sinner is
stored up for the righteous.

23 [a]Much food *is in* the [1]fallow
ground of the poor,
And for lack of justice there is
[2]waste.

24 [a]He who spares his rod hates his
son,
But he who loves him disciplines
him [1]promptly.

25 [a]The righteous eats to the
satisfying of his soul,
But the stomach of the wicked
shall be in want.

14

The wise woman builds her
house,
But the foolish pulls it down with
her hands.

2 He who walks in his uprightness
fears the LORD,
[a]But *he who is* perverse in his
ways despises Him.

3 In the mouth of a fool *is* a rod of
pride,
[a]But the lips of the wise will
preserve them.

4 Where no oxen *are*, the [1]trough
is clean;
But much increase *comes* by the
strength of an ox.

5 A [a]faithful witness does not lie,
But a false witness will utter [b]lies.

6 A scoffer seeks wisdom and does not *find it*,
But [a]knowledge *is* easy to him who understands.
7 Go from the presence of a foolish man,
When you do not perceive *in him* the lips of [a]knowledge.
8 The wisdom of the prudent *is* to understand his way,
But the folly of fools *is* deceit.

9 [a]Fools mock at [1]sin,
But among the upright *there is* favor.

10 The heart knows its own bitterness,
And a stranger does not share its joy.

11 [a]The house of the wicked will be overthrown,
But the tent of the upright will flourish.

12 [a]There is a way *that seems* right to a man,
But [b]its end *is* the way of [c]death.

13 Even in laughter the heart may sorrow,
And [a]the end of mirth *may be* grief.

14 The backslider in heart will be [a]filled with his own ways,
But a good man *will be satisfied* [1]from [b]above.

15 The simple believes every word,
But the prudent considers well his steps.
16 [a]A wise *man* fears and departs from evil,
But a fool rages and is self-confident.
17 A quick-tempered *man* acts foolishly,
And a man of wicked intentions is hated.
18 The simple inherit folly,
But the prudent are crowned with knowledge.
19 The evil will bow before the good,
And the wicked at the gates of the righteous.

20 [a]The poor *man* is hated even by his own neighbor,
But [1]the rich *has* many [b]friends.

5 [a]Rev. 1:5; 3:14 [b]Ex. 23:1; Deut. 19:16; Prov. 6:19; 12:17
6 [a]Prov. 8:9; 17:24
7 [a]Prov. 23:9
9 [a]Prov. 10:23 [1]Lit. *guilt*
11 [a]Job 8:15
12 [a]Prov. 16:25 [b]Rom. 6:21 [c]Prov. 12:15
13 [a]Prov. 5:4; Eccl. 2:1, 2
14 [a]Prov. 1:31; 12:15 [b]Prov. 13:2; 18:20 [1]Lit. *from above himself*
16 [a]Job 28:28; Ps. 34:14; Prov. 22:3
20 [a]Prov. 19:7 [b]Prov. 19:4 [1]Lit. *many are the lovers of the rich*
21 [a]Ps. 112:9; [Prov. 19:17]
23 [1]Lit. *talk of the lips*
25 [a][Ezek. 3:18–21] [1]*saves lives*
27 [a]Prov. 13:14
29 [a]Prov. 16:32; 19:11; Eccl. 7:9; James 1:19 [1]Lit. *short of spirit*
30 [a]Ps. 112:10 [b]Prov. 12:4; Hab. 3:16
31 [a]Prov. 17:5; Matt. 25:40; 1 John 3:17 [b][Job 31:15; Prov. 22:2]
32 [a]Gen. 49:18; Job 13:15; [Ps. 16:11; 73:24]; 2 Cor. 1:9; 5:8; [2 Tim. 4:18]
33 [a]Prov. 12:16
34 [a]Prov. 11:11 [1]*shame or disgrace*

21 He who despises his neighbor sins;
[a]But he who has mercy on the poor, happy *is* he.

22 Do they not go astray who devise evil?
But mercy and truth *belong* to those who devise good.

23 In all labor there is profit,
But [1]idle chatter *leads* only to poverty.

24 The crown of the wise is their riches,
But the foolishness of fools *is* folly.

25 A true witness [1]delivers [a]souls,
But a deceitful *witness* speaks lies.

26 In the fear of the LORD *there is* strong confidence,
And His children will have a place of refuge.
27 [a]The fear of the LORD *is* a fountain of life,
To turn *one* away from the snares of death.

28 In a multitude of people *is* a king's honor,
But in the lack of people *is* the downfall of a prince.

29 [a]*He who is* slow to wrath has great understanding,
But *he who is* [1]impulsive exalts folly.

30 A sound heart *is* life to the body,
But [a]envy *is* [b]rottenness to the bones.

31 [a]He who oppresses the poor reproaches [b]his Maker,
But he who honors Him has mercy on the needy.

32 The wicked is banished in his wickedness,
But [a]the righteous has a refuge in his death.

33 Wisdom rests in the heart of him who has understanding,
But [a]*what is* in the heart of fools is made known.

34 Righteousness exalts a [a]nation,
But sin *is* a [1]reproach to *any* people.

35 [a]The king's favor *is* toward a wise
servant,
But his wrath *is against* him who
causes shame.

15

A [a]soft answer turns away
wrath,
But [b]a harsh word stirs up anger.
2 The tongue of the wise uses
knowledge rightly,
[a]But the mouth of fools pours forth
foolishness.

3 [a]The eyes of the LORD *are* in every
place,
Keeping watch on the evil and the
good.

4 A [1]wholesome tongue *is* a tree of
life,
But perverseness in it breaks the
spirit.

5 [a]A fool despises his father's
instruction,
[b]But he who [1]receives correction
is prudent.

6 *In* the house of the righteous
there is much treasure,
But in the revenue of the wicked
is trouble.

7 The lips of the wise [1]disperse
knowledge,
But the heart of the fool *does* not
do so.

8 [a]The sacrifice of the wicked *is* an
abomination to the LORD,
But the prayer of the upright *is*
His delight.
9 The way of the wicked *is* an
abomination to the LORD,
But He loves him who [a]follows
righteousness.

10 [a]Harsh discipline *is* for him who
forsakes the way,
And [b]he who hates correction will
die.

11 [a]Hell[1] and [2]Destruction *are* before
the LORD;
So how much more [b]the hearts
of the sons of men.

12 [a]A scoffer does not love one who
corrects him,
Nor will he go to the wise.

13 [a]A merry heart makes a cheerful
[1]countenance,
But [b]by sorrow of the heart the
spirit is broken.

14 The heart of him who has
understanding seeks
knowledge,
But the mouth of fools feeds on
foolishness.

15 All the days of the afflicted *are*
evil,
[a]But he who is of a merry heart
has a continual feast.

16 [a]Better *is* a little with the fear of
the LORD,
Than great treasure with trouble.
17 [a]Better *is* a dinner of [1]herbs where
love is,
Than a fatted calf with hatred.

18 [a]A wrathful man stirs up strife,
But *he who is* slow to anger allays
contention.

19 [a]The way of the lazy *man is* like
a hedge of thorns,
But the way of the upright *is* a
highway.

20 [a]A wise son makes a father glad,
But a foolish man despises his
mother.

21 [a]Folly *is* joy *to him who is* destitute
of [1]discernment,
[b]But a man of understanding
walks uprightly.

22 [a]Without counsel, plans go awry,
But in the multitude of counselors
they are established.

23 A man has joy by the answer of
his mouth,
And [a]a word *spoken* [1]in due
season, how good *it is!*

24 [a]The way of life winds upward for
the wise,
That he may [b]turn away from
[1]hell below.

25 [a]The LORD will destroy the house
of the proud,
But [b]He will establish the
boundary of the widow.

26 [a]The thoughts of the wicked *are*
an abomination to the LORD,
[b]But *the words* of the pure *are*
pleasant.

27 [a]He who is greedy for gain
troubles his own house,
But he who hates bribes will live.

28 The heart of the righteous
[a]studies how to answer,

35 [a]Matt. 24:45–47

CHAPTER 15

1 [a]Prov. 25:15 [b]1 Sam. 25:10
2 [a]Prov. 12:23
3 [a]2 Chr. 16:9; Job 34:21; Prov. 5:21; Jer. 16:17; 32:19; Zech. 4:10; Heb. 4:13
4 [1]Lit. *healing*
5 [a]Prov. 10:1 [b]Prov. 13:18 [1]Lit. *keeps*
7 [1]*spread*
8 [a]Prov. 21:27; Eccl. 5:1; Is. 1:11; Jer. 6:20; Mic. 6:7
9 [a]Prov. 21:21
10 [a]1 Kin. 22:8 [b]Prov. 5:12
11 [a]Job 26:6; Ps. 139:8 [b]1 Sam. 16:7; 2 Chr. 6:30; Ps. 44:21; Acts 1:24 [1]Or *Sheol* [2]Heb. *Abaddon*
12 [a]Prov. 13:1; Amos 5:10; 2 Tim. 4:3
13 [a]Prov. 12:25 [b]Prov. 17:22 [1]*face*
15 [a]Prov. 17:22
16 [a]Ps. 37:16; Prov. 16:8; Eccl. 4:6; 1 Tim. 6:6
17 [a]Prov. 17:1 [1]Or *vegetables*
18 [a]Prov. 26:21
19 [a]Prov. 22:5
20 [a]Prov. 10:1
21 [a]Prov. 10:23 [b]Eph. 5:15 [1]Lit. *heart*
22 [a]Prov. 11:14
23 [a]Prov. 25:11; Is. 50:4 [1]Lit. *in its time*
24 [a]Phil. 3:20; [Col. 3:1, 2] [b]Prov. 14:16 [1]Or *Sheol*
25 [a]Prov. 12:7; Is. 2:11 [b]Ps. 68:5, 6
26 [a]Prov. 6:16, 18 [b]Ps. 37:30
27 [a]Is. 5:8; [Jer. 17:11]
28 [a]1 Pet. 3:15

But the mouth of the wicked
pours forth evil.

29 [a]The LORD *is* far from the wicked,
But [b]He hears the prayer of the
righteous.

30 The light of the eyes rejoices the
heart,
And a good report makes the
bones [1]healthy.

31 The ear that hears the rebukes of
life
Will abide among the wise.
32 He who disdains instruction
despises his own soul,
But he who heeds rebuke gets
understanding.
33 [a]The fear of the LORD *is* the
instruction of wisdom,
And [b]before honor *is* humility.

16 The [a]preparations[1] of the heart
belong to man,
[b]But the answer of the tongue *is*
from the LORD.

2 All the ways of a man *are* pure
in his own [a]eyes,
But the LORD weighs the spirits.

3 [a]Commit[1] your works to the LORD,
And your thoughts will be
established.

4 The [a]LORD has made all for
Himself,
[b]Yes, even the wicked for the day
of [1]doom.

5 [a]Everyone proud in heart *is* an
abomination to the LORD;
Though they join [1]forces, none
will go unpunished.

6 [a]In mercy and truth
Atonement is provided for
iniquity;
And [b]by the fear of the LORD *one*
departs from evil.

7 When a man's ways please the
LORD,
He makes even his enemies to be
at peace with him.

8 [a]Better *is* a little with
righteousness,
Than vast revenues without
justice.

9 [a]A man's heart plans his way,
[b]But the LORD directs his steps.

29 [a]Ps. 10:1; 34:16 [b]Ps. 145:18; [James 5:16]
30 [1]Lit. *fat*
33 [a]Prov. 1:7 [b]Prov. 18:12

CHAPTER 16

1 [a]Jer. 10:23 [b]Matt. 10:19 [1]*plans*
2 [a]Prov. 21:2
3 [a]Ps. 37:5; Prov. 3:6; [1 Pet. 5:7] [1]Lit. *Roll*
4 [a]Is. 43:7; Rom. 11:36 [b]Job 21:30; [Rom. 9:22] [1]Lit. *evil*
5 [a]Prov. 6:17; 8:13 [1]Lit. *hand to hand*
6 [a]Dan. 4:27; Luke 11:41 [b]Prov. 8:13; 14:16
8 [a]Ps. 37:16; Prov. 15:16
9 [a]Prov. 19:21 [b]Ps. 37:23; Prov. 20:24; Jer. 10:23
11 [a]Lev. 19:36 [1]*concern*
12 [a]Prov. 25:5
13 [a]Prov. 14:35
14 [a]Prov. 25:15
15 [a]Zech. 10:1
16 [a]Prov. 8:10, 11, 19
18 [1]*stumbling*
19 [1]*plunder*
20 [a]Ps. 34:8; Jer. 17:7

10 Divination *is* on the lips of the
king;
His mouth must not transgress in
judgment.
11 [a]Honest weights and scales *are* the
LORD'S;
All the weights in the bag *are* His
[1]work.
12 *It is* an abomination for kings to
commit wickedness,
For [a]a throne is established by
righteousness.
13 [a]Righteous lips *are* the delight of
kings,
And they love him who speaks
what is right.
14 As messengers of death *is* the
king's wrath,
But a wise man will [a]appease it.
15 In the light of the king's face *is*
life,
And his favor *is* like a [a]cloud of
the latter rain.

16 [a]How much better to get wisdom
than gold!
And to get understanding is to be
chosen rather than silver.

17 The highway of the upright *is* to
depart from evil;
He who keeps his way preserves
his soul.

18 Pride *goes* before destruction,
And a haughty spirit before [1]a
fall.
19 Better *to be* of a humble spirit
with the lowly,
Than to divide the [1]spoil with the
proud.

20 He who heeds the word wisely
will find good,
And whoever [a]trusts in the LORD,
happy *is* he.

21 The wise in heart will be called
prudent,
And sweetness of the lips
increases learning.

22 Understanding *is* a wellspring of
life to him who has it.
But the correction of fools *is* folly.

23 The heart of the wise teaches his
mouth,
And adds learning to his lips.

24 Pleasant words *are like* a
honeycomb,
Sweetness to the soul and health
to the bones.

25 There is a way *that seems* right
to a man,
But its end *is* the way of [a]death.

26 The person who labors, labors for
himself,
For his *hungry* mouth drives
[a]him *on.*

27 [1]An ungodly man digs up evil,
And *it is* on his lips like a burning
[a]fire.
28 A perverse man sows strife,
And [a]a whisperer separates the
best of friends.
29 A violent man entices his
neighbor,
And leads him in a way *that is*
not good.
30 He winks his eye to devise
perverse things;
He [1]purses his lips *and* brings
about evil.

31 [a]The silver-haired head *is* a crown
of glory,
If it is found in the way of
righteousness.

32 [a]*He who is* slow to anger *is* better
than the mighty,
And he who rules his spirit than
he who takes a city.

33 The lot is cast into the lap,
But its every decision *is* from the
LORD.

17 Better *is* [a]a dry morsel with
quietness,
Than a house full of [1]feasting
with strife.

2 A wise servant will rule over [a]a
son who causes shame,
And will share an inheritance
among the brothers.

3 The refining pot *is* for silver and
the furnace for gold,
[a]But the LORD tests the hearts.

4 An evildoer gives heed to false
lips;
A liar listens eagerly to a [1]spiteful
tongue.

5 [a]He who mocks the poor
reproaches his Maker;
[b]He who is glad at calamity will
not go unpunished.

6 [a]Children's children *are* the crown
of old men,
And the glory of children *is* their
father.

7 Excellent speech is not becoming
to a fool,
Much less lying lips to a prince.

8 A present *is* a precious stone in
the eyes of its possessor;
Wherever he turns, he prospers.

9 [a]He who covers a transgression
seeks love,
But [b]he who repeats a matter
separates friends.

10 [a]Rebuke is more effective for a
wise *man*
Than a hundred blows on a fool.

11 An evil *man* seeks only rebellion;
Therefore a cruel messenger will
be sent against him.

12 Let a man meet [a]a bear robbed
of her cubs,
Rather than a fool in his folly.

13 Whoever [a]rewards evil for good,
Evil will not depart from his
house.

14 The beginning of strife *is like*
releasing water;
Therefore [a]stop contention
before a quarrel starts.

15 [a]He who justifies the wicked, and
he who condemns the just,
Both of them alike *are* an
abomination to the LORD.

16 Why *is there* in the hand of a fool
the purchase price of wisdom,
Since *he has* no heart *for it?*

17 [a]A friend loves at all times,
And a brother is born for
adversity.

18 [a]A man devoid of [1]understanding
[2]shakes hands in a pledge,
And becomes [3]surety for his
friend.

19 He who loves transgression loves
strife,
And [a]he who exalts his gate seeks
destruction.

20 He who has a [1]deceitful heart
finds no good,
And he who has [a]a perverse
tongue falls into evil.

16:25 [a]Prov. 14:12
26 [a][Eccl. 6:7; John 6:35]
27 [a][James 3:6] [1]Lit. *A man of Belial*
28 [a]Prov. 17:9
30 [1]Lit. *compresses*
31 [a]Prov. 20:29
32 [a]Prov. 14:29; 19:11

CHAPTER 17

1 [a]Prov. 15:17 [1]Or *sacrificial meals*
2 [a]Prov. 10:5
3 [a]1 Chr. 29:17; Ps. 26:2; Prov. 15:11; Jer. 17:10; [Mal. 3:3]
4 [1]Lit. *destructive*
5 [a]Prov. 14:31 [b]Job 31:29; Prov. 24:17; Obad. 12; 1 Cor. 13:6
6 [a][Ps. 127:3; 128:3]
9 [a][Prov. 10:12; 1 Cor. 13:5–7; James 5:20] [b]Prov. 16:28
10 [a]Prov. 10:17; [Mic. 7:9]
12 [a]2 Sam. 17:8; Hos. 13:8
13 [a]Ps. 109:4, 5; Jer. 18:20; Rom. 12:17; 1 Thess. 5:15; [1 Pet. 3:9]
14 [a][Prov. 20:3; 1 Thess. 4:11]
15 [a]Ex. 23:7; Prov. 24:24; Is. 5:23
17 [a]Ruth 1:16; Prov. 18:24
18 [a]Prov. 6:1 [1]Lit. *heart* [2]Lit. *strikes the hands* [3]*guaranty* or *collateral*
19 [a]Prov. 16:18
20 [a]James 3:8 [1]*crooked*

21 He who begets a scoffer *does so*
to his sorrow,
And the father of a fool has no
joy.

22 A [a]merry heart [1]does good, *like*
medicine,
But a broken spirit dries the
bones.

23 A wicked *man* accepts a bribe
[1]behind the back
To pervert the ways of justice.

24 [a]Wisdom *is* in the sight of him who
has understanding,
But the eyes of a fool *are* on the
ends of the earth.

25 A [a]foolish son *is* a grief to his
father,
And bitterness to her who bore
him.

26 Also, to punish the righteous *is*
not good,
Nor to strike princes for *their*
uprightness.

27 [a]He who has knowledge spares his
words,
And a man of understanding is
of a calm spirit.
28 [a]Even a fool is counted wise when
he holds his peace;
When he shuts his lips, *he is*
considered perceptive.

18 A man who isolates himself
seeks his own desire;
He rages against all [1]wise
judgment.

2 A fool has no delight in
understanding,
But in expressing his [a]own heart.

3 When the wicked comes,
contempt comes also;
And with dishonor *comes*
reproach.

4 [a]The words of a man's mouth *are*
deep waters;
[b]The wellspring of wisdom *is* a
flowing brook.

5 *It is* not good to show partiality
to the wicked,
Or to overthrow the righteous in
[a]judgment.

6 A fool's lips enter into contention,
And his mouth calls for blows.
7 [a]A fool's mouth *is* his destruction,

22 [a]Prov. 12:25; 15:13, 15 [1]Or *makes medicine even better*

23 [1]Under cover, lit. *from the bosom*

24 [a]Eccl. 2:14

25 [a]Prov. 10:1; 15:20; 19:13

27 [a]Prov. 10:19; James 1:19

28 [a]Job 13:5

CHAPTER 18

1 [1]*sound wisdom*

2 [a]Eccl. 10:3

4 [a]Prov. 10:11 [b][James 3:17]

5 [a]Lev. 19:15; Deut. 1:17; 16:19; Ps. 82:2; Prov. 17:15

7 [a]Ps. 64:8; 140:9; Prov. 10:14 [b]Eccl. 10:12

8 [a]Prov. 12:18 [1]*gossip* or *slanderer* [2]A Jewish tradition *wounds* [3]Lit. *rooms of the belly*

10 [a]2 Sam. 22:2, 3, 33; Ps. 18:2; 61:3; 91:2; 144:2 [1]*secure*, lit. *set on high*

12 [a]Prov. 15:33; 16:18

16 [a]Gen. 32:20, 21; 1 Sam. 25:27; Prov. 17:8; 21:14

18 [a][Prov. 16:33]

20 [a]Prov. 12:14; 14:14

21 [a]Prov. 12:13; 13:3; Matt. 12:37

And his lips *are* the snare of his
[b]soul.
8 [a]The words of a [1]talebearer *are*
like [2]tasty trifles,
And they go down into the
[3]inmost body.

9 He who is slothful in his work
Is a brother to him who is a great
destroyer.

10 The name of the LORD *is* a strong
[a]tower;
The righteous run to it and are
[1]safe.
11 The rich man's wealth *is* his
strong city,
And like a high wall in his own
esteem.

12 [a]Before destruction the heart of a
man is haughty,
And before honor *is* humility.

13 He who answers a matter before
he hears *it*,
It *is* folly and shame to him.

14 The spirit of a man will sustain
him in sickness,
But who can bear a broken spirit?

15 The heart of the prudent acquires
knowledge,
And the ear of the wise seeks
knowledge.

16 [a]A man's gift makes room for him,
And brings him before great
men.

17 The first *one* to plead his cause
***seems* right,**
Until his neighbor comes and
examines him.

18 Casting [a]lots causes contentions
to cease,
And keeps the mighty apart.

19 A brother offended *is harder to*
***win* than a strong city,**
And contentions *are* like the bars
of a castle.

20 [a]A man's stomach shall be
satisfied from the fruit of his
mouth;
***From* the produce of his lips he**
shall be filled.

21 [a]Death and life *are* in the power
of the tongue,
And those who love it will eat its
fruit.

22 [a]*He who* finds a wife finds a good *thing*,
And obtains favor from the LORD.

23 The poor *man* uses entreaties,
But the rich answers [a]roughly.

24 A man *who has* friends [1]must himself be friendly,
[a]But there is a friend *who* sticks closer than a brother.

19

1 Better [a]*is* the poor who walks in his integrity
Than *one who is* perverse in his lips, and is a fool.

2 Also it is not good *for* a soul *to be* without knowledge,
And he sins who hastens with *his* feet.

3 The foolishness of a man twists his way,
And his heart frets against the LORD.

4 [a]Wealth makes many friends,
But the poor is separated from his friend.

5 A [a]false witness will not go unpunished,
And *he who* speaks lies will not escape.

6 Many entreat the favor of the nobility,
And every man *is* a friend to one who gives gifts.

7 [a]All the brothers of the poor hate him;
How much more do his friends go [b]far from him!
He may pursue *them with* words, *yet* they [1]abandon *him*.

8 He who gets [1]wisdom loves his own soul;
He who keeps understanding [a]will find good.

9 A false witness will not go unpunished,
And *he who* speaks lies shall perish.

10 Luxury is not fitting for a fool,
Much less [a]for a servant to rule over princes.

11 [a]The discretion of a man makes him slow to anger,
[b]And his glory *is* to overlook a transgression.

12 [a]The king's wrath *is* like the roaring of a lion,
But his favor *is* [b]like dew on the grass.

13 [a]A foolish son *is* the ruin of his father,
[b]And the contentions of a wife *are* a continual [1]dripping.

14 [a]Houses and riches *are* an inheritance from fathers,
But [b]a prudent wife *is* from the LORD.

15 [a]Laziness casts *one* into a deep sleep,
And an idle person will [b]suffer hunger.

16 [a]He who keeps the commandment keeps his soul,
But he who [1]is careless of his ways will die.

17 [a]He who has pity on the poor lends to the LORD,
And He will pay back what he has given.

18 [a]Chasten your son while there is hope,
And do not set your heart [1]on his destruction.

19 *A man of* great wrath will suffer punishment;
For if you rescue *him*, you will have to do it again.

20 Listen to counsel and receive instruction,
That you may be wise [a]in your latter days.

21 There are many plans in a man's heart,
[a]Nevertheless the LORD's counsel—that will stand.

22 What is desired in a man is [1]kindness,
And a poor man is better than a liar.

23 [a]The fear of the LORD *leads* to life,
And *he who has it* will abide in satisfaction;
He will not be visited with evil.

24 [a]A lazy *man* buries his hand in the [1]bowl,
And will not so much as bring it to his mouth again.

22 [a]Gen. 2:18; [Prov. 12:4; 19:14]
23 [a]James 2:3, 6
24 [a]Prov. 17:17; [John 15:14, 15] [1]So with Gr. mss., Syr., Tg., Vg.; MT *may come to ruin*

CHAPTER 19

1 [a]Prov. 28:6
4 [a]Prov. 14:20
5 [a]Ex. 23:1; Deut. 19:16–19; Prov. 6:19; 21:28
7 [a]Prov. 14:20 [b]Ps. 38:11 [1]Lit. *are not*
8 [a]Prov. 16:20 [1]Lit. *heart*
10 [a]Prov. 30:21, 22
11 [a]James 1:19 [b]Prov. 16:32; [Matt. 5:44]; Eph. 4:32; Col. 3:13
12 [a]Prov. 16:14 [b]Gen. 27:28; Deut. 33:28; Ps. 133:3; Hos. 14:5; Mic. 5:7
13 [a]Prov. 10:1 [b]Prov. 21:9, 19 [1]Irritation
14 [a]2 Cor. 12:14 [b]Prov. 18:22
15 [a]Prov. 6:9 [b]Prov. 10:4
16 [a]Prov. 13:13; 16:17; Luke 10:28; 11:28 [1]Is reckless, lit. *despises*
17 [a]Deut. 15:7, 8; Job 23:12, 13; Prov. 28:27; Eccl. 11:1; Matt. 10:42; 25:40; [2 Cor. 9:6–8]; Heb. 6:10
18 [a]Prov. 13:24 [1]Lit. *to put him to death;* a Jewish tradition *on his crying*
20 [a]Ps. 37:37
21 [a]Ps. 33:10, 11; Prov. 16:9; Is. 46:10; Heb. 6:17
22 [1]Lit. *loving-kindness*
23 [a]Prov. 14:27; [1 Tim. 4:8]
24 [a]Prov. 15:19 [1]LXX, Syr. *bosom;* Tg., Vg. *armpit*

25 Strike a scoffer, and the simple
[a]will become wary;
[b]Rebuke one who has
understanding, *and* he will
discern knowledge.

26 He who mistreats *his* father *and*
chases away *his* mother
Is [a]a son who causes shame and
brings reproach.

27 Cease listening to instruction, my
son,
And you will stray from the
words of knowledge.

28 A [1]disreputable witness scorns
justice,
And [a]the mouth of the wicked
devours iniquity.

29 Judgments are prepared for
scoffers,
[a]And beatings for the backs of
fools.

20

Wine [a]*is* a mocker,
Strong drink *is* a brawler,
And whoever is led astray by it
is not wise.

2 The [1]wrath of a king *is* like the
roaring of a lion;
Whoever provokes him to anger
sins *against* his own life.

3 [a]*It is* honorable for a man to stop
striving,
Since any fool can start a quarrel.

4 [a]The lazy *man* will not plow
because of winter;
[b]He will beg during harvest and
have nothing.

5 Counsel in the heart of man *is like*
deep water,
But a man of understanding will
draw it out.

6 Most men will proclaim each his
own [1]goodness,
But who can find a faithful man?

7 [a]The righteous *man* walks in his
integrity;
[b]His children *are* blessed after
him.

8 A king who sits on the throne of
judgment
Scatters all evil with his eyes.

9 [a]Who can say, "I have made my
heart clean,
I am pure from my sin"?

25 [a]Deut. 13:11 [b]Prov. 9:8
26 [a]Prov. 17:2
28 [a]Job 15:16 [1]Lit. *witness of Belial, worthless witness*
29 [a]Prov. 26:3

CHAPTER 20

1 [a]Gen. 9:21; Prov. 23:29–35; Is. 28:7; Hos. 4:11
2 [1]Lit. *fear* or *terror,* produced by the king's wrath
3 [a]Prov. 17:14
4 [a]Prov. 10:4 [b]Prov. 19:15
6 [1]Lit. *mercy*
7 [a]2 Cor. 1:12 [b]Ps. 37:26
9 [a][1 Kin. 8:46; 2 Chr. 6:36]; Job 9:30, 31; 14:4; [Ps. 51:5; Eccl. 7:20; Rom. 3:9; 1 John 1:8]
10 [a]Deut. 25:13
11 [a]Matt. 7:16
12 [a]Ex. 4:11; Ps. 94:9
13 [a]Rom. 12:11
14 [1]Lit. *evil, evil*
15 [a][Job 28:12–19; Prov. 3:13–15]
16 [a]Prov. 22:26
17 [a]Prov. 9:17
18 [a]Prov. 24:6 [b]Luke 14:31
19 [a]Prov. 11:13 [b]Rom. 16:18
20 [a]Ex. 21:17; Lev. 20:9; Prov. 30:11; Matt. 15:4 [b]Job 18:5, 6; Prov. 24:20
21 [a]Prov. 28:20 [b]Hab. 2:6
22 [a][Deut. 32:35]; Prov. 17:13; 24:29; [Rom. 12:17–19]; 1 Thess. 5:15; [1 Pet. 3:9] [b]2 Sam. 16:12 [1]*repay*

10 [a]Diverse weights *and* diverse
measures,
They *are* both alike, an
abomination to the LORD.

11 Even a child is [a]known by his
deeds,
Whether what he does *is* pure
and right.

12 [a]The hearing ear and the seeing
eye,
The LORD has made them both.

13 [a]Do not love sleep, lest you come
to poverty;
Open your eyes, *and* you will be
satisfied with bread.

14 "*It is* [1]good for nothing," cries the
buyer;
But when he has gone his way,
then he boasts.

15 There is gold and a multitude of
rubies,
But [a]the lips of knowledge *are* a
precious jewel.

16 [a]Take the garment of one who is
surety *for* a stranger,
And hold it as a pledge *when it*
is for a seductress.

17 [a]Bread gained by deceit *is* sweet
to a man,
But afterward his mouth will be
filled with gravel.

18 [a]Plans are established by counsel;
[b]By wise counsel wage war.

19 [a]He who goes about *as* a
talebearer reveals secrets;
Therefore do not associate with
one [b]who flatters with his lips.

20 [a]Whoever curses his father or his
mother,
[b]His lamp will be put out in deep
darkness.

21 [a]An inheritance gained hastily at
the beginning
[b]Will not be blessed at the end.

22 [a]Do not say, "I will [1]recompense
evil";
[b]Wait for the LORD, and He will
save you.

23 Diverse weights *are* an
abomination to the LORD,
And dishonest scales *are* not
good.

24 A man's steps *are* of the LORD;
How then can a man understand
his own way?

25 *It is* a snare for a man to devote
rashly *something as* holy,
And afterward to reconsider *his*
vows.

26 [a]A wise king sifts out the wicked,
And brings the threshing wheel
over them.

27 [a]The spirit of a man *is* the lamp
of the LORD,
Searching all the [1]inner depths of
his heart.

28 [a]Mercy and truth preserve the
king,
And by [1]lovingkindness he
upholds his throne.

29 The glory of young men *is* their
strength,
And [a]the splendor of old men *is*
their gray head.

30 Blows that hurt cleanse away
evil,
As *do* stripes the [1]inner depths of
the heart.

21 The king's heart *is* in the hand
of the LORD,
Like the [1]rivers of water;
He turns it wherever He wishes.

2 [a]Every way of a man *is* right in
his own eyes,
[b]But the LORD weighs the hearts.

3 [a]To do righteousness and justice
Is more acceptable to the LORD
than sacrifice.

4 [a]A haughty look, a proud heart,
And the [1]plowing of the wicked
are sin.

5 [a]The plans of the diligent *lead*
surely to plenty,
But *those of* everyone *who is*
hasty, surely to poverty.

6 [a]Getting treasures by a lying
tongue
[1]*Is* the fleeting fantasy of those
who seek death.

7 The violence of the wicked will
[1]destroy them,
Because they refuse to do justice.

8 The way of [1]a guilty man *is*
perverse;
But *as for* the pure, his work *is*
right.

9 Better to dwell in a corner of a
housetop,
Than in a house shared with [a]a
contentious woman.

10 [a]The soul of the wicked desires
evil;
His neighbor finds no favor in his
eyes.

11 When the scoffer is punished, the
simple is made wise;
But when the [a]wise is instructed,
he receives knowledge.

12 The righteous *God* wisely
considers the house of the
wicked,
Overthrowing the wicked for
their wickedness.

13 [a]Whoever shuts his ears to the cry
of the poor
Will also cry himself and not be
heard.

14 A gift in secret pacifies anger,
And a bribe [1]behind the back,
strong wrath.

15 *It is* a joy for the just to do justice,
But destruction *will come* to the
workers of iniquity.

16 A man who wanders from the
way of understanding
Will rest in the assembly of the
[a]dead.

17 He who loves pleasure *will be* a
poor man;
He who loves wine and oil will
not be rich.

18 The wicked *shall be* a ransom for
the righteous,
And the unfaithful for the
upright.

19 Better to dwell [1]in the wilderness,
Than with a contentious and
angry woman.

20 [a]*There is* desirable treasure,
And oil in the dwelling of the
wise,
But a foolish man squanders it.

21 [a]He who follows righteousness
and mercy
Finds life, righteousness and
honor.

26 [a]Ps. 101:8
27 [a]1 Cor. 2:11 [1]Lit. *rooms of the belly*
28 [a]Ps. 101:1; Prov. 21:21 [1]*mercy*
29 [a]Prov. 16:31
30 [1]Lit. *rooms of the belly*

CHAPTER 21

1 [1]*channels*
2 [a]Prov. 16:2 [b]Prov. 24:12; Luke 16:15
3 [a]1 Sam. 15:22; Prov. 15:8; Is. 1:11, 16, 17; Hos. 6:6; [Mic. 6:7, 8]
4 [a]Prov. 6:17 [1]Or *lamp*
5 [a]Prov. 10:4
6 [a]2 Pet. 2:3 [1]LXX *Pursue vanity on the snares of death;* Vg. *Is vain and foolish, and shall stumble on the snares of death;* Tg. *They shall be destroyed, and they shall fall who seek death*
7 [1]Lit. *drag them away*
8 [1]Or *The way of a man is perverse and strange;*
9 [a]Prov. 19:13
10 [a]James 4:5
11 [a]Prov. 19:25
13 [a][Matt. 7:2; 18:30–34]; James 2:13; 1 John 3:17
14 [1]Under cover, lit. *in the bosom*
16 [a]Ps. 49:14
19 [1]Lit. *in the land of the desert*
20 [a]Ps. 112:3; Prov. 8:21
21 [a]Prov. 15:9; Matt. 5:6; [Rom. 2:7]; 1 Cor. 15:58

22 A [a]wise *man* [1]scales the city of the mighty,
And brings down the trusted stronghold.

23 [a]Whoever guards his mouth and tongue
Keeps his soul from troubles.

24 A proud *and* haughty *man*—
"Scoffer" *is* his name;
He acts with arrogant pride.

25 The [a]desire of the lazy *man* kills him,
For his hands refuse to labor.
26 He covets greedily all day long,
But the righteous [a]gives and does not spare.

27 [a]The sacrifice of the wicked *is* an abomination;
How much more *when* he brings it with wicked intent!

28 A false witness shall perish,
But the man who hears *him* will speak endlessly.

29 A wicked man hardens his face,
But *as for* the upright, he [1]establishes his way.

30 [a]*There is* no wisdom or understanding
Or counsel against the LORD.

31 The horse *is* prepared for the day of battle,
But [a]deliverance *is* of the LORD.

22 A [a]*good* name is to be chosen rather than great riches,
Loving favor rather than silver and gold.

2 The [a]rich and the poor have this in common,
The [b]LORD *is* the maker of them all.

3 A prudent *man* foresees evil and hides himself,
But the simple pass on and are [a]punished.

4 By humility *and* the fear of the LORD
Are riches and honor and life.

5 Thorns *and* snares *are* in the way of the perverse;
He who guards his soul will be far from them.

22 [a]2 Sam. 5:6–9; Prov. 24:5; Eccl. 7:19; 9:15, 16 [1]Climbs over the walls of
23 [a]Prov. 12:13; 13:3; 18:21; [James 3:2]
25 [a]Prov. 13:4
26 [a][Prov. 22:9; Eph. 4:28]
27 [a]Prov. 15:8; Is. 66:3; Jer. 6:20; Amos 5:22
29 [1]Qr., LXX *understands*
30 [a]Is. 8:9, 10; [Jer. 9:23, 24]; Acts 5:39; 1 Cor. 3:19, 20
31 [a]Ps. 3:8; Jer. 3:23; [1 Cor. 15:57]

CHAPTER 22

1 [a][Prov. 10:7]; Eccl. 7:1
2 [a]Prov. 29:13 [b]Job 31:15; [Prov. 14:31]
3 [a]Prov. 27:12; Is. 26:20
6 [a]Eph. 6:4; 2 Tim. 3:15 [1]*Even*
7 [a]Prov. 18:23; James 2:6
8 [a]Job 4:8 [1]*trouble*
9 [a]2 Cor. 9:6 [b][Prov. 19:17] [1]Lit. *good*
10 [a]Ps. 101:5
11 [a]Ps. 101:6
13 [a]Prov. 26:13
14 [a]Prov. 2:16; 5:3; 7:5 [b]Eccl. 7:26
15 [a]Prov. 13:24; 23:13, 14

6 [a]Train up a child in the way he should go,
[1]And when he is old he will not depart from it.

7 The [a]rich rules over the poor,
And the borrower *is* servant to the lender.

8 He who sows iniquity will reap [a]sorrow,[1]
And the rod of his anger will fail.

9 [a]He who has a [1]generous eye will be [b]blessed,
For he gives of his bread to the poor.

10 [a]Cast out the scoffer, and contention will leave;
Yes, strife and reproach will cease.

11 [a]He who loves purity of heart
And has grace on his lips,
The king *will be* his friend.

12 The eyes of the LORD preserve knowledge,
But He overthrows the words of the faithless.

13 [a]The lazy *man* says, "*There is* a lion outside!
I shall be slain in the streets!"

14 [a]The mouth of an immoral woman *is* a deep pit;
[b]He who is abhorred by the LORD will fall there.

15 Foolishness *is* bound up in the heart of a child;
[a]The rod of correction will drive it far from him.

16 He who oppresses the poor to increase his *riches*,
And he who gives to the rich, *will* surely *come* to poverty.

Sayings of the Wise

17 Incline your ear and hear the words of the wise,
And apply your heart to my knowledge;
18 For *it is* a pleasant thing if you keep them within you;
Let them all be fixed upon your lips,
19 So that your trust may be in the LORD;
I have instructed you today, even you.

20 Have I not written to you
excellent things
Of counsels and knowledge,
21 [a]That I may make you know the
certainty of the words of truth,
[b]That you may answer words of
truth
To those who [1]send to you?

22 Do not rob the [a]poor because he
is poor,
Nor oppress the afflicted at the
gate;
23 [a]For the LORD will plead their
cause,
And plunder the soul of those
who plunder them.

24 Make no friendship with an
angry man,
And with a [a]furious man do not
go,
25 Lest you learn his ways
And set a snare for your soul.

26 [a]Do not be one of those who
[1]shakes hands in a pledge,
One of those who is [2]surety for
debts;
27 If you have nothing *with which*
to pay,
Why should he take away your
bed from under you?

28 [a]Do not remove the ancient
[1]landmark
Which your fathers have set.

29 Do you see a man *who* [1]excels in
his work?
He will stand before kings;
He will not stand before
[2]unknown *men*.

23

When you sit down to eat with
a ruler,
Consider carefully what *is* before
you;
2 And put a knife to your throat
If you *are* a man given to appetite.
3 Do not desire his delicacies,
For they *are* deceptive food.

4 [a]Do not overwork to be rich;
[b]Because of your own
understanding, cease!
5 [1]Will you set your eyes on that
which is not?
For *riches* certainly make
themselves wings;
They fly away like an eagle
toward heaven.

6 Do not eat the bread of [a]a[1] miser,
Nor desire his delicacies;
7 For as he thinks in his heart, so
is he.
"Eat and drink!" [a]he says to you,
But his heart is not with you.
8 The morsel you have eaten, you
will vomit up,
And waste your pleasant words.

9 [a]Do not speak in the hearing of a
fool,
For he will despise the wisdom
of your words.

10 Do not remove the ancient
[1]landmark,
Nor enter the fields of the
fatherless;
11 [a]For their Redeemer *is* mighty;
He will plead their cause against
you.

12 Apply your heart to instruction,
And your ears to words of
knowledge.

13 [a]Do not withhold correction from
a child,
For *if* you beat him with a rod,
he will not die.
14 You shall beat him with a rod,
And deliver his soul from [1]hell.

15 My son, if your heart is wise,
My heart will rejoice—indeed, I
myself;
16 Yes, my [1]inmost being will
rejoice
When your lips speak right
things.

17 [a]Do not let your heart envy
sinners,
But [b]*be zealous* for the fear of the
LORD all the day;
18 [a]For surely there is a [1]hereafter,
And your hope will not be cut off.

19 Hear, my son, and be wise;
And guide your heart in the way.
20 [a]Do not mix with winebibbers,
Or with gluttonous eaters of
meat;
21 For the drunkard and the glutton
will come to poverty,
And drowsiness will clothe *a man*
with rags.

22 [a]Listen to your father who begot
you,
And do not despise your mother
when she is old.

23 [a]Buy the truth, and do not sell *it*,
Also wisdom and instruction and
understanding.

---

21 [a]Luke 1:3, 4 [b]Prov. 25:13; 1 Pet. 3:15 [1]Or *send you*
22 [a]Ex. 23:6; Job 31:16–21; Zech. 7:10
23 [a]1 Sam. 24:12; Ps. 12:5; 140:12
24 [a]Prov. 29:22
26 [a]Prov. 11:15 [1]Lit. *strikes* [2]*guaranty*
28 [a]Deut. 19:14; 27:17; Job 24:2; Prov. 23:10 [1]*boundary*
29 [1]*is prompt in his business* [2]*obscure*

CHAPTER 23

4 [a][Prov. 28:20; Matt. 6:19; 1 Tim. 6:9, 10; Heb. 13:5] [b]Rom. 12:16
5 [1]Lit. *Will you cause your eyes to fly upon it and it is not?*
6 [a]Deut. 15:9; Prov. 28:22 [1]Lit. *one who has an evil eye*
7 [a]Prov. 12:2
9 [a]Prov. 9:8; Matt. 7:6
10 [1]*boundary*
11 [a]Prov. 22:23
13 [a]Prov. 13:24
14 [1]Or *Sheol*
16 [1]Lit. *kidneys*
17 [a]Ps. 37:1; Prov. 24:1, 19 [b]Prov. 28:14
18 [a][Ps. 37:37] [1]Future, lit. *latter end*
20 [a]Prov. 20:1; 23:29, 30; Is. 5:22; Matt. 24:49; [Luke 21:34]; Rom. 13:13; [Eph. 5:18]
22 [a]Prov. 1:8; Eph. 6:1
23 [a]Prov. 4:7; 18:15; [Matt. 13:44]

16 Have you found honey?
Eat only as much as you need,
Lest you be filled with it and
vomit.

17 Seldom set foot in your
neighbor's house,
Lest he become weary of you and
hate you.

18 [a]A man who bears false witness
against his neighbor
Is like a club, a sword, and a
sharp arrow.

19 Confidence in an unfaithful *man*
in time of trouble
Is like a bad tooth and a foot out
of joint.

20 *Like* one who takes away a
garment in cold weather,
And like vinegar on soda,
Is one who [a]sings songs to a
heavy heart.

21 [a]If your enemy is hungry, give him
bread to eat;
And if he is thirsty, give him
water to drink;

22 For *so* you will heap coals of fire
on his head,
[a]And the LORD will reward you.

23 The north wind brings forth rain,
And [a]a backbiting tongue an
angry countenance.

24 [a]*It is* better to dwell in a corner
of a housetop,
Than in a house shared with a
contentious woman.

25 *As* cold water to a weary soul,
So *is* [a]good news from a far
country.

26 A righteous *man* who falters
before the wicked
Is like a murky spring and a
[1]polluted well.

27 *It is* not good to eat much honey;
So [a]to seek one's own glory *is not*
glory.

28 [a]Whoever *has* no rule over his
own spirit
Is like a city broken down,
without walls.

26

1 As snow in summer [a]and rain
in harvest,
So honor is not fitting for a fool.

2 Like a flitting sparrow, like a
flying swallow,
So [a]a curse without cause shall
not alight.

3 [a]A whip for the horse,
A bridle for the donkey,
And a rod for the fool's back.

4 Do not answer a fool according
to his folly,
Lest you also be like him.

5 [a]Answer a fool according to his
folly,
Lest he be wise in his own eyes.

6 He who sends a message by the
hand of a fool
Cuts off *his own* feet *and* drinks
violence.

7 *Like* the legs of the lame that
hang limp
Is a proverb in the mouth of fools.

8 Like one who binds a stone in a
sling
Is he who gives honor to a fool.

9 *Like* a thorn *that* goes into the
hand of a drunkard
Is a proverb in the mouth of fools.

10 [1]The great *God* who formed
everything
Gives the fool *his* hire and the
transgressor *his* wages.

11 [a]As a dog returns to his own
vomit,
[b]*So* a fool repeats his folly.

12 [a]Do you see a man wise in his own
eyes?
There is more hope for a fool than
for him.

13 The lazy *man* says, "*There is* a
lion in the road!
A fierce lion *is* in the [1]streets!"

14 *As* a door turns on its hinges,
So *does* the lazy *man* on his bed.

15 The [a]lazy *man* buries his hand in
the [1]bowl;
It wearies him to bring it back to
his mouth.

16 The lazy *man is* wiser in his own
eyes
Than seven men who can answer
sensibly.

17 He who passes by *and* meddles
in a quarrel not his own
Is like one who takes a dog by
the ears.

18 Like a madman who throws
firebrands, arrows, and death,

19 *Is* the man *who* deceives his
neighbor,
And says, [a]"I was only joking!"

20 Where *there is* no wood, the fire
goes out;

---

18 [a]Ps. 57:4; Prov. 12:18
20 [a]Dan. 6:18
21 [a]Ex. 23:4, 5; 2 Kin. 6:22; 2 Chr. 28:15; Matt. 5:44; Rom. 12:20
22 [a]2 Sam. 16:12; [Matt. 6:4, 6]
23 [a]Ps. 101:5
24 [a]Prov. 19:13
25 [a]Prov. 15:30
26 [1]*ruined*
27 [a]Prov. 27:2; [Luke 14:11]
28 [a]Prov. 16:32

CHAPTER 26

1 [a]1 Sam. 12:17
2 [a]Num. 23:8; Deut. 23:5; 2 Sam. 16:12
3 [a]Ps. 32:9; Prov. 19:29
5 [a]Matt. 16:1–4; Rom. 12:16
10 [1]Heb. difficult in v. 10; ancient and modern translators differ greatly
11 [a]2 Pet. 2:22 [b]Ex. 8:15
12 [a]Prov. 29:20; Luke 18:11, 12; [Rev. 3:17]
13 [1]Or *plazas, squares*
15 [a]Prov. 19:24 [1]LXX, Syr. *bosom;* Tg., Vg. *armpit*
19 [a]Eph. 5:4

And where *there is* no
[1]talebearer, strife ceases.
21 [a]As charcoal *is* to burning coals,
and wood to fire,
So *is* a contentious man to kindle
strife.
22 The words of a [1]talebearer *are*
like [2]tasty trifles,
And they go down into the
[3]inmost body.

23 Fervent lips with a wicked heart
Are like earthenware covered
with silver dross.

24 He who hates, disguises *it* with
his lips,
And lays up deceit within
himself;
25 [a]When [1]he speaks kindly, do not
believe him,
For *there are* seven abominations
in his heart;
26 *Though his* hatred is covered by
deceit,
His wickedness will be revealed
before the assembly.

27 [a]Whoever digs a pit will fall
into it,
And he who rolls a stone will
have it roll back on him.

28 A lying tongue hates *those who
are* crushed by it,
And a flattering mouth works
[a]ruin.

27 Do[a] not boast about tomorrow,
For you do not know what a
day may bring forth.

2 [a]Let another man praise you, and
not your own mouth;
A stranger, and not your own
lips.

3 A stone *is* heavy and sand *is*
weighty,
But a fool's wrath *is* heavier than
both of them.

4 Wrath *is* cruel and anger a
torrent,
But [a]who *is* able to stand before
jealousy?

5 [a]Open rebuke *is* better
Than love carefully concealed.

6 Faithful *are* the wounds of a
friend,
But the kisses of an enemy *are*
[a]deceitful.

20 [1]*gossip* or *slanderer*, lit. *whisperer*
21 [a]Prov. 15:18
22 [1]*gossip* or *slanderer* [2]A Jewish tradition *wounds* [3]Lit. *rooms of the belly*
25 [a]Ps. 28:3; Prov. 26:23; Jer. 9:8 [1]Lit. *his voice is gracious*
27 [a]Esth. 7:10; Ps. 7:15; Prov. 28:10; Eccl. 10:8
28 [a]Prov. 29:5

CHAPTER 27

1 [a]Luke 12:19–21; James 4:13–16
2 [a]Prov. 25:27; 2 Cor. 10:12, 18; 12:11
4 [a]Prov. 6:34; 1 John 3:12
5 [a][Prov. 28:23]; Gal. 2:14
6 [a]Matt. 26:49
7 [1]*tramples on*
9 [1]Lit. *counsel of the soul*
10 [a]Prov. 17:17; 18:24
11 [a]Prov. 10:1; 23:15–26
12 [a]Prov. 22:3
15 [a]Prov. 19:13
16 [1]Lit. *hides*
18 [a]2 Kin. 18:31; Song 8:12; Is. 36:16; [1 Cor. 3:8; 9:7–13]; 2 Tim. 2:6 [1]*protects* or *tends*
20 [a]Prov. 30:15, 16; Hab. 2:5 [1]Or *Sheol* [2]Heb. *Abaddon*

7 A satisfied soul [1]loathes the
honeycomb,
But to a hungry soul every bitter
thing *is* sweet.

8 Like a bird that wanders from its
nest
Is a man who wanders from his
place.

9 Ointment and perfume delight
the heart,
And the sweetness of a man's
friend *gives delight* by [1]hearty
counsel.

10 Do not forsake your own friend
or your father's friend,
Nor go to your brother's house in
the day of your calamity;
[a]Better *is* a neighbor nearby than
a brother far away.

11 My son, be wise, and make my
heart glad,
[a]That I may answer him who
reproaches me.

12 A prudent *man* foresees evil *and*
hides himself;
The simple pass on *and* are
[a]punished.

13 Take the garment of him who is
surety for a stranger,
And hold it in pledge *when* he is
surety for a seductress.

14 He who blesses his friend with a
loud voice, rising early in the
morning,
It will be counted a curse to him.

15 A [a]continual dripping on a very
rainy day
And a contentious woman are
alike;
16 Whoever [1]restrains her restrains
the wind,
And grasps oil with his right
hand.

17 *As* iron sharpens iron,
So a man sharpens the
countenance of his friend.

18 [a]Whoever [1]keeps the fig tree will
eat its fruit;
So he who waits on his master
will be honored.

19 As in water face *reflects* face,
So a man's heart *reveals* the man.

20 [a]Hell[1] and [2]Destruction are never
full;

So [b]the eyes of man are never
satisfied.

21 [a]The refining pot *is* for silver and
the furnace for gold,
And a man *is valued* by what
others say of him.

22 [a]Though you grind a fool in a
mortar with a pestle along with
crushed grain,
Yet his foolishness will not
depart from him.

23 Be diligent to know the state of
your [a]flocks,
And attend to your herds;
24 For riches *are* not forever,
Nor does a crown *endure* to all
generations.
25 [a]*When* the hay is removed, and
the tender grass shows itself,
And the herbs of the mountains
are gathered in,
26 The lambs *will provide* your
clothing,
And the goats the price of a field;
27 *You shall have* enough goats'
milk for your food,
For the food of your household,
And the nourishment of your
maidservants.

28 The [a]wicked flee when no one
pursues,
But the righteous are bold as a
lion.

2 Because of the transgression of
a land, many *are* its princes;
But by a man of understanding
and knowledge
Right will be prolonged.

3 [a]A poor man who oppresses the
poor
Is like a driving rain [1]which
leaves no food.

4 [a]Those who forsake the law praise
the wicked,
[b]But such as keep the law contend
with them.

5 [a]Evil men do not understand
justice,
But [b]those who seek the LORD
understand all.

6 Better *is* the poor who walks in
his integrity
Than one perverse *in his* ways,
though he *be* rich.

7 Whoever keeps the law *is* a
discerning son,
But a companion of gluttons
shames his father.

8 One who increases his
possessions by usury and
extortion
Gathers it for him who will pity
the poor.

9 One who turns away his ear from
hearing the law,
[a]Even his prayer *is* an
abomination.

10 [a]Whoever causes the upright to go
astray in an evil way,
He himself will fall into his own
pit;
[b]But the blameless will inherit
good.

11 The rich man *is* wise in his own
eyes,
But the poor who has
understanding searches him
out.

12 When the righteous rejoice, *there*
is great [a]glory;
But when the wicked arise, men
[1]hide themselves.

13 [a]He who covers his sins will not
prosper,
But whoever confesses and
forsakes *them* will have mercy.

14 Happy *is* the man who is always
reverent,
But he who hardens his heart will
fall into calamity.

15 [a]*Like* a roaring lion and a
charging bear
[b]*Is* a wicked ruler over poor
people.

16 A ruler who lacks understanding
is a great [a]oppressor,
But he who hates covetousness
will prolong *his* days.

17 [a]A man burdened with bloodshed
will flee into a pit;
Let no one help him.

18 Whoever walks blamelessly will
be [1]saved,
But *he who is* perverse *in his*
ways will suddenly fall.

19 [a]He who tills his land will have
plenty of bread,
But he who follows frivolity will
have poverty enough!

20 [b]Eccl. 1:8; 4:8
21 [a]Prov. 17:3
22 [a]Prov. 23:35; 26:11; Jer. 5:3
23 [a]Prov. 24:27
25 [a]Ps. 104:14

CHAPTER 28

1 [a]Lev. 26:17, 36; Ps. 53:5
3 [a]Matt. 18:28 [1]Lit. *and there is no bread*
4 [a]Ps. 49:18; Rom. 1:32 [b]1 Kin. 18:18; Neh. 13:11, 15; Matt. 3:7; 14:4; Eph. 5:11
5 [a]Ps. 92:6; Is. 6:9; 44:18 [b]Ps. 119:100; Prov. 2:9; John 17:17; 1 Cor. 2:15; [1 John 2:20, 27]
9 [a]Ps. 66:18; 109:7; Prov. 15:8
10 [a]Ps. 7:15; Prov. 26:27 [b][Matt. 6:33; Heb. 6:12; 1 Pet. 3:9]
12 [a]Prov. 11:10; 29:2 [1]Lit. *will be searched for*
13 [a]Ps. 32:3–5; 1 John 1:8–10
15 [a]Prov. 19:12; 1 Pet. 5:8 [b]Ex. 1:14; Prov. 29:2; Matt. 2:16
16 [a]Eccl. 10:16; Is. 3:12
17 [a]Gen. 9:6
18 [1]*delivered*
19 [a]Prov. 12:11; 20:13

20 A faithful man will abound with
blessings,
[a]But he who hastens to be rich will
not go unpunished.

21 [a]To [1]show partiality *is* not good,
[b]Because for a piece of bread a
man will transgress.

22 A man with an evil eye hastens
after riches,
And does not consider that
[a]poverty will come upon him.

23 [a]He who rebukes a man will find
more favor afterward
Than he who flatters with the
tongue.

24 Whoever robs his father or his
mother,
And says, "*It is* no
transgression,"
The same [a]*is* companion to a
destroyer.

25 [a]He who is of a proud heart stirs
up strife,
[b]But he who trusts in the LORD will
be prospered.

26 He who [a]trusts in his own heart
is a fool,
But whoever walks wisely will be
delivered.

27 [a]He who gives to the poor will not
lack,
But he who hides his eyes will
have many curses.

28 When the wicked arise, [a]men
hide themselves;
But when they perish, the
righteous increase.

29 He[a] who is often rebuked, *and*
hardens *his* neck,
Will suddenly be destroyed, and
that without remedy.

2 When the righteous [1]are in
authority, the [a]people rejoice;
But when a wicked *man* rules,
[b]the people groan.

3 Whoever loves wisdom makes
his father rejoice,
But a companion of harlots
wastes *his* wealth.

4 The king establishes the land by
justice,
But he who receives bribes
overthrows it.

20 [a]Prov. 13:11; 20:21; 23:4; 1 Tim. 6:9
21 [a]Prov. 18:5 [b]Ezek. 13:19 [1]Lit. *recognize faces*
22 [a]Prov. 21:5
23 [a]Prov. 27:5, 6
24 [a]Prov. 18:9
25 [a]Prov. 13:10 [b]Prov. 29:25; 1 Tim. 6:6
26 [a]Prov. 3:5
27 [a]Deut. 15:7; Prov. 19:17; 22:9
28 [a]Job 24:4

CHAPTER 29

1 [a]2 Chr. 36:16; Prov. 6:15
2 [a]Esth. 8:15; Prov. 28:12 [b]Esth. 4:3 [1]*become great*
5 [a]Prov. 26:28
7 [a]Job 29:16; Ps. 41:1; Prov. 31:8, 9
8 [a]Prov. 11:11
9 [a]Matt. 11:17
10 [a]Gen. 4:5–8; 1 John 3:12 [1]Lit. *soul* or *life*
11 [a]Prov. 14:33 [1]Lit. *spirit*
13 [a][Matt. 5:45]
14 [a]Ps. 72:4; Is. 11:4
15 [a]Prov. 22:15
16 [a]Ps. 37:34; Prov. 21:12
18 [a]1 Sam. 3:1; Ps. 74:9; Amos 8:11, 12 [b]Prov. 8:32; John 13:17 [1]*prophetic vision*

5 A man who [a]flatters his neighbor
Spreads a net for his feet.

6 By transgression an evil man is
snared,
But the righteous sings and
rejoices.

7 The righteous [a]considers the
cause of the poor,
But the wicked does not
understand *such* knowledge.

8 Scoffers [a]set a city aflame,
But wise *men* turn away wrath.

9 *If* a wise man contends with a
foolish man,
[a]Whether *the fool* rages or laughs,
there is no peace.

10 [a]The bloodthirsty hate the
blameless,
But the upright seek his [1]well-
being.

11 A fool vents all his [a]feelings,[1]
But a wise *man* holds them back.

12 If a ruler pays attention to lies,
All his servants *become* wicked.

13 The poor *man* and the oppressor
have this in common:
[a]The LORD gives light to the eyes
of both.

14 The king who judges the [a]poor
with truth,
His throne will be established
forever.

15 The rod and rebuke give
[a]wisdom,
But a child left *to himself* brings
shame to his mother.

16 When the wicked are multiplied,
transgression increases;
But the righteous will see their
[a]fall.

17 Correct your son, and he will give
you rest;
Yes, he will give delight to your
soul.

18 [a]Where *there is* no [1]revelation, the
people cast off restraint;
But [b]happy *is* he who keeps the
law.

19 A servant will not be corrected
by mere words;
For though he understands, he
will not respond.

20 Do you see a man hasty in his
words?
[a]*There is* more hope for a fool than
for him.

21 He who pampers his servant from
childhood
Will have him as a son in the end.

22 [a]An angry man stirs up strife,
And a furious man abounds in
transgression.

23 [a]A man's pride will bring him low,
But the humble in spirit will
retain honor.

24 Whoever is a partner with a thief
hates his own life;
[a]He [1]swears to tell the truth, but
reveals nothing.

25 [a]The fear of man brings a snare,
But whoever trusts in the LORD
shall be [1]safe.

26 [a]Many seek the ruler's [1]favor,
But justice for man *comes* from
the LORD.

27 An unjust man *is* an abomination
to the righteous,
And *he who is* upright in the way
is an abomination to the
wicked.

The Wisdom of Agur

30 The words of Agur the son
of Jakeh, *his* utterance. This
man declared to Ithiel—to Ithiel
and Ucal:

2 [a]Surely I *am* more stupid than
any man,
And do not have the
understanding of a man.
3 I neither learned wisdom
Nor have [a]knowledge of the Holy
One.

4 [a]Who has ascended into heaven,
or descended?
[b]Who has gathered the wind in His
fists?
Who has bound the waters in a
garment?
Who has established all the ends
of the earth?
What *is* His name, and what *is*
His Son's name,
If you know?

5 [a]Every word of God *is* [1]pure;
[b]He *is* a shield to those who put
their trust in Him.
6 [a]Do not add to His words,
Lest He rebuke you, and you be
found a liar.

7 Two *things* I request of You
(Deprive me not before I die):
8 Remove falsehood and lies far
from me;
Give me neither poverty nor
riches—
[a]Feed me with the food allotted to
me;
9 [a]Lest I be full and deny *You*,
And say, "Who *is* the LORD?"
Or lest I be poor and steal,
And profane the name of my God.

10 Do not malign a servant to his
master,
Lest he curse you, and you be
found guilty.

11 *There is* a generation *that* curses
its [a]father,
And does not bless its mother.
12 *There is* a generation [a]*that is*
pure in its own eyes,
Yet is not washed from its
filthiness.
13 *There is* a generation—oh, how
[a]lofty are their eyes!
And their eyelids are [1]lifted up.
14 [a]*There is* a generation whose teeth
are like swords,
And whose fangs *are like* knives,
[b]To devour the poor from off the
earth,
And the needy from *among* men.

15 The leech has two daughters—
Give *and* Give!

There are three *things that* are
never satisfied,
Four never say, "Enough!":
16 [a]The[1] grave,
The barren womb,
The earth *that* is not satisfied
with water—
And the fire never says,
"Enough!"

17 [a]The eye *that* mocks *his* father,
And scorns obedience to *his*
mother,
The ravens of the valley will pick
it out,
And the young eagles will eat it.

18 There are three *things which* are
too wonderful for me,
Yes, four *which* I do not
understand:
19 The way of an eagle in the air,
The way of a serpent on a rock,

20 [a]Prov. 26:12
22 [a]Prov. 26:21
23 [a]Job 22:29; Prov. 15:33; 18:12; Is. 66:2; Dan. 4:30; Matt. 23:12; Luke 14:11; 18:14; Acts 12:23; [James 4:6–10; 1 Pet. 5:5, 6]
24 [a]Lev. 5:1 [1]Lit. *hears the adjuration* or *oath*
25 [a]Gen. 12:12; 20:2; Luke 12:4; John 12:42, 43 [1]*secure*, lit. *set on high*
26 [a]Ps. 20:9 [1]Lit. *face*

CHAPTER 30

2 [a]Ps. 73:22; Prov. 12:1
3 [a][Prov. 9:10]
4 [a][Ps. 68:18; John 3:13] [b]Job 38:4; Ps. 104:3; Is. 40:12
5 [a]Ps. 12:6; 19:8; 119:140 [b]Ps. 18:30; 84:11; 115:9–11 [1]*tested, refined, found pure*
6 [a]Deut. 4:2; 12:32; Rev. 22:18
8 [a]Job 23:12; Matt. 6:11; [Phil. 4:19]
9 [a]Deut. 8:12–14; Neh. 9:25, 26; Hos. 13:6
11 [a]Ex. 21:17; Prov. 20:20
12 [a][Prov. 16:2]; Is. 65:5; Luke 18:11; [Titus 1:15, 16]
13 [a]Ps. 131:1; Prov. 6:17; Is. 2:11; 5:15 [1]In arrogance
14 [a]Job 29:17; Ps. 52:2 [b]Ps. 14:4; Amos 8:4
16 [a]Prov. 27:20; Hab. 2:5 [1]Or *Sheol*
17 [a]Gen. 9:22; Lev. 20:9; Prov. 20:20

The way of a ship in the [1]midst
of the sea,
And the way of a man with a
virgin.

20 This *is* the way of an adulterous
woman:
She eats and wipes her mouth,
And says, "I have done no
wickedness."

21 For three *things* the earth is
perturbed,
Yes, for four it cannot bear up:
22 [a]For a servant when he reigns,
A fool when he is filled with food,
23 A [1]hateful *woman* when she is
married,
And a maidservant who succeeds
her mistress.

24 There are four *things which* are
little on the earth,
But they *are* exceedingly wise:
25 [a]The ants *are* a people not strong,
Yet they prepare their food in the
summer;
26 [a]The [1]rock badgers are a feeble
folk,
Yet they make their homes in the
crags;
27 The locusts have no king,
Yet they all advance in ranks;
28 The [1]spider skillfully grasps with
its hands,
And it is in kings' palaces.

29 There are three *things which* are
majestic in pace,
Yes, four *which* are stately in
walk:
30 A lion, *which is* mighty among
beasts
And does not turn away from
any;
31 A [1]greyhound,
A male goat also,
And [2]a king *whose* troops *are*
with him.

32 If you have been foolish in
exalting yourself,
Or if you have devised evil, [a]*put
your* hand on *your* mouth.
33 For *as* the churning of milk
produces butter,
And wringing the nose produces
blood,
So the forcing of wrath produces
strife.

The Words of King Lemuel's Mother

31 The words of King Lemuel,
the utterance which his
mother taught him:

2 What, my son?
And what, son of my womb?
And what, [a]son of my vows?
3 [a]Do not give your strength to
women,
Nor your ways [b]to that which
destroys kings.

4 [a]*It is* not for kings, O Lemuel,
It is not for kings to drink wine,
Nor for princes intoxicating
drink;
5 [a]Lest they drink and forget the
law,
And pervert the justice of all [1]the
afflicted.
6 [a]Give strong drink to him who is
perishing,
And wine to those who are bitter
of heart.
7 Let him drink and forget his
poverty,
And remember his misery no
more.

8 [a]Open your mouth for the
speechless,
In the cause of all *who are*
[1]appointed to die.
9 Open your mouth, [a]judge
righteously,
And [b]plead the cause of the poor
and needy.

The Virtuous Wife

10 [a]Who[1] can find a [2]virtuous wife?
For her worth *is* far above rubies.
11 The heart of her husband safely
trusts her;
So he will have no lack of gain.
12 She does him good and not evil
All the days of her life.
13 She seeks wool and flax,
And willingly works with her
hands.
14 She is like the merchant ships,
She brings her food from afar.
15 [a]She also rises while it is yet
night,
And [b]provides food for her
household,
And a portion for her
maidservants.
16 She considers a field and buys it;
From [1]her profits she plants a
vineyard.
17 She girds herself with strength,
And strengthens her arms.
18 She perceives that her
merchandise *is* good,
And her lamp does not go out by
night.
19 She stretches out her hands to the
distaff,
And her hand holds the spindle.

19 [1]Lit. *heart*
22 [a]Prov. 19:10; Eccl. 10:7
23 [1]Or *hated*
25 [a]Prov. 6:6
26 [a]Lev. 11:5; Ps. 104:18 [1]*rock hyraxes*
28 [1]Or *lizard*
31 [1]Or perhaps *strutting rooster*, lit. *girded of waist* [2]A Jewish tradition *a king against whom there is no uprising*
32 [a]Job 21:5; 40:4; Mic. 7:16

CHAPTER 31
2 [a]Is. 49:15
3 [a]Prov. 5:9 [b]Deut. 17:17; 1 Kin. 11:1; Neh. 13:26; Prov. 7:26; Hos. 4:11
4 [a]Eccl. 10:17
5 [a]Hos. 4:11 [1]Lit. *sons of affliction*
6 [a]Ps. 104:15
8 [a]Job 29:15, 16; Ps. 82 [1]Lit. *sons of passing away*
9 [a]Lev. 19:15; Deut. 1:16 [b]Job 29:12; Is. 1:17; Jer. 22:16
10 [a]Ruth 3:11; Prov. 12:4; 19:14 [1]Vv. 10–31 are an alphabetic acrostic in Hebrew; cf. Ps. 119 [2]Lit. *a wife of valor*, in the sense of all forms of excellence
15 [a]Prov. 20:13; Rom. 12:11 [b]Luke 12:42
16 [1]Lit. *the fruit of her hands*

20 [a]She extends her hand to the poor,
Yes, she reaches out her hands
to the needy.
21 She is not afraid of snow for her
household,
For all her household *is* clothed
with scarlet.
22 She makes tapestry for herself;
Her clothing *is* fine linen and
purple.
23 [a]Her husband is known in the
gates,
When he sits among the elders of
the land.
24 She makes linen garments and
sells *them*,
And supplies sashes for the
merchants.
25 Strength and honor *are* her
clothing;
She shall rejoice in time to come.

20 [a]Deut. 15:11; Job 31:16–20; Prov. 22:9; Rom. 12:13; Eph. 4:28; Heb. 13:16

23 [a]Prov. 12:4

26 She opens her mouth with
wisdom,
And on her tongue *is* the law of
kindness.
27 She watches over the ways of her
household,
And does not eat the bread of
idleness.
28 Her children rise up and call her
blessed;
Her husband *also*, and he praises
her:
29 "Many daughters have done well,
But you excel them all."
30 Charm *is* deceitful and beauty *is*
passing,
But a woman *who* fears the LORD,
she shall be praised.
31 Give her of the fruit of her hands,
And let her own works praise her
in the gates.

The Book of

Ecclesiastes

THE key word in Ecclesiastes is *vanity,* "the futile emptiness of trying to be happy apart from God." The Preacher (traditionally taken to be Solomon—1:1, 12—the wisest, richest, most influential king in Israel's history) looks at life "under the sun" (1:9) and, from the human perspective, declares it all to be empty. Power, popularity, prestige, pleasure—nothing can fill the God-shaped void in man's life but God Himself! But once seen from God's perspective, life takes on meaning and purpose, causing Solomon to exclaim, "Eat . . . drink . . . rejoice . . . do good . . . live joyfully . . . fear God . . . keep His commandments!" Skepticism and despair melt away when life is viewed as a daily gift from God.

The Hebrew title *Qoheleth* is a rare term, found only in Ecclesiastes (1:1, 2, 12; 7:27; 12:8–10). It comes from the word *qahal,* "to convoke an assembly, to assemble." Thus, it means "One Who Addresses an Assembly," "A Preacher." The Septuagint used the Greek word *Ekklesiastes* as its title for this book. Derived from the word *ekklesia,* "assembly," "congregation," "church," it simply means "Preacher." The Latin *Ecclesiastes* means "Speaker Before an Assembly."

CHAPTER 1

The Vanity of Life

THE words of the Preacher, the son of David, [a]king in Jerusalem.

2 "Vanity[a1] of vanities," says the
Preacher;
"Vanity of vanities, [b]all *is* vanity."

3 [a]What profit has a man from all
his labor
In which he [1]toils under the sun?
4 *One* generation passes away, and
another generation comes;
[a]But the earth abides forever.
5 [a]The sun also rises, and the sun
goes down,
And [1]hastens to the place where
it arose.
6 [a]The wind goes toward the south,
And turns around to the north;
The wind whirls about
continually,
And comes again on its circuit.
7 [a]All the rivers run into the sea,
Yet the sea *is* not full;
To the place from which the
rivers come,
There they return again.
8 All things *are* [1]full of labor;
Man cannot express *it.*
[a]The eye is not satisfied with
seeing,
Nor the ear filled with hearing.

9 [a]That which has been *is* what
will be,
That which *is* done is what will
be done,
And *there is* nothing new under
the sun.
10 Is there anything of which it may
be said,
"See, this *is* new"?
It has already been in ancient
times before us.
11 *There is* [a]no remembrance of
former *things,*
Nor will there be any
remembrance of *things* that are
to come
By *those* who will come after.

The Grief of Wisdom

12 I, the Preacher, was king over Israel in Jerusalem.
13 And I set my heart to seek and [a]search out by wisdom concerning all that is done under heaven; [b]this burdensome task God has given to the sons of man, by which they may be [1]exercised.
14 I have seen all the works that are done under the sun; and indeed, all *is* vanity and grasping for the wind.

1 [a]Prov. 1:1
2 [a]Ps. 39:5, 6; 62:9; 144:4; Eccl. 12:8 [b][Rom. 8:20, 21] [1]Or *Absurdity, Frustration, Futility, Nonsense;* and so throughout the book
3 [a]Eccl. 2:22; 3:9 [1]*labors*
4 [a]Ps. 104:5; 119:90
5 [a]Ps. 19:4–6 [1]Is eager for, lit. *panting*
6 [a]Eccl. 11:5; John 3:8
7 [a][Ps. 104:8, 9; Jer. 5:22]
8 [a]Prov. 27:20; Eccl. 4:8 [1]*wearisome*
9 [a]Eccl. 3:15
11 [a]Eccl. 2:16
13 [a][Eccl. 7:25; 8:16, 17] [b]Gen. 3:19; Eccl. 3:10 [1]Or *afflicted*

15 [a]*What is* crooked cannot be made
straight,
And what is lacking cannot be
numbered.

16 I communed with my heart,
saying, "Look, I have attained
greatness, and have gained [a]more
wisdom than all who were before
me in Jerusalem. My heart has
[1]understood great wisdom and
knowledge."
17 [a]And I set my heart to know
wisdom and to know madness and
folly. I perceived that this also is
grasping for the wind.

18 For [a]in much wisdom *is* much
grief,
And he who increases knowledge
increases sorrow.

The Vanity of Pleasure

2 I said [a]in my heart, "Come
now, I will test you with
[b]mirth; [1]therefore enjoy pleasure";
but surely, [c]this also *was* vanity.
2 I said of laughter—"Mad-
ness!"; and of mirth, "What does
it accomplish?"
3 [a]I searched in my heart *how* [1]to
gratify my flesh with wine, while
guiding my heart with wisdom,
and how to lay hold on folly, till I
might see what *was* [b]good for the
sons of men to do under heaven
all the days of their lives.
4 I made my works great, I built
myself [a]houses, and planted my-
self vineyards.
5 I made myself gardens and or-
chards, and I planted all *kinds* of
fruit trees in them.
6 I made myself water pools from
which to [1]water the growing trees
of the grove.
7 I acquired male and female ser-
vants, and had [1]servants born in
my house. Yes, I had greater pos-
sessions of herds and flocks than
all who were in Jerusalem before
me.
8 [a]I also gathered for myself sil-
ver and gold and the special trea-
sures of kings and of the prov-
inces. I acquired male and female
singers, the delights of the sons of
men, *and* [1]musical instruments of
all kinds.
9 [a]So I became great and [1]ex-
celled [b]more than all who were be-
fore me in Jerusalem. Also my wis-
dom remained with me.

10 Whatever my eyes desired I did
not keep from them.
I did not withhold my heart from
any pleasure,
For my heart rejoiced in all my
labor;
And [a]this was my [1]reward from
all my labor.
11 Then I looked on all the works
that my hands had done
And on the labor in which I had
toiled;
And indeed all *was* [a]vanity and
grasping for the wind.
There was no profit under the
sun.

The End of the Wise and the Fool

12 Then I turned myself to consider
wisdom [a]and madness and
folly;
For what *can* the man *do* who
succeeds the king?—
Only what he has already
[b]done.
13 Then I saw that wisdom [a]excels
folly
As light excels darkness.
14 [a]The wise man's eyes *are* in his
head,
But the fool walks in darkness.
Yet I myself perceived
That [b]the same event happens to
them all.

15 So I said in my heart,
"As it happens to the fool,
It also happens to me,
And why was I then more wise?"
Then I said in my heart,
"This also *is* vanity."
16 For *there is* [a]no more
remembrance of the wise than
of the fool forever,
Since all that now *is* will be
forgotten in the days to come.
And how does a wise *man* die?
As the fool!

17 Therefore I hated life because
the work that was done under the
sun *was* distressing to me, for all
is vanity and grasping for the
wind.
18 Then I hated all my labor in
which I had toiled under the sun,
because [a]I must leave it to the man
who will come after me.
19 And who knows whether he
will be wise or a fool? Yet he will
rule over all my labor in which I

---

15 [a]Eccl. 7:13
16 [a]1 Kin. 3:12, 13; Eccl. 2:9 [1]Lit. *seen*
17 [a]Eccl. 2:3, 12; 7:23, 25; [1 Thess. 5:21]
18 [a]Eccl. 12:12

CHAPTER 2

1 [a]Luke 12:19 [b]Prov. 14:13; [Eccl. 7:4; 8:15] [c]Eccl. 1:2 [1]*gladness*
3 [a]Eccl. 1:17 [b][Eccl. 3:12, 13; 5:18; 6:12] [1]Lit. *to draw my flesh*
4 [a]1 Kin. 7:1–12
6 [1]*Irrigate*
7 [1]Lit. *sons of my house*
8 [a]1 Kin. 9:28; 10:10, 14, 21 [1]Exact meaning unknown
9 [a]Eccl. 1:16 [b]2 Chr. 9:22 [1]Lit. *increased*
10 [a]Eccl. 3:22; 5:18; 9:9 [1]Lit. *portion*
11 [a]Eccl. 1:3, 14
12 [a]Eccl. 1:17; 7:25 [b]Eccl. 1:9
13 [a]Eccl. 7:11, 14, 19; 9:18; 10:10
14 [a]Prov. 17:24; Eccl. 8:1 [b]Ps. 49:10; Eccl. 9:2, 3, 11
16 [a]Eccl. 1:11; 4:16
18 [a]Ps. 49:10

toiled and in which I have shown
myself wise under the sun. This
also *is* vanity.
20 Therefore I turned my heart
and despaired of all the labor in
which I had toiled under the sun.
21 For there is a man whose labor
is with wisdom, knowledge, and
skill; yet he must leave his [1]heri-
tage to a man who has not labored
for it. This also *is* vanity and a
great evil.
22 [a]For what has man for all his
labor, and for the striving of his
heart with which he has toiled un-
der the sun?
23 For all his days *are* [a]sorrowful,
and his work burdensome; even in
the night his heart takes no rest.
This also is vanity.
24 [a]Nothing *is* better for a man
than that he should eat and drink,
and *that* his soul should enjoy
good in his labor. This also, I saw,
was from the hand of God.
25 For who can eat, or who can
have enjoyment, [1]more than I?
26 For *God* gives [a]wisdom and
knowledge and joy to a man who
is good in His sight; but to the sin-
ner He gives the work of gathering
and collecting, that [b]he may give
to *him who is* good before God.
This also *is* vanity and grasping
for the wind.

Everything Has Its Time

3 To everything *there is* a season,
A [a]time for every purpose under
heaven:

2 A time [1]to be born,
And [a]a time to die;
A time to plant,
And a time to pluck *what is*
planted;
3 A time to kill,
And a time to heal;
A time to break down,
And a time to build up;
4 A time to [a]weep,
And a time to laugh;
A time to mourn,
And a time to dance;
5 A time to cast away stones,
And a time to gather stones;
[a]A time to embrace,
And a time to refrain from
embracing;
6 A time to gain,
And a time to lose;
A time to keep,
And a time to throw away;
7 A time to tear,
And a time to sew;
[a]A time to keep silence,
And a time to [b]speak;
8 A time to love,
And a time to [a]hate;
A time of war,
And a time of peace.

The God-Given Task

9 [a]What profit has the worker
from that in which he labors?
10 [a]I have seen the God-given task
with which the sons of men are to
be occupied.
11 He has made everything beau-
tiful in its time. Also He has put
eternity in their hearts, except that
[a]no one can find out the work that
God does from beginning to end.
12 I know that nothing *is* [a]better
for them than to rejoice, and to do
good in their lives,
13 and also that [a]every man
should eat and drink and enjoy the
good of all his labor—it *is* the gift
of God.

14 I know that whatever God does,
It shall be forever.
[a]Nothing can be added to it,
And nothing taken from it.
God does *it*, that men should fear
before Him.
15 [a]That which is has already been,
And what is to be has already
been;
And God [1]requires an account of
[2]what is past.

Injustice Seems to Prevail

16 Moreover [a]I saw under the sun:

In the place of [1]judgment,
Wickedness *was* there;
And *in* the place of righteousness,
[2]Iniquity *was* there.

17 I said in my heart,

[a]"God shall judge the righteous and
the wicked,
For *there is* a time there for every
[1]purpose and for every work."

18 I said in my heart, "Concerning
the condition of the sons of men,
God tests them, that they may see
that they themselves are *like* ani-
mals."
19 [a]For what happens to the sons
of men also happens to animals;
one thing befalls them: as one dies,

21 [1]Lit. *portion*
22 [a]Eccl. 1:3; 3:9
23 [a]Job 5:7; 14:1
24 [a]Eccl. 3:12, 13, 22; Is. 56:12; Luke 12:19; 1 Cor. 15:32; [1 Tim. 6:17]
25 [1]So with MT, Tg., Vg.; some Heb. mss., LXX, Syr. *without Him*
26 [a]Job 32:8; Prov. 2:6; James 1:5 [b]Job 27:16, 17; Prov. 28:8

CHAPTER 3

1 [a]Eccl. 3:17; 8:6
2 [a]Job 14:5; Heb. 9:27 [1]Lit. *to bear*
4 [a]Rom. 12:15
5 [a]Joel 2:16; 1 Cor. 7:5
7 [a]Amos 5:13 [b]Prov. 25:11
8 [a]Prov. 13:5; Luke 14:26
9 [a]Eccl. 1:3
10 [a]Eccl. 1:13
11 [a]Job 5:9; Eccl. 7:23; 8:17; Rom. 11:33
12 [a]Eccl. 2:3, 24
13 [a]Eccl. 2:24
14 [a]James 1:17
15 [a]Eccl. 1:9 [1]Lit. *seeks* [2]*what is pursued*
16 [a]Eccl. 5:8 [1]*justice* [2]*Wickedness*
17 [a]Gen. 18:25; Ps. 96:13; Eccl. 11:9; [Matt. 16:27; Rom. 2:6–10; 2 Cor. 5:10; 2 Thess. 1:6–9] [1]*desire*
19 [a]Ps. 49:12, 20; 73:22; [Eccl. 2:16]

so dies the other. Surely, they all
have one breath; man has no ad-
vantage over animals, for all *is*
vanity.
20 All go to one place: [a]all are
from the dust, and all return to
dust.
21 [a]Who[1] knows the spirit of the
sons of men, which goes upward,
and the spirit of the animal, which
goes down to the earth?
22 [a]So I perceived that nothing *is*
better than that a man should re-
joice in his own works, for [b]that
is his [1]heritage. [c]For who can bring
him to see what will happen after
him?

4 Then I returned and consid-
ered all the [a]oppression that is
done under the sun:

And look! The tears of the
oppressed,
But they have no comforter—
[1]On the side of their oppressors
there is power,
But they have no comforter.
2 [a]Therefore I praised the dead who
were already dead,
More than the living who are still
alive.
3 [a]Yet, better than both *is he* who
has never existed,
Who has not seen the evil work
that is done under the sun.

The Vanity of Selfish Toil

4 Again, I saw that for all toil and
every skillful work a man is envied
by his neighbor. This also *is* vanity
and grasping for the wind.

5 [a]The fool folds his hands
And consumes his own flesh.
6 [a]Better a handful *with* quietness
Than both hands full, *together
with* toil and grasping for the
wind.

7 Then I returned, and I saw van-
ity under the sun:

8 There is one alone, without
[1]companion:
He has neither son nor brother.
Yet *there is* no end to all his
labors,
Nor is his [a]eye satisfied with
riches.
But [b]*he never asks,*
"For whom do I toil and deprive
myself of [c]good?"
This also *is* vanity and a [2]grave
misfortune.

The Value of a Friend

9 Two *are* better than one,
Because they have a good reward
for their labor.
10 For if they fall, one will lift up his
companion.
But woe to him *who is* alone
when he falls,
For *he has* no one to help him
up.
11 Again, if two lie down together,
they will keep warm;
But how can one be warm *alone?*
12 Though one may be overpowered
by another, two can withstand
him.
And a threefold cord is not
quickly broken.

Popularity Passes Away

13 Better a poor and wise youth
Than an old and foolish king who
will be admonished no more.
14 For he comes out of prison to be
king,
Although [1]he was born poor in
his kingdom.
15 I saw all the living who walk
under the sun;
They were with the second youth
who stands in his place.
16 *There was* no end of all the
people [1]over whom he was
made king;
Yet those who come afterward
will not rejoice in him.
Surely this also *is* vanity and
grasping for the wind.

Fear God, Keep Your Vows

5 Walk [a]prudently when you go
to the house of God; and draw
near to hear rather [b]than to give
the sacrifice of fools, for they do
not know that they do evil.

2 Do not be [a]rash with your mouth,
And let not your heart utter
anything hastily before God.
For God *is* in heaven, and you on
earth;
Therefore let your words [b]be
few.
3 For a dream comes through much
activity,
And [a]a fool's voice *is known* by
his many words.

4 [a]When you make a vow to God,
do not delay to [b]pay it;
For *He has* no pleasure in fools.
Pay what you have vowed—

20 [a]Gen. 3:19; Ps. 103:14

21 [a]Eccl. 12:7 [1]LXX, Syr., Tg., Vg. *Who knows whether the spirit . . . goes upward, and whether . . . goes downward to the earth?*

22 [a]Eccl. 2:24; 5:18 [b]Eccl. 2:10 [c]Eccl. 6:12; 8:7 [1]*portion* or *lot*

CHAPTER 4

1 [a]Job 35:9; Ps. 12:5; Eccl. 3:16; 5:8; Is. 5:7 [1]Lit. *At the hand*

2 [a]Job 3:17, 18

3 [a]Job 3:11–22; Eccl. 6:3; Luke 23:29

5 [a]Prov. 6:10; 24:33

6 [a]Prov. 15:16, 17; 16:8

8 [a]Prov. 27:20; Eccl. 5:10; [1 John 2:16] [b]Ps. 39:6 [c]Eccl. 2:18–21 [1]Lit. *a second* [2]Lit. *evil task*

14 [1]The youth

16 [1]Lit. *to all before whom he was to be*

CHAPTER 5

1 [a]Ex. 3:5; Is. 1:12 [b][1 Sam. 15:22]; Ps. 50:8; Prov. 15:8; 21:27; [Hos. 6:6]

2 [a]Prov. 20:25 [b]Prov. 10:19; Matt. 6:7

3 [a]Prov. 10:19

4 [a]Num. 30:2; Deut. 23:21–23; Ps. 50:14; 76:11 [b]Ps. 66:13, 14

5 [a]Better not to vow than to vow and not pay.

6 Do not let your [a]mouth cause your flesh to sin, [b]nor say before the messenger *of God* that it *was* an error. Why should God be angry at your [1]excuse and destroy the work of your hands?
7 For in the multitude of dreams and many words *there is* also vanity. But [a]fear God.

The Vanity of Gain and Honor

8 If you [a]see the oppression of the poor, and the violent [1]perversion of justice and righteousness in a province, do not marvel at the matter; for [b]high official watches over high official, and higher officials are over them.
9 Moreover the profit of the land is for all; *even* the king is served from the field.

10 He who loves silver will not be satisfied with silver;
Nor he who loves abundance, with increase.
This also *is* vanity.

11 When goods increase,
They increase who eat them;
So what profit have the owners
Except to see *them* with their eyes?

12 The sleep of a laboring man *is* sweet,
Whether he eats little or much;
But the abundance of the rich will not permit him to sleep.

13 [a]There is a severe evil *which* I have seen under the sun:
Riches kept for their owner to his hurt.
14 But those riches perish through [1]misfortune;
When he begets a son, *there is* nothing in his hand.
15 [a]As he came from his mother's womb, naked shall he return,
To go as he came;
And he shall take nothing from his labor
Which he may carry away in his hand.

16 And this also *is* a severe evil—
Just exactly as he came, so shall he go.
And [a]what profit has he [b]who has labored for the wind?
17 All his days [a]he also eats in darkness,
And *he has* much sorrow and sickness and anger.

18 Here is what I have seen: [a]*It is* good and fitting *for one* to eat and drink, and to enjoy the good of all his labor in which he toils under the sun all the days of his life which God gives him; [b]for it *is* his [1]heritage.
19 As for [a]every man to whom God has given riches and wealth, and given him power to eat of it, to receive his [1]heritage and rejoice in his labor—this *is* the [b]gift of God.
20 For he will not dwell unduly on the days of his life, because God keeps *him* busy with the joy of his heart.

6 There[a] is an evil which I have seen under the sun, and it *is* common among men:
2 A man to whom God has given riches and wealth and honor, [a]so that he lacks nothing for himself of all he desires; [b]yet God does not give him power to eat of it, but a foreigner consumes it. This *is* vanity, and it *is* an evil [1]affliction.
3 If a man begets a hundred *children* and lives many years, so that the days of his years are many, but his soul is not satisfied with goodness, or [a]indeed he has no burial, I say *that* [b]a [1]stillborn child *is* better than he—
4 for it comes in vanity and departs in darkness, and its name is covered with darkness.
5 Though it has not seen the sun or known *anything*, this has more rest than that man,
6 even if he lives a thousand years twice—but has not seen goodness. Do not all go to one [a]place?

7 [a]All the labor of man *is* for his mouth,
And yet the soul is not satisfied.
8 For what more has the wise *man* than the fool?
What does the poor man have,
Who knows *how* to walk before the living?
9 Better *is* [1]the [a]sight of the eyes than the wandering of [2]desire.

5 [a]Prov. 20:25; Acts 5:4
6 [a]Prov. 6:2 [b]1 Cor. 11:10 [1]Lit. *voice*
7 [a][Eccl. 12:13]
8 [a]Eccl. 3:16 [b][Ps. 12:5; 58:11; 82:1] [1]*wresting*
13 [a]Eccl. 6:1, 2
14 [1]Lit. *bad business*
15 [a]Job 1:21; Ps. 49:17; 1 Tim. 6:7
16 [a]Eccl. 1:3 [b]Prov. 11:29
17 [a]Ps. 127:2
18 [a]Eccl. 2:24; 3:12, 13; [1 Tim. 6:17] [b]Eccl. 2:10; 3:22 [1]Lit. *portion*
19 [a][Eccl. 6:2] [b]Eccl. 2:24; 3:13 [1]Lit. *portion*

CHAPTER 6

1 [a]Eccl. 5:13
2 [a]Job 21:10; Ps. 17:14; 73:7 [b]Luke 12:20 [1]*disease*
3 [a]2 Kin. 9:35; Is. 14:19, 20; Jer. 22:19 [b]Job 3:16; Ps. 58:8; Eccl. 4:3 [1]Or *miscarriage*
6 [a]Eccl. 2:14, 15
7 [a]Prov. 16:26
9 [a]Eccl. 11:9 [1]What the eyes see [2]Lit. *soul*

This also *is* vanity and grasping
for the wind.

10 Whatever one is, he has been
named [a]already,
For it is known that he *is* man;
[b]And he cannot contend with Him
who is mightier than he.
11 Since there are many things that
increase vanity,
How *is* man the better?

12 For who knows what *is* good
for man in life, [1]all the days of his
[2]vain life which he passes like [a]a
shadow? [b]Who can tell a man what
will happen after him under the
sun?

The Value of Practical Wisdom

7 A [a]good name *is* better than
precious ointment,
And the day of death than the day
of one's [b]birth;
2 Better to go to the house of
mourning
Than to go to the house of
feasting,
For that *is* the end of all men;
And the living will take *it* to
[a]heart.
3 [1]Sorrow *is* better than laughter,
[a]For by a sad countenance the
heart is made [2]better.
4 The heart of the wise *is* in the
house of mourning,
But the heart of fools *is* in the
house of mirth.

5 [a]*It is* better to [1]hear the rebuke of
the wise
Than for a man to hear the song
of fools.
6 [a]For like the [1]crackling of thorns
under a pot,
So *is* the laughter of the fool.
This also is vanity.
7 Surely oppression destroys a
wise *man's* reason,
[a]And a bribe [1]debases the heart.

8 The end of a thing *is* better than
its beginning;
[a]The patient in spirit *is* better than
the proud in spirit.
9 [a]Do not hasten in your spirit to be
angry,
For anger rests in the bosom of
fools.
10 Do not say,
"Why were the former days better
than these?"
For you do not inquire wisely
concerning this.

10 [a]Eccl. 1:9; 3:15 [b]Job 9:32; Is. 45:9; Jer. 49:19
12 [a]Ps. 102:11; James 4:14 [b]Ps. 39:6; Eccl. 3:22 [1]Lit. *the number of the days* [2]*futile*
CHAPTER 7
1 [a]Prov. 22:1 [b]Eccl. 4:2
2 [a][Ps. 90:12]
3 [a][2 Cor. 7:10] [1]*Vexation* or *Grief* [2]*well* or *pleasing*
5 [a]Ps. 141:5; [Prov. 13:18; 15:31, 32] [1]*listen to*
6 [a]Eccl. 2:2 [1]Lit. *sound*
7 [a]Ex. 23:8; Deut. 16:19; [Prov. 17:8, 23] [1]*destroys*
8 [a]Prov. 14:29; Gal. 5:22; Eph. 4:2
9 [a]Prov. 14:17; James 1:19
11 [a]Eccl. 11:7
12 [a]Eccl. 9:18 [b]Prov. 3:18 [1]A protective shade, lit. *shadow* [2]*advantage* or *profit*
13 [a]Job 12:14
14 [a]Deut. 28:47 [1]*alongside*
15 [a]Eccl. 8:12–14
16 [a]Prov. 25:16; Phil. 3:6 [b]Rom. 12:3
17 [a]Job 15:32; Ps. 55:23
18 [a]Eccl. 3:14; 5:7; 8:12, 13 [1]Lit. *come forth from all of them*
19 [a]Prov. 21:22; Eccl. 9:13–18
20 [a]1 Kin. 8:46; 2 Chr. 6:36; Prov. 20:9; Rom. 3:23; 1 John 1:8
23 [a]Rom. 1:22 [1]*tested*
24 [a]Job 28:12; 1 Tim. 6:16 [b]Rom. 11:33

11 Wisdom *is* good with an
inheritance,
And profitable [a]to those who see
the sun.
12 For wisdom *is* [1]a [a]defense *as*
money *is* a defense,
But the [2]excellence of knowledge
is that wisdom gives [b]life to
those who have it.

13 Consider the work of God;
For [a]who can make straight what
He has made crooked?
14 [a]In the day of prosperity be joyful,
But in the day of adversity
consider:
Surely God has appointed the one
[1]as well as the other,
So that man can find out nothing
that will come after him.

15 I have seen everything in my
days of vanity:

[a]There is a just *man* who perishes
in his righteousness,
And there is a wicked *man* who
prolongs *life* in his wickedness.

16 [a]Do not be overly righteous,
[b]Nor be overly wise:
Why should you destroy
yourself?
17 Do not be overly wicked,
Nor be foolish:
[a]Why should you die before your
time?
18 *It is* good that you grasp this,
And also not remove your hand
from the other;
For he who [a]fears God will
[1]escape them all.

19 [a]Wisdom strengthens the wise
More than ten rulers of the city.

20 [a]For *there is* not a just man on
earth who does good
And does not sin.

21 Also do not take to heart
everything people say,
Lest you hear your servant
cursing you.
22 For many times, also, your own
heart has known
That even you have cursed
others.

23 All this I have [1]proved by
wisdom.
[a]I said, "I will be wise";
But it *was* far from me.
24 [a]As for that which is far off and
[b]exceedingly deep,

Who can find it out?
25 [a]I applied my heart to know,
To search and seek out wisdom
and the reason *of things*,
To know the wickedness of folly,
Even of foolishness *and* madness.
26 [a]And I find more bitter than death
The woman whose heart *is* snares
and nets,
Whose hands *are* fetters.
[1]He who pleases God shall escape
from her,
But the sinner shall be trapped by
her.

27 "Here is what I have found," says
[a]the Preacher,
"*Adding* one thing to the other to
find out the reason,
28 Which my soul still seeks but I
cannot find:
[a]One man among a thousand I
have found,
But a woman among all these I
have not found.
29 Truly, this only I have found:
[a]That God made man upright,
But [b]they have sought out many
schemes."

8 Who *is* like a wise *man?*
And who knows the
interpretation of a thing?
[a]A man's wisdom makes his face
shine,
And [b]the [1]sternness of his face is
changed.

Obey Authorities for God's Sake

2 I *say*, "Keep the king's com-
mandment [a]for the sake of your
oath to God.
3 [a]"Do not be hasty to go from
his presence. Do not take your
stand for an evil thing, for he does
whatever pleases him."

4 Where the word of a king *is, there*
is power;
And [a]who may say to him, "What
are you doing?"
5 He who keeps his command will
experience nothing harmful;
And a wise man's heart [1]discerns
both time and judgment,
6 Because [a]for every matter there
is a time and judgment,
Though the misery of man
[1]increases greatly.
7 [a]For he does not know what will
happen;
So who can tell him when it will
occur?

8 [a]No one has power over the spirit
to retain the spirit,
And no one has power in the day
of death.
There is [b]no release from that
war,
And wickedness will not deliver
those who are given to it.

9 All this I have seen, and ap-
plied my heart to every work that
is done under the sun: *There is* a
time in which one man rules over
another to his own hurt.

Death Comes to All

10 Then I saw the wicked buried,
who had come and gone from the
place of holiness, and they were
[a]forgotten[1] in the city where they
had so done. This also *is* vanity.
11 [a]Because the sentence against
an evil work is not executed speed-
ily, therefore the heart of the sons
of men is fully set in them to do
evil.
12 [a]Though a sinner does evil a
hundred *times*, and his *days* are
prolonged, yet I surely know that
[b]it will be well with those who fear
God, who fear before Him.
13 But it will not be well with the
wicked; nor will he prolong *his*
days, *which are* as a shadow, be-
cause he does not fear before God.
14 There is a vanity which occurs
on earth, that there are just *men*
to whom it [a]happens according to
the work of the wicked; again,
there are wicked *men* to whom it
happens according to the work of
the [b]righteous. I said that this also
is vanity.
15 [a]So I commended enjoyment,
because a man has nothing better
under the sun than to eat, drink,
and be merry; for this will remain
with him in his labor *all* the days
of his life which God gives him un-
der the sun.
16 When I applied my heart to
know wisdom and to see the busi-
ness that is done on earth, even
though one sees no sleep day or
night,
17 then I saw all the work of God,
that [a]a man cannot find out the
work that is done under the sun.
For though a man labors to dis-
cover *it*, yet he will not find *it;*
moreover, though a wise *man* at-

---

25 [a]Eccl. 1:17
26 [a]Prov. 5:3, 4 [1]Lit. *He who is good before God*
27 [a]Eccl. 1:1, 2
28 [a]Job 33:23
29 [a]Gen. 1:27 [b]Gen. 3:6, 7

CHAPTER 8

1 [a]Prov. 4:8, 9; Acts 6:15 [b]Deut. 28:50 [1]Lit. *strength*
2 [a]Ex. 22:11; 2 Sam. 21:7; 1 Chr. 29:24; Ezek. 17:18; [Rom. 13:5]
3 [a]Eccl. 10:4
4 [a]1 Sam. 13:11, 13; Job 34:18
5 [1]Lit. *knows*
6 [a]Eccl. 3:1, 17 [1]*is great upon him*
7 [a]Prov. 24:22; Eccl. 6:12
8 [a]Ps. 49:6, 7; Job 14:5 [b]Deut. 20:5–8
10 [a]Eccl. 2:16; 9:5 [1]Some Heb. mss., LXX, Vg. *praised*
11 [a]Ps. 10:6; 50:21; Is. 26:10
12 [a]Is. 65:20; [Rom. 2:5–7] [b][Deut. 4:40; Ps. 37:11, 18, 19; Prov. 1:32, 33; Is. 3:10; Matt. 25:34, 41]
14 [a]Ps. 73:14 [b]Eccl. 2:14; 7:15; 9:1–3
15 [a]Eccl. 2:24
17 [a]Job 5:9; Ps. 73:16; Eccl. 3:11; Rom. 11:33

tempts to know *it,* he will not be
able to find *it.*

9 For I [1]considered all this in my
heart, so that I could declare
it all: [a]that the righteous and the
wise and their works *are* in the
hand of God. People know neither
love nor hatred *by* anything *they*
see before them.
2 [a]All things *come* alike to all:

One event *happens* to the
righteous and the wicked;
To the [1]good, the clean, and the
unclean;
To him who sacrifices and him
who does not sacrifice.
As is the good, so *is* the sinner;
He who takes an oath as *he* who
fears an oath.

3 This *is* an evil in all that is done
under the sun: that one thing *hap-*
pens to all. Truly the hearts of the
sons of men are full of evil; mad-
ness *is* in their hearts while they
live, and after that *they go* to the
dead.
4 But for him who is joined to all
the living there is hope, for a living
dog is better than a dead lion.

5 For the living know that they will
die;
But [a]the dead know nothing,
And they have no more reward,
For [b]the memory of them is
forgotten.
6 Also their love, their hatred, and
their envy have now perished;
Nevermore will they have a share
In anything done under the sun.

7 Go, [a]eat your bread with joy,
And drink your wine with a
merry heart;
For God has already accepted
your works.
8 Let your garments always be
white,
And let your head lack no oil.

9 [1]Live joyfully with the wife
whom you love all the days of your
vain life which He has given you
under the sun, all your days of
vanity; [a]for that *is* your portion in
life, and in the labor which you
perform under the sun.
10 [a]Whatever your hand finds to
do, do *it* with your [b]might; for
there is no work or device or
knowledge or wisdom in the grave
where you are going.
11 I returned [a]and saw under the
sun that—

The race *is* not to the swift,
Nor the battle to the strong,
Nor bread to the wise,
Nor riches to men of
understanding,
Nor favor to men of skill;
But time and [b]chance happen to
them all.
12 For [a]man also does not know his
time:
Like fish taken in a cruel net,
Like birds caught in a snare,
So the sons of men *are* [b]snared
in an evil time,
When it falls suddenly upon
them.

Wisdom Superior to Folly

13 This wisdom I have also seen
under the sun, and it *seemed* great
to me:
14 [a]*There was* a little city with few
men in it; and a great king came
against it, besieged it, and built
great [1]snares around it.
15 Now there was found in it a
poor wise man, and he by his wis-
dom delivered the city. Yet no one
remembered that same poor man.
16 Then I said:

"Wisdom *is* better than [a]strength.
Nevertheless [b]the poor man's
wisdom *is* despised,
And his words are not heard.
17 Words of the wise, *spoken*
quietly, *should be* heard
Rather than the shout of a ruler
of fools.
18 Wisdom *is* better than weapons
of war;
But [a]one sinner destroys much
good."

10 Dead[1] flies [2]putrefy the
perfumer's ointment,
And cause it to give off a foul
odor;
So does a little folly to one
respected for wisdom *and*
honor.
2 A wise man's heart *is* at his right
hand,
But a fool's heart at his left.
3 Even when a fool walks along the
way,
He lacks wisdom,
[a]And he shows everyone *that* he
is a fool.

CHAPTER 9

1 [a]Deut. 33:3; Job 12:10; Eccl. 8:14 [1]Lit. *put*
2 [a]Gen. 3:17–19; Job 21:7; Ps. 73:3, 12, 13; Mal. 3:15 [1]LXX, Syr., Vg. *good and bad,*
5 [a]Job 14:21; Is. 63:16 [b]Job 7:8–10; Eccl. 1:11; 2:16; 8:10; Is. 26:14
7 [a]Eccl. 8:15
9 [a]Eccl. 2:10 [1]Lit. *See life*
10 [a][Col. 3:17] [b]Rom. 12:11; Col. 3:23
11 [a]Jer. 9:23; Amos 2:14, 15 [b]1 Sam. 6:9
12 [a]Eccl. 8:7 [b]Prov. 29:6; Luke 12:20, 39; 17:26; 1 Thess. 5:3
14 [a]2 Sam. 20:16–22 [1]LXX, Syr., Vg. *bulwarks*
16 [a]Eccl. 7:12, 19 [b]Mark 6:2, 3
18 [a]Josh. 7:1–26; 2 Kin. 21:2–17

CHAPTER 10

1 [1]Lit. *Flies of death* [2]Tg., Vg. omit *putrefy*
3 [a]Prov. 13:16; 18:2

4 If the spirit of the ruler rises
against you,
[a]Do not leave your post;
For [b]conciliation[1] pacifies great
offenses.

5 There is an evil I have seen under
the sun,
As an error proceeding from the
ruler:
6 [a]Folly is set in [1]great dignity,
While the rich sit in a lowly place.
7 I have seen servants [a]on horses,
While princes walk on the ground
like servants.

8 [a]He who digs a pit will fall
into it,
And whoever breaks through a
wall will be bitten by a serpent.
9 He who quarries stones may be
hurt by them,
And he who splits wood may be
endangered by it.
10 If the ax is dull,
And one does not sharpen the
edge,
Then he must use more strength;
But wisdom [1]brings success.

11 A serpent may bite [a]when *it is* not
charmed;
The [1]babbler is no different.
12 [a]The words of a wise man's mouth
are gracious,
But [b]the lips of a fool shall
swallow him up;
13 The words of his mouth begin
with foolishness,
And the end of his talk *is* raving
madness.
14 [a]A fool also multiplies words.
No man knows what is to be;
Who can tell him [b]what will be
after him?
15 The labor of fools wearies them,
For they do not even know how
to go to the city!

16 [a]Woe to you, O land, when your
king *is* a child,
And your princes feast in the
morning!
17 Blessed *are* you, O land, when
your king *is* the son of nobles,
And your [a]princes feast at the
proper time—
For strength and not for
drunkenness!
18 Because of laziness the [1]building
decays,
And [a]through idleness of hands
the house leaks.
19 A feast is made for laughter,
And [a]wine makes merry;
But money answers everything.

20 [a]Do not curse the king, even in
your thought;
Do not curse the rich, even in
your bedroom;
For a bird of the air may carry
your voice,
And a bird in flight may tell the
matter.

The Value of Diligence

11 Cast your bread [a]upon the
waters,
[b]For you will find it after many
days.
2 [a]Give a serving [b]to seven, and also
to eight,
[c]For you do not know what evil
will be on the earth.

3 If the clouds are full of rain,
They empty *themselves* upon the
earth;
And if a tree falls to the south or
the north,
In the place where the tree falls,
there it shall lie.
4 He who observes the wind will
not sow,
And he who regards the clouds
will not reap.

5 As [a]you do not know what *is* the
way of the [1]wind,
[b]Or how the bones *grow* in the
womb of her who is with child,
So you do not know the works
of God who makes everything.
6 In the morning sow your seed,
And in the evening do not
withhold your hand;
For you do not know which will
prosper,
Either this or that,
Or whether both alike *will be*
good.

7 Truly the light is sweet,
And *it is* pleasant for the eyes [a]to
behold the sun;
8 But if a man lives many years
And [a]rejoices in them all,
Yet let him [b]remember the days
of darkness,
For they will be many.
All that is coming *is* vanity.

Seek God in Early Life

9 Rejoice, O young man, in your
youth,
And let your heart cheer you in
the days of your youth;

---

4 [a]Eccl. 8:3 [b]1 Sam. 25:24–33; Prov. 25:15 [1]Lit. *healing, health*
6 [a]Esth. 3:1 [1]*exalted positions*
7 [a]Prov. 19:10; 30:22
8 [a]Ps. 7:15; Prov. 26:27
10 [1]Lit. *is a successful advantage*
11 [a]Ps. 58:4, 5; Jer. 8:17 [1]Lit. *master of the tongue*
12 [a]Prov. 10:32; Luke 4:22 [b]Prov. 10:14; Eccl. 4:5
14 [a][Prov. 15:2]; Eccl. 5:3 [b]Eccl. 3:22; 8:7
16 [a]Is. 3:4, 5; 5:11
17 [a]Prov. 31:4; Is. 5:11
18 [a]Prov. 24:30–34 [1]Lit. *rafters sink*
19 [a]Judg. 9:13; Ps. 104:15; Eccl. 2:3
20 [a]Ex. 22:28; Acts 23:5

CHAPTER 11

1 [a]Is. 32:20 [b][Deut. 15:10; Prov. 19:17; Matt. 10:42; 2 Cor. 9:8; Gal. 6:9, 10; Heb. 6:10]
2 [a]Ps. 112:9; Matt. 5:42; Luke 6:30; [1 Tim. 6:18, 19] [b]Mic. 5:5 [c]Eph. 5:16
5 [a]John 3:8 [b]Ps. 139:14 [1]Or *spirit*
7 [a]Eccl. 7:11
8 [a]Eccl. 9:7 [b]Eccl. 12:1

[a]Walk in the [1]ways of your heart,
And [2]in the sight of your eyes;
But know that for all these
[b]God will bring you into
judgment.
10 Therefore remove [1]sorrow from
your heart,
And [a]put away evil from your
flesh,
[b]For childhood and [2]youth *are*
vanity.

12 Remember[a] now your Creator
in the days of your youth,
Before the [1]difficult days come,
And the years draw near [b]when
you say,
"I have no pleasure in them":
2 While the sun and the light,
The moon and the stars,
Are not darkened,
And the clouds do not return after
the rain;
3 In the day when the keepers of
the house tremble,
And the strong men bow down;
When the grinders cease because
they are few,
And those that look through the
windows grow dim;
4 When the doors are shut in the
streets,
And the sound of grinding is
low;
When one rises up at the sound
of a bird,
And all [a]the daughters of music
are brought low.
5 Also they are afraid of height,
And of terrors in the way;
When the almond tree blossoms,
The grasshopper is a burden,
And desire fails.
For man goes to [a]his eternal
home,
And [b]the mourners go about the
streets.

9 [a]Num. 15:39; Job 31:7; Eccl. 2:10 [b]Eccl. 3:17; 12:14; [Rom. 14:10] [1]Impulses [2]As you see to be best
10 [a]2 Cor. 7:1; 2 Tim. 2:22 [b]Ps. 39:5 [1]*vexation* [2]Prime of life
CHAPTER 12
1 [a]2 Chr. 34:3; Prov. 22:6; Lam. 3:27 [b]2 Sam. 19:35 [1]Lit. *evil*
4 [a]2 Sam. 19:35
5 [a]Job 17:13 [b]Gen. 50:10; Jer. 9:17
6 [1]So with Qr., Tg.; Kt. *removed;* LXX, Vg. *broken*
7 [a]Gen. 3:19; Job 34:15; Ps. 90:3 [b]Eccl. 3:21 [c]Num. 16:22; 27:16; Job 34:14; Is. 57:16; Zech. 12:1
8 [a]Ps. 62:9
9 [a]1 Kin. 4:32 [1]*arranged*
10 [1]Lit. *delightful*
11 [1]Lit. *masters of assemblies*
12 [a]Eccl. 1:18
13 [a][Deut. 6:2; 10:12]; Mic. 6:8
14 [a]Eccl. 11:9; Matt. 12:36; [Acts 17:30, 31; Rom. 2:16; 1 Cor. 4:5; 2 Cor. 5:10]

6 *Remember your Creator* before
the silver cord is [1]loosed,
Or the golden bowl is broken,
Or the pitcher shattered at the
fountain,
Or the wheel broken at the
well.
7 [a]Then the dust will return to the
earth as it was,
[b]And the spirit will return to God
[c]who gave it.

8 "Vanity[a] of vanities," says the
Preacher,
"All *is* vanity."

The Whole Duty of Man

9 And moreover, because the
Preacher was wise, he still taught
the people knowledge; yes, he
pondered and sought out *and* [a]set[1]
in order many proverbs.
10 The Preacher sought to find
[1]acceptable words; and *what was*
written *was* upright—words of
truth.
11 The words of the wise are like
goads, and the words of [1]scholars
are like well-driven nails, given by
one Shepherd.
12 And further, my son, be ad-
monished by these. Of making
many books *there is* no end, and
[a]much study *is* wearisome to the
flesh.
13 Let us hear the conclusion of
the whole matter:

[a]Fear God and keep His
commandments,
For this is man's all.
14 For [a]God will bring every work
into judgment,
Including every secret thing,
Whether good or evil.

The

Song of Solomon

THE Song of Solomon is a love song written by Solomon and abounding in metaphors and oriental imagery. Historically, it depicts the wooing and wedding of a shepherdess by King Solomon, and the joys and heartaches of wedded love.

Allegorically, it pictures Israel as God's betrothed bride (Hos. 2:19, 20), and the church as the bride of Christ. As human life finds its highest fulfillment in the love of man and woman, so spiritual life finds its highest fulfillment in the love of God for His people and Christ for His church.

The book is arranged like scenes in a drama with three main speakers: the bride (Shulamite), the king (Solomon), and a chorus (daughters of Jerusalem).

The Hebrew title *Shir Hashirim* comes from 1:1, "The song of songs." This is in the superlative and speaks of Solomon's most exquisite song. The Greek title *Asma Asmaton* and the Latin *Canticum Canticorum* also mean "Song of Songs" or "The Best Song." The name *Canticles* ("Songs") is derived from the Latin title. Because Solomon is mentioned in 1:1, the book is also known as the Song of Solomon.

THE [a]song of songs, which *is* Solomon's.

The Banquet

THE [1]SHULAMITE

2 Let him kiss me with the kisses
of his mouth—
[a]For [2]your love *is* better than wine.
3 Because of the fragrance of your
good ointments,
Your name *is* ointment poured
forth;
Therefore the virgins love you.
4 [a]Draw me away!

THE DAUGHTERS OF JERUSALEM

[b]We will run after [1]you.

THE SHULAMITE

The king [c]has brought me into his
chambers.

THE DAUGHTERS OF JERUSALEM

We will be glad and rejoice in
[2]you.

We will remember [1]your love
more than wine.

THE SHULAMITE

Rightly do they love [1]you.

5 I *am* dark, but lovely,
O daughters of Jerusalem,
Like the tents of Kedar,
Like the curtains of Solomon.
6 Do not look upon me, because I
am dark,
Because the sun has [1]tanned me.
My mother's sons were angry
with me;
They made me the keeper of the
vineyards,
But my own [a]vineyard I have not
kept.

(TO HER BELOVED)

7 Tell me, O you whom I love,
Where you feed *your flock,*
Where you make *it* rest at noon.
For why should I be as one who
[1]veils herself
By the flocks of your
companions?

THE BELOVED

8 If you do not know, [a]O fairest
among women,

CHAPTER 1

1 [a]1 Kin. 4:32
2 [a]Song 4:10 [1]A Palestinian young woman, Song 6:13. The speaker and audience are identified according to the number, gender, and person of the Hebrew words. Occasionally the identity is not certain. [2]Masc. sing.: the Beloved
4 [a]Hos. 11:4; John 6:44; 12:32 [b]Phil. 3:12–14 [c]Ps. 45:14, 15; John 14:2; Eph. 2:6 [1]Masc. sing.: the Beloved [2]Fem. sing.: the Shulamite
6 [a]Song 8:11, 12 [1]Lit. *looked upon me*
7 [1]LXX, Syr., Vg. *wanders*
8 [a]Song 5:9

[1]Follow in the footsteps of the flock,
And feed your little goats
Beside the shepherds' tents.
9 I have compared you, [a]my love,
[b]To my filly among Pharaoh's chariots.
10 [a]Your cheeks are lovely with ornaments,
Your neck with chains *of gold.*

THE DAUGHTERS OF JERUSALEM

11 We will make [1]you ornaments of gold
With studs of silver.

THE SHULAMITE

12 While the king *is* at his table,
My [1]spikenard sends forth its fragrance.
13 A bundle of myrrh *is* my beloved to me,
That lies all night between my breasts.
14 My beloved *is* to me a cluster of henna *blooms*
In the vineyards of En Gedi.

THE BELOVED

15 [a]Behold, you *are* fair, [1]my love!
Behold, you *are* fair!
You *have* dove's eyes.

THE SHULAMITE

16 Behold, you *are* [a]handsome, my beloved!
Yes, pleasant!
Also our [1]bed *is* green.
17 The beams of our houses *are* cedar,
And our rafters of fir.

2 I *am* the rose of Sharon,
And the lily of the valleys.

THE BELOVED

2 Like a lily among thorns,
So is my love among the daughters.

THE SHULAMITE

3 Like an apple tree among the trees of the woods,
So *is* my beloved among the sons.
I sat down in his shade with great delight,
And [a]his fruit *was* sweet to my taste.

8 [1]Lit. *Go out*
9 [a]Song 2:2, 10, 13; 4:1, 7; John 15:14 [b]2 Chr. 1:16
10 [a]Ezek. 16:11
11 [1]Fem. sing.: the Shulamite
12 [1]*perfume*
15 [a]Song 4:1; 5:12 [1]*my companion, friend*
16 [a]Song 5:10–16 [1]*couch*

CHAPTER 2
3 [a]Song 4:16; Rev. 22:1, 2
4 [1]Lit. *house of wine*
6 [a]Song 8:3
7 [a]Song 3:5; 8:4 [1]*adjure*
9 [a]Prov. 6:5; Song 2:17
14 [a]Song 5:2 [b]Song 8:13 [1]Lit. *appearance*
15 [a]Ps. 80:13; Ezek. 13:4; Luke 13:32

THE SHULAMITE TO THE DAUGHTERS OF JERUSALEM

4 He brought me to the [1]banqueting house,
And his banner over me *was* love.
5 Sustain me with cakes of raisins,
Refresh me with apples,
For I *am* lovesick.

6 [a]His left hand *is* under my head,
And his right hand embraces me.
7 [a]I [1]charge you, O daughters of Jerusalem,
By the gazelles or by the does of the field,
Do not stir up nor awaken love
Until it pleases.

The Beloved's Request

THE SHULAMITE

8 The voice of my beloved!
Behold, he comes
Leaping upon the mountains,
Skipping upon the hills.
9 [a]My beloved is like a gazelle or a young stag.
Behold, he stands behind our wall;
He is looking through the windows,
Gazing through the lattice.

10 My beloved spoke, and said to me:
"Rise up, my love, my fair one,
And come away.
11 For lo, the winter is past,
The rain is over *and* gone.
12 The flowers appear on the earth;
The time of singing has come,
And the voice of the turtledove
Is heard in our land.
13 The fig tree puts forth her green figs,
And the vines *with* the tender grapes
Give a good smell.
Rise up, my love, my fair one,
And come away!

14 "O my [a]dove, in the clefts of the rock,
In the secret *places* of the cliff,
Let me see your [1]face,
[b]Let me hear your voice;
For your voice *is* sweet,
And your face *is* lovely."

HER BROTHERS

15 Catch us [a]the foxes,
The little foxes that spoil the vines,
For our vines *have* tender grapes.

THE SHULAMITE

16 [a]My beloved *is* mine, and I *am* his.
He feeds *his flock* among the lilies.

(TO HER BELOVED)

17 [a]Until the day breaks
And the shadows flee away,
Turn, my beloved,
And be [b]like a gazelle
Or a young stag
Upon the mountains of [1]Bether.

A Troubled Night

THE SHULAMITE

3 By [a]night on my bed I sought the one I love;
I sought him, but I did not find him.
2 "I will rise now," *I said*,
"And go about the city;
In the streets and in the squares
I will seek the one I love."
I sought him, but I did not find him.
3 [a]The watchmen who go about the city found me;
I said,
"Have you seen the one I love?"

4 Scarcely had I passed by them,
When I found the one I love.
I held him and would not let him go,
Until I had brought him to the [a]house of my mother,
And into the [1]chamber of her who conceived me.

5 [a]I [1]charge you, O daughters of Jerusalem,
By the gazelles or by the does of the field,
Do not stir up nor awaken love
Until it pleases.

The Coming of Solomon

THE SHULAMITE

6 [a]Who *is* this coming out of the wilderness
Like pillars of smoke,
Perfumed with myrrh and frankincense,
With all the merchant's fragrant powders?
7 Behold, it *is* Solomon's couch,
With sixty valiant men around it,
Of the valiant of Israel.
8 They all hold swords,
Being expert in war.
Every man *has* his sword on his thigh
Because of fear in the night.

9 Of the wood of Lebanon
Solomon the King
Made himself a [1]palanquin:
10 He made its pillars *of* silver,
Its support *of* gold,
Its seat *of* purple,
Its interior paved *with* love
By the daughters of Jerusalem.
11 Go forth, O daughters of Zion,
And see King Solomon with the crown
With which his mother crowned him
On the day of his wedding,
The day of the gladness of his heart.

THE BELOVED

4 Behold, [a]you *are* fair, my love!
Behold, you *are* fair!
You *have* dove's eyes behind your veil.
Your hair *is* like a [b]flock of goats,
Going down from Mount Gilead.
2 [a]Your teeth *are* like a flock of shorn *sheep*
Which have come up from the washing,
Every one of which bears twins,
And none *is* [1]barren among them.
3 Your lips *are* like a strand of scarlet,
And your mouth is lovely.
[a]Your temples behind your veil
Are like a piece of pomegranate.
4 [a]Your neck *is* like the tower of David,
Built [b]for an armory,
On which hang a thousand [1]bucklers,
All shields of mighty men.
5 [a]Your two breasts *are* like two fawns,
Twins of a gazelle,
Which feed among the lilies.

6 [a]Until the day breaks
And the shadows flee away,
I will go my way to the mountain of myrrh
And to the hill of frankincense.

7 [a]You *are* all fair, my love,
And *there is* no spot in you.
8 Come with me from Lebanon, *my* spouse,
With me from Lebanon.
Look from the top of Amana,
From the top of Senir [a]and Hermon,

---

16 [a]Song 6:3
17 [a]Song 4:6 [b]Song 8:14 [1]Lit. *Separation*

CHAPTER 3

1 [a]Is. 26:9
3 [a]Song 5:7; Is. 21:6–8, 11, 12
4 [a]Song 8:2 [1]*room*
5 [a]Song 2:7; 8:4 [1]*adjure*
6 [a]Song 8:5
9 [1]A portable enclosed chair

CHAPTER 4

1 [a]Song 1:15; 5:12 [b]Song 6:5
2 [a]Song 6:6 [1]*bereaved*
3 [a]Song 6:7
4 [a]Song 7:4 [b]Neh. 3:19 [1]Small shields
5 [a]Prov. 5:19; Song 7:3
6 [a]Song 2:17
7 [a]Song 1:15; Eph. 5:27
8 [a]Deut. 3:9; 1 Chr. 5:23; Ezek. 27:5

From the lions' dens,
From the mountains of the leopards.

9 You have ravished my heart,
My sister, *my* spouse;
You have ravished my heart
With one *look* of your eyes,
With one link of your necklace.
10 How fair is your love,
My sister, *my* spouse!
[a]How much better than wine is your love,
And the [1]scent of your perfumes
Than all spices!
11 Your lips, O *my* spouse,
Drip as the honeycomb;
[a]Honey and milk *are* under your tongue;
And the fragrance of your garments
Is [b]like the fragrance of Lebanon.

12 A garden [1]enclosed
Is my sister, *my* spouse,
A spring shut up,
A fountain sealed.
13 Your plants *are* an orchard of pomegranates
With pleasant fruits,
Fragrant henna with spikenard,
14 Spikenard and saffron,
Calamus and cinnamon,
With all trees of frankincense,
Myrrh and aloes,
With all the chief spices—
15 A fountain of gardens,
A well of [a]living waters,
And streams from Lebanon.

THE SHULAMITE

16 Awake, O north *wind*,
And come, O south!
Blow upon my garden,
That its spices may flow out.
[a]Let my beloved come to his garden
And eat its pleasant [b]fruits.

THE BELOVED

5 I [a]have come to my garden, my [b]sister, *my* spouse;
I have gathered my myrrh with my spice;
[c]I have eaten my honeycomb with my honey;
I have drunk my wine with my milk.

(TO HIS FRIENDS)

Eat, O [d]friends!
Drink, yes, drink deeply,
O beloved ones!

The Shulamite's Troubled Evening

THE SHULAMITE

2 I sleep, but my heart is awake;
It is the voice of my beloved!
[a]He knocks, *saying*,
"Open for me, my sister, [1]my love,
My dove, my perfect one;
For my head is covered with dew,
My [2]locks with the drops of the night."

3 I have taken off my robe;
How can I put it on *again?*
I have washed my feet;
How can I [1]defile them?
4 My beloved put his hand
By the [1]latch *of the door*,
And my heart yearned for him.
5 I arose to open for my beloved,
And my hands dripped *with* myrrh,
My fingers with liquid myrrh,
On the handles of the lock.

6 I opened for my beloved,
But my beloved had turned away *and* was gone.
My [1]heart leaped up when he spoke.
[a]I sought him, but I could not find him;
I called him, but he gave me no answer.
7 [a]The watchmen who went about the city found me.
They struck me, they wounded me;
The keepers of the walls
Took my veil away from me.
8 I charge you, O daughters of Jerusalem,
If you find my beloved,
That you tell him I *am* lovesick!

THE DAUGHTERS OF JERUSALEM

9 What *is* your beloved
More than *another* beloved,
[a]O fairest among women?
What *is* your beloved
More than *another* beloved,
That you so [1]charge us?

THE SHULAMITE

10 My beloved *is* white and ruddy,
[1]Chief among ten thousand.
11 His head *is like* the finest gold;
His locks *are* wavy,
And black as a raven.
12 [a]His eyes *are* like doves
By the rivers of waters,
Washed with milk,
And [1]fitly set.

---

10 [a]Song 1:2, 4 [1]*fragrance*
11 [a]Prov. 24:13, 14; Song 5:1 [b]Gen. 27:27; Hos. 14:6, 7
12 [1]*locked* or *barred*
15 [a]Zech. 14:8; John 4:10; 7:38
16 [a]Song 5:1 [b]Song 7:13

CHAPTER 5

1 [a]Song 4:16 [b]Song 4:9 [c]Song 4:11 [d]Luke 15:7, 10; John 3:29
2 [a]Rev. 3:20 [1]*my companion, friend* [2]*curls* or *hair*
3 [1]*dirty*
4 [1]*opening*
6 [a]Song 3:1 [1]Lit. *soul*
7 [a]Song 3:3
9 [a]Song 1:8; 6:1 [1]*adjure*
10 [1]*Distinguished*
12 [a]Song 1:15; 4:1 [1]*sitting in a setting*

13 His cheeks *are* like a bed of
spices,
Banks of scented herbs.
His lips *are* lilies,
Dripping liquid myrrh.
14 His hands *are* rods of gold
Set with beryl.
His body *is* carved ivory
Inlaid *with* sapphires.
15 His legs *are* pillars of marble
Set on bases of fine gold.
His countenance *is* like Lebanon,
Excellent as the cedars.
16 His mouth *is* most sweet,
Yes, he *is* altogether lovely.
This *is* my beloved,
And this *is* my friend,
O daughters of Jerusalem!

THE DAUGHTERS OF JERUSALEM

6 Where has your beloved gone,
[a]O fairest among women?
Where has your beloved turned
aside,
That we may seek him with you?

THE SHULAMITE

2 My beloved has gone to his
[a]garden,
To the beds of spices,
To feed *his flock* in the gardens,
And to gather lilies.
3 [a]I *am* my beloved's,
And my beloved *is* mine.
He feeds *his flock* among the
lilies.

Praise of the Shulamite's Beauty

THE BELOVED

4 O my love, you *are as* beautiful
as Tirzah,
Lovely as Jerusalem,
Awesome as *an army* with
banners!
5 Turn your eyes away from me,
For they have [1]overcome me.
Your hair *is* [a]like a flock of goats
Going down from Gilead.
6 [a]Your teeth *are* like a flock of
sheep
Which have come up from the
washing;
Every one bears twins,
And none *is* [1]barren among them.
7 [a]Like a piece of pomegranate
Are your temples behind your
veil.

8 There are sixty queens
And eighty concubines,
And [a]virgins without number.
9 My dove, my [a]perfect one,
Is the only one,
The only one of her mother,
The favorite of the one who bore
her.
The daughters saw her
And called her blessed,
The queens and the concubines,
And they praised her.

10 Who is she who looks forth as the
morning,
Fair as the moon,
Clear as the sun,
[a]Awesome as *an army* with
banners?

THE SHULAMITE

11 I went down to the garden of nuts
To see the verdure of the valley,
[a]To see whether the vine had
budded
And the pomegranates had
bloomed.
12 Before I was even aware,
My soul had made me
As the chariots of [1]my noble
people.

THE BELOVED AND HIS FRIENDS

13 Return, return, O Shulamite;
Return, return, that we may look
upon you!

THE SHULAMITE

What would you see in the
Shulamite—
As it were, the dance of [1]the two
camps?

Expressions of Praise

THE BELOVED

7 How beautiful are your feet in
sandals,
[a]O prince's daughter!
The curves of your thighs *are* like
jewels,
The work of the hands of a
skillful workman.
2 Your navel *is* a rounded goblet;
It lacks no [1]blended beverage.
Your waist *is* a heap of wheat
Set about with lilies.
3 [a]Your two breasts *are* like two
fawns,
Twins of a gazelle.
4 [a]Your neck *is* like an ivory tower,
Your eyes *like* the pools in
Heshbon
By the gate of Bath Rabbim.

CHAPTER 6
1 [a]Song 1:8; 5:9
2 [a]Song 4:16; 5:1
3 [a]Song 2:16; 7:10
5 [a]Song 4:1 [1]*overwhelmed*
6 [a]Song 4:2 [1]*bereaved*
7 [a]Song 4:3
8 [a]Song 1:3
9 [a]Song 2:14; 5:2
10 [a]Song 6:4
11 [a]Song 7:12
12 [1]Heb. *Ammi Nadib*
13 [1]Heb. *Mahanaim*

CHAPTER 7
1 [a]Ps. 45:13
2 [1]Lit. *mixed* or *spiced drink*
3 [a]Song 4:5
4 [a]Song 4:4

Your nose *is* like the tower of
Lebanon
Which looks toward Damascus.
5 Your head *crowns* you like
Mount Carmel,
And the hair of your head *is* like
purple;
A king *is* held captive by *your*
tresses.

6 How fair and how pleasant you
are,
O love, with your delights!
7 This stature of yours is like a
palm tree,
And your breasts *like* its clusters.
8 I said, "I will go up to the palm
tree,
I will take hold of its branches."
Let now your breasts be like
clusters of the vine,
The fragrance of your [1]breath
like apples,
9 And the roof of your mouth like
the best wine.

THE SHULAMITE

The wine goes *down* smoothly for
my beloved,
[1]Moving gently the [2]lips of
sleepers.
10 [a]I *am* my beloved's,
And [b]his desire *is* toward me.

11 Come, my beloved,
Let us go forth to the field;
Let us lodge in the villages.
12 Let us get up early to the
vineyards;
Let us [a]see if the vine has
budded,
Whether the grape blossoms are
open,
And the pomegranates are in
bloom.
There I will give you my love.
13 The [a]mandrakes give off a
fragrance,
And at our gates [b]*are* pleasant
fruits,
All manner, new and old,
Which I have laid up for you, my
beloved.

8 Oh, that you were like my
brother,
Who nursed at my mother's
breasts!
If I should find you outside,
I would kiss you;
I would not be despised.
2 I would lead you *and* bring you
Into the [a]house of my mother,
She *who* used to instruct me.
I would cause you to drink of
[b]spiced wine,
Of the juice of my pomegranate.

(TO THE DAUGHTERS OF JERUSALEM)

3 [a]His left hand *is* under my head,
And his right hand embraces me.
4 [a]I charge you, O daughters of
Jerusalem,
Do not stir up nor awaken love
Until it pleases.

Love Renewed in Lebanon

A RELATIVE

5 [a]Who *is* this coming up from the
wilderness,
Leaning upon her beloved?

I awakened you under the apple
tree.
There your mother brought you
forth;
There she *who* bore you brought
you forth.

THE SHULAMITE TO HER BELOVED

6 [a]Set me as a seal upon your heart,
As a seal upon your arm;
For love *is as* strong as death,
[b]Jealousy *as* [1]cruel as [2]the grave;
Its flames *are* flames of fire,
[3]A most vehement flame.

7 Many waters cannot quench love,
Nor can the floods drown it.
[a]If a man would give for love
All the wealth of his house,
It would be utterly despised.

THE SHULAMITE'S BROTHERS

8 [a]We have a little sister,
And she has no breasts.
What shall we do for our sister
In the day when she is spoken
for?
9 If she *is* a wall,
We will build upon her
A battlement of silver;
And if she *is* a door,
We will enclose her
With boards of cedar.

THE SHULAMITE

10 I *am* a wall,
And my breasts like towers;
Then I became in his eyes
As one who found peace.
11 Solomon had a vineyard at Baal
Hamon;

---

8 [1]Lit. *nose*
9 [1]*Gliding over* [2]LXX, Syr., Vg. *lips and teeth.*
10 [a]Song 2:16; 6:3 [b]Ps. 45:11
12 [a]Song 6:11
13 [a]Gen. 30:14 [b]Song 2:3; 4:13, 16; Matt. 13:52

CHAPTER 8

2 [a]Song 3:4 [b]Prov. 9:2
3 [a]Song 2:6
4 [a]Song 2:7; 3:5
5 [a]Song 3:6
6 [a]Is. 49:16; Jer. 22:24; Hag. 2:23 [b]Prov. 6:34, 35 [1]*severe,* lit. *hard* [2]Or *Sheol* [3]Lit. *A flame of YAH,* poetic form of *YHWH, the LORD*
7 [a]Prov. 6:35
8 [a]Ezek. 23:33

[a]He leased the vineyard to keepers;
Everyone was to bring for its fruit
A thousand silver coins.

(TO SOLOMON)

12 My own vineyard *is* before me.
You, O Solomon, *may have* a thousand,
And those who tend its fruit two hundred.

THE BELOVED

13 You who dwell in the gardens,
The companions listen for your voice—
[a]Let me hear it!

THE SHULAMITE

14 [a]Make[1] haste, my beloved,
And [b]be like a gazelle
Or a young stag
On the mountains of spices.

11 [a]Matt. 21:33
13 [a]Song 2:14
14 [a]Rev. 22:17, 20 [b]Song 2:7, 9, 17 [1]*Hurry*, lit. *Flee*

The Book of

Isaiah

ISAIAH is like a miniature Bible. The first thirty-nine chapters (like the thirty-nine books of the Old Testament) are filled with judgment upon immoral and idolatrous men. Judah has sinned; the surrounding nations have sinned; the whole earth has sinned. Judgment must come, for God cannot allow such blatant sin to go unpunished forever. But the final twenty-seven chapters (like the twenty-seven books of the New Testament) declare a message of hope. The Messiah is coming as a Savior and a Sovereign to bear a cross and to wear a crown.

Isaiah's prophetic ministry, spanning the reigns of four kings of Judah, covers at least forty years.

Yesha'yahu and its shortened form *Yeshaiah* mean "Yahweh Is Salvation." This name is an excellent summary of the contents of the book. The Greek form in the Septuagint is *Hesaias*, and the Latin form is *Esaias* or *Isaias*.

THE [a]vision of Isaiah the son of
Amoz, which he saw concern-
ing Judah and Jerusalem in the
[b]days of Uzziah, Jotham, Ahaz,
and Hezekiah, kings of Judah.

The Wickedness of Judah

2 [a]Hear, O heavens, and give ear, O earth!
For the LORD has spoken:
"I have nourished and brought up children,
And they have rebelled against Me;
3 [a]The ox knows its owner
And the donkey its master's [1]crib;
But Israel [b]does not know,
My people do not [2]consider."

4 Alas, sinful nation,
A people [1]laden with iniquity,
[a]A [2]brood of evildoers,
Children who are corrupters!
They have forsaken the LORD,
They have provoked to anger
The Holy One of Israel,
They have turned away backward.

5 [a]Why should you be stricken again?
You will revolt more and more.
The whole head is sick,
And the whole heart faints.
6 From the sole of the foot even to the head,
There is no soundness in it,
But wounds and bruises and putrefying sores;
They have not been closed or bound up,
Or soothed with ointment.

7 [a]Your country *is* desolate,
Your cities *are* burned with fire;
Strangers devour your land in your presence;
And *it is* desolate, as overthrown by strangers.
8 So the daughter of Zion is left [a]as a [1]booth in a vineyard,
As a hut in a garden of cucumbers,
[b]As a besieged city.
9 [a]Unless the LORD of hosts
Had left to us a very small remnant,
We would have become like [b]Sodom,
We would have been made like Gomorrah.

10 Hear the word of the LORD,
You rulers [a]of Sodom;
Give ear to the law of our God,
You people of Gomorrah:
11 "To what purpose *is* the multitude of your [a]sacrifices to Me?"
Says the LORD.
"I have had enough of burnt offerings of rams
And the fat of fed cattle.
I do not delight in the blood of bulls,
Or of lambs or goats.

12 "When you come [a]to appear before Me,

CHAPTER 1
1 [a]Num. 12:6 [b]2 Chr. 26—32
2 [a]Jer. 2:12
3 [a]Jer. 8:7 [b]Jer. 9:3, 6 [1]*manger* or *feed trough* [2]*understand*
4 [a]Is. 57:3, 4; Matt. 3:7 [1]Lit. *heavy, weighed down* [2]*offspring, seed*
5 [a]Jer. 5:3
7 [a]Deut. 28:51, 52; 2 Chr. 36:19
8 [a]Job 27:18 [b]Jer. 4:17 [1]*shelter*
9 [a]2 Kin. 25:11, 22; Lam. 3:22 [b]Gen. 19:24; Rom. 9:29
10 [a]Deut. 32:32
11 [a][1 Sam. 15:22]
12 [a]Ex. 23:17

Who has required this from your
hand,
To trample My courts?
13 Bring no more [a]futile[1] sacrifices;
Incense is an abomination to Me.
The New Moons, the Sabbaths,
and [b]the calling of assemblies—
I cannot endure iniquity and the
sacred meeting.
14 Your [a]New Moons and your
[b]appointed feasts
My soul hates;
They are a trouble to Me,
I am weary of bearing *them*.
15 [a]When you [1]spread out your
hands,
I will hide My eyes from you;
[b]Even though you make many
prayers,
I will not hear.
Your hands are full of [2]blood.

16 "Wash[a] yourselves, make
yourselves clean;
Put away the evil of your doings
from before My eyes.
[b]Cease to do evil,
17 Learn to do good;
Seek justice,
Rebuke [1]the oppressor;
[2]Defend the fatherless,
Plead for the widow.

18 "Come now, and let us [a]reason
together,"
Says the LORD,
"Though your sins are like scarlet,
[b]They shall be as white as snow;
Though they are red like crimson,
They shall be as wool.
19 If you are willing and obedient,
You shall eat the good of the
land;
20 But if you refuse and rebel,
You shall be devoured by the
sword";
[a]For the mouth of the LORD has
spoken.

The Degenerate City

21 [a]How the faithful city
has become a [1]harlot!
It was full of justice;
Righteousness lodged in it,
But now [b]murderers.
22 [a]Your silver has become dross,
Your wine mixed with water.
23 [a]Your princes *are* rebellious,
And [b]companions of thieves;
[c]Everyone loves bribes,
And follows after rewards.
They [d]do not defend the
fatherless,
Nor does the cause of the widow
come before them.

24 Therefore the Lord says,
The LORD of hosts, the Mighty
One of Israel,
"Ah, [a]I will [1]rid Myself of My
adversaries,
And [2]take vengeance on My
enemies.
25 I will turn My hand against you,
And [a]thoroughly[1] purge away
your dross,
And take away all your alloy.
26 I will restore your judges [a]as at
the first,
And your counselors as at the
beginning.
Afterward [b]you shall be called
the city of righteousness, the
faithful city."

27 Zion shall be redeemed with
justice,
And her [1]penitents with
righteousness.
28 The [a]destruction of transgressors
and of sinners *shall be*
together,
And those who forsake the LORD
shall be consumed.
29 For [1]they shall be ashamed of the
[2]terebinth trees
Which you have desired;
And you shall be embarrassed
because of the gardens
Which you have chosen.
30 For you shall be as a terebinth
whose leaf fades,
And as a garden that has no
water.
31 [a]The strong shall be as tinder,
And the work of it as a spark;
Both will burn together,
And no one shall [b]quench *them*.

The Future House of God

2 The word that Isaiah the son
of Amoz saw concerning Ju-
dah and Jerusalem.

2 Now [a]it shall come to pass [b]in the
latter days
[c]*That* the mountain of the LORD's
house
Shall be established on the top of
the mountains,
And shall be exalted above the
hills;
And all nations shall flow to it.
3 Many people shall come and say,
[a]"Come, and let us go up to the
mountain of the LORD,
To the house of the God of Jacob;
He will teach us His ways,
And we shall walk in His paths."
[b]For out of Zion shall go forth the
law,

13 [a]Matt. 15:9 [b]Joel 1:14 [1]*worthless*
14 [a]Num. 28:11 [b]Lam. 2:6
15 [a]Prov. 1:28 [b]Ps. 66:18; Is. 59:1–3; Mic. 3:4 [1]Pray [2]*bloodshed*
16 [a]Jer. 4:14 [b]Rom. 12:9
17 [1]Some ancient vss. *the oppressed* [2]*Vindicate*
18 [a]Is. 43:26; Mic. 6:2 [b]Ps. 51:7; [Is. 43:25]; Rev. 7:14
20 [a]Is. 40:5; 58:14; Mic. 4:4; [Titus 1:2]
21 [a]Is. 57:3–9; Jer. 2:20 [b]Mic. 3:1–3 [1]Unfaithful
22 [a]Jer. 6:28
23 [a]Hos. 9:15 [b]Prov. 29:24 [c]Jer. 22:17 [d]Is. 10:2; Jer. 5:28; Ezek. 22:7; Zech. 7:10
24 [a]Deut. 28:63 [1]*be relieved of* [2]*avenge Myself*
25 [a]Is. 48:10; Ezek. 22:19–22; Mal. 3:3 [1]*refine with lye*
26 [a]Jer. 33:7–11 [b]Is. 33:5; Zech. 8:3
27 [1]Lit. *returners*
28 [a]Job 31:3; Ps. 9:5; [Is. 66:24; 2 Thess. 1:8, 9]
29 [1]So with MT, LXX, Vg.; some Heb. mss., Tg. *you* [2]Sites of pagan worship
31 [a]Ezek. 32:21 [b]Is. 66:24; Matt. 3:12; Mark 9:43

CHAPTER 2

2 [a]Mic. 4:1 [b]Gen. 49:1 [c]Ps. 68:15
3 [a]Jer. 50:5; [Zech. 8:21–23; 14:16–21] [b]Luke 24:47

And the word of the LORD from
Jerusalem.
4 He shall judge between the
nations,
And rebuke many people;
They shall beat their swords into
plowshares,
And their spears into pruning
[1]hooks;
Nation shall not lift up sword
against nation,
Neither shall they learn war
anymore.

The Day of the LORD

5 O house of Jacob, come and let
us [a]walk
In the light of the LORD.

6 For You have forsaken Your
people, the house of Jacob,
Because they are filled [a]with
eastern ways;
They *are* [b]soothsayers like the
Philistines,
[c]And they [1]are pleased with the
children of foreigners.
7 [a]Their land is also full of silver and
gold,
And there is no end to their
treasures;
Their land is also full of horses,
And there is no end to their
chariots.
8 [a]Their land is also full of idols;
They worship the work of their
own hands,
That which their own fingers
have made.
9 People bow down,
And each man humbles himself;
Therefore do not forgive them.

10 [a]Enter into the rock, and hide in
the dust,
From the terror of the LORD
And the glory of His majesty.
11 The [1]lofty looks of man shall be
[a]humbled,
The haughtiness of men shall be
bowed down,
And the LORD alone shall be
exalted [b]in that day.

12 For the day of the LORD of hosts
Shall come upon everything
proud and lofty,
Upon everything lifted up—
And it shall be brought low—
13 Upon all [a]the cedars of Lebanon
that are high and lifted up,
And upon all the oaks of Bashan;
14 [a]Upon all the high mountains,
And upon all the hills *that are*
lifted up;

4 [1]*knives*
5 [a]Eph. 5:8
6 [a]Num. 23:7 [b]Deut. 18:14 [c]Ps. 106:35 [1]Or *clap, shake hands to make bargains with the children*
7 [a]Deut. 17:16; Is. 30:16; 31:1; Mic. 5:10
8 [a]Is. 40:19, 20; Jer. 2:28
10 [a]Is. 2:19, 21; Rev. 6:15, 16
11 [a]Prov. 16:5; Is. 5:15 [b]Hos. 2:16 [1]*proud*
13 [a]Is. 14:8; Zech. 11:1, 2
14 [a]Is. 30:25
16 [a]1 Kin. 10:22; Is. 23:1, 14; 60:9
17 [1]*pride*
18 [1]Or *shall utterly vanish*
19 [a]Hos. 10:8; [Rev. 9:6] [b][2 Thess. 1:9] [c]Ps. 18:7; Is. 2:21; 13:13; 24:1, 19, 20; Hag. 2:6, 7; Heb. 12:26 [1]Lit. *dust*
22 [a]Ps. 146:3; Jer. 17:5 [b]Job 27:3 [1]Lit. *Cease yourselves from the man* [2]Lit. *in what is he to be esteemed*

CHAPTER 3
1 [a]2 Kin. 25:3; Is. 5:13; Jer. 37:21 [b]Lev. 26:26 [1]Every support
2 [a]2 Kin. 24:14; Is. 9:14, 15; Ezek. 17:12, 13
3 [1]Eminent looking men
4 [a]Eccl. 10:16 [1]*boys* [2]Or *capricious ones*

15 Upon every high tower,
And upon every fortified wall;
16 [a]Upon all the ships of Tarshish,
And upon all the beautiful sloops.
17 The [1]loftiness of man shall be
bowed down,
And the haughtiness of men shall
be brought low;
The LORD alone will be exalted
in that day,
18 But the idols [1]He shall utterly
abolish.

19 They shall go into the [a]holes of
the rocks,
And into the caves of the [1]earth,
[b]From the terror of the LORD
And the glory of His majesty,
When He arises [c]to shake the
earth mightily.

20 In that day a man will cast away
his idols of silver
And his idols of gold,
Which they made, *each* for
himself to worship,
To the moles and bats,
21 To go into the clefts of the rocks,
And into the crags of the rugged
rocks,
From the terror of the LORD
And the glory of His majesty,
When He arises to shake the
earth mightily.

22 [a]Sever[1] yourselves from such a
man,
Whose [b]breath *is* in his nostrils;
For [2]of what account is he?

Judgment on Judah and Jerusalem

3 For behold, the Lord,
the LORD of hosts,
[a]Takes away from Jerusalem and
from Judah
[b]The[1] stock and the store,
The whole supply of bread and
the whole supply of water;
2 [a]The mighty man and the man of
war,
The judge and the prophet,
And the diviner and the elder;
3 The captain of fifty and the
[1]honorable man,
The counselor and the skillful
artisan,
And the expert enchanter.

4 "I will give [a]children[1] *to be* their
princes,
And [2]babes shall rule over them.
5 The people will be oppressed,
Every one by another and every
one by his neighbor;

The child will be insolent toward
the [1]elder,
And the [2]base toward the
honorable."
6 When a man takes hold of his
brother
In the house of his father, *saying,*
"You have clothing;
You be our ruler,
And *let* these ruins *be* under your
[1]power,"
7 In that day he will protest, saying,
"I cannot cure *your* ills,
For in my house *is* neither food
nor clothing;
Do not make me a ruler of the
people."
8 For [a]Jerusalem stumbled,
And Judah is fallen,
Because their tongue and their
doings
Are against the LORD,
To provoke the eyes of His
glory.
9 The look on their countenance
witnesses against them,
And they declare their sin as
[a]Sodom;
They do not hide *it.*
Woe to their soul!
For they have brought evil upon
themselves.

10 "Say to the righteous [a]that *it shall
be* well *with them,*
[b]For they shall eat the fruit of their
doings.
11 Woe to the wicked! [a]*It shall be*
ill *with him,*
For the reward of his hands shall
be [1]given him.
12 *As for* My people, children *are*
their oppressors,
And women rule over them.
O My people! [a]Those who lead
you [1]cause *you* to err,
And destroy the way of your
paths."

Oppression and Luxury Condemned

13 The LORD stands up [a]to [1]plead,
And stands to judge the people.
14 The LORD will enter into
judgment
With the elders of His people
And His princes:
"For you have [1]eaten up [a]the
vineyard;
The plunder of the poor *is* in your
houses.
15 What do you mean by [a]crushing
My people
And grinding the faces of the
poor?"
Says the Lord GOD of hosts.

16 Moreover the LORD says:

"Because the daughters of Zion
are haughty,
And walk with [1]outstretched
necks
And [2]wanton eyes,
Walking and [3]mincing *as* they
go,
Making a jingling with their feet,
17 Therefore the Lord will strike
with [a]a scab
The crown of the head of the
daughters of Zion,
And the LORD will [b]uncover their
secret parts."

18 In that day the Lord will take
away the finery:
The jingling anklets, the [1]scarves,
and the [a]crescents;
19 The pendants, the bracelets, and
the veils;
20 The headdresses, the leg
ornaments, and the headbands;
The perfume boxes, the charms,
21 and the rings;
The nose jewels,
22 the festal apparel, and the
mantles;
The outer garments, the purses,
23 and the mirrors;
The fine linen, the turbans, and
the robes.

24 And so it shall be:
Instead of a sweet smell there will
be a stench;
Instead of a sash, a rope;
Instead of well-set hair,
[a]baldness;
Instead of a rich robe, a girding
of sackcloth;
And [1]branding instead of beauty.
25 Your men shall fall by the sword,
And your [1]mighty in the war.

26 [a]Her gates shall lament and
mourn,
And she *being* desolate [b]shall sit
on the ground.

4 And [a]in that day seven women
shall take hold of one man,
saying,
"We will [b]eat our own food and
wear our own apparel;
Only let us be called by your
name,
To take away [c]our reproach."

5 [1]*aged* [2]*despised, lightly esteemed*
6 [1]Lit. *hand*
8 [a]2 Chr. 36:16, 17; Mic. 3:12
9 [a]Gen. 13:13; Is. 1:10–15
10 [a][Deut. 28:1–14; Eccl. 8:12; Is. 54:17] [b]Ps. 128:2
11 [a][Ps. 11:6; Eccl. 8:12, 13] [1]*done to him*
12 [a]Is. 9:16 [1]*lead you astray*
13 [a]Is. 66:16; Hos. 4:1; Mic. 6:2 [1]*contend, plead His case*
14 [a]Matt. 21:33 [1]*burned*
15 [a]Mic. 3:2, 3
16 [1]Head held high [2]*seductive, ogling* [3]*tripping* or *skipping*
17 [a]Deut. 28:27 [b]Jer. 13:22
18 [a]Judg. 8:21, 26 [1]*headbands*
24 [a]Is. 22:12; Ezek. 27:31; Amos 8:10 [1]*burning scar*
25 [1]Lit. *strength*
26 [a]Jer. 14:2; Lam. 1:4 [b]Lam. 2:10

CHAPTER 4

1 [a]Is. 2:11, 17 [b]2 Thess. 3:12 [c]Luke 1:25

The Renewal of Zion

2 In that day [a]the Branch of the
LORD shall be beautiful and
glorious;
And the fruit of the earth *shall be*
excellent and appealing
For those of Israel who have
escaped.

3 And it shall come to pass that
he who is left in Zion and remains
in Jerusalem [a]will be called holy—
everyone who is [b]recorded among
the living in Jerusalem.
4 When [a]the Lord has washed
away the filth of the daughters of
Zion, and purged the [1]blood of Je-
rusalem from her midst, by the
spirit of judgment and by the spirit
of burning,
5 then the LORD will create above
every dwelling place of Mount
Zion, and above her assemblies, [a]a
cloud and smoke by day and [b]the
shining of a flaming fire by night.
For over all the glory there *will be*
a [1]covering.
6 And there will be a tabernacle
for shade in the daytime from the
heat, [a]for a place of refuge, and for
a shelter from storm and rain.

God's Disappointing Vineyard

5 Now let me sing to my
Well-beloved
A song of my Beloved [a]regarding
His vineyard:

My Well-beloved has a vineyard
[1]On a very fruitful hill.
2 He dug it up and cleared out its
stones,
And planted it with the choicest
vine.
He built a tower in its midst,
And also [1]made a winepress in it;
[a]So He expected *it* to bring forth
good grapes,
But it brought forth wild grapes.

3 "And now, O inhabitants of
Jerusalem and men of Judah,
[a]Judge, please, between Me and
My vineyard.
4 What more could have been done
to My vineyard
That I have not done in [a]it?
Why then, when I expected *it* to
bring forth *good* grapes,
Did it bring forth wild grapes?
5 And now, please let Me tell you
what I will do to My vineyard:

2 [a]Is. 12:1–6; [Jer. 23:5]; Zech. 3:8
3 [a]Is. 60:21 [b]Phil. 4:3
4 [a]Mal. 3:2, 3 [1]*bloodshed*
5 [a]Ex. 13:21, 22; Num. 9:15–23 [b]Zech. 2:5 [1]*canopy*
6 [a]Ps. 27:5; Is. 25:4

CHAPTER 5

1 [a]Ps. 80:8; Jer. 2:21; Matt. 21:33; Mark 12:1; Luke 20:9 [1]Lit. *In a horn, the son of fatness*
2 [a]Deut. 32:6 [1]Lit. *hewed out*
3 [a][Rom. 3:4]
4 [a]2 Chr. 36:15, 16; Jer. 2:5; 7:25, 26; Mic. 6:3; Matt. 23:37
5 [a]2 Chr. 36:19; Ps. 80:12; 89:40, 41
6 [a]2 Chr. 36:19–21 [b]Is. 7:19–25; Jer. 25:11 [1]*hoed*
7 [1]*wailing*
8 [a]Jer. 22:13–17; Mic. 2:2; Hab. 2:9–12 [1]Accumulate houses
9 [a]Is. 22:14
10 [a]Ezek. 45:11 [1]1 bath = 1/10 homer [2]1 homer = 1/10 ephah
11 [a]Prov. 23:29, 30; Eccl. 10:16, 17; Is. 5:22 [1]*pursue*
12 [a]Amos 6:5 [b]Job 34:27; Ps. 28:5
13 [a]2 Kin. 24:14–16 [b]Is. 1:3; 27:11; Hos. 4:6

[a]I will take away its hedge, and it
shall be burned;
And break down its wall, and it
shall be trampled down.
6 I will lay it [a]waste;
It shall not be pruned or [1]dug,
But there shall come up briers
and [b]thorns.
I will also command the clouds
That they rain no rain on it."

7 For the vineyard of the LORD of
hosts *is* the house of Israel,
And the men of Judah are His
pleasant plant.
He looked for justice, but behold,
oppression;
For righteousness, but behold, [1]a
cry *for help.*

Impending Judgment on Excesses

8 Woe to those who [1]join [a]house to
house;
They add field to field,
Till *there is* no place
Where they may dwell alone in
the midst of the land!
9 [a]In my hearing the LORD of hosts
said,
"Truly, many houses shall be
desolate,
Great and beautiful ones, without
inhabitant.
10 For ten acres of vineyard shall
yield one [a]bath,[1]
And a [2]homer of seed shall yield
one ephah."

11 [a]Woe to those who rise early in
the morning,
That they may [1]follow
intoxicating drink;
Who continue until night, *till*
wine inflames them!
12 [a]The harp and the strings,
The tambourine and flute,
And wine are in their feasts;
But [b]they do not regard the work
of the LORD,
Nor consider the operation of His
hands.

13 [a]Therefore my people have gone
into captivity,
Because *they have* no
[b]knowledge;
Their honorable men *are*
famished,
And their multitude dried up with
thirst.
14 Therefore Sheol has enlarged
itself
And opened its mouth beyond
measure;

Their glory and their multitude
and their pomp,
And he who is jubilant, shall
descend into it.
15 People shall be brought down,
[a]Each man shall be humbled,
And the eyes of the lofty shall be
humbled.
16 But the LORD of hosts shall be
[a]exalted in judgment,
And God who is holy shall be
hallowed in righteousness.
17 Then the lambs shall feed in their
pasture,
And in the waste places of [a]the
[1]fat ones strangers shall eat.

18 Woe to those who [1]draw iniquity
with cords of [2]vanity,
And sin as if with a cart rope;
19 [a]That say, "Let Him make speed
and hasten His work,
That we may see *it;*
And let the counsel of the Holy
One of Israel draw near and
come,
That we may know *it.*"

20 Woe to those who call evil good,
and good evil;
Who put darkness for light, and
light for darkness;
Who put bitter for sweet, and
sweet for bitter!

21 Woe to *those who are* [a]wise in
their own eyes,
And prudent in their own sight!

22 Woe to men mighty at drinking
wine,
Woe to men valiant for mixing
intoxicating drink,
23 Who [a]justify the wicked for a
bribe,
And take away justice from the
righteous man!

24 Therefore, [a]as the [1]fire devours
the stubble,
And the flame consumes the
chaff,
So [b]their root will be as
rottenness,
And their blossom will ascend
like dust;
Because they have rejected the
law of the LORD of hosts,
And despised the word of the
Holy One of Israel.
25 [a]Therefore the anger of the LORD
is aroused against His people;
He has stretched out His hand
against them
And stricken them,

15 [a]Is. 2:9, 11
16 [a]Is. 2:11
17 [a]Is. 10:16 [1]Lit. *fatlings, rich ones*
18 [1]*drag* [2]*emptiness* or *falsehood*
19 [a]Jer. 17:15; Amos 5:18
21 [a]Prov. 3:7; Rom. 1:22; 12:16; [1 Cor. 3:18–20]
23 [a]Ex. 23:8; Prov. 17:15; Is. 1:23; Mic. 3:11; 7:3
24 [a]Ex. 15:7 [b]Job 18:16 [1]Lit. *tongue of fire*
25 [a]2 Kin. 22:13, 17; Is. 66:15 [b]Ps. 18:7; Is. 64:3; Jer. 4:24; Nah. 1:5 [c]Is. 9:12, 17; Jer. 4:8; Dan. 9:16
26 [a]Is. 11:10, 12 [b]Is. 7:18; Zech. 10:8 [c]Mal. 1:11 [d]Joel 2:7
27 [a]Dan. 5:6
28 [a]Jer. 5:16 [1]Lit. *be regarded as*
30 [a]Is. 8:22; Jer. 4:23–28; Joel 2:10; Luke 21:25, 26 [1]*distress*

CHAPTER 6

1 [a]2 Kin. 15:7; 2 Chr. 26:23; Is. 1:1 [b]John 12:41; Rev. 4:2, 3; 20:11
2 [a]Ezek. 1:11
3 [a]Rev. 4:8 [b]Num. 14:21; Ps. 72:19

And [b]the hills trembled.
Their carcasses *were* as refuse in
the midst of the streets.

[c]For all this His anger is not
turned away,
But His hand *is* stretched out still.

26 [a]He will lift up a banner to the
nations from afar,
And will [b]whistle to them from
[c]the end of the earth;
Surely [d]they shall come with
speed, swiftly.
27 No one will be weary or stumble
among them,
No one will slumber or sleep;
Nor [a]will the belt on their loins
be loosed,
Nor the strap of their sandals be
broken;
28 [a]Whose arrows *are* sharp,
And all their bows bent;
Their horses' hooves will [1]seem
like flint,
And their wheels like a
whirlwind.
29 Their roaring *will be* like a lion,
They will roar like young lions;
Yes, they will roar
And lay hold of the prey;
They will carry *it* away safely,
And no one will deliver.
30 In that day they will roar against
them
Like the roaring of the sea.
And if *one* [a]looks to the land,
Behold, darkness *and* [1]sorrow;
And the light is darkened by the
clouds.

Isaiah Called to Be a Prophet

6 In the year that [a]King Uzziah
died, I [b]saw the Lord sitting on
a throne, high and lifted up, and
the train of His *robe* filled the tem-
ple.
2 Above it stood seraphim; each
one had six wings: with two he
covered his face, [a]with two he cov-
ered his feet, and with two he flew.
3 And one cried to another and
said:

[a]"Holy, holy, holy *is* the LORD of
hosts;
[b]The whole earth *is* full of His
glory!"

4 And the posts of the door were
shaken by the voice of him who
cried out, and the house was filled
with smoke.
5 So I said:

5 "Woe is me, for I am [1]undone!
Because I am a man of [a]unclean lips,
And I dwell in the midst of a people of unclean lips;
For my eyes have seen the King,
The LORD of hosts."

6 Then one of the seraphim flew
to me, having in his hand a live
coal *which* he had taken with the
tongs from [a]the altar.
7 And he [a]touched my mouth
with it, and said:

"Behold, this has touched your lips;
Your iniquity is taken away,
And your sin [1]purged."

8 Also I heard the voice of the
Lord, saying:

"Whom shall I send,
And who will go for [a]Us?"

Then I said, "Here *am* I! Send me."
9 And He said, "Go, and [a]tell this
people:

'Keep on hearing, but do not understand;
Keep on seeing, but do not perceive.'

10 "Make [a]the heart of this people dull,
And their ears heavy,
And shut their eyes;
[b]Lest they see with their eyes,
And hear with their ears,
And understand with their heart,
And return and be healed."

11 Then I said, "Lord, how long?"
And He answered:

[a]"Until the cities are laid waste and without inhabitant,
The houses are without a man,
The land is utterly desolate,
12 [a]The LORD has removed men far away,
And the forsaken places *are* many in the midst of the land.
13 But yet a tenth *will be* in it,
And will return and be for consuming,
As a terebinth tree or as an oak,
Whose stump *remains* when it is cut down.
So [a]the holy seed *shall be* its stump."

5 [a]Ex. 6:12, 30 [1]*destroyed, cut off*
6 [a]Rev. 8:3
7 [a]Jer. 1:9; Dan. 10:16 [1]*atoned for*
8 [a]Gen. 1:26
9 [a]Is. 43:8; Matt. 13:14; Mark 4:12; Luke 8:10; John 12:40; Acts 28:26; Rom. 11:8
10 [a]Ps. 119:70; Mark 6:1–6; Acts 7:51; Rom. 10:1–4 [b]Jer. 5:21
11 [a]Mic. 3:12
12 [a]2 Kin. 25:21; Is. 5:9
13 [a]Deut. 7:6; Ezra 9:2

CHAPTER 7

1 [a]2 Chr. 28 [b]2 Kin. 16:5, 9 [1]*conquer it*
2 [1]Lit. *settled upon*
3 [1]Lit. *A Remnant Shall Return*
4 [a]Ex. 14:13; Is. 30:15; Lam. 3:26 [1]*Be careful* [2]*be calm*
6 [1]*cause a sickening dread*
7 [a]2 Kin. 16:5; Is. 8:10; Acts 4:25, 26
8 [a]2 Sam. 8:6; 2 Kin. 17:6 [1]Lit. *shattered*
9 [a]2 Chr. 20:20; Is. 5:24
11 [a]Matt. 12:38 [1]Lit. *make the request deep or make it high above*

Isaiah Sent to King Ahaz

7 Now it came to pass in the days
of [a]Ahaz the son of Jotham, the
son of Uzziah, king of Judah, *that*
Rezin king of Syria and Pekah the
son of Remaliah, king of Israel,
went up to Jerusalem to *make* war
against [b]it, but could not [1]prevail
against it.
2 And it was told to the house of
David, saying, "Syria's forces are
[1]deployed in Ephraim." So his
heart and the heart of his peo-
ple were moved as the trees of
the woods are moved with the
wind.
3 Then the LORD said to Isaiah,
"Go out now to meet Ahaz, you
and [1]Shear-Jashub your son, at the
end of the aqueduct from the up-
per pool, on the highway to the
Fuller's Field,
4 "and say to him: [1]'Take heed,
and [2]be [a]quiet; do not fear or be
fainthearted for these two stubs of
smoking firebrands, for the fierce
anger of Rezin and Syria, and the
son of Remaliah.
5 'Because Syria, Ephraim, and
the son of Remaliah have plotted
evil against you, saying,
6 "Let us go up against Judah
and [1]trouble it, and let us make a
gap in its wall for ourselves, and
set a king over them, the son of
Tabel"—
7 'thus says the Lord GOD:

[a]"It shall not stand,
Nor shall it come to pass.
8 [a]For the head of Syria *is* Damascus,
And the head of Damascus *is* Rezin.
Within sixty-five years Ephraim will be [1]broken,
So that it will not *be* a people.
9 The head of Ephraim *is* Samaria,
And the head of Samaria *is* Remaliah's son.
[a]If you will not believe,
Surely you shall not be established." ' "

The Immanuel Prophecy

10 Moreover the LORD spoke
again to Ahaz, saying,
11 [a]"Ask a sign for yourself from
the LORD your God; [1]ask it either
in the depth or in the height
above."

12 But Ahaz said, "I will not ask,
nor will I test the LORD!"
13 Then he said, "Hear now, O
house of David! *Is it* a small thing
for you to weary men, but will you
weary my God also?
14 "Therefore the Lord Himself
will give you a sign: [a]Behold, the
virgin shall conceive and bear [b]a
Son, and shall call His name
[c]Immanuel.[1]
15 "Curds and honey He shall eat,
that He may know to refuse the
evil and choose the good.
16 [a]"For before the Child shall
know to refuse the evil and choose
the good, the land that you dread
will be forsaken by [b]both her
kings.
17 [a]"The LORD will bring the king
of Assyria upon you and your peo-
ple and your father's house—days
that have not come since the day
that [b]Ephraim departed from Ju-
dah."

18 And it shall come to pass in that
day
That the LORD [a]will whistle for
the fly
That *is* in the farthest part of the
rivers of Egypt,
And for the bee that *is* in the land
of Assyria.
19 They will come, and all of them
will rest
In the desolate valleys and in [a]the
clefts of the rocks,
And on all thorns and in all
pastures.

20 In the same day the Lord will
shave with a [a]hired [b]razor,
With those from beyond [1]the
River, with the king of Assyria,
The head and the hair of the legs,
And will also remove the beard.

21 It shall be in that day
That a man will keep alive a
young cow and two sheep;
22 So it shall be, from the
abundance of milk they give,
That he will eat curds;
For curds and honey everyone
will eat who is left in the land.

23 It shall happen in that day,
That wherever there could be a
thousand vines
Worth a thousand *shekels* of
silver,
[a]It will be for briers and thorns.

14 [a]Matt. 1:23; Luke 1:31; John 1:45; Rev. 12:5 [b]Is. 9:6] [c]Is. 8:8, 10 [1]Lit. *God-With-Us*

16 [a]Is. 8:4 [b]2 Kin. 15:30

17 [a]2 Chr. 28:19, 20; Is. 8:7, 8; 10:5, 6 [b]1 Kin. 12:16

18 [a]Is. 5:26

19 [a]Is. 2:19; Jer. 16:16

20 [a]Is. 10:5, 15 [b]2 Kin. 16:7; 2 Chr. 28:20 [1]The Euphrates

23 [a]Is. 5:6

CHAPTER 8

1 [a]Is. 30:8; Hab. 2:2 [1]Lit. *Speed the Spoil, Hasten the Booty*

2 [a]2 Kin. 16:10

4 [a]2 Kin. 17:6; Is. 7:16 [b]2 Kin. 15:29 [1]*knows how* [2]*plunder*

6 [a]John 9:7 [b]Is. 7:1, 2

7 [1]The Euphrates [2]Overflow

8 [a]Is. 30:28 [b]Is. 7:14; Matt. 1:23 [1]Lit. *be the fullness of* [2]Lit. *God-With-Us*

9 [a]Joel 3:9

24 With arrows and bows men will
come there,
Because all the land will become
briers and thorns.
25 And to any hill which could be
dug with the hoe,
You will not go there for fear of
briers and thorns;
But it will become a range for
oxen
And a place for sheep to roam.

Assyria Will Invade the Land

8 Moreover the LORD said to me,
"Take a large scroll, and [a]write
on it with a man's pen concerning
[1]Maher-Shalal-Hash-Baz.
2 "And I will take for Myself
faithful witnesses to record, [a]Uriah
the priest and Zechariah the son
of Jeberechiah."
3 Then I went to the prophetess,
and she conceived and bore a son.
Then the LORD said to me, "Call
his name Maher-Shalal-Hash-Baz;
4 [a]"for before the child [1]shall
have knowledge to cry 'My father'
and 'My mother,' [b]the riches of Da-
mascus and the [2]spoil of Samaria
will be taken away before the king
of Assyria."
5 The LORD also spoke to me
again, saying:

6 "Inasmuch as these people refused
The waters of [a]Shiloah that flow
softly,
And rejoice [b]in Rezin and in
Remaliah's son;
7 Now therefore, behold, the Lord
brings up over them
The waters of [1]the River, strong
and mighty—
The king of Assyria and all his
glory;
He will [2]go up over all his
channels
And go over all his banks.
8 He will pass through Judah,
He will overflow and pass over,
[a]He will reach up to the neck;
And the stretching out of his
wings
Will [1]fill the breadth of Your
land, O [b]Immanuel.[2]

9 "Be[a] shattered, O you peoples, and
be broken in pieces!
Give ear, all you from far
countries.
Gird yourselves, but be broken in
pieces;

Gird yourselves, but be broken in
pieces.
10 [a]Take counsel together, but it will
come to nothing;
Speak the word, [b]but it will not
stand,
[c]For [1]God *is* with us."

Fear God, Heed His Word

11 For the LORD spoke thus to me
with [1]a strong hand, and in-
structed me that I should not walk
in the way of this people, saying:

12 "Do not say, 'A conspiracy,'
Concerning all that this people
call a conspiracy,
Nor be afraid of their [1]threats,
nor be [2]troubled.
13 The LORD of hosts, Him you shall
hallow;
Let Him *be* your fear,
And *let* Him *be* your dread.
14 [a]He will be as a [1]sanctuary,
But [b]a stone of stumbling and a
rock of [2]offense
To both the houses of Israel,
As a trap and a snare to the
inhabitants of Jerusalem.
15 And many among them shall
[a]stumble;
They shall fall and be broken,
Be snared and [1]taken."

16 Bind up the testimony,
Seal the law among my disciples.
17 And I will wait on the LORD,
Who [a]hides His face from the
house of Jacob;
And I [b]will hope in Him.
18 [a]Here am I and the children whom
the LORD has given me!
We [b]*are* for signs and wonders
in Israel
From the LORD of hosts,
Who dwells in Mount Zion.

19 And when they say to you,
[a]"Seek those who are mediums
and wizards, [b]who whisper and
mutter," should not a people seek
their God? *Should they* [c]*seek* the
dead on behalf of the living?
20 [a]To the law and to the testi-
mony! If they do not speak accord-
ing to this word, *it is* because
[b]*there*[1] *is* no light in them.
21 They will pass through it hard-
pressed and hungry; and it shall
happen, when they are hungry,
that they will be enraged and
[a]curse [1]their king and their God,
and look upward.
22 Then they will look to the
earth, and see trouble and dark-
ness, gloom of anguish; and *they
will be* driven into darkness.

The Government of the Promised Son

9 Nevertheless [a]the gloom *will* not
be upon her who *is* distressed,
As when at [b]first He lightly
esteemed
The land of Zebulun and the land
of Naphtali,
And [c]afterward more heavily
oppressed *her*,
By the way of the sea, beyond the
Jordan,
In Galilee of the Gentiles.
2 [a]The people who walked in
darkness
Have seen a great light;
Those who dwelt in the land of
the shadow of death,
Upon them a light has shined.

3 You have multiplied the nation
And [1]increased its joy;
They rejoice before You
According to the joy of harvest,
As *men* rejoice [a]when they divide
the spoil.
4 For You have broken the yoke of
his burden
And the staff of his shoulder,
The rod of his oppressor,
As in the day of [a]Midian.
5 For every warrior's [1]sandal from
the noisy battle,
And garments rolled in blood,
[a]Will be used for burning *and* fuel
[2]of fire.

6 [a]For unto us a Child is born,
Unto us a [b]Son is given;
And [c]the government will be
upon His shoulder.
And His name will be called
[d]Wonderful, Counselor, [e]Mighty
God,
Everlasting Father, [f]Prince of
Peace.
7 Of the increase of *His*
government and peace
[a]*There will be* no end,
Upon the throne of David and
over His kingdom,
To order it and establish it with
judgment and justice
From that time forward, even
forever.
The [b]zeal of the LORD of hosts
will perform this.

The Punishment of Samaria

8 The Lord sent a word against
[a]Jacob,

---

10 [a]Is. 7:7 [b]Is. 7:14 [c]Rom. 8:31 [1]Heb. *Immanuel*

11 [1]Mighty power

12 [1]Lit. *fear* or *terror* [2]Lit. *in dread*

14 [a]Ezek. 11:16 [b]Luke 2:34; 20:17 [1]*holy abode* [2]*stumbling over*

15 [a]Matt. 21:44 [1]*captured*

17 [a]Is. 54:8 [b]Hab. 2:3

18 [a]Heb. 2:13 [b]Ps. 71:7

19 [a]1 Sam. 28:8 [b]Is. 29:4 [c]Ps. 106:28

20 [a]Luke 16:29 [b]Mic. 3:6 [1]Or *they have no dawn*

21 [a]Rev. 16:11 [1]Or *by their king and by their God*

CHAPTER 9

1 [a]Is. 8:22 [b]2 Kin. 15:29 [c]Matt. 4:13–16

2 [a]Matt. 4:16

3 [a]Judg. 5:30 [1]So with Qr., Tg.; Kt., Vg. *not increased joy;* LXX *Most of the people You brought down in Your joy*

4 [a]Judg. 7:22

5 [a]Is. 66:15 [1]*boot* [2]*for the fire*

6 [a][Luke 2:11] [b][John 3:16] [c][Matt. 28:18] [d]Judg. 13:18 [e]Titus 2:13 [f]Eph. 2:14

7 [a]Dan. 2:44 [b]Is. 37:32

8 [a]Gen. 32:28

And it has fallen on Israel.
9 All the people will know—
Ephraim and the inhabitant of Samaria—
Who say in pride and arrogance of heart:
10 "The bricks have fallen down,
But we will rebuild with hewn stones;
The sycamores are cut down,
But we will replace *them* with cedars."
11 Therefore the LORD shall set up
The adversaries of Rezin against him,
And spur his enemies on,
12 The Syrians before and the Philistines behind;
And they shall devour Israel with an open mouth.

For all this His anger is not turned away,
But His hand *is* [1]stretched out still.

13 For the people do not turn to Him who strikes them,
Nor do they seek the LORD of hosts.
14 Therefore the LORD will cut off head and tail from Israel,
Palm branch and bulrush [a]in one day.
15 The elder and honorable, he *is* the head;
The prophet who teaches lies, he *is* the tail.
16 For [a]the leaders of this people cause *them* to err,
And *those who are* led by them are destroyed.
17 Therefore the Lord [a]will have no joy in their young men,
Nor have mercy on their fatherless and widows;
For everyone *is* a hypocrite and an evildoer,
And every mouth speaks [1]folly.

[b]For all this His anger is not turned away,
But His hand *is* stretched out still.

18 For wickedness [a]burns as the fire;
It shall devour the briers and thorns,
And kindle in the thickets of the forest;
They shall mount up *like* rising smoke.
19 Through the wrath of the LORD of hosts
[a]The land is burned up,

12 [1]In judgment
14 [a]Rev. 18:8
16 [a]Is. 3:12; Mic. 3:1, 5, 9; Matt. 15:14
17 [a]Ps. 147:10 [b]Is. 5:25 [1]*foolishness*
18 [a]Ps. 83:14; [Is. 1:7; 10:17]; Nah. 1:10; Mal. 4:1
19 [a]Is. 8:22 [b]Mic. 7:2, 6
20 [a]Lev. 26:26 [b]Jer. 19:9 [1]*slice off* or *tear*
21 [a]2 Chr. 28:6, 8; Is. 11:13 [b]Is. 9:12, 17

CHAPTER 10

1 [a]Ps. 58:2
3 [a]Job 31:14 [b]Is. 13:6; Jer. 9:9; Hos. 9:7; Luke 19:44 [c]Is. 5:26
4 [a]Is. 24:22 [b]Is. 5:25 [1]Lit. *under*
5 [a]Jer. 51:20
6 [a]Is. 9:17 [b]2 Kin. 17:6; Jer. 34:22
7 [a]Gen. 50:20; Mic. 4:11, 12; Acts 2:23, 24
8 [a]2 Kin. 19:10

And the people shall be as fuel for the fire;
[b]No man shall spare his brother.
20 And he shall [1]snatch on the right hand
And be hungry;
He shall devour on the left hand
[a]And not be satisfied;
[b]Every man shall eat the flesh of his own arm.
21 Manasseh *shall devour* Ephraim, and Ephraim Manasseh;
Together they *shall be* [a]against Judah.

[b]For all this His anger is not turned away,
But His hand *is* stretched out still.

10 "Woe to those who [a]decree unrighteous decrees,
Who write misfortune,
Which they have prescribed
2 To rob the needy of justice,
And to take what is right from the poor of My people,
That widows may be their prey,
And *that* they may rob the fatherless.
3 [a]What will you do in [b]the day of punishment,
And in the desolation *which* will come from [c]afar?
To whom will you flee for help?
And where will you leave your glory?
4 Without Me they shall bow down among the [a]prisoners,
And they shall fall [1]among the slain."

[b]For all this His anger is not turned away,
But His hand *is* stretched out still.

Arrogant Assyria Also Judged

5 "Woe to Assyria, [a]the rod of My anger
And the staff in whose hand is My indignation.
6 I will send him against [a]an ungodly nation,
And against the people of My wrath
I will [b]give him charge,
To seize the spoil, to take the prey,
And to tread them down like the mire of the streets.
7 [a]Yet he does not mean so,
Nor does his heart think so;
But *it is* in his heart to destroy,
And cut off not a few nations.
8 [a]For he says,

'*Are* not my princes altogether
kings?
9 *Is* not [a]Calno [b]like Carchemish?
Is not Hamath like Arpad?
Is not Samaria [c]like Damascus?
10 As my hand has found the
kingdoms of the idols,
Whose carved images excelled
those of Jerusalem and
Samaria,
11 As I have done to Samaria and
her idols,
Shall I not do also to Jerusalem
and her idols?' "

12 Therefore it shall come to pass,
when the Lord has [1]performed all
His work [a]on Mount Zion and on
Jerusalem, *that He will say,* [b]"I
will punish the fruit of the arro-
gant heart of the king of Assyria,
and the glory of his haughty
looks."
13 [a]For he says:

"By the strength of my hand I have
done *it,*
And by my wisdom, for I am
prudent;
Also I have removed the
boundaries of the people,
And have robbed their treasuries;
So I have put down the
inhabitants like a [1]valiant *man.*
14 [a]My hand has found like a nest the
riches of the people,
And as one gathers eggs *that are*
left,
I have gathered all the earth;
And there was no one who moved
his wing,
Nor opened *his* mouth with even
a peep."

15 Shall [a]the ax boast itself against
him who chops with it?
Or shall the saw exalt itself
against him who saws with it?
As if a rod could wield *itself*
against those who lift it up,
Or as if a staff could lift up, *as if
it were* not wood!
16 Therefore the Lord, the [1]Lord of
hosts,
Will send leanness among his fat
ones;
And under his glory
He will kindle a burning
Like the burning of a fire.
17 So the Light of Israel will be for
a fire,
And his Holy One for a flame;
[a]It will burn and devour
His thorns and his briers in one
day.
18 And it will consume the glory of
his forest and of [a]his fruitful
field,
Both soul and body;
And they will be as when a sick
man wastes away.
19 Then the rest of the trees of his
forest
Will be so few in number
That a child may write them.

The Returning Remnant of Israel

20 And it shall come to pass in that
day
That the remnant of Israel,
And such as have escaped of the
house of Jacob,
[a]Will never again depend on him
who [1]defeated them,
But will depend on the LORD, the
Holy One of Israel, in truth.
21 The remnant will return, the
remnant of Jacob,
To the [a]Mighty God.
22 [a]For though your people, O Israel,
be as the sand of the sea,
[b]A remnant of them will return;
The destruction decreed shall
overflow with righteousness.
23 [a]For the Lord GOD of hosts
Will make a determined end
In the midst of all the land.

24 Therefore thus says the Lord
GOD of hosts: "O My people, who
dwell in Zion, [a]do not be afraid of
the Assyrian. He shall strike you
with a rod and lift up his staff
against you, in the manner of
[b]Egypt.
25 "For yet a very little while [a]and
the indignation will cease, as will
My anger in their destruction."
26 And the LORD of hosts will [1]stir
up [a]a scourge for him like the
slaughter of [b]Midian at the rock of
Oreb; [c]*as* His rod was on the sea,
so will He lift it up in the manner
of Egypt.

27 It shall come to pass in that day
That his burden will be taken
away from your shoulder,
And his yoke from your neck,
And the yoke will be destroyed
because of [a]the anointing oil.

28 He has come to Aiath,
He has passed Migron;
At Michmash he has attended to
his equipment.
29 They have gone [1]along [a]the ridge,

---

9 [a]Gen. 10:10; Amos 6:2 [b]2 Chr. 35:20 [c]2 Kin. 16:9
12 [a]2 Kin. 19:31; Is. 28:21 [b]2 Kin. 19:35; 2 Chr. 32:21; Jer. 50:18 [1]*completed*
13 [a][2 Kin. 19:22–24]; Is. 37:24–27; Ezek. 28:4; Dan. 4:30 [1]*mighty*
14 [a]Job 31:25
15 [a]Jer. 51:20
16 [1]So with Bg.; MT, DSS *YHWH (the LORD)*
17 [a]Is. 9:18
18 [a]2 Kin. 19:23
20 [a]2 Kin. 16:7 [1]Lit. *struck*
21 [a][Is. 9:6]
22 [a]Rom. 9:27, 28 [b]Is. 6:13
23 [a]Is. 28:22; Dan. 9:27; Rom. 9:28
24 [a]Is. 7:4; 12:2 [b]Ex. 14
25 [a]Is. 10:5; 26:20; Dan. 11:36
26 [a]2 Kin. 19:35 [b]Judg. 7:25; Is. 9:4 [c]Ex. 14:26, 27 [1]*arouse*
27 [a]Ps. 105:15; [1 John 2:20]
29 [a]1 Sam. 13:23 [1]Or *over the pass*

They have taken up lodging at
Geba.
Ramah is afraid,
[b]Gibeah of Saul has fled.
30 [1]Lift up your voice,
O daughter [a]of Gallim!
Cause it to be heard as far as
[b]Laish—
[2]O poor Anathoth!
31 [a]Madmenah has fled,
The inhabitants of Gebim seek
refuge.
32 As yet he will remain [a]at Nob that
day;
He will [b]shake his fist at the
mount of [c]the daughter of Zion,
The hill of Jerusalem.

33 Behold, the Lord,
The LORD of hosts,
Will lop off the bough with terror;
[a]Those of high stature *will be*
hewn down,
And the haughty will be humbled.
34 He will cut down the thickets of
the forest with iron,
And Lebanon will fall by the
Mighty One.

The Reign of Jesse's Offspring

11 There [a]shall come forth a [1]Rod
from the [2]stem of [b]Jesse,
And [c]a Branch shall [3]grow out of
his roots.
2 [a]The Spirit of the LORD shall rest
upon Him,
The Spirit of wisdom and
understanding,
The Spirit of counsel and might,
The Spirit of knowledge and of
the fear of the LORD.

3 His delight *is* in the fear of the
LORD,
And He shall not judge by the
sight of His eyes,
Nor decide by the hearing of His
ears;
4 But [a]with righteousness He shall
judge the poor,
And decide with equity for the
meek of the earth;
He shall [b]strike the earth with the
rod of His mouth,
And with the breath of His lips
He shall slay the wicked.
5 Righteousness shall be the belt of
His loins,
And faithfulness the belt of His
waist.

6 "The[a] wolf also shall dwell with
the lamb,
The leopard shall lie down with
the young goat,
The calf and the young lion and
the fatling together;
And a little child shall lead them.
7 The cow and the bear shall graze;
Their young ones shall lie down
together;
And the lion shall eat straw like
the ox.
8 The nursing child shall play by
the cobra's hole,
And the weaned child shall put
his hand in the viper's den.
9 [a]They shall not hurt nor destroy
in all My holy mountain,
For [b]the earth shall be full of the
knowledge of the LORD
As the waters cover the sea.

10 "And[a] in that day [b]there shall be
a Root of Jesse,
Who shall stand as a [c]banner to
the people;
For the [d]Gentiles shall seek Him,
And His resting place shall be
glorious."

11 It shall come to pass in that day
That the Lord shall set His hand
again the second time
To recover the remnant of His
people who are left,
[a]From Assyria and Egypt,
From Pathros and Cush,
From Elam and Shinar,
From Hamath and the [1]islands of
the sea.

12 He will set up a banner for the
nations,
And will [1]assemble the outcasts
of Israel,
And gather together [a]the
dispersed of Judah
From the four [2]corners of the
earth.
13 Also [a]the envy of Ephraim shall
depart,
And the adversaries of Judah
shall be cut off;
Ephraim shall not envy Judah,
And Judah shall not harass
Ephraim.
14 But they shall fly down upon the
shoulder of the Philistines
toward the west;
Together they shall plunder the
[1]people of the East;
[a]They shall lay their hand on
Edom and Moab;
And the people of Ammon shall
obey them.
15 The LORD [a]will utterly [1]destroy
the tongue of the Sea of Egypt;

29 [b]1 Sam. 11:4
30 [a]1 Sam. 25:44 [b]Judg. 18:7 [1]Or *Cry shrilly* [2]So with MT, Tg., Vg.; LXX, Syr. *Listen to her, O Anathoth*
31 [a]Josh. 15:31
32 [a]1 Sam. 21:1; Neh. 11:32 [b]Is. 13:2 [c]Is. 37:22
33 [a]Is. 37:24, 36–38; Ezek. 31:3; Amos 2:9

CHAPTER 11
1 [a][Zech. 6:12]; Rev. 5:5 [b][Is. 9:7; 11:10]; Matt. 1:5; [Acts 13:23] [c]Is. 4:2 [1]*Shoot* [2]*stock* or *trunk* [3]*be fruitful*
2 [a][Is. 42:1; 48:16; 61:1; Matt. 3:16]; Mark 1:10; Luke 3:22; [John 1:32]
4 [a]Rev. 19:11 [b]Job 4:9; Is. 30:28, 33; Mal. 4:6; 2 Thess. 2:8
6 [a]Hos. 2:18
9 [a]Job 5:23; Is. 65:25; Ezek. 34:25; Hos. 2:18 [b]Ps. 98:2, 3; Is. 45:6; Hab. 2:14
10 [a]Is. 2:11 [b]Is. 11:1; Rom. 15:12 [c]Is. 27:12, 13 [d]Rom. 15:10
11 [a]Is. 19:23–25; Hos. 11:11; Zech. 10:10 [1]Or *coastlands*
12 [a]John 7:35 [1]*gather* [2]Lit. *wings*
13 [a]Is. 9:21; Jer. 3:18; Ezek. 37:16, 17, 22; Hos. 1:11
14 [a]Is. 63:1; Dan. 11:41; Joel 3:19; Amos 9:12 [1]Lit. *sons*
15 [a]Is. 50:2; 51:10, 11; Zech. 10:10, 11 [1]So with MT, Vg.; LXX, Syr., Tg. *dry up*

With His mighty wind He will
shake His fist over [2]the River,
And strike it in the seven streams,
And make *men* cross over [3]dry-
shod.
16 [a]There will be a highway for the
remnant of His people
Who will be left from Assyria,
[b]As it was for Israel
In the day that he came up from
the land of Egypt.

A Hymn of Praise

12 And [a]in that day you will
say:

"O LORD, I will praise You;
Though You were angry with me,
Your anger is turned away, and
You comfort me.
2 Behold, God *is* my salvation,
I will trust and not be afraid;
[a]'For [b]YAH, the LORD, *is* my
strength and song;
He also has become my
salvation.' "
3 Therefore with joy you will draw
[a]water
From the wells of salvation.

4 And in that day you will say:

[a]"Praise the LORD, call upon His
name;
[b]Declare His deeds among the
peoples,
Make mention that His [c]name is
exalted.
5 [a]Sing to the LORD,
For He has done excellent things;
This *is* known in all the earth.
6 [a]Cry out and shout, O inhabitant
of Zion,
For great *is* [b]the Holy One of
Israel in your midst!"

Proclamation Against Babylon

13 The [a]burden[1] against Bab-
ylon which Isaiah the son of
Amoz saw.

2 "Lift[a] up a banner [b]on the high
mountain,
Raise your voice to them;
[c]Wave your hand, that they may
enter the gates of the nobles.
3 I have commanded My
[1]sanctified ones;
I have also called [a]My mighty
ones for My anger—
Those who [b]rejoice in My
exaltation."

15 [2]The Euphrates [3]Lit. *in sandals*
16 [a]Is. 19:23 [b]Ex. 14:29

CHAPTER 12

1 [a]Is. 2:11
2 [a]Ps. 83:18 [b]Ex. 15:2; Ps. 118:14
3 [a][John 4:10, 14; 7:37, 38]
4 [a]1 Chr. 16:8; Ps. 105:1 [b]Ps. 145:4–6 [c]Ps. 34:3
5 [a]Ex. 15:1; Ps. 98:1; Is. 24:14; 42:10, 11; 44:23
6 [a]Is. 52:9; 54:1; Zeph. 3:14, 15 [b]Ps. 89:18

CHAPTER 13

1 [a]Jer. 50; 51; Matt. 1:11; Rev. 14:8 [1]*oracle, prophecy*
2 [a]Is. 18:3 [b]Jer. 51:25 [c]Is. 10:32
3 [a]Joel 3:11 [b]Ps. 149:2 [1]*consecrated* or *set apart*
4 [a]Is. 17:12; Joel 3:14
5 [a]Is. 42:13 [b]Is. 24:1; 34:2 [1]Or *instruments*
6 [a]Is. 2:12; Ezek. 30:3; Amos 5:18; Zeph. 1:7; Rev. 6:17 [b]Is. 10:25; Job 31:23; Joel 1:15
8 [a]Ps. 48:6 [1]*Sharp pains*
9 [a]Mal. 4:1 [b]Ps. 104:35; Prov. 2:22
10 [a]Is. 24:21–23; Ezek. 32:7; Joel 2:31; Matt. 24:29; Mark 13:24; Luke 21:25
11 [a]Is. 26:21 [b][Is. 2:17] [1]Or *tyrants*
13 [a]Is. 34:4; 51:6; Hag. 2:6 [b]Ps. 110:5; Lam. 1:12
14 [1]*gathers*

4 The [a]noise of a multitude in the
mountains,
Like that of many people!
A tumultuous noise of the
kingdoms of nations gathered
together!
The LORD of hosts musters
The army for battle.
5 They come from a far country,
From the end of heaven—
The [a]LORD and His [1]weapons of
indignation,
To destroy the whole [b]land.

6 Wail, [a]for the day of the LORD *is*
at hand!
[b]It will come as destruction from
the Almighty.
7 Therefore all hands will be limp,
Every man's heart will melt,
8 And they will be afraid.
[a]Pangs[1] and sorrows will take
hold of *them;*
They will be in pain as a woman
in childbirth;
They will be amazed at one
another;
Their faces *will be like* flames.

9 Behold, [a]the day of the LORD
comes,
Cruel, with both wrath and fierce
anger,
To lay the land desolate;
And He will destroy [b]its sinners
from it.
10 For the stars of heaven and their
constellations
Will not give their light;
The sun will be [a]darkened in its
going forth,
And the moon will not cause its
light to shine.

11 "I will [a]punish the world for *its*
evil,
And the wicked for their iniquity;
[b]I will halt the arrogance of the
proud,
And will lay low the haughtiness
of the [1]terrible.
12 I will make a mortal more rare
than fine gold,
A man more than the golden
wedge of Ophir.
13 [a]Therefore I will shake the
heavens,
And the earth will move out of
her place,
In the wrath of the LORD of hosts
And in [b]the day of His fierce
anger.
14 It shall be as the hunted gazelle,
And as a sheep that no man
[1]takes up;

[a]Every man will turn to his own people,
And everyone will flee to his own land.
15 Everyone who is found will be thrust through,
And everyone who is captured will fall by the sword.
16 Their children also will be [a]dashed to pieces before their eyes;
Their houses will be plundered
And their wives [b]ravished.

17 "Behold,[a] I will stir up the Medes against them,
Who will not [1]regard silver;
And *as for* gold, they will not delight in it.
18 Also *their* bows will dash the young men to pieces,
And they will have no pity on the fruit of the womb;
Their eye will not spare children.
19 [a]And Babylon, the glory of kingdoms,
The beauty of the Chaldeans' pride,
Will be as when God overthrew [b]Sodom and Gomorrah.
20 [a]It will never be inhabited,
Nor will it be settled from generation to generation;
Nor will the Arabian pitch tents there,
Nor will the shepherds make their sheepfolds there.
21 [a]But wild beasts of the desert will lie there,
And their houses will be full of [1]owls;
Ostriches will dwell there,
And wild goats will caper there.
22 The hyenas will howl in their citadels,
And jackals in their pleasant palaces.
[a]Her time *is* near to come,
And her days will not be prolonged."

Mercy on Jacob

14 For the LORD [a]will have
mercy on Jacob, and [b]will
still choose Israel, and settle them
in their own land. [c]The strangers
will be joined with them, and they
will cling to the house of Jacob.
2 Then people will take them
[a]and bring them to their place, and
the house of Israel will possess
them for servants and maids in the
land of the LORD; they will take
them captive whose captives they
were, [b]and rule over their op-
pressors.

Fall of the King of Babylon

3 It shall come to pass in the day
the LORD gives you rest from your
sorrow, and from your fear and the
hard bondage in which you were
made to serve,
4 that you [a]will take up this prov-
erb against the king of Babylon,
and say:

"How the oppressor has ceased,
The [b]golden[1] city ceased!
5 The LORD has broken [a]the staff of the wicked,
The scepter of the rulers;
6 He who struck the people in wrath with a continual stroke,
He who ruled the nations in anger,
Is persecuted *and* no one hinders.
7 The whole earth is at rest *and* quiet;
They break forth into singing.
8 [a]Indeed the cypress trees rejoice over you,
And the cedars of Lebanon,
Saying, 'Since you [1]were cut down,
No woodsman has come up against us.'

9 "Hell[a1] from beneath is excited about you,
To meet *you* at your coming;
It stirs up the dead for you,
All the chief ones of the earth;
It has raised up from their thrones
All the kings of the nations.
10 They all shall [a]speak and say to you:
'Have you also become as weak as we?
Have you become like us?
11 Your pomp is brought down to Sheol,
And the sound of your stringed instruments;
The maggot is spread under you,
And worms cover you.'

The Fall of Lucifer

12 "How[a] you are fallen from heaven,
O [1]Lucifer, son of the morning!
How you are cut down to the ground,
You who weakened the nations!
13 For you have said in your heart:
[a]'I will ascend into heaven,
[b]I will exalt my throne above the stars of God;

---

14 [a]Jer. 50:16; 51:9
16 [a]Ps. 137:8, 9; Is. 13:18; 14:21; Hos. 10:14; Nah. 3:10 [b]Zech. 14:2
17 [a]Is. 21:2; Jer. 51:11, 28; Dan. 5:28, 31 [1]*esteem*
19 [a]Is. 14:4; Dan. 4:30; Rev. 18:11–16, 19, 21 [b]Gen. 19:24; Deut. 29:23; Jer. 50:40; Amos 4:11
20 [a]Jer. 50:3
21 [a]Is. 34:11–15; Zeph. 2:14; Rev. 18:2 [1]Or *howling creatures*
22 [a]Jer. 51:33

CHAPTER 14

1 [a]Ps. 102:13; Is. 49:13, 15; 54:7, 8 [b]Is. 41:8, 9; Zech. 1:17; 2:12 [c]Is. 60:4, 5, 10
2 [a]Is. 49:22; 60:9; 66:20 [b]Is. 60:14
4 [a]Is. 13:19; Hab. 2:6 [b]Rev. 18:16 [1]Or *insolent*
5 [a]Ps. 125:3
8 [a]Is. 55:12; Ezek. 31:16 [1]*have lain down*
9 [a]Ezek. 32:21 [1]Or *Sheol*
10 [a]Ezek. 32:21
12 [a]Is. 34:4; Luke 10:18; [Rev. 12:7–9] [1]Lit. *Day Star*
13 [a]Ezek. 28:2; Matt. 11:23 [b]Dan. 8:10; 2 Thess. 2:4

I will also sit on the [c]mount of
the congregation
[d]On the farthest sides of the north;
14 I will ascend above the heights of
the clouds,
[a]I will be like the Most High.'
15 Yet you [a]shall be brought down
to Sheol,
To the [1]lowest depths of the Pit.

16"Those who see you will gaze at
you,
And consider you, *saying:*
'*Is* this the man who made the
earth tremble,
Who shook kingdoms,
17 Who made the world as a
wilderness
And destroyed its cities,
Who [1]did not open the house of
his prisoners?'

18"All the kings of the nations,
All of them, sleep in glory,
Everyone in his own house;
19 But you are cast out of your grave
Like an [1]abominable branch,
Like the garment of those who
are slain,
[2]Thrust through with a sword,
Who go down to the stones of the
pit,
Like a corpse trodden underfoot.
20 You will not be joined with them
in burial,
Because you have destroyed your
land
And slain your people.
[a]The brood of evildoers shall
never be named.
21 Prepare slaughter for his children
[a]Because of the iniquity of their
fathers,
Lest they rise up and possess the
land,
And fill the face of the world with
cities."

Babylon Destroyed

22"For I will rise up against them,"
says the LORD of hosts,
"And cut off from Babylon [a]the
name and [b]remnant,
[c]And offspring and posterity,"
says the LORD.
23"I will also make it a possession
for the [a]porcupine,
And marshes of muddy water;
I will sweep it with the broom of
destruction," says the LORD of
hosts.

Assyria Destroyed

24 The LORD of hosts has sworn,
saying,

"Surely, as I have thought, so it
shall come to pass,
And as I have purposed, *so* it
shall [a]stand:
25 That I will break the [a]Assyrian
in My land,
And on My mountains tread him
underfoot.
Then [b]his yoke shall be removed
from them,
And his burden removed from
their shoulders.
26 This *is* the [a]purpose that is
purposed against the whole
earth,
And this *is* the hand that is
stretched out over all the
nations.
27 For the LORD of hosts has
[a]purposed,
And who will annul *it?*
His hand *is* stretched out,
And who will turn it back?"

Philistia Destroyed

28 This is the [1]burden which came
in the year that [a]King Ahaz died.

29"Do not rejoice, all you of Philistia,
[a]Because the rod that struck you
is broken;
For out of the serpent's roots will
come forth a viper,
[b]And its offspring *will be* a fiery
flying serpent.
30 The firstborn of the poor will
feed,
And the needy will lie down in
safety;
I will kill your roots with famine,
And it will slay your remnant.
31 Wail, O gate! Cry, O city!
All you of Philistia *are* dissolved;
For smoke will come from the
north,
And no one *will be* alone in his
[1]appointed times."

32 What will they answer the
messengers of the nation?
That [a]the LORD has founded Zion,
And [b]the poor of His people shall
take refuge in it.

Proclamation Against Moab

15 The [a]burden[1] against Moab.

Because in the night [b]Ar of [c]Moab
is laid waste
And destroyed,
Because in the night Kir of Moab
is laid waste
And destroyed,
2 He has gone up to the [1]temple and
Dibon,

---

13 [c]Ezek. 28:14 [d]Ps. 48:2
14 [a]Is. 47:8; 2 Thess. 2:4
15 [a]Ezek. 28:8; Matt. 11:23; Luke 10:15 [1]Lit. *recesses*
17 [1]Would not release
19 [1]*despised* [2]*Pierced*
20 [a]Job 18:19; Ps. 21:10; 109:13; Is. 1:4; 31:2
21 [a]Ex. 20:5; Lev. 26:39; Is. 13:16; Matt. 23:35
22 [a]Prov. 10:7; Is. 26:14; Jer. 51:62 [b]1 Kin. 14:10 [c]Job 18:19; Is. 47:9
23 [a]Is. 34:11; Zeph. 2:14
24 [a]Is. 43:13
25 [a]Mic. 5:5, 6; Zeph. 2:13 [b]Is. 10:27; Nah. 1:13
26 [a]Is. 23:9; Zeph. 3:6, 8
27 [a]2 Chr. 20:6; Job 9:12; 23:13; Ps. 33:11; Prov. 19:21; 21:30; Is. 43:13; Dan. 4:31, 35
28 [a]2 Kin. 16:20; 2 Chr. 28:27 [1]*oracle, prophecy*
29 [a]2 Chr. 26:6 [b]2 Kin. 18:8
31 [1]Or *ranks*
32 [a]Ps. 87:1, 5 [b]Zech. 11:11

CHAPTER 15

1 [a]2 Kin. 3:4 [b]Deut. 2:9; Num. 21:28 [c]Is. 15:1—16:14; Jer. 25:21; 48:1–47; Amos 2:1–3; Zeph. 2:8–11 [1]*oracle, prophecy*
2 [1]Heb. *bayith,* lit. *house*

To the high places to weep.
Moab will wail over Nebo and over Medeba;
[a]On all their heads *will be* baldness,
And every beard cut off.
3 In their streets they will clothe themselves with sackcloth;
On the tops of their houses
And in their streets
Everyone will wail, [a]weeping bitterly.
4 Heshbon and Elealeh will cry out,
Their voice shall be heard as far as [a]Jahaz;
Therefore the [1]armed soldiers of Moab will cry out;
His life will be burdensome to him.

5 "My[a] heart will cry out for Moab;
His fugitives *shall flee* to Zoar,
Like [1]a three-year-old heifer.
For [b]by the Ascent of Luhith
They will go up with weeping;
For in the way of Horonaim
They will raise up a cry of destruction,
6 For the waters [a]of Nimrim will be desolate,
For the green grass has withered away;
The grass fails, there is nothing green.
7 Therefore the abundance they have gained,
And what they have laid up,
They will carry away to the Brook of the Willows.
8 For the cry has gone all around the borders of Moab,
Its wailing to Eglaim
And its wailing to Beer Elim.
9 For the waters of [1]Dimon will be full of blood;
Because I will bring more upon [1]Dimon,
[a]Lions upon him who escapes from Moab,
And on the remnant of the land."

Moab Destroyed

16 Send [a]the lamb to the ruler of the land,
[b]From [1]Sela to the wilderness,
To the mount of the daughter of Zion.
2 For it shall be as a [a]wandering bird thrown out of the nest;
So shall be the daughters of Moab at the fords of the [b]Arnon.

3 "Take counsel, execute judgment;
Make your shadow like the night in the middle of the day;
Hide the outcasts,
Do not betray him who escapes.
4 Let My outcasts dwell with you, O Moab;
Be a shelter to them from the face of the [1]spoiler.
For the extortioner is at an end,
Devastation ceases,
The oppressors are consumed out of the land.
5 In mercy [a]the throne will be established;
And One will sit on it in truth, in the tabernacle of David,
[b]Judging and seeking justice and hastening [c]righteousness."

6 We have heard of the [a]pride of Moab—
He is very proud—
Of his haughtiness and his pride and his wrath;
[b]*But* his [1]lies *shall* not *be* so.
7 Therefore Moab shall [a]wail for Moab;
Everyone shall wail.
For the foundations [b]of Kir Hareseth you shall mourn;
Surely *they are* stricken.

8 For [a]the fields of Heshbon languish,
And [b]the vine of Sibmah;
The lords of the nations have broken down its choice plants,
Which have reached to Jazer
And wandered through the wilderness.
Her branches are stretched out,
They are gone over the [c]sea.
9 Therefore I will bewail the vine of Sibmah,
With the weeping of Jazer;
I will drench you with my tears,
[a]O Heshbon and Elealeh;
For [1]battle cries have fallen
Over your summer fruits and your harvest.

10 [a]Gladness is taken away,
And joy from the plentiful field;
In the vineyards there will be no singing,
Nor will there be shouting;
No treaders will tread out wine in the presses;
I have made their shouting cease.
11 Therefore [a]my [1]heart shall resound like a harp for Moab,
And my inner being for [2]Kir Heres.

12 And it shall come to pass,
When it is seen that Moab is weary on [a]the high place,

---

2 [a]Lev. 21:5; Jer. 48:37
3 [a]Jer. 48:38
4 [a]Num. 21:28; 32:3; Jer. 48:34 [1]So with MT, Tg., Vg.; LXX, Syr. *loins*
5 [a]Is. 16:11; Jer. 48:31 [b]Jer. 48:5 [1]Or *The Third Eglath*, an unknown city, Jer. 48:34
6 [a]Num. 32:36
9 [a]2 Kin. 17:25; Jer. 50:17 [1]So with MT, Tg.; DSS, Vg. *Dibon;* LXX *Rimon*

CHAPTER 16

1 [a]2 Kin. 3:4; Ezra 7:17 [b]2 Kin. 14:7; Is. 42:11 [1]Lit. *Rock*
2 [a]Prov. 27:8 [b]Num. 21:13
4 [1]*devastator*
5 [a][Is. 9:6, 7; 32:1; 55:4; Dan. 7:14; Mic. 4:7; Luke 1:33; Rev. 11:15] [b]Ps. 72:2 [c]Is. 9:7
6 [a]Jer. 48:29; Amos 2:1; Obad. 3, 4; Zeph. 2:8, 10 [b]Is. 28:15 [1]Lit. *vain talk*
7 [a]Jer. 48:20 [b]2 Kin. 3:25; Jer. 48:31
8 [a]Is. 24:7 [b]Is. 16:9 [c]Jer. 48:32
9 [a]Is. 15:4 [1]Or *shouting has*
10 [a]Is. 24:8; Jer. 48:33
11 [a]Is. 15:5; 63:15; Jer. 48:36; Hos. 11:8; Phil. 2:1 [1]Lit. *belly* [2]*Kir Hareseth*, v. 7
12 [a]Is. 15:2

That he will come to his
sanctuary to pray;
But he will not prevail.

13 This *is* the word which the
LORD has spoken concerning
Moab since that time.
14 But now the LORD has spoken,
saying, "Within three years, [a]as
the years of a hired man, the glory
of Moab will be despised with
all that great multitude, and the
remnant *will be* very small *and*
feeble."

Proclamation Against Syria and Israel

17 The [a]burden[1] against Damascus.

"Behold, Damascus will cease
from *being* a city,
And it will be a ruinous heap.
2 [1]The cities of [a]Aroer *are* forsaken;
They will be for flocks
Which lie down, and [b]no one will
make *them* afraid.
3 [a]The fortress also will cease from
Ephraim,
The kingdom from Damascus,
And the remnant of Syria;
They will be as the glory of the
children of Israel,"
Says the LORD of hosts.

4 "In that day it shall come to pass
That the glory of Jacob will
[1]wane,
And [a]the fatness of his flesh grow
lean.
5 [a]It shall be as when the harvester
gathers the grain,
And reaps the heads with his
arm;
It shall be as he who gathers
heads of grain
In the Valley of Rephaim.
6 [a]Yet gleaning grapes will be left
in it,
Like the shaking of an olive tree,
Two *or* three olives at the top of
the uppermost bough,
Four *or* five in its most fruitful
branches,"
Says the LORD God of Israel.

7 In that day a man will [a]look to
his Maker,
And his eyes will have respect for
the Holy One of Israel.
8 He will not look to the altars,
The work of his hands;
He will not respect what his
[a]fingers have made,
Nor the [1]wooden images nor the
incense altars.

9 In that day his strong cities will
be as a forsaken [1]bough
And [2]an uppermost branch,
Which they left because of the
children of Israel;
And there will be desolation.

10 Because you have forgotten [a]the
God of your salvation,
And have not been mindful of the
Rock of your [1]stronghold,
Therefore you will plant pleasant
plants
And set out foreign seedlings;
11 In the day you will make your
plant to grow,
And in the morning you will
make your seed to flourish;
But the harvest *will be* a heap of
ruins
In the day of grief and desperate
sorrow.

12 Woe to the multitude of many
people
Who make a noise [a]like the roar
of the seas,
And to the rushing of nations
That make a rushing like the
rushing of mighty waters!
13 The nations will rush like the
rushing of many waters;
But *God* will [a]rebuke them and
they will flee far away,
And [b]be chased like the chaff of
the mountains before the wind,
Like a rolling thing before the
whirlwind.
14 Then behold, at eventide, trouble!
And before the morning, he *is* no
more.
This *is* the portion of those who
plunder us,
And the lot of those who rob us.

Proclamation Against Ethiopia

18 Woe [a]to the land shadowed
with buzzing wings,
Which *is* beyond the rivers of
[1]Ethiopia,
2 Which sends ambassadors by
sea,
Even in vessels of reed on the
waters, *saying,*
"Go, swift messengers, to a nation
tall and smooth *of skin,*
To a people terrible from their
beginning onward,
A nation powerful and treading
down,
Whose land the rivers divide."

14 [a]Job 7:1; 14:6; Is. 21:16

CHAPTER 17

1 [a]Gen. 14:15; 15:2; 2 Kin. 16:9; Jer. 49:23; Amos 1:3–5; Zech. 9:1; Acts 9:2 [1]*oracle, prophecy*

2 [a]Num. 32:34 [b]Jer. 7:33 [1]So with MT, Vg.; LXX *It shall be forsaken forever;* Tg. *Its cities shall be forsaken and desolate*

3 [a]Is. 7:16; 8:4

4 [a]Is. 10:16 [1]*fade*

5 [a]Is. 17:11; Jer. 51:33; Joel 3:13; Matt. 13:30

6 [a]Deut. 4:27; Is. 24:13; Obad. 5

7 [a]Is. 10:20; Hos. 3:5; Mic. 7:7

8 [a]Is. 2:8; 31:7 [1]Heb. *Asherim,* Canaanite deities

9 [1]LXX *Hivites;* Tg. *laid waste;* Vg. *as the plows* [2]LXX *Amorites;* Tg. *in ruins;* Vg. *corn*

10 [a]Ps. 68:19; Is. 51:13 [1]*refuge*

12 [a]Is. 5:30; Jer. 6:23; Ezek. 43:2; Luke 21:25

13 [a]Ps. 9:5; Is. 41:11 [b]Ps. 83:13; Hos. 13:3

CHAPTER 18

1 [a]2 Kin. 19:9; Is. 20:4, 5; Ezek. 30:4, 5, 9; Zeph. 2:12; 3:10 [1]Heb. *Cush*

3 All inhabitants of the world and
dwellers on the earth:
[a]When he lifts up a banner on the
mountains, you see *it;*
And when he blows a trumpet,
you hear *it.*
4 For so the LORD said to me,
"I will take My rest,
And I will [1]look from My
dwelling place
Like clear heat in sunshine,
Like a cloud of dew in the heat
of harvest."
5 For before the harvest, when the
bud is perfect
And the sour grape is ripening in
the flower,
He will both cut off the sprigs
with pruning hooks
And take away *and* cut down the
branches.
6 They will be left together for the
mountain birds of prey
And for the beasts of the earth;
The birds of prey will summer on
them,
And all the beasts of the earth
will winter on them.

7 In that time [a]a present will be
brought to the LORD of hosts
[1]From a people tall and smooth *of
skin,*
And from a people terrible from
their beginning onward,
A nation powerful and treading
down,
Whose land the rivers divide—
To the place of the name of the
LORD of hosts,
To Mount Zion.

Proclamation Against Egypt

19 The [a]burden[1] against Egypt.

Behold, the LORD [b]rides on a swift
cloud,
And will come into Egypt;
[c]The idols of Egypt will [2]totter at
His presence,
And the heart of Egypt will melt
in its midst.

2 "I will [a]set Egyptians against
Egyptians;
Everyone will fight against his
brother,
And everyone against his
neighbor,
City against city, kingdom
against kingdom.
3 The spirit of Egypt will fail in its
midst;
I will destroy their counsel,
And they will [a]consult the idols
and the charmers,
The mediums and the sorcerers.
4 And the Egyptians I will give
[a]Into the hand of a cruel master,
And a fierce king will rule over
them,"
Says the Lord, the LORD of hosts.

5 [a]The waters will fail from the sea,
And the river will be wasted and
dried up.
6 The rivers will turn foul;
The brooks [a]of defense will be
emptied and dried up;
The reeds and rushes will wither.
7 The papyrus reeds by [1]the River,
by the mouth of the River,
And everything sown by the
River,
Will wither, be driven away, and
be no more.
8 The fishermen also will mourn;
All those will lament who cast
hooks into the River,
And they will languish who
spread nets on the waters.
9 Moreover those who work in
[a]fine flax
And those who weave fine fabric
will be ashamed;
10 And its foundations will be
broken.
All who make wages *will be*
troubled of soul.

11 Surely the princes of [a]Zoan *are*
fools;
Pharaoh's wise counselors give
foolish counsel.
[b]How do you say to Pharaoh, "I
am the son of the wise,
The son of ancient kings?"
12 [a]Where *are* they?
Where are your wise men?
Let them tell you now,
And let them know what the
LORD of hosts has [b]purposed
against Egypt.
13 The princes of Zoan have become
fools;
[a]The princes of [1]Noph are
deceived;
They have also [2]deluded Egypt,
Those who are the [3]mainstay of
its tribes.
14 The LORD has mingled [a]a
perverse spirit in her midst;
And they have caused Egypt to
err in all her work,
As a drunken man staggers in his
vomit.
15 Neither will there be *any* work for
Egypt,
Which [a]the head or tail,
Palm branch or bulrush, may do.

---

3 [a]Is. 5:26
4 [1]*watch*
7 [a]Ps. 68:31; 72:10; Is. 16:1; Zeph. 3:10; Mal. 1:11; Acts 8:27–38 [1]So with DSS, LXX, Vg.; MT omits *From;* Tg. *To*

CHAPTER 19

1 [a]Jer. 9:25, 26; Ezek. 29:1—30:19; Joel 3:19 [b]Ps. 18:10; 104:3; Matt. 26:64; Rev. 1:7 [c]Ex. 12:12; Jer. 43:12 [1]*oracle, prophecy* [2]Lit. *shake*
2 [a]Judg. 7:22; 1 Sam. 14:16, 20; 2 Chr. 20:23; Matt. 10:21, 36
3 [a]1 Chr. 10:13; Is. 8:19; 47:12; Dan. 2:2
4 [a]Is. 20:4; Jer. 46:26; Ezek. 29:19
5 [a]Is. 50:2; Jer. 51:36; Ezek. 30:12
6 [a]2 Kin. 19:24
7 [1]The Nile
9 [a]1 Kin. 10:28; Prov. 7:16; Ezek. 27:7
11 [a]Num. 13:22; Ps. 78:12, 43; Is. 30:4 [b]Gen. 41:38, 39; 1 Kin. 4:29, 30; Acts 7:22
12 [a]1 Cor. 1:20 [b]Ps. 33:11
13 [a]Jer. 2:16; Ezek. 30:13 [1]Ancient Memphis [2]Lit. *caused to stagger* [3]*cornerstone*
14 [a]1 Kin. 22:22; Is. 29:10
15 [a]Is. 9:14–16

16 In that day Egypt will [a]be like
women, and will be afraid and fear
because of the waving of the hand
of the LORD of hosts, [b]which He
waves over it.
17 And the land of Judah will be
a terror to Egypt; everyone who
makes mention of it will be afraid
in himself, because of the counsel
of the LORD of hosts which He has
[a]determined against it.

Egypt, Assyria, and Israel Blessed

18 In that day five cities in the
land of Egypt will [a]speak the lan-
guage of Canaan and [b]swear by
the LORD of hosts; one will be
called the City of [1]Destruction.
19 In that day [a]there will be an al-
tar to the LORD in the midst of the
land of Egypt, and a pillar to the
[b]LORD at its border.
20 And [a]it will be for a sign and
for a witness to the LORD of hosts
in the land of Egypt; for they will
cry to the LORD because of the op-
pressors, and He will send them a
[b]Savior and a Mighty One, and He
will deliver them.
21 Then the LORD will be known
to Egypt, and the Egyptians will
[a]know the LORD in that day, and
[b]will make sacrifice and offering;
yes, they will make a vow to the
LORD and perform *it*.
22 And the LORD will strike Egypt,
He will strike and [a]heal *it;* they
will return to the LORD, and He will
be entreated by them and heal
them.
23 In that day [a]there will be a
highway from Egypt to Assyria,
and the Assyrian will come into
Egypt and the Egyptian into As-
syria, and the Egyptians will
[b]serve with the Assyrians.
24 In that day Israel will be one
of three with Egypt and Assyria—
a blessing in the midst of the land,
25 whom the LORD of hosts shall
bless, saying, "Blessed *is* Egypt
My people, and Assyria [a]the work
of My hands, and Israel My inheri-
tance."

The Sign Against Egypt and Ethiopia

20 In the year that [a]Tartan[1]
came to Ashdod, when Sar-
gon the king of Assyria sent him,
and he fought against Ashdod and
took it,

16 [a]Jer. 51:30; Nah. 3:13 [b]Is. 11:15
17 [a]Is. 14:24; Dan. 4:35
18 [a]Zeph. 3:9 [b]Is. 45:23 [1]Some Heb. mss., Arab., DSS, Tg., Vg. *Sun;* LXX *Asedek*, lit. *Righteousness*
19 [a]Gen. 28:18; Ex. 24:4; Josh. 22:10, 26, 27; Is. 56:7; 60:7 [b]Ps. 68:31
20 [a]Josh. 4:20; 22:27 [b]Is. 43:11
21 [a][Is. 2:3, 4; 11:9] [b]Is. 56:7; 60:7; Zech. 14:16–18; Mal. 1:11
22 [a]Deut. 32:39; Is. 30:26; 57:18; [Heb. 12:11]
23 [a]Is. 11:16; 35:8; 49:11; 62:10 [b]Is. 27:13
25 [a]Deut. 14:2; Ps. 100:3; Is. 29:23; Hos. 2:23; [Eph. 2:10]

CHAPTER 20

1 [a]2 Kin. 18:17 [1]Or *the Commander in Chief*
2 [a]Zech. 13:4; Matt. 3:4 [b]1 Sam. 19:24; Mic. 1:8 [1]Lit. *loins*
3 [a]Is. 8:18
4 [a]Is. 19:4 [b]2 Sam. 10:4; Is. 3:17; Jer. 13:22; Mic. 1:11
5 [a]2 Kin. 18:21; Is. 30:3–5; 31:1; Ezek. 29:6, 7
6 [a]Is. 30:5, 7

CHAPTER 21

1 [a]Zech. 9:14 [1]*oracle, prophecy*
2 [a]Is. 33:1 [b]Is. 13:17; 22:6; Jer. 49:34
3 [a]Is. 15:5; 16:11 [b]Is. 13:8 [1]Lit. *bowed*
4 [a]Deut. 28:67
5 [a]Jer. 51:39; Dan. 5:5

2 at the same time the LORD
spoke by Isaiah the son of Amoz,
saying, "Go, and remove [a]the
sackcloth from your [1]body, and
take your sandals off your feet."
And he did so, [b]walking naked and
barefoot.
3 Then the LORD said, "Just as
My servant Isaiah has walked
naked and barefoot three years
[a]*for* a sign and a wonder against
Egypt and Ethiopia,
4 "so shall the [a]king of Assyria
lead away the Egyptians as
prisoners and the Ethiopians as
captives, young and old, naked
and barefoot, [b]with their buttocks
uncovered, to the shame of Egypt.
5 [a]"Then they shall be afraid and
ashamed of Ethiopia their expecta-
tion and Egypt their glory.
6 "And the inhabitant of this ter-
ritory will say in that day, 'Surely
such *is* our expectation, wherever
we flee for [a]help to be delivered
from the king of Assyria; and how
shall we escape?' "

The Fall of Babylon Proclaimed

21 The [1]burden against the Wil-
derness of the Sea.

As [a]whirlwinds in the South pass
through,
So it comes from the desert, from
a terrible land.
2 A distressing vision is declared
to me;
[a]The treacherous dealer deals
treacherously,
And the plunderer plunders.
[b]Go up, O Elam!
Besiege, O Media!
All its sighing I have made to
cease.

3 Therefore [a]my loins are filled
with pain;
[b]Pangs have taken hold of me, like
the pangs of a woman in
labor.
I was [1]distressed when *I* heard *it;*
I was dismayed when *I* saw *it*.
4 My heart wavered, fearfulness
frightened me;
[a]The night for which I longed He
turned into fear for me.
5 [a]Prepare the table,
Set a watchman in the tower,
Eat and drink.
Arise, you princes,
Anoint the shield!

6 For thus has the Lord said to me:
"Go, set a watchman,
Let him declare what he sees."
7 And he saw a chariot *with* a pair
of horsemen,
A chariot of donkeys, *and* a
chariot of camels,
And he listened earnestly with
great care.
8 [1]Then he cried, "A lion, my Lord!
I stand continually on the
[a]watchtower in the daytime;
I have sat at my post every night.
9 And look, here comes a chariot
of men *with* a pair of
horsemen!"
Then he answered and said,
[a]"Babylon is fallen, is fallen!
And [b]all the carved images of her
gods
He has broken to the ground."

10 [a]Oh, my threshing and the grain
of my floor!
That which I have heard from the
LORD of hosts,
The God of Israel,
I have declared to you.

Proclamation Against Edom

11 [a]The [1]burden against Dumah.

He calls to me out of [b]Seir,
"Watchman, what of the night?
Watchman, what of the night?"
12 The watchman said,
"The morning comes, and also the
night.
If you will inquire, inquire;
Return! Come back!"

Proclamation Against Arabia

13 [a]The [1]burden against Arabia.

In the forest in Arabia you will
lodge,
O you traveling companies [b]of
Dedanites.
14 O inhabitants of the land of
Tema,
Bring water to him who is thirsty;
With their bread they met him
who fled.
15 For they fled from the swords,
from the drawn sword,
From the bent bow, and from the
distress of war.

16 For thus the LORD has said to
me: "Within a year, [a]according to
the year of a hired man, all the
glory of [b]Kedar will fail;
17 "and the remainder of the num-
ber of archers, the mighty men of
the people of Kedar, will be dimin-
ished; for the LORD God of Israel
has spoken *it*."

Proclamation Against Jerusalem

22 The [1]burden against the Val-
ley of Vision.

What ails you now, that you have
all gone up to the housetops,
2 You who are full of noise,
A [1]tumultuous city, [a]a joyous
city?
Your slain *men are* not slain with
the sword,
Nor dead in battle.
3 All your rulers have fled together;
They are captured by the archers.
All who are found in you are
bound together;
They have fled from afar.
4 Therefore I said, "Look away
from me,
[a]I will weep bitterly;
Do not labor to comfort me
Because of the plundering of the
daughter of my people."

5 [a]For *it is* a day of trouble and
treading down and perplexity
[b]By the Lord GOD of hosts
In the Valley of Vision—
Breaking down the walls
And of crying to the mountain.
6 [a]Elam bore the quiver
With chariots of men *and*
horsemen,
And [b]Kir uncovered the shield.
7 It shall come to pass *that* your
choicest valleys
Shall be full of chariots,
And the horsemen shall set
themselves in array at the gate.

8 [a]He removed the [1]protection of
Judah.
You looked in that day to the
armor [b]of the House of the
Forest;
9 [a]You also saw the [1]damage to the
city of David,
That it was great;
And you gathered together the
waters of the lower pool.
10 You numbered the houses of
Jerusalem,
And the houses you broke down
To fortify the wall.
11 [a]You also made a reservoir
between the two walls
For the water of the old [b]pool.
But you did not look to its
Maker,
Nor did you have respect for Him
who fashioned it long ago.

8 [a]Hab. 2:1 [1]DSS *Then the observer cried, "My Lord!*
9 [a]Is. 13:19; 47:5, 9; 48:14; Jer. 51:8; Dan. 5:28, 31; Rev. 14:8; 18:2 [b]Is. 46:1; Jer. 50:2; 51:44
10 [a]Jer. 51:33; Mic. 4:13
11 [a]Gen. 25:14; 1 Chr. 1:30; Josh. 15:52 [b]Gen. 32:3; Jer. 49:7; Ezek. 35:2; Obad. 1 [1]*oracle, prophecy*
13 [a]Jer. 25:24; 49:28 [b]Gen. 10:7; 1 Chr. 1:9, 32; Jer. 25:23; Ezek. 27:15 [1]*oracle, prophecy*
16 [a]Is. 16:14 [b]Ps. 120:5; Song 1:5; Is. 42:11; 60:7; Ezek. 27:21

CHAPTER 22

1 [1]*oracle, prophecy*
2 [a]Is. 32:13 [1]*boisterous*
4 [a]Jer. 4:19
5 [a]Is. 37:3 [b]Lam. 1:5; 2:2
6 [a]Jer. 49:35 [b]Is. 15:1
8 [a]2 Kin. 18:15, 16 [b]1 Kin. 7:2; 10:17 [1]Lit. *covering*
9 [a]2 Kin. 20:20; 2 Chr. 32:4; Neh. 3:16 [1]Lit. *breaches* in the city walls
11 [a]Neh. 3:16 [b]2 Kin. 20:20; 2 Chr. 32:3, 4

12 And in that day the Lord GOD of hosts
[a]Called for weeping and for mourning,
[b]For baldness and for girding with sackcloth.
13 But instead, joy and gladness,
Slaying oxen and killing sheep,
Eating meat and [a]drinking wine:
[b]"Let us eat and drink, for tomorrow we die!"

14 [a]Then it was revealed in my hearing by the LORD of hosts,
"Surely for this iniquity there [b]will be no atonement for you,
Even to your death," says the Lord GOD of hosts.

The Judgment on Shebna

15 Thus says the Lord GOD of hosts:

"Go, proceed to this steward,
To [a]Shebna, who *is* over the house, *and say:*
16 'What have you here, and whom have you here,
That you have hewn a sepulcher here,
As he [a]who hews himself a sepulcher on high,
Who carves a tomb for himself in a rock?
17 Indeed, the LORD will throw you away violently,
O mighty man,
[a]And will surely seize you.
18 He will surely turn violently and toss you like a ball
Into a large country;
There you shall die, and there [a]your glorious chariots
Shall be the shame of your master's house.
19 So I will drive you out of your office,
And from your position [1]he will pull you down.

20 'Then it shall be in that day,
That I will call My servant [a]Eliakim the son of Hilkiah;
21 I will clothe him with your robe
And strengthen him with your belt;
I will commit your responsibility into his hand.
He shall be a father to the inhabitants of Jerusalem
And to the house of Judah.
22 The key of the house of David
I will lay on his [a]shoulder;
So he shall [b]open, and no one shall shut;
And he shall shut, and no one shall open.
23 I will fasten him *as* [a]a peg in a secure place,
And he will become a glorious throne to his father's house.

24 'They will hang on him all the
glory of his father's house, the off-
spring and the posterity, all ves-
sels of small quantity, from the
cups to all the pitchers.
25 'In that day,' says the LORD of
hosts, 'the peg that is fastened in
the secure place will be removed
and be cut down and fall, and the
burden that *was* on it will be cut
off; for the LORD has spoken.' "

Proclamation Against Tyre

23 The [a]burden[1] against Tyre.

Wail, you ships of Tarshish!
For it is laid waste,
So that there is no house, no harbor;
From the land of [2]Cyprus it is revealed to them.

2 Be still, you inhabitants of the coastland,
You merchants of Sidon,
[1]Whom those who cross the sea have filled.
3 And on great waters the grain of Shihor,
The harvest of [1]the River, *is* her revenue;
And [a]she is a marketplace for the nations.

4 Be ashamed, O Sidon;
For the sea has spoken,
The strength of the sea, saying,
"I do not labor, nor bring forth children;
Neither do I rear young men,
Nor bring up virgins."
5 [a]When the report *reaches* Egypt,
They also will be in agony at the report of Tyre.

6 Cross over to Tarshish;
Wail, you inhabitants of the coastland!
7 *Is* this your [a]joyous *city,*
Whose antiquity *is* from ancient days,
Whose feet carried her far off to dwell?
8 Who has taken this counsel against Tyre, [a]the crowning *city,*
Whose merchants *are* princes,

---

12 [a]Is. 32:11; Joel 1:13; 2:17 [b]Ezra 9:3; Is. 15:2; Mic. 1:16
13 [a]Is. 5:11, 22; 28:7, 8; Luke 17:26–29 [b]Is. 56:12; 1 Cor. 15:32
14 [a]Is. 5:9 [b]1 Sam. 3:14; Ezek. 24:13
15 [a]2 Kin. 18:37; Is. 36:3
16 [a]2 Sam. 18:18; 2 Chr. 16:14; Matt. 27:60
17 [a]Esth. 7:8
18 [a]Is. 2:7
19 [1]LXX omits *he will pull you down;* Syr., Tg., Vg. *I will pull you down*
20 [a]2 Kin. 18:18; Is. 36:3, 22; 37:2
22 [a]Is. 9:6 [b]Job 12:14; Rev. 3:7
23 [a]Ezra 9:8; Zech. 10:4

CHAPTER 23

1 [a]Jer. 25:22; 47:4; Ezek. 26—28; Amos 1:9; Zech. 9:2, 4 [1]*oracle, prophecy* [2]Heb. *Kittim,* western lands, especially Cyprus
2 [1]So with MT, Vg.; LXX, Tg. *Passing over the water;* DSS *Your messengers passing over the sea*
3 [a]Ezek. 27:3–23 [1]The Nile
5 [a]Is. 19:16
7 [a]Is. 22:2; 32:13
8 [a]Ezek. 28:2, 12

Whose traders *are* the honorable
of the earth?
9 The LORD of hosts has
[a]purposed it,
To [1]bring to dishonor the [b]pride
of all glory,
To bring into contempt all the
honorable of the earth.

10 Overflow through your land like
[1]the River,
O daughter of Tarshish;
There is no more [2]strength.
11 He stretched out His hand over
the sea,
He shook the kingdoms;
The LORD has given a
commandment [a]against
Canaan
To destroy its strongholds.
12 And He said, "You will rejoice no
more,
O you oppressed virgin daughter
of Sidon.
Arise, [a]cross over to Cyprus;
There also you will have no rest."

13 Behold, the land of the
[a]Chaldeans,
This people *which* was not;
Assyria founded it for [b]wild
beasts of the desert.
They set up its towers,
They raised up its palaces,
And brought it to ruin.

14 [a]Wail, you ships of Tarshish!
For your strength is laid waste.

15 Now it shall come to pass in
that day that Tyre will be forgotten
seventy years, according to the
days of one king. At the end of sev-
enty years it will happen to Tyre
as *in* the song of the harlot:

16 "Take a harp, go about the city,
You forgotten harlot;
Make sweet melody, sing many
songs,
That you may be remembered."

17 And it shall be, at the end of
seventy years, that the LORD will
deal with Tyre. She will return to
her hire, and [a]commit fornication
with all the kingdoms of the world
on the face of the earth.
18 Her gain and her pay [a]will be
set apart for the LORD; it will not
be treasured nor laid up, for her
gain will be for those who dwell
before the LORD, to eat sufficiently,
and for [1]fine clothing.

9 [a]Is. 14:26 [b]Job 40:11, 12; Is. 13:11; 24:4; Dan. 4:37 [1]*pollute*
10 [1]The Nile [2]*restraint*, lit. *belt*
11 [a]Zech. 9:2–4
12 [a]Ezek. 26:13, 14; Rev. 18:22
13 [a]Is. 47:1 [b]Ps. 72:9
14 [a]Ezek. 27:25–30
17 [a]Rev. 17:2
18 [a]Ex. 28:36; Zech. 14:20, 21 [1]*choice*

CHAPTER 24
2 [a]Hos. 4:9 [b]Ezek. 7:12, 13
4 [a]Is. 25:11 [1]*proud*
5 [a]Gen. 3:17; Num. 35:33; Is. 9:17; 10:6 [b]Is. 59:12 [c]1 Chr. 16:14–19; Ps. 105:7–12
6 [a]Mal. 4:6 [b]Is. 9:19 [1]Or *held guilty*
7 [a]Is. 16:8–10; Joel 1:10, 12
8 [a]Is. 5:12, 14; Jer. 7:34; 16:9; 25:10; Ezek. 26:13; Hos. 2:11; Rev. 18:22

Impending Judgment on the Earth

24 Behold, the LORD makes the
earth empty and makes it
waste,
Distorts its surface
And scatters abroad its
inhabitants.
2 And it shall be:
As with the people, so with the
[a]priest;
As with the servant, so with his
master;
As with the maid, so with her
mistress;
[b]As with the buyer, so with the
seller;
As with the lender, so with the
borrower;
As with the creditor, so with the
debtor.
3 The land shall be entirely
emptied and utterly plundered,
For the LORD has spoken this
word.

4 The earth mourns *and* fades
away,
The world languishes *and* fades
away;
The [a]haughty[1] people of the earth
languish.
5 [a]The earth is also defiled under its
inhabitants,
Because they have [b]transgressed
the laws,
Changed the ordinance,
Broken the [c]everlasting
covenant.
6 Therefore [a]the curse has
devoured the earth,
And those who dwell in it are
[1]desolate.
Therefore the inhabitants of the
earth are [b]burned,
And few men *are* left.

7 [a]The new wine fails, the vine
languishes,
All the merry-hearted sigh.
8 The mirth [a]of the tambourine
ceases,
The noise of the jubilant ends,
The joy of the harp ceases.
9 They shall not drink wine with a
song;
Strong drink is bitter to those
who drink it.
10 The city of confusion is broken
down;
Every house is shut up, so that
none may go in.
11 *There is* a cry for wine in the
streets,
All joy is darkened,

The mirth of the land is gone.
12 In the city desolation is left,
And the gate is stricken with
destruction.
13 When it shall be thus in the midst
of the land among the people,
[a]*It shall be* like the shaking of an
olive tree,
Like the gleaning of grapes when
the vintage is done.

14 They shall lift up their voice, they
shall sing;
For the majesty of the LORD
They shall cry aloud from the sea.
15 Therefore [a]glorify the LORD in the
dawning light,
[b]The name of the LORD God of
Israel in the coastlands of the
sea.
16 From the ends of the earth we
have heard songs:
"Glory to the righteous!"
But I said, [1]"I am ruined, ruined!
Woe to me!
[a]The treacherous dealers have
dealt treacherously,
Indeed, the treacherous dealers
have dealt very treacherously."

17 [a]Fear and the pit and the snare
Are upon you, O inhabitant of the
earth.
18 And it shall be
That he who flees from the noise
of the fear
Shall fall into the pit,
And he who comes up from the
midst of the pit
Shall be [1]caught in the snare;
For [a]the windows from on high
are open,
And [b]the foundations of the earth
are shaken.

19 [a]The earth is violently broken,
The earth is split open,
The earth is shaken exceedingly.
20 The earth shall [a]reel[1] to and fro
like a drunkard,
And shall totter like a hut;
Its transgression shall be heavy
upon it,
And it will fall, and not rise again.

21 It shall come to pass in that day
That the LORD will punish on
high the host of exalted ones,
And on the earth [a]the kings of the
earth.
22 They will be gathered together,
As prisoners are gathered in the
[1]pit,
And will be shut up in the prison;
After many days they will be
punished.
23 Then the [a]moon will be disgraced
And the sun ashamed;
For the LORD of hosts will [b]reign
On [c]Mount Zion and in Jerusalem
And before His elders, gloriously.

Praise to God

25 O LORD, You *are* my God.
[a]I will exalt You,
I will praise Your name,
[b]For You have done wonderful
things;
[c]*Your* counsels of old *are*
faithfulness *and* truth.
2 For You have made [a]a city a ruin,
A fortified city a ruin,
A palace of foreigners to be a city
no more;
It will never be rebuilt.
3 Therefore the strong people will
[a]glorify You;
The city of the [1]terrible nations
will fear You.
4 For You have been a strength to
the poor,
A strength to the needy in his
distress,
[a]A refuge from the storm,
A shade from the heat;
For the blast of the terrible ones
is as a storm *against* the wall.
5 You will reduce the noise of
aliens,
As heat in a dry place;
As heat in the shadow of a cloud,
The song of the terrible ones will
be [1]diminished.

6 And in [a]this mountain
[b]The LORD of hosts will make for
[c]all people
A feast of [1]choice pieces,
A feast of [2]wines on the lees,
Of fat things full of marrow,
Of well-refined wines on the lees.
7 And He will destroy on this
mountain
The surface of the covering cast
over all people,
And [a]the veil that is spread over
all nations.
8 He will [a]swallow up death
forever,
And the Lord GOD will [b]wipe
away tears from all faces;
The rebuke of His people
He will take away from all the
earth;
For the LORD has spoken.

9 And it will be said in that day:
"Behold, this *is* our God;

---

13 [a][Is. 17:5, 6; 27:12]
15 [a]Is. 25:3 [b]Mal. 1:11
16 [a]Is. 21:2; 33:1; Jer. 3:20; 5:11 [1]Lit. *Leanness to me, leanness to me*
17 [a]Jer. 48:43; Amos 5:19
18 [a]Gen. 7:11 [b]Ps. 18:7; 46:2; Is. 2:19, 21; 13:13 [1]Lit. *taken*
19 [a]Jer. 4:23
20 [a]Is. 19:14; 24:1; 28:7 [1]*stagger*
21 [a]Ps. 76:12
22 [1]*dungeon*
23 [a]Is. 13:10; 60:19; Ezek. 32:7; Joel 2:31; 3:15 [b]Rev. 19:4, 6 [c][Heb. 12:22]

CHAPTER 25
1 [a]Ex. 15:2 [b]Ps. 98:1 [c]Num. 23:19
2 [a]Is. 21:9; 23:13; Jer. 51:37
3 [a]Is. 24:15; Rev. 11:13 [1]*terrifying*
4 [a]Is. 4:6
5 [1]*humbled*
6 [a][Is. 2:2–4; 56:7] [b]Prov. 9:2; Matt. 22:4 [c][Dan. 7:14; Matt. 8:11] [1]Lit. *fat things* [2]*wines matured on the sediment*
7 [a]2 Cor. 3:15; [Eph. 4:18]
8 [a][Hos. 13:14; 1 Cor. 15:54; Rev. 20:14] [b]Is. 30:19; Rev. 7:17; 21:4

[a]We have waited for Him, and He will save us.
This is the LORD;
We have waited for Him;
[b]We will be glad and rejoice in His salvation."

10 For on this mountain the hand of the LORD will rest,
And [a]Moab shall be trampled down under Him,
As straw is trampled down for the refuse heap.
11 And He will spread out His hands in their midst
As a swimmer reaches out to swim,
And He will bring down their [a]pride
Together with the trickery of their hands.
12 The [a]fortress of the high fort of your walls
He will bring down, lay low,
And bring to the ground, down to the dust.

A Song of Salvation

26 In [a]that day this song will be sung in the land of Judah:

"We have a strong city;
[b]*God* will appoint salvation *for* walls and bulwarks.
2 [a]Open the gates,
That the righteous nation which [1]keeps the truth may enter in.
3 You will keep *him* in perfect [a]peace,
Whose mind *is* stayed *on You,*
Because he trusts in You.
4 Trust in the LORD forever,
[a]For in YAH, the LORD, *is* [1]everlasting strength.
5 For He brings [1]down those who dwell on high,
[a]The lofty city;
He lays it low,
He lays it low to the ground,
He brings it down to the dust.
6 The foot shall [1]tread it down—
The feet of the poor
And the steps of the needy."

7 The way of the just *is* uprightness;
[a]O Most Upright,
You [1]weigh the path of the just.
8 Yes, [a]in the way of Your judgments,
O LORD, we have [b]waited for You;
The desire of *our* soul *is* for Your name
And for the remembrance of You.
9 [a]With my soul I have desired You in the night,
Yes, by my spirit within me I will seek You early;
For when Your judgments *are* in the earth,
The inhabitants of the world will learn righteousness.

10 [a]Let grace be shown to the wicked,
Yet he will not learn righteousness;
In [b]the land of uprightness he will deal unjustly,
And will not behold the majesty of the LORD.
11 LORD, *when* Your hand is lifted up, [a]they will not see.
But they will see and be ashamed
For [1]*their* envy of people;
Yes, the fire of Your enemies shall devour them.

12 LORD, You will establish peace for us,
For You have also done all our works [1]in us.
13 O LORD our God, [a]masters besides You
Have had dominion over us;
But by You only we make mention of Your name.
14 *They are* dead, they will not live;
They are deceased, they will not rise.
Therefore You have punished and destroyed them,
And made all their memory to [a]perish.
15 You have increased the nation, O LORD,
You have [a]increased the nation;
You are glorified;
You have expanded all the [1]borders of the land.

16 LORD, [a]in trouble they have visited You,
They poured out a prayer *when* Your chastening *was* upon them.
17 As [a]a woman with child
Is in pain and cries out in her [1]pangs,
When she draws near the time of her delivery,
So have we been in Your sight, O LORD.
18 We have been with child, we have been in pain;
We have, as it were, [1]brought forth wind;
We have not accomplished any deliverance in the earth,

---

9 [a]Gen. 49:18; Is. 8:17; 26:8; [Titus 2:13] [b]Ps. 20:5
10 [a]Is. 16:14; Jer. 48:1–47; Ezek. 25:8–11; Amos 2:1–3; Zeph. 2:9
11 [a]Is. 24:4; 26:5
12 [a]Is. 26:5

CHAPTER 26

1 [a]Is. 2:11; 12:1 [b]Is. 60:18
2 [a]Ps. 118:19, 20 [1]Or *remains faithful*
3 [a]Is. 57:19; [Phil. 4:6, 7]
4 [a]Is. 12:2; 45:17 [1]Or *Rock of Ages*
5 [a]Is. 25:11, 12 [1]*low*
6 [1]*trample*
7 [a]Ps. 37:23 [1]Or *make level*
8 [a]Is. 64:5 [b]Is. 25:9; 33:2
9 [a]Ps. 63:6; Song 3:1; Is. 50:10; Luke 6:12
10 [a]Eccl. 8:12; [Rom. 2:4] [b]Ps. 143:10
11 [a]Job 34:27; Ps. 28:5; Is. 5:12 [1]Or *Your zeal for the people*
12 [1]Or *for us*
13 [a]2 Chr. 12:8
14 [a]Eccl. 9:5; Is. 14:22
15 [a]Is. 9:3 [1]Or *ends*
16 [a]Is. 37:3; Hos. 5:15
17 [a]Is. 13:8; [John 16:21] [1]*sharp pains*
18 [1]*given birth to*

Nor have [a]the inhabitants of the
world fallen.
19 [a]Your dead shall live;
Together with [1]my dead body
they shall arise.
[b]Awake and sing, you who dwell
in dust;
For your dew *is like* the dew of
herbs,
And the earth shall cast out the
dead.

Take Refuge from the Coming Judgment

20 Come, my people, [a]enter your
chambers,
And shut your doors behind you;
Hide yourself, as it were, [b]for a
little moment,
Until the indignation is past.
21 For behold, the LORD [a]comes out
of His place
To punish the inhabitants of the
earth for their iniquity;
The earth will also disclose her
[1]blood,
And will no more cover her slain.

27 In that day the LORD with His
severe sword, great and
strong,
Will punish Leviathan the fleeing
serpent,
[a]Leviathan that twisted serpent;
And He will slay [b]the reptile that
is in the sea.

The Restoration of Israel

2 In that day [a]sing to her,
[b]"A vineyard of [1]red wine!
3 [a]I, the LORD, keep it,
I water it every moment;
Lest any hurt it,
I keep it night and day.
4 Fury *is* not in Me.
Who would set [a]briers *and* thorns
Against Me in battle?
I would go through them,
I would burn them together.
5 Or let him take hold [a]of My
strength,
That he may [b]make peace
with Me;
And he shall make peace
with Me."

6 Those who come He shall cause
[a]to take root in Jacob;
Israel shall blossom and bud,
And fill the face of the world with
fruit.

7 [a]Has He struck [1]Israel as He
struck those who struck him?
Or has He been slain according
to the slaughter of those who
were slain by Him?
8 [a]In measure, by sending it away,
You contended with it.
[b]He removes *it* by His rough wind
In the day of the east wind.
9 Therefore by this the iniquity of
Jacob will be covered;
And this *is* all the fruit of taking
away his sin:
When he makes all the stones of
the altar
Like chalkstones that are beaten
to dust,
[1]Wooden images and incense
altars shall not stand.

10 Yet the fortified city *will be*
[a]desolate,
The habitation forsaken and left
like a wilderness;
There the calf will feed, and there
it will lie down
And consume its branches.
11 When its boughs are withered,
they will be broken off;
The women come *and* set them
on fire.
For [a]it *is* a people of no
understanding;
Therefore He who made them
will [b]not have mercy on them,
And [c]He who formed them will
show them no favor.

12 And it shall come to pass in that
day
That the LORD will thresh,
From the channel of [1]the River to
the Brook of Egypt;
And you will be [a]gathered one by
one,
O you children of Israel.

13 [a]So it shall be in that day:
[b]The great trumpet will be blown;
They will come, who are about to
perish in the land of Assyria,
And they who are outcasts in the
land of [c]Egypt,
And shall [d]worship the LORD in
the holy mount at Jerusalem.

Woe to Ephraim and Jerusalem

28 Woe to the crown of pride, to
the drunkards of Ephraim,
Whose glorious beauty *is* a fading
flower
Which *is* at the head of the
[1]verdant valleys,
To those who are overcome with
wine!

---

18 [a]Ps. 17:14
19 [a][Ezek. 37:1–14] [b][Dan. 12:2] [1]So with MT, Vg.; Syr., Tg. *their dead bodies;* LXX *those in the tombs*
20 [a]Ex. 12:22, 23 [b][Ps. 30:5]
21 [a]Mic. 1:3 [1]Or *bloodshed*

CHAPTER 27
1 [a]Ps. 74:13, 14 [b]Is. 51:9
2 [a]Is. 5:1 [b]Is. 5:7 [1]So with MT (Kittel's *Biblia Hebraica*), Bg., Vg.; MT (*Biblia Hebraica Stuttgartensia*), some Heb. mss., LXX *delight;* Tg. *choice vineyard*
3 [a]Is. 31:5
4 [a]2 Sam. 23:6
5 [a]Is. 25:4 [b]Job 22:21
6 [a]Is. 37:31
7 [a]Is. 10:12, 17; 30:30–33 [1]Lit. *him*
8 [a]Job 23:6 [b][Ps. 78:38]
9 [1]Heb. *Asherim,* Canaanite deities
10 [a]Is. 5:6, 17; 32:14
11 [a]Deut. 32:28 [b]Is. 9:17 [c]Deut. 32:18
12 [a][Is. 11:11; 56:8] [1]The Euphrates
13 [a]Is. 2:11 [b]Rev. 11:15 [c]Is. 19:21, 22 [d]Zech. 14:16

CHAPTER 28
1 [1]Lit. *valleys of fatness*

2 Behold, the Lord has a mighty
and strong one,
[a]Like a tempest of hail and a
destroying storm,
Like a flood of mighty waters
overflowing,
Who will bring *them* down to the
earth with *His* hand.
3 The crown of pride, the
drunkards of Ephraim,
Will be trampled underfoot;
4 And the glorious beauty is a
fading flower
Which *is* at the head of the
[1]verdant valley,
Like the first fruit before the
summer,
Which an observer sees;
He eats it up while it is still in
his hand.

5 In that day the LORD of hosts will
be
For a crown of glory and a
diadem of beauty
To the remnant of His people,
6 For a spirit of justice to him who
sits in judgment,
And for strength to those who
turn back the battle at the gate.

7 But they also [a]have erred through
wine,
And through intoxicating drink
are out of the way;
[b]The priest and the prophet have
erred through intoxicating
drink,
They are swallowed up by wine,
They are out of the way through
intoxicating drink;
They err in vision, they stumble
in judgment.
8 For all tables are full of vomit *and*
filth;
No place *is clean.*

9 "Whom[a] will he teach knowledge?
And whom will he make to
understand the message?
Those *just* weaned from milk?
Those *just* drawn from the
breasts?
10 [a]For precept *must be* upon
precept, precept upon precept,
Line upon line, line upon line,
Here a little, there a little."

11 For with [a]stammering lips and
another tongue
He will speak to this people,
12 To whom He said, "This *is* the
[a]rest *with which*
You may cause the weary to
rest,"

2 [a]Is. 30:30; Ezek. 13:11
4 [1]Lit. *valley of fatness*
7 [a]Prov. 20:1; Is. 5:11, 22; Hos. 4:11 [b]Is. 56:10, 12
9 [a]Jer. 6:10
10 [a][2 Chr. 36:15; Neh. 9:30; Jer. 25:3, 4; 35:15; 44:4]
11 [a]Is. 33:19; 1 Cor. 14:21
12 [a]Is. 30:15; Jer. 6:16; [Matt. 11:28, 29]
15 [a]Is. 9:15; Ezek. 13:22; Amos 2:4
16 [a]Gen. 49:24; Ps. 118:22; Is. 8:14, 15; Matt. 21:42; Mark 12:10; Luke 20:17; Acts 4:11; Rom. 9:33; 10:11; Eph. 2:20; 1 Pet. 2:6–8

And, "This *is* the refreshing";
Yet they would not hear.
13 But the word of the LORD was to
them,
"Precept upon precept, precept
upon precept,
Line upon line, line upon line,
Here a little, there a little,"
That they might go and fall
backward, and be broken
And snared and caught.

14 Therefore hear the word of the
LORD, you scornful men,
Who rule this people who *are* in
Jerusalem,
15 Because you have said, "We have
made a covenant with death,
And with Sheol we are in
agreement.
When the overflowing scourge
passes through,
It will not come to us,
[a]For we have made lies our refuge,
And under falsehood we have
hidden ourselves."

A Cornerstone in Zion

16 Therefore thus says the Lord
GOD:

"Behold, I lay in Zion [a]a stone for
a foundation,
A tried stone, a precious
cornerstone, a sure foundation;
Whoever believes will not act
hastily.
17 Also I will make justice the
measuring line,
And righteousness the plummet;
The hail will sweep away the
refuge of lies,
And the waters will overflow the
hiding place.
18 Your covenant with death will be
annulled,
And your agreement with Sheol
will not stand;
When the overflowing scourge
passes through,
Then you will be trampled down
by it.
19 As often as it goes out it will take
you;
For morning by morning it will
pass over,
And by day and by night;
It will be a terror just to
understand the report."

20 For the bed is too short to stretch
out *on,*
And the covering so narrow that
one cannot wrap himself *in it.*

21 For the LORD will rise up as *at*
Mount [a]Perazim,
He will be angry as in the Valley
of [b]Gibeon—
That He may do His work, [c]His
awesome work,
And bring to pass His act, His
[1]unusual act.
22 Now therefore, do not be
mockers,
Lest your bonds be made strong;
For I have heard from the Lord
GOD of hosts,
[a]A [1]destruction determined even
upon the whole earth.

Listen to the Teaching of God

23 Give ear and hear my voice,
Listen and hear my speech.
24 Does the plowman keep plowing
all day to sow?
Does he keep turning his soil and
breaking the clods?
25 When he has leveled its surface,
Does he not sow the black
cummin
And scatter the cummin,
Plant the wheat in rows,
The barley in the appointed
place,
And the [1]spelt in its place?
26 For He instructs him in right
judgment,
His God teaches him.
27 For the black cummin is not
threshed with a threshing
sledge,
Nor is a cartwheel rolled over the
cummin;
But the black cummin is beaten
out with a stick,
And the cummin with a rod.
28 Bread *flour* must be ground;
Therefore he does not thresh it
forever,
Break *it with* his cartwheel,
Or crush it *with* his horsemen.
29 This also comes from the LORD
of hosts,
[a]*Who* is wonderful in counsel *and*
excellent in [1]guidance.

Woe to Jerusalem

29 "Woe [a]to [1]Ariel, to Ariel, the
city [b]*where* David dwelt!
Add year to year;
Let feasts come around.
2 Yet I will distress Ariel;
There shall be heaviness and
sorrow,
And it shall be to Me as Ariel.
3 I will encamp against you all
around,
I will lay siege against you with
a mound,
And I will raise siegeworks
against you.
4 You shall be brought down,
You shall speak out of the
ground;
Your speech shall be low, out of
the dust;
Your voice shall be like a
medium's, [a]out of the ground;
And your speech shall whisper
out of the dust.

5 "Moreover the multitude of your
[a]foes
Shall be like fine dust,
And the multitude of the terrible
ones
Like [b]chaff that passes away;
Yes, it shall be [c]in an instant,
suddenly.
6 [a]You will be punished by the LORD
of hosts
With thunder and [b]earthquake
and great noise,
With storm and tempest
And the flame of devouring fire.
7 [a]The multitude of all the nations
who fight against [1]Ariel,
Even all who fight against her
and her fortress,
And distress her,
Shall be [b]as a dream of a night
vision.
8 [a]It shall even be as when a hungry
man dreams,
And look—he eats;
But he awakes, and his soul is
still empty;
Or as when a thirsty man dreams,
And look—he drinks;
But he awakes, and indeed *he is*
faint,
And his soul still craves:
So the multitude of all the nations
shall be,
Who fight against Mount Zion."

The Blindness of Disobedience

9 Pause and wonder!
Blind yourselves and be blind!
[a]They are drunk, [b]but not with
wine;
They stagger, but not with
intoxicating drink.
10 For [a]the LORD has poured out on
you
The spirit of deep sleep,
And has [b]closed your eyes,
namely, the prophets;
And He has covered your heads,
namely, [c]the seers.

11 The whole vision has become
to you like the words of a [1]book
[a]that is sealed, which *men* deliver

21 [a]2 Sam. 5:20; 1 Chr. 14:11 [b]Josh. 10:10, 12; 2 Sam. 5:25; 1 Chr. 14:16 [c][Lam. 3:33; Luke 19:41–44] [1]Lit. *foreign*
22 [a]Is. 10:22; Dan. 9:27 [1]Lit. *complete end*
25 [1]*rye*
29 [a]Ps. 92:5; Is. 9:6; Jer. 32:19 [1]*sound wisdom*

CHAPTER 29

1 [a]Ezek. 24:6, 9 [b]2 Sam. 5:9 [1]Jerusalem, lit. *Lion of God*
4 [a]Is. 8:19
5 [a]Is. 25:5 [b]Job 21:18; Is. 17:13 [c]Is. 30:13; 47:11; 1 Thess. 5:3
6 [a]Is. 28:2; 30:30 [b]1 Sam. 2:10; Zech. 14:4; Matt. 24:7; Mark 13:8; Luke 21:11; Rev. 16:18, 19
7 [a]Is. 37:36; Mic. 4:11, 12; Zech. 12:9 [b]Job 20:8 [1]Jerusalem
8 [a]Ps. 73:20
9 [a]Is. 28:7, 8 [b]Is. 51:21
10 [a]Ps. 69:23; Is. 6:9, 10; Mic. 3:6; Rom. 11:8 [b]Ps. 69:23; Is. 6:10 [c]1 Sam. 9:9; Is. 44:18; Mic. 3:6; [2 Thess. 2:9–12]
11 [a]Is. 8:16 [1]*scroll*

to one who is literate, saying, "Read this, please." [b]And he says, "I cannot, for it *is* sealed."

12 Then the book is delivered to one who [1]is illiterate, saying, "Read this, please." And he says, "I am not literate."

13 Therefore the Lord said:

[a]"Inasmuch as these people draw
near with their mouths
And honor Me [b]with their lips,
But have removed their hearts far
from Me,
And their fear toward Me is
taught by the commandment of
men,
14 [a]Therefore, behold, I will again do
a marvelous work
Among this people,
A marvelous work and a wonder;
[b]For the wisdom of their wise *men*
shall perish,
And the understanding of their
prudent *men* shall be hidden."

15 [a]Woe to those who seek deep to
hide their counsel far from the
LORD,
And their works are in the dark;
[b]They say, "Who sees us?" and,
"Who knows us?"
16 Surely you have things turned
around!
Shall the potter be esteemed as
the clay;
For shall the [a]thing made say of
him who made it,
"He did not make me"?
Or shall the thing formed say of
him who formed it,
"He has no understanding"?

Future Recovery of Wisdom

17 *Is* it not yet a very little while
Till [a]Lebanon shall be turned into
a fruitful field,
And the fruitful field be esteemed
as a forest?
18 [a]In that day the deaf shall hear the
words of the book,
And the eyes of the blind shall
see out of obscurity and out of
darkness.
19 [a]The humble also shall increase
their joy in the LORD,
And [b]the poor among men shall
rejoice
In the Holy One of Israel.
20 For the [1]terrible one is brought
to nothing,
[a]The scornful one is consumed,
And all who [b]watch for iniquity
are cut off—
21 Who make a man an offender by
a word,
And [a]lay a snare for him who
reproves in the gate,
And turn aside the just [b]by empty
words.

22 Therefore thus says the LORD, [a]who redeemed Abraham, concerning the house of Jacob:

"Jacob shall not now be [b]ashamed,
Nor shall his face now grow pale;
23 But when he sees his children,
[a]The work of My hands, in his
midst,
They will hallow My name,
And hallow the Holy One of
Jacob,
And fear the God of Israel.
24 These also [a]who erred in spirit
will come to understanding,
And those who complained will
learn doctrine."

Futile Confidence in Egypt

30 "Woe to the rebellious
children," says the LORD,
[a]"Who take counsel, but not of Me,
And who [1]devise plans, but not
of My Spirit,
[b]That they may add sin to sin;
2 [a]Who walk to go down to Egypt,
And [b]have not asked My advice,
To strengthen themselves in the
strength of Pharaoh,
And to trust in the shadow of
Egypt!
3 [a]Therefore the strength of
Pharaoh
Shall be your shame,
And trust in the shadow of Egypt
Shall be *your* humiliation.
4 For his princes were at [a]Zoan,
And his ambassadors came to
Hanes.
5 [a]They were all ashamed of a
people *who* could not benefit
them,
Or be help or benefit,
But a shame and also a
reproach."

6 [a]The [1]burden against the beasts of the South.

Through a land of trouble and
anguish,
From which *came* the lioness and
lion,
[b]The viper and fiery flying
serpent,
They will carry their riches on the
backs of young donkeys,

11 [b]Dan. 12:4, 9; [Matt. 13:11–16]; Rev. 5:1–5, 9
12 [1]Lit. *does not know books*
13 [a]Ps. 78:36; Ezek. 33:31; Matt. 15:8, 9; Mark 7:6, 7 [b]Col. 2:22
14 [a]Is. 6:9, 10; 28:21; Hab. 1:5 [b]Is. 44:25; Jer. 49:7; Obad. 8; 1 Cor. 1:19
15 [a]Is. 30:1 [b]Ps. 10:11; 94:7; Is. 47:10; Ezek. 8:12; Mal. 2:17
16 [a]Is. 45:9; Jer. 18:1–6; [Rom. 9:19–21]
17 [a]Is. 32:15
18 [a]Is. 35:5; Matt. 11:5; Mark 7:37
19 [a][Ps. 25:9; 37:11; Is. 11:4; 61:1; Matt. 5:5; 11:29] [b]Is. 14:30; [Matt. 5:3; 11:5; James 2:5]
20 [a]Is. 28:14 [b]Is. 59:4; Mic. 2:1 [1]*terrifying*
21 [a]Amos 5:10, 12 [b]Prov. 28:21
22 [a]Josh. 24:3 [b]Is. 45:17
23 [a][Is. 45:11; 49:20–26; Eph. 2:10]
24 [a]Is. 28:7

CHAPTER 30

1 [a]Is. 29:15 [b]Deut. 29:19 [1]Lit. *weave a web*
2 [a]Is. 31:1; Jer. 43:7 [b]Num. 27:21; Josh. 9:14; 1 Kin. 22:7; Jer. 21:2; 42:2, 20
3 [a]Is. 20:5; Jer. 37:5, 7
4 [a]Is. 19:11
5 [a]Jer. 2:36
6 [a]Is. 57:9; Hos. 8:9; 12:1 [b]Deut. 8:15; Is. 14:29 [1]*oracle, prophecy*

And their treasures on the humps
of camels,
To a people *who* shall not profit;
7 [a]For the Egyptians shall help in
vain and to no purpose.
Therefore I have called her
[1]Rahab-Hem-Shebeth.

A Rebellious People

8 Now go, [a]write it before them on
a tablet,
And note it on a scroll,
That it may be for time to come,
Forever and ever:
9 That [a]this *is* a rebellious people,
Lying children,
Children *who* will not hear the
law of the LORD;
10 [a]Who say to the seers, "Do not
see,"
And to the prophets, "Do not
prophesy to us right things;
[b]Speak to us smooth things,
prophesy deceits.
11 Get out of the way,
Turn aside from the path,
Cause the Holy One of Israel
To cease from before us."

12 Therefore thus says the Holy
One of Israel:

"Because you [a]despise this word,
And trust in oppression and
perversity,
And rely on them,
13 Therefore this iniquity shall be to
you
[a]Like a breach ready to fall,
A bulge in a high wall,
Whose breaking [b]comes
suddenly, in an instant.
14 And [a]He shall break it like the
breaking of the potter's vessel,
Which is broken in pieces;
He shall not spare.
So there shall not be found
among its fragments
[1]A shard to take fire from the
hearth,
Or to take water from the
cistern."

15 For thus says the Lord GOD, the
Holy One of Israel:

[a]"In returning and rest you shall be
saved;
In quietness and confidence shall
be your strength."
[b]But you would not,
16 And you said, "No, for we will
flee on horses"—
Therefore you shall flee!

7 [a]Jer. 37:7 [1]Lit. *Rahab Sits Idle*
8 [a]Hab. 2:2
9 [a]Deut. 32:20; Is. 1:2, 4; 65:2
10 [a]Is. 5:20; Jer. 11:21; Amos 2:12; Mic. 2:6 [b]1 Kin. 22:8, 13; Jer. 6:14; 23:17, 26; Ezek. 13:7; Mic. 2:11; Rom. 16:18; 2 Tim. 4:3, 4
12 [a]Lev. 26:43; Num. 15:31; Prov. 1:30; 13:13; Is. 5:24; Ezek. 20:13, 16, 24; Amos 2:4
13 [a]1 Kin. 20:30; Ps. 62:3, 4; Is. 58:12 [b]Is. 29:5
14 [a]Ps. 2:9; Jer. 19:11 [1]A piece of broken pottery
15 [a]Ps. 116:7; Is. 7:4; 28:12 [b]Matt. 23:37
17 [a]Lev. 26:36; Deut. 28:25; 32:30; Josh. 23:10; [Prov. 28:1] [1]A tree stripped of branches
18 [a]Is. 33:2 [b]Ps. 2:12; 34:8; Prov. 16:20; Jer. 17:7 [c]Is. 26:8
19 [a]Is. 65:9; [Ezek. 37:25, 28] [b]Is. 25:8 [c]Ps. 50:15; Is. 65:24; [Matt. 7:7–11]
20 [a]1 Kin. 22:27; Ps. 127:2 [b]Ps. 74:9; Amos 8:11 [1]*oppression*
21 [a]Josh. 1:7
22 [a]2 Chr. 31:1; Is. 2:20; 31:7 [b]Hos. 14:8
23 [a][Matt. 6:33]; 1 Tim. 6:8 [1]*rich*

And, "We will ride on swift
horses"—
Therefore those who pursue you
shall be swift!
17 [a]One thousand *shall flee* at the
threat of one,
At the threat of five you shall flee,
Till you are left as a [1]pole on top
of a mountain
And as a banner on a hill.

God Will Be Gracious

18 Therefore the LORD will wait, that
He may be [a]gracious to you;
And therefore He will be exalted,
that He may have mercy on
you.
For the LORD *is* a God of justice;
[b]Blessed *are* all those who [c]wait
for Him.

19 For the people [a]shall dwell in
Zion at Jerusalem;
You shall [b]weep no more.
He will be very gracious to you
at the sound of your cry;
When He hears it, He will
[c]answer you.
20 And *though* the Lord gives you
[a]The bread of adversity and the
water of [1]affliction,
Yet [b]your teachers will not be
moved into a corner anymore,
But your eyes shall see your
teachers.
21 Your ears shall hear a word
behind you, saying,
"This *is* the way, walk in it,"
Whenever you [a]turn to the right
hand
Or whenever you turn to the left.
22 [a]You will also defile the covering
of your images of silver,
And the ornament of your
molded images of gold.
You will throw them away as an
unclean thing;
[b]You will say to them, "Get
away!"

23 [a]Then He will give the rain for
your seed
With which you sow the ground,
And bread of the increase of the
earth;
It will be [1]fat and plentiful.
In that day your cattle will feed
In large pastures.
24 Likewise the oxen and the young
donkeys that work the ground
Will eat cured fodder,
Which has been winnowed with
the shovel and fan.

25 There will be [a]on every high
mountain
And on every high hill
Rivers *and* streams of waters,
In the day of the [b]great slaughter,
When the towers fall.
26 Moreover [a]the light of the moon
will be as the light of the sun,
And the light of the sun will be
sevenfold,
As the light of seven days,
In the day that the LORD binds up
the bruise of His people
And heals the stroke of their
wound.

Judgment on Assyria

27 Behold, the name of the LORD
comes from afar,
Burning *with* His anger,
And *His* burden *is* heavy;
His lips are full of indignation,
And His tongue like a devouring
fire.
28 [a]His breath is like an overflowing
stream,
[b]Which reaches up to the neck,
To sift the nations with the sieve
of futility;
And *there shall be* [c]a bridle in the
jaws of the people,
Causing *them* to err.

29 You shall have a song
As in the night *when* a holy
festival is kept,
And gladness of heart as when
one goes with a flute,
To come into [a]the mountain of the
LORD,
To [1]the Mighty One of Israel.
30 [a]The LORD will cause His glorious
voice to be heard,
And show the descent of His arm,
With the indignation of *His* anger
And the flame of a devouring fire,
With scattering, tempest, [b]and
hailstones.
31 For [a]through the voice of the
LORD
Assyria will be [1]beaten down,
As He strikes with the [b]rod.
32 And *in* every place where the
staff of punishment passes,
Which the LORD lays on him,
It will be with tambourines and
harps;
And in battles of [a]brandishing He
will fight with it.
33 [a]For Tophet *was* established of
old,
Yes, for the king it is prepared.
He has made *it* deep and large;
Its pyre *is* fire with much wood;

25 [a]Is. 2:14, 15 [b]Is. 2:10–21; 34:2
26 [a][Is. 60:19, 20; Rev. 21:23; 22:5]
28 [a]Is. 11:4; 2 Thess. 2:8 [b]Is. 8:8 [c]2 Kin. 19:28; Is. 37:29
29 [a][Is. 2:3] [1]Lit. *the Rock*
30 [a]Is. 29:6 [b]Is. 28:2
31 [a]Is. 14:25; 37:36 [b]Is. 10:5, 24 [1]Lit. *shattered*
32 [a]Is. 11:15
33 [a]2 Kin. 23:10; Jer. 7:31

CHAPTER 31

1 [a]Is. 30:1, 2 [b]Deut. 17:16; Ps. 20:7; Is. 2:7; 30:16 [c]Is. 9:13; Dan. 9:13; Amos 5:4–8
2 [a]Num. 23:19; Jer. 44:29 [1]*retract*
3 [a]Is. 20:6
4 [a]Num. 24:9; Hos. 11:10; Amos 3:8
5 [a]Deut. 32:11; Ps. 91:4
6 [a]Hos. 9:9
7 [a]Is. 2:20; 30:22 [b]1 Kin. 12:30

The breath of the LORD, like a
stream of brimstone,
Kindles it.

The Folly of Not Trusting God

31 Woe to those [a]who go down
to Egypt for help,
And [b]rely on horses,
Who trust in chariots because
they are many,
And in horsemen because they
are very strong,
But who do not look to the Holy
One of Israel,
[c]Nor seek the LORD!
2 Yet He also *is* wise and will bring
disaster,
And [a]will not [1]call back His
words,
But will arise against the house
of evildoers,
And against the help of those
who work iniquity.
3 Now the Egyptians *are* men, and
not God;
And their horses are flesh, and
not spirit.
When the LORD stretches out His
hand,
Both he who helps will fall,
And he who is helped will fall
down;
They all will perish [a]together.

God Will Deliver Jerusalem

4 For thus the LORD has spoken
to me:

[a]"As a lion roars,
And a young lion over his prey
(When a multitude of shepherds
is summoned against him,
He will not be afraid of their voice
Nor be disturbed by their noise),
So the LORD of hosts will come
down
To fight for Mount Zion and for
its hill.
5 [a]Like birds flying about,
So will the LORD of hosts defend
Jerusalem.
Defending, He will also deliver *it;*
Passing over, He will
preserve *it.*"

6 Return *to Him* against whom
the children of Israel have [a]deeply
revolted.
7 For in that day every man shall
[a]throw away his idols of silver and
his idols of gold—[b]sin, which your
own hands have made for your-
selves.

8 "Then Assyria shall [a]fall by a
sword not of man,
And a sword not of mankind shall
[b]devour him.
But he shall flee from the sword,
And his young men shall become
forced labor.
9 [a]He shall cross over to his
stronghold for fear,
And his princes shall be afraid of
the banner,"
Says the LORD,
Whose fire *is* in Zion
And whose furnace *is* in
Jerusalem.

A Reign of Righteousness

32 Behold, [a]a king will reign in
righteousness,
And princes will rule with justice.
2 A man will be as a hiding place
from the wind,
And [a]a [1]cover from the tempest,
As rivers of water in a dry place,
As the shadow of a great rock in
a weary land.
3 [a]The eyes of those who see will
not be dim,
And the ears of those who hear
will listen.
4 Also the heart of the [1]rash will
[a]understand knowledge,
And the tongue of the
stammerers will be ready to
speak plainly.

5 The foolish person will no longer
be called [1]generous,
Nor the miser said *to be*
bountiful;
6 For the foolish person will speak
foolishness,
And his heart will work [a]iniquity:
To practice ungodliness,
To utter error against the LORD,
To keep the hungry unsatisfied,
And he will cause the drink of the
thirsty to fail.
7 Also the schemes of the schemer
are evil;
He devises wicked plans
To destroy the poor with [a]lying
words,
Even when the needy speaks
justice.
8 But a [1]generous man devises
generous things,
And by generosity he shall stand.

Consequences of Complacency

9 Rise up, you women [a]who are at
ease,
Hear my voice;
You complacent daughters,
Give ear to my speech.

8 [a]2 Kin. 19:35, 36 [b]Is. 37:36
9 [a]Is. 37:37
CHAPTER 32
1 [a]Ps. 45:1
2 [a]Is. 4:6 [1]*shelter*
3 [a]Is. 29:18; 35:5
4 [a]Is. 29:24 [1]*hasty*
5 [1]*noble*
6 [a]Prov. 24:7–9
7 [a]Jer. 5:26–28; Mic. 7:3
8 [1]*noble*
9 [a]Is. 47:8; Amos 6:1; Zeph. 2:15
13 [a]Is. 7:23–25; Hos. 9:6 [b]Is. 22:2
14 [a]Is. 27:10
15 [a][Is. 11:2]; Ezek. 39:29; [Joel 2:28] [b]Ps. 107:35; Is. 29:17
17 [a]Ps. 119:165; Is. 2:4; Rom. 14:17; James 3:18
18 [a]Is. 11:10; 14:3; 30:15; [Hos. 2:18–23; Zech. 2:5; 3:10]
19 [a]Is. 30:30 [b]Zech. 11:2
20 [a][Eccl. 11:1]; Is. 30:23, 24
CHAPTER 33
1 [a]Is. 21:2; Hab. 2:8

10 In a year and *some* days
You will be troubled, you
complacent women;
For the vintage will fail,
The gathering will not come.
11 Tremble, you *women* who are at
ease;
Be troubled, you complacent
ones;
Strip yourselves, make
yourselves bare,
And gird *sackcloth* on *your*
waists.

12 People shall mourn upon their
breasts
For the pleasant fields, for the
fruitful vine.
13 [a]On the land of my people will
come up thorns *and* briers,
Yes, on all the happy homes *in*
[b]the joyous city;
14 [a]Because the palaces will be
forsaken,
The bustling city will be deserted.
The forts and towers will become
lairs forever,
A joy of wild donkeys, a pasture
of flocks—
15 Until [a]the Spirit is poured upon
us from on high,
And [b]the wilderness becomes a
fruitful field,
And the fruitful field is counted
as a forest.

The Peace of God's Reign

16 Then justice will dwell in the
wilderness,
And righteousness remain in the
fruitful field.
17 [a]The work of righteousness will be
peace,
And the effect of righteousness,
quietness and assurance
forever.
18 My people will dwell in a peaceful
habitation,
In secure dwellings, and in quiet
[a]resting places,
19 [a]Though hail comes down [b]on the
forest,
And the city is brought low in
humiliation.

20 Blessed *are* you who sow beside
all waters,
Who send out freely the feet of
[a]the ox and the donkey.

A Prayer in Deep Distress

33 Woe to you [a]who plunder,
though you *have* not *been*
plundered;
And you who deal treacherously,

though they have not dealt
treacherously with you!
[b]When you cease plundering,
You will be [c]plundered;
When you make an end of
dealing treacherously,
They will deal treacherously with
you.

2 O LORD, be gracious to us;
[a]We have waited for You.
Be [1]their arm every morning,
Our salvation also in the time of
trouble.
3 At the noise of the tumult the
people [a]shall flee;
When You lift Yourself up, the
nations shall be scattered;
4 And Your plunder shall be
gathered
Like the gathering of the
caterpillar;
As the running to and fro of
locusts,
He shall run upon them.
5 [a]The LORD is exalted, for He
dwells on high;
He has filled Zion with justice
and righteousness.
6 Wisdom and knowledge will be
the stability of your times,
And the strength of salvation;
The fear of the LORD *is* His
treasure.

7 Surely their valiant ones shall cry
outside,
[a]The ambassadors of peace shall
weep bitterly.
8 [a]The highways lie waste,
The traveling man ceases.
[b]He has broken the covenant,
[1]He has despised the [2]cities,
He regards no man.
9 [a]The earth mourns *and*
languishes,
Lebanon is shamed *and*
shriveled;
Sharon is like a wilderness,
And Bashan and Carmel shake
off *their fruits.*

Impending Judgment on Zion

10 "Now[a] I will rise," says the LORD;
"Now I will be exalted,
Now I will lift Myself up.
11 [a]You shall conceive chaff,
You shall bring forth stubble;
Your breath, *as* fire, shall devour
you.
12 And the people shall be *like* the
burnings of lime;
[a]*Like* thorns cut up they shall be
burned in the fire.

1 [b]Rev. 13:10 [c]Is. 10:12; 14:25; 31:8
2 [a]Is. 25:9; 26:8 [1]LXX omits *their;* Syr., Tg., Vg. *our*
3 [a]Is. 17:13
5 [a]Ps. 97:9
7 [a]2 Kin. 18:18, 37
8 [a]Judg. 5:6 [b]2 Kin. 18:13–17 [1]Tg. *They have been removed from their cities* [2]So with MT, Vg.; DSS *witnesses;* LXX omits *cities*
9 [a]Is. 24:4
10 [a]Ps. 12:5; Is. 2:19, 21
11 [a][Ps. 7:14; Is. 26:18; 59:4; James 1:15]
12 [a]Is. 9:18
13 [a]Ps. 48:10; Is. 49:1
14 [a]Is. 30:27, 30; Heb. 12:29
15 [a]Ps. 15:2; 24:3, 4; Is. 58:6–11 [b]Ps. 119:37
16 [1]Lit. *heights*
17 [a]Ps. 27:4
18 [a]1 Cor. 1:20
19 [a]2 Kin. 19:32 [b]Deut. 28:49, 50; Is. 28:11; Jer. 5:15 [1]Unintelligible speech
20 [a]Ps. 48:12 [b]Ps. 46:5; 125:1; Is. 32:18 [c]Is. 37:33 [d]Is. 54:2
21 [1]*ship*
22 [a][Acts 10:42] [b]Is. 1:10; 51:4, 7; James 4:12 [c]Ps. 89:18; Is. 25:9; 35:4; Zech. 9:9

13 Hear, [a]you *who are* afar off, what
I have done;
And you *who are* near,
acknowledge My might."

14 The sinners in Zion are afraid;
Fearfulness has seized the
hypocrites:
"Who among us shall dwell with
the devouring [a]fire?
Who among us shall dwell with
everlasting burnings?"
15 He who [a]walks righteously and
speaks uprightly,
He who despises the gain of
oppressions,
Who gestures with his hands,
refusing bribes,
Who stops his ears from hearing
of bloodshed,
And [b]shuts his eyes from seeing
evil:
16 He will dwell on [1]high;
His place of defense *will be* the
fortress of rocks;
Bread will be given him,
His water *will be* sure.

The Land of the Majestic King

17 Your eyes will see the King in His
[a]beauty;
They will see the land that is very
far off.
18 Your heart will meditate on
terror:
[a]"Where *is* the scribe?
Where *is* he who weighs?
Where *is* he who counts the
towers?"
19 [a]You will not see a fierce people,
[b]A people of obscure speech,
beyond perception,
Of a [1]stammering tongue *that*
you cannot understand.
20 [a]Look upon Zion, the city of our
appointed feasts;
Your eyes will see [b]Jerusalem, a
quiet home,
A tabernacle *that* will not be
taken down;
[c]Not one of [d]its stakes will ever
be removed,
Nor will any of its cords be
broken.
21 But there the majestic LORD *will*
be for us
A place of broad rivers *and*
streams,
In which no [1]galley with oars will
sail,
Nor majestic ships pass by
22 (For the LORD *is* our [a]Judge,
The LORD *is* our [b]Lawgiver,
[c]The LORD *is* our King;

He will save us);
23 Your tackle is loosed,
They could not strengthen their mast,
They could not spread the sail.

Then the prey of great plunder is divided;
The lame take the prey.
24 And the inhabitant will not say, "I am sick";
[a]The people who dwell in it *will be* forgiven *their* iniquity.

Judgment on the Nations

34 Come [a]near, you nations, to hear;
And heed, you people!
[b]Let the earth hear, and all that is in it,
The world and all things that come forth from it.
2 For the indignation of the LORD *is* against all nations,
And *His* fury against all their armies;
He has utterly destroyed them,
He has given them over to the [a]slaughter.
3 Also their slain shall be thrown out;
[a]Their stench shall rise from their corpses,
And the mountains shall be melted with their blood.
4 [a]All the host of heaven shall be dissolved,
And the heavens shall be rolled up like a scroll;
[b]All their host shall fall down
As the leaf falls from the vine,
And as [c]*fruit* falling from a fig tree.

5 "For [a]My sword shall be bathe[illegible]
heaven; [illegible] on
Indeed it [b]shall come d[illegible]
Edom, [illegible] My curse,
And on the peop[illegible]
for judgme[illegible]e LORD is filled
6 The [a]swo[illegible]
wit[illegible]e [1]overflowing with
[illegible]ness,
[illegible]ith the blood of lambs and goats,
With the fat of the kidneys of rams.
For [b]the LORD has a sacrifice in Bozrah,
And a great slaughter in the land of Edom.
7 The wild oxen shall come down with them,

And the young bulls with the mighty bulls;
Their land shall be soaked with blood,
And their dust [1]saturated with fatness."

8 For *it is* the day of the LORD's [a]vengeance,
The year of recompense for the cause of Zion.
9 [a]Its streams shall be turned into pitch,
And its dust into brimstone;
Its land shall become burning pitch.
10 It shall not be quenched night or day;
[a]Its smoke shall ascend forever.
[b]From generation to generation it shall lie waste;
No one shall pass through it forever and ever.
11 [a]But the [1]pelican and the [2]porcupine shall possess it,
Also the owl and the raven shall dwell in it.
And [b]He shall stretch out over it
The line of confusion and the stones of emptiness.
12 They shall call its nobles to the kingdom,
But none *shall be* there, and all its princes shall be nothing.

13 And [a]thorns shall come up in its palaces,
Nettles and brambles in its fortresses;
[b]It shall be a habitation of jackals,
A courtyard for ostriches.
14 The wild beasts of the desert shall also meet with the [1]jackals,
And the wild goat shall bleat to its companion;
Also [2]the night creature shall rest there,
And find for herself a place of rest.
15 There the arrow snake shall make her nest and lay *eggs*
And hatch, and gather *them* under her shadow;
There also shall the hawks be gathered,
Every one with her mate.

16 "Search from [a]the book of the LORD, and read:
Not one of these shall fail;
Not one shall lack her mate.
For My mouth has commanded it, and His Spirit has gathered them.
17 He has cast the lot for them,

24 [a]Is. 40:2; Jer. 50:20; Mic. 7:18, 19; 1 John 1:7–9

CHAPTER 34

1 [a]Ps. 49:1; Is. 41:1; 43:9 [b]Deut. 32:1; Is. 1:2
2 [a]Is. 13:5
3 [a]Joel 2:20; Amos 4:10
4 [a]Ps. 102:26; Is. 13:13; Ezek. 32:7, 8; Joel 2:31; Matt. 24:29; 2 Pet. 3:10 [b]Is. 14:12 [c]Rev. 6:12–14
5 [a]Deut. 32:41, 42; Jer. 46:10; Ezek. 21:3–5 [b]Is. 63:1; Jer. 49:7, 8, 20; Ezek. 25:12–14; 35:1–15; Amos 1:11, 12; Obad. 1–14; Mal. 1:4
6 [a]Is. 66:16 [b]Zeph. 1:7 [1]Lit. *fat*
7 [1]Lit. *made fat*
8 [a]Is. 63:4
9 [a]Deut. 29:23; Ps. 11:6; Is. 30:33
10 [illegible]:11; 18:18; 19:3 [b]Is. 13:20–22; 24:1; 34:10–15; Mal. 1:3, 4
11 [a]Is. 14:23; Zeph. 2:14; Rev. 18:2 [b]2 Kin. 21:13; Lam. 2:8 [1]Or *owl* [2]Or *hedgehog*
13 [a]Is. 32:13; Hos. 9:6 [b]Is. 13:21
14 [1]Lit. *howling creatures* [2]Heb. *lilith*
16 [a][Mal. 3:16]

And His hand has divided it
among them with a measuring
line.
They shall possess it forever;
From generation to generation
they shall dwell in it."

The Future Glory of Zion

35 The [a]wilderness and the
[1]wasteland shall be glad for
them,
And the [b]desert[2] shall rejoice and
blossom as the rose;
2 [a]It shall blossom abundantly and
rejoice,
Even with joy and singing.
The glory of Lebanon shall be
given to it,
The excellence of Carmel and
Sharon.
They shall see the [b]glory of the
LORD,
The excellency of our God.

3 [a]Strengthen the [1]weak hands,
And make firm the [2]feeble knees.
4 Say to those *who are* fearful-
hearted,
"Be strong, do not fear!
Behold, your God will come *with*
[a]vengeance,
With the recompense of God;
He will come and [b]save you."

5 Then the [a]eyes of the blind shall
be opened,
And [b]the ears of the deaf shall be
unstopped.
6 Then the [a]lame shall leap like a
deer,
And the [b]tongue of the dumb
sing.
For [c]waters shall burst forth in
the wilderness,
And streams in the desert.
7 The parched ground shall
become a pool,
And the thirsty land springs of
water;
In [a]the habitation of jackals,
where each lay,
There shall be grass with reeds
and rushes.

8 A [a]highway shall be there, and a
road,
And it shall be called the
Highway of Holiness.
[b]The unclean shall not pass
over it,
But it *shall be* for others.
Whoever walks the road,
although a fool,
Shall not go astray.
9 [a]No lion shall be there,

CHAPTER 35

1 [a]Is. 32:15; 55:12 [b]Is. 41:19; 51:3 [1]*desert* [2]Heb. *arabah*

2 [a]Is. 32:15 [b]Is. 40:5

3 [a]Job 4:3, 4; Heb. 12:12 [1]Lit. *sinking* [2]*tottering* or *stumbling*

4 [a]Is. 34:8 [b]Ps. 145:19; Is. 33:22

5 [a]Is. 29:18; Matt. 9:27; John 9:6, 7 [b][Matt. 11:5]

6 [a]Matt. 11:5; 15:30; John 5:8, 9; Acts 8:7 [b]Is. 32:4; Matt. 9:32; 12:22 [c]Is. 41:18; [John 7:38]

7 [a]Is. 34:13

8 [a]Is. 19:23 [b]Is. 52:1; Joel 3:17; [Matt. 7:13, 14]; 1 Pet. 1:15, 16; Rev. 21:27

9 [a]Lev. 26:6; [Is. 11:7, 9]; Ezek. 34:25

10 [a]Is. 51:11 [b]Is. 25:8; 30:19; 65:19; [Rev. 7:17; 21:4]

CHAPTER 36

1 [a]2 Kin. 18:13, 17; 2 Chr. 32:1

2 [1]A title, probably *Chief of Staff* or *Governor*

3 [a]Is. 22:20 [b]Is. 22:15

4 [a]2 Kin. 18:19

5 [1]Lit. *a word of the lips*

6 [a]Ezek. 29:6 [b]Ps. 146:3; Is. 30:3, 5, 7

Nor shall *any* ravenous beast go
up on it;
It shall not be found there.
But the redeemed shall walk
there,
10 And the [a]ransomed of the LORD
shall return,
And come to Zion with singing,
With everlasting joy on their
heads.
They shall obtain joy and
gladness,
And [b]sorrow and sighing shall
flee away.

Sennacherib Boasts Against the LORD

36 Now [a]it came to pass in the
fourteenth year of King
Hezekiah *that* Sennacherib king
of Assyria came up against all the
fortified cities of Judah and took
them.
2 Then the king of Assyria sent
the [1]Rabshakeh with a great army
from Lachish to King Hezekiah at
Jerusalem. And he stood by the
aqueduct from the upper pool, on
the highway to the Fuller's Field.
3 And [a]Eliakim the son of Hil-
kiah, who was over the household,
[b]Shebna the scribe, and Joah the
son of Asaph, the recorder, came
out to him.
4 [a]Then *the* Rabshakeh said to
them, "Say now to Hezekiah,
'Thus says the great king, the king
of Assyria: "What confidence is
this in which you trust?
5 "I say you speak of having
plans and power for war; but *they*
are [1]mere words. Now in whom do
you trust, that you rebel agai[illegible]
me?
6 "Look! You are trusting in the
o[illegible]ff of this broken reed, Egypt,
into [illegible]ich if a man leans, it will go
Pharao[illegible]hand and pierce it. So *is*
[b]trust in hi[illegible] of Egypt to all who
7 "But if you [illegible]
in the LORD our [illegible] to me, 'We trust
whose high places [illegible] is *it* not He
tars Hezekiah has taken [illegible]hose al-
said to Judah and Jerusalem [illegible] and
shall worship before this altar [illegible]
8 "Now therefore, I urge you,
give a pledge to my master the
king of Assyria, and I will give you
two thousand horses—if you are
able on your part to put riders on
them!
9 "How then will you repel one

30 "This *shall be* a sign to you:

You shall eat this year such as
grows of itself,
And the second year what
springs from the same;
Also in the third year sow and
reap,
Plant vineyards and eat the fruit
of them.
31 And the remnant who have
escaped of the house of Judah
Shall again take root downward,
And bear fruit upward.
32 For out of Jerusalem shall go a
remnant,
And those who escape from
Mount Zion.
The [a]zeal of the LORD of hosts
will do this.

33 "Therefore thus says the LORD
concerning the king of Assyria:

'He shall not come into this city,
Nor shoot an arrow there,
Nor come before it with shield,
Nor build a siege mound
against it.
34 By the way that he came,
By the same shall he return;
And he shall not come into this
city,'
Says the LORD.
35 'For I will [a]defend this city,
to save it
For My own sake and for My
servant [b]David's sake.'"

Sennacherib's Defeat and Death

36 Then the [a]angel[1] of the LORD
went out, and [2]killed in the camp
of the Assyrians one hundred and
eighty-five thousand; and when
people arose early in the morning,
there were the corpses—all dead.
37 So Sennacherib king of As-
syria departed and went away, re-
turned *home*, and remained at
Nineveh.
38 Now it came to pass, as he was
worshiping in the house of Nisroch
his god, that his sons Adramme-
lech and Sharezer struck him
down with the sword; and they es-
caped into the land of Ararat. Then
[a]Esarhaddon his son reigned in his
place.

Hezekiah's Life Extended

38 In [a]those days Hezekiah was
sick and near death. And
Isaiah the prophet, the son of

32 [a]2 Kin. 19:31; Is. 9:7; 59:17; Joel 2:18; Zech. 1:14

35 [a]2 Kin. 20:6; Is. 31:5; 38:6 [b]1 Kin. 11:13

36 [a]2 Kin. 19:35; Is. 10:12, 33, 34 [1]Or *Angel* [2]Lit. *struck*

38 [a]Ezra 4:2

CHAPTER 38

1 [a]2 Kin. 20:1–6, 9–11; 2 Chr. 32:24; Is. 38:1–8 [b]2 Sam. 17:23

3 [a]Neh. 13:14 [b]2 Kin. 18:5, 6; Ps. 26:3 [1]*whole* or *peaceful*

6 [a]2 Kin. 19:35–37; 2 Chr. 32:21; Is. 31:5; 37:35

7 [a]Judg. 6:17, 21, 36–40; 2 Kin. 20:8; Is. 7:11

11 [a]Ps. 27:13; 116:9 [1]Heb. *YAH, YAH* [2]LXX omits *among the inhabitants of the world* [3]So with some Heb. mss.; MT, Vg. *rest;* Tg. *land*

12 [a]Job 7:6

Amoz, went to him and said to
him, "Thus says the LORD: [b]'Set
your house in order, for you shall
die and not live.'"
2 Then Hezekiah turned his face
toward the wall, and prayed to the
LORD,
3 and said, [a]"Remember now, O
LORD, I pray, how I have walked
before You in truth and with a
[1]loyal heart, and have done *what*
is good in Your [b]sight." And Heze-
kiah wept bitterly.
4 And the word of the LORD came
to Isaiah, saying,
5 "Go and tell Hezekiah, 'Thus
says the LORD, the God of David
your father: "I have heard your
prayer, I have seen your tears;
surely I will add to your days fif-
teen years.
6 "I will deliver you and this city
from the hand of the king of As-
syria, and [a]I will defend this city."'
7 "And this *is* [a]the sign to you
from the LORD, that the LORD will
do this thing which He has spoken:
8 "Behold, I will bring the
shadow on the sundial, which has
gone down with the sun on the
sundial of Ahaz, ten degrees back-
ward." So the sun returned ten de-
grees on the dial by which it had
gone down.
9 This is the writing of Hezekiah
king of Judah, when he had been
sick and had recovered from his
sickness:

10 I said,
"In the prime of my life
I shall go to the gates of Sheol;
I am deprived of the remainder
of my years."
11 I said,
"I shall not see [1]YAH,
The LORD [a]in the land of the
living;
I shall observe man no more
[2]among the inhabitants of [3]the
world.
12 [a]My life span is gone,
Taken from me like a shepherd's
tent;
I have cut off my life like a
weaver.
He cuts me off from the loom;
From day until night You make
an end of me.
13 I have considered until
morning—
Like a lion,
So He breaks all my bones;

From day until night You make
an end of me.
14 Like a crane *or* a swallow, so I
chattered;
[a]I mourned like a dove;
My eyes fail *from looking*
upward.
O [1]LORD, I am oppressed;
[2]Undertake for me!

15 "What shall I say?
[1]He has both spoken to me,
And He Himself has done *it.*
I shall walk carefully all my years
[a]In the bitterness of my soul.
16 O Lord, by these *things men* live;
And in all these *things is* the life
of my spirit;
So You will restore me and make
me live.
17 Indeed *it was* for *my own* peace
That I had great bitterness;
But You have lovingly *delivered*
my soul from the pit of
corruption,
For You have cast all my sins
behind Your back.
18 For [a]Sheol cannot thank You,
Death cannot praise You;
Those who go down to the pit
cannot hope for Your truth.
19 The living, the living man, he
shall praise You,
As I *do* this day;
[a]The father shall make known
Your truth to the children.

20 "The LORD *was ready* to save me;
Therefore we will sing my songs
with stringed instruments
All the days of our life, in the
house of the LORD."

21 Now [a]Isaiah had said, "Let
them take a lump of figs, and apply
it as a poultice on the boil, and he
shall recover."
22 And [a]Hezekiah had said,
"What *is* the sign that I shall go
up to the house of the LORD?"

The Babylonian Envoys

39 At [a]that time [1]Merodach-
Baladan the son of Baladan,
king of Babylon, sent letters and
a present to Hezekiah, for he
heard that he had been sick and
had recovered.
2 [a]And Hezekiah was pleased
with them, and showed them the
house of his treasures—the silver
and gold, the spices and precious
ointment, and all his armory—all
that was found among his trea-
sures. There was nothing in his
house or in all his dominion that
Hezekiah did not show them.
3 Then Isaiah the prophet went
to King Hezekiah, and said to him,
"What did these men say, and
from where did they come to you?"
So Hezekiah said, "They came to
me from a [a]far country, from Bab-
ylon."
4 And he said, "What have they
seen in your house?" So Hezekiah
answered, "They have seen all that
is in my house; there is nothing
among my treasures that I have
not shown them."
5 Then Isaiah said to Hezekiah,
"Hear the word of the LORD of
hosts:
6 'Behold, the days are coming
[a]when all that *is* in your house, and
what your fathers have accumu-
lated until this day, shall be car-
ried to Babylon; nothing shall be
left,' says the LORD.
7 'And they shall take away
some of your [a]sons who will de-
scend from you, whom you will be-
get; and they shall be eunuchs in
the palace of the king of Bab-
ylon.'"
8 So Hezekiah said to Isaiah,
[a]"The word of the LORD which you
have spoken *is* good!" For he said,
"At least there will be peace and
truth in my days."

God's People Are Comforted

40 "Comfort, yes, comfort My
people!"
Says your God.
2 "Speak [1]comfort to Jerusalem, and
cry out to her,
That her warfare is ended,
That her iniquity is pardoned;
[a]For she has received from the
LORD's hand
Double for all her sins."

3 [a]The voice of one crying in the
wilderness:
[b]"Prepare the way of the LORD;
[c]Make straight [1]in the desert
A highway for our God.
4 Every valley shall be exalted
And every mountain and hill
brought low;
[a]The crooked places shall be made
[1]straight
And the rough places smooth;
5 The [a]glory of the LORD shall be
revealed,
And all flesh shall see *it* together;

14 [a]Is. 59:11; Ezek. 7:16; Nah. 2:7 [1]So with Bg.; MT, DSS *Lord* [2]*Be my surety*
15 [a]Job 7:11; 10:1; Is. 38:17 [1]So with MT, Vg.; DSS, Tg. *And shall I say to Him;* LXX omits first half of this verse
18 [a]Ps. 6:5; 30:9; 88:11; 115:17; [Eccl. 9:10]
19 [a]Deut. 4:9; 6:7; Ps. 78:3, 4
21 [a]2 Kin. 20:7
22 [a]2 Kin. 20:8

CHAPTER 39
1 [a]2 Kin. 20:12–19; 2 Chr. 32:31; Is. 39:1–8 [1]*Berodach-Baladan,* 2 Kin. 20:12
2 [a]2 Chr. 32:25, 31; Job 31:25
3 [a]Deut. 28:49; Jer. 5:15
6 [a]2 Kin. 24:13; 25:13–15; Jer. 20:5
7 [a]Dan. 1:1–7
8 [a]1 Sam. 3:18

CHAPTER 40
2 [a]Is. 61:7 [1]Lit. *to the heart of*
3 [a]Matt. 3:3; Mark 1:3; Luke 3:4–6; John 1:23 [b][Mal. 3:1; 4:5, 6] [c]Ps. 68:4 [1]So with MT, Tg., Vg.; LXX omits *in the desert*
4 [a]Is. 45:2 [1]Or *a plain*
5 [a]Is. 35:2

For the mouth of the LORD has
spoken."

6 The voice said, "Cry out!"
And [1]he said, "What shall I cry?"

[a]"All flesh *is* grass,
And all its loveliness *is* like the
flower of the field.
7 The grass withers, the flower
fades,
Because the breath of the LORD
blows upon it;
Surely the people *are* grass.
8 The grass withers, the flower
fades,
But [a]the word of our God stands
forever."

9 O Zion,
You who bring good tidings,
Get up into the high mountain;
O Jerusalem,
You who bring good tidings,
Lift up your voice with strength,
Lift *it* up, be not afraid;
Say to the cities of Judah,
"Behold your God!"

10 Behold, the Lord GOD shall come
[1]with a strong *hand,*
And [a]His arm shall rule for Him;
Behold, [b]His reward *is* with Him,
And His [2]work before Him.
11 He will [a]feed His flock like a
shepherd;
He will gather the lambs with His
arm,
And carry *them* in His bosom,
And gently lead those who are
with young.

12 [a]Who has measured the [1]waters in
the hollow of His hand,
Measured heaven with a [2]span
And calculated the dust of the
earth in a measure?
Weighed the mountains in scales
And the hills in a balance?
13 [a]Who has directed the Spirit of the
LORD,
Or *as* His counselor has taught
Him?
14 With whom did He take counsel,
and *who* instructed Him,
And [a]taught Him in the path of
justice?
Who taught Him knowledge,
And showed Him the way of
understanding?

15 Behold, the nations *are* as a drop
in a bucket,
And are counted as the small dust
on the scales;
Look, He lifts up the isles as a
very little thing.
16 And Lebanon *is* not sufficient to
burn,
Nor its beasts sufficient for a
burnt offering.
17 All nations before Him *are* as
[a]nothing,
And [b]they are counted by Him
less than nothing and
worthless.

18 To whom then will you [a]liken
God?
Or what likeness will you
compare to Him?
19 [a]The workman molds an image,
The goldsmith overspreads it
with gold,
And the silversmith casts silver
chains.
20 Whoever *is* too impoverished for
such [1]a contribution
Chooses a tree *that* will not rot;
He seeks for himself a skillful
workman
[a]To prepare a carved image *that*
will not totter.

21 [a]Have you not known?
Have you not heard?
Has it not been told you from the
beginning?
Have you not understood from
the foundations of the earth?
22 *It is* He who sits above the circle
of the earth,
And its inhabitants *are* like
grasshoppers,
Who [a]stretches out the heavens
like a curtain,
And spreads them out like a [b]tent
to dwell in.
23 He [1]brings the [a]princes to
nothing;
He makes the judges of the earth
useless.

24 Scarcely shall they be planted,
Scarcely shall they be sown,
Scarcely shall their stock take
root in the earth,
When He will also blow on them,
And they will wither,
And the whirlwind will take them
away like stubble.

25 "To[a] whom then will you liken Me,
Or *to whom* shall I be equal?"
says the Holy One.
26 Lift up your eyes on high,
And see who has created these
things,
Who brings out their host by
number;

6 [a]Job 14:2; James 1:10; 1 Pet. 1:24, 25 [1]So with MT, Tg.; DSS, LXX, Vg. *I*
8 [a][John 12:34]
10 [a]Is. 59:16, 18 [b]Is. 62:11; Rev. 22:12 [1]*in strength* [2]*recompense*
11 [a]Jer. 31:10; [Ezek. 34:23, 31]; Mic. 5:4; [John 10:11, 14–16; Heb. 13:20; 1 Pet. 2:25]
12 [a]Prov. 30:4 [1]So with MT, LXX, Vg.; DSS adds *of the sea;* Tg. adds *of the world* [2]A span=½ cubit, 9 inches; or the width of His hand
13 [a]Job 21:22; Rom. 11:34; [1 Cor. 2:16]
14 [a]Job 36:22, 23
17 [a]Dan. 4:35 [b]Ps. 62:9
18 [a]Ex. 8:10; 15:11; 1 Sam. 2:2; Is. 46:5; [Mic. 7:18]; Acts 17:29
19 [a]Ps. 115:4–8; Is. 41:7; 44:10; Hab. 2:18, 19
20 [a]1 Sam. 5:3, 4; Is. 41:7; 46:7; Jer. 10:3 [1]*an offering*
21 [a]Ps. 19:1; Is. 37:26; Acts 14:17; Rom. 1:19
22 [a]Job 9:8; Ps. 104:2; Is. 42:5; 44:24; Jer. 10:12 [b]Job 36:29; Ps. 19:4
23 [a]Job 12:21; Ps. 107:40; Is. 34:12; [1 Cor. 1:26–29] [1]*reduces*
25 [a][Deut. 4:15]; Is. 40:18; [John 14:9; Col. 1:15]

[a]He calls them all by name,
By the greatness of His might
And the strength of *His* power;
Not one is missing.

27 [a]Why do you say, O Jacob,
And speak, O Israel:
"My way is hidden from the LORD,
And my just claim is passed over
by my God"?
28 Have you not known?
Have you not heard?
The everlasting God, the LORD,
The Creator of the ends of the
earth,
Neither faints nor is weary.
[a]His understanding is
unsearchable.
29 He gives power to the weak,
And to *those who have* no might
He increases strength.
30 Even the youths shall faint and
be weary,
And the young men shall utterly
fall,
31 But those who [a]wait on the LORD
[b]Shall renew *their* strength;
They shall mount up with wings
like eagles,
They shall run and not be weary,
They shall walk and not faint.

Israel Assured of God's Help

41 "Keep [a]silence before Me,
O coastlands,
And let the people renew *their*
strength!
Let them come near, then let
them speak;
Let us [b]come near together for
judgment.

2 "Who raised up one [a]from the
east?
Who in righteousness called him
to His feet?
Who [b]gave the nations before
him,
And made *him* rule over kings?
Who gave *them* as the dust *to* his
sword,
As driven stubble to his bow?
3 Who pursued them, *and* passed
[1]safely
By the way *that* he had not gone
with his feet?
4 [a]Who has performed and done *it*,
Calling the generations from the
beginning?
'I, the LORD, am [b]the first;
And with the last I *am* [c]He.'"

5 The coastlands saw *it* and feared,
The ends of the earth were afraid;
They drew near and came.

6 [a]Everyone helped his neighbor,
And said to his brother,
[1]"Be of good courage!"
7 [a]So the craftsman encouraged the
[b]goldsmith;[1]
He who smooths *with* the
hammer *inspired* him who
strikes the anvil,
Saying, [2]"It *is* ready for the
soldering";
Then he fastened it with pegs,
[c]*That* it might not totter.

8 "But you, Israel, *are* My servant,
Jacob whom I have [a]chosen,
The descendants of Abraham My
[b]friend.
9 *You* whom I have taken from the
ends of the earth,
And called from its farthest
regions,
And said to you,
'You *are* My servant,
I have chosen you and have not
cast you away:
10 [a]Fear not, [b]for I *am* with you;
Be not dismayed, for I *am* your
God.
I will strengthen you,
Yes, I will help you,
I will uphold you with My
righteous right hand.'

11 "Behold, all those who were
incensed against you
Shall be [a]ashamed and disgraced;
They shall be as nothing,
And those who strive with you
shall perish.
12 You shall seek them and not find
them—
[1]Those who contended with you.
Those who war against you
Shall be as nothing,
As a nonexistent thing.
13 For I, the LORD your God, will
hold your right hand,
Saying to you, 'Fear not, I will
help you.'

14 "Fear not, you [a]worm Jacob,
You men of Israel!
I will help you," says the LORD
And your Redeemer, the Holy
One of Israel.
15 "Behold, [a]I will make you into a
new threshing sledge with
sharp teeth;
You shall thresh the mountains
and beat *them* small,
And make the hills like chaff.
16 You shall [a]winnow them, the
wind shall carry them away,
And the whirlwind shall scatter
them;

26 [a]Ps. 147:4
27 [a]Is. 54:7, 8
28 [a]Ps. 147:5; Eccl. 11:5; Rom. 11:33
31 [a]Is. 30:15; 49:23 [b][Job 17:9]; Ps. 103:5; [2 Cor. 4:8–10, 16]

CHAPTER 41

1 [a]Hab. 2:20; Zech. 2:13 [b]Is. 1:18
2 [a]Is. 46:11 [b]Gen. 14:14; Is. 45:1, 13
3 [1]Lit. *in peace*
4 [a]Is. 41:26 [b]Rev. 1:8, 17; 22:13 [c]Is. 43:10; 44:6
6 [a]Is. 40:19 [1]Lit. *Be strong*
7 [a]Is. 44:13 [b]Is. 40:19 [c]Is. 40:20 [1]*refiner* [2]Or *The soldering is good*
8 [a]Deut. 7:6; 10:15; Ps. 135:4; [Is. 43:1] [b]2 Chr. 20:7; James 2:23
10 [a]Is. 41:13, 14; 43:5 [b][Deut. 31:6]
11 [a]Ex. 23:22; Is. 45:24; 60:12; Zech. 12:3
12 [1]Lit. *Men of your strife*
14 [a]Job 25:6; Ps. 22:6
15 [a]Mic. 4:13; Hab. 3:12; [2 Cor. 10:4]
16 [a]Jer. 51:2

You shall rejoice in the LORD,
And [b]glory in the Holy One of Israel.

17 "The poor and needy seek water, but *there is* none,
Their tongues fail for thirst.
I, the LORD, will hear them;
I, the God of Israel, will not [a]forsake them.
18 I will open [a]rivers in desolate heights,
And fountains in the midst of the valleys;
I will make the [b]wilderness a pool of water,
And the dry land springs of water.
19 I will plant in the wilderness the cedar and the acacia tree,
The myrtle and the oil tree;
I will set in the [a]desert the cypress tree *and* the pine
And the box tree together,
20 [a]That they may see and know,
And consider and understand together,
That the hand of the LORD has done this,
And the Holy One of Israel has created it.

The Futility of Idols

21 "Present your case," says the LORD.
"Bring forth your strong *reasons*," says the [a]King of Jacob.
22 "Let[a] them bring forth and show us what will happen;
Let them show the [b]former things, what they *were*,
That we may [1]consider them,
And know the latter end of them;
Or declare to us things to come.
23 [a]Show the things that are to come hereafter,
That we may know that you *are* gods;
Yes, [b]do good or do evil,
That we may be dismayed and see *it* together.
24 Indeed [a]you *are* nothing,
And your work *is* nothing;
He who chooses you *is* an abomination.

25 "I have raised up one from the north,
And he shall come;
From the [1]rising of the sun [a]he shall call on My name;
[b]And he shall come against princes as *though* mortar,
As the potter treads clay.

16 [b]Is. 45:25
17 [a]Ps. 94:14; Rom. 11:2
18 [a]Is. 35:6, 7; 43:19; 44:3 [b]Ps. 107:35
19 [a]Is. 35:1
20 [a]Job 12:9; Is. 66:14
21 [a]Is. 43:15
22 [a]Is. 45:21 [b]Is. 43:9 [1]Lit. *set our heart on them*
23 [a]Is. 42:9; 44:7, 8; 45:3; [John 13:19] [b]Jer. 10:5
24 [a]Ps. 115:8; Is. 44:9; [Rom. 3:10–20; 1 Cor. 8:4]
25 [a]Ezra 1:2 [b]Is. 41:2; Jer. 50:3 [1]East
26 [a]Is. 43:9
27 [a]Is. 41:4 [b]Is. 40:9; Nah. 1:15
28 [a]Is. 63:5
29 [a]Is. 41:24 [1]So with MT, Vg.; DSS, Syr., Tg. *nothing;* LXX omits first line

CHAPTER 42

1 [a]Is. 43:10; 49:3, 6; Matt. 12:18; [Phil. 2:7] [b]Matt. 3:17; 17:5; Mark 1:11; Luke 3:22; Eph. 1:6 [c][Is. 11:2]; Matt. 3:16; [Luke 4:18, 19, 21]; John 3:34 [1]*Chosen*
3 [1]*dimly burning* [2]*extinguish*
4 [a][Gen. 49:10]
5 [a]Is. 44:24; Zech. 12:1 [b]Job 12:10; 33:4; Is. 57:16; Dan. 5:23; Acts 17:25
6 [a]Is. 43:1 [b]Is. 49:8 [c]Is. 49:6; Luke 2:32; [Acts 10:45; 13:47; Gal. 3:14]
7 [a]Is. 35:5

26 [a]Who has declared from the beginning, that we may know?
And former times, that we may say, '*He is* righteous'?
Surely *there is* no one who shows,
Surely *there is* no one who declares,
Surely *there is* no one who hears your words.
27 [a]The first time [b]*I said* to Zion,
'Look, there they are!'
And I will give to Jerusalem one who brings good tidings.
28 [a]For I looked, and *there was* no man;
I looked among them, but *there was* no counselor,
Who, when I asked of them, could answer a word.
29 [a]Indeed they *are* all [1]worthless;
Their works *are* nothing;
Their molded images *are* wind and confusion.

The Servant of the LORD

42 "Behold! [a]My Servant whom I uphold,
My [1]Elect One *in whom* My soul [b]delights!
[c]I have put My Spirit upon Him;
He will bring forth justice to the Gentiles.
2 He will not cry out, nor raise *His voice*,
Nor cause His voice to be heard in the street.
3 A bruised reed He will not break,
And [1]smoking flax He will not [2]quench;
He will bring forth justice for truth.
4 He will not fail nor be discouraged,
Till He has established justice in the earth;
[a]And the coastlands shall wait for His law."

5 Thus says God the LORD,
[a]Who created the heavens and stretched them out,
Who spread forth the earth and that which comes from it,
[b]Who gives breath to the people on it,
And spirit to those who walk on it:
6 "I,[a] the LORD, have called You in righteousness,
And will hold Your hand;
I will keep You [b]and give You as a covenant to the people,
As [c]a light to the Gentiles,
7 [a]To open blind eyes,

To [b]bring out prisoners from the
prison,
Those who sit in [c]darkness from
the prison house.
8 I *am* the LORD, that *is* My name;
And My [a]glory I will not give to
another,
Nor My praise to carved images.
9 Behold, the former things have
come to pass,
And new things I declare;
Before they spring forth I tell you
of them."

Praise to the LORD

10 [a]Sing to the LORD a new song,
And His praise from the ends of
the earth,
[b]You who go down to the sea, and
[1]all that is in it,
You coastlands and you
inhabitants of them!
11 Let the wilderness and its cities
lift up *their voice,*
The villages *that* Kedar inhabits.
Let the inhabitants of Sela sing,
Let them shout from the top of
the mountains.
12 Let them give glory to the LORD,
And declare His praise in the
coastlands.
13 The LORD shall go forth like a
mighty man;
He shall stir up *His* zeal like a
man of war.
He shall cry out, [a]yes, shout
aloud;
He shall prevail against His
enemies.

Promise of the LORD's Help

14 "I have held My peace a long time,
I have been still and restrained
Myself.
Now I will cry like a woman in
[1]labor,
I will pant and gasp at once.
15 I will lay waste the mountains
and hills,
And dry up all their vegetation;
I will make the rivers coastlands,
And I will dry up the pools.
16 I will bring the blind by a way
they did not know;
I will lead them in paths they
have not known.
I will make darkness light before
them,
And crooked places straight.
These things I will do for them,
And not forsake them.
17 They shall be [a]turned back,
They shall be greatly ashamed,
Who trust in carved images,
Who say to the molded images,

7 [b]Is. 61:1; Luke 4:18; [2 Tim. 2:26; Heb. 2:14] [c]Is. 9:2
8 [a]Ex. 20:3–5; Is. 48:11
10 [a]Ps. 33:3; 40:3; 98:1 [b]Ps. 107:23 [1]Lit. *its fullness*
13 [a]Is. 31:4
14 [1]*childbirth*
17 [a]Ps. 97:7; Is. 1:29; 44:11; 45:16
19 [a]Is. 43:8; Ezek. 12:2; [John 9:39, 41]
20 [a]Rom. 2:21
22 [1]Or *trapped in caves*
24 [a]Is. 65:2
25 [a]2 Kin. 25:9 [b]Is. 1:3; 5:13; Hos. 7:9 [c]Is. 29:13

CHAPTER 43

1 [a]Is. 43:5; 44:6 [b]Is. 42:6; 45:4
2 [a][Ps. 66:12; 91:3] [b][Deut. 31:6]; Jer. 30:11 [c]Dan. 3:25

'You *are* our gods.'
18 "Hear, you deaf;
And look, you blind, that you
may see.
19 [a]Who *is* blind but My servant,
Or deaf as My messenger *whom*
I send?
Who *is* blind as *he who is* perfect,
And blind as the LORD's servant?
20 Seeing many things, [a]but you do
not observe;
Opening the ears, but he does not
hear."

Israel's Obstinate Disobedience

21 The LORD is well pleased for His
righteousness' sake;
He will exalt the law and make
it honorable.
22 But this *is* a people robbed and
plundered;
All of them are [1]snared in holes,
And they are hidden in prison
houses;
They are for prey, and no one
delivers;
For plunder, and no one says,
"Restore!"
23 Who among you will give ear to
this?
Who will listen and hear for the
time to come?
24 Who gave Jacob for plunder, and
Israel to the robbers?
Was it not the LORD,
He against whom we have
sinned?
[a]For they would not walk in His
ways,
Nor were they obedient to His
law.
25 Therefore He has poured on him
the fury of His anger
And the strength of battle;
[a]It has set him on fire all around,
[b]Yet he did not know;
And it burned him,
Yet he did not take *it* to [c]heart.

The Redeemer of Israel

43 But now, thus says the LORD,
who created you, O Jacob,
And He who formed you,
O Israel:
"Fear not, [a]for I have redeemed
you;
[b]I have called *you* by your name;
You *are* Mine.
2 [a]When you pass through the
waters, [b]I *will be* with you;
And through the rivers, they shall
not overflow you.
When you [c]walk through the fire,
you shall not be burned,

Nor shall the flame scorch you.
3 For I *am* the LORD your God,
The Holy One of Israel, your Savior;
[a]I gave Egypt for your ransom,
Ethiopia and Seba in your place.
4 Since you were precious in My sight,
You have been honored,
And I have [a]loved you;
Therefore I will give men for you,
And people for your life.
5 [a]Fear not, for I *am* with you;
I will bring your descendants from the east,
And [b]gather you from the west;
6 I will say to the [a]north, 'Give them up!'
And to the south, 'Do not keep them back!'
Bring My sons from afar,
And My daughters from the ends of the earth—
7 Everyone who is [a]called by My name,
Whom [b]I have created for My glory;
I have formed him, yes, I have made him."

8 [a]Bring out the blind people who have eyes,
And the [b]deaf who have ears.
9 Let all the nations be gathered together,
And let the people be assembled.
[a]Who among them can declare this,
And show us former things?
Let them bring out their witnesses, that they may be justified;
Or let them hear and say, "*It is* truth."
10 "You[a] *are* My witnesses," says the LORD,
[b]"And My servant whom I have chosen,
That you may know and [c]believe Me,
And understand that I *am* He.
Before Me there was no God formed,
Nor shall there be after Me.
11 I, *even* I, [a]*am* the LORD,
And besides Me *there is* no savior.
12 I have declared and saved,
I have proclaimed,
And *there was* no [a]foreign *god* among you;
[b]Therefore you *are* My witnesses,"
Says the LORD, "that I *am* God.
13 [a]Indeed before the day *was*, I *am* He;
And *there is* no one who can deliver out of My hand;
I work, and who will [b]reverse it?"

14 Thus says the LORD, your Redeemer,
The Holy One of Israel:
"For your sake I will send to Babylon,
And bring them all down as fugitives—
The Chaldeans, who rejoice in their ships.
15 I *am* the LORD, your Holy One,
The Creator of Israel, your [a]King."

16 Thus says the LORD, who [a]makes a way in the sea
And a [b]path through the mighty waters,
17 Who [a]brings forth the chariot and horse,
The army and the power
(They shall lie down together, they shall not rise;
They are extinguished, they are quenched like a wick):
18 "Do[a] not remember the former things,
Nor consider the things of old.
19 Behold, I will do a [a]new thing,
Now it shall spring forth;
Shall you not know it?
[b]I will even make a road in the wilderness
And rivers in the desert.
20 The beast of the field will honor Me,
The jackals and the ostriches,
Because [a]I give waters in the wilderness
And rivers in the desert,
To give drink to My people, My chosen.
21 [a]This people I have formed for Myself;
They shall declare My [b]praise.

Pleading with Unfaithful Israel

22 "But you have not called upon Me, O Jacob;
And you [a]have been weary of Me, O Israel.
23 [a]You have not brought Me the sheep for your burnt offerings,
Nor have you honored Me with your sacrifices.
I have not caused you to serve with grain offerings,
Nor wearied you with incense.
24 You have bought Me no sweet cane with money,
Nor have you satisfied Me with the fat of your sacrifices;

3 [a][Prov. 11:8; 21:18]
4 [a]Is. 63:9
5 [a]Is. 41:10; 44:2; Jer. 30:10; 46:27, 28 [b]Is. 54:7
6 [a]Is. 49:12
7 [a]Is. 63:19; James 2:7 [b]Ps. 100:3; Is. 29:23; [John 3:2, 3; 2 Cor. 5:17; Eph. 2:10]
8 [a]Is. 6:9; 42:19; Ezek. 12:2 [b]Is. 29:18
9 [a]Is. 41:21, 22, 26
10 [a]Is. 44:8 [b]Is. 55:4 [c]Is. 41:4; 44:6
11 [a]Is. 45:21; Hos. 13:4
12 [a]Deut. 32:16; Ps. 81:9 [b]Is. 44:8
13 [a]Ps. 90:2; Is. 48:16 [b]Job 9:12; Is. 14:27
15 [a]Is. 41:20, 21
16 [a]Ex. 14:16, 21, 22; Ps. 77:19; Is. 51:10 [b]Josh. 3:13
17 [a]Ex. 14:4–9, 25
18 [a]Jer. 16:14
19 [a]Is. 42:9; 48:6; [2 Cor. 5:17; Rev. 21:5] [b]Ex. 17:6; Num. 20:11; Deut. 8:15; Ps. 78:16; Is. 35:1, 6
20 [a]Is. 48:21
21 [a]Ps. 102:18; Is. 42:12; [Luke 1:74, 75; Eph. 1:5, 6; 1 Pet. 2:9] [b]Jer. 13:11
22 [a]Mic. 6:3; Mal. 1:13; 3:14
23 [a]Amos 5:25

But you have burdened Me with
your sins,
You have [a]wearied Me with your
iniquities.

25 "I, *even* I, *am* He who [a]blots out
your transgressions [b]for My
own sake;
[c]And I will not remember your
sins.
26 Put Me in remembrance;
Let us contend together;
State your *case*, that you may be
[1]acquitted.
27 Your first father sinned,
And your [1]mediators have
transgressed against Me.
28 Therefore I will profane the
princes of the sanctuary;
[a]I will give Jacob to the curse,
And Israel to reproaches.

God's Blessing on Israel

44 "Yet hear now, O Jacob My
servant,
And Israel whom I have chosen.
2 Thus says the LORD who made
you
And formed you from the womb,
who will help you:
'Fear not, O Jacob My servant;
And you, Jeshurun, whom I have
chosen.
3 For I will pour water on him who
is thirsty,
And floods on the dry ground;
I will pour My Spirit on your
descendants,
And My blessing on your
offspring;
4 They will spring up among the
grass
Like willows by the
watercourses.'
5 One will say, 'I *am* the LORD's';
Another will call *himself* by the
name of Jacob;
Another will write *with* his hand,
'The LORD's,'
And name *himself* by the name
of Israel.

There Is No Other God

6 "Thus says the LORD, the King of
Israel,
And his Redeemer, the LORD of
hosts:
[a]'I *am* the First and I *am* the Last;
Besides Me *there is* no God.
7 And [a]who can proclaim as I do?
Then let him declare it and set it
in order for Me,
Since I appointed the ancient
people.
And the things that are coming
and shall come,
Let them show these to them.
8 Do not fear, nor be afraid;
[a]Have I not told you from that
time, and declared *it*?
[b]You *are* My witnesses.
Is there a God besides Me?
Indeed [c]*there is* no other Rock;
I know not *one*.'"

Idolatry Is Foolishness

9 [a]Those who make an image, all of
them *are* useless,
And their precious things shall
not profit;
They *are* their own witnesses;
[b]They neither see nor know, that
they may be ashamed.
10 Who would form a god or mold
an image
[a]*That* profits him nothing?
11 Surely all his companions would
be [a]ashamed;
And the workmen, they *are* mere
men.
Let them all be gathered together,
Let them stand up;
Yet they shall fear,
They shall be ashamed together.

12 [a]The blacksmith with the tongs
works one in the coals,
Fashions it with hammers,
And works it with the strength of
his arms.
Even so, he is hungry, and his
strength fails;
He drinks no water and is faint.

13 The craftsman stretches out *his*
rule,
He marks one out with chalk;
He fashions it with a plane,
He marks it out with the compass,
And makes it like the figure of a
man,
According to the beauty of a man,
that it may remain in the house.
14 He cuts down cedars for himself,
And takes the cypress and the
oak;
He [1]secures *it* for himself among
the trees of the forest.
He plants a pine, and the rain
nourishes *it*.

15 Then it shall be for a man to burn,
For he will take some of it and
warm himself;
Yes, he kindles *it* and bakes
bread;
Indeed he makes a god and
worships *it*;

24 [a]Ps. 95:10; Is. 1:14; 7:13; Ezek. 6:9; Mal. 2:17
25 [a]Is. 44:22; Jer. 50:20; [Acts 3:19] [b]Ezek. 36:22 [c]Is. 1:18; Jer. 31:34
26 [1]*Justified*
27 [1]*Interpreters*
28 [a]Ps. 79:4; Jer. 24:9; Dan. 9:11; Zech. 8:13

CHAPTER 44

6 [a]Is. 41:4; [Rev. 1:8, 17; 22:13]
7 [a]Is. 41:4, 22, 26
8 [a]Is. 41:22 [b]Is. 43:10, 12 [c]Deut. 4:35; 32:39; 1 Sam. 2:2; 2 Sam. 22:32; Is. 45:5; Joel 2:27
9 [a]Is. 41:24 [b]Ps. 115:4
10 [a]Is. 41:29; Jer. 10:5; Hab. 2:18; Acts 19:26
11 [a]Ps. 97:7; Is. 1:29; 42:17
12 [a]Is. 40:19; Jer. 10:3–5
14 [1]Lit. *appropriates*

He makes it a carved image, and
falls down to it.
16 He burns half of it in the fire;
With this half he eats meat;
He roasts a roast, and is satisfied.
He even warms *himself* and says,
"Ah! I am warm,
I have seen the fire."
17 And the rest of it he makes into
a god,
His carved image.
He falls down before it and
worships *it*,
Prays to it and says,
"Deliver me, for you *are* my god!"

18 [a]They do not know nor
understand;
For [b]He has [1]shut their eyes, so
that they cannot see,
And their hearts, so that they
cannot [c]understand.
19 And no one [a]considers in his
heart,
Nor *is there* knowledge nor
understanding to say,
"I have burned half of it in the fire,
Yes, I have also baked bread on
its coals;
I have roasted meat and eaten *it*;
And shall I make the rest of it an
abomination?
Shall I fall down before a block
of wood?"
20 He feeds on ashes;
[a]A deceived heart has turned him
aside;
And he cannot deliver his soul,
Nor say, "*Is there* not a [b]lie in my
right hand?"

Israel Is Not Forgotten

21 "Remember these, O Jacob,
And Israel, for you *are* My
servant;
I have formed you, you *are* My
servant;
O Israel, you will not be
[a]forgotten by Me!
22 [a]I have blotted out, like a thick
cloud, your transgressions,
And like a cloud, your sins.
Return to Me, for [b]I have
redeemed you."

23 [a]Sing, O heavens, for the LORD has
done *it!*
Shout, you lower parts of the
earth;
Break forth into singing, you
mountains,
O forest, and every tree in it!
For the LORD has redeemed
Jacob,
And [b]glorified Himself in Israel.

18 [a]Is. 45:20 [b][Ps. 81:12]; Is. 6:9, 10; 29:10; 2 Thess. 2:11 [c]Jer. 10:14 [1]Lit. *smeared over*
19 [a]Is. 46:8
20 [a]Job 15:31; Hos. 4:12; Rom. 1:21, 22; 2 Thess. 2:11; 2 Tim. 3:13 [b]Is. 57:11; 59:3, 4, 13; Rom. 1:25
21 [a]Is. 49:15
22 [a]Is. 43:25 [b]Is. 43:1; 1 Cor. 6:20; [1 Pet. 1:18, 19]
23 [a]Ps. 69:34; Is. 42:10; 49:13; Jer. 51:48; Rev. 18:20 [b]Is. 49:3; 60:21
24 [a]Is. 43:14 [b]Is. 43:1 [c]Job 9:8 [1]By Himself
25 [a]Is. 47:13 [b]Jer. 50:36 [c]2 Sam. 15:31; Job 5:12–14; Ps. 33:10; Is. 29:14; Jer. 51:57; 1 Cor. 1:20, 27
26 [a]Zech. 1:6; Matt. 5:18
27 [a]Jer. 50:38; 51:36
28 [a]2 Chr. 36:22; Ezra 1:1; Is. 45:13 [b]Ezra 6:7

CHAPTER 45
1 [a]Is. 44:28 [b]Ps. 73:23; Is. 41:13 [c]Dan. 5:30 [d]Job 12:21; Is. 45:5 [1]*strengthened* or *sustained*
2 [a]Is. 40:4 [b]Ps. 107:16 [1]Tg. *I will trample down the walls;* Vg. *I will humble the great ones of the earth* [2]DSS, LXX *mountains*
3 [a]Is. 41:23 [b]Ex. 33:12
4 [a]Is. 44:1

Judah Will Be Restored

24 Thus says the LORD, [a]your
Redeemer,
And [b]He who formed you from
the womb:
"I *am* the LORD, who makes all
things,
[c]Who stretches out the heavens
[1]all alone,
Who spreads abroad the earth by
Myself;
25 Who [a]frustrates the signs [b]of the
babblers,
And drives diviners mad;
Who turns wise men backward,
[c]And makes their knowledge
foolishness;
26 [a]Who confirms the word of His
servant,
And performs the counsel of His
messengers;
Who says to Jerusalem, 'You
shall be inhabited,'
To the cities of Judah, 'You shall
be built,'
And I will raise up her waste
places;
27 [a]Who says to the deep, 'Be dry!
And I will dry up your rivers';
28 Who says of [a]Cyrus, '*He is* My
shepherd,
And he shall perform all My
pleasure,
Saying to Jerusalem, [b]"You shall
be built,"
And to the temple, "Your
foundation shall be laid." '

Cyrus, God's Instrument

45 "Thus says the LORD to His
anointed,
To [a]Cyrus, whose [b]right hand I
have [1]held—
[c]To subdue nations before him
And [d]loose the armor of kings,
To open before him the double
doors,
So that the gates will not be shut:
2 'I will go before you
[a]And[1] make the [2]crooked places
straight;
[b]I will break in pieces the gates of
bronze
And cut the bars of iron.
3 I will give you the treasures of
darkness
And hidden riches of secret
places,
[a]That you may know that I, the
LORD,
Who [b]call *you* by your name,
Am the God of Israel.
4 For [a]Jacob My servant's sake,
And Israel My elect,

I have even called you by your
name;
I have named you, though you
have not known Me.
5 I [a]*am* the LORD, and [b]*there is* no
other;
There is no God besides Me.
[c]I will gird you, though you have
not known Me,
6 [a]That they may [b]know from the
rising of the sun to its setting
That *there is* none besides Me.
I *am* the LORD, and *there is* no
other;
7 I form the light and create
darkness,
I make peace and [a]create
calamity;
I, the LORD, do all these *things*.'

8 "Rain[a] down, you heavens, from
above,
And let the skies pour down
righteousness;
Let the earth open, let them bring
forth salvation,
And let righteousness spring up
together.
I, the LORD, have created it.

9 "Woe to him who strives with [a]his
Maker!
Let the potsherd *strive* with the
potsherds of the earth!
[b]Shall the clay say to him who
forms it, 'What are you
making?'
Or shall your handiwork *say*, 'He
has no hands'?
10 Woe to him who says to *his*
father, 'What are you
begetting?'
Or to the woman, 'What have you
brought forth?' "

11 Thus says the LORD,
The Holy One of Israel, and his
Maker:
[a]"Ask Me of things to come
concerning [b]My sons;
And concerning [c]the work of My
hands, you command Me.
12 [a]I have made the earth,
And [b]created man on it.
I—My hands—stretched out the
heavens,
And [c]all their host I have
commanded.
13 [a]I have raised him up in
righteousness,
And I will [1]direct all his ways;
He shall [b]build My city
And let My exiles go free,
[c]Not for price nor reward,"
Says the LORD of hosts.

The LORD, the Only Savior

14 Thus says the LORD:
[a]"The labor of Egypt and
merchandise of Cush
And of the Sabeans, men of
stature,
Shall come over to you, and they
shall be yours;
They shall walk behind you,
They shall come over [b]in chains;
And they shall bow down to you.
They will make supplication to
you, *saying*, [c]'Surely God *is* in
you,
And *there is* no other;
[d]*There is* no other God.' "

15 Truly You *are* God, [a]who hide
Yourself,
O God of Israel, the Savior!
16 They shall be [a]ashamed
And also disgraced, all of them;
They shall go in confusion
together,
Who are makers of idols.
17 [a]*But* Israel shall be saved by the
LORD
With an [b]everlasting salvation;
You shall not be ashamed or
[c]disgraced
Forever and ever.

18 For thus says the LORD,
[a]Who created the heavens,
Who is God,
Who formed the earth and
made it,
Who has established it,
Who did not create it [1]in vain,
Who formed it to be [b]inhabited:
[c]"I *am* the LORD, and *there is* no
other.
19 I have not spoken in [a]secret,
In a dark place of the earth;
I did not say to the seed of Jacob,
'Seek Me [1]in vain';
[b]I, the LORD, speak righteousness,
I declare things that are right.

20 "Assemble yourselves and come;
Draw near together,
You *who have* escaped from the
nations.
[a]They have no knowledge,
Who carry the wood of their
carved image,
And pray to a god *that* cannot
save.
21 Tell and bring forth *your case;*
Yes, let them take counsel
together.
[a]Who has declared this from
ancient time?
Who has told it from that time?
Have not I, the LORD?

5 [a]Deut. 4:35; 32:39; Is. 44:8 [b]Is. 45:14, 18 [c]Ps. 18:32
6 [a]Ps. 102:15; Is. 37:20; Mal. 1:11 [b][Is. 11:9; 52:10]
7 [a]Is. 31:2; 47:11; Amos 3:6
8 [a]Ps. 85:11
9 [a]Is. 64:8 [b]Jer. 18:6; Rom. 9:20, 21
11 [a]Is. 8:19 [b]Jer. 31:9 [c]Is. 29:23; 60:21; 64:8
12 [a]Is. 42:5; Jer. 27:5 [b]Gen. 1:26 [c]Gen. 2:1; Neh. 9:6
13 [a]Is. 41:2 [b]2 Chr. 36:22; Is. 44:28 [c][Rom. 3:24] [1]Or *make all his ways straight*
14 [a]Ps. 68:31; 72:10, 11; Is. 14:1; 49:23; 60:9, 10, 14, 16; Zech. 8:22, 23 [b]Ps. 149:8 [c]Jer. 16:19; Zech. 8:20–23; 1 Cor. 14:25 [d]Is. 45:5
15 [a]Ps. 44:24; Is. 57:17
16 [a]Is. 44:11
17 [a]Is. 26:4; [Rom. 11:26] [b]Is. 51:6 [c]Is. 29:22
18 [a]Is. 42:5 [b]Gen. 1:26; Ps. 115:16; Acts 17:26 [c]Is. 45:5 [1]Or *empty, a waste*
19 [a]Deut. 30:11 [b]Ps. 19:8; Is. 45:23; 63:1 [1]Or *in a waste place*
20 [a]Is. 44:9; 46:7; Jer. 10:5
21 [a]Is. 41:22; 43:9

[b]And *there is* no other God besides
Me,
A just God and a Savior;
There is none besides Me.

22 "Look to Me, and be saved,
[a]All you ends of the earth!
For I *am* God, and *there is* no
other.
23 [a]I have sworn by Myself;
The word has gone out of My
mouth *in* righteousness,
And shall not return,
That to Me every [b]knee shall
bow,
[c]Every tongue shall take an oath.
24 He shall say,
[1]'Surely in the LORD I have
[a]righteousness and strength.
To Him *men* shall come,
And [b]all shall be ashamed
Who are incensed against Him.
25 [a]In the LORD all the descendants
of Israel
Shall be justified, and [b]shall
glory.' "

Dead Idols and the Living God

46 Bel [a]bows down, Nebo
stoops;
Their idols were on the beasts
and on the cattle.
Your carriages *were* heavily
loaded,
[b]A burden to the weary *beast*.
2 They stoop, they bow down
together;
They could not deliver the
burden,
[a]But have themselves gone into
captivity.

3 "Listen to Me, O house of Jacob,
And all the remnant of the house
of Israel,
[a]Who have been upheld *by Me*
from [1]birth,
Who have been carried from the
womb:
4 Even to *your* old age, [a]I *am* He,
And *even* to gray hairs [b]I will
carry *you!*
I have made, and I will bear;
Even I will carry, and will deliver
you.

5 "To[a] whom will you liken Me, and
make *Me* equal
And compare Me, that we should
be alike?
6 [a]They lavish gold out of the bag,
And weigh silver on the scales;
They hire a [b]goldsmith, and he
makes it a god;

21 [b]Is. 44:8
22 [a]Ps. 22:27; 65:5
23 [a][Heb. 6:13] [b]Rom. 14:11 [c]Deut. 6:13
24 [a][1 Cor. 1:30] [b]Is. 41:11 [1]Or *Only in the LORD are all righteousness and strength*
25 [a]Is. 45:17 [b]1 Cor. 1:31

CHAPTER 46

1 [a]Jer. 50:2 [b]Jer. 10:5
2 [a]Jer. 48:7
3 [a]Ps. 71:6 [1]Lit. *the belly*
4 [a]Mal. 3:6 [b]Ps. 48:14
5 [a]Is. 40:18, 25
6 [a]Is. 40:19; 41:6 [b]Is. 44:12
7 [a]Jer. 10:5 [b]Is. 45:20
8 [a]Is. 44:19 [1]*be men*, take courage
9 [a]Deut. 32:7 [b]Is. 45:5, 21
10 [a]Is. 45:21; 48:3 [b]Ps. 33:11
11 [a]Is. 41:2, 25 [b]Is. 44:28 [c]Num. 23:19
12 [a]Ps. 76:5 [b][Rom. 10:3]
13 [a][Rom. 1:17] [b]Hab. 2:3 [c]Is. 62:11 [1]*delay*

CHAPTER 47

1 [a]Jer. 48:18 [b]Is. 3:26 [c]Jer. 25:12; 50:1—51:64 [1]*dainty*
2 [a]Ex. 11:5
3 [a]Is. 3:17; 20:4 [b][Rom. 12:19]

They prostrate themselves, yes,
they worship.
7 [a]They bear it on the shoulder, they
carry it
And set it in its place, and it
stands;
From its place it shall not move.
Though [b]*one* cries out to it, yet
it cannot answer
Nor save him out of his trouble.

8 "Remember this, and [1]show
yourselves men;
[a]Recall to mind, O you
transgressors.
9 [a]Remember the former things of
old,
For I *am* God, and [b]*there is* no
other;
I am God, and *there is* none
like Me,
10 [a]Declaring the end from the
beginning,
And from ancient times *things*
that are not *yet* done,
Saying, [b]'My counsel shall stand,
And I will do all My pleasure,'
11 Calling a bird of prey [a]from the
east,
The man [b]who executes My
counsel, from a far country.
Indeed [c]I have spoken *it;*
I will also bring it to pass.
I have purposed *it;*
I will also do it.

12 "Listen to Me, you [a]stubborn-
hearted,
[b]Who *are* far from righteousness:
13 [a]I bring My righteousness near, it
shall not be far off;
My salvation [b]shall not [1]linger.
And I will place [c]salvation in
Zion,
For Israel My glory.

The Humiliation of Babylon

47 "Come [a]down and [b]sit in the
dust,
O virgin daughter of [c]Babylon;
Sit on the ground without a
throne,
O daughter of the Chaldeans!
For you shall no more be called
Tender and [1]delicate.
2 [a]Take the millstones and grind
meal.
Remove your veil,
Take off the skirt,
Uncover the thigh,
Pass through the rivers.
3 [a]Your nakedness shall be
uncovered,
Yes, your shame will be seen;
[b]I will take vengeance,

And I will not arbitrate with a
man."

4 *As for* [a]our Redeemer, the LORD
of hosts *is* His name,
The Holy One of Israel.

5 "Sit in [a]silence, and go into
darkness,
O daughter of the Chaldeans;
[b]For you shall no longer be called
The Lady of Kingdoms.
6 [a]I was angry with My people;
[b]I have profaned My inheritance,
And given them into your hand.
You showed them no mercy;
[c]On the elderly you laid your yoke
very heavily.
7 And you said, 'I shall be [a]a lady
forever,'
So that you did not [b]take these
things to heart,
[c]Nor remember the latter end of
them.

8 "Therefore hear this now, *you who
are* given to pleasures,
Who dwell securely,
Who say in your heart,
'I *am*, and *there is* no one else
besides me;
I shall not sit *as* a widow,
Nor shall I know the loss of
children';
9 But these two *things* shall come
to you
[a]In a moment, in one day:
The loss of children, and
widowhood.
They shall come upon you in their
fullness
Because of the multitude of your
sorceries,
For the great abundance of your
enchantments.

10 "For you have trusted in your
wickedness;
You have said, 'No one [a]sees me';
Your wisdom and your
knowledge have [1]warped you;
And you have said in your
heart,
'I *am*, and *there is* no one else
besides me.'
11 Therefore evil shall come upon
you;
You shall not know from where
it arises.
And trouble shall fall upon you;
You will not be able [1]to put it off.
And [a]desolation shall come upon
you [b]suddenly,
Which you shall not know.

12 "Stand now with your
enchantments
And the multitude of your
sorceries,
In which you have labored from
your youth—
Perhaps you will be able to profit,
Perhaps you will prevail.
13 [a]You are wearied in the multitude
of your counsels;
Let now [b]the[1] astrologers, the
stargazers,
And [2]the monthly
prognosticators
Stand up and save you
From what shall come upon you.
14 Behold, they shall be [a]as stubble,
The fire shall [b]burn them;
They shall not deliver themselves
From the power of the flame;
It shall not *be* a coal to be
warmed by,
Nor a fire to sit before!
15 Thus shall they be to you
With whom you have labored,
[a]Your merchants from your youth;
They shall wander each one to his
[1]quarter.
No one shall save you.

Israel Refined for God's Glory

48 "Hear this, O house of Jacob,
Who are called by the name
of Israel,
And have come forth from the
wellsprings of Judah;
Who swear by the name of the
LORD,
And make mention of the God of
Israel,
But [a]not in truth or in
righteousness;
2 For they call themselves [a]after
the holy city,
And [b]lean on the God of Israel;
The LORD of hosts *is* His name:

3 "I have [a]declared the former
things from the beginning;
They went forth from My mouth,
and I caused them to hear it.
Suddenly I did *them*, [b]and they
came to pass.
4 Because I knew that you *were*
[1]obstinate,
And [a]your neck *was* an iron
sinew,
And your brow bronze,
5 Even from the beginning I have
declared *it* to you;
Before it came to pass I
proclaimed *it* to you,
Lest you should say, 'My idol has
done them,

4 [a]Jer. 50:34
5 [a]1 Sam. 2:9 [b]Is. 13:19; [Dan. 2:37]; Rev. 17:18
6 [a]2 Sam. 24:14 [b]Is. 43:28 [c]Deut. 28:49, 50
7 [a]Rev. 18:7 [b]Is. 42:25; 46:8 [c]Deut. 32:29; Jer. 5:31; Ezek. 7:2, 3
9 [a]Ps. 73:19; 1 Thess. 5:3; Rev. 18:8
10 [a]Is. 29:15; Ezek. 8:12; 9:9 [1]*led you astray*
11 [a]Is. 13:6; Jer. 51:8, 43; Luke 17:27; 1 Thess. 5:3 [b]Is. 29:5 [1]Lit. *to cover it* or *atone for it*
13 [a]Is. 57:10 [b]Is. 8:19; 44:25; 47:9; Dan. 2:2, 10 [1]Lit. *viewers of the heavens* [2]Lit. *those giving knowledge for new moons*
14 [a]Is. 5:24; Nah. 1:10; Mal. 4:1 [b][Is. 10:17]; Jer. 51:58
15 [a]Rev. 18:11 [1]*own side* or *way*

CHAPTER 48

1 [a]Is. 58:2; Jer. 4:2; 5:2
2 [a]Is. 52:1; 64:10 [b]Is. 10:20; Jer. 7:4; 21:2; Mic. 3:11; Rom. 2:17
3 [a]Is. 44:7, 8; 46:10 [b]Josh. 21:45; Is. 42:9
4 [a]Ex. 32:9; Deut. 31:27; Ezek. 2:4; 3:7 [1]Heb. *hard*

And my carved image and my
molded image
Have commanded them.'

6 "You have heard;
See all this.
And will you not declare *it*?
I have made you hear new things
from this time,
Even hidden things, and you did
not know them.
7 They are created now and not
from the beginning;
And before this day you have not
heard them,
Lest you should say, 'Of course I
knew them.'
8 Surely you did not hear,
Surely you did not know;
Surely from long ago your ear
was not opened.
For I knew that you would deal
very treacherously,
And were called [a]a transgressor
from the womb.

9 "For[a] My name's sake [b]I will [1]defer
My anger,
And *for* My praise I will restrain
it from you,
So that I do not cut you off.
10 Behold, [a]I have refined you, but
not as silver;
I have tested you in the [b]furnace
of affliction.
11 For My own sake, for My own
sake, I will do *it;*
For [a]how should *My name* be
profaned?
And [b]I will not give My glory to
another.

God's Ancient Plan to Redeem Israel

12 "Listen to Me, O Jacob,
And Israel, My called:
I *am* He, [a]I *am* the [b]First,
I *am* also the Last.
13 Indeed [a]My hand has laid the
foundation of the earth,
And My right hand has stretched
out the heavens;
When [b]I call to them,
They stand up together.

14 "All of you, assemble yourselves,
and hear!
Who among them has declared
these *things*?
[a]The LORD loves him;
[b]He shall do His pleasure on
Babylon,
And His arm *shall be against* the
Chaldeans.
15 I, *even* I, have spoken;
Yes, [a]I have called him,
I have brought him, and his way
will prosper.

16 "Come near to Me, hear this:
[a]I have not spoken in secret from
the beginning;
From the time that it was, I *was*
there.
And now [b]the Lord GOD and His
Spirit
[1]Have sent Me."

17 Thus says [a]the LORD, your
Redeemer,
The Holy One of Israel:
"I *am* the LORD your God,
Who teaches you to profit,
[b]Who leads you by the way you
should go.
18 [a]Oh, that you had heeded My
commandments!
[b]Then your peace would have
been like a river,
And your righteousness like the
waves of the sea.
19 [a]Your descendants also would
have been like the sand,
And the offspring of your body
like the grains of sand;
His name would not have been
cut off
Nor destroyed from before Me."

20 [a]Go forth from Babylon!
Flee from the Chaldeans!
With a voice of singing,
Declare, proclaim this,
Utter it to the end of the earth;
Say, "The LORD has [b]redeemed
His servant Jacob!"
21 And they [a]did not thirst
When He led them through the
deserts;
He [b]caused the waters to flow
from the rock for them;
He also split the rock, and the
waters gushed out.

22 "*There*[a] *is* no peace," says the
LORD, "for the wicked."

The Servant, the Light to the Gentiles

49 "Listen, [a]O coastlands, to Me,
And take heed, you peoples
from afar!
[b]The LORD has called Me from the
womb;
From the [1]matrix of My mother
He has made mention of My
name.
2 And He has made [a]My mouth like
a sharp sword;
[b]In the shadow of His hand He has
hidden Me,

8 [a]Ps. 58:3
9 [a]Ezek. 20:9, 14, 22, 44 [b]Ps. 78:38 [1]*delay*
10 [a]Ps. 66:10 [b]Deut. 4:20
11 [a]Ezek. 20:9 [b]Is. 42:8
12 [a]Deut. 32:39 [b][Rev. 22:13]
13 [a]Ps. 102:25 [b]Is. 40:26
14 [a]Is. 45:1 [b]Is. 44:28; 47:1–15
15 [a]Is. 45:1, 2
16 [a]Is. 45:19 [b]Zech. 2:8, 9, 11 [1]Heb. verb is sing.; or *Has sent Me and His Spirit*
17 [a]Is. 43:14 [b]Ps. 32:8
18 [a]Ps. 81:13 [b]Ps. 119:165
19 [a]Gen. 22:17
20 [a]Zech. 2:6, 7 [b][Ex. 19:4–6]
21 [a][Is. 41:17, 18] [b]Ex. 17:6
22 [a][Is. 57:21]
CHAPTER 49
1 [a]Is. 41:1 [b]Jer. 1:5 [1]Lit. *inward parts*
2 [a]Rev. 1:16; 2:12 [b]Is. 51:16

And made Me [c]a polished
shaft;
In His quiver He has
hidden Me."

3 "And He said to me,
[a]'You *are* My servant, O Israel,
[b]In whom I will be glorified.'
4 [a]Then I said, 'I have labored in
vain,
I have spent my strength for
nothing and in vain;
Yet surely my [1]just reward *is* with
the LORD,
And my [2]work with my God.' "

5 "And now the LORD says,
Who formed Me from the womb
to be His Servant,
To bring Jacob back to Him,
So that Israel [a]is [1]gathered to Him
(For I shall be glorious in the eyes
of the LORD,
And My God shall be My
strength),
6 Indeed He says,
'It is too small a thing that You
should be My Servant
To raise up the tribes of Jacob,
And to restore the preserved ones
of Israel;
I will also give You as a [a]light to
the Gentiles,
That You should be My salvation
to the ends of the earth.' "

7 Thus says the LORD,
The Redeemer of Israel, [1]their
Holy One,
[a]To Him [2]whom man despises,
To Him whom the nation abhors,
To the Servant of rulers:
[b]"Kings shall see and arise,
Princes also shall worship,
Because of the LORD who is
faithful,
The Holy One of Israel;
And He has chosen You."

8 Thus says the LORD:

"In an [a]acceptable[1] time I have
heard You,
And in the day of salvation I have
helped You;
I will [2]preserve You [b]and give
You
As a covenant to the people,
To restore the earth,
To cause them to inherit the
desolate [3]heritages;
9 That You may say [a]to the
prisoners, 'Go forth,'
To those who *are* in darkness,
'Show yourselves.'

"They shall feed along the roads,
And their pastures *shall be* on all
desolate heights.
10 They shall neither [a]hunger nor
thirst,
[b]Neither heat nor sun shall strike
them;
For He who has mercy on them
[c]will lead them,
Even by the springs of water He
will guide them.
11 [a]I will make each of My mountains
a road,
And My highways shall be
elevated.
12 Surely [a]these shall come from
afar;
Look! Those from the north and
the west,
And these from the land of
Sinim."

13 [a]Sing, O heavens!
Be joyful, O earth!
And break out in singing,
O mountains!
For the LORD has comforted His
people,
And will have mercy on His
afflicted.

God Will Remember Zion

14 [a]But Zion said, "The LORD has
forsaken me,
And my Lord has forgotten me."

15 "Can[a] a woman forget her nursing
child,
[1]And not have compassion on the
son of her womb?
Surely they may forget,
[b]Yet I will not forget you.
16 See, [a]I have inscribed you on the
palms *of My hands;*
Your walls *are* continually before
Me.
17 Your [1]sons shall make haste;
Your destroyers and those who
laid you waste
Shall go away from you.
18 [a]Lift up your eyes, look around
and see;
All these gather together *and*
come to you.
As I live," says the LORD,
"You shall surely clothe
yourselves with them all [b]as an
ornament,
And bind them *on you* as a bride
does.

19 "For your waste and desolate
places,
And the land of your destruction,

2 [c]Ps. 45:5
3 [a][Is. 41:8; 42:1; Zech. 3:8] [b]Is. 44:23; Matt. 12:18; [John 13:31, 32; 14:13; 15:8; 17:4; Eph. 1:6]
4 [a][Ezek. 3:19] [1]*justice* [2]*recompense*
5 [a]Matt. 23:37; [Rom. 11:25–29] [1]Qr., DSS, LXX *gathered to Him;* Kt. *not gathered*
6 [a]Is. 42:6; 51:4; [Luke 2:32]; Acts 13:47; [Gal. 3:14]
7 [a][Ps. 22:6; Is. 53:3; Matt. 26:67; 27:41]; Mark 15:29; Luke 23:35 [b][Is. 52:15] [1]Lit. *his* or *its* [2]Lit. *who is despised of soul*
8 [a]Ps. 69:13; 2 Cor. 6:2 [b]Is. 42:6 [1]*favorable* [2]*keep* [3]*inheritances*
9 [a]Is. 61:1; Zech. 9:12; Luke 4:18
10 [a]Is. 33:16; 48:21; Rev. 7:16 [b]Ps. 121:6 [c]Ps. 23:2; Is. 40:11; 48:17
11 [a]Is. 40:4
12 [a]Is. 43:5, 6
13 [a]Is. 44:23
14 [a]Is. 40:27
15 [a]Ps. 103:13; Mal. 3:17 [b]Rom. 11:29 [1]Lit. *From having compassion*
16 [a]Ex. 13:9; Song 8:6; Hag. 2:23
17 [1]DSS, LXX, Tg., Vg. *builders*
18 [a]Is. 60:4; John 4:35 [b]Prov. 17:6

[a]Will even now be too small for
the inhabitants;
And those who swallowed you up
will be far away.
20 [a]The children you will have,
[b]After you have lost the others,
Will say again in your ears,
'The place *is* too small for me;
Give me a place where I may
dwell.'
21 Then you will say in your heart,
'Who has begotten these for me,
Since I have lost my children and
am desolate,
A captive, and wandering to and
fro?
And who has brought these up?
There I was, left alone;
But these, where *were* they?' "

22 [a]Thus says the Lord GOD:

"Behold, I will lift My hand in an
oath to the nations,
And set up My [1]standard for the
peoples;
They shall bring your sons in
their [2]arms,
And your daughters shall be
carried on *their* shoulders;
23 [a]Kings shall be your foster fathers,
And their queens your nursing
mothers;
They shall bow down to you with
their faces to the earth,
And [b]lick up the dust of your feet.
Then you will know that I *am* the
LORD,
[c]For they shall not be ashamed
who wait for Me."

24 [a]Shall the prey be taken from the
mighty,
Or the captives [1]of the righteous
be delivered?

25 But thus says the LORD:

"Even the captives of the mighty
shall be taken away,
And the prey of the terrible be
delivered;
For I will contend with him who
contends with you,
And I will save your children.
26 I will [a]feed those who oppress
you with their own flesh,
And they shall be drunk with
their own [b]blood as with sweet
wine.
All flesh [c]shall know
That I, the LORD, *am* your Savior,
And your Redeemer, the Mighty
One of Jacob."

19 [a]Is. 54:1, 2; Zech. 10:10
20 [a]Is. 60:4 [b][Matt. 3:9; Rom. 11:11]
22 [a]Is. 60:4 [1]*banner* [2]Lit. *bosom*
23 [a]Ps. 72:11; Is. 52:15 [b]Ps. 72:9; Mic. 7:17 [c]Ps. 34:22; [Rom. 5:5]
24 [a]Matt. 12:29; Luke 11:21, 22 [1]So with MT, Tg.; DSS, Syr., Vg. *of the mighty;* LXX *unjustly*
26 [a]Is. 9:20 [b]Rev. 14:20 [c]Ps. 9:16; Is. 60:16

CHAPTER 50

1 [a]Deut. 24:1; Jer. 3:8 [b]Deut. 32:30; 2 Kin. 4:1; Neh. 5:5 [c]Is. 52:3
2 [a]Ps. 106:9; Nah. 1:4
3 [a]Ex. 10:21 [b]Is. 13:10; Rev. 6:12
4 [a]Ex. 4:11 [b]Matt. 11:28
5 [a]Ps. 40:6; Is. 35:5 [b]Matt. 26:39; Mark 14:36; Luke 22:42; John 8:29; 14:31; 15:10; Acts 26:19; [Phil. 2:8; Heb. 5:8; 10:7]
6 [a]Matt. 27:26; John 18:22 [b]Matt. 26:67; 27:30; Mark 14:65; 15:19 [c]Lam. 3:30
7 [a]Ezek. 3:8, 9; Luke 9:51
8 [a]Acts 2:24; [Rom. 8:32–34] [1]Lit. *master of My judgment*

The Servant, Israel's Hope

50 Thus says the LORD:

"Where *is* [a]the certificate of your
mother's divorce,
Whom I have put away?
Or which of My [b]creditors *is it*
to whom I have sold you?
For your iniquities [c]you have sold
yourselves,
And for your transgressions your
mother has been put away.
2 Why, when I came, *was there* no
man?
Why, when I called, *was there*
none to answer?
Is My hand shortened at all that
it cannot redeem?
Or have I no power to deliver?
Indeed with My [a]rebuke I dry up
the sea,
I make the rivers a wilderness;
Their fish stink because *there is*
no water,
And die of thirst.
3 [a]I clothe the heavens with
blackness,
[b]And I make sackcloth their
covering."

4 "The[a] Lord GOD has given Me
The tongue of the learned,
That I should know how to speak
A word in season to *him who is*
[b]weary.
He awakens Me morning by
morning,
He awakens My ear
To hear as the learned.
5 The Lord GOD [a]has opened My
ear;
And I was not [b]rebellious,
Nor did I turn away.
6 [a]I gave My back to those who
struck *Me*,
And [b]My cheeks to those who
plucked out the beard;
I did not hide My face from
shame and [c]spitting.

7 "For the Lord GOD will help Me;
Therefore I will not be disgraced;
Therefore [a]I have set My face like
a flint,
And I know that I will not be
ashamed.
8 [a]*He is* near who justifies Me;
Who will contend with Me?
Let us stand together.
Who *is* [1]My adversary?
Let him come near Me.
9 Surely the Lord GOD will
help Me;
Who *is* he *who* will condemn Me?

[a]Indeed they will all grow old like
a garment;
[b]The moth will eat them up.

10 "Who among you fears the LORD?
Who obeys the voice of His
Servant?
Who [a]walks in darkness
And has no light?
[b]Let him trust in the name of the
LORD
And rely upon his God.
11 Look, all you who kindle a fire,
Who encircle *yourselves* with
sparks:
Walk in the light of your fire and
in the sparks you have
kindled—
[a]This you shall have from My
hand:
You shall lie down [b]in torment.

The LORD Comforts Zion

51 "Listen to Me, [a]you who
[1]follow after righteousness,
You who seek the LORD:
Look to the rock *from which* you
were hewn,
And to the hole of the pit *from
which* you were dug.
2 [a]Look to Abraham your father,
And to Sarah *who* bore you;
[b]For I called him alone,
And [c]blessed him and increased
him."

3 For the LORD will [a]comfort Zion,
He will comfort all her waste
places;
He will make her wilderness like
Eden,
And her desert [b]like the garden
of the LORD;
Joy and gladness will be found
in it,
Thanksgiving and the voice of
melody.

4 "Listen to Me, My people;
And give ear to Me, O My nation:
[a]For law will proceed from Me,
And I will make My justice rest
[b]As a light of the peoples.
5 [a]My righteousness *is* near,
My salvation has gone forth,
[b]And My arms will judge the
peoples;
[c]The coastlands will wait
upon Me,
And [d]on My arm they will trust.
6 [a]Lift up your eyes to the heavens,
And look on the earth beneath.
For [b]the heavens will vanish
away like smoke,
[c]The earth will grow old like a
garment,
And those who dwell in it will die
in like manner;
But My salvation will be [d]forever,
And My righteousness will not be
[1]abolished.

7 "Listen to Me, you who know
righteousness,
You people [a]in whose heart *is* My
law:
[b]Do not fear the reproach of men,
Nor be afraid of their insults.
8 For [a]the moth will eat them up
like a garment,
And the worm will eat them like
wool;
But My righteousness will be
forever,
And My salvation from
generation to generation."

9 [a]Awake, awake, [b]put on strength,
O arm of the LORD!
Awake [c]as in the ancient days,
In the generations of old.
[d]*Are* You not *the arm* that cut
[e]Rahab apart,
And wounded the [f]serpent?
10 *Are* You not *the One* who [a]dried
up the sea,
The waters of the great deep;
That made the depths of the sea
a road
For the redeemed to cross over?
11 So [a]the ransomed of the LORD
shall return,
And come to Zion with singing,
With everlasting joy on their
heads.
They shall obtain joy and
gladness;
Sorrow and sighing shall flee
away.

12 "I, *even* I, *am* He [a]who comforts
you.
Who *are* you that you should be
afraid
[b]Of a man *who* will die,
And of the son of a man *who* will
be made [c]like grass?
13 And [a]you forget the LORD your
Maker,
[b]Who stretched out the heavens
And laid the foundations of the
earth;
You have feared continually
every day
Because of the fury of the
oppressor,
When *he has* prepared to destroy.

9 [a]Job 13:28; Ps. 102:26; Heb. 1:11 [b]Is. 51:6, 8
10 [a]Ps. 23:4 [b]2 Chr. 20:20
11 [a][John 9:39] [b]Ps. 16:4

CHAPTER 51

1 [a][Rom. 9:30–32] [1]*pursue*
2 [a]Rom. 4:1–3; Heb. 11:11 [b]Gen. 12:1 [c]Gen. 24:35; Deut. 1:10; Ezek. 33:24
3 [a]Is. 40:1; 52:9; Ps. 102:13 [b]Gen. 13:10; Joel 2:3
4 [a]Is. 2:3 [b]Is. 42:6
5 [a]Is. 46:13 [b]Ps. 67:4 [c]Is. 60:9 [d][Rom. 1:16]
6 [a]Is. 40:26 [b]Ps. 102:25, 26; Is. 13:13; 34:4; Matt. 24:35; Heb. 1:10–12; 2 Pet. 3:10 [c]Is. 24:19, 20; 50:9; Heb. 1:10–12 [d]Is. 45:17 [1]*broken*
7 [a]Ps. 37:31; Jer. 31:33; [Heb. 10:16] [b]Is. 25:8; 54:4; [Matt. 5:11, 12; 10:28; Acts 5:41]
8 [a]Is. 50:9
9 [a]Ps. 44:23 [b]Ps. 93:1 [c]Ps. 44:1 [d]Job 26:12; Ps. 89:10; Is. 30:7 [e]Ps. 87:4 [f]Ps. 74:13; Is. 27:1
10 [a]Ex. 14:21; Is. 63:11–13
11 [a]Is. 35:10; Jer. 31:11, 12
12 [a]2 Cor. 1:3 [b]Ps. 118:6; Is. 2:22 [c]Is. 40:6, 7; James 1:10; 1 Pet. 1:24
13 [a]Deut. 6:12; 8:11; Is. 17:10; Jer. 2:32 [b]Ps. 104:2

[c]And where *is* the fury of the
oppressor?
14 The captive exile hastens, that he
may be loosed,
[a]That he should not die in the pit,
And that his bread should not
fail.
15 But I *am* the LORD your God,
Who [a]divided the sea whose
waves roared—
The LORD of hosts *is* His name.
16 And [a]I have put My words in your
mouth;
[b]I have covered you with the
shadow of My hand,
[c]That I may [1]plant the heavens,
Lay the foundations of the earth,
And say to Zion, 'You *are* My
people.' "

God's Fury Removed

17 [a]Awake, awake!
Stand up, O Jerusalem,
You who [b]have drunk at the hand
of the LORD
The cup of His fury;
You have drunk the dregs of the
cup of trembling,
And drained *it* out.
18 *There is* no one to guide her
Among all the sons she has
brought forth;
Nor *is there any* who takes her
by the hand
Among all the sons she has
brought up.
19 [a]These two *things* have come to
you;
Who will be sorry for you?—
Desolation and destruction,
famine and sword—
[b]By whom will I comfort you?
20 [a]Your sons have fainted,
They lie at the head of all the
streets,
Like an antelope in a net;
They are full of the fury of the
LORD,
The rebuke of your God.

21 Therefore please hear this, you
afflicted,
And drunk [a]but not with wine.
22 Thus says your Lord,
The LORD and your God,
Who [a]pleads the cause of His
people:
"See, I have taken out of your
hand
The cup of trembling,
The dregs of the cup of My fury;
You shall no longer drink it.
23 [a]But I will put it into the hand of
those who afflict you,
Who have said to [1]you,
'Lie down, that we may walk over
you.'
And you have laid your body like
the ground,
And as the street, for those who
walk over."

God Redeems Jerusalem

52 Awake, awake!
Put on your strength,
O Zion;
Put on your beautiful garments,
O Jerusalem, the holy city!
For the uncircumcised [a]and the
unclean
Shall no longer come to you.
2 [a]Shake yourself from the dust,
arise;
Sit down, O Jerusalem!
[b]Loose yourself from the bonds of
your neck,
O captive daughter of Zion!

3 For thus says the LORD:

[a]"You have sold yourselves for
nothing,
And you shall be redeemed
[b]without money."

4 For thus says the Lord GOD:

"My people went down at first
Into [a]Egypt to [1]dwell there;
Then the Assyrian oppressed
them without cause.
5 Now therefore, what have I
here," says the LORD,
"That My people are taken away
for nothing?
Those who rule over them
[1]Make them wail," says the LORD,
"And My name *is* [a]blasphemed
continually every day.
6 Therefore My people shall know
My name;
Therefore *they shall know* in that
day
That I *am* He who speaks:
'Behold, *it is* I.' "

7 [a]How beautiful upon the
mountains
Are the feet of him who brings
good news,
Who proclaims peace,
Who brings glad tidings of good
things,
Who proclaims salvation,
Who says to Zion,
[b]"Your God reigns!"
8 Your watchmen shall lift up *their*
voices,
With their voices they shall sing
together;

13 [c]Job 20:7
14 [a]Zech. 9:11
15 [a]Job 26:12
16 [a]Deut. 18:18; Is. 59:21; John 3:34 [b]Ex. 33:22; Is. 49:2 [c]Is. 65:17 [1]*establish*
17 [a]Is. 52:1 [b]Job 21:20; Is. 29:9; Jer. 25:15; Rev. 14:10; 16:19
19 [a]Is. 47:9 [b]Amos 7:2
20 [a]Lam. 2:11
21 [a]Lam. 3:15
22 [a]Is. 3:12, 13; 49:25; Jer. 50:34
23 [a]Is. 14:2; Jer. 25:17, 26–28; Zech. 12:2 [1]Lit. *your soul*

CHAPTER 52

1 [a]Neh. 11:1; Is. 48:2; 64:10; Zech. 14:20, 21; Matt. 4:5; [Rev. 21:2–27]
2 [a]Is. 3:26 [b]Is. 9:4; 10:27; 14:25; Zech. 2:7
3 [a]Ps. 44:12; Jer. 15:13 [b]Is. 45:13
4 [a]Gen. 46:6 [1]As resident aliens
5 [a]Ezek. 36:20, 23; Rom. 2:24 [1]DSS *Mock;* LXX *Marvel and wail;* Tg. *Boast themselves;* Vg. *Treat them unjustly*
7 [a]Is. 40:9; 61:1; Nah. 1:15; Rom. 10:15; Eph. 6:15 [b]Ps. 93:1; Is. 24:23

For they shall see eye to eye
When the LORD brings back Zion.
9 Break forth into joy, sing together,
You waste places of Jerusalem!
For the LORD has comforted His people,
He has redeemed Jerusalem.
10 [a]The LORD has [1]made bare His holy arm
In the eyes of [b]all the nations;
And all the ends of the earth shall see
The salvation of our God.

11 [a]Depart! Depart! Go out from there,
Touch no unclean *thing;*
Go out from the midst of her,
[b]Be clean,
You who bear the vessels of the LORD.
12 For [a]you shall not go out with haste,
Nor go by flight;
[b]For the LORD will go before you,
[c]And the God of Israel *will be* your rear guard.

The Sin-Bearing Servant

13 Behold, [a]My Servant shall [1]deal prudently;
[b]He shall be exalted and [2]extolled and be very high.
14 Just as many were astonished at you,
So His [a]visage[1] was marred more than any man,
And His form more than the sons of men;
15 [a]So shall He [1]sprinkle many nations.
Kings shall shut their mouths at Him;
For [b]what had not been told them they shall see,
And what they had not heard they shall consider.

53 Who [a]has believed our report?
And to whom has the arm of the LORD been revealed?
2 For He shall grow up before Him as a tender plant,
And as a root out of dry ground.
He has no [1]form or [2]comeliness;
And when we see Him,
There is no [3]beauty that we should desire Him.
3 [a]He is despised and [1]rejected by men,
A Man of [2]sorrows and [b]acquainted with [3]grief.
And we hid, as it were, *our* faces from Him;
He was despised, and [c]we did not esteem Him.

4 Surely [a]He has borne our [1]griefs
And carried our [2]sorrows;
Yet we [3]esteemed Him stricken,
[4]Smitten by God, and afflicted.
5 But He *was* [a]wounded[1] for our transgressions,
He was [2]bruised for our iniquities;
The chastisement for our peace *was* upon Him,
And by His [b]stripes[3] we are healed.
6 All we like sheep have gone astray;
We have turned, every one, to his own way;
And the LORD [1]has laid on Him the iniquity of us all.

7 He was oppressed and He was afflicted,
Yet [a]He opened not His mouth;
[b]He was led as a lamb to the slaughter,
And as a sheep before its shearers is silent,
So He opened not His mouth.
8 He was [a]taken from [1]prison and from judgment,
And who will declare His generation?
For [b]He was cut off from the land of the living;
For the transgressions of My people He was stricken.
9 [a]And [1]they made His grave with the wicked—
But with the rich at His death,
Because He had done no violence,
Nor *was any* [b]deceit in His mouth.

10 Yet it pleased the LORD to [1]bruise Him;
He has put *Him* to grief.
When You make His soul [a]an offering for sin,
He shall see *His* seed, He shall prolong *His* days,
And the pleasure of the LORD shall prosper in His hand.
11 [1]He shall see the labor of His soul, *and* be satisfied.
By His knowledge [a]My righteous [b]Servant shall [c]justify many,
For He shall bear their iniquities.
12 [a]Therefore I will divide Him a portion with the great,
[b]And He shall divide the [1]spoil with the strong,

10 [a]Ps. 98:1–3 [b]Luke 3:6 [1]Revealed His power
11 [a]Is. 48:20 [b]Lev. 22:2
12 [a]Ex. 12:11, 33 [b]Mic. 2:13 [c]Ex. 14:19, 20
13 [a]Is. 42:1 [b]Phil. 2:9 [1]*prosper* [2]Lit. *be lifted up*
14 [a]Ps. 22:6, 7 [1]*appearance*
15 [a]Ezek. 36:25 [b]Rom. 15:21 [1]Or *startle*

CHAPTER 53

1 [a]John 12:38
2 [1]Stately form [2]*splendor* [3]Lit. *appearance*
3 [a]Ps. 22:6 [b][Heb. 4:15] [c][John 1:10, 11] [1]Or *forsaken* [2]Lit. *pains* [3]Lit. *sickness*
4 [a][Matt. 8:17] [1]Lit. *sicknesses* [2]Lit. *pains* [3]*reckoned* [4]*Struck down*
5 [a][Rom. 4:25] [b][1 Pet. 2:24, 25] [1]Or *pierced through* [2]*crushed* [3]Blows that cut in
6 [1]Lit. *has caused to land on Him*
7 [a]Matt. 26:63; 27:12–14 [b]Acts 8:32, 33
8 [a]Luke 23:1–25 [b][Dan. 9:26] [1]*confinement*
9 [a]Matt. 27:57–60 [b]1 Pet. 2:22 [1]Lit. *he* or *He*
10 [a][2 Cor. 5:21] [1]*crush*
11 [a][1 John 2:1] [b]Is. 42:1 [c][Rom. 5:15–18] [1]So with MT, Tg., Vg.; DSS, LXX *From the labor of His soul He shall see light*
12 [a]Ps. 2:8 [b]Col. 2:15 [1]*plunder*

Because He [c]poured out His soul
unto death,
And He was [d]numbered with the
transgressors,
And He bore the sin of many,
And [e]made intercession for the
transgressors.

A Perpetual Covenant of Peace

54 "Sing, O [a]barren,
You *who* have not borne!
Break forth into singing, and cry
aloud,
You *who* have not labored with
child!
For more *are* the children of the
desolate
Than the children of the married
woman," says the LORD.
2 "Enlarge[a] the place of your tent,
And let them stretch out the
curtains of your dwellings;
Do not spare;
Lengthen your cords,
And strengthen your stakes.
3 For you shall expand to the right
and to the left,
And your descendants will
[a]inherit the nations,
And make the desolate cities
inhabited.

4 "Do[a] not fear, for you will not be
ashamed;
Neither be disgraced, for you will
not be put to shame;
For you will forget the shame of
your youth,
And will not remember the
reproach of your widowhood
anymore.
5 [a]For your Maker *is* your husband,
The LORD of hosts *is* His name;
And your Redeemer *is* the Holy
One of Israel;
He is called [b]the God of the whole
earth.
6 For the LORD [a]has called you
Like a woman forsaken and
grieved in spirit,
Like a youthful wife when you
were refused,"
Says your God.
7 "For[a] a mere moment I have
forsaken you,
But with great mercies [b]I will
gather you.
8 With a little wrath I hid My face
from you for a moment;
[a]But with everlasting kindness I
will have mercy on you,"
Says the LORD, your Redeemer.

9 "For this *is* like the waters of
[a]Noah to Me;
For as I have sworn
That the waters of Noah would
no longer cover the earth,
So have I sworn
That I would not be angry with
[b]you, nor rebuke you.
10 For [a]the mountains shall depart
And the hills be removed,
[b]But My kindness shall not depart
from you,
Nor shall My covenant of peace
be removed,"
Says the LORD, who has mercy on
you.

11 "O you afflicted one,
Tossed with tempest, *and* not
comforted,
Behold, I will lay your stones with
[a]colorful gems,
And lay your foundations with
sapphires.
12 I will make your pinnacles of
rubies,
Your gates of crystal,
And all your walls of precious
stones.
13 All your children *shall be* [a]taught
by the LORD,
And [b]great *shall be* the peace of
your children.
14 In righteousness you shall be
established;
You shall be far from oppression,
for you shall not fear;
And from terror, for it shall not
come near you.
15 Indeed they shall surely
assemble, *but* not because
of Me.
Whoever assembles against you
shall [a]fall for your sake.

16 "Behold, I have created the
blacksmith
Who blows the coals in the fire,
Who brings forth an [1]instrument
for his work;
And I have created the [2]spoiler
to destroy.
17 No weapon formed against you
shall [a]prosper,
And every tongue *which* rises
against you in judgment
You shall condemn.
This *is* the heritage of the
servants of the LORD,
[b]And their righteousness *is*
from Me,"
Says the LORD.

An Invitation to Abundant Life

55 "Ho! [a]Everyone who thirsts,
Come to the waters;
And you who have no money,

12 [c]Is. 50:6 [Rom. 3:25] [d]Matt. 27:38; Mark 15:28; Luke 22:37; 2 Cor. 5:21 [e]Luke 23:34

CHAPTER 54

1 [a]Gal. 4:27
2 [a]Is. 49:19, 20
3 [a]Is. 14:2; 49:22, 23; 60:9
4 [a]Is. 41:10
5 [a]Jer. 3:14; Hos. 2:19 [b]Zech. 14:9; Rom. 3:29
6 [a]Is. 62:4
7 [a]Ps. 30:5; Is. 26:20; 60:10; 2 Cor. 4:17 [b][Is. 43:5; 56:8]
8 [a]Is. 55:3; Jer. 31:3
9 [a]Gen. 8:21; 9:11; [2 Pet. 3:6, 7] [b]Is. 12:1; Ezek. 39:29
10 [a]Ps. 46:2; Is. 51:6; Matt. 5:18 [b]2 Sam. 23:5; Ps. 89:33, 34; Is. 55:3; 59:21; 61:8
11 [a]1 Chr. 29:2; Job 28:16; Rev. 21:18, 19
13 [a]Jer. 31:34; [John 6:45; 1 Cor. 2:10]; 1 Thess. 4:9; [1 John 2:20] [b]Ps. 119:165
15 [a]Is. 41:11–16
16 [1]Or *weapon* [2]*destroyer*
17 [a]Is. 17:12–14; 29:8 [b]Is. 45:24, 25; 54:14

CHAPTER 55

1 [a][Matt. 5:6; John 4:14; 7:37; Rev. 21:6; 22:17]

[b]Come, buy and eat.
Yes, come, buy wine and milk
Without money and without
price.
2 Why do you [1]spend money for
what is not bread,
And your wages for *what* does
not satisfy?
Listen carefully to Me, and eat
what is good,
And let your soul delight itself
in abundance.
3 Incline your ear, and [a]come
to Me.
Hear, and your soul shall live;
[b]And I will make an everlasting
covenant with you—
The [c]sure mercies of David.
4 Indeed I have given him *as* [a]a
witness to the people,
[b]A leader and commander for the
people.
5 [a]Surely you shall call a nation you
do not know,
[b]And nations *who* do not know
you shall run to you,
Because of the LORD your God,
And the Holy One of Israel;
[c]For He has glorified you."

6 [a]Seek the LORD while He may be
[b]found,
Call upon Him while He is near.
7 [a]Let the [1]wicked forsake his
way,
And the unrighteous man [b]his
thoughts;
Let him return to the LORD,
[c]And He will have mercy on
him;
And to our God,
For He will abundantly pardon.

8 "For[a] My thoughts *are* not your
thoughts,
Nor *are* your ways My ways,"
says the LORD.
9 "For[a] *as* the heavens are higher
than the earth,
So are My ways higher than your
ways,
And My thoughts than your
thoughts.

10 "For [a]as the rain comes down, and
the snow from heaven,
And do not return there,
But water the earth,
And make it bring forth and bud,
That it may give seed to the sower
And bread to the eater,
11 [a]So shall My word be that goes
forth from My mouth;
It shall not return to Me [1]void,
But it shall accomplish what I
please,
And it shall [b]prosper *in the thing*
for which I sent it.

12 "For[a] you shall go out with joy,
And be led out with peace;
The mountains and the hills
Shall [b]break forth into singing
before you,
And [c]all the trees of the field shall
clap *their* hands.
13 [a]Instead of [b]the thorn shall come
up the cypress tree,
And instead of the brier shall
come up the myrtle tree;
And it shall be to the LORD [c]for
a name,
For an everlasting sign *that* shall
not be cut off."

Salvation for the Gentiles

56 Thus says the LORD:
"Keep justice, and do
righteousness,
[a]For My salvation *is* about to
come,
And My righteousness to be
revealed.
2 Blessed *is* the man *who* does this,
And the son of man *who* lays hold
on it;
[a]Who keeps from defiling the
Sabbath,
And keeps his hand from doing
any evil."

3 Do not let [a]the son of the
foreigner
Who has joined himself to the
LORD
Speak, saying,
"The LORD has utterly separated
me from His people";
Nor let the [b]eunuch say,
"Here I am, a dry tree."
4 For thus says the LORD:
"To the eunuchs who keep My
Sabbaths,
And choose what pleases Me,
And hold fast My covenant,
5 Even to them I will give in [a]My
house
And within My walls a place [b]and
a name
Better than that of sons and
daughters;
I will give [1]them an everlasting
name
That shall not be cut off.

6 "Also the sons of the foreigner
Who join themselves to the LORD,
to serve Him,
And to love the name of the LORD,
to be His servants—

1 [b][Matt. 13:44; Rev. 3:18]
2 [1]Lit. *weigh out silver*
3 [a]Matt. 11:28 [b]Is. 54:8; 61:8; Jer. 32:40 [c]2 Sam. 7:8; Ps. 89:28; [Acts 13:34]
4 [a][John 18:37; Rev. 1:5] [b][Jer. 30:9; Ezek. 34:23; Dan. 9:25]
5 [a]Is. 52:15; Eph. 2:11, 12 [b]Is. 60:5 [c]Is. 60:9
6 [a]Matt. 5:25; 25:11; John 7:34; 8:21; 2 Cor. 6:2; [Heb. 3:13] [b]Ps. 32:6; Is. 49:8
7 [a]Is. 1:16 [b]Is. 59:7; Zech. 8:17 [c]Ps. 130:7; Jer. 3:12 [1]Lit. *man of iniquity*
8 [a]2 Sam. 7:19
9 [a]Ps. 103:11
10 [a]Deut. 32:2
11 [a]Is. 45:23; Matt. 24:35 [b]Is. 46:9–11 [1]*empty,* without fruit
12 [a]Is. 35:10 [b]Ps. 98:8 [c]1 Chr. 16:33
13 [a]Is. 41:19 [b]Mic. 7:4 [c]Jer. 13:11

CHAPTER 56

1 [a]Is. 46:13; Matt. 3:2; 4:17; Rom. 13:11, 12
2 [a]Ex. 20:8–11; 31:13–17; Is. 58:13; Jer. 17:21, 22; Ezek. 20:12, 20
3 [a]Is. 14:1; [Eph. 2:12–19] [b]Deut. 23:1; Jer. 38:7; Acts 8:27
5 [a]1 Tim. 3:15 [b][1 John 3:1, 2] [1]Lit. *him*

Everyone who keeps from
defiling the Sabbath,
And holds fast My covenant—
7 Even them I will [a]bring to My
holy mountain,
And make them joyful in My
[b]house of prayer.
[c]Their burnt offerings and their
sacrifices
Will be [d]accepted on My altar;
For [e]My house shall be called a
house of prayer [f]for all
nations."
8 The Lord GOD, [a]who gathers the
outcasts of Israel, says,
[b]"Yet I will gather to him
Others besides those who are
gathered to him."

Israel's Irresponsible Leaders

9 [a]All you beasts of the field, come
to devour,
All you beasts in the forest.
10 His watchmen *are* [a]blind,
They are all ignorant;
[b]They *are* all dumb dogs,
They cannot bark;
[1]Sleeping, lying down, loving to
slumber.
11 Yes, *they are* [a]greedy[1] dogs
Which [b]never[2] have enough.
And they *are* shepherds
Who cannot understand;
They all look to their own way,
Every one for his own gain,
From his *own* territory.
12 "Come," *one says,* "I will bring
wine,
And we will fill ourselves with
intoxicating [a]drink;
[b]Tomorrow will be [c]as today,
And much more abundant."

Israel's Futile Idolatry

57 The righteous perishes,
And no man takes *it* to
heart;
[a]Merciful men *are* taken away,
[b]While no one considers
That the righteous is taken away
from [1]evil.
2 He shall enter into peace;
They shall rest in [a]their beds,
Each one walking *in* his
uprightness.

3 "But come here,
[a]You sons of the sorceress,
You offspring of the adulterer
and the harlot!
4 Whom do you ridicule?
Against whom do you make a
wide mouth
And stick out the tongue?

7 [a][Is. 2:2, 3; 60:11; Mic. 4:1, 2] [b]Matt. 21:13; Mark 11:17; Luke 19:46 [c][Rom. 12:1; Heb. 13:15; 1 Pet. 2:5] [d]Is. 60:7 [e]Matt. 21:13 [f][Mal. 1:11]
8 [a]Ps. 147:2; Is. 11:12; 27:12; 54:7 [b]Is. 60:3–11; 66:18–21; [John 10:16]
9 [a]Jer. 12:9
10 [a]Matt. 15:14 [b]Phil. 3:2 [1]Or *Dreaming*
11 [a]Is. 28:7; Ezek. 13:19; [Mic. 3:5, 11] [b]Ezek. 34:2–10 [1]Lit. *strong of soul* [2]Lit. *do not know satisfaction*
12 [a]Is. 28:7 [b]Ps. 10:6; Prov. 23:35; Is. 22:13; Luke 12:19; 1 Cor. 15:32 [c]2 Pet. 3:4

CHAPTER 57

1 [a]Ps. 12:1 [b]1 Kin. 14:13 [1]Lit. *the face of evil*
2 [a]2 Chr. 16:14
3 [a]Is. 1:4; Matt. 16:4
5 [a]2 Kin. 16:4 [b]2 Kin. 23:10; Ps. 106:37, 38; Jer. 7:31; Ezek. 16:20
6 [a]Jer. 3:9; Hab. 2:19 [b]Jer. 5:9, 29; 9:9
7 [a]Jer. 3:6; Ezek. 16:16 [b]Ezek. 23:41
8 [a]Ezek. 16:26 [1]Lit. *cut* [2]Lit. *hand,* a euphemism
9 [a]Hos. 7:11 [b]Ezek. 23:16, 40
10 [a]Jer. 2:25; 18:12
11 [a]Prov. 29:25; Is. 51:12, 13 [b]Ps. 50:21; Eccl. 8:11; Is. 42:14 [1]*remained silent*

Are you not children of
transgression,
Offspring of falsehood,
5 Inflaming yourselves with gods
[a]under every green tree,
[b]Slaying the children in the
valleys,
Under the clefts of the rocks?
6 Among the smooth [a]*stones* of the
stream
Is your portion;
They, they, *are* your lot!
Even to them you have poured a
drink offering,
You have offered a grain offering.
Should I receive comfort in
[b]these?

7 "On[a] a lofty and high mountain
You have set [b]your bed;
Even there you went up
To offer sacrifice.
8 Also behind the doors and their
posts
You have set up your
remembrance;
For you have uncovered yourself
to those other than Me,
And have gone up to them;
You have enlarged your bed
And [1]made *a covenant* with
them;
[a]You have loved their bed,
Where you saw *their* [2]nudity.
9 [a]You went to the king with
ointment,
And increased your perfumes;
You sent your [b]messengers far
off,
And *even* descended to Sheol.
10 You are wearied in the length of
your way;
[a]*Yet* you did not say, 'There is no
hope.'
You have found the life of your
hand;
Therefore you were not grieved.

11 "And [a]of whom have you been
afraid, or feared,
That you have lied
And not remembered Me,
Nor taken *it* to your heart?
Is it not because [b]I have [1]held My
peace from of old
That you do not fear Me?
12 I will declare your righteousness
And your works,
For they will not profit you.
13 When you cry out,
Let your collection *of idols* deliver
you.
But the wind will carry them all
away,
A breath will take *them.*

But he who puts his trust in Me
shall possess the land,
And shall inherit My holy
mountain."

Healing for the Backslider

14 And one shall say,
[a]"Heap it up! Heap it up!
Prepare the way,
Take the stumbling block out of
the way of My people."

15 For thus says the High and Lofty
One
Who inhabits eternity, [a]whose
name *is* Holy:
[b]"I dwell in the high and holy *place,*
[c]With him *who* has a contrite and
humble spirit,
[d]To revive the spirit of the humble,
And to revive the heart of the
contrite ones.
16 [a]For I will not contend forever,
Nor will I always be angry;
For the spirit would fail
before Me,
And the souls [b]*which* I have
made.
17 For the iniquity of [a]his
covetousness
I was angry and struck him;
[b]I hid and was angry,
[c]And he went on [1]backsliding in
the way of his heart.
18 I have seen his ways, and [a]will
heal him;
I will also lead him,
And restore comforts to him
And to [b]his mourners.

19 "I create [a]the fruit of the lips:
Peace, peace [b]to *him who is* far
off and to *him who is* near,"
Says the LORD,
"And I will heal him."
20 [a]But the wicked *are* like the
troubled sea,
When it cannot rest,
Whose waters cast up mire and
dirt.

21 "*There*[a] *is* no peace,"
Says my God, "for the wicked."

Fasting that Pleases God

58 "Cry aloud, [1]spare not;
Lift up your voice like a
trumpet;
[a]Tell My people their
transgression,
And the house of Jacob their sins.
2 Yet they seek Me daily,
And delight to know My ways,
As a nation that did
righteousness,
And did not forsake the
ordinance of their God.
They ask of Me the ordinances of
justice;
They take delight in approaching
God.
3 'Why[a] have we fasted,' *they say,*
'and You have not seen?
Why have we [b]afflicted our souls,
and You take no notice?'

"In fact, in the day of your fast you
find pleasure,
And [1]exploit all your laborers.
4 [a]Indeed you fast for strife and
debate,
And to strike with the fist of
wickedness.
You will not fast as *you do* this
day,
To make your voice heard on
high.
5 Is [a]it a fast that I have chosen,
[b]A day for a man to afflict his
soul?
Is it to bow down his head like a
bulrush,
And [c]to spread out sackcloth and
ashes?
Would you call this a fast,
And an acceptable day to the
LORD?

6 "*Is* this not the fast that I have
chosen:
To [a]loose the bonds of
wickedness,
[b]To undo the [1]heavy burdens,
[c]To let the oppressed go free,
And that you break every yoke?
7 *Is it* not [a]to share your bread with
the hungry,
And that you bring to your house
the poor who are [1]cast out;
[b]When you see the naked, that you
cover him,
And not hide yourself from [c]your
own flesh?
8 [a]Then your light shall break forth
like the morning,
Your healing shall spring forth
speedily,
And your righteousness shall go
before you;
[b]The glory of the LORD shall be
your rear guard.
9 Then you shall call, and the LORD
will answer;
You shall cry, and He will say,
'Here I *am.*'

"If you take away the yoke from
your midst,
The [1]pointing of the finger, and
[a]speaking wickedness,

14 [a]Is. 40:3; 62:10; Jer. 18:15
15 [a]Job 6:10; Luke 1:49 [b]Ps. 68:35; Zech. 2:13 [c]Ps. 34:18; 51:17; Is. 66:2 [d]Ps. 147:3; Is. 61:1–3
16 [a]Ps. 85:5; 103:9; [Mic. 7:18] [b]Num. 16:22; Job 34:14; Heb. 12:9
17 [a]Is. 2:7; 56:11; Jer. 6:13 [b]Is. 8:17; 45:15; 59:2 [c]Is. 9:13 [1]Or *turning back*
18 [a]Jer. 3:22 [b]Is. 61:2
19 [a]Is. 6:7; 51:16; 59:21; Heb. 13:15 [b]Acts 2:39; Eph. 2:17
20 [a]Job 15:20; Prov. 4:16; Jude 13
21 [a]Is. 48:22

CHAPTER 58

1 [a]Mic. 3:8 [1]*do not hold back*
3 [a]Mal. 3:13–18; Luke 18:12 [b]Lev. 16:29; 23:27 [1]Lit. *drive hard*
4 [a]1 Kin. 21:9
5 [a]Zech. 7:5 [b]Lev. 16:29 [c]Esth. 4:3; Job 2:8; Dan. 9:3
6 [a]Luke 4:18, 19 [b]Neh. 5:10–12 [c]Jer. 34:9 [1]Lit. *bonds of the yoke*
7 [a]Ezek. 18:7; Matt. 25:35 [b]Job 31:19–22; James 2:14–17 [c]Gen. 29:14; Neh. 5:5 [1]*wandering*
8 [a]Job 11:17 [b]Ex. 14:19; Is. 52:12
9 [a]Ps. 12:2; Is. 59:13 [1]Lit. *sending out of*

10 *If* you extend your soul to the hungry
And satisfy the afflicted soul,
Then your light shall dawn in the darkness,
And your [1]darkness shall be as the noonday.
11 The LORD will guide you continually,
And satisfy your soul in drought,
And strengthen your bones;
You shall be like a watered garden,
And like a spring of water, whose waters do not fail.
12 Those from among you
[a]Shall build the old waste places;
You shall raise up the foundations of many generations;
And you shall be called the Repairer of the Breach,
The Restorer of [1]Streets to Dwell In.

13 "If [a]you turn away your foot from the Sabbath,
From doing your pleasure on My holy day,
And call the Sabbath a delight,
The holy *day* of the LORD honorable,
And shall honor Him, not doing your own ways,
Nor finding your own pleasure,
Nor speaking *your own* words,
14 [a]Then you shall delight yourself in the LORD;
And I will cause you to [b]ride on the high hills of the earth,
And feed you with the heritage of Jacob your father.
[c]The mouth of the LORD has spoken."

Separated from God

59 Behold, the LORD's hand is not [a]shortened,
That it cannot save;
Nor His ear heavy,
That it cannot hear.
2 But your iniquities have separated you from your God;
And your sins have hidden *His* face from you,
So that He will [a]not hear.
3 For [a]your hands are defiled with [1]blood,
And your fingers with iniquity;
Your lips have spoken lies,
Your tongue has muttered perversity.

4 No one calls for justice,
Nor does *any* plead for truth.
They trust in [a]empty words and speak lies;
[b]They conceive [1]evil and bring forth iniquity.
5 They hatch vipers' eggs and weave the spider's web;
He who eats of their eggs dies,
And *from* that which is crushed a viper breaks out.

6 [a]Their webs will not become garments,
Nor will they cover themselves with their works;
Their works *are* works of iniquity,
And the act of violence *is* in their hands.
7 [a]Their feet run to evil,
And they make haste to shed [b]innocent blood;
[c]Their thoughts *are* thoughts of iniquity;
Wasting and [d]destruction *are* in their paths.
8 The way of [a]peace they have not known,
And *there is* no justice in their ways;
[b]They have made themselves crooked paths;
Whoever takes that way shall not know peace.

Sin Confessed

9 Therefore justice is far from us,
Nor does righteousness overtake us;
[a]We look for light, but there is darkness!
For brightness, *but* we walk in blackness!
10 [a]We grope for the wall like the blind,
And we grope as if *we had* no eyes;
We stumble at noonday as at twilight;
We are as dead *men* in desolate places.
11 We all growl like bears,
And [a]moan sadly like doves;
We look for justice, but *there is* none;
For salvation, *but* it is far from us.
12 For our [a]transgressions are multiplied before You,
And our sins testify against us;
For our transgressions *are* with us,
And *as for* our iniquities, we know them:
13 In transgressing and lying against the LORD,

58:10 [1]Or *gloom*
12 [a]Is. 61:4 [1]Lit. *Paths*
13 [a]Ex. 31:16, 17; 35:2, 3; Is. 56:2, 4, 6; Jer. 17:21–27
14 [a]Job 22:26; Is. 61:10 [b]Deut. 32:13; 33:29; Is. 33:16; Hab. 3:19 [c]Is. 1:20; 40:5; Mic. 4:4

CHAPTER 59

1 [a]Num. 11:23; Is. 50:2; Jer. 32:17
2 [a]Is. 1:15
3 [a]Is. 1:15, 21; Jer. 2:30, 34; Ezek. 7:23; Hos. 4:2 [1]*bloodshed*
4 [a]Is. 30:12; Jer. 7:4 [b]Job 15:35; Ps. 7:14; Is. 33:11 [1]*trouble*
6 [a]Job 8:14
7 [a]Prov. 1:16; Rom. 3:15 [b]Prov. 6:17 [c]Is. 55:7 [d]Rom. 3:16, 17
8 [a]Is. 57:20, 21 [b]Ps. 125:5; Prov. 2:15
9 [a]Jer. 8:15
10 [a]Deut. 28:29; Job 5:14; Amos 8:9
11 [a]Is. 38:14; Ezek. 7:16
12 [a]Is. 24:5; 58:1

And departing from our God,
Speaking oppression and revolt,
Conceiving and uttering [a]from the heart words of falsehood.
14 Justice is turned back,
And righteousness stands afar off;
For truth is fallen in the street,
And equity cannot enter.
15 So truth fails,
And he *who* departs from evil makes himself a [a]prey.

The Redeemer of Zion

Then the LORD saw *it,* and [1]it displeased Him
That *there was* no justice.
16 [a]He saw that *there was* no man,
And [b]wondered that *there was* no intercessor;
[c]Therefore His own arm brought salvation for Him;
And His own righteousness, it sustained Him.
17 [a]For He put on righteousness as a breastplate,
And a helmet of salvation on His head;
He put on the garments of vengeance for clothing,
And was clad with zeal as a cloak.
18 [a]According to *their* deeds, accordingly He will repay,
Fury to His adversaries,
Recompense to His enemies;
The coastlands He will fully repay.
19 [a]So shall they fear
The name of the LORD from the west,
And His glory from the rising of the sun;
When the enemy comes in [b]like a flood,
The Spirit of the LORD will lift up a standard against him.

20 "The[a] Redeemer will come to Zion,
And to those who turn from transgression in Jacob,"
Says the LORD.

21 "As[a] for Me," says the LORD,
"this *is* My covenant with them:
My Spirit who *is* upon you, and My
words which I have put in your
mouth, shall not depart from your
mouth, nor from the mouth of your
descendants, nor from the mouth
of your descendants' descen-
dants," says the LORD, "from this
time and forevermore."

13 [a]Matt. 12:34
15 [a]Is. 5:23; 10:2; 29:21; 32:7 [1]Lit. *it was evil in His eyes*
16 [a]Is. 41:28; 63:5; 64:7; Ezek. 22:30 [b]Mark 6:6 [c]Ps. 98:1; Is. 63:5
17 [a]Eph. 6:14, 17; 1 Thess. 5:8
18 [a]Is. 63:6; Rom. 2:6
19 [a]Ps. 113:3; Mal. 1:11 [b]Rev. 12:15
20 [a]Rom. 11:26
21 [a][Heb. 8:10; 10:16]

CHAPTER 60
1 [a]Eph. 5:14 [b]Mal. 4:2
3 [a]Is. 49:6, 23; Rev. 21:24
4 [a]Is. 49:18 [b]Is. 49:20–22
5 [a][Rom. 11:25–27]
6 [a]Gen. 25:4 [b]Gen. 25:3; Ps. 72:10 [c]Is. 61:6; Matt. 2:11
7 [a]Gen. 25:13 [b]Is. 56:7 [c]Is. 60:13; Hag. 2:7, 9
9 [a]Ps. 72:10 [b][Gal. 4:26] [c]Jer. 3:17 [d]Is. 55:5

The Gentiles Bless Zion

60 Arise, [a]shine;
For your light has come!
And [b]the glory of the LORD is risen upon you.
2 For behold, the darkness shall cover the earth,
And deep darkness the people;
But the LORD will arise over you,
And His glory will be seen upon you.
3 The [a]Gentiles shall come to your light,
And kings to the brightness of your rising.

4 "Lift[a] up your eyes all around, and see:
They all gather together, [b]they come to you;
Your sons shall come from afar,
And your daughters shall be nursed at *your* side.
5 Then you shall see and become radiant,
And your heart shall swell with joy;
Because [a]the abundance of the sea shall be turned to you,
The wealth of the Gentiles shall come to you.
6 The multitude of camels shall cover your *land,*
The dromedaries of Midian and [a]Ephah;
All those from [b]Sheba shall come;
They shall bring [c]gold and incense,
And they shall proclaim the praises of the LORD.
7 All the flocks of [a]Kedar shall be gathered together to you,
The rams of Nebaioth shall minister to you;
They shall ascend with [b]acceptance on My altar,
And [c]I will glorify the house of My glory.

8 "Who *are* these *who* fly like a cloud,
And like doves to their roosts?
9 [a]Surely the coastlands shall wait for Me;
And the ships of Tarshish *will come* first,
[b]To bring your sons from afar,
[c]Their silver and their gold with them,
To the name of the LORD your God,
And to the Holy One of Israel,
[d]Because He has glorified you.

10 "The[a] sons of foreigners shall
build up your walls,
[b]And their kings shall minister to
you;
For [c]in My wrath I struck you,
[d]But in My favor I have had mercy
on you.
11 Therefore your gates [a]shall be
open continually;
They shall not be shut day or
night,
That *men* may bring to you the
wealth of the Gentiles,
And their kings in procession.
12 [a]For the nation and kingdom
which will not serve you shall
perish,
And *those* nations shall be utterly
ruined.

13 "The[a] glory of Lebanon shall come
to you,
The cypress, the pine, and the
box tree together,
To beautify the place of My
sanctuary;
And I will make [b]the place of My
feet glorious.
14 Also the sons of those who
afflicted you
Shall come [a]bowing to you,
And all those who despised you
shall [b]fall prostrate at the soles
of your feet;
And they shall call you The City
of the LORD,
[c]Zion of the Holy One of Israel.

15 "Whereas you have been forsaken
and hated,
So that no one went through *you*,
I will make you an eternal
excellence,
A joy of many generations.
16 You shall drink the milk of the
Gentiles,
[a]And milk the breast of kings;
You shall know that [b]I, the LORD,
am your Savior
And your Redeemer, the Mighty
One of Jacob.

17 "Instead of bronze I will bring
gold,
Instead of iron I will bring silver,
Instead of wood, bronze,
And instead of stones, iron.
I will also make your officers
peace,
And your magistrates
righteousness.
18 Violence shall no longer be heard
in your land,
Neither [1]wasting nor destruction
within your borders;

10 [a]Is. 14:1, 2; 61:5; Zech. 6:15 [b]Is. 49:23; Rev. 21:24 [c]Is. 57:17 [d]Is. 54:7, 8
11 [a]Is. 26:2; 60:18; 62:10; Rev. 21:25, 26
12 [a]Is. 14:2; Zech. 14:17; Matt. 21:44
13 [a]Is. 35:2 [b]1 Chr. 28:2; Ps. 132:7
14 [a]Is. 45:14 [b]Is. 49:23; Rev. 3:9 [c][Heb. 12:22; Rev. 14:1]
16 [a]Is. 49:23 [b]Is. 43:3
18 [a]Is. 26:1 [1]*devastation*
19 [a]Rev. 21:23; 22:5 [b]Is. 41:16; 45:25; Zech. 2:5
20 [a]Amos 8:9
21 [a]Is. 52:1; Rev. 21:27 [b]Ps. 37:11; Matt. 5:5 [c]Is. 61:3; [Matt. 15:13; John 15:2] [d]Is. 29:23; [Eph. 2:10]
22 [a]Matt. 13:31, 32

CHAPTER 61

1 [a]Is. 11:2; Matt. 3:17; Luke 4:18, 19; John 1:32; 3:34 [b]Ps. 45:7; Matt. 11:5; Luke 7:22 [c]Ps. 147:3 [d]Is. 42:7; [Acts 10:43] [1]Lit. *bind up*
2 [a]Lev. 25:9 [b]Is. 34:8; Mal. 4:1, 3; [2 Thess. 1:7] [c]Is. 57:18; Jer. 31:13; Matt. 5:4
3 [a]Ps. 30:11 [b]Is. 60:21; [Jer. 17:7, 8] [c][John 15:8] [1]Lit. *appoint*
4 [a]Is. 49:8; 58:12; Ezek. 36:33; Amos 9:14

But you shall call [a]your walls
Salvation,
And your gates Praise.

God the Glory of His People

19 "The [a]sun shall no longer be your
light by day,
Nor for brightness shall the moon
give light to you;
But the LORD will be to you an
everlasting light,
And [b]your God your glory.
20 [a]Your sun shall no longer go
down,
Nor shall your moon withdraw
itself;
For the LORD will be your
everlasting light,
And the days of your mourning
shall be ended.
21 [a]Also your people *shall* all *be*
righteous;
[b]They shall inherit the land
forever,
[c]The branch of My planting,
[d]The work of My hands,
That I may be glorified.
22 [a]A little one shall become a
thousand,
And a small one a strong nation.
I, the LORD, will hasten it in its
time."

The Good News of Salvation

61 "The [a]Spirit of the Lord GOD
is upon Me,
Because the LORD [b]has
anointed Me
To preach good tidings to the
poor;
He has sent Me [c]to [1]heal the
brokenhearted,
To proclaim [d]liberty to the
captives,
And the opening of the prison to
those who are bound;
2 [a]To proclaim the acceptable year
of the LORD,
And [b]the day of vengeance of our
God;
[c]To comfort all who mourn,
3 To [1]console those who mourn in
Zion,
[a]To give them beauty for ashes,
The oil of joy for mourning,
The garment of praise for the
spirit of heaviness;
That they may be called trees of
righteousness,
[b]The planting of the LORD, [c]that
He may be glorified."

4 And they shall [a]rebuild the old
ruins,

They shall raise up the former
desolations,
And they shall repair the ruined
cities,
The desolations of many
generations.
5 [a]Strangers shall stand and feed
your flocks,
And the sons of the foreigner
Shall be your plowmen and your
vinedressers.
6 [a]But you shall be named the
priests of the LORD,
They shall call you the servants
of our God.
[b]You shall eat the riches of the
Gentiles,
And in their glory you shall
boast.
7 [a]Instead of your shame *you shall
have* double *honor*,
And *instead of* confusion they
shall rejoice in their portion.
Therefore in their land they shall
possess double;
Everlasting joy shall be theirs.

8 "For [a]I, the LORD, love justice;
[b]I hate robbery [1]for burnt offering;
I will direct their work in truth,
[c]And will make with them an
everlasting covenant.
9 Their descendants shall be
known among the Gentiles,
And their offspring among the
people.
All who see them shall
acknowledge them,
[a]That they *are* the posterity *whom*
the LORD has blessed."

10 [a]I will greatly rejoice in the LORD,
My soul shall be joyful in my
God;
For [b]He has clothed me with the
garments of salvation,
He has covered me with the robe
of righteousness,
[c]As a bridegroom decks *himself*
with ornaments,
And as a bride adorns *herself*
with her jewels.
11 For as the earth brings forth its
bud,
As the garden causes the things
that are sown in it to spring
forth,
So the Lord GOD will cause
[a]righteousness and [b]praise to
spring forth before all the
nations.

Assurance of Zion's Salvation

62 For Zion's sake I will not [1]hold
My peace,
And for Jerusalem's sake I will
not rest,
Until her righteousness goes
forth as brightness,
And her salvation as a lamp *that*
burns.
2 [a]The Gentiles shall see your
righteousness,
And all [b]kings your glory.
[c]You shall be called by a new
name,
Which the mouth of the LORD will
name.
3 You shall also be [a]a crown of
glory
In the hand of the LORD,
And a royal diadem
In the hand of your God.
4 [a]You shall no longer be termed
[b]Forsaken,[1]
Nor shall your land any more be
termed [c]Desolate;[2]
But you shall be called
[3]Hephzibah, and your land
[4]Beulah;
For the LORD delights in you,
And your land shall be married.
5 For *as* a young man marries a
virgin,
So shall your sons marry you;
And *as* the bridegroom rejoices
over the bride,
[a]*So* shall your God rejoice over
you.

6 [a]I have set watchmen on your
walls, O Jerusalem;
They shall [1]never hold their
peace day or night.
You who [2]make mention of the
LORD, do not keep silent,
7 And give Him no rest till He
establishes
And till He makes Jerusalem [a]a
praise in the earth.

8 The LORD has sworn by His right
hand
And by the arm of His strength:
"Surely I will no longer [a]give your
grain
As food for your enemies;
And the sons of the foreigner
shall not drink your new wine,
For which you have labored.
9 But those who have gathered it
shall eat it,
And praise the LORD;
Those who have brought it
together shall drink it [a]in My
holy courts."

10 Go through,
Go through the gates!
[a]Prepare the way for the people;

5 [a][Eph. 2:12]
6 [a]Ex. 19:6 [b]Is. 60:5, 11
7 [a]Is. 40:2; Zech. 9:12
8 [a]Ps. 11:7 [b]Is. 1:11, 13 [c]Gen. 17:7; Ps. 105:10; Is. 55:3; Jer. 32:40 [1]Or *in*
9 [a]Is. 65:23
10 [a]Hab. 3:18 [b]Ps. 132:9, 16 [c]Is. 49:18; Rev. 21:2
11 [a]Ps. 72:3; 85:11 [b]Is. 60:18; 62:7

CHAPTER 62

1 [1]*keep silent*
2 [a]Is. 60:3 [b]Ps. 102:15, 16; 138:4, 5; 148:11, 13 [c]Is. 62:4, 12; 65:15
3 [a]Is. 28:5; Zech. 9:16; 1 Thess. 2:19
4 [a]Hos. 1:10; 1 Pet. 2:10 [b]Is. 49:14; 54:6, 7 [c]Is. 54:1 [1]Heb. *Azubah* [2]Heb. *Shemamah* [3]Lit. *My Delight Is in Her* [4]Lit. *Married*
5 [a]Is. 65:19
6 [a]Is. 52:8; Jer. 6:17; Ezek. 3:17; 33:7 [1]*not be silent* [2]*remember*
7 [a]Is. 60:18; 61:11; Jer. 33:9; Zeph. 3:19, 20
8 [a]Lev. 26:16; Deut. 28:31, 33; Judg. 6:3–6; Is. 1:7; Jer. 5:17
9 [a]Deut. 12:12; 14:23, 26
10 [a]Is. 40:3; 57:14

Build up,
Build up the highway!
Take out the stones,
[b]Lift up a banner for the peoples!
11 Indeed the LORD has proclaimed
To the end of the world:
[a]"Say to the daughter of Zion,
'Surely your salvation is coming;
Behold, His [b]reward *is* with Him,
And His [1]work before Him.' "
12 And they shall call them The
Holy People,
The Redeemed of the LORD;
And you shall be called Sought
Out,
A City Not Forsaken.

The LORD in Judgment and Salvation

63 Who *is* this who comes from
Edom,
With dyed garments from
Bozrah,
This *One who is* [1]glorious in His
apparel,
Traveling in the greatness of His
strength?—

"I who speak in righteousness,
mighty to save."

2 Why [a]*is* Your apparel red,
And Your garments like one who
treads in the winepress?

3 "I have [a]trodden the winepress
alone,
And from the peoples no one *was*
with Me.
For I have trodden them in My
anger,
And trampled them in My fury;
Their blood is sprinkled upon My
garments,
And I have stained all My robes.
4 For the [a]day of vengeance *is* in
My heart,
And the year of My redeemed has
come.
5 [a]I looked, but [b]*there was* no one
to help,
And I wondered
That *there was* no one to uphold;
Therefore My own [c]arm brought
salvation for Me;
And My own fury, it
sustained Me.
6 I have trodden down the peoples
in My anger,
Made them drunk in My fury,
And brought down their strength
to the earth."

God's Mercy Remembered

7 I will mention the
lovingkindnesses of the LORD
And the praises of the LORD,
According to all that the LORD
has bestowed on us,
And the great goodness toward
the house of Israel,
Which He has bestowed on them
according to His mercies,
According to the multitude of His
lovingkindnesses.
8 For He said, "Surely they *are* My
people,
Children *who* will not lie."
So He became their Savior.
9 [a]In all their affliction He was
[1]afflicted,
[b]And the Angel of His Presence
saved them;
[c]In His love and in His pity He
redeemed them;
And [d]He bore them and carried
them
All the days of old.
10 But they [a]rebelled and [b]grieved
His Holy Spirit;
[c]So He turned Himself against
them as an enemy,
And He fought against them.

11 Then he [a]remembered the days of
old,
Moses *and* his people, *saying:*
"Where *is* He who [b]brought them
up out of the sea
With the [1]shepherd of His flock?
[c]Where *is* He who put His Holy
Spirit within them,
12 Who led *them* by the right hand
of Moses,
[a]With His glorious arm,
[b]Dividing the water before them
To make for Himself an
everlasting name,
13 [a]Who led them through the deep,
As a horse in the wilderness,
That they might not stumble?"

14 As a beast goes down into the
valley,
And the Spirit of the LORD causes
him to rest,
So You lead Your people,
[a]To make Yourself a glorious
name.

A Prayer of Penitence

15 [a]Look down from heaven,
And see [b]from Your habitation,
holy and glorious.
Where *are* Your zeal and Your
strength,
The yearning [c]of Your heart and
Your mercies toward me?
Are they restrained?
16 [a]Doubtless You *are* our Father,

---

10 [b]Is. 11:12
11 [a]Zech. 9:9; Matt. 21:5; John 12:15 [b]Is. 40:10; [Rev. 22:12] [1]*recompense*

CHAPTER 63
1 [1]Or *adorned*
2 [a][Rev. 19:13, 15]
3 [a]Lam. 1:15; Rev. 14:19, 20; 19:15
4 [a]Is. 34:8; 35:4; 61:2; Jer. 51:6
5 [a]Is. 41:28; 59:16 [b][John 16:32] [c]Ps. 98:1; Is. 59:16
9 [a]Judg. 10:16 [b]Ex. 14:19 [c]Deut. 7:7 [d]Ex. 19:4 [1]Kt., LXX, Syr. *not afflicted*
10 [a]Ex. 15:24 [b]Num. 14:11; Ps. 78:40; Acts 7:51; 1 Cor. 10:1–11 [c]Ex. 23:21; Ps. 106:40
11 [a]Ps. 106:44, 45 [b]Ex. 14:30 [c]Num. 11:17, 25, 29; Hag. 2:5 [1]MT, Vg. *shepherds*
12 [a]Ex. 15:6 [b]Ex. 14:21, 22; Josh. 3:16; Is. 11:15; 51:10
13 [a]Ps. 106:9
14 [a]2 Sam. 7:23
15 [a]Deut. 26:15; Ps. 80:14 [b]Ps. 33:14 [c]Jer. 31:20; Hos. 11:8
16 [a]Deut. 32:6

Though Abraham [b]was ignorant
of us,
And Israel does not acknowledge
us.
You, O LORD, *are* our Father;
Our Redeemer from Everlasting
is Your name.
17 O LORD, why have You [a]made us
stray from Your ways,
And hardened our heart from
Your fear?
Return for Your servants' sake,
The tribes of Your inheritance.
18 [a]Your holy people have possessed
it but a little while;
[b]Our adversaries have trodden
down Your sanctuary.
19 We have become *like* those of
old, over whom You never
ruled,
Those who were never called by
Your name.

64

Oh, that You would [1]rend the
heavens!
That You would come down!
That the mountains might shake
at Your [a]presence—
2 As fire burns brushwood,
As fire causes water to boil—
To make Your name known to
Your adversaries,
That the nations may tremble at
Your presence!
3 When [a]You did awesome things
for which we did not look,
You came down,
The mountains shook at Your
presence.
4 For since the beginning of the
world
[a]*Men* have not heard nor
perceived by the ear,
Nor has the eye seen any God
besides You,
Who acts for the one who waits
for Him.
5 You meet him who rejoices and
does righteousness,
Who remembers You in Your
ways.
You are indeed angry, for we
have sinned—
[a]In these ways we continue;
And we need to be saved.
6 But we are all like an unclean
thing,
And all [a]our righteousnesses *are*
like [1]filthy rags;
We all [b]fade as a leaf,
And our iniquities, like the wind,
Have taken us away.
7 And *there is* no one who calls on
Your name,
Who stirs himself up to take hold
of You;
For You have hidden Your face
from us,
And have [1]consumed us because
of our iniquities.
8 But now, O LORD,
You *are* our Father;
We *are* the clay, and You our
[a]potter;
And all we *are* the work of Your
hand.
9 Do not be furious, O LORD,
Nor remember iniquity forever;
Indeed, please look—we all *are*
Your people!
10 Your holy cities are a wilderness,
Zion is a wilderness,
Jerusalem a desolation.
11 Our holy and beautiful [1]temple,
Where our fathers praised You,
Is burned up with fire;
And all [a]our pleasant things [2]are
laid waste.
12 [a]Will You restrain Yourself
because of these *things,*
O LORD?
[b]Will You [1]hold Your peace, and
afflict us very severely?

The Righteousness of God's Judgment

65

"I was [a]sought by *those who*
did not ask *for Me;*
I was found by *those who* did not
seek Me.
I said, 'Here I am, here I am,'
To a nation *that* [b]was not called
by My name.
2 [a]I have stretched out My hands all
day long to a [b]rebellious
people,
Who [c]walk in a way *that is* not
good,
According to their own thoughts;
3 A people [a]who provoke Me to
anger continually to My face;
[b]Who sacrifice in gardens,
And burn incense on altars of
brick;
4 [a]Who sit among the graves,
And spend the night in the tombs;
[b]Who eat swine's flesh,
And the broth of [1]abominable
things is *in* their vessels;
5 [a]Who say, 'Keep to yourself,
Do not come near me,
For I am holier than you!'
These [1]*are* smoke in My nostrils,
A fire that burns all the day.
6 "Behold, [a]*it is* written before Me:
[b]I will not keep silence, [c]but will
repay—
Even repay into their bosom—

16 [b]Job 14:21
17 [a]Is. 6:9, 10; John 12:40
18 [a]Deut. 7:6 [b]Ps. 74:3–7; Is. 64:11

CHAPTER 64
1 [a]Ex. 19:18; Ps. 18:9; 144:5; Mic. 1:3, 4; [Hab. 3:13] [1]*tear open*
3 [a]Ex. 34:10
4 [a]Ps. 31:19
5 [a]Mal. 3:6
6 [a][Phil. 3:9] [b]Ps. 90:5, 6; Is.1:30 [1]Lit. *a filthy garment*
7 [1]Lit. *caused us to melt*
8 [a]Is. 29:16; 45:9; Jer. 18:6; [Rom. 9:20, 21]
11 [a]Ezek. 24:21 [1]Lit. *house* [2]*have become a ruin*
12 [a]Is. 42:14 [b]Ps. 83:1 [1]*keep silent*

CHAPTER 65
1 [a]Rom. 9:24; 10:20 [b]Is. 63:19
2 [a]Rom. 10:21 [b]Is. 1:2, 23 [c]Is. 42:24
3 [a]Deut. 32:21 [b]Is. 1:29
4 [a]Deut. 18:11 [b]Lev. 11:7; Is. 66:17 [1]Unclean meats, Lev. 7:18; 19:7
5 [a]Matt. 9:11; Luke 7:39; 18:9–12 [1]Cause My wrath to smoke
6 [a]Deut. 32:34 [b]Ps. 50:3 [c]Ps. 79:12

7 Your iniquities and [a]the iniquities
of your fathers together,"
Says the LORD,
[b]"Who have burned incense on the
mountains
[c]And blasphemed Me on the hills;
Therefore I will measure their
former work into their bosom."

8 Thus says the LORD:

"As the new wine is found in the
cluster,
And *one* says, 'Do not destroy it,
For [a]a blessing *is* in it,'
So will I do for My servants' sake,
That I may not destroy them [b]all.
9 I will bring forth descendants
from Jacob,
And from Judah an heir of My
mountains;
My [a]elect shall inherit it,
And My servants shall dwell
there.
10 [a]Sharon shall be a fold of flocks,
And [b]the Valley of Achor a place
for herds to lie down,
For My people who have
[c]sought Me.

11 "But you *are* those who forsake
the LORD,
Who forget [a]My holy mountain,
Who prepare [b]a table for [1]Gad,
And who furnish a drink offering
for [2]Meni.
12 Therefore I will number you for
the sword,
And you shall all bow down to
the slaughter;
[a]Because, when I called, you did
not answer;
When I spoke, you did not hear,
But did evil before My eyes,
And chose *that* in which I do not
delight."

13 Therefore thus says the Lord
GOD:

"Behold, My servants shall eat,
But you shall be hungry;
Behold, My servants shall drink,
But you shall be thirsty;
Behold, My servants shall rejoice,
But you shall be ashamed;
14 Behold, My servants shall sing
for joy of heart,
But you shall cry for sorrow of
heart,
And [a]wail for [1]grief of spirit.
15 You shall leave your name [a]as a
curse to [b]My chosen;
For the Lord GOD will slay you,
And [c]call His servants by another
name;
16 [a]So that he who blesses himself in
the earth
Shall bless himself in the God of
truth;
And [b]he who swears in the earth
Shall swear by the God of truth;
Because the former troubles are
forgotten,
And because they are hidden
from My eyes.

The Glorious New Creation

17 "For behold, I create [a]new heavens
and a new earth;
And the former shall not be
remembered or [1]come to mind.
18 But be glad and rejoice forever
in what I create;
For behold, I create Jerusalem *as*
a rejoicing,
And her people a joy.
19 [a]I will rejoice in Jerusalem,
And joy in My people;
The [b]voice of weeping shall no
longer be heard in her,
Nor the voice of crying.

20 "No more shall an infant from
there *live but a few* days,
Nor an old man who has not
fulfilled his days;
For the child shall die one
hundred years old,
[a]But the sinner *being* one hundred
years old shall be accursed.
21 [a]They shall build houses and
inhabit *them;*
They shall plant vineyards and
eat their fruit.
22 They shall not build and another
inhabit;
They shall not plant and [a]another
eat;
For [b]as the days of a tree, *so shall
be* the days of My people,
And [c]My elect shall long enjoy
the work of their hands.
23 They shall not labor in vain,
[a]Nor bring forth children for
trouble;
For [b]they *shall be* the
descendants of the blessed of
the LORD,
And their offspring with them.

24 "It shall come to pass
That [a]before they call, I will
answer;
And while they are still speaking,
I will [b]hear.
25 The [a]wolf and the lamb shall feed
together,

7 [a]Ex. 20:5 [b]Ezek. 18:6 [c]Is. 57:7; Ezek. 20:27, 28
8 [a]Joel 2:14 [b]Is. 1:9; Amos 9:8, 9
9 [a]Matt. 24:22
10 [a]Is. 33:9 [b]Josh. 7:24; Hos. 2:15 [c]Is. 55:6
11 [a]Is. 56:7 [b]Ezek. 23:41; [1 Cor. 10:21] [1]Lit. *Troop* or *Fortune;* a pagan deity [2]Lit. *Number* or *Destiny;* a pagan deity
12 [a]2 Chr. 36:15, 16; Prov. 1:24; Is. 41:28; 50:2; 66:4; Jer. 7:13
14 [a]Matt. 8:12; Luke 13:28 [1]Or *a broken spirit*
15 [a]Jer. 29:22; Zech. 8:13 [b]Is. 65:9, 22 [c][Acts 11:26]
16 [a]Ps. 72:17; Jer. 4:2 [b]Deut. 6:13; Zeph. 1:5
17 [a]Is. 51:16; 66:22; [2 Pet. 3:13]; Rev. 21:1 [1]Lit. *come upon the heart*
19 [a]Is. 62:4, 5 [b]Is. 35:10; 51:11; Rev. 7:17; 21:4
20 [a]Eccl. 8:12, 13; Is. 3:11; 22:14
21 [a]Ezek. 28:26; 45:4; Hos. 11:11; Amos 9:14
22 [a]Is. 62:8, 9 [b]Ps. 92:12 [c]Is. 65:9, 15
23 [a]Hos. 9:12 [b]Is. 61:9; [Jer. 32:38, 39; Acts 2:39]
24 [a]Ps. 91:15; Is. 58:9 [b]Is. 30:19; Dan. 9:20–23
25 [a]Is. 11:6–9

The lion shall eat straw like
the ox,
[b]And dust *shall be* the serpent's
food.
They shall not hurt nor destroy
in all My holy mountain,"
Says the LORD.

True Worship and False

66 Thus says the LORD:

[a]"Heaven *is* My throne,
And earth *is* My footstool.
Where *is* the house that you will
build Me?
And where *is* the place of My
rest?
2 For all those *things* My hand has
made,
And all those *things* exist,"
Says the LORD.
[a]"But on this *one* will I look:
[b]On *him who is* poor and of a
contrite spirit,
And who trembles at My word.

3 "He[a] who kills a bull *is as if* he
slays a man;
He who sacrifices a lamb, *as if* he
[b]breaks a dog's neck;
He who offers a grain offering, *as
if he offers* swine's blood;
He who burns incense, *as if* he
blesses an idol.
Just as they have chosen their
own ways,
And their soul delights in their
abominations,
4 So will I choose their delusions,
And bring their fears on them;
[a]Because, when I called, no one
answered,
When I spoke they did not hear;
But they did evil before My eyes,
And chose *that* in which I do not
delight."

The LORD Vindicates Zion

5 Hear the word of the LORD,
You who tremble at His word:
"Your brethren who [a]hated you,
Who cast you out for My name's
sake, said,
[b]'Let the LORD be glorified,
That [c]we may see your joy.'
But they shall be ashamed."

6 The sound of noise from the city!
A voice from the temple!
The voice of the LORD,
Who fully repays His enemies!

7 "Before she was in labor,
she gave birth;
Before her pain came,
She delivered a male child.
8 Who has heard such a thing?
Who has seen such things?
Shall the earth be made to give
birth in one day?
Or shall a nation be born at once?
For as soon as Zion was in labor,
She gave birth to her children.
9 Shall I bring to the time of birth,
and not cause delivery?" says
the LORD.
"Shall I who cause delivery shut
up *the womb?"* says your God.
10 "Rejoice with Jerusalem,
And be glad with her, all you who
love her;
Rejoice for joy with her, all you
who mourn for her;
11 That you may feed and be
satisfied
With the consolation of her
bosom,
That you may drink deeply and
be delighted
With the abundance of her
glory."

12 For thus says the LORD:

"Behold, [a]I will extend peace to
her like a river,
And the glory of the Gentiles like
a flowing stream.
Then you shall [b]feed;
On *her* sides shall you be
[c]carried,
And be dandled on *her* knees.
13 As one whom his mother
comforts,
So I will [a]comfort you;
And you shall be comforted in
Jerusalem."

The Reign and Indignation of God

14 When you see *this,* your heart
shall rejoice,
And [a]your bones shall flourish
like grass;
The hand of the LORD shall be
known to His servants,
And *His* indignation to His
enemies.
15 [a]For behold, the LORD will come
with fire
And with His chariots, like a
whirlwind,
To render His anger with fury,
And His rebuke with flames of
fire.
16 For by fire and by [a]His sword
The LORD will judge all flesh;
And the slain of the LORD shall
be [b]many.

---

25 [b]Gen. 3:14; Mic. 7:17

CHAPTER 66

1 [a]1 Kin. 8:27; 2 Chr. 6:18; Ps. 11:4; Matt. 5:34; Acts 17:24

2 [a]Ps. 34:18; [Is. 57:15; 61:1; Matt. 5:3, 4; Luke 18:13, 14] [b]Ps. 34:18; 51:17

3 [a][Is. 1:10–17; 58:1–7; Mic. 6:7, 8] [b]Deut. 23:18

4 [a]Prov. 1:24; Is. 65:12; Jer. 7:13

5 [a]Ps. 38:20; Is. 60:15; [Luke 6:22, 23] [b]Is. 5:19 [c][2 Thess. 1:10; Titus 2:13]

12 [a]Is. 48:18; 60:5 [b]Is. 60:16 [c]Is. 49:22; 60:4

13 [a]Is. 51:3; [2 Cor. 1:3, 4]

14 [a]Ezek. 37:1

15 [a]Is. 9:5; [2 Thess. 1:8]

16 [a]Is. 27:1 [b]Is. 34:6

17"Those[a] who sanctify themselves
and purify themselves,
To go to the gardens
[1]After an *idol* in the midst,
Eating swine's flesh and the
abomination and the mouse,
Shall [2]be consumed together,"
says the LORD.

18 "For I *know* their works and
their [a]thoughts. It shall be that I
will [b]gather all nations and
tongues; and they shall come and
see My glory.
19 [a]"I will set a sign among them;
and those among them who escape
I will send to the nations: *to* Tar-
shish and [1]Pul and Lud, who draw
the bow, and Tubal and Javan, *to*
the coastlands afar off who have
not heard My fame nor seen My
glory. [b]And they shall declare My
glory among the Gentiles.
20 "Then they shall [a]bring all your
brethren [b]for an offering to the
LORD out of all nations, on horses
and in chariots and in litters, on
mules and on camels, to My holy
mountain Jerusalem," says the
LORD, "as the children of Israel
bring an offering in a clean vessel
into the house of the LORD.
21 "And I will also take some of
them for [a]priests *and* Levites,"
says the LORD.

22"For as [a]the new heavens and the
new earth
Which I will make shall remain
before Me," says the LORD,
"So shall your descendants and
your name remain.
23 And [a]it shall come to pass
That from one New Moon to
another,
And from one Sabbath to
another,
[b]All flesh shall come to worship
before Me," says the LORD.

24"And they shall go forth and look
Upon the corpses of the men
Who have transgressed against
Me.
For their [a]worm does not die,
And their fire is not quenched.
They shall be an abhorrence to
all flesh."

17 [a]Is. 65:3–8 [1]Lit. *After one* [2]*come to an end*
18 [a]Is. 59:7 [b]Is. 45:22–25; Jer. 3:17
19 [a]Luke 2:34 [b]Mal. 1:11 [1]So with MT, Tg.; LXX *Put* (cf. Jer. 46:9)
20 [a]Is. 49:22 [b]Is. 18:7; [Rom. 15:16]
21 [a]Ex. 19:6; Is. 61:6; 1 Pet. 2:9; Rev. 1:6
22 [a]Is. 65:17; Heb. 12:26, 27; 2 Pet. 3:13; Rev. 21:1
23 [a]Zech. 14:16 [b]Zech. 14:17–21
24 [a]Is. 14:11; Mark 9:44, 46, 48

The Book of

Jeremiah

THE Book of Jeremiah is the prophecy of a man divinely called in his youth from the priest-city of Anathoth. A heartbroken prophet with a heartbreaking message, Jeremiah labors for more than forty years proclaiming a message of doom to the stiff-necked people of Judah. Despised and persecuted by his countrymen, Jeremiah bathes his harsh prophecies in tears of compassion. His broken heart causes him to write a broken book, which is difficult to arrange chronologically or topically. But through his sermons and signs he faithfully declares that surrender to God's will is the only way to escape calamity.

Yirmeyahu or *Yirmeyah* literally means "Yahweh Throws," perhaps in the sense of laying a foundation. It may effectively mean "Yahweh Establishes, Appoints, or Sends." The Greek form of the Hebrew name in the Septuagint is *Hieremias*, and the Latin form is *Jeremias*.

THE words of Jeremiah the son of Hilkiah, of the priests who *were* [a]in Anathoth in the land of Benjamin,
2 to whom the word of the LORD came in the days of [a]Josiah the son of Amon, king of Judah, [b]in the thirteenth year of his reign.
3 It came also in the days of [a]Jehoiakim the son of Josiah, king of Judah, [b]until the end of the eleventh year of Zedekiah the son of Josiah, king of Judah, [c]until the carrying away of Jerusalem captive [d]in the fifth month.

The Prophet Is Called

4 Then the word of the LORD came to me, saying:

5 "Before I [a]formed you in the womb
[b]I knew you;
Before you were born I
[c]sanctified[1] you;
I [2]ordained you a prophet to the nations."

6 Then said I:

[a]"Ah, Lord GOD!
Behold, I cannot speak, for I *am* a youth."

7 But the LORD said to me:

"Do not say, 'I *am* a youth,'
For you shall go to all to whom I send you,
And [a]whatever I command you, you shall speak.
8 [a]Do not be afraid of their faces,
For [b]I *am* with you to deliver you," says the LORD.

9 Then the LORD put forth His hand and [a]touched my mouth, and the LORD said to me:

"Behold, I have [b]put My words in your mouth.
10 [a]See, I have this day set you over the nations and over the kingdoms,
To [b]root out and to pull down,
To destroy and to throw down,
To build and to plant."

11 Moreover the word of the LORD came to me, saying, "Jeremiah, what do you see?" And I said, "I see a [1]branch of an almond tree."
12 Then the LORD said to me, "You have seen well, for I am [1]ready to perform My word."
13 And the word of the LORD came to me the second time, saying, "What do you see?" And I said, "I see [a]a boiling pot, and it is facing away from the north."
14 Then the LORD said to me:

"Out of the [a]north calamity shall break forth
On all the inhabitants of the land.

CHAPTER 1
1 [a]Josh. 21:18
2 [a]2 Kin. 21:24 [b]Jer. 25:3
3 [a]2 Kin. 23:34 [b]Jer. 39:2 [c]Jer. 52:12 [d]2 Kin. 25:8
5 [a]Is. 49:1, 5 [b]Ex. 33:12 [c][Luke 1:15] [1]*set you apart* [2]*appointed*
6 [a]Ex. 4:10; 6:12, 30
7 [a]Num. 22:20, 38
8 [a]Ezek. 2:6; 3:9 [b]Ex. 3:12
9 [a]Is. 6:7 [b]Is. 51:16
10 [a]1 Kin. 19:17 [b][2 Cor. 10:4, 5]
11 [1]Lit. *rod*
12 [1]Lit. *watching*
13 [a]Ezek. 11:3; 24:3
14 [a]Jer. 6:1

15 For behold, I am [a]calling
All the families of the kingdoms
of the north," says the LORD;
"They shall come and [b]each one
set his throne
At the entrance of the gates of
Jerusalem,
Against all its walls all around,
And against all the cities of
Judah.
16 I will utter My judgments
Against them concerning all their
wickedness,
Because [a]they have forsaken Me,
Burned [b]incense to other gods,
And worshiped the works of their
own [c]hands.

17 "Therefore [a]prepare yourself and
arise,
And speak to them all that I
command you.
[b]Do not be dismayed before their
faces,
Lest I dismay you before them.
18 For behold, I have made you this
day
[a]A fortified city and an iron pillar,
And bronze walls against the
whole land—
Against the kings of Judah,
Against its princes,
Against its priests,
And against the people of the
land.
19 They will fight against you,
But they shall not prevail against
you.
For I *am* with you," says the
LORD, "to deliver you."

God's Case Against Israel

2 Moreover the word of the LORD
came to me, saying,
2 "Go and cry in the hearing of
Jerusalem, saying, 'Thus says the
LORD:

"I remember you,
The kindness of your [a]youth,
The love of your betrothal,
[b]When you [1]went after Me in the
wilderness,
In a land not sown.
3 [a]Israel *was* holiness to the LORD,
[b]The firstfruits of His increase.
[c]All that devour him will offend;
Disaster will [d]come upon them,"
says the LORD.' "

4 Hear the word of the LORD, O
house of Jacob and all the families
of the house of Israel.
5 Thus says the LORD:

[a]"What injustice have your fathers
found in Me,
That they have gone far from Me,
[b]Have followed [1]idols,
And have become idolaters?
6 Neither did they say, 'Where *is*
the LORD,
Who [a]brought us up out of the
land of Egypt,
Who led us through [b]the
wilderness,
Through a land of deserts and
pits,
Through a land of drought and
the shadow of death,
Through a land that no one
crossed
And where no one dwelt?'
7 I brought you into [a]a bountiful
country,
To eat its fruit and its goodness.
But when you entered, you
[b]defiled My land
And made My heritage an
abomination.
8 The priests did not say, 'Where
is the LORD?'
And those who handle the [a]law
did not know Me;
The rulers also transgressed
against Me;
[b]The prophets prophesied by Baal,
And walked after *things that* do
not profit.

9 "Therefore [a]I will yet [1]bring
charges against you," says the
LORD,
"And against your children's
children I will bring charges.
10 For pass beyond the coasts of
[1]Cyprus and see,
Send to [2]Kedar and consider
diligently,
And see if there has been such *a*
[a]*thing.*
11 [a]Has a nation changed *its* gods,
Which *are* [b]not gods?
[c]But My people have changed
their Glory
For *what* does not profit.
12 Be astonished, O heavens, at this,
And be horribly afraid;
Be very desolate," says the LORD.
13 "For My people have committed
two evils:
They have forsaken Me, the
[a]fountain of living waters,
And hewn themselves cisterns—
broken cisterns that can hold
no water.

14 "*Is* Israel [a]a servant?
Is he a homeborn *slave?*
Why is he plundered?

15 [a]Jer. 6:22; 25:9 [b]Jer. 39:3
16 [a]Deut. 28:20 [b]Jer. 7:9 [c]Is. 37:19
17 [a]Job 38:3 [b]Ezek. 2:6
18 [a]Is. 50:7

CHAPTER 2

2 [a]Ezek. 16:8 [b]Deut. 2:7 [1]*followed*
3 [a][Ex. 19:5, 6] [b]Rev. 14:4 [c]Jer. 12:14 [d]Is. 41:11
5 [a]Is. 5:4 [b]2 Kin. 17:15 [1]*vanities* or *futilities*
6 [a]Is. 63:11 [b]Deut. 8:15; 32:10
7 [a]Num. 13:27 [b]Num. 35:33
8 [a]Rom. 2:20 [b]Jer. 23:13
9 [a]Mic. 6:2 [1]*contend with*
10 [a]Jer. 18:13 [1]Heb. *Kittim*, representative of western cultures [2]In northern Arabian desert, representative of eastern cultures
11 [a]Mic. 4:5 [b]Is. 37:19 [c]Rom. 1:23
13 [a]Ps. 36:9
14 [a][Ex. 4:22]

15 [a]The young lions roared at him,
and growled;
They made his land waste;
His cities are burned, without
inhabitant.
16 Also the people of [1]Noph and
[a]Tahpanhes
Have [2]broken the crown of your
head.
17 [a]Have you not brought this on
yourself,
In that you have forsaken the
LORD your God
When [b]He led you in the way?
18 And now why take [a]the road to
Egypt,
To drink the waters of [b]Sihor?
Or why take the road to [c]Assyria,
To drink the waters of [1]the River?
19 Your own wickedness will
[a]correct you,
And your backslidings will
rebuke you.
Know therefore and see that *it is*
an evil and bitter *thing*
That you have forsaken the LORD
your God,
And the [1]fear of Me *is* not in you,"
Says the Lord GOD of hosts.

20 "For of old I have [a]broken your
yoke *and* burst your bonds;
And [b]you said, 'I will not
[1]transgress,'
When [c]on every high hill and
under every green tree
You lay down, [d]playing the
harlot.
21 Yet I had [a]planted you a noble
vine, a seed of highest quality.
How then have you turned
before Me
Into [b]the degenerate plant of an
alien vine?
22 For though you wash yourself
with lye, and use much soap,
Yet your iniquity is [a]marked[1]
before Me," says the Lord GOD.

23 "How[a] can you say, 'I am not
[1]polluted,
I have not gone after the Baals'?
See your way in the valley;
Know what you have done:
You are a swift dromedary
breaking loose in her ways,
24 A wild donkey used to the
wilderness,
That sniffs at the wind in her
desire;
In her time of mating, who can
turn her away?
All those who seek her will not
weary themselves;
In her month they will find her.
25 Withhold your foot from being
unshod, and your throat from
thirst.
But you said, [a]'There is no hope.
No! For I have loved [b]aliens, and
after them I will go.'

26 "As the thief is ashamed when he
is found out,
So is the house of Israel ashamed;
They and their kings and their
princes, and their priests and
their [a]prophets,
27 Saying to a tree, 'You *are* my
father,'
And to a [a]stone, 'You gave birth
to me.'
For they have turned *their* back
to Me, and not *their* face.
But in the time of their [b]trouble
They will say, 'Arise and save us.'
28 But [a]where *are* your gods that
you have made for yourselves?
Let them arise,
If they [b]can save you in the time
of your [1]trouble;
For [c]*according to* the number of
your cities
Are your gods, O Judah.

29 "Why will you plead with Me?
You all have transgressed against
Me," says the LORD.
30 "In vain I have [a]chastened your
children;
They [b]received no correction.
Your sword has [c]devoured your
prophets
Like a destroying lion.

31 "O generation, see the word of the
LORD!
Have I been a wilderness to
Israel,
Or a land of darkness?
Why do My people say, 'We [1]are
lords;
[a]We will come no more to You'?
32 Can a virgin forget her
ornaments,
Or a bride her attire?
Yet My people [a]have forgotten
Me days without number.

33 "Why do you beautify your way
to seek love?
Therefore you have also taught
The wicked women your ways.
34 Also on your skirts is found
[a]The blood of the lives of the poor
innocents.
I have not found it by [1]secret
search,
But plainly on all these things.

15 [a]Is. 1:7; Jer. 50:17
16 [a]2 Kin. 23:29–37; Jer. 43:7–9 [1]Memphis in ancient Egypt [2]Or *grazed*
17 [a]Jer. 4:18 [b]Deut. 32:10
18 [a]Is. 30:1–3 [b]Josh. 13:3 [c]Hos. 5:13 [1]The Euphrates
19 [a]Is. 3:9; Jer. 4:18; Hos. 5:5 [1]*dread*
20 [a]Lev. 26:13 [b]Ex. 19:8; Josh. 24:18; Judg. 10:16; 1 Sam. 12:10 [c]Deut. 12:2; Is. 57:5, 7; Jer. 3:6 [d]Ex. 34:15 [1]Kt. *serve*
21 [a]Ex. 15:17; Ps. 44:2; 80:8; Is. 5:2 [b]Deut. 32:32; Is. 5:4
22 [a]Job 14:16, 17; Jer. 17:1, 2; Hos. 13:12 [1]*stained*
23 [a]Prov. 30:12 [1]*defiled*
25 [a]Is. 57:10; Jer. 18:12 [b]Jer. 3:13
26 [a]Is. 28:7; Jer. 5:31
27 [a]Jer. 3:9 [b]Judg. 10:10; Is. 26:16; Hos. 5:15
28 [a]Deut. 32:37; Judg. 10:14 [b]Is. 45:20 [c]2 Kin. 17:30, 31; Jer. 11:13 [1]Or *evil*
30 [a]Is. 9:13 [b]Is. 1:5; Jer. 5:3; 7:28 [c]Neh. 9:26; Jer. 26:20–24; Acts 7:52; 1 Thess. 2:15
31 [a]Deut. 32:15; Jer. 2:20, 25 [1]*have dominion*
32 [a]Ps. 106:21; Is. 17:10; Jer. 3:21; 13:25; Hos. 8:14
34 [a]2 Kin. 21:16; 24:4; Ps. 106:38; Jer. 7:6; 19:4 [1]*digging*

35 [a]Yet you say, 'Because I am
innocent,
Surely His anger shall turn
from me.'
Behold, [b]I will plead My case
against you,
[c]Because you say, 'I have not
sinned.'
36 [a]Why do you gad about so much
to change your way?
Also [b]you shall be ashamed of
Egypt [c]as you were ashamed of
Assyria.
37 Indeed you will go forth from
him
With your hands on [a]your head;
For the LORD has rejected your
trusted allies,
And you will [b]not prosper by
them.

Israel Is Shameless

3 "They say, 'If a man divorces his
wife,
And she goes from him
And becomes another man's,
[a]May he return to her again?'
Would not that [b]land be greatly
polluted?
But you have [c]played the harlot
with many lovers;
[d]Yet return to Me," says the LORD.

2 "Lift up your eyes to [a]the desolate
heights and see:
Where have you not [1]lain *with
men?*
[b]By the road you have sat for them
Like an Arabian in the
wilderness;
[c]And you have polluted the land
With your harlotries and your
wickedness.
3 Therefore the [a]showers have
been withheld,
And there has been no latter rain.
You have had a [b]harlot's
forehead;
You refuse to be ashamed.
4 Will you not from this time cry
to Me,
'My Father, You *are* [a]the guide of
[b]my youth?
5 [a]Will He remain angry forever?
Will He keep it to the end?'
Behold, you have spoken and
done evil things,
As you were able."

A Call to Repentance

6 The LORD said also to me in the
days of Josiah the king: "Have you
seen what [a]backsliding Israel has
done? She has [b]gone up on every
high mountain and under every
green tree, and there played the
harlot.
7 [a]"And I said, after she had
done all these *things*, 'Return to
Me.' But she did not return. And
her treacherous [b]sister Judah saw
it.
8 "Then I saw that [a]for all the
causes for which backsliding Is-
rael had committed adultery, I had
[b]put her away and given her a cer-
tificate of divorce; [c]yet her treach-
erous sister Judah did not fear, but
went and played the harlot also.
9 "So it came to pass, through
her casual harlotry, that she
[a]defiled the land and committed
adultery with [b]stones and trees.
10 "And yet for all this her treach-
erous sister Judah has not turned
to Me [a]with her whole heart, but
in pretense," says the LORD.
11 Then the LORD said to me,
[a]"Backsliding Israel has shown
herself more righteous than
treacherous Judah.
12 "Go and proclaim these words
toward [a]the north, and say:

'Return, backsliding Israel,' says
the LORD;
'I will not cause My anger to fall
on you.
For I *am* [b]merciful,' says the
LORD;
'I will not remain angry forever.
13 [a]Only acknowledge your iniquity,
That you have transgressed
against the LORD your God,
And have [b]scattered your
[1]charms
To [c]alien deities [d]under every
green tree,
And you have not obeyed My
voice,' says the LORD.

14 "Return, O backsliding chil-
dren," says the LORD; [a]"for I am
married to you. I will take you,
[b]one from a city and two from a
family, and I will bring you to
[c]Zion.
15 "And I will give you [a]shep-
herds according to My heart, who
will [b]feed you with knowledge and
understanding.
16 "Then it shall come to pass,
when you are multiplied and [a]in-
creased in the land in those days,"
says the LORD, "that they will say
no more, 'The ark of the covenant
of the LORD.' [b]It shall not come to

35 [a]Jer. 2:23, 29; Mal. 2:17; 3:8 [b]Jer. 2:9 [c][Prov. 28:13; 1 John 1:8, 10]
36 [a]Jer. 31:22; Hos. 5:13; 12:1 [b]Is. 30:3 [c]2 Chr. 28:16
37 [a]2 Sam. 13:19; Jer. 14:3, 4 [b]Jer. 37:7–10

CHAPTER 3

1 [a]Deut. 24:1–4 [b]Jer. 2:7 [c]Jer. 2:20; Ezek. 16:26 [d]Jer. 4:1; [Zech. 1:3]
2 [a]Deut. 12:2; Jer. 2:20; 3:21; 7:29 [b]Prov. 23:28 [c]Jer. 2:7 [1]Kt. *been violated*
3 [a]Lev. 26:19; Jer. 14:3–6 [b]Zeph. 3:5
4 [a]Ps. 71:17; Prov. 2:17 [b]Jer. 2:2; Hos. 2:15
5 [a]Ps. 103:9; [Is. 57:16]; Jer. 3:12
6 [a]Jer. 7:24 [b]Jer. 2:20
7 [a]2 Kin. 17:13 [b]Jer. 3:11; Ezek. 16:47, 48
8 [a]Ezek. 23:9 [b]2 Kin. 17:6; Is. 50:1 [c]Ezek. 23:11
9 [a]Jer. 2:7 [b]Is. 57:6; Jer. 2:27
10 [a]Jer. 12:2; Hos. 7:14
11 [a]Ezek. 16:51, 52
12 [a]2 Kin. 17:6 [b]Ps. 86:15; Jer. 12:15; 31:20; 33:26
13 [a]Lev. 26:40; Deut. 30:1, 2; [Prov. 28:13; 1 John 1:9] [b]Ezek. 16:15 [c]Jer. 2:25 [d]Deut. 12:2 [1]Lit. *ways*
14 [a]Jer. 31:32; Hos. 2:19, 20 [b]Jer. 31:6 [c][Rom. 11:5]
15 [a]Jer. 23:4; 31:10; [Ezek. 34:23]; Eph. 4:11 [b]Acts 20:28
16 [a]Is. 49:19; Jer. 23:3 [b]Is. 65:17

mind, nor shall they remember it, nor shall they visit *it*, nor shall it be made anymore.
17 "At that time Jerusalem shall be called The Throne of the LORD, and all the nations shall be gathered to it, [a]to the name of the LORD, to Jerusalem. No more shall they [b]follow[1] the dictates of their evil hearts.
18 "In those days [a]the house of Judah shall walk with the house of Israel, and they shall come together out of the land of [b]the north to [c]the land that I have given as an inheritance to your fathers.
19 "But I said:

'How can I put you among the children
And give you [a]a pleasant land,
A beautiful heritage of the hosts of nations?'

"And I said:

'You shall call Me, [b]"My Father,"
And not turn away from Me.'
20 Surely, *as* a wife treacherously departs from her [1]husband,
So [a]have you dealt treacherously with Me,
O house of Israel," says the LORD.

21 A voice was heard on [a]the desolate heights,
Weeping *and* supplications of the children of Israel.
For they have perverted their way;
They have forgotten the LORD their God.

22 "Return, you backsliding children,
And I will [a]heal your backslidings."

"Indeed we do come to You,
For You are the LORD our God.
23 [a]Truly, in vain *is salvation hoped for* from the hills,
And from the multitude of mountains;
[b]Truly, in the LORD our God
Is the salvation of Israel.
24 [a]For shame has devoured
The labor of our fathers from our youth—
Their flocks and their herds,
Their sons and their daughters.
25 We lie down in our shame,
And our [1]reproach covers us.
[a]For we have sinned against the LORD our God,
We and our fathers,
From our youth even to this day,
And [b]have not obeyed the voice of the LORD our God."

4

"If you will return, O Israel," says the LORD,
[a]"Return to Me;
And if you will put away your abominations out of My sight,
Then you shall not be moved.
2 [a]And you shall swear, 'The LORD lives,'
[b]In truth, in [1]judgment, and in righteousness;
[c]The nations shall bless themselves in Him,
And in Him they shall [d]glory."

3 For thus says the LORD to the men of Judah and Jerusalem:

[a]"Break up your [1]fallow ground,
And [b]do not sow among thorns.
4 [a]Circumcise yourselves to the LORD,
And take away the foreskins of your hearts,
You men of Judah and inhabitants of Jerusalem,
Lest My fury come forth like fire,
And burn so that no one can quench *it*,
Because of the evil of your doings."

An Imminent Invasion

5 Declare in Judah and proclaim in Jerusalem, and say:

[a]"Blow the trumpet in the land;
Cry, 'Gather together,'
And say, [b]'Assemble yourselves,
And let us go into the fortified cities.'
6 Set up the [1]standard toward Zion.
Take refuge! Do not delay!
For I will bring disaster from the [a]north,
And great destruction."

7 [a]The lion has come up from his thicket,
And [b]the destroyer of nations is on his way.
He has gone forth from his place
[c]To make your land desolate.
Your cities will be laid waste,
Without inhabitant.
8 For this, [a]clothe yourself with sackcloth,
Lament and wail.
For the fierce anger of the LORD
Has not turned back from us.

17 [a]Is. 60:9 [b]Deut. 29:19; Jer. 7:24 [1]*walk after the stubbornness* or *imagination*
18 [a]Is. 11:13; Jer. 50:4; Ezek. 37:16–22; Hos. 1:11 [b]Jer. 31:8 [c]Amos 9:15
19 [a]Ps. 106:24 [b]Is. 63:16; Jer. 3:4
20 [a]Is. 48:8 [1]Lit. *companion*
21 [a]Is. 15:2
22 [a]Jer. 30:17; 33:6; Hos. 6:1; 14:4
23 [a]Ps. 121:1, 2 [b]Ps. 3:8; Prov. 21:31; Jer. 17:14; 31:7; Jon. 2:9
24 [a]Jer. 11:13; 14:20; Hos. 9:10
25 [a]Ezra 9:6, 7 [b]Jer. 22:21 [1]*disgrace*

CHAPTER 4

1 [a]Jer. 3:1, 22; 15:19; Joel 2:12
2 [a]Deut. 10:20; Is. 45:23; 65:16; Jer. 12:16 [b]Is. 48:1; Zech. 8:8 [c][Gen. 22:18]; Ps. 72:18; Is. 65:16; Jer. 3:17; [Gal. 3:8] [d]Is. 45:25; Jer. 9:24; 1 Cor. 1:31; 2 Cor. 10:17 [1]*justice*
3 [a]Hos. 10:12 [b]Matt. 13:7 [1]*untilled*
4 [a]Deut. 10:16; 30:6; Jer. 9:25, 26; [Rom. 2:28, 29; Col. 2:11]
5 [a]Jer. 6:1; Hos. 8:1 [b]Josh. 10:20; Jer. 8:14
6 [a]Jer. 1:13–15; 6:1, 22; 50:17 [1]*banner*
7 [a]2 Kin. 24:1; Dan. 7:4 [b]Jer. 25:9; Ezek. 26:7–10 [c]Is. 1:7; 6:11; Jer. 2:15
8 [a]Is. 22:12; Jer. 6:26

9 "And it shall come to pass in that
day," says the LORD,
"*That* the heart of the king shall
perish,
And the heart of the princes;
The priests shall be astonished,
And the prophets shall wonder."

10 Then I said, "Ah, Lord GOD!
[a]Surely You have greatly deceived
this people and Jerusalem,
[b]Saying, 'You shall have peace,'
Whereas the sword reaches to the
[1]heart."

11 At that time it will be said
To this people and to Jerusalem,
[a]"A dry wind of the desolate
heights *blows* in the wilderness
Toward the daughter of My
people—
Not to fan or to cleanse—
12 A wind too strong for these will
come for Me;
Now [a]I will also speak judgment
against them."

13 "Behold, he shall come up like
clouds,
And [a]his chariots like a
whirlwind.
[b]His horses are swifter than
eagles.
Woe to us, for we are plundered!"
14 O Jerusalem, [a]wash your heart
from wickedness,
That you may be saved.
How long shall your evil thoughts
lodge within you?
15 For a voice declares [a]from Dan
And proclaims [1]affliction from
Mount Ephraim:
16 "Make mention to the nations,
Yes, proclaim against Jerusalem,
That watchers come from a [a]far
country
And raise their voice against the
cities of Judah.
17 [a]Like keepers of a field they are
against her all around,
Because she has been rebellious
against Me," says the LORD.
18 "Your[a] ways and your doings
Have procured these *things* for
you.
This *is* your wickedness,
Because it is bitter,
Because it reaches to your heart."

Sorrow for the Doomed Nation

19 O my [a]soul, my soul!
I am pained in my very heart!
My heart makes a noise in me;
I cannot hold my peace,

10 [a]2 Kin. 25:10–12; Ezek. 14:9; 2 Thess. 2:11 [b]Jer. 5:12; 14:13 [1]Lit. *soul*
11 [a]Jer. 51:1; Ezek. 17:10; Hos. 13:15
12 [a]Jer. 1:16
13 [a]Is. 5:28 [b]Deut. 28:49; Lam. 4:19; Hos. 8:1; Hab. 1:8
14 [a]Prov. 1:22; Is. 1:16; Jer. 13:27; James 4:8
15 [a]Jer. 8:16; 50:17 [1]Or *wickedness*
16 [a]Is. 39:3; Jer. 5:15
17 [a]2 Kin. 25:1, 4
18 [a]Ps. 107:17; Is. 50:1; Jer. 2:17, 19
19 [a]2 Kin. 25:11; 2 Chr. 36:20; Is. 15:5; 16:11; 21:3; 22:4; Jer. 9:1, 10; 20:9
20 [a]Ps. 42:7; Ezek. 7:26 [b]Jer. 10:20
21 [1]*banner*
22 [a]Jer. 9:3; 13:23; Rom. 16:19; 1 Cor. 14:20 [1]*foolish*
23 [a]Is. 24:19 [b]Gen. 1:2
24 [a]Is. 5:25; Jer. 10:10; Ezek. 38:20
25 [a]Jer. 9:10; 12:4; Zeph. 1:3
26 [a]Jer. 9:10
27 [a]Jer. 5:10, 18; 30:11; 46:28
28 [a]Jer. 12:4, 11; 14:2; Hos. 4:3 [b]Is. 5:30; 50:3; Joel 2:30, 31 [c]Is. 46:10, 11; [Dan. 4:35] [d][Num. 23:19]; Jer. 7:16; 23:30; 30:24

Because you have heard, O my
soul,
The sound of the trumpet,
The alarm of war.
20 [a]Destruction upon destruction is
cried,
For the whole land is plundered.
Suddenly [b]my tents are
plundered,
And my curtains in a moment.
21 How long will I see the [1]standard,
And hear the sound of the
trumpet?

22 "For My people *are* foolish,
They have not known Me.
They *are* [1]silly children,
And they have no understanding.
[a]They *are* wise to do evil,
But to do good they have no
knowledge."

23 [a]I beheld the earth, and indeed *it
was* [b]without form, and void;
And the heavens, they *had* no
light.
24 [a]I beheld the mountains, and
indeed they trembled,
And all the hills moved back and
forth.
25 I beheld, and indeed *there was* no
man,
And [a]all the birds of the heavens
had fled.
26 I beheld, and indeed the fruitful
land *was* a [a]wilderness,
And all its cities were broken
down
At the presence of the LORD,
By His fierce anger.

27 For thus says the LORD:

"The whole land shall be desolate;
[a]Yet I will not make a full end.
28 For this [a]shall the earth mourn,
And [b]the heavens above be black,
Because I have spoken.
I have [c]purposed and [d]will not
relent,
Nor will I turn back from it.
29 The whole city shall flee from the
noise of the horsemen and
bowmen.
They shall go into thickets and
climb up on the rocks.
Every city *shall be* forsaken,
And not a man shall dwell in it.

30 "And *when* you *are* plundered,
What will you do?
Though you clothe yourself with
crimson,
Though you adorn *yourself* with
ornaments of gold,

[a]Though you enlarge your eyes
with paint,
In vain you will make yourself
fair;
[b]*Your* lovers will despise you;
They will seek your life.

31 "For I have heard a voice as of a
woman in [1]labor,
The anguish as of her who brings
forth her first child,
The voice of the daughter of Zion
bewailing herself;
She [a]spreads her hands, *saying,*
'Woe *is* me now, for my soul is
[2]weary
Because of murderers!'

The Justice of God's Judgment

5 "Run to and fro through the streets
of Jerusalem;
See now and know;
And seek in her open places
[a]If you can find a man,
[b]If there is *anyone* who executes
[1]judgment,
Who seeks the truth,
[c]And I will pardon her.
2 [a]Though they say, '*As* [b]the LORD
lives,'
Surely they [c]swear falsely."

3 O LORD, *are* not [a]Your eyes on
the truth?
You have [b]stricken them,
But they have not grieved;
You have consumed them,
But [c]they have refused to receive
correction.
They have made their faces
harder than rock;
They have refused to return.

4 Therefore I said, "Surely these
are poor.
They are foolish;
For [a]they do not know the way
of the LORD,
The judgment of their God.
5 I will go to the great men and
speak to them,
For [a]they have known the way of
the LORD,
The judgment of their God."

But these have altogether
[b]broken the yoke
And burst the bonds.
6 Therefore [a]a lion from the forest
shall slay them,
[b]A wolf of the deserts shall destroy
them;
[c]A leopard will watch over their
cities.

30 [a]2 Kin. 9:30; Ezek. 23:40 [b]Jer. 22:20, 22; Lam. 1:2, 19; Ezek. 23:9, 10, 22
31 [a]Is. 1:15; Lam. 1:17 [1]*childbirth* [2]*faint*

CHAPTER 5

1 [a]Ezek. 22:30 [b]Gen. 18:23–32 [c]Gen. 18:26 [1]*justice*
2 [a]Is. 48:1; Titus 1:16 [b]Jer. 4:2 [c]Jer. 7:9
3 [a]2 Kin. 25:1; [2 Chr. 16:9; Jer. 16:17] [b]Is. 1:5; 9:13; Jer. 2:30 [c]Is. 9:13; Jer. 7:28; Zeph. 3:2
4 [a]Is. 27:11; Jer. 8:7; Hos. 4:6
5 [a]Mic. 3:1 [b]Ex. 32:25; Ps. 2:3; Jer. 2:20
6 [a]Jer. 4:7 [b]Ps. 104:20; Ezek. 22:27; Hab. 1:8; Zeph. 3:3 [c]Hos. 13:7
7 [a]Josh. 23:7; Jer. 12:16; Zeph. 1:5 [b]Deut. 32:21; Jer. 2:11; Gal. 4:8 [c]Deut. 32:15
8 [a]Jer. 13:27; 29:23; Ezek. 22:11
9 [a]Jer. 9:9
10 [a]Jer. 4:27 [1]*completely destroy*
11 [a]Jer. 3:6, 7, 20
12 [a]2 Chr. 36:16; Jer. 4:10 [b]Is. 28:15; 47:8; Jer. 23:17 [c]Jer. 14:13 [1]*disaster*
14 [a]Is. 24:6; Jer. 1:9; 23:29; Hos. 6:5; Zech. 1:6
15 [a]Deut. 28:49; Is. 5:26; Jer. 1:15; 6:22 [b]Is. 39:3; Jer. 4:16
17 [a]Lev. 26:16; Deut. 28:31, 33; Jer. 8:16; 50:7, 17

Everyone who goes out from
there shall be torn in pieces,
Because their transgressions are
many;
Their backslidings have
increased.

7 "How shall I pardon you for this?
Your children have forsaken Me
And [a]sworn by *those* [b]*that are*
not gods.
[c]When I had fed them to the full,
Then they committed adultery
And assembled themselves by
troops in the harlots' houses.
8 [a]They were *like* well-fed lusty
stallions;
Every one neighed after his
neighbor's wife.
9 Shall I not punish *them* for these
things?" says the LORD.
"And shall I not [a]avenge Myself on
such a nation as this?

10 "Go up on her walls and destroy,
But do not [1]make a [a]complete
end.
Take away her branches,
For they *are* not the LORD's.
11 For [a]the house of Israel and the
house of Judah
Have dealt very treacherously
with Me," says the LORD.

12 [a]They have lied about the LORD,
And said, [b]"*It is* not He.
[c]Neither will [1]evil come upon us,
Nor shall we see sword or famine.
13 And the prophets become wind,
For the word *is* not in them.
Thus shall it be done to them."

14 Therefore thus says the LORD
God of hosts:

"Because you speak this word,
[a]Behold, I will make My words in
your mouth fire,
And this people wood,
And it shall devour them.
15 Behold, I will bring a [a]nation
against you [b]from afar,
O house of Israel," says the LORD.
"It *is* a mighty nation,
It *is* an ancient nation,
A nation whose language you do
not know,
Nor can you understand what
they say.
16 Their quiver *is* like an open tomb;
They *are* all mighty men.
17 And they shall eat up your
[a]harvest and your bread,
Which your sons and daughters
should eat.

They shall eat up your flocks and
your herds;
They shall eat up your vines and
your fig trees;
They shall destroy your fortified
cities,
In which you trust, with the
sword.

18 "Nevertheless in those days,"
says the LORD, "I [a]will not [1]make
a complete end of you.
19 "And it will be when you say,
[a]'Why does the LORD our God do
all these *things* to us?' then you
shall answer them, 'Just as you
have [b]forsaken Me and served for-
eign gods in your land, so [c]you
shall serve aliens in a land *that is*
not yours.'

20 "Declare this in the house of Jacob
And proclaim it in Judah, saying,
21 'Hear this now, O [a]foolish people,
Without [1]understanding,
Who have eyes and see not,
And who have ears and hear not:
22 [a]Do you not fear Me?' says the
LORD.
'Will you not tremble at My
presence,
Who have placed the sand as the
[b]bound of the sea,
By a perpetual decree, that it
cannot pass beyond it?
And though its waves toss to and
fro,
Yet they cannot prevail;
Though they roar, yet they
cannot pass over it.
23 But this people has a defiant and
rebellious heart;
They have revolted and departed.
24 They do not say in their heart,
"Let us now fear the LORD our
God,
[a]Who gives rain, both the [b]former
and the latter, in its season.
[c]He reserves for us the appointed
weeks of the harvest."
25 [a]Your iniquities have turned these
things away,
And your sins have withheld
good from you.

26 'For among My people are found
wicked *men;*
They [a]lie in wait as one who sets
snares;
They set a trap;
They catch men.
27 As a cage is full of birds,
So their houses *are* full of deceit.

18 [a]Jer. 30:11; Amos 9:8 [1]*completely destroy*
19 [a]Deut. 29:24–29; 1 Kin. 9:8, 9; Jer. 13:22; 16:10–13 [b]Jer. 1:16; 2:13 [c]Deut. 28:48; Jer. 16:13
21 [a]Is. 6:9; Jer. 6:10; Ezek. 12:2; Matt. 13:14; John 12:40; Acts 28:26; Rom. 11:8 [1]Lit. *heart*
22 [a]Deut. 28:58; Ps. 119:120; Jer. 2:19; 10:7; [Rev. 15:4] [b]Job 26:10
24 [a]Ps. 147:8; Jer. 14:22; [Matt. 5:45]; Acts 14:17 [b]Deut. 11:14; Joel 2:23; James 5:7 [c][Gen. 8:22]
25 [a]Jer. 3:3
26 [a]Ps. 10:9; Prov. 1:11; Jer. 18:22; Hab. 1:15
28 [a]Deut. 32:15 [b]Is. 1:23; Jer. 7:6; 22:3; Zech. 7:10 [c]Job 12:6; Ps. 73:12 [1]Or *pass over* or *overlook*
29 [a]Jer. 5:9; Mal. 3:5
30 [a]Jer. 23:14; Hos. 6:10; 2 Tim. 4:3
31 [a]Jer. 14:14; Ezek. 13:6 [b]Mic. 2:11

CHAPTER 6

1 [a]Neh. 3:14 [b]Jer. 4:6
3 [a]2 Kin. 25:1–4; Jer. 4:17; 12:10
4 [a]Jer. 51:27; Joel 3:9 [b]Jer. 15:8; Zeph. 2:4
7 [a]Is. 57:20 [1]*gushes*

Therefore they have become
great and grown rich.
28 They have grown [a]fat, they are
sleek;
Yes, they [1]surpass the deeds of
the wicked;
They do not plead [b]the cause,
The cause of the fatherless;
[c]Yet they prosper,
And the right of the needy they
do not defend.
29 [a]Shall I not punish *them* for these
things?' says the LORD.
'Shall I not avenge Myself on such
a nation as this?'

30 "An astonishing and [a]horrible
thing
Has been committed in the land:
31 The prophets prophesy [a]falsely,
And the priests rule by their *own*
power;
And My people [b]love *to have it*
so.
But what will you do in the end?

Impending Destruction from the North

6 "O you children of Benjamin,
Gather yourselves to flee from
the midst of Jerusalem!
Blow the trumpet in Tekoa,
And set up a signal-fire in [a]Beth
Haccerem;
[b]For disaster appears out of the
north,
And great destruction.
2 I have likened the daughter of
Zion
To a lovely and delicate woman.
3 The [a]shepherds with their flocks
shall come to her.
They shall pitch *their* tents
against her all around.
Each one shall pasture in his own
place."

4 "Prepare[a] war against her;
Arise, and let us go up [b]at noon.
Woe to us, for the day goes away,
For the shadows of the evening
are lengthening.
5 Arise, and let us go by night,
And let us destroy her palaces."

6 For thus has the LORD of hosts
said:

"Cut down trees,
And build a mound against
Jerusalem.
This *is* the city to be punished.
She *is* full of oppression in her
midst.
7 [a]As a fountain [1]wells up with
water,

So she wells up with her wickedness.
[b]Violence and plundering are heard in her.
Before Me continually *are* [2]grief and wounds.
8 Be instructed, O Jerusalem,
Lest [a]My soul depart from you;
Lest I make you desolate,
A land not inhabited."

9 Thus says the LORD of hosts:

"They shall thoroughly glean as a vine the remnant of Israel;
As a grape-gatherer, put your hand back into the branches."

10 To whom shall I speak and give warning,
That they may hear?
Indeed their [a]ear *is* uncircumcised,
And they cannot give heed.
Behold, [b]the word of the LORD is a reproach to them;
They have no delight in it.
11 Therefore I am full of the fury of the LORD.
[a]I am weary of holding *it* in.
"I will pour it out [b]on the children outside,
And on the assembly of young men together;
For even the husband shall be taken with the wife,
The aged with *him who is* full of days.
12 And [a]their houses shall be turned over to others,
Fields and wives together;
For I will stretch out My hand
Against the inhabitants of the land," says the LORD.
13 "Because from the least of them even to the greatest of them,
Everyone *is* given to [a]covetousness;
And from the prophet even to the [b]priest,
Everyone deals falsely.
14 They have also [a]healed the [1]hurt of My people [2]slightly,
[b]Saying, 'Peace, peace!'
When *there is* no peace.
15 Were they [a]ashamed when they had committed abomination?
No! They were not at all ashamed;
Nor did they know how to blush.
Therefore they shall fall among those who fall;
At the time I punish them,
They shall be cast down," says the LORD.

7 [b]Ps. 55:9 [2]*sickness*
8 [a]Ezek. 23:18; Hos. 9:12
10 [a]Ex. 6:12; Jer. 5:21; 7:26; [Acts 7:51] [b]Jer. 8:9; 20:8
11 [a]Jer. 20:9 [b]Jer. 9:21
12 [a]Deut. 28:30; Jer. 8:10; 38:22
13 [a]Is. 56:11; Jer. 8:10; 22:17 [b]Jer. 5:31; 23:11; Mic. 3:5, 11
14 [a]Jer. 8:11–15; Ezek. 13:10 [b]Jer. 4:10; 23:17 [1]Lit. *crushing* [2]Superficially
15 [a]Jer. 3:3; 8:12
16 [a]Is. 8:20; Jer. 18:15; Mal. 4:4; Luke 16:29 [b]Matt. 11:29
17 [a]Is. 21:11; 58:1; Jer. 25:4; Ezek. 3:17; Hab. 2:1 [b]Deut. 4:1
19 [a]Is. 1:2 [b]Jer. 19:3, 15 [c]Prov. 1:31
20 [a]Ps. 40:6; 50:7–9; Is. 1:11; 66:3; Amos 5:21; Mic. 6:6, 7 [b]Is. 60:6 [c]Is. 43:24 [d]Jer. 7:21–23
22 [a]Jer. 1:15; 10:22; 50:41–43
23 [a]Is. 5:30
24 [a]Jer. 4:31; 13:21; 49:24 [1]*childbirth*

16 Thus says the LORD:

"Stand in the ways and see,
And ask for the [a]old paths, where the good way *is*,
And walk in it;
Then you will find [b]rest for your souls.
But they said, 'We will not walk *in it.*'
17 Also, I set [a]watchmen over you, *saying*,
[b]'Listen to the sound of the trumpet!'
But they said, 'We will not listen.'
18 Therefore hear, you nations,
And know, O congregation, what *is* among them.
19 [a]Hear, O earth!
Behold, I will certainly bring [b]calamity on this people—
[c]The fruit of their thoughts,
Because they have not heeded My words
Nor My law, but rejected it.
20 [a]For what purpose to Me
Comes frankincense [b]from Sheba,
And [c]sweet cane from a far country?
[d]Your burnt offerings *are* not acceptable,
Nor your sacrifices sweet to Me."

21 Therefore thus says the LORD:

"Behold, I will lay stumbling blocks before this people,
And the fathers and the sons together shall fall on them.
The neighbor and his friend shall perish."

22 Thus says the LORD:

"Behold, a people comes from the [a]north country,
And a great nation will be raised from the farthest parts of the earth.
23 They will lay hold on bow and spear;
They *are* cruel and have no mercy;
Their voice [a]roars like the sea;
And they ride on horses,
As men of war set in array against you, O daughter of Zion."

24 We have heard the report of it;
Our hands grow feeble.
[a]Anguish has taken hold of us,
Pain as of a woman in [1]labor.
25 Do not go out into the field,

Nor walk by the way.
Because of the sword of the enemy,
Fear *is* on every side.
26 O daughter of my people,
[a]Dress in sackcloth
[b]And roll about in ashes!
[c]Make mourning *as for* an only son, most bitter lamentation;
For the plunderer will suddenly come upon us.

27 "I have set you *as* an assayer *and* [a]a fortress among My people,
That you may know and test their way.
28 [a]They *are* all stubborn rebels, [b]walking as slanderers.
They are [c]bronze and iron,
They *are* all corrupters;
29 The bellows blow fiercely,
The lead is consumed by the fire;
The smelter refines in vain,
For the wicked are not drawn off.
30 *People* will call them [a]rejected silver,
Because the LORD has rejected them."

Trusting in Lying Words

7 The word that came to Jeremiah from the LORD, saying,
2 [a]"Stand in the gate of the
LORD's house, and proclaim there
this word, and say, 'Hear the word
of the LORD, all *you of* Judah who
enter in at these gates to worship
the LORD!' "
3 Thus says the LORD of hosts,
the God of Israel: [a]"Amend your
ways and your doings, and I will
cause you to dwell in this place.
4 [a]"Do not trust in these lying
words, saying, 'The temple of the
LORD, the temple of the LORD, the
temple of the LORD *are* these.'
5 "For if you thoroughly amend
your ways and your doings, if you
thoroughly [a]execute [1]judgment be-
tween a man and his neighbor,
6 "*if* you do not oppress the
stranger, the fatherless, and the
widow, and do not shed innocent
blood in this place, [a]or walk after
other gods to your hurt,
7 [a]"then I will cause you to dwell
in this place, in [b]the land that I
gave to your fathers forever and
ever.
8 "Behold, you trust in [a]lying
words that cannot profit.
9 [a]"Will you steal, murder, com-
mit adultery, swear falsely, burn
incense to Baal, and [b]walk after
other gods whom you do not
know,
10 [a]"and *then* come and stand be-
fore Me in this house [b]which is
called by My name, and say, 'We
are delivered to do all these
abominations'?
11 "Has [a]this house, which is
called by My name, become a [b]den
of thieves in your eyes? Behold, I,
even I, have seen *it*," says the
LORD.
12 "But go now to [a]My place
which *was* in Shiloh, [b]where I set
My name at the first, and see [c]what
I did to it because of the wicked-
ness of My people Israel.
13 "And now, because you have
done all these works," says the
LORD, "and I spoke to you, [a]rising
up early and speaking, but you did
not hear, and I [b]called you, but you
did not answer,
14 "therefore I will do to the
house which is called by My name,
in which you trust, and to this
place which I gave to you and your
fathers, as I have done to [a]Shiloh.
15 "And I will cast you out of My
sight, [a]as I have cast out all your
brethren—[b]the whole posterity of
Ephraim.
16 "Therefore [a]do not pray for this
people, nor lift up a cry or prayer
for them, nor make intercession to
Me; [b]for I will not hear you.
17 "Do you not see what they do
in the cities of Judah and in the
streets of Jerusalem?
18 [a]"The children gather wood,
the fathers kindle the fire, and the
women knead dough, to make
cakes for the queen of heaven; and
they [b]pour out drink offerings to
other gods, that they may provoke
Me to anger.
19 [a]"Do they provoke Me to an-
ger?" says the LORD. "*Do they* not
provoke themselves, to the shame
of their own faces?"
20 Therefore thus says the Lord
GOD: "Behold, My anger and My
fury will be poured out on this
place—on man and on beast, on
the trees of the field and on the
fruit of the ground. And it will
burn and not be quenched."
21 Thus says the LORD of hosts,
the God of Israel: [a]"Add your

26 [a]Jer. 4:8 [b]Jer. 25:34; Mic. 1:10 [c]Amos 8:10; [Zech. 12:10]
27 [a]Jer. 1:18
28 [a]Jer. 5:23 [b]Jer. 9:4 [c]Ezek. 22:18
30 [a]Is. 1:22; Jer. 7:29

CHAPTER 7

2 [a]Jer. 17:19; 26:2
3 [a]Jer. 4:1; 18:11; 26:13
4 [a]Jer. 7:8; Mic. 3:11
5 [a]1 Kin. 6:12; Jer. 21:12; 22:3 [1]*justice*
6 [a]Deut. 6:14, 15; Jer. 13:10
7 [a]Deut. 4:40 [b]Jer. 3:18
8 [a]Jer. 5:31; 14:13, 14
9 [a]1 Kin. 18:21; Hos. 4:1, 2; Zeph. 1:5 [b]Ex. 20:3; Jer. 7:6; 19:4
10 [a]Ezek. 23:39 [b]Jer. 7:11, 14; 32:34; 34:15
11 [a]Is. 56:7 [b]Matt. 21:13; Mark 11:17; Luke 19:46
12 [a]Josh. 18:1; Judg. 18:31 [b]Deut. 12:11 [c]1 Sam. 4:10; Ps. 78:60; Jer. 26:6
13 [a]2 Chr. 36:15; Jer. 11:7 [b]Prov. 1:24; Is. 65:12; 66:4
14 [a]1 Sam. 4:10, 11; Ps. 78:60; Jer. 26:6, 9
15 [a]2 Kin. 17:23 [b]Ps. 78:67; Hos. 7:13; 9:13; 12:1
16 [a]Ex. 32:10; Deut. 9:14; Jer. 11:14 [b]Jer. 15:1
18 [a]Jer. 44:17 [b]Jer. 19:13
19 [a]Deut. 32:16, 21
21 [a]Is. 1:11; Jer. 6:20; Hos. 8:13; Amos 5:21, 22

burnt offerings to your sacrifices
and eat meat.
22 [a]"For I did not speak to your
fathers, or command them in the
day that I brought them out of the
land of Egypt, concerning burnt
offerings or sacrifices.
23 "But this is what I commanded
them, saying, [a]'Obey My voice,
and [b]I will be your God, and you
shall be My people. And walk in
all the ways that I have com-
manded you, that it may be well
with you.'
24 [a]"Yet they did not obey or in-
cline their ear, but [b]followed[1] the
counsels *and* the [2]dictates of their
evil hearts, and [c]went[3] backward
and not forward.
25 "Since the day that your fa-
thers came out of the land of Egypt
until this day, I have even [a]sent to
you all My servants the prophets,
daily rising up early and sending
them.
26 [a]"Yet they did not obey Me or
incline their ear, but [b]stiffened
their neck. [c]They did worse than
their fathers.
27 "Therefore [a]you shall speak all
these words to them, but they will
not obey you. You shall also call
to them, but they will not answer
you.

Judgment on Obscene Religion

28 "So you shall say to them, 'This
is a nation that does not obey the
voice of the LORD their God [a]nor
receive correction. [b]Truth has per-
ished and has been cut off from
their mouth.
29 [a]'Cut off your hair and cast *it*
away, and take up a lamentation
on the desolate heights; for the
LORD has rejected and forsaken
the generation of His wrath.'
30 "For the children of Judah have
done evil in My sight," says the
LORD. [a]"They have set their abom-
inations in the house which is
called by My name, to [1]pollute it.
31 "And they have built the [a]high
places of Tophet, which *is* in the
Valley of the Son of Hinnom, to
[b]burn their sons and their daugh-
ters in the fire, [c]which I did not
command, nor did it come into My
heart.
32 "Therefore behold, [a]the days

22 [a][Hos. 6:6]
23 [a]Deut. 6:3 [b][Ex. 19:5, 6]
24 [a]Ps. 81:11 [b]Deut. 29:19 [c]Jer. 32:33 [1]*walked in* [2]*stubbornness* or *imagination* [3]Lit. *they were*
25 [a]2 Chr. 36:15
26 [a]Jer. 11:8 [b]Neh. 9:17 [c]Jer. 16:12
27 [a]Ezek. 2:7
28 [a]Jer. 5:3 [b]Jer. 9:3
29 [a]Mic. 1:16
30 [a]Dan. 9:27; 11:31 [1]*defile*
31 [a]2 Kin. 23:10 [b]Ps. 106:38 [c]Deut. 17:3
32 [a]Jer. 19:6 [b]2 Kin. 23:10
33 [a]Jer. 9:22; 19:11
34 [a]Is. 24:7, 8 [b]Lev. 26:33

CHAPTER 8

2 [a]2 Kin. 23:5 [b]Jer. 22:19
3 [a]Rev. 9:6 [1]*remnant*
5 [a]Jer. 7:24 [b]Jer. 9:6 [c]Jer. 5:3
6 [a]Ps. 14:2 [b]Mic. 7:2

are coming," says the LORD, "when
it will no more be called Tophet,
or the Valley of the Son of Hin-
nom, but the Valley of Slaughter;
[b]for they will bury in Tophet until
there is no room.
33 "The [a]corpses of this people
will be food for the birds of the
heaven and for the beasts of the
earth. And no one will frighten
them away.
34 "Then I will cause to [a]cease
from the cities of Judah and from
the streets of Jerusalem the voice
of mirth and the voice of gladness,
the voice of the bridegroom and
the voice of the bride. For [b]the land
shall be desolate.

8 "At that time," says the LORD,
"they shall bring out the bones
of the kings of Judah, and the
bones of its princes, and the bones
of the priests, and the bones of the
prophets, and the bones of the in-
habitants of Jerusalem, out of their
graves.
2 "They shall spread them before
the sun and the moon and all the
host of heaven, which they have
loved and which they have served
and after which they have walked,
which they have sought and
[a]which they have worshiped. They
shall not be gathered [b]nor buried;
they shall be like refuse on the face
of the earth.
3 "Then [a]death shall be chosen
rather than life by all the [1]residue
of those who remain of this evil
family, who remain in all the
places where I have driven them,"
says the LORD of hosts.

The Peril of False Teaching

4 "Moreover you shall say to
them, 'Thus says the LORD:

"Will they fall and not rise?
Will one turn away and not
return?
5 Why has this people [a]slidden
back,
Jerusalem, in a perpetual
backsliding?
[b]They hold fast to deceit,
[c]They refuse to return.
6 [a]I listened and heard,
But they do not speak aright.
[b]No man repented of his
wickedness,
Saying, 'What have I done?'

Everyone turned to his own
course,
As the horse rushes into the
battle.

7 "Even [a]the stork in the heavens
Knows her appointed times;
And the turtledove, the swift, and
the swallow
Observe the time of their coming.
But [b]My people do not know the
judgment of the LORD.

8 "How can you say, 'We *are* wise,
[a]And the law of the LORD *is* with
us'?
Look, the false pen of the scribe
certainly works falsehood.
9 [a]The wise men are ashamed,
They are dismayed and taken.
Behold, they have rejected the
word of the LORD;
So [b]what wisdom do they have?
10 Therefore [a]I will give their wives
to others,
And their fields to those who will
inherit *them;*
Because from the least even to
the greatest
Everyone is given to
[b]covetousness;
From the prophet even to the
priest
Everyone deals falsely.
11 For they have [a]healed the hurt of
the daughter of My people
[1]slightly,
Saying, [b]'Peace, peace!'
When *there is* no peace.
12 Were they [a]ashamed when they
had committed abomination?
No! They were not at all
ashamed,
Nor did they know how to blush.
Therefore they shall fall among
those who fall;
In the time of their punishment
They shall be cast down," says
the LORD.

13 "I will surely [1]consume them,"
says the LORD.
"No grapes *shall be* [a]on the vine,
Nor figs on the [b]fig tree,
And the leaf shall fade;
And *the things* I have given them
shall [c]pass away from
them." ' "

14 "Why do we sit still?
[a]Assemble yourselves,
And let us enter the fortified
cities,
And let us be silent there.

7 [a]Prov. 6:6–8; Song 2:12; Is. 1:3; Matt. 16:2, 3 [b]Jer. 5:4; 9:3
8 [a]Rom. 2:17
9 [a]Is. 19:11; Jer. 6:15; [1 Cor. 1:27] [b]Is. 44:25; Jer. 4:22
10 [a]Deut. 28:30; Amos 5:11; Zeph. 1:13 [b]Is. 56:11; 57:17; Jer. 6:13
11 [a]Jer. 6:14 [b]Ezek. 13:10 [1]Superficially
12 [a]Ps. 52:1, 7; Is. 3:9; Jer. 3:3; 6:15; Zeph. 3:5
13 [a]Jer. 5:17; 7:20; Joel 1:17 [b]Matt. 21:19; Luke 13:6 [c]Deut. 28:39, 40 [1]Or *take them away*
14 [a]Jer. 4:5 [b]Deut. 29:18; Ps. 69:21; Jer. 9:15; Lam. 3:19; Matt. 27:34 [1]Bitter or poisonous water
15 [a]Jer. 14:19
16 [a]Judg. 18:29; Jer. 4:15 [b]Jer. 47:3
17 [a]Ps. 58:4, 5
19 [a]Is. 39:3; Jer. 5:15
21 [a]Jer. 9:1 [b]Jer. 14:2; Joel 2:6; Nah. 2:10
22 [a]Gen. 37:25; Jer. 46:11

CHAPTER 9

1 [a]Is. 22:4; Jer. 10:19; Lam. 2:18

For the LORD our God has put us
to silence
And given us [b]water[1] of gall to
drink,
Because we have sinned against
the LORD.

15 "*We* [a]looked for peace, but no
good *came;*
And for a time of health, and
there was trouble!
16 The snorting of His horses was
heard from [a]Dan.
The whole land trembled at the
sound of the neighing of His
[b]strong ones;
For they have come and devoured
the land and all that is in it,
The city and those who dwell in
it."

17 "For behold, I will send serpents
among you,
Vipers which cannot be
[a]charmed,
And they shall bite you," says the
LORD.

The Prophet Mourns for the People

18 I would comfort myself in
sorrow;
My heart *is* faint in me.
19 Listen! The voice,
The cry of the daughter of my
people
From [a]a far country:
"*Is* not the LORD in Zion?
Is not her King in her?"

"Why have they provoked Me to
anger
With their carved images—
With foreign idols?"

20 "The harvest is past,
The summer is ended,
And we are not saved!"

21 [a]For the hurt of the daughter of
my people I am hurt.
I am [b]mourning;
Astonishment has taken hold of
me.
22 *Is there* no [a]balm in Gilead,
Is there no physician there?
Why then is there no recovery
For the health of the daughter of
my people?

9 Oh, [a]that my head were waters,
And my eyes a fountain of tears,
That I might weep day and night
For the slain of the daughter of
my people!
2 Oh, that I had in the wilderness

A lodging place for travelers;
That I might leave my people,
And go from them!
For [a]they *are* all adulterers,
An assembly of treacherous men.

3 "And *like* their bow [a]they have
bent their tongues *for* lies.
They are not valiant for the truth
on the earth.
For they proceed from [b]evil to
evil,
And they [c]do not know Me," says
the LORD.
4 "Everyone[a] take heed to his
[1]neighbor,
And do not trust any brother;
For every brother will utterly
supplant,
And every neighbor will [b]walk
with slanderers.
5 Everyone will [a]deceive his
neighbor,
And will not speak the truth;
They have taught their tongue to
speak lies;
They weary themselves to
commit iniquity.
6 Your dwelling place *is* in the
midst of deceit;
Through deceit they refuse to
know Me," says the LORD.

7 Therefore thus says the LORD
of hosts:

"Behold, [a]I will refine them and
[1]try them;
[b]For how shall I deal with the
daughter of My people?
8 Their tongue *is* an arrow shot out;
It speaks [a]deceit;
One speaks [b]peaceably to his
neighbor with his mouth,
But [1]in his heart he [2]lies in wait.
9 [a]Shall I not punish them for these
things?" says the LORD.
"Shall I not avenge Myself on such
a nation as this?"

10 I will take up a weeping and
wailing for the mountains,
And [a]for the [1]dwelling places of
the wilderness a lamentation,
Because they are burned up,
So that no one can pass through;
Nor can *men* hear the voice of the
cattle.
[b]Both the birds of the heavens and
the beasts have fled;
They are gone.

11 "I will make Jerusalem [a]a heap of
ruins, [b]a den of jackals.
I will make the cities of Judah
desolate, without an
inhabitant."

12 [a]Who *is* the wise man who may
understand this? And *who is he* to
whom the mouth of the LORD has
spoken, that he may declare it?
Why does the land perish *and* burn
up like a wilderness, so that no one
can pass through?
13 And the LORD said, "Because
they have forsaken My law which
I set before them, and have [a]not
obeyed My voice, nor walked ac-
cording to it,
14 "but they have [a]walked accord-
ing to the [1]dictates of their own
hearts and after the Baals, [b]which
their fathers taught them,"
15 therefore thus says the LORD of
hosts, the God of Israel: "Behold,
I will [a]feed them, this people, [b]with
wormwood, and give them [1]water
of gall to drink.
16 "I will [a]scatter them also
among the Gentiles, whom neither
they nor their fathers have known.
[b]And I will send a sword after
them until I have consumed them."

The People Mourn in Judgment

17 Thus says the LORD of hosts:

"Consider and call for [a]the
mourning women,
That they may come;
And send for skillful wailing
women,
That they may come.
18 Let them make haste
And take up a wailing for us,
That [a]our eyes may run with
tears,
And our eyelids gush with water.
19 For a voice of wailing is heard
from Zion:
'How we are plundered!
We are greatly ashamed,
Because we have forsaken the
land,
Because we have been cast out
of [a]our dwellings.' "
20 Yet hear the word of the LORD,
O women,
And let your ear receive the word
of His mouth;
Teach your daughters wailing,
And everyone her neighbor a
lamentation.
21 For death has come through our
windows,

2 [a]Jer. 5:7, 8; 23:10; Hos. 4:2
3 [a]Ps. 64:3; Is. 59:4; Jer. 9:8; Hos. 4:1, 2 [b]Jer. 4:22; 13:23 [c]Judg. 2:10; 1 Sam. 2:12; Jer. 4:22; Hos. 4:1; 1 Cor. 15:34
4 [a]Ps. 12:2; Prov. 26:24, 25; Jer. 9:8; Mic. 7:5, 6 [b]Ps. 15:3; Prov. 10:18; Jer. 6:28 [1]*friend*
5 [a]Ps. 36:3, 4; Is. 59:4
7 [a]Is. 1:25; Jer. 6:27; Mal. 3:3 [b]Hos. 11:8 [1]*test*
8 [a]Ps. 12:2 [b]Ps. 55:21 [1]Inwardly he [2]*sets his ambush*
9 [a]Is. 1:24; Jer. 5:9, 29
10 [a]Jer. 4:26; Hos. 4:3 [b]Jer. 4:25; Hos. 4:3 [1]Or *pastures*
11 [a]Is. 25:2; Jer. 19:3, 8; 26:9 [b]Is. 13:22; 34:13
12 [a]Ps. 107:43; Is. 42:23; Hos. 14:9
13 [a]Jer. 3:25; 7:24
14 [a]Jer. 7:24; 11:8; Rom. 1:21–24 [b]Gal. 1:14; 1 Pet. 1:18 [1]*stubbornness* or *imagination*
15 [a]Ps. 80:5 [b]Deut. 29:18; Jer. 8:14; 23:15; Lam. 3:15 [1]Bitter or poisonous water
16 [a]Lev. 26:33; Deut. 28:64; Jer. 15:2–4 [b]Lev. 26:33; Jer. 44:27; Ezek. 5:2
17 [a]2 Chr. 35:25; Job 3:8; Eccl. 12:5; Amos 5:16; Matt. 9:23
18 [a]Is. 22:4; Jer. 9:1; 14:17
19 [a]Lev. 18:28

Has entered our palaces,
To kill off [a]the children—[1]*no longer to be* outside!
And the young men—[2]*no longer* on the streets!

22 Speak, "Thus says the LORD:

'Even the carcasses of men shall fall [a]as refuse on the open field,
Like cuttings after the harvester,
And no one shall gather *them.*' "

23 Thus says the LORD:

[a]"Let not the wise *man* glory in his wisdom,
Let not the mighty *man* glory in his [b]might,
Nor let the rich *man* glory in his riches;
24 But [a]let him who glories glory in this,
That he understands and knows Me,
That I *am* the LORD, exercising lovingkindness, [1]judgment, and righteousness in the earth.
[b]For in these I delight," says the LORD.

25 "Behold, the days are coming,"
says the LORD, "that [a]I will punish
all *who are* circumcised with the
uncircumcised—
26 "Egypt, Judah, Edom, the peo-
ple of Ammon, Moab, and all *who*
are in the [a]farthest corners, who
dwell in the wilderness. For all
these nations *are* uncircumcised,
and all the house of Israel *are*
[b]uncircumcised in the heart."

Idols and the True God

10 Hear the word which the LORD speaks to you, O house of Israel.
2 Thus says the LORD:

[a]"Do not learn the way of the Gentiles;
Do not be dismayed at the signs of heaven,
For the Gentiles are dismayed at them.
3 For the customs of the peoples *are* [1]futile;
For [a]*one* cuts a tree from the forest,
The work of the hands of the workman, with the ax.
4 They decorate it with silver and gold;
They [a]fasten it with nails and hammers
So that it will not topple.
5 They *are* upright, like a palm tree,
And [a]they cannot speak;
They must be [b]carried,
Because they cannot go *by themselves.*
Do not be afraid of them,
For [c]they cannot do evil,
Nor can they do any good."

6 Inasmuch as *there is* none [a]like You, O LORD
(You *are* great, and Your name *is* great in might),
7 [a]Who would not fear You, O King of the nations?
For this is Your rightful due.
For [b]among all the wise *men* of the nations,
And in all their kingdoms,
There is none like You.
8 But they are altogether [a]dull-hearted and foolish;
A wooden idol *is* a [1]worthless doctrine.
9 Silver is beaten into plates;
It is brought from Tarshish,
And [a]gold from Uphaz,
The work of the craftsman
And of the hands of the metalsmith;
Blue and purple *are* their clothing;
They *are* all [b]the work of skillful *men.*
10 But the LORD *is* the true God;
He *is* [a]the living God and the [b]everlasting King.
At His wrath the earth will tremble,
And the nations will not be able to endure His indignation.

11 Thus you shall say to them:
[a]"The gods that have not made the
heavens and the earth [b]shall per-
ish from the earth and from under
these heavens."

12 He [a]has made the earth by His power,
He has [b]established the world by His wisdom,
And [c]has stretched out the heavens at His discretion.
13 [a]When He utters His voice,
There is a [1]multitude of waters in the heavens:
[b]"And He causes the vapors to ascend from the ends of the earth.
He makes lightning for the rain,

21 [a]2 Chr. 36:17; Jer. 6:11; 18:21; Ezek. 9:5, 6 [1]Lit. *from outside* [2]Lit. *from the square*
22 [a]Ps. 83:10; Is. 5:25; Jer. 8:1, 2
23 [a][Eccl. 9:11; Is. 47:10]; Ezek. 28:3–7 [b]Ps. 33:16–18
24 [a]Ps. 20:7; 44:8; Is. 41:16; Jer. 4:2; 1 Cor. 1:31; 2 Cor. 10:17; [Gal. 6:14] [b]Is. 61:8; Mic. 7:18 [1]*justice*
25 [a][Jer. 4:4; Rom. 2:28, 29]
26 [a]Jer. 25:23 [b]Lev. 26:41; Jer. 4:4; 6:10; Ezek. 44:7; [Rom. 2:28]

CHAPTER 10

2 [a][Lev. 18:3; 20:23; Deut. 12:30]
3 [a]Is. 40:19; 45:20 [1]Lit. *vanity*
4 [a]Is. 41:7
5 [a]Ps. 115:5; Is. 46:7; Jer. 10:5; 1 Cor. 12:2 [b]Ps. 115:7; Is. 46:1, 7 [c]Is. 41:23, 24
6 [a]Ex. 15:11; Deut. 33:26; Ps. 86:8, 10; Is. 46:5–9; Jer. 10:16
7 [a]Jer. 5:22; Rev. 15:4 [b]Ps. 89:6
8 [a]Ps. 115:8; Hab. 2:18 [1]*vain teaching*
9 [a]Dan. 10:5 [b]Ps. 115:4
10 [a]1 Tim. 6:17 [b]Ps. 10:16
11 [a]Ps. 96:5 [b]Is. 2:18; Zeph. 2:11
12 [a]Gen. 1:1, 6, 7; Jer. 51:15 [b]Ps. 93:1 [c]Job 9:8; Ps. 104:2; Is. 40:22
13 [a]Job 38:34 [b]Ps. 135:7 [1]Or *noise*

He brings the wind out of His
treasuries."

14 [a]Everyone is [b]dull-hearted,
without knowledge;
[c]Every metalsmith is put to shame
by an image;
[d]For his molded image *is*
falsehood,
And *there is* no breath in them.
15 They *are* futile, a work of errors;
In the time of their punishment
they shall perish.
16 [a]The Portion of Jacob *is* not like
them,
For He *is* the Maker of all *things*,
And [b]Israel *is* the tribe of His
inheritance;
[c]The LORD of hosts *is* His name.

The Coming Captivity of Judah

17 [a]Gather up your wares from the
land,
O [1]inhabitant of the fortress!

18 For thus says the LORD:

"Behold, I will [a]throw out at this
time
The inhabitants of the land,
And will distress them,
[b]That they may find *it so.*"

19 [a]Woe is me for my hurt!
My wound is severe.
But I say, [b]"Truly this *is* an
infirmity,
And [c]I must bear it."
20 [a]My tent is plundered,
And all my cords are broken;
My children have gone from me,
And they *are* [b]no more.
There is no one to pitch my tent
anymore,
Or set up my curtains.

21 For the shepherds have become
dull-hearted,
And have not sought the LORD;
Therefore they shall not prosper,
And all their flocks shall be
[a]scattered.
22 Behold, the noise of the report
has come,
And a great commotion out of the
[a]north country,
To make the cities of Judah
desolate, a [b]den of jackals.

23 O LORD, I know the [a]way of man
is not in himself;
It is not in man who walks to
direct his own steps.
24 O LORD, [a]correct me, but with
justice;
Not in Your anger, lest You bring
me to nothing.
25 [a]Pour out Your fury on the
Gentiles, [b]who do not know
You,
And on the families who do not
call on Your name;
For they have eaten up Jacob,
[c]Devoured him and consumed
him,
And made his dwelling place
desolate.

The Broken Covenant

11 The word that came to Jere-
miah from the LORD, saying,
2 "Hear the words of this cov-
enant, and speak to the men of Ju-
dah and to the inhabitants of Jeru-
salem;
3 "and say to them, 'Thus says
the LORD God of Israel: [a]"Cursed
is the man who does not obey the
words of this covenant
4 "which I commanded your fa-
thers in the day I brought them out
of the land of Egypt, [a]from the iron
furnace, saying, [b]'Obey My voice,
and do according to all that I com-
mand you; so shall you be My peo-
ple, and I will be your God,'
5 "that I may establish the [a]oath
which I have sworn to your fa-
thers, to give them [b]'a land flowing
with milk and honey,' as *it is* this
day."'" And I answered and said,
[1]"So be it, LORD."
6 Then the LORD said to me, "Pro-
claim all these words in the cities
of Judah and in the streets of Jeru-
salem, saying: 'Hear the words of
this covenant [a]and do them.
7 'For I earnestly exhorted your
fathers in the day I brought them
up out of the land of Egypt, until
this day, [a]rising early and exhort-
ing, saying, "Obey My voice."
8 [a]'Yet they did not obey or in-
cline their ear, but [b]everyone [1]fol-
lowed the dictates of his evil heart;
therefore I will bring upon them
all the words of this covenant,
which I commanded *them* to do,
but *which* they have not done.'"
9 And the LORD said to me, [a]"A
conspiracy has been found among
the men of Judah and among the
inhabitants of Jerusalem.
10 "They have turned back to [a]the
iniquities of their forefathers who
refused to hear My words, and
they have gone after other gods to

---

14 [a]Jer. 51:17 [b]Prov. 30:2 [c]Is. 42:17; 44:11 [d]Hab. 2:18
16 [a]Ps. 16:5; Jer. 51:19; Lam. 3:24 [b]Deut. 32:9; Ps. 74:2 [c]Is. 47:4
17 [a]Jer. 6:1 [1]Or *you who dwell under siege*
18 [a]1 Sam. 25:29; 2 Chr. 36:20 [b]Ezek. 6:10
19 [a]Jer. 8:21 [b]Ps. 77:10 [c]Mic. 7:9
20 [a]Jer. 4:20; Lam. 2:4 [b]Jer. 31:15; Lam. 1:5
21 [a]Jer. 23:2
22 [a]Jer. 5:15 [b]Jer. 9:11
23 [a]Prov. 16:1; 20:24
24 [a]Ps. 6:1; 38:1; Jer. 30:11
25 [a]Ps. 79:6, 7; Zeph. 3:8 [b]Job 18:21; 1 Thess. 4:5; [2 Thess. 1:8] [c]Jer. 8:16

CHAPTER 11

3 [a]Deut. 27:26; [Jer. 17:5]; Gal. 3:10
4 [a]Deut. 4:20; 1 Kin. 8:51 [b]Lev. 26:3; Deut. 11:27; Jer. 7:23
5 [a]Ex. 13:5; Deut. 7:12; Ps. 105:9; Jer. 32:22 [b]Ex. 3:8 [1]Heb. *Amen*
6 [a]Deut. 17:19; [Rom. 2:13]; James 1:22
7 [a]Jer. 35:15
8 [a]Jer. 7:26 [b]Jer. 13:10 [1]*walked in the stubbornness* or *imagination*
9 [a]Ezek. 22:25; Hos. 6:9
10 [a]1 Sam. 15:11; Jer. 3:10, 11; Ezek. 20:18

serve them; the house of Israel and
the house of Judah have broken
My covenant which I made with
their fathers."
11 Therefore thus says the LORD:
"Behold, I will surely bring calam-
ity on them which they will not be
able to [1]escape; and [a]though they
cry out to Me, I will not listen to
them.
12 "Then the cities of Judah and
the inhabitants of Jerusalem will
go and [a]cry out to the gods to
whom they offer incense, but they
will not save them at all in the time
of their trouble.
13 "For *according to* the number
of your [a]cities were your gods, O
Judah; and *according to* the num-
ber of the streets of Jerusalem you
have set up altars to *that* shameful
thing, altars to burn incense to
Baal.
14 "So [a]do not pray for this peo-
ple, or lift up a cry or prayer for
them; for I will not hear *them* in
the time that they cry out to Me
because of their trouble.

15 "What[a] has My beloved to do in
My house,
Having [b]done lewd deeds with
many?
And [c]the holy flesh has passed
from you.
When you do evil, then you
[d]rejoice.
16 The LORD called your name,
[a]Green Olive Tree, Lovely *and* of
Good Fruit.
With the noise of a great tumult
He has kindled fire on it,
And its branches are broken.

17 "For the LORD of hosts, [a]who
planted you, has pronounced
doom against you for the evil of
the house of Israel and of the
house of Judah, which they have
done against themselves to pro-
voke Me to anger in offering in-
cense to Baal."

Jeremiah's Life Threatened

18 Now the LORD gave me knowl-
edge *of it*, and I know *it*; for You
showed me their doings.
19 But I *was* like a docile lamb
brought to the slaughter; and I did
not know that they had devised
schemes against me, *saying*, "Let
us destroy the tree with its fruit,

11 [a]Ps. 18:41; Prov. 1:28; Is. 1:15; Jer. 14:12; Ezek. 8:18; Mic. 3:4; Zech. 7:13 [1]Lit. *go out*
12 [a]Deut. 32:37; Jer. 44:17
13 [a]2 Kin. 23:13; Jer. 2:28
14 [a]Ex. 32:10; Jer. 7:16; 14:11; [1 John 5:16]
15 [a]Ps. 50:16 [b]Ezek. 16:25 [c][Titus 1:15] [d]Prov. 2:14
16 [a]Ps. 52:8; [Rom. 11:17]
17 [a]Is. 5:2; Jer. 2:21; 12:2
19 [a]Ps. 83:4; Jer. 18:18 [b]Ps. 27:13
20 [a]1 Sam. 16:7; 1 Chr. 28:9; Ps. 7:9 [b]Jer. 15:15 [1]Most secret parts, lit. *kidneys*
21 [a]Jer. 1:1; 12:5, 6 [b]Is. 30:10; Amos 2:12; Mic. 2:6
22 [a]Jer. 9:21
23 [a]Jer. 23:12; Hos. 9:7; Mic. 7:4

CHAPTER 12

1 [a]Ezra 9:15; Ps. 51:4; Jer. 11:20 [b]Job 12:6; Jer. 5:27, 28; Hab. 1:4; Mal. 3:15
2 [a]Is. 29:13; Ezek. 33:31; Matt. 15:8; Mark 7:6 [1]Most secret parts, lit. *kidneys*
3 [a]Ps. 17:3 [b]Ps. 7:9; 11:5; Jer. 11:20 [c]Jer. 17:18; 50:27; James 5:5
4 [a]Jer. 23:10; Hos. 4:3 [b]Jer. 9:10; Hos. 4:3; Hab. 3:17 [c]Ps. 107:34

[a]and let us cut him off from [b]the
land of the living, that his name
may be remembered no more."

20 But, O LORD of hosts,
You who judge righteously,
[a]Testing the [1]mind and the heart,
Let me see Your [b]vengeance on
them,
For to You I have revealed my
cause.

21 "Therefore thus says the LORD
concerning the men of [a]Anathoth
who seek your life, saying, [b]'Do
not prophesy in the name of the
LORD, lest you die by our hand'—
22 "therefore thus says the LORD
of hosts: 'Behold, I will punish
them. The young men shall die by
the sword, their sons and their
daughters shall [a]die by famine;
23 'and there shall be no remnant
of them, for I will bring catastro-
phe on the men of Anathoth, *even*
[a]the year of their punishment.'"

Jeremiah's Question

12 Righteous [a]*are* You, O LORD,
when I plead with You;
Yet let me talk with You about
Your judgments.
[b]Why does the way of the wicked
prosper?
Why are those happy who deal
so treacherously?
2 You have planted them, yes, they
have taken root;
They grow, yes, they bear fruit.
[a]You *are* near in their mouth
But far from their [1]mind.
3 But You, O LORD, [a]know me;
You have seen me,
And You have [b]tested my heart
toward You.
Pull them out like sheep for the
slaughter,
And prepare them for [c]the day of
slaughter.
4 How long will [a]the land mourn,
And the herbs of every field
wither?
[b]The beasts and birds are
consumed,
[c]For the wickedness of those who
dwell there,
Because they said, "He will not
see our final end."

The LORD Answers Jeremiah

5 "If you have run with the footmen,
and they have wearied you,

Then how can you contend with horses?
And *if* in the land of peace,
In which you trusted, *they* wearied you,
Then how will you do in [a]the [1]floodplain of the Jordan?
6 For even [a]your brothers, the house of your father,
Even they have dealt treacherously with you;
Yes, they have called [1]a multitude after you.
[b]Do not believe them,
Even though they speak [2]smooth words to you.

7 "I have forsaken My house, I have left My heritage;
I have given the dearly beloved of My soul into the hand of her enemies.
8 My heritage is to Me like a lion in the forest;
It cries out against Me;
Therefore I have [a]hated it.
9 My [1]heritage *is* to Me *like* a speckled vulture;
The vultures all around *are* against her.
Come, assemble all the beasts of the field,
[a]Bring them to devour!

10 "Many [a]rulers[1] have destroyed [b]My vineyard,
They have [c]trodden My portion underfoot;
They have made My [2]pleasant portion a desolate wilderness.
11 They have made it [a]desolate;
Desolate, it mourns to Me;
The whole land is made desolate,
Because [b]no one takes *it* to heart.
12 The plunderers have come
On all the desolate heights in the wilderness,
For the sword of the LORD shall devour
From *one* end of the land to the *other* end of the land;
No flesh shall have peace.
13 [a]They have sown wheat but reaped thorns;
They have [1]put themselves to pain *but* do not profit.
But be ashamed of your harvest
Because of the fierce anger of the LORD."

14 Thus says the LORD: "Against
all My evil neighbors who [a]touch
the inheritance which I have
caused My people Israel to in-
herit—behold, I will [b]pluck them
out of their land and pluck out the
house of Judah from among them.
15 [a]"Then it shall be, after I have
plucked them out, that I will return
and have compassion on them
[b]and bring them back, everyone to
his heritage and everyone to his
land.
16 "And it shall be, if they will
learn carefully the ways of My
people, [a]to swear by My name, 'As
the LORD lives,' as they taught My
people to swear by Baal, then they
shall be [b]established in the midst
of My people.
17 "But if they do not [a]obey, I will
utterly pluck up and destroy that
nation," says the LORD.

Symbol of the Linen Sash

13 Thus the LORD said to me:
"Go and get yourself a linen
sash, and put it [1]around your
waist, but do not put it in water."
2 So I got a [1]sash according to
the word of the LORD, and put *it*
around my waist.
3 And the word of the LORD came
to me the second time, saying,
4 "Take the [1]sash that you ac-
quired, which *is* [2]around your
waist, and arise, go to the [3]Eu-
phrates, and hide it there in a hole
in the rock."
5 So I went and hid it by the
Euphrates, as the LORD com-
manded me.
6 Now it came to pass after many
days that the LORD said to me,
"Arise, go to the Euphrates, and
take from there the sash which I
commanded you to hide there."
7 Then I went to the Euphrates
and dug, and I took the [1]sash from
the place where I had hidden it;
and there was the sash, ruined. It
was profitable for nothing.
8 Then the word of the LORD
came to me, saying,
9 "Thus says the LORD: 'In this
manner [a]I will ruin the pride of Ju-
dah and the great [b]pride of Jerusa-
lem.
10 'This evil people, who [a]refuse
to hear My words, who [b]follow[1]
the dictates of their hearts, and
walk after other gods to serve
them and worship them, shall be
just like this sash which is profit-
able for nothing.
11 'For as the sash clings to the

5 [a]Josh. 3:15; 1 Chr. 12:15 [1]Or *thicket*
6 [a]Gen. 37:4–11; Job 6:15; Ps. 69:8; Jer. 9:4, 5 [b]Ps. 12:2; Prov. 26:25 [1]Or *abundantly* [2]Lit. *good*
8 [a]Hos. 9:15; Amos 6:8
9 [a]Lev. 26:22 [1]*inheritance*
10 [a]Jer. 6:3; 23:1 [b]Ps. 80:8–16; Is. 5:1–7 [c]Is. 63:18 [1]Lit. *shepherds* or *pastors* [2]*desired portion* of land
11 [a]Jer. 10:22; 22:6 [b]Is. 42:25
13 [a]Lev. 26:16; Deut. 28:38; Mic. 6:15; Hag. 1:6 [1]Or *strained*
14 [a]Jer. 2:3; 50:11, 12; Zech. 2:8 [b]Deut. 30:3; Ps. 106:47; Is. 11:11–16; Jer. 32:37
15 [a]Jer. 31:20; Lam. 3:32; Ezek. 28:25 [b]Amos 9:14
16 [a][Jer. 4:2]; Zeph. 1:5 [b][Eph. 2:20, 21; 1 Pet. 2:5]
17 [a]Ps. 2:8–12; Is. 60:12

CHAPTER 13

1 [1]Lit. *upon your loins*
2 [1]*waistband*
4 [1]*waistband* [2]Lit. *upon your loins* [3]Heb. *Perath*
7 [1]*waistband*
9 [a]Lev. 26:19 [b][Is. 2:10–17; 23:9]; Zeph. 3:11
10 [a]Jer. 16:12 [b]Jer. 7:24; 16:12 [1]*walk in the stubbornness* or *imagination*

waist of a man, so I have caused
the whole house of Israel and the
whole house of Judah to cling to
Me,' says the LORD, 'that [a]they may
become My people, [b]for renown,
for praise, and for [c]glory; but they
would [d]not hear.'

Symbol of the Wine Bottles

12 "Therefore you shall speak to
them this word: 'Thus says the
LORD God of Israel: "Every bottle
shall be filled with wine."' And
they will say to you, 'Do we not
certainly know that every bottle
will be filled with wine?'
13 "Then you shall say to them,
'Thus says the LORD: "Behold, I
will fill all the inhabitants of this
land—even the kings who sit on
David's throne, the priests, the
prophets, and all the inhabitants
of Jerusalem—[a]with drunkenness!
14 "And [a]I will dash them [1]one
against another, even the fathers
and the sons together," says the
LORD. "I will not pity nor spare nor
have mercy, but will destroy
them."'"

Pride Precedes Captivity

15 Hear and give ear:
Do not be proud,
For the LORD has spoken.
16 [a]Give glory to the LORD your God
Before He causes [b]darkness,
And before your feet stumble
On the dark mountains,
And while you are [c]looking for
light,
He turns it into [d]the shadow of
death
And makes *it* dense darkness.
17 But if you will not hear it,
My soul will [a]weep in secret for
your pride;
My eyes will weep bitterly
And run down with tears,
Because the LORD's flock has
been taken captive.

18 Say to [a]the king and to the queen
mother,
"Humble yourselves;
Sit down,
For your rule shall collapse, the
crown of your glory."
19 The cities of the South shall be
shut up,
And no one shall open *them;*
Judah shall be carried away
captive, all of it;

11 [a][Ex. 19:5, 6; Deut. 32:10, 11] [b]Jer. 33:9 [c]Is. 43:21 [d]Ps. 81:11; Jer. 7:13, 24, 26
13 [a]Ps. 60:3; 75:8; Is. 51:17; 63:6; Jer. 25:27; 51:7, 57
14 [a]2 Chr. 36:17; Ps. 2:9; Is. 9:20, 21; Jer. 19:9–11 [1]Lit. *a man against his brother*
16 [a]Josh. 7:19; Ps. 96:8; Mal. 2:2 [b]Is. 5:30; 8:22; Amos 8:9 [c]Is. 59:9 [d]Ps. 44:19; Jer. 2:6
17 [a]Ps. 119:136; Jer. 9:1; 14:17; Luke 19:41, 42
18 [a]2 Kin. 24:12; Jer. 22:26
20 [a]Jer. 10:22; 46:20
21 [a]Jer. 6:24 [1]*childbirth*
22 [a]Jer. 16:10 [b]Is. 47:2; Ezek. 16:37; Nah. 3:5 [1]Lit. *suffer violence*
24 [a]Lev. 26:33; Jer. 9:16; Ezek. 5:2, 12 [b]Ps. 1:4; Hos. 13:3
25 [a]Job 20:29; Ps. 11:6; Matt. 24:51 [b]Jer. 10:14
26 [a]Lam. 1:8; Ezek. 16:37; Hos. 2:10
27 [a]Jer. 5:7, 8 [b]Is. 65:7; Jer. 2:20; Ezek. 6:13

CHAPTER 14

2 [a]2 Kin. 25:3; Is. 3:26 [b]Jer. 8:21 [c]1 Sam. 5:12; Jer. 11:11; 46:12; Zech. 7:13
3 [a]Job 6:20; Ps. 40:14 [b]2 Sam. 15:30

It shall be wholly carried away
captive.
20 Lift up your eyes and see
Those who come from the [a]north.
Where *is* the flock *that* was given
to you,
Your beautiful sheep?
21 What will you say when He
punishes you?
For you have taught them
To be chieftains, to be head over
you.
Will not [a]pangs seize you,
Like a woman in [1]labor?
22 And if you say in your heart,
[a]"Why have these things come
upon me?"
For the greatness of your iniquity
[b]Your skirts have been uncovered,
Your heels [1]made bare.
23 Can the Ethiopian change his
skin or the leopard its spots?
Then may you also do good who
are accustomed to do evil.

24 "Therefore I will [a]scatter them
[b]like stubble
That passes away by the wind of
the wilderness.
25 [a]This is your lot,
The portion of your measures
from Me," says the LORD,
"Because you have forgotten Me
And trusted in [b]falsehood.
26 Therefore [a]I will uncover your
skirts over your face,
That your shame may appear.
27 I have seen your adulteries
And your *lustful* [a]neighings,
The lewdness of your harlotry,
Your abominations [b]on the hills
in the fields.
Woe to you, O Jerusalem!
Will you still not be made clean?"

Sword, Famine, and Pestilence

14 The word of the LORD that
came to Jeremiah concerning the droughts.

2 "Judah mourns,
And [a]her gates languish;
They [b]mourn for the land,
And [c]the cry of Jerusalem has
gone up.
3 Their nobles have sent their lads
for water;
They went to the cisterns *and*
found no water.
They returned with their vessels
empty;
They were [a]ashamed and
confounded
[b]And covered their heads.
4 Because the ground is parched,

For there was [a]no rain in the land,
The plowmen were ashamed;
They covered their heads.
5 Yes, the deer also gave birth in
the field,
But [1]left because there was no
grass.
6 And [a]the wild donkeys stood in
the desolate heights;
They sniffed at the wind like
jackals;
Their eyes failed because *there*
was no grass."

7 O LORD, though our iniquities
testify against us,
Do it [a]for Your name's sake;
For our backslidings are many,
We have sinned against You.
8 [a]O the Hope of Israel, his Savior
in time of trouble,
Why should You be like a
stranger in the land,
And like a traveler *who* turns
aside to tarry for a night?
9 Why should You be like a man
astonished,
Like a mighty one [a]*who* cannot
save?
Yet You, O LORD, [b]*are* in our
midst,
And we are called by Your name;
Do not leave us!

10 Thus says the LORD to this peo-
ple:

[a]"Thus they have loved to wander;
They have not restrained their
feet.
Therefore the LORD does not
accept them;
[b]He will remember their iniquity
now,
And punish their sins."

11 Then the LORD said to me, [a]"Do
not pray for this people, for *their*
good.
12 [a]"When they fast, I will not
hear their cry; and [b]when they of-
fer burnt offering and grain offer-
ing, I will not accept them. But [c]I
will consume them by the sword,
by the famine, and by the pes-
tilence."
13 [a]Then I said, "Ah, Lord GOD!
Behold, the prophets say to them,
'You shall not see the sword, nor
shall you have famine, but I will
give you [1]assured [b]peace in this
place.'"
14 And the LORD said to me, [a]"The
prophets prophesy lies in My
name. [b]I have not sent them, com-
manded them, nor spoken to them;
they prophesy to you a false vi-
sion, [1]divination, a worthless
thing, and the [c]deceit of their
heart.
15 "Therefore thus says the LORD
concerning the prophets who
prophesy in My name, whom I did
not send, [a]and who say, 'Sword
and famine shall not be in this
land'—'By sword and famine those
prophets shall be consumed!
16 'And the people to whom they
prophesy shall be cast out in the
streets of Jerusalem because of the
famine and the sword; [a]they will
have no one to bury them—them
nor their wives, their sons nor
their daughters—for I will pour
their wickedness on them.'
17 "Therefore you shall say this
word to them:

[a]'Let my eyes flow with tears night
and day,
And let them not cease;
[b]For the virgin daughter of my
people
Has been broken with a mighty
stroke, with a very severe blow.
18 If I go out to [a]the field,
Then behold, those slain with the
sword!
And if I enter the city,
Then behold, those sick from
famine!
Yes, both prophet and [b]priest go
about in a land they do not
know.'"

The People Plead for Mercy

19 [a]Have You utterly rejected Judah?
Has Your soul loathed Zion?
Why have You stricken us so that
[b]*there is* no healing for us?
[c]We looked for peace, but *there*
was no good;
And for the time of healing, and
there was trouble.
20 We acknowledge, O LORD, our
wickedness
And the iniquity of our [a]fathers,
For [b]we have sinned against You.
21 Do not abhor *us*, for Your name's
sake;
Do not disgrace the throne of
Your glory.
[a]Remember, do not break Your
covenant with us.
22 [a]Are there any among [b]the idols
of the nations that can cause
[c]rain?
Or can the heavens give showers?

4 [a]Jer. 3:3; Ezek. 22:24
5 [1]*abandoned* her young
6 [a]Job 39:5, 6; Jer. 2:24
7 [a]Ps. 25:11; Jer. 14:21
8 [a]Jer. 17:13
9 [a]Is. 59:1 [b]Ex. 29:45; Lev. 26:11; Ps. 46:5; Jer. 8:19
10 [a]Jer. 2:23–25 [b][Jer. 44:21–23]; Hos. 8:13
11 [a]Ex. 32:10; Jer. 7:16; 11:14
12 [a]Prov. 1:28; [Is. 1:15; 58:3–6]; Ezek. 8:18; Mic. 3:4; Zech. 7:13 [b]Jer. 6:20 [c]Jer. 9:16
13 [a]Jer. 4:10 [b]Jer. 8:11; 23:17 [1]*true*
14 [a]Jer. 27:10 [b]Jer. 29:8, 9 [c]Jer. 23:16; Ezek. 12:24 [1]Telling the future by signs and omens
15 [a]Jer. 5:12; Ezek. 14:10
16 [a]Ps. 79:2, 3; Jer. 7:32; 15:2, 3
17 [a]Jer. 9:1; 13:17; Lam. 1:16 [b]Is. 37:22; Jer. 8:21; Lam. 1:15; 2:13
18 [a]Jer. 6:25; Lam. 1:20; Ezek. 7:15 [b]Jer. 23:11
19 [a]Jer. 6:30; 7:29; 12:7; Lam. 5:22 [b]Jer. 15:18 [c]Job 30:26; Jer. 8:15; 1 Thess. 5:3
20 [a]Neh. 9:2; Ps. 32:5; Jer. 3:25 [b]Ps. 106:6; Jer. 8:14; 14:7; Dan. 9:8
21 [a]Ps. 106:45
22 [a]Zech. 10:1 [b]Deut. 32:21 [c]1 Kin. 17:1; Jer. 5:24

[d]*Are* You not He, O LORD our God?
Therefore we will wait for You,
Since You have made all these.

The LORD Will Not Relent

15 Then the LORD said to me,
[a]"*Even* if [b]Moses and [c]Sam-
uel stood before Me, My [1]mind
would not *be* favorable toward this
people. Cast *them* out of My sight,
and let them go forth.
2 "And it shall be, if they say to
you, 'Where should we go?' then
you shall tell them, 'Thus says the
LORD:

[a]"Such as *are* for death, to death;
And such as *are* for the sword,
to the sword;
And such as *are* for the famine,
to the famine;
And such as *are* for the [b]captivity,
to the captivity." '

3 "And I will [a]appoint over
them four forms *of destruction*,"
says the LORD: "the sword to slay,
the dogs to drag, [b]the birds of
the heavens and the beasts of the
earth to devour and destroy.
4 "I will hand them over to [a]trou-
ble, to all kingdoms of the earth,
because of [b]Manasseh the son of
Hezekiah, king of Judah, for what
he did in Jerusalem.

5 "For who will have pity on you,
O Jerusalem?
Or who will bemoan you?
Or who will turn aside to ask how
you are doing?
6 [a]You have forsaken Me," says the
LORD,
"You have [b]gone backward.
Therefore I will stretch out My
hand against you and destroy
you;
[c]I am [1]weary of relenting!
7 And I will winnow them with a
winnowing fan in the gates of
the land;
I will [a]bereave *them* of children;
I will destroy My people,
Since they [b]do not return from
their ways.
8 Their widows will be increased to
Me more than the sand of the
seas;
I will bring against them,
Against the mother of the young
men,
A plunderer at noonday;
I will cause anguish and terror to
fall on them [a]suddenly.

22 [d]Ps. 135:7

CHAPTER 15

1 [a]Ps. 99:6; Ezek. 14:14 [b]Ex.32:11–14; Num. 14:13–20; Ps. 99:6 [c]1 Sam. 7:9 [1]Lit. *soul was not toward*

2 [a]Jer. 43:11; Ezek. 5:2, 12; Zech. 11:9; [Rev. 13:10] [b]Jer. 9:16; 16:13

3 [a]Lev. 26:16, 21, 25; Jer. 12:3; Ezek. 14:21 [b]Jer. 7:33

4 [a]Deut. 28:25 [b]2 Kin. 24:3, 4

6 [a]Jer. 2:13 [b]Is. 1:4; Jer. 7:24 [c]Jer. 20:16; Zech. 8:14 [1]*tired*

7 [a]Jer. 18:21; Hos. 9:12–16 [b]Is. 9:13; Jer. 5:3; Amos 4:10, 11

8 [a]Is. 29:5

9 [a]1 Sam. 2:5; Is. 47:9 [b]Jer. 6:4; Amos 8:9

10 [a]Job 3:1; Jer. 20:14 [1]Or *land*

11 [a]Jer. 40:4, 5

13 [a]Ps. 44:12; Is. 52:3

14 [a]Deut. 28:36, 64; Jer. 16:13 [b]Deut. 32:22; Ps. 21:9; Jer. 17:4 [1]So with MT, Vg.; LXX, Syr., Tg. *cause you to serve* (cf. 17:4)

15 [a]Jer. 12:3 [b]Jer. 20:12 [c]Ps. 69:7–9; Jer. 20:8 [1]*attend to*

16 [a]Ezek. 3:1, 3; Rev. 10:9 [b][Job 23:12; Ps. 119:72]

17 [a]Ps. 26:4, 5

9 "She[a] languishes who has borne
seven;
She has breathed her last;
[b]Her sun has gone down
While *it was* yet day;
She has been ashamed and
confounded.
And the remnant of them I will
deliver to the sword
Before their enemies," says the
LORD.

Jeremiah's Dejection

10 [a]Woe is me, my mother,
That you have borne me,
A man of strife and a man of
contention to the whole [1]earth!
I have neither lent for interest,
Nor have men lent to me for
interest.
Every one of them curses me.

11 The LORD said:

"Surely it will be well with your
remnant;
Surely I will cause [a]the enemy to
intercede with you
In the time of adversity and in the
time of affliction.
12 Can anyone break iron,
The northern iron and the
bronze?
13 Your wealth and your treasures
I will give as [a]plunder without
price,
Because of all your sins,
Throughout your territories.
14 And I will [1]make *you* cross over
with your enemies
[a]Into a land *which* you do not
know;
For a [b]fire is kindled in My anger,
Which shall burn upon you."

15 O LORD, [a]You know;
Remember me and [1]visit me,
And [b]take vengeance for me on
my persecutors.
In Your enduring patience, do not
take me away.
Know that [c]for Your sake I have
suffered rebuke.
16 Your words were found, and I
[a]ate them,
And [b]Your word was to me the
joy and rejoicing of my heart;
For I am called by Your name,
O LORD God of hosts.
17 [a]I did not sit in the assembly of
the mockers,
Nor did I rejoice;
I sat alone because of Your hand,
For You have filled me with
indignation.

18 Why is my [a]pain perpetual
And my wound incurable,
Which refuses to be healed?
Will You surely be to me [b]like an
unreliable stream,
As waters *that* [1]fail?

The LORD Reassures Jeremiah

19 Therefore thus says the LORD:

[a]"If you return,
Then I will bring you back;
You shall [b]stand before Me;
If you [c]take out the precious from
the vile,
You shall be as My mouth.
Let them return to you,
But you must not return to them.
20 And I will make you to this
people a fortified bronze [a]wall;
And they will fight against you,
But [b]they shall not prevail against
you;
For I *am* with you to save you
And deliver you," says the LORD.
21 "I will deliver you from the hand
of the wicked,
And I will redeem you from the
grip of the terrible."

Jeremiah's Life-Style and Message

16 The word of the LORD also
came to me, saying,
2 "You shall not take a wife, nor
shall you have sons or daughters
in this place."
3 For thus says the LORD con-
cerning the sons and daughters
who are born in this place, and
concerning their mothers who
bore them and their fathers who
begot them in this land:
4 "They shall die [a]gruesome
deaths; they shall not be [b]la-
mented nor shall they be [c]buried,
but they shall be [d]like refuse on
the face of the earth. They shall
be consumed by the sword and by
famine, and their [e]corpses shall be
meat for the birds of heaven and
for the beasts of the earth."
5 For thus says the LORD: [a]"Do
not enter the house of mourning,
nor go to lament or bemoan them;
for I have taken away My peace
from this people," says the LORD,
"lovingkindness and mercies.
6 "Both the great and the small
shall die in this land. They shall
not be buried; [a]neither shall men
lament for them, [b]cut themselves,
nor [c]make themselves bald for
them.

18 [a]Job 34:6; Jer. 10:19; 30:15; Mic. 1:9 [b]Job 6:15 [1]Or *cannot be trusted*
19 [a]Jer. 4:1; Zech. 3:7 [b]1 Kin. 17:1; Jer. 15:1 [c]Jer. 6:29; Ezek. 22:26; 44:23
20 [a]Jer. 1:18; 6:27; Ezek. 3:9 [b]Ps. 46:7; Is. 41:10; Jer. 1:8, 19; 20:11; 37:21; 38:13; 39:11, 12

CHAPTER 16

4 [a]Jer. 15:2 [b]Jer. 22:18; 25:33 [c]Jer. 14:16; 19:11 [d]Ps. 83:10; Jer. 8:2; 9:22 [e]Ps. 79:2; Is. 18:6; Jer. 7:33; 34:20
5 [a]Ezek. 24:17, 22, 23
6 [a]Jer. 22:18 [b]Lev. 19:28; Deut. 14:1; Jer. 41:5; 47:5 [c]Is. 22:12; Jer. 7:29
7 [a]Prov. 31:6
9 [a]Is. 24:7, 8; Jer. 7:34; 25:10; Ezek. 26:13; Hos. 2:11; Rev. 18:23 [1]*rejoicing*
10 [a]Deut. 29:24; 1 Kin. 9:8; Jer. 5:19
11 [a]Deut. 29:25; 1 Kin. 9:9; 2 Chr. 7:22; Neh. 9:26–29; Jer. 22:9
12 [a]Jer. 7:26 [b]Jer. 3:17; 18:12 [1]*walks after the stubbornness* or *imagination*
13 [a]Deut. 4:26; 28:36, 63 [b]Jer. 15:14
14 [a]Is. 43:18; Jer. 23:7, 8; [Ezek. 37:21–25]
15 [a]Jer. 3:18 [b]Jer. 24:6; 30:3; 32:37
16 [a]Amos 4:2; Hab. 1:15

7 "Nor shall *men* break *bread* in
mourning for them, to comfort
them for the dead; nor shall *men*
give them the cup of consolation
to [a]drink for their father or their
mother.
8 "Also you shall not go into the
house of feasting to sit with them,
to eat and drink."
9 For thus says the LORD of hosts,
the God of Israel: "Behold, [a]I will
cause to cease from this place, be-
fore your eyes and in your days,
the voice of [1]mirth and the voice
of gladness, the voice of the bride-
groom and the voice of the bride.
10 "And it shall be, when you
show this people all these words,
and they say to you, [a]'Why has the
LORD pronounced all this great
disaster against us? Or what *is* our
iniquity? Or what *is* our sin that
we have committed against the
LORD our God?'
11 "then you shall say to them,
[a]'Because your fathers have for-
saken Me,' says the LORD; 'they
have walked after other gods and
have served them and worshiped
them, and have forsaken Me and
not kept My law.
12 'And you have done [a]worse
than your fathers, for behold,
[b]each one [1]follows the dictates of
his own evil heart, so that no one
listens to Me.
13 [a]'Therefore I will cast you out
of this land [b]into a land that you
do not know, neither you nor your
fathers; and there you shall serve
other gods day and night, where I
will not show you favor.'

God Will Restore Israel

14 "Therefore behold, the [a]days
are coming," says the LORD, "that
it shall no more be said, 'The LORD
lives who brought up the children
of Israel from the land of Egypt,'
15 "but, 'The LORD lives who
brought up the children of Israel
from the land of the [a]north and
from all the lands where He had
driven them.' For [b]I will bring
them back into their land which I
gave to their fathers.
16 "Behold, I will send for many
[a]fishermen," says the LORD, "and
they shall fish them; and afterward
I will send for many hunters, and
they shall hunt them from every

mountain and every hill, and out of the holes of the rocks.
17 "For My [a]eyes *are* on all their ways; they are not hidden from My face, nor is their iniquity hidden from My eyes.
18 "And first I will repay [a]double for their iniquity and their sin, because [b]they have defiled My land; they have filled My inheritance with the carcasses of their detestable and abominable idols."

19 O LORD, [a]my strength and my fortress,
[b]My refuge in the day of affliction,
The Gentiles shall come to You
From the ends of the earth and say,
"Surely our fathers have inherited lies,
Worthlessness and [c]unprofitable *things*."
20 Will a man make gods for himself,
[a]Which *are* not gods?

21 "Therefore behold, I will this once cause them to know,
I will cause them to know
My hand and My might;
And they shall know that [a]My name *is* the LORD.

Judah's Sin and Punishment

17 "The sin of Judah *is* [a]written with a [b]pen of iron;
With the point of a diamond *it is* [c]engraved
On the tablet of their heart,
And on the horns of your altars,
2 While their children remember
Their altars and their [a]wooden[1] images
By the green trees on the high hills.
3 O My mountain in the field,
I will give as plunder your wealth, all your treasures,
And your high places of sin within all your borders.
4 And you, even yourself,
Shall let go of your heritage which I gave you;
And I will cause you to serve your enemies
In [a]the land which you do not know;
For [b]you have kindled a fire in My anger *which* shall burn forever."

5 Thus says the LORD:

17 [a]Heb. 4:13
18 [a]Jer. 17:18 [b][Ezek. 43:7]
19 [a]Ps. 18:1, 2 [b]Jer. 17:17 [c]Is. 44:10
20 [a]Gal. 4:8
21 [a]Amos 5:8
CHAPTER 17
1 [a]Jer. 2:22 [b]Job 19:24 [c]2 Cor. 3:3
2 [a]Judg. 3:7 [1]Heb. *Asherim*, Canaanite deities
4 [a]Jer. 16:13 [b]Jer. 15:14
5 [a]Is. 30:1, 2; 31:1 [b]Is. 31:3 [1]Lit. *arm*
6 [a]Jer. 48:6 [b]Job 20:17 [c]Deut. 29:23
7 [a][Is. 30:18]
8 [a][Ps. 1:3] [1]Qr., Tg. *see*
9 [a][Eccl. 9:3] [1]Or *incurably sick*
10 [a]Rev. 2:23 [b]Rom. 2:6 [1]Most secret parts, lit. *kidneys*
11 [a]Ps. 55:23 [b]Luke 12:20 [1]Sits on eggs
13 [a]Jer. 14:8 [b][Is. 1:28] [c]Luke 10:20 [d]Jer. 2:13
14 [a]Deut. 10:21

[a]"Cursed *is* the man who trusts in man
And makes [b]flesh his [1]strength,
Whose heart departs from the LORD.
6 For he shall be [a]like a shrub in the desert,
And [b]shall not see when good comes,
But shall inhabit the parched places in the wilderness,
[c]*In* a salt land *which is* not inhabited.

7 "Blessed[a] *is* the man who trusts in the LORD,
And whose hope is the LORD.
8 For he shall be [a]like a tree planted by the waters,
Which spreads out its roots by the river,
And will not [1]fear when heat comes;
But its leaf will be green,
And will not be anxious in the year of drought,
Nor will cease from yielding fruit.

9 "The [a]heart *is* deceitful above all *things*,
And [1]desperately wicked;
Who can know it?
10 I, the LORD, [a]search the heart,
I test the [1]mind,
[b]Even to give every man according to his ways,
According to the fruit of his doings.

11 "*As* a partridge that [1]broods but does not hatch,
So is he who gets riches, but not by right;
It [a]will leave him in the midst of his days,
And at his end he will be [b]a fool."
12 A glorious high throne from the beginning
Is the place of our sanctuary.
13 O LORD, [a]the hope of Israel,
[b]All who forsake You shall be ashamed.

"Those who depart from Me
Shall be [c]written in the earth,
Because they have forsaken the LORD,
The [d]fountain of living waters."

Jeremiah Prays for Deliverance

14 Heal me, O LORD, and I shall be healed;
Save me, and I shall be saved,
For [a]You *are* my praise.

15 Indeed they say to me,
[a]"Where *is* the word of the LORD?
Let it come now!"
16 As for me, [a]I have not hurried
away from *being* a shepherd
who follows You,
Nor have I desired the woeful
day;
You know what came out of my
lips;
It was right there before You.
17 Do not be a terror to me;
[a]You *are* my hope in the day of
doom.
18 [a]Let them be ashamed who
persecute me,
But [b]do not let me be put to
shame;
Let them be dismayed,
But do not let me be dismayed.
Bring on them the day of doom,
And [c]destroy[1] them with double
destruction!

Hallow the Sabbath Day

19 Thus the LORD said to me: "Go
and stand in the gate of the chil-
dren of the people, by which the
kings of Judah come in and by
which they go out, and in all the
gates of Jerusalem;
20 "and say to them, [a]'Hear the
word of the LORD, you kings of Ju-
dah, and all Judah, and all the in-
habitants of Jerusalem, who enter
by these gates.
21 'Thus says the LORD: [a]"Take
heed to yourselves, and bear no
burden on the Sabbath day, nor
bring *it* in by the gates of Jeru-
salem;
22 "nor carry a burden out of your
houses on the Sabbath day, nor do
any work, but hallow the Sabbath
day, as I [a]commanded your fa-
thers.
23 [a]"But they did not obey nor in-
cline their ear, but [1]made their
neck stiff, that they might not hear
nor receive instruction.
24 "And it shall be, [a]if you heed
Me carefully," says the LORD, "to
bring no burden through the gates
of this city on the [b]Sabbath day,
but hallow the Sabbath day, to do
no work in it,
25 [a]"then shall enter the gates of
this city kings and princes sitting
on the throne of David, riding in
chariots and on horses, they and
their princes, accompanied by the
men of Judah and the inhabitants
of Jerusalem; and this city shall re-
main forever.
26 "And they shall come from the
cities of Judah and from [a]the
places around Jerusalem, from
the land of Benjamin and from
[b]the [1]lowland, from the mountains
and from [c]the [2]South, bringing
burnt offerings and sacrifices,
grain offerings and incense, bring-
ing [d]sacrifices of praise to the
house of the LORD.
27 "But if you will not heed Me
to hallow the Sabbath day, such
as not carrying a burden when en-
tering the gates of Jerusalem on
the Sabbath day, then [a]I will kin-
dle a fire in its gates, [b]and it shall
devour the palaces of Jerusalem,
and it shall not be [c]quenched." ' "

The Potter and the Clay

18 The word which came to
Jeremiah from the LORD,
saying:
2 "Arise and go down to the pot-
ter's house, and there I will cause
you to hear My words."
3 Then I went down to the pot-
ter's house, and there he was,
making something at the [1]wheel.
4 And the vessel that he [1]made
of clay was [2]marred in the hand
of the potter; so he made it again
into another vessel, as it seemed
good to the potter to make.
5 Then the word of the LORD
came to me, saying:
6 "O house of Israel, [a]can I not
do with you as this potter?" says
the LORD. "Look, [b]as the clay *is* in
the potter's hand, so *are* you in My
hand, O house of Israel!
7 "The instant I speak concern-
ing a nation and concerning a
kingdom, to [a]pluck up, to pull
down, and to destroy *it*,
8 [a]"if that nation against whom
I have spoken turns from its evil,
[b]I will relent of the disaster that I
thought to bring upon it.
9 "And the instant I speak con-
cerning a nation and concerning
a kingdom, to build and to plant
it,
10 "if it does evil in My sight so
that it does not obey My voice,
then I will relent concerning the
good with which I said I would
benefit it.
11 "Now therefore, speak to the

15 [a]Is. 5:19; Ezek. 12:22; 2 Pet. 3:4
16 [a]Jer. 1:4–12
17 [a]Jer. 16:19; Nah. 1:7
18 [a]Ps. 35:4; 70:2; Jer. 15:10; 18:18 [b]Ps. 25:2 [c]Jer. 11:20 [1]Lit. *crush*
20 [a]Ps. 49:1, 2; Jer. 19:3, 4
21 [a]Num. 15:32; Neh. 13:19; [John 5:9–12, 17; 7:22–24]
22 [a]Ex. 20:8; 31:13; Ezek. 20:12
23 [a]Jer. 7:24, 26 [1]Were stubborn
24 [a]Jer. 11:4; 26:3 [b]Ex. 16:23–30; 20:8–10; Num. 15:32–36; Deut. 5:12–14; Neh. 13:15; [Is. 58:13]
25 [a]Jer. 22:4
26 [a]Jer. 33:13 [b]Zech. 7:7 [c]Judg. 1:9 [d]Ps. 107:22; 116:17; Jer. 33:11 [1]Heb. *shephelah* [2]Heb. *Negev*
27 [a]Jer. 21:14; Lam. 4:11; Amos 1:4, 7, 10, 12 [b]2 Kin. 25:9; 2 Chr. 36:19; Jer. 39:8; 52:13; Amos 2:5 [c]Jer. 7:20; Ezek. 20:47

CHAPTER 18

3 [1]Potter's wheel
4 [1]*was making* [2]*ruined*
6 [a]Is. 45:9; Rom. 9:20, 21 [b]Is. 64:8
7 [a]Jer. 1:10
8 [a]Jer. 7:3–7; 12:16; [Ezek. 18:21; 33:11] [b][Ps. 106:45]; Jer. 26:3; [Hos. 11:8; Joel 2:13]; Jon. 3:10

men of Judah and to the inhabit-
ants of Jerusalem, saying, 'Thus
says the LORD: "Behold, I am fash-
ioning a disaster and devising a
plan against you. [a]Return now
every one from his evil way, and
make your ways and your doings
[b]good." ' "

God's Warning Rejected

12 And they said, [a]"That is hope-
less! So we will walk according to
our own plans, and we will every
one [1]obey the [b]dictates[2] of his evil
heart."
13 Therefore thus says the LORD:

[a]"Ask now among the Gentiles,
Who has heard such things?
The virgin of Israel has done [b]a
very horrible thing.
14 Will *a man* [1]leave the snow water
of Lebanon,
Which comes from the rock of the
field?
Will the cold flowing waters be
forsaken for strange waters?

15 "Because My people have
forgotten [a]Me,
They have burned incense to
worthless idols.
And they have caused themselves
to stumble in their ways,
From the [b]ancient paths,
To walk in pathways and not on
a highway,
16 To make their land [a]desolate *and*
a perpetual [b]hissing;
Everyone who passes by it will
be astonished
And shake his head.
17 [a]I will scatter them [b]as with an
east wind before the enemy;
[c]I will [1]show them the back and
not the face
In the day of their calamity."

Jeremiah Persecuted

18 Then they said, [a]"Come and let
us devise plans against Jeremiah;
[b]for the law shall not perish from
the priest, nor counsel from the
wise, nor the word from the
prophet. Come and let us attack
him with the tongue, and let us not
give heed to any of his words."

19 Give heed to me, O LORD,
And listen to the voice of those
who contend with me!
20 [a]Shall evil be repaid for good?

11 [a]2 Kin. 17:13; Is. 1:16–19; Jer. 4:1; Acts 26:20 [b]Jer. 7:3–7

12 [a]Is. 57:10; Jer. 2:25 [b]Jer. 3:17; 23:17 [1]Lit. *do* [2]*stubbornness* or *imagination*

13 [a]Is. 66:8; Jer. 2:10, 11; 1 Cor. 5:1 [b]Jer. 5:30; Hos. 6:10

14 [1]*forsake*

15 [a]Jer. 2:13, 32 [b]Jer. 6:16

16 [a]Jer. 19:8 [b]1 Kin. 9:8; Lam. 2:15; Mic. 6:16

17 [a]Jer. 13:24 [b]Ps. 48:7 [c]Jer. 2:27 [1]So with LXX, Syr., Tg., Vg.; MT *look them in*

18 [a]Jer. 11:19 [b]Lev. 10:11; Mal. 2:7; [John 7:48]

20 [a]Ps. 109:4 [b]Ps. 35:7; 57:6; Jer. 5:26 [c]Jer. 14:7—15:1 [1]*concerning*

21 [a]Ps. 109:9–20; Jer. 11:22; 14:16 [b]Jer. 15:7, 8; Ezek. 22:25

23 [a]Neh. 4:5; Ps. 35:14; 109:14; Is. 2:9; Jer. 11:20 [b]Jer. 7:20

CHAPTER 19

2 [a]Josh. 15:8; 2 Kin. 23:10; Jer. 7:31; 32:35

3 [a]Jer. 17:20 [b]1 Sam. 3:11; 2 Kin. 21:12

4 [a]Deut. 28:20; Is. 65:11; Jer. 2:13, 17, 19; 15:6; 17:13 [b]2 Kin. 21:12; Jer. 2:34; 7:6

5 [a]Num. 22:41; Jer. 7:31; 32:35

For they have [b]dug a pit for my
life.
Remember that I [c]stood before
You
To speak good [1]for them,
To turn away Your wrath from
them.
21 Therefore [a]deliver up their
children to the famine,
And pour out their *blood*
By the force of the sword;
Let their wives *become* widows
And [b]bereaved of their children.
Let their men be put to death,
Their young men *be* slain
By the sword in battle.
22 Let a cry be heard from their
houses,
When You bring a troop
suddenly upon them;
For they have dug a pit to take
me,
And hidden snares for my feet.
23 Yet, LORD, You know all their
counsel
Which is against me, to slay *me*.
[a]Provide no atonement for their
iniquity,
Nor blot out their sin from Your
sight;
But let them be overthrown
before You.
Deal *thus* with them
In the time of Your [b]anger.

The Sign of the Broken Flask

19 Thus says the LORD: "Go and
get a potter's earthen flask,
and *take* some of the elders of the
people and some of the elders of
the priests.
2 "And go out to [a]the Valley of
the Son of Hinnom, which *is* by
the entry of the Potsherd Gate; and
proclaim there the words that I
will tell you,
3 [a]"and say, 'Hear the word of
the LORD, O kings of Judah and in-
habitants of Jerusalem. Thus says
the LORD of hosts, the God of Is-
rael: "Behold, I will bring such a
catastrophe on this place, that
whoever hears of it, his ears will
[b]tingle.
4 "Because they [a]have forsaken
Me and made this an alien place,
because they have burned incense
in it to other gods whom neither
they, their fathers, nor the kings
of Judah have known, and have
filled this place with [b]the blood of
the innocents
5 [a]"(they have also built the high

places of Baal, to burn their sons
with fire *for* burnt offerings to
Baal, [b]which I did not command
or speak, nor did it come into My
mind),
6 "therefore behold, the days are
coming," says the LORD, "that this
place shall no more be called To-
phet or [a]the Valley of the Son of
Hinnom, but the Valley of Slaugh-
ter.
7 "And I will make void the
counsel of Judah and Jerusalem in
this place, [a]and I will cause them
to fall by the sword before their
enemies and by the hands of those
who seek their lives; their [b]corpses
I will give as meat for the birds of
the heaven and for the beasts of
the earth.
8 "I will make this city [a]desolate
and a hissing; everyone who
passes by it will be astonished and
hiss because of all its plagues.
9 "And I will cause them to eat
the [a]flesh of their sons and the
flesh of their daughters, and every-
one shall eat the flesh of his friend
in the siege and in the desperation
with which their enemies and
those who seek their lives shall
drive them to despair." '
10 [a]"Then you shall break the
flask in the sight of the men who
go with you,
11 "and say to them, 'Thus says
the LORD of hosts: [a]"Even so I will
break this people and this city, as
one breaks a potter's vessel, which
cannot be [1]made whole again; and
they shall [b]bury *them* in Tophet till
there is no place to bury.
12 "Thus I will do to this place,"
says the LORD, "and to its inhabit-
ants, and make this city like To-
phet.
13 "And the houses of Jerusalem
and the houses of the kings of Ju-
dah shall be defiled [a]like the place
of Tophet, because of all the
houses on whose [b]roofs they have
burned incense to all the host of
heaven, and [c]poured out drink of-
ferings to other gods." ' "
14 Then Jeremiah came from To-
phet, where the LORD had sent him
to prophesy; and he stood in [a]the
court of the Lord's house and said
to all the people,
15 "Thus says the LORD of hosts,
the God of Israel: 'Behold, I will
bring on this city and on all her
towns all the doom that I have pro-
nounced against it, because [a]they
have stiffened their necks that
they might not hear My words.' "

The Word of God to Pashhur

20 Now [a]Pashhur the son of
[b]Immer, the priest who *was*
also chief governor in the house
of the LORD, heard that Jeremiah
prophesied these things.
2 Then Pashhur struck Jeremiah
the prophet, and put him in the
stocks that *were* in the high [a]gate
of Benjamin, which *was* by the
house of the LORD.
3 And it happened on the next
day that Pashhur brought Jere-
miah out of the stocks. Then Jere-
miah said to him, "The LORD has
not called your name Pashhur, but
[1]Magor-Missabib.
4 "For thus says the LORD: 'Be-
hold, I will make you a terror to
yourself and to all your friends;
and they shall fall by the sword
of their enemies, and your eyes
shall see *it*. I will [a]give all Judah
into the hand of the king of Bab-
ylon, and he shall carry them cap-
tive to Babylon and slay them with
the sword.
5 'Moreover I [a]will deliver all the
wealth of this city, all its produce,
and all its precious things; all the
treasures of the kings of Judah I
will give into the hand of their
enemies, who will plunder them,
seize them, and [b]carry them to
Babylon.
6 'And you, Pashhur, and all who
dwell in your house, shall go into
captivity. You shall go to Babylon,
and there you shall die, and be
buried there, you and all your
friends, to whom you have [a]proph-
esied lies.' "

Jeremiah's Unpopular Ministry

7 O LORD, You [1]induced me, and I
was persuaded;
[a]You are stronger than I, and have
prevailed.
[b]I am [2]in derision daily;
Everyone mocks me.
8 For when I spoke, I cried out;
[a]I shouted, "Violence and
plunder!"
Because the word of the LORD
was made to me
A reproach and a derision daily.

5 [b]Lev. 18:21; 2 Kin. 17:17; Ps. 106:37, 38
6 [a]Josh. 15:8; Jer. 7:32
7 [a]Lev. 26:17; Deut. 28:25; Jer. 15:2, 9 [b]Ps. 79:2; Jer. 7:33; 16:4; 34:20
8 [a]Jer. 18:16; 49:13; 50:13
9 [a]Lev. 26:29; Deut. 28:53, 55; Is. 9:20; Lam. 4:10; Ezek. 5:10
10 [a]Jer. 51:63, 64
11 [a]Ps. 2:9; Is. 30:14; Jer. 13:14; Lam. 4:2; Rev. 2:27 [b]Jer. 7:32 [1]*restored*
13 [a]2 Kin. 23:10; Ps. 74:7; 79:1; Jer. 52:13; Ezek. 7:21, 22 [b]2 Kin. 23:12; Jer. 32:29; Zeph. 1:5 [c]Jer. 7:18; Ezek. 20:28
14 [a]2 Chr. 20:5; Jer. 26:2–8
15 [a]Neh. 9:17, 29; Jer. 7:26; 17:23

CHAPTER 20

1 [a]Ezra 2:37, 38 [b]1 Chr. 24:14
2 [a]Jer. 37:13; Zech. 14:10
3 [1]Lit. *Fear on Every Side*
4 [a]Jer. 21:4–10
5 [a]2 Kin. 20:17; 2 Chr. 36:10; Jer. 3:24; 27:21, 22 [b]Is. 39:6
6 [a]Jer. 14:13–15; Lam. 2:14
7 [a]Jer. 1:6, 7 [b]Job 12:4; Lam. 3:14 [1]*enticed* or *persuaded* [2]Lit. *a laughingstock all the day*
8 [a]Jer. 6:7

9 Then I said, "I will not make mention of Him,
Nor speak anymore in His name."
But *His word* was in my heart like a [a]burning fire
Shut up in my bones;
I was weary of holding *it* back,
And [b]I could not.
10 [a]For I heard many [1]mocking:
"Fear on every side!"
"Report," *they say,* "and we will report it!"
[b]All my acquaintances watched for my stumbling, *saying,*
"Perhaps he can be induced;
Then we will prevail against him,
And we will take our revenge on him."

11 But the LORD *is* [a]with me as a mighty, awesome One.
Therefore my persecutors will stumble, and will not [b]prevail.
They will be greatly ashamed, for they will not prosper.
Their [c]everlasting confusion will never be forgotten.
12 But, O LORD of hosts,
You who [a]test the righteous,
And see the [1]mind and heart,
[b]Let me see Your vengeance on them;
For I have pleaded my cause before You.

13 Sing to the LORD! Praise the LORD!
For [a]He has delivered the life of the poor
From the hand of evildoers.

14 [a]Cursed *be* the day in which I was born!
Let the day not be blessed in which my mother bore me!
15 Let the man *be* cursed
Who brought news to my father, saying,
"A male child has been born to you!"
Making him very glad.
16 And let that man be like the cities
Which the LORD [a]overthrew, and did not relent;
Let him [b]hear the cry in the morning
And the shouting at noon,
17 [a]Because he did not kill me from the womb,
That my mother might have been my grave,
And her womb always enlarged *with me.*
18 [a]Why did I come forth from the womb to [b]see [1]labor and sorrow,
That my days should be consumed with shame?

Jerusalem's Doom Is Sealed

21 The word which came to
Jeremiah from the LORD
when [a]King Zedekiah sent to him
[b]Pashhur the son of Melchiah, and
[c]Zephaniah the son of Maaseiah,
the priest, saying,
2 [a]"Please inquire of the LORD for
us, for [1]Nebuchadnezzar king of
Babylon makes war against us.
Perhaps the LORD will deal with us
according to all His wonderful
works, that *the king* may go away
from us."
3 Then Jeremiah said to them,
"Thus you shall say to Zedekiah,
4 'Thus says the LORD God of Is-
rael: "Behold, I will turn back the
weapons of war that *are* in your
hands, with which you fight
against the king of Babylon and
the [1]Chaldeans who besiege you
outside the walls; and [a]I will as-
semble them in the midst of this
city.
5 "I [a]Myself will fight against
you with an [b]outstretched hand
and with a strong arm, even in an-
ger and fury and great wrath.
6 "I will strike the inhabitants of
this city, both man and beast; they
shall die of a great pestilence.
7 "And afterward," says the
LORD, [a]"I will deliver Zedekiah
king of Judah, his servants and the
people, and such as are left in this
city from the pestilence and the
sword and the famine, into the
hand of Nebuchadnezzar king of
Babylon, into the hand of their en-
emies, and into the hand of those
who seek their life; and he shall
strike them with the edge of the
sword. [b]He shall not spare them,
or have pity or mercy." '
8 "Now you shall say to this peo-
ple, 'Thus says the LORD: "Behold,
[a]I set before you the way of life
and the way of death.
9 "He who [a]remains in this city
shall die by the sword, by famine,
and by pestilence; but he who goes
out and [1]defects to the Chaldeans
who besiege you, he shall [b]live,
and his life shall be as a prize to
him.

9 [a]Ps. 39:3 [b]Job 32:18
10 [a]Ps. 31:13 [b]Ps. 41:9; 55:13, 14 [1]*slandering*
11 [a]Jer. 1:18, 19 [b]Jer. 15:20; 17:18 [c]Jer. 23:40
12 [a][Jer. 11:20; 17:10] [b]Ps. 54:7; 59:10 [1]Most secret parts, lit. *kidneys*
13 [a]Ps. 35:9, 10; 109:30, 31
14 [a]Job 3:3
16 [a]Gen. 19:25 [b]Jer. 18:22
17 [a]Job 3:10, 11
18 [a]Job 3:20 [b]Lam. 3:1 [1]*toil*

CHAPTER 21

1 [a]2 Kin. 24:17, 18 [b]Jer. 38:1 [c]2 Kin. 25:18
2 [a]Jer. 37:3, 7 [1]Heb. *Nebuchadrezzar,* and so elsewhere in the book
4 [a]Is. 13:4 [1]Or *Babylonians,* and so elsewhere in the book
5 [a]Is. 63:10 [b]Ex. 6:6
7 [a]Jer. 37:17; 39:5; 52:9 [b]2 Chr. 36:17
8 [a]Deut. 30:15, 19
9 [a]Jer. 38:2 [b]Jer. 39:18 [1]Lit. *falls away to*

10 "For I have [a]set My face
against this city for adversity and
not for good," says the LORD. [b]"It
shall be given into the hand of the
king of Babylon, and he shall
[c]burn it with fire." '

Message to the House of David

11 "And concerning the house of
the king of Judah, *say*, 'Hear the
word of the LORD,
12 'O house of David! Thus says
the LORD:

[a]"Execute[1] judgment [b]in the
morning;
And deliver *him who is* plundered
Out of the hand of the oppressor,
Lest My fury go forth like fire
And burn so that no one can
quench *it*,
Because of the evil of your
doings.

13 "Behold, [a]I *am* against you,
O [1]inhabitant of the valley,
And rock of the plain," says the
LORD,
"Who say, [b]'Who shall come down
against us?
Or who shall enter our
dwellings?'
14 But I will punish you according
to the [a]fruit of your [1]doings,"
says the LORD;
"I will kindle a fire in its forest,
And [b]it shall devour all things
around it." ' "

22

Thus says the LORD: "Go
down to the house of the
king of Judah, and there speak this
word,
2 "and say, [a]'Hear the word of
the LORD, O king of Judah, you
who sit on the throne of David, you
and your servants and your people
who enter these gates!
3 'Thus says the LORD: [a]"Exe-
cute[1] judgment and righteousness,
and deliver the plundered out of
the hand of the oppressor. Do no
wrong and do no violence to the
stranger, the [b]fatherless, or the
widow, nor shed innocent blood in
this place.
4 "For if you indeed do this thing,
[a]then shall enter the gates of this
house, riding on horses and in
chariots, accompanied by servants
and people, kings who sit on the
throne of David.
5 "But if you will not [1]hear these

10 [a]Amos 9:4 [b]Jer. 38:3 [c]Jer. 34:2, 22; 37:10
12 [a]Zech. 7:9 [b]Ps. 101:8 [1]*Dispense justice*
13 [a][Ezek. 13:8] [b]Jer. 49:4 [1]*dweller*
14 [a]Is. 3:10, 11 [b]2 Chr. 36:19 [1]*deeds*

CHAPTER 22

2 [a]Jer. 17:20
3 [a]Jer. 21:12 [b]Jer. 7:6 [1]*Dispense justice*
4 [a]Jer. 17:25
5 [a]Matt. 23:38; Heb. 6:13, 17 [1]Obey
6 [a]Song 4:1
7 [a]Is. 37:24 [b]Jer. 21:14
8 [a]Deut. 29:24–26
9 [a]2 Chr. 34:25
10 [a]2 Kin. 22:20 [b]Jer. 14:17; 22:11
11 [a]1 Chr. 3:15 [b]2 Kin. 23:34 [1]Or *Jehoahaz*
13 [a]2 Kin. 23:35 [b]James 5:4 [1]Lit. *roof chambers, upper chambers*
14 [1]Lit. *roof chambers, upper chambers*

words, [a]I swear by Myself," says
the LORD, "that this house shall be-
come a desolation." ' "
6 For thus says the LORD to the
house of the king of Judah:

"You *are* [a]Gilead to Me,
The head of Lebanon;
Yet I surely will make you a
wilderness,
Cities *which* are not inhabited.
7 I will prepare destroyers against
you,
Everyone with his weapons;
They shall cut down [a]your choice
cedars
[b]And cast *them* into the fire.

8 "And many nations will pass
by this city; and everyone will say
to his neighbor, [a]'Why has the
LORD done so to this great city?'
9 "Then they will answer, [a]'Be-
cause they have forsaken the cov-
enant of the LORD their God, and
worshiped other gods and served
them.' "

10 Weep not for [a]the dead, nor
bemoan him;
Weep bitterly for him [b]who goes
away,
For he shall return no more,
Nor see his native country.

Message to the Sons of Josiah

11 For thus says the LORD con-
cerning [a]Shallum[1] the son of Jo-
siah, king of Judah, who reigned
instead of Josiah his father, [b]who
went from this place: "He shall not
return here anymore,
12 "but he shall die in the place
where they have led him captive,
and shall see this land no more.

13 "Woe[a] to him who builds his house
by unrighteousness
And his [1]chambers by injustice,
[b]*Who* uses his neighbor's service
without wages
And gives him nothing for his
work,
14 Who says, 'I will build myself a
wide house with spacious
[1]chambers,
And cut out windows for it,
Paneling *it* with cedar
And painting *it* with vermilion.'

15 "Shall you reign because you
enclose *yourself* in cedar?
Did not your father eat and drink,

And do justice and
righteousness?
Then [a]*it was* well with him.
16 He [1]judged the cause of the poor
and needy;
Then *it was* well.
Was not this knowing Me?" says
the LORD.
17 "Yet[a] your eyes and your heart *are*
for nothing but your
covetousness,
For shedding innocent blood,
And practicing oppression and
violence."

18 Therefore thus says the LORD
concerning Jehoiakim the son of
Josiah, king of Judah:

[a]"They shall not lament for him,
Saying, [b]'Alas, my brother!' or
'Alas, my sister!'
They shall not lament for him,
Saying, 'Alas, master!' or 'Alas,
his glory!'
19 [a]He shall be buried with the burial
of a donkey,
Dragged and cast out beyond the
gates of Jerusalem.

20 "Go up to Lebanon, and cry out,
And lift up your voice in Bashan;
Cry from Abarim,
For all your lovers are destroyed.
21 I spoke to you in your prosperity,
But you said, 'I will not hear.'
[a]This *has been* your manner from
your youth,
That you did not obey My voice.
22 The wind shall eat up all [a]your
[1]rulers,
And your lovers shall go into
captivity;
Surely then you will be ashamed
and humiliated
For all your wickedness.
23 O inhabitant of Lebanon,
Making your nest in the cedars,
How gracious will you be when
pangs come upon you,
Like [a]the pain of a woman in
[1]labor?

Message to Coniah

24 "As I live," says the LORD,
[a]"though [1]Coniah the son of Je-
hoiakim, king of Judah, [b]were the
[2]signet on My right hand, yet I
would pluck you off;
25 [a]"and I will give you into the
hand of those who seek your life,
and into the hand *of those* whose
face you fear—the hand of Nebu-
chadnezzar king of Babylon and
the hand of the [1]Chaldeans.
26 [a]"So I will cast you out, and
your mother who bore you, into
another country where you were
not born; and there you shall die.
27 "But to the land to which they
desire to return, there they shall
not return.

28 "Is this man [1]Coniah a despised,
broken idol—
[a]A vessel in which *is* no pleasure?
Why are they cast out, he and his
descendants,
And cast into a land which they
do not know?
29 [a]O earth, earth, earth,
Hear the word of the LORD!
30 Thus says the LORD:
'Write this man down as
[a]childless,
A man *who* shall not prosper in
his days;
For [b]none of his descendants
shall prosper,
Sitting on the throne of David,
And ruling anymore in Judah.'"

The Branch of Righteousness

23 "Woe [a]to the shepherds who
destroy and scatter the
sheep of My pasture!" says the
LORD.
2 Therefore thus says the LORD
God of Israel against the shep-
herds who feed My people: "You
have scattered My flock, driven
them away, and not attended to
them. [a]Behold, I will attend to you
for the evil of your doings," says
the LORD.
3 "But [a]I will gather the remnant
of My flock out of all countries
where I have driven them, and
bring them back to their folds; and
they shall be fruitful and increase.
4 "I will set up [a]shepherds over
them who will feed them; and they
shall fear no more, nor be dis-
mayed, nor shall they be lacking,"
says the LORD.

5 "Behold, [a]*the* days are coming,"
says the LORD,
"That I will raise to David a
Branch of righteousness;
A King shall reign and [1]prosper,
[b]And execute [2]judgment and
righteousness in the [3]earth.
6 [a]In His days Judah will be saved,
And Israel [b]will dwell safely;

15 [a]Ps. 128:2
16 [1]Defended
17 [a]Jer. 6:13; 8:10; Ezek. 19:6; [Luke 12:15–20]
18 [a]Jer. 16:4, 6 [b]1 Kin. 13:30
19 [a]1 Kin. 21:23, 24; 2 Chr. 36:6; Jer. 36:30; Dan. 1:2
21 [a]Jer. 3:24, 25; 32:30
22 [a]Jer. 23:1 [1]Lit. *shepherds*
23 [a]Jer. 6:24 [1]*childbirth*
24 [a]2 Kin. 24:6, 8; 1 Chr. 3:16; 2 Chr. 36:9; Jer. 37:1 [b]Song 8:6; Is. 49:16; Hag. 2:23 [1]Or *Jeconiah* or *Jehoiachin* [2]*signet ring*
25 [a]2 Kin. 24:15, 16; Jer. 34:20 [1]Or *Babylonians*
26 [a]2 Kin. 24:15; Jer. 10:18; 16:13
28 [a]Ps. 31:12; Jer. 48:38; Hos. 8:8 [1]See note at v. 24
29 [a]Deut. 32:1; Is. 1:2; 34:1; Mic. 1:2
30 [a]1 Chr. 3:16, 17; Matt. 1:12 [b]Ps. 94:20; Jer. 36:30

CHAPTER 23

1 [a]Is. 56:9–12; Jer. 10:21
2 [a]Ex. 32:34
3 [a]Is. 11:11, 12, 16; Jer. 32:37
4 [a]Jer. 3:15; [Ezek. 34:23]
5 [a]Is. 4:2; 11:1; 40:10, 11; Jer. 33:14; [Dan. 9:24; Zech. 6:12]; Matt. 1:1, 6; Luke 3:31; [John 1:45; 7:42] [b]Ps. 72:2; Is. 9:7; 32:1, 18; [Dan. 9:24] [1]*act wisely* [2]*justice* [3]*land*
6 [a]Deut. 33:28; Jer. 30:10; Zech. 14:11 [b]Jer. 32:37

Now [c]this *is* His name by which
He will be called:

[1]THE LORD OUR
RIGHTEOUSNESS.

7 "Therefore, behold, [a]*the* days
are coming," says the LORD, "that
they shall no longer say, 'As the
LORD lives who brought up the
children of Israel from the land of
Egypt,'
8 "but, 'As the LORD lives who
brought up and led the descen-
dants of the house of Israel from
the north country [a]and from all the
countries where I had driven
them.' And they shall dwell in their
own [b]land."

False Prophets and Empty Oracles

9 My heart within me is broken
Because of the prophets;
[a]All my bones shake.
I am like a drunken man,
And like a man whom wine has
overcome,
Because of the LORD,
And because of His holy words.
10 For [a]the land is full of adulterers;
For [b]because of a curse the land
mourns.
[c]The pleasant places of the
wilderness are dried up.
Their course of life is evil,
And their might *is* not right.

11 "For [a]both prophet and priest are
profane;
Yes, [b]in My house I have found
their wickedness," says the
LORD.
12 "Therefore[a] their way shall be to
them
Like slippery *ways;*
In the darkness they shall be
driven on
And fall in them;
For I [b]will bring disaster on them,
The year of their punishment,"
says the LORD.
13 "And I have seen [1]folly in the
prophets of Samaria:
[a]They prophesied by Baal
And [b]caused My people Israel to
err.
14 Also I have seen a horrible thing
in the prophets of Jerusalem:
[a]They commit adultery and walk
in lies;
They also [b]strengthen the hands
of evildoers,
So that no one turns back from
his wickedness.

6 [c]Is. 45:24; Jer. 33:16; [Dan. 9:24; Rom. 3:22; 1 Cor. 1:30] [1]Heb. *YHWH Tsidkenu*
7 [a]Is. 43:18, 19; Jer. 16:14
8 [a]Is. 43:5, 6; Ezek. 34:13; Amos 9:14, 15 [b]Gen. 12:7; Jer. 16:14, 15; 31:8
9 [a]Jer. 8:18; Hab. 3:16
10 [a]Jer. 9:2 [b]Hos. 4:2; Mal. 3:5 [c]Ps. 107:34; Jer. 9:10
11 [a]Jer. 6:13; Zeph. 3:4 [b]Jer. 7:30; 32:34; Ezek. 8:11; 23:39
12 [a]Ps. 35:6; [Prov. 4:19]; Jer. 13:16 [b]Jer. 11:23
13 [a]1 Kin. 18:18–21; Jer. 2:8 [b]Is. 9:16 [1]Lit. *distastefulness*
14 [a]Jer. 29:23 [b]Jer. 23:22; Ezek. 13:22, 23 [c]Gen. 18:20; Deut. 32:32; Is. 1:9, 10
15 [a]Deut. 29:18; Jer. 9:15 [1]Or *Pollution*
16 [a]Jer. 14:14; Ezek. 13:3, 6
17 [a]Jer. 8:11; Ezek. 13:10; Zech. 10:2 [b]Deut. 29:19; Jer. 3:17 [c]Jer. 5:12; Amos 9:10; Mic. 3:11 [1]*stubbornness* or *imagination*
18 [a]Job 15:8, 9; [Jer. 23:22; 1 Cor. 2:16]
19 [a]Jer. 25:32; 30:23; Amos 1:14
20 [a]2 Kin. 23:26, 27; Jer. 30:24 [b]Gen. 49:1
21 [a]Jer. 14:14; 23:32; 27:15
22 [a]Jer. 25:5

All of them are like [c]Sodom to
Me,
And her inhabitants like
Gomorrah.

15 "Therefore thus says the LORD
of hosts concerning the prophets:

'Behold, I will feed them with
[a]wormwood,
And make them drink the water
of gall;
For from the prophets of
Jerusalem
[1]Profaneness has gone out into all
the land.'"

16 Thus says the LORD of hosts:

"Do not listen to the words of the
prophets who prophesy to you.
They make you worthless;
[a]They speak a vision of their own
heart,
Not from the mouth of the LORD.
17 They continually say to those
who despise Me,
'The LORD has said, [a]"You shall
have peace"';
And *to* everyone who [b]walks
according to the [1]dictates of his
own heart, they say,
[c]'No evil shall come upon you.'"

18 For [a]who has stood in the counsel
of the LORD,
And has perceived and heard His
word?
Who has marked His word and
heard *it?*
19 Behold, a [a]whirlwind of the LORD
has gone forth in fury—
A violent whirlwind!
It will fall violently on the head
of the wicked.
20 The [a]anger of the LORD will not
turn back
Until He has executed and
performed the thoughts of His
heart.
[b]In the latter days you will
understand it perfectly.

21 "I[a] have not sent these prophets,
yet they ran.
I have not spoken to them, yet
they prophesied.
22 But if they had stood in My
counsel,
And had caused My people to
hear My words,
Then they would have [a]turned
them from their evil way
And from the evil of their doings.

23 "*Am* I a God near at hand," says
the LORD,
"And not a God afar off?
24 Can anyone [a]hide himself in
secret places,
So I shall not see him?" says the
LORD;
[b]"Do I not fill heaven and earth?"
says the LORD.

25 "I have heard what the proph-
ets have said who prophesy lies in
My name, saying, 'I have dreamed,
I have dreamed!'
26 "How long will *this* be in the
heart of the prophets who proph-
esy lies? Indeed *they are* prophets
of the deceit of their own heart,
27 "who try to make My people
forget My name by their dreams
which everyone tells his neighbor,
[a]as their fathers forgot My name
for Baal.

28 "The prophet who has a dream, let
him tell a dream;
And he who has My word, let him
speak My word faithfully.
What *is* the chaff to the wheat?"
says the LORD.
29 "*Is* not My word like a [a]fire?" says
the LORD,
"And like a hammer *that* breaks
the rock in pieces?

30 "Therefore behold, [a]I *am*
against the prophets," says the
LORD, "who steal My words every
one from his neighbor.
31 "Behold, I *am* [a]against the
prophets," says the LORD, "who
use their tongues and say, 'He
says.'
32 "Behold, I *am* against those
who prophesy false dreams," says
the LORD, "and tell them, and
cause My people to err by their
[a]lies and by [b]their recklessness. Yet
I did not send them or command
them; therefore they shall not
[c]profit this people at all," says the
LORD.
33 "So when these people or the
prophet or the priest ask you, say-
ing, 'What is [a]the [1]oracle of the
LORD?' you shall then say to them,
[2]'What oracle?' I will even forsake
you," says the LORD.
34 "And *as for* the prophet and the
priest and the people who say,
'The [1]oracle of the LORD!' I will
even punish that man and his
house.
35 "Thus every one of you shall
say to his neighbor, and every one
to his brother, 'What has the LORD
answered?' and, 'What has the
LORD spoken?'
36 "And the [1]oracle of the LORD
you shall mention no more. For
every man's word will be his ora-
cle, for you have [a]perverted the
words of the living God, the LORD
of hosts, our God.
37 "Thus you shall say to the
prophet, 'What has the LORD an-
swered you?' and, 'What has the
LORD spoken?'
38 "But since you say, 'The [1]oracle
of the LORD!' therefore thus says
the LORD: 'Because you say this
word, "The oracle of the LORD!"
and I have sent to you, saying, "Do
not say, 'The oracle of the LORD!' "
39 'therefore behold, I, even I,
[a]will utterly forget you and forsake
you, and the city that I gave you
and your fathers, and *will cast you*
out of My presence.
40 'And I will bring [a]an everlast-
ing reproach upon you, and a per-
petual [b]shame, which shall not be
forgotten.' "

The Sign of Two Baskets of Figs

24 The [a]LORD showed me, and
there were two baskets of
figs set before the temple of the
LORD, after Nebuchadnezzar [b]king
of Babylon had carried away cap-
tive [c]Jeconiah the son of Je-
hoiakim, king of Judah, and the
princes of Judah with the crafts-
men and smiths, from Jerusalem,
and had brought them to Babylon.
2 One basket *had* very good figs,
like the figs *that are* first ripe; and
the other basket *had* very bad figs
which could not be eaten, they
were so [a]bad.
3 Then the LORD said to me,
"What do you see, Jeremiah?"
And I said, "Figs, the good figs,
very good; and the bad, very bad,
which cannot be eaten, they are so
bad."
4 Again the word of the LORD
came to me, saying,
5 "Thus says the LORD, the God
of Israel: 'Like these good figs, so
will I [1]acknowledge those who are
carried away captive from Judah,

---

24 [a][Ps. 139:7]; Amos 9:2, 3 [b][1 Kin. 8:27]; Ps. 139:7
27 [a]Judg. 3:7
29 [a]Jer. 5:14
30 [a]Deut. 18:20; Ps. 34:16; Jer. 14:14, 15; Ezek. 13:8, 9
31 [a]Ezek. 13:9
32 [a]Jer. 20:6; 27:10; Lam. 2:14; 3:37 [b]Zeph. 3:4 [c]Jer. 7:8; Lam. 2:14
33 [a]Is. 13:1; Nah. 1:1; Hab. 1:1; Zech. 9:1; Mal. 1:1 [1]*burden, prophecy* [2]LXX, Tg., Vg. *'You are the burden.'*
34 [1]*burden, prophecy*
36 [a]Deut. 4:2 [1]*burden, prophecy*
38 [1]*burden, prophecy*
39 [a]Hos. 4:6
40 [a]Jer. 20:11; Ezek. 5:14, 15 [b]Mic. 3:5–7

CHAPTER 24

1 [a]Amos 7:1, 4; 8:1 [b]2 Kin. 24:12–16; 2 Chr. 36:10 [c]Jer. 22:24–28; 29:2
2 [a]Is. 5:4, 7; Jer. 29:17
5 [1]*regard*

whom I have sent out of this place
for *their own* good, into the land
of the Chaldeans.
6 'For I will set My eyes on them
for good, and [a]I will bring them
back to this land; [b]I will build
them and not pull *them* down, and
I will plant them and not pluck
them up.
7 'Then I will give them [a]a heart
to know Me, that I *am* the LORD;
and they shall be [b]My people, and
I will be their God, for they shall
return to Me [c]with their whole
heart.
8 'And as the bad [a]figs which
cannot be eaten, they are so bad'—
surely thus says the LORD—'so will
I give up Zedekiah the king of Ju-
dah, his princes, the [b]residue of Je-
rusalem who remain in this land,
and [c]those who dwell in the land
of Egypt.
9 'I will deliver them to [a]trouble
into all the kingdoms of the earth,
for *their* harm, [b]*to be* a reproach
and a byword, a taunt and a curse,
in all places where I shall drive
them.
10 'And I will send the sword, the
famine, and the pestilence among
them, till they are [1]consumed from
the land that I gave to them and
their fathers.' "

Seventy Years of Desolation

25 The word that came to Jere-
miah concerning all the peo-
ple of Judah, [a]in the fourth year
of [b]Jehoiakim the son of Josiah,
king of Judah (which *was* the first
year of Nebuchadnezzar king of
Babylon),
2 which Jeremiah the prophet
spoke to all the people of Judah
and to all the inhabitants of Jeru-
salem, saying:
3 [a]"From the thirteenth year of
Josiah the son of Amon, king of
Judah, even to this day, this *is* the
twenty-third year in which the
word of the LORD has come to me;
and I have spoken to you, rising
early and speaking, [b]but you have
not listened.
4 "And the LORD has sent to you
all His servants the prophets, [a]ris-
ing early and sending *them*, but
you have not listened nor inclined
your ear to hear.
5 "They said, [a]'Repent now every-

6 [a]Jer. 12:15; 29:10 [b]Jer. 32:41; 33:7; 42:10
7 [a][Deut. 30:6] [b]Jer. 30:22; 31:33; 32:38 [c]Jer. 29:13
8 [a]Jer. 29:17 [b]Jer. 39:9 [c]Jer. 44:1, 26–30
9 [a]Deut. 28:25, 37 [b]Ps. 44:13, 14
10 [1]*destroyed*

CHAPTER 25

1 [a]Jer. 36:1 [b]2 Kin. 24:1, 2
3 [a]Jer. 1:2 [b]Jer. 7:13; 11:7, 8, 10
4 [a]Jer. 7:13, 25
5 [a]Jer. 18:11
7 [a]Deut. 32:21
9 [a]Jer. 1:15 [b]Is. 45:1 [c]Jer. 18:16
10 [a]Rev. 18:23 [b]Eccl. 12:4 [1]Lit. *cause to perish from them*
11 [a]Jer. 29:10
12 [a]Ezra 1:1 [b]Is. 13:20 [1]Beginning circa 605 B.C. (2 Kin. 24:1) and ending circa 536 B.C. (Ezra 1:1)
14 [a]Jer. 50:9; 51:27, 28 [b]Jer. 51:27 [c]Jer. 27:7 [d]Jer. 50:29; 51:6, 24
15 [a]Rev. 14:10 [1]*wrath*

one of his evil way and his evil
doings, and dwell in the land that
the LORD has given to you and your
fathers forever and ever.
6 'Do not go after other gods to
serve them and worship them, and
do not provoke Me to anger with
the works of your hands; and I will
not harm you.'
7 "Yet you have not listened to
Me," says the LORD, "that you
might [a]provoke Me to anger with
the works of your hands to your
own hurt.
8 "Therefore thus says the LORD
of hosts: 'Because you have not
heard My words,
9 'behold, I will send and take
[a]all the families of the north,' says
the LORD, 'and Nebuchadnezzar
the king of Babylon, [b]My servant,
and will bring them against this
land, against its inhabitants, and
against these nations all around,
and will utterly destroy them, and
[c]make them an astonishment, a
hissing, and perpetual desolations.
10 'Moreover I will [1]take from
them the [a]voice of mirth and the
voice of gladness, the voice of
the bridegroom and the voice of
the bride, [b]the sound of the mill-
stones and the light of the lamp.
11 'And this whole land shall be
a desolation *and* an astonishment,
and these nations shall serve the
king of Babylon seventy [a]years.
12 'Then it will come to pass,
[a]when [1]seventy years are com-
pleted, *that* I will punish the king
of Babylon and that nation, the
land of the Chaldeans, for their in-
iquity,' says the LORD; [b]'and I will
make it a perpetual desolation.
13 'So I will bring on that land all
My words which I have pro-
nounced against it, all that is writ-
ten in this book, which Jeremiah
has prophesied concerning all the
nations.
14 [a]'(For many nations [b]and great
kings shall [c]be served by them
also; [d]and I will repay them ac-
cording to their deeds and accord-
ing to the works of their own
hands.)' "

Judgment on the Nations

15 For thus says the LORD God of
Israel to me: "Take this [a]wine cup
of [1]fury from My hand, and cause

all the nations, to whom I send
you, to drink it.
16 "And [a]they will drink and stag-
ger and go mad because of the
sword that I will send among
them."
17 Then I took the cup from the
LORD's hand, and made all the na-
tions drink, to whom the LORD had
sent me:
18 Jerusalem and the cities of Ju-
dah, its kings and its princes, to
make them [a]a desolation, an as-
tonishment, a hissing, and [b]a
curse, as *it is* this day;
19 Pharaoh king of Egypt, his ser-
vants, his princes, and all his peo-
ple;
20 all the mixed multitude, all
the kings of [a]the land of Uz, all
the kings of the land of the [b]Phi-
listines (namely, Ashkelon, Gaza,
Ekron, and [c]the remnant of Ash-
dod);
21 [a]Edom, Moab, and the people
of Ammon;
22 all the kings of [a]Tyre, all the
kings of Sidon, and the kings of
the coastlands which *are* across
the [b]sea;
23 [a]Dedan, Tema, Buz, and all
who are in the farthest corners;
24 all the kings of Arabia and all
the kings of the [a]mixed multitude
who dwell in the desert;
25 all the kings of Zimri, all the
kings of [a]Elam, and all the kings
of the [b]Medes;
26 [a]all the kings of the north, far
and near, one with another; and
all the kingdoms of the world
which *are* on the face of the earth.
Also the king of [1]Sheshach shall
drink after them.
27 "Therefore you shall say to
them, 'Thus says the LORD of hosts,
the God of Israel: [a]"Drink, [b]be
drunk, and vomit! Fall and rise no
more, because of the sword which
I will send among you." '
28 "And it shall be, if they refuse
to take the cup from your hand to
drink, then you shall say to them,
'Thus says the LORD of hosts: "You
shall certainly drink!
29 "For behold, [a]I begin to bring
calamity on the city [b]which is
called by My name, and should
you be utterly unpunished? You
shall not be unpunished, for [c]I will
call for a sword on all the inhabit-
ants of the earth," says the LORD
of hosts.'
30 "Therefore prophesy against
them all these words, and say to
them:

'The LORD will [a]roar from on high,
And utter His voice from [b]His
holy habitation;
He will roar mightily against [c]His
fold.
He will give [d]a shout, as those
who tread *the grapes,*
Against all the inhabitants of the
earth.
31 A noise will come to the ends of
the earth—
For the LORD has [a]a controversy
with the nations;
[b]He will plead His case with all
flesh.
He will give those *who are*
wicked to the sword,' says the
LORD."

32 Thus says the LORD of hosts:

"Behold, disaster shall go forth
From nation to nation,
And [a]a great whirlwind shall be
raised up
From the farthest parts of the
earth.

33 [a]"And at that day the slain of
the LORD shall be from *one* end of
the earth even to the *other* end
of the earth. They shall not be [b]la-
mented, [c]or gathered, or buried;
they shall become refuse on the
ground.

34 "Wail,[a] shepherds, and cry!
Roll about *in the ashes,*
You leaders of the flock!
For the days of your slaughter
and your dispersions are
fulfilled;
You shall fall like a precious
vessel.
35 And the shepherds will have no
[1]way to flee,
Nor the leaders of the flock to
escape.
36 A voice of the cry of the
shepherds,
And a wailing of the leaders to
the flock *will be heard.*
For the LORD has plundered their
pasture,
37 And the peaceful dwellings are
cut down
Because of the fierce anger of the
LORD.

16 [a]Jer. 51:7; Ezek. 23:34; Nah. 3:11
18 [a]Jer. 25:9, 11 [b]Jer. 24:9
20 [a]Job 1:1; Lam. 4:21 [b]Jer. 47:1–7; Ezek. 25:16, 17 [c]Is. 20:1
21 [a]Jer. 49:7
22 [a]Jer. 47:4; Zech. 9:2–4 [b]Jer. 49:23
23 [a]Is. 21:13; Jer. 49:7, 8
24 [a]Jer. 25:20; 50:37; Ezek. 30:5
25 [a]Gen. 10:22; Is. 11:11; Jer. 49:34 [b]Is. 13:17; Jer. 51:11, 28
26 [a]Jer. 50:9 [1]A code word for Babylon, Jer. 51:41
27 [a]Jer. 25:16; Hab. 2:16 [b]Is. 63:6
29 [a][Prov. 11:31]; Is. 10:12; Jer. 13:13; Ezek. 9:6; [Luke 23:31; 1 Pet. 4:17] [b]Dan. 9:18 [c]Ezek. 38:21
30 [a]Is. 42:13; Joel 3:16; Amos 1:2 [b]Ps. 11:4 [c]1 Kin. 9:3; Ps. 132:14 [d]Is. 16:9; Jer. 48:33
31 [a]Hos. 4:1; Mic. 6:2 [b]Is. 66:16; Joel 3:2
32 [a]Jer. 23:19; 30:23
33 [a]Is. 34:2, 3; 66:16 [b]Jer. 16:4, 6; Ezek. 39:4, 17 [c]Ps. 79:3; Jer. 8:2; Rev. 11:9
34 [a]Jer. 4:8; 6:26; Ezek. 27:30
35 [1]Or *refuge*

38 He has left His lair like the lion;
For their land is desolate
Because of the fierceness of the
Oppressor,
And because of His fierce anger."

Jeremiah Saved from Death

26 In the beginning of the reign
of Jehoiakim the son of Jo-
siah, king of Judah, this word
came from the LORD, saying,
2 "Thus says the LORD: 'Stand in
[a]the court of the LORD's house, and
speak to all the cities of Judah,
which come to worship *in* the
LORD's house, [b]all the words that
I command you to speak to them.
[c]Do not diminish a word.
3 [a]'Perhaps everyone will listen
and turn from his evil way, that I
may [b]relent concerning the calam-
ity which I purpose to bring on
them because of the evil of their
doings.'
4 "And you shall say to them,
'Thus says the LORD: [a]"If you will
not listen to Me, to walk in My law
which I have set before you,
5 "to heed the words of My ser-
vants the prophets [a]whom I sent
to you, both rising up early and
sending *them* (but you have not
heeded),
6 "then I will make this house
like [a]Shiloh, and will make this
city [b]a curse to all the nations of
the earth." ' "
7 So the priests and the prophets
and all the people heard Jeremiah
speaking these words in the house
of the LORD.
8 Now it happened, when Jere-
miah had made an end of speaking
all that the LORD had commanded
him to speak to all the people, that
the priests and the prophets and
all the people seized him, saying,
"You will surely die!
9 "Why have you prophesied in
the name of the LORD, saying, 'This
house shall be like Shiloh, and this
city shall be [a]desolate, without an
inhabitant'?" And all the people
were gathered against Jeremiah in
the house of the LORD.
10 When the princes of Judah
heard these things, they came up
from the king's house to the house
of the LORD and sat down in the
entry of the New Gate of the
LORD's *house*.
11 And the priests and the proph-
ets spoke to the princes and all the
people, saying, [1]"This man de-
serves to [a]die! For he has prophe-
sied against this city, as you have
heard with your ears."
12 Then Jeremiah spoke to all the
princes and all the people, saying:
"The LORD sent me to prophesy
against this house and against this
city with all the words that you
have heard.
13 "Now therefore, [a]amend your
ways and your doings, and obey
the voice of the LORD your God;
then the LORD will relent concern-
ing the doom that He has pro-
nounced against you.
14 "As for me, here [a]I am, in your
hand; do with me as seems good
and [1]proper to you.
15 "But know for certain that if
you put me to death, you will
surely bring innocent blood on
yourselves, on this city, and on its
inhabitants; for truly the LORD has
sent me to you to speak all these
words in your hearing."
16 So the princes and all the peo-
ple said to the priests and the
prophets, "This man does not de-
serve to die. For he has spoken to
us in the name of the LORD our
God."
17 [a]Then certain of the elders of
the land rose up and spoke to all
the assembly of the people, saying:
18 [a]"Micah of Moresheth prophe-
sied in the days of Hezekiah king
of Judah, and spoke to all the peo-
ple of Judah, saying, 'Thus says
the LORD of hosts:

[b]"Zion shall be plowed *like* a field,
Jerusalem shall become [c]heaps of
ruins,
And the mountain of the [1]temple
Like the [2]bare hills of the
forest." '

19 "Did Hezekiah king of Judah
and all Judah ever put him to
death? [a]Did he not fear the LORD
and [b]seek the LORD's favor? And
the LORD [c]relented concerning the
doom which He had pronounced
against them. [d]But we are doing
great evil against ourselves."
20 Now there was also a man who
prophesied in the name of the
LORD, Urijah the son of Shemaiah

CHAPTER 26
2 [a]2 Chr. 24:20, 21; Jer. 19:14 [b]Deut. 4:2; Jer. 43:1; Ezek. 3:10; Matt. 28:20; [Rev. 22:19] [c]Acts 20:27
3 [a]Is. 1:16–19; Jer. 36:3–7 [b]Jer. 18:8; Jon. 3:9
4 [a]Lev. 26:14, 15; Deut. 28:15; 1 Kin. 9:6; Is. 1:20; Jer. 17:27; 22:5
5 [a]Jer. 25:4; 29:19
6 [a]1 Sam. 4:10, 11; Ps. 78:60; Jer. 7:12, 14 [b]2 Kin. 22:19; Is. 65:15; Jer. 24:9
9 [a]Jer. 9:11
11 [a]Jer. 38:4 [1]Lit. *A judgment of death to this man*
13 [a]Jer. 7:3; [Joel 2:13]; Jon. 3:8
14 [a]Jer. 38:5 [1]*right*
17 [a]Acts 5:34
18 [a]Mic. 1:1 [b]Mic. 3:12 [c]Neh. 4:2; Ps. 79:1; Jer. 9:11 [1]Lit. *house* [2]Lit. *high places*
19 [a]2 Chr. 32:26; Is. 37:1, 4, 15–20 [b]2 Kin. 20:1–19 [c]Ex. 32:14; 2 Sam. 24:16; Jer. 18:8 [d][Acts 5:39]

of Kirjath Jearim, who prophesied
against this city and against this
land according to all the words of
Jeremiah.
21 And when Jehoiakim the king,
with all his mighty men and all the
princes, heard his words, the king
sought to put him to death; but
when Urijah heard *it*, he was
afraid and fled, and went to Egypt.
22 Then Jehoiakim the king sent
men to Egypt: Elnathan the son of
Achbor, and *other* men *who went*
with him to Egypt.
23 And they brought Urijah from
Egypt and brought him to Je-
hoiakim the king, who killed him
with the sword and cast his dead
body into the graves of the [1]com-
mon people.
24 Nevertheless [a]the hand of Ahi-
kam the son of Shaphan was with
Jeremiah, so that they should not
give him into the hand of the peo-
ple to put him to death.

Symbol of the Bonds and Yokes

27 In[1] the beginning of the
reign of [2]Jehoiakim the son
of Josiah, [a]king of Judah, this
word came to Jeremiah from the
LORD, saying,
2 "Thus says the LORD to me:
'Make for yourselves bonds and
yokes, [a]and put them on your
neck,
3 'and send them to the king of
Edom, the king of Moab, the king
of the Ammonites, the king of
Tyre, and the king of Sidon, by the
hand of the messengers who come
to Jerusalem to Zedekiah king of
Judah.
4 'And command them to say to
their masters, "Thus says the LORD
of hosts, the God of Israel—thus
you shall say to your masters:
5 [a]'I have made the earth, the
man and the beast that *are* on the
ground, by My great power and by
My outstretched arm, and [b]have
given it to whom it seemed proper
to Me.
6 [a]'And now I have given all
these lands into the hand of Nebu-
chadnezzar the king of Babylon,
[b]My servant; and [c]the beasts of the
field I have also given him to serve
him.
7 [a]'So all nations shall serve him
and his son and his son's son, [b]un-
til the time of his land comes; [c]and
then many nations and great kings
shall make him serve them.
8 'And it shall be, *that* the nation
and kingdom which will not serve
Nebuchadnezzar the king of Bab-
ylon, and which will not put its neck
under the yoke of the king of
Babylon, that nation I will punish,'
says the LORD, 'with the sword, the
famine, and the pestilence, until I
have consumed them by his hand.
9 'Therefore do not listen to your
prophets, your diviners, your
[1]dreamers, your soothsayers, or
your sorcerers, who speak to you,
saying, "You shall not serve the
king of Babylon."
10 'For they prophesy a [a]lie to you,
to remove you far from your land;
and I will drive you out, and you
will perish.
11 'But the nations that bring their
necks under the yoke of the king
of Babylon and serve him, I will
let them remain in their own land,'
says the LORD, 'and they shall till
it and dwell in it.'"'"
12 I also spoke to [a]Zedekiah king
of Judah according to all these
words, saying, "Bring your necks
under the yoke of the king of
Babylon, and serve him and his
people, and live!
13 [a]"Why will you die, you and
your people, by the sword, by the
famine, and by the pestilence, as
the LORD has spoken against the
nation that will not serve the king
of Babylon?
14 "Therefore [a]do not listen to the
words of the prophets who speak
to you, saying, 'You shall not serve
the king of Babylon,' for they
prophesy [b]a lie to you;
15 "for I have [a]not sent them,"
says the LORD, "yet they prophesy
a lie in My name, that I may drive
you out, and that you may perish,
you and the prophets who proph-
esy to you."
16 Also I spoke to the priests and
to all this people, saying, "Thus
says the LORD: 'Do not listen to
the words of your prophets who
prophesy to you, saying, "Behold,
[a]the vessels of the LORD's house
will now shortly be brought back
from Babylon"; for they prophesy a
lie to you.
17 'Do not listen to them; serve the

23 [1]Lit. *sons of the people*

24 [a]2 Kin. 22:12–14; Jer. 39:14; 40:5–7

CHAPTER 27

1 [a]Jer. 27:3, 12, 20; 28:1 [1]LXX omits v. 1. [2]So with MT, Tg., Vg.; some Heb. mss., Arab., Syr. *Zedekiah* (cf. 27:3, 12; 28:1)

2 [a]Jer. 28:10, 12; Ezek. 4:1; 12:3; 24:3

5 [a]Ps. 115:15; 146:6; Is. 45:12 [b]Deut. 9:29; Ps. 115:16; Jer. 32:17; Dan. 4:17, 25, 32

6 [a]Jer. 28:14 [b]Jer. 25:9; 43:10; Ezek. 29:18, 20 [c]Jer. 28:14; Dan. 2:38

7 [a]2 Chr. 36:20 [b]Jer. 25:12; 50:27; [Dan. 5:26]; Zech. 2:8, 9 [c]Jer. 25:14

9 [1]Lit. *dreams*

10 [a]Jer. 23:16, 32; 28:15

12 [a]Jer. 28:1; 38:17

13 [a][Prov. 8:36]; Jer. 27:8; 38:23; [Ezek. 18:31]

14 [a]Jer. 23:16 [b]Jer. 14:14; 23:21; 29:8, 9; Ezek. 13:22

15 [a]Jer. 23:21; 29:9

16 [a]2 Kin. 24:13; 2 Chr. 36:7, 10; Jer. 28:3; Dan. 1:2

king of Babylon, and live! Why
should this city be laid waste?
18 'But if they *are* prophets, and
if the word of the LORD is with
them, let them now make interces-
sion to the LORD of hosts, that the
vessels which are left in the house
of the LORD, *in* the house of the
king of Judah, and at Jerusalem,
do not go to Babylon.'
19 "For thus says the LORD of
hosts [a]concerning the pillars, con-
cerning the Sea, concerning the
carts, and concerning the remain-
der of the vessels that remain in
this city,
20 "which Nebuchadnezzar king
of Babylon did not take, when he
carried away [a]captive Jeconiah the
son of Jehoiakim, king of Judah,
from Jerusalem to Babylon, and all
the nobles of Judah and Jerusa-
lem—
21 "yes, thus says the LORD of
hosts, the God of Israel, concern-
ing the [a]vessels that remain in the
house of the LORD, and in the
house of the king of Judah and of
Jerusalem:
22 'They shall be [a]carried to Bab-
ylon, and there they shall be until
the day that I [b]visit them,' says the
LORD. 'Then [c]I will bring them up
and restore them to this place.' "

Hananiah's Falsehood and Doom

28 And [a]it happened in the
same year, at the beginning
of the reign of Zedekiah king of
Judah, in the [b]fourth year *and* in
the fifth month, *that* Hananiah the
son of [c]Azur the prophet, who *was*
from Gibeon, spoke to me in the
house of the LORD in the presence
of the priests and of all the people,
saying,
2 "Thus speaks the LORD of
hosts, the God of Israel, saying: 'I
have broken [a]the yoke of the king
of Babylon.
3 [a]'Within two full years I will
bring back to this place all the ves-
sels of the LORD's house, that
Nebuchadnezzar king of Babylon
[b]took away from this place and
carried to Babylon.
4 'And I will bring back to this
place [1]Jeconiah the son of Je-
hoiakim, king of Judah, with all
the captives of Judah who went to
Babylon,' says the LORD, 'for I will
break the yoke of the king of
Babylon.' "
5 Then the prophet Jeremiah
spoke to the prophet Hananiah in
the presence of the priests and in
the presence of all the people who
stood in the house of the LORD,
6 and the prophet Jeremiah said,
[a]"Amen! The LORD do so; the LORD
perform your words which you
have prophesied, to bring back the
vessels of the LORD's house and all
who were carried away captive,
from Babylon to this place.
7 "Nevertheless hear now this
word that I speak in your hearing
and in the hearing of all the peo-
ple:
8 "The prophets who have been
before me and before you of old
prophesied against many coun-
tries and great kingdoms—of war
and disaster and pestilence.
9 "As for [a]the prophet who
prophesies of [b]peace, when the
word of the prophet comes to pass,
the prophet will be known *as* one
whom the LORD has truly sent."
10 Then Hananiah the prophet
took the [a]yoke off the prophet
Jeremiah's neck and broke it.
11 And Hananiah spoke in the
presence of all the people, saying,
"Thus says the LORD: 'Even so I
will break the yoke of Nebuchad-
nezzar king of Babylon [a]from the
neck of all nations within the
space of two full years.' " And
the prophet Jeremiah went his
way.
12 Now the word of the LORD
came to Jeremiah, after Hananiah
the prophet had broken the yoke
from the neck of the prophet Jere-
miah, saying,
13 "Go and tell Hananiah, saying,
'Thus says the LORD: "You have
broken the yokes of wood, but you
have made in their place yokes of
iron."
14 'For thus says the LORD of
hosts, the God of Israel: [a]"I have
put a yoke of iron on the neck of
all these nations, that they may
serve Nebuchadnezzar king of
Babylon; and they shall serve him.
[b]I have given him the beasts of the
field also." ' "
15 Then the prophet Jeremiah
said to Hananiah the prophet,
"Hear now, Hananiah, the LORD

19 [a]1 Kin. 7:15; 2 Kin. 25:13–17; Jer. 52:17, 20, 21
20 [a]2 Kin. 24:14, 15; 2 Chr. 36:10, 18; Jer. 24:1
21 [a]Jer. 20:5
22 [a]2 Kin. 25:13; 2 Chr. 36:18 [b]2 Chr. 36:21; Jer. 29:10; 32:5 [c]Ezra 1:7; 7:19

CHAPTER 28

1 [a]Jer. 27:1 [b]Jer. 51:59 [c]Ezek. 11:1
2 [a]Jer. 27:12
3 [a]Jer. 27:16 [b]2 Kin. 24:13; Dan. 1:2
4 [1]*Jehoiachin*, 2 Kin. 24:12
6 [a]1 Kin. 1:36; Ps. 41:13; Jer. 11:5
9 [a]Deut. 18:22 [b]Jer. 23:17; Ezek. 13:10, 16
10 [a]Jer. 27:2
11 [a]Jer. 27:7
14 [a]Deut. 28:48; Jer. 27:7, 8 [b]Jer. 27:6

has not sent you, but [a]you make
this people trust in a [b]lie.
16 "Therefore thus says the LORD:
'Behold, I will cast you from the
face of the earth. This year you
shall [a]die, because you have
taught [b]rebellion against the
LORD.'"
17 So Hananiah the prophet died
the same year in the seventh
month.

Jeremiah's Letter to the Captives

29 Now these *are* the words of
the letter that Jeremiah the
prophet sent from Jerusalem to the
remainder of the elders who were
[a]carried away captive—to the
priests, the prophets, and all the
people whom Nebuchadnezzar
had carried away captive from Je-
rusalem to Babylon.
2 (This happened after [a]Jeco-
niah[1] the king, the [b]queen mother,
the [2]eunuchs, the princes of Ju-
dah and Jerusalem, the craftsmen,
and the smiths had departed from
Jerusalem.)
3 *The letter was sent* by the hand
of Elasah the son of [a]Shaphan, and
Gemariah the son of Hilkiah,
whom Zedekiah king of Judah
sent to Babylon, to Nebuchadnez-
zar king of Babylon, saying,

4 Thus says the LORD of hosts,
the God of Israel, to all who
were carried away captive,
whom I have caused to be
carried away from Jerusalem
to Babylon:
5 Build houses and dwell *in
them;* plant gardens and eat
their fruit.
6 Take wives and beget sons and
daughters; and take wives for
your sons and give your
daughters to husbands, so that
they may bear sons and
daughters—that you may be
increased there, and not
diminished.
7 And seek the peace of the city
where I have caused you to be
carried away captive, [a]and
pray to the LORD for it; for in
its peace you will have peace.
8 For thus says the LORD of hosts,
the God of Israel: Do not let
your prophets and your
diviners who are in your midst
[a]deceive you, nor listen to your
dreams which you cause to be
dreamed.
9 For they prophesy [a]falsely to
you in My name; I have not
sent them, says the LORD.
10 For thus says the LORD: After
[a]seventy years are completed
at Babylon, I will visit you and
perform My good word toward
you, and cause you to [b]return
to this place.
11 For I know the thoughts that I
think toward you, says the
LORD, thoughts of peace and
not of evil, to give you a future
and a hope.
12 Then you will [a]call upon Me
and go and pray to Me, and I
will [b]listen to you.
13 And [a]you will seek Me and find
Me, when you search for Me
[b]with all your heart.
14 [a]I will be found by you, says
the LORD, and I will bring you
back from your captivity; [b]I
will gather you from all the
nations and from all the places
where I have driven you, says
the LORD, and I will bring you
to the place from which I cause
you to be carried away captive.
15 Because you have said, "The
LORD has raised up prophets
for us in Babylon"—
16 [a]therefore thus says the LORD
concerning the king who sits
on the throne of David,
concerning all the people who
dwell in this city, and
concerning your brethren who
have not gone out with you into
captivity—
17 thus says the LORD of hosts:
Behold, I will send on them the
sword, the famine, and the
pestilence, and will make them
like [a]rotten figs that cannot be
eaten, they are so bad.
18 And I will pursue them with the
sword, with famine, and with
pestilence; and I [a]will deliver
them to trouble among all the
kingdoms of the earth—to be [b]a
curse, an astonishment, a
hissing, and a reproach among
all the nations where I have
driven them,
19 because they have not heeded
My words, says the LORD,
which [a]I sent to them by My

15 [a]Jer. 20:6; 29:31; Lam. 2:14; Ezek. 13:22; Zech. 13:3 [b]Jer. 27:10; 29:9
16 [a]Jer. 20:6 [b]Deut. 13:5; Jer. 29:32

CHAPTER 29

1 [a]Jer. 27:20
2 [a]2 Kin. 24:12–16; 2 Chr. 36:9, 10; Jer. 22:24–28 [b]2 Kin. 24:12, 15; Jer. 13:18 [1]*Jehoiachin,* 2 Kin. 24:12; 2 Chr. 36:10 [2]Or *officers*
3 [a]2 Chr. 34:8
7 [a]Ezra 6:10; Neh. 1:4–11; Dan. 9:16; 1 Tim. 2:2
8 [a]Jer. 14:14; 23:21; 27:14, 15; Eph. 5:6
9 [a]Jer. 28:15; 37:19
10 [a]2 Chr. 36:21–23; Ezra 1:1–4; Jer. 25:12; 27:22; Dan. 9:2; Zech. 7:5 [b][Jer. 24:6, 7]; Zeph. 2:7
12 [a]Ps. 50:15; Jer. 33:3; Dan. 9:3 [b]Ps. 145:19
13 [a]Lev. 26:39–42; Deut. 30:1–3 [b]1 Chr. 22:19; 2 Chr. 22:9; Jer. 24:7
14 [a][Deut. 4:7]; Ps. 32:6; 46:1; [Is. 55:6, 7]; Jer. 24:7 [b]Is. 43:5, 6; Jer. 23:8; 32:37
16 [a]Jer. 38:2, 3, 17–23
17 [a]Jer. 24:3, 8–10
18 [a]Deut. 28:25; 2 Chr. 29:8; Jer. 15:4; 24:9; 34:17; Ezek. 12:15 [b]Jer. 26:6; 42:18
19 [a]Jer. 25:4; 26:5; 35:15

servants the prophets, rising up
early and sending *them;*
neither would you heed, says
the LORD.
20 Therefore hear the word of the
LORD, all you of the captivity,
whom I have sent from
Jerusalem to Babylon.
21 Thus says the LORD of hosts,
the God of Israel, concerning
Ahab the son of Kolaiah, and
Zedekiah the son of Maaseiah,
who prophesy a [a]lie to you in
My name: Behold, I will deliver
them into the hand of
Nebuchadnezzar king of
Babylon, and he shall slay
them before your eyes.
22 [a]And because of them a curse
shall be taken up by all the
captivity of Judah who *are* in
Babylon, saying, "The LORD
make you like Zedekiah and
Ahab, [b]whom the king of
Babylon roasted in the fire";
23 because [a]they have done
disgraceful things in Israel,
have committed adultery with
their neighbors' wives, and
have spoken lying words in My
name, which I have not
commanded them. Indeed I
[b]know, and *am* a witness, says
the LORD.

24 You shall also speak to
Shemaiah the Nehelamite,
saying,
25 Thus speaks the LORD of hosts,
the God of Israel, saying: You
have sent letters in your name
to all the people who *are* at
Jerusalem, [a]to Zephaniah the
son of Maaseiah the priest, and
to all the priests, saying,
26 "The LORD has made you priest
instead of Jehoiada the priest,
so that there should be [a]officers
in the house of the LORD over
every man *who* is [b]demented
and considers himself a
prophet, that you should [c]put
him in prison and in the stocks.
27 Now therefore, why have you
not rebuked Jeremiah of
Anathoth who makes himself a
prophet to you?
28 For he has sent to us *in*
Babylon, saying, 'This
captivity is long; build houses
and dwell *in them,* and plant

21 [a]Jer. 14:14, 15; Lam. 2:14; 2 Pet. 2:1
22 [a]Gen. 48:20; Is. 65:15 [b]Dan. 3:6, 21
23 [a]Jer. 23:14 [b][Prov. 5:21; Jer. 16:17]; Mal. 3:5; [Heb. 4:13]
25 [a]2 Kin. 25:18; Jer. 21:1
26 [a]Jer. 20:1 [b]2 Kin. 9:11; Hos. 9:7; Mark 3:21; John 10:20; Acts 26:24; [2 Cor. 5:13] [c]Jer. 20:1, 2; Acts 16:24
31 [a]Jer. 28:15 [b]Ezek. 13:8–16, 22, 23
32 [a]Jer. 28:16 [1]*descendants,* lit. *seed*

CHAPTER 30

3 [a]Ps. 53:6; Jer. 29:14; 30:18; 32:44; Ezek. 39:25; Amos 9:14; Zeph. 3:20 [b]Jer. 16:15; Ezek. 20:42; 36:24
5 [1]*dread*
6 [a]Jer. 4:31; 6:24 [1]Lit. *male can give birth* [2]*childbirth*
7 [a][Is. 2:12]; Hos. 1:11; Joel 2:11; Amos 5:18; Zeph. 1:14 [b]Lam. 1:12; Dan. 9:12; 12:1

gardens and eat their fruit.'"
29 Now Zephaniah the priest read
this letter in the hearing of
Jeremiah the prophet.
30 Then the word of the LORD
came to Jeremiah, saying:
31 Send to all those in captivity,
saying, Thus says the LORD
concerning Shemaiah the
Nehelamite: Because
Shemaiah has prophesied to
you, [a]and I have not sent him,
and he has caused you to trust
in a [b]lie—
32 therefore thus says the LORD:
Behold, I will punish Shemaiah
the Nehelamite and his [1]family:
he shall not have anyone to
dwell among this people, nor
shall he see the good that I will
do for My people, says the
LORD, [a]because he has taught
rebellion against the LORD.

Restoration of Israel and Judah

30 The word that came to Jere-
miah from the LORD, saying,
2 "Thus speaks the LORD God of
Israel, saying: 'Write in a book for
yourself all the words that I have
spoken to you.
3 'For behold, the days are com-
ing,' says the LORD, 'that [a]I will
bring back from captivity My peo-
ple Israel and Judah,' says the
LORD. [b]'And I will cause them to
return to the land that I gave to
their fathers, and they shall pos-
sess it.'"
4 Now these *are* the words that
the LORD spoke concerning Israel
and Judah.
5 "For thus says the LORD:

'We have heard a voice of
trembling,
Of [1]fear, and not of peace.
6 Ask now, and see,
Whether a [1]man is ever in [2]labor
with child?
So why do I see every man *with*
his hands on his loins
[a]Like a woman in labor,
And all faces turned pale?
7 [a]Alas! For that day *is* great,
[b]So that none *is* like it;
And it *is* the time of Jacob's
trouble,
But he shall be saved out of it.
8 'For it shall come to pass in that
day,'

Says the LORD of hosts,
'*That* I will break his yoke from your neck,
And will burst your bonds;
Foreigners shall no more enslave them.
9 But they shall serve the LORD their God,
And [a]David their king,
Whom I will [b]raise up for them.

10 'Therefore [a]do not fear, O My servant Jacob,' says the LORD,
'Nor be dismayed, O Israel;
For behold, I will save you from afar,
And your seed [b]from the land of their captivity.
Jacob shall return, have rest and be quiet,
And no one shall make *him* afraid.
11 For I *am* with [a]you,' says the LORD, 'to save you;
[b]Though I make a full end of all nations where I have scattered you,
[c]Yet I will not make a complete end of you.
But I will correct you [d]in justice,
And will not let you go altogether unpunished.'

12 "For thus says the LORD:

[a]'Your affliction *is* incurable,
Your wound *is* severe.
13 *There is* no one to plead your cause,
That you may be bound up;
[a]You have no healing medicines.
14 [a]All your lovers have forgotten you;
They do not seek you;
For I have wounded you with the wound [b]of an enemy,
With the chastisement [c]of a cruel one,
For the multitude of your iniquities,
[d]*Because* your sins have increased.
15 Why [a]do you cry about your affliction?
Your sorrow *is* incurable.
Because of the multitude of your iniquities,
Because your sins have increased,
I have done these things to you.

16 'Therefore all those who devour you [a]shall be devoured;
And all your adversaries, every one of them, shall go into [b]captivity;
Those who plunder you shall become [c]plunder,
And all who prey upon you I will make a [d]prey.
17 [a]For I will restore health to you
And heal you of your wounds,' says the LORD,
'Because they called you an outcast *saying*:
"This *is* Zion;
No one seeks her." '

18 "Thus says the LORD:

'Behold, I will bring back the captivity of Jacob's tents,
And [a]have mercy on his dwelling places;
The city shall be built upon its own [1]mound,
And the palace shall remain according to its own plan.
19 Then [a]out of them shall proceed thanksgiving
And the voice of those who make merry;
[b]I will multiply them, and they shall not diminish;
I will also glorify them, and they shall not be small.
20 Their children also shall be [a]as before,
And their congregation shall be established before Me;
And I will punish all who oppress them.
21 Their nobles shall be from among them,
[a]And their governor shall come from their midst;
Then I will [b]cause him to draw near,
And he shall approach Me;
For who *is* this who pledged his heart to approach Me?' says the LORD.
22 'You shall be [a]My people,
And I will be your God.' "

23 Behold, the [a]whirlwind of the LORD
Goes forth with fury,
A [1]continuing whirlwind;
It will fall violently on the head of the wicked.
24 The fierce anger of the LORD will not return until He has done it,
And until He has performed the intents of His heart.

[a]In the latter days you will consider it.

---

9 [a]Is. 55:3; Ezek. 34:23; 37:24; Hos. 3:5 [b][Luke 1:69; Acts 2:30; 13:23]
10 [a]Is. 41:13; 43:5; 44:2; Jer. 46:27, 28 [b]Jer. 3:18
11 [a][Is. 43:2–5] [b]Amos 9:8 [c]Jer. 4:27; 46:27, 28 [d]Ps. 6:1; Is. 27:8; Jer. 10:24; 46:28
12 [a]2 Chr. 36:16; Jer. 15:18
13 [a]Jer. 8:22
14 [a]Jer. 22:20, 22; Lam. 1:2 [b]Job 13:24; 16:9; 19:11 [c]Job 30:21 [d]Jer. 5:6
15 [a]Jer. 15:18
16 [a]Ex. 23:22; Is. 41:11; Jer. 10:25 [b]Is. 14:2; Joel 3:8 [c]Is. 33:1; Ezek. 39:10 [d]Jer. 2:3
17 [a]Ex. 15:26; Ps. 107:20; Is. 30:26; Jer. 33:6
18 [a]Ps. 102:13 [1]*ruins*
19 [a]Ps. 126:1, 2; Is. 51:11; Jer. 31:4; Zeph. 3:14 [b]Is. 49:19–21; Jer. 23:3; 33:22; Zech. 10:8
20 [a]Is. 1:26
21 [a]Gen. 49:10 [b]Num. 16:5; Ps. 65:4
22 [a]Ex. 6:7; Jer. 32:38; Ezek. 36:28; Hos. 2:23; Zech. 13:9
23 [a]Jer. 23:19, 20; 25:32 [1]Or *sweeping*
24 [a]Gen. 49:1

The Remnant of Israel Saved

31 "At [a]the same time," says the LORD, [b]"I will be the God of all the families of Israel, and they shall be My people."
2 Thus says the LORD:

"The people who survived the sword
Found grace in the wilderness—
Israel, when [a]I went to give him rest."

3 The LORD has appeared [1]of old to me, *saying:*
"Yes, [a]I have loved you with [b]an everlasting love;
Therefore with lovingkindness I have [c]drawn you.
4 Again [a]I will build you, and you shall be rebuilt,
O virgin of Israel!
You shall again be adorned with your [b]tambourines,
And shall go forth in the dances of those who rejoice.
5 [a]You shall yet plant vines on the mountains of Samaria;
The planters shall plant and [1]eat *them* as ordinary food.
6 For there shall be a day
When the watchmen will cry on Mount Ephraim,
[a]'Arise, and let us go up *to* Zion,
To the LORD our God.'"

7 For thus says the LORD:

[a]"Sing with gladness for Jacob,
And shout among the chief of the nations;
Proclaim, give praise, and say,
'O LORD, save Your people,
The remnant of Israel!'
8 Behold, I will bring them [a]from the north country,
And [b]gather them from the ends of the earth,
Among them the blind and the lame,
The woman with child
And the one who labors with child, together;
A great throng shall return there.
9 [a]They shall come with weeping,
And with supplications I will lead them.
I will cause them to walk [b]by the rivers of waters,
In a straight way in which they shall not stumble;
For I am a Father to Israel,
And Ephraim *is* My [c]firstborn.

10 "Hear the word of the LORD, O nations,
And declare *it* in the [1]isles afar off, and say,
'He who scattered Israel [a]will gather him,
And keep him as a shepherd *does* his flock.'
11 For [a]the LORD has redeemed Jacob,
And ransomed him [b]from the hand of one stronger than he.
12 Therefore they shall come and sing in [a]the height of Zion,
Streaming to [b]the goodness of the LORD—
For wheat and new wine and oil,
For the young of the flock and the herd;
Their souls shall be like a [c]well-watered garden,
[d]And they shall sorrow no more at all.

13 "Then shall the virgin rejoice in the dance,
And the young men and the old, together;
For I will turn their mourning to joy,
Will comfort them,
And make them rejoice rather than sorrow.
14 I will [1]satiate the soul of the priests with abundance,
And My people shall be satisfied with My goodness, says the LORD."

Mercy on Ephraim

15 Thus says the LORD:

[a]"A voice was heard in [b]Ramah,
Lamentation *and* bitter [c]weeping,
Rachel weeping for her children,
Refusing to be comforted for her children,
Because [d]they *are* no more."

16 Thus says the LORD:

"Refrain your voice from [a]weeping,
And your eyes from tears;
For your work shall be rewarded, says the LORD,
And they shall come back from the land of the enemy.
17 There is [a]hope in your future, says the LORD,
That *your* children shall come back to their own border.

18 "I have surely heard Ephraim bemoaning himself:

CHAPTER 31
1 [a]Jer. 30:24 [b]Jer. 30:22
2 [a]Ex. 33:14; Num. 10:33; Deut. 1:33; Josh. 1:13; Ps. 95:11; Is. 63:14
3 [a]Deut. 4:37; 7:8; Mal. 1:2 [b]Is. 43:4; Rom. 11:28 [c]Hos. 11:4 [1]Lit. *from afar*
4 [a]Jer. 33:7 [b]Ex. 15:20; Judg. 11:34; Ps. 149:3
5 [a]Ps. 107:37; Is. 65:21; Ezek. 28:26; Amos 9:14 [1]Lit. *treat them as common*
6 [a][Is. 2:3; Jer. 31:12; 50:4, 5; Mic. 4:2]
7 [a]Is. 12:5, 6
8 [a]Jer. 3:12, 18; 23:8 [b]Deut. 30:4; Is. 43:6; Ezek. 20:34, 41; 34:13
9 [a][Ps. 126:5; Jer. 50:4] [b]Is. 35:8; 43:19; 49:10, 11 [c]Ex. 4:22
10 [a]Is. 40:11; Ezek. 34:12–14 [1]Or *coastlands*
11 [a]Is. 44:23; 48:20; Jer. 15:21; 50:19 [b]Is. 49:24
12 [a]Ezek. 17:23 [b]Hos. 3:5 [c]Is. 58:11 [d]Is. 35:10; 65:19; [John 16:22; Rev. 21:4]
14 [1]Fill to the full
15 [a]Matt. 2:17, 18 [b]Josh. 18:25; Judg. 4:5; Is. 10:29; Jer. 40:1 [c]Gen. 37:35 [d]Jer. 10:20
16 [a][Is. 25:8; 30:19]
17 [a]Jer. 29:11

'You have [a]chastised me, and I
was chastised,
Like an untrained bull;
[b]Restore me, and I will return,
For You *are* the LORD my God.
19 Surely, [a]after my turning, I
repented;
And after I was instructed, I
struck myself on the thigh;
I was [b]ashamed, yes, even
humiliated,
Because I bore the reproach of
my youth.'
20 *Is* Ephraim My dear son?
Is he a pleasant child?
For though I spoke against him,
I earnestly remember him still;
[a]Therefore My [1]heart yearns for
him;
[b]I will surely have mercy on him,
says the LORD.

21 "Set up signposts,
Make landmarks;
[a]Set your heart toward the
highway,
The way in *which* you went.
[1]Turn back, O virgin of Israel,
Turn back to these your cities.
22 How long will you [a]gad about,
O you [b]backsliding daughter?
For the LORD has created a new
thing in the earth—
A woman shall encompass a
man."

Future Prosperity of Judah

23 Thus says the LORD of hosts,
the God of Israel: "They shall
again use this speech in the land
of Judah and in its cities, when I
bring back their captivity: [a]'The
LORD bless you, O home of justice,
and [b]mountain of holiness!'
24 "And there shall dwell in Judah
itself, and [a]in all its cities together,
farmers and those going out with
flocks.
25 "For I have [1]satiated the weary
soul, and I have replenished every
sorrowful soul."
26 After this I awoke and looked
around, and my sleep was [a]sweet
to me.
27 "Behold, the days are coming,
says the LORD, that [a]I will sow the
house of Israel and the house of
Judah with the seed of man and
the seed of beast.
28 "And it shall come to pass, *that*
as I have [a]watched over them
[b]to pluck up, to break down, to
throw down, to destroy, and to af-

18 [a]Job 5:17; Ps. 94:12 [b]Ps. 80:3, 7, 19; Jer. 17:4; Lam. 5:21; [Acts 3:26]
19 [a]Deut. 30:2 [b]Ezek. 36:31
20 [a]Is. 63:15 [b][Hos. 14:4] [1]Lit. *inward parts*
21 [a]Jer. 50:5 [1]Or *Return*
22 [a]Jer. 2:18, 23, 36 [b]Jer. 3:6, 8, 11, 12, 14, 22
23 [a]Is. 1:26 [b][Zech. 8:3]
24 [a]Jer. 33:12
25 [1]*fully satisfied*
26 [a]Prov. 3:24
27 [a]Ezek. 36:9–11
28 [a]Jer. 44:27 [b]Jer. 1:10; 18:7 [c]Jer. 24:6
29 [a]Ezek. 18:2, 3
30 [a][Gal. 6:5, 7]
31 [a]Luke 22:20; Heb. 8:8–12; 10:16, 17
32 [a]Deut. 1:31 [1]So with MT, Tg., Vg.; LXX, Syr. *and I turned away from them*
33 [a]Jer. 32:40; Heb. 10:16 [b]Ps. 40:8; [2 Cor. 3:3] [c]Jer. 24:7; 30:22; 32:38 [1]Lit. *inward parts*
34 [a][John 6:45] [b][Acts 10:43; 13:39; Rom. 11:27]
35 [a]Gen. 1:14–18 [b]Is. 51:15 [c]Jer. 10:16
36 [a]Ps. 148:6

flict, so I will watch over them
[c]to build and to plant, says the
LORD.
29 [a]"In those days they shall say
no more:

'The fathers have eaten sour
grapes,
And the children's teeth are set
on edge.'

30 [a]"But every one shall die for his
own iniquity; every man who eats
the sour grapes, his teeth shall be
set on edge.

A New Covenant

31 "Behold, the [a]days are coming,
says the LORD, when I will make
a new covenant with the house of
Israel and with the house of Ju-
dah—
32 "not according to the covenant
that I made with their fathers in
the day *that* [a]I took them by the
hand to lead them out of the land
of Egypt, My covenant which they
broke, [1]though I was a husband to
them, says the LORD.
33 [a]"But this *is* the covenant that
I will make with the house of Israel
after those days, says the LORD: [b]I
will put My law in their minds, and
write it on their [1]hearts; [c]and I will
be their God, and they shall be My
people.
34 "No more shall every man
teach his neighbor, and every man
his brother, saying, 'Know the
LORD,' for [a]they all shall know Me,
from the least of them to the great-
est of them, says the LORD. For [b]I
will forgive their iniquity, and
their sin I will remember no
more."

35 Thus says the LORD,
[a]Who gives the sun for a light by
day,
The ordinances of the moon and
the stars for a light by night,
Who disturbs [b]the sea,
And its waves roar
[c](The LORD of hosts *is* His name):

36 "If [a]those ordinances depart
From before Me, says the LORD,
Then the seed of Israel shall also
cease
From being a nation before Me
forever."

37 Thus says the LORD:

[a]"If heaven above can be measured,
And the foundations of the earth
searched out beneath,
I will also [b]cast off all the seed
of Israel
For all that they have done, says
the LORD.

38 "Behold, the days are coming,
says the LORD, that the city shall
be built for the LORD [a]from the
Tower of Hananel to the Corner
Gate.
39 [a]"The surveyor's line shall
again extend straight forward over
the hill Gareb; then it shall turn
toward Goath.
40 "And the whole valley of the
dead bodies and of the ashes, and
all the fields as far as the Brook
Kidron, [a]to the corner of the Horse
Gate toward the east, [b]*shall be*
holy to the LORD. It shall not be
plucked up or thrown down any-
more forever."

Jeremiah Buys a Field

32 The word that came to Jere-
miah from the LORD [a]in the
tenth year of Zedekiah king of Ju-
dah, which was the eighteenth
year of Nebuchadnezzar.
2 For then the king of Babylon's
army besieged Jerusalem, and
Jeremiah the prophet was shut up
[a]in the court of the prison, which
was in the king of Judah's house.
3 For Zedekiah king of Judah
had shut him up, saying, "Why do
you [a]prophesy and say, 'Thus says
the LORD: [b]"Behold, I will give this
city into the hand of the king of
Babylon, and he shall take it;
4 "and Zedekiah king of Judah
[a]shall not escape from the hand of
the Chaldeans, but shall surely be
delivered into the hand of the king
of Babylon, and shall speak with
him [1]face to face, and see him [b]eye
to eye;
5 "then he shall [a]lead Zedekiah
to Babylon, and there he shall be
[b]until I visit him," says the LORD;
[c]"though you fight with the Chal-
deans, you shall not succeed" '?"
6 And Jeremiah said, "The word
of the LORD came to me, saying,
7 'Behold, Hanamel the son of
Shallum your uncle will come to
you, saying, "Buy my field which
is in Anathoth, for the [a]right of re-
demption *is* yours to buy *it*." '
8 "Then Hanamel my uncle's son
came to me in the court of the
prison according to the word of the
LORD, and said to me, 'Please buy
my field that *is* in Anathoth, which
is in the country of Benjamin; for
the right of inheritance *is* yours,
and the redemption yours; buy *it*
for yourself.' Then I knew that this
was the word of the LORD.
9 "So I bought the field from
Hanamel, the son of my uncle who
was in Anathoth, and [a]weighed
out to him the money—seventeen
shekels of silver.
10 "And I signed the [1]deed and
sealed *it*, took witnesses, and
weighed the money on the scales.
11 "So I took the purchase deed,
both that which was sealed *ac-
cording* to the law and custom, and
that which was open;
12 "and I gave the purchase deed
to [a]Baruch the son of Neriah, son
of Mahseiah, in the presence of
Hanamel my uncle's *son*, and in
the presence of the [b]witnesses who
signed the purchase deed, before
all the Jews who sat in the court
of the prison.
13 "Then I charged [a]Baruch be-
fore them, saying,
14 'Thus says the LORD of hosts,
the God of Israel: "Take these
deeds, both this purchase deed
which is sealed and this deed
which is open, and put them in an
earthen vessel, that they may last
many days."
15 'For thus says the LORD of
hosts, the God of Israel: "Houses
and fields and vineyards shall be
[a]possessed again in this land." '

Jeremiah Prays for Understanding

16 "Now when I had delivered the
purchase deed to Baruch the son
of Neriah, I prayed to the LORD,
saying:
17 'Ah, Lord GOD! Behold, [a]You
have made the heavens and the
earth by Your great power and
outstretched arm. [b]There is noth-
ing too [1]hard for You.
18 '*You* show [a]lovingkindness to
thousands, and repay the iniquity
of the fathers into the bosom of
their children after them—the

37 [a]Is. 40:12; Jer. 33:22 [b]Jer. 33:24–26; [Rom. 11:2–5, 26, 27]
38 [a]Neh. 3:1; 12:39; Zech. 14:10
39 [a]Ezek. 40:8; Zech. 2:1, 2
40 [a]2 Kin. 11:16; 2 Chr. 23:15; Neh. 3:28 [b][Joel 3:17]; Zech. 14:20

CHAPTER 32

1 [a]2 Kin. 25:1, 2; Jer. 39:1, 2
2 [a]Neh. 3:25; Jer. 33:1; 37:21; 39:14
3 [a]Jer. 26:8, 9 [b]Jer. 21:3–7; 34:2
4 [a]2 Kin. 25:4–7; Jer. 34:3; 38:18, 23; 39:5; 52:9 [b]Jer. 39:5 [1]Lit. *mouth to mouth*
5 [a]Jer. 27:22; 39:7; Ezek. 12:12, 13 [b]Jer. 27:22 [c]Jer. 21:4; 33:5
7 [a]Lev. 25:24, 25, 32; Ruth 4:4
9 [a]Gen. 23:16; Zech. 11:12
10 [1]Lit. *book*
12 [a]Jer. 36:4 [b]Is. 8:2
13 [a]Jer. 36:4
15 [a]Ezra 2:1; [Jer. 31:5, 12, 14]; Amos 9:14, 15; Zech. 3:10
17 [a]2 Kin. 19:15; Ps. 102:25; Is. 40:26–29; Jer. 27:5 [b]Gen. 18:14; Jer. 32:27; Zech. 8:6; Matt. 19:26; Mark 10:27; Luke 18:27 [1]*difficult*
18 [a]Ex. 20:6; 34:7; Deut. 5:9, 10

Great, [b]the Mighty God, whose
name *is* [c]the LORD of hosts.
19 '*You are* [a]great in counsel and
mighty in [1]work, for your [b]eyes
are open to all the ways of the sons
of men, [c]to give everyone accord-
ing to his ways and according to
the fruit of his doings.
20 'You have set signs and won-
ders in the land of Egypt, to this
day, and in Israel and among *other*
men; and You have made Yourself
[a]a name, as it is this day.
21 'You [a]have brought Your peo-
ple Israel out of the land of Egypt
with signs and wonders, with a
strong hand and an outstretched
arm, and with great terror;
22 'You have given them this land,
of which You swore to their fa-
thers to give them—[a]"a land flow-
ing with milk and honey."
23 'And they came in and took
possession of it, but [a]they have not
obeyed Your voice or walked in
Your law. They have done nothing
of all that You commanded them
to do; therefore You have caused
all this calamity to come upon
them.
24 'Look, the siege mounds! They
have come to the city to take it;
and the city has been given into
the hand of the Chaldeans who
fight against it, because of [a]the
sword and famine and pestilence.
What You have spoken has hap-
pened; there You see *it!*
25 'And You have said to me, O
Lord GOD, "Buy the field for
money, and take witnesses"!—yet
the city has been given into the
hand of the Chaldeans.' "

God's Assurance of the People's Return

26 Then the word of the LORD
came to Jeremiah, saying,
27 "Behold, I *am* the LORD, the
[a]God of all flesh. Is there anything
too hard for Me?
28 "Therefore thus says the LORD:
'Behold, I will give this city into
the hand of the Chaldeans, into the
hand of Nebuchadnezzar king of
Babylon, and he shall take it.
29 'And the Chaldeans who fight
against this city shall come and
[a]set fire to this city and burn it,
with the houses [b]on whose roofs
they have offered incense to Baal
and poured out drink offerings to
other gods, to provoke Me to an-
ger;
30 'because the children of Israel
and the children of Judah [a]have
done only evil before Me from
their youth. For the children of Is-
rael have provoked Me only to an-
ger with the work of their hands,'
says the LORD.
31 'For this city has been to Me *a
provocation of* My anger and My
fury from the day that they built
it, even to this day; [a]so I will re-
move it from before My face
32 'because of all the evil of the
children of Israel and the children
of Judah, which they have done to
provoke Me to anger—[a]they, their
kings, their princes, their priests,
[b]their prophets, the men of Judah,
and the inhabitants of Jerusalem.
33 'And they have turned to Me
the [a]back, and not the face; though
I taught them, [b]rising up early and
teaching *them*, yet they have not
listened to receive instruction.
34 'But they [a]set their abomina-
tions in [1]the house which is called
by My name, to defile it.
35 'And they built the high places
of Baal which *are* in the Valley of
the Son of Hinnom, to [a]cause their
sons and their daughters to pass
through *the fire* to [b]Molech,
[c]which I did not command them,
nor did it come into My mind that
they should do this abomination,
to cause Judah to sin.'
36 "Now therefore, thus says the
LORD, the God of Israel, concern-
ing this city of which you say, 'It
shall be delivered into the hand of
the king of Babylon by the sword,
by the famine, and by the pes-
tilence':
37 'Behold, I will [a]gather them out
of all countries where I have
driven them in My anger, in My
fury, and in great wrath; I will
bring them back to this place, and
I will cause them [b]to dwell safely.
38 'They shall be [a]My people, and
I will be their God;
39 'then I will [a]give them one
heart and one way, that they may
fear Me forever, for the good of
them and their children after them.
40 'And [a]I will make an everlast-
ing covenant with them, that I will

18 [b]Ps. 50:1; [Is. 9:6]; Jer. 20:11 [c]Jer. 10:16
19 [a]Is. 28:29 [b]Job 34:21; Ps. 33:13; Prov. 5:21; Jer. 16:17 [c]Ps. 62:12; Jer. 17:10; [Matt. 16:27; John 5:29] [1]*deed*
20 [a]Ex. 9:16; 1 Chr. 17:21; Is. 63:12; Jer. 13:11; Dan. 9:15
21 [a]Ex. 6:6; 2 Sam. 7:23; 1 Chr. 17:21; Ps. 136:11, 12
22 [a]Ex. 3:8, 17; Deut. 1:8; Ps. 105:9–11; Jer. 11:5
23 [a][Neh. 9:26]; Jer. 11:8; [Dan. 9:10–14]
24 [a]Jer. 14:12; Ezek. 14:21
27 [a][Num. 16:22]
29 [a]2 Chr. 36:19; Jer. 21:10; 37:8, 10; 52:13 [b]Jer. 19:13
30 [a]Deut. 9:7–12; Is. 63:10; Jer. 2:7; 3:25; 7:22–26; Ezek. 20:28
31 [a]2 Kin. 23:27; 24:3; Jer. 27:10
32 [a]Ezra 9:7; Is. 1:4, 6; Dan. 9:8 [b]Jer. 23:14
33 [a]Jer. 2:27; 7:24 [b]Jer. 7:13
34 [a]2 Kin. 21:1–7; Jer. 7:10–12, 30; 23:11; Ezek. 8:5, 6 [1]The temple
35 [a]2 Chr. 28:2, 3; 33:6; Jer. 7:31; 19:5 [b]Lev. 18:21; 1 Kin. 11:33; 2 Kin. 23:10; Acts 7:43 [c]Jer. 7:31
37 [a]Deut. 30:3; Jer. 23:3; 29:14; 31:10; 50:19; Ezek. 37:21 [b]Jer. 33:16
38 [a][Jer. 24:7; 30:22; 31:33]
39 [a][Jer. 24:7; Ezek. 11:19]
40 [a]Is. 55:3; Jer. 31:31; Ezek. 37:26

not turn away from doing them
good; but [b]I will put My fear in
their hearts so that they will not
depart from Me.
41 'Yes, [a]I will rejoice over them
to do them good, and [b]I will [1]as-
suredly plant them in this land,
with all My heart and with all My
soul.'
42 "For thus says the LORD: [a]'Just
as I have brought all this great ca-
lamity on this people, so I will
bring on them all the good that I
have promised them.
43 'And fields will be bought in
this land [a]of which you say, "*It is*
desolate, without man or beast; it
has been given into the hand of the
Chaldeans."
44 'Men will buy fields for money,
sign deeds and seal *them*, and take
witnesses, in [a]the land of Benja-
min, in the places around Jerusa-
lem, in the cities of Judah, in the
cities of the mountains, in the cit-
ies of the [1]lowland, and in the cit-
ies of the [2]South; for [b]I will cause
their captives to return,' says the
LORD."

Excellence of the Restored Nation

33 Moreover the word of the
LORD came to Jeremiah a
second time, while he was still
[a]shut up in the court of the prison,
saying,
2 "Thus says the LORD [a]who
made it, the LORD who formed it
to establish it [b](the[1] LORD *is* His
name):
3 [a]'Call to Me, and I will answer
you, and show you great and
[1]mighty things, which you do not
know.'
4 "For thus says the LORD, the
God of Israel, concerning the
houses of this city and the houses
of the kings of Judah, which have
been pulled down *to fortify* against
[a]the siege mounds and the sword:
5 'They come to fight with the
Chaldeans, but *only* to [a]fill their
places with the dead bodies of men
whom I will slay in My anger and
My fury, all for whose wickedness
I have hidden My face from this
city.
6 'Behold, [a]I will bring it health
and healing; I will heal them and
reveal to them the abundance of
peace and truth.

40 [b][Jer. 31:33]
41 [a]Deut. 30:9 [b]Amos 9:15 [1]*truly*
42 [a]Jer. 31:28
43 [a]Jer. 33:10
44 [a]Jer. 17:26 [b]Jer. 33:7, 11 [1]Heb. *shephelah* [2]Heb. *Negev*

CHAPTER 33

1 [a]Jer. 32:2, 3
2 [a]Is. 37:26 [b]Ex. 15:3 [1]Heb. *YHWH*
3 [a]Jer. 29:12 [1]*inaccessible*
4 [a]Is. 22:10
5 [a]2 Kin. 23:14
6 [a]Jer. 30:17
7 [a]Jer. 30:3; 32:44 [b]Is. 1:26
8 [a]Zech. 13:1
9 [a]Is. 62:7 [b]Is. 60:5
10 [a]Jer. 32:43
11 [a]Rev. 18:23 [b]Is. 12:4 [c]Lev. 7:12
12 [a]Is. 65:10
13 [a]Jer. 17:26; 32:44 [b]Lev. 27:32
14 [a]Jer. 23:5; 31:27, 31 [b]Jer. 29:10; 32:42

7 'And [a]I will cause the captives
of Judah and the captives of Israel
to return, and will rebuild those
places [b]as at the first.
8 'I will [a]cleanse them from all
their iniquity by which they have
sinned against Me, and I will par-
don all their iniquities by which
they have sinned and by which
they have transgressed against
Me.
9 [a]'Then it shall be to Me a name
of joy, a praise, and an honor be-
fore all nations of the earth, who
shall hear all the good that I do
to them; they shall [b]fear and
tremble for all the goodness and
all the prosperity that I provide
for it.'
10 "Thus says the LORD: 'Again
there shall be heard in this place—
[a]of which you say, "It *is* desolate,
without man and without beast"—
in the cities of Judah, in the streets
of Jerusalem that are desolate,
without man and without inhabit-
ant and without beast,
11 'the [a]voice of joy and the voice
of gladness, the voice of the bride-
groom and the voice of the bride,
the voice of those who will say:

[b]"Praise the LORD of hosts,
For the LORD *is* good,
For His mercy *endures* forever"—

and of those *who will* bring [c]the
sacrifice of praise into the house
of the LORD. For I will cause the
captives of the land to return as
at the first,' says the LORD.
12 "Thus says the LORD of hosts:
[a]'In this place which is desolate,
without man and without beast,
and in all its cities, there shall
again be a dwelling place of shep-
herds causing *their* flocks to lie
down.
13 [a]'In the cities of the mountains,
in the cities of the lowland, in the
cities of the South, in the land of
Benjamin, in the places around Je-
rusalem, and in the cities of Judah,
the flocks shall again [b]pass under
the hands of him who counts
them,' says the LORD.
14 [a]'Behold, the days are coming,'
says the LORD, 'that [b]I will perform
that good thing which I have
promised to the house of Israel and
to the house of Judah:

15 'In those days and at that time
I will cause to grow up to David
A [a]Branch of righteousness;
He shall execute judgment and
righteousness in the earth.
16 In those days Judah will be saved,
And Jerusalem will dwell safely.
And this *is the name* by which
she will be called:

[1]THE LORD OUR
RIGHTEOUSNESS.'

17 "For thus says the LORD: 'David
shall never [a]lack a man to sit on
the throne of the house of Israel;
18 'nor shall the [a]priests, the Le-
vites, lack a man to [b]offer burnt
offerings before Me, to [1]kindle
grain offerings, and to sacrifice
continually.' "

The Permanence of God's Covenant

19 And the word of the LORD came
to Jeremiah, saying,
20 "Thus says the LORD: 'If you
can break My covenant with the
day and My covenant with the
night, so that there will not be day
and night in their season,
21 'then [a]My covenant may also
be broken with David My servant,
so that he shall not have a son to
reign on his throne, and with the
Levites, the priests, My ministers.
22 'As [a]the host of heaven cannot
be numbered, nor the sand of the
sea measured, so will I [b]multiply
the descendants of David My ser-
vant and the [c]Levites who minister
to Me.' "
23 Moreover the word of the LORD
came to Jeremiah, saying,
24 "Have you not considered what
these people have spoken, saying,
'The two families which the LORD
has chosen, He has also cast them
off'? Thus they have [a]despised My
people, as if they should no more
be a nation before them.
25 "Thus says the LORD: 'If [a]My
covenant *is* not with day and night,
and if I have not [b]appointed the or-
dinances of heaven and earth,
26 [a]'then I will [b]cast away the de-
scendants of Jacob and David My
servant, *so* that I will not take *any*
of his descendants *to be* rulers
over the descendants of Abraham,
Isaac, and Jacob. For I will cause
their captives to return, and will
have mercy on them.' "

15 [a]Is. 4:2; 11:1; Jer. 23:5; Zech. 3:8; 6:12, 13
16 [1]Heb. *YHWH Tsidkenu;* cf. Jer. 23:5, 6
17 [a]2 Sam. 7:16; 1 Kin. 2:4; Ps. 89:29; [Luke 1:32]
18 [a]Num. 3:5–10; Deut. 18:1; 24:8; Josh. 3:3; Ezek. 44:15 [b][Rom. 12:1; 15:16; 1 Pet. 2:5, 9; Rev. 1:6] [1]*burn*
21 [a]2 Sam. 23:5; 2 Chr. 7:18; 21:7; Ps. 89:34
22 [a]Gen. 15:5; 22:17; Jer. 31:37 [b]Jer. 30:19; Ezek. 36:10, 11 [c]Is. 66:21; Jer. 33:18
24 [a]Neh. 4:2–4; Esth. 3:6–8; Ps. 44:13, 14; 83:4; Ezek. 36:2
25 [a]Gen. 8:22; Jer. 33:20 [b]Ps. 74:16; 104:19
26 [a]Jer. 31:37 [b]Rom. 11:1, 2

CHAPTER 34

1 [a]2 Kin. 25:1; Jer. 32:1, 2; 39:1; 52:4 [b]Jer. 1:15; 25:9; Dan. 2:37, 38
2 [a]2 Chr. 36:11, 12; Jer. 22:1, 2; 37:1, 2 [b]2 Kin. 25:9; Jer. 21:10; 32:3, 28
3 [a]2 Kin. 25:4, 5; Jer. 21:7; 52:7–11 [b]2 Kin. 25:6, 7; Jer. 32:4; 39:5, 6 [1]Lit. *mouth to mouth*
5 [a]2 Chr. 16:14; 21:19 [b]Dan. 2:46 [c]Jer. 22:18
7 [a]2 Kin. 18:13; 19:8; 2 Chr. 11:5, 9
8 [a]Ex. 21:2; Lev. 25:10; Neh. 5:1–13; Is. 58:6; Jer. 34:14, 17
9 [a]Neh. 5:11 [b]Lev. 25:39–46

Zedekiah Warned by God

34 The word which came to
Jeremiah from the LORD,
[a]when Nebuchadnezzar king of
Babylon and all his army, [b]all the
kingdoms of the earth under his
dominion, and all the people,
fought against Jerusalem and all
its cities, saying,
2 "Thus says the LORD, the God
of Israel: 'Go and [a]speak to Zede-
kiah king of Judah and tell him,
"Thus says the LORD: 'Behold, [b]I
will give this city into the hand of
the king of Babylon, and he shall
burn it with fire.
3 'And [a]you shall not escape
from his hand, but shall surely be
taken and delivered into his hand;
your eyes shall see the eyes of the
king of Babylon, he shall speak
with you [b]face[1] to face, and you
shall go to Babylon.' " '
4 "Yet hear the word of the LORD,
O Zedekiah king of Judah! Thus
says the LORD concerning you:
'You shall not die by the sword.
5 'You shall die in peace; as in
[a]the ceremonies of your fathers,
the former kings who were before
you, [b]so they shall burn incense
for you and [c]lament for you, *say-
ing,* "Alas, lord!" For I have
pronounced the word, says the
LORD.' "
6 Then Jeremiah the prophet
spoke all these words to Zedekiah
king of Judah in Jerusalem,
7 when the king of Babylon's
army fought against Jerusalem
and all the cities of Judah that
were left, against Lachish and
Azekah; for *only* [a]these fortified
cities remained of the cities of Ju-
dah.

Treacherous Treatment of Slaves

8 *This is* the word that came to
Jeremiah from the LORD, after
King Zedekiah had made a cov-
enant with all the people who *were*
at Jerusalem to proclaim [a]liberty
to them:
9 [a]that every man should set free
his male and female slave—a He-
brew man or woman—[b]that no one
should keep a Jewish brother in
bondage.
10 Now when all the princes and
all the people, who had entered

into the covenant, heard that
everyone should set free his male
and female slaves, that no one
should keep them in bondage any-
more, they obeyed and let *them*
go.
11 But afterward they changed
their minds and made the male
and female slaves return, whom
they had set free, and brought
them into subjection as male and
female slaves.
12 Therefore the word of the LORD
came to Jeremiah from the LORD,
saying,
13 "Thus says the LORD, the God
of Israel: 'I made a [a]covenant with
your fathers in the day that I
brought them out of the land of
Egypt, out of the house of bond-
age, saying,
14 "At the end of [a]seven years let
every man set free his Hebrew
brother, who [1]has been sold to
him; and when he has served you
six years, you shall let him go free
from you." But your fathers did
not obey Me nor incline their ear.
15 'Then you [1]recently turned and
did what was right in My sight—
every man proclaiming liberty to
his neighbor; and you [a]made a
covenant before Me [b]in the house
which is called by My name.
16 'Then you turned around and
[a]profaned My name, and every
one of you brought back his male
and female slaves, whom he had
set at liberty, at their pleasure, and
brought them back into subjection,
to be your male and female slaves.'
17 "Therefore thus says the LORD:
'You have not obeyed Me in pro-
claiming liberty, every one to his
brother and every one to his neigh-
bor. [a]Behold, I proclaim liberty to
you,' says the LORD—[b]'to the
sword, to pestilence, and to fam-
ine! And I will deliver you to [c]trou-
ble among all the kingdoms of the
earth.
18 'And I will give the men who
have transgressed My covenant,
who have not performed the words
of the covenant which they made
before Me, when [a]they cut the calf
in two and passed between the
parts of it—
19 'the princes of Judah, the
princes of Jerusalem, the [1]eu-
nuchs, the priests, and all the peo-

13 [a]Ex. 24:3, 7, 8; Deut. 5:2, 3, 27; Jer. 31:32

14 [a]Ex. 21:2; 23:10; Deut. 15:12; 1 Kin. 9:22 [1]Or *sold himself*

15 [a]2 Kin. 23:3; Neh. 10:29 [b]Jer. 7:10 [1]Lit. *today*

16 [a]Ex. 20:7; Lev. 19:12

17 [a]Lev. 26:34, 35; Esth. 7:10; Dan. 6:24; [Matt. 7:2; Gal. 6:7]; James 2:13 [b]Jer. 32:24, 36 [c]Deut. 28:25, 64; Jer. 29:18

18 [a]Gen. 15:10, 17

19 [1]Or *officers*

20 [a]2 Kin. 25:19–21; Jer. 22:25 [b]Deut. 28:26; 1 Sam. 17:44, 46; 1 Kin. 14:11; 16:4; Ps. 79:2; Jer. 7:33; 16:4; 19:7

21 [a]Jer. 37:5–11; 39:4–7

22 [a]Jer. 37:8, 10 [b]Jer. 38:3; 39:1, 2, 8; 52:7, 13 [c]Jer. 9:11; 44:2, 6

CHAPTER 35

2 [a]2 Sam. 4:2; 2 Kin. 10:15; 1 Chr. 2:55 [b]1 Kin. 6:5, 8; 1 Chr. 9:26, 33

4 [a]2 Kin. 12:9; 25:18; 1 Chr. 9:18, 19 [1]Lit. *threshold*

6 [a]2 Kin. 10:15, 23 [b]Lev. 10:9; Num. 6:2–4; Judg. 13:7, 14; Prov. 31:4; Ezek. 44:21; Luke 1:15

7 [a]Ex. 20:12; Eph. 6:2, 3

ple of the land who passed be-
tween the parts of the calf—
20 'I will [a]give them into the hand
of their enemies and into the hand
of those who seek their life. Their
[b]dead bodies shall be for meat for
the birds of the heaven and the
beasts of the earth.
21 'And I will give Zedekiah king
of Judah and his princes into the
hand of their enemies, into the
hand of those who seek their life,
and into the hand of the king of
Babylon's army [a]which has gone
back from you.
22 [a]'Behold, I will command,' says
the LORD, 'and cause them to re-
turn to this city. They will fight
against it [b]and take it and burn it
with fire; and [c]I will make the cit-
ies of Judah a desolation without
inhabitant.' "

The Obedient Rechabites

35 The word which came to
Jeremiah from the LORD in
the days of Jehoiakim the son of
Josiah, king of Judah, saying,
2 "Go to the house of the
[a]Rechabites, speak to them, and
bring them into the house of the
LORD, into one of [b]the chambers,
and give them wine to drink."
3 Then I took Jaazaniah the son
of Jeremiah, the son of Habazzi-
niah, his brothers and all his sons,
and the whole house of the Rech-
abites,
4 and I brought them into the
house of the LORD, into the cham-
ber of the sons of Hanan the son
of Igdaliah, a man of God, which
was by the chamber of the princes,
above the chamber of Maaseiah
the son of Shallum, [a]the keeper of
the [1]door.
5 Then I set before the sons of
the house of the Rechabites bowls
full of wine, and cups; and I said
to them, "Drink wine."
6 But they said, "We will drink
no wine, for [a]Jonadab the son of
Rechab, our father, commanded
us, saying, 'You shall drink [b]no
wine, you nor your sons, forever.
7 'You shall not build a house,
sow seed, plant a vineyard, nor
have *any of these;* but all your
days you shall dwell in tents, [a]that
you may live many days in the
land where you are sojourners.'

8 "Thus we have [a]obeyed the
voice of Jonadab the son of Re-
chab, our father, in all that he
charged us, to drink no wine all
our days, we, our wives, our sons,
or our daughters,
9 "nor to build ourselves houses
to dwell in; nor do we have vine-
yard, field, or seed.
10 "But we have dwelt in tents,
and have obeyed and done accord-
ing to all that Jonadab our father
commanded us.
11 "But it came to pass, when
Nebuchadnezzar king of Babylon
came up into the land, that we
said, 'Come, let us [a]go to Jerusa-
lem for fear of the army of the
Chaldeans and for fear of the army
of the Syrians.' So we dwell at Je-
rusalem."
12 Then came the word of the
LORD to Jeremiah, saying,
13 "Thus says the LORD of hosts,
the God of Israel: 'Go and tell the
men of Judah and the inhabitants
of Jerusalem, "Will you not [a]re-
ceive instruction to [1]obey My
words?" says the LORD.
14 "The words of Jonadab the son
of Rechab, which he commanded
his sons, not to drink wine, are
performed; for to this day they
drink none, and obey their father's
commandment. [a]But although I
have spoken to you, [b]rising early
and speaking, you did not [1]obey
Me.
15 "I have also sent to you all My
[a]servants the prophets, rising up
early and sending *them*, saying,
[b]'Turn now everyone from his evil
way, amend your doings, and do
not go after other gods to serve
them; then you will [c]dwell in the
land which I have given you and
your fathers.' But you have not in-
clined your ear, nor obeyed Me.
16 "Surely the sons of Jonadab
the son of Rechab have performed
the commandment of their [a]father,
which he commanded them, but
this people has not obeyed Me." '
17 "Therefore thus says the LORD
God of hosts, the God of Israel:
'Behold, I will bring on Judah and
on all the inhabitants of Jerusalem
all the doom that I have pro-
nounced against them; [a]because I
have spoken to them but they have
not heard, and I have called to
them but they have not an-
swered.' "
18 And Jeremiah said to the house
of the Rechabites, "Thus says the
LORD of hosts, the God of Israel:
'Because you have obeyed the
commandment of Jonadab your
father, and kept all his precepts
and done according to all that he
commanded you,
19 'therefore thus says the LORD of
hosts, the God of Israel: "Jonadab
the son of Rechab shall not lack a
man to [a]stand before Me for-
ever." ' "

The Scroll Read in the Temple

36 Now it came to pass in the
[a]fourth year of Jehoiakim
the son of Josiah, king of Judah,
that this word came to Jeremiah
from the LORD, saying:
2 "Take a [a]scroll of a book and
[b]write on it all the words that I
have spoken to you against Israel,
against Judah, and against [c]all the
nations, from the day I spoke to
you, from the days of [d]Josiah even
to this day.
3 "It [a]may be that the house of
Judah will hear all the adversities
which I purpose to bring upon
them, that everyone may [b]turn
from his evil way, that I may for-
give their iniquity and their sin."
4 Then Jeremiah [a]called Baruch
the son of Neriah; and [b]Baruch
wrote on a scroll of a book, [1]at the
instruction of Jeremiah, all the
words of the LORD which He had
spoken to him.
5 And Jeremiah commanded Bar-
uch, saying, "I *am* confined, I can-
not go into the house of the LORD.
6 "You go, therefore, and read
from the scroll which you have
written [1]at my instruction, the
words of the LORD, in the hearing
of the people in the LORD's house
on [a]the day of fasting. And you
shall also read them in the hearing
of all Judah who come from their
cities.
7 "It may be that they will pre-
sent their supplication before the
LORD, and everyone will turn from
his evil way. For great *is* the anger
and the fury that the LORD has pro-
nounced against this people."
8 And Baruch the son of Neriah
did according to all that Jeremiah

8 [a][Prov. 1:8, 9; 4:1, 2, 10; 6:20; Eph. 6:1; Col. 3:20]
11 [a]Jer. 4:5–7; 8:14
13 [a][Is. 28:9–12]; Jer. 6:10; 17:23; 32:33 [1]*listen to*
14 [a]2 Chr. 36:15 [b]Jer. 7:13; 25:3 [1]*listen to*
15 [a]Jer. 26:4, 5; 29:19 [b][Is. 1:16, 17]; Jer. 18:11; 25:5, 6; [Ezek. 18:30–32]; Acts 26:20 [c]Jer. 7:7; 25:5, 6
16 [a][Heb. 12:9]
17 [a]Prov. 1:24; Is. 65:12; 66:4; Jer. 7:13
19 [a][Ex. 20:12]; Jer. 15:19; [Luke 21:36; Eph. 6:2, 3]

CHAPTER 36

1 [a]2 Kin. 24:1; 2 Chr. 36:5–7; Jer. 25:1, 3; 45:1; Dan. 1:1
2 [a]Is. 8:1; Ezek. 2:9; Zech. 5:1 [b]Jer. 30:2; Hab. 2:2 [c]Jer. 25:15 [d]Jer. 25:3
3 [a]Jer. 26:3; Ezek. 12:3 [b][Deut. 30:2, 8; 1 Sam. 7:3]; Is. 55:7; Jer. 18:8; Jon. 3:8
4 [a]Jer. 32:12 [b]Jer. 45:1 [1]Lit. *from Jeremiah's mouth*
6 [a]Lev. 16:29; 23:27–32; Acts 27:9 [1]Lit. *from my mouth*

the prophet commanded him,
reading from the book the words
of the LORD in the LORD's house.
9 Now it came to pass in the fifth
year of Jehoiakim the son of Jo-
siah, king of Judah, in the ninth
month, *that* they proclaimed a fast
before the LORD to all the people
in Jerusalem, and to all the people
who came from the cities of Judah
to Jerusalem.
10 Then Baruch read from the
book the words of Jeremiah in the
house of the LORD, in the chamber
of Gemariah the son of Shaphan
the scribe, in the upper court at the
[a]entry of the New Gate of the
LORD's house, in the [1]hearing of all
the people.

The Scroll Read in the Palace

11 When Michaiah the son of
Gemariah, the son of Shaphan,
heard all the words of the LORD
from the book,
12 he then went down to the
king's house, into the scribe's
chamber; and there all the princes
were sitting—[a]Elishama the
scribe, Delaiah the son of Shema-
iah, [b]Elnathan the son of Achbor,
Gemariah the son of Shaphan,
Zedekiah the son of Hananiah,
and all the princes.
13 Then Michaiah declared to
them all the words that he had
heard when Baruch read the book
in the hearing of the people.
14 Therefore all the princes sent
Jehudi the son of Nethaniah, the
son of Shelemiah, the son of Cushi,
to Baruch, saying, "Take in your
hand the scroll from which you
have read in the hearing of the
people, and come." So Baruch the
son of Neriah took the scroll in his
hand and came to them.
15 And they said to him, "Sit
down now, and read it in our hear-
ing." So Baruch read *it* in their
hearing.
16 Now it happened, when they
had heard all the words, that they
looked in fear from one to another,
and said to Baruch, "We will
surely tell the king of all these
words."
17 And they asked Baruch, say-
ing, "Tell us now, how did you
write all these words—[1]at his in-
struction?"

10 [a]Jer. 26:10 [1]Lit. *ears*
12 [a]Jer. 41:1 [b]Jer. 26:22
17 [1]Lit. *with his mouth*
22 [a]Judg. 3:20; Amos 3:15
24 [a][Ps. 36:1]; Jer. 36:16 [b]Gen. 37:29, 34; 2 Sam. 1:11; 1 Kin. 21:27; 2 Kin. 19:1, 2; 22:11; Is. 36:22; 37:1; Jon. 3:6
26 [1]Or *son of Hammelech*
27 [1]Lit. *from Jeremiah's mouth*

18 So Baruch answered them, "He
proclaimed with his mouth all
these words to me, and I wrote
them with ink in the book."
19 Then the princes said to Bar-
uch, "Go and hide, you and Jere-
miah; and let no one know where
you are."

The King Destroys Jeremiah's Scroll

20 And they went to the king, into
the court; but they stored the scroll
in the chamber of Elishama the
scribe, and told all the words in
the hearing of the king.
21 So the king sent Jehudi to bring
the scroll, and he took it from
Elishama the scribe's chamber.
And Jehudi read it in the hearing
of the king and in the hearing of
all the princes who stood beside
the king.
22 Now the king was sitting in
[a]the winter house in the ninth
month, with *a fire* burning on the
hearth before him.
23 And it happened, when Jehudi
had read three or four columns,
that the king cut it with the
scribe's knife and cast *it* into the
fire that *was* on the hearth, until
all the scroll was consumed in the
fire that *was* on the hearth.
24 Yet they were [a]not afraid, nor
did they [b]tear their garments, the
king nor any of his servants who
heard all these words.
25 Nevertheless Elnathan, Dela-
iah, and Gemariah implored the
king not to burn the scroll; but he
would not listen to them.
26 And the king commanded Je-
rahmeel [1]the king's son, Seraiah
the son of Azriel, and Shelemiah
the son of Abdeel, to seize Baruch
the scribe and Jeremiah the
prophet, but the LORD hid them.

Jeremiah Rewrites the Scroll

27 Now after the king had burned
the scroll with the words which
Baruch had written [1]at the instruc-
tion of Jeremiah, the word of the
LORD came to Jeremiah, saying:
28 "Take yet another scroll, and
write on it all the former words
that were in the first scroll which
Jehoiakim the king of Judah has
burned.
29 "And you shall say to Je-
hoiakim king of Judah, 'Thus says

the LORD: "You have burned this
scroll, saying, [a]'Why have you
written in it that the king of Bab-
ylon will certainly come and de-
stroy this land, and cause man and
beast to [b]cease from here?'"
30 'Therefore thus says the LORD
concerning Jehoiakim king of Ju-
dah: [a]"He shall have no one to sit
on the throne of David, and his
dead body shall be [b]cast out to the
heat of the day and the frost of the
night.
31 "I will punish him, his [1]family,
and his servants for their iniquity;
and I will bring on them, on the
inhabitants of Jerusalem, and on
the men of Judah all the doom that
I have pronounced against them;
but they did not heed."'"
32 Then Jeremiah took another
scroll and gave it to Baruch the
scribe, the son of Neriah, who
wrote on it [1]at the instruction of
Jeremiah all the words of the book
which Jehoiakim king of Judah
had burned in the fire. And be-
sides, there were added to them
many similar words.

Zedekiah's Vain Hope

37 Now King [a]Zedekiah the son
of Josiah reigned instead of
Coniah the son of Jehoiakim,
whom Nebuchadnezzar king of
Babylon made king in the land of
Judah.
2 [a]But neither he nor his servants
nor the people of the land gave
heed to the words of the LORD
which He spoke by the prophet
Jeremiah.
3 And Zedekiah the king sent Je-
hucal the son of Shelemiah, and
[a]Zephaniah the son of Maaseiah,
the priest, to the prophet Jeremiah,
saying, [b]"Pray now to the LORD
our God for us."
4 Now Jeremiah was coming and
going among the people, for they
had not *yet* put him in prison.
5 Then [a]Pharaoh's army came up
from Egypt; and when the Chalde-
ans who were besieging Jerusalem
heard news of them, they departed
from Jerusalem.
6 Then the word of the LORD
came to the prophet Jeremiah,
saying,
7 "Thus says the LORD, the God
of Israel, 'Thus you shall say to the
king of Judah, [a]who sent you to
Me to inquire of Me: "Behold,
Pharaoh's army which has come
up to help you will return to Egypt,
to their own land.
8 [a]"And the Chaldeans shall
come back and fight against this
city, and take it and burn it with
fire."'
9 "Thus says the LORD: 'Do not
deceive yourselves, saying, "The
Chaldeans will surely depart from
us," for they will not depart.
10 [a]'For though you had defeated
the whole army of the Chaldeans
who fight against you, and there
remained *only* wounded men
among them, they would rise up,
every man in his tent, and burn the
city with fire.'"

Jeremiah Imprisoned

11 And it happened, when the
army of the Chaldeans left *the
siege* of Jerusalem for fear of Pha-
raoh's army,
12 that Jeremiah went out of Jeru-
salem to go into the land of Benja-
min to claim his property there
among the people.
13 And when he was in the Gate
of Benjamin, a captain of the
guard *was* there whose name *was*
Irijah the son of Shelemiah, the
son of Hananiah; and he seized
Jeremiah the prophet, saying,
"You are defecting to the Chal-
deans!"
14 Then Jeremiah said, [1]"False! I
am not defecting to the Chalde-
ans." But he did not listen to him.
So Irijah seized Jeremiah and
brought him to the princes.
15 Therefore the princes were an-
gry with Jeremiah, and they struck
him [a]and put him in prison in the
[b]house of Jonathan the scribe. For
they had made that the prison.
16 When Jeremiah entered [a]the
dungeon and the cells, and Jere-
miah had remained there many
days,
17 then Zedekiah the king sent
and took him *out*. The king asked
him secretly in his house, and said,
"Is there *any* word from the
LORD?" And Jeremiah said, "There
is." Then he said, "You shall be
[a]delivered into the hand of the
king of Babylon!"
18 Moreover Jeremiah said to

29 [a]Jer. 32:3 [b]Jer. 25:9–11; 26:9
30 [a]Jer. 22:30 [b]Jer. 22:19
31 [1]Lit. *seed*
32 [1]Lit. *from Jeremiah's mouth*

CHAPTER 37

1 [a]2 Kin. 24:17; 1 Chr. 3:15; 2 Chr. 36:10; Jer. 22:24
2 [a]2 Kin. 24:19, 20; 2 Chr. 36:12–16; [Prov. 29:12]
3 [a]Jer. 21:1, 2; 29:25; 52:24 [b]1 Kin. 13:6; Jer. 42:2; Acts 8:24
5 [a]2 Kin. 24:7; Jer. 37:7; Ezek. 17:15
7 [a]Is. 36:6; Jer. 21:2; Ezek. 17:17
8 [a]2 Chr. 36:19; Jer. 34:22
10 [a]Lev. 26:36–38; Is. 30:17; Jer. 21:4, 5
14 [1]*a lie*
15 [a]Jer. 20:2; [Matt. 21:35] [b]Gen. 39:20; 2 Chr. 16:10; 18:26; Jer. 38:26; Acts 5:18
16 [a]Jer. 38:6
17 [a]2 Kin. 25:4–7; Jer. 21:7; Ezek. 12:12, 13; 17:19–21

King Zedekiah, "What offense
have I committed against you,
against your servants, or against
this people, that you have put me
in prison?
19 "Where now *are* your prophets
who prophesied to you, saying,
'The king of Babylon will not come
against you or against this land'?
20 "Therefore please hear now, O
my lord the king. Please, let my
petition be accepted before you,
and do not make me return to the
house of Jonathan the scribe, lest
I die there."
21 Then Zedekiah the king com-
manded that they should commit
Jeremiah [a]to the court of the
prison, and that they should give
him daily a piece of bread from the
bakers' street, [b]until all the bread
in the city was gone. Thus Jere-
miah remained in the court of the
prison.

Jeremiah in the Dungeon

38 Now Shephatiah the son of
Mattan, Gedaliah the son of
Pashhur, [a]Jucal[1] the son of Shele-
miah, and [b]Pashhur the son of
Malchiah [c]heard the words that
Jeremiah had spoken to all the
people, saying,
2 "Thus says the LORD: [a]'He who
remains in this city shall die by the
sword, by famine, and by pesti-
lence; but he who goes over to the
Chaldeans shall live; his life shall
be as a prize to him, and he shall
live.'
3 "Thus says the LORD: [a]'This
city shall surely be [b]given into the
hand of the king of Babylon's
army, which shall take it.' "
4 Therefore the princes said to
the king, "Please, [a]let this man be
put to death, for thus he [1]weakens
the hands of the men of war who
remain in this city, and the hands
of all the people, by speaking such
words to them. For this man does
not seek the [2]welfare of this peo-
ple, but their harm."
5 Then Zedekiah the king said,
"Look, he *is* in your hand. For the
king can *do* nothing against you."
6 [a]So they took Jeremiah and
cast him into the dungeon of Mal-
chiah [1]the king's son, which *was*
in the court of the prison, and they
let Jeremiah down with ropes. And
in the dungeon *there was* no wa-
ter, but mire. So Jeremiah sank in
the mire.
7 [a]Now Ebed-Melech the Ethio-
pian, one of the [1]eunuchs, who was
in the king's house, heard that they
had put Jeremiah in the dungeon.
When the king was sitting at the
Gate of Benjamin,
8 Ebed-Melech went out of the
king's house and spoke to the
king, saying:
9 "My lord the king, these men
have done evil in all that they have
done to Jeremiah the prophet,
whom they have cast into the dun-
geon, and he is likely to die from
hunger in the place where he is.
For *there is* [a]no more bread in the
city."
10 Then the king commanded
Ebed-Melech the Ethiopian, say-
ing, "Take from here thirty men
with you, and lift Jeremiah the
prophet out of the dungeon before
he dies."
11 So Ebed-Melech took the men
with him and went into the house
of the king under the treasury, and
took from there old clothes and old
rags, and let them down by ropes
into the dungeon to Jeremiah.
12 Then Ebed-Melech the Ethio-
pian said to Jeremiah, "Please put
these old clothes and rags under
your armpits, under the ropes."
And Jeremiah did so.
13 So they pulled Jeremiah up
with ropes and lifted him out of
the dungeon. And Jeremiah re-
mained [a]in the court of the prison.

Zedekiah's Fears and Jeremiah's Advice

14 Then Zedekiah the king sent
and had Jeremiah the prophet
brought to him at the third en-
trance of the house of the LORD.
And the king said to Jeremiah, "I
will [a]ask you something. Hide
nothing from me."
15 Jeremiah said to Zedekiah, "If
I declare *it* to you, will you not
surely put me to death? And if I
give you advice, you will not listen
to me."
16 So Zedekiah the king swore se-
cretly to Jeremiah, saying, "*As* the
LORD lives, [a]who made our very
souls, I will not put you to death,
nor will I give you into the hand

21 [a]Jer. 32:2; 38:13, 28 [b]2 Kin. 25:3; Jer. 38:9; 52:6

CHAPTER 38

1 [a]Jer. 37:3 [b]Jer. 21:1 [c]Jer. 21:8 [1]*Jehucal*, Jer. 37:3

2 [a]Jer. 21:9

3 [a]Jer. 21:10; 32:3 [b]Jer. 34:2

4 [a]Jer. 26:11 [1]Is discouraging [2]Well-being; lit. *peace*

6 [a]Jer. 37:21; Lam. 3:55 [1]Or *son of Hammelech*

7 [a]Jer. 39:16 [1]Or *officers*

9 [a]Jer. 37:21

13 [a]Neh. 3:25; Jer. 37:21; Acts 23:35; 24:27; 28:16, 30

14 [a]Jer. 21:1, 2; 37:17

16 [a]Num. 16:22; Is. 57:16; Zech. 12:1; [Acts 17:25, 28]

of these men who seek your life."
17 Then Jeremiah said to Zede-
kiah, "Thus says the LORD, the God
of hosts, the God of Israel: 'If you
surely [a]surrender[1] [b]to the king of
Babylon's princes, then your soul
shall live; this city shall not be
burned with fire, and you and your
house shall live.
18 'But if you do not [1]surrender to
the king of Babylon's princes, then
this city shall be given into the
hand of the Chaldeans; they shall
burn it with fire, and [a]you shall not
escape from their hand.'"
19 And Zedekiah the king said to
Jeremiah, "I am afraid of the Jews
who have [a]defected to the Chalde-
ans, lest they deliver me into their
hand, and they [b]abuse me."
20 But Jeremiah said, "They shall
not deliver *you*. Please, obey the
voice of the LORD which I speak
to you. So it shall be [a]well with
you, and your soul shall live.
21 "But if you refuse to [1]surren-
der, this *is* the word that the LORD
has shown me:
22 'Now behold, all the [a]women
who are left in the king of Judah's
house *shall be* surrendered to the
king of Babylon's princes, and
those *women* shall say:

"Your close friends have [1]set upon
you
And prevailed against you;
Your feet have sunk in the mire,
And they have [2]turned away
again."

23 'So they shall surrender all
your wives and [a]children to the
Chaldeans. [b]You shall not escape
from their hand, but shall be taken
by the hand of the king of Babylon.
And you shall cause this city to be
burned with fire.'"
24 Then Zedekiah said to Jere-
miah, "Let no one know of these
words, and you shall not die.
25 "But if the princes hear that I
have talked with you, and they
come to you and say to you, 'De-
clare to us now what you have said
to the king, and also what the king
said to you; do not hide *it* from
us, and we will not put you to
death,'
26 "then you shall say to them, [a]'I
presented my request before the
king, that he would not make me
return [b]to Jonathan's house to die
there.'"
27 Then all the princes came to
Jeremiah and asked him. And he
told them according to all these
words that the king had com-
manded. So they stopped speaking
with him, for the conversation had
not been heard.
28 Now [a]Jeremiah remained in
the court of the prison until the day
that Jerusalem was taken. And he
was *there* when Jerusalem was
taken.

The Fall of Jerusalem

39 In the [a]ninth year of Zede-
kiah king of Judah, in the
tenth month, Nebuchadnezzar
king of Babylon and all his army
came against Jerusalem, and be-
sieged it.
2 In the [a]eleventh year of Zede-
kiah, in the fourth month, on the
ninth *day* of the month, the [1]city
was penetrated.
3 [a]Then all the princes of the
king of Babylon came in and
sat in the Middle Gate: Nergal-
Sharezer, Samgar-Nebo, Sarse-
chim, [1]Rabsaris, Nergal-Sarezer,
[2]Rabmag, with the rest of the
princes of the king of Babylon.
4 [a]So it was, when Zedekiah the
king of Judah and all the men of
war saw them, that they fled and
went out of the city by night, by
way of the king's garden, by the
gate between the two walls. And
he went out by way of the [1]plain.
5 But the Chaldean army pur-
sued them and [a]overtook Zede-
kiah in the plains of Jericho. And
when they had captured him, they
brought him up to Nebuchadnez-
zar king of Babylon, to [b]Riblah in
the land of Hamath, where he pro-
nounced judgment on him.
6 Then the king of Babylon killed
the sons of Zedekiah before his
[a]eyes in Riblah; the king of Bab-
ylon also killed all the [b]nobles of
Judah.
7 Moreover [a]he put out Zedeki-
ah's eyes, and bound him with
bronze [1]fetters to carry him off to
Babylon.
8 [a]And the Chaldeans burned the
king's house and the houses of the
people with [b]fire, and broke down
the [c]walls of Jerusalem.

17 [a]2 Kin. 24:12 [b]Jer. 39:3 [1]Lit. *go out*
18 [a]Jer. 32:4; 34:3 [1]Lit. *go out*
19 [a]Jer. 39:9 [b]1 Sam. 31:4
20 [a]Jer. 40:9
21 [1]Lit. *go out*
22 [a]Jer. 8:10 [1]Or *misled* [2]Deserted you
23 [a]Jer. 39:6; 41:10 [b]Jer. 39:5
26 [a]Jer. 37:20 [b]Jer. 37:15
28 [a][Ps. 23:4]; Jer. 37:21; 39:14

CHAPTER 39

1 [a]2 Kin. 25:1–12; Jer. 52:4; Ezek. 24:1, 2
2 [a]Jer. 1:3 [1]*city wall was breached*
3 [a]Jer. 1:15; 38:17 [1]A title, probably *Chief Officer;* also v. 13 [2]A title, probably *Troop Commander;* also v. 13
4 [a]2 Kin. 25:4; Is. 30:16; Jer. 52:7; Amos 2:14 [1]Or *Arabah;* the Jordan Valley
5 [a]Jer. 21:7; 32:4; 38:18, 23 [b]2 Kin. 23:33; Jer. 52:9, 26, 27
6 [a]Deut. 28:34 [b]Jer. 34:19–21
7 [a]2 Kin. 25:7; Jer. 52:11; Ezek. 12:13 [1]*chains*
8 [a]2 Kin. 25:9; Jer. 38:18; 52:13 [b]Jer. 21:10 [c]2 Kin. 25:10; Neh. 1:3; Jer. 52:14

9 [a]Then Nebuzaradan the captain of the guard carried away captive to Babylon the remnant of the people who remained in the city and those who [b]defected to him, with the rest of the people who remained.
10 But Nebuzaradan the captain of the guard left in the land of Judah the [a]poor people, who had nothing, and gave them vineyards and fields [1]at the same time.

Jeremiah Goes Free

11 Now Nebuchadnezzar king of Babylon gave charge concerning Jeremiah to Nebuzaradan the captain of the guard, saying,
12 "Take him and look after him, and do him no [a]harm; but do to him just as he says to you."
13 So Nebuzaradan the captain of the guard sent Nebushasban, Rabsaris, Nergal-Sharezer, Rabmag, and all the king of Babylon's chief officers;
14 then they sent *someone* [a]to take Jeremiah from the court of the prison, and committed him [b]to Gedaliah the son of [c]Ahikam, the son of Shaphan, that he should take him home. So he dwelt among the people.
15 Meanwhile the word of the LORD had come to Jeremiah while he was shut up in the court of the prison, saying,
16 "Go and speak to [a]Ebed-Melech the Ethiopian, saying, 'Thus says the LORD of hosts, the God of Israel: "Behold, [b]I will bring My words upon this city for adversity and not for good, and they shall be *performed* in that day before you.
17 "But I will deliver you in that day," says the LORD, "and you shall not be given into the hand of the men of whom you *are* afraid.
18 "For I will surely deliver you, and you shall not fall by the sword; but [a]your life shall be as a prize to you, [b]because you have put your trust in Me," says the LORD.' "

Jeremiah with Gedaliah the Governor

40 The word that came to Jeremiah from the LORD [a]after Nebuzaradan the captain of the guard had let him go from Ramah, when he had taken him bound in chains among all who were carried away captive from Jerusalem and Judah, who were carried away captive to Babylon.
2 And the captain of the guard took Jeremiah and [a]said to him: "The LORD your God has pronounced this doom on this place.
3 "Now the LORD has brought *it*, and has done just as He said. [a]Because you *people* have sinned against the LORD, and not obeyed His voice, therefore this thing has come upon you.
4 "And now look, I free you this day from the chains that [1]*were* on your hand. [a]If it seems good to you to come with me to Babylon, come, and I will look after you. But if it seems wrong for you to come with me to Babylon, remain here. See, [b]all the land *is* before you; wherever it seems good and convenient for you to go, go there."
5 Now while Jeremiah had not yet gone back, *Nebuzaradan said,* "Go back to [a]Gedaliah the son of Ahikam, the son of Shaphan, [b]whom the king of Babylon has made governor over the cities of Judah, and dwell with him among the people. Or go wherever it seems convenient for you to go." So the captain of the guard gave him rations and a gift and let him go.
6 [a]Then Jeremiah went to Gedaliah the son of Ahikam, to [b]Mizpah, and dwelt with him among the people who were left in the land.
7 [a]And when all the captains of the armies who *were* in the fields, they and their men, heard that the king of Babylon had made Gedaliah the son of Ahikam governor in the land, and had committed to him men, women, children, and [b]the poorest of the land who had not been carried away captive to Babylon,
8 then they came to Gedaliah at Mizpah—[a]Ishmael the son of Nethaniah, [b]Johanan and Jonathan the sons of Kareah, Seraiah the son of Tanhumeth, the sons of Ephai the Netophathite, and [c]Jezaniah[1] the son of a [d]Maachathite, they and their men.
9 And Gedaliah the son of Ahikam, the son of Shaphan, took an

9 [a]2 Kin. 25:8, 11, 12, 20 [b]Jer. 38:19
10 [a]Jer. 40:7 [1]Lit. *on that day*
12 [a]Jer. 1:18, 19; 15:20, 21
14 [a]Jer. 38:28 [b]Jer. 40:5 [c]2 Kin. 22:12, 14; 2 Chr. 34:20; Jer. 26:24
16 [a]Jer. 38:7, 12 [b]Jer. 21:10; [Dan. 9:12; Zech. 1:6]
18 [a]Jer. 21:9; 45:5 [b]1 Chr. 5:20; Ps. 37:40; [Jer. 17:7, 8]

CHAPTER 40

1 [a]Jer. 39:9, 11
2 [a]Jer. 50:7
3 [a]Deut. 29:24, 25; Jer. 50:7; Dan. 9:11; [Rom. 2:5]
4 [a]Jer. 39:12 [b]Gen. 20:15 [1]Or *are*
5 [a]Jer. 39:14 [b]2 Kin. 25:22; Jer. 41:10
6 [a]Jer. 39:14 [b]Judg. 20:1; 1 Sam. 7:5; 2 Chr. 16:6
7 [a]2 Kin. 25:23, 24 [b]Jer. 39:10
8 [a]Jer. 41:1–10 [b]Jer. 41:11; 43:2 [c]Jer. 42:1 [d]Deut. 3:14; Josh. 12:5; 2 Sam. 10:6 [1]*Jaazaniah,* 2 Kin. 25:23

oath before them and their men,
saying, "Do not be afraid to serve
the Chaldeans. Dwell in the land
and serve the king of Babylon, and
it shall be [a]well with you.
10 "As for me, I will indeed dwell
at Mizpah and serve the Chalde-
ans who come to us. But you,
gather wine and summer fruit and
oil, put *them* in your vessels, and
dwell in your cities that you have
taken."
11 Likewise, when all the Jews
who *were* in Moab, among the
Ammonites, in Edom, and who
were in all the countries, heard
that the king of Babylon had left
a remnant of Judah, and that he
had set over them Gedaliah the
son of Ahikam, the son of Sha-
phan,
12 then all the Jews [a]returned out
of all places where they had been
driven, and came to the land of Ju-
dah, to Gedaliah at Mizpah, and
gathered wine and summer fruit in
abundance.
13 Moreover Johanan the son of
Kareah and all the captains of the
forces that *were* in the fields came
to Gedaliah at Mizpah,
14 and said to him, [1]"Do you cer-
tainly know that [a]Baalis the king
of the Ammonites has sent Ish-
mael the son of Nethaniah to mur-
der you?" But Gedaliah the son of
Ahikam did not believe them.
15 Then Johanan the son of Ka-
reah spoke secretly to Gedaliah in
Mizpah, saying, "Let me go,
please, and I will kill Ishmael the
son of Nethaniah, and no one will
know *it*. Why should he murder
you, so that all the Jews who are
gathered to you would be scat-
tered, and the [a]remnant in Judah
perish?"
16 But Gedaliah the son of Ahi-
kam said to Johanan the son of
Kareah, "You shall not do this
thing, for you speak falsely con-
cerning Ishmael."

Insurrection Against Gedaliah

41 Now it came to pass in the
seventh month [a]*that* Ish-
mael the son of Nethaniah, the son
of Elishama, of the royal [1]family
and of the officers of the king,
came with ten men to Gedaliah the
son of Ahikam, at [b]Mizpah. And
there they ate bread together in
Mizpah.
2 Then Ishmael the son of Netha-
niah, and the ten men who were
with him, arose and [a]struck Geda-
liah the son of [b]Ahikam, the son
of Shaphan, with the sword, and
killed him whom the king of Bab-
ylon had made [c]governor over the
land.
3 Ishmael also struck down all
the Jews who were with him, *that
is*, with Gedaliah at Mizpah, and
the Chaldeans who were found
there, the men of war.
4 And it happened, on the second
day after he had killed Gedaliah,
when as yet no one knew *it*,
5 that certain men came from
Shechem, from Shiloh, and from
Samaria, eighty men [a]with their
beards shaved and their clothes
torn, having cut themselves, with
offerings and incense in their
hand, to bring *them* to [b]the house
of the LORD.
6 Now Ishmael the son of Netha-
niah went out from Mizpah to
meet them, weeping as he went
along; and it happened as he met
them that he said to them, "Come
to Gedaliah the son of Ahikam!"
7 So it was, when they came into
the midst of the city, that Ishmael
the son of Nethaniah [a]killed them
and cast them into the midst of a
[1]pit, he and the men who were
with him.
8 But ten men were found among
them who said to Ishmael, "Do not
kill us, for we have treasures of
wheat, barley, oil, and honey in the
field." So he desisted and did not
kill them among their brethren.
9 Now the [1]pit into which Ish-
mael had cast all the dead bodies
of the men whom he had slain, be-
cause of Gedaliah, *was* [a]the same
one Asa the king had made for fear
of Baasha king of Israel. Ishmael
the son of Nethaniah filled it with
the slain.
10 Then Ishmael carried away
captive all the [a]rest of the people
who *were* in Mizpah, [b]the king's
daughters and all the people who
remained in Mizpah, [c]whom Nebu-
zaradan the captain of the guard
had committed to Gedaliah the son
of Ahikam. And Ishmael the son
of Nethaniah carried them away

---

9 [a]Jer. 27:11; 38:17–20
12 [a]Jer. 43:5
14 [a]Jer. 41:10 [1]Or *Certainly you know that*
15 [a]Jer. 42:2

CHAPTER 41

1 [a]2 Kin. 25:25 [b]Jer. 40:6, 10 [1]Lit. *seed*
2 [a]2 Sam. 3:27; 20:9, 10; 2 Kin. 25:25; Ps. 41:9; 109:5; John 13:18 [b]Jer. 26:24 [c]Jer. 40:5
5 [a]Lev. 19:27, 28; Deut. 14:1; Is. 15:2 [b]1 Sam. 1:7; 2 Kin. 25:9; Neh. 10:34, 35
7 [a]Ps. 55:23; Is. 59:7; Ezek. 22:27; 33:24, 26 [1]Or *cistern*
9 [a]1 Kin. 15:22; 2 Chr. 16:6 [1]Or *cistern*
10 [a]Jer. 40:11, 12 [b]Jer. 43:6 [c]Jer. 40:7

captive and departed to go over to
[d]the Ammonites.
11 But when [a]Johanan the son of
Kareah and all the captains of the
forces that *were* with him heard
of all the evil that Ishmael the son
of Nethaniah had done,
12 they took all the men and went
to fight with Ishmael the son of
Nethaniah; and they found him by
[a]the great pool that *is* in Gibeon.
13 So it was, when all the people
who *were* with Ishmael saw Jo-
hanan the son of Kareah, and all
the captains of the forces who
were with him, that they were
glad.
14 Then all the people whom Ish-
mael had carried away captive
from Mizpah turned around and
came back, and went to Johanan
the son of Kareah.
15 But Ishmael the son of Netha-
niah escaped from Johanan with
eight men and went to the Am-
monites.
16 Then Johanan the son of Ka-
reah, and all the captains of the
forces that were with him, took
from Mizpah all the [a]rest of the
people whom he had recovered
from Ishmael the son of Nethaniah
after he had murdered Gedaliah
the son of Ahikam—the mighty
men of war and the women and
the children and the eunuchs,
whom he had brought back from
Gibeon.
17 And they departed and dwelt
in the habitation of [a]Chimham,
which is near Bethlehem, as they
went on their way to [b]Egypt,
18 because of the Chaldeans; for
they were afraid of them, because
Ishmael the son of Nethaniah had
murdered Gedaliah the son of Ahi-
kam, [a]whom the king of Babylon
had made governor in the land.

The Flight to Egypt Forbidden

42 Now all the captains of the
forces, [a]Johanan the son of
Kareah, Jezaniah the son of
Hoshaiah, and all the people, from
the least to the greatest, came near
2 and said to Jeremiah the
prophet, [a]"Please, let our petition
be acceptable to you, and [b]pray for
us to the LORD your God, for all
this remnant (since we are left *but*
[c]a few of many, as you can see),

10 [d]Jer. 40:14
11 [a]Jer. 40:7, 8, 13–16
12 [a]2 Sam. 2:13
16 [a]Jer. 40:11, 12; 43:4–7
17 [a]2 Sam. 19:37, 38 [b]Jer. 43:7
18 [a]Jer. 40:5

CHAPTER 42

1 [a]Jer. 40:8, 13; 41:11
2 [a]Jer. 15:11 [b]Ex. 8:28; 1 Sam. 7:8; 12:19; 1 Kin. 13:6; Is. 37:4; Jer. 37:3; Acts 8:24; [James 5:16] [c]Lev. 26:22; Deut. 28:62; Is. 1:9; Lam. 1:1
3 [a]Ezra 8:21
4 [a]1 Kin. 22:14; Jer. 23:28 [b]1 Sam. 3:17, 18; Ps. 40:10; Acts 20:20
5 [a]Gen. 31:50; Judg. 11:10; Jer. 43:2; Mic. 1:2; Mal. 2:14; 3:5
6 [a]Ex. 24:7; Deut. 5:27; Josh. 24:24 [b]Deut. 5:29, 33; 6:3; Jer. 7:23 [1]Lit. *good* [2]Lit. *evil*
10 [a]Jer. 24:6; 31:28; 33:7; Ezek. 36:36 [b]Deut. 32:36; [Jer. 18:8]
11 [a]Num. 14:9; 2 Chr. 32:7, 8; Is. 8:9, 10; 43:2, 5; Jer. 1:19; 15:20; Rom. 8:31
12 [a]Neh. 1:11; Ps. 106:46; Prov. 16:7
13 [a]Jer. 44:16
14 [a]Is. 31:1; Jer. 41:17; 43:7

3 "that the LORD your God may
show us [a]the way in which we
should walk and the thing we
should do."
4 Then Jeremiah the prophet
said to them, "I have heard. In-
deed, I will pray to the LORD your
God according to your words, and
it shall be, *that* [a]whatever the
LORD answers you, I will declare
it to you. I will [b]keep nothing back
from you."
5 So they said to Jeremiah, [a]"Let
the LORD be a true and faithful wit-
ness between us, if we do not do
according to everything which the
LORD your God sends us by you.
6 "Whether *it is* [1]pleasing or
[2]displeasing, we will [a]obey the
voice of the LORD our God to whom
we send you, [b]that it may be well
with us when we obey the voice
of the LORD our God."
7 And it happened after ten days
that the word of the LORD came to
Jeremiah.
8 Then he called Johanan the son
of Kareah, all the captains of the
forces which *were* with him, and
all the people from the least even
to the greatest,
9 and said to them, "Thus says
the LORD, the God of Israel, to
whom you sent me to present your
petition before Him:
10 'If you will still remain in this
land, then [a]I will build you and not
pull *you* down, and I will plant you
and not pluck *you* up. For I [b]relent
concerning the disaster that I have
brought upon you.
11 'Do not be afraid of the king
of Babylon, of whom you are
afraid; do not be afraid of him,'
says the LORD, [a]'for I *am* with you,
to save you and deliver you from
his hand.
12 'And [a]I will show you mercy,
that he may have mercy on you
and cause you to return to your
own land.'
13 "But if [a]you say, 'We will not
dwell in this land,' disobeying the
voice of the LORD your God,
14 "saying, 'No, but we will go to
the land of [a]Egypt where we shall
see no war, nor hear the sound of
the trumpet, nor be hungry for
bread, and there we will dwell'—
15 "Then hear now the word of
the LORD, O remnant of Judah!

Thus says the LORD of hosts, the
God of Israel: 'If you [a]wholly[1] set
[b]your faces to enter Egypt, and go
to dwell there,
16 'then it shall be *that* the [a]sword
which you feared shall overtake
you there in the land of Egypt; the
famine of which you were afraid
shall follow close after you there
in Egypt; and there you shall die.
17 'So shall it be with all the men
who set their faces to go to Egypt
to dwell there. They shall die by
the sword, by famine, and by pesti-
lence. And [a]none of them shall re-
main or escape from the disaster
that I will bring upon them.'
18 "For thus says the LORD of
hosts, the God of Israel: 'As My
anger and My fury have been
[a]poured out on the inhabitants of
Jerusalem, so will My fury be
poured out on you when you enter
Egypt. And [b]you shall be an oath,
an astonishment, a curse, and a re-
proach; and you shall see this
place no more.'
19 "The LORD has said concerning
you, O remnant of Judah, [a]'Do not
go to Egypt!' Know certainly that
I have [1]admonished you this day.
20 "For you [1]were hypocrites in
your hearts when you sent me to
the LORD your God, saying, 'Pray
for us to the LORD our God, and
according to all that the LORD your
God says, so declare to us and we
will do *it*.'
21 "And I have this day declared
it to you, but you have [a]not obeyed
the voice of the LORD your God,
or anything which He has sent you
by me.
22 "Now therefore, know cer-
tainly that you [a]shall die by the
sword, by famine, and by pesti-
lence in the place where you desire
to go to dwell."

Jeremiah Taken to Egypt

43 Now it happened, when
Jeremiah had stopped
speaking to all the people all the
[a]words of the LORD their God, for
which the LORD their God had sent
him to them, all these words,
2 [a]that Azariah the son of Ho-
shaiah, Johanan the son of Ka-
reah, and all the proud men spoke,
saying to Jeremiah, "You speak
falsely! The LORD our God has not

15 [a]Deut. 17:16; Jer. 44:12–14 [b]Luke 9:51 [1]Or *surely*
16 [a]Jer. 44:13, 27; Ezek. 11:8; Amos 9:1–4
17 [a]Jer. 44:14, 28
18 [a]2 Chr. 36:16–19; Jer. 7:20 [b]Deut. 29:21; Is. 65:15; Jer. 18:16; 24:9; 26:6; 29:18, 22; 44:12
19 [a]Deut. 17:16; Is. 30:1–7 [1]*warned*
20 [1]Lit. *used deceit against your souls*
21 [a]Is. 30:1–7
22 [a]Jer. 42:17; Ezek. 6:11

CHAPTER 43

1 [a]Jer. 42:9–18
2 [a]Jer. 42:1
3 [a]Jer. 36:4; 45:1 [1]Or *incited*
4 [a]2 Kin. 25:26
5 [a]Jer. 40:11, 12
6 [a]Jer. 41:10 [b]Jer. 39:10; 40:7
7 [a]Jer. 42:19 [b]Jer. 2:16; 44:1
8 [a]Jer. 44:1–30
9 [1]Or *mortar*
10 [a]Jer. 25:9; 27:6; Ezek. 29:18, 20
11 [a]Is. 19:1–25; Jer. 25:15–19; 44:13; 46:1, 2, 13–26; Ezek. 29:19, 20 [b]Jer. 15:2; Zech. 11:9
12 [a]Ex. 12:12; Is. 19:1; Jer. 46:25; Ezek. 30:13 [1]So with MT, Tg.; LXX, Syr., Vg. *He*

sent you to say, 'Do not go to
Egypt to dwell there.'
3 "But [a]Baruch the son of Neriah
has [1]set you against us, to deliver
us into the hand of the Chaldeans,
that they may put us to death or
carry us away captive to Bab-
ylon."
4 So Johanan the son of Kareah,
all the captains of the forces, and
all the people would [a]not obey the
voice of the LORD, to remain in the
land of Judah.
5 But Johanan the son of Kareah
and all the captains of the forces
took [a]all the remnant of Judah
who had returned to dwell in the
land of Judah, from all nations
where they had been driven—
6 men, women, children, [a]the
king's daughters, [b]and every per-
son whom Nebuzaradan the cap-
tain of the guard had left with Ged-
aliah the son of Ahikam, the son
of Shaphan, and Jeremiah the
prophet and Baruch the son of Ne-
riah.
7 [a]So they went to the land of
Egypt, for they did not obey the
voice of the LORD. And they went
as far as [b]Tahpanhes.
8 Then the [a]word of the LORD
came to Jeremiah in Tahpanhes,
saying,
9 "Take large stones in your
hand, and hide them in the sight
of the men of Judah, in the [1]clay
in the brick courtyard which *is* at
the entrance to Pharaoh's house in
Tahpanhes;
10 "and say to them, 'Thus says
the LORD of hosts, the God of Is-
rael: "Behold, I will send and bring
Nebuchadnezzar the king of Bab-
ylon, [a]My servant, and will set his
throne above these stones that I
have hidden. And he will spread
his royal pavilion over them.
11 [a]"When he comes, he shall
strike the land of Egypt *and deliver*
to death [b]*those appointed* for
death, and to captivity *those ap-
pointed* for captivity, and to the
sword *those appointed* for the
sword.
12 [1]"I will kindle a fire in the
houses of [a]the gods of Egypt, and
he shall burn them and carry them
away captive. And he shall array
himself with the land of Egypt, as
a shepherd puts on his garment,

and he shall go out from there in
peace.
13 "He shall also break the sacred
pillars of [1]Beth Shemesh that *are*
in the land of Egypt; and the
houses of the gods of the Egyp-
tians he shall burn with fire."'"

Israelites Will Be Punished in Egypt

44 The word that came to Jere-
miah concerning all the
Jews who dwell in the land of
Egypt, who dwell at [a]Migdol, at
[b]Tahpanhes, at [c]Noph,[1] and in the
country of [d]Pathros, saying,
2 "Thus says the LORD of hosts,
the God of Israel: 'You have seen
all the calamity that I have brought
on Jerusalem and on all the cities
of Judah; and behold, this day they
are [a]a desolation, and no one
dwells in them,
3 'because of their wickedness
which they have committed to pro-
voke Me to anger, in that they
went [a]to burn incense *and* to
[b]serve other gods whom they did
not know, they nor you nor your
fathers.
4 'However [a]I have sent to you
all My servants the prophets, ris-
ing early and sending *them,* say-
ing, "Oh, do not do this abomina-
ble thing that I hate!"
5 'But they did not listen or in-
cline their ear to turn from their
wickedness, to burn no incense to
other gods.
6 'So My fury and My anger were
poured out and kindled in the cit-
ies of Judah and in the streets of
Jerusalem; and they [1]are wasted
and desolate, as it is this day.'
7 "Now therefore, thus says the
LORD, the God of hosts, the God
of Israel: 'Why do you commit *this*
great evil [a]against yourselves, to
cut off from you man and woman,
child and infant, out of Judah,
leaving none to remain,
8 'in that you [a]provoke Me to
wrath with the works of your
hands, burning incense to other
gods in the land of Egypt where
you have gone to dwell, that you
may cut yourselves off and be [b]a
curse and a reproach among all
the nations of the earth?
9 'Have you forgotten the wick-
edness of your fathers, the wicked-
ness of the kings of Judah, the
wickedness of their wives, your
own wickedness, and the wicked-
ness of your wives, which they
committed in the land of Judah
and in the streets of Jerusalem?
10 'They have not been [a]hum-
bled,[1] to this day, nor have they
[b]feared; they have not walked in
My law or in My statutes that I set
before you and your fathers.'
11 "Therefore thus says the LORD
of hosts, the God of Israel: 'Behold,
[a]I will set My face against you for
catastrophe and for [1]cutting off all
Judah.
12 'And I will take the remnant of
Judah who have set their faces to
go into the land of Egypt to dwell
there, and [a]they shall all be con-
sumed *and* fall in the land of
Egypt. They shall be consumed by
the sword *and* by famine. They
shall die, from the least to the
greatest, by the sword and by fam-
ine; and [b]they shall be an oath, an
astonishment, a curse and a re-
proach!
13 [a]'For I will punish those who
dwell in the land of Egypt, as I
have punished Jerusalem, by the
sword, by famine, and by pesti-
lence,
14 'so that none of the remnant of
Judah who have gone into the land
of Egypt to dwell there shall es-
cape or survive, lest they return to
the land of Judah, to which they
[a]desire[1] to return and dwell. For
[b]none shall return except those
who escape.'"
15 Then all the men who knew
that their wives had burned in-
cense to other gods, with all the
women who stood by, a great mul-
titude, and all the people who
dwelt in the land of Egypt, in Path-
ros, answered Jeremiah, saying:
16 "*As for* the word that you have
spoken to us in the name of the
LORD, [a]we will not listen to you!
17 "But we will certainly do
[a]whatever has gone out of our own
mouth, to burn incense to the
[b]queen of heaven and pour out
drink offerings to her, as we have
done, we and our fathers, our
kings and our princes, in the cities
of Judah and in the streets of Jeru-
salem. For *then* we had plenty of
[1]food, were well-off, and saw no
trouble.

13 [1]Lit. *House of the Sun,* ancient On, later called Heliopolis

CHAPTER 44

1 [a]Ex. 14:2; Jer. 46:14 [b]Jer. 43:7; Ezek. 30:18 [c]Is. 19:13; Jer. 2:16; 46:14; Ezek. 30:13, 16; Hos. 9:6 [d]Is. 11:11; Ezek. 29:14; 30:14 [1]Ancient Memphis
2 [a]Is. 6:11; Jer. 4:7; 9:11; 34:22; Mic. 3:12
3 [a]Jer. 19:4 [b]Deut. 13:6; 32:17
4 [a]2 Chr. 36:15; Jer. 7:25; 25:4; 26:5; 29:19; Zech. 7:7
6 [1]Or *became a ruin*
7 [a]Num. 16:38; Jer. 7:19; [Ezek. 33:11]; Hab. 2:10
8 [a]2 Kin. 17:15–17; Jer. 25:6, 7; 44:3; 1 Cor. 10:21, 22 [b]1 Kin. 9:7, 8; 2 Chr. 7:20; Jer. 42:18
10 [a]2 Chr. 36:12; Jer. 6:15; 8:12; Dan. 5:22 [b][Prov. 28:14] [1]Lit. *crushed*
11 [a]Lev. 17:10; 20:5, 6; Jer. 21:10; Amos 9:4 [1]*destroying*
12 [a]Jer. 42:15–17, 22 [b]Is. 65:15; Jer. 42:18
13 [a]Jer. 43:11
14 [a]Jer. 22:26, 27 [b][Is. 4:2; 10:20]; Jer. 44:28; [Rom. 9:27] [1]Lit. *lift up their soul*
16 [a]Jer. 6:16
17 [a]Num. 30:12; Deut. 23:23; Judg. 11:36 [b]2 Kin. 17:16; Jer. 7:18 [1]Lit. *bread*

18 "But since we stopped burning
incense to the queen of heaven and
pouring out drink offerings to her,
we have lacked everything and
have been consumed by the sword
and by famine."
19 *The women also said,* [a]"And
when we burned incense to the
queen of heaven and poured out
drink offerings to her, did we
make cakes for her, to worship
her, and pour out drink offerings
to her without our husbands' *per-
mission?*"
20 Then Jeremiah spoke to all the
people—the men, the women, and
all the people who had given him
that answer—saying:
21 "The incense that you burned
in the cities of Judah and in the
streets of Jerusalem, you and your
fathers, your kings and your
princes, and the people of the land,
did not the LORD remember them,
and did it *not* come into His mind?
22 "So the LORD could no longer
bear *it*, because of the evil of
your doings *and* because of the
abominations which you com-
mitted. Therefore your land is a
desolation, an astonishment, a
curse, and without an inhabitant,
[a]as *it is* this day.
23 "Because you have burned in-
cense and because you have
sinned against the LORD, and have
not obeyed the voice of the LORD
or walked in His law, in His stat-
utes or in His testimonies, [a]there-
fore this calamity has happened to
you, as *at* this day."
24 Moreover Jeremiah said to all
the people and to all the women,
"Hear the word of the LORD, all Ju-
dah who *are* in the land of Egypt!
25 "Thus says the LORD of hosts,
the God of Israel, saying: 'You and
your wives have spoken with your
mouths and fulfilled with your
hands, saying, "We will surely
keep our vows that we have made,
to burn incense to the queen of
heaven and pour out drink offer-
ings to her." You will surely keep
your vows and perform your
vows!'
26 "Therefore hear the word of
the LORD, all Judah who dwell in
the land of Egypt: 'Behold, [a]I have
sworn by My [b]great name,' says
the LORD, 'that [c]My name shall no
more be named in the mouth of
any man of Judah in all the land
of Egypt, saying, "The Lord GOD
lives."
27 'Behold, I will watch over them
for adversity and not for good.
And all the men of Judah who *are*
in the land of Egypt [a]shall be con-
sumed by the sword and by
famine, until there is an end to
them.
28 'Yet [a]a small number who es-
cape the sword shall return from
the land of Egypt to the land of
Judah; and all the remnant of Ju-
dah, who have gone to the land of
Egypt to dwell there, shall know
whose words will stand, Mine or
theirs.
29 'And this *shall be* a sign to you,'
says the LORD, 'that I will punish
you in this place, that you may
know that My words will surely
[a]stand against you for adversity.'
30 "Thus says the LORD: 'Behold,
[a]I will give Pharaoh Hophra king
of Egypt into the hand of his ene-
mies and into the hand of those
who seek his life, as I gave [b]Zede-
kiah king of Judah into the hand
of Nebuchadnezzar king of Bab-
ylon, his enemy who sought his
life.'"

Assurance to Baruch

45 The [a]word that Jeremiah the
prophet spoke to [b]Baruch
the son of Neriah, when he had
written these words in a book [1]at
the instruction of Jeremiah, in the
[c]fourth year of Jehoiakim the son
of Josiah, king of Judah, saying,
2 "Thus says the LORD, the God
of Israel, to you, O Baruch:
3 'You said, "Woe is me now! For
the LORD has added grief to my
sorrow. I [a]fainted in my sighing,
and I find no rest."'
4 "Thus you shall say to him,
'Thus says the LORD: "Behold,
[a]what I have built I will break
down, and what I have planted I
will pluck up, that is, this whole
land.
5 "And do you seek great things
for yourself? Do not seek *them;* for
behold, [a]I will bring adversity on
all flesh," says the LORD. "But I
will give your [b]life to you as a prize
in all places, wherever you go."'"

19 [a]Jer. 7:18
22 [a]Jer. 25:11, 18, 38
23 [a]1 Kin. 9:9; Neh. 13:18; Jer. 44:2; Dan. 9:11, 12
26 [a]Gen. 22:16; Deut. 32:40, 41; Jer. 22:5; Amos 6:8; Heb. 6:13 [b]Jer. 10:6 [c]Neh. 9:5; Ps. 50:16; Ezek. 20:39
27 [a]Jer. 1:10; 31:28; Ezek. 7:6
28 [a]Is. 10:19; 27:12, 13
29 [a][Ps. 33:11]
30 [a]Jer. 46:25, 26; Ezek. 29:3; 30:21 [b]2 Kin. 25:4–7; Jer. 39:5

CHAPTER 45

1 [a]Jer. 36:1, 4, 32 [b]Jer. 32:12, 16; 43:3 [c]Jer. 25:1; 36:1; 46:2 [1]Lit. *from Jeremiah's mouth*
3 [a]Ps. 6:6; 69:3; [2 Cor. 4:1, 16; Gal. 6:9]
4 [a]Is. 5:5; Jer. 1:10; 11:17; 18:7–10; 31:28
5 [a]Jer. 25:17–26 [b]Jer. 21:9; 38:2; 39:18

Judgment on Egypt

46 The word of the LORD which came to Jeremiah the prophet against [a]the nations.
2 Against [a]Egypt.
[b]Concerning the army of Pharaoh Necho, king of Egypt, which was by the River Euphrates in Carchemish, and which Nebuchadnezzar king of Babylon [c]defeated in the [d]fourth year of Jehoiakim the son of Josiah, king of Judah:

3 "Order[1] the [2]buckler and shield,
And draw near to battle!
4 Harness the horses,
And mount up, you horsemen!
Stand forth with *your* helmets,
Polish the spears,
[a]Put on the armor!
5 Why have I seen them dismayed
and turned back?
Their mighty ones are beaten
down;
They have speedily fled,
And did not look back,
For [a]fear *was* all around," says
the LORD.
6 "Do not let the swift flee away,
Nor the mighty man escape;
They will [a]stumble and fall
Toward the north, by the River
Euphrates.

7 "Who *is* this coming up [a]like a
flood,
Whose waters move like the
rivers?
8 Egypt rises up like a flood,
And *its* waters move like the
rivers;
And he says, 'I will go up *and*
cover the earth,
I will destroy the city and its
inhabitants.'
9 Come up, O horses, and rage,
O chariots!
And let the mighty men come
forth:
[1]The Ethiopians and [2]the Libyans
who handle the shield,
And the Lydians [a]who handle
and bend the bow.
10 For this *is* [a]the day of the Lord
GOD of hosts,
A day of vengeance,
That He may avenge Himself on
His adversaries.
[b]The sword shall devour;
It shall be [1]satiated and made
drunk with their blood;
For the Lord GOD of hosts [c]has a
sacrifice
In the north country by the River
Euphrates.

11 "Go[a] up to Gilead and take balm,
[b]O virgin, the daughter of Egypt;
In vain you will use many
medicines;
[c]You shall not be cured.
12 The nations have heard of your
[a]shame,
And your cry has filled the land;
For the mighty man has stumbled
against the mighty;
They both have fallen together."

Babylonia Will Strike Egypt

13 The word that the LORD spoke
to Jeremiah the prophet, how
Nebuchadnezzar king of Babylon
would come *and* [a]strike the land
of Egypt.

14 "Declare in Egypt, and proclaim in
[a]Migdol;
Proclaim in [1]Noph and in
[b]Tahpanhes;
Say, 'Stand fast and prepare
yourselves,
For the sword devours all around
you.'
15 Why are your valiant *men* swept
away?
They did not stand
Because the LORD drove them
away.
16 He made many fall;
Yes, [a]one fell upon another.
And they said, 'Arise!
[b]Let us go back to our own people
And to the land of our nativity
From the oppressing sword.'
17 They cried there,
'Pharaoh, king of Egypt, *is but* a
noise.
He has passed by the appointed
time!'

18 "As I live," says the King,
[a]Whose name *is* the LORD of hosts,
"Surely as Tabor *is* among the
mountains
And as Carmel by the sea, *so* he
shall come.
19 O [a]you daughter dwelling in
Egypt,
Prepare yourself [b]to go into
captivity!
For [1]Noph shall be waste and
desolate, without inhabitant.

20 "Egypt *is* a very pretty [a]heifer,
But destruction comes, it comes
[b]from the north.

CHAPTER 46
1 [a]Jer. 25:15
2 [a]Jer. 25:17–19; Ezek. 29:2—32:32 [b]2 Kin. 23:33–35 [c]2 Kin. 23:29; 24:7; 2 Chr. 35:20 [d]Jer. 45:1
3 [1]*Set in order* [2]A small shield
4 [a]Is. 21:5; Jer. 51:11, 12; Joel 3:9; Nah. 2:1; 3:14
5 [a]Jer. 49:29
6 [a]Jer. 46:12, 16; Dan. 11:19
7 [a]Is. 8:7, 8; Jer. 47:2; Dan. 11:22
9 [a]Is. 66:19 [1]Heb. *Cush* [2]Heb. *Put*
10 [a]Is. 13:6; Joel 1:15 [b]Deut. 32:42; Is. 31:8; Jer. 12:12 [c]Is. 34:6; Zeph. 1:7; Ezek. 39:17 [1]Filled to the full
11 [a]Jer. 8:22 [b]Is. 47:1; Jer. 31:4, 21 [c]Ezek. 30:21
12 [a]Jer. 2:36; Nah. 3:8–10
13 [a]Is. 19:1; Jer. 43:10, 11; Ezek. 29:1–21
14 [a]Jer. 44:1 [b]Ezek. 30:18 [1]Ancient Memphis
16 [a]Lev. 26:36, 37; Jer. 46:6 [b]Jer. 51:9
18 [a]Is. 47:4; Jer. 48:15; Mal. 1:14
19 [a]Jer. 48:18 [b]Is. 20:4 [1]Ancient Memphis
20 [a]Hos. 10:11 [b]Jer. 1:14

21 Also her mercenaries are in her
midst like [1]fat bulls,
For they also are turned back,
They have fled away together.
They did not stand,
For [a]the day of their calamity had
come upon them,
The time of their punishment.
22 [a]Her noise shall go like a
serpent,
For they shall march with an
army
And come against her with axes,
Like those who chop wood.

23 "They shall [a]cut down her forest,"
says the LORD,
"Though it cannot be searched,
Because they *are* innumerable,
And more numerous than
[b]grasshoppers.
24 The daughter of Egypt shall be
ashamed;
She shall be delivered into the
hand
Of [a]the people of the north."

25 The LORD of hosts, the God of
Israel, says: "Behold, I will bring
punishment on [1]Amon of [a]No,[2]
and Pharaoh and Egypt, [b]with
their gods and their kings—Pha-
raoh and those who [c]trust in him.
26 [a]"And I will deliver them into
the hand of those who seek their
lives, into the hand of Nebuchad-
nezzar king of Babylon and the
hand of his servants. [b]Afterward
it shall be inhabited as in the days
of old," says the LORD.

God Will Preserve Israel

27 "But[a] do not fear, O My servant
Jacob,
And do not be dismayed, O Israel!
For behold, I will [b]save you from
afar,
And your offspring from the land
of their captivity;
Jacob shall return, have rest and
be at ease;
No one shall make *him* afraid.
28 Do not fear, O Jacob My
servant," says the LORD,
"For I *am* with you;
For I will make a complete end
of all the nations
To which I have driven you,
But I will not make [a]a complete
end of you.
I will rightly [b]correct you,
For I will not leave you wholly
unpunished."

21 [a][Ps. 37:13] [1]Lit. *calves of the stall*
22 [a][Is. 29:4]
23 [a]Is. 10:34 [b]Judg. 6:5; 7:12
24 [a]Jer. 1:15
25 [a]Ezek. 30:14–16 [b]Jer. 43:12, 13 [c]Is. 30:1–5; 31:1–3 [1]A sun god [2]Ancient Thebes
26 [a]Ezek. 32:11 [b]Ezek. 29:8–14
27 [a]Is. 41:13, 14; 43:5; 44:2 [b]Is. 11:11
28 [a]Amos 9:8, 9 [b]Jer. 30:11

CHAPTER 47

1 [a]Zeph. 2:4, 5 [b]Amos 1:6
2 [a]Is. 8:7, 8 [b]Jer. 1:14
3 [a]Jer. 8:16 [1]Lit. *From sinking hands*
4 [a]Is. 14:29–31 [b]Jer. 25:22 [c]Ezek. 25:16 [d]Gen. 10:14 [1]Cappadocia in Asia Minor
5 [a]Mic. 1:16 [b]Jer. 25:20
6 [a]Ezek. 21:3–5
7 [a]Ezek. 14:17 [b]Mic. 6:9 [1]Lit. *you*

CHAPTER 48

1 [a]Is. 15:1—16:14; 25:10 [b]Is. 15:2 [c]Num. 32:37 [1]Heb. *Misgab*
2 [a]Is. 16:14 [b]Jer. 49:3

Judgment on Philistia

47 The word of the LORD that
came to Jeremiah the
prophet [a]against the Philistines,
[b]before Pharaoh attacked Gaza.
2 Thus says the LORD:

"Behold, [a]waters rise [b]out of the
north,
And shall be an overflowing
flood;
They shall overflow the land and
all that is in it,
The city and those who dwell
within;
Then the men shall cry,
And all the inhabitants of the
land shall wail.
3 At the [a]noise of the stamping
hooves of his strong horses,
At the rushing of his chariots,
At the rumbling of his wheels,
The fathers will not look back for
their children,
[1]Lacking courage,
4 Because of the day that comes to
plunder all the [a]Philistines,
To cut off from [b]Tyre and Sidon
every helper who remains;
For the LORD shall plunder the
Philistines,
[c]The remnant of the country of
[d]Caphtor.[1]
5 [a]Baldness has come upon Gaza,
[b]Ashkelon is cut off
With the remnant of their valley.
How long will you cut yourself?

6 "O you [a]sword of the LORD,
How long until you are quiet?
Put yourself up into your
scabbard,
Rest and be still!
7 How can [1]it be quiet,
Seeing the LORD has [a]given it a
charge
Against Ashkelon and against the
seashore?
There He has [b]appointed it."

Judgment on Moab

48 Against [a]Moab.
Thus says the LORD of
hosts, the God of Israel:

"Woe to [b]Nebo!
For it is plundered,
[c]Kirjathaim is shamed *and* taken;
[1]The high stronghold is shamed
and dismayed—
2 [a]No more praise of Moab.
In [b]Heshbon they have devised
evil against her:

'Come, and let us cut her off as a nation.'
You also shall be cut down,
O [c]Madmen![1]
The sword shall pursue you;
3 A voice of crying *shall be* from [a]Horonaim:
'Plundering and great destruction!'

4 "Moab is destroyed;
[1]Her little ones have caused a cry to be heard;
5 [a]For in the Ascent of Luhith they ascend with continual weeping;
For in the descent of Horonaim the enemies have heard a cry of destruction.

6 "Flee, save your lives!
And be like [1]the [a]juniper in the wilderness.
7 For because you have trusted in your works and your [a]treasures,
You also shall be taken.
And [b]Chemosh shall go forth into captivity,
His [c]priests and his princes together.
8 And [a]the plunderer shall come against every city;
No one shall escape.
The valley also shall perish,
And the plain shall be destroyed,
As the LORD has spoken.

9 "Give[a] wings to Moab,
That she may flee and get away;
For her cities shall be desolate,
Without any to dwell in them.
10 [a]Cursed *is* he who does the work of the LORD deceitfully,
And cursed *is* he who keeps back his sword from blood.

11 "Moab has been at ease from [1]his youth;
He [a]has settled on his dregs,
And has not been emptied from vessel to vessel,
Nor has he gone into captivity.
Therefore his taste remained in him,
And his scent has not changed.

12 "Therefore behold, the days are coming," says the LORD,
"That I shall send him [1]wine-workers
Who will tip him over
And empty his vessels
And break the bottles.
13 Moab shall be ashamed of [a]Chemosh,

2 [c]Is. 10:31 [1]A city of Moab
3 [a]Is. 15:5; Jer. 48:5, 34
4 [1]So with MT, Tg., Vg.; LXX *Proclaim it in Zoar*
5 [a]Is. 15:5
6 [a]Jer. 17:6 [1]Or *Aroer*, a city of Moab
7 [a]Ps. 52:7; Is. 59:4; Jer. 9:23; [1 Tim. 6:17] [b]Num. 21:29; Judg. 11:24; Jer. 48:13 [c]Jer. 49:3
8 [a]Jer. 6:26
9 [a]Ps. 55:6
10 [a]Judg. 5:23; 1 Sam. 15:3, 9; 1 Kin. 20:42
11 [a]Zeph. 1:12 [1]Heb. uses masc. and fem. pronouns interchangeably in this chapter.
12 [1]Lit. *tippers* of wine bottles
13 [a]1 Kin. 11:7 [b]Hos. 10:6 [c]1 Kin. 12:29; 13:32–34; Hos. 8:5, 6
14 [a]Is. 16:6
15 [a][Is. 40:30, 31]; Jer. 50:27 [b]Jer. 46:18; 51:57; Mal. 1:14
17 [a]Is. 9:4; 14:4, 5
18 [a]Is. 47:1 [b]Num. 21:30; Josh. 13:9, 17; Is. 15:2; Jer. 48:22
19 [a]Deut. 2:36; Josh. 12:2; Is. 17:2 [b]1 Sam. 4:13, 14, 16
20 [a]Is. 16:7 [b]Num. 21:13
24 [a]Jer. 48:41; Amos 2:2
25 [a]Ps. 75:10; Zech. 1:19–21 [b]Ezek. 30:21 [1]Strength
26 [a]Jer. 25:15
27 [a]Zeph. 2:8

As the house of Israel [b]was ashamed of [c]Bethel, their confidence.
14 "How can you say, [a]'We *are* mighty
And strong men for the war'?
15 Moab is plundered and gone up *from* her cities;
Her chosen young men have [a]gone down to the slaughter,"
says [b]the King,
Whose name *is* the LORD of hosts.

16 "The calamity of Moab *is* near at hand,
And his affliction comes quickly.
17 Bemoan him, all you who are around him;
And all you who know his name,
Say, [a]'How the strong staff is broken,
The beautiful rod!'

18 "O [a]daughter inhabiting [b]Dibon,
Come down from *your* glory,
And sit in thirst;
For the plunderer of Moab has come against you,
He has destroyed your strongholds.
19 O inhabitant of [a]Aroer,
[b]Stand by the way and watch;
Ask him who flees
And her who escapes;
Say, 'What has happened?'
20 Moab is shamed, for he is broken down.
[a]Wail and cry!
Tell it in [b]Arnon, that Moab is plundered.

21 "And judgment has come on the plain country:
On Holon and Jahzah and Mephaath,
22 On Dibon and Nebo and Beth Diblathaim,
23 On Kirjathaim and Beth Gamul and Beth Meon,
24 On [a]Kerioth and Bozrah,
On all the cities of the land of Moab,
Far or near.
25 [a]The [1]horn of Moab is cut off,
And his [b]arm is broken," says the LORD.

26 "Make[a] him drunk,
Because he exalted *himself* against the LORD.
Moab shall wallow in his vomit,
And he shall also be in derision.
27 For [a]was not Israel a derision to you?

[b]Was he found among thieves?
For whenever you speak of him,
You shake *your head in* [c]scorn.
28 You who dwell in Moab,
Leave the cities and [a]dwell in the rock,
And be like [b]the dove *which* makes her nest
In the sides of the cave's mouth.

29 "We have heard the [a]pride of Moab
(He *is* exceedingly proud),
Of his loftiness and arrogance and [b]pride,
And of the haughtiness of his heart."

30 "I know his wrath," says the LORD,
"But it *is* not right;
[a]His [1]lies have made nothing right.
31 Therefore [a]I will wail for Moab,
And I will cry out for all Moab;
[1]I will mourn for the men of Kir Heres.
32 [a]O vine of Sibmah! I will weep for you with the weeping of [b]Jazer.
Your plants have gone over the sea,
They reach to the sea of Jazer.
The plunderer has fallen on your summer fruit and your vintage.
33 [a]Joy and gladness are taken
From the plentiful field
And from the land of Moab;
I have caused wine to [1]fail from the winepresses;
No one will tread with joyous shouting—
Not joyous shouting!

34 "From[a] the cry of Heshbon to [b]Elealeh and to Jahaz
They have uttered their voice,
[c]From Zoar to Horonaim,
Like [1]a three-year-old heifer;
For the waters of Nimrim also shall be desolate.

35 "Moreover," says the LORD,
"I will cause to cease in Moab
[a]The one who offers *sacrifices* in the [1]high places
And burns incense to his gods.
36 Therefore [a]My heart shall wail like flutes for Moab,
And like flutes My heart shall wail
For the men of Kir Heres.
Therefore [b]the riches they have acquired have perished.

37 "For [a]every head *shall be* bald, and every beard clipped;
On all the hands *shall be* cuts, and [b]on the loins sackcloth—

27 [b]Jer. 2:26 [c]Lam. 2:15; [Mic. 7:8–10]
28 [a]Ps. 55:6, 7 [b]Song 2:14
29 [a]Is. 16:6; Zeph. 2:8, 10 [b]Jer. 49:16
30 [a]Is. 16:6; Jer. 50:36 [1]*idle talk*
31 [a]Is. 15:5; 16:7, 11 [1]So with DSS, LXX, Vg.; MT *He*
32 [a]Is. 16:8, 9 [b]Num. 21:32; Is. 16:10
33 [a]Is. 16:10; Jer. 25:10; Joel 1:12 [1]*cease*
34 [a]Is. 15:4–6 [b]Num. 32:3, 37 [c]Is. 15:5, 6 [1]Or *The Third Eglath,* an unknown city, Is. 15:5
35 [a]Is. 15:2; 16:12 [1]Places for pagan worship
36 [a]Is. 15:5; 16:11 [b]Is. 15:7
37 [a]Is. 15:2, 3; Jer. 16:6; 41:5; 47:5 [b]Gen. 37:34; Is. 15:3; 20:2
38 [a]Is. 15:3 [b]Jer. 22:28
40 [a]Deut. 28:49; Jer. 49:22; Hos. 8:1; Hab. 1:8 [b]Is. 8:8
41 [a]Is. 13:8; 21:3; Jer. 30:6; Mic. 4:9, 10
42 [a]Ps. 83:4; Jer. 48:2
43 [a]Is. 24:17, 18; Lam. 3:47
44 [a]1 Kin. 19:17; Is. 24:18; Amos 5:19 [b]Jer. 11:23
45 [a]Num. 21:28, 29 [b]Num. 21:21, 26; Ps. 135:11 [c]Num. 24:17
46 [a]Num. 21:29
47 [a]Jer. 49:6, 39

38 A general lamentation
On all the [a]housetops of Moab,
And in its streets;
For I have [b]broken Moab like a vessel in which *is* no pleasure,"
says the LORD.
39 "They shall wail:
'How she is broken down!
How Moab has turned her back with shame!'
So Moab shall be a derision
And a dismay to all those about her."

40 For thus says the LORD:

"Behold, [a]one shall fly like an eagle,
And [b]spread his wings over Moab.
41 Kerioth is taken,
And the strongholds are surprised;
[a]The mighty men's hearts in Moab on that day shall be
Like the heart of a woman in birth pangs.
42 And Moab shall be destroyed [a]as a people,
Because he exalted *himself* against the LORD.
43 [a]Fear and the pit and the snare *shall be* upon you,
O inhabitant of Moab," says the LORD.
44 "He who flees from the fear shall fall into the pit,
And he who gets out of the pit shall be caught in the [a]snare.
For upon Moab, upon it [b]I will bring
The year of their punishment,"
says the LORD.

45 "Those who fled stood under the shadow of Heshbon
Because of exhaustion.
But [a]a fire shall come out of Heshbon,
A flame from the midst of [b]Sihon,
And [c]shall devour the brow of Moab,
The crown of the head of the sons of tumult.
46 [a]Woe to you, O Moab!
The people of Chemosh perish;
For your sons have been taken captive,
And your daughters captive.

47 "Yet I will bring back the captives of Moab
[a]In the latter days," says the LORD.

Thus far *is* the judgment of Moab.

Judgment on Ammon

49 Against the [a]Ammonites.
Thus says the LORD:

"Has Israel no sons?
Has he no heir?
Why *then* does [1]Milcom inherit
[b]Gad,
And his people dwell in its cities?
2 [a]Therefore behold, the days are
coming," says the LORD,
"That I will cause to be heard an
alarm of war
In [b]Rabbah of the Ammonites;
It shall be a desolate mound,
And her [1]villages shall be burned
with fire.
Then Israel shall take possession
of his inheritance," says the
LORD.

3 "Wail, O [a]Heshbon, for Ai is
plundered!
Cry, you daughters of Rabbah,
[b]Gird yourselves with sackcloth!
Lament and run to and fro by the
walls;
For [1]Milcom shall go into
captivity
With his [c]priests and his princes
together.
4 Why [a]do you boast in the valleys,
[1]Your flowing valley,
O [b]backsliding daughter?
Who trusted in her [c]treasures,
[d]*saying,*
'Who will come against me?'
5 Behold, I will bring fear upon
you,"
Says the Lord GOD of hosts,
"From all those who are around
you;
You shall be driven out, everyone
headlong,
And no one will gather those who
wander off.
6 But [a]afterward I will bring back
The captives of the people of
Ammon," says the LORD.

Judgment on Edom

7 [a]Against Edom.
Thus says the LORD of hosts:

[b]"*Is* wisdom no more in Teman?
[c]Has counsel perished from the
prudent?
Has their wisdom [d]vanished?
8 Flee, turn back, dwell in the
depths, O inhabitants of
[a]Dedan!
For I will bring the calamity of
Esau upon him,
The time *that* I will punish him.
9 [a]If grape-gatherers came to you,
Would they not leave *some*
gleaning grapes?
If thieves by night,
Would they not destroy until they
have enough?
10 [a]But I have made Esau bare;
I have uncovered his secret
places,
And he shall not be able to hide
himself.
His descendants are plundered,
His brethren and his neighbors,
And [b]he *is* no more.
11 Leave your fatherless children,
I will preserve *them* alive;
And let your widows trust in Me."

12 For thus says the LORD: "Be-
hold, [a]those whose judgment *was*
not to drink of the cup have as-
suredly drunk. And *are* you the
one who will altogether go un-
punished? You shall not go un-
punished, but you shall surely
drink *of it.*
13 "For [a]I have sworn by Myself,"
says the LORD, "that [b]Bozrah shall
become a desolation, a reproach,
a [1]waste, and a curse. And all its
cities shall be perpetual [2]wastes."

14 [a]I have heard a message from the
LORD,
And an ambassador has been
sent to the nations:
"Gather together, come against
her,
And rise up to battle!

15 "For indeed, I will make you small
among nations,
Despised among men.
16 Your fierceness has deceived
you,
The [a]pride of your heart,
O you who dwell in the clefts of
the rock,
Who hold the height of the hill!
[b]Though you make your [c]nest as
high as the eagle,
[d]I will bring you down from
there," says the LORD.

17 "Edom also shall be an
astonishment;
[a]Everyone who goes by it will be
astonished
And will hiss at all its plagues.
18 [a]As in the overthrow of Sodom
and Gomorrah
And their neighbors," says the
LORD,
"No one shall remain there,

CHAPTER 49
1 [a]Deut. 23:3, 4; 2 Chr. 20:1; Jer. 25:21; Ezek. 21:28–32; 25:1–7 [b]Amos 1:13–15; Zeph. 2:8–11 [1]Heb. *Malcam,* lit. *their king;* an Ammonite god, 1 Kin. 11:5; *Molech,* Lev. 18:21
2 [a]Amos 1:13–15 [b]Ezek. 25:5 [1]Lit. *daughters*
3 [a]Jer. 48:2 [b]Is. 32:11; Jer. 48:37 [c]Jer. 48:7 [1]See v. 1
4 [a]Jer. 9:23 [b]Jer. 3:14 [c]Jer. 48:7 [d]Jer. 21:13 [1]Lit. *Your valley is flowing*
6 [a]Jer. 48:47
7 [a]Gen. 25:30; 32:3; Is. 34:5, 6; Jer. 25:21; Ezek. 25:12–14; 35:1–15; Joel 3:19; Amos 1:11, 12; Obad. 1–9, 15, 16 [b]Gen. 36:11; Job 2:11 [c]Is. 19:11 [d]Jer. 8:9
8 [a]Is. 21:13; Jer. 25:23
9 [a]Obad. 5, 6
10 [a]Obad. 5, 6; Mal. 1:3 [b]Is. 17:14
12 [a]Jer. 25:29; Obad. 16
13 [a]Gen. 22:16; Is. 45:23; Jer. 44:26; Amos 6:8 [b]Gen. 36:33; 1 Chr. 1:44; Is. 34:6; 63:1; Amos 1:12 [1]*ruin* [2]*ruins*
14 [a]Obad. 1–4
16 [a]Jer. 48:29 [b]Obad. 3, 4 [c]Job 39:27; Is. 14:13–15 [d]Amos 9:2
17 [a]Jer. 18:16; 49:13; 50:13; Ezek. 35:7
18 [a]Gen. 19:24, 25; Deut. 29:23; Jer. 50:40; Amos 4:11; Zeph. 2:9

Nor shall a son of man dwell in
it.
19 "Behold,[a] he shall come up like a
lion from [b]the [1]floodplain of the
Jordan
Against the dwelling place of the
strong;
But I will suddenly make him run
away from her.
And who *is* a chosen *man that* I
may appoint over her?
For [c]who *is* like Me?
Who will arraign Me?
And [d]who *is* that shepherd
Who will withstand Me?"

20 [a]Therefore hear the counsel of the
LORD that He has taken against
Edom,
And His purposes that He has
proposed against the
inhabitants of Teman:
Surely the least of the flock shall
[1]draw them out;
Surely He shall make their
dwelling places desolate with
them.
21 [a]The earth shakes at the noise of
their fall;
At the cry its noise is heard at the
Red Sea.
22 Behold, [a]He shall come up and fly
like the eagle,
And spread His wings over
Bozrah;
The heart of the mighty men of
Edom in that day shall be
Like the heart of a woman in
birth pangs.

Judgment on Damascus

23 [a]Against Damascus.

[b]"Hamath and Arpad are shamed,
For they have heard bad news.
They are fainthearted;
[c]*There is* [1]trouble on the sea;
It cannot be quiet.
24 Damascus has grown feeble;
She turns to flee,
And fear has seized *her*.
[a]Anguish and sorrows have taken
her like a woman in [1]labor.
25 Why is [a]the city of praise not
deserted, the city of My joy?
26 [a]Therefore her young men shall
fall in her streets,
And all the men of war shall be
cut off in that day," says the
LORD of hosts.
27 "I[a] will kindle a fire in the wall of
Damascus,
And it shall consume the palaces
of Ben-Hadad."

19 [a]Jer. 50:44 [b]Josh. 3:15; Jer. 12:5 [c]Ex. 15:11; Is. 46:9 [d]Job 41:10 [1]Or *thicket*
20 [a]Is. 14:24, 27; Jer. 50:45 [1]Or *drag them away*
21 [a]Jer. 50:46; Ezek. 26:15, 18
22 [a]Jer. 48:40, 41
23 [a]Is. 17:1–3; Amos 1:3, 5; Zech. 9:1, 2 [b]Jer. 39:5; Zech. 9:2 [c][Is. 57:20] [1]*anxiety*
24 [a]Is. 13:8; Jer. 4:31; 6:24; 48:21 [1]*childbirth*
25 [a]Jer. 33:9
26 [a]Jer. 50:30; Amos 4:10
27 [a]Amos 1:4
28 [a]Gen. 25:13; Ps. 120:5; Is. 21:16, 17; Jer. 2:10; Ezek. 27:21 [b]Judg. 6:3; Job 1:3
29 [a]Ps. 120:5 [b]Jer. 46:5
31 [a]Ezek. 38:11 [b]Num. 23:9; Deut. 33:28; Mic. 7:16
32 [a]Ezek. 5:10 [1]Lit. *cut off at the corner*, Jer. 9:26; 25:23
33 [a]Jer. 9:11; 10:22; Zeph. 2:9, 12–15; Mal. 1:3
34 [a]Gen. 10:22; Jer. 25:25; Ezek. 32:24; Dan. 8:2 [b]2 Kin. 24:17, 18; Jer. 28:1
35 [a]Ps. 46:9; Is. 22:6 [1]Power

Judgment on Kedar and Hazor

28 [a]Against Kedar and against the
kingdoms of Hazor, which Nebu-
chadnezzar king of Babylon shall
strike.
Thus says the LORD:

"Arise, go up to Kedar,
And devastate [b]the men of the
East!
29 Their [a]tents and their flocks they
shall take away.
They shall take for themselves
their curtains,
All their vessels and their camels;
And they shall cry out to them,
[b]'Fear *is* on every side!'

30 "Flee, get far away! Dwell in the
depths,
O inhabitants of Hazor!" says the
LORD.
"For Nebuchadnezzar king of
Babylon has taken counsel
against you,
And has conceived a plan against
you.

31 "Arise, go up to [a]the wealthy
nation that dwells securely,"
says the LORD,
"Which has neither gates nor bars,
[b]Dwelling alone.
32 Their camels shall be for booty,
And the multitude of their cattle
for plunder.
I will [a]scatter to all winds those
[1]in the farthest corners,
And I will bring their calamity
from all its sides," says the
LORD.
33 "Hazor [a]shall be a dwelling for
jackals, a desolation forever;
No one shall reside there,
Nor son of man dwell in it."

Judgment on Elam

34 The word of the LORD that
came to Jeremiah the prophet
against [a]Elam, in the [b]beginning of
the reign of Zedekiah king of Ju-
dah, saying,
35 "Thus says the LORD of hosts:

'Behold, I will break [a]the [1]bow of
Elam,
The foremost of their might.
36 Against Elam I will bring the four
winds
From the four quarters of heaven,
And scatter them toward all those
winds;
There shall be no nations where
the outcasts of Elam will not go.

37 For I will cause Elam to be
dismayed before their enemies
And before those who seek their
life.
[a]I will bring disaster upon them,
My fierce anger,' says the LORD;
'And I will send the sword after
them
Until I have consumed them.
38 I will [a]set My throne in Elam,
And will destroy from there the
king and the princes,' says the
LORD.

39 'But it shall come to pass [a]in the
latter days:
I will bring back the captives of
Elam,' says the LORD."

Judgment on Babylon and Babylonia

50 The word that the LORD
spoke [a]against Babylon *and*
against the land of the Chaldeans
by Jeremiah the prophet.

2 "Declare among the nations,
Proclaim, and [1]set up a standard;
Proclaim—do not conceal *it*—
Say, 'Babylon is [a]taken, [b]Bel is
shamed.
[2]Merodach is broken in pieces;
[c]Her idols are humiliated,
Her images are broken in pieces.'
3 [a]For out of the north [b]a nation
comes up against her,
Which shall make her land
desolate,
And no one shall dwell therein.
They shall [1]move, they shall
depart,
Both man and beast.

4 "In those days and in that time,"
says the LORD,
"The children of Israel shall come,
[a]They and the children of Judah
together;
[b]With continual weeping they
shall come,
[c]And seek the LORD their God.
5 They shall ask the way to Zion,
With their faces toward it, *saying*,
'Come and let us join ourselves to
the LORD
In [a]a perpetual covenant
That will not be forgotten.'

6 "My people have been [a]lost sheep.
Their shepherds have led them
[b]astray;
They have turned them away *on*
[c]the mountains.
They have gone from mountain
to hill;
They have forgotten their resting
place.
7 All who found them have
[a]devoured them;
And [b]their adversaries said, [c]'We
have not offended,
Because they have sinned against
the LORD, [d]the habitation of
justice,
The LORD, [e]the hope of their
fathers.'

8 "Move[a] from the midst of Babylon,
Go out of the land of the
Chaldeans;
And be like the [1]rams before the
flocks.
9 [a]For behold, I will raise and cause
to come up against Babylon
An assembly of great nations
from the north country,
And they shall array themselves
against her;
From there she shall be captured.
Their arrows *shall be* like *those*
of [1]an expert warrior;
[b]None shall return in vain.
10 And Chaldea shall become
plunder;
[a]All who plunder her shall be
satisfied," says the LORD.

11 "Because[a] you were glad, because
you rejoiced,
You destroyers of My heritage,
Because you have grown fat [b]like
a heifer threshing grain,
And you [1]bellow like bulls,
12 Your mother shall be deeply
ashamed;
She who bore you shall be
ashamed.
Behold, the least of the nations
shall be a [a]wilderness,
A dry land and a desert.
13 Because of the wrath of the LORD
She shall not be inhabited,
[a]But she shall be wholly desolate.
[b]Everyone who goes by Babylon
shall be horrified
And hiss at all her plagues.

14 "Put[a] yourselves in array against
Babylon all around,
All you who bend the bow;
Shoot at her, spare no arrows,
For she has sinned against the
LORD.
15 Shout against her all around;
She has [a]given her hand,
Her foundations have fallen,
[b]Her walls are thrown down;
For [c]it *is* the vengeance of the
LORD.
Take vengeance on her.

37 [a]Jer. 9:16
38 [a]Jer. 43:10
39 [a]Jer. 48:47
CHAPTER 50
1 [a]Gen. 10:10; 11:9; 2 Kin. 17:24; Is. 13:1; 47:1; Dan. 1:1; Rev. 14:8
2 [a]Is. 21:9 [b]Is. 46:1; Jer. 51:44 [c]Jer. 43:12, 13 [1]*lift* [2]Or *Marduk;* a Babylonian god
3 [a]Jer. 51:48; Dan. 5:30, 31 [b]Is. 13:17, 18, 20 [1]Or *wander*
4 [a]Ezra 2:1; Is. 11:12, 13; Jer. 3:18; 31:31; 33:7; Hos. 1:11 [b]Ezra 3:12, 13; [Ps. 126:5]; Jer. 31:9; [Zech. 12:10] [c]Hos. 3:5
5 [a]Jer. 31:31
6 [a]Is. 53:6; [Ezek. 34:15, 16]; Matt. 9:36; 10:6; 1 Pet. 2:25 [b]Jer. 23:1; Ezek. 34:2 [c][Jer. 2:20; 3:6, 23]
7 [a]Ps. 79:7 [b]Jer. 40:2, 3; Zech. 11:5 [c]Jer. 2:3; Dan. 9:16 [d][Ps. 90:1; 91:1] [e]Ps. 22:4; Jer. 14:8; 17:13
8 [a]Is. 48:20; Jer. 51:6, 45; Zech. 2:6, 7; [Rev. 18:4] [1]*male goats*
9 [a]Jer. 15:14; 51:27 [b]2 Sam. 1:22 [1]So with some Heb. mss., LXX, Syr.; MT, Tg., Vg. *a warrior who makes childless*
10 [a][Rev. 17:16]
11 [a]Is. 47:6 [b]Hos. 10:11 [1]Or *neigh like steeds*
12 [a]Jer. 51:43
13 [a]Jer. 25:12 [b]Jer. 49:17
14 [a]Jer. 51:2
15 [a]1 Chr. 29:24; 2 Chr. 30:8; Lam. 5:6; Ezek. 17:18 [b]Jer. 51:58 [c]Jer. 51:6, 11

As she has done, so do to her.
16 Cut off the sower from Babylon,
And him who handles the sickle
at harvest time.
For fear of the oppressing sword
[a]Everyone shall turn to his own
people,
And everyone shall flee to his
own land.

17 "Israel *is like* [a]scattered sheep;
[b]The lions have driven *him* away.
First [c]the king of Assyria
devoured him;
Now at last this
[d]Nebuchadnezzar king of
Babylon has broken his
bones."

18 Therefore thus says the LORD
of hosts, the God of Israel:

"Behold, I will punish the king of
Babylon and his land,
As I have punished the king of
[a]Assyria.
19 [a]But I will bring back Israel to his
home,
And he shall feed on Carmel and
Bashan;
His soul shall be satisfied on
Mount Ephraim and Gilead.
20 In those days and in that time,"
says the LORD,
[a]"The iniquity of Israel shall be
sought, but *there shall be* none;
And the sins of Judah, but they
shall not be found;
For I will pardon those [b]whom I
preserve.

21 "Go up against the land of
Merathaim, against it,
And against the inhabitants of
[a]Pekod.
[1]Waste and utterly destroy them,"
says the LORD,
"And do [b]according to all that I
have commanded you.
22 [a]A sound of battle *is* in the land,
And of great destruction.
23 How [a]the hammer of the whole
earth has been cut apart and
broken!
How Babylon has become a
desolation among the nations!
I have laid a snare for you;
24 You have indeed been [a]trapped,
O Babylon,
And you were not aware;
You have been found and also
caught,
Because you have [b]contended
against the LORD.

16 [a]Is. 13:14; Jer. 51:9
17 [a]2 Kin. 24:10, 14 [b]Jer. 2:15 [c]2 Kin. 15:29; 17:6; 18:9–13 [d]2 Kin. 24:10–14; 25:1–7
18 [a]Is. 10:12; Ezek. 31:3, 11, 12; Nah. 3:7, 18, 19
19 [a]Is. 65:10; Jer. 33:12; Ezek. 34:13
20 [a]Num. 23:21; Is. 43:25; [Jer. 31:34; Mic. 7:19] [b]Is. 1:9
21 [a]Ezek. 23:23 [b]2 Sam. 16:11; 2 Kin. 18:25; 2 Chr. 36:23; Is. 10:6; 44:28; 48:14 [1]Or *Attack* with the sword
22 [a]Jer. 51:54
23 [a]Is. 14:6; Jer. 51:20–24
24 [a]Jer. 51:8, 31; Dan. 5:30 [b][Is. 45:9]
25 [a]Is. 13:5
27 [a]Ps. 22:12; Is. 34:7; Jer. 46:21 [b]Ps. 37:13; Jer. 48:44; Ezek. 7:7
28 [a]Ps. 149:6–9; Jer. 51:10
29 [a]Ps. 137:8; Jer. 51:56; [2 Thess. 1:6]; Rev. 18:6 [b][Is. 47:10] [1]Qr., some Heb. mss., LXX, Tg. add *to her*
30 [a]Is. 13:18; Jer. 49:26; 51:4
31 [1]So with MT, Tg.; LXX, Vg. *The time of your punishment*
32 [a]Is. 26:5; Mal. 4:1 [b]Jer. 21:14
34 [a]Prov. 23:11; Is. 43:14; Jer. 15:21; 31:11; Rev. 18:8 [b]Is. 47:4

25 The LORD has opened His
armory,
And has brought out [a]the
weapons of His indignation;
For this *is* the work of the Lord
GOD of hosts
In the land of the Chaldeans.
26 Come against her from the
farthest border;
Open her storehouses;
Cast her up as heaps of ruins,
And destroy her utterly;
Let nothing of her be left.
27 Slay all her [a]bulls,
Let them go down to the
slaughter.
Woe to them!
For their day has come, the time
of [b]their punishment.
28 The voice of those who flee and
escape from the land of
Babylon
[a]Declares in Zion the vengeance
of the LORD our God,
The vengeance of His temple.

29 "Call together the archers against
Babylon.
All you who bend the bow,
encamp against it all around;
Let none of them [1]escape.
[a]Repay her according to her work;
According to all she has done, do
to her;
[b]For she has been proud against
the LORD,
Against the Holy One of Israel.
30 [a]Therefore her young men shall
fall in the streets,
And all her men of war shall be
cut off in that day," says the
LORD.
31 "Behold, I *am* against you,
O most haughty one!" says the
Lord GOD of hosts;
"For your day has come,
[1]The time *that* I will punish you.
32 The most [a]proud shall stumble
and fall,
And no one will raise him up;
[b]I will kindle a fire in his cities,
And it will devour all around
him."

33 Thus says the LORD of hosts:

"The children of Israel *were*
oppressed,
Along with the children of
Judah;
All who took them captive have
held them fast;
They have refused to let them go.
34 [a]Their Redeemer *is* strong;
[b]The LORD of hosts *is* His name.

He will thoroughly plead their [c]case,
That He may give rest to the land,
And disquiet the inhabitants of Babylon.

35 "A sword *is* against the Chaldeans," says the LORD,
"Against the inhabitants of Babylon,
And [a]against her princes and [b]her wise men.
36 A sword *is* [a]against the soothsayers, and they will be fools.
A sword *is* against her mighty men, and they will be dismayed.
37 A sword *is* against their horses,
Against their chariots,
And against all [a]the mixed peoples who *are* in her midst;
And [b]they will become like women.
A sword *is* against her treasures, and they will be robbed.
38 [a]A [1]drought *is* against her waters, and they will be dried up.
For it *is* the land of carved images,
And they are insane with *their* idols.

39 "Therefore[a] the wild desert beasts shall dwell *there* with the jackals,
And the ostriches shall dwell in it.
[b]It shall be inhabited no more forever,
Nor shall it be dwelt in from generation to generation.
40 [a]As God overthrew Sodom and Gomorrah
And their neighbors," says the LORD,
"So no one shall reside there,
Nor son of man [b]dwell in it.

41 "Behold,[a] a people shall come from the north,
And a great nation and many kings
Shall be raised up from the ends of the earth.
42 [a]They shall hold the bow and the lance;
[b]They *are* cruel and shall not show mercy.
[c]Their voice shall roar like the sea;
They shall ride on horses,
Set in array, like a man for the battle,
Against you, O daughter of Babylon.

43 "The king of Babylon has [a]heard the report about them,
And his hands grow feeble;
Anguish has taken hold of him,
Pangs as of a woman in [b]childbirth.

44 "Behold,[a] he shall come up like a lion from the [1]floodplain of the Jordan
Against the dwelling place of the strong;
But I will make them suddenly run away from her.
And who *is a* chosen *man that* I may appoint over her?
For who *is* like Me?
Who will arraign Me?
And [b]who *is* that shepherd
Who will withstand Me?"

45 Therefore hear [a]the counsel of the LORD that He has taken against Babylon,
And His [b]purposes that He has proposed against the land of the Chaldeans:
[c]Surely the least of the flock shall draw them out;
Surely He will make their dwelling place desolate with them.
46 [a]At the noise of the taking of Babylon
The earth trembles,
And the cry is heard among the nations.

The Utter Destruction of Babylon

51 Thus says the LORD:
"Behold, I will raise up against [a]Babylon,
Against those who dwell in [1]Leb Kamai,
[b]A destroying wind.
2 And I will send [a]winnowers to Babylon,
Who shall winnow her and empty her land.
[b]For in the day of doom
They shall be against her all around.
3 Against *her* [a]let the archer bend his bow,
And lift himself up against *her* in his armor.
Do not spare her young men;
[b]Utterly destroy all her army.
4 Thus the slain shall fall in the land of the Chaldeans,
[a]And *those* thrust through in her streets.
5 For Israel is [a]not forsaken, nor Judah,

---

34 [c]Jer. 51:36; Mic. 7:9
35 [a]Dan. 5:30 [b]Is. 47:13; Jer. 51:57
36 [a]Is. 44:25; Jer. 48:30
37 [a]Jer. 25:20; Ezek. 30:5 [b]Jer. 51:30; Nah. 3:13
38 [a]Is. 44:27; Jer. 51:36; Rev. 16:12 [1]So with MT, Tg., Vg.; Syr. *sword;* LXX omits *A drought is*
39 [a]Is. 13:21, 22; 34:14; Jer. 51:37; Rev. 18:2 [b]Is. 13:20; Jer. 25:12
40 [a]Gen. 19:24, 25; Is. 13:19; Jer. 49:18; [Luke 17:28–30]; 2 Pet. 2:6; Jude 7 [b]Is. 13:20
41 [a]Is. 13:2–5; Jer. 6:22; 25:14; 51:27
42 [a]Jer. 6:23 [b]Is. 13:18 [c]Is. 5:30
43 [a]Jer. 51:31 [b]Jer. 6:24
44 [a]Jer. 49:19–21 [b]Job 41:10; Jer. 49:19 [1]Or *thicket*
45 [a][Ps. 33:11; Is. 14:24]; Jer. 51:10, 11 [b]Jer. 51:29 [c]Jer. 49:19, 20
46 [a]Rev. 18:9

CHAPTER 51

1 [a]Is. 47:1; Jer. 50:1 [b]2 Kin. 19:7; Jer. 4:11; Hos. 13:15 [1]Lit. *The Midst of Those Who Rise Up Against Me;* a code word for Chaldea, Babylonia
2 [a]Is. 41:16; Jer. 15:7; Matt. 3:12 [b]Jer. 50:14
3 [a]Jer. 50:14, 29 [b]Jer. 50:21
4 [a]Jer. 49:26; 50:30, 37
5 [a][Is. 54:7, 8; Jer. 33:24–26; 46:28]

By his God, the LORD of hosts,
Though their land was filled with
sin against the Holy One of
Israel."

6 [a]Flee from the midst of Babylon,
And every one save his life!
Do not be cut off in her iniquity,
For [b]this *is* the time of the LORD's
vengeance;
[c]He shall recompense her.
7 [a]Babylon *was* a golden cup in the
LORD's hand,
That made all the earth drunk.
[b]The nations drank her wine;
Therefore the nations [c]are
deranged.
8 Babylon has suddenly [a]fallen and
been destroyed.
[b]Wail for her!
[c]Take balm for her pain;
Perhaps she may be healed.

9 We would have healed Babylon,
But she is not healed.
Forsake her, and [a]let us go
everyone to his own country;
[b]For her judgment reaches to
heaven and is lifted up to the
skies.
10 The LORD has [a]revealed our
righteousness.
Come and let us [b]declare in Zion
the work of the LORD our God.

11 [a]Make[1] the arrows bright!
Gather the shields!
[b]The LORD has raised up the spirit
of the kings of the Medes.
[c]For His plan *is* against Babylon
to destroy it,
Because it *is* [d]the vengeance of
the LORD,
The vengeance for His temple.
12 [a]Set up the standard on the walls
of Babylon;
Make the guard strong,
Set up the watchmen,
Prepare the ambushes.
For the LORD has both devised
and done
What He spoke against the
inhabitants of Babylon.
13 [a]O you who dwell by many waters,
Abundant in treasures,
Your end has come,
The measure of your
covetousness.
14 [a]The LORD of hosts has sworn by
Himself:
"Surely I will fill you with men, [b]as
with locusts,
And they shall lift [c]up a shout
against you."

6 [a]Jer. 50:8; Rev. 18:4 [b]Jer. 50:15 [c]Jer. 25:14
7 [a]Jer. 25:15; Hab. 2:16; Rev. 17:4 [b]Rev. 14:8 [c]Jer. 25:16
8 [a]Is. 21:9; Jer. 50:2; Rev. 14:8; 18:2 [b][Is. 48:20]; Rev. 18:9, 11, 19 [c]Jer. 46:11
9 [a]Is. 13:14; Jer. 46:16; 50:16 [b]Ezra 9:6; Rev. 18:5
10 [a]Ps. 37:6; Mic. 7:9 [b][Is. 40:2]; Jer. 50:28
11 [a]Jer. 46:4, 9; Joel 3:9, 10 [b]Is. 13:17 [c]Jer. 50:45 [d]Jer. 50:28 [1]*Polish the arrows!*
12 [a]Nah. 2:1; 3:14
13 [a]Rev. 17:1, 15
14 [a]Jer. 49:13; Amos 6:8 [b]Jer. 51:27; Nah. 3:15 [c]Jer. 50:15
15 [a]Gen. 1:1, 6; Jer. 10:12–16 [b]Job 9:8; Ps. 104:2; Is. 40:22
16 [a]Ps. 135:7; Jer. 10:13
17 [a][Is. 44:18–20]; Jer. 10:14 [b]Jer. 50:2
20 [a]Is. 10:5, 15; Jer. 50:23
22 [a]2 Chr. 36:17; Is. 13:15, 16
24 [a]Jer. 50:15, 29
25 [a]Is. 13:2; Zech. 4:7

15 [a]He has made the earth by His
power;
He has established the world by
His wisdom,
And [b]stretched out the heaven by
His understanding.
16 When He utters *His* voice—
There is a multitude of waters in
the heavens:
[a]"He causes the vapors to ascend
from the ends of the earth;
He makes lightnings for the rain;
He brings the wind out of His
treasuries."

17 [a]Everyone is dull-hearted, without
knowledge;
Every metalsmith is put to shame
by the carved image;
[b]For his molded image is
falsehood,
And *there is* no breath in them.
18 They *are* futile, a work of errors;
In the time of their punishment
they shall perish.
19 The Portion of Jacob *is* not like
them,
For He *is* the Maker of all things;
And *Israel is* the tribe of His
inheritance.
The LORD of hosts *is* His name.

20 "You[a] *are* My battle-ax *and*
weapons of war:
For with you I will break the
nation in pieces;
With you I will destroy
kingdoms;
21 With you I will break in pieces
the horse and its rider;
With you I will break in pieces
the chariot and its rider;
22 With you also I will break in
pieces man and woman;
With you I will break in pieces
[a]old and young;
With you I will break in pieces
the young man and the maiden;
23 With you also I will break in
pieces the shepherd and his
flock;
With you I will break in pieces
the farmer and his yoke of
oxen;
And with you I will break in
pieces governors and rulers.

24 "And[a] I will repay Babylon
And all the inhabitants of
Chaldea
For all the evil they have done
In Zion in your sight," says the
LORD.

25 "Behold, I *am* against you,
[a]O destroying mountain,

Who destroys all the earth," says
the LORD.
"And I will stretch out My hand
against you,
Roll you down from the rocks,
[b]And make you a burnt mountain.
26 They shall not take from you a
stone for a corner
Nor a stone for a foundation,
[a]But you shall be desolate
forever," says the LORD.

27 [a]Set up a banner in the land,
Blow the trumpet among the
nations!
[b]Prepare the nations against her,
Call [c]the kingdoms together
against her:
Ararat, Minni, and Ashkenaz.
Appoint a general against her;
Cause the horses to come up like
the bristling locusts.
28 Prepare against her the nations,
With the kings of the Medes,
Its governors and all its rulers,
All the land of his dominion.
29 And the land will tremble and
sorrow;
For every [a]purpose of the LORD
shall be performed against
Babylon,
[b]To make the land of Babylon a
desolation without inhabitant.
30 The mighty men of Babylon have
ceased fighting,
They have remained in their
strongholds;
Their might has failed,
[a]They became *like* women;
They have burned her dwelling
places,
[b]The bars of her *gate* are broken.
31 [a]One runner will run to meet
another,
And one messenger to meet
another,
To show the king of Babylon that
his city is taken on *all* sides;
32 [a]The passages are blocked,
The reeds they have burned with
fire,
And the men of war are terrified.

33 For thus says the LORD of hosts,
the God of Israel:

"The daughter of Babylon *is* [a]like
a threshing floor
When [b]*it is* time to thresh her;
Yet a little while
[c]And the time of her harvest will
come."

34 "Nebuchadnezzar the king of
Babylon
Has [a]devoured me, he has
crushed me;
He has made me an [b]empty
vessel,
He has swallowed me up like a
monster;
He has filled his stomach with my
delicacies,
He has spit me out.
35 Let the violence *done* to me and
my flesh *be* upon Babylon,"
The inhabitant of Zion will say;
"And my blood be upon the
inhabitants of Chaldea!"
Jerusalem will say.

36 Therefore thus says the LORD:

"Behold, [a]I will plead your case
and take vengeance for you.
[b]I will dry up her sea and make
her springs dry.
37 [a]Babylon shall become a heap,
A dwelling place for jackals,
[b]An astonishment and a hissing,
Without an inhabitant.
38 They shall roar together like
lions,
They shall growl like lions'
whelps.
39 In their excitement I will prepare
their feasts;
[a]I will make them drunk,
That they may rejoice,
And sleep a perpetual sleep
And not awake," says the LORD.
40 "I will bring them down
Like lambs to the slaughter,
Like rams with male goats.

41 "Oh, how [a]Sheshach[1] is taken!
Oh, how [b]the praise of the whole
earth is seized!
How Babylon has become
desolate among the nations!
42 [a]The sea has come up over
Babylon;
She is covered with the multitude
of its waves.
43 [a]Her cities are a desolation,
A dry land and a wilderness,
A land where [b]no one dwells,
Through which no son of man
passes.
44 I will punish [a]Bel[1] in Babylon,
And I will bring out of his mouth
what he has swallowed;
And the nations shall not stream
to him anymore.
Yes, [b]the wall of Babylon shall
fall.

45 "My[a] people, go out of the midst
of her!

25 [b]Rev. 8:8
26 [a]Jer. 50:26, 40
27 [a]Is. 13:2; Jer. 50:2; 51:12 [b]Jer. 25:14 [c]Jer. 50:41, 42
29 [a]Jer. 50:45 [b]Is. 13:19, 20; 47:11; Jer. 50:13; 51:26, 43
30 [a]Is. 19:16; Jer. 48:41 [b]Is. 45:1, 2; Lam. 2:9; Amos 1:5; Nah. 3:13
31 [a]Jer. 50:24
32 [a]Jer. 50:38
33 [a]Is. 21:10; Dan. 2:35; Amos 1:3; Mic. 4:13 [b]Is. 41:15; Hab. 3:12 [c]Is. 17:15; Hos. 6:11; Joel 3:13; Rev. 14:15
34 [a]Jer. 50:17 [b]Is. 24:1–3
36 [a][Ps. 140:12]; Jer. 50:34 [b]Jer. 50:38
37 [a]Is. 13:22; Jer. 50:39; [Rev. 18:2] [b]Jer. 25:9, 11
39 [a]Jer. 51:57
41 [a]Jer. 25:26 [b]Is. 13:19; Jer. 49:25; [Dan. 4:30] [1]A code word for Babylon, Jer. 25:26
42 [a]Is. 8:7, 8; Jer. 51:55; Dan. 9:26
43 [a]Jer. 50:39, 40 [b]Is. 13:20
44 [a]Jer. 50:2; Is. 46:1 [b]Jer. 50:15 [1]A Babylonian god
45 [a]Is. 48:20; [Jer. 50:8, 28; 51:6; Rev. 18:4]

And let everyone deliver [1]himself
from the fierce anger of the
LORD.
46 And lest your heart faint,
And you fear [a]for the rumor that
will be heard in the land
(A rumor will come *one* year,
And after that, in *another* year
A rumor *will come,*
And violence in the land,
Ruler against ruler),
47 Therefore behold, the days are
coming
That I will bring judgment on the
carved images of Babylon;
Her whole land shall be ashamed,
And all her slain shall fall in her
midst.
48 Then [a]the heavens and the earth
and all that *is* in them
Shall sing joyously over Babylon;
[b]For the plunderers shall come to
her from the north," says the
LORD.

49 As Babylon *has caused* the slain
of Israel to fall,
So at Babylon the slain of all the
earth shall fall.
50 [a]You who have escaped the
sword,
Get away! Do not stand still!
[b]Remember the LORD afar off,
And let Jerusalem come to your
mind.

51 [a]We are ashamed because we
have heard reproach.
Shame has covered our faces,
For strangers [b]have come into the
[1]sanctuaries of the LORD's
house.

52 "Therefore behold, the days are
coming," says the LORD,
"That I will bring judgment on her
carved images,
And throughout all her land the
wounded shall groan.
53 [a]Though Babylon were to [1]mount
up to heaven,
And though she were to fortify
the height of her strength,
Yet from Me plunderers would
come to her," says the LORD.

54 [a]The sound of a cry *comes* from
Babylon,
And great destruction from the
land of the Chaldeans,
55 Because the LORD is plundering
Babylon
And silencing her loud voice,
Though her waves roar like great
waters,

45 [1]Lit. *his soul*

46 [a]2 Kin. 19:7; Is. 13:3–5

48 [a]Is. 44:23; 48:20; 49:13; Rev. 18:20 [b]Jer. 50:3, 41

50 [a]Jer. 44:28 [b][Deut. 4:29–31]; Ezek. 6:9

51 [a]Ps. 44:15; 79:4 [b]Ps. 74:3–8; Jer. 52:13; Lam. 1:10 [1]*holy places*

53 [a]Gen. 11:4; Job 20:6; [Ps. 139:8–10; Is. 14:12–14]; Jer. 49:16; Amos 9:2; Obad. 4 [1]*ascend*

54 [a]Jer. 50:22

56 [a]Ps. 94:1; Jer. 50:29

57 [a]Jer. 50:35 [b]Jer. 46:18; 48:15

58 [a]Jer. 50:15 [b]Hab. 2:13 [1]Lit. *laid utterly bare*

59 [a]Jer. 32:12

60 [a]Is. 30:8; Jer. 36:2

62 [a]Is. 13:20; 14:22, 23; Jer. 50:3, 39

63 [a]Jer. 19:10, 11; Rev. 18:21

And the noise of their voice is
uttered,
56 Because the plunderer comes
against her, against Babylon,
And her mighty men are taken.
Every one of their bows is
broken;
[a]For the LORD *is* the God of
recompense,
He will surely repay.

57 "And I will make drunk
Her princes and [a]wise men,
Her governors, her deputies, and
her mighty men.
And they shall sleep a perpetual
sleep
And not awake," says [b]the King,
Whose name *is* the LORD of hosts.

58 Thus says the LORD of hosts:

"The broad walls of Babylon shall
be utterly [a]broken,[1]
And her high gates shall be
burned with fire;
[b]The people will labor in vain,
And the nations, because of the
fire;
And they shall be weary."

Jeremiah's Command to Seraiah

59 The word which Jeremiah the
prophet commanded Seraiah the
son of [a]Neriah, the son of Mahse-
iah, when he went with Zedekiah
the king of Judah to Babylon in
the fourth year of his reign. And
Seraiah *was* the quartermaster.
60 So Jeremiah [a]wrote in a book
all the evil that would come upon
Babylon, all these words that are
written against Babylon.
61 And Jeremiah said to Seraiah,
"When you arrive in Babylon and
see it, and read all these words,
62 "then you shall say, 'O LORD,
You have spoken against this
place to cut it off, so that [a]none
shall remain in it, neither man nor
beast, but it shall be desolate for-
ever.'
63 "Now it shall be, when you
have finished reading this book,
[a]*that* you shall tie a stone to it and
throw it out into the Euphrates.
64 "Then you shall say, 'Thus
Babylon shall sink and not rise
from the catastrophe that I will
bring upon her. And they shall be
weary.' " Thus far *are* the words
of Jeremiah.

The Fall of Jerusalem Reviewed

52 Zedekiah *was* [a]twenty-one
years old when he became
king, and he reigned eleven years
in Jerusalem. His mother's name
was Hamutal the daughter of Jere-
miah of [b]Libnah.
2 He also did evil in the sight of
the LORD, according to all that Je-
hoiakim had done.
3 For because of the anger of the
LORD *this* happened in Jerusalem
and Judah, till He finally cast them
out from His presence. Then Zede-
kiah [a]rebelled against the king of
Babylon.
4 Now it came to pass in the
[a]ninth year of his reign, in the
tenth month, on the tenth *day* of
the month, *that* Nebuchadnezzar
king of Babylon and all his army
came against Jerusalem and en-
camped against it; and *they* built
a siege wall against it all around.
5 So the city was besieged until
the eleventh year of King Zed-
ekiah.
6 By the fourth month, on the
ninth day of the month, the famine
had become so severe in the city
that there was no food for the peo-
ple of the land.
7 Then the city wall was broken
through, and all the men of war
fled and went out of the city at
night by way of the gate between
the two walls, which *was* by the
king's garden, even though the
Chaldeans *were* near the city all
around. And they went by way of
the [1]plain.
8 But the army of the Chaldeans
pursued the king, and they over-
took Zedekiah in the plains of Jeri-
cho. All his army was scattered
from him.
9 [a]So they took the king and
brought him up to the king of
Babylon at Riblah in the land of
Hamath, and he pronounced judg-
ment on him.
10 [a]Then the king of Babylon
killed the sons of Zedekiah before
his eyes. And he killed all the
princes of Judah in Riblah.
11 He also [a]put out the eyes of
Zedekiah; and the king of Babylon
bound him in [1]bronze fetters, took
him to Babylon, and put him in
prison till the day of his death.

The Temple and City Plundered and Burned

12 [a]Now in the fifth month, on the
tenth *day* of the month ([b]which
was the nineteenth year of King
Nebuchadnezzar king of Babylon),
[c]Nebuzaradan, the captain of the
guard, *who* served the king of
Babylon, came to Jerusalem.
13 He burned the house of the
LORD and the king's house; all the
houses of Jerusalem, that is, all
the houses of the great, he burned
with fire.
14 And all the army of the Chalde-
ans who *were* with the captain of
the guard broke down all the walls
of Jerusalem all around.
15 [a]Then Nebuzaradan the cap-
tain of the guard carried away cap-
tive *some* of the poor people, the
rest of the people who remained
in the city, the defectors who had
deserted to the king of Babylon,
and the rest of the craftsmen.
16 But Nebuzaradan the captain
of the guard left *some* of the poor
of the land as vinedressers and
farmers.
17 [a]The [b]bronze pillars that *were*
in the house of the LORD, and the
carts and the bronze Sea that *were*
in the house of the LORD, the Chal-
deans broke in pieces, and carried
all their bronze to Babylon.
18 They also took away [a]the
pots, the shovels, the trimmers,
the [1]bowls, the spoons, and all the
bronze utensils with which the
priests ministered.
19 The basins, the firepans, the
bowls, the pots, the lampstands,
the spoons, and the cups, whatever
was solid gold and whatever *was*
solid silver, the captain of the
guard took away.
20 The two pillars, one Sea, the
twelve bronze bulls which *were*
under *it, and* the carts, which King
Solomon had made for the house
of the LORD—[a]the bronze of all
these articles was beyond mea-
sure.
21 Now *concerning* the [a]pillars:
the height of one pillar *was* eigh-
teen [1]cubits, a measuring line of
twelve cubits could measure its
circumference, and its thickness
was [2]four fingers; *it was* hollow.
22 A capital of bronze *was* on it;

CHAPTER 52
1 [a]2 Kin. 24:18; 2 Chr. 36:11 [b]Josh. 10:29; 2 Kin. 8:22; Is. 37:8
3 [a]2 Chr. 36:13
4 [a]2 Kin. 25:1; Jer. 39:1; Ezek. 24:1, 2; Zech. 8:19
7 [1]Or *Arabah;* the Jordan Valley
9 [a]2 Kin. 25:6; Jer. 32:4; 39:5
10 [a]Ezek. 12:13
11 [a]Ezek. 12:13 [1]*shackles*
12 [a]2 Kin. 25:8–21 [b]Jer. 52:29 [c]Jer. 39:9
15 [a]Jer. 39:9
17 [a]Jer. 27:19 [b]1 Kin. 7:15, 23, 27, 50
18 [a]Ex. 27:3; 1 Kin. 7:40, 45; 2 Kin. 25:14 [1]*basins*
20 [a]1 Kin. 7:47; 2 Kin. 25:16
21 [a]1 Kin. 7:15; 2 Kin. 25:17; 2 Chr. 3:15 [1]18 inches each 23 inches

and the height of one capital *was* five cubits, with a network and pomegranates all around the capital, all of bronze. The second pillar, with pomegranates was the same.

23 There were ninety-six pomegranates on the sides; [a]all the pomegranates, all around on the network, *were* one hundred.

The People Taken Captive to Babylonia

24 [a]The captain of the guard took Seraiah the chief priest, [b]Zephaniah the second priest, and the three doorkeepers.

25 He also took out of the city an [1]officer who had charge of the men of war, seven men of the king's close associates who were found in the city, the principal scribe of the army who mustered the people of the land, and sixty men of the people of the land who were found in the midst of the city.

26 And Nebuzaradan the captain of the guard took these and brought them to the king of Babylon at Riblah.

27 Then the king of Babylon struck them and put them to death at Riblah in the land of Hamath. Thus Judah was carried away captive from its own land.

28 [a]These *are* the people whom Nebuchadnezzar carried away captive: [b]in the seventh year, [c]three thousand and twenty-three Jews;

29 [a]in the eighteenth year of Nebuchadnezzar he carried away captive from Jerusalem eight hundred and thirty-two persons;

30 in the twenty-third year of Nebuchadnezzar, Nebuzaradan the captain of the guard carried away captive of the Jews seven hundred and forty-five persons. All the persons *were* four thousand six hundred.

Jehoiachin Released from Prison

31 [a]Now it came to pass in the thirty-seventh year of the captivity of Jehoiachin king of Judah, in the twelfth month, on the twenty-fifth *day* of the month, *that* [1]Evil-Merodach king of Babylon, in the first *year* of his reign, [b]lifted[2] up the head of Jehoiachin king of Judah and brought him out of prison.

32 And he spoke kindly to him and gave him a more prominent seat than those of the kings who *were* with him in Babylon.

33 So [1]Jehoiachin changed from his prison garments, [a]and he ate bread regularly before the king all the days of his life.

34 And as for his provisions, there was a regular ration given him by the king of Babylon, a portion for each day until the day of his death, all the days of his life.

23 [a]1 Kin. 7:20

24 [a]2 Kin. 25:18; 1 Chr. 6:14; Ezra 7:1 [b]Jer. 21:1; 29:25

25 [1]Lit. *eunuch*

28 [a]2 Kin. 24:2 [b]2 Kin. 24:12 [c]2 Kin. 24:14

29 [a]2 Kin. 25:11; Jer. 39:9

31 [a]2 Kin. 25:27–30 [b]Gen. 40:13, 20; Ps. 3:3; 27:6 [1]Or *Awil-Marduk;* lit. *The Man of Marduk* [2]Showed favor to

33 [a]2 Sam. 9:7, 13; 1 Kin. 2:7 [1]Lit. *he*

The Book of

Lamentations

LAMENTATIONS describes the funeral of a city. It is a tearstained portrait of the once proud Jerusalem, now reduced to rubble by the invading Babylonian hordes.

In a five-poem dirge, Jeremiah exposes his emotions. A death has occurred; Jerusalem lies barren. Jeremiah writes his lament in acrostic or alphabetical fashion. Beginning each chapter with the first letter *A* (aleph) he progresses verse by verse through the Hebrew alphabet, literally weeping from *A* to *Z*. And then, in the midst of this terrible holocaust, Jeremiah triumphantly cries out, "Great *is* Your faithfulness" (3:23). In the face of death and destruction, with life seemingly coming apart, Jeremiah turns tragedy into a triumph of faith. God has never failed him in the past. God has promised to remain faithful in the future. In the light of the God he knows and loves, Jeremiah finds hope and comfort.

The Hebrew title of this book comes from the first word of chapters 1, 2, and 4: *Ekah,* "Ah, how!" Another Hebrew word *Ginoth* ("Elegies" or "Lamentations") has also been used as the title because it better represents the contents of the book. The Greek title *Threnoi* means "Dirges" or "Laments," and the Latin title *Threni* ("Tears" or "Lamentations") was derived from this word. The subtitle in Jerome's Vulgate reads: *"Id est lamentationes Jeremiae prophetae,"* and this became the basis for the English title "The Lamentations of Jeremiah."

Jerusalem in Affliction

HOW lonely sits the city
That was full of people!
[a]*How* like a widow is she,
Who *was* great among the nations!
The [b]princess among the provinces
Has become a [1]slave!

2 She [a]weeps bitterly in the [b]night,
Her tears *are* on her cheeks;
Among all her lovers
She has none to comfort *her.*
All her friends have dealt treacherously with her;
They have become her enemies.

3 [a]Judah has gone into captivity,
Under affliction and hard servitude;
[b]She dwells among the [1]nations,
She finds no [c]rest;
All her persecutors overtake her in dire straits.

4 The roads to Zion mourn
Because no one comes to the [1]set feasts.
All her gates are [a]desolate;
Her priests sigh,
Her virgins are afflicted,
And she *is* in bitterness.

5 Her adversaries [a]have become [1]the master,
Her enemies prosper;
For the LORD has afflicted her
[b]Because of the multitude of her transgressions.
Her [c]children have gone into captivity before the enemy.

6 And from the daughter of Zion
All her splendor has departed.
Her princes have become like deer
That find no pasture,
That [1]flee without strength
Before the pursuer.

7 In the days of her affliction and roaming,
Jerusalem [a]remembers all her pleasant things
That she had in the days of old.
When her people fell into the hand of the enemy,

CHAPTER 1

1 [a]Is. 47:7–9 [b]1 Kin. 4:21; Ezra 4:20; Jer. 31:7 [1]Lit. *forced laborer*

2 [a]Jer. 13:17 [b]Job 7:3

3 [a]Jer. 52:27 [b]Lam. 2:9 [c]Deut. 28:65 [1]*Gentiles*

4 [a]Is. 27:10 [1]*appointed*

5 [a]Deut. 28:43 [b]Jer. 30:14, 15; Dan. 9:7, 16 [c]Jer. 52:28 [1]Lit. *her head*

6 [1]Lit. *are gone*

7 [a]Ps. 137:1

With no one to help her,
The adversaries saw her
And mocked at her [1]downfall.

8 [a]Jerusalem has sinned gravely,
Therefore she has become [1]vile.
All who honored her despise her
Because [b]they have seen her
nakedness;
Yes, she sighs and turns away.

9 Her uncleanness *is* in her skirts;
She [a]did not consider her destiny;
Therefore her collapse was
awesome;
She had no comforter.
"O LORD, behold my affliction,
For *the* enemy is exalted!"

10 The adversary has spread his
hand
Over all her [1]pleasant things;
For she has seen [a]the nations
enter her [2]sanctuary,
Those whom You commanded
[b]Not to enter Your assembly.

11 All her people sigh,
[a]They [1]seek bread;
They have given their [2]valuables
for food to restore life.
"See, O LORD, and consider,
For I am scorned."

12 "*Is it* nothing to you, all you who
[1]pass by?
Behold and see
[a]If there is any sorrow like my
sorrow,
Which has been brought on me,
Which the LORD has inflicted
In the day of His fierce anger.

13 "From above He has sent fire into
my bones,
And it overpowered them;
He has [a]spread a net for my feet
And turned me back;
He has made me desolate
And faint all the day.

14 "The[a] yoke of my transgressions
was [1]bound;
They were woven together by His
hands,
And thrust upon my neck.
He made my strength fail;
The Lord delivered me into the
hands of *those whom* I am not
able to withstand.

15 "The Lord has trampled underfoot
all my mighty *men* in my midst;
He has called an assembly
against me
To crush my young men;
[a]The Lord trampled *as* in a
winepress
The virgin daughter of Judah.

16 "For these *things* I weep;
My eye, [a]my eye overflows with
water;
Because the comforter, who
should restore my life,
Is far from me.
My children are desolate
Because the enemy prevailed."

17 [a]Zion [1]spreads out her hands,
But no one comforts her;
The LORD has commanded
concerning Jacob
That those [b]around him *become*
his adversaries;
Jerusalem has become an
unclean thing among them.

18 "The LORD is [a]righteous,
For I [b]rebelled against His
[1]commandment.
Hear now, all peoples,
And behold my sorrow;
My virgins and my young men
Have gone into captivity.

19 "I called for my lovers,
But they deceived me;
My priests and my elders
Breathed their last in the city,
While they sought food
To restore their life.

20 "See, O LORD, that I *am* in distress;
My [a]soul[1] is troubled;
My heart is overturned within
me,
For I have been very rebellious.
[b]Outside the sword bereaves,
At home *it is* like death.

21 "They have heard that I sigh,
But no one comforts me.
All my enemies have heard of my
trouble;
They are [a]glad that You have
done *it*.
Bring on [b]the day You have
[1]announced,
That they may become like me.

22 "Let[a] all their wickedness come
before You,
And do to them as You have done
to me
For all my transgressions;
For my sighs *are* many,
And my heart *is* faint."

7 [1]Vg. *Sabbaths*
8 [a][1 Kin. 8:46] [b]Jer. 13:22; Ezek. 16:37; Hos. 2:10 [1]LXX, Vg. *moved* or *removed*
9 [a]Deut. 32:29; Is. 47:7; Jer. 5:31
10 [a]Ps. 74:4–8; Is. 64:10, 11; Jer. 51:51 [b]Deut. 23:3; Neh. 13:1 [1]*desirable* [2]*holy place*, the temple
11 [a]Jer. 38:9; 52:6 [1]*hunt food* [2]*desirable things*
12 [a]Dan. 9:12 [1]Lit. *pass by this way*
13 [a]Ezek. 12:13; 17:20
14 [a]Deut. 28:48 [1]So with MT, Tg.; LXX, Syr., Vg. *watched over*
15 [a]Is. 63:3; [Rev. 14:19]
16 [a]Ps. 69:20; Eccl. 4:1; Jer. 13:17; Lam. 2:18
17 [a][Is. 1:15]; Jer. 4:31 [b]2 Kin. 24:2–4; Jer. 12:9 [1]Prays
18 [a]Neh. 9:33; Ps. 119:75; Dan. 9:7, 14 [b]1 Sam. 12:14, 15; Jer. 4:17 [1]Lit. *mouth*
20 [a]Job 30:27; Is. 16:11; Jer. 4:19; Lam. 2:11; Hos. 11:8 [b]Deut. 32:25; Ezek. 7:15 [1]Lit. *inward parts*
21 [a]Ps. 35:15; Jer. 48:27; 50:11; Lam. 2:15; Obad. 12 [b]Is. 13; [Jer. 46] [1]*proclaimed*
22 [a]Neh. 4:4, 5; Ps. 109:15; 137:7, 8; Jer. 30:16

God's Anger with Jerusalem

2 How the Lord has covered the
daughter of Zion
With a [a]cloud in His anger!
[b]He cast down from heaven to the
earth
[c]The beauty of Israel,
And did not remember [d]His
footstool
In the day of His anger.

2 The Lord has swallowed up and
has [a]not pitied
All the dwelling places of Jacob.
He has thrown down in His wrath
The strongholds of the daughter
of Judah;
He has brought *them* down to the
ground;
[b]He has profaned the kingdom
and its princes.

3 He has cut off in fierce anger
Every [1]horn of Israel;
[a]He has drawn back His right
hand
From before the enemy.
[b]He has blazed against Jacob like
a flaming fire
Devouring all around.

4 [a]Standing like an enemy, He has
bent His bow;
With His right hand, like an
adversary,
He has slain [b]all *who were*
pleasing to His eye;
On the tent of the daughter of
Zion,
He has poured out His fury like
fire.

5 [a]The Lord was like an enemy.
He has swallowed up Israel,
He has swallowed up all her
palaces;
[b]He has destroyed her
strongholds,
And has increased mourning and
lamentation
In the daughter of Judah.

6 He has done violence [a]to His
[1]tabernacle,
[b]*As if it were* a garden;
He has destroyed His place of
assembly;
The LORD has caused
The appointed feasts and
Sabbaths to be forgotten in
Zion.
In His burning indignation He
has [c]spurned the king and the
priest.

CHAPTER 2

1 [a][Lam. 3:44] [b]Matt. 11:23 [c]2 Sam. 1:19 [d]1 Chr. 28:2; Ps. 99:5; Ezek. 43:7

2 [a]Ps. 21:9; Lam. 3:43 [b]Ps. 89:39, 40; Is. 43:28

3 [a]Ps. 74:11; Jer. 21:4, 5 [b]Ps. 89:46 [1]Strength

4 [a]Is. 63:10 [b]Ezek. 24:25

5 [a]Jer. 30:14 [b]2 Kin. 25:9; Jer. 52:13; Lam. 2:2

6 [a]Ps. 80:12; 89:40; Is. 5:5; Jer. 7:14 [b]Is. 1:8; Jer. 52:13 [c]Is. 43:28 [1]Lit. *booth*

7 [a]Ezek. 24:21 [b]Ps. 74:3–8 [1]*delivered*

8 [a]Jer. 52:14 [b][2 Kin. 21:13; Is. 34:11; Amos 7:7–9] [1]*determined*

9 [a]Jer. 51:30 [b]Deut. 28:36; 2 Kin. 24:15; 25:7; Lam. 1:3; 4:20 [c]2 Chr. 15:3 [d]Ps. 74:9; Mic. 3:6 [1]*Gentiles* [2]Prophetic revelation

10 [a]Job 2:13; Is. 3:26 [b]Job 2:12; Ezek. 27:30 [c]Is. 15:3; Jon. 3:6–8 [1]A sign of mourning

11 [a]Ps. 6:7; Lam. 3:48 [b]Job 16:13; Ps. 22:14 [c]Lam. 4:4 [1]Lit. *inward parts* [2]Lit. *liver*

13 [a]Lam. 1:12; Dan. 9:12 [1]Or *bear witness to*

7 The Lord has spurned His altar,
He has [a]abandoned His
sanctuary;
He has [1]given up the walls of her
palaces
Into the hand of the enemy.
[b]They have made a noise in the
house of the LORD
As on the day of a set feast.

8 The LORD has [1]purposed to
destroy
The [a]wall of the daughter of Zion.
[b]He has stretched out a line;
He has not withdrawn His hand
from destroying;
Therefore He has caused the
rampart and wall to lament;
They languished together.

9 Her gates have sunk into the
ground;
He has destroyed and [a]broken
her bars.
[b]Her king and her princes *are*
among the [1]nations;
[c]The Law *is* no *more,*
And her [d]prophets find no [2]vision
from the LORD.

10 The elders of the daughter of
Zion
[a]Sit on the ground *and* keep
silence;
[1]They [b]throw dust on their heads
And [c]gird themselves with
sackcloth.
The virgins of Jerusalem
Bow their heads to the ground.

11 [a]My eyes fail with tears,
My [1]heart is troubled;
[b]My [2]bile is poured on the ground
Because of the destruction of the
daughter of my people,
Because [c]the children and the
infants
Faint in the streets of the city.

12 They say to their mothers,
"Where *is* grain and wine?"
As they swoon like the wounded
In the streets of the city,
As their life is poured out
In their mothers' bosom.

13 How shall I [a]console[1] you?
To what shall I liken you,
O daughter of Jerusalem?
What shall I compare with you,
that I may comfort you,
O virgin daughter of Zion?
For your ruin *is* spread wide as
the sea;
Who can heal you?

14 Your [a]prophets have seen for you
False and deceptive visions;
They have not [b]uncovered your
iniquity,
To bring back your captives,
But have envisioned for you false
[c]prophecies and delusions.

15 All who [1]pass by [a]clap *their*
hands at you;
They hiss [b]and shake their heads
At the daughter of Jerusalem:
"*Is* this the city that is called
[c]'The perfection of beauty,
The joy of the whole earth'?"

16 [a]All your enemies have opened
their mouth against you;
They hiss and gnash *their* teeth.
They say, [b]"We have swallowed
her up!
Surely this *is* the [c]day we have
waited for;
We have found *it*, [d]we have seen
it!"

17 The LORD has done what He
[a]purposed;
He has fulfilled His word
Which He commanded in days of
old.
He has thrown down and has not
pitied,
And He has caused an enemy to
[b]rejoice over you;
He has exalted the [1]horn of your
adversaries.

18 Their heart cried out to the Lord,
"O wall of the daughter of Zion,
[a]Let tears run down like a river
day and night;
Give yourself no relief;
Give [1]your eyes no rest.

19 "Arise, [a]cry out in the night,
At the beginning of the watches;
[b]Pour out your heart like water
before the face of the Lord.
Lift your hands toward Him
For the life of your young
children,
Who faint from hunger [c]at the
head of every street."

20 "See, O LORD, and consider!
To whom have You done this?
[a]Should the women eat their
offspring,
The children [1]they have cuddled?
Should the priest and prophet be
slain
In the sanctuary of the Lord?

21 "Young[a] and old lie
On the ground in the streets;

14 [a]Jer. 2:8; 23:25–29; 29:8, 9; 37:19 [b]Is. 58:1 [c]Jer. 23:33–36
15 [a]Ezek. 25:6 [b]Ps. 44:14 [c][Ps. 48:2; 50:2] [1]Lit. *pass by this way*
16 [a]Job 16:9, 10 [b]Ps. 56:2; 124:3 [c]Lam. 1:21 [d]Ps. 35:21
17 [a]Lev. 26:16 [b]Ps. 38:16 [1]Strength
18 [a]Jer. 14:17 [1]Lit. *the daughter of your eye*
19 [a]Ps. 119:147 [b]Ps. 42:4; 62:8 [c]Is. 51:20
20 [a]Lev. 26:29 [1]Vg. *a span long*
21 [a]2 Chr. 36:17 [b]Jer. 18:21
22 [a]Ps. 31:13 [b]Hos. 9:12 [c]Jer. 16:2–4; 44:7

CHAPTER 3
4 [a]Job 16:8 [b]Ps. 51:8
5 [1]*hardship* or *weariness*
6 [a][Ps. 88:5, 6; 143:3]
7 [a]Hos. 2:6
8 [a]Job 30:20
10 [a]Is. 38:13 [1]Lit. *secret places*
11 [a]Hos. 6:1
12 [a]Job 7:20; 16:12
13 [a]Job 6:4 [1]Lit. *sons of* [2]Lit. *kidneys*
14 [a]Jer. 20:7 [b]Job 30:9
15 [a]Jer. 9:15
16 [a][Prov. 20:17]

My virgins and my young men
Have fallen by the [b]sword;
You have slain *them* in the day
of Your anger,
You have slaughtered *and* not
pitied.

22 "You have invited as to a feast day
[a]The terrors that surround me.
In the day of the LORD's anger
There was no refugee or survivor.
[b]Those whom I have borne and
brought up
My enemies have [c]destroyed."

The Prophet's Anguish and Hope

3 I *am* the man *who* has seen
affliction by the rod of His
wrath.
2 He has led me and made *me* walk
In darkness and not *in* light.
3 Surely He has turned His hand
against me
Time and time again throughout
the day.

4 He has aged [a]my flesh and my
skin,
And [b]broken my bones.
5 He has besieged me
And surrounded *me* with
bitterness and [1]woe.
6 [a]He has set me in dark places
Like the dead of long ago.

7 [a]He has hedged me in so that I
cannot get out;
He has made my chain heavy.
8 Even [a]when I cry and shout,
He shuts out my prayer.
9 He has blocked my ways with
hewn stone;
He has made my paths crooked.

10 [a]He *has been* to me a bear lying
in wait,
Like a lion in [1]ambush.
11 He has turned aside my ways and
[a]torn me in pieces;
He has made me desolate.
12 He has bent His bow
And [a]set me up as a target for the
arrow.

13 He has caused [a]the [1]arrows of His
quiver
To pierce my [2]loins.
14 I have become the [a]ridicule of all
my people—
[b]Their taunting song all the day.
15 [a]He has filled me with bitterness,
He has made me drink
wormwood.

16 He has also broken my teeth
[a]with gravel,

And [1]covered me with ashes.
17 You have moved my soul far from peace;
I have forgotten [1]prosperity.
18 [a]And I said, "My strength and my hope
Have perished from the LORD."

19 Remember my affliction and roaming,
[a]The wormwood and the [1]gall.
20 My soul still remembers
And [1]sinks within me.
21 This I recall to my mind,
Therefore I have [a]hope.

22 [a]*Through* the LORD's mercies we are not consumed,
Because His compassions [b]fail not.
23 *They are* new [a]every morning;
Great *is* Your faithfulness.
24 "The LORD *is* my [a]portion," says my soul,
"Therefore I [b]hope in Him!"

25 The LORD *is* good to those who [a]wait for Him,
To the soul *who* seeks Him.
26 *It is* good that *one* should [a]hope [b]and wait quietly
For the salvation of the LORD.
27 [a]*It is* good for a man to bear
The yoke in his youth.

28 [a]Let him sit alone and keep silent,
Because *God* has laid *it* on him;
29 [a]Let him put his mouth in the dust—
There may yet be hope.
30 [a]Let him give *his* cheek to the one who strikes him,
And be full of reproach.

31 [a]For the Lord will not cast off forever.
32 Though He causes grief,
Yet He will show compassion
According to the multitude of His mercies.
33 For [a]He does not afflict [1]willingly,
Nor grieve the children of men.

34 To crush under one's feet
All the prisoners of the earth,
35 To turn aside the justice *due* a man
Before the face of the Most High,
36 Or subvert a man in his cause—
[a]The Lord does not approve.

37 Who *is* he [a]*who* speaks and it comes to pass,
When the Lord has not commanded *it*?
38 *Is it* not from the mouth of the Most High
That [a]woe and well-being proceed?
39 [a]Why should a living man [1]complain,
[b]A man for the punishment of his sins?

40 Let us search out and examine our ways,
And turn back to the LORD;
41 [a]Let us lift our hearts and hands
To God in heaven.
42 [a]We have transgressed and rebelled;
You have not pardoned.

43 You have covered *Yourself* with anger
And pursued us;
You have slain *and* not pitied.
44 You have covered Yourself with a cloud,
That prayer should not pass through.
45 You have made us an [a]offscouring and refuse
In the midst of the peoples.

46 [a]All our enemies
Have opened their mouths against us.
47 [a]Fear and a snare have come upon us,
[b]Desolation and destruction.
48 [a]My eyes overflow with rivers of water
For the destruction of the daughter of my people.

49 [a]My eyes flow and do not cease,
Without interruption,
50 Till the LORD from heaven
[a]Looks down and sees.
51 My eyes bring suffering to my soul
Because of all the daughters of my city.

52 My enemies [a]without cause
Hunted me down like a bird.
53 They [1]silenced my life [a]in the pit
And [b]threw [2]stones at me.
54 [a]The waters flowed over my head;
[b]I said, "I am cut off!"

55 [a]I called on Your name, O LORD,
From the lowest [b]pit.
56 [a]You have heard my voice:
"Do not hide Your ear
From my sighing, from my cry for help."

16 [1]Lit. *bent me down in*
17 [1]Lit. *good*
18 [a]Ps. 31:22
19 [a]Jer. 9:15 [1]*bitterness*
20 [1]Lit. *bowed down*
21 [a]Ps. 130:7
22 [a][Mal. 3:6] [b]Ps. 78:38
23 [a]Is. 33:2
24 [a]Ps. 16:5; 73:26; 119:57 [b]Mic. 7:7
25 [a]Is. 30:18
26 [a][Rom. 4:16–18] [b]Ps. 37:7
27 [a]Ps. 94:12
28 [a]Jer. 15:17
29 [a]Job 42:6
30 [a]Is. 50:6
31 [a]Ps. 77:7; 94:14
33 [a][Ezek. 33:11] [1]Lit. *from his heart*
36 [a][Hab. 1:13]
37 [a][Ps. 33:9–11]
38 [a]Job 2:10
39 [a]Prov. 19:3 [b]Mic. 7:9 [1]Or *murmur*
41 [a]Ps. 86:4
42 [a]Dan. 9:5
45 [a]1 Cor. 4:13
46 [a]Lam. 2:16
47 [a]Is. 24:17, 18 [b]Is. 51:19
48 [a]Jer. 4:19; 14:17
49 [a]Jer. 14:17
50 [a]Is. 63:15
52 [a]Ps. 35:7, 19
53 [a]Jer. 37:16 [b]Dan. 6:17 [1]LXX *put to death* [2]Lit. *a stone on*
54 [a]Ps. 69:2 [b]Is. 38:10
55 [a]Ps. 130:1 [b]Jer. 38:6–13
56 [a]Ps. 3:4

57 You [a]drew near on the day I
called on You,
And said, [b]"Do not fear!"

58 O Lord, You have [a]pleaded the
case for my soul;
[b]You have redeemed my life.
59 O LORD, You have seen [1]*how* I
am wronged;
[a]Judge my case.
60 You have seen all their
vengeance,
All their [a]schemes against me.

61 You have heard their reproach,
O LORD,
All their schemes against me,
62 The lips of my enemies
And their whispering against me
all the day.
63 Look at their [a]sitting down and
their rising up;
I *am* their taunting song.

64 [a]Repay them, O LORD,
According to the work of their
hands.
65 Give them [1]a veiled heart;
Your curse *be* upon them!
66 In Your anger,
Pursue and destroy them
[a]From under the heavens of the
[b]LORD.

The Degradation of Zion

4 How the gold has become dim!
How changed the fine gold!
The stones of the sanctuary are
[1]scattered
At the head of every street.

2 The precious sons of Zion,
[1]Valuable as fine gold,
How they are [2]regarded [a]as clay
pots,
The work of the hands of the
potter!
3 Even the jackals present their
breasts
To nurse their young;
But the daughter of my people *is*
cruel,
[a]Like ostriches in the wilderness.

4 The tongue of the infant clings
To the roof of its mouth for thirst;
[a]The young children ask for bread,
But no one breaks *it* for them.

5 Those who ate delicacies
Are desolate in the streets;
Those who were brought up in
scarlet
[a]Embrace ash heaps.

6 The punishment of the iniquity of
the daughter of my people
Is greater than the punishment of
the [a]sin of Sodom,
Which was [b]overthrown in a
moment,
With no hand to help her!

7 Her [1]Nazirites were [2]brighter
than snow
And whiter than milk;
They were more ruddy in body
than rubies,
Like sapphire in their
[3]appearance.

8 *Now* their appearance is blacker
than soot;
They go unrecognized in the
streets;
[a]Their skin clings to their bones,
It has become as dry as wood.

9 *Those* slain by the sword are
better off
Than *those* who die of hunger;
For these [a]pine away,
Stricken *for lack* of the fruits of
the [b]field.

10 The hands of the [a]compassionate
women
Have [1]cooked their [b]own
children;
They became [c]food for them
In the destruction of the daughter
of my people.

11 The LORD has fulfilled His fury,
[a]He has poured out His fierce
anger.
[b]He kindled a fire in Zion,
And it has devoured its
foundations.

12 The kings of the earth,
And all inhabitants of the world,
Would not have believed
That the adversary and the
enemy
Could [a]enter the gates of
Jerusalem—

13 [a]Because of the sins of her
prophets
And the iniquities of her priests,
[b]Who shed in her midst
The blood of the just.

14 They wandered blind in the
streets;
[a]They have defiled themselves
with blood,
[b]So that no one would touch their
garments.

57 [a]James 4:8 [b]Is. 41:10, 14; Dan. 10:12
58 [a]Ps. 35:1; Jer. 51:36 [b]Ps. 71:23
59 [a]Ps. 9:4 [1]Lit. *my wrong*
60 [a]Jer. 11:19
63 [a]Ps. 139:2
64 [a]Ps. 28:4; Jer. 11:20; 2 Tim. 4:14
65 [1]A Jewish tradition *sorrow of*
66 [a]Deut. 25:19; Jer. 10:11 [b]Ps. 8:3

CHAPTER 4

1 [1]Lit. *poured out*
2 [a]Is. 30:14; Jer. 19:11; [2 Cor. 4:7] [1]Lit. *Weighed against* [2]*reckoned*
3 [a]Job 39:14–17
4 [a]Ps. 22:15
5 [a]Job 24:8
6 [a]Ezek. 16:48 [b]Gen. 19:25; Jer. 20:16
7 [1]Or *nobles* [2]Or *purer* [3]Lit. *polishing*
8 [a]Job 19:20; Ps. 102:5
9 [a]Lev. 26:39; Ezek. 24:23 [b]Jer. 16:4
10 [a]Lev. 26:29; Deut. 28:57; 2 Kin. 6:29; Jer. 19:9; Lam. 2:20; Ezek. 5:10 [b]Is. 49:15 [c]Deut. 28:57 [1]*boiled*
11 [a]Jer. 7:20; Lam. 2:17; Ezek. 22:31 [b]Deut. 32:22; Jer. 21:14
12 [a]Jer. 21:13
13 [a]Jer. 5:31; Ezek. 22:26, 28; Zeph. 3:4 [b]Jer. 2:30; 26:8, 9; Matt. 23:31
14 [a]Jer. 2:34 [b]Num. 19:16

15 They cried out to them,
"Go away, [a]unclean!
Go away, go away,
Do not touch us!"
When they fled and wandered,
Those among the nations said,
"They shall no longer dwell *here.*"

16 The [1]face of the LORD scattered them;
He no longer regards them.
[a]*The people* do not respect the priests
Nor show favor to the elders.

17 Still [a]our eyes failed us,
Watching vainly for our help;
In our watching we watched
For a nation *that* could not save *us.*

18 [a]They [1]tracked our steps
So that we could not walk in our streets.
[b]Our end was near;
Our days were over,
For our end had come.

19 Our pursuers were [a]swifter
Than the eagles of the heavens.
They pursued us on the mountains
And lay in wait for us in the wilderness.

20 The [a]breath of our nostrils, the anointed of the LORD,
[b]Was caught in their pits,
Of whom we said, "Under his shadow
We shall live among the nations."

21 Rejoice and be glad, O daughter of [a]Edom,
You who dwell in the land of Uz!
[b]The cup shall also pass over to you
And you shall become drunk and make yourself naked.

22 [a]*The punishment of* your iniquity [1]is accomplished,
O daughter of Zion;
He will no longer send you into captivity.
[b]He will punish your iniquity,
O daughter of Edom;
He will uncover your sins!

A Prayer for Restoration

5 Remember, [a]O LORD, what has come upon us;
Look, and behold [b]our reproach!
2 [a]Our inheritance has been turned over to aliens,
And our houses to foreigners.
3 We have become orphans and waifs,
Our mothers *are* like [a]widows.
4 We pay for the water we drink,
And our wood comes at a price.
5 [a]*They* pursue at our [1]heels;
We labor *and* have no rest.
6 [a]We have given our hand [b]*to the* Egyptians
And the [c]Assyrians, to be satisfied with bread.
7 [a]Our fathers sinned *and are* no more,
But we bear their iniquities.
8 Servants rule over us;
There is none to deliver *us* from their hand.
9 We get our bread *at the risk* of our lives,
Because of the sword in the wilderness.

10 Our skin is hot as an oven,
Because of the fever of famine.
11 They [a]ravished the women in Zion,
The maidens in the cities of Judah.
12 Princes were hung up by their hands,
And elders were not respected.
13 Young men [a]ground at the millstones;
Boys staggered under *loads of* wood.
14 The elders have ceased *gathering at* the gate,
And the young men from their [a]music.

15 The joy of our heart has ceased;
Our dance has turned into [a]mourning.
16 [a]The crown has fallen *from* our head.
Woe to us, for we have sinned!
17 Because of this our heart is faint;
[a]Because of these *things* our eyes grow dim;
18 Because of Mount Zion which is [a]desolate,
With foxes walking about on it.

19 You, O LORD, [a]remain forever;
[b]Your throne from generation to generation.
20 [a]Why do You forget us forever,
And forsake us for so long a time?
21 [a]Turn us back to You, O LORD, and we will be [1]restored;
Renew our days as of old,
22 Unless You have utterly rejected us,
And are very angry with us!

---

15 [a]Lev. 13:45, 46
16 [a]Lam. 5:12 [1]Tg. *anger*
17 [a]2 Kin. 24:7
18 [a]2 Kin. 25:4 [b]Ezek. 7:2, 3, 6; Amos 8:2 [1]Lit. *hunted*
19 [a]Deut. 28:49
20 [a]Gen. 2:7 [b]Jer. 52:9; Ezek. 12:13
21 [a]Ps. 83:3–6 [b]Jer. 25:15; Obad. 10
22 [a][Is. 40:2; Jer. 33:7, 8] [b]Ps. 137:7 [1]*has been completed*

CHAPTER 5
1 [a]Ps. 89:50 [b]Ps. 79:4; Lam. 2:15
2 [a]Ps. 79:1
3 [a]Ex. 22:24; Jer. 15:8; 18:21
5 [a]Deut. 28:48; Jer. 28:14 [1]Lit. *necks*
6 [a]Gen. 24:2 [b]Hos. 9:3; 12:1 [c]Jer. 2:18; Hos. 5:13
7 [a]Jer. 31:29
11 [a]Is. 13:16; Zech. 14:2
13 [a]Judg. 16:21
14 [a]Is. 24:8; Jer. 7:34
15 [a]Jer. 25:10; Amos 8:10
16 [a]Job 19:9; Ps. 89:39; Jer. 13:18
17 [a]Ps. 6:7
18 [a]Is. 27:10
19 [a]Ps. 9:7; Hab. 1:12 [b]Ps. 45:6
20 [a]Ps. 13:1; 44:24
21 [a]Ps. 80:3, 7, 19; Jer. 31:18 [1]*returned*

The Book of

Ezekiel

EZEKIEL, a priest and a prophet, ministers during the darkest days of Judah's history: the seventy-year period of Babylonian captivity. Carried to Babylon before the final assault on Jerusalem, Ezekiel uses prophecies, parables, signs, and symbols to dramatize God's message to His exiled people. Though they are like dry bones in the sun, God will reassemble them and breathe life into the nation once again. Present judgment will be followed by future glory so that "you shall know that I *am* the LORD" (6:7).

The Hebrew name *Yehezke'l* means "God Strengthens" or "Strengthened by God." Ezekiel is indeed strengthened by God for the prophetic ministry to which he is called (3:8, 9). The name occurs twice in this book and nowhere else in the Old Testament. The Greek form in the Septuagint is *Iezekiel* and the Latin form in the Vulgate is *Ezechiel*.

Ezekiel's Vision of God

NOW it came to pass in the thir-
tieth year, in the fourth
month, on the fifth *day* of the
month, as I *was* among the cap-
tives by [a]the River Chebar, *that*
[b]the heavens were opened and I
saw [c]visions[1] of God.
2 On the fifth *day* of the month,
which *was* in the fifth year of King
Jehoiachin's captivity,
3 the word of the LORD came ex-
pressly to Ezekiel the priest, the
son of Buzi, in the land of the
[1]Chaldeans by the River Chebar;
and [a]the hand of the LORD was
upon him there.
4 Then I looked, and behold, [a]a
whirlwind was coming [b]out of the
north, a great cloud with raging fire
engulfing itself; and brightness
was all around it and radiating
out of its midst like the color of
amber, out of the midst of the
fire.
5 [a]Also from within it *came* the
likeness of four living creatures.
And [b]this *was* their appearance:
they had [c]the likeness of a man.
6 Each one had four faces, and
each one had four wings.
7 Their [1]legs *were* straight, and
the soles of their feet *were* like the
soles of calves' feet. They sparkled
[a]like the color of burnished
bronze.
8 [a]The hands of a man *were* un-
der their wings on their four sides;
and each of the four had faces and
wings.
9 Their wings touched one an-
other. *The creatures* did not turn
when they went, but each one
went straight [a]forward.
10 As for [a]the likeness of their
faces, *each* [b]had the face of a man;
each of the four had [c]the face of
a lion on the right side, [d]each of
the four had the face of an ox on
the left side, [e]and each of the four
had the face of an eagle.
11 Thus *were* their faces. Their
wings stretched upward; two
wings of each one touched one an-
other, and [a]two covered their bod-
ies.
12 And [a]each one went straight
forward; they went wherever the
spirit wanted to go, and they did
not turn when they went.
13 As for the likeness of the living
creatures, their appearance *was*
like burning coals of fire, [a]like the
appearance of torches going back
and forth among the living crea-
tures. The fire was bright, and out
of the fire went lightning.
14 And the living creatures ran
back and forth, [a]in appearance
like a flash of lightning.
15 Now as I looked at the living
creatures, behold, [a]a wheel *was* on
the earth beside each living crea-
ture with its four faces.

CHAPTER 1

1 [a]Ezek. 3:15, 23; 10:15 [b]Rev. 4:1; 19:11 [c]Ezek. 8:3 [1]So with MT, LXX, Vg.; Syr., Tg. *a vision*
3 [a]Ezek. 3:14, 22 [1]Or *Babylonians*, and so elsewhere in the book
4 [a]Jer. 23:19; 25:32 [b]Jer. 1:14
5 [a]Rev. 4:6–8 [b]Ezek. 10:8 [c]Ezek. 10:14
7 [a]Dan. 10:6 [1]Lit. *feet*
8 [a]Ezek. 10:8, 21
9 [a]Ezek. 1:12; 10:20–22
10 [a]Rev. 4:7 [b]Num. 2:10 [c]Num. 2:3 [d]Num. 2:18 [e]Num. 2:25
11 [a]Is. 6:2
12 [a]Ezek. 10:11, 22
13 [a]Rev. 4:5
14 [a][Matt. 24:27]
15 [a]Ezek. 10:9

16 [a]The appearance of the wheels
and their workings *was* [b]like the
color of beryl, and all four had the
same likeness. The appearance of
their workings *was*, as it were, a
wheel in the middle of a wheel.
17 When they moved, they went
toward any one of four directions;
they did not turn aside when they
went.
18 As for their rims, they were so
high they were awesome; and their
rims *were* [a]full of eyes, all around
the four of them.
19 [a]When the living creatures
went, the wheels went beside
them; and when the living crea-
tures were lifted up from the earth,
the wheels were lifted up.
20 Wherever the spirit wanted to
go, they went, *because* there the
spirit went; and the wheels were
lifted together with them, [a]for the
spirit of the [1]living creatures *was*
in the wheels.
21 When those went, *these* went;
when those stood, *these* stood; and
when those were lifted up from the
earth, the wheels were lifted up to-
gether with them, for the spirit of
the [1]living creatures *was* in the
wheels.
22 [a]The likeness of the [1]firmament
above the heads of the [2]living crea-
tures *was* like the color of an awe-
some [b]crystal, stretched out [c]over
their heads.
23 And under the firmament their
wings *spread out* straight, one to-
ward another. Each one had two
which covered one side, and each
one had two which covered the
other side of the body.
24 [a]When they went, I heard the
noise of their wings, [b]like the noise
of many waters, like [c]the voice of
the Almighty, a tumult like the
noise of an army; and when they
stood still, they let down their
wings.
25 A voice came from above the
firmament that *was* over their
heads; whenever they stood, they
let down their wings.
26 [a]And above the firmament over
their heads *was* the likeness of a
throne, [b]in appearance like a sap-
phire stone; on the likeness of the
throne *was* a likeness with the ap-
pearance of a man high above [c]it.
27 Also from the appearance of
His waist and upward [a]I saw, as
it were, the color of amber with
the appearance of fire all around
within it; and from the appearance
of His waist and downward I saw,
as it were, the appearance of fire
with brightness all around.
28 [a]Like the appearance of a rain-
bow in a cloud on a rainy day, so
was the appearance of the bright-
ness all around it. [b]This *was* the
appearance of the likeness of the
glory of the LORD.

Ezekiel Sent to Rebellious Israel

So when I saw *it*, [c]I fell on my
face, and I heard a voice of One
speaking.
2 And He said to me, "Son of
man, [a]stand on your feet, and
I will speak to you."
2 Then [a]the Spirit entered me
when He spoke to me, and set me
on my feet; and I heard Him who
spoke to me.
3 And He said to me: "Son of
man, I am sending you to the chil-
dren of Israel, to a rebellious na-
tion that has [a]rebelled against Me;
[b]they and their fathers have trans-
gressed against Me to this very
day.
4 [a]"For *they are* [1]impudent and
stubborn children. I am sending
you to them, and you shall say
to them, 'Thus says the Lord
GOD.'
5 [a]"As for them, whether they
hear or whether they refuse—for
they *are* a [b]rebellious house—yet
they [c]will know that a prophet has
been among them.
6 "And you, son of man, [a]do not
be afraid of them nor be afraid of
their words, though [b]briers and
thorns *are* with you and you dwell
among scorpions; [c]do not be afraid
of their words or dismayed by
their looks, [d]though they *are* a re-
bellious house.
7 [a]"You shall speak My words
to them, whether they hear or
whether they refuse, for they *are*
rebellious.
8 "But you, son of man, hear
what I say to you. Do not be rebel-
lious like that rebellious house;
open your mouth and [a]eat what I
give you."
9 Now when I looked, there was
[a]a hand stretched out to me; and

16 [a]Ezek. 10:9, 10 [b]Dan. 10:6
18 [a]Ezek. 10:12
19 [a]Ezek. 10:16, 17
20 [a]Ezek. 10:17 [1]Lit. *living creature;* LXX, Vg. *spirit of life;* Tg. *creatures*
21 [1]See note at v. 20
22 [a]Ezek. 10:1 [b]Rev. 4:6 [c]Ezek. 10:1 [1]Or *expanse* [2]So with LXX, Tg., Vg.; MT *living creature*
24 [a]Ezek. 3:13; 10:5 [b]Rev. 1:15 [c]Job 37:4, 5
26 [a]Ezek. 10:1 [b]Ex. 24:10, 16 [c]Ezek. 8:2
27 [a]Ezek. 8:2
28 [a]Rev. 4:3; 10:1 [b]Ezek. 3:23; 8:4 [c]Dan. 8:17

CHAPTER 2

1 [a]Dan. 10:11
2 [a]Ezek. 3:24
3 [a]Ezek. 5:6; 20:8, 13, 18 [b]Jer. 3:25
4 [a]Ezek. 3:7 [1]Lit. *stiff-faced and hard-hearted sons*
5 [a]Ezek. 3:11, 26, 27 [b]Ezek. 3:26 [c]Ezek. 33:33
6 [a]Jer. 1:8, 17 [b]Mic. 7:4 [c][1 Pet. 3:14] [d]Ezek. 3:9, 26, 27
7 [a]Jer. 1:7, 17
8 [a]Rev. 10:9
9 [a][Ezek. 8:3]

behold, [b]a scroll of a book *was*
in it.
10 Then He spread it before me;
and *there was* writing on the in-
side and on the outside, and writ-
ten on it *were* lamentations and
mourning and woe.
3 Moreover He said to me, "Son
of man, eat what you find; [a]eat
this scroll, and go, speak to the
house of Israel."
2 So I opened my mouth, and He
caused me to eat that scroll.
3 And He said to me, "Son of
man, feed your belly, and fill your
stomach with this scroll that I give
you." So I [a]ate, and it was in my
mouth [b]like honey in sweetness.
4 Then He said to me: "Son of
man, go to the house of Israel and
speak with My words to them.
5 "For you *are* not sent to a peo-
ple of unfamiliar speech and of
hard language, *but* to the house of
Israel,
6 "not to many people of unfa-
miliar speech and of hard lan-
guage, whose words you cannot
understand. Surely, [a]had I sent
you to them, they would have lis-
tened to you.
7 "But the house of Israel will not
listen to you, [a]because they will
not listen to Me; [b]for all the house
of Israel *are* [1]impudent and hard-
hearted.
8 "Behold, I have made your face
strong against their faces, and
your forehead strong against their
foreheads.
9 [a]"Like adamant stone, harder
than flint, I have made your fore-
head; [b]do not be afraid of them,
nor be dismayed at their looks,
though they *are* a rebellious
house."
10 Moreover He said to me: "Son
of man, receive into your heart all
My words that I speak to you, and
hear with your ears.
11 "And go, get to the captives,
to the children of your people,
and speak to them and tell
them, [a]'Thus says the Lord GOD,'
whether they hear, or whether
they refuse."
12 Then [a]the Spirit lifted me up,
and I heard behind me a great
thunderous voice: "Blessed *is* the
[b]glory of the LORD from His place!"
13 *I* also *heard* the [a]noise of the
wings of the living creatures that
touched one another, and the noise
of the wheels beside them, and a
great thunderous noise.
14 So the Spirit lifted me up and
took me away, and I went in bitter-
ness, in the [1]heat of my spirit; but
[a]the hand of the LORD was strong
upon me.
15 Then I came to the captives at
Tel Abib, who dwelt by the River
Chebar; and [a]I sat where they sat,
and remained there astonished
among them seven days.

Ezekiel Is a Watchman

16 Now it [a]came to pass at the end
of seven days that the word of the
LORD came to me, saying,
17 [a]"Son of man, I have made you
[b]a watchman for the house of Is-
rael; therefore hear a word from
My mouth, and give them [c]warn-
ing from Me:
18 "When I say to the wicked,
'You shall surely die,' and you give
him no warning, nor speak to
warn the wicked from his wicked
way, to save his life, that same
wicked *man* [a]shall die in his in-
iquity; but his blood I will require
at your hand.
19 "Yet, if you warn the wicked,
and he does not turn from his
wickedness, nor from his wicked
way, he shall die in his iniquity;
[a]but you have delivered your
soul.
20 "Again, when a [a]righteous *man*
turns from his righteousness and
commits iniquity, and I lay a stum-
bling block before him, he shall
die; because you did not give him
warning, he shall die in his sin,
and his righteousness which he
has done shall not be remembered;
but his blood I will require at your
hand.
21 "Nevertheless if you warn the
righteous *man* that the righteous
should not sin, and he does not sin,
he shall surely live because he
took warning; also you will have
delivered your soul."
22 [a]Then the hand of the LORD was
upon me there, and He said to me,
"Arise, go out [b]into the plain, and
there I shall talk with you."
23 So I arose and went out into the
plain, and behold, [a]the glory of the
LORD stood there, like the glory

9 [b]Jer. 36:2; Ezek. 3:1; Rev. 5:1–5; 10:8–11

CHAPTER 3

1 [a]Ezek. 2:8, 9
3 [a]Jer. 15:16; Rev. 10:9 [b]Ps. 19:10; 119:103
6 [a]Jon. 3:5–10; Matt. 11:21
7 [a]John 15:20, 21 [b]Ezek. 2:4 [1]Lit. *strong of forehead*
9 [a]Is. 50:7; Jer. 1:18; Mic. 3:8 [b]Jer. 1:8, 17; Ezek. 2:6
11 [a]Ezek. 2:5, 7
12 [a]1 Kin. 18:12; Ezek. 8:3; Acts 8:39 [b]Ezek. 1:28; 8:4
13 [a]Ezek. 1:24; 10:5
14 [a]2 Kin. 3:15; Ezek. 1:3; 8:1 [1]Or *anger*
15 [a]Job 2:13; Ps. 137:1
16 [a]Jer. 42:7
17 [a]Ezek. 33:7–9 [b]Is. 52:8; 56:10; Jer. 6:17 [c][Lev. 19:17; Prov. 14:25]; Is. 58:1
18 [a]Ezek. 33:6; [John 8:21, 24]
19 [a]Is. 49:4, 5; Ezek. 14:14, 20; Acts 18:6; 20:26; 1 Tim. 4:16
20 [a]Ps. 125:5; Ezek. 18:24; 33:18; Zeph. 1:6
22 [a]Ezek. 1:3 [b]Ezek. 8:4
23 [a]Ezek. 1:28; Acts 7:55

which I [b]saw by the River Chebar;
[c]and I fell on my face.
24 Then [a]the Spirit entered me
and set me on my feet, and spoke
with me and said to me: "Go, shut
yourself inside your house.
25 "And you, O son of man, surely
[a]they will put ropes on you and
bind you with them, so that you
cannot go out among them.
26 [a]"I will make your tongue cling
to the roof of your mouth, so that
you shall be mute and [b]not be [1]one
to rebuke them, [c]for they *are* a re-
bellious house.
27 [a]"But when I speak with you,
I will open your mouth, and you
shall say to them, [b]'Thus says the
Lord GOD.' He who hears, let him
hear; and he who refuses, let him
refuse; for they *are* a rebellious
house.

The Siege of Jerusalem Portrayed

4 "You also, son of man, take a
clay tablet and lay it before
you, and portray on it a city, Jeru-
salem.
2 [a]"Lay siege against it, build a
[b]siege wall against it, and heap up
a mound against it; set camps
against it also, and place battering
rams against it all around.
3 "Moreover take for yourself an
iron plate, and set it *as* an iron wall
between you and the city. Set your
face against it, and it shall be [a]be-
sieged, and you shall lay siege
against it. [b]This *will be* a sign to
the house of Israel.
4 "Lie also on your left side, and
lay the iniquity of the house of Is-
rael upon it. *According* to the num-
ber of the days that you lie on it,
you shall bear their iniquity.
5 "For I have laid on you the
years of their iniquity, according
to the number of the days, three
hundred and ninety days; [a]so you
shall bear the iniquity of the house
of Israel.
6 "And when you have com-
pleted them, lie again on your right
side; then you shall bear the in-
iquity of the house of Judah forty
days. I have laid on you a day for
each year.
7 "Therefore you shall set your
face toward the siege of Jerusa-
lem; your arm *shall be* uncovered,
and you shall prophesy against it.
8 [a]"And surely I will [1]restrain
you so that you cannot turn from
one side to another till you have
ended the days of your siege.
9 "Also take for yourself wheat,
barley, beans, lentils, millet, and
spelt; put them into one vessel, and
make bread of them for yourself.
During the number of days that
you lie on your side, three hundred
and ninety days, you shall eat it.
10 "And your food which you eat
shall be by weight, twenty shekels
a day; from time to time you shall
eat it.
11 "You shall also drink water by
measure, one-sixth of a hin; from
time to time you shall drink.
12 "And you shall eat it *as* barley
cakes; and bake it using fuel of hu-
man waste in their sight."
13 Then the LORD said, "So [a]shall
the children of Israel eat their de-
filed bread among the Gentiles,
where I will drive them."
14 So I said, [a]"Ah, Lord GOD! In-
deed I have never defiled myself
from my youth till now; I have
never eaten [b]what died of itself or
was torn by beasts, nor has [c]abom-
inable[1] flesh ever come into my
mouth."
15 Then He said to me, "See, I am
giving you cow dung instead of hu-
man waste, and you shall prepare
your bread over it."
16 Moreover He said to me, "Son
of man, surely I will cut off the
[a]supply of bread in Jerusalem;
they shall [b]eat bread by weight
and with anxiety, and shall [c]drink
water by measure and with dread,
17 "that they may lack bread and
water, and be dismayed with one
another, and [a]waste away because
of their iniquity.

A Sword Against Jerusalem

5 "And you, son of man, take a
sharp sword, take it as a bar-
ber's razor, [a]and pass *it* over your
head and your beard; then take
scales to weigh and divide the hair.
2 [a]"You shall burn with fire one-
third in the midst of [b]the city,
when [c]the days of the siege are fin-
ished; then you shall take one-
third and strike around *it* with the
sword, and one-third you shall
scatter in the wind: I will draw out
a sword after [d]them.

23 [b]Ezek. 1:1 [c]Ezek. 1:28
24 [a]Ezek. 2:2
25 [a]Ezek. 4:8
26 [a]Ezek. 24:27; Luke 1:20, 22 [b]Hos. 4:17; Amos 8:11 [c]Ezek. 2:5–7 [1]Lit. *one who rebukes*
27 [a]Ex. 4:11, 12; Ezek. 24:27; 33:22 [b]Ezek. 3:11

CHAPTER 4

2 [a]Jer. 6:6; Ezek. 21:22 [b]2 Kin. 25:1
3 [a]Jer. 39:1, 2; Ezek. 5:2 [b]Ezek. 12:6, 11; 24:24, 27
5 [a]Num. 14:34
8 [a]Ezek. 3:25 [1]Lit. *put ropes on*
13 [a]Dan. 1:8; Hos. 9:3
14 [a]Acts 10:14 [b]Ex. 22:31; Lev. 17:15; 22:8; Ezek. 44:31 [c]Deut. 14:3; Is. 65:4; 66:17 [1]Ritually unclean flesh, Lev. 7:18
16 [a]Lev. 26:26; Ps. 105:16; Is. 3:1; Ezek. 5:16; 14:13 [b]Ezek. 4:10, 11; 12:19 [c]Ezek. 4:11
17 [a]Lev. 26:39; Ezek. 24:23

CHAPTER 5

1 [a]Lev. 21:5; Is. 7:20; Ezek. 44:20
2 [a]Ezek. 5:12 [b]Ezek. 4:1 [c]Ezek. 4:8, 9 [d]Lev. 26:25; Lam. 1:20

3 [a]"You shall also take a small
number of them and bind them in
the edge of your *garment.*
4 "Then take some of them again
and [a]throw them into the midst of
the fire, and burn them in the fire.
From there a fire will go out into
all the house of Israel.
5 "Thus says the Lord GOD: 'This
is Jerusalem; I have set her in the
midst of the nations and the coun-
tries all around her.
6 'She has rebelled against My
judgments by doing wickedness
more than the nations, and against
My statutes more than the coun-
tries that *are* all around her; for
they have refused My judgments,
and they have not walked in My
statutes.'
7 "Therefore thus says the Lord
GOD: 'Because you have [1]multi-
plied *disobedience* more than the
nations that *are* all around you,
have not walked in My statutes
[a]nor kept My judgments, [2]nor even
done according to the judgments
of the nations that *are* all around
you'—
8 "therefore thus says the Lord
GOD: 'Indeed I, even I, *am* against
you and will execute judgments in
your midst in the sight of the na-
tions.
9 [a]'And I will do among you what
I have never done, and the like of
which I will never do again, be-
cause of all your abominations.
10 'Therefore fathers [a]shall eat
their sons in your midst, and sons
shall eat their fathers; and I will
execute judgments among you,
and all of you who remain I will
[b]scatter to all the winds.
11 'Therefore, *as* I live,' says the
Lord GOD, 'surely, because you
have [a]defiled My sanctuary with
all your [b]detestable things and
with all your abominations, there-
fore I will also diminish *you;* [c]My
eye will not spare, nor will I have
any pity.
12 [a]'One-third of you shall die of
the pestilence, and be consumed
with famine in your midst; and
one-third shall fall by the sword
all around you; and [b]I will scatter
another third to all the winds, and
I will draw out a sword after
[c]them.
13 'Thus shall My anger [a]be spent,
and I will [b]cause My fury to rest
upon them, [c]and I will be avenged;
[d]and they shall know that I, the
LORD, have spoken *it* in My zeal,
when I have spent My fury upon
them.
14 'Moreover [a]I will make you a
waste and a reproach among the
nations that *are* all around you, in
the sight of all who pass by.
15 'So [1]it shall be a [a]reproach, a
taunt, a [b]lesson, and an astonish-
ment to the nations that *are* all
around you, when I execute judg-
ments among you in anger and in
fury and in [c]furious rebukes. I, the
LORD, have spoken.
16 'When I [a]send against them the
terrible arrows of famine which
shall be for destruction, which I
will send to destroy you, I will in-
crease the famine upon you and
cut off your [b]supply of bread.
17 'So I will send against you fam-
ine and [a]wild beasts, and they will
bereave you. [b]Pestilence and blood
shall pass through you, and I will
bring the sword against you. I, the
LORD, have spoken.' "

Judgment on Idolatrous Israel

6 Now the word of the LORD
came to me, saying:
2 "Son of man, [a]set your face to-
ward the [b]mountains of Israel, and
prophesy against them,
3 "and say, 'O mountains of Is-
rael, hear the word of the Lord
GOD! Thus says the Lord GOD to
the mountains, to the hills, to the
ravines, and to the valleys: "In-
deed I, *even* I, will bring a sword
against you, and [a]I will destroy
your [1]high places.
4 "Then your altars shall be des-
olate, your incense altars shall be
broken, and [a]I will cast down your
slain *men* before your idols.
5 "And I will lay the corpses of
the children of Israel before their
idols, and I will scatter your bones
all around your altars.
6 "In all your dwelling places the
cities shall be laid waste, and the
[1]high places shall be desolate, so
that your altars may be laid waste
and made desolate, your idols may
be broken and made to cease, your
incense altars may be cut down,
and your works may be abolished.
7 "The slain shall fall in your

3 [a]Jer. 40:6; 52:16
4 [a]Jer. 41:1, 2; 44:14
7 [a]Jer. 2:10, 11 [1]Or *raged* [2]So with MT, LXX, Tg., Vg.; many Heb. mss., Syr. *but have done* (cf. 11:12)
9 [a][Amos 3:2]
10 [a]Jer. 19:9 [b]Zech. 2:6; 7:14
11 [a][Jer. 7:9–11] [b]Ezek. 11:21 [c]Ezek. 7:4, 9; 8:18; 9:10
12 [a]Ezek. 6:12 [b]Jer. 9:16 [c]Jer. 43:10, 11; 44:27
13 [a]Lam. 4:11 [b]Ezek. 21:17 [c]Is. 1:24 [d]Ezek. 36:6; 38:19
14 [a]Lev. 26:31
15 [a]Jer. 24:9 [b][Is. 26:9] [c]Ezek. 5:8; 25:17 [1]LXX, Syr., Tg., Vg. *you*
16 [a]Deut. 32:23 [b]Lev. 26:26
17 [a]Lev. 26:22 [b]Ezek. 38:22

CHAPTER 6

2 [a]Ezek. 20:46; 21:2; 25:2 [b]Ezek. 36:1
3 [a]Lev. 26:30 [1]Places for pagan worship
4 [a]Lev. 26:30
6 [1]Places for pagan worship

midst, and [a]you shall know that I
am the LORD.
8 [a]"Yet I will leave a remnant, so
that you may have *some* who es-
cape the sword among the nations,
when you are [b]scattered through
the countries.
9 "Then those of you who escape
will [a]remember Me among the na-
tions where they are carried cap-
tive, because [b]I was crushed by
their adulterous heart which has
departed from Me, and [c]by their
eyes which play the harlot after
their idols; [d]they will loathe them-
selves for the evils which they
committed in all their abomina-
tions.
10 "And they shall know that I *am*
the LORD; I have not said in vain
that I would bring this calamity
upon them."
11 'Thus says the Lord GOD:
[a]"Pound[1] your fists and stamp
your feet, and say, 'Alas, for all the
evil abominations of the house of
Israel! [b]For they shall fall by the
sword, by famine, and by pesti-
lence.
12 'He who is far off shall die by
the pestilence, he who is near shall
fall by the sword, and he who re-
mains and is besieged shall die by
the famine. [a]Thus will I spend My
fury upon them.
13 'Then you shall know that I *am*
the LORD, when their slain are
among their idols all around their
altars, [a]on every high hill, [b]on all
the mountaintops, [c]under every
green tree, and under every thick
oak, wherever they offered sweet
incense to all their idols.
14 'So I will [a]stretch out My hand
against them and make the land
desolate, yes, more desolate than
the wilderness toward [b]Diblah,
in all their dwelling places. Then
they shall know that I *am* the
LORD.' " ' "

Judgment on Israel Is Near

7 Moreover the word of the LORD
came to me, saying,
2 "And you, son of man, thus
says the Lord GOD to the land of
Israel:

[a]'An end! The end has come upon
the four corners of the land.
3 Now the end *has come* upon you,

7 [a]Ezek. 7:4, 9
8 [a]Jer. 44:28; Ezek. 5:2, 12; 12:16; 14:22 [b]Ezek. 5:12
9 [a][Deut. 4:29]; Ps. 137; Jer. 51:50 [b]Ps. 78:40; Is. 7:13; 43:24; Hos. 11:8 [c]Num. 15:39; Ezek. 20:7, 24 [d]Lev. 26:39; Job 42:6; Ezek. 20:43; 36:31
11 [a]Ezek. 21:14 [b]Ezek. 5:12 [1]Lit. *Strike your hands*
12 [a]Lam. 4:11, 22; Ezek. 5:13
13 [a]Jer. 2:20; 3:6 [b]1 Kin. 14:23; 2 Kin. 16:4; Ezek. 20:28; Hos. 4:13 [c]Is. 57:5
14 [a]Is. 5:25; Ezek. 14:13; 20:33, 34 [b]Num. 33:46

CHAPTER 7

2 [a]Ezek. 7:3, 5, 6; 11:13; Amos 8:2, 10; [Matt. 24:6, 13, 14]
3 [a][Rom. 2:6]
4 [a]Ezek. 5:11 [b]Ezek. 12:20
5 [a]2 Kin. 21:12, 13; Nah. 1:9
7 [a]Ezek. 7:10 [b]Zeph. 1:14, 15
8 [a]Ezek. 20:8, 21
9 [1]Lit. *give*
10 [a]Ezek. 7:7
11 [a]Jer. 6:7 [b]Jer. 16:5, 6; Ezek. 24:16, 22 [1]Or *their wealth*
12 [a]Prov. 20:14; 1 Cor. 7:30 [b]Is. 24:2

And I will send My anger against
you;
I will judge you [a]according to
your ways,
And I will repay you for all your
abominations.
4 [a]My eye will not spare you,
Nor will I have pity;
But I will repay your ways,
And your abominations will be in
your midst;
[b]Then you shall know that I *am*
the LORD!'

5 "Thus says the Lord GOD:

'A disaster, a singular [a]disaster;
Behold, it has come!
6 An end has come,
The end has come;
It has dawned for you;
Behold, it has come!
7 [a]Doom has come to you, you who
dwell in the land;
[b]The time has come,
A day of trouble *is* near,
And not of rejoicing in the
mountains.
8 Now upon you I will soon [a]pour
out My fury,
And spend My anger upon you;
I will judge you according to your
ways,
And I will repay you for all your
abominations.

9 'My eye will not spare,
Nor will I have pity;
I will [1]repay you according to
your ways,
And your abominations will be in
your midst.
Then you shall know that I *am*
the LORD who strikes.

10 'Behold, the day!
Behold, it has come!
[a]Doom has gone out;
The rod has blossomed,
Pride has budded.
11 [a]Violence has risen up into a rod
of wickedness;
None of them *shall remain,*
None of their multitude,
None of [1]them;
[b]Nor *shall there be* wailing for
them.
12 The time has come,
The day draws near.

'Let not the buyer [a]rejoice,
Nor the seller [b]mourn,
For wrath *is* on their whole
multitude.

13 For the seller shall not return to
what has been sold,
Though he may still be alive;
For the vision concerns the whole
multitude,
And it shall not turn back;
No one will strengthen himself
Who lives in iniquity.

14 'They have blown the trumpet and
made everyone ready,
But no one goes to battle;
For My wrath *is* on all their
multitude.
15 [a]The sword *is* outside,
And the pestilence and famine
within.
Whoever *is* in the field
Will die by the sword;
And whoever *is* in the city,
Famine and pestilence will
devour him.

16 'Those who [a]survive will escape
and be on the mountains
Like doves of the valleys,
All of them mourning,
Each for his iniquity.
17 Every [a]hand will be feeble,
And every knee will be *as* weak
as water.
18 They will also [a]be girded with
sackcloth;
Horror will cover them;
Shame *will be* on every face,
Baldness on all their heads.

19 'They will throw their silver into
the streets,
And their gold will be like refuse;
Their [a]silver and their gold will
not be able to deliver them
In the day of the wrath of the
LORD;
They will not satisfy their souls,
Nor fill their stomachs,
Because it became their
stumbling block of iniquity.

20 'As for the beauty of his
ornaments,
He set it in majesty;
[a]But they made from it
The images of their
abominations—
Their detestable things;
Therefore I have made it
Like refuse to them.
21 I will give it as [a]plunder
Into the hands of strangers,
And to the wicked of the earth
as spoil;
And they shall defile it.
22 I will turn My face from them,

15 [a]Deut. 32:25; Jer. 14:18; Lam. 1:20; Ezek. 5:12

16 [a]Ezra 9:15; Is. 37:31; Ezek. 6:8; 14:22

17 [a]Is. 13:7; Jer. 6:24; Ezek. 21:7; Heb. 12:12

18 [a]Is. 3:24; 15:2, 3; Jer. 48:37; Ezek. 27:31; Amos 8:10

19 [a]Prov. 11:4; Jer. 15:13; Zeph. 1:18

20 [a]Jer. 7:30

21 [a]2 Kin. 24:13; Jer. 20:5

23 [a]2 Kin. 21:16

24 [a]Ezek. 21:31; 28:7 [b]2 Chr. 7:20; Ezek. 24:21

25 [1]Lit. *Shuddering*

26 [a]Deut. 32:23; Is. 47:11; Jer. 4:20 [b]Ps. 74:9; Lam. 2:9; Ezek. 20:1, 3; Mic. 3:6

CHAPTER 8

1 [a]Ezek. 14:1; 20:1; 33:31 [b]Ezek. 1:3; 3:22

2 [a]Ezek. 1:26, 27 [b]Ezek. 1:4, 27

3 [a]Dan. 5:5 [b]Ezek. 3:14; Acts 8:39 [c]Ezek. 11:1, 24; 40:2 [d]Jer. 7:30; 32:34; Ezek. 5:11 [e]Ex. 20:4; Deut. 32:16, 21 [1]Arouses the LORD's jealousy

And they will defile My secret
place;
For robbers shall enter it and
defile it.

23 'Make a chain,
For [a]the land is filled with crimes
of blood,
And the city is full of violence.
24 Therefore I will bring the [a]worst
of the Gentiles,
And they will possess their
houses;
I will cause the pomp of the
strong to cease,
And their holy places shall be
[b]defiled.
25 [1]Destruction comes;
They will seek peace, but *there
shall be* none.
26 [a]Disaster will come upon disaster,
And rumor will be upon rumor.
[b]Then they will seek a vision from
a prophet;
But the law will perish from the
priest,
And counsel from the elders.

27 'The king will mourn,
The prince will be clothed with
desolation,
And the hands of the common
people will tremble.
I will do to them according to
their way,
And according to what they
deserve I will judge them;
Then they shall know that I *am*
the LORD!' "

Abominations in the Temple

8 And it came to pass in the sixth
year, in the sixth *month*, on the
fifth *day* of the month, as I sat in
my house with [a]the elders of Judah
sitting before me, that [b]the hand
of the Lord GOD fell upon me there.
2 [a]Then I looked, and there was
a likeness, like the appearance of
fire—from the appearance of His
waist and downward, fire; and
from His waist and upward, like
the appearance of brightness, [b]like
the color of amber.
3 He [a]stretched out the form of
a hand, and took me by a lock of
my hair; and [b]the Spirit lifted me
up between earth and heaven, and
[c]brought me in visions of God to
Jerusalem, to the door of the north
gate of the inner *court*, [d]where the
seat of the image of jealousy *was*,
which [e]provokes[1] to jealousy.

4 And behold, the [a]glory of the
God of Israel *was* there, like the
vision that I [b]saw in the plain.
5 Then He said to me, "Son of
man, lift your eyes now toward the
north." So I lifted my eyes toward
the north, and there, north of the
altar gate, was this image of jeal-
ousy in the entrance.
6 Furthermore He said to me,
"Son of man, do you see what they
are doing, the great [a]abominations
that the house of Israel commits
here, to make Me go far away from
My sanctuary? Now turn again,
you will see greater abomina-
tions."
7 So He brought me to the door
of the court; and when I looked,
there was a hole in the wall.
8 Then He said to me, "Son of
man, dig into the wall"; and when
I dug into the wall, there was a
door.
9 And He said to me, "Go in, and
see the wicked abominations
which they are doing there."
10 So I went in and saw, and
there—every [a]sort of [b]creeping
thing, abominable beasts, and all
the idols of the house of Israel,
[1]portrayed all around on the
walls.
11 And there stood before them
[a]seventy men of the elders of the
house of Israel, and in their midst
stood Jaazaniah the son of Sha-
phan. Each man had a censer in
his hand, and a thick cloud of in-
cense went up.
12 Then He said to me, "Son of
man, have you seen what the el-
ders of the house of Israel do in
the dark, every man in the room
of his idols? For they say, [a]'The
LORD does not see us, the LORD has
forsaken the land.' "
13 And He said to me, "Turn
again, *and* you will see greater
abominations that they are doing."
14 So He brought me to the door
of the north gate of the LORD's
house; and to my dismay, women
were sitting there weeping for
[1]Tammuz.
15 Then He said to me, "Have you
seen *this,* O son of man? Turn
again, you will see greater abomi-
nations than these."
16 So He brought me into the in-
ner court of the LORD's house; and
there, at the door of the temple of
the LORD, [a]between the porch and
the altar, [b]*were* about twenty-five
men [c]with their backs toward the
temple of the LORD and their faces
toward the east, and they were
worshiping [d]the sun toward the
east.
17 And He said to me, "Have you
seen *this,* O son of man? Is it a triv-
ial thing to the house of Judah to
commit the abominations which
they commit here? For they have
[a]filled the land with violence; then
they have returned to provoke Me
to anger. Indeed they put the
branch to their nose.
18 [a]"Therefore I also will act in
fury. My [b]eye will not spare nor
will I have pity; and though they
[c]cry in My ears with a loud voice,
I will not hear them."

The Wicked Are Slain

9 Then He called out in my hear-
ing with a loud voice, saying,
"Let those who have charge over
the city draw near, each *with* a
[1]deadly weapon in his hand."
2 And suddenly six men came
from the direction of the upper
gate, which faces north, each with
his [1]battle-ax in his hand. [a]One
man among them *was* clothed with
linen and had a writer's inkhorn
[2]at his side. They went in and
stood beside the bronze altar.
3 Now [a]the glory of the God of
Israel had gone up from the
cherub, where it had been, to the
threshold of the [1]temple. And He
called to the man clothed with
linen, who *had* the writer's ink-
horn at his side;
4 and the LORD said to him, "Go
through the midst of the city,
through the midst of Jerusalem,
and put [a]a mark on the foreheads
of the men [b]who sigh and cry over
all the abominations that are done
within it."
5 To the others He said in my
[1]hearing, "Go after him through
the city and [a]kill;[2] [b]do not let your
eye spare, nor have any pity.
6 [a]"Utterly[1] slay old *and* young
men, maidens and little children
and women; but [b]do not come near
anyone on whom *is* the mark; and
[c]begin at My sanctuary." [d]So they
began with the elders who *were*
before the [2]temple.

4 [a]Ezek. 3:12; 9:3 [b]Ezek. 1:28; 3:22, 23
6 [a]2 Kin. 23:4, 5
10 [a]Ex. 20:4 [b]Rom. 1:23 [1]Or *carved*
11 [a]Num. 11:16, 25
12 [a]Ezek. 9:9
14 [1]A Sumerian fertility god similar to the Gr. god Adonis
16 [a]Joel 2:17 [b]Ezek. 11:1 [c]Jer. 2:27; 32:33 [d]Deut. 4:19
17 [a]Ezek. 9:9
18 [a]Ezek. 5:13; 16:42; 24:13 [b]Ezek. 5:11; 7:4, 9; 9:5, 10 [c]Mic. 3:4

CHAPTER 9

1 [1]Or *destroying*
2 [a]Lev. 16:4 [1]Lit. *shattering weapon* [2]Lit. *upon his loins*
3 [a]Ezek. 3:23; 8:4; 10:4, 18; 11:22, 23 [1]Lit. *house*
4 [a]Rev. 7:2, 3; 9:4; 14:1 [b]Jer. 13:17
5 [a]Ezek. 7:9 [b]Ezek. 5:11 [1]Lit. *ears* [2]Lit. *strike*
6 [a]2 Chr. 36:17 [b]Rev. 9:4 [c]Jer. 25:29 [d]Ezek. 8:11, 12, 16 [1]Lit. *Slay to destruction* [2]Lit. *house*

7 Then He said to them, "Defile
the [1]temple, and fill the courts with
the slain. Go out!" And they went
out and killed in the city.
8 So it was, that while they were
killing them, I was left *alone*; and
I [a]fell on my face and cried out,
and said, [b]"Ah, Lord GOD! Will
You destroy all the remnant of Is-
rael in pouring out Your fury on
Jerusalem?"
9 Then He said to me, "The in-
iquity of the house of Israel and
Judah *is* exceedingly great, and
[a]the land is full of bloodshed, and
the city full of perversity; for they
say, [b]'The LORD has forsaken the
land, and [c]the LORD does not see!'
10 "And as for Me also, My [a]eye
will neither spare, nor will I have
pity, *but* [b]I will recompense their
deeds on their own head."
11 Just then, the man clothed with
linen, who *had* the inkhorn at his
side, reported back and said, "I
have done as You commanded
me."

The Glory Departs from the Temple

10 And I looked, and there in
the [a]firmament[1] that was
above the head of the cherubim,
there appeared something like a
sapphire stone, having the appear-
ance of the likeness of a throne.
2 [a]Then He spoke to the man
clothed with linen, and said, "Go
in among the wheels, under the
cherub, fill your hands with [b]coals
of fire from among the cherubim,
and [c]scatter *them* over the city."
And he went in as I watched.
3 Now the cherubim were stand-
ing on the [1]south side of the [2]tem-
ple when the man went in, and the
[a]cloud filled the inner court.
4 [a]Then the glory of the LORD
went up from the cherub, *and
paused* over the threshold of the
[1]temple; and [b]the house was filled
with the cloud, and the court was
full of the brightness of the LORD's
[c]glory.
5 And the [a]sound of the wings of
the cherubim was heard *even* in
the outer court, like [b]the voice of
Almighty God when He speaks.
6 Then it happened, when He
commanded the man clothed in
linen, saying, "Take fire from
among the wheels, from among
the cherubim," that he went in and
stood beside the wheels.
7 And the cherub stretched out
his hand from among the cheru-
bim to the fire that *was* among the
cherubim, and took *some of it* and
put *it* into the hands of the *man*
clothed with linen, who took *it* and
went out.
8 [a]The cherubim appeared to
have the form of a man's hand un-
der their wings.
9 [a]And when I looked, there were
four wheels by the cherubim, one
wheel by one cherub and another
wheel by each other cherub; the
wheels appeared *to have* the color
of a [b]beryl stone.
10 *As for* their appearance, all
four looked alike—as it were, a
wheel in the middle of a wheel.
11 [a]When they went, they went to-
ward *any of* their four directions;
they did not turn aside when they
went, but followed in the direction
the head was facing. They did not
turn aside when they went.
12 And their whole body, with
their back, their hands, their
wings, and the wheels that the four
had, *were* [a]full of eyes all around.
13 As for the wheels, they were
called in my [1]hearing, "Wheel."
14 [a]Each one had four faces: the
first face *was* the face of a cherub,
the second face the face of a man,
the third the face of a lion, and the
fourth the face of an eagle.
15 And the cherubim were lifted
up. This *was* [a]the living creature I
saw by the River Chebar.
16 [a]When the cherubim went, the
wheels went beside them; and
when the cherubim lifted their
wings to mount up from the earth,
the same wheels also did not turn
from beside them.
17 [a]When [1]*the cherubim* stood
still, *the wheels* stood still, and
when [2]*one* was lifted up, [3]*the other*
lifted itself up, for the spirit of the
living creature *was* in them.
18 Then [a]the glory of the LORD
[b]departed from the threshold of
the [1]temple and stood over the
cherubim.
19 And [a]the cherubim lifted their
wings and mounted up from the
earth in my sight. When they went
out, the wheels *were* beside them;
and they stood at the door of the

---

7 [1]Lit. *house*
8 [a]Num. 14:5; 16:4, 22, 45; Josh. 7:6 [b]Ezek. 11:13; Amos 7:2–6
9 [a]2 Kin. 21:16; Jer. 2:34; Ezek. 8:17 [b]Job 22:13; Ezek. 8:12 [c]Ps. 10:11; Is. 29:15
10 [a]Is. 65:6; Ezek. 5:11; 7:4; 8:18 [b]Ezek. 11:21; Hos. 9:7

CHAPTER 10

1 [a]Ezek. 1:22, 26 [1]*expanse*
2 [a]Ezek. 9:2, 3; Dan. 10:5 [b]Ps. 18:10–13; Is. 6:6; Ezek. 1:13 [c]Rev. 8:5
3 [a]1 Kin. 8:10, 11 [1]Lit. *right* [2]Lit. *house*
4 [a]Ezek. 1:28 [b]1 Kin. 8:10; Ezek. 43:5 [c]Ezek. 11:22, 23 [1]Lit. *house*
5 [a][Job 40:9]; Ezek. 1:24; [Rev. 10:3] [b][Ps. 29:3]
8 [a]Ezek. 1:8; 10:21
9 [a]Ezek. 1:15 [b]Ezek. 1:16
11 [a]Ezek. 1:17
12 [a]Rev. 4:6, 8
13 [1]Lit. *ears*
14 [a]1 Kin. 7:29, 36; Ezek. 1:6, 10, 11; Rev. 4:7
15 [a]Ezek. 1:3, 5
16 [a]Ezek. 1:19
17 [a]Ezek. 1:12, 20, 21 [1]Lit. *they* [2]Lit. *they were* [3]Lit. *they lifted them*
18 [a]Ezek. 10:4 [b]Hos. 9:12 [1]Lit. *house*
19 [a]Ezek. 11:22

[b]east gate of the LORD's house, and
the glory of the God of Israel *was*
above them.
20 [a]This *is* the living creature I
saw under the God of Israel [b]by
the River Chebar, and I knew they
were cherubim.
21 [a]Each one had four faces and
each one four wings, and the like-
ness of the hands of a man *was*
under their wings.
22 And [a]the likeness of their faces
was the same *as* the faces which
I had seen by the River Chebar,
their appearance and their per-
sons. [b]They each went straight for-
ward.

Judgment on Wicked Counselors

11 Then [a]the Spirit lifted me up
and brought me to [b]the East
Gate of the LORD's house, which
faces eastward; and there [c]at the
door of the gate were twenty-five
men, among whom I saw Jaaza-
niah the son of Azzur, and Pelatiah
the son of Benaiah, princes of the
people.
2 And He said to me: "Son of
man, these *are* the men who devise
iniquity and give wicked [1]counsel
in this city,
3 "who say, '*The time is* not
[a]near to build houses; [b]this *city is*
the [1]caldron, and we *are* the meat.'
4 "Therefore prophesy against
them, prophesy, O son of man!"
5 Then [a]the Spirit of the LORD fell
upon me, and said to me, "Speak!
'Thus says the LORD: "Thus you
have said, O house of Israel; for
[b]I know the things that come into
your mind.
6 [a]"You have multiplied your
slain in this city, and you have
filled its streets with the slain."
7 'Therefore thus says the Lord
GOD: [a]"Your slain whom you have
laid in its midst, they *are* the meat,
and this *city is* the caldron; [b]but I
shall bring you out of the midst
of it.
8 "You have [a]feared the sword;
and I will bring a sword upon
you," says the Lord GOD.
9 "And I will bring you out of its
midst, and deliver you into the
hands of strangers, and [a]execute
judgments on you.
10 [a]"You shall fall by the sword.
I will judge you at [b]the border of

19 [b]Ezek. 11:1
20 [a]Ezek. 1:22 [b]Ezek. 1:1
21 [a]Ezek. 1:6, 8; 10:14; 41:18, 19
22 [a]Ezek. 1:10 [b]Ezek. 1:9, 12

CHAPTER 11

1 [a]Ezek. 3:12, 14 [b]Ezek. 10:19 [c]Ezek. 8:16
2 [1]Advice
3 [a]Ezek. 12:22, 27; 2 Pet. 3:4 [b]Jer. 1:13; Ezek. 11:7, 11; 24:3, 6 [1]Pot
5 [a]Ezek. 2:2; 3:24 [b][Jer. 16:17; 17:10]
6 [a]Is. 1:15; Ezek. 7:23; 22:2–6, 9, 12, 27
7 [a]Ezek. 24:3, 6; Mic. 3:2, 3 [b]2 Kin. 25:18–22; Jer. 52:24–27; Ezek. 11:9
8 [a]Jer. 42:16
9 [a]Ezek. 5:8
10 [a]2 Kin. 25:19–21; Jer. 39:6; 52:10 [b]1 Kin. 8:65; 2 Kin. 14:25 [c]Ps. 9:16; Ezek. 6:7; 13:9, 14, 21, 23
11 [a]Ezek. 11:3, 7 [1]Pot
12 [a]Lev. 18:3, 24; Deut. 12:30, 31; Ezek. 8:10, 14, 16
13 [a]Acts 5:5 [b]Ezek. 9:8
16 [a]Ps. 90:1; 91:9; Is. 8:14; Jer. 29:7, 11 [1]*holy place*
17 [a]Is. 11:11–16; Jer. 3:12, 18; 24:5; Ezek. 20:41, 42; 28:5
18 [a]Ezek. 37:23
19 [a]Jer. 32:39; Ezek. 36:26; Zeph. 3:9 [b]Ps. 51:10; [Jer. 31:33]; Ezek. 18:31 [c]Zech. 7:12; [Rom. 2:4, 5] [1]Lit. *you* (pl.)
20 [a]Ps. 105:45 [b]Jer. 24:7; Ezek. 14:11; 36:28; 37:27

Israel. [c]Then you shall know that
I *am* the LORD.
11 [a]"This *city* shall not be your
[1]caldron, nor shall you be the meat
in its midst. I will judge you at the
border of Israel.
12 "And you shall know that I *am*
the LORD; for you have not walked
in My statutes nor executed My
judgments, but [a]have done accord-
ing to the customs of the Gentiles
which *are* all around you." ' "
13 Now it happened, while I was
prophesying, that [a]Pelatiah the
son of Benaiah died. Then [b]I fell
on my face and cried with a loud
voice, and said, "Ah, Lord GOD!
Will You make a complete end of
the remnant of Israel?"

God Will Restore Israel

14 Again the word of the LORD
came to me, saying,
15 "Son of man, your brethren,
your relatives, your countrymen,
and all the house of Israel in its
entirety, *are* those about whom the
inhabitants of Jerusalem have
said, 'Get far away from the LORD;
this land has been given to us as
a possession.'
16 "Therefore say, 'Thus says the
Lord GOD: "Although I have cast
them far off among the Gentiles,
and although I have scattered
them among the countries, [a]yet I
shall be a little [1]sanctuary for them
in the countries where they have
gone." '
17 "Therefore say, 'Thus says the
Lord GOD: [a]"I will gather you from
the peoples, assemble you from
the countries where you have been
scattered, and I will give you the
land of Israel." '
18 "And they will go there, and
they will take away all its [a]detest-
able things and all its abomina-
tions from there.
19 "Then [a]I will give them one
heart, and I will put [b]a new spirit
within [1]them, and take [c]the stony
heart out of their flesh, and give
them a heart of flesh,
20 [a]"that they may walk in My
statutes and keep My judgments
and do them; [b]and they shall be
My people, and I will be their God.
21 "But *as for those* whose hearts
follow the desire for their detest-
able things and their abominations,

[a]I will recompense their deeds on
their own heads," says the Lord
God.
22 So the cherubim [a]lifted up their
wings, with the wheels beside
them, and the glory of the God of
Israel *was* high above them.
23 And [a]the glory of the Lord
went up from the midst of the city
and stood [b]on the mountain,
[c]which *is* on the east side of the
city.
24 Then [a]the Spirit took me up
and brought me in a vision by the
Spirit of God into [1]Chaldea, to
those in captivity. And the vision
that I had seen went up from me.
25 So I spoke to those in captivity
of all the things the Lord had
shown me.

Judah's Captivity Portrayed

12 Now the word of the Lord
came to me, saying:
2 "Son of man, you dwell in the
midst of [a]a rebellious house, which
[b]has eyes to see but does not see,
and ears to hear but does not hear;
[c]for they *are* a rebellious house.
3 "Therefore, son of man, prepare your belongings for captivity,
and go into captivity by day in
their sight. You shall go from your
place into captivity to another
place in their sight. It may be that
they will consider, though they *are*
a rebellious house.
4 "By day you shall bring out
your belongings in their sight, as
though going into captivity; and at
evening you shall go in their sight,
like those who go into captivity.
5 "Dig through the wall in their
sight, and carry your belongings
out through it.
6 "In their sight you shall bear
them on *your* shoulders *and* carry
them out at twilight; you shall
cover your face, so that you cannot
see the ground, [a]for I have made
you a sign to the house of Israel."
7 So I did as I was commanded.
I brought out my belongings by
day, as though going into captivity, and at evening I dug through
the wall with my hand. I brought
them out at twilight, *and* I bore
them on *my* shoulder in their sight.
8 And in the morning the word
of the Lord came to me, saying,
9 "Son of man, has not the house
of Israel, [a]the rebellious house,
said to you, [b]'What are you doing?'
10 "Say to them, 'Thus says the
Lord God: "This [a]burden[1] *concerns* the prince in Jerusalem and
all the house of Israel who are
among them." '
11 "Say, [a]'I *am* a sign to you. As
I have done, so shall it be done to
them; [b]they shall be carried away
into captivity.'
12 "And [a]the prince who *is* among
them shall bear *his belongings* on
his shoulder at twilight and go out.
They shall dig through the wall to
carry *them* out through it. He shall
cover his face, so that he cannot
see the ground with *his* eyes.
13 "I will also spread My [a]net over
him, and he shall be caught in My
snare. [b]I will bring him to Babylon,
to the land of the Chaldeans; yet
he shall not see it, though he shall
die there.
14 [a]"I will scatter to every wind
all who *are* around him to help
him, and all his troops; and [b]I will
draw out the sword after them.
15 [a]"Then they shall know that I
am the Lord, when I scatter them
among the nations and disperse
them throughout the countries.
16 [a]"But I will spare a few of their
men from the sword, from famine,
and from pestilence, that they may
declare all their abominations
among the Gentiles wherever they
go. Then they shall know that I *am*
the Lord."

Judgment Not Postponed

17 Moreover the word of the Lord
came to me, saying,
18 "Son of man, [a]eat your bread
with [1]quaking, and drink your water with trembling and anxiety.
19 "And say to the people of the
land, 'Thus says the Lord God to
the inhabitants of Jerusalem *and*
to the land of Israel: "They shall
eat their bread with anxiety, and
drink their water with dread, so
that her land may [a]be emptied of
all who are in it, [b]because of the
violence of all those who dwell
in it.
20 "Then the cities that are inhabited shall be laid waste, and the
land shall become desolate; and
you shall know that I *am* the
Lord." ' "

21 [a]Ezek. 9:10
22 [a]Ezek. 1:19
23 [a]Ezek. 8:4; 9:3 [b]Zech. 14:4 [c]Ezek. 43:2
24 [a]Ezek. 8:3; 2 Cor. 12:2–4 [1]Or *Babylon*, and so elsewhere in the book

CHAPTER 12

2 [a]Is. 1:23; Ezek. 2:3, 6–8 [b]Is. 6:9; 42:20; Jer. 5:21; Matt. 13:13, 14; Mark 4:12; 8:18; [Luke 8:10; John 9:39–41; 12:40]; Acts 28:26; Rom. 11:8 [c]Ezek. 2:5
6 [a]Is. 8:18; Ezek. 4:3; 24:24
9 [a]Ezek. 2:5 [b]Ezek. 17:12; 24:19
10 [a]Mal. 1:1 [1]*oracle, prophecy*
11 [a]Ezek. 12:6 [b]2 Kin. 25:4, 5, 7
12 [a]2 Kin. 25:4; Jer. 39:4; 52:7; Ezek. 12:6
13 [a]Job 19:6; Jer. 52:9; Lam. 1:13; Ezek. 17:20 [b]2 Kin. 25:7; Jer. 52:11; Ezek. 17:16
14 [a]2 Kin. 25:4; Ezek. 5:10 [b]Ezek. 5:2, 12
15 [a][Ps. 9:16]; Ezek. 6:7, 14; 12:16, 20
16 [a]2 Kin. 25:11, 22; Ezek. 6:8–10
18 [a]Lam. 5:9; Ezek. 4:16 [1]*shaking*
19 [a]Jer. 10:22; Ezek. 6:6, 7, 14; Mic. 7:13; Zech. 7:14 [b]Ps. 107:34

21 And the word of the LORD came
to me, saying,
22 "Son of man, what *is* this prov-
erb *that* you *people* have about the
land of Israel, which says, [a]'The
days are prolonged, and every vi-
sion fails'?
23 "Tell them therefore, 'Thus
says the Lord GOD: "I will lay this
proverb to rest, and they shall no
more use it as a proverb in Israel."
But say to them, [a]"The days are
at hand, and the [1]fulfillment of
every vision.
24 "For [a]no more shall there be
any [b]false[1] vision or flattering
divination within the house of Is-
rael.
25 "For I *am* the LORD. I speak,
and [a]the word which I speak will
come to pass; it will no more be
postponed; for in your days, O re-
bellious house, I will say the word
and [b]perform it," says the Lord
GOD.' "
26 Again the word of the LORD
came to me, saying,
27 [a]"Son of man, look, the house
of Israel is saying, 'The vision that
he sees *is* [b]for many days *from
now,* and he prophesies of times
far off.'
28 [a]"Therefore say to them, 'Thus
says the Lord GOD: "None of My
words will be postponed any more,
but the word which I speak [b]will
be done," says the Lord GOD.' "

Woe to Foolish Prophets

13 And the word of the LORD
came to me, saying,
2 "Son of man, prophesy
[a]against the prophets of Israel who
prophesy, and say to [b]those who
prophesy out of their own [c]heart,[1]
'Hear the word of the LORD!' "
3 Thus says the Lord GOD: "Woe
to the foolish prophets, who follow
their own spirit and have seen
[1]nothing!
4 "O Israel, your prophets are
[a]like foxes in the deserts.
5 "You [a]have not gone up into
the [1]gaps to build a wall for the
house of Israel to stand in battle
on the day of the LORD.
6 [a]"They have envisioned futility
and false divination, saying, 'Thus
says the LORD!' But the LORD has
[b]not sent them; yet they hope that
the word may [1]be confirmed.

22 [a]Jer. 5:12; Ezek. 11:3; 12:27; Amos 6:3; 2 Pet. 3:4
23 [a]Ps. 37:13; Joel 2:1; Zeph. 1:14 [1]Lit. *word*
24 [a]Jer. 14:13–16; Ezek. 13:6; Zech. 13:2–4 [b]Lam. 2:14 [1]Lit. *vain*
25 [a][Is. 55:11]; Dan. 9:12; [Luke 21:33] [b]Num. 23:19; [Is. 14:24]
27 [a]Ezek. 12:22 [b]Dan. 10:14
28 [a]Ezek. 12:23, 25 [b]Jer. 4:7
CHAPTER 13
2 [a]Is. 28:7; Jer. 23:1–40; Lam. 2:14; Ezek. 22:25–28 [b]Ezek. 13:17 [c]Jer. 14:14; 23:16, 26 [1]Inspiration
3 [1]No vision
4 [a]Song 2:15
5 [a]Ps. 106:23; [Jer. 23:22]; Ezek. 22:30 [1]*breaches*
6 [a]Jer. 29:8; Ezek. 22:28 [b]Jer. 27:8–15 [1]Come true
9 [a]Jer. 23:30 [b]Jer. 20:3–6 [c]Ezra 2:59, 62; Neh. 7:5; [Ps. 69:28] [d]Jer. 20:3–6 [e]Ezek. 11:10, 12
10 [a]Jer. 6:14; 8:11 [b]Ezek. 22:28 [1]Or *whitewash*
11 [a]Ezek. 38:22
14 [a]Ezek. 13:9, 21, 23; 14:8
16 [a]Jer. 6:14; 8:11; 28:9; Ezek. 13:10
17 [a]Ezek. 20:46; 21:2

7 "Have you not seen a futile vi-
sion, and have you not spoken
false divination? You say, 'The
LORD says,' but I have not spoken."
8 Therefore thus says the Lord
GOD: "Because you have spoken
nonsense and envisioned lies,
therefore I *am* indeed against
you," says the Lord GOD.
9 "My hand will be [a]against the
prophets who envision futility and
who [b]divine lies; they shall not be
in the assembly of My people, [c]nor
be written in the record of the
house of Israel, [d]nor shall they en-
ter into the land of Israel. [e]Then
you shall know that I *am* the Lord
GOD.
10 "Because, indeed, because they
have seduced My people, saying,
[a]'Peace!' when *there is* no peace—
and one builds a wall, and they
[b]plaster[1] it with untempered *mor-
tar*—
11 "say to those who plaster *it*
with untempered *mortar,* that it
will fall. [a]There will be flooding
rain, and you, O great hailstones,
shall fall; and a stormy wind shall
tear *it* down.
12 "Surely, when the wall has
fallen, will it not be said to you,
'Where *is* the mortar with which
you plastered *it?*' "
13 Therefore thus says the Lord
GOD: "I will cause a stormy wind
to break forth in My fury; and
there shall be a flooding rain in My
anger, and great hailstones in fury
to consume *it.*
14 "So I will break down the wall
you have plastered with untem-
pered *mortar,* and bring it down
to the ground, so that its founda-
tion will be uncovered; it will fall,
and you shall be consumed in the
midst of it. [a]Then you shall know
that I *am* the LORD.
15 "Thus will I accomplish My
wrath on the wall and on those
who have plastered it with untem-
pered *mortar;* and I will say to you,
'The wall *is* no *more,* nor those
who plastered it,
16 '*that is,* the prophets of Israel
who prophesy concerning Jerusa-
lem, and who [a]see visions of peace
for her when *there is* no peace,' "
says the Lord GOD.
17 "Likewise, son of man, [a]set
your face against the daughters of

your people, [b]who prophesy out of
their own [1]heart; prophesy against
them,
18 "and say, 'Thus says the Lord
GOD: "Woe to the *women* who sew
magic charms [1]on their sleeves
and make veils for the heads of
people of every height to hunt
souls! Will you [a]hunt the souls of
My people, and keep yourselves
alive?
19 "And will you profane Me
among My people [a]for handfuls of
barley and for pieces of bread, kill-
ing people who should not die, and
keeping people alive who should
not live, by your lying to My peo-
ple who listen to lies?"
20 'Therefore thus says the Lord
GOD: "Behold, I *am* against your
magic charms by which you hunt
souls there like [1]birds. I will tear
them from your arms, and let the
souls go, the souls you hunt like
birds.
21 "I will also tear off your veils
and deliver My people out of your
hand, and they shall no longer be
as prey in your hand. [a]Then you
shall know that I *am* the LORD.
22 "Because with [a]lies you have
made the heart of the righteous
sad, whom I have not made sad;
and you have [b]strengthened the
hands of the wicked, so that he
does not turn from his wicked way
to save his life.
23 "Therefore [a]you shall no
longer envision futility nor prac-
tice divination; for I will deliver
My people out of your hand, and
you shall know that I *am* the
LORD." ' "

Idolatry Will Be Punished

14 Now [a]some of the elders of
Israel came to me and sat
before me.
2 And the word of the LORD came
to me, saying,
3 "Son of man, these men have
set up their idols in their hearts,
and put before them [a]that which
causes them to stumble into in-
iquity. [b]Should I let Myself be in-
quired of at all by them?
4 "Therefore speak to them, and
say to them, 'Thus says the Lord
GOD: "Everyone of the house of Is-
rael who sets up his idols in his
heart, and puts before him what
causes him to stumble into in-
iquity, and then comes to the
prophet, I the LORD will answer
him who comes, according to the
multitude of his idols,
5 "that I may seize the house of
Israel by their heart, because they
are all estranged from Me by their
idols." '
6 "Therefore say to the house of
Israel, 'Thus says the Lord GOD:
"Repent, turn away from your
idols, and [a]turn your faces away
from all your abominations.
7 "For anyone of the house of Is-
rael, or of the strangers who dwell
in Israel, who separates himself
from Me and sets up his idols in
his heart and puts before him what
causes him to stumble into in-
iquity, then comes to a prophet to
inquire of him concerning Me, I
the LORD will answer him by My-
self.
8 [a]"I will set My face against that
man and make him a [b]sign and a
proverb, and I will cut him off
from the midst of My people.
[c]Then you shall know that I *am*
the LORD.
9 "And if the prophet is induced
to speak anything, I the LORD
[a]have induced that prophet, and I
will stretch out My hand against
him and destroy him from among
My people Israel.
10 "And they shall bear their in-
iquity; the punishment of the
prophet shall be the same as the
punishment of the one who in-
quired,
11 "that the house of Israel may
[a]no longer stray from Me, nor be
profaned anymore with all their
transgressions, [b]but that they may
be My people and I may be their
God," says the Lord GOD.' "

Judgment on Persistent Unfaithfulness

12 The word of the LORD came
again to me, saying:
13 "Son of man, when a land sins
against Me by persistent unfaith-
fulness, I will stretch out My hand
against it; I will cut off its [a]supply
of bread, send famine on it, and
cut off man and beast from it.
14 [a]"Even *if* these three men,
Noah, Daniel, and Job, were
in it, they would deliver *only*

17 [b]Ezek. 13:2; Rev. 2:20 [1]Inspiration
18 [a][2 Pet. 2:14] [1]Lit. *over all the joints of My hands;* Vg. *under every elbow;* LXX, Tg. *on all elbows of the hands*
19 [a]1 Sam. 2:15–17; Prov. 28:21; Mic. 3:5; Rom. 16:18; 1 Pet. 5:2
20 [1]Lit. *flying ones*
21 [a]Ezek. 13:9
22 [a]Jer. 28:15 [b]Jer. 23:14
23 [a]Ezek. 12:24; 13:6; Mic. 3:5, 6; Zech. 13:3

CHAPTER 14

1 [a]2 Kin. 6:32; Ezek. 8:1; 20:1; 33:31
3 [a]Ezek. 7:19; Zeph. 1:3 [b]2 Kin. 3:13; Is. 1:15; Jer. 11:11; Ezek. 20:3, 31
6 [a]1 Sam. 7:3; Neh. 1:9; Is. 2:20; 30:22; 55:6, 7; Ezek. 18:30
8 [a]Lev. 17:10; 20:3, 5, 6; Jer. 44:11; Ezek. 15:7 [b]Num. 26:10; Deut. 28:37; Ezek. 5:15 [c]Ezek. 6:7; 13:14
9 [a]1 Kin. 22:23; Job 12:16; Is. 66:4; Jer. 4:10; 2 Thess. 2:11
11 [a]Ps. 119:67, 71; Jer. 31:18, 19; [Heb. 12:11]; 2 Pet. 2:15 [b]Ezek. 11:20; 37:27
13 [a]Lev. 26:26; 2 Kin. 25:3; Is. 3:1; Jer. 52:6; Ezek. 4:16; 5:16
14 [a]Jer. 15:1

themselves [b]by their righteous-
ness," says the Lord GOD.
15 "If I cause [a]wild beasts to pass
through the land, and they [1]empty
it, and make it so desolate that no
man may pass through because of
the beasts,
16 "*even* [a]*though* these three men
were [1]in it, *as* I live," says the Lord
GOD, "they would deliver neither
sons nor daughters; only they
would be delivered, and the land
would be [b]desolate.
17 "Or *if* [a]I bring a sword on that
land, and say, 'Sword, go through
the land,' and I [b]cut off man and
beast from it,
18 "even [a]*though* these three men
were in it, *as* I live," says the Lord
GOD, "they would deliver neither
sons nor daughters, but only they
themselves would be delivered.
19 "Or *if* I send [a]a pestilence into
that land and [b]pour out My fury
on it in blood, and cut off from it
man and beast,
20 "even [a]*though* Noah, Daniel,
and Job *were* in it, *as* I live," says
the Lord GOD, "they would deliver
neither son nor daughter; they
would deliver *only* themselves by
their righteousness."
21 For thus says the Lord GOD:
"How much more it shall be when
[a]I send My four [1]severe judgments
on Jerusalem—the sword and fam-
ine and wild beasts and pesti-
lence—to cut off man and beast
from it?
22 [a]"Yet behold, there shall be
left in it a remnant who will be
[b]brought out, *both* sons and
daughters; surely they will come
out to you, and [c]you will see their
ways and their doings. Then you
will be comforted concerning the
disaster that I have brought upon
Jerusalem, all that I have brought
upon it.
23 "And they will comfort you,
when you see their ways and their
doings; and you shall know that I
have done nothing [a]without cause
that I have done in it," says the
Lord GOD.

The Outcast Vine

15 Then the word of the LORD
came to me, saying:
2 "Son of man, how is the wood
of the vine *better* than any other

14 [b][Prov. 11:4]
15 [a]Lev. 26:22; Num. 21:6; Ezek. 5:17; 14:21 [1]Lit. *bereave it* of children
16 [a]Ezek. 14:14, 18, 20 [b]Ezek. 15:8; 33:28, 29 [1]Lit. *in the midst of it*
17 [a]Lev. 26:25; Ezek. 5:12; 21:3, 4; 29:8; 38:21 [b]Ezek. 25:13; Zeph. 1:3
18 [a]Ezek. 14:14
19 [a]2 Sam. 24:15; Ezek. 38:22 [b]Ezek. 7:8
20 [a]Ezek. 14:14
21 [a]Ezek. 5:17; 33:27; Amos 4:6–10; Rev. 6:8 [1]Lit. *evil*
22 [a]2 Kin. 25:11, 12; Ezra 2:1; Ezek. 12:16; 36:20 [b]Ezek. 6:8 [c]Ezek. 20:43
23 [a]Jer. 22:8, 9

CHAPTER 15

4 [a][John 15:6]
7 [a]Lev. 26:17; [Ps. 34:16]; Jer. 21:10; Ezek. 14:8 [b]Is. 24:18 [c]Ezek. 7:4

CHAPTER 16

2 [a]Is. 58:1; Ezek. 20:4; 22:2
3 [a]Ezek. 21:30 [b]Gen. 15:16; Deut. 7:1; Josh. 24:15; Ezek. 16:45 [1]*origin and your birth*
4 [a]Hos. 2:3
5 [1]*abhorred*
7 [a]Ex. 1:7; Deut. 1:10 [1]Lit. *a myriad*

wood, the vine branch which is
among the trees of the forest?
3 "Is wood taken from it to make
any object? Or can *men* make a
peg from it to hang any vessel on?
4 "Instead, [a]it is thrown into the
fire for fuel; the fire devours both
ends of it, and its middle is burned.
Is it useful for *any* work?
5 "Indeed, when it was whole, no
object could be made from it. How
much less will it be useful for *any*
work when the fire has devoured
it, and it is burned?
6 "Therefore thus says the Lord
GOD: 'Like the wood of the vine
among the trees of the forest,
which I have given to the fire for
fuel, so I will give up the inhab-
itants of Jerusalem;
7 'and [a]I will set My face against
them. [b]They will go out from *one*
fire, but *another* fire shall devour
them. [c]Then you shall know that
I *am* the LORD, when I set My face
against them.
8 'Thus I will make the land des-
olate, because they have persisted
in unfaithfulness,' says the Lord
GOD."

God's Love for Jerusalem

16 Again the word of the LORD
came to me, saying,
2 "Son of man, [a]cause Jerusalem
to know her abominations,
3 "and say, 'Thus says the Lord
GOD to Jerusalem: "Your [1]birth
[a]and your nativity *are* from the
land of Canaan; [b]your father *was*
an Amorite and your mother a Hit-
tite.
4 "*As for* your nativity, [a]on the
day you were born your navel cord
was not cut, nor were you washed
in water to cleanse *you;* you were
not rubbed with salt nor wrapped
in swaddling cloths.
5 "No eye pitied you, to do any
of these things for you, to have
compassion on you; but you were
thrown out into the open field,
when you yourself were [1]loathed
on the day you were born.
6 "And when I passed by you
and saw you struggling in your
own blood, I said to you in your
blood, 'Live!' Yes, I said to you in
your blood, 'Live!'
7 [a]"I made you [1]thrive like a
plant in the field; and you grew,

matured, and became very beauti-
ful. *Your* breasts were formed,
your hair grew, but you *were*
naked and bare.
8 "When I passed by you again
and looked upon you, indeed your
time *was* the time of love; [a]so I
spread [1]My wing over you and
covered your nakedness. Yes, I
[b]swore an oath to you and entered
into a [c]covenant with you, and
[d]you became Mine," says the Lord
GOD.
9 "Then I washed you in water;
yes, I thoroughly washed off your
blood, and I anointed you with
oil.
10 "I clothed you in embroidered
cloth and gave you sandals of
[1]badger skin; I clothed you with
fine linen and covered you with
silk.
11 "I adorned you with orna-
ments, [a]put bracelets on your
wrists, [b]and a chain on your neck.
12 "And I put a [1]jewel in your
nose, earrings in your ears, and a
beautiful crown on your head.
13 "Thus you were adorned with
gold and silver, and your clothing
was of fine linen, silk, and embroi-
dered cloth. [a]You ate *pastry of* fine
flour, honey, and oil. You were ex-
ceedingly [b]beautiful, and suc-
ceeded to royalty.
14 [a]"Your fame went out among
the nations because of your
beauty, for it *was* perfect through
My splendor which I had bestowed
on you," says the Lord GOD.

Jerusalem's Harlotry

15 [a]"But you trusted in your own
beauty, [b]played the harlot because
of your fame, and poured out your
harlotry on everyone passing by
who *would have* it.
16 [a]"You took some of your gar-
ments and adorned multicolored
[1]high places for yourself, and
played the harlot on them. *Such*
things should not happen, nor
be.
17 "You have also taken your
beautiful jewelry from My gold
and My silver, which I had given
you, and made for yourself male
images and played the harlot with
them.
18 "You took your embroidered
garments and covered them, and
you set My oil and My incense be-
fore them.
19 "Also [a]My food which I gave
you—the pastry of fine flour, oil,
and honey *which* I fed you—you
set it before them as [1]sweet in-
cense; and *so* it was," says the
Lord GOD.
20 [a]"Moreover you took your sons
and your daughters, whom you
bore to Me, and these you sacri-
ficed to them to be devoured. *Were*
your *acts* of harlotry a small mat-
ter,
21 "that you have slain My chil-
dren and offered them up to them
by causing them to pass through
the [a]*fire*?
22 "And in all your abominations
and acts of harlotry you did not
remember the days of your [a]youth,
[b]when you were naked and bare,
struggling in your blood.
23 "Then it was so, after all your
wickedness—'Woe, woe to you!'
says the Lord GOD—
24 "*that* [a]you also built for
yourself a shrine, and [b]made a
[1]high place for yourself in every
street.
25 "You built your high places [a]at
the head of every road, and made
your beauty to be abhorred. You
offered yourself to everyone who
passed by, and multiplied your
acts of harlotry.
26 "You also committed harlotry
with [a]the Egyptians, your very
fleshly neighbors, and increased
your acts of harlotry to [b]provoke
Me to anger.
27 "Behold, therefore, I stretched
out My hand against you, dimin-
ished your [1]allotment, and gave
you up to the will of those who
hate you, [a]the daughters of the
Philistines, who were ashamed of
your lewd behavior.
28 "You also played the harlot
with the [a]Assyrians, because you
were insatiable; indeed you played
the harlot with them and still were
not satisfied.
29 "Moreover you multiplied your
acts of harlotry as far as the land
of the trader, [a]Chaldea; and even
then you were not satisfied.
30 "How degenerate is your
heart!" says the Lord GOD, "seeing
you do all these *things*, the deeds
of a brazen harlot.

8 [a]Ruth 3:9 [b]Gen. 22:16–18 [c]Ex. 24:6–8 [d][Ex. 19:5] [1]Or *the corner of My garment*
10 [1]Or *dolphin* or *dugong*
11 [a]Gen. 24:22, 47 [b]Prov. 1:9
12 [1]Lit. *ring*
13 [a]Deut. 32:13, 14 [b]Ps. 48:2
14 [a]Lam. 2:15
15 [a]Mic. 3:11 [b]Is. 1:21; 57:8
16 [a]Ezek. 7:20 [1]Places for pagan worship
19 [a]Hos. 2:8 [1]Or *a sweet aroma*
20 [a]Jer. 7:31
21 [a]Jer. 19:5
22 [a]Jer. 2:2 [b]Ezek. 16:4–6
24 [a]Jer. 11:13 [b]Jer. 2:20; 3:2 [1]Place for pagan worship
25 [a]Prov. 9:14
26 [a]Ezek. 16:26; 20:7, 8 [b]Deut. 31:20
27 [a]Ezek. 16:57 [1]Allowance of food
28 [a]Jer. 2:18, 36
29 [a]Ezek. 23:14–17

Jerusalem's Adultery

31 [a]"You erected your shrine at
the head of every road, and built
your [1]high place in every street.
Yet you were not like a harlot, be-
cause you scorned [b]payment.
32 "*You are* an adulterous wife,
who takes strangers instead of her
husband.
33 "Men make payment to all har-
lots, but [a]you made your payments
to all your lovers, and [1]hired them
to come to you from all around for
your harlotry.
34 "You are the opposite of *other*
women in your harlotry, because
no one solicited you to be a harlot.
In that you gave payment but no
payment was given you, therefore
you are the opposite."

Jerusalem's Lovers Will Abuse Her

35 'Now then, O harlot, hear the
word of the LORD!
36 'Thus says the Lord GOD: "Be-
cause your filthiness was poured
out and your nakedness uncovered
in your harlotry with your lovers,
and with all your abominable
idols, and because of [a]the blood of
your children which you gave to
them,
37 "surely, therefore, [a]I will
gather all your lovers with whom
you took pleasure, all those you
loved, *and* all those you hated; I
will gather them from all around
against you and will uncover your
nakedness to them, that they may
see all your nakedness.
38 "And I will judge you as
[a]women who break wedlock or
[b]shed blood are judged; I will bring
blood upon you in fury and jeal-
ousy.
39 "I will also give you into their
hand, and they shall throw down
your shrines and break down
[a]your [1]high places. [b]They shall
also strip you of your clothes, take
your beautiful jewelry, and leave
you naked and bare.
40 [a]"They shall also bring up an
assembly against you, [b]and they
shall stone you with stones and
thrust you through with their
swords.
41 "They shall [a]burn your houses
with fire, and [b]execute judgments
on you in the sight of many
women; and I will make you [c]cease
playing the harlot, and you shall
no longer hire lovers.
42 "So [a]I will lay to rest My fury
toward you, and My jealousy shall
depart from you. I will be quiet,
and be angry no more.
43 "Because [a]you did not remem-
ber the days of your youth, but [1]ag-
itated Me with all these *things*,
surely [b]I will also recompense
your [2]deeds on *your own* head,"
says the Lord GOD. "And you shall
not commit lewdness in addition
to all your abominations.

More Wicked than Samaria and Sodom

44 "Indeed everyone who quotes
proverbs will use *this* proverb
against you: 'Like mother, like
daughter!'
45 "You *are* your mother's daugh-
ter, [1]loathing husband and chil-
dren; and you *are* the [a]sister of
your sisters, who loathed their
husbands and children; [b]your
mother *was* a Hittite and your fa-
ther an Amorite.
46 "Your elder sister *is* Samaria,
who dwells with her daughters to
the north of you; and [a]your youn-
ger sister, who dwells to the south
of you, *is* Sodom and her daugh-
ters.
47 "You did not walk in their
ways nor act according to their
abominations; but, as *if that were*
too little, [a]you became more cor-
rupt than they in all your ways.
48 "*As* I live," says the Lord GOD,
"neither [a]your sister Sodom nor
her daughters have done as you
and your daughters have done.
49 "Look, this was the iniquity of
your sister Sodom: She and her
daughter had pride, [a]fullness of
food, and abundance of idleness;
neither did she strengthen the
hand of the poor and needy.
50 "And they were haughty and
[a]committed abomination before
Me; therefore [b]I took them away
as [1]I saw *fit*.
51 "Samaria did not commit [a]half
of your sins; but you have multi-
plied your abominations more
than they, and [b]have justified your
sisters by all the abominations
which you have done.
52 "You who judged your sisters,

31 [a]Ezek. 16:24, 39 [b]Is. 52:3 [1]Place for pagan worship
33 [a]Hos. 8:9, 10 [1]Or *bribed*
36 [a]Jer. 2:34
37 [a]Lam. 1:8
38 [a]Lev. 20:10 [b]Gen. 9:6
39 [a]Ezek. 16:24, 31 [b]Hos. 2:3 [1]Places for pagan worship
40 [a]Ezek. 23:45–47 [b]John 8:5, 7
41 [a]Deut. 13:16 [b]Ezek. 5:8; 23:10, 48 [c]Ezek. 23:27
42 [a]Ezek. 5:13; 21:17
43 [a]Ps. 78:42 [b]Ezek. 9:10; 11:21; 22:31 [1]So with LXX, Syr., Tg., Vg.; MT *were agitated with Me* [2]Lit. *way*
45 [a]Ezek. 23:2–4 [b]Ezek. 16:3 [1]Or *despising*
46 [a]Is. 1:10
47 [a]Ezek. 5:6, 7
48 [a]Matt. 10:15; 11:24
49 [a]Gen. 13:10
50 [a]Gen. 13:13; 18:20; 19:5 [b]Gen. 19:24 [1]Vg. *you saw;* LXX *he saw;* Tg. *as was revealed to Me*
51 [a]Ezek. 23:11 [b]Jer. 3:8–11

bear your own shame also, be-
cause the sins which you com-
mitted were more abominable
than theirs; they are more righ-
teous than you. Yes, be disgraced
also, and bear your own shame,
because you justified your sisters.
53 [a]"When I bring back their cap-
tives, the captives of Sodom and
her daughters, and the captives of
Samaria and her daughters, then
I will also bring back [b]the captives
of your captivity among them,
54 "that you may bear your own
shame and be disgraced by all that
you did when [a]you comforted
them.
55 "When your sisters, Sodom
and her daughters, return to their
former state, and Samaria and her
daughters return to their former
state, then you and your daughters
will return to your former state.
56 "For your sister Sodom was not
a byword in your mouth in the
days of your pride,
57 "before your wickedness was
uncovered. It was like the time of
the [a]reproach of the daughters of
[1]Syria and all *those* around her,
and of [b]the daughters of the Philis-
tines, who despise you every-
where.
58 [a]"You have paid for your lewd-
ness and your abominations," says
the LORD.
59 'For thus says the Lord GOD: "I
will deal with you as you have
done, who [a]despised [b]the oath by
breaking the covenant.

An Everlasting Covenant

60 "Nevertheless I will [a]remember
My covenant with you in the days
of your youth, and I will establish
[b]an everlasting covenant with
you.
61 "Then [a]you will remember
your ways and be ashamed, when
you receive your older and your
younger sisters; for I will give
them to you for [b]daughters, [c]but
not because of My covenant with
you.
62 [a]"And I will establish My cov-
enant with you. Then you shall
know that I *am* the LORD,
63 "that you may [a]remember and
be ashamed, [b]and never open your
mouth anymore because of your
shame, when I provide you an
atonement for all you have done,"
says the Lord GOD.' "

The Eagles and the Vine

17 And the word of the LORD
came to me, saying,
2 "Son of man, pose a riddle, and
speak a [a]parable to the house of
Israel,
3 "and say, 'Thus says the Lord
GOD:

[a]"A great eagle with large wings
and long pinions,
Full of feathers of various colors,
Came to Lebanon
And [b]took from the cedar the
highest branch.
4 He cropped off its topmost young
twig
And carried it to a land of trade;
He set it in a city of merchants.
5 Then he took some of the seed
of the land
And planted it in [a]a fertile field;
He placed *it* by abundant waters
And set it [b]like a willow tree.
6 And it grew and became a
spreading vine [a]of low stature;
Its branches turned toward him,
But its roots were under it.
So it became a vine,
Brought forth branches,
And put forth shoots.

7 "But there was [1]another great
eagle with large wings and
many feathers;
And behold, [a]this vine bent its
roots toward him,
And stretched its branches
toward him,
From the garden terrace where it
had been planted,
That he might water it.
8 It was planted in [1]good soil by
many waters,
To bring forth branches, bear
fruit,
And become a majestic vine." '

9 "Say, 'Thus says the Lord GOD:

"Will it thrive?
[a]Will he not pull up its roots,
Cut off its fruit,
And leave it to wither?
All of its spring leaves will
wither,
And no great power or many
people
Will be needed to pluck it up by
its roots.
10 Behold, *it is* planted,

53 [a]Is. 1:9; [Ezek. 16:60] [b]Jer. 20:16
54 [a]Ezek. 14:22
57 [a]2 Kin. 16:5; 2 Chr. 28:18; Is. 7:1; Ezek. 5:14, 15; 22:4 [b]Ezek. 16:27 [1]Heb. *Aram;* so with MT, LXX, Tg., Vg.; many Heb. mss., Syr. *Edom*
58 [a]Ezek. 23:49
59 [a]Ezek. 17:13 [b]Deut. 29:12
60 [a]Lev. 26:42–45; Ps. 106:45 [b]Is. 55:3; Jer. 32:40; 50:5; Ezek. 37:26
61 [a]Jer. 50:4, 5; Ezek. 20:43; 36:31 [b]Is. 54:1; 60:4; [Gal. 4:26] [c]Jer. 31:31
62 [a]Hos. 2:19, 20
63 [a]Ezek. 36:31, 32; Dan. 9:7, 8 [b]Ps. 39:9; [Rom. 3:19]

CHAPTER 17

2 [a]Ezek. 20:49; 24:3
3 [a]Jer. 48:40; Ezek. 17:12; Hos. 8:1 [b]2 Kin. 24:12
5 [a]Deut. 8:7–9 [b]Is. 44:4
6 [a]Ezek. 17:14
7 [a]Ezek. 17:15 [1]So with LXX, Syr., Vg.; MT, Tg. *one*
8 [1]Lit. *a good field*
9 [a]2 Kin. 25:7

Will it thrive?
[a]Will it not utterly wither when the
east wind touches it?
It will wither in the garden
terrace where it grew." ' "

11 Moreover the word of the LORD
came to me, saying,
12 "Say now to [a]the rebellious
house: 'Do you not know what
these *things mean?*' Tell *them,* 'In-
deed [b]the king of Babylon went to
Jerusalem and took its king and
princes, and led them with him to
Babylon.
13 [a]'And he took the king's off-
spring, made a covenant with him,
[b]and put him under oath. He also
took away the mighty of the land,
14 'that the kingdom might be
[a]brought low and not lift itself up,
but that by keeping his covenant
it might stand.
15 'But [a]he rebelled against him
by sending his ambassadors to
Egypt, [b]that they might give him
horses and many people. [c]Will he
prosper? Will he who does such
things escape? Can he break a cov-
enant and still be delivered?
16 *'As* I live,' says the Lord GOD,
'surely [a]in the place *where* the
king *dwells* who made him king,
whose oath he despised and whose
covenant he broke—with him in
the midst of Babylon he shall die.
17 [a]'Nor will Pharaoh with *his*
mighty army and great company
do anything in the war, [b]when they
heap up a siege mound and build
a [1]wall to cut off many persons.
18 'Since he despised the oath by
breaking the covenant, and in fact
[a]gave[1] his hand and still did all
these *things,* he shall not escape.' "
19 Therefore thus says the Lord
GOD: "*As* I live, surely My oath
which he despised, and My cov-
enant which he broke, I will rec-
ompense on his own head.
20 "I will [a]spread My net over
him, and he shall be taken in My
snare. I will bring him to Babylon
and [b]try him there for the [1]treason
which he committed against Me.
21 [a]"All his [1]fugitives with all his
troops shall fall by the sword, and
those who remain shall be [b]scat-
tered to every wind; and you shall
know that I, the LORD, have spo-
ken."

Israel Exalted at Last

22 Thus says the Lord GOD: "I will
take also *one* of the highest
[a]branches of the high cedar and
set *it* out. I will crop off from the
topmost of its young twigs [b]a ten-
der one, and will [c]plant *it* on a high
and prominent mountain.
23 [a]"On the mountain height of Is-
rael I will plant it; and it will bring
forth boughs, and bear fruit, and
be a majestic cedar. [b]Under it will
dwell birds of every sort; in the
shadow of its branches they will
dwell.
24 "And all the trees of the field
shall know that I, the LORD, [a]have
brought down the high tree and
exalted the low tree, dried up the
green tree and made the dry tree
flourish; [b]I, the LORD, have spoken
and have done *it.*"

A False Proverb Refuted

18 The word of the LORD came
to me again, saying,
2 "What do you mean when you
use this proverb concerning the
land of Israel, saying:

'The [a]fathers have eaten sour
grapes,
And the children's teeth are set
on edge'?

3 *"As* I live," says the Lord GOD,
"you shall no longer use this prov-
erb in Israel.

4 "Behold, all souls are [a]Mine;
The soul of the father
As well as the soul of the son is
Mine;
[b]The soul who sins shall die.
5 But if a man is just
And does what is lawful and
right;
6 [a]If he has not eaten [1]on the
mountains,
Nor lifted up his eyes to the idols
of the house of Israel,
Nor [b]defiled his neighbor's wife,
Nor approached [c]a woman
during her impurity;
7 If he has not [a]oppressed anyone,
But has restored to the debtor his
[b]pledge;
Has robbed no one by violence,
But has [c]given his bread to the
hungry
And covered the naked with
[d]clothing;

10 [a]Hos. 13:15
12 [a]Ezek. 2:3–5; 12:9 [b]2 Kin. 24:11–16
13 [a]2 Kin. 24:17 [b]2 Chr. 36:13
14 [a]Ezek. 29:14
15 [a]2 Kin. 24:20 [b]Deut. 17:16 [c]Ezek. 17:9
16 [a]Ezek. 12:13
17 [a]Jer. 37:7 [b]Jer. 52:4 [1]Or *siege wall*
18 [a]1 Chr. 29:24 [1]Took an oath
20 [a]Ezek. 12:13 [b]Ezek. 20:36 [1]Lit. *unfaithful act*
21 [a]Ezek. 12:14 [b]Ezek. 12:15; 22:15 [1]So with MT, Vg.; many Heb. mss., Syr. *choice men;* Tg. *mighty men;* LXX omits *All his fugitives*
22 [a][Zech. 3:8] [b]Is. 53:2 [c][Ps. 2:6]
23 [a][Is. 2:2, 3] [b]Dan. 4:12
24 [a]Amos 9:11 [b]Ezek. 22:14

CHAPTER 18

2 [a]Lam. 5:7
4 [a]Num. 16:22; 27:16 [b][Rom. 6:23]
6 [a]Ezek. 22:9 [b]Lev. 18:20; 20:10 [c]Lev. 18:19; 20:18 [1]At the mountain shrines
7 [a]Ex. 22:21 [b]Deut. 24:12 [c]Deut. 15:7, 11 [d]Is. 58:7

8 If he has not [1]exacted [a]usury
Nor taken any increase,
But has withdrawn his hand from
iniquity
And [b]executed true [2]judgment
between man and man;
9 *If* he has walked in My statutes
And kept My judgments
faithfully—
He *is* just;
He shall surely [a]live!"
Says the Lord GOD.

10 "If he begets a son *who is* a robber
Or [a]a shedder of blood,
Who does any of these *things*
11 And does none of those *duties*,
But has eaten [1]on the mountains
Or defiled his neighbor's wife;
12 If he has oppressed the poor and
needy,
Robbed by violence,
Not restored the pledge,
Lifted his eyes to the idols,
Or [a]committed abomination;
13 If he has exacted usury
Or taken increase—
Shall he then live?
He shall not live!
If he has done any of these
abominations,
He shall surely die;
[a]His blood shall be upon him.

14 "*If*, however, he begets a son
Who sees all the sins which his
father has done,
And considers but does not do
likewise;
15 [a]*Who* has not eaten [1]on the
mountains,
Nor lifted his eyes to the idols of
the house of Israel,
Nor defiled his neighbor's wife;
16 Has not oppressed anyone,
Nor withheld a pledge,
Nor robbed by violence,
But has given his bread to the
hungry
And covered the naked with
clothing;
17 *Who* has withdrawn his hand
from [1]the poor
And not received usury or
increase,
But has executed My judgments
And walked in My statutes—
He shall not die for the iniquity
of his father;
He shall surely live!

18 "*As for* his father,
Because he cruelly oppressed,
Robbed his brother by violence,

8 [a]Ex. 22:25; Lev. 25:36; Deut. 23:19; Neh. 5:7; Ps. 15:5 [b]Deut. 1:16; Zech. 8:16 [1]Lent money at interest [2]*justice*
9 [a]Ezek. 20:11; Amos 5:4; [Hab. 2:4; Rom. 1:17]
10 [a]Gen. 9:6; Ex. 21:12; Num. 35:31
11 [1]At the mountain shrines
12 [a]2 Kin. 21:11; Ezek. 8:6, 17
13 [a]Lev. 20:9, 11–13, 16, 27; Ezek. 3:18; Acts 18:6
15 [a]Ezek. 18:6 [1]At the mountain shrines
17 [1]So with MT, Tg., Vg.; LXX *iniquity* (cf. v. 8)
18 [a]Ezek. 3:18
19 [a]Ex. 20:5; Deut. 5:9; 2 Kin. 23:26; 24:3, 4
20 [a]2 Kin. 14:6; 22:18–20; Ezek. 18:4 [b]Deut. 24:16; 2 Kin. 14:6; 2 Chr. 25:4; Jer. 31:29, 30 [c]1 Kin. 8:32; Is. 3:10, 11; [Matt. 16:27] [d]Rom. 2:6–9
21 [a]Ezek. 18:27; 33:12, 19
22 [a]Is. 43:25; Jer. 50:20; Ezek. 18:24; 33:16; Mic. 7:19 [b][Ps. 18:20–24]
23 [a]Lam. 3:33; [Ezek. 18:32; 33:11; 1 Tim. 2:4; 2 Pet. 3:9]
24 [a]1 Sam. 15:11; 2 Chr. 24:2, 17–22; Ezek. 3:20; 18:26; 33:18 [b][2 Pet. 2:20]
25 [a]Ezek. 18:29; 33:17, 20; Mal. 2:17; 3:13–15
26 [a]Ezek. 18:24
27 [a]Ezek. 18:21
28 [a]Ezek. 18:14

And did what *is* not good among
his people,
Behold, [a]he shall die for his
iniquity.

Turn and Live

19 "Yet you say, 'Why [a]should the
son not bear the guilt of the fa-
ther?' Because the son has done
what is lawful and right, and has
kept all My statutes and observed
them, he shall surely live.
20 [a]"The soul who sins shall die.
[b]The son shall not bear the guilt
of the father, nor the father bear
the guilt of the son. [c]The righteous-
ness of the righteous shall be upon
himself, [d]and the wickedness of
the wicked shall be upon himself.
21 "But [a]if a wicked man turns
from all his sins which he has com-
mitted, keeps all My statutes, and
does what is lawful and right, he
shall surely live; he shall not die.
22 [a]"None of the transgressions
which he has committed shall be
remembered against him; because
of the righteousness which he has
done, he shall [b]live.
23 [a]"Do I have any pleasure at all
that the wicked should die?" says
the Lord GOD, "*and* not that he
should turn from his ways and
live?
24 "But [a]when a righteous man
turns away from his righteousness
and commits iniquity, and does ac-
cording to all the abominations
that the wicked *man* does, shall he
live? [b]All the righteousness which
he has done shall not be remem-
bered; because of the unfaithful-
ness of which he is guilty and the
sin which he has committed, be-
cause of them he shall die.
25 "Yet you say, [a]'The way of the
Lord is not fair.' Hear now, O
house of Israel, is it not My way
which is fair, and your ways which
are not fair?
26 [a]"When a righteous *man* turns
away from his righteousness, com-
mits iniquity, and dies in it, it is
because of the iniquity which he
has done that he dies.
27 "Again, [a]when a wicked *man*
turns away from the wickedness
which he committed, and does
what is lawful and right, he pre-
serves himself alive.
28 "Because he [a]considers and

turns away from all the transgres-
sions which he committed, he shall
surely live; he shall not die.
29 [a]"Yet the house of Israel says,
'The way of the Lord is not fair.'
O house of Israel, is it not My ways
which are fair, and your ways
which are not fair?
30 [a]"Therefore I will judge you, O
house of Israel, every one accord-
ing to his ways," says the Lord
GOD. [b]"Repent, and turn from all
your transgressions, so that in-
iquity will not be your ruin.
31 [a]"Cast away from you all the
transgressions which you have
committed, and get yourselves a
[b]new heart and a new spirit. For
why should you die, O house of Is-
rael?
32 "For [a]I have no pleasure in the
death of one who dies," says the
Lord GOD. "Therefore turn and
[b]live!"

Israel Degraded

19 "Moreover [a]take up a lam-
entation for the princes of
Israel,
2 "and say:

'What *is* your mother?
A lioness:
She lay down among the lions;
Among the young lions she
nourished her cubs.
3 She brought up one of her cubs,
And [a]he became a young lion;
He learned to catch prey,
And he devoured men.
4 The nations also heard of him;
He was trapped in their pit,
And they brought him with
chains to the land of [a]Egypt.

5 'When she saw that she waited,
that her hope was lost,
She took [a]another of her cubs *and*
made him a young lion.
6 [a]He roved among the lions,
And [b]became a young lion;
He learned to catch prey;
He devoured men.
7 [1]He knew their desolate places,
And laid waste their cities;
The land with its fullness was
desolated
By the noise of his roaring.
8 [a]Then the nations set against him
from the provinces on every
side,
And spread their net over him;
[b]He was trapped in their pit.

29 [a]Ezek. 18:25
30 [a]Ezek. 7:3; 33:20 [b]Matt. 3:2; Rev. 2:5
31 [a]Is. 1:16; 55:7; Eph. 4:22, 23 [b]Ps. 51:10; Jer. 32:39; Ezek. 11:19; 36:26
32 [a]Lam. 3:33; Ezek. 33:11; [2 Pet. 3:9] [b][Prov. 4:2, 5, 6]

CHAPTER 19

1 [a]Ezek. 26:17; 27:2
3 [a]Ezek. 19:2; 2 Kin. 23:31, 32
4 [a]2 Kin. 23:33, 34; 2 Chr. 36:4
5 [a]2 Kin. 23:34
6 [a]2 Kin. 24:8, 9 [b]Ezek. 19:3
7 [1]LXX *He stood in insolence;* Tg. *He destroyed its palaces;* Vg. *He learned to make widows*
8 [a]2 Kin. 24:2, 11 [b]Ezek. 19:4
9 [a]2 Chr. 36:6; Jer. 22:18 [b]Ezek. 6:2 [1]Or *hooks*
10 [a]Ezek. 17:6 [b]Deut. 8:7–9 [1]Lit. *blood,* so with MT, Syr., Vg.; LXX *like a flower on a pomegranate tree;* Tg. *in your likeness*
11 [a]Ezek. 31:3; Dan. 4:11 [1]Or *many branches*
12 [a]Jer. 31:27, 28 [b]Ezek. 17:10; Hos. 13:5
14 [a]Judg. 9:15; 2 Kin. 24:20; Ezek. 17:18 [b]Lam. 2:5

CHAPTER 20

1 [a]Ezek. 8:1, 11, 12; 14:1
3 [a]Ezek. 7:26; 14:3
4 [a]Ezek. 16:2; 22:2; Matt. 23:32
5 [a]Ex. 6:6–8; Deut. 7:6

9 [a]They put him in a cage with
[1]chains,
And brought him to the king of
Babylon;
They brought him in nets,
That his voice should no longer
be heard on [b]the mountains of
Israel.

10 'Your mother *was* [a]like a vine in
your [1]bloodline,
Planted by the waters,
[b]Fruitful and full of branches
Because of many waters.
11 She had strong branches for
scepters of rulers.
[a]She towered in stature above the
thick branches,
And was seen in her height amid
the [1]dense foliage.
12 But she was [a]plucked up in fury,
She was cast down to the ground,
And the [b]east wind dried her
fruit.
Her strong branches were broken
and withered;
The fire consumed them.
13 And now she *is* planted in the
wilderness,
In a dry and thirsty land.
14 [a]Fire has come out from a rod of
her branches
And devoured her fruit,
So that she has no strong
branch— a scepter for ruling.' "

[b]This *is* a lamentation, and has
become a lamentation.

The Rebellions of Israel

20 It came to pass in the sev-
enth year, in the fifth *month,*
on the tenth *day* of the month, *that*
[a]certain of the elders of Israel
came to inquire of the LORD, and
sat before me.
2 Then the word of the LORD
came to me, saying,
3 "Son of man, speak to the el-
ders of Israel, and say to them,
'Thus says the Lord GOD: "Have
you come to inquire of Me? *As* I
live," says the Lord GOD, [a]"I will
not be inquired of by you." '
4 "Will you judge them, son of
man, will you judge *them?* Then
[a]make known to them the abomi-
nations of their fathers.
5 "Say to them, 'Thus says the
Lord GOD: "On the day when [a]I
chose Israel and raised My hand
in an oath to the descendants of
the house of Jacob, and made My-

self [b]known to them in the land of
Egypt, I raised My hand in an oath
to them, saying, [c]'I *am* the LORD
your God.'
6 "On that day I raised My hand
in an oath to them, [a]to bring them
out of the land of Egypt into a land
that I had searched out for them,
[b]'flowing with milk and honey,'
[c]the glory of all lands.
7 "Then I said to them, 'Each of
you, [a]throw away [b]the abomina-
tions which are before his eyes,
and do not defile yourselves with
[c]the idols of Egypt. I *am* the LORD
your God.'
8 "But they rebelled against Me
and would not [1]obey Me. They did
not all cast away the abominations
which were before their eyes, nor
did they forsake the idols of Egypt.
Then I said, 'I will [a]pour out My
fury on them and fulfill My anger
against them in the midst of the
land of Egypt.'
9 [a]"But I acted for My name's
sake, that it should not be pro-
faned before the Gentiles among
whom they *were,* in whose sight I
had made Myself [b]known to them,
to bring them out of the land of
Egypt.
10 "Therefore I [a]made them go
out of the land of Egypt and
brought them into the wilderness.
11 [a]"And I gave them My statutes
and [1]showed them My judgments,
[b]'which, *if* a man does, he shall live
by them.'
12 "Moreover I also gave them My
[a]Sabbaths, to be a sign between
them and Me, that they might
know that I *am* the LORD who sanc-
tifies them.
13 "Yet the house of Israel [a]re-
belled against Me in the wilder-
ness; they did not walk in My
statutes; they [b]despised My judg-
ments, [c]'which, *if* a man does, he
shall live by them'; and they
greatly [d]defiled My Sabbaths.
Then I said I would pour out My
fury on them in the [e]wilderness,
to consume them.
14 [a]"But I acted for My name's
sake, that it should not be pro-
faned before the Gentiles, in
whose sight I had brought them
out.
15 "So [a]I also raised My hand in
an oath to them in the wilderness,
that I would not bring them into
the land which I had given *them,*
[b]'flowing with milk and honey,'
[c]the glory of all lands,
16 [a]"because they despised My
judgments and did not walk in My
statutes, but profaned My Sab-
baths; for [b]their heart went after
their idols.
17 [a]"Nevertheless My eye spared
them from destruction. I did not
make an end of them in the wilder-
ness.
18 "But I said to their children in
the wilderness, 'Do not walk in the
statutes of your fathers, nor ob-
serve their judgments, nor defile
yourselves with their idols.
19 'I *am* the LORD your God:
[a]Walk in My statutes, keep My
judgments, and do them;
20 [a]'hallow My Sabbaths, and
they will be a sign between Me and
you, that you may know that I *am*
the LORD your God.'
21 "Notwithstanding, [a]the chil-
dren rebelled against Me; they
did not walk in My statutes, and
were not careful to observe My
judgments, [b]'which, *if* a man
does, he shall live by them'; but
they profaned My Sabbaths.
Then I said I would pour out
My fury on them and fulfill My
anger against them in the wilder-
ness.
22 "Nevertheless I [1]withdrew My
hand and acted for My name's
sake, that it should not be pro-
faned in the sight of the Gentiles,
in whose sight I had brought them
out.
23 "Also I raised My hand in an
oath to those in the wilderness,
that [a]I would scatter them among
the Gentiles and disperse them
throughout the countries,
24 [a]"because they had not exe-
cuted My judgments, but had de-
spised My statutes, profaned My
Sabbaths, and [b]their eyes were
fixed on their fathers' idols.
25 "Therefore [a]I also gave them
up to statutes *that were* not good,
and judgments by which they
could not live;
26 "and I pronounced them un-
clean because of their ritual gifts,
in that they caused all [1]their first-
born to pass [a]through *the fire,* that
I might make them desolate and

5 [b]Deut. 4:34 [c]Ex. 20:2
6 [a]Jer. 32:22 [b]Ex. 3:8 [c]Jer. 11:5; 32:22
7 [a]Ezek. 18:31 [b]2 Chr. 15:8 [c]Lev. 18:3
8 [a]Ezek. 7:8 [1]Lit. *listen to*
9 [a]Num. 14:13 [b]Josh. 2:10; 9:9, 10
10 [a]Ex. 13:18
11 [a]Neh. 9:13 [b]Lev. 18:5 [1]Lit. *made known to*
12 [a]Deut. 5:12
13 [a]Num. 14:22 [b]Prov. 1:25 [c]Lev. 18:5 [d]Ex. 16:27 [e]Num. 14:29
14 [a]Ezek. 20:9, 20
15 [a]Num. 14:28 [b]Ex. 3:8 [c]Ezek. 20:6
16 [a]Ezek. 20:13, 24 [b]Amos 5:25
17 [a][Ps. 78:38]
19 [a]Deut. 5:32
20 [a]Jer. 17:22
21 [a]Num. 25:1 [b]Lev. 18:5
22 [1]Refrained from judgment
23 [a]Lev. 26:33
24 [a]Ezek. 20:13, 16 [b]Ezek. 6:9
25 [a]Rom. 1:24
26 [a]Jer. 32:35 [1]Lit. *that open the womb*

that they [b]might know that I am
the LORD." '
27 "Therefore, son of man, speak
to the house of Israel, and say to
them, 'Thus says the Lord GOD: "In
this too your fathers have [a]blas-
phemed Me, by being unfaithful
to Me.
28 "When I brought them into the
land *concerning* which I had
raised My hand in an oath to give
them, and [a]they saw all the high
hills and all the thick trees, there
they offered their sacrifices and
provoked Me with their offerings.
There they also sent up their
[b]sweet aroma and poured out their
drink offerings.
29 "Then I said to them, 'What *is*
this [1]high place to which you go?'
So its name is called [2]Bamah to
this day." '
30 "Therefore say to the house of
Israel, 'Thus says the Lord GOD:
"Are you defiling yourselves in the
manner of your [a]fathers, and com-
mitting harlotry according to their
[b]abominations?
31 "For when you offer [a]your gifts
and make your sons pass through
the fire, you defile yourselves with
all your idols, even to this day. So
shall I be inquired of by you, O
house of Israel? *As* I live," says the
Lord GOD, "I will [b]not be inquired
of by you.
32 [a]"What you have in your mind
shall never be, when you say, 'We
will be like the Gentiles, like the
families in other countries, serving
wood and stone.'

God Will Restore Israel

33 "*As* I live," says the Lord
GOD, "surely with a mighty hand,
[a]with an outstretched arm, and
with fury poured out, I will rule
over you.
34 "I will bring you out from the
peoples and gather you out of the
countries where you are scattered,
with a mighty hand, with an out-
stretched arm, and with fury
poured out.
35 "And I will bring you into the
wilderness of the peoples, and
there [a]I will plead My case with
you face to face.
36 [a]"Just as I pleaded My case
with your fathers in the wilderness
of the land of Egypt, so I will plead
My case with you," says the Lord
GOD.
37 "I will make you [a]pass under
the rod, and I will bring you into
the bond of the [b]covenant;
38 [a]"I will purge the rebels from
among you, and those who trans-
gress against Me; I will bring them
out of the country where they
dwell, but [b]they shall not enter the
land of Israel. Then you will know
that I *am* the LORD.
39 "As for you, O house of Israel,"
thus says the Lord GOD: [a]"Go,
serve every one of you his idols—
and hereafter—if you will not obey
Me; [b]but profane My holy name no
more with your gifts and your
idols.
40 "For [a]on My holy mountain, on
the mountain height of Israel,"
says the Lord GOD, "there [b]all the
house of Israel, all of them in the
land, shall serve Me; there [c]I will
accept them, and there I will re-
quire your offerings and the first-
fruits of your [1]sacrifices, together
with all your holy things.
41 "I will accept you as a [a]sweet
aroma when I bring you out from
the peoples and gather you out of
the countries where you have been
scattered; and I will be hallowed
in you before the Gentiles.
42 [a]"Then you shall know that I
am the LORD, [b]when I bring you
into the land of Israel, into the
country *for* which I raised My
hand in an oath to give to your fa-
thers.
43 "And [a]there you shall remem-
ber your ways and all your doings
with which you were defiled; and
[b]you shall [1]loathe yourselves in
your own sight because of all the
evils that you have committed.
44 [a]"Then you shall know that I
am the LORD, when I have dealt
with you [b]for My name's sake, not
according to your wicked ways
nor according to your corrupt do-
ings, O house of Israel," says the
Lord GOD.' "

Fire in the Forest

45 Furthermore the word of the
LORD came to me, saying,
46 [a]"Son of man, set your face to-
ward the south; [1]preach against
the south and prophesy against the
forest land, the [2]South,

26 [b]Ezek. 6:7; 20:12, 20
27 [a]Rom. 2:24
28 [a]Ezek. 6:13 [b]Ezek. 16:19
29 [1]Place for pagan worship [2]Lit. *High Place*
30 [a]Judg. 2:19 [b]Jer. 7:26; 16:12
31 [a]Ezek. 16:20; 20:26 [b]Ezek. 20:3
32 [a]Ezek. 11:5
33 [a]Jer. 21:5
35 [a]Jer. 2:9, 35; Ezek. 17:20
36 [a]Num. 14:21–23, 28
37 [a]Lev. 27:32 [b]Ps. 89:30–34
38 [a]Ezek. 34:17 [b]Jer. 44:14
39 [a]Amos 4:4 [b]Is. 1:13–15
40 [a]Is. 2:2, 3 [b]Ezek. 37:22 [c]Zech. 8:20–22 [1]*offerings*
41 [a]Phil. 4:18
42 [a]Ezek. 36:23; 38:23 [b]Ezek. 11:17; 34:13; 36:24
43 [a]Ezek. 16:61 [b]Lev. 26:39 [1]Or *despise*
44 [a]Ezek. 24:24 [b]Ezek. 36:22
46 [a]Ezek. 21:2 [1]*proclaim,* lit. *drop* [2]Heb. *Negev*

47 "and say to the forest of the
South, 'Hear the word of the LORD!
Thus says the Lord GOD: "Behold,
[a]I will kindle a fire in you, and it
shall devour [b]every green tree and
every dry tree in you; the blazing
flame shall not be quenched, and
all faces [c]from the south to the
north shall be scorched by it.
48 "All flesh shall see that I, the
LORD, have kindled it; it shall not
be quenched." ' "
49 Then I said, "Ah, Lord GOD!
They say of me, 'Does he not speak
[a]parables?' "

Babylon, the Sword of God

21 And the word of the LORD
came to me, saying,
2 [a]"Son of man, set your face to-
ward Jerusalem, [b]preach[1] against
the holy places, and prophesy
against the land of Israel;
3 "and say to the land of Israel,
'Thus says the LORD: "Behold, I *am*
[a]against you, and I will draw My
sword out of its sheath and cut off
both [b]righteous and wicked from
you.
4 "Because I will cut off both
righteous and wicked from you,
therefore My sword shall go out
of its sheath against all flesh [a]from
south *to* north,
5 "that all flesh may know that
I, the LORD, have drawn My sword
out of its sheath; it [a]shall not re-
turn anymore." '
6 [a]"Sigh therefore, son of man,
with [1]a breaking heart, and sigh
with bitterness before their eyes.
7 "And it shall be when they say
to you, 'Why are you sighing?' that
you shall answer, 'Because of the
news; when it comes, every heart
will melt, [a]all hands will be feeble,
every spirit will faint, and all
knees will be weak *as* water. Be-
hold, it is coming and shall be
brought to pass,' says the Lord
GOD."
8 Again the word of the LORD
came to me, saying,
9 "Son of man, prophesy and
say, 'Thus says the LORD!' Say:

[a]'A sword, a sword is sharpened
And also polished!
10 Sharpened to make a dreadful
slaughter,
Polished to flash like lightning!
Should we then make mirth?
It despises the scepter of My son,
As it does all wood.
11 And He has given it to be
polished,
That it may be handled;
This sword is sharpened, and it
is polished
To be given into the hand of [a]the
slayer.'

12 "Cry and wail, son of man;
For it will be against My people,
Against all the princes of Israel.
Terrors including the sword will
be against My people;
Therefore [a]strike *your* thigh.

13 "Because *it is* [a]a testing,
And what if *the sword* despises
even the scepter?
[b]*The scepter* shall be no *more*,"

says the Lord GOD.

14 "You therefore, son of man,
prophesy,
And [a]strike *your* hands together.
The third time let the sword do
double *damage*.
It *is* the sword *that* slays,
The sword that slays the great
men,
That enters their [b]private
chambers.
15 I have set the point of the sword
against all their gates,
That the heart may melt and
many may stumble.
Ah! [a]*It is* made bright;
It is grasped for slaughter:

16 "Swords[a1] at the ready!
Thrust right!
Set your blade!
Thrust left—
Wherever your [2]edge is ordered!

17 "I also will [a]beat My fists together,
And [b]I will cause My fury to rest;
I, the LORD, have spoken."

18 The word of the LORD came to
me again, saying:
19 "And son of man, appoint for
yourself two ways for the sword
of the king of Babylon to go; both
of them shall go from the same
land. Make a sign; put *it* at the
head of the road to the city.
20 "Appoint a road for the sword
to go to [a]Rabbah of the Ammon-
ites, and to Judah, into fortified Je-
rusalem.

47 [a]Is. 9:18, 19; Jer. 21:14 [b]Luke 23:31 [c]Ezek. 21:4
49 [a]Ezek. 12:9; 17:2; Matt. 13:13; John 16:25

CHAPTER 21

2 [a]Ezek. 20:46 [b]Amos 7:16 [1]*proclaim,* lit. *drop*
3 [a]Jer. 21:13; Ezek. 5:8; Nah. 2:13; 3:5 [b]Job 9:22
4 [a]Jer. 12:12; Ezek. 20:47
5 [a][Is. 45:23; 55:11]
6 [a]Is. 22:4; Jer. 4:19; Luke 19:41 [1]Emotional distress, lit. *the breaking of your loins*
7 [a]Ezek. 7:17
9 [a]Deut. 32:41; Ezek. 5:1; 21:15, 28
11 [a]Ezek. 21:19
12 [a]Jer. 31:19
13 [a]Job 9:23; 2 Cor. 8:2 [b]Ezek. 21:27
14 [a]Num. 24:10; Ezek. 6:11 [b]1 Kin. 20:30
15 [a]Ezek. 21:10, 28
16 [a]Ezek. 14:17 [1]Lit. *Sharpen yourself!* or *Unite yourself!* [2]Lit. *face*
17 [a]Ezek. 22:13 [b]Ezek. 5:13; 16:42; 24:13
20 [a]Deut. 3:11; Jer. 49:2; Ezek. 25:5; Amos 1:14

21 "For the king of Babylon
stands at the parting of the road,
at the fork of the two roads, to use
divination: he shakes the arrows,
he consults the [1]images, he looks
at the liver.
22 "In his right hand is the divina-
tion for Jerusalem: to set up batter-
ing rams, to call for a slaughter,
to [a]lift the voice with shouting, [b]to
set battering rams against the
gates, to heap up a *siege* mound,
and to build a wall.
23 "And it will be to them like a
false divination in the eyes of
those who [a]have sworn oaths with
them; but he will bring their in-
iquity to remembrance, that they
may be taken.
24 "Therefore thus says the Lord
GOD: 'Because you have made
your iniquity to be remembered, in
that your transgressions are un-
covered, so that in all your do-
ings your sins appear—because
you have come to remembrance,
you shall be taken in hand.
25 'Now to you, O [a]profane,
wicked prince of Israel, [b]whose
day has come, whose iniquity *shall*
end,
26 'thus says the Lord GOD:

"Remove the turban, and take off
the crown;
Nothing *shall remain* the same.
[a]Exalt the humble, and humble the
exalted.
27 [1]Overthrown, overthrown,
I will make it overthrown!
[a]It shall be no *longer*,
Until He comes whose right it is,
And I will give it *to* [b]*Him*." '

A Sword Against the Ammonites

28 "And you, son of man, proph-
esy and say, 'Thus says the Lord
GOD [a]concerning the Ammonites
and concerning their reproach,'
and say:

'A sword, a sword *is* drawn,
Polished for slaughter,
For consuming, for flashing—
29 While they [a]see false visions for
you,
While they divine a lie to you,
To bring you on the necks of the
wicked, the slain
[b]Whose day has come,
Whose iniquity *shall* end.
30 'Return[a] *it* to its sheath.
[b]I will judge you
In the place where you were
created,
[c]In the land of your [1]nativity.
31 I will [a]pour out My indignation
on you;
I will [b]blow against you with the
fire of My wrath,
And deliver you into the hands
of brutal men *who are* skillful
to [c]destroy.
32 You shall be fuel for the fire;
Your blood shall be in the midst
of the land.
[a]You shall not be remembered,
For I the LORD have spoken.' "

Sins of Jerusalem

22 Moreover the word of the
LORD came to me, saying,
2 "Now, son of man, [a]will you
judge, will you judge [b]the bloody
city? Yes, show her all her abomi-
nations!
3 "Then say, 'Thus says the Lord
GOD: "The city sheds [a]blood in her
own midst, that her time may
come; and she makes idols within
herself to defile herself.
4 "You have become guilty by
the blood which you have [a]shed,
and have defiled yourself with the
idols which you have made. You
have caused your days to draw
near, and have come to *the end of*
your years; [b]therefore I have made
you a reproach to the nations, and
a mockery to all countries.
5 "*Those* near and *those* far from
you will mock you as [1]infamous
and full of tumult.
6 "Look, [a]the princes of Israel:
each one has used his [1]power to
shed blood in you.
7 "In you they have [a]made light
of father and mother; in your
midst they have [b]oppressed the
stranger; in you they have mis-
treated the [1]fatherless and the
widow.
8 "You have despised My holy
things and [a]profaned My Sab-
baths.
9 "In you are [a]men who slander
to cause bloodshed; [b]in you are
those who eat on the mountains;
in your midst they commit lewd-
ness.
10 "In you men [a]uncover their fa-
thers' nakedness; in you they vio-

21 [1]Heb. *teraphim*

22 [a]Jer. 51:14 [b]Ezek. 4:2

23 [a]Ezek. 17:16, 18

25 [a]Jer. 52:2 [b]Ezek. 21:29

26 [a]Luke 1:52

27 [a][Luke 1:32, 33] [b][Jer. 23:5, 6] [1]Or *Distortion, Ruin*

28 [a]Ezek. 25:1–7

29 [a]Ezek. 12:24; 13:6–9; 22:28 [b]Job 18:20

30 [a]Jer. 47:6, 7 [b]Gen. 15:14 [c]Ezek. 16:3 [1]Or *origin*

31 [a]Ezek. 7:8 [b]Ezek. 22:20, 21 [c]Hab. 1:6–10

32 [a]Ezek. 25:10

CHAPTER 22

2 [a]Ezek. 20:4 [b]Nah. 3:1

3 [a]Ezek. 24:6, 7

4 [a]2 Kin. 21:16 [b]Deut. 28:37

5 [1]Lit. *defiled of name*

6 [a]Is. 1:23 [1]Lit. *arm*

7 [a]Lev. 20:9 [b]Ex. 22:22 [1]Lit. *orphan*

8 [a]Lev. 19:30

9 [a]Lev. 19:16 [b]Ezek. 18:6, 11

10 [a]Lev. 18:7, 8

late women who are [b]set apart during their impurity.

11 "One commits abomination [a]with his neighbor's wife; [b]another lewdly defiles his daughter-in-law; and another in you violates his sister, his father's [c]daughter.

12 "In you [a]they take bribes to shed blood; [b]you take usury and increase; you have made profit from your neighbors by extortion, and [c]have forgotten Me," says the Lord GOD.

13 "Behold, therefore, I [a]beat My fists at the dishonest profit which you have made, and at the bloodshed which has been in your midst.

14 [a]"Can your heart endure, or can your hands remain strong, in the days when I shall deal with you? [b]I, the LORD, have spoken, and will do *it*.

15 [a]"I will scatter you among the nations, disperse you throughout the countries, and [b]remove your filthiness completely from you.

16 "You shall defile yourself in the sight of the nations; then [a]you shall know that I *am* the LORD." ' "

Israel in the Furnace

17 The word of the LORD came to me, saying,

18 "Son of man, [a]the house of Israel has become dross to Me; they *are* all bronze, tin, iron, and lead, in the midst of a [b]furnace; they have become dross from silver.

19 "Therefore thus says the Lord GOD: 'Because you have all become dross, therefore behold, I will gather you into the midst of Jerusalem.

20 '*As men* gather silver, bronze, iron, lead, and tin into the midst of a furnace, to blow fire on it, to [a]melt *it;* so I will gather *you* in My anger and in My fury, and I will leave *you there* and melt you.

21 'Yes, I will gather you and blow on you with the fire of My wrath, and you shall be melted in its midst.

22 'As silver is melted in the midst of a furnace, so shall you be melted in its midst; then you shall know that I, the LORD, have [a]poured out My fury on you.' "

Israel's Wicked Leaders

23 And the word of the LORD came to me, saying,

24 "Son of man, say to her: 'You *are* a land that is [a]not [1]cleansed or rained on in the day of indignation.'

25 [a]"The conspiracy of her [1]prophets in her midst is like a roaring lion tearing the prey; they [b]have devoured [2]people; [c]they have taken treasure and precious things; they have made many widows in her midst.

26 [a]"Her priests have [1]violated My law and [b]profaned My holy things; they have not [c]distinguished between the holy and unholy, nor have they made known *the difference* between the unclean and the clean; and they have hidden their eyes from My Sabbaths, so that I am profaned among them.

27 "Her [a]princes in her midst *are* like wolves tearing the prey, to shed blood, to destroy [1]people, and to get dishonest gain.

28 [a]"Her prophets plastered them with untempered *mortar,* [b]seeing false visions, and divining [c]lies for them, saying, 'Thus says the Lord GOD,' when the LORD had not spoken.

29 "The people of the land have used oppressions, committed robbery, and mistreated the poor and needy; and they wrongfully [a]oppress the stranger.

30 [a]"So I sought for a man among them who would [b]make a wall, and [c]stand in the gap before Me on behalf of the land, that I should not destroy it; but I found no one.

31 "Therefore I have [a]poured out My indignation on them; I have consumed them with the fire of My wrath; and I have recompensed [b]their deeds on their own heads," says the Lord GOD.

Two Harlot Sisters

23 The word of the LORD came again to me, saying:

2 "Son of man, there were [a]two women,
The daughters of one mother.
3 [a]They committed harlotry in Egypt,
They committed harlotry in [b]their youth;

10 [b]Lev. 18:19; 20:18
11 [a]Ezek. 18:11 [b]Lev. 18:15 [c]Lev. 18:9
12 [a]Ex. 23:8 [b]Ex. 22:25 [c]Ezek. 23:35
13 [a]Ezek. 21:17
14 [a]Ezek. 21:7 [b]Ezek. 17:24
15 [a]Deut. 4:27 [b]Ezek. 23:27, 48
16 [a]Ps. 9:16
18 [a]Is. 1:22 [b]Prov. 17:3
20 [a]Is. 1:25
22 [a]Ezek. 20:8, 33
24 [a]Ezek. 24:13 [1]So with MT, Syr., Vg.; LXX *showered upon*
25 [a]Hos. 6:9 [b]Matt. 23:14 [c]Mic. 3:11 [1]So with MT, Vg.; LXX *princes;* Tg. *scribes* [2]Lit. *souls*
26 [a]Mal. 2:8 [b]1 Sam. 2:29 [c]Lev. 10:10 [1]Lit. *done violence to*
27 [a]Is. 1:23 [1]Lit. *souls*
28 [a]Ezek. 13:10 [b]Ezek. 13:6, 7 [c]Jer. 23:25–32
29 [a]Ex. 23:9
30 [a]Jer. 5:1 [b]Ezek. 13:5 [c]Ps. 106:23
31 [a]Ezek. 22:22 [b]Ezek. 9:10

CHAPTER 23
2 [a]Ezek. 16:44–46
3 [a]Lev. 17:7 [b]Ezek. 16:22

Their breasts were there embraced,
Their virgin bosom was there pressed.
4 Their names: [1]Oholah the elder
and [2]Oholibah [a]her sister;
[b]They were Mine,
And they bore sons and daughters.
As for their names,
Samaria *is* Oholah, and
Jerusalem *is* Oholibah.

The Older Sister, Samaria

5 "Oholah played the harlot even though she was Mine;
And she lusted for her lovers, the neighboring [a]Assyrians,
6 *Who were* clothed in purple,
Captains and rulers,
All of them desirable young men,
Horsemen riding on horses.
7 Thus she committed her harlotry with them,
All of them choice men of Assyria;
And with all for whom she lusted,
With all their idols, she defiled herself.
8 She has never given up her harlotry *brought* [a]from Egypt,
For in her youth they had lain with her,
Pressed her virgin bosom,
And poured out their immorality upon her.

9 "Therefore I have delivered her
Into the hand of her lovers,
Into the hand of the [a]Assyrians,
For whom she lusted.
10 They uncovered her nakedness,
Took away her sons and daughters,
And slew her with the sword;
She became a byword among women,
For they had executed judgment on her.

The Younger Sister, Jerusalem

11 "Now [a]although her sister
Oholibah saw *this*, [b]she became
more corrupt in her lust than she,
and in her harlotry more corrupt
than her sister's harlotry.

12 "She lusted for the neighboring [a]Assyrians,
[b]Captains and rulers,
Clothed most gorgeously,
Horsemen riding on horses,
All of them desirable young men.
13 Then I saw that she was defiled;
Both *took* the same way.
14 But she increased her harlotry;
She looked at men portrayed on the wall,
Images of [a]Chaldeans portrayed in vermilion,
15 Girded with belts around their waists,
Flowing turbans on their heads,
All of them looking like captains,
In the manner of the Babylonians of Chaldea,
The land of their nativity.
16 [a]As soon as her eyes saw them,
She lusted for them
And sent [b]messengers to them in Chaldea.

17 "Then the [1]Babylonians came to her, into the bed of love,
And they defiled her with their immorality;
So she was defiled by them, [a]and alienated herself from them.
18 She revealed her harlotry and uncovered her nakedness.
Then [a]I [b]alienated Myself from her,
As I had alienated Myself from her sister.

19 "Yet she multiplied her harlotry
In calling to remembrance the days of her youth,
[a]When she had played the harlot in the land of Egypt.
20 For she lusted for her [1]paramours,
Whose flesh *is like* the flesh of donkeys,
And whose issue *is like* the issue of horses.
21 Thus you called to remembrance the lewdness of your youth,
When the [a]Egyptians pressed your bosom
Because of your youthful breasts.

Judgment on Jerusalem

22 "Therefore, Oholibah, thus
says the Lord GOD:

[a]'Behold, I will stir up your lovers against you,
From whom you have alienated yourself,
And I will bring them against you from every side:
23 The Babylonians,
All the Chaldeans,
[a]Pekod, Shoa, Koa,
[b]All the Assyrians with them,
All of them desirable young men,
Governors and rulers,
Captains and men of renown,
All of them riding on horses.

4 [a]Jer. 3:6, 7 [b]Ezek. 16:8, 20 [1]Lit. *Her Own Tabernacle* [2]Lit. *My Tabernacle Is in Her*

5 [a]2 Kin. 15:19; 16:7; 17:3; Ezek. 16:28; Hos. 5:13; 8:9, 10

8 [a]Ex. 32:4; 1 Kin. 12:28; 2 Kin. 10:29; 17:16; Ezek. 23:3, 19

9 [a]2 Kin. 17:3

11 [a]Jer. 3:8 [b]Jer. 3:8–11; Ezek. 16:51, 52

12 [a]2 Kin. 16:7, 8; Ezek. 16:28 [b]Ezek. 23:6, 23

14 [a]Jer. 50:2; Ezek. 8:10; 16:29

16 [a]2 Kin. 24:1 [b]Is. 57:9

17 [a]Ezek. 23:22, 28 [1]Lit. *sons of Babel*

18 [a]Jer. 6:8 [b]Ps. 78:59; 106:40; Jer. 12:8

19 [a]Lev. 18:3; Ezek. 23:2

20 [1]Illicit lovers

21 [a]Ezek. 16:26

22 [a]Ezek. 16:37–41; 23:28

23 [a]Jer. 50:21 [b]Ezek. 23:12

24 And they shall come against you
With chariots, wagons, and
war-horses,
With a horde of people.
They shall array against you
Buckler, shield, and helmet all
around.

'I will delegate judgment to them,
And they shall judge you
according to their judgments.
25 I will set My [a]jealousy against
you,
And they shall deal furiously with
you;
They shall remove your nose and
your ears,
And your remnant shall fall by
the sword;
They shall take your sons and
your daughters,
And your remnant shall be
devoured by fire.
26 [a]They shall also strip you of your
clothes
And take away your beautiful
jewelry.

27 'Thus [a]I will make you cease your
lewdness and your [b]harlotry
Brought from the land of Egypt,
So that you will not lift your eyes
to them,
Nor remember Egypt anymore.'

28 "For thus says the Lord GOD:
'Surely I will deliver you into the
hand of [a]those you hate, into the
hand *of those* [b]from whom you
alienated yourself.
29 [a]'They will deal hatefully with
you, take away all you have
worked for, and [b]leave you naked
and bare. The nakedness of your
harlotry shall be uncovered, both
your lewdness and your harlotry.
30 'I will do these *things* to you
because you have [a]gone as a harlot
after the Gentiles, because you
have become defiled by their idols.
31 'You have walked in the way
of your sister; therefore I will put
her [a]cup in your hand.'
32 "Thus says the Lord GOD:

'You shall drink of your sister's
cup,
The deep and wide one;
[a]You shall be laughed to scorn
And held in derision;
It contains much.
33 You will be filled with
drunkenness and sorrow,
The cup of horror and desolation,
The cup of your sister Samaria.
34 You shall [a]drink and drain it,
You shall break its [1]shards,
And tear at your own breasts;
For I have spoken,'
Says the Lord GOD.

35 "Therefore thus says the Lord
GOD:

'Because you [a]have forgotten Me
and [b]cast Me behind your back,
Therefore you shall bear the
penalty
Of your lewdness and your
harlotry.' "

Both Sisters Judged

36 The LORD also said to me: "Son
of man, will you [a]judge Oholah
and Oholibah? Then [b]declare to
them their abominations.
37 "For they have committed
adultery, and [a]blood *is* on their
hands. They have committed adul-
tery with their idols, and even sac-
rificed their sons [b]whom they bore
to Me, passing them through *the*
fire, to devour *them*.
38 "Moreover they have done this
to Me: They have [a]defiled My
sanctuary on the same day and
[b]profaned My Sabbaths.
39 "For after they had slain their
children for their idols, on the
same day they came into My sanc-
tuary to profane it; and indeed
[a]thus they have done in the midst
of My house.
40 "Furthermore you sent for men
to come from afar, [a]to whom a
messenger *was* sent; and there
they came. And you [b]washed your-
self for them, [c]painted your eyes,
and adorned yourself with orna-
ments.
41 "You sat on a stately [a]couch,
with a table prepared before it, [b]on
which you had set My incense and
My oil.
42 "The sound of a carefree multi-
tude *was* with her, and [1]Sabeans
were brought from the wilderness
with men of the common sort, who
put bracelets on their [2]wrists and
beautiful crowns on their heads.
43 "Then I said concerning *her*
who had grown old in adulteries,
'Will they commit harlotry with
her now, and she *with them?*'
44 "Yet they went in to her, as
men go in to a woman who plays

25 [a]Ex. 34:14; Ezek. 5:13; 8:17, 18; Zeph. 1:18
26 [a]Is. 3:18–23; Ezek. 16:39
27 [a]Ezek. 16:41; 22:15 [b]Ezek. 23:3, 19
28 [a]Jer. 21:7–10; Ezek. 16:37–41 [b]Ezek. 23:17
29 [a]Deut. 28:48; Ezek. 23:25, 26, 45–47 [b]Ezek. 16:39
30 [a]Ezek. 6:9
31 [a]2 Kin. 21:13; Jer. 7:14, 15; 25:15; Ezek. 23:33
32 [a]Ezek. 22:4, 5
34 [a]Ps. 75:8; Is. 51:17 [1]Earthenware fragments
35 [a]Is. 17:10; Jer. 3:21; Ezek. 22:12; Hos. 8:14; 13:6 [b]1 Kin. 14:9; Jer. 2:27; 32:33; Neh. 9:26
36 [a]Jer. 1:10; Ezek. 20:4; 22:2 [b]Is. 58:1; Ezek. 16:2; Mic. 3:8
37 [a]Ezek. 16:38 [b]Ezek. 16:20, 21, 36, 45; 20:26, 31
38 [a]2 Kin. 21:4, 7; Ezek. 5:11; 7:20 [b]Ezek. 22:8
39 [a]2 Kin. 21:2–8
40 [a]Is. 57:9 [b]Ruth 3:3 [c]2 Kin. 9:30; Jer. 4:30
41 [a]Esth. 1:6; Is. 57:7; Amos 2:8; 6:4 [b]Prov. 7:17; Ezek. 16:18, 19; Hos. 2:8
42 [1]Or *drunkards* [2]Lit. *hands*

the harlot; thus they went in to
Oholah and Oholibah, the lewd
women.
45 "But righteous men will [a]judge
them after the manner of adulter-
esses, and after the manner of
women who shed blood, because
they *are* adulteresses, and [b]blood
is on their hands.
46 "For thus says the Lord GOD:
[a]'Bring up an assembly against
them, give them up to trouble and
plunder.
47 [a]'The assembly shall stone
them with stones and [1]execute
them with their swords; [b]they shall
slay their sons and their daugh-
ters, and burn their houses with
fire.
48 'Thus [a]I will cause lewdness to
cease from the land, [b]that all
women may be taught not to prac-
tice your lewdness.
49 'They shall repay you for your
lewdness, and you shall [a]pay for
your idolatrous sins. [b]Then you
shall know that I *am* the Lord
GOD.' "

Symbol of the Cooking Pot

24 Again, in the ninth year, in
the tenth month, on the
tenth *day* of the month, the word
of the LORD came to me, saying,
2 "Son of man, write down the
name of the day, this very day—
the king of Babylon started his
siege against Jerusalem [a]this very
day.
3 [a]"And utter a parable to the re-
bellious house, and say to them,
'Thus says the Lord GOD:

[b]"Put on a pot, set *it* on,
And also pour water into it.
4 Gather pieces *of meat* in it,
Every good piece,
The thigh and the shoulder.
Fill *it* with choice [1]cuts;
5 Take the choice of the flock.
Also pile *fuel* bones under it,
Make it boil well,
And let the cuts simmer in it."

6 'Therefore thus says the Lord
GOD:

"Woe to [a]the bloody city,
To the pot whose scum *is* in it,
And whose scum is not gone
from it!
Bring it out piece by piece,
On which no [b]lot has fallen.
7 For her blood is in her midst;
She set it on top of a rock;
[a]She did not pour it on the ground,
To cover it with dust.
8 That it may raise up fury and take
vengeance,
[a]I have set her blood on top of a
rock,
That it may not be covered."

9 'Therefore thus says the Lord
GOD:

[a]"Woe to the bloody city!
I too will make the pyre great.
10 Heap on the wood,
Kindle the fire;
Cook the meat well,
Mix in the spices,
And let the [1]cuts be burned up.

11 "Then set the pot empty on the
coals,
That it may become hot and its
bronze may burn,
That [a]its filthiness may be melted
in it,
That its scum may be consumed.
12 She has [1]grown weary with [2]lies,
And her great scum has not gone
from her.
Let her scum *be* in the fire!
13 In your [a]filthiness *is* lewdness.
Because I have cleansed you, and
you were not cleansed,
You will [b]not be cleansed of your
filthiness anymore,
[c]Till I have caused My fury to rest
upon you.
14 [a]I, the LORD, have spoken *it;*
[b]It shall come to pass, and I will
do *it;*
I will not hold back,
[c]Nor will I spare,
Nor will I relent;
According to your ways
And according to your deeds
[1]They will judge you,"
Says the Lord GOD.' "

The Prophet's Wife Dies

15 Also the word of the LORD came
to me, saying,
16 "Son of man, behold, I take
away from you the desire of your
eyes with one stroke; yet you shall
[a]neither mourn nor weep, nor shall
your tears run down.
17 "Sigh in silence, [a]make no
mourning for the dead; [b]bind your
turban on your head, and [c]put your
sandals on your feet; [d]do not cover

45 [a]Ezek. 16:38 [b]Ezek. 23:37
46 [a]Ezek. 16:40
47 [a]Lev. 20:10; Ezek. 16:40 [b]2 Chr. 36:17, 19; Ezek. 24:21 [1]Lit. *cut down*
48 [a]Ezek. 22:15 [b]Deut. 13:11; Ezek. 22:15; 2 Pet. 2:6
49 [a]Is. 59:18; Ezek. 23:35 [b]Ezek. 20:38, 42, 44; 25:5

CHAPTER 24

2 [a]2 Kin. 25:1; Jer. 39:1; 52:4
3 [a]Ezek. 17:12 [b]Jer. 1:13; Ezek. 11:3
4 [1]Lit. *bones*
6 [a]2 Kin. 24:3, 4; Ezek. 22:2, 3, 27; Mic. 7:2; Nah. 3:1 [b]2 Sam. 8:2; Joel 3:3; Obad. 11; Nah. 3:10
7 [a]Lev. 17:13; Deut. 12:16
8 [a][Matt. 7:2]
9 [a]Ezek. 24:6; Nah. 3:1; Hab. 2:12
10 [1]Lit. *bones*
11 [a]Ezek. 22:15
12 [1]Or *wearied Me* [2]Or *toil*
13 [a]Ezek. 23:36–48 [b]Jer. 6:28–30; Ezek. 22:24 [c]Ezek. 5:13; 8:18; 16:42
14 [a][1 Sam. 15:29] [b]Num. 23:19; Ps. 33:9; Is. 55:11 [c]Ezek. 5:11 [1]LXX, Syr., Tg., Vg. *I*
16 [a]Jer. 16:5
17 [a]Jer. 16:5 [b]Lev. 10:6; 21:10 [c]2 Sam. 15:30 [d]Mic. 3:7

your [1]lips, and do not eat man's
bread *of sorrow*."
18 So I spoke to the people in the
morning, and at evening my wife
died; and the next morning I did
as I was commanded.
19 And the people said to me,
[a]"Will you not tell us what these
things signify to us, that you be-
have so?"
20 Then I answered them, "The
word of the LORD came to me, say-
ing,
21 'Speak to the house of Israel,
"Thus says the Lord GOD: 'Behold,
[a]I will profane My sanctuary,
[1]your arrogant boast, the desire of
your eyes, the [2]delight of your
soul; [b]and your sons and daugh-
ters whom you left behind shall
fall by the sword.
22 'And you shall do as I have
done; [a]you shall not cover *your*
[1]lips nor eat man's bread *of sor-
row*.
23 'Your turbans shall be on your
heads and your sandals on your
feet; [a]you shall neither mourn nor
weep, but [b]you shall pine away in
your iniquities and mourn with
one another.
24 'Thus [a]Ezekiel is a sign to you;
according to all that he has done
you shall do; [b]and when this
comes, [c]you shall know that I *am*
the Lord GOD.' "
25 'And you, son of man—*will it*
not *be* in the day when I take from
them [a]their stronghold, their joy
and their glory, the desire of their
eyes, and [1]that on which they set
their minds, their sons and their
daughters:
26 'on that day [a]one who escapes
will come to you to let *you* hear *it*
with *your* ears;
27 [a]'on that day your mouth will
be opened to him who has es-
caped; you shall speak and no
longer be mute. Thus you will be
a sign to them, and they shall
know that I *am* the LORD.' "

Proclamation Against Ammon

25 The word of the LORD came
to me, saying,
2 "Son of man, [a]set your face
[b]against the Ammonites, and
prophesy against them.
3 "Say to the Ammonites, 'Hear
the word of the Lord GOD! Thus
says the Lord GOD: [a]"Because you
said, 'Aha!' against My sanctuary
when it was profaned, and against
the land of Israel when it was
desolate, and against the house
of Judah when they went into cap-
tivity,
4 "indeed, therefore, I will de-
liver you as a possession to the
[1]men of the East, and they shall
set their encampments among you
and make their dwellings among
you; they shall eat your fruit, and
they shall drink your milk.
5 "And I will make [a]Rabbah [b]a
stable for camels and Ammon a
resting place for flocks. [c]Then you
shall know that I *am* the LORD."
6 'For thus says the Lord GOD:
"Because you [a]clapped *your*
hands, stamped your feet, and [b]re-
joiced in heart with all your dis-
dain for the land of Israel,
7 "indeed, therefore, I will
[a]stretch out My hand against you,
and give you as plunder to the na-
tions; I will cut you off from the
peoples, and I will cause you to
perish from the countries; I will
destroy you, and you shall know
that I *am* the LORD."

Proclamation Against Moab

8 'Thus says the Lord GOD: "Be-
cause [a]Moab and [b]Seir say, 'Look!
The house of Judah *is* like all the
nations,'
9 "therefore, behold, I will clear
the territory of Moab of cities, of
the cities on its frontier, the glory
of the country, Beth Jeshimoth,
Baal Meon, and [a]Kirjathaim.
10 [a]"To the men of the East I will
give it as a possession, together
with the Ammonites, that the Am-
monites [b]may not be remembered
among the nations.
11 "And I will execute judgments
upon Moab, and they shall know
that I *am* the LORD."

Proclamation Against Edom

12 'Thus says the Lord GOD: [a]"Be-
cause of what Edom did against
the house of Judah by taking ven-
geance, and has greatly offended
by avenging itself on them,"
13 'therefore thus says the Lord
GOD: "I will also stretch out My
hand against Edom, cut off man
and beast from it, and make it

17 [1]Lit. *moustache*
19 [a]Ezek. 12:9; 37:18
21 [a]Jer. 7:14; Lam. 2:7; Ezek. 7:20, 24 [b]Jer. 6:11; 16:3, 4; Ezek. 23:25, 47 [1]Lit. *the pride of your strength* [2]Lit. *compassion*
22 [a]Jer. 16:6, 7 [1]Lit. *moustache*
23 [a]Job 27:15; Ps. 78:64 [b]Lev. 26:39; Ezek. 33:10
24 [a]Is. 20:3; Ezek. 4:3; 12:6, 11; Luke 11:29, 30 [b]Jer. 17:15; John 13:19; 14:29 [c]Ezek. 6:7; 25:5
25 [a]Ps. 48:2; 50:2; Ezek. 24:21 [1]Lit. *the lifting up of their soul*
26 [a]Ezek. 33:21
27 [a]Ezek. 3:26; 33:22

CHAPTER 25

2 [a]Ezek. 35:2 [b]Jer. 49:1; Ezek. 21:28; Amos 1:13–15; Zeph. 2:9
3 [a]Ps. 70:2, 3; [Prov. 17:5]; Ezek. 26:2
4 [1]Lit. *sons*
5 [a]Deut. 3:11; 2 Sam. 12:26; Jer. 49:2; Ezek. 21:20 [b]Is. 17:2 [c]Ezek. 24:24
6 [a]Job 27:23; Lam. 2:15; Nah. 3:19; Zeph. 2:15 [b]Ezek. 36:5
7 [a]Ezek. 35:3
8 [a]Is. 15:6; Jer. 48:1; Amos 2:1, 2 [b]Ezek. 35:2, 5
9 [a]Num. 32:3, 38; Josh. 13:17; 1 Chr. 5:8; Jer. 48:23
10 [a]Ezek. 25:4 [b]Ezek. 21:32
12 [a]2 Chr. 28:17; Ps. 137:7; Jer. 49:7, 8; Amos 1:11; Obad. 10–14

desolate from Teman; [1]Dedan shall
fall by the sword.
14 [a]"I will lay My vengeance on
Edom by the hand of My people
Israel, that they may do in Edom
according to My anger and accord-
ing to My fury; and they shall
know My vengeance," says the
Lord GOD.

Proclamation Against Philistia

15 'Thus says the Lord GOD: [a]"Be-
cause [b]the Philistines dealt venge-
fully and took vengeance with [1]a
spiteful heart, to destroy because
of the [2]old hatred,"
16 'therefore thus says the Lord
GOD: [a]"I will stretch out My hand
against the Philistines, and I will
cut off the [b]Cherethites [c]and de-
stroy the remnant of the seacoast.
17 "I will [a]execute great ven-
geance on them with furious re-
bukes; [b]and they shall know that
I *am* the LORD, when I lay My ven-
geance upon them." ' "

Proclamation Against Tyre

26 And it came to pass in the
eleventh year, on the first
day of the month, *that* the word
of the LORD came to me, saying,
2 "Son of man, [a]because Tyre
has said against Jerusalem, [b]'Aha!
She is broken *who was* the gate-
way of the peoples; now she is
turned over to me; I shall be filled;
she is laid waste.'
3 "Therefore thus says the Lord
GOD: 'Behold, I *am* against you, O
Tyre, and will cause many nations
to come up against you, as the sea
causes its waves to come up.
4 'And they shall destroy the
walls of Tyre and break down her
towers; I will also scrape her dust
from her, and [a]make her like the
top of a rock.
5 'It shall be *a place for* spread-
ing nets [a]in the midst of the sea,
for I have spoken,' says the Lord
GOD; 'it shall become plunder for
the nations.
6 'Also her daughter *villages*
which *are* in the fields shall be
slain by the sword. [a]Then they
shall know that I am the LORD.'
7 "For thus says the Lord GOD:
'Behold, I will bring against Tyre
from the north [a]Nebuchadnezzar[1]
king of Babylon, [b]king of kings,
with horses, with chariots, and
with horsemen, and an army with
many people.
8 'He will slay with the sword
your daughter *villages* in the
fields; he will [a]heap up a siege
mound against you, build a wall
against you, and raise a [1]defense
against you.
9 'He will direct his battering
rams against your walls, and with
his axes he will break down your
towers.
10 'Because of the abundance of
his horses, their dust will cover
you; your walls will shake at the
noise of the horsemen, the wag-
ons, and the chariots, when he en-
ters your gates, as men enter a city
that has been breached.
11 'With the hooves of his [a]horses
he will trample all your streets; he
will slay your people by the sword,
and your strong pillars will fall to
the ground.
12 'They will plunder your riches
and pillage your merchandise;
they will break down your walls
and destroy your pleasant houses;
they will lay your stones, your tim-
ber, and your soil in the [a]midst of
the water.
13 [a]'I will put an end to the sound
of [b]your songs, and the sound of
your harps shall be heard no more.
14 [a]'I will make you like the top
of a rock; you shall be *a place for*
spreading nets, and you shall
never be rebuilt, for I the LORD
have spoken,' says the Lord GOD.
15 "Thus says the Lord GOD to
Tyre: 'Will the coastlands not
[a]shake at the sound of your fall,
when the wounded cry, when
slaughter is made in the midst of
you?
16 'Then all the [a]princes of the sea
will [b]come down from their
thrones, lay aside their robes, and
take off their embroidered gar-
ments; they will clothe themselves
with trembling; [c]they will sit on
the ground, [d]tremble *every* mo-
ment, and [e]be astonished at you.
17 'And they will take up a [a]lam-
entation for you, and say to you:

"How you have perished,
O one inhabited by seafaring
men,
O renowned city,

13 [1]Or *even to Dedan they shall fall*
14 [a]Is. 11:14
15 [a]Jer. 25:20; Amos 1—6 [b]2 Chr. 28:18 [1]Lit. *spite in soul* [2]Or *perpetual*
16 [a]Zeph. 2:4 [b]1 Sam. 30:14 [c]Jer. 47:4
17 [a]Ezek. 5:15 [b]Ps. 9:16

CHAPTER 26

2 [a]2 Sam. 5:11; Is. 23:1; Jer. 25:22; Amos 1:9; Zech. 9:2 [b]Ezek. 25:3
4 [a]Ezek. 26:14
5 [a]Ezek. 27:32
6 [a]Ezek. 25:5
7 [a]Jer. 27:3–6; Ezek. 29:18 [b]Ezra 7:12; Is. 10:8; Jer. 52:32; Dan. 2:37, 47 [1]Heb. *Nebuchadrezzar,* and so elsewhere in the book
8 [a]Jer. 52:4; Ezek. 21:22 [1]Lit. *a large shield*
11 [a]Hab. 1:8
12 [a]Ezek. 27:27, 32
13 [a]Is. 14:11; 24:8; Jer. 7:34; 25:10; Amos 6:5 [b]Is. 23:16; Ezek. 28:13; Rev. 18:22
14 [a]Ezek. 26:4, 5
15 [a]Jer. 49:21; Ezek. 27:28
16 [a]Is. 23:8 [b]Jon. 3:6 [c]Job 2:13 [d]Ezek. 32:10; Hos. 11:10 [e]Ezek. 27:35
17 [a]Ezek. 27:2–36; Rev. 18:9

Who was [b]strong at sea,
She and her inhabitants,
Who caused their terror *to be* on
all her inhabitants!
18 Now [a]the coastlands tremble on
the day of your fall;
Yes, the coastlands by the sea are
troubled at your departure." '

19 "For thus says the Lord GOD:
'When I make you a desolate city,
like cities that are not inhabited,
when I bring the deep upon you,
and great waters cover you,
20 'then I will bring you down
[a]with those who descend into the
Pit, to the people of old, and I will
make you dwell in the lowest part
of the earth, in places desolate
from antiquity, with those who go
down to the Pit, so that you may
never be inhabited; and I shall es-
tablish glory [b]in the land of the
living.
21 [a]'I will make you a terror, and
you *shall be* no *more;* [b]though you
are sought for, you will never be
found again,' says the Lord GOD."

Lamentation for Tyre

27 The word of the LORD came
again to me, saying,
2 "Now, son of man, [a]take up a
lamentation for Tyre,
3 "and say to Tyre, [a]'You who
[1]are situated at the entrance of the
sea, [b]merchant of the peoples on
many coastlands, thus says the
Lord GOD:

"O Tyre, you have said,
[c]'I *am* perfect in beauty.'
4 Your borders *are* in the midst of
the seas.
Your builders have perfected
your beauty.
5 They [1]made all *your* planks of fir
trees from [a]Senir;
They took a cedar from Lebanon
to make you a mast.
6 *Of* [a]oaks from Bashan they made
your oars;
The company of Ashurites have
inlaid your planks
With ivory from [b]the coasts of
[1]Cyprus.
7 Fine embroidered linen from
Egypt was what you spread for
your sail;
Blue and purple from the coasts
of Elishah was what covered
you.

17 [b]Josh. 19:29; Is. 23:4
18 [a]Ezek. 26:15
20 [a]Ezek. 32:18 [b]Ezek. 32:23
21 [a]Ezek. 27:36; 28:19 [b]Ps. 37:10, 36; Ezek. 28:19

CHAPTER 27

2 [a]Ezek. 26:17
3 [a]Ezek. 26:17; 28:2 [b]Is. 23:3 [c]Ezek. 28:12 [1]Lit. *sit* or *dwell*
5 [a]Deut. 3:9; 1 Chr. 5:23; Song 4:8 [1]*built*
6 [a]Is. 2:12, 13; Zech. 11:2 [b]Gen. 10:4; Is. 23:1, 12; Jer. 2:10 [1]Heb. *Kittim,* western lands, especially Cyprus
9 [a]Josh. 13:5; 1 Kin. 5:18; Ps. 83:7
10 [1]Heb. *Lud* [2]Heb. *Put*
11 [a]Ezek. 27:3
12 [a]Gen. 10:4; 2 Chr. 20:36; Ezek. 38:13
13 [a]Gen. 10:2; Is. 66:19; Ezek. 27:19 [b]Joel 3:3–6; Rev. 18:13
14 [a]Gen. 10:3; Ezek. 38:6
15 [a]Gen. 10:7; Is. 21:13
17 [a]Judg. 11:33; 1 Kin. 5:9, 11; Ezra 3:7; Acts 12:20 [b]Jer. 8:22
19 [1]LXX, Syr. *from Uzal*
20 [a]Gen. 25:3

8 "Inhabitants of Sidon and Arvad
were your oarsmen;
Your wise men, O Tyre, were in
you;
They became your pilots.
9 Elders of [a]Gebal and its wise men
Were in you to caulk your seams;
All the ships of the sea
And their oarsmen were in you
To market your merchandise.

10 "Those from Persia, [1]Lydia, and
[2]Libya
Were in your army as men of
war;
They hung shield and helmet in
you;
They gave splendor to you.
11 Men of Arvad with your army
were on your walls *all* around,
And the men of Gammad were in
your towers;
They hung their shields on your
walls *all* around;
They made [a]your beauty perfect.

12 [a]"Tarshish *was* your merchant
because of your many luxury
goods. They gave you silver, iron,
tin, and lead for your goods.
13 [a]"Javan, Tubal, and Meshech
were your traders. They bartered
[b]human lives and vessels of
bronze for your merchandise.
14 "Those from the house of [a]To-
garmah traded for your wares with
horses, steeds, and mules.
15 "The men of [a]Dedan *were* your
traders; many isles *were* the mar-
ket of your hand. They brought
you ivory tusks and ebony as pay-
ment.
16 "Syria *was* your merchant be-
cause of the abundance of goods
you made. They gave you for your
wares emeralds, purple, embroi-
dery, fine linen, corals, and rubies.
17 "Judah and the land of Israel
were your traders. They traded for
your merchandise wheat of [a]Min-
nith, millet, honey, oil, and [b]balm.
18 "Damascus *was* your merchant
because of the abundance of goods
you made, because of your many
luxury items, with the wine of Hel-
bon and with white wool.
19 "Dan and Javan paid for your
wares, [1]traversing back and forth.
Wrought iron, cassia, and cane
were among your merchandise.
20 [a]"Dedan *was* your merchant in
saddlecloths for riding.

21 "Arabia and all the princes of
[a]Kedar *were* your regular mer-
chants. They traded with you in
lambs, rams, and goats.
22 "The merchants of [a]Sheba and
Raamah *were* your merchants.
They traded for your wares the
choicest spices, all kinds of pre-
cious stones, and gold.
23 [a]"Haran, Canneh, Eden, the
merchants of [b]Sheba, Assyria, *and*
Chilmad *were* your merchants.
24 "These *were* your merchants in
choice items—in purple clothes, in
embroidered garments, in chests
of multicolored apparel, in sturdy
woven cords, which were in your
marketplace.

25 "The [a]ships of Tarshish were
carriers of your merchandise.
You were filled and very glorious
[b]in the midst of the seas.
26 Your oarsmen brought you into
many waters,
But [a]the east wind broke you in
the midst of the seas.

27 "Your [a]riches, wares, and
merchandise,
Your mariners and pilots,
Your caulkers and
merchandisers,
All your men of war who *are* in
you,
And the entire company which *is*
in your midst,
Will fall into the midst of the seas
on the day of your ruin.
28 The [a]common-land[1] will shake at
the sound of the cry of your
pilots.

29 "All [a]who handle the oar,
The mariners,
All the pilots of the sea
Will come down from their ships
and stand on the [1]shore.
30 They will make their voice heard
because of you;
They will cry bitterly and [a]cast
dust on their heads;
They [b]will roll about in ashes;
31 They will [a]shave themselves
completely bald because of
you,
Gird themselves with sackcloth,
And weep for you
With bitterness of heart *and*
bitter wailing.
32 In their wailing for you
They will [a]take up a lamentation,
And lament for you:
[b]'What *city is* like Tyre,
Destroyed in the midst of the sea?
33 'When[a] your wares went out by
sea,
You satisfied many people;
You enriched the kings of the
earth
With your many luxury goods
and your merchandise.
34 But [a]you are broken by the seas
in the depths of the waters;
[b]Your merchandise and the entire
company will fall in your midst.
35 [a]All the inhabitants of the isles
will be astonished at you;
Their kings will be greatly afraid,
And *their* countenance will be
troubled.
36 The merchants among the
peoples [a]will hiss at you;
[b]You will become a horror, and *be*
no [c]more forever.' " ' "

Proclamation Against the King of Tyre

28 The word of the LORD came
to me again, saying,
2 "Son of man, say to the prince
of Tyre, 'Thus says the Lord GOD:

"Because your heart *is* [a]lifted[1] up,
And [b]you say, 'I *am* a god,
I sit *in* the seat of gods,
[c]In the midst of the seas,'
[d]Yet you *are* a man, and not a god,
Though you set your heart as the
heart of a god
3 (Behold, [a]you *are* wiser than
Daniel!
There is no secret that can be
hidden from you!
4 With your wisdom and your
understanding
You have gained [a]riches for
yourself,
And gathered gold and silver into
your treasuries;
5 [a]By your great wisdom in trade
you have increased your riches,
And your heart is lifted up
because of your riches),"

6 'Therefore thus says the Lord
GOD:

"Because you have set your heart
as the heart of a god,
7 Behold, therefore, I will bring
[a]strangers against you,
[b]The most terrible of the nations;
And they shall draw their swords
against the beauty of your
wisdom,
And defile your splendor.

---

21 [a]Gen. 25:13; Is. 60:7; Jer. 49:28
22 [a]Gen. 10:7; 1 Kin. 10:1, 2; Ps. 72:10; Is. 60:6; Ezek. 38:13
23 [a]Gen. 11:31; 2 Kin. 19:12; Is. 37:12 [b]Gen. 25:3
25 [a]Ps. 48:7; Is. 2:16 [b]Ezek. 27:4
26 [a]Ps. 48:7; Jer. 18:17; Acts 27:14
27 [a][Prov. 11:4]
28 [a]Ezek. 26:15 [1]open lands or pasturelands
29 [a]Rev. 18:17 [1]Lit. *land*
30 [a]1 Sam. 4:12; 2 Sam. 1:2; Job 2:12; Lam. 2:10; Rev. 18:19 [b]Esth. 4:1, 3; Jer. 6:26; Jon. 3:6
31 [a]Is. 15:2; Jer. 16:6; Ezek. 29:18
32 [a]Ezek. 26:17 [b]Ezek. 26:4, 5; Rev. 18:18
33 [a]Rev. 18:19
34 [a]Ezek. 26:19 [b]Ezek. 27:27
35 [a]Is. 23:6; Ezek. 26:15, 16
36 [a]Jer. 18:16; Zeph. 2:15 [b]Ezek. 26:2 [c]Ps. 37:10, 36; Ezek. 28:19

CHAPTER 28

2 [a]Jer. 49:16; Ezek. 31:10 [b]Is. 14:14; 47:8; Ezek. 28:9; 2 Thess. 2:4 [c]Ezek. 27:3, 4 [d]Is. 31:3; Ezek. 28:9 [1]Proud
3 [a]Ezek. 14:14; Dan. 1:20; 2:20–23, 28; 5:11, 12; Zech. 9:3
4 [a]Ezek. 27:33; Zech. 9:1–3
5 [a]Ps. 62:10; Zech. 9:3
7 [a]Ezek. 26:7 [b]Ezek. 7:24; 21:31; 30:11; Hab. 1:6–8

8 They shall throw you down into
the [a]Pit,
And you shall die the death of the
slain
In the midst of the seas.

9 "Will you still [a]say before him who
slays you,
'I *am* a god'?
But you *shall be* a man, and not
a god,
In the hand of him who slays you.
10 You shall die the death of [a]the
uncircumcised
By the hand of aliens;
For I have spoken," says the Lord
GOD.'"

Lamentation for the King of Tyre

11 Moreover the word of the LORD
came to me, saying,
12 "Son of man, [a]take up a lamen-
tation for the king of Tyre, and
say to him, 'Thus says the Lord
GOD:

[b]"You *were* the seal of perfection,
Full of wisdom and perfect in
beauty.
13 You were in [a]Eden, the garden of
God;
Every precious stone *was* your
covering:
The sardius, topaz, and diamond,
Beryl, onyx, and jasper,
Sapphire, turquoise, and emerald
with gold.
The workmanship of [b]your
timbrels and pipes
Was prepared for you on the day
you were created.

14 "You *were* the anointed [a]cherub
who covers;
I established you;
You were on [b]the holy mountain
of God;
You walked back and forth in the
midst of fiery stones.
15 You *were* perfect in your ways
from the day you were created,
Till [a]iniquity was found in you.

16 "By the abundance of your trading
You became filled with violence
within,
And you sinned;
Therefore I cast you as a profane
thing
Out of the mountain of God;
And I destroyed you, [a]O covering
cherub,
From the midst of the fiery
stones.

8 [a]Is. 14:15
9 [a]Ezek. 28:2
10 [a]1 Sam. 17:26, 36; Ezek. 31:18; 32:19, 21, 25, 27
12 [a]Ezek. 27:2 [b]Ezek. 27:3; 28:3
13 [a]Gen. 2:8; Is. 51:3; Ezek. 31:8, 9; 36:35 [b]Ezek. 26:13
14 [a]Ex. 25:20; Ezek. 28:16 [b]Is. 14:13; Ezek. 20:40
15 [a][Is. 14:12]
16 [a]Ezek. 28:14
17 [a]Ezek. 28:2, 5 [1]Proud
19 [a]Ezek. 26:21 [b]Ezek. 27:36
21 [a]Ezek. 6:2; 25:2; 29:2 [b]Gen. 10:15, 19; Is. 23:2, 4, 12; Ezek. 27:8; 32:30
22 [a]Ex. 14:4, 17; Ezek. 39:13 [b]Ps. 9:16 [c]Ezek. 28:25
23 [a]Ezek. 38:22
24 [a]Num. 33:55; Josh. 23:13; Is. 55:13; Ezek. 2:6 [b]Ezek. 16:57; 25:6, 7
25 [a]Ps. 106:47; Is. 11:12, 13; Jer. 32:37; Ezek. 11:17; 20:41; 34:13; 37:21 [b]Ezek. 28:22

17 "Your [a]heart was [1]lifted up
because of your beauty;
You corrupted your wisdom for
the sake of your splendor;
I cast you to the ground,
I laid you before kings,
That they might gaze at you.

18 "You defiled your sanctuaries
By the multitude of your
iniquities,
By the iniquity of your trading;
Therefore I brought fire from
your midst;
It devoured you,
And I turned you to ashes upon
the earth
In the sight of all who saw you.
19 All who knew you among the
peoples are astonished at you;
[a]You have become a horror,
And *shall be* no [b]more
forever."'"

Proclamation Against Sidon

20 Then the word of the LORD
came to me, saying,
21 "Son of man, [a]set your face
[b]toward Sidon, and prophesy
against her,
22 "and say, 'Thus says the Lord
GOD:

[a]"Behold, I *am* against you,
O Sidon;
I will be glorified in your midst;
And [b]they shall know that I *am*
the LORD,
When I execute judgments in her
and am [c]hallowed in her.
23 [a]For I will send pestilence upon
her,
And blood in her streets;
The wounded shall be judged in
her midst
By the sword against her on
every side;
Then they shall know that I *am*
the LORD.

24 "And there shall no longer be
a pricking brier or [a]a painful thorn
for the house of Israel from among
all *who are* around them, who [b]de-
spise them. Then they shall know
that I *am* the Lord GOD."

Israel's Future Blessing

25 'Thus says the Lord GOD:
"When I have [a]gathered the house
of Israel from the peoples among
whom they are scattered, and am
[b]hallowed in them in the sight of

the Gentiles, then they will dwell
in their own land which I gave to
My servant Jacob.
26 "And they will [a]dwell [1]safely
there, [b]build houses, and [c]plant
vineyards; yes, they will dwell se-
curely, when I execute judgments
on all those around them who de-
spise them. Then they shall know
that I *am* the LORD their God." ' "

Proclamation Against Egypt

29 In the tenth year, in the
tenth *month,* on the twelfth
day of the month, the word of the
LORD came to me, saying,
2 "Son of man, [a]set your face
against Pharaoh king of Egypt,
and prophesy against him, and
[b]against all Egypt.
3 "Speak, and say, 'Thus says the
Lord GOD:

[a]"Behold, I *am* against you,
O Pharaoh king of Egypt,
O great [b]monster who lies in the
midst of his rivers,
[c]Who has said, 'My [1]River *is* my
own;
I have made *it* for myself.'
4 But [a]I will put hooks in your jaws,
And cause the fish of your rivers
to stick to your scales;
I will bring you up out of the
midst of your rivers,
And all the fish in your rivers will
stick to your scales.
5 I will leave you in the wilderness,
You and all the fish of your
rivers;
You shall fall on the [1]open [a]field;
[b]You shall not be picked up or
[2]gathered.
[c]I have given you as food
To the beasts of the field
And to the birds of the heavens.

6 "Then all the inhabitants of Egypt
Shall know that I *am* the LORD,
Because they have been a [a]staff
of reed to the house of Israel.
7 [a]When they took hold of you with
the hand,
You broke and tore all their
[1]shoulders;
When they leaned on you,
You broke and made all their
backs quiver."

8 'Therefore thus says the Lord
GOD: "Surely I will bring [a]a sword
upon you and cut off from you man
and beast.
9 "And the land of Egypt shall
become [a]desolate and waste; then
they will know that I *am* the LORD,
because he said, 'The River *is*
mine, and I have made *it.*'
10 "Indeed, therefore, I *am*
against you and against your riv-
ers, [a]and I will make the land of
Egypt utterly waste and desolate,
[b]from [1]Migdol *to* Syene, as far as
the border of Ethiopia.
11 [a]"Neither foot of man shall
pass through it nor foot of beast
pass through it, and it shall be
uninhabited forty years.
12 [a]"I will make the land of Egypt
desolate in the midst of the coun-
tries *that are* desolate; and among
the cities *that are* laid waste, her
cities shall be desolate forty years;
and I will [b]scatter the Egyptians
among the nations and disperse
them throughout the countries."
13 'Yet, thus says the Lord GOD:
"At the [a]end of forty years I will
gather the Egyptians from the peo-
ples among whom they were scat-
tered.
14 "I will bring back the captives
of Egypt and cause them to return
to the land of Pathros, to the land
of their origin, and there they shall
be a [a]lowly kingdom.
15 "It shall be the lowliest of king-
doms; it shall never again exalt it-
self above the nations, for I will
diminish them so that they will not
rule over the nations anymore.
16 "No longer shall it be [a]the con-
fidence of the house of Israel, but
will remind them of *their* iniquity
when they turned to follow them.
Then they shall know that I *am* the
Lord GOD." ' "

Babylonia Will Plunder Egypt

17 And it came to pass in the
twenty-seventh year, in the first
month, on the first *day* of the
month, *that* the word of the LORD
came to me, saying,
18 "Son of man, [a]Nebuchad-
nezzar king of Babylon caused his
army to labor strenuously against
Tyre; every head *was* made [b]bald,
and every shoulder rubbed raw;
yet neither he nor his army re-
ceived wages from Tyre, for the la-
bor which they expended on it.
19 "Therefore thus says the Lord
GOD: 'Surely I will give the land

26 [a]Jer. 23:6; Ezek. 36:28 [b]Is. 65:21; Jer. 32:15, 43, 44; Amos 9:13, 14 [c]Jer. 31:5; Amos 9:14 [1]securely

CHAPTER 29

2 [a]Ezek. 28:21 [b]Is. 19:1; Jer. 25:19; 46:2, 25; Ezek. 30:1—32:32; Joel 3:19
3 [a]Jer. 44:30; Ezek. 28:22; 29:10 [b]Ps. 74:13, 14; Is. 37:1; 51:9; Ezek. 32:2 [c]Ezek. 28:2 [1]The Nile
4 [a]2 Kin. 19:28; Is. 37:29; Ezek. 38:4
5 [a]Ezek. 32:4–6 [b]Jer. 8:2; 16:4; 25:33 [c]Jer. 7:33; 34:20; Ezek. 39:4 [1]Lit. *face of the field* [2]So with MT, LXX, Vg.; some Heb. mss., Tg. *buried*
6 [a]2 Kin. 18:21; Is. 36:6; Ezek. 17:15
7 [a]Jer. 37:5, 7, 11; Ezek. 17:17 [1]So with MT, Vg.; LXX, Syr. *hand*
8 [a]Jer. 46:13; Ezek. 14:17; 32:11–13
9 [a]Ezek. 30:7, 8
10 [a]Ezek. 30:12 [b]Ezek. 30:6 [1]Or *the tower*
11 [a]Jer. 43:11, 12; 46:19; Ezek. 32:13
12 [a]Jer. 25:15–19; 27:6–11; Ezek. 30:7, 26 [b]Jer. 46:19; Ezek. 30:23, 26
13 [a]Is. 19:23; Jer. 46:26
14 [a]Ezek. 17:6, 14
16 [a]Is. 30:2, 3; 36:4, 6; Lam. 4:17; Ezek. 17:15; 29:6
18 [a]Jer. 25:9; 27:6; Ezek. 26:7–12 [b]Jer. 48:37; Ezek. 27:31

of Egypt to [a]Nebuchadnezzar king
of Babylon; he shall take away her
wealth, carry off her spoil, and re-
move her pillage; and that will be
the wages for his army.
20 'I have given him the land of
Egypt *for* his labor, because they
[a]worked for Me,' says the Lord
GOD.
21 'In that day [a]I will cause the
[1]horn of the house of Israel to
spring forth, and I will [b]open your
mouth to speak in their midst.
Then they shall know that I *am* the
LORD.' "

Egypt and Her Allies Will Fall

30 The word of the LORD came
to me again, saying,
2 "Son of man, prophesy and
say, 'Thus says the Lord GOD:

[a]"Wail, 'Woe to the day!'
3 For [a]the day *is* near,
Even the day of the LORD *is* near;
It will be a day of clouds, the time
of the Gentiles.
4 The sword shall come upon
Egypt,
And great anguish shall be in
[1]Ethiopia,
When the slain fall in Egypt,
And they [a]take away her wealth,
And [b]her foundations are broken
down.

5 "Ethiopia, [1]Libya, [2]Lydia, [a]all
the mingled people, Chub, and the
men of the lands who are allied,
shall fall with them by the sword."
6 'Thus says the LORD:

"Those who uphold Egypt shall
fall,
And the pride of her power shall
come down.
[a]From [1]Migdol *to* Syene
Those within her shall fall by the
sword,"
Says the Lord GOD.

7 "They[a] shall be desolate in the
midst of the desolate countries,
And her cities shall be in the
midst of the cities *that are* laid
waste.
8 Then they will know that I *am* the
LORD,
When I have set a fire in Egypt
And all her helpers are destroyed.
9 On that day [a]messengers shall go
forth from Me in ships

19 [a]Jer. 43:10–13; Ezek. 30:10
20 [a]Is. 10:6, 7; 45:1–3; Jer. 25:9
21 [a]1 Sam. 2:10; Ps. 92:10; 132:17 [b]Ezek. 24:27; Amos 3:7, 8; [Luke 21:15] [1]Strength

CHAPTER 30

2 [a]Is. 13:6; 15:2; Ezek. 21:12; Joel 1:5, 11, 13
3 [a]Ezek. 7:7, 12; Joel 2:1; Obad. 15; Zeph. 1:7
4 [a]Ezek. 29:19 [b]Jer. 50:15 [1]Heb. *Cush*
5 [a]Jer. 25:20, 24 [1]Heb. *Put* [2]Heb. *Lud*
6 [a]Ezek. 29:10 [1]Or *the tower*
7 [a]Jer. 25:18–26; Ezek. 29:12
9 [a]Is. 18:1, 2 [1]Or *secure*
10 [a]Ezek. 29:19
11 [a]Ezek. 28:7; 31:12
12 [a]Is. 19:5, 6 [b]Is. 19:4
13 [a]Is. 19:1; Jer. 43:12; 46:25; Zech. 13:2 [b]Zech. 10:11 [c]Is. 19:16 [1]Ancient Memphis
14 [a]Is. 11:11; Jer. 44:1, 15; Ezek. 29:14 [b]Ps. 78:12, 43; Is. 19:11, 13 [c]Jer. 46:25; Ezek. 30:15, 16; Nah. 3:8–10 [1]Ancient Thebes
15 [a]Jer. 46:25 [1]Ancient Pelusium [2]Ancient Thebes
16 [a]Ezek. 30:8
17 [1]Ancient On, Heliopolis
18 [a]Jer. 2:16 [1]*Tahpanhes*, Jer. 43:7 [2]So with many Heb. mss., Bg., LXX, Syr., Tg., Vg.; MT *refrained*
19 [a][Ps. 9:16]; Ezek. 5:8; 25:11

To make the [1]careless Ethiopians
afraid,
And great anguish shall come
upon them,
As on the day of Egypt;
For indeed it is coming!"

10 'Thus says the Lord GOD:

[a]"I will also make a multitude of
Egypt to cease
By the hand of Nebuchadnezzar
king of Babylon.
11 He and his people with him, [a]the
most terrible of the nations,
Shall be brought to destroy the
land;
They shall draw their swords
against Egypt,
And fill the land with the slain.
12 [a]I will make the rivers dry,
And [b]sell the land into the hand
of the wicked;
I will make the land waste, and
all that is in it,
By the hand of aliens.
I, the LORD, have spoken."

13 'Thus says the Lord GOD:

"I will also [a]destroy the idols,
And cause the images to cease
from [1]Noph;
[b]There shall no longer be princes
from the land of Egypt;
[c]I will put fear in the land of Egypt.
14 I will make [a]Pathros desolate,
Set fire to [b]Zoan,
[c]And execute judgments in [1]No.
15 I will pour My fury on [1]Sin, the
strength of Egypt;
[a]I will cut off the multitude of [2]No,
16 And [a]set a fire in Egypt;
Sin shall have great pain,
No shall be split open,
And Noph *shall be in* distress
daily.
17 The young men of [1]Aven and Pi
Beseth shall fall by the sword,
And these *cities* shall go into
captivity.
18 [a]At [1]Tehaphnehes the day shall
also be [2]darkened,
When I break the yokes of Egypt
there.
And her arrogant strength shall
cease in her;
As for her, a cloud shall cover
her,
And her daughters shall go into
captivity.
19 Thus I will [a]execute judgments on
Egypt,
Then they shall know that I *am*
the LORD." ' "

Proclamation Against Pharaoh

20 And it came to pass in the elev-
enth year, in the first *month,* on
the seventh *day* of the month, *that*
the word of the LORD came to me,
saying,
21 "Son of man, I have [a]broken
the arm of Pharaoh king of Egypt;
and see, [b]it has not been bandaged
for healing, nor a [1]splint put on to
bind it, to make it strong enough
to hold a sword.
22 "Therefore thus says the Lord
GOD: 'Surely I *am* [a]against Pha-
raoh king of Egypt, and will
[b]break his arms, both the strong
one and the one that was broken;
and I will make the sword fall out
of his hand.
23 [a]'I will scatter the Egyptians
among the nations, and disperse
them throughout the countries.
24 'I will strengthen the arms of
the king of Babylon and put My
sword in his hand; but I will break
Pharaoh's arms, and he will groan
before him with the groanings of
a mortally wounded *man.*
25 'Thus I will strengthen the
arms of the king of Babylon, but
the arms of Pharaoh shall fall
down; [a]they shall know that I *am*
the LORD, when I put My sword
into the hand of the king of Bab-
ylon and he stretches it out against
the land of Egypt.
26 [a]'I will scatter the Egyptians
among the nations and disperse
them throughout the countries.
Then they shall know that I *am* the
LORD.'"

Egypt Cut Down Like a Great Tree

31 Now it came to pass in the
[a]eleventh year, in the third
month, on the first *day* of the
month, *that* the word of the LORD
came to me, saying,
2 "Son of man, say to Pharaoh
king of Egypt and to his multitude:

[a]'Whom are you like in your
greatness?
3 [a]Indeed Assyria *was* a cedar in
Lebanon,
With fine branches that shaded
the forest,
And of high stature;
And its top was among the thick
boughs.
4 [a]The waters made it grow;
Underground waters gave it
height,
With their rivers running around
the place where it was planted,
And sent out [1]rivulets to all the
trees of the field.
5 'Therefore [a]its height was exalted
above all the trees of the field;
Its boughs were multiplied,
And its branches became long
because of the abundance of
water,
As it sent them out.
6 All the [a]birds of the heavens
made their nests in its boughs;
Under its branches all the beasts
of the field brought forth their
young;
And in its shadow all great
nations [1]made their home.
7 'Thus it was beautiful in greatness
and in the length of its
branches,
Because its roots reached to
abundant waters.
8 The cedars in the [a]garden of God
could not hide it;
The fir trees were not like its
boughs,
And the [1]chestnut trees were not
like its branches;
No tree in the garden of God was
like it in beauty.
9 I made it beautiful with a
multitude of branches,
So that all the trees of Eden
envied it,
That *were* in the garden of God.'

10 "Therefore thus says the Lord
GOD: 'Because you have increased
in height, and it set its top among
the thick boughs, and [a]its heart
was [1]lifted up in its height,
11 'therefore I will deliver it into
the hand of the [a]mighty one of the
nations, and he shall surely deal
with it; I have driven it out for its
wickedness.
12 'And aliens, [a]the most terrible
of the nations, have cut it down
and left it; its branches have fallen
[b]on the mountains and in all the
valleys; its boughs lie [c]broken by
all the rivers of the land; and all
the peoples of the earth have gone
from under its shadow and left it.

13 'On [a]its ruin will remain all the
birds of the heavens,
And all the beasts of the field will
come to its branches—

21 [a]Jer. 48:25 [b]Jer. 46:11 [1]Lit. *bandage*
22 [a]Jer. 46:25; Ezek. 29:3 [b]Ps. 37:17
23 [a]Ezek. 29:12; 30:17, 18, 26
25 [a]Ps. 9:16
26 [a]Ezek. 29:12

CHAPTER 31

1 [a]Jer. 52:5, 6; Ezek. 30:20; 32:1
2 [a]Ezek. 31:18
3 [a]Is. 10:33, 34; Ezek. 17:3, 4, 22; 31:16; Dan. 4:10, 20–23
4 [a]Jer. 51:36; Ezek. 29:3–9 [1]Or *channels*
5 [a]Dan. 4:11
6 [a]Ezek. 17:23; 31:13; Dan. 4:12, 21; Matt. 13:32 [1]Lit. *dwelled*
8 [a]Gen. 2:8, 9; 13:10; Is. 51:3; Ezek. 28:13; 31:16, 18 [1]Or *plane,* Heb. *armon*
10 [a]2 Chr. 32:25; Is. 10:12; 14:13, 14; Ezek. 28:17; Dan. 5:20 [1]Proud
11 [a]Ezek. 30:10; Dan. 5:18, 19
12 [a]Ezek. 28:7; 30:11; 32:12 [b]Ezek. 32:5; 35:8 [c]Ezek. 30:24, 25
13 [a]Is. 18:6; Ezek. 32:4

14 'So that no trees by the waters
may ever again exalt themselves
for their height, nor set their tops
among the thick boughs, that no
tree which drinks water may ever
be high enough to reach up to
them.

'For [a]they have all been delivered
to death,
[b]To the depths of the earth,
Among the children of men who
go down to the Pit.'

15 "Thus says the Lord GOD: 'In
the day when it [a]went down to
[1]hell, I caused mourning. I covered
the deep because of it. I restrained
its rivers, and the great waters
were held back. I caused Lebanon
to [2]mourn for it, and all the trees
of the field wilted because of it.
16 'I made the nations [a]shake at
the sound of its fall, when I [b]cast
it down to [1]hell together with those
who descend into the Pit; and [c]all
the trees of Eden, the choice and
best of Lebanon, all that drink wa-
ter, [d]were comforted in the depths
of the earth.
17 'They also went down to hell
with it, with those *slain* by the
sword; and *those who were* its
strong arm [a]dwelt in its shadows
among the nations.
18 [a]'To which of the trees in Eden
will you then be likened in glory
and greatness? Yet you shall be
brought down with the trees of
Eden to the depths of the earth;
[b]you shall lie in the midst of the
uncircumcised, with *those* slain by
the sword. This *is* Pharaoh and
all his multitude,' says the Lord
GOD."

Lamentation for Pharaoh and Egypt

32 And it came to pass in the
twelfth year, in the [a]twelfth
month, on the first *day* of the
month, *that* the word of the LORD
came to me, saying,
2 "Son of man, [a]take up a lamen-
tation for Pharaoh king of Egypt,
and say to him:

[b]'You are like a young lion among
the nations,
And [c]you *are* like a monster in
the seas,
[d]Bursting forth in your rivers,
Troubling the waters with your
feet,
And [e]fouling their rivers.'

3 "Thus says the Lord GOD:

'I will therefore [a]spread My net
over you with a company of
many people,
And they will draw you up in My
net.
4 Then [a]I will leave you on the
land;
I will cast you out on the open
fields,
[b]And cause to [1]settle on you all the
birds of the heavens.
And with you I will fill the beasts
of the whole earth.
5 I will lay your flesh [a]on the
mountains,
And fill the valleys with your
carcass.

6 'I will also water the land with the
flow of your blood,
Even to the mountains;
And the riverbeds will be full of
you.
7 When *I* put out your light,
[a]I will cover the heavens, and
make its stars dark;
I will cover the sun with a cloud,
And the moon shall not give her
light.
8 All the [1]bright lights of the
heavens I will make dark over
you,
And bring darkness upon your
land,'
Says the Lord GOD.

9 'I will also trouble the hearts
of many peoples, when I bring
your destruction among the na-
tions, into the countries which you
have not known.
10 'Yes, I will make many peoples
astonished at you, and their kings
shall be horribly afraid of you
when I brandish My sword before
them; and [a]they shall tremble
every moment, every man for his
own life, in the day of your fall.'
11 [a]"For thus says the Lord GOD:
'The sword of the king of Babylon
shall come upon you.
12 'By the swords of the mighty
warriors, all of them [a]the most ter-
rible of the nations, I will cause
your multitude to fall.

[b]'They shall plunder the pomp of
Egypt,

14 [a]Ps. 82:7 [b]Ezek. 32:18
15 [a]Ezek. 32:22, 23 [1]Or *Sheol* [2]Lit. *be darkened*
16 [a]Ezek. 26:15; Hag. 2:7 [b]Is. 14:15; Ezek. 32:18 [c]Is. 14:8; Hab. 2:17 [d]Ezek. 32:31 [1]Or *Sheol*
17 [a]Lam. 4:20
18 [a]Ezek. 32:19 [b]Jer. 9:25, 26; Ezek. 28:10; 32:19, 21
CHAPTER 32
1 [a]Ezek. 31:1; 33:21
2 [a]Ezek. 27:2 [b]Jer. 4:7; Ezek. 19:2–6; Nah. 2:11–13 [c]Is. 27:1; Ezek. 29:3 [d]Jer. 46:7, 8 [e]Ezek. 34:18
3 [a]Ezek. 12:13; 17:20
4 [a]Ezek. 29:5 [b]Is. 18:6; Ezek. 31:13 [1]Lit. *sit* or *dwell*
5 [a]Ezek. 31:12
7 [a]Is. 13:10; Joel 2:31; 3:15; Amos 8:9; Matt. 24:29; Mark 13:24; Luke 21:25; Rev. 6:12, 13; 8:12
8 [1]Or *shining*
10 [a]Ezek. 26:16
11 [a]Jer. 46:26; Ezek. 30:4
12 [a]Ezek. 28:7; 30:11; 31:12 [b]Ezek. 29:19

And all its multitude shall be
destroyed.
13 Also I will destroy all its animals
From beside its great waters;
[a]The foot of man shall muddy
them no more,
Nor shall the hooves of animals
muddy them.
14 Then I will make their waters
[1]clear,
And make their rivers run like
oil,'
Says the Lord GOD.

15 'When I make the land of Egypt
desolate,
And the country is destitute of all
that once filled it,
When I strike all who dwell in it,
[a]Then they shall know that I *am*
the LORD.

16 'This *is* the [a]lamentation
With which they shall lament her;
The daughters of the nations
shall lament her;
They shall lament for her, for
Egypt,
And for all her multitude,'
Says the Lord GOD."

Egypt and Others Consigned to the Pit

17 It came to pass also in the
twelfth year, on the fifteenth *day*
of the month, [a]*that* the word of the
LORD came to me, saying:

18 "Son of man, wail over the
multitude of Egypt,
And [a]cast them down to the
depths of the earth,
Her and the daughters of the
famous nations,
With those who go down to the
Pit:
19 'Whom [a]do you surpass in
beauty?
[b]Go down, be placed with the
uncircumcised.'

20 "They shall fall in the midst of
those slain by the sword;
She is delivered to the sword,
[a]Drawing her and all her
multitudes.
21 [a]The strong among the mighty
Shall speak to him out of the
midst of hell
With those who help him:
'They have [b]gone down,
They lie with the uncircumcised,
slain by the sword.'

22 "Assyria[a] *is* there, and all her
company,

13 [a]Ezek. 29:11
14 [1]Lit. *sink;* settle, grow clear
15 [a]Ex. 7:5; 14:4, 18; Ps. 9:16; Ezek. 6:7
16 [a]2 Sam. 1:17; 2 Chr. 35:25; Jer. 9:17; Ezek. 26:17
17 [a]Ezek. 32:1; 33:21
18 [a]Ezek. 26:20; 31:14
19 [a]Jer. 9:25, 26; Ezek. 31:2, 18 [b]Ezek. 28:10
20 [a]Ps. 28:3
21 [a]Is. 1:31; 14:9, 10; Ezek. 32:27 [b]Ezek. 32:19, 25
22 [a]Ezek. 31:3, 16
23 [a]Is. 14:15 [b]Ezek. 32:24–27, 32
24 [a]Gen. 10:22; 14:1; Is. 11:11; Jer. 25:25; 49:34–39 [b]Ezek. 32:21 [c]Ezek. 32:23
25 [a]Ps. 139:8
26 [a]Gen. 10:2; Ezek. 27:13; 38:2, 3; 39:1 [b]Ezek. 32:19
27 [a]Is. 14:18, 19
29 [a]Is. 9:25, 26; 34:5, 6; Jer. 49:7–22; Ezek. 25:12–14

With their graves all around her,
All of them slain, fallen by the
sword.
23 [a]Her graves are set in the recesses
of the Pit,
And her company is all around
her grave,
All of them slain, fallen by the
sword,
Who [b]caused terror in the land
of the living.

24 "There *is* [a]Elam and all her
multitude,
All around her grave,
All of them slain, fallen by the
sword,
Who have [b]gone down
uncircumcised to the lower
parts of the earth,
[c]Who caused their terror in the
land of the living;
Now they bear their shame with
those who go down to the Pit.
25 They have set her [a]bed in the
midst of the slain,
With all her multitude,
With her graves all around it,
All of them uncircumcised, slain
by the sword;
Though their terror was caused
In the land of the living,
Yet they bear their shame
With those who go down to the
Pit;
It was put in the midst of the
slain.

26 "There *are* [a]Meshech and Tubal
and all their multitudes,
With all their graves around it,
All of them [b]uncircumcised, slain
by the sword,
Though they caused their terror
in the land of the living.
27 [a]They do not lie with the mighty
Who are fallen of the
uncircumcised,
Who have gone down to hell with
their weapons of war;
They have laid their swords
under their heads,
But their iniquities will be on
their bones,
Because of the terror of the
mighty in the land of the living.
28 Yes, you shall be broken in the
midst of the uncircumcised,
And lie with *those* slain by the
sword.

29 "There *is* [a]Edom,
Her kings and all her princes,
Who despite their might

Are laid beside *those* slain by the sword;
They shall lie with the uncircumcised,
And with those who go down to the Pit.
30 [a]There *are* the princes of the north,
All of them, and all the [b]Sidonians,
Who have gone down with the slain
In shame at the terror which they caused by their might;
They lie uncircumcised with *those* slain by the sword,
And bear their shame with those who go down to the Pit.

31 "Pharaoh will see them
And be [a]comforted over all his multitude,
Pharaoh and all his army,
Slain by the sword,"
Says the Lord GOD.

32 "For I have caused My terror in the land of the living;
And he shall be placed in the midst of the uncircumcised
With *those* slain by the sword,
Pharaoh and all his multitude,"
Says the Lord GOD.

The Watchman and His Message

33 Again the word of the LORD
came to me, saying,
2 "Son of man, speak to [a]the chil-
dren of your people, and say to
them: [b]'When I bring the sword
upon a land, and the people of the
land take a man from their terri-
tory and make him their [c]watch-
man,
3 'when he sees the sword com-
ing upon the land, if he blows the
trumpet and warns the people,
4 'then whoever hears the sound
of the trumpet and does [a]not take
warning, if the sword comes and
takes him away, [b]his blood shall
be on his *own* head.
5 'He heard the sound of the
trumpet, but did not take warning;
his blood shall be upon himself.
But he who takes warning will
[1]save his life.
6 'But if the watchman sees the
sword coming and does not blow
the trumpet, and the people are not
warned, and the sword comes and
takes *any* person from among
them, [a]he is taken away in his in-
iquity; but his blood I will require
at the watchman's hand.'
7 [a]"So you, son of man: I have
made you a watchman for the
house of Israel; therefore you shall
hear a word from My mouth and
warn them for Me.
8 "When I say to the wicked, 'O
wicked *man*, you shall surely die!'
and you do not speak to warn the
wicked from his way, that wicked
man shall die in his iniquity; but
his blood I will require at your
hand.
9 "Nevertheless if you warn the
wicked to turn from his way, and
he does not turn from his way, he
shall die in his iniquity; but you
have [1]delivered your soul.
10 "Therefore you, O son of man,
say to the house of Israel: 'Thus
you say, "If our transgressions and
our sins *lie* upon us, and we [a]pine[1]
away in them, [b]how can we then
live?" '
11 "Say to them: '*As* I live,' says
the Lord GOD, [a]'I have no pleasure
in the death of the wicked, but that
the wicked [b]turn from his way and
live. Turn, turn from your evil
ways! For [c]why should you die, O
house of Israel?'

The Fairness of God's Judgment

12 "Therefore you, O son of man,
say to the children of your people:
'The [a]righteousness of the righ-
teous man shall not deliver him in
the day of his transgression; as for
the wickedness of the wicked, [b]he
shall not fall because of it in the
day that he turns from his wicked-
ness; nor shall the righteous be
able to live because of *his righ-
teousness* in the day that he sins.'
13 "When I say to the righteous
that he shall surely live, [a]but he
trusts in his own righteousness
and commits iniquity, none of his
righteous works shall be remem-
bered; but because of the iniquity
that he has committed, he shall
die.
14 "Again, [a]when I say to the
wicked, 'You shall surely die,' if
he turns from his sin and does
[1]what is lawful and [2]right,
15 "*if* the wicked [a]restores the
pledge, [b]gives back what he has
stolen, and walks in [c]the statutes
of life without committing iniquity,

30 [a]Jer. 1:15; 25:26; Ezek. 38:6, 15; 39:2 [b]Jer. 25:22; Ezek. 28:21–23
31 [a]Ezek. 14:22; 31:16

CHAPTER 33

2 [a]Ezek. 3:11 [b]Ezek. 14:17 [c]2 Sam. 18:24, 25; 2 Kin. 9:17; Hos. 9:8
4 [a]2 Chr. 25:16; Jer. 6:17; Zech. 1:4 [b]Ezek. 18:13; 35:9; [Acts 18:6]
5 [1]Or *deliver his soul*
6 [a]Ezek. 33:8
7 [a]Is. 62:6; Ezek. 3:17–21
9 [1]Or *saved your life*
10 [a]Lev. 26:39; Ezek. 24:23 [b]Is. 49:14; Ezek. 37:11 [1]Or *waste away*
11 [a][2 Sam. 14:14; Lam. 3:33]; Ezek. 18:23, 32; Hos. 11:8; [2 Pet. 3:9] [b]Ezek. 18:21, 30; [Hos. 14:1, 4; Acts 3:19] [c][Is. 55:6, 7]; Jer. 3:22; Ezek. 18:30, 31; Hos. 14:1; [Acts 3:19]
12 [a]Ezek. 3:20; 18:24, 26 [b][2 Chr. 7:14]; Ezek. 8:21; 33:19
13 [a]Ezek. 3:20; 18:24
14 [a][Is. 55:7]; Jer. 18:7, 8; Ezek. 3:18, 19; 18:27; Hos. 14:1, 4 [1]*justice* [2]*righteousness*
15 [a]Ezek. 18:7 [b]Ex. 22:1–4; Lev. 6:2, 4, 5; Num. 5:6, 7; Luke 19:8 [c]Lev. 18:5; Ps. 119:59; 143:8; Ezek. 20:11, 13, 21

he shall surely live; he shall not
die.
16 [a]"None of his sins which he has
committed shall be remembered
against him; he has done what is
lawful and right; he shall surely
live.
17 [a]"Yet the children of your peo-
ple say, 'The way of the LORD is
not [1]fair.' But it is their way which
is not fair!
18 [a]"When the righteous turns
from his righteousness and com-
mits iniquity, he shall die because
of it.
19 "But when the wicked turns
from his wickedness and does
what is lawful and right, he shall
live because of it.
20 "Yet you say, [a]'The way of the
LORD is not [1]fair.' O house of Israel,
I will judge every one of you ac-
cording to his own ways."

The Fall of Jerusalem

21 And it came to pass in the
twelfth year [a]of our captivity, in
the tenth *month*, on the fifth *day*
of the month, [b]*that* one who had
escaped from Jerusalem came to
me and said, [c]"The city has been
[1]captured!"
22 Now [a]the hand of the LORD had
been upon me the evening before
the man came who had escaped.
And He had [b]opened my mouth;
so when he came to me in the
morning, my mouth was opened,
and I was no longer mute.

The Cause of Judah's Ruin

23 Then the word of the LORD
came to me, saying:
24 "Son of man, [a]they who inhabit
those [b]ruins in the land of Israel
are saying, [c]'Abraham was only
one, and he inherited the land.
[d]But we *are* many; the land has
been given to us as a [e]possession.'
25 "Therefore say to them, 'Thus
says the Lord GOD: [a]"You eat *meat*
with blood, you [b]lift up your eyes
toward your idols, and [c]shed
blood. Should you then possess the
[d]land?
26 "You rely on your sword, you
commit abominations, and you
[a]defile one another's wives. Should
you then possess the land?" '
27 "Say thus to them, 'Thus says
the Lord GOD: "*As* I live, surely

16 [a][Is. 1:18; 43:25]
17 [a]Ezek. 18:25, 29 [1]Or *equitable*
18 [a]Ezek. 18:26
20 [a]Ezek. 18:25, 29 [1]Or *equitable*
21 [a]Ezek. 1:2 [b]Ezek. 24:26 [c]2 Kin. 25:4 [1]Lit. *struck down*
22 [a]Ezek. 1:3; 8:1; 37:1 [b]Ezek. 24:27
24 [a]Ezek. 34:2 [b]Ezek. 36:4 [c]Is. 51:2 [d][Matt. 3:9] [e]Ezek. 11:15
25 [a]Lev. 3:17; 7:26; 17:10–14; 19:26 [b]Ezek. 18:6 [c]Ezek. 22:6, 9 [d]Deut. 29:28
26 [a]Ezek. 18:6; 22:11
27 [a]Ezek. 33:24 [b]Ezek. 39:4 [c]1 Sam. 13:6
28 [a]Jer. 44:2, 6, 22 [b]Ezek. 7:24; 24:21 [c]Ezek. 6:2, 3, 6 [1]Lit. *pride of her strength*
30 [a]Is. 29:13
31 [a]Ezek. 14:1 [b]Ezek. 8:1 [c]Is. 58:2 [d]Ps. 78:36, 37 [e][Matt. 13:22]
32 [a][Matt. 7:21–28]
33 [a]1 Sam. 3:20 [b]Ezek. 2:5

CHAPTER 34

2 [a]Zech. 11:17
3 [a]Zech. 11:16 [b]Ezek. 33:25, 26
4 [a]Zech. 11:16

[a]those who *are* in the ruins shall
fall by the sword, and the one who
is in the open field [b]I will give to
the beasts to be devoured, and
those who *are* in the strongholds
and [c]caves shall die of the pesti-
lence.
28 [a]"For I will make the land most
desolate, [1]her [b]arrogant strength
shall cease, and [c]the mountains of
Israel shall be so desolate that no
one will pass through.
29 "Then they shall know that I
am the LORD, when I have made
the land most desolate because of
all their abominations which they
have committed." '

Hearing and Not Doing

30 "As for you, son of man, the
children of your people are talking
about you beside the walls and in
the doors of the houses; and they
[a]speak to one another, everyone
saying to his brother, 'Please come
and hear what the word is that
comes from the LORD.'
31 "So [a]they come to you as peo-
ple do, they [b]sit before you *as* My
people, and they [c]hear your words,
but they do not do them; [d]for with
their mouth they show much love,
but [e]their hearts pursue their *own*
gain.
32 "Indeed you *are* to them as a
very lovely song of one who has
a pleasant voice and can play well
on an instrument; for they hear
your words, but they do [a]not do
them.
33 [a]"And when this comes to
pass—surely it will come—then
[b]they will know that a prophet has
been among them."

Irresponsible Shepherds

34 And the word of the LORD
came to me, saying,
2 "Son of man, prophesy against
the shepherds of Israel, prophesy
and say to them, 'Thus says the
Lord GOD to the shepherds: [a]"Woe
to the shepherds of Israel who feed
themselves! Should not the shep-
herds feed the flocks?
3 [a]"You eat the fat and clothe
yourselves with the wool; you
[b]slaughter the fatlings, *but* you do
not feed the flock.
4 [a]"The weak you have not
strengthened, nor have you healed

those who were sick, nor bound up
the broken, nor brought back what
was driven away, nor [b]sought
what was lost; but with [c]force and
[1]cruelty you have ruled them.
5 [a]"So they were [b]scattered be-
cause *there was* no shepherd; [c]and
they became food for all the beasts
of the field when they were scat-
tered.
6 "My sheep [a]wandered through
all the mountains, and on every
high hill; yes, My flock was scat-
tered over the whole face of the
earth, and no one was seeking or
searching *for them.*"
7 'Therefore, you shepherds,
hear the word of the LORD:
8 "*As* I live," says the Lord GOD,
"surely because My flock became
a prey, and My flock [a]became food
for every beast of the field, be-
cause *there was* no shepherd, nor
did My shepherds search for My
flock, [b]but the shepherds fed them-
selves and did not feed My
flock"—
9 'therefore, O shepherds, hear
the word of the LORD!
10 'Thus says the Lord GOD:
"Behold, I *am* [a]against the shep-
herds, and [b]I will require My flock
at their hand; I will cause them to
cease feeding the sheep, and the
shepherds shall [c]feed themselves
no more; for I will [d]deliver My
flock from their mouths, that they
may no longer be food for them."

God, the True Shepherd

11 'For thus says the Lord GOD:
"Indeed I Myself will search for
My sheep and seek them out.
12 "As a [a]shepherd seeks out his
flock on the day he is among his
scattered sheep, so will I seek out
My sheep and deliver them from
all the places where they were
scattered on [b]a cloudy and dark
day.
13 "And [a]I will bring them out
from the peoples and gather them
from the countries, and will bring
them to their own land; I will feed
them on the mountains of Israel,
[1]in the valleys and in all the inhab-
ited places of the country.
14 [a]"I will feed them in good pas-
ture, and their fold shall be on the
high mountains of Israel. [b]There
they shall lie down in a good fold
and feed in rich pasture on the
mountains of Israel.
15 "I will feed My flock, and I will
make them lie down," says the
Lord GOD.
16 [a]"I will seek what was lost and
bring back what was driven away,
bind up the broken and strengthen
what was sick; but I will destroy
[b]the fat and the strong, and feed
them [c]in judgment."
17 'And *as for* you, O My flock,
thus says the Lord GOD: [a]"Behold,
I shall judge between sheep and
sheep, between rams and goats.
18 "*Is it* too little for you to have
eaten up the good pasture, that
you must tread down with your
feet the [1]residue of your pasture—
and to have drunk of the clear wa-
ters, that you must foul the residue
with your feet?
19 "And *as for* My flock, they eat
what you have trampled with your
feet, and they drink what you have
fouled with your feet."
20 'Therefore thus says the Lord
GOD to them: [a]"Behold, I Myself
will judge between the fat and the
lean sheep.
21 "Because you have pushed
with side and shoulder, butted all
the weak ones with your horns,
and scattered them abroad,
22 "therefore I will save My flock,
and they shall no longer be a prey;
and I will judge between sheep and
sheep.
23 "I will establish one [a]shepherd
over them, and he shall feed
them—[b]My servant David. He
shall feed them and be their shep-
herd.
24 "And [a]I, the LORD, will be their
God, and My servant David [b]a
prince among them; I, the LORD,
have spoken.
25 [a]"I will make a covenant of
peace with them, and [b]cause wild
beasts to cease from the land; and
they [c]will dwell safely in the wil-
derness and sleep in the woods.
26 "I will make them and the
places all around [a]My hill [b]a bless-
ing; and I will [c]cause showers to
come down in their season; there
shall be [d]showers of blessing.
27 "Then [a]the trees of the field
shall yield their fruit, and the earth
shall yield her increase. They shall
be safe in their land; and they shall

4 [b]Luke 15:4 [c][1 Pet. 5:3] [1]*harshness* or *rigor*
5 [a]Ezek. 33:21 [b]Matt. 9:36 [c]Is. 56:9
6 [a]1 Pet. 2:25
8 [a]Ezek. 34:5, 6 [b]Ezek. 34:2, 10
10 [a]Jer. 21:13; 52:24–27 [b]Heb. 13:17 [c]Ezek. 34:2, 8 [d]Ezek. 13:23
12 [a]Jer. 31:10 [b]Ezek. 30:3
13 [a]Jer. 23:3 [1]Or *by the streams*
14 [a][John 10:9] [b]Jer. 33:12
16 [a]Mic. 4:6 [b]Is. 10:16 [c]Jer. 10:24
17 [a][Matt. 25:32]
18 [1]*remainder*
20 [a]Ezek. 34:17
23 [a][Is. 40:11] [b]Jer. 30:9
24 [a]Ex. 29:45 [b]Ezek. 37:24, 25
25 [a]Ezek. 37:26 [b]Is. 11:6–9 [c]Jer. 23:6
26 [a]Is. 56:7 [b]Zech. 8:13 [c]Lev. 26:4 [d]Ps. 68:9
27 [a]Is. 4:2

know that I *am* the LORD, when I
have [b]broken the bands of their
yoke and delivered them from the
hand of those who [c]enslaved them.
28 "And they shall no longer be
a prey for the nations, nor shall
beasts of the land devour them;
but [a]they shall dwell safely, and
no one shall make *them* afraid.
29 "I will raise up for them a [a]garden[1] of renown, and they shall [b]no
longer be consumed with hunger
in the land, [c]nor bear the shame
of the Gentiles anymore.
30 "Thus they shall know that [a]I,
the LORD their God, *am* with them,
and they, the house of Israel, *are*
[b]My people," says the Lord GOD.' "
31 "You are My [a]flock, the flock
of My pasture; you *are* men, *and*
I *am* your God," says the Lord
GOD.

Judgment on Mount Seir

35 Moreover the word of the
LORD came to me, saying,
2 "Son of man, set your face
against [a]Mount Seir and [b]prophesy against it,
3 "and say to it, 'Thus says the
Lord GOD:

"Behold, O Mount Seir, I *am*
against you;
[a]I will stretch out My hand against
you,
And make you [1]most desolate;
4 I shall lay your cities waste,
And you shall be desolate.
Then you shall know that I *am*
the LORD.

5 [a]"Because you have had an
[1]ancient hatred, and have shed *the
blood of* the children of Israel by
the power of the sword at the time
of their calamity, [b]*when* their iniquity *came to an* end,
6 "therefore, *as* I live," says the
Lord GOD, "I will prepare you for
[a]blood, and blood shall pursue
you; [b]since you have not hated
[1]blood, therefore blood shall pursue you.
7 "Thus I will make Mount Seir
[1]most desolate, and cut off from it
the [a]one who leaves and the one
who returns.
8 "And I will fill its mountains
with the slain; on your hills and
in your valleys and in all your ravines those who are slain by the
sword shall fall.
9 [a]"I will make you [1]perpetually
desolate, and your cities shall be
uninhabited; [b]then you shall know
that I *am* the LORD.
10 "Because you have said, 'These
two nations and these two countries shall be mine, and we will
[a]possess them,' although [b]the
LORD was there,
11 "therefore, *as* I live," says the
Lord GOD, "I will do [a]according to
your anger and according to the
envy which you showed in your
hatred against them; and I will
make Myself known among them
when I judge you.
12 [a]"Then you shall know that I
am the LORD. I have [b]heard all
your [c]blasphemies which you have
spoken against the mountains of
Israel, saying, 'They are desolate;
they are given to us to consume.'
13 "Thus [a]with your mouth you
have [1]boasted against Me and multiplied your [b]words against Me; I
have heard *them.*"
14 'Thus says the Lord GOD: [a]"The
whole earth will rejoice when I
make you desolate.
15 [a]"As you rejoiced because the
inheritance of the house of Israel
was desolate, [b]so I will do to you;
you shall be desolate, O Mount
Seir, as well as all of Edom—all
of it! Then they shall know that I
am the LORD." '

Blessing on Israel

36 "And you, son of man,
prophesy to the [a]mountains
of Israel, and say, 'O mountains of
Israel, hear the word of the LORD!
2 'Thus says the Lord GOD: "Because [a]the enemy has said of you,
'Aha! [b]The [1]ancient heights [c]have
become our possession,' " '
3 "therefore prophesy, and say,
'Thus says the Lord GOD: "Because
they made *you* desolate and swallowed you up on every side, so that
you became the possession of the
rest of the nations, [a]and you are
taken up by the lips of [b]talkers and
slandered by the people"—
4 'therefore, O mountains of Israel, hear the word of the Lord
GOD! Thus says the Lord GOD to
the mountains, the hills, the

27 [b]Jer. 2:20 [c]Jer. 25:14
28 [a]Jer. 30:10
29 [a][Is. 11:1] [b]Ezek. 36:29 [c]Ezek. 36:3, 6, 15 [1]Lit. *planting place*
30 [a]Ezek. 34:24 [b]Ezek. 14:11; 36:28
31 [a]Ps. 100:3

CHAPTER 35

2 [a]Ezek. 25:12–14 [b]Amos 1:11
3 [a]Ezek. 6:14 [1]Lit. *a desolation and a waste*
5 [a]Ezek. 25:12 [b]Ps. 137:7 [1]Or *everlasting*
6 [a]Is. 63:1–6 [b]Ps. 109:17 [1]Or *bloodshed*
7 [a]Judg. 5:6 [1]Lit. *a waste and a desolation*
9 [a]Jer. 49:13 [b]Ezek. 36:11 [1]Lit. *desolated forever*
10 [a]Ps. 83:4–12 [b][Ps. 48:1–3; 132:13, 14]
11 [a][James 2:13]
12 [a]Ps. 9:16 [b]Zeph. 2:8 [c]Is. 52:5
13 [a][1 Sam. 2:3] [b]Ezek. 36:3 [1]Lit. *made yourself great*
14 [a]Is. 65:13, 14
15 [a]Obad. 12, 15 [b]Lam. 4:21

CHAPTER 36

1 [a]Ezek. 6:2, 3
2 [a]Ezek. 25:3; 26:2 [b]Deut. 32:13 [c]Ezek. 35:10 [1]Or *everlasting*
3 [a]Deut. 28:37 [b]Ezek. 35:13

[1]rivers, the valleys, the desolate
wastes, and the cities that have
been forsaken, which [a]became
plunder and [b]mockery to the rest
of the nations all around—
5 'therefore thus says the Lord
GOD: [a]"Surely I have spoken in My
burning jealousy against the rest
of the nations and against all
Edom, [b]who gave My land to
themselves as a possession, with
wholehearted joy *and* [1]spiteful
minds, in order to plunder its open
country." '
6 "Therefore prophesy concerning the land of Israel, and say to
the mountains, the hills, the rivers,
and the valleys, 'Thus says the
Lord GOD: "Behold, I have spoken
in My jealousy and My fury, because you have [a]borne the shame
of the nations."
7 'Therefore thus says the Lord
GOD: "I have [a]raised My hand in
an oath that surely the nations that
are around you shall [b]bear their
own shame.
8 "But you, O mountains of Israel, you shall shoot forth your
branches and yield your fruit to
My people Israel, for they are
about to come.
9 "For indeed I *am* for you, and
I will turn to you, and you shall
be tilled and sown.
10 "I will multiply men upon you,
all the house of Israel, all of it; and
the cities shall be inhabited and
[a]the ruins rebuilt.
11 [a]"I will multiply upon you man
and beast; and they shall increase
and [1]bear young; I will make you
inhabited as in former times, and
do [b]better *for you* than at your beginnings. [c]Then you shall know
that I *am* the LORD.
12 "Yes, I will cause men to walk
on you, My people Israel; [a]they
shall take possession of you, and
you shall be their inheritance; no
more shall you [b]bereave them *of
children.*"
13 'Thus says the Lord GOD: "Because they say to you, [a]'You devour men and bereave your nation
of children,'
14 "therefore you shall devour
men no more, nor bereave your
nation anymore," says the Lord
GOD.
15 [a]"Nor will I let you hear the
taunts of the nations anymore, nor
bear the reproach of the peoples
anymore, nor shall you cause your
nation to stumble anymore," says
the Lord GOD.' "

The Renewal of Israel

16 Moreover the word of the LORD
came to me, saying:
17 "Son of man, when the house
of Israel dwelt in their own land,
[a]they defiled it by their own ways
and deeds; to Me their way was
like [b]the uncleanness of a woman
in her customary impurity.
18 "Therefore I poured out My
fury on them [a]for the blood they
had shed on the land, and for their
idols *with which* they had defiled it.
19 "So I [a]scattered them among
the nations, and they were dispersed throughout the countries; I
judged them [b]according to their
ways and their deeds.
20 "When they came to the nations, wherever they went, they
[a]profaned My holy name—when
they said of them, 'These *are* the
people of the LORD, *and* yet they
have gone out of His land.'
21 "But I had concern [a]for My
holy name, which the house of Israel had profaned among the nations wherever they went.
22 "Therefore say to the house of
Israel, 'Thus says the Lord GOD:
"I do not do *this* for your sake, O
house of Israel, [a]but for My holy
name's sake, which you have profaned among the nations wherever
you went.
23 "And I will sanctify My great
name, which has been profaned
among the nations, which you
have profaned in their midst; and
the nations shall know that I *am*
the LORD," says the Lord GOD,
"when I am [a]hallowed in you before their eyes.
24 "For [a]I will take you from
among the nations, gather you out
of all countries, and bring you into
your own land.
25 [a]"Then I will sprinkle clean water on you, and you shall be clean;
I will cleanse you [b]from all your
filthiness and from all your idols.
26 "I will give you a [a]new heart
and put a new spirit within you; I
will take the heart of stone out of

4 [a]Ezek. 34:8, 28 [b]Ps. 79:4; Jer. 48:27 [1]Or *ravines*
5 [a]Deut. 4:24; Ezek. 38:19 [b]Ezek. 35:10, 12 [1]Lit. *scorning souls*
6 [a]Ps. 74:10; 123:3, 4; Ezek. 34:29
7 [a]Ezek. 20:5 [b]Jer. 25:9, 15, 29
10 [a]Is. 58:12; 61:4; Amos 9:14
11 [a]Jer. 31:27; 33:12 [b]Job 42:12; Is. 51:3 [c]Ezek. 35:9; 37:6, 13 [1]Lit. *be fruitful*
12 [a]Obad. 17 [b]Jer. 15:7; Ezek. 22:12, 27
13 [a]Num. 13:32
15 [a]Is. 60:14; Ezek. 34:29
17 [a]Lev. 18:25, 27, 28; Jer. 2:7 [b]Lev. 15:19
18 [a]Ezek. 16:36, 38; 23:37
19 [a]Deut. 28:64; Ezek. 5:12; 22:15; Amos 9:9 [b]Ezek. 7:3; 18:30; 39:24; [Rom. 2:6]
20 [a]Is. 52:5; Ezek. 12:16; Rom. 2:24
21 [a]Ezek. 20:9, 14
22 [a]Ps. 106:8; Ezek. 20:44
23 [a]Is. 5:16; Ezek. 20:41; 28:22
24 [a]Is. 43:5, 6; Ezek. 34:13; 37:21
25 [a]Num. 19:17–19; Ps. 51:7; Is. 52:15; Heb. 9:13, 19; 10:22 [b]Jer. 33:8
26 [a]Ps. 51:10; Jer. 32:39; Ezek. 11:19; [John 3:3]

your flesh and give you a heart of
flesh.
27 "I will put My [a]Spirit within
you and cause you to walk in My
statutes, and you will keep My
judgments and do *them*.
28 [a]"Then you shall dwell in the
land that I gave to your fathers;
[b]you shall be My people, and I will
be your God.
29 "I will [a]deliver you from all
your uncleannesses. [b]I will call for
the grain and multiply it, and
[c]bring no famine upon you.
30 [a]"And I will multiply the fruit
of your trees and the increase of
your fields, so that you need never
again bear the reproach of famine
among the nations.
31 "Then [a]you will remember
your evil ways and your deeds that
were not good; and you [b]will
[1]loathe yourselves in your own
sight, for your iniquities and your
abominations.
32 [a]"Not for your sake do I do
this," says the Lord GOD, "let it be
known to you. Be ashamed and
confounded for your own ways, O
house of Israel!"
33 'Thus says the Lord GOD: "On
the day that I cleanse you from all
your iniquities, I will also enable
you to dwell in the cities, [a]and the
ruins shall be rebuilt.
34 "The desolate land shall be
tilled instead of lying desolate in
the sight of all who pass by.
35 "So they will say, 'This land
that was desolate has become like
the garden of [a]Eden; and the
wasted, desolate, and ruined
cities *are now* fortified *and* inhab-
ited.'
36 "Then the nations which are
left all around you shall know that
I, the LORD, have rebuilt the ruined
places *and* planted what was deso-
late. [a]I, the LORD, have spoken *it*,
and I will do *it*."
37 'Thus says the Lord GOD: [a]"I
will also let the house of Israel in-
quire of Me to do this for them: I
will [b]increase their men like a
flock.
38 "Like a [1]flock *offered as* holy
sacrifices, like the flock at Jerusa-
lem on its [2]feast days, so shall the
ruined cities be filled with flocks
of men. Then they shall know that
I *am* the LORD."'"

27 [a]Is. 44:3; 59:21; Ezek. 11:19; 37:14; [Joel 2:28, 29]
28 [a]Ezek. 28:25; 37:25 [b]Jer. 30:22; Ezek. 11:20; 37:27
29 [a]Zech. 13:1; [Matt. 1:21; Rom. 11:26] [b]Ps. 105:16 [c]Ezek. 34:27, 29; Hos. 2:21–23
30 [a]Lev. 26:4; Ezek. 34:27
31 [a]Ezek. 16:61, 63 [b]Lev. 26:39; Ezek. 6:9; 20:43 [1]*despise*
32 [a]Deut. 9:5
33 [a]Ezek. 36:10
35 [a]Is. 51:3; Ezek. 28:13; Joel 2:3
36 [a]Ezek. 17:24; 22:14; 37:14; Hos. 14:4–9
37 [a]Ezek. 14:3; 20:3, 31 [b]Ezek. 36:10
38 [1]Lit. *holy flock* [2]*appointed feasts*

CHAPTER 37

1 [a]Ezek. 1:3 [b]Ezek. 3:14; 8:3; 11:24; Acts 8:39
3 [a][Deut. 32:39; 1 Sam. 2:6; John 5:21; Rom. 4:17; 2 Cor. 1:9]
5 [a]Gen. 2:7; Ps. 104:29, 30; Ezek. 37:9, 10, 14
6 [a]Is. 49:23; Ezek. 6:7; 35:12; Joel 2:27; 3:17
9 [a][Ps. 104:30] [1]Breath of life
10 [a]Rev. 11:11 [1]Breath of life
11 [a]Jer. 33:24; Ezek. 36:10 [b]Ps. 141:7; Is. 49:14
12 [a]Deut. 32:39; 1 Sam. 2:6; Is. 26:19; 66:14; [Dan. 12:2]; Hos. 13:14 [b]Ezek. 36:24

The Dry Bones Live

37 The [a]hand of the LORD came
upon me and brought me out
[b]in the Spirit of the LORD, and set
me down in the midst of the valley;
and it *was* full of bones.
2 Then He caused me to pass by
them all around, and behold, *there
were* very many in the open valley;
and indeed *they were* very dry.
3 And He said to me, "Son of
man, can these bones live?" So I
answered, "O Lord GOD, [a]You
know."
4 Again He said to me, "Proph-
esy to these bones, and say to
them, 'O dry bones, hear the word
of the LORD!
5 'Thus says the Lord GOD to
these bones: "Surely I will [a]cause
breath to enter into you, and you
shall live.
6 "I will put sinews on you and
bring flesh upon you, cover you
with skin and put breath in you;
and you shall live. [a]Then you shall
know that I *am* the LORD." '"
7 So I prophesied as I was com-
manded; and as I prophesied,
there was a noise, and suddenly a
rattling; and the bones came to-
gether, bone to bone.
8 Indeed, as I looked, the sinews
and the flesh came upon them, and
the skin covered them over; but
there was no breath in them.
9 Also He said to me, "Prophesy
to the breath, prophesy, son of
man, and say to the [1]breath, 'Thus
says the Lord GOD: [a]"Come from
the four winds, O breath, and
breathe on these slain, that they
may live." '"
10 So I prophesied as He com-
manded me, [a]and [1]breath came
into them, and they lived, and
stood upon their feet, an exceed-
ingly great army.
11 Then He said to me, "Son of
man, these bones are the [a]whole
house of Israel. They indeed say,
[b]'Our bones are dry, our hope is
lost, and we ourselves are cut off!'
12 "Therefore prophesy and say
to them, 'Thus says the Lord GOD:
"Behold, [a]O My people, I will open
your graves and cause you to come
up from your graves, and [b]bring
you into the land of Israel.
13 "Then you shall know that I *am*
the LORD, when I have opened

your graves, O My people, and
brought you up from your graves.
14 "I [a]will put My Spirit in you,
and you shall live, and I will place
you in your own land. Then you
shall know that I, the LORD, have
spoken *it* and performed *it*," says
the LORD.' "

One Kingdom, One King

15 Again the word of the LORD
came to me, saying,
16 "As for you, son of man, [a]take
a stick for yourself and write on
it: 'For Judah and for [b]the children
of Israel, his companions.' Then
take another stick and write on it,
'For Joseph, the stick of Ephraim,
and *for* all the house of Israel, his
companions.'
17 "Then [a]join them one to an-
other for yourself into one stick,
and they will become one in your
hand.
18 "And when the children of
your people speak to you, saying,
[a]'Will you not show us what you
mean by these?'—
19 [a]"say to them, 'Thus says the
Lord GOD: "Surely I will take [b]the
stick of Joseph, which *is* in the
hand of Ephraim, and the tribes of
Israel, his companions; and I will
join them with it, with the stick
of Judah, and make them one
stick, and they will be one in My
hand." '
20 "And the sticks on which you
write will be in your hand [a]before
their eyes.
21 "Then say to them, 'Thus says
the Lord GOD: "Surely [a]I will take
the children of Israel from among
the nations, wherever they have
gone, and will gather them from
every side and bring them into
their own land;
22 "and [a]I will make them one na-
tion in the land, on the mountains
of Israel; and [b]one king shall be
king over them all; they shall no
longer be two nations, nor shall
they ever be divided into two king-
doms again.
23 [a]"They shall not defile them-
selves anymore with their idols,
nor with their detestable things,
nor with any of their transgres-
sions; but [b]I will deliver them from
all their dwelling places in which
they have sinned, and will cleanse

14 [a]Ezek. 36:27
16 [a]Num. 17:2, 3 [b]2 Chr. 11:12, 13, 16; 15:9; 30:11, 18
17 [a]Hos. 1:11
18 [a]Ezek. 12:9; 24:19
19 [a]Zech. 10:6 [b]Ezek. 37:16, 17
20 [a]Ezek. 12:3
21 [a]Ezek. 36:24
22 [a]Jer. 3:18 [b]Ezek. 34:23
23 [a]Ezek. 36:25 [b]Ezek. 36:28, 29
24 [a]Is. 40:11; [Luke 1:32]; 1 Pet. 2:25 [b][John 10:16] [c]Ezek. 36:27
25 [a]Ezek. 36:28; Rev. 21:3; 22:3 [b]Is. 60:21 [c]John 12:34
26 [a]Is. 55:3 [b]Ezek. 36:10 [c][2 Cor. 6:16] [1]Lit. *cut*
27 [a][John 1:14] [b]Ezek. 11:20
28 [a]Ezek. 36:23 [b]Ezek. 20:12

CHAPTER 38

2 [a]Ezek. 39:1 [b]Ezek. 35:2, 3 [c]Rev. 20:8 [d]Gen. 10:2 [e]Ezek. 32:26 [1]Tg., Vg., Aquila *the chief prince of Meshech,* also v. 3
4 [a]2 Kin. 19:28 [b]Is. 43:17 [c]Ezek. 23:12
5 [1]Heb. *Cush* [2]Heb. *Put*
6 [a]Gen. 10:2 [b]Ezek. 27:14
7 [a]Is. 8:9, 10
8 [a]Is. 24:22 [b]Is. 29:6

them. Then they shall be My peo-
ple, and I will be their God.
24 [a]"David My servant *shall be*
king over them, and [b]they shall all
have one shepherd; [c]they shall
also walk in My judgments and ob-
serve My statutes, and do them.
25 [a]"Then they shall dwell in the
land that I have given to Jacob My
servant, where your fathers dwelt;
and they shall dwell there, they,
their children, and their children's
children, [b]forever; and [c]My ser-
vant David *shall be* their prince
forever.
26 "Moreover I will [1]make [a]a cov-
enant of peace with them, and it
shall be an everlasting covenant
with them; I will establish them
and [b]multiply them, and I will set
My [c]sanctuary in their midst for-
evermore.
27 [a]"My tabernacle also shall be
with them; indeed I will be [b]their
God, and they shall be My people.
28 [a]"The nations also will know
that I, the LORD, [b]sanctify Israel,
when My sanctuary is in their
midst forevermore." ' "

Gog and Allies Attack Israel

38 Now the word of the LORD
came to me, saying,
2 [a]"Son of man, [b]set your face
against [c]Gog, of the land of [d]Ma-
gog, [1]the prince of Rosh, [e]Meshech,
and Tubal, and prophesy against
him,
3 "and say, 'Thus says the Lord
GOD: "Behold, I *am* against you,
O Gog, the prince of Rosh, Me-
shech, and Tubal.
4 [a]"I will turn you around, put
hooks into your jaws, and [b]lead
you out, with all your army,
horses, and horsemen, [c]all splen-
didly clothed, a great company
with bucklers and shields, all of
them handling swords.
5 "Persia, [1]Ethiopia, and [2]Libya
are with them, all of them *with*
shield and helmet;
6 [a]"Gomer and all its troops; the
house of [b]Togarmah *from* the far
north and all its troops—many
people *are* with you.
7 [a]"Prepare yourself and be
ready, you and all your companies
that are gathered about you; and
be a guard for them.
8 [a]"After many days [b]you will be

visited. In the latter years you will
come into the land of those
brought back from the sword [c]*and*
gathered from many people on
[d]the mountains of Israel, which
had long been desolate; they were
brought out of the nations, and
now all of them [e]dwell safely.
9 "You will ascend, coming [a]like
a storm, covering the [b]land like a
cloud, you and all your troops and
many peoples with you."
10 'Thus says the Lord GOD: "On
that day it shall come to pass *that*
thoughts will arise in your mind,
and you will make an evil plan:
11 "You will say, 'I will go up
against a land of [a]unwalled vil-
lages; I will [b]go to a peaceful peo-
ple, [c]who dwell [1]safely, all of them
dwelling without walls, and hav-
ing neither bars nor gates'—
12 "to take plunder and to take
booty, to stretch out your hand
against the waste places *that are*
again inhabited, [a]and against a
people gathered from the nations,
who have acquired livestock and
goods, who dwell in the midst of
the land.
13 [a]"Sheba, [b]Dedan, the mer-
chants [c]of Tarshish, and all [d]their
young lions will say to you, 'Have
you come to take plunder? Have
you gathered your army to take
booty, to carry away silver and
gold, to take away livestock and
goods, to take great plunder?' " '
14 "Therefore, son of man, proph-
esy and say to Gog, 'Thus says
the Lord GOD: [a]"On that day when
My people Israel [b]dwell safely, will
you not know *it?*
15 [a]"Then you will come from
your place out of the far north, you
and many peoples with you, all of
them riding on horses, a great
company and a mighty army.
16 "You will come up against My
people Israel like a cloud, to cover
the land. It will be in the latter days
that I will bring you against My
land, so that the nations may
[a]know Me, when I am [b]hallowed in
you, O Gog, before their eyes."
17 'Thus says the Lord GOD: "Are
you he of whom I have spoken in
former days by My servants the
prophets of Israel, who prophesied
for years in those days that I would
bring you against them?

Judgment on Gog

18 "And it will come to pass at the
same time, when Gog comes
against the land of Israel," says the
Lord GOD, "*that* My fury will show
in My face.
19 "For [a]in My jealousy [b]*and* in
the fire of My wrath I have spoken:
[c]'Surely in that day there shall be
a great [1]earthquake in the land of
Israel,
20 'so that [a]the fish of the sea, the
birds of the heavens, the beasts of
the field, all creeping things that
creep on the earth, and all men
who *are* on the face of the earth
shall shake at My presence. [b]The
mountains shall be thrown down,
the steep places shall fall, and
every wall shall fall to the ground.'
21 "I will [a]call for [b]a sword
against Gog throughout all My
mountains," says the Lord GOD.
[c]"Every man's sword will be
against his brother.
22 "And I will [a]bring him to judg-
ment with [b]pestilence and blood-
shed; [c]I will rain down on him, on
his troops, and on the many peo-
ples who *are* with him, flooding
rain, [d]great hailstones, fire, and
brimstone.
23 "Thus I will magnify Myself
and [a]sanctify Myself, [b]and I will
be known in the eyes of many na-
tions. Then they shall know that I
am the LORD." '

Gog's Armies Destroyed

39 "And [a]you, son of man,
prophesy against Gog, and
say, 'Thus says the Lord GOD: "Be-
hold, I *am* against you, O Gog, [1]the
prince of Rosh, Meshech, and Tu-
bal;
2 "and I will [a]turn you around
and lead you on, [b]bringing you up
from the far north, and bring you
against the mountains of Israel.
3 "Then I will knock the bow out
of your left hand, and cause the
arrows to fall out of your right
hand.
4 [a]"You shall [1]fall upon the
mountains of Israel, you and all
your troops and the peoples who
are with you; [b]I will give you to
birds of prey of every sort and *to*
the beasts of the field to be de-
voured.

8 [c]Ezek. 34:13 [d]Ezek. 36:1, 4 [e]Jer. 23:6; Ezek. 34:25; 39:26
9 [a]Is. 28:2 [b]Jer. 4:13
11 [a]Zech. 2:4 [b]Jer. 49:31 [c]Ezek. 38:8 [1]*securely*
12 [a]Ezek. 38:8
13 [a]Ezek. 27:22 [b]Ezek. 27:15, 20 [c]Ezek. 27:12 [d]Ezek. 19:3, 5
14 [a]Is. 4:1 [b]Jer. 23:6; Ezek. 38:8, 11; [Zech. 2:5, 8]
15 [a]Ezek. 39:2
16 [a]Ezek. 35:11 [b]Is. 5:16; 8:13; 29:23; Ezek. 28:22
19 [a]Deut. 32:21, 22; Ps. 18:7, 8; Ezek. 36:5, 6; [Nah. 1:2]; Heb. 12:29 [b]Ps. 89:46 [c]Joel 3:16; Hag. 2:6, 7; Rev. 16:18 [1]Lit. *shaking*
20 [a]Hos. 4:3 [b]Jer. 4:24; Nah. 1:5, 6
21 [a]Ps. 105:16 [b]Ezek. 14:17 [c]Judg. 7:22; 1 Sam. 14:20; 2 Chr. 20:23; Hag. 2:22
22 [a]Is. 66:16; Jer. 25:31 [b]Ezek. 5:17 [c]Ps. 11:6; Is. 30:30; Ezek. 13:11 [d]Rev. 16:21
23 [a]Ezek. 36:23 [b]Ps. 9:16; Ezek. 37:28; 38:16

CHAPTER 39

1 [a]Ezek. 38:2, 3 [1]Tg., Vg., Aquila *the chief prince of Meshech*
2 [a]Ezek. 38:8 [b]Ezek. 38:15
4 [a]Ezek. 38:4, 21 [b]Ezek. 33:27 [1]Be slain

5 "You shall [1]fall on [2]the open
field; for I have spoken," says the
Lord GOD.
6 [a]"And I will send fire on Magog
and on those who live [1]in security
in [b]the coastlands. Then they shall
know that I *am* the LORD.
7 [a]"So I will make My holy name
known in the midst of My people
Israel, and I will not *let them* [b]pro-
fane My holy name anymore.
[c]Then the nations shall know that
I am the LORD, the Holy One in Is-
rael.
8 [a]"Surely it is coming, and it
shall be done," says the Lord GOD.
"This *is* the day [b]of which I have
spoken.
9 "Then those who dwell in the
cities of Israel will go out and set
on fire and burn the weapons, both
the shields and bucklers, the bows
and arrows, the [1]javelins and
spears; and they will make fires
with them for seven years.
10 "They will not take wood from
the field nor cut down *any* from
the forests, because they will make
fires with the weapons; [a]and they
will plunder those who plundered
them, and pillage those who pil-
laged them," says the Lord GOD.

The Burial of Gog

11 "It will come to pass in that day
that I will give Gog a burial place
there in Israel, the valley of those
who pass by east of the sea; and
it will obstruct travelers, because
there they will bury Gog and all
his multitude. Therefore they will
call *it* the Valley of [1]Hamon Gog.
12 "For seven months the house
of Israel will be burying them, [a]in
order to cleanse the land.
13 "Indeed all the people of the
land will be burying, and they will
gain [a]renown for it on the day that
[b]I am glorified," says the Lord
GOD.
14 "They will set apart men regu-
larly employed, with the help of [1]a
search party, to pass through the
land and bury those bodies re-
maining on the ground, in order
[a]to cleanse it. At the end of seven
months they will make a search.
15 "The search party will pass
through the land; and *when any-
one* sees a man's bone, he shall
[1]set up a marker by it, till the buri-
ers have buried it in the Valley of
Hamon Gog.
16 "*The* name of *the* city *will* also
be [1]Hamonah. Thus they shall
[a]cleanse the land." '

A Triumphant Festival

17 "And as for you, son of man,
thus says the Lord GOD, [a]'Speak
to every sort of bird and to every
beast of the field:

[b]"Assemble yourselves and come;
Gather together from all sides to
My [c]sacrificial meal
Which I am sacrificing for you,
A great sacrificial meal [d]on the
mountains of Israel,
That you may eat flesh and drink
blood.
18 [a]You shall eat the flesh of the
mighty,
Drink the blood of the princes of
the earth,
Of rams and lambs,
Of goats and bulls,
All of them [b]fatlings of Bashan.
19 You shall eat fat till you are full,
And drink blood till you are
drunk,
At My sacrificial meal
Which I am sacrificing for you.
20 [a]You shall be filled at My table
With horses and riders,
[b]With mighty men
And with all the men of war,"
says the Lord GOD.

Israel Restored to the Land

21 [a]"I will set My glory among the
nations; all the nations shall see
My judgment which I have exe-
cuted, and [b]My hand which I have
laid on them.
22 [a]"So the house of Israel shall
know that I *am* the LORD their God
from that day forward.
23 [a]"The Gentiles shall know that
the house of Israel went into cap-
tivity for their iniquity; because
they were unfaithful to Me, there-
fore [b]I hid My face from them. I
[c]gave them into the hand of their
enemies, and they all fell by the
sword.
24 [a]"According to their unclean-
ness and according to their trans-
gressions I have dealt with them,
and hidden My face from them." '
25 "Therefore thus says the Lord
GOD: [a]'Now I will bring back the
captives of Jacob, and have mercy

5 [1]Be slain [2]Lit. *the face of the field*
6 [a]Ezek. 38:22; Amos 1:4, 7, 10; Nah. 1:6 [b]Ps. 72:10; Is. 66:19; Jer. 25:22 [1]*securely* or *confidently*
7 [a]Ezek. 39:25 [b]Lev. 18:21; Ezek. 36:23 [c]Ezek. 38:16
8 [a]Rev. 16:17; 21:6 [b]Ezek. 38:17
9 [1]Lit. *hand staffs*
10 [a]Is. 14:2; 33:1; Mic. 5:8; Hab. 2:8
11 [1]Lit. *The Multitude of Gog*
12 [a]Deut. 21:23; Ezek. 39:14, 16
13 [a]Jer. 33:9; Zeph. 3:19, 20 [b]Ezek. 28:22
14 [a]Ezek. 39:12 [1]Lit. *those who pass through*
15 [1]*build*
16 [a]Ezek. 39:12 [1]Lit. *Multitude*
17 [a]Is. 56:9; [Jer. 12:9]; Ezek. 39:4; Rev. 19:17, 18 [b]Is. 18:6 [c]Is. 34:6, 7; Jer. 46:10; Zeph. 1:7 [d]Ezek. 39:4
18 [a]Ezek. 29:5; Rev. 19:18 [b]Deut. 32:14; Ps. 22:12
20 [a]Ps. 76:5, 6; Ezek. 38:4; Hag. 2:22 [b]Rev. 19:18
21 [a]Ex. 9:16; Is. 37:20; Ezek. 36:23; 38:23 [b]Ex. 7:4
22 [a]Ex. 39:7, 28
23 [a]Jer. 22:8, 9; 44:22; Ezek. 36:18–20, 23 [b]Deut. 31:17; Is. 1:15; 59:2; Ezek. 39:29 [c]Lev. 26:25
24 [a]2 Kin. 17:7; Jer. 2:17, 19; 4:18; Ezek. 36:19
25 [a]Is. 27:12, 13; Jer. 30:3, 18; Ezek. 34:13; 36:24

on the [b]whole house of Israel; and
I will be jealous for My holy
name—
26 [a]'after they have borne their
shame, and all their unfaithfulness
in which they were unfaithful to
Me, when they [b]dwelt safely in
their *own* land and no one made
them afraid.
27 [a]'When I have brought them
back from the peoples and gath-
ered them out of their enemies'
lands, and I [b]am hallowed in them
in the sight of many nations,
28 [a]'then they shall know that I
am the LORD their God, who sent
them into captivity among the na-
tions, but also brought them back
to their land, and left none of them
[1]captive any longer.
29 [a]'And I will not hide My face
from them anymore; for I shall
have [b]poured out My Spirit on the
house of Israel,' says the Lord
GOD."

A New City, a New Temple

40 In the twenty-fifth year of
our captivity, at the begin-
ning of the year, on the tenth *day*
of the month, in the fourteenth
year after [a]the city was [1]captured,
on the very same day [b]the hand
of the LORD was upon me; and He
took me there.
2 [a]In the visions of God He took
me into the land of Israel and [b]set
me on a very high mountain; on
it toward the south *was* something
like the structure of a city.
3 He took me there, and behold,
there was a man whose appear-
ance *was* [a]like the appearance of
bronze. [b]He had a line of flax [c]and
a measuring rod in his hand, and
he stood in the gateway.
4 And the man said to me, [a]"Son
of man, look with your eyes and
hear with your ears, and [1]fix your
mind on everything I show you;
for you *were* brought here so that
I might show *them* to you. [b]De-
clare to the house of Israel every-
thing you see."
5 Now there was [a]a wall all
around the outside of the [1]temple.
In the man's hand was a measur-
ing rod six [2]cubits *long, each being*
a cubit and a handbreadth; and he
measured the width of the wall
structure, one rod; and the height,
one rod.

The Eastern Gateway of the Temple

6 Then he went to the gateway
which faced [a]east; and he went up
its stairs and measured the thresh-
old of the gateway, *which was* one
rod wide, and the other threshold
was one rod wide.
7 Each gate chamber *was* one
rod long and one rod wide; be-
tween the gate chambers *was a*
space of five cubits; and the
threshold of the gateway by the
vestibule of the inside gate *was*
one rod.
8 He also measured the vestibule
of the inside gate, one rod.
9 Then he measured the vesti-
bule of the gateway, eight cubits;
and the gateposts, two cubits. The
vestibule of the gate *was* on the
inside.
10 In the eastern gateway *were*
three gate chambers on one side
and three on the other; the three
were all the same size; also the
gateposts were of the same size on
this side and that side.
11 He measured the width of the
entrance to the gateway, ten cu-
bits; *and* the length of the gate,
thirteen cubits.
12 *There was* a [1]space in front of
the gate chambers, one cubit *on*
this side and one cubit on that side;
the gate chambers *were* six cubits
on this side and six cubits on that
side.
13 Then he measured the gateway
from the roof of *one* gate chamber
to the roof of the other; the width
was twenty-five cubits, as door
faces door.
14 He measured the gateposts,
sixty cubits high, and the court all
around the gateway *extended* to
the gatepost.
15 *From* the front of the entrance
gate to the front of the vesti-
bule of the inner gate *was* fifty
cubits.
16 *There were* [a]beveled window
frames in the gate chambers and
in their intervening archways on
the inside of the gateway all
around, and likewise in the vesti-
bules. *There were* windows all
around on the inside. And on each
gatepost *were* [b]palm trees.

25 [b]Jer. 31:1; Ezek. 20:40; Hos. 1:11
26 [a]Dan. 9:16 [b]Lev. 26:5, 6
27 [a]Ezek. 28:25, 26 [b]Ezek. 36:23, 24; 38:16
28 [a]Ezek. 34:30 [1]Lit. *there*
29 [a]Is. 54:8, 9 [b]Is. 32:15; Ezek. 36:27; 37:14; [Joel 2:28; Zech. 12:10]; Acts 2:17

CHAPTER 40

1 [a]2 Kin. 25:1–4; Jer. 39:2, 3; 52:4–7; Ezek. 33:21 [b]Ezek. 1:3; 3:14, 22; 37:1 [1]Lit. *struck*
2 [a]Ezek. 1:1; 3:14; 8:3; 37:1; Dan. 7:1, 7 [b][Is. 2:2, 3]; Ezek. 17:23; 20:40; 37:22; [Mic. 4:1]; Rev. 21:10
3 [a]Ezek. 1:7; Dan. 10:6; Rev. 1:15 [b]Ezek. 47:3; Zech. 2:1, 2 [c]Rev. 11:1; 21:15
4 [a]Ezek. 44:5 [b]Ezek. 43:10 [1]Lit. *set your heart*
5 [a][Is. 26:1]; Ezek. 42:20 [1]Lit. *house* [2]A royal cubit of about 21 inches
6 [a]Ezek. 43:1
12 [1]Lit. *border*
16 [a]1 Kin. 6:4; Ezek. 41:16, 26 [b]1 Kin. 6:29, 32, 35; 2 Chr. 3:5; Ezek. 40:22, 26, 31, 34, 37; 41:18–20, 25, 26

The Outer Court

17 Then he brought me into [a]the outer court; and *there were* [b]chambers and a pavement made all around the court; [c]thirty chambers faced the pavement.

18 The pavement was by the side of the gateways, corresponding to the length of the gateways; *this was* the lower pavement.

19 Then he measured the width from the front of the lower gateway to the front of the inner court exterior, one hundred cubits toward the east and the north.

The Northern Gateway

20 On the outer court was also a gateway facing north, and he measured its length and its width.

21 Its gate chambers, three on this side and three on that side, its gateposts and its archways, had the same measurements as the first gate; its length *was* fifty cubits and its width twenty-five cubits.

22 Its windows and those of its archways, and also its palm trees, *had* the same measurements as the gateway facing east; it was ascended by seven steps, and its archway *was* in front of it.

23 A gate of the inner court was opposite the northern gateway, just as the eastern *gateway;* and he measured from gateway to gateway, one hundred cubits.

The Southern Gateway

24 After that he brought me toward the south, and there a gateway was facing south; and he measured its gateposts and archways according to these same measurements.

25 *There were* windows in it and in its archways all around like those windows; its length *was* fifty cubits and its width twenty-five cubits.

26 Seven steps led up to it, and its archway *was* in front of them; and it had palm trees on its gateposts, one on this side and one on that side.

27 *There was* also a gateway on the inner court, facing south; and he measured from gateway to gateway toward the south, one hundred cubits.

17 [a]Ezek. 10:5; 42:1; 46:21; Rev. 11:2 [b]1 Kin. 6:5; 2 Chr. 31:11; Ezek. 40:38 [c]Ezek. 45:5

30 [a]Ezek. 40:21, 25, 33, 36

38 [a]2 Chr. 4:6

39 [a]Lev. 4:2, 3

Gateways of the Inner Court

28 Then he brought me to the inner court through the southern gateway; he measured the southern gateway according to these same measurements.

29 Also its gate chambers, its gateposts, and its archways *were* according to these same measurements; *there were* windows in it and in its archways all around; *it was* fifty cubits long and twenty-five cubits wide.

30 *There were* archways all around, [a]twenty-five cubits long and five cubits wide.

31 Its archways faced the outer court, palm trees *were* on its gateposts, and going up to it *were* eight steps.

32 And he brought me into the inner court facing east; he measured the gateway according to these same measurements.

33 Also its gate chambers, its gateposts, and its archways *were* according to these same measurements; and *there were* windows in it and in its archways all around; *it was* fifty cubits long and twenty-five cubits wide.

34 Its archways faced the outer court, and palm trees *were* on its gateposts on this side and on that side; and going up to it *were* eight steps.

35 Then he brought me to the north gateway and measured *it* according to these same measurements—

36 also its gate chambers, its gateposts, and its archways. It had windows all around; its length *was* fifty cubits and its width twenty-five cubits.

37 Its gateposts faced the outer court, palm trees *were* on its gateposts on this side and on that side, and going up to it *were* eight steps.

Where Sacrifices Were Prepared

38 *There was* a chamber and its entrance by the gateposts of the gateway, where they [a]washed the burnt offering.

39 In the vestibule of the gateway *were* two tables on this side and two tables on that side, on which to slay the burnt offering, [a]the sin

offering, and [b]the trespass offer-
ing.
40 At the outer side of the vesti-
bule, as one goes up to the en-
trance of the northern gateway,
were two tables; and on the other
side of the vestibule of the gateway
were two tables.
41 Four tables *were* on this side
and four tables on that side, by the
side of the gateway, eight tables
on which they slaughtered *the sac-
rifices.*
42 *There were* also four tables of
hewn stone for the burnt offering,
one cubit and a half long, one cubit
and a half wide, and one cubit
high; on these they laid the instru-
ments with which they slaugh-
tered the burnt offering and the
sacrifice.
43 Inside *were* hooks, a hand-
breadth wide, fastened all around;
and the flesh of the sacrifices *was*
on the tables.

Chambers for Singers and Priests

44 Outside the inner gate *were* the
chambers for [a]the singers in the
inner court, one facing south at
the side of the northern gateway,
and the other facing north at the
side of the southern gateway.
45 Then he said to me, "This
chamber which faces south *is* for
[a]the priests who have charge of the
temple.
46 "The chamber which faces
north *is* for the priests [a]who have
charge of the altar; these *are* the
sons of [b]Zadok, from the sons of
Levi, who come near the LORD to
minister to Him."

Dimensions of the Inner Court and Vestibule

47 And he measured the court,
one hundred cubits long and one
hundred cubits wide, foursquare.
The altar *was* in front of the tem-
ple.
48 Then he brought me to the [a]ves-
tibule of the temple and measured
the doorposts of the vestibule, five
cubits on this side and five cubits
on that side; and the width of the
gateway was three cubits on this
side and three cubits on that
side.
49 [a]The length of the vestibule
was twenty cubits, and the width
eleven cubits; and by the steps
which led up to it *there were* [b]pil-
lars by the doorposts, one on this
side and another on that side.

Dimensions of the Sanctuary

41 Then he [a]brought me into
the [1]sanctuary and mea-
sured the doorposts, six cubits
wide on one side and six cubits
wide on the other side—the width
of the tabernacle.
2 The width of the entryway *was*
ten cubits, and the side walls of the
entrance *were* five cubits on this
side and five cubits on the other
side; and he measured its length,
forty cubits, and its width, twenty
cubits.
3 Also he went inside and mea-
sured the doorposts, two cubits;
and the entrance, six cubits *high;*
and the width of the entrance,
seven cubits.
4 [a]He measured the length,
twenty cubits; and the width,
twenty cubits, beyond the sanctu-
ary; and he said to me, "This *is*
the Most Holy *Place.*"

The Side Chambers on the Wall

5 Next, he measured the wall of
the [1]temple, six cubits. The width
of each side chamber all around
the temple *was* four cubits on
every side.
6 [a]The side chambers *were* in
three stories, one above the other,
thirty chambers in each story; they
rested on [1]ledges which *were* for
the side chambers all around, that
they might be supported, but [b]not
fastened to the wall of the temple.
7 As one went up from story to
story, the side chambers [a]became
wider all around, because their
supporting ledges in the wall of the
temple ascended like steps; there-
fore the width of the structure in-
creased as one went up *from* the
lowest *story* to the highest by way
of the middle one.
8 I also saw an elevation all
around the temple; it was the foun-
dation of the side chambers, [a]a full
rod, *that is,* six cubits *high.*
9 The thickness of the outer wall
of the side chambers *was* five cu-
bits, and so also the remaining ter-
race by the place of the side cham-
bers of the [1]temple.

39 [b]Lev. 5:6; 6:6; 7:1
44 [a]1 Chr. 6:31, 32; 16:41–43; 25:1–7
45 [a]Lev. 8:35; Num. 3:27, 28, 32, 38; 18:5; 1 Chr. 9:23; 2 Chr. 13:11; Ps. 134:1
46 [a]Lev. 6:12, 13; Num. 18:5; Ezek. 44:15 [b]1 Kin. 2:35; Ezek. 43:19; 44:15, 16
48 [a]1 Kin. 6:3; 2 Chr. 3:4
49 [a]1 Kin. 6:3 [b]1 Kin. 7:15–22; 2 Chr. 3:17; Jer. 52:17–23; [Rev. 3:12]

CHAPTER 41

1 [a]Ezek. 40:2, 3, 17 [1]Heb. *heykal;* the main room in the temple, the holy place, Ex. 26:33
4 [a]1 Kin. 6:20; 2 Chr. 3:8
5 [1]Lit. *house*
6 [a]1 Kin. 6:5–10 [b]1 Kin. 6:6, 10 [1]Lit. *the wall*
7 [a]1 Kin. 6:8
8 [a]Ezek. 40:5
9 [1]Lit. *house*

10 And between *it and* the *wall*
chambers was a width of twenty
cubits all around the temple on
every side.
11 The doors of the side chambers
opened on the terrace, one door
toward the north and another to-
ward the south; and the width of
the terrace *was* five cubits all
around.

The Building at the Western End

12 The building that faced the sep-
arating courtyard at its western
end *was* seventy cubits wide; the
wall of the building *was* five cubits
thick all around, and its length
ninety cubits.

Dimensions and Design of the Temple Area

13 So he measured the temple,
one [a]hundred cubits long; and the
separating courtyard with the
building and its walls *was* one
hundred cubits long;
14 also the width of the eastern
face of the temple, including the
separating courtyard, *was* one
hundred cubits.
15 He measured the length of the
building behind it, facing the sepa-
rating courtyard, with its [a]galleries
on the one side and on the other
side, one hundred cubits, as well
as the inner [1]temple and the
porches of the court,
16 their doorposts and [a]the bev-
eled window frames. And the gal-
leries all around their three stories
opposite the threshold were pan-
eled with [b]wood from the ground
to the windows—the windows
were covered—
17 from the space above the door,
even to the inner [1]room, as well
as outside, and on every wall all
around, inside and outside, by
measure.
18 And *it was* made [a]with cheru-
bim and [b]palm trees, a palm tree
between cherub and cherub. *Each*
cherub had two faces,
19 [a]so that the face of a man *was*
toward a palm tree on one side,
and the face of a young lion to-
ward a palm tree on the other side;
thus *it was* made throughout the
temple all around.
20 From the floor to the space
above the door, and on the wall
of the sanctuary, cherubim and
palm trees *were* carved.
21 The [a]doorposts of the temple
were square, *as was* the front of
the sanctuary; their appearance
was similar.
22 [a]The altar *was* of wood, three
cubits high, and its length two cu-
bits. Its corners, its length, and its
sides *were* of wood; and he said
to me, "This *is* [b]the table that *is*
[c]before the LORD."
23 [a]The temple and the sanctuary
had two doors.
24 The doors had two [a]panels
apiece, two folding panels: two
panels for one door and two panels
for the other *door.*
25 Cherubim and palm trees *were*
carved on the doors of the temple
just as they *were* carved on the
walls. A wooden canopy *was* on
the front of the vestibule outside.
26 *There were* [a]beveled window
frames and palm trees on one side
and on the other, on the sides of
the vestibule—also on the side
chambers of the temple and on the
canopies.

The Chambers for the Priests

42 Then he [a]brought me out
into the outer court, by the
way toward the [b]north; and he
brought me into [c]the chamber
which *was* opposite the separating
courtyard, and which *was* oppo-
site the building toward the north.
2 Facing the length, *which was*
one hundred cubits (the width was
fifty cubits), was the north door.
3 Opposite the inner court of
twenty *cubits,* and opposite the
[a]pavement of the outer court, *was*
[b]gallery against gallery in three
stories.
4 In front of the chambers, to-
ward the inside, *was* a walk ten
cubits wide, at a distance of one
cubit; and their doors faced north.
5 Now the upper chambers *were*
shorter, because the galleries took
away *space* from them more than
from the lower and middle stories
of the building.
6 For they *were* in three *stories*
and did not have pillars like the
pillars of the courts; therefore *the
upper level* was [1]shortened more
than the lower and middle levels
from the ground up.

13 [a]Ezek. 40:47
15 [a]Ezek. 42:3, 5 [1]Or *sanctuary*
16 [a]1 Kin. 6:4; Ezek. 40:16, 25 [b]1 Kin. 6:15
17 [1]Lit. *house;* the Most Holy Place
18 [a]1 Kin. 6:29; 2 Chr. 3:7 [b]2 Chr. 3:5; Ezek. 40:16
19 [a]Ezek. 1:10; 10:14
21 [a]1 Kin. 6:33; Ezek. 40:9, 14, 16; 41:1
22 [a]Ex. 30:1–3; 1 Kin. 6:20; Rev. 8:3 [b]Ex. 25:23, 30; Lev. 24:6; Ezek. 23:41; 44:16; Mal. 1:7, 12 [c]Ex. 30:8
23 [a]1 Kin. 6:31–35
24 [a]1 Kin. 6:34
26 [a]Ezek. 40:16
CHAPTER 42
1 [a]Ezek. 41:1 [b]Ezek. 40:20 [c]Ezek. 41:12, 15
3 [a]Ezek. 40:17 [b]Ezek. 41:15, 16; 42:5
6 [1]Or *narrowed*

7 And a wall which *was* outside
ran parallel to the chambers, at the
front of the chambers, toward the
outer court; its length *was* fifty cu-
bits.
8 The length of the chambers to-
ward the outer court *was* fifty cu-
bits, whereas that facing the tem-
ple *was* one [a]hundred cubits.
9 At the lower chambers *was* the
entrance on the east side, as one
goes into them from the outer
court.
10 Also *there were* chambers in
the thickness of the wall of the
court toward the east, opposite the
separating courtyard and opposite
the building.
11 [a]*There was* a walk in front of
them also, and their appearance
was like the chambers which *were*
toward the north; they *were* as
long and as wide as the others, and
all their exits and entrances *were*
according to plan.
12 And corresponding to the
doors of the chambers that *were*
facing south, as one enters them,
there was a door in front of the
walk, the way directly in front of
the wall toward the east.
13 Then he said to me, "The north
chambers *and* the south chambers,
which *are* opposite the separating
courtyard, *are* the holy chambers
where the priests who approach
the LORD [a]shall eat the most holy
offerings. There they shall lay the
most holy offerings—[b]the grain of-
fering, the sin offering, and the
trespass offering—for the place *is*
holy.
14 [a]"When the priests enter them,
they shall not go out of the holy
chamber into the outer court; but
there they shall leave their gar-
ments in which they minister, for
they *are* holy. They shall put on
other garments; then they may
approach *that* which *is* for the
people."

Outer Dimensions of the Temple

15 Now when he had finished
measuring the inner [1]temple, he
brought me out through the
gateway that faces toward
the [a]east, and measured it all
around.
16 He measured the east side with
the [1]measuring rod, five hundred

8 [a]Ezek. 41:13, 14

11 [a]Ezek. 42:4

13 [a]Lev. 6:16, 26; 24:9; Ezek. 43:19 [b]Lev. 2:3, 10; 6:14, 17, 25

14 [a]Ezek. 44:19

15 [a]Ezek. 40:6; 43:1 [1]Lit. *house*

16 [1]About 10.5 feet, Ezek. 40:5

20 [a][Is. 60:18]; Ezek. 40:5; Zech. 2:5 [b]Ezek. 45:2; Rev. 21:16 [1]Or *profane*

CHAPTER 43

1 [a]Ezek. 10:19; 46:1

2 [a]Ezek. 11:23 [b]Ezek. 1:24; Rev. 1:15; 14:2 [c]Ezek. 10:4; Rev. 18:1

3 [a]Ezek. 1:4–28 [b]Jer. 1:10; Ezek. 9:1, 5; 32:18 [c]Ezek. 1:28; 3:23 [1]Some Heb. mss., Vg. *He*

4 [a]Ezek. 10:19; 11:23 [1]Lit. *house*

5 [a]Ezek. 3:12, 14; 8:3; 2 Cor. 12:2–4 [b]Ezek. 40:34; 1 Kin. 8:10, 11 [1]Lit. *house*

6 [a]Ezek. 1:26; 40:3

7 [a]Ps. 99:1; Is. 60:13 [b]1 Chr. 28:2; Ps. 99:5 [c]Ex. 29:45; Ps. 68:16; 132:14; Ezek. 37:26–28; Joel 3:17; [John 1:14; 2 Cor. 6:16] [d]Ezek. 39:7 [e]Lev. 26:30; Jer. 16:18; Ezek. 6:5, 13 [1]Unfaithful idolatry

8 [a]2 Kin. 16:14; 21:4, 5, 7; Ezek. 8:3; 23:39; 44:7

rods by the measuring rod all
around.
17 He measured the north side,
five hundred rods by the measur-
ing rod all around.
18 He measured the south side,
five hundred rods by the measur-
ing rod.
19 He came around to the west
side *and* measured five hundred
rods by the measuring rod.
20 He measured it on the four
sides; [a]it had a wall all around,
[b]five hundred *cubits* long and five
hundred wide, to separate the holy
areas from the [1]common.

The Temple, the LORD's Dwelling Place

43 Afterward he brought me to
the gate, the gate [a]that faces
toward the east.
2 [a]And behold, the glory of the
God of Israel came from the way
of the east. [b]His voice *was* like the
sound of many waters; [c]and the
earth shone with His glory.
3 *It was* [a]like the appearance of
the vision which I saw—like the vi-
sion which I saw when [1]I came [b]to
destroy the city. The visions *were*
like the vision which I saw [c]by the
River Chebar; and I fell on my
face.
4 [a]And the glory of the LORD
came into the [1]temple by way of
the gate which faces toward the
east.
5 [a]The Spirit lifted me up and
brought me into the inner court;
and behold, [b]the glory of the LORD
filled the [1]temple.
6 Then I heard *Him* speaking to
me from the temple, while [a]a man
stood beside me.
7 And He said to me, "Son of
man, *this is* [a]the place of My
throne and [b]the place of the soles
of My feet, [c]where I will dwell in
the midst of the children of Israel
forever. [d]No more shall the house
of Israel defile My holy name, they
nor their kings, by their [1]harlotry
or with [e]the carcasses of their
kings on their high places.
8 [a]"When they set their thresh-
old by My threshold, and their
doorpost by My doorpost, with a
wall between them and Me, they
defiled My holy name by the
abominations which they com-

mitted; therefore I have consumed
them in My anger.
9 "Now let them put their harlo-
try and the carcasses of their kings
far away from Me, and I will dwell
in their midst forever.
10 "Son of man, [a]describe the
[1]temple to the house of Israel, that
they may be ashamed of their in-
iquities; and let them measure the
pattern.
11 "And if they are ashamed of all
that they have done, make known
to them the design of the [1]temple
and its arrangement, its exits and
its entrances, its entire design and
all its [a]ordinances, all its forms
and all its laws. Write *it* down in
their sight, so that they may keep
its whole design and all its ordi-
nances, and [b]perform them.
12 "This *is* the law of the [1]temple:
The whole area surrounding [a]the
mountaintop *is* most holy. Behold,
this *is* the law of the temple.

Dimensions of the Altar

13 "These are the measurements
of the [a]altar in cubits [b](the [1]*cubit*
is one cubit and a handbreadth):
the base one cubit high and one
cubit wide, with a rim all around
its edge of one span. This *is* the
height of the altar:
14 "from the base on the ground
to the lower ledge, two cubits; the
width of the ledge, one cubit; from
the smaller ledge to the larger
ledge, four cubits; and the width
of the ledge, *one* cubit.
15 "The altar hearth *is* four cubits
high, with four [a]horns extending
upward from the [1]hearth.
16 "The altar hearth *is* twelve cu-
bits long, twelve wide, [a]square at
its four corners;
17 "the ledge, fourteen *cubits* long
and fourteen wide on its four sides,
with a rim of half a cubit around
it; its base, one cubit all around;
and [a]its steps face toward the
east."

Consecrating the Altar

18 And He said to me, "Son of
man, thus says the Lord GOD:
'These *are* the ordinances for the
altar on the day when it is made,
for sacrificing [a]burnt offerings
on it, and for [b]sprinkling blood
on it.

10 [a]Ezek. 40:4 [1]Lit. *house*
11 [a]Ezek. 44:5 [b]Ezek. 11:20 [1]Lit. *house*
12 [a]Ezek. 40:2 [1]Lit. *house*
13 [a]Ex. 27:1–8; 2 Chr. 4:1 [b]Ezek. 41:8 [1]A royal cubit of about 21 inches
15 [a]Ex. 27:2; Lev. 9:9; 1 Kin. 1:50 [1]Heb. *ariel*
16 [a]Ex. 27:1
17 [a]Ex. 20:26
18 [a]Ex. 40:29 [b]Lev. 1:5, 11; [Heb. 9:21, 22]
19 [a]Ex. 29:10; Lev. 8:14; Ezek. 45:18, 19 [b]Ezek. 44:15, 16 [c]1 Kin. 2:35; Ezek. 40:46
21 [a]Ex. 29:14; Lev. 4:12 [b]Heb. 13:11 [1]Lit. *house*
24 [a]Lev. 2:13; Num. 18:19; [Mark 9:49, 50; Col. 4:6]
25 [a]Ex. 29:35; Lev. 8:33
26 [1]Lit. *fill its hands* [2]LXX, Syr. *themselves*
27 [a]Lev. 9:1–4 [b]Ezek. 20:40, 41; [Rom. 12:1; 1 Pet. 2:5]

CHAPTER 44

1 [a]Ezek. 43:1
2 [a]Ezek. 43:2–4
3 [a]Gen. 31:54; Ex. 24:9–11; [1 Cor. 10:18] [b]Ezek. 46:2, 8

19 'You shall give [a]a young bull
for a sin offering to [b]the priests,
the Levites, who are of the seed
of [c]Zadok, who approach Me to
minister to Me,' says the Lord
GOD.
20 'You shall take some of its
blood and put *it* on the four horns
of the altar, on the four corners of
the ledge, and on the rim around
it; thus you shall cleanse it and
make atonement for it.
21 'Then you shall also take the
bull of the sin offering, and [a]burn
it in the appointed place of the
[1]temple, [b]outside the sanctuary.
22 'On the second day you shall
offer a kid of the goats without
blemish for a sin offering; and they
shall cleanse the altar, as they
cleansed *it* with the bull.
23 'When you have finished
cleansing *it*, you shall offer a
young bull without blemish, and a
ram from the flock without blem-
ish.
24 'When you offer them before
the LORD, [a]the priests shall throw
salt on them, and they will offer
them up *as* a burnt offering to the
LORD.
25 'Every day for [a]seven days you
shall prepare a goat *for* a sin offer-
ing; they shall also prepare a
young bull and a ram from the
flock, both without blemish.
26 'Seven days they shall make
atonement for the altar and purify
it, and so [1]consecrate [2]*it*.
27 [a]'When these days are over it
shall be, on the eighth day and
thereafter, that the priests shall of-
fer your burnt offerings and your
peace offerings on the altar; and I
will [b]accept you,' says the Lord
GOD."

The East Gate and the Prince

44 Then He brought me back to
the outer gate of the sanctu-
ary [a]which faces toward the east,
but it *was* shut.
2 And the LORD said to me, "This
gate shall be shut; it shall not be
opened, and no man shall enter by
it, [a]because the LORD God of Israel
has entered by it; therefore it shall
be shut.
3 "*As for* the [a]prince, *because* he
is the prince, he may sit in it to
[b]eat bread before the LORD; he

shall enter by way of the vestibule of the gateway, and go out the same way."

Those Admitted to the Temple

4 Also He brought me by way of the north gate to the front of the [1]temple; so I looked, and [a]behold, the glory of the LORD filled the house of the LORD; [b]and I fell on my face.

5 And the LORD said to me, [a]"Son of man, [1]mark well, see with your eyes and hear with your ears, all that I say to you concerning all the [b]ordinances of the house of the LORD and all its laws. Mark well who may enter the house and all who go out from the sanctuary.

6 "Now say to the [a]rebellious, to the house of Israel, 'Thus says the Lord GOD: "O house of Israel, [b]let Us have no more of all your abominations.

7 [a]"When you brought in [b]foreigners, [c]uncircumcised in heart and uncircumcised in flesh, to be in My sanctuary to defile it—My house—and when you offered [d]My food, [e]the fat and the blood, then they broke My covenant because of all your abominations.

8 "And you have not [a]kept charge of My holy things, but you have set *others* to keep charge of My sanctuary for you."

9 'Thus says the Lord GOD: [a]"No foreigner, uncircumcised in heart or uncircumcised in flesh, shall enter My sanctuary, including any foreigner who *is* among the children of Israel.

Laws Governing Priests

10 [a]"And the Levites who went far from Me, when Israel went astray, who strayed away from Me after their idols, they shall bear their iniquity.

11 "Yet they shall be ministers in My sanctuary, [a]*as* gatekeepers of the house and ministers of the house; [b]they shall slay the burnt offering and the sacrifice for the people, and [c]they shall stand before them to minister to them.

12 "Because they ministered to them before their idols and [a]caused[1] the house of Israel to fall into iniquity, therefore I have [b]raised My hand in an oath against them," says the Lord GOD, "that they shall bear their iniquity.

13 [a]"And they shall not come near Me to minister to Me as priest, nor come near any of My holy things, nor into the Most Holy *Place;* but they shall [b]bear their shame and their abominations which they have committed.

14 "Nevertheless I will make them [a]keep charge of the temple, for all its work, and for all that has to be done in it.

15 [a]"But the priests, the Levites, [b]the sons of Zadok, who kept charge of My sanctuary [c]when the children of Israel went astray from Me, they shall come near Me to minister to Me; and they [d]shall stand before Me to offer to Me the [e]fat and the blood," says the Lord GOD.

16 "They shall [a]enter My sanctuary, and they shall come near [b]My table to minister to Me, and they shall keep My charge.

17 "And it shall be, whenever they enter the gates of the inner court, that [a]they shall put on linen garments; no wool shall come upon them while they minister within the gates of the inner court or within the house.

18 [a]"They shall have linen turbans on their heads and linen trousers on their bodies; they shall not clothe themselves with *anything that causes* sweat.

19 "When they go out to the outer court, to the *outer* court to the people, [a]they shall take off their garments in which they have ministered, leave them in the holy chambers, and put on other garments; and in their holy garments they shall [b]not sanctify the people.

20 [a]"They shall neither shave their heads nor let their hair grow [b]long, but they shall keep their hair well trimmed.

21 [a]"No priest shall drink wine when he enters the inner court.

22 "They shall not take as wife a [a]widow or a divorced woman, but take virgins of the descendants of the house of Israel, or widows of priests.

23 "And [a]they shall teach My people *the difference* between the holy and the unholy, and cause

---

4 [a]Ezek. 3:23; 43:5 [b]Ezek. 1:28; 43:3 [1]Lit. *house*
5 [a]Ezek. 40:4 [b]Ezek. 43:10, 11 [1]Lit. *set your heart*
6 [a]Ezek. 2:5 [b]1 Pet. 4:3
7 [a]Acts 21:28 [b]Lev. 22:25 [c]Lev. 26:41 [d]Lev. 21:17 [e]Lev. 3:16
8 [a]Lev. 22:2
9 [a]Ezek. 44:7
10 [a]2 Kin. 23:8
11 [a]1 Chr. 26:1–19 [b]2 Chr. 29:34; 30:17 [c]Num. 16:9
12 [a]Is. 9:16 [b]Ps. 106:26 [1]Lit. *became a stumbling block of iniquity to the house of Israel*
13 [a]2 Kin. 23:9 [b]Ezek. 32:30
14 [a]Num. 18:4
15 [a]Ezek. 40:46 [b][1 Sam. 2:35] [c]Ezek. 44:10 [d]Deut. 10:8 [e]Ezek. 44:7
16 [a]Num. 18:5, 7, 8 [b]Ezek. 41:22
17 [a]Ex. 28:39–43; 39:27–29
18 [a]Ex. 28:40; 39:28
19 [a]Ezek. 42:14 [b]Lev. 6:27
20 [a]Lev. 21:5 [b]Num. 6:5
21 [a]Lev. 10:9
22 [a]Lev. 21:7, 13, 14
23 [a]Mal. 2:6–8

them to [b]discern between the un-
clean and the clean.
24 [a]"In controversy they shall
stand as judges, *and* judge it ac-
cording to My judgments. They
shall keep My laws and My stat-
utes in all My appointed meetings,
[b]and they shall hallow My Sab-
baths.
25 "They shall not defile *them-
selves* by coming near a dead per-
son. Only for father or mother, for
son or daughter, for brother or un-
married sister may they defile
themselves.
26 [a]"After he is cleansed, they
shall count seven days for him.
27 "And on the day that he goes
to the sanctuary to minister in the
sanctuary, [a]he must offer his sin
offering [b]in the inner court," says
the Lord GOD.
28 "It shall be, in regard to their
inheritance, *that* I [a]*am* their inher-
itance. You shall give them no
[b]possession in Israel, for I *am* their
possession.
29 [a]"They shall eat the grain of-
fering, the sin offering, and the
trespass offering; [b]every dedi-
cated thing in Israel shall be
theirs.
30 "The [a]best[1] of all firstfruits of
any kind, and every sacrifice of
any kind from all your sacrifices,
shall be the priest's; also you [b]shall
give to the priest the first of your
ground meal, [c]to cause a blessing
to rest on your house.
31 "The priests shall not eat any-
thing, bird or beast, that [a]died nat-
urally or was torn *by wild beasts.*

The Holy District

45 "Moreover, when you [a]di-
vide the land by lot into in-
heritance, you shall [b]set apart a
district for the LORD, a holy section
of the land; its length *shall be*
twenty-five thousand *cubits,* and
the width ten thousand. It *shall be*
holy throughout its territory all
around.
2 "Of this there shall be a square
plot for the sanctuary, [a]five hun-
dred by five hundred *rods,* with
fifty cubits around it for an open
space.
3 "So this is the district you shall
measure: twenty-five thousand *cu-
bits* long and ten thousand wide;
[a]in it shall be the sanctuary, the
Most Holy *Place.*
4 "It shall be [a]a holy *section* of
the land, belonging to the priests,
the ministers of the sanctuary,
who come near to minister to the
LORD; it shall be a place for their
houses and a holy place for the
sanctuary.
5 [a]"*An area* twenty-five thou-
sand *cubits* long and ten thousand
wide shall belong to the Levites,
the ministers of the [1]temple; they
shall have [b]twenty[2] chambers as
a possession.

Properties of the City and the Prince

6 [a]"You shall appoint as the
property of the city *an area* five
thousand *cubits* wide and twenty-
five thousand long, adjacent to the
district of the holy *section;* it shall
belong to the whole house of Is-
rael.
7 [a]"The prince shall have *a sec-
tion* on one side and the other of
the holy district and the city's
property; and bordering on the
holy district and the city's prop-
erty, extending westward on the
west side and eastward on the east
side, the length *shall be* side by
side with one of the *tribal* portions,
from the west border to the east
border.
8 "The land shall be his posses-
sion in Israel; and [a]My princes
shall no more oppress My people,
but they shall give *the rest of* the
land to the house of Israel, accord-
ing to their tribes."

Laws Governing the Prince

9 'Thus says the Lord GOD:
[a]"Enough, O princes of Israel!
[b]Remove violence and plundering,
execute justice and righteousness,
and stop dispossessing My peo-
ple," says the Lord GOD.
10 "You shall have [a]honest scales,
an honest ephah, and an honest
bath.
11 "The ephah and the bath shall
be of the same measure, so that
the bath contains one-tenth of a
homer, and the ephah one-tenth of
a homer; their measure shall be ac-
cording to the homer.
12 "The [a]shekel *shall be* twenty
gerahs; twenty shekels, twenty-

23 [b]Lev. 20:25
24 [a]Deut. 17:8, 9; 1 Chr. 23:4; 2 Chr. 19:8–10 [b]Ezek. 22:26
26 [a]Num. 6:10; 19:11, 13–19
27 [a]Lev. 5:3, 6; Num. 6:9–11 [b]Ezek. 44:17
28 [a]Num. 18:20; Deut. 10:9; 18:1, 2; Josh. 13:14, 33 [b]Ezek. 45:4
29 [a]Lev. 7:6 [b]Lev. 27:21, 28; Num. 18:14
30 [a]Ex. 13:2; 22:29; 23:19; Num. 3:13; 18:12 [b]Num. 15:20; Neh. 10:37 [c]Prov. 3:9; [Mal. 3:10] [1]Lit. *first*
31 [a]Ex. 22:31; Lev. 22:8; Deut. 14:21; Ezek. 4:14

CHAPTER 45

1 [a]Num. 26:52–56; Ezek. 47:22 [b]Ezek. 48:8, 9
2 [a]Ezek. 42:20
3 [a]Ezek. 48:10
4 [a]Ezek. 48:10, 11
5 [a]Ezek. 48:13 [b]Ezek. 40:17 [1]Lit. *house* [2]So with MT, Tg., Vg.; LXX *a possession, cities of dwelling*
6 [a]Ezek. 48:15
7 [a]Ezek. 48:21
8 [a][Is. 11:3–5]; Jer. 22:17; Ezek. 22:27
9 [a]Ezek. 44:6 [b]Jer. 22:3; Zech. 8:16
10 [a]Lev. 19:36; Deut. 25:15; Prov. 16:11; Amos 8:4–6; Mic. 6:10, 11
12 [a]Ex. 30:13; Lev. 27:25; Num. 3:47

five shekels, *and* fifteen shekels shall be your mina.

13 "This *is* the offering which you shall offer: you shall give one-sixth of an ephah from a homer of wheat, and one-sixth of an ephah from a homer of barley.

14 "The ordinance concerning oil, the bath of oil, *is* one-tenth of a bath from a kor. A kor *is* a homer or ten baths, for ten baths *are* a homer.

15 "And one lamb shall be given from a flock of two hundred, from the rich pastures of Israel. These shall be for grain offerings, burnt offerings, and peace offerings, [a]to make atonement for them," says the Lord GOD.

16 "All the people of the land shall give this offering for the prince in Israel.

17 "Then it shall be the [a]prince's part *to give* burnt offerings, grain offerings, and drink offerings, at the feasts, the New Moons, the Sabbaths, and at all the appointed seasons of the house of Israel. He shall prepare the sin offering, the grain offering, the burnt offering, and the peace offerings to make atonement for the house of Israel."

Keeping the Feasts

18 'Thus says the Lord GOD: "In the first *month,* on the first *day* of the month, you shall take a young bull without blemish and [a]cleanse the sanctuary.

19 [a]"The priest shall take some of the blood of the sin offering and put *it* on the doorposts of the [1]temple, on the four corners of the ledge of the altar, and on the gateposts of the gate of the inner court.

20 "And so you shall do on the seventh *day* of the month [a]for everyone who has sinned unintentionally or in ignorance. Thus you shall make atonement for the temple.

21 [a]"In the first *month,* on the fourteenth day of the month, you shall observe the Passover, a feast of seven days; unleavened bread shall be eaten.

22 "And on that day the prince shall prepare for himself and for all the people of the land [a]a bull *for* a sin offering.

23 "On the [a]seven days of the feast he shall prepare a burnt offering to the LORD, seven bulls and seven rams without blemish, daily for seven days, [b]and a kid of the goats daily *for* a sin offering.

24 [a]"And he shall prepare a grain offering of one ephah for each bull and one ephah for each ram, together with a hin of oil for each ephah.

25 "In the seventh *month,* on the fifteenth day of the month, at the [a]feast, he shall do likewise for seven days, according to the sin offering, the burnt offering, the grain offering, and the oil."

The Manner of Worship

46 'Thus says the Lord GOD: "The gateway of the inner court that faces toward the east shall be shut the six [a]working days; but on the Sabbath it shall be opened, and on the day of the New Moon it shall be opened.

2 [a]"The prince shall enter by way of the vestibule of the gateway from the outside, and stand by the gatepost. The priests shall prepare his burnt offering and his peace offerings. He shall worship at the threshold of the gate. Then he shall go out, but the gate shall not be shut until evening.

3 "Likewise the people of the land shall worship at the entrance to this gateway before the LORD on the Sabbaths and the New Moons.

4 "The burnt offering that [a]the prince offers to the LORD on the [b]Sabbath day *shall be* six lambs without blemish, and a ram without blemish;

5 [a]"and the grain offering *shall be one* ephah for a ram, and the grain offering for the lambs, [1]as much as he wants to give, as well as a hin of oil with every ephah.

6 "On the day of the New Moon *it shall be* a young bull without blemish, six lambs, and a ram; they shall be without blemish.

7 "He shall prepare a grain offering of an ephah for a bull, an ephah for a ram, [1]as much as he wants to give for the lambs, and a hin of oil with every ephah.

8 [a]"When the prince enters, he shall go in by way of the vestibule of the gateway, and go out the same way.

---

15 [a]Lev. 1:4; 6:30
17 [a]Ezek. 46:4–12
18 [a]Lev. 16:16, 33; Ezek. 43:22, 26
19 [a]Lev. 16:18–20; Ezek. 43:20 [1]Lit. *house*
20 [a]Lev. 4:27; Ps. 19:12
21 [a]Ex. 12:18; Lev. 23:5, 6; Num. 9:2, 3; 28:16, 17; Deut. 16:1
22 [a]Lev. 4:14
23 [a]Lev. 23:8 [b]Num. 28:15, 22, 30; 29:5, 11, 16, 19
24 [a]Num. 28:12–15; Ezek. 46:5, 7
25 [a]Lev. 23:34; Num. 29:12; Deut. 16:13; 2 Chr. 5:3; 7:8, 10

CHAPTER 46

1 [a]Ex. 20:9
2 [a]Ezek. 44:3
4 [a]Ezek. 45:17 [b]Num. 28:9, 10
5 [a]Num. 28:12; Ezek. 45:24; 46:7, 11 [1]Lit. *the gift of his hand*
7 [1]Lit. *as much as his hand can reach*
8 [a]Ezek. 44:3; 46:2

9 "But when the people of the
land [a]come before the LORD on the
appointed feast days, whoever en-
ters by way of the north [b]gate to
worship shall go out by way of the
south gate; and whoever enters by
way of the south gate shall go out
by way of the north gate. He shall
not return by way of the gate
through which he came, but shall
go out through the opposite gate.
10 "The prince shall then be in
their midst. When they go in, he
shall go in; and when they go out,
he shall go out.
11 "At the festivals and the ap-
pointed feast days [a]the grain offer-
ing shall be an ephah for a bull,
an ephah for a ram, as much as
he wants to give for the lambs, and
a hin of oil with every ephah.
12 "Now when the prince makes
a voluntary burnt offering or vol-
untary peace offering to the LORD,
the gate that faces toward the east
[a]shall then be opened for him; and
he shall prepare his burnt offering
and his peace offerings as he did
on the Sabbath day. Then he shall
go out, and after he goes out the
gate shall be shut.
13 [a]"You shall daily make a burnt
offering to the LORD *of* a lamb of
the first year without blemish; you
shall prepare it [1]every morning.
14 "And you shall prepare a grain
offering with it every morning, a
sixth of an ephah, and a third of
a hin of oil to moisten the fine
flour. This grain offering is a per-
petual ordinance, to be made regu-
larly to the LORD.
15 "Thus they shall prepare the
lamb, the grain offering, and the
oil, *as* a [a]regular burnt offering
every morning."

The Prince and Inheritance Laws

16 'Thus says the Lord GOD: "If
the prince gives a gift *of some* of
his inheritance to any of his sons,
it shall belong to his sons; it is their
possession by inheritance.
17 "But if he gives a gift of some
of his inheritance to one of his ser-
vants, it shall be his until [a]the year
of liberty, after which it shall re-
turn to the prince. But his inheri-
tance shall belong to his sons; it
shall become theirs.
18 "Moreover [a]the prince shall not
take any of the people's inheri-
tance by evicting them from their
property; he shall provide an in-
heritance for his sons from his
own property, so that none of My
people may be scattered from his
property." ' "

How the Offerings Were Prepared

19 Now he brought me through
the entrance, which *was* at the side
of the gate, into the holy [a]cham-
bers of the priests which face to-
ward the north; and there a place
was situated at their extreme west-
ern end.
20 And he said to me, "This *is* the
place where the priests shall [a]boil
the trespass offering and the sin
offering, *and* where they shall
[b]bake the grain offering, so that
they do not bring *them* out into
the outer court [c]to sanctify the
people."
21 Then he brought me out into
the outer court and caused me to
pass by the four corners of the
court; and in fact, in every corner
of the court *there was another*
court.
22 In the four corners of the court
were enclosed courts, forty *cubits*
long and thirty wide; all four cor-
ners *were* the same size.
23 *There was* a row *of building*
stones all around in them, all
around the four of them; and
[1]cooking hearths were made under
the rows of stones all around.
24 And he said to me, "These *are*
the [1]kitchens where the ministers
of the [2]temple shall [a]boil the sacri-
fices of the people."

The Healing Waters and Trees

47 Then he brought me back to
the door of the [1]temple; and
there was [a]water, flowing from un-
der the threshold of the temple to-
ward the east, for the front of the
temple faced east; the water was
flowing from under the right side
of the temple, south of the altar.
2 He brought me out by way of
the north gate, and led me around
on the outside to the outer gateway
that faces [a]east; and there was wa-
ter, running out on the right side.
3 And when [a]the man went out
to the east with the line in his
hand, he measured one thousand

9 [a]Ex. 23:14–17; 34:23; Deut. 16:16, 17; Ps. 84:7; Mic. 6:6 [b]Ezek. 48:31, 33
11 [a]Ezek. 46:5, 7
12 [a]Ezek. 44:3; 46:1, 2, 8
13 [a]Ex. 29:38; Num. 28:3–5 [1]Lit. *morning by morning*
15 [a]Ex. 29:42; Num. 28:6
17 [a]Lev. 25:10
18 [a]Ezek. 45:8
19 [a]Ezek. 42:13
20 [a]2 Chr. 35:13 [b]Lev. 2:4, 5, 7 [c]Ezek. 44:19
23 [1]Lit. *boiling places*
24 [a]Ezek. 46:20 [1]Lit. *house of those who boil* [2]Lit. *house*

CHAPTER 47

1 [a]Ps. 46:4; Is. 30:25; 55:1; [Jer. 2:13]; Joel 3:18; Zech. 13:1; 14:8; [Rev. 22:1, 17] [1]Lit. *house*
2 [a]Ezek. 44:1, 2
3 [a]Ezek. 40:3

cubits, and he brought me through
the waters; the water *came up to*
my ankles.
4 Again he measured one thou-
sand and brought me through the
waters; the water *came up to my*
knees. Again he measured one
thousand and brought me through;
the water *came up to my* waist.
5 Again he measured one thou-
sand, *and it was* a river that I could
not cross; for the water was too
deep, water in which one must
swim, a river that could not be
crossed.
6 He said to me, "Son of man,
have you seen *this?*" Then he
brought me and returned me to the
bank of the river.
7 When I returned, there, along
the bank of the river, *were* very
many [a]trees on one side and the
other.
8 Then he said to me: "This wa-
ter flows toward the eastern re-
gion, goes down into the [1]valley,
and enters the sea. *When it*
reaches the sea, *its* waters are
healed.
9 "And it shall be *that* every liv-
ing thing that moves, wherever
[1]the rivers go, will live. There will
be a very great multitude of fish,
because these waters go there; for
they will be healed, and everything
will live wherever the river goes.
10 "It shall be *that* fishermen will
stand by it from En Gedi to En
Eglaim; they will be *places* for
spreading their nets. Their fish will
be of the same kinds as the fish
[a]of the Great Sea, exceedingly
many.
11 "But its swamps and marshes
will not be healed; they will be
given over to salt.
12 [a]"Along the bank of the river,
on this side and that, will grow all
kinds of trees used for food; [b]their
leaves will not wither, and their
fruit will not fail. They will bear
fruit every month, because their
water flows from the sanctuary.
Their fruit will be for food, and
their leaves for [c]medicine."[1]

Borders of the Land

13 Thus says the Lord GOD:
"These *are* the [a]borders by which
you shall divide the land as an in-
heritance among the twelve tribes
of Israel. [b]Joseph *shall have two*
portions.
14 "You shall inherit it equally
with one another; for I [a]raised My
hand in an oath to give it to your
fathers, and this land shall [b]fall to
you as your inheritance.
15 "This *shall be* the border of the
land on the north: from the Great
Sea, *by* [a]the road to Hethlon, as
one goes to [b]Zedad,
16 [a]"Hamath, [b]Berothah, Sibraim
(which *is* between the border of
Damascus and the border of Ha-
math), to Hazar Hatticon (which *is*
on the border of Hauran).
17 "Thus the boundary shall be
from the Sea to [a]Hazar Enan, the
border of Damascus; and as for the
north, northward, it is the border
of Hamath. *This is* the north side.
18 "On the east side you shall
mark out the border from between
Hauran and Damascus, and be-
tween Gilead and the land of Is-
rael, along the Jordan, and along
the eastern side of the sea. *This is*
the east side.
19 "The south side, toward the
[1]South, *shall be* from Tamar to
[a]the waters of [2]Meribah by Ka-
desh, along the brook to the Great
Sea. *This is* the south side, toward
the South.
20 "The west side *shall be* the
Great Sea, from the *southern*
boundary until one comes to a
point opposite Hamath. This *is* the
west side.
21 "Thus you shall [a]divide this
land among yourselves according
to the tribes of Israel.
22 "It shall be that you will divide
it by [a]lot as an inheritance for
yourselves, [b]and for the strangers
who dwell among you and who
bear children among you. [c]They
shall be to you as native-born
among the children of Israel; they
shall have an inheritance with you
among the tribes of Israel.
23 "And it shall be *that* in what-
ever tribe the stranger dwells,
there you shall give *him* his inheri-
tance," says the Lord GOD.

Division of the Land

48 "Now these *are* the names
of the tribes: [a]From the
northern border along the road to
Hethlon at the entrance of Ha-

7 [a][Is. 60:13, 21; 61:3; Ezek. 47:12; Rev. 22:2]
8 [1]Or *Arabah,* The Jordan Valley
9 [1]Lit. *two rivers*
10 [a]Num. 34:3; Josh. 23:4; Ezek. 48:28
12 [a]Ezek. 47:7; [Rev. 22:2] [b]Job 18:16; [Ps. 1:3; Jer. 17:8] [c][Rev. 22:2] [1]Or *healing*
13 [a]Num. 34:1–29 [b]Gen. 48:5; 1 Chr. 5:1; Ezek. 48:4, 5
14 [a]Gen. 12:7; 13:15; 15:7; 17:8; 26:3; 28:13; Deut. 1:8; Ezek. 20:5, 6, 28, 42 [b]Ezek. 48:29
15 [a]Ezek. 48:1 [b]Num. 34:7, 8
16 [a]Num. 34:8 [b]2 Sam. 8:8
17 [a]Num. 34:9; Ezek. 48:1
19 [a]Num. 20:13; Deut. 32:51; Ps. 81:7; Ezek. 48:28 [1]Heb. *Negev* [2]Lit. *Strife*
21 [a]Ezek. 45:1
22 [a]Num. 26:55, 56 [b][Eph. 3:6; Rev. 7:9, 10] [c][Acts 11:18; 15:9; Gal. 3:28; Eph. 2:12–14; Col. 3:11]

CHAPTER 48

1 [a]Ezek. 47:15

math, to Hazar Enan, the border
of Damascus northward, in the di-
rection of Hamath, *there shall be*
one *section for* [b]Dan from its east
to its west side;
2 "by the border of Dan, from the
east side to the west, one *section*
for [a]Asher;
3 "by the border of Asher, from
the east side to the west, one *sec-*
tion for [a]Naphtali;
4 "by the border of Naphtali,
from the east side to the west, one
section for [a]Manasseh;
5 "by the border of Manasseh,
from the east side to the west, one
section for [a]Ephraim;
6 "by the border of Ephraim,
from the east side to the west, one
section for [a]Reuben;
7 "by the border of Reuben, from
the east side to the west, one *sec-*
tion for [a]Judah;
8 "by the border of Judah, from
the east side to the west, shall be
[a]the district which you shall set
apart, twenty-five thousand *cubits*
in width, and *in* length the same
as one of the *other* portions, from
the east side to the west, with the
[b]sanctuary in the center.
9 "The district that you shall set
apart for the LORD *shall be* twenty-
five thousand *cubits* in length and
ten thousand in width.
10 "To these—to the priests—the
holy district shall belong: on the
north twenty-five thousand *cubits*
in length, on the west ten thousand
in width, on the east ten thousand
in width, and on the south twenty-
five thousand in length. The sanc-
tuary of the LORD shall be in the
center.
11 [a]"*It shall be* for the priests of
the sons of Zadok, who are sancti-
fied, who have kept My charge,
who did not go astray when the
children of Israel went astray, [b]as
the Levites went astray.
12 "And *this* district of land that
is set apart shall be to them a thing
most [a]holy by the border of the
Levites.
13 "Opposite the border of the
priests, the [a]Levites *shall have an*
area twenty-five thousand *cubits*
in length and ten thousand in
width; its entire length *shall be*
twenty-five thousand and its width
ten thousand.

1 [b]Josh. 19:40–48
2 [a]Josh. 19:24–31
3 [a]Josh. 19:32–39
4 [a]Josh. 13:29–31; 17:1–11, 17, 18
5 [a]Josh. 16:5–10; 17:8–10, 14–18
6 [a]Josh. 13:15–23
7 [a]Josh. 15:1–63; 19:9
8 [a]Ezek. 45:1–6 [b][Is. 12:6; 33:20–22]; Ezek. 45:3, 4
11 [a]Ezek. 40:46; 44:15 [b]Ezek. 44:10, 12
12 [a]Ezek. 45:4
13 [a]Ezek. 45:5
14 [a]Ex. 22:29; Lev. 27:10, 28, 33; Ezek. 44:30
15 [a]Ezek. 45:6 [b]Ezek. 42:20
19 [a]Ezek. 45:6
21 [a]Ezek. 34:24; 45:7; 48:22 [b]Ezek. 48:8, 10 [1]Lit. *house*

14 [a]"And they shall not sell or ex-
change any of it; they may not
alienate this best *part* of the land,
for *it is* holy to the LORD.
15 [a]"The five thousand *cubits*
in width that remain, along the
edge of the twenty-five thousand,
shall be [b]for general use by the
city, for dwellings and common-
land; and the city shall be in the
center.
16 "These *shall be* its measure-
ments: the north side four thou-
sand five hundred *cubits*, the
south side four thousand five hun-
dred, the east side four thousand
five hundred, and the west side
four thousand five hundred.
17 "The common-land of the city
shall be: to the north two hundred
and fifty *cubits*, to the south two
hundred and fifty, to the east two
hundred and fifty, and to the west
two hundred and fifty.
18 "The rest of the length, along-
side the district of the holy *section*,
shall be ten thousand *cubits* to the
east and ten thousand to the west.
It shall be adjacent to the district
of the holy *section*, and its produce
shall be food for the workers of
the city.
19 [a]"The workers of the city, from
all the tribes of Israel, shall culti-
vate it.
20 "The entire district *shall be*
twenty-five thousand *cubits* by
twenty-five thousand *cubits*,
foursquare. You shall set apart the
holy district with the property of
the city.
21 [a]"The rest *shall belong* to the
prince, on one side and on the
other of the holy district and of
the city's property, next to the
twenty-five thousand *cubits* of
the *holy* district as far as the
eastern border, and westward
next to the twenty-five thousand
as far as the western border, adja-
cent to the *tribal* portions; *it shall*
belong to the prince. It shall be the
holy district, [b]and the sanctuary
of the [1]temple *shall be* in the
center.
22 "Moreover, apart from the pos-
session of the Levites and the pos-
session of the city *which are* in the
midst of what *belongs* to the
prince, *the area* between the bor-
der of Judah and the border of

[a]Benjamin shall belong to the
prince.
23 "As for the rest of the tribes,
from the east side to the west, Ben-
jamin *shall have* one *section;*
24 "by the border of Benjamin,
from the east side to the west,
[a]Simeon *shall have* one *section;*
25 "by the border of Simeon, from
the east side to the west, [a]Issachar
shall have one *section;*
26 "by the border of Issachar,
from the east side to the west,
[a]Zebulun *shall have* one *section;*
27 "by the border of Zebulun,
from the east side to the west,
[a]Gad *shall have* one *section;*
28 "by the border of Gad, on the
south side, toward the [1]South, the
border shall be from Tamar *to*
[a]the waters of [2]Meribah *by* Ka-
desh, along the brook to the [b]Great
Sea.
29 [a]"This *is* the land which you
shall divide by lot as an inheri-
tance among the tribes of Israel,
and these *are* their portions," says
the Lord GOD.

The Gates of the City and Its Name

30 "These *are* the exits of the city.
On the north side, measuring four
thousand five hundred *cubits*
31 [a]"(the gates of the city *shall be*
named after the tribes of Israel),
the three gates northward: one
gate for Reuben, one gate for Ju-
dah, and one gate for Levi;
32 "on the east side, four thou-
sand five hundred *cubits,* three
gates: one gate for Joseph, one
gate for Benjamin, and one gate
for Dan;
33 "on the south side, measuring
four thousand five hundred *cubits,*
three gates: one gate for Simeon,
one gate for Issachar, and one gate
for Zebulun;
34 "on the west side, four thou-
sand five hundred *cubits* with their
three gates: one gate for Gad, one
gate for Asher, and one gate for
Naphtali.
35 "All the way around *shall be*
eighteen thousand *cubits;* [a]and the
name of the city from *that* day
shall be: [b]THE[1] LORD *IS* THERE."

22 [a]Josh. 18:21–28
24 [a]Josh. 19:1–9
25 [a]Josh. 19:17–23
26 [a]Josh. 19:10–16
27 [a]Josh. 13:24–28
28 [a]Gen. 14:7; 2 Chr. 20:2; Ezek. 47:19 [b]Ezek. 47:10, 15, 19, 20 [1]Heb. *Negev* [2]Lit. *Strife*
29 [a]Ezek. 47:14, 21, 22
31 [a][Rev. 21:10–14]
35 [a]Jer. 23:6; 33:16 [b]Is. 12:6; 14:32; 24:23; Jer. 3:17; 8:19; 14:9; Ezek. 35:10; Joel 3:21; Zech. 2:10; Rev. 21:3; 22:3 [1]Heb. *YHWH Shammah*

The Book of

Daniel

DANIEL'S life and ministry bridge the entire seventy-year period of Babylonian captivity. Deported to Babylon at the age of sixteen, and handpicked for government service, Daniel becomes God's prophetic mouthpiece to the gentile and Jewish world declaring God's present and eternal purpose. Nine of the twelve chapters in his book revolve around dreams, including God-given visions involving trees, animals, beasts, and images. In both his personal adventures and prophetic visions, Daniel shows God's guidance, intervention, and power in the affairs of men.

The name *Daniye'l* or *Dani'el* means "God Is My Judge," and the book is, of course, named after the author and principal character. The Greek form *Daniel* in the Septuagint is the basis for the Latin and English titles.

Daniel and His Friends Obey God

IN the third year of the reign
of [a]Jehoiakim king of Judah,
Nebuchadnezzar king of Bab-
ylon came to Jerusalem and be-
sieged it.
2 And the Lord gave Jehoiakim
king of Judah into his hand, with
[a]some of the articles of [1]the house
of God, which he carried [b]into the
land of Shinar to the house of his
god; [c]and he brought the articles
into the treasure house of his god.
3 Then the king instructed Ash-
penaz, the master of his eunuchs,
to bring [a]some of the children of
Israel and some of the king's de-
scendants and some of the nobles,
4 young men [a]in whom *there*
was no blemish, but good-looking,
gifted in all wisdom, possessing
knowledge and quick to under-
stand, who *had* ability to serve in
the king's palace, and [b]whom they
might teach the language and [1]lit-
erature of the Chaldeans.
5 And the king appointed for
them a daily provision of the
king's delicacies and of the wine
which he drank, and three years
of training for them, so that at the
end of *that time* they might [a]serve
before the king.
6 Now from among those of the
sons of Judah were Daniel, Hana-
niah, Mishael, and Azariah.
7 [a]To them the chief of the eu-
nuchs gave names: [b]he gave Dan-
iel *the name* Belteshazzar; to
Hananiah, Shadrach; to Mish-
ael, Meshach; and to Azariah,
Abed-Nego.
8 But Daniel purposed in his
heart that he would not defile him-
self [a]with the portion of the king's
delicacies, nor with the wine
which he drank; therefore he re-
quested of the chief of the eunuchs
that he might not defile himself.
9 Now [a]God had brought Daniel
into the favor and [1]goodwill of the
chief of the eunuchs.
10 And the chief of the eunuchs
said to Daniel, "I fear my lord the
king, who has appointed your food
and drink. For why should he see
your faces looking worse than the
young men who *are* your age?
Then you would endanger my
head before the king."
11 So Daniel said to [1]the steward
whom the chief of the eunuchs had
set over Daniel, Hananiah, Mish-
ael, and Azariah,
12 "Please test your servants for
ten days, and let them give us
vegetables to eat and water to
drink.
13 "Then let our appearance be
examined before you, and the ap-
pearance of the young men who
eat the portion of the king's delica-
cies; and as you see fit, *so* deal
with your servants."
14 So he consented with them in
this matter, and tested them ten
days.
15 And at the end of ten days their
features appeared better and fatter

CHAPTER 1

1 [a]2 Kin. 24:1, 2; 2 Chr. 36:5–7; Jer. 25:1; 52:12–30

2 [a]2 Chr. 36:7; Jer. 27:19, 20; Dan. 5:2 [b]Gen. 10:10; 11:2; Is. 11:11; Zech. 5:11 [c]2 Chr. 36:7 [1]The temple

3 [a]2 Kin. 20:17, 18; Is. 39:7

4 [a]Lev. 24:19, 20 [b]Acts 7:22 [1]Lit. *writing* or *book*

5 [a]Gen. 41:46; 1 Sam. 16:22; 1 Kin. 10:8; Dan. 1:19

7 [a]Gen. 41:45; 2 Kin. 24:17 [b]Dan. 2:26; 4:8; 5:12

8 [a]Lev. 11:47; Deut. 32:38; Ezek. 4:13; Hos. 9:3

9 [a]Gen. 39:21; 1 Kin. 8:50; [Job 5:15, 16]; Ps. 106:46; [Prov. 16:7]; Acts 7:10; 27:3 [1]*kindness*

11 [1]Or *Melzar*

in flesh than all the young men
who ate the portion of the king's
delicacies.
16 Thus [1]the steward took away
their portion of delicacies and the
wine that they were to drink, and
gave them vegetables.
17 As for these four young men,
[a]God gave them [b]knowledge and
skill in all literature and wisdom;
and Daniel had [c]understanding in
all visions and dreams.
18 Now at the end of the days,
when the king had said that they
should be brought in, the chief of
the eunuchs brought them in be-
fore Nebuchadnezzar.
19 Then the king [1]interviewed
them, and among them all none
was found like Daniel, Hananiah,
Mishael, and Azariah; therefore
[a]they served before the king.
20 [a]And in all matters of wisdom
and understanding about which
the king examined them, he found
them ten times better than all the
magicians *and* astrologers who
were in all his realm.
21 [a]Thus Daniel continued until
the first year of King Cyrus.

Nebuchadnezzar's Dream

2 Now in the second year
of Nebuchadnezzar's reign,
Nebuchadnezzar had dreams;
[a]and his spirit was *so* troubled
that [b]his sleep left him.
2 [a]Then the king gave the com-
mand to call the magicians, the as-
trologers, the sorcerers, and the
Chaldeans to tell the king his
dreams. So they came and stood
before the king.
3 And the king said to them, "I
have had a dream, and my spirit
is anxious to [1]know the dream."
4 Then the Chaldeans spoke to
the king in Aramaic, [a]"O[1] king,
live forever! Tell your servants the
dream, and we will give the inter-
pretation."
5 The king answered and said to
the Chaldeans, "My [1]decision is
firm: if you do not make known
the dream to me, and its interpre-
tation, you shall be [a]cut in pieces,
and your houses shall be made an
ash heap.
6 [a]"However, if you tell the
dream and its interpretation, you
shall receive from me gifts, re-
wards, and great honor. Therefore
tell me the dream and its inter-
pretation."
7 They answered again and said,
"Let the king tell his servants the
dream, and we will give its inter-
pretation."
8 The king answered and said, "I
know for certain that you would
gain time, because you see that my
decision is firm:
9 "if you do not make known the
dream to me, *there is only* one de-
cree for you! For you have agreed
to speak lying and corrupt words
before me till the [1]time has
changed. Therefore tell me the
dream, and I shall know that you
can [2]give me its interpretation."
10 The Chaldeans answered the
king, and said, "There is not a man
on earth who can tell the king's
matter; therefore no king, lord, or
ruler has *ever* asked such things
of any magician, astrologer, or
Chaldean.
11 "*It is* a [1]difficult thing that the
king requests, and there is no
other who can tell it to the king
[a]except the gods, whose dwelling
is not with flesh."
12 For this reason the king was
angry and very furious, and gave
the command to destroy all the
wise *men* of Babylon.
13 So the decree went out, and
they began killing the wise *men;*
and they sought [a]Daniel and his
companions, to kill *them.*

God Reveals Nebuchadnezzar's Dream

14 Then with counsel and wisdom
Daniel answered Arioch, the cap-
tain of the king's guard, who had
gone out to kill the wise *men* of
Babylon;
15 he answered and said to Arioch
the king's captain, "Why is the de-
cree from the king so [1]urgent?"
Then Arioch made the decision
known to Daniel.
16 So Daniel went in and asked
the king to give him time, that he
might tell the king the inter-
pretation.
17 Then Daniel went to his house,
and made the decision known to
Hananiah, Mishael, and Azariah,
his companions,
18 [a]that they might seek mercies

16 [1]Or *Melzar*

17 [a]1 Kin. 3:12, 28; 2 Chr. 1:10–12; [Luke 21:15; James 1:5–7] [b]Acts 7:22 [c]Num. 12:6; 2 Chr. 26:5; Dan. 5:11, 12, 14; 10:1

19 [a]Gen. 41:46; [Prov. 22:29]; Dan. 1:5 [1]Lit. *talked with them*

20 [a]1 Kin. 10:1

21 [a]Dan. 6:28; 10:1

CHAPTER 2

1 [a]Gen. 40:5–8; 41:1, 8; Job 33:15–17; Dan. 2:3; 4:5 [b]Esth. 6:1; Dan. 6:18

2 [a]Gen. 41:8; Ex. 7:11; Is. 47:12, 13; Dan. 1:20; 2:10, 27; 4:6; 5:7

3 [1]Or *understand*

4 [a]1 Kin. 1:31; Dan. 3:9; 5:10; 6:6, 21 [1]The original language of Daniel 2:4b through 7:28 is Aramaic.

5 [a]2 Kin. 10:27; Ezra 6:11; Dan. 3:29 [1]The command

6 [a]Dan. 5:16

9 [1]Situation [2]Or *declare to me*

11 [a]Gen. 41:39; Dan. 5:11 [1]Or *rare*

13 [a]Dan. 1:19, 20

15 [1]Or *harsh*

18 [a][Dan. 9:9; Matt. 18:19]

from the God of heaven concern-
ing this secret, so that Daniel and
his companions might not perish
with the rest of the wise *men* of
Babylon.
19 Then the secret was revealed
to Daniel [a]in a night vision. So
Daniel blessed the God of heaven.
20 Daniel answered and said:

[a]"Blessed be the name of God
forever and ever,
[b]For wisdom and might are His.
21 And He changes [a]the times and
the seasons;
[b]He removes kings and raises up
kings;
[c]He gives wisdom to the wise
And knowledge to those who
have understanding.
22 [a]He reveals deep and secret
things;
[b]He knows what *is* in the
darkness,
And [c]light dwells with Him.

23 "I thank You and praise You,
O God of my fathers;
You have given me wisdom and
might,
And have now made known to
me what we [a]asked of You,
For You have made known to us
the king's [1]demand."

Daniel Explains the Dream

24 Therefore Daniel went to Ari-
och, whom the king had appointed
to destroy the wise *men* of Bab-
ylon. He went and said thus to
him: "Do not destroy the wise *men*
of Babylon; take me before the
king, and I will tell the king the
interpretation."
25 Then Arioch quickly brought
Daniel before the king, and said
thus to him, "I have found a man
of the [1]captives of Judah, who will
make known to the king the inter-
pretation."
26 The king answered and said to
Daniel, whose name *was* Belte-
shazzar, "Are you able to make
known to me the dream which I
have seen, and its interpretation?"
27 Daniel answered in the pres-
ence of the king, and said, "The
secret which the king has de-
manded, the wise *men*, the astrolo-
gers, the magicians, and the sooth-
sayers cannot declare to the king.
28 [a]"But there is a God in heaven
who reveals secrets, and He has
made known to King Nebuchad-
nezzar [b]what will be in the latter
days. Your dream, and the visions
of your head upon your bed, were
these:
29 "As for you, O king, thoughts
came *to* your *mind while* on your
bed, *about* what would come to
pass after this; [a]and He who re-
veals secrets has made known to
you what will be.
30 [a]"But as for me, this secret has
not been revealed to me because
I have more wisdom than anyone
living, but for *our* sakes who make
known the interpretation to the
king, [b]and that you may [1]know the
thoughts of your heart.
31 "You, O king, were watching;
and behold, a great image! This
great image, whose splendor *was*
excellent, stood before you; and its
form *was* awesome.
32 [a]"This image's head *was* of fine
gold, its chest and arms of silver,
its belly and [1]thighs of bronze,
33 "its legs of iron, its feet partly
of iron and partly of [1]clay.
34 "You watched while a stone
was cut out [a]without hands, which
struck the image on its feet of iron
and clay, and broke them in
pieces.
35 [a]"Then the iron, the clay, the
bronze, the silver, and the gold
were crushed together, and be-
came [b]like chaff from the summer
threshing floors; the wind carried
them away so that [c]no trace of
them was found. And the stone
that struck the image [d]became a
great mountain [e]and filled the
whole earth.
36 "This *is* the dream. Now we
will tell the interpretation of it be-
fore the king.
37 [a]"You, O king, *are* a king of
kings. [b]For the God of heaven has
given you a kingdom, power,
strength, and glory;
38 [a]"and wherever the children of
men dwell, or the beasts of the
field and the birds of the heaven,
He has given *them* into your hand,
and has made you ruler over them
all—[b]you *are* this head of gold.
39 "But after you shall arise [a]an-
other kingdom [b]inferior to yours;
then another, a third kingdom of
bronze, which shall rule over all
the earth.

19 [a]Num. 12:6; Job 33:15; [Prov. 3:32]; Amos 3:7
20 [a]Ps. 113:2 [b][1 Chr. 29:11, 12; Job 12:13; Ps. 147:5; Jer. 32:19; Matt. 6:13; Rom. 11:33]
21 [a]Ps. 31:15; Esth. 1:13; Dan. 2:9; 7:25 [b]Job 12:18; [Ps. 75:6, 7; Jer. 27:5; Dan. 4:35] [c]1 Kin. 3:9, 10; 4:29; [James 1:5]
22 [a]Job 12:22; Ps. 25:14; [Prov. 3:22] [b]Job 26:6; Ps. 139:12; [Is. 45:7; Jer. 23:24; Heb. 4:13] [c][Ps. 36:9]; Dan. 5:11, 14; [1 Tim. 6:16; James 1:17; 1 John 1:5]
23 [a]Ps. 21:2, 4; Dan. 2:18, 29, 30 [1]Lit. *word*
25 [1]Lit. *sons of the captivity*
28 [a]Gen. 40:8; Amos 4:13 [b]Gen. 49:1; Is. 2:2; Dan. 10:14; Mic. 4:1
29 [a][Dan. 2:22, 28]
30 [a]Acts 3:12 [b]Dan. 2:47 [1]Understand
32 [a]Dan. 2:38, 45 [1]Or *sides*
33 [1]Or *baked clay*, also vv. 34, 35, 42
34 [a]Dan. 8:25; [Zech. 4:6]; 2 Cor. 5:1; Heb. 9:24
35 [a]Dan. 7:23–27; [Rev. 16:14] [b]Ps. 1:4; Is. 17:13; 41:15, 16; Hos. 13:3 [c]Ps. 37:10, 36 [d][Is. 2:2, 3]; Mic. 4:1 [e]Ps. 80:9
37 [a]Ezra 7:12; Is. 47:5; Jer. 27:6, 7; Ezek. 26:7; Hos. 8:10 [b]Ezra 1:2
38 [a]Ps. 50:10, 11; Jer. 27:6; Dan. 4:21, 22 [b]Dan. 2:32
39 [a]Dan. 5:28, 31 [b]Dan. 2:32

40 "And [a]the fourth kingdom shall
be as strong as iron, inasmuch as
iron breaks in pieces and shatters
everything; and like iron that
crushes, *that kingdom* will break
in pieces and crush all the others.
41 "Whereas you saw the feet and
toes, partly of potter's clay and
partly of iron, the kingdom shall
be divided; yet the strength of the
iron shall be in it, just as you saw
the iron mixed with ceramic clay.
42 "And *as* the toes of the feet
were partly of iron and partly of
clay, [a]so the kingdom shall be
partly strong and partly [1]frag-
ile.
43 "As you saw iron mixed with
ceramic clay, they will mingle with
the seed of men; but they will not
adhere to one another, just as iron
does not mix with clay.
44 "And in the days of these kings
[a]the God of heaven will set up a
kingdom [b]which shall never be de-
stroyed; and the kingdom shall not
be left to other people; [c]it shall
[1]break in pieces and [2]consume all
these kingdoms, and it shall stand
forever.
45 [a]"Inasmuch as you saw that the
stone was cut out of the mountain
without hands, and that it broke
in pieces the iron, the bronze, the
clay, the silver, and the gold—the
great God has made known to
the king what will come to pass
after this. The dream is certain,
and its interpretation is sure."

Daniel and His Friends Promoted

46 [a]Then King Nebuchadnezzar
fell on his face, prostrate before
Daniel, and commanded that they
should present an offering [b]and in-
cense to him.
47 The king answered Daniel, and
said, "Truly [a]your God *is* the God
of [b]gods, the Lord of kings, and a
revealer of secrets, since you could
reveal this secret."
48 [a]Then the king promoted Dan-
iel [b]and gave him many great gifts;
and he made him ruler over the
whole province of Babylon, and
[c]chief administrator over all the
wise *men* of Babylon.
49 Also Daniel petitioned the
king, [a]and he set Shadrach, Me-
shach, and Abed-Nego over the af-
fairs of the province of Babylon;
but Daniel [b]*sat* in [1]the gate of the
king.

The Image of Gold

3 Nebuchadnezzar the king
made an image of gold, whose
height *was* [1]sixty cubits *and* its
width six cubits. He set it up in the
plain of Dura, in the province of
Babylon.
2 And King Nebuchadnezzar
sent *word* to gather together the
satraps, the administrators, the
governors, the counselors, the
treasurers, the judges, the mag-
istrates, and all the officials of the
provinces, to come to the dedi-
cation of the image which King
Nebuchadnezzar had set up.
3 So the satraps, the administra-
tors, the governors, the counsel-
ors, the treasurers, the judges, the
magistrates, and all the officials of
the provinces gathered together
for the dedication of the image that
King Nebuchadnezzar had set up;
and they stood before the image
that Nebuchadnezzar had set up.
4 Then a herald cried [1]aloud: "To
you it is commanded, [a]O peoples,
nations, and languages,
5 "*that* at the time you hear the
sound of the horn, flute, harp, lyre,
and psaltery, in symphony with all
kinds of music, you shall fall down
and worship the gold image that
King Nebuchadnezzar has set up;
6 "and whoever does not fall
down and worship shall [a]be cast
immediately into the midst of a
burning fiery furnace."
7 So at that time, when all the
people heard the sound of the
horn, flute, harp, *and* lyre, in sym-
phony with all kinds of music, all
the people, nations, and languages
fell down *and* worshiped the gold
image which King Nebuchadnez-
zar had set up.

Daniel's Friends Disobey the King

8 Therefore at that time certain
Chaldeans [a]came forward and ac-
cused the Jews.
9 They spoke and said to King
Nebuchadnezzar, [a]"O king, live
forever!
10 "You, O king, have made a de-
cree that everyone who hears the
sound of the horn, flute, harp, lyre,
and psaltery, in symphony with all

40 [a]Dan. 7:7, 23
42 [a]Dan. 7:24 [1]Or *brittle*
44 [a]Dan. 2:28, 37 [b]Is. 9:6, 7; Ezek. 37:25; Dan. 4:3, 34; 6:26; 7:14, 27; Mic. 4:7; [Luke 1:32, 33] [c]Ps. 2:9; Is. 60:12; Dan. 2:34, 35; [1 Cor. 15:24] [1]Or *crush* [2]Lit. *put an end to*
45 [a]Dan. 2:35; Is. 28:16
46 [a]Dan. 3:5, 7; Acts 10:25; 14:13; Rev. 19:10; 22:8 [b]Lev. 26:31; Ezra 6:10
47 [a]Dan. 3:28, 29; 4:34–37 [b][Deut. 10:17]
48 [a][Prov. 14:35; 21:1] [b]Dan. 2:6 [c]Dan. 4:9; 5:11
49 [a]Dan. 1:7; 3:12 [b]Esth. 2:19, 21; 3:2; Amos 5:15 [1]The king's court
CHAPTER 3
1 [1]About 90 feet
4 [a]Dan. 4:1; 6:25 [1]Lit. *with strength*
6 [a]Jer. 29:22; Ezek. 22:18–22; Matt. 13:42, 50; Rev. 9:2; 13:15; 14:11
8 [a]Ezra 4:12–16; Esth. 3:8, 9; Dan. 6:12, 13
9 [a]Dan. 2:4; 5:10; 6:6, 21

kinds of music, shall fall down and
worship the gold image;
11 "and whoever does not fall
down and worship shall be cast
into the midst of a burning fiery
furnace.
12 [a]"There are certain Jews whom
you have set over the affairs of the
province of Babylon: Shadrach,
Meshach, and Abed-Nego; these
men, O king, have [b]not paid due
regard to you. They do not serve
your gods or worship the gold im-
age which you have set up."
13 Then Nebuchadnezzar, in
[a]rage and fury, gave the command
to bring Shadrach, Meshach, and
Abed-Nego. So they brought these
men before the king.
14 Nebuchadnezzar spoke, saying
to them, "*Is it* true, Shadrach,
Meshach, and Abed-Nego, *that*
you do not serve my gods or wor-
ship the gold image which I have
set up?
15 "Now if you are ready at the
time you hear the sound of the
horn, flute, harp, lyre, *and* psal-
tery, in symphony with all kinds
of music, and you fall down and
worship the image which I have
made, [a]*good!* But if you do not
worship, you shall be cast immedi-
ately into the midst of a burning
fiery furnace. [b]And who *is* the god
who will deliver you from my
hands?"
16 Shadrach, Meshach, and Abed-
Nego answered and said to the
king, "O Nebuchadnezzar, [a]we
have no need to answer you in this
matter.
17 "If that *is the case,* our [a]God
whom we serve is able to [b]deliver
us from the burning fiery furnace,
and He will deliver *us* from your
hand, O king.
18 "But if not, let it be known to
you, O king, that we do not serve
your gods, nor will we [a]worship
the gold image which you have
set up."

Saved in Fiery Trial

19 Then Nebuchadnezzar was full
of fury, and the expression on his
face changed toward Shadrach,
Meshach, and Abed-Nego. He
spoke and commanded that they
heat the furnace seven times more
than it was usually heated.

12 [a]Dan. 2:49 [b]Dan. 1:8; 6:12, 13
13 [a]Dan. 2:12; 3:19
15 [a]Ex. 32:32; Luke 13:9 [b]Ex. 5:2; 2 Kin. 18:35; Is. 36:18–20; Dan. 2:47
16 [a][Matt. 10:19]
17 [a]Job 5:19; [Ps. 27:1, 2; Is. 26:3, 4]; Jer. 1:8; 15:20, 21; Dan. 6:19–22 [b]1 Sam. 17:37; Jer. 1:8; 15:20, 21; 42:11; Dan. 6:16, 19–22; Mic. 7:7; 2 Cor. 1:10
18 [a]Job 13:15
22 [1]Or *harsh*
24 [1]High officials
25 [a][Ps. 91:3–9]; Is. 43:2 [b]Job 1:6; 38:7; [Ps. 34:7]; Dan. 3:28 [1]Or *a son of the gods*
26 [a][Dan. 4:2, 3, 17, 34, 35] [1]Lit. *door*
27 [a][Is. 43:2]; Heb. 11:34
28 [a][Ps. 34:7, 8]; Is. 37:36; [Jer. 17:7]; Dan. 6:22, 23; Acts 5:19; 12:7 [1]Or *angel*

20 And he commanded certain
mighty men of valor who *were* in
his army to bind Shadrach, Me-
shach, and Abed-Nego, *and* cast
them into the burning fiery fur-
nace.
21 Then these men were bound in
their coats, their trousers, their
turbans, and their *other* garments,
and were cast into the midst of the
burning fiery furnace.
22 Therefore, because the king's
command was [1]urgent, and the
furnace exceedingly hot, the flame
of the fire killed those men who
took up Shadrach, Meshach, and
Abed-Nego.
23 And these three men, Sha-
drach, Meshach, and Abed-Nego,
fell down bound into the midst of
the burning fiery furnace.
24 Then King Nebuchadnezzar
was astonished; and he rose in
haste *and* spoke, saying to his
[1]counselors, "Did we not cast
three men bound into the midst of
the fire?" They answered and said
to the king, "True, O king."
25 "Look!" he answered, "I see
four men loose, [a]walking in the
midst of the fire; and they are not
hurt, and the form of the fourth is
like [b]the[1] Son of God."

Nebuchadnezzar Praises God

26 Then Nebuchadnezzar went
near the [1]mouth of the burning
fiery furnace *and* spoke, saying,
"Shadrach, Meshach, and Abed-
Nego, servants of the [a]Most High
God, come out, and come *here.*"
Then Shadrach, Meshach, and
Abed-Nego came from the midst
of the fire.
27 And the satraps, administra-
tors, governors, and the king's
counselors gathered together, and
they saw these men [a]on whose
bodies the fire had no power; the
hair of their head was not singed
nor were their garments affected,
and the smell of fire was not on
them.
28 Nebuchadnezzar spoke, say-
ing, "Blessed be the God of Sha-
drach, Meshach, and Abed-Nego,
who sent His [a]Angel[1] and deliv-
ered His servants who trusted in
Him, and they have frustrated the
king's word, and yielded their bod-
ies, that they should not serve nor

worship any god except their own
God!
29 [a]"Therefore I make a decree
that any people, nation, or lan-
guage which speaks anything
amiss against the [b]God of Sha-
drach, Meshach, and Abed-Nego
shall be [c]cut in pieces, and their
houses shall be made an ash heap;
[d]because there is no other God
who can deliver like this."
30 Then the king [1]promoted Sha-
drach, Meshach, and Abed-Nego
in the province of Babylon.

Nebuchadnezzar's Second Dream

4 Nebuchadnezzar the king,

[a]To all peoples, nations, and
languages that dwell in all the
earth:

Peace be multiplied to you.

2 I thought it good to declare the
signs and wonders [a]that the
Most High God has worked for
me.

3 [a]How great *are* His signs,
And how mighty His wonders!
His kingdom *is* [b]an everlasting
kingdom,
And His dominion *is* from
generation to generation.

4 I, Nebuchadnezzar, was at rest
in my house, and flourishing in
my palace.
5 I saw a dream which made me
afraid, [a]and the thoughts on my
bed and the visions of my head
[b]troubled me.
6 Therefore I issued a decree to
bring in all the wise *men* of
Babylon before me, that they
might make known to me the
interpretation of the dream.
7 [a]Then the magicians, the
astrologers, the Chaldeans,
and the soothsayers came in,
and I told them the dream; but
they did not make known to me
its interpretation.
8 But at last Daniel came before
me [a](his name *is* Belteshazzar,
according to the name of my
god; [b]in him *is* the Spirit of the
Holy God), and I told the dream
before him, *saying*:
9 "Belteshazzar, [a]chief of the
magicians, because I know that
the Spirit of the Holy God *is* in
you, and no secret troubles
you, explain to me the visions
of my dream that I have seen,
and its interpretation.
10 "These *were* the visions of my
head *while* on my bed:

I was looking, and behold,
[a]A tree in the midst of the earth,
And its height *was* great.
11 The tree grew and became
strong;
Its height reached to the heavens,
And it could be seen to the ends
of all the earth.
12 Its leaves *were* lovely,
Its fruit abundant,
And in it *was* food for all.
[a]The beasts of the field found
shade under it,
The birds of the heavens dwelt in
its branches,
And all flesh was fed from it.

13 "I saw in the visions of my
head *while* on my bed, and
there was [a]a watcher, [b]a holy
one, coming down from
heaven.
14 He cried [1]aloud and said thus:

[a]'Chop down the tree and cut off
its branches,
Strip off its leaves and scatter its
fruit.
[b]Let the beasts get out from
under it,
And the birds from its branches.
15 Nevertheless leave the stump and
roots in the earth,
Bound with a band of iron and
bronze,
In the tender grass of the field.
Let it be wet with the dew of
heaven,
And *let* him graze with the beasts
On the grass of the earth.
16 Let his heart be changed from
that of a man,
Let him be given the heart of a
beast,
And let seven [a]times[1] pass over
him.

17 'This decision *is* by the decree of
the watchers,
And the sentence by the word of
the holy ones,
In order [a]that the living may
know
[b]That the Most High rules in the
kingdom of men,

29 [a]Dan. 6:26 [b]Dan. 2:46, 47; 4:34–37 [c]Ezra 6:11; Dan. 2:5 [d]Dan. 6:27
30 [1]Lit. *caused to prosper*

CHAPTER 4

1 [a]Ezra 4:17; Dan. 3:4; 6:25
2 [a]Dan. 3:26
3 [a]2 Sam. 7:16; Ps. 89:35–37; Dan. 6:27; 7:13, 14; [Luke 1:31–33] [b][Dan. 2:44; 4:34; 6:26]
5 [a]Dan. 2:28, 29 [b]Dan. 2:1
7 [a]Dan. 2:2
8 [a]Dan. 1:7 [b]Is. 63:11; Dan. 2:11; 4:18; 5:11, 14
9 [a]Dan. 2:48; 5:11
10 [a]Ezek. 31:3; Dan. 4:20
12 [a]Jer. 27:6; Ezek. 17:23; 31:6; Lam. 4:20
13 [a][Dan. 4:17, 23] [b]Deut. 33:2; Ps. 89:7; Dan. 8:13; Zech. 14:5; Jude 14
14 [a]Ezek. 31:10–14; Dan. 4:23; [Matt. 3:10; 7:19; Luke 13:7–9] [b]Ezek. 31:12, 13; Dan. 4:12 [1]Lit. *with strength*
16 [a]Dan. 11:13; 12:7 [1]Possibly *years*
17 [a]Ps. 9:16; 83:18 [b]Dan. 2:21; 4:25, 32; 5:21

[c]Gives it to whomever He will,
And sets over it the [d]lowest of
men.'

18 "This dream I, King
Nebuchadnezzar, have seen.
Now you, Belteshazzar,
declare its interpretation,
[a]since all the wise *men* of my
kingdom are not able to make
known to me the
interpretation; but you *are*
able, [b]for the Spirit of the Holy
God is in you."

Daniel Explains the Second Dream

19 Then Daniel, [a]whose name was
Belteshazzar, was astonished
for a time, and his thoughts
[b]troubled him. *So* the king
spoke, and said, "Belteshazzar,
do not let the dream or its
interpretation trouble you."
Belteshazzar answered and
said,
"My lord, *may* [c]the dream
[1]concern those who hate you,
and its interpretation [2]concern
your enemies!
20 [a]The tree that you saw, which
grew and became strong,
whose height reached to the
heavens and which *could be*
seen by all the earth,
21 whose leaves *were* lovely and
its fruit abundant, in which *was*
food for all, under which the
beasts of the field dwelt, and
in whose branches the birds of
the heaven had their home—
22 [a]it *is* you, O king, who have
grown and become strong; for
your greatness has grown and
reaches to the heavens, [b]and
your dominion to the end of the
earth.
23 [a]And inasmuch as the king saw
a watcher, a holy one, coming
down from heaven and saying,
'Chop down the tree and
destroy it, but leave its stump
and roots in the earth, *bound*
with a band of iron and bronze
in the tender grass of the field;
let it be wet with the dew of
heaven, [b]and let him graze with
the beasts of the field, till seven
[1]times pass over him';
24 this is the interpretation, O
king, and this is the decree of
the Most High, which has come
upon my lord the king:
25 They shall [a]drive you from
men, your dwelling shall be
with the beasts of the field, and
they shall make you [b]eat grass
like oxen. They shall wet you
with the dew of heaven, and
seven [1]times shall pass over
you, [c]till you know that the
Most High rules in the kingdom
of men, and [d]gives it to
whomever He chooses.
26 And inasmuch as they gave the
command to leave the stump
and roots of the tree, your
kingdom shall be assured to
you, after you come to know
that [a]Heaven[1] rules.
27 Therefore, O king, let my
advice be acceptable to you;
[a]break off your sins by *being*
righteous, and your iniquities
by showing mercy to *the* poor.
[b]Perhaps there may be [c]a
[1]lengthening of your
prosperity."

Nebuchadnezzar's Humiliation

28 All *this* came upon King
Nebuchadnezzar.
29 At the end of the twelve months
he was walking [1]about the
royal palace of Babylon.
30 The king [a]spoke, saying, "Is
not this great Babylon, that I
have built for a royal dwelling
by my mighty power and for
the honor of my majesty?"
31 [a]While the word *was still* in the
king's mouth, [b]a voice fell from
heaven: "King
Nebuchadnezzar, to you it is
spoken: the kingdom has
departed from you!
32 And [a]they shall drive you from
men, and your dwelling *shall*
be with the beasts of the field.
They shall make you eat grass
like oxen; and seven [1]times
shall pass over you, until you
know that the Most High rules
in the kingdom of men, and
gives it to whomever He
chooses."
33 That very hour the word was
fulfilled concerning
Nebuchadnezzar; he was
driven from men and ate grass
like oxen; his body was wet
with the dew of heaven till his

17 [c]Jer. 27:5–7; Ezek. 29:18–20; Dan. 2:37; 5:18 [d]1 Sam. 2:8; Dan. 11:21
18 [a]Gen. 41:8, 15; Dan. 5:8, 15 [b]Dan. 4:8, 9; 5:11, 14
19 [a]Dan. 4:8 [b]Jer. 4:19; Dan. 7:15, 28; 8:27 [c]2 Sam. 18:32; Jer. 29:7; Dan. 4:24; 10:16 [1]*be for* [2]*for*
20 [a]Dan. 4:10–12
22 [a]Dan. 2:37, 38 [b]Jer. 27:6–8
23 [a]Dan. 4:13–15 [b]Dan. 5:21 [1]Possibly *years*
25 [a]Dan. 4:32; 5:21 [b]Ps. 106:20 [c]Ps. 83:18; Dan. 4:2, 17, 32 [d]Jer. 27:5 [1]Possibly *years*
26 [a]Matt. 21:25; Luke 15:18 [1]God
27 [a][Prov. 28:13]; Is. 55:7; Ezek. 18:21, 22; [Rom. 2:9–11; 1 Pet. 4:8] [b][Ps. 41:1–3]; Is. 58:6, 7, 10 [c]1 Kin. 21:29 [1]*prolonging*
29 [1]Or *upon*
30 [a]Prov. 16:18; Is. 13:19; Dan. 5:20
31 [a]Dan. 5:5; Luke 12:20 [b]Dan. 4:24
32 [a][Dan. 4:25] [1]Possibly *years*

hair had grown like eagles'
feathers and his nails like
birds' *claws.*

Nebuchadnezzar Praises God

34 And [a]at the end of the [1]time I,
Nebuchadnezzar, lifted my
eyes to heaven, and my
understanding returned to me;
and I blessed the Most High
and praised and honored Him
[b]who lives forever:

For His dominion *is* [c]an
everlasting dominion,
And His kingdom *is* from
generation to generation.
35 [a]All the inhabitants of the earth
are reputed as nothing;
[b]He does according to His will in
the army of heaven
And *among* the inhabitants of the
earth.
[c]No one can restrain His hand
Or say to Him, [d]"What have You
done?"

36 At the same time my reason
returned to me, [a]and for the
glory of my kingdom, my
honor and splendor returned to
me. My counselors and nobles
resorted to me, I was [b]restored
to my kingdom, and excellent
majesty was [c]added to me.
37 Now I, Nebuchadnezzar,
[a]praise and extol and honor the
King of heaven, [b]all of whose
works *are* truth, and His ways
justice. [c]And those who walk in
pride He is able to put down.

Belshazzar's Feast

5 Belshazzar the king [a]made a
great feast for a thousand of
his lords, and drank wine in the
presence of the thousand.
2 While he tasted the wine, Bel-
shazzar gave the command to
bring the gold and silver vessels
[a]which his [1]father Nebuchadnez-
zar had taken from the temple
which *had been* in Jerusalem, that
the king and his lords, his wives,
and his concubines might drink
from them.
3 Then they brought the gold
[a]vessels that had been taken from
the temple of the house of God
which *had been* in Jerusalem; and
the king and his lords, his wives,

34 [a]Dan. 4:26 [b]Ps. 102:24–27; Dan. 6:26; 12:7; [Rev. 4:10] [c][Ps. 10:16]; Dan. 2:44; 7:14; Mic. 4:7; [Luke 1:33] [1]Lit. *days*
35 [a]Ps. 39:5; Is. 40:15, 17 [b]Ps. 115:3; 135:6; Dan. 6:27 [c]Job 34:29; Is. 43:13 [d]Job 9:12; Is. 45:9; Jer. 18:6; Rom. 9:20; [1 Cor. 2:16]
36 [a]Dan. 4:26 [b]2 Chr. 20:20 [c]Job 42:12; [Prov. 22:4; Matt. 6:33]
37 [a]Dan. 2:46, 47; 3:28, 29 [b]Deut. 32:4; [Ps. 33:4]; Is. 5:16; [Rev. 15:3] [c]Ex. 18:11; Job 40:11, 12; Dan. 5:20

CHAPTER 5

1 [a]Esth. 1:3; Is. 22:12–14
2 [a]2 Kin. 24:13; 25:15; Ezra 1:7–11; Jer. 52:19; Dan. 1:2 [1]Or *ancestor*
3 [a]2 Chr. 36:10
4 [a]Is. 42:8; Dan. 5:23; Rev. 9:20
5 [a]Dan. 4:31
6 [a]Ezek. 7:17; 21:7
7 [a]Dan. 4:6, 7; 5:11, 15 [b]Is. 47:13 [c]Dan. 6:2, 3 [1]Lit. *with strength*
8 [a]Gen. 41:8; Dan. 2:27; 4:7; 5:15
9 [a]Job 18:11; Is. 21:2–4; Jer. 6:24; Dan. 2:1; 5:6 [1]*perplexed*
11 [a]Dan. 2:48; 4:8, 9, 18 [1]Or *ancestor*
12 [a]Dan. 1:7; 4:8 [1]Lit. *untying knots*

and his concubines drank from
them.
4 They drank wine, [a]and praised
the gods of gold and silver, bronze
and iron, wood and stone.
5 [a]In the same hour the fingers
of a man's hand appeared and
wrote opposite the lampstand on
the plaster of the wall of the king's
palace; and the king saw the part
of the hand that wrote.
6 Then the king's countenance
changed, and his thoughts trou-
bled him, so that the joints of
his hips were loosened and his
[a]knees knocked against each
other.
7 [a]The king cried [1]aloud to bring
in [b]the astrologers, the Chaldeans,
and the soothsayers. The king
spoke, saying to the wise *men* of
Babylon, "Whoever reads this
writing, and tells me its interpreta-
tion, shall be clothed with purple
and *have* a chain of gold around
his neck; [c]and he shall be the third
ruler in the kingdom."
8 Now all the king's wise *men*
came, [a]but they could not read the
writing, or make known to the
king its interpretation.
9 Then King Belshazzar was
greatly [a]troubled, his countenance
was changed, and his lords were
[1]astonished.
10 The queen, because of the
words of the king and his lords,
came to the banquet hall. The
queen spoke, saying, "O king, live
forever! Do not let your thoughts
trouble you, nor let your counte-
nance change.
11 [a]"There is a man in your king-
dom in whom *is* the Spirit of the
Holy God. And in the days of your
[1]father, light and understanding
and wisdom, like the wisdom of
the gods, were found in him; and
King Nebuchadnezzar your [1]fa-
ther—your father the king—made
him chief of the magicians, as-
trologers, Chaldeans, *and* sooth-
sayers.
12 "Inasmuch as an excellent
spirit, knowledge, understanding,
interpreting dreams, solving rid-
dles, and [1]explaining enigmas
were found in this Daniel, [a]whom
the king named Belteshazzar, now
let Daniel be called, and he will
give the interpretation."

The Writing on the Wall Explained

13 Then Daniel was brought in be-
fore the king. The king spoke, and
said to Daniel, "*Are* you that Dan-
iel [1]who is one of the captives from
Judah, whom my [2]father the king
brought from Judah?
14 "I have heard of you, that [a]the
[1]Spirit of God *is* in you, and *that*
light and understanding and excel-
lent wisdom are found in you.
15 "Now [a]the wise *men*, the as-
trologers, have been brought in be-
fore me, that they should read this
writing and make known to me its
interpretation, but they could not
give the interpretation of the thing.
16 "And I have heard of you, that
you can give interpretations and
[1]explain enigmas. [a]Now if you can
read the writing and make known
to me its interpretation, you shall
be clothed with purple and *have*
a chain of gold around your neck,
and shall be the third ruler in the
kingdom."
17 Then Daniel answered, and
said before the king, "Let your
gifts be for yourself, and give your
rewards to another; yet I will read
the writing to the king, and make
known to him the interpretation.
18 "O king, [a]the Most High God
gave Nebuchadnezzar your [1]fa-
ther a kingdom and majesty, glory
and honor.
19 "And because of the majesty
that He gave him, [a]all peoples, na-
tions, and languages trembled and
feared before him. Whomever he
wished, he [b]executed; whomever
he wished, he kept alive; whom-
ever he wished, he set up; and
whomever he wished, he put
down.
20 [a]"But when his heart was lifted
up, and his spirit was hardened in
pride, he was deposed from his
kingly throne, and they took his
glory from him.
21 "Then he was [a]driven from the
sons of men, his heart was made
like the beasts, and his dwelling
was with the wild donkeys. They
fed him with grass like oxen, and
his body was wet with the dew of
heaven, [b]till he [1]knew that the
Most High God rules in the king-
dom of men, and appoints over it
whomever He chooses.
22 "But you his son, Belshazzar,
[a]have not humbled your heart, al-
though you knew all this.
23 [a]"And you have [1]lifted yourself
up against the Lord of heaven.
They have brought the [b]vessels of
[2]His house before you, and you
and your lords, your wives and
your concubines, have drunk wine
from them. And you have praised
the gods of silver and gold, bronze
and iron, wood and stone, [c]which
do not see or hear or know; and
the God who *holds* your breath in
His hand [d]and owns all your ways,
you have not glorified.
24 "Then the [1]fingers of the hand
were sent from Him, and this writ-
ing was written.
25 "And this is the inscription that
was written:

[1]MENE, MENE, [2]TEKEL,
[3]UPHARSIN.

26 "This *is* the interpretation of
each word. MENE: God has num-
bered your kingdom, and finished
it;
27 "TEKEL: [a]You have been
weighed in the balances, and
found wanting;
28 "PERES: Your kingdom has
been divided, and given to the
[a]Medes and [b]Persians."[1]
29 Then Belshazzar gave the com-
mand, and they clothed Daniel
with purple and *put* a chain of gold
around his neck, and made a proc-
lamation concerning him [a]that he
should be the third ruler in the
kingdom.

Belshazzar's Fall

30 [a]That very night Belshazzar,
king of the Chaldeans, was slain.
31 [a]And Darius the Mede received
the kingdom, *being* about sixty-
two years old.

The Plot Against Daniel

6 It pleased Darius to set over
the kingdom one hundred and
twenty satraps, to be over the
whole kingdom;
2 and over these, three gover-
nors, of whom Daniel *was* one,
that the satraps might give ac-
count to them, so that the king
would suffer no loss.
3 Then this Daniel distinguished
himself above the governors and

13 [1]Lit. *who is of the sons of the captivity* [2]Or *ancestor*
14 [a]Dan. 4:8, 9, 18; 5:11, 12 [1]Or *spirit of the gods*
15 [a]Dan. 5:7, 8
16 [a]Dan. 5:7, 29 [1]Lit. *untie knots*
18 [a]Jer. 27:5–7; Dan. 2:37, 38; 4:17, 22, 25 [1]Or *ancestor*
19 [a]Jer. 27:7 [b]Dan. 2:12, 13; 3:6
20 [a]Ex. 9:17; Job 15:25; Is. 14:13–15; Dan. 4:30, 37
21 [a]Job 30:3–7; Dan. 4:32, 33 [b]Ex. 9:14–16; Ps. 83:17, 18; Ezek. 17:24; [Dan. 4:17, 34, 35] [1]Recognized
22 [a]Ex. 10:3; 2 Chr. 33:23; 36:12
23 [a]Dan. 5:3, 4 [b]Ex. 40:9; Num. 18:3; Is. 52:11; Heb. 9:21 [c]Ps. 115:5, 6; Is. 37:19; Hab. 2:18, 19; Acts 17:24–26; Rom. 1:21 [d]Ps. 139:3; Prov. 20:24; [Jer. 10:23] [1]Exalted [2]The temple
24 [1]Lit. *palm*
25 [1]Lit. *a mina* (50 shekels) from the verb "to number" [2]Lit. *a shekel* from the verb "to weigh" [3]Lit. *and half-shekels* from the verb "to divide"; pl. of *Peres*, v. 28
27 [a]Job 31:6; Ps. 62:9; Jer. 6:30
28 [a]Is. 21:2; Dan. 5:31; 9:1 [b]Dan. 6:28; Acts 2:9 [1]Aram. *Paras*, consonant with *Peres*
29 [a]Dan. 5:7, 16
30 [a]Jer. 51:31, 39, 57
31 [a]Dan. 2:39; 9:1

satraps, [a]because an excellent
spirit *was* in him; and the king
gave thought to setting him over
the whole realm.
4 [a]So the governors and satraps
sought to find *some* charge against
Daniel concerning the kingdom;
but they could find no charge or
fault, because he *was* faithful; nor
was there any error or fault found
in him.
5 Then these men said, "We shall
not find any charge against this
Daniel unless we find *it* against
him concerning the law of his
God."
6 So these governors and satraps
thronged before the king, and said
thus to him: [a]"King Darius, live
forever!
7 "All the governors of the king-
dom, the administrators and sa-
traps, the counselors and advisors,
have [a]consulted together to estab-
lish a royal statute and to make a
firm decree, that whoever petitions
any god or man for thirty days, ex-
cept you, O king, shall be cast into
the den of lions.
8 "Now, O king, establish the de-
cree and sign the writing, so that
it cannot be changed, according to
the [a]law of the Medes and Per-
sians, which [1]does not alter."
9 Therefore King Darius signed
the written decree.

Daniel in the Lions' Den

10 Now when Daniel knew that
the writing was signed, he went
home. And in his upper room, with
his windows open [a]toward Jerusa-
lem, he knelt down on his knees
[b]three times that day, and prayed
and gave thanks before his God,
as was his custom since early
days.
11 Then these men assembled and
found Daniel praying and making
supplication before his God.
12 [a]And they went before the
king, and spoke concerning the
king's decree: "Have you not
signed a decree that every man
who petitions any god or man
within thirty days, except you, O
king, shall be cast into the den of
lions?" The king answered and
said, "The thing *is* true, [b]according
to the law of the Medes and Per-
sians, which [1]does not alter."
13 So they answered and said be-
fore the king, "That Daniel, [a]who
is [1]one of the captives from Judah,
[b]does not show due regard for you,
O king, or for the decree that you
have signed, but makes his peti-
tion three times a day."
14 And the king, when he heard
these words, [a]was greatly dis-
pleased with himself, and set *his*
heart on Daniel to deliver him; and
he [1]labored till the going down of
the sun to deliver him.
15 Then these men [1]approached
the king, and said to the king,
"Know, O king, that *it is* [a]the law
of the Medes and Persians that no
decree or statute which the king
establishes may be changed."
16 So the king gave the command,
and they brought Daniel and cast
him into the den of lions. *But* the
king spoke, saying to Daniel,
"Your God, whom you serve con-
tinually, He will deliver you."
17 [a]Then a stone was brought and
laid on the mouth of the den, [b]and
the king sealed it with his own sig-
net ring and with the signets of his
lords, that the purpose concerning
Daniel might not be changed.

Daniel Saved from the Lions

18 Now the king went to his pal-
ace and spent the night fasting;
and no [1]musicians were brought
before him. [a]Also his sleep [2]went
from him.
19 Then the [a]king arose very early
in the morning and went in haste
to the den of lions.
20 And when he came to the den,
he cried out with a [1]lamenting
voice to Daniel. The king spoke,
saying to Daniel, "Daniel, servant
of the living God, [a]has your God,
whom you serve continually, been
able to deliver you from the lions?"
21 Then Daniel said to the king,
[a]"O king, live forever!
22 [a]"My God sent His angel and
[b]shut the lions' mouths, so that
they have not hurt me, because I
was found innocent before Him;
and also, O king, I have done no
wrong before you."
23 Now the king was exceedingly
glad for him, and commanded that
they should take Daniel up out of
the den. So Daniel was taken up
out of the den, and no injury what-

CHAPTER 6
3 [a]Dan. 5:12
4 [a]Eccl. 4:4
6 [a]Neh. 2:3; Dan. 2:4; 6:21
7 [a]Ps. 59:3; 62:4; 64:2–6
8 [a]Esth. 1:19; 8:8; Dan. 6:12, 15 [1]Lit. *does not pass away*
10 [a]1 Kin. 8:29, 30, 46–48; Ps. 5:7; Jon. 2:4 [b]Ps. 55:17; Acts 2:1, 2, 15; [Phil. 4:6]; 1 Thess. 5:17, 18
12 [a]Dan. 3:8–12; Acts 16:19–21 [b]Esth. 1:19; Dan. 6:8, 15 [1]Lit. *does not pass away*
13 [a]Dan. 1:6; 5:13 [b]Esth. 3:8; Dan. 3:12; Acts 5:29 [1]Lit. *of the sons of the captivity*
14 [a]Mark 6:26 [1]*strove*
15 [a]Esth. 8:8; Ps. 94:20, 21; Dan. 6:8, 12 [1]Lit. *thronged before*
17 [a]Lam. 3:53 [b]Matt. 27:66
18 [a]Esth. 6:1; Ps. 77:4; Dan. 2:1 [1]Exact meaning unknown [2]Or *fled*
19 [a]Dan. 3:24
20 [a]Gen. 18:14; Num. 11:23; Jer. 32:17; Dan. 3:17; [Luke 1:37] [1]Or *grieved*
21 [a]Dan. 2:4; 6:6
22 [a]Num. 20:16; Is. 63:9; Dan. 3:28; Acts 12:11; [Heb. 1:14] [b]Ps. 91:11–13; 2 Tim. 4:17; Heb. 11:33

ever was found on him, [a]because
he believed in his God.

Darius Honors God

24 And the king gave the command, [a]and they brought those
men who had accused Daniel, and
they cast *them* into the den of
lions—them, [b]their children, and
their wives; and the lions overpowered them, and broke all their
bones in pieces before they ever
came to the bottom of the den.
25 [a]Then King Darius wrote:

To all peoples, nations, and
languages that dwell in all the
earth:

Peace be multiplied to you.

26 [a]I make a decree that in every
dominion of my kingdom *men
must* [b]tremble and fear before
the God of Daniel.

[c]For He *is* the living God,
And steadfast forever;
His kingdom *is the one* which
shall not be [d]destroyed,
And His dominion *shall endure* to
the end.
27 He delivers and rescues,
[a]And He works signs and wonders
In heaven and on earth,
Who has delivered Daniel from
the [1]power of the lions.

28 So this Daniel prospered in the
reign of Darius [a]and in the reign
of [b]Cyrus the Persian.

Vision of the Four Beasts

7 In the first year of Belshazzar
king of Babylon, [a]Daniel [1]had
a dream and [b]visions of his head
while on his bed. Then he wrote
down the dream, telling [2]the main
facts.
2 Daniel spoke, saying, "I saw in
my vision by night, and behold, the
four winds of heaven were stirring
up the Great Sea.
3 "And four great beasts [a]came
up from the sea, each different
from the other.
4 "The first *was* [a]like a lion, and
had eagle's wings. I watched till
its wings were plucked off; and it
was lifted up from the earth and
made to stand on two feet like a
man, and a [b]man's heart was given
to it.
5 [a]"And suddenly another beast,
a second, like a bear. It was raised
up on one side, and *had* three ribs
in its mouth between its teeth. And
they said thus to it: 'Arise, devour
much flesh!'
6 "After this I looked, and there
was another, like a leopard, which
had on its back four wings of a
bird. The beast also had [a]four
heads, and dominion was given
to it.
7 "After this I saw in the night
visions, and behold, [a]a fourth
beast, dreadful and terrible, exceedingly strong. It had huge iron
teeth; it was devouring, breaking
in pieces, and trampling the residue with its feet. It *was* different
from all the beasts that *were* before it, [b]and it had ten horns.
8 "I was considering the horns,
and [a]there was another horn, a little one, coming up among them,
before whom three of the first
horns were plucked out by the
roots. And there, in this horn, *were*
eyes like the eyes [b]of a man, [c]and
a mouth speaking [1]pompous
words.

Vision of the Ancient of Days

9 "I[a] watched till thrones were [1]put
in place,
And [b]the Ancient of Days was
seated;
[c]His garment *was* white as snow,
And the hair of His head *was* like
pure wool.
His throne *was* a fiery flame,
[d]Its wheels a burning fire;
10 [a]A fiery stream issued
And came forth from before Him.
[b]A thousand thousands ministered
to Him;
Ten thousand times ten thousand
stood before Him.
[c]The [1]court was seated,
And the books were opened.

11 "I watched then because of the
sound of the [1]pompous words
which the horn was speaking; [a]I
watched till the beast was slain,
and its body destroyed and given
to the burning flame.
12 "As for the rest of the beasts,
they had their dominion taken
away, yet their lives were prolonged for a season and a time.

---

23 [a]Heb. 11:33
24 [a]Deut. 19:18, 19; Esth. 7:10 [b]Deut. 24:16; 2 Kin. 14:6; Esth. 9:10
25 [a]Ezra 1:1, 2; Esth. 3:12; 8:9; Dan. 4:1
26 [a]Ezra 6:8–12; 7:13; Dan. 3:29 [b]Ps. 99:1 [c]Dan. 4:34; 6:20; Hos. 1:10; Rom. 9:26 [d]Dan. 2:44; 4:3; 7:14, 27; [Luke 1:33]
27 [a]Dan. 4:2, 3 [1]Lit. *hand*
28 [a]Dan. 1:21 [b]Ezra 1:1, 2

CHAPTER 7

1 [a]Num. 12:6; [Amos 3:7] [b][Dan. 2:28] [1]Lit. *saw* [2]Lit. *the head* or *chief of the words*
3 [a]Dan. 7:17; Rev. 13:1; 17:8
4 [a]Deut. 28:49; 2 Sam. 1:23; Jer. 48:40; Ezek. 17:3; Hab. 1:8 [b]Dan. 4:16, 34
5 [a]Dan. 2:39
6 [a]Dan. 8:8, 22
7 [a]Dan. 2:40 [b]Dan. 2:41; Rev. 12:3; 13:1
8 [a]Dan. 8:9 [b]Rev. 9:7 [c]Ps. 12:3; Rev. 13:5, 6 [1]Lit. *great things*
9 [a][Rev. 20:4] [b]Ps. 90:2 [c]Ps. 104:2; Rev. 1:14 [d]Ezek. 1:15 [1]Or *set up*
10 [a]Ps. 50:3; Is. 30:33; 66:15 [b]Deut. 33:2; 1 Kin. 22:19; Ps. 68:17; Rev. 5:11 [c]Dan. 12:1; [Rev. 20:11–15] [1]Or *judgment*
11 [a][Rev. 19:20; 20:10] [1]Lit. *great*

13 "I was watching in the night
visions,
And behold, [a]One like the Son of
Man,
Coming with the clouds of
heaven!
He came to the Ancient of Days,
And they brought Him near
before Him.
14 [a]Then to Him was given dominion
and glory and a kingdom,
That all [b]peoples, nations, and
languages should serve Him.
His dominion *is* [c]an everlasting
dominion,
Which shall not pass away,
And His kingdom *the one*
Which shall not be destroyed.

Daniel's Visions Interpreted

15 "I, Daniel, was grieved in my
spirit [1]within *my* body, and the vi-
sions of my head troubled me.
16 "I came near to one of those
who stood by, and asked him the
truth of all this. So he told me and
made known to me the interpreta-
tion of these things:
17 'Those great beasts, which are
four, *are* four [1]kings *which* arise
out of the earth.
18 'But [a]the saints of the Most
High shall receive the kingdom,
and possess the kingdom forever,
even forever and ever.'
19 "Then I wished to know the
truth about the fourth beast, which
was different from all the others,
exceedingly dreadful, *with* its
teeth of iron and its nails of
bronze, *which* devoured, broke in
pieces, and trampled the residue
with its feet;
20 "and the ten horns that *were*
on its head, and the other *horn*
which came up, before which
three fell, namely, that horn
which had eyes and a mouth
which spoke [1]pompous words,
whose appearance *was* greater
than his fellows.
21 "I was watching; [a]and the same
horn was making war against the
saints, and prevailing against
them,
22 "until the Ancient of Days
came, [a]and a judgment was
made *in favor* of the saints of the
Most High, and the time came for
the saints to possess the kingdom.
23 "Thus he said:

13 [a][Matt. 24:30; 26:64; Mark 13:26; 14:62; Luke 21:27; Rev. 1:7, 13; 14:14]
14 [a][Matt. 28:18; John 3:35, 36; 1 Cor. 15:27; Eph. 1:22; Phil. 2:9–11; Rev. 1:6; 11:15] [b]Dan. 3:4 [c]Mic. 4:7; [Luke 1:33]; John 12:34; Heb. 12:28
15 [1]Lit. *in the midst of its sheath*
17 [1]Representing their kingdoms, v. 23
18 [a]Is. 60:12–14
20 [1]Lit. *great things*
21 [a]Rev. 11:7; 13:7; 17:14
22 [a][Rev. 1:6]
23 [a]Dan. 2:40
24 [a]Rev. 13:1; 17:12
25 [a]Rev. 13:1–6 [b]Rev. 17:6 [c]Dan. 2:21 [d]Rev. 13:7; 18:24 [e]Rev. 12:14 [1]Lit. *wear out*
26 [a][Dan. 2:35; 7:10, 22] [b]Rev. 19:20
27 [a]Dan. 7:14, 18, 22 [b][Luke 1:33, 34] [c]Is. 60:12
28 [a]Dan. 8:27 [b]Luke 2:19, 51 [1]Lit. *word*

CHAPTER 8

1 [a]Dan. 7:1 [1]The Hebrew language resumes in Dan. 8:1.
2 [a]Esth. 1:2; 2:8 [1]Or *Susa* [2]Or *fortified palace*
3 [a]Dan. 7:5

'The fourth beast shall be
[a]A fourth kingdom on earth,
Which shall be different from all
other kingdoms,
And shall devour the whole earth,
Trample it and break it in pieces.
24 [a]The ten horns *are* ten kings
Who shall arise from this
kingdom.
And another shall rise after them;
He shall be different from the first
ones,
And shall subdue three kings.
25 [a]He shall speak *pompous* words
against the Most High,
Shall [b]persecute[1] the saints of the
Most High,
And shall [c]intend to change times
and law.
Then [d]*the saints* shall be given
into his hand
[e]For a time and times and half a
time.

26 'But[a] the court shall be seated,
And they shall [b]take away his
dominion,
To consume and destroy *it*
forever.
27 Then the [a]kingdom and
dominion,
And the greatness of the
kingdoms under the whole
heaven,
Shall be given to the people, the
saints of the Most High.
[b]His kingdom *is* an everlasting
kingdom,
[c]And all dominions shall serve
and obey Him.'

28 "This *is* the end of the [1]account.
As for me, Daniel, [a]my thoughts
greatly troubled me, and my coun-
tenance changed; but I [b]kept the
matter in my heart."

Vision of a Ram and a Goat

8 In[1] the third year of the reign
of King Belshazzar a vision ap-
peared *to* me—to me, Daniel—
after the one that appeared to me
[a]the first time.
2 I saw in the vision, and it so
happened while I was looking, that
I *was* in [a]Shushan,[1] the [2]citadel,
which *is* in the province of Elam;
and I saw in the vision that I was
by the River Ulai.
3 Then I lifted my eyes and saw,
and there, standing beside the
river, was a ram which had two
horns, and the two horns *were*
high; but one *was* [a]higher than the

other, and the higher one came up last.

4 I saw the ram pushing westward, northward, and southward, so that no animal could [1]withstand him; nor *was there any* that could deliver from his hand, [a]but he did according to his will and became great.

5 And as I was considering, suddenly a male goat came from the west, across the surface of the whole earth, without touching the ground; and the goat *had* a notable [a]horn between his eyes.

6 Then he came to the ram that had two horns, which I had seen standing beside the river, and ran at him with furious power.

7 And I saw him confronting the ram; he was moved with rage against him, [1]attacked the ram, and broke his two horns. There was no power in the ram to withstand him, but he cast him down to the ground and trampled him; and there was no one that could deliver the ram from his hand.

8 Therefore the male goat grew very great; but when he became strong, the large horn was broken, and in place of it [a]four notable ones came up toward the four winds of heaven.

9 [a]And out of one of them came a little horn which grew exceedingly great toward the south, [b]toward the east, and toward the [c]Glorious *Land*.

10 [a]And it grew up to [b]the host of heaven; and [c]it cast down *some* of the host and *some* of the stars to the ground, and trampled them.

11 [a]He even exalted *himself* as high as [b]the Prince of the host; [c]and by him [d]the daily *sacrifices* were taken away, and the place of [1]His sanctuary was cast down.

12 Because of transgression, [a]an army was given over *to the horn* to oppose the daily *sacrifices;* and he cast [b]truth down to the ground. He [c]did *all this* and prospered.

13 Then I heard [a]a holy one speaking; and *another* holy one said to that certain *one* who was speaking, "How long *will* the vision *be, concerning* the daily *sacrifices* and the transgression [1]of desolation, the giving of both the sanctuary and the host to be trampled underfoot?"

14 And he said to me, "For two thousand three hundred [1]days; then the sanctuary shall be cleansed."

Gabriel Interprets the Vision

15 Then it happened, when I, Daniel, had seen the vision and [a]was seeking the meaning, that suddenly there stood before me [b]one having the appearance of a man.

16 And I heard a man's voice [a]between *the banks of* the Ulai, who called, and said, [b]"Gabriel, make this *man* understand the vision."

17 So he came near where I stood, and when he came I was afraid and [a]fell on my face; but he said to me, "Understand, son of man, that the vision *refers* to the time of the end."

18 [a]Now, as he was speaking with me, I was in a deep sleep with my face to the ground; [b]but he touched me, and stood me upright.

19 And he said, "Look, I am making known to you what shall happen in the latter time of the indignation; [a]for at the appointed time the end *shall be.*

20 "The ram which you saw, having the two horns—*they are* the kings of Media and Persia.

21 "And the [1]male goat *is* the [2]kingdom of Greece. The large horn that *is* between its eyes [a]*is* the first king.

22 [a]"As for the broken *horn* and the four that stood up in its place, four kingdoms shall arise out of that nation, but not with its power.

23 "And in the latter time of their
kingdom,
When the transgressors have
reached their fullness,
A king shall arise,
[a]Having fierce [1]features,
Who understands sinister
schemes.
24 His power shall be mighty, [a]but
not by his own power;
He shall destroy [1]fearfully,
[b]And shall prosper and thrive;
[c]He shall destroy the mighty, and
also the holy people.

25 "Through[a] his cunning
He shall cause deceit to prosper
under his [1]rule;

4 [a]Dan. 5:19 [1]Lit. *stand before him*
5 [a]Dan. 8:8, 21; 11:3
7 [1]Lit. *struck*
8 [a]Dan. 7:6; 8:22; 11:4
9 [a]Dan. 11:21 [b]Dan. 11:25 [c]Ps. 48:2
10 [a]Dan. 11:28 [b]Is. 14:13; Jer. 48:26 [c]Rev. 12:4
11 [a]2 Kin. 19:22, 23; 2 Chr. 32:15–17; Is. 37:23; Dan. 8:25; 11:36, 37 [b]Josh. 5:14 [c]Ezek. 46:14; Dan. 11:31; 12:11 [d]Ex. 29:38 [1]The temple
12 [a]Dan. 11:31 [b]Ps. 119:43; Is. 59:14 [c]Dan. 8:4; 11:36
13 [a]Dan. 4:13, 23; 1 Pet. 1:12 [1]Or *making desolate*
14 [1]Lit. *evening-mornings*
15 [a]1 Pet. 1:10 [b]Ezek. 1:26
16 [a]Dan. 12:6, 7 [b]Dan. 9:21; Luke 1:19, 26
17 [a]Ezek. 1:28; 44:4; Dan. 2:46; Rev. 1:17
18 [a]Dan. 10:9; Luke 9:32 [b]Ezek. 2:2; Dan. 10:10, 16, 18
19 [a]Hab. 2:3
21 [a]Dan. 11:3 [1]*shaggy male* [2]Lit. *king*, representing his kingdom, Dan. 7:17, 23
22 [a]Dan. 11:4
23 [a]Deut. 28:50 [1]Lit. *countenance*
24 [a]Rev. 17:13 [b]Dan. 11:36 [c]Dan. 7:25 [1]Or *extraordinarily*
25 [a]Dan. 11:21 [1]Lit. *hand*

[b]And he shall exalt *himself* in his
heart.
He shall destroy many in *their*
prosperity.
[c]He shall even rise against the
Prince of princes;
But he shall be [d]broken without
human [1]means.

26 "And the vision of the evenings
and mornings
Which was told is true;
[a]Therefore seal up the vision,
For *it refers* to many days *in the*
future."

27 [a]And I, Daniel, fainted and was
sick for days; afterward I arose
and went about the king's busi-
ness. I was [1]astonished by the vi-
sion, but no one understood it.

Daniel's Prayer for the People

9 In the first year [a]of Darius the
son of Ahasuerus, of the lin-
eage of the Medes, who was
made king over the realm of the
Chaldeans—
2 in the first year of his reign I,
Daniel, understood by the books
the number of the years *specified*
by the word of the LORD through
[a]Jeremiah the prophet, that He
would accomplish seventy years in
the desolations of Jerusalem.
3 [a]Then I set my face toward the
Lord God to make request by
prayer and supplications, with
fasting, sackcloth, and ashes.
4 And I prayed to the LORD my
God, and made confession, and
said, "O [a]Lord, great and awesome
God, who keeps His covenant and
mercy with those who love Him,
and with those who keep His com-
mandments,
5 [a]"we have sinned and com-
mitted iniquity, we have done
wickedly and rebelled, even by
departing from Your precepts and
Your judgments.
6 [a]"Neither have we heeded
Your servants the prophets, who
spoke in Your name to our kings
and our princes, to our fathers and
all the people of the land.
7 "O Lord, [a]righteousness *be-*
longs to You, but to us shame of
face, as *it is* this day—to the men
of Judah, to the inhabitants of Je-
rusalem and all Israel, those near
and those far off in all the coun-

25 [b]Dan. 8:11–13; 11:36; 12:7 [c]Dan. 11:36; Rev. 19:19, 20 [d]Job 34:20; Lam. 4:6 [1]Lit. *hand*
26 [a]Ezek. 12:27; Dan. 12:4, 9; Rev. 22:10
27 [a]Dan. 7:28; 8:17; Hab. 3:16 [1]*amazed*

CHAPTER 9

1 [a]Dan. 1:21
2 [a]2 Chr. 36:21; Ezra 1:1; Jer. 25:11, 12; 29:10; Zech. 7:5
3 [a]Neh. 1:4; Dan. 6:10; 10:15
4 [a]Ex. 20:6
5 [a]1 Kin. 8:47, 48; Neh. 9:33; Ps. 106:6; Is. 64:5–7; Jer. 14:7
6 [a]2 Chr. 36:15; Jer. 44:4, 5
7 [a]Neh. 9:33
9 [a][Neh. 9:17; Ps. 130:4, 7]
11 [a]Is. 1:3–6; Jer. 8:5–10 [b]Lev. 26:14; Neh. 1:6; Ps. 106:6
12 [a]Is. 44:26; Jer. 44:2–6; Lam. 2:17; Zech. 1:6 [b]Lam. 1:12; 2:13; Ezek. 5:9; [Amos 3:2]
13 [a]Lev. 26:14–45; Deut. 28:15–68; Lam. 2:17 [b]Job 36:13; Is. 9:13; Jer. 2:30; Hos. 7:7
14 [a]Jer. 31:28; 44:27 [b]Neh. 9:33
15 [a]Ex. 32:11; 1 Kin. 8:51; Neh. 1:10 [b]Ex. 14:18; Neh. 9:10; Jer. 32:20
16 [a]1 Sam. 12:7; Ps. 31:1; Mic. 6:4, 5 [b]Ps. 87:1–3; Dan. 9:20; Joel 3:17; Zech. 8:3 [c]Ex. 20:5 [d]Ps. 122:6; Jer. 29:7; Lam. 2:16 [e]Ps. 79:4

tries to which You have driven
them, because of the unfaithful-
ness which they have committed
against You.
8 "O Lord, to us *belongs* shame
of face, to our kings, our princes,
and our fathers, because we have
sinned against You.
9 [a]"To the Lord our God *belong*
mercy and forgiveness, though we
have rebelled against Him.
10 "We have not obeyed the voice
of the LORD our God, to walk in
His laws, which He set before us
by His servants the prophets.
11 "Yes, [a]all Israel has trans-
gressed Your law, and has de-
parted so as not to obey Your
voice; therefore the curse and the
oath written in the [b]Law of Moses
the servant of God have been
poured out on us, because we have
sinned against Him.
12 "And He has [a]confirmed His
words, which He spoke against us
and against our judges who judged
us, by bringing upon us a great
disaster; [b]for under the whole
heaven such has never been done
as what has been done to Jerusa-
lem.
13 [a]"As *it is* written in the Law of
Moses, all this disaster has come
upon us; [b]yet we have not made
our prayer before the LORD our
God, that we might turn from our
iniquities and understand Your
truth.
14 "Therefore the LORD has [a]kept
the disaster in mind, and brought
it upon us; for [b]the LORD our God
is righteous in all the works which
He does, though we have not
obeyed His voice.
15 "And now, O Lord our God,
[a]who brought Your people out of
the land of Egypt with a mighty
hand, and made Yourself [b]a name,
as *it is* this day—we have sinned,
we have done wickedly!
16 "O Lord, [a]according to all Your
righteousness, I pray, let Your an-
ger and Your fury be turned away
from Your city Jerusalem, [b]Your
holy mountain; because for our
sins, [c]and for the iniquities of our
fathers, [d]Jerusalem and Your peo-
ple [e]*are* a reproach to all *those*
around us.
17 "Now therefore, our God, hear
the prayer of Your servant, and his

supplications, [a]and [b]for the Lord's
sake [1]cause Your face to shine on
[2]Your sanctuary, [c]which is deso-
late.
18 [a]"O my God, incline Your ear
and hear; open Your eyes [b]and see
our desolations, and the city
[c]which is called by Your name; for
we do not present our supplica-
tions before You because of our
righteous deeds, but because of
Your great mercies.
19 "O Lord, hear! O Lord, forgive!
O Lord, listen and act! Do not de-
lay for Your own sake, my God,
for Your city and Your people are
called by Your name."

The Seventy-Weeks Prophecy

20 Now while I *was* speaking,
praying, and confessing my sin
and the sin of my people Israel,
and presenting my supplication
before the LORD my God for the
holy mountain of my God,
21 yes, while I *was* speaking in
prayer, the man [a]Gabriel, whom I
had seen in the vision at the begin-
ning, [1]being caused to fly swiftly,
reached me about the time of the
evening offering.
22 And he informed *me,* and
talked with me, and said, "O Dan-
iel, I have now come forth to give
you skill to understand.
23 "At the beginning of your sup-
plications the [1]command went out,
and I have come to tell *you,* for you
are greatly [a]beloved; therefore
[b]consider the matter, and under-
stand the vision:

24 "Seventy [1]weeks are determined
For your people and for your holy city,
To finish the transgression,
[2]To make an end of sins,
[a]To make reconciliation for iniquity,
[b]To bring in everlasting righteousness,
To seal up vision and prophecy,
[c]And to anoint [3]the Most Holy.

25 "Know therefore and understand,
That from the going forth of the command
To restore and build Jerusalem
Until [a]Messiah [b]the Prince,
There shall be seven weeks and sixty-two weeks;
The [1]street shall be built again, and the [2]wall,
Even in troublesome times.

26 "And after the sixty-two weeks
[a]Messiah shall [1]be cut off, [b]but not for Himself;
And [c]the people of the prince who is to come
[d]Shall destroy the city and the sanctuary.
The end of it *shall be* with a flood,
And till the end of the war desolations are determined.
27 Then he shall confirm [a]a [1]covenant with [b]many for one week;
But in the middle of the week
He shall bring an end to sacrifice and offering.
And on the wing of abominations shall be one who makes desolate,
[c]Even until the consummation, which is determined,
Is poured out on the [2]desolate."

Vision of the Glorious Man

10 In the third year of Cyrus
king of Persia a message
was revealed to Daniel, whose
[a]name was called Belteshazzar.
The message *was* true, [1]but the ap-
pointed time *was* long; and he un-
derstood the message, and had
understanding of the vision.
2 In those days I, Daniel, was
mourning three full weeks.
3 I ate no [1]pleasant food, no meat
or wine came into my mouth, nor
did I anoint myself at all, till three
whole weeks were fulfilled.
4 Now on the twenty-fourth day
of the first month, as I was by the
side of the great river, that *is,* the
[1]Tigris,
5 I lifted my eyes and looked, and
behold, a certain man clothed in
[a]linen, whose waist *was* [b]girded
with gold of Uphaz!
6 His body *was* like beryl, his
face like the appearance of light-
ning, his eyes like torches of fire,
his arms and feet like burnished
bronze in color, [a]and the sound of
his words like the voice of a multi-
tude.
7 And I, Daniel, alone saw the vi-
sion, for the men who were with
me did not see the vision; but a
great terror fell upon them, so that
they fled to hide themselves.

17 [a]Num. 6:24–26; Ps. 80:3, 7, 19 [b]Lam. 5:18 [c][John 16:24] [1]Be gracious [2]The temple
18 [a]Is. 37:17 [b]Ex. 3:7 [c]Jer. 25:29
21 [a]Dan. 8:16; Luke 1:19, 26 [1]Or *being weary with weariness*
23 [a]Dan. 10:11, 19 [b]Matt. 24:15 [1]Lit. *word*
24 [a]2 Chr. 29:24; [Is. 53:10]; Acts 10:43; [Rom. 5:10]; Heb. 9:12, 14 [b]Rev. 14:6 [c]Ps. 45:7 [1]Lit. *sevens,* and so throughout the chapter [2]So with Qr., LXX, Syr., Vg.; Kt., Theodotion *To seal up* [3]The Most Holy Place
25 [a]Luke 2:1, 2; John 1:41; 4:25 [b]Is. 55:4 [1]Or *open square* [2]Or *moat*
26 [a][Is. 53:8]; Matt. 27:50; Mark 9:12; 15:37; [Luke 23:46; 24:26]; John 19:30; Acts 8:32 [b][1 Pet. 2:21] [c]Matt. 22:7 [d]Matt. 24:2; Mark 13:2; Luke 19:43, 44 [1]Suffer the death penalty
27 [a]Is. 42:6 [b][Matt. 26:28] [c]Dan. 11:36 [1]Or *treaty* [2]Or *desolator*

CHAPTER 10
1 [a]Dan. 1:7 [1]Or *and of great conflict;*
3 [1]*desirable*
4 [1]Heb. *Hiddekel*
5 [a]Ezek. 9:2; 10:2 [b]Rev. 1:13; 15:6
6 [a][Rev. 1:15]

8 Therefore I was left alone when
I saw this great vision, and no
strength remained in me; for my
[1]vigor was turned to [2]frailty in me,
and I retained no strength.
9 Yet I heard the sound of his
words; and while I heard the
sound of his words I was in a deep
sleep on my face, with my face to
the ground.

Prophecies Concerning Persia and Greece

10 [a]Suddenly, a hand touched me,
which made me tremble on my
knees and *on* the palms of my
hands.
11 And he said to me, "O Daniel,
[a]man greatly beloved, understand
the words that I speak to you, and
stand upright, for I have now been
sent to you." While he was speak-
ing this word to me, I stood trem-
bling.
12 Then he said to me, [a]"Do not
fear, Daniel, for from the first day
that you set your heart to under-
stand, and to humble yourself be-
fore your God, [b]your words were
heard; and I have come because
of your words.
13 [a]"But the prince of the king-
dom of Persia withstood me
twenty-one days; and behold, [b]Mi-
chael, one of the chief princes,
came to help me, for I had been
left alone there with the kings of
Persia.
14 "Now I have come to make you
understand what will happen to
your people [a]in the latter days, [b]for
the vision *refers* to *many* days yet
to come."
15 When he had spoken such
words to me, [a]I [1]turned my face
toward the ground and became
speechless.
16 And suddenly, [a]*one* having the
likeness of the [1]sons of men
[b]touched my lips; then I opened
my mouth and spoke, saying to
him who stood before me, "My
lord, because of the vision [c]my sor-
rows have [2]overwhelmed me, and
I have retained no strength.
17 "For how can this servant of
my lord talk with you, my lord?
As for me, no strength remains in
me now, nor is any breath left in
me."
18 Then again, *the one* having the

8 [1]Lit. *splendor* [2]Lit. *ruin*
10 [a]Dan. 9:21
11 [a]Dan. 9:23
12 [a]Rev. 1:17 [b]Dan. 9:3, 4, 22, 23; Acts 10:4
13 [a]Dan. 10:20 [b]Dan. 10:21; 12:1; Jude 9; [Rev. 12:7]
14 [a]Gen. 49:1; Deut. 31:29; Dan. 2:28 [b]Dan. 8:26; 10:1
15 [a]Dan. 8:18; 10:9 [1]Lit. *set*
16 [a]Dan. 8:15 [b]Jer. 1:9; Dan. 10:10 [c]Dan. 10:8, 9 [1]Theodotion, Vg. *the son;* LXX *a hand* [2]Or *turned upon*
19 [a]Dan. 10:11 [b]Judg. 6:23; Is. 43:1; Dan. 10:12
20 [a]Dan. 10:13
21 [a]Dan. 10:13; Jude 9; [Rev. 12:7]

CHAPTER 11

1 [a]Dan. 9:1 [b]Dan. 5:31
3 [a]Dan. 7:6; 8:5 [b]Dan. 8:4; 11:16, 36
4 [a]Jer. 49:36; Ezek. 37:9; Dan. 7:2; 8:8; Zech. 2:6; Rev. 7:1 [b]Dan. 8:22
6 [1]Lit. *arm*

likeness of a man touched me and
strengthened me.
19 [a]And he said, "O man greatly
beloved, [b]fear not! Peace *be* to
you; be strong, yes, be strong!"
So when he spoke to me I was
strengthened, and said, "Let my
lord speak, for you have strength-
ened me."
20 Then he said, "Do you know
why I have come to you? And now
I must return to fight [a]with the
prince of Persia; and when I have
gone forth, indeed the prince of
Greece will come.
21 "But I will tell you what is
noted in the Scripture of Truth.
(No one upholds me against these,
[a]except Michael your prince.
11 "Also [a]in the first year of
[b]Darius the Mede, I, *even*
I, stood up to confirm and
strengthen him.)
2 "And now I will tell you the
truth: Behold, three more kings
will arise in Persia, and the fourth
shall be far richer than *them* all;
by his strength, through his riches,
he shall stir up all against the
realm of Greece.
3 "Then [a]a mighty king shall
arise, who shall rule with great do-
minion, and [b]do according to his
will.
4 "And when he has arisen, [a]his
kingdom shall be broken up and
divided toward the four winds of
heaven, but not among his poster-
ity [b]nor according to his dominion
with which he ruled; for his king-
dom shall be uprooted, even for
others besides these.

Warring Kings of North and South

5 "Also the king of the South
shall become strong, as well as *one*
of his princes; and he shall gain
power over him and have domin-
ion. His dominion *shall be* a great
dominion.
6 "And at the end of *some* years
they shall join forces, for the
daughter of the king of the South
shall go to the king of the North
to make an agreement; but she
shall not retain the power of her
[1]authority, and neither he nor his
[1]authority shall stand; but she
shall be given up, with those who
brought her, and with him who
begot her, and with him who

strengthened her in *those* times.

7 "But from a branch of her roots *one* shall arise in his place, who shall come with an army, enter the fortress of the king of the North, and deal with them and prevail.

8 "And he shall also carry their gods captive to Egypt, with their [1]princes *and* their precious articles of silver and gold; and he shall continue *more* years than the king of the North.

9 "Also *the king of the North* shall come to the kingdom of the king of the South, but shall return to his own land.

10 "However his sons shall stir up strife, and assemble a multitude of great forces; and *one* shall certainly come [a]and overwhelm and pass through; then he shall return [b]to his fortress and stir up strife.

11 "And the king of the South shall be [a]moved with rage, and go out and fight with him, with the king of the North, who shall muster a great multitude; but the [b]multitude shall be given into the hand of his *enemy*.

12 "When he has taken away the multitude, his heart will be [1]lifted up; and he will cast down tens of thousands, but he will not prevail.

13 "For the king of the North will return and muster a multitude greater than the former, and shall certainly come at the end of some years with a great army and much equipment.

14 "Now in those times many shall rise up against the king of the South. Also, [1]violent men of your people shall exalt themselves [2]in fulfillment of the vision, but they shall [a]fall.

15 "So the king of the North shall come and [a]build a siege mound, and take a fortified city; and the [1]forces of the South shall not withstand *him*. Even his choice troops *shall have* no strength to resist.

16 "But he who comes against him [a]shall do according to his own will, and [b]no one shall stand against him. He shall stand in the Glorious Land with destruction in his [1]power.

17 "He shall also [a]set his face to enter with the strength of his whole kingdom, and [1]upright ones with him; thus shall he do. And he shall give him the daughter of women to destroy it; but she shall not stand *with him,* [b]or be for him.

18 "After this he shall turn his face to the coastlands, and shall take many. But a ruler shall bring the reproach against them to an end; and with the reproach removed, he shall turn back on him.

19 "Then he shall turn his face toward the fortress of his own land; but he shall [a]stumble and fall, [b]and not be found.

20 "There shall arise in his place one who imposes taxes *on* the glorious kingdom; but within a few days he shall be destroyed, but not in anger or in battle.

21 "And in his place [a]shall arise a vile person, to whom they will not give the honor of royalty; but he shall come in peaceably, and seize the kingdom by intrigue.

22 "With the [1]force of a [a]flood they shall be swept away from before him and be broken, [b]and also the prince of the covenant.

23 "And after the league *is made* with him [a]he shall act deceitfully, for he shall come up and become strong with a small *number of* people.

24 "He shall enter peaceably, even into the richest places of the province; and he shall do *what* his fathers have not done, nor his forefathers: he shall disperse among them the plunder, [1]spoil, and riches; and he shall devise his plans against the strongholds, but *only* for a time.

25 "He shall stir up his power and his courage against the king of the South with a great army. And the king of the South shall be stirred up to battle with a very great and mighty army; but he shall not stand, for they shall devise plans against him.

26 "Yes, those who eat of the portion of his delicacies shall destroy him; his army shall [1]be swept away, and many shall fall down slain.

27 "Both these kings' hearts *shall be* bent on evil, and they shall speak lies at the same table; but it shall not prosper, for the end *will* still *be* at the [a]appointed time.

28 "While returning to his land with great riches, his heart shall

8 [1]Or *molded images*
10 [a]Is. 8:8; Jer. 46:7, 8; 51:42; Dan. 9:26; 11:26, 40 [b]Dan. 11:7
11 [a]Prov. 16:14 [b][Ps. 33:10, 16]
12 [1]Proud
14 [a]Job 9:13 [1]Or *robbers,* lit. *sons of breakage* [2]Lit. *to establish*
15 [a]Jer. 6:6; Ezek. 4:2; 17:17 [1]Lit. *arms*
16 [a]Dan. 8:4, 7 [b]Josh. 1:5 [1]Lit. *hand*
17 [a]2 Kin. 12:17; 2 Chr. 20:3; Ezek. 4:3, 7 [b]Dan. 9:26 [1]Or *bring equitable terms*
19 [a]Ps. 27:2; Jer. 46:6 [b]Job 20:8; Ps. 37:36; Ezek. 26:21
21 [a]Dan. 7:8
22 [a]Dan. 9:26 [b]Dan. 8:10, 11 [1]Lit. *arms*
23 [a]Dan. 8:25
24 [1]*booty*
26 [1]Or *overflow*
27 [a]Dan. 8:19; Hab. 2:3

be *moved* against the holy cov-
enant; so he shall do *damage* and
return to his own land.

The Northern King's Blasphemies

29 "At the appointed time he shall
return and go toward the south;
but it shall not be like the former
or the latter.
30 [a]"For ships from [1]Cyprus shall
come against him; therefore he
shall be grieved, and return in rage
against the holy covenant, and do
damage. So he shall return and
show regard for those who forsake
the holy covenant.
31 "And [1]forces shall be mustered
by him, [a]and they shall defile the
sanctuary fortress; then they shall
take away the daily *sacrifices*, and
place *there* the abomination of
desolation.
32 "Those who do wickedly
against the covenant he shall [1]cor-
rupt with flattery; but the people
who know their God shall be
strong, and carry out *great ex-
ploits*.
33 "And those of the people who
understand shall instruct many;
yet *for many* days they shall fall
by sword and flame, by captivity
and plundering.
34 "Now when they fall, they shall
be aided with a little help; but
many shall join with them by [1]in-
trigue.
35 "And *some* of those of under-
standing shall fall, [a]to refine them,
purify *them*, and make *them*
white, *until* the time of the end; be-
cause *it is* still for the appointed
time.
36 "Then the king shall do ac-
cording to his own will: he shall
[a]exalt and magnify himself above
every god, shall speak blasphe-
mies against the God of gods,
and shall prosper till the wrath
has been accomplished; for
what has been determined shall be
done.
37 "He shall regard neither the
[1]God of his fathers nor the desire
of women, [a]nor regard any god;
for he shall exalt himself above
them all.
38 "But in their place he shall
honor a god of fortresses; and a
god which his fathers did not
know he shall honor with gold and
silver, with precious stones and
pleasant things.
39 "Thus he shall act against the
strongest fortresses with a foreign
god, which he shall acknowledge,
and advance *its* glory; and he shall
cause them to rule over many, and
divide the land for [1]gain.

The Northern King's Conquests

40 "At the [a]time of the end the
king of the South shall attack him;
and the king of the North shall
come against him [b]like a whirl-
wind, with chariots, [c]horsemen,
and with many ships; and he shall
enter the countries, overwhelm
them, and pass through.
41 "He shall also enter the Glo-
rious Land, and many *coun-
tries* shall be overthrown; but
these shall escape from his hand:
[a]Edom, Moab, and the [1]prominent
people of Ammon.
42 "He shall stretch out his hand
against the countries, and the land
of [a]Egypt shall not escape.
43 "He shall have power over the
treasures of gold and silver, and
over all the precious things of
Egypt; also the Libyans and Ethio-
pians *shall follow* [a]at his heels.
44 "But news from the east and
the north shall trouble him; there-
fore he shall go out with great fury
to destroy and annihilate many.
45 "And he shall plant the tents
of his palace between the seas and
[a]the glorious holy mountain; [b]yet
he shall come to his end, and no
one will help him.

Prophecy of the End Time

12 "At that time Michael shall
stand up,
The great prince who stands
watch over the sons of your
people;
[a]And there shall be a time of
trouble,
Such as never was since there
was a nation,
Even to that time.
And at that time your people
[b]shall be delivered,
Every one who is found [c]written
in the book.
2 And many of those who sleep in
the dust of the earth shall
awake,
[a]Some to everlasting life,

30 [a]Gen. 10:4; Num. 24:24; Is. 23:1, 12; Jer. 2:10 [1]Heb. *Kittim*, western lands, especially Cyprus
31 [a]Dan. 8:11–13; 12:11 [1]Lit. *arms*
32 [1]*pollute*
34 [1]Or *slipperiness, flattery*
35 [a][Deut. 8:16; Prov. 17:3]; Dan. 12:10; Zech. 13:9; Mal. 3:2, 3
36 [a]Dan. 7:8, 25
37 [a]Is. 14:13; 2 Thess. 2:4 [1]Or *gods*
39 [1]*profit*
40 [a]Dan. 11:27, 35; 12:4, 9 [b]Is. 21:1 [c]Ezek. 38:4; Rev. 9:16
41 [a]Is. 11:14 [1]Lit. *chief of the sons of Ammon*
42 [a]Joel 3:19
43 [a]Ex. 11:8
45 [a]Ps. 48:2 [b]Rev. 19:20

CHAPTER 12

1 [a]Is. 26:20; Jer. 30:7; Ezek. 5:9; Dan. 9:12; Matt. 24:21; Mark 13:19 [b]Rom. 11:26 [c]Ex. 32:32; Ps. 56:8
2 [a][Matt. 25:46; John 5:28, 29; Acts 24:15]

Some to shame [b]and everlasting
[1]contempt.
3 Those who are wise shall [a]shine
Like the brightness of the
firmament,
[b]And those who turn many to
righteousness
[c]Like the stars forever and ever.

4 "But you, Daniel, [a]shut up the
words, and seal the book until the
time of the end; many shall [b]run
to and fro, and knowledge shall in-
crease."
5 Then I, Daniel, looked; and
there stood two others, one on this
riverbank and the other on that
[a]riverbank.
6 And *one* said to the man
clothed in [a]linen, who *was* above
the waters of the river, [b]"How long
shall the fulfillment of these won-
ders *be*?"
7 Then I heard the man clothed
in linen, who *was* above the waters
of the river, when he [a]held up his
right hand and his left hand to
heaven, and swore by Him [b]who
lives forever, [c]that *it shall be* for
a time, times, and half *a time*; [d]and
when the power of [e]the holy peo-
ple has been completely shat-
tered, all these *things* shall be fin-
ished.
8 Although I heard, I did not un-
derstand. Then I said, "My lord,
what *shall be* the end of these
things?"
9 And he said, "Go *your way*,
Daniel, for the words *are* closed
up and sealed till the time of the
end.
10 [a]"Many shall be purified, made
white, and refined, [b]but the wicked
shall do wickedly; and none of the
wicked shall understand, but [c]the
wise shall understand.
11 "And from the time *that* the
daily *sacrifice* is taken away, and
the abomination of desolation is
set up, *there shall be* one thousand
two hundred and ninety days.
12 "Blessed *is* he who waits, and
comes to the one thousand three
hundred and thirty-five days.
13 "But you, go *your way* till the
end; [a]for you shall rest, [b]and will
arise to your inheritance at the end
of the days."

2 [b][Is. 66:24; Rom. 9:21] [1]Lit. *abhorrence*
3 [a]Prov. 3:35; Dan. 11:33, 35; Matt. 13:43 [b]Prov. 11:30; [James 5:19, 20] [c]1 Cor. 15:41
4 [a]Is. 8:16; Dan. 12:9; Rev. 22:10 [b]Amos 8:12
5 [a]Dan. 10:4
6 [a]Ezek. 9:2; Dan. 10:5 [b]Dan. 8:13; 12:8; Matt. 24:3; Mark 13:4
7 [a]Deut. 32:40 [b]Dan. 4:34 [c]Dan. 7:25; Rev. 12:14 [d]Luke 21:24 [e]Dan. 8:24
10 [a]Zech. 13:9 [b]Is. 32:6, 7; Rev. 22:11 [c]Dan. 12:3; Hos. 14:9; John 7:17; 8:47
13 [a]Is. 57:2; Rev. 14:13 [b]Ps. 1:5

The Book of

Hosea

HOSEA, whose name means "Salvation," ministers to the northern kingdom of Israel (also called Ephraim, after its largest tribe). Outwardly, the nation is enjoying a time of prosperity and growth; but inwardly, moral corruption and spiritual adultery permeate the people. Hosea, instructed by God to marry a woman named Gomer, finds his domestic life to be an accurate and tragic dramatization of the unfaithfulness of God's people. During his half century of prophetic ministry, Hosea repeatedly echoes his threefold message: God abhors the sins of His people; judgment is certain; but God's loyal love stands firm.

The names Hosea, Joshua, and Jesus are all derived from the same Hebrew root word. The word *hoshea* means "salvation," but "Joshua" and "Jesus" include an additional idea: "Yahweh Is Salvation." As God's messenger, Hosea offers the possibility of salvation if only the nation will turn from idolatry back to God.

Israel's last king, Hoshea, has the same name as the prophet even though the English Bible spells them differently. Hosea in the Greek and Latin is *Osee.*

CHAPTER 1

THE word of the LORD that came
to Hosea the son of Beeri, in
the days of [a]Uzziah, [b]Jotham,
[c]Ahaz, *and* [d]Hezekiah, kings of Ju-
dah, and in the days of [e]Jeroboam
the son of Joash, king of Israel.

The Family of Hosea

2 When the LORD began to speak
by Hosea, the LORD said to Hosea:

[a]"Go, take yourself a wife of
harlotry
And children of harlotry,
For [b]the land has committed
great [1]harlotry
By departing from the LORD."

3 So he went and took Gomer the
daughter of Diblaim, and she con-
ceived and bore him a son.
4 Then the LORD said to him:

"Call his name Jezreel,
For in a little *while*
[a]I will avenge the bloodshed of
Jezreel on the house of Jehu,
[b]And bring an end to the kingdom
of the house of Israel.
5 [a]It shall come to pass in that day
That I will break the bow of Israel
in the Valley of Jezreel."

6 And she conceived again and
bore a daughter. Then *God* said to
him:

"Call her name [1]Lo-Ruhamah,
[a]For I will no longer have mercy
on the house of Israel,
[2]But I will utterly take them away.
7 [a]Yet I will have mercy on the
house of Judah,
Will save them by the LORD their
God,
And [b]will not save them by bow,
Nor by sword or battle,
By horses or horsemen."

8 Now when she had weaned Lo-
Ruhamah, she conceived and bore
a son.
9 Then *God* said:

"Call his name [1]Lo-Ammi,
For you *are* not My people,
And I will not be your *God.*

The Restoration of Israel

10 "Yet [a]the number of the children
of Israel
Shall be as the sand of the sea,
Which cannot be measured or
numbered.
[b]And it shall come to pass
In the place where it was said to
them,
'You *are* [1]not My [c]people,'
There it shall be said to them,
'*You are* [d]sons of the living God.'
11 [a]Then the children of Judah and
the children of Israel

---

1 [a]Amos 1:1 [b]2 Chr. 27 [c]2 Chr. 28 [d]2 Chr. 29:1—32:33 [e]2 Kin. 13:13;14:23–29
2 [a]Hos. 3:1 [b]Jer. 2:13 [1]Spiritual adultery
4 [a]2 Kin. 10:11 [b]2 Kin.15:8–10; 17:6, 23; 18:11
5 [a]2 Kin. 15:29
6 [a]2 Kin. 17:6 [1]Lit. *No-Mercy* [2]Or *That I may forgive them at all*
7 [a]2 Kin. 19:29–35 [b][Zech. 4:6]
9 [1]Lit. *Not-My-People*
10 [a]Gen. 22:17; 32:12 [b]1 Pet. 2:10 [c]Rom. 9:26 [d][John 1:12] [1]Heb. *lo-ammi,* v. 9
11 [a]Is. 11:11–13

Shall be gathered together,
And appoint for themselves one head;
And they shall come up out of the land,
For great *will be* the day of Jezreel!

2 Say to your brethren, [1]'My people,'
And to your sisters, [2]'Mercy *is* shown.'

God's Unfaithful People

2 "Bring[1] charges against your mother, [2]bring charges;
For [a]she *is* not My wife, nor *am* I her Husband!
Let her put away her [b]harlotries from her sight,
And her adulteries from between her breasts;
3 Lest [a]I strip her naked
And expose her, as in the day she was [b]born,
And make her like a wilderness,
And set her like a dry land,
And slay her with [c]thirst.

4 "I will not have mercy on her children,
For they *are* the [a]children of harlotry.
5 For their mother has played the harlot;
She who conceived them has behaved shamefully.
For she said, 'I will go after my lovers,
[a]Who give *me* my bread and my water,
My wool and my linen,
My oil and my drink.'

6 "Therefore, behold,
[a]I will hedge up your way with thorns,
And [1]wall her in,
So that she cannot find her paths.
7 She will [1]chase her lovers,
But not overtake them;
Yes, she will seek them, but not find *them*.
Then she will say,
[a]'I will go and return to my [b]first husband,
For then *it was* better for me than now.'
8 For she did not [a]know
That I gave her grain, new wine, and oil,
And multiplied her silver and gold—
Which they prepared for Baal.

CHAPTER 2

1 [1]Heb. *Ammi*, Hos. 1:9, 10 [2]Heb. *Ruhamah*, Hos. 1:6

2 [a]Is. 50:1 [b]Ezek. 16:25 [1]Or *Contend with* [2]Or *contend*

3 [a]Jer. 13:22, 26; Ezek. 16:37–39 [b]Ezek. 16:4–7, 22 [c]Jer. 14:3; Amos 8:11–13

4 [a]John 8:41

5 [a]Ezek. 23:5; Hos. 2:8, 12

6 [a]Job 19:8; Lam. 3:7, 9 [1]Lit. *wall up her wall*

7 [a]Luke 15:17, 18 [b]Is. 54:5–8; Jer. 2:2; 3:1; Ezek. 16:8; 23:4 [1]Or *pursue*

8 [a]Is. 1:3; Ezek. 16:19

10 [a]Ezek. 16:37

11 [a]Jer. 7:34; 16:9; Hos. 3:4; Amos 5:21; 8:10

14 [1]Lit. *to her heart*

15 [a]Josh. 7:26 [b]Jer. 2:1–3; Ezek. 16:8–14 [c]Ex. 15:1

16 [1]Heb. *Ishi* [2]Heb. *Baali*

17 [a]Ex. 23:13; Josh. 23:7; Ps. 16:4

18 [a]Job 5:23; Is. 11:6–9; Ezek. 34:25

9 "Therefore I will return and take away
My grain in its time
And My new wine in its season,
And will take back My wool and My linen,
Given to cover her nakedness.
10 Now [a]I will uncover her lewdness in the sight of her lovers,
And no one shall deliver her from My hand.
11 [a]I will also cause all her mirth to cease,
Her feast days,
Her New Moons,
Her Sabbaths—
All her appointed feasts.

12 "And I will destroy her vines and her fig trees,
Of which she has said,
'These *are* my wages that my lovers have given me.'
So I will make them a forest,
And the beasts of the field shall eat them.
13 I will punish her
For the days of the Baals to which she burned incense.
She decked herself with her earrings and jewelry,
And went after her lovers;
But Me she forgot," says the LORD.

God's Mercy on His People

14 "Therefore, behold, I will allure her,
Will bring her into the wilderness,
And speak [1]comfort to her.
15 I will give her her vineyards from there,
And [a]the Valley of Achor as a door of hope;
She shall sing there,
As in [b]the days of her youth,
[c]As in the day when she came up from the land of Egypt.

16 "And it shall be, in that day,"
Says the LORD,
"*That* you will call Me [1]'My Husband,'
And no longer call Me [2]'My Master,'
17 For [a]I will take from her mouth the names of the Baals,
And they shall be remembered by their name no more.
18 In that day I will make a [a]covenant for them
With the beasts of the field,
With the birds of the air,

And *with* the creeping things of the ground.
Bow and sword of battle [b]I will shatter from the earth,
To make them [c]lie down safely.
19 "I will betroth you to Me forever;
Yes, I will betroth you to Me
In righteousness and justice,
In lovingkindness and mercy;
20 I will betroth you to Me in faithfulness,
And [a]you shall know the LORD.

21 "It shall come to pass in that day
That [a]I will answer," says the LORD;
"I will answer the heavens,
And they shall answer the earth.
22 The earth shall answer
With grain,
With new wine,
And with oil;
They shall answer [1]Jezreel.
23 Then [a]I will sow her for Myself in the earth,
[b]And I will have mercy on *her who had* [1]not obtained mercy;
Then [c]I will say to *those who were* [2]not My people,
'You *are* [3]My people!'
And they shall say, '*You are* my God!' "

Israel Will Return to God

3 Then the LORD said to me, "Go
again, love a woman *who is*
loved by a [a]lover[1] and is commit-
ting adultery, just like the love of
the LORD for the children of Israel,
who look to other gods and love
the raisin cakes *of the pagans*."
2 So I bought her for myself for
fifteen *shekels* of silver, and one
and one-half homers of barley.
3 And I said to her, "You shall
[a]stay with me many days; you
shall not play the harlot, nor shall
you have a man—so, too, *will* I *be*
toward you."
4 For the children of Israel shall
abide many days [a]without king or
prince, without sacrifice or sacred
pillar, without [b]ephod or [c]tera-
phim.
5 Afterward the children of Is-
rael shall return and [a]seek the
LORD their God and [b]David their
king. They shall fear the LORD and
His goodness in the [c]latter days.

God's Charge Against Israel

4 Hear the word of the LORD,
You children of Israel,
For the LORD *brings* a [a]charge[1] against the inhabitants of the land:
"There is no truth or mercy
Or [b]knowledge of God in the land.
2 *By* swearing and lying,
Killing and stealing and committing adultery,
They break all restraint,
With bloodshed [1]upon bloodshed.
3 Therefore [a]the land will mourn;
And [b]everyone who dwells there will waste away
With the beasts of the field
And the birds of the air;
Even the fish of the sea will be taken away.

4 "Now let no man contend, or rebuke another;
For your people *are* like those [a]who contend with the priest.
5 Therefore you shall stumble [a]in the day;
The prophet also shall stumble with you in the night;
And I will destroy your mother.
6 [a]My people are destroyed for lack of knowledge.
Because you have rejected knowledge,
I also will reject you from being priest for Me;
[b]Because you have forgotten the law of your God,
I also will forget your children.

7 "The more they increased,
The more they sinned against Me;
[a]I[1] will change [2]their glory into shame.
8 They eat up the sin of My people;
They set their [1]heart on their iniquity.
9 And it shall be: [a]like people, like priest.
So I will punish them for their ways,
And [1]reward them for their deeds.
10 For [a]they shall eat, but not have enough;
They shall commit harlotry, but not increase;
Because they have ceased obeying the LORD.

The Idolatry of Israel

11 "Harlotry, wine, and new wine [a]enslave the heart.
12 My people ask counsel from their [a]wooden *idols*,
And their [1]staff informs them.

---

18 [b]Is. 2:4 [c]Lev. 26:5
20 [a][Jer. 31:33, 34]
21 [a]Zech. 8:12
22 [1]Lit. *God Will Sow*
23 [a]Jer. 31:27 [b]Hos. 1:6 [c]Hos. 1:10 [1]Heb. *lo-ruhamah* [2]Heb. *lo-ammi* [3]Heb. *ammi*

CHAPTER 3
1 [a]Jer. 3:20 [1]Lit. *friend* or *husband*
3 [a]Deut. 21:13
4 [a]Hos. 10:3 [b]Ex. 28:4–12 [c]Judg. 17:5; 18:14, 17
5 [a]Jer. 50:4 [b]Jer. 30:9 [c][Is. 2:2, 3]

CHAPTER 4
1 [a]Is. 1:18 [b]Jer. 4:22 [1]A legal complaint
2 [1]Lit. *touching*
3 [a]Amos 5:16; 8:8 [b]Zeph. 1:3
4 [a]Deut. 17:12
5 [a]Jer. 15:8
6 [a]Is. 5:13 [b]Ezek. 22:26
7 [a]1 Sam. 2:30 [1]So with MT, LXX, Vg.; scribal tradition, Syr., Tg. *They will change* [2]So with MT, LXX, Syr., Tg., Vg.; scribal tradition *My glory*
8 [1]Desires
9 [a]Is. 24:2 [1]*repay*
10 [a]Lev. 26:26
11 [a]Is. 5:12; 28:7
12 [a]Jer. 2:27 [1]Diviner's rod

For [b]the spirit of harlotry has
caused *them* to stray,
And they have played the harlot
against their God.
13 [a]They offer sacrifices on the
mountaintops,
And burn incense on the hills,
Under oaks, poplars, and
terebinths,
Because their shade *is* good.
[b]Therefore your daughters
commit harlotry,
And your brides commit adultery.

14 "I will not punish your daughters
when they commit harlotry,
Nor your brides when they
commit adultery;
For *the men* themselves go apart
with harlots,
And offer sacrifices with a [a]ritual
harlot.
Therefore people *who* do not
understand will be trampled.

15 "Though you, Israel, play the
harlot,
Let not Judah offend.
[a]Do not come up to Gilgal,
Nor go up to [b]Beth[1] Aven,
[c]Nor swear an oath, *saying*, 'As
the LORD lives'—

16 "For Israel [a]is stubborn
Like a stubborn calf;
Now the LORD will let them
forage
Like a lamb in [1]open country.

17 "Ephraim *is* joined to idols,
[a]Let him alone.
18 Their drink [1]is rebellion,
They commit harlotry
continually.
[a]Her [2]rulers [3]dearly love dishonor.
19 [a]The wind has wrapped her up in
its wings,
And [b]they shall be ashamed
because of their sacrifices.

Impending Judgment on Israel and Judah

5 "Hear this, O priests!
Take heed, O house of Israel!
Give ear, O house of the king!
For [1]yours *is* the judgment,
Because [a]you have been a snare
to Mizpah
And a net spread on Tabor.
2 The revolters are [a]deeply
involved in slaughter,
Though I rebuke them all.
3 [a]I know Ephraim,
And Israel is not hidden from Me;

12 [b]Is. 44:19, 20
13 [a]Is. 1:29; 57:5, 7; Jer. 2:20; Ezek. 6:13; 20:28 [b]Amos 7:17; [Rom. 1:28–32]
14 [a]Deut. 23:18
15 [a]Hos. 9:15; 12:11 [b]1 Kin. 12:29; Josh. 7:2; Hos. 10:8 [c]Jer. 5:2; 44:26; Amos 8:14 [1]Lit. *House of Idolatry* or *Wickedness*
16 [a]Jer. 3:6; 7:24; 8:5; Zech. 7:11 [1]Lit. *a large place*
17 [a]Matt. 15:14
18 [a]Mic. 3:11 [1]Or *has turned aside* [2]Lit. *shields* [3]Heb. difficult; a Jewish tradition *shamefully love, 'Give!'*
19 [a]Jer. 51:1 [b]Is. 1:29

CHAPTER 5

1 [a]Hos. 6:9 [1]Or *to you*
2 [a]Is. 29:15; Hos. 4:2; 6:9
3 [a]Amos 3:2; 5:12 [b]Hos. 4:17
4 [a]Hos. 4:12 [1]Or *Their deeds will not allow them to turn*
5 [a]Hos. 7:10
6 [a]Prov. 1:28; Is. 1:15; Jer. 11:11; Ezek. 8:18; Mic. 3:4; John 7:34
7 [a]Is. 48:8; Jer. 3:20; Hos. 6:7 [1]Lit. *strange*
8 [a]Hos. 8:1; Joel 2:1 [b]Is. 10:30 [c]Josh. 7:2
10 [a]Deut. 19:14; 27:17
11 [a]Deut. 28:33 [b]Mic. 6:16
12 [a]Prov. 12:4
13 [a]Jer. 30:12–15 [b]2 Kin. 15:19; Hos. 7:11; 10:6
14 [a]Ps. 7:2; Lam. 3:10; Hos. 13:7, 8 [b]Ps. 50:22

For now, O Ephraim, [b]you
commit harlotry;
Israel is defiled.

4 "They[1] do not direct their deeds
Toward turning to their God,
For [a]the spirit of harlotry is in
their midst,
And they do not know the LORD.
5 The [a]pride of Israel testifies to his
face;
Therefore Israel and Ephraim
stumble in their iniquity;
Judah also stumbles with them.

6 "With their flocks and herds
[a]They shall go to seek the LORD,
But they will not find *Him*;
He has withdrawn Himself from
them.
7 They have [a]dealt treacherously
with the LORD,
For they have begotten [1]pagan
children.
Now a New Moon shall devour
them and their heritage.

8 "Blow[a] the ram's horn in Gibeah,
The trumpet in Ramah!
[b]Cry aloud *at* [c]Beth Aven,
'*Look* behind you, O Benjamin!'
9 Ephraim shall be desolate in the
day of rebuke;
Among the tribes of Israel I make
known what is sure.

10 "The princes of Judah are like
those who [a]remove a
landmark;
I will pour out my wrath on them
like water.
11 Ephraim is [a]oppressed *and*
broken in judgment,
Because he willingly walked by
[b]*human* precept.
12 Therefore I *will be* to Ephraim
like a moth,
And to the house of Judah [a]like
rottenness.

13 "When Ephraim saw his sickness,
And Judah *saw* his [a]wound,
Then Ephraim went [b]to Assyria
And sent to King Jareb;
Yet he cannot cure you,
Nor heal you of your wound.
14 For [a]I *will be* like a lion to
Ephraim,
And like a young lion to the
house of Judah.
[b]I, *even* I, will tear *them* and go
away;
I will take *them* away, and no one
shall rescue.
15 I will return again to My place

Till they [1]acknowledge their
offense.
Then they will seek My face;
In their affliction they will
earnestly seek Me."

A Call to Repentance

6 Come,[a] and let us return to the
LORD;
For [b]He has torn, but [c]He will
heal us;
He has stricken, but He will [1]bind
us up.
2 [a]After two days He will revive us;
On the third day He will raise us
up,
That we may live in His sight.
3 [a]Let us know,
Let us pursue the knowledge of
the LORD.
His going forth is established [b]as
the morning;
[c]He will come to us [d]like the rain,
Like the latter *and* former rain to
the earth.

Impenitence of Israel and Judah

4 "O Ephraim, what shall I do to
you?
O Judah, what shall I do to you?
For your faithfulness is like a
morning cloud,
And like the early dew it goes
away.
5 Therefore I have hewn *them* by
the prophets,
I have slain them by [a]the words
of My mouth;
And [1]your judgments *are like*
light *that* goes forth.
6 For I desire [a]mercy[1] and [b]not
sacrifice,
And the [c]knowledge of God more
than burnt offerings.

7 "But like [1]men they transgressed
the covenant;
There they dealt treacherously
with Me.
8 [a]Gilead *is* a city of evildoers
And [1]defiled with blood.
9 As bands of robbers lie in wait
for a man,
So the company of [a]priests
[b]murder on the way to
Shechem;
Surely they commit [c]lewdness.
10 I have seen a horrible thing in the
house of Israel:
There *is* the [1]harlotry of Ephraim;
Israel is defiled.
11 Also, O Judah, a harvest is
appointed for you,
When I return the captives of My
people.

7 "When I would have healed
Israel,
Then the iniquity of Ephraim was
uncovered,
And the wickedness of Samaria.
For [a]they have committed fraud;
A thief comes in;
A band of robbers [1]takes spoil
outside.
2 They [1]do not consider in their
hearts
That [a]I remember all their
wickedness;
Now their own deeds have
surrounded them;
They are before My face.
3 They make a [a]king glad with their
wickedness,
And princes [b]with their lies.

4 "They[a] *are* all adulterers.
Like an oven heated by a baker—
He ceases stirring *the fire* after
kneading the dough,
Until it is leavened.
5 In the day of our king
Princes have made *him* sick,
[1]inflamed with [a]wine;
He stretched out his hand with
scoffers.
6 They prepare their heart like an
oven,
While they lie in wait;
[1]Their baker sleeps all night;
In the morning it burns like a
flaming fire.
7 They are all hot, like an oven,
And have devoured their judges;
All their kings have fallen.
[a]None among them calls upon Me.

8 "Ephraim [a]has mixed himself
among the peoples;
Ephraim is a cake unturned.
9 [a]Aliens have devoured his
strength,
But he does not know *it;*
Yes, gray hairs are here and there
on him,
Yet he does not know *it.*
10 And the [a]pride of Israel testifies
to his face,
But [b]they do not return to the
LORD their God,
Nor seek Him for all this.

Futile Reliance on the Nations

11 "Ephraim[a] also is like a silly dove,
without [1]sense—
[b]They call to Egypt,
They go to [c]Assyria.
12 Wherever they go, I will [a]spread
My net on them;

15 [1]Lit. *become guilty* or *bear punishment*

CHAPTER 6

1 [a]Is. 1:18; Acts 10:43 [b]Deut. 32:39; Hos. 5:14 [c]Jer. 30:17; Hos. 14:4 [1]Bandage
2 [a]Luke 24:46; Acts 10:40; [1 Cor. 15:4]
3 [a]Is. 54:13 [b]2 Sam. 23:4 [c]Ps. 72:6; Joel 2:23 [d]Job 29:23
5 [a][Jer. 23:29] [1]Or *the judgments on you*
6 [a]Matt. 9:13; 12:7 [b]Is. 1:12, 13; [Mic. 6:6–8] [c][John 17:3] [1]Or *faithfulness* or *loyalty*
7 [1]Or *Adam*
8 [a]Hos. 12:11 [1]Lit. *foot-tracked*
9 [a]Hos. 5:1 [b]Jer. 7:9, 10; Hos. 4:2 [c]Ezek. 22:9; 23:27; Hos. 2:10
10 [1]Spiritual adultery

CHAPTER 7

1 [a]Ezek. 23:4–8; Hos. 5:1 [1]*plunders*
2 [a]Ps. 25:7; Jer. 14:10; 17:1; Hos. 8:13; 9:9; Amos 8:7 [1]Lit. *do not say to*
3 [a]Hos. 1:1 [b]Mic. 7:3; [Rom. 1:32]
4 [a]Jer. 9:2; 23:10
5 [a]Is. 28:1, 7 [1]Lit. *with the heat of*
6 [1]So with MT, Vg.; Syr., Tg. *Their anger;* LXX *Ephraim*
7 [a]Is. 64:7
8 [a]Ps. 106:35
9 [a]Is. 1:7; 42:25; Hos. 8:7
10 [a]Hos. 5:5 [b]Is. 9:13
11 [a]Hos. 11:11 [b]Is. 30:3 [c]Hos. 5:13; 8:9 [1]Lit. *heart*
12 [a]Ezek. 12:13

I will bring them down like birds
of the air;
I will chastise them
[b]According to what their
congregation has heard.

13 "Woe to them, for they have fled
from Me!
Destruction to them,
Because they have transgressed
against Me!
Though [a]I redeemed them,
Yet they have spoken lies against
Me.
14 [a]They did not cry out to Me with
their heart
When they wailed upon their
beds.

"They [1]assemble together for
grain and new [b]wine,
[2]They rebel against Me;
15 Though I disciplined *and*
strengthened their arms,
Yet they devise evil against Me;
16 They return, *but* not [1]to the Most
High;
[a]They are like a treacherous bow.
Their princes shall fall by the
sword
For the [b]cursings of their tongue.
This *shall be* their derision [c]in the
land of Egypt.

The Apostasy of Israel

8 "Set the [1]trumpet to your mouth!
He shall come [a]like an eagle
against the house of the LORD,
Because they have transgressed
My covenant
And rebelled against My law.
2 [a]Israel will cry to Me,
'My God, [b]we know You!'
3 Israel has rejected the good;
The enemy will pursue him.

4 "They[a] set up kings, but not by Me;
They made princes, but I did not
acknowledge *them*.
From their silver and gold
They made idols for themselves—
That they might be cut off.
5 Your [1]calf [2]is rejected,
O Samaria!
My anger is aroused against
them—
[a]How long until they attain to
innocence?
6 For from Israel *is* even this:
A [a]workman made it, and it *is* not
God;
But the calf of Samaria shall be
broken to pieces.

7 "They[a] sow the wind,
And reap the whirlwind.

12 [b]Lev. 26:14
13 [a]Mic. 6:4
14 [a]Job 35:9, 10 [b]Amos 2:8 [1]So with MT, Tg.; Vg. *thought upon;* LXX *slashed themselves for* (cf. 1 Kin. 18:28) [2]So with MT, Syr., Tg.; LXX omits *They rebel against Me;* Vg. *They departed from Me*
16 [a]Ps. 78:57 [b]Ps. 73:9 [c]Hos. 8:13; 9:3 [1]Or *upward*

CHAPTER 8

1 [a]Deut. 28:49 [1]*ram's horn,* Heb. *shophar*
2 [a]Ps. 78:34 [b]Titus 1:16
4 [a]2 Kin. 15:23, 25
5 [a]Jer. 13:27 [1]Golden calf image [2]Or *has rejected you*
6 [a]Is. 40:19
7 [a]Prov. 22:8 [b]Hos. 7:9
8 [a]2 Kin. 17:6 [b]Jer. 22:28; 25:34
9 [a]Jer. 2:24 [b]Ezek. 16:33, 34
10 [a]Ezek. 16:37; 22:20 [b]Is. 10:8 [1]Or *begin to diminish* [2]Or *oracle* or *proclamation*
12 [a][Deut. 4:6–8]
13 [a]Zech. 7:6 [b]Jer. 14:10 [c]Amos 8:7
14 [a]Deut. 32:18 [b]Is. 29:23 [c]Num. 32:17 [d]Jer. 17:27 [1]Or *palaces* [2]Or *citadels*

CHAPTER 9

1 [a]Is. 22:12, 13 [b]Jer. 44:17
3 [a][Lev. 25:23] [b]Hos. 7:16; 8:13 [c]Ezek. 4:13

The stalk has no bud;
It shall never produce meal.
If it should produce,
[b]Aliens would swallow it up.
8 [a]Israel is swallowed up;
Now they are among the Gentiles
[b]Like a vessel in which *is* no
pleasure.
9 For they have gone up to Assyria,
Like [a]a wild donkey alone by
itself;
Ephraim [b]has hired lovers.
10 Yes, though they have hired
among the nations,
Now [a]I will gather them;
And they shall [1]sorrow a little,
Because of the [2]burden of [b]the
king of princes.

11 "Because Ephraim has made many
altars for sin,
They have become for him altars
for sinning.
12 I have written for him [a]the great
things of My law,
But they were considered a
strange thing.
13 *For* the sacrifices of My offerings
[a]they sacrifice flesh and eat *it*,
[b]*But* the LORD does not accept
them.
[c]Now He will remember their
iniquity and punish their sins.
They shall return to Egypt.

14 "For[a] Israel has forgotten [b]his
Maker,
And has built [1]temples;
Judah also has multiplied
[c]fortified cities;
But [d]I will send fire upon his
cities,
And it shall devour his [2]palaces."

Judgment of Israel's Sin

9 Do[a] not rejoice, O Israel, with joy
like *other* peoples,
For you have played the harlot
against your God.
You have made love *for* [b]hire on
every threshing floor.
2 The threshing floor and the
winepress
Shall not feed them,
And the new wine shall fail in
her.

3 They shall not dwell in [a]the
LORD's land,
[b]But Ephraim shall return to
Egypt,
And [c]shall eat unclean *things* in
Assyria.
4 They shall not offer wine
offerings to the LORD,

Nor [a]shall their [b]sacrifices be
pleasing to Him.
It shall be like bread of mourners
to them;
All who eat it shall be defiled.
For their bread *shall be* for their
own life;
It shall not come into the house
of the LORD.
5 What will you do in the appointed
day,
And in the day of the feast of the
LORD?
6 For indeed they are gone because
of destruction.
Egypt shall gather them up;
Memphis shall bury them.
[a]Nettles shall possess their
valuables of silver;
Thorns *shall be* in their tents.

7 The [a]days of punishment have
come;
The days of recompense have
come.
Israel knows!
The prophet *is* a [b]fool,
[c]The spiritual man *is* insane,
Because of the greatness of your
iniquity and great enmity.
8 The [a]watchman of Ephraim *is*
with my God;
But the prophet *is* a [1]fowler's
snare in all his ways—
Enmity in the house of his God.
9 [a]They are deeply corrupted,
As in the days of [b]Gibeah.
He will remember their iniquity;
He will punish their sins.

10 "I found Israel
Like grapes in the [a]wilderness;
I saw your fathers
As the [b]firstfruits on the fig tree
in its first season.
But they went to [c]Baal Peor,
And [1]separated themselves *to*
that shame;
[d]They became an abomination
like the thing they loved.
11 *As for* Ephraim, their glory shall
fly away like a bird—
No birth, no pregnancy, and no
conception!
12 Though they bring up their
children,
Yet I will bereave them to the last
man.
Yes, [a]woe to them when I depart
from them!
13 Just [a]as I saw Ephraim like Tyre,
planted in a pleasant place,
So Ephraim will bring out his
children to the murderer."

14 Give them, O LORD—
What will You give?
Give them [a]a miscarrying womb
And dry breasts!

15 "All their wickedness *is* in [a]Gilgal,
For there I hated them.
Because of the evil of their deeds
I will drive them from My house;
I will love them no more.
[b]All their princes *are* rebellious.
16 Ephraim is [a]stricken,
Their root is dried up;
They shall bear no fruit.
Yes, were they to bear children,
I would kill the darlings of their
womb."

17 My God will [a]cast them away,
Because they did not obey Him;
And they shall be [b]wanderers
among the nations.

Israel's Sin and Captivity

10 Israel [a]empties *his* vine;
He brings forth fruit for
himself.
According to the multitude of his
fruit
[b]He has increased the altars;
According to the bounty of his
land
They have embellished *his* sacred
pillars.
2 Their heart is [a]divided;[1]
Now they are held guilty.
He will break down their altars;
He will ruin their sacred pillars.

3 For now they say,
"We have no king,
Because we did not fear the LORD.
And as for a king, what would he
do for us?"
4 They have spoken words,
Swearing falsely in making a
covenant.
Thus judgment springs up [a]like
hemlock in the furrows of the
field.

5 The inhabitants of Samaria fear
Because of the [a]calf[1] of Beth
Aven.
For its people mourn for it,
And [2]its priests shriek for it—
Because its [b]glory has departed
from it.
6 *The idol* also shall be carried to
Assyria
As a present for King [a]Jareb.
Ephraim shall receive shame,
And Israel shall be ashamed of
his own counsel.

4 [a]Jer. 6:20 [b]Hos. 8:13; Amos 5:22
6 [a]Is. 5:6; 7:23; Hos. 10:8
7 [a]Is. 10:3; Jer. 10:15; Mic. 7:4; Luke 21:22 [b]Lam. 2:14; [Ezek. 13:3, 10] [c]Mic. 2:11
8 [a]Jer. 6:17; 31:6; Ezek. 3:17; 33:7 [1]One who catches birds in a trap or snare
9 [a]Hos. 10:9 [b]Judg. 19:22
10 [a]Jer. 2:2 [b]Is. 28:4; Mic. 7:1 [c]Num. 25:3; Ps. 106:28 [d]Ps. 81:12 [1]Or *dedicated*
12 [a]Deut. 31:17; Hos. 7:13
13 [a]Ezek. 26—28
14 [a]Luke 23:29
15 [a]Hos. 4:15; 12:11 [b]Is. 1:23; Hos. 5:2
16 [a]Hos. 5:11
17 [a]2 Kin. 17:20; [Zech. 10:6] [b]Lev. 26:33

CHAPTER 10

1 [a]Nah. 2:2 [b]Jer. 2:28; Hos. 8:11; 12:11
2 [a]1 Kin. 18:21; Zeph. 1:5; [Matt. 6:24] [1]Divided in loyalty
4 [a]Deut. 31:16, 17; 2 Kin. 17:3, 4; Amos 5:7
5 [a]1 Kin. 12:28, 29; Hos. 8:5, 6; 13:2 [b]Hos. 9:11 [1]Lit. *calves, images* [2]*idolatrous priests*
6 [a]Hos. 5:13

7 *As for* Samaria, her king is cut
off
Like a twig on the water.
8 Also the [a]high places of [1]Aven,
[b]the sin of Israel,
Shall be destroyed.
The thorn and thistle shall grow
on their altars;
[c]They shall say to the mountains,
"Cover us!"
And to the hills, "Fall on us!"

9 "O Israel, you have sinned from
the days of [a]Gibeah;
There they stood.
The [b]battle in Gibeah against the
children of [1]iniquity
Did not [2]overtake them.
10 When *it is* My desire, I will
chasten them.
[a]Peoples shall be gathered against
them
When I bind them [1]for their two
transgressions.
11 Ephraim *is* [a]a trained heifer
That loves to thresh *grain;*
But I harnessed her fair neck,
I will make Ephraim [1]pull *a plow.*
Judah shall plow;
Jacob shall break his clods."

12 Sow for yourselves
righteousness;
Reap in mercy;
[a]Break up your fallow ground,
For *it is* time to seek the LORD,
Till He [b]comes and rains
righteousness on you.

13 [a]You have plowed wickedness;
You have reaped iniquity.
You have eaten the fruit of lies,
Because you trusted in your own
way,
In the multitude of your mighty
men.
14 Therefore tumult shall arise
among your people,
And all your fortresses shall be
plundered
As Shalman plundered Beth
Arbel in the day of battle—
A mother dashed in pieces upon
her children.
15 Thus it shall be done to you,
O Bethel,
Because of your great
wickedness.
At dawn the king of Israel
Shall be cut off utterly.

God's Continuing Love for Israel

11 "When Israel *was* a [1]child, I
loved him,
And out of Egypt [a]I called My
[b]son.
2 [1]As they called them,
So they [a]went [2]from them;
They sacrificed to the Baals,
And burned incense to carved
images.

3 "I[a] taught Ephraim to walk,
Taking them by [1]their arms;
But they did not know that [b]I
healed them.
4 I drew them with [1]gentle cords,
With bands of love,
And [a]I was to them as those who
take the yoke from their [2]neck.
[b]I stooped *and* fed them.

5 "He shall not return to the land of
Egypt;
But the Assyrian shall be his
king,
Because they refused to repent.
6 And the sword shall slash in his
cities,
Devour his districts,
And consume *them,*
Because of their own counsels.
7 My people are bent on
[a]backsliding from Me.
Though [1]they call [2]to the Most
High,
None at all exalt *Him.*

8 "How[a] can I give you up, Ephraim?
How can I hand you over, Israel?
How can I make you like
[b]Admah?
How can I set you like Zeboiim?
My heart [1]churns within Me;
My sympathy is stirred.
9 I will not execute the fierceness
of My anger;
I will not again destroy Ephraim.
[a]For I *am* God, and not man,
The Holy One in your midst;
And I will not [1]come with terror.

10 "They shall walk after the LORD.
[a]He will roar like a lion.
When He roars,
Then *His* sons shall come
trembling from the west;
11 They shall come trembling like a
bird from Egypt,
[a]Like a dove from the land of
Assyria.
[b]And I will let them dwell in their
houses,"
Says the LORD.

God's Charge Against Ephraim

12 "Ephraim has encircled Me with
lies,

8 [a]Hos. 4:15 [b]Deut. 9:21; 1 Kin. 13:34 [c]Is. 2:19; Luke 23:30; Rev. 6:16 [1]Lit. *Idolatry* or *Wickedness*
9 [a]Hos. 9:9 [b]Judg. 20 [1]So with many Heb. mss., LXX, Vg.; MT *unruliness* [2]Or *overcome*
10 [a]Jer. 16:16 [1]Or *in their two habitations*
11 [a][Jer. 50:11; Hos. 4:16; Mic. 4:13] [1]Lit. *to ride*
12 [a]Jer. 4:3 [b]Hos. 6:3
13 [a][Job 4:8; Prov. 22:8; Gal. 6:7, 8]

CHAPTER 11

1 [a]Matt. 2:15 [b]Ex. 4:22, 23 [1]Or *youth*
2 [a]2 Kin. 17:13–15 [1]So with MT, Vg.; LXX *Just as I called them;* Tg. interprets as *I sent prophets to a thousand of them.* [2]So with MT, Tg., Vg.; LXX *from My face*
3 [a]Deut. 1:31; 32:10, 11 [b]Ex. 15:26 [1]Some Heb. mss., LXX, Syr., Vg. *My arms*
4 [a]Lev. 26:13 [b]Ex. 16:32; Ps. 78:25 [1]Lit. *cords of a man* [2]Lit. *jaws*
7 [a]Jer. 3:6, 7; 8:5 [1]The prophets [2]Or *upward*
8 [a]Jer. 9:7 [b]Gen. 14:8; 19:24, 25; Deut. 29:23 [1]Lit. *turns over*
9 [a]Num. 23:19 [1]Or *enter a city*
10 [a]Is. 31:4; [Joel 3:16]; Amos 1:2
11 [a]Is. 11:11; 60:8; Hos. 7:11 [b]Ezek. 28:25, 26; 34:27, 28

And the house of Israel with
deceit;
But Judah still walks with God,
Even with the [1]Holy One *who is*
faithful.

12 "Ephraim [a]feeds on the
wind,
And pursues the east wind;
He daily increases lies and
[1]desolation.
[b]Also they make a [2]covenant with
the Assyrians,
And [c]oil is carried to Egypt.

2 "The[a] LORD also *brings* a [1]charge
against Judah,
And will punish Jacob according
to his ways;
According to his deeds He will
recompense him.
3 He took his brother [a]by the heel
in the womb,
And in his strength he [b]struggled
with God.
4 Yes, he struggled with the Angel
and prevailed;
He wept, and sought favor from
Him.
He found Him *in* [a]Bethel,
And there He spoke to us—
5 That is, the LORD God of hosts.
The LORD *is* His [a]memorable
name.
6 [a]So you, by *the help of* your God,
return;
Observe mercy and justice,
And wait on your God
continually.

7 "A cunning [1]Canaanite!
[a]Deceitful scales *are* in his hand;
He loves to oppress.
8 And Ephraim said,
[a]'Surely I have become rich,
I have found wealth for myself;
In all my labors
They shall find in me no iniquity
that *is* sin.'

9 "But I *am* the LORD your God,
Ever since the land of Egypt;
[a]I will again make you dwell in
tents,
As in the days of the appointed
feast.
10 [a]I have also spoken by the
prophets,
And have multiplied visions;
I have given [1]symbols [2]through
the witness of the prophets."

11 Though [a]Gilead *has* idols—
Surely they are [1]vanity—
Though they sacrifice bulls in
[b]Gilgal,
Indeed their altars *shall be* heaps
in the furrows of the field.

12 Jacob [a]fled to the country of
Syria;
[b]Israel served for a spouse,
And for a wife he tended *sheep*.
13 [a]By a prophet the LORD brought
Israel out of Egypt,
And by a prophet he was
preserved.
14 Ephraim [a]provoked *Him* to anger
most bitterly;
Therefore his Lord will leave the
guilt of his bloodshed upon
him,
[b]And return his reproach upon
him.

Relentless Judgment on Israel

13 When Ephraim spoke,
trembling,
He exalted *himself* in Israel;
But when he offended through
Baal *worship*, he died.
2 Now they sin more and more,
And have made for themselves
molded images,
Idols of their silver, according to
their skill;
All of it *is* the work of craftsmen.
They say of them,
"Let [1]the men who sacrifice [2]kiss
the calves!"
3 Therefore they shall be like the
morning cloud
And like the early dew that
passes away,
[a]Like chaff blown off from a
threshing floor
And like smoke from a chimney.

4 "Yet [a]I *am* the LORD your God
Ever since the land of Egypt,
And you shall know no God but
Me;
For [b]*there is* no savior besides
Me.
5 [a]I [1]knew you in the wilderness,
[b]In the land of [2]great drought.
6 [a]When they had pasture, they
were filled;
They were filled and their heart
was exalted;
Therefore they forgot Me.

7 "So [a]I will be to them like a lion;
Like [b]a leopard by the road I will
lurk;
8 I will meet them [a]like a bear
deprived *of her cubs*;
I will tear open their rib cage,

12 [1]Or *holy ones*

CHAPTER 12

1 [a]Job 15:2, 3; Hos. 8:7 [b]2 Kin. 17:4; Hos. 8:9 [c]Is. 30:6 [1]*ruin* [2]Or *treaty*
2 [a]Hos. 4:1; Mic. 6:2 [1]A legal complaint
3 [a]Gen. 25:26 [b]Gen. 32:24–28
4 [a][Gen. 28:12–19; 35:9–15]
5 [a]Ex. 3:15
6 [a]Hos. 14:1; Mic. 6:8
7 [a]Prov. 11:1; Amos 8:5; Mic. 6:11 [1]Or *merchant*
8 [a]Ps. 62:10; Hos. 13:6; Rev. 3:17
9 [a]Lev. 23:42
10 [a]2 Kin. 17:13; Jer. 7:25 [1]Or *parables* [2]Lit. *by the hand*
11 [a]Hos. 6:8 [b]Hos. 9:15 [1]*worthless*
12 [a]Gen. 28:5; Deut. 26:5 [b]Gen. 29:20, 28
13 [a]Ex. 12:50, 51; 13:3; Ps. 77:20; Is. 63:11, 12; Mic. 6:4
14 [a]Ezek. 18:10–13 [b]Dan. 11:18; Mic. 6:16

CHAPTER 13

2 [1]Or *those who offer human sacrifice* [2]Worship with kisses
3 [a]Ps. 1:4; Is. 17:13; Dan. 2:35
4 [a]Is. 43:11 [b]Is. 43:11; 45:21, 22; [1 Tim. 2:5]
5 [a]Deut. 2:7; 32:10 [b]Deut. 8:15 [1]Cared for you [2]Lit. *droughts*
6 [a]Deut. 8:12, 14; 32:13–15; Jer. 5:7
7 [a]Lam. 3:10; Hos. 5:14 [b]Jer. 5:6
8 [a]2 Sam. 17:8; Prov. 17:12

And there I will devour them like
a lion.
The [1]wild beast shall tear them.

9 "O Israel, [1]you are destroyed,
But [2]your help *is* from Me.
10 [1]I will be your King;
[a]Where *is any other,*
That he may save you in all your
cities?
And your judges to whom [b]you
said,
'Give me a king and princes'?
11 [a]I gave you a king in My anger,
And took *him* away in My wrath.

12 "The[a] iniquity of Ephraim *is* bound
up;
His sin *is* stored up.
13 [a]The sorrows of a woman in
childbirth shall come upon him.
He *is* an unwise son,
For he should not stay long where
children are born.

14 "I will ransom them from the
[1]power of [2]the grave;
I will redeem them from death.
[a]O Death, [3]I will be your plagues!
O [4]Grave, [5]I will be your
destruction!
[b]Pity is hidden from My eyes."

15 Though he is fruitful among *his*
brethren,
[a]An east wind shall come;
The wind of the LORD shall come
up from the wilderness.
Then his spring shall become dry,
And his fountain shall be dried
up.
He shall plunder the treasury of
every desirable prize.
16 Samaria [1]is held guilty,
For she has [a]rebelled against her
God.
They shall fall by the sword,
Their infants shall be dashed in
pieces,
And their women with child
[b]ripped open.

Israel Restored at Last

14 O Israel, [a]return to the LORD
your God,
For you have stumbled because
of your iniquity;
2 Take words with you,
And return to the LORD.
Say to Him,
"Take away all iniquity;
Receive *us* graciously,
For we will offer the [a]sacrifices[1]
of our lips.
3 Assyria shall [a]not save us,
[b]We will not ride on horses,
Nor will we say anymore to the
work of our hands,
'*You are* our gods.'
[c]For in You the fatherless finds
mercy."

4 "I will heal their [a]backsliding,
I will [b]love them freely,
For My anger has turned away
from him.
5 I will be like the [a]dew to
Israel;
He shall [1]grow like the lily,
And [2]lengthen his roots like
Lebanon.
6 His branches shall [1]spread;
[a]His beauty shall be like an olive
tree,
And [b]his fragrance like
Lebanon.
7 [a]Those who dwell under his
shadow shall return;
They shall be revived *like* grain,
And [1]grow like a vine.
Their [2]scent *shall be* like the wine
of Lebanon.

8 "Ephraim *shall say,*
'What have I to do anymore with
idols?'
I have heard and observed him.
I *am* like a green cypress tree;
[a]Your fruit is found in Me."

9 Who *is* wise?
Let him understand these
things.
Who is prudent?
Let him know them.
For [a]the ways of the LORD *are*
right;
The righteous walk in them,
But transgressors stumble in
them.

---

8 [1]Lit. *beast of the field*
9 [1]Lit. *it* or *he destroyed you* [2]Lit. *in your help*
10 [a]Deut. 32:38 [b]1 Sam. 8:5, 6 [1]LXX, Syr., Tg., Vg. *Where is your king?*
11 [a]1 Sam. 8:7; 10:17–24
12 [a]Deut. 32:34, 35
13 [a]Is. 13:8
14 [a][1 Cor. 15:54, 55] [b]Jer. 15:6 [1]Lit. *hand* [2]Or *Sheol* [3]LXX *where is your punishment?* [4]Or *Sheol* [5]LXX *where is your sting?*
15 [a]Jer. 4:11, 12
16 [a]2 Kin. 18:12 [b]2 Kin. 15:16 [1]LXX *shall be disfigured*

CHAPTER 14

1 [a][Joel 2:13]
2 [a][Heb. 13:15] [1]Lit. *bull calves;* LXX *fruit*
3 [a]Hos. 7:11; 10:13; 12:1 [b][Ps. 33:17] [c]Ps. 10:14; 68:5
4 [a]Jer. 14:7 [b][Eph. 1:6]
5 [a]Prov. 19:12 [1]Lit. *bud* or *sprout* [2]Lit. *strike*
6 [a]Ps. 52:8; 128:3 [b]Gen. 27:27 [1]Lit. *go*
7 [a]Dan. 4:12 [1]Lit. *bud* or *sprout* [2]Lit. *remembrance*
8 [a][John 15:4]
9 [a][Prov. 10:29]

The Book of

Joel

DISASTER strikes the southern kingdom of Judah without warning. An ominous black cloud descends upon the land—the dreaded locusts. In a matter of hours, every living green thing has been stripped bare. Joel, God's spokesman during the reign of Joash (835–796 B.C.), seizes this occasion to proclaim God's message. Although the locust plague has been a terrible judgment for sin, God's future judgments during the day of the Lord will make that plague pale by comparison. In that day, God will destroy His enemies, but bring unparalleled blessing to those who faithfully obey Him.

The Hebrew name *Yo'el* means "Yahweh Is God." This name is appropriate to the theme of the book, which emphasizes God's sovereign work in history. The courses of nature and nations are in His hand. The Greek equivalent is *Ioel*, and the Latin is *Joel*.

THE word of the LORD that came
to [a]Joel the son of Pethuel.

The Land Laid Waste

2 Hear this, you elders,
And give ear, all you inhabitants
of the land!
[a]Has *anything like* this happened
in your days,
Or even in the days of your
fathers?
3 [a]Tell your children about it,
Let your children *tell* their
children,
And their children another
generation.

4 [a]What the chewing [1]locust left,
the [b]swarming locust has
eaten;
What the swarming locust left,
the crawling locust has eaten;
And what the crawling locust left,
the consuming locust has
eaten.

5 Awake, you [a]drunkards, and
weep;
And wail, all you drinkers of
wine,
Because of the new wine,
[b]For it has been cut off from your
mouth.
6 For [a]a nation has come up against
My land,
Strong, and without number;
[b]His teeth *are* the teeth of a lion,
And he has the fangs of a [1]fierce
lion.
7 He has [a]laid waste My vine,
And [1]ruined My fig tree;
He has stripped it bare and
thrown *it* away;
Its branches are made white.

8 [a]Lament like a virgin girded with
sackcloth
For [b]the husband of her youth.
9 [a]The grain offering and the drink
offering
Have been cut off from the house
of the LORD;
The priests [b]mourn, who minister
to the LORD.
10 The field is wasted,
[a]The land mourns;
For the grain is ruined,
[b]The new wine is dried up,
The oil fails.

11 [a]Be ashamed, you farmers,
Wail, you vinedressers,
For the wheat and the barley;
Because the harvest of the field
has perished.
12 [a]The vine has dried up,
And the fig tree has withered;
The pomegranate tree,
The palm tree also,
And the apple tree—
All the trees of the field are
withered;
Surely [b]joy has withered away
from the sons of men.

Mourning for the Land

13 [a]Gird yourselves and lament, you
priests;
Wail, you who minister before
the altar;
Come, lie all night in sackcloth,
You who minister to my God;

CHAPTER 1

1 [a]Acts 2:16

2 [a]Jer. 30:7; Joel 2:2

3 [a]Ex. 10:2; Ps. 78:4; Is. 38:19

4 [a]Deut. 28:38; Joel 2:25; Amos 4:9 [b]Is. 33:4 [1]Exact identity of these locusts unknown

5 [a]Is. 5:11; 28:1; Hos. 7:5 [b]Is. 32:10

6 [a]Prov. 30:25; Joel 2:2, 11, 25 [b]Rev. 9:8 [1]Or *lioness*

7 [a]Is. 5:6; Amos 4:9 [1]Or *splintered*

8 [a]Is. 22:12 [b]Prov. 2:17; Jer. 3:4

9 [a]Hos. 9:4; Joel 1:13; 2:14 [b]Joel 2:17

10 [a]Jer. 12:11; Hos. 3:4 [b]Is. 24:7

11 [a]Jer. 14:3, 4; Amos 5:16

12 [a]Joel 1:10; Hab. 3:17 [b]Is. 16:10; 24:11; Jer. 48:33

13 [a]Jer. 4:8; Ezek. 7:18

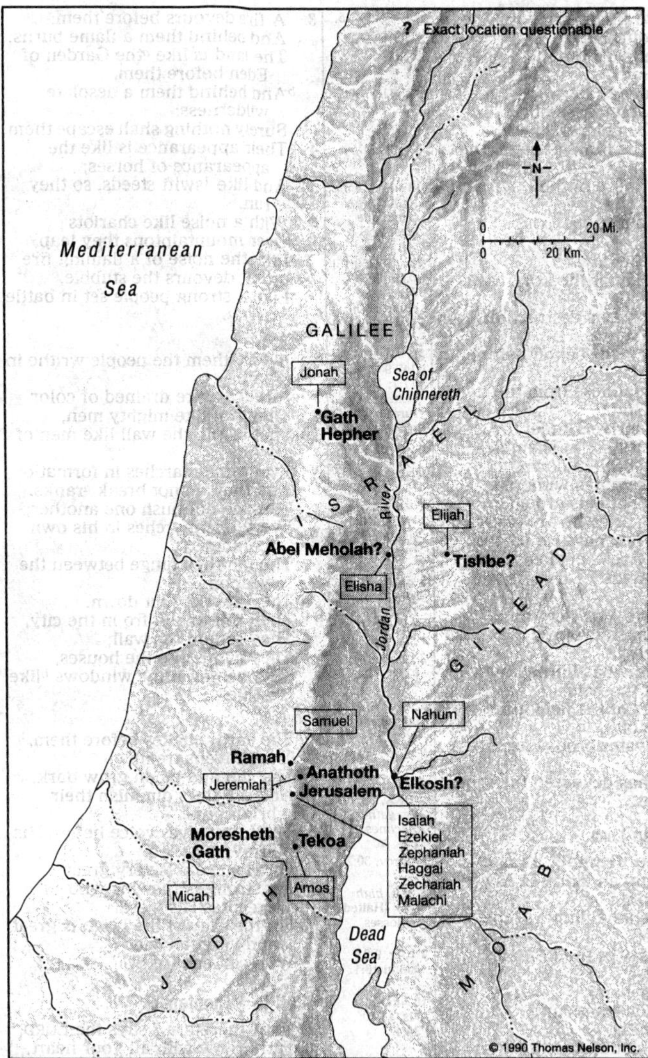

The Prophets of Israel and Judah. From the Scriptures we can learn where a number of the prophets were born or where they prophesied. We know that some prophets had homes in the South, but prophesied to the North. Others, such as Jonah in the North, extended his ministry beyond his homeland to the foreign city of Nineveh. For still others, such as Joel, Obadiah, and Habakkuk, geographical information is lacking. The home of Nahum is indicated only by his designation as "the Elkoshite"; and although we know Hosea was from the North, the exact location of his home and ministry are unknown.

For the grain offering and the
drink offering
Are withheld from the house of
your God.
14 [a]Consecrate a fast,
Call [b]a sacred assembly;
Gather the elders
And [c]call the inhabitants of the
land
Into the house of the LORD your
God,
And cry out to the LORD.

15 [a]Alas for the day!
For [b]the day of the LORD *is* at
hand;
It shall come as destruction from
the Almighty.
16 Is not the food [a]cut off before our
eyes,
[b]Joy and gladness from the house
of our God?
17 The seed shrivels under the clods,
Storehouses are in shambles;
Barns are broken down,
For the grain has withered.
18 How [a]the animals groan!
The herds of cattle are restless,
Because they have no pasture;
Even the flocks of sheep [1]suffer
punishment.

19 O LORD, [a]to You I cry out;
For [b]fire has devoured the [1]open
pastures,
And a flame has burned all the
trees of the field.
20 The beasts of the field also [a]cry
out to You,
For [b]the water brooks are dried
up,
And fire has devoured the [1]open
pastures.

The Day of the LORD

2 Blow [a]the [1]trumpet in Zion,
And [b]sound an alarm in My holy
mountain!
Let all the inhabitants of the land
tremble;
For [c]the day of the LORD is
coming,
For it is at hand:
2 [a]A day of darkness and
gloominess,
A day of clouds and thick
darkness,
Like the morning *clouds* spread
over the mountains.
[b]A people *come*, great and strong,
[c]The like of whom has never been;
Nor will there ever be any *such*
after them,
Even for many successive
generations.

14 [a]Joel 2:15, 16 [b]Lev. 23:36 [c]2 Chr. 20:13
15 [a][Jer. 30:7] [b]Is. 13:6
16 [a]Is. 3:1 [b]Deut. 12:7
18 [a]Hos. 4:3 [1]LXX, Vg. *are made desolate*
19 [a][Ps. 50:15] [b]Jer. 9:10 [1]Lit. *pastures of the wilderness*
20 [a]Ps. 104:21; 147:9 [b]1 Kin. 17:7; 18:5 [1]Lit. *pastures of the wilderness*

CHAPTER 2

1 [a]Jer. 4:5 [b]Num. 10:5 [c][Obad. 15] [1]*ram's horn*
2 [a]Amos 5:18 [b]Joel 1:6; 2:11, 25 [c]Dan. 9:12; 12:1
3 [a]Is. 51:3 [b]Zech. 7:14
4 [a]Rev. 9:7 [1]Or *horsemen*
5 [a]Rev. 9:9
6 [a]Nah. 2:10 [1]LXX, Tg., Vg. *gather blackness*
7 [a]Prov. 30:27
8 [1]Lit. *highway* [2]Halted by losses
9 [a]Jer. 9:21 [b]John 10:1
10 [a]Ps. 18:7 [b]Is. 13:10; 34:4
11 [a]Jer. 25:30 [b]Rev. 18:8 [c]Amos 5:18 [d][Mal. 3:2]
12 [a]Jer. 4:1
13 [a][Ps. 34:18; 51:17] [b]Gen. 37:34 [c][Ex. 34:6]

3 A fire devours before them,
And behind them a flame burns;
The land *is* like [a]the Garden of
Eden before them,
[b]And behind them a desolate
wilderness;
Surely nothing shall escape them.
4 [a]Their appearance is like the
appearance of horses;
And like [1]swift steeds, so they
run.
5 [a]With a noise like chariots
Over mountaintops they leap,
Like the noise of a flaming fire
that devours the stubble,
Like a strong people set in battle
array.

6 Before them the people writhe in
pain;
[a]All faces [1]are drained of color.
7 They run like mighty men,
They climb the wall like men of
war;
Every one marches in formation,
And they do not break [a]ranks.
8 They do not push one another;
Every one marches in his own
[1]column.
Though they lunge between the
weapons,
They are not [2]cut down.
9 They run to and fro in the city,
They run on the wall;
They climb into the houses,
They [a]enter at the windows [b]like
a thief.

10 [a]The earth quakes before them,
The heavens tremble;
[b]The sun and moon grow dark,
And the stars diminish their
brightness.
11 [a]The LORD gives voice before His
army,
For His camp is very great;
[b]For strong *is the One* who
executes His word.
For the [c]day of the LORD *is* great
and very terrible;
[d]Who can endure it?

A Call to Repentance

12 "Now, therefore," says the LORD,
[a]"Turn to Me with all your heart,
With fasting, with weeping, and
with mourning."
13 So [a]rend your heart, and not
[b]your garments;
Return to the LORD your God,
For He *is* [c]gracious and merciful,
Slow to anger, and of great
kindness;
And He relents from doing harm.

14 [a]Who knows *if* He will turn and
relent,
And leave [b]a blessing behind
Him—
[c]A grain offering and a drink
offering
For the LORD your God?

15 [a]Blow the [1]trumpet in Zion,
[b]Consecrate a fast,
Call a sacred assembly;
16 Gather the people,
[a]Sanctify the congregation,
Assemble the elders,
Gather the children and nursing
babes;
[b]Let the bridegroom go out from
his chamber,
And the bride from her dressing
room.
17 Let the priests, who minister to
the LORD,
Weep [a]between the porch and the
altar;
Let them say, [b]"Spare Your
people, O LORD,
And do not give Your heritage to
reproach,
That the nations should [1]rule over
them.
[c]Why should they say among the
peoples,
'Where *is* their God?' "

The Land Refreshed

18 Then the LORD will [a]be zealous
for His land,
And pity His people.
19 The LORD will answer and say to
His people,
"Behold, I will send you [a]grain and
new wine and oil,
And you will be satisfied by them;
I will no longer make you a
reproach among the nations.

20 "But [a]I will remove far from you
[b]the northern *army*,
And will drive him away into a
barren and desolate land,
With his face toward the eastern
sea
And his back [c]toward the western
sea;
His stench will come up,
And his foul odor will rise,
Because he has done [1]monstrous
things."

21 Fear not, O land;
Be glad and rejoice,
For the LORD has done
[1]marvelous things!
22 Do not be afraid, you beasts of
the field;
For [a]the open pastures are
springing up,
And the tree bears its fruit;
The fig tree and the vine yield
their strength.
23 Be glad then, you children of
Zion,
And [a]rejoice in the LORD your
God;
For He has given you the [1]former
rain faithfully,
And He [b]will cause the rain to
come down for you—
The former rain,
And the latter rain in the first
month.
24 The threshing floors shall be full
of wheat,
And the vats shall overflow with
new wine and oil.

25 "So I will restore to you the years
[a]that the swarming [1]locust has
eaten,
The crawling locust,
The consuming locust,
And the chewing locust,
My great army which I sent
among you.
26 You shall [a]eat in plenty and be
satisfied,
And praise the name of the LORD
your God,
Who has dealt wondrously with
you;
And My people shall never be put
to [b]shame.
27 Then you shall know that I *am*
[a]in the midst of Israel:
[b]I *am* the LORD your God
And there is no other.
My people shall never be put to
shame.

God's Spirit Poured Out

28 "And[a] it shall come to pass
afterward
That [b]I will pour out My Spirit on
all flesh;
[c]Your sons and your [d]daughters
shall prophesy,
Your old men shall dream
dreams,
Your young men shall see
visions.
29 And also on *My* [a]menservants
and on *My* maidservants
I will pour out My Spirit in those
days.

30 "And [a]I will show wonders in the
heavens and in the earth:
Blood and fire and pillars of
smoke.

14 [a]Josh. 14:12; 2 Sam. 12:22; 2 Kin. 19:4; Jer. 26:3; Jon. 3:9 [b]Hag. 2:19 [c]Joel 1:9, 13
15 [a]Num. 10:3; 2 Kin. 10:20 [b]Joel 1:14 [1]*ram's horn*
16 [a]Ex. 19:10 [b]Ps. 19:5
17 [a]Matt. 23:35 [b]Ex. 32:11, 12; [Is. 37:20]; Amos 7:2, 5 [c]Ps. 42:10 [1]Or *speak a proverb against them*
18 [a][Is. 60:10; 63:9, 15]
19 [a]Jer. 31:12; Hos. 2:21, 22; Joel 1:10; [Mal. 3:10]
20 [a]Ex. 10:19 [b]Jer. 1:14, 15 [c]Deut. 11:24 [1]Lit. *great*
21 [1]Lit. *great*
22 [a]Joel 1:19
23 [a]Deut. 11:14; Is. 41:16; Jer. 5:24; Hab. 3:18; Zech. 10:7 [b]Lev. 26:4; Hos. 6:3; Zech. 10:1; James 5:7 [1]Or *teacher of righteousness*
25 [a]Joel 1:4–7; 2:2–11 [1]Exact identity of these locusts unknown
26 [a]Lev. 26:5; Deut. 11:15; Is. 62:9 [b]Is. 45:17
27 [a]Lev. 26:11, 12; [Joel 3:17, 21] [b][Is. 45:5, 6]
28 [a]Ezek. 39:29; Acts 2:17–21 [b]Zech. 12:10 [c]Is. 54:13 [d]Acts 21:9
29 [a][1 Cor. 12:13; Gal. 3:28]
30 [a]Matt. 24:29; Mark 13:24, 25; Luke 21:11, 25, 26; Acts 2:19

31 [a]The sun shall be turned into
darkness,
And the moon into blood,
[b]Before the coming of the great
and awesome day of the LORD.
32 And it shall come to pass
That [a]whoever calls on the name
of the LORD
Shall be [1]saved.
For [b]in Mount Zion and in
Jerusalem there shall be
[2]deliverance,
As the LORD has said,
Among [c]the remnant whom the
LORD calls.

God Judges the Nations

3 "For behold, [a]in those days and
at that time,
When I bring back the captives
of Judah and Jerusalem,
2 [a]I will also gather all nations,
And bring them down to the
Valley of Jehoshaphat;
And I [b]will enter into judgment
with them there
On account of My people, My
heritage Israel,
Whom they have scattered
among the nations;
They have also divided up My
land.
3 They have [a]cast lots for My
people,
Have given a boy *as payment* for
a harlot,
And sold a girl for wine, that they
may drink.

4 "Indeed, what have you to do with
Me,
[a]O Tyre and Sidon, and all the
coasts of Philistia?
Will you [1]retaliate against Me?
But if you [2]retaliate against Me,
Swiftly and speedily I will return
your [3]retaliation upon your
own head;
5 Because you have taken My
silver and My gold,
And have carried into your
temples My [1]prized
possessions.
6 Also the people of Judah and the
people of Jerusalem
You have sold to the Greeks,
That you may remove them far
from their borders.

7 "Behold, [a]I will raise them
Out of the place to which you
have sold them,
And will return your [1]retaliation
upon your own head.
8 I will sell your sons and your
daughters
Into the hand of the people of
Judah,
And they will sell them to the
[a]Sabeans,[1]
To a people [b]far off;
For the LORD has spoken."

9 [a]Proclaim this among the nations:
"Prepare for war!
Wake up the mighty men,
Let all the men of war draw near,
Let them come up.
10 [a]Beat your plowshares into
swords
And your [1]pruning hooks into
spears;
[b]Let the weak say, 'I *am* strong.' "
11 Assemble and come, all you
nations,
And gather together all around.
Cause [a]Your mighty ones to go
down there, O LORD.

12 "Let the nations be wakened, and
come up to the Valley of
Jehoshaphat;
For there I will sit to [a]judge all
the surrounding nations.
13 [a]Put in the sickle, for [b]the harvest
is ripe.
Come, go down;
For the [c]winepress is full,
The vats overflow—
For their wickedness *is* great."

14 Multitudes, multitudes in the
valley of decision!
For [a]the day of the LORD *is* near
in the valley of decision.
15 The sun and moon will grow
dark,
And the stars will diminish their
brightness.
16 The LORD also will roar from
Zion,
And utter His voice from
Jerusalem;
The heavens and earth will
shake;
[a]But the LORD will be a shelter for
His people,
And the strength of the children
of Israel.

17 "So you shall know that I *am* the
LORD your God,
Dwelling in Zion My [a]holy
mountain.
Then Jerusalem shall be holy,
And no aliens shall ever pass
through her again."

---

31 [a]Is. 13:9, 10; 34:4 [b][Mal. 4:1, 5, 6]
32 [a]Rom. 10:13 [b]Is. 46:13 [c][Mic. 4:7] [1]Or *delivered* [2]Or *salvation*

CHAPTER 3
1 [a]Jer. 30:3
2 [a]Zech. 14:2 [b]Is. 66:16
3 [a]Nah. 3:10
4 [a]Amos 1:6–8 [1]Or *render Me repayment* [2]Or *repay Me* [3]Or *repayment*
5 [1]Lit. *precious good things*
7 [a]Jer. 23:8 [1]Or *repayment*
8 [a]Ezek. 23:42 [b]Jer. 6:20 [1]Lit. *Shebaites,* Is. 60:6; Ezek. 27:22
9 [a]Ezek. 38:7
10 [a][Is. 2:4] [b]Zech. 12:8 [1]*pruning knives*
11 [a]Is. 13:3
12 [a]Is. 2:4
13 [a]Rev. 14:15 [b]Jer. 51:33 [c][Is. 63:3]
14 [a]Joel 2:1
16 [a][Is. 51:5, 6]
17 [a]Zech. 8:3

God Blesses His People

18 And it will come to pass in that
day
That the mountains shall drip
with new wine,
The hills shall flow with milk,
And all the brooks of Judah shall
be flooded with water;
A [a]fountain shall flow from the
house of the LORD
And water the Valley of
[1]Acacias.

18 [a]Ps. 46:4; Ezek. 47:1; Zech. 14:8; [Rev. 22:1] [1]Heb. *Shittim*

21 [a]Is. 4:4

19 "Egypt shall be a desolation,
And Edom a desolate wilderness,
Because of violence *against* the
people of Judah,
For they have shed innocent
blood in their land.
20 But Judah shall abide forever,
And Jerusalem from generation
to generation.
21 For I will [a]acquit them of the guilt
of bloodshed, whom I had not
acquitted;
For the LORD dwells in Zion."

The Book of

Amos

AMOS prophesies during a period of national optimism in Israel. Business is booming and boundaries are bulging. But below the surface, greed and injustice are festering. Hypocritical religious motions have replaced true worship, creating a false sense of security and a growing callousness to God's disciplining hand. Famine, drought, plagues, death, destruction—nothing can force the people to their knees.

Amos, the farmer-turned-prophet, lashes out at sin unflinchingly, trying to visualize the nearness of God's judgment and mobilize the nation to repentance. The nation, like a basket of rotting fruit, stands ripe for judgment because of its hypocrisy and spiritual indifference.

The name *Amos* is derived from the Hebrew root *amas,* "to lift a burden, to carry." Thus, his name means "Burden" or "Burden-Bearer." Amos lives up to the meaning of his name by bearing up under his divinely given burden of declaring judgment to rebellious Israel. The Greek and Latin titles are both transliterated in English as *Amos.*

THE words of Amos, who was among the [a]sheepbreeders of [b]Tekoa, which he saw concerning Israel in the days of [c]Uzziah king of Judah, and in the days of [d]Jeroboam the son of Joash, king of Israel, two years before the [e]earthquake.

2 And he said:

"The LORD [a]roars from Zion,
And utters His voice from
Jerusalem;
The pastures of the shepherds
mourn,
And the top of [b]Carmel withers."

Judgment on the Nations

3 Thus says the LORD:

"For three transgressions of
[a]Damascus, and for four,
I will not turn away its
punishment,
Because they have [b]threshed
Gilead with implements of iron.
4 [a]But I will send a fire into the
house of Hazael,
Which shall devour the palaces
of [b]Ben-Hadad.
5 I will also break the *gate* [a]bar of
Damascus,
And cut off the inhabitant from
the Valley of Aven,
And the one who [1]holds the
scepter from [2]Beth Eden.

CHAPTER 1

1 [a]2 Kin. 3:4; Amos 7:14 [b]2 Sam. 14:2 [c]2 Chr. 26:1–23 [d]Amos 7:10 [e]Zech. 14:5

2 [a]Joel 3:16 [b]1 Sam. 25:2

3 [a]Is. 8:4; 17:1–3 [b]2 Kin. 10:32, 33

4 [a]Jer. 49:27; 51:30 [b]2 Kin. 6:24

5 [a]Jer. 51:30 [1]Rules [2]Lit. *House of Eden*

6 [a]Jer. 47:1, 5

7 [a]Jer. 47:1

8 [a]Zeph. 2:4 [b]Ps. 81:14 [c]Ezek. 25:16

9 [a]Is. 23:1–18

The people of Syria shall go
captive to Kir,"
Says the LORD.

6 Thus says the LORD:

"For three transgressions of
[a]Gaza, and for four,
I will not turn away its
punishment,
Because they took captive the
whole captivity
To deliver *them* up to Edom.
7 [a]But I will send a fire upon the wall
of Gaza,
Which shall devour its palaces.
8 I will cut off the inhabitant [a]from
Ashdod,
And the one who holds the
scepter from Ashkelon;
I will [b]turn My hand against
Ekron,
And [c]the remnant of the
Philistines shall perish,"
Says the Lord GOD.

9 Thus says the LORD:

"For three transgressions of [a]Tyre,
and for four,
I will not turn away its
punishment,
Because they delivered up the
whole captivity to Edom,
And did not remember the
covenant of brotherhood.

10 But I will send a fire upon the wall
of Tyre,
Which shall devour its palaces."

11 Thus says the LORD:

"For three transgressions of
[a]Edom, and for four,
I will not turn away its
punishment,
Because he pursued his [b]brother
with the sword,
And cast off all pity;
His anger tore perpetually,
And he kept his wrath forever.
12 But [a]I will send a fire upon
Teman,
Which shall devour the palaces
of Bozrah."

13 Thus says the LORD:

"For three transgressions of [a]the
people of Ammon, and for four,
I will not turn away its
punishment,
Because they ripped open the
women with child in Gilead,
That they might enlarge their
territory.
14 But I will kindle a fire in the wall
of [a]Rabbah,
And it shall devour its palaces,
[b]Amid shouting in the day of
battle,
And a tempest in the day of the
whirlwind.
15 [a]Their king shall go into captivity,
He and his princes together,"
Says the LORD.

2 Thus says the LORD:

[a]"For three transgressions of Moab,
and for four,
I will not turn away its
punishment,
Because he [b]burned the bones of
the king of Edom to lime.
2 But I will send a fire upon Moab,
And it shall devour the palaces
of [a]Kerioth;
Moab shall die with tumult,
With shouting *and* trumpet
sound.
3 And I will cut off [a]the judge from
its midst,
And slay all its princes with him,"
Says the LORD.

Judgment on Judah

4 Thus says the LORD:

"For three transgressions of
[a]Judah, and for four,
I will not turn away its
punishment,
[b]Because they have despised the
law of the LORD,
And have not kept His
commandments.
[c]Their lies lead them astray,
Lies [d]which their fathers
followed.
5 [a]But I will send a fire upon
Judah,
And it shall devour the palaces
of Jerusalem."

Judgment on Israel

6 Thus says the LORD:

"For three transgressions of
[a]Israel, and for four,
I will not turn away its
punishment,
Because [b]they sell the righteous
for silver,
And the [c]poor for a pair of
sandals.
7 They [1]pant after the dust of the
earth *which is* on the head of
the poor,
And [a]pervert the way of the
humble.
[b]A man and his father go in to the
same girl,
[c]To defile My holy name.
8 They lie down [a]by every altar on
clothes [b]taken in pledge,
And drink the wine of [1]the
condemned *in* the house of
their god.

9 "Yet *it was* I *who* destroyed the
[a]Amorite before them,
Whose height *was* like the
[b]height of the cedars,
And he *was as* strong as the oaks;
Yet I [c]destroyed his fruit above
And his roots beneath.
10 Also *it was* [a]I *who* brought you
up from the land of Egypt,
And [b]led you forty years through
the wilderness,
To possess the land of the
Amorite.
11 I raised up some of your sons as
[a]prophets,
And some of your young men as
[b]Nazirites.
Is it not so, O you children of
Israel?"
Says the LORD.
12 "But you gave the Nazirites wine
to drink,
And commanded the prophets
[a]saying,
'Do not prophesy!'

---

11 [a]Is. 21:11 [b]Obad. 10–12
12 [a]Obad. 9, 10
13 [a]Ezek. 25:2
14 [a]Deut. 3:11 [b]Amos 2:2
15 [a]Jer. 49:3

CHAPTER 2

1 [a]Zeph. 2:8–11 [b]2 Kin. 3:26, 27
2 [a]Jer. 48:24, 41
3 [a]Num. 24:17
4 [a]Hos. 12:2 [b]Lev. 26:14 [c]Jer. 16:19 [d]Ezek. 20:13, 16, 18
5 [a]Hos. 8:14
6 [a]2 Kin. 17:7–18; 18:12 [b]Is. 29:21 [c]Amos 4:1; 5:11; 8:6
7 [a]Amos 5:12 [b]Ezek. 22:11 [c]Lev. 20:3 [1]Or *trample on*
8 [a]1 Cor. 8:10 [b]Ex. 22:26 [1]Or *those punished by fines*
9 [a]Num. 21:25 [b]Ezek. 31:3 [c][Mal. 4:1]
10 [a]Ex. 12:51 [b]Deut. 2:7
11 [a]Num. 12:6 [b]Num. 6:2, 3
12 [a]Is. 30:10

13 "Behold,[a] I am [1]weighed down by
you,
As a cart full of sheaves [2]is
weighed down.
14 [a]Therefore [1]flight shall perish
from the swift,
The strong shall not strengthen
his power,
[b]Nor shall the mighty [2]deliver
himself;
15 He shall not stand who handles
the bow,
The swift of foot shall not
[1]escape,
Nor shall he who rides a horse
deliver himself.
16 The most [1]courageous men of
might
Shall flee naked in that day,"
Says the LORD.

Authority of the Prophet's Message

3 Hear this word that the LORD
has spoken against you, O chil-
dren of Israel, against the whole
family which I brought up from the
land of Egypt, saying:

2 "You[a] only have I known of all the
families of the earth;
[b]Therefore I will punish you for all
your iniquities."

3 Can two walk together, unless
they are agreed?
4 Will a lion roar in the forest,
when he has no prey?
Will a young lion [1]cry out of his
den, if he has caught nothing?
5 Will a bird fall into a snare on
the earth, where there is no
[1]trap for it?
Will a snare spring up from the
earth, if it has caught nothing
at all?
6 If a [1]trumpet is blown in a city,
will not the people be afraid?
[a]If there is calamity in a city, will
not the LORD have done *it?*

7 Surely the Lord GOD does
nothing,
Unless [a]He reveals His secret to
His servants the prophets.
8 A lion has roared!
Who will not fear?
The Lord GOD has spoken!
[a]Who can but prophesy?

Punishment of Israel's Sins

9 "Proclaim in the palaces at
[1]Ashdod,
And in the palaces in the land of
Egypt, and say:

'Assemble on the mountains of
Samaria;
See great tumults in her midst,
And the [2]oppressed within her.
10 For they [a]do not know to do
right,'
Says the LORD,
'Who store up violence and
[1]robbery in their palaces.' "

11 Therefore thus says the Lord
GOD:

"An adversary *shall be* all around
the land;
He shall sap your strength from
you,
And your palaces shall be
plundered."

12 Thus says the LORD:

"As a shepherd [1]takes from the
mouth of a lion
Two legs or a piece of an ear,
So shall the children of Israel be
taken out
Who dwell in Samaria—
In the corner of a bed and [2]on the
edge of a couch!
13 Hear and testify against the
house of Jacob,"
Says the Lord GOD, the God of
hosts,
14 "That in the day I punish Israel for
their transgressions,
I will also visit *destruction* on the
altars of [a]Bethel;
And the horns of the altar shall
be cut off
And fall to the ground.
15 I will [1]destroy [a]the winter house
along with [b]the summer house;
The [c]houses of ivory shall perish,
And the great houses shall have
an end,"
Says the LORD.

4 Hear this word, you [a]cows of
Bashan, who *are* on the
mountain of Samaria,
Who oppress the [b]poor,
Who crush the needy,
Who say to [1]your husbands,
"Bring *wine*, let us [c]drink!"
2 [a]The Lord GOD has sworn by His
holiness:
"Behold, the days shall come upon
you
When He will take you away
[b]with fishhooks,
And your posterity with
fishhooks.
3 [a]You will go out *through* broken
walls,

---

13 [a]Is. 1:14 [1]Or *tottering under* [2]Or *totters*
14 [a]Jer. 46:6 [b]Ps. 33:16; Jer. 9:23 [1]Or *the place of refuge* [2]Lit. *save his soul* or *life*
15 [1]Or *save*
16 [1]Lit. *strong of his heart among the mighty*

CHAPTER 3

2 [a][Gen. 18:19; Ex. 19:5, 6; Deut. 7:6; Ps. 147:19] [b]Jer. 14:10; Ezek. 20:36; Dan. 9:12; Matt. 11:22; [Rom. 2:9]
4 [1]Lit. *give his voice*
5 [1]Or *bait* or *lure*
6 [a]Is. 45:7 [1]*ram's horn*
7 [a]Gen. 6:13; 18:17; [Jer. 23:22]; Dan. 9:22; [John 15:15]
8 [a]Jer. 20:9; [Mic. 3:8]; Acts 4:20; 1 Cor. 9:16
9 [1]So with MT; LXX *Assyria* [2]Or *oppression*
10 [a]Ps. 14:4; Jer. 4:22; Amos 5:7; 6:12 [1]Or *devastation*
12 [1]Or *snatches* [2]Heb. uncertain, possibly *on the cover*
14 [a]2 Kin. 23:15; Hos. 10:5–8, 14, 15; Amos 4:4
15 [a]Jer. 36:22 [b]Judg. 3:20 [c]1 Kin. 22:39; Ps. 45:8 [1]Lit. *strike*

CHAPTER 4

1 [a]Ps. 22:12; Ezek. 39:18 [b]Amos 2:6 [c]Prov. 23:20 [1]Lit. *their masters* or *lords*
2 [a]Ps. 89:35 [b]Jer. 16:16; Ezek. 29:4; Hab. 1:15
3 [a]Ezek. 12:5

Each one straight ahead of her,
And you will [1]be cast into
Harmon,"
Says the LORD.

4 "Come[a] to Bethel and transgress,
At [b]Gilgal multiply transgression;
[c]Bring your sacrifices every
morning,
[d]Your tithes every three [1]days.
5 [a]Offer a sacrifice of thanksgiving
with leaven,
Proclaim *and* announce [b]the
freewill offerings;
For this you love,
You children of Israel!"
Says the Lord GOD.

Israel Did Not Accept Correction

6 "Also I gave you [1]cleanness of
teeth in all your cities.
And lack of bread in all your
places;
[a]Yet you have not returned to
Me,"
Says the LORD.

7 "I also withheld rain from you,
When *there were* still three
months to the harvest.
I made it rain on one city,
I withheld rain from another city.
One part was rained upon,
And where it did not rain the part
withered.
8 So two *or* three cities wandered
to another city to drink water,
But they were not satisfied;
Yet you have not returned to
Me,"
Says the LORD.

9 "I[a] blasted you with blight and
mildew.
When your gardens increased,
Your vineyards,
Your fig trees,
And your olive trees,
[b]The locust devoured *them;*
Yet you have not returned to
Me,"
Says the LORD.

10 "I sent among you a plague [a]after
the manner of Egypt;
Your young men I killed with a
sword,
Along with your captive horses;
I made the stench of your camps
come up into your nostrils;
Yet you have not returned to
Me,"
Says the LORD.

3 [1]Or *cast them*

4 [a]Ezek. 20:39; Amos 3:14 [b]Hos. 4:15 [c]Num. 28:3; Amos 5:21, 22 [d]Deut. 14:28 [1]Or *years,* Deut. 14:28

5 [a]Lev. 7:13 [b]Lev. 22:18; Deut. 12:6

6 [a]2 Chr. 28:22; Is. 26:11; Jer. 5:3; Hag. 2:17 [1]Hunger

9 [a]Deut. 28:22; Hag. 2:17 [b]Joel 1:4, 7; Amos 7:1, 2

10 [a]Ex. 9:3, 6; Lev. 26:25; Deut. 28:27, 60; Ps. 78:50

11 [a]Gen. 19:24, 25; Deut. 29:23; Is. 13:19; Jer. 49:18; Lam. 4:6

12 [a]Jer. 5:22

13 [a]Ps. 139:2; Dan. 2:28 [b]Mic. 1:3 [c]Is. 47:4; Jer. 10:16 [1]Or *spirit* [2]Or *His*

CHAPTER 5

1 [a]Jer. 7:29; 9:10, 17; Ezek. 19:1

4 [a][Deut. 4:29; 2 Chr. 15:2; Jer. 29:13] [b][Is. 55:3]

5 [a]1 Kin. 12:28, 29; Amos 4:4 [b]Gen. 21:31–33; Amos 8:14 [c]Hos. 4:15

6 [a][Is. 55:3, 6, 7; Amos 5:14]

11 "I overthrew *some* of you,
As God overthrew [a]Sodom and
Gomorrah,
And you were like a firebrand
plucked from the burning;
Yet you have not returned to
Me,"
Says the LORD.

12 "Therefore thus will I do to you,
O Israel;
Because I will do this to you,
[a]Prepare to meet your God,
O Israel!"

13 For behold,
He who forms mountains,
And creates the [1]wind,
[a]Who declares to man what [2]his
thought *is,*
And makes the morning
darkness,
[b]Who treads the high places of the
earth—
[c]The LORD God of hosts *is* His
name.

A Lament for Israel

5 Hear this word which I [a]take
up against you, a lamentation,
O house of Israel:

2 The virgin of Israel has fallen;
She will rise no more.
She lies forsaken on her land;
There is no one to raise her up.

3 For thus says the Lord GOD:

"The city that goes out by a
thousand
Shall have a hundred left,
And that which goes out by a
hundred
Shall have ten left to the house
of Israel."

A Call to Repentance

4 For thus says the LORD to the
house of Israel:

[a]"Seek Me [b]and live;
5 But do not seek [a]Bethel,
Nor enter Gilgal,
Nor pass over to [b]Beersheba;
For Gilgal shall surely go into
captivity,
And [c]Bethel shall come to
nothing.
6 [a]Seek the LORD and live,
Lest He break out like fire *in* the
house of Joseph,
And devour *it,*
With no one to quench *it* in
Bethel—

7 You who [a]turn justice to
wormwood,
And lay righteousness to rest in
the earth!"
8 He made the [a]Pleiades and Orion;
He turns the shadow of death into
morning
[b]And makes the day dark as night;
He [c]calls for the waters of the sea
And pours them out on the face
of the earth;
[d]The LORD *is* His name.
9 He [1]rains ruin upon the strong,
So that fury comes upon the
fortress.

10 [a]They hate the one who rebukes
in the gate,
And they [b]abhor the one who
speaks uprightly.
11 [a]Therefore, because you [1]tread
down the poor
And take grain [2]taxes from him,
Though [b]you have built houses of
hewn stone,
Yet you shall not dwell in them;
You have planted [3]pleasant
vineyards,
But you shall not drink wine from
them.
12 For I [a]know your manifold
transgressions
And your mighty sins:
[b]Afflicting the just *and* taking
bribes;
[c]Diverting the poor *from justice* at
the gate.
13 Therefore [a]the prudent keep
silent at that time,
For it *is* an evil time.

14 Seek good and not evil,
That you may live;
So the LORD God of hosts will be
with you,
[a]As you have spoken.
15 [a]Hate evil, love good;
Establish justice in the gate.
[b]It may be that the LORD God of
hosts
Will be gracious to the remnant
of Joseph.

The Day of the LORD

16 Therefore the LORD God of
hosts, the Lord, says this:

"*There shall be* wailing in all
streets,
And they shall say in all the
highways,
'Alas! Alas!'
They shall call the farmer to
mourning,
[a]And skillful lamenters to wailing.
17 In all vineyards *there shall be*
wailing,
For [a]I will pass through you,"
Says the LORD.

18 [a]Woe to you who desire the day
of the LORD!
For what good *is* [b]the day of the
LORD to you?
It *will be* darkness, and not light.
19 It *will be* [a]as though a man fled
from a lion,
And a bear met him!
Or *as though* he went into the
house,
Leaned his hand on the wall,
And a serpent bit him!
20 *Is* not the day of the LORD
darkness, and not light?
Is it not very dark, with no
brightness in it?

21 "I[a] hate, I despise your feast days,
And [b]I do not savor your sacred
assemblies.
22 [a]Though you offer Me burnt
offerings and your grain
offerings,
I will not accept *them*,
Nor will I regard your fattened
peace offerings.
23 Take away from Me the noise of
your songs,
For I will not hear the melody of
your stringed instruments.
24 [a]But let justice run down like
water,
And righteousness like a mighty
stream.

25 "Did[a] you offer Me sacrifices and
offerings
In the wilderness forty years,
O house of Israel?
26 You also carried [1]Sikkuth[2] [a]your
king
And [2]Chiun, your idols,
The star of your gods,
Which you made for yourselves.
27 Therefore I will send you into
captivity [a]beyond Damascus,"
Says the LORD, [b]whose name *is*
the God of hosts.

Warnings to Zion and Samaria

6 Woe [a]to you *who are* at [b]ease in
Zion,
And [c]trust in Mount Samaria,
Notable persons in the [d]chief
nation,
To whom the house of Israel
comes!
2 [a]Go over to [b]Calneh and see;

7 [a]Amos 6:12
8 [a]Job 9:9; 38:31 [b]Ps. 104:20 [c]Job 38:34 [d][Amos 4:13]
9 [1]Or *flashes forth destruction*
10 [a]Is. 29:21; 66:5 [b]1 Kin. 22:8
11 [a]Amos 2:6 [b]Mic. 6:15 [1]*trample* [2]Or *tribute* [3]*desirable*
12 [a]Hos. 5:3 [b]Amos 2:6 [c]Is. 29:21
13 [a]Amos 6:10
14 [a]Mic. 3:11
15 [a]Rom. 12:9 [b]Joel 2:14
16 [a]Jer. 9:17
17 [a]Ex. 12:12
18 [a]Is. 5:19 [b]Joel 2:2
19 [a]Jer. 48:44
21 [a]Is. 1:11–16 [b]Lev. 26:31
22 [a]Mic. 6:6, 7
24 [a]Mic. 6:8
25 [a]Deut. 32:17
26 [a]1 Kin. 11:33 [1]LXX, Vg. *tabernacle of Moloch* [2]A pagan deity
27 [a]2 Kin. 17:6 [b]Amos 4:13

CHAPTER 6

1 [a]Luke 6:24 [b]Zeph. 1:12 [c]Is. 31:1 [d]Ex. 19:5
2 [a]Jer. 2:10 [b]Is. 10:9

And from there go to [c]Hamath
the great;
Then go down to Gath of the
Philistines.
[d]*Are you* better than these
kingdoms?
Or is their territory greater than
your territory?

3 *Woe to* you who [a]put far off the
day of [b]doom,
[c]Who cause [d]the seat of violence
to come near;
4 Who lie on beds of ivory,
Stretch out on your couches,
Eat lambs from the flock
And calves from the midst of the
stall;
5 [a]Who sing idly to the sound of
stringed instruments,
And invent for yourselves
[b]musical instruments [c]like
David;
6 Who [a]drink wine from bowls,
And anoint yourselves with the
best ointments,
[b]But are not grieved for the
affliction of Joseph.
7 Therefore they shall now go
[a]captive as the first of the
captives,
And those who recline at
banquets shall be removed.

8 [a]The Lord GOD has sworn by
Himself,
The LORD God of hosts says:
"I abhor [b]the pride of Jacob,
And hate his palaces;
Therefore I will deliver up *the*
city
And all that is in it."

9 Then it shall come to pass, that
if ten men remain in one house,
they shall die.
10 And when [1]a relative *of the*
dead, with one who will burn *the*
bodies, picks up the [2]bodies to take
them out of the house, he will say
to one inside the house, "*Are there*
any more with you?" Then some-
one will say, "None." And he will
say, [a]"Hold your tongue! [b]For we
dare not mention the name of the
LORD."

11 For behold, [a]the LORD gives a
command:
[b]He will break the great house into
bits,
And the little house into pieces.

12 Do horses run on rocks?
Does *one* plow *there* with oxen?
Yet [a]you have turned justice into
gall,
And the fruit of righteousness
into wormwood,
13 You who rejoice over [1]Lo Debar,
Who say, "Have we not taken
[2]Karnaim for ourselves
By our own strength?"

14 "But, behold, [a]I will raise up a
nation against you,
O house of Israel,"
Says the LORD God of hosts;
"And they will afflict you from the
[b]entrance of Hamath
To the Valley of the Arabah."

Vision of the Locusts

7 Thus the Lord GOD showed me:
Behold, He formed locust
swarms at the [1]beginning of the
late crop; indeed *it was* the late
crop after the king's mowings.
2 And so it was, when they had
finished eating the grass of the
land, that I said:

"O Lord GOD, forgive, I pray!
[a]Oh,[1] that Jacob may stand,
For he *is* small!"
3 *So* [a]the LORD relented concerning
this.
"It shall not be," said the LORD.

Vision of the Fire

4 Thus the Lord GOD showed me:
Behold, the Lord GOD called [1]for
conflict by fire, and it consumed
the great deep and devoured the
[2]territory.
5 Then I said:

"O Lord GOD, cease, I pray!
[a]Oh, that Jacob may stand,
For he *is* small!"
6 *So* the LORD relented concerning
this.
"This also shall not be," said the
Lord GOD.

Vision of the Plumb Line

7 Thus He showed me: Behold,
the Lord stood on a wall *made*
with a plumb line, with a plumb
line in His hand.
8 And the LORD said to me,
"Amos, what do you see?" And I
said, "A plumb line." Then the
Lord said:

"Behold, [a]I am setting a plumb line
In the midst of My people Israel;
[b]I will not pass by them anymore.

---

2 [c]1 Kin. 8:65; 2 Kin. 18:34 [d]Nah. 3:8
3 [a]Is. 56:12; Ezek. 12:27; Amos 9:10; Matt. 24:37–39 [b]Amos 5:18 [c]Amos 5:12 [d]Ps. 94:20
5 [a]Is. 5:12; Amos 5:23 [b]1 Chr. 15:16; 16:42 [c]1 Chr. 23:5
6 [a]Amos 2:8; 4:1 [b]Gen. 37:25
7 [a]Amos 5:27
8 [a]Gen. 22:16; Jer. 51:14; Amos 4:2; 8:7; Heb. 6:13–17 [b]Ps. 47:4; Ezek. 24:21; Amos 8:7
10 [a]Amos 5:13 [b]Amos 8:3 [1]Lit. *his loved one* or *uncle* [2]Lit. *bones*
11 [a]Is. 55:11 [b]2 Kin. 25:9; Amos 3:15
12 [a]1 Kin. 21:7–13; Is. 59:13, 14; Hos. 10:4; Amos 5:7, 11, 12
13 [1]Lit. *Nothing* [2]Lit. *Horns*, a symbol of strength
14 [a]Jer. 5:15 [b]Num. 34:7, 8; 1 Kin. 8:65; 2 Kin. 14:25

CHAPTER 7

1 [1]Lit. *beginning of the sprouting of*
2 [a]Is. 51:19 [1]Or *How shall Jacob stand*
3 [a]Deut. 32:36; Jer. 26:19; Hos. 11:8; Amos 5:15; Jon. 3:10; [James 5:16]
4 [1]*to contend* [2]Lit. *portion*
5 [a]Amos 7:2, 3
8 [a]2 Kin. 21:13; Is. 28:17; 34:11; Lam. 2:8 [b]Mic. 7:18

9 [a]The [1]high places of Isaac shall be desolate,
And the [2]sanctuaries of Israel shall be laid waste.
[b]I will rise with the sword against the house of Jeroboam."

Amaziah's Complaint

10 Then Amaziah the [a]priest of
[b]Bethel sent to [c]Jeroboam king of
Israel, saying, "Amos has con-
spired against you in the midst of
the house of Israel. The land is not
able to [1]bear all his words.
11 "For thus Amos has said:

'Jeroboam shall die by the sword,
And Israel shall surely be led away [a]captive
From their own land.' "

12 Then Amaziah said to Amos:

"Go, you seer!
Flee to the land of Judah.
There eat bread,
And there prophesy.
13 But [a]never again prophesy at Bethel,
[b]For it *is* the king's [1]sanctuary,
And it *is* the royal [2]residence."

14 Then Amos answered, and said
to Amaziah:

"I *was* no prophet,
Nor *was* I [a]a son of a prophet,
But I *was* a [b]sheepbreeder
And a tender of sycamore fruit.
15 Then the LORD took me [1]as I followed the flock,
And the LORD said to me,
'Go, [a]prophesy to My people Israel.'
16 Now therefore, hear the word of the LORD:
You say, 'Do not prophesy against Israel,
And [a]do not [1]spout against the house of Isaac.'

17 "Therefore[a] thus says the
LORD:

[b]'Your wife shall be a harlot in the city;
Your sons and daughters shall fall by the sword;
Your land shall be divided by *survey* line;
You shall die in a [c]defiled land;
And Israel shall surely be led away captive
From his own land.' "

9 [a]Gen. 46:1 [b]2 Kin.15:8–
10 [1]Places of pagan worship [2]Or *holy places*

10 [a]1 Kin. 12:31, 32; 13:33 [b]Amos 4:4 [c]2 Kin. 14:23 [1]Or *endure*

11 [a]Amos 5:27; 6:7

13 [a]Amos 2:12 [b]1 Kin. 12:29, 32 [1]Or *holy place* [2]Lit. *house*

14 [a]1 Kin. 20:35 [b]Zech. 13:5

15 [a]Amos 3:8 [1]Lit. *from behind*

16 [a]Ezek. 21:2 [1]Lit. *drip*

17 [a]Jer. 28:12; 29:21, 32 [b]Zech. 14:2 [c]Hos. 9:3

CHAPTER 8

2 [a]Ezek. 7:2 [b]Amos 7:8

3 [a]Amos 5:23 [b]Amos 6:9, 10

4 [1]Or *trample on,* Amos 2:7

5 [a]Neh. 13:15 [b]Mic. 6:10, 11 [c]Lev. 19:35, 36 [1]Lit. *open*

6 [a]Amos 2:6

7 [a]Amos 6:8 [b]Hos. 7:2; 8:13

8 [a]Hos. 4:3 [b]Amos 9:5 [1]The Nile; some Heb. mss., LXX, Tg., Syr., Vg. *River* (cf. 9:5); MT *the light*

9 [a]Job 5:14 [1]Lit. *a day of light*

10 [a]Ezek. 7:18 [b]Ezek. 27:31 [c][Zech. 12:10]

Vision of the Summer Fruit

8 Thus the Lord GOD showed me:
Behold, a basket of summer
fruit.
2 And He said, "Amos, what do
you see?" So I said, "A basket of
summer fruit." Then the LORD said
to me:

[a]"The end has come upon My people Israel;
[b]I will not pass by them anymore.
3 And [a]the songs of the temple
Shall be wailing in that day,"
Says the Lord GOD—
"Many dead bodies everywhere,
[b]They shall be thrown out in silence."

4 Hear this, you who [1]swallow up the needy,
And make the poor of the land fail,

5 Saying:

"When will the New Moon be past,
That we may sell grain?
And [a]the Sabbath,
That we may [1]trade wheat?
[b]Making the ephah small and the shekel large,
Falsifying the scales by [c]deceit,
6 That we may buy the poor for [a]silver,
And the needy for a pair of sandals—
Even sell the bad wheat?"

7 The LORD has sworn by [a]the pride of Jacob:
"Surely [b]I will never forget any of their works.
8 [a]Shall the land not tremble for this,
And everyone mourn who dwells in it?
All of it shall swell like [1]the River,
Heave and subside
[b]Like the River of Egypt.

9 "And it shall come to pass in that day," says the Lord GOD,
[a]"That I will make the sun go down at noon,
And I will darken the earth in [1]broad daylight;
10 I will turn your feasts into [a]mourning,
[b]And all your songs into lamentation;
[c]I will bring sackcloth on every waist,
And baldness on every head;

I will make it like mourning for
an only *son*,
And its end like a bitter day.

11 "Behold, the days are coming,"
says the Lord GOD,
"That I will send a famine on the
land,
Not a famine of bread,
Nor a thirst for water,
But [a]of hearing the words of the
LORD.
12 They shall wander from sea to
sea,
And from north to east;
They shall run to and fro, seeking
the word of the LORD,
But shall [a]not find *it*.

13 "In that day the fair virgins
And strong young men
Shall faint from thirst.
14 Those who [a]swear by [b]the [1]sin of
Samaria,
Who say,
'As your god lives, O Dan!'
And, 'As the way of [c]Beersheba
lives!'
They shall fall and never rise
again."

The Destruction of Israel

9 I saw the Lord standing by the
altar, and He said:

"Strike the [1]doorposts, that the
thresholds may shake,
And [a]break them on the heads of
them all.
I will slay the last of them with
the sword.
[b]He who flees from them shall not
get away,
And he who escapes from them
shall not be delivered.

2 "Though[a] they dig into [1]hell,
From there My hand shall take
them;
[b]Though they climb up to heaven,
From there I will bring them
down;
3 And though they [a]hide
themselves on top of Carmel,
From there I will search and take
them;
Though they hide from My sight
at the bottom of the sea,
From there I will command the
serpent, and it shall bite them;
4 Though they go into captivity
before their enemies,
From there [a]I will command the
sword,
And it shall slay them.

11 [a]1 Sam. 3:1; 2 Chr. 15:3; Ps. 74:9; Ezek. 7:26; Mic. 3:6
12 [a]Hos. 5:6
14 [a]Hos. 4:15 [b]Deut. 9:21 [c]Amos 5:5 [1]Or *Ashima*, a Syrian goddess

CHAPTER 9

1 [a]Ps. 68:21; Hab. 3:13 [b]Amos 2:14 [1]Capitals of the pillars
2 [a]Ps. 139:8; Jer. 23:24 [b]Job 20:6; Jer. 51:53; Obad. 4; Matt. 11:23 [1]Or *Sheol*
3 [a]Jer. 23:24
4 [a]Lev. 26:33 [b]Lev. 17:10; Jer. 21:10; 39:16; 44:11
5 [a]Ps. 104:32; 144:5; Is. 64:1; Mic. 1:4 [b]Amos 8:8 [1]The Nile
6 [a]Ps. 104:3, 13 [b]Amos 5:8 [c]Amos 4:13; 5:27 [1]Or *stairs*
7 [a]Jer. 47:4 [b]Deut. 2:23 [c]Amos 1:5 [1]Lit. *sons of the Ethiopians* [2]Crete
8 [a]Jer. 44:27; Amos 9:4 [b]Jer. 5:10; 30:11; [Joel 2:32]; Amos 3:12; [Obad. 16, 17]
9 [a][Is. 65:8–16] [1]*shake* [2]Lit. *pebble*
10 [a][Is. 28:15]; Jer. 5:12; Amos 6:3
11 [a]Acts 15:16–18 [1]Lit. *booth;* a figure of a deposed dynasty [2]Lit. *wall up its breaches*
12 [a]Obad. 19 [b]Num. 24:18; Is. 11:14 [1]LXX *mankind*

[b]I will set My eyes on them for
harm and not for good."

5 The Lord GOD of hosts,
He who touches the earth and it
[a]melts,
[b]And all who dwell there
mourn;
All of it shall swell like [1]the
River,
And subside like the River of
Egypt.
6 He who builds His [a]layers[1] in the
sky,
And has founded His strata in the
earth;
Who [b]calls for the waters of the
sea,
And pours them out on the face
of the earth—
[c]The LORD *is* His name.

7 "*Are* you not like the [1]people of
Ethiopia to Me,
O children of Israel?" says the
LORD.
"Did I not bring up Israel from the
land of Egypt,
The [a]Philistines from [b]Caphtor,[2]
And the Syrians from [c]Kir?

8 "Behold, [a]the eyes of the Lord GOD
are on the sinful kingdom,
And I [b]will destroy it from the
face of the earth;
Yet I will not utterly destroy the
house of Jacob,"
Says the LORD.

9 "For surely I will command,
And will [1]sift the house of Israel
among all nations,
As *grain* is sifted in a sieve;
[a]Yet not the smallest [2]grain shall
fall to the ground.
10 All the sinners of My people shall
die by the sword,
[a]Who say, 'The calamity shall not
overtake nor confront us.'

Israel Will Be Restored

11 "On[a] that day I will raise up
The [1]tabernacle of David, which
has fallen down,
And [2]repair its damages;
I will raise up its ruins,
And rebuild it as in the days of
old;
12 [a]That they may possess the
remnant of [b]Edom,[1]
And all the Gentiles who are
called by My name,"
Says the LORD who does this
thing.

13 "Behold, [a]the days are coming,"
says the LORD,
"When the plowman shall
overtake the reaper,
And the treader of grapes him
who sows seed;
[b]The mountains shall drip with
sweet wine,
And all the hills shall flow *with*
it.
14 [a]I will bring back the captives of
My people Israel;
[b]They shall build the waste cities
and inhabit *them*;
They shall plant vineyards and
drink wine from them;
They shall also make gardens
and eat fruit from them.
15 I will plant them in their land,
[a]And no longer shall they be
pulled up
From the land I have given
them,"
Says the LORD your God.

13 [a]Lev. 26:5 [b]Joel 3:18
14 [a]Ps. 53:6; Is. 60:4; Jer. 30:3, 18 [b]Is. 61:4
15 [a]Is. 60:21; Ezek. 34:28; 37:25

The Book of

Obadiah

A STRUGGLE that began in the womb between twin brothers, Esau and Jacob, eventuates in a struggle between their respective descendants, the Edomites and the Israelites. For the Edomites' stubborn refusal to aid Israel, first during the time of wilderness wandering (Num. 20:14–21) and later during a time of invasion, they are roundly condemned by Obadiah. This little-known prophet describes their crimes, tries their case, and pronounces their judgment: total destruction.

The Hebrew name *Obadyah* means "Worshiper of Yahweh" or "Servant of Yahweh." The Greek title in the Septuagint is *Obdiou,* and the Latin title in the Vulgate is *Abdias.*

The Coming Judgment on Edom

THE vision of Obadiah.

Thus says the Lord GOD
[a]concerning Edom
[b](We have heard a report from the LORD,
And a messenger has been sent among the nations, *saying,*
"Arise, and let us rise up against her for battle"):

2 "Behold, I will make you small among the nations;
You shall be greatly despised.
3 The [a]pride of your heart has deceived you,
You who dwell in the clefts of the rock,
Whose habitation is high;
[b]*You* who say in your heart,
'Who will bring me down to the ground?'
4 [a]Though you ascend *as* high as the eagle,
And though you [b]set your nest among the stars,
From there I will bring you down," says the LORD.

5 "If [a]thieves had come to you,
If robbers by night—
Oh, how you will be cut off!—
Would they not have stolen till they had enough?
If grape-gatherers had come to you,
[b]Would they not have left *some* gleanings?

6 "Oh, how Esau shall be searched out!
How his hidden treasures shall be sought after!
7 All the men in your confederacy
Shall force you to the border;
[a]The men at peace with you
Shall deceive you *and* prevail against you.
Those who eat your bread shall lay a [1]trap for you.
[b]No[2] one is aware of it.

8 "Will[a] I not in that day," says the LORD,
"Even destroy the wise *men* from Edom,
And understanding from the mountains of Esau?
9 Then your [a]mighty men,
O [b]Teman, shall be dismayed,
To the end that everyone from the mountains of Esau
May be cut off by slaughter.

Edom Mistreated His Brother

10 "For [a]violence against your brother Jacob,
Shame shall cover you,
And [b]you shall be cut off forever.
11 In the day that you [a]stood on the other side—
In the day that strangers carried captive his forces,
When foreigners entered his gates
And [b]cast lots for Jerusalem—
Even you *were* as one of them.

12 "But you should not have [a]gazed[1] on the day of your brother
[2]In the day of his captivity;
Nor should you have [b]rejoiced over the children of Judah
In the day of their destruction;
Nor should you have spoken proudly
In the day of distress.

CHAPTER 1

1 [a]Is. 21:11; Ezek. 25:12; Joel 3:19; Mal. 1:3 [b]Jer. 49:14–16; Obad. 1–4
3 [a]Is. 16:6; Jer. 49:16 [b]Is. 14:13–15; Rev. 18:7
4 [a]Job 20:6 [b]Hab. 2:9; Mal. 1:4
5 [a]Jer. 49:9 [b]Deut. 24:21
7 [a]Jer. 38:22 [b]Is. 19:11; Jer. 49:7 [1]Or *wound* or *plot* [2]Or *There is no understanding in him*
8 [a][Job 5:12–14]; Is. 29:14
9 [a]Ps. 76:5 [b]Gen. 36:11; 1 Chr. 1:45; Job 2:11; Jer. 49:7
10 [a]Gen. 27:41; Ezek. 25:12; Amos 1:11 [b]Ezek. 35:9; Joel 3:19
11 [a]Ps. 83:5–8; Amos 1:6, 9 [b]Joel 3:3; Nah. 3:10
12 [a]Mic. 4:11; 7:10 [b][Prov. 17:5]; Ezek. 35:15; 36:5 [1]Gloated over [2]Lit. *On the day he became a foreigner*

13 You should not have entered the
gate of My people
In the day of their calamity.
Indeed, you should not have
[1]gazed on their affliction
In the day of their calamity,
Nor laid *hands* on their substance
In the day of their calamity.
14 You should not have stood at the
crossroads
To cut off those among them who
escaped;
Nor should you have [1]delivered
up those among them who
remained
In the day of distress.

15 "For[a] the day of the LORD upon all
the nations *is* near;
[b]As you have done, it shall be done
to you;
Your [1]reprisal shall return upon
your own head.
16 [a]For as you drank on My holy
mountain,
So shall all the nations drink
continually;
Yes, they shall drink, and
swallow,
And they shall be as though they
had never been.

Israel's Final Triumph

17 "But on Mount Zion there [a]shall
be [1]deliverance,
And there shall be holiness;
The house of Jacob shall possess
their possessions.
18 The house of Jacob shall be a fire,
And the house of Joseph [a]a flame;
But the house of Esau *shall be*
stubble;
They shall kindle them and
devour them,
And no survivor shall *remain* of
the house of Esau,"
For the LORD has spoken.

19 The [1]South [a]shall possess the
mountains of Esau,
[b]And the Lowland shall possess
Philistia.
They shall possess the fields of
Ephraim
And the fields of Samaria.
Benjamin *shall possess* Gilead.
20 And the captives of this host of
the children of Israel
Shall possess the land of the
Canaanites
As [a]far as Zarephath.
The captives of Jerusalem who
are in Sepharad
[b]Shall possess the cities of the
[1]South.
21 Then [a]saviors[1] shall come to
Mount Zion
To judge the mountains of Esau,
And the [b]kingdom shall be the
LORD's.

13 [1]Gloated over
14 [1]Handed over to the enemy
15 [a]Ezek. 30:3; [Joel 1:15; 2:1, 11, 31; Amos 5:18, 20] [b]Jer. 50:29; 51:56; Hab. 2:8 [1]Or *reward*
16 [a]Joel 3:17
17 [a]Is. 14:1, 2; Joel 2:32; Amos 9:8 [1]Or *salvation*
18 [a]Is. 5:24; 9:18, 19; Zech. 12:6
19 [a]Is. 11:14; Amos 9:12 [b]Zeph. 2:7 [1]Heb. *Negev*
20 [a]1 Kin. 17:9; Luke 4:26 [b]Jer. 32:44 [1]Heb. *Negev*
21 [a][James 5:20] [b]Ps. 22:28; [Dan. 2:44; 7:14; Zech. 14:9; Rev. 11:15] [1]*deliverers*

The Book of

Jonah

NINEVEH is northeast; Tarshish is west. When God calls Jonah to preach repentance to the wicked Ninevites, the prophet knows that God's mercy may follow. He turns down the assignment and heads for Tarshish instead. But once God has dampened his spirits (by tossing him out of the boat and into the water) and has demonstrated His protection (by moving him out of the water and into the fish), Jonah realizes God is serious about His command. Nineveh must hear the word of the Lord; therefore Jonah goes. Although the preaching is a success, the preacher comes away angry and discouraged and he must learn firsthand of God's compassion for sinful men.

Yonah is the Hebrew word for "dove." The Septuagint hellenized this word into *Ionas,* and the Latin Vulgate used the title *Jonas.*

Jonah's Disobedience

NOW the word of the LORD
came to [a]Jonah the son of
Amittai, saying,
2 "Arise, go to [a]Nineveh, that
[b]great city, and cry out against it;
for [c]their wickedness has come up
before Me."
3 But Jonah arose to flee to
Tarshish from the presence of the
LORD. He went down to [a]Joppa,
and found a ship going to Tarshish;
so he paid the fare, and went
down into it, to go with them to
[b]Tarshish [c]from the presence of
the LORD.

The Storm at Sea

4 But [a]the LORD [1]sent out a great
wind on the sea, and there was a
mighty tempest on the sea, so that
the ship was about to be broken
up.
5 Then the mariners were afraid;
and every man cried out to his god,
and threw the cargo that *was* in
the ship into the sea, to lighten [1]the
load. But Jonah had gone down
[a]into the lowest parts of the ship,
had lain down, and was fast
asleep.
6 So the captain came to him,
and said to him, "What do you
mean, sleeper? Arise, [a]call on your
God; [b]perhaps your God will consider
us, so that we may not perish."
7 And they said to one another,
"Come, let us [a]cast lots, that we
may know for whose cause this
trouble *has come* upon us." So
they cast lots, and the lot fell on
Jonah.
8 Then they said to him, [a]"Please
tell us! For whose cause *is* this
trouble upon us? What is your occupation?
And where do you come
from? What is your country? And
of what people are you?"
9 So he said to them, "I *am* a Hebrew;
and I fear [1]the LORD, the God
of heaven, [a]who made the sea and
the dry *land.*"

Jonah Thrown into the Sea

10 Then the men were exceedingly
afraid, and said to him,
"Why have you done this?" For the
men knew that he fled from the
presence of the LORD, because he
had told them.
11 Then they said to him, "What
shall we do to you that the sea may
be calm for us?"—for the sea was
growing more tempestuous.
12 And he said to them, [a]"Pick me
up and [1]throw me into the sea;
then the sea will become calm for
you. For I know that this great
tempest *is* because of me."
13 Nevertheless the men rowed
hard to return to land, [a]but they
could not, for the sea continued to
grow more tempestuous against
them.
14 Therefore they cried out to the
LORD and said, "We pray, O LORD,
please do not let us perish for this
man's life, and [a]do not charge us
with innocent blood; for You,

CHAPTER 1

1 [a]2 Kin. 14:25; Matt. 12:39–41; 16:4; Luke 11:29, 30, 32

2 [a]Is. 37:37 [b]Gen. 10:11, 12; 2 Kin. 19:36; Jon. 4:11; Nah. 1:1; Zeph. 2:13 [c]Gen. 18:20; Hos. 7:2

3 [a]Josh. 19:46; 2 Chr. 2:16; Ezra 3:7; Acts 9:36, 43 [b]Is. 23:1 [c]Gen. 4:16; Job 1:12; 2:7

4 [a]Ps. 107:25 [1]Lit. *hurled*

5 [a]1 Sam. 24:3 [1]Lit. *from upon them*

6 [a]Ps. 107:28 [b]Joel 2:14

7 [a]Josh. 7:14; 1 Sam. 14:41, 42; Prov. 16:33

8 [a]Josh. 7:19; 1 Sam. 14:43

9 [a][Neh. 9:6]; Ps. 146:6; Acts 17:24 [1]Heb. *YHWH*

12 [a]John 11:50 [1]Lit. *hurl*

13 [a][Prov. 21:30]

14 [a]Deut. 21:8

O LORD, [b]have done as it pleased You."

15 So they picked up Jonah and threw him into the sea, [a]and the sea ceased from its raging.

16 Then the men [a]feared the LORD exceedingly, and offered a sacrifice to the LORD and took vows.

Jonah's Prayer and Deliverance

17 Now the LORD had prepared a great fish to swallow Jonah. And [a]Jonah was in the belly of the fish three days and three nights.

2 Then Jonah prayed to the LORD his God from the fish's belly.

2 And he said:

"I [a]cried out to the LORD because
of my affliction,
[b]And He answered me.

"Out of the belly of Sheol I cried,
And You heard my voice.
3 [a]For You cast me into the deep,
Into the heart of the seas,
And the floods surrounded me;
[b]All Your billows and Your waves
passed over me.
4 [a]Then I said, 'I have been cast out
of Your sight;
Yet I will look again [b]toward
Your holy temple.'
5 The [a]waters surrounded me, *even*
to my soul;
The deep closed around me;
Weeds were wrapped around my
head.
6 I went down to the [1]moorings of
the mountains;
The earth with its bars *closed*
behind me forever;
Yet You have brought up my [a]life
from the pit,
O LORD, my God.

7 "When my soul fainted within me,
I remembered the LORD;
[a]And my prayer went *up* to You,
Into Your holy temple.

8 "Those who regard [a]worthless
idols
Forsake their own [1]Mercy.
9 But I will [a]sacrifice to You
With the voice of thanksgiving;
I will pay what I have [b]vowed.
[c]Salvation *is* of the [d]LORD."

10 So the LORD spoke to the fish, and it vomited Jonah onto dry *land*.

14 [b]Ps. 115:3; [Dan. 4:35]
15 [a][Ps. 89:9; 107:29]; Luke 8:24
16 [a]Mark 4:41; Acts 5:11
17 [a][Matt. 12:40; Luke 11:30]

CHAPTER 2

2 [a]1 Sam. 30:6; Ps. 120:1; Lam. 3:55 [b]Ps. 65:2
3 [a]Ps. 88:6 [b]Ps. 42:7
4 [a]Ps. 31:22; Jer. 7:15 [b]1 Kin. 8:38; 2 Chr. 6:38; Ps. 5:7
5 [a]Ps. 69:1; Lam. 3:54
6 [a]Job 33:28; [Ps. 16:10; Is. 38:17] [1]*foundations* or *bases*
7 [a]2 Chr. 30:27; Ps. 18:6
8 [a]2 Kin. 17:15; Ps. 31:6; Jer. 10:8 [1]Or *Loving-kindness*
9 [a]Ps. 50:14, 23; Jer. 33:11; Hos. 14:2 [b]Job 22:27; [Eccl. 5:4, 5] [c]Ps. 3:8; [Is. 45:17] [d][Jer. 3:23]

CHAPTER 3

3 [1]Exact meaning unknown
4 [a][Deut. 18:22]
5 [a][Matt. 12:41; Luke 11:32]
6 [a]Job 2:8
7 [a]2 Chr. 20:3; Dan. 3:29; Joel 2:15 [1]Lit. *great ones*
8 [a]Is. 58:6 [b]Is. 59:6
9 [a]2 Sam. 12:22; Joel 2:14; Amos 5:15
10 [a]Ex. 32:14; Jer. 18:8; Amos 7:3, 6

Jonah Preaches at Nineveh

3 Now the word of the LORD came to Jonah the second time, saying,

2 "Arise, go to Nineveh, that great city, and preach to it the message that I tell you."

3 So Jonah arose and went to Nineveh, according to the word of the LORD. Now Nineveh was an exceedingly great city, [1]a three-day journey *in extent*.

4 And Jonah began to enter the city on the first day's walk. Then [a]he cried out and said, "Yet forty days, and Nineveh shall be overthrown!"

The People of Nineveh Believe

5 So the [a]people of Nineveh believed God, proclaimed a fast, and put on sackcloth, from the greatest to the least of them.

6 Then word came to the king of Nineveh; and he arose from his throne and laid aside his robe, covered *himself* with sackcloth [a]and sat in ashes.

7 [a]And he caused *it* to be proclaimed and published throughout Nineveh by the decree of the king and his [1]nobles, saying,

Let neither man nor beast, herd
nor flock, taste anything; do
not let them eat, or drink water.
8 But let man and beast be
covered with sackcloth, and
cry mightily to God; yes, [a]let
every one turn from his evil
way and from [b]the violence
that is in his hands.
9 [a]Who can tell *if* God will turn
and relent, and turn away from
His fierce anger, so that we
may not perish?

10 [a]Then God saw their works, that they turned from their evil way; and God relented from the disaster that He had said He would bring upon them, and He did not do it.

Jonah's Anger and God's Kindness

4 But it displeased Jonah exceedingly, and he became angry.

2 So he prayed to the LORD, and said, "Ah, LORD, was not this what

I said when I was still in my coun-
try? Therefore I [a]fled previously
to Tarshish; for I know that You
are a [b]gracious and merciful God,
slow to anger and abundant in
lovingkindness, One who relents
from doing harm.
3 [a]"Therefore now, O LORD,
please take my life from me, for
[b]*it is* better for me to die than to
live!"
4 Then the LORD said, "*Is it* right
for you to be angry?"
5 So Jonah went out of the city
and sat on the east side of the city.
There he made himself a shelter
and sat under it in the shade, till
he might see what would become
of the city.
6 And the LORD God prepared a
[1]plant and made it come up over
Jonah, that it might be shade for
his head to deliver him from his
misery. So Jonah [2]was very grate-
ful for the plant.
7 But as morning dawned the
next day God prepared a worm,
and it *so* damaged the plant that
it withered.
8 And it happened, when the sun
arose, that God prepared a vehe-
ment east wind; and the sun beat
on Jonah's head, so that he grew
faint. Then he wished death for
himself, and said, [a]"*It is* better for
me to die than to live."
9 Then God said to Jonah, "*Is it*
right for you to be angry about the
plant?" And he said, "*It is* right for
me to be angry, even to death!"
10 But the LORD said, "You have
had pity on the plant for which you
have not labored, nor made it
grow, which [1]came up in a night
and perished in a night.
11 "And should I not pity Nin-
eveh, [a]that great city, in which are
more than one hundred and
twenty thousand persons [b]who
cannot discern between their right
hand and their left—and much
livestock?"

CHAPTER 4

2 [a]Jon. 1:3 [b]Ex. 34:6; Num. 14:18; Ps. 86:5, 15; Joel 2:13

3 [a]1 Kin. 19:4; Job 6:8, 9 [b]Jon. 4:8

6 [1]Heb. *kikayon,* exact identity unknown [2]Lit. *rejoiced with great joy*

8 [a]Jon. 4:3

10 [1]Lit. *was a son of a night*

11 [a]Jon. 1:2; 3:2, 3 [b]Deut. 1:39; Is. 7:16

The Book of

Micah

MICAH, called from his rustic home to be a prophet, leaves his familiar surroundings to deliver a stern message of judgment to the princes and people of Jerusalem. Burdened by the abusive treatment of the poor by the rich and influential, the prophet turns his verbal rebukes upon any who would use their social or political power for personal gain. One-third of Micah's book exposes the sins of his countrymen; another third pictures the punishment God is about to send; and the final third holds out the hope of restoration once that discipline has ended. Through it all, God's righteous demands upon His people are clear: "to do justly, to love mercy, and to walk humbly with your God" (6:8).

The name *Michayahu* ("Who Is Like Yahweh?") is shortened to *Michaia.* In 7:18, Micah hints at his own name with the phrase "Who *is* a God like You?" The Greek and Latin titles of this book are *Michaias* and *Micha.*

THE word of the LORD that came to [a]Micah of Moresheth in the days of [b]Jotham, Ahaz, *and* Hezekiah, kings of Judah, which he saw concerning Samaria and Jerusalem.

The Coming Judgment on Israel

2 Hear, all you peoples!
Listen, O earth, and all that is in it!
Let the Lord GOD be a witness against you,
The Lord from [a]His holy temple.

3 For behold, the LORD is coming out of His place;
He will come down
And tread on the high places of the earth.
4 [a]The mountains will melt under Him,
And the valleys will split
Like wax before the fire,
Like waters poured down a steep place.
5 All this is for the transgression of Jacob
And for the sins of the house of Israel.
What *is* the transgression of Jacob?
Is it not Samaria?
And what *are* the [a]high places of Judah?
Are they not Jerusalem?

6 "Therefore I will make Samaria [a]a heap of ruins in the field,
Places for planting a vineyard;
I will pour down her stones into the valley,
And I will [b]uncover her foundations.
7 All her carved images shall be beaten to pieces,
And all her [a]pay as a harlot shall be burned with the fire;
All her idols I will lay desolate,
For she gathered *it* from the pay of a harlot,
And they shall return to the [b]pay of a harlot."

Mourning for Israel and Judah

8 Therefore I will wail and howl,
I will go stripped and naked;
[a]I will make a wailing like the jackals
And a mourning like the ostriches,
9 For her wounds *are* incurable.
For [a]it has come to Judah;
It has come to the gate of My people—
To Jerusalem.

10 [a]Tell *it* not in Gath,
Weep not at all;
In [1]Beth Aphrah
Roll yourself in the dust.
11 Pass by in naked shame, you inhabitant of [1]Shaphir;
The inhabitant of [2]Zaanan does not go out.
Beth Ezel mourns;
Its place to stand is taken away from you.

CHAPTER 1

1 [a][2 Pet. 1:21]; Jer. 26:18 [b]2 Kin. 15:5, 7, 32–38; 2 Chr. 27:1–9; Is. 1:1; Hos. 1:1

2 [a][Ps. 11:4]

4 [a]Amos 9:5

5 [a]Deut. 32:13; 33:29; Amos 4:13

6 [a]2 Kin. 19:25; Mic. 3:12 [b]Ezek. 13:14

7 [a]Hos. 2:5 [b]Deut. 23:18; Is. 23:17

8 [a]Ps. 102:6

9 [a]2 Kin. 18:13; Is. 8:7, 8

10 [a]2 Sam. 1:20 [1]Lit. *House of Dust*

11 [1]Lit. *Beautiful* [2]Lit. *Going Out*

12 For the inhabitant of [1]Maroth
[2]pined for good,
But [a]disaster came down from the LORD
To the gate of Jerusalem.
13 O inhabitant of [a]Lachish,
Harness the chariot to the swift steeds
(She *was* the beginning of sin to the daughter of Zion),
For the transgressions of Israel were [b]found in you.
14 Therefore you shall [a]give presents to [1]Moresheth Gath;
The houses of [b]Achzib[2] *shall be* a lie to the kings of Israel.
15 I will yet bring an heir to you,
O inhabitant of [a]Mareshah;[1]
The glory of Israel shall come to [b]Adullam.[2]
16 Make yourself [a]bald and cut off your hair,
Because of your [b]precious children;
Enlarge your baldness like an eagle,
For they shall go from you into [c]captivity.

Woe to Evildoers

2 Woe to those who devise iniquity,
And [1]work out evil on their beds!
At [a]morning light they practice it,
Because it is in the power of their hand.
2 They [a]covet fields and take *them* by violence,
Also houses, and seize *them*.
So they oppress a man and his house,
A man and his inheritance.

3 Therefore thus says the LORD:

"Behold, against this [a]family I am devising [b]disaster,
From which you cannot remove your necks;
Nor shall you walk haughtily,
For this *is* an evil time.
4 In that day *one* shall take up a proverb against you,
And [a]lament with a bitter lamentation, saying:
'We are utterly destroyed!
He has changed the [1]heritage of my people;
How He has removed *it* from me!
To [2]a turncoat He has divided our fields.'"

5 Therefore you will have no [1]one to determine boundaries by lot
In the assembly of the LORD.

12 [a]Is. 59:9–11; Jer. 14:19; Amos 3:6 [1]Lit. *Bitterness* [2]Lit. *was sick*

13 [a]Josh. 10:3; 2 Kin. 14:19; 18:14; Is. 36:2 [b]Ezek. 23:11

14 [a]2 Sam. 8:2 [b]Josh. 15:44 [1]Lit. *Possession of Gath* [2]Lit. *Lie*

15 [a]Josh. 15:44 [b]2 Chr. 11:7 [1]Lit. *Inheritance* [2]Lit. *Refuge*

16 [a]Job 1:20 [b]Lam. 4:5 [c]2 Kin. 17:6; Amos 7:11, 17; [Mic. 4:10]

CHAPTER 2

1 [a]Hos. 7:6, 7 [1]Plan

2 [a]Is. 5:8

3 [a]Ex. 20:5; Jer. 8:3; Amos 3:1, 2 [b]Amos 5:13

4 [a]2 Sam. 1:17 [1]Lit. *portion* [2]Lit. *one turning back*, an apostate

5 [1]Lit. *one casting a surveyor's line*

6 [1]Or *preach*, lit. *drip words* [2]Lit. *to these* [3]Vg. *He shall not take shame*

10 [a]Deut. 12:9 [b]Lev. 18:25

11 [a]Is. 30:10; Jer. 5:30, 31; 2 Tim. 4:3, 4 [1]Or *preach*, lit. *drip* [2]*concerning*

12 [a][Mic. 4:6, 7] [b]Jer. 31:10 [c]Ezek. 33:22; 36:37 [1]Heb. *Bozrah*

13 [a][Hos. 3:5] [b]Is. 52:12

Lying Prophets

6 "Do not prattle," *you say to those* who [1]prophesy.
So they shall not prophesy [2]to you;
[3]They shall not return insult for insult.
7 *You who are* named the house of Jacob:
"Is the Spirit of the LORD restricted?
Are these His doings?
Do not My words do good
To him who walks uprightly?

8 "Lately My people have risen up as an enemy—
You pull off the robe with the garment
From those who trust *you*, as they pass by,
Like men returned from war.
9 The women of My people you cast out
From their pleasant houses;
From their children
You have taken away My glory forever.

10 "Arise and depart,
For this *is* not *your* [a]rest;
Because it is [b]defiled, it shall destroy,
Yes, with utter destruction.
11 If a man should walk in a false spirit
And speak a lie, *saying*,
'I will [1]prophesy to you [2]of wine and drink,'
Even he would be the [a]prattler of this people.

Israel Restored

12 "I[a] will surely assemble all of you, O Jacob,
I will surely gather the remnant of Israel;
I will put them together [b]like sheep of [1]the fold,
Like a flock in the midst of their pasture;
[c]They shall make a loud noise because of *so many* people.
13 The one who breaks open will come up before them;
They will break out,
Pass through the gate,
And go out by it;
[a]Their king will pass before them,
[b]With the LORD at their head."

Wicked Rulers and Prophets

3 And I said:
"Hear now, O heads of Jacob,

And you [a]rulers of the house of
Israel:
[b]*Is it* not for you to know justice?
2 You who hate good and love evil;
Who strip the skin from [1]My
people,
And the flesh from their bones;
3 Who also [a]eat the flesh of My
people,
Flay their skin from them,
Break their bones,
And chop *them* in pieces
Like *meat* for the pot,
[b]Like flesh in the caldron."

4 Then [a]they will cry to the LORD,
But He will not hear them;
He will even hide His face from
them at that time,
Because they have been evil in
their deeds.

5 Thus says the LORD [a]concerning
the prophets
Who make my people stray;
Who chant [1]"Peace"
[2]While they [b]chew with their
teeth,
But who prepare war against him
[c]Who puts nothing into their
mouths:
6 "Therefore[a] you shall have night
without [1]vision,
And you shall have darkness
without divination;
The sun shall go down on the
prophets,
And the day shall be dark for
[b]them.
7 So the seers shall be ashamed,
And the diviners abashed;
Indeed they shall all cover their
lips;
[a]For *there is* no answer from
God."

8 But truly I am full of power by
the Spirit of the LORD,
And of justice and might,
[a]To declare to Jacob his
transgression
And to Israel his sin.
9 Now hear this,
You heads of the house of Jacob
And rulers of the house of Israel,
Who abhor justice
And [1]pervert all equity,
10 [a]Who build up Zion with
[b]bloodshed
And Jerusalem with iniquity:
11 [a]Her heads judge for a bribe,
[b]Her priests teach for pay,
And her prophets divine for
[1]money.
[c]Yet they lean on the LORD, and
say,
"Is not the LORD among us?
No harm can come upon us."
12 Therefore because of you
Zion shall be [a]plowed *like* a field,
[b]Jerusalem shall become heaps of
ruins,
And [c]the mountain of the [1]temple
Like the bare hills of the forest.

The LORD's Reign in Zion

4 Now [a]it shall come to pass in the
latter days
That the mountain of the LORD's
house
Shall be established on the top of
the mountains,
And shall be exalted above the
hills;
And peoples shall flow to it.
2 Many nations shall come and say,
"Come, and let us go up to the
mountain of the LORD,
To the house of the God of Jacob;
He will teach us His ways,
And we shall walk in His paths."
For out of Zion the law shall go
forth,
And the word of the LORD from
Jerusalem.
3 He shall judge between many
peoples,
And rebuke strong nations afar
off;
They shall beat their swords into
[a]plowshares,
And their spears into [1]pruning
hooks;
Nation shall not lift up sword
against nation,
[b]Neither shall they learn war
anymore.

4 [a]But everyone shall sit under his
vine and under his fig tree,
And no one shall make *them*
afraid;
For the mouth of the LORD of
hosts has spoken.
5 For all people walk each in the
name of his god,
But [a]we will walk in the name of
the LORD our God
Forever and ever.

Zion's Future Triumph

6 "In that day," says the LORD,
[a]"I will assemble the lame,
[b]I will gather the outcast
And those whom I have afflicted;
7 I will make the lame [a]a remnant,
And the outcast a strong nation;
So the LORD [b]will reign over them
in Mount Zion

CHAPTER 3

1 [a]Ezek. 22:27 [b]Ps. 82:1–5; Jer. 5:4, 5
2 [1]Lit. *them*
3 [a]Ps. 14:4; 27:2; Zeph. 3:3 [b]Ezek. 11:3, 6, 7
4 [a]Ps. 18:41; Prov. 1:28; Is. 1:15; Jer. 11:11
5 [a]Is. 56:10, 11; Jer. 6:13; Ezek. 13:10, 19 [b]Matt. 7:15 [c]Ezek. 13:18 [1]All is well [2]For those who feed them
6 [a]Is. 8:20–22; 29:10–12 [b]Is. 29:10; [Jer. 23:33–40]; Ezek. 13:23 [1]Prophetic revelation
7 [a]Amos 8:11
8 [a]Is. 58:1
9 [1]Lit. *twist*
10 [a]Jer. 22:13, 17 [b]Ezek. 22:27; Hab. 2:12
11 [a]Is. 1:23; Mic. 7:3 [b]Jer. 6:13 [c]Is. 48:2; Jer. 7:4 [1]Lit. *silver*
12 [a]Jer. 26:18 [b]Ps. 79:1; Jer. 9:11 [c]Mic. 4:1, 2 [1]Lit. *house*

CHAPTER 4

1 [a]Is. 2:2–4; Ezek. 17:22; Dan. 2:28; 10:14; Hos. 3:5
3 [a]Is. 2:4; Joel 3:10 [b]Ps. 72:7 [1]*pruning knives*
4 [a]1 Kin. 4:25; Zech. 3:10
5 [a]Zech. 10:12
6 [a]Ezek. 34:16 [b]Ps. 147:2
7 [a]Mic. 2:12 [b][Is. 9:6; 24:23; Luke 1:33; Rev. 11:15]

From now on, even forever.
8 And you, O tower of the flock,
The stronghold of the daughter of Zion,
To you shall it come,
Even the former dominion shall come,
The kingdom of the daughter of Jerusalem."

9 Now why do you cry aloud?
[a]*Is there* no king in your midst?
Has your counselor perished?
For [b]pangs have seized you like a woman in [1]labor.
10 Be in pain, and labor to bring forth,
O daughter of Zion,
Like a woman in birth pangs.
For now you shall go forth from the city,
You shall dwell in the field,
And to [a]Babylon you shall go.
There you shall be delivered;
There the [b]LORD will [c]redeem you
From the hand of your enemies.

11 [a]Now also many nations have gathered against you,
Who say, "Let her be defiled,
And let our eye [b]look upon Zion."
12 But they do not know [a]the thoughts of the LORD,
Nor do they understand His counsel;
For He will gather them [b]like sheaves to the threshing floor.

13 "Arise[a] and [b]thresh, O daughter of Zion;
For I will make your horn iron,
And I will make your hooves bronze;
You shall [c]beat in pieces many peoples;
[d]I will consecrate their gain to the LORD,
And their substance to [e]the Lord of the whole earth."

5 Now gather yourself in troops,
O daughter of troops;
He has laid siege against us;
They will [a]strike the judge of Israel with a rod on the cheek.

The Coming Messiah

2 "But you, [a]Bethlehem [b]Ephrathah,
Though you are little [c]among the [d]thousands of Judah,
Yet out of you shall come forth to Me
The One to be [e]Ruler in Israel,
[f]Whose goings forth *are* from of old,
From [1]everlasting."

3 Therefore He shall give them up,
Until the time *that* [a]she who is in labor has given birth;
Then [b]the remnant of His brethren
Shall return to the children of Israel.
4 And He shall stand and [a]feed[1] *His flock*
In the strength of the LORD,
In the majesty of the name of the LORD His God;
And they shall abide,
For now He [b]shall be great
To the ends of the earth;
5 And this *One* [a]shall be peace.

Judgment on Israel's Enemies

When the Assyrian comes into our land,
And when he treads in our palaces,
Then we will raise against him
Seven shepherds and eight princely men.
6 They shall [1]waste with the sword the land of Assyria,
And the land of [a]Nimrod at its entrances;
Thus He shall [b]deliver *us* from the Assyrian,
When he comes into our land
And when he treads within our borders.

7 Then [a]the remnant of Jacob
Shall be in the midst of many peoples,
[b]Like dew from the LORD,
Like showers on the grass,
That [1]tarry for no man
Nor [2]wait for the sons of men.
8 And the remnant of Jacob
Shall be among the Gentiles,
In the midst of many peoples,
Like a [a]lion among the beasts of the forest,
Like a young lion among flocks of sheep,
Who, if he passes through,
Both treads down and tears in pieces,
And none can deliver.
9 Your hand shall be lifted against your adversaries,
And all your enemies shall be [1]cut off.

10 "And it shall be in that day," says the LORD,

---

9 [a]Jer. 8:19 [b]Is. 13:8; Jer. 30:6 [1]*childbirth*
10 [a]2 Chr. 36:20; Amos 5:27 [b][Is. 45:13; Mic. 7:8–12] [c]Ezra 1:1–3; 2:1; Ps. 18:17
11 [a]Lam. 2:16 [b]Obad. 12
12 [a][Is. 55:8, 9] [b]Is. 21:10
13 [a]Jer. 51:33; [Zech. 12:1–8; 14:14] [b]Is. 41:15 [c]Dan. 2:44 [d]Is. 18:7 [e]Zech. 4:14

CHAPTER 5

1 [a]1 Kin. 22:24; Job 16:10; Lam. 3:30; Matt. 27:30; Mark 15:19
2 [a]Is. 11:1; Matt. 2:6; Luke 2:4, 11; John 7:42 [b]Gen. 35:19; 48:7; Ruth 4:11 [c]1 Sam. 23:23 [d]Ex. 18:25 [e][Gen. 49:10; Is. 9:6] [f]Ps. 90:2; [John 1:1] [1]Lit. *the days of eternity*
3 [a]Hos. 11:8; Mic. 4:10 [b]Mic. 4:7; 7:18
4 [a][Is. 40:11; 49:9; Ezek. 34:13–15, 23, 24]; Mic. 7:14 [b]Ps. 72:8; Is. 52:13; Zech. 9:10; [Luke 1:32] [1]*shepherd*
5 [a][Is. 9:6]; Luke 2:14; [Eph. 2:14; Col. 1:20]
6 [a]Gen. 10:8–11 [b]Is. 14:25; Luke 1:71 [1]*devastate*
7 [a]Mic. 5:3 [b]Gen. 27:28; Deut. 32:2; Ps. 72:6; Hos. 14:5 [1]*wait* [2]*delay*
8 [a]Gen. 49:9; Num. 24:9
9 [1]*destroyed*

"That I will [a]cut[1] off your [b]horses
from your midst
And destroy your [c]chariots.
11 I will cut off the cities of your land
And throw down all your
strongholds.
12 I will cut off sorceries from your
hand,
And you shall have no
[a]soothsayers.
13 [a]Your carved images I will also cut
off,
And your sacred pillars from
your midst;
You shall [b]no more worship the
work of your hands;
14 I will pluck your [1]wooden images
from your midst;
Thus I will destroy your cities.
15 And I will [a]execute vengeance in
anger and fury
On the nations that have not
[1]heard."

God Pleads with Israel

6 Hear now what the LORD says:

"Arise, plead your case before the
mountains,
And let the hills hear your voice.
2 [a]Hear, O you mountains, [b]the
LORD's complaint,
And you strong foundations of
the earth;
For [c]the LORD has a complaint
against His people,
And He will [1]contend with Israel.

3 "O My people, what [a]have I done
to you?
And how have I [b]wearied you?
Testify against Me.
4 [a]For I brought you up from the
land of Egypt,
I redeemed you from the house
of bondage;
And I sent before you Moses,
Aaron, and Miriam.
5 O My people, remember now
What [a]Balak king of Moab
counseled,
And what Balaam the son of Beor
answered him,
From [1]Acacia Grove to Gilgal,
That you may know [b]the
righteousness of the LORD."

6 With what shall I come before the
LORD,
And bow myself before the High
God?
Shall I come before Him with
burnt offerings,
With calves a year old?
7 [a]Will the LORD be pleased with
thousands of rams,
Ten thousand [b]rivers of oil?
[c]Shall I give my firstborn *for* my
transgression,
[1]The fruit of my body *for* the sin
of my soul?

8 He has [a]shown you, O man, what
is good;
And what does the LORD require
of you
But [b]to do justly,
To love [1]mercy,
And to walk humbly with your
God?

Punishment of Israel's Injustice

9 The LORD's voice cries to the
city—
Wisdom shall see Your name:

"Hear the rod!
Who has appointed it?
10 Are there yet the treasures of
wickedness
In the house of the wicked,
And the short measure *that is* an
abomination?
11 Shall I count pure *those* with [a]the
wicked scales,
And with the bag of deceitful
weights?
12 For her rich men are full of
[a]violence,
Her inhabitants have spoken lies,
And [b]their tongue is deceitful in
their mouth.

13 "Therefore I will also [a]make *you*
sick by striking you,
By making *you* desolate because
of your sins.
14 [a]You shall eat, but not be satisfied;
[1]Hunger *shall be* in your midst.
[2]You may carry *some* away, but
shall not save *them;*
And what you do rescue I will
give over to the sword.

15 "You shall [a]sow, but not reap;
You shall tread the olives, but not
anoint yourselves with oil;
And *make* sweet wine, but not
drink wine.
16 For the statutes of [a]Omri are
[b]kept;
All the works of Ahab's house *are*
done;
And you walk in their counsels,
That I may make you a
[1]desolation,
And your inhabitants a hissing.
Therefore you shall bear the
[c]reproach of [2]My people."

---

10 [a]Zech. 9:10 [b]Deut. 17:16 [c]Is. 2:7; 22:18 [1]*destroy*
12 [a]Is. 2:6
13 [a]Zech. 13:2 [b]Is. 2:8
14 [1]Heb. *Asherim,* Canaanite deities
15 [a][2 Thess. 1:8] [1]*obeyed*

CHAPTER 6

2 [a]Ps. 50:1, 4 [b]Hos. 12:2 [c][Is. 1:18] [1]*bring charges against*
3 [a]Jer. 2:5, 31 [b]Is. 43:22, 23
4 [a][Deut. 4:20]
5 [a]Num. 22:5, 6 [b]Judg. 5:11 [1]Heb. *Shittim,* Num. 25:1; Josh. 2:1; 3:1
7 [a]Is. 1:11 [b]Job 29:6 [c]2 Kin. 16:3 [1]*My own child*
8 [a][Deut. 10:12] [b]Gen. 18:19 [1]Or *loving-kindness*
11 [a]Hos. 12:7
12 [a]Mic. 2:1, 2 [b]Jer. 9:2–6, 8
13 [a]Lev. 26:16
14 [a]Lev. 26:26 [1]Or *Emptiness* or *Humiliation* [2]Tg., Vg. *You shall take hold*
15 [a]Amos 5:11
16 [a]1 Kin. 16:25, 26 [b]Hos. 5:11 [c]Is. 25:8 [1]Or *object of horror* [2]So with MT, Tg., Vg.; LXX *nations*

Sorrow for Israel's Sins

7 Woe is me!
For I am like those who gather summer fruits,
Like those who [a]glean vintage grapes;
There is no cluster to eat
Of the first-ripe fruit *which* [b]my soul desires.
2 The [a]faithful[1] *man* has perished from the earth,
And *there is* no one upright among men.
They all lie in wait for blood;
[b]Every man hunts his brother with a net.

3 That they may successfully do evil with both hands—
The prince asks *for gifts,*
The judge *seeks* a [a]bribe,
And the great *man* utters his evil desire;
So they scheme together.
4 The best of them *is* [a]like a brier;
The most upright *is sharper* than a thorn hedge;
The day of your watchman and your punishment comes;
Now shall be their perplexity.

5 [a]Do not trust in a friend;
Do not put your confidence in a companion;
Guard the doors of your mouth
From her who lies in your [b]bosom.
6 For [a]son dishonors father,
Daughter rises against her mother,
Daughter-in-law against her mother-in-law;
A man's enemies *are* the men of his own household.
7 Therefore I will look to the LORD;
I will [a]wait for the God of my salvation;
My God will hear me.

Israel's Confession and Comfort

8 [a]Do not rejoice over me, my enemy;
[b]When I fall, I will arise;
When I sit in darkness,
The LORD *will be* a light to me.
9 [a]I will bear the indignation of the LORD,
Because I have sinned against Him,
Until He pleads my [b]case
And executes justice for me.
He will bring me forth to the light;
I will see His righteousness.
10 Then *she who is* my enemy will see,
And [a]shame will cover her who said to me,
[b]"Where is the LORD your God?"
My eyes will see her;
Now she will be trampled down
Like mud in the streets.

11 *In* the day when your [a]walls are to be built,
In that day [1]the decree shall go far and wide.
12 *In* that day [a]they[1] shall come to you
From Assyria and the [2]fortified cities,
From the [3]fortress to [4]the River,
From sea to sea,
And mountain *to* mountain.
13 Yet the land shall be desolate
Because of those who dwell in it,
And [a]for the fruit of their deeds.

God Will Forgive Israel

14 Shepherd Your people with Your staff,
The flock of Your heritage,
Who dwell [1]solitarily *in* a [a]woodland,
In the midst of Carmel;
Let them feed *in* Bashan and Gilead,
As in days of old.

15 "As[a] in the days when you came out of the land of Egypt,
I will show [1]them [b]wonders."

16 The nations [a]shall see and be ashamed of all their might;
[b]They shall put *their* hand over *their* mouth;
Their ears shall be deaf.
17 They shall lick the [a]dust like a serpent;
[b]They shall crawl from their holes like [1]snakes of the earth.
[c]They shall be afraid of the LORD our God,
And shall fear because of You.
18 [a]Who *is* a God like You,
[b]Pardoning iniquity
And passing over the transgression of [c]the remnant of His heritage?

[d]He does not retain His anger forever,
Because He delights *in* [e]mercy.[1]

CHAPTER 7

1 [a]Is. 17:6 [b]Is. 28:4; Hos. 9:10
2 [a]Ps. 12:1; Is. 57:1 [b]Hab. 1:15 [1]Or *loyal*
3 [a]Amos 5:12; Mic. 3:11
4 [a]Is. 55:13; Ezek. 2:6
5 [a]Jer. 9:4 [b]Deut. 28:56
6 [a]Matt. 10:36; Mark 3:21; Luke 8:19; John 7:5
7 [a]Ps. 130:5; Is. 25:9; Lam. 3:24, 25
8 [a]Prov. 24:17; Obad. 12; [Acts 10:43] [b]Ps. 37:24; [Prov. 24:16]; 2 Cor. 4:9
9 [a]Lam. 3:39, 40; [2 Cor. 5:21] [b]Jer. 50:34
10 [a]Ps. 35:26 [b]Ps. 42:3
11 [a]Is. 54:11; [Amos 9:11] [1]Or *the boundary shall be extended*
12 [a][Is. 11:16; 19:23–25] [1]Lit. *he,* collective of the captives [2]Heb. *arey mazor,* possibly *cities of Egypt* [3]Heb. *mazor,* possibly *Egypt* [4]The Euphrates
13 [a]Jer. 21:14
14 [a]Is. 37:24 [1]Alone
15 [a]Ps. 68:22; 78:12 [b]Ex. 34:10 [1]Lit. *him,* collective for the captives
16 [a]Is. 26:11 [b]Job 21:5
17 [a]Ps. 72:9; [Is. 49:23] [b]Ps. 18:45 [c]Jer. 33:9 [1]Lit. *crawlers*
18 [a]Ex. 15:11 [b]Ex. 34:6, 7, 9; Is. 43:25; Jer. 50:20 [c]Mic. 4:7 [d]Ps. 103:8, 9, 13; [Is. 57:16] [e][Ezek. 33:11] [1]Or *loving-kindness*

19 He will again have compassion
on us,
And will subdue our
iniquities.

You will cast all [1]our sins
Into the depths of the sea.
20 [a]You will give truth to Jacob
And [1]mercy to Abraham,
[b]Which You have sworn to our
fathers
From days of old.

19 [1]Lit. *their*

20 [a]Luke 1:72, 73 [b]Ps. 105:9 [1]Or *loving-kindness*

The Book of Nahum

"**FOR** everyone to whom much is given, from him much will be required" (Luke 12:48). Nineveh had been given the privilege of knowing the one true God. Under Jonah's preaching this great gentile city had repented, and God had graciously stayed His judgment. However, a hundred years later, Nahum proclaims the downfall of this same city. The Assyrians have forgotten their revival and have returned to their habits of violence, idolatry, and arrogance. As a result, Babylon will so destroy the city that no trace of it will remain—a prophecy fulfilled in painful detail.

The Hebrew word *nahum* ("comfort," "consolation") is a shortened form of Nehemiah ("Comfort of Yahweh"). The destruction of the capital city of Assyria is a message of comfort and consolation to Judah and all who live in fear of the cruelty of the Assyrians. The title of this book in the Greek and Latin Bibles is *Naoum* and *Nahum*.

THE [1]burden [a]against Nineveh. The book of the vision of Nahum the Elkoshite.

God's Wrath on His Enemies

2 God *is* [a]jealous, and the LORD avenges;
The LORD avenges and *is* furious.
The LORD will take vengeance on His adversaries,
And He reserves *wrath* for His enemies;
3 The LORD *is* [a]slow to anger and [b]great in power,
And will not at all acquit *the wicked.*

[c]The LORD has His way
In the whirlwind and in the storm,
And the clouds *are* the dust of His feet.
4 [a]He rebukes the sea and makes it dry,
And dries up all the rivers.
[b]Bashan and Carmel wither,
And the flower of Lebanon wilts.
5 The mountains quake before Him,
The hills melt,
And the earth [1]heaves at His presence,
Yes, the world and all who dwell in it.

6 Who can stand before His indignation?
And [a]who can endure the fierceness of His anger?
His fury is poured out like fire,
And the rocks are thrown down by Him.

7 [a]The LORD *is* good,
A stronghold in the day of trouble;
And [b]He knows those who trust in Him.
8 But with an overflowing flood
He will make an utter end of its place,
And darkness will pursue His enemies.

9 [a]What do you [1]conspire against the LORD?
[b]He will make an utter end *of it*.
Affliction will not rise up a second time.
10 For while tangled [a]*like* thorns,
[b]And while drunken *like* drunkards,
[c]They shall be devoured like stubble fully dried.
11 From you comes forth *one*
Who plots evil against the LORD,
A [1]wicked counselor.

12 Thus says the LORD:

"Though *they are* [1]safe, and likewise many,
Yet in this manner they will be [a]cut down
When he passes through.
Though I have afflicted you,
I will afflict you no more;

CHAPTER 1

1 [a]2 Kin. 19:36; Jon. 1:2; Nah. 2:8; Zeph. 2:13 [1]*oracle, prophecy*

2 [a]Ex. 20:5; Josh. 24:19

3 [a]Ex. 34:6, 7; Neh. 9:17; Ps. 103:8 [b][Job 9:4] [c]Ps. 18:17

4 [a]Josh. 3:15, 16; Ps. 106:9; Is. 50:2; Matt. 8:26 [b]Is. 33:9

5 [1]Tg. *burns*

6 [a]Jer. 10:10; [Mal. 3:2]

7 [a]Ps. 25:8; 37:39, 40; 100:5; [Jer. 33:11]; Lam. 3:25 [b]Ps. 1:6; John 10:14; 2 Tim. 2:19

9 [a]Ps. 2:1; Nah. 1:11 [b]1 Sam. 3:12 [1]Or *devise*

10 [a]2 Sam. 23:6; Mic. 7:4 [b]Is. 56:12; Nah. 3:11 [c]Is. 5:24; 10:17; Mal. 4:1

11 [1]Lit. *counselor of Belial*

12 [a][Is. 10:16–19, 33, 34] [1]Or *at peace* or *complete*

13 For now I will break off his yoke
from you,
And burst your bonds apart."

14 The LORD has given a command
concerning you:
[1]"Your name shall be perpetuated
no longer.
Out of the house of your gods
I will cut off the carved image and
the molded image.
I will dig your [a]grave,
For you are [b]vile."[2]

15 Behold, on the mountains
The [a]feet of him who brings good
tidings,
Who proclaims peace!
O Judah, keep your appointed
feasts,
Perform your vows.
For the [1]wicked one shall no
more pass through you;
He is [b]utterly cut off.

The Destruction of Nineveh

2 He[1] who scatters has come up
before your face.
Man the fort!
Watch the road!
Strengthen *your* flanks!
Fortify *your* power mightily.

2 For the LORD will restore the
excellence of Jacob
Like the excellence of Israel,
For the emptiers have emptied
them out
And ruined their vine branches.

3 The shields of his mighty men *are*
made red,
The valiant men *are* in scarlet.
The chariots *come* with flaming
torches
In the day of his preparation,
And [1]the spears are
brandished.
4 The chariots rage in the streets,
They jostle one another in the
broad roads;
They seem like torches,
They run like lightning.

5 He remembers his nobles;
They stumble in their walk;
They make haste to her walls,
And the defense is prepared.
6 The gates of the rivers are
opened,
And the palace is dissolved.
7 [1]It is decreed:
She shall be led away captive,
She shall be brought up;
And her maidservants shall lead
her as with the voice of doves,
Beating their breasts.

8 Though Nineveh of old *was* like
a pool of water,
Now they flee away.
[1]"Halt! Halt!" *they cry;*
But no one turns back.
9 [1]Take spoil of silver!
Take spoil of [a]gold!
There is no end of treasure,
Or wealth of every desirable
prize.
10 She is empty, desolate, and
waste!
The heart melts, and the knees
shake;
Much pain *is* in every side,
And all their faces [1]are drained
of color.

11 Where *is* the dwelling of the
[a]lions,
And the feeding place of the
young lions,
Where the lion walked, the
lioness *and* lion's cub,
And no one made *them* afraid?
12 The lion tore in pieces enough for
his cubs,
[1]Killed for his lionesses,
[a]Filled his caves with prey,
And his dens with [2]flesh.

13 "Behold, [a]I *am* against you,"
says the LORD of hosts, "I will burn
[1]your chariots in smoke, and the
sword shall devour your young
lions; I will cut off your prey from
the earth, and the voice of your
[b]messengers shall be heard no
more."

The Woe of Nineveh

3 Woe to the [a]bloody city!
It *is* all full of lies *and* robbery.
Its [1]victim never departs.
2 The noise of a whip
And the noise of rattling wheels,
Of galloping horses,
Of [1]clattering chariots!
3 Horsemen charge with bright
sword and glittering spear.
There is a multitude of slain,
A great number of bodies,
Countless corpses—
They stumble over the corpses—
4 Because of the multitude of
[1]harlotries of the [2]seductive
harlot,
[a]The mistress of sorceries,
Who sells nations through her
harlotries,

14 [a]Ezek. 32:22, 23 [b]Nah. 3:6 [1]Lit. *No more of your name shall be fruitful* [2]Or *contemptible*

15 [a]Is. 40:9; 52:7; Rom. 10:15 [b]Is. 29:7, 8 [1]Lit. *one of Belial*

CHAPTER 2

1 [1]Vg. *He who destroys*

3 [1]Lit. *the cypresses are shaken;* LXX, Syr. *the horses rush about;* Vg. *the drivers are stupefied*

7 [1]Heb. *Huzzab*

8 [1]Lit. *Stand*

9 [a]Ezek. 7:19; Zeph. 1:18 [1]*Plunder*

10 [1]LXX, Tg., Vg. *gather blackness;* Joel 2:6

11 [a]Job 4:10, 11; Ezek. 19:2–7

12 [a]Is. 10:6; Jer. 51:34 [1]Lit. *Strangled* [2]Torn flesh

13 [a]Jer. 21:13; Ezek. 5:8; Nah. 3:5 [b]2 Kin. 18:17–25; 19:9–13, 23 [1]Lit. *her*

CHAPTER 3

1 [a]Ezek. 22:2, 3; 24:6–9; Hab. 2:12 [1]Lit. *prey*

2 [1]*bounding* or *jolting*

4 [a]Is. 47:9–12; Rev. 18:2, 3 [1]Spiritual unfaithfulness [2]Lit. *goodly charm,* in a bad sense

And families through her
sorceries.

5 "Behold, I *am* [a]against you," says
the LORD of hosts;
[b]"I will lift your skirts over your
face,
I will show the nations your
nakedness,
And the kingdoms your shame.
6 I will cast abominable filth upon
you,
Make you [a]vile,[1]
And make you [b]a spectacle.
7 It shall come to pass *that* all who
look upon you
[a]Will flee from you, and say,
[b]'Nineveh is laid waste!
[c]Who will bemoan her?'
Where shall I seek comforters for
you?"

8 [a]Are you better than [b]No[1] Amon
That was situated by the [2]River,
That had the waters around her,
Whose rampart *was* the sea,
Whose wall *was* the sea?
9 Ethiopia and Egypt *were* her
strength,
And *it was* boundless;
[a]Put and Lubim were [1]your
helpers.
10 Yet she *was* carried away,
She went into captivity;
[a]Her young children also were
dashed to pieces
[b]At the head of every street;
They [c]cast lots for her honorable
men,
And all her great men were
bound in chains.
11 You also will be [a]drunk;
You will be hidden;
You also will seek refuge from
the enemy.

12 All your strongholds *are* [a]fig trees
with ripened figs:
If they are shaken,
They fall into the mouth of the
eater.

13 Surely, [a]your people in your
midst *are* women!
The gates of your land are wide
open for your enemies;
Fire shall devour the [b]bars of
your *gates*.

14 Draw your water for the
siege!
[a]Fortify your strongholds!
Go into the clay and tread the
mortar!
Make strong the brick kiln!
15 There the fire will devour you,
The sword will cut you off;
It will eat you up like a
[a]locust.

Make yourself many—like the
locust!
Make yourself many— like the
swarming locusts!
16 You have multiplied your
[a]merchants more than the stars
of heaven.
The locust plunders and flies
away.
17 [a]Your commanders *are* like
swarming locusts,
And your generals like great
grasshoppers,
Which camp in the hedges on a
cold day;
When the sun rises they flee
away,
And the place where they *are* is
not known.

18 [a]Your shepherds slumber, O [b]king
of Assyria;
Your nobles rest *in the dust*.
Your people are [c]scattered on the
mountains,
And no one gathers them.
19 Your injury *has* no healing,
[a]Your wound is severe.
[b]All who hear news of you
Will clap *their* hands over you,
For upon whom has not your
wickedness passed
continually?

5 [a]Jer. 50:31; Ezek. 26:3; Nah. 2:13 [b]Is. 47:2, 3; Jer. 13:26
6 [a]Nah. 1:14 [b]Heb. 10:33 [1]*despicable*
7 [a]Rev. 18:10 [b]Jon. 3:3; 4:11 [c]Is. 51:19; Jer. 15:5
8 [a]Amos 6:2 [b]Jer. 46:25; Ezek. 30:14–16 [1]Ancient Thebes; Tg., Vg. *populous Alexandria* [2]Lit. *rivers*, the Nile and the surrounding canals
9 [a]Gen. 10:6; Jer. 46:9; Ezek. 27:10 [1]LXX *her*
10 [a]Ps. 137:9; Is. 13:16; Hos. 13:16 [b]Lam. 2:19 [c]Joel 3:3; Obad. 11
11 [a]Is. 49:26; Jer. 25:27; Nah. 1:10
12 [a]Rev. 6:12, 13
13 [a]Is. 19:16; Jer. 50:37; 51:30 [b]Ps. 147:13; Jer. 51:30
14 [a]Nah. 2:1
15 [a]Joel 1:4
16 [a]Rev. 18:3, 11–19
17 [a]Rev. 9:7
18 [a]Ex. 15:16; Ps. 76:5, 6; Is. 56:10; Jer. 51:57 [b]Jer. 50:18; Ezek. 31:3 [c]1 Kin. 22:17; Is. 13:14
19 [a]Jer. 46:11; Mic. 1:9 [b]Job 27:23; Lam. 2:15; Zeph. 2:15

The Book of Habakkuk

HABAKKUK ministers during the "death throes" of the nation of Judah. Although repeatedly called to repentance, the nation stubbornly refuses to change her sinful ways. Habakkuk, knowing the hardheartedness of his countrymen, asks God how long this intolerable condition can continue. God replies that the Babylonians will be His chastening rod upon the nation—an announcement that sends the prophet to his knees. He acknowledges that the just in any generation shall live by faith (2:4), not by sight. Habakkuk concludes by praising God's wisdom even though he does not fully understand God's ways.

Habaqquq is an unusual Hebrew name derived from the verb *habaq*, "embrace." Thus his name probably means "One Who Embraces" or "Clings." At the end of his book this name becomes appropriate because Habakkuk chooses to cling firmly to God regardless of what happens to his nation (3:16–19). The Greek title in the Septuagint is *Ambakouk*, and the Latin title in Jerome's Vulgate is *Habacuc*.

THE [1]burden which the prophet Habakkuk saw.

The Prophet's Question

2 O LORD, how long shall I cry,
[a]And You will not hear?
Even cry out to You, [b]"Violence!"
And You will [c]not save.
3 Why do You show me iniquity,
And cause *me* to see [1]trouble?
For plundering and violence *are* before me;
There is strife, and contention arises.
4 Therefore the law is powerless,
And justice never goes forth.
For the [a]wicked surround the righteous;
Therefore perverse judgment proceeds.

The LORD's Reply

5 "Look[a] among the nations and watch—
Be utterly astounded!
For *I will* work a work in your days
Which you would not believe, though it were told *you*.
6 For indeed I am [a]raising up the Chaldeans,
A bitter and hasty [b]nation
Which marches through the breadth of the earth,
To possess dwelling places *that are* not theirs.
7 They are terrible and dreadful;
Their judgment and their dignity proceed from themselves.
8 Their horses also are [a]swifter than leopards,
And more fierce than evening wolves.
Their [1]chargers [2]charge ahead;
Their cavalry comes from afar;
They fly as the [b]eagle *that* hastens to eat.
9 "They all come for violence;
Their faces are set *like* the east wind.
They gather captives like sand.
10 They scoff at kings,
And princes are scorned by them.
They deride every stronghold,
For they heap up earthen *mounds* and seize it.
11 Then *his* [1]mind changes, and he transgresses;
He commits offense,
[a]*Ascribing* this power to his god."

The Prophet's Second Question

12 Are You not [a]from everlasting,
O LORD my God, my Holy One?
We shall not die.
O LORD, [b]You have appointed them for judgment;
O Rock, You have marked them for [c]correction.
13 *You are* of purer eyes than to behold evil,
And cannot look on wickedness.

CHAPTER 1

1 [1]*oracle, prophecy*

2 [a]Lam. 3:8 [b]Mic. 2:1, 2; 3:1–3 [c][Job 21:5–16]

3 [1]Or *toil*

4 [a]Jer. 12:1

5 [a]Is. 29:14; Ezek. 12:22–28

6 [a]Deut. 28:49, 50; 2 Kin. 24:2; 2 Chr. 36:17; Jer. 4:11–13; Mic. 4:10 [b]Ezek. 7:24; 21:31

8 [a]Jer. 4:13 [b]Job 9:26; 39:29, 30; Lam. 4:19; Ezek. 17:3; Hos. 8:1; Matt. 24:28; Luke 17:37 [1]Lit. *horsemen* [2]Lit. *spring about*

11 [a]Dan. 5:4 [1]Lit. *spirit* or *wind*

12 [a]Deut. 33:27; Ps. 90:2; 93:2; Mal. 3:6 [b]Is. 10:5–7; Mal. 3:5 [c]Jer. 25:9

Why do You look on those who
deal treacherously,
And hold Your tongue when the
wicked devours
A *person* more righteous than he?
14 *Why* do You make men like fish
of the sea,
Like creeping things *that have* no
ruler over them?

15 They take up all of them with a
hook,
They catch them in their net,
And gather them in their dragnet.
Therefore they rejoice and are
glad.
16 Therefore [a]they sacrifice to their
net,
And burn incense to their
dragnet;
Because by them their share *is*
[1]sumptuous
And their food plentiful.
17 Shall they therefore empty their
net,
And continue to slay nations
without pity?

2 I will [a]stand my watch
And set myself on the rampart,
And watch to see what He will
say to me,
And what I will answer when I
am corrected.

The Just Live by Faith

2 Then the LORD answered me
and said:

[a]"Write the vision
And make *it* plain on tablets,
That he may run who reads it.
3 For [a]the vision *is* yet for an
appointed time;
But at the end it will speak, and
it will [b]not lie.
Though it tarries, [c]wait for it;
Because it will [d]surely come,
It will not tarry.

4 "Behold the proud,
His soul is not upright in him;
But the [a]just shall live by his
faith.

Woe to the Wicked

5 "Indeed, because he transgresses
by wine,
He is a proud man,
And he does not stay at home.
Because he [a]enlarges his desire
as [1]hell,
And he *is* like death, and cannot
be satisfied,
He gathers to himself all nations

16 [a]Deut. 8:17 [1]Lit. *fat*

CHAPTER 2

1 [a]Is. 21:8, 11

2 [a]Is. 8:1

3 [a]Dan. 8:17, 19; 10:14 [b]Ezek. 12:24, 25 [c][Heb. 10:37, 38] [d]Ps. 27:13, 14; [James 5:7, 8; 2 Pet. 3:9]

4 [a][John 3:36]; Rom. 1:17; Heb. 10:38

5 [a]Prov. 27:20; 30:16; Is. 5:11–15 [1]Or *Sheol*

6 [a]Mic. 2:4 [1]Syr., Vg. *thick clay*

7 [1]Lit. *those who bite you*

8 [a]Is. 33:1; Jer. 27:7; Ezek. 39:10; Zech. 2:8 [1]Or *bloodshed*

9 [a]Jer. 49:16; Obad. 4 [1]Lit. *hand of evil*

13 [1]Lit. *for what satisfies fire*, for what is of no lasting value

15 [a]Hos. 7:5 [1]Lit. *Attaching* or *Joining* [2]Lit. *their*

16 [1]DSS, LXX *reel!*; Syr., Vg. *fall fast asleep!*

And heaps up for himself all
peoples.
6 "Will not all these [a]take up a
proverb against him,
And a taunting riddle against
him, and say,
'Woe to him who increases
What is not his—how long?
And to him who loads himself
with [1]many pledges'?
7 Will not [1]your creditors rise up
suddenly?
Will they not awaken who
oppress you?
And you will become their booty.
8 [a]Because you have plundered
many nations,
All the remnant of the people
shall plunder you,
Because of men's [1]blood
And the violence of the land *and*
the city,
And of all who dwell in it.

9 "Woe to him who covets evil gain
for his house,
That he may [a]set his nest on high,
That he may be delivered from
the [1]power of disaster!
10 You give shameful counsel to
your house,
Cutting off many peoples,
And sin *against* your soul.
11 For the stone will cry out from
the wall,
And the beam from the timbers
will answer it.

12 "Woe to him who builds a town
with bloodshed,
Who establishes a city by
iniquity!
13 Behold, *is it* not of the LORD of
hosts
That the peoples labor [1]to feed
the fire,
And nations weary themselves in
vain?
14 For the earth will be filled
With the knowledge of the glory
of the LORD,
As the waters cover the sea.

15 "Woe to him who gives drink to
his neighbor,
[1]Pressing *him* to your [a]bottle,
Even to make *him* drunk,
That you may look on [2]his
nakedness!
16 You are filled with shame instead
of glory.
You also—drink!
And [1]be exposed as
uncircumcised!

The cup of the LORD's right hand
will be turned against you,
And utter shame will be on your
glory.
17 For the violence *done to* Lebanon
will cover you,
And the plunder of beasts *which*
made them afraid,
Because of men's blood
And the violence of the land *and*
the city,
And of all who dwell in it.

18 "What profit is the image, that its
maker should carve it,
The molded image, a teacher of
lies,
That the maker of its mold should
trust in it,
To make mute idols?
19 Woe to him who says to wood,
'Awake!'
To silent stone, 'Arise! It shall
teach!'
Behold, it is overlaid with gold
and silver,
Yet in it there is no breath at all.

20 "But[a] the LORD is in His holy
temple.
Let all the earth keep silence
before Him."

The Prophet's Prayer

3 A prayer of Habakkuk the
prophet, on [1]Shigionoth.

2 O LORD, I have heard Your
speech *and* was afraid;
O LORD, revive Your work in the
midst of the years!
In the midst of the years make *it*
known;
In wrath remember mercy.

3 God came from Teman,
The Holy One from Mount Paran.
Selah

His glory covered the heavens,
And the earth was full of His
praise.
4 *His* brightness was like the light;
He had rays *flashing* from His
hand,
And there His power *was* hidden.
5 Before Him went pestilence,
And fever followed at His feet.

6 He stood and measured the earth;
He looked and startled the
nations.
[a]And the everlasting mountains
were scattered,
The perpetual hills bowed.
His ways *are* everlasting.
7 I saw the tents of Cushan in
affliction;
The curtains of the land of Midian
trembled.

8 O LORD, were You displeased
with the rivers,
Was Your anger against the
rivers,
Was Your wrath against the sea,
That You rode on Your horses,
Your chariots of salvation?
9 Your bow was made quite ready;
Oaths were sworn over *Your*
[1]arrows. Selah

You divided the earth with rivers.
10 The mountains saw You *and*
trembled;
The overflowing of the water
passed by.
The deep uttered its voice,
And [a]lifted its hands on high.
11 The [a]sun and moon stood still in
their habitation;
At the light of Your arrows they
went,
At the shining of Your glittering
spear.

12 You marched through the land in
indignation;
You [1]trampled the nations in
anger.
13 You went forth for the salvation
of Your people,
For salvation with Your
Anointed.
You struck the head from the
house of the wicked,
By laying bare from foundation
to neck. Selah

14 You thrust through with his own
arrows
The head of his villages.
They came out like a whirlwind
to scatter me;
Their rejoicing was like feasting
on the poor in secret.
15 [a]You walked through the sea with
Your horses,
Through the heap of great
waters.

16 When I heard, [a]my body
trembled;
My lips quivered at *the* voice;
Rottenness entered my bones;
And I trembled in myself,
That I might rest in the day of
trouble.
When he comes up to the people,

20 [a]Zeph. 1:7; Zech. 2:13

CHAPTER 3

1 [1]Exact meaning unknown

6 [a]Nah. 1:5

9 [1]Lit. *tribes* or *rods,* cf. v. 14

10 [a]Ex. 14:22

11 [a]Josh. 10:12–14

12 [1]Or *threshed*

15 [a]Ps. 77:19; Hab. 3:8

16 [a]Ps. 119:120

He will invade them with his
troops.

A Hymn of Faith

17 Though the fig tree may not
blossom,
Nor fruit be on the vines;
Though the labor of the olive may
fail,
And the fields yield no food;
Though the flock may be cut off
from the fold,
And there be no herd in the
stalls—

18 Yet I will [a]rejoice in the
LORD,
I will joy in the God of my
salvation.

19 [1]The LORD God is my strength;
He will make my feet like [a]deer's
feet,
And He will make me [b]walk on
my high hills.

To the Chief Musician. With
my stringed instruments.

18 [a]Is. 41:16; 61:10
19 [a]2 Sam. 22:34; Ps. 18:33 [b]Deut. 32:13; 33:29 [1]Heb. *YHWH Adonai*

The Book of

Zephaniah

DURING Judah's hectic political and religious history, reform comes from time to time. Zephaniah's forceful prophecy may be a factor in the reform that occurs during Josiah's reign—a "revival" that produces outward change, but does not fully remove the inward heart of corruption which characterizes the nation. Zephaniah hammers home his message repeatedly that the day of the Lord, Judgment Day, is coming when the malignancy of sin will be dealt with. Israel and her gentile neighbors will soon experience the crushing hand of God's wrath. But after the chastening process is complete, blessing will come in the person of the Messiah, who will be the cause for praise and singing.

Tsephan-yah means "Yahweh Hides" or "Yahweh Has Hidden." Zephaniah was evidently born during the latter part of the reign of King Manasseh. His name may mean that he was "hidden" from Manasseh's atrocities. The Greek and Latin title is *Sophonias*.

THE word of the LORD which came to Zephaniah the son of Cushi, the son of Gedaliah, the son of Amariah, the son of Hezekiah, in the days of [a]Josiah the son of Amon, king of Judah.

The Great Day of the LORD

2 "I will [1]utterly consume
everything
From the face of the land,"
Says the LORD;
3 "I[a] will consume man and beast;
I will consume the birds of the
heavens,
The fish of the sea,
And the [1]stumbling blocks along
with the wicked.
I will cut off man from the face
of the [2]land,"
Says the LORD.

4 "I will stretch out My hand against
Judah,
And against all the inhabitants of
Jerusalem.
[1]I will cut off every trace of Baal
from this place,
The names of the [a]idolatrous[2]
priests with the *pagan* priests—
5 Those [a]who worship the host of
heaven on the housetops;
Those who worship and swear
oaths by the LORD,
But who *also* swear [b]by [1]Milcom;
6 [a]Those who have turned back
from *following* the LORD,
And [b]have not sought the LORD,
nor inquired of Him."

7 [a]Be silent in the presence of the
Lord GOD;
[b]For the day of the LORD *is* at
hand,
For [c]the LORD has prepared a
sacrifice;
He has [1]invited His guests.

8 "And it shall be,
In the day of the LORD's sacrifice,
That I will punish [a]the princes
and the king's children,
And all such as are clothed with
foreign apparel.
9 In the same day I will punish
All those who [a]leap over the
threshold,
Who fill their masters' houses
with violence and deceit.

10 "And there shall be on that day,"
says the LORD,
"The sound of a mournful cry from
[a]the Fish Gate,
A wailing from the Second
Quarter,
And a loud crashing from the
hills.
11 [a]Wail, you inhabitants of
[1]Maktesh!
For all the merchant people are
cut down;
All those who handle money are
cut off.

CHAPTER 1

1 [a]2 Kin. 22:1, 2

2 [1]Lit. *make a complete end of*, Jer. 8:13

3 [a]Hos. 4:3 [1]Idols [2]*ground*

4 [a]Hos. 10:5 [1]Fulfilled in 2 Kin. 23:4, 5 [2]Heb. *chemarim*

5 [a]2 Kin. 23:12 [b]Josh. 23:7 [1]Or *Malcam*, an Ammonite god, 1 Kin. 11:5; Jer. 49:1; *Molech*, Lev. 18:21

6 [a]Is. 1:4 [b]Hos. 7:7

7 [a]Zech. 2:13 [b]Is. 13:6 [c]Jer. 46:10 [1]Lit. *set apart, consecrated*

8 [a]Jer. 39:6

9 [a]1 Sam. 5:5

10 [a]2 Chr. 33:14

11 [a]James 5:1 [1]A market district of Jerusalem, lit. *Mortar*

12 "And it shall come to pass at that time
That I will search Jerusalem with lamps,
And punish the men
Who are [a]settled[1] in complacency,
[b]Who say in their heart,
'The LORD will not do good,
Nor will He do evil.'
13 Therefore their goods shall become booty,
And their houses a desolation;
They shall build houses, but not inhabit *them;*
They shall plant vineyards, but [a]not drink their wine."

14 [a]The great day of the LORD *is* near;
It is near and hastens quickly.
The noise of the day of the LORD is bitter;
There the mighty men shall cry out.
15 [a]That day *is* a day of wrath,
A day of trouble and distress,
A day of devastation and desolation,
A day of darkness and gloominess,
A day of clouds and thick darkness,
16 A day of [a]trumpet and alarm
Against the fortified cities
And against the high towers.

17 "I will bring distress upon men,
And they shall [a]walk like blind men,
Because they have sinned against the LORD;
Their blood shall be poured out like dust,
And their flesh like refuse."

18 [a]Neither their silver nor their gold
Shall be able to deliver them
In the day of the LORD's wrath;
But the whole land shall be devoured
By the fire of His jealousy,
For He will make speedy riddance
Of all those who dwell in the land.

A Call to Repentance

2 Gather[a] yourselves together, yes, gather together,
O [1]undesirable nation,
2 Before the decree is issued,
Or the day passes like chaff,
Before the LORD's fierce anger comes upon you,
Before the day of the LORD's anger comes upon you!
3 [a]Seek the LORD, [b]all you meek of the earth,
Who have upheld His justice.
Seek righteousness, seek humility.
[c]It may be that you will be hidden
In the day of the LORD's anger.

Judgment on Nations

4 For [a]Gaza shall be forsaken,
And Ashkelon desolate;
They shall drive out Ashdod [b]at noonday,
And Ekron shall be uprooted.
5 Woe to the inhabitants of [a]the seacoast,
The nation of the Cherethites!
The word of the LORD *is* against you,
O [b]Canaan, land of the Philistines:
"I will destroy you;
So there shall be no inhabitant."

6 The seacoast shall be pastures,
With [1]shelters for shepherds [a]and folds for flocks.
7 The coast shall be for [a]the remnant of the house of Judah;
They shall feed *their* flocks there;
In the houses of Ashkelon they shall lie down at evening.
For the LORD their God will [b]intervene[1] for them,
And [c]return their captives.

8 "I[a] have heard the reproach of Moab,
And [b]the insults of the people of Ammon,
With which they have reproached My people,
And [c]made arrogant threats against their borders.
9 Therefore, as I live,"
Says the LORD of hosts, the God of Israel,
"Surely [a]Moab shall be like Sodom,
And [b]the people of Ammon like Gomorrah—
[c]Overrun[1] with weeds and saltpits,
And a [2]perpetual desolation.
The residue of My people shall plunder them,
And the remnant of My people shall possess them."

10 This they shall have [a]for their pride,
Because they have reproached and made arrogant threats
Against the people of the LORD of hosts.

---

12 [a]Jer. 48:11; Amos 6:1 [b]Ps. 94:7 [1]Lit. *on their lees;* like the dregs of wine
13 [a]Deut. 28:39
14 [a]Jer. 30:7; Joel 2:1, 11
15 [a]Is. 22:5
16 [a]Is. 27:13; Jer. 4:19
17 [a]Deut. 28:29
18 [a]Ezek. 7:19

CHAPTER 2

1 [a]2 Chr. 20:4; Joel 1:14; 2:16 [1]Or *shameless*
3 [a]Ps. 105:4; Amos 5:6 [b]Ps. 76:9 [c]Joel 2:14; Amos 5:14, 15
4 [a]Jer. 47:1, 5; Amos 1:7, 8; Zech. 9:5 [b]Jer. 6:4
5 [a]Ezek. 25:15–17 [b]Josh. 13:3
6 [a]Is. 17:2 [1]Underground huts or cisterns, lit. *excavations*
7 [a][Mic. 5:7, 8] [b]Luke 1:68 [c]Jer. 29:14 [1]Lit. *visit them*
8 [a]Jer. 48:27; Amos 2:1–3 [b]Ezek. 25:3; Amos 1:13 [c]Jer. 49:1
9 [a]Is. 15:1–9; Jer. 48:1–47 [b]Amos 1:13 [c]Deut. 29:23 [1]Lit. *Possessed by nettles* [2]Or *permanent ruin*
10 [a]Is. 16:6

11 The LORD *will be* awesome to
them,
For He will reduce to nothing all
the gods of the earth;
[a]*People* shall worship Him,
Each one from his place,
Indeed all [b]the shores of the
nations.

12 "You[a] Ethiopians also,
You shall be slain by [b]My
sword."

13 And He will stretch out His hand
against the north,
[a]Destroy Assyria,
And make Nineveh a desolation,
As dry as the wilderness.
14 The herds shall lie down in her
midst,
[a]Every beast of the nation.
Both the [b]pelican and the bittern
Shall lodge on the capitals *of* her
pillars;
Their voice shall sing in the
windows;
Desolation *shall be* at the
threshold;
For He will lay bare the [c]cedar
work.
15 This is the rejoicing city
[a]That dwelt securely,
[b]That said in her heart,
"I *am it,* and *there is* none besides
me."
How has she become a
desolation,
A place for beasts to lie down!
Everyone who passes by her
[c]Shall hiss and [d]shake his fist.

The Wickedness of Jerusalem

3 Woe to her who is rebellious and
polluted,
To the oppressing city!
2 She has not obeyed *His* voice,
She has not received correction;
She has not trusted in the LORD,
She has not drawn near to her
God.

3 [a]Her princes in her midst *are*
roaring lions;
Her judges *are* [b]evening wolves
That leave not a bone till
morning.
4 Her [a]prophets are insolent,
treacherous people;
Her priests have [1]polluted the
sanctuary,
They have done [b]violence to the
law.
5 The LORD *is* righteous in her
midst,
He will do no unrighteousness.
[1]Every morning He brings His
justice to light;
He never fails,
But [a]the unjust knows no shame.

6 "I have cut off nations,
Their fortresses are devastated;
I have made their streets
desolate,
With none passing by.
Their cities are destroyed;
There is no one, no inhabitant.
7 [a]I said, 'Surely you will fear Me,
You will receive instruction'—
So that her dwelling would not
be cut off,
Despite everything for which I
punished her.
But [1]they rose early and
[b]corrupted all their deeds.

A Faithful Remnant

8 "Therefore [a]wait for Me," says the
LORD,
"Until the day I rise up [1]for
plunder;
My determination *is* to [b]gather
the nations
To My assembly of kingdoms,
To pour on them My indignation,
All My fierce anger;
All the earth [c]shall be devoured
With the fire of My jealousy.

9 "For then I will restore to the
peoples [a]a pure [1]language,
That they all may call on the
name of the LORD,
To serve Him with one accord.
10 [a]From beyond the rivers of
Ethiopia
My worshipers,
The daughter of My dispersed
ones,
Shall bring My offering.
11 In that day you shall not be
shamed for any of your deeds
In which you transgress against
Me;
For then I will take away from
your midst
Those who [a]rejoice in your pride,
And you shall no longer be
haughty
In My holy mountain.
12 I will leave in your midst
[a]A meek and humble people,
And they shall trust in the name
of the LORD.
13 [a]The remnant of Israel [b]shall do
no unrighteousness
[c]And speak no lies,
Nor shall a deceitful tongue be
found in their mouth;

11 [a]Mal. 1:11 [b]Gen. 10:5
12 [a]Is. 18:1–7; Ezek. 30:4, 5 [b]Ps. 17:13
13 [a]Is. 10:5–27; 14:24–27; Mic. 5:5, 6
14 [a]Is. 13:21 [b]Is. 14:23; 34:11 [c]Jer. 22:14
15 [a]Is. 47:8 [b]Rev. 18:7 [c]Lam. 2:15 [d]Nah. 3:19

CHAPTER 3

3 [a]Ezek. 22:27 [b]Jer. 5:6; Hab. 1:8
4 [a]Hos. 9:7 [b]Ezek. 22:26; Mal. 2:7, 8 [1]Or *profaned*
5 [a]Jer. 3:3 [1]Lit. *Morning by morning*
7 [a]Jer. 8:6 [b]Gen. 6:12 [1]They were eager
8 [a]Prov. 20:22; Mic. 7:7; Hab. 2:3 [b]Is. 66:18; Ezek. 38:14–23; Joel 3:2; Mic. 4:12; Matt. 25:32 [c]Zeph. 1:18 [1]LXX, Syr. *for witness;* Tg. *for the day of My revelation for judgment;* Vg. *for the day of My resurrection that is to come*
9 [a]Is. 19:18; 57:19 [1]Lit. *lip*
10 [a]Ps. 68:31; Is. 18:1; Acts 8:27
11 [a]Is. 2:12; 5:15; Matt. 3:9
12 [a]Is. 14:32; Zech. 13:8, 9
13 [a]Is. 10:20–22; [Mic. 4:7] [b]Is. 60:21 [c]Zech. 8:3, 16; Rev. 14:5

For [d]they shall feed *their* flocks
and lie down,
And no one shall make *them*
afraid."

Joy in God's Faithfulness

14 [a]Sing, O daughter of Zion!
Shout, O Israel!
Be glad and rejoice with all *your*
heart,
O daughter of Jerusalem!
15 The LORD has taken away your
judgments,
He has cast out your enemy.
[a]The King of Israel, the LORD, [b]*is*
in your midst;
You shall [1]see disaster no more.
16 In that day [a]it shall be said to
Jerusalem:
"Do not fear;
Zion, [b]let not your hands be
weak.
17 The LORD your God [a]in your
midst,
The Mighty One, will save;
[b]He will rejoice over you with
gladness,
He will quiet *you* with His love,
He will rejoice over you with
singing."
18 "I will gather those who [a]sorrow
over the appointed assembly,
Who are among you,
To whom its reproach *is* a
burden.
19 Behold, at that time
I will deal with all who afflict you;
I will save the [a]lame,
And gather those who were
driven out;
I will appoint them for praise and
fame
In every land where they were
put to shame.
20 At that time [a]I will bring you
back,
Even at the time I gather you;
For I will give you [1]fame and
praise
Among all the peoples of the
earth,
When I return your captives
before your eyes,"
Says the LORD.

13 [d]Ezek. 34:13–15, 28

14 [a]Is. 12:6

15 [a][John 1:49] [b]Ezek. 48:35; [Rev. 7:15] [1]So with Heb. mss., LXX, Bg.; MT, Vg. *fear*

16 [a]Is. 35:3, 4 [b]Job 4:3; Heb. 12:12

17 [a]Zeph. 3:5, 15 [b]Deut. 30:9; Is. 62:5; 65:19; Jer. 32:41

18 [a]Lam. 2:6

19 [a][Ezek. 34:16; Mic. 4:6, 7]

20 [a]Is. 11:12; Ezek. 28:25; Amos 9:14 [1]Lit. *a name*

The Book of

Haggai

WITH the Babylonian exile in the past, and a newly returned group of Jews back in the land, the work of rebuilding the temple can begin. However, sixteen years after the process is begun, the people have yet to finish the project, for their personal affairs have interfered with God's business. Haggai preaches a fiery series of sermonettes designed to stir up the nation to finish the temple. He calls the builders to renewed courage in the Lord, renewed holiness of life, and renewed faith in God who controls the future.

The etymology and meaning of *Haggay* is uncertain, but it is probably derived from the Hebrew word *hag,* "festival." It may also be an abbreviated form of *haggiah,* "festival of Yahweh." Thus, Haggai's name means "Festal" or "Festive," possibly because he was born on the day of a major feast, such as Tabernacles (Haggai's second message takes place during that feast, 2:1). The title in the Septuagint is *Aggaios* and in the Vulgate it is *Aggaeus*.

The Command to Build God's House

IN [a]the second year of King Darius, in the sixth month, on the
first day of the month, the word
of the LORD came by [b]Haggai the
prophet to [c]Zerubbabel the son of
Shealtiel, governor of Judah, and
to [d]Joshua the son of [e]Jehozadak,
the high priest, saying,
2 "Thus speaks the LORD of
hosts, saying: 'This people says,
"The time has not come, the time
that the LORD's house should be
built." ' "
3 Then the word of the LORD
[a]came by Haggai the prophet, saying,
4 "*Is it* [a]time for you yourselves
to dwell in your paneled houses,
and this [1]temple *to lie* in ruins?"
5 Now therefore, thus says the
LORD of hosts: [a]"Consider your
ways!

6 "You have [a]sown much, and bring
in little;
You eat, but do not have enough;
You drink, but you are not filled
with drink;
You clothe yourselves, but no one
is warm;
And [b]he who earns wages,
Earns wages *to put* into a bag
with holes."

7 Thus says the LORD of hosts:
"Consider your ways!
8 "Go up to the [a]mountains and
bring wood and build the [1]temple,
that I may take pleasure in it and
be glorified," says the LORD.
9 [a]"*You* looked for much, but indeed *it came to* little; and when
you brought it home, [b]I blew it
away. Why?" says the LORD of
hosts. "Because of My house that
is in ruins, while every one of you
runs to his own house.
10 "Therefore [a]the heavens above
you withhold the dew, and the
earth withholds its fruit.
11 "For I [a]called for a drought on
the land and the mountains, on the
grain and the new wine and the
oil, on whatever the ground brings
forth, on men and livestock, and
on [b]all the labor of *your* hands."

The People's Obedience

12 [a]Then Zerubbabel the son of
Shealtiel, and Joshua the son of
Jehozadak, the high priest, with all
the remnant of the people, obeyed
the voice of the LORD their God,
and the words of Haggai the
prophet, as the LORD their God had
sent him; and the people feared the
presence of the LORD.
13 Then Haggai, the LORD's messenger, spoke the LORD's message
to the people, saying, [a]"I *am* with
you, says the LORD."
14 So [a]the LORD stirred up the

CHAPTER 1

1 [a]Ezra 4:24; Hag. 2:10; Zech. 1:1, 7 [b]Ezra 5:1; 6:14 [c]1 Chr. 3:19; Ezra 2:2; Neh. 7:7; Zech. 4:6; Matt. 1:12, 13 [d]Ezra 5:2, 3; Zech. 6:11 [e]1 Chr. 6:15

3 [a]Ezra 5:1

4 [a]2 Sam. 7:2 [1]Lit. *house*

5 [a]Lam. 3:40

6 [a]Deut. 28:38–40; Hos. 8:7; Hag. 1:9, 10; 2:16, 17 [b]Zech. 8:10

8 [a]Ezra 3:7 [1]Lit. *house*

9 [a]Hag. 2:16 [b]Hag. 2:17

10 [a]Lev. 26:19; Deut. 28:23; 1 Kin. 8:35; Joel 1:18–20

11 [a]1 Kin. 17:1; 2 Kin. 8:1 [b]Hag. 2:17

12 [a]Ezra 5:2

13 [a][Matt. 28:20; Rom. 8:31]

14 [a]2 Chr. 36:22; Ezra 1:1

spirit of Zerubbabel the son of
Shealtiel, [b]governor of Judah, and
the spirit of Joshua the son of Je-
hozadak, the high priest, and the
spirit of all the remnant of the peo-
ple; [c]and they came and worked
on the house of the LORD of hosts,
their God,
15 on the twenty-fourth day of the
sixth month, in the second year of
King Darius.

The Coming Glory of God's House

2 In the seventh *month,* on the
twenty-first of the month, the
word of the LORD came [1]by Haggai
the prophet, saying:
2 "Speak now to Zerubbabel the
son of Shealtiel, governor of Ju-
dah, and to Joshua the son of Je-
hozadak, the high priest, and to
the remnant of the people, saying:
3 [a]'Who is left among you who
saw this [1]temple in its former
glory? And how do you see it now?
In comparison with it, [b]*is this* not
in your eyes as nothing?
4 'Yet now [a]be strong, Zerubba-
bel,' says the LORD; 'and be strong,
Joshua, son of Jehozadak, the high
priest; and be strong, all you peo-
ple of the land,' says the LORD, 'and
work; for I *am* with you,' says the
LORD of hosts.
5 [a]'*According to* the word that I
covenanted with you when you
came out of Egypt, so [b]My Spirit
remains among you; do not fear!'
6 "For thus says the LORD of
hosts: [a]'Once more (it *is* a little
while) [b]I will shake heaven and
earth, the sea and dry land;
7 'and I will shake all nations,
and they shall come to [a]the [1]Desire
of All Nations, and I will fill this
[2]temple with [b]glory,' says the LORD
of hosts.
8 'The silver *is* Mine, and the
gold *is* Mine,' says the LORD of
hosts.
9 [a]'The glory of this latter [1]tem-
ple shall be greater than the for-
mer,' says the LORD of hosts. 'And
in this place I will give [b]peace,'
says the LORD of hosts."

The People Are Defiled

10 On the twenty-fourth *day* of the
ninth *month,* in the second year
of Darius, the word of the LORD
came by Haggai the prophet, say-
ing,
11 "Thus says the LORD of hosts:
'Now, [a]ask the priests *concerning
the* law, saying,
12 "If one carries holy meat in the
fold of his garment, and with the
edge he touches bread or stew,
wine or oil, or any food, will it be-
come holy?" ' " Then the priests
answered and said, "No."
13 And Haggai said, "If *one who
is* [a]unclean *because* of a dead body
touches any of these, will it be un-
clean?" So the priests answered
and said, "It shall be unclean."
14 Then Haggai answered and
said, [a]" 'So is this people, and so
is this nation before Me,' says the
LORD, 'and so is every work of
their hands; and what they offer
there is unclean.

Promised Blessing

15 'And now, carefully [a]consider
from this day forward: from before
stone was laid upon stone in the
temple of the LORD—
16 'since those *days,* [a]when *one*
came to a heap of twenty ephahs,
there were *but* ten; when *one* came
to the wine vat to draw out fifty
baths from the press, there were
but twenty.
17 [a]'I struck you with blight and
mildew and hail [b]in all the labors
of your hands; [c]yet you did not
turn to Me,' says the LORD.
18 'Consider now from this day
forward, from the twenty-fourth
day of the ninth month, from [a]the
day that the foundation of the
LORD's temple was laid—consider
it:
19 [a]'Is the seed still in the barn?
As yet the vine, the fig tree, the
pomegranate, and the olive tree
have not yielded *fruit. But* from
this day I will [b]bless *you.*' "

Zerubbabel Chosen as a Signet

20 And again the word of the LORD
came to Haggai on the twenty-
fourth day of the month, saying,
21 "Speak to Zerubbabel, [a]gover-
nor of Judah, saying:

[b]'I will shake heaven and earth.
22 [a]I will overthrow the throne of
kingdoms;
I will destroy the strength of the
Gentile kingdoms.

14 [b]Hag. 2:21 [c]Ezra 5:2, 8; Neh. 4:6

CHAPTER 2

1 [1]Lit. *by the hand of*

3 [a]Ezra 3:12, 13 [b]Zech. 4:10 [1]Lit. *house*

4 [a]Deut. 31:23; 1 Chr. 22:13; 28:20; Zech. 8:9; Eph. 6:10

5 [a]Ex. 29:45, 46 [b][Neh. 9:20]; Is. 63:11, 14

6 [a]Heb. 12:26 [b][Joel 3:16]

7 [a]Gen. 49:10; Mal. 3:1 [b]1 Kin. 8:11; Is. 60:7; Zech. 2:5 [1]Or *desire of all nations* [2]Lit. *house*

9 [a][John 1:14] [b]Ps. 85:8, 9; Luke 2:14; [Eph. 2:14] [1]Lit. *house*

11 [a]Lev. 10:10, 11; Deut. 33:10; Mal. 2:7

13 [a]Lev. 22:4–6; Num. 19:11, 22

14 [a][Titus 1:15]

15 [a]Hag. 1:5, 7; 2:18

16 [a]Hag. 1:6, 9; Zech. 8:10

17 [a]Deut. 28:22; 1 Kin. 8:37; Amos 4:9 [b]Hag. 1:11 [c]Jer. 5:3; Amos 4:6–11

18 [a]Ezra 5:1, 2, 16; Zech. 8:9

19 [a]Zech. 8:12 [b]Ps. 128:1–6; Jer. 31:12, 14; [Mal. 3:10]

21 [a]Ezra 5:2; Hag. 1:1, 14; Zech. 4:6–10 [b]Hag. 2:6, 7; [Heb. 12:26, 27]

22 [a][Dan. 2:44; Rev. 19:11–21]

[b]I will overthrow the chariots
And those who ride in them;
The horses and their riders shall
come down,
Every one by the sword of his
brother.

23 'In that day,' says the LORD of
hosts, 'I will take you, Zerubbabel
My servant, the son of Shealtiel,'
says the LORD, [a]'and will make you
like a signet *ring;* for [b]I have cho-
sen you,' says the LORD of hosts."

22 [b]Ps. 46:9; Ezek. 39:20; Mic. 5:10; Zech. 9:10

23 [a]Song 8:6; Jer. 22:24 [b]Is. 42:1; 43:10

The Book of

Zechariah

FOR a dozen years or more, the task of rebuilding the temple has been half completed. Zechariah is commissioned by God to encourage the people in their unfinished responsibility. Rather than exhorting them to action with strong words of rebuke, Zechariah seeks to encourage them to action by reminding them of the future importance of the temple. The temple must be built, for one day the Messiah's glory will inhabit it. But future blessing is contingent upon present obedience. The people are not merely building a building; they are building the future. With that as their motivation, they can enter into the building project with wholehearted zeal, for their Messiah is coming.

Zekar-yah means "Yahweh Remembers" or "Yahweh Has Remembered." This theme dominates the whole book: Israel will be blessed because Yahweh remembers the covenant He made with the fathers. The Greek and Latin version of his name is *Zacharias.*

A Call to Repentance

IN the eighth month [a]of the second year of Darius, the word of the LORD came [b]to Zechariah the son of Berechiah, the son of [c]Iddo the prophet, saying,
2 "The LORD has been very angry with your fathers.
3 "Therefore say to them, 'Thus says the LORD of hosts: "Return [a]to Me," says the LORD of hosts, "and I will return to you," says the LORD of hosts.
4 "Do not be like your fathers, [a]to whom the former prophets preached, saying, 'Thus says the LORD of hosts: [b]"Turn now from your evil ways and your evil deeds." ' But they did not hear nor heed Me," says the LORD.
5 "Your fathers, where *are* they?
And the prophets, do they live forever?
6 Yet surely [a]My words and My statutes,
Which I commanded My servants the prophets,
Did they not overtake your fathers?

"So they returned and said:

[b]'Just as the LORD of hosts determined to do to us,
According to our ways and according to our deeds,
So He has dealt with us.' " ' "

Vision of the Horses

7 On the twenty-fourth day of the eleventh month, which is the month Shebat, in the second year of Darius, the word of the LORD came to Zechariah the son of Berechiah, the son of Iddo the prophet:
8 I saw by night, and behold, [a]a man riding on a red horse, and it stood among the myrtle trees in the hollow; and behind him *were* [b]horses: red, sorrel, and white.
9 Then I said, [a]"My lord, what *are* these?" So the angel who talked with me said to me, "I will show you what they *are.*"
10 And the man who stood among the myrtle trees answered and said, [a]"These *are the ones* whom the LORD has sent to walk to and fro throughout the earth."
11 [a]So they answered the Angel of the LORD, who stood among the myrtle trees, and said, "We have walked to and fro throughout the earth, and behold, all the earth is [1]resting quietly."

The LORD Will Comfort Zion

12 Then the Angel of the LORD answered and said, "O LORD of hosts, [a]how long will You not have mercy on Jerusalem and on the cities of Judah, against which You

CHAPTER 1

1 [a]Ezra 4:24; 6:15; Hag. 1:1; Zech. 7:1 [b]Ezra 5:1; 6:14; Zech. 7:1; Matt. 23:35; Luke 11:51 [c]Neh. 12:4, 16

3 [a]Is. 31:6; 44:22; [Mic. 7:19; Mal. 3:7–10; Luke 15:20; James 4:8]

4 [a]2 Chr. 36:15, 16 [b]Is. 31:6; Jer. 3:12; 18:11; Ezek. 18:30; [Hos. 14:1]

6 [a][Is. 55:11] [b]Lam. 1:18; 2:17

8 [a]Is. 55:13; Zech. 6:2; [Rev. 6:4] [b][Zech. 6:2–7; Rev. 6:2]

9 [a]Zech. 4:4, 5, 13; 6:4

10 [a][Heb. 1:14]

11 [a][Ps. 103:20, 21] [1]Lit. *sitting and quiet*

12 [a]Ps. 74:10; Jer. 12:4; Hab. 1:2

were angry [b]these seventy years?"
13 And the LORD answered the angel who talked to me, *with* [a]good *and* comforting words.
14 So the angel who spoke with me said to me, [1]"Proclaim, saying, 'Thus says the LORD of hosts:

"I am [a]zealous[2] for Jerusalem
And for Zion with great [3]zeal.
15 I am exceedingly angry with the nations at ease;
For [a]I was a little angry,
And they helped—*but* with evil *intent*."

16 'Therefore thus says the LORD:

[a]"I am returning to Jerusalem with mercy;
My [b]house [c]shall be built in it,"
says the LORD of hosts,
"And [d]a *surveyor's* line shall be stretched out over Jerusalem." '

17 "Again proclaim, saying, 'Thus says the LORD of hosts:

"My cities shall again [1]spread out through prosperity;
[a]The LORD will again comfort Zion,
And [b]will again choose Jerusalem." ' "

Vision of the Horns

18 Then I raised my eyes and looked, and there *were* four [a]horns.
19 And I said to the angel who talked with me, "What *are* these?" So he answered me, [a]"These *are* the [1]horns that have scattered Judah, Israel, and Jerusalem."
20 Then the LORD showed me four craftsmen.
21 And I said, "What are these coming to do?" So he said, "These *are* the [a]horns that scattered Judah, so that no one could lift up his head; but [1]the craftsmen are coming to terrify them, to cast out the horns of the nations that [b]lifted up *their* horn against the land of Judah to scatter it."

Vision of the Measuring Line

2 Then I raised my eyes and looked, and behold, [a]a man with a measuring line in his hand.
2 So I said, "Where are you going?" And he said to me, [a]"To measure Jerusalem, *to* see what *is* its width and what *is* its length."
3 And there *was* the angel who talked with me, going out; and another angel was coming out to meet him,
4 who said to him, "Run, speak to this young man, saying: [a]'Jerusalem shall be inhabited *as* towns without walls, because of the multitude of men and livestock in it.
5 'For I,' says the LORD, 'will be [a]a wall of fire all around her, [b]and I will be the glory in her midst.' "

Future Joy of Zion and Many Nations

6 "Up, up! Flee [a]from the land of the north," says the LORD; "for I have [b]spread you abroad like the four winds of heaven," says the LORD.
7 "Up, Zion! [a]Escape, you who dwell with the daughter of Babylon."
8 For thus says the LORD of hosts: "He sent Me after glory, to the nations which plunder you; for he who [a]touches you touches the [1]apple of His eye.
9 "For surely I will [a]shake My hand against them, and they shall become [1]spoil for their servants. Then [b]you will know that the LORD of hosts has sent Me.
10 [a]"Sing and rejoice, O daughter of Zion! For behold, I am coming and I [b]will dwell in your midst," says the LORD.
11 [a]"Many nations shall be joined to the LORD [b]in that day, and they shall become [c]My people. And I will dwell in your midst. Then [d]you will know that the LORD of hosts has sent Me to you.
12 "And the LORD will [a]take possession of Judah as His inheritance in the Holy Land, and will again choose Jerusalem.
13 [a]"Be silent, all flesh, before the LORD, for He is aroused [b]from His holy habitation!"

Vision of the High Priest

3 Then he showed me [a]Joshua the high priest standing before the Angel of the LORD, and [b]Satan[1] standing at his right hand to oppose him.
2 And the LORD said to Satan, [a]"The LORD rebuke you, Satan! The LORD who [b]has chosen Jerusa-

---

12 [b]Jer. 25:11, 12; 29:10
13 [a]Jer. 29:10
14 [a]Zech. 8:2 [1]Lit. *Cry out* [2]Or *jealous* [3]Or *jealousy*
15 [a]Is. 47:6
16 [a][Zech. 2:10; 8:3] [b]Ezra 6:14, 15 [c]Is. 44:28 [d]Zech. 2:1–3
17 [a][Is. 40:1, 2; 51:3] [b]Zech. 2:12 [1]Or *overflow with good*
18 [a][Lam. 2:17]
19 [a]Ezra 4:1, 4, 7 [1]Kingdoms or powers
21 [a][Ps. 75:10] [b]Ps. 75:4, 5 [1]Lit. *these*

CHAPTER 2
1 [a]Jer. 31:39
2 [a]Rev. 11:1
4 [a]Jer. 31:27
5 [a][Is. 26:1] [b][Is. 60:19]
6 [a]Is. 48:20 [b]Deut. 28:64
7 [a]Is. 48:20
8 [a]Deut. 32:10 [1]Lit. *pupil*
9 [a]Is. 19:16 [b]Zech. 4:9 [1]*booty* or *plunder*
10 [a]Is. 12:6 [b][Lev. 26:12]
11 [a][Is. 2:2, 3] [b]Zech. 3:10 [c]Ex. 12:49 [d]Ezek. 33:33
12 [a][Deut. 32:9]
13 [a]Hab. 2:20 [b]Ps. 68:5

CHAPTER 3
1 [a]Hag. 1:1 [b]Ps. 109:6 [1]Lit. *the Adversary*
2 [a][Jude 9] [b][Rom. 8:33]

lem rebuke you! [c]*Is* this not a
brand plucked from the fire?"
3 Now Joshua was clothed with
[a]filthy garments, and was standing
before the Angel.
4 Then He answered and spoke
to those who stood before Him,
saying, "Take away the filthy gar-
ments from him." And to him He
said, "See, I have removed your in-
iquity from you, [a]and I will clothe
you with rich robes."
5 And I said, "Let them put a
clean [a]turban on his head." So
they put a clean turban on his
head, and they put the clothes on
him. And the Angel of the LORD
stood by.

The Coming Branch

6 Then the Angel of the LORD ad-
monished Joshua, saying,
7 "Thus says the LORD of hosts:

'If you will walk in My ways,
And if you will [a]keep My
command,
Then you shall also [b]judge My
house,
And likewise have charge of My
courts;
I will give you places to walk
Among these who [c]stand here.

8 'Hear, O Joshua, the high priest,
You and your companions who
sit before you,
For they are [a]a[1] wondrous sign;
For behold, I am bringing forth
[b]My Servant the [c]BRANCH.
9 For behold, the stone
That I have laid before Joshua:
[a]Upon the stone *are* [b]seven eyes.
Behold, I will engrave its
inscription,'
Says the LORD of hosts,
'And [c]I will remove the iniquity
of that land in one day.
10 [a]In that day,' says the LORD of
hosts,
'Everyone will invite his neighbor
[b]Under his vine and under his fig
tree.' "

Vision of the Lampstand and Olive Trees

4 Now [a]the angel who talked
with me came back and wak-
ened me, [b]as a man who is wak-
ened out of his sleep.
2 And he said to me, "What do
you see?" So I said, "I am looking,
and there *is* [a]a lampstand of solid

2 [c]Amos 4:11
3 [a]Ezra 9:15; Is. 64:6
4 [a]Gen. 3:21; Is. 61:10
5 [a]Ex. 29:6
7 [a]Lev. 8:35; Ezek. 44:16 [b]Deut. 17:9, 12 [c]Zech. 3:4
8 [a]Ps. 71:7 [b]Is. 42:1 [c]Is. 11:1; 53:2; Jer. 23:5; 33:15; Zech. 6:12 [1]Lit. *men of a sign* or *wonder*
9 [a][Zech. 4:10; Rev. 5:6] [b]Ps. 118:22 [c]Jer. 31:34; 50:20; Zech. 3:4
10 [a]Zech. 2:11 [b]1 Kin. 4:25; Is. 36:16; Mic. 4:4

CHAPTER 4

1 [a]Zech. 1:9; 2:3 [b]Dan. 8:18
2 [a]Rev. 1:12 [b]Ex. 25:37; [Rev. 4:5]
3 [a]Rev. 11:3, 4
6 [a]Hag. 1:1 [b]Is. 30:1; Hos. 1:7; Hag. 2:4, 5
7 [a]Ps. 114:4, 6; Is. 40:4; Jer. 51:25; Nah. 1:5; Zech. 14:4, 5; [Matt. 21:21] [b]Ps. 118:22 [c]Ezra 3:10, 11, 13; Ps. 84:11
9 [a]Ezra 3:8–10; 5:16; Hag. 2:18 [b]Ezra 6:14, 15; Zech. 6:12, 13 [c]Zech. 2:9, 11; 6:15 [d][Is. 43:16]; Zech. 2:8 [1]Lit. *house*
10 [a]Neh. 4:2–4; Amos 7:2, 5; Hag. 2:3 [b]2 Chr. 16:9; Prov. 15:3; Zech. 3:9 [1]Lit. *plummet stone*
11 [a]Zech. 4:3; Rev. 11:4
12 [1]Lit. *into the hands of*
14 [a]Rev. 11:4 [b]Zech. 3:1–7 [1]Lit. *sons of fresh oil*

gold with a bowl on top of it, [b]and
on the *stand* seven lamps with
seven pipes to the seven lamps.
3 [a]"Two olive trees *are* by it, one
at the right of the bowl and the
other at its left."
4 So I answered and spoke to the
angel who talked with me, saying,
"What *are* these, my lord?"
5 Then the angel who talked with
me answered and said to me, "Do
you not know what these are?"
And I said, "No, my lord."
6 So he answered and said to
me:

"This *is* the word of the LORD to
[a]Zerubbabel:
[b]'Not by might nor by power, but
by My Spirit,'
Says the LORD of hosts.
7 'Who *are* you, [a]O great mountain?
Before Zerubbabel *you shall
become* a plain!
And he shall bring forth [b]the
capstone
[c]With shouts of "Grace, grace to
it!" ' "

8 Moreover the word of the LORD
came to me, saying:
9 "The hands of Zerubbabel
[a]Have laid the foundation of this
[1]temple;
His hands [b]shall also finish *it*.
Then [c]you will know
That the [d]LORD of hosts has sent
Me to you.
10 For who has despised the day of
[a]small things?
For these seven rejoice to see
The [1]plumb line in the hand of
Zerubbabel.
[b]They are the eyes of the LORD,
Which scan to and fro throughout
the whole earth."

11 Then I answered and said to
him, "What *are* these [a]two olive
trees—at the right of the lamp-
stand and at its left?"
12 And I further answered and
said to him, "What *are these* two
olive branches that *drip* [1]into the
receptacles of the two gold pipes
from which the golden *oil* drains?"
13 Then he answered me and said,
"Do you not know what these
are?" And I said, "No, my lord."
14 So he said, [a]"These *are* the two
[1]anointed ones, [b]who stand beside
the Lord of the whole earth."

Vision of the Flying Scroll

5 Then I turned and raised my eyes, and saw there a flying [a]scroll.

2 And he said to me, "What do you see?" So I answered, "I see a flying scroll. Its length *is* twenty cubits and its width ten cubits."

3 Then he said to me, "This *is* the [a]curse that goes out over the face of the whole earth: 'Every thief shall be expelled,' according *to* this side of *the scroll;* and, 'Every perjurer shall be expelled,' according *to* that side of it."

4 "I will send out *the curse,*" says
the LORD of hosts;
"It shall enter the house of the
[a]thief
And the house of [b]the one who
swears falsely by My name.
It shall remain in the midst of his
house
And consume [c]it, with its timber
and stones."

Vision of the Woman in a Basket

5 Then the angel who talked with me came out and said to me, "Lift your eyes now, and see what this *is* that goes forth."

6 So I asked, "What *is* it?" And he said, "It *is* a [1]basket that is going forth." He also said, "This *is* their resemblance throughout the earth:

7 "Here *is* a lead disc lifted up, and this *is* a woman sitting inside the basket";

8 then he said, "This *is* Wickedness!" And he thrust her down into the basket, and threw the lead [1]cover over its mouth.

9 Then I raised my eyes and looked, and there *were* two women, coming with the wind in their wings; for they had wings like the wings of a [a]stork, and they lifted up the basket between earth and heaven.

10 So I said to the [a]angel who talked with me, "Where are they carrying the basket?"

11 And he said to me, "To [a]build a house for it in [b]the land of [1]Shinar; when it is ready, *the basket* will be set there on its base."

CHAPTER 5

1 [a]Jer. 36:2; Ezek. 2:9; Rev. 5:1
3 [a]Mal. 4:6
4 [a]Ex. 20:15; Lev. 19:11 [b]Ex. 20:7; Lev. 19:12; Is. 48:1; Jer. 5:2; Zech. 8:17; Mal. 3:5 [c]Lev. 14:34, 35; Job 18:15
6 [1]Heb. *ephah,* a measuring container, and so elsewhere
8 [1]Lit. *stone*
9 [a]Lev. 11:13, 19; Ps. 104:17; Jer. 8:7
10 [a]Zech. 5:5
11 [a]Jer. 29:5, 28 [b]Gen. 10:10; Is. 11:11; Dan. 1:2 [1]Babylon

CHAPTER 6

2 [a]Zech. 1:8; Rev. 6:4 [b]Rev. 6:5
4 [a]Zech. 5:10
5 [a][Ps. 104:4; Heb. 1:7, 14] [b]1 Kin. 22:19; Dan. 7:10; Zech. 4:14; Luke 1:19
6 [a]Jer. 1:14; Ezek. 1:4 [1]The chariot
7 [a]Gen. 13:17; Zech. 1:10
8 [a]Eccl. 10:4
11 [a]Ex. 29:6 [b]Ezra 3:2; Hag. 1:1; Zech. 3:1 [1]Lit. *crowns*
12 [a]John 1:45 [b]Is. 4:2; 11:1; Jer. 23:5; 33:15; Zech. 3:8 [1]Lit. *sprout up*

Vision of the Four Chariots

6 Then I turned and raised my eyes and looked, and behold, four chariots *were* coming from between two mountains, and the mountains *were* mountains of bronze.

2 With the first chariot *were* [a]red horses, with the second chariot [b]black horses,

3 with the third chariot white horses, and with the fourth chariot dappled horses—strong *steeds.*

4 Then I answered [a]and said to the angel who talked with me, "What *are* these, my lord?"

5 And the angel answered and said to me, [a]"These *are* four spirits of heaven, who go out from *their* [b]station before the Lord of all the earth.

6 [1]"The one with the black horses is going to [a]the north country, the white are going after them, and the dappled are going toward the south country."

7 Then the strong *steeds* went out, eager to go, that they might [a]walk to and fro throughout the earth. And He said, "Go, walk to and fro throughout the earth." So they walked to and fro throughout the earth.

8 And He called to me, and spoke to me, saying, "See, those who go toward the north country have given rest to My [a]Spirit in the north country."

The Command to Crown Joshua

9 Then the word of the LORD came to me, saying:

10 "Receive *the gift* from the captives—from Heldai, Tobijah, and Jedaiah, who have come from Babylon—and go the same day and enter the house of Josiah the son of Zephaniah.

11 "Take the silver and gold, make [a]an[1] elaborate crown, and set *it* on the head of [b]Joshua the son of Jehozadak, the high priest.

12 "Then speak to him, saying, 'Thus says the LORD of hosts, saying:

"Behold, [a]the Man whose name *is*
the [b]BRANCH!
From His place He shall [1]branch
out,

[c]And He shall build the temple of
the LORD;
13 Yes, He shall build the temple of
the LORD.
He [a]shall bear the glory,
And shall sit and rule on His
throne;
So [b]He shall be a priest on His
throne,
And the counsel of peace shall be
between [1]them both." '

14 "Now the [1]elaborate crown
shall be [a]for a memorial in the
temple of the LORD [2]for Helem, To-
bijah, Jedaiah, and Hen the son of
Zephaniah.
15 "Even [a]those from afar shall
come and build the temple of the
LORD. Then you shall know that
the LORD of hosts has sent Me to
you. And *this* shall come to pass
if you diligently obey the voice of
the LORD your God."

Obedience Better than Fasting

7 Now in the fourth year of King
Darius it came to pass *that* the
word of the LORD came to Zecha-
riah, on the fourth day of the ninth
month, Chislev,
2 when [1]*the people* sent [2]She-
rezer, with Regem-Melech and
his men, *to* [3]the house of God, [4]to
pray before the LORD,
3 *and* to [a]ask the priests who
were in the house of the LORD of
hosts, and the prophets, saying,
"Should I weep in [b]the fifth month
and [1]fast as I have done for so
many years?"
4 Then the word of the LORD of
hosts came to me, saying,
5 "Say to all the people of the
land, and to the priests: 'When you
[a]fasted and mourned in the fifth
[b]and seventh *months* [c]during
those seventy years, did you really
fast [d]for Me—for Me?
6 [a]'When you eat and when you
drink, do you not eat and drink *for
yourselves?*
7 '*Should you* not *have obeyed*
the words which the LORD pro-
claimed through the [a]former
prophets when Jerusalem and
the cities around it were in-
habited and prosperous, and [b]the
[1]South and the Lowland were in-
habited?' "

12 [c][Eph. 2:20]
13 [a]Is. 22:24 [b]Ps. 110:4 [1]Both offices
14 [a]Ex. 12:14 [1]Lit. *crowns* [2]So with MT, Tg., Vg.; Syr. *for Heldai* (cf. v. 10); LXX *for the patient ones*
15 [a]Is. 57:19

CHAPTER 7

2 [1]Lit. *they*, cf. v. 5 [2]Or *Sar-Ezer* [3]Heb. *Bethel* [4]Or *to entreat the favor of*
3 [a]Mal. 2:7 [b]Zech. 8:19 [1]Lit. *consecrate myself*
5 [a][Is. 58:1–9] [b]Jer. 41:1 [c]Zech. 1:12 [d][Rom. 14:6]
6 [a]1 Chr. 29:22
7 [a]Zech. 1:4 [b]Jer. 17:26 [1]Heb. *Negev*
9 [a]Jer. 7:28 [1]Or *lovingkindness*
10 [a]Ex. 22:22 [b]Mic. 2:1
11 [a]Neh. 9:29 [b]Jer. 17:23 [1]Lit. *gave a stubborn* or *rebellious shoulder* [2]Lit. *made their ears heavy*
12 [a]Ezek. 11:19 [b]Neh. 9:29, 30 [c]Dan. 9:11, 12
13 [a]Prov. 1:24–28
14 [a]Deut. 4:27; 28:64

CHAPTER 8

2 [a]Zech. 1:14 [1]Or *jealous* [2]Or *jealousy* [3]Lit. *heat* or *rage*
3 [a]Zech. 1:16 [b]Zech. 2:10, 11 [c]Is. 1:21 [d][Is. 2:2, 3] [e]Jer. 31:23

Disobedience Resulted in Captivity

8 Then the word of the LORD
came to Zechariah, saying,
9 "Thus says the LORD of hosts:

[a]'Execute true justice,
Show [1]mercy and compassion
Everyone to his brother.
10 [a]Do not oppress the widow or the
fatherless,
The alien or the poor.
[b]Let none of you plan evil in his
heart
Against his brother.'

11 "But they refused to heed,
[a]shrugged[1] their shoulders, and
[b]stopped[2] their ears so that they
could not hear.
12 "Yes, they made their [a]hearts
like flint, [b]refusing to hear the law
and the words which the LORD of
hosts had sent by His Spirit
through the former prophets.
[c]Thus great wrath came from the
LORD of hosts.
13 "Therefore it happened, *that*
just as He proclaimed and they
would not hear, so [a]they called out
and I would not listen," says the
LORD of hosts.
14 "But [a]I scattered them with a
whirlwind among all the nations
which they had not known. Thus
the land became desolate after
them, so that no one passed
through or returned; for they made
the pleasant land desolate."

Jerusalem, Holy City of the Future

8 Again the word of the LORD of
hosts came, saying,
2 "Thus says the LORD of hosts:

[a]'I am [1]zealous for Zion with great
[2]zeal;
With great [3]fervor I am zealous
for her.'

3 "Thus says the LORD:

[a]'I will return to Zion,
And [b]dwell in the midst of
Jerusalem.
Jerusalem [c]shall be called the
City of Truth,
[d]The Mountain of the LORD of
hosts,
[e]The Holy Mountain.'

4 "Thus says the LORD of hosts:

[a]'Old men and old women shall again sit
In the streets of Jerusalem,
Each one with his staff in his hand
Because of [1]great age.
5 The streets of the city
Shall be [a]full of boys and girls
Playing in its streets.'

6 "Thus says the LORD of hosts:

'If it is [1]marvelous in the eyes of the remnant of this people in these days,
[a]Will it also be marvelous in My eyes?'
Says the LORD of hosts.

7 "Thus says the LORD of hosts:

'Behold, [a]I will save My people from the land of the [1]east
And from the land of the [2]west;
8 I will [a]bring them *back*,
And they shall dwell in the midst of Jerusalem.
[b]They shall be My people
And I will be their God,
[c]In truth and righteousness.'

9 "Thus says the LORD of hosts:

[a]'Let your hands be strong,
You who have been hearing in these days
These words by the mouth of [b]the prophets,
Who *spoke* in [c]the day the foundation was laid
For the house of the LORD of hosts,
That the temple might be built.
10 For before these days
There were no [a]wages for man nor any hire for beast;
There was no peace from the enemy for whoever went out or came in;
For I set all men, everyone, against his neighbor.

11 [a]'But now I *will* not *treat* the remnant of this people as in the former days,' says the LORD of hosts.

12 'For[a] the [1]seed *shall be* prosperous,
The vine shall give its fruit,
[b]The ground shall give her increase,
And [c]the heavens shall give their dew—
I will cause the remnant of this people
To possess all these.
13 And it shall come to pass
That just as you were [a]a curse among the nations,
O house of Judah and house of Israel,
So I will save you, and [b]you shall be a blessing.
Do not fear,
Let your hands be strong.'

14 "For thus says the LORD of hosts:

[a]'Just as I determined to [1]punish you
When your fathers provoked Me to wrath,'
Says the LORD of hosts,
[b]'And I would not relent,
15 So again in these days
I am determined to do good
To Jerusalem and to the house of Judah.
Do not fear.
16 These *are* the things you shall [a]do:
[b]Speak each man the truth to his neighbor;
Give judgment in your gates for truth, justice, and peace;
17 [a]Let none of you think evil in [1]your heart against your neighbor;
And do not love a false oath.
For all these *are things* that I hate,'
Says the LORD."

18 Then the word of the LORD of hosts came to me, saying,
19 "Thus says the LORD of hosts:

[a]'The fast of the fourth *month*,
[b]The fast of the fifth,
[c]The fast of the seventh,
[d]And the fast of the tenth,
Shall be [e]joy and gladness and cheerful feasts
For the house of Judah.
[f]Therefore love truth and peace.'

20 "Thus says the LORD of hosts:

'Peoples shall yet come,
Inhabitants of many cities;
21 The inhabitants of one *city* shall go to another, saying,
[a]"Let us continue to go and pray before the LORD,
And seek the LORD of hosts.
I myself will go also."

4 [a]1 Sam. 2:31; Is. 65:20 [1]Lit. *many days.*
5 [a]Jer. 30:19, 20
6 [a][Gen. 18:14; Luke 1:37] [1]Or *wonderful*
7 [a]Ps. 107:3; Is. 11:11; Ezek. 37:21 [1]Lit. *rising sun* [2]Lit. *setting sun*
8 [a]Zeph. 3:20; Zech. 10:10 [b][Jer. 30:22; 31:1, 33; Zech. 13:9] [c]Jer. 4:2
9 [a]1 Chr. 22:13; Is. 35:4; Hag. 2:4 [b]Ezra 5:1, 2; 6:14; Zech. 4:9 [c]Hag. 2:18
10 [a]Hag. 1:6, 9
11 [a][Ps. 103:9]; Is. 12:1; Hag. 2:15–19
12 [a]Joel 2:22 [b]Ps. 67:6 [c]Hag. 1:10 [1]Lit. *seed of peace*
13 [a]Jer. 42:18 [b]Gen. 12:2; Ruth 4:11, 12; Is. 19:24, 25; Ezek. 34:26; [Zeph. 3:20]
14 [a]Jer. 31:28 [b][2 Chr. 36:16] [1]Lit. *bring calamity to you*
16 [a]Zech. 7:9, 10 [b]Ps. 15:2; [Prov. 12:17–19]; Zech. 8:3; [Eph. 4:25]
17 [a]Prov. 3:29; Jer. 4:14; Zech. 7:10 [1]Lit. *his*
19 [a]Jer. 52:6 [b]Jer. 52:12 [c]2 Kin. 25:25; Jer. 41:1, 2 [d]Jer. 52:4 [e]Esth. 8:17 [f]Zech. 8:16; Luke 1:74, 75
21 [a][Is. 2:2, 3; Mic. 4:1, 2]

22 Yes, [a]many peoples and strong
nations
Shall come to seek the LORD of
hosts in Jerusalem,
And to pray before the LORD.'

23 "Thus says the LORD of hosts:
'In those days ten men [a]from every
language of the nations shall
[b]grasp the [1]sleeve of a Jewish man,
saying, "Let us go with you, for
we have heard [c]*that* God *is* with
you." ' "

Israel Defended Against Enemies

9 The [1]burden of the word of the
LORD
Against the land of Hadrach,
And [a]Damascus its resting place
(For [b]the eyes of men
And all the tribes of Israel
Are on the LORD);
2 Also *against* [a]Hamath, *which*
borders on it,
And *against* [b]Tyre and [c]Sidon,
though they are very [d]wise.

3 For Tyre built herself a tower,
Heaped up silver like the dust,
And gold like the mire of the
streets.
4 Behold, [a]the LORD will cast her
out;
He will destroy [b]her power in the
sea,
And she will be devoured by fire.

5 Ashkelon shall see *it* and fear;
Gaza also shall be very
sorrowful;
And [a]Ekron, for He dried up her
expectation.
The king shall perish from Gaza,
And Ashkelon shall not be
inhabited.

6 "A[1] mixed race shall settle [a]in
Ashdod,
And I will cut off the pride of the
[b]Philistines.
7 I will take away the blood from
his mouth,
And the abominations from
between his teeth.
But he who remains, even he
shall be for our God,
And shall be like a leader in
Judah,
And Ekron like a Jebusite.
8 [a]I will camp around My house
Because of the army,
Because of him who passes by
and him who returns.

22 [a]Is. 60:3; 66:23; [Zech. 14:16–21]

23 [a]Is. 3:6 [b][Is. 45:14] [c]1 Cor. 14:25 [1]Lit. *wing,* corner of a garment

CHAPTER 9

1 [a]Is. 17:1; Jer. 23:33 [b]Amos 1:3–5 [1]*oracle, prophecy*

2 [a]Jer. 49:23 [b]Is. 23; Jer. 25:22; 47:4; Ezek. 26; Amos 1:9, 10 [c]1 Kin. 17:9 [d]Ezek. 28:3

4 [a]Is. 23:1 [b]Ezek. 26:17

5 [a]Zeph. 2:4, 5

6 [a]Amos 1:8; Zeph. 2:4 [b]Ezek. 25:15–17 [1]Lit. *An illegitimate one*

8 [a][Ps. 34:7]

9 [a]Zeph. 3:14, 15; Zech. 2:10 [b][Ps. 110:1; Is. 9:6, 7; Jer. 23:5, 6]; Matt. 21:5; Mark 11:7, 9; Luke 19:38; John 12:15

10 [a]Hos. 1:7; Mic. 5:10 [b]Ps. 46:9; Is. 2:4; Hos. 2:18; Mic. 4:3 [c]Ps. 72:8

11 [a]Is. 42:7

12 [a]Is. 49:9; Jer. 17:13; Heb. 6:18–20 [b]Is. 61:7

14 [a]Ps. 18:14; Hab. 3:11 [b]Is. 21:1

15 [a]Is. 37:35; Zech. 12:8 [1]Sacrificial basins

16 [a]Jer. 31:10, 11 [b]Is. 62:3; Mal. 3:17 [1]Lit. *stones*

No more shall an oppressor pass
through them,
For now I have seen with My
eyes.

The Coming King

9 "Rejoice [a]greatly, O daughter of
Zion!
Shout, O daughter of Jerusalem!
Behold, [b]your King is coming to
you;
He *is* just and having salvation,
Lowly and riding on a donkey,
A colt, the foal of a donkey.
10 I [a]will cut off the chariot from
Ephraim
And the horse from Jerusalem;
The [b]battle bow shall be cut off.
He shall speak peace to the
nations;
His dominion *shall be* [c]'from sea
to sea,
And from the River to the ends
of the earth.'

God Will Save His People

11 "As for you also,
Because of the blood of your
covenant,
I will set your [a]prisoners free
from the waterless pit.
12 Return to the stronghold,
[a]You prisoners of hope.
Even today I declare
That I will restore [b]double to you.
13 For I have bent Judah, My *bow,*
Fitted the bow with Ephraim,
And raised up your sons, O Zion,
Against your sons, O Greece,
And made you like the sword of
a mighty man."

14 Then the LORD will be seen over
them,
And [a]His arrow will go forth like
lightning.
The Lord GOD will blow the
trumpet,
And go [b]with whirlwinds from
the south.
15 The LORD of hosts will [a]defend
them;
They shall devour and subdue
with slingstones.
They shall drink *and* roar as if
with wine;
They shall be filled *with blood*
like [1]basins,
Like the corners of the altar.
16 The LORD their God will [a]save
them in that day,
As the flock of His people.
For [b]they *shall be like* the [1]jewels
of a crown,

[c]Lifted like a banner over His
land—
17 For [a]how great is [1]its goodness
And how great [1]its [b]beauty!
[c]Grain shall make the young men
thrive,
And new wine the young women.

Restoration of Judah and Israel

10 Ask [a]the LORD for [b]rain
In [c]the time of the [1]latter
rain.
The LORD will make [2]flashing
clouds;
He will give them showers of
rain,
Grass in the field for everyone.

2 For the [a]idols[1] speak delusion;
The diviners envision [b]lies,
And tell false dreams;
They [c]comfort in vain.
Therefore *the people* wend their
way like [d]sheep;
They are [2]in trouble [e]because
there is no shepherd.

3 "My anger is kindled against the
[a]shepherds,
[b]And I will punish the [1]goatherds.
For the LORD of hosts [c]will visit
His flock,
The house of Judah,
And [d]will make them as His royal
horse in the battle.
4 From him comes [a]the
cornerstone,
From him [b]the tent peg,
From him the battle bow,
From him every [1]ruler together.
5 They shall be like mighty men,
Who [a]tread down *their enemies*
In the mire of the streets in the
battle.
They shall fight because the LORD
is with them,
And the riders on horses shall be
put to shame.

6 "I will strengthen the house of
Judah,
And I will save the house of
Joseph.
[a]I will bring them back,
Because I [b]have mercy on them.
They shall be as though I had not
cast them aside;
For I *am* the LORD their God,
And I [c]will hear them.
7 *Those of* Ephraim shall be like a
mighty man,
And their [a]heart shall rejoice as
if with wine.
Yes, their children shall see *it* and
be glad;

16 [c]Is. 11:12
17 [a][Ps. 31:19] [b][Ps. 45:1–16] [c]Joel 3:18 [1]Lit. *His*

CHAPTER 10

1 [a][Jer. 14:22] [b][Deut. 11:13, 14] [c][Joel 2:23] [1]Spring rain [2]Or *lightning flashes*
2 [a]Jer. 10:8 [b]Jer. 27:9; [Ezek. 13] [c]Job 13:4 [d]Jer. 50:6, 17 [e]Ezek. 34:5–8; Matt. 9:36; Mark 6:34 [1]Heb. *teraphim* [2]*afflicted*
3 [a]Jer. 25:34–36; Ezek. 34:2; Zech. 11:17 [b]Ezek. 34:17 [c]Luke 1:68 [d]Song 1:9 [1]Leaders
4 [a]Is. 28:16 [b]Is. 22:23 [1]Or *despot*
5 [a]Ps. 18:42
6 [a]Jer. 3:18; Ezek. 37:21 [b]Hos. 1:7; Zech. 1:16 [c]Zech. 13:9
7 [a]Ps. 104:15
8 [a]Is. 5:26 [b]Is. 49:19; Ezek. 36:37; Zech. 2:4
9 [a]Hos. 2:23 [b]Deut. 30:1 [1]Or *scatter*
10 [a]Is. 11:11; Hos. 11:11 [b]Is. 49:19, 20
11 [a]Is. 11:15 [b]Is. 14:25; Zeph. 2:13 [c]Ezek. 30:13 [1]The Nile
12 [a]Mic. 4:5

CHAPTER 11

1 [a]Zech. 10:10
2 [a]Ezek. 31:3 [b]Is. 32:19
3 [a]Jer. 25:34–36 [1]Or *floodplain, thicket*
5 [a][Jer. 2:3]; 50:7 [b]Deut. 29:19; Hos. 12:8; 1 Tim. 6:9

Their heart shall rejoice in the
LORD.
8 I will [a]whistle for them and
gather them,
For I will redeem them;
[b]And they shall increase as they
once increased.

9 "I[a] will [1]sow them among the
peoples,
And they shall [b]remember Me in
far countries;
They shall live, together with
their children,
And they shall return.
10 [a]I will also bring them back from
the land of Egypt,
And gather them from Assyria.
I will bring them into the land of
Gilead and Lebanon,
[b]Until no *more room* is found for
them.
11 [a]He shall pass through the sea
with affliction,
And strike the waves of the sea:
All the depths of [1]the River shall
dry up.
Then [b]the pride of Assyria shall
be brought down,
And [c]the scepter of Egypt shall
depart.

12 "So I will strengthen them in the
LORD,
And [a]they shall walk up and
down in His name,"
Says the LORD.

Desolation of Israel

11 Open [a]your doors,
O Lebanon,
That fire may devour your
cedars.
2 Wail, O cypress, for the [a]cedar
has fallen,
Because the mighty *trees* are
ruined.
Wail, O oaks of Bashan,
[b]For the thick forest has come
down.
3 *There is* the sound of wailing
[a]shepherds!
For their glory is in ruins.
There is the sound of roaring
lions!
For the [1]pride of the Jordan is in
ruins.

Prophecy of the Shepherds

4 Thus says the LORD my God,
"Feed the flock for slaughter,
5 "whose owners slaughter them
and [a]feel no guilt; those who sell
them [b]say, 'Blessed be the LORD,

for I am rich'; and their shepherds
do [c]not pity them.
6 "For I will no longer pity the
inhabitants of the land," says the
LORD. "But indeed I will give
everyone into his neighbor's hand
and into the hand of his king. They
shall [1]attack the land, and I will
not deliver *them* from their hand."
7 So I fed the flock for slaughter,
[1]in particular [a]the poor of the
flock. I took for myself two staffs:
the one I called [2]Beauty, and the
other I called [3]Bonds; and I fed the
flock.
8 I [1]dismissed the three shep-
herds [a]in one month. My soul
loathed them, and their soul also
abhorred me.
9 Then I said, "I will not feed
you. [a]Let what is dying die, and
what is perishing perish. Let those
that are left eat each other's flesh."
10 And I took my staff, [1]Beauty,
and cut it in two, that I might break
the covenant which I had made
with all the peoples.
11 So it was broken on that day.
Thus [a]the[1] poor of the flock, who
were watching me, knew that it
was the word of the LORD.
12 Then I said to them, "If it is
[1]agreeable to you, give *me* my
wages; and if not, refrain." So they
[a]weighed out for my wages thirty
pieces of silver.
13 And the LORD said to me,
"Throw it to the [a]potter"—that
princely price they set on me. So
I took the thirty *pieces* of silver
and threw them into the house of
the LORD for the potter.
14 Then I cut in two my other
staff, [1]Bonds, that I might break
the brotherhood between Judah
and Israel.
15 And the LORD said to me,
[a]"Next, take for yourself the im-
plements of a foolish shepherd.
16 "For indeed I will raise up a
shepherd in the land *who* will not
care for those who are cut off, nor
seek the young, nor heal those that
are broken, nor feed those that still
stand. But he will eat the flesh of
the fat and tear their hooves in
[a]pieces.

17 "Woe[a] to the worthless shepherd,
Who leaves the flock!
A sword *shall be* against his arm
And against his right eye;
His arm shall completely
wither,
And his right eye shall be totally
blinded."

The Coming Deliverance of Judah

12 The [1]burden of the word of
the LORD against Israel.
Thus says the LORD, [a]who
stretches out the heavens, lays the
foundation of the earth, and
[b]forms the spirit of man within
him:
2 "Behold, I will make Jerusalem
[a]a cup of [1]drunkenness to all the
surrounding peoples, when they
lay siege against Judah and Jeru-
salem.
3 [a]"And it shall happen in that
day that I will make Jerusalem [b]a
very heavy stone for all peoples;
all who would heave it away will
surely be cut in pieces, though all
nations of the earth are gathered
against it.
4 "In that day," says the LORD,
[a]"I will strike every horse with
confusion, and its rider with mad-
ness; I will open My eyes on the
house of Judah, and will strike
every horse of the peoples with
blindness.
5 "And the governors of Judah
shall say in their heart, 'The in-
habitants of Jerusalem *are* my
strength in the LORD of hosts, their
God.'
6 "In that day I will make the
governors of Judah [a]like a firepan
in the woodpile, and like a fiery
torch in the sheaves; they shall de-
vour all the surrounding peoples
on the right hand and on the left,
but Jerusalem shall be inhabited
again in her own place—Jerusa-
lem.
7 "The LORD will save the tents
of Judah first, so that the glory of
the house of David and the glory
of the inhabitants of Jerusalem
shall not become greater than that
of Judah.
8 "In that day the LORD will de-
fend the inhabitants of Jerusalem;
the one who is feeble among them
in that day shall be like David, and
the house of David *shall be* like
God, like the Angel of the LORD be-
fore them.
9 "It shall be in that day *that* I

5 [c]Ezek. 34:2, 3
6 [1]Lit. *strike*
7 [a]Jer. 39:10; Zeph. 3:12; Matt. 11:5 [1]So with MT, Tg., Vg.; LXX *for the Canaanites* [2]Or *Grace* [3]Or *Unity*
8 [a]Hos. 5:7 [1]Or *destroyed*, lit. *cut off*
9 [a]Jer. 15:2
10 [1]Or *Grace*
11 [a]Zeph. 3:12; Matt. 27:50; Mark 15:37; Luke 23:46; Acts 8:32 [1]So with MT, Tg., Vg.; LXX *the Canaanites*
12 [a]Gen. 37:28; Ex. 21:32; Matt. 26:15; 27:9, 10 [1]*good in your sight*
13 [a]Matt. 27:3–10; Acts 1:18, 19
14 [1]Or *Unity*
15 [a]Is. 56:11; Ezek. 34:2
16 [a]Ezek. 34:1–10; Mic. 3:1–3
17 [a]Jer. 23:1; Ezek. 34:2; Zech. 10:2; 11:15; John 10:12, 13

CHAPTER 12

1 [a]Is. 42:5; 44:24 [b]Num. 16:22; [Eccl. 12:7; Is. 57:16]; Heb. 12:9 [1]*oracle, prophecy*
2 [a]Is. 51:17 [1]Lit. *reeling*
3 [a]Zech. 12:4, 6, 8; 13:1 [b]Matt. 21:44
4 [a]Ps. 76:6; Ezek. 38:4
6 [a]Is. 10:17, 18; Obad. 18; Zech. 11:1

will seek to [a]destroy all the nations
that come against Jerusalem.

Mourning for the Pierced One

10 [a]"And I will pour on the house
of David and on the inhabitants of
Jerusalem the Spirit of grace and
supplication; then they will [b]look
on Me whom they pierced. Yes,
they will mourn for Him [c]as one
mourns for *his* only *son*, and
grieve for Him as one grieves for
a firstborn.
11 "In that day there shall be a
great [a]mourning in Jerusalem,
[b]like the mourning at Hadad Rimmon
in the plain of [1]Megiddo.
12 [a]"And the land shall mourn,
every family by itself: the family
of the house of David by itself, and
their wives by themselves; the
family of the house of [b]Nathan by
itself, and their wives by themselves;
13 "the family of the house of Levi
by itself, and their wives by themselves;
the family of Shimei by itself,
and their wives by themselves;
14 "all the families that remain,
every family by itself, and their
wives by themselves.

Idolatry Cut Off

13 "In that [a]day [b]a fountain
shall be opened for the house
of David and for the inhabitants
of Jerusalem, for sin and for [c]uncleanness.
2 "It shall be in that day," says
the LORD of hosts, "*that* I will [a]cut
off the names of the idols from the
land, and they shall no longer be
remembered. I will also cause [b]the
prophets and the unclean spirit to
depart from the land.
3 "It shall come to pass *that* if
anyone still prophesies, then his
father and mother who begot him
will say to him, 'You shall [a]not
live, because you have spoken lies
in the name of the LORD.' And his
father and mother who begot him
[b]shall thrust him through when he
prophesies.
4 "And it shall be in that day *that*
[a]every prophet will be ashamed of
his vision when he prophesies;
they will not wear [b]a robe of
coarse hair to deceive.
5 [a]"But he will say, 'I *am* no
prophet, I *am* a farmer; for a man
taught me to keep cattle from my
youth.'
6 "And *one* will say to him,
'What are these wounds between
your [1]arms?' Then he will answer,
'*Those* with which I was wounded
in the house of my friends.'

The Shepherd Savior

7 "Awake, O sword, against [a]My
Shepherd,
Against the Man [b]who is My
Companion,"
Says the LORD of hosts.
[c]"Strike the Shepherd,
And the sheep will be scattered;
Then I will turn My hand against
[d]the little ones.
8 And it shall come to pass in all
the land,"
Says the LORD,
"*That* [a]two-thirds in it shall be cut
off *and* die,
[b]But *one*-third shall be left in it:
9 I will bring the *one*-third [a]through
the fire,
Will [b]refine them as silver is
refined,
And test them as gold is tested.
[c]They will call on My name,
And I will answer them.
[d]I will say, 'This *is* My people';
And each one will say, 'The LORD
is my God.'"

The Day of the LORD

14 Behold, [a]the day of the LORD
is coming,
And your [1]spoil will be divided
in your midst.
2 For [a]I will gather all the nations
to battle against Jerusalem;
The city shall be taken,
The houses [1]rifled,
And the women ravished.
Half of the city shall go into
captivity,
But the remnant of the people
shall not be cut off from the
city.

3 Then the LORD will go forth
And fight against those nations,
As He fights in the day of battle.
4 And in that day His feet will stand
[a]on the Mount of Olives,
Which faces Jerusalem on the
east.
And the Mount of Olives shall be
split in two,
From east to west,
[b]*Making* a very large valley;

9 [a]Hag. 2:22
10 [a][Joel 2:28, 29] [b]John 19:34, 37; 20:27 [c]Jer. 6:26
11 [a][Rev. 1:7] [b]2 Kin. 23:29 [1]Heb. *Megiddon*
12 [a][Matt. 24:30] [b]Luke 3:31

CHAPTER 13

1 [a][Rev. 21:6, 7] [b][Heb. 9:14] [c]Ezek. 36:25
2 [a]Ex. 23:13 [b]Jer. 23:14, 15
3 [a]Deut. 18:20 [b]Deut. 13:6–11
4 [a][Mic. 3:6, 7] [b]2 Kin. 1:8
5 [a]Amos 7:14
6 [1]Or *hands*
7 [a]Is. 40:11 [b][John 10:30] [c]Matt. 26:31, 56, 67 [d]Luke 12:32
8 [a]Ezek. 5:2, 4, 12 [b][Rom. 11:5]
9 [a]Is. 48:10 [b]1 Pet. 1:6, 7 [c]Ps. 50:15 [d]Hos. 2:23

CHAPTER 14

1 [a][Is. 13:6, 9] [1]*plunder* or *booty*
2 [a]Zech. 12:2, 3 [1]Or *plundered*
4 [a]Ezek. 11:23 [b]Joel 3:12

Half of the mountain shall move
toward the north
And half of it toward the south.

5 Then you shall flee *through* My
mountain valley,
For the mountain valley shall
reach to Azal.
Yes, you shall flee
As you fled from the [a]earthquake
In the days of Uzziah king of
Judah.

[b]Thus the LORD my God will come,
And [c]all the saints with [1]You.

6 It shall come to pass in that day
That there will be no light;
The [1]lights will diminish.
7 It shall be one day
[a]Which is known to the LORD—
Neither day nor night.
But at [b]evening time it shall
happen
That it will be light.

8 And in that day it shall be
That living [a]waters shall flow
from Jerusalem,
Half of them toward [1]the eastern
sea
And half of them toward [2]the
western sea;
In both summer and winter it
shall occur.
9 And the LORD shall be [a]King over
all the earth.
In that day it shall be—
[b]"The LORD *is* one,"
And His name one.

10 All the land shall be turned into
a plain from Geba to Rimmon
south of Jerusalem. [1]*Jerusalem*
shall be raised up and [a]inhabited
in her place from Benjamin's Gate
to the place of the First Gate and
the Corner Gate, [b]and *from* the
Tower of Hananel to the king's
winepresses.

11 *The people* shall dwell in it;
And [a]no longer shall there be
utter destruction,
[b]But Jerusalem shall be safely
inhabited.

12 And this shall be the plague
with which the LORD will strike all
the people who fought against Je-
rusalem:

Their flesh shall [1]dissolve while
they stand on their feet,
Their eyes shall dissolve in their
sockets,
And their tongues shall dissolve
in their mouths.

13 It shall come to pass in that day
That [a]a great panic from the
LORD will be among them.
Everyone will seize the hand of
his neighbor,
And raise [b]his hand against his
neighbor's hand;
14 Judah also will fight at
Jerusalem.
[a]And the wealth of all the
surrounding nations
Shall be gathered together:
Gold, silver, and apparel in great
abundance.

15 [a]Such also shall be the plague
On the horse *and* the mule,
On the camel and the donkey,
And on all the cattle that will be
in those camps.
So *shall* this plague *be*.

The Nations Worship the King

16 And it shall come to pass *that*
everyone who is left of all the na-
tions which came against Jerusa-
lem shall [a]go up from year to year
to [b]worship the King, the LORD of
hosts, and to keep [c]the Feast of
Tabernacles.
17 [a]And it shall be *that* whichever
of the families of the earth do not
come up to Jerusalem to worship
the King, the LORD of hosts, on
them there will be no rain.
18 If the family of [a]Egypt will not
come up and enter in, [b]they *shall
have* no *rain;* they shall receive the
plague with which the LORD strikes
the nations who do not come up
to keep the Feast of Tabernacles.
19 This shall be the [1]punishment
of Egypt and the punishment of all
the nations that do not come up
to keep the Feast of Tabernacles.
20 In that day [a]"HOLINESS TO
THE LORD" shall be *engraved* on
the bells of the horses. The [b]pots
in the LORD's house shall be like
the bowls before the altar.
21 Yes, [1]every pot in Jerusalem
and Judah shall be holiness to the
LORD of hosts. Everyone who sac-
rifices shall come and take them
and cook in them. In that day there
shall no longer be a [a]Canaanite [b]in
the house of the LORD of hosts.

5 [a]Is. 29:6; Amos 1:1 [b][Ps. 96:13]; Is. 66:15, 16; Matt. 24:30, 31; 25:31; Jude 14 [c]Joel 3:11 [1]Or *you;* LXX, Tg., Vg. *Him*
6 [1]Lit. *glorious ones*
7 [a]Matt. 24:36 [b]Is. 30:26
8 [a]Ezek. 47:1–12; Joel 3:18; [John 7:38; Rev. 22:1, 2] [1]The Dead Sea [2]The Mediterranean Sea
9 [a][Jer. 23:5, 6; Rev. 11:15] [b][Eph. 4:5, 6]; Deut. 6:4
10 [a]Jer. 30:18; Zech. 12:6 [b]Neh. 3:1; Jer. 31:38 [1]Lit. *She*
11 [a]Jer. 31:40 [b]Jer. 23:6; Ezek. 34:25–28; Hos. 2:18
12 [1]Lit. *decay*
13 [a]1 Sam. 14:15, 20 [b]Judg. 7:22; 2 Chr. 20:23; Ezek. 38:21
14 [a]Ezek. 39:10, 17
15 [a]Zech. 14:12
16 [a][Is. 2:2, 3; 60:6–9; 66:18–21; Mic. 4:1, 2] [b]Is. 27:13 [c]Lev. 23:34–44; Neh. 8:14; Hos. 12:9; John 7:2
17 [a]Is. 60:12
18 [a]Is. 19:21 [b]Deut. 11:10
19 [1]Lit. *sin*
20 [a]Ex. 28:36; 39:30; Is. 23:18; Jer. 2:3 [b]Ezek. 46:20
21 [a]Is. 35:8; Ezek. 44:9; Joel 3:17; Rev. 21:27; 22:15 [b][Eph. 2:19–22] [1]Or *on every pot . . . shall be engraved "HOLINESS TO THE LORD OF HOSTS"*

The Book of

Malachi

MALACHI, a prophet in the days of Nehemiah, directs his message of judgment to a people plagued with corrupt priests, wicked practices, and a false sense of security in their privileged relationship with God. Using the question-and-answer method, Malachi probes deeply into their problems of hypocrisy, infidelity, mixed marriages, divorce, false worship, and arrogance. So sinful has the nation become that God's words to the people no longer have any impact. For four hundred years after Malachi's ringing condemnations, God remains silent. Only with the coming of John the Baptist (prophesied in 3:1) does God again communicate to His people through a prophet's voice.

The meaning of the name *Mal'aki* ("My Messenger") is probably a shortened form of *Mal'akya,* "Messenger of Yahweh," and it is appropriate to the book which speaks of the coming of the "messenger of the covenant" ("messenger" is mentioned three times in 2:7; 3:1). The Septuagint used the title *Malachias* even though it also translated it "by the hand of his messenger." The Latin title is *Maleachi.*

THE [1]burden of the word of the LORD to Israel [2]by Malachi.

Israel Beloved of God

2 "I[a] have loved you," says the
LORD.
"Yet you say, 'In what way have
You loved us?'
Was not Esau Jacob's brother?"
Says the LORD.
"Yet [b]Jacob I have loved;
3 But Esau I have hated,
And [a]laid waste his mountains
and his heritage
For the jackals of the
wilderness."

4 Even though Edom has said,
"We have been impoverished,
But we will return and build the
desolate places,"

Thus says the LORD of hosts:

"They may build, but I will [a]throw
down;
They shall be called the Territory
of Wickedness,
And the people against whom the
LORD will have indignation
forever.
5 Your eyes shall see,
And you shall say,
[a]'The LORD is magnified beyond
the border of Israel.'

Polluted Offerings

6 "A son [a]honors *his* father,
And a servant *his* master.
[b]If then I am the Father,
Where *is* My honor?
And if I *am* a Master,
Where *is* My reverence?
Says the LORD of hosts
To you priests who despise My
name.
[c]Yet you say, 'In what way have
we despised Your name?'

7 "You offer [a]defiled food on My
altar,
But say,
'In what way have we defiled
You?'
By saying,
[b]'The table of the LORD is
[1]contemptible.'
8 And [a]when you offer the blind as
a sacrifice,
Is it not evil?
And when you offer the lame and
sick,
Is it not evil?
Offer it then to your governor!
Would he be pleased with you?
Would he [b]accept[1] you
favorably?"
Says the LORD of hosts.

9 "But now entreat God's favor,
That He may be gracious to us.

CHAPTER 1

1 [1]*oracle, prophecy* [2]Lit. *by the hand of*

2 [a]Deut. 4:37; 7:8; 23:5; Is. 41:8, 9; [Jer. 31:3]; John 15:12 [b]Rom. 9:13

3 [a]Jer. 49:18; Ezek. 35:9, 15

4 [a]Jer. 49:16–18

5 [a]Ps. 35:27; Mic. 5:4

6 [a][Ex. 20:12]; Prov. 30:11, 17; [Matt. 15:4–8; Eph. 6:2, 3] [b][Is. 63:16; 64:8]; Jer. 31:9; Luke 6:46 [c]Mal. 2:14

7 [a]Deut. 15:21 [b]Ezek. 41:22 [1]Or *to be despised*

8 [a]Lev. 22:22; Deut. 15:19–23 [b][Job 42:8] [1]Lit. *lift up your face*

[a]*While* this is being *done* by your hands,
Will He accept you favorably?"
Says the LORD of hosts.
10 "Who *is there* even among you who would shut the doors,
[a]So that you would not kindle fire *on* My altar in vain?
I have no pleasure in you,"
Says the LORD of hosts,
[b]"Nor will I accept an offering from your hands.
11 For [a]from the rising of the sun, even to its going down,
My name *shall be* great [b]among the Gentiles;
[c]In every place [d]incense *shall be* offered to My name,
And a pure offering;
[e]For My name shall be great among the nations,"
Says the LORD of hosts.

12 "But you profane it,
In that you say,
[a]'The table of the [1]LORD is defiled;
And its fruit, its food, *is* contemptible.'
13 You also say,
'Oh, what a [a]weariness!'
And you sneer at it,"
Says the LORD of hosts.
"And you bring the stolen, the lame, and the sick;
Thus you bring an offering!
[b]Should I accept this from your hand?"
Says the LORD.
14 "But cursed *be* [a]the deceiver
Who has in his flock a male,
And takes a vow,
But sacrifices to the Lord [b]what is blemished—
For [c]I *am* a great King,"
Says the LORD of hosts,
"And My name *is to be* feared among the nations.

Corrupt Priests

2 "And now, O [a]priests, this commandment is for you.
2 [a]If you will not hear,
And if you will not take *it* to heart,
To give glory to My name,"
Says the LORD of hosts,
"I will send a curse upon you,
And I will curse your blessings.
Yes, I have cursed them [b]already,
Because you do not take *it* to heart.

3 "Behold, I will rebuke your descendants
And spread [a]refuse on your faces,
The refuse of your solemn feasts;
And *one* will [b]take you away [1]with it.
4 Then you shall know that I have sent this commandment to you,
That My covenant with Levi may continue,"
Says the LORD of hosts.
5 "My[a] covenant was with him, *one* of life and peace,
And I gave them to him [b]*that he might* fear *Me;*
So he feared Me
And was reverent before My name.
6 [a]The[1] law of truth was in his mouth,
And [2]injustice was not found on his lips.
He walked with Me in peace and equity,
And [b]turned many away from iniquity.

7 "For[a] the lips of a priest should keep knowledge,
And *people* should seek the law from his mouth;
[b]For he is the messenger of the LORD of hosts.
8 But you have departed from the way;
You [a]have caused many to stumble at the law.
[b]You have corrupted the covenant of Levi,"
Says the LORD of hosts.
9 "Therefore [a]I also have made you contemptible and base
Before all the people,
Because you have not kept My ways
But have shown [b]partiality in the law."

Treachery of Infidelity

10 [a]Have we not all one Father?
[b]Has not one God created us?
Why do we deal treacherously with one another
By profaning the covenant of the fathers?
11 Judah has dealt treacherously,
And an abomination has been committed in Israel and in Jerusalem,
For Judah has [a]profaned
The LORD's holy *institution* which He loves:
He has married the daughter of a foreign god.
12 May the LORD cut off from the tents of Jacob
The man who does this, being [1]awake and aware,

9 [a]Hos. 13:9
10 [a]1 Cor. 9:13 [b]Is. 1:11
11 [a]Is. 59:19 [b]Is. 60:3, 5 [c]1 Tim. 2:8 [d]Rev. 8:3 [e]Is. 66:18, 19
12 [a]Mal. 1:7 [1]So with Bg.; MT *Lord*
13 [a]Is. 43:22 [b]Lev. 22:20
14 [a]Mal. 1:8 [b]Lev. 22:18–20 [c]Ps. 47:2

CHAPTER 2

1 [a]Mal. 1:6
2 [a][Lev. 26:14, 15; Deut. 28:15] [b]Mal. 3:9
3 [a]Ex. 29:14 [b]1 Kin. 14:10 [1]Lit. *to it*
5 [a]Num. 25:12; Ezek. 34:25 [b]Deut. 33:9
6 [a]Deut. 33:10 [b]Jer. 23:22; [James 5:20] [1]Or *True instruction* [2]Or *unrighteousness*
7 [a]Num. 27:21; Deut. 17:8–11; Jer. 18:18 [b][Gal. 4:14]
8 [a]Jer. 18:15 [b]Num. 25:12, 13; Neh. 13:29; Ezek. 44:10
9 [a]1 Sam. 2:30 [b]Deut. 1:17; Mic. 3:11; 1 Tim. 5:21
10 [a]Jer. 31:9; 1 Cor. 8:6; [Eph. 4:6] [b]Job 31:15
11 [a]Ezra 9:1, 2; Neh. 13:23
12 [1]Talmud, Vg. *teacher and student*

Yet [a]who brings an offering to the
LORD of hosts!

13 And this is the second thing you
do:
You cover the altar of the LORD
with tears,
With weeping and crying;
So He does not regard the
offering anymore,
Nor receive *it* with goodwill from
your hands.
14 Yet you say, "For what
reason?"
Because the LORD has been
witness
Between you and [a]the wife of
your youth,
With whom you have dealt
treacherously;
[b]Yet she is your companion
And your wife by covenant.
15 But [a]did He not make *them* one,
Having a remnant of the Spirit?
And why one?
He seeks [b]godly offspring.
Therefore take heed to your
spirit,
And let none deal treacherously
with the wife of his youth.

16 "For [a]the LORD God of Israel says
That He hates divorce,
For it covers one's garment with
violence,"
Says the LORD of hosts.
"Therefore take heed to your
spirit,
That you do not deal
treacherously."

17 [a]You have wearied the LORD with
your words;
Yet you say,
"In what way have we wearied
Him?"
In that you say,
[b]"Everyone who does evil
Is good in the sight of the LORD,
And He delights in them,"
Or, "Where *is* the God of justice?"

The Coming Messenger

3 "Behold, [a]I send My messenger,
And he will [b]prepare the way
before Me.
And the Lord, whom you seek,
Will suddenly come to His
temple,
[c]Even the Messenger of the
covenant,
In whom you delight.
Behold, [d]He is coming,"
Says the LORD of hosts.

2 "But who can endure [a]the day of
His coming?
And [b]who can stand when He
appears?
For [c]He *is* like a refiner's fire
And like launderers' soap.
3 [a]He will sit as a refiner and a
purifier of silver;
He will purify the sons of Levi,
And [1]purge them as gold and
silver,
That they may [b]offer to the LORD
An offering in righteousness.

4 "Then [a]the offering of Judah and
Jerusalem
Will be [1]pleasant to the LORD,
As in the days of old,
As in former years.
5 And I will come near you for
judgment;
I will be a swift witness
Against sorcerers,
Against adulterers,
[a]Against perjurers,
Against those who [b]exploit wage
earners and [c]widows and
orphans,
And against those who turn away
an alien—
Because they do not fear Me,"
Says the LORD of hosts.

6 "For I *am* the LORD, [a]I do not
change;
[b]Therefore you are not consumed,
O sons of Jacob.
7 Yet from the days of [a]your
fathers
You have gone away from My
ordinances
And have not kept *them.*
[b]Return to Me, and I will return
to you,"
Says the LORD of hosts.
[c]"But you said,
'In what way shall we return?'

Do Not Rob God

8 "Will a man rob God?
Yet you have robbed Me!
But you say,
'In what way have we robbed
You?'
[a]In tithes and offerings.
9 You are cursed with a curse,
For you have robbed Me,
Even this whole nation.
10 [a]Bring all the tithes into the
[b]storehouse,
That there may be food in My
house,
And try Me now in this,"
Says the LORD of hosts,

12 [a]Neh. 13:29
14 [a]Prov. 5:18; Jer. 9:2; Mal. 3:5 [b]Prov. 2:17
15 [a]Gen. 2:24; Matt. 19:4, 5 [b]Ezra 9:2; [1 Cor. 7:14]
16 [a]Deut. 24:1; [Matt. 5:31; 19:6–8]
17 [a]Is. 43:22, 24 [b]Is. 5:20; Zeph. 1:12

CHAPTER 3

1 [a]Matt. 11:10; Mark 1:2; Luke 1:76; 7:27; John 1:23; 2:14, 15 [b][Is. 40:3] [c]Is. 63:9 [d]Hab. 2:7
2 [a]Jer. 10:10; Joel 2:11; Nah. 1:6; [Mal. 4:1] [b]Is. 33:14; Ezek. 22:14; Rev. 6:17 [c]Is. 4:4; Zech. 13:9; [Matt. 3:10–12; 1 Cor. 3:13–15]
3 [a]Is. 1:25; Dan. 12:10; Zech. 13:9 [b][1 Pet. 2:5] [1]Or *refine*
4 [a]Mal. 1:11 [1]*pleasing*
5 [a]Lev. 19:12; Zech. 5:4; [James 5:12] [b]Lev. 19:13; James 5:4 [c]Ex. 22:22
6 [a][Num. 23:19; Rom. 11:29; James 1:17] [b][Lam. 3:22]
7 [a]Acts 7:51 [b]Zech. 1:3 [c]Mal. 1:6
8 [a]Neh. 13:10–12
10 [a]Prov. 3:9, 10 [b]1 Chr. 26:20

"If I will not open for you the
[c]windows of heaven
And [d]pour out for you such
blessing
That *there will* not *be room*
enough *to receive it.*

11 "And I will rebuke [a]the devourer
for your sakes,
So that he will not destroy the
fruit of your ground,
Nor shall the vine fail to bear fruit
for you in the field,"
Says the LORD of hosts;
12 "And all nations will call you
blessed,
For you will be [a]a delightful
land,"
Says the LORD of hosts.

The People Complain Harshly

13 "Your[a] words have been [1]harsh
against Me,"
Says the LORD,
"Yet you say,
'What have we spoken against
You?'
14 [a]You have said,
'It is useless to serve God;
What profit *is it* that we have kept
His ordinance,
And that we have walked as
mourners
Before the LORD of hosts?
15 So now [a]we call the proud
blessed,
For those who do wickedness are
[1]raised up;
They even [b]tempt God and go
free.' "

A Book of Remembrance

16 Then those [a]who feared the LORD
[b]spoke to one another,
And the LORD listened and heard
them;
So [c]a book of remembrance was
written before Him
For those who fear the LORD
And who [1]meditate on His name.

17 "They[a] shall be Mine," says the
LORD of hosts,
"On the day that I make them My
[b]jewels.[1]
And [c]I will spare them
As a man spares his own son who
serves him."
18 [a]Then you shall again discern
Between the righteous and the
wicked,
Between one who serves God
And one who does not serve Him.

The Great Day of God

4 "For behold, [a]the day is coming,
Burning like an oven,
And all [b]the proud, yes, all who
do wickedly will be [c]stubble.
And the day which is coming
shall burn them up,"
Says the LORD of hosts,
"That will [d]leave them neither root
nor branch.
2 But to you who [a]fear My
name
The [b]Sun of Righteousness shall
arise
With healing in His wings;
And you shall go out
And grow fat like stall-fed
calves.
3 [a]You shall trample the wicked,
For they shall be ashes under the
soles of your feet
On the day that I do *this,*"
Says the LORD of hosts.

4 "Remember the [a]Law of Moses,
My servant,
Which I commanded him in
Horeb for all Israel,
With [b]*the* statutes and
judgments.
5 Behold, I will send you [a]Elijah the
prophet
[b]Before the coming of the great
and dreadful day of the
LORD.
6 And he will turn
The hearts of the fathers to the
children,
And the hearts of the children to
their fathers,
Lest I come and [a]strike the earth
with [b]a curse."

10 [c]Gen. 7:11 [d]2 Chr. 31:10
11 [a]Amos 4:9
12 [a]Dan. 8:9
13 [a]Mal. 2:17 [1]Lit. *strong*
14 [a]Job 21:14
15 [a]Ps. 73:12 [b]Ps. 95:9 [1]Lit. *built*
16 [a]Ps. 66:16 [b]Heb. 3:13 [c]Ps. 56:8 [1]Or *esteem*
17 [a]Ex. 19:5; Deut. 7:6; Is. 43:21; [1 Pet. 2:9] [b]Is. 62:3 [c]Ps. 103:13 [1]Lit. *special treasure*
18 [a][Ps. 58:11]

CHAPTER 4

1 [a]Ps. 21:9; [Nah. 1:5, 6; Mal. 3:2, 3; 2 Pet. 3:7] [b]Mal. 3:18 [c]Is. 5:24; Obad. 18 [d]Amos 2:9
2 [a]Mal. 3:16 [b]Matt. 4:16; Luke 1:78; Acts 10:43; 2 Cor. 4:6; Eph. 5:14
3 [a]Mic. 7:10
4 [a]Ex. 20:3 [b]Deut. 4:10
5 [a][Matt. 11:14; 17:10–13; Mark 9:11–13; Luke 1:17]; John 1:21 [b]Joel 2:31
6 [a]Zech. 14:12 [b]Zech. 5:3

The
New Testament

Words of Christ in Red

The Gospel According to

Matthew

MATTHEW is the gospel written by a Jew to Jews about a Jew. Matthew is the writer, his countrymen are the readers, and Jesus Christ is the subject. Matthew's design is to present Jesus as the King of the Jews, the long-awaited Messiah. Through a carefully selected series of Old Testament quotations, Matthew documents Jesus Christ's claim to be the Messiah. His genealogy, baptism, messages, and miracles all point to the same inescapable conclusion: Christ is King. Even in His death, seeming defeat is turned to victory by the Resurrection, and the message again echoes forth: the King of the Jews lives.

At an early date this gospel was given the title *Kata Matthaion,* "According to Matthew." As this title suggests, other gospel accounts were known at that time (the word "Gospel" was added later). Matthew ("Gift of the Lord") was also surnamed Levi (Mark 2:14; Luke 5:27).

CHAPTER 1

The Genealogy of Jesus Christ

THE book of the [a]genealogy[1] of
Jesus Christ, [b]the Son of David,
[c]the Son of Abraham:
2 [a]Abraham begot Isaac, [b]Isaac
begot Jacob, and Jacob begot [c]Ju-
dah and his brothers.
3 [a]Judah begot Perez and Zerah
by Tamar, [b]Perez begot Hezron,
and Hezron begot Ram.
4 Ram begot Amminadab, Am-
minadab begot Nahshon, and
Nahshon begot Salmon.
5 Salmon begot [a]Boaz by Rahab,
Boaz begot Obed by Ruth, Obed
begot Jesse,
6 and [a]Jesse begot David the
king.
[b]David the king begot Solomon
by her [1]*who had been the wife* of
Uriah.
7 [a]Solomon begot Rehoboam,
Rehoboam begot [b]Abijah, and
Abijah begot [1]Asa.
8 Asa begot [a]Jehoshaphat, Je-
hoshaphat begot Joram, and
Joram begot [b]Uzziah.
9 Uzziah begot Jotham, Jotham
begot [a]Ahaz, and Ahaz begot
Hezekiah.
10 [a]Hezekiah begot Manasseh,
Manasseh begot [1]Amon, and
Amon begot [b]Josiah.
11 [a]Josiah begot [1]Jeconiah and his
brothers about the time they were
[b]carried away to Babylon.
12 And after they were brought to
Babylon, [a]Jeconiah begot Sheal-
tiel, and Shealtiel begot [b]Zerub-
babel.
13 Zerubbabel begot Abiud,
Abiud begot Eliakim, and Eliakim
begot Azor.
14 Azor begot Zadok, Zadok be-
got Achim, and Achim begot Eliud.
15 Eliud begot Eleazar, Eleazar
begot Matthan, and Matthan begot
Jacob.
16 And Jacob begot Joseph the
husband of [a]Mary, of whom was
born Jesus who is called Christ.
17 So all the generations from
Abraham to David *are* fourteen
generations, from David until the
captivity in Babylon *are* fourteen
generations, and from the captiv-
ity in Babylon until the Christ *are*
fourteen generations.

Christ Born of Mary

18 Now the [a]birth of Jesus Christ
was as follows: After His mother
Mary was betrothed to Joseph, be-
fore they came together, she was
found with child [b]of the Holy
Spirit.
19 Then Joseph her husband, be-
ing [1]a just *man,* and not wanting
[a]to make her a public example,
was minded to put her away se-
cretly.
20 But while he thought about
these things, behold, an angel of
the Lord appeared to him in a

---

1 [a]Luke 3:23 [b]John 7:42 [c]Gen. 12:3; 22:18 [1]Lit. *generation*
2 [a]Gen. 21:2, 12 [b]Gen. 25:26; 28:14 [c]Gen. 29:35
3 [a]Gen. 38:27; 49:10 [b]Ruth 4:18–22
5 [a]Ruth 2:1; 4:1–13
6 [a]1 Sam. 16:1 [b]2 Sam. 7:12; 12:24 [1]Words in italic type have been added for clarity. They are not found in the original Greek.
7 [a]1 Chr. 3:10 [b]2 Chr. 11:20 [1]NU *Asaph*
8 [a]1 Chr. 3:10 [b]2 Kin. 15:13
9 [a]2 Kin. 15:38
10 [a]2 Kin. 20:21 [b]1 Kin. 13:2 [1]NU *Amos*
11 [a]1 Chr. 3:15, 16 [b]2 Kin. 24:14–16 [1]Or *Coniah* or *Jehoiachin*
12 [a]1 Chr. 3:17 [b]Ezra 3:2
16 [a]Matt. 13:55
18 [a]Luke 1:27 [b]Luke 1:35
19 [a]Deut. 24:1 [1]*an upright*

dream, saying, "Joseph, son of Da-
vid, do not be afraid to take to you
Mary your wife, [a]for that which is
[1]conceived in her is of the Holy
Spirit.
21 [a]"And she will bring forth a
Son, and you shall call His name
[1]JESUS, [b]for He will save His people
from their sins."
22 So all this was done that it
might be fulfilled which was spo-
ken by the Lord through the
prophet, saying:
23 [a]*"Behold,*[1] *the virgin shall be
with child, and bear a Son, and
they shall call His name Imman-
uel,"* which is translated, "God
with us."
24 Then Joseph, being aroused
from sleep, did as the angel of the
Lord commanded him and took to
him his wife,
25 and [1]did not know her till she
had brought forth [a]her[2] firstborn
Son. And he called His name
JESUS.

Wise Men from the East

2 Now after [a]Jesus was born in
Bethlehem of Judea in the days
of Herod the king, behold, [1]wise
men [b]from the East came to Jeru-
salem,
2 saying, [a]"Where is He who has
been born King of the Jews? For
we have seen [b]His star in the
East and have come to worship
Him."
3 When Herod the king heard
this, he was troubled, and all Jeru-
salem with him.
4 And when he had gathered all
[a]the chief priests and [b]scribes of
the people together, [c]he inquired
of them where the Christ was to
be born.
5 So they said to him, "In Bethle-
hem of Judea, for thus it is written
by the prophet:

6 *'But[a] you, Bethlehem, in the land
of Judah,
Are not the least among the
rulers of Judah;
For out of you shall come a Ruler
[b] Who will shepherd My people
Israel.'"*

7 Then Herod, when he had se-
cretly called the [1]wise men, deter-
mined from them what time the
[a]star appeared.
8 And he sent them to Bethlehem
and said, "Go and search carefully
for the young Child, and when you
have found *Him,* bring back word
to me, that I may come and wor-
ship Him also."
9 When they heard the king, they
departed; and behold, the star
which they had seen in the East
went before them, till it came and
stood over where the young Child
was.
10 When they saw the star, they
rejoiced with exceedingly great
joy.
11 And when they had come into
the house, they saw the young
Child with Mary His mother, and
fell down and worshiped Him. And
when they had opened their
treasures, [a]they presented gifts
to Him: gold, frankincense, and
myrrh.
12 Then, being divinely warned
[a]in a dream that they should not
return to Herod, they departed for
their own country another way.

The Flight into Egypt

13 Now when they had departed,
behold, an angel of the Lord ap-
peared to Joseph in a dream, say-
ing, "Arise, take the young Child
and His mother, flee to Egypt, and
stay there until I bring you word;
for Herod will seek the young
Child to destroy Him."
14 When he arose, he took the
young Child and His mother by
night and departed for Egypt,
15 and was there until the death
of Herod, that it might be fulfilled
which was spoken by the Lord
through the prophet, saying, [a]*"Out
of Egypt I called My Son."*

Massacre of the Innocents

16 Then Herod, when he saw that
he was deceived by the wise men,
was exceedingly angry; and he
sent forth and put to death all the
male children who were in Bethle-
hem and in all its districts, from
two years old and under, accord-
ing to the time which he had deter-
mined from the wise men.
17 Then was fulfilled what was
spoken by Jeremiah the prophet,
saying:

20 [a]Luke 1:35 [1]Lit. *begotten*

21 [a][Is. 7:14; 9:6, 7]; Luke 1:31; 2:21 [b]Luke 2:11; John 1:29; [Acts 4:12; 5:31; 13:23, 38; Rom. 5:18, 19; Col. 1:20–23] [1]Lit. *Savior*

23 [a]Is. 7:14 [1]Words in oblique type in the New Testament are quoted from the Old Testament.

25 [a]Ex. 13:2; Luke 2:7, 21 [1]Kept her a virgin [2]NU *a Son*

CHAPTER 2

1 [a]Mic. 5:2; Luke 2:4–7 [b]Gen. 25:6; 1 Kin. 4:30 [1]Gr. *magoi*

2 [a]Luke 2:11 [b][Num. 24:17; Is. 60:3]

4 [a]2 Chr. 36:14 [b]2 Chr. 34:13 [c]Mal. 2:7

6 [a]Mic. 5:2; John 7:42 [b]Gen. 49:10; [Rev. 2:27]

7 [a]Num. 24:17 [1]Gr. *magoi*

11 [a]Ps. 72:10; Is. 60:6

12 [a][Job 33:15, 16]; Matt. 1:20

15 [a]Num. 24:8; Hos. 11:1

18 *"A [a]voice was heard in Ramah,*
Lamentation, weeping, and *great*
mourning,
Rachel weeping for her children,
Refusing to be comforted,
Because they are no more."

The Home in Nazareth

19 Now when Herod was dead,
behold, an angel of the Lord ap-
peared in a dream to Joseph in
Egypt,
20 [a]saying, "Arise, take the young
Child and His mother, and go to
the land of Israel, for those who
[b]sought the young Child's life are
dead."
21 Then he arose, took the young
Child and His mother, and came
into the land of Israel.
22 But when he heard that Arche-
laus was reigning over Judea in-
stead of his father Herod, he was
afraid to go there. And being
warned by God in a [a]dream, he
turned aside [b]into the region of
Galilee.
23 And he came and dwelt in a
city called [a]Nazareth, that it might
be fulfilled [b]which was spoken by
the prophets, "He shall be called
a Nazarene."

John the Baptist Prepares the Way

3 In those days [a]John the Baptist
came preaching [b]in the wilder-
ness of Judea,
2 and saying, "Repent, for [a]the
kingdom of heaven is at hand!"
3 For this is he who was spoken
of by the prophet Isaiah, saying:

[a]*"The voice of one crying in the*
wilderness:
[b]*'Prepare the way of the* LORD;
Make His paths straight.'"

4 Now [a]John himself was clothed
in camel's hair, with a leather belt
around his waist; and his food was
[b]locusts and [c]wild honey.
5 [a]Then Jerusalem, all Judea,
and all the region around the Jor-
dan went out to him
6 [a]and were baptized by him in
the Jordan, confessing their sins.
7 But when he saw many of the
Pharisees and Sadducees coming
to his baptism, he said to them,
[a]"Brood of vipers! Who warned
you to flee from [b]the wrath to
come?
8 "Therefore bear fruits worthy
of repentance,
9 "and do not think to say to
yourselves, [a]'We have Abraham as
our father.' For I say to you that
God is able to raise up children to
Abraham from these stones.
10 "And even now the ax is laid
to the root of the trees. [a]Therefore
every tree which does not bear
good fruit is cut down and thrown
into the fire.
11 [a]"I indeed baptize you with wa-
ter unto repentance, but He who
is coming after me is mightier than
I, whose sandals I am not worthy
to carry. [b]He will baptize you with
the Holy Spirit [1]and fire.
12 [a]"His winnowing fan *is* in His
hand, and He will thoroughly
clean out His threshing floor, and
gather His wheat into the barn; but
He will [b]burn up the chaff with un-
quenchable fire."

John Baptizes Jesus

13 [a]Then Jesus came [b]from Gali-
lee to John at the Jordan to be bap-
tized by him.
14 And John *tried to* prevent Him,
saying, "I need to be baptized by
You, and are You coming to me?"
15 But Jesus answered and said to
him, "Permit *it to be* so now, for
thus it is fitting for us to fulfill all
righteousness." Then he allowed
Him.
16 [a]When He had been baptized,
Jesus came up immediately from
the water; and behold, the heavens
were opened to Him, and [1]He saw
[b]the Spirit of God descending like
a dove and alighting upon Him.
17 [a]And suddenly a voice *came*
from heaven, saying, [b]"This is My
beloved Son, in whom I am well
pleased."

Satan Tempts Jesus

4 Then [a]Jesus was led up by [b]the
Spirit into the wilderness to be
tempted by the devil.
2 And when He had fasted forty
days and forty nights, afterward
He was hungry.
3 Now when the tempter came to
Him, he said, "If You are the Son
of God, command that these stones
become bread."

18 [a]Jer. 31:15
20 [a]Luke 2:39 [b]Matt. 2:16
22 [a]Matt. 2:12, 13, 19 [b]Luke 2:39
23 [a]John 1:45, 46 [b]Judg. 13:5

CHAPTER 3

1 [a]Mark 1:3–8 [b]Josh. 14:10
2 [a]Dan. 2:44
3 [a]Is. 40:3 [b]Luke 1:76
4 [a]Mark 1:6 [b]Lev. 11:22 [c]1 Sam. 14:25, 26
5 [a]Mark 1:5
6 [a]Acts 19:4, 18
7 [a]Matt. 12:34 [b][1 Thess. 1:10]
9 [a]John 8:33
10 [a]Matt. 7:19
11 [a]Luke 3:16 [b][Acts 2:3, 4] [1]M omits *and fire*
12 [a]Mal. 3:3 [b]Matt. 13:30
13 [a]Mark 1:9–11 [b]Matt. 2:22
16 [a]Mark 1:10 [b]John 1:32 [1]Or *he*
17 [a]John 12:28 [b]Ps. 2:7

CHAPTER 4

1 [a]Mark 1:12 [b]Ezek. 3:14

4 But He answered and said, "It
is written, [a]*'Man shall not live by
bread alone, but by every word
that proceeds from the mouth of
God.'* "
5 Then the devil took Him up
[a]into the holy city, set Him on the
pinnacle of the temple,
6 and said to Him, "If You are
the Son of God, throw Yourself
down. For it is written:

[a]*'He shall give His angels charge*
over you,'

and,

[b]*'In their hands they shall bear you*
up,
Lest you dash your foot against
a stone.' "

7 Jesus said to him, "It is written
again, [a]*'You shall not* [1]*tempt the*
LORD your God.' "
8 Again, the devil took Him up
on an exceedingly high mountain,
and [a]showed Him all the kingdoms
of the world and their glory.
9 And he said to Him, "All these
things I will give You if You will
fall down and worship me."
10 Then Jesus said to him,
[1]"Away with you, Satan! For it is
written, [a]*'You shall worship the*
LORD your God, and Him only you
shall serve.' "
11 Then the devil [a]left Him, and
behold, [b]angels came and minis-
tered to Him.

Jesus Begins His Galilean Ministry

12 [a]Now when Jesus heard that
John had been put in prison, He
departed to Galilee.
13 And leaving Nazareth, He
came and dwelt in Capernaum,
which is by the sea, in the regions
of Zebulun and Naphtali,
14 that it might be fulfilled which
was spoken by Isaiah the prophet,
saying:

15 *"The*[a] *land of Zebulun and the*
land of Naphtali,
By the way of the sea, beyond the
Jordan,
Galilee of the Gentiles:
16 [a]*The people who sat in darkness*
have seen a great light,
And upon those who sat in the
region and shadow of death
Light has dawned."

17 [a]From that time Jesus began to
preach and to say, [b]"Repent, for
the kingdom of heaven [1]is at
hand."

Four Fishermen Called as Disciples

18 [a]And Jesus, walking by the Sea
of Galilee, saw two brothers, Si-
mon [b]called Peter, and Andrew his
brother, casting a net into the sea;
for they were fishermen.
19 Then He said to them, "Follow
Me, and [a]I will make you fishers
of men."
20 [a]They immediately left *their*
nets and followed Him.
21 [a]Going on from there, He saw
two other brothers, James *the son*
of Zebedee, and John his brother,
in the boat with Zebedee their fa-
ther, mending their nets. He called
them,
22 and immediately they left the
boat and their father, and followed
Him.

Jesus Heals a Great Multitude

23 And Jesus went about all Gali-
lee, [a]teaching in their synagogues,
preaching [b]the gospel of the king-
dom, [c]and healing all kinds of sick-
ness and all kinds of disease
among the people.
24 Then [1]His fame went through-
out all Syria; and they [a]brought to
Him all sick people who were af-
flicted with various diseases and
torments, and those who were
demon-possessed, epileptics, and
paralytics; and He healed them.
25 [a]Great multitudes followed
Him—from Galilee, and *from*
[1]Decapolis, Jerusalem, Judea, and
beyond the Jordan.

The Beatitudes

5 And seeing the multitudes, [a]He
went up on a mountain, and
when He was seated His disciples
came to Him.
2 Then He opened His mouth and
[a]taught them, saying:

3 "Blessed[a] *are* the poor in spirit,
For theirs is the kingdom of
heaven.

4 [a]Deut. 8:3
5 [a]Neh. 11:1, 18
6 [a]Ps. 91:11 [b]Ps. 91:12
7 [a]Deut. 6:16 [1]*test*
8 [a][1 John 2:15–17]
10 [a]Deut. 6:13; 10:20 [1]M *Get behind Me*
11 [a][James 4:7] [b][Heb. 1:14]
12 [a]John 4:43
15 [a]Is. 9:1, 2
16 [a]Luke 2:32
17 [a]Mark 1:14, 15 [b]Matt. 3:2; 10:7 [1]*has drawn near*
18 [a]Mark 1:16–20 [b]John 1:40–42
19 [a]Luke 5:10
20 [a]Mark 10:28
21 [a]Mark 1:19
23 [a]Matt. 9:35 [b][Matt. 24:14] [c]Mark 1:34
24 [a]Luke 4:40 [1]Lit. *the report of Him*
25 [a]Mark 3:7, 8 [1]Lit. *Ten Cities*

CHAPTER 5

1 [a]Mark 3:13
2 [a][Matt. 7:29]
3 [a]Luke 6:20–23

4 [a]Blessed *are* those who mourn,
For they shall be comforted.
5 [a]Blessed *are* the meek,
For [b]they shall inherit the [1]earth.
6 Blessed *are* those who [a]hunger and thirst for righteousness,
[b]For they shall be filled.
7 Blessed *are* the merciful,
[a]For they shall obtain mercy.
8 [a]Blessed *are* the pure in heart,
For [b]they shall see God.
9 Blessed *are* the peacemakers,
For they shall be called sons of God.
10 [a]Blessed *are* those who are persecuted for righteousness' sake,
For theirs is the kingdom of heaven.

11 [a]"Blessed are you when they revile and persecute you, and say all kinds of [b]evil against you falsely for My sake.
12 [a]"Rejoice and be exceedingly glad, for great *is* your reward in heaven, for [b]so they persecuted the prophets who were before you.

Believers Are Salt and Light

13 "You are the salt of the earth; [a]but if the salt loses its flavor, how shall it be seasoned? It is then good for nothing but to be thrown out and trampled underfoot by men.
14 [a]"You are the light of the world. A city that is set on a hill cannot be hidden.
15 "Nor do they [a]light a lamp and put it under a basket, but on a lampstand, and it gives light to all *who are* in the house.
16 "Let your light so shine before men, [a]that they may see your good works and [b]glorify your Father in heaven.

Christ Fulfills the Law

17 [a]"Do not think that I came to destroy the Law or the Prophets. I did not come to destroy but to fulfill.
18 "For assuredly, I say to you, [a]till heaven and earth pass away, one [1]jot or one [2]tittle will by no means pass from the law till all is fulfilled.
19 [a]"Whoever therefore breaks one of the least of these commandments, and teaches men so, shall be called least in the kingdom of heaven; but whoever does and teaches *them,* he shall be called great in the kingdom of heaven.
20 "For I say to you, that unless your righteousness exceeds [a]*the righteousness* of the scribes and Pharisees, you will by no means enter the kingdom of heaven.

Murder Begins in the Heart

21 "You have heard that it was said to those [1]of old, [a]*'You shall not murder,* and whoever murders will be in danger of the judgment.'
22 "But I say to you that [a]whoever is angry with his brother [1]without a cause shall be in danger of the judgment. And whoever says to his brother, [b]'Raca!'[2] shall be in danger of the council. But whoever says, [3]'You fool!' shall be in danger of [4]hell fire.
23 "Therefore [a]if you bring your gift to the altar, and there remember that your brother has something against you,
24 [a]"leave your gift there before the altar, and go your way. First be reconciled to your brother, and then come and offer your gift.
25 [a]"Agree with your adversary quickly, [b]while you are on the way with him, lest your adversary deliver you to the judge, the judge hand you over to the officer, and you be thrown into prison.
26 "Assuredly, I say to you, you will by no means get out of there till you have paid the last penny.

Adultery in the Heart

27 "You have heard that it was said [1]to those of old, [a]*'You shall not commit adultery.'*
28 "But I say to you that whoever [a]looks at a woman to lust for her has already committed adultery with her in his heart.
29 [a]"If your right eye causes you to [1]sin, [b]pluck it out and cast *it* from you; for it is more profitable for you that one of your members perish, than for your whole body to be cast into hell.
30 "And if your right hand causes you to [1]sin, cut it off and cast *it* from you; for it is more profitable for you that one of your members perish, than for your whole body to be cast into hell.

4 [a]Rev. 21:4
5 [a]Ps. 37:11 [b][Rom. 4:13] [1]Or *land*
6 [a]Luke 1:53 [b][Is. 55:1; 65:13]
7 [a]Ps. 41:1
8 [a]Ps. 15:2; 24:4 [b]1 Cor. 13:12
10 [a]1 Pet. 3:14
11 [a]Luke 6:22 [b]1 Pet. 4:14
12 [a]1 Pet. 4:13, 14 [b]Acts 7:52
13 [a]Luke 14:34
14 [a][John 8:12]
15 [a]Luke 8:16
16 [a]1 Pet. 2:12 [b][John 15:8]
17 [a]Rom. 10:4
18 [a]Luke 16:17 [1]Gr. *iota,* Heb. *yod,* the smallest letter [2]The smallest stroke in a Heb. letter
19 [a][James 2:10]
20 [a][Rom. 10:3]
21 [a]Ex. 20:13; Deut. 5:17 [1]*in ancient times*
22 [a][1 John 3:15] [b][James 2:20; 3:6] [1]NU omits *without a cause* [2]Lit., in Aram., *Empty head* [3]Gr. *More* [4]Gr. *Gehenna*
23 [a]Matt. 8:4
24 [a][Job 42:8]
25 [a]Luke 12:58, 59 [b][Is. 55:6]
27 [a]Ex. 20:14; Deut. 5:18 [1]NU, M omit *to those of old*
28 [a]Prov. 6:25
29 [a]Mark 9:43 [b][Col. 3:5] [1]Lit. *stumble* or *offend*
30 [1]Lit. *stumble* or *offend*

Marriage Is Sacred and Binding

31 "Furthermore it has been said, [a]'Whoever divorces his wife, let him give her a certificate of divorce.'

32 "But I say to you that [a]whoever divorces his wife for any reason except [1]sexual immorality causes her to commit adultery; and whoever marries a woman who is divorced commits adultery.

Jesus Forbids Oaths

33 "Again you have heard that [a]it was said to those of [1]old, [b]'You shall not swear falsely, but [c]shall perform your oaths to the Lord.'

34 "But I say to you, [a]do not swear at all: neither by heaven, for it is [b]God's throne;

35 "nor by the earth, for it is His footstool; nor by Jerusalem, for it is the city of [a]the great King.

36 "Nor shall you swear by your head, because you cannot make one hair white or black.

37 [a]"But let [1]your 'Yes' be 'Yes,' and your 'No,' 'No.' For whatever is more than these is from the evil one.

Go the Second Mile

38 "You have heard that it was said, [a]*'An eye for an eye and a tooth for a tooth.'*

39 [a]"But I tell you not to resist an evil person. [b]But whoever slaps you on your right cheek, turn the other to him also.

40 "If anyone wants to sue you and take away your tunic, let him have *your* cloak also.

41 "And whoever [a]compels you to go one mile, go with him two.

42 "Give to him who asks you, and [a]from him who wants to borrow from you do not turn away.

Love Your Enemies

43 "You have heard that it was said, [a]*'You shall love your neighbor* [b]and hate your enemy.'

44 [1]"But I say to you, [a]love your enemies, bless those who curse you, [b]do good to those who hate you, and pray [c]for those who spitefully use you and persecute you,

45 "that you may be sons of your Father in heaven; for [a]He makes His sun rise on the evil and on the good, and sends rain on the just and on the unjust.

46 [a]"For if you love those who love you, what reward have you? Do not even the tax collectors do the same?

47 "And if you greet your [1]brethren only, what do you do more *than others?* Do not even the [2]tax collectors do so?

48 [a]"Therefore you shall be perfect, just [b]as your Father in heaven is perfect.

Do Good to Please God

6 "Take heed that you do not do your charitable deeds before men, to be seen by them. Otherwise you have no reward from your Father in heaven.

2 "Therefore, [a]when you do a charitable deed, do not sound a trumpet before you as the hypocrites do in the synagogues and in the streets, that they may have glory from men. Assuredly, I say to you, they have their reward.

3 "But when you do a charitable deed, do not let your left hand know what your right hand is doing,

4 "that your charitable deed may be in secret; and your Father who sees in secret [a]will Himself reward you [1]openly.

The Model Prayer

5 "And when you pray, you shall not be like the [1]hypocrites. For they love to pray standing in the synagogues and on the corners of the streets, that they may be seen by men. Assuredly, I say to you, they have their reward.

6 "But you, when you pray, [a]go into your room, and when you have shut your door, pray to your Father who *is* in the secret *place;* and your Father who sees in secret will reward you [1]openly.

7 "And when you pray, [a]do not use vain repetitions as the heathen *do.* [b]For they think that they will be heard for their many words.

8 "Therefore do not be like them. For your Father [a]knows the things you have need of before you ask Him.

9 "In this [a]manner, therefore, pray:

---

31 [a]Deut. 24:1
32 [a][Luke 16:18] [1]Or *fornication*
33 [a]Matt. 23:16 [b]Lev. 19:12 [c]Deut. 23:23 [1]*ancient times*
34 [a]James 5:12 [b]Is. 66:1
35 [a]Ps. 48:2
37 [a][Col. 4:6] [1]Lit. *your word be yes yes*
38 [a]Ex. 21:24; Lev. 24:20; Deut. 19:21
39 [a]Luke 6:29 [b]Is. 50:6
41 [a]Matt. 27:32
42 [a]Luke 6:30–34
43 [a]Lev. 19:18 [b]Deut. 23:3–6
44 [a]Luke 6:27 [b][Rom. 12:20] [c]Acts 7:60 [1]NU *But I say to you, love your enemies and pray for those who persecute you*
45 [a]Job 25:3
46 [a]Luke 6:32
47 [1]M *friends* [2]NU *Gentiles*
48 [a][Col. 1:28; 4:12] [b]Eph. 5:1

CHAPTER 6

2 [a]Rom. 12:8
4 [a]Luke 14:12–14 [1]NU omits *openly*
5 [1]*pretenders*
6 [a]2 Kin. 4:33 [1]NU omits *openly*
7 [a]Eccl. 5:2 [b]1 Kin. 18:26
8 [a][Rom. 8:26, 27]
9 [a]Luke 11:2–4

[b]Our Father in heaven,
Hallowed be Your [c]name.
10 Your kingdom come.
[a]Your will be done
On earth [b]as *it is* in heaven.
11 Give us this day our [a]daily bread.
12 And [a]forgive us our debts,
As we forgive our debtors.
13 [a]And do not lead us into
temptation,
But [b]deliver us from the evil one.
[1]For Yours is the kingdom and the
power and the glory forever.
Amen.

14 [a]"For if you forgive men their
trespasses, your heavenly Father
will also forgive you.
15 "But [a]if you do not forgive men
their trespasses, neither will your
Father forgive your trespasses.

Fasting to Be Seen Only by God

16 "Moreover, [a]when you fast, do
not be like the [1]hypocrites, with a
sad countenance. For they dis-
figure their faces that they may
appear to men to be fasting. As-
suredly, I say to you, they have
their reward.
17 "But you, when you fast,
[a]anoint your head and wash your
face,
18 "so that you do not appear to
men to be fasting, but to your Fa-
ther who *is* in the secret *place;* and
your Father who sees in secret will
reward you [1]openly.

Lay Up Treasures in Heaven

19 [a]"Do not lay up for yourselves
treasures on earth, where moth
and rust destroy and where thieves
break in and steal;
20 [a]"but lay up for yourselves
treasures in heaven, where neither
moth nor rust destroys and where
thieves do not break in and steal.
21 "For where your treasure is,
there your heart will be also.

The Lamp of the Body

22 [a]"The lamp of the body is the
eye. If therefore your eye is [1]good,
your whole body will be full of
light.
23 "But if your eye is [1]bad, your
whole body will be full of dark-
ness. If therefore the light that is
in you is darkness, how great *is*
that darkness!

9 [b][Matt. 5:9, 16] [c]Mal. 1:11
10 [a]Matt. 26:42 [b]Ps. 103:20
11 [a]Prov. 30:8
12 [a][Matt. 18:21, 22]
13 [a][2 Pet. 2:9] [b]John 17:15 [1]NU omits the rest of v. 13.
14 [a]Mark 11:25
15 [a]Matt. 18:35
16 [a]Is. 58:3–7 [1]*pretenders*
17 [a]Ruth 3:3
18 [1]NU, M omit *openly*
19 [a]Prov. 23:4
20 [a]Matt. 19:21
22 [a]Luke 11:34, 35 [1]Clear, or healthy
23 [1]Evil, or unhealthy
24 [a]Luke 16:9, 11, 13 [b][Gal. 1:10] [1]Lit., in Aram., *riches*
25 [a]Luke 12:22
26 [a]Luke 12:24
27 [1]About 18 inches [2]*height*
29 [1]*dressed*
33 [a][1 Tim. 4:8]

CHAPTER 7
1 [a]Rom. 14:3 [1]Condemn
2 [a]Luke 6:38 [1]Condemnation
3 [a]Luke 6:41

You Cannot Serve God and Riches

24 [a]"No one can serve two mas-
ters; for either he will hate the one
and love the other, or else he will
be loyal to the one and despise the
other. [b]You cannot serve God and
[1]mammon.

Do Not Worry

25 "Therefore I say to you, [a]do not
worry about your life, what you
will eat or what you will drink; nor
about your body, what you will put
on. Is not life more than food and
the body more than clothing?
26 [a]"Look at the birds of the air,
for they neither sow nor reap nor
gather into barns; yet your heav-
enly Father feeds them. Are you
not of more value than they?
27 "Which of you by worrying can
add one [1]cubit to his [2]stature?
28 "So why do you worry about
clothing? Consider the lilies of the
field, how they grow: they neither
toil nor spin;
29 "and yet I say to you that even
Solomon in all his glory was not
[1]arrayed like one of these.
30 "Now if God so clothes the
grass of the field, which today is,
and tomorrow is thrown into the
oven, *will He* not much more
clothe you, O you of little faith?
31 "Therefore do not worry, say-
ing, 'What shall we eat?' or 'What
shall we drink?' or 'What shall we
wear?'
32 "For after all these things the
Gentiles seek. For your heavenly
Father knows that you need all
these things.
33 "But [a]seek first the kingdom of
God and His righteousness, and all
these things shall be added to
you.
34 "Therefore do not worry about
tomorrow, for tomorrow will
worry about its own things. Suffi-
cient for the day *is* its own trouble.

Do Not Judge

7 "Judge[1] [a]not, that you be not
judged.
2 "For with what [1]judgment you
judge, you will be judged; [a]and
with the measure you use, it will
be measured back to you.
3 [a]"And why do you look at the
speck in your brother's eye, but do

not consider the plank in your own
eye?
4 "Or how can you say to your
brother, 'Let me remove the speck
from your eye'; and look, a plank
is in your own eye?
5 "Hypocrite! First remove the
plank from your own eye, and then
you will see clearly to remove the
speck from your brother's eye.
6 [a]"Do not give what is holy to
the dogs; nor cast your pearls be-
fore swine, lest they trample them
under their feet, and turn and tear
you in pieces.

Keep Asking, Seeking, Knocking

7 [a]"Ask, and it will be given to
you; seek, and you will find;
knock, and it will be opened to
you.
8 "For [a]everyone who asks re-
ceives, and he who seeks finds,
and to him who knocks it will be
opened.
9 [a]"Or what man is there among
you who, if his son asks for bread,
will give him a stone?
10 "Or if he asks for a fish, will
he give him a serpent?
11 "If you then, [a]being evil, know
how to give good gifts to your chil-
dren, how much more will your
Father who is in heaven give good
things to those who ask Him!
12 "Therefore, [a]whatever you
want men to do to you, do also to
them, for [b]this is the Law and the
Prophets.

The Narrow Way

13 [a]"Enter by the narrow gate; for
wide *is* the gate and broad *is* the
way that leads to destruction, and
there are many who go in by it.
14 [1]"Because narrow *is* the gate
and [2]difficult *is* the way which
leads to life, and there are few who
find it.

You Will Know Them by Their Fruits

15 [a]"Beware of false prophets,
[b]who come to you in sheep's cloth-
ing, but inwardly they are rav-
enous wolves.
16 [a]"You will know them by their
fruits. [b]Do men gather grapes from
thornbushes or figs from thistles?
17 "Even so, [a]every good tree
bears good fruit, but a bad tree
bears bad fruit.

6 [a]Prov. 9:7, 8
7 [a][Mark 11:24]
8 [a]Prov. 8:17
9 [a]Luke 11:11
11 [a]Gen. 6:5; 8:21
12 [a]Luke 6:31 [b]Gal. 5:14
13 [a]Luke 13:24
14 [1]NU, M *How narrow . . . !* [2]*confined*
15 [a]Jer. 23:16 [b]Mic. 3:5
16 [a]Matt. 7:20; 12:33 [b]Luke 6:43
17 [a]Matt. 12:33
19 [a][John 15:2, 6]
21 [a]Luke 6:46 [b]Rom. 2:13
22 [a]Num. 24:4
23 [a][2 Tim. 2:19] [b]Ps. 5:5; 6:8
24 [a]Luke 6:47–49
28 [a]Matt. 13:54
29 [a][John 7:46]
CHAPTER 8
2 [a]Mark 1:40–45 [b]John 9:38

18 "A good tree cannot bear bad
fruit, nor *can* a bad tree bear good
fruit.
19 [a]"Every tree that does not bear
good fruit is cut down and thrown
into the fire.
20 "Therefore by their fruits you
will know them.

I Never Knew You

21 "Not everyone who says to Me,
[a]'Lord, Lord,' shall enter the king-
dom of heaven, but he who [b]does
the will of My Father in heaven.
22 "Many will say to Me in that
day, 'Lord, Lord, have we [a]not
prophesied in Your name, cast out
demons in Your name, and done
many wonders in Your name?'
23 "And [a]then I will declare to
them, 'I never knew you; [b]depart
from Me, you who practice law-
lessness!'

Build on the Rock

24 "Therefore [a]whoever hears
these sayings of Mine, and does
them, I will liken him to a wise
man who built his house on the
rock:
25 "and the rain descended, the
floods came, and the winds blew
and beat on that house; and it did
not fall, for it was founded on the
rock.
26 "But everyone who hears these
sayings of Mine, and does not do
them, will be like a foolish man
who built his house on the sand:
27 "and the rain descended, the
floods came, and the winds blew
and beat on that house; and it fell.
And great was its fall."
28 And so it was, when Jesus had
ended these sayings, that [a]the peo-
ple were astonished at His teach-
ing,
29 [a]for He taught them as one
having authority, and not as the
scribes.

Jesus Cleanses a Leper

8 When He had come down from
the mountain, great multitudes
followed Him.
2 [a]And behold, a leper came and
[b]worshiped Him, saying, "Lord, if
You are willing, You can make me
clean."
3 Then Jesus put out *His* hand
and touched him, saying, "I am

willing; be cleansed." Immediately
his leprosy [a]was cleansed.
4 And Jesus said to him, [a]"See
that you tell no one; but go your
way, show yourself to the priest,
and offer the gift that [b]Moses
[c]commanded, as a testimony to
them."

Jesus Heals a Centurion's Servant

5 [a]Now when Jesus had entered
Capernaum, a [b]centurion came to
Him, pleading with Him,
6 saying, "Lord, my servant is ly-
ing at home paralyzed, dreadfully
tormented."
7 And Jesus said to him, "I will
come and heal him."
8 The centurion answered and
said, "Lord, [a]I am not worthy that
You should come under my roof.
But only [b]speak a word, and my
servant will be healed.
9 "For I also am a man under au-
thority, having soldiers under me.
And I say to this *one*, 'Go,' and he
goes; and to another, 'Come,' and
he comes; and to my servant, 'Do
this,' and he does *it*."
10 When Jesus heard *it*, He mar-
veled, and said to those who fol-
lowed, "Assuredly, I say to you, I
have not found such great faith,
not even in Israel!
11 "And I say to you that [a]many
will come from east and west, and
sit down with Abraham, Isaac, and
Jacob in the kingdom of heaven.
12 "But [a]the sons of the kingdom
[b]will be cast out into outer dark-
ness. There will be weeping and
gnashing of teeth."
13 Then Jesus said to the centu-
rion, "Go your way; and as you
have believed, *so* let it be done for
you." And his servant was healed
that same hour.

Peter's Mother-in-Law Healed

14 [a]Now when Jesus had come
into Peter's house, He saw [b]his
wife's mother lying sick with a
fever.
15 So He touched her hand, and
the fever left her. And she arose
and served [1]them.

Many Healed After Sabbath Sunset

16 [a]When evening had come, they
brought to Him many who were
demon-possessed. And He cast out
the spirits with a word, and healed
all who were sick,
17 that it might be fulfilled which
was spoken by Isaiah the prophet,
saying:

> [a]*"He Himself took our infirmities*
> *And bore our sicknesses."*

The Cost of Discipleship

18 And when Jesus saw great mul-
titudes about Him, He gave a com-
mand to depart to the other side.
19 [a]Then a certain scribe came
and said to Him, "Teacher, I will
follow You wherever You go."
20 And Jesus said to him, "Foxes
have holes and birds of the air
have nests, but the Son of Man has
nowhere to lay *His* head."
21 [a]Then another of His disciples
said to Him, "Lord, [b]let me first go
and bury my father."
22 But Jesus said to him, "Follow
Me, and let the dead bury their
own dead."

Wind and Wave Obey Jesus

23 Now when He got into a boat,
His disciples followed Him.
24 [a]And suddenly a great tempest
arose on the sea, so that the boat
was covered with the waves. But
He was asleep.
25 Then His disciples came to *Him*
and awoke Him, saying, "Lord,
save us! We are perishing!"
26 But He said to them, "Why are
you fearful, O you of little faith?"
Then [a]He arose and rebuked the
winds and the sea, and there was
a great calm.
27 So the men marveled, saying,
[1]"Who can this be, that even the
winds and the sea obey Him?"

Two Demon-Possessed Men Healed

28 [a]When He had come to the
other side, to the country of the
[1]Gergesenes, there met Him two
demon-possessed *men*, coming out
of the tombs, exceedingly fierce,
so that no one could pass that way.
29 And suddenly they cried out,
saying, "What have we to do with
You, Jesus, You Son of God? Have
You come here to torment us be-
fore the time?"
30 Now a good way off from them
there was a herd of many swine
feeding.

3 [a]Matt. 11:5; Luke 4:27
4 [a]Matt. 9:30; Mark 5:43; Luke 4:41; 8:56; 9:21 [b]Lev. 14:3, 4, 10; Mark 1:44; Luke 5:14 [c]Lev. 14:4–32; Deut. 24:8
5 [a]Luke 7:1–3 [b]Matt. 27:54; Acts 10:1
8 [a]Luke 15:19, 21 [b]Ps. 107:20
11 [a][Gen. 12:3; Is. 2:2, 3; 11:10]; Mal. 1:11; Luke 13:29; [Acts 10:45; 11:18; 14:27; Rom. 15:9–13; Eph. 3:6]
12 [a][Matt. 21:43] [b]Matt. 13:42, 50; 22:13; 24:51; 25:30; Luke 13:28; 2 Pet. 2:17; Jude 13
14 [a]Matt. 8:14–16; Mark 1:29–31; Luke 4:38, 39 [b]1 Cor. 9:5
15 [1]NU, M *Him*
16 [a]Mark 1:32–34; Luke 4:40, 41
17 [a]Is. 53:4; 1 Pet. 2:24
19 [a]Matt. 8:19–22; Luke 9:57, 58
21 [a]Luke 9:59, 60 [b]1 Kin. 19:20
24 [a]Mark 4:37; Luke 8:23–25
26 [a]Ps. 65:7; 89:9; 107:29
27 [1]Lit. *What sort of man is this*
28 [a]Mark 5:1–4; Luke 8:26–33 [1]NU *Gadarenes*

31 So the demons begged Him,
saying, "If You cast us out, [1]permit
us to go away into the herd of
swine."
32 And He said to them, "Go." So
when they had come out, they
went into the herd of swine. And
suddenly the whole herd of swine
ran violently down the steep place
into the sea, and perished in the
water.
33 Then those who kept *them* fled;
and they went away into the city
and told everything, including
what *had happened* to the demon-
possessed *men.*
34 And behold, the whole city
came out to meet Jesus. And when
they saw Him, [a]they begged *Him*
to depart from their region.

Jesus Forgives and Heals a Paralytic

9 So He got into a boat, crossed
over, [a]and came to His own
city.
2 [a]Then behold, they brought to
Him a paralytic lying on a bed.
[b]When Jesus saw their faith, He
said to the paralytic, "Son, be of
good cheer; your sins are forgiven
you."
3 And at once some of the scribes
said within themselves, "This Man
blasphemes!"
4 But Jesus, [a]knowing their
thoughts, said, "Why do you think
evil in your hearts?
5 "For which is easier, to say,
'*Your* sins are forgiven you,' or to
say, 'Arise and walk'?
6 "But that you may know that
the Son of Man has power on earth
to forgive sins"—then He said to
the paralytic, "Arise, take up your
bed, and go to your house."
7 And he arose and departed to
his house.
8 Now when the multitudes saw
it, they [a]marveled[1] and glorified
God, who had given such power
to men.

Matthew the Tax Collector

9 [a]As Jesus passed on from
there, He saw a man named Mat-
thew sitting at the tax office. And
He said to him, "Follow Me." So
he arose and followed Him.
10 [a]Now it happened, as Jesus sat
at the table in the house, *that* be-
hold, many tax collectors and sin-
ners came and sat down with Him
and His disciples.
11 And when the Pharisees saw *it*,
they said to His disciples, "Why
does your Teacher eat with [a]tax
collectors and [b]sinners?"
12 When Jesus heard *that*, He
said to them, "Those who are well
have no need of a physician, but
those who are sick.
13 "But go and learn what *this*
means: [a]'*I desire mercy and not*
sacrifice.' For I did not come to call
the righteous, [b]but sinners, [1]to re-
pentance."

Jesus Is Questioned About Fasting

14 Then the disciples of John
came to Him, saying, [a]"Why do we
and the Pharisees fast [1]often, but
Your disciples do not fast?"
15 And Jesus said to them, "Can
[a]the [1]friends of the bridegroom
mourn as long as the bridegroom
is with them? But the days will
come when the bridegroom will be
taken away from them, and [b]then
they will fast.
16 "No one puts a piece of un-
shrunk cloth on an old garment;
for [1]the patch pulls away from the
garment, and the tear is made
worse.
17 "Nor do they put new wine into
old wineskins, or else the wine-
skins [1]break, the wine is spilled,
and the wineskins are ruined. But
they put new wine into new wine-
skins, and both are preserved."

A Girl Restored to Life and a Woman Healed

18 [a]While He spoke these things
to them, behold, a ruler came and
worshiped Him, saying, "My
daughter has just died, but come
and lay Your hand on her and she
will live."
19 So Jesus arose and followed
him, and so *did* His [a]disciples.
20 [a]And suddenly, a woman who
had a flow of blood for twelve
years came from behind and
[b]touched the hem of His garment.
21 For she said to herself, "If only
I may touch His garment, I shall
be made well."
22 But Jesus turned around, and
when He saw her He said, "Be of
good cheer, daughter; [a]your faith
has made you well." And the

31 [1]NU *send us into*
34 [a]Deut. 5:25; 1 Kin. 17:18; Amos 7:12; Luke 5:8; Acts 16:39

CHAPTER 9

1 [a]Matt. 4:13; 11:23; Mark 5:21
2 [a]Mark 2:3–12; Luke 5:18–26 [b]Matt. 8:10
4 [a]Ps. 139:2; Matt. 12:25; Mark 12:15; Luke 5:22; 6:8; 9:47; 11:17
8 [a]Matt. 8:27; John 7:15 [1]NU *were afraid*
9 [a]Mark 2:14; Luke 5:27
10 [a]Mark 2:15; Luke 5:29
11 [a]Matt. 11:19; Mark 2:16; Luke 5:30; 15:2 [b][Gal. 2:15]
13 [a]Hos. 6:6; [Mic. 6:6–8]; Matt. 12:7 [b]Mark 2:17; Luke 5:32; 1 Tim. 1:15 [1]NU omits *to repentance*
14 [a]Mark 2:18; Luke 5:33–35; 18:12 [1]NU brackets *often* as disputed.
15 [a]John 3:29 [b]Acts 13:2, 3; 14:23 [1]Lit. *sons of the bridechamber*
16 [1]Lit. *that which is put on*
17 [1]*burst*
18 [a]Mark 5:22–43; Luke 8:41–56
19 [a]Matt. 10:2–4
20 [a]Mark 5:25; Luke 8:43 [b]Num. 15:38; Deut. 22:12; Matt. 14:36; 23:5; Mark 6:56
22 [a]Matt. 9:29; 15:28; Mark 5:34; 10:52; Luke 7:50; 8:48; 17:19; 18:42

woman was made well from that
hour.
23 [a]When Jesus came into the rul-
er's house, and saw [b]the flute play-
ers and the noisy crowd wailing,
24 He said to them, [a]"Make room,
for the girl is not dead, but sleep-
ing." And they ridiculed Him.
25 But when the crowd was put
outside, He went in and [a]took her
by the hand, and the girl arose.
26 And the [a]report of this went out
into all that land.

Two Blind Men Healed

27 When Jesus departed from
there, [a]two blind men followed
Him, crying out and saying, [b]"Son
of David, have mercy on us!"
28 And when He had come into
the house, the blind men came to
Him. And Jesus said to them, "Do
you believe that I am able to do
this?" They said to Him, "Yes,
Lord."
29 Then He touched their eyes,
saying, "According to your faith
let it be to you."
30 And their eyes were opened.
And Jesus sternly warned them,
saying, [a]"See *that* no one knows
it."
31 [a]But when they had departed,
they [1]spread the news about Him
in all that [2]country.

A Mute Man Speaks

32 [a]As they went out, behold, they
brought to Him a man, mute and
demon-possessed.
33 And when the demon was cast
out, the mute spoke. And the mul-
titudes marveled, saying, "It was
never seen like this in Israel!"
34 But the Pharisees said, [a]"He
casts out demons by the ruler of
the demons."

The Compassion of Jesus

35 Then Jesus went about all the
cities and villages, [a]teaching in
their synagogues, preaching the
gospel of the kingdom, and heal-
ing every sickness and every dis-
ease [1]among the people.
36 [a]But when He saw the multi-
tudes, He was moved with com-
passion for them, because they
were [1]weary and scattered, [b]like
sheep having no shepherd.
37 Then He said to His disciples,

23 [a]Mark 5:38 [b]2 Chr. 35:25
24 [a]Acts 20:10
25 [a]Mark 1:31
26 [a]Matt. 4:24
27 [a]Matt. 20:29–34 [b]Luke 18:38, 39
30 [a]Matt. 8:4
31 [a]Mark 7:36 [1]Lit. *made Him known* [2]Lit. *land*
32 [a]Matt. 12:22, 24
34 [a]Luke 11:15
35 [a]Matt. 4:23 [1]NU omits *among the people*
36 [a]Mark 6:34 [b]Num. 27:17 [1]NU, M *harassed*
37 [a]Luke 10:2
38 [a]2 Thess. 3:1

CHAPTER 10
1 [a]Luke 6:13
2 [a]John 1:42
3 [1]NU omits *Lebbaeus, whose surname was*
4 [a]Acts 1:13 [b]John 13:2, 26 [1]NU *Cananaean*
5 [a]Matt. 4:15 [b]John 4:9
6 [a]Matt. 15:24 [b]Jer. 50:6
7 [a]Luke 9:2 [b]Matt. 3:2 [1]*has drawn near*
8 [a][Acts 8:18] [1]NU *raise the dead, cleanse the lepers* [2]M omits *raise the dead*
9 [a]1 Sam. 9:7 [b]Mark 6:8
10 [a]1 Tim. 5:18
11 [a]Luke 10:8
13 [a]Luke 10:5 [b]Ps. 35:13
14 [a]Mark 6:11 [b]Acts 13:51

[a]"The harvest truly *is* plentiful, but
the laborers *are* few.
38 [a]"Therefore pray the Lord of
the harvest to send out laborers
into His harvest."

The Twelve Apostles

10 And [a]when He had called
His twelve disciples to *Him,*
He gave them power *over* unclean
spirits, to cast them out, and to
heal all kinds of sickness and all
kinds of disease.
2 Now the names of the twelve
apostles are these: first, Simon,
[a]who is called Peter, and Andrew
his brother; James the *son* of Zebe-
dee, and John his brother;
3 Philip and Bartholomew;
Thomas and Matthew the tax col-
lector; James the *son* of Alphaeus,
and [1]Lebbaeus, whose surname
was Thaddaeus;
4 [a]Simon the [1]Cananite, and Ju-
das [b]Iscariot, who also betrayed
Him.

Sending Out the Twelve

5 These twelve Jesus sent out
and commanded them, saying:
[a]"Do not go into the way of the
Gentiles, and do not enter a city
of [b]the Samaritans.
6 [a]"But go rather to the [b]lost
sheep of the house of Israel.
7 [a]"And as you go, preach, say-
ing, [b]'The kingdom of heaven [1]is
at hand.'
8 "Heal the sick, [1]cleanse the lep-
ers, [2]raise the dead, cast out de-
mons. [a]Freely you have received,
freely give.
9 [a]"Provide neither gold nor sil-
ver nor [b]copper in your money
belts,
10 "nor bag for *your* journey, nor
two tunics, nor sandals, nor staffs;
[a]for a worker is worthy of his food.
11 [a]"Now whatever city or town
you enter, inquire who in it is wor-
thy, and stay there till you go out.
12 "And when you go into a
household, greet it.
13 [a]"If the household is worthy,
let your peace come upon it. [b]But
if it is not worthy, let your peace
return to you.
14 [a]"And whoever will not receive
you nor hear your words, when
you depart from that house or city,
[b]shake off the dust from your feet.

15 "Assuredly, I say to you, [a]it will
be more tolerable for the land of
Sodom and Gomorrah in the day
of judgment than for that city!

Persecutions Are Coming

16 [a]"Behold, I send you out as
sheep in the midst of wolves.
[b]Therefore be wise as serpents and
[c]harmless[1] as doves.
17 "But beware of men, for [a]they
will deliver you up to councils and
[b]scourge you in their synagogues.
18 [a]"You will be brought before
governors and kings for My sake,
as a testimony to them and to the
Gentiles.
19 [a]"But when they deliver you
up, do not worry about how or
what you should speak. For [b]it will
be given to you in that hour what
you should speak;
20 [a]"for it is not you who speak,
but the Spirit of your Father who
speaks in you.
21 [a]"Now brother will deliver up
brother to death, and a father *his*
child; and children will rise up
against parents and cause them to
be put to death.
22 "And [a]you will be hated by all
for My name's sake. [b]But he who
endures to the end will be saved.
23 [a]"When they persecute you in
this city, flee to another. For as-
suredly, I say to you, you will not
have [b]gone through the cities of Is-
rael [c]before the Son of Man comes.
24 [a]"A disciple is not above *his*
teacher, nor a servant above his
master.
25 "It is enough for a disciple that
he be like his teacher, and a ser-
vant like his master. If [a]they have
called the master of the house
[1]Beelzebub, how much more *will
they call* those of his house-
hold!
26 "Therefore do not fear them.
[a]For there is nothing covered that
will not be revealed, and hidden
that will not be known.

Jesus Teaches the Fear of God

27 "Whatever I tell you in the
dark, [a]speak in the light; and what
you hear in the ear, preach on the
housetops.
28 [a]"And do not fear those who
kill the body but cannot kill the
soul. But rather [b]fear Him who is
able to destroy both soul and body
in [1]hell.
29 "Are not two [a]sparrows sold
for a [1]copper coin? And not one
of them falls to the ground apart
from your Father's will.
30 [a]"But the very hairs of your
head are all numbered.
31 "Do not fear therefore; you are
of more value than many spar-
rows.

Confess Christ Before Men

32 [a]"Therefore whoever confesses
Me before men, [b]him I will also
confess before My Father who is
in heaven.
33 [a]"But whoever denies Me be-
fore men, him I will also deny be-
fore My Father who is in heaven.

Christ Brings Division

34 [a]"Do not think that I came to
bring peace on earth. I did not
come to bring peace but a sword.
35 "For I have come to [a]'*set*[1] *a
man against his father, a daugh-
ter against her mother, and a
daughter-in-law against her
mother-in-law*';
36 "and [a]'*a man's enemies will be
those of his own household.*'
37 [a]"He who loves father or
mother more than Me is not wor-
thy of Me. And he who loves son
or daughter more than Me is not
worthy of Me.
38 [a]"And he who does not take his
cross and follow after Me is not
worthy of Me.
39 [a]"He who finds his life will lose
it, and he who loses his life for My
sake will find it.

A Cup of Cold Water

40 [a]"He who receives you receives
Me, and he who receives Me re-
ceives Him who sent Me.
41 [a]"He who receives a prophet in
the name of a prophet shall receive
a prophet's reward. And he who
receives a righteous man in the
name of a righteous man shall re-
ceive a righteous man's reward.
42 [a]"And whoever gives one of
these little ones only a cup of cold
water in the name of a disciple,
assuredly, I say to you, he shall by
no means lose his reward."

15 [a]Matt. 11:22, 24
16 [a]Luke 10:3 [b]Eph. 5:15 [c][Phil. 2:14–16] [1]*innocent*
17 [a]Mark 13:9 [b]Acts 5:40; 22:19; 26:11
18 [a]2 Tim. 4:16
19 [a]Luke 12:11, 12; 21:14, 15 [b]Ex. 4:12
20 [a]2 Sam. 23:2
21 [a]Mic. 7:6
22 [a]Luke 21:17 [b]Mark 13:13
23 [a]Acts 8:1 [b][Mark 13:10] [c]Matt. 16:28
24 [a]John 15:20
25 [a]John 8:48, 52 [1]NU, M *Beelzebul;* a Philistine deity, 2 Kin. 1:2, 3
26 [a]Mark 4:22
27 [a]Acts 5:20
28 [a]Luke 12:4 [b]Luke 12:5 [1]Gr. *Gehenna*
29 [a]Luke 12:6, 7 [1]Gr. *assarion,* a coin worth about 1/16 of a denarius
30 [a]Luke 21:18
32 [a]Luke 12:8 [b][Rev. 3:5]
33 [a]2 Tim. 2:12
34 [a][Luke 12:49]
35 [a]Mic. 7:6 [1]*alienate a man from*
36 [a]John 13:18
37 [a]Luke 14:26
38 [a][Mark 8:34]
39 [a]John 12:25
40 [a]Luke 9:48
41 [a]1 Kin. 17:10
42 [a]Mark 9:41

John the Baptist Sends Messengers to Jesus

11 Now it came to pass, when
Jesus finished commanding
His twelve disciples, that He de-
parted from there to [a]teach and to
preach in their cities.
2 [a]And when John had heard [b]in
prison about the works of Christ,
he [1]sent two of his disciples
3 and said to Him, "Are You [a]the
Coming One, or do we look for an-
other?"
4 Jesus answered and said to
them, "Go and tell John the things
which you hear and see:
5 [a]"*The* blind see and *the* lame
walk; *the* lepers are cleansed and
the deaf hear; *the* dead are raised
up and [b]*the* poor have the gospel
preached to them.
6 "And blessed is he who is not
[a]offended because of Me."
7 [a]As they departed, Jesus began
to say to the multitudes concern-
ing John: "What did you go out
into the wilderness to see? [b]A reed
shaken by the wind?
8 "But what did you go out to
see? A man clothed in soft gar-
ments? Indeed, those who wear
soft *clothing* are in kings' houses.
9 "But what did you go out to
see? A prophet? Yes, I say to you,
[a]and more than a prophet.
10 "For this is *he* of whom it is
written:

[a]'Behold, I send My messenger
before Your face,
Who will prepare Your way
before You.'

11 "Assuredly, I say to you,
among those born of women there
has not risen one greater than
John the Baptist; but he who is
least in the kingdom of heaven is
greater than he.
12 [a]"And from the days of John
the Baptist until now the kingdom
of heaven suffers violence, and the
violent take it by force.
13 [a]"For all the prophets and the
law prophesied until John.
14 "And if you are willing to re-
ceive *it*, he is [a]Elijah who is to
come.
15 [a]"He who has ears to hear, let
him hear!
16 [a]"But to what shall I liken this
generation? It is like children sit-
ting in the marketplaces and call-
ing to their companions,
17 "and saying:

'We played the flute for you,
And you did not dance;
We mourned to you,
And you did not [1]lament.'

18 "For John came neither eating
nor drinking, and they say, 'He has
a demon.'
19 "The Son of Man came eating
and drinking, and they say, 'Look,
a glutton and a [1]winebibber, [a]a
friend of tax collectors and sin-
ners!' [b]But wisdom is justified by
her [2]children."

Woe to the Impenitent Cities

20 [a]Then He began to rebuke the
cities in which most of His mighty
works had been done, because
they did not repent:
21 "Woe to you, Chorazin! Woe to
you, Bethsaida! For if the mighty
works which were done in you had
been done in Tyre and Sidon, they
would have repented long ago [a]in
sackcloth and ashes.
22 "But I say to you, [a]it will be
more tolerable for Tyre and Sidon
in the day of judgment than for
you.
23 "And you, Capernaum, [a]who[1]
are exalted to heaven, will be
brought down to Hades; for if the
mighty works which were done in
you had been done in Sodom, it
would have remained until this
day.
24 "But I say to you [a]that it shall
be more tolerable for the land of
Sodom in the day of judgment
than for you."

Jesus Gives True Rest

25 [a]At that time Jesus answered
and said, "I thank You, Father,
Lord of heaven and earth, that
[b]You have hidden these things
from *the* wise and prudent [c]and
have revealed them to babes.
26 "Even so, Father, for so it
seemed good in Your sight.
27 [a]"All things have been deliv-
ered to Me by My Father, and no
one knows the Son except the Fa-
ther. [b]Nor does anyone know the

CHAPTER 11
1 [a]Luke 23:5
2 [a]Luke 7:18–35 [b]Matt. 4:12; 14:3 [1]NU *sent by his*
3 [a]John 6:14
5 [a]Is. 29:18; 35:4–6 [b]Is. 61:1
6 [a][Rom. 9:32]
7 [a]Luke 7:24 [b][Eph. 4:14]
9 [a]Luke 1:76; 20:6
10 [a]Mal. 3:1
12 [a]Luke 16:16
13 [a]Mal. 4:4–6
14 [a]Luke 1:17
15 [a]Luke 8:8
16 [a]Luke 7:31
17 [1]Lit. *beat your breast*
19 [a]Matt. 9:10 [b]Luke 7:35 [1]*wine drinker* [2]NU *works*
20 [a]Luke 10:13–15, 18
21 [a]Jon. 3:6–8
22 [a]Matt. 10:15; 11:24
23 [a]Is. 14:13 [1]NU *will you be exalted to heaven? No, you will be*
24 [a]Matt. 10:15
25 [a]Luke 10:21, 22 [b]Ps. 8:2 [c]Matt. 16:17
27 [a]Matt. 28:18 [b]John 1:18; 6:46; 10:15

Father except the Son, and *the one* to whom the Son wills to reveal *Him.*
28 "Come to [a]Me, all *you* who labor and are heavy laden, and I will give you rest.
29 "Take My yoke upon you [a]and learn from Me, for I am [1]gentle and [b]lowly in heart, [c]and you will find rest for your souls.
30 [a]"For My yoke *is* easy and My burden is light."

Jesus Is Lord of the Sabbath

12 At that time [a]Jesus went through the grainfields on the Sabbath. And His disciples were hungry, and began to [b]pluck heads of grain and to eat.
2 And when the Pharisees saw *it,* they said to Him, "Look, Your disciples are doing what is not lawful to do on the Sabbath!"
3 But He said to them, "Have you not read [a]what David did when he was hungry, he and those who were with him:
4 "how he entered the house of God and ate [a]the showbread which was not lawful for him to eat, nor for those who were with him, [b]but only for the priests?
5 "Or have you not read in the [a]law that on the Sabbath the priests in the temple [1]profane the Sabbath, and are blameless?
6 "Yet I say to you that in this place there is [a]*One* greater than the temple.
7 "But if you had known what *this* means, [a]*'I desire mercy and not sacrifice,'* you would not have condemned the guiltless.
8 "For the Son of Man is Lord [1]even of the Sabbath."

Healing on the Sabbath

9 [a]Now when He had departed from there, He went into their synagogue.
10 And behold, there was a man who had a withered hand. And they asked Him, saying, [a]"Is it lawful to heal on the Sabbath?"—that they might accuse Him.
11 Then He said to them, "What man is there among you who has one sheep, and if it falls into a pit on the Sabbath, will not lay hold of it and lift *it* out?
12 "Of how much more value then is a man than a sheep? Therefore it is lawful to do good on the Sabbath."
13 Then He said to the man, "Stretch out your hand." And he stretched *it* out, and it was restored as whole as the other.
14 Then [a]the Pharisees went out and plotted against Him, how they might destroy Him.

Behold, My Servant

15 But when Jesus knew *it,* [a]He withdrew from there. [b]And great [1]multitudes followed Him, and He healed them all.
16 Yet He [a]warned them not to make Him known,
17 that it might be fulfilled which was spoken by Isaiah the prophet, saying:

18 *"Behold!* [a] *My Servant whom I*
have chosen,
My Beloved [b]*in whom My soul is*
well pleased!
I will put My Spirit upon Him,
And He will declare justice to the
Gentiles.
19 *He will not quarrel nor cry out,*
Nor will anyone hear His voice
in the streets.
20 *A bruised reed He will not break,*
And smoking flax He will not
quench,
Till He sends forth justice to
victory;
21 *And in His name Gentiles will*
trust."

A House Divided Cannot Stand

22 [a]Then one was brought to Him who was demon-possessed, blind and mute; and He healed him, so that the [1]blind and mute man both spoke and saw.
23 And all the multitudes were amazed and said, "Could this be the [a]Son of David?"
24 [a]Now when the Pharisees heard *it* they said, "This *fellow* does not cast out demons except by [1]Beelzebub, the ruler of the demons."
25 But Jesus [a]knew their thoughts, and said to them: "Every kingdom divided against itself is brought to desolation, and every city or house divided against itself will not stand.
26 "If Satan casts out Satan, he is

---

28 [a][John 6:35–37]
29 [a][John 13:15]; Eph. 4:2; [Phil. 2:5; 1 Pet. 2:21; 1 John 2:6] [b]Zech. 9:9; [Phil. 2:7, 8] [c]Jer. 6:16 [1]*meek*
30 [a][1 John 5:3]

CHAPTER 12

1 [a]Mark 2:23; Luke 6:1–5 [b]Deut. 23:25
3 [a]Ex. 31:15; 35:2; 1 Sam. 21:6
4 [a]Ex. 25:30; Lev. 24:5 [b]Ex. 29:32; Lev. 8:31; 24:9
5 [a]Num. 28:9; [John 7:22] [1]*desecrate*
6 [a][2 Chr. 6:18; Is. 66:1, 2; Mal. 3:1]; Matt. 12:41, 42
7 [a][1 Sam. 15:22; Hos. 6:6; Mic. 6:6–8]; Matt. 9:13
8 [1]NU, M omit *even*
9 [a]Mark 3:1–6; Luke 6:6–11
10 [a]Luke 13:14; 14:3; John 9:16
14 [a]Ps. 2:2; Matt. 27:1; Mark 3:6; [Luke 6:11]; John 5:18; 10:39; 11:53
15 [a]Matt. 10:23; Mark 3:7 [b]Matt. 19:2 [1]NU brackets *multitudes* as disputed.
16 [a]Matt. 8:4; 9:30; 17:9
18 [a]Is. 42:1–4; 49:3 [b]Matt. 3:17; 17:5
22 [a]Matt. 9:32; [Mark 3:11]; Luke 11:14, 15 [1]NU omits *blind and*
23 [a]Matt. 9:27; 21:9
24 [a]Matt. 9:34; Mark 3:22; Luke 11:15 [1]NU, M *Beelzebul,* a Philistine deity
25 [a]Matt. 9:4; John 2:25; Rev. 2:23

divided against himself. How then will his kingdom stand?

27 "And if I cast out demons by Beelzebub, by whom do your sons cast *them* out? Therefore they shall be your judges.

28 "But if I cast out demons by the Spirit of God, [a]surely the kingdom of God has come upon you.

29 [a]"Or how can one enter a strong man's house and plunder his goods, unless he first binds the strong man? And then he will plunder his house.

30 "He who is not with Me is against Me, and he who does not gather with Me scatters abroad.

The Unpardonable Sin

31 "Therefore I say to you, [a]every sin and blasphemy will be forgiven men, [b]but the blasphemy *against* the Spirit will not be forgiven men.

32 "Anyone who [a]speaks a word against the Son of Man, [b]it will be forgiven him; but whoever speaks against the Holy Spirit, it will not be forgiven him, either in this age or in the *age* to come.

A Tree Known by Its Fruit

33 "Either make the tree good and [a]its fruit good, or else make the tree bad and its fruit bad; for a tree is known by *its* fruit.

34 [a]"Brood[1] of vipers! How can you, being evil, speak good things? [b]For out of the abundance of the heart the mouth speaks.

35 "A good man out of the good treasure [1]of his heart brings forth good things, and an evil man out of the evil treasure brings forth evil things.

36 "But I say to you that for every idle word men may speak, they will give account of it in the day of judgment.

37 "For by your words you will be justified, and by your words you will be condemned."

The Scribes and Pharisees Ask for a Sign

38 [a]Then some of the scribes and Pharisees answered, saying, "Teacher, we want to see a sign from You."

39 But He answered and said to them, "An evil and [a]adulterous generation seeks after a sign, and no sign will be given to it except the sign of the prophet Jonah.

40 [a]"For as Jonah was three days and three nights in the belly of the great fish, so will the Son of Man be three days and three nights in the heart of the earth.

41 [a]"The men of Nineveh will rise up in the judgment with this generation and [b]condemn it, [c]because they repented at the preaching of Jonah; and indeed a greater than Jonah *is* here.

42 [a]"The queen of the South will rise up in the judgment with this generation and condemn it, for she came from the ends of the earth to hear the wisdom of Solomon; and indeed a greater than Solomon *is* here.

An Unclean Spirit Returns

43 [a]"When an unclean spirit goes out of a man, [b]he goes through dry places, seeking rest, and finds none.

44 "Then he says, 'I will return to my house from which I came.' And when he comes, he finds *it* empty, swept, and put in order.

45 "Then he goes and takes with him seven other spirits more wicked than himself, and they enter and dwell there; [a]and the last *state* of that man is worse than the first. So shall it also be with this wicked generation."

Jesus' Mother and Brothers Send for Him

46 While He was still talking to the multitudes, [a]behold, His mother and [b]brothers stood outside, seeking to speak with Him.

47 Then one said to Him, "Look, [a]Your mother and Your brothers are standing outside, seeking to speak with You."

48 But He answered and said to the one who told Him, "Who is My mother and who are My brothers?"

49 And He stretched out His hand toward His disciples and said, "Here are My mother and My [a]brothers!

50 "For [a]whoever does the will of

---

28 [a][Dan. 2:44; 7:14; Luke 1:33]; 11:20; [17:20, 21; 1 John 3:8]

29 [a]Is. 49:24; [Luke 11:21–23]

31 [a]Mark 3:28–30; Luke 12:10; [Heb. 6:4–6; 10:26, 29; 1 John 5:16] [b]Acts 7:51

32 [a]Matt. 11:19; 13:55; John 7:12, 52 [b]1 Tim. 1:13

33 [a]Matt. 7:16–18; Luke 6:43, 44; [John 15:4–7]

34 [a]Matt. 3:7; 23:33; Luke 3:7 [b]1 Sam. 24:13; Is. 32:6; [Matt. 15:18]; Luke 6:45; Eph. 4:29; [James 3:2–12] [1]*Offspring*

35 [1]NU, M omit *of his heart*

38 [a]Matt. 16:1; Mark 8:11; Luke 11:16; John 2:18; 1 Cor. 1:22

39 [a]Is. 57:3; Matt. 16:4; Mark 8:38; [Luke 11:29–32]; John 4:48

40 [a]Jon. 1:17; Luke 24:46; 1:13

41 [a]Luke 11:32 [b]Jer. 3:11 [c]Jon. 3:5

42 [a]1 Kin. 10:1–13

43 [a]Luke 11:24–26 [b][1 Pet. 5:8]

45 [a][2 Pet. 2:20–22]

46 [a]Luke 8:19–21 [b]John 2:12; 7:3, 5

47 [a]Matt. 13:55, 56

49 [a]John 20:17

50 [a]John 15:14

My Father in heaven is My brother and sister and mother."

The Parable of the Sower

13 On the same day Jesus went out of the house [a]and sat by the sea.

2 [a]And great multitudes were gathered together to Him, so that [b]He got into a boat and sat; and the whole multitude stood on the shore.

3 Then He spoke many things to them in parables, saying: [a]"Behold, a sower went out to sow.

4 "And as he sowed, some *seed* fell by the wayside; and the birds came and devoured them.

5 "Some fell on stony places, where they did not have much earth; and they immediately sprang up because they had no depth of earth.

6 "But when the sun was up they were scorched, and because they had no root they withered away.

7 "And some fell among thorns, and the thorns sprang up and choked them.

8 "But others fell on good ground and yielded a crop: some [a]a hundredfold, some sixty, some thirty.

9 [a]"He who has ears to hear, let him hear!"

The Purpose of Parables

10 And the disciples came and said to Him, "Why do You speak to them in parables?"

11 He answered and said to them, "Because [a]it has been given to you to know the [1]mysteries of the kingdom of heaven, but to them it has not been given.

12 [a]"For whoever has, to him more will be given, and he will have abundance; but whoever does not have, even what he has will be taken away from him.

13 "Therefore I speak to them in parables, because seeing they do not see, and hearing they do not hear, nor do they understand.

14 "And in them the prophecy of Isaiah is fulfilled, which says:

[a]*'Hearing you will hear and shall*
not understand,
And seeing you will see and not
[b]*perceive;*

15 *For the hearts of this people have*
grown dull.
Their ears [a]*are hard of hearing,*
And their eyes they have [b]*closed,*
Lest they should see with their
eyes and hear with their ears,
Lest they should understand with
their hearts and turn,
So that I [1]*should* [c]*heal them.'*

16 "But [a]blessed *are* your eyes for they see, and your ears for they hear;

17 "for assuredly, I say to you [a]that many prophets and righteous *men* desired to see what you see, and did not see *it*, and to hear what you hear, and did not hear *it*.

The Parable of the Sower Explained

18 [a]"Therefore hear the parable of the sower:

19 "When anyone hears the word [a]of the kingdom, and does not understand *it*, then the wicked *one* comes and snatches away what was sown in his heart. This is he who received seed by the wayside.

20 "But he who received the seed on stony places, this is he who hears the word and immediately [a]receives it with joy;

21 "yet he has no root in himself, but endures only for a while. For when [a]tribulation or persecution arises because of the word, immediately [b]he stumbles.

22 "Now [a]he who received seed [b]among the thorns is he who hears the word, and the cares of this world and the deceitfulness of riches choke the word, and he becomes unfruitful.

23 "But he who received seed on the good ground is he who hears the word and understands *it*, who indeed bears [a]fruit and produces: some a hundredfold, some sixty, some thirty."

The Parable of the Wheat and the Tares

24 Another parable He put forth to them, saying: "The kingdom of heaven is like a man who sowed good seed in his field;

25 "but while men slept, his enemy came and sowed tares among the wheat and went his way.

26 "But when the grain had

CHAPTER 13

1 [a]Matt. 13:1–15; Mark 4:1–12; Luke 8:4–10

2 [a]Luke 8:4 [b]Luke 5:3

3 [a]Luke 8:5

8 [a]Gen. 26:12; Matt. 13:23

9 [a]Matt. 11:15; Mark 4:9; Rev. 2:7, 11, 17, 29; 3:6, 13, 22

11 [a][Matt. 11:25; 16:17]; Mark 4:10, 11; [John 6:65; 1 Cor. 2:10; Col. 1:27; 1 John 2:20, 27] [1]*secret* or *hidden truths*

12 [a]Matt. 25:29; Mark 4:25; Luke 8:18; 19:26

14 [a]Is. 6:9, 10; Ezek. 12:2; Mark 4:12; Luke 8:10; John 12:40; Acts 28:26, 27; Rom. 11:8; [2 Cor. 3:14, 15] [b][John 3:36]

15 [a]Ps. 119:70; Zech. 7:11; 2 Tim. 4:4; Heb. 5:11 [b]Luke 19:42 [c]Acts 28:26, 27 [1]NU, M *would*

16 [a][Prov. 20:12; Matt. 16:17]; Luke 10:23, 24; [John 20:29]

17 [a]John 8:56; Heb. 11:13; 1 Pet. 1:10, 11

18 [a]Mark 4:13–20; Luke 8:11–15

19 [a]Matt. 4:23

20 [a]Is. 58:2; Ezek. 33:31, 32; John 5:35

21 [a][Acts 14:22] [b]Matt. 11:6; 2 Tim. 1:15

22 [a]Matt. 19:23; Mark 10:23; Luke 18:24; 1 Tim. 6:9; 2 Tim. 4:10 [b]Jer. 4:3

23 [a][John 15:5]; Phil. 1:11; Col. 1:6

sprouted and produced a crop,
then the tares also appeared.
27 "So the servants of the owner
came and said to him, 'Sir, did you
not sow good seed in your field?
How then does it have tares?'
28 "He said to them, 'An enemy
has done this.' The servants said
to him, 'Do you want us then to
go and gather them up?'
29 "But he said, 'No, lest while
you gather up the tares you also
uproot the wheat with them.
30 'Let both grow together until
the harvest, and at the time of
harvest I will say to the reapers,
"First gather together the tares
and bind them in bundles to burn
them, but [a]gather the wheat into
my barn." ' "

The Parable of the Mustard Seed

31 Another parable He put forth
to them, saying: [a]"The kingdom of
heaven is like a mustard seed,
which a man took and sowed in
his field,
32 "which indeed is the least of all
the seeds; but when it is grown it
is greater than the herbs and be-
comes a [a]tree, so that the birds of
the air come and nest in its
branches."

The Parable of the Leaven

33 [a]Another parable He spoke to
them: "The kingdom of heaven is
like leaven, which a woman took
and hid in three [1]measures of meal
till [b]it was all leavened."

Prophecy and the Parables

34 [a]All these things Jesus spoke to
the multitude in parables; and
without a parable He did not speak
to them,
35 that it might be fulfilled which
was spoken by the prophet, say-
ing:

[a]"I will open My mouth in parables;
[b]I will utter things kept secret from
the foundation of the world."

The Parable of the Tares Explained

36 Then Jesus sent the multitude
away and went into the house.
And His disciples came to Him,
saying, "Explain to us the parable
of the tares of the field."
37 He answered and said to them:
"He who sows the good seed is the
Son of Man.
38 [a]"The field is the world, the
good seeds are the sons of
the kingdom, but the tares are [b]the
sons of the wicked *one.*
39 "The enemy who sowed them
is the devil, [a]the harvest is the end
of the age, and the reapers are the
angels.
40 "Therefore as the tares are
gathered and burned in the fire, so
it will be at the end of this age.
41 "The Son of Man will send out
His angels, [a]and they will gather
out of His kingdom all things that
offend, and those who practice
lawlessness,
42 [a]"and will cast them into the
furnace of fire. [b]There will be wail-
ing and gnashing of teeth.
43 [a]"Then the righteous will shine
forth as the sun in the kingdom of
their Father. [b]He who has ears to
hear, let him hear!

The Parable of the Hidden Treasure

44 "Again, the kingdom of heaven
is like treasure hidden in a field,
which a man found and hid; and
for joy over it he goes and [a]sells
all that he has and [b]buys that field.

The Parable of the Pearl of Great Price

45 "Again, the kingdom of heaven
is like a merchant seeking beauti-
ful pearls,
46 "who, when he had found [a]one
pearl of great price, went and sold
all that he had and bought it.

The Parable of the Dragnet

47 "Again, the kingdom of heaven
is like a dragnet that was cast into
the sea and [a]gathered some of
every kind,
48 "which, when it was full, they
drew to shore; and they sat down
and gathered the good into ves-
sels, but threw the bad away.
49 "So it will be at the end of the
age. The angels will come forth,
[a]separate the wicked from among
the just,
50 "and cast them into the furnace
of fire. There will be wailing and
gnashing of teeth."
51 [1]Jesus said to them, "Have you
understood all these things?" They
said to Him, "Yes, [2]Lord."

30 [a]Matt. 3:12
31 [a][Is. 2:2, 3; Mic. 4:1]; Mark 4:30; Luke 13:18, 19
32 [a]Ps. 104:12; Ezek. 17:22–24; 31:3–9; Dan. 4:12
33 [a]Luke 13:20, 21 [b][1 Cor. 5:6; Gal. 5:9] [1]Gr. *sata,* same as a Heb. *seah;* approximately 2 pecks in all
34 [a]Mark 4:33, 34; John 10:6; 16:25
35 [a]Ps. 78:2 [b]Rom. 16:25, 26; 1 Cor. 2:7; Eph. 3:9; Col. 1:26
38 [a]Matt. 24:14; 28:19; Mark 16:15; Luke 24:47; Rom. 10:18; Col. 1:6 [b]Gen. 3:15; John 8:44; Acts 13:10
39 [a]Joel 3:13; Rev. 14:15
41 [a]Matt. 18:7; 2 Pet. 2:1, 2
42 [a]Matt. 3:12; Rev. 19:20; 20:10 [b]Matt. 8:12; 13:50
43 [a][Dan. 12:3; 1 Cor. 15:42, 43, 58] [b]Matt. 13:9
44 [a]Phil. 3:7, 8 [b][Is. 55:1; Rev. 3:18]
46 [a]Prov. 2:4; 3:14, 15; 8:10, 19
47 [a]Matt. 22:9, 10
49 [a]Matt. 25:32
51 [1]NU omits *Jesus said to them* [2]NU omits *Lord*

52 Then He said to them, "There-
fore every [1]scribe instructed [2]con-
cerning the kingdom of heaven is
like a householder who brings out
of his treasure [a]*things* new and
old."

Jesus Rejected at Nazareth

53 Now it came to pass, when
Jesus had finished these parables,
that He departed from there.
54 [a]When He had come to His own
country, He taught them in their
synagogue, so that they were as-
tonished and said, "Where did this
Man get this wisdom and *these*
mighty works?
55 [a]"Is this not the carpenter's
son? Is not His mother called
Mary? And [b]His brothers [c]James,
[1]Joses, Simon, and Judas?
56 "And His sisters, are they not
all with us? Where then did this
Man get all these things?"
57 So they [a]were offended at Him.
But Jesus said to them, [b]"A
prophet is not without honor ex-
cept in his own country and in his
own house."
58 Now [a]He did not do many
mighty works there because of
their unbelief.

John the Baptist Beheaded

14 At that time [a]Herod the te-
trarch heard the report
about Jesus
2 and said to his servants, "This
is John the Baptist; he is risen from
the dead, and therefore these pow-
ers are at work in him."
3 [a]For Herod had laid hold of
John and bound him, and put *him*
in prison for the sake of Herodias,
his brother Philip's wife.
4 Because John had said to him,
[a]"It is not lawful for you to have
her."
5 And although he wanted to put
him to death, he feared the multi-
tude, [a]because they counted him
as a prophet.
6 But when Herod's birthday was
celebrated, the daughter of Hero-
dias danced before them and
pleased Herod.
7 Therefore he promised with an
oath to give her whatever she
might ask.
8 So she, having been prompted
by her mother, said, "Give me
John the Baptist's head here on a
platter."
9 And the king was sorry; never-
theless, because of the oaths and
because of those who sat with him,
he commanded *it* to be given to
her.
10 So he sent and had John be-
headed in prison.
11 And his head was brought on
a platter and given to the girl, and
she brought *it* to her mother.
12 Then his disciples came and
took away the body and buried it,
and went and told Jesus.

Feeding the Five Thousand

13 [a]When Jesus heard *it*, He de-
parted from there by boat to a de-
serted place by Himself. But when
the multitudes heard it, they fol-
lowed Him on foot from the cities.
14 And when Jesus went out He
saw a great multitude; and He
[a]was moved with compassion for
them, and healed their sick.
15 [a]When it was evening, His dis-
ciples came to Him, saying, "This
is a deserted place, and the hour
is already late. Send the multi-
tudes away, that they may go into
the villages and buy themselves
food."
16 But Jesus said to them, "They
do not need to go away. You give
them something to eat."
17 And they said to Him, "We
have here only five loaves and two
fish."
18 He said, "Bring them here to
Me."
19 Then He commanded the multi-
tudes to sit down on the grass. And
He took the five loaves and the two
fish, and looking up to heaven, [a]He
blessed and broke and gave the
loaves to the disciples; and the dis-
ciples gave to the multitudes.
20 So they all ate and were filled,
and they took up twelve baskets
full of the fragments that re-
mained.
21 Now those who had eaten were
about five thousand men, besides
women and children.

Jesus Walks on the Sea

22 Immediately Jesus [1]made His
disciples get into the boat and go
before Him to the other side, while
He sent the multitudes away.

---

52 [a]Song 7:13 [1]A scholar of the Old Testament [2]Or *for*
54 [a]Ps. 22:22; Matt. 2:23; Mark 6:1; Luke 4:16; John 7:15
55 [a]Is. 49:7; Mark 6:3; [Luke 3:23]; John 6:42 [b]Matt. 12:46 [c]Mark 15:40 [1]NU *Joseph*
57 [a]Matt. 11:6; Mark 6:3, 4 [b]Luke 4:24; John 4:44
58 [a]Mark 6:5, 6; John 5:44, 46, 47

CHAPTER 14

1 [a]Mark 6:14–29; Luke 9:7–9
3 [a]Matt. 4:12; Mark 6:17; Luke 3:19, 20
4 [a]Lev. 18:16; 20:21
5 [a]Matt. 21:26; Luke 20:6
13 [a]Matt. 10:23; 12:15; Mark 6:32–44; Luke 9:10–17; John 6:1, 2
14 [a]Matt. 9:36; Mark 6:34
15 [a]Mark 6:35; Luke 9:12
19 [a]1 Sam. 9:13; Matt. 15:36; 26:26; Mark 6:41; 8:7; 14:22; Luke 24:30; Acts 27:35; [Rom. 14:6]
22 [1]*invited, strongly urged*

23 [a]And when He had sent the
multitudes away, He went up on
the mountain by Himself to pray.
[b]Now when evening came, He was
alone there.
24 But the boat was now [1]in the
middle of the sea, tossed by the
waves, for the wind was contrary.
25 Now in the fourth watch of the
night Jesus went to them, walking
on the sea.
26 And when the disciples saw
Him [a]walking on the sea, they
were troubled, saying, "It is a
ghost!" And they cried out for fear.
27 But immediately Jesus spoke to
them, saying, [1]"Be of good [a]cheer!
[2]It is I; do not be afraid."
28 And Peter answered Him and
said, "Lord, if it is You, command
me to come to You on the water."
29 So He said, "Come." And when
Peter had come down out of the
boat, he walked on the water to
go to Jesus.
30 But when he saw [1]that the wind
was boisterous, he was afraid; and
beginning to sink he cried out, saying,
"Lord, save me!"
31 And immediately Jesus
stretched out *His* hand and caught
him, and said to him, "O you of
[a]little faith, why did you doubt?"
32 And when they got into the
boat, the wind ceased.
33 Then those who were in the
boat [1]came and worshiped Him,
saying, "Truly [a]You are the Son
of God."

Many Touch Him and Are Made Well

34 [a]When they had crossed over,
they came [1]to the land of Gennesaret.
35 And when the men of that
place recognized Him, they sent
out into all that surrounding region,
brought to Him all who were
sick,
36 and begged Him that they
might only [a]touch the hem of His
garment. And [b]as many as touched
it were made perfectly well.

Defilement Comes from Within

15 Then [a]the scribes and Pharisees
who were from Jerusalem
came to Jesus, saying,
2 [a]"Why do Your disciples transgress
the tradition of the elders?

23 [a]Mark 6:46 [b]John 6:16
24 [1]NU *many furlongs away from the land*
26 [a]Job 9:8
27 [a]Acts 23:11; 27:22, 25, 36 [1]*Take courage* [2]Lit. *I am*
30 [1]NU brackets *that* and *boisterous* as disputed.
31 [a]Matt. 6:30; 8:26
33 [a]Ps. 2:7 [1]NU omits *came and*
34 [a]Mark 6:53 [1]NU *to land at*
36 [a][Mark 5:24–34] [b][Luke 6:19]

CHAPTER 15

1 [a]Mark 7:1
2 [a]Mark 7:5
4 [a][Deut. 5:16] [b]Ex. 21:17
5 [a]Mark 7:11, 12
6 [1]NU omits *or mother* [2]NU *word*
7 [a]Mark 7:6
8 [a]Is. 29:13 [1]NU omits *draw near to Me with their mouth, And*
9 [a][Col. 2:18–22]
10 [a]Mark 7:14
11 [a][Acts 10:15]
13 [a][John 15:2]
14 [a]Luke 6:39
15 [a]Mark 7:17
16 [a]Matt. 16:9
17 [a][1 Cor. 6:13]
18 [a][James 3:6]
19 [a]Prov. 6:14

For they do not wash their hands
when they eat bread."
3 He answered and said to them,
"Why do you also transgress the
commandment of God because of
your tradition?
4 "For God commanded, saying,
[a]*'Honor your father and your
mother'*; and, [b]*'He who curses father
or mother, let him be put to
death.'*
5 "But you say, 'Whoever says to
his father or mother, [a]"Whatever
profit you might have received
from me *is* a gift *to God*"—
6 'then he need not honor his father
[1]or mother.' Thus you have
made the [2]commandment of God
of no effect by your tradition.
7 [a]"Hypocrites! Well did Isaiah
prophesy about you, saying:

8 *'These[a] people [1]draw near to Me
with their mouth,
And honor Me with their lips,
But their heart is far from Me.*
9 *And in vain they worship Me,
[a]Teaching as doctrines the
commandments of men.'* "

10 [a]When He had called the multitude
to *Himself*, He said to them,
"Hear and understand:
11 [a]"Not what goes into the mouth
defiles a man; but what comes out
of the mouth, this defiles a man."
12 Then His disciples came and
said to Him, "Do You know that
the Pharisees were offended when
they heard this saying?"
13 But He answered and said,
[a]"Every plant which My heavenly
Father has not planted will be uprooted.
14 "Let them alone. [a]They are
blind leaders of the blind. And if
the blind leads the blind, both will
fall into a ditch."
15 [a]Then Peter answered and said
to Him, "Explain this parable to
us."
16 So Jesus said, [a]"Are you also
still without understanding?
17 "Do you not yet understand
that [a]whatever enters the mouth
goes into the stomach and is eliminated?
18 "But [a]those things which proceed
out of the mouth come from
the heart, and they defile a man.
19 [a]"For out of the heart proceed

evil thoughts, murders, adulteries,
fornications, thefts, false witness,
blasphemies.
20 "These are *the things* which
defile a man, but to eat with un-
washed hands does not defile a
man."

A Gentile Shows Her Faith

21 [a]Then Jesus went out from
there and departed to the region
of Tyre and Sidon.
22 And behold, a woman of Ca-
naan came from that region and
cried out to Him, saying, "Have
mercy on me, O Lord, [a]Son of
David! My daughter is severely
demon-possessed."
23 But He answered her not a
word. And His disciples came and
urged Him, saying, "Send her
away, for she cries out after
us."
24 But He answered and said, [a]"I
was not sent except to the lost
sheep of the house of Israel."
25 Then she came and worshiped
Him, saying, "Lord, help me!"

21 [a]Mark 7:24–30
22 [a]Matt. 1:1; 22:41, 42
24 [a]Matt. 10:5, 6; [Rom. 15:8]
26 [a]Matt. 7:6; Phil. 3:2
28 [a]Luke 7:9
29 [a]Matt. 15:29–31; Mark 7:31–37 [b]Matt. 4:18
30 [a]Is. 35:5, 6; Matt. 11:5; Luke 7:22 [b]Mark 7:25; Luke 7:38; 8:41; 10:39 [1]*crippled*
31 [1]*crippled*

26 But He answered and said, "It
is not good to take the children's
bread and throw *it* to the little
[a]dogs."
27 And she said, "Yes, Lord, yet
even the little dogs eat the crumbs
which fall from their masters' ta-
ble."
28 Then Jesus answered and said
to her, "O woman, [a]great *is* your
faith! Let it be to you as you de-
sire." And her daughter was
healed from that very hour.

Jesus Heals Great Multitudes

29 [a]Jesus departed from there,
[b]skirted the Sea of Galilee, and
went up on the mountain and sat
down there.
30 [a]Then great multitudes came to
Him, having with them *the* lame,
blind, mute, [1]maimed, and many
others; and they laid them down
at Jesus' [b]feet, and He healed
them.
31 So the multitude marveled
when they saw *the* mute speaking,
the [1]maimed made whole, *the*

Jesus' Ministry Beyond Galilee. Near Tyre, Jesus cast out a demon from the daughter of a Syro-Phoenician woman (Mark 7:24–30). Peter made his great confession at Caesarea Philippi (Matt. 16:13–19). Jesus returned to Galilee via the Decapolis region, crossing the Jordan River south of the Sea of Galilee.

lame walking, and *the* blind see-
ing; and they [a]glorified the God of
Israel.

Feeding the Four Thousand

32 [a]Now Jesus called His disciples
to *Himself* and said, "I have com-
passion on the multitude, because
they have now continued with Me
three days and have nothing to eat.
And I do not want to send them
away hungry, lest they faint on the
way."
33 [a]Then His disciples said to
Him, "Where could we get enough
bread in the wilderness to fill such
a great multitude?"
34 Jesus said to them, "How many
loaves do you have?" And they
said, "Seven, and a few little
fish."
35 So He commanded the multi-
tude to sit down on the ground.
36 And [a]He took the seven loaves
and the fish and [b]gave thanks,
broke *them* and gave *them* to His
disciples; and the disciples *gave* to
the multitude.
37 So they all ate and were filled,
and they took up seven large bas-
kets full of the fragments that were
left.
38 Now those who ate were four
thousand men, besides women and
children.
39 [a]And He sent away the multi-
tude, got into the boat, and came
to the region of [1]Magdala.

The Pharisees and Sadducees Seek a Sign

16 Then the [a]Pharisees and
Sadducees came, and testing
Him asked that He would show
them a sign from heaven.
2 He answered and said to them,
"When it is evening you say, *'It
will be* fair weather, for the sky is
red';
3 "and in the morning, *'It will be*
foul weather today, for the sky is
red and threatening.' [1]Hypocrites!
You know how to discern the face
of the sky, but you cannot *discern*
the signs of the times.
4 [a]"A wicked and adulterous
generation seeks after a sign, and
no sign shall be given to it except
the sign of [1]the prophet Jonah."
And He left them and departed.

31 [a]Luke 5:25, 26; 19:37, 38
32 [a]Mark 8:1–10
33 [a]2 Kin. 4:43
36 [a]Matt. 14:19; 26:27; Luke 22:17, 19; John 6:11, 23; Acts 27:35; [Rom. 14:6] [b]1 Sam. 9:13; Luke 22:19
39 [a]Mark 8:10 [1]NU *Magadan*

CHAPTER 16

1 [a]Matt. 12:38; Mark 8:11; Luke 11:16; 12:54–56; 1 Cor. 1:22
3 [1]NU omits *Hypocrites*
4 [a]Prov. 30:12; Matt. 12:39; Luke 11:29; 24:46 [1]NU omits *the prophet*
5 [a]Mark 8:14
6 [a]Mark 8:15; Luke 12:1 [1]*yeast*
8 [1]NU *have no bread*
9 [a]Matt. 14:15–21; Mark 6:30–44; Luke 9:10–17; John 6:1–14
10 [a]Matt. 15:32–38; Mark 8:1–9
11 [1]*yeast*
12 [1]*teaching*
13 [a]Mark 8:27; Luke 9:18
14 [a]Matt. 14:2; Luke 9:7–9 [b]Matt. 21:11
15 [a]John 6:67
16 [a]Matt. 14:33; Mark 8:29; Luke 9:20; John 6:69; 11:27; Acts 8:37; 9:20; Heb. 1:2, 5; 1 John 4:15
17 [a][Eph. 2:8] [b][Matt. 11:27; 1 Cor. 2:10]; Gal. 1:16
18 [a]John 1:42 [b]Acts 2:41; [Eph. 2:20; Rev. 21:14] [c]Job 33:17; Ps. 9:13; 107:18; Is. 38:10 [1]*be victorious*
19 [a]Matt. 18:18; John 20:23

The Leaven of the Pharisees and Sadducees

5 Now [a]when His disciples had
come to the other side, they had
forgotten to take bread.
6 Then Jesus said to them,
[a]"Take heed and beware of the
[1]leaven of the Pharisees and the
Sadducees."
7 And they reasoned among
themselves, saying, *"It is* because
we have taken no bread."
8 But Jesus, being aware of *it,*
said to them, "O you of little faith,
why do you reason among your-
selves because you [1]have brought
no bread?
9 [a]"Do you not yet understand,
or remember the five loaves of the
five thousand and how many bas-
kets you took up?
10 [a]"Nor the seven loaves of the
four thousand and how many
large baskets you took up?
11 "How is it you do not under-
stand that I did not speak to you
concerning bread?—*but* to beware
of the [1]leaven of the Pharisees and
Sadducees."
12 Then they understood that He
did not tell *them* to beware of the
leaven of bread, but of the [1]doc-
trine of the Pharisees and Sad-
ducees.

Peter Confesses Jesus as the Christ

13 When Jesus came into the re-
gion of Caesarea Philippi, He
asked His disciples, saying, [a]"Who
do men say that I, the Son of Man,
am?"
14 So they said, [a]"Some *say* John
the Baptist, some Elijah, and oth-
ers Jeremiah or [b]one of the proph-
ets."
15 He said to them, "But who do
[a]you say that I am?"
16 Simon Peter answered and
said, [a]"You are the Christ, the Son
of the living God."
17 Jesus answered and said to
him, "Blessed are you, Simon Bar-
Jonah, [a]for flesh and blood has not
revealed *this* to you, but [b]My Fa-
ther who is in heaven.
18 "And I also say to you that [a]you
are Peter, and [b]on this rock I will
build My church, and [c]the gates of
Hades shall not [1]prevail against it.
19 [a]"And I will give you the keys

of the kingdom of heaven, and
whatever you bind on earth [1]will
be bound in heaven, and whatever
you loose on earth will be loosed
in heaven."
20 [a]Then He commanded His dis-
ciples that they should tell no one
that He was Jesus the Christ.

Jesus Predicts His Death and Resurrection

21 From that time Jesus began [a]to
show to His disciples that He must
go to Jerusalem, and suffer many
things from the elders and chief
priests and scribes, and be killed,
and be raised the third day.
22 Then Peter took Him aside and
began to rebuke Him, saying,
[1]"Far be it from You, Lord; this
shall not happen to You!"
23 But He turned and said to Pe-
ter, "Get behind Me, [a]Satan! [b]You
are [1]an offense to Me, for you are
not mindful of the things of God,
but the things of men."

Take Up the Cross and Follow Him

24 [a]Then Jesus said to His disci-
ples, "If anyone desires to come
after Me, let him deny himself, and
take up his cross, and [b]follow Me.
25 "For [a]whoever desires to save
his life will lose it, but whoever
loses his life for My sake will find
it.
26 "For what [a]profit is it to a man
if he gains the whole world, and
loses his own soul? Or [b]what will
a man give in exchange for his
soul?
27 "For [a]the Son of Man will come
in the glory of His Father [b]with His
angels, [c]and then He will reward
each according to his works.

Jesus Transfigured on the Mount

28 "Assuredly, I say to you, [a]there
are some standing here who shall
not taste death till they see the Son
of Man coming in His kingdom."

17 Now [a]after six days Jesus
took Peter, James, and John
his brother, led them up on a high
mountain by themselves;
2 and He was transfigured before
them. His face shone like the sun,
and His clothes became as white
as the light.
3 And behold, Moses and Elijah
appeared to them, talking with
Him.
4 Then Peter answered and said
to Jesus, "Lord, it is good for us
to be here; if You wish, [1]let us
make here three tabernacles: one
for You, one for Moses, and one
for Elijah."
5 [a]While he was still speaking,
behold, a bright cloud over-
shadowed them; and suddenly a
voice came out of the cloud, say-
ing, [b]"This is My beloved Son, [c]in
whom I am well pleased. [d]Hear
Him!"
6 [a]And when the disciples heard
it, they fell on their faces and were
greatly afraid.
7 But Jesus came and [a]touched
them and said, "Arise, and do not
be afraid."
8 When they had lifted up their
eyes, they saw no one but Jesus
only.
9 Now as they came down from
the mountain, Jesus commanded
them, saying, "Tell the vision to no
one until the Son of Man is risen
from the dead."
10 And His disciples asked Him,
saying, [a]"Why then do the scribes
say that Elijah must come first?"
11 Jesus answered and said to
them, "Indeed, Elijah is coming
[1]first and will [a]restore all things.
12 [a]"But I say to you that Elijah
has come already, and they [b]did
not know him but did to him what-
ever they wished. Likewise [c]the
Son of Man is also about to suffer
at their hands."
13 [a]Then the disciples understood
that He spoke to them of John the
Baptist.

A Boy Is Healed

14 [a]And when they had come to
the multitude, a man came to Him,
kneeling down to Him and saying,
15 "Lord, have mercy on my son,
for he is [1]an epileptic and suffers
severely; for he often falls into the
fire and often into the water.
16 "So I brought him to Your dis-
ciples, but they could not cure
him."
17 Then Jesus answered and said,
"O [1]faithless and [a]perverse gener-
ation, how long shall I be with
you? How long shall I bear with
you? Bring him here to Me."

---

19 [1]Or *will have been bound . . . will have been loosed*
20 [a]Luke 9:21
21 [a]Luke 9:22; 18:31; 24:46
22 [1]Lit. *Merciful to You* (May God be merciful)
23 [a]Matt. 4:10 [b][Rom. 8:7] [1]*a stumbling block*
24 [a][2 Tim. 3:12] [b][1 Pet. 2:21]
25 [a]John 12:25
26 [a]Luke 12:20, 21 [b]Ps. 49:7, 8
27 [a]Mark 8:38 [b][Dan. 7:10] [c]Rom. 2:6
28 [a]Luke 9:27

CHAPTER 17

1 [a]Mark 9:2–8
4 [1]NU *I will make*
5 [a]2 Pet. 1:17 [b]Mark 1:11 [c]Matt. 3:17; 12:18 [d][Deut. 18:15, 19]
6 [a]2 Pet. 1:18
7 [a]Dan. 8:18
10 [a]Mal. 4:5
11 [a][Mal. 4:6] [1]NU omits *first*
12 [a]Mark 9:12, 13 [b]Matt. 14:3, 10 [c]Matt. 16:21
13 [a]Matt. 11:14
14 [a]Mark 9:14–28
15 [1]Lit. *moonstruck*
17 [a]Phil. 2:15 [1]*unbelieving*

18 And Jesus [a]rebuked the de-
mon, and it came out of him; and
the child was cured from that very
hour.
19 Then the disciples came to
Jesus privately and said, "Why
could we not cast it out?"
20 So Jesus said to them, "Be-
cause of your [1]unbelief; for as-
suredly, I say to you, [a]if you have
faith as a mustard seed, you will
say to this mountain, 'Move from
here to there,' and it will move;
and nothing will be impossible for
you.
21 [1]"However, this kind does not
go out except by prayer and fast-
ing."

Jesus Again Predicts His Death and Resurrection

22 [a]Now while they were [1]staying
in Galilee, Jesus said to them, "The
Son of Man is about to be betrayed
into the hands of men,
23 "and they will kill Him, and the
third day He will be raised up."
And they were exceedingly [a]sor-
rowful.

Peter and His Master Pay Their Taxes

24 [a]When they had come to
[1]Capernaum, those who received
the [2]*temple* tax came to Peter and
said, "Does your Teacher not pay
the *temple* tax?"
25 He said, "Yes." And when he
had come into the house, Jesus an-
ticipated him, saying, "What do
you think, Simon? From whom do
the kings of the earth take customs
or taxes, from their sons or from
[a]strangers?"
26 Peter said to Him, "From stran-
gers." Jesus said to him, "Then the
sons are free.
27 "Nevertheless, lest we offend
them, go to the sea, cast in a hook,
and take the fish that comes up
first. And when you have opened
its mouth, you will find a [1]piece
of money; take that and give it to
them for Me and you."

Who Is the Greatest?

18 At [a]that time the disciples
came to Jesus, saying, "Who
then is greatest in the kingdom of
heaven?"
2 Then Jesus called a little [a]child
to Him, set him in the midst of
them,
3 and said, "Assuredly, I say to
you, [a]unless you are converted and
become as little children, you will
by no means enter the kingdom of
heaven.
4 [a]"Therefore whoever humbles
himself as this little child is the
greatest in the kingdom of heaven.
5 [a]"Whoever receives one little
child like this in My name receives
Me.

Jesus Warns of Offenses

6 [a]"But whoever causes one of
these little ones who believe in Me
to sin, it would be better for him
if a millstone were hung around
his neck, and he were drowned in
the depth of the sea.
7 "Woe to the world because of
[1]offenses! For [a]offenses must
come, but [b]woe to that man by
whom the offense comes!
8 [a]"If your hand or foot causes
you to sin, cut it off and cast *it*
from you. It is better for you to en-
ter into life lame or maimed, rather
than having two hands or two feet,
to be cast into the everlasting fire.
9 "And if your eye causes you to
sin, pluck it out and cast *it* from
you. It is better for you to enter
into life with one eye, rather than
having two eyes, to be cast into
[1]hell fire.

The Parable of the Lost Sheep

10 "Take heed that you do not de-
spise one of these little ones, for I
say to you that in heaven [a]their an-
gels always [b]see the face of My Fa-
ther who is in heaven.
11 [a]"For[1] the Son of Man has
come to save that which was lost.
12 [a]"What do you think? If a man
has a hundred sheep, and one of
them goes astray, does he not
leave the ninety-nine and go to the
mountains to seek the one that is
straying?
13 "And if he should find it, as-
suredly, I say to you, he rejoices
more over that *sheep* than over the
ninety-nine that did not go astray.
14 "Even so it is not the [a]will of
your Father who is in heaven that
one of these little ones should per-
ish.

18 [a]Luke 4:41
20 [a]Luke 17:6 [1]NU *little faith*
21 [1]NU omits v. 21.
22 [a]Mark 8:31 [1]NU *gathering together*
23 [a]John 16:6; 19:30
24 [a]Mark 9:33 [1]NU *Capharnaum,* here and elsewhere [2]Lit. *double drachma*
25 [a][Is. 60:10–17]
27 [1]Gr. *stater,* the exact temple tax for two

CHAPTER 18

1 [a]Luke 9:46–48; 22:24–27
2 [a]Matt. 19:14
3 [a]Luke 18:16
4 [a][Matt. 20:27; 23:11]
5 [a][Matt. 10:42]
6 [a]Mark 9:42
7 [a][1 Cor. 11:19] [b]Matt. 26:24; 27:4, 5 [1]*enticements to sin*
8 [a]Matt. 5:29, 30
9 [1]Gr. *Gehenna*
10 [a][Heb. 1:14] [b]Luke 1:19
11 [a]Luke 9:56 [1]NU omits v. 11.
12 [a]Luke 15:4–7
14 [a][1 Tim. 2:4]

Dealing with a Sinning Brother

15 "Moreover [a]if your brother sins against you, go and tell him his fault between you and him alone. If he hears you, [b]you have gained your brother.

16 "But if he will not hear, take with you one or two more, that [a]*'by the mouth of two or three witnesses every word may be established.'*

17 "And if he refuses to hear them, tell *it* to the church. But if he refuses even to hear the church, let him be to you like a [a]heathen and a tax collector.

18 "Assuredly, I say to you, [a]whatever you bind on earth will be bound in heaven, and whatever you loose on earth will be loosed in heaven.

19 [a]"Again[1] I say to you that if two of you agree on earth concerning anything that they ask, [b]it will be done for them by My Father in heaven.

20 "For where two or three are gathered [a]together in My name, I am there in the midst of them."

The Parable of the Unforgiving Servant

21 Then Peter came to Him and said, "Lord, how often shall my brother sin against me, and I forgive him? [a]Up to seven times?"

22 Jesus said to him, "I do not say to you, [a]up to seven times, but up to seventy times seven.

23 "Therefore the kingdom of heaven is like a certain king who wanted to settle accounts with his servants.

24 "And when he had begun to settle accounts, one was brought to him who owed him ten thousand talents.

25 "But as he was not able to pay, his master commanded [a]that he be sold, with his wife and children and all that he had, and that payment be made.

26 "The servant therefore fell down before him, saying, 'Master, have patience with me, and I will pay you all.'

27 "Then the master of that servant was moved with compassion, released him, and forgave him the debt.

28 "But that servant went out and found one of his fellow servants who owed him a hundred denarii; and he laid hands on him and took *him* by the throat, saying, 'Pay me what you owe!'

29 "So his fellow servant fell down [1]at his feet and begged him, saying, 'Have patience with me, and I will pay you [2]all.'

30 "And he would not, but went and threw him into prison till he should pay the debt.

31 "So when his fellow servants saw what had been done, they were very grieved, and came and told their master all that had been done.

32 "Then his master, after he had called him, said to him, 'You wicked servant! I forgave you [a]all that debt because you begged me.

33 'Should you not also have had compassion on your fellow servant, just as I had pity on you?'

34 "And his master was angry, and delivered him to the torturers until he should pay all that was due to him.

35 [a]"So My heavenly Father also will do to you if each of you, from his heart, does not forgive his brother [1]his trespasses."

Marriage and Divorce

19 Now it came to pass, [a]when Jesus had finished these sayings, *that* He departed from Galilee and came to the region of Judea beyond the Jordan.

2 [a]And great multitudes followed Him, and He healed them there.

3 The Pharisees also came to Him, testing Him, and saying to Him, "Is it lawful for a man to divorce his wife for *just* any reason?"

4 And He answered and said to them, "Have you not read that He who [1]made *them* at the beginning [a]*'made them male and female,'*

5 "and said, [a]*'For this reason a man shall leave his father and mother and be joined to his wife, and [b]the two shall become one flesh'*?

6 "So then, they are no longer two but one flesh. Therefore what God has joined together, let not man separate."

7 They said to Him, [a]"Why then

---

15 [a]Lev. 19:17; [Luke 17:3, 4; Gal. 6:1]; 2 Thess. 3:15; [James 5:19] [b][James 5:20]; 1 Pet. 3:1
16 [a]Deut. 17:6; 19:15; John 8:17; 2 Cor. 13:1; 1 Tim. 5:19; Heb. 10:28
17 [a]Rom. 16:17; 1 Cor. 5:9; [2 Thess. 3:6, 14; 2 John 10]
18 [a]Matt. 16:19; [John 20:22, 23; 1 Cor. 5:4]
19 [a][1 Cor. 1:10] [b][1 John 3:22; 5:14] [1]NU, M *Again, assuredly, I say*
20 [a]Acts 20:7; 1 Cor. 14:26
21 [a]Luke 17:4
22 [a][Matt. 6:14; Mark 11:25]; Col. 3:13
25 [a]Ex. 21:2; Lev. 25:39; 2 Kin. 4:1; Neh. 5:5, 8
29 [1]NU omits *at his feet* [2]NU, M omit *all*
32 [a]Luke 7:41–43
35 [a]Prov. 21:13; Matt. 6:12; Mark 11:26; James 2:13 [1]NU omits *his trespasses*

CHAPTER 19

1 [a]Matt. 19:1–9; Mark 10:1–12; John 10:40
2 [a]Matt. 12:15
4 [a]Gen. 1:27; 5:2; [Mal. 2:15] [1]NU *created*
5 [a]Gen. 2:24; Mark 10:5–9; Eph. 5:31 [b][1 Cor. 6:16; 7:2]
7 [a]Deut. 24:1–4; Matt. 5:31

did Moses command to give a cer-
tificate of divorce, and to put her
away?"
8 He said to them, "Moses, be-
cause of the [a]hardness of your
hearts, permitted you to divorce
your [b]wives, but from the begin-
ning it was not so.
9 [a]"And I say to you, whoever di-
vorces his wife, except for [1]sexual
immorality, and marries another,
commits adultery; and whoever
marries her who is divorced com-
mits adultery."
10 His disciples said to Him, [a]"If
such is the case of the man with
his wife, it is better not to marry."

Jesus Teaches on Celibacy

11 But He said to them, [a]"All
cannot accept this saying, but
only *those* to whom it has been
given:
12 "For there are [1]eunuchs who
were born thus from *their* mother's
womb, and [a]there are eunuchs
who were made eunuchs by men,
and there are eunuchs who have
made themselves eunuchs for
the kingdom of heaven's sake. He
who is able to accept *it*, let him
accept *it*."

Jesus Blesses Little Children

13 [a]Then little children were
brought to Him that He might put
His hands on them and pray, but
the disciples rebuked them.
14 But Jesus said, "Let the little
children come to Me, and do not
forbid them; for [a]of such is the
kingdom of heaven."
15 And He laid *His* hands on them
and departed from there.

Jesus Counsels the Rich Young Ruler

16 [a]Now behold, one came and
said to Him, [b]"Good[1] Teacher,
what good thing shall I do that I
may have eternal life?"
17 So He said to him, [1]"Why do
you call Me good? [2]No one *is* [a]good
but One, *that is*, God. But if you
want to enter into life, [b]keep the
commandments."
18 He said to Him, "Which ones?"
Jesus said, [a]"*'You shall not mur-
der,' 'You shall not commit adul-
tery,' 'You shall not steal,' 'You
shall not bear false witness,'*
19 [a]*'Honor your father and your
mother,'* and, [b]*'You shall love your
neighbor as yourself.'* "
20 The young man said to Him,
"All these things I have [a]kept
[1]from my youth. What do I still
lack?"
21 Jesus said to him, "If you want
to be perfect, [a]go, sell what you
have and give to the poor, and you
will have treasure in heaven; and
come, follow Me."
22 But when the young man heard
that saying, he went away sorrow-
ful, for he had great possessions.

With God All Things Are Possible

23 Then Jesus said to His disci-
ples, "Assuredly, I say to you that
[a]it is hard for a rich man to enter
the kingdom of heaven.
24 "And again I say to you, it is
easier for a camel to go through
the eye of a needle than for a rich
man to enter the kingdom of God."
25 When His disciples heard *it*,
they were greatly astonished, say-
ing, "Who then can be saved?"
26 But Jesus looked at *them* and
said to them, "With men this is im-
possible, but [a]with God all things
are possible."
27 Then Peter answered and said
to Him, "See, [a]we have left all and
followed You. Therefore what
shall we have?"
28 So Jesus said to them, "As-
suredly I say to you, that in the
regeneration, when the Son of
Man sits on the throne of His
glory, [a]you who have followed Me
will also sit on twelve thrones,
judging the twelve tribes of Israel.
29 [a]"And everyone who has left
houses or brothers or sisters or fa-
ther or mother [1]or wife or children
or [2]lands, for My name's sake,
shall receive a hundredfold, and
inherit eternal life.
30 [a]"But many *who are* first will
be last, and the last first.

The Parable of the Workers in the Vineyard

20 "For the kingdom of heaven
is like a landowner who
went out early in the morning to
hire laborers for his vineyard.
2 "Now when he had agreed with
the laborers for a denarius a day,
he sent them into his vineyard.
3 "And he went out about the

8 [a]Heb. 3:15 [b]Mal. 2:16
9 [a][Matt. 5:32] [1]Or *fornication*
10 [a][Prov. 21:19]
11 [a][1 Cor. 7:2, 7, 9, 17]
12 [a][1 Cor. 7:32] [1]Emasculated men
13 [a]Luke 18:15
14 [a]Matt. 18:3, 4
16 [a]Mark 10:17–30 [b]Luke 10:25 [1]NU omits *Good*
17 [a]Nah. 1:7 [b]Lev. 18:5 [1]NU *Why do you ask Me about what is good?* [2]NU *There is One who is good. But*
18 [a]Ex. 20:13–16
19 [a]Ex. 20:12–16; Deut. 5:16–20 [b]Lev. 19:18
20 [a][Phil. 3:6, 7] [1]NU omits *from my youth*
21 [a]Acts 2:45; 4:34, 35
23 [a][1 Tim. 6:9]
26 [a]Jer. 32:17
27 [a]Deut. 33:9
28 [a]Luke 22:28–30
29 [a]Mark 10:29, 30 [1]NU omits *or wife* [2]Lit. *fields*
30 [a]Luke 13:30

third hour and saw others stand-
ing idle in the marketplace,
4 "and said to them, 'You also go
into the vineyard, and whatever is
right I will give you.' So they went.
5 "Again he went out about the
sixth and the ninth hour, and did
likewise.
6 "And about the eleventh hour
he went out and found others
standing [1]idle, and said to them,
'Why have you been standing here
idle all day?'
7 "They said to him, 'Because no
one hired us.' He said to them,
'You also go into the vineyard,
[1]and whatever is right you will re-
ceive.'
8 "So when evening had come,
the owner of the vineyard said to
his steward, 'Call the laborers and
give them *their* wages, beginning
with the last to the first.'
9 "And when those came who
were hired about the eleventh
hour, they each received a de-
narius.
10 "But when the first came, they
supposed that they would receive
more; and they likewise received
each a denarius.
11 "And when they had received
it, they [1]complained against the
landowner,
12 "saying, 'These last *men* have
worked *only* one hour, and you
made them equal to us who have
borne the burden and the heat of
the day.'
13 "But he answered one of them
and said, 'Friend, I am doing you
no wrong. Did you not agree with
me for a denarius?
14 'Take *what is* yours and go
your way. I wish to give to this last
man *the same* as to you.
15 [a]'Is it not lawful for me to do
what I wish with my own things?
Or [b]is your eye evil because I am
good?'
16 [a]"So the last will be first, and
the first last. [b]For[1] many are
called, but few chosen."

Jesus a Third Time Predicts His Death and Resurrection

17 [a]Now Jesus, going up to Jeru-
salem, took the twelve disciples
aside on the road and said to them,
18 [a]"Behold, we are going up to
Jerusalem, and the Son of Man
will be betrayed to the chief priests
and to the scribes; and they will
condemn Him to death,
19 [a]"and deliver Him to the Gen-
tiles to [b]mock and to [c]scourge and
to [d]crucify. And the third day He
will [e]rise again."

Greatness Is Serving

20 [a]Then the mother of [b]Zebedee's
sons came to Him with her sons,
kneeling down and asking some-
thing from Him.
21 And He said to her, "What do
you wish?" She said to Him,
"Grant that these two sons of mine
[a]may sit, one on Your right hand
and the other on the left, in Your
kingdom."
22 But Jesus answered and said,
"You do not know what you ask.
Are you able to drink [a]the cup that
I am about to drink, [1]and be bap-
tized with [b]the baptism that I am
baptized with?" They said to Him,
"We are able."
23 So He said to them, [a]"You will
indeed drink My cup, [1]and be bap-
tized with the baptism that I am
baptized with; but to sit on My
right hand and on My left is not
Mine to give, but *it is for those*
for whom it is prepared by My Fa-
ther."
24 [a]And when the ten heard *it*,
they were greatly displeased with
the two brothers.
25 But Jesus called them to *Him-
self* and said, "You know that the
rulers of the Gentiles lord it over
them, and those who are great ex-
ercise authority over them.
26 "Yet [a]it shall not be so among
you; but [b]whoever desires to be-
come great among you, let him be
your servant.
27 [a]"And whoever desires to be
first among you, let him be your
slave—
28 [a]"just as the [b]Son of Man did
not come to be served, [c]but to
serve, and [d]to give His life a ran-
som [e]for many."

Two Blind Men Receive Their Sight

29 [a]Now as they went out of Jeri-
cho, a great multitude followed
Him.
30 And behold, [a]two blind men sit-
ting by the road, when they heard

CHAPTER 20
6 [1]NU omits *idle*
7 [1]NU omits the rest of v. 7.
11 [1]*grumbled*
15 [a][Rom. 9:20, 21] [b]Deut. 15:9
16 [a]Matt. 19:30 [b]Matt. 22:14 [1]NU omits the rest of v. 16.
17 [a]Mark 10:32–34
18 [a]Matt. 16:21; 26:47–57
19 [a]Matt. 27:2 [b]Matt. 26:67, 68; 27:29, 41 [c]Matt. 27:26 [d]Acts 3:13–15 [e]Matt. 28:5, 6
20 [a]Mark 10:35–45 [b]Matt. 4:21; 10:2
21 [a][Matt. 19:28]
22 [a]Luke 22:42 [b]Luke 12:50 [1]NU omits *and be baptized with the baptism that I am baptized with*
23 [a][Acts 12:2] [1]NU omits *and be baptized with the baptism that I am baptized with*
24 [a]Mark 10:41
26 [a][1 Pet. 5:3] [b]Matt. 23:11
27 [a][Matt. 18:4]
28 [a]John 13:4 [b][Phil. 2:6, 7] [c]Luke 22:27 [d][Is. 53:10, 11] [e][Rom. 5:15, 19]
29 [a]Mark 10:46–52
30 [a]Matt. 9:27

that Jesus was passing by, cried
out, saying, "Have mercy on us, O
Lord, [b]Son of David!"
31 Then the multitude [a]warned
them that they should be quiet; but
they cried out all the more, saying,
"Have mercy on us, O Lord, Son
of David!"
32 So Jesus stood still and called
them, and said, "What do you
want Me to do for you?"
33 They said to Him, "Lord, that
our eyes may be opened."
34 So Jesus had [a]compassion and
touched their eyes. And immedi-
ately their eyes received sight, and
they followed Him.

The Triumphal Entry

21 Now [a]when they drew near
Jerusalem, and came to
[1]Bethphage, at [b]the Mount of
Olives, then Jesus sent two disci-
ples,
2 saying to them, "Go into the
village opposite you, and immedi-
ately you will find a donkey tied,
and a colt with her. Loose *them*
and bring *them* to Me.
3 "And if anyone says anything
to you, you shall say, 'The Lord
has need of them,' and immedi-
ately he will send them."
4 [1]All this was done that it might
be fulfilled which was spoken by
the prophet, saying:

5 *"Tell[a] the daughter of Zion,*
'Behold, your King is coming to
you,
Lowly, and sitting on a donkey,
A colt, the foal of a donkey.'"

6 [a]So the disciples went and did
as Jesus commanded them.
7 They brought the donkey and
the colt, [a]laid their clothes on
them, [1]and set *Him* on them.
8 And a very great multitude
spread their clothes on the road;
[a]others cut down branches from
the trees and spread *them* on the
road.
9 Then the multitudes who went
before and those who followed
cried out, saying:

"Hosanna to the Son of David!
[a]'*Blessed is He who comes in the*
name of the LORD!'
Hosanna in the highest!"

10 [a]And when He had come into
Jerusalem, all the city was moved,
saying, "Who is this?"
11 So the multitudes said, "This is
Jesus, [a]the prophet from Nazareth
of Galilee."

Jesus Cleanses the Temple

12 [a]Then Jesus went into the tem-
ple [1]of God and drove out all those
who bought and sold in the temple,
and overturned the tables of the
[b]money changers and the seats of
those who sold doves.
13 And He said to them, "It is writ-
ten, [a]'*My house shall be called a*
house of prayer,' but you have
made it a [b]'*den of thieves.*'"
14 Then *the* blind and *the* lame
came to Him in the temple, and He
healed them.
15 But when the chief priests and
scribes saw the wonderful things
that He did, and the children cry-
ing out in the temple and saying,
"Hosanna to the [a]Son of David!"
they were [1]indignant
16 and said to Him, "Do You hear
what these are saying?" And Jesus
said to them, "Yes. Have you never
read,

[a]'*Out of the mouth of babes and*
nursing infants
You have perfected praise'?"

17 Then He left them and [a]went
out of the city to Bethany, and He
lodged there.

The Fig Tree Withered

18 [a]Now in the morning, as He re-
turned to the city, He was hungry.
19 [a]And seeing a fig tree by the
road, He came to it and found
nothing on it but leaves, and said
to it, "Let no fruit grow on you
ever again." Immediately the fig
tree withered away.

The Lesson of the Withered Fig Tree

20 [a]And when the disciples saw *it*,
they marveled, saying, "How did
the fig tree wither away so soon?"
21 So Jesus answered and said to
them, "Assuredly, I say to you, [a]if
you have faith and [b]do not doubt,
you will not only do what was
done to the fig tree, [c]but also if you
say to this mountain, 'Be removed

30 [b][2 Sam. 7:14–17; Ps. 89:3–5, 19–37; Is. 11:10–12; Ezek. 37:21–25]; Matt. 1:1; Luke 1:31, 32; [Acts 15:14–17]
31 [a]Matt. 19:13
34 [a]Matt. 9:36; 14:14; 15:32; 18:27

CHAPTER 21

1 [a]Mark 11:1–10; Luke 19:29–38 [b][Zech. 14:4] [1]M *Bethsphage*
4 [1]NU omits *All*
5 [a]Is. 62:11; Zech. 9:9; John 12:15
6 [a]Mark 11:4
7 [a]2 Kin. 9:13 [1]NU *and He sat*
8 [a]Lev. 23:40; John 12:13
9 [a]Ps. 118:26; Matt. 23:39
10 [a]John 2:13, 15
11 [a][Deut. 18:15, 18]; Matt. 2:23; 16:14; Luke 4:16–29; John 6:14; 7:40; 9:17; [Acts 3:22, 23]
12 [a]Mal. 3:1; Mark 11:15–18; Luke 19:45–47; John 2:13–16 [b]Deut. 14:25 [1]NU omits *of God*
13 [a]Is. 56:7 [b]Jer. 7:11
15 [a]Matt. 1:1; John 7:42 [1]*angry*
16 [a]Ps. 8:2; Matt. 11:25
17 [a]Matt. 26:6; Mark 11:1, 11, 12; 14:3; Luke 19:29; 24:50; John 11:1, 18; 12:1
18 [a]Mark 11:12–14, 20–24
19 [a]Mark 11:13
20 [a]Mark 11:20
21 [a]Matt. 17:20 [b]James 1:6 [c]1 Cor. 13:2

and be cast into the sea,' it will be
done.
22 "And [a]whatever things you ask
in prayer, believing, you will re-
ceive."

Jesus' Authority Questioned

23 [a]Now when He came into the
temple, the chief priests and the
elders of the people confronted
Him as He was teaching, and
[b]said, "By what authority are You
doing these things? And who gave
You this authority?"
24 But Jesus answered and said to
them, "I also will ask you one
thing, which if you tell Me, I like-
wise will tell you by what author-
ity I do these things:
25 "The [a]baptism of [b]John—
where was it from? From heaven
or from men?" And they reasoned
among themselves, saying, "If we
say, 'From heaven,' He will say to
us, 'Why then did you not believe
him?'
26 "But if we say, 'From men,' we
[a]fear the multitude, [b]for all count
John as a prophet."
27 So they answered Jesus and
said, "We do not know." And He
said to them, "Neither will I tell
you by what authority I do these
things.

The Parable of the Two Sons

28 "But what do you think? A man
had two sons, and he came to the
first and said, 'Son, go, work today
in my [a]vineyard.'
29 "He answered and said, 'I will
not,' but afterward he regretted it
and went.
30 "Then he came to the second
and said likewise. And he an-
swered and said, 'I *go,* sir,' but he
did not go.
31 "Which of the two did the will
of *his* father?" They said to Him,
"The first." Jesus said to them,
[a]"Assuredly, I say to you that tax
collectors and harlots enter the
kingdom of God before you.
32 "For [a]John came to you in the
way of righteousness, and you did
not believe him; [b]but tax collectors
and harlots believed him; and
when you saw *it,* you did not
afterward [1]relent and believe him.

The Parable of the Wicked Vinedressers

33 "Hear another parable: There
was a certain landowner [a]who
planted a vineyard and set a hedge
around it, dug a winepress in it and
built a tower. And he leased it to
vinedressers and [b]went into a far
country.
34 "Now when vintage-time drew
near, he sent his servants to the
vinedressers, that they might re-
ceive its fruit.
35 [a]"And the vinedressers took
his servants, beat one, killed one,
and stoned another.
36 "Again he sent other servants,
more than the first, and they did
likewise to them.
37 "Then last of all he sent his
[a]son to them, saying, 'They will re-
spect my son.'
38 "But when the vinedressers
saw the son, they said among
themselves, [a]'This is the heir.
[b]Come, let us kill him and seize his
inheritance.'
39 [a]"So they took him and cast
him out of the vineyard and killed
him.
40 "Therefore, when the owner of
the vineyard comes, what will he
do to those vinedressers?"
41 [a]They said to Him, [b]"He will
destroy those wicked men miser-
ably, [c]and lease *his* vineyard to
other vinedressers who will [1]ren-
der to him the fruits in their sea-
sons."
42 Jesus said to them, "Have you
never read in the Scriptures:

[a]'The stone which the builders rejected
Has become the chief cornerstone.
This was the LORD's doing,
And it is marvelous in our eyes'?

43 "Therefore I say to you, [a]the
kingdom of God will be taken from
you and given to a nation bearing
the fruits of it.
44 "And [a]whoever falls on this
stone will be broken; but on
whomever it falls, [b]it will grind
him to powder."
45 Now when the chief priests and
Pharisees heard His parables, they
[1]perceived that He was speaking
of them.

22 [a]Matt. 7:7–11; Mark 11:24; Luke 11:9; [John 15:7; James 5:16; 1 John 3:22; 5:14]
23 [a]Mark 11:27–33; Luke 20:1–8 [b]Ex. 2:14; Acts 4:7; 7:27
25 [a][John 1:29–34] [b]John 1:15–28
26 [a]Matt. 14:5; 21:46; Luke 20:6 [b]Matt. 14:5; Mark 6:20
28 [a]Matt. 20:1; 21:33
31 [a]Luke 7:29, 37–50
32 [a]Luke 3:1–12; 7:29 [b]Luke 3:12, 13 [1]*regret it*
33 [a]Ps. 80:9; Mark 12:1–12; Luke 20:9–19 [b]Matt. 25:14
35 [a]2 Chr. 24:21; 36:16; [Matt. 23:34, 37; Acts 7:52; 1 Thess. 2:15]; Heb. 11:36, 37
37 [a][John 3:16]
38 [a][Ps. 2:8; Heb. 1:2] [b][Ps. 2:2]; John 11:53; Acts 4:27
39 [a][Matt. 26:50]; Mark 14:46; Luke 22:54; John 18:12; [Acts 2:23]
41 [a]Luke 20:16 [b][Luke 21:24] [c][Matt. 8:11; Acts 13:46; Rom. 9; 10] [1]*give*
42 [a]Ps. 118:22, 23; Is. 28:16; Mark 12:10; Luke 20:17; Acts 4:11; [Rom. 9:33]; Eph. 2:20; [1 Pet. 2:6, 7]
43 [a][Matt. 8:12]; Acts 13:46
44 [a]Is. 8:14, 15; Zech. 12:3; Luke 20:18; [Rom. 9:33]; 1 Pet. 2:8 [b][Is. 60:12; Dan. 2:44]
45 [1]*knew*

46 But when they sought to lay hands on Him, they [a]feared the multitudes, because [b]they took Him for a prophet.

The Parable of the Wedding Feast

22 And Jesus answered [a]and spoke to them again by parables and said:

2 "The kingdom of heaven is like a certain king who arranged a marriage for his son,

3 "and sent out his servants to call those who were invited to the wedding; and they were not willing to come.

4 "Again, he sent out other servants, saying, 'Tell those who are invited, "See, I have prepared my dinner; [a]my oxen and fatted cattle *are* killed, and all things *are* ready. Come to the wedding." '

5 "But they made light of it and went their ways, one to his own farm, another to his business.

6 "And the rest seized his servants, treated *them* [1]spitefully, and killed *them*.

7 "But when the king heard *about it*, he was furious. And he sent out [a]his armies, destroyed those murderers, and burned up their city.

8 "Then he said to his servants, 'The wedding is ready, but those who were invited were not [a]worthy.

9 'Therefore go into the highways, and as many as you find, invite to the wedding.'

10 "So those servants went out into the highways and [a]gathered together all whom they found, both bad and good. And the wedding *hall* was filled with guests.

11 "But when the king came in to see the guests, he saw a man there [a]who did not have on a wedding garment.

12 "So he said to him, 'Friend, how did you come in here without a wedding garment?' And he was [a]speechless.

13 "Then the king said to the servants, 'Bind him hand and foot, [1]take him away, and cast *him* [a]into outer darkness; there will be weeping and gnashing of teeth.'

14 [a]"For many are called, but few *are* chosen."

The Pharisees: Is It Lawful to Pay Taxes to Caesar?

15 [a]Then the Pharisees went and plotted how they might entangle Him in *His* talk.

16 And they sent to Him their disciples with the [a]Herodians, saying, "Teacher, we know that You are true, and teach the way of God in truth; nor do You care about anyone, for You do not [1]regard the person of men.

17 "Tell us, therefore, what do You think? Is it lawful to pay taxes to Caesar, or not?"

18 But Jesus [1]perceived their wickedness, and said, "Why do you test Me, *you* hypocrites?

19 "Show Me the tax money." So they brought Him a denarius.

20 And He said to them, "Whose image and inscription *is* this?"

21 They said to Him, "Caesar's." And He said to them, [a]"Render[1] therefore to Caesar the things that are [b]Caesar's, and to God the things that are [c]God's."

22 When they had heard *these words*, they marveled, and left Him and went their way.

The Sadducees: What About the Resurrection?

23 [a]The same day the Sadducees, [b]who say there is no resurrection, came to Him and asked Him,

24 saying: "Teacher, [a]Moses said that if a man dies, having no children, his brother shall marry his wife and raise up offspring for his brother.

25 "Now there were with us seven brothers. The first died after he had married, and having no offspring, left his wife to his brother.

26 "Likewise the second also, and the third, even to the seventh.

27 "Last of all the woman died also.

28 "Therefore, in the resurrection, whose wife of the seven will she be? For they all had her."

29 Jesus answered and said to them, "You are [1]mistaken, [a]not knowing the Scriptures nor the power of God.

30 "For in the resurrection they neither marry nor are given in marriage, but [a]are like angels [1]of God in heaven.

46 [a]Matt. 21:26; Mark 11:18, 32 [b]Matt. 21:11; Luke 7:16; John 7:40

CHAPTER 22

1 [a]Luke 14:16; [Rev. 19:7–9]

4 [a]Prov. 9:2

6 [1]*insolently*

7 [a][Dan. 9:26]

8 [a]Matt. 10:11

10 [a]Matt. 13:38, 47, 48; [Acts 28:28]

11 [a][2 Cor. 5:3; Eph. 4:24; Col. 3:10, 12; Rev. 3:4; 16:15; 19:8]

12 [a][Rom. 3:19]

13 [a]Matt. 8:12; 25:30; Luke 13:28 [1]NU omits *take him away, and*

14 [a]Matt. 20:16

15 [a]Mark 12:13–17; Luke 20:20–26

16 [a]Mark 3:6; 8:15; 12:13 [1]Lit. *look at the face of*

18 [1]*knew*

21 [a]Matt. 17:25 [b][Rom. 13:1–7; 1 Pet. 2:13–15] [c][1 Cor. 3:23; 6:19, 20; 12:27] [1]*Pay*

23 [a]Mark 12:18–27; Luke 20:27–40 [b]Acts 23:8

24 [a]Deut. 25:5

29 [a]John 20:9 [1]*deceived*

30 [a][1 John 3:2] [1]NU omits *of God*

31 "But concerning the resurrection of the dead, have you not read what was spoken to you by God, saying,
32 [a]*'I am the God of Abraham, the God of Isaac, and the God of Jacob'*? God is not the God of the dead, but of the living."
33 And when the multitudes heard *this*, [a]they were astonished at His teaching.

The Scribes: Which Is the First Commandment of All?

34 [a]But when the Pharisees heard that He had silenced the Sadducees, they gathered together.
35 Then one of them, [a]a lawyer, asked *Him a question*, testing Him, and saying,
36 "Teacher, which *is* the great commandment in the law?"
37 Jesus said to him, [a]"*'You shall love the* LORD *your God with all your heart, with all your soul, and with all your mind.'*
38 "This is *the* first and great commandment.
39 "And *the* second *is* like it: [a]*'You shall love your neighbor as yourself.'*
40 [a]"On these two commandments hang all the Law and the Prophets."

Jesus: How Can David Call His Descendant Lord?

41 [a]While the Pharisees were gathered together, Jesus asked them,
42 saying, "What do you think about the Christ? Whose Son is He?" They said to Him, "*The* [a]*Son* of David."
43 He said to them, "How then does David in the Spirit call Him *'Lord,'* saying:

44 *'The*[a] LORD *said to my Lord,*
"Sit at My right hand,
Till I make Your enemies Your footstool"'?

45 "If David then calls Him *'Lord,'* how is He his Son?"
46 [a]And no one was able to answer Him a word, [b]nor from that day on did anyone dare question Him anymore.

32 [a]Ex. 3:6, 15
33 [a]Matt. 7:28
34 [a]Mark 12:28–31
35 [a]Luke 7:30; 10:25; 11:45, 46, 52; 14:3
37 [a]Deut. 6:5; 10:12; 30:6
39 [a]Lev. 19:18
40 [a][Matt. 7:12]
41 [a]Luke 20:41–44
42 [a]Matt. 1:1; 21:9
44 [a]Ps. 110:1
46 [a]Luke 14:6 [b]Mark 12:34

CHAPTER 23
2 [a]Neh. 8:4, 8
3 [a][Rom. 2:19] [1]NU omits *to observe*
4 [a]Luke 11:46
5 [a][Matt. 6:1–6, 16–18]
6 [a]Luke 11:43; 20:46 [1]Or *place of honor*
8 [a][James 3:1] [1]*Leader* [2]NU omits *the Christ*
9 [a][Mal. 1:6]
11 [a]Matt. 20:26, 27
12 [a]Luke 14:11; 18:14 [1]*put down* [2]*lifted up*
13 [a]Luke 11:52
14 [a]Mark 12:40 [1]NU omits v. 14.
15 [1]Gr. *Gehenna*
16 [a]Matt. 15:14; 23:24

Woe to the Scribes and Pharisees

23 Then Jesus spoke to the multitudes and to His disciples,
2 saying: [a]"The scribes and the Pharisees sit in Moses' seat.
3 "Therefore whatever they tell you [1]to observe, *that* observe and do, but do not do according to their works; for [a]they say, and do not do.
4 [a]"For they bind heavy burdens, hard to bear, and lay *them* on men's shoulders; but they *themselves* will not move them with one of their fingers.
5 "But all their works they do to [a]be seen by men. They make their phylacteries broad and enlarge the borders of their garments.
6 [a]"They love the [1]best places at feasts, the best seats in the synagogues,
7 "greetings in the marketplaces, and to be called by men, 'Rabbi, Rabbi.'
8 [a]"But you, do not be called 'Rabbi'; for One is your [1]Teacher, [2]the Christ, and you are all brethren.
9 "Do not call anyone on earth your father; [a]for One is your Father, He who is in heaven.
10 "And do not be called teachers; for One is your Teacher, the Christ.
11 "But [a]he who is greatest among you shall be your servant.
12 [a]"And whoever exalts himself will be [1]humbled, and he who humbles himself will be [2]exalted.
13 "But [a]woe to you, scribes and Pharisees, hypocrites! For you shut up the kingdom of heaven against men; for you neither go in *yourselves*, nor do you allow those who are entering to go in.
14 [1]"Woe to you, scribes and Pharisees, hypocrites! [a]For you devour widows' houses, and for a pretense make long prayers. Therefore you will receive greater condemnation.
15 "Woe to you, scribes and Pharisees, hypocrites! For you travel land and sea to win one proselyte, and when he is won, you make him twice as much a son of [1]hell as yourselves.
16 "Woe to you, [a]blind guides,

who say, [b]'Whoever swears by the
temple, it is nothing; but whoever
swears by the gold of the temple,
he is obliged *to perform it.*'
17 "Fools and blind! For which is
greater, the gold [a]or the temple
that [1]sanctifies the gold?
18 "And, 'Whoever swears by the
altar, it is nothing; but whoever
swears by the gift that is on it, he
is obliged *to perform it.*'
19 "Fools and blind! For which is
greater, the gift [a]or the altar that
sanctifies the gift?
20 "Therefore he who [1]swears by
the altar, swears by it and by all
things on it.
21 "He who swears by the temple,
swears by it and by [a]Him who
[1]dwells in it.
22 "And he who swears by
heaven, swears by [a]the throne of
God and by Him who sits on it.
23 "Woe to you, scribes and Phar-
isees, hypocrites! [a]For you pay
tithe of mint and anise and cum-
min, and [b]have neglected the
weightier *matters* of the law: jus-
tice and mercy and faith. These
you ought to have done, without
leaving the others undone.
24 "Blind guides, who strain out
a gnat and swallow a camel!
25 "Woe to you, scribes and Phar-
isees, hypocrites! [a]For you cleanse
the outside of the cup and dish, but
inside they are full of extortion
and [1]self-indulgence.
26 "Blind Pharisee, first cleanse
the inside of the cup and dish, that
the outside of them may be clean
also.
27 "Woe to you, scribes and Phar-
isees, hypocrites! [a]For you are like
whitewashed tombs which indeed
appear beautiful outwardly, but in-
side are full of dead *men's* bones
and all uncleanness.
28 "Even so you also outwardly
appear righteous to men, but in-
side you are full of hypocrisy and
lawlessness.
29 [a]"Woe to you, scribes and
Pharisees, hypocrites! Because
you build the tombs of the proph-
ets and [1]adorn the monuments of
the righteous,
30 "and say, 'If we had lived in the
days of our fathers, we would not
have been partakers with them in
the blood of the prophets.'

16 [b][Matt. 5:33, 34]
17 [a]Ex. 30:29 [1]NU *sanctified*
19 [a]Ex. 29:37
20 [1]Swears an oath
21 [a]1 Kin. 8:13 [1]M *dwelt*
22 [a]Matt. 5:34
23 [a]Luke 11:42; 18:12 [b][Hos. 6:6]
25 [a]Luke 11:39 [1]M *unrighteousness*
27 [a]Acts 23:3
29 [a]Luke 11:47, 48 [1]*decorate*
31 [a][Acts 7:51, 52]
32 [a][1 Thess. 2:16]
33 [a]Matt. 3:7; 12:34 [1]*offspring*
34 [a]Luke 11:49 [b]Acts 7:54–60; 22:19 [c]2 Cor. 11:24, 25
35 [a]Rev. 18:24 [b]Gen. 4:8 [c]2 Chr. 24:20, 21
37 [a]Luke 13:34, 35 [b]2 Chr. 24:20, 21; 36:15, 16 [c]Deut. 32:11, 12 [d]Ps. 17:8; 91:4
39 [a]Ps. 118:26

CHAPTER 24
1 [a]Mark 13:1
2 [a]Luke 19:44
3 [a]Mark 13:3 [b][1 Thess. 5:1–3]

31 "Therefore you are witnesses
against yourselves that [a]you are
sons of those who murdered the
prophets.
32 [a]"Fill up, then, the measure of
your fathers' *guilt.*
33 "Serpents, [a]brood[1] of vipers!
How can you escape the con-
demnation of hell?
34 [a]"Therefore, indeed, I send you
prophets, wise men, and scribes:
[b]*some* of them you will kill and
crucify, and [c]*some* of them you
will scourge in your synagogues
and persecute from city to city,
35 [a]"that on you may come all the
righteous blood shed on the earth,
[b]from the blood of righteous Abel
to [c]the blood of Zechariah, son of
Berechiah, whom you murdered
between the temple and the altar.
36 "Assuredly, I say to you, all
these things will come upon this
generation.

Jesus Laments over Jerusalem

37 [a]"O Jerusalem, Jerusalem, the
one who kills the prophets [b]and
stones those who are sent to her!
How often [c]I wanted to gather
your children together, as a hen
gathers her chicks [d]under *her*
wings, but you were not willing!
38 "See! Your house is left to you
desolate;
39 "for I say to you, you shall see
Me no more till you say, [a]*'Blessed
is He who comes in the name of
the LORD!'* "

Jesus Predicts the Destruction of the Temple

24 Then [a]Jesus went out and
departed from the temple,
and His disciples came up to show
Him the buildings of the temple.
2 And Jesus said to them, "Do
you not see all these things? As-
suredly, I say to you, [a]not *one*
stone shall be left here upon an-
other, that shall not be thrown
down."

The Signs of the Times and the End of the Age

3 Now as He sat on the Mount
of Olives, [a]the disciples came to
Him privately, saying, [b]"Tell us,
when will these things be? And

what *will be* the sign of Your
coming, and of the end of the
age?"
4 And Jesus answered and said
to them: [a]"Take heed that no one
deceives you.
5 "For [a]many will come in My
name, saying, 'I am the Christ,'
[b]and will deceive many.
6 "And you will hear of [a]wars
and rumors of wars. See that you
are not troubled; for [1]all *these
things* must come to pass, but the
end is not yet.
7 "For [a]nation will rise against
nation, and kingdom against king-
dom. And there will be [b]famines,
[1]pestilences, and earthquakes in
various places.
8 "All these *are* the beginning of
sorrows.
9 [a]"Then they will deliver you up
to tribulation and kill you, and you
will be hated by all nations for My
name's sake.
10 "And then many will be of-
fended, will betray one another,
and will hate one another.
11 "Then [a]many false prophets
will rise up and [b]deceive many.
12 "And because lawlessness will
abound, the love of many will
grow [a]cold.
13 [a]"But he who endures to the
end shall be saved.
14 "And this [a]gospel of the king-
dom [b]will be preached in all the
world as a witness to all the na-
tions, and then the end will come.

The Great Tribulation

15 [a]"Therefore when you see the
[b]'*abomination of desolation,*' spo-
ken of by Daniel the prophet,
standing in the holy place" [c](who-
ever reads, let him understand),
16 "then let those who are in Ju-
dea flee to the mountains.
17 "Let him who is on the house-
top not go down to take anything
out of his house.
18 "And let him who is in the field
not go back to get his clothes.
19 "But [a]woe to those who are
pregnant and to those who are
nursing babies in those days!
20 "And pray that your flight may
not be in winter or on the Sabbath.
21 "For [a]then there will be great
tribulation, such as has not been
since the beginning of the world

4 [a][Col. 2:8, 18]
5 [a]John 5:43 [b]Matt. 24:11
6 [a][Rev. 6:2–4] [1]NU omits *all*
7 [a]Hag. 2:22 [b]Rev. 6:5, 6 [1]NU omits *pestilences*
9 [a]Matt. 10:17
11 [a]2 Pet. 2:1 [b][1 Tim. 4:1]
12 [a][2 Thess. 2:3]
13 [a]Matt. 10:22
14 [a]Matt. 4:23 [b]Rom. 10:18
15 [a]Mark 13:14 [b]Dan. 9:27; 11:31; 12:11 [c]Dan. 9:23
19 [a]Luke 23:29
21 [a]Dan. 9:26
22 [a]Is. 65:8, 9 [1]*chosen ones'*
23 [a]Luke 17:23
24 [a][2 Thess. 2:9] [b][2 Tim. 2:19]
27 [a]Luke 17:24
28 [a]Luke 17:37
29 [a][Dan. 7:11] [b]Ezek. 32:7
30 [a][Dan. 7:13, 14] [b]Zech. 12:12
31 [a][1 Cor. 15:52] [1]*chosen ones*
32 [a]Luke 21:29
33 [a][James 5:9] [1]Or *He*
34 [a][Matt. 10:23; 16:28; 23:36]
35 [a]Luke 21:33

until this time, no, nor ever shall
be.
22 "And unless those days were
shortened, no flesh would be
saved; [a]but for the [1]elect's sake
those days will be shortened.
23 [a]"Then if anyone says to you,
'Look, here *is* the Christ!' or
'There!' do not believe *it*.
24 "For [a]false christs and false
prophets will rise and show great
signs and wonders to deceive, [b]if
possible, even the elect.
25 "See, I have told you before-
hand.
26 "Therefore if they say to you,
'Look, He is in the desert!' do not
go out; *or* 'Look, *He is* in the inner
rooms!' do not believe *it*.
27 [a]"For as the lightning comes
from the east and flashes to the
west, so also will the coming of the
Son of Man be.
28 [a]"For wherever the carcass is,
there the eagles will be gathered
together.

The Coming of the Son of Man

29 [a]"Immediately after the tribu-
lation of those days [b]the sun will
be darkened, and the moon will
not give its light; the stars will fall
from heaven, and the powers of
the heavens will be shaken.
30 [a]"Then the sign of the Son of
Man will appear in heaven, [b]and
then all the tribes of the earth will
mourn, and they will see the Son
of Man coming on the clouds of
heaven with power and great
glory.
31 [a]"And He will send His angels
with a great sound of a trumpet,
and they will gather together His
[1]elect from the four winds, from
one end of heaven to the other.

The Parable of the Fig Tree

32 "Now learn [a]this parable from
the fig tree: When its branch has
already become tender and puts
forth leaves, you know that sum-
mer *is* near.
33 "So you also, when you see all
these things, know [a]that [1]it is
near—at the doors!
34 "Assuredly, I say to you, [a]this
generation will by no means pass
away till all these things take
place.
35 [a]"Heaven and earth will pass

away, but My words will by no
means pass away.

No One Knows the Day or Hour

36 [a]"But of that day and hour no
one knows, not even the angels of
[1]heaven, [b]but My Father only.
37 "But as the days of Noah *were*,
so also will the coming of the Son
of Man be.
38 [a]"For as in the days before the
flood, they were eating and drink-
ing, marrying and giving in mar-
riage, until the day that Noah en-
tered the ark,
39 "and did not know until the
flood came and took them all
away, so also will the coming of
the Son of Man be.
40 [a]"Then two *men* will be in the
field: one will be taken and the
other left.
41 "Two *women will be* grinding
at the mill: one will be taken and
the other left.
42 [a]"Watch therefore, for you do
not know what [1]hour your Lord is
coming.
43 [a]"But know this, that if the
master of the house had known
what [1]hour the thief would come,
he would have watched and not al-
lowed his house to be broken into.
44 [a]"Therefore you also be ready,
for the Son of Man is coming at
an hour you do not expect.

The Faithful Servant and the Evil Servant

45 [a]"Who then is a faithful and
wise servant, whom his master
made ruler over his household, to
give them food [1]in due season?
46 [a]"Blessed *is* that servant whom
his master, when he comes, will
find so doing.
47 "Assuredly, I say to you that
[a]he will make him ruler over all
his goods.
48 "But if that evil servant says in
his heart, 'My master [a]is delaying
[1]his coming,'
49 "and begins to beat *his* fellow
servants, and to eat and drink with
the drunkards,
50 "the master of that servant will
come on a day when he is not look-
ing for *him* and at an hour that he
is [a]not aware of,
51 "and will cut him in two and
appoint *him* his portion with the
hypocrites. [a]There shall be weep-
ing and gnashing of teeth.

The Parable of the Wise and Foolish Virgins

25 "Then the kingdom of
heaven shall be likened to
ten virgins who took their lamps
and went out to meet [a]the bride-
groom.
2 [a]"Now five of them were wise,
and five *were* foolish.
3 "Those who *were* foolish took
their lamps and took no oil with
them,
4 "but the wise took oil in their
vessels with their lamps.
5 "But while the bridegroom was
delayed, [a]they all slumbered and
slept.
6 "And at midnight [a]a cry was
heard: 'Behold, the bridegroom [1]is
coming; go out to meet him!'
7 "Then all those virgins arose
and [a]trimmed their lamps.
8 "And the foolish said to the
wise, 'Give us *some* of your oil, for
our lamps are going out.'
9 "But the wise answered, say-
ing, '*No,* lest there should not be
enough for us and you; but go
rather to those who sell, and buy
for yourselves.'
10 "And while they went to buy,
the bridegroom came, and those
who were ready went in with him
to the wedding; and [a]the door was
shut.
11 "Afterward the other virgins
came also, saying, [a]'Lord, Lord,
open to us!'
12 "But he answered and said,
'Assuredly, I say to you, [a]I do not
know you.'
13 [a]"Watch therefore, for you
[b]know neither the day nor the
hour [1]in which the Son of Man is
coming.

The Parable of the Talents

14 [a]"For *the kingdom of heaven is*
[b]like a man traveling to a far coun-
try, *who* called his own servants
and delivered his goods to them.
15 "And to one he gave five tal-
ents, to another two, and to an-
other one, [a]to each according to
his own ability; and immediately
he went on a journey.

36 [a]Acts 1:7 [b]Zech. 14:7 [1]NU adds *nor the Son*
38 [a][Gen. 6:3–5]
40 [a]Luke 17:34
42 [a]Matt. 25:13 [1]NU *day*
43 [a]Luke 12:39 [1]Lit. *watch of the night*
44 [a][1 Thess. 5:6]
45 [a]Luke 12:42–46 [1]*at the right time*
46 [a]Rev. 16:15
47 [a]Matt. 25:21, 23
48 [a][2 Pet. 3:4–9] [1]NU omits *his coming*
50 [a]Mark 13:32
51 [a]Matt. 8:12; 25:30

CHAPTER 25

1 [a][Eph. 5:29, 30]
2 [a]Matt. 13:47; 22:10
5 [a]1 Thess. 5:6
6 [a][1 Thess. 4:16] [1]NU omits *is coming*
7 [a]Luke 12:35
10 [a]Luke 13:25
11 [a][Matt. 7:21–23]
12 [a][Hab. 1:13]
13 [a]Mark 13:35 [b]Matt. 24:36, 42 [1]NU omits the rest of v. 13.
14 [a]Luke 19:12–27 [b]Matt. 21:33
15 [a][Rom. 12:6]

16 "Then he who had received the
five talents went and traded with
them, and made another five tal-
ents.
17 "And likewise he who *had re-
ceived* two gained two more also.
18 "But he who had received one
went and dug in the ground, and
hid his lord's money.
19 "After a long time the lord of
those servants came and settled
accounts with them.
20 "So he who had received five
talents came and brought five
other talents, saying, 'Lord, you
delivered to me five talents; look,
I have gained five more talents be-
sides them.'
21 "His lord said to him, 'Well
done, good and faithful servant;
you were [a]faithful over a few
things, [b]I will make you ruler over
many things. Enter into [c]the joy of
your lord.'
22 "He also who had received two
talents came and said, 'Lord, you
delivered to me two talents; look,
I have gained two more talents be-
sides them.'
23 "His lord said to him, [a]'Well
done, good and faithful servant;
you have been faithful over a few
things, I will make you ruler over
many things. Enter into [b]the joy
of your lord.'
24 "Then he who had received the
one talent came and said, 'Lord, I
knew you to be a hard man, reap-
ing where you have not sown, and
gathering where you have not
scattered seed.
25 'And I was afraid, and went
and hid your talent in the ground.
Look, *there* you have *what is*
yours.'
26 "But his lord answered and
said to him, 'You [a]wicked and lazy
servant, you knew that I reap
where I have not sown, and gather
where I have not scattered seed.
27 'So you ought to have depos-
ited my money with the bankers,
and at my coming I would have
received back my own with inter-
est.
28 'Therefore take the talent from
him, and give *it* to him who has
ten talents.
29 [a]'For to everyone who has,
more will be given, and he will
have abundance; but from him
who does not have, even what he
has will be taken away.
30 'And cast the unprofitable ser-
vant [a]into the outer darkness.
[b]There will be weeping and
[c]gnashing of teeth.'

The Son of Man Will Judge the Nations

31 [a]"When the Son of Man comes
in His glory, and all the [1]holy an-
gels with Him, then He will sit on
the throne of His glory.
32 [a]"All the nations will be gath-
ered before Him, and [b]He will sep-
arate them one from another, as
a shepherd divides *his* sheep from
the goats.
33 "And He will set the [a]sheep on
His right hand, but the goats on
the left.
34 "Then the King will say to
those on His right hand, 'Come,
you blessed of My Father, [a]inherit
the kingdom [b]prepared for you
from the foundation of the world:
35 [a]'for I was hungry and you
gave Me food; I was thirsty and
you gave Me drink; [b]I was a
stranger and you took Me in;
36 'I *was* [a]naked and you clothed
Me; I was sick and you visited Me;
[b]I was in prison and you came to
Me.'
37 "Then the righteous will an-
swer Him, saying, 'Lord, when did
we see You hungry and feed *You*,
or thirsty and give *You* drink?
38 'When did we see You a
stranger and take *You* in, or naked
and clothe *You*?
39 'Or when did we see You sick,
or in prison, and come to You?'
40 "And the King will answer and
say to them, 'Assuredly, I say to
you, [a]inasmuch as you did *it* to one
of the least of these My brethren,
you did *it* to Me.'
41 "Then He will also say to those
on the left hand, [a]'Depart from Me,
you cursed, [b]into the everlasting
fire prepared for [c]the devil and his
angels:
42 'for I was hungry and you gave
Me no food; I was thirsty and you
gave Me no drink;
43 'I was a stranger and you did
not take Me in, naked and you did
not clothe Me, sick and in prison
and you did not visit Me.'
44 "Then they also will answer

21 [a][Luke 16:10; 1 Cor. 4:2; 2 Tim. 4:7, 8] [b][Matt. 24:47; 25:34, 46; Luke 12:44; 22:29, 30; Rev. 3:21; 21:7] [c][2 Tim. 2:12; Heb. 12:2; 1 Pet. 1:8]
23 [a]Matt. 24:45, 47; 25:21 [b][Ps. 16:11; John 15:10, 11]
26 [a]Matt. 18:32; Luke 19:22
29 [a]Matt. 13:12; Mark 4:25; Luke 8:18; [John 15:2]
30 [a]Matt. 8:12; 22:13; [Luke 13:28] [b]Matt. 7:23; 8:12; 24:51 [c]Ps. 112:10
31 [a][Zech. 14:5]; Matt. 16:27; Mark 8:38; Acts 1:11; [1 Thess. 4:16]; 2 Thess. 1:7; [Jude 14]; Rev. 1:7 [1]NU omits *holy*
32 [a][Rom. 14:10; 2 Cor. 5:10; Rev. 20:12] [b]Ezek. 20:38
33 [a]Ps. 79:13; 100:3; [John 10:11, 27, 28]
34 [a][Rom. 8:17; 1 Pet. 1:4, 9; Rev. 21:7] [b]Matt. 20:23; Mark 10:40; 1 Cor. 2:9; Heb. 11:16
35 [a]Is. 58:7; Ezek. 18:7, 16; [James 1:27; 2:15, 16] [b]Job 31:32; [Heb. 13:2]; 3 John 5
36 [a]Is. 58:7; Ezek. 18:7, 16; [James 2:15, 16] [b]2 Tim. 1:16
40 [a]Prov. 14:31; Matt. 10:42; Mark 9:41; Heb. 6:10
41 [a]Ps. 6:8; Matt. 7:23; Luke 13:27 [b]Matt. 13:40, 42 [c][2 Pet. 2:4]; Jude 6

[1]Him, saying, 'Lord, when did we
see You hungry or thirsty or a
stranger or naked or sick or in
prison, and did not minister to
You?'
45 "Then He will answer them,
saying, 'Assuredly, I say to you,
[a]inasmuch as you did not do *it* to
one of the least of these, you did
not do *it* to Me.'
46 "And [a]these will go away into
everlasting punishment, but the
righteous into eternal life."

The Plot to Kill Jesus

26 Now it came to pass, when
Jesus had finished all these
sayings, *that* He said to His disci-
ples,
2 [a]"You know that after two days
is the Passover, and the Son of
Man will be delivered up to be cru-
cified."
3 [a]Then the chief priests, [1]the
scribes, and the elders of the peo-
ple assembled at the palace of the
high priest, who was called Caia-
phas,
4 and [a]plotted to take Jesus by
[1]trickery and kill *Him*.
5 But they said, "Not during the
feast, lest there be an uproar
among the [a]people."

The Anointing at Bethany

6 And when Jesus was in [a]Beth-
any at the house of Simon the
leper,
7 a woman came to Him having
an alabaster flask of very costly
fragrant oil, and she poured *it* on
His head as He sat *at the table*.
8 [a]But when His disciples saw *it*,
they were indignant, saying, "Why
this waste?
9 "For this fragrant oil might
have been sold for much and given
to *the* poor."
10 But when Jesus was aware of
it, He said to them, "Why do you
trouble the woman? For she has
done a good work for Me.
11 [a]"For you have the poor with
you always, but [b]Me you do not
have always.
12 "For in pouring this fragrant oil
on My body, she did *it* for My
[a]burial.
13 "Assuredly, I say to you, wher-
ever this gospel is preached in the
whole world, what this woman has

44 [1]NU, M omit *Him*
45 [a]Prov. 14:31
46 [a][Dan. 12:2]

CHAPTER 26

2 [a]Luke 22:1, 2
3 [a]John 11:47 [1]NU omits *the scribes*
4 [a]Acts 4:25–28 [1]*deception*
5 [a]Matt. 21:26
6 [a]Mark 14:3–9
8 [a]John 12:4
11 [a][Deut. 15:11] [b][John 13:33; 14:19; 16:5, 28; 17:11]
12 [a]John 19:38–42
14 [a]Mark 14:10, 11; Luke 22:3–6 [b]Matt. 10:4
15 [a]Zech. 11:12
17 [a]Ex. 12:6, 18–20
18 [a]Luke 9:51
20 [a]Mark 14:17–21
21 [a]John 6:70, 71; 13:21
23 [a]Ps. 41:9
24 [a]1 Cor. 15:3 [b]Luke 17:1 [c]John 17:12
26 [a]Mark 14:22–25 [b]1 Cor. 11:23–25 [c][1 Pet. 2:24] [1]M *gave thanks for*

done will also be told as a memo-
rial to her."

Judas Agrees to Betray Jesus

14 [a]Then one of the twelve, called
[b]Judas Iscariot, went to the chief
priests
15 and said, [a]"What are you will-
ing to give me if I deliver Him to
you?" And they counted out to him
thirty pieces of silver.
16 So from that time he sought op-
portunity to betray Him.

Jesus Celebrates Passover with His Disciples

17 [a]Now on the first *day of the*
Feast of Unleavened Bread the
disciples came to Jesus, saying to
Him, "Where do You want us to
prepare for You to eat the Pass-
over?"
18 And He said, "Go into the city
to a certain man, and say to him,
'The Teacher says, [a]"My time is at
hand; I will keep the Passover at
your house with My disciples." ' "
19 So the disciples did as Jesus
had directed them; and they pre-
pared the Passover.
20 [a]When evening had come, He
sat down with the twelve.
21 Now as they were eating, He
said, "Assuredly, I say to you, one
of you will [a]betray Me."
22 And they were exceedingly
sorrowful, and each of them began
to say to Him, "Lord, is it I?"
23 He answered and said, [a]"He
who dipped *his* hand with Me in
the dish will betray Me.
24 "The Son of Man indeed goes
just [a]as it is written of Him, but
[b]woe to that man by whom the Son
of Man is betrayed! [c]It would have
been good for that man if he had
not been born."
25 Then Judas, who was betray-
ing Him, answered and said,
"Rabbi, is it I?" He said to him,
"You have said it."

Jesus Institutes the Lord's Supper

26 [a]And as they were eating,
[b]Jesus took bread, [1]blessed and
broke *it*, and gave *it* to the disci-
ples and said, "Take, eat; [c]this is
My body."
27 Then He took the cup, and gave

thanks, and gave *it* to them, say-
ing, [a]"Drink from it, all of you.
28 "For [a]this is My blood [b]of the
[1]new covenant, which is shed
[c]for many for the [2]remission of
sins.
29 "But [a]I say to you, I will not
drink of this fruit of the vine from
now on [b]until that day when I
drink it new with you in My Fa-
ther's kingdom."
30 [a]And when they had sung a
hymn, they went out to the Mount
of Olives.

Jesus Predicts Peter's Denial

31 Then Jesus said to them, [a]"All
of you will [b]be [1]made to stumble
because of Me this night, for it is
written:

> [c]'*I will strike the Shepherd,*
> *And the sheep of the flock will*
> *be scattered.*'

32 "But after I have been raised,
[a]I will go before you to Galilee."
33 Peter answered and said to
Him, "Even if all are [1]made to
stumble because of You, I will
never be made to stumble."
34 Jesus said to him, [a]"Assuredly,
I say to you that this night, before
the rooster crows, you will deny
Me three times."
35 Peter said to Him, "Even if I
have to die with You, I will not
deny You!" And so said all the dis-
ciples.

The Prayer in the Garden

36 [a]Then Jesus came with them to
a place called Gethsemane, and
said to the disciples, "Sit here
while I go and pray over there."
37 And He took with Him Peter
and [a]the two sons of Zebedee, and
He began to be sorrowful and
deeply distressed.
38 Then He said to them, [a]"My
soul is exceedingly sorrowful,
even to death. Stay here and watch
with Me."
39 He went a little farther and fell
on His face, and [a]prayed, saying,
[b]"O My Father, if it is possible, [c]let
this cup pass from Me; neverthe-
less, [d]not as I will, but as You
will."
40 Then He came to the disciples
and found them sleeping, and said
to Peter, "What? Could you not
watch with Me one hour?
41 [a]"Watch and pray, lest you en-
ter into temptation. [b]The spirit in-
deed *is* willing, but the flesh *is*
weak."
42 Again, a second time, He went
away and prayed, saying, "O My
Father, [1]if this cup cannot pass
away from Me unless I drink it,
Your will be done."
43 And He came and found them
asleep again, for their eyes were
heavy.
44 So He left them, went away
again, and prayed the third time,
saying the same words.
45 Then He came to His disciples
and said to them, "Are *you* still
sleeping and resting? Behold, the
hour [1]is at hand, and the Son of
Man is being [a]betrayed into the
hands of sinners.
46 "Rise, let us be going. See, My
betrayer is at hand."

Betrayal and Arrest in Gethsemane

47 And [a]while He was still speak-
ing, behold, Judas, one of the
twelve, with a great multitude with
swords and clubs, came from the
chief priests and elders of the peo-
ple.
48 Now His betrayer had given
them a sign, saying, "Whomever
I kiss, He is the One; seize Him."
49 Immediately he went up to
Jesus and said, "Greetings, Rabbi!"
[a]and kissed Him.
50 But Jesus said to him, [a]"Friend,
why have you come?" Then they
came and laid hands on Jesus and
took Him.
51 And suddenly, [a]one of those
who were with Jesus stretched out
his hand and drew his sword,
struck the servant of the high
priest, and cut off his ear.
52 But Jesus said to him, "Put
your sword in its place, [a]for all
who take the sword will [1]perish by
the sword.
53 "Or do you think that I cannot
now pray to My Father, and He
will provide Me with [a]more than
twelve legions of angels?
54 "How then could the Scriptures
be fulfilled, [a]that it must happen
thus?"
55 In that hour Jesus said to the

27 [a]Mark 14:23
28 [a][Ex. 24:8] [b]Jer. 31:31 [c]Matt. 20:28 [1]NU omits *new* [2]*forgiveness*
29 [a]Mark 14:25 [b]Acts 10:41
30 [a]Mark 14:26–31
31 [a]John 16:32 [b][Matt. 11:6] [c]Zech. 13:7 [1]*caused to take offense at Me*
32 [a]Matt. 28:7, 10, 16
33 [1]*caused to take offense at You*
34 [a]John 13:38
36 [a]Mark 14:32–35
37 [a]Matt. 4:21; 17:1
38 [a]John 12:27
39 [a][Heb. 5:7–9] [b]John 12:27 [c]Matt. 20:22 [d]John 5:30; 6:38
41 [a]Luke 22:40, 46 [b][Gal. 5:17]
42 [1]NU *if this may not pass away unless*
45 [a]Matt. 17:22, 23; 20:18, 19 [1]*has drawn near*
47 [a]Acts 1:16
49 [a]2 Sam. 20:9
50 [a]Ps. 41:9; 55:13
51 [a]John 18:10
52 [a]Rev. 13:10 [1]M *die*
53 [a]Dan. 7:10
54 [a]Is. 50:6; 53:2–11

multitudes, "Have you come out,
as against a robber, with swords
and clubs to take Me? I sat daily
with you, teaching in the temple,
and you did not seize Me.
56 "But all this was done that the
[a]Scriptures of the prophets might
be fulfilled." Then [b]all the disciples
forsook Him and fled.

Jesus Faces the Sanhedrin

57 [a]And those who had laid hold
of Jesus led *Him* away to Caiaphas
the high priest, where the scribes
and the elders were assembled.
58 But [a]Peter followed Him at a
distance to the high priest's court-
yard. And he went in and sat with
the servants to see the end.
59 Now the chief priests, [1]the el-
ders, and all the council sought
[a]false testimony against Jesus to
put Him to death,
60 [1]but found none. Even though
[a]many false witnesses came for-
ward, they found none. But at last
[b]two [2]false witnesses came for-
ward
61 and said, "This *fellow* said, [a]'I
am able to destroy the temple of
God and to build it in three days.'"
62 [a]And the high priest arose and
said to Him, "Do You answer
nothing? What *is it* these men tes-
tify against You?"
63 But [a]Jesus kept silent. And the
high priest answered and said to
Him, [b]"I put You under oath by the
living God: Tell us if You are the
Christ, the Son of God!"
64 Jesus said to him, "*It is as* you
said. Nevertheless, I say to you,
[a]hereafter you will see the Son of
Man [b]sitting at the right hand of
the Power, and coming on the
clouds of heaven."
65 [a]Then the high priest tore his
clothes, saying, "He has spoken
blasphemy! What further need
do we have of witnesses? Look,
now you have heard His [b]blas-
phemy!
66 "What do you think?" They an-
swered and said, [a]"He is deserving
of death."
67 [a]Then they spat in His face and
beat Him; and [b]others struck *Him*
with [1]the palms of their hands,
68 saying, [a]"Prophesy to us,
Christ! Who is the one who struck
You?"

56 [a]Lam. 4:20 [b]John 18:15
57 [a]John 18:12, 19–24
58 [a]John 18:15, 16
59 [a]Ps. 35:11 [1]NU omits *the elders*
60 [a]Mark 14:55 [b]Deut. 19:15 [1]NU *but found none, even though many false witnesses came forward.* [2]NU omits *false witnesses*
61 [a]John 2:19
62 [a]Mark 14:60
63 [a]Is. 53:7 [b]Lev. 5:1
64 [a]Dan. 7:13 [b][Acts 7:55]
65 [a]2 Kin. 18:37 [b]John 10:30–36
66 [a]Lev. 24:16
67 [a]Is. 50:6; 53:3 [b]Luke 22:63–65 [1]Or *rods,*
68 [a]Mark 14:65
69 [a]John 18:16–18, 25–27
73 [a]Luke 22:59
74 [a]Mark 14:71 [1]*call down curses* [2]Swear oaths
75 [a]Matt. 26:34

CHAPTER 27

1 [a]John 18:28
2 [a]Acts 3:13 [1]NU omits *Pontius*
3 [a]Matt. 26:14 [b]Matt. 26:15
5 [a]Acts 1:18

Peter Denies Jesus, and Weeps Bitterly

69 [a]Now Peter sat outside in the
courtyard. And a servant girl came
to him, saying, "You also were
with Jesus of Galilee."
70 But he denied it before *them*
all, saying, "I do not know what
you are saying."
71 And when he had gone out to
the gateway, another *girl* saw him
and said to those *who were* there,
"This *fellow* also was with Jesus
of Nazareth."
72 But again he denied with an
oath, "I do not know the Man!"
73 And a little later those who
stood by came up and said to Pe-
ter, "Surely you also are *one* of
them, for your [a]speech betrays
you."
74 Then [a]he began to [1]curse and
[2]swear, *saying*, "I do not know the
Man!" Immediately a rooster
crowed.
75 And Peter remembered the
word of Jesus who had said to him,
[a]"Before the rooster crows, you
will deny Me three times." So he
went out and wept bitterly.

Jesus Handed Over to Pontius Pilate

27 When morning came, [a]all
the chief priests and elders
of the people plotted against Jesus
to put Him to death.
2 And when they had bound
Him, they led Him away and [a]de-
livered Him to [1]Pontius Pilate the
governor.

Judas Hangs Himself

3 [a]Then Judas, His betrayer, see-
ing that He had been condemned,
was remorseful and brought back
the thirty [b]pieces of silver to the
chief priests and elders,
4 saying, "I have sinned by be-
traying innocent blood." And they
said, "What *is that* to us? You see
to it!"
5 Then he threw down the pieces
of silver in the temple and [a]de-
parted, and went and hanged him-
self.
6 But the chief priests took the
silver pieces and said, "It is not
lawful to put them into the trea-
sury, because they are the price of
blood."

7 And they consulted together and bought with them the potter's field, to bury strangers in.
8 Therefore that field has been called [a]the Field of Blood to this day.
9 Then was fulfilled what was spoken by Jeremiah the prophet, saying, [a]*"And they took the thirty pieces of silver, the value of Him who was priced,* whom they of the children of Israel priced,
10 *"and [a]gave them for the potter's field, as the* Lord *directed me."*

Jesus Faces Pilate

11 Now Jesus stood before the governor. [a]And the governor asked Him, saying, "Are You the King of the Jews?" Jesus said to him, [b]*"It is as* you say."
12 And while He was being accused by the chief priests and elders, [a]He answered nothing.
13 Then Pilate said to Him, [a]"Do You not hear how many things they testify against You?"
14 But He answered him not one word, so that the governor marveled greatly.

Taking the Place of Barabbas

15 [a]Now at the feast the governor was accustomed to releasing to the multitude one prisoner whom they wished.
16 And at that time they had a notorious prisoner called [1]Barabbas.
17 Therefore, when they had gathered together, Pilate said to them, "Whom do you want me to release to you? Barabbas, or Jesus who is called Christ?"
18 For he knew that they had handed Him over because of [a]envy.
19 While he was sitting on the judgment seat, his wife sent to him, saying, "Have nothing to do with that just Man, for I have suffered many things today in a dream because of Him."
20 [a]But the chief priests and elders persuaded the multitudes that they should ask for Barabbas and destroy Jesus.
21 The governor answered and said to them, "Which of the two do you want me to release to you?" They said, [a]"Barabbas!"

8 [a]Acts 1:19
9 [a]Zech. 11:12
10 [a]Jer. 32:6–9; Zech. 11:12, 13
11 [a]Mark 15:2–5 [b]John 18:37
12 [a]John 19:9
13 [a]Matt. 26:62
15 [a]Luke 23:17–25
16 [1]NU *Jesus Barabbas*
18 [a]Matt. 21:38
20 [a]Acts 3:14
21 [a]Acts 3:14
23 [a]Acts 3:13
24 [a]Deut. 21:6–8 [1]*an uproar* [2]NU omits *just*
25 [a]Josh. 2:19
26 [a][Is. 50:6; 53:5] [1]*flogged* with a Roman scourge
27 [a]Mark 15:16–20 [1]The governor's headquarters [2]*cohort*
28 [a]John 19:2 [b]Luke 23:11
29 [a]Is. 53:3 [1]Lit. *woven*
30 [a]Matt. 26:67
31 [a]Is. 53:7
32 [a]Heb. 13:12 [b]Mark 15:21
33 [a]John 19:17
34 [a]Ps. 69:21 [1]NU omits *sour*
35 [a]Luke 23:34 [1]NU, M omit the rest of v. 35.

22 Pilate said to them, "What then shall I do with Jesus who is called Christ?" *They* all said to him, "Let Him be crucified!"
23 Then the governor said, [a]"Why, what evil has He done?" But they cried out all the more, saying, "Let Him be crucified!"
24 When Pilate saw that he could not prevail at all, but rather *that* a [1]tumult was rising, he [a]took water and washed *his* hands before the multitude, saying, "I am innocent of the blood of this [2]just Person. You see *to it.*"
25 And all the people answered and said, [a]"His blood *be* on us and on our children."
26 Then he released Barabbas to them; and when [a]he had [1]scourged Jesus, he delivered *Him* to be crucified.

The Soldiers Mock Jesus

27 [a]Then the soldiers of the governor took Jesus into the [1]Praetorium and gathered the whole [2]garrison around Him.
28 And they [a]stripped Him and [b]put a scarlet robe on Him.
29 [a]When they had [1]twisted a crown of thorns, they put *it* on His head, and a reed in His right hand. And they bowed the knee before Him and mocked Him, saying, "Hail, King of the Jews!"
30 Then [a]they spat on Him, and took the reed and struck Him on the head.
31 And when they had mocked Him, they took the robe off Him, put His *own* clothes on Him, [a]and led Him away to be crucified.

The King on a Cross

32 [a]Now as they came out, [b]they found a man of Cyrene, Simon by name. Him they compelled to bear His cross.
33 [a]And when they had come to a place called Golgotha, that is to say, Place of a Skull,
34 [a]they gave Him [1]sour wine mingled with gall to drink. But when He had tasted *it,* He would not drink.
35 [a]Then they crucified Him, and divided His garments, casting lots, [1]that it might be fulfilled which was spoken by the prophet:

[b]*"They divided My garments*
among them,
And for My clothing they cast
lots."
36 [a]Sitting down, they kept watch
over Him there.
37 And they [a]put up over His head
the accusation written against
Him:

THIS IS JESUS THE KING OF
THE JEWS.

38 [a]Then two robbers were cruci-
fied with Him, one on the right and
another on the left.
39 And [a]those who passed by
blasphemed Him, wagging their
heads
40 and saying, [a]"You who destroy
the temple and build *it* in three
days, save Yourself! [b]If You are
the Son of God, come down from
the cross."
41 Likewise the chief priests also,
mocking with the [1]scribes and el-
ders, said,
42 "He [a]saved others; Himself He
cannot save. [1]If He is the King of
Israel, let Him now come down
from the cross, and we will believe
[2]Him.
43 [a]"He trusted in God; let Him
deliver Him now if He will have
Him; for He said, 'I am the Son of
God.' "
44 [a]Even the robbers who were
crucified with Him reviled Him
with the same thing.

Jesus Dies on the Cross

45 [a]Now from the sixth hour until
the ninth hour there was darkness
over all the land.
46 And about the ninth hour
[a]Jesus cried out with a loud voice,
saying, "Eli, Eli, lama sabach-
thani?" that is, [b]*"My God, My*
God, why have You forsaken
Me?"
47 Some of those who stood there,
when they heard *that*, said, "This
Man is calling for Elijah!"
48 Immediately one of them ran
and took a sponge, [a]filled *it* with
sour wine and put *it* on a reed, and
offered it to Him to drink.
49 The rest said, "Let Him alone;
let us see if Elijah will come to save
Him."
50 And Jesus [a]cried out again with
a loud voice, and [b]yielded up His
spirit.
51 Then, behold, [a]the veil of the
temple was torn in two from top
to bottom; and the earth quaked,
and the rocks were split,
52 and the graves were opened;
and many bodies of the saints who
had fallen asleep were raised;
53 and coming out of the graves
after His resurrection, they went
into the holy city and appeared to
many.
54 [a]So when the centurion and
those with him, who were guard-
ing Jesus, saw the earthquake and
the things that had happened, they
feared greatly, saying, [b]"Truly this
was the Son of God!"
55 And many women [a]who fol-
lowed Jesus from Galilee, minis-
tering to Him, were there looking
on from afar,
56 [a]among whom were Mary
Magdalene, Mary the mother of
James and [1]Joses, and the mother
of Zebedee's sons.

Jesus Buried in Joseph's Tomb

57 Now [a]when evening had come,
there came a rich man from Ari-
mathea, named Joseph, who him-
self had also become a disciple of
Jesus.
58 This man went to Pilate and
asked for the body of Jesus. Then
Pilate commanded the body to be
given to him.
59 When Joseph had taken the
body, he wrapped it in a clean
linen cloth,
60 and [a]laid it in his new tomb
which he had hewn out of the rock;
and he rolled a large stone against
the door of the tomb, and de-
parted.
61 And Mary Magdalene was
there, and the other Mary, sitting
[1]opposite the tomb.

Pilate Sets a Guard

62 On the next day, which fol-
lowed the Day of Preparation, the
chief priests and Pharisees gath-
ered together to Pilate,
63 saying, "Sir, we remember,
while He was still alive, how that
deceiver said, [a]'After three days I
will rise.'
64 "Therefore command that the
tomb be made secure until the

35 [b]Ps. 22:18
36 [a]Matt. 27:54
37 [a]John 19:19
38 [a]Is. 53:9, 12
39 [a]Mark 15:29
40 [a]John 2:19 [b]Matt. 26:63
41 [1]M *scribes, the Pharisees, and the elders*
42 [a][John 3:14, 15] [1]NU omits *If* [2]NU, M *in Him*
43 [a]Ps. 22:8
44 [a]Luke 23:39–43
45 [a]Mark 15:33–41
46 [a][Heb. 5:7] [b]Ps. 22:1
48 [a]Ps. 69:21
50 [a]Luke 23:46 [b][John 10:18]
51 [a]Ex. 26:31
54 [a]Mark 15:39 [b]Matt. 14:33
55 [a]Luke 8:2, 3
56 [a]Mark 15:40, 47; 16:9 [1]NU *Joseph*
57 [a]John 19:38–42
60 [a]Is. 53:9
61 [1]*in front of*
63 [a]Mark 8:31; 10:34

third day, lest His disciples come
[1]by night and steal Him *away*, and
say to the people, 'He has risen
from the dead.' So the last decep-
tion will be worse than the first."
65 Pilate said to them, "You have
a guard; go your way, make *it* as
secure as you know how."
66 So they went and made the
tomb secure, [a]sealing the stone
and setting the guard.

He Is Risen

28 Now [a]after the Sabbath, as
the first *day* of the week be-
gan to dawn, Mary Magdalene
[b]and the other Mary came to see
the tomb.
2 And behold, there was a great
earthquake; for [a]an angel of the
Lord descended from heaven, and
came and rolled back the stone
[1]from the door, and sat on it.
3 [a]His countenance was like
lightning, and his clothing as
white as snow.
4 And the guards shook for fear
of him, and became like [a]dead
men.
5 But the angel answered and
said to the women, "Do not be
afraid, for I know that you seek
Jesus who was crucified.
6 "He is not here; for He is risen,
[a]as He said. Come, see the place
where the Lord lay.
7 "And go quickly and tell His
disciples that He is risen from the
dead, and indeed [a]He is going be-
fore you into Galilee; there you
will see Him. Behold, I have told
you."
8 So they went out quickly from
the tomb with fear and great joy,
and ran to bring His disciples
word.

The Women Worship the Risen Lord

9 And [1]as they went to tell His
disciples, behold, [a]Jesus met them,
saying, "Rejoice!" So they came
and held Him by the feet and wor-
shiped Him.
10 Then Jesus said to them, "Do
not be afraid. Go *and* tell [a]My
brethren to go to Galilee, and there
they will see Me."

The Soldiers Are Bribed

11 Now while they were going, be-
hold, some of the guard came into
the city and reported to the chief
priests all the things that had hap-
pened.
12 When they had assembled with
the elders and consulted together,
they gave a large sum of money
to the soldiers,
13 saying, "Tell them, 'His disci-
ples came at night and stole Him
away while we slept.'
14 "And if this comes to the gover-
nor's ears, we will appease him
and make you secure."
15 So they took the money and did
as they were instructed; and this
saying is commonly reported
among the Jews until this day.

The Great Commission

16 Then the eleven disciples went
away into Galilee, to the mountain
[a]which Jesus had appointed for
them.
17 When they saw Him, they wor-
shiped Him; but some [a]doubted.
18 And Jesus came and spoke to
them, saying, [a]"All authority has
been given to Me in heaven and
on earth.
19 [a]"Go [1]therefore and [b]make dis-
ciples of all the nations, baptizing
them in the name of the Father
and of the Son and of the Holy
Spirit,
20 [a]"teaching them to observe all
things that I have commanded
you; and lo, I am [b]with you always,
even to the end of the age."
[1]Amen.

64 [1]NU omits *by night*
66 [a]Dan. 6:17

CHAPTER 28

1 [a]Luke 24:1–10 [b]Matt. 27:56, 61
2 [a]Mark 16:5 [1]NU omits *from the door*
3 [a]Dan. 7:9; 10:6
4 [a]Rev. 1:17
6 [a]Matt. 12:40; 16:21; 17:23; 20:19
7 [a]Mark 16:7
9 [a]John 20:14 [1]NU omits *as they went to tell His disciples*
10 [a]John 20:17
16 [a]Matt. 26:32; 28:7, 10
17 [a]John 20:24–29
18 [a][Dan. 7:13, 14]
19 [a]Mark 16:15 [b]Luke 24:47 [1]M omits *therefore*
20 [a][Acts 2:42] [b][Acts 4:31; 18:10; 23:11] [1]NU omits *Amen*

The Gospel According to

Mark

THE message of Mark's gospel is captured in a single verse: "For even the Son of Man did not come to be served, but to serve, and to give His life a ransom for many" (10:45). Chapter by chapter, the book unfolds the dual focus of Christ's life: service and sacrifice.

Mark portrays Jesus as a Servant on the move, instantly responsive to the will of the Father. By preaching, teaching, and healing, He ministers to the needs of others even to the point of death. After the Resurrection, He commissions His followers to continue His work in His power—servants following in the steps of the perfect Servant.

The ancient title for this gospel was *Kata Markon,* "According to Mark." The author is best known by his Latin name *Marcus,* but in Jewish circles he was called by his Hebrew name *John.* Acts 12:12, 25 refer to him as "John whose surname was Mark."

CHAPTER 1

John the Baptist Prepares the Way

THE [a]beginning of the gospel
of Jesus Christ, [b]the Son of
God.
2 As it is written in [1]the Proph-
ets:

> [a]*"Behold, I send My messenger*
> *before Your face,*
> *Who will prepare Your way*
> *before You."*

3 *"The[a] voice of one crying in the*
> *wilderness:*
> *'Prepare the way of the* LORD;
> *Make His paths straight.'* "

4 [a]John came baptizing in the
wilderness and preaching a bap-
tism of repentance [1]for the remis-
sion of sins.
5 [a]Then all the land of Judea, and
those from Jerusalem, went out to
him and were all baptized by him
in the Jordan River, confessing
their sins.
6 Now John was [a]clothed with
camel's hair and with a leather belt
around his waist, and he ate lo-
custs and wild honey.
7 And he preached, saying,
[a]"There comes One after me who
is mightier than I, whose sandal
strap I am not worthy to stoop
down and loose.
8 [a]"I indeed baptized you with
water, but He will baptize you
[b]with the Holy Spirit."

John Baptizes Jesus

9 [a]It came to pass in those days
that Jesus came from Nazareth of
Galilee, and was baptized by John
in the Jordan.
10 [a]And immediately, coming up
[1]from the water, He saw the heav-
ens [2]parting and the Spirit [b]de-
scending upon Him like a dove.
11 Then a voice came from
heaven, [a]"You are My beloved
Son, in whom I am well pleased."

Satan Tempts Jesus

12 [a]Immediately the Spirit [1]drove
Him into the wilderness.
13 And He was there in the wilder-
ness forty days, tempted by Satan,
and was with the wild beasts; [a]and
the angels ministered to Him.

Jesus Begins His Galilean Ministry

14 [a]Now after John was put in
prison, Jesus came to Galilee,
[b]preaching the gospel [1]of the king-
dom of God,
15 and saying, [a]"The time is ful-
filled, and [b]the kingdom of God [1]is
at hand. Repent, and believe in the
gospel."

Four Fishermen Called as Disciples

16 [a]And as He walked by the Sea
of Galilee, He saw Simon and An-
drew his brother casting a net into

---

1 [a]Luke 3:22 [b]Matt. 14:33
2 [a]Mal. 3:1 [1]NU *Isaiah the prophet*
3 [a]Is. 40:3
4 [a]Matt. 3:1 [1]Or *because of forgiveness*
5 [a]Matt. 3:5
6 [a]Matt. 3:4
7 [a]John 1:27
8 [a]Acts 1:5; 11:16 [b]Is. 44:3
9 [a]Matt. 3:13–17
10 [a]Matt. 3:16 [b]Acts 10:38 [1]NU *out of* [2]*torn open*
11 [a]Matt. 3:17; 12:18
12 [a]Matt. 4:1–11 [1]*sent Him out*
13 [a]Matt. 4:10, 11
14 [a]Matt. 4:12 [b]Matt. 4:23 [1]NU omits *of the kingdom*
15 [a][Gal. 4:4] [b]Matt. 3:2; 4:17 [1]*has drawn near*
16 [a]Luke 5:2–11

the sea; for they were fishermen.
17 Then Jesus said to them, "Fol-
low Me, and I will make you be-
come [a]fishers of men."
18 [a]They immediately left their
nets and followed Him.
19 When He had gone a little far-
ther from there, He saw James the
son of Zebedee, and John his
brother, who also *were* in the boat
mending their nets.
20 And immediately He called
them, and they left their father
Zebedee in the boat with the hired
servants, and went after Him.

Jesus Casts Out an Unclean Spirit

21 [a]Then they went into Caper-
naum, and immediately on the
Sabbath He entered the [b]syna-
gogue and taught.
22 [a]And they were astonished at
His teaching, for He taught them
as one having authority, and not
as the scribes.
23 Now there was a man in their
synagogue with an [a]unclean spirit.
And he cried out,
24 saying, "Let *us* alone! [a]What
have we to do with You, Jesus of
Nazareth? Did You come to de-
stroy us? I [b]know who You are—
the [c]Holy One of God!"
25 But Jesus [a]rebuked him, say-
ing, [1]"Be quiet, and come out of
him!"
26 And when the unclean spirit
[a]had convulsed him and cried out
with a loud voice, he came out of
him.
27 Then they were all amazed, so
that they questioned among them-
selves, saying, [1]"What is this?
What new [2]doctrine *is* this? For
with authority He commands even
the unclean spirits, and they obey
Him."
28 And immediately His [a]fame
spread throughout all the region
around Galilee.

Peter's Mother-in-Law Healed

29 [a]Now as soon as they had come
out of the synagogue, they entered
the house of Simon and Andrew,
with James and John.
30 But Simon's wife's mother lay
sick with a fever, and they told
Him about her at once.
31 So He came and took her by
the hand and lifted her up, and im-
mediately the fever left her. And
she served them.

Many Healed After Sabbath Sunset

32 [a]At evening, when the sun had
set, they brought to Him all who
were sick and those who were
demon-possessed.
33 And the whole city was gath-
ered together at the door.
34 Then He healed many who
were sick with various diseases,
and [a]cast out many demons; and
He [b]did not allow the demons to
speak, because they knew Him.

Preaching in Galilee

35 Now [a]in the morning, having
risen a long while before daylight,
He went out and departed to a [1]sol-
itary place; and there He [b]prayed.
36 And Simon and those *who*
were with Him searched for Him.
37 When they found Him, they
said to Him, [a]"Everyone [b]is look-
ing for You."
38 But He said to them, [a]"Let us
go into the next towns, that I may
preach there also, because [b]for this
purpose I have come forth."
39 [a]And He was preaching in their
synagogues throughout all Galilee,
and [b]casting out demons.

Jesus Cleanses a Leper

40 [a]Now a leper came to Him,
imploring Him, kneeling down to
Him and saying to Him, "If You
are willing, You can make me
clean."
41 Then Jesus, moved with [a]com-
passion, stretched out *His* hand
and touched him, and said to him,
"I am willing; be cleansed."
42 As soon as He had spoken,
[a]immediately the leprosy left him,
and he was cleansed.
43 And He strictly warned him
and sent him away at once,
44 and said to him, "See that you
say nothing to anyone; but go your
way, show yourself to the priest,
and offer for your cleansing those
things [a]which Moses commanded,
as a testimony to them."
45 [a]However, he went out and be-
gan to proclaim *it* freely, and to
spread the matter, so that Jesus
could no longer openly enter the
city, but was outside in deserted

17 [a]Matt. 13:47, 48
18 [a]Matt. 19:27; [Luke 14:26]
21 [a]Matt. 4:13; Luke 4:31–37 [b]Ps. 22:22; Matt. 4:23; Luke 4:16; 13:10
22 [a]Matt. 7:28, 29; 13:54
23 [a][Matt. 12:43]; Mark 5:2; 7:25; Luke 4:33
24 [a]Matt. 8:28, 29; Mark 5:7, 8; Luke 8:28 [b]Mark 3:11; Luke 4:41; James 2:19 [c]Ps. 16:10
25 [a][Luke 4:39] [1]Lit. *Be muzzled*
26 [a]Mark 9:20
27 [1]NU *What is this? A new doctrine with authority. He* [2]*teaching*
28 [a]Matt. 4:24; 9:31
29 [a]Matt. 8:14, 15; Luke 4:38, 39
32 [a]Matt. 8:16, 17; Luke 4:40, 41
34 [a]Matt. 9:33; Luke 13:32 [b]Mark 3:12; Luke 4:41; Acts 16:17, 18
35 [a]Luke 4:42, 43 [b]Matt. 26:39, 44; Mark 6:46; Luke 5:16; 6:12; 9:28, 29; Heb. 5:7 [1]*deserted*
37 [a]Matt. 4:25; John 3:26; 12:19 [b][Heb. 11:6]
38 [a]Luke 4:43 [b][Is. 61:1, 2; Mark 10:45; John 16:28; 17:4, 8]
39 [a]Ps. 22:22; Matt. 4:23; 9:35; Mark 1:21; 3:1; Luke 4:44 [b]Mark 5:8, 13; 7:29, 30
40 [a]Matt. 8:2–4; Luke 5:12–14
41 [a]Luke 7:13
42 [a]Matt. 15:28; Mark 5:29
44 [a]Lev. 14:1–32
45 [a]Matt. 28:15; Luke 5:15

places; [b]and they came to Him from every direction.

Jesus Forgives and Heals a Paralytic

2 And again [a]He entered Capernaum after *some* days, and it was heard that He was in the house.

2 [1]Immediately many gathered together, so that there was no longer room to receive *them,* not even near the door. And He preached the word to them.

3 Then they came to Him, bringing a [a]paralytic who was carried by four *men.*

4 And when they could not come near Him because of the crowd, they uncovered the roof where He was. So when they had broken through, they let down the bed on which the paralytic was lying.

5 When Jesus saw their faith, He said to the paralytic, "Son, your sins are forgiven you."

6 And some of the scribes were sitting there and reasoning in their hearts,

7 "Why does this *Man* speak blasphemies like this? [a]Who can forgive sins but God alone?"

8 But immediately, when Jesus perceived in His spirit that they reasoned thus within themselves, He said to them, "Why do you reason about these things in your hearts?

9 [a]"Which is easier, to say to the paralytic, '*Your* sins are forgiven you,' or to say, 'Arise, take up your bed and walk'?

10 "But that you may know that the Son of Man has [1]power on earth to forgive sins"—He said to the paralytic,

11 "I say to you, arise, take up your bed, and go to your house."

12 Immediately he arose, took up the bed, and went out in the presence of them all, so that all were amazed and [a]glorified God, saying, "We never saw *anything* like this!"

Matthew the Tax Collector

13 [a]Then He went out again by the sea; and all the multitude came to Him, and He taught them.

14 [a]As He passed by, He saw Levi the *son* of Alphaeus sitting at the tax office. And He said to him, [b]"Follow Me." So he arose and [c]followed Him.

15 [a]Now it happened, as He was dining in *Levi's* house, that many tax collectors and sinners also sat together with Jesus and His disciples; for there were many, and they followed Him.

16 And when the scribes [1]and Pharisees saw Him eating with the tax collectors and sinners, they said to His disciples, "How *is it* that He eats and drinks with tax collectors and sinners?"

17 When Jesus heard *it,* He said to them, [a]"Those who are well have no need of a physician, but those who are sick. I did not come to call *the* righteous, but sinners, [1]to repentance."

Jesus Is Questioned About Fasting

18 [a]The disciples of John and of the Pharisees were fasting. Then they came and said to Him, "Why do the disciples of John and of the Pharisees fast, but Your disciples do not fast?"

19 And Jesus said to them, "Can the [1]friends of the bridegroom fast while the bridegroom is with them? As long as they have the bridegroom with them they cannot fast.

20 "But the days will come when the bridegroom will be [a]taken away from them, and then they will fast in those days.

21 "No one sews a piece of unshrunk cloth on an old garment; or else the new piece pulls away from the old, and the tear is made worse.

22 "And no one puts new wine into old wineskins; or else the new wine bursts the wineskins, the wine is spilled, and the wineskins are ruined. But new wine must be put into new wineskins."

Jesus Is Lord of the Sabbath

23 [a]Now it happened that He went through the grainfields on the Sabbath; and as they went His disciples began [b]to pluck the heads of grain.

24 And the Pharisees said to Him, "Look, why do they do what is [a]not lawful on the Sabbath?"

25 But He said to them, "Have you never read [a]what David did when

---

45 [b]Mark 2:2, 13; 3:7; Luke 5:17; John 6:2

CHAPTER 2

1 [a]Matt. 9:1

2 [1]NU omits *Immediately*

3 [a]Matt. 4:24; 8:6; Acts 8:7; 9:33

7 [a]Job 14:4; Is. 43:25; Dan. 9:9

9 [a]Matt. 9:5

10 [1]*authority*

12 [a]Matt. 15:31; [Phil. 2:11]

13 [a]Matt. 9:9

14 [a]Matt. 9:9–13; Luke 5:27–32 [b]Matt. 4:19; 8:22; 19:21; John 1:43; 12:26; 21:22 [c]Luke 18:28

15 [a]Matt. 9:10

16 [1]NU *of the*

17 [a]Matt. 9:12, 13; 18:11; Luke 5:31, 32; 19:10 [1]NU omits *to repentance*

18 [a]Matt. 9:14–17; Luke 5:33–38

19 [1]Lit. *sons of the bridechamber*

20 [a]Acts 1:9; 13:2, 3; 14:23

23 [a]Matt. 12:1–8; Luke 6:1–5 [b]Deut. 23:25

24 [a]Ex. 20:10; 31:15

25 [a]1 Sam. 21:1–6

he was in need and hungry, he and
those with him:
26 "how he went into the house
of God *in the days* of Abiathar the
high priest, and ate the show-
bread, [a]which is not lawful to eat
except for the priests, and also
gave some to those who were with
him?"
27 And He said to them, "The Sab-
bath was made for man, and not
man for the [a]Sabbath.
28 "Therefore [a]the Son of Man is
also Lord of the Sabbath."

Healing on the Sabbath

3 And [a]He entered the syna-
gogue again, and a man was
there who had a withered hand.
2 So they [a]watched Him closely,
whether He would [b]heal him on
the Sabbath, so that they might
[1]accuse Him.
3 And He said to the man who
had the withered hand, [1]"Step for-
ward."
4 Then He said to them, "Is it
lawful on the Sabbath to do good
or to do evil, to save life or to kill?"
But they kept silent.
5 And when He had looked
around at them with anger, being
grieved by the [a]hardness of their
hearts, He said to the man,
"Stretch out your hand." And he
stretched *it* out, and his hand was
restored [1]as whole as the other.
6 [a]Then the Pharisees went out
and immediately plotted with [b]the
Herodians against Him, how they
might destroy Him.

A Great Multitude Follows Jesus

7 But Jesus withdrew with His
disciples to the sea. And a great
multitude from Galilee followed
Him, [a]and from Judea
8 and Jerusalem and Idumea and
beyond the Jordan; and those from
Tyre and Sidon, a great multitude,
when they heard how [a]many
things He was doing, came to Him.
9 So He told His disciples that a
small boat should be kept ready
for Him because of the multitude,
lest they should crush Him.
10 For He healed [a]many, so that
as many as had afflictions pressed
about Him to [b]touch Him.
11 [a]And the unclean spirits, when-
ever they saw Him, fell down be-
fore Him and cried out, saying,
[b]"You are the Son of God."
12 But [a]He sternly warned them
that they should not make Him
known.

The Twelve Apostles

13 [a]And He went up on the moun-
tain and called to *Him* those He
Himself wanted. And they came to
Him.
14 Then He appointed twelve,
[1]that they might be with Him and
that He might send them out to
preach,
15 and to have [1]power [2]to heal
sicknesses and to cast out demons:
16 [1]Simon, [a]to whom He gave the
name Peter;
17 James the *son* of Zebedee and
John the brother of James, to
whom He gave the name Boa-
nerges, that is, "Sons of Thunder";
18 Andrew, Philip, Bartholomew,
Matthew, Thomas, James the *son*
of Alphaeus, Thaddaeus, Simon
the Cananite;
19 and Judas Iscariot, who also
betrayed Him. And they went into
a house.

A House Divided Cannot Stand

20 Then the multitude came to-
gether again, [a]so that they could
not so much as eat bread.
21 But when His [a]own people
heard *about this,* they went out to
lay hold of Him, [b]for they said, "He
is out of His mind."
22 And the scribes who came
down from Jerusalem said, [a]"He
has Beelzebub," and, "By the
[b]ruler of the demons He casts out
demons."
23 [a]So He called them to *Himself*
and said to them in parables:
"How can Satan cast out Satan?
24 "If a kingdom is divided
against itself, that kingdom cannot
stand.
25 "And if a house is divided
against itself, that house cannot
stand.
26 "And if Satan has risen up
against himself, and is divided, he
cannot stand, but has an end.
27 [a]"No one can enter a strong
man's house and plunder his
goods, unless he first binds the
strong man. And then he will plun-
der his house.

26 [a]Lev. 24:5–9
27 [a]Deut. 5:14
28 [a]Matt. 12:8

CHAPTER 3

1 [a]Luke 6:6–11
2 [a]Luke 14:1; 20:20 [b]Luke 13:14 [1]*bring charges against*
3 [1]Lit. *Arise into the midst*
5 [a]Zech. 7:12 [1]NU omits *as whole as the other*
6 [a]Mark 12:13 [b]Matt. 22:16
7 [a]Luke 6:17
8 [a]Mark 5:19
10 [a]Luke 7:21 [b]Matt. 9:21; 14:36
11 [a]Luke 4:41 [b]Matt. 8:29; 14:33
12 [a]Mark 1:25, 34
13 [a]Luke 9:1
14 [1]NU adds *whom He also named apostles*
15 [1]*authority* [2]NU omits *to heal sicknesses and*
16 [a]John 1:42 [1]NU *and He appointed the twelve: Simon . . .*
20 [a]Mark 6:31
21 [a]Mark 6:3 [b]John 7:5; 10:20
22 [a]Matt. 9:34; 10:25 [b][John 12:31; 14:30; 16:11]
23 [a]Matt. 12:25–29
27 [a][Is. 49:24, 25]

The Unpardonable Sin

28 [a]"Assuredly, I say to you, all
sins will be forgiven the sons of
men, and whatever blasphemies
they may utter;
29 "but he who blasphemes
against the Holy Spirit never has
forgiveness, but is subject to eter-
nal condemnation"—
30 because they [a]said, "He has an
unclean spirit."

Jesus' Mother and Brothers Send for Him

31 [a]Then His brothers and His
mother came, and standing out-
side they sent to Him, calling Him.
32 And a multitude was sitting
around Him; and they said to Him,
"Look, Your mother and Your
brothers [1]are outside seeking
You."
33 But He answered them, saying,
"Who is My mother, or My broth-
ers?"
34 And He looked around in a cir-
cle at those who sat about Him,
and said, "Here are My mother
and My brothers!
35 "For whoever does the [a]will of
God is My brother and My sister
and mother."

The Parable of the Sower

4 And [a]again He began to teach
by the sea. And a great multi-
tude was gathered to Him, so that
He got into a boat and sat *in it* on
the sea; and the whole multitude
was on the land facing the sea.
2 Then He taught them many
things by parables, [a]and said to
them in His teaching:
3 "Listen! Behold, a sower went
out to sow.
4 "And it happened, as he sowed,
that some *seed* fell by the wayside;
and the birds [1]of the air came and
devoured it.
5 "Some fell on stony ground,
where it did not have much earth;
and immediately it sprang up be-
cause it had no depth of earth.
6 "But when the sun was up it
was scorched, and because it had
no root it withered away.
7 "And some *seed* fell among
thorns; and the thorns grew up
and choked it, and it yielded no
[1]crop.
8 "But other *seed* fell on good
ground and yielded a crop that
sprang up, increased and pro-
duced: some thirtyfold, some sixty,
and some a hundred."
9 And He said [1]to them, "He who
has ears to hear, let him hear!"

The Purpose of Parables

10 [a]But when He was alone, those
around Him with the twelve asked
Him about the parable.
11 And He said to them, "To you
it has been given to [a]know the
[1]mystery of the kingdom of God;
but to [b]those who are outside, all
things come in parables,
12 "so that

[a]'*Seeing they may see and not*
perceive,
And hearing they may hear and
not understand;
Lest they should turn,
And their sins be forgiven
them.' "

The Parable of the Sower Explained

13 And He said to them, "Do you
not understand this parable? How
then will you understand all the
parables?
14 [a]"The sower sows the word.
15 "And these are the ones by the
wayside where the word is sown.
When they hear, Satan comes im-
mediately and takes away the
word that was sown in their
hearts.
16 "These likewise are the ones
sown on stony ground who, when
they hear the word, immediately
receive it with gladness;
17 "and they have no root in
themselves, and so endure only for
a time. Afterward, when tribula-
tion or persecution arises for the
word's sake, immediately they
stumble.
18 "Now these are the ones sown
among thorns; *they are* the ones
who hear the word,
19 "and the [a]cares of this world,
[b]the deceitfulness of riches, and
the desires for other things enter-
ing in choke the word, and it be-
comes unfruitful.
20 "But these are the ones sown
on good ground, those who hear
the word, [1]accept *it*, and bear

---

28 [a]Matt. 12:31, 32; Luke 12:10; [1 John 5:16]
30 [a]Matt. 9:34; John 7:20; 8:48, 52; 10:20
31 [a]Matt. 12:46–50; Luke 8:19–21
32 [1]NU, M add *and Your sisters*
35 [a]Eph. 6:6; Heb. 10:36; 1 Pet. 4:2; [1 John 2:17]

CHAPTER 4

1 [a]Matt. 13:1–15; Luke 8:4–10
2 [a]Mark 12:38
4 [1]NU, M omit *of the air*
7 [1]Lit. *fruit*
9 [1]NU, M omit *to them*
10 [a]Matt. 13:10; Luke 8:9
11 [a][Matt. 11:25; 1 Cor. 2:10–16; 2 Cor. 4:6] [b][1 Cor. 5:12, 13; Col. 4:5; 1 Thess. 4:12; 1 Tim. 3:7] [1]*secret* or *hidden truths*
12 [a]Is. 6:9, 10; 43:8; Jer. 5:21; Ezek. 12:2; Matt. 13:14; Luke 8:10; John 12:40; Rom. 11:8
14 [a]Matt. 13:18–23; Luke 8:11–15
19 [a]Luke 21:34 [b]Prov. 23:5; Eccl. 5:13; Luke 18:24; 1 Tim. 6:9, 10, 17
20 [1]*receive*

[a]fruit: some thirtyfold, some sixty, and some a hundred."

Light Under a Basket

21 [a]Also He said to them, "Is a lamp brought to be put under a basket or under a bed? Is it not to be set on a lampstand?

22 [a]"For there is nothing hidden which will not be revealed, nor has anything been kept secret but that it should come to light.

23 [a]"If anyone has ears to hear, let him hear."

24 Then He said to them, "Take heed what you hear. [a]With the same measure you use, it will be measured to you; and to you who hear, more will be given.

25 [a]"For whoever has, to him more will be given; but whoever does not have, even what he has will be taken away from him."

The Parable of the Growing Seed

26 And He said, [a]"The kingdom of God is as if a man should [1]scatter seed on the ground,

27 "and should sleep by night and rise by day, and the seed should sprout and [a]grow, he himself does not know how.

28 "For the earth [a]yields crops by itself: first the blade, then the head, after that the full grain in the head.

29 "But when the grain ripens, immediately [a]he puts in the sickle, because the harvest has come."

The Parable of the Mustard Seed

30 Then He said, [a]"To what shall we liken the kingdom of God? Or with what parable shall we picture it?

31 "*It is* like a mustard seed which, when it is sown on the ground, is smaller than all the seeds on earth;

32 "but when it is sown, it grows up and becomes greater than all herbs, and shoots out large branches, so that the birds of the air may nest under its shade."

Jesus' Use of Parables

33 [a]And with many such parables He spoke the word to them as they were able to hear *it.*

34 But without a parable He did not speak to them. And when they were alone, [a]He explained all things to His disciples.

Wind and Wave Obey Jesus

35 [a]On the same day, when evening had come, He said to them, "Let us cross over to the other side."

36 Now when they had left the multitude, they took Him along in the boat as He was. And other little boats were also with Him.

37 And a great windstorm arose, and the waves beat into the boat, so that it was already filling.

38 But He was in the stern, asleep on a pillow. And they awoke Him and said to Him, [a]"Teacher, [b]do You not care that we are perishing?"

39 Then He arose and [a]rebuked the wind, and said to the sea, [b]"Peace,[1] be still!" And the wind ceased and there was a great calm.

40 But He said to them, "Why are you so fearful? [a]How[1] *is it* that you have no faith?"

41 And they feared exceedingly, and said to one another, "Who can this be, that even the wind and the sea obey Him!"

A Demon-Possessed Man Healed

5 Then [a]they came to the other side of the sea, to the country of the [1]Gadarenes.

2 And when He had come out of the boat, immediately there met Him out of the tombs a man with an [a]unclean spirit,

3 who had *his* dwelling among the tombs; and no one could bind [1]him, not even with chains,

4 because he had often been bound with shackles and chains. And the chains had been pulled apart by him, and the shackles broken in pieces; neither could anyone tame him.

5 And always, night and day, he was in the mountains and in the tombs, crying out and cutting himself with stones.

6 When he saw Jesus from afar, he ran and worshiped Him.

7 And he cried out with a loud voice and said, "What have I to do with You, Jesus, Son of the Most High God? I [a]implore[1] You by God that You do not torment me."

20 [a][John 15:2, 5; Rom. 7:4] **21** [a]Matt. 5:15; Luke 8:16; 11:33 **22** [a]Eccl. 12:14; Matt. 10:26, 27; Luke 12:3; [1 Cor. 4:5] **23** [a]Matt. 11:15; 13:9, 43; Mark 4:9; Luke 8:8; 14:35; Rev. 3:6, 13, 22; 13:9 **24** [a]Matt. 7:2; Luke 6:38; 2 Cor. 9:6 **25** [a]Matt. 13:12; 25.29; Luke 8:18; 19:26 **26** [a][Matt. 13:24–30, 36–43]; Luke 8:1 [1]*sow* **27** [a][2 Cor. 3:18; 2 Pet. 3:18] **28** [a][John 12:24] **29** [a][Mark 13:30, 39]; Rev. 14:15 **30** [a]Matt. 13:31, 32; Luke 13:18, 19; [Acts 2:41; 4:4; 5:14; 19:20] **33** [a]Matt. 13:34, 35; [John 16:12] **34** [a]Luke 24:27, 45 **35** [a]Matt. 8:18, 23–27; Luke 8:22, 25 **38** [a][Matt. 23:8–10] [b]Ps. 44:23 **39** [a]Mark 9:25; Luke 4:39 [b]Ps. 65:7; 89:9; 93:4; 104:6, 7; Matt. 8:26; Luke 8:24 [1]Lit. *Be quiet* **40** [a]Matt. 14:31, 32; Luke 8:25 [1]NU *Have you still no faith?*

CHAPTER 5

1 [a]Matt. 8:28–34; Luke 8:26–37 [1]NU *Gerasenes* **2** [a]Mark 1:23; 7:25; [Rev. 16:13, 14] **3** [1]NU adds *anymore* **7** [a]Matt. 26:63; Mark 1:24; Acts 19:13 [1]*adjure*

8 For He said to him, [a]"Come out
of the man, unclean spirit!"
9 Then He asked him, "What *is*
your name?" And he answered,
saying, "My name *is* Legion; for
we are many."
10 Also he begged Him earnestly
that He would not send them out
of the country.
11 Now a large herd of [a]swine
was feeding there near the moun-
tains.
12 So all the demons begged Him,
saying, "Send us to the swine, that
we may enter them."
13 And [1]at once Jesus gave them
permission. Then the unclean spir-
its went out and entered the swine
(there were about two thousand);
and the herd ran violently down
the steep place into the sea, and
drowned in the sea.
14 So those who fed the swine
fled, and they told *it* in the city and
in the country. And they went out
to see what it was that had hap-
pened.
15 Then they came to Jesus, and
saw the one *who had been* [a]demon-
possessed and had the legion, [b]sit-
ting and [c]clothed and in his right
mind. And they were afraid.
16 And those who saw it told them
how it happened to him *who had
been* demon-possessed, and about
the swine.
17 Then [a]they began to plead with
Him to depart from their region.
18 And when He got into the
boat, [a]he who had been demon-
possessed begged Him that he
might be with Him.
19 However, Jesus did not permit
him, but said to him, "Go home to
your friends, and tell them what
great things the Lord has done for
you, and how He has had compas-
sion on you."
20 And he departed and began to
[a]proclaim in [1]Decapolis all that
Jesus had done for him; and all
[b]marveled.

A Girl Restored to Life and a Woman Healed

21 [a]Now when Jesus had crossed
over again by boat to the other
side, a great multitude gathered to
Him; and He was by the sea.
22 [a]And behold, one of the rulers
of the synagogue came, Jairus by
name. And when he saw Him, he
fell at His feet
23 and begged Him earnestly, say-
ing, "My little daughter lies at the
point of death. Come and [a]lay
Your hands on her, that she may
be healed, and she will live."
24 So *Jesus* went with him, and a
great multitude followed Him and
thronged Him.
25 Now a certain woman [a]had a
flow of blood for twelve years,
26 and had suffered many things
from many physicians. She had
spent all that she had and was no
better, but rather grew worse.
27 When she heard about Jesus,
she came behind *Him* in the crowd
and [a]touched His garment.
28 For she said, "If only I may
touch His clothes, I shall be made
well."
29 Immediately the fountain of
her blood was dried up, and she
felt in *her* body that she was
healed of the [1]affliction.
30 And Jesus, immediately know-
ing in Himself that [a]power had
gone out of Him, turned around in
the crowd and said, "Who touched
My clothes?"
31 But His disciples said to Him,
"You see the multitude thronging
You, and You say, 'Who touched
Me?' "
32 And He looked around to see
her who had done this thing.
33 But the woman, [a]fearing and
trembling, knowing what had hap-
pened to her, came and fell down
before Him and told Him the
whole truth.
34 And He said to her, "Daughter,
[a]your faith has made you well. [b]Go
in peace, and be healed of your af-
fliction."
35 [a]While He was still speak-
ing, *some* came from the ruler
of the synagogue's *house* who
said, "Your daughter is dead.
Why trouble the Teacher any fur-
ther?"
36 As soon as Jesus heard the
word that was spoken, He said to
the ruler of the synagogue, "Do
not be afraid; only [a]believe."
37 And He permitted no one to fol-
low Him except Peter, James, and
John the brother of James.
38 Then He came to the house of
the ruler of the synagogue, and

8 [a]Mark 1:25; 9:25; [Acts 16:18]
11 [a]Lev. 11:7, 8; Deut. 14:8; Luke 15:15, 16
13 [1]NU *He gave*
15 [a]Matt. 4:24; 8:16; Mark 1:32 [b]Luke 10:39 [c][Is. 61:10]
17 [a]Matt. 8:34; Acts 16:39
18 [a]Luke 8:38, 39
20 [a]Ex. 15:2; Ps. 66:16 [b]Matt. 9:8, 33; John 5:20; 7:21; Acts 3:12; 4:13 [1]Lit. *Ten Cities*
21 [a]Matt. 9:1; Luke 8:40
22 [a]Matt. 9:18–26; Luke 8:41–56; Acts 13:15
23 [a]Matt. 8:15; Mark 6:5; 7:32; 8:23, 25; 16:18; Luke 4:40; Acts 9:17; 28:8
25 [a]Lev. 15:19, 25; Matt. 9:20
27 [a]Matt. 14:35, 36; Mark 3:10; 6:56
29 [1]*suffering*
30 [a]Luke 6:19; 8:46
33 [a][Ps. 89:7]
34 [a]Matt. 9:22; Mark 10:52; Acts 14:9 [b]1 Sam. 1:17; 20:42; 2 Kin. 5:19; Luke 7:50; 8:48; Acts 16:36; [James 2:16]
35 [a]Luke 8:49
36 [a][Mark 9:23; John 11:40]

saw [1]a tumult and those who [a]wept
and wailed loudly.
39 When He came in, He said to
them, "Why make this commotion
and weep? The child is not dead,
but [a]sleeping."
40 And they ridiculed Him. [a]But
when He had put them all outside,
He took the father and the mother
of the child, and those *who were*
with Him, and entered where the
child was lying.
41 Then He took the child by the
hand, and said to her, "Talitha,
cumi," which is translated, "Little
girl, I say to you, arise."
42 Immediately the girl arose and
walked, for she was twelve years
of age. And they were [a]overcome
with great amazement.
43 But [a]He commanded them
strictly that no one should know
it, and said that *something* should
be given her to eat.

Jesus Rejected at Nazareth

6 Then [a]He went out from there
and came to His own country,
and His disciples followed Him.
2 And when the Sabbath had
come, He began to teach in the
synagogue. And many hearing
Him were [a]astonished, saying,
[b]"Where *did* this Man *get* these
things? And what wisdom *is* this
which is given to Him, that such
mighty works are performed by
His hands!
3 "Is this not the carpenter, the
Son of Mary, and [a]brother of
James, Joses, Judas, and Simon?
And are not His sisters here with
us?" So they [b]were offended at
Him.
4 But Jesus said to them, [a]"A
prophet is not without honor ex-
cept in his own country, among his
own relatives, and in his own
house."
5 [a]Now He could do no mighty
work there, except that He laid His
hands on a few sick people and
healed *them.*
6 And [a]He marveled because of
their unbelief. [b]Then He went
about the villages in a circuit,
teaching.

Sending Out the Twelve

7 [a]And He called the twelve to
Himself, and began to send them
out [b]two *by* two, and gave them
power over unclean spirits.
8 He commanded them to take
nothing for the journey except a
staff—no bag, no bread, no copper
in *their* money belts—
9 but [a]to wear sandals, and not
to put on two tunics.
10 [a]Also He said to them, "In
whatever place you enter a house,
stay there till you depart from that
place.
11 [a]"And [1]whoever will not re-
ceive you nor hear you, when you
depart from there, [b]shake off the
dust under your feet as a testimony
against them. [2]Assuredly, I say to
you, it will be more tolerable for
Sodom and Gomorrah in the day
of judgment than for that city!"
12 So they went out and preached
that *people* should repent.
13 And they cast out many de-
mons, [a]and anointed with oil many
who were sick, and healed *them.*

John the Baptist Beheaded

14 [a]Now King Herod heard *of*
Him, for His name had become
well known. And he said, "John
the Baptist is risen from the dead,
and therefore [b]these powers are at
work in him."
15 [a]Others said, "It is Elijah." And
others said, "It is [1]the Prophet, [b]or
like one of the prophets."
16 [a]But when Herod heard, he
said, "This is John, whom I be-
headed; he has been raised from
the dead!"
17 For Herod himself had sent and
laid hold of John, and bound him
in prison for the sake of Herodias,
his brother Philip's wife; for he
had married her.
18 Because John had said to
Herod, [a]"It is not lawful for you
to have your brother's wife."
19 Therefore Herodias [1]held it
against him and wanted to kill
him, but she could not;
20 for Herod [a]feared John, know-
ing that he *was* a just and holy
man, and he protected him. And
when he heard him, he [1]did many
things, and heard him gladly.
21 [a]Then an opportune day came
when Herod [b]on his birthday gave
a feast for his nobles, the high offi-
cers, and the chief *men* of Galilee.
22 And when Herodias' daughter

38 [a]Acts 9:39 [1]*an uproar*
39 [a]John 11:4, 11
40 [a]Acts 9:40
42 [a]Mark 1:27; 7:37
43 [a][Matt. 8:4; 12:16–19; 17:9]

CHAPTER 6

1 [a]Matt. 13:54
2 [a]Matt. 7:28 [b]John 6:42
3 [a]Matt. 12:46 [b][Matt. 11:6]
4 [a]John 4:44
5 [a]Gen. 19:22; 32:25
6 [a]Is. 59:16 [b]Matt. 9:35
7 [a]Mark 3:13, 14 [b][Eccl. 4:9, 10]
9 [a][Eph. 6:15]
10 [a]Matt. 10:11
11 [a]Matt. 10:14 [b]Acts 13:51; 18:6 [1]NU *whatever place* [2]NU omits the rest of v. 11.
13 [a][James 5:14]
14 [a]Luke 9:7–9 [b]Luke 19:37
15 [a]Mark 8:28 [b]Matt. 21:11 [1]NU, M *a prophet, like one*
16 [a]Luke 3:19
18 [a]Lev. 18:16; 20:21
19 [1]*held a grudge*
20 [a]Matt. 14:5; 21:26 [1]NU *was very perplexed, yet*
21 [a]Matt. 14:6 [b]Gen. 40:20

herself came in and danced, and
pleased Herod and those who sat
with him, the king said to the girl,
"Ask me whatever you want, and
I will give *it* to you."
23 He also swore to her, [a]"What-
ever you ask me, I will give you,
up to half my kingdom."
24 So she went out and said to her
mother, "What shall I ask?" And
she said, "The head of John the
Baptist!"
25 Immediately she came in with
haste to the king and asked, say-
ing, "I want you to give me at once
the head of John the Baptist on a
platter."
26 [a]And the king was exceedingly
sorry; *yet*, because of the oaths
and because of those who sat with
him, he did not want to refuse her.
27 Immediately the king sent an
executioner and commanded his
head to be brought. And he went
and beheaded him in prison,
28 brought his head on a platter,
and gave it to the girl; and the girl
gave it to her mother.
29 When his disciples heard *of it*,
they came and [a]took away his
corpse and laid it in a tomb.

Feeding the Five Thousand

30 [a]Then the apostles gathered to
Jesus and told Him all things, both
what they had done and what they
had taught.
31 [a]And He said to them, "Come
aside by yourselves to a deserted
place and rest a while." For [b]there
were many coming and going, and
they did not even have time to eat.
32 [a]So they departed to a deserted
place in the boat by themselves.
33 But [1]the multitudes saw them
departing, and many [a]knew Him
and ran there on foot from all the
cities. They arrived before them
and came together to Him.
34 [a]And Jesus, when He came out,
saw a great multitude and was
moved with compassion for them,
because they were like [b]sheep not
having a shepherd. So [c]He began
to teach them many things.
35 [a]When the day was now far
spent, His disciples came to Him
and said, "This is a deserted place,
and already the hour *is* late.
36 "Send them away, that they
may go into the surrounding coun-

23 [a]Esth. 5:3, 6; 7:2
26 [a]Matt. 14:9
29 [a]1 Kin. 13:29, 30; Matt. 27:58–61; Acts 8:2
30 [a]Luke 9:10
31 [a]Matt. 14:13 [b]Mark 3:20
32 [a]Matt. 14:13–21; Luke 9:10–17; John 6:5–13
33 [a][Col. 1:6] [1]NU, M *they*
34 [a]Matt. 9:36; 14:14; [Heb. 5:2] [b]Num. 27:17; 1 Kin. 22:17; 2 Chr. 18:16; Zech. 10:2 [c][Is. 48:17; 61:1–3]; Luke 9:11
35 [a]Matt. 14:15; Luke 9:12
36 [1]NU *something to eat* and omits the rest of v. 36.
37 [a]Num. 11:13, 22; 2 Kin. 4:43
38 [a]Matt. 14:17; Luke 9:13; John 6:9
39 [a]Matt. 15:35; Mark 8:6
41 [a]John 11:41, 42 [b]1 Sam. 9:13; Matt. 15:36; 26:26; Mark 8:7; Luke 24:30
44 [1]NU, M omit *about*
45 [a]Matt. 14:22–32; John 6:15–21 [1]*invited, strongly urged*
46 [a]Mark 1:35; Luke 5:16
48 [a]Luke 24:28
49 [a]Matt. 14:26; Luke 24:37
50 [a]Matt. 9:2; John 16:33 [b]Is. 41:10 [1]*Take courage*
51 [a]Ps. 107:29

try and villages and buy them-
selves [1]bread; for they have noth-
ing to eat."
37 But He answered and said to
them, "You give them something
to eat." And they said to Him,
[a]"Shall we go and buy two hun-
dred denarii worth of bread and
give them *something* to eat?"
38 But He said to them, "How
many loaves do you have? Go and
see." And when they found out
they said, [a]"Five, and two fish."
39 Then He [a]commanded them to
make them all sit down in groups
on the green grass.
40 So they sat down in ranks, in
hundreds and in fifties.
41 And when He had taken the
five loaves and the two fish, He
[a]looked up to heaven, [b]blessed and
broke the loaves, and gave *them*
to His disciples to set before them;
and the two fish He divided among
them all.
42 So they all ate and were filled.
43 And they took up twelve bas-
kets full of fragments and of the
fish.
44 Now those who had eaten the
loaves were [1]about five thousand
men.

Jesus Walks on the Sea

45 [a]Immediately He [1]made His
disciples get into the boat and go
before Him to the other side, to
Bethsaida, while He sent the multi-
tude away.
46 And when He had sent them
away, He [a]departed to the moun-
tain to pray.
47 Now when evening came, the
boat was in the middle of the sea;
and He *was* alone on the land.
48 Then He saw them straining at
rowing, for the wind was against
them. Now about the fourth watch
of the night He came to them,
walking on the sea, and [a]would
have passed them by.
49 And when they saw Him walk-
ing on the sea, they supposed it
was a [a]ghost, and cried out;
50 for they all saw Him and were
troubled. But immediately He
talked with them and said to them,
[a]"Be[1] of good cheer! It is I; do not
be [b]afraid."
51 Then He went up into the boat
to them, and the wind [a]ceased.

And they were greatly [b]amazed in
themselves beyond measure, and
marveled.
52 For [a]they had not understood
about the loaves, because their
[b]heart was hardened.

Many Touch Him and Are Made Well

53 [a]When they had crossed over,
they came to the land of Gennes-
aret and anchored there.
54 And when they came out of the
boat, immediately [1]the people rec-
ognized Him,
55 ran through that whole sur-
rounding region, and began to
carry about on beds those who
were sick to wherever they heard
He was.
56 Wherever He entered, into vil-
lages, cities, or the country, they
laid the sick in the marketplaces,
and begged Him that [a]they might
just touch the [b]hem of His gar-
ment. And as many as touched
Him were made well.

Defilement Comes from Within

7 Then [a]the Pharisees and some
of the scribes came together to
Him, having come from Jeru-
salem.
2 Now [1]when they saw some of
His disciples eat bread with de-
filed, that is, with [a]unwashed
hands, [2]they found fault.
3 For the Pharisees and all the
Jews do not eat unless they wash
their hands [1]in a special way, hold-
ing the [a]tradition of the elders.
4 *When they come* from the
marketplace, they do not eat un-
less they wash. And there are
many other things which they
have received and hold, *like* the
washing of cups, pitchers, copper
vessels, and couches.
5 [a]Then the Pharisees and
scribes asked Him, "Why do
Your disciples not walk according
to the tradition of the elders,
but eat bread with unwashed
hands?"
6 He answered and said to them,
"Well did Isaiah prophesy of you
[a]hypocrites, as it is written:

[b]'This people honors Me with their
lips,
But their heart is far from Me.

7 *And in vain they worship Me,*
Teaching as doctrines the
commandments of men.'

8 "For laying aside the com-
mandment of God, you hold the
tradition of men—[1]the washing of
pitchers and cups, and many other
such things you do."
9 He said to them, "*All too* well
[a]you [1]reject the commandment of
God, that you may keep your tradi-
tion.
10 "For Moses said, [a]*'Honor your*
father and your mother'; and, [b]*'He*
who curses father or mother, let
him be put to death.'
11 "But you say, 'If a man says to
his father or mother, [a]"Whatever
profit you might have received
from me *is* Corban"—' (that is, a
gift *to God*),
12 "then you no longer let him do
anything for his father or his
mother,
13 "making the word of God of no
effect through your tradition
which you have handed down.
And many such things you do."
14 [a]When He had called all the
multitude to *Himself*, He said to
them, "Hear Me, everyone, and
[b]understand:
15 "There is nothing that enters a
man from outside which can defile
him; but the things which come
out of him, those are the things
that [a]defile a man.
16 [a]"If[1] anyone has ears to hear,
let him hear!"
17 [a]When He had entered a house
away from the crowd, His disciples
asked Him concerning the parable.
18 So He said to them, [a]"Are you
thus without understanding also?
Do you not perceive that whatever
enters a man from outside cannot
defile him,
19 "because it does not enter his
heart but his stomach, and is elimi-
nated, [1]*thus* purifying all foods?"
20 And He said, [a]"What comes out
of a man, that defiles a man.
21 [a]"For from within, out of the
heart of men, [b]proceed evil
thoughts, [c]adulteries, [d]fornica-
tions, murders,
22 "thefts, [a]covetousness, wicked-
ness, [b]deceit, [c]lewdness, an evil
eye, [d]blasphemy, [e]pride, fool-
ishness.

---

51 [b]Mark 1:27; 2:12; 5:42; 7:37
52 [a]Mark 8:17, 18 [b]Mark 3:5; 16:14
53 [a]Matt. 14:34–36
54 [1]Lit. *they*
56 [a]Matt. 9:20 [b]Num. 15:38, 39

CHAPTER 7

1 [a]Matt. 15:1–20
2 [a]Matt. 15:20 [1]NU omits *when* [2]NU omits *they found fault*
3 [a]Gal. 1:14 [1]Lit. *with the fist*
5 [a]Matt. 15:2
6 [a]Matt. 23:13–29 [b]Is. 29:13
8 [1]NU omits the rest of v. 8.
9 [a]Prov. 1:25 [1]*set aside*
10 [a]Ex. 20:12; Deut. 5:16 [b]Ex. 21:17
11 [a]Matt. 15:5; 23:18
14 [a]Matt. 15:10 [b]Matt. 16:9, 11, 12
15 [a]Is. 59:3
16 [a]Matt. 11:15 [1]NU omits v. 16.
17 [a]Matt. 15:15
18 [a][Heb. 5:11–14]
19 [1]NU sets off the final phrase as Mark's comment that Jesus has declared all foods clean.
20 [a]Ps. 39:1
21 [a]Gen. 6:5; 8:21 [b][Gal. 5:19–21] [c]2 Pet. 2:14 [d]1 Thess. 4:3
22 [a]Luke 12:15 [b]Rom. 1:28, 29 [c]1 Pet. 4:3 [d]Rev. 2:9 [e]1 John 2:16

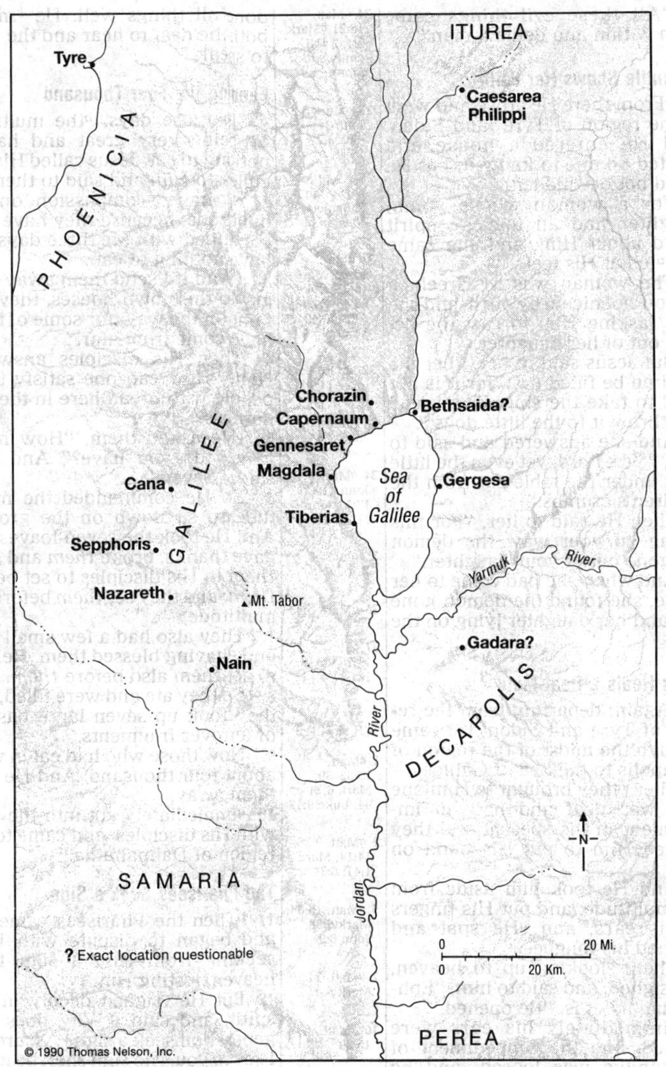

Cities of the Galilean Ministry. Jesus began His public ministry at Cana, where He graced a wedding party with His presence and turned water into wine (John 2:1–11). In the synagogue of Nazareth, Jesus announced that He was the fulfillment of Isaiah's prophecy (Luke 4:16–22). But His hometown rejected Him, so He established His base of ministry in Capernaum, a prosperous fishing town situated along an international trade route. The Sea of Galilee was the setting for many miracles.

23 "All these evil things come from within and defile a man."

A Gentile Shows Her Faith

24 [a]From there He arose and went to the region of Tyre [1]and Sidon. And He entered a house and wanted no one to know *it*, but He could not be [b]hidden.

25 For a woman whose young daughter had an unclean spirit heard about Him, and she came and [a]fell at His feet.

26 The woman was a [1]Greek, a [2]Syro-Phoenician by birth, and she kept [3]asking Him to cast the demon out of her daughter.

27 But Jesus said to her, "Let the children be filled first, for it is not good to take the children's bread and throw *it* to the little dogs."

28 And she answered and said to Him, "Yes, Lord, yet even the little dogs under the table eat from the children's crumbs."

29 Then He said to her, "For this saying go your way; the demon has gone out of your daughter."

30 And when she had come to her house, she found the demon gone out, and her daughter lying on the bed.

Jesus Heals a Deaf-Mute

31 [a]Again, departing from the region of Tyre and Sidon, He came through the midst of the region of Decapolis to the Sea of Galilee.

32 Then [a]they brought to Him one who was deaf and had an impediment in his speech, and they begged Him to put His hand on him.

33 And He took him aside from the multitude, and put His fingers in his ears, and [a]He spat and touched his tongue.

34 Then, [a]looking up to heaven, [b]He sighed, and said to him, "Ephphatha," that is, "Be opened."

35 [a]Immediately his ears were opened, and the [1]impediment of his tongue was loosed, and he spoke plainly.

36 Then [a]He commanded them that they should tell no one; but the more He commanded them, the more widely they proclaimed *it*.

37 And they were [a]astonished beyond measure, saying, "He has done all things well. He [b]makes both the deaf to hear and the mute to speak."

Feeding the Four Thousand

8 In those days, [a]the multitude being very great and having nothing to eat, Jesus called His disciples *to Him* and said to them,

2 "I have [a]compassion on the multitude, because they have now continued with Me three days and have nothing to eat.

3 "And if I send them away hungry to their own houses, they will faint on the way; for some of them have come from afar."

4 Then His disciples answered Him, "How can one satisfy these people with bread here in the wilderness?"

5 [a]He asked them, "How many loaves do you have?" And they said, "Seven."

6 So He commanded the multitude to sit down on the ground. And He took the seven loaves and gave thanks, broke *them* and gave *them* to His disciples to set before *them*; and they set *them* before the multitude.

7 They also had a few small fish; and [a]having blessed them, He said to set them also before *them*.

8 So they ate and were filled, and they took up seven large baskets of leftover fragments.

9 Now those who had eaten were about four thousand. And He sent them away,

10 [a]immediately got into the boat with His disciples, and came to the region of Dalmanutha.

The Pharisees Seek a Sign

11 [a]Then the Pharisees came out and began to dispute with Him, seeking from Him a sign from heaven, testing Him.

12 But He [a]sighed deeply in His spirit, and said, "Why does this generation seek a sign? Assuredly, I say to you, [b]no sign shall be given to this generation."

Beware of the Leaven of the Pharisees and Herod

13 And He left them, and getting into the boat again, departed to the other side.

24 [a]Matt. 15:21 [b]Mark 2:1, 2 [1]NU omits *and Sidon*

25 [a]Mark 5:22; John 11:32; Rev. 1:17

26 [1]*Gentile* [2]A Syrian of Phoenicia [3]*begging*

31 [a]Matt. 15:29; Mark 15:37; Luke 23:46; 24:46; Acts 10:40; 1 Cor. 15:4

32 [a]Matt. 9:32; Luke 11:14

33 [a]Mark 8:23; John 9:6

34 [a]Mark 6:41; John 11:41; 17:1 [b]John 11:33, 38

35 [a]Is. 35:5, 6 [1]Lit. *bond*

36 [a]Mark 5:43

37 [a]Mark 6:51; 10:26 [b]Matt. 12:22

CHAPTER 8

1 [a]Matt. 15:32–39; Mark 6:34–44; Luke 9:12

2 [a]Matt. 9:36; 14:14; Mark 1:41; 6:34

5 [a]Matt. 15:34; Mark 6:38; John 6:9

7 [a]Matt. 14:19; Mark 6:41

10 [a]Matt. 15:39

11 [a]Matt. 12:38; 16:1; Luke 11:16; John 2:18; 6:30; 1 Cor. 1:22

12 [a]Mark 7:34 [b]Matt. 12:39

14 [a]Now [1]the disciples had forgotten to take bread, and they did not have more than one loaf with them in the boat.
15 [a]Then He charged them, saying, "Take heed, beware of the [1]leaven of the Pharisees and the leaven of Herod."
16 And they reasoned among themselves, saying, "*It is* because we have no bread."
17 But Jesus, being aware of *it*, said to them, "Why do you reason because you have no bread? [a]Do you not yet perceive nor understand? Is your heart [1]still hardened?
18 "Having eyes, do you not see? And having ears, do you not hear? And do you not remember?
19 [a]"When I broke the five loaves for the five thousand, how many baskets full of fragments did you take up?" They said to Him, "Twelve."
20 "Also, [a]when I broke the seven for the four thousand, how many large baskets full of fragments did you take up?" And they said, "Seven."
21 So He said to them, "How *is it* [a]you do not understand?"

A Blind Man Healed at Bethsaida

22 Then He came to Bethsaida; and they brought a [a]blind man to Him, and begged Him to [b]touch him.
23 So He took the blind man by the hand and led him out of the town. And when [a]He had spit on his eyes and put His hands on him, He asked him if he saw anything.
24 And he looked up and said, "I see men like trees, walking."
25 Then He put *His* hands on his eyes again and made him look up. And he was restored and saw everyone clearly.
26 Then He sent him away to his house, saying, [1]"Neither go into the town, [a]nor tell anyone in the town."

Peter Confesses Jesus as the Christ

27 [a]Now Jesus and His disciples went out to the towns of Caesarea Philippi; and on the road He asked His disciples, saying to them, "Who do men say that I am?"
28 So they answered, [a]"John the Baptist; but some *say*, [b]Elijah; and others, one of the prophets."
29 He said to them, "But who do you say that I am?" Peter answered and said to Him, [a]"You are the Christ."
30 [a]Then He strictly warned them that they should tell no one about Him.

14 [a]Matt. 16:5 [1]NU, M *they*
15 [a]Matt. 16:6; Luke 12:1 [1]*yeast*
17 [a]Mark 6:52; 16:14 [1]NU omits *still*
19 [a]Matt. 14:20; Mark 6:43; Luke 9:17; John 6:13
20 [a]Matt. 15:37
21 [a][Mark 6:52]
22 [a]Matt. 9:27; John 9:1 [b]Luke 18:15
23 [a]Mark 7:33
26 [a]Matt. 8:4; Mark 5:43; 7:36 [1]NU *"Do not even go into the town."*
27 [a]Matt. 16:13–16; Luke 9:18–20
28 [a]Matt. 14:2 [b]Mark 6:14, 15; Luke 9:7, 8
29 [a]John 1:41; 4:42; 6:69; 11:27; Acts 2:36; 8:37; 9:20
30 [a]Matt. 8:4; 16:20; Luke 9:21
31 [a][Is. 53:3–11]; Matt. 16:21; 20:19; Luke 18:31–33; 1 Pet. 1:11 [b]Mark 10:33 [c]Mark 9:31; 10:34
33 [a]Mark 16:14; [Rev. 3:19] [1]*setting your mind on*
34 [a][Matt. 10:38]; Luke 14:27
35 [a]Matt. 10:39; Luke 17:33; John 12:25
38 [a]Matt. 10:33; Luke 9:26; 12:9 [b]Rom. 1:16; 2 Tim. 1:8, 9; 2:12

CHAPTER 9

1 [a]Matt. 16:28; Mark 13:26; Luke 9:27; Acts 7:55, 56; Rev. 20:4 [b][Matt. 24:30] [1]*having come*
2 [a]Matt. 17:1–8; Luke 9:28–36

Jesus Predicts His Death and Resurrection

31 And [a]He began to teach them that the Son of Man must suffer many things, and be [b]rejected by the elders and chief priests and scribes, and be [c]killed, and after three days rise again.
32 He spoke this word openly. Then Peter took Him aside and began to rebuke Him.
33 But when He had turned around and looked at His disciples, He [a]rebuked Peter, saying, "Get behind Me, Satan! For you are not [1]mindful of the things of God, but the things of men."

Take Up the Cross and Follow Him

34 When He had called the people to *Himself*, with His disciples also, He said to them, [a]"Whoever desires to come after Me, let him deny himself, and take up his cross, and follow Me.
35 "For [a]whoever desires to save his life will lose it, but whoever loses his life for My sake and the gospel's will save it.
36 "For what will it profit a man if he gains the whole world, and loses his own soul?
37 "Or what will a man give in exchange for his soul?
38 [a]"For whoever [b]is ashamed of Me and My words in this adulterous and sinful generation, of him the Son of Man also will be ashamed when He comes in the glory of His Father with the holy angels."

Jesus Transfigured on the Mount

9 And He said to them, [a]"Assuredly, I say to you that there are some standing here who will not taste death till they see [b]the kingdom of God [1]present with power."
2 [a]Now after six days Jesus took

Peter, James, and John, and led them up on a high mountain apart by themselves; and He was transfigured before them.

3 His clothes became shining, exceedingly [a]white, like snow, such as no launderer on earth can whiten them.

4 And Elijah appeared to them with Moses, and they were talking with Jesus.

5 Then Peter answered and said to Jesus, "Rabbi, it is good for us to be here; and let us make three tabernacles: one for You, one for Moses, and one for Elijah"—

6 because he did not know what to say, for they were greatly afraid.

7 And a [a]cloud came and overshadowed them; and a voice came out of the cloud, saying, "This is [b]My beloved Son. [c]Hear Him!"

8 Suddenly, when they had looked around, they saw no one anymore, but only Jesus with themselves.

9 [a]Now as they came down from the mountain, He commanded them that they should tell no one the things they had seen, till the Son of Man had risen from the dead.

10 So they kept this word to themselves, questioning [a]what the rising from the dead meant.

11 And they asked Him, saying, "Why do the scribes say [a]that Elijah must come first?"

12 Then He answered and told them, "Indeed, Elijah is coming first and restores all things. And [a]how is it written concerning the Son of Man, that He must suffer many things and [b]be treated with contempt?

13 "But I say to you that [a]Elijah has also come, and they did to him whatever they wished, as it is written of him."

A Boy Is Healed

14 [a]And when He came to the disciples, He saw a great multitude around them, and scribes disputing with them.

15 Immediately, when they saw Him, all the people were greatly amazed, and running to *Him*, greeted Him.

16 And He asked the scribes, "What are you discussing with them?"

17 Then [a]one of the crowd answered and said, "Teacher, I brought You my son, who has a mute spirit.

18 "And wherever it seizes him, it throws him down; he foams at the mouth, gnashes his teeth, and becomes rigid. So I spoke to Your disciples, that they should cast it out, but they could not."

19 He answered him and said, "O [a]faithless[1] generation, how long shall I be with you? How long shall I [2]bear with you? Bring him to Me."

20 Then they brought him to Him. And [a]when he saw Him, immediately the spirit convulsed him, and he fell on the ground and wallowed, foaming at the mouth.

21 So He asked his father, "How long has this been happening to him?" And he said, "From childhood.

22 "And often he has thrown him both into the fire and into the water to destroy him. But if You can do anything, have compassion on us and help us."

23 Jesus said to him, [a]"If[1] you can believe, all things *are* possible to him who believes."

24 Immediately the father of the child cried out and said with tears, "Lord, I believe; [a]help my unbelief!"

25 When Jesus saw that the people came running together, He [a]rebuked the unclean spirit, saying to it: "Deaf and dumb spirit, I command you, come out of him and enter him no more!"

26 Then *the spirit* cried out, convulsed him greatly, and came out of him. And he became as one dead, so that many said, "He is dead."

27 But Jesus took him by the hand and lifted him up, and he arose.

28 [a]And when He had come into the house, His disciples asked Him privately, "Why could we not cast it out?"

29 So He said to them, "This kind can come out by nothing but [a]prayer [1]and fasting."

---

3 [a]Dan. 7:9; Matt. 28:3
7 [a]Ex. 40:34; 1 Kin. 8:10; Acts 1:9; Rev. 1:7 [b]Ps. 2:7; [Is. 42:1]; Matt. 3:17; Mark 1:11; Luke 1:35; 3:22; 2 Pet. 1:17 [c]Acts 3:22
9 [a]Matt. 17:9–13; Mark 16:6; Luke 24:6, 7, 46
10 [a]John 2:19–22
11 [a]Mal. 4:5; Matt. 17:10
12 [a]Ps. 22:6; Is. 53:3; Dan. 9:26 [b]Luke 23:11; Phil. 2:7
13 [a]Mal. 4:5; Matt. 11:14; 17:12; Luke 1:17
14 [a]Matt. 17:14–19; Luke 9:37–42
17 [a]Matt. 17:14; Luke 9:38
19 [a]John 4:48 [1]*unbelieving* [2]*put up with*
20 [a]Mark 1:26; Luke 9:42
23 [a]Matt. 17:20; Mark 11:23; Luke 17:6; John 11:40 [1]NU *"'If You can!' All things*
24 [a]Luke 17:5
25 [a]Mark 1:25
28 [a]Matt. 17:19
29 [a][James 5:16] [1]NU omits *and fasting*

Jesus Again Predicts His Death and Resurrection

30 Then they departed from there and passed through Galilee, and He did not want anyone to know *it*.
31 [a]For He taught His disciples and said to them, "The Son of Man is being betrayed into the hands of men, and they will [b]kill Him. And after He is killed, He will [c]rise the third day."
32 But they [a]did not understand this saying, and were afraid to ask Him.

Who Is the Greatest?

33 [a]Then He came to Capernaum. And when He was in the house He asked them, "What was it you [1]disputed among yourselves on the road?"
34 But they kept silent, for on the road they had [a]disputed among themselves who *would be the* [b]greatest.
35 And He sat down, called the twelve, and said to them, [a]"If anyone desires to be first, he shall be last of all and servant of all."
36 Then [a]He took a little child and set him in the midst of them. And when He had taken him in His arms, He said to them,
37 "Whoever receives one of these little children in My name receives Me; and [a]whoever receives Me, receives not Me but Him who sent Me."

Jesus Forbids Sectarianism

38 [a]Now John answered Him, saying, "Teacher, we saw someone who does not follow us casting out demons in Your name, and we forbade him because he does not follow us."
39 But Jesus said, "Do not forbid him, [a]for no one who works a miracle in My name can soon afterward speak evil of Me.
40 "For [a]he who is not against [1]us is on [2]our side.
41 [a]"For whoever gives you a cup of water to drink in My name, because you belong to Christ, assuredly, I say to you, he will by no means lose his reward.

Jesus Warns of Offenses

42 [a]"But whoever causes one of these little ones who believe in Me [1]to stumble, it would be better for him if a millstone were hung around his neck, and he were thrown into the sea.
43 [a]"If your hand causes you to sin, cut it off. It is better for you to enter into life [1]maimed, rather than having two hands, to go to [2]hell, into the fire that shall never be quenched—
44 [1]"where

> [a]*'Their worm does not die,*
> *And the fire is not quenched.'*

45 "And if your foot causes you to sin, cut it off. It is better for you to enter life lame, rather than having two feet, to be cast into [1]hell, [2]into the fire that shall never be quenched—
46 "where

> [a]*'Their worm does not die,*
> *And the fire is not quenched.'*

47 "And if your eye causes you to sin, pluck it out. It is better for you to enter the kingdom of God with one eye, rather than having two eyes, to be cast into [1]hell fire—
48 "where

> [a]*'Their worm does not die,*
> *And the [b]fire is not quenched.'*

Tasteless Salt Is Worthless

49 "For everyone will be [a]seasoned with fire, [b]and[1] every sacrifice will be seasoned with salt.
50 [a]"Salt *is* good, but if the salt loses its flavor, how will you season it? [b]Have salt in yourselves, and [c]have peace with one another."

Marriage and Divorce

10 Then [a]He arose from there and came to the region of Judea by the other side of the Jordan. And multitudes gathered to Him again, and as He was accustomed, He taught them again.
2 [a]The Pharisees came and asked Him, "Is it lawful for a man to divorce *his* wife?" testing Him.

---

31 [a]Luke 9:44 [b]Matt. 16:21; 27:50 [c]1 Cor. 15:4
32 [a]Luke 2:50; 18:34
33 [a]Matt. 18:1–5 [1]*discussed*
34 [a][Prov. 13:10] [b]Luke 22:24; 23:46; 24:46
35 [a]Luke 22:26, 27
36 [a]Mark 10:13–16
37 [a]Matt. 10:40
38 [a]Num. 11:27–29
39 [a]1 Cor. 12:3
40 [a][Matt. 12:30] [1]M *you* [2]M *your*
41 [a]Matt. 10:42
42 [a]Luke 17:1, 2 [1]To fall into sin
43 [a]Matt. 5:29, 30; 18:8, 9 [1]*crippled* [2]Gr. *Gehenna*
44 [a]Is. 66:24 [1]NU omits v. 44.
45 [1]Gr. *Gehenna* [2]NU omits the rest of v. 45 and all of v. 46.
46 [a]Is. 66:24
47 [1]Gr. *Gehenna*
48 [a]Is. 66:24 [b]Jer. 7:20
49 [a][Matt. 3:11] [b]Lev. 2:13 [1]NU omits the rest of v. 49.
50 [a]Matt. 5:13 [b]Col. 4:6 [c]Rom. 12:18; 14:19

CHAPTER 10

1 [a]Matt. 19:1–9
2 [a]Matt. 19:3

3 And He answered and said to
them, "What did Moses command
you?"
4 They said, [a]"Moses permitted
a man to write a certificate of di-
vorce, and to dismiss *her.*"
5 And Jesus answered and said
to them, "Because of the hardness
of your heart he wrote you this
[1]precept.
6 "But from the beginning of the
creation, God [a]*'made them male
and female.'*
7 [a]*'For this reason a man shall
leave his father and mother and be
joined to his wife,*
8 *'and the two shall become one
flesh'*; so then they are no longer
two, but one flesh.
9 "Therefore what God has
joined together, let not man sepa-
rate."
10 In the house His disciples also
asked Him again about the same
matter.
11 So He said to them, [a]"Whoever
divorces his wife and marries an-
other commits adultery against
her.
12 "And if a woman divorces her
husband and marries another, she
commits adultery."

Jesus Blesses Little Children

13 [a]Then they brought little chil-
dren to Him, that He might touch
them; but the disciples rebuked
those who brought *them.*
14 But when Jesus saw *it*, He was
greatly displeased and said to
them, "Let the little children come
to Me, and do not forbid them; for
[a]of such is the kingdom of God.
15 "Assuredly, I say to you, [a]who-
ever does not receive the kingdom
of God as a little child will [b]by no
means enter it."
16 And He took them up in His
arms, laid *His* hands on them, and
blessed them.

Jesus Counsels the Rich Young Ruler

17 [a]Now as He was going out on
the road, one came running, knelt
before Him, and asked Him,
"Good Teacher, what shall I [b]do
that I may inherit eternal life?"
18 So Jesus said to him, "Why do
you call Me good? No one *is* good
but One, *that is,* [a]God.
19 "You know the command-
ments: [a]*'Do not commit adultery,'
'Do not murder,' 'Do not steal,' 'Do
not bear false witness,'* 'Do not de-
fraud,' *'Honor your father and
your mother.'* "
20 And he answered and said
to Him, "Teacher, all these things
I have [a]kept from my youth."
21 Then Jesus, looking at him,
loved him, and said to him, "One
thing you lack: Go your way, [a]sell
whatever you have and give to the
poor, and you will have [b]treasure
in heaven; and come, [c]take up the
cross, and follow Me."
22 But he was sad at this word,
and went away sorrowful, for he
had great possessions.

With God All Things Are Possible

23 [a]Then Jesus looked around and
said to His disciples, "How hard
it is for those who have riches to
enter the kingdom of God!"
24 And the disciples were aston-
ished at His words. But Jesus an-
swered again and said to them,
"Children, how hard it is [1]for those
[a]who trust in riches to enter the
kingdom of God!
25 "It is easier for a camel to go
through the eye of a needle than
for a [a]rich man to enter the king-
dom of God."
26 And they were greatly aston-
ished, saying among themselves,
"Who then can be saved?"
27 But Jesus looked at them and
said, "With men *it is* impossible,
but not [a]with God; for with God
all things are possible."
28 [a]Then Peter began to say to
Him, "See, we have left all and fol-
lowed You."
29 So Jesus answered and said,
"Assuredly, I say to you, there
is no one who has left house
or brothers or sisters or father or
mother [1]or wife or children or
[2]lands, for My sake and the gos-
pel's,
30 [a]"who shall not receive a hun-
dredfold now in this time—houses
and brothers and sisters and moth-
ers and children and lands, with
[b]persecutions—and in the age to
come, eternal life.
31 [a]"But many *who are* first will
be last, and the last first."

4 [a]Deut. 24:1–4; Matt. 5:31; 19:7
5 [1]*command*
6 [a]Gen. 1:27; 5:2
7 [a]Gen. 2:24; [1 Cor. 6:16]; Eph. 5:31
11 [a]Ex. 20:14; [Matt. 5:32; 19:9]; Luke 16:18; [Rom. 7:3]; 1 Cor. 7:10, 11
13 [a]Matt. 19:13–15; Luke 18:15–17
14 [a][1 Cor. 14:20; 1 Pet. 2:2]
15 [a]Matt. 18:3, 4; 19:14; Luke 18:17 [b]Luke 13:28
17 [a]Matt. 19:16–30; Luke 18:18–30 [b]John 6:28; Acts 2:37
18 [a]1 Sam. 2:2
19 [a]Ex. 20:12–16; Deut. 5:16–20; [Rom. 13:9; James 2:10, 11]
20 [a]Phil. 3:6
21 [a][Luke 12:33; 16:9] [b]Matt. 6:19, 20; 19:21 [c][Mark 8:34]
23 [a]Matt. 19:23; [Mark 4:19]; Luke 18:24
24 [a]Job 31:24; Ps. 52:7; 62:10; [Prov. 11:28; 1 Tim. 6:17] [1]NU omits *for those who trust in riches*
25 [a][Matt. 13:22; 19:24]
27 [a]Job 42:2; Jer. 32:17; Matt. 19:26; Luke 1:37
28 [a]Matt. 19:27; Luke 18:28
29 [1]NU omits *or wife* [2]Lit. *fields*
30 [a]2 Chr. 25:9; Luke 18:29, 30 [b]1 Thess. 3:3; 2 Tim. 3:12; [1 Pet. 4:12, 13]
31 [a]Matt. 19:30; 20:16; Luke 13:30

Jesus a Third Time Predicts His Death and Resurrection

32 [a]Now they were on the road,
going up to Jerusalem, and Jesus
was going before them; and they
were amazed. And as they fol-
lowed they were afraid. [b]Then He
took the twelve aside again and
began to tell them the things that
would happen to Him:
33 "Behold, we are going up to Je-
rusalem, and the Son of Man will
be betrayed to the chief priests and
to the scribes; and they will con-
demn Him to death and deliver
Him to the Gentiles;
34 "and they will mock Him, and
[1]scourge Him, and spit on Him,
and kill Him. And the third day He
will rise again."

Greatness Is Serving

35 [a]Then James and John, the
sons of Zebedee, came to Him,
saying, "Teacher, we want You to
do for us whatever we ask."
36 And He said to them, "What do
you want Me to do for you?"
37 They said to Him, "Grant us
that we may sit, one on Your right
hand and the other on Your left,
in Your glory."
38 But Jesus said to them, "You
do not know what you ask. Are
you able to drink the [a]cup that I
drink, and be baptized with the
[b]baptism that I am baptized with?"
39 They said to Him, "We are
able." So Jesus said to them,
[a]"You will indeed drink the cup
that I drink, and with the baptism
I am baptized with you will be bap-
tized;
40 "but to sit on My right hand
and on My left is not Mine to give,
but *it is for those* [a]for whom it is
prepared."
41 [a]And when the ten heard *it*,
they began to be greatly dis-
pleased with James and John.
42 But Jesus called them to *Him-
self* and said to them, [a]"You know
that those who are considered rul-
ers over the Gentiles lord it over
them, and their great ones exercise
authority over them.
43 [a]"Yet it shall not be so among
you; but whoever desires to be-
come great among you shall be
your servant.
44 "And whoever of you desires
to be first shall be slave of all.
45 "For even [a]the Son of Man did
not come to be served, but to serve,
and [b]to give His life a ransom for
many."

Jesus Heals Blind Bartimaeus

46 [a]Now they came to Jericho. As
He went out of Jericho with His
disciples and a great multitude,
blind Bartimaeus, the son of Ti-
maeus, sat by the road begging.
47 And when he heard that it was
Jesus of Nazareth, he began to cry
out and say, "Jesus, [a]Son of David,
[b]have mercy on me!"
48 Then many warned him to be
quiet; but he cried out all the more,
"Son of David, have mercy on
me!"
49 So Jesus stood still and com-
manded him to be called. Then
they called the blind man, saying
to him, "Be of good cheer. Rise,
He is calling you."
50 And throwing aside his gar-
ment, he rose and came to Jesus.
51 So Jesus answered and said to
him, "What do you want Me to do
for you?" The blind man said to
Him, [1]"Rabboni, that I may receive
my sight."
52 Then Jesus said to him, "Go
your way; [a]your faith has [1]made
you well." And immediately he re-
ceived his sight and followed Jesus
on the road.

The Triumphal Entry

11 Now [a]when they drew near
Jerusalem, to [1]Bethphage
and Bethany, at the Mount of Ol-
ives, He sent two of His disciples;
2 and He said to them, "Go into
the village opposite you; and as
soon as you have entered it you
will find a colt tied, on which no
one has sat. Loose it and bring *it*.
3 "And if anyone says to you,
'Why are you doing this?' say, 'The
Lord has need of it,' and immedi-
ately he will send it here."
4 So they went their way, and
found [1]the colt tied by the door
outside on the street, and they
loosed it.
5 But some of those who stood
there said to them, "What are you
doing, loosing the colt?"
6 And they spoke to them just as

32 [a]Matt. 20:17–19; Luke 18:31–33 [b]Mark 8:31; 9:31; Luke 9:22; 18:31
34 [1]*flog Him* with a Roman scourge
35 [a][James 4:3]
38 [a]Matt. 26:39, 42; Mark 14:36; Luke 22:42; John 18:11 [b]Luke 12:50
39 [a]Matt. 10:17, 18, 21, 22; 24:9; John 16:33; Acts 12:2; Rev. 1:9
40 [a][Matt. 25:34; John 17:2, 6, 24; Rom. 8:30; Heb. 11:16]
41 [a]Matt. 20:24
42 [a]Luke 22:25
43 [a]Matt. 20:26, 28; Mark 9:35; Luke 9:48
45 [a]Luke 22:27; John 13:14; [Phil. 2:7, 8] [b]Matt. 20:28; [2 Cor. 5:21; 1 Tim. 2:5, 6; Titus 2:14]
46 [a]Matt. 20:29–34; Luke 18:35–43
47 [a]Jer. 23:5; Matt. 22:42; Rom. 1:3, 4; Rev. 22:16 [b]Matt. 15:22; Luke 17:13
51 [1]Lit. *My Great One*
52 [a]Matt. 9:22; Mark 5:34 [1]Lit. *saved you*

CHAPTER 11

1 [a]Matt. 21:1–9; Luke 19:29; John 2:13 [1]M *Bethsphage*
4 [1]NU, M *a*

Jesus had commanded. So they let
them go.
7 Then they brought the colt to
Jesus and threw their clothes on
it, and He sat on it.
8 [a]And many spread their clothes
on the road, and others cut down
leafy branches from the trees and
spread *them* on the road.
9 Then those who went before
and those who followed cried out,
saying:

"Hosanna!
[a]'*Blessed is He who comes in the*
name of the LORD!'
10 Blessed *is* the kingdom of our
father David
That comes [1]in the name of the
Lord!
[a]Hosanna in the highest!"

11 [a]And Jesus went into Jerusa-
lem and into the temple. So when
He had looked around at all things,
as the hour was already late, He
went out to Bethany with the
twelve.

The Fig Tree Withered

12 [a]Now the next day, when they
had come out from Bethany, He
was hungry.
13 [a]And seeing from afar a fig tree
having leaves, He went to see if
perhaps He would find something
on it. When He came to it, He
found nothing but leaves, for it
was not the season for figs.
14 In response Jesus said to it,
"Let no one eat fruit from you ever
again." And His disciples heard *it*.

Jesus Cleanses the Temple

15 [a]So they came to Jerusalem.
Then Jesus went into the temple
and began to drive out those who
bought and sold in the temple, and
overturned the tables of the money
changers and the seats of those
who sold [b]doves.
16 And He would not allow any-
one to carry wares through the
temple.
17 Then He taught, saying to
them, "Is it not written, [a]'*My house*
shall be called a house of prayer
for all nations'? But you have
made it a [b]'*den of thieves*.'"
18 And [a]the scribes and chief
priests heard it and sought how

8 [a]Matt. 21:8
9 [a]Ps. 118:25, 26; Matt. 21:9
10 [a]Ps. 148:1 [1]NU omits *in the name of the Lord*
11 [a]Matt. 21:12
12 [a]Matt. 21:18–22
13 [a]Matt. 21:19
15 [a]Mal. 3:1; Matt. 21:12–16; Luke 19:45–47; John 2:13–16 [b]Lev. 14:22
17 [a]Is. 56:7 [b]Jer. 7:11
18 [a]Ps. 2:2; Matt. 21:45, 46; Luke 19:47 [b]Matt. 7:28; Mark 1:22; 6:2; Luke 4:32
20 [a]Matt. 21:19–22
23 [a]Matt. 17:20; 21:21; Luke 17:6
24 [a]Matt. 7:7; Luke 11:9; [John 14:13; 15:7; 16:24; James 1:5, 6]
25 [a]Matt. 6:14; 18:23–35; Eph. 4:32; [Col. 3:13]
26 [a]Matt. 6:15; 18:35 [1]NU omits v. 26.
27 [a]Matt. 21:23–27; Luke 20:1–8
28 [a]John 5:27
30 [a][Mark 1:4, 5, 8]; Luke 7:29, 30

they might destroy Him; for they
feared Him, because [b]all the peo-
ple were astonished at His teach-
ing.
19 When evening had come, He
went out of the city.

The Lesson of the Withered Fig Tree

20 [a]Now in the morning, as they
passed by, they saw the fig tree
dried up from the roots.
21 And Peter, remembering, said
to Him, "Rabbi, look! The fig tree
which You cursed has withered
away."
22 So Jesus answered and said to
them, "Have faith in God.
23 "For [a]assuredly, I say to you,
whoever says to this mountain, 'Be
removed and be cast into the sea,'
and does not doubt in his heart,
but believes that those things he
says will be done, he will have
whatever he says.
24 "Therefore I say to you, [a]what-
ever things you ask when you
pray, believe that you receive
them, and you will have *them*.

Forgiveness and Prayer

25 "And whenever you stand
praying, [a]if you have anything
against anyone, forgive him, that
your Father in heaven may also
forgive you your trespasses.
26 [1]"But [a]if you do not forgive,
neither will your Father in heaven
forgive your trespasses."

Jesus' Authority Questioned

27 Then they came again to Jeru-
salem. [a]And as He was walking in
the temple, the chief priests, the
scribes, and the elders came to
Him.
28 And they said to Him, "By what
[a]authority are You doing these
things? And who gave You this au-
thority to do these things?"
29 But Jesus answered and said to
them, "I also will ask you one
question; then answer Me, and I
will tell you by what authority I
do these things:
30 "The [a]baptism of John—was it
from heaven or from men? Answer
Me."
31 And they reasoned among
themselves, saying, "If we say,
'From heaven,' He will say, 'Why
then did you not believe him?'

32 "But if we say, 'From men' "—
they feared the people, for [a]all
counted John to have been a
prophet indeed.
33 So they answered and said to
Jesus, "We do not know." And
Jesus answered and said to them,
"Neither will I tell you by what au-
thority I do these things."

The Parable of the Wicked Vinedressers

12 Then [a]He began to speak to
them in parables: "A man
planted a vineyard and set a hedge
around *it*, dug *a place for* the wine
vat and built a tower. And he
leased it to [1]vinedressers and went
into a far country.
2 "Now at vintage-time he sent
a servant to the vinedressers, that
he might receive some of the fruit
of the vineyard from the vine-
dressers.
3 "And they took *him* and beat
him and sent *him* away empty-
handed.
4 "Again he sent them another
servant, [1]and at him they threw
stones, wounded *him* in the head,
and sent *him* away shamefully
treated.
5 "And again he sent another,
and him they killed; and many oth-
ers, [a]beating some and killing
some.
6 "Therefore still having one son,
his beloved, he also sent him to
them last, saying, 'They will re-
spect my son.'
7 "But those [1]vinedressers said
among themselves, 'This is the
heir. Come, let us kill him, and the
inheritance will be ours.'
8 "So they took him and [a]killed
him and cast *him* out of the vine-
yard.
9 "Therefore what will the owner
of the vineyard do? He will come
and destroy the vinedressers, and
give the vineyard to others.
10 "Have you not even read this
Scripture:

[a]*'The stone which the builders*
rejected
Has become the chief
cornerstone.
11 *This was the* LORD*'s doing,*
And it is marvelous in our
eyes'?"

32 [a]Matt. 3:5; 14:5; Mark 6:20

CHAPTER 12

1 [a]Matt. 21:33–46; Luke 20:9–19 [1]*tenant farmers*

4 [1]NU omits *and at him they threw stones*

5 [a]2 Chr. 36:16

7 [1]*tenant farmers*

8 [a][Acts 2:23]

10 [a]Ps. 118:22, 23

12 [a]Matt. 21:45, 46; Mark 11:18; John 7:25, 30, 44

13 [a]Matt. 22:15–22; Luke 20:20–26

14 [a]Acts 18:26 [1]Court no man's favor [2]Lit. *look at the face of men*

15 [a]Matt. 23:28; Luke 12:1

17 [a][Eccl. 5:4, 5] [1]*Pay*

18 [a]Matt. 22:23–33; Luke 20:27–38 [b]Acts 23:8

19 [a]Deut. 25:5

12 [a]And they sought to lay hands
on Him, but feared the multitude,
for they knew He had spoken the
parable against them. So they left
Him and went away.

The Pharisees: Is It Lawful to Pay Taxes to Caesar?

13 [a]Then they sent to Him some
of the Pharisees and the Herodi-
ans, to catch Him in *His* words.
14 When they had come, they said
to Him, "Teacher, we know that
You are true, and [1]care about no
one; for You do not [2]regard the
person of men, but teach the [a]way
of God in truth. Is it lawful to pay
taxes to Caesar, or not?
15 "Shall we pay, or shall we not
pay?" But He, knowing their [a]hy-
pocrisy, said to them, "Why do you
test Me? Bring Me a denarius that
I may see *it*."
16 So they brought *it*. And He said
to them, "Whose image and in-
scription *is* this?" They said to
Him, "Caesar's."
17 And Jesus answered and said
to them, [1]"Render to Caesar the
things that are Caesar's, and to
[a]God the things that are God's."
And they marveled at Him.

The Sadducees: What About the Resurrection?

18 [a]Then *some* Sadducees, [b]who
say there is no resurrection, came
to Him; and they asked Him, say-
ing:
19 "Teacher, [a]Moses wrote to us
that if a man's brother dies, and
leaves *his* wife behind, and leaves
no children, his brother should
take his wife and raise up off-
spring for his brother.
20 "Now there were seven broth-
ers. The first took a wife; and dy-
ing, he left no offspring.
21 "And the second took her, and
he died; nor did he leave any off-
spring. And the third likewise.
22 "So the seven had her and left
no offspring. Last of all the woman
died also.
23 "Therefore, in the resurrection,
when they rise, whose wife will
she be? For all seven had her as
wife."
24 Jesus answered and said to
them, "Are you not therefore

[1]mistaken, because you do not
know the Scriptures nor the power
of God?
25 "For when they rise from the
dead, they neither marry nor are
given in marriage, but [a]are like an-
gels in heaven.
26 "But concerning the dead, that
they [a]rise, have you not read in the
book of Moses, in the *burning* bush
passage, how God spoke to him,
saying, [b]*'I am the God of Abra-*
ham, the God of Isaac, and the God
of Jacob'?
27 "He is not the God of the dead,
but the God of the living. You are
therefore greatly [1]mistaken."

The Scribes: Which Is the First Commandment of All?

28 [a]Then one of the scribes came,
and having heard them reasoning
together, [1]perceiving that He had
answered them well, asked Him,
"Which is the [2]first commandment
of all?"
29 Jesus answered him, "The
[1]first of all the commandments *is:*
[a]*'Hear, O Israel, the* LORD *our God,*
the LORD *is one.*
30 *'And you shall* [a]*love the* LORD
your God with all your heart, with
all your soul, with all your mind,
and with all your strength.' [1]This
is the first commandment.
31 "And the second, like *it, is* this:
[a]*'You shall love your neighbor as*
yourself.' There is no other com-
mandment greater than [b]these."
32 So the scribe said to Him,
"Well *said,* Teacher. You have
spoken the truth, for there is one
God, [a]and there is no other but He.
33 "And to love Him with all the
heart, with all the understanding,
[1]with all the soul, and with all the
strength, and to love one's neigh-
bor as oneself, [a]is more than all
the whole burnt offerings and sac-
rifices."
34 Now when Jesus saw that he
answered wisely, He said to him,
"You are not far from the kingdom
of God." [a]But after that no one
dared question Him.

Jesus: How Can David Call His Descendant Lord?

35 [a]Then Jesus answered and
said, while He taught in the tem-
ple, "How *is it* that the scribes say
that the Christ is the Son of David?
36 "For David himself said [a]by the
Holy Spirit:

[b]*'The* LORD *said to my Lord,*
"Sit at My right hand,
Till I make Your enemies Your
footstool."'

37 "Therefore David himself calls
Him *'Lord'*; how is He *then* his
[a]Son?" And the common people
heard Him gladly.

Beware of the Scribes

38 Then [a]He said to them in His
teaching, [b]"Beware of the scribes,
who desire to go around in long
robes, [c]*love* greetings in the
marketplaces,
39 "the [a]best seats in the syna-
gogues, and the best places at
feasts,
40 [a]"who devour widows' houses,
and [1]for a pretense make long
prayers. These will receive greater
condemnation."

The Widow's Two Mites

41 [a]Now Jesus sat opposite the
treasury and saw how the people
put money [b]into the treasury. And
many *who were* rich put in much.
42 Then one poor widow came
and threw in two [1]mites, which
make a [2]quadrans.
43 So He called His disciples to
Himself and said to them, "As-
suredly, I say to you that [a]this poor
widow has put in more than all
those who have given to the trea-
sury;
44 "for they all put in out of their
abundance, but she out of her pov-
erty put in all that she had, [a]her
whole livelihood."

Jesus Predicts the Destruction of the Temple

13 Then [a]as He went out of the
temple, one of His disciples
said to Him, "Teacher, see what
manner of stones and what build-
ings *are here!*"
2 And Jesus answered and said
to him, "Do you see these great
buildings? [a]Not *one* stone shall be
left upon another, that shall not be
thrown down."

24 [1]Or *deceived*
25 [a][1 Cor. 15:42, 49, 52]
26 [a][Rev. 20:12, 13] [b]Ex. 3:6, 15
27 [1]Or *deceived*
28 [a]Matt. 22:34–40 [1]NU *seeing* [2]*foremost*
29 [a]Deut. 6:4, 5 [1]*foremost*
30 [a][Deut. 10:12; 30:6] [1]NU omits the rest of v. 30.
31 [a]Lev. 19:18 [b][Rom. 13:9]
32 [a]Deut. 4:39
33 [a][Hos. 6:6] [1]NU omits *with all the soul*
34 [a]Matt. 22:46
35 [a]Luke 20:41–44
36 [a]2 Sam. 23:2 [b]Ps. 110:1
37 [a][Acts 2:29–31]
38 [a]Mark 4:2 [b]Matt. 23:1–7 [c]Matt. 23:7
39 [a]Luke 14:7
40 [a]Matt. 23:14 [1]*for appearance' sake*
41 [a]Luke 21:1–4 [b]2 Kin. 12:9
42 [1]Gr. *lepta,* very small copper coins [2]A Roman coin
43 [a][2 Cor. 8:12]
44 [a]Deut. 24:6

CHAPTER 13

1 [a]Luke 21:5–36
2 [a]Luke 19:44

The Signs of the Times and the End of the Age

3 Now as He sat on the Mount
of Olives opposite the temple, [a]Pe-
ter, [b]James, [c]John, and [d]Andrew
asked Him privately,
4 [a]"Tell us, when will these
things be? And what *will be* the
sign when all these things will be
fulfilled?"
5 And Jesus, answering them,
began to say: [a]"Take heed that no
one deceives you.
6 "For many will come in My
name, saying, 'I am *He*,' and will
deceive many.
7 "But when you hear of wars
and rumors of wars, do not be
troubled; for *such things* must
happen, but the end *is* not yet.
8 "For nation will rise against na-
tion, and [a]kingdom against king-
dom. And there will be earth-
quakes in various places, and
there will be famines [1]and trou-
bles. [b]These *are* the beginnings of
[2]sorrows.
9 "But [a]watch out for yourselves,
for they will deliver you up to
councils, and you will be beaten
in the synagogues. You will [1]be
brought before rulers and kings
for My sake, for a testimony to
them.
10 "And [a]the gospel must first be
preached to all the nations.
11 [a]"But when they arrest *you* and
deliver you up, do not worry be-
forehand, [1]or premeditate what
you will speak. But whatever is
given you in that hour, speak that;
for it is not you who speak, [b]but
the Holy Spirit.
12 "Now [a]brother will betray
brother to death, and a father *his*
child; and children will rise up
against parents and cause them to
be put to death.
13 [a]"And you will be hated by all
for My name's sake. But [b]he who
[1]endures to the end shall be saved.

The Great Tribulation

14 [a]"So when you see the [b]*'abom-
ination of desolation,'* [1]spoken of
by Daniel the prophet, standing
where it ought not" (let the reader
understand), "then [c]let those who
are in Judea flee to the mountains.
15 "Let him who is on the house-
top not go down into the house,
nor enter to take anything out of
his house.
16 "And let him who is in the field
not go back to get his clothes.
17 [a]"But woe to those who are preg-
nant and to those who are nurs-
ing babies in those days!
18 "And pray that your flight may
not be in winter.
19 [a]"For *in* those days there will
be tribulation, such as has not
been since the beginning of the
creation which God created until
this time, nor ever shall be.
20 "And unless the Lord had
shortened those days, no flesh
would be saved; but for the elect's
sake, whom He chose, He short-
ened the days.
21 [a]"Then if anyone says to you,
'Look, here *is* the Christ!' or,
'Look, *He is* there!' do not believe
it.
22 "For false christs and false
prophets will rise and show signs
and [a]wonders to deceive, if possi-
ble, even the [1]elect.
23 "But [a]take heed; see, I have
told you all things beforehand.

The Coming of the Son of Man

24 [a]"But in those days, after that
tribulation, the sun will be dark-
ened, and the moon will not give
its light;
25 "the stars of heaven will fall,
and the powers in the heavens will
be [a]shaken.
26 [a]"Then they will see the Son of
Man coming in the clouds with
great power and glory.
27 "And then He will send His an-
gels, and gather together His [1]elect
from the four winds, from the far-
thest part of earth to the farthest
part of heaven.

The Parable of the Fig Tree

28 [a]"Now learn this parable from
the fig tree: When its branch has
already become tender, and puts
forth leaves, you know that sum-
mer is near.
29 "So you also, when you see
these things happening, know that
[1]it is near—at the doors!
30 "Assuredly, I say to you, this
generation will by no means pass
away till all these things take
place.

3 [a]Matt. 16:18 [b]Mark 1:19 [c]Mark 1:19 [d]John 1:40
4 [a]Matt. 24:3
5 [a]Eph. 5:6
8 [a]Hag. 2:22 [b]Matt. 24:8 [1]NU omits *and troubles* [2]Lit. *birth pangs*
9 [a]Matt. 10:17, 18; 24:9 [1]NU, M *stand*
10 [a]Matt. 24:14
11 [a]Luke 12:11; 21:12–17 [b]Acts 2:4; 4:8, 31 [1]NU omits *or premeditate*
12 [a]Mic. 7:6
13 [a]Luke 21:17 [b]Matt. 10:22; 24:13 [1]*bears patiently*
14 [a]Matt. 24:15 [b]Dan. 9:27; 11:31; 12:11 [c]Luke 21:21 [1]NU omits *spoken of by Daniel the prophet*
17 [a]Luke 21:23
19 [a]Dan. 9:26; 12:1
21 [a]Luke 17:23; 21:8
22 [a]Rev. 13:13, 14 [1]*chosen ones*
23 [a][2 Pet. 3:17]
24 [a]Zeph. 1:15
25 [a]Is. 13:10; 34:4
26 [a][Dan. 7:13, 14]
27 [1]*chosen ones*
28 [a]Luke 21:29
29 [1]Or *He*

31 "Heaven and earth will pass
away, but [a]My words will by no
means pass away.

No One Knows the Day or Hour

32 "But of that day and hour [a]no
one knows, not even the angels in
heaven, nor the Son, but only the
[b]Father.
33 [a]"Take heed, watch and pray;
for you do not know when the time
is.
34 [a]"*It is* like a man going to a far
country, who left his house and
gave [b]authority to his servants,
and to each his work, and com-
manded the doorkeeper to watch.
35 [a]"Watch therefore, for you do
not know when the master of the
house is coming—in the evening,
at midnight, at the crowing of the
rooster, or in the morning—
36 "lest, coming suddenly, he find
you sleeping.
37 "And what I say to you, I say
to all: Watch!"

The Plot to Kill Jesus

14 After [a]two days it was the
Passover and [b]*the Feast* of
Unleavened Bread. And the chief
priests and the scribes sought how
they might take Him by [1]trickery
and put *Him* to death.
2 But they said, "Not during the
feast, lest there be an uproar of the
people."

The Anointing at Bethany

3 [a]And being in Bethany at the
house of Simon the leper, as He
sat at the table, a woman came
having an alabaster flask of very
costly [1]oil of spikenard. Then she
broke the flask and poured *it* on
His head.
4 But there were some who were
indignant among themselves, and
said, "Why was this fragrant oil
wasted?
5 "For it might have been sold for
more than three hundred [a]denarii
and given to the poor." And they
[b]criticized[1] her sharply.
6 But Jesus said, "Let her alone.
Why do you trouble her? She has
done a good work for Me.
7 [a]"For you have the poor with
you always, and whenever you
wish you may do them good; [b]but
Me you do not have always.
8 "She has done what she could.
She has come beforehand to
anoint My body for burial.
9 "Assuredly, I say to you, wher-
ever this gospel is [a]preached in the
whole world, what this woman has
done will also be told as a memo-
rial to her."

Judas Agrees to Betray Jesus

10 [a]Then Judas Iscariot, one of the
twelve, went to the chief priests to
betray Him to them.
11 And when they heard *it*, they
were glad, and promised to give
him money. So he sought how he
might conveniently betray Him.

Jesus Celebrates the Passover with His Disciples

12 [a]Now on the first day of Un-
leavened Bread, when they [1]killed
the Passover *lamb*, His disciples
said to Him, "Where do You want
us to go and prepare, that You may
eat the Passover?"
13 And He sent out two of His dis-
ciples and said to them, "Go into
the city, and a man will meet you
carrying a pitcher of water; follow
him.
14 "Wherever he goes in, say to
the master of the house, 'The
Teacher says, "Where is the guest
room in which I may eat the Pass-
over with My disciples?"'
15 "Then he will show you a
large upper room, furnished *and*
prepared; there make ready for
us."
16 So His disciples went out, and
came into the city, and found it just
as He had said to them; and they
prepared the Passover.
17 [a]In the evening He came with
the twelve.
18 Now as they sat and ate, Jesus
said, "Assuredly, I say to you, [a]one
of you who eats with Me will be-
tray Me."
19 And they began to be sorrow-
ful, and to say to Him one by one,
"*Is* it I?" [1]And another *said*, "*Is* it
I?"
20 He answered and said to them,
"*It is* one of the twelve, who dips
with Me in the dish.
21 [a]"The Son of Man indeed goes
just as it is written of Him, but woe
to that man by whom the Son of
Man is betrayed! It would have

31 [a]Is. 40:8; [2 Pet. 3:7, 10, 12]
32 [a]Matt. 25:13 [b]Matt. 24:36; Acts 1:7
33 [a]Matt. 24:42; 25:13; Luke 12:40; 21:34; [Rom. 13:11]; 1 Thess. 5:6; 1 Pet. 4:7
34 [a]Matt. 24:45; 25:14 [b][Matt. 16:19]
35 [a]Matt. 24:42, 44

CHAPTER 14

1 [a]Matt. 26:2–5; Luke 22:1, 2; John 11:55; 13:1 [b]Ex. 12:1–27; Mark 14:12 [1]*deception*
3 [a]Matt. 26:6; Luke 7:37; John 12:1, 3 [1]Perfume of pure nard
5 [a]Matt. 18:28; Mark 12:15 [b]Matt. 20:11; John 6:61 [1]*scolded*
7 [a]Deut. 15:11; Matt. 26:11; John 12:8 [b][John 7:33; 8:21; 14:2, 12; 16:10, 17, 28]
9 [a]Matt. 28:19, 20; Mark 16:15; Luke 24:47
10 [a]Ps. 41:9; 55:12–14; Matt. 10:2–4
12 [a]Ex. 12:8; Matt. 26:17–19; Luke 22:7–13 [1]*sacrificed*
17 [a]Matt. 26:20–24; Luke 22:14, 21–23
18 [a]Ps. 41:9; Matt. 26:46; Mark 14:42; John 6:70, 71; 13:18
19 [1]NU omits the rest of v. 19.
21 [a]Matt. 26:24; Luke 22:22; Acts 1:16–20

been good for that man if he had
never been born."

Jesus Institutes the Lord's Supper

22 [a]And as they were eating, Jesus
took bread, blessed and broke *it,*
and gave *it* to them and said,
"Take, [1]eat; this is My [b]body."
23 Then He took the cup, and
when He had given thanks He
gave *it* to them, and they all drank
from it.
24 And He said to them, "This is
My blood of the [1]new covenant,
which is shed for many.
25 "Assuredly, I say to you, I will
no longer drink of the fruit of the
vine until that day when I drink it
new in the kingdom of God."
26 [a]And when they had sung [1]a
hymn, they went out to the Mount
of Olives.

Jesus Predicts Peter's Denial

27 [a]Then Jesus said to them, "All
of you will be made to stumble
[1]because of Me this night, for it is
written:

[b]'I will strike the Shepherd,
And the sheep will be scattered.'

28 "But [a]after I have been raised,
I will go before you to Galilee."
29 [a]Peter said to Him, "Even if all
are made to [1]stumble, yet I *will* not
be."
30 Jesus said to him, "Assuredly,
I say to you that today, *even* this
night, before the rooster crows
twice, you will deny Me three
times."
31 But he spoke more vehemently,
"If I have to die with You, I will
not deny You!" And they all said
likewise.

The Prayer in the Garden

32 [a]Then they came to a place
which was named Gethsemane;
and He said to His disciples, "Sit
here while I pray."
33 And He [a]took Peter, James,
and John with Him, and He began
to be troubled and deeply dis-
tressed.
34 Then He said to them, [a]"My
soul is exceedingly sorrowful,
even to death. Stay here and
watch."
35 He went a little farther, and fell
on the ground, and prayed that if
it were possible, the hour might
pass from Him.
36 And He said, [a]"Abba, Father,
[b]all things *are* possible for You.
Take this cup away from Me;
[c]nevertheless, not what I will, but
what You *will.*"
37 Then He came and found them
sleeping, and said to Peter, "Si-
mon, are you sleeping? Could you
not watch one hour?
38 [a]"Watch and pray, lest you en-
ter into temptation. [b]The spirit in-
deed *is* willing, but the flesh *is*
weak."
39 Again He went away and
prayed, and spoke the same words.
40 And when He returned, He
found them asleep again, for their
eyes were heavy; and they did not
know what to answer Him.
41 Then He came the third time
and said to them, "Are you still
sleeping and resting? It is enough!
[a]The hour has come; behold, the
Son of Man is being betrayed into
the hands of sinners.
42 [a]"Rise, let us be going. See, My
betrayer is at hand."

Betrayal and Arrest in Gethsemane

43 [a]And immediately, while He
was still speaking, Judas, one of
the twelve, with a great multitude
with swords and clubs, came from
the chief priests and the scribes
and the elders.
44 Now His betrayer had given
them a signal, saying, "Whomever
I [a]kiss, He is the One; seize Him
and lead *Him* away safely."
45 As soon as he had come, imme-
diately he went up to Him and said
to Him, "Rabbi, Rabbi!" and
kissed Him.
46 Then they laid their hands on
Him and took Him.
47 And one of those who stood by
drew his sword and struck the ser-
vant of the high priest, and cut off
his ear.
48 [a]Then Jesus answered and said
to them, "Have you come out, as
against a robber, with swords and
clubs to take Me?
49 "I was daily with you in the
temple [a]teaching, and you did not
seize Me. But [b]the Scriptures must
be fulfilled."

22 [a]Matt. 26:26–29; Luke 22:17–20; 1 Cor. 11:23–25 [b][1 Pet. 2:24] [1]NU omits *eat*
24 [1]NU omits *new*
26 [a]Matt. 26:30 [1]Or *hymns*
27 [a]Matt. 26:31–35; Mark 14:50; John 16:32 [b][Is. 53:5, 10]; Zech. 13:7 [1]NU omits *because of Me this night*
28 [a]Matt. 28:16; Mark 16:7; John 21:1
29 [a]Matt. 26:33, 34; Luke 22:33, 34; John 13:37, 38 [1]*fall away*
32 [a]Matt. 26:36–46; Luke 22:40–46; John 18:1
33 [a]Mark 5:37; 9:2; 13:3
34 [a]Is. 53:3, 4; Matt. 26:38; John 12:27
36 [a]Rom. 8:15; Gal. 4:6 [b][Heb. 5:7] [c]Is. 50:5; John 5:30; 6:38
38 [a]Luke 21:36 [b][Rom. 7:18, 21–24; Gal. 5:17]
41 [a]John 13:1; 17:1
42 [a]Matt. 26:46; Mark 14:18; Luke 9:44; John 13:21; 18:1, 2
43 [a]Ps. 3:1; Matt. 26:47–56; Luke 22:47–53; John 18:3–11
44 [a][Prov. 27:6]
48 [a]Matt. 26:55; Luke 22:52
49 [a]Matt. 21:23 [b]Ps. 22:6; Is. 53:7; Luke 22:37; 24:44

50 [a]Then they all forsook Him and
fled.

A Young Man Flees Naked

51 Now a certain young man fol-
lowed Him, having a linen cloth
thrown around *his* naked *body.*
And the young men laid hold of
him,
52 and he left the linen cloth and
fled from them naked.

Jesus Faces the Sanhedrin

53 [a]And they led Jesus away to
the high priest; and with him were
[b]assembled all the [c]chief priests,
the elders, and the scribes.
54 But [a]Peter followed Him at a
distance, right into the courtyard
of the high priest. And he sat with
the servants and warmed himself
at the fire.
55 [a]Now the chief priests and all
the council sought testimony
against Jesus to put Him to death,
but found none.
56 For many bore [a]false witness
against Him, but their testimonies
[1]did not agree.
57 Then some rose up and bore
false witness against Him, saying,
58 "We heard Him say, [a]'I will de-
stroy this temple made with hands,
and within three days I will build
another made without hands.' "
59 But not even then did their tes-
timony agree.
60 [a]And the high priest stood up
in the midst and asked Jesus, say-
ing, "Do You answer nothing?
What *is it* these men testify against
You?"
61 But [a]He kept silent and an-
swered nothing. [b]Again the high
priest asked Him, saying to Him,
"Are You the Christ, the Son of
the Blessed?"
62 Jesus said, "I am. [a]And you will
see the Son of Man sitting at the
right hand of the Power, and com-
ing with the clouds of heaven."
63 Then the high priest tore his
clothes and said, "What further
need do we have of witnesses?
64 "You have heard the [a]blas-
phemy! What do you think?" And
they all condemned Him to be de-
serving of [b]death.
65 Then some began to [a]spit on
Him, and to blindfold Him, and to
beat Him, and to say to Him,
"Prophesy!" And the officers
[1]struck Him with the palms of their
hands.

Peter Denies Jesus, and Weeps

66 [a]Now as Peter was below in the
courtyard, one of the servant girls
of the high priest came.
67 And when she saw Peter warm-
ing himself, she looked at him and
said, "You also were with [a]Jesus
of Nazareth."
68 But he denied it, saying, "I nei-
ther know nor understand what
you are saying." And he went out
on the porch, and a rooster
crowed.
69 [a]And the servant girl saw him
again, and began to say to those
who stood by, "This is one of
them."
70 But he denied it again. [a]And a
little later those who stood by said
to Peter again, "Surely you are *one*
of them; [b]for you are a Galilean,
[1]and your [2]speech shows *it.*"
71 Then he began to curse and
swear, "I do not know this Man
of whom you speak!"
72 [a]A second time *the* rooster
crowed. Then Peter called to mind
the word that Jesus had said to
him, "Before the rooster crows
twice, you will deny Me three
times." And when he thought
about it, he wept.

Jesus Faces Pilate

15 Immediately, [a]in the morn-
ing, the chief priests held a
consultation with the elders and
scribes and the whole council; and
they bound Jesus, led *Him* away,
and [b]delivered *Him* to Pilate.
2 [a]Then Pilate asked Him, "Are
You the King of the Jews?" He an-
swered and said to him, "*It is as*
you say."
3 And the chief priests accused
Him of many things, but He [a]an-
swered nothing.
4 [a]Then Pilate asked Him again,
saying, "Do You answer nothing?
See how many things [1]they testify
against You!"
5 [a]But Jesus still answered noth-
ing, so that Pilate marveled.

Taking the Place of Barabbas

6 Now [a]at the feast he was accus-
tomed to releasing one prisoner to

---

50 [a]Ps. 88:8
53 [a]Matt. 26:57–68 [b]Mark 15:1 [c]John 7:32; 18:3; 19:6
54 [a]John 18:15
55 [a]Matt. 26:59
56 [a]Ex. 20:16 [1]*were not consistent*
58 [a]John 2:19
60 [a]Matt. 26:62
61 [a]Is. 53:7 [b]Luke 22:67–71
62 [a]Luke 22:69
64 [a]John 10:33, 36 [b]John 19:7
65 [a]Is. 50:6; 52:14 [1]NU *received Him with slaps*
66 [a]John 18:16–18, 25–27
67 [a]John 1:45
69 [a]Matt. 26:71
70 [a]Luke 22:59 [b]Acts 2:7 [1]NU omits the rest of v. 70. [2]*accent*
72 [a]Matt. 26:75

CHAPTER 15

1 [a]Ps. 2:2 [b]Acts 3:13
2 [a]Matt. 27:11–14
3 [a]John 19:9
4 [a]Matt. 27:13 [1]NU *of which they accuse You*
5 [a]Is. 53:7
6 [a]Matt. 27:15–26

them, whomever they requested.
7 And there was one named
Barabbas, *who was* chained with
his fellow rebels; they had com-
mitted murder in the rebellion.
8 Then the multitude, [1]crying
aloud, began to ask *him to do* just
as he had always done for them.
9 But Pilate answered them, say-
ing, "Do you want me to release
to you the King of the Jews?"
10 For he knew that the chief
priests had handed Him over be-
cause of envy.
11 But [a]the chief priests stirred up
the crowd, so that he should rather
release Barabbas to them.
12 Pilate answered and said to
them again, "What then do you
want me to do *with Him* whom you
call the [a]King of the Jews?"
13 So they cried out again, "Cru-
cify Him!"
14 Then Pilate said to them,
"Why, [a]what evil has He done?"
But they cried out all the more,
"Crucify Him!"
15 [a]So Pilate, wanting to gratify
the crowd, released Barabbas to
them; and he delivered Jesus, after
he had scourged *Him,* to be [b]cruci-
fied.

The Soldiers Mock Jesus

16 [a]Then the soldiers led Him
away into the hall called [1]Praeto-
rium, and they called together the
whole garrison.
17 And they clothed Him with
purple; and they twisted a crown
of thorns, put it on His *head,*
18 and began to salute Him, "Hail,
King of the Jews!"
19 Then they [a]struck Him on the
head with a reed and spat on Him;
and bowing the knee, they wor-
shiped Him.
20 And when they had [a]mocked
Him, they took the purple off Him,
put His own clothes on Him, and
led Him out to crucify Him.

The King on a Cross

21 [a]Then they compelled a certain
man, Simon a Cyrenian, the father
of Alexander and Rufus, as he was
coming out of the country and
passing by, to bear His cross.
22 [a]And they brought Him to the
place Golgotha, which is trans-
lated, Place of a Skull.
23 [a]Then they gave Him wine min-
gled with myrrh to drink, but He
did not take *it.*
24 And when they crucified Him,
[a]they divided His garments, cast-
ing lots for them to determine
what every man should take.
25 Now [a]it was the third hour, and
they crucified Him.
26 And [a]the inscription of His [1]ac-
cusation was written above:

THE KING OF THE JEWS.

27 [a]With Him they also crucified
two robbers, one on His right and
the other on His left.
28 [1]So the Scripture was fulfilled
which says, [a]*"And He was num-
bered with the transgressors."*
29 And [a]those who passed by
blasphemed Him, [b]wagging their
heads and saying, "Aha! [c]*You* who
destroy the temple and build *it* in
three days,
30 "save Yourself, and come
down from the cross!"
31 Likewise the chief priests also,
[a]mocking among themselves with
the scribes, said, "He saved [b]oth-
ers; Himself He cannot save.
32 "Let the Christ, the King of Is-
rael, descend now from the cross,
that we may see and [1]believe."
Even [a]those who were crucified
with Him reviled Him.

Jesus Dies on the Cross

33 Now [a]when the sixth hour had
come, there was darkness over the
whole land until the ninth hour.
34 And at the ninth hour Jesus
cried out with a loud voice, saying,
"Eloi, Eloi, lama sabachthani?"
which is translated, [a]*"My God, My
God, why have You forsaken Me?"*
35 Some of those who stood by,
when they heard *that,* said, "Look,
He is calling for Elijah!"
36 Then [a]someone ran and filled
a sponge full of sour wine, put *it*
on a reed, and [b]offered *it* to Him
to drink, saying, "Let Him alone;
let us see if Elijah will come to take
Him down."
37 [a]And Jesus cried out with a
loud voice, and breathed His last.
38 Then [a]the veil of the temple
was torn in two from top to bot-
tom.
39 So [a]when the centurion, who
stood opposite Him, saw that [1]He

8 [1]NU *going up*
11 [a]Acts 3:14
12 [a]Mic. 5:2
14 [a]1 Pet. 2:21–23
15 [a]Matt. 27:26 [b][Is. 53:8]
16 [a]Matt. 27:27–31 [1]The governor's headquarters
19 [a][Is. 50:6; 52:14; 53:5]
20 [a]Luke 22:63; 23:11
21 [a]Matt. 27:32
22 [a]John 19:17–24
23 [a]Matt. 27:34
24 [a]Ps. 22:18
25 [a]John 19:14
26 [a]Matt. 27:37 [1]*crime*
27 [a]Luke 22:37
28 [a]Is. 53:12 [1]NU omits v. 28.
29 [a]Ps. 22:6, 7; 69:7 [b]Ps. 109:25 [c]John 2:19–21
31 [a]Luke 18:32 [b]John 11:43, 44
32 [a]Matt. 27:44 [1]M *believe Him*
33 [a]Luke 23:44–49
34 [a]Ps. 22:1
36 [a]John 19:29 [b]Ps. 69:21
37 [a]Matt. 27:50
38 [a]Ex. 26:31–33
39 [a]Luke 23:47 [1]NU *He thus breathed His last*

cried out like this and breathed His
last, he said, "Truly this Man was
the Son of God!"
40 [a]There were also women look-
ing on [b]from afar, among whom
were Mary Magdalene, Mary the
mother of James the Less and of
Joses, and Salome,
41 who also [a]followed Him and
ministered to Him when He was
in Galilee, and many other women
who came up with Him to Jeru-
salem.

Jesus Buried in Joseph's Tomb

42 [a]Now when evening had come,
because it was the Preparation
Day, that is, the day before the
Sabbath,
43 Joseph of Arimathea, a promi-
nent council member, who [a]was
himself waiting for the kingdom of
God, coming and taking courage,
went in to Pilate and asked for the
body of Jesus.
44 Pilate marveled that He was al-
ready dead; and summoning the
centurion, he asked him if He had
been dead for some time.
45 So when he found out from the
centurion, he granted the body to
Joseph.
46 [a]Then he bought fine linen,
took Him down, and wrapped Him
in the linen. And he laid Him in a
tomb which had been hewn out of
the rock, and rolled a stone against
the door of the tomb.
47 And Mary Magdalene and
Mary *the mother* of Joses ob-
served where He was laid.

He Is Risen

16 Now [a]when the Sabbath was
past, Mary Magdalene,
Mary *the mother* of James, and
Salome [b]bought spices, that they
might come and anoint Him.
2 [a]Very early in the morning, on
the first *day* of the week, they
came to the tomb when the sun
had risen.
3 And they said among them-
selves, "Who will roll away the
stone from the door of the tomb
for us?"
4 But when they looked up, they
saw that the stone had been rolled
away—for it was very large.
5 [a]And entering the tomb, they
saw a young man clothed in a long
white robe sitting on the right side;
and they were alarmed.
6 [a]But he said to them, "Do not
be alarmed. You seek Jesus of
Nazareth, who was crucified. He
is risen! He is not here. See the
place where they laid Him.
7 "But go, tell His disciples—and
Peter—that He is going [1]before
you into Galilee; there you will see
Him, [a]as He said to you."
8 So they went out [1]quickly and
fled from the tomb, for they trem-
bled and were amazed. [a]And they
said nothing to anyone, for they
were afraid.

Mary Magdalene Sees the Risen Lord

9 [1]Now when *He* rose early on
the first *day* of the week, He ap-
peared first to Mary Magdalene,
[a]out of whom He had cast seven
demons.
10 [a]She went and told those who
had been with Him, as they
mourned and wept.
11 [a]And when they heard that He
was alive and had been seen by
her, they did not believe.

Jesus Appears to Two Disciples

12 After that, He appeared in an-
other form [a]to two of them as they
walked and went into the country.
13 And they went and told *it* to
the rest, *but* they did not believe
them either.

The Great Commission

14 [a]Later He appeared to the
eleven as they sat at the table; and
He rebuked their unbelief and
hardness of heart, because they
did not believe those who had seen
Him after He had risen.
15 [a]And He said to them, "Go into
all the world [b]and preach the gos-
pel to every creature.
16 [a]"He who believes and is bap-
tized will be saved; [b]but he who
does not believe will be con-
demned.
17 "And these [a]signs will follow
those who [1]believe: [b]In My name
they will cast out demons; [c]they
will speak with new tongues;
18 [a]"they[1] will take up serpents;
and if they drink anything deadly,
it will by no means hurt them;
[b]they will lay hands on the sick,
and they will recover."

40 [a]Matt. 27:55 [b]Ps. 38:11
41 [a]Luke 8:2, 3
42 [a]John 19:38–42
43 [a]Luke 2:25, 38; 23:51
46 [a]Matt. 27:59, 60

CHAPTER 16

1 [a]John 20:1–8 [b]Luke 23:56
2 [a]Luke 24:1
5 [a]John 20:11, 12
6 [a]Matt. 28:6
7 [a]Matt. 26:32; 28:16, 17 [1]*ahead of*
8 [a]Matt. 28:8 [1]NU, M omit *quickly*
9 [a]Luke 8:2 [1]Vv. 9–20 are bracketed in NU as not in the original text. They are lacking in Codex Sinaiticus and Codex Vaticanus, although nearly all other mss. of Mark contain them.
10 [a]Luke 24:10
11 [a]Luke 24:11, 41
12 [a]Luke 24:13–35
14 [a]1 Cor. 15:5
15 [a]Matt. 28:19 [b][Col. 1:23]
16 [a][John 3:18, 36] [b][John 12:48]
17 [a]Acts 5:12 [b]Luke 10:17 [c][Acts 2:4] [1]*have believed*
18 [a]Acts 28:3–6 [b]James 5:14 [1]NU *and in their hands they will*

Christ Ascends to God's Right Hand

19 So then, [a]after the Lord had
spoken to them, He was [b]received
up into heaven, and [c]sat down at
the right hand of God.
20 And they went out and
preached everywhere, the Lord
working with *them* [a]and confirm-
ing the word through the accom-
panying signs. Amen.

19 [a]Acts 1:2, 3 [b]Luke 9:51; 24:51 [c][Ps. 110:1]
20 [a][Heb. 2:4]

The Gospel According to

Luke

LUKE, a physician, writes with the compassion and warmth of a family doctor as he carefully documents the perfect humanity of the Son of Man, Jesus Christ. Luke emphasizes Jesus' ancestry, birth, and early life before moving carefully and chronologically through His earthly ministry. Growing belief and growing opposition develop side by side. Those who believe are challenged to count the cost of discipleship. Those who oppose will not be satisfied until the Son of Man hangs lifeless on a cross. But the Resurrection insures that His purpose will be fulfilled: "to seek and to save that which was lost" (19:10).

Kata Loukan, "According to Luke," is the ancient title that was added to this gospel at a very early date. The Greek name *Luke* appears only three times in the New Testament (Col. 4:14; 2 Tim. 4:11; Philem. 24).

Dedication to Theophilus

INASMUCH as many have taken
in hand to set in order a narra-
tive of those [a]things which
[1]have been fulfilled among us,
2 just as those who [a]from the be-
ginning were [b]eyewitnesses and
ministers of the word [c]delivered
them to us,
3 it seemed good to me also, hav-
ing [1]had perfect understanding of
all things from the very first, to
write to you an orderly account,
[a]most excellent Theophilus,
4 [a]that you may know the cer-
tainty of those things in which you
were instructed.

John's Birth Announced to Zacharias

5 There was [a]in the days of
Herod, the king of Judea, a certain
priest named Zacharias, [b]of the
division of [c]Abijah. His [d]wife *was*
of the daughters of Aaron, and her
name *was* Elizabeth.
6 And they were both righteous
before God, walking in all the
commandments and ordinances of
the Lord blameless.
7 But they had no child, be-
cause Elizabeth was barren, and
they were both well advanced in
years.
8 So it was, that while he was
serving as priest before God in the
order of his division,
9 according to the custom of the
priesthood, [1]his lot fell [a]to burn in-
cense when he went into the tem-
ple of the Lord.
10 [a]And the whole multitude of
the people was praying outside at
the hour of incense.
11 Then an angel of the Lord ap-
peared to him, standing on the
right side of [a]the altar of incense.
12 And when Zacharias saw *him,*
[a]he was troubled, and fear fell
upon him.
13 But the angel said to him, "Do
not be afraid, Zacharias, for your
prayer is heard; and your wife
Elizabeth will bear you a son,
and [a]you shall call his name
John.
14 "And you will have joy and
gladness, and [a]many will rejoice
at his birth.
15 "For he will be [a]great in the
sight of the Lord, and [b]shall drink
neither wine nor strong drink. He
will also be filled with the Holy
Spirit, [c]even from his mother's
womb.
16 "And he will turn many of the
children of Israel to the Lord their
God.
17 [a]"He will also go before Him
in the spirit and power of Elijah,
'to turn the hearts of the fathers
to the children,' and the disobedi-
ent to the wisdom of the just, to
make ready a people prepared for
the Lord."
18 And Zacharias said to the an-
gel, [a]"How shall I know this? For

CHAPTER 1

1 [a]John 20:31 [1]Or *are most surely believed*

2 [a]Acts 1:21, 22 [b]Acts 1:2 [c]Heb. 2:3

3 [a]Acts 1:1 [1]Lit. *accurately followed*

4 [a][John 20:31]

5 [a]Matt. 2:1 [b]1 Chr. 24:1, 10 [c]Neh. 12:4 [d]Lev. 21:13, 14

9 [a]Ex. 30:7, 8 [1]*he was chosen by lot*

10 [a]Lev. 16:17

11 [a]Ex. 30:1

12 [a]Luke 2:9

13 [a]Luke 1:57, 60, 63

14 [a]Luke 1:58

15 [a][Luke 7:24–28] [b]Num. 6:3 [c]Jer. 1:5

17 [a]Mal. 4:5, 6; Matt. 3:2; 11:14

18 [a]Gen. 17:17

I am an old man, and my wife is
well advanced in years."
19 And the angel answered and
said to him, "I am [a]Gabriel, who
stands in the presence of God, and
was sent to speak to you and bring
you [1]these glad [b]tidings.
20 "But behold, [a]you will be mute
and not able to speak until the day
these things take place, because
you did not believe my words
which will be fulfilled in their own
time."
21 And the people waited for
Zacharias, and marveled that he
lingered so long in the temple.
22 But when he came out, he could
not speak to them; and they per-
ceived that he had seen a vision
in the temple, for he beckoned to
them and remained speechless.
23 So it was, as soon as [a]the days
of his service were completed, that
he departed to his own house.
24 Now after those days his wife
Elizabeth conceived; and she hid
herself five months, saying,
25 "Thus the Lord has dealt with
me, in the days when He looked
on *me*, to [a]take away my reproach
among people."

Christ's Birth Announced to Mary

26 Now in the sixth month the an-
gel Gabriel was sent by God to a
city of Galilee named Nazareth,
27 to a virgin [a]betrothed to a man
whose name was Joseph, of the
house of David. The virgin's name
was Mary.
28 And having come in, the angel
said to her, [a]"Rejoice, highly fa-
vored *one*, [b]the Lord *is* with you;
[1]blessed *are* you among women!"
29 But [1]when she saw *him*, [a]she
was troubled at his saying, and
considered what manner of greet-
ing this was.
30 Then the angel said to her, "Do
not be afraid, Mary, for you have
found [a]favor with God.
31 [a]"And behold, you will con-
ceive in your womb and bring
forth a Son, and [b]shall call His
name JESUS.
32 "He will be great, [a]and will
be called the Son of the Highest;
and [b]the Lord God will give
Him the [c]throne of His [d]father
David.
33 [a]"And He will reign over the
house of Jacob forever, and of His
kingdom there will be no end."
34 Then Mary said to the angel,
"How can this be, since I [1]do not
know a man?"
35 And the angel answered and
said to her, [a]"*The* Holy Spirit will
come upon you, and the power of
the Highest will overshadow you;
therefore, also, that Holy One who
is to be born will be called [b]the Son
of God.
36 "Now indeed, Elizabeth your
relative has also conceived a son
in her old age; and this is now the
sixth month for her who was
called barren.
37 "For [a]with God nothing will be
impossible."
38 Then Mary said, "Behold the
maidservant of the Lord! Let it be
to me according to your word."
And the angel departed from her.

Mary Visits Elizabeth

39 Now Mary arose in those days
and went into the hill country with
haste, [a]to a city of Judah,
40 and entered the house of
Zacharias and greeted Elizabeth.
41 And it happened, when Eliza-
beth heard the greeting of Mary,
that the babe leaped in her womb;
and Elizabeth was [a]filled with the
Holy Spirit.
42 Then she spoke out with a loud
voice and said, [a]"Blessed *are* you
among women, and blessed *is* the
fruit of your womb!
43 "But why *is* this *granted* to me,
that the mother of my Lord should
come to me?
44 "For indeed, as soon as the
voice of your greeting sounded in
my ears, the babe leaped in my
womb for joy.
45 [a]"Blessed *is* she who [1]believed,
for there will be a fulfillment of
those things which were told her
from the Lord."

The Song of Mary

46 And Mary said:

[a]"My soul [1]magnifies the Lord,
47 And my spirit has [a]rejoiced in
[b]God my Savior.
48 For [a]He has regarded the lowly
state of His maidservant;
For behold, henceforth [b]all
generations will call me
blessed.

19 [a]Dan. 8:16 [b]Luke 2:10 [1]*this good news*
20 [a]Ezek. 3:26; 24:27
23 [a]2 Kin. 11:5
25 [a]Gen. 30:23
27 [a]Matt. 1:18
28 [a]Dan. 9:23 [b]Judg. 6:12 [1]NU omits *blessed are you among women*
29 [a]Luke 1:12 [1]NU omits *when she saw him*
30 [a]Luke 2:52
31 [a]Is. 7:14 [b]Luke 2:21
32 [a]Mark 5:7 [b]2 Sam. 7:12, 13, 16 [c]2 Sam. 7:14–17 [d]Matt. 1:1
33 [a][Dan. 2:44]
34 [1]Am a virgin
35 [a]Matt. 1:20 [b][Heb. 1:2, 8]
37 [a]Jer. 32:17
39 [a]Josh. 21:9
41 [a]Acts 6:3
42 [a]Judg. 5:24
45 [a]John 20:29 [1]Or *believed that there*
46 [a]1 Sam. 2:1–10 [1]Declares the greatness of
47 [a]Hab. 3:18 [b]1 Tim. 1:1; 2:3
48 [a]Ps. 138:6 [b]Luke 11:27

49 For He who is mighty [a]has done
great things for me,
And [b]holy *is* His name.
50 And [a]His mercy *is* on those who
fear Him
From generation to generation.
51 [a]He has shown strength with His
arm;
[b]He has scattered *the* proud in the
imagination of their hearts.
52 [a]He has put down the mighty from
their thrones,
And exalted *the* lowly.
53 He has [a]filled *the* hungry with
good things,
And *the* rich He has sent away
empty.
54 He has helped His [a]servant Israel,
[b]In remembrance of *His* mercy,
55 [a]As He spoke to our [b]fathers,
To Abraham and to his [c]seed
forever."

56 And Mary remained with her
about three months, and returned
to her house.

Birth of John the Baptist

57 Now Elizabeth's full time came
for her to be delivered, and she
brought forth a son.
58 When her neighbors and rela-
tives heard how the Lord had
shown great mercy to her, they
[a]rejoiced with her.

Circumcision of John the Baptist

59 So it was, [a]on the eighth day,
that they came to circumcise the
child; and they would have called
him by the name of his father,
Zacharias.
60 His mother answered and said,
[a]"No; he shall be called John."
61 But they said to her, "There is
no one among your relatives who
is called by this name."
62 So they made signs to his fa-
ther—what he would have him
called.
63 And he asked for a writing tab-
let, and wrote, saying, "His name
is John." So they all marveled.
64 Immediately his mouth was
opened and his tongue *loosed*, and
he spoke, praising God.
65 Then fear came on all who
dwelt around them; and all these
sayings were discussed through-
out all the hill country of Judea.
66 And all those who heard *them*
[a]kept *them* in their hearts, saying,
"What kind of child will this be?"
And [b]the hand of the Lord was
with him.

Zacharias' Prophecy

67 Now his father Zacharias [a]was
filled with the Holy Spirit, and
prophesied, saying:

68 "Blessed[a] *is* the Lord God of Israel,
For [b]He has visited and redeemed
His people,
69 [a]And has raised up a horn of
salvation for us
In the house of His servant David,
70 [a]As He spoke by the mouth of His
holy prophets,
Who *have been* [b]since the world
began,
71 That we should be saved from our
enemies
And from the hand of all who
hate us,
72 [a]To perform the mercy *promised*
to our fathers
And to remember His holy
covenant,
73 [a]The oath which He swore to our
father Abraham:
74 To grant us that we,
Being delivered from the hand of
our enemies,
Might [a]serve Him without fear,
75 [a]In holiness and righteousness
before Him all the days of our
life.

76 "And you, child, will be called the
[a]prophet of the Highest;
For [b]you will go before the face
of the Lord to prepare His
ways,
77 To give [a]knowledge of salvation
to His people
By the remission of their sins,
78 Through the tender mercy of our
God,
With which the [1]Dayspring from
on high [2]has visited us;
79 [a]To give light to those who sit in
darkness and the shadow of
death,
To [b]guide our feet into the way
of peace."

80 So [a]the child grew and became
strong in spirit, and [b]was in the
deserts till the day of his manifes-
tation to Israel.

Christ Born of Mary

2 And it came to pass in those
days *that* a decree went out

49 [a]Ps. 71:19; 126:2, 3 [b]Ps. 111:9; Rev. 4:8
50 [a]Gen. 17:7; Ex. 20:6; 34:6, 7; Ps. 103:17
51 [a]Ps. 98:1; 118:15; Is. 40:10 [b]Ps. 33:10; [1 Pet. 5:5]
52 [a]1 Sam. 2:7, 8
53 [a][Matt. 5:6]
54 [a]Is. 41:8 [b]Ps. 98:3; [Jer. 31:3]
55 [a]Gen. 17:19; Ps. 132:11; [Gal. 3:16] [b][Rom. 11:28] [c]Gen. 17:7
58 [a][Rom. 12:15]
59 [a]Gen. 17:12; Lev. 12:3; Luke 2:21; Phil. 3:5
60 [a]Luke 1:13, 63
66 [a]Luke 2:19 [b]Gen. 39:2; Acts 11:21
67 [a]Joel 2:28
68 [a]1 Kin. 1:48; Ps. 106:48 [b]Ex. 3:16
69 [a]2 Sam. 22:3; Ps. 132:17; Ezek. 29:21
70 [a]Jer. 23:5; Rom. 1:2 [b]Acts 3:21
72 [a]Lev. 26:42
73 [a]Gen. 12:3; 22:16–18; [Heb. 6:13]
74 [a][Rom. 6:18; Heb. 9:14]
75 [a]Jer. 32:39; [Eph. 4:24; 2 Thess. 2:13]
76 [a]Matt. 3:3; 11:9; Mark 3:2, 3; Luke 3:4; John 1:23 [b]Is. 40:3; Mal. 3:1; Matt. 11:10
77 [a][Jer. 31:34; Mark 1:4]; Luke 3:3
78 [1]Lit. *Dawn;* the Messiah [2]NU *shall visit*
79 [a]Is. 9:2; Matt. 4:16; [Acts 26:18; 2 Cor. 4:6; Eph. 5:14] [b][John 10:4; 14:27; 16:33]
80 [a]Luke 2:40 [b]Matt. 3:1

from Caesar Augustus that all the
world should be registered.
2 [a]This census first took place
while Quirinius was governing
Syria.
3 So all went to be registered,
everyone to his own city.
4 Joseph also went up from Gali-
lee, out of the city of Nazareth, into
Judea, to [a]the city of David, which
is called Bethlehem, [b]because he
was of the house and lineage of
David,
5 to be registered with Mary, [a]his
betrothed [1]wife, who was with
child.
6 So it was, that while they were
there, the days were completed for
her to be delivered.
7 And [a]she brought forth her
firstborn Son, and wrapped Him
in swaddling cloths, and laid Him
in a [1]manger, because there was
no room for them in the inn.

Glory in the Highest

8 Now there were in the same
country shepherds living out in the
fields, keeping watch over their
flock by night.
9 And [1]behold, an angel of the
Lord stood before them, and the
glory of the Lord shone around
them, [a]and they were greatly
afraid.
10 Then the angel said to them,
[a]"Do not be afraid, for behold, I
bring you good tidings of great joy
[b]which will be to all people.
11 [a]"For there is born to you this
day in the city of David [b]a Savior,
[c]who is Christ the Lord.
12 "And this *will be* the sign to
you: You will find a Babe wrapped
in swaddling cloths, lying in a
[1]manger."
13 [a]And suddenly there was with
the angel a multitude of the heav-
enly host praising God and saying:

14 "Glory[a] to God in the highest,
And on earth [b]peace, [c]goodwill[1]
toward men!"

15 So it was, when the angels had
gone away from them into heaven,
that the shepherds said to one an-
other, "Let us now go to Bethle-
hem and see this thing that has
come to pass, which the Lord has
made known to us."
16 And they came with haste and
found Mary and Joseph, and the
Babe lying in a manger.
17 Now when they had seen *Him*,
they made [1]widely known the say-
ing which was told them concern-
ing this Child.
18 And all those who heard *it*
marveled at those things which
were told them by the shepherds.
19 [a]But Mary kept all these things
and pondered *them* in her heart.
20 Then the shepherds returned,
glorifying and [a]praising God for
all the things that they had heard
and seen, as it was told them.

Circumcision of Jesus

21 [a]And when eight days were
completed [1]for the circumcision of
the Child, His name was called
[b]JESUS, the name given by the an-
gel [c]before He was conceived in
the womb.

Jesus Presented in the Temple

22 Now when [a]the days of her pu-
rification according to the law of
Moses were completed, they
brought Him to Jerusalem to pre-
sent *Him* to the Lord
23 [a](as it is written in the law of
the Lord, [b]*"Every male who opens
the womb shall be called holy to
the LORD"*),
24 and to offer a sacrifice accord-
ing to what is said in the law of
the Lord, [a]*"A pair of turtledoves
or two young pigeons."*

Simeon Sees God's Salvation

25 And behold, there was a man
in Jerusalem whose name was
Simeon, and this man was just and
devout, [a]waiting for the Consola-
tion of Israel, and the Holy Spirit
was upon him.
26 And it had been revealed to
him by the Holy Spirit that he
would not [a]see death before he had
seen the Lord's Christ.
27 So he came [a]by the Spirit into
the temple. And when the parents
brought in the Child Jesus, to do
for Him according to the custom
of the law,
28 he took Him up in his arms and
blessed God and said:

29 "Lord, [a]now You are letting Your
servant depart in peace,

CHAPTER 2

2 [a]Acts 5:37
4 [a]1 Sam. 16:1 [b]Matt. 1:16
5 [a][Matt. 1:18] [1]NU omits *wife*
7 [a]Matt. 1:25 [1]*feed trough*
9 [a]Luke 1:12 [1]NU omits *behold*
10 [a]Luke 1:13, 30 [b]Gen. 12:3
11 [a]Is. 9:6 [b]Matt. 1:21 [c]Acts 2:36
12 [1]*feed trough*
13 [a]Dan. 7:10
14 [a]Luke 19:38 [b]Is. 57:19 [c][Eph. 2:4, 7] [1]NU *toward men of goodwill*
17 [1]NU omits *widely*
19 [a]Gen. 37:11
20 [a]Luke 19:37
21 [a]Lev. 12:3 [b][Matt. 1:21] [c]Luke 1:31 [1]NU *for His circumcision*
22 [a]Lev. 12:2–8
23 [a]Deut. 18:4 [b]Ex. 13:2, 12, 15
24 [a]Lev. 12:2, 8
25 [a]Mark 15:43
26 [a][Heb. 11:5]
27 [a]Matt. 4:1
29 [a]Gen. 46:30

According to Your word;
30 For my eyes [a]have seen Your salvation
31 Which You have prepared before the face of all peoples,
32 [a]A light to *bring* revelation to the Gentiles,
And the glory of Your people Israel."

33 [1]And Joseph and His mother
marveled at those things which
were spoken of Him.
34 Then Simeon blessed them,
and said to Mary His mother, "Be-
hold, this *Child* is destined for the
[a]fall and rising of many in Israel,
and for [b]a sign which will be spo-
ken against
35 "(yes, [a]a sword will pierce
through your own soul also), that
the thoughts of many hearts may
be revealed."

Anna Bears Witness to the Redeemer

36 Now there was one, Anna, a
prophetess, the daughter of Pha-
nuel, of the tribe of [a]Asher. She
was of a great age, and had lived
with a husband seven years from
her virginity;
37 and this woman *was* a widow
[1]of about eighty-four years, who
did not depart from the temple,
but served *God* with fastings and
prayers [a]night and day.
38 And coming in that instant she
gave thanks to [1]the Lord, and
spoke of Him to all those who
[a]looked for redemption in Jeru-
salem.

The Family Returns to Nazareth

39 So when they had performed
all things according to the law of
the Lord, they returned to Galilee,
to their *own* city, Nazareth.
40 [a]And the Child grew and be-
came strong [1]in spirit, filled with
wisdom; and the grace of God was
upon Him.

The Boy Jesus Amazes the Scholars

41 His parents went to [a]Jerusalem
[b]every year at the Feast of the
Passover.
42 And when He was twelve years
old, they went up to Jerusalem ac-
cording to the [a]custom of the feast.
43 When they had finished the
[a]days, as they returned, the Boy
Jesus lingered behind in Jerusa-
lem. And [1]Joseph and His mother
did not know *it;*
44 but supposing Him to have
been in the company, they went a
day's journey, and sought Him
among *their* relatives and acquain-
tances.
45 So when they did not find Him,
they returned to Jerusalem, seek-
ing Him.
46 Now so it was *that* after three
days they found Him in the temple,
sitting in the midst of the teachers,
both listening to them and asking
them questions.
47 And [a]all who heard Him were
astonished at His understanding
and answers.
48 So when they saw Him, they
were amazed; and His mother said
to Him, "Son, why have You done
this to us? Look, Your father and
I have sought You anxiously."
49 And He said to them, "Why did
you seek Me? Did you not know
that I must be [a]about [b]My Father's
business?"
50 But [a]they did not understand
the statement which He spoke to
them.

Jesus Advances in Wisdom and Favor

51 Then He went down with them
and came to Nazareth, and was
[1]subject to them, but His mother
[a]kept all these things in her heart.
52 And Jesus [a]increased in wis-
dom and stature, [b]and in favor
with God and men.

John the Baptist Prepares the Way

3 Now in the fifteenth year of the
reign of Tiberius Caesar, [a]Pon-
tius Pilate being governor of Ju-
dea, Herod being tetrarch of Gali-
lee, his brother Philip tetrarch of
Iturea and the region of Trachoni-
tis, and Lysanias tetrarch of Abi-
lene,
2 [1]while [a]Annas and Caiaphas
were high priests, the word of God
came to [b]John the son of Zacharias
in the wilderness.
3 [a]And he went into all the re-
gion around the Jordan, preaching
a baptism of repentance [b]for the
remission of sins,
4 as it is written in the book of
the words of Isaiah the prophet,
saying:

---

30 [a][Is. 52:10]
32 [a]Acts 10:45; 13:47; 28:28
33 [1]NU *And His father and mother*
34 [a][1 Pet. 2:7, 8] [b]Acts 4:2; 17:32; 28:22
35 [a]Ps. 42:10
36 [a]Josh. 19:24
37 [a]1 Tim. 5:5 [1]NU *until she was eighty-four*
38 [a]Mark 15:43 [1]NU *God*
40 [a]Luke 1:80; 2:52 [1]NU omits *in spirit*
41 [a]John 4:20 [b]Deut. 16:1, 16
42 [a]Ex. 23:14, 15
43 [a]Ex. 12:15 [1]NU *His parents*
47 [a]Matt. 7:28; 13:54; 22:33
49 [a]John 9:4 [b][Luke 4:22, 32]
50 [a]John 7:15, 46
51 [a]Dan. 7:28 [1]*obedient*
52 [a][Col. 2:2, 3] [b]1 Sam. 2:26

CHAPTER 3

1 [a]Matt. 27:2
2 [a]Acts 4:6 [b]Luke 1:13 [1]NU, M *in the high priesthood of Annas and Caiaphas*
3 [a]Mark 1:4 [b]Luke 1:77

[a]"The voice of one crying in the
wilderness:
'Prepare the way of the LORD*;*
Make His paths straight.
5 *Every valley shall be filled*
And every mountain and hill
brought low;
The crooked places shall be made
straight
And the rough ways smooth;
6 *And [a]all flesh shall see the*
salvation of God.'"

John Preaches to the People

7 Then he said to the multitudes
that came out to be baptized by
him, [a]"Brood[1] of vipers! Who
warned you to flee from the wrath
to come?
8 "Therefore bear fruits [a]worthy
of repentance, and do not begin to
say to yourselves, 'We have Abra-
ham as *our* father.' For I say to
you that God is able to raise up
children to Abraham from these
stones.
9 "And even now the ax is laid
to the root of the trees. Therefore
[a]every tree which does not bear
good fruit is cut down and thrown
into the fire."
10 So the people asked him, say-
ing, [a]"What shall we do then?"
11 He answered and said to them,
[a]"He who has two tunics, let him
give to him who has none; and he
who has food, [b]let him do like-
wise."
12 Then [a]tax collectors also came
to be baptized, and said to him,
"Teacher, what shall we do?"
13 And he said to them, [a]"Collect
no more than what is appointed
for you."
14 Likewise the soldiers asked
him, saying, "And what shall we
do?" So he said to them, "Do not
[1]intimidate anyone [a]or accuse
falsely, and be content with your
wages."
15 Now as the people were in ex-
pectation, and all reasoned in their
hearts about John, whether he was
the Christ *or* not,
16 John answered, saying to all,
[a]"I indeed baptize you with water;
but One mightier than I is coming,
whose sandal strap I am not wor-
thy to loose. He will [b]baptize you
with the Holy Spirit and fire.
17 "His winnowing fan *is* in His
hand, and He will thoroughly
clean out His threshing floor, and
[a]gather the wheat into His barn;
but the chaff He will burn with un-
quenchable fire."
18 And with many other exhorta-
tions he preached to the people.
19 [a]But Herod the tetrarch, being
rebuked by him concerning Hero-
dias, his [1]brother Philip's wife, and
for all the evils which Herod had
done,
20 also added this, above all, that
he shut John up in prison.

John Baptizes Jesus

21 When all the people were bap-
tized, [a]it came to pass that Jesus
also was baptized; and while He
prayed, the heaven was opened.
22 And the Holy Spirit descended
in bodily form like a dove upon
Him, and a voice came from
heaven which said, "You are My
beloved Son; in You I am [a]well
pleased."

The Genealogy of Jesus Christ

23 Now Jesus Himself began *His*
ministry at [a]about thirty years of
age, being (as was supposed) [b]*the*
son of Joseph, *the son* of Heli,
24 *the son* of Matthat, *the son* of
Levi, *the son* of Melchi, *the son* of
Janna, *the son* of Joseph,
25 *the son* of Mattathiah, *the son*
of Amos, *the son* of Nahum, *the*
son of Esli, *the son* of Naggai,
26 *the son* of Maath, *the son* of
Mattathiah, *the son* of Semei, *the*
son of Joseph, *the son* of Judah,
27 *the son* of Joannas, *the son* of
Rhesa, *the son* of [a]Zerubbabel, *the*
son of Shealtiel, *the son* of Neri,
28 *the son* of Melchi, *the son* of
Addi, *the son* of Cosam, *the son*
of Elmodam, *the son* of Er,
29 *the son* of Jose, *the son* of El-
iezer, *the son* of Jorim, *the son* of
Matthat, *the son* of Levi,
30 *the son* of Simeon, *the son* of
Judah, *the son* of Joseph, *the son*
of Jonan, *the son* of Eliakim,
31 *the son* of Melea, *the son* of
Menan, *the son* of Mattathah, *the*
son of [a]Nathan, [b]*the son* of David,
32 [a]*the son* of Jesse, *the son* of
Obed, *the son* of Boaz, *the son* of
Salmon, *the son* of Nahshon,
33 *the son* of Amminadab, *the son*
of Ram, *the son* of Hezron, *the son*
of Perez, *the son* of Judah,

4 [a]Is. 40:3–5; Matt. 3:3; Mark 1:3
6 [a]Ps. 98:2; Is. 52:10; Luke 2:10; [Rom. 10:8–18]
7 [a]Matt. 3:7; 12:34; 23:33 [1]*Offspring*
8 [a][2 Cor. 7:9–11]
9 [a]Matt. 7:19; Luke 13:6–9
10 [a]Luke 3:12, 14; [Acts 2:37, 38; 16:30, 31]
11 [a]Luke 11:41; 2 Cor. 8:14; James 2:15, 16; [1 John 3:17; 4:20] [b]Is. 58:7; [1 Tim. 6:17, 18]
12 [a]Matt. 21:32; Luke 7:29
13 [a]Luke 19:8
14 [a]Ex. 20:16; 23:1; Lev. 19:11 [1]Lit. *shake down* for money
16 [a]Matt. 3:11, 12; Mark 1:7, 8 [b]John 7:39; 20:22; Acts 2:1–4
17 [a]Mic. 4:12; Matt. 13:24–30
19 [a]Matt. 14:3; Mark 6:17 [1]NU *brother's wife*
21 [a]Matt. 3:13–17; John 1:32
22 [a]Ps. 2:7; [Is. 42:1]; Matt. 3:17; 17:5; Mark 1:11; Luke 1:35; 9:35; 2 Pet. 1:17
23 [a][Num. 4:3, 35, 39, 43, 47] [b]Matt. 13:55; John 6:42
27 [a]Ezra 2:2; 3:8
31 [a]Zech. 12:12 [b]2 Sam. 5:14; 7:12; 1 Chr. 3:5; 17:11; Is. 9:7; Jer. 23:5
32 [a]Ruth 4:18–22; 1 Chr. 2:10–12; Is. 11:1, 10

34 *the son* of Jacob, *the son* of
Isaac, *the son* of Abraham, [a]*the
son* of Terah, *the son* of Nahor,
35 *the son* of Serug, *the son* of
Reu, *the son* of Peleg, *the son* of
Eber, *the son* of Shelah,
36 [a]*the son* of Cainan, *the son* of
[b]Arphaxad, [c]*the son* of Shem, *the
son* of Noah, *the son* of Lamech,
37 *the son* of Methuselah, *the son*
of Enoch, *the son* of Jared, *the son*
of Mahalalel, *the son* of Cainan,
38 *the son* of Enosh, *the son* of
Seth, *the son* of Adam, [a]*the son*
of God.

Satan Tempts Jesus

4 Then [a]Jesus, being filled with
the Holy Spirit, returned from
the Jordan and [b]was led by the
Spirit [1]into the wilderness,
2 being [1]tempted for forty days
by the devil. And [a]in those days
He ate nothing, and afterward,
when they had ended, He was hun-
gry.
3 And the devil said to Him, "If
You are [a]the Son of God, com-
mand this stone to become bread."
4 But Jesus answered him, say-
ing, "It is written, [a]*'Man shall not
live by bread alone, [1]but by every
word of God.'* "
5 [1]Then the devil, taking Him up
on a high mountain, showed Him
all the kingdoms of the world in a
moment of time.
6 And the devil said to Him, "All
this authority I will give You, and
their glory; for [a]*this* has been de-
livered to me, and I give it to
whomever I wish.
7 "Therefore, if You will worship
before me, all will be Yours."
8 And Jesus answered and said
to him, [1]"Get behind Me, Satan!
[2]For it is written, [a]*'You shall wor-
ship the LORD your God, and Him
only you shall serve.'* "
9 [a]Then he brought Him to Jeru-
salem, set Him on the pinnacle of
the temple, and said to Him, "If
You are the Son of God, throw
Yourself down from here.
10 "For it is written:

[a]*'He shall give His angels charge
over you,
To keep you,'*

11 "and,

34 [a]Gen. 11:24, 26–30; 12:3
36 [a]Gen. 11:12 [b]Gen. 10:22, 24; 11:10–13 [c]Gen. 5:6–32; 9:27; 11:10
38 [a]Gen. 5:1, 2

CHAPTER 4

1 [a]Matt. 4:1–11 [b]Luke 2:27 [1]NU *in*
2 [a]Ex. 34:28 [1]*tested*
3 [a]John 20:31
4 [a]Deut. 8:3 [1]NU omits *but by every word of God*
5 [1]NU *And taking Him up, he showed Him*
6 [a][Rev. 13:2, 7]
8 [a]Deut. 6:13; 10:20 [1]NU omits *Get behind Me, Satan* [2]NU, M omit *For*
9 [a]Matt. 4:5–7
10 [a]Ps. 91:11
11 [a]Ps. 91:12
12 [a]Deut. 6:16 [1]*test*
13 [a][Heb. 4:15] [1]*testing*
14 [a]Matt. 4:12 [b]John 4:43 [c]Acts 10:37 [d]Matt. 4:24
15 [a]Matt. 4:23 [b]Is. 52:13
16 [a]Mark 6:1 [b]Acts 13:14–16; 17:2
18 [a]Is. 49:8, 9; 61:1, 2 [b][Dan. 9:24] [1]NU omits *to heal the brokenhearted* [2]*downtrodden*
21 [a]Acts 13:29
22 [a][Ps. 45:2] [b]John 6:42

[a]*'In their hands they shall bear you
up,
Lest you dash your foot against
a stone.'* "

12 And Jesus answered and said
to him, "It has been said, [a]*'You
shall not [1]tempt the LORD your
God.'* "
13 Now when the devil had ended
every [1]temptation, he departed
from Him [a]until an opportune
time.

Jesus Begins His Galilean Ministry

14 [a]Then Jesus returned [b]in the
power of the Spirit to [c]Galilee, and
[d]news of Him went out through all
the surrounding region.
15 And He [a]taught in their syna-
gogues, [b]being glorified by all.

Jesus Rejected at Nazareth

16 So He came to [a]Nazareth,
where He had been brought up.
And as His custom was, [b]He went
into the synagogue on the Sabbath
day, and stood up to read.
17 And He was handed the book
of the prophet Isaiah. And when
He had opened the book, He found
the place where it was written:

18 *"The[a] Spirit of the LORD is upon
Me,
Because He has anointed Me
To preach the gospel to the poor;
He has sent Me [1]to heal the
brokenhearted,
To proclaim liberty to the
captives
And recovery of sight to the
blind,
To [b]set at liberty those who are
[2]oppressed;*
19 *To proclaim the acceptable year
of the LORD."*

20 Then He closed the book, and
gave *it* back to the attendant and
sat down. And the eyes of all who
were in the synagogue were fixed
on Him.
21 And He began to say to them,
"Today this Scripture is [a]fulfilled
in your hearing."
22 So all bore witness to Him, and
[a]marveled at the gracious words
which proceeded out of His mouth.
And they said, [b]"Is this not Jo-
seph's son?"
23 He said to them, "You will

surely say this proverb to Me,
'Physician, heal yourself! What-
ever we have heard done in [a]Ca-
pernaum,[1] do also here in [b]Your
country.' "
24 Then He said, "Assuredly, I say
to you, no [a]prophet is accepted in
his own country.
25 "But I tell you truly, [a]many
widows were in Israel in the days
of Elijah, when the heaven was
shut up three years and six
months, and there was a great
famine throughout all the land;
26 "but to none of them was Elijah
sent except to [1]Zarephath, *in the
region* of Sidon, to a woman *who
was* a widow.
27 [a]"And many lepers were in Is-
rael in the time of Elisha the
prophet, and none of them was
cleansed except Naaman the Syr-
ian."
28 So all those in the synagogue,
when they heard these things,
were [a]filled with [1]wrath,
29 [a]and rose up and thrust Him
out of the city; and they led Him
to the brow of the hill on which
their city was built, that they might
throw Him down over the cliff.
30 Then [a]passing through the
midst of them, He went His way.

Jesus Casts Out an Unclean Spirit

31 Then [a]He went down to Ca-
pernaum, a city of Galilee, and was
teaching them on the Sabbaths.
32 And they were [a]astonished at
His teaching, [b]for His word was
with authority.
33 [a]Now in the synagogue there
was a man who had a spirit of an
unclean demon. And he cried out
with a loud voice,
34 saying, "Let *us* alone! What
have we to do with You, Jesus of
Nazareth? Did You come to de-
stroy us? [a]I know who You are—
[b]the Holy One of God!"
35 But Jesus rebuked him, saying,
[1]"Be quiet, and come out of him!"
And when the demon had thrown
him in *their* midst, it came out of
him and did not hurt him.
36 Then they were all amazed and
spoke among themselves, saying,
"What a word this *is!* For with au-
thority and power He commands
the unclean spirits, and they come
out."
37 And the report about Him went
out into every place in the sur-
rounding region.

Peter's Mother-in-Law Healed

38 [a]Now He arose from the syna-
gogue and entered Simon's house.
But Simon's wife's mother was
[1]sick with a high fever, and they
[b]made request of Him concerning
her.
39 So He stood over her and [a]re-
buked the fever, and it left her. And
immediately she arose and served
them.

Many Healed After Sabbath Sunset

40 [a]When the sun was setting, all
those who had any that were sick
with various diseases brought
them to Him; and He laid His
hands on every one of them and
healed them.
41 [a]And demons also came out of
many, crying out and saying,
[b]"You are [1]the Christ, the Son of
God!" And He, [c]rebuking *them,*
did not allow them to [2]speak, for
they knew that He was the Christ.

Jesus Preaches in Galilee

42 [a]Now when it was day, He de-
parted and went into a deserted
place. And the crowd sought Him
and came to Him, and tried to keep
Him from leaving them;
43 but He said to them, "I must
[a]preach the kingdom of God to the
other cities also, because for this
purpose I have been sent."
44 [a]And He was preaching in the
synagogues of [1]Galilee.

Four Fishermen Called as Disciples

5 So [a]it was, as the multitude
pressed about Him to [b]hear the
word of God, that He stood by the
Lake of Gennesaret,
2 and saw two boats standing by
the lake; but the fishermen had
gone from them and were washing
their nets.
3 Then He got into one of the
boats, which was Simon's, and
asked him to put out a little from
the land. And He [a]sat down and
taught the multitudes from the
boat.
4 When He had stopped speak-
ing, He said to Simon, [a]"Launch

23 [a]Matt. 4:13; 11:23 [b]Matt. 13:54; Mark 6:1 [1]NU *Capharnanum,* here and elsewhere
24 [a]Matt. 13:57; Mark 6:4; John 4:44
25 [a]1 Kin. 17:9; James 5:17
26 [1]Gr. *Sarepta*
27 [a]2 Kin. 5:1–14
28 [a]Luke 6:11 [1]*rage*
29 [a]Luke 17:25; John 8:37; 10:31
30 [a]John 8:59; 10:39
31 [a]Is. 9:1; Matt. 4:13; Mark 1:21
32 [a]Matt. 7:28, 29 [b]Luke 4:36; [John 6:63; 7:46; 8:26, 28, 38, 47; 12:49, 50]
33 [a]Mark 1:23
34 [a]Luke 4:41 [b]Ps. 16:10; Is. 49:7; Dan. 9:24; Luke 1:35
35 [1]Lit. *Be muzzled*
38 [a]Matt. 8:14, 15; Mark 1:29–31 [b]Mark 5:23 [1]*afflicted with*
39 [a]Luke 8:24
40 [a]Matt. 8:16, 17; Mark 1:32–34
41 [a]Mark 1:34; 3:11; Acts 8:7 [b]Mark 8:29 [c]Mark 1:25, 34; 3:11; Luke 4:34, 35 [1]NU omits *the Christ* [2]Or *say that they knew*
42 [a]Mark 1:35–38; Luke 9:10
43 [a]Mark 1:14; [John 9:4]
44 [a]Matt. 4:23; 9:35; Mark 1:39 [1]NU *Judea*

CHAPTER 5

1 [a]Matt. 4:18–22; Mark 1:16–20; John 1:40–42 [b]Acts 13:44
3 [a]John 8:2
4 [a]John 21:6

out into the deep and let down
your nets for a catch."
5 But Simon answered and said
to Him, "Master, we have toiled all
night and caught [a]nothing; never-
theless [b]at Your word I will let
down the net."
6 And when they had done this,
they caught a great number of fish,
and their net was breaking.
7 So they signaled to *their* part-
ners in the other boat to come and
help them. And they came and
filled both the boats, so that they
began to sink.
8 When Simon Peter saw *it*, he
fell down at Jesus' knees, saying,
[a]"Depart from me, for I am a sinful
man, O Lord!"
9 For he and all who were with
him were [a]astonished at the catch
of fish which they had taken;
10 and so also *were* James and
John, the sons of Zebedee, who
were partners with Simon. And Je-
sus said to Simon, "Do not be
afraid. [a]From now on you will
catch men."
11 So when they had brought their
boats to land, [a]they [1]forsook all
and followed Him.

Jesus Cleanses a Leper

12 [a]And it happened when He was
in a certain city, that behold, a
man who was full of [b]leprosy saw
Jesus; and he fell on *his* face and
[1]implored Him, saying, "Lord, if
You are willing, You can make me
clean."
13 Then He put out *His* hand and
touched him, saying, "I am willing;
be cleansed." [a]Immediately the
leprosy left him.
14 [a]And He charged him to tell no
one, "But go and show yourself to
the priest, and make an offering
for your cleansing, as a testimony
to them, [b]just as Moses com-
manded."
15 However, [a]the report went
around concerning Him all the
more; and [b]great multitudes came
together to hear, and to be healed
by Him of their infirmities.
16 [a]So He Himself *often* withdrew
into the wilderness and [b]prayed.

Jesus Forgives and Heals a Paralytic

17 Now it happened on a certain
day, as He was teaching, that there
were Pharisees and teachers of the
law sitting by, who had come out
of every town of Galilee, Judea,
and Jerusalem. And the power of
the Lord was *present* [1]to heal
them.
18 [a]Then behold, men brought on
a bed a man who was paralyzed,
whom they sought to bring in and
lay before Him.
19 And when they could not find
how they might bring him in, be-
cause of the crowd, they went up
on the housetop and let him down
with *his* bed through the tiling into
the midst [a]before Jesus.
20 When He saw their faith, He
said to him, "Man, your sins are
forgiven you."
21 [a]And the scribes and the Phari-
sees began to reason, saying,
"Who is this who speaks blasphe-
mies? [b]Who can forgive sins but
God alone?"
22 But when Jesus [a]perceived
their thoughts, He answered and
said to them, "Why are you rea-
soning in your hearts?
23 "Which is easier, to say, 'Your
sins are forgiven you,' or to say,
'Rise up and walk'?
24 "But that you may know that
the Son of Man has power on earth
to forgive sins"—He said to the
man who was paralyzed, [a]"I say
to you, arise, take up your bed, and
go to your house."
25 Immediately he rose up before
them, took up what he had been
lying on, and departed to his own
house, [a]glorifying God.
26 And they were all amazed, and
they [a]glorified God and were filled
with fear, saying, "We have seen
strange things today!"

Matthew the Tax Collector

27 [a]After these things He went out
and saw a tax collector named
Levi, sitting at the tax office. And
He said to him, [b]"Follow Me."
28 So he left all, rose up, and [a]fol-
lowed Him.
29 [a]Then Levi gave Him a great
feast in his own house. And [b]there
were a great number of tax collec-
tors and others who sat down with
them.
30 [1]And their scribes and the
Pharisees [2]complained against His
disciples, saying, [a]"Why do You

5 [a]John 21:3 [b]Ps. 33:9
8 [a]2 Sam. 6:9; 1 Kin. 17:18
9 [a]Mark 5:42; 10:24, 26
10 [a]Matt. 4:19; Mark 1:17
11 [a]Matt. 4:20; 19:27; [Mark 1:18; 8:34, 35; Luke 9:59–62]; John 12:26 [1]*left behind*
12 [a]Matt. 8:2–4; Mark 1:40–44 [b]Lev. 13:14 [1]*begged*
13 [a]Matt. 20:34; Luke 8:44; John 5:9
14 [a]Matt. 8:4; Luke 17:14 [b]Lev. 13:1–3; 14:2–32
15 [a]Mark 1:45 [b]Matt. 4:25; Mark 3:7; John 6:2
16 [a]Luke 9:10 [b]Matt. 14:23; Mark 1:35; Luke 6:12; 9:18; 11:1
17 [1]NU *with Him to heal*
18 [a]Matt. 9:2–8; Mark 2:3–12
19 [a]Matt. 15:30
21 [a]Matt. 9:3; 26:65; Mark 2:6, 7; John 10:33 [b]Ps. 32:5; 130:4; Is. 43:25
22 [a]Luke 9:47; John 2:25
24 [a]Mark 2:11; 5:41; Luke 7:14
25 [a]Luke 17:15, 18; Acts 3:8
26 [a]Luke 1:65; 7:16
27 [a]Matt. 9:9–17; Mark 2:13–22 [b][Mark 8:34]; Luke 9:59; John 12:26; 21:19, 22
28 [a]Matt. 4:22; 19:27; Mark 10:28
29 [a]Matt. 9:9, 10; Mark 2:15 [b]Luke 15:1
30 [a]Matt. 11:19; Luke 15:2; Acts 23:9 [1]NU *But the Pharisees and their scribes* [2]*grumbled*

eat and drink with tax collectors
and sinners?"
31 Jesus answered and said to
them, "Those who are well have
no need of a physician, but those
who are sick.
32 [a]"I have not come to call *the*
righteous, but sinners, to repen-
tance."

Jesus Is Questioned About Fasting

33 Then they said to Him, [a]"Why[1]
do the disciples of John fast often
and make prayers, and likewise
those of the Pharisees, but Yours
eat and drink?"
34 And He said to them, "Can you
make the friends of the bride-
groom fast while the [a]bridegroom
is with them?
35 "But the days will come when
the bridegroom will be taken away
from them; then they will fast in
those days."
36 [a]Then He spoke a parable to
them: "No one [1]puts a piece from
a new garment on an old one; oth-
erwise the new makes a tear, and
also the piece that was *taken* out
of the new does not match the old.
37 "And no one puts new wine
into old wineskins; or else the new
wine will burst the wineskins and
be spilled, and the wineskins will
be ruined.
38 "But new wine must be put into
new wineskins, [1]and both are pre-
served.
39 "And no one, having drunk old
wine, [1]immediately desires new;
for he says, 'The old is [2]better.'"

Jesus Is Lord of the Sabbath

6 Now [a]it happened [1]on the sec-
ond Sabbath after the first that
He went through the grainfields.
And His disciples plucked the
heads of grain and ate *them*, rub-
bing *them* in *their* hands.
2 And some of the Pharisees said
to them, "Why are you doing
[a]what is not lawful to do on the
Sabbath?"
3 But Jesus answering them said,
"Have you not even read this,
[a]what David did when he was hun-
gry, he and those who were with
him:
4 "how he went into the house
of God, took and ate the show-
bread, and also gave some to those

32 [a]Matt. 9:13; 1 Tim. 1:15
33 [a]Matt. 9:14; Mark 2:18; Luke 7:33 [1]NU omits *Why do*, making the verse a statement
34 [a]John 3:29
36 [a]Matt. 9:16, 17; Mark 2:21, 22 [1]NU *tears a piece from a new garment and puts it on an old one*
38 [1]NU omits *and both are preserved*
39 [1]NU omits *immediately* [2]NU *good*
CHAPTER 6
1 [a]Matt. 12:1–8; Mark 2:23–28 [1]NU *on a Sabbath that He went*
2 [a]Ex. 20:10
3 [a]1 Sam. 21:6
4 [a]Lev. 24:9
6 [a]Matt. 12:9–14; Mark 3:1–6; Luke 13:14; 14:3; John 9:16
7 [a]Luke 13:14; 14:1–6 [b]Luke 20:20
8 [a]Matt. 9:4; John 2:24, 25
9 [a]John 7:23 [1]M *to kill*
10 [1]NU, M *him* [2]NU omits *as whole as the other*
12 [a]Matt. 14:23; Mark 1:35; Luke 5:16; 9:18; 11:1
13 [a]John 6:70 [b]Matt. 10:1
14 [a]John 1:42
16 [a]Jude 1 [b]Luke 22:3–6
17 [a]Matt. 4:25; Mark 3:7, 8

with him, [a]which is not lawful for
any but the priests to eat?"
5 And He said to them, "The Son
of Man is also Lord of the Sab-
bath."

Healing on the Sabbath

6 [a]Now it happened on another
Sabbath, also, that He entered the
synagogue and taught. And a man
was there whose right hand was
withered.
7 So the scribes and Pharisees
watched Him closely, whether He
would [a]heal on the Sabbath, that
they might find an [b]accusation
against Him.
8 But He [a]knew their thoughts,
and said to the man who had the
withered hand, "Arise and stand
here." And he arose and stood.
9 Then Jesus said to them, "I will
ask you one thing: [a]Is it lawful on
the Sabbath to do good or to do
evil, to save life or [1]to destroy?"
10 And when He had looked
around at them all, He said to [1]the
man, "Stretch out your hand."
And he did so, and his hand was
restored [2]as whole as the other.
11 But they were filled with rage,
and discussed with one another
what they might do to Jesus.

The Twelve Apostles

12 Now it came to pass in those
days that He went out to the moun-
tain to pray, and continued all
night in [a]prayer to God.
13 And when it was day, He called
His disciples to *Himself*; [a]and from
them He chose [b]twelve whom He
also named apostles:
14 Simon, [a]whom He also named
Peter, and Andrew his brother;
James and John; Philip and Bar-
tholomew;
15 Matthew and Thomas; James
the *son* of Alphaeus, and Simon
called the Zealot;
16 Judas [a]*the son* of James, and
[b]Judas Iscariot who also became
a traitor.

Jesus Heals a Great Multitude

17 And He came down with them
and stood on a level place with a
crowd of His disciples [a]and a great
multitude of people from all Judea
and Jerusalem, and from the sea-
coast of Tyre and Sidon, who came

to hear Him and be healed of their
diseases,
18 as well as those who were tor-
mented with unclean spirits. And
they were healed.
19 And the whole multitude
[a]sought to [b]touch Him, for [c]power
went out from Him and healed
them all.

The Beatitudes

20 Then He lifted up His eyes to-
ward His disciples, and said:

[a]"Blessed *are you* poor,
For yours is the kingdom of
God.
21 [a]Blessed *are you* who hunger now,
For you shall be [b]filled.[1]
[c]Blessed *are you* who weep now,
For you shall [d]laugh.
22 [a]Blessed are you when men hate
you,
And when they [b]exclude you,
And revile *you*, and cast out
your name as evil,
For the Son of Man's sake.
23 [a]Rejoice in that day and leap for
joy!
For indeed your reward *is* great
in heaven,
For [b]in like manner their
fathers did to the prophets.

Jesus Pronounces Woes

24 "But[a] woe to you [b]who are rich,
For [c]you have received your
consolation.
25 [a]Woe to you who are full,
For you shall hunger.
[b]Woe to you who laugh now,
For you shall mourn and [c]weep.
26 [a]Woe [1]to you when [2]all men speak
well of you,
For so did their fathers to the
false prophets.

Love Your Enemies

27 [a]"But I say to you who hear:
Love your enemies, do good to
those who hate you,
28 [a]"bless those who curse you,
and [b]pray for those who spitefully
use you.
29 [a]"To him who strikes you on
the *one* cheek, offer the other also.
[b]And from him who takes away
your cloak, do not withhold *your*
tunic either.
30 [a]"Give to everyone who asks of
you. And from him who takes
away your goods do not ask *them*
back.
31 [a]"And just as you want men to
do to you, you also do to them like-
wise.
32 [a]"But if you love those who
love you, what credit is that to
you? For even sinners love those
who love them.
33 "And if you do good to those
who do good to you, what credit
is that to you? For even sinners do
the same.
34 [a]"And if you lend *to those* from
whom you hope to receive back,
what credit is that to you? For even
sinners lend to sinners to receive
as much back.
35 "But [a]love your enemies, [b]do
good, and [c]lend, [1]hoping for noth-
ing in return; and your reward will
be great, and [d]you will be sons of
the Most High. For He is kind to
the unthankful and evil.
36 [a]"Therefore be merciful, just as
your Father also is merciful.

Do Not Judge

37 [a]"Judge not, and you shall not
be judged. Condemn not, and you
shall not be condemned. [b]Forgive,
and you will be forgiven.
38 [a]"Give, and it will be given to
you: good measure, pressed down,
shaken together, and running over
will be put into your [b]bosom. For
[c]with the same measure that you
use, it will be measured back to
you."
39 And He spoke a parable to
them: [a]"Can the blind lead the
blind? Will they not both fall into
the ditch?
40 [a]"A disciple is not above his
teacher, but everyone who is per-
fectly trained will be like his
teacher.
41 [a]"And why do you look at the
speck in your brother's eye, but do
not perceive the plank in your own
eye?
42 "Or how can you say to your
brother, 'Brother, let me remove
the speck that *is* in your eye,' when
you yourself do not see the plank
that *is* in your own eye? Hypocrite!
First remove the plank from your
own eye, and then you will see
clearly to remove the speck that
is in your brother's eye.

19 [a]Matt. 9:21; 14:36 [b]Mark 5:27, 28 [c]Luke 8:46
20 [a]Matt. 5:3–12; [11:5]
21 [a]Is. 55:1; 65:13 [b][Rev. 7:16] [c][Is. 61:3] [d]Ps. 126:5 [1]*satisfied*
22 [a]1 Pet. 2:19; 3:14; 4:14 [b][John 16:2]
23 [a]James 1:2 [b]Acts 7:51
24 [a]James 5:1–6 [b]Luke 12:21 [c]Luke 16:25
25 [a][Is. 65:13] [b][Prov. 14:13] [c]James 4:9
26 [a][John 15:19] [1]NU, M omit *to you* [2]M omits *all*
27 [a]Rom. 12:20
28 [a]Rom. 12:14 [b]Acts 7:60
29 [a]Matt. 5:39–42 [b][1 Cor. 6:7]
30 [a]Deut. 15:7, 8
31 [a]Matt. 7:12
32 [a]Matt. 5:46
34 [a]Matt. 5:42
35 [a][Rom. 13:10] [b]Heb. 13:16 [c]Ps. 37:26 [d]Matt. 5:46 [1]*expecting*
36 [a]Matt. 5:48
37 [a]Matt. 7:1–5 [b]Matt. 18:21–35
38 [a][Prov. 19:17; 28:27] [b]Ps. 79:12 [c]James 2:13
39 [a]Matt. 15:14; 23:16
40 [a][John 13:16; 15:20]
41 [a]Matt. 7:3

A Tree Is Known by Its Fruit

43 [a]"For a good tree does not bear bad fruit, nor does a bad tree bear good fruit.

44 "For [a]every tree is known by its own fruit. For *men* do not gather figs from thorns, nor do they gather grapes from a bramble bush.

45 [a]"A good man out of the good treasure of his heart brings forth good; and an evil man out of the evil [1]treasure of his heart brings forth evil. For out [b]of the abundance of the heart his mouth speaks.

Build on the Rock

46 [a]"But why do you call Me 'Lord, Lord,' and not do the things which I say?

47 [a]"Whoever comes to Me, and hears My sayings and does them, I will show you whom he is like:

48 "He is like a man building a house, who dug deep and laid the foundation on the rock. And when the flood arose, the stream beat vehemently against that house, and could not shake it, for it was [1]founded on the rock.

49 "But he who heard and did nothing is like a man who built a house on the earth without a foundation, against which the stream beat vehemently; and immediately it [1]fell. And the ruin of that house was great."

Jesus Heals a Centurion's Servant

7 Now when He concluded all His sayings in the hearing of the people, He [a]entered Capernaum.

2 And a certain centurion's servant, who was dear to him, was sick and ready to die.

3 So when he heard about Jesus, he sent elders of the Jews to Him, pleading with Him to come and heal his servant.

4 And when they came to Jesus, they begged Him earnestly, saying that the one for whom He should do this was deserving,

5 "for he loves our nation, and has built us a synagogue."

6 Then Jesus went with them. And when He was already not far from the house, the centurion sent friends to Him, saying to Him, "Lord, do not trouble Yourself, for I am not worthy that You should enter under my roof.

7 "Therefore I did not even think myself worthy to come to You. But [a]say the word, and my servant will be healed.

8 "For I also am a man placed under [a]authority, having soldiers under me. And I say to one, 'Go,' and he goes; and to another, 'Come,' and he comes; and to my servant, 'Do this,' and he does *it*."

9 When Jesus heard these things, He marveled at him, and turned around and said to the crowd that followed Him, "I say to you, I have not found such great faith, not even in Israel!"

10 And those who were sent, returning to the house, found the servant well [1]who had been sick.

Jesus Raises the Son of the Widow of Nain

11 Now it happened, the day after, *that* He went into a city called Nain; and many of His disciples went with Him, and a large crowd.

12 And when He came near the gate of the city, behold, a dead man was being carried out, the only son of his mother; and she was a widow. And a large crowd from the city was with her.

13 When the Lord saw her, He had [a]compassion on her and said to her, [b]"Do not weep."

14 Then He came and touched the open coffin, and those who carried *him* stood still. And He said, "Young man, I say to you, [a]arise."

15 So he who was dead [a]sat up and began to speak. And He [b]presented him to his mother.

16 [a]Then fear [1]came upon all, and they [b]glorified God, saying, [c]"A great prophet has risen up among us"; and, [d]"God has visited His people."

17 And this report about Him went throughout all Judea and all the surrounding region.

John the Baptist Sends Messengers to Jesus

18 [a]Then the disciples of John reported to him concerning all these things.

---

43 [a]Matt. 7:16–18, 20
44 [a]Matt. 12:33
45 [a]Matt. 12:35 [b]Prov. 15:2, 28; 16:23; 18:21; Matt. 12:34 [1]NU omits *treasure of his heart*
46 [a]Mal. 1:6; Matt. 7:21; 25:11; Luke 13:25
47 [a]Matt. 7:24–27; [John 14:21]; James 1:22–25
48 [1]NU *well built*
49 [1]NU *collapsed*

CHAPTER 7

1 [a]Matt. 8:5–13
7 [a]Ps. 33:9; 107:20
8 [a][Mark 13:34]
10 [1]NU omits *who had been sick*
13 [a]Lam. 3:32; John 11:35; [Heb. 4:15] [b]Luke 8:52
14 [a]Mark 5:41; Luke 8:54; John 11:43; Acts 9:40; [Rom. 4:17]
15 [a]Matt. 11:5; Luke 8:55; John 11:44 [b]1 Kin. 17:23; 2 Kin. 4:36
16 [a]Luke 1:65 [b]Luke 5:26 [c]Luke 24:19; John 4:19; 6:14; 9:17 [d]Luke 1:68 [1]*seized them all*
18 [a]Matt. 11:2–19

19 And John, calling two of his disciples to *him*, sent *them* to [1]Jesus, saying, "Are You [a]the Coming One, or [2]do we look for another?"

20 When the men had come to Him, they said, "John the Baptist has sent us to You, saying, 'Are You the Coming One, or do we look for another?' "

21 And that very hour He cured many of [1]infirmities, afflictions, and evil spirits; and to many blind He gave sight.

22 [a]Jesus answered and said to them, "Go and tell John the things you have seen and heard: [b]that *the* blind [c]see, *the* lame [d]walk, *the* lepers are [e]cleansed, *the* deaf [f]hear, *the* dead are raised, [g]*the* poor have the gospel preached to them.

23 "And blessed is *he* who is not [1]offended because of Me."

24 [a]When the messengers of John had departed, He began to speak to the multitudes concerning John: "What did you go out into the wilderness to see? A reed shaken by the wind?

25 "But what did you go out to see? A man clothed in soft garments? Indeed those who are gorgeously appareled and live in luxury are in kings' courts.

26 "But what did you go out to see? A prophet? Yes, I say to you, and more than a prophet.

27 "This is *he* of whom it is written:

> [a]'*Behold, I send My messenger*
> *before Your face,*
> *Who will prepare Your way*
> *before You.*'

28 "For I say to you, among those born of women there is [1]not a [a]greater prophet than John the Baptist; but he who is least in the kingdom of God is greater than he."

29 And when all the people heard *Him*, even the tax collectors [1]justified God, [a]having been baptized with the baptism of John.

30 But the Pharisees and [1]lawyers rejected [a]the will of God for themselves, not having been baptized by him.

31 [1]And the Lord said, [a]"To what then shall I liken the men of this generation, and what are they like?

32 "They are like children sitting in the marketplace and calling to one another, saying:

> 'We played the flute for you,
> And you did not dance;
> We mourned to you,
> And you did not weep.'

33 "For [a]John the Baptist came [b]neither eating bread nor drinking wine, and you say, 'He has a demon.'

34 "The Son of Man has come [a]eating and drinking, and you say, 'Look, a glutton and a [1]winebibber, a friend of tax collectors and sinners!'

35 [a]"But wisdom is justified by all her children."

A Sinful Woman Forgiven

36 [a]Then one of the Pharisees asked Him to eat with him. And He went to the Pharisee's house, and sat down to eat.

37 And behold, a woman in the city who was a sinner, when she knew that *Jesus* sat at the table in the Pharisee's house, brought an alabaster flask of fragrant oil,

38 and stood at His feet behind *Him* weeping; and she began to wash His feet with her tears, and wiped *them* with the hair of her head; and she kissed His feet and anointed *them* with the fragrant oil.

39 Now when the Pharisee who had invited Him saw *this*, he spoke to himself, saying, [a]"This Man, if He were a prophet, would know who and what manner of woman *this is* who is touching Him, for she is a sinner."

40 And Jesus answered and said to him, "Simon, I have something to say to you." So he said, "Teacher, say it."

41 "There was a certain creditor who had two debtors. One owed five hundred [a]denarii, and the other fifty.

42 "And when they had nothing with which to repay, he freely forgave them both. Tell Me, therefore, which of them will love him more?"

43 Simon answered and said, "I

19 [a][Mic. 5:2; Zech. 9:9; Mal. 3:1–3] [1]NU *the Lord* [2]*should we expect*

21 [1]*illnesses*

22 [a]Matt. 11:4 [b]Is. 35:5 [c]John 9:7 [d]Matt. 15:31 [e]Luke 17:12–14 [f]Mark 7:37 [g][Is. 61:1–3; Luke 4:18]

23 [1]*caused to stumble*

24 [a]Matt. 11:7

27 [a]Is. 40:3; Mal. 3:1; Matt. 11:10; Mark 1:2

28 [a][Luke 1:15] [1]NU *none greater than John;*

29 [a]Matt. 3:5; Luke 3:12 [1]*declared the righteousness of*

30 [a]Acts 20:27 [1]*the experts in the law*

31 [a]Matt. 11:16 [1]NU, M omit *And the Lord said*

33 [a]Matt. 3:1 [b][Matt. 3:4]; Luke 1:15

34 [a]Luke 15:2 [1]An excessive drinker

35 [a]Matt. 11:19

36 [a]Matt. 26:6; Mark 14:3; John 11:2

39 [a]Luke 15:2

41 [a]Matt. 18:28; Mark 6:37

suppose the *one* whom he forgave
more." And He said to him, "You
have rightly judged."
44 Then He turned to the woman
and said to Simon, "Do you see
this woman? I entered your house;
you gave Me no [a]water for My feet,
but she has washed My feet with
her tears and wiped *them* with the
hair of her head.
45 "You gave Me no [a]kiss, but this
woman has not ceased to kiss My
feet since the time I came in.
46 [a]"You did not anoint My head
with oil, but this woman has
anointed My feet with fragrant oil.
47 [a]"Therefore I say to you, her
sins, *which are* many, are forgiven,
for she loved much. But to whom
little is forgiven, *the same* loves lit-
tle."
48 Then He said to her, [a]"Your
sins are forgiven."
49 And those who sat at the table
with Him began to say to them-
selves, [a]"Who is this who even for-
gives sins?"
50 Then He said to the woman,
[a]"Your faith has saved you. Go in
peace."

Many Women Minister to Jesus

8 Now it came to pass, after-
ward, that He went through
every city and village, preaching
and [1]bringing the glad tidings of
the kingdom of God. And the
twelve *were* with Him,
2 and [a]certain women who had
been healed of evil spirits and [1]in-
firmities—Mary called Magda-
lene, [b]out of whom had come
seven demons,
3 and Joanna the wife of Chuza,
Herod's steward, and Susanna,
and many others who provided for
[1]Him from their [2]substance.

The Parable of the Sower

4 [a]And when a great multitude
had gathered, and they had come
to Him from every city, He spoke
by a parable:
5 "A sower went out to sow his
seed. And as he sowed, some fell
by the wayside; and it was tram-
pled down, and the birds of the air
devoured it.
6 "Some fell on rock; and as soon
as it sprang up, it withered away
because it lacked moisture.
7 "And some fell among thorns,
and the thorns sprang up with it
and choked it.
8 "But others fell on good
ground, sprang up, and yielded [1]a
crop a hundredfold." When He
had said these things He cried,
[a]"He who has ears to hear, let him
hear!"

The Purpose of Parables

9 [a]Then His disciples asked Him,
saying, "What does this parable
mean?"
10 And He said, "To you it has
been given to know the [1]mysteries
of the kingdom of God, but to the
rest *it is given* in parables, that

[a]*'Seeing they may not see,*
And hearing they may not
understand.'

The Parable of the Sower Explained

11 [a]"Now the parable is this: The
seed is the [b]word of God.
12 "Those by the wayside are the
ones who hear; then the devil
comes and takes away the word
out of their hearts, lest they should
believe and be saved.
13 "But the ones on the rock *are*
those who, when they hear, re-
ceive the word with joy; and these
have no root, who believe for a
while and in time of [1]temptation
fall away.
14 "Now the ones *that* fell among
thorns are those who, when they
have heard, go out and are choked
with cares, [a]riches, and pleasures
of life, and bring no fruit to matu-
rity.
15 "But the ones *that* fell on the
good ground are those who, hav-
ing heard the word with a noble
and good heart, keep *it* and bear
fruit with [a]patience.[1]

The Parable of the Revealed Light

16 [a]"No one, when he has lit a
lamp, covers it with a vessel or
puts *it* under a bed, but sets *it* on
a lampstand, that those who enter
may see the [b]light.
17 [a]"For nothing is secret that will
not be [b]revealed, nor *anything* hid-
den that will not be known and
come to light.
18 "Therefore take heed how you
hear. [a]For whoever has, to him

44 [a]Gen. 18:4; 19:2; 43:24; Judg. 19:21; 1 Tim. 5:10
45 [a]Rom. 16:16
46 [a]2 Sam. 12:20; Ps. 23:5; Eccl. 9:8; Dan. 10:3
47 [a][1 Tim. 1:14]
48 [a]Matt. 9:2; Mark 2:5
49 [a]Matt. 9:3; [Mark 2:7]; Luke 5:21
50 [a]Matt. 9:22; Mark 5:34; 10:52; Luke 8:48; 18:42

CHAPTER 8

1 [1]*proclaiming the good news*
2 [a]Matt. 27:55; Mark 15:40, 41; Luke 23:49, 55 [b]Matt. 27:56; Mark 16:9 [1]*sicknesses*
3 [1]NU, M *them* [2]*possessions*
4 [a]Matt. 13:2–9; Mark 4:1–9
8 [a]Matt. 11:15; Mark 7:16; Luke 14:35; Rev. 2:7, 11, 17, 29; 3:6, 13, 22; 13:9 [1]Lit. *fruit*
9 [a]Matt. 13:10–23; Mark 4:10–20
10 [a]Is. 6:9; Matt. 13:14; Acts 28:26 [1]*secret* or *hidden truths*
11 [a]Matt. 13:18; Mark 4:14; [1 Pet. 1:23] [b]Luke 5:1; 11:28
13 [1]*testing*
14 [a]Matt. 19:23; 1 Tim. 6:9, 10
15 [a][Rom. 2:7; Heb. 10:36–39; James 5:7, 8] [1]*endurance*
16 [a]Matt. 5:15; Mark 4:21; Luke 11:33 [b]Matt. 5:14
17 [a]Matt. 10:26; Luke 12:2; [1 Cor. 4:5] [b][Eccl. 12:14; 2 Cor. 5:10]
18 [a]Matt. 25:29

more will be given; and whoever
does not have, even what he
[1]seems to [b]have will be taken from
him."

Jesus' Mother and Brothers Come to Him

19 [a]Then His mother and brothers
came to Him, and could not ap-
proach Him because of the crowd.
20 And it was told Him *by some,*
who said, "Your mother and Your
brothers are standing outside, de-
siring to see You."
21 But He answered and said to
them, "My mother and My broth-
ers are these who hear the word
of God and do it."

Wind and Wave Obey Jesus

22 [a]Now it happened, on a certain
day, that He got into a boat with
His disciples. And He said to them,
"Let us cross over to the other side
of the lake." And they launched
out.
23 But as they sailed He fell
asleep. And a windstorm came
down on the lake, and they were
filling *with water,* and were in
[1]jeopardy.
24 And they came to Him and
awoke Him, saying, "Master, Mas-
ter, we are perishing!" Then He
arose and rebuked the wind and
the raging of the water. And they
ceased, and there was a calm.
25 But He said to them, [a]"Where
is your faith?" And they were
afraid, and marveled, saying to
one another, [b]"Who can this be?
For He commands even the winds
and water, and they obey Him!"

A Demon-Possessed Man Healed

26 [a]Then they sailed to the coun-
try of the [1]Gadarenes, which is op-
posite Galilee.
27 And when He stepped out on
the land, there met Him a certain
man from the city who had de-
mons [1]for a long time. And he
wore no clothes, nor did he live in
a house but in the tombs.
28 When he saw Jesus, he [a]cried
out, fell down before Him, and
with a loud voice said, [b]"What
have I to do with [c]You, Jesus, Son
of the Most High God? I beg You,
do not torment me!"
29 For He had commanded the un-
clean spirit to come out of the man.
For it had often seized him, and
he was kept under guard, bound
with chains and shackles; and he
broke the bonds and was driven
by the demon into the wilderness.
30 Jesus asked him, saying,
"What is your name?" And he
said, "Legion," because many de-
mons had entered him.
31 And they begged Him that He
would not command them to go
out [a]into the abyss.
32 Now a herd of many [a]swine
was feeding there on the moun-
tain. So they begged Him that He
would permit them to enter them.
And He permitted them.
33 Then the demons went out of
the man and entered the swine,
and the herd ran violently down
the steep place into the lake and
drowned.
34 When those who fed *them* saw
what had happened, they fled and
told *it* in the city and in the coun-
try.
35 Then they went out to see what
had happened, and came to Jesus,
and found the man from whom the
demons had departed, [a]sitting at
the [b]feet of Jesus, clothed and in
his [c]right mind. And they were
afraid.
36 They also who had seen *it* told
them by what means he who had
been demon-possessed was
[1]healed.
37 [a]Then the whole multitude of
the surrounding region of the
[1]Gadarenes [b]asked Him to [c]depart
from them, for they were seized
with great [d]fear. And He got into
the boat and returned.
38 Now [a]the man from whom the
demons had departed begged Him
that he might be with Him. But Je-
sus sent him away, saying,
39 "Return to your own house,
and tell what great things God has
done for you." And he went his
way and proclaimed throughout
the whole city what great things
Jesus had done for him.

A Girl Restored to Life and a Woman Healed

40 So it was, when Jesus returned,
that the multitude welcomed Him,
for they were all waiting for Him.
41 [a]And behold, there came a man

18 [b]Matt. 13:12 [1]*thinks that he has*
19 [a]Ps. 69:8; Matt. 12:46–50; Mark 3:31–35
22 [a]Matt. 8:23–27; Mark 4:36–41
23 [1]*danger*
25 [a]Luke 9:41 [b]Luke 4:36; 5:26
26 [a]Matt. 8:28–34; Mark 5:1–17 [1]NU *Gerasenes*
27 [1]NU *and for a long time wore no clothes*
28 [a]Mark 1:26; 9:26 [b]Mark 1:23, 24 [c]Luke 4:41
31 [a]Rom. 10:7; [Rev. 20:1, 3]
32 [a]Lev. 11:7; Deut. 14:8
35 [a][Matt. 11:28] [b]Matt. 28:9; Mark 7:25; Luke 10:39; 17:16; John 11:32 [c][2 Tim. 1:7]
36 [1]*delivered*
37 [a]Matt. 8:34 [b]Mark 1:24; Luke 4:34 [c]Job 21:14; Acts 16:39 [d]Luke 5:26 [1]NU *Gerasenes*
38 [a]Mark 5:18–20
41 [a]Matt. 9:18–26; Mark 5:22–43

named Jairus, and he was a ruler
of the synagogue. And he fell
down at Jesus' feet and begged
Him to come to his house,
42 for he had an only daughter
about twelve years of age, and she
[a]was dying. But as He went, the
multitudes thronged Him.
43 [a]Now a woman, having a [b]flow
of blood for twelve years, who had
spent all her livelihood on physi-
cians and could not be healed by
any,
44 came from behind and
[a]touched the border of His gar-
ment. And immediately her flow of
blood stopped.
45 And Jesus said, "Who touched
Me?" When all denied it, Peter
[1]and those with him said, "Master,
the multitudes throng and press
You, [2]and You say, 'Who touched
Me?' "
46 But Jesus said, "Somebody
touched Me, for I perceived [a]power
going out from Me."
47 Now when the woman saw that
she was not hidden, she came
trembling; and falling down before
Him, she declared to Him in the
presence of all the people the rea-
son she had touched Him and how
she was healed immediately.
48 And He said to her, "Daughter,
[1]be of good cheer; [a]your faith has
made you well. [b]Go in peace."
49 [a]While He was still speaking,
someone came from the ruler of
the synagogue's *house*, saying to
him, "Your daughter is dead. Do
not trouble the [1]Teacher."
50 But when Jesus heard *it*, He an-
swered him, saying, "Do not be
afraid; [a]only believe, and she will
be made well."
51 When He came into the house,
He permitted no one to go [1]in ex-
cept [2]Peter, James, and John, and
the father and mother of the girl.
52 Now all wept and mourned for
her; but He said, [a]"Do not weep;
she is not dead, [b]but sleeping."
53 And they ridiculed Him, know-
ing that she was dead.
54 But He [1]put them all outside,
took her by the hand and called,
saying, "Little girl, [a]arise."
55 Then her spirit returned, and
she arose immediately. And He
commanded that she be given
something to eat.
56 And her parents were aston-
ished, but [a]He charged them to tell
no one what had happened.

Sending Out the Twelve

9 Then [a]He called His twelve dis-
ciples together and [b]gave them
power and authority over all de-
mons, and to cure diseases.
2 [a]He sent them to preach the
kingdom of God and to heal the
sick.
3 [a]And He said to them, "Take
nothing for the journey, neither
staffs nor bag nor bread nor
money; and do not have two tunics
apiece.
4 [a]"Whatever house you enter,
stay there, and from there depart.
5 [a]"And whoever will not receive
you, when you go out of that city,
[b]shake off the very dust from your
feet as a testimony against them."
6 [a]So they departed and went
through the towns, preaching the
gospel and healing everywhere.

Herod Seeks to See Jesus

7 [a]Now Herod the tetrarch heard
of all that was done by Him; and
he was perplexed, because it was
said by some that John had risen
from the dead,
8 and by some that Elijah had ap-
peared, and by others that one of
the old prophets had risen again.
9 Herod said, "John I have be-
headed, but who is this of whom
I hear such things?" [a]So he sought
to see Him.

Feeding the Five Thousand

10 [a]And the apostles, when they
had returned, told Him all that
they had done. [b]Then He took
them and went aside privately into
a deserted place belonging to the
city called Bethsaida.
11 But when the multitudes knew
it, they followed Him; and He re-
ceived them and spoke to them
about the kingdom of God, and
healed those who had need of
healing.
12 [a]When the day began to wear
away, the twelve came and said to
Him, "Send the multitude away,
that they may go into the sur-
rounding towns and country, and
lodge and get provisions; for we
are in a deserted place here."

42 [a]Luke 7:2
43 [a]Matt. 9:20 [b]Luke 15:19–22
44 [a]Mark 6:56; Luke 5:13
45 [1]NU omits *and those with him* [2]NU omits the rest of v. 45.
46 [a]Mark 5:30; Luke 6:19
48 [a]Mark 5:34; Luke 7:50 [b]John 8:11 [1]NU omits *be of good cheer*
49 [a]Mark 5:35 [1]NU adds *anymore*
50 [a][Mark 11:22–24]
51 [1]NU adds *with Him* [2]NU, M *Peter, John, and James*
52 [a]Luke 7:13 [b][John 11:11, 13]
54 [a]Luke 7:14; John 11:43 [1]NU omits *put them all outside*
56 [a]Matt. 8:4; 9:30; Mark 5:43

CHAPTER 9

1 [a]Matt. 10:1, 2; Mark 3:13; 6:7 [b]Mark 16:17, 18; [John 14:12]
2 [a]Matt. 10:7, 8; Mark 6:12; Luke 10:1, 9
3 [a]Matt. 10:9–15; Mark 6:8–11; Luke 10:4–12; 22:35
4 [a]Matt. 10:11; Mark 6:10
5 [a]Matt. 10:14 [b]Luke 10:11; Acts 13:51
6 [a]Mark 6:12; Luke 8:1
7 [a]Matt. 14:1, 2; Mark 6:14
9 [a]Luke 23:8
10 [a]Mark 6:30 [b]Matt. 14:13
12 [a]Matt. 14:15; Mark 6:35; John 6:1, 5

13 But He said to them, "You give
them something to eat." And they
said, "We have no more than five
loaves and two fish, unless we go
and buy food for all these people."
14 For there were about five thou-
sand men. Then He said to His dis-
ciples, "Make them sit down in
groups of fifty."
15 And they did so, and made
them all sit down.
16 Then He took the five loaves
and the two fish, and looking up
to heaven, He [a]blessed and broke
them, and gave *them* to the disci-
ples to set before the multitude.
17 So they all ate and were [1]filled,
and twelve baskets of the leftover
fragments were taken up by them.

Peter Confesses Jesus as the Christ

18 [a]And it happened, as He was
alone praying, *that* His disciples
joined Him, and He asked them,
saying, "Who do the crowds say
that I am?"
19 So they answered and said,
[a]"John the Baptist, but some *say*
Elijah; and others *say* that one of
the old prophets has risen again."
20 He said to them, "But who do
you say that I am?" [a]Peter an-
swered and said, "The Christ of
God."

Jesus Predicts His Death and Resurrection

21 [a]And He strictly warned and
commanded them to tell this to no
one,
22 saying, [a]"The Son of Man must
suffer many things, and be re-
jected by the elders and chief
priests and scribes, and be killed,
and be raised the third day."

Take Up the Cross and Follow Him

23 [a]Then He said to *them* all, "If
anyone desires to come after Me,
let him deny himself, and take up
his cross [1]daily, and follow Me.
24 [a]"For whoever desires to save
his life will lose it, but whoever
loses his life for My sake will
save it.
25 [a]"For what profit is it to a man
if he gains the whole world, and
is himself destroyed or lost?
26 [a]"For whoever is ashamed of
Me and My words, of him the Son
of Man will be [b]ashamed when He
comes in His *own* glory, and *in His*
Father's, and of the holy angels.

Jesus Transfigured on the Mount

27 [a]"But I tell you truly, there are
some standing here who shall not
taste death till they see the king-
dom of God."
28 [a]Now it came to pass, about
eight days after these sayings, that
He took Peter, John, and James
and went up on the mountain to
pray.
29 As He prayed, the appearance
of His face was altered, and His
robe *became* white *and* glistening.
30 And behold, two men talked
with Him, who were [a]Moses and
[b]Elijah,
31 who appeared in glory and
spoke of His [1]decease which He
was about to accomplish at Jeru-
salem.
32 But Peter and those with him
[a]were heavy with sleep; and when
they were fully awake, they saw
His glory and the two men who
stood with Him.
33 Then it happened, as they were
parting from Him, *that* Peter said
to Jesus, "Master, it is good for us
to be here; and let us make three
[1]tabernacles: one for You, one for
Moses, and one for Elijah"—not
knowing what he said.
34 While he was saying this, a
cloud came and overshadowed
them; and they were fearful as
they entered the [a]cloud.
35 And a voice came out of the
cloud, saying, [a]"This is [1]My be-
loved Son. [b]Hear Him!"
36 When the voice had ceased, Je-
sus was found alone. [a]But they
kept quiet, and told no one in those
days any of the things they had
seen.

A Boy Is Healed

37 [a]Now it happened on the next
day, when they had come down
from the mountain, that a great
multitude met Him.
38 Suddenly a man from the mul-
titude cried out, saying, "Teacher,
I implore You, look on my son, for
he is my only child.
39 "And behold, a spirit seizes
him, and he suddenly cries out; it
convulses him so that he foams *at*

16 [a]Luke 22:19; 24:30
17 [1]*satisfied*
18 [a]Matt. 16:13–16; Mark 8:27–29
19 [a]Matt. 14:2
20 [a]Matt. 16:16; John 6:68, 69
21 [a]Matt. 8:4; 16:20; Mark 8:30
22 [a]Matt. 16:21; 17:22; Luke 18:31–33; 23:46; 24:46
23 [a]Matt. 10:38; 16:24; Mark 8:34; Luke 14:27 [1]M omits *daily*
24 [a]Matt. 10:39; Luke 17:33; [John 12:25]
25 [a]Matt. 16:26; Mark 8:36; [Luke 16:19–31]; Acts 1:18, 25
26 [a][Rom. 1:16] [b]Matt. 10:33; Mark 8:38; Luke 12:9; 2 Tim. 2:12
27 [a]Matt. 16:28; Mark 9:1; Acts 7:55, 56; Rev. 20:4
28 [a]Matt. 17:1–8; Mark 9:2–8
30 [a]Heb. 11:23–29 [b]2 Kin. 2:1–11
31 [1]Death, lit. *departure*
32 [a]Dan. 8:18; 10:9; Matt. 26:40, 43; Mark 14:40
33 [1]*tents*
34 [a]Ex. 13:21; Acts 1:9
35 [a]Ps. 2:7; [Is. 42:1; Matt. 3:17; 12:18]; Mark 1:11; Luke 3:22 [b]Acts 3:22 [1]NU *My Son, the Chosen One*
36 [a]Matt. 17:9; Mark 9:9
37 [a]Matt. 17:14–18; Mark 9:14–27

the mouth; and it departs from
him with great difficulty, bruising
him.
40 "So I implored Your disciples
to cast it out, but they could not."
41 Then Jesus answered and said,
"O [1]faithless and perverse genera-
tion, how long shall I be with you
and [2]bear with you? Bring your
son here."
42 And as he was still coming, the
demon threw him down and con-
vulsed *him*. Then Jesus rebuked
the unclean spirit, healed the child,
and gave him back to his father.

Jesus Again Predicts His Death

43 And they were all amazed at
the majesty of God. But while
everyone marveled at all the
things which Jesus did, He said to
His disciples,
44 [a]"Let these words sink down
into your ears, for the Son of Man
is about to be betrayed into the
hands of men."
45 [a]But they did not understand
this saying, and it was hidden from
them so that they did not perceive
it; and they were afraid to ask Him
about this saying.

Who Is the Greatest?

46 [a]Then a dispute arose among
them as to which of them would
be greatest.
47 And Jesus, [a]perceiving the
thought of their heart, took a [b]little
child and set him by Him,
48 and said to them, [a]"Whoever
receives this little child in My
name receives Me; and [b]whoever
receives Me [c]receives Him who
sent Me. [d]For he who is least
among you all will be great."

Jesus Forbids Sectarianism

49 [a]Now John answered and said,
"Master, we saw someone casting
out demons in Your name, and we
forbade him because he does not
follow with us."
50 But Jesus said to him, "Do not
forbid *him*, for [a]he who is not
against [1]us is on [2]our side."

A Samaritan Village Rejects the Savior

51 Now it came to pass, when the
time had come for [a]Him to be re-
ceived up, that He steadfastly set
His face to go to Jerusalem,
52 and sent messengers before
His face. And as they went, they
entered a village of the Samari-
tans, to prepare for Him.
53 But [a]they did not receive Him,
because His face was *set* for the
journey to Jerusalem.
54 And when His disciples [a]James
and John saw *this*, they said,
"Lord, do You want us to com-
mand fire to come down from
heaven and consume them, [1]just
as [b]Elijah did?"
55 But He turned and rebuked
them, [1]and said, "You do not know
what manner of [a]spirit you are of.
56 [1]"For [a]the Son of Man did not
come to destroy men's lives but to
save *them*." And they went to an-
other village.

The Cost of Discipleship

57 [a]Now it happened as they jour-
neyed on the road, *that* someone
said to Him, "Lord, I will follow
You wherever You go."
58 And Jesus said to him, "Foxes
have holes and birds of the air
have nests, but the Son of Man
[a]has nowhere to lay *His* head."
59 [a]Then He said to another, "Fol-
low Me." But he said, "Lord, let
me first go and bury my father."
60 Jesus said to him, "Let the dead
bury their own dead, but you go
and preach the kingdom of God."
61 And another also said, "Lord,
[a]I will follow You, but let me first
go *and* bid them farewell who are
at my house."
62 But Jesus said to him, "No one,
having put his hand to the plow,
and looking back, is [a]fit for the
kingdom of God."

The Seventy Sent Out

10 After these things the Lord
appointed [1]seventy others
also, and [a]sent them two by two
before His face into every city and
place where He Himself was about
to go.
2 Then He said to them, [a]"The
harvest truly *is* great, but the la-
borers *are* few; therefore [b]pray the
Lord of the harvest to send out la-
borers into His harvest.
3 "Go your way; [a]behold, I send
you out as lambs among wolves.

41 [1]*unbelieving* [2]*put up with*
44 [a]Matt. 17:22; Mark 10:33; 14:53; Luke 22:54; John 18:12
45 [a]Mark 9:32; Luke 2:50; 18:34
46 [a]Matt. 18:1–5; Mark 9:33–37; Luke 22:24
47 [a]Matt. 9:4; John 2:24, 25 [b]Luke 18:17
48 [a]Matt. 18:5 [b]Matt. 10:40; Mark 9:37; John 12:44 [c]John 13:20 [d][Matt. 23:11, 12]; 1 Cor. 15:9; Eph. 3:8
49 [a]Mark 9:38–40
50 [a]Matt. 12:30; Luke 11:23 [1]NU *you* [2]NU *your*
51 [a]Is. 50:7; Mark 16:19; Acts 1:2
53 [a]John 4:4, 9
54 [a]Mark 3:17 [b]2 Kin. 1:10, 12 [1]NU omits *just as Elijah did*
55 [a][Rom. 8:15; 2 Tim. 1:7] [1]NU omits the rest of v. 55.
56 [a]Luke 19:10; John 3:17; 12:47 [1]NU omits *For the Son of Man did not come to destroy men's lives but to save them.*
57 [a]Matt. 8:19–22
58 [a]Luke 2:7; 8:23
59 [a]Matt. 8:21, 22
61 [a]1 Kin. 19:20
62 [a]2 Tim. 4:10

CHAPTER 10

1 [a]Matt. 10:1; Mark 6:7 [1]NU *seventy-two others*
2 [a]Matt. 9:37, 38; John 4:35 [b][1 Cor. 3:9]; 2 Thess. 3:1
3 [a]Matt. 10:16

4 [a]"Carry neither money bag, knapsack, nor sandals; and [b]greet no one along the road.
5 [a]"But whatever house you enter, first say, 'Peace to this house.'
6 "And if a son of peace is there, your peace will rest on it; if not, it will return to you.
7 [a]"And remain in the same house, [b]eating and drinking such things as they give, for [c]the laborer is worthy of his wages. Do not go from house to house.
8 "Whatever city you enter, and they receive you, eat such things as are set before you.
9 [a]"And heal the sick there, and say to them, [b]'The kingdom of God has come near to you.'
10 "But whatever city you enter, and they do not receive you, go out into its streets and say,
11 [a]'The very dust of your city which clings to [1]us we wipe off against you. Nevertheless know this, that the kingdom of God has come near you.'
12 [1]"But I say to you that [a]it will be more tolerable in that Day for Sodom than for that city.

Woe to the Impenitent Cities

13 [a]"Woe to you, Chorazin! Woe to you, Bethsaida! [b]For if the mighty works which were done in you had been done in Tyre and Sidon, they would have repented long ago, sitting in sackcloth and ashes.
14 "But it will be more tolerable for Tyre and Sidon at the judgment than for you.
15 [a]"And you, Capernaum, [1]who are [b]exalted to heaven, [c]will be brought down to Hades.
16 [a]"He who hears you hears Me, [b]he who rejects you rejects Me, and [c]he who rejects Me rejects Him who sent Me."

The Seventy Return with Joy

17 Then [a]the [1]seventy returned with joy, saying, "Lord, even the demons are subject to us in Your name."
18 And He said to them, [a]"I saw Satan fall like lightning from heaven.
19 "Behold, [a]I give you the authority to trample on serpents and scorpions, and over all the power of the enemy, and nothing shall by any means hurt you.
20 "Nevertheless do not rejoice in this, that the spirits are subject to you, but [1]rather rejoice because [a]your names are written in heaven."

Jesus Rejoices in the Spirit

21 [a]In that hour Jesus rejoiced in the Spirit and said, "I thank You, Father, Lord of heaven and earth, that You have hidden these things from *the* wise and prudent and revealed them to babes. Even so, Father, for so it seemed good in Your sight.
22 [a]"All[1] things have been delivered to Me by My Father, and [b]no one knows who the Son is except the Father, and who the Father is except the Son, and *the one* to whom the Son wills to reveal *Him.*"
23 Then He turned to *His* disciples and said privately, [a]"Blessed *are* the eyes which see the things you see;
24 "for I tell you [a]that many prophets and kings have desired to see what you see, and have not seen *it*, and to hear what you hear, and have not heard *it.*"

The Parable of the Good Samaritan

25 And behold, a certain [1]lawyer stood up and tested Him, saying, [a]"Teacher, what shall I do to inherit eternal life?"
26 He said to him, "What is written in the law? What is your reading *of it?*"
27 So he answered and said, [a]"*'You shall love the* LORD *your God with all your heart, with all your soul, with all your strength, and with all your mind,'* and [b]*'your neighbor as yourself.'*"
28 And He said to him, "You have answered rightly; do this and [a]you will live."
29 But he, wanting to [a]justify himself, said to Jesus, "And who is my neighbor?"
30 Then Jesus answered and said: "A certain *man* went down from Jerusalem to Jericho, and fell among [1]thieves, who stripped him of his clothing, wounded *him,* and departed, leaving *him* half dead.
31 "Now by chance a certain

4 [a]Luke 9:3–5 [b]2 Kin. 4:29
5 [a]Matt. 10:12
7 [a]Matt. 10:11 [b]1 Cor. 10:27 [c]1 Tim. 5:18
9 [a]Mark 3:15 [b]Matt. 3:2; 10:7
11 [a]Acts 13:51 [1]NU *our feet*
12 [a]Matt. 10:15; 11:24 [1]NU, M omit *But*
13 [a]Matt. 11:21–23 [b]Ezek. 3:6
15 [a]Matt. 11:23 [b]Is. 14:13–15 [c]Ezek. 26:20 [1]NU *will you be exalted to heaven? You will be thrust down to Hades!*
16 [a]John 13:20 [b]1 Thess. 4:8 [c]John 5:23
17 [a]Luke 10:1 [1]NU *seventy-two*
18 [a]John 12:31
19 [a]Mark 16:18
20 [a]Is. 4:3 [1]NU, M omit *rather*
21 [a]Matt. 11:25–27
22 [a]John 3:35; 5:27; 17:2 [b][John 1:18; 6:44, 46] [1]M *And turning to the disciples He said, "All*
23 [a]Matt. 13:16, 17
24 [a]1 Pet. 1:10, 11
25 [a]Matt. 19:16–19; 22:35 [1]*expert in the law*
27 [a]Deut. 6:5 [b]Lev. 19:18
28 [a]Ezek. 20:11, 13, 21
29 [a]Luke 16:15
30 [1]*robbers*

priest came down that road. And
when he saw him, [a]he passed by
on the other side.
32 "Likewise a Levite, when he ar-
rived at the place, came and
looked, and passed by on the other
side.
33 "But a certain [a]Samaritan, as
he journeyed, came where he was.
And when he saw him, he had
[b]compassion.
34 "So he went to *him* and ban-
daged his wounds, pouring on oil
and wine; and he set him on his
own animal, brought him to an
inn, and took care of him.
35 "On the next day, [1]when he de-
parted, he took out two [a]denarii,
gave *them* to the innkeeper, and
said to him, 'Take care of him; and
whatever more you spend, when I
come again, I will repay you.'
36 "So which of these three do
you think was neighbor to him
who fell among the thieves?"
37 And he said, "He who showed
mercy on him." Then Jesus said
to him, [a]"Go and do likewise."

Mary and Martha Worship and Serve

38 Now it happened as they went
that He entered a certain village;
and a certain woman named [a]Mar-
tha welcomed Him into her house.
39 And she had a sister called
Mary, [a]who also [b]sat at [1]Jesus' feet
and heard His word.
40 But Martha was distracted with
much serving, and she approached
Him and said, "Lord, do You not
care that my sister has left me to
serve alone? Therefore tell her to
help me."
41 And [1]Jesus answered and said
to her, "Martha, Martha, you are
worried and troubled about many
things.
42 "But [a]one thing is needed, and
Mary has chosen that good part,
which will not be taken away from
her."

The Model Prayer

11 Now it came to pass, as He
was praying in a certain
place, when He ceased, *that* one
of His disciples said to Him, "Lord,
teach us to pray, as John also
taught his disciples."
2 So He said to them, "When you
pray, say:

[a]Our[1] Father [2]in heaven,
Hallowed be Your name.
Your kingdom come.
[3]Your will be done
On earth as *it is* in heaven.
3 Give us day by day our daily
bread.
4 And [a]forgive us our sins,
For we also forgive everyone who
is indebted to us.
And do not lead us into
temptation,
[1]But deliver us from the evil one."

A Friend Comes at Midnight

5 And He said to them, "Which
of you shall have a friend, and go
to him at midnight and say to him,
'Friend, lend me three loaves;
6 'for a friend of mine has come
to me on his journey, and I have
nothing to set before him';
7 "and he will answer from
within and say, 'Do not trouble
me; the door is now shut, and my
children are with me in bed; I can-
not rise and give to you'?
8 "I say to you, [a]though he will
not rise and give to him because
he is his friend, yet because of his
persistence he will rise and give
him as many as he needs.

Keep Asking, Seeking, Knocking

9 [a]"So I say to you, ask, and it
will be given to you; [b]seek, and
you will find; knock, and it will be
opened to you.
10 "For everyone who asks re-
ceives, and he who seeks finds,
and to him who knocks it will be
opened.
11 [a]"If a son asks for [1]bread from
any father among you, will he give
him a stone? Or if *he asks* for a
fish, will he give him a serpent in-
stead of a fish?
12 "Or if he asks for an egg, will
he offer him a scorpion?
13 "If you then, being evil, know
how to give [a]good gifts to your
children, how much more will *your*
heavenly Father give the Holy
Spirit to those who ask Him!"

A House Divided Cannot Stand

14 [a]And He was casting out a de-
mon, and it was mute. So it was,
when the demon had gone out,
that the mute spoke; and the mul-
titudes marveled.
15 But some of them said, [a]"He

31 [a]Ps. 38:11
33 [a]John 4:9 [b]Luke 15:20
35 [a]Matt. 20:2 [1]NU omits *when he departed*
37 [a]Prov. 14:21; [Matt. 9:13; 12:7]
38 [a]John 11:1; 12:2, 3
39 [a][1 Cor. 7:32–40] [b]Luke 8:35; Acts 22:3 [1]NU *the Lord's*
41 [1]NU *the Lord*
42 [a][Ps. 27:4; John 6:27]

CHAPTER 11

2 [a]Matt. 6:9–13 [1]NU omits *Our* [2]NU omits *in heaven* [3]NU omits the rest of v. 2.
4 [a][Eph. 4:32] [1]NU omits *But deliver us from the evil one*
8 [a][Luke 18:1–5]
9 [a]Ps. 50:14, 15; Jer. 33:3; [Matt. 7:7; 21:22; Mark 11:24; John 15:7; James 1:5, 6; 1 John 3:22; 5:14, 15] [b]Is. 55:6
11 [a]Matt. 7:9 [1]NU omits *bread from any father among you, will he give him a stone? Or if he asks for*
13 [a]James 1:17
14 [a]Matt. 9:32–34; 12:22, 24
15 [a]Matt. 9:34; 12:24

casts out demons by [1]Beelzebub,
the ruler of the demons."
16 Others, testing *Him*, [a]sought
from Him a sign from heaven.
17 [a]But [b]He, knowing their
thoughts, said to them: "Every
kingdom divided against itself is
brought to desolation, and a house
divided against a house falls.
18 "If Satan also is divided against
himself, how will his kingdom
stand? Because you say I cast out
demons by Beelzebub.
19 "And if I cast out demons by
Beelzebub, by whom do your sons
cast *them* out? Therefore they will
be your judges.
20 "But if I cast out demons [a]with
the finger of God, surely the king-
dom of God has come upon you.
21 [a]"When a strong man, fully
armed, guards his own palace, his
goods are in peace.
22 "But [a]when a stronger than he
comes upon him and overcomes
him, he takes from him all his ar-
mor in which he trusted, and di-
vides his [1]spoils.
23 [a]"He who is not with Me is
against Me, and he who does not
gather with Me scatters.

An Unclean Spirit Returns

24 [a]"When an unclean spirit goes
out of a man, he goes through dry
places, seeking rest; and finding
none, he says, 'I will return to my
house from which I came.'
25 "And when he comes, he finds
it swept and put in order.
26 "Then he goes and takes with
him seven other spirits more
wicked than himself, and they en-
ter and dwell there; and [a]the last
state of that man is worse than the
first."

Keeping the Word

27 And it happened, as He spoke
these things, that a certain woman
from the crowd raised her voice
and said to Him, [a]"Blessed *is* the
womb that bore You, and *the*
breasts which nursed You!"
28 But He said, [a]"More than that,
blessed *are* those who hear the
word of God and keep it!"

Seeking a Sign

29 [a]And while the crowds were
thickly gathered together, He be-
gan to say, "This is an evil genera-
tion. It seeks a [b]sign, and no sign
will be given to it except the sign
of Jonah [1]the prophet.
30 "For as [a]Jonah became a sign
to the Ninevites, so also the Son
of Man will be to this generation.
31 [a]"The queen of the South will
rise up in the judgment with the
men of this generation and con-
demn them, for she came from the
ends of the earth to hear the wis-
dom of Solomon; and indeed a
[b]greater than Solomon *is* here.
32 "The men of Nineveh will rise
up in the judgment with this gener-
ation and condemn it, for [a]they re-
pented at the preaching of Jonah;
and indeed a greater than Jonah
is here.

The Lamp of the Body

33 [a]"No one, when he has lit a
lamp, puts *it* in a secret place or
under a [b]basket, but on a lamp-
stand, that those who come in may
see the light.
34 [a]"The lamp of the body is the
eye. Therefore, when your eye is
[1]good, your whole body also is full
of light. But when *your eye* is [2]bad,
your body also *is* full of darkness.
35 "Therefore take heed that the
light which is in you is not dark-
ness.
36 "If then your whole body *is* full
of light, having no part dark, *the*
whole *body* will be full of light, as
when the bright shining of a lamp
gives you light."

Woe to the Pharisees and Lawyers

37 And as He spoke, a certain
Pharisee asked Him to dine with
him. So He went in and sat down
to eat.
38 [a]When the Pharisee saw *it*, he
marveled that He had not first
washed before dinner.
39 [a]Then the Lord said to him,
"Now you Pharisees make the out-
side of the cup and dish clean, but
[b]your inward part is full of [1]greed
and wickedness.
40 "Foolish ones! Did not [a]He who
made the outside make the inside
also?
41 [a]"But rather give alms of [1]such
things as you have; then indeed all
things are clean to you.
42 [a]"But woe to you Pharisees!

15 [1]NU, M *Beelzebul*
16 [a]Matt. 12:38; 16:1; Mark 8:11
17 [a]Matt. 12:25–29; Mark 3:23–27 [b]Matt. 9:4; John 2:25
20 [a]Ex. 8:19
21 [a]Matt. 12:29; Mark 3:27
22 [a][Is. 53:12; Col. 2:15] [1]*plunder*
23 [a]Matt. 12:30; Mark 9:40
24 [a]Matt. 12:43–45; Mark 1:27; 3:11; 5:13; Acts 5:16; 8:7
26 [a]John 5:14; [Heb. 6:4–6; 10:26; 2 Pet. 2:20]
27 [a]Luke 1:28, 48
28 [a]Ps. 1:1, 2; 112:1; 119:1, 2; Is. 48:17, 18; [Matt. 7:21; Luke 8:21]; James 1:25
29 [a]Matt. 12:38–42 [b]1 Cor. 1:22 [1]NU omits *the prophet*
30 [a]Jon. 1:17; 2:10; 3:3–10; Luke 24:46; Acts 10:40; 1 Cor. 15:4
31 [a]1 Kin. 10:1–9; 2 Chr. 9:1–8 [b][Is. 9:6; Rom. 9:5]
32 [a]Jon. 3:5
33 [a]Matt. 5:15; Mark 4:21; Luke 8:16 [b]Matt. 5:15
34 [a]Matt. 6:22, 23 [1]Clear, or healthy [2]Evil, or unhealthy
38 [a]Matt. 15:2; Mark 7:2, 3
39 [a]Matt. 23:25 [b]Gen. 6:5; Titus 1:15 [1]Lit. *eager grasping* or *robbery*
40 [a]Gen. 1:26, 27
41 [a]Is. 58:7; Dan. 4:27; [Luke 12:33; 16:9] [1]Or *what is inside*
42 [a]Matt. 23:23

For you tithe the mint and rue and all
manner of herbs, and [b]pass by jus-
tice and the [c]love of God. These
you ought to have done, without
leaving the others undone.
43 [a]"Woe to you Pharisees! For
you love the [1]best seats in the syn-
agogues and greetings in the
marketplaces.
44 [a]"Woe to you, [1]scribes and
Pharisees, hypocrites! [b]For you
are like graves which are not seen,
and the men who walk over *them*
are not aware *of them*."
45 Then one of the lawyers an-
swered and said to Him, "Teacher,
by saying these things You re-
proach us also."
46 And He said, "Woe to you also,
lawyers! [a]For you load men with
burdens hard to bear, and you
yourselves do not touch the bur-
dens with one of your fingers.
47 [a]"Woe to you! For you build the
tombs of the prophets, and your
fathers killed them.
48 "In fact, you bear witness that
you approve the deeds of your fa-
thers; for they indeed killed them,
and you build their tombs.
49 "Therefore the wisdom of God
also said, [a]'I will send them proph-
ets and apostles, and *some* of them
they will kill and persecute,'
50 "that the blood of all the proph-
ets which was shed from the foun-
dation of the world may be re-
quired of this generation,
51 [a]"from the blood of Abel to [b]the
blood of Zechariah who perished
between the altar and the temple.
Yes, I say to you, it shall be re-
quired of this generation.
52 [a]"Woe to you lawyers! For you
have taken away the key of knowl-
edge. You did not enter in your-
selves, and those who were enter-
ing in you hindered."
53 [1]And as He said these things
to them, the scribes and the Phari-
sees began to assail *Him* vehe-
mently, and to cross-examine Him
about many things,
54 lying in wait for Him, [1]and
[a]seeking to catch Him in some-
thing He might say, [2]that they
might accuse Him.

Beware of Hypocrisy

12 In [a]the meantime, when an
innumerable multitude of
people had gathered together, so
that they trampled one another, He
began to say to His disciples first
of all, [b]"Beware of the [1]leaven of
the Pharisees, which is hypocrisy.
2 [a]"For there is nothing covered
that will not be revealed, nor hid-
den that will not be known.
3 "Therefore whatever you have
spoken in the dark will be heard
in the light, and what you have
spoken in the ear in inner rooms
will be proclaimed on the house-
tops.

Jesus Teaches the Fear of God

4 [a]"And I say to you, [b]My
friends, do not be afraid of those
who kill the body, and after that
have no more that they can do.
5 "But I will show you whom you
should fear: Fear Him who, after
He has killed, has power to cast
into hell; yes, I say to you, [a]fear
Him!
6 "Are not five sparrows sold for
two [1]copper coins? And [a]not one
of them is forgotten before God.
7 "But the very hairs of your
head are all numbered. Do not fear
therefore; you are of more value
than many sparrows.

Confess Christ Before Men

8 [a]"Also I say to you, whoever
confesses Me [b]before men, him the
Son of Man also will confess be-
fore the angels of God.
9 "But he who [a]denies Me before
men will be denied before the an-
gels of God.
10 "And [a]anyone who speaks a
word against the Son of Man, it
will be forgiven him; but to him
who blasphemes against the Holy
Spirit, it will not be forgiven.
11 [a]"Now when they bring you to
the synagogues and magistrates
and authorities, do not worry
about how or what you should an-
swer, or what you should say.
12 "For the Holy Spirit will [a]teach
you in that very hour what you
ought to say."

The Parable of the Rich Fool

13 Then one from the crowd said
to Him, "Teacher, tell my brother
to divide the inheritance with me."
14 But He said to him, [a]"Man, who

42 [b][Mic. 6:7, 8] [c]John 5:42
43 [a]Matt. 23:6; Mark 12:38, 39; Luke 14:7; 20:46 [1]Or *places of honor*
44 [a]Matt. 23:27 [b]Ps. 5:9 [1]NU omits *scribes and Pharisees, hypocrites*
46 [a]Matt. 23:4
47 [a]Matt. 23:29; Acts 7:52
49 [a]Prov. 1:20; Matt. 23:34
51 [a]Gen. 4:8; 2 Chr. 36:16 [b]2 Chr. 24:20, 21
52 [a]Matt. 23:13
53 [1]NU *And when He left there*
54 [a]Mark 12:13 [1]NU omits *and seeking* [2]NU omits *that they might accuse Him*

CHAPTER 12

1 [a]Matt. 16:6; Mark 8:15 [b]Matt. 16:12; Luke 11:39 [1]*yeast*
2 [a]Matt. 10:26; Mark 4:22; Luke 8:17; [1 Cor. 4:5]
4 [a]Is. 51:7, 8, 12, 13; Jer. 1:8; Matt. 10:28 [b][John 15:13–15]
5 [a]Ps. 119:120
6 [a]Matt. 6:26 [1]Gr. *assarion*, a coin worth about 1/16 of a denarius
8 [a]1 Sam. 2:30; Matt. 10:32; [Mark 8:38; Rom. 10:9; 2 Tim. 2:12; 1 John 2:23] [b]Ps. 119:46
9 [a]Matt. 10:33; [Mark 8:38; 2 Tim. 2:12]
10 [a][Matt. 12:31, 32; Mark 3:28; 1 John 5:16]
11 [a]Matt. 6:25; 10:19; Mark 13:11
12 [a][John 14:26]
14 [a][John 18:36]

made Me a judge or an arbitrator over you?"
15 And He said to them, [a]"Take heed and beware of [1]covetousness, for one's life does not consist in the abundance of the things he possesses."
16 Then He spoke a parable to them, saying: "The ground of a certain rich man yielded plentifully.
17 "And he thought within himself, saying, 'What shall I do, since I have no room to store my crops?'
18 "So he said, 'I will do this: I will pull down my barns and build greater, and there I will store all my crops and my goods.
19 'And I will say to my soul, [a]"Soul, you have many goods laid up for many years; take your ease; [b]eat, drink, *and* be merry." '
20 "But God said to him, 'Fool! This night [a]your soul will be required of you; [b]then whose will those things be which you have provided?'
21 "So *is* he who lays up treasure for himself, [a]and is not rich toward God."

Do Not Worry

22 Then He said to His disciples, "Therefore I say to you, [a]do not worry about your life, what you will eat; nor about the body, what you will put on.
23 "Life is more than food, and the body *is more* than clothing.
24 "Consider the ravens, for they neither sow nor reap, which have neither storehouse nor barn; and [a]God feeds them. Of how much more value are you than the birds?
25 "And which of you by worrying can add one cubit to his stature?
26 "If you then are not able to do *the* least, why [1]are you anxious for the rest?
27 "Consider the lilies, how they grow: they neither toil nor spin; and yet I say to you, even [a]Solomon in all his glory was not [1]arrayed like one of these.
28 "If then God so clothes the grass, which today is in the field and tomorrow is thrown into the oven, how much more *will He clothe* you, O *you* of [a]little faith?
29 "And do not seek what you should eat or what you should drink, nor have an anxious mind.
30 "For all these things the nations of the world seek after, and your Father [a]knows that you need these things.
31 [a]"But seek [1]the kingdom of God, and all these things shall be added to you.
32 "Do not fear, little flock, for [a]it is your Father's good pleasure to give you the kingdom.
33 [a]"Sell what you have and give [b]alms; [c]provide yourselves money bags which do not grow old, a treasure in the heavens that does not fail, where no thief approaches nor moth destroys.
34 "For where your treasure is, there your heart will be also.

The Faithful Servant and the Evil Servant

35 [a]"Let your waist be girded and [b]*your* lamps burning;
36 "and you yourselves be like men who wait for their master, when he will return from the wedding, that when he comes and knocks they may open to him immediately.
37 [a]"Blessed *are* those servants whom the master, when he comes, will find watching. Assuredly, I say to you that he will gird himself and have them sit down *to eat,* and will come and serve them.
38 "And if he should come in the second watch, or come in the third watch, and find *them* so, blessed are those servants.
39 [a]"But know this, that if the master of the house had known what hour the thief would come, he would [1]have watched and not allowed his house to be broken into.
40 [a]"Therefore you also be ready, for the Son of Man is coming at an hour you do not expect."
41 Then Peter said to Him, "Lord, do You speak this parable *only* to us, or to all *people?*"
42 And the Lord said, [a]"Who then is that faithful and wise steward, whom *his* master will make ruler over his household, to give *them their* portion of food [1]in due season?
43 "Blessed *is* that servant whom

15 [a][1 Tim. 6:6–10] [1]NU *all covetousness*
19 [a]Eccl. 11:9; 1 Cor. 15:32; James 5:5 [b][Eccl. 2:24; 3:13; 5:18; 8:15]
20 [a]Job 27:8; Ps. 52:7; [James 4:14] [b]Ps. 39:6; Jer. 17:11
21 [a][Matt. 6:20; Luke 12:33; 1 Tim. 6:18, 19; James 2:5; 5:1–5]
22 [a]Matt. 6:25–33
24 [a]Job 38:41; Ps. 147:9
26 [1]*do you worry*
27 [a]1 Kin. 10:4–7; 2 Chr. 9:3–6 [1]*clothed*
28 [a]Matt. 6:30; 8:26; 14:31; 16:8
30 [a]Matt. 6:31, 32
31 [a]Matt. 6:33 [1]NU *His kingdom, and these things*
32 [a][Dan. 7:18, 27]; Zech. 13:7; [Matt. 11:25, 26; Luke 22:29, 30]
33 [a]Matt. 19:21; Acts 2:45; 4:34 [b]Luke 11:41 [c]Matt. 6:20; Luke 16:9; [1 Tim. 6:19]
35 [a][Eph. 6:14; 1 Pet. 1:13] [b][Matt. 25:1–13]
37 [a]Matt. 24:46
39 [a]Matt. 24:43; 1 Thess. 5:2; [2 Pet. 3:10]; Rev. 3:3; 16:15 [1]NU *not have allowed*
40 [a]Matt. 24:44; 25:13; Mark 13:33; [Luke 21:34, 36]; 1 Thess. 5:6; [2 Pet. 3:12]
42 [a]Matt. 24:45, 46; 25:21; [1 Cor. 4:2] [1]*at the right time*

his master will find so doing when
he comes.
44 [a]"Truly, I say to you that he
will make him ruler over all that
he has.
45 [a]"But if that servant says in his
heart, 'My master is delaying his
coming,' and begins to beat the
male and female servants, and to
eat and drink and be drunk,
46 "the master of that servant will
come on a [a]day when he is not
looking for *him*, and at an hour
when he is not aware, and will cut
him in two and appoint *him* his
portion with the unbelievers.
47 "And [a]that servant who [b]knew
his master's will, and did not pre-
pare *himself* or do according to his
will, shall be beaten with many
stripes.
48 [a]"But he who did not know, yet
committed things deserving of
stripes, shall be beaten with few.
For everyone to whom much is
given, from him much will be re-
quired; and to whom much has
been committed, of him they will
ask the more.

Christ Brings Division

49 [a]"I came to send fire on the
earth, and how I wish it were al-
ready kindled!
50 "But [a]I have a baptism to be
baptized with, and how distressed
I am till it is [b]accomplished!
51 [a]"Do *you* suppose that I came
to give peace on earth? I tell you,
not at all, [b]but rather division.
52 [a]"For from now on five in one
house will be divided: three
against two, and two against three.
53 [a]"Father will be divided against
son and son against father, mother
against daughter and daughter
against mother, mother-in-law
against her daughter-in-law and
daughter-in-law against her
mother-in-law."

Discern the Time

54 Then He also said to the multi-
tudes, [a]"Whenever you see a cloud
rising out of the west, immediately
you say, 'A shower is coming'; and
so it is.
55 "And when you see the [a]south
wind blow, you say, 'There will be
hot weather'; and there is.

44 [a]Matt. 24:47; 25:21; [Rev. 3:21]
45 [a]Matt. 24:48; 2 Pet. 3:3, 4
46 [a]1 Thess. 5:3
47 [a]Num. 15:30; Deut. 25:2; [John 9:41; 15:22; Acts 17:30] [b][James 4:17]
48 [a][Lev. 5:17]; Num. 15:29; [1 Tim. 1:13]
49 [a]Luke 12:51
50 [a]Matt. 20:18, 22, 23; Mark 10:38 [b]John 12:27; 19:30
51 [a]Matt. 10:34–36 [b]Mic. 7:6; John 7:43; 9:16; 10:19; Acts 14:4
52 [a]Matt. 10:35; Mark 13:12
53 [a]Matt. 10:21, 36
54 [a]Matt. 16:2, 3
55 [a]Job 37:17
56 [a]Luke 19:41–44
58 [a]Prov. 25:8; Matt. 5:25, 26 [b][Ps. 32:6; Is. 55:6]

CHAPTER 13

1 [1]*mixed*
6 [a]Is. 5:2; Matt. 21:19
7 [1]*waste*
9 [a][John 15:2] [1]NU *And if it bears fruit after that, well. But if not, you can*

56 "Hypocrites! You can discern
the face of the sky and of the earth,
but how *is it* you do not discern
[a]this time?

Make Peace with Your Adversary

57 "Yes, and why, even of your-
selves, do you not judge what is
right?
58 [a]"When you go with your ad-
versary to the magistrate, make
every effort [b]along the way to set-
tle with him, lest he drag you to
the judge, the judge deliver you to
the officer, and the officer throw
you into prison.
59 "I tell you, you shall not depart
from there till you have paid the
very last mite."

Repent or Perish

13 There were present at that
season some who told Him
about the Galileans whose blood
Pilate had [1]mingled with their sac-
rifices.
2 And Jesus answered and said
to them, "Do you suppose that
these Galileans were worse sin-
ners than all *other* Galileans, be-
cause they suffered such things?
3 "I tell you, no; but unless you
repent you will all likewise perish.
4 "Or those eighteen on whom
the tower in Siloam fell and killed
them, do you think that they were
worse sinners than all *other* men
who dwelt in Jerusalem?
5 "I tell you, no; but unless you
repent you will all likewise per-
ish."

The Parable of the Barren Fig Tree

6 He also spoke this parable: [a]"A
certain *man* had a fig tree planted
in his vineyard, and he came seek-
ing fruit on it and found none.
7 "Then he said to the keeper of
his vineyard, 'Look, for three
years I have come seeking fruit on
this fig tree and find none. Cut it
down; why does it [1]use up the
ground?'
8 "But he answered and said to
him, 'Sir, let it alone this year
also, until I dig around it and fertil-
ize *it*.
9 [1]'And if it bears fruit, *well*. But
if not, after that you can [a]cut it
down.'"

A Spirit of Infirmity

10 Now He was teaching in one
of the synagogues on the Sabbath.
11 And behold, there was a
woman who had a spirit of infirm-
ity eighteen years, and was bent
over and could in no way [1]raise
herself up.
12 But when Jesus saw her, He
called *her* to *Him* and said to her,
"Woman, you are loosed from
your [a]infirmity."
13 [a]And He laid *His* hands on her,
and immediately she was made
straight, and glorified God.
14 But the ruler of the synagogue
answered with indignation, be-
cause Jesus had [a]healed on the
Sabbath; and he said to the crowd,
[b]"There are six days on which men
ought to work; therefore come and
be healed on them, and [c]not on the
Sabbath day."
15 The Lord then answered him
and said, [1]"Hypocrite! [a]Does not
each one of you on the Sabbath
loose his ox or donkey from the
stall, and lead *it* away to water it?
16 "So ought not this woman, [a]be-
ing a daughter of Abraham, whom
Satan has bound—think of it—for
eighteen years, be loosed from this
bond on the Sabbath?"
17 And when He said these things,
all His adversaries were put to
shame; and all the multitude re-
joiced for all the glorious things
that were [a]done by Him.

The Parable of the Mustard Seed

18 [a]Then He said, "What is the
kingdom of God like? And to what
shall I compare it?
19 "It is like a mustard seed,
which a man took and put in his
garden; and it grew and became
a [1]large tree, and the birds of the
air nested in its branches."

The Parable of the Leaven

20 And again He said, "To what
shall I liken the kingdom of God?
21 "It is like [1]leaven, which a
woman took and hid in three
[a]measures[2] of meal till it was all
leavened."

The Narrow Way

22 [a]And He went through the
cities and villages, teaching, and
journeying toward Jerusalem.
23 Then one said to Him, "Lord,
are there [a]few who are saved?"
And He said to them,
24 [a]"Strive to enter through the
narrow gate, for [b]many, I say to
you, will seek to enter and will not
be able.
25 [a]"When once the Master of the
house has risen up and [b]shut the
door, and you begin to stand out-
side and knock at the door, saying,
[c]'Lord, Lord, open for us,' and He
will answer and say to you, [d]'I do
not know you, where you are
from,'
26 "then you will begin to say,
'We ate and drank in Your pres-
ence, and You taught in our
streets.'
27 [a]"But He will say, 'I tell you I
do not know you, where you are
from. [b]Depart from Me, all you
workers of iniquity.'
28 [a]"There will be weeping and
gnashing of teeth, [b]when you see
Abraham and Isaac and Jacob and
all the prophets in the kingdom of
God, and yourselves thrust out.
29 "They will come from the east
and the west, from the north and
the south, and sit down in the king-
dom of God.
30 [a]"And indeed there are last
who will be first, and there are first
who will be last."
31 [1]On that very day some Phari-
sees came, saying to Him, "Get out
and depart from here, for Herod
wants to kill You."
32 And He said to them, "Go, tell
that fox, 'Behold, I cast out de-
mons and perform cures today and
tomorrow, and the third *day* [a]I
shall be [1]perfected.'
33 "Nevertheless I must journey
today, tomorrow, and the *day* fol-
lowing; for it cannot be that a
prophet should perish outside of
Jerusalem.

Jesus Laments over Jerusalem

34 [a]"O Jerusalem, Jerusalem, the
one who kills the prophets and
stones those who are sent to her!
How often I wanted to gather your
children together, as a hen *gathers*
her brood under *her* wings, but
you were not willing!
35 "See! [a]Your house is left to you
desolate; and [1]assuredly, I say to

11 [1]*straighten up*
12 [a]Luke 7:21; 8:2
13 [a]Mark 16:18; Acts 9:17
14 [a][Luke 6:6–11; 14:1–6]; John 5:16 [b]Ex. 20:9; 23:12 [c]Matt. 12:10; Mark 3:2; Luke 6:7; 14:3
15 [a][Matt. 7:5; 23:13]; Luke 14:5 [1]NU, M *Hypocrites*
16 [a]Luke 19:9
17 [a]Mark 5:19, 20
18 [a]Matt. 13:31, 32; Mark 4:30–32
19 [1]NU omits *large*
21 [a]Matt. 13:33 [1]*yeast* [2]Gr. *sata,* same as Heb. *seah;* approximately 2 pecks in all
22 [a]Matt. 9:35; Mark 6:6
23 [a][Matt. 7:14; 20:16]
24 [a][Matt. 7:13] [b][John 7:34; 8:21; 13:33; Rom. 9:31]
25 [a][Ps. 32:6]; Is. 55:6 [b]Matt. 25:10; Rev. 22:11 [c]Luke 6:46 [d]Matt. 7:23; 25:12
27 [a][Matt. 7:23; 25:41] [b]Ps. 6:8; [Matt. 25:41]; Titus 1:16
28 [a]Matt. 8:12; 13:42; 24:51 [b]Matt. 8:11
30 [a][Matt. 19:30; 20:16]; Mark 10:31
31 [1]NU *In that very hour*
32 [a]Luke 24:46; Acts 10:40; 1 Cor. 15:4; [Heb. 2:10; 5:9; 7:28] [1]Resurrected
34 [a]Matt. 23:37–39; 2 Chr. 24:20, 21; 36:15, 16
35 [a]Lev. 26:31, 32; Ps. 69:25; Is. 1:7; Jer. 22:5; Dan. 9:27; Mic. 3:12 [1]NU, M omit *assuredly*

you, you shall not see Me until
the time comes when you say,
[b]*'Blessed is He who comes in the*
name of the LORD!' "

A Man with Dropsy Healed on the Sabbath

14 Now it happened, as He
went into the house of one
of the rulers of the Pharisees to eat
bread on the Sabbath, that they
watched Him closely.
2 And behold, there was a cer-
tain man before Him who had
dropsy.
3 And Jesus, answering, spoke to
the lawyers and Pharisees, saying,
[a]"Is it lawful to heal on the [1]Sab-
bath?"
4 But they kept silent. And He
took *him* and healed him, and let
him go.
5 Then He answered them, say-
ing, [a]"Which of you, having a
[1]donkey or an ox that has fallen
into a pit, will not immediately pull
him out on the Sabbath day?"
6 And they could not answer
Him regarding these things.

Take the Lowly Place

7 So He told a parable to those
who were invited, when He noted
how they chose the best places,
saying to them:
8 "When you are invited by any-
one to a wedding feast, do not sit
down in the best place, lest one
more honorable than you be in-
vited by him;
9 "and he who invited you and
him come and say to you, 'Give
place to this man,' and then you
begin with shame to take the low-
est place.
10 [a]"But when you are invited, go
and sit down in the lowest place,
so that when he who invited you
comes he may say to you, 'Friend,
go up higher.' Then you will have
glory in the presence of those who
sit at the table with you.
11 [a]"For whoever exalts himself
will be [1]humbled, and he who
humbles himself will be exalted."
12 Then He also said to him who
invited Him, "When you give a
dinner or a supper, do not ask your
friends, your brothers, your rela-
tives, nor rich neighbors, lest they
also invite you back, and you be
repaid.
13 "But when you give a feast, in-
vite [a]*the* poor, *the* [1]maimed, *the*
lame, *the* blind.
14 "And you will be [a]blessed, be-
cause they cannot repay you; for
you shall be repaid at the resur-
rection of the just."

The Parable of the Great Supper

15 Now when one of those who sat
at the table with Him heard these
things, he said to Him, [a]"Blessed
is he who shall eat [1]bread in the
kingdom of God!"
16 [a]Then He said to him, "A cer-
tain man gave a great supper and
invited many,
17 "and [a]sent his servant at sup-
per time to say to those who were
invited, 'Come, for all things are
now ready.'
18 "But they all with one *accord*
began to make excuses. The first
said to him, 'I have bought a piece
of ground, and I must go and see
it. I ask you to have me excused.'
19 "And another said, 'I have
bought five yoke of oxen, and I am
going to test them. I ask you to
have me excused.'
20 "Still another said, 'I have mar-
ried a wife, and therefore I cannot
come.'
21 "So that servant came and re-
ported these things to his master.
Then the master of the house, be-
ing angry, said to his servant, 'Go
out quickly into the streets and
lanes of the city, and bring in here
the poor and *the* [1]maimed and *the*
lame and *the* blind.'
22 "And the servant said, 'Master,
it is done as you commanded, and
still there is room.'
23 "Then the master said to the
servant, 'Go out into the highways
and hedges, and compel *them* to
come in, that my house may be
filled.
24 'For I say to you [a]that none of
those men who were invited shall
taste my supper.' "

Leaving All to Follow Christ

25 Now great multitudes went
with Him. And He turned and said
to them,
26 [a]"If anyone comes to Me [b]and
does not hate his father and

---

35 [b]Ps. 118:26; Matt. 21:9; Mark 11:10; Luke 19:38; John 12:13

CHAPTER 14

3 [a]Matt. 12:10 [1]NU adds *or not*

5 [a][Ex. 23:5; Deut. 22:4]; Luke 13:15 [1]NU, M *son*

10 [a]Prov. 25:6, 7

11 [a]Job 22:29; Ps. 18:27; Prov. 29:23; Matt. 23:12; Luke 18:14; James 4:6; [1 Pet. 5:5] [1]*put down*

13 [a]Neh. 8:10, 12 [1]*crippled*

14 [a][Matt. 25:34–40]

15 [a]Rev. 19:9 [1]M *dinner*

16 [a]Matt. 22:2–14

17 [a]Prov. 9:2, 5

21 [1]*crippled*

24 [a][Matt. 21:43; 22:8; Acts 13:46]

26 [a]Deut. 13:6; 33:9; Matt. 10:37 [b]Rom. 9:13

mother, wife and children, broth-
ers and sisters, [c]yes, and his own
life also, he cannot be My disciple.
27 "And [a]whoever does not bear
his cross and come after Me can-
not be My disciple.
28 "For [a]which of you, intending
to build a tower, does not sit down
first and count the cost, whether
he has *enough* to finish *it*—
29 "lest, after he has laid the foun-
dation, and is not able to finish,
all who see *it* begin to mock him,
30 "saying, 'This man began to
build and was not able to finish.'
31 "Or what king, going to make
war against another king, does not
sit down first and consider
whether he is able with ten thou-
sand to meet him who comes
against him with twenty thou-
sand?
32 "Or else, while the other is still
a great way off, he sends a delega-
tion and asks conditions of peace.
33 "So likewise, whoever of you
[a]does not forsake all that he has
cannot be My disciple.

Tasteless Salt Is Worthless

34 [a]"Salt *is* good; but if the salt
has lost its flavor, how shall it be
seasoned?
35 "It is neither fit for the land nor
for the [1]dunghill, *but* men throw
it out. He who has ears to hear,
let him hear!"

The Parable of the Lost Sheep

15 Then [a]all the tax collectors
and the sinners drew near to
Him to hear Him.
2 And the Pharisees and scribes
complained, saying, "This Man
[1]receives sinners [a]and eats with
them."
3 So He spoke this parable to
them, saying:
4 [a]"What man of you, having a
hundred sheep, if he loses one of
them, does not leave the ninety-
nine in the wilderness, and go af-
ter the one which is lost until he
finds it?
5 "And when he has found *it*, he
lays *it* on his shoulders, rejoicing.
6 "And when he comes home, he
calls together *his* friends and
neighbors, saying to them, [a]'Re-
joice with me, for I have found my
sheep [b]which was lost!'
7 "I say to you that likewise there
will be more joy in heaven over
one sinner who repents [a]than over
ninety-nine [1]just persons who
[b]need no repentance.

The Parable of the Lost Coin

8 "Or what woman, having ten
silver [1]coins, if she loses one coin,
does not light a lamp, sweep the
house, and search carefully until
she finds *it*?
9 "And when she has found *it*,
she calls *her* friends and neighbors
together, saying, 'Rejoice with me,
for I have found the piece which I
lost!'
10 "Likewise, I say to you, there
is joy in the presence of the angels
of God over one sinner who re-
pents."

The Parable of the Lost Son

11 Then He said: "A certain man
had two sons.
12 "And the younger of them said
to *his* father, 'Father, give me the
portion of goods that falls *to me*.'
So he divided to them [a]*his* live-
lihood.
13 "And not many days after, the
younger son gathered all together,
journeyed to a far country, and
there wasted his possessions with
[1]prodigal living.
14 "But when he had spent all,
there arose a severe famine in that
land, and he began to be in want.
15 "Then he went and joined him-
self to a citizen of that country,
and he sent him into his fields to
feed swine.
16 "And he would gladly have
filled his stomach with the [1]pods
that the swine ate, and no one gave
him *anything*.
17 "But when he came to himself,
he said, 'How many of my father's
hired servants have bread enough
and to spare, and I perish with
hunger!
18 'I will arise and go to my father,
and will say to him, "Father, [a]I
have sinned against heaven and
before you,
19 "and I am no longer worthy to
be called your son. Make me like
one of your hired servants." '
20 "And he arose and came to his
father. But [a]when he was still a
great way off, his father saw him

26 [c]Rev. 12:11
27 [a]Matt. 16:24; Mark 8:34; Luke 9:23; [2 Tim. 3:12]
28 [a]Prov. 24:27
33 [a]Matt. 19:27
34 [a]Matt. 5:13; [Mark 9:50]
35 [1]*rubbish heap*

CHAPTER 15

1 [a][Matt. 9:10–13]
2 [a]Acts 11:3; Gal. 2:12 [1]*welcomes*
4 [a]Matt. 18:12–14; 1 Pet. 2:25
6 [a][Rom. 12:15] [b][Luke 19:10; 1 Pet. 2:10, 25]
7 [a][Luke 5:32] [b][Mark 2:17] [1]*upright*
8 [1]Gr. *drachma*, a valuable coin often worn in a ten-piece garland by married women
12 [a]Mark 12:44
13 [1]*wasteful*
16 [1]*carob pods*
18 [a]Ex. 9:27; 10:16; Num. 22:34; Josh. 7:20; 1 Sam. 15:24, 30; 26:21; 2 Sam. 12:13; 24:10, 17; Ps. 51:4; Matt. 27:4
20 [a][Jer. 3:12]; Matt. 9:36; [Acts 2:39; Eph. 2:13, 17]

and had compassion, and ran and
fell on his neck and kissed him.
21 "And the son said to him, 'Father, I have sinned against heaven
[a]and in your sight, and am no
longer worthy to be called your
son.'
22 "But the father said to his servants, [1]'Bring out the best robe and
put *it* on him, and put a ring on
his hand and sandals on *his* feet.
23 'And bring the fatted calf here
and kill *it*, and let us eat and be
merry;
24 [a]'for this my son was dead and
is alive again; he was lost and is
found.' And they began to be
merry.
25 "Now his older son was in the
field. And as he came and drew
near to the house, he heard music
and dancing.
26 "So he called one of the servants and asked what these things
meant.
27 "And he said to him, 'Your
brother has come, and because he
has received him safe and sound,
your father has killed the fatted
calf.'
28 "But he was angry and would
not go in. Therefore his father
came out and pleaded with him.
29 "So he answered and said to
his father, 'Lo, these many years
I have been serving you; I never
transgressed your commandment
at any time; and yet you never
gave me a young goat, that I might
make merry with my friends.
30 'But as soon as this son of
yours came, who has devoured
your livelihood with harlots, you
killed the fatted calf for him.'
31 "And he said to him, 'Son, you
are always with me, and all that I
have is yours.
32 'It was right that we should
make merry and be glad, [a]for your
brother was dead and is alive
again, and was lost and is found.' "

The Parable of the Unjust Steward

16 He also said to His disciples:
"There was a certain rich
man who had a steward, and an
accusation was brought to him
that this man was [1]wasting his
goods.
2 "So he called him and said to
him, 'What is this I hear about
you? Give an [a]account of your
stewardship, for you can no longer
be steward.'
3 "Then the steward said within
himself, 'What shall I do? For my
master is taking the stewardship
away from me. I cannot dig; I am
ashamed to beg.
4 'I have resolved what to do,
that when I am put out of the
stewardship, they may receive me
into their houses.'
5 "So he called every one of his
master's debtors to *him*, and said
to the first, 'How much do you owe
my master?'
6 "And he said, 'A hundred
[1]measures of oil.' So he said to
him, 'Take your bill, and sit down
quickly and write fifty.'
7 "Then he said to another, 'And
how much do you owe?' So he
said, 'A hundred [1]measures of
wheat.' And he said to him, 'Take
your bill, and write eighty.'
8 "So the master commended the
unjust steward because he had
dealt shrewdly. For the sons of this
world are more shrewd in their
generation than [a]the sons of light.
9 "And I say to you, [a]make
friends for yourselves by unrighteous [1]mammon, that when [2]you
fail, they may receive you into an
everlasting home.
10 [a]"He who *is* faithful in *what is*
least is faithful also in much; and
he who is unjust in *what is* least
is unjust also in much.
11 "Therefore if you have not
been faithful in the unrighteous
mammon, who will commit to your
trust the true *riches*?
12 "And if you have not been
faithful in what is another man's,
who will give you what is your
[a]own?
13 [a]"No servant can serve two
masters; for either he will hate the
one and love the other, or else he
will be loyal to the one and despise
the other. You cannot serve God
and mammon."

The Law, the Prophets, and the Kingdom

14 Now the Pharisees, [a]who were
lovers of money, also heard all
these things, and they [1]derided
Him.

---

21 [a]Ps. 51:4
22 [1]NU *Quickly bring*
24 [a]Matt. 8:22; Luke 9:60; 15:32; Rom. 11:15; [Eph. 2:1, 5; 5:14; Col. 2:13; 1 Tim. 5:6]
32 [a]Luke 15:24

CHAPTER 16

1 [1]*squandering*
2 [a][Rom. 14:12; 2 Cor. 5:10; 1 Pet. 4:5, 6]
6 [1]Gr. *batos*, same as Heb. *bath;* 8 or 9 gallons each
7 [1]Gr. *koros*, same as Heb. *kor;* 10 or 12 bushels each
8 [a][John 12:36; Eph. 5:8]; 1 Thess. 5:5
9 [a]Dan. 4:27; [Matt. 6:19; 19:21]; Luke 11:41; [1 Tim. 6:17–19] [1]Lit., in Aram., *wealth* [2]NU *it fails*
10 [a]Matt. 25:21; Luke 19:17
12 [a][1 Pet. 1:3, 4]
13 [a]Matt. 6:24; Gal. 1:10
14 [a]Matt. 23:14 [1]Lit. *turned up their nose at*

15 And He said to them, "You are
those who [a]justify yourselves [b]be-
fore men, but [c]God knows your
hearts. For [d]what is highly es-
teemed among men is an abomina-
tion in the sight of God.
16 [a]"The law and the prophets
were until John. Since that time
the kingdom of God has been
preached, and everyone is press-
ing into it.
17 [a]"And it is easier for heaven
and earth to pass away than for
one [1]tittle of the law to fail.
18 [a]"Whoever divorces his wife
and marries another commits
adultery; and whoever marries her
who is divorced from *her* husband
commits adultery.

The Rich Man and Lazarus

19 "There was a certain rich man
who was clothed in purple and fine
linen and [1]fared sumptuously
every day.
20 "But there was a certain beggar
named Lazarus, full of sores, who
was laid at his gate,
21 "desiring to be fed with [1]the
crumbs which fell from the rich
man's table. Moreover the dogs
came and licked his sores.
22 "So it was that the beggar died,
and was carried by the angels to
[a]Abraham's bosom. The rich man
also died and was buried.
23 "And being in torments in
Hades, he lifted up his eyes and
saw Abraham afar off, and Laza-
rus in his bosom.
24 "Then he cried and said, 'Fa-
ther Abraham, have mercy on me,
and send Lazarus that he may dip
the tip of his finger in water and
[a]cool my tongue; for I [b]am tor-
mented in this flame.'
25 "But Abraham said, 'Son, [a]re-
member that in your lifetime you
received your good things, and
likewise Lazarus evil things; but
now he is comforted and you are
tormented.
26 'And besides all this, between
us and you there is a great gulf
fixed, so that those who want to
pass from here to you cannot, nor
can those from there pass to us.'
27 "Then he said, 'I beg you there-
fore, father, that you would send
him to my father's house,
28 'for I have five brothers, that
he may testify to them, lest they
also come to this place of torment.'
29 "Abraham said to him, [a]'They
have Moses and the prophets; let
them hear them.'
30 "And he said, 'No, father Abra-
ham; but if one goes to them from
the dead, they will repent.'
31 "But he said to him, [a]'If they
do not hear Moses and the proph-
ets, [b]neither will they be per-
suaded though one rise from the
dead.'"

Jesus Warns of Offenses

17 Then He said to the disci-
ples, [a]"It is impossible that
no [1]offenses should come, but
[b]woe *to him* through whom they
do come!
2 "It would be better for him if
a millstone were hung around his
neck, and he were thrown into the
sea, than that he should [1]offend
one of these little ones.
3 "Take heed to yourselves. [a]If
your brother sins [1]against you,
[b]rebuke him; and if he repents, for-
give him.
4 "And if he sins against you
seven times in a day, and seven
times in a day returns [1]to you, say-
ing, 'I repent,' you shall forgive
him."

Faith and Duty

5 And the apostles said to the
Lord, "Increase our faith."
6 [a]So the Lord said, "If you have
faith as a mustard seed, you can
say to this mulberry tree, 'Be
pulled up by the roots and be
planted in the sea,' and it would
obey you.
7 "And which of you, having a
servant plowing or tending sheep,
will say to him when he has come
in from the field, 'Come at once
and sit down to eat'?
8 "But will he not rather say to
him, 'Prepare something for my
supper, and gird yourself [a]and
serve me till I have eaten and
drunk, and afterward you will eat
and drink'?
9 "Does he thank that servant
because he did the things that
were commanded [1]him? I think
not.
10 "So likewise you, when you
have done all those things which

15 [a]Luke 10:29 [b][Matt. 6:2, 5, 16] [c]Ps. 7:9 [d]1 Sam. 16:7
16 [a]Matt. 3:1–12; 4:17; 11:12, 13
17 [a]Is. 40:8; 51:6 [1]The smallest stroke in a Heb. letter
18 [a]1 Cor. 7:10, 11
19 [1]*lived in luxury*
21 [1]NU *what fell*
22 [a]Matt. 8:11
24 [a]Zech. 14:12 [b][Mark 9:42–48]
25 [a]Luke 6:24
29 [a]Acts 15:21; 17:11
31 [a][John 5:46] [b]John 12:10, 11

CHAPTER 17

1 [a][1 Cor. 11:19] [b][2 Thess. 1:6] [1]*stumbling blocks*
2 [1]*cause one of these little ones to stumble*
3 [a][Matt. 18:15, 21] [b][Prov. 17:10] [1]NU omits *against you*
4 [1]M omits *to you*
6 [a][Mark 9:23; 11:23]
8 [a][Luke 12:37]
9 [1]NU omits the rest of v. 9; M omits *him*

you are commanded, say, 'We are
[a]unprofitable servants. We have
done what was our duty to do.' "

Ten Lepers Cleansed

11 Now it happened [a]as He went
to Jerusalem that He passed
through the midst of Samaria and
Galilee.
12 Then as He entered a certain
village, there met Him ten men
who were lepers, [a]who stood afar
off.
13 And they lifted up *their* voices
and said, "Jesus, Master, have
mercy on us!"
14 So when He saw *them*, He
said to them, [a]"Go, show your-
selves to the priests." And so it
was that as they went, they were
cleansed.
15 And one of them, when he saw
that he was healed, returned, and
with a loud voice [a]glorified God,
16 and fell down on *his* face at His
feet, giving Him thanks. And he
was a [a]Samaritan.
17 So Jesus answered and said,
"Were there not ten cleansed? But
where *are* the nine?
18 "Were there not any found who
returned to give glory to God ex-
cept this foreigner?"
19 [a]And He said to him, "Arise, go
your way. Your faith has made
you well."

The Coming of the Kingdom

20 Now when He was asked by
the Pharisees when the kingdom
of God would come, He answered
them and said, "The kingdom of
God does not come with obser-
vation;
21 [a]"nor will they say, [1]'See here!'
or 'See there!' For indeed, [b]the
kingdom of God is [2]within you."
22 Then He said to the disciples,
[a]"The days will come when you
will desire to see one of the days
of the Son of Man, and you will
not see *it*.
23 [a]"And they will say to you,
[1]'Look here!' or 'Look there!' Do
not go after *them* or follow *them*.
24 [a]"For as the lightning that
flashes out of one *part* under
heaven shines to the other *part*
under heaven, so also the Son of
Man will be in His day.
25 [a]"But first He must suffer many
things and be [b]rejected by this
generation.
26 [a]"And as it [b]was in the [c]days
of [d]Noah, so it will be also in the
days of the Son of Man:
27 "They ate, they drank, they
married wives, they were given in
marriage, until the [a]day that Noah
entered the ark, and the flood
came and [b]destroyed them all.
28 [a]"Likewise as it was also in the
days of Lot: They ate, they drank,
they bought, they sold, they
planted, they built;
29 "but on [a]the day that Lot went
out of Sodom it rained fire and
brimstone from heaven and de-
stroyed *them* all.
30 "Even so will it be in the day
when the Son of Man [a]is revealed.
31 "In that day, he [a]who is on the
housetop, and his [1]goods *are* in the
house, let him not come down to
take them away. And likewise the
one who is in the field, let him not
turn back.
32 [a]"Remember Lot's wife.
33 [a]"Whoever seeks to save his
life will lose it, and whoever loses
his life will preserve it.
34 [a]"I tell you, in that night there
will be two [1]*men* in one bed: the
one will be taken and the other will
be left.
35 [a]"Two *women* will be grinding
together: the one will be taken and
the other left.
36 [1]"Two *men* will be in the field:
the one will be taken and the other
left."
37 And they answered and said to
Him, [a]"Where, Lord?" So He said
to them, "Wherever the body is,
there the eagles will be gathered
together."

The Parable of the Persistent Widow

18 Then He spoke a parable to
them, that men [a]always
ought to pray and not lose heart,
2 saying: "There was in a certain
city a judge who did not fear God
nor [1]regard man.
3 "Now there was a widow in
that city; and she came to him,
saying, [1]'Get justice for me from
my adversary.'
4 "And he would not for a while;
but afterward he said within him-
self, 'Though I do not fear God nor
regard man,

10 [a]Rom. 3:12; 11:35
11 [a]Luke 9:51, 52
12 [a]Lev. 13:46
14 [a]Matt. 8:4
15 [a]Luke 5:25; 18:43
16 [a]2 Kin. 17:24
19 [a]Matt. 9:22
21 [a]Luke 17:23 [b][Rom. 14:17] [1]NU reverses *here* and *there* [2]*in your midst*
22 [a]Matt. 9:15
23 [a]Matt. 24:23 [1]NU reverses *here* and *there*
24 [a]Matt. 24:27
25 [a]Mark 8:31; 9:31; 10:33 [b]Luke 9:22
26 [a]Matt. 24:37–39 [b][Gen. 6:5–7] [c][Gen. 6:8–13] [d]1 Pet. 3:20
27 [a]Gen. 7:1–16 [b]Gen. 7:19–23
28 [a]Gen. 19
29 [a]Gen. 19:16, 24, 29
30 [a][2 Thess. 1:7]
31 [a]Mark 13:15 [1]*possessions*
32 [a]Gen. 19:26
33 [a]Matt. 10:39; 16:25
34 [a][1 Thess. 4:17] [1]Or *people*
35 [a]Matt. 24:40, 41
36 [1]NU, M omit v. 36.
37 [a]Matt. 24:28

CHAPTER 18

1 [a]Luke 11:5–10
2 [1]*respect*
3 [1]*Avenge me on*

5 [a]"yet because this widow trou-
bles me I will [1]avenge her, lest by
her continual coming she weary
me.'"
6 Then the Lord said, "Hear what
the unjust judge said.
7 "And [a]shall God not avenge
His own elect who cry out day and
night to Him, though He bears
long with them?
8 "I tell you [a]that He will avenge
them speedily. Nevertheless, when
the Son of Man comes, will He re-
ally find faith on the earth?"

The Parable of the Pharisee and the Tax Collector

9 Also He spoke this parable to
some [a]who trusted in themselves
that they were righteous, and de-
spised others:
10 "Two men went up to the tem-
ple to pray, one a Pharisee and the
other a tax collector.
11 "The Pharisee [a]stood and
prayed thus with himself, [b]'God, I
thank You that I am not like other
men—extortioners, unjust, adul-
terers, or even as this tax collector.
12 'I fast twice a week; I give tithes
of all that I possess.'
13 "And the tax collector, stand-
ing afar off, would not so much as
raise *his* eyes to heaven, but beat
his breast, saying, 'God, be merci-
ful to me a sinner!'
14 "I tell you, this man went down
to his house justified *rather* than
the other; [a]for everyone who ex-
alts himself will be [1]humbled, and
he who humbles himself will be
exalted."

Jesus Blesses Little Children

15 [a]Then they also brought infants
to Him that He might touch them;
but when the disciples saw *it*, they
rebuked them.
16 But Jesus called them to *Him*
and said, "Let the little children
come to Me, and do not forbid
them; for [a]of such is the kingdom
of God.
17 [a]"Assuredly, I say to you, who-
ever does not receive the kingdom
of God as a little child will by no
means enter it."

Jesus Counsels the Rich Young Ruler

18 [a]Now a certain ruler asked
Him, saying, "Good Teacher, what

5 [a]Luke 11:8 [1]*vindicate*
7 [a]Rev. 6:10
8 [a]Heb. 10:37; [2 Pet. 3:8, 9]
9 [a]Prov. 30:12; Luke 10:29; 16:15
11 [a]Ps. 135:2 [b]Is. 1:15; 58:2; Rev. 3:17
14 [a]Job 22:29; Matt. 23:12; Luke 14:11; [James 4:6; 1 Pet. 5:5] [1]*put down*
15 [a]Matt. 19:13–15; Mark 10:13–16
16 [a]Matt. 18:3; 1 Cor. 14:20; 1 Pet. 2:2
17 [a]Matt. 18:3; 19:14; Mark 10:15
18 [a]Matt. 19:16–29; Mark 10:17–30
19 [a]Ps. 86:5; 119:68
20 [a]Ex. 20:12–16; Deut. 5:16–20; Mark 10:19; Rom. 13:9 [b]Eph. 6:2; Col. 3:20
21 [a]Phil. 3:6
22 [a]Matt. 6:19, 20; 19:21; [1 Tim. 6:19]
24 [a]Prov. 11:28; Matt. 19:23; Mark 10:23
27 [a]Job 42:2; Jer. 32:17; Zech. 8:6; Matt. 19:26; Luke 1:37
28 [a]Matt. 19:27 [1]NU *our own*
29 [a]Deut. 33:9
30 [a]Job 42:10
31 [a]Matt. 16:21; 17:22; 20:17; Mark 10:32; Luke 9:51 [b]Ps. 22; [Is. 53] [1]*fulfilled*
32 [a]Matt. 26:67; 27:2, 29, 41; Mark 14:65; 15:1, 19, 20, 31; Luke 23:1; John 18:28; Acts 3:13

shall I do to inherit eternal life?"
19 So Jesus said to him, "Why do
you call Me good? No one *is* good
but [a]One, *that is*, God.
20 "You know the command-
ments: [a]*'Do not commit adultery,'
'Do not murder,' 'Do not steal,' 'Do
not bear false witness,'* [b]*'Honor
your father and your mother.'*"
21 And he said, "All [a]these things
I have kept from my youth."
22 So when Jesus heard these
things, He said to him, "You still
lack one thing. [a]Sell all that you
have and distribute to the poor,
and you will have treasure in
heaven; and come, follow Me."
23 But when he heard this, he be-
came very sorrowful, for he was
very rich.

With God All Things Are Possible

24 And when Jesus saw that he
became very sorrowful, He said,
[a]"How hard it is for those who
have riches to enter the kingdom
of God!
25 "For it is easier for a camel to
go through the eye of a needle than
for a rich man to enter the king-
dom of God."
26 And those who heard it said,
"Who then can be saved?"
27 But He said, [a]"The things
which are impossible with men are
possible with God."
28 [a]Then Peter said, "See, we
have left [1]all and followed You."
29 So He said to them, "As-
suredly, I say to you, [a]there is no
one who has left house or parents
or brothers or wife or children, for
the sake of the kingdom of God,
30 [a]"who shall not receive many
times more in this present time,
and in the age to come eternal
life."

Jesus a Third Time Predicts His Death and Resurrection

31 [a]Then He took the twelve aside
and said to them, "Behold, we are
going up to Jerusalem, and all
things [b]that are written by the
prophets concerning the Son of
Man will be [1]accomplished.
32 "For [a]He will be delivered to
the Gentiles and will be mocked
and insulted and spit upon.
33 "They will scourge *Him* and

kill Him. And the third day He will
rise again."
34 [a]But they understood none of
these things; this saying was hid-
den from them, and they did not
know the things which were spo-
ken.

A Blind Man Receives His Sight

35 [a]Then it happened, as He was
coming near Jericho, that a certain
blind man sat by the road begging.
36 And hearing a multitude pass-
ing by, he asked what it meant.
37 So they told him that Jesus of
Nazareth was passing by.
38 And he cried out, saying, "Je-
sus, [a]Son of David, have mercy on
me!"
39 Then those who went before
warned him that he should be
quiet; but he cried out all the more,
"Son of David, have mercy on
me!"
40 So Jesus stood still and com-
manded him to be brought to Him.
And when he had come near, He
asked him,
41 saying, "What do you want Me
to do for you?" He said, "Lord, that
I may receive my sight."
42 Then Jesus said to him, "Re-
ceive your sight; [a]your faith has
made you well."
43 And immediately he received
his sight, and followed Him, [a]glori-
fying God. And all the people,
when they saw *it*, gave praise to
God.

Jesus Comes to Zacchaeus' House

19 Then *Jesus* entered and
passed through [a]Jericho.
2 Now behold, *there was* a man
named Zacchaeus who was a chief
tax collector, and he was rich.
3 And he sought to [a]see who Je-
sus was, but could not because of
the crowd, for he was of short stat-
ure.
4 So he ran ahead and climbed
up into a sycamore tree to see Him,
for He was going to pass that *way*.
5 And when Jesus came to the
place, He looked up [1]and saw him,
and said to him, "Zacchaeus,
[2]make haste and come down, for
today I must stay at your house."
6 So he [1]made haste and came
down, and received Him joyfully.
7 But when they saw *it*, they all
[1]complained, saying, [a]"He has
gone to be a guest with a man who
is a sinner."
8 Then Zacchaeus stood and said
to the Lord, "Look, Lord, I give
half of my goods to the [a]poor; and
if I have taken anything from any-
one by [b]false accusation, [c]I restore
fourfold."
9 And Jesus said to him, "Today
salvation has come to this house,
because [a]he also is [b]a son of Abra-
ham;
10 [a]"for the Son of Man has come
to seek and to save that which was
lost."

The Parable of the Minas

11 Now as they heard these
things, He spoke another parable,
because He was near Jerusalem
and because [a]they thought the
kingdom of God would appear im-
mediately.
12 [a]Therefore He said: "A certain
nobleman went into a far country
to receive for himself a kingdom
and to return.
13 "So he called ten of his ser-
vants, delivered to them ten
[1]minas, and said to them, 'Do busi-
ness till I come.'
14 [a]"But his citizens hated him,
and sent a delegation after him,
saying, 'We will not have this *man*
to reign over us.'
15 "And so it was that when he
returned, having received the
kingdom, he then commanded
these servants, to whom he had
given the money, to be called to
him, that he might know how
much every man had gained by
trading.
16 "Then came the first, saying,
'Master, your mina has earned ten
minas.'
17 "And he said to him, [a]'Well
done, good servant; because you
were [b]faithful in a very little, have
authority over ten cities.'
18 "And the second came, saying,
'Master, your mina has earned five
minas.'
19 "Likewise he said to him, 'You
also be over five cities.'
20 "Then another came, saying,
'Master, here is your mina, which
I have kept put away in a hand-
kerchief.
21 [a]'For I feared you, because you

34 [a]Mark 9:32; Luke 2:50; 9:45; [John 10:6; 12:16]
35 [a]Matt. 20:29–34; Mark 10:46–52
38 [a]Matt. 9:27
42 [a]Luke 17:19
43 [a]Luke 5:26; Acts 4:21; 11:18

CHAPTER 19

1 [a]Josh. 6:26; 1 Kin. 16:34
3 [a]John 12:21
5 [1]NU omits *and saw him* [2]*hurry*
6 [1]*hurried*
7 [a]Matt. 9:11; Luke 5:30; 15:2 [1]*grumbled*
8 [a][Ps. 41:1] [b]Luke 3:14 [c]Ex. 22:1; Lev. 6:5; Num. 5:7; 1 Sam. 12:3; 2 Sam. 12:6
9 [a]Luke 3:8; 13:16; [Rom. 4:16; Gal. 3:7] [b][Luke 13:16]
10 [a]Matt. 18:11; [Luke 5:32; Rom. 5:8]
11 [a]Acts 1:6
12 [a]Matt. 25:14–30; Mark 13:34
13 [1]Gr. *mna*, same as Heb. *minah*, each worth about three months' salary
14 [a][John 1:11]
17 [a]Matt. 25:21, 23 [b]Luke 16:10
21 [a]Matt. 25:24

are [1]an austere man. You collect
what you did not deposit, and reap
what you did not sow.'
22 "And he said to him, [a]'Out of
your own mouth I will judge you,
you wicked servant. [b]You knew
that I was an austere man, collect-
ing what I did not deposit and
reaping what I did not sow.
23 'Why then did you not put my
money in the bank, that at my
coming I might have collected it
with interest?'
24 "And he said to those who
stood by, 'Take the mina from him,
and give *it* to him who has ten mi-
nas.'
25 ("But they said to him, 'Master,
he has ten minas.')
26 'For I say to you, [a]that to every-
one who has will be given; and
from him who does not have, even
what he has will be taken away
from him.
27 'But bring here those enemies
of mine, who did not want me to
reign over them, and slay *them* be-
fore me.' "

The Triumphal Entry

28 When He had said this, [a]He
went on ahead, going up to Jerusa-
lem.
29 [a]And it came to pass, when He
drew near to [1]Bethphage and
[b]Bethany, at the mountain called
[c]Olivet, *that* He sent two of His
disciples,
30 saying, "Go into the village op-
posite *you,* where as you enter you
will find a colt tied, on which no
one has ever sat. Loose it and
bring *it here.*
31 "And if anyone asks you, 'Why
are you loosing *it?*' thus you shall
say to him, 'Because the Lord has
need of it.' "
32 So those who were sent went
their way and found *it* just [a]as He
had said to them.
33 But as they were loosing the
colt, the owners of it said to them,
"Why are you loosing the colt?"
34 And they said, "The Lord has
need of him."
35 Then they brought him to Je-
sus. [a]And they threw their own
clothes on the colt, and they set
Jesus on him.
36 And as He went, *many* spread
their clothes on the road.
37 Then, as He was now drawing
near the descent of the Mount of
Olives, the whole multitude of the
disciples began to [a]rejoice and
praise God with a loud voice for
all the mighty works they had
seen,
38 saying:

[a]" *'Blessed is the King who comes in*
the name of the LORD!'
[b]Peace in heaven and glory in the
highest!"

39 And some of the Pharisees
called to Him from the crowd,
"Teacher, rebuke Your disciples."
40 But He answered and said to
them, "I tell you that if these
should keep silent, [a]the stones
would immediately cry out."

Jesus Weeps over Jerusalem

41 Now as He drew near, He saw
the city and [a]wept over it,
42 saying, "If you had known,
even you, especially in this [a]your
day, the things *that* [b]*make* for
your [c]peace! But now they are hid-
den from your eyes.
43 "For days will come upon you
when your enemies will [a]build an
embankment around you, sur-
round you and close you in on
every side,
44 [a]"and level you, and your chil-
dren within you, to the ground;
and [b]they will not leave in you one
stone upon another, [c]because you
did not know the time of your visi-
tation."

Jesus Cleanses the Temple

45 [a]Then He went into the temple
and began to drive out those who
[1]bought and sold in it,
46 saying to them, "It is written,
[a]*'My house* [1]*is a house of prayer,'*
but you have made it a [b]*'den of*
thieves.' "
47 And He [a]was teaching daily in
the temple. But [b]the chief priests,
the scribes, and the leaders of the
people sought to destroy Him,
48 and were unable to do any-
thing; for all the people were very
attentive to [a]hear Him.

Jesus' Authority Questioned

20 Now [a]it happened on one of
those days, as He taught the

21 [1]a *severe*
22 [a]2 Sam. 1:16; Job 15:6; [Matt. 12:37] [b]Matt. 25:26
26 [a]Matt. 13:12; 25:29; Mark 4:25; Luke 8:18
28 [a]Mark 10:32
29 [a]Matt. 21:1; Mark 11:1 [b]Matt. 26:6; John 12:1 [c]John 8:1; Acts 1:12 [1]M *Bethsphage*
32 [a]Luke 22:13
35 [a]2 Kin. 9:13; Matt. 21:7; Mark 11:7
37 [a]Luke 13:17; 18:43
38 [a]Ps. 118:26; Luke 13:35 [b]Luke 2:14; [Eph. 2:14]
40 [a]Hab. 2:11
41 [a]Is. 53:3; John 11:35
42 [a]Ps. 95:7, 8; Heb. 3:13 [b][Luke 1:77–79; Acts 10:36] [c][Rom. 5:1]
43 [a]Is. 29:3, 4; Jer. 6:3, 6; Luke 21:20
44 [a]1 Kin. 9:7, 8; Mic. 3:12 [b]Matt. 24:2; Mark 13:2; Luke 21:6 [c][Dan. 9:24; Luke 1:68, 78; 1 Pet. 2:12]
45 [a]Mal. 3:1; Matt. 21:12, 13; Mark 11:11, 15–17; John 2:13–16 [1]NU *were selling, saying*
46 [a]Is. 56:7 [b]Jer. 7:11 [1]NU *shall be*
47 [a]Luke 21:37; 22:53 [b]Mark 11:18; Luke 20:19; John 7:19; 8:37
48 [a]Luke 21:38

CHAPTER 20

1 [a]Matt. 21:23–27; Mark 11:27–33

people in the temple and preached the gospel, *that* the chief priests and the scribes, together with the elders, confronted *Him*

2 and spoke to Him, saying, "Tell us, [a]by what authority are You doing these things? Or who is he who gave You this authority?"

3 But He answered and said to them, "I also will ask you one thing, and answer Me:

4 "The [a]baptism of John—was it from heaven or from men?"

5 And they reasoned among themselves, saying, "If we say, 'From heaven,' He will say, 'Why [1]then did you not believe him?'

6 "But if we say, 'From men,' all the people will stone us, [a]for they are persuaded that John was a prophet."

7 So they answered that they did not know where *it was* from.

8 And Jesus said to them, "Neither will I tell you by what authority I do these things."

The Parable of the Wicked Vinedressers

9 Then He began to tell the people this parable: [a]"A certain man planted a vineyard, leased it to [1]vinedressers, and went into a far country for a long time.

10 "Now at [1]vintage-time he [a]sent a servant to the vinedressers, that they might give him some of the fruit of the vineyard. But the vinedressers beat him and sent *him* away empty-handed.

11 "Again he sent another servant; and they beat him also, treated *him* shamefully, and sent *him* away empty-handed.

12 "And again he sent a third; and they wounded him also and cast *him* out.

13 "Then the owner of the vineyard said, 'What shall I do? I will send my beloved son. Probably they will respect *him* when they see him.'

14 "But when the vinedressers saw him, they reasoned among themselves, saying, 'This is the [a]heir. Come, [b]let us kill him, that the inheritance may be [c]ours.'

15 "So they cast him out of the vineyard and [a]killed *him*. Therefore what will the owner of the vineyard do to them?

16 "He will come and destroy those vinedressers and give the vineyard to [a]others." And when they heard *it* they said, "Certainly not!"

17 Then He looked at them and said, "What then is this that is written:

[a]'The stone which the builders rejected
Has become the chief cornerstone'?

18 "Whoever falls on that stone will be [a]broken; but [b]on whomever it falls, it will grind him to powder."

19 And the chief priests and the scribes that very hour sought to lay hands on Him, but they [1]feared the people—for they knew He had spoken this parable against them.

The Pharisees: Is It Lawful to Pay Taxes to Caesar?

20 [a]So they watched *Him*, and sent spies who pretended to be righteous, that they might seize on His words, in order to deliver Him to the power and the authority of the governor.

21 Then they asked Him, saying, [a]"Teacher, we know that You say and teach rightly, and You do not show personal favoritism, but teach the way of God in truth:

22 "Is it lawful for us to pay taxes to Caesar or not?"

23 But He perceived their craftiness, and said to them, [1]"Why do you test Me?

24 "Show Me a denarius. Whose image and inscription does it have?" They answered and said, "Caesar's."

25 And He said to them, [a]"Render[1] therefore to Caesar the things that are Caesar's, and to God the things that are God's."

26 But they could not catch Him in His words in the presence of the people. And they marveled at His answer and kept silent.

The Sadducees: What About the Resurrection?

27 [a]Then some of the Sadducees, [b]who deny that there is a resurrection, came to *Him* and asked Him,

2 [a]Acts 4:7; 7:27
4 [a]John 1:26, 31
5 [1]NU, M omit *then*
6 [a]Matt. 14:5; 21:26; Mark 6:20; Luke 7:24–30
9 [a]Ps. 80:8; Matt. 21:33–46; Mark 12:1–12 [1]*tenant farmers*
10 [a]2 Kin. 17:13, 14; 2 Chr. 36:15, 16; [Acts 7:52; 1 Thess. 2:15] [1]Lit. *the season*
14 [a][Heb. 1:1–3] [b]Matt. 27:21–23 [c]John 11:47, 48
15 [a]Luke 23:33; Acts 2:22, 23; 3:15
16 [a][John 1:11–13]; Rom. 11:1, 11; 1 Cor. 6:15; Gal. 2:17; 3:21; 6:14
17 [a]Ps. 118:22; Matt. 21:42; 1 Pet. 2:7, 8
18 [a]Is. 8:14, 15 [b][Dan. 2:34, 35, 44, 45]; Matt. 21:44
19 [1]M *were afraid—for*
20 [a]Matt. 22:15
21 [a]Matt. 22:16; Mark 12:14
23 [1]NU omits *Why do you test Me?*
25 [a]Matt. 17:24–27; Rom. 13:7; [1 Pet. 2:13–17] [1]*Pay*
27 [a]Matt. 22:23–33; Mark 12:18–27 [b]Acts 23:6, 8

28 saying: "Teacher, Moses wrote to us *that* if a man's brother dies, having a wife, and he dies without children, his brother should take his wife and raise up offspring for his brother.

29 "Now there were seven brothers. And the first took a wife, and died without children.

30 "And the second [1]took her as wife, and he died childless.

31 "Then the third took her, and in like manner the seven [1]also; and they left no children, and died.

32 "Last of all the woman died also.

33 "Therefore, in the resurrection, whose wife does she become? For all seven had her as wife."

34 Jesus answered and said to them, "The sons of this age marry and are given in marriage.

35 "But those who are [a]counted worthy to attain that age, and the resurrection from the dead, neither marry nor are given in marriage;

36 "nor can they die anymore, for [a]they are equal to the angels and are sons of God, [b]being sons of the resurrection.

37 "But even Moses showed in the *burning* bush *passage* that the dead are raised, when he called the Lord [a]'*the God of Abraham, the God of Isaac, and the God of Jacob.*'

38 "For He is not the God of the dead but of the living, for [a]all live to Him."

39 Then some of the scribes answered and said, "Teacher, You have spoken well."

40 But after that they dared not question Him anymore.

Jesus: How Can David Call His Descendant Lord?

41 And He said to them, [a]"How can they say that the Christ is the Son of David?

42 "Now David himself said in the Book of Psalms:

[a]'The LORD said to my Lord,
"Sit at My right hand,
43 *Till I make Your enemies Your*
footstool."'

44 "Therefore David calls Him '*Lord*'; [a]how is He then his Son?"

Beware of the Scribes

45 [a]Then, in the hearing of all the people, He said to His disciples,

46 [a]"Beware of the scribes, who desire to go around in long robes, [b]love greetings in the marketplaces, the best seats in the synagogues, and the best places at feasts,

47 [a]"who devour widows' houses, and for a [b]pretense make long prayers. These will receive greater condemnation."

The Widow's Two Mites

21 And He looked up [a]and saw the rich putting their gifts into the treasury,

2 and He saw also a certain [a]poor widow putting in two [b]mites.[1]

3 So He said, "Truly I say to you [a]that this poor widow has put in more than all;

4 "for all these out of their abundance have put in offerings [1]for God, but she out of her poverty put in [a]all the livelihood that she had."

Jesus Predicts the Destruction of the Temple

5 [a]Then, as some spoke of the temple, how it was [1]adorned with beautiful stones and donations, He said,

6 "These things which you see—the days will come in which [a]not *one* stone shall be left upon another that shall not be thrown down."

The Signs of the Times and the End of the Age

7 So they asked Him, saying, "Teacher, but when will these things be? And what sign *will there be* when these things are about to take place?"

8 And He said: [a]"Take heed that you not be deceived. For many will come in My name, saying, 'I am *He*,' and, 'The time has drawn near.' [1]Therefore do not [2]go after them.

9 "But when you hear of [a]wars and commotions, do not be terrified; for these things must come to pass first, but the end *will not come* immediately."

10 [a]Then He said to them, "Nation

30 [1]NU omits the rest of v. 30.
31 [1]NU, M *also left no children*
35 [a]Phil. 3:11
36 [a][1 Cor. 15:42, 49, 52; 1 John 3:2] [b]Rom. 8:23
37 [a]Ex. 3:1–6, 15; Acts 7:30–32
38 [a][Rom. 6:10, 11; 14:8, 9; Heb. 11:16]
41 [a]Matt. 22:41–46; Mark 12:35–37
42 [a]Ps. 110:1; Acts 2:34, 35
44 [a]Acts 13:22, 23; Rom. 1:3; 9:4, 5
45 [a]Matt. 23:1–7; Mark 12:38–40
46 [a]Matt. 23:5 [b]Luke 11:43; 14:7
47 [a]Matt. 23:14 [b][Matt. 6:5, 6]

CHAPTER 21

1 [a]Mark 12:41–44
2 [a][2 Cor. 6:10] [b]Mark 12:42 [1]Gr. *lepta*, very small copper coins
3 [a][2 Cor. 8:12]
4 [a][2 Cor. 8:12] [1]NU omits *for God*
5 [a]Matt. 24:1; Mark 13:1 [1]*decorated*
6 [a]Is. 64:10, 11; Lam. 2:6–9; Mic. 3:12; Luke 19:41–44
8 [a]Matt. 24:4; Mark 13:5; Eph. 5:6; 2 Thess. 2:3; [1 John 4:1] [1]NU omits *Therefore* [2]*follow*
9 [a]Rev. 6:4
10 [a]Matt. 24:7

will rise against nation, and king-
dom against kingdom.
11 "And there will be great
[a]earthquakes in various places,
and famines and pestilences; and
there will be fearful sights and
great signs from heaven.
12 [a]"But before all these things,
they will lay their hands on you
and persecute *you*, delivering *you*
up to the synagogues and [b]prisons.
[c]You will be brought before kings
and rulers [d]for My name's sake.
13 "But [a]it will turn out for you
as an occasion for testimony.
14 [a]"Therefore settle *it* in your
hearts not to meditate beforehand
on what you will [1]answer;
15 "for I will give you a mouth and
wisdom [a]which all your adversar-
ies will not be able to contradict
or [1]resist.
16 [a]"You will be betrayed even by
parents and brothers, relatives and
friends; and they will put [b]*some* of
you to death.
17 "And [a]you will be hated by all
for My name's sake.
18 [a]"But not a hair of your head
shall be lost.
19 "By your patience possess your
souls.

The Destruction of Jerusalem

20 [a]"But when you see Jerusalem
surrounded by armies, then know
that its desolation is near.
21 "Then let those who are in Ju-
dea flee to the mountains, let those
who are in the midst of her depart,
and let not those who are in the
country enter her.
22 "For these are the days of ven-
geance, that [a]all things which are
written may be fulfilled.
23 [a]"But woe to those who are
pregnant and to those who are
nursing babies in those days! For
there will be great distress in the
land and wrath upon this people.
24 "And they will fall by the edge
of the sword, and be led away cap-
tive into all nations. And Jerusa-
lem will be trampled by Gentiles
[a]until the times of the Gentiles are
fulfilled.

The Coming of the Son of Man

25 [a]"And there will be signs in the
sun, in the moon, and in the stars;
and on the earth distress of na-
tions, with perplexity, the sea and
the waves roaring;
26 "men's hearts failing them
from fear and the expectation of
those things which are coming on
the earth, [a]for the powers of the
heavens will be shaken.
27 "Then they will see the Son of
Man [a]coming in a cloud with
power and great glory.
28 "Now when these things begin
to happen, look up and lift up your
heads, because [a]your redemption
draws near."

The Parable of the Fig Tree

29 [a]Then He spoke to them a para-
ble: "Look at the fig tree, and all
the trees.
30 "When they are already bud-
ding, you see and know for your-
selves that summer is now near.
31 "So you also, when you see
these things happening, know that
the kingdom of God is near.
32 "Assuredly, I say to you, this
generation will by no means pass
away till all things take place.
33 [a]"Heaven and earth will pass
away, but My [b]words will by no
means pass away.

The Importance of Watching

34 "But [a]take heed to yourselves,
lest your hearts be weighed down
with [1]carousing, drunkenness, and
[b]cares of this life, and that Day
come on you unexpectedly.
35 "For [a]it will come as a snare
on all those who dwell on the face
of the whole earth.
36 [a]"Watch therefore, and [b]pray
always that you may [1]be counted
[c]worthy to escape all these things
that will come to pass, and [d]to
stand before the Son of Man."
37 [a]And in the daytime He was
teaching in the temple, but [b]at
night He went out and stayed on
the mountain called Olivet.
38 Then early in the morning all
the people came to Him in the tem-
ple to hear Him.

The Plot to Kill Jesus

22 Now [a]the Feast of Unleav-
ened Bread drew near,
which is called Passover.
2 And [a]the chief priests and the
scribes sought how they might kill
Him, for they feared the people.

---

11 [a]Rev. 6:12
12 [a][Rev. 2:10] [b]Acts 4:3; 5:18; 12:4; 16:24 [c]Acts 25:23 [d]1 Pet. 2:13
13 [a][Phil. 1:12–14, 28]
14 [a]Luke 12:11 [1]*say in defense*
15 [a]Acts 6:10 [1]*withstand*
16 [a]Mic. 7:6 [b]Acts 7:59; 12:2
17 [a]Matt. 10:22
18 [a]Matt. 10:30
20 [a]Mark 13:14
22 [a][Dan. 9:24–27]
23 [a]Matt. 24:19
24 [a][Dan. 9:27; 12:7]
25 [a][2 Pet. 3:10–12]
26 [a]Matt. 24:29
27 [a]Rev. 1:7; 14:14
28 [a][Rom. 8:19, 23]
29 [a]Mark 13:28
33 [a]Matt. 24:35 [b]Is. 40:8
34 [a]1 Thess. 5:6 [b]Luke 8:14 [1]*dissipation*
35 [a]Rev. 3:3; 16:15
36 [a]Matt. 24:42; 25:13 [b]Luke 18:1 [c]Luke 20:35 [d][Eph. 6:13] [1]NU *have strength to*
37 [a]John 8:1, 2 [b]Luke 22:39

CHAPTER 22

1 [a]Matt. 26:2–5
2 [a]John 11:47

3 [a]Then Satan entered Judas,
surnamed Iscariot, who was num-
bered among the [b]twelve.
4 So he went his way and con-
ferred with the chief priests and
captains, how he might betray
Him to them.
5 And they were glad, and
[a]agreed to give him money.
6 So he promised and sought op-
portunity to [a]betray Him to them
in the absence of the multitude.

Jesus and His Disciples Prepare the Passover

7 [a]Then came the Day of Un-
leavened Bread, when the Pass-
over must be [1]killed.
8 And He sent Peter and John,
saying, "Go and prepare the Pass-
over for us, that we may eat."
9 So they said to Him, "Where
do You want us to prepare?"
10 And He said to them, "Behold,
when you have entered the city, a
man will meet you carrying a
pitcher of water; follow him into
the house which he enters.
11 "Then you shall say to the mas-
ter of the house, 'The Teacher says
to you, "Where is the guest room
where I may eat the Passover with
My disciples?"'
12 "Then he will show you a large,
furnished upper room; there make
ready."
13 So they went and [a]found it just
as He had said to them, and they
prepared the Passover.

Jesus Institutes the Lord's Supper

14 [a]When the hour had come, He
sat down, and the [1]twelve apostles
with Him.
15 Then He said to them, "With
fervent desire I have desired to eat
this Passover with you before I
suffer;
16 "for I say to you, I will no
longer eat of it [a]until it is fulfilled
in the kingdom of God."
17 Then He took the cup, and gave
thanks, and said, "Take this and
divide *it* among yourselves;
18 "for [a]I say to you, [1]I will not
drink of the fruit of the vine until
the kingdom of God comes."
19 [a]And He took bread, gave
thanks and broke *it*, and gave *it*
to them, saying, "This is My [b]body
which is given for you; [c]do this in
remembrance of Me."
20 Likewise He also *took* the cup
after supper, saying, [a]"This cup *is*
the new covenant in My blood,
which is shed for you.
21 [a]"But behold, the hand of My
betrayer *is* with Me on the table.
22 [a]"And truly the Son of Man
goes [b]as it has been determined,
but woe to that man by whom He
is betrayed!"
23 [a]Then they began to question
among themselves, which of them
it was who would do this thing.

The Disciples Argue About Greatness

24 [a]Now there was also a dispute
among them, as to which of them
should be considered the greatest.
25 [a]And He said to them, "The
kings of the Gentiles exercise lord-
ship over them, and those who ex-
ercise authority over them are
called 'benefactors.'
26 [a]"But not so *among* you; on the
contrary, [b]he who is greatest
among you, let him be as the youn-
ger, and he who governs as he who
serves.
27 [a]"For who *is* greater, he who
sits at the table, or he who serves?
Is it not he who sits at the table?
Yet [b]I am among you as the One
who serves.
28 "But you are those who have
continued with Me in [a]My trials.
29 "And [a]I bestow upon you a
kingdom, just as My Father be-
stowed *one* upon Me,
30 "that [a]you may eat and drink
at My table in My kingdom, [b]and
sit on thrones judging the twelve
tribes of Israel."

Jesus Predicts Peter's Denial

31 [1]And the Lord said, "Simon, Si-
mon! Indeed, [a]Satan has asked for
you, that he may [b]sift *you* as
wheat.
32 "But [a]I have prayed for you,
that your faith should not fail; and
when you have returned to *Me*,
[b]strengthen your brethren."
33 But he said to Him, "Lord, I am
ready to go with You, both to
prison and to death."
34 [a]Then He said, "I tell you, Pe-
ter, the rooster shall not crow this
day before you will deny three
times that you know Me."

---

3 [a]Mark 14:10, 11 [b]Matt. 10:2–4
5 [a]Zech. 11:12
6 [a]Ps. 41:9
7 [a]Matt. 26:17–19 [1]Sacrificed
13 [a]Luke 19:32
14 [a]Mark 14:17 [1]NU omits *twelve*
16 [a][Rev. 19:9]
18 [a]Mark 14:25 [1]NU adds *from now on*
19 [a]Matt. 26:26 [b][1 Pet. 2:24] [c]1 Cor. 11:23–26
20 [a]1 Cor. 10:16
21 [a]John 13:21, 26, 27
22 [a]Matt. 26:24 [b]Acts 2:23
23 [a]John 13:22, 25
24 [a]Mark 9:34
25 [a]Mark 10:42–45
26 [a][1 Pet. 5:3] [b]Luke 9:48
27 [a][Luke 12:37] [b]Phil. 2:7
28 [a][Heb. 2:18; 4:15]
29 [a]Matt. 24:47
30 [a][Matt. 8:11] [b][Rev. 3:21]
31 [a]1 Pet. 5:8 [b]Amos 9:9 [1]NU omits *And the Lord said*
32 [a][John 17:9, 11, 15] [b]John 21:15–17
34 [a]John 13:37, 38

Supplies for the Road

35 [a]And He said to them, "When I sent you without money bag, knapsack, and sandals, did you lack anything?" So they said, "Nothing."
36 Then He said to them, "But now, he who has a money bag, let him take *it*, and likewise a knapsack; and he who has no sword, let him sell his garment and buy one.
37 "For I say to you that this which is written must still be [1]accomplished in Me: [a]*'And He was numbered with the transgressors.'* For the things concerning Me have an end."
38 So they said, "Lord, look, here *are* two swords." And He said to them; "It is enough."

The Prayer in the Garden

39 [a]Coming out, [b]He went to the Mount of Olives, as He was accustomed, and His disciples also followed Him.
40 [a]When He came to the place, He said to them, "Pray that you may not enter into temptation."
41 [a]And He was withdrawn from them about a stone's throw, and He knelt down and prayed,
42 saying, "Father, if it is Your will, take this cup away from Me; nevertheless [a]not My will, but Yours, be done."
43 [1]Then [a]an angel appeared to Him from heaven, strengthening Him.
44 [a]And being in agony, He prayed more earnestly. Then His sweat became like great drops of blood falling down to the ground.
45 When He rose up from prayer, and had come to His disciples, He found them sleeping from sorrow.
46 Then He said to them, "Why [a]do you sleep? Rise and [b]pray, lest you enter into temptation."

Betrayal and Arrest in Gethsemane

47 And while He was still speaking, [a]behold, a multitude; and he who was called [b]Judas, one of the twelve, went before them and drew near to Jesus to kiss Him.
48 But Jesus said to him, "Judas, are you betraying the Son of Man with a [a]kiss?"
49 When those around Him saw what was going to happen, they said to Him, "Lord, shall we strike with the sword?"
50 And [a]one of them struck the servant of the high priest and cut off his right ear.
51 But Jesus answered and said, "Permit even this." And He touched his ear and healed him.
52 [a]Then Jesus said to the chief priests, captains of the temple, and the elders who had come to Him, "Have you come out, as against a [b]robber, with swords and clubs?
53 "When I was with you daily in the [a]temple, you did not try to seize Me. But this is your [b]hour, and the power of darkness."

Peter Denies Jesus, and Weeps Bitterly

54 [a]Having arrested Him, they led *Him* and brought Him into the high priest's house. [b]But Peter followed at a distance.
55 [a]Now when they had kindled a fire in the midst of the courtyard and sat down together, Peter sat among them.
56 And a certain servant girl, seeing him as he sat by the fire, looked intently at him and said, "This man was also with Him."
57 But he denied [1]Him, saying, "Woman, I do not know Him."
58 [a]And after a little while another saw him and said, "You also are of them." But Peter said, "Man, I am not!"
59 [a]Then after about an hour had passed, another confidently affirmed, saying, "Surely this *fellow* also was with Him, for he is a [b]Galilean."
60 But Peter said, "Man, I do not know what you are saying!" Immediately, while he was still speaking, [1]the rooster crowed.
61 And the Lord turned and looked at Peter. Then [a]Peter remembered the word of the Lord, how He had said to him, [b]"Before the rooster [1]crows, you will deny Me three times."
62 So Peter went out and wept bitterly.

Jesus Mocked and Beaten

63 [a]Now the men who held Jesus mocked Him and [b]beat Him.

35 [a]Matt. 10:9
37 [a]Is. 53:12 [1]*fulfilled*
39 [a]John 18:1 [b]Luke 21:37
40 [a]Mark 14:32–42
41 [a]Matt. 26:39
42 [a]John 4:34; 5:30; 6:38; 8:29
43 [a]Matt. 4:11 [1]NU brackets vv. 43 and 44 as not in the original text.
44 [a][Heb. 5:7]
46 [a]Luke 9:32 [b]Luke 22:40
47 [a]John 18:3–11 [b]Acts 1:16, 17
48 [a][Prov. 27:6]
50 [a]Matt. 26:51
52 [a]Matt. 26:55 [b]Luke 23:32
53 [a]Luke 19:47, 48 [b][John 12:27]
54 [a]Matt. 26:57 [b]John 18:15
55 [a]Mark 14:66–72
57 [1]NU *it*
58 [a]John 18:25
59 [a]Mark 14:70 [b]Acts 1:11; 2:7
60 [1]NU, M *a rooster*
61 [a]Matt. 26:75 [b]John 13:38 [1]NU adds *today*
63 [a]Ps. 69:1, 4, 7–9 [b]Is. 50:6

64 [1]And having blindfolded Him,
they [a]struck Him on the face and
asked Him, saying, "Prophesy!
Who is the one who struck You?"
65 And many other things they
blasphemously spoke against Him.

Jesus Faces the Sanhedrin

66 [a]As soon as it was day, [b]the el-
ders of the people, both chief
priests and scribes, came together
and led Him into their council, say-
ing,
67 [a]"If You are the Christ, tell us."
But He said to them, "If I tell you,
you will [b]by no means believe.
68 "And if I [1]also ask *you,* you will
by no means answer [2]Me or let
Me go.
69 [a]"Hereafter the Son of Man
will sit on the right hand of the
power of God."
70 Then they all said, "Are You
then the Son of God?" So He said
to them, [a]"You *rightly* say that I
am."
71 [a]And they said, "What further
testimony do we need? For we
have heard it ourselves from His
own mouth."

Jesus Handed Over to Pontius Pilate

23 Then [a]the whole multitude
of them arose and led Him
to [b]Pilate.
2 And they began to [a]accuse
Him, saying, "We found this *fellow*
[b]perverting [1]the nation, and [c]for-
bidding to pay taxes to Caesar, say-
ing [d]that He Himself is Christ, a
King."
3 [a]Then Pilate asked Him, say-
ing, "Are You the King of the
Jews?" He answered him and said,
"*It is as* you say."
4 So Pilate said to the chief
priests and the crowd, [a]"I find no
fault in this Man."
5 But they were the more fierce,
saying, "He stirs up the people,
teaching throughout all Judea, be-
ginning from [a]Galilee to this
place."

Jesus Faces Herod

6 When Pilate heard [1]of Galilee,
he asked if the Man were a Gali-
lean.
7 And as soon as he knew that
He belonged to [a]Herod's jurisdic-
tion, he sent Him to Herod, who
was also in Jerusalem at that time.
8 Now when Herod saw Jesus,
[a]he was exceedingly glad; for he
had desired for a long *time* to see
Him, because [b]he had heard many
things about Him, and he hoped
to see some miracle done by Him.
9 Then he questioned Him with
many words, but He answered him
[a]nothing.
10 And the chief priests and
scribes stood and vehemently ac-
cused Him.
11 [a]Then Herod, with his [1]men of
war, treated Him with contempt
and mocked *Him,* arrayed Him in
a gorgeous robe, and sent Him
back to Pilate.
12 That very day [a]Pilate and
Herod became friends with each
other, for previously they had been
at enmity with each other.

Taking the Place of Barabbas

13 [a]Then Pilate, when he had
called together the chief priests,
the rulers, and the people,
14 said to them, [a]"You have
brought this Man to me, as one
who misleads the people. And in-
deed, [b]having examined *Him* in
your presence, I have found no
fault in this Man concerning those
things of which you accuse Him;
15 "no, neither did Herod, for [1]I
sent you back to him; and indeed
nothing deserving of death has
been done by Him.
16 [a]"I will therefore chastise Him
and release *Him*"
17 [a](for[1] it was necessary for him
to release one to them at the feast).
18 And [a]they all cried out at once,
saying, "Away with this *Man,* and
release to us Barabbas"—
19 who had been thrown into
prison for a certain rebellion made
in the city, and for murder.
20 Pilate, therefore, wishing to re-
lease Jesus, again called out to
them.
21 But they shouted, saying, "Cru-
cify *Him,* crucify Him!"
22 Then he said to them the third
time, "Why, what evil has He
done? I have found no reason for
death in Him. I will therefore chas-
tise Him and let *Him* go."
23 But they were insistent, de-
manding with loud voices that He
be crucified. And the voices of

64 [a]Zech. 13:7 [1]NU *And having blindfolded Him, they asked Him*
66 [a]Matt. 27:1 [b]Acts 4:26
67 [a]Matt. 26:63–66 [b]Luke 20:5–7
68 [1]NU omits *also* [2]NU omits the rest of v. 68.
69 [a]Heb. 1:3; 8:1
70 [a]Matt. 26:64; 27:11
71 [a]Mark 14:63

CHAPTER 23
1 [a]John 18:28 [b]Luke 3:1; 13:1
2 [a]Acts 24:2 [b]Acts 17:7 [c]Matt. 17:27 [d]John 19:12 [1]NU *our*
3 [a]1 Tim. 6:13
4 [a][1 Pet. 2:22]
5 [a]John 7:41
6 [1]NU omits *of Galilee*
7 [a]Luke 3:1; 9:7; 13:31
8 [a]Luke 9:9 [b]Matt. 14:1
9 [a]John 19:9
11 [a]Is. 53:3 [1]*troops*
12 [a]Acts 4:26, 27
13 [a]Mark 15:14
14 [a]Luke 23:1, 2 [b]Luke 23:4
15 [1]NU *he sent Him back to us*
16 [a]John 19:1
17 [a]John 18:39 [1]NU omits v. 17.
18 [a]Acts 3:13–15

these men [1]and of the chief priests
prevailed.
24 So [a]Pilate gave sentence that it
should be as they requested.
25 [a]And he released [1]to them the
one they requested, who for rebel-
lion and murder had been thrown
into prison; but he delivered Jesus
to their will.

The King on a Cross

26 [a]Now as they led Him away,
they laid hold of a certain man, Si-
mon a Cyrenian, who was coming
from the country, and on him they
laid the cross that he might bear
it after Jesus.
27 And a great multitude of the
people followed Him, and women
who also mourned and lamented
Him.
28 But Jesus, turning to them,
said, "Daughters of Jerusalem, do
not weep for Me, but weep for
yourselves and for your children.
29 [a]"For indeed the days are com-
ing in which they will say, 'Blessed
are the barren, wombs that never
bore, and breasts which never
nursed!'
30 "Then they will begin [a]*'to say*
to the mountains, "Fall on us!" and
to the hills, "Cover us!"'
31 [a]"For if they do these things in
the green wood, what will be done
in the dry?"
32 [a]There were also two others,
criminals, led with Him to be put
to death.
33 And [a]when they had come to
the place called Calvary, there
they crucified Him, and the crimi-
nals, one on the right hand and the
other on the left.
34 [1]Then Jesus said, "Father, [a]for-
give them, for [b]they do not know
what they do." And [c]they divided
His garments and cast lots.
35 And [a]the people stood looking
on. But even the [b]rulers with them
sneered, saying, "He saved others;
let Him save Himself if He is the
Christ, the chosen of God."
36 The soldiers also mocked Him,
coming and offering Him [a]sour
wine,
37 and saying, "If You are the
King of the Jews, save Yourself."
38 [a]And an inscription also was
[1]written over Him in letters of
Greek, Latin, and Hebrew:

THIS IS THE KING OF THE
JEWS.

39 [a]Then one of the criminals who
were hanged blasphemed Him,
saying, [1]"If You are the Christ,
save Yourself and us."
40 But the other, answering, re-
buked him, saying, "Do you not
even fear God, seeing you are un-
der the same condemnation?
41 "And we indeed justly, for we
receive the due reward of our
deeds; but this Man has done
[a]nothing wrong."
42 Then he said [1]to Jesus, "Lord,
remember me when You come into
Your kingdom."
43 And Jesus said to him, "As-
suredly, I say to you, today you
will be with Me in [a]Paradise."

Jesus Dies on the Cross

44 [a]Now it [1]was about the sixth
hour, and there was darkness over
all the earth until the ninth hour.
45 Then the sun was [1]darkened,
and [a]the veil of the temple was
torn in [2]two.
46 And when Jesus had cried out
with a loud voice, He said, "Father,
[a]*'into Your hands I commit My*
spirit.'" [b]Having said this, He
breathed His last.
47 [a]So when the centurion saw
what had happened, he glorified
God, saying, "Certainly this was
a righteous Man!"
48 And the whole crowd who
came together to that sight, seeing
what had been done, beat their
breasts and returned.
49 [a]But all His acquaintances, and
the women who followed Him
from Galilee, stood at a distance,
watching these things.

Jesus Buried in Joseph's Tomb

50 [a]Now behold, *there was* a man
named Joseph, a council member,
a good and just man.
51 He had not consented to their
decision and deed. *He was* from
Arimathea, a city of the Jews,
[a]who[1] himself was also waiting for
the kingdom of God.
52 This man went to Pilate and
asked for the body of Jesus.
53 [a]Then he took it down,
wrapped it in linen, and laid it in
a tomb *that was* hewn out of the

23 [1]NU omits *and of the chief priests*
24 [a]Mark 15:15
25 [a]Is. 53:8 [1]NU, M omit *to them*
26 [a]Matt. 27:32
29 [a]Matt. 24:19
30 [a]Hos. 10:8; Rev. 6:16, 17; 9:6
31 [a][Jer. 25:29]
32 [a]Is. 53:9, 12
33 [a]John 19:17–24
34 [a]1 Cor. 4:12 [b]Acts 3:17 [c]Matt. 27:35 [1]NU brackets the first sentence as a later addition.
35 [a]Ps. 22:17 [b]Matt. 27:39
36 [a]Ps. 69:21
38 [a]John 19:19 [1]NU omits *written* and *in letters of Greek, Latin, and Hebrew*
39 [a]Mark 15:32 [1]NU *Are You not the Christ? Save*
41 [a][Heb. 7:26]
42 [1]NU *"Jesus, remember me*
43 [a][Rev. 2:7]
44 [a]Matt. 27:45–56 [1]NU adds *already*
45 [a]Matt. 27:51 [1]NU *obscured* [2]*the middle*
46 [a]Ps. 31:5 [b]John 19:30
47 [a]Mark 15:39
49 [a]Ps. 38:11
50 [a]Matt. 27:57–61
51 [a]Luke 2:25, 38 [1]NU *who was waiting*
53 [a]Mark 15:46

rock, where no one had ever lain
before.
54 That day was [a]the Preparation,
and the Sabbath drew near.
55 And the women [a]who had
come with Him from Galilee fol-
lowed after, and [b]they observed
the tomb and how His body was
laid.
56 Then they returned and [a]pre-
pared spices and fragrant oils.
And they rested on the Sab-
bath [b]according to the command-
ment.

He Is Risen

24 Now [a]on the first *day* of the
week, very early in the
morning, they, [1]and certain *other*
women with them, came to the
tomb [b]bringing the spices which
they had prepared.
2 [a]But they found the stone
rolled away from the tomb.
3 [a]Then they went in and did
not find the body of the Lord
Jesus.
4 And it happened, as they were
[1]greatly perplexed about this, that
[a]behold, two men stood by them
in shining garments.
5 Then, as they were afraid and
bowed *their* faces to the earth,
they said to them, "Why do you
seek the living among the dead?
6 "He is not here, but is risen!
[a]Remember how He spoke to you
when He was still in Galilee,
7 "saying, 'The Son of Man must
be [a]delivered into the hands of sin-
ful men, and be crucified, and the
third day rise again.' "
8 And [a]they remembered His
words.
9 [a]Then they returned from the
tomb and told all these things to
the eleven and to all the rest.
10 It was Mary Magdalene, [a]Jo-
anna, Mary *the mother* of James,
and the other *women* with them,
who told these things to the apos-
tles.
11 [a]And their words seemed to
them like [1]idle tales, and they did
not believe them.
12 [a]But Peter arose and ran to the
tomb; and stooping down, he saw
the linen cloths [1]lying by them-
selves; and he departed, marvel-
ing to himself at what had hap-
pened.

The Road to Emmaus

13 [a]Now behold, two of them were
traveling that same day to a village
called Emmaus, which was [1]seven
miles from Jerusalem.
14 And they talked together of all
these things which had happened.
15 So it was, while they conversed
and reasoned, that [a]Jesus Him-
self drew near and went with
them.
16 But [a]their eyes were restrained,
so that they did not know Him.
17 And He said to them, "What
kind of conversation *is* this that
you have with one another as you
[1]walk and are sad?"
18 Then the one [a]whose name was
Cleopas answered and said to
Him, "Are You the only stranger
in Jerusalem, and have You not
known the things which happened
there in these days?"
19 And He said to them, "What
things?" So they said to Him, "The
things concerning Jesus of Naza-
reth, [a]who was a Prophet [b]mighty
in deed and word before God and
all the people,
20 [a]"and how the chief priests and
our rulers delivered Him to be con-
demned to death, and crucified
Him.
21 "But we were hoping [a]that it
was He who was going to redeem
Israel. Indeed, besides all this, to-
day is the third day since these
things happened.
22 "Yes, and [a]certain women of
our company, who arrived at the
tomb early, astonished us.
23 "When they did not find His
body, they came saying that they
had also seen a vision of angels
who said He was alive.
24 "And [a]certain of those *who*
were with us went to the tomb and
found *it* just as the women had
said; but Him they did not see."
25 Then He said to them, "O fool-
ish ones, and slow of heart to be-
lieve in all that the prophets have
spoken!
26 [a]"Ought not the Christ to have
suffered these things and to enter
into His [b]glory?"
27 And beginning at [a]Moses and
[b]all the Prophets, He [1]expounded
to them in all the Scriptures the
things concerning Himself.

54 [a]Matt. 27:62
55 [a]Luke 8:2 [b]Mark 15:47
56 [a]Mark 16:1 [b]Ex. 20:10

CHAPTER 24

1 [a]John 20:1–8 [b]Luke 23:56 [1]NU omits *and certain other women with them*
2 [a]Mark 16:4
3 [a]Mark 16:5
4 [a]John 20:12 [1]NU omits *greatly*
6 [a]Luke 9:22
7 [a]Luke 9:44; 11:29, 30; 18:31–33
8 [a]John 2:19–22
9 [a]Mark 16:10
10 [a]Luke 8:3
11 [a]Luke 24:25 [1]*nonsense*
12 [a]John 20:3–6 [1]NU omits *lying*
13 [a]Mark 16:12 [1]Lit. *60 stadia*
15 [a][Matt. 18:20]
16 [a]John 20:14; 21:4
17 [1]NU *walk? And they stood still, looking sad.*
18 [a]John 19:25
19 [a]Matt. 21:11 [b]Acts 7:22
20 [a]Acts 13:27, 28
21 [a]Luke 1:68; 2:38
22 [a]Mark 16:10
24 [a]Luke 24:12
26 [a]Acts 17:2, 3 [b][1 Pet. 1:10–12]
27 [a][Deut. 18:15] [b][Is. 7:14; 9:6] [1]*explained*

The Disciples' Eyes Opened

28 Then they drew near to the vil-
lage where they were going, and
[a]He [1]indicated that He would have
gone farther.
29 But [a]they constrained Him,
saying, [b]"Abide with us, for it is
toward evening, and the day is far
spent." And He went in to stay
with them.
30 Now it came to pass, as [a]He sat
at the table with them, that He
took bread, blessed and broke *it*,
and gave it to them.
31 Then their eyes were opened
and they knew Him; and He van-
ished from their sight.
32 And they said to one another,
"Did not our heart burn within us
while He talked with us on the
road, and while He opened the
Scriptures to us?"
33 So they rose up that very hour
and returned to Jerusalem, and
found the eleven and those *who
were* with them gathered together,
34 saying, "The Lord is risen in-
deed, and [a]has appeared to Si-
mon!"
35 And they told about the things
that had happened on the road,
and how He was [1]known to them
in the breaking of bread.

Jesus Appears to His Disciples

36 [a]Now as they said these things,
Jesus Himself stood in the midst
of them, and said to them, "Peace
to you."
37 But they were terrified and
frightened, and supposed they had
seen [a]a spirit.
38 And He said to them, "Why are
you troubled? And why do doubts
arise in your hearts?
39 "Behold My hands and My feet,
that it is I Myself. [a]Handle Me and
see, for a [b]spirit does not have
flesh and bones as you see I have."
40 [1]When He had said this, He
showed them His hands and His
feet.
41 But while they still did not be-
lieve [a]for joy, and marveled, He
said to them, [b]"Have you any food
here?"
42 So they gave Him a piece of a
broiled fish [1]and some honey-
comb.
43 [a]And He took *it* and ate in their
presence.

The Scriptures Opened

44 Then He said to them, [a]"These
are the words which I spoke to you
while I was still with you, that all
things must be fulfilled which
were written in the Law of Moses
and *the* Prophets and *the* Psalms
concerning Me."
45 And [a]He opened their under-
standing, that they might compre-
hend the Scriptures.
46 Then He said to them, [a]"Thus
it is written, [1]and thus it was nec-
essary for the Christ to suffer and
to rise from the dead the third
day,
47 "and that repentance and [a]re-
mission of sins should be preached
in His name [b]to all nations, begin-
ning at Jerusalem.
48 "And [a]you are witnesses of
these things.
49 [a]"Behold, I send the Promise of
My Father upon you; but tarry in
the city [1]of Jerusalem until you
are endued with power from on
high."

The Ascension

50 And He led them out [a]as far as
Bethany, and He lifted up His
hands and blessed them.
51 [a]Now it came to pass, while He
blessed them, that He was parted
from them and carried up into
heaven.
52 [a]And they worshiped Him, and
returned to Jerusalem with great
joy,
53 and were continually [a]in the
temple [1]praising and blessing God.
[2]Amen.

28 [a]Mark 6:48 [1]*acted as if*
29 [a]Gen. 19:2, 3 [b][John 14:23]
30 [a]Matt. 14:19
34 [a]1 Cor. 15:5
35 [1]*recognized*
36 [a]Mark 16:14
37 [a]Mark 6:49
39 [a]John 20:20, 27 [b][1 Cor. 15:50]
40 [1]Some printed New Testaments omit v. 40. It is found in nearly all Gr. mss.
41 [a]Gen. 45:26 [b]John 21:5
42 [1]NU omits *and some honeycomb*
43 [a]Acts 10:39–41
44 [a]Matt. 16:21; 17:22; 20:18
45 [a]Acts 16:14
46 [a]Acts 17:3 [1]NU *that the Christ should suffer and rise*
47 [a]Acts 5:31; 10:43; 13:38; 26:18 [b][Jer. 31:34]
48 [a][Acts 1:8]
49 [a]Joel 2:28 [1]NU omits *of Jerusalem*
50 [a]Acts 1:12
51 [a]Mark 16:19
52 [a]Matt. 28:9
53 [a]Acts 2:46 [1]NU omits *praising and* [2]NU omits *Amen.*

The Gospel According to

John

JUST as a coin has two sides, both valid, so Jesus Christ has two natures, both valid. Luke presents Christ in His humanity as the Son of Man; John portrays Him in His deity as the Son of God. John's purpose is crystal clear: to set forth Christ in His deity in order to spark believing faith in his readers. John's gospel is topical, not primarily chronological, and it revolves around seven miracles and seven "I am" statements of Christ.

Following an extended eyewitness description of the Upper Room meal and discourse, John records events leading up to the Resurrection, the final climactic proof that Jesus is who He claims to be—the Son of God.

The title of the Fourth Gospel follows the same format as the titles of the synoptic Gospels: *Kata Ioannen*, "According to John." As with the others, the word "Gospel" was added later. *Ioannes* is derived from the Hebrew name *Johanan*, "Yahweh Has Been Gracious."

The Eternal Word

IN the beginning [a]was the Word,
and the [b]Word was [c]with God,
and the Word was [d]God.
2 [a]He was in the beginning with
God.
3 [a]All things were made through
Him, and without Him nothing
was made that was made.
4 [a]In Him was life, and [b]the life
was the light of men.
5 And [a]the light shines in the
darkness, and the darkness did not
[1]comprehend it.

John's Witness: The True Light

6 There was a [a]man sent from
God, whose name *was* John.
7 This man came for a [a]witness,
to bear witness of the Light, that
all through him might [b]believe.
8 He was not that Light, but *was*
sent to bear witness of that [a]Light.
9 [a]That[1] was the true Light which
gives light to every man coming
into the world.
10 He was in the world, and the
world was made through Him, and
[a]the world did not know Him.
11 [a]He came to His [1]own, and His
[2]own did not receive Him.
12 But [a]as many as received Him,
to them He gave the [1]right to become children of God, to those
who believe in His name:
13 [a]who were born, not of blood,

CHAPTER 1
1 [a]1 John 1:1 [b]Rev. 19:13 [c][John 17:5] [d][1 John 5:20]
2 [a]Gen. 1:1
3 [a][Col. 1:16, 17]
4 [a][1 John 5:11] [b]John 8:12; 9:5; 12:46
5 [a][John 3:19] [1]Or *overcome*
6 [a]Matt. 3:1–17
7 [a]John 3:25–36; 5:33–35 [b][John 3:16]
8 [a]Is. 9:2; 49:6
9 [a]Is. 49:6 [1]Or *That was the true Light which, coming into the world, gives light to every man.*
10 [a]Heb. 1:2
11 [a][Luke 19:14] [1]His own things or domain [2]His own people
12 [a]Gal. 3:26 [1]*authority*
13 [a][1 Pet. 1:23]
14 [a]Rev. 19:13 [b]Gal. 4:4 [c]Heb. 2:11 [d]Is. 40:5 [e][John 8:32; 14:6; 18:37]
15 [a]John 3:32 [b][Matt. 3:11] [c][Col. 1:17]

nor of the will of the flesh, nor of
the will of man, but of God.

The Word Becomes Flesh

14 [a]And the Word [b]became [c]flesh
and dwelt among us, and [d]we beheld His glory, the glory as of the
only begotten of the Father, [e]full
of grace and truth.
15 [a]John bore witness of Him and
cried out, saying, "This was He of
whom I said, [b]'He who comes after
me [1]is preferred before me, [c]for He
was before me.' "
16 [1]And of His [a]fullness we have
all received, and grace for grace.
17 For [a]the law was given through
Moses, *but* [b]grace and [c]truth came
through Jesus Christ.
18 [a]No one has seen God at any
time. [b]The only begotten [1]Son,
who is in the bosom of the Father,
He has declared *Him*.

A Voice in the Wilderness

19 Now this is [a]the testimony of
John, when the Jews sent priests
and Levites from Jerusalem to ask
him, "Who are you?"
20 [a]He confessed, and did not
deny, but confessed, "I am not the
Christ."

[1]*ranks higher than I* **16** [a][Col. 1:19; 2:9] [1]NU *For*
17 [a][Ex. 20:1] [b][Rom. 5:21; 6:14] [c][John 8:32; 14:6; 18:37] **18** [a]Ex. 33:20 [b]1 John 4:9 [1]NU *God*
19 [a]John 5:33 **20** [a]Luke 3:15

21 And they asked him, "What
then? Are you Elijah?" He said, "I
am not." "Are you [a]the Prophet?"
And he answered, "No."
22 Then they said to him, "Who
are you, that we may give an
answer to those who sent us?
What do you say about your-
self?"
23 He said: [a]"I *am*

[b]'*The voice of one crying in the*
wilderness:
"Make straight the way of the
LORD,"'

as the prophet Isaiah said."
24 Now those who were sent were
from the Pharisees.
25 And they asked him, saying,
"Why then do you baptize if you
are not the Christ, nor Elijah, nor
the Prophet?"
26 John answered them, saying,
[a]"I baptize with water, [b]but there
stands One among you whom you
do not know.
27 [a]"It is He who, coming after
me, [1]is preferred before me, whose
sandal strap I am not worthy to
loose."
28 These things were done [a]in
[1]Bethabara beyond the Jordan,
where John was baptizing.

The Lamb of God

29 The next day John saw Jesus
coming toward him, and said, "Be-
hold! [a]The Lamb of God [b]who
takes away the sin of the world!
30 "This is He of whom I said, 'Af-
ter me comes a Man who [1]is pre-
ferred before me, for He was be-
fore me.'
31 "I did not know Him; but that
He should be revealed to Israel,
[a]therefore I came baptizing with
water."
32 [a]And John bore witness, say-
ing, "I saw the Spirit descending
from heaven like a dove, and He
remained upon Him.
33 "I did not know Him, but He
who sent me to baptize with water
said to me, 'Upon whom you see
the Spirit descending, and remain-
ing on Him, [a]this is He who bap-
tizes with the Holy Spirit.'
34 "And I have seen and testified
that this is the [a]Son of God."

21 [a]Deut. 18:15, 18
23 [a]Matt. 3:3 [b]Is. 40:3
26 [a]Matt. 3:11 [b]Mal. 3:1
27 [a]Acts 19:4 [1]*ranks higher than I*
28 [a]Judg. 7:24 [1]NU, M *Bethany*
29 [a]Rev. 5:6–14 [b][1 Pet. 2:24]
30 [1]*ranks higher than I*
31 [a]Matt. 3:6
32 [a]Mark 1:10
33 [a]Matt. 3:11
34 [a]John 11:27
36 [a]John 1:29
37 [a]Matt. 4:20, 22
40 [a]Matt. 4:18
41 [1]Lit. *Anointed One*
42 [a]Matt. 16:18 [1]NU *John* [2]Gr. *Petros,* usually translated *Peter*
43 [a]John 6:5; 12:21, 22; 14:8, 9
44 [a]John 12:21
45 [a]John 21:2 [b]Luke 24:27 [c][Zech. 6:12] [d][Matt. 2:23] [e]Luke 3:23
46 [a]John 7:41, 42, 52
47 [a]Ps. 32:2; 73:1

The First Disciples

35 Again, the next day, John stood
with two of his disciples.
36 And looking at Jesus as He
walked, he said, [a]"Behold the
Lamb of God!"
37 The two disciples heard him
speak, and they [a]followed Jesus.
38 Then Jesus turned, and seeing
them following, said to them,
"What do you seek?" They said to
Him, "Rabbi" (which is to say,
when translated, Teacher), "where
are You staying?"
39 He said to them, "Come and
see." They came and saw where
He was staying, and remained
with Him that day (now it was
about the tenth hour).
40 One of the two who heard
John *speak,* and followed Him,
was [a]Andrew, Simon Peter's
brother.
41 He first found his own brother
Simon, and said to him, "We have
found the [1]Messiah" (which is
translated, the Christ).
42 And he brought him to Jesus.
Now when Jesus looked at him, He
said, "You are Simon the son of
[1]Jonah. [a]You shall be called Ce-
phas" (which is translated, [2]A
Stone).

Philip and Nathanael

43 The following day Jesus
wanted to go to Galilee, and He
found [a]Philip and said to him,
"Follow Me."
44 Now [a]Philip was from Beth-
saida, the city of Andrew and Pe-
ter.
45 Philip found [a]Nathanael and
said to him, "We have found Him
of whom [b]Moses in the law, and
also the [c]prophets, wrote—Jesus
[d]of Nazareth, the [e]son of Joseph."
46 And Nathanael said to him,
[a]"Can anything good come out of
Nazareth?" Philip said to him,
"Come and see."
47 Jesus saw Nathanael coming
toward Him, and said of him, "Be-
hold, [a]an Israelite indeed, in whom
is no deceit!"
48 Nathanael said to Him, "How
do You know me?" Jesus an-
swered and said to him, "Before
Philip called you, you were
under the fig tree, I saw you."
49 Nathanael answered and said

to Him, "Rabbi, [a]You are the Son
of God! You are [b]the King of Is-
rael!"
50 Jesus answered and said to
him, "Because I said to you, 'I saw
you under the fig tree,' do you be-
lieve? You will see greater things
than these."
51 And He said to him, "Most as-
suredly, I say to you, [a]hereafter[1]
you shall see heaven open, and the
angels of God ascending and de-
scending upon the Son of Man."

Water Turned to Wine

2 On the third day there was a
[a]wedding in [b]Cana of Galilee,
and the [c]mother of Jesus was
there.
2 Now both Jesus and His disci-
ples were invited to the wedding.
3 And when they ran out of wine,
the mother of Jesus said to Him,
"They have no wine."
4 Jesus said to her, [a]"Woman,
[b]what does your concern have to
do with Me? [c]My hour has not yet
come."
5 His mother said to the servants,
"Whatever He says to you, do *it*."
6 Now there were set there six
waterpots of stone, [a]according to
the manner of purification of the
Jews, containing twenty or thirty
gallons apiece.
7 Jesus said to them, "Fill the
waterpots with water." And they
filled them up to the brim.
8 And He said to them, "Draw
some out now, and take *it* to the
master of the feast." And they
took *it*.
9 When the master of the feast
had tasted [a]the water that was
made wine, and did not know
where it came from (but the ser-
vants who had drawn the water
knew), the master of the feast
called the bridegroom.
10 And he said to him, "Every
man at the beginning sets out the
good wine, and when the *guests*
have well drunk, then the inferior.
You have kept the good wine until
now!"
11 This [a]beginning of signs Jesus
did in Cana of Galilee, [b]and [1]mani-
fested His glory; and His disciples
believed in Him.
12 After this He went down to
[a]Capernaum, He, His mother, [b]His
brothers, and His disciples; and
they did not stay there many days.

Jesus Cleanses the Temple

13 [a]Now the Passover of the Jews
was at hand, and Jesus went up
to Jerusalem.
14 [a]And He found in the temple
those who sold oxen and sheep
and doves, and the money chang-
ers [1]doing business.
15 When He had made a whip of
cords, He drove them all out of the
temple, with the sheep and the
oxen, and poured out the chang-
ers' money and overturned the ta-
bles.
16 And He said to those who sold
doves, "Take these things away!
Do not make [a]My Father's house
a house of merchandise!"
17 Then His disciples remem-
bered that it was written, [a]"*Zeal
for Your house* [1]*has eaten Me up.*"
18 So the Jews answered and said
to Him, [a]"What sign do You show
to us, since You do these things?"
19 Jesus answered and said to
them, [a]"Destroy this temple, and
in three days I will raise it up."
20 Then the Jews said, "It has
taken forty-six years to build this
temple, and will You raise it up in
three days?"
21 But He was speaking [a]of the
temple of His body.
22 Therefore, when He had risen
from the dead, [a]His disciples re-
membered that He had said this [1]to
them; and they believed the Scrip-
ture and the word which Jesus had
said.

The Discerner of Hearts

23 Now when He was in Jerusa-
lem at the Passover, during the
feast, many believed in His name
when they saw the [a]signs which
He did.
24 But Jesus did not commit Him-
self to them, because He [a]knew all
men,
25 and had no need that anyone
should testify of man, for [a]He
knew what was in man.

The New Birth

3 There was a man of the Phari-
sees named Nicodemus, a ruler
of the Jews.
2 [a]This man came to Jesus by

49 [a]Matt. 14:33; [b]Matt 21:5
51 [a]Gen. 28:12 [1]NU omits *hereafter*

CHAPTER 2

1 [a][Heb. 13:4] [b]John 4:46 [c]John 19:25
4 [a]John 19:26 [b]2 Sam. 16:10 [c]John 7:6, 8, 30; 8:20
6 [a][Mark 7:3]
9 [a]John 4:46
11 [a]John 4:54 [b][John 1:14] [1]*revealed*
12 [a]Matt. 4:13 [b]Matt. 12:46; 13:55
13 [a]Deut. 16:1–6
14 [a]Mark 11:15, 17 [1]Lit. *sitting*
16 [a]Luke 2:49
17 [a]Ps. 69:9 [1]NU, M *will eat*
18 [a]Matt. 12:38
19 [a]Matt. 26:61; 27:40
21 [a][1 Cor. 3:16; 6:19]
22 [a]Luke 24:8 [1]NU, M omit *to them*
23 [a][Acts 2:22]
24 [a]Rev. 2:23
25 [a]Matt. 9:4

CHAPTER 3

2 [a]John 7:50; 19:39

night and said to Him, "Rabbi, we
know that You are a teacher come
from God; for [b]no one can do these
signs that You do unless [c]God is
with him."
3 Jesus answered and said to
him, "Most assuredly, I say to you,
[a]unless one is born [1]again, he can-
not see the kingdom of God."
4 Nicodemus said to Him, "How
can a man be born when he is
old? Can he enter a second time
into his mother's womb and be
born?"
5 Jesus answered, "Most as-
suredly, I say to you, [a]unless one
is born of water and the Spirit, he
cannot enter the kingdom of God.
6 "That which is born of the flesh
is [a]flesh, and that which is born
of the Spirit is spirit.
7 "Do not marvel that I said to
you, 'You must be born again.'
8 [a]"The wind blows where it
wishes, and you hear the sound of
it, but cannot tell where it comes
from and where it goes. So is
everyone who is born of the
Spirit."
9 Nicodemus answered and said
to Him, [a]"How can these things
be?"
10 Jesus answered and said to
him, "Are you the teacher of Is-
rael, and do not know these
things?
11 [a]"Most assuredly, I say to you,
We speak what We know and tes-
tify what We have seen, and [b]you
do not receive Our witness.
12 "If I have told you earthly
things and you do not believe, how
will you believe if I tell you heav-
enly things?
13 [a]"No one has ascended to
heaven but He who came down
from heaven, *that is,* the Son of
Man [1]who is in heaven.
14 [a]"And as Moses lifted up the
serpent in the wilderness, even so
[b]must the Son of Man be lifted up,
15 "that whoever [a]believes in Him
should [1]not perish but [b]have eter-
nal life.
16 [a]"For God so loved the world
that He gave His only begotten
[b]Son, that whoever believes in
Him should not perish but have
everlasting life.
17 [a]"For God did not send His Son
into the world to condemn the

2 [b]John 9:16, 33 [c][Acts 10:38]
3 [a][1 Pet. 1:23] [1]Or *from above*
5 [a][Acts 2:38]
6 [a]1 Cor. 15:50
8 [a]Eccl. 11:5
9 [a]John 6:52, 60
11 [a][Matt. 11:27] [b]John 3:32; 8:14
13 [a]Eph. 4:9 [1]NU omits *who is in heaven*
14 [a]Num. 21:9 [b]John 8:28; 12:34; 19:18
15 [a]John 6:47 [b]John 3:36 [1]NU omits *not perish but*
16 [a]Rom. 5:8 [b][Is. 9:6]
17 [a]Luke 9:56
18 [a]John 5:24; 6:40, 47; 20:31
19 [a][John 1:4, 9–11]
20 [a]Eph. 5:11, 13
21 [a]1 Cor. 15:10
22 [a]John 4:1, 2
23 [a]1 Sam. 9:4 [b]Matt. 3:5, 6
24 [a]Matt. 4:12; 14:3
26 [a]John 1:7, 15, 27, 34 [b]Mark 2:2; 3:10; 5:24
27 [a]1 Cor. 3:5, 6; 4:7
28 [a]John 1:19–27 [b]Mal. 3:1
29 [a][2 Cor. 11:2] [b]Song 5:1
30 [a][Is. 9:7]
31 [a]John 3:13; 8:23 [b]Matt. 28:18 [c]1 Cor. 15:47

world, but that the world through
Him might be saved.
18 [a]"He who believes in Him is not
condemned; but he who does not
believe is condemned already, be-
cause he has not believed in the
name of the only begotten Son of
God.
19 "And this is the condemnation,
[a]that the light has come into the
world, and men loved darkness
rather than light, because their
deeds were evil.
20 "For [a]everyone practicing evil
hates the light and does not come
to the light, lest his deeds should
be exposed.
21 "But he who does the truth
comes to the light, that his deeds
may be clearly seen, that they have
been [a]done in God."

John the Baptist Exalts Christ

22 After these things Jesus and
His disciples came into the land of
Judea, and there He remained with
them [a]and baptized.
23 Now John also was baptizing
in Aenon near [a]Salim, because
there was much water there. [b]And
they came and were baptized.
24 For [a]John had not yet been
thrown into prison.
25 Then there arose a dispute be-
tween *some* of John's disciples and
the Jews about purification.
26 And they came to John and
said to him, "Rabbi, He who was
with you beyond the Jordan, [a]to
whom you have testified—behold,
He is baptizing, and all [b]are com-
ing to Him!"
27 John answered and said, [a]"A
man can receive nothing unless it
has been given to him from
heaven.
28 "You yourselves bear me wit-
ness, that I said, [a]'I am not the
Christ,' but, [b]'I have been sent be-
fore Him.'
29 [a]"He who has the bride is the
bridegroom; but [b]the friend of the
bridegroom, who stands and hears
him, rejoices greatly because of
the bridegroom's voice. Therefore
this joy of mine is fulfilled.
30 [a]"He must increase, but I *must*
decrease.
31 [a]"He who comes from above [b]is
above all; [c]he who is of the earth
is earthly and speaks of the earth.

[d]He who comes from heaven is
above all.
32 "And [a]what He has seen and
heard, that He testifies; and no one
receives His testimony.
33 "He who has received His testi-
mony [a]has certified that God is
true.
34 [a]"For He whom God has sent
speaks the words of God, for God
does not give the Spirit [b]by mea-
sure.
35 [a]"The Father loves the Son,
and has given all things into His
hand.
36 [a]"He who believes in the Son
has everlasting life; and he who
does not believe the Son shall not
see life, but the [b]wrath of God
abides on him."

A Samaritan Woman Meets Her Messiah

4 Therefore, when the Lord
knew that the Pharisees had
heard that Jesus made and [a]bap-
tized more disciples than John
2 (though Jesus Himself did not
baptize, but His disciples),
3 He left Judea and departed
again to Galilee.
4 But He needed to go through
Samaria.
5 So He came to a city of Sa-
maria which is called Sychar, near
the plot of ground that [a]Jacob
[b]gave to his son Joseph.
6 Now Jacob's well was there.
Jesus therefore, being wearied
from *His* journey, sat thus by the
well. It was about the sixth hour.
7 A woman of Samaria came to
draw water. Jesus said to her,
"Give Me a drink."
8 For His disciples had gone
away into the city to buy food.
9 Then the woman of Samaria
said to Him, "How is it that You,
being a Jew, ask a drink from me,
a Samaritan woman?" For [a]Jews
have no dealings with [b]Samari-
tans.
10 Jesus answered and said to her,
"If you knew the [a]gift of God, and
who it is who says to you, 'Give
Me a drink,' you would have asked
Him, and He would have given you
[b]living water."
11 The woman said to Him, "Sir,
You have nothing to draw with,

31 [d]John 6:33
32 [a]John 3:11; 15:15
33 [a]1 John 5:10
34 [a]John 7:16 [b]John 1:16
35 [a][Heb. 2:8]
36 [a]John 3:16, 17; 6:47 [b]Rom. 1:18

CHAPTER 4

1 [a]John 3:22, 26
5 [a]Gen. 33:19 [b]Gen. 48:22
9 [a]Acts 10:28 [b]2 Kin. 17:24
10 [a][Rom. 5:15] [b]Is. 12:3; 44:3
14 [a][John 6:35, 58] [b]John 7:37, 38
15 [a]John 6:34, 35; 17:2, 3
19 [a]Luke 7:16, 39; 24:19
20 [a]Judg. 9:7 [b]Deut. 12:5, 11
21 [a]1 Tim. 2:8
22 [a][2 Kin. 17:28–41] [b][Rom. 3:1; 9:4, 5]
23 [a][Heb. 13:10–14] [b]Phil. 3:3 [c][John 1:17]
24 [a]2 Cor. 3:17
25 [a]Deut. 18:15 [b]John 4:29, 39
26 [a]Matt. 26:63, 64

and the well is deep. Where then
do You get that living water?
12 "Are You greater than our
father Jacob, who gave us the
well, and drank from it himself,
as well as his sons and his live-
stock?"
13 Jesus answered and said to her,
"Whoever drinks of this water will
thirst again,
14 "but [a]whoever drinks of the
water that I shall give him will
never thirst. But the water that I
shall give him [b]will become in him
a fountain of water springing up
into everlasting life."
15 [a]The woman said to Him, "Sir,
give me this water, that I may not
thirst, nor come here to draw."
16 Jesus said to her, "Go, call your
husband, and come here."
17 The woman answered and said,
"I have no husband." Jesus said
to her, "You have well said, 'I have
no husband,'
18 "for you have had five hus-
bands, and the one whom you now
have is not your husband; in that
you spoke truly."
19 The woman said to Him, "Sir,
[a]I perceive that You are a prophet.
20 "Our fathers worshiped on
[a]this mountain, and you *Jews* say
that in [b]Jerusalem is the place
where one ought to worship."
21 Jesus said to her, "Woman, be-
lieve Me, the hour is coming [a]when
you will neither on this mountain,
nor in Jerusalem, worship the Fa-
ther.
22 "You worship [a]what you do not
know; we know what we worship,
for [b]salvation is of the Jews.
23 "But the hour is coming, and
now is, when the true worshipers
will [a]worship the Father in [b]spirit
[c]and truth; for the Father is seek-
ing such to worship Him.
24 [a]"God *is* Spirit, and those who
worship Him must worship in
spirit and truth."
25 The woman said to Him, "I
know that Messiah [a]is coming"
(who is called Christ). "When He
comes, [b]He will tell us all things."
26 Jesus said to her, [a]"I who speak
to you am *He*."

The Whitened Harvest

27 And at this *point* His disciples
came, and they marveled that He

talked with a woman; yet no
one said, "What do You seek?"
or, "Why are You talking with
her?"
28 The woman then left her water-
pot, went her way into the city, and
said to the men,
29 "Come, see a Man [a]who told
me all things that I ever did. Could
this be the Christ?"
30 Then they went out of the city
and came to Him.
31 In the meantime His disciples
urged Him, saying, "Rabbi, eat."
32 But He said to them, "I have
food to eat of which you do not
know."
33 Therefore the disciples said to
one another, "Has anyone brought
Him *anything* to eat?"
34 Jesus said to them, [a]"My food
is to do the will of Him who sent
Me, and to [b]finish His work.
35 "Do you not say, 'There are still
four months and *then* comes [a]the
harvest'? Behold, I say to you, lift
up your eyes and look at the fields,
[b]for they are already white for har-
vest!
36 [a]"And he who reaps receives
wages, and gathers fruit for eter-
nal life, that [b]both he who sows
and he who reaps may rejoice to-
gether.
37 "For in this the saying is
true: [a]'One sows and another
reaps.'
38 "I sent you to reap that for
which you have not labored; [a]oth-
ers have labored, and you have
entered into their labors."

The Savior of the World

39 And many of the Samaritans of
that city believed in Him [a]because
of the word of the woman who tes-
tified, "He told me all that I *ever*
did."
40 So when the Samaritans had
come to Him, they urged Him to
stay with them; and He stayed
there two days.
41 And many more believed be-
cause of His own [a]word.
42 Then they said to the woman,
"Now we believe, not because of
what you said, for [a]we ourselves
have heard *Him* and we know that
this is indeed [1]the Christ, the Sav-
ior of the world."

29 [a]John 4:25

34 [a]Ps. 40:7, 8; Heb. 10:9 [b]Job 23:12; [John 6:38; 17:4; 19:30]

35 [a]Gen. 8:22 [b]Matt. 9:37; Luke 10:2

36 [a]Dan. 12:3; Rom. 6:22 [b]1 Thess. 2:19

37 [a]1 Cor. 3:5–9

38 [a]Jer. 44:4; [1 Pet. 1:12]

39 [a]John 4:29

41 [a]Luke 4:32; [John 6:63]

42 [a]John 17:8; 1 John 4:14 [1]NU omits *the Christ*

44 [a]Matt. 13:57; Mark 6:4; Luke 4:24

45 [a]John 2:13, 23; 3:2 [b]Deut. 16:16

46 [a]John 2:1, 11 [1]*royal official*

48 [a]John 6:30; Rom. 15:19; 1 Cor. 1:22; 2 Cor. 12:12; [2 Thess. 2:9]; Heb. 2:4

CHAPTER 5

1 [a]Lev. 23:2; Deut. 16:16 [b]John 2:13

2 [a]Neh. 3:1, 32; 12:39 [1]NU *Bethzatha*

Welcome at Galilee

43 Now after the two days He de-
parted from there and went to Gal-
ilee.
44 For [a]Jesus Himself testified
that a prophet has no honor in his
own country.
45 So when He came to Galilee,
the Galileans received Him, [a]hav-
ing seen all the things He did in
Jerusalem at the feast; [b]for they
also had gone to the feast.

A Nobleman's Son Healed

46 So Jesus came again to Cana
of Galilee [a]where He had made the
water wine. And there was a cer-
tain [1]nobleman whose son was
sick at Capernaum.
47 When he heard that Jesus had
come out of Judea into Galilee, he
went to Him and implored Him to
come down and heal his son, for
he was at the point of death.
48 Then Jesus said to him, [a]"Un-
less you *people* see signs and won-
ders, you will by no means be-
lieve."
49 The nobleman said to Him,
"Sir, come down before my child
dies!"
50 Jesus said to him, "Go your
way; your son lives." So the man
believed the word that Jesus spoke
to him, and he went his way.
51 And as he was now going
down, his servants met him and
told *him*, saying, "Your son lives!"
52 Then he inquired of them the
hour when he got better. And they
said to him, "Yesterday at the sev-
enth hour the fever left him."
53 So the father knew that *it was*
at the same hour in which Jesus
said to him, "Your son lives." And
he himself believed, and his whole
household.
54 This again *is* the second sign
Jesus did when He had come out
of Judea into Galilee.

A Man Healed at the Pool of Bethesda

5 After [a]this there was a feast of
the Jews, and Jesus [b]went up
to Jerusalem.
2 Now there is in Jerusalem [a]by
the Sheep *Gate* a pool, which is
called in Hebrew, [1]Bethesda, hav-
ing five porches.
3 In these lay a great multitude

of sick people, blind, lame, [1]para-
lyzed, [2]waiting for the moving of
the water.
4 For an angel went down at a
certain time into the pool and
stirred up the water; then whoever
stepped in first, after the stirring
of the water, was made well of
whatever disease he had.
5 Now a certain man was there
who had an infirmity thirty-eight
years.
6 When Jesus saw him lying
there, and knew that he already
had been *in that condition* a long
time, He said to him, "Do you want
to be made well?"
7 The sick man answered Him,
"Sir, I have no man to put me into
the pool when the water is stirred
up; but while I am coming, another
steps down before me."
8 Jesus said to him, [a]"Rise, take
up your bed and walk."
9 And immediately the man was
made well, took up his bed, and
walked. And [a]that day was the
Sabbath.
10 The Jews therefore said to him
who was cured, "It is the Sabbath;
[a]it is not lawful for you to carry
your bed."
11 He answered them, "He who
made me well said to me, 'Take
up your bed and walk.'"
12 Then they asked him, "Who is
the Man who said to you, 'Take up
your bed and walk'?"
13 But the one who was [a]healed
did not know who it was, for Jesus
had withdrawn, a multitude being
in *that* place.
14 Afterward Jesus found him in
the temple, and said to him, "See,
you have been made well. [a]Sin no
more, lest a worse thing come
upon you."
15 The man departed and told the
Jews that it was Jesus who had
made him well.

Honor the Father and the Son

16 For this reason the Jews [a]per-
secuted Jesus, [1]and sought to kill
Him, because He had done these
things on the Sabbath.
17 But Jesus answered them,
[a]"My Father has been working un-
til now, and I have been working."
18 Therefore the Jews [a]sought all
the more to kill Him, because He
not only broke the Sabbath, but
also said that God was His Father,
[b]making Himself equal with
God.
19 Then Jesus answered and said
to them, "Most assuredly, I say to
you, [a]the Son can do nothing of
Himself, but what He sees the Fa-
ther do; for whatever He does, the
Son also does in like manner.
20 "For [a]the Father loves the Son,
and [b]shows Him all things that He
Himself does; and He will show
Him greater works than these, that
you may marvel.
21 "For as the Father raises the
dead and gives life to *them*, [a]even
so the Son gives life to whom He
will.
22 "For the Father judges no one,
but [a]has committed all judgment
to the Son,
23 "that all should honor the Son
just as they honor the Father. [a]He
who does not honor the Son does
not honor the Father who sent
Him.

Life and Judgment Are Through the Son

24 "Most assuredly, I say to you,
[a]he who hears My word and be-
lieves in Him who sent Me has
everlasting life, and shall not come
into judgment, [b]but has passed
from death into life.
25 "Most assuredly, I say to you,
the hour is coming, and now is,
when [a]the dead will hear the voice
of the Son of God; and those who
hear will live.
26 "For [a]as the Father has life in
Himself, so He has granted the Son
to have [b]life in Himself,
27 "and [a]has given Him authority
to execute judgment also, [b]because
He is the Son of Man.
28 "Do not marvel at this; for the
hour is coming in which all who
are in the graves will [a]hear His
voice
29 [a]"and come forth—[b]those who
have done good, to the resur-
rection of life, and those who have
done evil, to the resurrection of
condemnation.
30 [a]"I can of Myself do nothing.
As I hear, I judge; and My judg-
ment is righteous, because [b]I do
not seek My own will but the will
of the Father who sent Me.

3 [1]*withered* [2]NU omits the rest of v. 3 and all of v. 4.
8 [a]Matt. 9:6; Mark 2:11; Luke 5:24
9 [a]John 9:14
10 [a]Ex. 20:10; Neh. 13:19; Jer. 17:21, 22; Matt. 12:2; Mark 2:24; Luke 6:2
13 [a]Luke 13:14; 22:51
14 [a]Matt. 12:45; [Mark 2:5]; John 8:11
16 [a]Luke 4:29; John 8:37; 10:39 [1]NU omits *and sought to kill Him*
17 [a][John 9:4; 17:4]
18 [a]John 7:1, 19 [b]John 10:30; Phil. 2:6
19 [a]Matt. 26:39; John 5:30; 6:38; 8:28; 12:49; 14:10
20 [a]Matt. 3:17; John 3:35; 2 Pet. 1:17 [b][Matt. 11:27]
21 [a]Luke 7:14; 8:54; [John 11:25]
22 [a]Matt. 11:27; 28:18; [John 3:35; 17:2; Acts 17:31; 1 Pet. 4:5]
23 [a]Luke 10:16; 1 John 2:23
24 [a]John 3:16, 18; 6:47 [b][1 John 3:14]
25 [a][Eph. 2:1, 5; Col. 2:13]
26 [a]Ps. 36:9 [b][John 1:4; 14:6]; 1 Cor. 15:45
27 [a]John 9:39; [Acts 10:42; 17:31] [b]Dan. 7:13
28 [a][1 Thess. 4:15–17]
29 [a]Is. 26:19; [1 Cor. 15:52] [b]Dan. 12:2; Matt. 25:46; Acts 24:15
30 [a]John 5:19 [b]Matt. 26:39; John 4:34; 6:38

The Fourfold Witness

31 [a]"If I bear witness of Myself,
My witness is not [1]true.
32 [a]"There is another who bears
witness of Me, and I know that the
witness which He witnesses of Me
is true.
33 "You have sent to John, [a]and
he has borne witness to the truth.
34 "Yet I do not receive testimony
from man, but I say these things
that you may be saved.
35 "He was the burning and [a]shin-
ing lamp, and [b]you were willing
for a time to rejoice in his light.
36 "But [a]I have a greater witness
than John's; for [b]the works which
the Father has given Me to finish—
the very [c]works that I do—bear
witness of Me, that the Father has
sent Me.
37 "And the Father Himself, who
sent Me, [a]has testified of Me. You
have neither heard His voice at
any time, [b]nor seen His form.
38 "But you do not have His word
abiding in you, because whom He
sent, Him you do not believe.
39 [a]"You search the Scriptures,
for in them you think you have
eternal life; and [b]these are they
which testify of Me.
40 [a]"But you are not willing to
come to Me that you may have life.
41 [a]"I do not receive honor from
men.
42 "But I know you, that you do
not have the love of God in you.
43 "I have come in My Father's
name, and you do not receive Me;
if another comes in his own name,
him you will receive.
44 [a]"How can you believe, who re-
ceive honor from one another, and
do not seek [b]the honor that *comes*
from the only God?
45 "Do not think that I shall ac-
cuse you to the Father; [a]there is
one who accuses you—Moses, in
whom you trust.
46 "For if you believed Moses, you
would believe Me; [a]for he wrote
about Me.
47 "But if you [a]do not believe his
writings, how will you believe My
words?"

Feeding the Five Thousand

6 After [a]these things Jesus
went over the Sea of Galilee,
which is *the Sea* of [b]Tiberias.
2 Then a great multitude fol-
lowed Him, because they saw His
signs which He performed on
those who were [a]diseased.[1]
3 And Jesus went up on the
mountain, and there He sat with
His disciples.
4 [a]Now the Passover, a feast of
the Jews, was near.
5 [a]Then Jesus lifted up *His* eyes,
and seeing a great multitude com-
ing toward Him, He said to [b]Philip,
"Where shall we buy bread, that
these may eat?"
6 But this He said to test him, for
He Himself knew what He would
do.
7 Philip answered Him, [a]"Two
hundred denarii worth of bread is
not sufficient for them, that every
one of them may have a little."
8 One of His disciples, [a]Andrew,
Simon Peter's brother, said to
Him,
9 "There is a lad here who has
five barley loaves and two small
fish, [a]but what are they among so
many?"
10 Then Jesus said, "Make the
people sit down." Now there was
much grass in the place. So the
men sat down, in number about
five thousand.
11 And Jesus took the loaves, and
when He had given thanks He
distributed *them* [1]to the disciples,
and the disciples to those sitting
down; and likewise of the fish, as
much as they wanted.
12 So when they were filled, He
said to His disciples, "Gather up
the fragments that remain, so that
nothing is lost."
13 Therefore they gathered *them*
up, and filled twelve baskets with
the fragments of the five barley
loaves which were left over by
those who had eaten.
14 Then those men, when they
had seen the sign that Jesus did,
said, "This is truly [a]the Prophet
who is to come into the world."

Jesus Walks on the Sea

15 Therefore when Jesus per-
ceived that they were about to
come and take Him by force to
make Him [a]king, He departed
again to the mountain by Himself
alone.

31 [a]John 8:14 [1]*valid* as testimony
32 [a][Matt. 3:17]
33 [a][John 1:15, 19, 27, 32]
35 [a]2 Pet. 1:19 [b]Mark 6:20
36 [a]1 John 5:9 [b]John 3:2; 10:25; 17:4 [c]John 9:16; 10:38
37 [a]Matt. 3:17 [b]1 John 4:12
39 [a]Is. 8:20; 34:16 [b]Luke 24:27
40 [a][John 1:11; 3:19]
41 [a]1 Thess. 2:6
44 [a]John 12:43 [b][Rom. 2:29]
45 [a]Rom. 2:12
46 [a]Deut. 18:15, 18
47 [a]Luke 16:29, 31

CHAPTER 6

1 [a]Mark 6:32 [b]John 6:23; 21:1
2 [a]Matt. 4:23; 8:16; 9:35; 14:36; 15:30; 19:2 [1]*sick*
4 [a]Deut. 16:1
5 [a]Matt. 14:14 [b]John 1:43
7 [a]Num. 11:21, 22
8 [a]John 1:40
9 [a]2 Kin. 4:43
11 [1]NU omits *to the disciples, and the disciples*
14 [a]Gen. 49:10
15 [a][John 18:36]

16 [a]Now when evening came, His
disciples went down to the sea,
17 got into the boat, and went over
the sea toward Capernaum. And
it was already dark, and Jesus had
not come to them.
18 Then the sea arose because a
great wind was blowing.
19 So when they had rowed about
[1]three or four miles, they saw Je-
sus walking on the sea and draw-
ing near the boat; and they were
[a]afraid.
20 But He said to them, [a]"It is I;
do not be afraid."
21 Then they willingly received
Him into the boat, and immedi-
ately the boat was at the land
where they were going.

The Bread from Heaven

22 On the following day, when the
people who were standing on the
other side of the sea saw that there
was no other boat there, except
[1]that one [2]which His disciples had
entered, and that Jesus had not en-
tered the boat with His disciples,
but His disciples had gone away
alone—
23 however, other boats came
from Tiberias, near the place
where they ate bread after the
Lord had given thanks—
24 when the people therefore saw
that Jesus was not there, nor His
disciples, they also got into boats
and came to Capernaum, [a]seeking
Jesus.
25 And when they found Him on
the other side of the sea, they said
to Him, "Rabbi, when did You
come here?"
26 Jesus answered them and said,
"Most assuredly, I say to you, you
seek Me, not because you saw the
signs, but because you ate of the
loaves and were filled.
27 [a]"Do not labor for the food
which perishes, but [b]for the food
which endures to everlasting life,
which the Son of Man will give
you, [c]because God the Father has
set His seal on Him."
28 Then they said to Him, "What
shall we do, that we may work the
works of God?"
29 Jesus answered and said to
them, [a]"This is the work of God,
that you believe in Him whom He
sent."
30 Therefore they said to Him,
[a]"What sign will You perform
then, that we may see it and be-
lieve You? What work will You
do?
31 [a]"Our fathers ate the manna in
the desert; as it is written, [b]*'He
gave them bread from heaven to
eat.'*"
32 Then Jesus said to them, "Most
assuredly, I say to you, Moses did
not give you the bread from
heaven, but [a]My Father gives you
the true bread from heaven.
33 "For the bread of God is He
who comes down from heaven and
gives life to the world."
34 [a]Then they said to Him, "Lord,
give us this bread always."
35 And Jesus said to them, [a]"I am
the bread of life. [b]He who comes
to Me shall never hunger, and he
who believes in Me shall never
[c]thirst.
36 [a]"But I said to you that you
have seen Me and yet [b]do not be-
lieve.
37 [a]"All that the Father gives Me
will come to Me, and [b]the one who
comes to Me I will [1]by no means
cast out.
38 "For I have come down from
heaven, [a]not to do My own will,
[b]but the will of Him who sent Me.
39 "This is the will of the Father
who sent Me, [a]that of all He has
given Me I should lose nothing, but
should raise it up at the last day.
40 "And this is the will of Him
who sent Me, [a]that everyone who
sees the Son and believes in Him
may have everlasting life; and I
will raise him up at the last day."

Rejected by His Own

41 The Jews then [1]complained
about Him, because He said, "I am
the bread which came down from
heaven."
42 And they said, [a]"Is not this Je-
sus, the son of Joseph, whose fa-
ther and mother we know? How
is it then that He says, 'I have come
down from heaven'?"
43 Jesus therefore answered and
said to them, [1]"Do not murmur
among yourselves.
44 [a]"No one can come to Me un-
less the Father who sent Me
[b]draws him; and I will raise him
up at the last day.

16 [a]Matt. 14:23; Mark 6:47
19 [a]Matt. 17:6 [1]Lit. *25 or 30 stadia*
20 [a]Is. 43:1, 2
22 [1]NU omits *that* [2]NU omits *which His disciples had entered*
24 [a]Mark 1:37; Luke 4:42
27 [a]Matt. 6:19 [b]John 4:14; [Eph. 2:8, 9] [c]Ps. 2:7; Is. 42:1; Matt. 3:17; 17:5; Mark 1:11; 9:7; Luke 3:22; 9:35; John 5:37; Acts 2:22; 2 Pet. 1:17
29 [a]1 Thess. 1:3; James 2:22; [1 John 3:23]; Rev. 2:26
30 [a]Matt. 12:38; 16:1; Mark 8:11; 1 Cor. 1:22
31 [a]Ex. 16:15; Num. 11:7; 1 Cor. 10:3 [b]Ex. 16:4, 15; Neh. 9:15; Ps. 78:24
32 [a]John 3:13, 16
34 [a]John 4:15
35 [a]John 6:48, 58 [b]John 4:14; 7:37; Rev. 7:16 [c]Is. 55:1, 2
36 [a]John 6:26, 64; 15:24 [b]John 10:26
37 [a]John 6:45 [b][Matt. 24:24; John 10:28, 29]; 2 Tim. 2:19; 1 John 2:19 [1]*certainly not*
38 [a]Matt. 26:39; John 5:30 [b]John 4:34
39 [a]John 10:28; 17:12; 18:9
40 [a]John 3:15, 16; 4:14; 6:27, 47, 54
41 [1]*grumbled*
42 [a]Matt. 13:55; Mark 6:3; Luke 4:22
43 [1]*Stop grumbling*
44 [a]Song 1:4 [b][Eph. 2:8, 9; Phil. 1:29; 2:12, 13]

45 "It is written in the prophets,
[a]'*And they shall all be taught by*
God.' [b]Therefore everyone who
[1]has heard and learned from the
Father comes to Me.
46 [a]"Not that anyone has seen the
Father, [b]except He who is from
God; He has seen the Father.
47 "Most assuredly, I say to you,
[a]he who believes [1]in Me has ever-
lasting life.
48 [a]"I am the bread of life.
49 [a]"Your fathers ate the manna
in the wilderness, and are dead.
50 [a]"This is the bread which
comes down from heaven, that one
may eat of it and not die.
51 "I am the living bread [a]which
came down from heaven. If any-
one eats of this bread, he will live
forever; and [b]the bread that I shall
give is My flesh, which I shall give
for the life of the world."
52 The Jews therefore [a]quarreled
among themselves, saying, "How
can this Man give us *His* flesh to
eat?"
53 Then Jesus said to them, "Most
assuredly, I say to you, unless [a]you
eat the flesh of the Son of Man and
drink His blood, you have no life
in you.
54 [a]"Whoever eats My flesh and
drinks My blood has eternal life,
and I will raise him up at the last
day.
55 "For My flesh is [1]food indeed,
and My blood is [2]drink indeed.
56 "He who eats My flesh and
drinks My blood [a]abides in Me,
and I in him.
57 "As the living Father sent Me,
and I live because of the Father,
so he who feeds on Me will live
because of Me.
58 [a]"This is the bread which came
down from heaven—not [b]as your
fathers ate the manna, and are
dead. He who eats this bread will
live forever."
59 These things He said in the
synagogue as He taught in Caper-
naum.

Many Disciples Turn Away

60 [a]Therefore many of His disci-
ples, when they heard *this*, said,
"This is a [1]hard saying; who can
understand it?"
61 When Jesus knew in Himself
that His disciples [1]complained
about this, He said to them, "Does
this [2]offend you?
62 [a]"*What* then if you should see
the Son of Man ascend where He
was before?
63 [a]"It is the Spirit who gives life;
the [b]flesh profits nothing. The
[c]words that I speak to you are
spirit, and *they* are life.
64 "But [a]there are some of you
who do not believe." For [b]Jesus
knew from the beginning who they
were who did not believe, and who
would betray Him.
65 And He said, "Therefore [a]I
have said to you that no one can
come to Me unless it has been
granted to him by My Father."
66 [a]From that *time* many of His
disciples went [1]back and walked
with Him no more.
67 Then Jesus said to the twelve,
"Do you also want to go away?"
68 But Simon Peter answered
Him, "Lord, to whom shall we go?
You have [a]the words of eternal
life.
69 [a]"Also we have come to believe
and know that You are the [1]Christ,
the Son of the living God."
70 Jesus answered them, [a]"Did I
not choose you, the twelve, [b]and
one of you is a devil?"
71 He spoke of [a]Judas Iscariot, *the*
son of Simon, for it was he who
would [b]betray Him, being one of
the twelve.

Jesus' Brothers Disbelieve

7 After these things Jesus
walked in Galilee; for He did
not want to walk in Judea, [a]be-
cause the [1]Jews sought to kill Him.
2 [a]Now the Jews' Feast of Taber-
nacles was at hand.
3 [a]His brothers therefore said to
Him, "Depart from here and go
into Judea, that Your disciples also
may see the works that You are
doing.
4 "For no one does anything in
secret while he himself seeks to be
known openly. If You do these
things, show Yourself to the
world."
5 For [a]even His [b]brothers did not
believe in Him.
6 Then Jesus said to them, [a]"My
time has not yet come, but your
time is always ready.
7 [a]"The world cannot hate you,

45 [a]Is. 54:13 [b]John 6:37 [1]M *hears and has learned*
46 [a]John 1:18 [b]Matt. 11:27
47 [a][John 3:16, 18] [1]NU omits *in Me*
48 [a]John 6:33, 35
49 [a]John 6:31, 58
50 [a]John 6:51, 58
51 [a]John 3:13 [b]Heb. 10:5
52 [a]John 7:43; 9:16; 10:19
53 [a]Matt. 26:26
54 [a]John 4:14; 6:27, 40
55 [1]NU *true food* [2]NU *true drink*
56 [a][1 John 3:24; 4:15, 16]
58 [a]John 6:49–51 [b]Ex. 16:14–35
60 [a]John 6:66 [1]*difficult*
61 [1]*grumbled* [2]*make you stumble*
62 [a]Acts 1:9; 2:32, 33
63 [a]2 Cor. 3:6 [b]John 3:6 [c][John 6:68; 14:24]
64 [a]John 6:36 [b]John 2:24, 25; 13:11
65 [a]John 6:37, 44, 45
66 [a]Luke 9:62 [1]Or *away;* lit. *to the back*
68 [a]Acts 5:20
69 [a]Luke 9:20 [1]NU *Holy One of God.*
70 [a]Luke 6:13 [b][John 13:27]
71 [a]John 12:4; 13:2, 26 [b]Matt. 26:14–16

CHAPTER 7

1 [a]John 5:18; 7:19, 25; 8:37, 40 [1]The ruling authorities
2 [a]Lev. 23:34
3 [a]Matt. 12:46
5 [a]Ps. 69:8 [b]Mark 3:21
6 [a]John 2:4; 8:20
7 [a][John 15:19]

but it hates Me [b]because I testify
of it that its works are evil.
8 "You go up to this feast. I am
not [1]yet going up to this feast, [a]for
My time has not yet fully come."
9 When He had said these things
to them, He remained in Galilee.

The Heavenly Scholar

10 But when His brothers had
gone up, then He also went up to
the feast, not openly, but as it were
in secret.
11 Then [a]the Jews sought Him at
the feast, and said, "Where is He?"
12 And [a]there was much com-
plaining among the people con-
cerning Him. [b]Some said, "He is
good"; others said, "No, on the
contrary, He deceives the people."
13 However, no one spoke openly
of Him [a]for fear of the Jews.
14 Now about the middle of the
feast Jesus went up into the temple
and [a]taught.
15 [a]And the Jews marveled, say-
ing, "How does this Man know let-
ters, having never studied?"
16 [1]Jesus answered them and
said, [a]"My doctrine is not Mine,
but His who sent Me.
17 [a]"If anyone wills to do His will,
he shall know concerning the doc-
trine, whether it is from God or
whether I speak on My own *au-
thority.*
18 [a]"He who speaks from himself
seeks his own glory; but He who
[b]seeks the glory of the One who
sent Him is true, and [c]no unrigh-
teousness is in Him.
19 [a]"Did not Moses give you the
law, yet none of you keeps the
law? [b]Why do you seek to kill
Me?"
20 The people answered and said,
[a]"You have a demon. Who is seek-
ing to kill You?"
21 Jesus answered and said to
them, "I did one work, and you all
marvel.
22 [a]"Moses therefore gave you
circumcision (not that it is from
Moses, [b]but from the fathers), and
you circumcise a man on the Sab-
bath.
23 "If a man receives circumcision
on the Sabbath, so that the law of
Moses should not be broken, are
you angry with Me because [a]I

7 [b]John 3:19
8 [a]John 8:20 [1]NU omits *yet*
11 [a]John 11:56
12 [a]John 9:16; 10:19 [b]Luke 7:16
13 [a][John 9:22; 12:42; 19:38]
14 [a]Mark 6:34
15 [a]Matt. 13:54
16 [a]John 3:11 [1]NU, M *So Jesus*
17 [a]John 3:21; 8:43
18 [a]John 5:41 [b]John 8:50 [c][2 Cor. 5:21]
19 [a]Deut. 33:4 [b]Matt. 12:14
20 [a]John 8:48, 52
22 [a]Lev. 12:3 [b]Gen. 17:9–14
23 [a]John 5:8, 9, 16
24 [a]Prov. 24:23
25 [a]Matt. 21:38; 26:4
26 [a]John 7:48 [1]NU omits *truly*
27 [a]Luke 4:22
28 [a]John 8:14 [b]John 5:43 [c]Rom. 3:4 [d]John 1:18; 8:55
29 [a]Matt. 11:27 [1]NU, M omit *But*
30 [a]Mark 11:18 [b]John 7:32, 44; 8:20; 10:39
31 [a]Matt. 12:23
33 [a]John 13:33 [b][1 Pet. 3:22] [1]NU, M omit *to them*
34 [a]Hos. 5:6 [b][Matt. 5:20]
35 [a]James 1:1

made a man completely well on
the Sabbath?
24 [a]"Do not judge according to ap-
pearance, but judge with righteous
judgment."

Could This Be the Christ?

25 Now some of them from Jeru-
salem said, "Is this not He whom
they seek to [a]kill?
26 "But look! He speaks boldly,
and they say nothing to Him. [a]Do
the rulers know indeed that this is
[1]truly the Christ?
27 [a]"However, we know where
this Man is from; but when the
Christ comes, no one knows where
He is from."
28 Then Jesus cried out, as He
taught in the temple, saying,
[a]"You both know Me, and you
know where I am from; and [b]I
have not come of Myself, but He
who sent Me [c]is true, [d]whom you
do not know.
29 [1]"But [a]I know Him, for I am
from Him, and He sent Me."
30 Therefore [a]they sought to take
Him; but [b]no one laid a hand on
Him, because His hour had not yet
come.
31 And [a]many of the people be-
lieved in Him, and said, "When the
Christ comes, will He do more
signs than these which this *Man*
has done?"

Jesus and the Religious Leaders

32 The Pharisees heard the crowd
murmuring these things concern-
ing Him, and the Pharisees and the
chief priests sent officers to take
Him.
33 Then Jesus said [1]to them, [a]"I
shall be with you a little while
longer, and *then* I [b]go to Him who
sent Me.
34 "You [a]will seek Me and not
find *Me,* and where I am you [b]can-
not come."
35 Then the Jews said among
themselves, "Where does He in-
tend to go that we shall not find
Him? Does He intend to go to [a]the
Dispersion among the Greeks and
teach the Greeks?
36 "What is this thing that He
said, 'You will seek Me and not
find Me, and where I am you can-
not come'?"

The Promise of the Holy Spirit

37 [a]On the last day, that great
day of the feast, Jesus stood and
cried out, saying, [b]"If anyone
thirsts, let him come to Me and
drink.
38 [a]"He who believes in Me, as the
Scripture has said, [b]out of his
heart will flow rivers of living wa-
ter."
39 [a]But this He spoke concern-
ing the Spirit, whom those [1]be-
lieving in Him would receive;
for the [2]Holy Spirit was not yet
given, because Jesus was not yet
[b]glorified.

Who Is He?

40 Therefore [1]many from the
crowd, when they heard this say-
ing, said, "Truly this is [a]the
Prophet."
41 Others said, "This is [a]the
Christ." But some said, "Will the
Christ come out of Galilee?
42 [a]"Has not the Scripture said
that the Christ comes from the
seed of David and from the town
of Bethlehem, [b]where David
was?"
43 So [a]there was a division among
the people because of Him.
44 Now [a]some of them wanted to
take Him, but no one laid hands
on Him.

Rejected by the Authorities

45 Then the officers came to the
chief priests and Pharisees, who
said to them, "Why have you not
brought Him?"
46 The officers answered, [a]"No
man ever spoke like this Man!"
47 Then the Pharisees answered
them, "Are you also deceived?
48 "Have any of the rulers or the
Pharisees believed in Him?
49 "But this crowd that does not
know the law is accursed."
50 Nicodemus [a](he who came to
[1]Jesus [2]by night, being one of
them) said to them,
51 [a]"Does our law judge a man be-
fore it hears him and knows what
he is doing?"
52 They answered and said to
him, "Are you also from Galilee?
Search and look, for [a]no prophet
[1]has arisen out of Galilee."

An Adulteress Faces the Light of the World

53 [1]And everyone went to his *own*
house.
8 But Jesus went to the Mount
of Olives.
2 Now [1]early in the morning He
came again into the temple, and
all the people came to Him; and
He sat down and [a]taught them.
3 Then the scribes and Pharisees
brought to Him a woman caught
in adultery. And when they had set
her in the midst,
4 they said to Him, "Teacher,
[1]this woman was caught in [a]adul-
tery, in the very act.
5 [a]"Now [1]Moses, in the law, com-
manded us [2]that such should be
stoned. But what do You [3]say?"
6 This they said, testing Him,
that they [a]might have *something*
of which to accuse Him. But Jesus
stooped down and wrote on the
ground with *His* finger, [1]as though
He did not hear.
7 So when they continued asking
Him, He [1]raised Himself up and
said to them, [a]"He who is without
sin among you, let him throw a
stone at her first."
8 And again He stooped down
and wrote on the ground.
9 Then those who heard *it,* [a]be-
ing[1] convicted by *their* conscience,
went out one by one, beginning
with the oldest *even* to the last.
And Jesus was left alone, and the
woman standing in the midst.
10 When Jesus had raised Himself
up [1]and saw no one but the
woman, He said to her, "Woman,
where are those accusers [2]of
yours? Has no one condemned
you?"
11 She said, "No one, Lord." And
Jesus said to her, [a]"Neither do I
condemn you; go [1]and [b]sin no
more."
12 Then Jesus spoke to them
again, saying, [a]"I am the light of
the world. He who [b]follows Me
shall not walk in darkness, but
have the light of life."

Jesus Defends His Self-Witness

13 The Pharisees therefore said to
Him, [a]"You bear witness of Your-

37 [a]Lev. 23:36 [b][Is. 55:1]
38 [a]Deut. 18:15 [b]Is. 12:3; 43:20; 44:3; 55:1
39 [a]Is. 44:3 [b]John 12:16; 13:31; 17:5 [1]NU *who believed* [2]NU omits *Holy*
40 [a]Deut. 18:15, 18 [1]NU *some*
41 [a]John 4:42; 6:69
42 [a]Mic. 5:2 [b]1 Sam. 16:1, 4
43 [a]John 7:12
44 [a]John 7:30
46 [a]Luke 4:22
50 [a]John 3:1, 2; 19:39 [1]Lit. *Him* [2]NU *before*
51 [a]Deut. 1:16, 17; 19:15
52 [a][Is. 9:1, 2] [1]NU *is to rise*
53 [1]NU brackets 7:53 through 8:11 as not in the original text. They are present in over 900 mss. of John.

CHAPTER 8

2 [a]John 8:20; 18:20 [1]M *very early*
4 [a]Ex. 20:14 [1]M *we found this woman*
5 [a]Lev. 20:10 [1]M *in our law Moses commanded* [2]NU, M *to stone such* [3]M adds *about her*
6 [a]Matt. 22:15 [1]NU, M omit *as though He did not hear*
7 [a]Deut. 17:7 [1]M *He looked up*
9 [a]Rom. 2:22 [1]NU, M omit *being convicted by their conscience*
10 [1]NU omits *and saw no one but the woman;* M *He saw her and said,* [2]NU, M omit *of yours*
11 [a][John 3:17] [b][John 5:14] [1]NU, M add *from now on*

12 [a]John 1:4; 9:5; 12:35 [b]1 Thess. 5:5 **13** [a]John 5:31

self; Your witness is not [1]true."
14 Jesus answered and said to
them, "Even if I bear witness of
Myself, My witness is true, for I
know where I came from and
where I am going; but [a]you do not
know where I come from and
where I am going.
15 [a]"You judge according to the
flesh; [b]I judge no one.
16 "And yet if I do judge, My judg-
ment is true; for [a]I am not alone,
but I *am* with the Father who sent
Me.
17 [a]"It is also written in your law
that the testimony of two men is
true.
18 "I am One who bears witness
of Myself, and [a]the Father who
sent Me bears witness of Me."
19 Then they said to Him, "Where
is Your Father?" Jesus answered,
[a]"You know neither Me nor My
Father. [b]If you had known Me, you
would have known My Father
also."
20 These words Jesus spoke in
[a]the treasury, as He taught in the
temple; and [b]no one laid hands on
Him, for [c]His hour had not yet
come.

Jesus Predicts His Departure

21 Then Jesus said to them again,
"I am going away, and [a]you will
seek Me, and [b]will die in your sin.
Where I go you cannot come."
22 So the Jews said, "Will He kill
Himself, because He says, 'Where
I go you cannot come'?"
23 And He said to them, [a]"You are
from beneath; I am from above.
[b]You are of this world; I am not
of this world.
24 [a]"Therefore I said to you that
you will die in your sins; [b]for if you
do not believe that I am *He*, you
will die in your sins."
25 Then they said to Him, "Who
are You?" And Jesus said to them,
"Just what I [a]have been saying to
you from the beginning.
26 "I have many things to say and
to judge concerning you, but [a]He
who sent Me is true; and [b]I speak
to the world those things which I
heard from Him."
27 They did not understand that
He spoke to them of the Father.
28 Then Jesus said to them,
"When you [a]lift[1] up the Son of

13 [1]*valid* as testimony
14 [a]John 7:28; 9:29
15 [a]John 7:24 [b][John 3:17; 12:47; 18:36]
16 [a]John 16:32
17 [a]Deut. 17:6; 19:15
18 [a]John 5:37
19 [a]John 16:3 [b]John 14:7
20 [a]Mark 12:41, 43 [b]John 2:4; 7:30 [c]John 7:8
21 [a]John 7:34; 13:33 [b]John 8:24
23 [a]John 3:31 [b]1 John 4:5
24 [a]John 8:21 [b][Mark 16:16]
25 [a]John 4:26
26 [a]John 7:28 [b]John 3:32; 15:15
28 [a]John 3:14; 12:32; 19:18 [b][Rom. 1:4] [c]John 5:19, 30 [d]John 3:11 [1]Crucify
29 [a]John 14:10 [b]John 8:16; 16:32 [c]John 4:34; 5:30; 6:38
30 [a]John 7:31; 10:42; 11:45
31 [a][John 14:15, 23]
32 [a][John 1:14, 17; 14:6] [b][Rom. 6:14, 18, 22]
33 [a][Matt. 3:9]
34 [a]2 Pet. 2:19
35 [a]Gal. 4:30
36 [a]Gal. 5:1
37 [a]John 7:19
38 [a][John 3:32; 5:19, 30; 14:10, 24] [1]NU *heard from*
39 [a]Matt. 3:9 [b][Rom. 2:28]
40 [a]John 8:37 [b]John 8:26
41 [a]Is. 63:16
42 [a]1 John 5:1 [b]John 16:27; 17:8, 25 [c]Gal. 4:4
43 [a][John 7:17]

Man, [b]then you will know that I
am *He*, and [c]*that* I do nothing of
Myself; but [d]as My Father taught
Me, I speak these things.
29 "And [a]He who sent Me is with
Me. [b]The Father has not left Me
alone, [c]for I always do those things
that please Him."
30 As He spoke these words,
[a]many believed in Him.

The Truth Shall Make You Free

31 Then Jesus said to those Jews
who believed Him, "If you [a]abide
in My word, you are My disciples
indeed.
32 "And you shall know the
[a]truth, and [b]the truth shall make
you free."
33 They answered Him, [a]"We are
Abraham's descendants, and have
never been in bondage to anyone.
How *can* You say, 'You will be
made free'?"
34 Jesus answered them, "Most
assuredly, I say to you, [a]whoever
commits sin is a slave of sin.
35 "And [a]a slave does not abide
in the house forever, *but* a son
abides forever.
36 [a]"Therefore if the Son makes
you free, you shall be free indeed.

Abraham's Seed and Satan's

37 "I know that you are Abra-
ham's descendants, but [a]you seek
to kill Me, because My word has
no place in you.
38 [a]"I speak what I have seen with
My Father, and you do what you
have [1]seen with your father."
39 They answered and said to
Him, [a]"Abraham is our father." Je-
sus said to them, [b]"If you were
Abraham's children, you would do
the works of Abraham.
40 [a]"But now you seek to kill Me,
a Man who has told you the truth
[b]which I heard from God. Abra-
ham did not do this.
41 "You do the deeds of your fa-
ther." Then they said to Him, "We
were not born of fornication; [a]we
have one Father—God."
42 Jesus said to them, [a]"If God
were your Father, you would love
Me, for [b]I proceeded forth and
came from God; [c]nor have I come
of Myself, but He sent Me.
43 [a]"Why do you not understand

My speech? Because you are not
able to listen to My word.
44 [a]"You are of *your* father the
devil, and the [b]desires of your fa-
ther you want to [c]do. He was a
murderer from the beginning, and
[d]does not stand in the truth, be-
cause there is no truth in him.
When he speaks a lie, he speaks
from his own *resources,* for he is
a liar and the father of it.
45 "But because I tell the truth,
you do not believe Me.
46 "Which of you convicts Me of
sin? And if I tell the truth, why do
you not believe Me?
47 [a]"He who is of God hears God's
words; therefore you do not hear,
because you are not of God."

Before Abraham Was, I AM

48 Then the Jews answered and
said to Him, "Do we not say rightly
that You are a Samaritan and
[a]have a demon?"
49 Jesus answered, "I do not have
a demon; but I honor My Father,
and [a]you dishonor Me.
50 "And [a]I do not seek My *own*
glory; there is One who seeks and
judges.
51 "Most assuredly, I say to you,
[a]if anyone keeps My word he shall
never see death."
52 Then the Jews said to Him,
"Now we know that You [a]have a
demon! [b]Abraham is dead, and the
prophets; and You say, 'If anyone
keeps My word he shall never
taste death.'
53 "Are You greater than our fa-
ther Abraham, who is dead? And
the prophets are dead. [a]Who do
You make Yourself out to be?"
54 Jesus answered, [a]"If I honor
Myself, My honor is nothing. [b]It is
My Father who honors Me, of
whom you say that He is [1]your
God.
55 "Yet [a]you have not known
Him, but I know Him. And if I say,
'I do not know Him,' I shall be a
liar like you; but I do know Him
and [b]keep His word.
56 "Your father Abraham [a]re-
joiced to see My day, [b]and he saw
it and was glad."
57 Then the Jews said to Him,
"You are not yet fifty years old,
and have You seen Abraham?"
58 Jesus said to them, "Most as-
suredly, I say to you, [a]before Abra-
ham was, [b]I AM."
59 Then [a]they took up stones to
throw at Him; but Jesus hid Him-
self and went out of the temple,
[b]going[1] through the midst of them,
and so passed by.

A Man Born Blind Receives Sight

9 Now as *Jesus* passed by, He
saw a man who was blind from
birth.
2 And His disciples asked Him,
saying, "Rabbi, [a]who sinned, this
man or his parents, that he was
born blind?"
3 Jesus answered, "Neither this
man nor his parents sinned, [a]but
that the works of God should be
revealed in him.
4 [a]"I[1] must work the works of
Him who sent Me while it is [b]day;
the night is coming when no one
can work.
5 "As long as I am in the world,
[a]I am the light of the world."
6 When He had said these things,
[a]He spat on the ground and made
clay with the saliva; and He
anointed the eyes of the blind man
with the clay.
7 And He said to him, "Go, wash
[a]in the pool of Siloam" (which is
translated, Sent). So [b]he went and
washed, and came back seeing.
8 Therefore the neighbors and
those who previously had seen
that he was [1]blind said, "Is not this
he who sat and begged?"
9 Some said, "This is he." Others
said, [1]"He is like him." He said, "I
am *he.*"
10 Therefore they said to him,
"How were your eyes opened?"
11 He answered and said, [a]"A
Man called Jesus made clay and
anointed my eyes and said to me,
'Go to [1]the pool of Siloam and
wash.' So I went and washed, and
I received sight."
12 Then they said to him, "Where
is He?" He said, "I do not know."

The Pharisees Excommunicate the Healed Man

13 They brought him who for-
merly was blind to the Pharisees.
14 Now it was a Sabbath when Je-
sus made the clay and opened his
eyes.
15 Then the Pharisees also asked

44 [a]Matt. 13:38; 1 John 3:8 [b]1 John 2:16, 17 [c][1 John 3:8–10, 15] [d][Jude 6]
47 [a]Luke 8:15; John 10:26; 1 John 4:6
48 [a]John 7:20; 10:20
49 [a]John 5:41
50 [a]John 5:41; 7:18; [Phil. 2:6–8]
51 [a]John 5:24; 11:26
52 [a]John 7:20; 10:20 [b]Zech. 1:5; Heb. 11:13
53 [a]John 10:33; 19:7
54 [a]John 5:31, 32 [b]John 5:41; Acts 3:13 [1]NU, M *our*
55 [a]John 7:28, 29 [b][John 15:10]
56 [a]Luke 10:24 [b]Matt. 13:17; Heb. 11:13
58 [a]Mic. 5:2; John 17:5; Heb. 7:3; Rev. 22:13 [b]Ex. 3:14; Is. 43:13; John 17:5, 24; Col. 1:17; Rev. 1:8
59 [a]John 10:31; 11:8 [b]Luke 4:30; John 10:39 [1]NU omits the rest of v. 59.

CHAPTER 9

2 [a]Luke 13:2; John 9:34; Acts 28:4
3 [a]John 11:4
4 [a][John 4:34; 5:19, 36; 17:4] [b]John 11:9, 10; 12:35; Gal. 6:10 [1]NU *We*
5 [a][John 1:5, 9; 3:19; 8:12; 12:35, 46]
6 [a]Mark 7:33; 8:23
7 [a]Neh. 3:15; Is. 8:6; Luke 13:4; John 9:11 [b]2 Kin. 5:14
8 [1]NU *a beggar*
9 [1]NU *"No, but he is like him."*
11 [a]John 9:6, 7 [1]NU omits *the pool of*

him again how he had received his
sight. He said to them, "He put
clay on my eyes, and I washed,
and I see."
16 Therefore some of the Phari-
sees said, "This Man is not from
God, because He does not [1]keep
the Sabbath." Others said, [a]"How
can a man who is a sinner do such
signs?" And [b]there was a division
among them.
17 They said to the blind man
again, "What do you say about
Him because He opened your
eyes?" He said, [a]"He is a prophet."
18 But the Jews did not believe
concerning him, that he had been
blind and received his sight, until
they called the parents of him who
had received his sight.
19 And they asked them, saying,
"Is this your son, who you say was
born blind? How then does he now
see?"
20 His parents answered them
and said, "We know that this is our
son, and that he was born blind;
21 "but by what means he now
sees we do not know, or who
opened his eyes we do not know.
He is of age; ask him. He will
speak for himself."
22 His parents said these *things*
because [a]they feared the Jews, for
the Jews had agreed already that
if anyone confessed *that* He *was*
Christ, he [b]would be put out of the
synagogue.
23 Therefore his parents said, "He
is of age; ask him."
24 So they again called the man
who was blind, and said to him,
[a]"Give God the glory! [b]We know
that this Man is a sinner."
25 He answered and said,
"Whether He is a sinner *or not* I
do not know. One thing I know:
that though I was blind, now I
see."
26 Then they said to him again,
"What did He do to you? How did
He open your eyes?"
27 He answered them, "I told you
already, and you did not listen.
Why do you want to hear *it* again?
Do you also want to become His
disciples?"
28 Then they reviled him and said,
"You are His disciple, but we are
Moses' disciples.
29 "We know that God [a]spoke to

16 [a]John 3:2; 9:33 [b]John 7:12, 43; 10:19 [1]*observe*
17 [a][John 4:19; 6:14]
22 [a]John 7:13; 12:42; 19:38; Acts 5:13 [b]John 16:2
24 [a]Josh. 7:19; 1 Sam. 6:5; Ezra 10:11; Rev. 11:13 [b]John 9:16
29 [a]Ex. 19:19, 20; 33:11; 34:29; Num. 12:6–8 [b][John 5:45–47] [c]John 7:27, 28; 8:14
30 [a]John 3:10
31 [a]Job 27:9; 35:12; Ps. 18:41; Prov. 1:28; 15:29; 28:9; Is. 1:15; Jer. 11:11; 14:12; Ezek. 8:18; Mic. 3:4; Zech. 7:13; [James 5:16]
33 [a]John 3:2; 9:16
34 [a]Ps. 51:5; John 9:2 [1]Excommunicated him
35 [a]John 5:14 [b]John 1:7; 16:31 [c]Matt. 14:33; 16:16; Mark 1:1; John 10:36; 1 John 5:13 [1]NU *Man*
37 [a]John 4:26
38 [a]Matt. 8:2
39 [a][John 3:17; 5:22, 27; 12:47] [b]Matt. 13:13; 15:14
40 [a][Rom. 2:19]
41 [a]John 15:22, 24
CHAPTER 10
3 [a]John 20:16

[b]Moses; *as for* this *fellow*, [c]we do
not know where He is from."
30 The man answered and said to
them, [a]"Why, this is a marvelous
thing, that you do not know where
He is from; yet He has opened my
eyes!
31 "Now we know that [a]God does
not hear sinners; but if anyone is
a worshiper of God and does His
will, He hears him.
32 "Since the world began it has
been unheard of that anyone
opened the eyes of one who was
born blind.
33 [a]"If this Man were not from
God, He could do nothing."
34 They answered and said to
him, [a]"You were completely born
in sins, and are you teaching us?"
And they [1]cast him out.

True Vision and True Blindness

35 Jesus heard that they had cast
him out; and when He had [a]found
him, He said to him, "Do you [b]be-
lieve in [c]the Son of [1]God?"
36 He answered and said, "Who
is He, Lord, that I may believe in
Him?"
37 And Jesus said to him, "You
have both seen Him and [a]it is He
who is talking with you."
38 Then he said, "Lord, I believe!"
And he [a]worshiped Him.
39 And Jesus said, [a]"For judgment
I have come into this world, [b]that
those who do not see may see, and
that those who see may be made
blind."
40 Then *some* of the Pharisees
who were with Him heard these
words, [a]and said to Him, "Are we
blind also?"
41 Jesus said to them, [a]"If you
were blind, you would have no sin;
but now you say, 'We see.' There-
fore your sin remains.

Jesus the True Shepherd

10 "Most assuredly, I say to
you, he who does not enter
the sheepfold by the door, but
climbs up some other way, the
same is a thief and a robber.
2 "But he who enters by the door
is the shepherd of the sheep.
3 "To him the doorkeeper opens,
and the sheep hear his voice; and
he calls his own sheep by [a]name
and leads them out.

4 "And when he brings out his
own sheep, he goes before them;
and the sheep follow him, for they
know his voice.
5 "Yet they will by no means fol-
low a [a]stranger, but will flee from
him, for they do not know the
voice of strangers."
6 Jesus used this illustration, but
they did not understand the things
which He spoke to them.

Jesus the Good Shepherd

7 Then Jesus said to them again,
"Most assuredly, I say to you, I am
the door of the sheep.
8 "All who *ever* came [1]before Me
are thieves and robbers, but the
sheep did not hear them.
9 [a]"I am the door. If anyone
enters by Me, he will be saved,
and will go in and out and find pas-
ture.
10 "The thief does not come ex-
cept to steal, and to kill, and to de-
stroy. I have come that they may
have life, and that they may have
it more abundantly.
11 [a]"I am the good shepherd. The
good shepherd gives His life for
the sheep.
12 "But a [1]hireling, *he who is* not
the shepherd, one who does not
own the sheep, sees the wolf com-
ing and [a]leaves the sheep and
flees; and the wolf catches the
sheep and scatters them.
13 "The hireling flees because he
is a hireling and does not care
about the sheep.
14 "I am the good shepherd; and
[a]I know My *sheep,* and [b]am known
by My own.
15 [a]"As the Father knows Me,
even so I know the Father; [b]and I
lay down My life for the sheep.
16 "And [a]other sheep I have
which are not of this fold; them
also I must bring, and they will
hear My voice; [b]and there will be
one flock *and* one shepherd.
17 "Therefore My Father [a]loves
Me, [b]because I lay down My life
that I may take it again.
18 "No one takes it from Me, but
I lay it down of Myself. I [a]have
power to lay it down, and I have
power to take it again. [b]This com-
mand I have received from My Fa-
ther."
19 Therefore [a]there was a division
again among the Jews because of
these sayings.
20 And many of them said, [a]"He
has a demon and is [1]mad. Why do
you listen to Him?"
21 Others said, "These are not the
words of one who has a demon.
[a]Can a demon [b]open the eyes of
the blind?"

The Shepherd Knows His Sheep

22 Now it was the Feast of Dedica-
tion in Jerusalem, and it was win-
ter.
23 And Jesus walked in the tem-
ple, [a]in Solomon's porch.
24 Then the Jews surrounded Him
and said to Him, "How long do
You keep us in [1]doubt? If You are
the Christ, tell us plainly."
25 Jesus answered them, "I told
you, and you do not believe. [a]The
works that I do in My Father's
name, they [b]bear witness of Me.
26 "But [a]you do not believe, be-
cause you are not of My sheep, [1]as
I said to you.
27 [a]"My sheep hear My voice, and
I know them, and they follow Me.
28 "And I give them eternal life,
and they shall never perish; nei-
ther shall anyone snatch them out
of My hand.
29 [a]"My Father, [b]who has given
them to Me, is greater than all; and
no one is able to snatch *them* out
of My Father's hand.
30 [a]"I and *My* Father are one."

Renewed Efforts to Stone Jesus

31 Then [a]the Jews took up stones
again to stone Him.
32 Jesus answered them, "Many
good works I have shown you
from My Father. For which of
those works do you stone Me?"
33 The Jews answered Him, say-
ing, "For a good work we do not
stone You, but for [a]blasphemy,
and because You, being a Man,
[b]make Yourself God."
34 Jesus answered them, "Is it not
written in your law, [a]*'I said, "You
are gods"'*?
35 "If He called them gods, [a]to
whom the word of God came (and
the Scripture [b]cannot be broken),
36 "do you say of Him [a]whom the
Father sanctified and [b]sent into
the world, 'You are blaspheming,'

5 [a][2 Cor. 11:13–15]
8 [1]M omits *before Me*
9 [a][John 14:6; Eph. 2:18]
11 [a]Gen. 49:24; Is. 40:11; Ezek. 34:23; [Heb. 13:20]; 1 Pet. 2:25; 5:4; Rev. 7:17
12 [a]Zech. 11:16, 17 [1]*hired man*
14 [a]Is. 40:11; Nah. 1:7; Zech. 13:7; John 6:64; 2 Tim. 2:19 [b]2 Tim. 1:12
15 [a]Matt. 11:27 [b]Matt. 27:50; Mark 15:37; Luke 23:46; [John 15:13; 19:30]; 1 John 3:16
16 [a]Is. 42:6; 56:8; Acts 10:45; 11:18; 13:46 [b]Ezek. 37:22; John 11:52; 17:20; Eph. 2:13–18; 1 Pet. 2:25
17 [a]John 5:20 [b][Is. 53:7, 8, 12; Heb. 2:9]
18 [a]Matt. 26:53; [John 2:19; 5:26] [b][John 6:38; 14:31; 17:4; Acts 2:24, 32]
19 [a]John 7:43; 9:16
20 [a]John 7:20 [1]*insane*
21 [a][Ex. 4:11] [b]John 9:6, 7, 32, 33
23 [a]Acts 3:11; 5:12
24 [1]Suspense
25 [a]John 5:36; 10:38 [b]Matt. 11:4; John 2:11; 20:30
26 [a][John 8:47] [1]NU omits *as I said to you*
27 [a]John 10:4, 14
29 [a]John 14:28 [b][John 17:2, 6, 12, 24]
30 [a]John 17:11, 21–24
31 [a]John 8:59
33 [a]Matt. 9:3 [b]John 5:18
34 [a]Ps. 82:6
35 [a]Matt. 5:17, 18 [b]1 Pet. 1:25
36 [a]John 6:27 [b]John 3:17

[c]because I said, 'I am [d]the Son of
God'?
37 [a]"If I do not do the works of
My Father, do not believe Me;
38 "but if I do, though you do not
believe Me, [a]believe the works,
that you may know and [1]believe
[b]that the Father *is* in Me, and I in
Him."
39 [a]Therefore they sought again
to seize Him, but He escaped out
of their hand.

The Believers Beyond Jordan

40 And He went away again be-
yond the Jordan to the place
[a]where John was baptizing at first,
and there He stayed.
41 Then many came to Him and
said, "John performed no sign,
[a]but all the things that John spoke
about this Man were true."
42 And many believed in Him
there.

The Death of Lazarus

11 Now a certain *man* was sick,
Lazarus of Bethany, the
town of [a]Mary and her sister Mar-
tha.
2 [a]It was *that* Mary who
anointed the Lord with fragrant oil
and wiped His feet with her hair,
whose brother Lazarus was sick.
3 Therefore the sisters sent to
Him, saying, "Lord, behold, he
whom You love is sick."
4 When Jesus heard *that*, He
said, "This sickness is not unto
death, but for the glory of God,
that the Son of God may be glori-
fied through it."
5 Now Jesus loved Martha and
her sister and Lazarus.
6 So, when He heard that he was
sick, [a]He stayed two more days in
the place where He was.
7 Then after this He said to *the*
disciples, "Let us go to Judea
again."
8 *The* disciples said to Him,
"Rabbi, lately the Jews sought to
[a]stone You, and are You going
there again?"
9 Jesus answered, "Are there not
twelve hours in the day? [a]If any-
one walks in the day, he does not
stumble, because he sees the [b]light
of this world.
10 "But [a]if one walks in the night,
he stumbles, because the light is
not in him."
11 These things He said, and after
that He said to them, "Our friend
Lazarus [a]sleeps, but I go that I may
wake him up."
12 Then His disciples said,
"Lord, if he sleeps he will get
well."
13 However, Jesus spoke of his
death, but they thought that He
was speaking about taking rest in
sleep.
14 Then Jesus said to them
plainly, "Lazarus is dead.
15 "And I am glad for your sakes
that I was not there, that you may
believe. Nevertheless let us go to
him."
16 Then [a]Thomas, who is called
the Twin, said to his fellow disci-
ples, "Let us also go, that we may
die with Him."

I Am the Resurrection and the Life

17 So when Jesus came, He found
that he had already been in the
tomb four days.
18 Now Bethany was near Jerusa-
lem, about [1]two miles away.
19 And many of the Jews had
joined the women around Martha
and Mary, to comfort them con-
cerning their brother.
20 Then Martha, as soon as she
heard that Jesus was coming, went
and met Him, but Mary was sitting
in the house.
21 Now Martha said to Jesus,
"Lord, if You had been here, my
brother would not have died.
22 "But even now I know that
[a]whatever You ask of God, God
will give You."
23 Jesus said to her, "Your
brother will rise again."
24 Martha said to Him, [a]"I know
that he will rise again in the resur-
rection at the last day."
25 Jesus said to her, "I am [a]the
resurrection and the life. [b]He who
believes in Me, though he may
[c]die, he shall live.
26 "And whoever lives and be-
lieves in Me shall never die. Do
you believe this?"
27 She said to Him, "Yes, Lord, [a]I
believe that You are the Christ, the
Son of God, who is to come into
the world."

36 [c]John 5:17, 18 [d]Luke 1:35
37 [a]John 10:25; 15:24
38 [a]John 5:36 [b]John 14:10, 11 [1]NU *understand*
39 [a]John 7:30, 44
40 [a]John 1:28
41 [a][John 1:29, 36; 3:28–36; 5:33]

CHAPTER 11

1 [a]Luke 10:38, 39; John 11:5, 19
2 [a]Matt. 26:7
6 [a]John 10:40
8 [a]John 8:59; 10:31
9 [a]Luke 13:33; John 9:4; 12:35 [b]Is. 9:2
10 [a]John 12:35
11 [a]Deut. 31:16; [Dan. 12:2]; Matt. 9:24; Acts 7:60; [1 Cor. 15:18, 51]
16 [a]Matt. 10:3; Mark 3:18; Luke 6:15; John 14:5; 20:26–28; Acts 1:13
18 [1]Lit. *15 stadia*
22 [a][John 9:31; 11:41]
24 [a][Luke 14:14; John 5:29]
25 [a]John 5:21; 6:39, 40, 44; [Rev. 1:18] [b]John 3:16, 36; 1 John 5:10 [c]1 Cor. 15:22; [Heb. 9:27]
27 [a]Matt. 16:16; Luke 2:11; John 4:42; 6:14, 69

Jesus and Death, the Last Enemy

28 And when she had said these
things, she went her way and se-
cretly called Mary her sister, say-
ing, "The Teacher has come and
is calling for you."
29 As soon as she heard *that*, she
arose quickly and came to Him.
30 Now Jesus had not yet come
into the town, but [1]was in the place
where Martha met Him.
31 [a]Then the Jews who were with
her in the house, and comforting
her, when they saw that Mary rose
up quickly and went out, followed
her, [1]saying, "She is going to the
tomb to weep there."
32 Then, when Mary came where
Jesus was, and saw Him, she [a]fell
down at His feet, saying to Him,
[b]"Lord, if You had been here, my
brother would not have died."
33 Therefore, when Jesus saw her
weeping, and the Jews who came
with her weeping, He groaned in
the spirit and was troubled.
34 And He said, "Where have you
laid him?" They said to Him,
"Lord, come and see."
35 [a]Jesus wept.
36 Then the Jews said, "See how
He loved him!"
37 And some of them said, "Could
not this Man, [a]who opened the
eyes of the blind, also have kept
this man from dying?"

Lazarus Raised from the Dead

38 Then Jesus, again groaning
in Himself, came to the tomb. It
was a cave, and a [a]stone lay
against it.
39 Jesus said, "Take away the
stone." Martha, the sister of him
who was dead, said to Him, "Lord,
by this time there is a stench, for
he has been *dead* four days."
40 Jesus said to her, "Did I not say
to you that if you would believe
you would [a]see the glory of God?"
41 Then they took away the stone
[1]*from the place* where the dead
man was lying. And Jesus lifted up
His eyes and said, "Father, I thank
You that You have heard Me.
42 "And I know that You always
hear Me, but [a]because of the peo-
ple who are standing by I said *this*,
that they may believe that You
sent Me."

30 [1]NU *was still*
31 [a]John 11:19, 33 [1]NU *supposing that she was going*
32 [a]Mark 5:22; 7:25; Rev. 1:17 [b]John 11:21
35 [a]Luke 19:41
37 [a]John 9:6, 7
38 [a]Matt. 27:60, 66; Mark 15:46; Luke 24:2; John 20:1
40 [a][John 11:4, 23]
41 [1]NU omits *from the place where the dead man was lying*
42 [a]John 12:30; 17:21
44 [a]John 19:40 [b]John 20:7
45 [a]John 2:23; 10:42; 12:11, 18
46 [a]John 5:15
47 [a]Ps. 2:2; Matt. 26:3; Mark 14:1; Luke 22:2 [b]John 12:19; Acts 4:16
49 [a]Matt. 26:3; Luke 3:2; John 18:14; Acts 4:6
50 [a]John 18:14 [1]NU *you*
52 [a]Is. 49:6; Acts 10:45; 11:18; 13:46; [1 John 2:2] [b]Ps. 22:27; John 10:16; [Eph. 2:14–17]
53 [a]Matt. 26:4; Luke 6:11; 19:47; 22:2; John 5:16
54 [a]John 4:1, 3; 7:1 [b]2 Chr. 13:19
55 [a]Matt. 26:1; Mark 14:1; Luke 22:1; John 2:13; 5:1; 6:4 [b]Num. 9:10, 13; 31:19, 20; 2 Chr. 30:17; Luke 2:22
56 [a]John 7:11

43 Now when He had said these
things, He cried with a loud voice,
"Lazarus, come forth!"
44 And he who had died came out
bound hand and foot with [a]grave-
clothes, and [b]his face was wrapped
with a cloth. Jesus said to them,
"Loose him, and let him go."

The Plot to Kill Jesus

45 Then many of the Jews who
had come to Mary, [a]and had seen
the things Jesus did, believed in
Him.
46 But some of them went away
to the Pharisees and [a]told them the
things Jesus did.
47 [a]Then the chief priests and the
Pharisees gathered a council and
said, [b]"What shall we do? For this
Man works many signs.
48 "If we let Him alone like this,
everyone will believe in Him, and
the Romans will come and
take away both our place and
nation."
49 And one of them, [a]Caiaphas,
being high priest that year, said
to them, "You know nothing
at all,
50 [a]"nor do you consider that it is
expedient for [1]us that one man
should die for the people, and not
that the whole nation should per-
ish."
51 Now this he did not say on his
own *authority;* but being high
priest that year he prophesied that
Jesus would die for the nation,
52 and [a]not for that nation only,
but [b]also that He would gather to-
gether in one the children of God
who were scattered abroad.
53 Then, from that day on, they
plotted to [a]put Him to death.
54 [a]Therefore Jesus no longer
walked openly among the Jews,
but went from there into the coun-
try near the wilderness, to a city
called [b]Ephraim, and there re-
mained with His disciples.
55 [a]And the Passover of the Jews
was near, and many went from the
country up to Jerusalem before the
Passover, to [b]purify themselves.
56 [a]Then they sought Jesus, and
spoke among themselves as they
stood in the temple, "What do you
think—that He will not come to the
feast?"
57 Now both the chief priests and

the Pharisees had given a com-
mand, that if anyone knew where
He was, he should report *it*, that
they might [a]seize Him.

The Anointing at Bethany

12 Then, six days before the
Passover, Jesus came to
Bethany, [a]where Lazarus was
[1]who had been dead, whom He
had raised from the dead.
2 [a]There they made Him a sup-
per; and Martha served, but Laza-
rus was one of those who sat at
the table with Him.
3 Then [a]Mary took a pound of
very costly oil of [b]spikenard,
anointed the feet of Jesus, and
wiped His feet with her hair. And
the house was filled with the fra-
grance of the oil.
4 But one of His disciples, [a]Judas
Iscariot, Simon's *son*, who would
betray Him, said,
5 "Why was this fragrant oil not
sold for [1]three hundred denarii
and given to the poor?"
6 This he said, not that he cared
for the poor, but because he was
a thief, and [a]had the money box;
and he used to take what was put
in it.
7 But Jesus said, "Let her alone;
[1]she has kept this for the day of
My burial.
8 "For [a]the poor you have with
you always, but Me you do not
have always."

The Plot to Kill Lazarus

9 Now a great many of the Jews
knew that He was there; and they
came, not for Jesus' sake only, but
that they might also see Lazarus,
[a]whom He had raised from the
dead.
10 [a]But the chief priests plotted to
put Lazarus to death also,
11 [a]because on account of him
many of the Jews went away and
believed in Jesus.

The Triumphal Entry

12 [a]The next day a great multitude
that had come to the feast, when
they heard that Jesus was coming
to Jerusalem,
13 took branches of palm trees
and went out to meet Him, and
cried out:

"Hosanna!
[a]'*Blessed is He who comes in the*
name of the LORD!'
The King of Israel!"

14 [a]Then Jesus, when He had
found a young donkey, sat on it;
as it is written:

15 "*Fear*[a] *not, daughter of Zion;*
Behold, your King is coming,
Sitting on a donkey's colt."

16 [a]His disciples did not under-
stand these things at first; [b]but
when Jesus was glorified, [c]then
they remembered that these things
were written about Him and *that*
they had done these things to
Him.
17 Therefore the people, who
were with Him when He called
Lazarus out of his tomb and raised
him from the dead, bore witness.
18 [a]For this reason the people also
met Him, because they heard that
He had done this sign.
19 The Pharisees therefore said
among themselves, [a]"You see that
you are accomplishing nothing.
Look, the world has gone after
Him!"

The Fruitful Grain of Wheat

20 Now there [a]were certain
Greeks among those [b]who came
up to worship at the feast.
21 Then they came to Philip, [a]who
was from Bethsaida of Galilee, and
asked him, saying, "Sir, we wish
to see Jesus."
22 Philip came and told Andrew,
and in turn Andrew and Philip told
Jesus.
23 But Jesus answered them, say-
ing, [a]"The hour has come that the
Son of Man should be glorified.
24 "Most assuredly, I say to you,
[a]unless a grain of wheat falls into
the ground and dies, it remains
alone; but if it dies, it produces
much [1]grain.
25 [a]"He who loves his life will lose
it, and he who hates his life in this
world will keep it for eternal life.
26 "If anyone serves Me, let him
[a]follow Me; and [b]where I am, there
My servant will be also. If anyone
serves Me, him My Father will
honor.

57 [a]Matt. 26:14–16

CHAPTER 12

1 [a]Matt. 21:17; John 11:1, 43 [1]NU omits *who had been dead*
2 [a]Matt. 26:6; Mark 14:3; Luke 10:38–41
3 [a]Luke 10:38, 39; John 11:2 [b]Song 1:12
4 [a]John 13:26
5 [1]About one year's wages for a worker
6 [a]John 13:29
7 [1]NU *that she may keep*
8 [a]Deut. 15:11; Matt. 26:11; Mark 14:7; John 17:11
9 [a]John 11:43, 44
10 [a]Luke 16:31
11 [a]John 11:45; 12:18
12 [a]Matt. 21:4–9; Mark 11:7–10; Luke 19:35–38
13 [a]Ps. 118:25, 26
14 [a]Matt. 21:7
15 [a]Is. 40:9; Zech. 9:9
16 [a]Luke 18:34 [b]John 7:39; 12:23 [c][John 14:26]
18 [a]John 12:11
19 [a]John 11:47, 48
20 [a]Mark 7:26; Acts 17:4 [b]1 Kin. 8:41, 42; Acts 8:27
21 [a]John 1:43, 44; 14:8–11
23 [a]Matt. 26:18, 45; John 13:32; Acts 3:13
24 [a][Rom. 14:9]; 1 Cor. 15:36 [1]Lit. *fruit*
25 [a]Matt. 10:39; Mark 8:35; Luke 9:24
26 [a][Matt. 16:24] [b]John 14:3; 17:24; [1 Thess. 4:17]

Jesus Predicts His Death on the Cross

27 [a]"Now My soul is troubled, and
what shall I say? 'Father, save Me
from this hour'? [b]But for this pur-
pose I came to this hour.
28 "Father, glorify Your name."
[a]Then a voice came from heaven,
saying, "I have both glorified *it*
and will glorify *it* again."
29 Therefore the people who
stood by and heard *it* said that it
had thundered. Others said, "An
angel has spoken to Him."
30 Jesus answered and said,
[a]"This voice did not come because
of Me, but for your sake.
31 "Now is the judgment of this
world; now [a]the ruler of this world
will be cast out.
32 "And I, [a]if I am [1]lifted up from
the earth, will draw [b]all *peoples* to
Myself."
33 [a]This He said, signifying by
what death He would die.
34 The people answered Him,
[a]"We have heard from the law that
the Christ remains forever; and
how *can* You say, 'The Son of Man
must be lifted up'? Who is this Son
of Man?"
35 Then Jesus said to them, "A lit-
tle while longer [a]the light is with
you. [b]Walk while you have the
light, lest darkness overtake you;
[c]he who walks in darkness does
not know where he is going.
36 "While you have the light, be-
lieve in the light, that you may be-
come [a]sons of light." These things
Jesus spoke, and departed, and
[b]was hidden from them.

Who Has Believed Our Report?

37 But although He had done so
many [a]signs before them, they did
not believe in Him,
38 that the word of Isaiah the
prophet might be fulfilled, which
he spoke:

> [a]"*Lord, who has believed our*
> *report?*
> *And to whom has the arm of the*
> *LORD been revealed?*"

39 Therefore they could not be-
lieve, because Isaiah said again:

40 "*He[a] has blinded their eyes and*
hardened their hearts,
[b]*Lest they should see with their*
eyes,
Lest they should understand with
their hearts and turn,
So that I should heal them."

41 [a]These things Isaiah said
[1]when he saw His glory and spoke
of Him.

Walk in the Light

42 Nevertheless even among the
rulers many believed in Him, but
[a]because of the Pharisees they did
not confess *Him*, lest they should
be put out of the synagogue;
43 [a]for they loved the praise of
men more than the praise of God.
44 Then Jesus cried out and said,
[a]"He who believes in Me, [b]believes
not in Me [c]but in Him who sent
Me.
45 "And [a]he who sees Me sees
Him who sent Me.
46 [a]"I have come *as* a light into
the world, that whoever believes
in Me should not abide in dark-
ness.
47 "And if anyone hears My
words and does not [1]believe, [a]I do
not judge him; for [b]I did not come
to judge the world but to save the
world.
48 [a]"He who rejects Me, and does
not receive My words, has that
which judges him—[b]the word that
I have spoken will judge him in the
last day.
49 "For [a]I have not spoken on My
own *authority;* but the Father who
sent Me gave Me a command,
[b]what I should say and what I
should speak.
50 "And I know that His com-
mand is everlasting life. Therefore,
whatever I speak, just as the Fa-
ther has told Me, so I [a]speak."

Jesus Washes the Disciples' Feet

13 Now [a]before the Feast of the
Passover, when Jesus knew
that [b]His hour had come that He
should depart from this world to
the Father, having loved His own
who were in the world, He [c]loved
them to the end.
2 And [1]supper being ended, [a]the
devil having already put it into the
heart of Judas Iscariot, Simon's
son, to betray Him,

---

27 [a][Matt. 26:38, 39] [b]Luke 22:53
28 [a]Matt. 3:17; 17:5
30 [a]John 11:42
31 [a][2 Cor. 4:4]
32 [a]John 3:14; 8:28 [b][Rom. 5:18] [1]Crucified
33 [a]John 18:32; 21:19
34 [a]Mic. 4:7
35 [a][John 1:9; 7:33; 8:12] [b]Eph. 5:8 [c][1 John 2:9–11]
36 [a]Luke 16:8 [b]John 8:59
37 [a]John 11:47
38 [a]Is. 53:1
40 [a]Is. 6:9, 10 [b]Matt. 13:14
41 [a]Is. 6:1 [1]NU *because*
42 [a]John 7:13; 9:22
43 [a]John 5:41, 44
44 [a]Mark 9:37 [b][John 3:16, 18, 36; 11:25, 26] [c][John 5:24]
45 [a][John 14:9]
46 [a]John 1:4, 5; 8:12; 12:35, 36
47 [a]John 5:45 [b]John 3:17 [1]NU *keep them*
48 [a][Luke 10:16] [b]Deut. 18:18, 19
49 [a]John 8:38 [b]Deut. 18:18
50 [a]John 5:19; 8:28

CHAPTER 13

1 [a]Matt. 26:2 [b]John 12:23; 17:1 [c]John 15:9
2 [a]Luke 22:3 [1]NU *during supper*

3 Jesus, knowing [a]that the Father had given all things into His hands, and that He [b]had come from God and [c]was going to God,
4 [a]rose from supper and laid aside His garments, took a towel and girded Himself.
5 After that, He poured water into a basin and began to wash the disciples' feet, and to wipe *them* with the towel with which He was girded.
6 Then He came to Simon Peter. And *Peter* said to Him, [a]"Lord, are You washing my feet?"
7 Jesus answered and said to him, "What I am doing you [a]do not understand now, [b]but you will know after this."
8 Peter said to Him, "You shall never wash my feet!" Jesus answered him, [a]"If I do not wash you, you have no part with Me."
9 Simon Peter said to Him, "Lord, not my feet only, but also *my* hands and *my* head!"
10 Jesus said to him, "He who is bathed needs only to wash *his* feet, but is completely clean; and [a]you are clean, but not all of you."
11 For [a]He knew who would betray Him; therefore He said, "You are not all clean."
12 So when He had washed their feet, taken His garments, and sat down again, He said to them, "Do you [1]know what I have done to you?
13 [a]"You call Me Teacher and Lord, and you say well, for *so* I am.
14 [a]"If I then, *your* Lord and Teacher, have washed your feet, [b]you also ought to wash one another's feet.
15 "For [a]I have given you an example, that you should do as I have done to you.
16 [a]"Most assuredly, I say to you, a servant is not greater than his master; nor is he who is sent greater than he who sent him.
17 [a]"If you know these things, blessed are you if you do them.

Jesus Identifies His Betrayer

18 "I do not speak concerning all of you. I know whom I have chosen; but that the [a]Scripture may be fulfilled, [b]*'He who eats [1]bread with Me has lifted up his heel against Me.'*
19 [a]"Now I tell you before it comes, that when it does come to pass, you may believe that I am *He.*
20 [a]"Most assuredly, I say to you, he who receives whomever I send receives Me; and he who receives Me receives Him who sent Me."
21 [a]When Jesus had said these things, [b]He was troubled in spirit, and testified and said, "Most assuredly, I say to you, [c]one of you will betray Me."
22 Then the disciples looked at one another, perplexed about whom He spoke.
23 Now [a]there was [1]leaning on Jesus' bosom one of His disciples, whom Jesus loved.
24 Simon Peter therefore motioned to him to ask who it was of whom He spoke.
25 Then, leaning [1]back on Jesus' breast, he said to Him, "Lord, who is it?"
26 Jesus answered, "It is he to whom I shall give a piece of bread when I have dipped *it.*" And having dipped the bread, He gave *it* to [a]Judas Iscariot, *the son* of Simon.
27 [a]Now after the piece of bread, Satan entered him. Then Jesus said to him, "What you do, do quickly."
28 But no one at the table knew for what reason He said this to him.
29 For some thought, because [a]Judas had the money box, that Jesus had said to him, "Buy *those things* we need for the feast," or that he should give something to the poor.
30 Having received the piece of bread, he then went out immediately. And it was night.

The New Commandment

31 So, when he had gone out, Jesus said, [a]"Now the Son of Man is glorified, and [b]God is glorified in Him.
32 "If God is glorified in Him, God will also glorify Him in Himself, and [a]glorify Him immediately.
33 "Little children, I shall be with you a [a]little while longer. You will seek Me; [b]and as I said to the Jews, 'Where I am going, you cannot come,' so now I say to you.

---

3 [a]Acts 2:36 [b]John 8:42; 16:28 [c]John 17:11; 20:17
4 [a][Luke 22:27]
6 [a]Matt. 3:14
7 [a]John 12:16; 16:12 [b]John 13:19
8 [a][1 Cor. 6:11]
10 [a][John 15:3]
11 [a]John 6:64; 18:4
12 [1]*understand*
13 [a]Matt. 23:8, 10
14 [a]Luke 22:27 [b][Rom. 12:10]
15 [a][1 Pet. 2:21–24]
16 [a]Matt. 10:24
17 [a][James 1:25]
18 [a]John 15:25; 17:12 [b]Ps. 41:9 [1]NU *My bread has*
19 [a]John 14:29; 16:4
20 [a]Matt. 10:40
21 [a]Luke 22:21 [b]John 12:27 [c]1 John 2:19
23 [a]John 19:26; 20:2; 21:7, 20 [1]*reclining*
25 [1]NU, M add *thus*
26 [a]John 6:70, 71; 12:4
27 [a]Luke 22:3
29 [a]John 12:6
31 [a]John 12:23 [b][1 Pet. 4:11]
32 [a]John 12:23
33 [a]John 12:35; 14:19; 16:16–19 [b][John 7:34; 8:21]

34 [a]"A new commandment I give
to you, that you love one another;
as I have loved you, that you also
love one another.
35 [a]"By this all will know that you
are My disciples, if you have love
for one another."

Jesus Predicts Peter's Denial

36 Simon Peter said to Him,
"Lord, where are You going?" Je-
sus answered him, "Where I [a]am
going you cannot follow Me now,
but [b]you shall follow Me after-
ward."
37 Peter said to Him, "Lord, why
can I not follow You now? I will
[a]lay down my life for Your sake."
38 Jesus answered him, "Will you
lay down your life for My sake?
Most assuredly, I say to you, the
rooster shall not [a]crow till you
have denied Me three times.

The Way, the Truth, and the Life

14 "Let [a]not your heart be trou-
bled; you believe in God, be-
lieve also in Me.
2 "In My Father's house are
many [1]mansions; if *it were* not *so,*
[2]I would have told you. [a]I go to pre-
pare a place for you.
3 "And if I go and prepare a
place for you, [a]I will come again
and receive you to Myself; that
[b]where I am, *there* you may be
also.
4 "And where I go you know,
and the way you know."
5 [a]Thomas said to Him, "Lord,
we do not know where You are go-
ing, and how can we know the
way?"
6 Jesus said to him, "I am [a]the
way, [b]the truth, and [c]the life. [d]No
one comes to the Father [e]except
through Me.

The Father Revealed

7 [a]"If you had known Me, you
would have known My Father
also; and from now on you know
Him and have seen Him."
8 Philip said to Him, "Lord, show
us the Father, and it is sufficient
for us."
9 Jesus said to him, "Have I been
with you so long, and yet you have
not known Me, Philip? [a]He who
has seen Me has seen the Father;

34 [a]1 Thess. 4:9
35 [a]1 John 2:5
36 [a]John 13:33; 14:2; 16:5 [b]2 Pet. 1:14
37 [a]Mark 14:29–31
38 [a]John 18:25–27

CHAPTER 14

1 [a][John 14:27; 16:22, 24]
2 [a]John 13:33, 36 [1]Lit. *dwellings* [2]NU *would I have told you that I go* or *I would have told you; for I go*
3 [a][Acts 1:11] [b][John 12:26]
5 [a]Matt. 10:3
6 [a][Heb. 9:8; 10:19, 20] [b][John 1:14, 17; 8:32; 18:37] [c][John 11:25] [d]1 Tim. 2:5 [e][John 10:7–9]
7 [a]John 8:19
9 [a]Col. 1:15
10 [a]John 10:38; 14:11, 20 [b]John 5:19; 14:24
11 [a]John 5:36; 10:38
12 [a]Luke 10:17
13 [a]Matt. 7:7 [b]John 13:31
14 [1]NU *ask Me*
15 [a]1 John 5:3 [1]NU *you will keep*
16 [a]Rom. 8:15 [1]*Comforter,* Gr. *Parakletos*
17 [a][1 John 4:6; 5:7] [b][1 Cor. 2:14] [c][1 John 2:27]
18 [a][Matt. 28:20] [b][John 14:3, 28]
19 [a]John 16:16, 22 [b][1 Cor. 15:20]
20 [a]John 10:38; 14:11
21 [a]1 John 2:5 [1]*reveal*
22 [a]Luke 6:16

so how can you say, 'Show us the
Father'?
10 "Do you not believe that [a]I am
in the Father, and the Father in
Me? The words that I speak to you
[b]I do not speak on My own *author-
ity;* but the Father who dwells in
Me does the works.
11 "Believe Me that I *am* in the Fa-
ther and the Father in Me, [a]or else
believe Me for the sake of the
works themselves.

The Answered Prayer

12 [a]"Most assuredly, I say to you,
he who believes in Me, the works
that I do he will do also; and
greater *works* than these he will
do, because I go to My Father.
13 [a]"And whatever you ask in My
name, that I will do, that the Father
may be [b]glorified in the Son.
14 "If you [1]ask anything in My
name, I will do *it.*

Jesus Promises Another Helper

15 [a]"If you love Me, [1]keep My com-
mandments.
16 "And I will pray the Father,
and [a]He will give you another
[1]Helper, that He may abide with
you forever—
17 [a]"the Spirit of truth, [b]whom the
world cannot receive, because it
neither sees Him nor knows Him;
but you know Him, for He dwells
with you [c]and will be in you.
18 [a]"I will not leave you orphans;
[b]I will come to you.

Indwelling of the Father and the Son

19 "A little while longer and the
world will see Me no more, but
[a]you will see Me. [b]Because I live,
you will live also.
20 "At that day you will know that
[a]I *am* in My Father, and you in Me,
and I in you.
21 [a]"He who has My command-
ments and keeps them, it is he who
loves Me. And he who loves Me
will be loved by My Father, and I
will love him and [1]manifest Myself
to him."
22 [a]Judas (not Iscariot) said to
Him, "Lord, how is it that You will
manifest Yourself to us, and not
to the world?"
23 Jesus answered and said to
him, "If anyone loves Me, he will
keep My word; and My Father will

love him, [a]and We will come to
him and make Our home with him.
24 "He who does not love Me does
not keep My words; and [a]the word
which you hear is not Mine but the
Father's who sent Me.

The Gift of His Peace

25 "These things I have spoken to
you while being present with you.
26 "But [a]the [1]Helper, the Holy
Spirit, whom the Father will [b]send
in My name, [c]He will teach you all
things, and bring to your [d]remem-
brance all things that I said to you.
27 [a]"Peace I leave with you, My
peace I give to you; not as the
world gives do I give to you. Let
not your heart be troubled, neither
let it be afraid.
28 "You have heard Me [a]say to
you, 'I am going away and coming
back to you.' If you loved Me, you
would rejoice because [1]I said, [b]'I
am going to the Father,' for [c]My
Father is greater than I.
29 "And [a]now I have told you be-
fore it comes, that when it does
come to pass, you may believe.
30 "I will no longer talk much
with you, [a]for the ruler of this
world is coming, and he has [b]noth-
ing in Me.
31 "But that the world may know
that I love the Father, and [a]as the
Father gave Me commandment, so
I do. Arise, let us go from here.

The True Vine

15 "I am the true vine, and My
Father is the vinedresser.
2 [a]"Every branch in Me that does
not bear fruit He [1]takes away; and
every *branch* that bears fruit He
prunes, that it may bear [b]more
fruit.
3 [a]"You are already clean be-
cause of the word which I have
spoken to you.
4 [a]"Abide in Me, and I in you. As
the branch cannot bear fruit of it-
self, unless it abides in the vine,
neither can you, unless you abide
in Me.
5 "I am the vine, you *are* the
branches. He who abides in Me,
and I in him, bears much [a]fruit; for
without Me you can do [b]nothing.
6 "If anyone does not abide in
Me, [a]he is cast out as a branch and
is withered; and they gather them
and throw *them* into the fire, and
they are burned.
7 "If you abide in Me, and My
words [a]abide in you, [b]you[1] will ask
what you desire, and it shall be
done for you.
8 [a]"By this My Father is glorified,
that you bear much fruit; [b]so you
will be My disciples.

Love and Joy Perfected

9 "As the Father [a]loved Me, I also
have loved you; abide in My love.
10 [a]"If you keep My command-
ments, you will abide in My love,
just as I have kept My Father's
commandments and abide in His
love.
11 "These things I have spoken to
you, that My joy may remain in
you, and [a]*that* your joy may be
full.
12 [a]"This is My [b]commandment,
that you love one another as I have
loved you.
13 [a]"Greater love has no one than
this, than to lay down one's life for
his friends.
14 [a]"You are My friends if you do
whatever I command you.
15 "No longer do I call you ser-
vants, for a servant does not know
what his master is doing; but I
have called you friends, [a]for all
things that I heard from My Father
I have made known to you.
16 [a]"You did not choose Me, but
I chose you and [b]appointed you
that you should go and bear fruit,
and *that* your fruit should remain,
that whatever you ask the Father
[c]in My name He may give you.
17 "These things I command you,
that you love one another.

The World's Hatred

18 [a]"If the world hates you, you
know that it hated Me before *it
hated* you.
19 [a]"If you were of the world, the
world would love its own. Yet [b]be-
cause you are not of the world, but
I chose you out of the world, there-
fore the world hates you.
20 "Remember the word that I
said to you, [a]'A servant is not
greater than his master.' If they
persecuted Me, they will also per-
secute you. [b]If they kept My word,
they will keep yours also.
21 "But [a]all these things they will

23 [a]Rev. 3:20; 21:3
24 [a]John 5:19
26 [a]Luke 24:49 [b]John 15:26 [c]1 Cor. 2:13 [d]John 2:22; 12:16 [1]*Comforter,* Gr. *Parakletos*
27 [a][Phil. 4:7]
28 [a]John 14:3, 18 [b]John 16:16 [c][Phil. 2:6] [1]NU omits *I said*
29 [a]John 13:19
30 [a][John 12:31] [b][Heb. 4:15]
31 [a]John 10:18

CHAPTER 15

2 [a]Matt. 15:13 [b][Matt. 13:12] [1]Or *lifts up*
3 [a][John 13:10; 17:17]
4 [a][Col. 1:23]
5 [a]Hos. 14:8 [b]2 Cor. 3:5
6 [a]Matt. 3:10
7 [a]1 John 2:14 [b]John 14:13; 16:23 [1]NU omits *you will*
8 [a][Matt. 5:16] [b]John 8:31
9 [a]John 5:20; 17:26
10 [a]John 14:15
11 [a]1 John 1:4
12 [a]1 John 3:11 [b]Rom. 12:9
13 [a]1 John 3:16
14 [a][Matt. 12:50; 28:20]
15 [a]Gen. 18:17
16 [a]John 6:70; 13:18; 15:19 [b][Col. 1:6] [c]John 14:13; 16:23, 24
18 [a]1 John 3:13
19 [a]1 John 4:5 [b]John 17:14
20 [a]John 13:16 [b]Ezek. 3:7
21 [a]Matt. 10:22; 24:9

do to you for My name's sake, be-
cause they do not know Him who
sent Me.
22 [a]"If I had not come and spoken
to them, they would have no sin,
[b]but now they have no excuse for
their sin.
23 [a]"He who hates Me hates My
Father also.
24 "If I had not done among them
[a]the works which no one else did,
they would have no sin; but now
they have [b]seen and also hated
both Me and My Father.
25 "But *this happened* that the
word might be fulfilled which is
written in their law, [a]*'They hated
Me without a cause.'*

The Coming Rejection

26 [a]"But when the [1]Helper comes,
whom I shall send to you from the
Father, the Spirit of truth who pro-
ceeds from the Father, [b]He will tes-
tify of Me.
27 "And [a]you also will bear wit-
ness, because [b]you have been with
Me from the beginning.

16 "These things I have spoken
to you, that you [a]should not
be made to stumble.
2 [a]"They will put you out of the
synagogues; yes, the time is com-
ing [b]that whoever kills you will
think that he offers God service.
3 "And [a]these things they will do
[1]to you because they have not
known the Father nor Me.
4 "But these things I have told
you, that when [1]the time comes,
you may remember that I told you
of them. And these things I did not
say to you at the beginning, be-
cause I was with you.

The Work of the Holy Spirit

5 "But now I [a]go away to Him
who sent Me, and none of you asks
Me, 'Where are You going?'
6 "But because I have said these
things to you, [a]sorrow has filled
your heart.
7 "Nevertheless I tell you the
truth. It is to your advantage that
I go away; for if I do not go away,
the Helper will not come to you;
but [a]if I depart, I will send Him to
you.
8 "And when He has [a]come, He
will convict the world of sin, and
of righteousness, and of judgment:

22 [a]John 9:41; 15:24 [b][Rom. 1:20; James 4:17]
23 [a]1 John 2:23
24 [a]John 3:2 [b]John 14:9
25 [a]Ps. 35:19; 69:4; 109:3–5
26 [a]Luke 24:49; [John 14:17]; Acts 2:4, 33 [b]1 John 5:6 [1]*Comforter*, Gr. *Parakletos*
27 [a]Luke 24:48; 1 Pet. 5:1; 2 Pet. 1:16 [b]Matt. 3:14; Luke 1:2; 1 John 1:1

CHAPTER 16

1 [a]Matt. 11:6
2 [a]John 9:22 [b]Acts 8:1
3 [a]John 8:19; 15:21; Acts 13:27; Rom. 10:2 [1]NU, M omit *to you*
4 [1]NU *their*
5 [a]John 7:33; 13:33; 14:28; 17:11
6 [a]Matt. 17:23; [John 16:20, 22]
7 [a]Acts 2:33
8 [a]Acts 1:8; 2:1–4, 37
9 [a]Acts 2:22
10 [a]Acts 2:32 [b]John 5:32
11 [a]Acts 26:18 [b][Luke 10:18]
12 [a]Mark 4:33
13 [a][John 14:17] [b]John 14:26; Acts 11:28; Rev. 1:19
14 [a]John 15:26
15 [a]Matt. 11:27; John 3:35 [1]NU, M *takes of Mine and will declare*
16 [a]John 7:33; 12:35; 13:33; 14:19; 19:40–42; 20:19 [b]John 13:3
18 [1]*understand*
20 [a]Mark 16:10; Luke 23:48; 24:17 [b]Luke 24:32, 41
21 [a]Gen. 3:16; Is. 13:8; 26:17; 42:14; 1 Thess. 5:3

9 [a]"of sin, because they do not
believe in Me;
10 [a]"of righteousness, [b]because I
go to My Father and you see Me
no more;
11 [a]"of judgment, because [b]the
ruler of this world is judged.
12 "I still have many things to say
to you, [a]but you cannot bear *them*
now.
13 "However, when He, [a]the Spirit
of truth, has come, [b]He will guide
you into all truth; for He will not
speak on His own *authority*, but
whatever He hears He will speak;
and He will tell you things to
come.
14 [a]"He will glorify Me, for He
will take of what is Mine and de-
clare *it* to you.
15 [a]"All things that the Father has
are Mine. Therefore I said that He
[1]will take of Mine and declare *it*
to you.

Sorrow Will Turn to Joy

16 "A [a]little while, and you will
not see Me; and again a little
while, and you will see Me, [b]be-
cause I go to the Father."
17 Then *some* of His disciples said
among themselves, "What is this
that He says to us, 'A little while,
and you will not see Me; and again
a little while, and you will see Me';
and, 'because I go to the Father'?"
18 They said therefore, "What is
this that He says, 'A little while'?
We do not [1]know what He is say-
ing."
19 Now Jesus knew that they de-
sired to ask Him, and He said to
them, "Are you inquiring among
yourselves about what I said, 'A
little while, and you will not see
Me; and again a little while, and
you will see Me'?
20 "Most assuredly, I say to you
that you will weep and [a]lament,
but the world will rejoice; and you
will be sorrowful, but your sorrow
will be turned into [b]joy.
21 [a]"A woman, when she is in la-
bor, has sorrow because her hour
has come; but as soon as she has
given birth to the child, she no
longer remembers the anguish, for
joy that a human being has been
born into the world.
22 "Therefore you now have sor-
row; but I will see you again and

[a]your heart will rejoice, and your
joy no one will take from you.
23 "And in that day you will ask
Me nothing. [a]Most assuredly, I say
to you, whatever you ask the Fa-
ther in My name He will give you.
24 "Until now you have asked
nothing in My name. Ask, and you
will receive, [a]that your joy may be
[b]full.

Jesus Christ Has Overcome the World

25 "These things I have spoken to
you in figurative language; but the
time is coming when I will no
longer speak to you in figurative
language, but I will tell you
[a]plainly about the Father.
26 "In that day you will ask in My
name, and I do not say to you that
I shall pray the Father for you;
27 [a]"for the Father Himself loves
you, because you have loved Me,
and [b]have believed that I came
forth from God.
28 [a]"I came forth from the Father
and have come into the world.
Again, I leave the world and go to
the Father."
29 His disciples said to Him, "See,
now You are speaking plainly, and
using no figure of speech!
30 "Now we are sure that [a]You
know all things, and have no need
that anyone should question You.
By this [b]we believe that You came
forth from God."
31 Jesus answered them, "Do you
now believe?
32 [a]"Indeed the hour is coming,
yes, has now come, that you will
be scattered, [b]each to his [1]own,
and will leave Me alone. And [c]yet
I am not alone, because the Father
is with Me.
33 "These things I have spoken to
you, that [a]in Me you may have
peace. [b]In the world you [1]will have
tribulation; but be of good cheer,
[c]I have overcome the world."

Jesus Prays for Himself

17 Jesus spoke these words,
lifted up His eyes to heaven,
and said: "Father, [a]the hour has
come. Glorify Your Son, that Your
Son also may glorify You,
2 [a]"as You have given Him au-
thority over all flesh, that He
[1]should give eternal life to as many
[b]as You have given Him.

22 [a]1 Pet. 1:8
23 [a]Matt. 7:7
24 [a]John 17:13 [b]John 15:11
25 [a]John 7:13
27 [a][John 14:21, 23] [b]John 3:13
28 [a]John 13:1, 3; 16:5, 10, 17
30 [a]John 21:17 [b]John 17:8
32 [a]Matt. 26:31, 56 [b]John 20:10 [c]John 8:29 [1]*own things or place*
33 [a][Eph. 2:14] [b]2 Tim. 3:12 [c]Rom. 8:37 [1]NU, M omit *will*

CHAPTER 17
1 [a]John 12:23
2 [a]John 3:35 [b]John 6:37, 39; 17:6, 9, 24 [1]M *shall*
3 [a]Jer. 9:23, 24 [b]1 Cor. 8:4 [c]John 3:34
4 [a]John 13:31 [b]John 4:34; 19:30 [c]John 14:31
5 [a]Phil. 2:6 [1]Lit. *alongside*
6 [a]Ps. 22:22 [b]John 6:37 [c]Ezek. 18:4 [1]*revealed*
8 [a]John 8:28 [b]John 8:42; 16:27, 30 [c]Deut. 18:15, 18
9 [a][1 John 5:19]
10 [a]John 16:15
11 [a]John 13:1 [b][1 Pet. 1:5] [c]John 10:30 [1]NU, M *keep them through Your name which You have given Me*
12 [a]Heb. 2:13 [b]1 John 2:19 [c]John 6:70 [d]Ps. 41:9; 109:8 [1]NU omits *in the world* [2]NU *Your name which You gave Me. And I guarded them; (or it:)* [3]*destroyed* [4]*destruction*
14 [a]John 15:19 [b]John 8:23
15 [a]1 John 5:18

3 "And [a]this is eternal life, that
they may know You, [b]the only true
God, and Jesus Christ [c]whom You
have sent.
4 [a]"I have glorified You on the
earth. [b]I have finished the work
[c]which You have given Me to do.
5 "And now, O Father, glorify Me
together [1]with Yourself, with the
glory [a]which I had with You before
the world was.

Jesus Prays for His Disciples

6 [a]"I have [1]manifested Your
name to the men [b]whom You have
given Me out of the world. [c]They
were Yours, You gave them to Me,
and they have kept Your word.
7 "Now they have known that all
things which You have given Me
are from You.
8 "For I have given to them the
words [a]which You have given Me;
and they have received *them*, [b]and
have known surely that I came
forth from You; and they have be-
lieved that [c]You sent Me.
9 "I pray for them. [a]I do not pray
for the world but for those whom
You have given Me, for they are
Yours.
10 "And all Mine are Yours, and
[a]Yours are Mine, and I am glori-
fied in them.
11 [a]"Now I am no longer in the
world, but these are in the world,
and I come to You. Holy Father,
[b]keep[1] through Your name those
whom You have given Me, that
they may be one [c]as We *are*.
12 "While I was with them [1]in the
world, [a]I kept them in [2]Your
name. Those whom You gave Me
I have kept; and [b]none of them is
[3]lost [c]except the son of [4]perdition,
[d]that the Scripture might be ful-
filled.
13 "But now I come to You, and
these things I speak in the world,
that they may have My joy fulfilled
in themselves.
14 "I have given them Your word;
[a]and the world has hated them be-
cause they are not of the world,
[b]just as I am not of the world.
15 "I do not pray that You should
take them out of the world, but
[a]that You should keep them from
the evil one.
16 "They are not of the world, just
as I am not of the world.

17 [a]"Sanctify[1] them by Your truth.
[b]Your word is truth.
18 [a]"As You sent Me into the
world, I also have sent them into
the world.
19 "And [a]for their sakes I sanctify
Myself, that they also may be
sanctified by the truth.

Jesus Prays for All Believers

20 "I do not pray for these alone,
but also for those who [1]will believe
in Me through their word;
21 [a]"that they all may be one, as
[b]You, Father, *are* in Me, and I in
You; that they also may be one in
Us, that the world may believe that
You sent Me.
22 "And the [a]glory which You
gave Me I have given them, [b]that
they may be one just as We are
one:
23 "I in them, and You in Me;
[a]that they may be made perfect in
one, and that the world may know
that You have sent Me, and have
loved them as You have loved Me.
24 [a]"Father, I desire that they also
whom You gave Me may be with
Me where I am, that they may be-
hold My glory which You have
given Me; [b]for You loved Me be-
fore the foundation of the world.
25 "O righteous Father! [a]The
world has not known You, but [b]I
have known You; and [c]these have
known that You sent Me.
26 [a]"And I have declared to them
Your name, and will declare *it*,
that the love [b]with which You
loved Me may be in them, and I
in them."

Betrayal and Arrest in Gethsemane

18 When Jesus had spoken
these words, [a]He went out
with His disciples over [b]the Brook
Kidron, where there was a garden,
which He and His disciples en-
tered.
2 And Judas, who betrayed Him,
also knew the place; [a]for Jesus of-
ten met there with His disciples.
3 [a]Then Judas, having received a
detachment *of troops*, and officers
from the chief priests and Phari-
sees, came there with lanterns,
torches, and weapons.
4 Jesus therefore, [a]knowing all
things that would come upon Him,
went forward and said to them,
"Whom are you seeking?"
5 They answered Him, [a]"Jesus
[1]of Nazareth." Jesus said to them,
"I am *He*." And Judas, who [b]be-
trayed Him, also stood with them.
6 Now when He said to them, "I
am *He*," they drew back and fell
to the ground.
7 Then He asked them again,
"Whom are you seeking?" And
they said, "Jesus of Nazareth."
8 Jesus answered, "I have told
you that I am *He*. Therefore, if you
seek Me, let these go their way,"
9 that the saying might be ful-
filled which He spoke, [a]"Of those
whom You gave Me I have lost
none."
10 [a]Then Simon Peter, having a
sword, drew it and struck the high
priest's servant, and cut off his
right ear. The servant's name was
Malchus.
11 So Jesus said to Peter, "Put
your sword into the sheath. Shall
I not drink [a]the cup which My Fa-
ther has given Me?"

Before the High Priest

12 Then the detachment *of troops*
and the captain and the officers of
the Jews arrested Jesus and bound
Him.
13 And [a]they led Him away to
[b]Annas first, for he was the father-
in-law of [c]Caiaphas who was high
priest that year.
14 [a]Now it was Caiaphas who ad-
vised the Jews that it was [1]expedi-
ent that one man should die for the
people.

Peter Denies Jesus

15 [a]And Simon Peter followed Je-
sus, and so *did* [b]another[1] disciple.
Now that disciple was known to
the high priest, and went with Je-
sus into the courtyard of the high
priest.
16 [a]But Peter stood at the door
outside. Then the other disciple,
who was known to the high priest,
went out and spoke to her who
kept the door, and brought Peter
in.
17 Then the servant girl who kept
the door said to Peter, "You are
not also *one* of this Man's disci-
ples, are you?" He said, "I am
[a]not."

17 [a][Eph. 5:26] [b]Ps. 119:9, 142, 151 [1]*Set them apart*
18 [a]John 4:38; 20:21
19 [a][Heb. 10:10]
20 [1]NU, M omit *will*
21 [a][Gal. 3:28] [b]John 10:38; 17:11, 23
22 [a]1 John 1:3 [b][2 Cor. 3:18]
23 [a][Col. 3:14]
24 [a][1 Thess. 4:17] [b]John 17:5
25 [a]John 15:21 [b]John 7:29; 8:55; 10:15 [c]John 3:17; 17:3, 8, 18, 21, 23
26 [a]John 17:6 [b]John 15:9

CHAPTER 18

1 [a]Mark 14:26, 32 [b]2 Sam. 15:23
2 [a]Luke 21:37; 22:39
3 [a]Luke 22:47–53
4 [a]John 6:64; 13:1, 3; 19:28
5 [a]Matt. 21:11 [b]Ps. 41:9 [1]Lit. *the Nazarene*
9 [a][John 6:39; 17:12]
10 [a]Matt. 26:51
11 [a]Matt. 20:22; 26:39
13 [a]Matt. 26:57 [b]Luke 3:2 [c]Matt. 26:3
14 [a]John 11:50 [1]*advantageous*
15 [a]Mark 14:54 [b]John 20:2–5 [1]M *the other*
16 [a]Matt. 26:69
17 [a]Matt. 26:34

18 Now the servants and officers who had made a fire of coals stood there, for it was cold, and they warmed themselves. And Peter stood with them and warmed himself.

Jesus Questioned by the High Priest

19 The high priest then asked Jesus about His disciples and His doctrine.

20 Jesus answered him, [a]"I spoke openly to the world. I always taught [b]in synagogues and [c]in the temple, where [1]the Jews always meet, and in secret I have said nothing.

21 "Why do you ask Me? Ask [a]those who have heard Me what I said to them. Indeed they know what I said."

22 And when He had said these things, one of the officers who stood by [a]struck[1] Jesus with the palm of his hand, saying, "Do You answer the high priest like that?"

23 Jesus answered him, "If I have spoken evil, bear witness of the evil; but if well, why do you strike Me?"

24 [a]Then Annas sent Him bound to [b]Caiaphas the high priest.

Peter Denies Twice More

25 Now Simon Peter stood and warmed himself. [a]Therefore they said to him, "You are not also *one* of His disciples, are you?" He denied *it* and said, "I am not!"

26 One of the servants of the high priest, a relative *of him* whose ear Peter cut off, said, "Did I not see you in the garden with Him?"

27 Peter then denied again; and [a]immediately a rooster crowed.

In Pilate's Court

28 [a]Then they led Jesus from Caiaphas to the Praetorium, and it was early morning. [b]But they themselves did not go into the [1]Praetorium, lest they should be defiled, but that they might eat the Passover.

29 [a]Pilate then went out to them and said, "What accusation do you bring against this Man?"

30 They answered and said to him, "If He were not [1]an evildoer, we would not have delivered Him up to you."

31 Then Pilate said to them, "You take Him and judge Him according to your law." Therefore the Jews said to him, "It is not lawful for us to put anyone to death,"

32 [a]that the saying of Jesus might be fulfilled which He spoke, [b]signifying by what death He would die.

33 [a]Then Pilate entered the [1]Praetorium again, called Jesus, and said to Him, "Are You the King of the Jews?"

34 Jesus answered him, "Are you speaking for yourself about this, or did others tell you this concerning Me?"

35 Pilate answered, "Am I a Jew? Your own nation and the chief priests have delivered You to me. What have You done?"

36 [a]Jesus answered, [b]"My kingdom is not of this world. If My kingdom were of this world, My servants would fight, so that I should not be delivered to the Jews; but now My kingdom is not from here."

37 Pilate therefore said to Him, "Are You a king then?" Jesus answered, "You say *rightly* that I am a king. For this cause I was born, and for this cause I have come into the world, [a]that I should bear [b]witness to the truth. Everyone who [c]is of the truth [d]hears My voice."

38 Pilate said to Him, "What is truth?" And when he had said this, he went out again to the Jews, and said to them, [a]"I find no fault in Him at all.

Taking the Place of Barabbas

39 [a]"But you have a custom that I should release someone to you at the Passover. Do you therefore want me to release to you the King of the Jews?"

40 [a]Then they all cried again, saying, "Not this Man, but Barabbas!" [b]Now Barabbas was a robber.

The Soldiers Mock Jesus

19 So then [a]Pilate took Jesus and scourged *Him*.

2 And the soldiers twisted a crown of thorns and put *it* on His head, and they put on Him a purple robe.

3 [1]Then they said, "Hail, King of the Jews!" And they [a]struck Him with their hands.

20 [a]Luke 4:15 [b]John 6:59 [c]Mark 14:49 [1]NU *all the Jews meet*
21 [a]Mark 12:37
22 [a]Jer. 20:2 [1]Lit. *gave Jesus a slap.*
24 [a]Matt. 26:57 [b]John 11:49
25 [a]Luke 22:58–62
27 [a]John 13:38
28 [a]Mark 15:1 [b]Acts 10:28; 11:3 [1]The governor's headquarters
29 [a]Matt. 27:11–14
30 [1]*a criminal*
32 [a]Matt. 20:17–19; 26:2 [b]John 3:14; 8:28; 12:32, 33
33 [a]Matt. 27:11 [1]The governor's headquarters
36 [a]1 Tim. 6:13 [b][Dan. 2:44; 7:14]
37 [a][Matt. 5:17; 20:28] [b]Is. 55:4 [c][John 14:6] [d]John 8:47; 10:27
38 [a]John 19:4, 6
39 [a]Luke 23:17–25
40 [a]Acts 3:14 [b]Luke 23:19
CHAPTER 19
1 [a]Matt. 20:19; 27:26
3 [a]Is. 50:6 [1]NU *And they came up to Him and said*

4 Pilate then went out again, and
said to them, "Behold, I am bring-
ing Him out to you, [a]that you may
know that I find no fault in Him."

Pilate's Decision

5 Then Jesus came out, wearing
the crown of thorns and the purple
robe. And *Pilate* said to them, "Be-
hold the Man!"
6 [a]Therefore, when the chief
priests and officers saw Him, they
cried out, saying, "Crucify *Him*,
crucify *Him!*" Pilate said to them,
"You take Him and crucify *Him*,
for I find no fault in Him."
7 The Jews answered him, [a]"We
have a law, and according to [1]our
law He ought to die, because [b]He
made Himself the Son of God."
8 Therefore, when Pilate heard
that saying, he was the more
afraid,
9 and went again into the Praeto-
rium, and said to Jesus, "Where
are You from?" [a]But Jesus gave
him no answer.
10 Then Pilate said to Him, "Are
You not speaking to me? Do You
not know that I have [1]power to
crucify You, and [1]power to release
You?"
11 Jesus answered, [a]"You could
have no power at all against Me
unless it had been given you from
above. Therefore [b]the one who de-
livered Me to you has the greater
sin."
12 From then on Pilate sought to
release Him, but the Jews cried
out, saying, "If you let this Man
go, you are not Caesar's friend.
[a]Whoever makes himself a king
speaks against Caesar."
13 [a]When Pilate therefore heard
that saying, he brought Jesus out
and sat down in the judgment seat
in a place that is called *The*
Pavement, but in Hebrew, Gab-
batha.
14 Now [a]it was the Preparation
Day of the Passover, and about the
sixth hour. And he said to the
Jews, "Behold your King!"
15 But they cried out, "Away with
Him, away with *Him!* Crucify
Him!" Pilate said to them, "Shall
I crucify your King?" The chief
priests answered, [a]"We have no
king but Caesar!"
16 [a]Then he delivered Him to
them to be crucified. So they took
Jesus [1]and led *Him* away.

The King on a Cross

17 [a]And He, bearing His cross,
[b]went out to a place called *the
Place* of a Skull, which is called
in Hebrew, Golgotha,
18 where they crucified Him, and
[a]two others with Him, one on ei-
ther side, and Jesus in the center.
19 [a]Now Pilate wrote a title and
put *it* on the cross. And the writing
was:

JESUS OF NAZARETH, THE
KING OF THE JEWS.

20 Then many of the Jews read
this title, for the place where Jesus
was crucified was near the city;
and it was written in Hebrew,
Greek, *and* Latin.
21 Therefore the chief priests of
the Jews said to Pilate, "Do not
write, 'The King of the Jews,' but,
'He said, "I am the King of the
Jews."'"
22 Pilate answered, "What I have
written, I have written."
23 [a]Then the soldiers, when they
had crucified Jesus, took His gar-
ments and made four parts, to
each soldier a part, and also the
tunic. Now the tunic was without
seam, woven from the top in one
piece.
24 They said therefore among
themselves, "Let us not tear it, but
cast lots for it, whose it shall be,"
that the Scripture might be ful-
filled which says:

[a]"*They divided My garments*
among them,
And for My clothing they cast
lots."

Therefore the soldiers did these
things.

Behold Your Mother

25 [a]Now there stood by the cross
of Jesus His mother, and His moth-
er's sister, Mary the *wife* of [b]Clo-
pas, and Mary Magdalene.
26 When Jesus therefore saw His
mother, and [a]the disciple whom
He loved standing by, He said to
His mother, [b]"Woman, behold
your son!"
27 Then He said to the disciple,

4 [a]Is. 53:9; John 18:33, 38; 1 Pet. 2:22–24
6 [a]Acts 3:13
7 [a]Lev. 24:16 [b]Matt. 26:63–66; John 5:18; 10:33 [1]NU *the law*
9 [a]Is. 53:7; Matt. 27:12, 14; Luke 23:9
10 [1]*authority*
11 [a][Luke 22:53]; John 7:30 [b]John 3:27; Rom. 13:1
12 [a]Luke 23:2; John 18:33; Acts 17:7
13 [a]Deut. 1:17; 1 Sam. 15:24; Prov. 29:25; Is. 51:12; Acts 4:19
14 [a]Matt. 27:62; John 19:31, 42
15 [a][Gen. 49:10]
16 [a]Matt. 27:26, 31; Mark 15:15; Luke 23:24 [1]NU omits *and led Him away*
17 [a]Matt. 27:31, 33; Mark 15:21, 22; Luke 23:26, 33 [b]Num. 15:36; Heb. 13:12
18 [a]Ps. 22:16–18; Is. 53:12; Matt. 20:19; 26:2
19 [a]Matt. 27:37; Mark 15:26; Luke 23:38
23 [a]Matt. 27:35; Mark 15:24; Luke 23:34
24 [a]Ps. 22:18
25 [a]Matt. 27:55; Mark 15:40; Luke 2:35; 23:49 [b]Luke 24:18
26 [a]John 13:23; 20:2; 21:7, 20, 24 [b]John 2:4

"Behold your mother!" And from
that hour that disciple took her [a]to
his own *home.*

It Is Finished

28 After this, Jesus, [1]knowing that
all things were now accomplished,
[a]that the Scripture might be ful-
filled, said, "I thirst!"
29 Now a vessel full of sour wine
was sitting there; and [a]they filled
a sponge with sour wine, put *it* on
hyssop, and put *it* to His mouth.
30 So when Jesus had received the
sour wine, He said, [a]"It is fin-
ished!" And bowing His head, He
gave up His spirit.

Jesus' Side Is Pierced

31 [a]Therefore, because it was the
Preparation *Day,* [b]that the bodies
should not remain on the cross on
the Sabbath (for that Sabbath was
a [c]high day), the Jews asked Pilate
that their legs might be broken,
and *that* they might be taken
away.
32 Then the soldiers came and
broke the legs of the first and of
the other who was crucified with
Him.
33 But when they came to Jesus
and saw that He was already dead,
they did not break His legs.
34 But one of the soldiers pierced
His side with a spear, and immedi-
ately [a]blood and water came out.
35 And he who has seen has testi-
fied, and his testimony is [a]true;
and he knows that he is telling the
truth, so that you may [b]believe.
36 For these things were done that
the Scripture should be fulfilled,
[a]*"Not one of His bones shall be
broken."*
37 And again another Scripture
says, [a]*"They shall look on Him
whom they pierced."*

Jesus Buried in Joseph's Tomb

38 [a]After this, Joseph of Arima-
thea, being a disciple of Jesus, but
secretly, [b]for fear of the Jews,
asked Pilate that he might take
away the body of Jesus; and Pilate
gave *him* permission. So he came
and took the body of Jesus.
39 And [a]Nicodemus, who at first
came to Jesus by night, also came,
bringing a mixture of [b]myrrh and
aloes, about a hundred pounds.
40 Then they took the body of Je-
sus, and [a]bound it in strips of linen
with the spices, as the custom of
the Jews is to bury.
41 Now in the place where He was
crucified there was a garden, and
in the garden a new tomb in which
no one had yet been laid.
42 So [a]there they laid Jesus, [b]be-
cause of the Jews' Preparation
Day, for the tomb was nearby.

The Empty Tomb

20 Now on the [a]first *day* of the
week Mary Magdalene went
to the tomb early, while it was still
dark, and saw *that* the [b]stone had
been taken away from the tomb.
2 Then she ran and came to Si-
mon Peter, and to the [a]other disci-
ple, [b]whom Jesus loved, and said
to them, "They have taken away
the Lord out of the tomb, and we
do not know where they have laid
Him."
3 [a]Peter therefore went out, and
the other disciple, and were going
to the tomb.
4 So they both ran together, and
the other disciple outran Peter and
came to the tomb first.
5 And he, stooping down and
looking in, saw [a]the linen cloths
lying *there;* yet he did not go in.
6 Then Simon Peter came, fol-
lowing him, and went into the
tomb; and he saw the linen cloths
lying *there,*
7 and [a]the [1]handkerchief that
had been around His head, not ly-
ing with the linen cloths, but
folded together in a place by itself.
8 Then the [a]other disciple, who
came to the tomb first, went in
also; and he saw and believed.
9 For as yet they did not [1]know
the [a]Scripture, that He must rise
again from the dead.
10 Then the disciples went away
again to their own homes.

Mary Magdalene Sees the Risen Lord

11 [a]But Mary stood outside by the
tomb weeping, and as she wept
she stooped down *and looked* into
the tomb.
12 And she saw two angels in
white sitting, one at the head and
the other at the feet, where the
body of Jesus had lain.
13 Then they said to her,

27 [a]John 1:11; 16:32
28 [a]Ps. 22:15 [1]M *seeing*
29 [a]Matt. 27:48, 50
30 [a]John 17:4
31 [a]Mark 15:42 [b]Deut. 21:23 [c]Ex. 12:16
34 [a][1 John 5:6, 8]
35 [a]John 21:24 [b][John 20:31]
36 [a][Ex. 12:46; Num. 9:12]; Ps. 34:20
37 [a]Zech. 12:10; 13:6
38 [a]Luke 23:50–56 [b][John 7:13; 9:22; 12:42]
39 [a]John 3:1, 2; 7:50 [b]Matt. 2:11
40 [a]John 20:5, 7
42 [a]Is. 53:9 [b]John 19:14, 31

CHAPTER 20
1 [a]Matt. 28:1–8 [b]Matt. 27:60, 66; 28:2
2 [a]John 21:23, 24 [b]John 13:23; 19:26; 21:7, 20, 24
3 [a]Luke 24:12
5 [a]John 19:40
7 [a]John 11:44 [1]*face cloth*
8 [a]John 21:23, 24
9 [a]Ps. 16:10 [1]*understand*
11 [a]Mark 16:5

"Woman, why are you weeping?"
She said to them, "Because they
have taken away my Lord, and I
do not know where they have laid
Him."
14 [a]Now when she had said this,
she turned around and saw Jesus
standing *there,* and [b]did not know
that it was Jesus.
15 Jesus said to her, "Woman,
why are you weeping? Whom are
you seeking?" She, supposing Him
to be the gardener, said to Him,
"Sir, if You have carried Him
away, tell me where You have laid
Him, and I will take Him away."
16 Jesus said to her, [a]"Mary!" She
turned and said to [1]Him, "Rab-
boni!" (which is to say, Teacher).
17 Jesus said to her, "Do not cling
to Me, for I have not yet [a]ascended
to My Father; but go to [b]My breth-
ren and say to them, [c]'I am ascend-
ing to My Father and your Father,
and *to* [d]My God and your God.'"
18 [a]Mary Magdalene came and
told the [1]disciples that she had
seen the Lord, and *that* He had
spoken these things to her.

The Apostles Commissioned

19 [a]Then, the same day at eve-
ning, being the first *day* of the
week, when the doors were shut
where the disciples were [1]assem-
bled, for [b]fear of the Jews, Jesus
came and stood in the midst, and
said to them, [c]"Peace *be* with
you."
20 When He had said this, He
[a]showed them *His* hands and His
side. [b]Then the disciples were glad
when they saw the Lord.
21 So Jesus said to them again,
"Peace to you! [a]As the Father has
sent Me, I also send you."
22 And when He had said this, He
breathed on *them,* and said to
them, "Receive the Holy Spirit.
23 [a]"If you forgive the sins of any,
they are forgiven them; if you re-
tain the *sins* of any, they are re-
tained."

Seeing and Believing

24 Now Thomas, [a]called the Twin,
one of the twelve, was not with
them when Jesus came.
25 The other disciples therefore
said to him, "We have seen the
Lord." So he said to them, "Unless
I see in His hands the print of the
nails, and put my finger into the
print of the nails, and put my hand
into His side, I will not believe."
26 And after eight days His dis-
ciples were again inside, and
Thomas with them. Jesus came,
the doors being shut, and stood in
the midst, and said, "Peace to
you!"
27 Then He said to Thomas,
"Reach your finger here, and look
at My hands; and [a]reach your
hand *here,* and put *it* into My side.
Do not be [b]unbelieving, but be-
lieving."
28 And Thomas answered and
said to Him, "My Lord and my
God!"
29 Jesus said to him, [1]"Thomas,
because you have seen Me, you
have believed. [a]Blessed *are* those
who have not seen and *yet* have be-
lieved."

That You May Believe

30 And [a]truly Jesus did many
other signs in the presence of His
disciples, which are not written in
this book;
31 [a]but these are written that [b]you
may believe that Jesus [c]is the
Christ, the Son of God, [d]and that
believing you may have life in His
name.

Breakfast by the Sea

21 After these things Jesus
showed Himself again to the
disciples at the [a]Sea of Tiberias,
and in this way He showed *Him-
self:*
2 Simon Peter, [a]Thomas called
the Twin, [b]Nathanael of [c]Cana in
Galilee, [d]the *sons* of Zebedee, and
two others of His disciples were to-
gether.
3 Simon Peter said to them, "I
am going fishing." They said to
him, "We are going with you
also." They went out and [1]immedi-
ately got into the boat, and that
night they caught nothing.
4 But when the morning had now
come, Jesus stood on the shore; yet
the disciples [a]did not know that it
was Jesus.
5 Then [a]Jesus said to them, "Chil-
dren, have you any food?" They
answered Him, "No."
6 And He said to them, [a]"Cast

14 [a]Matt. 28:9 [b]John 21:4
16 [a]John 10:3 [1]NU adds *in Hebrew*
17 [a]Heb. 4:14 [b]Heb. 2:11 [c]John 16:28; 17:11 [d]Eph. 1:17
18 [a]Luke 24:10, 23 [1]NU *disciples, "I have seen the Lord,"*
19 [a]Luke 24:36 [b]John 9:22; 19:38 [c]John 14:27; 16:33 [1]NU omits *assembled*
20 [a]Acts 1:3 [b]John 16:20, 22
21 [a]John 17:18, 19
23 [a]Matt. 16:19; 18:18
24 [a]John 11:16
27 [a]1 John 1:1 [b]Mark 16:14
29 [a]1 Pet. 1:8 [1]NU, M omit *Thomas*
30 [a]John 21:25
31 [a]Luke 1:4 [b]1 John 5:13 [c]Luke 2:11 [d]John 3:15, 16; 5:24

CHAPTER 21
1 [a]John 6:1
2 [a]John 20:24 [b]John 1:45–51 [c]John 2:1 [d]Matt. 4:21
3 [1]NU omits *immediately*
4 [a]John 20:14
5 [a]Luke 24:41
6 [a]Luke 5:4, 6, 7

the net on the right side of the
boat, and you will find *some.*" So
they cast, and now they were not
able to draw it in because of the
multitude of fish.
7 Therefore [a]that disciple whom
Jesus loved said to Peter, "It is the
Lord!" Now when Simon Peter
heard that it was the Lord, he put
on *his* outer garment (for he had
removed it), and plunged into the
sea.
8 But the other disciples came in
the little boat (for they were not
far from land, but about two hun-
dred cubits), dragging the net with
fish.
9 Then, as soon as they had come
to land, they saw a fire of coals
there, and fish laid on it, and
bread.
10 Jesus said to them, "Bring
some of the fish which you have
just caught."
11 Simon Peter went up and
dragged the net to land, full of
large fish, one hundred and fifty-
three; and although there were so
many, the net was not broken.
12 Jesus said to them, [a]"Come *and*
eat breakfast." Yet none of the dis-
ciples dared ask Him, "Who are
You?"—knowing that it was the
Lord.
13 Jesus then came and took the
bread and gave it to them, and
likewise the fish.
14 This *is* now [a]the third time Je-
sus showed Himself to His disci-
ples after He was raised from the
dead.

Jesus Restores Peter

15 So when they had eaten break-
fast, Jesus said to Simon Peter,
"Simon, *son* of [1]Jonah, do you love
Me more than these?" He said to
Him, "Yes, Lord; You know that I
[2]love You." He said to him, [a]"Feed
My lambs."
16 He said to him again a second
time, "Simon, *son* of [1]Jonah, do
you love Me?" He said to Him,
"Yes, Lord; You know that I [2]love
You." [a]He said to him, "Tend My
[b]sheep."
17 He said to him the third time,
"Simon, *son* of [1]Jonah, do you
[2]love Me?" Peter was grieved be-
cause He said to him the third
time, "Do you [2]love Me?" And he
said to Him, "Lord, [a]You know all
things; You know that I [2]love
You." Jesus said to him, "Feed My
sheep.
18 [a]"Most assuredly, I say to you,
when you were younger, you
girded yourself and walked where
you wished; but when you are old,
you will stretch out your hands,
and another will gird you and
carry *you* where you do not wish."
19 This He spoke, signifying [a]by
what death he would glorify God.
And when He had spoken this, He
said to him, [b]"Follow Me."

The Beloved Disciple and His Book

20 Then Peter, turning around,
saw the disciple [a]whom Jesus
loved following, [b]who also had
leaned on His breast at the supper,
and said, "Lord, who is the one
who betrays You?"
21 Peter, seeing him, said to Jesus,
"But Lord, what *about* this man?"
22 Jesus said to him, "If I [1]will that
he remain [a]till I come, what *is that*
to you? You follow Me."
23 Then this saying went out
among the brethren that this dis-
ciple would not die. Yet Jesus
did not say to him that he would
not die, but, "If I will that he re-
main till I come, what *is that* to
you?"
24 This is the disciple who [a]testi-
fies of these things, and wrote
these things; and we know that his
testimony is true.
25 [a]And there are also many other
things that Jesus did, which if they
were written one by one, [b]I sup-
pose that even the world itself
could not contain the books that
would be written. Amen.

7 [a]John 13:23; 20:2
12 [a]Acts 10:41
14 [a]John 20:19, 26
15 [a]Acts 20:28; 1 Tim. 4:6; 1 Pet. 5:2 [1]NU *John* [2]*have affection for*
16 [a]Matt. 2:6; Acts 20:28; Heb. 13:20; 1 Pet. 2:25; 5:2, 4 [b]Ps. 79:13; Matt. 10:16; 15:24; 25:33; 26:31 [1]NU *John* [2]*have affection for*
17 [a]John 2:24, 25; 16:30 [1]NU *John* [2]*have affection for*
18 [a]John 13:36; Acts 12:3, 4
19 [a]2 Pet. 1:13, 14 [b][Matt. 4:19; 16:24]; John 21:22
20 [a]John 13:23; 20:2 [b]John 13:25
22 [a][Matt. 16:27, 28; 25:31; 1 Cor. 4:5; 11:26; Rev. 2:25; 3:11; 22:7, 20] [1]*desire*
24 [a]John 19:35; 3 John 12
25 [a]John 20:30 [b]Amos 7:10

The Acts

of the Apostles

JESUS' last recorded words have come to be known as the Great Commission: "You shall be witnesses to Me in Jerusalem, and in all Judea and Samaria, and to the end of the earth" (1:8). The Book of Acts, written by Luke, is the story of the men and women who took that commission seriously and began to spread the news of a risen Savior to the most remote corners of the known world.

Each section of the book (1—7; 8—12; 13—28) focuses on a particular audience, a key personality, and a significant phase in the expansion of the gospel message.

As the second volume in a two-part work by Luke, this book probably had no separate title. But all available Greek manuscripts designate it by the title *Praxeis*, "Acts," or by an expanded title like "The Acts of the Apostles." *Praxeis* was commonly used in Greek literature to summarize the accomplishments of outstanding men. While the apostles are mentioned collectively at several points, this book really records the acts of Peter (1—12) and of Paul (13—28).

Prologue

THE former account I made, O
[a]Theophilus, of all that Jesus
began both to do and teach,
2 [a]until the day in which [1]He was
taken up, after He through the
Holy Spirit [b]had given command-
ments to the apostles whom He
had chosen,
3 [a]to whom He also presented
Himself alive after His suffering by
many [1]infallible proofs, being seen
by them during forty days and
speaking of the things pertaining
to the kingdom of God.

The Holy Spirit Promised

4 [a]And being assembled together
with *them*, He commanded them
not to depart from Jerusalem, but
to wait for the Promise of the Fa-
ther, "which," *He said*, "you have
[b]heard from Me;
5 [a]"for John truly baptized with
water, [b]but you shall be baptized
with the Holy Spirit not many days
from now."
6 Therefore, when they had
come together, they asked Him,
saying, "Lord, will You at this time
restore the kingdom to Israel?"
7 And He said to them, [a]"It is not
for you to [b]know times or seasons
which the Father has put in His
own authority.
8 [a]"But you shall receive power
[b]when the Holy Spirit has come
upon you; and [c]you shall be [1]wit-
nesses to Me in Jerusalem, and in
all Judea and [d]Samaria, and to the
[e]end of the earth."

Jesus Ascends to Heaven

9 [a]Now when He had spoken
these things, while they watched,
[b]He was taken up, and a cloud re-
ceived Him out of their sight.
10 And while they looked stead-
fastly toward heaven as He went
up, behold, two men stood by them
[a]in white apparel,
11 who also said, "Men of Galilee,
why do you stand gazing up into
heaven? This *same* Jesus, who was
taken up from you into heaven,
[a]will so come in like manner as
you saw Him go into heaven."

The Upper Room Prayer Meeting

12 [a]Then they returned to Jerusa-
lem from the mount called Olivet,
which is near Jerusalem, a Sab-
bath day's journey.
13 And when they had entered,
they went up [a]into the upper room
where they were staying: [b]Peter,

CHAPTER 1

1 [a]Luke 1:3
2 [a]Mark 16:19 [b]Matt. 28:19 [1]He ascended into heaven.
3 [a]Mark 16:12, 14 [1]*unmistakable*
4 [a]Luke 24:49 [b][John 14:16, 17, 26; 15:26]
5 [a]Matt. 3:11 [b][Joel 2:28]
7 [a]1 Thess. 5:1 [b]Matt. 24:36
8 [a][Acts 2:1, 4] [b]Luke 24:49 [c]Luke 24:48 [d]Acts 8:1, 5, 14 [e]Col. 1:23 [1]NU *My witnesses*
9 [a]Luke 24:50, 51 [b]Acts 1:2
10 [a]John 20:12
11 [a]Dan. 7:13
12 [a]Luke 24:52
13 [a]Acts 9:37, 39; 20:8 [b]Matt. 10:2–4

James, John, and Andrew; Philip
and Thomas; Bartholomew and
Matthew; James *the son* of Al-
phaeus and [c]Simon the Zealot; and
[d]Judas *the son* of James.
14 [a]These all continued with one
[1]accord in prayer [2]and supplica-
tion, with [b]the women and Mary
the mother of Jesus, and with [c]His
brothers.

Matthias Chosen

15 And in those days Peter stood
up in the midst of the [1]disciples
(altogether the number [a]of names
was about a hundred and twenty),
and said,
16 "Men *and* brethren, this Scrip-
ture had to be fulfilled, [a]which the
Holy Spirit spoke before by the
mouth of David concerning Judas,
[b]who became a guide to those who
arrested Jesus;
17 "for [a]he was numbered with us
and obtained a part in [b]this min-
istry."
18 [a](Now this man purchased a
field with [b]the [1]wages of iniquity;
and falling headlong, he burst
open in the middle and all his [2]en-
trails gushed out.
19 And it became known to all
those dwelling in Jerusalem; so
that field is called in their own lan-
guage, Akel Dama, that is, Field
of Blood.)
20 "For it is written in the Book
of Psalms:

[a]'Let his dwelling place be
[1]desolate,
And let no one live in it';

and,

[b]'Let another take his [2]office.'

21 "Therefore, of these men who
have accompanied us all the time
that the Lord Jesus went in and
out among us,
22 "beginning from the baptism of
John to that day when [a]He was
taken up from us, one of these
must [b]become a witness with us of
His resurrection."
23 And they proposed two: Joseph
called [a]Barsabas, who was sur-
named Justus, and Matthias.
24 And they prayed and said,
"You, O Lord, [a]who know the
hearts of all, show which of these
two You have chosen
25 [a]"to take part in this ministry
and apostleship from which Judas
by transgression fell, that he might
go to his own place."
26 And they cast their lots, and
the lot fell on Matthias. And he
was numbered with the eleven
apostles.

Coming of the Holy Spirit

2 When [a]the Day of Pentecost
had fully come, [b]they were all
[1]with one accord in one place.
2 And suddenly there came a
sound from heaven, as of a rushing
mighty wind, and [a]it filled the
whole house where they were sit-
ting.
3 Then there appeared to them
[1]divided tongues, as of fire, and
one sat upon each of them.
4 And [a]they were all filled with
the Holy Spirit and began [b]to
speak with other tongues, as the
Spirit gave them utterance.

The Crowd's Response

5 And there were dwelling in Je-
rusalem Jews, [a]devout men, from
every nation under heaven.
6 And when this sound occurred,
the [a]multitude came together, and
were confused, because everyone
heard them speak in his own lan-
guage.
7 Then they were all amazed and
marveled, saying to one another,
"Look, are not all these who speak
[a]Galileans?
8 "And how *is it that* we hear,
each in our own [1]language in
which we were born?
9 "Parthians and Medes and
Elamites, those dwelling in Meso-
potamia, Judea and [a]Cappadocia,
Pontus and Asia,
10 "Phrygia and Pamphylia,
Egypt and the parts of Libya ad-
joining Cyrene, visitors from
Rome, both Jews and proselytes,
11 "Cretans and [1]Arabs—we hear
them speaking in our own tongues
the wonderful works of God."
12 So they were all amazed and
perplexed, saying to one another,
"Whatever could this mean?"
13 Others mocking said, "They
are full of new wine."

13 [c]Luke 6:15 [d]Jude 1
14 [a]Acts 2:1, 46 [b]Luke 23:49, 55 [c]Matt. 13:55 [1]*purpose* or *mind* [2]NU omits *and supplication*
15 [a]Luke 22:32; Rev. 3:4 [1]NU *brethren*
16 [a]Ps. 41:9 [b]Matt. 26:47; Mark 14:43; Luke 22:47; John 18:3
17 [a]Matt. 10:4 [b]Acts 1:25
18 [a]Matt. 27:3–10 [b]Matt. 18:7; 26:14, 15, 24; Mark 14:21; Luke 22:22; John 17:12 [1]*reward of unrighteousness* [2]*intestines*
20 [a]Ps. 69:25 [b]Ps. 109:8 [1]*deserted* [2]Gr. *episkopen*, position of overseer
22 [a]Acts 1:9 [b]Acts 1:8; 2:32
23 [a]Acts 15:22
24 [a]1 Sam. 16:7; Jer. 17:10; Acts 1:2
25 [a]Acts 1:17

CHAPTER 2

1 [a]Lev. 23:15; Deut. 16:9; Acts 20:16; 1 Cor. 16:8 [b]Acts 1:14 [1]NU *together*
2 [a]Acts 4:31
3 [1]Or *tongues as of fire, distributed and resting on each*
4 [a]Matt. 3:11; 5:6; 10:20; Luke 3:16; John 14:16; 16:7–15; Acts 1:5 [b]Mark 16:17; Acts 10:46; 19:6; [1 Cor. 12:10, 28, 30; 13:1]
5 [a]Luke 2:25; Acts 8:2
6 [a]Acts 4:32
7 [a]Matt. 26:73; Acts 1:11
8 [1]*dialect*
9 [a]1 Pet. 1:1
11 [1]*Arabians*

Peter's Sermon

14 But Peter, standing up with the eleven, raised his voice and said to them, "Men of Judea and all who dwell in Jerusalem, let this be known to you, and heed my words.
15 "For these are not drunk, as you suppose, [a]since it is *only* [1]the third hour of the day.
16 "But this is what was spoken by the prophet Joel:

17 *'And[a] it shall come to pass in the last days, says God,*
[b]That I will pour out of My Spirit on all flesh;
Your sons and [c]your daughters shall prophesy,
Your young men shall see visions,
Your old men shall dream dreams.
18 *And on My menservants and on My maidservants*
I will pour out My Spirit in those days;
[a]And they shall prophesy.
19 *[a]I will show wonders in heaven above*
And signs in the earth beneath:
Blood and fire and vapor of smoke.
20 *[a]The sun shall be turned into darkness,*
And the moon into blood,
Before the coming of the great and awesome day of the LORD.
21 *And it shall come to pass*
That [a]whoever calls on the name of the LORD
Shall be saved.'

22 "Men of Israel, hear these words: Jesus of Nazareth, a Man attested by God to you [a]by miracles, wonders, and signs which God did through Him in your midst, as you yourselves also know—

15 [a]1 Thess. 5:7 [1]9 A.M.
17 [a]Is. 44:3; Ezek. 11:19; Joel 2:28–32; [Zech. 12:10; John 7:38] [b]Acts 10:45 [c]Acts 21:9
18 [a]Acts 21:4, 9; 1 Cor. 12:10
19 [a]Joel 2:30
20 [a]Is. 13:10; Ezek. 32:7; Matt. 24:29; Mark 13:24, 25; Luke 21:25; Rev. 6:12
21 [a]Rom. 10:13
22 [a]Is. 50:5; John 3:2; 5:6; Acts 10:38

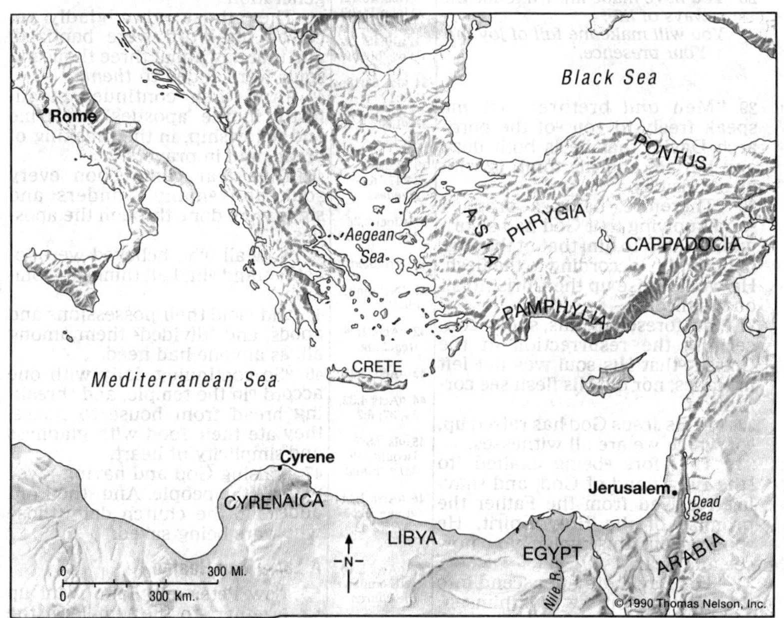

The Nations of Pentecost. In the first Christian century, Jewish communities were located primarily in the eastern part of the Roman Empire, where Greek was the common language, but also existed as far west as Italy and as far east as Babylonia. In addition to people from the nations shown here, those present on the Day of Pentecost (Acts 2:9–11) included visitors from Mesopotamia and even farther east, from Parthia, Media, and Elam (present-day Iran).

23 "Him, [a]being delivered by the
determined purpose and fore-
knowledge of God, [b]you [1]have
taken by lawless hands, have cru-
cified, and put to death;
24 [a]"whom God raised up, having
[1]loosed the [2]pains of death, be-
cause it was not possible that He
should be held by it.
25 "For David says concerning
Him:

[a]'I foresaw the LORD always before
my face,
For He is at my right hand, that
I may not be shaken.
26 *Therefore my heart rejoiced, and*
my tongue was glad;
Moreover my flesh also will rest
in hope.
27 *For You will not leave my soul*
in Hades,
Nor will You allow Your Holy
One to see [a]corruption.
28 *You have made known to me the*
ways of life;
You will make me full of joy in
Your presence.'

29 "Men *and* brethren, let *me*
speak freely to you [a]of the patri-
arch David, that he is both dead
and buried, and his tomb is with
us to this day.
30 "Therefore, being a prophet,
[a]and knowing that God had sworn
with an oath to him that of the fruit
of his body, [1]according to the flesh,
He would raise up the Christ to sit
on his throne,
31 "he, foreseeing this, spoke con-
cerning the resurrection of the
Christ, [a]that His soul was not left
in Hades, nor did His flesh see cor-
ruption.
32 [a]"This Jesus God has raised up,
[b]of which we are all witnesses.
33 "Therefore [a]being exalted [1]to
[b]the right hand of God, and [c]hav-
ing received from the Father the
promise of the Holy Spirit, He
[d]poured out this which you now
see and hear.
34 "For David did not ascend into
the heavens, but he says himself:

[a]'The LORD said to my Lord,
"Sit at My right hand,
35 *Till I make Your enemies Your*
footstool."'

23 [a]Luke 22:22 [b]Acts 5:30 [1]NU omits *have taken*
24 [a][Rom. 8:11] [1]*destroyed* or *abolished* [2]Lit. *birth pangs*
25 [a]Ps. 16:8–11
27 [a]Acts 13:30–37
29 [a]Acts 13:36
30 [a]Ps. 132:11 [1]NU *He would seat one on his throne,*
31 [a]Ps. 16:10
32 [a]Acts 2:24 [b]Acts 1:8; 3:15
33 [a][Acts 5:31] [b][Heb. 10:12] [c][John 14:26] [d]Acts 2:1–11, 17; 10:45 [1]Possibly *by*
34 [a]Ps. 68:18; 110:1
37 [a]Luke 3:10, 12, 14
38 [a]Luke 24:47 [1]*forgiveness*
39 [a]Joel 2:28, 32 [b]Eph. 2:13
40 [1]*crooked*
41 [1]NU omits *gladly*
42 [a]Acts 1:14 [1]*teaching*
43 [a]Acts 2:22
44 [a]Acts 4:32, 34, 37; 5:2
45 [a]Is. 58:7 [1]*would sell* [2]*distributed*
46 [a]Acts 1:14 [b]Luke 24:53 [c]Acts 2:42; 20:7
47 [a]Acts 5:14 [1]NU omits *to the church*

CHAPTER 3

1 [a]Acts 2:46 [b]Ps. 55:17
2 [a]Acts 14:8

36 "Therefore let all the house of
Israel know assuredly that God
has made this Jesus, whom you
crucified, both Lord and Christ."
37 Now when they heard *this,*
[a]they were cut to the heart, and
said to Peter and the rest of the
apostles, "Men *and* brethren, what
shall we do?"
38 Then Peter said to them, [a]"Re-
pent, and let every one of you be
baptized in the name of Jesus
Christ for the [1]remission of sins;
and you shall receive the gift of
the Holy Spirit.
39 "For the promise is to you and
[a]to your children, and [b]to all who
are afar off, as many as the Lord
our God will call."

A Vital Church Grows

40 And with many other words he
testified and exhorted them, say-
ing, "Be saved from this [1]perverse
generation."
41 Then those who [1]gladly re-
ceived his word were baptized;
and that day about three thousand
souls were added *to them.*
42 [a]And they continued stead-
fastly in the apostles' [1]doctrine
and fellowship, in the breaking of
bread, and in prayers.
43 Then fear came upon every
soul, and [a]many wonders and
signs were done through the apos-
tles.
44 Now all who believed were to-
gether, and [a]had all things in com-
mon,
45 and [1]sold their possessions and
goods, and [a]divided[2] them among
all, as anyone had need.
46 [a]So continuing daily with one
accord [b]in the temple, and [c]break-
ing bread from house to house,
they ate their food with gladness
and simplicity of heart,
47 praising God and having favor
with all the people. And [a]the Lord
added [1]to the church daily those
who were being saved.

A Lame Man Healed

3 Now Peter and John went up
together [a]to the temple at the
hour of prayer, [b]the ninth *hour.*
2 And [a]a certain man lame from
his mother's womb was carried,
whom they laid daily at the gate
of the temple which is called Beau-

tiful, [b]to [1]ask alms from those who
entered the temple;
3 who, seeing Peter and John
about to go into the temple, asked
for alms.
4 And fixing his eyes on him,
with John, Peter said, "Look at
us."
5 So he gave them his attention,
expecting to receive something
from them.
6 Then Peter said, "Silver and
gold I do not have, but what I do
have I give you: [a]In the name of
Jesus Christ of Nazareth, rise up
and walk."
7 And he took him by the right
hand and lifted *him* up, and imme-
diately his feet and ankle bones re-
ceived strength.
8 So he, [a]leaping up, stood and
walked and entered the temple
with them—walking, leaping, and
praising God.
9 [a]And all the people saw him
walking and praising God.
10 Then they knew that it was he
who [a]sat begging alms at the Beau-
tiful Gate of the temple; and they
were filled with wonder and
amazement at what had happened
to him.

Preaching in Solomon's Portico

11 Now as the lame man who was
healed held on to Peter and John,
all the people ran together to them
in the porch [a]which is called Sol-
omon's, greatly amazed.
12 So when Peter saw *it*, he re-
sponded to the people: "Men of Is-
rael, why do you marvel at this?
Or why look so intently at us, as
though by our own power or godli-
ness we had made this man walk?
13 [a]"The God of Abraham, Isaac,
and Jacob, the God of our fathers,
[b]glorified His Servant Jesus,
whom you [c]delivered up and
[d]denied in the presence of Pilate,
when he was determined to let
Him go.
14 "But you denied [a]the Holy One
[b]and the Just, and [c]asked for a
murderer to be granted to you,
15 "and killed the [1]Prince of life,
[a]whom God raised from the dead,
[b]of which we are witnesses.
16 [a]"And His name, through faith
in His name, has made this man
strong, whom you see and know.
Yes, the faith which *comes*
through Him has given him this
perfect soundness in the presence
of you all.
17 "Yet now, brethren, I know
that [a]you did *it* in ignorance, as
did also your rulers.
18 "But [a]those things which God
foretold [b]by the mouth of all His
prophets, that the Christ would
suffer, He has thus fulfilled.
19 [a]"Repent therefore and be con-
verted, that your sins may be
blotted out, so that times of re-
freshing may come from the pres-
ence of the Lord,
20 "and that He may send [1]Jesus
Christ, who was [2]preached to you
before,
21 [a]"whom heaven must receive
until the times of [b]restoration of
all things, [c]which God has spoken
by the mouth of all His holy proph-
ets since [1]the world began.
22 "For Moses truly said to the fa-
thers, [a]*'The* LORD *your God will
raise up for you a Prophet like me
from your brethren. Him you shall
hear in all things, whatever He
says to you.*
23 *'And it shall be that every soul
who will not hear that Prophet
shall be utterly destroyed from
among the people.'*
24 "Yes, and [a]all the prophets,
from Samuel and those who fol-
low, as many as have spoken, have
also [1]foretold these days.
25 [a]"You are sons of the prophets,
and of the covenant which God
made with our fathers, saying to
Abraham, [b]*'And in your seed all
the families of the earth shall be
blessed.'*
26 "To you [a]first, God, having
raised up His Servant Jesus, sent
Him to bless you, [b]in turning away
every one *of you* from your iniqui-
ties."

Peter and John Arrested

4 Now as they spoke to the peo-
ple, the priests, the captain of
the temple, and the [a]Sadducees
came upon them,
2 being greatly disturbed that
they taught the people and
preached in Jesus the resurrection
from the dead.
3 And they laid hands on them,
and put *them* in custody until the

2 [b]John 9:8 [1]Beg
6 [a]Acts 4:10
8 [a]Is. 35:6
9 [a]Acts 4:16, 21
10 [a]John 9:8
11 [a]John 10:23
13 [a]John 5:30 [b]John 7:39; 12:23; 13:31 [c]Matt. 27:2 [d]Matt. 27:20
14 [a]Mark 1:24 [b]Acts 7:52 [c]John 18:40
15 [a]Acts 2:24 [b]Acts 2:32 [1]Or *Originator*
16 [a]Matt. 9:22
17 [a]Luke 23:34
18 [a]Acts 26:22 [b]1 Pet. 1:10
19 [a][Acts 2:38; 26:20]
20 [1]NU, M *Christ Jesus* [2]NU, M *ordained for you before*
21 [a]Acts 1:11 [b]Matt. 17:11 [c]Luke 1:70 [1]Or *time*
22 [a]Deut. 18:15, 18, 19
24 [a]Luke 24:25 [1]NU, M *proclaimed*
25 [a][Rom. 9:4, 8] [b]Gen. 12:3; 18:18; 22:18; 26:4; 28:14
26 [a][Rom. 1:16; 2:9] [b]Matt. 1:21

CHAPTER 4

1 [a]Matt. 22:23

next day, for it was already eve-
ning.
4 However, many of those who
heard the word believed; and the
number of the men came to be
about five thousand.

Addressing the Sanhedrin

5 And it came to pass, on the
next day, that their rulers, elders,
and scribes,
6 as well as [a]Annas the high
priest, Caiaphas, John, and Alex-
ander, and as many as were of the
family of the high priest, were
gathered together at Jerusalem.
7 And when they had set them
in the midst, they asked, [a]"By
what power or by what name have
you done this?"
8 [a]Then Peter, filled with the
Holy Spirit, said to them, "Rulers
of the people and elders of Israel:
9 "If we this day are judged for
a good deed *done* to a helpless
man, by what means he has been
made well,
10 "let it be known to you all, and
to all the people of Israel, [a]that by
the name of Jesus Christ of Naza-
reth, whom you crucified, [b]whom
God raised from the dead, by Him
this man stands here before you
whole.
11 "This is the [a]*'stone which was
rejected by you builders, which
has become the chief cornerstone.'*
12 [a]"Nor is there salvation in any
other, for there is no other name
under heaven given among men
by which we must be saved."

The Name of Jesus Forbidden

13 Now when they saw the bold-
ness of Peter and John, [a]and per-
ceived that they were uneducated
and untrained men, they mar-
veled. And they realized that they
had been with Jesus.
14 And seeing the man who had
been healed [a]standing with them,
they could say nothing against it.
15 But when they had com-
manded them to go aside out of
the council, they conferred among
themselves,
16 saying, [a]"What shall we do to
these men? For, indeed, that a
[1]notable miracle has been done
through them *is* [b]evident[2] to all
who dwell in Jerusalem, and we
cannot deny *it.*
17 "But so that it spreads no fur-
ther among the people, let us se-
verely threaten them, that from
now on they speak to no man in
this name."
18 [a]So they called them and com-
manded them not to speak at all
nor teach in the name of Jesus.
19 But Peter and John answered
and said to them, [a]"Whether it is
right in the sight of God to listen
to you more than to God, you
judge.
20 [a]"For we cannot but speak the
things which [b]we have seen and
heard."
21 So when they had further
threatened them, they let them go,
finding no way of punishing them,
[a]because of the people, since they
all [b]glorified God for [c]what had
been done.
22 For the man was over forty
years old on whom this miracle of
healing had been performed.

Prayer for Boldness

23 And being let go, [a]they went to
their own *companions* and re-
ported all that the chief priests and
elders had said to them.
24 So when they heard that, they
raised their voice to God with one
accord and said: "Lord, [a]You *are*
God, who made heaven and earth
and the sea, and all that is in them,
25 "who [1]by the mouth of Your
servant David have said:

[a]*'Why did the nations rage,*
And the people plot vain things?
26 *The kings of the earth took their*
stand,
And the rulers were gathered
together
Against the LORD *and against His*
Christ.'

27 "For [a]truly against [b]Your holy
Servant Jesus, [c]whom You
anointed, both Herod and Pontius
Pilate, with the Gentiles and the
people of Israel, were gathered to-
gether
28 [a]"to do whatever Your hand
and Your purpose determined be-
fore to be done.
29 "Now, Lord, look on their
threats, and grant to Your servants

6 [a]Luke 3:2; John 11:49; 18:13
7 [a]Ex. 2:14; Matt. 21:23; Acts 7:27
8 [a]Luke 12:11, 12
10 [a]Acts 2:22; 3:6, 16 [b]Acts 2:24
11 [a]Ps. 118:22; Is. 28:16; Matt. 21:42
12 [a]Is. 42:1, 6, 7; 53:11; Dan. 9:24; [Matt. 1:21; John 14:6; Acts 10:43; 1 Tim. 2:5, 6]
13 [a]Matt. 11:25; [1 Cor. 1:27]
14 [a]Acts 3:11
16 [a]John 11:47 [b]Acts 3:7–10 [1]*remarkable sign* [2]*well known*
18 [a]Acts 5:28, 40
19 [a]Acts 5:29
20 [a]Acts 1:8; 2:32 [b]Acts 22:15; [1 John 1:1, 3]
21 [a]Matt. 21:26; Luke 20:6, 19; 22:2; Acts 5:26 [b]Matt. 15:31 [c]Acts 3:7, 8
23 [a]Acts 2:44–46; 12:12
24 [a]Ex. 20:11; 2 Kin. 19:15; Neh. 9:6; Ps. 146:6
25 [a]Ps. 2:1, 2 [1]NU *through the Holy Spirit, by the mouth of our father, Your servant David,*
27 [a]Matt. 26:3; Luke 22:2; 23:1, 8 [b][Luke 1:35] [c]Luke 4:18; John 10:36
28 [a]Acts 2:23; 3:18

[a]that with all boldness they may
speak Your word,
30 "by stretching out Your hand
to heal, [a]and that signs and won-
ders may be done [b]through the
name of [c]Your holy Servant Je-
sus."
31 And when they had prayed,
[a]the place where they were assem-
bled together was shaken; and
they were all filled with the Holy
Spirit, [b]and they spoke the word
of God with boldness.

Sharing in All Things

32 Now the multitude of those
who believed [a]were of one heart
and one soul; [b]neither did anyone
say that any of the things he pos-
sessed was his own, but they had
all things in common.
33 And with [a]great power the
apostles gave [b]witness to the res-
urrection of the Lord Jesus. And
[c]great grace was upon them all.
34 Nor was there anyone among
them who lacked; [a]for all who
were possessors of lands or houses
sold them, and brought the pro-
ceeds of the things that were sold,
35 [a]and laid *them* at the apostles'
feet; [b]and they distributed to each
as anyone had need.
36 And [1]Joses, who was also
named Barnabas by the apostles
(which is translated Son of [2]En-
couragement), a Levite of the
country of Cyprus,
37 [a]having land, sold *it*, and
brought the money and laid *it* at
the apostles' feet.

Lying to the Holy Spirit

5 But a certain man named Ana-
nias, with Sapphira his wife,
sold a possession.
2 And he kept back *part* of the
proceeds, his wife also being
aware *of it*, and brought a certain
part and laid *it* at the apostles' feet.
3 [a]But Peter said, "Ananias, why
has [b]Satan filled your heart to lie
to the Holy Spirit and keep back
part of the price of the land for
yourself?
4 "While it remained, was it not
your own? And after it was sold,
was it not in your own control?
Why have you conceived this thing
in your heart? You have not lied
to men but to God."
5 Then Ananias, hearing these
words, [a]fell down and breathed his
last. So great fear came upon all
those who heard these things.
6 And the young men arose and
[a]wrapped him up, carried *him* out,
and buried *him*.
7 Now it was about three hours
later when his wife came in, not
knowing what had happened.
8 And Peter answered her, "Tell
me whether you sold the land for
so much?" She said, "Yes, for so
much."
9 Then Peter said to her, "How
is it that you have agreed together
[a]to test the Spirit of the Lord?
Look, the feet of those who have
buried your husband *are* at the
door, and they will carry you out."
10 [a]Then immediately she fell
down at his feet and breathed her
last. And the young men came in
and found her dead, and carrying
her out, buried *her* by her hus-
band.
11 [a]So great fear came upon all
the church and upon all who heard
these things.

Continuing Power in the Church

12 And [a]through the hands of the
apostles many signs and wonders
were done among the people. [b]And
they were all with one accord in
Solomon's Porch.
13 Yet [a]none of the rest dared join
them, [b]but the people esteemed
them highly.
14 And believers were increas-
ingly added to the Lord, multi-
tudes of both men and women,
15 so that they brought the sick
out into the streets and laid *them*
on beds and couches, [a]that at least
the shadow of Peter passing by
might fall on some of them.
16 Also a multitude gathered from
the surrounding cities to Jerusa-
lem, bringing [a]sick people and
those who were tormented by un-
clean spirits, and they were all
healed.

Imprisoned Apostles Freed

17 [a]Then the high priest rose up,
and all those who *were* with him
(which is the sect of the Saddu-
cees), and they were filled with
[1]indignation,
18 [a]and laid their hands on the

29 [a]Acts 4:13, 31; 9:27; 13:46; 14:3; 19:8; 26:26; Eph. 6:19
30 [a]Acts 2:43; 5:12 [b]Acts 3:6, 16 [c]Acts 4:27
31 [a]Matt. 5:6; Acts 2:2, 4; 16:26 [b]Acts 4:29
32 [a]Acts 5:12; Rom. 15:5, 6; 2 Cor. 13:11; Phil. 1:27; 2:2; 1 Pet. 3:8 [b]Acts 2:44
33 [a][Acts 1:8] [b]Acts 1:22 [c]Rom. 6:15
34 [a][Matt. 19:21]; Acts 2:45
35 [a]Acts 4:37; 5:2 [b]Acts 2:45; 6:1
36 [1]NU *Joseph* [2]Or *Consolation*
37 [a]Acts 4:34, 35; 5:1, 2

CHAPTER 5

3 [a]Num. 30:2; Deut. 23:21; Eccl. 5:4 [b]Matt. 4:10; Luke 22:3; John 13:2, 27
5 [a]Ezek. 11:13; Acts 5:10, 11
6 [a]John 19:40
9 [a]Matt. 4:7; Acts 5:3, 4
10 [a]Ezek. 11:13; Acts 5:5
11 [a]Acts 2:43; 5:5; 19:17
12 [a]Acts 2:43; 4:30; 6:8; 14:3; 15:12; [Rom. 15:19]; 2 Cor. 12:12; Heb. 2:4 [b]Acts 3:11; 4:32
13 [a]John 9:22 [b]Acts 2:47; 4:21
15 [a]Matt. 9:21; 14:36; Acts 19:12
16 [a]Mark 16:17, 18; [John 14:12]
17 [a]Matt. 3:7; Acts 4:1, 2, 6 [1]*jealousy*
18 [a]Luke 21:12; Acts 4:3; 16:37

apostles and put them in the com-
mon prison.
19 But at night [a]an angel of the
Lord opened the prison doors and
brought them out, and said,
20 "Go, stand in the temple and
speak to the people [a]all the words
of this life."
21 And when they heard *that*,
they entered the temple early in
the morning and taught. [a]But the
high priest and those with him
came and called the [1]council to-
gether, with all the [2]elders of the
children of Israel, and sent to the
prison to have them brought.

Apostles on Trial Again

22 But when the officers came and
did not find them in the prison,
they returned and reported,
23 saying, "Indeed we found the
prison shut securely, and the
guards standing [1]outside before
the doors; but when we opened
them, we found no one inside!"
24 Now when [1]the high priest,
[a]the captain of the temple, and the
chief priests heard these things,
they wondered what the outcome
would be.
25 So one came and told them,
[1]saying, "Look, the men whom
you put in prison are standing in
the temple and teaching the peo-
ple!"
26 Then the captain went with the
officers and brought them without
violence, [a]for they feared the peo-
ple, lest they should be stoned.
27 And when they had brought
them, they set *them* before the
council. And the high priest asked
them,
28 saying, [a]"Did we not strictly
command you not to teach in this
name? And look, you have filled
Jerusalem with your doctrine,
[b]and intend to bring this Man's
[c]blood on us!"
29 But Peter and the *other* apos-
tles answered and said: [a]"We
ought to obey God rather than
men.
30 [a]"The God of our fathers raised
up Jesus whom you murdered by
[b]hanging on a tree.
31 [a]"Him God has exalted to His
right hand *to be* [b]Prince and [c]Sav-
ior, [d]to give repentance to Israel
and forgiveness of sins.
32 "And [a]we are His witnesses to
these things, and *so* also *is* the
Holy Spirit [b]whom God has given
to those who obey Him."

Gamaliel's Advice

33 When they heard *this*, they
were [a]furious[1] and plotted to kill
them.
34 Then one in the council stood
up, a Pharisee named [a]Gamaliel,
a teacher of the law held in respect
by all the people, and commanded
them to put the apostles outside for
a little while.
35 And he said to them: "Men of
Israel, [1]take heed to yourselves
what you intend to do regarding
these men.
36 "For some time ago Theudas
rose up, claiming to be somebody.
A number of men, about four hun-
dred, [1]joined him. He was slain,
and all who obeyed him were scat-
tered and came to nothing.
37 "After this man, Judas of Gali-
lee rose up in the days of the cen-
sus, and drew away many people
after him. He also perished, and
all who obeyed him were dis-
persed.
38 "And now I say to you, keep
away from these men and let them
alone; for if this plan or this work
is of men, it will come to nothing;
39 [a]"but if it is of God, you cannot
overthrow it—lest you even be
found [b]to fight against God."
40 And they agreed with him, and
when they had [a]called for the
apostles [b]and beaten *them*, they
commanded that they should not
speak in the name of Jesus, and
let them go.
41 So they departed from the pres-
ence of the council, [a]rejoicing that
they were counted worthy to suffer
shame for [1]His name.
42 And daily [a]in the temple, and
in every house, [b]they did not cease
teaching and preaching Jesus *as*
the Christ.

Seven Chosen to Serve

6 Now in those days, [a]when *the
number of* the disciples was
multiplying, there arose a com-
plaint against the Hebrews by the
[b]Hellenists,[1] because their widows
were neglected [c]in the daily distri-
bution.

19 [a]Acts 12:7; 16:26
20 [a][John 6:63, 68; 17:3]
21 [a]Acts 4:5, 6 [1]Sanhedrin [2]*council of elders* or *senate*
23 [1]NU, M omit *outside*
24 [a]Acts 4:1; 5:26 [1]NU omits *the high priest*
25 [1]NU, M omit *saying*
26 [a]Matt. 21:26
28 [a]Acts 4:17, 18 [b]Acts 2:23, 36 [c]Matt. 23:35
29 [a]Acts 4:19
30 [a]Acts 3:13, 15 [b][1 Pet. 2:24]
31 [a][Acts 2:33, 36] [b]Acts 3:15 [c]Matt. 1:21 [d]Luke 24:47
32 [a]John 15:26, 27 [b]Acts 2:4; 10:44
33 [a]Acts 2:37; 7:54 [1]*cut to the quick*
34 [a]Acts 22:3
35 [1]*be careful*
36 [1]*followed*
39 [a]1 Cor. 1:25 [b]Acts 7:51; 9:5
40 [a]Acts 4:18 [b]Matt. 10:17
41 [a][1 Pet. 4:13–16] [1]NU *the name;* M *the name of Jesus*
42 [a]Acts 2:46 [b]Acts 4:20, 29

CHAPTER 6

1 [a]Acts 2:41; 4:4 [b]Acts 9:29; 11:20 [c]Acts 4:35; 11:29 [1]Greek-speaking Jews

2 Then the twelve summoned the
multitude of the disciples and said,
[a]"It is not desirable that we should
leave the word of God and serve
tables.
3 "Therefore, brethren, [a]seek out
from among you seven men of
good reputation, full of the Holy
Spirit and wisdom, whom we may
appoint over this [b]business;
4 "but we [a]will give ourselves
continually to prayer and to the
ministry of the word."
5 And the saying pleased the
whole multitude. And they chose
Stephen, [a]a man full of faith and
the Holy Spirit, and [b]Philip, Proch-
orus, Nicanor, Timon, Parmenas,
and [c]Nicolas, a proselyte from An-
tioch,
6 whom they set before the apos-
tles; and [a]when they had prayed,
[b]they laid hands on them.
7 Then [a]the word of God spread,
and the number of the disciples
multiplied greatly in Jerusalem,
and a great many [b]of the priests
were obedient to the faith.

Stephen Accused of Blasphemy

8 And Stephen, full of [1]faith and
power, did great [a]wonders and
signs among the people.
9 Then there arose some from
what is called the Synagogue of
the Freedmen (Cyrenians, Alexan-
drians, and those from Cilicia and
Asia), disputing with Stephen.
10 And [a]they were not able to re-
sist the wisdom and the Spirit by
which he spoke.
11 [a]Then they secretly induced
men to say, "We have heard him
speak blasphemous words against
Moses and God."
12 And they stirred up the peo-
ple, the elders, and the scribes;
and they came upon *him*, seized
him, and brought *him* to the
council.
13 They also set up false witnesses
who said, "This man does not
cease to speak [1]blasphemous
words against this holy place and
the law;
14 [a]"for we have heard him say
that this Jesus of Nazareth will de-
stroy this place and change the
customs which Moses delivered to
us."
15 And all who sat in the council,
looking steadfastly at him, saw his
face as the face of an angel.

Stephen's Address: The Call of Abraham

7 Then the high priest said, "Are
these things so?"
2 And he said, [a]"Brethren and fa-
thers, listen: The [b]God of glory ap-
peared to our father Abraham
when he was in Mesopotamia, be-
fore he dwelt in [c]Haran,
3 "and said to him, [a]*'Get out of
your country and from your rela-
tives, and come to a land that I will
show you.'*
4 "Then [a]he came out of the land
of the Chaldeans and dwelt in
Haran. And from there, when his
father was [b]dead, He moved him
to this land in which you now
dwell.
5 "And *God* gave him no inheri-
tance in it, not even *enough* to set
his foot on. But even when *Abra-
ham* had no child, [a]He promised
to give it to him for a possession,
and to his descendants after him.
6 "But God spoke in this way:
[a]that his descendants would dwell
in a foreign land, and that they
would bring them into [b]bondage
and oppress *them* four hundred
years.
7 [a]*'And the nation to whom they
will be in bondage I will [b]judge,'*
said God, [c]*'and after that they
shall come out and serve Me in this
place.'*
8 [a]"Then He gave him the cov-
enant of circumcision; [b]and so
Abraham begot Isaac and circum-
cised him on the eighth day; [c]and
Isaac *begot* Jacob, and [d]Jacob *be-
got* the twelve patriarchs.

The Patriarchs in Egypt

9 [a]"And the patriarchs, becom-
ing envious, [b]sold Joseph into
Egypt. [c]But God was with him
10 "and delivered him out of all
his troubles, [a]and gave him favor
and wisdom in the presence of
Pharaoh, king of Egypt; and he
made him governor over Egypt
and all his house.
11 [a]"Now a famine and great
[1]trouble came over all the land of
Egypt and Canaan, and our fathers
found no sustenance.

---

2 [a]Ex. 18:17
3 [a]Deut. 1:13; 1 Tim. 3:7 [b]Phil. 1:1; 1 Tim. 3:8–13
4 [a]Acts 2:42
5 [a]Acts 6:3; 11:24 [b]Acts 8:5, 26; 21:8 [c]Rev. 2:6, 15
6 [a]Acts 1:24 [b]Num. 8:10; 27:18; Deut. 34:9; [Mark 5:23; Acts 8:17; 9:17; 13:3; 19:6; 1 Tim. 4:14; 2 Tim. 1:6]; Heb. 6:2
7 [a]Acts 12:24; Col. 1:6 [b]John 12:42
8 [a]Acts 2:43; 5:12; 8:15; 14:3 [1]NU *grace*
10 [a]Ex. 4:12; Is. 54:17; Luke 21:15
11 [a]1 Kin. 21:10, 13; Matt. 26:59, 60
13 [1]NU omits *blasphemous*
14 [a]Acts 10:38; 25:8

CHAPTER 7

2 [a]Acts 22:1 [b]Ps. 29:3; 1 Cor. 2:8 [c]Gen. 11:31, 32
3 [a]Gen. 12:1
4 [a]Gen. 11:31; 15:7; Heb. 11:8–10 [b]Gen. 11:32
5 [a]Gen. 12:7; 13:15; 15:3, 18; 17:8; 26:3
6 [a]Gen. 15:13, 14, 16; 47:11, 12 [b]Ex. 1:8–14; 12:40, 41; Gal. 3:17
7 [a]Gen. 15:14 [b]Ex. 14:13–31 [c]Ex. 3:12; Josh. 3:1–17
8 [a]Gen. 17:9–14 [b]Gen. 21:1–5 [c]Gen. 25:21–26 [d]Gen. 29:31—30:24; 35:18, 22–26
9 [a]Gen. 37:4, 11, 28; Ps. 105:17 [b]Gen. 37:28 [c]Gen. 39:2, 21, 23
10 [a]Gen. 41:38–44
11 [a]Gen. 41:54; 42:5 [1]*affliction*

12 [a]"But when Jacob heard that
there was grain in Egypt, he sent
out our fathers first.
13 "And the [a]second *time* Joseph
was made known to his brothers,
and Joseph's family became
known to the Pharaoh.
14 [a]"Then Joseph sent and called
his father Jacob and [b]all his rela-
tives to *him*, [1]seventy-five people.
15 [a]"So Jacob went down to
Egypt; [b]and he died, he and our
fathers.
16 "And [a]they were carried back
to Shechem and laid in [b]the tomb
that Abraham bought for a sum of
money from the sons of Hamor,
the father of Shechem.

God Delivers Israel by Moses

17 "But when [a]the time of the
promise drew near which God had
sworn to Abraham, [b]the people
grew and multiplied in Egypt
18 "till another king [a]arose who
did not know Joseph.
19 "This man dealt treacherously
with our people, and oppressed
our forefathers, [a]making them ex-
pose their babies, so that they
might not live.
20 [a]"At this time Moses was born,
and [b]was well pleasing to God; and
he was brought up in his father's
house for three months.
21 "But [a]when he was set out,
[b]Pharaoh's daughter took him
away and brought him up as her
own son.
22 "And Moses was learned in all
the wisdom of the Egyptians, and
was [a]mighty in words and deeds.
23 [a]"Now when he was forty
years old, it came into his heart
to visit his brethren, the children
of Israel.
24 "And seeing one of *them* suffer
wrong, he defended and avenged
him who was oppressed, and
struck down the Egyptian.
25 "For he supposed that his
brethren would have understood
that God would deliver them by his
hand, but they did not understand.
26 "And the next day he appeared
to two of them as they were fight-
ing, and *tried to* reconcile them,
saying, 'Men, you are brethren;
why do you wrong one another?'
27 "But he who did his neighbor
wrong pushed him away, saying,
[a]*'Who made you a ruler and a
judge over us?*
28 *'Do you want to kill me as you
did the Egyptian yesterday?'*
29 [a]"Then, at this saying, Moses
fled and became a dweller in the
land of Midian, where he [b]had two
sons.
30 [a]"And when forty years had
passed, an Angel [1]of the Lord ap-
peared to him in a flame of fire in
a bush, in the wilderness of Mount
Sinai.
31 "When Moses saw *it*, he mar-
veled at the sight; and as he drew
near to observe, the voice of the
Lord came to him,
32 "*saying,* [a]*'I am the God of your
fathers—the God of Abraham, the
God of Isaac, and the God of Ja-
cob.'* And Moses trembled and
dared not look.
33 [a]*'Then the* LORD *said to him,
"Take your sandals off your feet,
for the place where you stand is
holy ground.*
34 *"I have surely* [a]*seen the op-
pression of My people who are in
Egypt; I have heard their groaning
and have come down to deliver
them. And now come, I will* [b]*send
you to Egypt."'*
35 "This Moses whom they re-
jected, saying, [a]*'Who made you a
ruler and a judge?'* is the one God
sent *to be* a ruler and a deliverer
[b]by the hand of the Angel who ap-
peared to him in the bush.
36 [a]"He brought them out, after he
had [b]shown wonders and signs in
the land of Egypt, [c]and in the Red
Sea, [d]and in the wilderness forty
years.

Israel Rebels Against God

37 "This is that Moses who said
to the children of Israel, [a]*'The*
LORD *your God will raise up for
you a Prophet like me from your
brethren.* [b]*Him*[1] *you shall hear.'*
38 [a]"This is he who was in the
[1]congregation in the wilderness
with [b]the Angel who spoke to him
on Mount Sinai, and *with* our fa-
thers, [c]the one who received the
living [d]oracles[2] to give to us,
39 "whom our fathers [a]would not
obey, but rejected. And in their
hearts they turned back to Egypt,
40 [a]"saying to Aaron, *'Make us
gods to go before us; as for this*

12 [a]Gen. 42:1, 2
13 [a]Gen. 45:4, 16
14 [a]Gen. 45:9, 27 [b]Deut. 10:22 [1]Or *seventy*, Ex. 1:5
15 [a]Gen. 46:1–7 [b]Gen. 49:33
16 [a]Josh. 24:32 [b]Gen. 23:16
17 [a]Gen. 15:13 [b]Ex. 1:7–9
18 [a]Ex. 1:8
19 [a]Ex. 1:22
20 [a]Ex. 2:1, 2 [b]Heb. 11:23
21 [a]Ex. 2:3, 4 [b]Ex. 2:5–10
22 [a]Luke 24:19
23 [a]Ex. 2:11, 12
27 [a]Ex. 2:14
29 [a]Heb. 11:27 [b]Ex. 2:15, 21, 22; 4:20; 18:3
30 [a]Ex. 3:1–10 [1]NU omits *of the Lord*
32 [a]Ex. 3:6, 15
33 [a]Ex. 3:5, 7, 8, 10
34 [a]Ex. 2:24, 25 [b]Ps. 105:26
35 [a]Ex. 2:14 [b]Ex. 14:21
36 [a]Ex. 12:41; 33:1 [b]Ps. 105:27 [c]Ex. 14:21 [d]Ex. 16:1, 35
37 [a]Deut. 18:15, 18, 19 [b]Matt. 17:5 [1]NU, M omit *Him you shall hear*
38 [a]Ex. 19:3 [b]Gal. 3:19 [c]Deut. 5:27 [d]Heb. 5:12 [1]Gr. *ekklesia, assembly* or *church* [2]*sayings*
39 [a]Ps. 95:8–11
40 [a]Ex. 32:1, 23

Moses who brought us out of the
land of Egypt, we do not know
what has become of him.'
41 [a]"And they made a calf in those
days, offered sacrifices to the idol,
and [b]rejoiced in the works of their
own hands.
42 "Then [a]God turned and gave
them up to worship [b]the host of
heaven, as it is written in the book
of the Prophets:

[c]*'Did you offer Me slaughtered*
animals and sacrifices during
forty years in the wilderness,
O house of Israel?
43 *You also took up the tabernacle*
of Moloch,
And the star of your god
Remphan,
Images which you made to
worship;
And [a]*I will carry you away*
beyond Babylon.'

God's True Tabernacle

44 "Our fathers had the taberna-
cle of witness in the wilderness, as
He appointed, instructing Moses
[a]to make it according to the pat-
tern that he had seen,
45 [a]"which our fathers, having re-
ceived it in turn, also brought with
Joshua into the land possessed by
the Gentiles, [b]whom God drove out
before the face of our fathers until
the [c]days of David,
46 [a]"who found favor before God
and [b]asked to find a dwelling for
the God of Jacob.
47 [a]"But Solomon built Him a
house.
48 "However, [a]the Most High does
not dwell in temples made with
hands, as the prophet says:

49 *'Heaven*[a] *is My throne,*
And earth is My footstool.
What house will you build for
Me? says the LORD,
Or what is the place of My rest?
50 *Has My hand not* [a]*made all these*
things?'

Israel Resists the Holy Spirit

51 "*You* [a]stiff-necked[1] and [b]uncir-
cumcised in heart and ears! You
always resist the Holy Spirit; as
your fathers *did*, so do you.
52 [a]"Which of the prophets did
your fathers not persecute? And
they killed those who foretold the
coming of [b]the Just One, of whom
you now have become the betray-
ers and murderers,
53 [a]"who have received the law by
the direction of angels and have
not kept *it*."

Stephen the Martyr

54 [a]When they heard these things
they were [1]cut to the heart, and
they gnashed at him with *their*
teeth.
55 But he, [a]being full of the Holy
Spirit, gazed into heaven and saw
the [b]glory of God, and Jesus stand-
ing at the right hand of God,
56 and said, "Look! [a]I see the
heavens opened and the [b]Son of
Man standing at the right hand of
God!"
57 Then they cried out with a loud
voice, stopped their ears, and ran
at him with one accord;
58 and they cast *him* out of the city
and stoned *him*. And [a]the wit-
nesses laid down their clothes at
the feet of a young man named
Saul.
59 And they stoned Stephen as he
was calling on *God* and saying,
"Lord Jesus, [a]receive my spirit."
60 Then he knelt down and cried
out with a loud voice, [a]"Lord, do
not charge them with this sin."
And when he had said this, he fell
asleep.

Saul Persecutes the Church

8 Now Saul was consenting to
his death. At that time a great
persecution arose against the
church which was at Jerusalem;
and [a]they were all scattered
throughout the regions of Judea
and Samaria, except the apostles.
2 And devout men carried Ste-
phen *to his burial*, and [a]made great
lamentation over him.
3 As for Saul, [a]he made havoc of
the church, entering every house,
and dragging off men and women,
committing *them* to prison.

Christ Is Preached in Samaria

4 Therefore [a]those who were scat-
tered went everywhere preach-
ing the word.
5 Then [a]Philip went down to [1]the
city of Samaria and preached
Christ to them.
6 And the multitudes with one

41 [a]Ex. 32:2–4; Deut. 9:16; Ps. 106:19 [b]Ex. 32:6, 18, 19
42 [a]Ps. 81:12; [2 Thess. 2:11] [b]Deut. 4:19; 2 Kin. 21:3 [c]Amos 5:25–27
43 [a]2 Chr. 36:11–21; Jer. 25:9–12
44 [a]Ex. 25:40; [Heb. 8:5]
45 [a]Deut. 32:49; Josh. 3:14; 18:1; 23:9 [b]Neh. 9:24; Ps. 44:2 [c]2 Sam. 6:2–15
46 [a]2 Sam. 7:1–13; 1 Kin. 8:17 [b]1 Chr. 22:7; Ps. 132:4, 5
47 [a]1 Kin. 6:1–38; 8:20, 21; 2 Chr. 3:1–17
48 [a]1 Kin. 8:27; 2 Chr. 2:6; Acts 17:24
49 [a]Is. 66:1, 2; Matt. 5:34
50 [a]Ps. 102:25
51 [a]Ex. 32:9; Is. 6:10 [b]Lev. 26:41 [1]*stubborn*
52 [a]2 Chr. 36:16; Matt. 21:35; 23:35; 1 Thess. 2:15 [b]Acts 3:14; 22:14; 1 John 2:1
53 [a]Ex. 20:1; Deut. 33:2; Acts 7:38; Gal. 3:19; Heb. 2:2
54 [a]Acts 5:33 [1]*furious*
55 [a]Matt. 5:8; 16:28; Mark 9:1; Luke 9:27; Acts 6:5 [b][Ex. 24:17]
56 [a]Matt. 3:16 [b]Dan. 7:13
58 [a]Acts 22:20
59 [a]Ps. 31:5
60 [a]Matt. 5:44; Luke 23:34

CHAPTER 8

1 [a]John 16:2; Acts 8:4; 11:19
2 [a]Gen. 23:2
3 [a]Acts 7:58; 1 Cor. 15:9; Gal. 1:13; Phil. 3:6; 1 Tim. 1:13
4 [a]Matt. 10:23
5 [a]Acts 6:5; 8:26, 30 [1]*Or a*

accord heeded the things spoken
by Philip, hearing and seeing the
miracles which he did.
7 For [a]unclean spirits, crying
with a loud voice, came out of
many who were possessed; and
many who were paralyzed and
lame were healed.
8 And there was great joy in that
city.

The Sorcerer's Profession of Faith

9 But there was a certain man
called Simon, who previously
[a]practiced [1]sorcery in the city and
[b]astonished the [2]people of Samaria,
claiming that he was someone great,
10 to whom they all gave heed,
from the least to the greatest, saying,
"This man is the great power
of God."
11 And they heeded him because
he had astonished them with his
[1]sorceries for a long time.
12 But when they believed Philip
as he preached the things [a]concerning
the kingdom of God and
the name of Jesus Christ, both men
and women were baptized.
13 Then Simon himself also believed;
and when he was baptized
he continued with Philip, and was
amazed, seeing the miracles and
signs which were done.

The Sorcerer's Sin

14 Now when the [a]apostles who
were at Jerusalem heard that Samaria
had received the word of
God, they sent Peter and John to
them,
15 who, when they had come
down, prayed for them [a]that they
might receive the Holy Spirit.
16 For [a]as yet He had fallen upon
none of them. [b]They had only been
baptized in [c]the name of the Lord
Jesus.
17 Then [a]they laid hands on them,
and they received the Holy Spirit.
18 And when Simon saw that
through the laying on of the apostles'
hands the Holy Spirit was
given, he offered them money,
19 saying, "Give me this power
also, that anyone on whom I lay
hands may receive the Holy
Spirit."
20 But Peter said to him, "Your
money perish with you, because
[a]you thought that [b]the gift of
God could be purchased with
money!
21 "You have neither part nor
portion in this matter, for your
[a]heart is not right in the sight of
God.
22 "Repent therefore of this your
wickedness, and pray God [a]if perhaps
the thought of your heart
may be forgiven you.
23 "For I see that you are [a]poisoned
by bitterness and bound by
iniquity."
24 Then Simon answered and
said, [a]"Pray to the Lord for me,
that none of the things which you
have spoken may come upon me."
25 So when they had testified and
preached the word of the Lord,
they returned to Jerusalem,
preaching the gospel in many villages
of the Samaritans.

Christ Is Preached to an Ethiopian

26 Now an angel of the Lord
spoke to [a]Philip, saying, "Arise
and go toward the south along the
road which goes down from Jerusalem
to Gaza." This is [1]desert.
27 So he arose and went. And behold,
[a]a man of Ethiopia, a eunuch
of great authority under Candace
the queen of the Ethiopians, who
had charge of all her treasury, and
[b]had come to Jerusalem to worship,
28 was returning. And sitting in
his chariot, he was reading Isaiah
the prophet.
29 Then the Spirit said to Philip,
"Go near and overtake this chariot."
30 So Philip ran to him, and heard
him reading the prophet Isaiah,
and said, "Do you understand
what you are reading?"
31 And he said, "How can I, unless
someone guides me?" And he
asked Philip to come up and sit
with him.
32 The place in the Scripture
which he read was this:

[a]*"He was led as a sheep to the*
slaughter;
And as a lamb before its shearer
is silent,
[b]*So He opened not His mouth.*
33 *In His humiliation His [a]justice*
was taken away,

7 [a]Mark 16:17
9 [a]Acts 8:11; 13:6 [b]Acts 5:36 [1]*magic* [2]Or *nation*
11 [1]*magic arts*
12 [a]Acts 1:3; 8:4
14 [a]Acts 5:12, 29, 40
15 [a]Acts 2:38; 19:2
16 [a]Acts 19:2 [b]Matt. 28:19; Acts 2:38 [c]Acts 10:48; 19:5
17 [a]Acts 6:6; 19:6; Heb. 6:2
20 [a]2 Kin. 5:16; Is. 55:1; Dan. 5:17; [Matt. 10:8] [b][Acts 2:38; 10:45; 11:17]
21 [a]Jer. 17:9
22 [a]Dan. 4:27; 2 Tim. 2:25
23 [a]Heb. 12:15
24 [a]Gen. 20:7, 17; Ex. 8:8; Num. 21:7; 1 Kin. 13:6; Job 42:8; James 5:16
26 [a]Acts 6:5 [1]Or *a deserted place*
27 [a]Ps. 68:31; 87:4; Is. 56:3; Zeph. 3:10 [b]1 Kin. 8:41, 42; John 12:20
32 [a]Is. 53:7, 8 [b]Matt. 26:62, 63; 27:12, 14; John 19:9
33 [a]Luke 23:1–25

And who will declare His
generation?
For His life is [b]taken from the
earth."

34 So the eunuch answered Philip
and said, "I ask you, of whom does
the prophet say this, of himself or
of some other man?"
35 Then Philip opened his mouth,
[a]and beginning at this Scripture,
preached Jesus to him.
36 Now as they went down the
road, they came to some water.
And the eunuch said, "See, *here*
is water. [a]What hinders me from
being baptized?"
37 [1]Then Philip said, [a]"If you be-
lieve with all your heart, you
may." And he answered and said,
[b]"I believe that Jesus Christ is the
Son of God."
38 So he commanded the chariot
to stand still. And both Philip and
the eunuch went down into the wa-
ter, and he baptized him.
39 Now when they came up out of
the water, [a]the Spirit of the Lord
caught Philip away, so that the eu-
nuch saw him no more; and he
went on his way rejoicing.
40 But Philip was found at
[1]Azotus. And passing through, he
preached in all the cities till he
came to [a]Caesarea.

The Damascus Road: Saul Converted

9 Then [a]Saul, still breathing
threats and murder against the
disciples of the Lord, went to the
high priest
2 and asked [a]letters from him to
the synagogues of Damascus, so
that if he found any who were of
the Way, whether men or women,
he might bring them bound to Je-
rusalem.
3 [a]As he journeyed he came near
Damascus, and suddenly a light
shone around him from heaven.
4 Then he fell to the ground, and
heard a voice saying to him, "Saul,
Saul, [a]why are you persecuting
Me?"
5 And he said, "Who are You,
Lord?" Then the Lord said, "I am
Jesus, whom you are persecuting.
[1]It *is* hard for you to kick against
the goads."
6 So he, trembling and aston-
ished, said, "Lord, what do You
want me to do?" Then the Lord
said to him, "Arise and go into the
city, and you will be told what you
must do."
7 And [a]the men who journeyed
with him stood speechless, hearing
a voice but seeing no one.
8 Then Saul arose from the
ground, and when his eyes were
opened he saw no one. But they
led him by the hand and brought
him into Damascus.
9 And he was three days without
sight, and neither ate nor drank.

Ananias Baptizes Saul

10 Now there was a certain disci-
ple at Damascus [a]named Ananias;
and to him the Lord said in a vi-
sion, "Ananias." And he said,
"Here I am, Lord."
11 So the Lord *said* to him, "Arise
and go to the street called Straight,
and inquire at the house of Judas
for *one* called Saul [a]of Tarsus, for
behold, he is praying.
12 "And in a vision he has seen a
man named Ananias coming in
and putting *his* hand on him, so
that he might receive his sight."
13 Then Ananias answered,
"Lord, I have heard from many
about this man, [a]how much [1]harm
he has done to Your saints in Jeru-
salem.
14 "And here he has authority
from the chief priests to bind all
[a]who call on Your name."
15 But the Lord said to him,
"Go, for [a]he is a chosen vessel of
Mine to bear My name before
[b]Gentiles, [c]kings, and the [d]chil-
dren[1] of Israel.
16 "For [a]I will show him how
many things he must suffer for My
[b]name's sake."
17 [a]And Ananias went his way
and entered the house; and [b]laying
his hands on him he said, "Brother
Saul, the Lord [1]Jesus, who ap-
peared to you on the road as you
came, has sent me that you may
receive your sight and [c]be filled
with the Holy Spirit."
18 Immediately there fell from his
eyes *something* like scales, and he
received his sight at once; and he
arose and was baptized.
19 So when he had received food,
he was strengthened. [a]Then Saul

33 [b]Luke 23:33–46
35 [a]Luke 24:27
36 [a]Acts 10:47; 16:33
37 [a][Mark 16:16] [b]Matt. 16:16 [1]NU, M omit v. 37. It is found in Western texts, including the Latin tradition.
39 [a]Ezek. 3:12, 14
40 [a]Acts 21:8 [1]Same as Heb. *Ashdod*

CHAPTER 9

1 [a]Acts 7:57; 8:1, 3; 26:10, 11
2 [a]Acts 22:5
3 [a]1 Cor. 15:8
4 [a][Matt. 25:40]
5 [1]NU, M omit the rest of v. 5 and begin v. 6 with *But arise and go*
7 [a][Acts 22:9; 26:13]
10 [a]Acts 22:12
11 [a]Acts 21:39; 22:3
13 [a]Acts 9:1 [1]*bad things*
14 [a]Acts 7:59; 9:2, 21
15 [a]Eph. 3:7, 8 [b]Rom. 1:5; 11:13 [c]Acts 25:22, 23; 26:1 [d]Rom. 1:16; 9:1–5 [1]Lit. *sons*
16 [a]Acts 20:23 [b]2 Cor. 4:11
17 [a]Acts 22:12, 13 [b]Acts 8:17 [c]Acts 2:4; 4:31; 8:17; 13:52 [1]M omits *Jesus*
19 [a]Acts 26:20

spent some days with the disciples
at Damascus.

Saul Preaches Christ

20 Immediately he preached [1]the
Christ in the synagogues, that He
is the Son of God.
21 Then all who heard were
amazed, and said, [a]"Is this not he
who destroyed those who called
on this name in Jerusalem, and has
come here for that purpose, so that
he might bring them bound to the
chief priests?"
22 But Saul increased all the more
in strength, [a]and confounded the
Jews who dwelt in Damascus,
proving that this *Jesus* is the
Christ.

Saul Escapes Death

23 Now after many days were
past, [a]the Jews plotted to kill him.
24 [a]But their plot became known
to Saul. And they watched the
gates day and night, to kill him.
25 Then the disciples took him by
night and [a]let *him* down through
the wall in a large basket.

Saul at Jerusalem

26 And [a]when Saul had come to
Jerusalem, he tried to join the dis-
ciples; but they were all afraid of
him, and did not believe that he
was a disciple.
27 [a]But Barnabas took him and
brought *him* to the apostles. And
he declared to them how he had
seen the Lord on the road, and that
He had spoken to him, [b]and how
he had preached boldly at Damas-
cus in the name of Jesus.
28 So [a]he was with them at Jeru-
salem, coming in and going out.
29 And he spoke boldly in the
name of the Lord Jesus and dis-
puted against the [a]Hellenists,[1] [b]but
they attempted to kill him.
30 When the brethren found out,
they brought him down to Caes-
area and sent him out to Tarsus.

The Church Prospers

31 [a]Then the [1]churches through-
out all Judea, Galilee, and Samaria
had peace and were [b]edified.[2] And
walking in the [c]fear of the Lord
and in the [d]comfort of the Holy
Spirit, they were [e]multiplied.

20 [1]NU *Jesus*
21 [a]Acts 8:3; 9:13; Gal. 1:13, 23
22 [a]Acts 18:28
23 [a]Acts 23:12; 2 Cor. 11:26
24 [a]2 Cor. 11:32
25 [a]Josh. 2:15; 1 Sam. 19:12
26 [a]Acts 22:17–20; 26:20; Gal. 1:17, 18
27 [a]Acts 4:36; 13:2 [b]Acts 9:20, 22
28 [a]Gal. 1:18
29 [a]Acts 6:1; 11:20 [b]Acts 9:23; 2 Cor. 11:26 [1]Greek-speaking Jews
31 [a]Acts 5:11; 8:1; 16:5 [b][Eph. 4:16, 29] [c]Ps. 34:9 [d]John 14:16 [e]Acts 16:5 [1]NU *church . . . was* [2]*built up*
32 [a]Acts 8:14
34 [a][Acts 3:6, 16; 4:10]
35 [a]1 Chr. 5:16; 27:29; Is. 33:9; 35:2; 65:10 [b]Acts 11:21; 15:19
36 [a]1 Tim. 2:10; Titus 3:8 [1]Lit., in Aram., *Gazelle* [2]Lit., in Gr., *Gazelle*
37 [a]Acts 1:13; 9:39
40 [a]Matt. 9:25 [b]Luke 22:41; Acts 7:60 [c]Mark 5:41, 42; John 11:43
42 [a]John 11:45
43 [a]Acts 10:6

CHAPTER 10
1 [a]Acts 8:40; 23:23

Aeneas Healed

32 Now it came to pass, as Peter
went [a]through all *parts of the*
country, that he also came down
to the saints who dwelt in Lydda.
33 There he found a certain man
named Aeneas, who had been
bedridden eight years and was
paralyzed.
34 And Peter said to him, "Ae-
neas, [a]Jesus the Christ heals you.
Arise and make your bed." Then
he arose immediately.
35 So all who dwelt at Lydda and
[a]Sharon saw him and [b]turned to
the Lord.

Dorcas Restored to Life

36 At Joppa there was a certain
disciple named [1]Tabitha, which is
translated [2]Dorcas. This woman
was full [a]of good works and
charitable deeds which she did.
37 But it happened in those days
that she became sick and died.
When they had washed her, they
laid *her* in [a]an upper room.
38 And since Lydda was near
Joppa, and the disciples had heard
that Peter was there, they sent two
men to him, imploring *him* not to
delay in coming to them.
39 Then Peter arose and went
with them. When he had come,
they brought *him* to the upper
room. And all the widows stood by
him weeping, showing the tunics
and garments which Dorcas had
made while she was with them.
40 But Peter [a]put them all out, and
[b]knelt down and prayed. And turn-
ing to the body he [c]said, "Tabitha,
arise." And she opened her eyes,
and when she saw Peter she sat
up.
41 Then he gave her *his* hand and
lifted her up; and when he had
called the saints and widows, he
presented her alive.
42 And it became known through-
out all Joppa, [a]and many believed
on the Lord.
43 So it was that he stayed many
days in Joppa with [a]Simon, a tan-
ner.

Cornelius Sends a Delegation

10 There was a certain man in
[a]Caesarea called Cornelius,

a centurion of what was called the
Italian [1]Regiment,
2 [a]a devout *man* and one who
[b]feared God with all his house-
hold, who gave [1]alms generously
to the people, and prayed to God
always.
3 About [1]the ninth hour of the
day [a]he saw clearly in a vision an
angel of God coming in and saying
to him, "Cornelius!"
4 And when he observed him, he
was afraid, and said, "What is it,
lord?" So he said to him, "Your
prayers and your alms have come
up for a memorial before God.
5 "Now [a]send men to Joppa, and
send for Simon whose surname is
Peter.
6 "He is lodging with [a]Simon, a
tanner, whose house is by the sea.
[b]He[1] will tell you what you must
do."
7 And when the angel who spoke
to him had departed, Cornelius
called two of his household ser-
vants and a devout soldier from
among those who waited on him
continually.
8 So when he had explained all
these things to them, he sent them
to Joppa.

Peter's Vision

9 The next day, as they went on
their journey and drew near the
city, [a]Peter went up on the house-
top to pray, about [1]the sixth hour.
10 Then he became very hungry
and wanted to eat; but while they
made ready, he fell into a trance
11 and [a]saw heaven opened and
an object like a great sheet bound
at the four corners, descending to
him and let down to the earth.
12 In it were all kinds of four-
footed animals of the earth, wild
beasts, creeping things, and birds
of the air.
13 And a voice came to him,
"Rise, Peter; kill and eat."
14 But Peter said, "Not so, Lord!
[a]For I have never eaten anything
common or unclean."
15 And a voice *spoke* to him again
the second time, [a]"What God has
[1]cleansed you must not call com-
mon."
16 This was done three times. And
the object was taken up into
heaven again.

Summoned to Caesarea

17 Now while Peter [1]wondered
within himself what this vision
which he had seen meant, behold,
the men who had been sent from
Cornelius had made inquiry for Si-
mon's house, and stood before the
gate.
18 And they called and asked
whether Simon, whose surname
was Peter, was lodging there.
19 While Peter thought about the
vision, [a]the Spirit said to him, "Be-
hold, three men are seeking you.
20 [a]"Arise therefore, go down and
go with them, doubting nothing;
for I have sent them."
21 Then Peter went down to the
men [1]who had been sent to him
from Cornelius, and said, "Yes, I
am he whom you seek. For what
reason have you come?"
22 And they said, "Cornelius *the*
centurion, a just man, one who
fears God and [a]has a good reputa-
tion among all the nation of the
Jews, was divinely instructed by
a holy angel to summon you to his
house, and to hear words from
you."
23 Then he invited them in and
lodged *them*. On the next day Pe-
ter went away with them, [a]and
some brethren from Joppa accom-
panied him.

Peter Meets Cornelius

24 And the following day they en-
tered Caesarea. Now Cornelius
was waiting for them, and had
called together his relatives and
close friends.
25 As Peter was coming in, Cor-
nelius met him and fell down at
his feet and worshiped *him*.
26 But Peter lifted him up, saying,
[a]"Stand up; I myself am also a
man."
27 And as he talked with him, he
went in and found many who had
come together.
28 Then he said to them, "You
know how [a]unlawful it is for a
Jewish man to keep company with
or go to one of another nation. But
[b]God has shown me that I should
not call any man common or un-
clean.
29 "Therefore I came without ob-
jection as soon as I was sent for.

1 [1]*Cohort*
2 [a]Acts 8:2; 9:22; 22:12 [b][Acts 10:22, 35; 13:16, 26] [1]*charitable gifts*
3 [a]Acts 10:30; 11:13 [1]3 P.M.
5 [a]Acts 11:13, 14
6 [a]Acts 9:43 [b]Acts 11:14 [1]NU, M omit the rest of v. 6.
9 [a]Acts 10:9–32; 11:5–14 [1]Noon
11 [a]Ezek. 1:1; Matt. 3:16; Acts 7:56; Rev. 4:1; 19:11
14 [a]Lev. 11:4; 20:25; Deut. 14:3, 7; Ezek. 4:14
15 [a][Matt. 15:11; Mark 7:19]; Acts 10:28; [Rom. 14:14]; 1 Cor. 10:25; [1 Tim. 4:4; Titus 1:15] [1]Declared clean
17 [1]*was perplexed*
19 [a]Acts 11:12
20 [a]Acts 15:7–9
21 [1]NU, M omit *who had been sent to him from Cornelius*
22 [a]Acts 22:12
23 [a]Acts 10:45; 11:12
26 [a]Acts 14:14, 15; Rev. 19:10; 22:8
28 [a]John 4:9; 18:28; Acts 11:3; Gal. 2:12 [b][Acts 10:14, 35; 15:8, 9]

I ask, then, for what reason have
you sent for me?"
30 So Cornelius said, [1]"Four days
ago I was fasting until this hour;
and at the ninth hour I prayed in
my house, and behold, [a]a man
stood before me [b]in bright cloth-
ing,
31 "and said, 'Cornelius, [a]your
prayer has been heard, and [b]your
[1]alms are remembered in the sight
of God.
32 'Send therefore to Joppa and
call Simon here, whose surname
is Peter. He is lodging in the house
of Simon, a tanner, by the sea.
[1]When he comes, he will speak to
you.'
33 "So I sent to you immediately,
and you have done well to come.
Now therefore, we are all present
before God, to hear all the things
commanded you by God."

Preaching to Cornelius' Household

34 Then Peter opened *his* mouth
and said: [a]"In truth I perceive that
God shows no partiality.
35 "But [a]in every nation whoever
fears Him and works righteous-
ness is [b]accepted by Him.
36 "The word which *God* sent to
the [1]children of Israel, [a]preaching
peace through Jesus Christ—[b]He
is Lord of all—
37 "that word you know, which
was proclaimed throughout all Ju-
dea, and [a]began from Galilee after
the baptism which John preached:
38 "how [a]God anointed Jesus of
Nazareth with the Holy Spirit and
with power, who [b]went about do-
ing good and healing all who were
oppressed by the devil, [c]for God
was with Him.
39 "And we are [a]witnesses of all
things which He did both in the
land of the Jews and in Jerusalem,
whom [1]they [b]killed by hanging on
a tree.
40 "Him [a]God raised up on the
third day, and showed Him openly,
41 [a]"not to all the people, but to
witnesses chosen before by God,
even to us [b]who ate and drank with
Him after He arose from the dead.
42 "And [a]He commanded us to
preach to the people, and to testify
[b]that it is He who was ordained by
God *to be* Judge [c]of the living and
the dead.
43 [a]"To Him all the prophets wit-
ness that, through His name,
[b]whoever believes in Him will re-
ceive [c]remission[1] of sins."

The Holy Spirit Falls on the Gentiles

44 While Peter was still speaking
these words, [a]the Holy Spirit fell
upon all those who heard the
word.
45 [a]And [1]those of the circumcision
who believed were astonished, as
many as came with Peter, [b]be-
cause the gift of the Holy Spirit
had been poured out on the Gen-
tiles also.
46 For they heard them speak
with tongues and magnify God.
Then Peter answered,
47 "Can anyone forbid water, that
these should not be baptized who
have received the Holy Spirit [a]just
as we *have?*"
48 [a]And he commanded them to
be baptized [b]in the name of the
Lord. Then they asked him to stay
a few days.

Peter Defends God's Grace

11 Now the apostles and breth-
ren who were in Judea
heard that the Gentiles had also re-
ceived the word of God.
2 And when Peter came up to Je-
rusalem, [a]those of the circumci-
sion contended with him,
3 saying, [a]"You went in to uncir-
cumcised men [b]and ate with
them!"
4 But Peter explained *it* to them
[a]in order from the beginning, say-
ing:
5 [a]"I was in the city of Joppa
praying; and in a trance I saw a
vision, an object descending like
a great sheet, let down from
heaven by four corners; and it
came to me.
6 "When I observed it intently
and considered, I saw four-footed
animals of the earth, wild beasts,
creeping things, and birds of the
air.
7 "And I heard a voice saying to
me, 'Rise, Peter; kill and eat.'
8 "But I said, 'Not so, Lord! For
nothing common or unclean has at
any time entered my mouth.'
9 "But the voice answered me
again from heaven, 'What God

30 [a]Acts 1:10 [b]Matt. 28:3 [1]NU *Four days ago to this hour, at the ninth hour*
31 [a]Dan. 10:12 [b]Heb. 6:10 [1]*charitable gifts*
32 [1]NU omits the rest of v. 32.
34 [a]Deut. 10:17
35 [a][Eph. 2:13] [b]Ps. 15:1, 2
36 [a]Is. 57:19 [b]Rom. 10:12 [1]Lit. *sons*
37 [a]Luke 4:14
38 [a]Luke 4:18 [b]Matt. 4:23 [c]John 3:2; 8:29
39 [a]Acts 1:8 [b]Acts 2:23 [1]NU, M *they also*
40 [a]Acts 2:24
41 [a][John 14:17, 19, 22; 15:27] [b]Luke 24:30, 41–43
42 [a]Matt. 28:19 [b]John 5:22, 27 [c]1 Pet. 4:5
43 [a]Zech. 13:1 [b]Gal. 3:22 [c]Acts 13:38, 39 [1]*forgiveness*
44 [a]Acts 4:31
45 [a]Acts 10:23 [b]Acts 11:18 [1]The Jews
47 [a]Acts 2:4; 10:44; 11:17; 15:8
48 [a]1 Cor. 1:14–17 [b]Acts 2:38; 8:16; 19:5

CHAPTER 11
2 [a]Acts 10:45
3 [a]Acts 10:28 [b]Gal. 2:12
4 [a]Luke 1:3
5 [a]Acts 10:9

has cleansed you must not call
common.'
10 "Now this was done three
times, and all were drawn up again
into heaven.
11 "At that very moment, three
men stood before the house where
I was, having been sent to me from
Caesarea.
12 "Then [a]the Spirit told me to go
with them, doubting nothing.
Moreover [b]these six brethren ac-
companied me, and we entered the
man's house.
13 [a]"And he told us how he had
seen an angel standing in his
house, who said to him, 'Send men
to Joppa, and call for Simon whose
surname is Peter,
14 'who will tell you words by
which you and all your household
will be saved.'
15 "And as I began to speak, the
Holy Spirit fell upon them, [a]as
upon us at the beginning.
16 "Then I remembered the word
of the Lord, how He said, [a]'John
indeed baptized with water, but
[b]you shall be baptized with the
Holy Spirit.'
17 [a]"If therefore God gave them
the same gift as *He gave* us when
we believed on the Lord Jesus
Christ, [b]who was I that I could
withstand God?"
18 When they heard these things
they became silent; and they glori-
fied God, saying, [a]"Then God has
also granted to the Gentiles repen-
tance to life."

Barnabas and Saul at Antioch

19 [a]Now those who were scattered
after the persecution that arose
over Stephen traveled as far as
Phoenicia, Cyprus, and Antioch,
preaching the word to no one but
the Jews only.
20 But some of them were men
from Cyprus and Cyrene, who,
when they had come to Antioch,
spoke to [a]the Hellenists, preaching
the Lord Jesus.
21 And [a]the hand of the Lord was
with them, and a great number be-
lieved and [b]turned to the Lord.
22 Then news of these things
came to the ears of the church in
Jerusalem, and they sent out [a]Bar-
nabas to go as far as Antioch.
23 When he came and had seen

12 [a][John 16:13]; Acts 10:19; 15:7 [b]Acts 10:23

13 [a]Acts 10:30

15 [a]Acts 2:1–4; 15:7–9

16 [a]Matt. 3:11; Mark 1:8; John 1:26, 33; Acts 1:5; 19:4 [b]Is. 44:3

17 [a][Acts 15:8, 9] [b]Acts 10:47

18 [a]Is. 42:1, 6; 49:6; Luke 2:32; John 11:52; Rom. 10:12, 13; 15:9, 16

19 [a]Acts 8:1, 4

20 [a]Acts 6:1; 9:29

21 [a]Luke 1:66; Acts 2:47 [b]Acts 9:35; 14:1

22 [a]Acts 4:36; 9:27

23 [a]Acts 13:43; 14:22

24 [a]Acts 6:5 [b]Acts 5:14; 11:21

25 [a]Acts 9:11, 30

27 [a]Acts 2:17; 13:1; 15:32; 21:9; 1 Cor. 12:28; Eph. 4:11

28 [a]John 16:13; Acts 21:10 [b]Acts 18:2

29 [a]Rom. 15:26; 1 Cor. 16:1; 2 Cor. 9:1

30 [a]Acts 12:25

CHAPTER 12

2 [a]Matt. 4:21; 20:23

3 [a]Ex. 12:15; 23:15; Acts 20:6

4 [a]John 21:18 [1]Gr. *tetrads,* squads of four

5 [1]NU *constantly* or *earnestly*

the grace of God, he was glad, and
[a]encouraged them all that with
purpose of heart they should con-
tinue with the Lord.
24 For he was a good man, [a]full
of the Holy Spirit and of faith.
[b]And a great many people were
added to the Lord.
25 Then Barnabas departed for
[a]Tarsus to seek Saul.
26 And when he had found him,
he brought him to Antioch. So it
was that for a whole year they as-
sembled with the church and
taught a great many people. And
the disciples were first called
Christians in Antioch.

Relief to Judea

27 And in these days [a]prophets
came from Jerusalem to Antioch.
28 Then one of them, named [a]Ag-
abus, stood up and showed by the
Spirit that there was going to be
a great famine throughout all the
world, which also happened in the
days of [b]Claudius Caesar.
29 Then the disciples, each ac-
cording to his ability, determined
to send [a]relief to the brethren
dwelling in Judea.
30 [a]This they also did, and sent it
to the elders by the hands of Bar-
nabas and Saul.

Herod's Violence to the Church

12 Now about that time Herod
the king stretched out *his*
hand to harass some from the
church.
2 Then he killed James [a]the
brother of John with the sword.
3 And because he saw that it
pleased the Jews, he proceeded
further to seize Peter also. Now it
was *during* [a]the Days of Unleav-
ened Bread.
4 So [a]when he had arrested him,
he put *him* in prison, and delivered
him to four [1]squads of soldiers to
keep him, intending to bring him
before the people after Passover.

Peter Freed from Prison

5 Peter was therefore kept in
prison, but [1]constant prayer was
offered to God for him by the
church.
6 And when Herod was about to
bring him out, that night Peter was
sleeping, bound with two chains

between two soldiers; and the
guards before the door were [1]keep-
ing the prison.
7 Now behold, [a]an angel of the
Lord stood by *him*, and a light
shone in the prison; and he struck
Peter on the side and raised him
up, saying, "Arise quickly!" And
his chains fell off *his* hands.
8 Then the angel said to him,
"Gird yourself and tie on your san-
dals"; and so he did. And he said
to him, "Put on your garment and
follow me."
9 So he went out and followed
him, and [a]did not know that what
was done by the angel was real,
but thought [b]he was seeing a vi-
sion.
10 When they were past the first
and the second guard posts, they
came to the iron gate that leads to
the city, [a]which opened to them of
its own accord; and they went out
and went down one street, and im-
mediately the angel departed from
him.
11 And when Peter had come to
himself, he said, "Now I know for
certain that [a]the Lord has sent His
angel, and [b]has delivered me from
the hand of Herod and *from* all
the expectation of the Jewish peo-
ple."
12 So, when he had considered
this, [a]he came to the house of
Mary, the mother of [b]John whose
surname was Mark, where many
were gathered together [c]praying.
13 And as Peter knocked at the
door of the gate, a girl named
Rhoda came to answer.
14 When she recognized Peter's
voice, because of *her* gladness she
did not open the gate, but ran in
and announced that Peter stood
before the gate.
15 But they said to her, "You are
beside yourself!" Yet she kept in-
sisting that it was so. So they said,
[a]"It is his angel."
16 Now Peter continued knock-
ing; and when they opened *the
door* and saw him, they were as-
tonished.
17 But [a]motioning to them with
his hand to keep silent, he de-
clared to them how the Lord had
brought him out of the prison. And
he said, "Go, tell these things to
James and to the brethren." And
he departed and went to another
place.
18 Then, as soon as it was day,
there was no small [1]stir among the
soldiers about what had become of
Peter.
19 But when Herod had searched
for him and not found him, he ex-
amined the guards and com-
manded that *they* should be put to
death. And he went down from Ju-
dea to Caesarea, and stayed *there*.

Herod's Violent Death

20 Now Herod had been very an-
gry with the people of [a]Tyre and
Sidon; but they came to him with
one accord, and having made Blas-
tus [1]the king's personal aide their
friend, they asked for peace, be-
cause [b]their country was [2]supplied
with food by the king's *country*.
21 So on a set day Herod, arrayed
in royal apparel, sat on his throne
and gave an oration to them.
22 And the people kept shouting,
"The voice of a god and not of a
man!"
23 Then immediately an angel of
the Lord [a]struck him, because [b]he
did not give glory to God. And he
was eaten by worms and [1]died.
24 But [a]the word of God grew and
multiplied.

Barnabas and Saul Appointed

25 And [a]Barnabas and Saul re-
turned [1]from Jerusalem when they
had [b]fulfilled *their* ministry, and
they also [c]took with them [d]John
whose surname was Mark.

13 Now [a]in the church that was
at Antioch there were cer-
tain prophets and teachers: [b]Bar-
nabas, Simeon who was called
Niger, [c]Lucius of Cyrene, Manaen
who had been brought up with
Herod the tetrarch, and Saul.
2 As they ministered to the Lord
and fasted, the Holy Spirit said,
[a]"Now separate to Me Barnabas
and Saul for the work [b]to which I
have called them."
3 Then, [a]having fasted and
prayed, and laid hands on them,
they sent *them* away.

Preaching in Cyprus

4 So, being sent out by the Holy
Spirit, they went down to Seleucia,

6 [1]*guarding*
7 [a]Acts 5:19
9 [a]Ps. 126:1 [b]Acts 10:3, 17; 11:5
10 [a]Acts 5:19; 16:26
11 [a][Ps. 34:7]; Dan. 3:28; 6:22; [Heb. 1:14] [b]Job 5:19; [Ps. 33:18, 19; 34:22; 41:2]; 2 Cor. 1:10; [2 Pet. 2:9]
12 [a]Acts 4:23 [b]Acts 13:5, 13; 15:37; 2 Tim. 4:11; Philem. 24; 1 Pet. 5:13 [c]Acts 12:5
15 [a]Gen. 48:16; [Matt. 18:10]
17 [a]Acts 13:16; 19:33; 21:40
18 [1]*disturbance*
20 [a]Matt. 11:21 [b]1 Kin. 5:11; Ezra 3:7; Ezek. 27:17 [1]*who was in charge of the king's bedchamber* [2]Lit. *nourished*
23 [a]1 Sam. 25:38; 2 Sam. 24:16, 17; 2 Kin. 19:35; Acts 5:19 [b]Ps. 115:1 [1]*breathed his last*
24 [a]Is. 55:11; Acts 6:7; 19:20
25 [a]Acts 11:30 [b]Acts 11:30 [c]Acts 13:5, 13 [d]Acts 12:12; 15:37 [1]NU, M *to*

CHAPTER 13
1 [a]Acts 14:26 [b]Acts 11:22 [c]Rom. 16:21
2 [a]Num. 8:14; Acts 9:15; 22:21; Rom. 1:1; Gal. 1:15; 2:9 [b]Matt. 9:38; Acts 14:26; Rom. 10:15; Eph. 3:7, 8; 1 Tim. 2:7; 2 Tim. 1:11; Heb. 5:4
3 [a]Matt. 9:15; Mark 2:20; Luke 5:35; Acts 6:6

and from there they sailed to [a]Cy-
prus.
5 And when they arrived in
Salamis, [a]they preached the word
of God in the synagogues of the
Jews. They also had [b]John as *their*
assistant.
6 Now when they had gone
through [1]the island to Paphos,
they found [a]a certain sorcerer, a
false prophet, a Jew whose name
was Bar-Jesus,
7 who was with the proconsul,
Sergius Paulus, an intelligent man.
This man called for Barnabas and
Saul and sought to hear the word
of God.
8 But [a]Elymas the sorcerer (for
so his name is translated) [1]with-
stood them, seeking to turn the
proconsul away from the faith.
9 Then Saul, who also *is called*
Paul, [a]filled with the Holy Spirit,
looked intently at him
10 and said, "O full of all deceit
and all fraud, [a]*you* son of the devil,
you enemy of all righteousness,
will you not cease perverting the
straight ways of the Lord?
11 "And now, indeed, [a]the hand of
the Lord *is* upon you, and you shall
be blind, not seeing the sun for a
time." And immediately a dark
mist fell on him, and he went
around seeking someone to lead
him by the hand.
12 Then the proconsul believed,
when he saw what had been done,
being astonished at the teaching of
the Lord.

At Antioch in Pisidia

13 Now when Paul and his party
set sail from Paphos, they came to
Perga in Pamphylia; and [a]John,
departing from them, returned to
Jerusalem.
14 But when they departed from

4 [a]Acts 4:36
5 [a][Acts 13:46] [b]Acts 12:25; 15:37
6 [a]Acts 8:9 [1]NU *the whole island*
8 [a]Ex. 7:11; 2 Tim. 3:8 [1]*opposed*
9 [a]Acts 2:4; 4:8
10 [a]Matt. 13:38; John 8:44; [1 John 3:8]
11 [a]Ex. 9:3; 1 Sam. 5:6; Job 19:21; Ps. 32:4; Heb. 10:31
13 [a]Acts 15:38

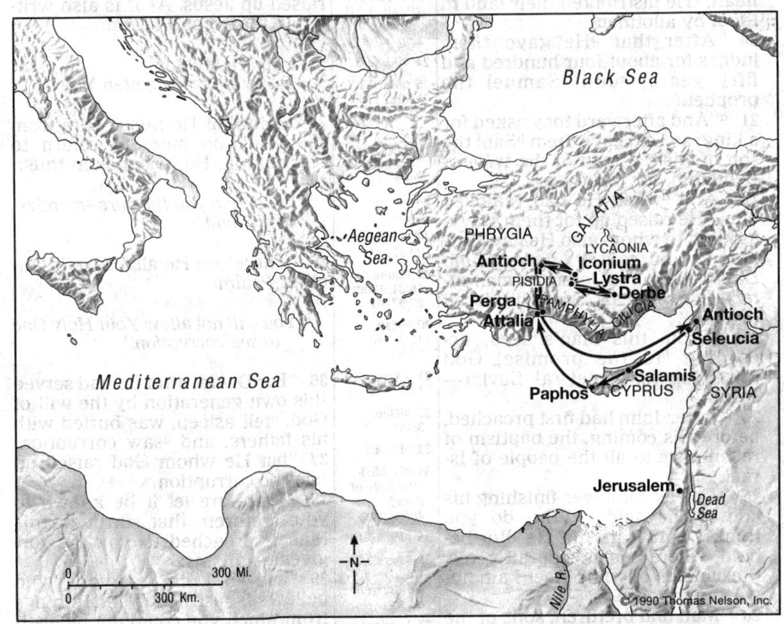

Paul Goes to Galatia (The First Missionary Journey, Acts 13; 14). Sent out from the church at Antioch (Acts 13:1–3), Paul and Barnabas went to the cities of Galatia in Asia Minor. The Jewish synagogues in these cities provided Paul a platform for preaching the gospel. At times, however, he even encountered opposition from the synagogues.

Perga, they came to Antioch in Pi-
sidia, and [a]went into the syna-
gogue on the Sabbath day and sat
down.
15 And [a]after the reading of the
Law and the Prophets, the rulers
of the synagogue sent to them,
saying, "Men *and* brethren, if you
have [b]any word of [1]exhortation for
the people, say on."
16 Then Paul stood up, and mo-
tioning with *his* hand said, "Men
of Israel, and [a]you who fear God,
listen:
17 "The God of this people [1]Israel
[a]chose our fathers, and exalted the
people [b]when they dwelt as
strangers in the land of Egypt, and
with [2]an uplifted arm He [c]brought
them out of it.
18 "Now [a]for a time of about forty
years He put up with their ways
in the wilderness.
19 "And when He had destroyed
[a]seven nations in the land of Ca-
naan, [b]He distributed their land to
them by allotment.
20 "After that [a]He gave *them*
judges for about four hundred and
fifty years, [b]until Samuel the
prophet.
21 [a]"And afterward they asked for
a king; so God gave them [b]Saul the
son of Kish, a man of the tribe of
Benjamin, for forty years.
22 "And [a]when He had removed
him, [b]He raised up for them David
as king, to whom also He gave tes-
timony and said, [c]'*I have found
David* the *son* of Jesse, [d]*a man af-
ter My own heart,* who will do all
My will.'
23 [a]"From this man's seed, ac-
cording [b]to *the* promise, God
raised up for Israel [c]a[1] Savior—
Jesus—
24 [a]"after John had first preached,
before His coming, the baptism of
repentance to all the people of Is-
rael.
25 "And as John was finishing his
course, he said, [a]'Who do you
think I am? I am not *He.* But be-
hold, [b]there comes One after me,
the sandals of whose feet I am not
worthy to loose.'
26 "Men *and* brethren, sons of the
[1]family of Abraham, and [a]those
among you who fear God, [b]to you
the [2]word of this salvation has
been sent.
27 "For those who dwell in Jeru-
salem, and their rulers, [a]because
they did not know Him, nor even
the voices of the Prophets which
are read every Sabbath, have ful-
filled *them* in condemning *Him.*
28 [a]"And though they found no
cause for death *in Him,* they asked
Pilate that He should be put to
death.
29 [a]"Now when they had fulfilled
all that was written concerning
Him, [b]they took *Him* down from
the tree and laid *Him* in a tomb.
30 [a]"But God raised Him from the
dead.
31 [a]"He was seen for many days
by those who came up with Him
from Galilee to Jerusalem, who are
His witnesses to the people.
32 "And we declare to you glad
tidings—[a]that promise which was
made to the fathers.
33 "God has fulfilled this for us
their children, in that He has
raised up Jesus. As it is also writ-
ten in the second Psalm:

[a]'*You are My Son,*
Today I have begotten You.'

34 "And that He raised Him from
the dead, no more to return to
[1]corruption, He has spoken thus:

[a]'*I will give you the sure* [2]*mercies*
of David.'

35 "Therefore He also says in an-
other *Psalm:*

[a]'*You will not allow Your Holy One*
to see corruption.'

36 "For David, after he had served
[1]his own generation by the will of
God, [a]fell asleep, was buried with
his fathers, and [2]saw corruption;
37 "but He whom God raised up
[1]saw no corruption.
38 "Therefore let it be known to
you, brethren, that [a]through this
Man is preached to you the for-
giveness of sins;
39 "and [a]by Him everyone who
believes is justified from all things
from which you could not be justi-
fied by the law of Moses.
40 "Beware therefore, lest what
has been spoken in the prophets
come upon you:

14 [a]Acts 16:13
15 [a]Luke 4:16 [b]Heb. 13:22 [1]*encouragement*
16 [a]Acts 10:35
17 [a]Deut. 7:6–8 [b]Acts 7:17 [c]Ex. 14:8 [1]M omits *Israel* [2]*Mighty power*
18 [a]Num. 14:34
19 [a]Deut. 7:1 [b]Josh. 14:1, 2; 19:51
20 [a]Judg. 2:16 [b]1 Sam. 3:20
21 [a]1 Sam. 8:5 [b]1 Sam. 10:20–24
22 [a]1 Sam. 15:23, 26, 28 [b]1 Sam. 16:1, 12, 13 [c]Ps. 89:20 [d]1 Sam. 13:14
23 [a]Is. 11:1 [b]Ps. 132:11 [c][Matt. 1:21] [1]M *salvation, after*
24 [a][Luke 3:3]
25 [a]Mark 1:7 [b]John 1:20, 27
26 [a]Ps. 66:16 [b]Matt. 10:6 [1]*stock* [2]*message*
27 [a]Luke 23:34
28 [a]Matt. 27:22, 23
29 [a]Luke 18:31 [b]Matt. 27:57–61
30 [a]Matt. 12:39, 40; 28:6
31 [a]Acts 1:3, 11
32 [a][Gen. 3:15]
33 [a]Ps. 2:7
34 [a]Is. 55:3 [1]*the state of decay* [2]*blessings*
35 [a]Ps. 16:10
36 [a]Acts 2:29 [1]*in his* [2]*underwent decay*
37 [1]*underwent no decay*
38 [a]Jer. 31:34
39 [a][Is. 53:11]

41 '*Behold,*[a] *you despisers,*
Marvel and perish!
For I work a work in your days,
A work which you will by no
means believe,
Though one were to declare it to
you.' "

Blessing and Conflict at Antioch

42 [1]So when the Jews went out
of the synagogue, the Gentiles
begged that these words might be
preached to them the next Sab-
bath.
43 Now when the congregation
had broken up, many of the Jews
and devout proselytes followed
Paul and Barnabas, who, speaking
to them, [a]persuaded them to con-
tinue in [b]the grace of God.
44 On the next Sabbath almost the
whole city came together to hear
the word of God.
45 But when the Jews saw the
multitudes, they were filled with
envy; and contradicting and blas-
pheming, they [a]opposed the things
spoken by Paul.
46 Then Paul and Barnabas grew
bold and said, [a]"It was necessary
that the word of God should be
spoken to you first; but [b]since you
reject it, and judge yourselves
unworthy of everlasting life, be-
hold, [c]we turn to the Gentiles.
47 "For so the Lord has com-
manded us:

[a]'*I have set you as a light to the*
Gentiles,
That you should be for salvation
to the ends of the earth.' "

48 Now when the Gentiles heard
this, they were glad and glorified
the word of the Lord. [a]And as
many as had been appointed to
eternal life believed.
49 And the word of the Lord was
being spread throughout all the re-
gion.
50 But the Jews stirred up the de-
vout and prominent women and
the chief men of the city, [a]raised
up persecution against Paul and
Barnabas, and expelled them from
their region.
51 [a]But they shook off the dust
from their feet against them, and
came to Iconium.
52 And the disciples [a]were filled
with joy and [b]with the Holy Spirit.

41 [a]Hab. 1:5
42 [1]Or *And when they went out of the synagogue of the Jews;* NU *And when they went out of the synagogue, they begged*
43 [a]Acts 11:23 [b]Titus 2:11; Heb. 12:15; 1 Pet. 5:12
45 [a]Acts 18:6; 1 Pet. 4:4; Jude 10
46 [a]Matt. 10:6; Acts 3:26; Rom. 1:16 [b]Ex. 32:10; Deut. 32:21; Is. 55:5; Matt. 21:43; Rom. 10:19 [c]Acts 18:6
47 [a]Is. 42:6; 49:6; Luke 2:32
48 [a][Acts 2:47]
50 [a]Acts 7:52; 2 Tim. 3:11
51 [a]Matt. 10:14; Mark 6:11; [Luke 9:5]
52 [a]Matt. 5:12; John 16:22 [b]Acts 2:4; 4:8, 31; 13:9

CHAPTER 14

1 [a]John 7:35; Acts 18:4; Rom. 1:14, 16; 1 Cor. 1:22
2 [1]embittered [2]Lit. *souls*
3 [a]Mark 16:20; Acts 4:29; 20:32; Heb. 2:4 [b]Acts 5:12
4 [a]Luke 12:51 [b]Acts 13:2, 3
5 [a]2 Tim. 3:11
6 [a]Matt. 10:23
8 [a]Acts 3:2
9 [1]Lit. *Who*
10 [a][Is. 35:6]
11 [a]Acts 8:10; 28:6
12 [1]*Jupiter* [2]*Mercury*
13 [a]Dan. 2:46
14 [a]Num. 14:6; Matt. 26:65; Mark 14:63

At Iconium

14 Now it happened in Iconium
that they went together to
the synagogue of the Jews, and so
spoke that a great multitude both
of the Jews and of the [a]Greeks be-
lieved.
2 But the unbelieving Jews
stirred up the Gentiles and [1]poi-
soned their [2]minds against the
brethren.
3 Therefore they stayed there a
long time, speaking boldly in the
Lord, [a]who was bearing witness to
the word of His grace, granting
signs and [b]wonders to be done by
their hands.
4 But the multitude of the city
was [a]divided: part sided with the
Jews, and part with the [b]apostles.
5 And when a violent attempt
was made by both the Gentiles and
Jews, with their rulers, [a]to abuse
and stone them,
6 they became aware of it and
[a]fled to Lystra and Derbe, cities of
Lycaonia, and to the surrounding
region.
7 And they were preaching the
gospel there.

Idolatry at Lystra

8 [a]And in Lystra a certain
man without strength in his feet
was sitting, a cripple from his
mother's womb, who had never
walked.
9 *This* man heard Paul speaking.
[1]Paul, observing him intently and
seeing that he had faith to be
healed,
10 said with a loud voice, [a]"Stand
up straight on your feet!" And he
leaped and walked.
11 Now when the people saw
what Paul had done, they raised
their voices, saying in the Lycao-
nian *language,* [a]"The gods have
come down to us in the likeness
of men!"
12 And Barnabas they called
[1]Zeus, and Paul, [2]Hermes, because
he was the chief speaker.
13 Then the priest of Zeus, whose
temple was in front of their city,
brought oxen and garlands to the
gates, [a]intending to sacrifice with
the multitudes.
14 But when the apostles Barna-
bas and Paul heard this, [a]they tore

their clothes and ran in among the
multitude, crying out
15 and saying, "Men, [a]why are
you doing these things? [b]We also
are men with the same nature as
you, and preach to you that you
should turn from [c]these useless
things [d]to the living God, [e]who
made the heaven, the earth, the
sea, and all things that are in them,
16 [a]"who in bygone generations
allowed all nations to walk in their
own ways.
17 [a]"Nevertheless He did not
leave Himself without witness, in
that He did good, [b]gave us rain
from heaven and fruitful seasons,
filling our hearts with [c]food and
gladness."
18 And with these sayings they
could scarcely restrain the multi-
tudes from sacrificing to them.

Stoning, Escape to Derbe

19 [a]Then Jews from Antioch and
Iconium came there; and having
persuaded the multitudes, [b]they
stoned Paul *and* dragged *him* out
of the city, supposing him to be
[c]dead.
20 However, when the disciples
gathered around him, he rose up
and went into the city. And the
next day he departed with Barna-
bas to Derbe.

Strengthening the Converts

21 And when they had preached
the gospel to that city [a]and made
many disciples, they returned to
Lystra, Iconium, and Antioch,
22 strengthening the souls of the
disciples, [a]exhorting *them* to con-
tinue in the faith, and *saying,* [b]"We
must through many tribulations
enter the kingdom of God."
23 So when they had [a]appointed
elders in every church, and prayed
with fasting, they commended
them to the Lord in whom they had
believed.
24 And after they had passed
through Pisidia, they came to Pam-
phylia.
25 Now when they had preached
the word in Perga, they went down
to Attalia.
26 From there they sailed to Anti-
och, where they had been com-
mended to the grace of God for the
work which they had completed.

15 [a]Acts 10:26 [b]James 5:17 [c]1 Sam. 12:21; Jer. 8:19; 14:22; Amos 2:4; 1 Cor. 8:4 [d]1 Thess. 1:9 [e]Gen. 1:1; Ex. 20:11; Ps. 146:6; Acts 4:24; 17:24; Rev. 14:7
16 [a]Ps. 81:12; Mic. 4:5; 1 Pet. 4:3
17 [a]Acts 17:24–27; Rom. 1:19, 20 [b]Lev. 26:4; Deut. 11:14; [Matt. 5:45] [c]Ps. 145:16
19 [a]Acts 13:45, 50; 14:2–5; 1 Thess. 2:14 [b]Acts 14:5; 2 Cor. 11:25; 2 Tim. 3:11 [c][2 Cor. 12:1–4]
21 [a]Matt. 28:19
22 [a]Acts 11:23 [b]Matt. 10:38; Luke 22:28; [Rom. 8:17; 2 Tim. 2:12; 3:12]
23 [a]Matt. 9:15; Mark 2:20; Luke 5:35; 2 Cor. 8:19; Titus 1:5
27 [a]Acts 15:4, 12 [b]1 Cor. 16:9; 2 Cor. 2:12; Col. 4:3; Rev. 3:8

CHAPTER 15

1 [a]Gal. 2:12 [b]John 7:22; Acts 15:5; Gal. 5:2; Phil. 3:2; [Col. 2:8, 11, 16]
2 [a]Gal. 2:1
3 [a]Acts 20:38; 21:5; Rom. 15:24; 1 Cor. 16:6, 11; 2 Cor. 1:16; Titus 3:13; 3 John 6 [b]Acts 14:27; 15:4, 12
7 [a]Acts 10:20
8 [a]1 Chr. 28:9; Acts 1:24 [b]Acts 2:4; 10:44, 47 [1]*bore witness to*
9 [a]Rom. 10:12 [b]Acts 10:15, 28
10 [a]Matt. 23:4; Gal. 5:1

27 Now when they had come and
gathered the church together,
[a]they reported all that God had
done with them, and that He had
[b]opened the door of faith to the
Gentiles.
28 So they stayed there a long
time with the disciples.

Conflict over Circumcision

15 And [a]certain *men* came
down from Judea and taught
the brethren, [b]"Unless you are
circumcised according to the
custom of Moses, you cannot be
saved."
2 Therefore, when Paul and Bar-
nabas had no small dissension and
dispute with them, they deter-
mined that [a]Paul and Barnabas
and certain others of them should
go up to Jerusalem, to the apostles
and elders, about this question.
3 So, [a]being sent on their way by
the church, they passed through
Phoenicia and Samaria, [b]describ-
ing the conversion of the Gentiles;
and they caused great joy to all the
brethren.
4 And when they had come to Je-
rusalem, they were received by the
church and the apostles and the
elders; and they reported all things
that God had done with them.
5 But some of the sect of the
Pharisees who believed rose up,
saying, "It is necessary to circum-
cise them, and to command *them*
to keep the law of Moses."

The Jerusalem Council

6 Now the apostles and elders
came together to consider this
matter.
7 And when there had been
much dispute, Peter rose up and
said to them: [a]"Men and brethren,
you know that a good while ago
God chose among us, that by my
mouth the Gentiles should hear the
word of the gospel and believe.
8 "So God, [a]who knows the
heart, [1]acknowledged them by
[b]giving them the Holy Spirit, just
as *He did* to us,
9 [a]"and made no distinction be-
tween us and them, [b]purifying
their hearts by faith.
10 "Now therefore, why do you
test God [a]by putting a yoke on the
neck of the disciples which neither

our fathers nor we were able to
bear?
11 "But [a]we believe that through
the grace of the Lord Jesus [1]Christ
we shall be saved in the same man-
ner as they."
12 Then all the multitude kept si-
lent and listened to Barnabas and
Paul declaring how many miracles
and wonders God had [a]worked
through them among the Gentiles.
13 And after they had [1]become si-
lent, [a]James answered, saying,
"Men *and* brethren, listen to me:
14 [a]"Simon has declared how God
at the first visited the Gentiles to
take out of them a people for His
name.
15 "And with this the words of the
prophets agree, just as it is written:

16 *'After[a] this I will return*
And will rebuild the tabernacle of
David, which has fallen down;
I will rebuild its ruins,
And I will set it up;
17 *So that the rest of mankind may*
seek the LORD,
Even all the Gentiles who are
called by My name,
Says the [1]LORD who does all
these things.'

18 [1]"Known to God from eternity
are all His works.
19 "Therefore [a]I judge that we
should not trouble those from
among the Gentiles who [b]are turn-
ing to God,
20 "but that we [a]write to them to
abstain [b]from things polluted by
idols, [c]*from* [1]sexual immorality,
[d]*from* things strangled, and *from*
blood.
21 "For Moses has had through-
out many generations those who
preach him in every city, [a]being
read in the synagogues every Sab-
bath."

The Jerusalem Decree

22 Then it pleased the apostles
and elders, with the whole church,
to send chosen men of their own
company to Antioch with Paul and
Barnabas, *namely*, Judas who was
also named [a]Barsabas,[1] and Silas,
leading men among the brethren.
23 They wrote this *letter* by them:

The apostles, the elders, and
the brethren,

To the brethren who are of the
Gentiles in Antioch, Syria, and
Cilicia:

Greetings.

24 Since we have heard that
[a]some who went out from us
have troubled you with words,
[b]unsettling your souls,
[1]saying, "*You must* be
circumcised and keep the
law"—to whom we gave no
such commandment—
25 it seemed good to us, being
assembled with one [1]accord, to
send chosen men to you with
our beloved Barnabas and
Paul,
26 [a]men who have risked their
lives for the name of our Lord
Jesus Christ.
27 We have therefore sent Judas
and Silas, who will also report
the same things by word of
mouth.
28 For it seemed good to the Holy
Spirit, and to us, to lay upon
you no greater burden than
these necessary things:
29 [a]that you abstain from things
offered to idols, [b]from blood,
from things strangled, and
from [c]sexual[1] immorality. If
you keep yourselves from
these, you will do well.

Farewell.

Continuing Ministry in Syria

30 So when they were sent off,
they came to Antioch; and when
they had gathered the multitude
together, they delivered the letter.
31 When they had read it, they re-
joiced over its encouragement.
32 Now Judas and Silas, them-
selves being [a]prophets also, [b]ex-
horted and strengthened the breth-
ren with many words.
33 And after they had stayed
there for a time, they were [a]sent
back with greetings from the
brethren to [1]the apostles.
34 [1]However, it seemed good to
Silas to remain there.
35 [a]Paul and Barnabas also re-
mained in Antioch, teaching and
preaching the word of the Lord,
with many others also.

---

11 [a]Rom. 3:4; 5:15 [1]NU, M omit *Christ*
12 [a]Acts 14:27; 15:3, 4
13 [a]Acts 12:17 [1]*stopped speaking*
14 [a]Acts 15:7
16 [a]Amos 9:11, 12
17 [1]NU *LORD, who makes these things*
18 [1]NU (continuing v. 17) *known from eternity (of old).'*
19 [a]Acts 15:28; 21:25 [b]1 Thess. 1:9
20 [a]Acts 21:25 [b][1 Cor. 8:1; 10:20, 28] [c][1 Cor. 6:9] [d]Lev. 3:17 [1]Or *fornication*
21 [a]Acts 13:15, 27
22 [a]Acts 1:23 [1]NU, M *Barsabbas*
24 [a]Titus 1:10, 11 [b]Gal. 1:7; 5:10 [1]NU omits *saying, "You must be circumcised and keep the law"*
25 [1]*purpose* or *mind*
26 [a]Acts 13:50; 14:19
29 [a]Acts 15:20; 21:25 [b]Lev. 17:14 [c]Col. 3:5 [1]Or *fornication*
32 [a]Eph. 4:11 [b]Acts 14:22; 18:23
33 [a]Heb. 11:31 [1]NU *those who had sent them*
34 [1]NU, M omit v. 34.
35 [a]Acts 13:1

Division over John Mark

36 Then after some days Paul said
to Barnabas, "Let us now go back
and visit our brethren in every city
where we have preached the word
of the Lord, *and see* how they are
doing."
37 Now Barnabas [1]was deter-
mined to take with them [a]John
called Mark.
38 But Paul insisted that they
should not take with them [a]the one
who had departed from them in
Pamphylia, and had not gone with
them to the work.
39 Then the contention became so
sharp that they parted from one
another. And so Barnabas took
Mark and sailed to [a]Cyprus;
40 but Paul chose Silas and de-
parted, [a]being [1]commended by the
brethren to the grace of God.
41 And he went through Syria
and Cilicia, [a]strengthening the
churches.

Timothy Joins Paul and Silas

16 Then he came to [a]Derbe and
Lystra. And behold, a cer-
tain disciple was there, [b]named
Timothy, [c]*the* son of a certain Jew-
ish woman who believed, but his
father *was* Greek.
2 He was well spoken of by the
brethren who were at Lystra and
Iconium.
3 Paul wanted to have him go on
with him. And he [a]took *him* and
circumcised him because of the
Jews who were in that region, for
they all knew that his father was
Greek.
4 And as they went through the
cities, they delivered to them the
[a]decrees to keep, [b]which were de-
termined by the apostles and el-
ders at Jerusalem.
5 [a]So the churches were
strengthened in the faith, and in-
creased in number daily.

The Macedonian Call

6 Now when they had gone
through Phrygia and the region of
[a]Galatia, they were forbidden by
the Holy Spirit to preach the word
in [1]Asia.
7 After they had come to Mysia,
they tried to go into Bithynia, but
the [1]Spirit did not permit them.
8 So passing by Mysia, they
[a]came down to Troas.
9 And a vision appeared to Paul
in the night. A [a]man of Macedonia
stood and pleaded with him, say-
ing, "Come over to Macedonia and
help us."
10 Now after he had seen the vi-
sion, immediately we sought to go
[a]to Macedonia, concluding that the
Lord had called us to preach the
gospel to them.

Lydia Baptized at Philippi

11 Therefore, sailing from Troas,
we ran a straight course to Sam-
othrace, and the next *day* came to
Neapolis,
12 and from there to [a]Philippi,
which is the [1]foremost city of that
part of Macedonia, a colony. And
we were staying in that city for
some days.
13 And on the Sabbath day we
went out of the city to the river-
side, where prayer was custom-
arily made; and we sat down and
spoke to the women who met
there.
14 Now a certain woman named
Lydia heard *us*. She was a seller
of purple from the city of [a]Thya-
tira, who worshiped God. [b]The
Lord opened her heart to heed the
things spoken by Paul.
15 And when she and her house-
hold were baptized, she begged *us*,
saying, "If you have judged me to
be faithful to the Lord, come to my
house and stay." So [a]she per-
suaded us.

Paul and Silas Imprisoned

16 Now it happened, as we went
to prayer, that a certain slave girl
[a]possessed with a spirit of div-
ination met us, who brought her
masters [b]much profit by fortune-
telling.
17 This girl followed Paul and us,
and cried out, saying, "These men
are the servants of the Most High
God, who proclaim to us the way
of salvation."
18 And this she did for many days.
But Paul, [a]greatly [1]annoyed,
turned and said to the spirit, "I
command you in the name of Jesus
Christ to come out of her." [b]And
he came out that very hour.
19 But [a]when her masters saw

37 [a]Acts 12:12, 25; Col. 4:10; 2 Tim. 4:11; Philem. 24 [1]*resolved*
38 [a]Acts 13:13
39 [a]Acts 4:36; 13:4
40 [a]Acts 11:23; 14:26 [1]*committed*
41 [a]Acts 16:5

CHAPTER 16

1 [a]Acts 14:6 [b]Acts 19:22; Rom. 16:21; 1 Cor. 4:17; 16:10; Phil. 1:1; 2:19; 1 Thess. 3:2; 2 Tim. 1:2 [c]2 Tim. 1:5; 3:15
3 [a][1 Cor. 9:20; Gal. 2:3; 5:2]
4 [a]Acts 15:19–21 [b]Acts 15:28, 29
5 [a]Acts 2:47; 15:41
6 [a]Acts 18:23; Gal. 1:1, 2 [1]The Roman province of Asia
7 [1]NU adds *of Jesus*
8 [a]Acts 16:11; 20:5; 2 Cor. 2:12; 2 Tim. 4:13
9 [a]Acts 10:30
10 [a]2 Cor. 2:13
12 [a]Acts 20:6; Phil. 1:1; 1 Thess. 2:2 [1]Lit. *first*
14 [a]Rev. 1:11; 2:18, 24 [b]Luke 24:45
15 [a]Gen. 19:3; 33:11; Judg. 19:21; Luke 24:29; [Heb. 13:2]
16 [a]Lev. 19:31; 20:6, 27; Deut. 18:11; 1 Sam. 28:3, 7; 2 Kin. 21:6; 1 Chr. 10:13; Is. 8:19 [b]Acts 19:24
18 [a]Mark 1:25, 34 [b]Mark 16:17 [1]*distressed*
19 [a]Acts 16:16; 19:25, 26

that their hope of profit was gone,
they seized Paul and Silas and
[b]dragged *them* into the market-
place to the authorities.
20 And they brought them to the
magistrates, and said, "These men,
being Jews, [a]exceedingly trouble
our city;
21 "and they teach customs which
are not lawful for us, being Ro-
mans, to receive or observe."
22 Then the multitude rose up to-
gether against them; and the mag-
istrates tore off their clothes [a]and
commanded *them* to be beaten
with rods.
23 And when they had laid many
stripes on them, they threw *them*
into prison, commanding the jailer
to keep them securely.
24 Having received such a charge,
he put them into the inner prison
and fastened their feet in the
stocks.

The Philippian Jailer Saved

25 But at midnight Paul and Silas
were praying and singing hymns
to God, and the prisoners were lis-
tening to them.
26 [a]Suddenly there was a great
earthquake, so that the founda-
tions of the prison were shaken;
and immediately [b]all the doors
were opened and everyone's
chains were loosed.
27 And the keeper of the prison,
awaking from sleep and seeing the
prison doors open, supposing the
prisoners had fled, drew his sword
and was about to kill himself.
28 But Paul called with a loud
voice, saying, "Do yourself no
harm, for we are all here."

19 [b]Matt. 10:18
20 [a]1 Kin. 18:17; Acts 17:8
22 [a]2 Cor. 6:5; 11:23, 25; 1 Thess. 2:2
26 [a]Acts 4:31 [b]Acts 5:19; 12:7, 10

Paul Goes to Greece (The Second Missionary Journey, Acts 15:39—18:22). Starting from Jerusalem, Paul took Silas to visit again the churches of Galatia. Young Timothy joined them in Lystra. Then they went to Macedonia and Achaia, present-day Greece. On this journey the Philippian jailer was saved, the Bereans "searched the Scriptures daily" (Acts 17:11), and Paul preached at the Areopagus.

29 Then he called for a light, ran
in, and fell down trembling before
Paul and Silas.
30 And he brought them out and
said, [a]"Sirs, what must I do to be
saved?"
31 So they said, [a]"Believe on the
Lord Jesus Christ, and you will be
saved, you and your household."
32 Then they spoke the word of
the Lord to him and to all who
were in his house.
33 And he took them the same
hour of the night and washed *their*
stripes. And immediately he and
all his family were baptized.
34 Now when he had brought
them into his house, [a]he set food
before them; and he rejoiced, hav-
ing believed in God with all his
household.

Paul Refuses to Depart Secretly

35 And when it was day, the mag-
istrates sent the [1]officers, saying,
"Let those men go."
36 So the keeper of the prison re-
ported these words to Paul, saying,
"The magistrates have sent to let
you go. Now therefore depart, and
go in peace."
37 But Paul said to them, "They
have beaten us openly, uncon-
demned [a]Romans, *and* have
thrown *us* into prison. And now do
they put us out secretly? No in-
deed! Let them come themselves
and get us out."
38 And the officers told these
words to the magistrates, and they
were afraid when they heard that
they were Romans.
39 Then they came and pleaded
with them and brought *them* out,
and [a]asked *them* to depart from
the city.
40 So they went out of the prison
[a]and entered *the house of* Lydia;
and when they had seen the breth-
ren, they encouraged them and de-
parted.

Preaching Christ at Thessalonica

17 Now when they had passed
through Amphipolis and
Apollonia, they came to [a]Thessa-
lonica, where there was a syna-
gogue of the Jews.
2 Then Paul, as his custom was,
[a]went in to them, and for three
Sabbaths [b]reasoned with them
from the Scriptures,
3 explaining and demonstrating
[a]that the Christ had to suffer and
rise again from the dead, and *say-
ing*, "This Jesus whom I preach to
you is the Christ."
4 [a]And some of them were per-
suaded; and a great multitude of
the devout Greeks, and not a few
of the leading women, joined Paul
and [b]Silas.

Assault on Jason's House

5 But the Jews [1]who were not
persuaded, [2]becoming [a]envious,
took some of the evil men from the
marketplace, and gathering a mob,
set all the city in an uproar and
attacked the house of [b]Jason, and
sought to bring them out to the
people.
6 But when they did not find
them, they dragged Jason and
some brethren to the rulers of the
city, crying out, [a]"These who have
turned the world upside down
have come here too.
7 "Jason has [1]harbored them,
and these are all acting contrary
to the decrees of Caesar, [a]saying
there is another king—Jesus."
8 And they troubled the crowd
and the rulers of the city when
they heard these things.
9 So when they had taken secu-
rity from Jason and the rest, they
let them go.

Ministering at Berea

10 Then [a]the brethren immedi-
ately sent Paul and Silas away by
night to Berea. When they arrived,
they went into the synagogue of
the Jews.
11 These were more [1]fair-minded
than those in Thessalonica, in that
they received the word with all
readiness, and [a]searched the
Scriptures daily *to find out*
whether these things were so.
12 Therefore many of them be-
lieved, and also not a few of the
Greeks, prominent women as well
as men.
13 But when the Jews from Thes-
salonica learned that the word of
God was preached by Paul at
Berea, they came there also and
stirred up the crowds.
14 [a]Then immediately the breth-

30 [a]Luke 3:10; Acts 2:37; 9:6; 22:10
31 [a][John 3:16, 36; 6:47; Acts 13:38, 39; Rom. 10:9–11; 1 John 5:10]
34 [a]Matt. 5:4; Luke 5:29; 19:6
35 [1]*lictors*, lit. *rod bearers*
37 [a]Acts 22:25–29
39 [a]Matt. 8:34
40 [a]Acts 16:14

CHAPTER 17

1 [a]Acts 17:11, 13; 20:4; 27:2; Phil. 4:16; 1 Thess. 1:1; 2 Thess. 1:1; 2 Tim. 4:10
2 [a]Luke 4:16; Acts 9:20; 13:5, 14; 14:1; 16:13; 19:8 [b]1 Thess. 2:1–16
3 [a]Luke 24:26, 46; Acts 18:5, 28; Gal. 3:1
4 [a]Acts 28:24 [b]Acts 15:22, 27, 32, 40
5 [a]Acts 13:45 [b]Acts 17:6, 7, 9; Rom. 16:21 [1]NU omits *who were not persuaded* [2]M omits *becoming envious*
6 [a][Acts 16:20]
7 [a]Luke 23:2; John 19:12; 1 Pet. 2:13 [1]*welcomed*
10 [a]Acts 9:25; 17:14
11 [a]Is. 34:16; Luke 16:29; John 5:39 [1]Lit. *noble*
14 [a]Matt. 10:23

ren sent Paul away, to go to the
sea; but both Silas and Timothy re-
mained there.
15 So those who conducted Paul
brought him to Athens; and [a]re-
ceiving a command for Silas and
Timothy to come to him with all
speed, they departed.

The Philosophers at Athens

16 Now while Paul waited for
them at Athens, [a]his spirit was
provoked within him when he saw
that the city was [1]given over to
idols.
17 Therefore he reasoned in the
synagogue with the Jews and with
the *Gentile* worshipers, and in the
marketplace daily with those who
happened to be there.
18 [1]Then certain Epicurean and
Stoic philosophers encountered
him. And some said, "What does
this [2]babbler want to say?" Others
said, "He seems to be a proclaimer
of foreign gods," because he
preached to them [a]Jesus and the
resurrection.
19 And they took him and brought
him to the [1]Areopagus, saying,
"May we know what this new doc-
trine *is* of which you speak?
20 "For you are bringing some
strange things to our ears. There-
fore we want to know what these
things mean."
21 For all the Athenians and the
foreigners who were there spent
their time in nothing else but ei-
ther to tell or to hear some new
thing.

Addressing the Areopagus

22 Then Paul stood in the midst
of the [1]Areopagus and said, "Men
of Athens, I perceive that in all
things you are very religious;
23 "for as I was passing through
and considering the objects of
your worship, I even found an al-
tar with this inscription:

TO THE UNKNOWN GOD.

Therefore, the One whom you
worship without knowing, Him I
proclaim to you:
24 [a]"God, who made the world
and everything in it, since He is
[b]Lord of heaven and earth, [c]does
not dwell in temples made with
hands.
25 "Nor is He worshiped with
men's hands, as though He needed
anything, since He [a]gives to all life,
breath, and all things.
26 "And He has made from one
[1]blood every nation of men to
dwell on all the face of the earth,
and has determined their preap-
pointed times and [a]the boundaries
of their dwellings,
27 [a]"so that they should seek the
Lord, in the hope that they might
grope for Him and find Him,
[b]though He is not far from each
one of us;
28 "for [a]in Him we live and move
and have our being, [b]as also some
of your own poets have said, 'For
we are also His offspring.'
29 "Therefore, since we are the
offspring of God, [a]we ought not to
think that the Divine Nature is like
gold or silver or stone, some-
thing shaped by art and man's de-
vising.
30 "Truly, [a]these times of igno-
rance God overlooked, but [b]now
commands all men everywhere to
repent,
31 "because He has appointed a
day on which [a]He will judge the
world in righteousness by the Man
whom He has ordained. He has
given assurance of this to all by
[b]raising Him from the dead."
32 And when they heard of the
resurrection of the dead, some
mocked, while others said, "We
will hear you again on this *mat-
ter.*"
33 So Paul departed from among
them.
34 However, some men joined him
and believed, among them Diony-
sius the Areopagite, a woman
named Damaris, and others with
them.

Ministering at Corinth

18 After these things Paul de-
parted from Athens and
went to Corinth.
2 And he found a certain Jew
named [a]Aquila, born in Pontus,
who had recently come from Italy
with his wife Priscilla (because
Claudius had commanded all the
Jews to depart from Rome); and
he came to them.
3 So, because he was of the same
trade, he stayed with them [a]and

15 [a]Acts 18:5
16 [a]2 Pet. 2:8 [1]*full of idols*
18 [a]1 Cor. 15:12 [1]NU, M add *also* [2]Lit. *seed picker,* an idler who makes a living picking up scraps
19 [1]Lit. *Hill of Ares,* or *Mars' Hill*
22 [1]Lit. *Hill of Ares,* or *Mars' Hill*
24 [a]Is. 42:5; Acts 14:15 [b]Deut. 10:14; Ps. 115:16; Matt. 11:25 [c]1 Kin. 8:27; Acts 7:48–50
25 [a]Gen. 2:7; Is. 42:5; Dan. 5:23
26 [a]Deut. 32:8; Job 12:23; Dan. 4:35 [1]NU omits *blood*
27 [a][Rom. 1:20] [b]Deut. 4:7; Ps. 139:7, 10; Jer. 23:23, 24; [Acts 14:17]
28 [a][Col. 1:17; Heb. 1:3] [b]Titus 1:12
29 [a]Ps. 115:4–7; Is. 40:18, 19; Rom. 1:23
30 [a]Acts 14:16; [Rom. 3:25] [b]Luke 24:47; Acts 26:20; [Titus 2:11, 12]; 1 Pet. 1:14; 4:3
31 [a]Ps. 9:8; 96:13; 98:9; John 5:22, 27; Acts 10:42; Rom. 2:16 [b]Acts 2:24

CHAPTER 18

2 [a]Rom. 16:3; 1 Cor. 16:19; 2 Tim. 4:19
3 [a]Acts 20:34; 1 Cor. 4:12; 9:14; 2 Cor. 11:7; 12:13; 1 Thess. 2:9; 4:11; 2 Thess. 3:8

worked; for by occupation they
were tentmakers.
4 [a]And he reasoned in the syna-
gogue every Sabbath, and per-
suaded both Jews and Greeks.
5 [a]When Silas and Timothy had
come from Macedonia, Paul was
[b]compelled [1]by the Spirit, and tes-
tified to the Jews *that* Jesus *is* the
Christ.
6 But [a]when they opposed him
and blasphemed, [b]he shook *his*
garments and said to them, [c]"Your
blood *be* upon your *own* heads; [d]I
am clean. [e]From now on I will go
to the Gentiles."
7 And he departed from there
and entered the house of a certain
man named [1]Justus, *one* who wor-
shiped God, whose house was next
door to the synagogue.
8 [a]Then Crispus, the ruler of the
synagogue, believed on the Lord
with all his household. And many
of the Corinthians, hearing, be-
lieved and were baptized.
9 Now [a]the Lord spoke to Paul
in the night by a vision, "Do not
be afraid, but speak, and do not
keep silent;
10 [a]"for I am with you, and no one
will attack you to hurt you; for I
have many people in this city."
11 And he continued *there* a year
and six months, teaching the word
of God among them.
12 When Gallio was proconsul of
Achaia, the Jews with one accord
rose up against Paul and brought
him to the [1]judgment seat,
13 saying, "This *fellow* persuades
men to worship God contrary to
the law."
14 And when Paul was about to
open *his* mouth, Gallio said to the
Jews, "If it were a matter of
wrongdoing or wicked crimes, O
Jews, there would be reason why
I should bear with you.
15 "But if it is a [a]question of
words and names and your own
law, look *to it* yourselves; for I do
not want to be a judge of such *mat-
ters*."
16 And he drove them from the
judgment seat.
17 Then [1]all the Greeks took
[a]Sosthenes, the ruler of the syna-
gogue, and beat *him* before the
judgment seat. But Gallio took no
notice of these things.

4 [a]Acts 17:2
5 [a]Acts 17:14, 15 [b]Acts 18:28 [1]Or *in his spirit* or *in the Spirit*
6 [a]Acts 13:45 [b]Neh. 5:13; Matt. 10:14; Acts 13:51 [c]Lev. 20:9, 11, 12; 2 Sam. 1:16; 1 Kin. 2:33; Ezek. 18:13; 33:4, 6, 8; Matt. 27:25; Acts 20:26 [d][Ezek. 3:18, 19] [e]Acts 13:46–48; 28:28
7 [1]NU *Titius Justus*
8 [a]1 Cor. 1:14
9 [a]Acts 23:11
10 [a]Jer. 1:18, 19
12 [1]Gr. *bema*
15 [a]Acts 23:29; 25:19
17 [a]1 Cor. 1:1 [1]NU *they all*
18 [a]Num. 6:2, 5, 9, 18; Acts 21:24 [b]Rom. 16:1 [1]Lit. *many days*
21 [a]Acts 19:21; 20:16 [b]1 Cor. 4:19; Heb. 6:3; James 4:15 [1]NU omits *I must by all means keep this coming feast in Jerusalem*
22 [a]Acts 8:40 [1]To Jerusalem
23 [a]Gal. 1:2 [b]Acts 14:22; 15:32, 41 [1]*successively*
24 [a]Acts 19:1; 1 Cor. 1:12; 3:4; 16:12; Titus 3:13
25 [a]Rom. 12:11 [b][Matt. 3:1–11; Mark 1:7, 8; Luke 3:16, 17; 7:29; John 1:26, 33]; Acts 19:3
27 [a]1 Cor. 3:6
28 [a]Acts 9:22; 17:3; 18:5

CHAPTER 19

1 [a]1 Cor. 1:12; 3:5, 6; Titus 3:13

Paul Returns to Antioch

18 So Paul still remained [1]a good
while. Then he took leave of the
brethren and sailed for Syria, and
Priscilla and Aquila *were* with
him. [a]He had *his* hair cut off at
[b]Cenchrea, for he had taken a
vow.
19 And he came to Ephesus, and
left them there; but he himself en-
tered the synagogue and reasoned
with the Jews.
20 When they asked *him* to stay
a longer time with them, he did not
consent,
21 but took leave of them, saying,
[a]"I[1] must by all means keep this
coming feast in Jerusalem; but I
will return again to you, [b]God will-
ing." And he sailed from Ephesus.
22 And when he had landed at
[a]Caesarea, and [1]gone up and
greeted the church, he went down
to Antioch.
23 After he had spent some time
there, he departed and went over
the region of [a]Galatia and Phrygia
[1]in order, [b]strengthening all the
disciples.

Ministry of Apollos

24 [a]Now a certain Jew named
Apollos, born at Alexandria, an el-
oquent man *and* mighty in the
Scriptures, came to Ephesus.
25 This man had been instructed
in the way of the Lord; and being
[a]fervent in spirit, he spoke and
taught accurately the things of the
Lord, [b]though he knew only the
baptism of John.
26 So he began to speak boldly in
the synagogue. When Aquila and
Priscilla heard him, they took him
aside and explained to him the
way of God more accurately.
27 And when he desired to cross
to Achaia, the brethren wrote, ex-
horting the disciples to receive
him; and when he arrived, [a]he
greatly helped those who had be-
lieved through grace;
28 for he vigorously refuted the
Jews publicly, [a]showing from the
Scriptures that Jesus is the Christ.

Paul at Ephesus

19 And it happened, while
[a]Apollos was at Corinth,
that Paul, having passed through

[b]the upper regions, came to Ephe-
sus. And finding some disciples
2 he said to them, "Did you
receive the Holy Spirit when you
believed?" So they said to him,
[a]"We have not so much as heard
whether there is a Holy Spirit."
3 And he said to them, "Into
what then were you baptized?" So
they said, [a]"Into John's baptism."
4 Then Paul said, [a]"John indeed
baptized with a baptism of repen-
tance, saying to the people that
they should believe on Him who
would come after him, that is, on
Christ Jesus."
5 When they heard *this*, they
were baptized [a]in the name of the
Lord Jesus.
6 And when Paul had [a]laid hands
on them, the Holy Spirit came
upon them, and [b]they spoke with
tongues and prophesied.
7 Now the men were about
twelve in all.
8 [a]And he went into the syna-
gogue and spoke boldly for three
months, reasoning and persuading
[b]concerning the things of the king-
dom of God.
9 But [a]when some were hard-
ened and did not believe, but
spoke evil [b]of the Way before the
multitude, he departed from them
and withdrew the disciples, rea-
soning daily in the school of Ty-
rannus.
10 And [a]this continued for two
years, so that all who dwelt in Asia
heard the word of the Lord Jesus,
both Jews and Greeks.

Miracles Glorify Christ

11 Now [a]God worked unusual
miracles by the hands of Paul,
12 [a]so that even handkerchiefs or
aprons were brought from his
body to the sick, and the diseases
left them and the evil spirits went
out of them.
13 [a]Then some of the itinerant
Jewish exorcists [b]took it upon
themselves to call the name of the
Lord Jesus over those who had
evil spirits, saying, [1]"We [2]exorcise
you by the Jesus whom Paul
[c]preaches."
14 Also there were seven sons of
Sceva, a Jewish chief priest, who
did so.
15 And the evil spirit answered
and said, "Jesus I know, and Paul
I know; but who are you?"
16 Then the man in whom the
evil spirit was leaped on them,
[1]overpowered them, and prevailed
against [2]them, so that they fled
out of that house naked and
wounded.
17 This became known both to all
Jews and Greeks dwelling in
Ephesus; and [a]fear fell on them all,
and the name of the Lord Jesus
was magnified.
18 And many who had believed
came [a]confessing and telling their
deeds.
19 Also, many of those who had
practiced magic brought their
books together and burned *them*
in the sight of all. And they
counted up the value of them, and
it totaled fifty thousand *pieces* of
silver.
20 [a]So the word of the Lord grew
mightily and prevailed.

The Riot at Ephesus

21 [a]When these things were ac-
complished, Paul [b]purposed in the
Spirit, when he had passed
through [c]Macedonia and Achaia,
to go to Jerusalem, saying, "After
I have been there, [d]I must also see
Rome."
22 So he sent into Macedonia two
of those who ministered to him,
[a]Timothy and [b]Erastus, but he
himself stayed in Asia for a time.
23 And [a]about that time there
arose a great commotion about
[b]the Way.
24 For a certain man named De-
metrius, a silversmith, who made
silver shrines of [1]Diana, brought
[a]no small profit to the craftsmen.
25 He called them together with
the workers of similar occupation,
and said: "Men, you know that we
have our prosperity by this trade.
26 "Moreover you see and hear
that not only at Ephesus, but
throughout almost all Asia, this
Paul has persuaded and turned
away many people, saying that
[a]they are not gods which are made
with hands.
27 "So not only is this trade of
ours in danger of falling into disre-
pute, but also the temple of the
great goddess Diana may be de-
spised and [1]her magnificence

1 [b]Acts 18:23
2 [a]1 Sam. 3:7; Acts 8:16
3 [a]Luke 7:29; Acts 18:25
4 [a]Matt. 3:11; Mark 1:4, 7, 8; Luke 3:16; [John 1:15, 26, 27]; Acts 13:24
5 [a]Matt. 28:19; Acts 8:12, 16; 10:48
6 [a]Acts 6:6; 8:17 [b]Mark 16:17; Acts 2:4; 10:46
8 [a]Acts 17:2; 18:4 [b]Acts 1:3; 28:23
9 [a]2 Tim. 1:15; 2 Pet. 2:2; Jude 10 [b]Acts 9:2; 19:23; 22:4; 24:14
10 [a]Acts 19:8; 20:31
11 [a]Mark 16:20; Acts 14:3
12 [a]2 Kin. 4:29; Acts 5:15
13 [a]Matt. 12:27; Luke 11:19 [b]Mark 9:38; Luke 9:49 [c]1 Cor. 1:23; 2:2 [1]NU *I* [2]*adjure*, solemnly command
16 [1]M *and they overpowered them* [2]NU *both of them*
17 [a]Luke 1:65; 7:16; Acts 2:43; 5:5, 11
18 [a]Matt. 3:6
20 [a]Acts 6:7; 12:24
21 [a]Rom. 15:25; Gal. 2:1 [b]Acts 20:22; 2 Cor. 1:16 [c]Acts 20:1; 1 Cor. 16:5 [d]Acts 18:21; 23:11; Rom. 1:13; 15:22–29
22 [a]1 Tim. 1:2 [b]Rom. 16:23; 2 Tim. 4:20
23 [a]2 Cor. 1:8 [b]Acts 9:2
24 [a]Acts 16:16, 19 [1]Gr. *Artemis*
26 [a]Deut. 4:28; Ps. 115:4; Is. 44:10–20; Jer. 10:3; Acts 17:29; 1 Cor. 8:4; 10:19; Rev. 9:20
27 [1]NU *she be deposed from her magnificence*

destroyed, whom all Asia and the
world worship."
28 Now when they heard *this*,
they were full of wrath and cried
out, saying, "Great *is* Diana of the
Ephesians!"
29 So the whole city was filled
with confusion, and rushed into
the theater with one accord, having seized [a]Gaius and [b]Aristarchus, Macedonians, Paul's travel
companions.
30 And when Paul wanted to go
in to the people, the disciples
would not allow him.
31 Then some of the [1]officials of
Asia, who were his friends, sent
to him pleading that he would not
venture into the theater.
32 Some therefore cried one thing
and some another, for the assembly was confused, and most of
them did not know why they had
come together.
33 And they drew Alexander out
of the multitude, the Jews putting
him forward. And [a]Alexander
[b]motioned with his hand, and
wanted to make his defense to the
people.
34 But when they found out that
he was a Jew, all with one voice
cried out for about two hours,
"Great *is* Diana of the Ephesians!"
35 And when the city clerk had
quieted the crowd, he said: "Men
of Ephesus, what man is there who
does not know that the city of the
Ephesians is temple guardian of
the great goddess [1]Diana, and of
the *image* which fell down from
[2]Zeus?

29 [a]Acts 20:4; Rom. 16:23; 1 Cor. 1:14; 3 John 1 [b]Acts 20:4; 27:2; Col. 4:10; Philem. 24

31 [1]*Asiarchs, rulers of Asia,* the province

33 [a]1 Tim. 1:20; 2 Tim. 4:14 [b]Acts 12:17

35 [1]Gr. *Artemis* [2]*heaven*

Asia and Greece Revisited (Paul's Third Missionary Journey, Acts 18:23—21:16). Paul visited the churches of Galatia for a third time, and then settled in Ephesus for more than two years. Upon leaving Ephesus, Paul traveled again to Macedonia and Achaia (Greece) for a three-month stay. He returned to Asia by way of Macedonia.

On this third journey Paul wrote 1 Corinthians from Ephesus, 2 Corinthians from Macedonia, and the letter to the Romans from Corinth.

36 "Therefore, since these things
cannot be denied, you ought to be
quiet and do nothing rashly.
37 "For you have brought these
men here who are neither robbers
of temples nor blasphemers of
[1]your goddess.
38 "Therefore, if Demetrius and
his fellow craftsmen have a [1]case
against anyone, the courts are
open and there are proconsuls. Let
them bring charges against one
another.
39 "But if you have any other in-
quiry to make, it shall be deter-
mined in the lawful assembly.
40 "For we are in danger of being
[1]called in question for today's up-
roar, there being no reason which
we may give to account for this
disorderly gathering."
41 And when he had said these
things, he dismissed the assembly.

Journeys in Greece

20 After the uproar had ceased,
Paul called the disciples to
himself, embraced *them*, and [a]de-
parted to go to Macedonia.
2 Now when he had gone over
that region and encouraged them
with many words, he came to
[a]Greece
3 and stayed three months. And
[a]when the Jews plotted against
him as he was about to sail to
Syria, he decided to return
through Macedonia.
4 And Sopater of Berea accom-
panied him to Asia—also [a]Aristar-
chus and Secundus of the Thessa-
lonians, and [b]Gaius of Derbe, and
[c]Timothy, and [d]Tychicus and
[e]Trophimus of Asia.
5 These men, going ahead,
waited for us at [a]Troas.
6 But we sailed away from Phi-
lippi after [a]the Days of Unleav-
ened Bread, and in five days joined
them [b]at Troas, where we stayed
seven days.

Ministering at Troas

7 Now on [a]the first *day* of the
week, when the disciples came to-
gether [b]to break bread, Paul, ready
to depart the next day, spoke to
them and continued his message
until midnight.
8 There were many lamps [a]in the
upper room where [1]they were
gathered together.
9 And in a window sat a certain
young man named Eutychus, who
was sinking into a deep sleep. He
was overcome by sleep; and as
Paul continued speaking, he fell
down from the third story and was
taken up dead.
10 But Paul went down, [a]fell on
him, and embracing *him* said,
[b]"Do not trouble yourselves, for
his life is in him."
11 Now when he had come up,
had broken bread and eaten, and
talked a long while, even till day-
break, he departed.
12 And they brought the young
man in alive, and they were not a
little comforted.

From Troas to Miletus

13 Then we went ahead to the ship
and sailed to Assos, there intend-
ing to take Paul on board; for so
he had [1]given orders, intending
himself to go on foot.
14 And when he met us at Assos,
we took him on board and came
to Mitylene.
15 We sailed from there, and the
next *day* came opposite Chios. The
following *day* we arrived at Samos
and stayed at Trogyllium. The next
day we came to Miletus.
16 For Paul had decided to sail
past Ephesus, so that he would not
have to spend time in Asia; for [a]he
was hurrying [b]to be at Jerusalem,
if possible, on [c]the Day of Pente-
cost.

The Ephesian Elders Exhorted

17 From Miletus he sent to Ephe-
sus and called for the elders of the
church.
18 And when they had come to
him, he said to them: "You know,
[a]from the first day that I came to
Asia, in what manner I always
lived among you,
19 "serving the Lord with all hu-
mility, with many tears and trials
which happened to me [a]by the
plotting of the Jews;
20 "how [a]I kept back nothing that
was helpful, but proclaimed it to
you, and taught you publicly and
from house to house,
21 [a]"testifying to Jews, and also
to Greeks, [b]repentance toward

37 [1]NU *our*
38 [1]Lit. *matter*
40 [1]Or *charged with rebellion concerning today*

CHAPTER 20

1 [a]1 Cor. 16:5; 1 Tim. 1:3
2 [a]Acts 17:15; 18:1
3 [a]Acts 9:23; 23:12; 25:3; 2 Cor. 11:26
4 [a]Acts 19:29; Col. 4:10 [b]Acts 19:29 [c]Acts 16:1 [d]Eph. 6:21; Col. 4:7; 2 Tim. 4:12; Titus 3:12 [e]Acts 21:29; 2 Tim. 4:20
5 [a]2 Cor. 2:12; 2 Tim. 4:13
6 [a]Ex. 12:14, 15 [b]Acts 16:8; 2 Cor. 2:12; 2 Tim. 4:13
7 [a]1 Cor. 16:2; Rev. 1:10 [b]Acts 2:42, 46; 20:11; 1 Cor. 10:16
8 [a]Acts 1:13 [1]NU, M *we*
10 [a]1 Kin. 17:21; 2 Kin. 4:34 [b]Matt. 9:23, 24; Mark 5:39
13 [1]*arranged it*
16 [a]Acts 18:21; 19:21; 21:4 [b]Acts 24:17 [c]Acts 2:1; 1 Cor. 16:8
18 [a]Acts 18:19; 19:1, 10; 20:4, 16
19 [a]Acts 20:3
20 [a]Acts 20:27
21 [a]Acts 18:5; 19:10 [b]Mark 1:15

God and faith toward our Lord
Jesus Christ.
22 "And see, now [a]I go bound in
the spirit to Jerusalem, not know-
ing the things that will happen to
me there,
23 "except that [a]the Holy Spirit
testifies in every city, saying that
chains and tribulations await me.
24 [1]"But [a]none of these things
move me; nor do I count my life
dear to myself, [b]so that I may fin-
ish my [2]race with joy, [c]and the
ministry [d]which I received from
the Lord Jesus, to testify to the
gospel of the grace of God.
25 "And indeed, now I know that
you all, among whom I have gone
preaching the kingdom of God,
will see my face no more.
26 "Therefore I testify to you this
day that I *am* [a]innocent[1] of the
blood of all *men*.
27 "For I have not [1]shunned to de-
clare to you [a]the whole counsel of
God.
28 [a]"Therefore take heed to your-
selves and to all the flock, among
which the Holy Spirit [b]has made
you overseers, to shepherd the
church [1]of God [c]which He pur-
chased [d]with His own blood.
29 "For I know this, that after my
departure [a]savage wolves will
come in among you, not sparing
the flock.
30 "Also [a]from among yourselves
men will rise up, speaking [1]per-
verse things, to draw away the dis-
ciples after themselves.
31 "Therefore watch, and remem-
ber that [a]for three years I did not
cease to warn everyone night and
day with tears.
32 "So now, brethren, I commend
you to God and [a]to the word of His
grace, which is able [b]to build you
up and give you [c]an inheritance
among all those who are sanc-
tified.
33 "I have coveted no one's silver
or gold or apparel.
34 [1]"Yes, you yourselves know
[a]that these hands have provided
for my necessities, and for those
who were with me.
35 "I have shown you in every
way, [a]by laboring like this, that
you must support the weak. And
remember the words of the Lord
Jesus, that He said, 'It is more

22 [a]Acts 19:21
23 [a]Acts 21:4, 11
24 [a]Acts 21:13 [b]2 Tim. 4:7 [c]Acts 1:17 [d]Gal. 1:1 [1]NU *But I do not count my life of any value or dear to myself* [2]*course*
26 [a]Acts 18:6 [1]Lit. *clean*
27 [a]Luke 7:30 [1]*avoided declaring*
28 [a]1 Pet. 5:2 [b]1 Cor. 12:28 [c]Eph. 1:7, 14 [d]Heb. 9:14 [1]M *of the Lord and God*
29 [a]Matt. 7:15
30 [a]1 Tim. 1:20 [1]*misleading*
31 [a]Acts 19:8, 10; 24:17
32 [a]Heb. 13:9 [b]Acts 9:31 [c][Heb. 9:15]
34 [a]Acts 18:3 [1]NU, M omit *Yes*
35 [a]Rom. 15:1
37 [a]Acts 21:13 [b]Gen. 45:14 [1]Lit. *much*

CHAPTER 21
4 [a][Acts 20:23; 21:12] [1]NU *the disciples*
5 [a]Acts 9:40; 20:36
6 [a]John 1:11
8 [a]Acts 8:40; 21:16 [b]Eph. 4:11 [c]Acts 6:5 [1]NU omits *who were Paul's companions*
9 [a]Joel 2:28
10 [a]Acts 11:28
11 [a]Acts 20:23; 21:33; 22:25

blessed to give than to receive.'"
36 And when he had said these
things, he knelt down and prayed
with them all.
37 Then they all [a]wept [1]freely, and
[b]fell on Paul's neck and kissed
him,
38 sorrowing most of all for the
words which he spoke, that they
would see his face no more. And
they accompanied him to the ship.

Warnings on the Journey to Jerusalem

21 Now it came to pass, that
when we had departed from
them and set sail, running a
straight course we came to Cos,
the following *day* to Rhodes, and
from there to Patara.
2 And finding a ship sailing over
to Phoenicia, we went aboard and
set sail.
3 When we had sighted Cyprus,
we passed it on the left, sailed to
Syria, and landed at Tyre; for
there the ship was to unload her
cargo.
4 And finding [1]disciples, we
stayed there seven days. [a]They
told Paul through the Spirit not to
go up to Jerusalem.
5 When we had come to the end
of those days, we departed and
went on our way; and they all ac-
companied us, with wives and chil-
dren, till *we were* out of the city.
And [a]we knelt down on the shore
and prayed.
6 When we had taken our leave
of one another, we boarded the
ship, and they returned [a]home.
7 And when we had finished *our*
voyage from Tyre, we came to
Ptolemais, greeted the brethren,
and stayed with them one day.
8 On the next *day* we [1]who were
Paul's companions departed and
came to [a]Caesarea, and entered
the house of Philip [b]the evangelist,
[c]who was *one* of the seven, and
stayed with him.
9 Now this man had four virgin
daughters [a]who prophesied.
10 And as we stayed many days,
a certain prophet named [a]Agabus
came down from Judea.
11 When he had come to us, he
took Paul's belt, bound his *own*
hands and feet, and said, "Thus
says the Holy Spirit, [a]'So shall the
Jews at Jerusalem bind the man

who owns this belt, and deliver
him into the hands of the Gen-
tiles.' "
12 Now when we heard these
things, both we and those from
that place pleaded with him not to
go up to Jerusalem.
13 Then Paul answered, [a]"What
do you mean by weeping and
breaking my heart? For I am ready
not only to be bound, but also to
die at Jerusalem for the name of
the Lord Jesus."
14 So when he would not be per-
suaded, we ceased, saying, [a]"The
will of the Lord be done."

Paul Urged to Make Peace

15 And after those days we
[1]packed and went up to Jerusalem.
16 Also some of the disciples from
Caesarea went with us and
brought with them a certain
Mnason of Cyprus, an early
disciple, with whom we were to
lodge.
17 [a]And when we had come to Je-
rusalem, the brethren received us
gladly.
18 On the following *day* Paul went
in with us to [a]James, and all the
elders were present.
19 When he had greeted them, [a]he
told in detail those things which
God had done among the Gentiles
[b]through his ministry.
20 And when they heard *it*, they
glorified the Lord. And they said
to him, "You see, brother, how
many myriads of Jews there are
who have believed, and they are
all [a]zealous for the law;
21 "but they have been informed
about you that you teach all the
Jews who are among the Gentiles
to forsake Moses, saying that they
ought not to circumcise *their* chil-
dren nor to walk according to the
customs.
22 [1]"What then? The assembly
must certainly meet, for they will
hear that you have come.
23 "Therefore do what we tell
you: We have four men who have
taken a vow.
24 "Take them and be purified
with them, and pay their expenses
so that they may [a]shave *their*
heads, and that all may know that
those things of which they were in-
formed concerning you are noth-
ing, but *that* you yourself also
walk orderly and keep the law.
25 "But concerning the Gentiles
who believe, [a]we have written *and*
decided [1]that they should observe
no such thing, except that they
should keep themselves from
things offered to idols, from blood,
from things strangled, and from
[2]sexual immorality."

Arrested in the Temple

26 Then Paul took the men, and
the next day, having been purified
with them, [a]entered the temple [b]to
announce the [1]expiration of the
days of purification, at which time
an offering should be made for
each one of them.
27 Now when the seven days were
almost ended, [a]the Jews from
Asia, seeing him in the temple,
stirred up the whole crowd and
[b]laid hands on him,
28 crying out, "Men of Israel,
help! This is the man [a]who teaches
all *men* everywhere against the
people, the law, and this place; and
furthermore he also brought
Greeks into the temple and has de-
filed this holy place."
29 (For they had [1]previously seen
[a]Trophimus the Ephesian with him
in the city, whom they supposed
that Paul had brought into the tem-
ple.)
30 And [a]all the city was disturbed;
and the people ran together, seized
Paul, and dragged him out of the
temple; and immediately the doors
were shut.
31 Now as they were [a]seeking to
kill him, news came to the com-
mander of the [1]garrison that all Je-
rusalem was in an uproar.
32 [a]He immediately took soldiers
and centurions, and ran down to
them. And when they saw the
commander and the soldiers, they
stopped beating Paul.
33 Then the [a]commander came
near and took him, and [b]com-
manded *him* to be bound with two
chains; and he asked who he was
and what he had done.
34 And some among the multitude
cried one thing and some another.
So when he could not ascertain the
truth because of the tumult, he
commanded him to be taken into
the barracks.

13 [a]Acts 20:24, 37
14 [a]Matt. 6:10; 26:42; Luke 11:2; 22:42
15 [1]*made preparations*
17 [a]Acts 15:4
18 [a]Acts 15:13; Gal. 1:19; 2:9
19 [a]Acts 15:4, 12; Rom. 15:18, 19 [b]Acts 1:17; 20:24; 1 Tim. 2:7
20 [a]Acts 15:1; 22:3; [Rom. 10:2]; Gal. 1:14
22 [1]NU *What then is to be done? They will certainly hear*
24 [a]Num. 6:2, 13, 18; Acts 18:18
25 [a]Acts 15:19, 20, 29 [1]NU omits *that they should observe no such thing, except* [2]*fornication*
26 [a]John 11:55; Acts 21:24; 24:18 [b]Num. 6:13; Acts 24:18 [1]*completion*
27 [a]Acts 20:19; 24:18 [b]Acts 26:21
28 [a][Matt. 24:15]; Acts 6:13; 24:6
29 [a]Acts 20:4 [1]M omits *previously*
30 [a]2 Kin. 11:15; Acts 16:19; 26:21
31 [a]2 Cor. 11:23 [1]*cohort*
32 [a]Acts 23:27; 24:7
33 [a]Acts 24:7 [b]Acts 20:23; 21:11; Eph. 6:20; 2 Tim. 1:16; 2:9

35 When he reached the stairs, he
had to be carried by the soldiers
because of the violence of the mob.
36 For the multitude of the people
followed after, crying out, [a]"Away
with him!"

Addressing the Jerusalem Mob

37 Then as Paul was about to be
led into the barracks, he said to
the commander, "May I speak to
you?" He replied, "Can you speak
Greek?
38 [a]"Are you not the Egyptian
who some time ago stirred up a re-
bellion and led the four thousand
assassins out into the wilderness?"
39 But Paul said, [a]"I am a Jew
from Tarsus, in Cilicia, a citizen
of no [1]mean city; and I implore
you, permit me to speak to the peo-
ple."
40 So when he had given him per-
mission, Paul stood on the stairs
and [a]motioned with his hand to the
people. And when there was a
great silence, he spoke to *them* in
the [b]Hebrew language, saying,
22 "Brethren[a] and fathers, hear
my defense before you
now."
2 And when they heard that he
spoke to them in the [a]Hebrew lan-
guage, they kept all the more si-
lent. Then he said:
3 [a]"I am indeed a Jew, born in
Tarsus of Cilicia, but brought up
in this city [b]at the feet of [c]Gama-
liel, taught [d]according to the strict-
ness of our fathers' law, and [e]was
zealous toward God [f]as you all are
today.
4 [a]"I persecuted this Way to the
death, binding and delivering into
prisons both men and women,
5 "as also the high priest bears
me witness, and [a]all the council of
the elders, [b]from whom I also re-
ceived letters to the brethren, and
went to Damascus [c]to bring in
chains even those who were there
to Jerusalem to be punished.
6 "Now [a]it happened, as I jour-
neyed and came near Damascus at
about noon, suddenly a great light
from heaven shone around me.
7 "And I fell to the ground and
heard a voice saying to me, 'Saul,
Saul, why are you persecuting
Me?'
8 "So I answered, 'Who are You,

36 [a]John 19:15
38 [a]Acts 5:36
39 [a]Acts 9:11; 22:3 [1]*insignificant*
40 [a]Acts 12:17 [b]Acts 22:2

CHAPTER 22

1 [a]Acts 7:2
2 [a]Acts 21:40
3 [a]2 Cor. 11:22 [b]Deut. 33:3 [c]Acts 5:34 [d]Acts 23:6; 26:5 [e]Gal. 1:14 [f][Rom. 10:2]
4 [a]1 Tim. 1:13
5 [a]Acts 23:14; 24:1; 25:15 [b]Luke 22:66 [c]Acts 9:2
6 [a]Acts 9:3; 26:12, 13
9 [a]Acts 9:7 [1]NU omits *and were afraid*
12 [a]Acts 9:17 [b]Acts 10:22 [c]1 Tim. 3:7
14 [a]Acts 3:13; 5:30 [b]Acts 9:15; 26:16 [c]Acts 3:14; 7:52 [d]1 Cor. 9:1; 15:8 [e]Gal. 1:12
15 [a]Acts 23:11 [b]Acts 4:20; 26:16
16 [a]Heb. 10:22 [b]Rom. 10:13
17 [a]Acts 9:26; 26:20
18 [a]Acts 22:14 [b]Matt. 10:14
19 [a]Acts 8:3; 22:4 [b]Matt. 10:17
20 [a]Acts 7:54—8:1 [b]Luke 11:48 [1]NU omits *to his death*
21 [a]Acts 9:15

Lord?' And He said to me, 'I am
Jesus of Nazareth, whom you are
persecuting.'
9 "And [a]those who were with me
indeed saw the light [1]and were
afraid, but they did not hear the
voice of Him who spoke to me.
10 "So I said, 'What shall I do,
Lord?' And the Lord said to me,
'Arise and go into Damascus, and
there you will be told all things
which are appointed for you to do.'
11 "And since I could not see for
the glory of that light, being led
by the hand of those who were
with me, I came into Damascus.
12 "Then [a]a certain Ananias, a de-
vout man according to the law,
[b]having a good testimony with all
the [c]Jews who dwelt *there*,
13 "came to me; and he stood and
said to me, 'Brother Saul, receive
your sight.' And at that same hour
I looked up at him.
14 "Then he said, [a]'The God of our
fathers [b]has chosen you that you
should [c]know His will, and [d]see
the Just One, [e]and hear the voice
of His mouth.
15 [a]'For you will be His witness to
all men of [b]what you have seen
and heard.
16 'And now why are you waiting?
Arise and be baptized, [a]and wash
away your sins, [b]calling on the
name of the Lord.'
17 "Now [a]it happened, when I re-
turned to Jerusalem and was pray-
ing in the temple, that I was in a
trance
18 "and [a]saw Him saying to me,
[b]'Make haste and get out of Jeru-
salem quickly, for they will not re-
ceive your testimony concerning
Me.'
19 "So I said, 'Lord, [a]they know
that in every synagogue I impris-
oned and [b]beat those who believe
on You.
20 [a]'And when the blood of Your
martyr Stephen was shed, I also
was standing by [b]consenting [1]to
his death, and guarding the clothes
of those who were killing him.'
21 "Then He said to me, 'Depart,
[a]for I will send you far from here
to the Gentiles.' "

Paul's Roman Citizenship

22 And they listened to him until
this word, and *then* they raised

their voices and said, [a]"Away with
such a *fellow* from the earth, for
[b]he is not fit to live!"
23 Then, as they cried out and
[1]tore off *their* clothes and threw
dust into the air,
24 the commander ordered him to
be brought into the barracks, and
said that he should be examined
under scourging, so that he might
know why they shouted so against
him.
25 And as they bound him with
thongs, Paul said to the centurion
who stood by, [a]"Is it lawful for you
to scourge a man who is a Roman,
and uncondemned?"
26 When the centurion heard
that, he went and told the com-
mander, saying, "Take care what
you do, for this man is a Roman."
27 Then the commander came and
said to him, "Tell me, are you a
Roman?" He said, "Yes."
28 The commander answered,
"With a large sum I obtained this
citizenship." And Paul said, "But
I was born *a citizen*."
29 Then immediately those who
were about to examine him with-
drew from him; and the com-
mander was also afraid after he
found out that he was a Roman,
and because he had bound him.

The Sanhedrin Divided

30 The next day, because he
wanted to know for certain why
he was accused by the Jews, he
released him from *his* bonds,
and commanded the chief priests
and all their council to appear, and
brought Paul down and set him be-
fore them.

23 Then Paul, looking earnestly
at the council, said, "Men
and brethren, [a]I have lived in all
good conscience before God until
this day."
2 And the high priest Ananias
commanded those who stood by
him [a]to strike him on the mouth.
3 Then Paul said to him, "God
will strike you, *you* whitewashed
wall! For you sit to judge me ac-
cording to the law, and [a]do you
command me to be struck contrary
to the law?"
4 And those who stood by said,
"Do you revile God's high priest?"
5 Then Paul said, [a]"I did not
know, brethren, that he was the
high priest; for it is written, [b]'*You
shall not speak evil of a ruler of
your people.*' "
6 But when Paul perceived that
one part were Sadducees and the
other Pharisees, he cried out in the
council, "Men *and* brethren, [a]I am
a Pharisee, the son of a Pharisee;
[b]concerning the hope and resur-
rection of the dead I am being
judged!"
7 And when he had said this, a
dissension arose between the
Pharisees and the Sadducees; and
the assembly was divided.
8 [a]For Sadducees say that there
is no resurrection—and no angel
or spirit; but the Pharisees confess
both.
9 Then there arose a loud outcry.
And the scribes of the Pharisees'
party arose and protested, saying,
[a]"We find no evil in this man; [1]but
[b]if a spirit or an angel has spoken
to him, [c]let us not fight against
God."
10 Now when there arose a great
dissension, the commander, fear-
ing lest Paul might be pulled to
pieces by them, commanded the
soldiers to go down and take him
by force from among them, and
bring *him* into the barracks.

The Plot Against Paul

11 But [a]the following night the
Lord stood by him and said, [1]"Be
of good cheer, Paul; for as you
have testified for Me in [b]Jerusa-
lem, so you must also bear witness
at [c]Rome."
12 And when it was day, [a]some of
the Jews banded together and
bound themselves under an oath,
saying that they would neither eat
nor drink till they had [b]killed Paul.
13 Now there were more than
forty who had formed this con-
spiracy.
14 They came to the chief priests
and [a]elders, and said, "We have
bound ourselves under a great
oath that we will eat nothing until
we have killed Paul.
15 "Now you, therefore, together
with the council, suggest to the
commander that he be brought
down to you [1]tomorrow, as though
you were going to make further in-
quiries concerning him; but we are

22 [a]Acts 21:36; 1 Thess. 2:16 [b]Acts 25:24
23 [1]Lit. *threw*
25 [a]Acts 16:37

CHAPTER 23

1 [a]Acts 24:16; 1 Cor. 4:4; 2 Cor. 1:12; 4:2; 2 Tim. 1:3; Heb. 13:18
2 [a]1 Kin. 22:24; Jer. 20:2; John 18:22
3 [a]Lev. 19:35; Deut. 25:1, 2; John 7:51
5 [a]Lev. 5:17, 18 [b]Ex. 22:28; Eccl. 10:20; 2 Pet. 2:10
6 [a]Acts 26:5; Phil. 3:5 [b]Acts 24:15, 21; 26:6; 28:20
8 [a]Matt. 22:23; Mark 12:18; Luke 20:27
9 [a]Acts 25:25; 26:31 [b]John 12:29; Acts 22:6, 7, 17, 18 [c]Acts 5:39 [1]NU *what if a spirit or an angel has spoken to him?* omitting the last clause
11 [a]Acts 18:9; 27:23, 24 [b]Acts 21:18, 19; 22:1–21 [c]Acts 28:16, 17, 23 [1]*Take courage*
12 [a]Acts 23:21, 30; 25:3 [b]Acts 9:23, 24; 25:3; 26:21; 27:42; 1 Thess. 2:15
14 [a]Acts 4:5, 23; 6:12; 22:5; 24:1; 25:15
15 [1]NU omits *tomorrow*

ready to kill him before he comes
near."
16 So when Paul's sister's son
heard of their ambush, he went
and entered the barracks and told
Paul.
17 Then Paul called one of the
centurions to *him* and said, "Take
this young man to the commander,
for he has something to tell him."
18 So he took him and brought
him to the commander and said,
"Paul the prisoner called me to
him and asked *me* to bring this
young man to you. He has something to say to you."
19 Then the commander took him
by the hand, went aside, and asked
privately, "What is it that you have
to tell me?"
20 And he said, [a]"The Jews have
agreed to ask that you bring Paul
down to the council tomorrow, as
though they were going to inquire
more fully about him.
21 "But do not yield to them, for
more than forty of them lie in wait
for him, men who have bound
themselves by an oath that they
will neither eat nor drink till they
have killed him; and now they are
ready, waiting for the promise
from you."
22 So the commander let the
young man depart, and commanded *him*, "Tell no one that you
have revealed these things to me."

Sent to Felix

23 And he called for two centurions, saying, "Prepare two hundred soldiers, seventy horsemen,
and two hundred spearmen to go
to [a]Caesarea at the third hour of
the night;
24 "and provide mounts to set
Paul on, and bring *him* safely to
Felix the governor."
25 He wrote a letter in the following manner:
26 Claudius Lysias,

To the most excellent governor
Felix:

Greetings.

27 [a]This man was seized by the
Jews and was about to be killed
by them. Coming with the
troops I rescued him, having

20 [a]Acts 23:12
23 [a]Acts 8:40; 23:33
27 [a]Acts 21:30, 33; 24:7
28 [a]Acts 22:30
29 [a]Acts 18:15; 25:19 [b]Acts 25:25; 26:31
30 [a]Acts 23:20 [b]Acts 24:8; 25:6 [1]NU *there would be a plot against the man*
33 [a]Acts 8:40 [b]Acts 23:26–30
34 [a]Acts 6:9; 21:39
35 [a]Acts 24:1, 10; 25:16 [b]Matt. 27:27 [1]Headquarters

CHAPTER 24

1 [a]Acts 21:27 [b]Acts 23:2, 30, 35; 25:2
2 [1]Or *reforms are*
4 [1]*graciousness*
5 [a]Luke 23:2; Acts 6:13; 16:20; 17:6; 21:28; 1 Pet. 2:12, 15

learned that he was a Roman.
28 [a]And when I wanted to know
the reason they accused him, I
brought him before their
council.
29 I found out that he was accused
[a]concerning questions of their
law, [b]but had nothing charged
against him deserving of death
or chains.
30 And [a]when it was told me that
[1]the Jews lay in wait for the
man, I sent him immediately to
you, and [b]also commanded his
accusers to state before you the
charges against him.

Farewell.

31 Then the soldiers, as they were
commanded, took Paul and
brought *him* by night to Antipatris.
32 The next day they left the
horsemen to go on with him, and
returned to the barracks.
33 When they came to [a]Caesarea
and had delivered the [b]letter to the
governor, they also presented Paul
to him.
34 And when the governor had
read *it*, he asked what province he
was from. And when he understood that *he was* from [a]Cilicia,
35 he said, [a]"I will hear you when
your accusers also have come."
And he commanded him to be kept
in [b]Herod's [1]Praetorium.

Accused of Sedition

24 Now after [a]five days [b]Ananias the high priest came
down with the elders and a certain
orator *named* Tertullus. These
gave evidence to the governor
against Paul.
2 And when he was called upon,
Tertullus began his accusation,
saying: "Seeing that through you
we enjoy great peace, and [1]prosperity is being brought to this nation by your foresight,
3 "we accept *it* always and in all
places, most noble Felix, with all
thankfulness.
4 "Nevertheless, not to be tedious to you any further, I beg you
to hear, by your [1]courtesy, a few
words from us.
5 [a]"For we have found this man
a plague, a creator of dissension
among all the Jews throughout the

world, and a ringleader of the sect
of the Nazarenes.
6 [a]"He even tried to profane the
temple, and we seized him, [1]and
wanted [b]to judge him according to
our law.
7 [a]"But the commander Lysias
came by and with great violence
took *him* out of our hands,
8 [a]"commanding his accusers to
come to you. By examining him
yourself you may ascertain all
these things of which we accuse
him."
9 And the Jews also [1]assented,
maintaining that these things were
so.

The Defense Before Felix

10 Then Paul, after the governor
had nodded to him to speak, an-
swered: "Inasmuch as I know that
you have been for many years a
judge of this nation, I do the more
cheerfully answer for myself,
11 "because you may ascertain
that it is no more than twelve days
since I went up to Jerusalem [a]to
worship.
12 [a]"And they neither found me in
the temple disputing with anyone
nor inciting the crowd, either in
the synagogues or in the city.
13 "Nor can they prove the things
of which they now accuse me.
14 "But this I confess to you, that
according to [a]the Way which they
call a sect, so I worship the [b]God
of my fathers, believing all things
which are written in [c]the Law and
in the Prophets.
15 [a]"I have hope in God, which
they themselves also accept, [b]that
there will be a resurrection [1]of *the*
dead, both of *the* just and *the* un-
just.
16 [a]"This *being* so, I myself al-
ways strive to have a conscience
without offense toward God and
men.
17 "Now after many years [a]I came
to bring alms and offerings to my
nation,
18 [a]"in the midst of which some
Jews from Asia found me [b]purified
in the temple, neither with a mob
nor with tumult.
19 [a]"They ought to have been here
before you to object if they had
anything against me.
20 "Or else let those who are *here*
themselves say [1]if they found any
wrongdoing in me while I stood
before the council,
21 "unless *it is* for this one state-
ment which I cried out, standing
among them, [a]'Concerning the res-
urrection of the dead I am being
judged by you this day.' "

Felix Procrastinates

22 But when Felix heard these
things, having more accurate
knowledge of *the* [a]Way, he ad-
journed the proceedings and said,
"When [b]Lysias the commander
comes down, I will make a deci-
sion on your case."
23 So he commanded the centu-
rion to keep Paul and to let *him*
have liberty, and [a]told him not to
forbid any of his friends to provide
for or visit him.
24 And after some days, when Fe-
lix came with his wife Drusilla,
who was Jewish, he sent for Paul
and heard him concerning the
[a]faith in Christ.
25 Now as he reasoned about
righteousness, self-control, and
the judgment to come, Felix was
afraid and answered, "Go away
for now; when I have a convenient
time I will call for you."
26 Meanwhile he also hoped that
[a]money would be given him by
Paul, [1]that he might release him.
Therefore he sent for him more of-
ten and conversed with him.
27 But after two years Porcius
Festus succeeded Felix; and Felix,
[a]wanting to do the Jews a favor,
left Paul bound.

Paul Appeals to Caesar

25 Now when Festus had come
to the province, after three
days he went up from [a]Caesarea
to Jerusalem.
2 [a]Then the [1]high priest and the
chief men of the Jews informed
him against Paul; and they peti-
tioned him,
3 asking a favor against him, that
he would summon him to Jerusa-
lem—[a]while *they* lay in ambush
along the road to kill him.
4 But Festus answered that Paul
should be kept at Caesarea, and
that he himself was going *there*
shortly.
5 "Therefore," he said, "let those

6 [a]Acts 21:28 [b]John 18:31 [1]NU ends the sentence here and omits the rest of v. 6, all of v. 7, and the first clause of v. 8.
7 [a]Acts 21:33; 23:10
8 [a]Acts 23:30
9 [1]NU, M *joined the attack*
11 [a]Acts 21:15, 18, 26, 27; 24:17
12 [a]Acts 25:8; 28:17
14 [a]Amos 8:14; Acts 9:2; 24:22 [b]2 Tim. 1:3 [c]Acts 26:22; 28:23
15 [a]Acts 23:6; 26:6, 7; 28:20 [b][Dan. 12:2; John 5:28, 29; 11:24] [1]NU omits *of the dead*
16 [a]Acts 23:1
17 [a]Acts 11:29, 30; Rom. 15:25–28; 1 Cor. 16:1–4; 2 Cor. 8:1–4; 9:1, 2, 12; Gal. 2:10
18 [a]Acts 21:27; 26:21 [b]Acts 21:26
19 [a][Acts 23:30; 25:16]
20 [1]NU, M *what wrongdoing they found*
21 [a][Acts 23:6; 24:15; 28:20]
22 [a]Acts 9:2; 18:26; 19:9, 23; 22:4 [b]Acts 23:26; 24:7
23 [a]Acts 23:16; 27:3; 28:16
24 [a][John 3:15; 5:24; 11:25; 12:46; 20:31; Rom. 10:9]
26 [a]Ex. 23:8 [1]NU omits *that he might release him*
27 [a]Ex. 23:2; Acts 12:3; 23:35; 25:9, 14

CHAPTER 25

1 [a]Acts 8:40; 25:4, 6, 13
2 [a]Acts 24:1; 25:15 [1]NU *chief priests*
3 [a]Acts 23:12, 15

who have authority among you go
down with *me* and accuse this
man, to see [a]if there is any fault
in him."
6 And when he had remained
among them more than ten days,
he went down to Caesarea. And
the next day, sitting on the judg-
ment seat, he commanded Paul to
be brought.
7 When he had come, the Jews
who had come down from Jerusa-
lem stood about [a]and laid many se-
rious complaints against Paul,
which they could not prove,
8 while he answered for himself,
[a]"Neither against the law of the
Jews, nor against the temple, nor
against Caesar have I offended in
anything at all."
9 But Festus, [a]wanting to do the
Jews a favor, answered Paul and
said, [b]"Are you willing to go up
to Jerusalem and there be judged
before me concerning these
things?"
10 So Paul said, "I stand at Cae-
sar's judgment seat, where I ought
to be judged. To the Jews I have
done no wrong, as you very well
know.
11 [a]"For if I am an offender, or
have committed anything deserv-
ing of death, I do not object to dy-
ing; but if there is nothing in these
things of which these men accuse
me, no one can deliver me to them.
[b]I appeal to Caesar."
12 Then Festus, when he had con-
ferred with the council, answered,
"You have appealed to Caesar? To
Caesar you shall go!"

Paul Before Agrippa

13 And after some days King
Agrippa and Bernice came to
Caesarea to greet Festus.
14 When they had been there
many days, Festus laid Paul's case
before the king, saying: [a]"There is
a certain man left a prisoner by Fe-
lix,
15 [a]"about whom the chief priests
and the elders of the Jews in-
formed *me*, when I was in Jerusa-
lem, asking for a judgment against
him.
16 [a]"To them I answered, 'It is
not the custom of the Romans to
deliver any man [1]to destruction be-
fore the accused meets the accu-
sers face to face, and has opportu-
nity to answer for himself con-
cerning the charge against him.'
17 "Therefore when they had
come together, [a]without any delay,
the next day I sat on the judgment
seat and commanded the man to
be brought in.
18 "When the accusers stood up,
they brought no accusation
against him of such things as I
[1]supposed,
19 [a]"but had some questions
against him about their own reli-
gion and about a certain Jesus,
who had died, whom Paul affirmed
to be alive.
20 "And because I was uncertain
of such questions, I asked whether
he was willing to go to Jerusalem
and there be judged concerning
these matters.
21 "But when Paul [a]appealed to be
reserved for the decision of Augus-
tus, I commanded him to be kept
till I could send him to Caesar."
22 Then [a]Agrippa said to Festus,
"I also would like to hear the man
myself." "Tomorrow," he said,
"you shall hear him."
23 So the next day, when Agrippa
and Bernice had come with great
[1]pomp, and had entered the audi-
torium with the commanders and
the prominent men of the city, at
Festus' command [a]Paul was
brought in.
24 And Festus said: "King
Agrippa and all the men who are
here present with us, you see this
man about whom [a]the whole as-
sembly of the Jews petitioned me,
both at Jerusalem and here, crying
out that he was [b]not fit to live any
longer.
25 "But when I found that [a]he had
committed nothing deserving of
death, [b]and that he himself had ap-
pealed to Augustus, I decided to
send him.
26 "I have nothing certain to write
to my lord concerning him. There-
fore I have brought him out before
you, and especially before you,
King Agrippa, so that after the
examination has taken place I may
have something to write.
27 "For it seems to me unreason-
able to send a prisoner and not to
specify the charges against him."

5 [a]Acts 18:14; 25:18
7 [a]Mark 15:3; Luke 23:2, 10; Acts 24:5, 13
8 [a]Acts 6:13; 24:12; 28:17
9 [a]Acts 12:2; 24:27 [b]Acts 25:20
11 [a]Acts 18:14; 23:29; 25:25; 26:31 [b]Acts 26:32; 28:19
14 [a]Acts 24:27
15 [a]Acts 24:1; 25:2, 3
16 [a]Acts 25:4, 5 [1]NU omits *to destruction*, although it is implied
17 [a]Matt. 27:19; Acts 25:6, 10
18 [1]*suspected*
19 [a]Acts 18:14, 15; 23:29
21 [a]Acts 25:11, 12
22 [a]Acts 9:15
23 [a]Acts 9:15 [1]*pageantry*
24 [a]Acts 25:2, 3, 7 [b]Acts 21:36; 22:22
25 [a]Acts 23:9, 29; 26:31 [b]Acts 25:11, 12

Paul's Early Life

26 Then Agrippa said to Paul,
"You are permitted to speak
for yourself." So Paul stretched
out his hand and answered for
himself:
2 "I think myself [a]happy, King
Agrippa, because today I shall an-
swer [b]for myself before you con-
cerning all the things of which I
am [c]accused by the Jews,
3 "especially because you are ex-
pert in all customs and questions
which have to do with the Jews.
Therefore I beg you to hear me pa-
tiently.
4 "My manner of life from my
youth, which was spent from
the beginning among my own
nation at Jerusalem, all the Jews
know.
5 "They knew me from the first,
if they were willing to testify,
that according to [a]the strictest
sect of our religion I lived a Phar-
isee.
6 [a]"And now I stand and am
judged for the hope of [b]the prom-
ise made by God to our fathers.
7 "To this *promise* [a]our twelve
tribes, earnestly serving *God*
[b]night and day, [c]hope to attain. For
this hope's sake, King Agrippa, I
am accused by the Jews.
8 "Why should it be thought in-
credible by you that God raises the
dead?
9 [a]"Indeed, I myself thought I
must do many things [1]contrary to
the name of [b]Jesus of Nazareth.
10 [a]"This I also did in Jerusalem,
and many of the saints I shut up
in prison, having received author-
ity [b]from the chief priests; and
when they were put to death, I cast
my vote against *them.*
11 [a]"And I punished them often in
every synagogue and compelled
them to blaspheme; and being ex-
ceedingly enraged against them, I
persecuted *them* even to foreign
cities.

Paul Recounts His Conversion

12 [a]"While thus occupied, as I
journeyed to Damascus with au-
thority and commission from the
chief priests,
13 "at midday, O king, along the
road I saw a light from heaven,
brighter than the sun, shining
around me and those who jour-
neyed with me.
14 "And when we all had fallen
to the ground, I heard a voice
speaking to me and saying in the
Hebrew language, 'Saul, Saul, why
are you persecuting Me? *It is* hard
for you to kick against the goads.'
15 "So I said, 'Who are You,
Lord?' And He said, 'I am Jesus,
whom you are persecuting.
16 'But rise and stand on your
feet; for I have appeared to you for
this purpose, [a]to make you a min-
ister and a witness both of the
things which you have seen and
of the things which I will yet reveal
to you.
17 'I will [1]deliver you from the
Jewish people, as well as *from* the
Gentiles, [a]to whom I [2]now send
you,
18 [a]'to open their eyes, *in order* [b]to
turn *them* from darkness to light,
and *from* the power of Satan to
God, [c]that they may receive for-
giveness of sins and [d]an inheri-
tance among those who are [e]sancti-
fied[1] by faith in Me.'

Paul's Post-Conversion Life

19 "Therefore, King Agrippa, I
was not disobedient to the heav-
enly vision,
20 "but [a]declared first to those in
Damascus and in Jerusalem, and
throughout all the region of Judea,
and *then* to the Gentiles, that they
should repent, turn to God, and do
[b]works befitting repentance.
21 "For these reasons the Jews
seized me in the temple and tried
to kill *me.*
22 "Therefore, having obtained
help from God, to this day I stand,
witnessing both to small and great,
saying no other things than those
[a]which the prophets and [b]Moses
said would come—
23 [a]"that the Christ would suffer,
[b]that He would be the first to rise
from the dead, and [c]would pro-
claim light to the *Jewish* people
and to the Gentiles."

Agrippa Parries Paul's Challenge

24 Now as he thus made his de-
fense, Festus said with a loud
voice, "Paul, [a]you are beside your-
self! Much learning is driving you
mad!"

CHAPTER 26

2 [a][1 Pet. 3:14; 4:14] [b][1 Pet. 3:15, 16] [c]Acts 21:28; 24:5, 6

5 [a]Phil. 3:5

6 [a]Acts 23:6 [b]Acts 13:32

7 [a]James 1:1 [b]1 Thess. 3:10 [c]Phil. 3:11

9 [a]1 Tim. 1:12, 13 [b]Acts 2:22; 10:38 [1]*against*

10 [a]Acts 8:1–3; 9:13 [b]Acts 9:14

11 [a]Acts 22:19

12 [a]Acts 9:3–8; 22:6–11; 26:12–18

16 [a]Acts 22:15

17 [a]Acts 22:21 [1]*rescue* [2]NU, M omit *now*

18 [a]Is. 35:5; 42:7, 16 [b]1 Pet. 2:9 [c]Luke 1:77 [d]Col. 1:12 [e]Acts 20:32 [1]*set apart*

20 [a]Acts 9:19, 20, 22; 11:26 [b]Matt. 3:8

22 [a]Rom. 3:21 [b]John 5:46

23 [a]Luke 24:26 [b]1 Cor. 15:20, 23 [c]Luke 2:32

24 [a][1 Cor. 1:23; 2:13, 14; 4:10]

25 But he said, "I am not [1]mad, most noble Festus, but speak the words of truth and reason.

26 "For the king, before whom I also speak freely, [a]knows these things; for I am convinced that none of these things escapes his attention, since this thing was not done in a corner.

27 "King Agrippa, do you believe the prophets? I know that you do believe."

28 Then Agrippa said to Paul, "You almost persuade me to become a Christian."

29 And Paul said, [a]"I would to God that not only you, but also all who hear me today, might become both almost and altogether such as I am, except for these chains."

30 When he had said these things, the king stood up, as well as the governor and Bernice and those who sat with them;

31 and when they had gone aside, they talked among themselves, saying, [a]"This man is doing nothing deserving of death or chains."

32 Then Agrippa said to Festus, "This man might have been set [a]free [b]if he had not appealed to Caesar."

The Voyage to Rome Begins

27 And when [a]it was decided that we should sail to Italy, they delivered Paul and some other prisoners to *one* named Julius, a centurion of the Augustan Regiment.

2 So, entering a ship of Adramyttium, we put to sea, meaning to sail along the coasts of Asia. [a]Aristarchus, a Macedonian of Thessalonica, was with us.

3 And the next *day* we landed at Sidon. And Julius [a]treated Paul kindly and gave *him* liberty to go to his friends and receive care.

4 When we had put to sea from there, we sailed under *the shelter of* Cyprus, because the winds were contrary.

5 And when we had sailed over the sea which is off Cilicia and Pamphylia, we came to Myra, *a city* of Lycia.

6 There the centurion found [a]an Alexandrian ship sailing to Italy, and he put us on board.

7 When we had sailed slowly many days, and arrived with difficulty off Cnidus, the wind not permitting us to proceed, we sailed under *the shelter of* [a]Crete off Salmone.

8 Passing it with difficulty, we came to a place called Fair Havens, near the city of Lasea.

Paul's Warning Ignored

9 Now when much time had been spent, and sailing was now dangerous [a]because [1]the Fast was already over, Paul advised them,

10 saying, "Men, I perceive that this voyage will end with disaster and much loss, not only of the cargo and ship, but also our lives."

11 Nevertheless the centurion was more persuaded by the helmsman and the owner of the ship than by the things spoken by Paul.

12 And because the harbor was not suitable to winter in, the majority advised to set sail from there also, if by any means they could reach Phoenix, a harbor of Crete opening toward the southwest and northwest, *and* winter *there*.

In the Tempest

13 When the south wind blew softly, supposing that they had obtained *their* desire, putting out to sea, they sailed close by Crete.

14 But not long after, a tempestuous head wind arose, called [1]Euroclydon.

15 So when the ship was caught, and could not head into the wind, we let *her* [1]drive.

16 And running under *the shelter of* an island called [1]Clauda, we secured the skiff with difficulty.

17 When they had taken it on board, they used cables to undergird the ship; and fearing lest they should run aground on the [1]Syrtis *Sands*, they struck sail and so were driven.

18 And because we were exceedingly tempest-tossed, the next *day* they lightened the ship.

19 On the third day [a]we threw the ship's tackle overboard with our own hands.

20 Now when neither sun nor stars appeared for many days, and no small tempest beat on *us*, all hope that we would be saved was finally given up.

---

25 [1]*out of my mind*
26 [a]Acts 26:3
29 [a]1 Cor. 7:7
31 [a]Acts 23:9, 29; 25:25
32 [a]Acts 28:18 [b]Acts 25:11

CHAPTER 27

1 [a]Acts 25:12, 25
2 [a]Acts 19:29
3 [a]Acts 24:23; 28:16
6 [a]Acts 28:11
7 [a]Acts 2:11; 27:12, 21; Titus 1:5, 12
9 [a]Lev. 16:29–31; 23:27–29; Num. 29:7 [1]The Day of Atonement, late September or early October
14 [1]A southeast wind that stirs up broad waves; NU *Euraquilon*, a northeaster
15 [1]*be driven*
16 [1]NU *Cauda*
17 [1]M *Syrtes*
19 [a]Jon. 1:5

21 But after long abstinence from
food, then Paul stood in the midst
of them and said, "Men, you
should have listened to me, and
not have sailed from Crete and in-
curred this disaster and loss.
22 "And now I urge you to take
[1]heart, for there will be no loss of
life among you, but only of the
ship.
23 [a]"For there stood by me this
night an angel of the God to whom
I belong and [b]whom I serve,
24 "saying, 'Do not be afraid,
Paul; you must be brought before
Caesar; and indeed God has
granted you all those who sail with
you.'
25 "Therefore take heart, men,
[a]for I believe God that it will be
just as it was told me.
26 "However, [a]we must run
aground on a certain island."

22 [1]courage

23 [a]Acts 18:9; 23:11; 2 Tim. 4:17 [b]Dan. 6:16; Rom. 1:9; 2 Tim. 1:3

25 [a]Luke 1:45; Rom. 4:20, 21; 2 Tim. 1:12

26 [a]Acts 28:1

29 [1]Or *wished*

27 Now when the fourteenth night
had come, as we were driven up
and down in the Adriatic *Sea*,
about midnight the sailors sensed
that they were drawing near some
land.
28 And they took soundings and
found *it* to be twenty fathoms; and
when they had gone a little farther,
they took soundings again and
found *it* to be fifteen fathoms.
29 Then, fearing lest we should
run aground on the rocks, they
dropped four anchors from the
stern, and [1]prayed for day to
come.
30 And as the sailors were seeking
to escape from the ship, when they
had let down the skiff into the sea,
under pretense of putting out an-
chors from the prow,
31 Paul said to the centurion and
the soldiers, "Unless these men

On to Rome (Paul's Fourth Journey, Acts 27:1—28:16). In Jerusalem following his third missionary journey, Paul struggled with Jews who accused him of profaning the temple (Acts 21:26–34). He was placed in Roman custody in Caesarea for two years, but after appealing to Caesar, was sent by ship to Rome. After departing the island of Crete, Paul's party was shipwrecked on Malta by a great storm. Three months later he finally arrived at the imperial city.

stay in the ship, you cannot be
saved."
32 Then the soldiers cut away
the ropes of the skiff and let it fall
off.
33 And as day was about to dawn,
Paul implored *them* all to take
food, saying, "Today is the four-
teenth day you have waited and
continued without food, and eaten
nothing.
34 "Therefore I urge you to take
nourishment, for this is for your
survival, [a]since not a hair will fall
from the head of any of you."
35 And when he had said these
things, he took bread and [a]gave
thanks to God in the presence of
them all; and when he had broken
it he began to eat.
36 Then they were all encouraged,
and also took food themselves.
37 And in all we were two hun-
dred and seventy-six [a]persons on
the ship.
38 So when they had eaten
enough, they lightened the ship
and threw out the wheat into the
sea.

Shipwrecked on Malta

39 When it was day, they did not
recognize the land; but they ob-
served a bay with a beach, onto
which they planned to run the ship
if possible.
40 And they [1]let go the anchors
and left *them* in the sea, mean-
while loosing the rudder ropes;
and they hoisted the mainsail to
the wind and made for shore.
41 But striking [1]a place where two
seas met, [a]they ran the ship
aground; and the prow stuck fast
and remained immovable, but the
stern was being broken up by the
violence of the waves.
42 And the soldiers' plan was to
kill the prisoners, lest any of
them should swim away and
escape.
43 But the centurion, wanting to
save Paul, kept them from *their*
purpose, and commanded that
those who could swim should
jump *overboard* first and get to
land,
44 and the rest, some on boards
and some on *parts* of the ship. And
so it was [a]that they all escaped
safely to land.

Paul's Ministry on Malta

28 Now when they had es-
caped, they then found out
that [a]the island was called Malta.
2 And the [a]natives[1] showed us
unusual kindness; for they kindled
a fire and made us all welcome,
because of the rain that was falling
and because of the cold.
3 But when Paul had gathered a
bundle of sticks and laid *them* on
the fire, a viper came out because
of the heat, and fastened on his
hand.
4 So when the natives saw the
creature hanging from his hand,
they said to one another, "No
doubt this man is a murderer,
whom, though he has escaped the
sea, yet justice does not allow to
live."
5 But he shook off the creature
into the fire and [a]suffered no harm.
6 However, they were expecting
that he would swell up or suddenly
fall down dead. But after they had
looked for a long time and saw no
harm come to him, they changed
their minds and [a]said that he was
a god.
7 In that region there was an es-
tate of the [1]leading citizen of the
island, whose name was Publius,
who received us and entertained
us courteously for three days.
8 And it happened that the father
of Publius lay sick of a fever and
dysentery. Paul went in to him and
[a]prayed, and [b]he laid his hands on
him and healed him.
9 So when this was done, the rest
of those on the island who had dis-
eases also came and were healed.
10 They also honored us in many
[a]ways; and when we departed,
they provided such things as were
[b]necessary.

Arrival at Rome

11 After three months we sailed
in [a]an Alexandrian ship whose
figurehead was the [1]Twin Broth-
ers, which had wintered at the is-
land.
12 And landing at Syracuse, we
stayed three days.
13 From there we circled round
and reached Rhegium. And after
one day the south wind blew; and
the next day we came to Puteoli,

34 [a]1 Kin. 1:52; [Matt. 10:30; Luke 12:7; 21:18]
35 [a]1 Sam. 9:13; Matt. 15:36; Mark 8:6; John 6:11; [1 Tim. 4:3, 4]
37 [a]Acts 2:41; 7:14; Rom. 13:1; 1 Pet. 3:20
40 [1]*cast off*
41 [a]2 Cor. 11:25 [1]A reef
44 [a]Acts 27:22, 31

CHAPTER 28

1 [a]Acts 27:26
2 [a]Acts 28:4; Rom. 1:14; 1 Cor. 14:11; Col. 3:11 [1]Lit. *barbarians*
5 [a]Mark 16:18; Luke 10:19
6 [a]Acts 12:22; 14:11
7 [1]Magistrate
8 [a]Acts 9:40; [James 5:14, 15] [b]Matt. 9:18; Mark 5:23; 6:5; 7:32; 16:18; Luke 4:40; Acts 19:11, 12; [1 Cor. 12:9, 28]
10 [a]Matt. 15:6; 1 Tim. 5:17 [b][Phil. 4:19]
11 [a]Acts 27:6 [1]Gr. *Dioskouroi,* Zeus's sons Castor and Pollux

14 where we found [a]brethren, and
were invited to stay with them
seven days. And so we went to-
ward Rome.
15 And from there, when the
brethren heard about us, they
came to meet us as far as Appii
Forum and Three Inns. When Paul
saw them, he thanked God and
took courage.
16 Now when we came to Rome,
the centurion delivered the prison-
ers to the captain of the guard; but
[a]Paul was permitted to dwell by
himself with the soldier who
guarded him.

Paul's Ministry at Rome

17 And it came to pass after three
days that Paul called the leaders
of the Jews together. So when they
had come together, he said to
them: "Men *and* brethren, [a]though
I have done nothing against our
people or the customs of our fa-
thers, yet [b]I was delivered as a
prisoner from Jerusalem into the
hands of the Romans,
18 "who, [a]when they had exam-
ined me, wanted to let *me* go, be-
cause there was no cause for put-
ting me to death.
19 "But when the [1]Jews spoke
against *it*, [a]I was compelled to ap-
peal to Caesar, not that I had any-
thing of which to accuse my na-
tion.
20 "For this reason therefore I
have called for you, to see *you* and
speak with *you*, because [a]for the
hope of Israel I am bound with
[b]this chain."
21 Then they said to him, "We nei-
ther received letters from Judea
concerning you, nor have any of
the brethren who came reported or
spoken any evil of you.
22 "But we desire to hear from
you what you think; for concern-
ing this sect, we know that [a]it is
spoken against everywhere."
23 So when they had appointed
him a day, many came to him at
his lodging, [a]to whom he ex-
plained and solemnly testified of
the kingdom of God, persuading
them concerning Jesus [b]from both
the Law of Moses and the Proph-
ets, from morning till evening.
24 And [a]some were persuaded by
the things which were spoken, and
some disbelieved.
25 So when they did not agree
among themselves, they departed
after Paul had said one word: "The
Holy Spirit spoke rightly through
Isaiah the prophet to [1]our fathers,
26 "saying,

[a]*'Go to this people and say:*
"Hearing you will hear, and shall
not understand;
And seeing you will see, and not
perceive;
27 *For the hearts of this people have*
grown dull.
Their ears are hard of hearing,
And their eyes they have closed,
Lest they should see with their
eyes and hear with their ears,
Lest they should understand with
their hearts and turn,
So that I should heal them."'

28 "Therefore let it be known to
you that the salvation of God has
been sent [a]to the Gentiles, and
they will hear it!"
29 [1]And when he had said these
words, the Jews departed and had
a great dispute among themselves.
30 Then Paul dwelt two whole
years in his own rented house, and
received all who came to him,
31 [a]preaching the kingdom of God
and teaching the things which con-
cern the Lord Jesus Christ with
all confidence, no one forbidding
him.

14 [a]Rom. 1:8
16 [a]Acts 23:11; 24:25; 27:3
17 [a]Acts 23:29; 24:12, 13; 26:31 [b]Acts 21:33
18 [a]Acts 22:24; 24:10; 25:8; 26:32
19 [a]Acts 25:11, 21, 25 [1]The ruling authorities
20 [a]Acts 26:6, 7 [b]Acts 26:29; Eph. 3:1; 4:1; 6:20; 2 Tim. 1:8, 16; Philem. 10, 13
22 [a]Luke 2:34; Acts 24:5, 14; [1 Pet. 2:12; 3:16; 4:14, 16]
23 [a]Luke 24:27; [Acts 17:3; 19:8] [b]Acts 26:6, 22
24 [a]Acts 14:4; 19:9
25 [1]NU *your*
26 [a]Is. 6:9, 10; Jer. 5:21; Ezek. 12:2; Matt. 13:14, 15; Mark 4:12; Luke 8:10; John 12:40, 41; Rom. 11:8
28 [a]Is. 42:1, 6; 49:6; Matt. 21:41; Luke 2:32; Rom. 11:11
29 [1]NU omits v. 29.
31 [a]Acts 4:31; Eph. 6:19

The Epistle of Paul the Apostle to the

Romans

ROMANS, Paul's greatest work, is placed first among his thirteen epistles in the New Testament. While the four Gospels present the words and works of Jesus Christ, Romans explores the significance of His sacrificial death. Using a question-and-answer format, Paul records the most systematic presentation of doctrine in the Bible. Romans is more than a book of theology; it is also a book of practical exhortation. The good news of Jesus Christ is more than facts to be believed; it is also a life to be lived—a life of righteousness befitting the person, "justified freely by [God's] grace through the redemption that is in Christ Jesus" (3:24).

Although some manuscripts omit "in Rome" in 1:7, 15, the title *Pros Romaious,* "To the Romans," has been associated with the epistle almost from the beginning.

Greeting

PAUL, a bondservant of Jesus
Christ, [a]called *to be* an apostle,
[b]separated to the gospel of God
2 [a]which He promised before
[b]through His prophets in the Holy
Scriptures,
3 concerning His Son Jesus
Christ our Lord, who [1]was [a]born
of the seed of David according to
the flesh,
4 *and* [a]declared *to be* the Son of
God with power according [b]to the
Spirit of holiness, by the resur-
rection from the dead.
5 Through Him [a]we have re-
ceived grace and apostleship for
[b]obedience to the faith among all
nations [c]for His name,
6 among whom you also are the
called of Jesus Christ;

7 To all who are in Rome, be-
loved of God, [a]called *to be* saints:

[b]Grace to you and peace from
God our Father and the Lord Jesus
Christ.

Desire to Visit Rome

8 First, [a]I thank my God through
Jesus Christ for you all, that [b]your
faith is spoken of throughout the
whole world.
9 For [a]God is my witness, [b]whom
I serve [1]with my spirit in the gos-
pel of His Son, that [c]without ceas-
ing I make mention of you always
in my prayers,
10 making request if, by some
means, now at last I may find a
way in the will of God to come to
you.
11 For I long to see you, that [a]I
may impart to you some spiritual
gift, so that you may be estab-
lished—
12 that is, that I may be encour-
aged together with you by [a]the
mutual faith both of you and me.
13 Now I do not want you to be
unaware, brethren, that I often
planned to come to you (but [a]was
hindered until now), that I might
have some [b]fruit among you
also, just as among the other Gen-
tiles.
14 I am a debtor both to Greeks
and to barbarians, both to wise
and to unwise.
15 So, as much as is in me, *I am*
ready to preach the gospel to you
who are in Rome also.

The Just Live by Faith

16 For [a]I am not ashamed of the
gospel [1]of Christ, for [b]it is the
power of God to salvation for
everyone who believes, [c]for the
Jew first and also for the Greek.
17 For [a]in it the righteousness of
God is revealed from faith to faith;
as it is written, [b]*"The just shall live
by faith."*

CHAPTER 1

1 [a]1 Tim. 1:11 [b]Acts 9:15; 13:2

2 [a]Acts 26:6 [b]Gal. 3:8

3 [a]Gal. 4:4 [1]*came*

4 [a]Acts 9:20; 13:33 [b][Heb. 9:14]

5 [a]Eph. 3:8 [b]Acts 6:7 [c]Acts 9:15

7 [a]1 Cor. 1:2, 24 [b]1 Cor. 1:3

8 [a]1 Cor. 1:4 [b]Rom. 16:19

9 [a]Rom. 9:1 [b]Acts 27:23 [c]1 Thess. 3:10 [1]Or *in*

11 [a]Rom. 15:29

12 [a]Titus 1:4

13 [a][1 Thess. 2:18] [b]Phil. 4:17

16 [a]Ps. 40:9, 10 [b]1 Cor. 1:18, 24 [c]Acts 3:26 [1]NU omits *of Christ*

17 [a]Rom. 3:21; 9:30 [b]Hab. 2:4

God's Wrath on Unrighteousness

18 [a]For the wrath of God is re-
vealed from heaven against all un-
godliness and [b]unrighteousness of
men, who [1]suppress the truth in
unrighteousness,
19 because [a]what may be known
of God is [1]manifest [2]in them, for
[b]God has shown *it* to them.
20 For since the creation of the
world [a]His invisible *attributes* are
clearly seen, being understood by
the things that are made, *even* His
eternal power and [1]Godhead, so
that they are without excuse,
21 because, although they knew
God, they did not glorify *Him* as
God, nor were thankful, but [a]be-
came futile in their thoughts, and
their foolish hearts were dark-
ened.
22 [a]Professing to be wise, they be-
came fools,
23 and changed the glory of the
[a]incorruptible [b]God into an image
made like [1]corruptible man—and
birds and four-footed animals and
creeping things.
24 [a]Therefore God also gave them
up to uncleanness, in the lusts of
their hearts, [b]to dishonor their
bodies [c]among themselves,
25 who exchanged [a]the truth of
God [b]for the lie, and worshiped
and served the creature rather
than the Creator, who is blessed
forever. Amen.
26 For this reason God gave them
up to [a]vile passions. For even their
[1]women exchanged the natural
use for what is against nature.
27 Likewise also the [1]men, leaving
the natural use of the [2]woman,
burned in their lust for one an-
other, [1]men with [1]men committing
what is shameful, and receiving in
themselves the penalty of their er-
ror which was due.
28 And even as they did not like
to retain God in *their* knowledge,
God gave them over to a debased
mind, to do those things [a]which
are not fitting;
29 being filled with all unrigh-
teousness, [1]sexual immorality,
wickedness, [2]covetousness, [3]mali-
ciousness; full of envy, murder,
strife, deceit, evil-mindedness;
they are whisperers,
30 backbiters, haters of God, vio-
lent, proud, boasters, inventors of
evil things, disobedient to parents,
31 [1]undiscerning, untrustworthy,
unloving, [2]unforgiving, unmer-
ciful;
32 who, [a]knowing the righteous
judgment of God, that those who
practice such things [b]are deserv-
ing of death, not only do the same
but also [c]approve of those who
practice them.

God's Righteous Judgment

2 Therefore you are [a]inexcus-
able, O man, whoever you are
who judge, [b]for in whatever you
judge another you condemn your-
self; for you who judge practice
the same things.
2 But we know that the judgment
of God is according to truth
against those who practice such
things.
3 And do you think this, O man,
you who judge those practicing
such things, and doing the same,
that you will escape the judgment
of God?
4 Or do you despise [a]the riches
of His goodness, [b]forbearance, and
[c]longsuffering, [d]not knowing that
the goodness of God leads you to
repentance?
5 But in accordance with your
hardness and your [1]impenitent
heart [a]you are [2]treasuring up for
yourself wrath in the day of wrath
and revelation of the righteous
judgment of God,
6 who [a]*"will render to each one*
according to his deeds":
7 eternal life to those who by pa-
tient continuance in doing good
seek for glory, honor, and immor-
tality;
8 but to those who are self-
seeking and [a]do not obey the truth,
but obey unrighteousness—indig-
nation and wrath,
9 tribulation and anguish, on
every soul of man who does evil,
of the Jew [a]first and also of the
[1]Greek;
10 [a]but glory, honor, and peace to
everyone who works what is good,
to the Jew first and also to the
Greek.
11 For [a]there is no partiality with
God.
12 For as many as have sinned
without law will also perish with-

18 [a][Acts 17:30] [b]2 Thess. 2:10 [1]*hold down*
19 [a][Acts 14:17; 17:24] [b][John 1:9] [1]*evident* [2]*among*
20 [a]Ps. 19:1–6 [1]*divine nature, deity*
21 [a]Jer. 2:5
22 [a]Jer. 10:14
23 [a]1 Tim. 1:17; 6:15, 16 [b]Deut. 4:16–18 [1]*perishable*
24 [a]Eph. 4:18, 19 [b]1 Cor. 6:18 [c]Lev. 18:22
25 [a]1 Thess. 1:9 [b]Is. 44:20
26 [a]Lev. 18:22 [1]Lit. *females*
27 [1]Lit. *males* [2]Lit. *female*
28 [a]Eph. 5:4
29 [1]NU omits *sexual immorality* [2]*greed* [3]*malice*
31 [1]*without understanding* [2]NU omits *unforgiving*
32 [a][Rom. 2:2] [b][Rom. 6:21] [c]Hos. 7:3

CHAPTER 2

1 [a][Rom. 1:20] [b][Matt. 7:1–5]
4 [a][Eph. 1:7, 18; 2:7] [b][Rom. 3:25] [c]Ex. 34:6 [d]Is. 30:18
5 [a][Deut. 32:34] [1]*unrepentant* [2]*storing*
6 [a]Ps. 62:12; Prov. 24:12
8 [a][2 Thess. 1:8]
9 [a]1 Pet. 4:17 [1]Gentile
10 [a][1 Pet. 1:7]
11 [a]Deut. 10:17

out law, and as many as have
sinned in the law will be judged
by the law
13 (for [a]not the hearers of the law
are just in the sight of God, but the
doers of the law will be justified;
14 for when Gentiles, who do not
have the law, by nature do the
things in the law, these, although
not having the law, are a law to
themselves,
15 who show the [a]work of the law
written in their hearts, their [b]con-
science also bearing witness, and
between themselves *their* thoughts
accusing or else excusing *them*)
16 [a]in the day when God will
judge the secrets of men [b]by Jesus
Christ, [c]according to my gospel.

The Jews Guilty as the Gentiles

17 [1]Indeed [a]you are called a Jew,
and [b]rest[2] on the law, [c]and make
your boast in God,
18 and [a]know *His* will, and [b]ap-
prove the things that are excellent,
being instructed out of the law,
19 and [a]are confident that you
yourself are a guide to the blind,
a light to those who are in dark-
ness,
20 an instructor of the foolish, a
teacher of babes, [a]having the form
of knowledge and truth in the law.
21 [a]You, therefore, who teach an-
other, do you not teach yourself?
You who preach that a man should
not steal, do you steal?
22 You who say, "Do not commit
adultery," do you commit adul-
tery? You who abhor idols, [a]do
you rob temples?
23 You who [a]make your boast in
the law, do you dishonor God
through breaking the law?
24 For [a]*"the name of God is* [b]*blas-
phemed among the Gentiles be-
cause of you,"* as it is written.

Circumcision of No Avail

25 [a]For circumcision is indeed
profitable if you keep the law; but
if you are a breaker of the law,
your circumcision has become
uncircumcision.
26 Therefore, [a]if an uncircum-
cised man keeps the righteous re-
quirements of the law, will not his
uncircumcision be counted as cir-
cumcision?
27 And will not the physically

13 [a][James 1:22, 25]
15 [a]1 Cor. 5:1 [b]Acts 24:25
16 [a][Matt. 25:31] [b]Acts 10:42; 17:31 [c]1 Tim. 1:11
17 [a]John 8:33 [b]Mic. 3:11 [c]Is. 48:1, 2 [1]NU *But if* [2]*rely*
18 [a]Deut. 4:8 [b]Phil. 1:10
19 [a]Matt. 15:14
20 [a][2 Tim. 3:5]
21 [a]Matt. 23:3
22 [a]Mal. 3:8
23 [a]Rom. 2:17; 9:4
24 [a]Ezek. 16:27 [b]Is. 52:5; Ezek. 36:22
25 [a][Gal. 5:3]
26 [a][Acts 10:34]
27 [a]Matt. 12:41 [1]Lit. *letter*
28 [a][Gal. 6:15]
29 [a][1 Pet. 3:4] [b]Phil. 3:3 [c]Deut. 30:6 [d][1 Cor. 4:5] [1]A play on words—*Jew* is literally *praise.*

CHAPTER 3

2 [a]Deut. 4:5–8 [1]*sayings,* Scriptures
3 [a]Heb. 4:2 [b][2 Tim. 2:13]
4 [a]Job 40:8 [b][John 3:33] [c]Ps. 62:9 [d]Ps. 51:4 [1]Found true
5 [a]Gal. 3:15
6 [a][Gen. 18:25]
8 [a]Rom. 5:20 [1]Lit. *judgment*
9 [a]Gal. 3:22
10 [a]Ps. 14:1–3; 53:1–3; Eccl. 7:20

uncircumcised, if he fulfills the
law, [a]judge you who, *even* with
your [1]written *code* and circumci-
sion, *are* a transgressor of the law?
28 For [a]he is not a Jew who *is one*
outwardly, nor *is* circumcision that
which *is* outward in the flesh;
29 but *he is* a Jew [a]who *is one* in-
wardly; and [b]circumcision *is that*
of the heart, [c]in the Spirit, not in
the letter; [d]whose [1]praise *is* not
from men but from God.

God's Judgment Defended

3 What advantage then has the
Jew, or what *is* the profit of cir-
cumcision?
2 Much in every way! Chiefly be-
cause [a]to them were committed the
[1]oracles of God.
3 For what if [a]some did not be-
lieve? [b]Will their unbelief make
the faithfulness of God without ef-
fect?
4 [a]Certainly not! Indeed, let [b]God
be [1]true but [c]every man a liar. As
it is written:

[d]*"That You may be justified in Your
words,
And may overcome when You
are judged."*

5 But if our unrighteousness
demonstrates the righteousness of
God, what shall we say? *Is* God un-
just who inflicts wrath? [a](I speak
as a man.)
6 Certainly not! For then [a]how
will God judge the world?
7 For if the truth of God has in-
creased through my lie to His
glory, why am I also still judged
as a sinner?
8 And *why* not *say,* [a]"Let us do
evil that good may come"?—as we
are slanderously reported and as
some affirm that we say. Their
[1]condemnation is just.

All Have Sinned

9 What then? Are we better *than
they?* Not at all. For we have previ-
ously charged both Jews and
Greeks that [a]they are all under sin.
10 As it is written:

[a]*"There is none righteous, no, not
one;*
11 *There is none who understands;
There is none who seeks after
God.*

12 *They have all turned aside;*
They have together become
unprofitable;
There is none who does good, no,
not one."
13 "*Their*[a] *throat is an open* [1]*tomb;*
With their tongues they have
practiced deceit";
[b]"*The poison of asps is under their*
lips";
14 "*Whose*[a] *mouth is full of cursing*
and bitterness."
15 "*Their*[a] *feet are swift to shed*
blood;
16 *Destruction and misery are in*
their ways;
17 *And the way of peace they have*
not known."
18 "*There*[a] *is no fear of God before*
their eyes."

19 Now we know that whatever
[a]the law says, it says to those who
are under the law, that [b]every
mouth may be stopped, and all the
world may become [1]guilty before
God.
20 Therefore [a]by the deeds of the
law no flesh will be justified in His
sight, for by the law *is* the knowl-
edge of sin.

God's Righteousness Through Faith

21 But now [a]the righteousness of
God apart from the law is re-
vealed, [b]being witnessed by the
Law [c]and the Prophets,
22 even the righteousness of God,
through faith in Jesus Christ, to all
[1]and on all who believe. For [a]there
is no difference;
23 for [a]all have sinned and fall
short of the glory of God,
24 being justified [1]freely [a]by His
grace [b]through the redemption
that is in Christ Jesus,
25 whom God set forth [a]*as* a [1]pro-
pitiation [b]by His blood, through
faith, to demonstrate His righ-
teousness, because in His forbear-
ance God had passed over [c]the
sins that were previously com-
mitted,
26 to demonstrate at the present
time His righteousness, that He
might be just and the justifier of
the one who has faith in Jesus.

Boasting Excluded

27 [a]Where *is* boasting then? It is
excluded. By what law? Of works?
No, but by the law of faith.

13 [a]Ps. 5:9 [b]Ps. 140:3 [1]*grave*
14 [a]Ps. 10:7
15 [a]Prov. 1:16; Is. 59:7, 8
18 [a]Ps. 36:1
19 [a]John 10:34 [b]Job 5:16 [1]*accountable*
20 [a][Gal. 2:16]
21 [a]Acts 15:11 [b]John 5:46 [c]1 Pet. 1:10
22 [a][Col. 3:11] [1]NU omits *and on all*
23 [a]Gal. 3:22
24 [a][Eph. 2:8] [b][Heb. 9:12, 15] [1]*without any cost*
25 [a]Lev. 16:15 [b]Col. 1:20 [c]Acts 14:16; 17:30 [1]*mercy seat*
27 [a][1 Cor. 1:29]
28 [a]Gal. 2:16 [1]*declared righteous*
30 [a][Gal. 3:8, 20]

CHAPTER 4

1 [a]Is. 51:2 [b]James 2:21 [1]Or *(fore)father according to the flesh has found?*
2 [a]Rom. 3:20, 27
3 [a]Gen. 15:6 [1]*imputed, credited, reckoned, counted*
4 [a]Rom. 11:6 [1]*according to*
5 [a][Eph. 2:8, 9] [b]Josh. 24:2
6 [a]Ps. 32:1, 2
7 [a]Ps. 32:1, 2
11 [a]Gen. 17:10 [b]Luke 19:9

28 Therefore we conclude [a]that a
man is [1]justified by faith apart
from the deeds of the law.
29 Or *is He* the God of the Jews
only? *Is He* not also the God of the
Gentiles? Yes, of the Gentiles also,
30 since [a]*there is* one God who
will justify the circumcised by
faith and the uncircumcised
through faith.
31 Do we then make void the law
through faith? Certainly not! On
the contrary, we establish the law.

Abraham Justified by Faith

4 What then shall we say that
[a]Abraham our [b]father[1] has
found according to the flesh?
2 For if Abraham was [a]justified
by works, he has *something* to
boast about, but not before God.
3 For what does the Scripture
say? [a]"*Abraham believed God,*
and it was [1]*accounted to him for*
righteousness."
4 Now [a]to him who works, the
wages are not counted [1]as grace
but [1]as debt.

David Celebrates the Same Truth

5 But to him who [a]does not work
but believes on Him who justifies
[b]the ungodly, his faith is ac-
counted for righteousness,
6 just as David also [a]describes
the blessedness of the man to
whom God imputes righteousness
apart from works:

7 "*Blessed*[a] *are those whose lawless*
deeds are forgiven,
And whose sins are covered;
8 *Blessed is the man to whom the*
LORD shall not impute sin."

Abraham Justified Before Circumcision

9 *Does* this blessedness then
come upon the circumcised *only,*
or upon the uncircumcised also?
For we say that faith was ac-
counted to Abraham for righ-
teousness.
10 How then was it accounted?
While he was circumcised, or
uncircumcised? Not while circum-
cised, but while uncircumcised.
11 And [a]he received the sign of
circumcision, a seal of the righ-
teousness of the faith which *he had*
while still uncircumcised, that [b]he

might be the father of all those
who believe, though they are
uncircumcised, that righteousness
might be imputed to them also,
12 and the father of circumcision
to those who not only *are* of the
circumcision, but who also walk in
the steps of the faith which our fa-
ther [a]Abraham *had while still*
uncircumcised.

The Promise Granted Through Faith

13 For the promise that he would
be the [a]heir of the world *was* not
to Abraham or to his seed through
the law, but through the righteous-
ness of faith.
14 For [a]if those who are of the law
are heirs, faith is made void and
the promise made of no effect,
15 because [a]the law brings about
wrath; for where there is no law
there is no transgression.
16 Therefore *it is* of faith that *it*
might be [a]according to grace, [b]so
that the promise might be [1]sure to
all the seed, not only to those who
are of the law, but also to those
who are of the faith of Abraham,
[c]who is the father of us all
17 (as it is written, [a]*"I have made*
you a father of many nations") in
the presence of Him whom he be-
lieved—God, [b]who gives life to the
dead and calls those [c]things
which do not exist as though they
did;
18 who, contrary to hope, in hope
believed, so that he became the fa-
ther of many nations, according to
what was spoken, [a]*"So shall your*
descendants be."
19 And not being weak in faith,
[a]he did not consider his own body,
already dead (since he was about
a hundred years old), [b]and the
deadness of Sarah's womb.
20 He did not waver at the prom-
ise of God through unbelief, but
was strengthened in faith, giving
glory to God,
21 and being fully convinced that
what He had promised [a]He was
also able to perform.
22 And therefore [a]*"it was ac-*
counted to him for righteousness."
23 Now [a]it was not written for his
sake alone that it was imputed to
him,
24 but also for us. It shall be im-
puted to us who believe [a]in Him
who raised up Jesus our Lord from
the dead,
25 [a]who was delivered up because
of our offenses, and [b]was raised
because of our justification.

Faith Triumphs in Trouble

5 Therefore, [a]having been justi-
fied by faith, [1]we have [b]peace
with God through our Lord Jesus
Christ,
2 [a]through whom also we have
access by faith into this grace [b]in
which we stand, and [c]rejoice in
hope of the glory of God.
3 And not only *that,* but [a]we also
glory in tribulations, [b]knowing
that tribulation produces [1]per-
severance;
4 [a]and perseverance, [1]character;
and character, hope.
5 [a]Now hope does not disap-
point, [b]because the love of God has
been poured out in our hearts by
the Holy Spirit who was given
to us.

Christ in Our Place

6 For when we were still without
strength, [1]in due time [a]Christ died
for the ungodly.
7 For scarcely for a righteous
man will one die; yet perhaps for
a good man someone would even
dare to die.
8 But [a]God demonstrates His
own love toward us, in that while
we were still sinners, Christ died
for us.
9 Much more then, having now
been justified [a]by His blood, we
shall be saved [b]from wrath
through Him.
10 For [a]if when we were enemies
[b]we were reconciled to God
through the death of His Son,
much more, having been recon-
ciled, we shall be saved [c]by His
life.
11 And not only *that,* but we also
[a]rejoice in God through our Lord
Jesus Christ, through whom we
have now received the reconcilia-
tion.

Death in Adam, Life in Christ

12 Therefore, just as [a]through one
man sin entered the world, and
[b]death through sin, and thus death
spread to all men, because all
sinned—

12 [a]Rom. 4:18–22
13 [a]Gen. 17:4–6; 22:17
14 [a]Gal. 3:18
15 [a]Rom. 3:20
16 [a][Rom. 3:24] [b][Gal. 3:22] [c]Is. 51:2 [1]*certain*
17 [a]Gen. 17:5 [b][Rom. 8:11] [c]Rom. 9:26
18 [a]Gen. 15:5
19 [a]Gen. 17:17 [b]Heb. 11:11
21 [a][Heb. 11:19]
22 [a]Gen. 15:6
23 [a]Rom. 15:4
24 [a]Acts 2:24
25 [a]Is. 53:4, 5 [b][1 Cor. 15:17]

CHAPTER 5

1 [a]Is. 32:17 [b][Eph. 2:14] [1]Some ancient mss. *let us have*
2 [a][Eph. 2:18; 3:12] [b]1 Cor. 15:1 [c]Heb. 3:6
3 [a]Matt. 5:11, 12 [b]James 1:3 [1]*endurance*
4 [a][James 1:12] [1]*approved character*
5 [a]Phil. 1:20 [b]2 Cor. 1:22
6 [a][Rom. 4:25; 5:8; 8:32] [1]*at the right time*
8 [a][John 3:16; 15:13]
9 [a]Eph. 2:13 [b]1 Thess. 1:10
10 [a][Rom. 8:32] [b]2 Cor. 5:18 [c]John 14:19
11 [a][Gal. 4:9]
12 [a][1 Cor. 15:21] [b]Gen. 2:17

13 (For until the law sin was in the
world, but [a]sin is not imputed
when there is no law.
14 Nevertheless death reigned
from Adam to Moses, even over
those who had not sinned accord-
ing to the likeness of the transgres-
sion of Adam, [a]who is a type of
Him who was to come.
15 But the free gift *is* not like the
[1]offense. For if by the one man's
offense many died, much more the
grace of God and the gift by the
grace of the one Man, Jesus Christ,
abounded [a]to many.
16 And the gift *is* not like *that*
which came through the one who
sinned. For the judgment *which*
came from one *offense resulted* in
condemnation, but the free gift
which came from many [1]offenses
resulted in justification.
17 For if by the one man's [1]offense
death reigned through the one,
much more those who receive
abundance of grace and of the gift
of righteousness will reign in life
through the One, Jesus Christ.)
18 Therefore, as through [1]one
man's offense *judgment* came to
all men, resulting in condemna-
tion, even so through [a]one[2] Man's
righteous act *the free gift came* [b]to
all men, resulting in justification
of life.
19 For as by one man's disobedi-
ence many were made sinners, so
also by [a]one Man's obedience
many will be made righteous.
20 Moreover [a]the law entered that
the offense might abound. But
where sin abounded, grace
[b]abounded much more,
21 so that as sin reigned in death,
even so grace might reign through
righteousness to eternal life
through Jesus Christ our Lord.

Dead to Sin, Alive to God

6 What shall we say then? [a]Shall
we continue in sin that grace
may abound?
2 Certainly not! How shall we
who [a]died to sin live any longer
in it?
3 Or do you not know that [a]as
many of us as were baptized into
Christ Jesus [b]were baptized into
His death?
4 Therefore we were [a]buried
with Him through baptism into

13 [a]1 John 3:4
14 [a][1 Cor. 15:21, 22]
15 [a][Is. 53:11] [1]*trespass* or *false step*
16 [1]*trespasses*
17 [1]*trespass*
18 [a][1 Cor. 15:21, 45] [b][John 12:32] [1]Or *one trespass* [2]Or *one righteous act*
19 [a][Phil. 2:8]
20 [a]John 15:22 [b]1 Tim. 1:14

CHAPTER 6
1 [a]Rom. 3:8; 6:15
2 [a][Gal. 2:19]
3 [a][Gal. 3:27] [b][1 Cor. 15:29]
4 [a]Col. 2:12 [b]1 Cor. 6:14 [c]John 2:11 [d][Gal. 6:15]
5 [a]Phil. 3:10
6 [a]Gal. 2:20; 5:24; 6:14 [b]Col. 2:11 [1]*rendered inoperative*
7 [a]1 Pet. 4:1 [1]*cleared*
8 [a]2 Tim. 2:11
9 [a]Rev. 1:18
10 [a]Heb. 9:27 [b]Luke 20:38
11 [a][Rom. 6:2; 7:4, 6] [b][Gal. 2:19] [1]*consider*
12 [a]Ps. 19:13
13 [a]Col. 3:5 [b]1 Pet. 2:24; 4:2 [1]Or *weapons*
14 [a][Gal. 5:18]
15 [a]1 Cor. 9:21
16 [a]2 Pet. 2:19
17 [a]2 Tim. 1:13 [1]*entrusted*
18 [a]John 8:32

death, that [b]just as Christ was
raised from the dead by [c]the glory
of the Father, [d]even so we also
should walk in newness of life.
5 [a]For if we have been united to-
gether in the likeness of His death,
certainly we also shall be *in the*
likeness of *His* resurrection,
6 knowing this, that [a]our old man
was crucified with *Him,* that [b]the
body of sin might be [1]done away
with, that we should no longer be
slaves of sin.
7 For [a]he who has died has been
[1]freed from sin.
8 Now [a]if we died with Christ, we
believe that we shall also live with
Him,
9 knowing that [a]Christ, having
been raised from the dead, dies no
more. Death no longer has domin-
ion over Him.
10 For *the death* that He died, [a]He
died to sin once for all; but *the life*
that He lives, [b]He lives to God.
11 Likewise you also, [1]reckon
yourselves to be [a]dead indeed to
sin, but [b]alive to God in Christ
Jesus our Lord.
12 [a]Therefore do not let sin reign
in your mortal body, that you
should obey it in its lusts.
13 And do not present your
[a]members *as* [1]instruments of un-
righteousness to sin, but [b]present
yourselves to God as being alive
from the dead, and your members
as [1]instruments of righteousness
to God.
14 For [a]sin shall not have domin-
ion over you, for you are not under
law but under grace.

From Slaves of Sin to Slaves of God

15 What then? Shall we sin [a]be-
cause we are not under law but un-
der grace? Certainly not!
16 Do you not know that [a]to
whom you present yourselves
slaves to obey, you are that one's
slaves whom you obey, whether of
sin *leading* to death, or of obedi-
ence *leading* to righteousness?
17 But God be thanked that
though you were slaves of sin, yet
you obeyed from the heart [a]that
form of doctrine to which you
were [1]delivered.
18 And [a]having been set free from
sin, you became slaves of righ-
teousness.

19 I speak in human *terms* because of the weakness of your flesh. For just as you presented your members *as* slaves of uncleanness, and of lawlessness *leading* to *more* lawlessness, so now present your members *as* slaves *of* righteousness [1]for holiness.

20 For when you were [a]slaves of sin, you were free in regard to righteousness.

21 [a]What fruit did you have then in the things of which you are now ashamed? For [b]the end of those things *is* death.

22 But now [a]having been set free from sin, and having become slaves of God, you have your fruit [1]to holiness, and the end, everlasting life.

23 For [a]the wages of sin *is* death, but [b]the [1]gift of God *is* eternal life in Christ Jesus our Lord.

Freed from the Law

7 Or do you not know, brethren (for I speak to those who know the law), that the law [1]has dominion over a man as long as he lives?

2 For [a]the woman who has a husband is bound by the law to *her* husband as long as he lives. But if the husband dies, she is released from the law of *her* husband.

3 So then [a]if, while *her* husband lives, she marries another man, she will be called an adulteress; but if her husband dies, she is free from that law, so that she is no adulteress, though she has married another man.

4 Therefore, my brethren, you also have become [a]dead to the law through the body of Christ, that you may be married to another—to Him who was raised from the dead, that we should [b]bear fruit to God.

5 For when we were in the flesh, the sinful passions which were aroused by the law [a]were at work in our members [b]to bear fruit to death.

6 But now we have been delivered from the law, having died to what we were held by, so that we should serve [a]in the newness of the Spirit and not *in* the oldness of the letter.

Sin's Advantage in the Law

7 What shall we say then? *Is* the law sin? Certainly not! On the contrary, [a]I would not have known sin except through the law. For I would not have known covetousness unless the law had said, [b]*"You shall not covet."*

8 But [a]sin, taking opportunity by the commandment, produced in me all *manner of evil* desire. For [b]apart from the law sin *was* dead.

9 I was alive once without the law, but when the commandment came, sin revived and I died.

10 And the commandment, [a]which *was* to *bring* life, I found to *bring* death.

11 For sin, taking occasion by the commandment, deceived me, and by it killed *me*.

12 Therefore [a]the law *is* holy, and the commandment holy and just and good.

Law Cannot Save from Sin

13 Has then what is good become death to me? Certainly not! But sin, that it might appear sin, was producing death in me through what is good, so that sin through the commandment might become exceedingly sinful.

14 For we know that the law is spiritual, but I am carnal, [a]sold under sin.

15 For what I am doing, I do not understand. [a]For what I will to do, that I do not practice; but what I hate, that I do.

16 If, then, I do what I will not to do, I agree with the law that *it is* good.

17 But now, *it is* no longer I who do it, but sin that dwells in me.

18 For I know that [a]in me (that is, in my flesh) nothing good dwells; for to will is present with me, but *how* to perform what is good I do not find.

19 For the good that I will *to do*, I do not do; but the evil I will not *to do*, that I practice.

20 Now if I do what I will not *to do*, it is no longer I who do it, but sin that dwells in me.

21 I find then a law, that evil is present with me, the one who wills to do good.

22 For I [a]delight in the law of

---

19 [1]*unto sanctification*
20 [a]John 8:34
21 [a]Jer. 12:13; Ezek. 16:63; Rom. 7:5 [b]Rom. 1:32; Gal. 6:8
22 [a][John 8:32]; Rom. 6:18; 8:2 [1]*unto sanctification*
23 [a]Gen. 2:17 [b]Rom. 2:7; 1 Pet. 1:4 [1]*free gift*

CHAPTER 7

1 [1]*rules*
2 [a]1 Cor. 7:39
3 [a][Matt. 5:32]
4 [a]Rom. 8:2; Gal. 2:19; 5:18; [Col. 2:14] [b]Gal. 5:22
5 [a]Rom. 6:13 [b]Rom. 6:21; Gal. 5:19; James 1:15
6 [a]Rom. 2:29; 2 Cor. 3:6
7 [a]Rom. 3:20 [b]Ex. 20:17; Deut. 5:21; Acts 20:33
8 [a]Rom. 4:15 [b]1 Cor. 15:56
10 [a]Lev. 18:5; Ezek. 20:11, 13, 21; Luke 10:28; Rom. 10:5; 2 Cor. 3:7; Gal. 3:12
12 [a]Ps. 19:8
14 [a]1 Kin. 21:20, 25; 2 Kin. 17:17; Rom. 6:16
15 [a]Rom. 7:19; [Gal. 5:17]
18 [a][Gen. 6:5; 8:21]
22 [a]Ps. 1:2

God according to [b]the inward man.
23 But [a]I see another law in [b]my
members, warring against the law
of my mind, and bringing me into
captivity to the law of sin which
is in my members.
24 O wretched man that I am!
Who will deliver me [a]from this
body of death?
25 [a]I thank God—through Jesus
Christ our Lord! So then, with the
mind I myself serve the law of
God, but with the flesh the law of
sin.

Free from Indwelling Sin

8 *There is* therefore now no
condemnation to those who
are in Christ Jesus, [a]who[1] do not
walk according to the flesh, but ac-
cording to the Spirit.
2 For [a]the law of [b]the Spirit of
life in Christ Jesus has made me
free from [c]the law of sin and death.
3 For [a]what the law could not do
in that it was weak through the
flesh, [b]God *did* by sending His own
Son in the likeness of sinful flesh,
on account of sin: He condemned
sin in the flesh,
4 that the righteous requirement
of the law might be fulfilled in us
who [a]do not walk according to the
flesh but according to the Spirit.
5 For [a]those who live according
to the flesh set their minds on the
things of the flesh, but those *who
live* according to the Spirit, [b]the
things of the Spirit.
6 For [a]to be [1]carnally minded *is*
death, but to be spiritually minded
is life and peace.
7 Because [a]the [1]carnal mind *is*
enmity against God; for it is not
subject to the law of God, [b]nor in-
deed can be.
8 So then, those who are in the
flesh cannot please God.
9 But you are not in the flesh but
in the Spirit, if indeed the Spirit
of God dwells in you. Now if any-
one does not have the Spirit of
Christ, he is not His.
10 And if Christ *is* in you, the body
is dead because of sin, but the
Spirit *is* life because of righ-
teousness.
11 But if the Spirit of [a]Him who
raised Jesus from the dead dwells
in you, [b]He who raised Christ from
the dead will also give life to your
mortal bodies [1]through His Spirit
who dwells in you.

Sonship Through the Spirit

12 [a]Therefore, brethren, we are
debtors—not to the flesh, to live
according to the flesh.
13 For [a]if you live according to the
flesh you will die; but if by the
Spirit you [b]put to death the deeds
of the body, you will live.
14 For [a]as many as are led by the
Spirit of God, these are sons of
God.
15 For [a]you did not receive the
spirit of bondage again [b]to fear,
but you received the [c]Spirit of
adoption by whom we cry out,
[d]"Abba,[1] Father."
16 [a]The Spirit Himself bears wit-
ness with our spirit that we are
children of God,
17 and if children, then [a]heirs—
heirs of God and joint heirs with
Christ, [b]if indeed we suffer with
Him, that we may also be glorified
together.

From Suffering to Glory

18 For I consider that [a]the suffer-
ings of this present time are not
worthy *to be compared* with the
glory which shall be revealed
in us.
19 For [a]the earnest expectation of
the creation eagerly waits for the
revealing of the sons of God.
20 For [a]the creation was subjected
to futility, not willingly, but be-
cause of Him who subjected *it* in
hope;
21 because the creation itself also
will be delivered from the bondage
of [1]corruption into the glorious
[a]liberty of the children of God.
22 For we know that the whole
creation [a]groans and labors with
birth pangs together until now.
23 Not only *that*, but we also who
have [a]the firstfruits of the Spirit,
[b]even we ourselves groan [c]within
ourselves, eagerly waiting for the
adoption, the [d]redemption of our
body.
24 For we were saved in this hope,
but [a]hope that is seen is not hope;
for why does one still hope for
what he sees?
25 But if we hope for what we do
not see, we eagerly wait for *it* with
perseverance.

22 [b][2 Cor. 4:16]
23 [a][Gal. 5:17] [b]Rom. 6:13, 19
24 [a][1 Cor. 15:51, 52]
25 [a]1 Cor. 15:57

CHAPTER 8

1 [a]Gal. 5:16 [1]NU omits the rest of v. 1.
2 [a]Rom. 6:18, 22 [b][1 Cor. 15:45] [c]Rom. 7:24, 25
3 [a]Acts 13:39 [b][2 Cor. 5:21]
4 [a]Gal. 5:16, 25
5 [a]John 3:6 [b][Gal. 5:22–25]
6 [a]Gal. 6:8 [1]*fleshly*
7 [a]James 4:4 [b]1 Cor. 2:14 [1]*fleshly*
11 [a]Acts 2:24 [b]1 Cor. 6:14 [1]Or *because of*
12 [a][Rom. 6:7, 14]
13 [a]Gal. 6:8 [b]Eph. 4:22
14 [a][Gal. 5:18]
15 [a]Heb. 2:15 [b]2 Tim. 1:7 [c][Is. 56:5] [d]Mark 14:36 [1]Lit., in Aram., *Father*
16 [a]Eph. 1:13
17 [a]Acts 26:18 [b]Phil. 1:29
18 [a]2 Cor. 4:17
19 [a][2 Pet. 3:13]
20 [a]Gen. 3:17–19
21 [a][2 Cor. 3:17] [1]*decay*
22 [a]Jer. 12:4, 11
23 [a]2 Cor. 5:5 [b]2 Cor. 5:2, 4 [c][Luke 20:36] [d]Eph. 1:14; 4:30
24 [a]Heb. 11:1

26 Likewise the Spirit also helps
in our weaknesses. For [a]we do not
know what we should pray for
as we ought, but [b]the Spirit Him-
self makes intercession [1]for us
with groanings which cannot be
uttered.
27 Now [a]He who searches the
hearts knows what the mind of the
Spirit *is,* because He makes inter-
cession for the saints [b]according
to *the will of* God.
28 And we know that all things
work together for good to those
who love God, to those [a]who are
the called according to *His* pur-
pose.
29 For whom [a]He foreknew, [b]He
also predestined [c]*to be* conformed
to the image of His Son, [d]that He
might be the firstborn among
many brethren.
30 Moreover whom He predes-
tined, these He also [a]called; whom
He called, these He also [b]justified;
and whom He justified, these He
also [c]glorified.

God's Everlasting Love

31 What then shall we say to these
things? [a]If God *is* for us, who *can
be* against us?
32 [a]He who did not spare His own
Son, but [b]delivered Him up for us
all, how shall He not with Him also
freely give us all things?
33 Who shall bring a charge
against God's elect? [a]*It is* God who
justifies.
34 [a]Who *is* he who condemns? *It
is* Christ who died, and further-
more is also risen, [b]who is even
at the right hand of God, [c]who also
makes intercession for us.
35 Who shall separate us from the
love of Christ? *Shall* tribulation, or
distress, or persecution, or famine,
or nakedness, or peril, or sword?
36 As it is written:

> [a]*"For Your sake we are killed all
> day long;
> We are accounted as sheep for
> the slaughter."*

37 [a]Yet in all these things we are
more than conquerors through
Him who loved us.
38 For I am persuaded that neither
death nor life, nor angels nor
[a]principalities nor powers, nor
things present nor things to come,
39 nor height nor depth, nor any
other created thing, shall be able
to separate us from the love of God
which is in Christ Jesus our Lord.

Israel's Rejection of Christ

9 I [a]tell the truth in Christ, I am
not lying, my conscience also
bearing me witness in the Holy
Spirit,
2 [a]that I have great sorrow and
continual grief in my heart.
3 For [a]I could wish that I myself
were accursed from Christ for my
brethren, my [1]countrymen accord-
ing to the flesh,
4 who are Israelites, [a]to whom
pertain the adoption, [b]the glory,
[c]the covenants, [d]the giving of the
law, [e]the service *of God,* and [f]the
promises;
5 [a]of whom *are* the fathers and
from [b]whom, according to the
flesh, Christ *came,* [c]who is over all,
the eternally blessed God. Amen.

Israel's Rejection and God's Purpose

6 [a]But it is not that the word of
God has taken no effect. For [b]they
are not all Israel who *are* of Israel,
7 [a]nor *are they* all children be-
cause they are the seed of Abra-
ham; but, [b]*"In Isaac your seed
shall be called."*
8 That is, those who *are* the chil-
dren of the flesh, these *are* not the
children of God; but [a]the children
of the promise are counted as the
seed.
9 For this *is* the word of promise:
[a]*"At this time I will come and Sa-
rah shall have a son."*
10 And not only *this,* but when
[a]Rebecca also had conceived by
one man, *even* by our father Isaac
11 (for *the children* not yet being
born, nor having done any good
or evil, that the purpose of God ac-
cording to election might stand,
not of works but of [a]Him who
calls),
12 it was said to her, [a]*"The older
shall serve the younger."*
13 As it is written, [a]*"Jacob I have
loved, but Esau I have hated."*

Israel's Rejection and God's Justice

14 What shall we say then? [a]*Is
there* unrighteousness with God?
Certainly not!

26 [a]Matt. 20:22 [b]Eph. 6:18 [1]NU omits *for us*
27 [a]1 Chr. 28:9 [b]1 John 5:14
28 [a]2 Tim. 1:9
29 [a]2 Tim. 2:19 [b]Eph. 1:5, 11 [c][2 Cor. 3:18] [d]Heb. 1:6
30 [a][1 Pet. 2:9; 3:9] [b][Gal. 2:16] [c]John 17:22
31 [a]Num. 14:9
32 [a]Rom. 5:6, 10 [b][Rom. 4:25]
33 [a]Is. 50:8, 9
34 [a]John 3:18 [b]Mark 16:19 [c]Heb. 7:25; 9:24
36 [a]Ps. 44:22
37 [a]1 Cor. 15:57
38 [a][Eph. 1:21]

CHAPTER 9

1 [a]2 Cor. 1:23
2 [a]Rom. 10:1
3 [a]Ex. 32:32 [1]Or *relatives*
4 [a]Ex. 4:22 [b]1 Sam. 4:21 [c]Acts 3:25 [d]Ps. 147:19 [e]Heb. 9:1, 6 [f][Acts 2:39; 13:32]
5 [a]Deut. 10:15 [b][Luke 1:34, 35; 3:23] [c]Jer. 23:6
6 [a]Num. 23:19 [b][Gal. 6:16]
7 [a][Gal. 4:23] [b]Gen. 21:12
8 [a]Gal. 4:28
9 [a]Gen. 18:10, 14
10 [a]Gen. 25:21
11 [a][Rom. 4:17; 8:28]
12 [a]Gen. 25:23
13 [a]Mal. 1:2, 3
14 [a]Deut. 32:4

15 For He says to Moses, [a]*"I will
have mercy on whomever I will
have mercy, and I will have com-
passion on whomever I will have
compassion."*
16 So then *it is* not of him who
wills, nor of him who runs, but of
God who shows mercy.
17 For [a]the Scripture says to the
Pharaoh, [b]*"For this very purpose
I have raised you up, that I may
show My power in you, and that
My name may be declared in all
the earth."*
18 Therefore He has mercy on
whom He wills, and whom He
wills He [a]hardens.
19 You will say to me then, "Why
does He still find fault? For [a]who
has resisted His will?"
20 But indeed, O man, who are
you to reply against God? [a]Will the
thing formed say to him who
formed *it*, "Why have you made
me like this?"
21 Does not the [a]potter have
power over the clay, from the
same lump to make [b]one vessel for
honor and another for dishonor?
22 *What* if God, wanting to show
His wrath and to make His power
known, endured with much long-
suffering [a]the vessels of wrath
[b]prepared for destruction,
23 and that He might make known
[a]the riches of His glory on the ves-
sels of mercy, which He had [b]pre-
pared beforehand for glory,
24 *even* us whom He [a]called, [b]not
of the Jews only, but also of the
Gentiles?
25 As He says also in Hosea:

[a]*"I will call them My people, who
were not My people,
And her beloved, who was not
beloved."*
26 *"And*[a] *it shall come to pass in the
place where it was said to them,
'You are not My people,'
There they shall be called sons of
the living God."*

27 Isaiah also cries out concerning
Israel:

[a]*"Though the number of the
children of Israel be as the sand
of the sea,*
[b]*The remnant will be saved.*
28 *For* [1]*He will finish the work and
cut it short in righteousness,*
[a]*Because the* LORD *will make a
short work upon the earth."*
29 And as Isaiah said before:

[a]*"Unless the* LORD *of* [1]*Sabaoth had
left us a seed,*
[b]*We would have become like
Sodom,
And we would have been made
like Gomorrah."*

Present Condition of Israel

30 What shall we say then? [a]That
Gentiles, who did not pursue righ-
teousness, have attained to righ-
teousness, [b]even the righteousness
of faith;
31 but Israel, [a]pursuing the law of
righteousness, [b]has not attained to
the law [1]of righteousness.
32 Why? Because *they did* not
seek it by faith, but as it were, [1]by
the works of the law. For [a]they
stumbled at that stumbling stone.
33 As it is written:

[a]*"Behold, I lay in Zion a stumbling
stone and rock of offense,
And* [b]*whoever believes on Him
will not be put to shame."*

Israel Needs the Gospel

10 Brethren, my heart's desire
and prayer to God for [1]Israel
is that they may be saved.
2 For I bear them witness [a]that
they have a zeal for God, but not
according to knowledge.
3 For they being ignorant of
[a]God's righteousness, and seeking
to establish their own [b]righteous-
ness, have not submitted to the
righteousness of God.
4 For [a]Christ *is* the end of the law
for righteousness to everyone who
believes.
5 For Moses writes about the
righteousness which is of the law,
[a]*"The man who does those things
shall live by them."*
6 But the righteousness of faith
speaks in this way, [a]*"Do not say
in your heart, 'Who will ascend
into heaven?'"* (that is, to bring
Christ down *from above*)
7 or, [a]*" 'Who will descend into
the abyss?'"* (that is, to bring
Christ up from the dead).
8 But what does it say? [a]*"The
word is near you, in your mouth
and in your heart"* (that is, the

15 [a]Ex. 33:19
17 [a]Gal. 3:8 [b]Ex. 9:16
18 [a]Ex. 4:21
19 [a]2 Chr. 20:6
20 [a]Is. 29:16
21 [a]Prov. 16:4 [b]2 Tim. 2:20
22 [a][1 Thess. 5:9] [b][1 Pet. 2:8]
23 [a][Col. 1:27] [b][Rom. 8:28–30]
24 [a][Rom. 8:28] [b]Rom. 3:29
25 [a]Hos. 2:23
26 [a]Hos. 1:10
27 [a]Is. 10:22, 23 [b]Rom. 11:5
28 [a]Is. 10:23; 28:22 [1]NU *the* LORD *will finish the work and cut it short upon the earth*
29 [a]Is. 1:9 [b]Is. 13:19 [1]Lit., in Heb., *Hosts*
30 [a]Rom. 4:11 [b]Rom. 1:17; 3:21; 10:6
31 [a][Rom. 10:2–4] [b][Gal. 5:4] [1]NU omits *of righteousness*
32 [a][1 Cor. 1:23] [1]NU *by works*, omitting *of the law*
33 [a]Is. 8:14; 28:16 [b]Rom. 5:5; 10:11

CHAPTER 10

1 [1]NU *them*
2 [a]Acts 21:20
3 [a][Rom. 1:17] [b][Phil. 3:9]
4 [a][Gal. 3:24; 4:5]
5 [a]Lev. 18:5
6 [a]Deut. 30:12–14
7 [a]Deut. 30:13
8 [a]Deut. 30:14

word of faith which we preach):
9 that [a]if you confess with your
mouth the Lord Jesus and believe
in your heart that God has raised
Him from the dead, you will be
saved.
10 For with the heart one believes
unto righteousness, and with the
mouth confession is made unto
salvation.
11 For the Scripture says, [a]"*Who-
ever believes on Him will not be
put to shame.*"
12 For [a]there is no distinction be-
tween Jew and Greek, for [b]the
same Lord over all [c]is rich to all
who call upon Him.
13 For [a]"*whoever calls [b]on the
name of the* LORD *shall be saved.*"

Israel Rejects the Gospel

14 How then shall they call on
Him in whom they have not be-
lieved? And how shall they believe
in Him of whom they have not
heard? And how shall they hear
[a]without a preacher?
15 And how shall they preach un-
less they are sent? As it is written:

[a]"*How beautiful are the feet of
those who [1]preach the gospel
of peace,
Who bring glad tidings of good
things!*"

16 But they have not all obeyed
the gospel. For Isaiah says,
[a]"LORD, *who has believed our re-
port?*"
17 So then faith *comes* by hearing,
and hearing by the word of God.
18 But I say, have they not heard?
Yes indeed:

[a]"*Their sound has gone out to all
the earth,
[b]And their words to the ends of
the world.*"

19 But I say, did Israel not know?
First Moses says:

[a]"*I will provoke you to jealousy by
those who are not a nation,
I will move you to anger by a
[b]foolish nation.*"

20 But Isaiah is very bold and
says:

9 [a]Matt. 10:32; Luke 12:8; Acts 8:37; Rom. 14:9; [1 Cor. 12:3]; Phil. 2:11
11 [a]Is. 28:16; Jer. 17:7; Rom. 9:33
12 [a]Acts 15:9; Rom. 3:22, 29; Gal. 3:28 [b]Acts 10:36; 1 Tim. 2:5 [c]Eph. 1:7
13 [a]Joel 2:32; Acts 2:21 [b]Acts 9:14
14 [a]Acts 8:31; Titus 1:3
15 [a]Is. 52:7; Nah. 1:15 [1]NU omits *preach the gospel of peace, Who*
16 [a]Is. 53:1; John 12:38
18 [a]Ps. 19:4; Matt. 24:14; Mark 16:15; Rom. 1:8; Col. 1:6, 23; 1 Thess. 1:8 [b]Matt. 4:8
19 [a]Deut. 32:21; Rom. 11:11 [b]Titus 3:3
20 [a]Is. 65:1; Rom. 9:30
21 [a]Is. 65:2
CHAPTER 11
1 [a]Ps. 94:14; Jer. 46:28 [b]1 Sam. 12:22; Jer. 31:37 [c]2 Cor. 11:22; Phil. 3:5
2 [a][Rom. 8:29]
3 [a]1 Kin. 19:10, 14
4 [a]1 Kin. 19:18
5 [a]2 Kin. 19:4; Rom. 9:27
6 [a]Rom. 4:4 [1]NU omits the rest of v. 6.
7 [a]Rom. 9:31 [b]Mark 6:52; Rom. 9:18; 11:25; 2 Cor. 3:14
8 [a]Is. 29:10, 13 [b]Deut. 29:3, 4; Is. 6:9; Matt. 13:13, 14; John 12:40; Acts 28:26, 27
9 [a]Ps. 69:22, 23

[a]"*I was found by those who did not
seek Me;
I was made manifest to those who
did not ask for Me.*"

21 But to Israel he says:

[a]"*All day long I have stretched out
My hands
To a disobedient and contrary
people.*"

Israel's Rejection Not Total

11 I say then, [a]has God cast
away His people? [b]Certainly
not! For [c]I also am an Israelite, of
the seed of Abraham, *of* the tribe
of Benjamin.
2 God has not cast away His peo-
ple whom [a]He foreknew. Or do
you not know what the Scripture
says of Elijah, how he pleads with
God against Israel, saying,
3 [a]"LORD, *they have killed Your
prophets and torn down Your al-
tars, and I alone am left, and they
seek my life*"?
4 But what does the divine re-
sponse say to him? [a]"*I have re-
served for Myself seven thousand
men who have not bowed the knee
to Baal.*"
5 [a]Even so then, at this present
time there is a remnant according
to the election of grace.
6 And [a]if by grace, then *it is* no
longer of works; otherwise grace
is no longer grace. [1]But if *it is* of
works, it is no longer grace; other-
wise work is no longer work.
7 What then? [a]Israel has not ob-
tained what it seeks; but the elect
have obtained it, and the rest were
[b]blinded.
8 Just as it is written:

[a]"*God has given them a spirit of
stupor,
[b]Eyes that they should not see
And ears that they should not
hear,
To this very day.*"

9 And David says:

[a]"*Let their table become a snare
and a trap,
A stumbling block and a
recompense to them.*
10 *Let their eyes be darkened, so
that they do not see,
And bow down their back
always.*"

Israel's Rejection Not Final

11 I say then, have they stumbled that they should fall? Certainly not! But [a]through their [1]fall, to provoke them to [b]jealousy, salvation *has come* to the Gentiles.

12 Now if their [1]fall *is* riches for the world, and their failure riches for the Gentiles, how much more their fullness!

13 For I speak to you Gentiles; inasmuch as [a]I am an apostle to the Gentiles, I magnify my ministry,

14 if by any means I may provoke to jealousy *those who are* my flesh and [a]save some of them.

15 For if their being cast away *is* the reconciling of the world, what *will* their acceptance *be* [a]but life from the dead?

16 For if [a]the firstfruit *is* holy, the lump *is* also *holy;* and if the root *is* holy, so *are* the branches.

17 And if [a]some of the branches were broken off, [b]and you, being a wild olive tree, were grafted in among them, and with them became a partaker of the root and [1]fatness of the olive tree,

18 [a]do not boast against the branches. But if you do boast, *remember that* you do not support the root, but the root supports you.

19 You will say then, "Branches were broken off that I might be grafted in."

20 Well *said.* Because of [a]unbelief they were broken off, and you stand by faith. Do not be haughty, but fear.

21 For if God did not spare the natural branches, He may not spare you either.

22 Therefore consider the goodness and severity of God: on those who fell, severity; but toward you, [1]goodness, [a]if you continue in *His* goodness. Otherwise [b]you also will be cut off.

23 And they also, [a]if they do not continue in unbelief, will be grafted in, for God is able to graft them in again.

24 For if you were cut out of the olive tree which is wild by nature, and were grafted contrary to nature into a cultivated olive tree, how much more will these, who *are* natural *branches,* be grafted into their own olive tree?

25 For I do not desire, brethren, that you should be ignorant of this mystery, lest you should be [a]wise in your own [1]opinion, that [b]blindness in part has happened to Israel [c]until the fullness of the Gentiles has come in.

26 And so all Israel will be [1]saved, as it is written:

[a]"The Deliverer will come out of Zion,
And He will turn away ungodliness from Jacob;
27 *For [a]this is My covenant with them,*
When I take away their sins."

28 Concerning the gospel *they are* enemies for your sake, but concerning the election *they are* [a]beloved for the sake of the fathers.

29 For the gifts and the calling of God *are* [a]irrevocable.

30 For as you [a]were once disobedient to God, yet have now obtained mercy through their disobedience,

31 even so these also have now been disobedient, that through the mercy shown you they also may obtain mercy.

32 For God has [1]committed them [a]all to disobedience, that He might have mercy on all.

33 Oh, the depth of the riches both of the wisdom and knowledge of God! How unsearchable *are* His judgments and His ways past finding out!

34 *"For who has known the [a]mind of the LORD?*
Or [b]who has become His counselor?"
35 *"Or [a] who has first given to Him*
And it shall be repaid to him?"

36 For [a]of Him and through Him and to Him *are* all things, [b]to whom *be* glory forever. Amen.

Living Sacrifices to God

12 I [a]beseech[1] you therefore, brethren, by the mercies of God, that you present your bodies [b]a living sacrifice, holy, acceptable to God, *which is* your [2]reasonable service.

2 And [a]do not be conformed to this world, but [b]be transformed by the renewing of your mind, that

11 [a]Is. 42:6, 7; Acts 28:28 [b]Deut. 32:21; Acts 13:46; Rom. 10:19 [1]*trespass*
12 [1]*trespass*
13 [a]Acts 9:15; 22:21; Gal. 1:16; 2:7–9; Eph. 3:8
14 [a]1 Cor. 9:22; 1 Tim. 4:16; James 5:20
15 [a][Is. 26:16–19]
16 [a]Lev. 23:10; [James 1:18]
17 [a]Jer. 11:16; [John 15:2] [b]Acts 2:39; [Eph. 2:12] [1]*richness*
18 [a][1 Cor. 10:12]
20 [a]Heb. 3:19
22 [a]1 Cor. 15:2; Heb. 3:6, 14 [b][John 15:2] [1]NU adds *of God*
23 [a][2 Cor. 3:16]
25 [a]Rom. 12:16 [b]2 Cor. 3:14 [c]Luke 21:24; John 10:16; Rom. 11:12 [1]*estimation*
26 [a]Ps. 14:7; Is. 59:20, 21 [1]Or *delivered*
27 [a]Is. 27:9; Heb. 8:12
28 [a]Deut. 7:8; 10:15; Rom. 9:5
29 [a]Num. 23:19
30 [a][Eph. 2:2]
32 [a]Rom. 3:9; [Gal. 3:22] [1]*shut them all up in*
34 [a]Is. 40:13; Jer. 23:18; 1 Cor. 2:16 [b]Job 36:22
35 [a]Job 41:11
36 [a][1 Cor. 8:6; 11:12]; Col. 1:16; Heb. 2:10 [b]Heb. 13:21

CHAPTER 12

1 [a]1 Cor. 1:10; 2 Cor. 10:1–4 [b]Phil. 4:18; Heb. 10:18, 20 [1]*urge* [2]*rational*
2 [a]Matt. 13:22; Gal. 1:4; 1 John 2:15 [b]Eph. 4:23; [Titus 3:5]

you may [c]prove what *is* that good
and acceptable and perfect will of
God.

Serve God with Spiritual Gifts

3 For I say, [a]through the grace
given to me, to everyone who is
among you, [b]not to think *of himself*
more highly than he ought to
think, but to think soberly, as God
has dealt [c]to each one a measure
of faith.
4 For [a]as we have many mem-
bers in one body, but all the mem-
bers do not have the same func-
tion,
5 so [a]we, *being* many, are one
body in Christ, and individually
members of one another.
6 Having then gifts differing ac-
cording to the grace that is [a]given
to us, *let us use them:* if prophecy,
let us [b]*prophesy* in proportion to
our faith;
7 or ministry, *let us use it* in *our*
ministering; [a]he who teaches, in
teaching;
8 [a]he who exhorts, in exhorta-
tion; [b]he who gives, with liberality;
[c]he who leads, with diligence; he
who shows mercy, [d]with cheerful-
ness.

Behave Like a Christian

9 [a]*Let* love *be* without hypocrisy.
[b]Abhor what is evil. Cling to what
is good.
10 [a]*Be* kindly affectionate to one
another with brotherly love, [b]in
honor giving preference to one an-
other;
11 not lagging in diligence, fer-
vent in spirit, serving the Lord;
12 [a]rejoicing in hope, [b]patient[1] in
tribulation, [c]continuing steadfastly
in prayer;
13 [a]distributing to the needs of the
saints, [b]given[1] to hospitality.
14 [a]Bless those who persecute
you; bless and do not curse.
15 [a]Rejoice with those who re-
joice, and weep with those who
weep.
16 [a]Be of the same mind toward
one another. [b]Do not set your mind
on high things, but associate with
the humble. Do not be wise in your
own opinion.
17 [a]Repay no one evil for evil.
[b]Have[1] regard for good things in
the sight of all men.

2 [c][1 Thess. 4:3]
3 [a]Gal. 2:9 [b]Prov. 25:27 [c][Eph. 4:7]
4 [a]1 Cor. 12:12–14
5 [a][1 Cor. 10:17]
6 [a][John 3:27] [b]Acts 11:27
7 [a]Eph. 4:11
8 [a]Acts 15:32 [b][Matt. 6:1–3] [c][Acts 20:28] [d]2 Cor. 9:7
9 [a]1 Tim. 1:5 [b]Ps. 34:14
10 [a]Heb. 13:1 [b]Phil. 2:3
12 [a]Luke 10:20 [b]Luke 21:19 [c]Luke 18:1 [1]*persevering*
13 [a]1 Cor. 16:1 [b]1 Tim. 3:2 [1]Lit. *pursuing*
14 [a][Matt. 5:44]
15 [a][1 Cor. 12:26]
16 [a][Phil. 2:2; 4:2] [b]Jer. 45:5
17 [a][Matt. 5:39] [b]2 Cor. 8:21 [1]Or *Provide good*
18 [a]Heb. 12:14
19 [a]Lev. 19:18 [b]Deut. 32:35
20 [a]Prov. 25:21, 22
21 [a][Rom. 12:1, 2]

CHAPTER 13

1 [a]1 Pet. 2:13
2 [a][Titus 3:1] [1]Lit. *receive*
3 [a]1 Pet. 2:14
5 [a]Eccl. 8:2 [b][1 Pet. 2:13, 19]
7 [a]Matt. 22:21
8 [a][Gal. 5:13, 14]
9 [a]Ex. 20:13–17; Deut. 5:17–21 [1]NU omits *"You shall not bear false witness,"*

18 If it is possible, as much as de-
pends on you, [a]live peaceably with
all men.
19 Beloved, [a]do not avenge your-
selves, but *rather* give place to
wrath; for it is written, [b]*"Ven-*
geance is Mine, I will repay," says
the Lord.
20 Therefore

[a]*"If your enemy is hungry, feed*
him;
If he is thirsty, give him a drink;
For in so doing you will heap
coals of fire on his head."

21 Do not be overcome by evil, but
[a]overcome evil with good.

Submit to Government

13 Let every soul be [a]subject to
the governing authorities.
For there is no authority except
from God, and the authorities that
exist are appointed by God.
2 Therefore whoever resists [a]the
authority resists the ordinance of
God, and those who resist will
[1]bring judgment on themselves.
3 For rulers are not a terror to
good works, but to evil. Do you
want to be unafraid of the author-
ity? [a]Do what is good, and you will
have praise from the same.
4 For he is God's minister to you
for good. But if you do evil, be
afraid; for he does not bear the
sword in vain; for he is God's min-
ister, an avenger to *execute* wrath
on him who practices evil.
5 Therefore [a]*you* must be sub-
ject, not only because of wrath
[b]but also for conscience' sake.
6 For because of this you also
pay taxes, for they are God's min-
isters attending continually to this
very thing.
7 [a]Render therefore to all their
due: taxes to whom taxes *are due,*
customs to whom customs, fear to
whom fear, honor to whom honor.

Love Your Neighbor

8 Owe no one anything except to
love one another, for [a]he who
loves another has fulfilled the law.
9 For the commandments, [a]*"You*
shall not commit adultery," "You
shall not murder," "You shall not
steal," [1]*"You shall not bear false*
witness," "You shall not covet,"

and if *there is* any other command-
ment, are *all* summed up in this
saying, namely, [b]*"You shall love*
your neighbor as yourself."
10 Love does no harm to a neigh-
bor; therefore [a]love *is* the fulfill-
ment of the law.

Put on Christ

11 And *do* this, knowing the time,
that now *it is* high time [a]to awake
out of sleep; for now our salvation
is nearer than when we *first* be-
lieved.
12 The night is far spent, the day
is at hand. [a]Therefore let us cast
off the works of darkness, and [b]let
us put on the armor of light.
13 [a]Let us walk [1]properly, as in
the day, [b]not in revelry and drunk-
enness, [c]not in lewdness and lust,
[d]not in strife and envy.
14 But [a]put on the Lord Jesus
Christ, and [b]make no provision for
the flesh, to *fulfill its* lusts.

The Law of Liberty

14 Receive[a] one who is weak in
the faith, *but* not to disputes
over doubtful things.
2 For one believes he [a]may eat
all things, but he who is weak eats
only vegetables.
3 Let not him who eats despise
him who does not eat, and [a]let not
him who does not eat judge him
who eats; for God has received
him.
4 [a]Who are you to judge anoth-
er's servant? To his own master he
stands or falls. Indeed, he will be
made to stand, for God is able to
make him stand.
5 [a]One person esteems *one* day
above another; another esteems
every day *alike*. Let each be fully
convinced in his own mind.
6 He who [a]observes the day, ob-
serves *it* to the Lord; [1]and he who
does not observe the day, to the
Lord he does not observe *it*. He
who eats, eats to the Lord, for [b]he
gives God thanks; and he who
does not eat, to the Lord he does
not eat, and gives God thanks.
7 For [a]none of us lives to himself,
and no one dies to himself.
8 For if we [a]live, we live to the
Lord; and if we die, we die to the
Lord. Therefore, whether we live
or die, we are the Lord's.
9 For [a]to this end Christ died
[1]and rose and lived again, that He
might be [b]Lord of both the dead
and the living.
10 But why do you judge your
brother? Or why do you show con-
tempt for your brother? For [a]we
shall all stand before the judgment
seat of [1]Christ.
11 For it is written:

> [a]*"As I live, says the* LORD,
> *Every knee shall bow to Me,*
> *And every tongue shall confess*
> *to God."*

12 So then [a]each of us shall give
account of himself to God.
13 Therefore let us not judge one
another [1]anymore, but rather re-
solve this, [a]not to put a stumbling
block or a cause to fall in *our*
brother's way.

The Law of Love

14 I know and am convinced by
the Lord Jesus [a]that *there is* noth-
ing unclean of itself; but to him
who considers anything to be un-
clean, to him *it is* unclean.
15 Yet if your brother is grieved
because of *your* food, you are no
longer walking in love. [a]Do not de-
stroy with your food the one for
whom Christ died.
16 [a]Therefore do not let your good
be spoken of as evil;
17 [a]for the kingdom of God is not
eating and drinking, but righteous-
ness and [b]peace and joy in the
Holy Spirit.
18 For he who serves Christ in
[1]these things [a]*is* acceptable to God
and approved by men.
19 [a]Therefore let us pursue the
things *which make* for peace and
the things by which [b]one may [1]ed-
ify another.
20 [a]Do not destroy the work of
God for the sake of food. [b]All
things indeed *are* pure, [c]but *it is*
evil for the man who eats with [1]of-
fense.
21 *It is* good neither to eat [a]meat
nor drink wine nor *do anything* by
which your brother stumbles [1]or
is offended or is made weak.
22 [1]Do you have faith? Have *it* to
yourself before God. [a]Happy *is* he
who does not condemn himself in
what he approves.

9 [b]Lev. 19:18
10 [a][Matt. 7:12; 22:39, 40]
11 [a][1 Cor. 15:34]
12 [a]Eph. 5:11 [b][Eph. 6:11, 13]
13 [a]Phil. 4:8 [b]Prov. 23:20 [c][1 Cor. 6:9] [d]James 3:14 [1]*decently*
14 [a]Gal. 3:27 [b][Gal. 5:16]

CHAPTER 14
1 [a][1 Cor. 8:9; 9:22]
2 [a][Titus 1:15]
3 [a][Col. 2:16]
4 [a]James 4:11, 12
5 [a]Gal. 4:10
6 [a]Gal. 4:10 [b][1 Tim. 4:3] [1]NU omits the rest of this sentence.
7 [a][Gal. 2:20]
8 [a]2 Cor. 5:14, 15
9 [a]2 Cor. 5:15 [b]Acts 10:36 [1]NU omits *and rose*
10 [a]2 Cor. 5:10 [1]NU *God*
11 [a]Is. 45:23
12 [a]1 Pet. 4:5
13 [a]1 Cor. 8:9 [1]*any longer*
14 [a]1 Cor. 10:25
15 [a]1 Cor. 8:11
16 [a][Rom. 12:17]
17 [a]1 Cor. 8:8 [b][Rom. 8:6]
18 [a]2 Cor. 8:21 [1]NU *this thing*
19 [a]Rom. 12:18 [b]1 Cor. 14:12 [1]*build up*
20 [a]Rom. 14:15 [b]Acts 10:15 [c]1 Cor. 8:9–12 [1]A feeling of giving offense
21 [a]1 Cor. 8:13 [1]NU omits the rest of v. 21.
22 [a][1 John 3:21] [1]NU *The faith which you have—have*

23 But he who doubts is con-
demned if he eats, because *he does*
not *eat* from faith; for [a]whatever
is not from faith is [1]sin.

Bearing Others' Burdens

15 We [a]then who are strong
ought to bear with the [1]scru-
ples of the weak, and not to please
ourselves.
2 [a]Let each of us please *his*
neighbor for *his* good, leading to
[1]edification.
3 [a]For even Christ did not please
Himself; but as it is written, [b]*"The*
reproaches of those who re-
proached You fell on Me."
4 For [a]whatever things were
written before were written for our
learning, that we through the [1]pa-
tience and comfort of the Scrip-
tures might have hope.
5 [a]Now may the God of patience
and comfort grant you to be like-
minded toward one another, ac-
cording to Christ Jesus,
6 that you may [a]with one mind
and one mouth glorify the God and
Father of our Lord Jesus Christ.

Glorify God Together

7 Therefore [a]receive one an-
other, just [b]as Christ also received
[1]us, to the glory of God.
8 Now I say that [a]Jesus Christ
has become a [1]servant to the cir-
cumcision for the truth of God, [b]to
confirm the promises *made* to the
fathers,
9 and [a]that the Gentiles might
glorify God for *His* mercy, as it is
written:

[b]*"For this reason I will confess to*
You among the Gentiles,
And sing to Your name."

10 And again he says:

[a]*"Rejoice, O Gentiles, with His*
people!"

11 And again:

[a]*"Praise the* LORD, *all you Gentiles!*
Laud Him, all you peoples!"

12 And again, Isaiah says:

[a]*"There shall be a root of Jesse;*
And He who shall rise to reign
over the Gentiles,
In Him the Gentiles shall hope."

13 Now may the God of hope fill
you with all [a]joy and peace in be-
lieving, that you may abound in
hope by the power of the Holy
Spirit.

From Jerusalem to Illyricum

14 Now [a]I myself am confident
concerning you, my brethren, that
you also are full of goodness,
[b]filled with all knowledge, able
also to admonish [1]one another.
15 Nevertheless, brethren, I have
written more boldly to you on
some points, as reminding you,
[a]because of the grace given to me
by God,
16 that [a]I might be a minister of
Jesus Christ to the Gentiles, minis-
tering the gospel of God, that the
[b]offering [1]of the Gentiles might be
acceptable, sanctified by the Holy
Spirit.
17 Therefore I have reason to
glory in Christ Jesus [a]in the things
which pertain to God.
18 For I will not dare to speak of
any of those things [a]which Christ
has not accomplished through me,
in word and deed, [b]to make the
Gentiles obedient—
19 [a]in mighty signs and wonders,
by the power of the Spirit of God,
so that from Jerusalem and round
about to Illyricum I have fully
preached the gospel of Christ.
20 And so I have made it my aim
to preach the gospel, not where
Christ was named, [a]lest I should
build on another man's foun-
dation,
21 but as it is written:

[a]*"To whom He was not announced,*
they shall see;
And those who have not heard
shall understand."

Plan to Visit Rome

22 For this reason [a]I also have
been much hindered from coming
to you.
23 But now no longer having a
place in these parts, and [a]having
a great desire these many years to
come to you,
24 whenever I journey to Spain, [1]I
shall come to you. For I hope to
see you on my journey, [a]and to be
helped on my way there by you,

23 [a]Titus 1:15 [1]M puts Rom. 16:25–27 here.

CHAPTER 15

1 [a]Rom. 14:1; [Gal. 6:1, 2]; 1 Thess. 5:14 [1]*weaknesses*
2 [a]1 Cor. 9:22; 10:24, 33; 2 Cor. 13:9 [1]*building up*
3 [a]Matt. 26:39; [Phil. 2:5–8] [b]Ps. 69:9
4 [a]Rom. 4:23, 24; 1 Cor. 10:11; 2 Tim. 3:16, 17 [1]*perseverance*
5 [a]1 Cor. 1:10; Phil. 1:27
6 [a]Acts 4:24
7 [a]Rom. 14:1, 3 [b]Rom. 5:2 [1]NU, M *you*
8 [a]Matt. 15:24; Acts 3:26 [b][Rom. 4:16]; 2 Cor. 1:20 [1]*minister*
9 [a]John 10:16 [b]2 Sam. 22:50; Ps. 18:49
10 [a]Deut. 32:43
11 [a]Ps. 117:1
12 [a]Is. 11:1, 10
13 [a]Rom. 12:12; 14:17
14 [a]2 Pet. 1:12 [b]1 Cor. 1:5; 8:1, 7, 10 [1]M *others*
15 [a]Rom. 1:5; 12:3
16 [a]Acts 9:15; Rom. 11:13 [b][Is. 66:20] [1]Consisting of
17 [a]Heb. 2:17; 5:1
18 [a]Acts 15:12; 21:19; 2 Cor. 3:5; Gal. 2:8 [b]Rom. 1:5
19 [a]Acts 19:11
20 [a]1 Cor. 3:10; [2 Cor. 10:13, 15, 16]
21 [a]Is. 52:15
22 [a]Rom. 1:13; 1 Thess. 2:17, 18
23 [a]Acts 19:21; 23:11; Rom. 1:10, 11
24 [a]Acts 15:3 [1]NU omits *I shall come to you* and joins *Spain* with the next sentence.

if first I may [b]enjoy your *company*
for a while.
25 But now [a]I am going to Jerusa-
lem to [1]minister to the saints.
26 For [a]it pleased those from
Macedonia and Achaia to make a
certain contribution for the poor
among the saints who are in Jeru-
salem.
27 It pleased them indeed, and
they are their debtors. For [a]if the
Gentiles have been partakers of
their spiritual things, [b]their duty is
also to minister to them in material
things.
28 Therefore, when I have per-
formed this and have sealed to
them [a]this fruit, I shall go by way
of you to Spain.
29 [a]But I know that when I come
to you, I shall come in the fullness
of the blessing [1]of the gospel of
Christ.
30 Now I beg you, brethren,
through the Lord Jesus Christ, and
[a]through the love of the Spirit,
[b]that you strive together with me
in prayers to God for me,
31 [a]that I may be delivered from
those in Judea who [1]do not be-
lieve, and that [b]my service for Je-
rusalem may be acceptable to the
saints,
32 [a]that I may come to you with
joy [b]by the will of God, and may
[c]be refreshed together with you.
33 Now [a]the God of peace *be* with
you all. Amen.

Sister Phoebe Commended

16 I commend to you Phoebe
our sister, who is a servant
of the church in [a]Cenchrea,
2 [a]that you may receive her in
the Lord [b]in a manner worthy of
the saints, and assist her in what-
ever business she has need of you;
for indeed she has been a helper
of many and of myself also.

Greeting Roman Saints

3 Greet [a]Priscilla and Aquila, my
fellow workers in Christ Jesus,
4 who risked their own necks for
my life, to whom not only I give
thanks, but also all the churches
of the Gentiles.
5 Likewise *greet* [a]the church that
is in their house. Greet my beloved
Epaenetus, who is [b]the firstfruits
of [1]Achaia to Christ.
6 Greet Mary, who labored much
for us.
7 Greet Andronicus and Junia,
my countrymen and my fellow
prisoners, who are of note among
the [a]apostles, who also [b]were in
Christ before me.
8 Greet Amplias, my beloved in
the Lord.
9 Greet Urbanus, our fellow
worker in Christ, and Stachys, my
beloved.
10 Greet Apelles, approved in
Christ. Greet those who are of the
household of Aristobulus.
11 Greet Herodion, my [1]country-
man. Greet those who are of the
household of Narcissus who are in
the Lord.
12 Greet Tryphena and Tryphosa,
who have labored in the Lord.
Greet the beloved Persis, who la-
bored much in the Lord.
13 Greet Rufus, [a]chosen in the
Lord, and his mother and mine.
14 Greet Asyncritus, Phlegon,
Hermas, Patrobas, Hermes, and
the brethren who are with them.
15 Greet Philologus and Julia,
Nereus and his sister, and Olym-
pas, and all the saints who are with
them.
16 [a]Greet one another with a holy
kiss. [1]The churches of Christ greet
you.

Avoid Divisive Persons

17 Now I urge you, brethren, note
those [a]who cause divisions and of-
fenses, contrary to the doctrine
which you learned, and [b]avoid
them.
18 For those who are such do not
serve our Lord [1]Jesus Christ, but
[a]their own belly, and [b]by smooth
words and flattering speech de-
ceive the hearts of the simple.
19 For [a]your obedience has be-
come known to all. Therefore I am
glad on your behalf; but I want you
to be [b]wise in what is good, and
[1]simple concerning evil.
20 And [a]the God of peace [b]will
crush Satan under your feet
shortly. [c]The grace of our Lord
Jesus Christ *be* with you. Amen.

Greetings from Paul's Friends

21 [a]Timothy, my fellow worker,
and [b]Lucius, [c]Jason, and [d]Sosipa-
ter, my countrymen, greet you.

24 [b]Rom. 1:12
25 [a]Acts 19:21 [1]*serve*
26 [a]1 Cor. 16:1
27 [a]Rom. 11:17 [b]1 Cor. 9:11
28 [a]Phil. 4:17
29 [a][Rom. 1:11] [1]NU omits *of the gospel*
30 [a]Phil. 2:1 [b]2 Cor. 1:11
31 [a]2 Tim. 3:11; 4:17 [b]2 Cor. 8:4 [1]*are disobedient*
32 [a]Rom. 1:10 [b]Acts 18:21 [c]1 Cor. 16:18
33 [a]1 Cor. 14:33

CHAPTER 16

1 [a]Acts 18:18
2 [a]Phil. 2:29 [b]Phil. 1:27
3 [a]Acts 18:2, 18, 26
5 [a]1 Cor. 16:19 [b]1 Cor. 16:15 [1]NU *Asia*
7 [a]Acts 1:13, 26 [b]Gal. 1:22
11 [1]Or *relative*
13 [a]2 John 1
16 [a]1 Cor. 16:20 [1]NU *All the churches*
17 [a][Acts 15:1] [b][1 Cor. 5:9]
18 [a]Phil. 3:19 [b]Col. 2:4 [1]NU, M omit *Jesus*
19 [a]Rom. 1:8 [b]Matt. 10:16 [1]*innocent*
20 [a]Rom. 15:33 [b]Gen. 3:15 [c]1 Cor. 16:23
21 [a]Acts 16:1 [b]Acts 13:1 [c]Acts 17:5 [d]Acts 20:4

22 I, Tertius, who wrote *this* epis-
tle, greet you in the Lord.
23 [a]Gaius, my host and *the host*
of the whole church, greets you.
[b]Erastus, the treasurer of the
city, greets you, and Quartus, a
brother.
24 [a]The[1] grace of our Lord Jesus
Christ *be* with you all. Amen.

Benediction

25 [1]Now [a]to Him who is able to
establish you [b]according to my
gospel and the preaching of Jesus
Christ, [c]according to the revelation
of the mystery [d]kept secret since
the world began
26 but [a]now made manifest, and
by the prophetic Scriptures made
known to all nations, according to
the commandment of the everlast-
ing God, for [b]obedience to the
faith—
27 to [a]God, alone wise, *be* glory
through Jesus Christ forever.
Amen.

23 [a]1 Cor. 1:14 [b]Acts 19:22
24 [a]1 Thess. 5:28 [1]NU omits v. 24.
25 [a][Eph. 3:20] [b]Rom. 2:16 [c]Eph. 1:9 [d]Col. 1:26; 2:2; 4:3 [1]M puts Rom. 16:25–27 after Rom. 14:23.
26 [a]Eph. 1:9 [b]Rom. 1:5
27 [a]Jude 25

The First Epistle of Paul the Apostle to the

Corinthians

CORINTH, the most important city in Greece during Paul's day, was a bustling hub of worldwide commerce, degraded culture, and idolatrous religion. There Paul founded a church (Acts 18:1–17), and two of his letters are addressed "To the church of God which is at Corinth" (1:2; 2 Cor. 1:1).

First Corinthians reveals the problems, pressures, and struggles of a church called out of a pagan society. Paul addresses a variety of problems in the lifestyle of the Corinthian church: factions, lawsuits, immorality, questionable practices, abuse of the Lord's Supper, and spiritual gifts. In addition to words of discipline, Paul shares words of counsel in answer to questions raised by the Corinthian believers.

The oldest recorded title of this epistle is *Pros Korinthious A,* in effect, the "First to the Corinthians." The *A* was no doubt a later addition to distinguish this book from Second Corinthians.

CHAPTER 1

Greeting

PAUL, [a]called *to be* an apostle of Jesus Christ [b]through the will of God, and [c]Sosthenes *our* brother,

2 To the church of God which is at Corinth, to those who [a]are [1]sanctified in Christ Jesus, [b]called *to be* saints, with all who in every place call on the name of Jesus Christ [c]our Lord, [d]both theirs and ours:

3 [a]Grace to you and peace from God our Father and the Lord Jesus Christ.

Spiritual Gifts at Corinth

4 [a]I thank my God always concerning you for the grace of God which was given to you by Christ Jesus,
5 that you were enriched in every thing by Him [a]in all [1]utterance and all knowledge,
6 even as [a]the testimony of Christ was confirmed [1]in you,
7 so that you come short in no gift, eagerly [a]waiting for the revelation of our Lord Jesus Christ,
8 [a]who will also confirm you to the end, [b]*that you may be* blameless in the day of our Lord Jesus Christ.
9 [a]God *is* faithful, by whom you were called into [b]the fellowship of His Son, Jesus Christ our Lord.

Sectarianism Is Sin

10 Now I plead with you, brethren, by the name of our Lord Jesus Christ, [a]that you all [1]speak the same thing, and *that* there be no [2]divisions among you, but *that* you be perfectly joined together in the same mind and in the same judgment.
11 For it has been declared to me concerning you, my brethren, by those of Chloe's *household,* that there are [1]contentions among you.
12 Now I say this, that [a]each of you says, "I am of Paul," or "I am of [b]Apollos," or "I am of [c]Cephas," or "I am of Christ."
13 [a]Is Christ divided? Was Paul crucified for you? Or were you baptized in the name of Paul?
14 I thank God that I baptized [a]none of you except [b]Crispus and [c]Gaius,
15 lest anyone should say that I had baptized in my own name.
16 Yes, I also baptized the household of [a]Stephanas. Besides, I do

---

CHAPTER 1
1 [a]Rom. 1:1 [b]2 Cor. 1:1 [c]Acts 18:17
2 [a][Acts 15:9] [b]Rom. 1:7 [c][1 Cor. 8:6] [d][Rom. 3:22] [1]*set apart*
3 [a]Rom. 1:7
4 [a]Rom. 1:8
5 [a][1 Cor. 12:8] [1]*speech*
6 [a]2 Tim. 1:8 [1]Or *among*
7 [a]Phil. 3:20
8 [a]1 Thess. 3:13; 5:23 [b]Col. 1:22; 2:7
9 [a]Is. 49:7 [b][John 15:4]
10 [a]2 Cor. 13:11 [1]Have a uniform testimony [2]*schisms* or *dissensions*
11 [1]*quarrels*
12 [a]1 Cor. 3:4 [b]Acts 18:24 [c]John 1:42
13 [a]2 Cor. 11:4
14 [a]John 4:2 [b]Acts 18:8 [c]Rom. 16:23
16 [a]1 Cor. 16:15, 17

not know whether I baptized any
other.
17 For Christ did not send me to
baptize, but to preach the gospel,
[a]not with wisdom of words, lest
the cross of Christ should be made
of no effect.

Christ the Power and Wisdom of God

18 For the [1]message of the cross
is [a]foolishness to [b]those who are
perishing, but to us [c]who are being
saved it is the [d]power of God.
19 For it is written:

[a]*"I will destroy the wisdom of the*
wise,
And bring to nothing the
understanding of the prudent."

20 [a]Where *is* the wise? Where *is*
the scribe? Where *is* the [1]disputer
of this age? [b]Has not God made
foolish the wisdom of this world?
21 For since, in the [a]wisdom of
God, the world through wisdom
did not know God, it pleased God
through the foolishness of the
message preached to save those
who believe.
22 For [a]Jews request a sign, and
Greeks seek after wisdom;
23 but we preach Christ crucified,
[a]to the Jews a [1]stumbling block
and to the [2]Greeks [b]foolishness,
24 but to those who are called,
both Jews and Greeks, Christ [a]the
power of God and [b]the wisdom of
God.
25 Because the foolishness of God
is wiser than men, and the weak-
ness of God is stronger than men.

Glory Only in the Lord

26 For [1]you see your calling,
brethren, [a]that not many wise ac-
cording to the flesh, not many
mighty, not many [2]noble, *are*
called.
27 But [a]God has chosen the fool-
ish things of the world to put to
shame the wise, and God has cho-
sen the weak things of the world
to put to shame the things which
are mighty;
28 and the [1]base things of the
world and the things which are de-
spised God has chosen, and the
things which are not, to bring to
nothing the things that are,
29 that no flesh should glory in
His presence.
30 But of Him you are in Christ
Jesus, who became for us wisdom
from God—and [a]righteousness
and sanctification and redemp-
tion—
31 that, as it is written, [a]*"He who*
glories, let him glory in the LORD."

Christ Crucified

2 And I, brethren, when I came
to you, did not come with ex-
cellence of speech or of wisdom
declaring to you the [1]testimony of
God.
2 For I determined not to know
anything among you [a]except Jesus
Christ and Him crucified.
3 [a]I was with you [b]in weakness,
in fear, and in much trembling.
4 And my speech and my preach-
ing [a]*were* not with persuasive
words of [1]human wisdom, [b]but in
demonstration of the Spirit and of
power,
5 that your faith should not be in
the wisdom of men but in the
[a]power of God.

Spiritual Wisdom

6 However, we speak wisdom
among those who are mature, yet
not the wisdom of this age, nor of
the rulers of this age, who are com-
ing to nothing.
7 But we speak the wisdom of
God in a mystery, the hidden *wis-*
dom which God [1]ordained before
the ages for our glory,
8 which none of the rulers of this
age knew; for [a]had they known,
they would not have [b]crucified the
Lord of glory.
9 But as it is written:

[a]*"Eye has not seen, nor ear heard,*
Nor have entered into the heart
of man
The things which God has
prepared for those who love
Him."

10 But [a]God has revealed *them* to
us through His Spirit. For the
Spirit searches all things, yes, the
deep things of God.
11 For what man knows the things
of a man except the [a]spirit of the
man which is in him? [b]Even so no
one knows the things of God ex-
cept the Spirit of God.

17 [a][1 Cor. 2:1, 4, 13]
18 [a]1 Cor. 2:14 [b]2 Cor. 2:15 [c][1 Cor. 15:2] [d]Rom. 1:16; 1 Cor. 1:24 [1]Lit. *word*
19 [a]Is. 29:14
20 [a]Is. 19:12; 33:18 [b]Job 12:17; Matt. 13:22; 1 Cor. 2:6, 8; 3:18, 19 [1]*debater*
21 [a]Dan. 2:20; [Rom. 11:33]
22 [a]Matt. 12:38; Mark 8:11; John 2:18; 4:48
23 [a]Is. 8:14; Luke 2:34; John 6:60; Gal. 5:11; [1 Pet. 2:8] [b][1 Cor. 2:14] [1]Gr. *skandalon, offense* [2]NU *Gentiles*
24 [a][Rom. 1:4] [b]Col. 2:3
26 [a]John 7:48 [1]*consider* [2]*well-born*
27 [a]Ps. 8:2; Matt. 11:25
28 [1]*insignificant or lowly*
30 [a]Jer. 23:5; 33:16; [2 Cor. 5:21; Phil. 3:9]
31 [a]Jer. 9:23, 24; 2 Cor. 10:17

CHAPTER 2

1 [1]NU *mystery*
2 [a]1 Cor. 1:23; Gal. 6:14
3 [a]Acts 18:1 [b][2 Cor. 4:7]
4 [a]2 Pet. 1:16 [b]Rom. 15:19; 1 Cor. 4:20 [1]NU omits *human*
5 [a]Rom. 1:16; 1 Thess. 1:5
7 [1]*predetermined*
8 [a]Luke 23:34 [b]Matt. 27:33–50
9 [a][Is. 64:4; 65:17]
10 [a]Matt. 11:25; 13:11; 16:17; [Gal. 1:12; Eph. 3:3, 5]
11 [a]Job 32:8; Eccl. 12:7; [1 Cor. 6:20; James 2:26] [b]Rom. 11:33

12 Now we have received, not the
spirit of the world, but [a]the Spirit
who is from God, that we might
know the things that have been
freely given to us by God.
13 These things we also speak, not
in words which man's wisdom
teaches but which the [1]Holy Spirit
teaches, comparing spiritual
things with spiritual.
14 [a]But the natural man does not
receive the things of the Spirit of
God, for they are foolishness to
him; nor can he know *them*, be-
cause they are spiritually dis-
cerned.
15 But he who is spiritual judges
all things, yet he himself is *rightly*
judged by no one.
16 For [a]*"who has known the mind*
of the LORD *that he may instruct*
Him?" [b]But we have the mind of
Christ.

Sectarianism Is Carnal

3 And I, brethren, could not
speak to you as to spiritual
people but as to carnal, as to
[a]babes in Christ.
2 I fed you with [a]milk and not
with solid food; [b]for until now you
were not able *to receive it*, and
even now you are still not able;
3 for you are still carnal. For
where *there are* envy, strife, and
divisions among you, are you not
carnal and [1]behaving like *mere*
men?
4 For when one says, "I am of
Paul," and another, "I *am* of Apol-
los," are you not carnal?

Watering, Working, Warning

5 Who then is Paul, and who *is*
Apollos, but [a]ministers through
whom you believed, as the Lord
gave to each one?
6 [a]I planted, [b]Apollos watered,
[c]but God gave the increase.
7 So then [a]neither he who plants
is anything, nor he who waters,
but God who gives the increase.
8 Now he who plants and he who
waters are one, [a]and each one will
receive his own reward according
to his own labor.
9 For [a]we are God's fellow work-
ers; you are God's field, *you are*
[b]God's building.
10 [a]According to the grace of God
which was given to me, as a wise
master builder I have laid [b]the
foundation, and another builds on
it. But let each one take heed how
he builds on it.
11 For no other foundation can
anyone lay than [a]that which is
laid, [b]which is Jesus Christ.
12 Now if anyone builds on this
foundation *with* gold, silver, pre-
cious stones, wood, hay, straw,
13 each one's work will become
clear; for the Day [a]will declare it,
because [b]it will be revealed by fire;
and the fire will test each one's
work, of what sort it is.
14 If anyone's work which he has
built on *it* endures, he will receive
a reward.
15 If anyone's work is burned, he
will suffer loss; but he himself will
be saved, yet so as through fire.
16 [a]Do you not know that you are
the temple of God and *that* the
Spirit of God dwells in you?
17 If anyone [1]defiles the temple of
God, God will destroy him. For the
temple of God is holy, which *tem-*
ple you are.

Avoid Worldly Wisdom

18 [a]Let no one deceive himself. If
anyone among you seems to be
wise in this age, let him become a
fool that he may become wise.
19 For the wisdom of this world
is foolishness with God. For it is
written, [a]*"He catches the wise in*
their own craftiness";
20 and again, [a]*"The* LORD *knows*
the thoughts of the wise, that they
are futile."
21 Therefore let no one boast in
men. For [a]all things are yours:
22 whether Paul or Apollos or Ce-
phas, or the world or life or death,
or things present or things to
come—all are yours.
23 And [a]you *are* Christ's, and
Christ *is* God's.

Stewards of the Mysteries of God

4 Let a man so consider us, as
[a]servants of Christ [b]and stew-
ards of the mysteries of God.
2 Moreover it is required in stew-
ards that one be found faithful.
3 But with me it is a very small
thing that I should be judged by
you or by a human [1]court. In fact,
I do not even judge myself.
4 For I know of nothing against

12 [a][Rom. 8:15]
13 [1]NU omits *Holy*
14 [a]Matt. 16:23
16 [a]Is. 40:13 [b][John 15:15]

CHAPTER 3

1 [a]Heb. 5:13
2 [a]1 Pet. 2:2 [b]John 16:12
3 [1]Lit. *walking according to man*
5 [a]2 Cor. 3:3, 6; 4:1; 5:18; 6:4
6 [a]Acts 18:4 [b]Acts 18:24–27 [c][2 Cor. 3:5]
7 [a][Gal. 6:3]
8 [a]Ps. 62:12
9 [a]2 Cor. 6:1 [b][Eph. 2:20–22]
10 [a]Rom. 1:5 [b]1 Cor. 4:15
11 [a]Is. 28:16 [b]Eph. 2:20
13 [a]1 Pet. 1:7 [b]Luke 2:35
16 [a]2 Cor. 6:16
17 [1]*destroys*
18 [a]Prov. 3:7
19 [a]Job 5:13
20 [a]Ps. 94:11
21 [a][2 Cor. 4:5]
23 [a]2 Cor. 10:7

CHAPTER 4

1 [a]Col. 1:25 [b]Titus 1:7
3 [1]Lit. *day*

myself, yet I am not justified by
this; but He who judges me is the
Lord.
5 [a]Therefore judge nothing be-
fore the time, until the Lord comes,
who will both bring to [b]light the
hidden things of darkness and [c]re-
veal the [1]counsels of the hearts.
[d]Then each one's praise will come
from God.

Fools for Christ's Sake

6 Now these things, brethren, I
have figuratively transferred to
myself and Apollos for your sakes,
that you may learn in us not
to think beyond what is written,
that none of you may be [1]puffed
up on behalf of one against the
other.
7 For who [1]makes you differ *from*
another? And [a]what do you have
that you did not receive? Now if
you did indeed receive *it*, why do
you boast as if you had not re-
ceived *it*?
8 You are already full! [a]You are
already rich! You have reigned as
kings without us—and indeed I
could wish you did reign, that we
also might reign with you!
9 For I think that God has dis-
played us, the apostles, last, as
men condemned to death; for we
have been made a [a]spectacle[1] to
the world, both to angels and to
men.
10 We *are* [a]fools for Christ's sake,
but you *are* wise in Christ! [b]We *are*
weak, but you *are* strong! You *are*
distinguished, but we *are* dis-
honored!
11 To the present hour we both
hunger and thirst, and we are
poorly clothed, and beaten, and
homeless.
12 [a]And we labor, working with
our own hands. [b]Being reviled, we
bless; being persecuted, we en-
dure;
13 being defamed, we [1]entreat.
[a]We have been made as the filth
of the world, the offscouring of all
things until now.

Paul's Paternal Care

14 I do not write these things to
shame you, but [a]as my beloved
children I warn *you*.
15 For though you might have ten
thousand instructors in Christ, yet
you do not *have* many fathers; for
[a]in Christ Jesus I have begotten
you through the gospel.
16 Therefore I urge you, [a]imitate
me.
17 For this reason I have sent
[a]Timothy to you, [b]who is my be-
loved and faithful son in the Lord,
who will [c]remind you of my ways
in Christ, as I [d]teach everywhere
[e]in every church.
18 [a]Now some are [1]puffed up, as
though I were not coming to you.
19 [a]But I will come to you shortly,
[b]if the Lord wills, and I will know,
not the word of those who are
puffed up, but the power.
20 For [a]the kingdom of God *is* not
in word but in [b]power.
21 What do you want? [a]Shall I
come to you with a rod, or in love
and a spirit of gentleness?

Immorality Defiles the Church

5 It is actually reported *that*
there is sexual immorality
among you, and such sexual im-
morality as is not even [1]named
among the Gentiles—that a man
has his father's [a]wife!
2 [a]And you are [1]puffed up, and
have not rather [b]mourned, that he
who has done this deed might be
taken away from among you.
3 [a]For I indeed, as absent in body
but present in spirit, have already
judged (as though I were present)
him who has so done this deed.
4 In the [a]name of our Lord Jesus
Christ, when you are gathered to-
gether, along with my spirit, [b]with
the power of our Lord Jesus
Christ,
5 [a]deliver such a one to [b]Satan
for the destruction of the flesh,
that his spirit may be saved in the
day of the Lord [1]Jesus.
6 [a]Your glorying is not good. Do
you not know that [b]a little leaven
leavens the whole lump?
7 Therefore [1]purge out the old
leaven, that you may be a new
lump, since you truly are un-
leavened. For indeed [a]Christ,
our [b]Passover, was sacrificed [2]for
us.
8 Therefore [a]let us keep the feast,
[b]not with old leaven, nor [c]with the
leaven of malice and wickedness,
but with the unleavened *bread* of
sincerity and truth.

---

5 [a]Matt. 7:1 [b]Matt. 10:26 [c]1 Cor. 3:13 [d]Rom. 2:29 [1]*motives*
6 [1]*arrogant*
7 [a]John 3:27 [1]*distinguishes you*
8 [a]Rev. 3:17
9 [a]Heb. 10:33 [1]Lit. *theater*
10 [a]Acts 17:18; 26:24 [b]2 Cor. 13:9
12 [a]Acts 18:3; 20:34 [b]Matt. 5:44
13 [a]Lam. 3:45 [1]*exhort, encourage*
14 [a]1 Thess. 2:11
15 [a]Gal. 4:19
16 [a][1 Cor. 11:1]
17 [a]Acts 19:22 [b]1 Tim. 1:2, 18 [c]1 Cor. 11:2 [d]1 Cor. 7:17 [e]1 Cor. 14:33
18 [a]1 Cor. 5:2 [1]*arrogant*
19 [a]Acts 19:21; 20:2 [b]Acts 18:21
20 [a]1 Thess. 1:5 [b]1 Cor. 2:4
21 [a]2 Cor. 10:2

CHAPTER 5

1 [a]Lev. 18:6–8 [1]NU omits *named*
2 [a]1 Cor. 4:18 [b]2 Cor. 7:7–10 [1]*arrogant*
3 [a]Col. 2:5
4 [a][Matt. 18:20] [b][John 20:23]
5 [a]1 Tim. 1:20 [b][Acts 26:18] [1]NU omits *Jesus*
6 [a]1 Cor. 3:21 [b]Gal. 5:9
7 [a]Is. 53:7 [b]John 19:14 [1]*clean out* [2]NU omits *for us*
8 [a]Ex. 12:15 [b]Deut. 16:3 [c]Matt. 16:6

Immorality Must Be Judged

9 I wrote to you in my epistle [a]not
to [1]keep company with sexually
immoral people.
10 Yet *I* certainly *did* not *mean*
with the sexually immoral people
of this world, or with the covetous,
or extortioners, or idolaters, since
then you would need to go [a]out of
the world.
11 But now I have written to you
not to keep company [a]with anyone
named a brother, who is sexually
immoral, or covetous, or an idola-
ter, or a reviler, or a drunkard, or
an extortioner—[b]not even to eat
with such a person.
12 For what *have* I *to do* with
judging those also who are out-
side? Do you not judge those who
are inside?
13 But those who are outside God
judges. Therefore [a]*"put away from
yourselves the evil person."*

Do Not Sue the Brethren

6 Dare any of you, having a mat-
ter against another, go to law
before the unrighteous, and not
before the [a]saints?
2 Do you not know that [a]the
saints will judge the world? And
if the world will be judged by you,
are you unworthy to judge the
smallest matters?
3 Do you not know that we shall
[a]judge angels? How much more,
things that pertain to this life?
4 If then you have [1]judgments
concerning things pertaining to
this life, do you appoint those who
are least esteemed by the church
to judge?
5 I say this to your shame. Is it
so, that there is not a wise man
among you, not even one, who will
be able to judge between his breth-
ren?
6 But brother goes to law against
brother, and that before un-
believers!
7 Now therefore, it is already an
utter failure for you that you go
to law against one another. [a]Why
do you not rather accept wrong?
Why do you not rather *let your-
selves* be cheated?
8 No, you yourselves do wrong
and cheat, and *you do* these things
to your brethren!
9 Do you not know that the un-
righteous will not inherit the king-
dom of God? Do not be deceived.
[a]Neither fornicators, nor idolaters,
nor adulterers, nor [1]homosexuals,
nor [2]sodomites,
10 nor thieves, nor covetous, nor
drunkards, nor revilers, nor extor-
tioners will inherit the kingdom of
God.
11 And such were [a]some of you.
[b]But you were washed, but you
were [1]sanctified, but you were
justified in the name of the Lord
Jesus and by the Spirit of our God.

Glorify God in Body and Spirit

12 [a]All things are lawful for me,
but all things are not [1]helpful. All
things are lawful for me, but I will
not be brought under the power of
[2]any.
13 [a]Foods for the stomach and the
stomach for foods, but God will de-
stroy both it and them. Now the
body *is* not for [b]sexual immorality
but [c]for the Lord, [d]and the Lord
for the body.
14 And [a]God both raised up the
Lord and will also raise us up [b]by
His power.
15 Do you not know that [a]your
bodies are members of Christ?
Shall I then take the members of
Christ and make *them* members of
a harlot? Certainly not!
16 Or do you not know that he
who is joined to a harlot is one
body *with her?* For [a]*"the two,"* He
says, *"shall become one flesh."*
17 [a]But he who is joined to the
Lord is one spirit *with Him.*
18 [a]Flee sexual immorality. Every
sin that a man does is outside the
body, but he who commits sexual
immorality sins [b]against his own
body.
19 Or [a]do you not know that your
body is the temple of the Holy
Spirit *who is* in you, whom you
have from God, [b]and you are not
your own?
20 For [a]you were bought at a
price; therefore glorify God in
your body [1]and in your spirit,
which are God's.

Principles of Marriage

7 Now concerning the things of
which you wrote to me: [a]*It is*

---

9 [a]2 Cor. 6:14 [1]*associate*
10 [a]John 17:15
11 [a]Matt. 18:17 [b]Gal. 2:12
13 [a]Deut. 13:5; 17:7, 12; 19:19; 21:21; 22:21, 24; 24:7

CHAPTER 6

1 [a]Dan. 7:22
2 [a]Ps. 49:14
3 [a]2 Pet. 2:4
4 [1]*courts*
7 [a][Prov. 20:22]
9 [a]Gal. 5:21 [1]*catamites,* those submitting to homosexuals [2]*male homosexuals*
11 [a][1 Cor. 12:2] [b]Heb. 10:22 [1]*set apart*
12 [a]1 Cor. 10:23 [1]*profitable* [2]Or *anything*
13 [a]Matt. 15:17 [b]Gal. 5:19 [c]1 Thess. 4:3 [d][Eph. 5:23]
14 [a]2 Cor. 4:14 [b]Eph. 1:19
15 [a]Rom. 12:5
16 [a]Gen. 2:24
17 [a][John 17:21–23]
18 [a]Heb. 13:4 [b]Rom. 1:24
19 [a]2 Cor. 6:16 [b]Rom. 14:7
20 [a]2 Pet. 2:1 [1]NU omits the rest of v. 20.

CHAPTER 7

1 [a]1 Cor. 7:8, 26

good for a man not to touch a
woman.
2 Nevertheless, because of sex-
ual immorality, let each man have
his own wife, and let each woman
have her own husband.
3 [a]Let the husband render to his
wife the affection due her, and
likewise also the wife to her hus-
band.
4 The wife does not have author-
ity over her own body, but the hus-
band *does.* And likewise the hus-
band does not have authority over
his own body, but the wife *does.*
5 [a]Do not deprive one another
except with consent for a time,
that you may give yourselves to
fasting and prayer; and come to-
gether again so that [b]Satan does
not tempt you because of your lack
of self-control.
6 But I say this as a concession,
[a]not as a commandment.
7 For [a]I wish that all men were
even as I myself. But each one has
his own gift from God, one in this
manner and another in that.
8 But I say to the unmarried and
to the widows: [a]It is good for them
if they remain even as I am;
9 but [a]if they cannot exercise
self-control, let them marry. For it
is better to marry than to burn
with passion.

Keep Your Marriage Vows

10 Now to the married I com-
mand, *yet* not I but the [a]Lord: [b]A
wife is not to depart from *her* hus-
band.
11 But even if she does depart, let
her remain unmarried or be recon-
ciled to *her* husband. And a hus-
band is not to divorce *his* wife.
12 But to the rest I, not the Lord,
say: If any brother has a wife who
does not believe, and she is willing
to live with him, let him not di-
vorce her.
13 And a woman who has a hus-
band who does not believe, if he
is willing to live with her, let her
not divorce him.
14 For the unbelieving husband is
sanctified by the wife, and the
unbelieving wife is sanctified by
the husband; otherwise [a]your chil-
dren would be unclean, but now
they are holy.
15 But if the unbeliever departs,
let him depart; a brother or a sister
is not under bondage in such
cases. But God has called us [a]to
peace.
16 For how do you know, O wife,
whether you will [a]save *your* hus-
band? Or how do you know, O
husband, whether you will save
your wife?

Live as You Are Called

17 But as God has distributed to
each one, as the Lord has called
each one, so let him walk. And [a]so
I [1]ordain in all the churches.
18 Was anyone called while cir-
cumcised? Let him not become
uncircumcised. Was anyone called
while uncircumcised? [a]Let him not
be circumcised.
19 [a]Circumcision is nothing and
uncircumcision is nothing, but
[b]keeping the commandments of
God *is what matters.*
20 Let each one remain in the
same calling in which he was
called.
21 Were you called *while* a slave?
Do not be concerned about it; but
if you can be made free, rather
use *it.*
22 For he who is called in the Lord
while a slave is [a]the Lord's freed-
man. Likewise he who is called
while free is [b]Christ's slave.
23 [a]You were bought at a price;
do not become slaves of men.
24 Brethren, let each one remain
with [a]God in that *state* in which
he was called.

To the Unmarried and Widows

25 Now concerning virgins: [a]I
have no commandment from the
Lord; yet I give judgment as one
[b]whom the Lord in His mercy *has
made* [c]trustworthy.
26 I suppose therefore that this is
good because of the present dis-
tress—[a]that *it is* good for a man
to remain as he is:
27 Are you bound to a wife? Do
not seek to be loosed. Are you
loosed from a wife? Do not seek
a wife.
28 But even if you do marry, you
have not sinned; and if a virgin
marries, she has not sinned. Never-
theless such will have trouble in
the flesh, but I would spare you.
29 But [a]this I say, brethren, the

3 [a]Ex. 21:10
5 [a]Joel 2:16 [b]1 Thess. 3:5
6 [a]2 Cor. 8:8
7 [a]Acts 26:29
8 [a]1 Cor. 7:1, 26
9 [a]1 Tim. 5:14
10 [a]Mark 10:6–10 [b]Mal. 2:14; [Matt. 5:32]
14 [a]Ezra 9:2; Mal. 2:15
15 [a]Rom. 12:18
16 [a]Rom. 11:14; 1 Pet. 3:1
17 [a]1 Cor. 4:17 [1]*direct*
18 [a]Acts 15:1
19 [a][Rom. 2:27, 29; Gal. 3:28; 5:6; 6:15; Col. 3:11] [b][John 15:14]
22 [a][John 8:36]; Rom. 6:18; Philem. 16 [b][1 Cor. 9:21; Gal. 5:13]; Eph. 6:6; Col. 3:24; 1 Pet. 2:16
23 [a]Lev. 25:42; 1 Cor. 6:20; 1 Pet. 1:18, 19; Rev. 5:9
24 [a][Eph. 6:5–8; Col. 3:22–24]
25 [a]2 Cor. 8:8 [b]2 Cor. 4:1; 1 Tim. 1:13, 16 [c]1 Tim. 1:12
26 [a]1 Cor. 7:1, 8
29 [a][Rom. 13:11]; 1 Cor. 7:31; 1 Pet. 4:7; [2 Pet. 3:8, 9]

time *is* short, so that from now on
even those who have wives should
be as though they had none,
30 those who weep as though they
did not weep, those who rejoice as
though they did not rejoice, those
who buy as though they did not
possess,
31 and those who use this world
as not [a]misusing *it.* For [b]the form
of this world is passing away.
32 But I want you to be without
[1]care. [a]He who is unmarried [2]cares
for the things of the Lord—how he
may please the Lord.
33 But he who is married cares
about the things of the world—
how he may please *his* wife.
34 There is a difference between
a wife and a virgin. The unmarried
woman [a]cares about the things of
the Lord, that she may be holy
both in body and in spirit. But she
who is married cares about the
things of the world—how she may
please *her* husband.
35 And this I say for your own
profit, not that I may put a leash
on you, but for what is proper, and
that you may serve the Lord with-
out distraction.
36 But if any man thinks he is be-
having improperly toward his
[1]virgin, if she is past the flower of
youth, and thus it must be, let him
do what he wishes. He does not
sin; let them marry.
37 Nevertheless he who stands
steadfast in his heart, having no
necessity, but has power over his
own will, and has so determined
in his heart that he will keep his
[1]virgin, does well.
38 [a]So then he who gives [1]*her* in
marriage does well, but he who
does not give *her* in marriage does
better.
39 [a]A wife is bound by law as long
as her husband lives; but if her
husband dies, she is at liberty to
be married to whom she wishes,
[b]only in the Lord.
40 But she is happier if she re-
mains as she is, [a]according to my
judgment—and [b]I think I also have
the Spirit of God.

Be Sensitive to Conscience

8 Now [a]concerning things of-
fered to idols: We know that
we all have [b]knowledge. [c]Knowl-
edge [1]puffs up, but love [2]edifies.
2 And [a]if anyone thinks that he
knows anything, he knows noth-
ing yet as he ought to know.
3 But if anyone loves God, this
one is known by Him.
4 Therefore concerning the eat-
ing of things offered to idols, we
know that [a]an idol *is* nothing in
the world, [b]and that *there is* no
other God but one.
5 For even if there are [a]so-called
gods, whether in heaven or on
earth (as there are many gods and
many lords),
6 yet [a]for us *there is* one God, the
Father, [b]of whom *are* all things,
and we for Him; and [c]one Lord
Jesus Christ, [d]through whom *are*
all things, and [e]through whom we
live.
7 However, *there is* not in every-
one that knowledge; for some,
[a]with consciousness of the idol,
until now eat *it* as a thing offered
to an idol; and their conscience,
being weak, is [b]defiled.
8 But [a]food does not commend us
to God; for neither if we eat are
we the better, nor if we do not eat
are we the worse.
9 But [a]beware lest somehow this
liberty of yours become [b]a [1]stum-
bling block to those who are weak.
10 For if anyone sees you who
have knowledge eating in an idol's
temple, will not [a]the conscience
of him who is weak be embold-
ened to eat those things offered to
idols?
11 And [a]because of your knowl-
edge shall the weak brother per-
ish, for whom Christ died?
12 But [a]when you thus sin against
the brethren, and wound their
weak conscience, you sin against
Christ.
13 Therefore, [a]if food makes my
brother stumble, I will never again
eat meat, lest I make my brother
stumble.

A Pattern of Self-Denial

9 Am [a]I not an apostle? Am I not
free? [b]Have I not seen Jesus
Christ our Lord? [c]Are you not my
work in the Lord?
2 If I am not an apostle to others,
yet doubtless I am to you. For you
are [a]the [1]seal of my apostleship in
the Lord.

---

31 [a]1 Cor. 9:18 [b][1 John 2:17]
32 [a]1 Tim. 5:5 [1]*concern* [2]*is concerned about*
34 [a]Luke 10:40
36 [1]Or *virgin daughter*
37 [1]Or *virgin daughter*
38 [a]Heb. 13:4 [1]NU *his own virgin*
39 [a]Rom. 7:2 [b]2 Cor. 6:14
40 [a]1 Cor. 7:6, 25 [b]1 Thess. 4:8

CHAPTER 8

1 [a]Acts 15:20 [b]Rom. 14:14 [c]Rom. 14:3 [1]*makes arrogant* [2]*builds up*
2 [a][1 Cor. 13:8–12]
4 [a]Is. 41:24 [b]Deut. 4:35, 39; 6:4
5 [a][John 10:34]
6 [a]Mal. 2:10 [b]Acts 17:28 [c]John 13:13 [d]John 1:3 [e]Rom. 5:11
7 [a][1 Cor. 10:28] [b]Rom. 14:14, 22
8 [a][Rom. 14:17]
9 [a]Gal. 5:13 [b]Rom. 14:13, 21 [1]*cause of offense*
10 [a]1 Cor. 10:28
11 [a]Rom. 14:15, 20
12 [a]Matt. 25:40
13 [a]Rom. 14:21

CHAPTER 9

1 [a]Acts 9:15 [b]1 Cor. 15:8 [c]1 Cor. 3:6; 4:15
2 [a]2 Cor. 12:12 [1]*certification*

3 My defense to those who examine me is this:
4 [a]Do we have no [1]right to eat and drink?
5 Do we have no right to take along [1]a believing wife, as *do* also the other apostles, [a]the brothers of the Lord, and [b]Cephas?
6 Or *is it* only Barnabas and I [a]*who* have no right to refrain from working?
7 Who ever [a]goes to war at his own expense? Who [b]plants a vineyard and does not eat of its fruit? Or who [c]tends a flock and does not drink of the milk of the flock?
8 Do I say these things as a *mere* man? Or does not the law say the same also?
9 For it is written in the law of Moses, [a]*"You shall not muzzle an ox while it treads out the grain."* Is it oxen God is concerned about?
10 Or does He say *it* altogether for our sakes? For our sakes, no doubt, *this* is written, that [a]he who plows should plow in hope, and he who threshes in hope should be partaker of his hope.
11 [a]If we have sown spiritual things for you, *is it* a great thing if we reap your material things?
12 If others are partakers of *this* right over you, *are* we not even more? [a]Nevertheless we have not used this right, but endure all things [b]lest we hinder the gospel of Christ.
13 [a]Do you not know that those who minister the holy things eat *of the things* of the [b]temple, and those who serve at the altar partake of *the offerings of* the altar?
14 Even so [a]the Lord has commanded [b]that those who preach the gospel should live from the gospel.
15 But [a]I have used none of these things, nor have I written these things that it should be done so to me; for [b]it *would be* better for me to die than that anyone should make my boasting void.
16 For if I preach the gospel, I have nothing to boast of, for [a]necessity is laid upon me; yes, woe is me if I do not preach the gospel!
17 For if I do this willingly, [a]I have a reward; but if against my will, [b]I have been entrusted with a stewardship.
18 What is my reward then? That [a]when I preach the gospel, I may present the gospel [1]of Christ without charge, that I [b]may not abuse my authority in the gospel.

Serving All Men

19 For though I am [a]free from all *men,* [b]I have made myself a servant to all, [c]that I might win the more;
20 and [a]to the Jews I became as a Jew, that I might win Jews; to those *who are* under the law, as under the [1]law, that I might win those *who are* under the law;
21 [a]to [b]those *who are* without law, as without law [c](not being without [1]law toward God, but under [2]law toward Christ), that I might win those *who are* without law;
22 [a]to the weak I became [1]as weak, that I might win the weak. [b]I have become all things to all *men,* [c]that I might by all means save some.
23 Now this I do for the gospel's sake, that I may be partaker of it with *you.*

Striving for a Crown

24 Do you not know that those who run in a race all run, but one receives the prize? [a]Run in such a way that you may [1]obtain *it.*
25 And everyone who competes *for the prize* [1]is temperate in all things. Now they *do it* to obtain a perishable crown, but we *for* [a]an imperishable *crown.*
26 Therefore I run thus: [a]not with uncertainty. Thus I fight: not as *one who* beats the air.
27 [a]But I discipline my body and [b]bring *it* into subjection, lest, when I have preached to others, I myself should become [c]disqualified.

Old Testament Examples

10 Moreover, brethren, I do not want you to be unaware that all our fathers were under [a]the cloud, all passed through [b]the sea,
2 all were baptized into Moses in the cloud and in the sea,
3 all ate the same [a]spiritual food,
4 and all drank the same [a]spiritual drink. For they drank of that spiritual Rock that followed them, and that Rock was Christ.
5 But with most of them God was

4 [a][1 Thess. 2:6, 9] [1]*authority*
5 [a]Matt. 13:55 [b]Matt. 8:14 [1]Lit. *a sister, a wife*
6 [a]Acts 4:36
7 [a]2 Cor. 10:4 [b]Deut. 20:6 [c]John 21:15
9 [a]Deut. 25:4
10 [a]2 Tim. 2:6
11 [a]Rom. 15:27
12 [a][Acts 18:3; 20:33] [b]2 Cor. 11:12
13 [a]Lev. 6:16, 26; 7:6, 31 [b]Num. 18:8–31
14 [a]Matt. 10:10 [b]Rom. 10:15
15 [a]Acts 18:3; 20:33 [b]2 Cor. 11:10
16 [a][Rom. 1:14]
17 [a]1 Cor. 3:8, 14; 9:18 [b]Gal. 2:7
18 [a]1 Cor. 10:33 [b]1 Cor. 7:31; 9:12 [1]NU omits *of Christ*
19 [a]1 Cor. 9:1 [b]Gal. 5:13 [c]Matt. 18:15
20 [a]Acts 16:3; 21:23–26 [1]NU adds *though not being myself under the law*
21 [a][Gal. 2:3; 3:2] [b][Rom. 2:12, 14] [c][1 Cor. 7:22] [1]NU *God's law* [2]NU *Christ's law*
22 [a]Rom. 14:1; 15:1 [b]1 Cor. 10:33 [c]Rom. 11:14 [1]NU omits *as*
24 [a]Gal. 2:2 [1]*win*
25 [a]James 1:12 [1]*exercises self-control*
26 [a]2 Tim. 2:5
27 [a][Rom. 8:13] [b][Rom. 6:18] [c]Jer. 6:30

CHAPTER 10

1 [a]Ex. 13:21, 22 [b]Ex. 14:21, 22, 29
3 [a]Ex. 16:4, 15, 35
4 [a]Ex. 17:5–7

not well pleased, for *their bodies*
[a]were scattered in the wilderness.
6 Now these things became our
examples, to the intent that we
should not lust after evil things as
[a]they also lusted.
7 [a]And do not become idolaters
as *were* some of them. As it is writ-
ten, [b]*"The people sat down to eat
and drink, and rose up to play."*
8 [a]Nor let us commit sexual im-
morality, as [b]some of them did,
and [c]in one day twenty-three thou-
sand fell;
9 nor let us [1]tempt Christ, as
[a]some of them also tempted, and
[b]were destroyed by serpents;
10 nor complain, as [a]some of them
also complained, and [b]were de-
stroyed by [c]the destroyer.
11 Now [1]all these things happened
to them as examples, and [a]they
were written for our [2]admonition,
[b]upon whom the ends of the ages
have come.
12 Therefore [a]let him who thinks
he stands take heed lest he fall.
13 No temptation has overtaken
you except such as is common to
man; but [a]God *is* faithful, [b]who
will not allow you to be tempted
beyond what you are able, but
with the temptation will also make
the way of escape, that you may
be able to [1]bear *it*.

Flee from Idolatry

14 Therefore, my beloved, [a]flee
from idolatry.
15 I speak as to [a]wise men; judge
for yourselves what I say.
16 [a]The cup of blessing which we
bless, is it not the [1]communion of
the blood of Christ? [b]The bread
which we break, is it not the com-
munion of the body of Christ?
17 For [a]we, *though* many, are one
bread *and* one body; for we all par-
take of that one bread.
18 Observe [a]Israel [b]after the flesh:
[c]Are not those who eat of the sacri-
fices [1]partakers of the altar?
19 What am I saying then? [a]That
an idol is anything, or what is of-
fered to idols is anything?
20 Rather, that the things which
the Gentiles [a]sacrifice [b]they sacri-
fice to demons and not to God, and
I do not want you to have fellow-
ship with demons.
21 [a]You cannot drink the cup of
the Lord and [b]the cup of demons;
you cannot partake of the
[c]Lord's table and of the table of
demons.
22 Or do we [a]provoke the Lord to
jealousy? [b]Are we stronger than
He?

All to the Glory of God

23 All things are lawful [1]for me,
but not all things are [a]helpful; all
things are lawful [1]for me, but not
all things [2]edify.
24 Let no one seek his own, but
each one [a]the other's *well-being*.
25 [a]Eat whatever is sold in the
meat market, asking no questions
for conscience' sake;
26 for [a]*"the earth is the* LORD's,
and all its fullness."
27 If any of those who do not be-
lieve invites you *to dinner*, and you
desire to go, [a]eat whatever is set
before you, asking no question for
conscience' sake.
28 But if anyone says to you,
"This was offered to idols," do not
eat it [a]for the sake of the one who
told you, and for conscience' sake;
[1]for [b]*"the earth is the* LORD's, *and
all its fullness."*
29 "Conscience," I say, not your
own, but that of the other. For
[a]why is my liberty judged by an-
other *man's* conscience?
30 But if I partake with thanks,
why am I evil spoken of for *the
food* [a]over which I give thanks?
31 [a]Therefore, whether you eat or
drink, or whatever you do, do all
to the glory of God.
32 [a]Give no offense, either to the
Jews or to the Greeks or to the
church of God,
33 just [a]as I also please all *men*
in all *things*, not seeking my own
profit, but the *profit* of many, that
they may be saved.

11 Imitate[a] me, just as I also *im-
itate* Christ.

Head Coverings

2 Now I praise you, brethren,
that you remember me in all things
and keep the traditions just as I
delivered *them* to you.
3 But I want you to know that
[a]the head of every man is Christ,
[b]the head of woman *is* man, and
[c]the head of Christ *is* God.
4 Every man praying or [a]prophe-

5 [a]Num. 14:29, 37; 26:65
6 [a]Num. 11:4, 34
7 [a]1 Cor. 5:11; 10:14 [b]Ex. 32:6
8 [a]Rev. 2:14 [b]Num. 25:1–9 [c]Ps. 106:29
9 [a]Ex. 17:2, 7 [b]Num. 21:6–9 [1]*test*
10 [a]Ex. 16:2 [b]Num. 14:37 [c]Ex. 12:23
11 [a]Rom. 15:4 [b]Phil. 4:5 [1]NU omits *all* [2]*instruction*
12 [a]Rom. 11:20
13 [a]1 Cor. 1:9 [b]Ps. 125:3 [1]*endure*
14 [a]2 Cor. 6:17
15 [a]1 Cor. 8:1
16 [a]Matt. 26:26–28 [b]Acts 2:42 [1]*fellowship* or *sharing*
17 [a]1 Cor. 12:12, 27
18 [a]Rom. 4:12 [b]Rom. 4:1 [c]Lev. 3:3; 7:6, 14 [1]*fellowshippers* or *sharers*
19 [a]1 Cor. 8:4
20 [a]Lev. 17:7 [b]Deut. 32:17
21 [a]2 Cor. 6:15, 16 [b]Deut. 32:38 [c][1 Cor. 11:23–29]
22 [a]Deut. 32:21 [b]Ezek. 22:14
23 [a]1 Cor. 6:12 [1]NU omits *for me* [2]*build up*
24 [a]Phil. 2:4
25 [a][1 Tim. 4:4]
26 [a]Ps. 24:1
27 [a]Luke 10:7, 8
28 [a][1 Cor. 8:7, 10, 12] [b]Ps. 24:1 [1]NU omits the rest of v. 28.
29 [a]Rom. 14:16
30 [a]Rom. 14:6
31 [a]Col. 3:17
32 [a]Rom. 14:13
33 [a]Rom. 15:2

CHAPTER 11

1 [a]Eph. 5:1
3 [a]Eph. 1:22; 4:15; 5:23 [b]Gen. 3:16 [c]John 14:28
4 [a]1 Cor. 12:10

sying, having *his* head covered,
dishonors his head.
5 But every woman who prays or
prophesies with *her* head uncov-
ered dishonors her head, for that
is one and the same as if her head
were [a]shaved.
6 For if a woman is not covered,
let her also be shorn. But if it is
[a]shameful for a woman to be shorn
or shaved, let her be covered.
7 For a man indeed ought not to
cover *his* head, since [a]he is the im-
age and glory of God; but woman
is the glory of man.
8 For man is not from woman,
but woman [a]from man.
9 Nor was man created for the
woman, but woman [a]for the man.
10 For this reason the woman
ought to have *a symbol of* author-
ity on *her* head, because of the an-
gels.
11 Nevertheless, [a]neither *is* man
independent of woman, nor
woman independent of man, in the
Lord.
12 For as woman *came* from man,
even so man also *comes* through
woman; but all things are from
God.
13 Judge among yourselves. Is it
proper for a woman to pray to God
with her head uncovered?
14 Does not even nature itself
teach you that if a man has long
hair, it is a dishonor to him?
15 But if a woman has long hair,
it is a glory to her; for *her* hair is
given [1]to her for a covering.
16 But [a]if anyone seems to be con-
tentious, we have no such custom,
[b]nor *do* the churches of God.

Conduct at the Lord's Supper

17 Now in giving these instruc-
tions I do not praise *you,* since you
come together not for the better
but for the worse.
18 For first of all, when you come
together as a church, [a]I hear that
there are divisions among you,
and in part I believe it.
19 For [a]there must also be factions
among you, [b]that those who are
approved may be [1]recognized
among you.
20 Therefore when you come to-
gether in one place, it is not to eat
the Lord's Supper.
21 For in eating, each one takes
his own supper ahead of *others;*
and one is hungry and [a]another is
drunk.
22 What! Do you not have houses
to eat and drink in? Or do you de-
spise [a]the church of God and
[b]shame [1]those who have nothing?
What shall I say to you? Shall I
praise you in this? I do not praise
you.

Institution of the Lord's Supper

23 For [a]I received from the Lord
that which I also delivered to you:
[b]that the Lord Jesus on the *same*
night in which He was betrayed
took bread;
24 and when He had given thanks,
He broke *it* and said, [1]"Take, eat;
this is My body which is [2]broken
for you; do this in remembrance
of Me."
25 In the same manner *He* also
took the cup after supper, saying,
"This cup is the new covenant in
My blood. This do, as often as you
drink *it,* in remembrance of Me."
26 For as often as you eat this
bread and drink this cup, you pro-
claim the Lord's death [a]till He
comes.

Examine Yourself

27 Therefore whoever eats [a]this
bread or drinks *this* cup of the
Lord in an unworthy manner will
be guilty of the body and [1]blood
of the Lord.
28 But [a]let a man examine him-
self, and so let him eat of the bread
and drink of the cup.
29 For he who eats and drinks [1]in
an unworthy manner eats and
drinks judgment to himself, not
discerning the [2]Lord's body.
30 For this reason many *are* weak
and sick among you, and many
[1]sleep.
31 For [a]if we would judge our-
selves, we would not be judged.
32 But when we are judged, [a]we
are chastened by the Lord, that we
may not be condemned with the
world.
33 Therefore, my brethren, when
you [a]come together to eat, wait for
one another.
34 But if anyone is hungry, let him
eat at home, lest you come to-
gether for judgment. And the rest
I will set in order when I come.

5 [a]Deut. 21:12
6 [a]Num. 5:18
7 [a]Gen. 1:26, 27; 5:1; 9:6; James 3:9
8 [a]Gen. 2:21–23; 1 Tim. 2:13
9 [a]Gen. 2:18
11 [a][Gal. 3:28]
15 [1]M omits *to her*
16 [a]1 Tim. 6:4 [b]1 Cor. 7:17
18 [a]1 Cor. 1:10–12; 3:3
19 [a]Matt. 18:7; Luke 17:1; 1 Tim. 4:1; 2 Pet. 2:1 [b][Deut. 13:3]; Luke 2:35; 1 John 2:19 [1]Lit. *manifest, evident*
21 [a]2 Pet. 2:13; Jude 12
22 [a]1 Cor. 10:32 [b]James 2:6 [1]The poor
23 [a]1 Cor. 15:3; Gal. 1:12; Col. 3:24 [b]Matt. 26:26–28; Mark 14:22–24; Luke 22:17–20; 1 Cor. 10:16
24 [1]NU omits *Take, eat* [2]NU omits *broken*
26 [a]John 14:3; [Acts 1:11]
27 [a][John 6:51] [1]NU, M *the blood*
28 [a]Matt. 26:22; 2 Cor. 13:5; Gal. 6:4
29 [1]NU omits *in an unworthy manner* [2]NU omits *Lord's*
30 [1]Are dead
31 [a][Ps. 32:5; 1 John 1:9]
32 [a]2 Sam. 7:14; Ps. 94:12; [Heb. 12:5–10; Rev. 3:19]
33 [a]1 Cor. 14:26

Spiritual Gifts: Unity in Diversity

12 Now [a]concerning spiritual
gifts, brethren, I do not want
you to be ignorant:
2 You know [a]that[1] you were Gen-
tiles, carried away to these [b]dumb[2]
idols, however you were led.
3 Therefore I make known to you
that no one speaking by the Spirit
of God calls Jesus [1]accursed, and
[a]no one can say that Jesus is Lord
except by the Holy Spirit.
4 [a]There are [1]diversities of gifts,
but [b]the same Spirit.
5 [a]There are differences of minis-
tries, but the same Lord.
6 And there are diversities of ac-
tivities, but it is the same God [a]who
works [1]all in all.
7 But the manifestation of the
Spirit is given to each one for the
profit *of all:*
8 for to one is given [a]the word
of wisdom through the Spirit, to
another [b]the word of knowledge
through the same Spirit,
9 [a]to another faith by the same
Spirit, to another [b]gifts of healings
by [1]the same Spirit,
10 [a]to another the working of mir-
acles, to another [b]prophecy, to an-
other [c]discerning of spirits, to an-
other [d]*different* kinds of tongues,
to another the interpretation of
tongues.
11 But one and the same Spirit
works all these things, [a]distribut-
ing to each one individually [b]as He
wills.

Unity and Diversity in One Body

12 For [a]as the body is one and has
many members, but all the mem-
bers of that one body, being many,
are one body, [b]so also *is* Christ.
13 For [a]by one Spirit we were all
baptized into one body—[b]whether
Jews or Greeks, whether slaves or
free—and [c]have all been made to
drink [1]into one Spirit.
14 For in fact the body is not one
member but many.
15 If the foot should say, "Because
I am not a hand, I am not of the
body," is it therefore not of the
body?
16 And if the ear should say, "Be-
cause I am not an eye, I am not
of the body," is it therefore not of
the body?
17 If the whole body *were* an eye,
where *would be* the hearing? If the
whole *were* hearing, where *would
be* the smelling?
18 But now [a]God has set the mem-
bers, each one of them, in the body
[b]just as He pleased.
19 And if they *were* all one mem-
ber, where *would* the body *be?*
20 But now indeed *there are* many
members, yet one body.
21 And the eye cannot say to the
hand, "I have no need of you"; nor
again the head to the feet, "I have
no need of you."
22 No, much rather, those mem-
bers of the body which seem to be
weaker are necessary.
23 And those *members* of the
body which we think to be less
honorable, on these we bestow
greater honor; and our un-
presentable *parts* have greater
modesty,
24 but our presentable *parts* have
no need. But God composed the
body, having given greater honor
to that *part* which lacks it,
25 that there should be no [1]schism
in the body, but *that* the members
should have the same care for one
another.
26 And if one member suffers, all
the members suffer with *it;* or if
one member is honored, all the
members rejoice with *it.*
27 Now [a]you are the body of
Christ, and [b]members individ-
ually.
28 And [a]God has appointed these
in the church: first [b]apostles, sec-
ond [c]prophets, third teachers, after
that [d]miracles, then [e]gifts of heal-
ings, [f]helps, [g]administrations, vari-
eties of tongues.
29 *Are* all apostles? *Are* all proph-
ets? *Are* all teachers? *Are* all work-
ers of miracles?
30 Do all have gifts of healings?
Do all speak with tongues? Do all
interpret?
31 But [a]earnestly desire the [1]best
gifts. And yet I show you a more
excellent way.

The Greatest Gift

13 Though I speak with the
tongues of men and of an-
gels, but have not love, I have be-
come sounding brass or a clanging
cymbal.

CHAPTER 12

1 [a]1 Cor. 12:4; 14:1, 37
2 [a]Eph. 2:11 [b]Ps. 115:5 [1]NU, M *that when* [2]*mute, silent*
3 [a]Matt. 16:17 [1]Gr. *anathema*
4 [a]Rom. 12:3–8 [b]Eph. 4:4 [1]*allotments or various kinds*
5 [a]Rom. 12:6
6 [a]1 Cor. 15:28 [1]*all things in*
8 [a]1 Cor. 2:6, 7 [b]Rom. 15:14
9 [a]2 Cor. 4:13 [b]Mark 3:15; 16:18 [1]NU *one*
10 [a]Mark 16:17 [b]Rom. 12:6 [c]1 John 4:1 [d]Acts 2:4–11
11 [a]Rom. 12:6 [b][John 3:8]
12 [a]Rom. 12:4, 5 [b][Gal. 3:16]
13 [a][Rom. 6:5] [b]Col. 3:11 [c][John 7:37–39] [1]NU omits *into*
18 [a]1 Cor. 12:28 [b]Rom. 12:3
25 [1]*division*
27 [a]Rom. 12:5 [b]Eph. 5:30
28 [a]Eph. 4:11 [b][Eph. 2:20; 3:5] [c]Acts 13:1 [d]1 Cor. 12:10, 29 [e]1 Cor. 12:9, 30 [f]Num. 11:17 [g]Rom. 12:8
31 [a]1 Cor. 14:1, 39 [1]NU *greater*

2 And though I have *the gift of*
[a]prophecy, and understand all
mysteries and all knowledge, and
though I have all faith, [b]so that I
could remove mountains, but have
not love, I am nothing.
3 And [a]though I bestow all my
goods to feed *the poor*, and though
I give my body [1]to be burned, but
have not love, it profits me noth-
ing.
4 [a]Love suffers long *and* is [b]kind;
love [c]does not envy; love does not
parade itself, is not [1]puffed up;
5 does not behave rudely, [a]does
not seek its own, is not provoked,
[1]thinks no evil;
6 [a]does not rejoice in iniquity,
but [b]rejoices in the truth;
7 [a]bears all things, believes all
things, hopes all things, endures
all things.
8 Love never fails. But whether
there are prophecies, they will fail;
whether *there are* tongues, they
will cease; whether *there is* knowl-
edge, it will vanish away.
9 [a]For we know in part and we
prophesy in part.
10 But when that which is [1]perfect
has come, then that which is in
part will be done away.
11 When I was a child, I spoke as
a child, I understood as a child, I
thought as a child; but when I be-
came a man, I put away childish
things.
12 For [a]now we see in a mirror,
dimly, but then [b]face to face. Now
I know in part, but then I shall
know just as I also am known.
13 And now abide faith, hope,
love, these three; but the greatest
of these *is* love.

Prophecy and Tongues

14 Pursue love, and [a]desire
spiritual *gifts*, [b]but espe-
cially that you may prophesy.
2 For he who [a]speaks in a tongue
does not speak to men but to God,
for no one understands *him;* how-
ever, in the spirit he speaks mys-
teries.
3 But he who prophesies speaks
[a]edification and [b]exhortation and
comfort to men.
4 He who speaks in a tongue edi-
fies himself, but he who prophe-
sies edifies the church.
5 I wish you all spoke with
tongues, but even more that you
prophesied; [1]for he who prophe-
sies *is* greater than he who speaks
with tongues, unless indeed he in-
terprets, that the church may re-
ceive edification.

Tongues Must Be Interpreted

6 But now, brethren, if I come to
you speaking with tongues, what
shall I profit you unless I speak to
you either by [a]revelation, by
knowledge, by prophesying, or by
teaching?
7 Even things without life,
whether flute or harp, when they
make a sound, unless they make
a distinction in the sounds, how
will it be known what is piped or
played?
8 For if the trumpet makes an
uncertain sound, who will prepare
for battle?
9 So likewise you, unless you ut-
ter by the tongue words easy to un-
derstand, how will it be known
what is spoken? For you will be
speaking into the air.
10 There are, it may be, so many
kinds of languages in the world,
and none of them *is* without [1]sig-
nificance.
11 Therefore, if I do not know the
meaning of the language, I shall
be a [1]foreigner to him who speaks,
and he who speaks *will be* a for-
eigner to me.
12 Even so you, since you are
[1]zealous for spiritual *gifts, let it be*
for the [2]edification of the church
that you seek to excel.
13 Therefore let him who speaks
in a tongue pray that he may [a]in-
terpret.
14 For if I pray in a tongue, my
spirit prays, but my understanding
is unfruitful.
15 What is *the conclusion* then? I
will pray with the spirit, and I will
also pray with the understanding.
[a]I will sing with the spirit, and I
will also sing [b]with the under-
standing.
16 Otherwise, if you bless with the
spirit, how will he who occupies
the place of the uninformed say
"Amen" [a]at your giving of thanks,
since he does not understand what
you say?
17 For you indeed give thanks
well, but the other is not edified.

CHAPTER 13

2 [a]1 Cor. 12:8–10, 28; 14:1 [b]Matt. 17:20; 21:21

3 [a]Matt. 6:1, 2 [1]NU *so I may boast*

4 [a]Prov. 10:12; 17:9 [b]Eph. 4:32 [c]Gal. 5:26 [1]*arrogant*

5 [a]1 Cor. 10:24 [1]*keeps no accounts of evil*

6 [a]Rom. 1:32 [b]2 John 4

7 [a]Gal. 6:2

9 [a]1 Cor. 8:2; 13:12

10 [1]*complete*

12 [a]Phil. 3:12 [b][1 John 3:2]

CHAPTER 14

1 [a]1 Cor. 12:31; 14:39 [b]Num. 11:25, 29

2 [a]Acts 2:4; 10:46

3 [a]Rom. 14:19; 15:2 [b]1 Tim. 4:13

5 [1]NU *and*

6 [a]1 Cor. 14:26

10 [1]*meaning*

11 [1]Lit. *barbarian*

12 [1]*eager* [2]*building up*

13 [a]1 Cor. 12:10

15 [a]Col. 3:16 [b]Ps. 47:7

16 [a]1 Cor. 11:24

18 I thank my God I speak with tongues more than you all;
19 yet in the church I would rather speak five words with my understanding, that I may teach others also, than ten thousand words in a tongue.

Tongues a Sign to Unbelievers

20 Brethren, [a]do not be children in understanding; however, in malice [b]be babes, but in understanding be mature.
21 [a]In the law it is written:

[b]"With men of other tongues and other lips
I will speak to this people;
And yet, for all that, they will not hear Me,"

says the Lord.
22 Therefore tongues are for a [a]sign, not to those who believe but to unbelievers; but prophesying is not for unbelievers but for those who believe.
23 Therefore if the whole church comes together in one place, and all speak with tongues, and there come in *those who are* uninformed or unbelievers, [a]will they not say that you are [1]out of your mind?
24 But if all prophesy, and an unbeliever or an uninformed person comes in, he is convinced by all, he is convicted by all.
25 [1]And thus the secrets of his heart are revealed; and so, falling down on *his* face, he will worship God and report [a]that God is truly among you.

Order in Church Meetings

26 How is it then, brethren? Whenever you come together, each of you has a psalm, [a]has a teaching, has a tongue, has a revelation, has an interpretation. [b]Let all things be done for [1]edification.
27 If anyone speaks in a tongue, *let there be* two or at the most three, *each* in turn, and let one interpret.
28 But if there is no interpreter, let him keep silent in church, and let him speak to himself and to God.
29 Let two or three prophets speak, and [a]let the others judge.
30 But if *anything* is revealed to another who sits by, [a]let the first keep silent.
31 For you can all prophesy one by one, that all may learn and all may be encouraged.
32 And [a]the spirits of the prophets are subject to the prophets.
33 For God is not *the author* of [1]confusion but of peace, [a]as in all the churches of the saints.
34 [a]Let [1]your women keep silent in the churches, for they are not permitted to speak; but *they are* to be submissive, as the [b]law also says.
35 And if they want to learn something, let them ask their own husbands at home; for it is shameful for women to speak in church.
36 Or did the word of God come *originally* from you? Or *was it* you only that it reached?
37 [a]If anyone thinks himself to be a prophet or spiritual, let him acknowledge that the things which I write to you are the commandments of the Lord.
38 But [1]if anyone is ignorant, let him be ignorant.
39 Therefore, brethren, [a]desire earnestly to prophesy, and do not forbid to speak with tongues.
40 [a]Let all things be done decently and in order.

The Risen Christ, Faith's Reality

15 Moreover, brethren, I declare to you the gospel [a]which I preached to you, which also you received and [b]in which you stand,
2 [a]by which also you are saved, if you hold fast that word which I preached to you—unless [b]you believed in vain.
3 For [a]I delivered to you first of all that [b]which I also received: that Christ died for our sins [c]according to the Scriptures,
4 and that He was buried, and that He rose again the third day [a]according to the Scriptures,
5 [a]and that He was seen by [1]Cephas, then [b]by the twelve.
6 After that He was seen by over five hundred brethren at once, of whom the greater part remain to the present, but some have [1]fallen asleep.
7 After that He was seen by James, then [a]by all the apostles.

20 [a]Ps. 131:2 [b][1 Pet. 2:2]
21 [a]John 10:34 [b]Is. 28:11, 12
22 [a]Mark 16:17
23 [a]Acts 2:13 [1]*insane*
25 [a]Is. 45:14 [1]NU omits *And thus*
26 [a]1 Cor. 12:8–10; 14:6 [b][2 Cor. 12:19] [1]*building up*
29 [a]1 Cor. 12:10
30 [a][1 Thess. 5:19, 20]
32 [a]1 John 4:1
33 [a]1 Cor. 11:16 [1]*disorder*
34 [a]1 Tim. 2:11 [b]Gen. 3:16 [1]NU omits *your*
37 [a]2 Cor. 10:7
38 [1]NU *if anyone does not recognize this, he is not recognized.*
39 [a]1 Cor. 12:31
40 [a]1 Cor. 14:33

CHAPTER 15

1 [a][Gal. 1:11] [b][Rom. 5:2; 11:20]
2 [a]Rom. 1:16 [b]Gal. 3:4
3 [a]1 Cor. 11:2, 23 [b][Gal. 1:12] [c]Ps. 22:15
4 [a]Ps. 16:9–11; 68:18; 110:1
5 [a]Luke 24:34 [b]Matt. 28:17 [1]Peter
6 [1]Died
7 [a]Acts 1:3, 4

8 [a]Then last of all He was seen
by me also, as by one born out of
due time.
9 For I am [a]the least of the apos-
tles, who am not worthy to be
called an apostle, because [b]I perse-
cuted the church of God.
10 But [a]by the grace of God I am
what I am, and His grace toward
me was not in vain; but I labored
more abundantly than they all,
[b]yet not I, but the grace of God
which was with me.
11 Therefore, whether *it was* I or
they, so we preach and so you be-
lieved.

The Risen Christ, Our Hope

12 Now if Christ is preached that
He has been raised from the dead,
how do some among you say that
there is no resurrection of the
dead?
13 But if there is no resurrection
of the dead, [a]then Christ is not
risen.
14 And if Christ is not risen, then
our preaching *is* empty and your
faith *is* also empty.
15 Yes, and we are found false
witnesses of God, because [a]we
have testified of God that He
raised up Christ, whom He did not
raise up—if in fact the dead do not
rise.
16 For if *the* dead do not rise, then
Christ is not risen.
17 And if Christ is not risen, your
faith *is* futile; [a]you are still in your
sins!
18 Then also those who have
[1]fallen [a]asleep in Christ have per-
ished.
19 [a]If in this life only we have
hope in Christ, we are of all men
the most pitiable.

The Last Enemy Destroyed

20 But now [a]Christ is risen from
the dead, *and* has become [b]the
firstfruits of those who have
[1]fallen asleep.
21 For [a]since by man *came* death,
[b]by Man also *came* the resur-
rection of the dead.
22 For as in Adam all die, even so
in Christ all shall [a]be made alive.
23 But [a]each one in his own order:
Christ the firstfruits, afterward
those *who are* Christ's at His com-
ing.

8 [a][Acts 9:3–8; 22:6–11; 26:12–18]; 1 Cor. 9:1
9 [a]2 Cor. 12:11; Eph. 3:8; 1 Tim. 1:15 [b]Acts 8:3
10 [a]Eph. 3:7, 8 [b]Matt. 10:20; Rom. 15:18; Gal. 2:8; Phil. 2:13
13 [a][1 Thess. 4:14]
15 [a]Acts 2:24
17 [a][Rom. 4:25]
18 [a]Job 14:12; Ps. 13:3 [1]Died
19 [a]1 Cor. 4:9; 2 Tim. 3:12
20 [a]Acts 2:24; 1 Pet. 1:3 [b]Acts 26:23; 1 Cor. 15:23; Rev. 1:5 [1]Died
21 [a]Gen. 3:19; Ezek. 18:4; Rom. 5:12; 6:23; Heb. 9:27 [b]John 11:25
22 [a][John 5:28, 29]
23 [a][1 Thess. 4:15–17]
24 [a][Dan. 2:44; 7:14, 27; 2 Pet. 1:11]
25 [a]Ps. 110:1; Matt. 22:44
26 [a][2 Tim. 1:10; Rev. 20:14; 21:4]
27 [a]Ps. 8:6
28 [a][Phil. 3:21] [b]1 Cor. 3:23; 11:3; 12:6
30 [a]2 Cor. 11:26 [1]*danger*
31 [a]1 Thess. 2:19 [b]Rom. 8:36
32 [a]2 Cor. 1:8 [b]Eccl. 2:24; Is. 22:13; 56:12; Luke 12:19
33 [a][1 Cor. 5:6]
34 [a]Rom. 13:11; Eph. 5:14 [b][1 Thess. 4:5] [c]1 Cor. 6:5
35 [a]Ezek. 37:3
36 [a]John 12:24
39 [1]NU, M omit *of flesh*
40 [1]*heavenly*

24 Then *comes* the end, when He
delivers [a]the kingdom to God the
Father, when He puts an end to all
rule and all authority and power.
25 For He must reign [a]till He has
put all enemies under His feet.
26 [a]The last enemy *that* will be
destroyed *is* death.
27 For [a]*"He has put all things un-
der His feet."* But when He says
"all things are put under *Him,*" *it
is* evident that He who put all
things under Him is excepted.
28 [a]Now when all things are made
subject to Him, then [b]the Son Him-
self will also be subject to Him
who put all things under Him, that
God may be all in all.

Effects of Denying the Resurrection

29 Otherwise, what will they do
who are baptized for the dead, if
the dead do not rise at all? Why
then are they baptized for the
dead?
30 And [a]why do we stand in [1]jeop-
ardy every hour?
31 I affirm, by [a]the boasting in you
which I have in Christ Jesus our
Lord, [b]I die daily.
32 If, in the manner of men, [a]I
have fought with beasts at Ephe-
sus, what advantage *is it* to me?
If *the* dead do not rise, [b]*"Let us
eat and drink, for tomorrow we
die!"*
33 Do not be deceived: [a]"Evil com-
pany corrupts good habits."
34 [a]Awake to righteousness, and
do not sin; [b]for some do not have
the knowledge of God. [c]I speak
this to your shame.

A Glorious Body

35 But someone will say, [a]"How
are the dead raised up? And with
what body do they come?"
36 Foolish one, [a]what you sow is
not made alive unless it dies.
37 And what you sow, you do not
sow that body that shall be, but
mere grain—perhaps wheat or
some other *grain.*
38 But God gives it a body as He
pleases, and to each seed its own
body.
39 All flesh *is* not the same flesh,
but *there is* one *kind* [1]*of* flesh of
men, another flesh of animals, an-
other of fish, *and* another of birds.
40 *There are* also [1]celestial bodies

and [2]terrestrial bodies; but the
glory of the celestial *is* one, and
the *glory* of the terrestrial *is* an-
other.
41 *There is* one glory of the sun,
another glory of the moon, and an-
other glory of the stars; for *one*
star differs from *another* star in
glory.
42 [a]So also *is* the resurrection of
the dead. *The body* is sown in cor-
ruption, it is raised in incorruption.
43 [a]It is sown in dishonor, it is
raised in glory. It is sown in weak-
ness, it is raised in power.
44 It is sown a natural body, it is
raised a spiritual body. There is a
natural body, and there is a spiri-
tual body.
45 And so it is written, [a]*"The first
man Adam became a living be-
ing."* [b]The last Adam *became* [c]a
life-giving spirit.
46 However, the spiritual is not
first, but the natural, and after-
ward the spiritual.
47 [a]The first man *was* of the earth,
[b]*made*[1] of dust; the second Man *is*
[2]the Lord [c]from heaven.
48 As *was* the [1]*man* of dust, so
also *are* those *who are* [1]*made* of
dust; [a]and as *is* the heavenly *Man*,
so also *are* those *who are* heav-
enly.
49 And [a]as we have borne the
image of the *man* of dust, [b]we[1]
shall also bear the image of the
heavenly *Man*.

Our Final Victory

50 Now this I say, brethren, that
[a]flesh and blood cannot inherit the
kingdom of God; nor does corrup-
tion inherit incorruption.
51 Behold, I tell you a [1]mystery:
[a]We shall not all sleep, [b]but we
shall all be changed—
52 in a moment, in the twinkling
of an eye, at the last trumpet. [a]For
the trumpet will sound, and the
dead will be raised incorruptible,
and we shall be changed.
53 For this corruptible must put on
incorruption, and [a]this mortal
must put on immortality.
54 So when this corruptible has
put on incorruption, and this mor-
tal has put on immortality, then
shall be brought to pass the saying
that is written: [a]*"Death is swal-
lowed up in victory."*
55 *"O*[a][1] *Death, where is your sting?
O Hades, where is your victory?"*
56 The sting of death *is* sin, and
[a]the strength of sin *is* the law.
57 [a]But thanks *be* to God, who
gives us [b]the victory through our
Lord Jesus Christ.
58 [a]Therefore, my beloved breth-
ren, be steadfast, immovable, al-
ways abounding in the work of the
Lord, knowing [b]that your labor is
not in vain in the Lord.

Collection for the Saints

16 Now concerning [a]the collec-
tion for the saints, as I have
given orders to the churches of Ga-
latia, so you must do also:
2 [a]On the first *day* of the week
let each one of you lay something
aside, storing up as he may pros-
per, that there be no collections
when I come.
3 And when I come, [a]whomever
you approve by *your* letters I will
send to bear your gift to Jeru-
salem.
4 [a]But if it is fitting that I go also,
they will go with me.

Personal Plans

5 Now I will come to you [a]when
I pass through Macedonia (for I am
passing through Macedonia).
6 And it may be that I will re-
main, or even spend the winter
with you, that you may [a]send me
on my journey, wherever I go.
7 For I do not wish to see you
now on the way; but I hope to stay
a while with you, [a]if the Lord per-
mits.
8 But I will tarry in Ephesus until
[a]Pentecost.
9 For [a]a great and effective door
has opened to me, and [b]*there are*
many adversaries.
10 And [a]if Timothy comes, see
that he may be with you without
fear; for [b]he does the work of the
Lord, as I also *do*.
11 [a]Therefore let no one despise
him. But send him on his journey
[b]in peace, that he may come to me;
for I am waiting for him with the
brethren.
12 Now concerning *our* brother
[a]Apollos, I strongly urged him to
come to you with the brethren, but
he was quite unwilling to come at

40 [2]*earthly*
42 [a][Dan. 12:3]
43 [a][Phil. 3:21]
45 [a]Gen. 2:7 [b][Rom. 5:14] [c]John 5:21; 6:57
47 [a]John 3:31 [b]Gen. 2:7; 3:19 [c]John 3:13 [1]*earthy* [2]NU omits *the Lord*
48 [a]Phil. 3:20 [1]*earthy*
49 [a]Gen. 5:3 [b]Rom. 8:29 [1]M *let us also bear*
50 [a][John 3:3, 5]
51 [a][1 Thess. 4:15] [b][Phil. 3:21] [1]*hidden truth*
52 [a]Matt. 24:31
53 [a]2 Cor. 5:4
54 [a]Is. 25:8
55 [a]Hos. 13:14 [1]NU *O Death, where is your victory? O Death, where is your sting?*
56 [a][Rom. 3:20; 4:15; 7:8]
57 [a][Rom. 7:25] [b][1 John 5:4]
58 [a]2 Pet. 3:14 [b][1 Cor. 3:8]

CHAPTER 16

1 [a]Gal. 2:10
2 [a]Acts 20:7
3 [a]2 Cor. 3:1; 8:18
4 [a]2 Cor. 8:4, 19
5 [a]2 Cor. 1:15, 16
6 [a]Acts 15:3
7 [a]James 4:15
8 [a]Lev. 23:15–22
9 [a]Acts 14:27 [b]Acts 19:9
10 [a]Acts 19:22 [b]Phil. 2:20
11 [a]1 Tim. 4:12 [b]Acts 15:33
12 [a]1 Cor. 1:12; 3:5

this time; however, he will come
when he has a convenient time.

Final Exhortations

13 [a]Watch, [b]stand fast in the faith,
be brave, [c]be strong.
14 [a]Let all *that* you *do* be done
with love.
15 I urge you, brethren—you
know [a]the household of Stepha-
nas, that it is [b]the firstfruits of
Achaia, and *that* they have de-
voted themselves to [c]the ministry
of the saints—
16 [a]that you also submit to such,
and to everyone who works and
[b]labors with *us*.
17 I am glad about the coming of
Stephanas, Fortunatus, and Achai-
cus, [a]for what was lacking on your
part they supplied.
18 [a]For they refreshed my spirit
and yours. Therefore [b]acknowl-
edge such men.

Greetings and a Solemn Farewell

19 The churches of Asia greet you.
Aquila and Priscilla greet you
heartily in the Lord, [a]with the
church that is in their house.
20 All the brethren greet you.
[a]Greet one another with a holy
kiss.
21 [a]The salutation with my own
hand—Paul's.
22 If anyone [a]does not love the
Lord Jesus Christ, [b]let him be [1]ac-
cursed. [c]O[2] Lord, come!
23 [a]The grace of our Lord Jesus
Christ *be* with you.
24 My love *be* with you all in
Christ Jesus. Amen.

13 [a]Matt. 24:42 [b]Phil. 1:27; 4:1 [c][Eph. 3:16; 6:10]
14 [a][1 Pet. 4:8]
15 [a]1 Cor. 1:16 [b]Rom. 16:5 [c]2 Cor. 8:4
16 [a]Heb. 13:17 [b][Heb. 6:10]
17 [a]2 Cor. 11:9
18 [a]Col. 4:8 [b]Phil. 2:29
19 [a]Rom. 16:5
20 [a]Rom. 16:16
21 [a]Col. 4:18
22 [a]Eph. 6:24 [b]Gal. 1:8, 9 [c]Jude 14, 15 [1]Gr. *anathema* [2]Aram. *Marana tha;* possibly *Maran atha, Our Lord has come*

23 [a]Rom. 16:20

The Second Epistle of Paul the Apostle to the

Corinthians

SINCE Paul's first letter, the Corinthian church had been swayed by false teachers who stirred the people against Paul. They claimed he was fickle, proud, unimpressive in appearance and speech, dishonest, and unqualified as an apostle of Jesus Christ. Paul sent Titus to Corinth to deal with these difficulties, and upon his return, rejoiced to hear of the Corinthians' change of heart. Paul wrote this letter to express his thanksgiving for the repentant majority and to appeal to the rebellious minority to accept his authority. Throughout the book he defends his conduct, character, and calling as an apostle of Jesus Christ.

To distinguish this epistle from First Corinthians, it was given the title *Pros Korinthious B*, the "Second to the Corinthians." The *A* and *B* were probably later additions to *Pros Korinthious*.

Greeting

PAUL, [a]an apostle of Jesus
Christ by the will of God, and
[b]Timothy *our* brother,

To the church of God which is
at Corinth, [c]with all the saints who
are in all Achaia:

2 [a]Grace to you and peace from
God our Father and the Lord Jesus
Christ.

Comfort in Suffering

3 [a]Blessed *be* the God and Father
of our Lord Jesus Christ, the Father of mercies and God of all comfort,
4 who [a]comforts us in all our
tribulation, that we may be able to
comfort those who are in any
[1]trouble, with the comfort with
which we ourselves are comforted
by God.
5 For as [a]the sufferings of Christ
abound in us, so our [1]consolation
also abounds through Christ.
6 Now if we are afflicted, [a]*it is*
for your consolation and salvation,
which is effective for enduring the
same sufferings which we also suffer. Or if we are comforted, *it is*
for your consolation and salvation.
7 And our hope for you *is* steadfast, because we know that [a]as you
are partakers of the sufferings, so
also *you will partake* of the consolation.

CHAPTER 1

1 [a]1 Cor. 1:1; Eph. 1:1; Col. 1:1; 1 Tim. 1:1; 2 Tim. 1:1 [b]Acts 16:1; 1 Cor. 16:10 [c]Phil. 1:1; Col. 1:2
2 [a]Rom. 1:7
3 [a]Eph. 1:3; 1 Pet. 1:3
4 [a]Is. 51:12; 66:13; 2 Cor. 7:6, 7, 13 [1]*tribulation*
5 [a][Acts 9:4]; 2 Cor. 4:10; Phil. 3:10; Col. 1:24 [1]*comfort*
6 [a]2 Cor. 4:15; 12:15; Eph. 3:1, 13; 2 Tim. 2:10
7 [a][Rom. 8:17; 2 Tim. 2:12]
8 [a]Acts 19:23; 1 Cor. 15:32; 16:9 [1]*tribulation*
9 [a]Jer. 17:5, 7
10 [a][2 Pet. 2:9] [1]NU *shall*
11 [a]Rom. 15:30; Phil. 1:19; Philem. 22 [b]2 Cor. 4:15; 9:11 [1]M *your behalf*
12 [a]2 Cor. 2:17 [b][1 Cor. 2:4] [1]The opposite of duplicity

Delivered from Suffering

8 For we do not want you to be
ignorant, brethren, of [a]our [1]trouble
which came to us in Asia: that we
were burdened beyond measure,
above strength, so that we despaired even of life.
9 Yes, we had the sentence of
death in ourselves, that we should
[a]not trust in ourselves but in God
who raises the dead,
10 [a]who delivered us from so
great a death, and [1]does deliver us;
in whom we trust that He will still
deliver *us*,
11 you also [a]helping together in
prayer for us, that thanks may be
given by many persons on [1]our behalf [b]for the gift *granted* to us
through many.

Paul's Sincerity

12 For our boasting is this: the testimony of our conscience that we
conducted ourselves in the world
in [1]simplicity and [a]godly sincerity,
[b]not with fleshly wisdom but by
the grace of God, and more abundantly toward you.
13 For we are not writing any
other things to you than what you

read or understand. Now I trust
you will understand, even to the
end
14 (as also you have understood
us in part), [a]that we are your boast
as [b]you also *are* ours, in the day
of the Lord Jesus.

Sparing the Church

15 And in this confidence [a]I in-
tended to come to you before, that
you might have [b]a second bene-
fit—
16 to pass by way of you to Mace-
donia, [a]to come again from Mace-
donia to you, and be helped by you
on my way to Judea.
17 Therefore, when I was plan-
ning this, did I do it lightly? Or the
things I plan, do I plan [a]according
to the flesh, that with me there
should be Yes, Yes, and No, No?
18 But *as* God *is* [a]faithful, our
[1]word to you was not Yes and No.
19 For [a]the Son of God, Jesus
Christ, who was preached among
you by us—by me, [b]Silvanus, and
[c]Timothy—was not Yes and No,
[d]but in Him was Yes.
20 [a]For all the promises of God in
Him *are* Yes, and in Him Amen,
to the glory of God through us.
21 Now He who establishes us
with you in Christ and [a]has
anointed us *is* God,
22 who [a]also has sealed us and
[b]given us the Spirit in our hearts
as a guarantee.
23 Moreover [a]I call God as witness
against my soul, [b]that to spare you
I came no more to Corinth.
24 Not [a]that we [1]have dominion
over your faith, but are fellow
workers for your joy; for [b]by faith
you stand.

2 But I determined this within
myself, [a]that I would not come
again to you in sorrow.
2 For if I make you [a]sorrowful,
then who is he who makes me glad
but the one who is made sorrowful
by me?

Forgive the Offender

3 And I wrote this very thing to
you, lest, when I came, [a]I should
have sorrow over those from
whom I ought to have joy, [b]having
confidence in you all that my joy
is *the joy* of you all.
4 For out of much [1]affliction
and anguish of heart I wrote
to you, with many tears, [a]not that
you should be grieved, but that
you might know the love which I
have so abundantly for you.
5 But [a]if anyone has caused grief,
he has not [b]grieved me, but all of
you to some extent—not to be too
severe.
6 This punishment which *was in-
flicted* [a]by the majority *is* sufficient
for such a man,
7 [a]so that, on the contrary, you
ought rather to forgive and com-
fort *him,* lest perhaps such a one
be swallowed up with too much
sorrow.
8 Therefore I urge you to re-
affirm *your* love to him.
9 For to this end I also wrote, that
I might put you to the test, whether
you are [a]obedient in all things.
10 Now whom you forgive any-
thing, I also *forgive.* For [1]if indeed
I have forgiven anything, I have
forgiven that one for your sakes
in the presence of Christ,
11 lest Satan should take advan-
tage of us; for we are not ignorant
of his devices.

Triumph in Christ

12 Furthermore, [a]when I came to
Troas to *preach* Christ's gospel,
and [b]a [1]door was opened to me by
the Lord,
13 [a]I had no rest in my spirit, be-
cause I did not find Titus my
brother; but taking my leave of
them, I departed for Macedonia.
14 Now thanks *be* to God who al-
ways leads us in triumph in Christ,
and through us [1]diffuses the fra-
grance of His knowledge in every
place.
15 For we are to God the fra-
grance of Christ [a]among those
who are being saved and [b]among
those who are perishing.
16 [a]To the one *we are* the aroma
of death *leading* to death, and to
the other the aroma of life *leading*
to life. And [b]who *is* sufficient for
these things?
17 For we are not, as [1]so many,
[a]peddling[2] the word of God; but
as [b]of sincerity, but as from God,
we speak in the sight of God in
Christ.

14 [a]2 Cor. 5:12 [b]Phil. 2:16
15 [a]1 Cor. 4:19 [b]Rom. 1:11; 15:29
16 [a]1 Cor. 16:3–6
17 [a]2 Cor. 10:2; 11:18
18 [a]1 John 5:20 [1]*message*
19 [a]Mark 1:1 [b]1 Pet. 5:12 [c]2 Cor. 1:1 [d][Heb. 13:8]
20 [a][Rom. 15:8, 9]
21 [a][1 John 2:20, 27]
22 [a][Eph. 4:30] [b][Eph. 1:14]
23 [a]Gal. 1:20 [b]1 Cor. 4:21
24 [a][1 Pet. 5:3] [b]Rom. 11:20 [1]*rule*

CHAPTER 2

1 [a]2 Cor. 1:23
2 [a]2 Cor. 7:8
3 [a]2 Cor. 12:21 [b]Gal. 5:10
4 [a][2 Cor. 2:9; 7:8, 12] [1]*tribulation*
5 [a][1 Cor. 5:1] [b]Gal. 4:12
6 [a]1 Cor. 5:4, 5
7 [a]Gal. 6:1
9 [a]2 Cor. 7:15; 10:6
10 [1]NU *indeed, what I have forgiven, if I have forgiven anything, I did it for your sakes*
12 [a]Acts 16:8 [b]1 Cor. 16:9 [1]Opportunity
13 [a]2 Cor. 7:6, 13; 8:6
14 [1]*manifests*
15 [a][1 Cor. 1:18] [b][2 Cor. 4:3]
16 [a]Luke 2:34 [b][1 Cor. 15:10]
17 [a]2 Pet. 2:3 [b]2 Cor. 1:12 [1]M *the rest* [2]*adulterating for gain*

Christ's Epistle

3 Do [a]we begin again to com-
mend ourselves? Or do we
need, as some *others,* [b]epistles of
commendation to you or *letters* of
commendation from you?
2 [a]You are our epistle written in
our hearts, known and read by all
men;
3 clearly *you are* an epistle of
Christ, [a]ministered by us, written
not with ink but by the Spirit of
the living God, not [b]on tablets of
stone but [c]on tablets of flesh, *that*
is, of the heart.

The Spirit, Not the Letter

4 And we have such trust
through Christ toward God.
5 [a]Not that we are sufficient of
ourselves to think of anything as
being from ourselves, but [b]our suf-
ficiency *is* from God,
6 who also made us sufficient as
[a]ministers of [b]the new covenant,
not [c]of the letter but of the [1]Spirit;
for [d]the letter kills, [e]but the Spirit
gives life.

Glory of the New Covenant

7 But if [a]the ministry of death,
[b]written *and* engraved on stones,
was glorious, [c]so that the children
of Israel could not look steadily at
the face of Moses because of the
glory of his countenance, which
glory was passing away,
8 how will [a]the ministry of the
Spirit not be more glorious?
9 For if the ministry of con-
demnation *had* glory, the ministry
[a]of righteousness exceeds much
more in glory.
10 For even what was made glori-
ous had no glory in this respect,
because of the glory that excels.
11 For if what is passing away
was glorious, what remains *is*
much more glorious.
12 Therefore, since we have such
hope, [a]we use great boldness of
speech—
13 unlike Moses, [a]*who* put a veil
over his face so that the children
of Israel could not look steadily at
[b]the end of what was passing
away.
14 But [a]their minds were blinded.
For until this day the same veil re-
mains unlifted in the reading of the
Old Testament, because the *veil* is
taken away in Christ.
15 But even to this day, when Mo-
ses is read, a veil lies on their
heart.
16 Nevertheless [a]when one turns
to the Lord, [b]the veil is taken
away.
17 Now [a]the Lord is the Spirit; and
where the Spirit of the Lord *is,*
there *is* [b]liberty.
18 But we all, with unveiled face,
beholding [a]as in a mirror [b]the
glory of the Lord, [c]are being trans-
formed into the same image from
glory to glory, just as [1]by the Spirit
of the Lord.

The Light of Christ's Gospel

4 Therefore, since we have this
ministry, [a]as we have received
mercy, we [b]do not lose heart.
2 But we have renounced the hid-
den things of shame, not walking
in craftiness nor [1]handling the
word of God deceitfully, but by
manifestation of the truth [a]com-
mending ourselves to every man's
conscience in the sight of God.
3 But even if our gospel is veiled,
[a]it is veiled to those who are per-
ishing,
4 whose minds [a]the god of this
age [b]has blinded, who do not be-
lieve, lest [c]the light of the gospel
of the glory of Christ, [d]who is the
image of God, should shine on
them.
5 [a]For we do not preach our-
selves, but Christ Jesus the Lord,
and [b]ourselves your bondservants
for Jesus' sake.
6 For it is the God [a]who com-
manded light to shine out of dark-
ness, who has [b]shone in our hearts
to *give* the light of the knowledge
of the glory of God in the face of
Jesus Christ.

Cast Down but Unconquered

7 But we have this treasure in
earthen vessels, [a]that the excel-
lence of the power may be of God
and not of us.
8 *We are* [a]hard-pressed on every
side, yet not crushed; *we are* per-
plexed, but not in despair;
9 persecuted, but not [a]forsaken;
[b]struck down, but not destroyed—
10 [a]always carrying about in the
body the dying of the Lord Jesus,

CHAPTER 3

1 [a]2 Cor. 5:12; 10:12, 18; 12:11 [b]Acts 18:27
2 [a]1 Cor. 9:2
3 [a]1 Cor. 3:5 [b]Ex. 24:12; 31:18; 32:15 [c]Ps. 40:8
5 [a][John 15:5] [b]1 Cor. 15:10
6 [a]1 Cor. 3:5 [b]Jer. 31:31 [c]Rom. 2:27 [d]Gal. 3:10 [e]John 6:63 [1]Or *spirit*
7 [a]Rom. 7:10 [b]Ex. 34:1 [c]Ex. 34:29
8 [a][Gal. 3:5]
9 [a][Rom. 1:17; 3:21]
12 [a]Eph. 6:19
13 [a]Ex. 34:33–35 [b][Gal. 3:23]
14 [a]Acts 28:26
16 [a]Rom. 11:23 [b]Is. 25:7
17 [a][1 Cor. 15:45] [b]Gal. 5:1, 13
18 [a]1 Cor. 13:12 [b][2 Cor. 4:4, 6] [c][Rom. 8:29, 30] [1]Or *from the Lord, the Spirit*

CHAPTER 4

1 [a]1 Cor. 7:25 [b]2 Cor. 4:16
2 [a]2 Cor. 5:11 [1]*adulterating the word of God*
3 [a][1 Cor. 1:18]
4 [a]John 12:31 [b]John 12:40 [c][2 Cor. 3:8, 9] [d][John 1:18]
5 [a]1 Cor. 1:13 [b]1 Cor. 9:19
6 [a]Gen. 1:3 [b]2 Pet. 1:19
7 [a]1 Cor. 2:5
8 [a]2 Cor. 1:8; 7:5
9 [a][Heb. 13:5] [b]Ps. 37:24
10 [a]Phil. 3:10

[b]that the life of Jesus also may be
manifested in our body.
11 For we who live [a]are always de-
livered to death for Jesus' sake,
that the life of Jesus also may be
manifested in our mortal flesh.
12 So then death is working in us,
but life in you.
13 And since we have [a]the same
spirit of faith, according to what
is written, [b]*"I believed and there-
fore I spoke,"* we also believe and
therefore speak,
14 knowing that [a]He who raised
up the Lord Jesus will also raise
us up with Jesus, and will present
us with you.
15 For [a]all things *are* for your
sakes, that [b]grace, having spread
through the many, may cause
thanksgiving to abound to the
glory of God.

Seeing the Invisible

16 Therefore we [a]do not lose
heart. Even though our outward
man is perishing, yet the inward
man is [b]being renewed day by day.
17 For [a]our light affliction, which
is but for a moment, is working for
us a far more exceeding *and* eter-
nal weight of glory,
18 [a]while we do not look at the
things which are seen, but at the
things which are not seen. For
the things which are seen *are* tem-
porary, but the things which are
not seen *are* eternal.

Assurance of the Resurrection

5 For we know that if [a]our
earthly [1]house, *this* tent, is de-
stroyed, we have a building from
God, a house [b]not made with
hands, eternal in the heavens.
2 For in this [a]we groan, earnestly
desiring to be clothed with our
[1]habitation which is from heaven,
3 if indeed, [a]having been clothed,
we shall not be found naked.
4 For we who are in *this* tent
groan, being burdened, not be-
cause we want to be unclothed,
[a]but further clothed, that mortality
may be swallowed up by life.
5 Now He who has prepared us
for this very thing *is* God, who also
[a]has given us the Spirit as [1]a guar-
antee.
6 So *we are* always confident,
knowing that while we are at
home in the body we are absent
from the Lord.
7 For [a]we walk by faith, not by
sight.
8 We are confident, yes, [a]well
pleased rather to be absent from
the body and to be present with
the Lord.

The Judgment Seat of Christ

9 Therefore we make it our aim,
whether present or absent, to be
well pleasing to Him.
10 [a]For we must all appear before
the judgment seat of Christ, [b]that
each one may receive the things
done in the body, according to
what he has done, whether good
or bad.
11 Knowing, therefore, [a]the terror
of the Lord, we persuade men; but
we are well known to God, and I
also trust are well known in your
consciences.

Be Reconciled to God

12 For [a]we do not commend our-
selves again to you, but give you
opportunity [b]to boast on our be-
half, that you may have *an answer*
for those who boast in appearance
and not in heart.
13 For [a]if we are beside ourselves,
it is for God; or if we are of sound
mind, *it is* for you.
14 For the love of Christ compels
us, because we judge thus: that [a]if
One died for all, then all died;
15 and He died for all, [a]that those
who live should live no longer for
themselves, but for Him who died
for them and rose again.
16 [a]Therefore, from now on, we
regard no one according to the
flesh. Even though we have known
Christ according to the flesh, [b]yet
now we know *Him thus* no longer.
17 Therefore, if anyone [a]*is* in
Christ, *he is* [b]a new creation; [c]old
things have passed away; behold,
all things have become [d]new.
18 Now all things *are* of God,
[a]who has reconciled us to Himself
through Jesus Christ, and has
given us the ministry of recon-
ciliation,
19 that is, that [a]God was in Christ
reconciling the world to Himself,
not [1]imputing their trespasses to
them, and has committed to us the
word of reconciliation.

---

10 [b]Rom. 8:17
11 [a]Rom. 8:36
13 [a]2 Pet. 1:1 [b]Ps. 116:10
14 [a][Rom. 8:11]
15 [a]Col. 1:24 [b]1 Cor. 9:19; 2 Cor. 1:11
16 [a]2 Cor. 4:1; Gal. 6:9 [b][Is. 40:29, 31; Col. 3:10]
17 [a]Matt. 5:12; Rom. 8:18; 1 Pet. 1:6
18 [a]Rom. 8:24; [2 Cor. 5:7; Heb. 11:1, 13]

CHAPTER 5

1 [a]Job 4:19; 1 Cor. 15:47; 2 Cor. 4:7 [b]Mark 14:58; Acts 7:48; Heb. 9:11, 24 [1]Physical body
2 [a]Rom. 8:23; 2 Cor. 5:4 [1]*dwelling*
3 [a]Rev. 3:18
4 [a]1 Cor. 15:53
5 [a]Rom. 8:23; [2 Cor. 1:22]; Eph. 1:14 [1]*down payment, earnest*
7 [a]Rom. 8:24; Heb. 11:1
8 [a]Phil. 1:23
10 [a]Matt. 16:27; Acts 10:42; Rom. 2:16; 14:10, 12 [b]Gal. 6:7; Eph. 6:8
11 [a][Heb. 10:31; 12:29; Jude 23]
12 [a]2 Cor. 3:1 [b]2 Cor. 1:14; Phil. 1:26
13 [a]Mark 3:21; 2 Cor. 11:1, 16; 12:11
14 [a][Rom. 5:15; 6:6; Gal. 2:20; Col. 3:3]
15 [a][Rom. 6:11]
16 [a]2 Cor. 10:3 [b][Matt. 12:50]
17 [a][John 6:63] [b][Rom. 8:9] [c]Is. 43:18; 65:17; [Eph. 4:24]; Rev. 21:4 [d][Rom. 6:3–10; Col. 3:3]
18 [a]Rom. 5:10; [Eph. 2:16; Col. 1:20]
19 [a][Rom. 3:24] [1]*reckoning*

20 Now then, we are [a]ambassa-
dors for Christ, as though God
were pleading through us: we im-
plore *you* on Christ's behalf, be
reconciled to God.
21 For [a]He made Him who knew
no sin *to be* sin for us, that we
might become [b]the righteousness
of God in Him.

Marks of the Ministry

6 We then, *as* [a]workers together
with Him also [b]plead with *you*
not to receive the grace of God in
vain.
2 For He says:

[a]"*In an acceptable time I have*
heard you,
And in the day of salvation I have
helped you."

Behold, now *is* the accepted time;
behold, now *is* the day of sal-
vation.
3 [a]We give no offense in any-
thing, that our ministry may not
be blamed.
4 But in all *things* we commend
ourselves [a]as ministers of God: in
much [1]patience, in tribulations, in
needs, in distresses,
5 [a]in stripes, in imprisonments,
in tumults, in labors, in sleepless-
ness, in fastings;
6 by purity, by knowledge, by
longsuffering, by kindness, by the
Holy Spirit, by [1]sincere love,
7 [a]by the word of truth, by [b]the
power of God, by [c]the armor of
righteousness on the right hand
and on the left,
8 by honor and dishonor, by evil
report and good report; as deceiv-
ers, and *yet* true;
9 as unknown, and [a]*yet* well
known; [b]as dying, and behold we
live; [c]as chastened, and *yet* not
killed;
10 as sorrowful, yet always rejoic-
ing; as poor, yet making many
[a]rich; as having nothing, and *yet*
possessing all things.

Be Holy

11 O Corinthians! [1]We have spo-
ken openly to you, [a]our heart is
wide open.
12 You are not restricted by us,
but [a]you are restricted by your
own affections.
13 Now in return for the same [a](I
speak as to children), you also be
open.
14 [a]Do not be unequally yoked to-
gether with unbelievers. For [b]what
[1]fellowship has righteousness with
lawlessness? And what [2]commu-
nion has light with darkness?
15 And what accord has Christ
with Belial? Or what part has a be-
liever with an unbeliever?
16 And what agreement has the
temple of God with idols? For
[a]you[1] are the temple of the living
God. As God has said:

[b]"*I will dwell in them*
And walk among them.
I will be their God,
And they shall be My people."

17 Therefore

[a]"*Come out from among them*
And be separate, says the Lord.
Do not touch what is unclean,
And I will receive you."
18 "*I* [a]*will be a Father to you,*
And you shall be My [b]*sons and*
daughters,
Says the LORD *Almighty.*"

7 Therefore,[a] having these prom-
ises, beloved, let us cleanse
ourselves from all filthiness of the
flesh and spirit, perfecting holi-
ness in the fear of God.

The Corinthians' Repentance

2 Open *your hearts* to us. We
have wronged no one, we have
corrupted no one, [a]we have
cheated no one.
3 I do not say *this* to condemn;
for [a]I have said before that you are
in our hearts, to die together and
to live together.
4 [a]Great *is* my boldness of
speech toward you, [b]great *is* my
boasting on your behalf. [c]I am
filled with comfort. I am exceed-
ingly joyful in all our tribulation.
5 For indeed, [a]when we came to
Macedonia, our bodies had no rest,
but [b]we were troubled on every
side. [c]Outside *were* conflicts, in-
side *were* fears.
6 Nevertheless [a]God, who com-
forts the downcast, comforted us
by [b]the coming of Titus,
7 and not only by his coming, but
also by the [1]consolation with

20 [a]Eph. 6:20
21 [a]Is. 53:6, 9 [b][Rom. 1:17; 3:21]

CHAPTER 6

1 [a]1 Cor. 3:9 [b]2 Cor. 5:20
2 [a]Is. 49:8
3 [a]Rom. 14:13
4 [a]1 Cor. 4:1 [1]*endurance*
5 [a]2 Cor. 11:23
6 [1]Lit. *un-hypocritical*
7 [a]2 Cor. 7:14 [b]1 Cor. 2:4 [c]2 Cor. 10:4
9 [a]2 Cor. 4:2; 5:11 [b]1 Cor. 4:9, 11 [c]Ps. 118:18
10 [a][2 Cor. 8:9]
11 [a]2 Cor. 7:3 [1]Lit. *Our mouth is open*
12 [a]2 Cor. 12:15
13 [a]1 Cor. 4:14
14 [a]1 Cor. 5:9 [b]Eph. 5:6, 7, 11 [1]*in common* [2]*fellowship*
16 [a][1 Cor. 3:16, 17; 6:19] [b]Ezek. 37:26, 27 [1]NU *we*
17 [a]Is. 52:11
18 [a]2 Sam. 7:14 [b][Rom. 8:14]

CHAPTER 7

1 [a][1 John 3:3]
2 [a]Acts 20:33
3 [a]2 Cor. 6:11, 12
4 [a]2 Cor. 3:12 [b]1 Cor. 1:4 [c]Phil. 2:17
5 [a]2 Cor. 2:13 [b]2 Cor. 4:8 [c]Deut. 32:25
6 [a]2 Cor. 1:3, 4 [b]2 Cor. 2:13; 7:13
7 [1]*comfort*

which he was comforted in you,
when he told us of your earnest
desire, your mourning, your zeal
for me, so that I rejoiced even
more.
8 For even if I made you [a]sorry
with my letter, I do not regret it;
[b]though I did regret it. For I per-
ceive that the same epistle made
you sorry, though only for a while.
9 Now I rejoice, not that you
were made sorry, but that your
sorrow led to repentance. For you
were made sorry in a godly man-
ner, that you might suffer loss
from us in nothing.
10 For [a]godly sorrow produces re-
pentance *leading* to salvation, not
to be regretted; [b]but the sorrow of
the world produces death.
11 For observe this very thing,
that you sorrowed in a godly man-
ner: What diligence it produced in
you, *what* [a]clearing *of yourselves,*
what indignation, *what* fear, *what*
vehement desire, *what* zeal, *what*
vindication! In all *things* you
proved yourselves to be [b]clear in
this matter.
12 Therefore, although I wrote to
you, *I did* not *do it* for the sake of
him who had done the wrong, nor
for the sake of him who suffered
wrong, [a]but that our care for you
in the sight of God might appear
to you.

The Joy of Titus

13 Therefore we have been com-
forted in your comfort. And we re-
joiced exceedingly more for the
joy of Titus, because his spirit [a]has
been refreshed by you all.
14 For if in anything I have
boasted to him about you, I am not
ashamed. But as we spoke all
things to you in truth, even so our
boasting to Titus was found true.
15 And his affections are greater
for you as he remembers [a]the obe-
dience of you all, how with fear
and trembling you received him.
16 Therefore I rejoice that [a]I have
confidence in you in everything.

Excel in Giving

8 Moreover, brethren, we make
known to you the grace of God
bestowed on the churches of
Macedonia:

8 [a]2 Cor. 2:2 [b]2 Cor. 2:4
10 [a]2 Sam. 12:13; Ps. 32:10; Matt. 26:75 [b]Prov. 17:22
11 [a]Eph. 5:11 [b]2 Cor. 2:5–11
12 [a]2 Cor. 2:4
13 [a]Rom. 15:32
15 [a]2 Cor. 2:9; Phil. 2:12
16 [a]2 Cor. 2:3; 8:22; 2 Thess. 3:4; Philem. 8, 21

CHAPTER 8

2 [a]Mark 12:44
4 [a]Acts 11:29; 24:17; Rom. 15:25, 26; 1 Cor. 16:1, 3, 4; 2 Cor. 9:1 [1]NU, M omit *that we would receive,* thus changing text to *urgency for the favor and fellowship*
5 [a][Rom. 12:1, 2] [b][Eph. 6:6]
6 [a]2 Cor. 8:17; 12:18
7 [a][1 Cor. 1:5; 12:13] [b]2 Cor. 9:8
8 [a]1 Cor. 7:6
9 [a]Matt. 8:20; Luke 9:58; Phil. 2:6, 7 [b]Rom. 9:23; [Eph. 1:7; Rev. 3:18]
10 [a]1 Cor. 7:25, 40 [b][Prov. 19:17; Matt. 10:42; 1 Tim. 6:18, 19; Heb. 13:16] [c]1 Cor. 16:2; 2 Cor. 9:2
12 [a]Mark 12:43, 44; Luke 21:3, 4; 2 Cor. 9:7
15 [a]Ex. 16:18

2 that in a great trial of affliction
the abundance of their joy and
[a]their deep poverty abounded in
the riches of their liberality.
3 For I bear witness that accord-
ing to *their* ability, yes, and be-
yond *their* ability, *they were* freely
willing,
4 imploring us with much ur-
gency [1]that we would receive the
gift and [a]the fellowship of the min-
istering to the saints.
5 And not *only* as we had hoped,
but they first [a]gave themselves to
the Lord, and *then* to us by the
[b]will of God.
6 So [a]we urged Titus, that as he
had begun, so he would also com-
plete this grace in you as well.
7 But as [a]you abound in every-
thing—in faith, in speech, in
knowledge, in all diligence, and in
your love for us—*see* [b]that you
abound in this grace also.

Christ Our Pattern

8 [a]I speak not by commandment,
but I am testing the sincerity of
your love by the diligence of oth-
ers.
9 For you know the grace of our
Lord Jesus Christ, [a]that though He
was rich, yet for your sakes He be-
came poor, that you through His
poverty might become [b]rich.
10 And in this [a]I give advice:
[b]It is to your advantage not only
to be doing what you began
and [c]were desiring to do a year
ago;
11 but now you also must com-
plete the doing *of it;* that as *there*
was a readiness to desire *it,* so
there also *may be* a completion out
of what *you* have.
12 For [a]if there is first a willing
mind, *it is* accepted according to
what one has, *and* not according
to what he does not have.
13 For *I do* not *mean* that others
should be eased and you bur-
dened;
14 but by an equality, *that* now at
this time your abundance *may*
supply their lack, that their abun-
dance also may supply your lack—
that there may be equality.
15 As it is written, [a]*"He who gath-*
ered much had nothing left over,
and he who gathered little had no
lack."

Collection for the Judean Saints

16 But thanks *be* to God who [1]puts
the same earnest care for you into
the heart of Titus.
17 For he not only accepted the
exhortation, but being more dili-
gent, he went to you of his own
accord.
18 And we have sent with him [a]the
brother whose praise *is* in the gos-
pel throughout all the churches,
19 and not only *that,* but who was
also [a]chosen by the churches to
travel with us with this gift, which
is administered by us [b]to the glory
of the Lord Himself and *to show*
your ready mind,
20 avoiding this: that anyone
should blame us in this lavish gift
which is administered by us—
21 [a]providing honorable things,
not only in the sight of the Lord,
but also in the sight of men.
22 And we have sent with them
our brother whom we have often
proved diligent in many things, but
now much more diligent, because
of the great confidence which *we
have* in you.
23 If *anyone inquires* about [a]Titus,
he is my partner and fellow worker
concerning you. Or if our brethren
are inquired about, they are [b]mes-
sengers[1] of the churches, the glory
of Christ.
24 Therefore show to them, [1]and
before the churches the proof of
your love and of our [a]boasting on
your behalf.

Administering the Gift

9 Now concerning [a]the minister-
ing to the saints, it is super-
fluous for me to write to you;
2 for I know your willingness,
about which I boast of you to the
Macedonians, that Achaia was
ready a [a]year ago; and your zeal
has stirred up the majority.
3 [a]Yet I have sent the brethren,
lest our boasting of you should be
in vain in this respect, that, as I
said, you may be ready;
4 lest if *some* Macedonians come
with me and find you unprepared,
we (not to mention you!) should
be ashamed of this [1]confident
boasting.
5 Therefore I thought it neces-
sary to [1]exhort the brethren to go
to you ahead of time, and prepare
your generous gift beforehand,
which *you had* previously prom-
ised, that it may be ready as *a
matter of* generosity and not as a
[2]grudging obligation.

The Cheerful Giver

6 [a]But this *I say:* He who sows
sparingly will also reap sparingly,
and he who sows [1]bountifully will
also reap [1]bountifully.
7 *So let* each one *give* as he pur-
poses in his heart, [a]not grudgingly
or of [1]necessity; for [b]God loves a
cheerful giver.
8 [a]And God *is* able to make all
grace abound toward you, that
you, always having all sufficiency
in all *things,* may have an abun-
dance for every good work.
9 As it is written:

[a]"He has dispersed abroad,
He has given to the poor;
His righteousness endures
forever."

10 Now [1]may He who [a]supplies
seed to the sower, and bread for
food, [2]supply and multiply the
seed you have *sown* and increase
the fruits of your [b]righteousness,
11 while *you are* enriched in
everything for all liberality,
[a]which causes thanksgiving
through us to God.
12 For the administration of this
service not only [a]supplies the
needs of the saints, but also is
abounding through many thanks-
givings to God,
13 while, through the proof of this
ministry, they [a]glorify God for the
obedience of your confession to
the gospel of Christ, and for *your*
liberal [b]sharing with them and all
men,
14 and by their prayer for you,
who long for you because of the
exceeding [a]grace of God in you.
15 Thanks *be* to God [a]for His in-
describable gift!

The Spiritual War

10 Now [a]I, Paul, myself am
pleading with you by the
meekness and gentleness of
Christ—[b]who in presence *am*
lowly among you, but being absent
am bold toward you.

16 [1]NU *has put*
18 [a]1 Cor. 16:3; 2 Cor. 12:18
19 [a]Acts 14:23; 1 Cor. 16:3, 4 [b]2 Cor. 4:15
21 [a]Rom. 12:17; Phil. 4:8; 1 Pet. 2:12
23 [a]2 Cor. 7:13, 14 [b][John 13:16]; Phil. 2:25 [1]Lit. *apostles,* "sent ones"
24 [a]2 Cor. 7:4, 14; 9:2 [1]NU, M omit *and*

CHAPTER 9

1 [a]Acts 11:29; Rom. 15:26; 1 Cor. 16:1; 2 Cor. 8:4; Gal. 2:10
2 [a]2 Cor. 8:10
3 [a]2 Cor. 8:6, 17
4 [1]NU *confidence.*
5 [1]*encourage* [2]Lit. *covetousness*
6 [a]Prov. 11:24; 22:9; Gal. 6:7, 9 [1]*with blessings*
7 [a]Deut. 15:7 [b]Deut. 15:10; 1 Chr. 29:17; [Prov. 11:25]; Rom. 12:8; [2 Cor. 8:12] [1]*compulsion*
8 [a][Prov. 11:24]
9 [a]Ps. 112:9
10 [a]Is. 55:10 [b]Hos. 10:12 [1]NU omits *may* [2]NU *will supply*
11 [a]2 Cor. 1:11
12 [a]2 Cor. 8:14
13 [a][Matt. 5:16] [b][Heb. 13:16]
14 [a]2 Cor. 8:1
15 [a][John 3:16; 4:10; Rom. 6:23; 8:32; Eph. 2:8; James 1:17]

CHAPTER 10

1 [a]Rom. 12:1 [b]1 Thess. 2:7

2 But I beg *you* [a]that when I am
present I may not be bold with that
confidence by which I intend to be
bold against some, who think of
us as if we walked according to the
flesh.
3 For though we walk in the
flesh, we do not war according to
the flesh.
4 [a]For the weapons [b]of our war-
fare *are* not [1]carnal but [c]mighty in
God [d]for pulling down strong-
holds,
5 [a]casting down arguments and
every high thing that exalts itself
against the knowledge of God,
bringing every thought into captiv-
ity to the obedience of Christ,
6 [a]and being ready to punish all
disobedience when [b]your obedi-
ence is fulfilled.

Reality of Paul's Authority

7 [a]Do you look at things accord-
ing to the outward appearance? [b]If
anyone is convinced in himself
that he is Christ's, let him again
consider this in himself, that just
as he *is* Christ's, even [1]so [c]we *are*
Christ's.
8 For even if I should boast some-
what more [a]about our authority,
which the Lord gave [1]us for [2]edi-
fication and not for your destruc-
tion, [b]I shall not be ashamed—
9 lest I seem to terrify you by let-
ters.
10 "For *his* letters," they say, "*are*
weighty and powerful, but [a]*his*
bodily presence *is* weak, and *his*
[b]speech contemptible."
11 Let such a person consider this,
that what we are in word by letters
when we are absent, such *we will*
also *be* in deed when we are pres-
ent.

Limits of Paul's Authority

12 [a]For we dare not class our-
selves or compare ourselves with
those who commend themselves.
But they, measuring themselves by
themselves, and comparing them-
selves among themselves, are not
wise.
13 [a]We, however, will not boast
beyond measure, but within the
limits of the sphere which God ap-
pointed us—a sphere which espe-
cially includes you.
14 For we are not overextending
ourselves (as though *our authority*
did not extend to you), [a]for it was
to you that we came with the gos-
pel of Christ;
15 not boasting of things beyond
measure, *that is,* [a]in other men's
labors, but having hope, *that* as
your faith is increased, we shall be
greatly enlarged by you in our
sphere,
16 to preach the gospel in the *re-
gions* beyond you, *and* not to boast
in another man's sphere of ac-
complishment.
17 But [a]"*he who glories, let him
glory in the* LORD."
18 For [a]not he who commends
himself is approved, but [b]whom
the Lord commends.

Concern for Their Faithfulness

11 Oh, that you would bear
with me in a little [a]folly—
and indeed you do bear with me.
2 For I am [a]jealous for you with
godly jealousy. For [b]I have be-
trothed you to one husband, [c]that
I may present *you* [d]*as* a chaste vir-
gin to Christ.
3 But I fear, lest somehow, as
[a]the serpent deceived Eve by his
craftiness, so your minds [b]may be
corrupted from the [1]simplicity that
is in Christ.
4 For if he who comes preaches
another Jesus whom we have not
preached, or *if* you receive a differ-
ent spirit which you have not re-
ceived, or a [a]different gospel
which you have not accepted—you
may well put up with it!

Paul and False Apostles

5 For I consider that [a]I am not
at all inferior to the most eminent
apostles.
6 Even though [a]*I am* untrained in
speech, yet *I am* not [b]in knowl-
edge. But [c]we have [1]been thor-
oughly manifested among you in
all things.
7 Did I commit sin in [1]humbling
myself that you might be exalted,
because I preached the gospel of
God to you [a]free of charge?
8 I robbed other churches, taking
wages *from them* to minister to
you.
9 And when I was present with
you, and in need, [a]I was a burden
to no one, for what I lacked [b]the

---

2 [a]1 Cor. 4:21; 2 Cor. 13:2, 10
4 [a]Eph. 6:13 [b]1 Cor. 9:7; [2 Cor. 6:7]; 1 Tim. 1:18 [c]Acts 7:22 [d]Jer. 1:10; [2 Cor. 10:8; 13:10] [1]*of the flesh*
5 [a]1 Cor. 1:19
6 [a]2 Cor. 13:2, 10 [b]2 Cor. 7:15
7 [a][John 7:24]; 2 Cor. 5:12 [b]1 Cor. 1:12; 14:37 [c][Rom. 14:8]; 1 Cor. 3:23 [1]NU *as we are.*
8 [a]2 Cor. 13:10 [b]2 Cor. 7:14 [1]NU omits *us* [2]*building up*
10 [a]1 Cor. 2:3, 4; 2 Cor. 12:7; Gal. 4:13 [b][1 Cor. 1:17]; 2 Cor. 11:6
12 [a]2 Cor. 5:12
13 [a]2 Cor. 10:15
14 [a]1 Cor. 3:5, 6
15 [a]Rom. 15:20
17 [a]Is. 65:16; Jer. 9:24; 1 Cor. 1:31
18 [a]Prov. 27:2 [b]Rom. 2:29; [1 Cor. 4:5]

CHAPTER 11

1 [a]Matt. 17:17; 2 Cor. 11:4, 16, 19
2 [a]Gal. 4:17 [b]Hos. 2:19; [Eph. 5:26] [c]Col. 1:28 [d]Lev. 21:13
3 [a]Gen. 3:4, 13; John 8:44; 1 Thess. 3:5; 1 Tim. 2:14; [Rev. 12:9, 15] [b]Eph. 6:24 [1]NU adds *and purity*
4 [a]Gal. 1:6–8
5 [a][1 Cor. 15:10]; 2 Cor. 12:11; Gal. 2:6
6 [a][1 Cor. 1:17] [b][1 Cor. 12:8; Eph. 3:4] [c][2 Cor. 12:12] [1]NU omits *been*
7 [a]Acts 18:3; 1 Cor. 9:18; 2 Cor. 12:13 [1]*putting myself down*
9 [a]Acts 20:33 [b]Phil. 4:10

brethren who came from Macedo-
nia supplied. And in everything I
kept myself from being burden-
some to you, and so I will keep *my-*
self.
10 [a]As the truth of Christ is in me,
[b]no one shall stop me from this
boasting in the regions of Achaia.
11 Why? [a]Because I do not love
you? God knows!
12 But what I do, I will also con-
tinue to do, [a]that I may cut off the
opportunity from those who desire
an opportunity to be regarded just
as we are in the things of which
they boast.
13 For such [a]*are* false apostles,
[b]deceitful workers, transforming
themselves into apostles of Christ.
14 And no wonder! For Satan him-
self transforms himself into [a]an
angel of light.
15 Therefore *it is* no great thing
if his ministers also transform
themselves into ministers of righ-
teousness, [a]whose end will be ac-
cording to their works.

Reluctant Boasting

16 I say again, let no one think me
a fool. If otherwise, at least receive
me as a fool, that I also may boast
a little.
17 What I speak, [a]I speak not ac-
cording to the Lord, but as it were,
foolishly, in this confidence of
boasting.
18 Seeing that many boast accord-
ing to the flesh, I also will boast.
19 For you put up with fools
gladly, [a]since you *yourselves* are
wise!
20 For you put up with it [a]if one
brings you into bondage, if one de-
vours *you,* if one takes *from you,*
if one exalts himself, if one strikes
you on the face.
21 To *our* shame [a]I say that we
were too weak for that! But [b]in
whatever anyone is bold—I speak
foolishly—I am bold also.

Suffering for Christ

22 Are they [a]Hebrews? So *am* I.
Are they Israelites? So *am* I. Are
they the seed of Abraham? So
am I.
23 Are they ministers of Christ?—
I speak as a fool—I *am* more: [a]in
labors more abundant, [b]in stripes
above measure, in prisons more
frequently, [c]in deaths often.
24 From the Jews five times I re-
ceived [a]forty [b]*stripes* minus one.
25 Three times I was [a]beaten with
rods; [b]once I was stoned; three
times I [c]was shipwrecked; a night
and a day I have been in the deep;
26 *in* journeys often, *in* perils of
waters, *in* perils of robbers, [a]*in*
perils of *my own* countrymen, [b]*in*
perils of the Gentiles, *in* perils in
the city, *in* perils in the wilderness,
in perils in the sea, *in* perils among
false brethren;
27 in weariness and toil, [a]in sleep-
lessness often, [b]in hunger and
thirst, in [c]fastings often, in cold
and nakedness—
28 besides the other things, what
comes upon me daily: [a]my deep
concern for all the churches.
29 [a]Who is weak, and I am not
weak? Who is made to stumble,
and I do not burn *with indig-*
nation?
30 If I must boast, [a]I will boast in
the things which concern my [1]in-
firmity.
31 [a]The God and Father of our
Lord Jesus Christ, [b]who is blessed
forever, knows that I am not lying.
32 [a]In Damascus the governor,
under Aretas the king, was guard-
ing the city of the Damascenes
with a garrison, desiring to arrest
me;
33 but I was let down in a basket
through a window in the wall, and
escaped from his hands.

The Vision of Paradise

12 It is [1]doubtless not profitable
for me to boast. I will come
to [a]visions and [b]revelations of the
Lord:
2 I know a man [a]in Christ who
fourteen years ago—whether in
the body I do not know, or whether
out of the body I do not know, God
knows—such a one [b]was caught
up to the third heaven.
3 And I know such a man—
whether in the body or out of the
body I do not know, God knows—
4 how he was caught up into
[a]Paradise and heard inexpressible
words, which it is not lawful for a
man to utter.
5 Of such a one I will boast; yet

10 [a]Rom. 1:9; 9:1 [b]1 Cor. 9:15
11 [a]2 Cor. 6:11; 12:15
12 [a]1 Cor. 9:12
13 [a]Phil. 1:15 [b]Phil. 3:2
14 [a]Gal. 1:8
15 [a][Phil. 3:19]
17 [a]1 Cor. 7:6
19 [a]1 Cor. 4:10
20 [a][Gal. 2:4; 4:3, 9; 5:1]
21 [a]2 Cor. 10:10 [b]Phil. 3:4
22 [a]Phil. 3:4–6
23 [a]1 Cor. 15:10 [b]Acts 9:16 [c]1 Cor. 15:30
24 [a]Deut. 25:3 [b]2 Cor. 6:5
25 [a]Acts 16:22, 23; 21:32 [b]Acts 14:5, 19 [c]Acts 27:1–44
26 [a]Acts 9:23, 24; 13:45, 50; 17:5, 13 [b]Acts 14:5, 19; 19:23; 27:42
27 [a]Acts 20:31 [b]1 Cor. 4:11 [c]Acts 9:9; 13:2, 3; 14:23
28 [a]Acts 20:18
29 [a][1 Cor. 8:9, 13; 9:22]
30 [a][2 Cor. 12:5, 9, 10] [1]*weakness*
31 [a]1 Thess. 2:5 [b]Rom. 9:5
32 [a]Acts 9:19–25

CHAPTER 12

1 [a]Acts 16:9; 18:9; 22:17, 18; 23:11; 26:13–15; 27:23 [b][Gal. 1:12; 2:2] [1]NU *necessary, though not profitable, to boast*
2 [a]Rom. 16:7 [b]Acts 22:17
4 [a]Luke 23:43

of myself I will not [a]boast, except
in my infirmities.
6 For though I might desire to
boast, I will not be a fool; for I will
speak the truth. But I refrain, lest
anyone should think of me above
what he sees me *to be* or hears
from me.

The Thorn in the Flesh

7 And lest I should be exalted
above measure by the abundance
of the revelations, a [a]thorn in the
flesh was given to me, [b]a messen-
ger of Satan to [1]buffet me, lest I
be exalted above measure.
8 [a]Concerning this thing I
pleaded with the Lord three times
that it might depart from me.
9 And He said to me, "My grace
is sufficient for you, for My
strength is made perfect in weak-
ness." Therefore most gladly [a]I
will rather boast in my infirmities,
[b]that the power of Christ may rest
upon me.
10 Therefore [a]I take pleasure in
infirmities, in reproaches, in
needs, in persecutions, in dis-
tresses, for Christ's sake. [b]For
when I am weak, then I am strong.

Signs of an Apostle

11 I have become [a]a fool [1]in boast-
ing; you have compelled me. For
I ought to have been commended
by you; for [b]in nothing was I be-
hind the most eminent apostles,
though [c]I am nothing.
12 [a]Truly the signs of an apostle
were accomplished among you
with all perseverance, in signs and
[b]wonders and mighty [c]deeds.
13 For what is it in which you
were inferior to other churches,
except that I myself was not bur-
densome to you? Forgive me this
wrong!

Love for the Church

14 [a]Now *for* the third time I am
ready to come to you. And I will
not be burdensome to you; for [b]I
do not seek yours, but you. [c]For
the children ought not to lay up
for the parents, but the parents for
the children.
15 And I will very gladly spend
and be spent [a]for your souls;
though [b]the more abundantly I
love you, the less I am loved.
16 But be that *as it may,* [a]I did
not burden you. Nevertheless,
being crafty, I caught you by cun-
ning!
17 Did I take advantage of you by
any of those whom I sent to you?
18 I urged Titus, and sent our
[a]brother with *him.* Did Titus take
advantage of you? Did we not
walk in the same spirit? Did *we*
not *walk* in the same steps?
19 [a]Again,[1] do you think that we
excuse ourselves to you? [b]We
speak before God in Christ. [c]But
we do all things, beloved, for your
edification.
20 For I fear lest, when I come, I
shall not find you such as I wish,
and *that* [a]I shall be found by you
such as you do not wish; lest *there
be* contentions, jealousies, out-
bursts of wrath, selfish ambitions,
backbitings, whisperings, con-
ceits, tumults;
21 lest, when I come again, my
God [a]will humble me among you,
and I shall mourn for many [b]who
have sinned before and have not
repented of the uncleanness, [c]for-
nication, and lewdness which they
have practiced.

Coming with Authority

13 This *will be* [a]the third
time I am coming to you.
[b]*"By the mouth of two or three wit-
nesses every word shall be estab-
lished."*
2 [a]I have told you before, and
foretell as if I were present the sec-
ond time, and now being absent
[1]I write to those [b]who have sinned
before, and to all the rest, that if I
come again [c]I will not spare—
3 since you seek a proof of Christ
[a]speaking in me, who is not weak
toward you, but mighty [b]in you.
4 [a]For though He was crucified
in weakness, yet [b]He lives by the
power of God. For [c]we also are
weak in Him, but we shall live with
Him by the power of God toward
you.
5 Examine yourselves *as to*
whether you are in the faith. Test
yourselves. Do you not know your-
selves, [a]that Jesus Christ is in
you?—unless indeed you [1]are [b]dis-
qualified.
6 But I trust that you will know
that we are not disqualified.

5 [a]2 Cor. 11:30
7 [a]Ezek. 28:24 [b]Job 2:7 [1]*beat*
8 [a]Matt. 26:44
9 [a]2 Cor. 11:30 [b][1 Pet. 4:14]
10 [a][Rom. 5:3; 8:35] [b]2 Cor. 13:4
11 [a]2 Cor. 5:13; 11:1, 16; 12:6 [b]2 Cor. 11:5 [c]1 Cor. 3:7; 13:2; 15:9 [1]NU omits *in boasting*
12 [a]Rom. 15:18 [b]Acts 15:12 [c]Acts 14:8–10; 16:16–18; 19:11, 12; 20:6–12; 28:1–10
14 [a]2 Cor. 1:15; 13:1, 2 [b][1 Cor. 10:24–33] [c]1 Cor. 4:14
15 [a][2 Tim. 2:10] [b]2 Cor. 6:12, 13
16 [a]2 Cor. 11:9
18 [a]2 Cor. 8:18
19 [a]2 Cor. 5:12 [b][Rom. 9:1, 2] [c]1 Cor. 10:33 [1]NU *You have been thinking for a long time that we*
20 [a]1 Cor. 4:21
21 [a]2 Cor. 2:1, 4 [b]2 Cor. 13:2 [c]1 Cor. 5:1

CHAPTER 13

1 [a]2 Cor. 12:14 [b]Deut. 17:6; 19:15
2 [a]2 Cor. 10:2 [b]2 Cor. 12:21 [c]2 Cor. 1:23; 10:11 [1]NU omits *I write*
3 [a]Matt. 10:20 [b][1 Cor. 9:2]
4 [a][1 Pet. 3:18] [b][Rom. 1:4; 6:4] [c][2 Cor. 10:3, 4]
5 [a][Gal. 4:19] [b]1 Cor. 9:27 [1]*do not stand the test*

Paul Prefers Gentleness

7 Now [1]I pray to God that you
do no evil, not that we should ap-
pear approved, but that you should
do what is honorable, though [a]we
may seem disqualified.
8 For we can do nothing against
the truth, but for the truth.
9 For we are glad [a]when we are
weak and you are strong. And this
also we pray, [b]that you may be
made complete.
10 [a]Therefore I write these things
being absent, lest being present I
should use sharpness, according to
the [b]authority which the Lord has
given me for edification and not
for destruction.

Greetings and Benediction

11 Finally, brethren, farewell. Be-
come complete. [a]Be of good com-
fort, be of one mind, live in peace;
and the God of love [b]and peace
will be with you.
12 [a]Greet one another with a holy
kiss.
13 All the saints greet you.
14 [a]The grace of the Lord Jesus
Christ, and the love of God, and
[b]the [1]communion of the Holy
Spirit *be* with you all. Amen.

7 [a]2 Cor. 6:9 [1]NU *we*
9 [a]1 Cor. 4:10 [b]1 Cor. 1:10; 2 Cor. 13:11; Eph. 4:12; [1 Thess. 3:10]
10 [a]1 Cor. 4:21 [b]1 Cor. 5:4; 2 Cor. 10:8
11 [a]Rom. 12:16, 18 [b]Rom. 15:33; Eph. 6:23
12 [a]Rom. 16:16
14 [a]Rom. 16:24 [b]Phil. 2:1 [1]*fellowship*

The Epistle of Paul the Apostle to the

Galatians

THE Galatians, having launched their Christian experience by faith, seem content to leave their voyage of faith and chart a new course based on works—a course Paul finds disturbing. His letter to the Galatians is a vigorous attack against the gospel of works and a defense of the gospel of faith.

Paul begins by setting forth his credentials as an apostle with a message from God: blessing comes from God on the basis of faith, not law. The law declares men guilty and imprisons them; faith sets men free to enjoy liberty in Christ. But liberty is not license. Freedom in Christ means freedom to produce the fruits of righteousness through a Spirit-led life-style.

The book is called *Pros Galatas,* "To the Galatians," and it is the only letter of Paul that is specifically addressed to a number of churches ("To the churches of Galatia," 1:2). The name *Galatians* was given to this Celtic people because they originally lived in Gaul before their migration to Asia Minor.

Greeting

PAUL, an apostle (not from men
nor through man, but [a]through
Jesus Christ and God the Fa-
ther [b]who raised Him from the
dead),
2 and all the brethren who are
with me,

To the churches of Galatia:

3 Grace to you and peace from
God the Father and our Lord Jesus
Christ,
4 [a]who gave Himself for our sins,
that He might deliver us [b]from this
present evil age, according to the
will of our God and Father,
5 to whom *be* glory forever and
ever. Amen.

Only One Gospel

6 I marvel that you are turning
away so soon [a]from Him who
called you in the grace of Christ,
to a different gospel,
7 [a]which is not another; but there
are some [b]who trouble you and
want to [c]pervert[1] the gospel of
Christ.
8 But even if [a]we, or an angel
from heaven, preach any other
gospel to you than what we have
preached to you, let him be [1]ac-
cursed.
9 As we have said before, so now
I say again, if anyone preaches
any other gospel to you [a]than what
you have received, let him be ac-
cursed.
10 For [a]do I now [b]persuade men,
or God? Or [c]do I seek to please
men? For if I still pleased men, I
would not be a bondservant of
Christ.

Call to Apostleship

11 [a]But I make known to you,
brethren, that the gospel which
was preached by me is not accord-
ing to man.
12 For [a]I neither received it from
man, nor was I taught *it,* but *it*
came [b]through the revelation of
Jesus Christ.
13 For you have heard of my for-
mer conduct in Judaism, how [a]I
persecuted the church of God be-
yond measure and [b]*tried to* de-
stroy it.
14 And I advanced in Judaism be-
yond many of my contemporaries
in my own nation, [a]being more ex-
ceedingly zealous [b]for the tradi-
tions of my fathers.
15 But when it pleased God, [a]who

CHAPTER 1

1 [a]Acts 9:6 [b]Acts 2:24
4 [a][Matt. 20:28] [b]Heb. 2:5
6 [a][Rom. 8:28]; Gal. 1:15; 5:8
7 [a]2 Cor. 11:4 [b]Acts 15:1; Gal. 5:10, 12 [c]2 Cor. 2:17 [1]*distort*
8 [a]1 Cor. 16:22 [1]Gr. *anathema*
9 [a]Deut. 4:2
10 [a][1 Cor. 10:33]; 1 Thess. 2:4 [b]1 Sam. 24:7 [c]1 Thess. 2:4
11 [a][Rom. 2:16]; 1 Cor. 15:1
12 [a]1 Cor. 15:1 [b][Eph. 3:3–5]
13 [a]Acts 9:1 [b]Acts 8:3; 22:4, 5
14 [a]Acts 26:9; Phil. 3:6 [b]Jer. 9:14; Matt. 15:2; Mark 7:3; [Col. 2:8]
15 [a]Is. 49:1, 5; Jer. 1:5; Acts 9:15; Rom. 1:1; Gal. 1:6

separated me from my mother's
womb and called *me* through His
grace,
16 [a]to reveal His Son in me, that
[b]I might preach Him among the
Gentiles, I did not immediately
confer with [c]flesh and blood,
17 nor did I go up to Jerusalem to
those *who were* apostles before
me; but I went to Arabia, and re-
turned again to Damascus.

Contacts at Jerusalem

18 Then after three years [a]I went
up to Jerusalem to see [1]Peter, and
remained with him fifteen days.
19 But [a]I saw none of the other
apostles except [b]James, the Lord's
brother.
20 (Now *concerning* the things
which I write to you, indeed, be-
fore God, I do not lie.)
21 [a]Afterward I went into the re-
gions of Syria and Cilicia.
22 And I was unknown by face to
the churches of Judea which [a]*were*
in Christ.
23 But they were [a]hearing only,
"He who formerly [b]persecuted us
now preaches the faith which he
once *tried to* destroy."
24 And they [a]glorified God in me.

Defending the Gospel

2 Then after fourteen years [a]I
went up again to Jerusalem
with Barnabas, and also took Titus
with *me.*
2 And I went up [1]by revelation,
and communicated to them that
gospel which I preach among the
Gentiles, but [a]privately to those
who were of reputation, lest by
any means [b]I might run, or had
run, in vain.
3 Yet not even Titus who *was*
with me, being a Greek, was com-
pelled to be circumcised.
4 And *this occurred* because of
[a]false brethren secretly brought in
(who came in by stealth to spy out
our [b]liberty which we have in
Christ Jesus, [c]that they might
bring us into bondage),
5 to whom we did not yield sub-
mission even for an hour, that [a]the
truth of the gospel might continue
with you.
6 But from those [a]who seemed to
be something—whatever they
were, it makes no difference to me;
[b]God [1]shows personal favoritism
to no man—for those who seemed
to be something [c]added nothing to
me.
7 But on the contrary, [a]when
they saw that the gospel for the
uncircumcised [b]had been com-
mitted to me, as *the gospel* for the
circumcised *was* to Peter
8 (for He who worked effectively
in Peter for the apostleship to the
[a]circumcised [b]also [c]worked effec-
tively in me toward the Gentiles),
9 and when James, [1]Cephas, and
John, who seemed to be [a]pillars,
perceived [b]the grace that had been
given to me, they gave me and Bar-
nabas the right hand of fellowship,
[c]that we *should go* to the Gentiles
and they to the circumcised.
10 *They desired* only that we
should remember the poor, [a]the
very thing which I also was eager
to do.

No Return to the Law

11 [a]Now when [1]Peter had come to
Antioch, I [2]withstood him to his
face, because he was to be blamed;
12 for before certain men came
from James, [a]he would eat with
the Gentiles; but when they came,
he withdrew and separated him-
self, fearing [1]those who were of
the circumcision.
13 And the rest of the Jews also
played the hypocrite with him, so
that even Barnabas was carried
away with their hypocrisy.
14 But when I saw that they were
not straightforward about [a]the
truth of the gospel, I said to Peter
[b]before *them* all, [c]"If you, being a
Jew, live in the manner of Gentiles
and not as the Jews, [1]why do you
compel Gentiles to live as [2]Jews?
15 [a]"We *who are* Jews by nature,
and not [b]sinners of the Gentiles,
16 [a]"knowing that a man is not
[1]justified by the works of the law
but [b]by faith in Jesus Christ, even
we have believed in Christ Jesus,
that we might be justified by faith
in Christ and not [c]by the works of
the law; for by the works of the
law no flesh shall be justified.
17 "But if, while we seek to be
justified by Christ, we ourselves
also are found [a]sinners, *is* Christ
therefore a minister of sin? Cer-
tainly not!

16 [a][2 Cor. 4:5–7] [b]Acts 9:15 [c]Matt. 16:17
18 [a]Acts 9:26 [1]NU *Cephas*
19 [a]1 Cor. 9:5 [b]Matt. 13:55
21 [a]Acts 9:30
22 [a]Rom. 16:7
23 [a]Acts 9:20, 21 [b]Acts 8:3
24 [a]Acts 11:18

CHAPTER 2

1 [a]Acts 15:2
2 [a]Acts 15:1–4 [b]Phil. 2:16 [1]*because of*
4 [a]Acts 15:1, 24 [b]Gal. 3:25; 5:1, 13 [c]Gal. 4:3, 9
5 [a][Gal. 1:6; 2:14; 3:1]
6 [a]Gal. 2:9; 6:3 [b]Acts 10:34 [c]2 Cor. 11:5; 12:11 [1]Lit. *does not receive the face of a man*
7 [a]Acts 9:15; 13:46; 22:21 [b]1 Thess. 2:4
8 [a]1 Pet. 1:1 [b]Acts 9:15 [c][Gal. 3:5]
9 [a]Matt. 16:18 [b]Rom. 1:5 [c]Acts 13:3 [1]Peter
10 [a]Acts 11:30
11 [a]Acts 15:35 [1]NU *Cephas* [2]*opposed*
12 [a][Acts 10:28; 11:2, 3] [1]Jewish Christians
14 [a]Gal. 1:6; 2:5 [b]1 Tim. 5:20 [c][Acts 10:28] [1]NU *how can you* [2]Some interpreters stop the quotation here.
15 [a][Acts 15:10] [b]Matt. 9:11
16 [a]Acts 13:38, 39 [b]Rom. 1:17 [c]Ps. 143:2 [1]*declared righteous*
17 [a][1 John 3:8]

18 "For if I build again those
things which I destroyed, I make
myself a transgressor.
19 "For I [a]through the law [b]died
to the law that I might [c]live to God.
20 "I have been [a]crucified with
Christ; it is no longer I who live,
but Christ lives in me; and the *life*
which I now live in the flesh [b]I live
by faith in the Son of God, [c]who
loved me and gave Himself for me.
21 "I do not set aside the grace of
God; for [a]if righteousness *comes*
through the law, then Christ died
[1]in vain."

Justification by Faith

3 O foolish Galatians! Who has
bewitched you [1]that you
should not obey the truth, before
whose eyes Jesus Christ was
clearly portrayed [2]among you as
crucified?
2 This only I want to learn from
you: Did you receive the Spirit by
the works of the law, [a]or by the
hearing of faith?
3 Are you so foolish? [a]Having be-
gun in the Spirit, are you now be-
ing made perfect by [b]the flesh?
4 [a]Have you suffered so [1]many
things in vain—if indeed *it was* in
vain?
5 Therefore He who supplies the
Spirit to you and works miracles
among you, *does He do it* by the
works of the law, or by the hearing
of faith?—
6 just as Abraham [a]*"believed
God, and it was accounted to him
for righteousness."*
7 Therefore know that *only*
[a]those who are of faith are sons
of Abraham.
8 And [a]the Scripture, foreseeing
that God would justify the Gentiles
by faith, preached the gospel to
Abraham beforehand, *saying,* [b]*"In
you all the nations shall be
blessed."*
9 So then those who *are* of faith
are blessed with believing Abra-
ham.

The Law Brings a Curse

10 For as many as are of the
works of the law are under the
curse; for it is written, [a]*"Cursed is
everyone who does not continue
in all things which are written in
the book of the law, to do them."*
11 But that no one is [1]justified by
the law in the sight of God *is* evi-
dent, for [a]*"the just shall live by
faith."*
12 Yet [a]the law is not of faith, but
[b]*"the man who does them shall
live by them."*
13 [a]Christ has redeemed us from
the curse of the law, having be-
come a curse for us (for it is writ-
ten, [b]*"Cursed is everyone who
hangs on a tree"*),
14 [a]that the blessing of Abraham
might come upon the [b]Gentiles in
Christ Jesus, that we might receive
[c]the promise of the Spirit through
faith.

The Changeless Promise

15 Brethren, I speak in the man-
ner of men: [a]Though *it is* only a
man's covenant, yet *if it is* con-
firmed, no one annuls or adds
to it.
16 Now to Abraham and his Seed
were the promises made. He does
not say, "And to seeds," as of
many, but as of [a]one, [b]*"And to
your Seed,"* who is [c]Christ.
17 And this I say, *that* the law,
[a]which was four hundred and
thirty years later, cannot annul the
covenant that was confirmed be-
fore by God [1]in Christ, [b]that it
should make the promise of no ef-
fect.
18 For if [a]the inheritance *is* of the
law, [b]*it is* no longer of promise;
but God gave *it* to Abraham by
promise.

Purpose of the Law

19 What purpose then *does* the
law *serve?* [a]It was added because
of transgressions, till the [b]Seed
should come to whom the promise
was made; *and it was* [c]appointed
through angels by the hand [d]of a
mediator.
20 Now a mediator does not *medi-
ate* for one *only,* [a]but God is one.
21 *Is* the law then against the
promises of God? Certainly not!
For if there had been a law given
which could have given life, truly
righteousness would have been by
the law.
22 But the Scripture has confined
[a]all under sin, [b]that the promise by
faith in Jesus Christ might be
given to those who believe.

19 [a]Rom. 8:2 [b][Rom. 6:2, 14; 7:4]; 1 Cor. 9:20 [c][Rom. 6:11] **20** [a][Rom. 6:6; Gal. 5:24; 6:14] [b]Rom. 6:8–11; 2 Cor. 5:15; [Eph. 2:4–6; Col. 3:1–4] [c]Is. 53:12; Eph. 5:2 **21** [a]Heb. 7:11 [1]*for nothing*

CHAPTER 3

1 [1]NU omits *that you should not obey the truth* [2]NU omits *among you* **2** [a]Rom. 10:16, 17 **3** [a][Gal. 4:9] [b]Heb. 7:16 **4** [a]Heb. 10:35 [1]Or *great* **6** [a]Gen. 15:6 **7** [a]John 8:39 **8** [a]Rom. 9:17 [b]Gen. 12:3; 18:18; 22:18; 26:4; 28:14 **10** [a]Deut. 27:26 **11** [a]Hab. 2:4; Rom. 1:17; Heb. 10:38 [1]*declared righteous* **12** [a]Rom. 4:4, 5 [b]Lev. 18:5; Rom. 10:5 **13** [a][Rom. 8:3] [b]Deut. 21:23 **14** [a][Rom. 4:1–5, 9, 16; Gal. 3:28] [b]Is. 42:1, 6; 49:6; Luke 2:32; Rom. 3:29, 30 [c]Is. 32:15 **15** [a]Heb. 9:17 **16** [a]Gen. 22:18 [b]Gen. 12:3, 7; 13:15; 24:7 [c][1 Cor. 12:12] **17** [a]Gen. 15:13; Ex. 12:40; Acts 7:6 [b][Rom. 4:13] [1]NU omits *in Christ* **18** [a][Rom. 8:17] [b]Rom. 4:14 **19** [a]John 15:22 [b]Gal. 4:4 [c]Acts 7:53 [d]Ex. 20:19; Deut. 5:5 **20** [a][Rom. 3:29] **22** [a]Rom. 11:32 [b]Rom. 4:11

23 But before faith came, we were
kept under guard by the law, [1]kept
for the faith which would after-
ward be revealed.
24 Therefore [a]the law was our [1]tu-
tor *to bring us* to Christ, [b]that we
might be justified by faith.
25 But after faith has come, we are
no longer under a tutor.

Sons and Heirs

26 For you [a]are all sons of God
through faith in Christ Jesus.
27 For [a]as many of you as were
baptized into Christ [b]have put on
Christ.
28 [a]There is neither Jew nor
Greek, [b]there is neither slave nor
free, there is neither male nor fe-
male; for you are all [c]one in Christ
Jesus.
29 And [a]if you *are* Christ's, then
you are Abraham's [b]seed, and
[c]heirs according to the promise.

4 Now I say *that* the heir, as long
as he is a child, does not differ
at all from a slave, though he is
master of all,
2 but is under guardians and
stewards until the time appointed
by the father.
3 Even so we, when we were chil-
dren, [a]were in bondage under the
elements of the world.
4 But [a]when the fullness of the
time had come, God sent forth His
Son, [b]born[1] [c]of a woman, [d]born
under the law,
5 [a]to redeem those who were un-
der the law, [b]that we might receive
the adoption as sons.
6 And because you are sons, God
has sent forth [a]the Spirit of His
Son into your hearts, crying out,
[1]"Abba, Father!"
7 Therefore you are no longer a
slave but a son, [a]and if a son, then
an heir [1]of God [2]through Christ.

Fears for the Church

8 But then, indeed, [a]when you
did not know God, [b]you served
those which by nature are not
gods.
9 But now [a]after you have known
God, or rather are known by God,
[b]how *is it that* you turn again to
[c]the weak and beggarly elements,
to which you desire again to be in
bondage?
10 [a]You observe days and months
and seasons and years.
11 I am afraid for you, [a]lest I have
labored for you in vain.
12 Brethren, I urge you to become
like me, for I *became* like you.
[a]You have not injured me at all.
13 You know that [a]because of
physical infirmity I preached the
gospel to you at the first.
14 And my trial which was in my
flesh you did not despise or reject,
but you received me [a]as an [1]angel
of God, [b]*even* as Christ Jesus.
15 [1]What then was the blessing
you *enjoyed*? For I bear you wit-
ness that, if possible, you would
have plucked out your own eyes
and given them to me.
16 Have I therefore become
your enemy because I tell you the
truth?
17 They [a]zealously court you, *but*
for no good; yes, they want to ex-
clude you, that you may be zealous
for them.
18 But it is good to be zealous in
a good thing always, and not only
when I am present with you.
19 [a]My little children, for whom I
labor in birth again until Christ is
formed in you,
20 I would like to be present with
you now and to change my tone;
for I have doubts about you.

Two Covenants

21 Tell me, you who desire to be
under the law, do you not hear the
law?
22 For it is written that Abraham
had two sons: [a]the one by a bond-
woman, [b]the other by a free-
woman.
23 But he *who was* of the bond-
woman [a]was born according to the
flesh, [b]and he of the freewoman
through promise,
24 which things are symbolic. For
these are [1]the two covenants: the
one from Mount [a]Sinai which
gives birth to bondage, which is
Hagar—
25 for this Hagar is Mount Sinai
in Arabia, and corresponds to Je-
rusalem which now is, and is in
bondage with her children—
26 but the [a]Jerusalem above
is free, which is the mother of
us all.
27 For it is written:

23 [1]Lit. *confined*
24 [a]Rom. 10:4 [b]Acts 13:39 [1]In a household, the guardian responsible for the care and discipline of the children
26 [a]John 1:12
27 [a][Rom. 6:3] [b]Rom. 10:12; 13:14
28 [a]Col. 3:11 [b][1 Cor. 12:13] [c][Eph. 2:15, 16]
29 [a]Gen. 21:10 [b]Rom. 4:11 [c]Rom. 8:17
CHAPTER 4
3 [a]Col. 2:8, 20
4 [a][Gen. 49:10] [b][John 1:14] [c]Gen. 3:15 [d]Luke 2:21, 27 [1]Or *made*
5 [a][Matt. 20:28] [b][John 1:12]
6 [a][Rom. 5:5; 8:9, 15, 16] [1]Lit., in Aram., *Father*
7 [a][Rom. 8:16, 17] [1]NU *through God* [2]NU omits *through Christ*
8 [a]Eph. 2:12 [b]Rom. 1:25
9 [a][1 Cor. 8:3] [b]Col. 2:20 [c]Heb. 7:18
10 [a]Rom. 14:5
11 [a]1 Thess. 3:5
12 [a]2 Cor. 2:5
13 [a]1 Cor. 2:3
14 [a]Mal. 2:7 [b][Luke 10:16] [1]Or *messenger*
15 [1]NU *Where*
17 [a]Rom. 10:2
19 [a]1 Cor. 4:15
22 [a]Gen. 16:15 [b]Gen. 21:2
23 [a]Rom. 9:7, 8 [b]Heb. 11:11
24 [a]Deut. 33:2 [1]NU, M omit *the*
26 [a][Is. 2:2]

[a]*"Rejoice, O barren,*
You who do not bear!
Break forth and shout,
You who are not in labor!
For the desolate has many more
children
Than she who has a husband."

28 Now [a]we, brethren, as Isaac
was, are [b]children of promise.
29 But, as [a]he who was born ac-
cording to the flesh then perse-
cuted him *who was born* according
to the Spirit, [b]even so *it is* now.
30 Nevertheless what does [a]the
Scripture say? [b]*"Cast out the*
bondwoman and her son, for [c]*the*
son of the bondwoman shall not
be heir with the son of the free-
woman."
31 So then, brethren, we are not
children of the bondwoman but of
the free.

Christian Liberty

5 [a]Stand[1] fast therefore in the
liberty by which Christ has
made us free, and do not be entan-
gled again with a [b]yoke of bond-
age.
2 Indeed I, Paul, say to you that
[a]if you become circumcised, Christ
will profit you nothing.
3 And I testify again to every
man who becomes circumcised
[a]that he is [1]a debtor to keep the
whole law.
4 [a]You have become estranged
from Christ, you who *attempt to*
be justified by law; [b]you have
fallen from grace.
5 For we through the Spirit ea-
gerly [a]wait for the hope of righ-
teousness by faith.
6 For [a]in Christ Jesus neither cir-
cumcision nor uncircumcision
avails anything, but [b]faith working
through love.

Love Fulfills the Law

7 You [a]ran well. Who hindered
you from obeying the truth?
8 This persuasion does not *come*
from Him who calls you.
9 [a]A little leaven leavens the
whole lump.
10 I have confidence in you, in the
Lord, that you will have no other
mind; but he who troubles you
shall bear his judgment, whoever
he is.
11 And I, brethren, if I still preach

27 [a]Is. 54:1
28 [a]Gal. 3:29 [b]Acts 3:25
29 [a]Gen. 21:9 [b]Gal. 5:11
30 [a][Gal. 3:8, 22] [b]Gen. 21:10, 12 [c][John 8:35]

CHAPTER 5

1 [a]Phil. 4:1 [b]Acts 15:10 [1]NU *For freedom Christ has made us free; stand fast therefore, and*
2 [a]Acts 15:1
3 [a][Rom. 2:25] [1]*obligated*
4 [a][Rom. 9:31] [b]Heb. 12:15
5 [a]Rom. 8:24
6 [a][Gal. 6:15] [b]1 Thess. 1:3
7 [a]1 Cor. 9:24
9 [a]1 Cor. 5:6
11 [a]1 Cor. 15:30 [b][1 Cor. 1:23]
12 [a]Josh. 7:25 [b]Acts 15:1, 2 [1]*mutilate themselves*
13 [a]1 Cor. 8:9 [b]1 Pet. 2:16 [c]1 Cor. 9:19
14 [a]Matt. 7:12; 22:40 [b]Lev. 19:18
16 [a]Rom. 6:12
17 [a]Rom. 7:18, 22, 23; 8:5 [b]Rom. 7:15
18 [a][Rom. 6:14; 7:4; 8:14]
19 [a]Eph. 5:3, 11 [1]NU omits *adultery* [2]*sexual immorality*
21 [a]1 Cor. 6:9, 10 [1]NU omits *murders*
22 [a][John 15:2] [b][Col. 3:12–15] [c]Rom. 15:14 [d]1 Cor. 13:7
23 [a]1 Tim. 1:9 [1]*meekness*
24 [a]Rom. 6:6
25 [a][Rom. 8:4, 5]
26 [a]Phil. 2:3

CHAPTER 6

1 [1]*caught*

circumcision, [a]why do I still suffer
persecution? Then [b]the offense of
the cross has ceased.
12 [a]I could wish that those [b]who
trouble you would even [1]cut them-
selves off!
13 For you, brethren, have been
called to liberty; only [a]do not *use*
liberty as an [b]opportunity for the
flesh, but [c]through love serve one
another.
14 For [a]all the law is fulfilled in
one word, *even* in this: [b]*"You shall*
love your neighbor as yourself."
15 But if you bite and devour one
another, beware lest you be con-
sumed by one another!

Walking in the Spirit

16 I say then: [a]Walk in the Spirit,
and you shall not fulfill the lust of
the flesh.
17 For [a]the flesh lusts against the
Spirit, and the Spirit against the
flesh; and these are contrary to
one another, [b]so that you do not
do the things that you wish.
18 But [a]if you are led by the Spirit,
you are not under the law.
19 Now [a]the works of the flesh are
evident, which are: [1]adultery, [2]for-
nication, uncleanness, lewdness,
20 idolatry, sorcery, hatred, con-
tentions, jealousies, outbursts of
wrath, selfish ambitions, dissen-
sions, heresies,
21 envy, [1]murders, drunkenness,
revelries, and the like; of which I
tell you beforehand, just as I also
told *you* in time past, that [a]those
who practice such things will not
inherit the kingdom of God.
22 But [a]the fruit of the Spirit is
[b]love, joy, peace, longsuffering,
kindness, [c]goodness, [d]faithful-
ness,
23 [1]gentleness, self-control.
[a]Against such there is no law.
24 And those *who are* Christ's
[a]have crucified the flesh with its
passions and desires.
25 [a]If we live in the Spirit, let us
also walk in the Spirit.
26 [a]Let us not become conceited,
provoking one another, envying
one another.

Bear and Share the Burdens

6 Brethren, if a man is [1]over-
taken in any trespass, you who

are spiritual restore such a one
in a spirit of [a]gentleness, con-
sidering yourself lest you also be
tempted.
2 [a]Bear one another's burdens,
and so fulfill [b]the law of Christ.
3 For [a]if anyone thinks himself
to be something, when [b]he is noth-
ing, he deceives himself.
4 But [a]let each one examine his
own work, and then he will have
rejoicing in himself alone, and [b]not
in another.
5 For [a]each one shall bear his
own load.

Be Generous and Do Good

6 [a]Let him who is taught the
word share in all good things with
him who teaches.
7 Do not be deceived, God is not
mocked; for [a]whatever a man
sows, that he will also reap.
8 For he who sows to his flesh
will of the flesh reap corruption,
but he who sows to the Spirit will
of the Spirit reap [a]everlasting life.
9 And [a]let us not grow weary
while doing good, for in due sea-
son we shall reap [b]if we do not lose
heart.
10 [a]Therefore, as we have oppor-
tunity, [b]let us do good to all, [c]espe-
cially to those who are of the
household of faith.

1 [a]Eph. 4:2
2 [a]Acts 20:35; Rom. 15:1; 1 Thess. 5:14 [b][James 2:8]
3 [a]Rom. 12:3 [b][2 Cor. 3:5; James 1:22]
4 [a]1 Cor. 11:28 [b]Luke 18:11
5 [a][Rom. 2:6]
6 [a]1 Cor. 9:11, 14
7 [a][Rom. 2:6]
8 [a][Rom. 6:8]
9 [a]1 Cor. 15:58; 2 Cor. 4:1; 2 Thess. 3:13 [b][Matt. 24:13]; Heb. 12:3, 5; [James 5:7, 8]
10 [a]Prov. 3:27; [John 9:4; 12:35] [b]Titus 3:8 [c]Rom. 12:13
12 [a]Gal. 5:11; Phil. 3:8
14 [a][1 Cor. 1:18] [b][Gal. 2:20]; Col. 2:20 [1]Or *which*, the cross
15 [a][Rom. 2:26, 28]; 1 Cor. 7:19; [Gal. 5:6]

Glory Only in the Cross

11 See with what large letters I
have written to you with my own
hand!
12 As many as desire to make a
good showing in the flesh, these
would compel you to be circum-
cised, [a]only that they may not suf-
fer persecution for the cross of
Christ.
13 For not even those who are cir-
cumcised keep the law, but they
desire to have you circumcised
that they may boast in your flesh.
14 But God forbid that I should
boast except in the [a]cross of our
Lord Jesus Christ, by [1]whom the
world has been crucified to me,
and [b]I to the world.
15 For [a]in Christ Jesus neither cir-
cumcision nor uncircumcision
avails anything, but a new cre-
ation.

Blessing and a Plea

16 And as many as walk accord-
ing to this rule, peace and mercy
be upon them, and upon the Israel
of God.
17 From now on let no one trouble
me, for I bear in my body the
marks of the Lord Jesus.
18 Brethren, the grace of our Lord
Jesus Christ *be* with your spirit.
Amen.

The Epistle of Paul the Apostle to the

Ephesians

EPHESIANS is addressed to a group of believers who are rich beyond measure in Jesus Christ, yet living as beggars, and only because they are ignorant of their wealth. Paul begins by describing in chapters 1—3 the contents of the Christian's heavenly "bank account": adoption, acceptance, redemption, forgiveness, wisdom, inheritance, the seal of the Holy Spirit, life, grace, citizenship—in short, every spiritual blessing. In chapters 4—6 the Christian learns a spiritual walk rooted in his spiritual wealth. "For we are His workmanship, created in Christ Jesus [1—3] for good works, . . . that we should walk in them [4—6]" (2:10).

The traditional title of this epistle is *Pros Ephesious,* "To the Ephesians." Many ancient manuscripts, however, omit *en Epheso,* "in Ephesus," in 1:1. This has led a number of scholars to challenge the traditional view that this message was directed specifically to the Ephesians. The encyclical theory proposes that it was a circular letter sent by Paul to the churches of Asia. It is argued that Ephesians is really a Christian treatise designed for general use: it involves no controversy and deals with no specific problems in any particular church. Some scholars accept an ancient tradition that Ephesians is Paul's letter to the Laodiceans (Col. 4:16), but there is no way to be sure. If Ephesians began as a circular letter, it eventually became associated with Ephesus, the foremost of the Asian churches. Another plausible option is that this epistle was directly addressed to the Ephesians, but written in such a way as to make it helpful for all the churches in Asia.

Greeting

PAUL, an apostle of Jesus
Christ by the will of God,

To the saints who are in Ephe-
sus, and faithful in Christ Jesus:

2 Grace to you and peace from
God our Father and the Lord Jesus
Christ.

Redemption in Christ

3 [a]Blessed *be* the God and Father
of our Lord Jesus Christ, who has
blessed us with every spiritual
blessing in the heavenly *places* in
Christ,
4 just as [a]He chose us in Him [b]be-
fore the foundation of the world,
that we should [c]be holy and with-
out blame before Him in love,
5 [a]having predestined us to
[b]adoption as sons by Jesus Christ
to Himself, [c]according to the good
pleasure of His will,
6 to the praise of the glory of His
grace, [a]by which He [1]made us ac-
cepted in [b]the Beloved.
7 [a]In Him we have redemption
through His blood, the forgiveness
of sins, according to [b]the riches of
His grace
8 which He made to abound to-
ward us in all wisdom and [1]pru-
dence,
9 [a]having made known to us the
mystery of His will, according to
His good pleasure [b]which He pur-
posed in Himself,
10 that in the dispensation of [a]the
fullness of the times [b]He might
gather together in one [c]all things
in Christ, [1]both which are in
heaven and which are on earth—
in Him.
11 [a]In Him also we have obtained
an inheritance, being predestined

CHAPTER 1
3 [a]2 Cor. 1:3
4 [a]Rom. 8:28 [b]1 Pet. 1:2 [c]Luke 1:75
5 [a]Acts 13:48; [Rom. 8:29] [b]John 1:12 [c][1 Cor. 1:21]
6 [a][Rom. 3:24] [b]Matt. 3:17 [1]Lit. *bestowed grace (favor) upon us*
7 [a][Heb. 9:12] [b][Rom. 3:24, 25]
8 [1]*understanding*
9 [a][Rom. 16:25] [b][2 Tim. 1:9]
10 [a]Gal. 4:4 [b]1 Cor. 3:22 [c]Eph. 3:15; [Phil. 2:9; Col. 1:16, 20] [1]NU, M omit *both*
11 [a]Rom. 8:17

according to [b]the purpose of Him
who works all things according to
the counsel of His will,
12 [a]that we [b]who first trusted in
Christ should be to the praise of
His glory.
13 In Him you also *trusted*, after
you heard [a]the word of truth, the
gospel of your salvation; in whom
also, having believed, [b]you were
sealed with the Holy Spirit of
promise,
14 [a]who[1] is the [2]guarantee of our
inheritance [b]until the redemption
of [c]the purchased possession, [d]to
the praise of His glory.

Prayer for Spiritual Wisdom

15 Therefore I also, [a]after I heard
of your faith in the Lord Jesus and
your love for all the saints,
16 [a]do not cease to give thanks for
you, making mention of you in my
prayers:
17 that [a]the God of our Lord Jesus
Christ, the Father of glory, [b]may
give to you the spirit of wisdom
and revelation in the knowledge of
Him,
18 [a]the eyes of your [1]understand-
ing being enlightened; that you
may know what is [b]the hope of His
calling, what are the riches of the
glory of His inheritance in the
saints,
19 and what *is* the exceeding
greatness of His power toward us
who believe, [a]according to the
working of His mighty power
20 which He worked in Christ
when [a]He raised Him from the
dead and [b]seated *Him* at His right
hand in the heavenly *places*,
21 [a]far above all [b]principality[1] and
[2]power and [3]might and dominion,
and every name that is named, not
only in this age but also in that
which is to come.
22 And [a]He put all *things* under
His feet, and gave Him [b]*to be* head
over all *things* to the church,
23 [a]which is His body, [b]the full-
ness of Him [c]who fills all in all.

By Grace Through Faith

2 And [a]you *He made alive*, [b]who
were dead in trespasses and
sins,
2 [a]in which you once walked ac-
cording to the [1]course of this
world, according to [b]the prince of

11 [b]Is. 46:10
12 [a]2 Thess. 2:13 [b]James 1:18
13 [a]John 1:17 [b][2 Cor. 1:22]
14 [a]2 Cor. 5:5 [b]Rom. 8:23 [c][Acts 20:28] [d]1 Pet. 2:9 [1]NU *which* [2]*down payment, earnest*
15 [a]Col. 1:4; Philem. 5
16 [a]Rom. 1:9
17 [a]John 20:17; Rom. 15:6 [b]Is. 11:2; Col. 1:9
18 [a]Acts 26:18; 2 Cor. 4:6; Heb. 6:4 [b]Eph. 2:12 [1]NU, M *hearts*
19 [a]Col. 2:12
20 [a]Acts 2:24 [b]Ps. 110:1
21 [a]Is. 9:6, 7; Luke 1:32, 33; Phil. 2:9, 10; Rev. 19:12 [b][Rom. 8:38, 39] [1]*rule* [2]*authority* [3]*power*
22 [a]Ps. 8:6; 110:1; Matt. 28:18; 1 Cor. 15:27 [b]Heb. 2:7
23 [a]Rom. 12:5 [b]Col. 2:9 [c][1 Cor. 12:6]

CHAPTER 2

1 [a]Eph. 2:5; Col. 2:13 [b]Eph. 4:18
2 [a]Col. 1:21 [b][John 12:31]; Eph. 6:12 [c]Col. 3:6 [1]Gr. *aion, aeon*
3 [a]1 Pet. 4:3 [b]Gal. 5:16 [c][Ps. 51:5]
4 [a]Ps. 103:8–11; Rom. 10:12 [b]John 3:16; 1 John 4:9, 10
5 [a]Rom. 5:6, 8 [b][Rom. 6:4, 5]
6 [a]Eph. 1:20
7 [a]Titus 3:4
8 [a][2 Tim. 1:9] [b]Rom. 4:16 [c][John 1:12, 13]
9 [a]Rom. 4:4, 5; 11:6 [b]Rom. 3:27
10 [a]Is. 19:25
11 [a][Rom. 2:28; Col. 2:11]

the power of the air, the spirit who
now works in [c]the sons of dis-
obedience,
3 [a]among whom also we all once
conducted ourselves in [b]the lusts
of our flesh, fulfilling the desires
of the flesh and of the mind, and
[c]were by nature children of wrath,
just as the others.
4 But God, [a]who is rich in mercy,
because of His [b]great love with
which He loved us,
5 [a]even when we were dead in
trespasses, [b]made us alive to-
gether with Christ (by grace you
have been saved),
6 and raised *us* up together, and
made *us* sit together [a]in the heav-
enly *places* in Christ Jesus,
7 that in the ages to come He
might show the exceeding riches
of His grace in [a]*His* kindness to-
ward us in Christ Jesus.
8 [a]For by grace you have been
saved [b]through faith, and that not
of yourselves; [c]*it is* the gift of God,
9 not of [a]works, lest anyone
should [b]boast.
10 For we are [a]His workmanship,
created in Christ Jesus for good
works, which God prepared be-
forehand that we should walk in
them.

Brought Near by His Blood

11 Therefore remember that you,
once Gentiles in the flesh—who
are called Uncircumcision by what
is called [a]the Circumcision made
in the flesh by hands—
12 that at that time you were with-
out Christ, being aliens from the
commonwealth of Israel and
strangers from the covenants of
promise, having no hope and with-
out God in the world.
13 But now in Christ Jesus you
who once were far off have been
brought near by the blood of
Christ.

Christ Our Peace

14 For He Himself is our peace,
who has made both one, and has
broken down the middle wall of
separation,
15 having abolished in His flesh
the enmity, *that is*, the law of com-
mandments *contained* in ordi-
nances, so as to create in Himself

one [a]new man *from* the two, *thus* making peace,
16 and that He might [a]reconcile them both to God in one body through the cross, thereby [b]putting to death the enmity.
17 And He came and preached peace to you who were afar off and to those who were near.
18 For [a]through Him we both have access [b]by one Spirit to the Father.

Christ Our Cornerstone

19 Now, therefore, you are no longer strangers and foreigners, but fellow citizens with the saints and members of the household of God,
20 having been [a]built [b]on the foundation of the [c]apostles and prophets, Jesus Christ Himself being [d]the chief corner*stone*,
21 in whom the whole building, being fitted together, grows into [a]a holy temple in the Lord,
22 [a]in whom you also are being built together for a [b]dwelling place of God in the Spirit.

The Mystery Revealed

3 For this reason I, Paul, the prisoner of Christ Jesus for you Gentiles—
2 if indeed you have heard of the [1]dispensation of the grace of God [a]which was given to me for you,
3 [a]how that by revelation [b]He made known to me the mystery (as I have briefly written already,
4 by which, when you read, you may understand my knowledge in the mystery of Christ),
5 which in other ages was not made known to the sons of men, as it has now been revealed by the Spirit to His holy apostles and prophets:
6 that the Gentiles [a]should be fellow heirs, of the same body, and partakers of His promise in Christ through the gospel,
7 [a]of which I became a minister [b]according to the gift of the grace of God given to me by [c]the effective working of His power.

Purpose of the Mystery

8 To me, [a]who am less than the least of all the saints, this grace was given, that I should preach among the Gentiles [b]the unsearchable riches of Christ,
9 and to make all see what *is* the [1]fellowship of the mystery, which from the beginning of the ages has been hidden in God who [a]created all things [2]through Jesus Christ;
10 [a]to the intent that now [b]the [1]manifold wisdom of God might be made known by the church [c]to the [2]principalities and powers in the heavenly *places*,
11 [a]according to the eternal purpose which He accomplished in Christ Jesus our Lord,
12 in whom we have boldness and access [a]with confidence through faith in Him.
13 [a]Therefore I ask that you do not lose heart at my tribulations for you, [b]which is your glory.

Appreciation of the Mystery

14 For this reason I bow my knees to the [a]Father [1]of our Lord Jesus Christ,
15 from whom the whole family in heaven and earth is named,
16 that He would grant you, [a]according to the riches of His glory, [b]to be strengthened with might through His Spirit in [c]the inner man,
17 [a]that Christ may dwell in your hearts through faith; that you, [b]being rooted and grounded in love,
18 [a]may be able to comprehend with all the saints [b]what *is* the width and length and depth and height—
19 to know the love of Christ which passes knowledge; that you may be filled [a]with all the fullness of God.
20 Now [a]to Him who is able to do exceedingly abundantly [b]above all that we ask or think, [c]according to the power that works in us,
21 [a]to Him *be* glory in the church by Christ Jesus to all generations, forever and ever. Amen.

Walk in Unity

4 I, therefore, the prisoner [1]of the Lord, [2]beseech you to [a]walk worthy of the calling with which you were called,
2 with all lowliness and gentleness, with longsuffering, bearing with one another in love,
3 endeavoring to keep the unity

15 [a]Gal. 6:15
16 [a][Col. 1:20–22] [b][Rom. 6:6]
18 [a]John 10:9 [b]1 Cor. 12:13
20 [a]1 Pet. 2:4 [b]Matt. 16:18 [c]1 Cor. 12:28 [d]Ps. 118:22
21 [a]1 Cor. 3:16, 17
22 [a]1 Pet. 2:5 [b]John 17:23

CHAPTER 3

2 [a]Acts 9:15 [1]*stewardship*
3 [a]Acts 22:17, 21; 26:16 [b][Rom. 11:25; 16:25]
6 [a]Gal. 3:28, 29
7 [a]Rom. 15:16 [b]Rom. 1:5 [c]Rom. 15:18
8 [a][1 Cor. 15:9] [b][Col. 1:27; 2:2, 3]
9 [a]Heb. 1:2 [1]NU, M *stewardship* (dispensation) [2]NU omits *through Jesus Christ*
10 [a]1 Pet. 1:12 [b][1 Tim. 3:16] [c]Col. 1:16; 2:10, 15 [1]*variegated* or *many-sided* [2]*rulers*
11 [a][Eph. 1:4, 11]
12 [a]Heb. 4:16; 10:19, 35
13 [a]Phil. 1:14 [b]2 Cor. 1:6
14 [a]Eph. 1:3 [1]NU omits *of our Lord Jesus Christ*
16 [a][Phil. 4:19] [b]Col. 1:11 [c]Rom. 7:22
17 [a]John 14:23 [b]Col. 1:23
18 [a]Eph. 1:18 [b]Rom. 8:39
19 [a]Eph. 1:23
20 [a]Rom. 16:25 [b]1 Cor. 2:9 [c]Col. 1:29
21 [a]Rom. 11:36

CHAPTER 4

1 [a]1 Thess. 2:12 [1]Lit. *in* [2]*exhort, encourage*

of the Spirit [a]in the bond of peace.
4 [a]*There is* one body and one
Spirit, just as you were called in
one hope of your calling;
5 [a]one Lord, [b]one faith, [c]one bap-
tism;
6 [a]one God and Father of all, who
is above all, and [b]through all, and
in [1]you all.

Spiritual Gifts

7 But [a]to each one of us grace
was given according to the mea-
sure of Christ's gift.
8 Therefore He says:

[a]*"When He ascended on high,*
He led captivity captive,
And gave gifts to men."

9 [a](Now this, *"He ascended"*—
what does it mean but that He also
[1]first descended into the lower
parts of the earth?
10 He who descended is also the
One [a]who ascended far above all
the heavens, [b]that He might fill all
things.)
11 And He Himself gave some *to
be* apostles, some prophets, some
evangelists, and some pastors and
teachers,
12 for the equipping of the saints
for the work of ministry, [a]for the
[1]edifying of [b]the body of Christ,
13 till we all come to the unity of
the faith [a]and of the knowledge of
the Son of God, to [b]a perfect man,
to the measure of the stature of the
fullness of Christ;
14 that we should no longer be
[a]children, tossed to and fro and
carried about with every wind of
doctrine, by the trickery of men,
in the cunning craftiness of [b]de-
ceitful plotting,
15 but, speaking the truth in love,
may grow up in all things into Him
who is the [a]head—Christ—
16 [a]from whom the whole body,
joined and knit together by what
every joint supplies, according to
the effective working by which
every part does its share, causes
growth of the body for the edifying
of itself in love.

The New Man

17 This I say, therefore, and testify
in the Lord, that you should [a]no
longer walk as [1]the rest of the Gen-
tiles walk, in the futility of their
mind,
18 having their understanding
darkened, being alienated from
the life of God, because of the ig-
norance that is in them, because
of the [a]blindness of their heart;
19 [a]who, being past feeling, [b]have
given themselves over to lewd-
ness, to work all uncleanness with
greediness.
20 But you have not so learned
Christ,
21 if indeed you have heard Him
and have been taught by Him, as
the truth is in Jesus:
22 that you [a]put off, concerning
your former conduct, the old man
which grows corrupt according to
the deceitful lusts,
23 and [a]be renewed in the spirit
of your mind,
24 and that you [a]put on the new
man which was created according
to God, in true righteousness and
holiness.

Do Not Grieve the Spirit

25 Therefore, putting away lying,
[a]*"Let each one of you speak truth
with his neighbor,"* for [b]we are
members of one another.
26 [a]*"Be angry, and do not sin"*: do
not let the sun go down on your
wrath,
27 [a]nor give [1]place to the devil.
28 Let him who stole steal no
longer, but rather [a]let him labor,
working with *his* hands what is
good, that he may have something
[b]to give him who has need.
29 [a]Let no corrupt word proceed
out of your mouth, but [b]what is
good for necessary [1]edification,
[c]that it may impart grace to the
hearers.
30 And [a]do not grieve the Holy
Spirit of God, by whom you were
sealed for the day of redemption.
31 [a]Let all bitterness, wrath, an-
ger, [1]clamor, and [b]evil speaking
be put away from you, [c]with all
malice.
32 And [a]be kind to one another,
tenderhearted, [b]forgiving one an-
other, even as God in Christ for-
gave you.

Walk in Love

5 Therefore[a] be imitators of God
as dear [b]children.

---

3 [a]Col. 3:14
4 [a]Rom. 12:5
5 [a]1 Cor. 1:13 [b]Jude 3 [c][Heb. 6:6]
6 [a]Mal. 2:10 [b]Rom. 11:36 [1]NU omits *you;* M *us*
7 [a][1 Cor. 12:7, 11]
8 [a]Ps. 68:18
9 [a]John 3:13; 20:17 [1]NU omits *first*
10 [a]Acts 1:9 [b][Eph. 1:23]
12 [a]1 Cor. 14:26 [b]Col. 1:24 [1]*building up*
13 [a]Col. 2:2 [b]1 Cor. 14:20
14 [a]1 Cor. 14:20 [b]Rom. 16:18
15 [a]Eph. 1:22
16 [a]Col. 2:19
17 [a]Eph. 2:2; 4:22 [1]NU omits *the rest of*
18 [a]Rom. 1:21
19 [a]1 Tim. 4:2 [b]1 Pet. 4:3
22 [a]Col. 3:8
23 [a][Rom. 12:2]
24 [a][Rom. 6:4; 7:6; 12:2]
25 [a]Zech. 8:16 [b]Rom. 12:5
26 [a]Ps. 4:4; 37:8
27 [a][Rom. 12:19] [1]*an opportunity*
28 [a]Acts 20:35 [b]Luke 3:11
29 [a]Col. 3:8 [b]1 Thess. 5:11 [c]Col. 3:16 [1]*building up*
30 [a]Is. 7:13
31 [a]Col. 3:8, 19 [b]James 4:11 [c]Titus 3:3 [1]*loud quarreling*
32 [a]2 Cor. 6:10 [b][Mark 11:25]

CHAPTER 5

1 [a]Luke 6:36 [b]1 Pet. 1:14–16

2 And [a]walk in love, [b]as Christ
also has loved us and given Him-
self for us, an offering and a sacri-
fice to God [c]for a sweet-smelling
aroma.
3 But fornication and all [a]un-
cleanness or [b]covetousness, let it
not even be named among you, as
is fitting for saints;
4 [a]neither filthiness, nor [b]foolish
talking, nor coarse jesting, [c]which
are not fitting, but rather [d]giving
of thanks.
5 For [1]this you know, that no for-
nicator, unclean person, nor cov-
etous man, who is an idolater, has
any [a]inheritance in the kingdom of
Christ and God.
6 Let no one deceive you with
empty words, for because of these
things the wrath of God comes
upon the sons of disobedience.
7 Therefore do not be [a]partakers
with them.

Walk in Light

8 For you were once darkness,
but now *you are* [a]light in the Lord.
Walk as children of light
9 (for [a]the fruit of the [1]Spirit *is*
in all goodness, righteousness, and
truth),
10 [a]finding out what is acceptable
to the Lord.
11 And have [a]no fellowship with
the unfruitful works of darkness,
but rather [1]expose *them.*
12 [a]For it is shameful even to
speak of those things which are
done by them in secret.
13 But [a]all things that are [1]ex-
posed are made manifest by the
light, for whatever makes manifest
is light.
14 Therefore He says:

[a]"Awake, you who sleep,
Arise from the dead,
And Christ will give you light."

Walk in Wisdom

15 [a]See then that you walk [1]cir-
cumspectly, not as fools but as
wise,
16 [a]redeeming the time, [b]because
the days are evil.
17 [a]Therefore do not be unwise,
but [b]understand [c]what the will of
the Lord *is.*
18 And [a]do not be drunk with
wine, in which is dissipation; but
be filled with the Spirit,
19 speaking to one another [a]in
psalms and hymns and spiritual
songs, singing and making [b]mel-
ody in your heart to the Lord,
20 [a]giving thanks always for all
things to God the Father [b]in the
name of our Lord Jesus Christ,
21 [a]submitting to one another in
the fear of [1]God.

Marriage—Christ and the Church

22 Wives, [a]submit to your own
husbands, as to the Lord.
23 For [a]the husband is head of the
wife, as also [b]Christ is head of the
church; and He is the Savior of
the body.
24 Therefore, just as the church is
subject to Christ, so *let* the wives
be to their own husbands [a]in
everything.
25 [a]Husbands, love your wives,
just as Christ also loved the church
and [b]gave Himself for her,
26 that He might [1]sanctify and
cleanse her [a]with the washing of
water [b]by the word,
27 [a]that He might present her to
Himself a glorious church, [b]not
having spot or wrinkle or any such
thing, but that she should be holy
and without blemish.
28 So husbands ought to love their
own wives as their own bodies; he
who loves his wife loves himself.
29 For no one ever hated his own
flesh, but nourishes and cherishes
it, just as the Lord *does* the church.
30 For [a]we are members of His
body, [1]of His flesh and of His
bones.
31 [a]*"For this reason a man shall
leave his father and mother and be
joined to his wife, and the [b]two
shall become one flesh."*
32 This is a great mystery, but I
speak concerning Christ and the
church.
33 Nevertheless [a]let each one of
you in particular so love his own
wife as himself, and let the wife
see that she [b]respects *her* husband.

Children and Parents

6 Children, [a]obey your parents
in the Lord, for this is right.
2 [a]*"Honor your father and
mother,"* which is the first com-
mandment with promise:

---

2 [a]1 Thess. 4:9 [b]Gal. 1:4 [c]2 Cor. 2:14, 15
3 [a]Col. 3:5–7 [b][Luke 12:15]
4 [a]Matt. 12:34, 35 [b]Titus 3:9 [c]Rom. 1:28 [d]Phil. 4:6
5 [a]1 Cor. 6:9, 10 [1]NU *know this*
7 [a]1 Tim. 5:22
8 [a]1 Thess. 5:5
9 [a]Gal. 5:22 [1]NU *light*
10 [a][Rom. 12:1, 2]
11 [a]2 Cor. 6:14 [1]*reprove*
12 [a]Rom. 1:24
13 [a][John 3:20, 21] [1]*reproved*
14 [a][Is. 26:19; 60:1]
15 [a]Col. 4:5 [1]*carefully*
16 [a]Col. 4:5 [b]Eccl. 11:2
17 [a]Col. 4:5 [b][Rom. 12:2] [c]1 Thess. 4:3
18 [a]Prov. 20:1; 23:31
19 [a]Acts 16:25 [b]James 5:13
20 [a]Ps. 34:1 [b][1 Pet. 2:5]
21 [a][Phil. 2:3] [1]NU *Christ*
22 [a]Col. 3:18—4:1
23 [a][1 Cor. 11:3] [b]Col. 1:18
24 [a]Titus 2:4, 5
25 [a]Col. 3:19 [b]Acts 20:28
26 [a]John 3:5 [b][John 15:3; 17:17] [1]*set it apart*
27 [a]Col. 1:22 [b]Song 4:7
30 [a]Gen. 2:23 [1]NU omits the rest of v. 30.
31 [a]Gen. 2:24 [b][1 Cor. 6:16]
33 [a]Col. 3:19 [b]1 Pet. 3:1, 6

CHAPTER 6

1 [a]Col. 3:20
2 [a]Deut. 5:16

3 *"that it may be well with you
and you may live long on the
earth."*
4 And [a]you, fathers, do not pro-
voke your children to wrath, but
[b]bring them up in the training and
admonition of the Lord.

Bondservants and Masters

5 [a]Bondservants, be obedient to
those who are your masters ac-
cording to the flesh, [b]with fear and
trembling, [c]in sincerity of heart, as
to Christ;
6 [a]not with eyeservice, as men-
pleasers, but as bondservants of
Christ, doing the will of God from
the heart,
7 with goodwill doing service, as
to the Lord, and not to men,
8 [a]knowing that whatever good
anyone does, he will receive the
same from the Lord, whether *he
is* a slave or free.
9 And you, masters, do the same
things to them, giving up threaten-
ing, knowing that [1]your own [a]Mas-
ter also is in heaven, and [b]there
is no partiality with Him.

The Whole Armor of God

10 Finally, my brethren, be strong
in the Lord and in the power of
His might.
11 [a]Put on the whole armor of
God, that you may be able to stand
against the [1]wiles of the devil.
12 For we do not wrestle against
flesh and blood, but against [a]prin-
cipalities, against powers, against
[b]the rulers of [1]the darkness of this
age, against spiritual *hosts* of
wickedness in the heavenly *places*.
13 [a]Therefore take up the whole
armor of God, that you may be
able to withstand [b]in the evil day,
and having done all, to stand.
14 Stand therefore, [a]having
girded your waist with truth, [b]hav-
ing put on the breastplate of righ-
teousness,
15 [a]and having shod your feet
with the preparation of the gospel
of peace;
16 above all, taking [a]the shield of
faith with which you will be able
to quench all the fiery darts of the
wicked one.
17 And [a]take the helmet of salva-
tion, and [b]the sword of the Spirit,
which is the word of God;
18 [a]praying always with all prayer
and supplication in the Spirit, [b]be-
ing watchful to this end with all
perseverance and [c]supplication for
all the saints—
19 and for me, that utterance may
be given to me, [a]that I may open
my mouth boldly to make known
the mystery of the gospel,
20 for which [a]I am an ambassador
in chains; that in it I may speak
boldly, as I ought to speak.

A Gracious Greeting

21 But that you also may know
my affairs *and* how I am doing,
[a]Tychicus, a beloved brother and
[b]faithful minister in the Lord, will
make all things known to you;
22 [a]whom I have sent to you for
this very purpose, that you may
know our affairs, and *that* he may
[b]comfort your hearts.
23 Peace to the brethren, and love
with faith, from God the Father
and the Lord Jesus Christ.
24 Grace *be* with all those who
love our Lord Jesus Christ in sin-
cerity. Amen.

4 [a]Col. 3:21 [b]Gen. 18:19
5 [a][1 Tim. 6:1] [b]2 Cor. 7:15 [c]1 Chr. 29:17
6 [a]Col. 3:22
8 [a]Rom. 2:6
9 [a]Col. 4:1 [b]Rom. 2:11 [1]NU *He who is both their Master and yours is*
11 [a][2 Cor. 6:7] [1]*schemings*
12 [a]Rom. 8:38 [b]Luke 22:53 [1]NU *this darkness,*
13 [a][2 Cor. 10:4] [b]Eph. 5:16
14 [a]Is. 11:5 [b]Is. 59:17
15 [a]Is. 52:7
16 [a]1 John 5:4
17 [a]1 Thess. 5:8 [b][Heb. 4:12]
18 [a]Luke 18:1 [b][Matt. 26:41] [c]Phil. 1:4
19 [a]Col. 4:3
20 [a]2 Cor. 5:20
21 [a]Acts 20:4 [b]1 Cor. 4:1, 2
22 [a]Col. 4:8 [b]2 Cor. 1:6

The Epistle of Paul the Apostle to the

Philippians

PAUL writes a thank-you note to the believers at Philippi for their help in his hour of need, and he uses the occasion to send along some instruction on Christian unity. His central thought is simple: Only in Christ are real unity and joy possible. With Christ as your model of humility and service, you can enjoy a oneness of purpose, attitude, goal, and labor—a truth which Paul illustrates from his own life, and one the Philippians desperately need to hear. Within their own ranks, fellow workers in the Philippian church are at odds, hindering the work in proclaiming new life in Christ. Because of this, Paul exhorts the church to "stand fast . . . be of the same mind . . . rejoice in the Lord always . . . but in everything by prayer and supplication, with thanksgiving, let your requests be made known . . . and the peace of God, which surpasses all understanding, will guard your hearts and minds through Christ Jesus" (4:1, 2, 4, 6,7).

This epistle is called *Pros Philippesious,* "To the Philippians." The church at Philippi was the first church Paul founded in Macedonia.

CHAPTER 1

Greeting

PAUL and Timothy, bond-
servants of Jesus Christ,

To all the saints in Christ Jesus
who are in Philippi, with the
[1]bishops and [a]deacons:

2 Grace to you and peace from
God our Father and the Lord Jesus
Christ.

Thankfulness and Prayer

3 [a]I thank my God upon every re-
membrance of you,
4 always in [a]every prayer of
mine making request for you all
with joy,
5 [a]for your fellowship in the gos-
pel from the first day until now,
6 being confident of this very
thing, that He who has begun [a]a
good work in you will complete *it*
until the day of Jesus Christ;
7 just as it is right for me to think
this of you all, because I have you
in my heart, inasmuch as both in
my chains and in the defense and
confirmation of the gospel, you all
are partakers with me of grace.
8 For God is my witness, how
greatly I long for you all with the
affection of Jesus Christ.
9 And this I pray, that your love
may abound still more and more
in knowledge and all discernment,
10 that you may approve the
things that are excellent, that you
may be sincere and without of-
fense till the day of Christ,
11 being filled with the fruits of
righteousness [a]which *are* by Jesus
Christ, [b]to the glory and praise of
God.

Christ Is Preached

12 But I want you to know, breth-
ren, that the things *which hap-
pened* to me have actually turned
out for the furtherance of the gos-
pel,
13 so that it has become evident
[a]to the whole [1]palace guard, and
to all the rest, that my chains are
in Christ;
14 and most of the brethren in the
Lord, having become confident by
my chains, are much more bold to
speak the word without fear.
15 Some indeed preach Christ
even from envy and strife, and
some also from goodwill:
16 [1]The former preach Christ
from selfish ambition, not sin-
cerely, supposing to add affliction
to my chains;
17 but the latter out of love, know-
ing that I am appointed for the de-
fense of the gospel.
18 What then? Only *that* in every

1 [a][1 Tim. 3:8–13] [1]Lit. *overseers*
3 [a]1 Cor. 1:4
4 [a]Eph. 1:16; 1 Thess. 1:2
5 [a][Rom. 12:13]
6 [a][John 6:29]
11 [a][Eph. 2:10]; Col. 1:6 [b]John 15:8
13 [a]Phil. 4:22 [1]Or *Praetorium*
16 [1]NU reverses vv. 16 and 17.

way, whether in pretense or in
truth, Christ is preached; and in
this I rejoice, yes, and will rejoice.

To Live Is Christ

19 For I know that [a]this will turn
out for my deliverance through
your prayer and the supply of the
Spirit of Jesus Christ,
20 according to my earnest expec-
tation and hope that in nothing I
shall be ashamed, but [a]with all
boldness, as always, so now also
Christ will be magnified in my
body, whether by life [b]or by death.
21 For to me, to live *is* Christ, and
to die *is* gain.
22 But if *I* live on in the flesh, this
will mean fruit from *my* labor; yet
what I shall choose I [1]cannot tell.
23 [1]For I am hard-pressed be-
tween the two, having a [a]desire to
depart and be with Christ, *which*
is [b]far better.
24 Nevertheless to remain in the
flesh *is* more needful for you.
25 And being confident of this, I
know that I shall remain and con-
tinue with you all for your prog-
ress and joy of faith,
26 that [a]your rejoicing for me may
be more abundant in Jesus Christ
by my coming to you again.

Striving and Suffering for Christ

27 Only [a]let your conduct be wor-
thy of the gospel of Christ, so that
whether I come and see you or am
absent, I may hear of your affairs,
that you stand fast in one spirit,
[b]with one mind [c]striving together
for the faith of the gospel,
28 and not in any way terrified by
your adversaries, which is to them
a proof of perdition, but [1]to you
of salvation, and that from God.
29 For to you [a]it has been granted
on behalf of Christ, [b]not only to
believe in Him, but also to [c]suffer
for His sake,
30 [a]having the same conflict
[b]which you saw in me and now
hear *is* in me.

Unity Through Humility

2 Therefore if *there is* any [1]con-
solation in Christ, if any com-
fort of love, if any fellowship of the
Spirit, if any [a]affection and mercy,
2 [a]fulfill my joy [b]by being like-
minded, having the same love, *be-*
ing of [c]one accord, of one mind.
3 [a]*Let* nothing *be done* through
selfish ambition or conceit, but [b]in
lowliness of mind let each esteem
others better than himself.
4 [a]Let each of you look out not
only for his own interests, but also
for the interests of [b]others.

The Humbled and Exalted Christ

5 [a]Let this mind be in you which
was also in Christ Jesus,
6 who, [a]being in the form of God,
did not consider it [1]robbery to be
equal with God,
7 [a]but [1]made Himself of no repu-
tation, taking the form [b]of a
bondservant, *and* [c]coming in the
likeness of men.
8 And being found in appearance
as a man, He humbled Himself and
[a]became [b]obedient to *the point of*
death, even the death of the cross.
9 [a]Therefore God also [b]has
highly exalted Him and [c]given
Him the name which is above
every name,
10 [a]that at the name of Jesus every
knee should bow, of those in
heaven, and of those on earth, and
of those under the earth,
11 and [a]*that* every tongue should
confess that Jesus Christ *is* Lord,
to the glory of God the Father.

Light Bearers

12 Therefore, my beloved, [a]as you
have always obeyed, not as in my
presence only, but now much more
in my absence, [b]work out your
own salvation with [c]fear and trem-
bling;
13 for [a]it is God who works in you
both to will and to do [b]for *His* good
pleasure.
14 Do all things [a]without [1]com-
plaining and [b]disputing,[2]
15 that you may become blame-
less and [1]harmless, children of
God without fault in the midst of
a crooked and perverse genera-
tion, among whom you shine as
[a]lights in the world,
16 holding fast the word of life, so
that [a]I may rejoice in the day of
Christ that [b]I have not run in vain
or labored in [c]vain.
17 Yes, and if [a]I am being poured
out *as a drink offering* on the sacri-
fice [b]and service of your faith, [c]I
am glad and rejoice with you all.

---

19 [a]Job 13:16, LXX
20 [a]Eph. 6:19, 20 [b][Rom. 14:8]
22 [1]*do not know*
23 [a][2 Cor. 5:2, 8] [b][Ps. 16:11] [1]NU, M *But*
26 [a]2 Cor. 1:14
27 [a]Eph. 4:1 [b]Eph. 4:3 [c]Jude 3
28 [1]NU *of your salvation*
29 [a][Matt. 5:11, 12] [b]Eph. 2:8 [c][2 Tim. 3:12]
30 [a]Col. 1:29; 2:1 [b]Acts 16:19–40

CHAPTER 2

1 [a]Col. 3:12 [1]Or *encouragement*
2 [a]John 3:29 [b]Rom. 12:16 [c]Phil. 4:2
3 [a]Gal. 5:26 [b]Rom. 12:10
4 [a]1 Cor. 13:5 [b]Rom. 15:1, 2
5 [a][Matt. 11:29]
6 [a]2 Cor. 4:4 [1]Or *something to be held onto to be equal*
7 [a]Ps. 22:6 [b]Is. 42:1 [c][John 1:14] [1]*emptied Himself* of His privileges
8 [a]Matt. 26:39 [b]Heb. 5:8
9 [a]Heb. 2:9 [b]Acts 2:33 [c]Eph. 1:21
10 [a]Is. 45:23
11 [a]John 13:13
12 [a]Phil. 1:5, 6; 4:15 [b]John 6:27, 29 [c]Eph. 6:5
13 [a]Heb. 13:20, 21 [b]Eph. 1:5
14 [a]1 Pet. 4:9 [b]Rom. 14:1 [1]*grumbling* [2]*arguing*
15 [a]Matt. 5:15, 16 [1]*innocent*
16 [a]2 Cor. 1:14 [b]Gal. 2:2 [c]1 Thess. 3:5
17 [a]2 Tim. 4:6 [b]Rom. 15:16 [c]2 Cor. 7:4

18 For the same reason you also be glad and rejoice with me.

Timothy Commended

19 But I trust in the Lord Jesus to send [a]Timothy to you shortly, that I also may be encouraged when I know your [1]state.
20 For I have no one [a]like-minded, who will sincerely care for your state.
21 For all seek their own, not the things which are of Christ Jesus.
22 But you know his proven character, [a]that as a son with *his* father he served with me in the gospel.
23 Therefore I hope to send him at once, as soon as I see how it goes with me.
24 But I trust in the Lord that I myself shall also come shortly.

Epaphroditus Praised

25 Yet I considered it necessary to send to you [a]Epaphroditus, my brother, fellow worker, and [b]fellow soldier, [c]but your messenger and [d]the one who ministered to my need;
26 [a]since he was longing for you all, and was distressed because you had heard that he was sick.
27 For indeed he was sick almost unto death; but God had mercy on him, and not only on him but on me also, lest I should have sorrow upon sorrow.
28 Therefore I sent him the more eagerly, that when you see him again you may rejoice, and I may be less sorrowful.
29 Receive him therefore in the Lord with all gladness, and hold such men in esteem;
30 because for the work of Christ he came close to death, [1]not regarding his life, [a]to supply what was lacking in your service toward me.

All for Christ

3 Finally, my brethren, [a]rejoice in the Lord. For me to write the same things to you *is* not tedious, but for you *it is* safe.
2 [a]Beware of dogs, beware of [b]evil workers, [c]beware of the mutilation!
3 For we are [a]the circumcision, [b]who worship [1]God in the Spirit, rejoice in Christ Jesus, and have no confidence in the flesh,
4 though [a]I also might have confidence in the flesh. If anyone else thinks he may have confidence in the flesh, I [b]more so:
5 circumcised the eighth day, of the stock of Israel, [a]*of* the tribe of Benjamin, [b]a Hebrew of the Hebrews; concerning the law, [c]a Pharisee;
6 concerning zeal, [a]persecuting the church; concerning the righteousness which is in the law, blameless.
7 But [a]what things were gain to me, these I have counted loss for Christ.
8 Yet indeed I also count all things loss [a]for the excellence of the knowledge of Christ Jesus my Lord, for whom I have suffered the loss of all things, and count them as rubbish, that I may gain Christ
9 and be found in Him, not having [a]my own righteousness, which *is* from the law, but [b]that which *is* through faith in Christ, the righteousness which is from God by faith;
10 that I may know Him and the [a]power of His resurrection, and [b]the fellowship of His sufferings, being conformed to His death,
11 if, by any means, I may [a]attain[1] to the resurrection from the dead.

Pressing Toward the Goal

12 Not that I have already [a]attained,[1] or am already [b]perfected; but I press on, that I may lay hold of that for which Christ Jesus has also laid hold of me.
13 Brethren, I do not count myself to have [1]apprehended; but one thing *I do*, [a]forgetting those things which are behind and [b]reaching forward to those things which are ahead,
14 [a]I press toward the goal for the prize of [b]the upward call of God in Christ Jesus.
15 Therefore let us, as many as are [a]mature, [b]have this mind; and if in anything you think otherwise, [c]God will reveal even this to you.
16 Nevertheless, to *the degree* that we have already [1]attained, [a]let us walk [b]by the same [2]rule, let us be of the same mind.

19 [a]Rom. 16:21 [1]*condition*
20 [a]2 Tim. 3:10
22 [a]1 Cor. 4:17
25 [a]Phil. 4:18 [b]Philem. 2 [c]2 Cor. 8:23 [d]2 Cor. 11:9
26 [a]Phil. 1:8
30 [a]1 Cor. 16:17 [1]*risking*

CHAPTER 3

1 [a]1 Thess. 5:16
2 [a]Gal. 5:15 [b]Ps. 119:115 [c]Rom. 2:28
3 [a]Deut. 30:6 [b]Rom. 7:6 [1]NU, M *in the Spirit of God*
4 [a]2 Cor. 5:16; 11:18 [b]2 Cor. 11:22, 23
5 [a]Rom. 11:1 [b]2 Cor. 11:22 [c]Acts 23:6
6 [a]Acts 8:3; 22:4, 5; 26:9–11
7 [a]Matt. 13:44
8 [a]Jer. 9:23
9 [a]Rom. 10:3 [b]Rom. 1:17
10 [a]Eph. 1:19, 20 [b][Rom. 6:3–5]
11 [a]Acts 26:6–8 [1]Lit. *arrive at*
12 [a][1 Tim. 6:12, 19] [b]Heb. 12:23 [1]*obtained it*
13 [a]Luke 9:62 [b]Heb. 6:1 [1]*laid hold of it*
14 [a]2 Tim. 4:7 [b]Heb. 3:1
15 [a]1 Cor. 2:6 [b]Gal. 5:10 [c]Hos. 6:3
16 [a]Gal. 6:16 [b]Rom. 12:16; 15:5 [1]*arrived* [2]NU omits *rule* and the rest of v. 16.

Our Citizenship in Heaven

17 Brethren, [a]join in following my
example, and note those who so
walk, as [b]you have us for a pattern.
18 For many walk, of whom I have
told you often, and now tell you
even weeping, *that they are* [a]the
enemies of the cross of Christ:
19 [a]whose end *is* destruction,
[b]whose god *is their* belly, and
[c]*whose* glory *is* in their shame—
[d]who set their mind on earthly
things.
20 For [a]our citizenship is in
heaven, [b]from which we also [c]ea-
gerly wait for the Savior, the Lord
Jesus Christ,
21 [a]who will transform our lowly
body that it may be [b]conformed to
His glorious body, [c]according to
the working by which He is able
even to [d]subdue all things to Him-
self.

4 Therefore, my beloved and
[a]longed-for brethren, [b]my joy
and crown, so [c]stand fast in the
Lord, beloved.

Be United, Joyful, and in Prayer

2 I implore Euodia and I implore
Syntyche [a]to be of the same mind
in the Lord.
3 [1]And I urge you also, true com-
panion, help these women who
[a]labored with me in the gospel,
with Clement also, and the rest of
my fellow workers, whose names
are in [b]the Book of Life.
4 [a]Rejoice in the Lord always.
Again I will say, rejoice!
5 Let your [1]gentleness be known
to all men. [a]The Lord *is* at hand.
6 [a]Be anxious for nothing, but in
everything by prayer and suppli-
cation, with [b]thanksgiving, let
your requests be made known to
God;
7 and [a]the peace of God, which
surpasses all understanding, will
guard your hearts and minds
through Christ Jesus.

Meditate on These Things

8 Finally, brethren, whatever
things are [a]true, whatever things
are [b]noble, whatever things *are*
[c]just, [d]whatever things *are* pure,
whatever things *are* [e]lovely, what-
ever things *are* of good report, if
there is any virtue and if *there is*

17 [a][1 Cor. 4:16; 11:1] [b]Titus 2:7, 8
18 [a]Gal. 1:7
19 [a]2 Cor. 11:15 [b]1 Tim. 6:5 [c]Hos. 4:7 [d]Rom. 8:5
20 [a]Eph. 2:6, 19 [b]Acts 1:11 [c]1 Cor. 1:7
21 [a][1 Cor. 15:43–53] [b]1 John 3:2 [c]Eph. 1:19 [d][1 Cor. 15:28]

CHAPTER 4

1 [a]Phil. 1:8 [b]2 Cor. 1:14 [c]Phil. 1:27
2 [a]Phil. 2:2; 3:16
3 [a]Rom. 16:3 [b]Luke 10:20 [1]NU, M *Yes*
4 [a]Rom. 12:12
5 [a][James 5:7–9] [1]*graciousness* or *forbearance*
6 [a]Matt. 6:25 [b][1 Thess. 5:17, 18]
7 [a][John 14:27]
8 [a]Eph. 4:25 [b]2 Cor. 8:21 [c]Deut. 16:20 [d]1 Thess. 5:22 [e]1 Cor. 13:4–7
9 [a]Rom. 15:33
10 [a]2 Cor. 11:9 [1]*you have revived your care*
11 [a]1 Tim. 6:6, 8
12 [a]1 Cor. 4:11 [1]*live humbly* [2]*live in prosperity*
13 [a]John 15:5 [1]NU *Him who*
14 [a]Phil. 1:7
15 [a]2 Cor. 11:8, 9
17 [a]Titus 3:14
18 [a]Phil. 2:25 [b]Heb. 13:16 [c]2 Cor. 9:12 [1]Or *have received all*
19 [a]Ps. 23:1
20 [a]Rom. 16:27
21 [a]Gal. 1:2
23 [1]NU *your spirit*

anything praiseworthy—meditate
on these things.
9 The things which you learned
and received and heard and saw
in me, these do, and [a]the God of
peace will be with you.

Philippian Generosity

10 But I rejoiced in the Lord
greatly that now at last [a]your[1] care
for me has flourished again;
though you surely did care, but
you lacked opportunity.
11 Not that I speak in regard to
need, for I have learned in what-
ever state I am, [a]to be content:
12 [a]I know how to [1]be abased, and
I know how to [2]abound. Every-
where and in all things I have
learned both to be full and to be
hungry, both to abound and to suf-
fer need.
13 I can do all things [a]through
[1]Christ who strengthens me.
14 Nevertheless you have done
well that [a]you shared in my dis-
tress.
15 Now you Philippians know
also that in the beginning of the
gospel, when I departed from
Macedonia, [a]no church shared
with me concerning giving and re-
ceiving but you only.
16 For even in Thessalonica you
sent *aid* once and again for my ne-
cessities.
17 Not that I seek the gift, but I
seek [a]the fruit that abounds to
your account.
18 Indeed I [1]have all and abound.
I am full, having received from
[a]Epaphroditus the things *sent*
from you, [b]a sweet-smelling
aroma, [c]an acceptable sacrifice,
well pleasing to God.
19 And my God [a]shall supply all
your need according to His riches
in glory by Christ Jesus.
20 [a]Now to our God and Father *be*
glory forever and ever. Amen.

Greeting and Blessing

21 Greet every saint in Christ
Jesus. The brethren [a]who are with
me greet you.
22 All the saints greet you, but
especially those who are of Cae-
sar's household.
23 The grace of our Lord Jesus
Christ be with [1]you all. Amen.

The Epistle of Paul the Apostle to the

Colossians

IF Ephesians can be labeled the epistle portraying the "church of Christ," then Colossians must surely be the "Christ of the church." Ephesians focuses on the body; Colossians focuses on the Head. Like Ephesians, the little Book of Colossians divides neatly in half with the first portion doctrinal (1 and 2) and the second practical (3 and 4). Paul's purpose is to show that Christ is preeminent—first and foremost in everything—and the Christian's life should reflect that priority. Because believers are rooted in Him, alive in Him, hidden in Him, and complete in Him, it is utterly inconsistent for them to live life without Him. Clothed in His love, with His peace ruling in their hearts, they are equipped to make Christ first in every area of life.

This epistle became known as *Pros Kolossaeis,* "To the Colossians," because of 1:2. Paul also wanted it to be read in the neighboring church at Laodicea (4:16).

PAUL, [a]an apostle of Jesus
Christ by the will of God, and
Timothy our brother,
2 To the saints [a]and faithful
brethren in Christ *who are* in Colosse:

[b]Grace to you and peace from
God our Father [1]and the Lord
Jesus Christ.

Their Faith in Christ

3 [a]We give thanks to the God and
Father of our Lord Jesus Christ,
praying always for you,
4 [a]since we heard of your faith
in Christ Jesus and of [b]your love
for all the saints;
5 because of the hope [a]which is
laid up for you in heaven, of which
you heard before in the word of
the truth of the gospel,
6 which has come to you, [a]as *it
has* also in all the world, and [b]is
bringing forth [1]fruit, as *it is* also
among you since the day you
heard and knew [c]the grace of God
in truth;
7 as you also learned from [a]Epaphras, our dear fellow servant,
who is [b]a faithful minister of
Christ on your behalf,
8 who also declared to us your
[a]love in the Spirit.

CHAPTER 1

1 [a]Eph. 1:1
2 [a]1 Cor. 4:17 [b]Gal. 1:3 [1]NU omits *and the Lord Jesus Christ*
3 [a]Phil. 1:3
4 [a]Eph. 1:15 [b][Heb. 6:10]
5 [a][1 Pet. 1:4]
6 [a]Matt. 24:14 [b]John 15:16 [c]Eph. 3:2 [1]NU, M add *and growing*
7 [a]Philem. 23 [b]2 Cor. 11:23
8 [a]Rom. 15:30
9 [a]Eph. 1:15–17 [b]1 Cor. 1:5 [c][Rom. 12:2] [d]Eph. 1:8
10 [a]Eph. 4:1 [b]1 Thess. 4:1 [c]Heb. 13:21 [d]2 Pet. 3:18
11 [a][Eph. 3:16; 6:10] [b]Eph. 4:2 [c][Acts 5:41]
12 [a][Eph. 5:20] [b]Eph. 1:11
13 [a]Eph. 6:12 [b]2 Pet. 1:11 [1]*transferred*
14 [a]Eph. 1:7 [1]NU, M omit *through His blood*
15 [a]2 Cor. 4:4 [b]Rev. 3:14
16 [a]Heb. 1:2, 3 [b][Eph. 1:20, 21]

Preeminence of Christ

9 [a]For this reason we also, since
the day we heard it, do not cease
to pray for you, and to ask [b]that
you may be filled with [c]the knowledge of His will [d]in all wisdom and
spiritual understanding;
10 [a]that you may walk worthy of
the Lord, [b]fully pleasing *Him,* [c]being fruitful in every good work
and increasing in the [d]knowledge
of God;
11 [a]strengthened with all might,
according to His glorious power,
[b]for all patience and longsuffering
[c]with joy;
12 [a]giving thanks to the Father
who has qualified us to be partakers of [b]the inheritance of the saints
in the light.
13 He has delivered us from [a]the
power of darkness [b]and [1]conveyed
us into the kingdom of the Son of
His love,
14 [a]in whom we have redemption
[1]through His blood, the forgiveness of sins.
15 He is [a]the image of the invisible
God, [b]the firstborn over all creation.
16 For [a]by Him all things were
created that are in heaven and that
are on earth, visible and invisible,
whether thrones or [b]dominions or

[1]principalities or [2]powers. All
things were created [c]through Him
and for Him.
17 [a]And He is before all things,
and in Him [b]all things consist.
18 And [a]He is the head of the
body, the church, who is the begin-
ning, [b]the firstborn from the dead,
that in all things He may have the
preeminence.

Reconciled in Christ

19 For it pleased *the Father that*
[a]in Him all the fullness should
dwell,
20 and [a]by Him to reconcile [b]all
things to Himself, by Him, whether
things on earth or things in
heaven, [c]having made peace
through the blood of His cross.
21 And you, [a]who once were
alienated and enemies in your
mind [b]by wicked works, yet now
He has [c]reconciled
22 [a]in the body of His flesh
through death, [b]to present you
holy, and blameless, and above re-
proach in His sight—
23 if indeed you continue [a]in the
faith, grounded and steadfast, and
are [b]not moved away from the
hope of the gospel which you
heard, [c]which was preached to
every creature under heaven, [d]of
which I, Paul, became a minister.

Sacrificial Service for Christ

24 [a]I now rejoice in my sufferings
[b]for you, and fill up in my flesh
[c]what is lacking in the afflictions
of Christ, for [d]the sake of His body,
which is the church,
25 of which I became a minister
according to [a]the [1]stewardship
from God which was given to me
for you, to fulfill the word of God,
26 [a]the [1]mystery which has been
hidden from ages and from gener-
ations, [b]but now has been revealed
to His saints.
27 [a]To them God willed to make
known what are [b]the riches of the
glory of this mystery among the
Gentiles: [1]which is [c]Christ in you,
[d]the hope of glory.
28 Him we preach, [a]warning
every man and teaching every
man in all wisdom, [b]that we may
present every man perfect in
Christ Jesus.
29 To this *end* I also labor, striving
according to His working which
works in me [a]mightily.

Not Philosophy but Christ

2 For I want you to know what
a great [a]conflict[1] I have for you
and those in Laodicea, and *for* as
many as have not seen my face in
the flesh,
2 that their hearts may be en-
couraged, being knit together in
love, and *attaining* to all riches of
the full assurance of understand-
ing, to the knowledge of the mys-
tery of God, [1]both of the Father
and of Christ,
3 [a]in whom are hidden all the
treasures of wisdom and knowl-
edge.
4 Now this I say [a]lest anyone
should deceive you with persua-
sive words.
5 For [a]though I am absent in the
flesh, yet I am with you in spirit,
rejoicing [1]to see [b]your *good* order
and the [c]steadfastness of your
faith in Christ.
6 [a]As you therefore have re-
ceived Christ Jesus the Lord, so
walk in Him,
7 [a]rooted and built up in Him and
established in the faith, as you
have been taught, abounding [1]in
it with thanksgiving.
8 Beware lest anyone [1]cheat you
through philosophy and empty de-
ceit, according to [a]the tradition of
men, according to the [b]basic prin-
ciples of the world, and not ac-
cording to Christ.
9 For [a]in Him dwells all the full-
ness of the Godhead [1]bodily;
10 and you are complete in Him,
who is the [a]head of all [1]principality
and power.

Not Legalism but Christ

11 In Him you were also [a]circum-
cised with the circumcision made
without hands, by [b]putting off the
body [1]of the sins of the flesh, by
the circumcision of Christ,
12 [a]buried with Him in baptism, in
which you also were raised with
Him through [b]faith in the working
of God, [c]who raised Him from the
dead.
13 And you, being dead in your
trespasses and the uncircumcision

16 [c]Heb. 2:10 [1]*rulers* [2]*authorities*
17 [a][John 17:5] [b]Heb. 1:3
18 [a]Eph. 1:22 [b]Rev. 1:5
19 [a]John 1:16
20 [a]Eph. 2:14 [b]2 Cor. 5:18 [c]Eph. 1:10
21 [a][Eph. 2:1] [b]Titus 1:15 [c]2 Cor. 5:18, 19
22 [a]2 Cor. 5:18 [b][Eph. 5:27]
23 [a]Eph. 3:17 [b][John 15:6] [c]Col. 1:6 [d]Col. 1:25
24 [a]2 Cor. 7:4 [b]Eph. 3:1, 13 [c][2 Cor. 1:5; 12:15] [d]Eph. 1:23
25 [a]Gal. 2:7 [1]*dispensation* or *administration*
26 [a][1 Cor. 2:7] [b][2 Tim. 1:10] [1]*secret* or *hidden truth*
27 [a]2 Cor. 2:14 [b]Rom. 9:23 [c][Rom. 8:10, 11] [d]1 Tim. 1:1 [1]M *who*
28 [a]Acts 20:20 [b]Eph. 5:27
29 [a]Eph. 3:7

CHAPTER 2

1 [a]Phil. 1:30 [1]*struggle*
2 [1]NU omits *both of the Father and*
3 [a]1 Cor. 1:24, 30
4 [a]Rom. 16:18
5 [a]1 Thess. 2:17 [b]1 Cor. 14:40 [c]1 Pet. 5:9 [1]Lit. *and seeing*
6 [a]1 Thess. 4:1
7 [a]Eph. 2:21 [1]NU omits *in it*
8 [a]Gal. 1:14 [b]Gal. 4:3, 9, 10 [1]Lit. *plunder you* or *take you captive*
9 [a][John 1:14] [1]*in bodily form*
10 [a][Eph. 1:20, 21] [1]*rule and authority*
11 [a]Deut. 10:16 [b]Rom. 6:6; 7:24 [1]NU omits *of the sins*

12 [a]Rom. 6:4 [b]Eph. 1:19, 20 [c]Acts 2:24

of your flesh, He has made alive
together with Him, having for-
given you all trespasses,
14 [a]having wiped out the [1]hand-
writing of requirements that was
against us, which was contrary to
us. And He has taken it out of the
way, having nailed it to the cross.
15 [a]Having disarmed [b]principali-
ties and powers, He made a public
spectacle of them, triumphing over
them in it.
16 So let no one [a]judge you in food
or in drink, or regarding a [1]festival
or a new moon or sabbaths,
17 [a]which are a shadow of things
to come, but the [1]substance is of
Christ.
18 Let no one cheat you of your
reward, taking delight in *false* hu-
mility and worship of angels, in-
truding into those things which he
has [1]not seen, vainly puffed up by
his fleshly mind,
19 and not holding fast to [a]the
Head, from whom all the body,
nourished and knit together by
joints and ligaments, [b]grows with
the increase *that is* from God.
20 [1]Therefore, if you [a]died with
Christ from the basic principles of
the world, [b]why, as *though* living
in the world, do you subject your-
selves to regulations—
21 [a]"Do not touch, do not taste, do
not handle,"
22 which all concern things which
perish with the using—[a]according
to the commandments and doc-
trines of men?
23 [a]These things indeed have an
appearance of wisdom in self-
imposed religion, *false* humility,
and [1]neglect of the body, *but are*
of no value against the indulgence
of the flesh.

Not Carnality but Christ

3 If then you were [a]raised with
Christ, seek those things which
are above, [b]where Christ is, sitting
at the right hand of God.
2 Set your mind on things above,
not on things on the [a]earth.
3 [a]For you died, [b]and your life is
hidden with Christ in God.
4 [a]When Christ *who is* [b]our life
appears, then you also will appear
with Him in [c]glory.
5 [a]Therefore put to death [b]your
members which are on the earth:

14 [a][Eph. 2:15, 16] [1]*certificate of debt with its*
15 [a][Is. 53:12] [b]Eph. 6:12
16 [a]Rom. 14:3 [1]*feast day*
17 [a]Heb. 8:5; 10:1 [1]Lit. *body*
18 [1]NU omits *not*
19 [a]Eph. 4:15 [b]Eph. 1:23; 4:16
20 [a]Rom. 6:2–5 [b]Gal. 4:3, 9 [1]NU, M omit *Therefore*
21 [a]1 Tim. 4:3
22 [a]Titus 1:14
23 [a]1 Tim. 4:8 [1]*severe treatment, asceticism*

CHAPTER 3

1 [a]Col. 2:12 [b]Eph. 1:20
2 [a][Matt. 6:19–21]
3 [a][Rom. 6:2] [b][2 Cor. 5:7]
4 [a][1 John 3:2] [b]John 14:6 [c]1 Cor. 15:43
5 [a][Rom. 8:13] [b][Rom. 6:13] [c]Eph. 5:3 [d]Eph. 4:19; 5:3, 5
6 [a]Rom. 1:18 [b][Eph. 2:2]
7 [a]1 Cor. 6:11
8 [a]Eph. 4:22
10 [a]Rom. 12:2 [b][Rom. 8:29] [c][Eph. 2:10]
11 [a]Gal. 3:27, 28 [b]Eph. 1:23
12 [a][1 Pet. 1:2] [b]1 John 3:17
13 [a][Mark 11:25]
14 [a]1 Pet. 4:8 [b][1 Cor. 13] [c]Eph. 4:3
15 [a][John 14:27] [b]1 Cor. 7:15 [c]Eph. 4:4 [d][1 Thess. 5:18]
16 [a]Eph. 5:19
17 [a]1 Cor. 10:31
18 [a]1 Pet. 3:1 [b][Eph. 5:22–6:9]
19 [a][Eph. 5:25] [b]Eph. 4:31
20 [a]Eph. 6:1 [b]Eph. 5:24

[c]fornication, uncleanness, passion,
evil desire, and covetousness,
[d]which is idolatry.
6 [a]Because of these things the
wrath of God is coming upon [b]the
sons of disobedience,
7 [a]in which you yourselves once
walked when you lived in them.
8 [a]But now you yourselves are to
put off all these: anger, wrath, mal-
ice, blasphemy, filthy language out
of your mouth.
9 Do not lie to one another, since
you have put off the old man with
his deeds,
10 and have put on the new *man*
who [a]is renewed in knowledge
[b]according to the image of Him
who [c]created him,
11 where there is neither [a]Greek
nor Jew, circumcised nor uncir-
cumcised, barbarian, Scythian,
slave *nor* free, [b]but Christ *is* all and
in all.

Character of the New Man

12 Therefore, [a]as *the* elect of God,
holy and beloved, [b]put on tender
mercies, kindness, humility, meek-
ness, longsuffering;
13 [a]bearing with one another, and
forgiving one another, if anyone
has a complaint against another;
even as Christ forgave you, so you
also *must do.*
14 [a]But above all these things [b]put
on love, which is the [c]bond of per-
fection.
15 And let [a]the peace of God rule
in your hearts, [b]to which also you
were called [c]in one body; and [d]be
thankful.
16 Let the word of Christ dwell in
you richly in all wisdom, teaching
and admonishing one another [a]in
psalms and hymns and spiritual
songs, singing with grace in your
hearts to the Lord.
17 And [a]*whatever* you do in word
or deed, *do* all in the name of the
Lord Jesus, giving thanks to God
the Father through Him.

The Christian Home

18 [a]Wives, submit to your own
husbands, [b]as is fitting in the Lord.
19 [a]Husbands, love your wives
and do not be [b]bitter toward them.
20 [a]Children, obey your parents
[b]in all things, for this is well pleas-
ing to the Lord.

21 [a]Fathers, do not provoke your
children, lest they become dis-
couraged.
22 [a]Bondservants, obey in all
things your masters according to
the flesh, not with eyeservice, as
men-pleasers, but in sincerity of
heart, fearing God.
23 [a]And whatever you do, do it
heartily, as to the Lord and not to
men,
24 [a]knowing that from the Lord
you will receive the reward of the
inheritance; [b]for[1] you serve the
Lord Christ.
25 But he who does wrong will be
repaid for what he has done, and
[a]there is no partiality.

4 Masters,[a] give your bond-
servants what is just and fair,
knowing that you also have a Mas-
ter in heaven.

Christian Graces

2 [a]Continue earnestly in prayer,
being vigilant in it [b]with thanks-
giving;
3 [a]meanwhile praying also for
us, that God would [b]open to us a
door for the word, to speak [c]the
[1]mystery of Christ, [d]for which I am
also in chains,
4 that I may make it manifest, as
I ought to speak.
5 [a]Walk in [b]wisdom toward
those *who are* outside, [c]redeeming
the time.
6 *Let* your speech always *be*
[a]with grace, [b]seasoned with salt,
[c]that you may know how you
ought to answer each one.

Final Greetings

7 [a]Tychicus, a beloved brother,
faithful minister, and fellow ser-
vant in the Lord, will tell you all
the news about me.
8 [a]I am sending him to you for
this very purpose, that [1]he may
know your circumstances and
comfort your hearts,
9 with [a]Onesimus, a faithful and
beloved brother, who is *one* of you.
They will make known to you all
things which *are happening* here.
10 [a]Aristarchus my fellow pris-
oner greets you, with [b]Mark the
cousin of Barnabas (about whom
you received instructions: if he
comes to you, welcome him),
11 and Jesus who is called Justus.
These *are my* only fellow workers
for the kingdom of God who are
of the circumcision; they have
proved to be a comfort to me.
12 [a]Epaphras, who is *one* of you,
a bondservant of Christ, greets
you, always [b]laboring fervently for
you in prayers, that you may stand
[c]perfect and [1]complete in all the
will of God.
13 For I bear him witness that he
has a great [1]zeal for you, and those
who are in Laodicea, and those in
Hierapolis.
14 [a]Luke the beloved physician
and [b]Demas greet you.
15 Greet the brethren who are in
Laodicea, and [1]Nymphas and [a]the
church that *is* in [2]his house.

Closing Exhortations and Blessing

16 Now when [a]this epistle is read
among you, see that it is read also
in the church of the Laodiceans,
and that you likewise read the
epistle from Laodicea.
17 And say to [a]Archippus, "Take
heed to [b]the ministry which you
have received in the Lord, that you
may fulfill it."
18 [a]This salutation by my own
hand—Paul. [b]Remember my
chains. Grace *be* with you. Amen.

21 [a]Eph. 6:4
22 [a]Eph. 6:5
23 [a][Eccl. 9:10]
24 [a]Eph. 6:8 [b]1 Cor. 7:22 [1]NU omits *for*
25 [a]Rom. 2:11

CHAPTER 4

1 [a]Eph. 6:9
2 [a]Luke 18:1 [b]Col. 2:7
3 [a]Eph. 6:19 [b]1 Cor. 16:9 [c]Eph. 3:3, 4; 6:19 [d]Eph. 6:20 [1]*hidden truth*
5 [a]Eph. 5:15 [b][Matt. 10:16] [c]Eph. 5:16
6 [a]Eccl. 10:12 [b]Mark 9:50 [c]1 Pet. 3:15
7 [a]2 Tim. 4:12
8 [a]Eph. 6:22 [1]NU *you may know our circumstances and he may comfort*
9 [a]Philem. 10
10 [a]Acts 19:29; 20:4; 27:2 [b]2 Tim. 4:11
12 [a]Philem. 23 [b]Rom. 15:30 [c]Matt. 5:48 [1]NU *fully assured*
13 [1]NU *concern*
14 [a]2 Tim. 4:11 [b]2 Tim. 4:10
15 [a]Rom. 16:5 [1]NU *Nympha* [2]NU *her*
16 [a]1 Thess. 5:27
17 [a]Philem. 2 [b]2 Tim. 4:5
18 [a]1 Cor. 16:21 [b]Heb. 13:3

The First Epistle of Paul the Apostle to the

Thessalonians

PAUL has many pleasant memories of the days he spent with the infant Thessalonian church. Their faith, hope, love, and perseverance in the face of persecution are exemplary. Paul's labors as a spiritual parent to the fledgling church have been richly rewarded, and his affection is visible in every line of his letter.

Paul encourages them to excel in their newfound faith, to increase in their love for one another, and to rejoice, pray, and give thanks always. He closes his letter with instruction regarding the return of the Lord, whose advent signifies hope and comfort for believers both living and dead.

Because this is the first of Paul's two canonical letters to the church at Thessalonica, it received the title *Pros Thessalonikeis A,* the "First to the Thessalonians."

Greeting

PAUL, [a]Silvanus, and Timothy,

To the church of the [b]Thessalo-
nians in God the Father and the
Lord Jesus Christ:

Grace to you and peace [1]from
God our Father and the Lord Jesus
Christ.

Their Good Example

2 [a]We give thanks to God always
for you all, making mention of you
in our prayers,
3 remembering without ceasing
[a]your work of faith, [b]labor of love,
and patience of hope in our Lord
Jesus Christ in the sight of our God
and Father,
4 knowing, beloved brethren,
[a]your election by God.
5 For [a]our gospel did not come
to you in word only, but also in
power, [b]and in the Holy Spirit [c]and
in much assurance, as you know
what kind of men we were among
you for your sake.
6 And [a]you became followers of
us and of the Lord, having re-
ceived the word in much affliction,
[b]with joy of the Holy Spirit,
7 so that you became examples
to all in Macedonia and Achaia
who believe.

CHAPTER 1

1 [a]1 Pet. 5:12 [b]Acts 17:1–9 [1]NU omits *from God our Father and the Lord Jesus Christ*
2 [a]Rom. 1:8; 2 Thess. 1:3
3 [a]John 6:29 [b]Rom. 16:6
4 [a]Col. 3:12
5 [a]Mark 16:20 [b]2 Cor. 6:6 [c]Heb. 2:3
6 [a]1 Cor. 4:16; 11:1 [b]Acts 5:41; 13:52; 2 Cor. 6:10; Gal. 5:22
8 [a]Rom. 10:18 [b]Rom. 1:8; 16:19; 2 Cor. 2:14; 2 Thess. 1:4
9 [a]1 Thess. 2:1 [b]1 Cor. 12:2
10 [a][Rom. 2:7] [b]Matt. 3:7; Rom. 5:9

CHAPTER 2

2 [a]Acts 14:5; 16:19–24; Phil. 1:30 [b]Acts 17:1–9 [1]NU, M omit *even*
3 [a]2 Cor. 7:2
4 [a]1 Cor. 7:25 [b]Titus 1:3 [c]Gal. 1:10 [d]Prov. 17:3
5 [a]2 Cor. 2:17

8 For from you the word of the
Lord [a]has sounded forth, not only
in Macedonia and Achaia, but also
[b]in every place. Your faith toward
God has gone out, so that we do
not need to say anything.
9 For they themselves declare
concerning us [a]what manner of
entry we had to you, [b]and how you
turned to God from idols to serve
the living and true God,
10 and [a]to wait for His Son from
heaven, whom He raised from the
dead, *even* Jesus who delivers us
[b]from the wrath to come.

Paul's Conduct

2 For you yourselves know,
brethren, that our coming to
you was not in vain.
2 But [1]even after we had suffered
before and were spitefully treated
at [a]Philippi, as you know, we were
[b]bold in our God to speak to you
the gospel of God in much conflict.
3 [a]For our exhortation *did* not
come from error or uncleanness,
nor *was it* in deceit.
4 But as [a]we have been approved
by God [b]to be entrusted with the
gospel, even so we speak, [c]not as
pleasing men, but God [d]who tests
our hearts.
5 For [a]neither at any time did we
use flattering words, as you know,

nor a [1]cloak for covetousness—[b]God *is* witness.
6 [a]Nor did we seek glory from men, either from you or from others, when [b]we might have [c]made demands [d]as apostles of Christ.
7 But [a]we were gentle among you, just as a nursing *mother* cherishes her own children.
8 So, affectionately longing for you, we were well pleased [a]to impart to you not only the gospel of God, but also [b]our own lives, because you had become dear to us.
9 For you remember, brethren, our [a]labor and toil; for laboring night and day, [b]that we might not be a burden to any of you, we preached to you the gospel of God.
10 [a]You *are* witnesses, and God *also*, [b]how devoutly and justly and blamelessly we behaved ourselves among you who believe;
11 as you know how we exhorted, and comforted, and [1]charged every one of you, as a father *does* his own children,
12 [a]that you would walk worthy of God [b]who calls you into His own kingdom and glory.

Their Conversion

13 For this reason we also thank God [a]without ceasing, because when you [b]received the word of God which you heard from us, you welcomed *it* [c]not *as* the word of men, but as it is in truth, the word of God, which also effectively [d]works in you who believe.
14 For you, brethren, became imitators [a]of the churches of God which are in Judea in Christ Jesus. For [b]you also suffered the same things from your own countrymen, just as they *did* from the Judeans,
15 [a]who killed both the Lord Jesus and [b]their own prophets, and have persecuted us; and they do not please God [c]and are [1]contrary to all men,
16 [a]forbidding us to speak to the Gentiles that they may be saved, so as always [b]to fill up *the measure of* their sins; [c]but wrath has come upon them to the uttermost.

Longing to See Them

17 But we, brethren, having been taken away from you for a short time [a]in presence, not in heart, endeavored more eagerly to see your face with great desire.
18 Therefore we wanted to come to you—even I, Paul, time and again—but [a]Satan hindered us.
19 For [a]what *is* our hope, or joy, or [b]crown of rejoicing? *Is it* not even you in the [c]presence of our Lord Jesus Christ [d]at His coming?
20 For you are our glory and joy.

Concern for Their Faith

3 Therefore, when we could no longer endure it, we thought it good to be left in Athens alone,
2 and sent [a]Timothy, our brother and minister of God, and our fellow laborer in the gospel of Christ, to establish you and encourage you concerning your faith,
3 [a]that no one should be shaken by these afflictions; for you yourselves know that [b]we are appointed to this.
4 [a]For, in fact, we told you before when we were with you that we would suffer tribulation, just as it happened, and you know.
5 For this reason, when I could no longer endure it, I sent to know your faith, [a]lest by some means the tempter had tempted you, and [b]our labor might be in vain.

Encouraged by Timothy

6 [a]But now that Timothy has come to us from you, and brought us good news of your faith and love, and that you always have good remembrance of us, greatly desiring to see us, [b]as we also *to see* you—
7 therefore, brethren, in all our affliction and distress [a]we were comforted concerning you by your faith.
8 For now we live, if you [a]stand fast in the Lord.
9 For what thanks can we render to God for you, for all the joy with which we rejoice for your sake before our God,
10 night and day praying exceedingly that we may see your face [a]and perfect what is lacking in your faith?

Prayer for the Church

11 Now may our God and Father Himself, and our Lord Jesus Christ, [a]direct our way to you.

5 [b]Rom. 1:9 [1]*pretext for greed*
6 [a]1 Tim. 5:17 [b]1 Cor. 9:4 [c]2 Cor. 11:9 [d]1 Cor. 9:1
7 [a]1 Cor. 2:3
8 [a]Rom. 1:11 [b]2 Cor. 12:15
9 [a]Acts 18:3; 20:34, 35 [b]2 Cor. 12:13
10 [a]1 Thess. 1:5 [b]2 Cor. 7:2
11 [1]NU, M *implored*
12 [a]Eph. 4:1 [b]1 Cor. 1:9
13 [a]1 Thess. 1:2, 3 [b]Mark 4:20 [c][Gal. 4:14] [d][1 Pet. 1:23]
14 [a]Gal. 1:22 [b]Acts 17:5
15 [a]Acts 2:23 [b]Matt. 5:12; 23:34, 35 [c]Esth. 3:8 [1]*hostile*
16 [a]Luke 11:52 [b]Gen. 15:16 [c]Matt. 24:6
17 [a]1 Cor. 5:3
18 [a]Rom. 1:13; 15:22
19 [a]2 Cor. 1:14 [b]Prov. 16:31 [c]Jude 24 [d]1 Cor. 15:23

CHAPTER 3

2 [a]Rom. 16:21
3 [a]Eph. 3:13 [b]Acts 9:16; 14:22
4 [a]Acts 20:24
5 [a]1 Cor. 7:5 [b]Gal. 2:2
6 [a]Acts 18:5 [b]Phil. 1:8
7 [a]2 Cor. 1:4
8 [a]Phil. 4:1
10 [a]2 Cor. 13:9
11 [a]Mark 1:3

12 And may the Lord make you increase and [a]abound in love to one another and to all, just as we *do* to you,
13 so that He may establish [a]your hearts blameless in holiness before our God and Father at the coming of our Lord Jesus Christ with all His saints.

Plea for Purity

4 Finally then, brethren, we urge and exhort in the Lord Jesus [a]that you should abound more and more, [b]just as you received from us how you ought to walk and to please God;
2 for you know what commandments we gave you through the Lord Jesus.
3 For this is [a]the will of God, [b]your sanctification: [c]that you should abstain from sexual immorality;
4 [a]that each of you should know how to possess his own vessel in sanctification and honor,
5 [a]not in passion of lust, [b]like the Gentiles [c]who do not know God;
6 that no one should take advantage of and defraud his brother in this matter, because the Lord [a]*is* the avenger of all such, as we also forewarned you and testified.
7 For God did not call us to uncleanness, [a]but in holiness.
8 [a]Therefore he who rejects *this* does not reject man, but God, [b]who[1] has also given us His Holy Spirit.

A Brotherly and Orderly Life

9 But concerning brotherly love you have no need that I should write to you, for [a]you yourselves are taught by God [b]to love one another;
10 and indeed you do so toward all the brethren who are in all Macedonia. But we urge you, brethren, [a]that you increase more and more;
11 that you also aspire to lead a quiet life, [a]to mind your own business, and [b]to work with your own hands, as we commanded you,
12 [a]that you may walk properly toward those who are outside, and *that* you may lack nothing.

The Comfort of Christ's Coming

13 But I do not want you to be ignorant, brethren, concerning those who have fallen [1]asleep, lest you sorrow [a]as others [b]who have no hope.
14 For [a]if we believe that Jesus died and rose again, even so God will bring with Him [b]those who [1]sleep in Jesus.
15 For this we say to you [a]by the word of the Lord, that [b]we who are alive *and* remain until the coming of the Lord will by no means precede those who are [1]asleep.
16 For [a]the Lord Himself will descend from heaven with a shout, with the voice of an archangel, and with [b]the trumpet of God. [c]And the dead in Christ will rise first.
17 [a]Then we who are alive *and* remain shall be caught up together with them [b]in the clouds to meet the Lord in the air. And thus [c]we shall always be with the Lord.
18 [a]Therefore comfort one another with these words.

The Day of the Lord

5 But concerning [a]the times and the seasons, brethren, you have no need that I should write to you.
2 For you yourselves know perfectly that [a]the day of the Lord so comes as a thief in the night.
3 For when they say, "Peace and safety!" then [a]sudden destruction comes upon them, [b]as labor pains upon a pregnant woman. And they shall not escape.
4 [a]But you, brethren, are not in darkness, so that this Day should overtake you as a thief.
5 You are all [a]sons of light and sons of the day. We are not of the night nor of darkness.
6 [a]Therefore let us not sleep, as others *do*, but [b]let us watch and be [1]sober.
7 For [a]those who sleep, sleep at night, and those who get drunk [b]are drunk at night.
8 But let us who are of the day be sober, [a]putting on the breastplate of faith and love, and *as* a helmet the hope of salvation.
9 For [a]God did not appoint us to wrath, [b]but to obtain salvation through our Lord Jesus Christ,

12 [a]Phil. 1:9
13 [a]2 Thess. 2:17

CHAPTER 4

1 [a]1 Cor. 15:58 [b]Phil. 1:27
3 [a][Rom. 12:2] [b]Eph. 5:27 [c][1 Cor. 6:15–20]
4 [a]Rom. 6:19
5 [a]Col. 3:5 [b]Eph. 4:17, 18 [c]1 Cor. 15:34
6 [a]2 Thess. 1:8
7 [a]Lev. 11:44
8 [a]Luke 10:16 [b]1 Cor. 2:10 [1]NU *who also gives*
9 [a][Jer. 31:33, 34] [b]Matt. 22:39
10 [a]1 Thess. 3:12
11 [a]2 Thess. 3:11 [b]Acts 20:35
12 [a]Rom. 13:13
13 [a]Lev. 19:28 [b][Eph. 2:12] [1]Died
14 [a]1 Cor. 15:13 [b]1 Cor. 15:20, 23 [1]Or *through Jesus sleep*
15 [a]1 Kin. 13:17; 20:35 [b]1 Cor. 15:51, 52 [1]Dead
16 [a][Matt. 24:30, 31] [b][1 Cor. 15:52] [c][1 Cor. 15:23]
17 [a][1 Cor. 15:51–53] [b]Acts 1:9 [c]John 14:3; 17:24
18 [a]1 Thess. 5:11

CHAPTER 5

1 [a]Matt. 24:3
2 [a][2 Pet. 3:10]
3 [a]Is. 13:6–9 [b]Hos. 13:13
4 [a]1 John 2:8
5 [a]Eph. 5:8
6 [a]Matt. 25:5 [b][1 Pet. 5:8] [1]*self-controlled*
7 [a][Luke 21:34] [b]Acts 2:15
8 [a]Eph. 6:14
9 [a]Rom. 9:22 [b][2 Thess. 2:13]

10 [a]who died for us, that whether
we wake or sleep, we should live
together with Him.
11 Therefore [1]comfort each other
and [2]edify one another, just as you
also are doing.

Various Exhortations

12 And we urge you, brethren, [a]to
recognize those who labor among
you, and are over you in the Lord
and [1]admonish you,
13 and to esteem them very highly
in love for their work's sake. [a]Be
at peace among yourselves.
14 Now we [1]exhort you, brethren,
[a]warn those who are [2]unruly,
[b]comfort the fainthearted, [c]uphold
the weak, [d]be patient with all.
15 [a]See that no one renders evil
for evil to anyone, but always
[b]pursue what is good both for
yourselves and for all.
16 [a]Rejoice always,
17 [a]pray without ceasing,
18 in everything give thanks; for
this is the will of God in Christ
Jesus for you.
19 [a]Do not quench the Spirit.
20 [a]Do not despise prophecies.
21 [a]Test all things; [b]hold fast what
is good.
22 Abstain from every form of
evil.

Blessing and Admonition

23 Now may [a]the God of peace
Himself [b]sanctify[1] you completely;
and may your whole spirit, soul,
and body [c]be preserved blameless
at the coming of our Lord Jesus
Christ.
24 He who calls you *is* [a]faithful,
who also will [b]do *it*.
25 Brethren, pray for us.
26 Greet all the brethren with a
holy kiss.
27 I charge you by the Lord that
this [1]epistle be read to all the [2]holy
brethren.
28 The grace of our Lord Jesus
Christ *be* with you. Amen.

10 [a]2 Cor. 5:15
11 [1]Or *encourage* [2]*build one another up*
12 [a]1 Cor. 16:18 [1]*instruct* or *warn*
13 [a]Mark 9:50
14 [a]2 Thess. 3:6, 7, 11 [b]Heb. 12:12 [c]Rom. 14:1; 15:1 [d]Gal. 5:22 [1]*encourage* [2]*insubordinate* or *idle*
15 [a]Lev. 19:18 [b]Gal. 6:10
16 [a][2 Cor. 6:10]
17 [a]Eph. 6:18
19 [a]Eph. 4:30
20 [a]1 Cor. 14:1, 31
21 [a]1 John 4:1 [b]Phil. 4:8
23 [a]Phil. 4:9 [b]1 Thess. 3:13 [c]1 Cor. 1:8, 9 [1]*set you apart*

24 [a][1 Cor. 10:13] [b]Phil. 1:6   **27** [1]*letter* [2]NU omits *holy*

The Second Epistle of Paul the Apostle to the

Thessalonians

SINCE Paul's first letter, the seeds of false doctrine have been sown among the Thessalonians, causing them to waver in their faith. Paul removes these destructive seeds and again plants the seeds of truth. He begins by commending the believers on their faithfulness in the midst of persecution and encouraging them that present suffering will be repaid with future glory. Therefore, in the midst of persecution, expectation can be high.

Paul then deals with the central matter of his letter: a misunderstanding spawned by false teachers regarding the coming day of the Lord. Despite reports to the contrary, that Day has not yet come, and Paul recounts the events that must first take place. Laboring for the gospel, rather than lazy resignation, is the proper response.

As the second letter in Paul's Thessalonian correspondence, this was entitled *Pros Thessalonikeis B*, the "Second to the Thessalonians."

Greeting

PAUL, Silvanus, and Timothy,
To the church of the Thessalonians in God our Father and the Lord Jesus Christ:

2 [a]Grace to you and peace from
God our Father and the Lord Jesus
Christ.

God's Final Judgment and Glory

3 We are bound to thank God al-
ways for you, brethren, as it is fit-
ting, because your faith grows ex-
ceedingly, and the love of every
one of you all abounds toward
each other,
4 so that [a]we ourselves boast of
you among the churches of God
[b]for your patience and faith [c]in all
your persecutions and [1]tribula-
tions that you endure,
5 *which is* [a]manifest[1] evidence of
the righteous judgment of God,
that you may be counted worthy
of the kingdom of God, [b]for which
you also suffer;
6 [a]since *it is* a righteous thing
with God to repay with [1]tribulation
those who trouble you,
7 and to *give* you who are trou-
bled [a]rest with us when [b]the Lord
Jesus is revealed from heaven with
His mighty angels,
8 in flaming fire taking ven-
geance on those who do not know
God, and on those who do not obey
the gospel of our Lord Jesus
Christ.
9 [a]These shall be punished with
everlasting destruction from the
presence of the Lord and [b]from the
glory of His power,
10 when He comes, in that Day,
[a]to be [b]glorified in His saints and
to be admired among all those who
[1]believe, because our testimony
among you was believed.
11 Therefore we also pray always
for you that our God would [a]count
you worthy of *this* calling, and ful-
fill all the good pleasure of *His*
goodness and [b]the work of faith
with power,
12 [a]that the name of our Lord
Jesus Christ may be glorified in
you, and you in Him, according to
the grace of our God and the Lord
Jesus Christ.

The Great Apostasy

2 Now, brethren, [a]concerning
the coming of our Lord Jesus
Christ [b]and our gathering together
to Him, we ask you,

CHAPTER 1

2 [a]1 Cor. 1:3
4 [a]2 Cor. 7:4; [1 Thess. 2:19] [b]1 Thess. 1:3 [c]1 Thess. 2:14 [1]*afflictions*
5 [a]Phil. 1:28 [b]1 Thess. 2:14 [1]*plain*
6 [a]Rev. 6:10 [1]*affliction*
7 [a]Rev. 14:13 [b][1 Thess. 4:16]; Jude 14
9 [a]Phil. 3:19; 1 Thess. 5:3 [b]Deut. 33:2
10 [a]Matt. 25:31 [b]Is. 49:3; John 17:10; 1 Thess. 2:12 [1]NU, M *have believed*
11 [a]Col. 1:12 [b]1 Thess. 1:3
12 [a][Col. 3:17]

CHAPTER 2

1 [a]Mark 13:26; [1 Thess. 4:15–17] [b]Matt. 24:31

2 [a]not to be soon shaken in mind
or troubled, either by spirit or by
word or by letter, as if from us,
as though the day of [1]Christ had
come.
3 Let no one deceive you by any
means; for *that Day will not come*
[a]unless the falling away comes
first, and [b]the man of [1]sin is re-
vealed, [c]the son of perdition,
4 who opposes and [a]exalts him-
self [b]above all that is called God
or that is worshiped, so that he sits
[1]as God in the temple of God,
showing himself that he is God.
5 Do you not remember that
when I was still with you I told you
these things?
6 And now you know what is re-
straining, that he may be revealed
in his own time.
7 For [a]the [1]mystery of lawless-
ness is already at work; only [2]He
who now restrains *will do so* until
[2]He is taken out of the way.
8 And then the lawless one will
be revealed, [a]whom the Lord will
consume [b]with the breath of His
mouth and destroy [c]with the
brightness of His coming.
9 The coming of the *lawless one*
is [a]according to the working of Sa-
tan, with all power, [b]signs, and ly-
ing wonders,
10 and with all unrighteous decep-
tion among [a]those who perish, be-
cause they did not receive [b]the
love of the truth, that they might
be saved.
11 And [a]for this reason God will
send them strong delusion, [b]that
they should believe the lie,
12 that they all may be con-
demned who did not believe the
truth but [a]had pleasure in unrigh-
teousness.

Stand Fast

13 But we are [1]bound to give
thanks to God always for you,
brethren beloved by the Lord, be-
cause God [a]from the beginning
[b]chose you for salvation [c]through
[2]sanctification by the Spirit and
belief in the truth,
14 to which He called you by
our gospel, for [a]the obtaining
of the glory of our Lord Jesus
Christ.
15 Therefore, brethren, [a]stand fast
and hold [b]the traditions which you

2 [a]Matt. 24:4 [1]NU *the Lord*
3 [a]1 Tim. 4:1 [b]Dan. 7:25; 8:25; 11:36; 2 Thess. 2:8; Rev. 13:5 [c]John 17:12 [1]NU *lawlessness*
4 [a]Is. 14:13, 14; Ezek. 28:2 [b]1 Cor. 8:5 [1]NU omits *as God*
7 [a]1 John 2:18 [1]*hidden truth* [2]Or *he*
8 [a]Dan. 7:10 [b]Is. 11:4; Rev. 2:16; 19:15 [c]Heb. 10:27
9 [a]John 8:41 [b]Deut. 13:1
10 [a]2 Cor. 2:15 [b]1 Cor. 16:22
11 [a]Rom. 1:28 [b]1 Tim. 4:1
12 [a]Rom. 1:32; 1 Cor. 13:6
13 [a]Eph. 1:4 [b]1 Thess. 1:4 [c]1 Thess. 4:7; [1 Pet. 1:2] [1]*under obligation* [2]*being set apart by*
14 [a]1 Pet. 5:10
15 [a]1 Cor. 16:13 [b]Rom. 6:17; 1 Cor. 11:2; 2 Thess. 3:6; Jude 3 [1]*letter*
16 [a][Rev. 1:5] [b]Titus 3:7; 1 Pet. 1:3
17 [a]1 Cor. 1:8 [1]*strengthen*

CHAPTER 3

1 [a]Eph. 6:19
2 [a]Rom. 15:31 [b]Acts 28:24
3 [a]1 Cor. 1:9; 1 Thess. 5:24 [b]John 17:15
4 [a]2 Cor. 7:16
5 [a]1 Chr. 29:18
6 [a]Rom. 16:17 [b]1 Cor. 5:1 [c]1 Thess. 4:11 [1]NU, M *they*
8 [a]1 Thess. 2:9 [1]Lit. *for nothing*
9 [a]1 Cor. 9:4, 6–14
11 [a]1 Tim. 5:13; 1 Pet. 4:15
12 [a]Eph. 4:28; 1 Thess. 4:11, 12 [1]*encourage*

were taught, whether by word or
our [1]epistle.
16 Now may our Lord Jesus
Christ Himself, and our God and
Father, [a]who has loved us and
given *us* everlasting consolation
and [b]good hope by grace,
17 comfort your hearts [a]and [1]es-
tablish you in every good word
and work.

Pray for Us

3 Finally, brethren, [a]pray for us,
that the word of the Lord may
run *swiftly* and be glorified, just
as *it is* with you,
2 and [a]that we may be delivered
from unreasonable and wicked
men; [b]for not all have faith.
3 But [a]the Lord is faithful, who
will establish you and [b]guard *you*
from the evil one.
4 And [a]we have confidence in the
Lord concerning you, both that
you do and will do the things we
command you.
5 Now may [a]the Lord direct your
hearts into the love of God and
into the patience of Christ.

Warning Against Idleness

6 But we command you, breth-
ren, in the name of our Lord Jesus
Christ, [a]that you withdraw [b]from
every brother who walks [c]dis-
orderly and not according to the
tradition which [1]he received
from us.
7 For you yourselves know how
you ought to follow us, for we were
not disorderly among you;
8 nor did we eat anyone's bread
[1]free of charge, but worked with
[a]labor and toil night and day, that
we might not be a burden to any
of you,
9 not because we do not have
[a]authority, but to make ourselves
an example of how you should fol-
low us.
10 For even when we were with
you, we commanded you this: If
anyone will not work, neither shall
he eat.
11 For we hear that there are some
who walk among you in a dis-
orderly manner, not working at
all, but are [a]busybodies.
12 Now those who are such we
command and [1]exhort through our
Lord Jesus Christ [a]that they work

in quietness and eat their own
bread.
13 But as *for* you, brethren, [a]do
not grow weary *in* doing good.
14 And if anyone does not obey
our word in this [1]epistle, note that
person and [a]do not keep company
with him, that he may be ashamed.
15 [a]Yet do not count *him* as an en-
emy, [b]but [1]admonish *him* as a
brother.

13 [a]Gal. 6:9
14 [a]Matt. 18:17 [1]*letter*
15 [a]Lev. 19:17 [b]Titus 3:10 [1]*warn*
16 [a]Rom. 15:33
17 [a]1 Cor. 16:21 [1]*letter*
18 [a]Rom. 16:20, 24

Benediction

16 Now may [a]the Lord of peace
Himself give you peace always in
every way. The Lord *be* with you
all.
17 [a]The salutation of Paul with my
own hand, which is a sign in every
[1]epistle; so I write.
18 [a]The grace of our Lord Jesus
Christ *be* with you all. Amen.

The First Epistle of Paul the Apostle to

Timothy

PAUL, the aged and experienced apostle, writes to the young pastor Timothy who is facing a heavy burden of responsibility in the church at Ephesus. The task is challenging: false doctrine must be erased, public worship safeguarded, and mature leadership developed. In addition to the conduct of the church, Paul talks pointedly about the conduct of the minister. Timothy must be on his guard lest his youthfulness become a liability, rather than an asset, to the gospel. He must be careful to avoid false teachers and greedy motives, pursuing instead righteousness, godliness, faith, love, perseverance, and the gentleness that befits a man of God.

The Greek title for this letter is *Pros Timotheon A,* the "First to Timothy." *Timothy* means "honoring God" or "honored by God," and probably was given to him by his mother Eunice.

Greeting

PAUL, an apostle of Jesus
Christ, by the commandment
of God our Savior and the Lord
Jesus Christ, our hope,

2 To Timothy, a [a]true son in the
faith:

[b]Grace, mercy, *and* peace from
God our Father and Jesus Christ
our Lord.

No Other Doctrine

3 As I urged you [a]when I went
into Macedonia—remain in Ephe-
sus that you may [1]charge some
[b]that they teach no other doctrine,
4 [a]nor give heed to fables and
endless genealogies, which cause
disputes rather than godly edifica-
tion which is in faith.
5 Now [a]the purpose of the com-
mandment is love [b]from a pure
heart, *from* a good conscience, and
from [1]sincere faith,
6 from which some, having
strayed, have turned aside to [a]idle
talk,
7 desiring to be teachers of the
law, understanding neither what
they say nor the things which they
affirm.
8 But we know that the law *is*
[a]good if one uses it lawfully,
9 knowing this: that the law is
not made for a righteous person,
but for *the* lawless and insubordi-
nate, for *the* ungodly and for sin-
ners, for *the* unholy and profane,
for murderers of fathers and mur-
derers of mothers, for manslayers,
10 for fornicators, for sodomites,
for kidnappers, for liars, for per-
jurers, and if there is any other
thing that is [1]contrary to sound
doctrine,
11 according to the glorious gos-
pel of the [a]blessed God which was
[b]committed to my trust.

Glory to God for His Grace

12 And I thank Christ Jesus our
Lord who has [a]enabled me, [b]be-
cause He counted me faithful,
[c]putting *me* into the ministry,
13 although [a]I was formerly a
blasphemer, a persecutor, and an
[1]insolent man; but I obtained
mercy because [b]I did *it* ignorantly
in unbelief.
14 [a]And the grace of our Lord was
exceedingly abundant, [b]with faith
and love which are in Christ Jesus.
15 [a]This *is* a faithful saying and
worthy of all acceptance, that
[b]Christ Jesus came into the world
to save sinners, of whom I am
chief.
16 However, for this reason I ob-
tained mercy, that in me first Jesus
Christ might show all longsuffer-

CHAPTER 1

2 [a]Titus 1:4 [b]Gal. 1:3

3 [a]Acts 20:1, 3 [b]Gal. 1:6, 7 [1]*command*

4 [a]Titus 1:14

5 [a]Rom. 13:8–10 [b]Eph. 6:24 [1]Lit. *unhypocritical*

6 [a]1 Tim. 6:4, 20

8 [a]Rom. 7:12, 16

10 [1]*opposed*

11 [a]1 Tim. 6:15 [b]1 Cor. 9:17

12 [a]1 Cor. 15:10 [b]1 Cor. 7:25 [c]Col. 1:25

13 [a]Acts 8:3 [b]John 4:21 [1]*violently arrogant*

14 [a]Rom. 5:20 [b]2 Tim. 1:13; 2:22

15 [a]2 Tim. 2:11 [b]Matt. 1:21; 9:13

ing, as a pattern to those who are
going to believe on Him for ever-
lasting life.
17 Now to [a]the King eternal, [b]im-
mortal, [c]invisible, to [1]God [d]who
alone is wise, [e]*be* honor and glory
forever and ever. Amen.

Fight the Good Fight

18 This [1]charge I commit to you,
son Timothy, according to the
prophecies previously made con-
cerning you, that by them you
may wage the good warfare,
19 having faith and a good con-
science, which some having re-
jected, concerning the faith have
suffered shipwreck,
20 of whom are [a]Hymenaeus and
[b]Alexander, whom I delivered to
Satan that they may learn not to
[c]blaspheme.

Pray for All Men

2 Therefore I [1]exhort first of all
that supplications, prayers, in-
tercessions, *and* giving of thanks
be made for all men,
2 [a]for kings and [b]all who are in
[1]authority, that we may lead a
quiet and peaceable life in all god-
liness and [2]reverence.
3 For this *is* [a]good and accept-
able in the sight [b]of God our Sav-
ior,
4 [a]who desires all men to be
saved [b]and to come to the knowl-
edge of the truth.
5 [a]For *there is* one God and [b]one
Mediator between God and men,
the Man Christ Jesus,
6 [a]who gave Himself a ransom
for all, to be testified in due time,
7 [a]for which I was appointed a
preacher and an apostle—I am
speaking the truth [1]in Christ *and*
not lying—[b]a teacher of the Gen-
tiles in faith and truth.

Men and Women in the Church

8 I desire therefore that the men
pray [a]everywhere, [b]lifting up holy
hands, without wrath and doubt-
ing;
9 in like manner also, that the
[a]women adorn themselves in mod-
est apparel, with propriety and
[1]moderation, not with braided hair
or gold or pearls or costly clothing,
10 [a]but, which is proper for
women professing godliness, with
good works.
11 Let a woman learn in silence
with all submission.
12 And [a]I do not permit a woman
to teach or to have authority over
a man, but to be in silence.
13 For Adam was formed first,
then Eve.
14 And Adam was not deceived,
but the woman being deceived, fell
into transgression.
15 Nevertheless she will be saved
in childbearing if they continue in
faith, love, and holiness, with self-
control.

Qualifications of Overseers

3 This *is* a faithful saying: If a
man desires the position of a
[1]bishop, he desires a good work.
2 A bishop then must be blame-
less, the husband of one wife, tem-
perate, sober-minded, of good be-
havior, hospitable, able to teach;
3 not [1]given to wine, not violent,
[2]not greedy for money, but gentle,
not quarrelsome, not [3]covetous;
4 one who rules his own house
well, having *his* children in sub-
mission with all reverence
5 (for if a man does not know
how to rule his own house, how
will he take care of the church of
God?);
6 not a [1]novice, lest being puffed
up with pride he fall into the *same*
condemnation as the devil.
7 Moreover he must have a good
testimony among those who are
outside, lest he fall into reproach
and the [a]snare of the devil.

Qualifications of Deacons

8 Likewise deacons *must be* rev-
erent, not double-tongued, [a]not
given to much wine, not greedy for
money,
9 holding the [1]mystery of the
faith with a pure conscience.
10 But let these also first be tested;
then let them serve as deacons, be-
ing *found* blameless.
11 Likewise, *their* wives *must be*
reverent, not [1]slanderers, temper-
ate, faithful in all things.
12 Let deacons be the husbands of
one wife, ruling *their* children and
their own houses well.
13 For those who have served well
as deacons [a]obtain for themselves

17 [a]Ps. 10:16 [b]Rom. 1:23 [c]Heb. 11:27 [d]Rom. 16:27 [e]1 Chr. 29:11 [1]NU *the only God,*
18 [1]*command*
20 [a]2 Tim. 2:17, 18 [b]2 Tim. 4:14 [c]Acts 13:45

CHAPTER 2

1 [1]*encourage*
2 [a]Ezra 6:10 [b][Rom. 13:1] [1]*a prominent place* [2]*dignity*
3 [a]Rom. 12:2 [b]2 Tim. 1:9
4 [a]Ezek. 18:23, 32; John 3:17; 1 Tim. 4:10; Titus 2:11; 2 Pet. 3:9 [b][John 17:3]
5 [a]1 Cor. 8:6; Gal. 3:20 [b][Heb. 9:15]
6 [a]Mark 10:45
7 [a]Eph. 3:7, 8; 1 Tim. 1:11; 2 Tim. 1:11 [b][Gal. 1:15, 16] [1]NU omits *in Christ*
8 [a]Luke 23:34 [b]Ps. 134:2
9 [a]1 Pet. 3:3 [1]*discretion*
10 [a]1 Pet. 3:4
12 [a]1 Cor. 14:34; Titus 2:5

CHAPTER 3

1 [1]Lit. *overseer*
3 [1]*addicted* [2]NU omits *not greedy for money* [3]*loving money*
6 [1]*new convert*
7 [a]1 Tim. 6:9; 2 Tim. 2:26
8 [a]Ezek. 44:21
9 [1]*hidden truth*
11 [1]*malicious gossips*
13 [a]Matt. 25:21

a good standing and great boldness in the faith which is in Christ Jesus.

The Great Mystery

14 These things I write to you, though I hope to come to you shortly;

15 but if I am delayed, *I write* so that you may know how you ought to conduct yourself in the house of God, which is the church of the living God, the pillar and [1]ground of the truth.

16 And without controversy great is the [1]mystery of godliness:

[a]God[2] was manifested in the flesh,
[b]Justified in the Spirit,
[c]Seen by angels,
[d]Preached among the Gentiles,
[e]Believed on in the world,
[f]Received up in glory.

The Great Apostasy

4 Now the Spirit [1]expressly says that in latter times some will depart from the faith, giving heed [a]to deceiving spirits and doctrines of demons,

2 [a]speaking lies in hypocrisy, having their own conscience [b]seared with a hot iron,

3 forbidding to marry, *and commanding* to abstain from foods which God created to be received with thanksgiving by those who believe and know the truth.

4 For every creature of God *is* good, and nothing is to be refused if it is received with thanksgiving;

5 for it is [1]sanctified by the word of God and prayer.

A Good Servant of Jesus Christ

6 If you instruct the brethren in these things, you will be a good minister of Jesus Christ, [a]nourished in the words of faith and of the good doctrine which you have carefully followed.

7 But [a]reject profane and old wives' fables, and [b]exercise yourself toward godliness.

8 For [a]bodily exercise profits a little, but godliness is profitable for all things, [b]having promise of the life that now is and of that which is to come.

9 This *is* a faithful saying and worthy of all acceptance.

10 For to this *end* [1]we both labor and suffer reproach, because we trust in the living God, [a]who is *the* Savior of all men, especially of those who believe.

11 These things command and teach.

Take Heed to Your Ministry

12 Let no one [1]despise your youth, but be an [a]example to the believers in word, in conduct, in love, [2]in spirit, in faith, in purity.

13 Till I come, give attention to reading, to exhortation, to [1]doctrine.

14 [a]Do not neglect the gift that is in you, which was given to you by prophecy [b]with the laying on of the hands of the eldership.

15 Meditate on these things; give yourself entirely to them, that your progress may be evident to all.

16 Take heed to yourself and to the doctrine. Continue in them, for in doing this you will save both yourself and those who hear you.

Treatment of Church Members

5 Do not rebuke an older man, but exhort *him* as a father, younger men as brothers,

2 older women as mothers, younger women as sisters, with all purity.

Honor True Widows

3 Honor widows who are really widows.

4 But if any widow has children or grandchildren, let them first learn to show piety at home and [a]to repay their parents; for this is [1]good and acceptable before God.

5 Now she who is really a widow, and left alone, trusts in God and continues in supplications and prayers [a]night and day.

6 But she who lives in [1]pleasure is dead while she lives.

7 And these things command, that they may be blameless.

8 But if anyone does not provide for his own, [a]and especially for those of his household, [b]he has denied the faith [c]and is worse than an unbeliever.

9 Do not let a widow under sixty years old be taken into the number, *and not unless* she has been the wife of one man,

---

15 [1]*foundation, mainstay*

16 [a][John 1:14; 1 Pet. 1:20; 1 John 1:2; 3:5, 8] [b][Matt. 3:16; Rom. 1:4] [c]Matt. 28:2 [d]Acts 10:34; Rom. 10:18 [e]Rom. 16:26; 2 Cor. 1:19; Col. 1:6, 23 [f]Luke 24:51 [1]*hidden truth* [2]NU *Who*

CHAPTER 4

1 [a]2 Tim. 3:13; Rev. 16:14 [1]*explicitly*

2 [a]Matt. 7:15 [b]Eph. 4:19

5 [1]*set apart*

6 [a]2 Tim. 3:14

7 [a]2 Tim. 2:16; Titus 1:14 [b]Heb. 5:14

8 [a]1 Cor. 8:8 [b]Ps. 37:9

10 [a]Ps. 36:6 [1]NU *we labor and strive,*

12 [a]Phil. 3:17; Titus 2:7; 1 Pet. 5:3 [1]*look down on your youthfulness* [2]NU omits *in spirit*

13 [1]*teaching*

14 [a]2 Tim. 1:6 [b]Acts 6:6; 1 Tim. 5:22

CHAPTER 5

4 [a]Gen. 45:10 [1]NU, M omit *good and*

5 [a]Acts 26:7

6 [1]*indulgence*

8 [a]Is. 58:7; 2 Cor. 12:14 [b]2 Tim. 3:5 [c]Matt. 18:17

10 well reported for good works:
if she has brought up children, if
she has lodged strangers, if she
has washed the saints' feet, if she
has relieved the afflicted, if she has
diligently followed every good
work.
11 But [1]refuse *the* younger wid-
ows; for when they have begun to
grow wanton against Christ, they
desire to marry,
12 having condemnation because
they have cast off their first [1]faith.
13 And besides they learn *to be*
idle, wandering about from house
to house, and not only idle but also
gossips and busybodies, saying
things which they ought not.
14 Therefore I desire that *the*
younger *widows* marry, bear chil-
dren, manage the house, give no
opportunity to the adversary to
speak reproachfully.
15 For some have already turned
aside after Satan.
16 If any believing [1]man or
woman has widows, let them [2]re-
lieve them, and do not let the
church be burdened, that it may
relieve those who are really wid-
ows.

Honor the Elders

17 Let the elders who rule well be
counted worthy of double honor,
especially those who labor in the
word and doctrine.
18 For the Scripture says, [a]*"You*
shall not muzzle an ox while it
treads out the grain," and, [b]"The
laborer *is* worthy of his wages."
19 Do not receive an accusation
against an elder except [a]from two
or three witnesses.
20 Those who are sinning rebuke
in the presence of all, that the rest
also may fear.
21 I charge *you* before God and
the Lord Jesus Christ and the
[1]elect angels that you observe
these things without [a]prejudice,
doing nothing with partiality.
22 Do not lay hands on anyone
hastily, nor [a]share in other peo-
ple's sins; keep yourself pure.
23 No longer drink only water, but
use a little wine for your stomach's
sake and your frequent [1]infir-
mities.
24 Some men's sins are [a]clearly
evident, preceding *them* to judg-
ment, but those of some *men* fol-
low later.
25 Likewise, the good works *of*
some are clearly evident, and
those that are otherwise cannot be
hidden.

Honor Masters

6 Let as many [a]bondservants
as are under the yoke count
their own masters worthy of all
honor, so that the name of God
and *His* doctrine may not be blas-
phemed.
2 And those who have believing
masters, let them not despise *them*
because they are brethren, but
rather serve *them* because those
who are benefited are believers
and beloved. Teach and exhort
these things.

Error and Greed

3 If anyone teaches otherwise
and does not consent to [a]whole-
some words, *even* the words of our
Lord Jesus Christ, [b]and to the
[1]doctrine which accords with god-
liness,
4 he is proud, knowing nothing,
but is obsessed with disputes and
arguments over words, from
which come envy, strife, reviling,
evil suspicions,
5 [1]useless wranglings of men of
corrupt minds and destitute of the
truth, who suppose that godliness
is a *means of* gain. [2]From [a]such
withdraw yourself.
6 Now godliness with [a]content-
ment is great gain.
7 For we brought nothing into
this world, [1]*and it is* [a]certain we
can carry nothing out.
8 And having food and clothing,
with these we shall be [a]content.
9 But those who desire to be rich
fall into temptation and a snare,
and *into* many foolish and harmful
lusts which drown men in destruc-
tion and perdition.
10 For the love of money is a root
of all *kinds of* evil, for which some
have strayed from the faith in their
greediness, and pierced them-
selves through with many sor-
rows.

The Good Confession

11 But you, O man of God, flee
these things and pursue righteous-

---

11 [1]Refuse to enroll
12 [1]Or *solemn promise*
16 [1]NU omits *man or* [2]*give aid to*
18 [a]Deut. 25:4; 1 Cor. 9:7–9 [b]Lev. 19:13; Deut. 24:15; Matt. 10:10; Luke 10:7; 1 Cor. 9:14
19 [a]Deut. 17:6; 19:15; Matt. 18:16
21 [a]Deut. 1:17 [1]*chosen*
22 [a]Eph. 5:6, 7; 2 John 11
23 [1]*illnesses*
24 [a]Gal. 5:19–21

CHAPTER 6

1 [a]Eph. 6:5; Titus 2:9; 1 Pet. 2:18
3 [a]2 Tim. 1:13 [b]Titus 1:1 [1]*teaching*
5 [a]2 Tim. 3:5 [1]NU, M *constant friction* [2]NU omits the rest of v. 5.
6 [a]Phil. 4:11; Heb. 13:5
7 [a]Job 1:21; Ps. 49:17; Eccl. 5:15 [1]NU omits *and it is certain*
8 [a]Prov. 30:8, 9

ness, godliness, faith, love, patience, gentleness.
12 Fight the good fight of faith, lay hold on eternal life, to which you were also called and have confessed the good confession in the presence of many witnesses.
13 I urge you in the sight of God who gives life to all things, and *before* Christ Jesus [a]who witnessed the good confession before Pontius Pilate,
14 that you keep *this* commandment without spot, blameless until our Lord Jesus Christ's appearing,
15 which He will manifest in His own time, *He who is* the blessed and only [1]Potentate, the King of kings and Lord of lords,
16 who alone has immortality, dwelling in [a]unapproachable light, [b]whom no man has seen or can see, to whom *be* honor and everlasting power. Amen.

13 [a]Matt. 27:2; John 18:36, 37
15 [1]*Sovereign*
16 [a]Dan. 2:22 [b]John 6:46
17 [a]Jer. 9:23; 48:7 [b]Eccl. 5:18, 19
19 [a][Matt. 6:20, 21; 19:21]
20 [a][2 Tim. 1:12, 14] [b]Titus 1:14 [1]*empty chatter*

Instructions to the Rich

17 Command those who are rich in this present age not to be haughty, nor to trust in uncertain [a]riches but in the living God, who gives us richly all things [b]to enjoy.
18 *Let them* do good, that they be rich in good works, ready to give, willing to share,
19 [a]storing up for themselves a good foundation for the time to come, that they may lay hold on eternal life.

Guard the Faith

20 O Timothy! [a]Guard what was committed to your trust, [b]avoiding the profane *and* [1]idle babblings and contradictions of what is falsely called knowledge—
21 by professing it some have strayed concerning the faith. Grace *be* with you. Amen.

The Second Epistle of Paul the Apostle to

Timothy

PRISON is the last place from which to expect a letter of encouragement, but that is where Paul's second letter to Timothy originates. He begins by assuring Timothy of his continuing love and prayers, and reminds him of his spiritual heritage and responsibilities. Only the one who perseveres, whether as a soldier, athlete, farmer, or minister of Jesus Christ, will reap the reward. Paul warns Timothy that his teaching will come under attack as men desert the truth for ear-itching words (4:3). But Timothy has Paul's example to guide him and God's Word to fortify him as he faces growing opposition and glowing opportunities in the last days.

Paul's last epistle received the title *Pros Timotheon B,* the "Second to Timothy." When Paul's epistles were collected together the *B* was probably added to distinguish this letter from the first letter he wrote to Timothy.

Greeting

PAUL, an apostle of [1]Jesus
Christ by the will of God, ac-
cording to the [a]promise of life
which is in Christ Jesus,
2 To Timothy, a [a]beloved son:

Grace, mercy, *and* peace from
God the Father and Christ Jesus
our Lord.

Timothy's Faith and Heritage

3 I thank God, whom I serve with
a pure conscience, as *my* [a]fore-
fathers *did,* as without ceasing I
remember you in my prayers
night and day,
4 greatly desiring to see you, be-
ing mindful of your tears, that I
may be filled with joy,
5 when I call to remembrance
[a]the [1]genuine faith that is in you,
which dwelt first in your grand-
mother Lois and [b]your mother
Eunice, and I am persuaded is in
you also.
6 Therefore I remind you [a]to stir
up the gift of God which is in you
through the laying on of my hands.
7 For [a]God has not given us a
spirit of fear, [b]but of power and
of love and of a sound mind.

Not Ashamed of the Gospel

8 [a]Therefore do not be ashamed
of [b]the testimony of our Lord, nor
of me [c]His prisoner, but share with
me in the sufferings for the gospel
according to the power of God,
9 who has saved us and called *us*
with a holy calling, [a]not according
to our works, but [b]according to His
own purpose and grace which was
given to us in Christ Jesus [c]before
time began,
10 but [a]has now been revealed by
the appearing of our Savior Jesus
Christ, *who* has abolished death
and brought life and immortality
to light through the gospel,
11 [a]to which I was appointed a
preacher, an apostle, and a teacher
[1]of the Gentiles.
12 For this reason I also suffer
these things; nevertheless I am not
ashamed, [a]for I know whom I have
believed and am persuaded that
He is able to keep what I have
committed to Him until that Day.

Be Loyal to the Faith

13 [a]Hold fast [b]the pattern of
[c]sound words which you have
heard from me, in faith and love
which are in Christ Jesus.
14 That good thing which was
committed to you, keep by the
Holy Spirit who dwells in us.
15 This you know, that all those
in Asia have turned away from me,
among whom are Phygellus and
Hermogenes.

CHAPTER 1

1 [a]Titus 1:2 [1]NU, M *Christ Jesus*
2 [a]1 Tim. 1:2; 2 Tim. 2:1; Titus 1:4
3 [a]Acts 24:14
5 [a]1 Tim. 1:5; 4:6 [b]Acts 16:1 [1]Lit. *unhypocritical*
6 [a]1 Tim. 4:14
7 [a]John 14:27; Rom. 8:15; 1 John 4:18 [b][Acts 1:8]
8 [a][Mark 8:38; Luke 9:26; Rom. 1:16]; 2 Tim. 1:12, 16 [b]1 Tim. 2:6 [c]Eph. 3:1; 2 Tim. 1:16
9 [a][Rom. 3:20]; Eph. 2:8, 9 [b]Rom. 8:28 [c]Rom. 16:25; Eph. 1:4; Titus 1:2
10 [a]Eph. 1:9
11 [a]Acts 9:15 [1]NU omits *of the Gentiles*
12 [a]1 Pet. 4:19
13 [a]2 Tim. 3:14; Titus 1:9 [b]Rom. 2:20; 6:17 [c]1 Tim. 6:3

16 The Lord grant mercy to the
[a]household of Onesiphorus, for he
often refreshed me, and was not
ashamed of my chain;
17 but when he arrived in Rome,
he sought me out very zealously
and found *me*.
18 The Lord [a]grant to him that he
may find mercy from the Lord [b]in
that Day—and you know very well
how many ways he [c]ministered [1]*to
me* at Ephesus.

Be Strong in Grace

2 You therefore, [a]my son, [b]be
strong in the grace that is in
Christ Jesus.
2 And the things that you have
heard from me among many wit-
nesses, commit these to faithful
men who will be able to teach oth-
ers also.
3 You therefore must [a]endure[1]
hardship [b]as a good soldier of Je-
sus Christ.
4 [a]No one engaged in warfare en-
tangles himself with the affairs of
this life, that he may please him
who enlisted him as a soldier.
5 And also [a]if anyone competes
in athletics, he is not crowned un-
less he competes according to the
rules.
6 The hardworking farmer must
be first to partake of the crops.
7 Consider what I say, and [1]may
the Lord [a]give you understanding
in all things.
8 Remember that Jesus Christ,
[a]of the seed of David, [b]was raised
from the dead [c]according to my
gospel,
9 [a]for which I suffer trouble as
an evildoer, [b]*even* to the point of
chains; [c]but the word of God is not
chained.
10 Therefore [a]I endure all things
for the sake of the [1]elect, [b]that they
also may obtain the salvation
which is in Christ Jesus with eter-
nal glory.
11 *This is* a faithful saying:

For [a]if we died with *Him*,
We shall also live with *Him*.
12 [a]If we endure,
We shall also reign with *Him*.
[b]If we deny *Him*,
He also will deny us.
13 If we are faithless,
He remains faithful;
He [a]cannot deny Himself.

16 [a]2 Tim. 4:19
18 [a]Mark 9:41 [b]2 Thess. 1:10 [c]Heb. 6:10 [1]*to me* from Vg., a few Gr. mss.

CHAPTER 2

1 [a]1 Tim. 1:2 [b]Eph. 6:10
3 [a]2 Tim. 4:5 [b]1 Tim. 1:18 [1]NU *You must share*
4 [a][2 Pet. 2:20]
5 [a][1 Cor. 9:25]
7 [a]Prov. 2:6 [1]NU *the Lord will give you*
8 [a]Rom. 1:3, 4 [b]1 Cor. 15:4 [c]Rom. 2:16
9 [a]Acts 9:16 [b]Eph. 3:1 [c]Acts 28:31
10 [a]Eph. 3:13 [b]2 Cor. 1:6 [1]*chosen ones*
11 [a]Rom. 6:5, 8
12 [a][Rom. 5:17; 8:17] [b]Matt. 10:33
13 [a]Num. 23:19
14 [a]Titus 3:9 [1]*battle*
15 [a]2 Pet. 1:10
16 [1]*empty chatter* [2]*lead*
17 [a]1 Tim. 1:20
18 [a]1 Cor. 15:12
19 [a][1 Cor. 3:11] [b][Nah. 1:7] [1]NU, M *the Lord*
20 [a]Rom. 9:21
21 [a]2 Tim. 3:17 [1]*set apart*
22 [a]1 Tim. 6:11
24 [a]Titus 3:2 [b]Titus 1:9 [c]1 Tim. 3:3
25 [a]Gal. 6:1 [b]Acts 8:22 [c]1 Tim. 2:4
26 [a]1 Tim. 3:7

CHAPTER 3

1 [a]1 Tim. 4:1 [1]*times of stress*

Approved and Disapproved Workers

14 Remind *them* of these things,
[a]charging *them* before the Lord
not to [1]strive about words to no
profit, to the ruin of the hearers.
15 [a]Be diligent to present yourself
approved to God, a worker who
does not need to be ashamed,
rightly dividing the word of truth.
16 But shun profane *and* [1]idle bab-
blings, for they will [2]increase to
more ungodliness.
17 And their message will spread
like cancer. [a]Hymenaeus and Phi-
letus are of this sort,
18 who have strayed concerning
the truth, [a]saying that the resur-
rection is already past; and they
overthrow the faith of some.
19 Nevertheless [a]the solid founda-
tion of God stands, having this
seal: "The Lord [b]knows those who
are His," and, "Let everyone who
names the name of [1]Christ depart
from iniquity."
20 But in a great house there are
not only [a]vessels of gold and sil-
ver, but also of wood and clay,
some for honor and some for dis-
honor.
21 Therefore if anyone cleanses
himself from the latter, he will be
a vessel for honor, [1]sanctified and
useful for the Master, [a]prepared
for every good work.
22 [a]Flee also youthful lusts; but
pursue righteousness, faith, love,
peace with those who call on the
Lord out of a pure heart.
23 But avoid foolish and ignorant
disputes, knowing that they gener-
ate strife.
24 And [a]a servant of the Lord
must not quarrel but be gentle to
all, [b]able to teach, [c]patient,
25 [a]in humility correcting those
who are in opposition, [b]if God
perhaps will grant them repen-
tance, [c]so that they may know the
truth,
26 and *that* they may come to
their senses *and* [a]*escape* the snare
of the devil, having been taken
captive by him to *do* his will.

Perilous Times and Perilous Men

3 But know this, that [a]in the last
days [1]perilous times will come:
2 For men will be lovers of them-
selves, lovers of money, boasters,

proud, blasphemers, disobedient
to parents, unthankful, unholy,
3 unloving, [1]unforgiving, slan-
derers, without self-control, brutal,
despisers of good,
4 [a]traitors, headstrong, haughty,
lovers of pleasure rather than lov-
ers of God,
5 [a]having a form of godliness but
[b]denying its power. And [c]from
such people turn away!
6 For [a]of this sort are those who
creep into households and make
captives of gullible women loaded
down with sins, led away by vari-
ous lusts,
7 always learning and never able
[a]to come to the knowledge of the
truth.
8 [a]Now as Jannes and Jambres
resisted Moses, so do these also re-
sist the truth: [b]men of corrupt
minds, [c]disapproved concerning
the faith;
9 but they will progress no fur-
ther, for their folly will be manifest
to all, [a]as theirs also was.

The Man of God and the Word of God

10 [a]But you have carefully fol-
lowed my doctrine, manner of life,
purpose, faith, longsuffering, love,
perseverance,
11 persecutions, afflictions, which
happened to me [a]at Antioch, [b]at
Iconium, [c]at Lystra—what perse-
cutions I endured. And [d]out of
them all the Lord delivered me.
12 Yes, and [a]all who desire to live
godly in Christ Jesus will suffer
persecution.
13 [a]But evil men and impostors
will grow worse and worse, de-
ceiving and being deceived.
14 But you must [a]continue in the
things which you have learned and
been assured of, knowing from
whom you have learned *them*,
15 and that from childhood you
have known [a]the Holy Scriptures,
which are able to make you wise
for salvation through faith which
is in Christ Jesus.
16 [a]All Scripture *is* given by inspi-
ration of God, [b]and *is* profitable for
doctrine, for reproof, for correc-
tion, for [1]instruction in righ-
teousness,
17 [a]that the man of God may be
complete, [b]thoroughly equipped
for every good work.

3 [1]*irreconcilable*
4 [a]2 Pet. 2:10
5 [a]Titus 1:16 [b]1 Tim. 5:8 [c]2 Thess. 3:6
6 [a]Matt. 23:14
7 [a]1 Tim. 2:4
8 [a]Ex. 7:11, 12, 22; 8:7; 9:11 [b]1 Tim. 6:5 [c]Rom. 1:28
9 [a]Ex. 7:11, 12; 8:18; 9:11
10 [a]1 Tim. 4:6
11 [a]Acts 13:44–52 [b]Acts 14:1–6, 19 [c]Acts 14:8–20 [d]Ps. 34:19
12 [a][Ps. 34:19]
13 [a]2 Thess. 2:11
14 [a]2 Tim. 1:13
15 [a]John 5:39
16 [a][2 Pet. 1:20] [b]Rom. 4:23; 15:4 [1]*training, discipline*
17 [a]1 Tim. 6:11 [b]2 Tim. 2:21

CHAPTER 4

1 [a]1 Tim. 5:21 [b]Acts 10:42 [1]NU omits *therefore* [2]NU *and by*
2 [a]Titus 2:15 [b]1 Tim. 5:20 [c]1 Tim. 4:13
3 [a]2 Tim. 3:1 [b]1 Tim. 1:10 [c]2 Tim. 3:6
4 [a]1 Tim. 1:4
5 [a]2 Tim. 1:8 [b]Acts 21:8
6 [a]Phil. 2:17 [b][Phil. 1:23]
7 [a]1 Cor. 9:24–27
8 [a]James 1:12 [b]John 5:22 [c]2 Tim. 1:12
10 [a]Col. 4:14 [b]1 John 2:15
11 [a]Acts 12:12, 25; 15:37–39
12 [a]Acts 20:4
14 [a]1 Tim. 1:20

Preach the Word

4 I [a]charge *you* [1]therefore before
God and the Lord Jesus Christ,
[b]who will judge the living and the
dead [2]at His appearing and His
kingdom:
2 Preach the word! Be ready in
season *and* out of season. [a]Con-
vince, [b]rebuke, [c]exhort, with all
longsuffering and teaching.
3 [a]For the time will come when
they will not endure [b]sound doc-
trine, [c]but according to their own
desires, *because* they have itching
ears, they will heap up for them-
selves teachers;
4 and they will turn *their* ears
away from the truth, and [a]be
turned aside to fables.
5 But you be watchful in all
things, [a]endure afflictions, do the
work of [b]an evangelist, fulfill your
ministry.

Paul's Valedictory

6 For [a]I am already being poured
out as a drink offering, and the
time of [b]my departure is at hand.
7 [a]I have fought the good fight, I
have finished the race, I have kept
the faith.
8 Finally, there is laid up for me
[a]the crown of righteousness,
which the Lord, the righteous
[b]Judge, will give to me [c]on that
Day, and not to me only but also
to all who have loved His appear-
ing.

The Abandoned Apostle

9 Be diligent to come to me
quickly;
10 for [a]Demas has forsaken me,
[b]having loved this present world,
and has departed for Thessalo-
nica—Crescens for Galatia, Titus
for Dalmatia.
11 Only Luke is with me. Get
[a]Mark and bring him with you, for
he is useful to me for ministry.
12 And [a]Tychicus I have sent to
Ephesus.
13 Bring the cloak that I left with
Carpus at Troas when you come—
and the books, especially the
parchments.
14 [a]Alexander the coppersmith
did me much harm. May the Lord
repay him according to his works.
15 You also must beware of him,

for he has greatly resisted our words.
16 At my first defense no one stood with me, but all forsook me. [a]May it not be charged against them.

The Lord Is Faithful

17 [a]But the Lord stood with me and strengthened me, [b]so that the message might be preached fully through me, and *that* all the Gentiles might hear. Also I was delivered [c]out of the mouth of the lion.
18 [a]And the Lord will deliver me from every evil work and preserve *me* for His heavenly kingdom. [b]To Him *be* glory forever and ever. Amen!

Come Before Winter

19 Greet [a]Prisca and Aquila, and the household of [b]Onesiphorus.
20 [a]Erastus stayed in Corinth, but [b]Trophimus I have left in Miletus sick.
21 Do your utmost to come before winter. Eubulus greets you, as well as Pudens, Linus, Claudia, and all the brethren.

Farewell

22 The Lord [1]Jesus Christ be with your spirit. Grace be with you. Amen.

16 [a]Acts 7:60; [1 Cor. 13:5]
17 [a]Deut. 31:6; Acts 23:11 [b]Acts 9:15; Phil. 1:12 [c]1 Sam. 17:37; Ps. 22:21
18 [a]Ps. 121:7; [2 Pet. 2:9] [b]Rom. 11:36; Gal. 1:5; Heb. 13:21; 2 Pet. 3:18
19 [a]Acts 18:2; Rom. 16:3 [b]2 Tim. 1:16
20 [a]Acts 19:22; Rom. 16:23 [b]Acts 20:4; 21:29
22 [1]NU omits *Jesus Christ*

The Epistle of Paul the Apostle to

Titus

TITUS, a young pastor, faces the unenviable assignment of setting in order the church at Crete. Paul writes advising him to appoint elders, men of proven spiritual character in their homes and businesses, to oversee the work of the church. But elders are not the only individuals in the church who are required to excel spiritually. Men and women, young and old, each have their vital functions to fulfill in the church if they are to be living examples of the doctrine they profess. Throughout his letter to Titus, Paul stresses the necessary, practical working out of salvation in the daily lives of both the elders and the congregation. Good works are desirable and profitable for all believers.

This third Pastoral Epistle is simply titled *Pros Titon,* "To Titus." Ironically, this was also the name of the Roman general who destroyed Jerusalem in A.D. 70 and succeeded his father Vespasian as emperor.

Greeting

PAUL, a bondservant of God
and an apostle of Jesus Christ,
according to the faith of God's
elect and [a]the acknowledgment of
the truth [b]which accords with god-
liness,
2 in hope of eternal life which
God, who [a]cannot lie, promised
before time began,
3 but has in due time manifested
His word through preaching,
which was committed to me ac-
cording to the commandment of
God our Savior;

4 To [a]Titus, a true son in *our*
common faith:

Grace, mercy, *and* peace from
God the Father and [1]the Lord Je-
sus Christ our Savior.

Qualified Elders

5 For this reason I left you in
Crete, that you should [a]set in order
the things that are lacking, and ap-
point elders in every city as I com-
manded you—
6 if a man is blameless, the hus-
band of one wife, [a]having faithful
children not accused of [1]dissipa-
tion or insubordination.
7 For a [1]bishop must be blame-
less, as a steward of God, not self-
willed, not quick-tempered, [a]not
given to wine, not violent, not
greedy for money,
8 but hospitable, a lover of what
is good, sober-minded, just, holy,
self-controlled,
9 holding fast the faithful word
as he has been taught, that he may
be able, by sound doctrine, both
to exhort and convict those who
contradict.

The Elders' Task

10 For there are many insubordi-
nate, both idle [a]talkers and deceiv-
ers, especially those of the cir-
cumcision,
11 whose mouths must be
stopped, who subvert whole
households, teaching things
which they ought not, [a]for the sake
of dishonest gain.
12 [a]One of them, a prophet of their
own, said, "Cretans *are* always
liars, evil beasts, lazy gluttons."
13 This testimony is true. [a]There-
fore rebuke them sharply, that
they may be sound in the faith,
14 not giving heed to Jewish fa-
bles and [a]commandments of men
who turn from the truth.
15 [a]To the pure all things are pure,
but to those who are defiled and
unbelieving nothing is pure; but
even their mind and conscience
are defiled.
16 They profess to [a]know God, but
[b]in works they deny Him, being
[1]abominable, disobedient, [c]and
disqualified for every good work.

CHAPTER 1

1 [a]2 Tim. 2:25 [b][1 Tim. 3:16]
2 [a]Num. 23:19
4 [a]2 Cor. 2:13; 8:23; Gal. 2:3; 2 Tim. 4:10 [1]NU *Christ Jesus*
5 [a]1 Cor. 11:34
6 [a]1 Tim. 3:2–4; Titus 1:6–8 [1]*debauchery,* lit. *incorrigibility*
7 [a]Lev. 10:9 [1]Lit. *overseer*
10 [a]James 1:26
11 [a]1 Tim. 6:5
12 [a]Acts 17:28
13 [a]2 Cor. 13:10; 2 Tim. 4:2
14 [a]Is. 29:13
15 [a]Luke 11:41; Rom. 14:14, 20; 1 Cor. 6:12
16 [a]Matt. 7:20–23; 25:12; 1 John 2:4 [b][2 Tim. 3:5, 7] [c]Rom. 1:28 [1]*detestable*

Qualities of a Sound Church

2 But as for you, speak the things
which are proper for sound
doctrine:
2 that the older men be sober,
reverent, temperate, sound in
faith, in love, in patience;
3 the older women likewise, that
they be reverent in behavior, not
slanderers, not given to much
wine, teachers of good things—
4 that they admonish the young
women to love their husbands, to
love their children,
5 to be discreet, chaste, [a]home-
makers, good, [b]obedient to their
own husbands, [c]that the word of
God may not be blasphemed.
6 Likewise, exhort the young
men to be sober-minded,
7 in all things showing yourself
to be [a]a pattern of good works; in
doctrine *showing* integrity, rever-
ence, [b]incorruptibility,[1]
8 sound speech that cannot be
condemned, that one who is an op-
ponent may be ashamed, having
nothing evil to say of [1]you.
9 *Exhort* [a]bondservants to be
obedient to their own masters, to
be well pleasing in all *things,* not
answering back,
10 not [1]pilfering, but showing all
good [2]fidelity, that they may adorn
the doctrine of God our Savior in
all things.

Trained by Saving Grace

11 For [a]the grace of God that
brings salvation has appeared to
all men,
12 teaching us that, denying un-
godliness and worldly lusts, we
should live soberly, righteously,
and godly in the present age,
13 [a]looking for the blessed [b]hope
and glorious appearing of our
great God and Savior Jesus Christ,
14 [a]who gave Himself for us, that
He might redeem us from every
lawless deed [b]and purify for Him-
self [c]*His* own special people, zeal-
ous for good works.
15 Speak these things, [a]exhort,
and rebuke with all authority. Let
no one despise you.

Graces of the Heirs of Grace

3 Remind them [a]to be subject to
rulers and authorities, to obey,
[b]to be ready for every good work,

CHAPTER 2

5 [a]1 Tim. 5:14 [b]1 Cor. 14:34; 1 Tim. 2:11 [c]Rom. 2:24

7 [a]Phil. 3:17; 1 Tim. 4:12 [b]Eph. 6:24 [1]NU omits *incorruptibility*

8 [1]NU, M *us*

9 [a]Eph. 6:5; 1 Tim. 6:1

10 [1]*thieving* [2]*honesty*

11 [a][Rom. 5:15]

13 [a]1 Cor. 1:7 [b][Col. 3:4]

14 [a]Is. 53:12; Gal. 1:4 [b]Ezek. 37:23; [Heb. 1:3; 9:14; 1 John 1:7] [c]Ex. 15:16

15 [a]1 Tim. 4:13; 5:20; 2 Tim. 4:2

CHAPTER 3

1 [a][Rom. 13:1]; 1 Pet. 2:13 [b]Col. 1:10

3 [a]1 Cor. 6:11; 1 Pet. 4:3

4 [a]Titus 2:11 [b]1 Tim. 2:3

5 [a][Rom. 3:20]; Eph. 2:4–9 [b]John 3:3

6 [a]Ezek. 36:26

7 [a][Matt. 25:34]; Mark 10:17; [Rom. 8:17, 23, 24; Titus 1:2]

8 [a]1 Tim. 1:15

9 [a]1 Tim. 1:4; 2 Tim. 2:23

10 [a]Matt. 18:17 [1]*warning*

12 [a]Acts 20:4; Eph. 6:21; Col. 4:7; 2 Tim. 4:12

13 [a]Acts 18:24; 1 Cor. 16:12

2 to speak evil of no one, to be
peaceable, gentle, showing all hu-
mility to all men.
3 For [a]we ourselves were also
once foolish, disobedient, de-
ceived, serving various lusts and
pleasures, living in malice and
envy, hateful and hating one an-
other.
4 But when [a]the kindness and the
love of [b]God our Savior toward
man appeared,
5 [a]not by works of righteousness
which we have done, but accord-
ing to His mercy He saved us,
through [b]the washing of regenera-
tion and renewing of the Holy
Spirit,
6 [a]whom He poured out on us
abundantly through Jesus Christ
our Savior,
7 that having been justified by
His grace [a]we should become heirs
according to the hope of eternal
life.
8 [a]This is a faithful saying, and
these things I want you to affirm
constantly, that those who have
believed in God should be careful
to maintain good works. These
things are good and profitable to
men.

Avoid Dissension

9 But [a]avoid foolish disputes,
genealogies, contentions, and
strivings about the law; for they
are unprofitable and useless.
10 [a]Reject a divisive man after the
first and second [1]admonition,
11 knowing that such a person is
warped and sinning, being self-
condemned.

Final Messages

12 When I send Artemas to you,
or [a]Tychicus, be diligent to come
to me at Nicopolis, for I have de-
cided to spend the winter there.
13 Send Zenas the lawyer and
[a]Apollos on their journey with
haste, that they may lack nothing.
14 And let our *people* also learn
to maintain good works, to *meet*
urgent needs, that they may not be
unfruitful.

Farewell

15 All who *are* with me greet you.
Greet those who love us in the
faith. Grace *be* with you all. Amen.

The Epistle of Paul the Apostle to

Philemon

DOES Christian brotherly love really work, even in situations of extraordinary tension and difficulty? Will it work, for example, between a prominent slave owner and one of his runaway slaves? Paul has no doubt! He writes a "postcard" to Philemon, his beloved brother and fellow worker, on behalf of Onesimus—a deserter, thief, and formerly worthless slave, but now Philemon's brother in Christ. With much tact and tenderness, Paul asks Philemon to receive Onesimus back with the same gentleness with which he would receive Paul himself. Any debt Onesimus owes, Paul promises to make good. Knowing Philemon, Paul is confident that brotherly love and forgiveness will carry the day.

Since this letter is addressed to Philemon in verse 1, it becomes known as *Pros Philemona,* "To Philemon." Like First and Second Timothy and Titus, it is addressed to an individual, but unlike the Pastoral Epistles, Philemon is also addressed to a family and a church (v. 2).

Greeting

PAUL, a [a]prisoner of Christ Je-
sus, and Timothy *our* brother,
To Philemon our beloved *friend*
and fellow laborer,
2 to [1]the beloved Apphia, [a]Ar-
chippus our fellow soldier, and to
the church in your house:
3 Grace to you and peace from
God our Father and the Lord Jesus
Christ.

Philemon's Love and Faith

4 [a]I thank my God, making men-
tion of you always in my prayers,
5 [a]hearing of your love and faith
which you have toward the Lord
Jesus and toward all the saints,
6 that the sharing of your faith
may become effective [a]by the ac-
knowledgment of [b]every good
thing which is in [1]you in Christ Je-
sus.
7 For we [1]have great [2]joy and
[3]consolation in your love, because
the [4]hearts of the saints have been
refreshed by you, brother.

The Plea for Onesimus

8 Therefore, though I might be
very bold in Christ to command
you what is fitting,
9 *yet* for love's sake I rather ap-
peal *to you*—being such a one as
Paul, the aged, and now also a
prisoner of Jesus Christ—
10 I appeal to you for my son
[a]Onesimus, whom I have begot-
ten *while* in my chains,
11 who once was unprofitable to
you, but now is profitable to you
and to me.
12 I am sending him [1]back. You
therefore receive him, that is, my
own [2]heart,
13 whom I wished to keep with
me, that on your behalf he might
minister to me in my chains for the
gospel.
14 But without your consent I
wanted to do nothing, [a]that your
good deed might not be by com-
pulsion, as it were, but volun-
tary.
15 For perhaps he departed for a
while for this *purpose*, that you
might receive him forever,
16 no longer as a slave but more
than a slave—a beloved brother,
especially to me but how much
more to you, both in the [a]flesh and
in the Lord.

Philemon's Obedience Encouraged

17 If then you count me as a part-
ner, receive him as *you would* me.

CHAPTER 1
1 [a]Eph. 3:1
2 [a]Col. 4:17 [1]NU *our sister Apphia*
4 [a]Eph. 1:16; 1 Thess. 1:2; 2 Thess. 1:3
5 [a]Eph. 1:15; Col. 1:4; 1 Thess. 3:6
6 [a]Phil. 1:9; [Col. 1:9; 3:10; James 2:14–17] [b][1 Thess. 5:18] [1]NU, M *us*
7 [1]NU *had* [2]M *thanksgiving* [3]*comfort* [4]Lit. *inward parts,* heart, liver, and lungs
10 [a]Col. 4:9
12 [1]NU *back to you in person, that is, my own heart,* [2]See v. 7.
14 [a]2 Cor. 9:7; 1 Pet. 5:2
16 [a]Eph. 6:5; Col. 3:22

18 But if he has wronged you or
owes anything, put that on my ac-
count.
19 I, Paul, am writing with my
own [a]hand. I will repay—not to
mention to you that you owe me
even your own self besides.
20 Yes, brother, let me have joy
from you in the Lord; refresh my
heart in the Lord.
21 [a]Having confidence in your
obedience, I write to you, knowing
that you will do even more than I
say.

19 [a]1 Cor. 16:21
21 [a]2 Cor. 7:16
22 [a]Phil. 1:25; 2:24 [b]2 Cor. 1:11
23 [a]Col. 1:7; 4:12
24 [a]Acts 12:12, 25; 15:37–39 [b]Acts 19:29; 27:2 [c]Col. 4:14 [d]2 Tim. 4:11
25 [a]2 Tim. 4:22

22 But, meanwhile, also prepare a
guest room for me, for [a]I trust that
[b]through your prayers I shall be
granted to you.

Farewell

23 [a]Epaphras, my fellow prisoner
in Christ Jesus, greets you,
24 *as do* [a]Mark, [b]Aristarchus,
[c]Demas, [d]Luke, my fellow la-
borers.
25 [a]The grace of our Lord Jesus
Christ *be* with your spirit. Amen.

The Epistle to the

Hebrews

MANY Jewish believers, having stepped out of Judaism into Christianity, want to reverse their course in order to escape persecution by their countrymen. The writer of Hebrews exhorts them to "go on to perfection" (6:1). His appeal is based on the superiority of Christ over the Judaic system. Christ is better than the angels, for they worship Him. He is better than Moses, for He created him. He is better than the Aaronic priesthood, for His sacrifice was once for all time. He is better than the law, for He mediates a better covenant. In short, there is more to be gained in Christ than to be lost in Judaism. Pressing on in Christ produces tested faith, self-discipline, and a visible love seen in good works.

Although the King James Version uses the title "The Epistle of Paul the Apostle to the Hebrews," there is no early manuscript evidence to support it. The oldest and most reliable title is simply *Pros Ebraious,* "To Hebrews."

God's Supreme Revelation

GOD, who [1]at various times and
[a]in various ways spoke in time
past to the fathers by the
prophets,
2 has in these last days spoken
to us by *His* Son, whom He has
appointed heir of all things,
through whom also He made the
[1]worlds;
3 [a]who being the brightness of
His glory and the express [b]image
of His person, and [c]upholding all
things by the word of His power,
[d]when He had [1]by Himself [2]purged
[3]our sins, [e]sat down at the right
hand of the Majesty on high,
4 having become so much better
than the angels, as [a]He has by inheritance
obtained a more excellent
name than they.

The Son Exalted Above Angels

5 For to which of the angels did
He ever say:

[a]*"You are My Son,*
Today I have begotten You"?

And again:

[b]*"I will be to Him a Father,*
And He shall be to Me a Son"?

6 But when He again brings [a]the
firstborn into the world, He says:

[b]*"Let all the angels of God worship*
Him."

7 And of the angels He says:

[a]*"Who makes His angels spirits*
And His ministers a flame of
fire."

8 But to the Son *He says:*

[a]*"Your throne, O God, is forever*
and ever;
A [1]scepter of righteousness is the
scepter of Your kingdom.
9 *You have loved righteousness*
and hated lawlessness;
Therefore God, Your God, [a]has
anointed You
With the oil of gladness more
than Your companions."

10 And:

[a]*"You,* LORD, *in the beginning laid*
the foundation of the earth,
And the heavens are the work of
Your hands.
11 [a]*They will perish, but You remain;*
And [b]they will all grow old like
a garment;
12 *Like a cloak You will fold them*
up,
And they will be changed.
But You are the [a]same,
And Your years will not fail."

13 But to which of the angels has
He ever said:

[a]*"Sit at My right hand,*
Till I make Your enemies Your
footstool"?

CHAPTER 1

1 [a]Num. 12:6, 8; Joel 2:28 [1]Or *in many portions*
2 [1]Or *ages,* Gr. *aiones,* aeons
3 [a]John 1:14 [b]2 Cor. 4:4; Col. 1:15 [c]Col. 1:17 [d][Heb. 7:27] [e]Ps. 110:1 [1]NU omits *by Himself* [2]*cleansed* [3]NU omits *our*
4 [a]Is. 9:6, 7; Luke 1:32, 33; [Phil. 2:9, 10]
5 [a]Ps. 2:7; Acts 13:33; Heb. 5:5 [b]2 Sam. 7:14
6 [a]Ps. 89:27; [Rom. 8:29] [b]Deut. 32:43, LXX, DSS; Ps. 97:7; 1 Pet. 3:22; Rev. 5:11–13
7 [a]Ps. 104:4
8 [a]Ps. 45:6, 7 [1]A ruler's staff
9 [a]Is. 61:1, 3
10 [a]Ps. 102:25–27
11 [a][Is. 34:4] [b]Is. 50:9; 51:6; Heb. 8:13
12 [a]Heb. 13:8
13 [a]Ps. 110:1; Matt. 22:44; Heb. 1:3

14 [a]Are they not all ministering
spirits sent forth to minister for
those who will [b]inherit salvation?

Do Not Neglect Salvation

2 Therefore we must give [1]the
more earnest heed to the
things we have heard, lest we drift
away.
2 For if the word [a]spoken
through angels proved steadfast,
and [b]every transgression and
disobedience received a just [1]re-
ward,
3 [a]how shall we escape if we ne-
glect so great a salvation, [b]which
at the first began to be spoken by
the Lord, and was [c]confirmed to
us by those who heard *Him,*
4 [a]God also bearing witness
[b]both with signs and wonders,
with various miracles, and [c]gifts[1]
of the Holy Spirit, [d]according to
His own will?

The Son Made Lower than Angels

5 For He has not put [a]the world
to come, of which we speak, in
subjection to angels.
6 But one testified in a certain
place, saying:

[a]*"What is man that You are*
mindful of him,
Or the son of man that You take
care of him?
7 *You have made him* [1]*a little lower*
than the angels;
You have crowned him with
glory and honor,
[2]*And set him over the works of*
Your hands.
8 [a]*You have put all things in*
subjection under his feet."

For in that He put all in subjection
under him, He left nothing *that is*
not put under him. But now [b]we
do not yet see all things put under
him.
9 But we see Jesus, [a]who was
made [1]a little lower than the an-
gels, for the suffering of death
[b]crowned with glory and honor,
that He, by the grace of God, might
taste death [c]for everyone.

Bringing Many Sons to Glory

10 For it was fitting for Him, [a]for
whom *are* all things and by whom
are all things, in bringing many
sons to glory, to make the captain
of their salvation [b]perfect through
sufferings.
11 For [a]both He who [1]sanctifies
and those who are being sanctified
[b]*are* all of one, for which reason
[c]He is not ashamed to call them
brethren,
12 saying:

[a]*"I will declare Your name to My*
brethren;
In the midst of the assembly I will
sing praise to You."

13 And again:

[a]*"I will put My trust in Him."*

And again:

[b]*"Here am I and the children whom*
God has given Me."

14 Inasmuch then as the children
have partaken of flesh and blood,
He [a]Himself likewise shared in the
same, [b]that through death He
might destroy him who had the
power of [c]death, that is, the devil,
15 and release those who
[a]through fear of death were all
their lifetime subject to bondage.
16 For indeed He does not [1]give
aid to angels, but He does [2]give aid
to the seed of Abraham.
17 Therefore, in all things He had
[a]to be made like *His* brethren, that
He might be [b]a merciful and faith-
ful High Priest in things *pertaining*
to God, to make propitiation for
the sins of the people.
18 [a]For in that He Himself has suf-
fered, being [1]tempted, He is able
to aid those who are tempted.

The Son Was Faithful

3 Therefore, holy brethren, par-
takers of the heavenly calling,
consider the Apostle and High
Priest of our confession, Christ Je-
sus,
2 who was faithful to Him who
appointed Him, as [a]Moses also
was faithful in all His house.
3 For this One has been counted
worthy of more glory than Moses,
inasmuch as [a]He who built the
house has more honor than the
house.
4 For every house is built by
someone, but [a]He who built all
things *is* God.
5 [a]And Moses indeed *was* faith-

14 [a]Ps. 103:20 [b]Rom. 8:17

CHAPTER 2

1 [1]*all the more careful attention*

2 [a]Acts 7:53 [b]Num. 15:30 [1]*retribution or penalty*

3 [a]Heb. 10:28 [b]Matt. 4:17 [c]Luke 1:2

4 [a]Mark 16:20 [b]Acts 2:22, 43 [c]1 Cor. 12:4, 7, 11 [d]Eph. 1:5, 9 [1]*distributions*

5 [a][2 Pet. 3:13]

6 [a]Ps. 8:4–6

7 [1]Or *for a little while* [2]NU, M omit the rest of v. 7.

8 [a]Matt. 28:18 [b]1 Cor. 15:25, 27

9 [a]Phil. 2:7–9 [b]Acts 2:33; 3:13 [c][John 3:16] [1]Or *for a little while*

10 [a]Col. 1:16 [b]Heb. 5:8, 9; 7:28

11 [a]Heb. 10:10 [b]Acts 17:26 [c]Matt. 28:10 [1]*sets apart*

12 [a]Ps. 22:22

13 [a]2 Sam. 22:3; Is. 8:17 [b]Is. 8:18

14 [a]John 1:14 [b]Col. 2:15 [c]2 Tim. 1:10

15 [a][Luke 1:74]

16 [1]Or *take on the nature of* [2]Or *take on*

17 [a]Phil. 2:7 [b][Heb. 4:15; 5:1–10]

18 [a][Heb. 4:15, 16] [1]*tested*

CHAPTER 3

2 [a]Num. 12:7

3 [a]Zech. 6:12, 13

4 [a][Eph. 2:10]

5 [a]Heb. 3:2

ful in all His house as [b]a servant,
[c]for a testimony of those things
which would be spoken *afterward,*
6 but Christ as [a]a Son over His
own house, [b]whose house we are
[c]if we hold fast the confidence and
the rejoicing of the hope [1]firm to
the end.

Be Faithful

7 Therefore, as [a]the Holy Spirit
says:

[b]"Today, if you will hear His voice,
8 *Do not harden your hearts as in*
the rebellion,
In the day of trial in the
wilderness,
9 *Where your fathers tested Me,*
tried Me,
And saw My works forty years.
10 *Therefore I was angry with that*
generation,
And said, 'They always go astray
in their heart,
And they have not known My
ways.'
11 *So I swore in My wrath,*
'They shall not enter My rest.' "

12 Beware, brethren, lest there be
in any of you an evil heart of unbe-
lief in departing from the living
God;
13 but [1]exhort one another daily,
while it is called *"Today,"* lest any
of you be hardened through the
deceitfulness of sin.
14 For we have become partakers
of Christ if we hold the beginning
of our confidence steadfast to the
end,
15 while it is said:

[a]"Today, if you will hear His voice,
Do not harden your hearts as in
the rebellion."

Failure of the Wilderness Wanderers

16 [a]For who, having heard, re-
belled? Indeed, *was it* not all who
came out of Egypt, *led* by Moses?
17 Now with whom was He angry
forty years? *Was it* not with those
who sinned, [a]whose corpses fell in
the wilderness?
18 And [a]to whom did He swear
that they would not enter His rest,
but to those who did not obey?
19 So we see that they could not
enter in because of [a]unbelief.

5 [b]Ex. 14:31; Num. 12:7 [c]Deut. 18:15, 18, 19
6 [a]Ps. 2:7; 110:4; Heb. 1:2 [b][1 Cor. 3:16]; 1 Tim. 3:15 [c][Matt. 10:22] [1]NU omits *firm to the end*
7 [a]Acts 1:16 [b]Ps. 95:7–11; Heb. 3:15; 4:7
13 [1]*encourage*
15 [a]Ps. 95:7, 8
16 [a]Num. 14:2, 11, 30; Deut. 1:35, 36, 38
17 [a]Num. 14:22, 23
18 [a]Num. 14:30
19 [a]Num. 14:1–39; 1 Cor. 10:11, 12

CHAPTER 4

1 [a]2 Cor. 6:1; [Gal. 5:4]; Heb. 12:15
2 [1]NU, M *since they were not united by faith with those who heeded it*
3 [a]Ps. 95:11; Heb. 3:11
4 [a]Gen. 2:2; Ex. 20:11; 31:17
5 [a]Ps. 95:11
7 [a]Ps. 95:7, 8
8 [a]Josh. 22:4 [1]Gr. *Jesus,* same as Heb. *Joshua*
11 [a]2 Pet. 1:10
12 [a]Ps. 147:15 [b]Is. 49:2 [c]Eph. 6:17; Rev. 2:12 [d][John 12:48]; 1 Cor. 14:24, 25
13 [a]2 Chr. 16:9; Ps. 33:13–15; 90:8 [b]Job 26:6; Prov. 15:11

The Promise of Rest

4 Therefore, since a promise re-
mains of entering His rest, [a]let
us fear lest any of you seem to
have come short of it.
2 For indeed the gospel was
preached to us as well as to them;
but the word which they heard did
not profit them, [1]not being mixed
with faith in those who heard *it.*
3 For we who have believed do
enter that rest, as He has said:

[a]"So I swore in My wrath,
'They shall not enter My rest,' "

although the works were finished
from the foundation of the world.
4 For He has spoken in a certain
place of the seventh *day* in this
way: *[a]"And God rested on the sev-*
enth day from all His works";
5 and again in this *place:* *[a]"They*
shall not enter My rest."
6 Since therefore it remains that
some *must* enter it, and those to
whom it was first preached did not
enter because of disobedience,
7 again He designates a certain
day, saying in David, *"Today,"* af-
ter such a long time, as it has been
said:

[a]"Today, if you will hear His voice,
Do not harden your hearts."

8 For if [1]Joshua had [a]given them
rest, then He would not afterward
have spoken of another day.
9 There remains therefore a rest
for the people of God.
10 For he who has entered His rest
has himself also ceased from his
works as God *did* from His.

The Word Discovers Our Condition

11 [a]Let us therefore be diligent to
enter that rest, lest anyone fall ac-
cording to the same example of
disobedience.
12 For the word of God *is* [a]living
and powerful, and [b]sharper than
any [c]two-edged sword, piercing
even to the division of soul and
spirit, and of joints and marrow,
and is [d]a discerner of the thoughts
and intents of the heart.
13 [a]And there is no creature hid-
den from His sight, but all things
are [b]naked and open to the eyes

of Him to whom we *must give* ac-
count.

Our Compassionate High Priest

14 Seeing then that we have a
great [a]High Priest who has passed
through the heavens, Jesus the
Son of God, [b]let us hold fast *our*
confession.
15 For [a]we do not have a High
Priest who cannot sympathize
with our weaknesses, but [b]was in
all *points* tempted as *we are,* [c]*yet*
without sin.
16 [a]Let us therefore come boldly
to the throne of grace, that we may
obtain mercy and find grace to
help in time of need.

Qualifications for High Priesthood

5 For every high priest taken
from among men [a]is appointed
for men in things *pertaining* to
God, that he may offer both gifts
and sacrifices for sins.
2 He can [1]have compassion on
those who are ignorant and going
astray, since he himself is also
subject to [a]weakness.
3 Because of this he is required
as for the people, so also for [a]him-
self, to offer *sacrifices* for sins.
4 And no man takes this honor
to himself, but he who is called by
God, just as [a]Aaron *was.*

A Priest Forever

5 [a]So also Christ did not glorify
Himself to become High Priest, *but*
it was He who said to Him:

[b]*"You are My Son,*
Today I have begotten You."

6 As *He* also *says* in another
place:

[a]*"You are a priest forever*
According to the order of
Melchizedek";

7 who, in the days of His flesh,
when He had [a]offered up prayers
and supplications, [b]with vehement
cries and tears to Him [c]who was
able to save Him from death, and
was heard [d]because of His godly
fear,
8 though He was a Son, *yet* He
learned [a]obedience by the things
which He suffered.

14 [a]Heb. 2:17; 7:26 [b]Heb. 10:23
15 [a]Is. 53:3–5 [b]Luke 22:28 [c]2 Cor. 5:21; Heb. 7:26
16 [a][Eph. 2:18; Heb. 10:19, 22]

CHAPTER 5

1 [a]Heb. 2:17; 8:3
2 [a]Heb. 7:28 [1]*deal gently with*
3 [a]Lev. 9:7; 16:6; [Heb. 7:27; 9:7]
4 [a]Ex. 28:1; Num. 16:40; 1 Chr. 23:13
5 [a]John 8:54 [b]Ps. 2:7
6 [a]Ps. 110:4; Heb. 7:17
7 [a]Matt. 26:39, 42, 44; Mark 14:36, 39; Luke 22:41, 44 [b]Ps. 22:1 [c]Matt. 26:53 [d]Matt. 26:39
8 [a]Phil. 2:8
9 [a]Heb. 2:10
10 [a]Ps. 110:4
11 [a][John 16:12]; Heb. 7:1–22 [b][Matt. 13:15]
12 [a]1 Cor. 3:1–3; 1 Pet. 2:2 [1]*sayings, Scriptures*
13 [a]Eph. 4:14
14 [a]Is. 7:15; Phil. 1:9 [1]*mature* [2]*practice*

CHAPTER 6

1 [a]Heb. 5:12 [b][Heb. 9:14] [1]*maturity*
2 [a]John 3:25; Acts 19:3–5 [b][Acts 8:17] [c]Acts 17:31 [d]Acts 24:25
3 [1]M *let us do*
4 [a][John 4:10]; Eph. 2:8 [b][Gal. 3:2, 5]; Heb. 2:4
6 [a]Heb. 10:29 [1]Or *and have fallen away*
7 [a]Ps. 65:10
8 [a]Is. 5:6

9 And [a]having been perfected,
He became the author of eternal
salvation to all who obey Him,
10 called by God as High Priest
[a]*"according to the order of Mel-*
chizedek,"
11 of whom [a]we have much to say,
and hard to explain, since you
have become [b]dull of hearing.

Spiritual Immaturity

12 For though by this time you
ought to be teachers, you need
someone to teach you again the
first principles of the [1]oracles of
God; and you have come to need
[a]milk and not solid food.
13 For everyone who partakes
only of milk *is* unskilled in the
word of righteousness, for he is [a]a
babe.
14 But solid food belongs to those
who are [1]of full age, *that is,* those
who by reason of [2]use have their
senses exercised [a]to discern both
good and evil.

The Peril of Not Progressing

6 Therefore, [a]leaving the discus-
sion of the elementary *princi-*
ples of Christ, let us go on to [1]per-
fection, not laying again the
foundation of repentance from
[b]dead works and of faith toward
God,
2 [a]of the doctrine of baptisms, [b]of
laying on of hands, [c]of resur-
rection of the dead, [d]and of eternal
judgment.
3 And this [1]we will do if God per-
mits.
4 For *it is* impossible for those
who were once enlightened, and
have tasted [a]the heavenly gift, and
[b]have become partakers of the
Holy Spirit,
5 and have tasted the good word
of God and the powers of the age
to come,
6 [1]if they fall away, to renew
them again to repentance, [a]since
they crucify again for themselves
the Son of God, and put *Him* to
an open shame.
7 For the earth which drinks in
the rain that often comes upon it,
and bears herbs useful for those
by whom it is cultivated, [a]receives
blessing from God;
8 [a]but if it bears thorns and
briers, *it is* rejected and near to

being cursed, whose end *is* to be
burned.

A Better Estimate

9 But, beloved, we are confident
of better things concerning you,
yes, things that accompany salva-
tion, though we speak in this man-
ner.
10 For [a]God *is* not unjust to forget
[b]your work and [1]labor of love
which you have shown toward His
name, *in that* you have [c]minis-
tered to the saints, and do min-
ister.
11 And we desire that each one of
you show the same diligence [a]to
the full assurance of hope until the
end,
12 that you do not become [1]slug-
gish, but imitate those who
through faith and patience [a]inherit
the promises.

God's Infallible Purpose in Christ

13 For when God made a promise
to Abraham, because He could
swear by no one greater, [a]He
swore by Himself,
14 saying, [a]*"Surely blessing I will
bless you, and multiplying I will
multiply you."*
15 And so, after he had patiently
endured, he obtained the [a]promise.
16 For men indeed swear by the
greater, and [a]an oath for confirma-
tion *is* for them an end of all dis-
pute.
17 Thus God, determining to show
more abundantly to [a]the heirs of
promise [b]the [1]immutability of His
counsel, [2]confirmed *it* by an oath,
18 that by two [1]immutable things,
in which it *is* impossible for God
to [a]lie, we [2]might have strong con-
solation, who have fled for refuge
to lay hold of the hope [b]set before
us.
19 This *hope* we have as an an-
chor of the soul, both sure and
steadfast, [a]and which enters the
Presence *behind* the veil,
20 [a]where the forerunner has en-
tered for us, *even* Jesus, [b]having
become High Priest forever ac-
cording to the order of Mel-
chizedek.

The King of Righteousness

7 For this [a]Melchizedek, king of
Salem, priest of the Most High
God, who met Abraham returning
from the slaughter of the kings and
blessed him,
2 to whom also Abraham gave a
tenth part of all, first being trans-
lated "king of righteousness," and
then also king of Salem, meaning
"king of peace,"
3 without father, without mother,
without genealogy, having neither
beginning of days nor end of life,
but made like the Son of God, re-
mains a priest continually.
4 Now consider how great this
man *was,* to whom even the patri-
arch Abraham gave a tenth of the
[1]spoils.
5 And indeed [a]those who are of
the sons of Levi, who receive the
priesthood, have a commandment
to receive tithes from the people
according to the law, that is, from
their brethren, though they have
come from the loins of Abraham;
6 but he whose genealogy is not
derived from them received tithes
from Abraham [a]and blessed [b]him
who had the promises.
7 Now beyond all contradiction
the lesser is blessed by the better.
8 Here mortal men receive tithes,
but there he *receives them,* [a]of
whom it is witnessed that he lives.
9 Even Levi, who receives tithes,
paid tithes through Abraham, so
to speak,
10 for he was still in the loins of
his father when Melchizedek met
him.

Need for a New Priesthood

11 [a]Therefore, if perfection were
through the Levitical priesthood
(for under it the people received
the law), what further need *was
there* that another priest should
rise according to the order of Mel-
chizedek, and not be called ac-
cording to the order of Aaron?
12 For the priesthood being
changed, of necessity there is also
a change of the law.
13 For He of whom these things
are spoken belongs to another
tribe, from which no man has [1]of-
ficiated at the altar.
14 For *it is* evident that [a]our Lord
arose from [b]Judah, of which tribe
Moses spoke nothing concerning
[1]priesthood.
15 And it is yet far more evident

---

10 [a]Rom. 3:4 [b]1 Thess. 1:3 [c]Rom. 15:25; Heb.10:32–34 [1]NU omits *labor of*

11 [a]Col. 2:2

12 [a]Heb. 10:36 [1]*lazy*

13 [a]Gen. 22:16, 17; Luke 1:73

14 [a]Gen. 22:16, 17

15 [a]Gen. 12:4; 21:5

16 [a]Ex. 22:11

17 [a]Rom. 8:17; Heb. 11:9 [b]Rom. 11:29 [1]*unchangeableness of His purpose* [2]*guaranteed*

18 [a]Num. 23:19; 1 Sam. 15:29; Titus 1:2 [b][Col. 1:5]; Heb. 3:6; 7:19; 12:1 [1]*unchangeable* [2]M omits *might*

19 [a]Lev. 16:2, 15; Heb. 9:3, 7

20 [a][John 14:2; Heb. 4:14] [b]Gen. 14:17–19; Ps. 110:4; Heb. 3:1; 5:10, 11

CHAPTER 7

1 [a]Gen. 14:18–20; Heb. 7:6

4 [1]*plunder*

5 [a]Num. 18:21–26; 2 Chr. 31:4

6 [a]Gen. 14:19, 20 [b][Rom. 4:13]

8 [a]Heb. 5:6; 6:20; [Rev. 1:18]

11 [a][Rom. 7:7–14]; Gal. 2:21; Heb. 7:18; 8:7

13 [1]*served*

14 [a]Gen. 49:8–10; Num. 24:17; Is. 1:1; Mic. 5:2; Matt. 1:3; 2:6; Rev. 5:5 [b]Matt. 1:2 [1]NU *priests*

if, in the likeness of Melchizedek,
there arises another priest
16 who has come, not according
to the law of a fleshly command-
ment, but according to the power
of an endless life.
17 For [1]He testifies:

[a]*"You are a priest forever*
According to the order of
Melchizedek."

18 For on the one hand there is an
annulling of the former command-
ment because of [a]its weakness and
unprofitableness,
19 for [a]the law made nothing [1]per-
fect; on the other hand, *there is the*
bringing in of [b]a better hope,
through which [c]we draw near to
God.

Greatness of the New Priest

20 And inasmuch as *He was* not
made priest without an oath
21 (for they have become priests
without an oath, but He with an
oath by Him who said to Him:

[a]*"The LORD has sworn*
And will not relent,
'You are a priest [1]*forever*
According to the order of
Melchizedek' "),

22 by so much more Jesus has be-
come a [1]surety of a [a]better cov-
enant.
23 Also there were many priests,
because they were prevented by
death from continuing.
24 But He, because He continues
forever, has an unchangeable
priesthood.
25 Therefore He is also [a]able to
save [1]to the uttermost those who
come to God through Him, since
He always lives [b]to make interces-
sion for them.
26 For such a High Priest was fit-
ting for us, [a]*who is* holy, [1]harm-
less, undefiled, separate from sin-
ners, [b]and has become higher than
the heavens;
27 who does not need daily, as
those high priests, to offer up sac-
rifices, first for His [a]own sins and
then for the people's, for this He
did once for all when He offered
up Himself.
28 For the law appoints as high
priests men who have weakness,

17 [a]Ps. 110:4; Heb. 5:6; 6:20; 7:21 [1]NU *it is testified*
18 [a][Rom. 8:3]; Gal. 3:21; Heb. 7:11
19 [a][Acts 13:39]; Rom. 3:20; 7:7; Gal. 2:16; 3:21; Heb. 9:9; 10:1 [b]Heb. 6:18, 19 [c]Lam. 3:57; Rom. 5:2; [Eph. 2:18]; Heb. 4:16; James 4:8 [1]*complete*
21 [a]Ps. 110:4; Heb. 5:6; 7:17 [1]NU ends the quotation after *forever.*
22 [a]Heb. 8:6 [1]*guarantee*
25 [a]Jude 24 [b]Rom. 8:34; 1 Tim. 2:5; Heb. 9:24; 1 John 2:1 [1]*completely* or *forever*
26 [a][2 Cor. 5:21]; Heb. 4:15 [b]Eph. 1:20 [1]*innocent*
27 [a]Lev. 9:7; 16:6; Heb. 5:3

CHAPTER 8

1 [a]Ps. 68:18; 110:1; Eph. 1:20; Col. 3:1; Heb. 2:17; 3:1; 10:12
2 [a]Heb. 9:8, 12 [b]Heb. 9:11, 24 [1]Lit. *holies*
3 [a][Rom. 4:25; 5:6, 8; Gal. 2:20; Eph. 5:2]; Heb. 5:1; 8:4 [b][Eph. 5:2; Heb. 9:14]
5 [a]Heb. 9:23, 24 [b]Col. 2:17; Heb. 10:1 [c]Ex. 25:40
6 [a][2 Cor. 3:6–8] [b][Luke 22:20]; Heb. 7:22
7 [a]Ex. 3:8; 19:5
8 [a]Jer. 31:31–34
10 [a]Jer. 31:33; Rom. 11:27; Heb. 10:16 [b]Zech. 8:8

but the word of the oath, which
came after the law, *appoints* the
Son who has been perfected for-
ever.

The New Priestly Service

8 Now *this is* the main point of
the things we are saying: We
have such a High Priest, [a]who is
seated at the right hand of the
throne of the Majesty in the heav-
ens,
2 a Minister of [a]the [1]sanctuary
and of [b]the true tabernacle which
the Lord erected, and not man.
3 For [a]every high priest is ap-
pointed to offer both gifts and sac-
rifices. Therefore [b]*it is* necessary
that this One also have something
to offer.
4 For if He were on earth, He
would not be a priest, since there
are priests who offer the gifts ac-
cording to the law;
5 who serve [a]the copy and [b]sha-
dow of the heavenly things, as Mo-
ses was divinely instructed when
he was about to make the taberna-
cle. For He said, [c]*"See that you*
make all things according to the
pattern shown you on the moun-
tain."
6 But now [a]He has obtained a
more excellent ministry, inasmuch
as He is also Mediator of a [b]better
covenant, which was established
on better promises.

A New Covenant

7 For if that [a]first *covenant* had
been faultless, then no place would
have been sought for a second.
8 Because finding fault with
them, He says: [a]*"Behold, the days*
are coming, says the LORD, when
I will make a new covenant with
the house of Israel and with the
house of Judah—
9 *"not according to the covenant*
that I made with their fathers in
the day when I took them by the
hand to lead them out of the land
of Egypt; because they did not con-
tinue in My covenant, and I dis-
regarded them, says the LORD.
10 *"For this is the covenant that I*
will make with the house of Israel
after those days, says the [a]*LORD: I*
will put My laws in their mind and
write them on their hearts; and [b]*I*

will be their God, and they shall
be My people.
11 [a]*"None of them shall teach his*
neighbor, and none his brother,
saying, 'Know the [b]*LORD,' for all*
shall know Me, from the least of
them to the greatest of them.
12 *"For I will be merciful to their*
unrighteousness, [a]*and their sins*
[1]*and their lawless deeds I will re-*
member no more."
13 [a]In that He says, *"A new cov-*
enant," He has made the first ob-
solete. Now what is becoming ob-
solete and growing old is ready
to vanish away.

The Earthly Sanctuary

9 Then indeed, even the first *cov-*
enant had ordinances of divine
service and [a]the earthly sanctuary.
2 For a tabernacle was pre-
pared: the first *part,* in which *was*
the lampstand, the table, and the
showbread, which is called the
[1]sanctuary;
3 [a]and behind the second veil,
the part of the tabernacle which
is called the Holiest of All,
4 which had the [a]golden censer
and [b]the ark of the covenant over-
laid on all sides with gold, in which
were [c]the golden pot that had the
manna, [d]Aaron's rod that budded,
and [e]the tablets of the covenant;
5 and [a]above it were the cheru-
bim of glory overshadowing the
mercy seat. Of these things we
cannot now speak in detail.

Limitations of the Earthly Service

6 Now when these things had
been thus prepared, [a]the priests al-
ways went into the first part of the
tabernacle, performing *the ser-*
vices.
7 But into the second part the
high priest *went* alone [a]once a
year, not without blood, which he
offered for [b]himself and *for* the
people's sins *committed* in ig-
norance;
8 the Holy Spirit indicating this,
that [a]the way into the Holiest of
All was not yet made manifest
while the first tabernacle was still
standing.
9 It *was* symbolic for the present
time in which both gifts and sacri-
fices are offered [a]which cannot
make him who performed the ser-

11 [a]Is. 54:13; John 6:45; [1 John 2:27] [b]Jer. 31:34
12 [a]Rom. 11:27 [1]NU omits *and their lawless deeds*
13 [a][2 Cor. 5:17]; Heb. 1:11

CHAPTER 9

1 [a]Ex. 25:8; [Heb. 8:2; 9:11, 24]
2 [1]*holy place,* lit. *holies*
3 [a]Ex. 26:31–35; 40:3
4 [a]Lev. 16:12 [b]Ex. 25:10 [c]Ex. 16:33 [d]Num.17:1–10 [e]Ex. 25:16; 34:29; Deut. 10:2–5
5 [a]Ex. 25:17, 20; Lev. 16:2; 1 Kin. 8:7
6 [a]Num. 18:2–6; 28:3
7 [a]Ex. 30:10; Lev. 16:34; Heb. 10:3 [b]Heb. 5:3
8 [a][John 14:6; Heb. 10:20]
9 [a][Gal. 3:21]; Heb. 7:19
10 [a]Lev. 11:2; Col. 2:16 [b]Num. 19:7 [c]Eph. 2:15 [1]Lit. *baptisms*
11 [a][Eph. 1:3–11]; Heb. 10:1 [1]NU *that have come*
12 [a]Heb. 10:4 [b]Is. 53:12; Eph. 1:7 [c]Zech. 3:9 [d][Dan. 9:24]
13 [a]Lev. 16:14, 15; Heb. 9:19; 10:4 [b]Num. 19:2 [1]*sets apart* [2]*cleansing*
14 [a]1 John 1:7 [b]Heb. 6:1 [c]Luke 1:74 [1]*blemish*
15 [a]Rom. 3:25 [b]Heb. 3:1
17 [a]Gal. 3:15
18 [a]Ex. 24:6
19 [a]Ex. 24:5, 6 [b]Lev. 14:4, 7; Num. 19:6, 18 [1]*command*
20 [a][Matt. 26:28] [b]Ex. 24:3–8
21 [a]Ex. 29:12, 36

vice perfect in regard to the con-
science—
10 *concerned* only with [a]foods and
drinks, [b]various [1]washings, [c]and
fleshly ordinances imposed until
the time of reformation.

The Heavenly Sanctuary

11 But Christ came *as* High Priest
of [a]the good things [1]to come, with
the greater and more perfect tab-
ernacle not made with hands, that
is, not of this creation.
12 Not [a]with the blood of goats
and calves, but [b]with His own
blood He entered the Most Holy
Place [c]once for all, [d]having ob-
tained eternal redemption.
13 For if [a]the blood of bulls and
goats and [b]the ashes of a heifer,
sprinkling the unclean, [1]sanctifies
for the [2]purifying of the flesh,
14 how much more shall the blood
of Christ, who through the eternal
Spirit offered Himself without
[1]spot to God, [a]cleanse your con-
science from [b]dead works [c]to serve
the living God?
15 And for this reason [a]He is the
Mediator of the new covenant, by
means of death, for the redemp-
tion of the transgressions under
the first covenant, that [b]those who
are called may receive the promise
of the eternal inheritance.

The Mediator's Death Necessary

16 For where there *is* a testament,
there must also of necessity be the
death of the testator.
17 For [a]a testament *is* in force af-
ter men are dead, since it has no
power at all while the testator
lives.
18 [a]Therefore not even the first
covenant was dedicated without
blood.
19 For when Moses had spoken
every [1]precept to all the people ac-
cording to the law, [a]he took the
blood of calves and goats, [b]with
water, scarlet wool, and hyssop,
and sprinkled both the book itself
and all the people,
20 saying, [a]*"This is the* [b]*blood of*
the covenant which God has com-
manded you."
21 Then likewise [a]he sprinkled
with blood both the tabernacle and
all the vessels of the ministry.
22 And according to the law al-

most all things are [1]purified with blood, and [a]without shedding of blood there is no [2]remission.

Greatness of Christ's Sacrifice

23 Therefore *it was* necessary that [a]the copies of the things in the heavens should be [1]purified with these, but the heavenly things themselves with better sacrifices than these.
24 For [a]Christ has not entered the holy places made with hands, *which are* [1]copies of [b]the true, but into heaven itself, now [c]to appear in the presence of God for us;
25 not that He should offer Himself often, as [a]the high priest enters the Most Holy Place every year with blood of another—
26 He then would have had to suffer often since the foundation of the world; but now, once at the end of the ages, He has appeared to put away sin by the sacrifice of Himself.
27 [a]And as it is appointed for men to die once, [b]but after this the judgment,
28 so [a]Christ was [b]offered once to bear the sins [c]of many. To those who [d]eagerly wait for Him He will appear a second time, apart from sin, for salvation.

Animal Sacrifices Insufficient

10 For the law, having a [a]shadow of the good things to come, *and* not the very image of the things, [b]can never with these same sacrifices, which they offer continually year by year, make those who approach perfect.
2 For then would they not have ceased to be offered? For the worshipers, once [1]purified, would have had no more consciousness of sins.
3 But in those *sacrifices there is* a reminder of sins every year.
4 For [a]*it is* not possible that the blood of bulls and goats could take away sins.

Christ's Death Fulfills God's Will

5 Therefore, when He came into the world, He said:

[a]*"Sacrifice and offering You did not desire,*
But a body You have prepared for Me.
6 *In burnt offerings and sacrifices for sin*
You had no pleasure.
7 *Then I said, 'Behold, I have come—*
In the volume of the book it is written of Me—
To do Your will, O God.' "

8 Previously saying, *"Sacrifice and offering, burnt offerings, and offerings for sin You did not desire, nor had pleasure in them"* (which are offered according to the law),
9 then He said, *"Behold, I have come to do Your will, [1]O God."* He takes away the first that He may establish the second.
10 [a]By that will we have been [1]sanctified [b]through the offering of the body of Jesus Christ once *for all.*

Christ's Death Perfects the Sanctified

11 And every priest stands [a]ministering daily and offering repeatedly the same sacrifices, which can never take away sins.
12 [a]But this Man, after He had offered one sacrifice for sins forever, sat down [b]at the right hand of God,
13 from that time waiting [a]till His enemies are made His footstool.
14 For by one offering He has perfected forever those who are being [1]sanctified.
15 But the Holy Spirit also witnesses to us; for after He had said before,
16 [a]*"This is the covenant that I will make with them after those days, says the* LORD: *I will put My laws into their hearts, and in their minds I will write them,"*
17 *then He adds,* [a]*"Their sins and their lawless deeds I will remember no more."*
18 Now where there is [1]remission of these, *there is* no longer an offering for sin.

Hold Fast Your Confession

19 Therefore, brethren, having [a]boldness[1] to enter [b]the Holiest by the blood of Jesus,
20 by a new and [a]living way which He consecrated for us, through the veil, that is, His flesh,

22 [a]Lev. 17:11 [1]*cleansed* [2]*forgiveness*
23 [a]Heb. 8:5 [1]*cleansed*
24 [a]Heb. 6:20 [b]Heb. 8:2 [c]Rom. 8:34 [1]*representations*
25 [a]Heb. 9:7
27 [a]Gen. 3:19; Eccl. 3:20 [b][2 Cor. 5:10]; 1 John 4:17
28 [a]Rom. 6:10 [b]Is. 53:12; 1 Pet. 2:24 [c]Matt. 26:28 [d]1 Cor. 1:7; Titus 2:13

CHAPTER 10

1 [a]Heb. 8:5 [b]Heb. 7:19; 9:9
2 [1]*cleansed*
4 [a]Mic. 6:6, 7
5 [a]Ps. 40:6–8
9 [1]NU, M omit *O God*
10 [a]John 17:19; [Eph. 5:26; Heb. 2:11; 10:14, 29; 13:12] [b][Heb. 9:12] [1]*set apart*
11 [a]Num. 28:3
12 [a]Col. 3:1; Heb. 1:3 [b]Ps. 110:1
13 [a]Ps. 110:1; Heb. 1:13
14 [1]*set apart*
16 [a]Jer. 31:33, 34; Heb. 8:10
17 [a]Jer. 31:34
18 [1]*forgiveness*
19 [a][Eph. 2:18]; Heb. 4:16 [b]Heb. 9:8, 12 [1]*confidence*
20 [a]John 14:6; [Heb. 7:24, 25]

21 and *having* a High Priest over
the house of God,
22 let us [a]draw near with a true
heart [b]in full assurance of faith,
having our hearts sprinkled from
an evil conscience and our bodies
washed with pure water.
23 Let us hold fast the confession
of *our* hope without wavering, for
[a]He who promised *is* faithful.
24 And let us consider one an-
other in order to stir up love and
good works,
25 [a]not forsaking the assembling
of ourselves together, as *is* the
manner of some, but exhorting *one
another*, and [b]so much the more
as you see [c]the Day approaching.

The Just Live by Faith

26 For [a]if we sin willfully [b]after we
have received the knowledge of
the truth, there [c]no longer remains
a sacrifice for sins,
27 but a certain fearful expecta-
tion of judgment, and [a]fiery
indignation which will devour the
adversaries.
28 Anyone who has rejected Mo-
ses' law dies without mercy on the
testimony of two or three [a]wit-
nesses.
29 [a]Of how much worse punish-
ment, do you suppose, will he be
thought worthy who has trampled
the Son of God underfoot,
[b]counted the blood of the covenant
by which he was sanctified a com-
mon thing, [c]and insulted the Spirit
of grace?
30 For we know Him who said,
[a]*"Vengeance is Mine, I will re-
pay,"* [1]says the Lord. And again,
[b]*"The* LORD *will judge His people."*
31 [a]It is a fearful thing to fall into
the hands of the living God.
32 But [a]recall the former days in
which, after you were [1]illumi-
nated, you endured a great struggle
with sufferings:
33 partly while you were made [a]a
spectacle both by reproaches and
tribulations, and partly while [b]you
became companions of those who
were so treated;
34 for you had compassion on [1]me
[a]in my chains, and [b]joyfully ac-
cepted the plundering of your
[2]goods, knowing that [c]you have a
better and an enduring possession
for yourselves [3]in heaven.

22 [a]Heb. 7:19; 10:1 [b]Eph. 3:12
23 [a]1 Cor. 1:9; 10:13
25 [a]Acts 2:42 [b]Rom. 13:11 [c]Phil. 4:5
26 [a]Num. 15:30 [b]2 Pet. 2:20 [c]Heb. 6:6
27 [a]Zeph. 1:18
28 [a]Deut. 17:2–6; 19:15
29 [a][Heb. 2:3] [b]1 Cor. 11:29 [c][Matt. 12:31]
30 [a]Deut. 32:35 [b]Deut. 32:36 [1]NU omits *says the Lord*
31 [a][Luke 12:5]
32 [a]Gal. 3:4 [1]*enlightened*
33 [a]1 Cor. 4:9 [b]Phil. 1:7
34 [a]2 Tim. 1:16 [b]Matt. 5:12 [c]Matt. 6:20 [1]NU *the prisoners* instead of *me in my chains* [2]*possessions* [3]NU omits *in heaven*
35 [a]Matt. 5:12
36 [a]Luke 21:19 [b][Col. 3:24]
37 [a]Luke 18:8 [b]Hab. 2:3, 4 [1]Or *that which* [2]*delay*
38 [a]Rom. 1:17 [1]NU *My just one*
39 [a]2 Pet. 2:20 [b]Acts 16:31 [1]*destruction*

CHAPTER 11
1 [a]Rom. 8:24 [1]*realization* [2]Or *confidence*
3 [a]Ps. 33:6 [1]Or *ages*, Gr. *aiones*, aeons
4 [a]Gen. 4:3–5 [b]Heb. 12:24
5 [a]Gen. 5:21–24
7 [a]Gen. 6:13–22 [b]1 Pet. 3:20 [c]Rom. 3:22
8 [a]Gen. 12:1–4

35 Therefore do not cast away
your confidence, [a]which has great
reward.
36 [a]For you have need of endur-
ance, so that after you have done
the will of God, [b]you may receive
the promise:

37 *"For* [a]*yet a little while,*
And [b]*He*[1] *who is coming will*
come and will not [2]*tarry.*
38 *Now* [a]*the*[1] *just shall live by faith;*
But if anyone draws back,
My soul has no pleasure in him."

39 But we are not of those [a]who
draw back to [1]perdition, but of
those who [b]believe to the saving
of the soul.

By Faith We Understand

11 Now faith is the [1]substance
of things hoped for, the [2]evi-
dence [a]of things not seen.
2 For by it the elders obtained a
good testimony.
3 By faith we understand that
[a]the [1]worlds were framed by the
word of God, so that the things
which are seen were not made of
things which are visible.

Faith at the Dawn of History

4 By faith [a]Abel offered to God
a more excellent sacrifice than
Cain, through which he obtained
witness that he was righteous, God
testifying of his gifts; and through
it he being dead still [b]speaks.
5 By faith Enoch was taken away
so that he did not see death, [a]*"and
was not found, because God had
taken him"*; for before he was
taken he had this testimony, that
he pleased God.
6 But without faith *it is* impossi-
ble to please *Him*, for he who
comes to God must believe that He
is, and *that* He is a rewarder of
those who diligently seek Him.
7 By faith [a]Noah, being divinely
warned of things not yet seen,
moved with godly fear, [b]prepared
an ark for the saving of his house-
hold, by which he condemned the
world and became heir of [c]the
righteousness which is according
to faith.

Faithful Abraham

8 By faith [a]Abraham obeyed
when he was called to go out to

the place which he would receive
as an inheritance. And he went
out, not knowing where he was go-
ing.
9 By faith he dwelt in the land
of promise as *in* a foreign country,
[a]dwelling in tents with Isaac and
Jacob, [b]the heirs with him of the
same promise;
10 for he waited for [a]the city
which has foundations, [b]whose
builder and maker *is* God.
11 By faith [a]Sarah herself also re-
ceived strength to conceive seed,
and [b]she[1] bore a child when she
was past the age, because she
judged Him [c]faithful who had
promised.
12 Therefore from one man, and
him as good as [a]dead, were born
as many as the [b]stars of the sky
in multitude—innumerable as the
sand which is by the seashore.

The Heavenly Hope

13 These all died in faith, [a]not
having received the [b]promises, but
[c]having seen them afar off [1]were
assured of them, embraced *them*
and [d]confessed that they were
strangers and pilgrims on the
earth.
14 For those who say such things
[a]declare plainly that they seek a
homeland.
15 And truly if they had called to
mind [a]that *country* from which
they had come out, they would
have had opportunity to return.
16 But now they desire a better,
that is, a heavenly *country*. There-
fore God is not ashamed [a]to be
called their God, for He has [b]pre-
pared a city for them.

The Faith of the Patriarchs

17 By faith Abraham, [a]when he
was tested, offered up Isaac, and
he who had received the promises
offered up his only begotten *son*,
18 [1]of whom it was said, [a]*"In Isaac
your seed shall be called,"*
19 concluding that God [a]*was* able
to raise *him* up, even from the
dead, from which he also received
him in a figurative sense.
20 By faith [a]Isaac blessed Jacob
and Esau concerning things to
come.
21 By faith Jacob, when he was
dying, [a]blessed each of the sons of
Joseph, and worshiped, *leaning* on
the top of his staff.
22 By faith [a]Joseph, when he was
dying, made mention of the depar-
ture of the children of Israel, and
gave instructions concerning his
bones.

The Faith of Moses

23 By faith [a]Moses, when he was
born, was hidden three months by
his parents, because they saw *he
was* a beautiful child; and they
were not afraid of the king's [b]com-
mand.
24 By faith [a]Moses, when he be-
came of age, refused to be called
the son of Pharaoh's daughter,
25 choosing rather to suffer afflic-
tion with the people of God than
to enjoy the [1]passing pleasures of
sin,
26 esteeming [a]the [1]reproach of
Christ greater riches than the trea-
sures [2]in Egypt; for he looked to
the [b]reward.
27 By faith [a]he forsook Egypt, not
fearing the wrath of the king; for
he endured as seeing Him who is
invisible.
28 By faith [a]he kept the Passover
and the sprinkling of blood, lest
he who destroyed the firstborn
should touch them.
29 By faith [a]they passed through
the Red Sea as by dry *land*,
whereas the Egyptians, attempting
to do so, were drowned.

By Faith They Overcame

30 By faith [a]the walls of Jericho
fell down after they were encircled
for seven days.
31 By faith [a]the harlot Rahab did
not perish with those who [1]did not
believe, when [b]she had received
the spies with peace.
32 And what more shall I say? For
the time would fail me to tell of
[a]Gideon and [b]Barak and [c]Samson
and [d]Jephthah, also *of* [e]David and
[f]Samuel and the prophets:
33 who through faith subdued
kingdoms, worked righteousness,
obtained promises, [a]stopped the
mouths of lions,
34 [a]quenched the violence of fire,
escaped the edge of the sword, out
of weakness were made strong,
became valiant in battle, turned to
flight the armies of the aliens.

9 [a]Gen. 12:8; 13:3, 18; 18:1, 9 [b]Heb. 6:17
10 [a][Heb. 12:22; 13:14] [b][Rev. 21:10]
11 [a]Gen. 17:19; 18:11–14; 21:1, 2 [b]Luke 1:36 [c]Heb. 10:23 [1]NU omits *she bore a child*
12 [a]Rom. 4:19 [b]Gen. 15:5; 22:17; 32:12
13 [a]Heb. 11:39 [b]Gen. 12:7 [c]John 8:56 [d]Ps. 39:12 [1]NU, M omit *were assured of them*
14 [a]Heb. 13:14
15 [a]Gen. 11:31
16 [a]Ex. 3:6, 15; 4:5 [b][Rev. 21:2]
17 [a]James 2:21
18 [a]Gen. 21:12 [1]*to*
19 [a]Rom. 4:17
20 [a]Gen. 27:26–40
21 [a]Gen. 48:1, 5, 16, 20
22 [a]Gen. 50:24, 25
23 [a]Ex. 2:1–3 [b]Ex. 1:16, 22
24 [a]Ex. 2:11–15
25 [1]*temporary*
26 [a]Heb. 13:13 [b]Rom. 8:18 [1]*reviling because of* [2]NU, M *of*
27 [a]Ex. 10:28
28 [a]Ex. 12:21
29 [a]Ex. 14:22–29
30 [a]Josh. 6:20
31 [a]Josh. 2:9; 6:23 [b]Josh. 2:1 [1]*were disobedient*
32 [a]Judg. 6:11; 7:1–25 [b]Judg. 4:6–24 [c]Judg. 13:24—16:31 [d]Judg. 11:1–29; 12:1–7 [e]1 Sam. 16:17 [f]1 Sam. 7:9–14
33 [a]Dan. 6:22
34 [a]Dan. 3:23–28

35 [a]Women received their dead
raised to life again. Others were
[b]tortured, not accepting deliver-
ance, that they might obtain a bet-
ter resurrection.
36 Still others had trial of mock-
ings and scourgings, yes, and [a]of
chains and imprisonment.
37 [a]They were stoned, they were
sawn in two, [1]were tempted, were
slain with the sword. [b]They wan-
dered about [c]in sheepskins and
goatskins, being destitute, af-
flicted, tormented—
38 of whom the world was not
worthy. They wandered in deserts
and mountains, [a]*in* dens and caves
of the earth.
39 And all these, [a]having obtained
a good testimony through faith,
did not receive the promise,
40 God having provided some-
thing better for us, that they
should not be [a]made perfect apart
from us.

The Race of Faith

12 Therefore we also, since we
are surrounded by so great
a cloud of witnesses, [a]let us lay
aside every weight, and the sin
which so easily ensnares *us*, and
[b]let us run [c]with endurance the
race that is set before us,
2 looking unto Jesus, the [1]author
and [2]finisher of *our* faith, [a]who for
the joy that was set before Him
[b]endured the cross, despising the
shame, and [c]has sat down at the
right hand of the throne of God.

The Discipline of God

3 [a]For consider Him who en-
dured such hostility from sinners
against Himself, [b]lest you become
weary and discouraged in your
souls.
4 [a]You have not yet resisted to
bloodshed, striving against sin.
5 And you have forgotten the ex-
hortation which speaks to you as
to sons:

[a]"My son, do not despise the
[1]chastening of the LORD,
Nor be discouraged when you are
rebuked by Him;
6 *For [a]whom the LORD loves He*
chastens,
And scourges every son whom
He receives."

35 [a]1 Kin. 17:22 [b]Acts 22:25
36 [a]Gen. 39:20
37 [a]1 Kin. 21:13 [b]2 Kin. 1:8 [c]Zech. 13:4 [1]NU omits *were tempted*
38 [a]1 Kin. 18:4, 13; 19:9
39 [a]Heb. 11:2, 13
40 [a]Heb. 5:9

CHAPTER 12

1 [a]Col. 3:8 [b]1 Cor. 9:24 [c]Rom. 12:12
2 [a]Luke 24:26 [b]Phil. 2:8 [c]Ps. 110:1 [1]*originator* [2]*perfecter*
3 [a]Matt. 10:24 [b]Gal. 6:9
4 [a][1 Cor. 10:13]
5 [a]Prov. 3:11, 12 [1]*discipline*
6 [a]Rev. 3:19
7 [a]Deut. 8:5 [b]Prov. 13:24; 19:18; 23:13 [1]NU, M *It is for discipline that you endure; God*
8 [a]1 Pet. 5:9
9 [a][Job 12:10]
10 [a]Lev. 11:44
11 [a]James 3:17, 18 [1]*discipline*
12 [a]Is. 35:3
14 [a]Ps. 34:14 [b]Matt. 5:8
15 [a]Heb. 4:1 [b]Deut. 29:18
16 [a][1 Cor. 6:13–18] [b]Gen. 25:33 [1]*godless*
17 [a]Gen. 27:30–40
18 [a]Deut. 4:11; 5:22 [1]NU *to that which* [2]NU *gloom*
19 [a]Ex. 20:18–26

7 [a]If[1] you endure chastening,
God deals with you as with sons;
for what [b]son is there whom a fa-
ther does not chasten?
8 But if you are without chasten-
ing, [a]of which all have become
partakers, then you are illegiti-
mate and not sons.
9 Furthermore, we have had hu-
man fathers who corrected *us*, and
we paid *them* respect. Shall we not
much more readily be in subjec-
tion to [a]the Father of spirits and
live?
10 For they indeed for a few days
chastened *us* as seemed *best* to
them, but He for *our* profit, [a]that
we may be partakers of His holi-
ness.
11 Now no [1]chastening seems to
be joyful for the present, but pain-
ful; nevertheless, afterward it
yields [a]the peaceable fruit of righ-
teousness to those who have been
trained by it.

Renew Your Spiritual Vitality

12 Therefore [a]strengthen the
hands which hang down, and the
feeble knees,
13 and make straight paths for
your feet, so that what is lame may
not be *dislocated*, but rather be
healed.
14 [a]Pursue peace with all *people*,
and holiness, [b]without which no
one will see the Lord:
15 looking carefully lest anyone
[a]fall short of the grace of God; lest
any [b]root of bitterness springing
up cause trouble, and by this many
become defiled;
16 lest there *be* any [a]fornicator or
[1]profane person like Esau, [b]who
for one morsel of food sold his
birthright.
17 For you know that afterward,
when he wanted to inherit the
blessing, he was [a]rejected, for he
found no place for repentance,
though he sought it diligently with
tears.

The Glorious Company

18 For you have not come [1]to [a]the
mountain that may be touched and
that burned with fire, and to black-
ness and [2]darkness and tempest,
19 and the sound of a trumpet and
the voice of words, so that those
who heard *it* [a]begged that the

word should not be spoken to them
anymore.
20 (For they could not endure
what was commanded: [a]*"And if so
much as a beast touches the moun-
tain, it shall be stoned* [1]*or shot
with an arrow."*
21 And so terrifying was the sight
that Moses said, [a]*"I am exceed-
ingly afraid* and trembling.")
22 But you have come to Mount
Zion and to the city of the living
God, the heavenly Jerusalem, to
an innumerable company of an-
gels,
23 to the [1]general assembly and
church of [a]the firstborn [b]*who are*
registered in heaven, to God [c]the
Judge of all, to the spirits of just
men [d]made perfect,
24 to Jesus [a]the Mediator of the
new covenant, and to [b]the blood
of sprinkling that speaks better
things [c]than *that of* Abel.

Hear the Heavenly Voice

25 See that you do not refuse Him
who speaks. For [a]if they did not
escape who refused Him who
spoke on earth, much more *shall
we not escape* if we turn away
from Him who *speaks* from
heaven,
26 whose voice then shook the
earth; but now He has promised,
saying, [a]*"Yet once more I* [1]*shake
not only the earth, but also
heaven."*
27 Now this, *"Yet once more,"* in-
dicates the [a]removal of those
things that are being shaken, as
of things that are made, that the
things which cannot be shaken
may remain.
28 Therefore, since we are receiv-
ing a kingdom which cannot be
shaken, let us have grace, by
which we [1]may [a]serve God accept-
ably with reverence and godly
fear.
29 For [a]our God *is* a consuming
fire.

Concluding Moral Directions

13 Let [a]brotherly love continue.
2 [a]Do not forget to enter-
tain strangers, for by so *doing*
[b]some have unwittingly enter-
tained angels.
3 [a]Remember the prisoners as if
chained with them—those who are
mistreated—since you yourselves
are in the body also.
4 [a]Marriage *is* honorable among
all, and the bed undefiled; [b]but for-
nicators and adulterers God will
judge.
5 *Let your* conduct *be* without
covetousness; *be* content with
such things as you have. For He
Himself has said, [a]*"I will never
leave you nor forsake you."*
6 So we may boldly say:

[a]*"The* LORD *is my helper;
I will not fear.
What can man do to me?"*

Concluding Religious Directions

7 Remember those who [1]rule
over you, who have spoken the
word of God to you, whose faith
follow, considering the outcome of
their conduct.
8 Jesus Christ *is* [a]the same yes-
terday, today, and forever.
9 Do not be carried [1]about with
various and strange doctrines. For
it is good that the heart be estab-
lished by grace, not with foods
which have not profited those who
have been occupied with them.
10 We have an altar from which
those who serve the tabernacle
have no right to eat.
11 For the bodies of those ani-
mals, whose blood is brought into
the sanctuary by the high priest for
sin, are burned outside the camp.
12 Therefore Jesus also, that He
might [1]sanctify the people with His
own blood, suffered outside the
gate.
13 Therefore let us go forth to
Him, outside the camp, bearing
[a]His reproach.
14 For here we have no continuing
city, but we seek the one to come.
15 [a]Therefore by Him let us con-
tinually offer [b]the sacrifice of
praise to God, that is, [c]the fruit of
our lips, [1]giving thanks to His
name.
16 [a]But do not forget to do good
and to share, for [b]with such sacri-
fices God is well pleased.
17 [a]Obey those who [1]rule over
you, and be submissive, for [b]they
watch out for your souls, as those
who must give account. Let them
do so with joy and not with grief,

20 [a]Ex. 19:12, 13 [1]NU, M omit the rest of v. 20.
21 [a]Deut. 9:19
23 [a][James 1:18] [b]Luke 10:20 [c]Gen. 18:25; Ps. 50:6; 94:2 [d][Phil. 3:12] [1]*festal gathering*
24 [a]1 Tim. 2:5; Heb. 8:6; 9:15 [b]Ex. 24:8 [c]Gen. 4:10; Heb. 11:4
25 [a]Heb. 2:2, 3
26 [a]Hag. 2:6 [1]NU *will shake*
27 [a][Is. 34:4; 54:10; 65:17; Rom. 8:19, 21]; 1 Cor. 7:31; Heb. 1:10
28 [a]Heb. 13:15, 21 [1]M omits *may*
29 [a]Ex. 24:17

CHAPTER 13

1 [a]Rom. 12:10
2 [a]Matt. 25:35; Rom. 12:13 [b]Gen. 18:1–22; 19:1
3 [a]Matt. 25:36; Heb. 10:34
4 [a]Prov. 5:18, 19 [b]1 Cor. 6:9; Gal. 5:19, 21; 1 Thess. 4:6
5 [a]Gen. 28:15; Deut. 31:6, 8; Josh. 1:5
6 [a]Ps. 27:1; 118:6
7 [1]*lead*
8 [a][John 8:58]; 2 Cor. 1:19; Heb. 1:12
9 [1]NU, M *away*
12 [1]*set apart*
13 [a]1 Pet. 4:14
15 [a]Eph. 5:20 [b]Lev. 7:12 [c]Is. 57:19; Hos. 14:2 [1]Lit. *confessing*
16 [a]Rom. 12:13 [b]2 Cor. 9:12; Phil. 4:18
17 [a]Phil. 2:29 [b]Is. 62:6; Ezek. 3:17; Acts 20:28 [1]*lead*

for that would be unprofitable for
you.

Prayer Requested

18 [a]Pray for us; for we are confi-
dent that we have [b]a good con-
science, in all things desiring to
live honorably.
19 But I especially urge *you* to do
this, that I may be restored to you
the sooner.

Benediction, Final Exhortation, Farewell

20 Now may [a]the God of peace
[b]who brought up our Lord Jesus
from the dead, [c]that great Shep-
herd of the sheep, [d]through the
blood of the everlasting covenant,
21 make you [1]complete in every
good work to do His will, [a]working
in [2]you what is well pleasing in His
sight, through Jesus Christ, to
whom *be* glory forever and ever.
Amen.
22 And I appeal to you, brethren,
bear with the word of exhortation,
for I have written to you in few
words.
23 Know that *our* brother Timothy
has been set free, with whom I
shall see you if he comes shortly.
24 Greet all those who [1]rule over
you, and all the saints. Those from
Italy greet you.
25 Grace *be* with you all. Amen.

18 [a]Eph. 6:19 [b]Acts 23:1
20 [a]Rom. 5:1, 2, 10; 15:33 [b]Ps. 16:10, 11; Hos. 6:2; Rom. 4:24 [c]Ps. 23:1; Is. 40:11; 63:11; John 10:11; 1 Pet. 2:25; 5:4 [d]Zech. 9:11; Heb. 10:29
21 [a]Phil. 2:13 [1]*perfect* [2]NU, M *us*
24 [1]*lead*

The Epistle of

James

FAITH without works cannot be called faith. "Faith without works is dead" (2:26), and a dead faith is worse than no faith at all. Faith must work; it must produce; it must be visible. Verbal faith is not enough; mental faith is insufficient. Faith must be there, but it must be more. It must inspire action. Throughout his epistle to Jewish believers, James integrates true faith and everyday practical experience by stressing that true faith must manifest itself in works of faith.

Faith endures trials. Trials come and go, but a strong faith will face them head-on and develop endurance. Faith understands temptations. It will not allow us to consent to our lust and slide into sin. Faith obeys the Word. It will not merely hear and not do. Faith produces doers. Faith harbors no prejudice. For James, faith and favoritism cannot coexist. Faith displays itself in works. Faith is more than mere words; it is more than knowledge; it is demonstrated by obedience; and it overtly responds to the promises of God. Faith controls the tongue. This small but immensely powerful part of the body must be held in check. Faith can do it. Faith acts wisely. It gives us the ability to choose wisdom that is heavenly and to shun wisdom that is earthly. Faith produces separation from the world and submission to God. It provides us with the ability to resist the Devil and humbly draw near to God. Finally, faith waits patiently for the coming of the Lord. Through trouble and trial it stifles complaining.

The name *Iakobos* (James) in 1:1 is the basis for the early title *Iakobou Epistole,* "Epistle of James." *Iakobos* is the Greek form of the Hebrew name Jacob, a Jewish name common in the first century.

Greeting to the Twelve Tribes

JAMES, [a]a bondservant of God
and of the Lord Jesus Christ,

To the twelve tribes which are
scattered abroad:

Greetings.

Profiting from Trials

2 My brethren, [a]count it all joy
[b]when you fall into various trials,
3 [a]knowing that the testing of
your faith produces [1]patience.
4 But let patience have *its* perfect
work, that you may be [1]perfect and
complete, lacking nothing.
5 [a]If any of you lacks wisdom,
[b]let him ask of God, who gives to
all liberally and without reproach,
and [c]it will be given to him.
6 [a]But let him ask in faith, with
no doubting, for he who doubts is
like a wave of the sea driven and
tossed by the wind.
7 For let not that man suppose
that he will receive anything from
the Lord;
8 *he is* [a]a double-minded man,
unstable in all his ways.

The Perspective of Rich and Poor

9 Let the lowly brother glory in
his exaltation,
10 but the rich in his humiliation,
because [a]as a flower of the field
he will pass away.
11 For no sooner has the sun risen
with a burning heat than it withers
the grass; its flower falls, and its
beautiful appearance perishes. So
the rich man also will fade away
in his pursuits.

Loving God Under Trials

12 [a]Blessed *is* the man who en-
dures temptation; for when he has

CHAPTER 1

1 [a]Acts 12:17

2 [a]Acts 5:41 [b]1 Pet. 1:6

3 [a]Rom. 5:3–5 [1]*endurance or perseverance*

4 [1]*mature*

5 [a]1 Kin. 3:9; James 3:17 [b]Prov. 2:3–6; Matt. 7:7 [c]Jer. 29:12

6 [a][Mark 11:23, 24]; Acts 10:20

8 [a]James 4:8

10 [a]Job 14:2

12 [a]Job 5:17; Luke 6:22; Heb. 10:36; James 5:11; [1 Pet. 3:14; 4:14]

been approved, he will receive [b]the
crown of life [c]which the Lord has
promised to those who love Him.
13 Let no one say when he is
tempted, "I am tempted by God";
for God cannot be tempted by evil,
nor does He Himself tempt any-
one.
14 But each one is tempted when
he is drawn away by his own de-
sires and enticed.
15 Then, [a]when desire has con-
ceived, it gives birth to sin; and sin,
when it is full-grown, [b]brings forth
death.
16 Do not be deceived, my be-
loved brethren.
17 [a]Every good gift and every per-
fect gift is from above, and comes
down from the Father of lights,
[b]with whom there is no variation
or shadow of turning.
18 [a]Of His own will He brought us
forth by the [b]word of truth, [c]that
we might be a kind of firstfruits
of His creatures.

Qualities Needed in Trials

19 [1]So then, my beloved brethren,
let every man be swift to hear,
[a]slow to speak, [b]slow to wrath;
20 for the wrath of man does not
produce the righteousness of God.

Doers—Not Hearers Only

21 Therefore [a]lay aside all filthi-
ness and [1]overflow of wickedness,
and receive with meekness the im-
planted word, [b]which is able to
save your souls.
22 But [a]be doers of the word, and
not hearers only, deceiving your-
selves.
23 For [a]if anyone is a hearer of the
word and not a doer, he is like a
man observing his natural face in
a mirror;
24 for he observes himself, goes
away, and immediately forgets
what kind of man he was.
25 But [a]he who looks into the per-
fect law of liberty and continues
in it, and is not a forgetful hearer
but a doer of the work, [b]this one
will be blessed in what he does.
26 If anyone [1]among you thinks
he is religious, and [a]does not bridle
his tongue but deceives his own
heart, this one's religion *is* useless.
27 [a]Pure and undefiled religion
before God and the Father is this:

12 [b][1 Cor. 9:25] [c]Matt. 10:22
15 [a]Job 15:35 [b][Rom. 5:12; 6:23]
17 [a]John 3:27 [b]Num. 23:19
18 [a]John 1:13 [b][1 Pet. 1:3, 23] [c][Eph. 1:12, 13]
19 [a]Prov. 10:19; 17:27 [b]Prov. 14:17; 16:32 [1]NU *Know this* or *This you know*
21 [a]Col. 3:8 [b]Acts 13:26 [1]*abundance*
22 [a]Matt. 7:21–28
23 [a]Luke 6:47
25 [a]James 2:12 [b]John 13:17
26 [a]Ps. 34:13 [1]NU omits *among you*
27 [a]Matt. 25:34–36 [b]Is. 1:17 [c][Rom. 12:2]

CHAPTER 2

1 [a]1 Cor. 2:8 [b]Lev. 19:15
2 [1]*bright* [2]*vile*
3 [1]Lit. *look upon*
4 [1]*differentiated*
5 [a]1 Cor. 1:27 [b]Luke 12:21 [c]Ex. 20:6
6 [a]1 Cor. 11:22 [b]Acts 13:50
7 [a]1 Pet. 4:16
8 [a]Lev. 19:18
9 [a]Deut. 1:17 [1]Lit. *receive the face*
10 [a]Gal. 3:10 [b]Deut. 27:26
11 [a]Ex. 20:14; Deut. 5:18 [b]Ex. 20:13; Deut. 5:17
12 [a]James 1:25
13 [a]Job 22:6 [b]Prov. 21:13 [c]Mic. 7:18 [d]Rom. 12:8
14 [a]Matt. 7:21–23, 26; 21:28–32

[b]to visit orphans and widows in
their trouble, [c]*and* to keep oneself
unspotted from the world.

Beware of Personal Favoritism

2 My brethren, do not hold the
faith of our Lord Jesus Christ,
[a]*the Lord* of glory, with [b]partiality.
2 For if there should come into
your assembly a man with gold
rings, in [1]fine apparel, and there
should also come in a poor man
in [2]filthy clothes,
3 and you [1]pay attention to the
one wearing the fine clothes and
say to him, "You sit here in a good
place," and say to the poor man,
"You stand there," or, "Sit here at
my footstool,"
4 have you not [1]shown partiality
among yourselves, and become
judges with evil thoughts?
5 Listen, my beloved brethren:
[a]Has God not chosen the poor of
this world *to be* [b]rich in faith and
heirs of the kingdom [c]which He
promised to those who love Him?
6 But [a]you have dishonored the
poor man. Do not the rich oppress
you [b]and drag you into the courts?
7 Do they not blaspheme that
noble name by which you are
[a]called?
8 If you really fulfill *the* royal
law according to the Scripture,
[a]"*You shall love your neighbor as
yourself,*" you do well;
9 but if you [1]show partiality, you
commit sin, and are convicted by
the law as [a]transgressors.
10 For whoever shall keep the
whole law, and yet [a]stumble in one
point, [b]he is guilty of all.
11 For He who said, [a]"*Do not com-
mit adultery,*" also said, [b]"*Do not
murder.*" Now if you do not com-
mit adultery, but you do murder,
you have become a transgressor of
the law.
12 So speak and so do as those
who will be judged by [a]the law of
liberty.
13 For [a]judgment is without mercy
to the one who has shown [b]no
[c]mercy. [d]Mercy triumphs over
judgment.

Faith Without Works Is Dead

14 [a]What *does it* profit, my breth-
ren, if someone says he has faith

but does not have works? Can
faith save him?
15 [a]If a brother or sister is naked
and destitute of daily food,
16 and [a]one of you says to them,
"Depart in peace, be warmed and
filled," but you do not give them
the things which are needed for
the body, what *does it* profit?
17 Thus also faith by itself, if it
does not have works, is dead.
18 But someone will say, "You
have faith, and I have works."
[a]Show me your faith without [1]your
works, [b]and I will show you my
faith by [2]my works.
19 You believe that there is one
God. You do well. Even the de-
mons believe—and tremble!
20 But do you want to know, O
foolish man, that faith without
works is [1]dead?
21 Was not Abraham our father
justified by works [a]when he of-
fered Isaac his son on the altar?
22 Do you see [a]that faith was
working together with his works,
and by [b]works faith was made
[1]perfect?
23 And the Scripture was fulfilled
which says, *[a]"Abraham believed
God, and it was [1]accounted to him
for righteousness."* And he was
called [b]the friend of God.
24 You see then that a man is jus-
tified by works, and not by faith
only.
25 Likewise, [a]was not Rahab the
harlot also justified by works
when she received the messengers
and sent *them* out another way?
26 For as the body without the
spirit is dead, so faith without
works is dead also.

The Untamable Tongue

3 My brethren, [a]let not many of
you become teachers, [b]know-
ing that we shall receive a stricter
judgment.
2 For [a]we all stumble in many
things. [b]If anyone does not stum-
ble in word, [c]he *is* a [1]perfect man,
able also to bridle the whole body.
3 [1]Indeed, [a]we put bits in horses'
mouths that they may obey us, and
we turn their whole body.
4 Look also at ships: although
they are so large and are driven
by fierce winds, they are turned by

15 [a]Luke 3:11
16 [a][1 John 3:17, 18]
18 [a]Heb. 6:10 [b]James 3:13 [1]NU omits *your* [2]NU omits *my*
20 [1]NU *useless*
21 [a]Gen. 22:9, 10, 12, 16–18
22 [a]Heb. 11:17 [b]John 8:39 [1]*complete*
23 [a]Gen. 15:6 [b]2 Chr. 20:7 [1]*credited*
25 [a]Heb. 11:31

CHAPTER 3

1 [a][Matt. 23:8] [b]Luke 6:37
2 [a]1 Kin. 8:46 [b]Ps. 34:13 [c][Matt. 12:34–37] [1]*mature*
3 [a]Ps. 32:9 [1]NU *Now if*
5 [a]Prov. 12:18; 15:2 [b]Ps. 12:3; 73:8
6 [a]Prov. 16:27 [b][Matt. 12:36; 15:11, 18] [1]*unrighteousness* [2]*existence* [3]Gr. *Gehenna*
8 [a]Ps. 140:3
9 [a]Gen. 1:26; 5:1; 9:6 [1]*likeness*
12 [a]Matt. 7:16–20 [1]NU *Neither can a salty spring produce fresh water.*
13 [a]Gal. 6:4
14 [a]Rom. 13:13 [b]Rom. 2:17 [1]*selfish ambition*
15 [a]Phil. 3:19
16 [a]1 Cor. 3:3
17 [a]1 Cor. 2:6, 7 [b]James 2:1 [c]Rom. 12:9
18 [a]Prov. 11:18

CHAPTER 4

1 [1]*battles*

a very small rudder wherever the
pilot desires.
5 Even so [a]the tongue is a little
member and [b]boasts great things.
See how great a forest a little fire
kindles!
6 And [a]the tongue *is* a fire, a
world of [1]iniquity. The tongue is
so set among our members that it
[b]defiles the whole body, and sets
on fire the course of [2]nature; and
it is set on fire by [3]hell.
7 For every kind of beast and
bird, of reptile and creature of the
sea, is tamed and has been tamed
by mankind.
8 But no man can tame the
tongue. *It is* an unruly evil, [a]full
of deadly poison.
9 With it we bless our God and
Father, and with it we curse men,
who have been made [a]in the [1]simil-
itude of God.
10 Out of the same mouth proceed
blessing and cursing. My brethren,
these things ought not to be so.
11 Does a spring send forth fresh
water and bitter from the same
opening?
12 Can a [a]fig tree, my brethren,
bear olives, or a grapevine bear
figs? [1]Thus no spring yields both
salt water and fresh.

Heavenly Versus Demonic Wisdom

13 [a]Who *is* wise and understand-
ing among you? Let him show by
good conduct *that* his works *are
done* in the meekness of wisdom.
14 But if you have [a]bitter envy and
[1]self-seeking in your hearts, [b]do
not boast and lie against the truth.
15 [a]This wisdom does not descend
from above, but *is* earthly, sensual,
demonic.
16 For [a]where envy and self-
seeking *exist*, confusion and every
evil thing *are* there.
17 But [a]the wisdom that is from
above is first pure, then peaceable,
gentle, willing to yield, full of
mercy and good fruits, [b]without
partiality [c]and without hypocrisy.
18 [a]Now the fruit of righteousness
is sown in peace by those who
make peace.

Pride Promotes Strife

4 Where do [1]wars and fights
come from among you? Do
they not *come* from your *desires*

for pleasure [a]that war in your
members?
2 You lust and do not have. You
murder and covet and cannot ob-
tain. You fight and [1]war. [2]Yet you
do not have because you do not
ask.
3 [a]You ask and do not receive,
[b]because you ask amiss, that you
may spend *it* on your pleasures.
4 [1]Adulterers and adulteresses!
Do you not know that [a]friendship
with the world is enmity with God?
[b]Whoever therefore wants to be a
friend of the world makes himself
an enemy of God.
5 Or do you think that the Scrip-
ture says in vain, [a]"The Spirit who
dwells in us yearns jealously"?
6 But He gives more grace.
Therefore He says:

[a]"*God resists the proud,*
But gives grace to the humble."

Humility Cures Worldliness

7 Therefore submit to God. [a]Re-
sist the devil and he will flee from
you.
8 [a]Draw near to God and He will
draw near to you. [b]Cleanse *your*
hands, *you* sinners; and [c]purify
your hearts, *you* double-minded.
9 [a]Lament and mourn and weep!
Let your laughter be turned to
mourning and *your* joy to gloom.
10 [a]Humble yourselves in the
sight of the Lord, and He will lift
you up.

Do Not Judge a Brother

11 [a]Do not speak evil of one an-
other, brethren. He who speaks
evil of a brother [b]and judges his
brother, speaks evil of the law and
judges the law. But if you judge
the law, you are not a doer of the
law but a judge.
12 There is one [1]Lawgiver, [a]who
is able to save and to destroy.
[b]Who[2] are you to judge [3]another?

Do Not Boast About Tomorrow

13 Come now, you who say, "To-
day or tomorrow [1]we will go to
such and such a city, spend a year
there, buy and sell, and make a
profit";
14 whereas you do not know what
will happen tomorrow. For what *is*
your life? [a]It is even a vapor that
appears for a little time and then
vanishes away.
15 Instead you *ought* to say, [a]"If
the Lord wills, we shall live and
do this or that."
16 But now you boast in your ar-
rogance. [a]All such boasting is evil.
17 Therefore, [a]to him who knows
to do good and does not do *it*, to
him it is sin.

Rich Oppressors Will Be Judged

5 Come now, *you* [a]rich, weep
and howl for your miseries
that are coming upon *you!*
2 Your [a]riches [1]are corrupted,
and [b]your garments are moth-
eaten.
3 Your gold and silver are cor-
roded, and their corrosion will be
a witness against you and will eat
your flesh like fire. [a]You have
heaped up treasure in the last
days.
4 Indeed [a]the wages of the labor-
ers who mowed your fields, which
you kept back by fraud, cry out;
and [b]the cries of the reapers have
reached the ears of the Lord of
[1]Sabaoth.
5 You have lived on the earth in
pleasure and [1]luxury; you have
[2]fattened your hearts [3]as in a day
of slaughter.
6 You have condemned, you
have murdered the just; he does
not resist you.

Be Patient and Persevering

7 Therefore be patient, brethren,
until the coming of the Lord. See
how the farmer waits for the pre-
cious fruit of the earth, waiting pa-
tiently for it until it receives the
early and latter rain.
8 You also be patient. Establish
your hearts, for the coming of the
Lord [1]is at hand.
9 Do not [1]grumble against one
another, brethren, lest you be
[2]condemned. Behold, the Judge is
standing at the door!
10 [a]My brethren, take the proph-
ets, who spoke in the name of the
Lord, as an example of suffering
and [b]patience.
11 Indeed [a]we count them blessed
who [b]endure. You have heard of
[c]the perseverance of Job and seen
[d]the end *intended* by the Lord—

1 [a]Rom. 7:23
2 [1]*battle* [2]NU, M omit *Yet*
3 [a]Job 27:8, 9 [b][Ps. 66:18]
4 [a]1 John 2:15 [b]Gal. 1:4 [1]NU omits *Adulterers and*
5 [a]Gen. 6:5
6 [a]Prov. 3:34
7 [a][Eph. 4:27; 6:11]
8 [a]2 Chr. 15:2 [b]Is. 1:16 [c]1 Pet. 1:22
9 [a]Matt. 5:4
10 [a]Job 22:29
11 [a]1 Pet. 2:1–3 [b][Matt. 7:1–5]
12 [a][Matt. 10:28] [b]Rom. 14:4 [1]NU adds *and Judge* [2]NU, M *But who* [3]NU *a neighbor*
13 [1]M *let us*
14 [a]Job 7:7
15 [a]Acts 18:21
16 [a]1 Cor. 5:6
17 [a][Luke 12:47]

CHAPTER 5

1 [a][Luke 6:24]
2 [a]Matt. 6:19 [b]Job 13:28 [1]*have rotted*
3 [a]Rom. 2:5
4 [a]Lev. 19:13 [b]Deut. 24:15 [1]Lit., in Heb., *Hosts*
5 [1]*indulgence* [2]Lit. *nourished* [3]NU omits *as*
8 [1]*has drawn near*
9 [1]Lit. *groan* [2]NU, M *judged*
10 [a]Matt. 5:12 [b]Heb. 10:36
11 [a][Ps. 94:12] [b][James 1:12] [c]Job 1:21, 22; 2:10 [d]Job 42:10

that [e]the Lord is very compassion-
ate and merciful.
12 But above all, my brethren, [a]do
not swear, either by heaven or by
earth or with any other oath. But
let your "Yes" be "Yes," and *your*
"No," "No," lest you fall into
[1]judgment.

Meeting Specific Needs

13 Is anyone among you suffer-
ing? Let him [a]pray. Is anyone
cheerful? [b]Let him sing psalms.
14 Is anyone among you sick? Let
him call for the elders of the
church, and let them pray over
him, [a]anointing him with oil in the
name of the Lord.
15 And the prayer of faith will
save the sick, and the Lord will
raise him up. [a]And if he has com-
mitted sins, he will be forgiven.
16 [1]Confess *your* trespasses to one
another, and pray for one another,
that you may be healed. [a]The ef-
fective, [2]fervent prayer of a righ-
teous man avails much.
17 Elijah was a man [a]with a na-
ture like ours, and [b]he prayed ear-
nestly that it would not rain; and
it did not rain on the land for three
years and six months.
18 And he prayed [a]again, and the
heaven gave rain, and the earth
produced its fruit.

Bring Back the Erring One

19 Brethren, if anyone among you
wanders from the truth, and some-
one [a]turns him back,
20 let him know that he who turns
a sinner from the error of his way
[a]will save [1]a soul from death and
[b]cover a multitude of sins.

11 [e]Num. 14:18
12 [a]Matt. 5:34–37 [1]M *hypocrisy*
13 [a]Ps. 50:14, 15 [b]Eph. 5:19
14 [a]Mark 6:13; 16:18
15 [a]Is. 33:24
16 [a]Num. 11:2 [1]NU *Therefore confess your sins* [2]*supplication*
17 [a]Acts 14:15 [b]1 Kin. 17:1; 18:1
18 [a]1 Kin. 18:1, 42
19 [a]Matt. 18:15; Gal. 6:1
20 [a]Rom. 11:14; 1 Cor. 1:21; James 1:21 [b]Prov. 10:12; [1 Pet. 4:8] [1]NU *his soul*

The First Epistle of

Peter

PERSECUTION can cause either growth or bitterness in the Christian life. Response determines the result. In writing to Jewish believers struggling in the midst of persecution, Peter encourages them to conduct themselves courageously for the Person and program of Christ. Both their character and conduct must be above reproach. Having been born again to a living hope, they are to imitate the Holy One who has called them. The fruit of that character will be conduct rooted in submission: citizens to government, servants to masters, wives to husbands, husbands to wives, and Christians to one another. Only after submission is fully understood does Peter deal with the difficult area of suffering. The Christians are not to "think it strange concerning the fiery trial which is to try you, as though some strange thing happened to you" (4:12), but are to rejoice as partakers of the suffering of Christ. That response to life is truly the climax of one's submission to the good hand of God.

This epistle begins with the phrase *Petros apostolos Iesou Christou,* "Peter, an apostle of Jesus Christ." This is the basis of the early title *Petrou A,* the "First of Peter."

Greeting to the Elect Pilgrims

PETER, an apostle of Jesus
Christ,

To the [1]pilgrims [a]of the Disper-
sion in Pontus, Galatia, Cappado-
cia, Asia, and Bithynia,
2 [a]elect [b]according to the fore-
knowledge of God the Father, [c]in
sanctification of the Spirit, for
[d]obedience and [e]sprinkling of the
blood of Jesus Christ:

[f]Grace to you and peace be
multiplied.

A Heavenly Inheritance

3 [a]Blessed *be* the God and Father
of our Lord Jesus Christ, who [b]ac-
cording to His abundant mercy
[c]has begotten us again to a living
hope [d]through the resurrection of
Jesus Christ from the dead,
4 to an inheritance [1]incorruptible
and undefiled and that does not
fade away, [a]reserved in heaven for
you,
5 [a]who are kept by the power of
God through faith for salvation
ready to be revealed in the last
time.
6 [a]In this you greatly rejoice,
though now [b]for a little while, if

CHAPTER 1

1 [a]John 7:35; James 1:1 [1]*sojourners,* temporary residents

2 [a]Eph. 1:4 [b][Rom. 8:29]; 1 Pet. 1:20 [c]2 Thess. 2:13 [d]Rom. 1:5 [e]Is. 52:15; Heb. 10:22; 12:24 [f]Rom. 1:7

3 [a]Eph. 1:3 [b]Gal. 6:16; Titus 3:5 [c][John 3:3, 5] [d]1 Cor. 15:20; 1 Pet. 3:21

4 [a]Col. 1:5 [1]*imperishable*

5 [a]John 10:28; [Phil. 4:7]

6 [a]Matt. 5:12 [b]2 Cor. 4:17 [c]James 1:2; 1 Pet. 4:12 [1]*distressed*

7 [a]James 1:3 [b]Job 23:10 [c][Rom. 2:7]

8 [a]1 John 4:20 [b]John 20:29 [1]M *known*

11 [a]2 Pet. 1:21

12 [a]Eph. 3:10 [1]NU, M *you*

need be, [c]you have been [1]grieved
by various trials,
7 that [a]the genuineness of your
faith, *being* much more precious
than gold that perishes, though [b]it
is tested by fire, [c]may be found to
praise, honor, and glory at the rev-
elation of Jesus Christ,
8 [a]whom having not [1]seen you
love. [b]Though now you do not see
Him, yet believing, you rejoice
with joy inexpressible and full of
glory,
9 receiving the end of your
faith—the salvation of *your* souls.
10 Of this salvation the prophets
have inquired and searched care-
fully, who prophesied of the grace
that would come to you,
11 searching what, or what man-
ner of time, [a]the Spirit of Christ
who was in them was indicating
when He testified beforehand the
sufferings of Christ and the glories
that would follow.
12 To them it was revealed that,
not to themselves, but to [1]us they
were ministering the things which
now have been reported to you
through those who have preached
the gospel to you by the Holy
Spirit sent from heaven—things
which [a]angels desire to look into.

Living Before God Our Father

13 Therefore gird up the loins of
your mind, be sober, and rest *your*
hope fully upon the grace that is
to be brought to you at the revela-
tion of Jesus Christ;
14 as obedient children, not [a]con-
forming yourselves to the former
lusts, *as* in your ignorance;
15 [a]but as He who called you *is*
holy, you also be holy in all *your*
conduct,
16 because it is written, [a]*"Be holy,*
for I am holy."
17 And if you call on the Father,
who [a]without partiality judges ac-
cording to each one's work, con-
duct yourselves throughout the
time of your [1]stay *here* in fear;
18 knowing that you were not re-
deemed with [1]corruptible things,
like silver or gold, from your aim-
less conduct *received* by tradition
from your fathers,
19 but [a]with the precious blood of
Christ, [b]as of a lamb without blem-
ish and without spot.
20 [a]He indeed was foreordained
before the foundation of the world,
but was [1]manifest [b]in these last
times for you
21 who through Him believe in
God, [a]who raised Him from the
dead and [b]gave Him glory, so that
your faith and hope are in God.

The Enduring Word

22 Since you [a]have purified your
souls in obeying the truth [1]through
the Spirit in [2]sincere [b]love of the
brethren, love one another fer-
vently with a pure heart,
23 [a]having been born again, not of
[1]corruptible seed but [2]incorrupt-
ible, [b]through the word of God
which lives and abides [3]forever,
24 because

[a]*"All flesh is as grass,*
And all [1]the glory of man as the
flower of the grass.
The grass withers,
And its flower falls away,
25 [a]*But the [1]word of the LORD*
endures forever."

[b]Now this is the word which by the
gospel was preached to you.

2 Therefore, [a]laying aside all
malice, all deceit, hypocrisy,
envy, and all evil speaking,
2 [a]as newborn babes, desire the
pure [b]milk of the word, that you
may grow [1]thereby,
3 if indeed you have [a]tasted that
the Lord *is* gracious.

The Chosen Stone and His Chosen People

4 Coming to Him *as to* a living
stone, [a]rejected indeed by men, but
chosen by God *and* precious,
5 you also, as living stones, are
being built up a spiritual house, a
holy priesthood, to offer up spiri-
tual sacrifices acceptable to God
through Jesus Christ.
6 Therefore it is also contained
in the Scripture,

[a]*"Behold, I lay in Zion*
A chief cornerstone, elect,
precious,
And he who believes on Him will
by no means be put to shame."

7 Therefore, to you who believe,
He is precious; but to those who
[1]are disobedient,

[a]*"The stone which the builders*
rejected
Has become the chief
cornerstone,"

8 and

[a]*"A stone of stumbling*
And a rock of offense."

[b]They stumble, being disobedient
to the word, [c]to which they also
were appointed.
9 But you *are* a chosen genera-
tion, a royal priesthood, a holy na-
tion, His own special people, that
you may proclaim the praises of
Him who called you out of [a]dark-
ness into His marvelous light;
10 [a]who once *were* not a people
but *are* now the people of God,
who had not obtained mercy but
now have obtained mercy.

Living Before the World

11 Beloved, I beg *you* as sojourn-
ers and pilgrims, abstain from
fleshly lusts [a]which war against
the soul,
12 [a]having your conduct honor-
able among the Gentiles, that
when they speak against you as
evildoers, [b]they may, by *your*

14 [a][Rom. 12:2]
15 [a][2 Cor. 7:1]
16 [a]Lev. 11:44, 45; 19:2; 20:7
17 [a]Acts 10:34 [1]*sojourning, dwelling* as resident aliens
18 [1]*perishable*
19 [a]Acts 20:28 [b]Ex. 12:5
20 [a]Rom. 3:25 [b]Gal. 4:4 [1]*revealed*
21 [a]Acts 2:24 [b]Acts 2:33
22 [a]Acts 15:9 [b]Heb. 13:1 [1]NU omits *through the Spirit* [2]Lit. *unhypocritical*
23 [a]John 1:13 [b]James 1:18 [1]*perishable* [2]*imperishable* [3]NU omits *forever*
24 [a]Is. 40:6–8 [1]NU *its glory as*
25 [a]Is. 40:8 [b][John 1:1] [1]*spoken word*

CHAPTER 2

1 [a]Heb. 12:1
2 [a][Matt. 18:3; 19:14] [b]1 Cor. 3:2 [1]NU adds *up to salvation*
3 [a]Heb. 6:5
4 [a]Ps. 118:22
6 [a]Is. 28:16
7 [a]Ps. 118:22 [1]NU *disbelieve*
8 [a]Is. 8:14 [b]1 Cor. 1:23 [c]Rom. 9:22
9 [a][Acts 26:18]
10 [a]Hos. 1:9, 10; 2:23
11 [a]James 4:1
12 [a]Phil. 2:15 [b]Matt. 5:16; 9:8

good works which they observe,
glorify God in the day of visitation.

Submission to Government

13 [a]Therefore submit yourselves
to every [1]ordinance of man for the
Lord's sake, whether to the king
as supreme,
14 or to governors, as to those
who are sent by him for the punishment
of evildoers and *for the*
praise of those who do good.
15 For this is the will of God, that
by doing good you may put to silence
the ignorance of foolish
men—
16 [a]as free, yet not [b]using liberty
as a cloak for [1]vice, but as bondservants
of God.
17 Honor all *people.* Love the
brotherhood. Fear [a]God. Honor
the king.

Submission to Masters

18 [a]Servants, *be* submissive to
your masters with all fear, not only
to the good and gentle, but also to
the harsh.
19 For this *is* [a]commendable, if because
of conscience toward God
one endures grief, suffering
wrongfully.
20 For [a]what credit *is it* if, when
you are beaten for your faults, you
take it patiently? But when you do
good and suffer, if you take it patiently,
this *is* commendable before
God.
21 For [a]to this you were called, because
Christ also suffered for [1]us,
[b]leaving [2]us an example, that you
should follow His steps:

22 *"Who[a] committed no sin,*
Nor was deceit found in His
mouth";

23 [a]who, when He was reviled, did
not revile in return; when He suffered,
He did not threaten, but
[b]committed *Himself* to Him who
judges righteously;
24 [a]who Himself bore our sins in
His own body on the tree, [b]that we,
having died to sins, might live for
righteousness—[c]by whose [1]stripes
you were healed.
25 For [a]you were like sheep going
astray, but have now returned [b]to

13 [a]Matt. 22:21 [1]*institution*
16 [a]Rom. 6:14, 20, 22; 1 Cor. 7:22; [Gal. 5:1] [b]Gal. 5:13 [1]*wickedness*
17 [a]Prov. 24:21
18 [a]Eph. 6:5–8
19 [a]Matt. 5:10
20 [a]Luke 6:32–34
21 [a]Matt. 16:24; 1 Thess. 3:3, 4 [b][1 John 2:6] [1]NU *you* [2]NU, M *you*
22 [a]Is. 53:9; 2 Cor. 5:21
23 [a]Is. 53:7; Heb. 12:3; 1 Pet. 3:9 [b]Luke 23:46
24 [a]Is. 53:4, 11; 1 Cor. 15:3; [Heb. 9:28] [b]Rom. 7:6 [c]Is. 53:5 [1]*wounds*
25 [a]Is. 53:5, 6 [b]Is. 40:11; [Ezek. 34:23]; Zech. 13:7 [1]Gr. *Episkopos*

CHAPTER 3

1 [a]Gen. 3:16; 1 Cor. 14:34; Eph. 5:22; Col. 3:18 [b]1 Cor. 7:16 [c]Matt. 18:15
2 [a]1 Pet. 2:12; 3:6
3 [a]Is. 3:18; 1 Tim. 2:9
4 [a]Rom. 2:29 [1]*imperishable*
6 [a]Gen. 18:12
7 [a]1 Cor. 7:3; [Eph. 5:25]; Col. 3:19 [b]1 Cor. 12:23 [c]Job 42:8
8 [1]NU *humble*
9 [a][Prov. 17:13] [b]Matt. 5:44 [c]Matt. 25:34
10 [a]Ps. 34:12–16 [b]James 1:26 [1]*restrain*
11 [a]Ps. 37:27

the Shepherd and [1]Overseer of
your souls.

Submission to Husbands

3 Wives, likewise, *be* [a]submissive
to your own husbands,
that even if some do not obey the
word, [b]they, without a word, may
[c]be won by the conduct of their
wives,
2 [a]when they observe your
chaste conduct *accompanied* by
fear.
3 [a]Do not let your adornment be
merely outward—arranging the
hair, wearing gold, or putting on
fine apparel—
4 rather *let it be* [a]the hidden person
of the heart, with the [1]incorruptible
beauty of a gentle and
quiet spirit, which is very precious
in the sight of God.
5 For in this manner, in former
times, the holy women who trusted
in God also adorned themselves,
being submissive to their own husbands,
6 as Sarah obeyed Abraham,
[a]calling him lord, whose daughters
you are if you do good and are not
afraid with any terror.

A Word to Husbands

7 [a]Husbands, likewise, dwell
with *them* with understanding,
giving honor to the wife, [b]as to the
weaker vessel, and as *being* heirs
together of the grace of life, [c]that
your prayers may not be hindered.

Called to Blessing

8 Finally, all *of you be* of one
mind, having compassion for one
another; love as brothers, *be*
tenderhearted, *be* [1]courteous;
9 [a]not returning evil for evil or
reviling for reviling, but on the
contrary [b]blessing, knowing that
you were called to this, [c]that you
may inherit a blessing.
10 For

[a]*"He who would love life*
And see good days,
[b]*Let him* [1]*refrain his tongue from evil,*
And his lips from speaking deceit.
11 *Let him* [a]*turn away from evil and*
do good;

[b]Let him seek peace and pursue it.
12 *For the eyes of the LORD are on the righteous,*
[a]And His ears are open to their prayers;
But the face of the LORD is against those who do evil."

Suffering for Right and Wrong

13 [a]And who *is* he who will harm
you if you become followers of
what is good?
14 [a]But even if you should suffer
for righteousness' sake, *you are*
blessed. [b]*"And do not be afraid of*
their threats, nor be troubled."
15 But [1]sanctify [2]the Lord God in
your hearts, and always [a]*be* ready
to *give* a defense to everyone who
asks you a reason for the [b]hope
that is in you, with meekness and
fear;
16 [a]having a good conscience, that
when they defame you as evil-
doers, those who revile your
good conduct in Christ may be
ashamed.
17 For *it is* better, if it is the will
of God, to suffer for doing good
than for doing evil.

Christ's Suffering and Ours

18 For Christ also suffered once
for sins, the just for the unjust, that
He might bring [1]us to God, being
put to death in the flesh but made
alive by the Spirit,
19 by whom also He went and
preached to the spirits in prison,
20 who formerly were disobedi-
ent, [1]when once the Divine long-
suffering waited in the days of
Noah, while *the* ark was being
prepared, in which a few, that is,
eight souls, were saved through
water.
21 [a]There is also an antitype
which now saves us—baptism
[b](not the removal of the filth of the
flesh, [c]but the answer of a good
conscience toward God), through
the resurrection of Jesus Christ,
22 who has gone into heaven and
[a]is at the right hand of God, [b]an-
gels and authorities and powers
having been made subject to Him.

4 Therefore, since Christ suf-
fered [1]for us in the flesh, arm
yourselves also with the same
mind, for he who has suffered in
the flesh has ceased from sin,
2 that he no longer should live
the rest of *his* time in the flesh for
the lusts of men, [a]but for the will
of God.
3 For we *have spent* enough of
our past [1]lifetime in doing the will
of the Gentiles—when we walked
in lewdness, lusts, drunkenness,
revelries, drinking parties, and
abominable idolatries.
4 In regard to these, they think
it strange that you do not run with
them in the same flood of dissipa-
tion, speaking evil of *you.*
5 They will give an account to
Him who is ready [a]to judge the liv-
ing and the dead.
6 For this reason [a]the gospel was
preached also to those who are
dead, that they might be judged ac-
cording to men in the flesh, but
[b]live according to God in the spirit.

Serving for God's Glory

7 But [a]the end of all things is at
hand; therefore be serious and
watchful in your prayers.
8 And above all things have fer-
vent love for one another, for
[a]*"love will cover a multitude of*
sins."
9 [a]*Be* hospitable to one another
[b]without grumbling.
10 [a]As each one has received a
gift, minister it to one another, [b]as
good stewards of [c]the manifold
grace of God.
11 [a]If anyone speaks, *let him*
speak as the [1]oracles of God. If
anyone ministers, *let him do it* as
with the ability which God sup-
plies, that [b]in all things God may
be glorified through Jesus Christ,
to whom belong the glory and
the [2]dominion forever and ever.
Amen.

Suffering for God's Glory

12 Beloved, do not think it strange
concerning the fiery trial which is
to try you, as though some strange
thing happened to you;
13 but rejoice [a]to the extent that
you partake of Christ's sufferings,
that [b]when His glory is revealed,
you may also be glad with exceed-
ing joy.
14 If you are [1]reproached for the
name of Christ, [a]blessed *are you,*

11 [b]Rom. 12:18
12 [a]John 9:31
13 [a]Prov. 16:7
14 [a]James 1:12 [b]Is. 8:12
15 [a]Ps. 119:46 [b][Titus 3:7] [1]*set apart* [2]NU *Christ as Lord*
16 [a]1 Tim. 1:5; Heb. 13:18; 1 Pet. 3:21
18 [1]NU, M *you*
20 [1]NU, M *when the longsuffering of God waited patiently*
21 [a]Acts 16:33; Eph. 5:26 [b][Titus 3:5] [c][Rom. 10:10]
22 [a]Ps. 110:1 [b]Rom. 8:38; Heb. 1:6

CHAPTER 4

1 [1]NU omits *for us*
2 [a]John 1:13
3 [1]NU *time*
5 [a]Acts 10:42; Rom. 14:9; 2 Tim. 4:1
6 [a]1 Pet. 1:12; 3:19 [b][Rom. 8:9, 13]; Gal. 5:25
7 [a]Rom. 13:11; Heb. 9:26; James 5:8, 9; 1 John 2:18
8 [a][Prov. 10:12]; 1 Cor. 13:4; James 5:20
9 [a]1 Tim. 3:2; Heb. 13:2 [b]2 Cor. 9:7
10 [a]Rom. 12:6–8 [b]Matt. 24:45; 1 Cor. 4:1, 2 [c][1 Cor. 12:4]
11 [a]Eph. 4:29 [b][1 Cor. 10:31]; Eph. 5:20 [1]*utterances* [2]*sovereignty*
13 [a]James 1:2 [b]2 Tim. 2:12
14 [a]Matt. 5:11; Luke 6:22; Acts 5:41 [1]*insulted* or *reviled*

for the Spirit of glory and of God
rests upon you. [2]On their part He
is blasphemed, [b]but on your part
He is glorified.
15 But let none of you suffer as a
murderer, a thief, an evildoer, or
as a [1]busybody in other people's
matters.
16 Yet if *anyone suffers* as a Chris-
tian, let him not be ashamed, but
let him glorify God in this [1]matter.
17 For the time *has come* [a]for
judgment to begin at the house of
God; and if *it begins* with us first,
[b]what will *be* the end of those who
do not obey the gospel of God?
18 Now

> [a]*"If the righteous one is scarcely*
> *saved,*
> *Where will the ungodly and the*
> *sinner appear?"*

19 Therefore let those who suffer
according to the will of God
[a]commit their souls *to Him* in do-
ing good, as to a faithful Creator.

Shepherd the Flock

5 The elders who are among you
I exhort, I who am a fellow
elder and a [a]witness of the suffer-
ings of Christ, and also a partaker
of the [b]glory that will be revealed:
2 [a]Shepherd the flock of God
which is among you, serving as
overseers, [b]not by compulsion but
[1]willingly, [c]not for dishonest gain
but eagerly;
3 nor as [a]being [1]lords over [b]those
entrusted to you, but [c]being exam-
ples to the flock;
4 and when [a]the Chief Shepherd
appears, you will receive [b]the
crown of glory that does not fade
away.

Submit to God, Resist the Devil

5 Likewise you younger people,
submit yourselves to *your* elders.
Yes, [a]all of *you* be submissive to
one another, and be clothed with
humility, for

> [b]*"God resists the proud,*
> *But* [c]*gives grace to the humble."*

6 Therefore humble yourselves
under the mighty hand of God,
that He may exalt you in due time,
7 casting all your care upon Him,
for He cares for you.
8 Be [1]sober, be [2]vigilant; [3]be-
cause your adversary the devil
walks about like a roaring lion,
seeking whom he may devour.
9 Resist him, steadfast in the
faith, knowing that the same suf-
ferings are experienced by your
brotherhood in the world.
10 But [1]may the God of all grace,
[a]who called [2]us to His eternal
glory by Christ Jesus, after you
have suffered a while, [3]perfect,
establish, strengthen, and settle
you.
11 [a]To Him *be* the glory and the
dominion forever and ever. Amen.

Farewell and Peace

12 By [a]Silvanus, our faithful
brother as I consider him, I have
written to you briefly, exhort-
ing and testifying [b]that this is the
true grace of God in which you
stand.
13 She who is in Babylon, elect to-
gether with *you*, greets you; and
so does [a]Mark my son.
14 Greet one another with a kiss
of love. Peace to you all who are
in Christ Jesus. Amen.

---

14 [b]Matt. 5:16 [2]NU omits the rest of v. 14.
15 [1]*meddler*
16 [1]NU *name*
17 [a]Is. 10:12 [b]Luke 10:12
18 [a]Prov. 11:31
19 [a]2 Tim. 1:12

CHAPTER 5

1 [a]Matt. 26:37 [b]Rom. 8:17, 18
2 [a]Acts 20:28 [b]1 Cor. 9:17 [c]1 Tim. 3:3 [1]NU adds *according to God*
3 [a]Ezek. 34:4 [b]Ps. 33:12 [c]Phil. 3:17 [1]*masters*
4 [a]Heb. 13:20 [b]2 Tim. 4:8
5 [a]Eph. 5:21 [b]Prov. 3:34 [c]Is. 57:15
8 [1]*self-controlled* [2]*watchful* [3]NU, M omit *because*
10 [a]1 Cor. 1:9 [1]NU *the God of all grace,* [2]NU, M *you* [3]NU *will perfect*
11 [a]Rev. 1:6
12 [a]2 Cor. 1:19 [b]Acts 20:24
13 [a]Acts 12:12, 25; 15:37, 39

The Second Epistle of

Peter

FIRST Peter deals with problems from the outside; Second Peter deals with problems from the inside. Peter writes to warn the believers about the false teachers who are peddling damaging doctrine. He begins by urging them to keep close watch on their personal lives. The Christian life demands diligence in pursuing moral excellence, knowledge, self-control, perseverance, godliness, brotherly kindness, and selfless love. By contrast, the false teachers are sensual, arrogant, greedy, and covetous. They scoff at the thought of future judgment and live their lives as if the present would be the pattern for the future. Peter reminds them that although God may be longsuffering in sending judgment, ultimately it will come. In view of that fact, believers should live lives of godliness, blamelessness, and steadfastness.

The statement of authorship in 1:1 is very clear: "Simon Peter, a bondservant and apostle of Jesus Christ." To distinguish this epistle from the first by Peter it was given the Greek title *Petrou B,* the "Second of Peter."

Greeting the Faithful

SIMON Peter, a bondservant
and [a]apostle of Jesus Christ,
To those who have [1]obtained
[b]like[2] precious faith with us by the
righteousness of our God and Savior Jesus Christ:
2 [a]Grace and peace be multiplied
to you in the knowledge of God
and of Jesus our Lord,
3 as His [a]divine power has given
to us all things that *pertain* to life
and godliness, through the knowledge of Him [b]who called us by
glory and virtue,
4 [a]by which have been given to
us exceedingly great and precious
promises, that through these you
may be [b]partakers of the divine
nature, having escaped the [1]corruption *that is* in the world
through lust.

Fruitful Growth in the Faith

5 But also for this very reason,
[a]giving all diligence, add to your
faith virtue, to virtue [b]knowledge,
6 to knowledge self-control, to
self-control [1]perseverance, to perseverance godliness,
7 to godliness brotherly kindness, and [a]to brotherly kindness
love.
8 For if these things are yours
and abound, *you will be* neither
[1]barren [a]nor unfruitful in the
knowledge of our Lord Jesus
Christ.
9 For he who lacks these things
is [a]shortsighted, even to blindness,
and has forgotten that he was
cleansed from his old sins.
10 Therefore, brethren, be even
more diligent [a]to make your call
and election sure, for if you do
these things you will never stumble;
11 for so an entrance will be supplied to you abundantly into the
everlasting kingdom of our Lord
and Savior Jesus Christ.

Peter's Approaching Death

12 For this reason [a]I will not be
negligent to remind you always of
these things, [b]though you know
and are established in the present
truth.
13 Yes, I think it is right, [a]as long
as I am in this [1]tent, [b]to stir you
up by reminding *you,*
14 [a]knowing that shortly I *must*
[1]put off my tent, just as [b]our Lord
Jesus Christ showed me.
15 Moreover I will be careful to
ensure that you always have a reminder of these things after my
[1]decease.

CHAPTER 1

1 [a]Gal. 2:8 [b]Eph. 4:5 [1]*received* [2]*faith of the same value*
2 [a]Dan. 4:1
3 [a]1 Pet. 1:5 [b]1 Thess. 2:12; 2 Thess. 2:14; 1 Pet. 5:10
4 [a]2 Cor. 1:20; 7:1 [b][2 Cor. 3:18] [1]*depravity*
5 [a]2 Pet. 3:18 [b]2 Pet. 1:2
6 [1]*patience*
7 [a]Gal. 6:10
8 [a][John 15:2] [1]*useless*
9 [a]1 John 2:9–11
10 [a]2 Cor. 13:5; 1 John 3:19
12 [a]Phil. 3:1; 1 John 2:21; Jude 5 [b]1 Pet. 5:12
13 [a][2 Cor. 5:1, 4]; 2 Pet. 1:14 [b]2 Pet. 3:1 [1]Body
14 [a][2 Cor. 5:1; 2 Tim. 4:6] [b]John 13:36; 21:18, 19 [1]Die and leave this body
15 [1]Lit. *exodus, departure*

The Trustworthy Prophetic Word

16 For we did not follow [a]cun-
ningly devised fables when we
made known to you the [b]power
and [c]coming of our Lord Jesus
Christ, but were [d]eyewitnesses of
His majesty.
17 For He received from God the
Father honor and glory when such
a voice came to Him from the Ex-
cellent Glory: [a]"This is My beloved
Son, in whom I am well pleased."
18 And we heard this voice which
came from heaven when we were
with Him on [a]the holy mountain.
19 [1]And so we have the prophetic
word confirmed, which you do
well to heed as a [a]light that shines
in a dark place, [b]until [c]the day
dawns and the morning star rises
in your [d]hearts;
20 knowing this first, that [a]no
prophecy of Scripture is of any pri-
vate [1]interpretation,
21 for [a]prophecy never came by
the will of man, [b]but [1]holy men of
God spoke *as they were* moved by
the Holy Spirit.

Destructive Doctrines

2 But there were also false
prophets among the people,
even as there will be [a]false teach-
ers among you, who will secretly
bring in destructive heresies, even
denying the Lord who bought
them, *and* bring on themselves
swift destruction.
2 And many will follow their de-
structive ways, because of whom
the way of truth will be blas-
phemed.
3 By covetousness they will ex-
ploit you with deceptive words; for
a long time their judgment has not
been idle, and their destruction
[1]does not slumber.

Doom of False Teachers

4 For if God did not spare the an-
gels who sinned, but cast *them*
down to [1]hell and delivered *them*
into chains of darkness, to be re-
served for judgment;
5 and did not spare the ancient
world, but saved Noah, *one of*
eight *people*, a preacher of righ-
teousness, bringing in the flood on
the world of the ungodly;
6 and turning the cities of
[a]Sodom and Gomorrah into ashes,
condemned *them* to destruction,
making *them* an example to those
who afterward would live un-
godly;
7 and [a]delivered righteous Lot,
who was oppressed by the filthy
conduct of the wicked
8 (for that righteous man, dwell-
ing among them, [a]tormented *his*
righteous soul from day to day by
seeing and hearing *their* lawless
deeds)—
9 *then* [a]the Lord knows how to
deliver the godly out of tempta-
tions and to reserve the unjust un-
der punishment for the day of
judgment,
10 and especially [a]those who walk
according to the flesh in the lust
of uncleanness and despise au-
thority. [b]*They are* presumptuous,
self-willed. They are not afraid to
speak evil of [1]dignitaries,
11 whereas [a]angels, who are
greater in power and might, do not
bring a reviling accusation against
them before the Lord.

Depravity of False Teachers

12 But these, [a]like natural brute
beasts made to be caught and de-
stroyed, speak evil of the things
they do not understand, and will
utterly perish in their own cor-
ruption,
13 [a]*and* will receive the wages of
unrighteousness, *as* those who
count it pleasure [b]to [1]carouse in
the daytime. [c]*They are* spots and
blemishes, [2]carousing in their own
deceptions while [d]they feast with
you,
14 having eyes full of [1]adultery
and that cannot cease from sin, en-
ticing unstable souls. [a]*They have*
a heart trained in covetous prac-
tices, *and are* accursed children.
15 They have forsaken the right
way and gone astray, following
the way of [a]Balaam the *son* of
Beor, who loved the wages of un-
righteousness;
16 but he was rebuked for his in-
iquity: a dumb donkey speaking
with a man's voice restrained the
madness of the prophet.
17 [a]These are wells without water,
[1]clouds carried by a tempest, for
whom is reserved the blackness of
darkness [2]forever.

16 [a]1 Cor. 1:17 [b][Matt. 28:18; Eph. 1:19–22] [c][1 Pet. 5:4] [d]Matt. 17:1–5; Luke 1:2
17 [a]Ps. 2:7; Is. 42:1; Matt. 17:5; Mark 9:7; Luke 1:35; 9:35
18 [a]Matt. 17:1
19 [a][John 1:4, 5, 9] [b]Prov. 4:18 [c]Rev. 2:28; 22:16 [d][2 Cor. 4:5–7] [1]Or *We also have the more sure prophetic word*
20 [a][Rom. 12:6] [1]Or *origin*
21 [a]Jer. 23:26; [2 Tim. 3:16] [b]2 Sam. 23:2; Luke 1:70; Acts 1:16; 3:18; 1 Pet. 1:11 [1]NU *men spoke from God*

CHAPTER 2

1 [a]Matt. 24:5, 24; 1 Tim. 4:1, 2
3 [1]M *will not*
4 [1]Lit. *Tartarus*
6 [a]Gen. 19:1–26; Jude 7
7 [a]Gen. 19:16, 29
8 [a]Ps. 119:139
9 [a]Ps. 34:15–19; 1 Cor. 10:13; Rev. 3:10
10 [a]Jude 4, 7, 8 [b]Ex. 22:28; Jude 8 [1]*glorious ones*, lit. *glories*
11 [a]Jude 9
12 [a]Jude 10
13 [a]Phil. 3:19 [b]Rom. 13:13 [c]Jude 12 [d]1 Cor. 11:20, 21 [1]*revel* [2]*reveling*
14 [a]Jude 11 [1]Lit. *an adulteress*
15 [a]Num. 22:5, 7; Deut. 23:4; Neh. 13:2; Jude 11; Rev. 2:14
17 [a]Jude 12, 13 [1]NU *and mists* [2]NU omits *forever*

Deceptions of False Teachers

18 For when they speak great
swelling *words* of emptiness, they
allure through the lusts of the
flesh, through lewdness, the ones
who [1]have actually escaped from
those who live in error.
19 While they promise them lib-
erty, they themselves are slaves of
[1]corruption; [a]for by whom a per-
son is overcome, by him also he
is brought into [2]bondage.
20 For if, after they [a]have escaped
the pollutions of the world through
the knowledge of the Lord and
Savior Jesus Christ, they are
[b]again entangled in them and over-
come, the latter end is worse for
them than the beginning.
21 For [a]it would have been better
for them not to have known the
way of righteousness, than having
known *it*, to turn from the holy
commandment delivered to
them.
22 But it has happened to them ac-
cording to the true proverb: [a]*"A
dog returns to his own vomit,"*
and, "a sow, having washed, to her
wallowing in the mire."

God's Promise Is Not Slack

3 Beloved, I now write to you
this second epistle (in *both of*
which [a]I stir up your pure minds
by way of reminder),
2 that you may be mindful of the
words [a]which were spoken before
by the holy prophets, [b]and of the
commandment of [1]us, the apostles
of the Lord and Savior,
3 knowing this first: that scoffers
will come in the last days, [a]walk-
ing according to their own lusts,
4 and saying, "Where is the
promise of His coming? For since
the fathers fell asleep, all things
continue as *they were* from the be-
ginning of [a]creation."
5 For this they willfully forget:
that [a]by the word of God the heav-
ens were of old, and the earth
[b]standing out of water and in the
water,
6 [a]by which the world *that* then
existed perished, being flooded
with water.
7 But [a]the heavens and the earth
which are now preserved by the
same word, are reserved for [b]fire

18 [1]NU *are barely escaping*
19 [a]John 8:34 [1]*depravity* [2]*slavery*
20 [a]Matt. 12:45 [b][Heb. 6:4–6]
21 [a]Luke 12:47
22 [a]Prov. 26:11

CHAPTER 3

1 [a]2 Pet. 1:13
2 [a]2 Pet. 1:21 [b]Jude 17 [1]NU, M *the apostles of your Lord and Savior* or *your apostles of the Lord and Savior*
3 [a]2 Pet. 2:10
4 [a]Gen. 6:1–7
5 [a]Gen. 1:6, 9 [b]Ps. 24:2; 136:6
6 [a]Gen. 7:11, 12, 21–23
7 [a]2 Pet. 3:10, 12 [b][2 Thess. 1:8] [1]*destruction*
8 [a]Ps. 90:4
9 [a]Hab. 2:3 [b]Is. 30:18 [c]Ezek. 33:11 [d][Rom. 2:4] [1]NU *you*
10 [a]Rev. 3:3; 16:15 [b]Ps. 102:25, 26 [1]NU *laid bare*, lit. *found*
11 [a]1 Pet. 1:15
12 [a]1 Cor. 1:7, 8 [b]Ps. 50:3 [c]Mic. 1:4
13 [a]Is. 65:17; 66:22 [b]Rev. 21:1
14 [a]1 Cor. 1:8; 15:58
15 [a]Rom. 2:4
16 [a]1 Cor. 15:24 [b]2 Tim. 3:16
17 [a]Mark 13:23 [b]Eph. 4:14
18 [a]Eph. 4:15 [b]2 Tim. 4:18

until the day of judgment and
[1]perdition of ungodly men.
8 But, beloved, do not forget this
one thing, that with the Lord one
day *is* as a thousand years, and [a]a
thousand years as one day.
9 [a]The Lord is not slack concern-
ing *His* promise, as some count
slackness, but [b]is longsuffering to-
ward [1]us, [c]not willing that any
should perish but [d]that all should
come to repentance.

The Day of the Lord

10 But [a]the day of the Lord will
come as a thief in the night, in
which [b]the heavens will pass away
with a great noise, and the ele-
ments will melt with fervent heat;
both the earth and the works that
are in it will be [1]burned up.
11 Therefore, since all these
things will be dissolved, what
manner *of persons* ought you to be
[a]in holy conduct and godliness,
12 [a]looking for and hastening the
coming of the day of God, because
of which the heavens will [b]be dis-
solved, being on fire, and the ele-
ments will [c]melt with fervent heat?
13 Nevertheless we, according to
His promise, look for [a]new heav-
ens and a [b]new earth in which
righteousness dwells.

Be Steadfast

14 Therefore, beloved, looking
forward to these things, be diligent
[a]to be found by Him in peace,
without spot and blameless;
15 and consider *that* [a]the long-
suffering of our Lord *is* salva-
tion—as also our beloved brother
Paul, according to the wisdom
given to him, has written to you,
16 as also in all his [a]epistles,
speaking in them of these things,
in which are some things hard to
understand, which untaught and
unstable *people* twist to their own
destruction, as *they do* also the
[b]rest of the Scriptures.
17 You therefore, beloved, [a]since
you know *this* beforehand, [b]be-
ware lest you also fall from your
own steadfastness, being led away
with the error of the wicked;
18 [a]but grow in the grace and
knowledge of our Lord and Savior
Jesus Christ. [b]To Him *be* the glory
both now and forever. Amen.

The First Epistle of

John

GOD is light; God is love; and God is life. John is enjoying a delightful fellowship with that God of light, love, and life, and he desperately desires that his spiritual children enjoy the same fellowship.

God is light. Therefore, to engage in fellowship with Him we must walk in light and not in darkness. As we walk in the light, we will regularly confess our sins, allowing the blood of Christ to continually cleanse us. Two major roadblocks to hinder this walk will be falling in love with the world and falling for the alluring lies of false teachers.

God is love. Since we are His children we must walk in love. In fact, John says that if we do not love, we do not know God. Love is more than just words; it is actions. Love is giving, not getting. Biblical love is unconditional in its nature. Christ's love fulfilled those qualities and when that brand of love characterizes us, we will be free of self-condemnation and experience confidence before God.

God is life. Those who fellowship with Him must possess His quality of life. Spiritual life begins with spiritual birth which occurs through faith in Jesus Christ. Faith in Jesus Christ infuses us with God's life—eternal life.

Although the apostle John's name is not found in this book, it was given the title *Ioannou A,* the "First of John."

What Was Heard, Seen, and Touched

THAT [a]which was from the be-
ginning, which we have heard,
which we have [b]seen with our
eyes, [c]which we have looked upon,
and [d]our hands have handled, con-
cerning the [e]Word of life—
2 [a]the life [b]was manifested, and
we have seen, [c]and bear witness,
and declare to you that eternal life
which was [d]with the Father and
was manifested to us—
3 that which we have seen and
heard we declare to you, that you
also may have fellowship with us;
and truly our fellowship *is* [a]with
the Father and with His Son Jesus
Christ.
4 And these things we write to
you [a]that [1]your joy may be full.

Fellowship with Him and One Another

5 [a]This is the message which we
have heard from Him and declare
to you, that [b]God is light and in
Him is no darkness at all.
6 [a]If we say that we have fellow-
ship with Him, and walk in dark-
ness, we lie and do not practice the
truth.
7 But if we [a]walk in the light as
He is in the light, we have fellow-
ship with one another, and [b]the
blood of Jesus Christ His Son
cleanses us from all sin.
8 If we say that we have no sin,
we deceive ourselves, and the
truth is not in us.
9 If we [a]confess our sins, He is
[b]faithful and just to forgive us *our*
sins and to [c]cleanse us from all un-
righteousness.
10 If we say that we have not
sinned, we [a]make Him a liar, and
His word is not in us.

2 My little children, these things
I write to you, so that you may
not sin. And if anyone sins, [a]we
have an Advocate with the Father,
Jesus Christ the righteous.
2 And [a]He Himself is the propiti-
ation for our sins, and not for ours
only but [b]also for the whole world.

The Test of Knowing Him

3 Now by this we know that we
know Him, if we keep His com-
mandments.
4 He who says, "I know Him,"
and does not keep His command-

CHAPTER 1

1 [a][John 1:1] [b]John 1:14 [c]2 Pet. 1:16 [d]Luke 24:39 [e][John 1:1, 4, 14]
2 [a]John 1:4 [b]Rom. 16:26 [c]John 21:24 [d][John 1:1, 18; 16:28]
3 [a]1 Cor. 1:9
4 [a]John 15:11; 16:24 [1]NU, M *our*
5 [a]1 John 3:11 [b][1 Tim. 6:16]
6 [a][1 John 2:9–11]
7 [a]Is. 2:5 [b][1 Cor. 6:11]
9 [a]Prov. 28:13 [b][Rom. 3:24–26] [c]Ps. 51:2
10 [a]1 John 5:10

CHAPTER 2

1 [a]Heb. 7:25; 9:24
2 [a][Rom. 3:25] [b]John 1:29

ments, is a [a]liar, and the truth is
not in him.
5 But [a]whoever keeps His word,
truly the love of God [1]is perfected
[b]in him. By this we know that we
are in Him.
6 [a]He who says he abides in Him
[b]ought himself also to walk just as
He walked.
7 [1]Brethren, I write no new com-
mandment to you, but an old com-
mandment which you have had
[a]from the beginning. The old
commandment is the word which
you heard [2]from the beginning.
8 Again, [a]a new commandment
I write to you, which thing is true
in Him and in you, [b]because the
darkness is passing away, and [c]the
true light is already shining.
9 [a]He who says he is in the light,
and hates his brother, is in dark-
ness until now.
10 [a]He who loves his brother
abides in the light, and [b]there is
no cause for stumbling in him.
11 But he who [a]hates his brother
is in darkness and [b]walks in dark-
ness, and does not know where he
is going, because the darkness has
blinded his eyes.

Their Spiritual State

12 I write to you, little children,
Because [a]your sins are forgiven
you for His name's sake.
13 I write to you, fathers,
Because you have known Him
who is [a]from the beginning.
I write to you, young men,
Because you have overcome
the wicked one.
I write to you, little children,
Because you have [b]known the
Father.
14 I have written to you, fathers,
Because you have known Him
who is from the beginning.
I have written to you, young men,
Because [a]you are strong, and
the word of God abides in
you,
And you have overcome the
wicked one.

Do Not Love the World

15 [a]Do not love the world or the
things in the world. [b]If anyone
loves the world, the love of the Fa-
ther is not in him.
16 For all that *is* in the world—the
lust of the flesh, [a]the lust of the
eyes, and the pride of life—is not
of the Father but is of the world.
17 And [a]the world is passing
away, and the lust of it; but he who
does the will of God abides for-
ever.

Deceptions of the Last Hour

18 [a]Little children, [b]it is the last
hour; and as you have heard that
[c]the[1] Antichrist is coming, [d]even
now many antichrists have come,
by which we know [e]that it is the
last hour.
19 [a]They went out from us, but
they were not of us; for [b]if they
had been of us, they would have
continued with us; but *they went*
out [c]that they might be made man-
ifest, that none of them were of us.
20 But [a]you have an anointing
[b]from the Holy One, and [c]you[1]
know all things.
21 I have not written to you be-
cause you do not know the truth,
but because you know it, and that
no lie is of the truth.
22 [a]Who is a liar but he who de-
nies that [b]Jesus is the Christ? He
is antichrist who denies the Father
and the Son.
23 [a]Whoever denies the Son does
not have the [b]Father either; [c]he
who acknowledges the Son has the
Father also.

Let Truth Abide in You

24 Therefore let that abide in you
[a]which you heard from the begin-
ning. If what you heard from the
beginning abides in you, [b]you also
will abide in the Son and in the
Father.
25 [a]And this is the promise that
He has promised us—eternal life.
26 These things I have written to
you concerning those who *try to*
[1]deceive you.
27 But the [a]anointing which you
have received from Him abides in
you, and [b]you do not need that
anyone teach you; but as the same
anointing [c]teaches you concerning
all things, and is true, and is not
a lie, and just as it has taught you,
you [1]will abide in Him.

The Children of God

28 And now, little children, abide
in Him, that [1]when He appears, we
may have [a]confidence and not be

4 [a]Rom. 3:4
5 [a]John 14:21, 23 [b][1 John 4:12] [1]*has been completed*
6 [a]John 15:4 [b]1 Pet. 2:21
7 [a]1 John 3:11, 23; 4:21 [1]NU *Beloved* [2]NU omits *from the beginning*
8 [a]John 13:34; 15:12 [b]Rom. 13:12 [c][John 1:9; 8:12; 12:35]
9 [a][1 Cor. 13:2]
10 [a][1 John 3:14] [b]2 Pet. 1:10
11 [a][1 John 2:9; 3:15; 4:20] [b]John 12:35
12 [a][1 Cor. 6:11]
13 [a]John 1:1 [b][Rom. 8:15–17]
14 [a]Eph. 6:10
15 [a][Rom. 12:2] [b]James 4:4
16 [a][Eccl. 5:10, 11]
17 [a]1 Cor. 7:31
18 [a]John 21:5 [b]1 Pet. 4:7 [c]2 Thess. 2:3 [d]2 John 7 [e]1 Tim. 4:1 [1]NU omits *the*
19 [a]Deut. 13:13 [b]Matt. 24:24 [c]1 Cor. 11:19
20 [a]2 Cor. 1:21 [b]Acts 3:14 [c][John 16:13] [1]NU *you all know.*
22 [a]2 John 7 [b]1 John 4:3
23 [a]John 15:23 [b]John 5:23 [c]1 John 4:15; 5:1
24 [a]2 John 5, 6 [b]John 14:23
25 [a]John 3:14–16; 6:40; 17:2, 3
26 [1]*lead you astray*
27 [a][John 14:16; 16:13] [b][Jer. 31:33] [c][John 14:16] [1]NU omits *will*
28 [a]1 John 3:21; 4:17; 5:14 [1]NU *if*

ashamed before Him at His coming.

29 [a]If you know that He is righteous, you know that [b]everyone who practices righteousness is born of Him.

3 Behold [a]what manner of love the Father has bestowed on us, that [b]we should be called children of [1]God! Therefore the world does not know [2]us, [c]because it did not know Him.

2 Beloved, [a]now we are children of God; and [b]it has not yet been revealed what we shall be, but we know that when He is revealed, [c]we shall be like Him, for [d]we shall see Him as He is.

3 [a]And everyone who has this hope in Him purifies himself, just as He is pure.

Sin and the Child of God

4 Whoever commits sin also commits lawlessness, and [a]sin is lawlessness.

5 And you know [a]that He was manifested [b]to take away our sins, and [c]in Him there is no sin.

6 Whoever abides in Him does not sin. Whoever sins has neither seen Him nor known Him.

7 Little children, let no one deceive you. He who practices righteousness is righteous, just as He is righteous.

8 [a]He who sins is of the devil, for the devil has sinned from the beginning. For this purpose the Son of God was manifested, [b]that He might destroy the works of the devil.

9 Whoever has been [a]born of God does not sin, for [b]His seed remains in him; and he cannot sin, because he has been born of God.

The Imperative of Love

10 In this the children of God and the children of the devil are manifest: Whoever does not practice righteousness is not of God, nor *is* he who does not love his brother.

11 For this is the message that you heard from the beginning, [a]that we should love one another,

12 not as [a]Cain *who* was of the wicked one and murdered his brother. And why did he murder him? Because his works were evil and his brother's righteous.

29 [a]Acts 22:14 [b]1 John 3:7, 10

CHAPTER 3

1 [a][1 John 4:10] [b][John 1:12] [c]John 15:18, 21; 16:3 [1]NU adds *And we are.* [2]M *you*

2 [a][Rom. 8:15, 16] [b][Rom. 8:18, 19, 23] [c]Rom. 8:29 [d][Ps. 16:11]

3 [a]1 John 4:17

4 [a]Rom. 4:15

5 [a]1 John 1:2; 3:8 [b]John 1:29 [c][2 Cor. 5:21]

8 [a]Matt. 13:38 [b]Luke 10:18

9 [a]John 1:3; 3:3 [b]1 Pet. 1:23

11 [a][John 13:34; 15:12]

12 [a]Gen. 4:4, 8

13 [a][John 15:18; 17:14]

14 [1]NU omits *his brother*

15 [a]Matt. 5:21 [b][Gal. 5:20, 21]

16 [a][John 3:16] [b]John 10:11; 15:13

17 [a]Deut. 15:7

18 [a]Ezek. 33:31

19 [a]John 18:37 [1]NU *shall know* [2]*persuade, set at rest*

20 [a][1 Cor. 4:4, 5]

21 [a][1 John 2:28; 5:14]

22 [a]Ps. 34:15 [b]John 8:29

23 [a]Matt. 22:39 [1]M omits *us*

24 [a]John 14:23 [b]John 14:21; 17:21 [c]Rom. 8:9, 14, 16

CHAPTER 4

1 [a]1 Cor. 14:29 [b]Matt. 24:5

2 [a]1 Cor. 12:3

13 Do not marvel, my brethren, if [a]the world hates you.

14 We know that we have passed from death to life, because we love the brethren. He who does not love [1]*his* brother abides in death.

15 [a]Whoever hates his brother is a murderer, and you know that [b]no murderer has eternal life abiding in him.

The Outworking of Love

16 [a]By this we know love, [b]because He laid down His life for us. And we also ought to lay down *our* lives for the brethren.

17 But [a]whoever has this world's goods, and sees his brother in need, and shuts up his heart from him, how does the love of God abide in him?

18 My little children, [a]let us not love in word or in tongue, but in deed and in truth.

19 And by this we [1]know [a]that we are of the truth, and shall [2]assure our hearts before Him.

20 [a]For if our heart condemns us, God is greater than our heart, and knows all things.

21 Beloved, if our heart does not condemn us, [a]we have confidence toward God.

22 And [a]whatever we ask we receive from Him, because we keep His commandments [b]and do those things that are pleasing in His sight.

23 And this is His commandment: that we should believe on the name of His Son Jesus Christ [a]and love one another, as He gave [1]us commandment.

The Spirit of Truth and the Spirit of Error

24 Now [a]he who keeps His commandments [b]abides in Him, and He in him. And [c]by this we know that He abides in us, by the Spirit whom He has given us.

4 Beloved, do not believe every spirit, but [a]test the spirits, whether they are of God; because [b]many false prophets have gone out into the world.

2 By this you know the Spirit of God: [a]Every spirit that confesses that Jesus Christ has come in the flesh is of God,

3 and every spirit that does not

confess [1]that Jesus [2]Christ has
come in the flesh is not of God.
And this is the *spirit* of the Anti-
christ, which you have heard was
coming, and is now already in the
world.
4 You are of God, little children,
and have overcome them, because
He who is in you is greater than
[a]he who is in the world.
5 [a]They are of the world. There-
fore they speak *as* of the world,
and [b]the world hears them.
6 We are of God. He who knows
God hears us; he who is not of God
does not hear us. [a]By this we know
the spirit of truth and the spirit of
error.

Knowing God Through Love

7 [a]Beloved, let us love one an-
other, for love is of God; and
everyone who [b]loves is born of
God and knows God.
8 He who does not love does not
know God, for God is love.
9 [a]In this the love of God was
manifested toward us, that God
has sent His only begotten [b]Son
into the world, that we might live
through Him.
10 In this is love, [a]not that we
loved God, but that He loved us
and sent His Son [b]*to be* the propiti-
ation for our sins.
11 Beloved, [a]if God so loved us,
we also ought to love one another.

Seeing God Through Love

12 [a]No one has seen God at any
time. If we love one another, God
abides in us, and His love has been
perfected in us.
13 [a]By this we know that we abide
in Him, and He in us, because He
has given us of His Spirit.
14 And [a]we have seen and testify
that [b]the Father has sent the Son
as Savior of the world.
15 [a]Whoever confesses that Jesus
is the Son of God, God abides in
him, and he in God.
16 And we have known and be-
lieved the love that God has for us.
God is love, and [a]he who abides
in love abides in God, and God [b]in
him.

The Consummation of Love

17 Love has been perfected
among us in this: that [a]we may
have boldness in the day of judg-
ment; because as He is, so are we
in this world.
18 There is no fear in love; but
perfect love casts out fear, because
fear involves torment. But he who
fears has not been made perfect
in love.
19 [a]We love [1]Him because He first
loved us.

Obedience by Faith

20 [a]If someone says, "I love God,"
and hates his brother, he is a liar;
for he who does not love his
brother whom he has seen, [1]how
can he love God [b]whom he has not
seen?
21 And [a]this commandment we
have from Him: that he who loves
God *must* love his brother also.

5 Whoever believes that [a]Jesus
is the Christ is [b]born of God,
and everyone who loves Him who
begot also loves him who is begot-
ten of Him.
2 By this we know that we love
the children of God, when we love
God and [a]keep His command-
ments.
3 [a]For this is the love of God, that
we keep His commandments. And
[b]His commandments are not bur-
densome.
4 For [a]whatever is born of God
overcomes the world. And this is
the victory that [b]has overcome the
world—[1]our faith.
5 Who is he who overcomes the
world, but [a]he who believes that
Jesus is the Son of God?

The Certainty of God's Witness

6 This is He who came [a]by water
and blood—Jesus Christ; not only
by water, but by water and blood.
[b]And it is the Spirit who bears wit-
ness, because the Spirit is truth.
7 For there are three that bear
witness [1]in heaven: the Father,
[a]the Word, and the Holy Spirit;
[b]and these three are one.
8 And there are three that bear
witness on earth: [a]the Spirit, the
water, and the blood; and these
three agree as one.
9 If we receive [a]the witness of
men, the witness of God is greater;
[b]for this is the witness of [1]God
which He has testified of His Son.
10 He who believes in the Son of

3 [1]NU omits *that* [2]NU omits *Christ has come in the flesh*
4 [a]John 14:30; 16:11
5 [a]John 3:31 [b]John 15:19; 17:14
6 [a][1 Cor. 2:12–16]
7 [a]1 John 3:10, 11, 23 [b]1 Thess. 4:9
9 [a]Rom. 5:8 [b]John 3:16
10 [a]Titus 3:5 [b]1 John 2:2
11 [a]Matt. 18:33
12 [a]John 1:18
13 [a]John 14:20
14 [a]John 1:14 [b]John 3:17; 4:42
15 [a][Rom. 10:9]
16 [a][1 John 3:24] [b][John 14:23]
17 [a]1 John 2:28
19 [a]1 John 4:10 [1]NU omits *Him*
20 [a][1 John 2:4] [b]1 John 4:12 [1]NU *he cannot*
21 [a][Matt. 5:43, 44; 22:39]

CHAPTER 5

1 [a]1 John 2:22; 4:2, 15 [b]John 1:13
2 [a]John 15:10
3 [a]John 14:15 [b]Matt. 11:30; 23:4
4 [a]John 16:33 [b]1 John 2:13; 4:4 [1]M *your*
5 [a]1 Cor. 15:57
6 [a]John 1:31–34 [b][John 14:17]
7 [a][John 1:1] [b]John 10:30 [1]NU, M omit the words from *in heaven* (v. 7) through *on earth* (v. 8). Only 4 or 5 very late mss. contain these words in Greek.
8 [a]John 15:26
9 [a]John 5:34, 37; 8:17, 18 [b][Matt. 3:16, 17] [1]NU *God, that*

God [a]has the witness in himself;
he who does not believe God [b]has
made Him a liar, because he has
not believed the testimony that
God has given of His Son.
11 And this is the testimony: that
God has given us eternal life, and
this life is in His Son.
12 [a]He who has the Son has [1]life;
he who does not have the Son of
God does not have [1]life.
13 These things I have written to
you who believe in the name of the
Son of God, that you may know
that you have eternal life, [1]and
that you may *continue to* believe
in the name of the Son of God.

Confidence and Compassion in Prayer

14 Now this is the confidence that
we have in Him, that [a]if we ask
anything according to His will, He
hears us.
15 And if we know that He hears
us, whatever we ask, we know that
we have the petitions that we have
asked of Him.
16 If anyone sees his brother sin-
ning a sin *which does* not *lead* to
death, he will ask, and [a]He will
give him life for those who commit
sin not *leading* to death. [b]There is
sin *leading* to death. [c]I do not say
that he should pray about that.
17 [a]All unrighteousness is sin, and
there is sin not *leading* to death.

Knowing the True—Rejecting the False

18 We know that [a]whoever is born
of God does not sin; but he who
has been born of God [b]keeps[1]
[2]himself, and the wicked one does
not touch him.
19 We know that we are of God,
and [a]the whole world lies *under*
the sway of the wicked one.
20 And we know that the [a]Son of
God has come and [b]has given us
an understanding, [c]that we may
know Him who is true; and we are
in Him who is true, in His Son Je-
sus Christ. [d]This is the true God
[e]and eternal life.
21 Little children, keep yourselves
from idols. Amen.

10 [a][Rom. 8:16] [b]John 3:18, 33

12 [a][John 3:15, 36; 6:47; 17:2, 3] [1]Or *the life*

13 [1]NU omits the rest of v. 13.

14 [a][1 John 2:28; 3:21, 22]

16 [a]Job 42:8 [b][Matt. 12:31] [c]Jer. 7:16; 14:11

17 [a]1 John 3:4

18 [a][1 Pet. 1:23]; 1 John 3:9 [b]James 1:27 [1]*guards* [2]NU *him*

19 [a]John 12:31; 17:15; Gal. 1:4

20 [a]1 John 4:2 [b]Luke 24:45 [c]John 17:3; Rev. 3:7 [d]Is. 9:6 [e]1 John 5:11, 12

The Second Epistle of

John

"**LET** him who thinks he stands take heed lest he fall" (1 Cor. 10:12). These words of the apostle Paul could well stand as a subtitle for John's little epistle. The recipients, a chosen lady and her children, were obviously standing. They were walking in truth, remaining faithful to the commandments they had received from the Father. John is deeply pleased to be able to commend them. But he takes nothing for granted. Realizing that standing is just one step removed from falling, he hesitates not at all to issue a reminder: "love one another" (v. 5). The apostle admits that this is not new revelation, but he views it sufficiently important to repeat. Loving one another, he stresses, is equivalent to walking according to God's commandments.

John indicates, however, that this love must be discerning. It is not a naive, unthinking, open to anything and anyone kind of love. Biblical love is a matter of choice; it is dangerous and foolish to float through life with undiscerning love. False teachers abound who do not acknowledge Christ as having come in the flesh. It is false charity to open the door to false teaching. We must have fellowship with God. We must have fellowship with Christians. But we must not have fellowship with false teachers.

The "elder" of verse 1 has been traditionally identified with the apostle John, resulting in the Greek title *Ioannou B,* the "Second of John."

Greeting the Elect Lady

THE Elder,
To the [1]elect lady and her chil-
dren, whom I love in truth, and not
only I, but also all those who have
known [a]the truth,
2 because of the truth which
abides in us and will be with us
forever:

3 [a]Grace, mercy, *and* peace will
be with [1]you from God the Father
and from the Lord Jesus Christ,
the Son of the Father, in truth and
love.

Walk in Christ's Commandments

4 I [a]rejoiced greatly that I have
found *some* of your children walk-
ing in truth, as we received com-
mandment from the Father.
5 And now I plead with you,
lady, not as though I wrote a new
commandment to you, but that
which we have had from the
beginning: [a]that we love one an-
other.
6 [a]This is love, that we walk ac-
cording to His commandments.
This is the commandment, that [b]as
you have heard from the begin-
ning, you should walk in it.

Beware of Antichrist Deceivers

7 For [a]many deceivers have gone
out into the world [b]who do not
confess Jesus Christ *as* coming in
the flesh. [c]This is a deceiver and
an antichrist.
8 [a]Look to yourselves, [b]that [1]we
do not lose those things we
worked for, but *that* [1]we may re-
ceive a full reward.
9 [a]Whoever [1]transgresses and
does not abide in the doctrine of
Christ does not have God. He who
abides in the doctrine of Christ has
both the Father and the Son.
10 If anyone comes to you and
[a]does not bring this doctrine, do
not receive him into your house
nor greet him;

CHAPTER 1

1 [a]Col. 1:5 [1]*chosen*
3 [a]Rom. 1:7; 1 Tim. 1:2 [1]NU, M *us*
4 [a]1 Thess. 2:19, 20; 3 John 3, 4
5 [a][John 13:34, 35; 15:12, 17]; 1 John 3:11; 4:7, 11
6 [a]John 14:15; 1 John 2:5; 5:3 [b]1 John 2:24
7 [a]1 John 2:19; 4:1 [b]1 John 4:2 [c]1 John 2:22
8 [a]Mark 13:9 [b]Gal. 3:4 [1]NU *you*
9 [a]John 7:16; 8:31; 1 John 2:19, 23, 24 [1]NU *goes ahead*
10 [a]1 Kin. 13:16; Rom. 16:17; 2 Thess. 3:6, 14; Titus 3:10

11 for he who greets him shares
in his evil deeds.

John's Farewell Greeting

12 [a]Having many things to write
to you, I did not wish *to do so*
with paper and ink; but I hope
to come to you and speak face
to face, [b]that our joy may be
full.
13 [a]The children of your elect sis-
ter greet you. Amen.

12 [a]3 John 13, 14 [b]John 17:13
13 [a]1 Pet. 5:13

The Third Epistle of

John

IN Third John the apostle encourages fellowship with Christian brothers. Following his expression of love for Gaius, John assures him of his prayers for his health and voices his joy over Gaius's persistent walk in truth and for the manner in which he shows hospitality and support for missionaries who have come to his church.

But not everyone in the church feels the same way. Diotrephes' heart is one hundred and eighty degrees removed from Gaius's heart. He is no longer living in love. Pride has taken precedence in his life. He has refused a letter John has written for the church, fearing that his authority might be superseded by that of the apostle. He also has accused John of evil words and refused to accept missionaries. He forbids others to do so and even expels them from the church if they disobey him. John uses this negative example as an opportunity to encourage Gaius to continue his hospitality. Demetrius has a good testimony and may even be one of those turned away by Diotrephes. He is widely known for his good character and his loyalty to the truth. Here he is well commended by John and stands as a positive example for Gaius.

The Greek titles of First, Second, and Third John are *Ioannou A, B,* and *G.* The *G* is gamma, the third letter of the Greek alphabet; *Ioannou G* means the "Third of John."

Greeting to Gaius

THE Elder,
To the beloved Gaius, [a]whom
I love in truth:

2 Beloved, I pray that you may
prosper in all things and be in
health, just as your soul pros-
pers.
3 For I [a]rejoiced greatly when
brethren came and testified of the
truth *that is* in you, just as you
walk in the truth.
4 I have no greater [a]joy than to
hear that [b]my children walk in
[1]truth.

Gaius Commended for Generosity

5 Beloved, you do faithfully
whatever you do for the brethren
[1]and for strangers,
6 who have borne witness of
your love before the church. *If* you
send them forward on their jour-
ney in a manner worthy of God,
you will do well,
7 because they went forth for His
name's sake, [a]taking nothing from
the Gentiles.
8 We therefore ought to [a]receive[1]
such, that we may become fellow
workers for the truth.

Diotrephes and Demetrius

9 I wrote to the church, but Di-
otrephes, who loves to have the
preeminence among them, does
not receive us.
10 Therefore, if I come, I will call
to mind his deeds which he does,
[a]prating[1] against us with malicious
words. And not content with that,
he himself does not receive the
brethren, and forbids those who
wish to, putting *them* out of the
church.
11 Beloved, [a]do not imitate what
is evil, but what is good. [b]He who
does good is of God, [1]but he who
does evil has not seen [c]God.
12 Demetrius [a]has a *good* testi-
mony from all, and from the truth
itself. And we also [1]bear witness,
[b]and you know that our testimony
is true.

CHAPTER 1

1 [a]2 John 1
3 [a]2 John 4
4 [a]1 Thess. 2:19, 20; 2 John 4 [b][1 Cor. 4:15] [1]NU *the truth*
5 [1]NU *and especially for*
7 [a]1 Cor. 9:12, 15
8 [a]Matt. 10:40; Rom. 12:13; Heb. 13:2; 1 Pet. 4:9 [1]NU *support*
10 [a]Prov. 10:8, 10 [1]*talking nonsense*
11 [a]Ps. 34:14; 37:27; Rom. 14:19; 1 Thess. 5:15; 1 Tim. 6:11; 2 Tim. 2:22 [b][1 John 2:29; 3:10] [c][1 John 3:10] [1]NU, M omit *but*
12 [a]Acts 6:3; 1 Tim. 3:7 [b]John 19:35; 21:24 [1]*testify*

Farewell Greeting

13 [a]I had many things to write, but
I do not wish to write to you with
pen and ink;
14 but I hope to see you shortly,
and we shall speak face to
face. Peace to you. Our friends
greet you. Greet the friends by
name.

13 [a]2 John 12

The Epistle of

Jude

FIGHT! Contend! Do battle! When apostasy arises, when false teachers emerge, when the truth of God is attacked, it is time to fight for the faith. Only believers who are spiritually "in shape" can answer the summons. At the beginning of his letter Jude focuses on the believers' common salvation, but then feels compelled to challenge them to contend for the faith. The danger is real. False teachers have crept into the church, turning God's grace into unbounded license to do as they please. Jude reminds such men of God's past dealings with unbelieving Israel, disobedient angels, and wicked Sodom and Gomorrah. In the face of such danger Christians should not be caught off guard. The challenge is great, but so is the God who is able to keep them from stumbling.

The Greek title *Iouda,* "Of Jude," comes from the name *Ioudas* which appears in verse 1. This name, which can be translated Jude or Judas, was popular in the first century because of Judas Maccabaeus (died 160 B.C.), a leader of the Jewish resistance against Syria during the Maccabean revolt.

Greeting to the Called

JUDE, a bondservant of Jesus
Christ, and [a]brother of James,

To those who are [b]called,
[1]sanctified by God the Father, and
[c]preserved in Jesus Christ:

2 Mercy, [a]peace, and love be
multiplied to you.

Contend for the Faith

3 Beloved, while I was very dili-
gent to write to you [a]concerning
our common salvation, I found it
necessary to write to you exhort-
ing [b]you to contend earnestly for
the faith which was once for all
delivered to the saints.
4 For certain men have crept in
unnoticed, who long ago were
marked out for this condemnation,
ungodly men, who turn the grace
of our God into lewdness and deny
the only Lord [1]God and our Lord
Jesus Christ.

Old and New Apostates

5 But I want to remind you,
though you once knew this, that
[a]the Lord, having saved the people
out of the land of Egypt, afterward
destroyed those who did not be-
lieve.
6 And the angels who did not
keep their [1]proper domain, but left
their own abode, He has reserved
in everlasting chains under dark-
ness for the judgment of the great
day;
7 as [a]Sodom and Gomorrah, and
the cities around them in a similar
manner to these, having given
themselves over to sexual immo-
rality and gone after strange flesh,
are set forth as an example, suffer-
ing the [1]vengeance of eternal fire.
8 [a]Likewise also these dreamers
defile the flesh, reject authority,
and [b]speak evil of [1]dignitaries.
9 Yet Michael the archangel, in
[1]contending with the devil, when
he disputed about the body of Mo-
ses, dared not bring against him
a reviling accusation, but said,
[a]"The Lord rebuke you!"
10 [a]But these speak evil of what-
ever they do not know; and what-
ever they know naturally, like
brute beasts, in these things they
corrupt themselves.
11 Woe to them! For they have
gone in the way [a]of Cain, [b]have
run greedily in the error of Balaam
for profit, and perished [c]in the re-
bellion of Korah.

Apostates Depraved and Doomed

12 These are [1]spots in your love
feasts, while they feast with you
without fear, serving *only* them-

CHAPTER 1

1 [a]Acts 1:13 [b]Rom. 1:7 [c]John 17:11, 12 [1]NU *beloved*

2 [a]1 Pet. 1:2; 2 Pet. 1:2

3 [a]Titus 1:4 [b]Phil. 1:27

4 [1]NU omits *God*

5 [a]Ex. 12:51; 1 Cor. 10:5–10; Heb. 3:16

6 [1]*own*

7 [a]Gen. 19:24; 2 Pet. 2:6 [1]*punishment*

8 [a]2 Pet. 2:10 [b]Ex. 22:28 [1]*glorious ones*, lit. *glories*

9 [a]Zech. 3:2 [1]*arguing*

10 [a]2 Pet. 2:12

11 [a]Gen. 4:3–8; Heb. 11:4; 1 John 3:12 [b]Num. 31:16; 2 Pet. 2:15; Rev. 2:14 [c]Num. 16:1–3, 31–35

12 [1]*stains*, or *hidden reefs*

selves. *They are* clouds without
water, carried [2]about by the winds;
late autumn trees without fruit,
twice dead, pulled up by the roots;
13 [a]raging waves of the sea,
[b]foaming up their own shame;
wandering stars [c]for whom is re-
served the blackness of darkness
forever.
14 Now Enoch, the seventh from
Adam, prophesied about these
men also, saying, "Behold, the
Lord comes with ten thousands of
His saints,
15 "to execute judgment on all, to
convict all who are ungodly
among them of all their ungodly
deeds which they have committed
in an ungodly way, and of all the
[a]harsh things which ungodly sin-
ners have spoken against Him."

Apostates Predicted

16 These are grumblers, com-
plainers, walking according to
their own lusts; and they [a]mouth
great swelling *words,* [b]flattering
people to gain advantage.
17 [a]But you, beloved, remember
the words which were spoken be-
fore by the apostles of our Lord
Jesus Christ:
18 how they told you that [a]there
would be mockers in the last time
who would walk according to their
own ungodly lusts.
19 These are [1]sensual persons,
who cause divisions, not having
the Spirit.

Maintain Your Life with God

20 But you, beloved, [a]building
yourselves up on your most holy
faith, [b]praying in the Holy Spirit,
21 keep yourselves in the love of
God, [a]looking for the mercy of our
Lord Jesus Christ unto eternal life.
22 And on some have compassion,
[1]making a distinction;
23 but [a]others save [1]with fear,
[b]pulling *them* out of the [2]fire, hat-
ing even [c]the garment defiled by
the flesh.

Glory to God

24 [a]Now to Him who is able to keep
[1]you from stumbling,
And [b]to present *you* faultless
Before the presence of His glory
with exceeding joy,
25 To [1]God our Savior,
[2]Who alone is wise,
Be glory and majesty,
Dominion and [3]power,
Both now and forever.
Amen.

12 [2]NU, M *along*
13 [a]Is. 57:20 [b][Phil. 3:19] [c]2 Pet. 2:17
15 [a]1 Sam. 2:3
16 [a]2 Pet. 2:18 [b]Prov. 28:21
17 [a]2 Pet. 3:2
18 [a][1 Tim. 4:1]
19 [1]*soulish* or *worldly*
20 [a]Col. 2:7 [b][Rom. 8:26]
21 [a]Titus 2:13
22 [1]NU *who are doubting* (or *making distinctions*)
23 [a]Rom. 11:14 [b]Amos 4:11 [c][Zech. 3:4, 5] [1]NU omits *with fear* [2]NU adds *and on some have mercy with fear*
24 [a][Eph. 3:20] [b]Col. 1:22 [1]M *them*
25 [1]NU *the only God our* [2]NU *Through Jesus Christ our Lord, Be glory* [3]NU adds *Before all time,*

The Revelation

of Jesus Christ

JUST as Genesis is the book of beginnings, Revelation is the book of consummation. In it, the divine program of redemption is brought to fruition, and the holy name of God is vindicated before all creation. Although there are numerous prophecies in the Gospels and Epistles, Revelation is the only New Testament book that focuses primarily on prophetic events. Its title means "unveiling" or "disclosure." Thus, the book is an unveiling of the character and program of God. Penned by John during his exile on the island of Patmos, Revelation centers around visions and symbols of the resurrected Christ, who alone has authority to judge the earth, to remake it, and to rule it in righteousness.

The title of this book in the Greek text is *Apokalypsis Ioannou,* "Revelation of John." It is also known as the Apocalypse, a transliteration of the word *apokalypsis,* meaning "unveiling," "disclosure," or "revelation." Thus, the book is an unveiling of that which otherwise could not be known. A better title comes from the first verse: *Apokalypsis Iesou Christou,* "Revelation of Jesus Christ." This could be taken as a revelation which came from Christ or as a revelation which is about Christ—both are appropriate. Because of the unified contents of this book, it should not be called Revelations.

CHAPTER 1

Introduction and Benediction

THE Revelation of Jesus Christ,
[a]which God gave Him to show
His servants—things which
must [1]shortly take place. And [b]He
sent and signified *it* by His angel
to His servant John,
2 [a]who bore witness to the word
of God, and to the testimony of
Jesus Christ, to all things [b]that he
saw.
3 [a]Blessed *is* he who reads and
those who hear the words of this
prophecy, and keep those things
which are written in it; for [b]the
time *is* near.

Greeting the Seven Churches

4 John, to the seven churches
which are in Asia:

Grace to you and peace from
Him [a]who is and [b]who was and
who is to come, [c]and from the
seven Spirits who are before His
throne,
5 and from Jesus Christ, [a]the
faithful [b]witness, the [c]firstborn
from the dead, and [d]the ruler over
the kings of the earth. To Him
[e]who [1]loved us [f]and washed us
from our sins in His own blood,
6 and has [a]made us [1]kings and
priests to His God and Father, [b]to
Him *be* glory and dominion forever and ever. Amen.
7 Behold, He is coming with
[a]clouds, and every eye will see
Him, even [b]they who pierced Him.
And all the tribes of the earth will
mourn because of Him. Even so,
Amen.
8 [a]"I am the Alpha and the
Omega, [1]*the* Beginning and *the*
End," says the [2]Lord, [b]"who is and
who was and who is to come, the
[c]Almighty."

Vision of the Son of Man

9 I, John, [1]both your brother and
[a]companion in the tribulation and
[b]kingdom and patience of Jesus

1 [a]John 3:32 [b]Rev. 22:6 [1]*quickly* or *swiftly*
2 [a]1 Cor. 1:6 [b]1 John 1:1
3 [a]Luke 11:28 [b]James 5:8
4 [a]Ex. 3:14 [b]John 1:1 [c][Is. 11:2]
5 [a]John 8:14 [b]Is. 55:4 [c][Col. 1:18] [d]Rev. 17:14 [e]John 13:34 [f]Heb. 9:14 [1]NU *loves us and freed;* M *loves us and washed*
6 [a]1 Pet. 2:5, 9 [b]1 Tim. 6:16 [1]NU, M *a kingdom*
7 [a]Matt. 24:30 [b]Zech. 12:10–14
8 [a]Is. 41:4 [b]Rev. 4:8; 11:17 [c]Is. 9:6

[1]NU, M omit *the Beginning and the End* [2]NU, M *Lord God* **9** [a]Phil. 1:7 [b][2 Tim. 2:12] [1]NU, M omit *both*

Christ, was on the island that is
called Patmos for the word of God
and for the testimony of Jesus
Christ.
10 [a]I was in the Spirit on [b]the
Lord's Day, and I heard behind me
[c]a loud voice, as of a trumpet,
11 saying, [1]"I am the Alpha and
the Omega, the First and the Last,"
and, "What you see, write in a
book and send *it* to the seven
churches [2]which are in Asia: to
Ephesus, to Smyrna, to Pergamos,
to Thyatira, to Sardis, to Phila-
delphia, and to Laodicea."
12 Then I turned to see the voice
that spoke with me. And having
turned [a]I saw seven golden lamp-
stands,
13 [a]and in the midst of the seven
lampstands [b]*One* like the Son of
Man, [c]clothed with a garment
down to the feet and [d]girded about
the chest with a golden band.
14 His head and [a]hair *were* white
like wool, as white as snow, and
[b]His eyes like a flame of fire;
15 [a]His feet *were* like fine brass,
as if refined in a furnace, and [b]His
voice as the sound of many waters;
16 [a]He had in His right hand seven
stars, [b]out of His mouth went a
sharp two-edged sword, [c]and His
countenance *was* like the sun shin-
ing in its strength.
17 And [a]when I saw Him, I fell at
His feet as dead. But [b]He laid His
right hand on me, saying [1]to me,
"Do not be afraid; [c]I am the First
and the Last.
18 [a]"I *am* He who lives, and was
dead, and behold, [b]I am alive for-
evermore. Amen. And [c]I have the
keys of [1]Hades and of Death.
19 [1]"Write the things which you
have [a]seen, [b]and the things which
are, [c]and the things which will
take place after this.
20 "The [1]mystery of the seven
stars which you saw in My right
hand, and the seven golden lamp-
stands: The seven stars are [a]the
[2]angels of the seven churches, and
[b]the seven lampstands [3]which you
saw are the seven churches.

The Loveless Church

2 "To the [1]angel of the church of
Ephesus write,
'These things says [a]He who
holds the seven stars in His right
hand, [b]who walks in the midst of
the seven golden lampstands:
2 [a]"I know your works, your
labor, your [1]patience, and that
you cannot [2]bear those who are
evil. And [b]you have tested those
[c]who say they are apostles and
are not, and have found them
liars;
3 "and you have persevered and
have patience, and have labored
for My name's sake and have [a]not
become weary.
4 "Nevertheless I have *this*
against you, that you have left
your first love.
5 "Remember therefore from
where you have fallen; repent and
do the first works, [a]or else I will
come to you quickly and remove
your lampstand from its place—
unless you repent.
6 "But this you have, that you
hate the deeds of the Nicolaitans,
which I also hate.
7 [a]"He who has an ear, let him
hear what the Spirit says to the
churches. To him who overcomes
I will give [b]to eat from [c]the tree
of life, which is in the midst of the
Paradise of God."'

The Persecuted Church

8 "And to the [1]angel of the
church in Smyrna write,
'These things says [a]the First
and the Last, who was dead, and
came to life:
9 "I know your works, tribula-
tion, and poverty (but you are
[a]rich); and *I know* the blasphemy
of [b]those who say they are Jews
and are not, [c]but *are* a [1]synagogue
of Satan.
10 [a]"Do not fear any of those
things which you are about to suf-
fer. Indeed, the devil is about to
throw *some* of you into prison, that
you may be tested, and you will
have tribulation ten days. [b]Be
faithful until death, and I will give
you [c]the crown of life.
11 [a]"He who has an ear, let him
hear what the Spirit says to the
churches. He who overcomes shall
not be hurt by [b]the second
death."'

10 [a]Acts 10:10 [b]Acts 20:7 [c]Rev. 4:1 **11** [1]NU, M omit *"I am the Alpha and the Omega, the First and the Last," and,* [2]NU, M omit *which are in Asia* **12** [a]Ex. 25:37 **13** [a]Rev. 2:1 [b]Ezek. 1:26 [c]Dan. 10:5 [d]Rev. 15:6 **14** [a]Dan. 7:9 [b]Dan. 10:6 **15** [a]Ezek. 1:7 [b]Ezek. 1:24; 43:2 **16** [a]Rev. 1:20; 2:1; 3:1 [b]Is. 49:2 [c]Matt. 17:2 **17** [a]Ezek. 1:28 [b]Dan. 8:18; 10:10, 12 [c]Is. 41:4; 44:6; 48:12 [1]NU, M omit *to me* **18** [a]Rom. 6:9 [b]Rev. 4:9 [c]Ps. 68:20 [1]Lit. *Unseen;* the unseen realm **19** [a]Rev. 1:9–18 [b]Rev. 2:1 [c]Rev. 4:1 [1]NU, M *Therefore, write* **20** [a]Rev. 2:1 [b]Zech. 4:2 [1]*hidden truth* [2]Or *messengers* [3]NU, M omit *which you saw*

CHAPTER 2

1 [a]Rev. 1:16 [b]Rev. 1:13 [1]Or *messenger* **2** [a]Ps. 1:6 [b]1 John 4:1 [c]2 Cor. 11:13 [1]*perseverance* [2]*endure* **3** [a]Gal. 6:9 **5** [a]Matt. 21:41 **7** [a]Matt. 11:15 [b][Rev. 22:2, 14] [c][Gen. 2:9; 3:22] **8** [a]Rev. 1:8, 17, 18 [1]Or *messenger* **9** [a]Luke 12:21 [b]Rom. 2:17 [c]Rev. 3:9 [1]*congregation* **10** [a]Matt. 10:22 [b]Matt. 24:13 [c]James 1:12

11 [a]Rev. 13:9 [b][Rev. 20:6, 14; 21:8]

sea of glass, like crystal. [b]And in
the midst of the throne, and
around the throne, *were* four living
creatures full of eyes in front and
in back.
7 [a]The first living creature *was*
like a lion, the second living crea-
ture like a calf, the third living
creature had a face like a man, and
the fourth living creature *was* like
a flying eagle.
8 *The* four living creatures, each
having [a]six wings, were full of
eyes around and within. And they
do not rest day or night, saying:

[b]"Holy,[1] holy, holy,
[c]Lord God Almighty,
[d]Who was and is and is to come!"

9 Whenever the living creatures
give glory and honor and thanks
to Him who sits on the throne,
[a]who lives forever and ever,
10 [a]the twenty-four elders fall
down before Him who sits on the
throne and worship Him who lives
forever and ever, and cast their
crowns before the throne, saying:

11 "You[a] are worthy, [1]O Lord,
To receive glory and honor and
power;
[b]For You created all things,
And by [c]Your will they [2]exist and
were created."

The Lamb Takes the Scroll

5 And I saw in the right *hand* of
Him who sat on the throne [a]a
scroll written inside and on the
back, [b]sealed with seven seals.
2 Then I saw a strong angel pro-
claiming with a loud voice, [a]"Who
is worthy to open the scroll and
to loose its seals?"
3 And no one in heaven or on the
earth or under the earth was able
to open the scroll, or to look at it.
4 So I wept much, because no
one was found worthy to open
[1]and read the scroll, or to look
at it.
5 But one of the elders said to
me, "Do not weep. Behold, [a]the
Lion of the tribe of [b]Judah, [c]the
Root of David, has [d]prevailed to
open the scroll [e]and [1]to loose its
seven seals."
6 And I looked, [1]and behold, in
the midst of the throne and of the
four living creatures, and in the
midst of the elders, stood [a]a Lamb
as though it had been slain, having
seven horns and [b]seven eyes,
which are [c]the seven Spirits of God
sent out into all the earth.
7 Then He came and took the
scroll out of the right hand [a]of Him
who sat on the throne.

Worthy Is the Lamb

8 Now when He had taken the
scroll, [a]the four living creatures
and the twenty-four elders fell
down before the Lamb, each hav-
ing a harp, and golden bowls full
of incense, which are the [b]prayers
of the saints.
9 And [a]they sang a new song,
saying:

[b]"You are worthy to take the scroll,
And to open its seals;
For You were slain,
And [c]have redeemed us to God
[d]by Your blood
Out of every tribe and tongue and
people and nation,
10 And have made [1]us [a]kings[2] and
[b]priests to our God;
And [3]we shall reign on the earth."

11 Then I looked, and I heard the
voice of many angels around the
throne, the living creatures, and
the elders; and the number of them
was ten thousand times ten thou-
sand, and thousands of thousands,
12 saying with a loud voice:

"Worthy is the Lamb who was
slain
To receive power and riches and
wisdom,
And strength and honor and
glory and blessing!"

13 And [a]every creature which is
in heaven and on the earth and un-
der the earth and such as are in
the sea, and all that are in them, I
heard saying:

[b]"Blessing and honor and glory and
power
Be to Him [c]who sits on the throne,
And to the Lamb, forever and
ever!"[1]

14 Then the four living creatures
said, "Amen!" And the [1]twenty-
four elders fell down and wor-
shiped [2]Him who lives forever and
ever.

---

6 [b]Ezek. 1:5
7 [a]Ezek. 1:10; 10:14
8 [a]Is. 6:2 [b]Is. 6:3 [c]Rev. 1:8 [d]Rev. 1:4 [1]M has *holy* nine times.
9 [a]Rev. 1:18
10 [a]Rev. 5:8, 14; 7:11; 11:16; 19:4
11 [a]Rev. 1:6; 5:12 [b]Gen. 1:1 [c]Col. 1:16 [1]NU, M *our Lord and God* [2]NU, M *existed*

CHAPTER 5

1 [a]Ezek. 2:9, 10 [b]Is. 29:11
2 [a]Rev. 4:11; 5:9
4 [1]NU, M omit *and read*
5 [a]Gen. 49:9 [b]Heb. 7:14 [c]Is. 11:1, 10 [d]Rev. 3:21 [e]Rev. 6:1 [1]NU, M omit *to loose*
6 [a][John 1:29] [b]Zech. 3:9; 4:10 [c]Rev. 1:4; 3:1; 4:5 [1]NU, M *I saw in the midst . . . a Lamb standing*
7 [a]Rev. 4:2
8 [a]Rev. 4:8–10; 19:4 [b]Rev. 8:3
9 [a]Rev. 14:3 [b]Rev. 4:11 [c]John 1:29 [d][Heb. 9:12]
10 [a]Ex. 19:6 [b]Is. 61:6 [1]NU, M *them* [2]NU *a kingdom* [3]NU, M *they*
13 [a]Phil. 2:10 [b]1 Chr. 29:11 [c]Rev. 4:2, 3; 6:16; 20:11 [1]M adds *Amen*
14 [1]NU, M omit *twenty-four* [2]NU, M omit *Him who lives forever and ever*

First Seal: The Conqueror

6 Now [a]I saw when the Lamb
opened one of the [1]seals; and
I heard [b]one of the four living crea-
tures saying with a voice like thun-
der, "Come and see."
2 And I looked, and behold, [a]a
white horse. [b]He who sat on it had
a bow; [c]and a crown was given to
him, and he went out [d]conquering
and to conquer.

Second Seal: Conflict on Earth

3 When He opened the second
seal, [a]I heard the second living
creature saying, "Come [1]and see."
4 [a]Another horse, fiery red, went
out. And it was granted to the one
who sat on it to [b]take peace from
the earth, and that *people* should
kill one another; and there was
given to him a great sword.

Third Seal: Scarcity on Earth

5 When He opened the third seal,
[a]I heard the third living creature
say, "Come and see." So I looked,
and behold, [b]a black horse, and he
who sat on it had a pair of [c]scales[1]
in his hand.
6 And I heard a voice in the midst
of the four living creatures saying,
"A [1]quart of wheat for a [2]denarius,
and three quarts of barley for a de-
narius; and [a]do not harm the oil
and the wine."

Fourth Seal: Widespread Death on Earth

7 When He opened the fourth
seal, [a]I heard the voice of the
fourth living creature saying,
"Come and see."
8 [a]So I looked, and behold, a pale
horse. And the name of him who
sat on it was Death, and Hades fol-
lowed with him. And [1]power was
given to them over a fourth of the
earth, [b]to kill with sword, with
hunger, with death, [c]and by the
beasts of the earth.

Fifth Seal: The Cry of the Martyrs

9 When He opened the fifth seal,
I saw under [a]the altar [b]the souls
of those who had been slain [c]for
the word of God and for [d]the testi-
mony which they held.
10 And they cried with a loud
voice, saying, [a]"How long, O Lord,
[b]holy and true, [c]until You judge
and avenge our blood on those
who dwell on the earth?"
11 Then a [a]white robe was given
to each of them; and it was said
to them [b]that they should rest a lit-
tle while longer, until both *the
number of* their fellow servants
and their brethren, who would be
killed as they *were,* was com-
pleted.

Sixth Seal: Cosmic Disturbances

12 I looked when He opened the
sixth seal, [a]and [1]behold, there was
a great earthquake; and [b]the sun
became black as sackcloth of hair,
and the [2]moon became like blood.
13 [a]And the stars of heaven fell to
the earth, as a fig tree drops its late
figs when it is shaken by a mighty
wind.
14 [a]Then the sky [1]receded as a
scroll when it is rolled up, and
[b]every mountain and island was
moved out of its place.
15 And the [a]kings of the earth, the
great men, [1]the rich men, the com-
manders, the mighty men, every
slave and every free man, [b]hid
themselves in the caves and in the
rocks of the mountains,
16 [a]and said to the mountains and
rocks, "Fall on us and hide us from
the face of Him who [b]sits on the
throne and from the wrath of the
Lamb!
17 "For the great day of His wrath
has come, [a]and who is able to
stand?"

The Sealed of Israel

7 After these things I saw four
angels standing at the four cor-
ners of the earth, [a]holding the four
winds of the earth, [b]that the wind
should not blow on the earth, on
the sea, or on any tree.
2 Then I saw another angel as-
cending from the east, having the
seal of the living God. And he cried
with a loud voice to the four angels
to whom it was granted to harm
the earth and the sea,
3 saying, [a]"Do not harm the
earth, the sea, or the trees till we
have sealed the servants of our
God [b]on their foreheads."
4 [a]And I heard the number of
those who were sealed. [b]One hun-
dred *and* forty-four thousand [c]of

CHAPTER 6

1 [a][Rev. 5:5–7, 12; 13:8] [b]Rev. 4:7 [1]NU, M *seven seals*
2 [a]Zech. 1:8; 6:3 [b]Ps. 45:4, 5, LXX [c]Zech. 6:11 [d]Matt. 24:5
3 [a]Rev. 4:7 [1]NU, M omit *and see*
4 [a]Zech. 1:8; 6:2 [b]Matt. 24:6, 7
5 [a]Rev. 4:7 [b]Zech. 6:2, 6 [c]Matt. 24:7 [1]*balances*
6 [a]Rev. 7:3; 9:4 [1]Gr. *choinix,* about 1 quart [2]About 1 day's wage for a worker
7 [a]Rev. 4:7
8 [a]Zech. 6:3 [b]Ezek. 5:12, 17; 14:21; 29:5 [c]Lev. 26:22 [1]*authority*
9 [a]Rev. 8:3 [b][Rev. 20:4] [c]Rev. 1:2, 9 [d]2 Tim. 1:8
10 [a]Zech. 1:12 [b]Rev. 3:7 [c]Rev. 11:18
11 [a]Rev. 3:4, 5; 7:9 [b]Heb. 11:40
12 [a]Matt. 24:7 [b]Joel 2:10, 31; 3:15 [1]NU, M omit *behold* [2]NU, M *whole moon*
13 [a]Rev. 8:10; 9:1
14 [a]Is. 34:4 [b]Rev. 16:20 [1]Or *split apart*
15 [a]Ps. 2:2–4 [b]Is. 2:10, 19, 21; 24:21 [1]NU, M *the commanders, the rich men,*
16 [a]Luke 23:29, 30 [b]Rev. 20:11
17 [a]Zeph. 1:14

CHAPTER 7

1 [a]Dan. 7:2 [b]Rev. 7:3; 8:7; 9:4
3 [a]Rev. 6:6 [b]Rev. 22:4
4 [a]Rev. 9:16 [b]Rev. 14:1, 3 [c]Gen. 49:1–27

all the tribes of the children of Is-
rael *were* sealed:

5 of the tribe of Judah
twelve thousand *were* sealed;
of the tribe of Reuben
twelve thousand *were* [1]sealed;
of the tribe of Gad
twelve thousand *were* sealed;
6 of the tribe of Asher
twelve thousand *were* sealed;
of the tribe of Naphtali
twelve thousand *were* sealed;
of the tribe of Manasseh
twelve thousand *were* sealed;
7 of the tribe of Simeon
twelve thousand *were* sealed;
of the tribe of Levi
twelve thousand *were* sealed;
of the tribe of Issachar
twelve thousand *were* sealed;
8 of the tribe of Zebulun
twelve thousand *were* sealed;
of the tribe of Joseph
twelve thousand *were* sealed;
of the tribe of Benjamin
twelve thousand *were* sealed.

A Multitude from the Great Tribulation

9 After these things I looked, and
behold, [a]a great multitude which
no one could number, [b]of all na-
tions, tribes, peoples, and tongues,
standing before the throne and be-
fore the Lamb, [c]clothed with white
robes, with palm branches in their
hands,
10 and crying out with a loud
voice, saying, [a]"Salvation *belongs*
to our God [b]who sits on the throne,
and to the Lamb!"
11 [a]All the angels stood around
the throne and the elders and the
four living creatures, and fell on
their faces before the throne and
[b]worshiped God,
12 [a]saying:

"Amen! Blessing and glory and
wisdom,
Thanksgiving and honor and
power and might,
Be to our God forever and ever.
Amen."

13 Then one of the elders an-
swered, saying to me, "Who are
these arrayed in [a]white robes, and
where did they come from?"
14 And I said to him, [1]"Sir, you
know." So he said to me, [a]"These
are the ones who come out of the
great tribulation, and [b]washed

5 [1]NU, M omit *sealed* in vv. 5b–8b.
9 [a]Is. 60:1–5; Rom. 11:25 [b]Rev. 5:9 [c]Rev. 3:5, 18; 4:4; 6:11
10 [a]Ps. 3:8; Is. 43:11; Jer. 3:23; Hos. 13:4; Rev. 19:1 [b]Rev. 5:13
11 [a]Rev. 4:6 [b]Rev. 4:11; 5:9, 12, 14; 11:16
12 [a]Rev. 5:13, 14
13 [a]Rev. 7:9
14 [a]Rev. 6:9 [b]Is. 1:18; Zech. 3:3–5; [Heb. 9:14] [1]NU, M *My lord*
15 [a]Is. 4:5, 6; Rev. 21:3
16 [a]Ps. 121:5; Is. 49:10 [b]Ps. 121:6; Rev. 21:4
17 [a]Ps. 23:1; Matt. 2:6; [John 10:11, 14] [b]Is. 25:8; Matt. 5:4; Rev. 21:4 [1]NU, M *fountains of the waters of life*

CHAPTER 8

1 [a]Rev. 6:1
2 [a][Matt. 18:10]; Luke 1:19 [b]2 Chr. 29:25–28
3 [a]Rev. 5:8 [b]Ex. 30:1; Rev. 8:3
4 [a]Ps. 141:2; Luke 1:10
5 [a]Ex. 19:16; Rev. 11:19; 16:18 [b]Rev. 4:5 [c]2 Sam. 22:8; 1 Kin. 19:11; Acts 4:31
7 [a]Ex. 9:23; Is. 28:2; Ezek. 38:22; Joel 2:30 [b]Rev. 16:2 [c]Is. 2:13; Rev. 9:4,15–18 [1]NU, M add *and a third of the earth was burned up*
8 [a]Jer. 51:25; Amos 7:4 [b]Ex. 7:17; Rev. 11:6; 16:3 [c]Ezek. 14:19

their robes and made them white
in the blood of the Lamb.
15 "Therefore they are before the
throne of God, and serve Him day
and night in His temple. And He
who sits on the throne will [a]dwell
among them.
16 [a]"They shall neither hunger
anymore nor thirst anymore; [b]the
sun shall not strike them, nor any
heat;
17 "for the Lamb who is in the
midst of the throne [a]will shepherd
them and lead them to [1]living
fountains of waters. [b]And God will
wipe away every tear from their
eyes."

Seventh Seal: Prelude to the Seven Trumpets

8 When[a] He opened the seventh
seal, there was silence in
heaven for about half an hour.
2 [a]And I saw the seven angels
who stand before God, [b]and to
them were given seven trumpets.
3 Then another angel, having a
golden censer, came and stood at
the altar. He was given much in-
cense, that he should offer *it* with
[a]the prayers of all the saints upon
[b]the golden altar which was before
the throne.
4 And [a]the smoke of the incense,
with the prayers of the saints, as-
cended before God from the an-
gel's hand.
5 Then the angel took the censer,
filled it with fire from the altar, and
threw *it* to the earth. And [a]there
were noises, thunderings, [b]light-
nings, [c]and an earthquake.
6 So the seven angels who had
the seven trumpets prepared them-
selves to sound.

First Trumpet: Vegetation Struck

7 The first angel sounded: [a]And
hail and fire followed, mingled
with blood, and they were thrown
[b]to the [1]earth. And a third [c]of the
trees were burned up, and all
green grass was burned up.

Second Trumpet: The Seas Struck

8 Then the second angel
sounded: [a]And *something* like a
great mountain burning with fire
was thrown into the sea, [b]and a
third of the sea [c]became blood.

9 [a]And a third of the living creatures in the sea died, and a third of the ships were destroyed.

Third Trumpet: The Waters Struck

10 Then the third angel sounded: [a]And a great star fell from heaven, burning like a torch, [b]and it fell on a third of the rivers and on the springs of water.

11 [a]The name of the star is Wormwood. [b]A third of the waters became wormwood, and many men died from the water, because it was made bitter.

Fourth Trumpet: The Heavens Struck

12 [a]Then the fourth angel sounded: And a third of the sun was struck, a third of the moon, and a third of the stars, so that a third of them were darkened. A third of the day [1]did not shine, and likewise the night.

13 And I looked, [a]and I heard an [1]angel flying through the midst of heaven, saying with a loud voice, [b]"Woe, woe, woe to the inhabitants of the earth, because of the remaining blasts of the trumpet of the three angels who are about to sound!"

Fifth Trumpet: The Locusts from the Bottomless Pit

9 Then the fifth angel sounded: [a]And I saw a star fallen from heaven to the earth. To him was given the key to [b]the [1]bottomless pit.

2 And he opened the bottomless pit, and smoke arose out of the pit like the smoke of a great furnace. So the [a]sun and the air were darkened because of the smoke of the pit.

3 Then out of the smoke locusts came upon the earth. And to them was given power, [a]as the scorpions of the earth have power.

4 They were commanded [a]not to harm [b]the grass of the earth, or any green thing, or any tree, but only those men who do not have [c]the seal of God on their foreheads.

5 And [1]they were not given *authority* to kill them, [a]but to torment them *for* five months. Their torment *was* like the torment of a scorpion when it strikes a man.

6 In those days [a]men will seek death and will not find it; they will desire to die, and death will flee from them.

7 [a]The shape of the locusts was like horses prepared for battle. [b]On their heads were crowns of something like gold, [c]and their faces *were* like the faces of men.

8 They had hair like women's hair, and [a]their teeth were like lions' *teeth.*

9 And they had breastplates like breastplates of iron, and the sound of their wings *was* [a]like the sound of chariots with many horses running into battle.

10 They had tails like scorpions, and there were stings in their tails. Their power *was* to hurt men five months.

11 And they had as king over them [a]the angel of the bottomless pit, whose name in Hebrew *is* [1]Abaddon, but in Greek he has the name [2]Apollyon.

12 [a]One woe is past. Behold, still two more woes are coming after these things.

Sixth Trumpet: The Angels from the Euphrates

13 Then the sixth angel sounded: And I heard a voice from the four horns of the [a]golden altar which is before God,

14 saying to the sixth angel who had the trumpet, "Release the four angels who are bound [a]at the great river Euphrates."

15 So the four angels, who had been prepared for the hour and day and month and year, were released to kill a [a]third of mankind.

16 Now [a]the number of the army [b]of the horsemen *was* two hundred million; [c]I heard the number of them.

17 And thus I saw the horses in the vision: those who sat on them had breastplates of fiery red, hyacinth blue, and sulfur yellow; [a]and the heads of the horses *were* like the heads of lions; and out of their mouths came fire, smoke, and brimstone.

18 By these three *plagues* a third of mankind was killed—by the fire and the smoke and the brimstone which came out of their mouths.

19 For [1]their power is in their

9 [a]Rev. 16:3
10 [a]Is. 14:12; Rev. 6:13; 9:1 [b]Rev. 14:7; 16:4
11 [a]Ruth 1:20 [b]Ex. 15:23
12 [a]Is. 13:10; Joel 2:31; Amos 8:9; Matt. 24:29; Rev. 6:12 [1]*had no light*
13 [a]Rev. 14:6; 19:17 [b]Rev. 9:12; 11:14; 12:12 [1]NU, M *eagle*

CHAPTER 9

1 [a]Luke 10:18; Rev. 8:10 [b]Luke 8:31; Rev. 9:2, 11; 17:8 [1]Lit. *shaft of the abyss*
2 [a]Joel 2:2, 10
3 [a]Ex. 10:4; Judg. 7:12
4 [a]Rev. 6:6 [b]Rev. 8:7 [c]Ex. 12:23; Ezek. 9:4; Rev. 7:2, 3
5 [a][Rev. 9:10; 11:7] [1]The locusts
6 [a]Job 3:21; 7:15; Is. 2:19; Jer. 8:3; Rev. 6:16
7 [a]Joel 2:4 [b]Nah. 3:17 [c]Dan. 7:8
8 [a]Joel 1:6
9 [a]Jer. 47:3; Joel 2:5–7
11 [a]Eph. 2:2 [1]Lit. *Destruction* [2]Lit. *Destroyer*
12 [a]Rev. 8:13; 11:14
13 [a]Rev. 8:3
14 [a]Gen. 15:18; Deut. 1:7; Josh. 1:4; Rev. 16:12
15 [a]Rev. 8:7–9; 9:18
16 [a]Ps. 68:17; Dan. 7:10 [b]Ezek. 38:4 [c]Rev. 7:4
17 [a]1 Chr. 12:8; Is. 5:28, 29
19 [1]NU, M *the power of the horses*

mouth and in their tails; [a]for their
tails *are* like serpents, having
heads; and with them they do
harm.
20 But the rest of mankind, who
were not killed by these plagues,
[a]did not repent of the works of
their hands, that they should not
worship [b]demons, [c]and idols of
gold, silver, brass, stone, and
wood, which can neither see nor
hear nor walk.
21 And they did not repent of their
murders [a]or their [1]sorceries or
their sexual immorality or their
thefts.

The Mighty Angel with the Little Book

10 I saw still another mighty
angel coming down from
heaven, clothed with a cloud. [a]And
a rainbow *was* on [b]his head, his
face *was* like the sun, and [c]his feet
like pillars of fire.
2 He had a little book open in his
hand. [a]And he set his right foot on
the sea and *his* left *foot* on the
land,
3 and cried with a loud voice, as
when a lion roars. When he cried
out, [a]seven thunders uttered their
voices.
4 Now when the seven thunders
[1]uttered their voices, I was about
to write; but I heard a voice from
heaven saying [2]to me, [a]"Seal up
the things which the seven thun-
ders uttered, and do not write
them."
5 The angel whom I saw stand-
ing on the sea and on the land
[a]raised up his [1]hand to heaven
6 and swore by Him who lives
forever and ever, [a]who created
heaven and the things that are in
it, the earth and the things that are
in it, and the sea and the things
that are in it, [b]that there should be
delay no longer,
7 but [a]in the days of the sounding
of the seventh angel, when he is
about to sound, the mystery of
God would be finished, as He de-
clared to His servants the proph-
ets.

John Eats the Little Book

8 Then the voice which I heard
from heaven spoke to me again
and said, "Go, take the little book
which is open in the hand of the
angel who stands on the sea and
on the earth."
9 So I went to the angel and said
to him, "Give me the little book."
And he said to me, [a]"Take and eat
it; and it will make your stomach
bitter, but it will be as sweet as
honey in your mouth."
10 Then I took the little book out
of the angel's hand and ate it, [a]and
it was as sweet as honey in my
mouth. But when I had eaten it,
[b]my stomach became bitter.
11 And [1]he said to me, "You must
prophesy again about many peo-
ples, nations, tongues, and kings."

The Two Witnesses

11 Then I was given [a]a reed like
a measuring rod. [1]And the
angel stood, saying, [b]"Rise and
measure the temple of God, the
altar, and those who worship
there.
2 "But leave out [a]the court which
is outside the temple, and do not
measure it, [b]for it has been given
to the Gentiles. And they will
[c]tread the holy city underfoot *for*
[d]forty-two months.
3 "And I will give *power* to my
two [a]witnesses, [b]and they will
prophesy [c]one thousand two hun-
dred and sixty days, clothed in
sackcloth."
4 These are the [a]two olive trees
and the two lampstands standing
before the [1]God of the earth.
5 And if anyone wants to harm
them, [a]fire proceeds from their
mouth and devours their enemies.
[b]And if anyone wants to harm
them, he must be killed in this
manner.
6 These [a]have power to shut
heaven, so that no rain falls in the
days of their prophecy; and they
have power over waters to turn
them to blood, and to strike the
earth with all plagues, as often as
they desire.

The Witnesses Killed

7 When they [a]finish their testi-
mony, [b]the beast that ascends [c]out
of the bottomless pit [d]will make
war against them, overcome them,
and kill them.
8 And their dead bodies *will lie*
in the street of [a]the great city
which spiritually is called Sodom

19 [a]Is. 9:15
20 [a]Deut. 31:29 [b]1 Cor. 10:20 [c]Dan. 5:23
21 [a]Rev. 21:8; 22:15 [1]NU, M *drugs*

CHAPTER 10

1 [a]Rev. 4:3 [b]Rev. 1:16 [c]Rev. 1:15
2 [a]Matt. 28:18
3 [a]Ps. 29:3–9
4 [a]Dan. 8:26; 12:4, 9 [1]NU, M *sounded,* [2]NU, M omit *to me*
5 [a]Dan. 12:7 [1]NU, M *right hand*
6 [a]Rev. 4:11 [b]Rev. 16:17
7 [a]Rev. 11:15
9 [a]Jer. 15:16
10 [a]Ezek. 3:3 [b]Ezek. 2:10
11 [1]NU, M *they*

CHAPTER 11

1 [a]Ezek. 40:3—42:20 [b]Num. 23:18 [1]NU, M omit *And the angel stood*
2 [a]Ezek. 40:17, 20 [b]Ps. 79:1 [c]Dan. 8:10 [d]Rev. 12:6; 13:5
3 [a]Rev. 20:4 [b]Rev. 19:10 [c]Rev. 12:6
4 [a]Zech. 4:2, 3, 11, 14 [1]NU, M *Lord*
5 [a]2 Kin. 1:10–12 [b]Num. 16:29
6 [a]1 Kin. 17:1
7 [a]Luke 13:32 [b]Rev. 13:1, 11; 17:8 [c]Rev. 9:1, 2 [d]Dan. 7:21
8 [a]Rev. 14:8

and Egypt, [b]where also [1]our Lord
was crucified.
9 [a]Then *those* from the peoples,
tribes, tongues, and nations [1]will
see their dead bodies three-and-a-
half days, [b]and not allow their
dead bodies to be put into graves.
10 [a]And those who dwell on the
earth will rejoice over them, make
merry, [b]and send gifts to one an-
other, [c]because these two prophets
tormented those who dwell on the
earth.

The Witnesses Resurrected

11 [a]Now after the three-and-a-half
days [b]the breath of life from God
entered them, and they stood on
their feet, and great fear fell on
those who saw them.
12 And [1]they heard a loud voice
from heaven saying to them,
"Come up here." [a]And they as-
cended to heaven [b]in a cloud, [c]and
their enemies saw them.
13 In the same hour [a]there was a
great earthquake, [b]and a tenth of
the city fell. In the earthquake
seven thousand people were
killed, and the rest were afraid
[c]and gave glory to the God of
heaven.
14 [a]The second woe is past. Be-
hold, the third woe is coming
quickly.

Seventh Trumpet: The Kingdom Proclaimed

15 Then [a]the seventh angel
sounded: [b]And there were loud
voices in heaven, saying, [c]"The
[1]kingdoms of this world have be-
come *the kingdoms* of our Lord
and of His Christ, [d]and He shall
reign forever and ever!"
16 And [a]the twenty-four elders
who sat before God on their
thrones fell on their faces and
[b]worshiped God,
17 saying:

"We give You thanks, O Lord God
Almighty,
The One [a]who is and who was
[1]and who is to come,
Because You have taken Your
great power [b]and reigned.
18 The nations were [a]angry, and
Your [1]wrath has come,
And the time of the [b]dead, that
they should be judged,
And that You should reward
Your servants the prophets and
the saints,
And those who fear Your name,
small and great,
And should destroy those who
destroy the earth."

19 Then [a]the temple of God was
opened in heaven, and the ark of
[1]His covenant was seen in His tem-
ple. And [b]there were lightnings,
noises, thunderings, an earth-
quake, [c]and great hail.

The Woman, the Child, and the Dragon

12 Now a great sign appeared
in heaven: a woman clothed
with the sun, with the moon under
her feet, and on her head a garland
of twelve stars.
2 Then being with child, she
cried out [a]in labor and in pain to
give birth.
3 And another sign appeared in
heaven: behold, [a]a great, fiery red
dragon having seven heads and
ten horns, and seven diadems on
his heads.
4 [a]His tail drew a third [b]of the
stars of heaven [c]and threw them
to the earth. And the dragon stood
[d]before the woman who was ready
to give birth, [e]to devour her Child
as soon as it was born.
5 She bore a male Child [a]who
was to rule all nations with a rod
of iron. And her Child was [b]caught
up to God and His throne.
6 Then [a]the woman fled into the
wilderness, where she has a place
prepared by God, that they should
feed her there [b]one thousand two
hundred and sixty days.

Satan Thrown Out of Heaven

7 And war broke out in heaven:
[a]Michael and his angels fought
[b]with the dragon; and the dragon
and his angels fought,
8 but they [1]did not prevail, nor
was a place found for [2]them in
heaven any longer.
9 So [a]the great dragon was cast
out, [b]that serpent of old, called
the Devil and Satan, [c]who de-
ceives the whole world; [d]he was
cast to the earth, and his angels
were cast out with him.
10 Then I heard a loud voice say-

8 [b]Heb. 13:12 [1]NU, M *their*
9 [a]Rev. 17:15 [b]Ps. 79:2, 3 [1]NU, M *see . . . and will not allow*
10 [a]Rev. 12:12 [b]Esth. 9:19, 22 [c]Rev. 16:10
11 [a]Rev. 11:9 [b]Ezek. 37:5, 9, 10
12 [a]Is. 14:13 [b]Acts 1:9 [c]2 Kin. 2:11, 12 [1]M *I*
13 [a]Rev. 6:12; 8:5; 11:19; 16:18 [b]Rev. 16:19 [c]Rev. 14:7; 16:9; 19:7
14 [a]Rev. 8:13; 9:12
15 [a]Rev. 8:2; 10:7 [b]Is. 27:13 [c]Rev. 12:10 [d]Ex. 15:18 [1]NU, M *kingdom . . . has become the kingdom*
16 [a]Rev. 4:4 [b]Rev. 4:11; 5:9, 12, 14; 7:11
17 [a]Rev. 16:5 [b]Rev. 19:6 [1]NU, M omit *and who is to come*
18 [a]Ps. 2:1 [b]Dan. 7:10 [1]*anger*
19 [a]Rev. 4:1; 15:5, 8 [b]Rev. 8:5 [c]Rev. 16:21 [1]M *the covenant of the Lord*

CHAPTER 12

2 [a]Is. 26:17; 66:6–9
3 [a]Rev. 13:1; 17:3, 7, 9
4 [a]Rev. 9:10, 19 [b]Rev. 8:7, 12 [c]Dan. 8:10 [d]Rev. 12:2 [e]Matt. 2:16
5 [a]Ps. 2:9 [b]Acts 1:9–11
6 [a]Rev. 12:4, 14 [b]Rev. 11:3; 13:5
7 [a]Dan. 10:13, 21; 12:1 [b]Rev. 20:2
8 [1]*were not strong enough* [2]M *him*
9 [a]John 12:31 [b]Gen. 3:1, 4 [c]Rev. 20:3 [d]Rev. 9:1

ing in heaven, [a]"Now salvation,
and strength, and the kingdom of
our God, and the power of His
Christ have come, for the accuser
of our brethren, [b]who accused
them before our God day and
night, has been cast down.
11 "And [a]they overcame him by
the blood of the Lamb and by the
word of their testimony, [b]and they
did not love their lives to the death.
12 "Therefore [a]rejoice, O heavens,
and you who dwell in them! [b]Woe
to the inhabitants of the earth and
the sea! For the devil has come
down to you, having great wrath,
[c]because he knows that he has a
short time."

The Woman Persecuted

13 Now when the dragon saw that
he had been cast to the earth, he
persecuted [a]the woman who gave
birth to the male *Child.*
14 [a]But the woman was given two
wings of a great eagle, [b]that she
might fly [c]into the wilderness to
her place, where she is nourished
[d]for a time and times and half a
time, from the presence of the ser-
pent.
15 So the serpent [a]spewed water
out of his mouth like a flood after
the woman, that he might cause
her to be carried away by the
flood.
16 But the earth helped the
woman, and the earth opened its
mouth and swallowed up the flood
which the dragon had spewed out
of his mouth.
17 And the dragon was enraged
with the woman, and he went to
make war with the rest of her off-
spring, who keep the command-
ments of God and have the testi-
mony of Jesus [1]Christ.

The Beast from the Sea

13 Then [1]I stood on the sand of
the sea. And I saw [a]a beast
rising up out of the sea, [b]having
[2]seven heads and ten horns, and
on his horns ten crowns, and on
his heads a [c]blasphemous name.
2 Now the beast which I saw was
like a leopard, his feet were like
the feet of a bear, and his mouth
like the mouth of a lion. The
[a]dragon gave him his power, his
throne, and great authority.
3 And *I saw* one of his heads [a]as
if it had been mortally wounded,
and his deadly wound was healed.
And [b]all the world marveled and
followed the beast.
4 So they worshiped the dragon
who gave authority to the beast;
and they worshiped the beast, say-
ing, [a]"Who *is* like the beast? Who
is able to make war with him?"
5 And he was given [a]a mouth
speaking great things and blas-
phemies, and he was given author-
ity to [1]continue for [b]forty-two
months.
6 Then he opened his mouth in
blasphemy against God, to blas-
pheme His name, [a]His tabernacle,
and those who dwell in heaven.
7 It was granted to him [a]to make
war with the saints and to over-
come them. And [b]authority was
given him over every [1]tribe,
tongue, and nation.
8 All who dwell on the earth will
worship him, [a]whose names have
not been written in the Book of
Life of the Lamb slain [b]from the
foundation of the world.
9 [a]If anyone has an ear, let him
hear.
10 [a]He who leads into captivity
shall go into captivity; [b]he who
kills with the sword must be killed
with the sword. [c]Here is the [1]pa-
tience and the faith of the saints.

The Beast from the Earth

11 Then I saw another beast [a]com-
ing up out of the earth, and he had
two horns like a lamb and spoke
like a dragon.
12 And he exercises all the au-
thority of the first beast in his pres-
ence, and causes the earth and
those who dwell in it to worship
the first beast, [a]whose deadly
wound was healed.
13 [a]He performs great signs, [b]so
that he even makes fire come
down from heaven on the earth in
the sight of men.
14 [a]And he deceives [1]those who
dwell on the earth [b]by those signs
which he was granted to do in the
sight of the beast, telling those
who dwell on the earth to make
an image to the beast who was
wounded by the sword [c]and lived.
15 He was granted *power* to give
breath to the image of the beast,

---

10 [a]Rev. 11:15 [b]Zech. 3:1
11 [a]Rom. 16:20 [b]Luke 14:26
12 [a]Ps. 96:11 [b]Rev. 8:13 [c]Rev. 10:6
13 [a]Rev. 12:5
14 [a]Ex. 19:4 [b]Rev. 12:6 [c]Rev. 17:3 [d]Dan. 7:25; 12:7
15 [a]Is. 59:19
17 [1]NU, M omit *Christ*

CHAPTER 13

1 [a]Dan. 7:2, 7 [b]Rev. 12:3 [c]Rev. 17:3 [1]NU *he* [2]NU, M *ten horns and seven heads*
2 [a]Rev. 12:3, 9; 13:4, 12
3 [a]Rev. 13:12, 14 [b]Rev. 17:8
4 [a]Rev. 18:18
5 [a]Dan. 7:8, 11, 20, 25; 11:36 [b]Rev. 11:2 [1]M *make war*
6 [a][Col. 2:9]
7 [a]Dan. 7:21 [b]Rev. 11:18 [1]NU, M add *and people*
8 [a]Ex. 32:32 [b]Rev. 17:8
9 [a]Rev. 2:7
10 [a]Is. 33:1 [b]Gen. 9:6 [c]Rev. 14:12 [1]*perseverance*
11 [a]Rev. 11:7
12 [a]Rev. 13:3, 4
13 [a]Matt. 24:24 [b]1 Kin. 18:38
14 [a]Rev. 12:9 [b]2 Thess. 2:9 [c]2 Kin. 20:7 [1]M *my own people*

that the image of the beast should
both speak [a]and cause as many as
would not worship the image of
the beast to be killed.
16 He causes all, both small and
great, rich and poor, free and
slave, [a]to receive a mark on their
right hand or on their foreheads,
17 and that no one may buy or sell
except one who has [1]the mark or
[a]the name of the beast, [b]or the
number of his name.
18 [a]Here is wisdom. Let him who
has [b]understanding calculate [c]the
number of the beast, [d]for it is the
number of a man: His number *is*
666.

The Lamb and the 144,000

14 Then I looked, and behold,
[1]a [a]Lamb standing on Mount
Zion, and with Him [b]one hundred
and forty-four thousand, [2]having
His Father's name [c]written on
their foreheads.
2 And I heard a voice from
heaven, [a]like the voice of many
waters, and like the voice of loud
thunder. And I heard the sound of
[b]harpists playing their harps.
3 They sang as it were a new
song before the throne, before the
four living creatures, and the el-
ders; and no one could learn that
song [a]except the hundred *and*
forty-four thousand who were re-
deemed from the earth.
4 These are the ones who were
not defiled with women, [a]for they
are virgins. These are the ones
[b]who follow the Lamb wherever
He goes. These [c]were [1]redeemed
from *among* men, [d]*being* firstfruits
to God and to the Lamb.
5 And [a]in their mouth was found
no [1]deceit, for [b]they are without
fault [2]before the throne of God.

The Proclamations of Three Angels

6 Then I saw another angel
[a]flying in the midst of heaven,
[b]having the everlasting gospel to
preach to those who dwell on the
earth—[c]to every nation, tribe,
tongue, and people—
7 saying with a loud voice,
[a]"Fear God and give glory to Him,
for the hour of His judgment has
come; [b]and worship Him who
made heaven and earth, the sea
and springs of water."

15 [a]Rev. 16:2
16 [a]Rev. 7:3; 14:9; 20:4
17 [a]Rev. 14:9–11 [b]Rev. 15:2 [1]NU, M *the mark, the name*
18 [a]Rev. 17:9 [b][1 Cor. 2:14] [c]Rev. 15:2 [d]Rev. 21:17

CHAPTER 14

1 [a]Rev. 5:6 [b]Rev. 7:4; 14:3 [c]Rev. 7:3; 22:4 [1]NU, M *the* [2]NU, M add *His name and*
2 [a]Rev. 1:15; 19:6 [b]Rev. 5:8
3 [a]Rev. 5:9
4 [a][2 Cor. 11:2] [b]Rev. 3:4; 7:17 [c]Rev. 5:9 [d]James 1:18 [1]M adds *by Jesus*
5 [a]Ps. 32:2 [b]Eph. 5:27 [1]NU, M *falsehood* [2]NU, M omit the rest of v. 5.
6 [a]Rev. 8:13 [b]Eph. 3:9 [c]Rev. 13:7
7 [a]Rev. 11:18 [b]Neh. 9:6
8 [a]Is. 21:9 [b]Jer. 51:7 [1]NU *Babylon the great is fallen, is fallen, which has made;* M *Babylon the great is fallen. She has made*
9 [a]Rev. 13:14, 15; 14:11 [b]Rev. 13:16
10 [a]Ps. 75:8 [b]Rev. 18:6 [c]Rev. 16:19 [d]Rev. 20:10 [e]2 Thess. 1:7
11 [a]Is. 34:8–10
12 [a]Rev. 13:10 [b]Rev. 12:17 [1]*steadfastness, perseverance* [2]NU, M omit *here are those*
13 [a]Eccl. 4:1, 2 [b]1 Cor. 15:18 [c]Heb. 4:9, 10 [d][1 Cor. 3:11–15; 15:58] [1]NU, M omit *to me*
15 [a]Rev. 16:17 [b]Joel 3:13 [c]Jer. 51:33 [1]NU, M omit *for You*
18 [a]Rev. 16:8

8 And another angel followed,
saying, [a]"Babylon[1] is fallen, is
fallen, that great city, because [b]she
has made all nations drink of the
wine of the wrath of her forni-
cation."
9 Then a third angel followed
them, saying with a loud voice, [a]"If
anyone worships the beast and his
image, and receives *his* [b]mark on
his forehead or on his hand,
10 "he himself [a]shall also drink of
the wine of the wrath of God,
which is [b]poured out full strength
into [c]the cup of His indignation.
[d]He shall be tormented with [e]fire
and brimstone in the presence of
the holy angels and in the pres-
ence of the Lamb.
11 "And [a]the smoke of their tor-
ment ascends forever and ever;
and they have no rest day or night,
who worship the beast and his im-
age, and whoever receives the
mark of his name."
12 [a]Here is the [1]patience of the
saints; [b]here[2] *are* those who keep
the commandments of God and the
faith of Jesus.
13 Then I heard a voice from
heaven saying [1]to me, "Write:
[a]'Blessed *are* the dead [b]who die in
the Lord from now on.'" "Yes,"
says the Spirit, [c]"that they may
rest from their labors, and their
works follow [d]them."

Reaping the Earth's Harvest

14 Then I looked, and behold, a
white cloud, and on the cloud sat
One like the Son of Man, having
on His head a golden crown, and
in His hand a sharp sickle.
15 And another angel [a]came out
of the temple, crying with a loud
voice to Him who sat on the cloud,
[b]"Thrust in Your sickle and reap,
for the time has come [1]for You to
reap, for the harvest [c]of the earth
is ripe."
16 So He who sat on the cloud
thrust in His sickle on the earth,
and the earth was reaped.

Reaping the Grapes of Wrath

17 Then another angel came out
of the temple which is in heaven,
he also having a sharp sickle.
18 And another angel came out
from the altar, [a]who had power
over fire, and he cried with a loud

cry to him who had the sharp
sickle, saying, [b]"Thrust in your
sharp sickle and gather the clus-
ters of the vine of the earth, for
her grapes are fully ripe."
19 So the angel thrust his sickle
into the earth and gathered the
vine of the earth, and threw *it* into
[a]the great winepress of the wrath
of God.
20 And [a]the winepress was tram-
pled [b]outside the city, and blood
came out of the winepress, [c]up to
the horses' bridles, for one thou-
sand six hundred [1]furlongs.

Prelude to the Bowl Judgments

15 Then [a]I saw another sign in
heaven, great and marvel-
ous: [b]seven angels having the
seven last plagues, [c]for in them the
wrath of God is complete.
2 And I saw *something* like [a]a
sea of glass [b]mingled with fire, and
those who have the victory over
the beast, [c]over his image and
[1]over his mark *and* over the [d]num-
ber of his name, standing on the
sea of glass, [e]having harps of God.
3 They sing [a]the song of Moses,
the servant of God, and the song
of the [b]Lamb, saying:

[c]"Great and marvelous *are* Your
works,
Lord God Almighty!
[d]Just and true *are* Your ways,
O King of the [1]saints!
4 [a]Who shall not fear You, O Lord,
and glorify Your name?
For *You* alone *are* [b]holy.
For [c]all nations shall come and
worship before You,
For Your judgments have been
manifested."

5 After these things I looked, and
[1]behold, [a]the [2]temple of the taber-
nacle of the testimony in heaven
was opened.
6 And out of the [1]temple came
the seven angels having the seven
plagues, [a]clothed in pure bright
linen, and having their chests
girded with golden bands.
7 [a]Then one of the four living
creatures gave to the seven angels
seven golden bowls full of the
wrath of God [b]who lives forever
and ever.
8 [a]The temple was filled with
smoke [b]from the glory of God and

18 [b]Joel 3:13
19 [a]Rev. 19:15
20 [a]Is. 63:3
[b]Heb. 13:12
[c]Is. 34:3 [1]Lit. *stadia,* about 184 miles in all

CHAPTER 15

1 [a]Rev. 12:1, 3
[b]Rev. 21:9
[c]Rev. 14:10
2 [a]Rev. 4:6
[b][Matt. 3:11]
[c]Rev. 13:14, 15 [d]Rev. 13:17 [e]Rev. 5:8 [1]NU, M omit *over his mark*
3 [a]Ex. 15:1–21
[b]Rev. 15:3
[c]Deut. 32:3, 4
[d]Ps. 145:17
[1]NU, M *nations*
4 [a]Ex. 15:14
[b]Lev. 11:44
[c]Is. 66:23
5 [a]Num. 1:50
[1]NU, M omit *behold*
[2]*sanctuary,* the inner shrine
6 [a]Ex. 28:6
[1]*sanctuary,* the inner shrine
7 [a]Rev. 4:6
[b]1 Thess. 1:9
8 [a]Ex. 19:18; 40:34
[b]2 Thess. 1:9

CHAPTER 16

1 [a]Rev. 15:1
[b]Rev. 14:10
[1]NU, M *seven bowls*
2 [a]Rev. 8:7
[b]Ex. 9:9–11
[c]Rev. 13:15–17; 14:9 [d]Rev. 13:14 [1]*severe and malignant,* lit. *bad and evil*
3 [a]Rev. 8:8; 11:6 [b]Ex. 7:17–21 [c]Rev. 8:9
4 [a]Rev. 8:10
[b]Ex. 7:17–20
5 [a]Rev. 15:3, 4
[b]Rev. 1:4, 8
[1]NU, M omit *O Lord* [2]NU, M *was, the Holy One*
6 [a]Matt. 23:34
[b]Rev. 11:18
[c]Is. 49:26
[1]NU, M omit *For*
7 [a]Rev. 15:3
[b]Rev. 13:10; 19:2 [1]NU, M omit *another from*

from His power, and no one was
able to enter the temple till the
seven plagues of the seven angels
were completed.
16 Then I heard a loud voice
from the temple saying [a]to
the seven angels, "Go and pour out
the [1]bowls [b]of the wrath of God
on the earth."

First Bowl: Loathsome Sores

2 So the first went and poured
out his bowl [a]upon the earth, and
a [1]foul and [b]loathsome sore came
upon the men [c]who had the mark
of the beast and those [d]who wor-
shiped his image.

Second Bowl: The Sea Turns to Blood

3 Then the second angel poured
out his bowl [a]on the sea, and [b]it
became blood as of a dead *man;*
[c]and every living creature in the
sea died.

Third Bowl: The Waters Turn to Blood

4 Then the third angel poured
out his bowl [a]on the rivers and
springs of water, [b]and they be-
came blood.
5 And I heard the angel of the
waters saying:

[a]"You are righteous, [1]O Lord,
The One [b]who is and who [2]was
and who is to be,
Because You have judged these
things.
6 For [a]they have shed the blood [b]of
saints and prophets,
[c]And You have given them blood
to drink.
[1]For it is their just due."

7 And I heard [1]another from the
altar saying, "Even so, [a]Lord God
Almighty, [b]true and righteous *are*
Your judgments."

Fourth Bowl: Men Are Scorched

8 Then the fourth angel poured
out his bowl [a]on the sun, [b]and
power was given to him to scorch
men with fire.
9 And men were scorched with
great heat, and they [a]blasphemed
the name of God who has power
over these plagues; [b]and they did
not repent [c]and give Him glory.

8 [a]Rev. 8:12 [b]Rev. 9:17, 18 9 [a]Rev. 16:11 [b]Dan. 5:22 [c]Rev. 11:13

Fifth Bowl: Darkness and Pain

10 Then the fifth angel poured out
his bowl [a]on the throne of the
beast, [b]and his kingdom became
full of darkness; [c]and they gnawed
their tongues because of the pain.
11 They blasphemed the God of
heaven because of their pains and
their sores, and did not repent of
their deeds.

Sixth Bowl: Euphrates Dried Up

12 Then the sixth angel poured
out his bowl [a]on the great river
Euphrates, [b]and its water was
dried up, [c]so that the way of the
kings from the east might be pre-
pared.
13 And I saw three unclean [a]spir-
its like frogs *coming* out of the
mouth of [b]the dragon, out of the
mouth of the beast, and out of
the mouth of [c]the false prophet.
14 For they are spirits of demons,
[a]performing signs, *which* go out to
the kings [1]of the earth and of [b]the
whole world, to gather them to
[c]the battle of that great day of God
Almighty.
15 [a]"Behold, I am coming as a
thief. Blessed *is* he who watches,
and keeps his garments, [b]lest he
walk naked and they see his
shame."
16 [a]And they gathered them to-
gether to the place called in He-
brew, [1]Armageddon.

Seventh Bowl: The Earth Utterly Shaken

17 Then the seventh angel poured
out his bowl into the air, and a loud
voice came out of the temple of
heaven, from the throne, saying,
[a]"It is done!"
18 And [a]there were noises and
thunderings and lightnings; [b]and
there was a great earthquake, such
a mighty and great earthquake [c]as
had not occurred since men were
on the earth.
19 Now [a]the great city was di-
vided into three parts, and the cit-
ies of the nations fell. And [b]great
Babylon [c]was remembered before
God, [d]to give her the cup of the
wine of the fierceness of His
wrath.
20 Then [a]every island fled away,
and the mountains were not found.

10 [a]Rev. 13:2 [b]Rev. 8:12; 9:2 [c]Rev. 11:10
12 [a]Rev. 9:14 [b]Jer. 50:38 [c]Is. 41:2, 25; 46:11
13 [a]1 John 4:1 [b]Rev. 12:3, 9 [c]Rev. 13:11, 14; 19:20; 20:10
14 [a]2 Thess. 2:9 [b]Luke 2:1 [c]Rev. 17:14; 19:19; 20:8 [1]NU, M omit *of the earth and*
15 [a]Matt. 24:43 [b]2 Cor. 5:3
16 [a]Rev. 19:19 [1]Lit. *Mount Megiddo;* M *Megiddo*
17 [a]Rev. 10:6; 21:6
18 [a]Rev. 4:5 [b]Rev. 11:13 [c]Dan. 12:1
19 [a]Rev. 14:8 [b]Rev. 17:5, 18 [c]Rev. 14:8; 18:5 [d]Is. 51:17
20 [a]Rev. 6:14; 20:11

CHAPTER 17

1 [a]Rev. 1:1; 21:9 [b]Rev. 16:19 [c]Nah. 3:4 [d]Jer. 51:13 [1]NU, M omit *to me*
2 [a]Rev. 2:22; 18:3, 9 [b]Jer. 51:7
3 [a]Rev. 12:6, 14; 21:10 [b]Rev. 12:3 [c]Rev. 13:1
4 [a]Rev. 18:12, 16 [b]Dan. 11:38 [c]Jer. 51:7 [d]Rev. 14:8 [1]M *the fornication of the earth*
5 [a]2 Thess. 2:7
6 [a]Rev. 18:24 [b]Rev. 13:15 [c]Rev. 6:9, 10
7 [1]*hidden truth*
8 [a]Rev. 11:7 [b]Rev. 13:10; 17:11 [c]Rev. 3:10 [d]Rev. 13:3 [e]Rev. 13:8 [1]*destruction*

21 And great hail from heaven fell
upon men, *each hailstone* about
the weight of a talent. Men blas-
phemed God because of the plague
of the hail, since that plague was
exceedingly great.

The Scarlet Woman and the Scarlet Beast

17 Then [a]one of the seven an-
gels who had the seven
bowls came and talked with me,
saying [1]to me, "Come, [b]I will show
you the judgment of [c]the great har-
lot [d]who sits on many waters,
2 [a]"with whom the kings of the
earth committed fornication, and
[b]the inhabitants of the earth were
made drunk with the wine of her
fornication."
3 So he carried me away in the
Spirit [a]into the wilderness. And I
saw a woman sitting [b]on a scarlet
beast *which was* full of [c]names of
blasphemy, having seven heads
and ten horns.
4 The woman [a]was arrayed in
purple and scarlet, [b]and adorned
with gold and precious stones
and pearls, [c]having in her hand a
golden cup [d]full of abominations
and the filthiness of [1]her fornica-
tion.
5 And on her forehead a name
was written:

[a]MYSTERY, BABYLON THE
GREAT, THE MOTHER OF
HARLOTS AND OF THE
ABOMINATIONS OF THE
EARTH.

6 I saw [a]the woman, drunk [b]with
the blood of the saints and with
the blood of [c]the martyrs of Jesus.
And when I saw her, I marveled
with great amazement.

The Meaning of the Woman and the Beast

7 But the angel said to me, "Why
did you marvel? I will tell you the
[1]mystery of the woman and of the
beast that carries her, which has
the seven heads and the ten horns.
8 "The beast that you saw was,
and is not, and [a]will ascend out of
the bottomless pit and [b]go to [1]per-
dition. And those who [c]dwell on
the earth [d]will marvel, [e]whose
names are not written in the Book
of Life from the foundation of the

world, when they see the beast
that was, and is not, and [2]yet is.
9 [a]"Here *is* the mind which has
wisdom: [b]The seven heads are
seven mountains on which the
woman sits.
10 "There are also seven kings.
Five have fallen, one is, *and* the
other has not yet come. And when
he comes, he must [a]continue a
short time.
11 "The [a]beast that was, and is
not, is himself also the eighth, and
is of the seven, and is going to
[1]perdition.
12 [a]"The ten horns which you saw
are ten kings who have received
no kingdom as yet, but they re-
ceive authority for one hour as
kings with the beast.
13 "These are of one mind, and
they will give their power and au-
thority to the beast.
14 [a]"These will make war with the
Lamb, and the Lamb will [b]over-
come them, [c]for He is Lord of lords
and King of kings; [d]and those *who
are* with Him *are* called, chosen,
and faithful."
15 Then he said to me, [a]"The wa-
ters which you saw, where the har-
lot sits, [b]are peoples, multitudes,
nations, and tongues.
16 "And the ten horns which you
[1]saw on the beast, [a]these will hate
the harlot, make her [b]desolate
[c]and naked, eat her flesh and
[d]burn her with fire.
17 [a]"For God has put it into their
hearts to fulfill His purpose, to be
of one mind, and to give their king-
dom to the beast, [b]until the words
of God are fulfilled.
18 "And the woman whom you
saw [a]is that great city [b]which
reigns over the kings of the earth."

The Fall of Babylon the Great

18 After[a] these things I saw an-
other angel coming down
from heaven, having great author-
ity, [b]and the earth was illuminated
with his glory.
2 And he cried [1]mightily with a
loud voice, saying, [a]"Babylon the
great is fallen, is fallen, and [b]has
become a dwelling place of de-
mons, a prison for every foul spirit,
and [c]a cage for every unclean and
hated bird!
3 "For all the nations [a]have

8 [2]NU, M *shall be present*
9 [a]Rev. 13:18 [b]Rev. 13:1
10 [a]Rev. 13:5
11 [a]Rev. 13:3, 12, 14; 17:8 [1]*destruction*
12 [a]Dan. 7:20
14 [a]Rev. 16:14; 19:19 [b]Rev. 19:20 [c]1 Tim. 6:15 [d]Jer. 50:44
15 [a]Is. 8:7 [b]Rev. 13:7
16 [a]Jer. 50:41 [b]Rev. 18:17, 19 [c]Ezek. 16:37, 39 [d]Rev. 18:8 [1]NU, M *saw, and the beast*
17 [a]2 Thess. 2:11 [b]Rev. 10:7
18 [a]Rev. 11:8; 16:19 [b]Rev. 12:4

CHAPTER 18

1 [a]Rev. 17:1, 7 [b]Ezek. 43:2
2 [a]Is. 13:19; 21:9 [b]Is. 13:21; 34:11, 13–15 [c]Is. 14:23 [1]NU, M omit *mightily*
3 [a]Rev. 14:8 [b]Is. 47:15 [1]Lit. *strengths*
4 [a]Is. 48:20
5 [a]Gen. 18:20 [b]Rev. 16:19 [1]NU, M *have been heaped up*
6 [a]Ps. 137:8 [b]Rev. 14:10 [c]Rev. 16:19 [1]NU, M omit *to you*
7 [a]Ezek. 28:2–8 [b]Is. 47:7, 8 [1]*sensually*
8 [a]Rev. 18:10 [b]Rev. 17:16 [c]Jer. 50:34 [1]NU, M *has judged*
9 [a]Ezek. 26:16; 27:35 [b]Jer. 50:46 [c]Rev. 19:3
10 [a]Is. 21:9 [b]Rev. 18:17, 19
11 [a]Ezek. 27:27–34
12 [a]Rev. 17:4
13 [a]Ezek. 27:13

drunk of the wine of the wrath of
her fornication, the kings of the
earth have committed fornication
with her, [b]and the merchants of
the earth have become rich
through the [1]abundance of her lux-
ury."
4 And I heard another voice from
heaven saying, [a]"Come out of
her, my people, lest you share
in her sins, and lest you receive
of her plagues.
5 [a]"For her sins [1]have reached to
heaven, and [b]God has remem-
bered her iniquities.
6 [a]"Render to her just as she ren-
dered [1]to you, and repay her dou-
ble according to her works; [b]in the
cup which she has mixed, [c]mix
double for her.
7 [a]"In the measure that she glori-
fied herself and lived [1]luxuriously,
in the same measure give her tor-
ment and sorrow; for she says in
her heart, 'I sit *as* [b]queen, and am
no widow, and will not see sor-
row.'
8 "Therefore her plagues will
come [a]in one day—death and
mourning and famine. And [b]she
will be utterly burned with fire,
[c]for strong *is* the Lord God who
[1]judges her.

The World Mourns Babylon's Fall

9 [a]"The kings of the earth who
committed fornication and lived
luxuriously with her [b]will weep
and lament for her, [c]when they see
the smoke of her burning,
10 "standing at a distance for fear
of her torment, saying, [a]'Alas, alas,
that great city Babylon, that
mighty city! [b]For in one hour your
judgment has come.'
11 "And [a]the merchants of the
earth will weep and mourn over
her, for no one buys their mer-
chandise anymore:
12 [a]"merchandise of gold and sil-
ver, precious stones and pearls,
fine linen and purple, silk and
scarlet, every kind of citron wood,
every kind of object of ivory, every
kind of object of most precious
wood, bronze, iron, and marble;
13 "and cinnamon and incense,
fragrant oil and frankincense,
wine and oil, fine flour and wheat,
cattle and sheep, horses and chari-
ots, and bodies and [a]souls of men.

14 "The fruit that your soul longed
for has gone from you, and all the
things which are rich and splendid
have [1]gone from you, and you
shall find them no more at all.
15 "The merchants of these
things, who became rich by her,
will stand at a distance for fear of
her torment, weeping and wailing,
16 "and saying, 'Alas, alas, [a]that
great city [b]that was clothed in fine
linen, purple, and scarlet, and
adorned with gold and precious
stones and pearls!
17 [a]'For in one hour such great
riches [1]came to nothing.' [b]Every
shipmaster, all who travel by ship,
sailors, and as many as trade on
the sea, stood at a distance
18 [a]"and cried out when they saw
the smoke of her burning, saying,
[b]'What *is* like this great city?'
19 [a]"They threw dust on their
heads and cried out, weeping and
wailing, and saying, 'Alas, alas,
that great city, in which all who
had ships on the sea became rich
by her wealth! [b]For in one hour
she [1]is made desolate.'
20 [a]"Rejoice over her, O heaven,
and *you* [1]holy apostles and proph-
ets, for [b]God has avenged you on
her!"

Finality of Babylon's Fall

21 Then a mighty angel took up
a stone like a great millstone and
threw *it* into the sea, saying,
[a]"Thus with violence the great city
Babylon shall be thrown down,
and [b]shall not be found anymore.
22 [a]"The sound of harpists, musi-
cians, flutists, and trumpeters shall
not be heard in you anymore. No
craftsman of any craft shall be
found in you anymore, and the
sound of a millstone shall not be
heard in you anymore.
23 [a]"The light of a lamp shall not
shine in you anymore, [b]and the
voice of bridegroom and bride
shall not be heard in you anymore.
For [c]your merchants were the
great men of the earth, [d]for by
your sorcery all the nations were
deceived.
24 "And [a]in her was found the
blood of prophets and saints, and
of all who [b]were slain on the
earth."

14 [1]NU, M *been lost to you*
16 [a]Rev. 17:18 [b]Rev. 17:4
17 [a]Rev. 18:10 [b]Is. 23:14 [1]*have been laid waste*
18 [a]Ezek. 27:30 [b]Rev. 13:4
19 [a]Josh. 7:6 [b]Rev. 18:8 [1]*have been laid waste*
20 [a]Jer. 51:48 [b]Luke 11:49 [1]NU, M *saints and apostles*
21 [a]Jer. 51:63, 64 [b]Rev. 12:8; 16:20
22 [a]Jer. 7:34; 16:9; 25:10
23 [a]Jer. 25:10 [b]Jer. 7:34; 16:9 [c]Is. 23:8 [d]2 Kin. 9:22
24 [a]Rev. 16:6; 17:6 [b]Jer. 51:49

CHAPTER 19

1 [a]Rev. 11:15; 19:6 [b]Rev. 4:11 [1]NU, M add *something like* [2]NU, M omit *the Lord*
2 [a]Rev. 15:3; 16:7 [b]Deut. 32:43
3 [a]Is. 34:10
4 [a]Rev. 4:4, 6, 10 [b]1 Chr. 16:36
5 [a]Ps. 134:1 [b]Rev. 11:18 [1]NU, M omit *both*
6 [a]Ezek. 1:24 [b]Rev. 11:15 [1]NU, M *our*
7 [a][Matt. 22:2; 25:10]
8 [a]Ezek. 16:10 [b]Ps. 132:9
9 [a]Luke 14:15 [b]Rev. 22:6
10 [a]Rev. 22:8 [b]Acts 10:26 [c][Heb. 1:14] [d]1 John 5:10 [e]Luke 24:27
11 [a]Rev. 15:5 [b]Rev. 6:2; 19:19, 21

Heaven Exults over Babylon

19 After these things [a]I [1]heard
a loud voice of a great multi-
tude in heaven, saying, "Alleluia!
[b]Salvation and glory and honor
and power *belong* to [2]the Lord our
God!
2 "For [a]true and righteous *are*
His judgments, because He has
judged the great harlot who cor-
rupted the earth with her fornica-
tion; and He [b]has avenged on her
the blood of His servants *shed* by
her."
3 Again they said, "Alleluia!
[a]Her smoke rises up forever and
ever!"
4 And [a]the twenty-four elders
and the four living creatures fell
down and worshiped God who sat
on the throne, saying, [b]"Amen! Al-
leluia!"
5 Then a voice came from the
throne, saying, [a]"Praise our God,
all you His servants and those
who fear Him, [b]both[1] small and
great!"
6 [a]And I heard, as it were, the
voice of a great multitude, as the
sound of many waters and as
the sound of mighty thunderings,
saying, "Alleluia! For [b]the[1] Lord
God Omnipotent reigns!
7 "Let us be glad and rejoice and
give Him glory, for [a]the marriage
of the Lamb has come, and His
wife has made herself ready."
8 And [a]to her it was granted to
be arrayed in fine linen, clean and
bright, [b]for the fine linen is the
righteous acts of the saints.
9 Then he said to me, "Write:
[a]'Blessed *are* those who are called
to the marriage supper of the
Lamb!'" And he said to me,
[b]"These are the true sayings of
God."
10 And [a]I fell at his feet to worship
him. But he said to me, [b]"See *that
you do* not *do that!* I am your [c]fel-
low servant, and of your breth-
ren [d]who have the testimony
of Jesus. Worship God! For the
[e]testimony of Jesus is the spirit of
prophecy."

Christ on a White Horse

11 [a]Now I saw heaven opened,
and behold, [b]a white horse. And
He who sat on him *was* called

[c]Faithful and True, and [d]in righ-
teousness He judges and makes
war.
12 [a]His eyes *were* like a flame of
fire, and on His head *were* many
crowns. [b]He [1]had a name written
that no one knew except Him-
self.
13 [a]He *was* clothed with a robe
dipped in blood, and His name is
called [b]The Word of God.
14 [a]And the armies in heaven,
[b]clothed in [1]fine linen, white and
clean, followed Him on white
horses.
15 Now [a]out of His mouth goes a
[1]sharp sword, that with it He
should strike the nations. And [b]He
Himself will rule them with a rod
of iron. [c]He Himself treads the
winepress of the fierceness and
wrath of Almighty God.
16 And [a]He has on *His* robe and
on His thigh a name written:

[b]KING OF KINGS AND LORD OF
LORDS.

The Beast and His Armies Defeated

17 Then I saw an angel standing
in the sun; and he cried with a loud
voice, saying to all the birds that
fly in the midst of heaven, [a]"Come
and gather together for the [1]sup-
per of the great God,
18 [a]"that you may eat the flesh of
kings, the flesh of captains, the
flesh of mighty men, the flesh of
horses and of those who sit on
them, and the flesh of all *people*,
[1]free and slave, both small and
great."
19 [a]And I saw the beast, the kings
of the earth, and their armies,
gathered together to make war
against Him who sat on the horse
and against His army.
20 [a]Then the beast was captured,
and with him the false prophet
who worked signs in his presence,
by which he deceived those who
received the mark of the beast and
[b]those who worshiped his image.
[c]These two were cast alive into the
lake of fire [d]burning with brim-
stone.
21 And the rest [a]were killed with
the sword which proceeded from
the mouth of Him who sat on the
horse. [b]And all the birds [c]were
filled with their flesh.

11 [c]Rev. 3:7, 14 [d]Ps. 96:13; Is. 11:4
12 [a]Dan. 10:6; Rev. 1:14 [b]Rev. 2:17; 19:16 [1]M adds *names written, and*
13 [a]Is. 63:2, 3 [b][John 1:1, 14]
14 [a]Rev. 14:20 [b]Matt. 28:3 [1]NU, M *pure white linen*
15 [a]Is. 11:4; 2 Thess. 2:8; Rev. 1:16 [b]Ps. 2:8, 9 [c]Is. 63:3–6; Rev. 14:20 [1]M *sharp two-edged*
16 [a]Rev. 2:17; 19:12 [b]Dan. 2:47
17 [a]1 Sam. 17:44; Jer. 12:9; Ezek. 39:17 [1]NU, M *great supper of God*
18 [a]Ezek. 39:18–20 [1]NU, M *both free*
19 [a]Rev. 16:13–16
20 [a]Rev. 16:13 [b]Rev. 13:8, 12, 13 [c]Is. 30:33; Dan. 7:11 [d]Rev. 14:10
21 [a]Rev. 19:15 [b]Rev. 19:17, 18 [c]Rev. 17:16

CHAPTER 20

1 [a]Rev. 1:18; 9:1
2 [a]Is. 24:22; 2 Pet. 2:4; Jude 6
3 [a]Dan. 6:17; Matt. 27:66 [b]Rev. 12:9; 20:8, 10
4 [a]Dan. 7:9; Matt. 19:28; Luke 22:30 [b]Dan. 7:22; [1 Cor. 6:2, 3] [c]Rev. 6:9 [d]Rev. 13:12 [e]Rev. 13:15 [f]John 14:19 [g]Rom. 8:17; 2 Tim. 2:12 [1]M *the*
6 [a][Rev. 2:11; 20:14] [b]Is. 61:6; 1 Pet. 2:9; Rev. 1:6 [c]Rev. 20:4
8 [a]Rev. 12:9; 20:3, 10 [b]Ezek. 38:2; 39:1, 6 [c]Rev. 16:14
9 [a]Is. 8:8; Ezek. 38:9, 16

Satan Bound 1000 Years

20 Then I saw an angel coming
down from heaven, [a]having
the key to the bottomless pit and
a great chain in his hand.
2 He laid hold of [a]the dragon,
that serpent of old, who is *the*
Devil and Satan, and bound him
for a thousand years;
3 and he cast him into the bot-
tomless pit, and shut him up, and
[a]set a seal on him, [b]so that he
should deceive the nations no
more till the thousand years were
finished. But after these things he
must be released for a little while.

The Saints Reign with Christ 1000 Years

4 And I saw [a]thrones, and they
sat on them, and [b]judgment was
committed to them. Then *I saw*
[c]the souls of those who had been
beheaded for their witness to Jesus
and for the word of God, [d]who had
not worshiped the beast [e]or his im-
age, and had not received *his* mark
on their foreheads or on their
hands. And they [f]lived and
[g]reigned with Christ for [1]a thou-
sand years.
5 But the rest of the dead did not
live again until the thousand years
were finished. This *is* the first res-
urrection.
6 Blessed and holy *is* he who has
part in the first resurrection. Over
such [a]the second death has no
power, but they shall be [b]priests
of God and of Christ, [c]and shall
reign with Him a thousand years.

Satanic Rebellion Crushed

7 Now when the thousand years
have expired, Satan will be re-
leased from his prison
8 and will go out [a]to deceive the
nations which are in the four cor-
ners of the earth, [b]Gog and Magog,
[c]to gather them together to battle,
whose number *is* as the sand of the
sea.
9 [a]They went up on the breadth
of the earth and surrounded the
camp of the saints and the beloved
city. And fire came down from
God out of heaven and devoured
them.
10 The devil, who deceived them,
was cast into the lake of fire and

brimstone [a]where[1] the beast and
the false prophet *are*. And they
[b]will be tormented day and night
forever and ever.

The Great White Throne Judgment

11 Then I saw a great white throne
and Him who sat on it, from whose
face [a]the earth and the heaven fled
away. [b]And there was found no
place for them.
12 And I saw the dead, [a]small and
great, standing before [1]God, [b]and
books were opened. And another
[c]book was opened, which is *the
Book* of Life. And the dead were
judged [d]according to their works,
by the things which were written
in the books.
13 The sea gave up the dead who
were in it, [a]and Death and Hades
delivered up the dead who were
in them. [b]And they were judged,
each one according to his works.
14 Then [a]Death and Hades were
cast into the lake of fire. [b]This is
the second [1]death.
15 And anyone not found written
in the Book of Life [a]was cast into
the lake of fire.

All Things Made New

21 Now [a]I saw a new heaven
and a new earth, [b]for the
first heaven and the first earth had
passed away. Also there was no
more sea.
2 Then I, [1]John, saw [a]the holy
city, New Jerusalem, coming down
out of heaven from God, prepared
[b]as a bride adorned for her hus-
band.
3 And I heard a loud voice from
heaven saying, "Behold, [a]the tab-
ernacle of God *is* with men, and
He will dwell with them, and they
shall be His people. God Himself
will be with them *and be* their God.
4 [a]"And God will wipe away
every tear from their eyes; [b]there
shall be no more death, [c]nor sor-
row, nor crying. There shall be no
more pain, for the former things
have passed away."
5 Then [a]He who sat on the throne
said, [b]"Behold, I make all things
new." And He said [1]to me, "Write,
for [c]these words are true and faith-
ful."
6 And He said to me, [a]"It[1] is
done! [b]I am the Alpha and the
Omega, the Beginning and the
End. [c]I will give of the fountain of
the water of life freely to him who
thirsts.
7 "He who overcomes [1]shall in-
herit all things, and [a]I will be his
God and he shall be My son.
8 [a]"But the cowardly, [1]unbeliev-
ing, abominable, murderers, sex-
ually immoral, sorcerers, idola-
ters, and all liars shall have their
part in [b]the lake which burns with
fire and brimstone, which is the
second death."

The New Jerusalem

9 Then one of [a]the seven angels
who had the seven bowls filled
with the seven last plagues came
[1]to me and talked with me, saying,
"Come, I will show you [b]the [2]bride,
the Lamb's wife."
10 And he carried me away [a]in the
Spirit to a great and high moun-
tain, and showed me [b]the [1]great
city, the [2]holy Jerusalem, descend-
ing out of heaven from God,
11 [a]having the glory of God. Her
light *was* like a most precious
stone, like a jasper stone, clear as
crystal.
12 Also she had a great and high
wall with [a]twelve gates, and
twelve angels at the gates, and
names written on them, which are
the names of the twelve tribes of
the children of Israel:
13 [a]three gates on the east, three
gates on the north, three gates on
the south, and three gates on the
west.
14 Now the wall of the city had
twelve foundations, and [a]on them
were the [1]names of the twelve
apostles of the Lamb.
15 And he who talked with me
[a]had a gold reed to measure the
city, its gates, and its wall.
16 The city is laid out as a square;
its length is as great as its breadth.
And he measured the city with the
reed: twelve thousand [1]furlongs.
Its length, breadth, and height are
equal.
17 Then he measured its wall: one
hundred *and* forty-four cubits, *ac-
cording* to the measure of a man,
that is, of an angel.
18 The construction of its wall

10 [a]Rev. 19:20; 20:14, 15 [b]Rev. 14:10 [1]NU, M *where also*
11 [a]2 Pet. 3:7 [b]Dan. 2:35
12 [a]Rev. 19:5 [b]Dan. 7:10 [c]Ps. 69:28 [d]Matt. 16:27 [1]NU, M *the throne*
13 [a]Rev. 1:18; 6:8; 21:4 [b]Rev. 2:23; 20:12
14 [a]1 Cor. 15:26 [b]Rev. 21:8 [1]NU, M *death, the lake of fire.*
15 [a]Rev. 19:20

CHAPTER 21

1 [a][2 Pet. 3:13] [b]Rev. 20:11
2 [a]Is. 52:1 [b]2 Cor. 11:2 [1]NU, M omit *John*
3 [a]Lev. 26:11
4 [a]Is. 25:8 [b]1 Cor. 15:26 [c]Is. 35:10; 51:11; 65:19
5 [a]Rev. 4:2, 9; 20:11 [b]Is. 43:19 [c]Rev. 19:9; 22:6 [1]NU, M omit *to me*
6 [a]Rev. 10:6; 16:17 [b]Rev. 1:8; 22:13 [c]John 4:10 [1]M omits *It is done*
7 [a]Zech. 8:8 [1]M *I shall give him these things*
8 [a]1 Cor. 6:9 [b]Rev. 20:14 [1]M adds *and sinners,*
9 [a]Rev. 15:1 [b]Rev. 19:7; 21:2 [1]NU, M omit *to me* [2]M *woman, the Lamb's bride*
10 [a]Rev. 1:10 [b]Ezek. 48 [1]NU, M omit *great* [2]NU, M *holy city, Jerusalem*
11 [a]Rev. 15:8; 21:23; 22:5
12 [a]Ezek. 48:31–34
13 [a]Ezek. 48:31–34
14 [a]Eph. 2:20 [1]NU, M *twelve names*
15 [a]Ezek. 40:3
16 [1]Lit. *stadia,* about 1,380 miles in all

was *of* jasper; and the city *was*
pure gold, like clear glass.
19 [a]The foundations of the wall of
the city *were* adorned with all
kinds of precious stones: the first
foundation *was* jasper, the second
sapphire, the third chalcedony, the
fourth emerald,
20 the fifth sardonyx, the sixth
sardius, the seventh chrysolite, the
eighth beryl, the ninth topaz, the
tenth chrysoprase, the eleventh ja-
cinth, and the twelfth amethyst.
21 The twelve gates *were* twelve
[a]pearls: each individual gate was
of one pearl. [b]And the street of the
city *was* pure gold, like transpar-
ent glass.

The Glory of the New Jerusalem

22 [a]But I saw no temple in it, for
the Lord God Almighty and the
Lamb are its temple.
23 [a]The city had no need of the
sun or of the moon to shine [1]in it,
for the [2]glory of God illuminated
it. The Lamb *is* its light.
24 [a]And the nations [1]of those who
are saved shall walk in its light,
and the kings of the earth bring
their glory and honor [2]into it.
25 [a]Its gates shall not be shut at
all by day [b](there shall be no night
there).
26 [a]And they shall bring the glory
and the honor of the nations
into [1]it.
27 But [a]there shall by no means
enter it anything [1]that defiles, or
causes an abomination or a lie, but
only those who are written in the
Lamb's [b]Book of Life.

The River of Life

22 And he showed me [a]a [1]pure
river of water of life, clear
as crystal, proceeding from the
throne of God and of the Lamb.
2 [a]In the middle of its street, and
on either side of the river, *was* [b]the
tree of life, which bore twelve
fruits, each *tree* yielding its fruit
every month. The leaves of the tree
were [c]for the healing of the na-
tions.
3 And [a]there shall be no more
curse, [b]but the throne of God and
of the Lamb shall be in it, and His
[c]servants shall serve Him.
4 [a]They shall see His face, and
[b]His name *shall be* on their fore-
heads.
5 [a]There shall be no night there:
They need no lamp nor [b]light of
the sun, for [c]the Lord God gives
them light. [d]And they shall reign
forever and ever.

The Time Is Near

6 Then he said to me, [a]"These
words *are* faithful and true." And
the Lord God of the [1]holy prophets
[b]sent His angel to show His ser-
vants the things which must
[c]shortly take place.
7 [a]"Behold, I am coming quickly!
[b]Blessed *is* he who keeps the
words of the prophecy of this
book."
8 Now I, John, [1]saw and heard
these things. And when I heard
and saw, [a]I fell down to worship
before the feet of the angel who
showed me these things.
9 Then he said to me, [a]"See *that*
you do not *do that*. [1]For I am your
fellow servant, and of your breth-
ren the prophets, and of those who
keep the words of this book. Wor-
ship God."
10 [a]And he said to me, "Do not
seal the words of the prophecy of
this book, [b]for the time is at hand.
11 "He who is unjust, let him be
unjust still; he who is filthy, let him
be filthy still; he who is righteous,
let him [1]be righteous still; he who
is holy, let him be holy still."

Jesus Testifies to the Churches

12 "And behold, I am coming
quickly, and [a]My reward *is* with
Me, [b]to give to every one accord-
ing to his work.
13 [a]"I am the Alpha and the
Omega, *the* [1]Beginning and *the*
End, the First and the Last."
14 [a]Blessed *are* those who [1]do His
commandments, that they may
have the right [b]to the tree of life,
[c]and may enter through the gates
into the city.
15 [1]But [a]outside *are* [b]dogs and
sorcerers and sexually immoral
and murderers and idolaters, and
whoever loves and practices a lie.

19 [a]Is. 54:11
21 [a]Matt. 13:45, 46 [b]Rev. 22:2
22 [a]John 4:21, 23
23 [a]Is. 24:23; 60:19, 20 [1]NU, M omit *in it* [2]M *very glory*
24 [a]Is. 60:3, 5; 66:12 [1]NU, M omit *of those who are saved* [2]M *of the nations to Him*
25 [a]Is. 60:11 [b]Is. 60:20
26 [a]Rev. 21:24 [1]M adds *that they may enter in.*
27 [a]Joel 3:17 [b]Phil. 4:3 [1]NU, M *profane, nor one who causes*

CHAPTER 22

1 [a]Ezek. 47:1 [1]NU, M omit *pure*
2 [a]Ezek. 47:12 [b]Gen. 2:9 [c]Rev. 21:24
3 [a]Zech. 14:11 [b]Ezek. 48:35 [c]Rev. 7:15
4 [a][Matt. 5:8] [b]Rev. 14:1
5 [a]Rev. 21:23 [b]Rev. 7:15 [c]Ps. 36:9 [d]Dan. 7:18, 27
6 [a]Rev. 19:9 [b]Rev. 1:1 [c]Heb. 10:37 [1]NU, M *spirits of the prophets*
7 [a][Rev. 3:11] [b]Rev. 1:3
8 [a]Rev. 19:10 [1]NU, M *am the one who heard and saw*
9 [a]Rev. 19:10 [1]NU, M omit *For*
10 [a]Dan. 8:26 [b]Rev. 1:3
11 [1]NU, M *do right*
12 [a]Is. 40:10; 62:11 [b]Rev. 20:12
13 [a]Is. 41:4 [1]NU, M *First and the Last, the Beginning and the End.*
14 [a]Dan. 12:12 [b][Prov. 11:30] [c]Rev. 21:27 [1]NU *wash their robes,*
15 [a]1 Cor. 6:9 [b]Phil. 3:2 [1]NU, M omit *But*

16 [a]"I, Jesus, have sent My angel
to testify to you these things in the
churches. [b]I am the Root and the
Offspring of David, [c]the Bright and
Morning Star."
17 And the Spirit and [a]the bride
say, "Come!" And let him who
hears say, "Come!" [b]And let him
who thirsts come. Whoever desires, let him take the water of life
freely.

A Warning

18 [1]For I testify to everyone who
hears the words of the prophecy
of this book: [a]If anyone adds to
these things, [2]God will add to him
the plagues that are written in this
book;
19 and if anyone takes away from
the words of the book of this
prophecy, [a]God[1] shall take away
his part from the [2]Book of Life,
from the holy city, and *from* the
things which are written in this
book.

I Am Coming Quickly

20 He who testifies to these things
says, "Surely I am coming
quickly." Amen. Even so, come,
Lord Jesus!
21 The grace of our Lord Jesus
Christ *be* [1]with you all. Amen.

16 [a]Rev. 1:1 [b]Rev. 5:5 [c]Num. 24:17
17 [a][Rev. 21:2, 9] [b]Is. 55:1; Rev. 21:6
18 [a]Deut. 4:2; 12:32; Prov. 30:6 [1]NU, M omit *For* [2]M *may God add*
19 [a]Ex. 32:33 [1]M *may God take away* [2]NU, M *tree of life*
21 [1]NU *with all;* M *with all the saints*

Additional Study Helps
and
Concordance

Teachings and Illustrations of Christ

Subject	Reference
Abiding in Christ	John 15:4–10
Ability	Matt. 25:14, 15
Ablution	Matt. 6:17, 18
Abode	John 14:23
Abraham	John 8:37, 56
Abstinence	Luke 21:34
Abundant life	John 10:10
Access to God	John 10:7, 9
Accountability	Luke 12:47, 48
Accusation, false	Matt. 5:11
Adultery	Matt. 5:27, 28
Adversity	Luke 24:46
Affliction	Matt. 24:7–12
Agreement	Matt. 18:19
Altar	Matt. 23:18, 19
Ambition	Luke 22:25–30
Angels	Matt. 13:39, 41
Anger	Matt. 5:22
Anxiety	Luke 12:22–31
Apostasy	Matt. 13:18–22 Luke 8:13
Apostles	Luke 11:49
Appearance	Matt. 6:16
Appearance, outward	Matt. 23:27, 28
Authority	Matt. 21:24 Luke 10:19
Avarice	Luke 12:16–21
Backsliding	Luke 9:62
Baptism	Matt. 28:19 Acts 1:5
Beatitudes	Matt. 5:3–11
Beelzebub	Matt. 10:25
Begging	Luke 16:3
Beneficence	Matt. 5:42
Betrayal	Matt. 26:21
Bigotry	Luke 18:9–14
Birds	Matt. 8:20
Blasphemy	Matt. 12:31, 32
Blessings	Matt. 5:3–11
Blind guides	Matt. 15:14
Borrowing	Matt. 5:42
Bread of life	John 6:32–35
Brothers	Matt. 23:8
Builders	Matt. 7:24 Luke 6:47–49
Burdens	Luke 11:46
Burial	Matt. 8:22
Caesar	Matt. 22:21
Call of God	Matt. 20:16
Called ones	Matt. 22:14
Capital and labor	Matt. 20:1–15
Capital punishment	Matt. 26:52
Care of God	Matt. 6:30, 33
Caution	Mark 4:24
Celibacy	Matt. 19:11, 12
Character	John 1:47
Charity	Luke 12:33
Cheating	Mark 10:19
Chosen	Matt. 22:14
Church	Matt. 18:17
Circumcision	John 7:22, 23
Cleansing	John 15:3
Coin	Matt. 22:19–21
Coldness	Matt. 24:12
Communication	Luke 24:17
Compassion	Matt. 15:32 Luke 10:33
Compromise	Matt. 5:25, 26
Conceit	Luke 18:10–12
Conduct, Christian	Matt. 5:16
Confessing Christ	Matt. 10:32, 33
Confession of sin	Luke 18:13, 14
Confidence	Mark 10:24
Conflict	Matt. 10:34–36
Conscience	John 8:7–9
Contention	Matt. 18:15–17
Contentment	John 6:43
Conversion	Matt. 13:15
Convict	John 16:8
Corruption, moral	Luke 11:39
Courage	Matt. 9:22
Covenant	Mark 14:24
Coveting	Mark 7:21, 22
Cross-bearing	Matt. 10:38
Crucifixion	Luke 9:22
Cup of water	Matt. 10:42
Dancing	Luke 15:25–27
Daniel	Matt. 24:15
Darkness	Luke 11:35
David	Matt. 12:3
Day	John 11:9
Deaf	Matt. 13:13–15
Death	Luke 9:22 John 8:51
Debts	Matt. 18:24
Deceivers	Matt. 24:4, 5
Decision	Matt. 6:24
Defilement	Matt. 15:11, 18, 19
Devil	Matt. 13:38, 39
Diligence	John 9:4
Disbelief	John 5:38
Discernment	Matt. 16:2, 3
Discipleship	Luke 14:33
Disputes	Mark 9:33, 34
Distress	Luke 21:23, 25
Divorce	Matt. 5:31, 32
Doctrine	Mark 7:7
Doubt	Matt. 21:21
Drunkard	Luke 7:34
Drunkenness	Luke 21:34
Dullness	Matt. 13:13
Duty	Luke 17:10
Dwelling places	John 14:2, 3
Earth	Matt. 5:18
Earthquakes	Mark 13:8
Economy	Matt. 15:37 John 6:12
Elect	Matt. 24:24, 31
Election	Matt. 25:34
Elijah	Matt. 17:11, 12
Employer	Matt. 20:1–16
Encouragement	Matt. 9:2
Endowments	Matt. 25:14, 15
Endurance	Matt. 10:22 Luke 21:19
Enemies	Matt. 5:43, 44
Eternal life	Matt. 19:29
Eternal sin	Mark 3:29
Etiquette	Luke 10:8
Evil	Matt. 15:19
Exaltation	Matt. 23:12
Example	John 13:15
Excuses	Luke 14:18–20
Extravagance	Luke 15:11–14
Fainting	Mark 8:2, 3
Faith	Matt. 6:25 Mark 11:22 Luke 7:50
Faithfulness	Matt. 25:21
Faithlessness	Matt. 25:24–30
False prophets	Matt. 24:11
False witness	Matt. 19:18
Farm	Matt. 22:2–6
Fasting	Matt. 6:16–18
Faultfinding	Matt. 7:3–5
Faults	Matt. 18:15
Fear of God	Matt. 10:28
Feast	Luke 14:8
Feet washing	John 13:12–15
Fellowship	Matt. 8:11
Flattery	Luke 6:26
Flesh	John 6:53
Flock	Matt. 26:31

Subject	*Reference*
Following Christ	Matt. 10:37, 38
Food	Matt. 6:11
	Matt. 6:25
	John 6:27
Fool	Matt. 5:22
Formalism	Matt. 23:23–28
Forsaking all	Luke 14:33
Foxes	Luke 9:58
Friends	Luke 11:5–8
Frugality	John 6:12
Fruitfulness	Matt. 13:23
Fruitlessness	Luke 13:6–9
Generosity	Matt. 25:34–40
Gentiles	Matt. 10:5–7
Gentleness	Matt. 5:5
Giving	Luke 6:38
Gladness	Luke 15:32
Glorifying God	Matt. 5:16
Gluttony	Luke 21:34
God	Matt. 19:17, 26
Godlessness	John 5:42, 44
Golden Rule	Matt. 7:12
Gospel	Luke 4:18
Grace	2 Cor. 12:9
Greatness	Matt. 5:19
Grumble	John 6:43
Guidance	John 16:13
Hairs numbered	Matt. 10:30
Hand of God	John 10:27–29
Happiness	Matt. 5:12
	John 13:16, 17
Harlots	Matt. 21:31
Harvest	Matt. 9:37, 38
Hatred	John 15:18, 19
Healing	Matt. 10:7, 8
	Mark 2:17
Heart	Matt. 13:19
Heaven	Luke 16:17
	John 3:13
Hell	Matt. 5:22
	Matt. 10:28
Helper	John 14:16
	John 15:26
Helpless	John 6:44
Hireling	John 10:11–13
Holy Spirit	John 14:26
Home	Mark 5:19
Honesty	Mark 10:19
	Luke 8:15
Honor of men	Matt. 6:2
Honor of parents	Matt. 15:3–6
Hospitality	Luke 14:12–14
Humility	Matt. 11:29
	John 13:14
Hunger, spiritual	Matt. 5:6
	Luke 6:21
Hypocrisy	Matt. 6:5
	Luke 6:42
Ignorance	Matt. 22:29
Immortality	Matt. 25:46
	John 11:25, 26
Impartiality of God	Matt. 5:45
Inconsistency	Matt. 7:3–5
	Luke 6:41, 42
Indecision	Luke 9:62
Indifference	Matt. 24:12
Industry	John 4:36
Infidelity	John 3:18
Influence	Matt. 5:13
Ingratitude	Luke 17:17, 18
Innocence	Matt. 10:16
Insincerity	Luke 16:15
Inspiration	Luke 12:12
Instability	Matt. 7:26, 27
Instruction	John 6:45
Insufficiency	Mark 10:21
Integrity	Luke 16:10
Intercession	John 17:9
Investment	Matt. 6:19, 20
Jealousy	Luke 15:25–30
John the Baptist	Luke 7:24–28
Jonah	Matt. 12:39–41
Joy	Matt. 25:21
	Luke 15:7, 10
Judge not	Matt. 7:1, 2
Judgment	Matt. 11:24
Judgment day	Matt. 25:31–46
Justice	John 5:30
Justification, self	Luke 16:15
Killing	Matt. 5:21, 22
Kindness	Luke 10:30–35
Kingdom	Luke 7:28
	John 18:36
Kiss	Luke 7:45
Knowledge	John 8:31, 32
Labor	Matt. 20:1–14
Laughter	Luke 6:21
Law	Luke 16:16
Lawsuit	Matt. 5:25, 40
Lawyers	Luke 11:46
Leaven	Matt. 16:6
	Luke 13:20, 21
Lending	Luke 6:34, 35
Lepers	Matt. 10:7, 8
Levite	Luke 10:30–32
Liars	John 8:44, 45
Liberality	Luke 6:30, 38
Liberty	Luke 4:18
Life	Matt. 6:25
	John 5:40
Light	Luke 11:33
	John 8:12
Living water	John 4:10
Log	Luke 6:41, 42
Loneliness	John 16:32
Lord's Supper	Matt. 26:26–29
Loss of soul	Matt. 16:25, 26
Lost opportunity	Matt. 25:7–12
Love	Matt. 22:37–40
Lukewarmness	Matt. 26:40, 41
Lunatic	Matt. 17;14, 15
Lust	Mark 4:18, 19
Magistrates	Luke 12:11, 58
Mammon	Matt. 6:24
Marriage	Matt. 19:4–6
	Mark 12:25
Martyrdom	John 16:1–3
Mary's choice	Luke 10:41, 42
Memorial	Matt. 26:13
Mercy	Matt. 5:7
	Luke 16:24
Minister	Luke 10:2
Miracles	Matt. 12:28
Money lender, creditor	Luke 7:41, 42
Moses	Matt. 19:8
Moses' Law	John 7:19
Mother	Matt. 10:37
Mourn	Matt. 5:4
Murder	Matt. 15:19
Mysteries of Heaven	Matt. 13:11
Narrow way	Matt. 7:13, 14
Neglect	Luke 12:47
Neighbor	Matt. 19:19
Neutrality	Matt. 12:30
New birth	John 3:3, 5–8
Noah	Luke 17:26, 27
Oath	Matt. 5:33–37
Obedience	Matt. 12:50
Offering	Matt. 5:25
Offerings	Luke 21:3, 4
Opportunity	Matt. 5:25
Parables	Mark 4:11, 12
Paradise	Luke 23:43
Pardoning	Luke 6:37
Parents	Matt. 10:21
Patriotism	Matt. 22:21
Peace	Mark 9:50
Peacemakers	Matt. 5:9
Penitence	Luke 18:13
Perception	John 8:43
Perfection	Matt. 5:48
Persecution	Matt. 24:9
Perseverance	Matt. 10:22
Pharisaism	Matt. 23:2–33
Pharisee and tax collector	Luke 18:10–14
Pharisees	Matt. 5:20
Philanthropy	Luke 11:41
Physician	Matt. 9:12
Piety	John 1:47
Pleasing God	John 8:29
Pleasures	Luke 8:14
Poison	Mark 16:17, 18
Poll tax	Matt. 22:19–21
Polygamy	Matt. 19:8, 9
Poor	Mark 14:7
Power	Matt. 6:13
Prayer	Matt. 6:9–13
	Matt. 7:7–11
Preaching	Mark 16:15, 16

Subject	Reference
Procrastination	Matt. 25:3
Profit and loss	Matt. 16:26
Prophets	Matt. 7:15
	Matt. 10:41
Proselyte	Luke 23:15
Protection	Luke 18:3
Providence	Matt. 6:25–33
Prudence	Matt. 10:16–20
Punishment	Matt. 21:41
Purity	Matt. 5:8
Ransom	Matt. 20:28
Reaping	John 4:35–38
Receiving Christ	Mark 9:37
Reconciliation	Matt. 5:23, 24
Regeneration	Matt. 19:28
Rejecting Christ	John 3:18
Rejoicing	Luke 10:20
Release	Luke 4:18
Religion	Matt. 25:34–36
	Mark 7:6–8
Repentance	Matt. 11:21
	Luke 13:28
Reproof	Matt. 11:21–23
Resignation	Matt. 26:39
Responsibility	Luke 12:47, 48
Rest	Matt. 11:28–30
	Matt. 26:45
Resurrection	John 6:40
Retaliation	Matt. 5:39–44
Retribution	Matt. 23:34, 35
Reward	Matt. 10:42
Riches	Mark 4:19
Righteousness	Matt. 5:6, 20
	John 16:10
Robbers	Luke 10:30
	John 10:1
Robbery	Matt. 23:25
Sabbath	Matt. 12:5–8
Sackcloth	Matt. 11:21
Sacrifice	Matt. 12:7
Sacrilege	Matt. 21:13
Sadducees	Matt. 16:6
Salt	Matt. 5:13
	Mark 9:50
Salvation	Luke 19:19
	John 4:22
Samaritan	Luke 10:30–35
Sanctification	John 17:17
Satan	Matt. 4:10
	Mark 4:15
Scripture	Matt. 21:42
	Luke 4:21
Secrecy	Luke 12:2, 3
Security	Luke 6:47, 48
Seduction	Mark 13:22
Seeking the kingdom	Matt. 6:19, 20
Self-condemnation	Matt. 23:29–32
	Luke 19:20–24
Self-control	Matt. 5:21
Self-deception	Luke 12:16–21
Self-denial	Matt. 16:24–26
Self-exaltation	Matt. 23:12
Self-examination	Matt. 7:3–5
Selfishness	Luke 6:32–35
Self-righteousness	Matt. 23:23–27
Self-sacrifice	Matt. 16:25
Serpents	Matt. 23:33
	John 3:14
Service	Luke 22:27
Sheep	Luke 15:4–7
Shepherd	John 10:1–18
Sickness	Matt. 10:8
Signs	Luke 11:16
	John 4:48
Silence	Matt. 17:9
Sin	Matt. 26:28
	John 8:34
Sincerity	Matt. 5:13–16
Skepticism	John 20:27, 29
Slaves	Matt. 18:23
	John 15:15
Sleep	Mark 4:26, 27
	Mark 13:35, 36
Slothfulness	Matt. 25:26–30
Son of Man	Luke 9:22
Sorrow	Matt. 19:22
	John 16:6
Soul	Matt. 10:28
	Luke 12:19, 20
Soul winners	Matt. 4:19
Sowing	Mark 4:14
Speech	John 8:43
Spirit	Matt. 26:41
	Mark 5:8
Statement	Matt. 5:37
Steadfastness	Matt. 10:22
Stealing	Matt. 19:18
Steward	Luke 12:42, 43
	Luke 16:1–8
Stewardship	Luke 19:13–27
Stomach	Matt. 15:17
Strife	Luke 22:24
Stubbornness	John 5:40
Stumbling block	Matt. 23:13
Submission	Matt. 26:39, 42
Suffering	Matt. 26:38
Supper, The Lord's	Luke 22:14–20
Swearing	Matt. 23:16–22
Talents	Matt. 18:24
Taxes	Matt. 22:19–21
Tax collectors	Matt. 5:46, 47
Teaching	Matt. 28:19, 20
	John 13:13–15
Temperance	Luke 21:34
Temptations	Matt. 4:1–11
	Luke 8:13
Thieves	Matt. 6:19
	John 10:1, 8
Timidness	Mark 4:40
Tithes	Luke 18:11, 12
Traditions	Mark 7:9, 13
Transgressions	Matt. 15:2
Treasures	Matt. 6:19–21
Tribulation	Matt. 24:9
	John 16:33
Truth	John 14:6
Unbelievers	Luke 12:46
Uncharitableness	John 7:24
Unchastity	Matt. 5:31, 32
Uncleanness	Matt. 23:27
Unity	John 17:20, 21
Unpardonable sin	Matt. 12:31, 32
Vengeance	Matt. 5:39, 40
Vine	John 15:1, 4, 5
Visions	Matt. 17:9
Walks of Life	John 8:12
	John 12:35
War	Matt. 24:26
Watchfulness	Matt. 24:42, 44
	Luke 12:37–40
Wedding	Luke 14:8–10
Widow	Mark 12:43, 44
Wine	Luke 5:37–39
Wisdom	Luke 21:15
Witness	John 8:14
Witness, false	Matt. 19:18
Witnessing	Acts 1:8
Wives	Luke 14:20, 26
Worker	Matt. 10:10
Worldliness	Luke 21:34
Worm	Mark 9:43–48
Worries of the world	Matt. 13:22
Worship	Matt. 4:10
Yoke	Matt. 11:28, 29
Zacchaeus	Luke 19:5
Zeal	John 2:17

The Parables of Jesus Christ

Parable	*Matthew*	*Mark*	*Luke*
1. Lamp Under a Basket	5:14–16	4:21, 22	8:16, 17 11:33–36
2. A Wise Man Builds on Rock and a Foolish Man Builds on Sand	7:24–27		6:47–49
3. Unshrunk (New) Cloth on an Old Garment	9:16	2:21	5:36
4. New Wine in Old Wineskins	9:17	2:22	5:37, 38
5. The Sower	13:3–23	4:2–20	8:4–15
6. The Tares (Weeds)	13:24–30		
7. The Mustard Seed	13:31, 32	4:30–32	13:18, 19
8. The Leaven	13:33		13:20, 21
9. The Hidden Treasure	13:44		
10. The Pearl of Great Price	13:45, 46		
11. The Dragnet	13:47–50		
12. The Lost Sheep	18:12–14		15:3–7
13. The Unforgiving Servant	18:23–35		
14. The Workers in the Vineyard	20:1–16		
15. The Two Sons	21:28–32		
16. The Wicked Vinedressers	21:33–45	12:1–12	20:9–19
17. The Wedding Feast	22:2–14		
18. The Fig Tree	24:32–44	13:28–32	21:29–33
19. The Wise and Foolish Virgins	25:1–13		
20. The Talents	25:14–30		
21. The Growing Seed		4:26–29	
22. The Absent Householder		13:33–37	
23. The Creditor and Two Debtors			7:41–43
24. The Good Samaritan			10:30–37
25. A Friend in Need			11:5–13
26. The Rich Fool			12:16–21
27. The Faithful Servant and the Evil Servant			12:35–40
28. Faithful and Wise Steward			12:42–48
29. The Barren Fig Tree			13:6–9
30. The Great Supper			14:16–24
31. Building a Tower and a King Making War			14:25–35
32. The Lost Coin			15:8–10
33. The Lost Son			15:11–32
34. The Unjust Steward			16:1–13
35. The Rich Man and Lazarus			16:19–31
36. Unprofitable Servants			17:7–10
37. The Persistent Widow			18:1–8
38. The Pharisee and the Tax Collector			18:9–14
39. The Minas (Pounds)			19:11–27

The Miracles of Jesus Christ

Miracle	Matthew	Mark	Luke	John
1. Cleansing a Leper	8:2	1:40	5:12	
2. Healing a Centurion's Servant (of paralysis)	8:5		7:1	
3. Healing Peter's Mother-in-law	8:14	1:30	4:38	
4. Healing the Sick at Evening	8:16	1:32	4:40	
5. Stilling the Storm	8:23	4:35	8:22	
6. Demons Entering a Herd of Swine	8:28	5:1	8:26	
7. Healing a Paralytic	9:2	2:3	5:18	
8. Raising the Ruler's Daughter	9:18, 23	5:22, 35	8:40, 49	
9. Healing the Hemorrhaging Woman	9:20	5:25	8:43	
10. Healing Two Blind Men	9:27			
11. Curing a Demon-possessed, Mute Man	9:32			
12. Healing a Man's Withered Hand	12:9	3:1	6:6	
13. Curing a Demon-possessed, Blind and Mute Man	12:22		11:14	
14. Feeding the Five Thousand	14:13	6:30	9:10	6:1
15. Walking on the Sea	14:25	6:48		6:19
16. Healing the Gentile Woman's Daughter	15:21	7:24		
17. Feeding the Four Thousand	15:32	8:1		
18. Healing the Epileptic Boy	17:14	9:17	9:38	
19. Temple Tax in the Fish's Mouth	17:24			
20. Healing Two Blind Men	20:30	10:46	18:35	
21. Withering the Fig Tree	21:18	11:12		
22. Casting Out an Unclean Spirit		1:23	4:33	
23. Healing a Deaf Mute		7:31		
24. Healing a Blind Paralytic at Bethsaida		8:22		
25. Escape from the Hostile Multitude			4:30	
26. Draught of Fish			5:1	
27. Raising of a Widow's Son at Nain			7:11	
28. Healing the Infirm, Bent Woman			13:11	
29. Healing the Man with Dropsy			14:1	
30. Cleansing the Ten Lepers			17:11	
31. Restoring a Servant's Ear			22:51	
32. Turning Water into Wine				2:1
33. Healing the Nobleman's Son (of fever)				4:46
34. Healing an Infirm Man at Bethesda				5:1
35. Healing the Man Born Blind				9:1
36. Raising of Lazarus				11:43
37. Second Draught of Fish				21:1

Read Your Bible Through in a Year

A systematic division of the books of the Bible, primarily for reading.

JANUARY

Date	MORNING MATT.	EVENING GEN.
1	1	1, 2, 3
2	2	4, 5, 6
3	3	7, 8, 9
4	4	10, 11, 12
5	5: 1–26	13, 14, 15
6	5:27–48	16, 17
7	6: 1–18	18, 19
8	6:19–34	20, 21, 22
9	7	23, 24
10	8: 1–17	25, 26
11	8:18–34	27, 28
12	9: 1–17	29, 30
13	9:18–38	31, 32
14	10: 1–20	33, 34, 35
15	10:21–42	36, 37, 38
16	11	39, 40
17	12: 1–23	41, 42
18	12:24–50	43, 44, 45
19	13: 1–30	46, 47, 48
20	13:31–58	49, 50
		EX.
21	14: 1–21	1, 2, 3
22	14:22–36	4, 5, 6
23	15: 1–20	7, 8
24	15:21–39	9, 10, 11
25	16	12, 13
26	17	14, 15
27	18: 1–20	16, 17, 18
28	18:21–35	19, 20
29	19	21, 22
30	20: 1–16	23, 24
31	20:17–34	25, 26

FEBRUARY

Date	MORNING MATT.	EVENING EX.
1	21: 1–22	27, 28
2	21:23–46	29, 30
3	22: 1–22	31, 32, 33
4	22:23–46	34, 35
5	23: 1–22	36, 37, 38
6	23:23–39	39, 40
		LEV.
7	24: 1–28	1, 2, 3
8	24:29–51	4, 5
9	25: 1–30	6, 7
10	25:31–46	8, 9, 10
11	26: 1–25	11, 12
12	26:26–50	13
13	26:51–75	14
14	27: 1–26	15, 16
15	27:27–50	17, 18
16	27:51–66	19, 20
17	28	21, 22
	MARK	
18	1: 1–22	23, 24
19	1:23–45	25
20	2	26, 27
		NUM.
21	3: 1–19	1, 2
22	3:20–35	3, 4
23	4: 1–20	5, 6
24	4:21–41	7, 8
25	5: 1–20	9, 10, 11
26	5:21–43	12, 13, 14
27	6: 1–29	15, 16
28	6:30–56	17, 18, 19
29	7: 1–13	20, 21, 22

MARCH

Date	MORNING MARK	EVENING NUM.
1	7:14–37	23, 24, 25
2	8: 1–21	26, 27
3	8:22–38	28, 29, 30
4	9: 1–29	31, 32, 33
5	9:30–50	34, 35, 36
		DEUT.
6	10: 1–31	1, 2
7	10:32–52	3, 4
8	11: 1–18	5, 6, 7
9	11:19–33	8, 9, 10
10	12: 1–27	11, 12, 13
11	12:28–44	14, 15, 16
12	13: 1–20	17, 18, 19
13	13:21–37	20, 21, 22
14	14: 1–26	23, 24, 25
15	14:27–53	26, 27
16	14:54–72	28, 29
17	15: 1–25	30, 31
18	15:26–47	32, 33, 34
		JOSH.
19	16	1, 2, 3
	LUKE	
20	1: 1–20	4, 5, 6
21	1:21–38	7, 8, 9
22	1:39–56	10, 11, 12
23	1:57–80	13, 14, 15
24	2: 1–24	16, 17, 18
25	2:25–52	19, 20, 21
26	3	22, 23, 24
		JUDG.
27	4: 1–30	1, 2, 3
28	4:31–44	4, 5, 6
29	5: 1–16	7, 8
30	5:17–39	9, 10
31	6: 1–26	11, 12

APRIL

Date	MORNING LUKE	EVENING JUDG.
1	6:27–49	13, 14, 15
2	7: 1–30	16, 17, 18
3	7:31–50	19, 20, 21
		RUTH
4	8: 1–25	1, 2, 3, 4
		1 SAM.
5	8:26–56	1, 2, 3
6	9: 1–17	4, 5, 6
7	9:18–36	7, 8, 9
8	9:37–62	10, 11, 12
9	10: 1–24	13, 14
10	10:25–42	15, 16
11	11: 1–28	17, 18
12	11:29–54	19, 20, 21
13	12: 1–31	22, 23, 24
14	12:32–59	25, 26
15	13: 1–22	27, 28, 29
16	13:23–35	30, 31
		2 SAM.
17	14: 1–24	1, 2
18	14:25–35	3, 4, 5
19	15: 1–10	6, 7, 8
20	15:11–32	9, 10, 11
21	16	12, 13
22	17: 1–19	14, 15
23	17:20–37	16, 17, 18
24	18: 1–23	19, 20
25	18:24–43	21, 22
26	19: 1–27	23, 24
		1 KIN.
27	19:28–48	1, 2
28	20: 1–26	3, 4, 5
29	20:27–47	6, 7
30	21: 1–19	8, 9

MAY

Date	MORNING LUKE	EVENING 1 KIN.
1	21:20–38	10, 11
2	22: 1–20	12, 13
3	22:21–46	14, 15
4	22:47–71	16, 17, 18
5	23: 1–25	19, 20
6	23:26–56	21, 22
		2 KIN.
7	24: 1–35	1, 2, 3
8	24:36–53	4, 5, 6
	JOHN	
9	1: 1–28	7, 8, 9
10	1:29–51	10, 11, 12
11	2	13, 14
12	3: 1–18	15, 16
13	3:19–38	17, 18
14	4: 1–30	19, 20, 21
15	4:31–54	22, 23
16	5: 1–24	24, 25
		1 CHR.
17	5:25–47	1, 2, 3
18	6: 1–21	4, 5, 6
19	6:22–44	7, 8, 9
20	6:45–71	10, 11, 12
21	7: 1–27	13, 14, 15
22	7:28–53	16, 17, 18
23	8: 1–27	19, 20, 21
24	8:28–59	22, 23, 24
25	9: 1–23	25, 26, 27
26	9:24–41	28, 29
		2 CHR.
27	10: 1–23	1, 2, 3
28	10:24–42	4, 5, 6
29	11: 1–29	7, 8, 9
30	11:30–57	10, 11, 12
31	12: 1–26	13, 14

JUNE

Date	MORNING JOHN	EVENING 2 CHR.
1	12:27–50	15, 16
2	13: 1–20	17, 18
3	13:21–38	19, 20
4	14	21, 22
5	15	23, 24
6	16	25, 26, 27
7	17	28, 29
8	18: 1–18	30, 31
9	18:19–40	32, 33
10	19: 1–22	34, 35, 36
		EZRA
11	19:23–42	1, 2
12	20	3, 4, 5
13	21	6, 7, 8
	ACTS	
14	1	9, 10
		NEH.
15	2: 1–21	1, 2, 3
16	2:22–47	4, 5, 6
17	3	7, 8, 9
18	4: 1–22	10, 11
19	4:23–37	12, 13
		ESTH.
20	5: 1–21	1, 2
21	5:22–42	3, 4, 5
22	6	6, 7, 8
23	7: 1–21	9, 10
		JOB
24	7:22–43	1, 2
25	7:44–60	3, 4
26	8: 1–25	5, 6, 7
27	8:26–40	8, 9, 10
28	9: 1–21	11, 12, 13
29	9:22–43	14, 15, 16
30	10: 1–23	17, 18, 19

JULY

Date	MORNING	EVENING
	ACTS	**JOB**
1	10:24–48	20, 21
2	11	22, 23, 24
3	12	25, 26, 27
4	13: 1–25	28, 29
5	13:26–52	30, 31
6	14	32, 33
7	15: 1–21	34, 35
8	15:22–41	36, 37
9	16: 1–21	38, 39, 40
10	16:22–40	41, 42
		PS.
11	17: 1–15	1, 2, 3
12	17:16–34	4, 5, 6
13	18	7, 8, 9
14	19: 1–20	10, 11, 12
15	19:21–41	13, 14, 15
16	20: 1–16	16, 17
17	20:17–38	18, 19
18	21: 1–17	20, 21, 22
19	21:18–40	23, 24, 25
20	22	26, 27, 28
21	23: 1–15	29, 30
22	23:16–35	31, 32
23	24	33, 34
24	25	35, 36
25	26	37, 38, 39
26	27: 1–26	40, 41, 42
27	27:27–44	43, 44, 45
28	28	46, 47, 48
	ROM.	
29	1	49, 50
30	2	51, 52, 53
31	3	54, 55, 56

AUGUST

Date	MORNING	EVENING
	ROM.	**PS.**
1	4	57, 58, 59
2	5	60, 61, 62
3	6	63, 64, 65
4	7	66, 67
5	8: 1–21	68, 69
6	8:22–39	70, 71
7	9: 1–15	72, 73
8	9:16–33	74, 75, 76
9	10	77, 78
10	11: 1–18	79, 80
11	11:19–36	81, 82, 83
12	12	84, 85, 86
13	13	87, 88
14	14	89, 90
15	15: 1–13	91, 92, 93
16	15:14–33	94, 95, 96
17	16	97, 98, 99
	1 COR.	
18	1	100, 101, 102
19	2	103, 104
20	3	105, 106
21	4	107, 108, 109
22	5	110, 111, 112
23	6	113, 114, 115
24	7: 1–19	116, 117, 118
25	7:20–40	119: 1–88
26	8	119: 89–176
27	9	120, 121, 122
28	10: 1–18	123, 124, 125
29	10:19–33	126, 127, 128
30	11: 1–16	129, 130, 131
31	11:17–34	132, 133, 134

SEPTEMBER

Date	MORNING	EVENING
	1 COR.	**PS.**
1	12	135, 136
2	13	137, 138, 139
3	14: 1–20	140, 141, 142
4	14:21–40	143, 144, 145
5	15: 1–28	146, 147
6	15:29–58	148, 149, 150
		PROV.
7	16	1, 2
	2 COR.	
8	1	3, 4, 5
9	2	6, 7
10	3	8, 9
11	4	10, 11, 12
12	5	13, 14, 15
13	6	16, 17, 18
14	7	19, 20, 21
15	8	22, 23, 24
16	9	25, 26
17	10	27, 28, 29
18	11: 1–15	30, 31
		ECCL.
19	11:16–33	1, 2, 3
20	12	4, 5, 6
21	13	7, 8, 9
	GAL.	
22	1	10, 11, 12
		SONG
23	2	1, 2, 3
24	3	4, 5
25	4	6, 7, 8
		IS.
26	5	1, 2
27	6	3, 4
	EPH.	
28	1	5, 6
29	2	7, 8
30	3	9, 10

OCTOBER

Date	MORNING	EVENING
	EPH.	**IS.**
1	4	11, 12, 13
2	5: 1–16	14, 15, 16
3	5:17–33	17, 18, 19
4	6	20, 21, 22
	PHIL.	
5	1	23, 24, 25
6	2	26, 27
7	3	28, 29
8	4	30, 31
	COL.	
9	1	32, 33
10	2	34, 35, 36
11	3	37, 38
12	4	39, 40
	1 THESS.	
13	1	41, 42
14	2	43, 44
15	3	45, 46
16	4	47, 48, 49
17	5	50, 51, 52
	2 THESS.	
18	1	53, 54, 55
19	2	56, 57, 58
20	3	59, 60, 61
	1 TIM.	
21	1	62, 63, 64
22	2	65, 66
		JER.
23	3	1, 2
24	4	3, 4, 5
25	5	6, 7, 8
26	6	9, 10, 11
	2 TIM.	
27	1	12, 13, 14
28	2	15, 16, 17
29	3	18, 19
30	4	20, 21
	TITUS	
31	1	22, 23

NOVEMBER

Date	MORNING	EVENING
	TITUS	**JER.**
1	2	24, 25, 26
2	3	27, 28, 29
3	**PHILEM.**	30, 31
	HEB.	
4	1	32, 33
5	2	34, 35, 36
6	3	37, 38, 39
7	4	40, 41, 42
8	5	43, 44, 45
9	6	46, 47
10	7	48, 49
11	8	50
12	9	51, 52
		LAM.
13	10: 1–18	1, 2
14	10:19–39	3, 4, 5
		EZEK.
15	11: 1–19	1, 2
16	11:20–40	3, 4
17	12	5, 6, 7
18	13	8, 9, 10
	JAMES	
19	1	11, 12, 13
20	2	14, 15
21	3	16, 17
22	4	18, 19
23	5	20, 21
	1 PET.	
24	1	22, 23
25	2	24, 25, 26
26	3	27, 28, 29
27	4	30, 31, 32
28	5	33, 34
	2 PET.	
29	1	35, 36
30	2	37, 38, 39

DECEMBER

Date	MORNING	EVENING
	2 PET.	**EZEK.**
1	3	40, 41
	1 JOHN	
2	1	42, 43, 44
3	2	45, 46
4	3	47, 48
		DAN.
5	4	1, 2
6	5	3, 4
7	**2 JOHN**	5, 6, 7
8	**3 JOHN**	8, 9, 10
9	**JUDE**	11, 12
	REV.	**HOS.**
10	1	1, 2, 3, 4
11	2	5, 6, 7, 8
12	3	9, 10, 11
13	4	12, 13, 14
14	5	**JOEL**
		AMOS
15	6	1, 2, 3
16	7	4, 5, 6
17	8	7, 8, 9
18	9	**OBAD.**
19	10	**JON.**
		MIC.
20	11	1, 2, 3
21	12	4, 5
22	13	6, 7
23	14	**NAH.**
24	15	**HAB.**
25	16	**ZEPH.**
26	17	**HAG.**
		ZECH.
27	18	1, 2, 3, 4
28	19	5, 6, 7, 8
29	20	9, 10, 11, 12
30	21	13, 14
31	22	**MAL.**

Harmony of the Gospels

Date	Event	Location	Matthew	Mark	Luke	John
INTRODUCTIONS TO JESUS CHRIST						
	(1) Luke's Introduction				1:1–4	
	(2) Pre-fleshly state of Christ					1:1–18
	(3) Genealogy of Jesus Christ		1:1–17		3:23–38	
BIRTH, INFANCY, AND ADOLESCENCE OF JESUS AND JOHN THE BAPTIST						
7 B.C.	(1) Announcement of Birth of John	Jerusalem (Temple)			1:5–25	
7 or 6 B.C.	(2) Announcement of Birth of Jesus to the Virgin	Nazareth			1:26–38	
c. 5 B.C.	(3) Song of Elizabeth to Mary	Hill Country of Judea			1:39–45	
	(4) Mary's Song of Praise				1:46–56	
5 B.C.	(5) Birth, Infancy, and Purpose for Future of John the Baptist	Judea			1:57–80	
	(6) Announcement of Jesus' Birth to Joseph	Nazareth	1:18–25			
5–4 B.C.	(7) Birth of Jesus Christ	Bethlehem	1:24, 25		2:1–7	
	(8) Proclamation by the Angels	Near Bethlehem			2:8–14	
	(9) The Visit of Homage by Shepherds	Bethlehem			2:15–20	
	(10) Jesus' Circumcision	Bethlehem			2:21	
4 B.C.	(11) First Temple Visit with Acknowledgments by Simeon and Anna	Jerusalem			2:22–38	
	(12) Visit of the Wise Men	Jerusalem & Bethlehem	2:1–12			
	(13) Flight into Egypt and Massacre of Innocents	Bethlehem, Jerusalem & Egypt	2:13–18			
	(14) From Egypt to Nazareth with Jesus		2:19–23		2:39	
Afterward	(15) Childhood of Jesus	Nazareth			2:40, 51	
A.D. 7–8	(16) Jesus, 12 Years Old, Visits the Temple	Jerusalem			2:41–50	
Afterward	(17) 18-Year Account of Jesus' Adolescence and Adulthood	Nazareth			2:51, 52	
TRUTHS ABOUT JOHN THE BAPTIST						
c. A.D. 25–27	(1) John's Ministry Begins	Judean Wilderness	3:1	1:1–4	3:1, 2	1:19–28
	(2) Man and Message		3:2–12	1:2–8	3:3–14	
	(3) His Picture of Jesus		3:11, 12	1:7, 8	3:15–18	1:26, 27
	(4) His Courage		14:4–12		3:19, 20	
BEGINNING OF JESUS' MINISTRY						
c. A.D. 27	(1) Jesus Baptized	Jordan River	3:13–17	1:9–11	3:21–23	1:29–34
	(2) Jesus Tempted	Wilderness	4:1–11	1:12, 13	4:1–13	
	(3) Calls First Disciples	Beyond Jordan				1:35–51
	(4) The First Miracle	Cana in Galilee				2:1–11

Date	Event	Location	Matthew	Mark	Luke	John
	(5) First Stay in Capernaum	(Capernaum is "His" city)				2:12
A.D. 27	(6) First Cleansing of the Temple	Jerusalem				2:13–22
	(7) Received at Jerusalem	Judea				2:23–25
	(8) Teaches Nicodemus about Second Birth	Judea				3:1–21
	(9) Co-Ministry with John	Judea				3:22–30
	(10) Leaves for Galilee	Judea	4:12	1:14	4:14	4:1–4
	(11) Samaritan Woman at Jacob's Well	Samaria				4:5–42
	(12) Returns to Galilee			1:15	4:15	4:43–45
THE GALILEAN MINISTRY OF JESUS						
A.D. 27–29						
A.D. 27	(1) Healing of the Nobleman's Son	Cana				4:46–54
	(2) Rejected at Nazareth	Nazareth			4:16–30	
	(3) Moved to Capernaum	Capernaum	4:13–17			
	(4) Four Become Fishers of Men	Sea of Galilee	4:18–22	1:16–20	5:1–11	
	(5) Demoniac Healed on the Sabbath Day	Capernaum		1:21–28	4:31–37	
	(6) Peter's Mother-in-Law Cured, Plus Others	Capernaum	8:14–17	1:29–34	4:38–41	
c. A.D. 27	(7) First Preaching Tour of Galilee	Galilee	4:23–25	1:35–39	4:42–44	
	(8) Leper Healed and Response Recorded	Galilee	8:1–4	1:40–45	5:12–16	
	(9) Paralytic Healed	Capernaum	9:1–8	2:1–12	5:17–26	
	(10) Matthew's Call and Reception Held	Capernaum	9:9–13	2:13–17	5:27–32	
	(11) Disciples Defended via a Parable	Capernaum	9:14–17	2:18–22	5:33–39	
A.D. 28	(12) Goes to Jerusalem for Second Passover; Heals Lame Man	Jerusalem				5:1–47
	(13) Plucked Grain Precipitates Sabbath Controversy	En Route to Galilee	12:1–8	2:23–28	6:1–5	
	(14) Withered Hand Healed Causes Another Sabbath Controversy	Galilee	12:9–14	3:1–6	6:6–11	
	(15) Multitudes Healed	Sea of Galilee	12:15–21	3:7–12	6:17–19	
	(16) Twelve Apostles Selected After a Night of Prayer	Near Capernaum		3:13–19	6:12–16	
	(17) Sermon on the Mt.	Near Capernaum	5:1—7:29		6:20–49	
	(18) Centurion's Servant Healed	Capernaum	8:5–13		7:1–10	
	(19) Raises Widow's Son from Dead	Nain			7:11–17	
	(20) Jesus Allays John's Doubts	Galilee	11:2–19		7:18–35	
	(21) Woes Upon the Privileged		11:20–30			
	(22) A Sinful Woman Anoints Jesus	Simon's House, Capernaum			7:36–50	
	(23) Another Tour of Galilee	Galilee			8:1–3	
	(24) Jesus Accused of Blasphemy	Capernaum	12:22–27	3:20–30	11:14–23	

Date	Event	Location	Matthew	Mark	Luke	John
A.D. 28	(25) Jesus' Answer to a Demand for a Sign	Capernaum	12:38–45		11:24–26, 29–36	
	(26) Mother, Brothers Seek Audience	Capernaum	12:46–50	3:31–35	8:19–21	
	(27) Famous Parables of Sower, Seed, Tares, Mustard Seed, Leaven, Treasure, Pearl, Dragnet, Lamp Told	By Sea of Galilee	13:1–52	4:1–34	8:4–18	
	(28) Sea Made Serene	Sea of Galilee	8:23–27	4:35–41	8:22–25	
	(29) Gadarene Demoniac Healed	E. Shore of Galilee	8:28–34	5:1–20	8:26–39	
	(30) Jairus's Daughter Raised and Woman with Hemorrhage Healed		9:18–26	5:21–43	8:40–56	
	(31) Two Blind Men's Sight Restored		9:27–31			
	(32) Mute Demoniac Healed		9:32–34			
	(33) Nazareth's Second Rejection of Christ	Nazareth	13:53–58	6:1–6		
	(34) Twelve Sent Out		9:35—11:1	6:7–13	9:1–6	
	(35) Fearful Herod Beheads John	Galilee	14:1–12	6:14–29	9:7–9	
Spring A.D. 29	(36) Return of 12, Jesus Withdraws, 5,000 Fed	Near Bethsaida	14:13–21	6:30–44	9:10–17	6:1–14
	(37) Walks on the Water	Sea of Galilee	14:22–33	6:45–52		6:15–21
	(38) Sick of Gennesaret Healed	Gennesaret	14:34–36	6:53–56		
	(39) Peak of Popularity Passes in Galilee	Capernaum				6:22–71 7:1
A.D. 29	(40) Traditions Attacked		15:1–20	7:1–23		
	(41) Aborted Retirement in Phoenicia: Syro-Phoenician Healed	Phoenicia	15:21–28	7:24–30		
	(42) Afflicted Healed	Decapolis	15:29–31	7:31–37		
	(43) 4,000 Fed	Decapolis	15:32–39	8:1–9		
	(44) Pharisees Increase Attack	Magdala	16:1–4	8:10–13		
	(45) Disciples' Carelessness Condemned; Blind Man Healed		16:5–12	8:14–26		
	(46) Peter Confesses Jesus Is the Christ	Near Caesarea Philippi	16:13–20	8:27–30	9:18–21	
	(47) Jesus Foretells His Death	Caesarea Philippi	16:21–26	8:31–38	9:22–25	
	(48) Kingdom Promised		16:27, 28	9:1	9:26, 27	
	(49) The Transfiguration	Mountain Unnamed	17:1–13	9:2–13	9:28–36	
	(50) Epileptic Healed	Mt. of Transfiguration	17:14–21	9:14–29	9:37–42	
	(51) Again Tells of Death, Resurrection	Galilee	17:22, 23	9:30–32	9:43–45	
	(52) Taxes Paid	Capernaum	17:24–27			
	(53) Disciples Contend About Greatness; Jesus Defines; also Patience, Loyalty, Forgiveness	Capernaum	18:1–35	9:33–50	9:46–62	
	(54) Jesus Rejects Brothers' Advice	Galilee				7:2–9
c. Sept. A.D. 29	(55) Galilee Departure and Samaritan Rejection		19:1		9:51–56	7:10
	(56) Cost of Discipleship		8:18–22		9:57–62	

Date	Event	Location	Matthew	Mark	Luke	John
LAST JUDEAN AND PEREAN MINISTRY OF JESUS						
A.D. 29–30 Oct. A.D. 29	(1) Feast of Tabernacles	Jerusalem				7:2, 10–52
	(2) Forgiveness of Adulteress	Jerusalem				7:53—8:11
A.D. 29	(3) Christ—the Light of the World	Jerusalem				8:12–20
	(4) Pharisees Can't Meet the Prophecy Thus Try to Destroy the Prophet	Jerusalem—Temple				8:21–59
	(5) Man Born Blind Healed: Following Consequences	Jerusalem				9:1–41
	(6) Parable of the Good Shepherd	Jerusalem				10:1–21
	(7) The Service of the Seventy	Probably Judea			10:1–24	
	(8) Lawyer Hears the Story of the Good Samaritan	Judea (?)			10:25–37	
	(9) The Hospitality of Martha and Mary	Bethany			10:38–42	
	(10) Another Lesson on Prayer	Judea (?)			11:1–13	
	(11) Accused of Connection with Beelzebub				11:14–36	
	(12) Judgment Against Lawyers and Pharisees				11:37–54	
	(13) Jesus Deals with Hypocrisy, Covetousness, Worry, and Alertness				12:1–59	
	(14) Repent or Perish				13:1–5	
	(15) Barren Fig Tree				13:6–9	
	(16) Crippled Woman Healed on Sabbath				13:10–17	
	(17) Parables of Mustard Seed and Leaven	Probably Perea			13:18–21	
Winter A.D. 29	(18) Feast of Dedication	Jerusalem				10:22–39
	(19) Withdrawal Beyond Jordan					10:40–42
	(20) Begins Teaching Return to Jerusalem with Special Words About Herod	Perea			13:22–35	
	(21) Meal with a Pharisee Ruler Occasions Healing Man with Dropsy; Parables of Ox, Best Places, and Great Supper				14:1–24	
	(22) Demands of Discipleship	Perea			14:25–35	
	(23) Parables of Lost Sheep, Coin, Son				15:1–32	
	(24) Parables of Unjust Steward, Rich Man and Lazarus				16:1–31	
	(25) Lessons on Service, Faith, Influence				17:1–10	
	(26) Resurrection of Lazarus	Perea to Bethany				11:1–44
	(27) Reaction to It: Withdrawal of Jesus					11:45–54
A.D. 30	(28) Begins Last Journey to Jerusalem via Samaria & Galilee	Samaria, Galilee			17:11	
	(29) Heals Ten Lepers				17:12–19	

Date	Event	Location	Matthew	Mark	Luke	John
A.D. 30	(30) Lessons on the Coming Kingdom				17:20–37	
	(31) Parables: Persistent Widow, Pharisee and Tax Collector				18:1–14	
	(32) Doctrine on Divorce		19:1–12	10:1–12		
	(33) Jesus Blesses Children: Objections	Perea	19:13–15	10:13–16	18:15–17	
	(34) Rich Young Ruler	Perea	19:16–30	10:17–31	18:18–30	
	(35) Laborers of the 11th Hour		20:1–16			
	(36) Foretells Death and Resurrection	Near Jordan	20:17–19	10:32–34	18:31–34	
	(37) Ambition of James and John		20:20–28	10:35–45		
	(38) Blind Bartimaeus Healed	Jericho		10:46–52	18:35–43	
	(39) Interview with Zacchaeus	Jericho			19:1–10	
	(40) Parable: the Minas	Jericho			19:11–27	
	(41) Returns to Home of Mary and Martha	Bethany				11:55—12:1
	(42) Plot to Kill Lazarus	Bethany				12:9–11
JESUS' FINAL WEEK OF WORK AT JERUSALEM						
Spring A.D. 30 Sunday	(1) Triumphal Entry	Bethany, Jerusalem, Bethany	21:1–9	11:1–11	19:28–44	12:12–19
Monday	(2) Fig Tree Cursed and Temple Cleansed	Bethany to Jerusalem	21:10–19	11:12–18	19:45–48	
	(3) The Attraction of Sacrifice	Jerusalem				12:20–50
Tuesday	(4) Withered Fig Tree Testifies	Bethany to Jerusalem	21:20–22	11:19–26		
	(5) Sanhedrin Challenges Jesus. Answered by Parables: Two Sons, Wicked Vinedressers and Marriage Feast	Jerusalem	21:23—22:14	11:27—12:12	20:1–19	
	(6) Tribute to Caesar	Jerusalem	22:15–22	12:13–17	20:20–26	
	(7) Sadducees Question the Resurrection	Jerusalem	22:23–33	12:18–27	20:27–40	
	(8) Pharisees Question Commandments	Jerusalem	22:34–40	12:28–34		
	(9) Jesus and David	Jerusalem	22:41–46	12:35–37	20:41–44	
	(10) Jesus' Last Sermon	Jerusalem	23:1–39	12:38–40	20:45–47	
	(11) Widow's Mite	Jerusalem		12:41–44	21:1–4	
	(12) Jesus Tells of the Future	Mt. of Olives	24:1–51	13:1–37	21:5–36	
	(13) Parables: Ten Virgins, Talents, The Day of Judgment	Mt. of Olives	25:1–46			
	(14) Jesus Tells Date of Crucifixion		26:1–5	14:1, 2	22:1, 2	
	(15) Anointing by Mary at Simon's Feast	Bethany	26:6–13	14:3–9		12:2–8
	(16) Judas Contracts the Betrayal		26:14–16	14:10, 11	22:3–6	
Thursday	(17) Preparation for the Passover	Jerusalem	26:17–19	14:12–16	22:7–13	
Thursday P.M.	(18) Passover Eaten, Jealousy Rebuked	Jerusalem	26:20	14:17	22:14–16, 24–30	
	(19) Feet Washed	Upper Room				13:1–20
	(20) Judas Revealed, Defects	Upper Room	26:21–25	14:18–21	22:21–23	13:21–30

Date	Event	Location	Matthew	Mark	Luke	John
Thursday P.M.	(21) Jesus Warns About Further Desertion; Cries of Loyalty	Upper Room	26:31–35	14:27–31	22:31–38	13:31–38
	(22) Institution of the Lord's Supper	Upper Room	26:26–29	14:22–25	22:17–20	
	(23) Last Speech to the Apostles and Intercessory Prayer	Jerusalem				14:1—17:26
Thursday-Friday	(24) The Grief of Gethsemane	Mt. of Olives	26:30, 36–46	14:36, 32–42	22:39–46	18:1
Friday	(25) Betrayal, Arrest, Desertion	Gethsemane	26:47–56	14:43–52	22:47–53	18:2–12
	(26) First Examined by Annas	Jerusalem				18:12–14, 19–23
	(27) Trial by Caiaphas and Council; Following Indignities	Jerusalem	26:57, 59–68	14:53, 55–65	22:54, 63–65	18:24
	(28) Peter's Triple Denial	Jerusalem	26:58, 69–75	14:54, 66–72	22:54–62	18:15–18, 25–27
	(29) Condemnation by the Council	Jerusalem	27:1	15:1	22:66–71	
	(30) Suicide of Judas	Jerusalem	27:3–10			
	(31) First Appearance Before Pilate	Jerusalem	27:2, 11–14	15:1–5	23:1–7	18:28–38
	(32) Jesus Before Herod	Jerusalem			23:6–12	
	(33) Second Appearance Before Pilate	Jerusalem	27:15–26	15:6–15	23:13–25	18:39—19:16
	(34) Mockery by Roman Soldiers	Jerusalem	27:27–30	15:16–19		
	(35) Led to Golgotha	Jerusalem	27:31–34	15:20–23	23:26–33	19:16, 17
	(36) 6 Events of First 3 Hours on Cross	Calvary	27:35–44	15:24–32	23:33–43	19:18–27
	(37) Last 3 Hours on Cross	Calvary	27:45–50	15:33–37	23:44–46	19:28–30
	(38) Events Attending Jesus' Death		27:51–56	15:38–41	23:45, 47–49	
	(39) Burial of Jesus	Jerusalem	27:57–60	15:42–46	23:50–54	19:31–42
Friday-Saturday	(40) Tomb Sealed	Jerusalem	27:61–66		23:55, 56	
	(41) Women Watch	Jerusalem		15:47		

THE RESURRECTION THROUGH THE ASCENSION

Date	Event	Location	Matthew	Mark	Luke	John
A.D. 30 Dawn of First Day (Sunday, "Lord's Day")	(1) Women Visit the Tomb	Near Jerusalem	28:1–10	16:1–8	24:1–11	
	(2) Peter and John; See the Empty Tomb				24:12	20:1–10
	(3) Jesus' Appearance to Mary Magdalene	Jerusalem		16:9–11		20:11–18
	(4) Jesus' Appearance to the Other Women	Jerusalem	28:9, 10			
	(5) Guards' Report of the Resurrection		28:11–15			
Sunday Afternoon	(6) Jesus' Appearance to Two Disciples on Way to Emmaus			16:12, 13	24:13–35	
Late Sunday	(7) Jesus' Appearance to Ten Disciples Without Thomas	Jerusalem			24:36–43	20:19–25
One Week Later	(8) Appearance to Disciples with Thomas	Jerusalem				20:26–31
During 40 Days until Ascension	(9) Jesus' Appearance to Seven Disciples by Sea of Galilee	Galilee				21:1–25
	(10) Great Commission		28:16–20	16:14–18	24:44–49	
	(11) The Ascension	Mt. Olivet		16:19, 20	24:50–53	

Concordance

The Concordance includes proper names and significant topics, defined by phrases and scripture references. Occasionally, a keyword applies to more than one Bible person, place, or topic. This is the case with "Abijah," for whom the Concordance lists four different persons by that name. The second, third, and following occurrences are distinguished by the dash ("———").

— A —

AARON

Ancestry and family of, Ex 6:16–20, 23
Helper and prophet to Moses, Ex 4:13–31; 7:1, 2
Appears before Pharaoh, Ex 5:1–4
Performs miracles, Ex 7:9, 10, 19, 20
Supports Moses' hands, Ex 17:10–12
Ascends Mt. Sinai; sees God's glory, Ex 19:24; 24:1, 9, 10
Judges Israel in Moses' absence, Ex 24:14
Chosen by God as priest, Ex 28:1
Consecrated, Ex 29; Lev 8
Duties prescribed, Ex 30:7–10
Tolerates Israel's idolatry, Ex 32
Priestly ministry begins, Lev 9
Sons offer profane fire; Aaron's humble response, Lev 10
Conspires against Moses, Num 12:1–16
Rebelled against by Korah, Num 16
Intercedes to stop plague, Num 16:45–48
Rod buds to confirm his authority, Num 17:1–10
With Moses, fails at Meribah, Num 20:1–13
Dies; son succeeds him as priest, Num 20:23–29
His priesthood compared:
with Melchizedek's, Heb 7:11–19
with Christ's, Heb 9:6–15, 23–28

ABADDON

Angel of the bottomless pit, Rev 9:11

ABASED

I know how to be *a* ....Phil 4:12

ABBA

And He said, "*A* ....Mark 14:36
by whom we cry out, "*A* .....Rom 8:15
crying out, "*A* ....Gal 4:6

ABED-NEGO

Name given to Azariah, a Hebrew captive, Dan 1:7
Appointed by Nebuchadnezzar, Dan 2:49
Refuses to serve idols; cast into furnace but delivered, Dan 3:12–30

ABEL

Adam's second son, Gen 4:2
His offering accepted, Gen 4:4
Murdered by Cain, Gen 4:8
His sacrifice offered by faith, Heb 11:4

ABEL BETH MAACHAH

Captured by Tiglath-Pileser, 2 Kin 15:29
Refuge of Sheba; saved from destruction, 2 Sam 20:14–22
Seized by Ben-Hadad, 1 Kin 15:20

ABHOR

My soul shall not *a*..........Lev 26:11
Therefore I *a* myself..........Job 42:6
nations will *a* him..........Prov 24:24
a the pride of Jacob ....Amos 6:8
A what is evil ....Rom 12:9

ABHORRED

a His own inheritance ....Ps 106:40
he who is *a* by the ....Prov 22:14
and their soul also *a* ....Zech 11:8

ABHORRENCE

They shall be an *a*.............Is 66:24

ABHORRENT

you have made us *a*..............Ex 5:21

ABHORS

So that his life *a* ....Job 33:20

ABIATHAR

A priest who escapes Saul at Nob, 1 Sam 22:20–23
Becomes high priest under David, 1 Sam 23:6, 9–12
Remains faithful to David, 2 Sam 15:24–29
Informs David about Ahithophel, 2 Sam 15:34–36
Supports Adonijah's usurpation, 1 Kin 1:7, 9, 25
Deposed by Solomon, 1 Kin 2:26, 27, 35

ABIDE

nor *a* in its paths ....Job 24:13
LORD, who may *a* ....Ps 15:1
He shall *a* before God ....Ps 61:7
the Most High shall *a*...........Ps 91:1
"If you *a* in My word..........John 8:31
And a slave does not *a* ......John 8:35
Helper, that He may *a* .....John 14:16
A in Me and I in you ....John 15:4
If you *a* in Me ....John 15:7
a in My love.......................John 15:9
And now *a* faith ....1 Cor 13:13
does the love of God *a* .....1 John 3:17
we know that we *a* ....1 John 4:13

ABIDES

He who *a* from of old ....Ps 55:19
He who *a* in Me ....John 15:5
lives and *a* forever ....1 Pet 1:23
will of God *a* forever ....1 John 2:17

ABIDING

not have His word *a* ....John 5:38
has eternal life *a* ....1 John 3:15

ABIEZRITES

Relatives of Gideon; rally to his call, Judg 6:11, 24, 34

ABIGAIL

Wise wife of foolish Nabal, 1 Sam 25:3
Appeases David and becomes his wife, 1 Sam 25:14–42
Mother of Chileab, 2 Sam 3:3

ABIHU

Second son of Aaron, Ex 6:23
Offers profane fire and dies, Lev 10:1–7

ABIJAH

Samuel's second son; follows corrupt ways, 1 Sam 8:2, 3
——— Descendant of Aaron; head of an office of priests, 1 Chr 24:3, 10
Zechariah belongs to division of, Luke 1:5
——— Son of Jeroboam I, 1 Kin 14:1–18
——— Another name for King Abijam, 2 Chr 11:20

ABIJAM (or Abijah)

King of Judah, 1 Kin 14:31
Follows the sins of his father, 1 Kin 15:1–7
Defeats Jeroboam and takes cities, 2 Chr 13:13–20

ABILITY

who had *a* to serve ....Dan 1:4
according to his own *a* .....Matt 25:15
and beyond their *a* ....2 Cor 8:3
a which God supplies ....1 Pet 4:11

ABIMELECH

King of Gerar; takes Sarah in ignorance, Gen 20:1–18
Makes treaty with Abraham, Gen 21:22–34
——— A second king of Gerar; sends Isaac away, Gen 26:1–16
Makes treaty with Isaac, Gen 26:17–33
——— Gideon's son by a concubine, Judg 8:31
Conspires to become king, Judg 9

ABINADAB

A man of Kirjath Jearim in whose house the ark was kept, 1 Sam 7:1, 2
—— The second of Jesse's eight sons, 1 Sam 16:8
Serves in Saul's army, 1 Sam 17:13
—— A son of Saul slain at Mt. Gilboa, 1 Sam 31:1–8
Bones of, buried by men of Jabesh, 1 Chr 10:1–12

ABIRAM

Reubenite who conspired against Moses, Num 16:1–50

ABISHAG

A Shunammite employed as David's nurse, 1 Kin 1:1–4, 15
Witnessed David's choice of Solomon as successor, 1 Kin 1:15–31
Adonijah slain for desiring to marry her, 1 Kin 2:13–25

ABISHAI

David's nephew; joins Joab in blood-revenge against Abner, 2 Sam 2:18–24
Loyal to David during Absalom's and Sheba's rebellion, 2 Sam 16:9–12; 20:1–6, 10
Rebuked by David, 2 Sam 16:9–12; 19:21–23
His exploits, 2 Sam 21:16, 17; 23:18; 1 Chr 18:12, 13

ABLE

you are *a* to number ....Gen 15:5
shall give as he is *a* ....Deut 16:17
For who is *a* to judge ....1 Kin 3:9
"The LORD is *a* ....2 Chr 25:9
Who then is *a* to stand ......Job 41:10
God whom we serve is *a* .....Dan 3:17
God is *a* to raise up ....Matt 3:9
believe that I am *a* ....Matt 9:28
fear Him who is *a* ....Matt 10:28
Are you *a* to drink the .....Matt 20:22
beyond what you are *a* ....1 Cor 10:13
And God is *a* to make ....2 Cor 9:8
may be *a* to comprehend .....Eph 3:18
persuaded that He is *a* ......2 Tim 1:12
learning and never *a* ....2 Tim 3:7
being tempted, He is *a* ....Heb 2:18
that God was *a* to ....Heb 11:19
to Him who is *a* ....Jude 24
has come, and who is *a* ......Rev 6:17

ABNER

Saul's cousin; commander of his army, 1 Sam 14:50, 51
Rebuked by David, 1 Sam 26:5, 14–16
Supports Ishbosheth; defeated by David's men; kills Asahel, 2 Sam 2:8–32
Makes covenant with David, 2 Sam 3:6–21
Killed by Joab; mourned by David, 2 Sam 3:22–39

ABODE

but left their own *a* ....Jude 6

ABOLISHED

your works may be *a* ....Ezek 6:6
having *a* in His flesh ....Eph 2:15
Christ, who has *a* ....2 Tim 1:10

ABOMINABLE

not make yourselves *a* ......Lev 11:43
They have done *a* ....Ps 14:1
your grave like an *a* ....Is 14:19
Oh, do not do this *a* ....Jer 44:4
they deny Him, being *a* .....Titus 1:16
and *a* idolatries ....1 Pet 4:3
unbelieving, *a* ....Rev 21:8

ABOMINATION

every shepherd is an *a* ......Gen 46:34
If we sacrifice the *a* ....Ex 8:26
You have made me an *a* ....Ps 88:8
yes, seven are an *a* ....Prov 6:16
wickedness is an *a* ....Prov 8:7
Dishonest scales are an *a* ....Prov 11:1
the scoffer is an *a* ....Prov 24:9
prayer is an *a* ....Prov 28:9
An unjust man is an *a* ......Prov 29:27
incense is an *a* ....Is 1:13
and place there the *a* ....Dan 11:31
the *a* of desolation ....Dan 12:11
the '*a* of desolation,' ....Matt 24:15
among men is an *a* ....Luke 16:15

ABOMINATIONS

to follow the *a* ....Deut 18:9
delights in their *a* ....Is 66:3
will put away your *a* ....Jer 4:1
your harlotry, your *a* ....Jer 13:27
will see greater *a* ....Ezek 8:6
a which they commit ....Ezek 8:17
you, throw away the *a* ......Ezek 20:7
show her all her *a* ....Ezek 22:2
a golden cup full of *a* ....Rev 17:4
of the *a* of the earth ....Rev 17:5

ABOUND

lawlessness will *a* ....Matt 24:12
the offense might *a* ....Rom 5:20
sin that grace may *a* ....Rom 6:1
thanksgiving to *a* ....2 Cor 4:15
to make all grace *a* ....2 Cor 9:8
and I know how to *a* ....Phil 4:12
that you should *a* ....1 Thess 4:1
things are yours and *a* ....2 Pet 1:8

ABOUNDED

But where sin *a* ....Rom 5:20

ABOUNDING

and *a* in mercy ....Ps 103:8
immovable, always *a* ......1 Cor 15:58

ABOVE

that is in heaven *a* ....Ex 20:4
"He sent from *a* ....2 Sam 22:17
A it stood seraphim ....Is 6:2
nor a servant *a* his master ..Matt 10:24
He who comes from *a* ....John 3:31
I am from *a* ....John 8:23
been given you from *a* .....John 19:11
who is *a* all ....Eph 4:6
the name which is *a* ....Phil 2:9
things which are *a* ....Col 3:1
perfect gift is from *a* ....James 1:17

ABRAHAM

Ancestry and family, Gen 11:26–31
Receives God's call; enters Canaan, Gen 12:1–6
Promised Canaan by God; pitched tent near Bethel, Gen 12:7, 8
Deceives Egyptians concerning Sarai, Gen 12:11–20
Separates from Lot; inherits Canaan, Gen 13
Rescues Lot from captivity, Gen 14:11–16
Gives a tithe to Melchizedek; refuses spoil, Gen 14:18–24
Covenant renewed; promised a son, Gen 15
Takes Hagar as concubine; Ishmael born, Gen 16
Name changed from Abram; circumcision commanded, Gen 17
Entertains Lord and angels, Gen 18:1–15
Intercedes for Sodom, Gen 18:16–33
Deceives Abimelech concerning Sarah, Gen 20
Birth of Isaac, Gen 21:1–7
Sends Hagar and Ishmael away, Gen 21:9–14
Offers Isaac in obedience to God, Gen 22:1–19
Finds wife for Isaac, Gen 24
Marries Keturah; fathers other children; dies, Gen 25:1–10
Friend of God, 2 Chr 20:7
Justified by faith, Rom 4:1–12
Father of true believers, Rom 4:11–25
In the line of faith, Heb 11:8–10
Eternal home of, in heaven, Luke 16:19–25

ABRAM

See ABRAHAM

ABSALOM

Son of David, 2 Sam 3:3
Kills Amnon for raping Tamar; flees from David, 2 Sam 13:20–39
Returns through Joab's intrigue; reconciled to David, 2 Sam 14
Attempts to usurp throne, 2 Sam 15:1—18:8
Caught and killed by Joab, 2 Sam 18:9–18
Mourned by David, 2 Sam 18:19—19:8

ABSENT

For I indeed, as *a* ....1 Cor 5:3
in the body we are *a* ....2 Cor 5:6

ABSTAIN

we write to them to *a* .....Acts 15:20
A from every form ....1 Thess 5:22
and commanding to *a* ....1 Tim 4:3
a from fleshly lusts ....1 Pet 2:11

ABUNDANCE

is the sound of *a* ....1 Kin 18:41
workmen with you in *a* ....1 Chr 22:15
and *a* of peace ....Ps 72:7
eyes bulge with *a* ....Ps 73:7
nor he who loves *a* ....Eccl 5:10
delight itself in *a* ....Is 55:2
For out of the *a* ....Matt 12:34
put in out of their *a* ....Mark 12:44
not consist in the *a* ....Luke 12:15
of affliction the *a* ....2 Cor 8:2
above measure by the *a* .....2 Cor 12:7
rich through the *a* ....Rev 18:3

ABUNDANT

Longsuffering and *a* ....Ps 86:15
slow to anger and *a* ....Jon 4:2
in labors more *a* ....2 Cor 11:23
Lord was exceedingly *a* ....1 Tim 1:14
a mercy has begotten ....1 Pet 1:3

ABUNDANTLY

a satisfied with the ....Ps 36:8
may have it more *a* ....John 10:10
to do exceedingly *a* ....Eph 3:20
to show more *a* to the ....Heb 6:17

ACACIA GROVE

Spies sent from, Josh 2:1
Israel's last camp before crossing the Jordan, Josh 3:1

ACCEPT

For I will *a* him ....Job 42:8
a your burnt sacrifice ....Ps 20:3
offering, I will not *a* ....Jer 14:12
Should I *a* this from ....Mal 1:13

ACCEPTABLE

sought to find *a* ....Eccl 12:10
a time I have heard ....Is 49:8
proclaim the *a* year ....Is 61:2
proclaim the *a* year ....Luke 4:19
is that good and *a* ....Rom 12:2
finding out what is *a* ....Eph 5:10
For this is good and *a* ....1 Tim 2:3
spiritual sacrifices *a* ....1 Pet 2:5

ACCEPTABLY

we may serve God *a* ....Heb 12:28

ACCEPTED

Behold, now is the *a* ....2 Cor 6:2
by which He made us *a* ....Eph 1:6

ACCESS

we have *a* by faith ....Rom 5:2
we have boldness and *a* ....Eph 3:12

ACCOMPLISHED

today the LORD has *a* .....1 Sam 11:13
A desire *a* is sweet to ....Prov 13:19
must still be *a* ....Luke 22:37
all things were now *a* ......John 19:28

ACCORD

and Israel with one *a* ....Josh 9:2
serve Him with one *a* ....Zeph 3:9
continued with one *a* ....Acts 1:14
daily with one *a* ....Acts 2:46
what *a* has Christ with .....2 Cor 6:15
love, being of one *a* ....Phil 2:2

ACCOUNT

they will give *a* ....Matt 12:36
The former *a* I made ....Acts 1:1
each of us shall give *a* .....Rom 14:12
put that on my *a* ....Philem 18
those who must give *a* ....Heb 13:17

ACCOUNTED

and He *a* it to him ....Gen 15:6
And that was *a* to him ....Ps 106:31
his faith is *a* ....Rom 4:5
a as sheep for the ....Rom 8:36
and it was *a* to him ....Gal 3:6
and it was *a* to him ....James 2:23

ACCURSED

he who is hanged is *a* ......Deut 21:23
regarding the *a* things ....Josh 7:1
years old shall be *a* ....Is 65:20
not know the law is *a* ....John 7:49
that I myself were *a* ....Rom 9:3
calls Jesus *a*, and no one ....1 Cor 12:3
let him be *a* ....Gal 1:8

ACCUSATION

they wrote an *a* against ....Ezra 4:6
over His head the *a* ....Matt 27:37
they might find an *a* ....Luke 6:7
Do not receive an *a* ....1 Tim 5:19
not bring a reviling *a* ....2 Pet 2:11

ACCUSE

anyone or *a* falsely ....Luke 3:14
they began to *a* Him ....Luke 23:2
think that I shall *a* ....John 5:45

ACCUSED

forward and *a* the Jews ....Dan 3:8
while He was being *a* ......Matt 27:12

ACCUSER

a of our brethren ....Rev 12:10

ACCUSING

their thoughts *a* or else ......Rom 2:15

ACHAIA

Visited by Paul, Acts 18:1, 12
Apollos preaches in, Acts 18:24–28
Gospel proclaimed throughout, 1 Thess 1:7, 8

ACHAN (or Achar)

Sin of, caused Israel's defeat, Josh 7:1–15
Stoned to death, Josh 7:16–25
Sin of, recalled, Josh 22:20
Also called Achar, 1 Chr 2:7

ACHISH

A king of Gath, 1 Sam 21:10–15
David seeks refuge with, 1 Sam 27:1–12
Forced by Philistine lords to expel David, 1 Sam 29:1–11
Receives Shimei's servants, 1 Kin 2:39, 40

ACHOR, VALLEY OF

Site of Achan's stoning, Josh 7:24–26
On Judah's boundary, Josh 15:7
Promises concerning, Is 65:10

ACHSAH

A daughter of Caleb, 1 Chr 2:49
Given to Othniel, Josh 15:16–19
Given springs of water, Judg 1:12–15

ACKNOWLEDGE

did he *a* his brothers ....Deut 33:9
a my transgressions ....Ps 51:3
in all your ways *a* ....Prov 3:6
and Israel does not *a* ....Is 63:16
a your iniquity ....Jer 3:13
let him *a* that the things ...1 Cor 14:37

ACKNOWLEDGED

of Israel, and God *a* them .....Ex 2:25
a my sin to You ....Ps 32:5

ACKNOWLEDGES

there is no one who *a* ....Ps 142:4
he who *a* the Son has .....1 John 2:23

ACQUAINT

a yourself with Him ....Job 22:21

ACQUAINTANCES

You have put away my *a* ....Ps 88:8

All my *a* watched for ....Jer 20:10
But all His *a* ....Luke 23:49

ACQUAINTED

and are *a* with all my ways ....Ps 139:3
a Man of sorrows and *a* ....Is 53:3

ACQUIT

at all *a* the wicked ....Nah 1:3

ACT

seen every great *a* ....Deut 11:7
is time for You to *a* ....Ps 119:126
His *a*, His unusual *a* ....Is 28:21
in the very *a* ....John 8:4

ACTIONS

by Him *a* are weighed ......1 Sam 2:3

ACTS

LORD, the righteous *a* ....Judg 5:11
His *a* to the children ....Ps 103:7
declare Your mighty *a* ....Ps 145:4
of Your awesome *a* ....Ps 145:6

ADAM

Creation of, Gen 1:26, 27; 2:7
Given dominion over the earth, Gen 1:28–30
Given a wife, Gen 2:18–25
Temptation, fall, and exile from Eden, Gen 3
Children of, Gen 4:1, 2; 5:3, 4
Transgression results in sin and death, Rom 5:12–14
——— Last or second Adam, an appellation of Christ, Rom 5:14, 15; 1 Cor 15:20–24, 45–48

ADD

You shall not *a* ....Deut 4:2
Do not *a* to His words ....Prov 30:6

ADDED

things shall be *a* ....Matt 6:33
And the Lord *a* to the ....Acts 2:47
many people were *a* ....Acts 11:24
It was *a* because of ....Gal 3:19

ADMINISTERS

a justice for the ....Deut 10:18

ADMONISH

also to *a* one another ....Rom 15:14
a him as a brother ....2 Thess 3:15

ADMONISHED

further, my son, be *a* ....Eccl 12:12
Angel of the LORD *a* ....Zech 3:6

ADMONISHING

a one another in ....Col 3:16

ADMONITION

were written for our *a* .....1 Cor 10:11
in the training and *a* ....Eph 6:4

ADONIJAH

David's fourth son, 2 Sam 3:2, 4
Attempts to usurp throne, 1 Kin 1:5–53
Desires Abishag as wife, 1 Kin 2:13–18
Executed by Solomon, 1 Kin 2:19–25

ADONI-ZEDEK

An Amorite king of Jerusalem, Josh 10:1–5

Defeated and slain by Joshua, Josh 10:6–27

ADONIRAM (or Adoram)

Official under David, Solomon, and Rehoboam, 2 Sam 20:24; 1 Kin 5:14; 12:18
Stoned by angry Israelites, 1 Kin 12:18
Called Hadoram, 2 Chr 10:18

ADOPTION

the Spirit of *a* ....Rom 8:15
waiting for the *a* ....Rom 8:23
to whom pertain the *a* ....Rom 9:4
we might receive the *a* ....Gal 4:5
a as sons by Jesus ....Eph 1:5

ADORN

a the monuments ....Matt 23:29
also, that the women *a* ......1 Tim 2:9

ADORNED

By His Spirit He *a* ....Job 26:13
You shall again be *a* ....Jer 31:4
temple, how it was *a* ....Luke 21:5
also *a* themselves ....1 Pet 3:5
prepared as a bride *a* ....Rev 21:2

ADRIFT

A among the dead ....Ps 88:5

ADULTERER

the *a* and the adulteress ......Lev 20:10
The eye of the *a* ....Job 24:15

ADULTERERS

the land is full of *a* ....Jer 23:10
nor idolaters, nor *a* ....1 Cor 6:9
a God will judge ....Heb 13:4
A and adulteresses ....James 4:4

ADULTERIES

I have seen your *a* ....Jer 13:27
her sight, and her *a* ....Hos 2:2
evil thoughts, *a* ....Mark 7:21

ADULTEROUS

evil and *a* generation ....Matt 12:39

ADULTERY

You shall not commit *a* ......Ex 20:14
Whoever commits *a* ....Prov 6:32
Israel had committed *a* ....Jer 3:8
already committed *a* ....Matt 5:28
is divorced commits *a* ....Matt 5:32
another commits *a* ....Mark 10:11
a woman caught in *a* ....John 8:3
those who commit *a* ....Rev 2:22

ADVANTAGE

a will it be to You ....Job 35:3
man has no *a* over ....Eccl 3:19
a that I go away ....John 16:7
What *a* then has the ....Rom 3:1
Satan should take *a* ....2 Cor 2:11
no one should take *a* ......1 Thess 4:6
people to gain *a* ....Jude 16

ADVERSARIES

The *a* of the LORD ....1 Sam 2:10
rid Myself of My *a* ....Is 1:24
a will not be able ....Luke 21:15
and there are many *a* ....1 Cor 16:9
terrified by your *a* ....Phil 1:28
will devour the *a* ....Heb 10:27

ADVERSARY

in the way as an *a* ....Num 22:22
battle he become our *a* .....1 Sam 29:4
how long will the *a* ....Ps 74:10
a has spread his hand ....Lam 1:10
Agree with your *a* ....Matt 5:25
justice for me from my *a* ....Luke 18:3
opportunity to the *a* ....1 Tim 5:14
your *a* the devil walks ....1 Pet 5:8

ADVERSITIES

you from all your *a* ....1 Sam 10:19
known my soul in *a* ....Ps 31:7

ADVERSITY

them with every *a* ....2 Chr 15:6
I shall never be in *a* ....Ps 10:6
from the days of *a* ....Ps 94:13
brother is born for *a* ....Prov 17:17
faint in the day of *a* ....Prov 24:10
the day of *a* consider ....Eccl 7:14
you the bread of *a* ....Is 30:20

ADVICE

And blessed is your *a* .....1 Sam 25:33
in this I give my *a* ....2 Cor 8:10

ADVOCATE

we have an *A* with the ....1 John 2:1

AFAR

and worship from *a* ....Ex 24:1
sons shall come from *a* ....Is 60:4
and not a God *a* ....Jer 23:23
and saw Abraham *a* ....Luke 16:23
to all who are *a* ....Acts 2:39
to you who were *a* ....Eph 2:17
but having seen them *a* ....Heb 11:13

AFFAIRS

he will guide his *a* ....Ps 112:5
I may hear of your *a* ....Phil 1:27
himself with the *a* ....2 Tim 2:4

AFFECTION

to his wife the *a* ....1 Cor 7:3
for you all with the *a* ....Phil 1:8
if any *a* and mercy ....Phil 2:1

AFFECTIONATE

Be kindly *a* to one ....Rom 12:10

AFFIRM

you to *a* constantly ....Titus 3:8

AFFLICT

a them with their ....Ex 1:11
oath to *a* her soul ....Num 30:13
may be bound to *a* you ......Judg 16:6
a the descendants ....1 Kin 11:39
will hear, and *a* them ....Ps 55:19
a Your heritage ....Ps 94:5
a man to *a* his soul ....Is 58:5
to destroy, and to *a* ....Jer 31:28
For He does not *a* ....Lam 3:33
deal with all who *a* ....Zeph 3:19

AFFLICTED

"Why have You *a* ....Num 11:11
and the Almighty has *a* ......Ruth 1:21
To him who is *a* ....Job 6:14
hears the cry of the *a* ....Job 34:28
You *a* the peoples ....Ps 44:2
Before I was *a* ....Ps 119:67
I am *a* very much ....Ps 119:107

Many a time they have *a* .....Ps 129:1
the cause of the *a* ....Ps 140:12
days of the *a* are evil ....Prov 15:15
Smitten by God, and *a* ....Is 53:4
oppressed and He was *a* ....Is 53:7
"O you *a* one ....Is 54:11
Why have we *a* our ....Is 58:3
and satisfy the *a* ....Is 58:10
her virgins are *a* ....Lam 1:4
she has relieved the *a* ....1 Tim 5:10
being destitute, *a* ....Heb 11:37

AFFLICTING

A the just and taking ....Amos 5:12

AFFLICTION

in the land of my *a* ....Gen 41:52
the bread of *a* ....Deut 16:3
indeed look on the *a* ....1 Sam 1:11
LORD saw that the *a* ....2 Kin 14:26
a take hold of me ....Job 30:16
days of *a* confront me ....Job 30:27
held in the cords of *a* ....Job 36:8
of death, bound in *a* ....Ps 107:10
is my comfort in my *a* ....Ps 119:50
and it is an evil *a* ....Eccl 6:2
a He was afflicted ....Is 63:9
refuge in the day of *a* ....Jer 16:19
"O LORD, behold my *a* ....Lam 1:9
not grieved for the *a* ....Amos 6:6
For our light *a* ....2 Cor 4:17
supposing to add *a* ....Phil 1:16
the word in much *a* ....1 Thess 1:6

AFRAID

garden, and I was *a* ....Gen 3:10
saying, "Do not be *a* ....Gen 15:1
his face, for he was *a* ....Ex 3:6
none will make you *a* ....Lev 26:6
of whom you are *a* ....Deut 7:19
I will not be *a* ....Ps 3:6
ungodliness made me *a* ....Ps 18:4
Do not be *a* when one ....Ps 49:16
Whenever I am *a* ....Ps 56:3
farthest parts are *a* ....Ps 65:8
nor be *a* of their threats ....Is 8:12
no one will make them *a* ....Is 17:2
that you should be *a* ....Is 51:12
dream which made me *a* ....Dan 4:5
do not be *a* ....Matt 14:27
if you do evil, be *a* ....Rom 13:4
do good and are not *a* ....1 Pet 3:6

AFTERWARD

A he will let you go ....Ex 11:1
a we will speak ....Job 18:2
a receive me to glory ....Ps 73:24
you shall follow Me *a* ....John 13:36
the firstfruits, *a* ....1 Cor 15:23

AGAG

A king of Amalek in Balaam's prophecy, Num 24:7
——— Amalekite king spared by Saul, but slain by Samuel, 1 Sam 15:8, 9, 20–24, 32, 33

AGAIN

day He will rise *a* ....Matt 20:19
'You must be born *a* ....John 3:7
to renew them *a* ....Heb 6:6
having been born *a* ....1 Pet 1:23

AGAINST

his hand shall be *a* ....Gen 16:12
I will set My face *a* ....Lev 20:3

come to 'set a man *a* ....Matt 10:35
or house divided *a* ....Matt 12:25
not with Me is *a* Me ....Matt 12:30
blasphemy *a* the Spirit ......Matt 12:31
For nation will rise *a* ....Matt 24:7
out, as *a* a robber ....Matt 26:55
I have sinned *a* ....Luke 15:18
lifted up his heel *a* ....John 13:18
LORD and *a* His Christ ......Acts 4:26
to kick *a* the goads ....Acts 9:5
all men everywhere *a* ......Acts 21:28
let us not fight *a* ....Acts 23:9
a the promises of God ....Gal 3:21
we do not wrestle *a* ....Eph 6:12
I have a few things *a* ....Rev 2:20

AGE

well advanced in *a*..........Gen 18:11
Israel were dim with *a* ......Gen 48:10
the flower of their *a*........1 Sam 2:33
the grave at a full *a* ....Job 5:26
a is as nothing ....Ps 39:5
and in the *a* to come ......Mark 10:30
"The sons of this *a* ....Luke 20:34
He is of *a* ....John 9:21
who are of full *a*............Heb 5:14
the powers of the *a* ....Heb 6:5

AGED

Wisdom is with *a* ....Job 12:12
a one as Paul, the *a* ....Philem 9

AGES

ordained before the *a* ....1 Cor 2:7
in other *a* was not ....Eph 3:5
at the end of the *a* ....Heb 9:26

AGONY

And being in *a* ....Luke 22:44

AGREE

A with your adversary ......Matt 5:25
that if two of you *a* ....Matt 18:19
testimonies did not *a* ......Mark 14:56
and these three *a* ....1 John 5:8

AGREED

unless they are *a* ....Amos 3:3
they were glad, and *a* ....Luke 22:5

AGREEMENT

with Sheol we are in *a* ....Is 28:15
the North to make an *a* ......Dan 11:6
what *a* has the temple ......2 Cor 6:16

AHAB

A wicked king of Israel, 1 Kin 16:29
Marries Jezebel; promotes Baal worship, 1 Kin 16:31–33; 18:17–46
Denounced by Elijah, 1 Kin 17:1
Wars against Ben-Hadad, 1 Kin 20:1–43
Covets Naboth's vineyard, 1 Kin 21:1–16
Death predicted; repentance delays judgment, 1 Kin 21:17–29
Goes to war in spite of Micaiah's warning; killed in battle, 1 Kin. 22:1–37
Prophecy concerning, fulfilled, 1 Kin 22:38
—— Lying prophet, Jer 29:21–23

AHASUERUS

The father of Darius the Mede, Dan 9:1
—— Persian king, probably Xerxes I, 486–465 B.C., Ezra 4:6; Esth 1:1
Makes Esther queen, Esth 2:16, 17
Orders Jews annihilated, by Haman's advice, Esth 3:8–15
Reverses decree at Esther's request, Esth 7; 8
Exalts Mordecai, Esth 10:1–3

AHAZ

King of Judah; pursues idolatry; submits to Assyrian rule; desecrates the temple, 2 Kin 16
Defeated by Syria and Israel, 2 Chr 28:5–15
Comforted by Isaiah; refuses to ask a sign, Is 7:1–17

AHAZIAH

King of Israel; son of Ahab and Jezebel; worships Baal, 1 Kin 22:51–53
Falls through lattice; calls on Baal-Zebub; dies according to Elijah's word, 2 Kin 1:2–18
—— King of Judah; Ahab's son-in-law; reigns wickedly, 2 Kin 8:25–29; 2 Chr 22:1–6
Killed by Jehu, 2 Kin 9:27–29; 2 Chr 22:7–9

AHIJAH

A prophet of Shiloh who foretells division of Solomon's kingdom, 1 Kin 11:29–39
Foretells elimination of Jeroboam's line, 1 Kin 14:1–18
A writer of prophecy, 2 Chr 9:29

AHIKAM

Sent in Josiah's mission to Huldah, 2 Kin 22:12–14
Protects Jeremiah, Jer 26:24
The father of Gedaliah, governor under Nebuchadnezzar, 2 Kin 25:22; Jer 39:14

AHIMAAZ

A son of Zadok the high priest, 1 Chr 6:8, 9
Warns David of Absalom's plans, 2 Sam 15:27, 36
First to tell David of Absalom's defeat, 2 Sam 18:19–30

AHIMELECH

High priest in Saul's reign; helps David, 1 Sam 21:1–9
Betrayed and killed by Doeg; son Abiathar escapes, 1 Sam 22:9–20
David writes concerning, Ps 52:title

AHINOAM

Wife of David, 1 Sam 25:43; 27:3; 30:5, 18
Mother of Amnon, 2 Sam 3:2

AHITHOPHEL

David's counselor, 2 Sam 15:12
Joins Absalom's insurrection; counsels him, 2 Sam 15:31; 16:20–23
His counsel rejected; commits suicide, 2 Sam 17:1–23

AI

Israel defeated at, Josh 7:2–5
Israel destroys completely, Josh 8:1–28

AIDE

the king's personal *a* ....Acts 12:20

AIJALON

Amorites not driven from, Judg 1:35
Miracle there, Josh 10:12, 13
City of refuge, 1 Chr 6:66–69
Fortified by Rehoboam, 2 Chr 11:5, 10
Captured by Philistines, 2 Chr 28:18

AIR

the birds of the *a* ....Gen 1:26
of the *a* have nests ....Luke 9:58
as one who beats the *a* ......1 Cor 9:26
be speaking into the *a* ....1 Cor 14:9
of the power of the *a* ....Eph 2:2
meet the Lord in the *a* ....1 Thess 4:17
his bowl into the *a* ....Rev 16:17

AKEL DAMA

Field called "Field of Blood," Acts 1:19

AKRABBIM

An "ascent" on the south of the Dead Sea, Num 34:4
One border of Judah, Josh 15:3

ALARM

to sound the *a* against .....2 Chr 13:12
A day of trumpet and *a* .....Zeph 1:16

ALEXANDER

A member of the high-priestly family, Acts 4:6
—— A Jew in Ephesus, Acts 19:33, 34
—— An apostate condemned by Paul, 1 Tim 1:19, 20

ALEXANDRIA

Men of, persecute Stephen, Acts 6:9
Paul sails in ship of, Acts 27:6

ALIEN

because you were an *a* ......Deut 23:7
I am an *a* in their ....Job 19:15
who turn away an *a* ....Mal 3:5

ALIENATED

a herself from them ....Ezek 23:17
darkened, being *a* ....Eph 4:18
you, who once were *a* ....Col 1:21

ALIENS

For we are *a* and ....1 Chr 29:15
For I have loved *a* ....Jer 2:25
A have devoured his ....Hos 7:9
without Christ, being *a* ....Eph 2:12
the armies of the *a* ....Heb 11:34

ALIKE

All things come *a* ....Eccl 9:2
esteems every day *a* ....Rom 14:5

ALIVE

in the ark remained *a* ....Gen 7:23
with them went down *a* ....Num 16:33
LORD your God are *a* ....Deut 4:4
I kill and I make *a* ....Deut 32:39
Let them go down *a* ....Ps 55:15
he preserves himself *a* .....Ezek 18:27
heard that He was *a* ....Mark 16:11
son was dead and is *a* .....Luke 15:24
presented Himself *a* ....Acts 1:3
dead indeed to sin, but *a*.....Rom 6:11
I was *a* once without ....Rom 7:9
all shall be made *a*........1 Cor 15:22
trespasses, made us *a* ....Eph 2:5
flesh, He has made *a* ....Col 2:13

that we who are *a* ....1 Thess 4:15
the flesh but made *a* ....1 Pet 3:18
and behold, I am *a* ....Rev 1:18
a name that you are *a* ....Rev 3:1
These two were cast *a* ......Rev 19:20

ALL

for this is man's *a* ....Eccl 12:13

ALLELUIA

Again they said, "*A* ....Rev 19:3

ALLOW

a Your Holy One ....Ps 16:10
a My faithfulness ....Ps 89:33
nor do you *a* those ....Matt 23:13
a Your Holy One ....Acts 2:27
who will not *a* ....1 Cor 10:13

ALLOWED

bygone generations *a* ....Acts 14:16

ALLURE

behold, I will *a* ....Hos 2:14
they *a* through the lusts .....2 Pet 2:18

ALMOND

a blossoms on one ....Ex 25:33
a tree blossoms ....Eccl 12:5

ALMOST

for me, my feet had *a* ....Ps 73:2
a persuade me to ....Acts 26:28
a all things are ....Heb 9:22

ALMS

But rather give *a* ....Luke 11:41
you have and give *a* ....Luke 12:33
I came to bring *a* ....Acts 24:17

ALOES

with myrrh and *a* ....Ps 45:8
my bed with myrrh, *a* ....Prov 7:17
mixture of myrrh and *a* .....John 19:39

ALPHA

I am the *A* and the ....Rev 1:8
I am the *A* and the ....Rev 22:13

ALTAR

Then Noah built an *a* ....Gen 8:20
An *a* of earth you ....Ex 20:24
a shall be kept ....Lev 6:9
it to you upon the *a* ....Lev 17:11
offering for the *a* ....Num 7:84
called the *a* Witness ....Josh 22:34
and tear down the *a* ....Judg 6:25
"Go up, erect an *a* ....2 Sam 24:18
cried out against the *a* .....1 Kin 13:2
I will go to the *a* ....Ps 43:4
there will be an *a* ....Is 19:19
Lord has spurned His *a* ....Lam 2:7
you cover the *a* ....Mal 2:13
your gift to the *a* ....Matt 5:23
swears by the *a* ....Matt 23:18
I even found an *a* ....Acts 17:23
the offerings of the *a* ....1 Cor 9:13
partakers of the *a* ....1 Cor 10:18
We have an *a* from ....Heb 13:10
Isaac his son on the *a* ....James 2:21
and stood at the *a* ....Rev 8:3

ALTARS

a Hezekiah has taken ....2 Kin 18:22
Even Your *a*, O LORD ....Ps 84:3

on the horns of your *a* ....Jer 17:1
a shall be broken ....Ezek 6:4
has made many *a* ....Hos 8:11
a shall be heaps ....Hos 12:11
destruction on the *a* ....Amos 3:14
and torn down Your *a* ....Rom 11:3

ALTERED

of His face was *a* ....Luke 9:29

ALWAYS

delight, rejoicing *a* ....Prov 8:30
the poor with you *a* ....Matt 26:11
Me you do not have *a* ....Matt 26:11
lo, I am with you *a* ....Matt 28:20
'Son, you are *a* ....Luke 15:31
men *a* ought to pray ....Luke 18:1
immovable, *a* abounding ...1 Cor 15:58
Rejoice in the Lord *a* ....Phil 4:4
thus we shall *a* ....1 Thess 4:17
a be ready to give a ....1 Pet 3:15

AM

to Moses, "I *A* WHO I *A* ......Ex 3:14
First and I *a* the Last ....Is 44:6
in My name, I *a* there ......Matt 18:20
I *a* the bread of life ....John 6:35
I *a* the light of the ....John 8:12
I *a* from above ....John 8:23
Abraham was, I *A* ....John 8:58
I *a* the door ....John 10:9
I *a* the good shepherd ....John 10:11
I *a* the resurrection ....John 11:25
to him, "I *a* the way ....John 14:6
of God I *a* what I *a* ....1 Cor 15:10

AMALEK

Grandson of Esau, Gen 36:11, 12
A chief of Edom, Gen 36:16
First among nations, Num 24:20

AMALEKITES

Destruction predicted, Ex 17:14; Deut 25:17–19
Defeated by Israel, Ex 17:8–13; Judg 7:12–25; 1 Sam 14:47, 48; 27:8, 9; 1 Chr 4:42, 43
Overcome Israel, Num 14:39–45; Judg 3:13

AMASA

Commands Absalom's rebels, 2 Sam 17:25
Made David's commander, 2 Sam 19:13
Treacherously killed by Joab, 2 Sam 20:9–12
Death avenged, 1 Kin 2:28–34

AMAZED

trembled and were *a* ....Mark 16:8

AMAZIAH

King of Judah; kills his father's assassinators, 2 Kin 14:1–6; 2 Chr 25:1–4
Hires troops from Israel; is rebuked by a man of God; sends troops home, 2 Chr 25:5–10
Defeats Edomites; worships their gods, 2 Chr 25:11–16
Wars with Israel, 2 Kin 14:8–14; 2 Chr 25:17–24
Killed by conspirators, 2 Chr 25:25–28

AMBASSADOR

but a faithful *a* ....Prov 13:17
for which I am an *a* ....Eph 6:20

AMBASSADORS

which sends *a* by sea ....Is 18:2
cry outside, the *a* ....Is 33:7
we are *a* for Christ ....2 Cor 5:20

AMBITION

Christ from selfish *a* ....Phil 1:16
through selfish *a* ....Phil 2:3

AMEN

uninformed say "*A* ....1 Cor 14:16
are Yes, and in Him *A* ......2 Cor 1:20
creatures said, "*A* ....Rev 5:14

AMEND

A your ways and your ....Jer 7:3
from his evil way, *a* ....Jer 35:15

AMMON

A nation fathered by Lot, Gen 19:36, 38

AMMONITES

Excluded from assembly for hostility to Israel, Deut 23:3–6
Propose cruel treaty; conquered by Saul, 1 Sam 11:1–3, 11
Abuse David's ambassadors; conquered by his army, 2 Sam 10:1–14
Harass postexilic Jews, Neh 4:3, 7, 8
Defeated by Israel and Judah, Judg 11:4–33; 2 Chr 20:1–25; 27:5, 6
Prophecies concerning, Ps 83:1–18; Jer 25:9–21; Ezek 25:1–7; Amos 1:13–15; Zeph 2:9–11

AMNON

A son of David, 2 Sam 3:2
Rapes his half sister, 2 Sam 13:1–18
Killed by Absalom, 2 Sam 13:19–29

AMON

King of Judah, 2 Kin 21:18, 19
Follows evil, 2 Chr 33:22, 23
Killed by conspiracy, 2 Kin 21:23, 24
——— A governor of Samaria, 1 Kin 22:10, 26

AMORITES

Defeated by Joshua, Josh 10:1–43
Not driven out of Canaan, Judg 1:34–36
Put to forced labor under Solomon, 1 Kin 9:20, 21

AMOS

A prophet of Israel, Amos 1:1
Pronounces judgment against nations, Amos 1:1–3, 15
Denounces Israel's sins, Amos 4:1—7:9
Condemns Amaziah, the priest of Bethel, Amos 7:10–17
Predicts Israel's downfall, Amos 9:1–10
Foretells great blessings, Amos 9:11–15

AMRAM

Son of Kohath, Num 3:17–19
The father of Aaron, Moses and Miriam, Ex 6:18–20; 1 Chr 6:3

ANAKIM

A race of giants; very strong, Num 13:28–33; Deut 2:10, 11, 21
Defeated
by Joshua, Josh 10:36–39; 11:21
by Caleb, Josh 14:6–15

ANANIAS

Disciple at Jerusalem; slain for lying to God, Acts 5:1–11

——A Christian disciple at Damascus, Acts 9:10–19; 22:12–16

——A Jewish high priest, Acts 23:1–5

ANATHOTH

A Levitical city in Benjamin, Josh 21:18

Jeremiah's birthplace; he buys property there, Jer 1:1; 32:6–15

To be invaded by Assyria, Is 10:30

ANCHOR

ANCIENT

ANDREW

A disciple of John the Baptist, then of Christ, Matt 4:18, 19; John 1:40–42

Enrolled among the Twelve, Matt 10:2

Mentioned, Mark 13:3, 4; John 6:8, 9; 12:20–22; Acts 1:13

ANGEL

ANGELS

ANGER

ANGRY

ANGUISH

ANIMAL

ANIMALS

ANISE

ANNA

Aged prophetess, Luke 2:36–38

ANNAS

A Jewish high priest, Luke 3:2

Christ appeared before, John 18:12–24

Peter and John appeared before, Acts 4:6

ANNUL

ANNULLING

ANNULS

ANOINT

ANOINTED

ANOINTING

ANOTHER

that you love one *a* ....John 13:34
and He will give you *a* .....John 14:16
'Let *a* take his ....Acts 1:20

ANSWER

will give Pharaoh an *a* ......Gen 41:16
a I should take back ....2 Sam 24:13
Him, he could not *a* ....Job 9:3
Call, and I will *a* ....Job 13:22
how shall I *a* Him ....Job 31:14
and you shall *a* ....Job 40:7
the day that I call, *a* ....Ps 102:2
In Your faithfulness *a* ....Ps 143:1
a turns away wrath ....Prov 15:1
A man has joy by the *a* .....Prov 15:23
He who gives a right *a* .....Prov 24:26
a a fool according ....Prov 26:4
was there none to *a* ....Is 50:2
for there is no *a* ....Mic 3:7
or what you should *a* ......Luke 12:11
you may have an *a* ....2 Cor 5:12
ought to *a* each one ....Col 4:6

ANSWERS

a a matter before he ....Prov 18:13
but the rich *a* ....Prov 18:23
money *a* everything ....Eccl 10:19

ANT

Go to the *a* ....Prov 6:6

ANTICHRIST

heard that the *A* ....1 John 2:18
a who denies the ....1 John 2:22
is the spirit of the *A* ....1 John 4:3
is a deceiver and an *a* ....2 John 7

ANTIOCH

——— In Syria:
First Gentile church established, Acts 11:19–21
Disciples first called "Christians" in, Acts 11:26
Church commissions Paul, Acts 13:1–4; 15:35–41
Church troubled by Judaizers, Acts 15:1–4; Gal 2:11–21
——— In Pisidia:
Paul visits; Jews reject the gospel, Acts 13:14, 42–51

ANTITYPE

a which now saves us ....1 Pet 3:21

ANXIETIES

the multitude of my *a* ....Ps 94:19
Try me, and know my *a* ......Ps 139:23

ANXIETY

A in the heart of man ......Prov 12:25
eat their bread with *a* ......Ezek 12:19

ANXIOUS

drink, nor have an *a* ....Luke 12:29
Be *a* for nothing ....Phil 4:6

APART

that you shall set *a* ....Ex 13:12
she shall be set *a* ....Lev 15:19
the LORD has set *a* ....Ps 4:3
justified by faith *a* ....Rom 3:28

APHEK

A town in the Plain of Sharon, Josh 12:18
Site of Philistine camp, 1 Sam 4:1; 29:1
——— A city in Jezreel, 1 Kin 20:26–30
Syria's defeat prophesied here, 2 Kin 13:14–19

APOLLOS

An Alexandrian Jew; instructed by Aquila and Priscilla and sent to Achaia, Acts 18:24–28
Referred to as having ministered in Corinth, 1 Cor 1:12; 3:4, 22; 4:6; 16:12

APOLLYON

Angel of the bottomless pit, Rev 9:11

APOSTLE

called to be an *a* ....Rom 1:1
inasmuch as I am an *a* ......Rom 11:13
Am I not an *a* ....1 Cor 9:1
the signs of an *a* were .....2 Cor 12:12
a preacher and an *a* ....1 Tim 2:7
consider the *A* ....Heb 3:1

APOSTLES

of the twelve *a* ....Matt 10:2
whom He also named *a* .....Luke 6:13
displayed us, the *a* ....1 Cor 4:9
am the least of the *a* ....1 Cor 15:9
to the most eminent *a* ....2 Cor 11:5
themselves into *a* ....2 Cor 11:13
none of the other *a* ....Gal 1:19
gave some to be *a* ....Eph 4:11
who say they are *a* ....Rev 2:2
heaven, and you holy *a* ....Rev 18:20

APOSTLESHIP

in this ministry and *a* ....Acts 1:25
received grace and *a* ....Rom 1:5
are the seal of my *a* ....1 Cor 9:2
in Peter for the *a* ....Gal 2:8

APPAREL

is glorious in His *a* ....Is 63:1
clothed with foreign *a* ....Zeph 1:8
by them in white *a* ....Acts 1:10
themselves in modest *a* ....1 Tim 2:9
gold rings, in fine *a* ....James 2:2
or putting on fine *a* ....1 Pet 3:3

APPEAL

I *a* to Caesar ....Acts 25:11
love's sake I rather *a* ....Philem 9

APPEAR

and let the dry land *a* ....Gen 1:9
all your males shall *a* ....Ex 23:17
all Israel comes to *a* ....Deut 31:11
shall I come and *a* ....Ps 42:2
Let Your work *a* ....Ps 90:16
He shall *a* in His ....Ps 102:16
doings your sins *a* ....Ezek 21:24
faces that they may *a* ....Matt 6:16
also outwardly *a* ....Matt 23:28
kingdom of God would *a* ...Luke 19:11
For we must all *a* ....2 Cor 5:10
for Him He will *a* ....Heb 9:28
and the sinner *a* ....1 Pet 4:18

APPEARANCE

Do not look at his *a* ....1 Sam 16:7
a is blacker than soot ....Lam 4:8

As He prayed, the *a* ....Luke 9:29
judge according to *a* ....John 7:24
those who boast in *a* ....2 Cor 5:12
to the outward *a* ....2 Cor 10:7
found in *a* as a man ....Phil 2:8
indeed have an *a* ....Col 2:23

APPEARED

an angel of the Lord *a* ....Luke 1:11
who *a* in glory and ....Luke 9:31
brings salvation has *a* ....Titus 2:11
of the ages, He has *a* ....Heb 9:26

APPEARING

Lord Jesus Christ's *a* ....1 Tim 6:14
been revealed by the *a* ....2 Tim 1:10
and the dead at His *a* ....2 Tim 4:1
who have loved His *a* ....2 Tim 4:8
hope and glorious *a* ....Titus 2:13

APPEARS

can stand when He *a* ....Mal 3:2
who is our life *a* ....Col 3:4
the Chief Shepherd *a* ....1 Pet 5:4
in Him, that when He *a* ....1 John 2:28

APPETITE

or satisfy the *a* ....Job 38:39
are a man given to *a* ....Prov 23:2

APPLE

He kept him as the *a* ....Deut 32:10
And my law as the *a* ....Prov 7:2
Like an *a* tree among ....Song 2:3
touches the *a* of His eye ......Zech 2:8

APPLES

fitly spoken is like *a* ....Prov 25:11
refresh me with *a* ....Song 2:5

APPLIED

a my heart to know ....Eccl 7:25

APPOINT

I will even *a* terror ....Lev 26:16
a each of them to his ....Num 4:19
a me ruler over the ....2 Sam 6:21
a salvation for walls ....Is 26:1
For God did not *a* ....1 Thess 5:9
a elders in every city ....Titus 1:5

APPOINTED

You have *a* his limits ....Job 14:5
To release those *a* ....Ps 102:20
And as it is *a* for men ....Heb 9:27

APPROACH

a anyone who is near ....Lev 18:6
And cause to *a* You ....Ps 65:4
year, make those who *a* ....Heb 10:1

APPROACHING

take delight in *a* God ....Is 58:2
as you see the Day *a* ....Heb 10:25

APPROVE

their posterity who *a* ....Ps 49:13
do the same but also *a* ....Rom 1:32
a the things that ....Rom 2:18
a the things that are ....Phil 1:10

APPROVED

to God and *a* by men ....Rom 14:18
to present yourself *a* ....2 Tim 2:15
when he has been *a* ....James 1:12

AQUILA
Paul's host in Corinth, Acts 18:2, 3
Travels to Syria and Ephesus with Paul, Acts 18:18, 19
Instructs Apollos, Acts 18:24–26
Esteemed by Paul, Rom 16:3, 4

AR
A chief Moabite city, Num 21:15
On Israel's route, Deut 2:18
Destroyed by Sihon, Num 21:28
Destroyed by God, Is 15:1

ARABIA
Pays tribute to Solomon, 1 Kin 10:14, 15
Plunders Jerusalem, 2 Chr 21:16, 17
Defeated by Uzziah, 2 Chr 26:1, 7
Denounced by prophets, Is 21:13–17

ARARAT
Site of ark's landing, Gen 8:4
Assassins flee to, 2 Kin 19:37; Is 37:38

ARAUNAH (or Ornan)
A Jebusite, 2 Sam 24:15–25
His threshing floor bought by David, 2 Sam 24:18–25
becomes site of temple, 2 Chr 3:1
Also called Ornan, 1 Chr 21:18–28

ARBITRATOR
a judge or an *a* over .... Luke 12:14

ARCHANGEL
with the voice of an *a* ..... 1 Thess 4:16
Yet Michael the *a* .... Jude 9

ARCHELAUS
Son of Herod the Great, Matt 2:22

AREOPAGUS
Paul preaches at, Acts 17:18–34

ARGUMENTS
fill my mouth with *a* .... Job 23:4
casting down *a* and .... 2 Cor 10:5

ARIEL
Ezra's friend, Ezra 8:15–17
——— Name applied to Jerusalem, Is 29:1, 2, 7

ARISE
needy, now I will *a* .... Ps 12:5
A for our help .... Ps 44:26
Let God *a* .... Ps 68:1
A, shine; for your light .... Is 60:1
But the LORD will *a* .... Is 60:2
Righteousness shall *a* .... Mal 4:2
I will *a* and go to .... Luke 15:18
you who sleep, *a* .... Eph 5:14

ARISTARCHUS
A Macedonian Christian, Acts 19:29
Accompanies Paul, Acts 20:1, 4
Imprisoned with Paul, Col 4:10

ARK
Make yourself an *a* .... Gen 6:14
she took an *a* of bulrushes .... Ex 2:3
Bezalel made the *a* .... Ex 37:1
seat which is on the *a* .... Lev 16:2
Let us bring the *a* .... 1 Sam 4:3
golden censer and the *a* .... Heb 9:4
of Noah, while the *a* .... 1 Pet 3:20
in heaven, and the *a* .... Rev 11:19

ARM
with an outstretched *a* .... Ex 6:6
"Has the LORD's *a* .... Num 11:23
With him is an *a* .... 2 Chr 32:8
a that has no strength .... Job 26:2
Have you an *a* like God .... Job 40:9
Break the *a* of the .... Ps 10:15
You have a mighty *a* .... Ps 89:13
a have gained Him the .... Ps 98:1
a shall rule for Him .... Is 40:10
therefore His own *a* .... Is 59:16
strength with His *a* .... Luke 1:51
with an uplifted *a* .... Acts 13:17
a yourselves also with .... 1 Pet 4:1

ARMAGEDDON
See MEGIDDO
Possible site of final battle, Rev 16:16

ARMED
You have *a* me with ...... 2 Sam 22:40
a strong man, fully *a* .... Luke 11:21

ARMIES
make captains of the *a* ...... Deut 20:9
"I defy the *a* .... 1 Sam 17:10
any number to His *a* .... Job 25:3
not go out with our *a* .... Ps 60:10
And he sent out his *a* .... Matt 22:7
surrounded by *a* .... Luke 21:20
And the *a* in heaven .... Rev 19:14
the earth, and their *a* .... Rev 19:19

ARMOR
but he put his *a* .... 1 Sam 17:54
spears, put on the *a* .... Jer 46:4
let us put on the *a* .... Rom 13:12
Put on the whole *a* .... Eph 6:11

ARMS
are the everlasting *a* ...... Deut 33:27
into the clash of *a* .... Job 39:21
It is God who *a* .... Ps 18:32
My *a* will judge the .... Is 51:5
wounds between your *a* ..... Zech 13:6
took them up in His *a* ..... Mark 10:16
took Him up in his *a* .... Luke 2:28

ARMY
the multitude of an *a* .... Ps 33:16
an exceedingly great *a* ..... Ezek 37:10
the number of the *a* .... Rev 9:16

ARNON
Boundary between Moab and Ammon, Num 21:13, 26
Border of Reuben, Deut 3:12, 16
Ammonites reminded of, Judg 11:18–26

AROER
A town in east Jordan; rebuilt by Gadites, Num 32:34; Deut 2:36
Assigned to Reuben, Deut 3:12
Ruled by Amorites, Josh 12:2; 13:9, 10, 16

AROMA
smelled a soothing *a* .... Gen 8:21
To the one we are the *a* ..... 2 Cor 2:16
for a sweet-smelling *a* .... Eph 5:2
a sweet-smelling *a* .... Phil 4:18

AROUSED
the LORD was greatly *a* .... Num 11:10
his wrath was *a* .... Job 32:2
Then Joseph, being *a* .... Matt 1:24

ARPHAXAD
A son of Shem, Gen 10:22, 24
Born two years after the flood, Gen 11:10–13
An ancestor of Christ, Luke 3:36

ARRAYED
his glory was not *a* .... Matt 6:29
"Who are these *a* .... Rev 7:13
The woman was *a* .... Rev 17:4

ARROGANCE
Pride and *a* and the .... Prov 8:13
I will halt the *a* .... Is 13:11

ARROGANT
the fruit of the *a* .... Is 10:12
sanctuary, your *a* boast .... Ezek 24:21

ARROW
deliverance and the *a* ...... 2 Kin 13:17
a cannot make him flee ..... Job 41:28
make ready their *a* .... Ps 11:2
a that flies by day .... Ps 91:5
a sword, and a sharp *a* ..... Prov 25:18
Their tongue is an *a* .... Jer 9:8
as a target for the *a* .... Lam 3:12

ARROWS
He sent out *a* and .... 2 Sam 22:15
a pierce me deeply .... Ps 38:2
There He broke the *a* .... Ps 76:3
Like *a* in the hand of .... Ps 127:4
He has caused the *a* .... Lam 3:13
were sworn over Your *a* .... Hab 3:9

ARTAXERXES
Artaxerxes I, king of Persia (465–425 B.C.), authorizes Ezra's mission to Jerusalem, Ezra 7:1–28
Temporarily halts rebuilding program at Jerusalem, Ezra 4:7–23
Authorizes Nehemiah's mission, Neh 2:1–10
Permits Nehemiah to return, Neh 13:6

ARTEMIS
Worship of, at Ephesus, creates uproar, Acts 19:23–41

ASA
Third king of Judah; restores true worship, 1 Kin 15:8–15; 2 Chr 14—15
Hires Ben-Hadad against Baasha; rebuked by a prophet, 1 Kin 15:16–22; 2 Chr 16:1–10
Diseased, seeks physicians rather than the Lord, 2 Chr 16:12
Death and burial, 2 Chr 16:13, 14

ASAHEL
David's nephew; captain in his army; noted for valor, 2 Sam 2:18; 23:24; 1 Chr 2:16; 27:7
Killed by Abner, 2 Sam 2:19–23
Avenged by Joab, 2 Sam 3:27, 30

ASAPH
A Levite choir leader under David and Solomon, 1 Chr 15:16–19; 16:1–7; 2 Chr 5:6, 12

Twelve Psalms assigned to, 2 Chr 29:30; Ps 50; 73—83

ASCEND

Who may *a* into the ....Ps 24:3
If I *a* into heaven ....Ps 139:8
'I will *a* into heaven ....Is 14:13
a as high as the eagle ....Obad 4
see the Son of Man *a*..........John 6:62

ASCENDED

You have *a* on high ....Ps 68:18
Who has *a* into heaven ....Prov 30:4
No one has *a* ....John 3:13
"When He *a* on high ....Eph 4:8
also the One who *a* ....Eph 4:10
And they *a* to heaven ....Rev 11:12

ASCENDING

angels of God were *a* ....Gen 28:12
the angels of God *a* ....John 1:51

ASCRIBE

a greatness to our God ....Deut 32:3
a righteousness ....Job 36:3
A strength to God ....Ps 68:34

ASENATH

Daughter of Poti-Pherah and wife of Joseph, Gen 41:45
Mother of Manasseh and Ephraim, Gen 41:50–52; 46:20

ASHAMED

I am too *a* and ....Ezra 9:6
all my enemies be *a* ....Ps 6:10
Let me not be *a* ....Ps 25:2
who waits on You be *a* ....Ps 25:3
The wise men are *a* ....Jer 8:9
forsake You shall be *a* ....Jer 17:13
And Israel shall be *a* ....Hos 10:6
For whoever is *a* ....Mark 8:38
am not *a* of the gospel ....Rom 1:16
nothing I shall be *a* ....Phil 1:20
Therefore God is not *a* ....Heb 11:16
in Christ may be *a* ....1 Pet 3:16
let him not be *a* ....1 Pet 4:16
and not be *a* before ....1 John 2:28

ASHDOD

One of five Philistine cities, Josh 13:3
Seat of Dagon worship, 1 Sam 5:1–8
Opposes Nehemiah, Neh 4:7
Women of, marry Jews, Neh 13:23, 24
Called Azotus, Acts 8:40

ASHER

Jacob's second son by Zilpah, Gen 30:12, 13
Goes to Egypt with Jacob, Gen 46:8, 17
Blessed by Jacob, Gen 49:20
——Tribe of:
Census of, Num 1:41; 26:47
Slow to fight against Canaanites, Judg 1:31, 32; 5:17
Among Gideon's army, Judg 6:35; 7:23
A godly remnant among, 2 Chr 30:11

ASHERAH

The female counterpart of Baal, Judg 3:7; 1 Kin 18:19
Image of, erected by Manasseh in the temple, 2 Kin 21:7
Vessels of, destroyed by Josiah, 2 Kin 23:4
——Translated "wooden images," idols used in the worship of Asherah, Ex 34:13; Deut 12:3; 16:21; 1 Kin 16:32, 33; 2 Kin 23:6, 7

ASHES

are proverbs of *a* ....Job 13:12
become like dust and *a* ....Job 30:19
For I have eaten *a* ....Ps 102:9
He feeds on *a* ....Is 44:20
sackcloth and sat in *a* ....Jon 3:6
in sackcloth and *a* ....Luke 10:13
and the *a* of a heifer ....Heb 9:13

ASHKELON

One of five Philistine cities, Josh 13:3; Jer 47:5, 7
Captured by Judah, Judg 1:18
Men of, killed by Samson, Judg 14:19, 20
Repossessed by Philistines, 1 Sam 6:17; 2 Sam 1:20
Doom of, pronounced by the prophets, Jer 47:5, 7; Amos 1:8; Zeph 2:4, 7; Zech 9:5

ASHTAROTH

A city in Bashan; residence of King Og, Deut 1:4; Josh 12:4
Captured by Israel, Josh 9:10
——A general designation of the Canaanite female deities, 1 Sam 7:3, 4; 31:10

ASHTORETH

A mother-goddess worshiped by the Philistines, 1 Sam 31:10
Israel ensnared by, Judg 2:13; 10:6
Worshiped by Solomon, 1 Kin 11:5, 33
Destroyed by Josiah, 2 Kin 23:13

ASIA

Paul forbidden to preach in, Acts 16:6
Paul's later ministry in, Acts 19:1–26
Seven churches of, Rev 1:4, 11

ASIDE

lay something *a*, storing ....1 Cor 16:2
lay *a* all filthiness ....James 1:21
Therefore, laying *a* ....1 Pet 2:1

ASK

"Why is it that you *a* ....Gen 32:29
when your children *a* ....Josh 4:6
"*A* a sign for yourself ....Is 7:11
They shall *a* the way ....Jer 50:5
the young children *a* ....Lam 4:4
A the LORD for rain in ....Zech 10:1
whatever things you *a* ....Matt 21:22
a, and it will be ....Luke 11:9
that whatever You *a* ....John 11:22
a anything in My ....John 14:14
in that day you will *a* ....John 16:23
something, let them *a* ....1 Cor 14:35
above all that we *a* ....Eph 3:20
wisdom, let him *a* ....James 1:5
But let him *a* in faith ....James 1:6
because you do not *a* ....James 4:2
hears us, whatever we *a* ....1 John 5:15

ASKS

For everyone who *a* ....Matt 7:8
if his son *a* for bread ....Matt 7:9
Or if he *a* for a fish ....Luke 11:11

ASLEEP

down, and was fast *a* ....Jon 1:5
But He was *a* ....Matt 8:24
but some have fallen *a* ....1 Cor 15:6
those who are *a* ....1 Thess 4:15
the fathers fell *a* ....2 Pet 3:4

ASSEMBLED

of the God of Israel *a* ....Ezra 9:4
behold, the kings *a* ....Ps 48:4

ASSEMBLING

not forsaking the *a* ....Heb 10:25

ASSEMBLY

to kill this whole *a* ....Ex 16:3
It is a sacred *a* ....Lev 23:36
a I will praise You ....Ps 22:22
I have hated the *a* ....Ps 26:5
also in the *a* of the ....Ps 89:5
to be feared in the *a* ....Ps 89:7
will rest in the *a* of the ....Prov 21:16
fast, call a sacred *a* ....Joel 1:14
people, sanctify the *a* ....Joel 2:16
a I will sing praise ....Heb 2:12
to the general *a* ....Heb 12:23
come into your *a* ....James 2:2

ASSHUR

One of the sons of Shem; progenitor of the Assyrians, Gen 10:22; 1 Chr 1:17
——The chief god of the Assyrians; seen in names like Ashurbanipal (Osnapper), Ezra 4:10
——A city in Assyria or the nation of Assyria, Num 24:22, 24

ASSURANCE

night, and have no *a* ....Deut 28:66
riches of the full *a* ....Col 2:2
Spirit and in much *a* ....1 Thess 1:5
to the full *a* of hope ....Heb 6:11
a true heart in full *a* ....Heb 10:22

ASSURE

a our hearts before ....1 John 3:19

ASSURED

I will give you *a* peace ....Jer 14:13
learned and been *a* ....2 Tim 3:14

ASSYRIA (or Asshur)

Founded by Nimrod, Gen 10:8–12; Mic 5:6
Agent of God's purposes, Is 7:17–20; 10:5, 6
Attacks and finally conquers Israel, 2 Kin 15:19, 20, 29; 17:3–41
Invades and threatens Judah, 2 Kin 18:13–37
Hezekiah prays for help against; army miraculously slain, 2 Kin 19:1–35
Prophecies concerning, Num 24:22–24; Is 10:12–19; 14:24, 25; 19:23–25; Hos 10:6; 11:5; Nah 3:1–19

ASTONISHED

Just as many were *a* ....Is 52:14
that the people were *a* ....Matt 7:28
who heard Him were *a* ....Luke 2:47

ASTONISHMENT

you shall become an *a* ....Deut 28:37
a has taken hold ....Jer 8:21

ASTRAY

is a people who go *a* ....Ps 95:10
a fool, shall not go *a* ....Is 35:8
Their lies lead them *a* ....Amos 2:4

and one of them goes *a*.....Matt 18:12
'They always go *a* ....Heb 3:10
like sheep going *a* ....1 Pet 2:25

ATHALIAH

Daughter of Ahab and Jezebel, 2 Kin 8:18, 26; 2 Chr 22:2, 3
Kills royal children; usurps throne, 2 Kin 11:1–3; 2 Chr 22:10, 11
Killed in priestly uprising, 2 Kin 11:4–16; 2 Chr 23:1–21

ATHENS

Paul preaches in, Acts 17:15–34
Paul resides in, 1 Thess 3:1

ATONEMENT

a year he shall make *a* ....Ex 30:10
priest shall make *a*..........Lev 16:30
the blood that makes *a* ......Lev 17:11
for it is the Day of *A* ....Lev 23:28
what shall I make *a* ....2 Sam 21:3
offerings to make *a*.........Neh 10:33
a is provided for ....Prov 16:6
there will be no *a* ....Is 22:14
I provide you an *a* ....Ezek 16:63

ATTAIN

It is high, I cannot *a* ....Ps 139:6
understanding will *a* ....Prov 1:5
How long until they *a* ....Hos 8:5
worthy to *a* that age ....Luke 20:35
by any means, I may *a* ....Phil 3:11

ATTEND

just cause, O LORD, *a* ....Ps 17:1
And *a* to the voice of ....Ps 86:6
behold, I will *a* ....Jer 23:2

ATTENTION

My son, give *a* to my ....Prov 4:20
Till I come, give *a* ....1 Tim 4:13
and you pay *a* to the ....James 2:3

ATTENTIVE

Let Your ears be *a* ....Ps 130:2
the people were very *a*.....Luke 19:48

ATTESTED

a Man *a* by God to you ....Acts 2:22

AUSTERE

because you are an *a* ....Luke 19:21

AUTHOR

For God is not the *a* ....1 Cor 14:33
He became the *a*...............Heb 5:9
unto Jesus, the *a* ....Heb 12:2

AUTHORITIES

a that exist are ....Rom 13:1
of God, angels and *a* ....1 Pet 3:22

AUTHORITY

Jew, wrote with full *a* ....Esth 9:29
the righteous are in *a* ....Prov 29:2
them as one having *a* ....Matt 7:29
who are great exercise *a* ...Matt 20:25
"All *a* has been given ......Matt 28:18
a I will give You ....Luke 4:6
and has given Him *a* ....John 5:27
You have given Him *a* ....John 17:2
has put in His own *a* ....Acts 1:7
For there is no *a* ....Rom 13:1

to have a symbol of *a* ....1 Cor 11:10
and all who are in *a* ....1 Tim 2:2
and rebuke with all *a* ....Titus 2:15
defile the flesh, reject *a* ....Jude 8

AUTUMN

a trees without fruit ....Jude 12

AVAILS

nor uncircumcision *a* ....Gal 5:6
of a righteous man *a* ....James 5:16

AVEN

The city of On in Egypt near Cairo; known as Heliopolis, Gen 41:45; Ezek 30:17
——A name contemptuously applied to Bethel, Hos 10:5, 8
——Valley in Syria, Amos 1:5

AVENGE

for He will *a* the ....Deut 32:43
you that He will *a* ....Luke 18:8
Beloved, do not *a* ....Rom 12:19
a our blood on those ....Rev 6:10

AVENGER

The *a* of blood ....Num 35:19
the enemy and the *a* ....Ps 8:2
God's minister, an *a* ....Rom 13:4
the Lord is the *a* ....1 Thess 4:6

AVENGES

It is God who *a* ....2 Sam 22:48
When He *a* blood ....Ps 9:12

AWAKE

be satisfied when I *a* ....Ps 17:15
I lie *a* ....Ps 102:7
A, lute and harp ....Ps 108:2
My eyes are *a* through .....Ps 119:148
A, O north wind ....Song 4:16
but my heart is *a* ....Song 5:2
of the earth shall *a* ....Dan 12:2
it is high time to *a* ....Rom 13:11
A to righteousness ....1 Cor 15:34
"*A*, you who sleep ....Eph 5:14

AWAY

the wind drives *a*...............Ps 1:4
Do not cast me *a* ....Ps 51:11
A time to cast *a* ....Eccl 3:5
fair one, and come *a* ....Song 2:10
and the shadows flee *a* ......Song 2:17
minded to put her *a* ....Matt 1:19
and earth will pass *a* ....Matt 24:35
and steal Him *a* ....Matt 27:64
the rich He has sent *a* ....Luke 1:53
of God who takes *a* ....John 1:29
"I am going *a*................John 8:21
they cried out, "*A* ....John 19:15
"They have taken *a* ....John 20:2
crying out, "*A* ....Acts 21:36
the veil is taken *a* ....2 Cor 3:14
Barnabas was carried *a* ......Gal 2:13
unless the falling *a* ....2 Thess 2:3
in Asia have turned *a* ....2 Tim 1:15
heard, lest we drift *a* ....Heb 2:1
if they fall *a* ....Heb 6:6
which can never take *a* .....Heb 10:11
that does not fade *a* ....1 Pet 5:4
the world is passing *a* ......1 John 2:17
and the heaven fled *a* ....Rev 20:11
if anyone takes *a* ....Rev 22:19
God shall take *a* ....Rev 22:19

AWE

the world stand in *a* ....Ps 33:8
my heart stands in *a* ....Ps 119:161

AWESOME

a is this place ....Gen 28:17
a thing that I will do ....Ex 34:10
God, the great and *a* ....Deut 7:21
God, mighty and *a* ....Deut 10:17
Angel of God, very *a* ....Judg 13:6
a deeds for Your land ....2 Sam 7:23
heaven, O great and *a* ....Neh 1:5
hand shall teach You *a* ....Ps 45:4
By *a* deeds in ....Ps 65:5
a are Your works ....Ps 66:3
He is *a* in His doing ....Ps 66:5
O God, You are more *a* ....Ps 68:35
He is *a* to the kings ....Ps 76:12
Your great and *a* name ....Ps 99:3
of the might of Your *a* ....Ps 145:6
When You did *a* things ....Is 64:3
with me as a mighty, *a* ....Jer 20:11
her collapse was *a* ....Lam 1:9
"O Lord, great and *a* ....Dan 9:4

AWL

his ear with an *a* ....Ex 21:6
you shall take an *a* ....Deut 15:17

AX

a stroke with the *a* ....Deut 19:5
Abimelech took an *a* ....Judg 9:48
a tree, the iron *a* ....2 Kin 6:5
If the *a* is dull ....Eccl 10:10
a boast itself against ....Is 10:15
And even now the *a* ....Matt 3:10

AZARIAH

A prophet who encourages King Asa, 2 Chr 15:1–8
——Son of King Jehoshaphat, 2 Chr 21:2
——King of Judah, 2 Kin 15:1
——A high priest who rebukes King Uzziah, 2 Chr 26:16–20
——Chief priest in the time of Hezekiah, 2 Chr 31:9, 10
——The Hebrew name of Abed-Nego, Dan 1:7

AZEKAH

Camp of Goliath, 1 Sam 17:1, 4, 17
Besieged by Nebuchadnezzar, Jer 34:7

AZMAVETH

A village near Jerusalem, Neh 12:29
Also called Beth Azmaveth, Neh 7:28

—B—

BAAL (or Baals)

Deities of Canaanite polytheism, Judg 10:10–14
The male god of the Phoenicians and Canaanites; the counterpart of the female Ashtaroth, 2 Kin 23:5
Nature of the worship of, 1 Kin 18:26, 28; 19:18; Ps 106:28; Jer 7:9; 19:5; Hos 9:10; 13:1, 2
Worshiped by Israelites, Num 25:1–5; Judg 2:11–14; 3:7; 6:28–32; 1 Kin 16:31, 32; 2 Kin 21:3; Jer 11:13; Hos 2:8
Ahaz makes images to, 2 Chr 28:1–4

Overthrown by Elijah, 1 Kin 18:17–40 by Josiah, 2 Kin 23:4, 5
Denounced by prophets, Jer 19:4–6; Ezek 16:1, 2, 20, 21
Historic retrospect, Rom 11:4

BAAL PEOR (or Baal of Peor)

A Moabite god; worshiped by Israelites, Num 25:1–9

BAAL PERAZIM

Site of David's victory over the Philistines, 2 Sam 5:18–20
Same as Perazim, Is 28:21

BAAL-ZEBUB

A Philistine god at Ekron, 2 Kin 1:2
Ahaziah inquires of, 2 Kin 1:2, 6, 16
Also called Beelzebub, Matt 10:25; 12:24

BAALAH

A town also known as Kirjath Jearim, Josh 15:9, 10

BAALS

Deities of Canaanite polytheism, Judg 10:10–14
Ensnare Israelites, Judg 2:11–14; 3:7
Ahaz makes images to, 2 Chr 28:1–4

BAANAH

A murderer of Ishbosheth, 2 Sam 4:1–12

BAASHA

Usurps throne of Israel; his evil reign; wars with Judah, 1 Kin 15:16—16:7

BABBLER

b is no different .... Eccl 10:11
"What does this *b* .... Acts 17:18

BABBLINGS

the profane and idle *b* ..... 1 Tim 6:20

BABE

the *b* leaped in my .... Luke 1:44
You will find a *B* .... Luke 2:12
for he is a *b* .... Heb 5:13

BABEL, TOWER OF

A huge brick structure intended to magnify man and preserve the unity of the race, Gen 11:1–4
Objectives of, thwarted by God, Gen 11:5–9

BABES

Out of the mouth of *b* .... Ps 8:2
b shall rule over them .... Is 3:4
revealed them to *b* .... Matt 11:25
'Out of the mouth of *b* ...... Matt 21:16
a teacher of *b* .... Rom 2:20
as to carnal, as to *b* .... 1 Cor 3:1
as newborn *b* .... 1 Pet 2:2

BABYLON

Built by Nimrod; Tower of Babel, Gen 10:8–10; 11:1–9
Descriptions of, Is 13:19; 14:4; Jer 51:44; Dan 4:30
Jews carried captive to, 2 Kin 25:1–21; 2 Chr 36:5–21
Inhabitants of, described, Is 47:1, 9–13; Jer 50:35–38; Dan 5:1–3
Prophecies concerning, Is 13:1–22; Jer 21:1–7; 25:9–12; 27:5–8; 29:10; Jer 50:1–46; Dan 2:31–38; 7:2–4
The prophetic city, Rev 14:8; 16:19; 17:1—18:24

BACK

Jordan turned *b* .... Ps 114:3
but a rod is for the *b* .... Prov 10:13
for the fool's *b* .... Prov 26:3
I gave My *b* to those .... Is 50:6
cast Me behind your *b* ..... Ezek 23:35
found Him, bring *b* word ..... Matt 2:8
plow, and looking *b* .... Luke 9:62
they drew *b* and fell .... John 18:6
I am sending him *b* .... Philem 12
of those who draw *b* .... Heb 10:39
someone turns him *b* ...... James 5:19
inside and on the *b* .... Rev 5:1

BACKBITERS

b, haters of God .... Rom 1:30

BACKBITING

b tongue an angry .... Prov 25:23

BACKSLIDER

The *b* in heart will be .... Prov 14:14

BACKSLIDINGS

b will rebuke you .... Jer 2:19
And I will heal your *b* .... Jer 3:22
b have increased .... Jer 5:6
for our *b* are many .... Jer 14:7

BACKWARD

fell off the seat *b* .... 1 Sam 4:18
shadow ten degrees *b* ..... 2 Kin 20:11

BAD

speak to you either *b* ...... Gen 24:50
good for *b* or *b* for good ..... Lev 27:10
b tree bears *b* fruit .... Matt 7:17

BAG

is sealed up in a *b* .... Job 14:17
wages to put into a *b* .... Hag 1:6
nor *b* for your .... Matt 10:10

BAKE

b twelve cakes with it .... Lev 24:5

BAKED

b unleavened cakes .... Ex 12:39
b unleavened bread .... 1 Sam 28:24

BAKER

the butler and the *b* .... Gen 40:1

BAKERS

of bread from the *b* .... Jer 37:21

BAKES

kindles it and *b* bread .... Is 44:15

BALAAM

Sent by Balak to curse Israel, Num 22:5–7; Josh 24:9
Hindered by talking donkey, Num 22:22–35; 2 Pet 2:16
Curse becomes a blessing, Deut 23:4, 5; Josh 24:10
Prophecies of, Num 23:7–10, 18–24; 24:3–9, 15–24
NT references to, 2 Pet 2:15, 16; Jude 11; Rev 2:14

BALAK

A Moabite king, Num 22:4
Hires Balaam to curse Israel, Num 22—24

BALANCE

b is an abomination .... Prov 11:1
small dust on the *b* .... Is 40:15

BALANCES

falsifying the *b* .... Amos 8:5

BALD

shall not make any *b* .... Lev 21:5
every head shall be *b* .... Jer 48:37
completely *b* because ...... Ezek 27:31

BALDHEAD

Go up, you *b* .... 2 Kin 2:23

BALM

a little *b* and a .... Gen 43:11
no *b* in Gilead .... Jer 8:22

BAND

A *b* of robbers takes .... Hos 7:1
with a golden *b* .... Rev 1:13

BANDAGED

him, and *b* his wounds ..... Luke 10:34

BANKERS

my money with the *b* ...... Matt 25:27

BANNERS

we will set up our *b* .... Ps 20:5
They set up their *b* .... Ps 74:4
as an army with *b* .... Song 6:4

BANQUET

b that I have prepared .... Esth 5:4
companions make a *b* .... Job 41:6
lords, came to the *b* .... Dan 5:10

BANQUETING

He brought me to the *b* ...... Song 2:4

BANQUETS

b shall be removed .... Amos 6:7

BAPTISM

coming to his *b* .... Matt 3:7
b that I am baptized .... Matt 20:22
The *b* of John .... Matt 21:25
But I have a *b* .... Luke 12:50
said, "Into John's *b* .... Acts 19:3
with Him through *b* .... Rom 6:4
Lord, one faith, one *b* .... Eph 4:5
buried with Him in *b* .... Col 2:12
now saves us—*b* .... 1 Pet 3:21

BAPTISMS

of the doctrine of *b* .... Heb 6:2

BAPTIZE

I indeed *b* you with .... Matt 3:11
"Why then do you *b* .... John 1:25
Himself did not *b* .... John 4:2
did not send me to *b* .... 1 Cor 1:17

You shall *b* him with a .....Prov 23:14
b their swords into ....Is 2:4
you shall *b* in pieces ....Mic 4:13
spat in His face and *b*.........Matt 26:67
but *b* his breast ....Luke 18:13

BEATEN

and you will be *b* ....Mark 13:9
his will, shall be *b* ....Luke 12:47
Three times I was *b* ....2 Cor 11:25
when you are *b* for your.....1 Pet 2:20

BEAUTIFUL

but Rachel was *b* ....Gen 29:17
B in elevation ....Ps 48:2
has made everything *b* ....Eccl 3:11
my love, you are as *b* ....Song 6:4
of the LORD shall be *b* ....Is 4:2
How *b* upon the ....Is 52:7
indeed appear *b* ....Matt 23:27
begging alms at the *B* ....Acts 3:10
they saw he was a *b* ....Heb 11:23

BEAUTIFY

b the humble with ....Ps 149:4
b the place of My ....Is 60:13

BEAUTY

for glory and for *b* ....Ex 28:2
"The *b* of Israel is ....2 Sam 1:19
To behold the *b* ....Ps 27:4
and *b* is passing ....Prov 31:30
see the King in His *b* ....Is 33:17
no *b* that we should ....Is 53:2
the one I called *B* ....Zech 11:7
Do not let your *b* ....1 Pet 3:3
the incorruptible *b* ....1 Pet 3:4

BECAME

b a living being ....Gen 2:7
to the Jews I *b* ....1 Cor 9:20
for I *b* like you ....Gal 4:12

BED

house, if I make my *b* ....Job 17:13
I remember You on my *b* ....Ps 63:6
if I make my *b* in hell ....Ps 139:8
Also our *b* is green ....Song 1:16
b is too short to stretch ....Is 28:20
you have set your *b* ....Is 57:7
"Arise, take up your *b*..............Matt 9:6
be two men in one *b* ....Luke 17:34
and the *b* undefiled ....Heb 13:4

BEDS

sing aloud on their *b* ....Ps 149:5
shall rest in their *b* ....Is 57:2
who lie on *b* of ivory ....Amos 6:4

BEE

Egypt, and for the *b* ....Is 7:18

BEELZEBUB

Jesus accused of serving, Matt 10:25; 12:24–27

BEER LAHAI ROI

Angel meets Hagar there, Gen 16:7–14
Isaac dwells in, Gen 24:62

BEERSHEBA

God appears there to Hagar, Gen 21:14–19
to Isaac, Gen 26:23–25
to Jacob, Gen 46:1–5
to Elijah, 1 Kin 19:3–7
Oaths sworn there by Abraham, Gen 21:31–33
by Isaac, Gen 26:26–33

BEFOREHAND

do not worry *b* ....Mark 13:11
told you all things *b*...........Mark 13:23
not to meditate *b* ....Luke 21:14
when He testified *b* ....1 Pet 1:11

BEG

I would *b* mercy of my ....Job 9:15
I am ashamed to *b* ....Luke 16:3
b you as sojourners ....1 Pet 2:11

BEGAN

Then men *b* to call on ....Gen 4:26
since the world *b* ....Luke 1:70

BEGETS

b a scoffer does ....Prov 17:21
b a wise child will ....Prov 23:24
b a hundred children ....Eccl 6:3

BEGGAR

and lifts the *b* ....1 Sam 2:8
there was a certain *b* ....Luke 16:20

BEGGARLY

weak and *b* elements ....Gal 4:9

BEGINNING

b God created the ....Gen 1:1
Though your *b* was ....Job 8:7
of the LORD is the *b* ....Ps 111:10
that God does from *b* ....Eccl 3:11
who made them at the *b* ....Matt 19:4
In the *b* was the Word ....John 1:1
This *b* of signs Jesus ....John 2:11
a murderer from the *b* ....John 8:44
with Me from the *b* ....John 15:27
the *b*, the firstborn ....Col 1:18
having neither *b* ....Heb 7:3
True Witness, the *B* ....Rev 3:14
and the Omega, the *B* ....Rev 21:6

BEGOTTEN

I have *b* You ....Ps 2:7
heart, 'Who has *b* ....Is 49:21
glory as of the only *b* ....John 1:14
Christ Jesus I have *b* ....1 Cor 4:15
abundant mercy has *b* ....1 Pet 1:3
loves him who is *b* ....1 John 5:1

BEGUILING

b unstable souls ....2 Pet 2:14

BEGUN

Having *b* in the Spirit ....Gal 3:3
that He who has *b* ....Phil 1:6

BEHALF

to speak on God's *b* ....Job 36:2
you on Christ's *b* ....2 Cor 5:20
has been granted on *b* ....Phil 1:29

BEHAVE

I will *b* wisely in a ....Ps 101:2
does not *b* rudely ....1 Cor 13:5

BEHAVED

sent him, and *b* wisely ....1 Sam 18:5
and blamelessly we *b* ....1 Thess 2:10

BEHAVIOR

of good *b*, hospitable ....1 Tim 3:2
they be reverent in *b* ....Titus 2:3

BEHEADED

he sent and had John *b* ....Matt 14:10
those who had been *b* ....Rev 20:4

BEHEMOTH

Described, Job 40:15–24

BEHOLD

the eyes to *b* the sun ....Eccl 11:7
B, you are fair ....Song 1:15
B, the virgin shall ....Is 7:14
Judah, "*B* your God ....Is 40:9
B the Lamb of God ....John 1:36
I am, that they may *b* ....John 17:24
to them, "*B* the Man ....John 19:5
B what manner of love ....1 John 3:1

BEHOLDING

with unveiled face, *b* ....2 Cor 3:18

BEING

man became a living *b* ....Gen 2:7
God while I have my *b* ....Ps 104:33
move and have our *b* ....Acts 17:28
who, *b* in the form of....................Phil 2:6

BEL

Patron god of Babylon, Is 46:1; Jer 50:2; 51:44

BELIEF

by the Spirit and *b* ....2 Thess 2:13

BELIEVE

B in the LORD your God ...2 Chr 20:20
tears, "Lord, I *b* ....Mark 9:24
b that you receive ....Mark 11:24
because they did not *b*..........Mark 16:14
have no root, who *b* ....Luke 8:13
and slow of heart to *b* ....Luke 24:25
to those who *b* ....John 1:12
how will you *b* ....John 3:12
sent, Him you do not *b* ....John 5:38
we may see it and *b* ....John 6:30
to him, "Do you *b* ....John 9:35
this, that they may *b* ....John 11:42
you *b* in God ....John 14:1
written that you may *b* ....John 20:31
King Agrippa, do you *b*..........Acts 26:27
the Lord Jesus and *b* ....Rom 10:9
And how shall they *b* ....Rom 10:14
a wife who does not *b* ....1 Cor 7:12
I spoke," we also *b* ....2 Cor 4:13
given to those who *b* ....Gal 3:22
Christ, not only to *b* ....Phil 1:29
comes to God must *b* ....Heb 11:6
b that there is one ....James 2:19
Even the demons *b* ....James 2:19
Beloved, do not *b* ....1 John 4:1

BELIEVED

And he *b* in the LORD ....Gen 15:6
b that I would see the ....Ps 27:13
Who has *b* our report ....Is 53:1
of that city *b* in Him ....John 4:39
seen Me, you have *b* ....John 20:29
who heard the word *b* ....Acts 4:4
of those who *b* were of ....Acts 4:32
Holy Spirit when you *b* ....Acts 19:2
"Abraham *b* God ....Rom 4:3
I know whom I have *b* ....2 Tim 1:12

BELIEVERS

be an example to the *b* ....1 Tim 4:12
are benefited are *b* ....1 Tim 6:2

BELIEVES

The simple *b* every ....Prov 14:15
He who *b* and is ....Mark 16:16
that whoever *b* in Him ......John 3:16
He who *b* in the Son ......John 3:36
with the heart one *b* ....Rom 10:10
b all things ....1 Cor 13:7

BELIEVING

you ask in prayer, *b* ....Matt 21:22
blessed with *b* Abraham ....Gal 3:9

BELLY

On your *b* you shall go ....Gen 3:14
And Jonah was in the *b* ....Jon 1:17
three nights in the *b* ....Matt 12:40
whose god is their *b* ....Phil 3:19

BELONG

To the Lord our God *b* ....Dan 9:9
My name, because you *b* ....Mark 9:41

BELOVED

"The *b* of the Lord ....Deut 33:12
so He gives His *b* ....Ps 127:2
of myrrh is my *b* ....Song 1:13
My *b* is mine ....Song 2:16
b more than another ....Song 5:9
Where has your *b* ....Song 6:1
leaning upon her *b* ....Song 8:5
a song of my *B* ....Is 5:1
for you are greatly *b* ....Dan 9:23
"This is My *b* ....Matt 3:17
election they are *b* ....Rom 11:28
us accepted in the *B* ....Eph 1:6
Luke the *b* physician ....Col 4:14
than a slave as a *b* ....Philem 16
"This is My *b* ....2 Pet 1:17
our *b* brother Paul ....2 Pet 3:15
the saints and the *b* ....Rev 20:9

BELSHAZZAR

King of Babylon; Daniel interprets his dream, Dan 5

BELT

with a leather *b* ....Matt 3:4
us, he took Paul's *b* ....Acts 21:11

BELTESHAZZAR

Daniel's Babylonian name, Dan 1:7

BEMOAN

Or who will *b* you ....Jer 15:5
for the dead, nor *b* ....Jer 22:10

BEN-AMMI

Son of Lot; father of the Ammonites, Gen 19:38

BEN-HADAD

Ben-Hadad I, king of Damascus; hired by Asa, king of Judah, to attack Baasha, king of Israel, 1 Kin 15:18–21
——— Ben-Hadad II, king of Damascus; makes war on Ahab, king of Israel, 1 Kin 20
Falls in siege against Samaria, 2 Kin 6:24–33; 7:6–20
Killed by Hazael, 2 Kin 8:7–15
——— Ben-Hadad III, king of Damascus; loses all Israelite conquests made by Hazael, his father, 2 Kin 13:3–25

BEN-ONI

Rachel's name for Benjamin, Gen 35:16–18

BENAIAH

The son of Jehoiada; a mighty man, 2 Sam 23:20–23
Faithful to David, 2 Sam 15:18; 20:23
Escorts Solomon to the throne, 1 Kin 1:38–40
Executes Adonijah, Joab and Shimei, 1 Kin 2:25, 29–34, 46
——— A Pirathonite; another of David's mighty men, 2 Sam 23:30
Divisional commander, 1 Chr 27:14

BEND

The wicked *b* their bow ....Ps 11:2

BENEATH

and on the earth *b* ....Deut 4:39
"You are from *b* ....John 8:23

BENEFACTORS

them are called '*b* ....Luke 22:25

BENEFIT

That I may see the *b* ....Ps 106:5
people who could not *b* ....Is 30:5
might have a second *b* ......2 Cor 1:15

BENJAMIN

Jacob's youngest son, Gen 35:16–20
Taken to Egypt against Jacob's wishes, Gen 42—45
Jacob's prophecy concerning, Gen 49:27
——— Tribe of:
Families of, Num 26:38–41
Territory allotted to, Josh 18:11–28
Attacked by remaining tribes for condoning sin of Gibeah, Judg 20:12–48
Wives provided for remnant of, Judg 21:1–23
Tribe of Saul, 1 Sam 9:1, 2
of Paul, Phil 3:5

BENT

behold, this vine *b* ....Ezek 17:7

BEREA

A city of Macedonia; visited by Paul, Acts 17:10–15

BEREAVE

I will *b* them of ....Jer 15:7
no more shall you *b* ....Ezek 36:12
children, yet I will *b* ....Hos 9:12

BERNICE

Sister of Herod Agrippa II, Acts 25:13, 23
Hears Paul's defense, Acts 26:1–30

BERODACH-BALADAN

See MERODACH-BALADAN
A king of Babylon, 2 Kin 20:12–19

BESEECH

Return, we *b* You ....Ps 80:14
b you therefore ....Rom 12:1
of the LORD, *b* you to ....Eph 4:1

BESIDE

He leads me *b* the ....Ps 23:2
"Paul, you are *b* ....Acts 26:24
For if we are *b* ....2 Cor 5:13

BEST

with the *b* ointments ....Amos 6:6
'Bring out the *b* ....Luke 15:22
earnestly desire the *b* ......1 Cor 12:31

BESTOW

LORD, that He may *b* ....Ex 32:29
b greater honor ....1 Cor 12:23

BESTOWED

love the Father has *b* ....1 John 3:1

BETH HORON

Twin towns of Ephraim, Josh 16:3, 5
Fortified by Solomon, 2 Chr 8:3–5
Prominent in battles, Josh 10:10–14; 1 Sam 13:18

BETH PEOR

Town near Pisgah, Deut 3:29
Moses buried near, Deut 34:6
Assigned to Reubenites, Josh 13:15, 20

BETH SHAN (or Beth Shean)

A town in Issachar, Josh 17:11–16
Saul's corpse hung up at, 1 Sam 31:10–13; 2 Sam 21:12–14

BETH SHEMESH

Ark brought to, 1 Sam 6:12–19
Joash defeats Amaziah at, 2 Kin 14:11
Taken by Philistines, 2 Chr 28:18

BETHABARA

A place beyond the Jordan where John baptized, John 1:28

BETHANY

A town on the Mt. of Olives, Luke 19:29
Home of Lazarus, John 11:1
Home of Simon, the leper, Matt 26:6
Jesus visits there, Mark 11:1, 11, 12
Scene of the Ascension, Luke 24:50, 51

BETHEL

Abram settles near, Gen 12:7, 8
Site of Abram's altar, Gen 13:3, 4
Site of Jacob's vision of the ladder, Gen 28:10–19
Jacob returns to, Gen 35:1–15
Samuel judges there, 1 Sam 7:15, 16
Site of worship and sacrifice, 1 Sam 10:3
Center of idolatry, 1 Kin 12:28–33
Josiah destroys altars of, 2 Kin 23:4, 15–20
Denounced by prophets, 1 Kin 13:1–10; Amos 7:10–13; Jer 48:13; Hos 10:15

BETHESDA

Jerusalem pool, John 5:2–4

BETHLEHEM

Originally called Ephrath, Gen 35:16
Rachel buried there, Gen 35:19
Home of Naomi and Boaz, Ruth 1:1, 19; 4:9–11
Home of David, 1 Sam 16:1–18

Predicted place of Messiah's birth, Mic 5:2
Christ born there, Matt 2:1; Luke 2:4–7; John 7:42
Infants of, killed by Herod, Matt 2:16–18

BETHPHAGE

Village near Bethany, Mark 11:1
Near Mt. of Olives, Matt 21:1

BETHSAIDA

A city of Galilee, Mark 6:45
Home of Andrew, Peter and Philip, John 1:44; 12:21
Blind man healed there, Mark 8:22, 23
5,000 fed nearby, Luke 9:10–17
Unbelief of, denounced, Matt 11:21; Luke 10:13

BETRAY

the outcasts, do not *b* ....Is 16:3
you, one of you will *b* ......Matt 26:21
Now brother will *b* ....Mark 13:12

BETRAYED

Man is about to be *b* ....Matt 17:22
in which He was *b* ....1 Cor 11:23

BETRAYER

See, My *b* is at ....Matt 26:46

BETRAYING

"Judas, are you *b* ....Luke 22:48

BETRAYS

who is the one who *b* ......John 21:20

BETROTH

"You shall *b* a wife ....Deut 28:30
"I will *b* you to Me ....Hos 2:19

BETROTHED

to a virgin *b* to a man ....Luke 1:27
For I have *b* you to ....2 Cor 11:2

BETTER

b than sacrifice ....1 Sam 15:22
It is *b* to trust in ....Ps 118:8
B is a little with the ....Prov 15:16
B is a dry morsel ....Prov 17:1
B is the poor who ....Prov 19:1
B to dwell in ....Prov 21:19
b is a neighbor ....Prov 27:10
B a handful with ....Eccl 4:6
Two are *b* than one ....Eccl 4:9
B a poor and wise ....Eccl 4:13
were the former days *b* ....Eccl 7:10
features appeared *b* ....Dan 1:15
For it is *b* to marry ....1 Cor 7:9
Christ, which is far *b* ....Phil 1:23
b than the angels ....Heb 1:4
b things concerning ....Heb 6:9
b things than that ....Heb 12:24

BEULAH

A symbol of true Israel, Is 62:4, 5

BEWARE

"*B* of false prophets ....Matt 7:15
b of evil workers ....Phil 3:2
B lest anyone cheat ....Col 2:8

BEWITCHED

b you that you should ....Gal 3:1

BEYOND

b what is written ....1 Cor 4:6
b their ability ....2 Cor 8:3
advanced in Judaism *b* ....Gal 1:14

BEZALEL

Hur's grandson, 1 Chr 2:20
Tabernacle builder, Ex 31:1–11; 35:30–35

BILDAD

One of Job's friends, Job 2:11
Makes three speeches, Job 8:1–22; 18:1–21; 25:1–6

BILHAH

Rachel's maid, Gen 29:29
The mother of Dan and Naphtali, Gen 30:1–8
Commits incest with Reuben, Gen 35:22

BILLOWS

b have gone over me ....Ps 42:7
all Your *b* and Your ....Jon 2:3

BIND

b the cluster of the ....Job 38:31
b the wild ox in the ....Job 39:10
b them around your ....Prov 3:3
B them on your fingers ....Prov 7:3
B up the testimony ....Is 8:16
but He will *b* us up ....Hos 6:1
and whatever you *b* ....Matt 16:19
'*B* him hand and foot ....Matt 22:13
b heavy burdens ....Matt 23:4

BIRD

the blood of the *b* ....Lev 14:52
with him as with a *b* ....Job 41:5
soul, "Flee as a *b* ....Ps 11:1
has escaped as a *b* ....Ps 124:7
b hastens to the snare ....Prov 7:23
for a *b* of the air may ....Eccl 10:20
fly away like a *b* ....Hos 9:11
unclean and hated *b* ....Rev 18:2

BIRDS

b will eat your flesh ....Gen 40:19
b make their nests ....Ps 104:17
b caught in a snare ....Eccl 9:12
Look at the *b* ....Matt 6:26
"Foxes have holes and *b* .....Matt 8:20

BIRTH

heaven, who gives it *b* ....Job 38:29
makes the deer give *b* ....Ps 29:9
the day of one's *b* ....Eccl 7:1
bring to the time of *b* ....Is 66:9
the deer also gave *b* ....Jer 14:5
Now the *b* of Jesus ....Matt 1:18
will rejoice at his *b* ....Luke 1:14
who was blind from *b* ....John 9:1
conceived, it gives *b* ......James 1:15

BIRTHDAY

which was Pharaoh's *b* .....Gen 40:20
b gave a feast for his ....Mark 6:21

BIRTHRIGHT

"Sell me your *b* ....Gen 25:31
Esau despised his *b* ....Gen 25:34
according to his *b* ....Gen 43:33
of food sold his *b* ....Heb 12:16

BISHOP

the position of a *b* ....1 Tim 3:1
b must be blameless ....Titus 1:7

BIT

and they *b* the people ....Num 21:6
be harnessed with *b* ....Ps 32:9

BITE

A serpent may *b* ....Eccl 10:11
But if you *b* and ....Gal 5:15

BITHYNIA

The Spirit keeps Paul from, Acts 16:7
Peter writes to Christians of, 1 Pet 1:1

BITS

the great house into *b* ....Amos 6:11
Indeed, we put *b* ....James 3:3

BITTER

made their lives *b* ....Ex 1:14
b herbs they ....Ex 12:8
to those who are *b* ....Prov 31:6
who put *b* for sweet ....Is 5:20
and do not be *b* ....Col 3:19
But if you have *b* ....James 3:14
make your stomach *b* ....Rev 10:9

BITTERLY

has dealt very *b* ....Ruth 1:20
And Hezekiah wept *b* ....2 Kin 20:3
he went out and wept *b* .....Matt 26:75

BITTERNESS

man dies in the *b* ....Job 21:25
heart knows its own *b* ......Prov 14:10
all my years in the *b* ....Is 38:15
you are poisoned by *b* ....Acts 8:23
b springing up cause ....Heb 12:15

BLACK

My skin grows *b* ....Job 30:30
wavy, and *b* as a raven .....Song 5:11
one hair white or *b* ....Matt 5:36
a *b* horse ....Rev 6:5
and the sun became *b* ....Rev 6:12

BLACKNESS

the heavens with *b* ....Is 50:3
whom is reserved the *b* ....Jude 13

BLACKSMITH

The *b* with the tongs ....Is 44:12
I have created the *b* ....Is 54:16

BLADE

went in after the *b* ....Judg 3:22
first the *b* ....Mark 4:28

BLAME

that anyone should *b* ....2 Cor 8:20
be holy and without *b* ....Eph 1:4

BLAMELESS

You shall be *b* ....Deut 18:13
and that man was *b* ....Job 1:1
when You speak, and *b* ....Ps 51:4
Let my heart be *b* ....Ps 119:80
end, that you may be *b* ....1 Cor 1:8
which is in the law, *b* ....Phil 3:6
you holy, and *b* ....Col 1:22
your hearts *b* in ....1 Thess 3:13
body be preserved *b* ....1 Thess 5:23
bishop then must be *b* ....1 Tim 3:2
deacons, being found *b* ....1 Tim 3:10
without spot and *b* ....2 Pet 3:14

BLAMELESSLY

b we behaved ... 1 Thess 2:10

BLASPHEME

b Your name forever ... Ps 74:10
compelled them to *b* ... Acts 26:11
may learn not to *b* ... 1 Tim 1:20
b that noble name ... James 2:7
God, to *b* His name ... Rev 13:6

BLASPHEMED

a foolish people has *b* ... Ps 74:18
b continually every ... Is 52:5
who passed by *b* Him ... Matt 27:39
who were hanged *b* ... Luke 23:39
The name of God is *b* ... Rom 2:24
doctrine may not be *b* ... 1 Tim 6:1
On their part He is *b* ... 1 Pet 4:14
great heat, and they *b* ... Rev 16:9

BLASPHEMER

I was formerly a *b* ... 1 Tim 1:13

BLASPHEMERS

boasters, proud, *b* ... 2 Tim 3:2

BLASPHEMES

b the name of the LORD ... Lev 24:16
"This Man *b* ... Matt 9:3

BLASPHEMIES

false witness, *b* ... Matt 15:19
is this who speaks *b* ... Luke 5:21
great things and *b* ... Rev 13:5

BLASPHEMY

but the *b* against ... Matt 12:31
"He has spoken *b* ... Matt 26:65
was full of names of *b* ... Rev 17:3

BLAST

By the *b* of God they ... Job 4:9
for the *b* of the ... Is 25:4

BLASTED

"I *b* you with blight ... Amos 4:9

BLEATING

"What then is this *b* ... 1 Sam 15:14

BLEMISH

shall be without *b* ... Ex 12:5
LORD, a ram without *b* ... Lev 6:6
be holy and without *b* ... Eph 5:27
as of a lamb without *b* ... 1 Pet 1:19

BLEMISHED

to the Lord what is *b* ... Mal 1:14

BLESS

b those who *b* you ... Gen 12:3
You go unless You *b* ... Gen 32:26
"The LORD *b* you and ... Num 6:24
b the LORD at all ... Ps 34:1
b You while I live ... Ps 63:4
b His holy name ... Ps 103:1
b the house of Israel ... Ps 115:12
b those who fear the ... Ps 115:13
b you in the name of ... Ps 129:8
I will abundantly *b* ... Ps 132:15
b those who curse ... Luke 6:28
B those who persecute ... Rom 12:14
Being reviled, we *b* ... 1 Cor 4:12
With it we *b* our God ... James 3:9

BLESSED

And God *b* them ... Gen 1:22
the earth shall be *b* ... Gen 12:3
b be those who ... Gen 27:29
indeed he shall be *b* ... Gen 27:33
B is he who ... Num 24:9
B shall be the ... Deut 28:4
You have *b* the work of ... Job 1:10
B is the man who walks ... Ps 1:1
B is the man to whom ... Ps 32:2
B is the nation whose ... Ps 33:12
B is he who considers ... Ps 41:1
B are those who keep ... Ps 106:3
B is he who comes ... Ps 118:26
b who fears the LORD ... Ps 128:4
rise up and call her *b* ... Prov 31:28
will call you *b* ... Mal 3:12
B are the poor in ... Matt 5:3
B are those who mourn ... Matt 5:4
B are the meek ... Matt 5:5
B are those who hunger ... Matt 5:6
B are the merciful ... Matt 5:7
B are the pure in ... Matt 5:8
B are the peacemakers ... Matt 5:9
B are those who are ... Matt 5:10
B are you when they ... Matt 5:11
b is he who is ... Matt 11:6
b are your eyes ... Matt 13:16
B is He who comes ... Matt 21:9
hand, 'Come, you *b* ... Matt 25:34
Jesus took bread, *b* ... Matt 26:26
b are you among women ... Luke 1:28
know these things, *b* ... John 13:17
B are those who have ... John 20:29
'It is more *b* to give ... Acts 20:35
the Creator, who is *b* ... Rom 1:25
all, the eternally *b* ... Rom 9:5
B be the God and ... Eph 1:3
b God which was ... 1 Tim 1:11
the lesser is *b* ... Heb 7:7
this one will be *b* ... James 1:25
B is he who reads ... Rev 1:3
'*B* are the dead who ... Rev 14:13
B is he who watches ... Rev 16:15
B are those who are ... Rev 19:9
B and holy is he who ... Rev 20:6
B is he who keeps the ... Rev 22:7
B are those who do His ... Rev 22:14

BLESSING

and you shall be a *b* ... Gen 12:2
I will command My *b* ... Lev 25:21
before you today a *b* ... Deut 11:26
The *b* of a perishing ... Job 29:13
Your *b* is upon Your ... Ps 3:8
The *b* of the LORD ... Prov 10:22
shall be showers of *b* ... Ezek 34:26
relent, and leave a *b* ... Joel 2:14
and you shall be a *b* ... Zech 8:13
the fullness of the *b* ... Rom 15:29
b which we bless ... 1 Cor 10:16
that the *b* of Abraham ... Gal 3:14
with every spiritual *b* ... Eph 1:3
cultivated, receives *b* ... Heb 6:7
to inherit the *b* ... Heb 12:17
honor and glory and *b* ... Rev 5:12

BLESSINGS

of the law, the *b* ... Josh 8:34
B are on the head of ... Prov 10:6

BLIGHT

"I blasted you with *b* ... Amos 4:9
I struck you with *b* ... Hag 2:17

BLIND

I was eyes to the *b* ... Job 29:15
B yourselves and be ... Is 29:9
To open *b* eyes ... Is 42:7
I will bring the *b* ... Is 42:16
b people who have eyes ... Is 43:8
His watchmen are *b* ... Is 56:10
They wandered *b* ... Lam 4:14
when you offer the *b* ... Mal 1:8
The *b* see ... Matt 11:5
b leads the *b* ... Matt 15:14
of sight to the *b* ... Luke 4:18
to Him, "Are we *b* ... John 9:40
miserable, poor, *b* ... Rev 3:17

BLINDED

b their eyes and ... John 12:40
and the rest were *b* ... Rom 11:7
of this age has *b* ... 2 Cor 4:4
the darkness has *b* ... 1 John 2:11

BLINDS

a bribe, for a bribe *b* ... Deut 16:19

BLOOD

of your brother's *b* ... Gen 4:10
b shall be shed ... Gen 9:6
you are a husband of *b* ... Ex 4:25
b that makes atonement ... Lev 17:11
b sustains its life ... Lev 17:14
do not cover my *b* ... Job 16:18
is there in my *b* ... Ps 30:9
And condemn innocent *b* ... Ps 94:21
hands are full of *b* ... Is 1:15
also disclose her *b* ... Is 26:21
And the moon into *b* ... Joel 2:31
For this is My *b* ... Matt 26:28
called the Field of *B* ... Matt 27:8
"His *b* be on us and ... Matt 27:25
new covenant in My *b* ... Luke 22:20
were born, not of *b* ... John 1:13
b has eternal life ... John 6:54
b every nation of men ... Acts 17:26
with His own *b* ... Acts 20:28
propitiation by His *b* ... Rom 3:25
justified by His *b* ... Rom 5:9
through His *b* ... Eph 1:7
brought near by the *b* ... Eph 2:13
against flesh and *b* ... Eph 6:12
peace through the *b* ... Col 1:20
"This is the *b* ... Heb 9:20
are purified with *b* ... Heb 9:22
of *b* there is no ... Heb 9:22
the Holiest by the *b* ... Heb 10:19
sprinkling of the *b* ... 1 Pet 1:2
with the precious *b* ... 1 Pet 1:19
b of Jesus Christ His ... 1 John 1:7
our sins in His own *b* ... Rev 1:5
us to God by Your *b* ... Rev 5:9
them white in the *b* ... Rev 7:14
overcame him by the *b* ... Rev 12:11
a robe dipped in *b* ... Rev 19:13

BLOODSHED

me from the guilt of *b* ... Ps 51:14
the land is full of *b* ... Ezek 9:9
build up Zion with *b* ... Mic 3:10

BLOODTHIRSTY

The LORD abhors the *b* ... Ps 5:6
B and deceitful men ... Ps 55:23

BLOSSOM

Israel shall *b* and bud ... Is 27:6

and *b* as the rose ....Is 35:1
the fig tree may not *b* ....Hab 3:17

BLOT

say that He would *b* ....2 Kin 14:27
from my sins, and *b* ....Ps 51:9
and I will not *b* ....Rev 3:5

BLOTTED

Let them be *b* out of ....Ps 69:28
I have *b* out ....Is 44:22
your sins may be *b* ....Acts 3:19

BLOW

an east wind to *b* ....Ps 78:26
B upon my garden ....Song 4:16
with a very severe *b* ....Jer 14:17

BLOWS

B that hurt cleanse ....Prov 20:30
breath of the LORD *b* ....Is 40:7
The wind *b* where it ....John 3:8

BOANERGES

Surname of James and John, Mark 3:17

BOAST

puts on his armor *b* ......1 Kin 20:11
soul shall make its *b* ....Ps 34:2
God we *b* all day long ....Ps 44:8
and make your *b* ....Rom 2:17
that we are your *b* ....2 Cor 1:14
you, and not to *b* ....2 Cor 10:16
that I also may *b* ....2 Cor 11:16
lest anyone should *b* ....Eph 2:9
your hearts, do not *b* ....James 3:14

BOASTERS

God, violent, proud, *b* ....Rom 1:30
lovers of money, *b* ....2 Tim 3:2

BOASTFUL

b shall not stand ....Ps 5:5
I was envious of the *b* ....Ps 73:3

BOASTING

Where is *b* then ....Rom 3:27
should make my *b* ....1 Cor 9:15
you, great is my *b* ....2 Cor 7:4
All such *b* is evil ....James 4:16

BOASTS

Whoever falsely *b* ....Prov 25:14

BOAZ

A wealthy Bethlehemite, Ruth 2:1, 4–18
Husband of Ruth, Ruth 4:10–13
Ancestor of Christ, Matt 1:5
——— Pillar of the temple, 1 Kin 7:21

BODIES

valley of the dead *b* ....Jer 31:40
b a living sacrifice ....Rom 12:1
not know that your *b* ....1 Cor 6:15
also celestial *b* ....1 Cor 15:40
wives as their own *b* ....Eph 5:28
and chariots, and *b* ....Rev 18:13

BODILY

b form like a dove ....Luke 3:22
b presence is weak ....2 Cor 10:10
of the Godhead *b* ....Col 2:9
b exercise ....1 Tim 4:8

BODY

b clings to the ground ....Ps 44:25
b is carved ivory ....Song 5:14
b was wet with the dew ......Dan 4:33
of the *b* is the eye ....Matt 6:22
those who kill the *b* ....Matt 10:28
this is My *b* ....Matt 26:26
and asked for the *b* ....Matt 27:58
around his naked *b* ....Mark 14:51
of the temple of His *b* ....John 2:21
deliver me from this *b* ....Rom 7:24
redemption of our *b* ....Rom 8:23
members in one *b* ....Rom 12:4
and the Lord for the *b* ....1 Cor 6:13
against his own *b* ....1 Cor 6:18
not know that your *b* ....1 Cor 6:19
glorify God in your *b* ....1 Cor 6:20
But I discipline my *b* ....1 Cor 9:27
one bread and one *b* ....1 Cor 10:17
b which is broken ....1 Cor 11:24
be guilty of the *b* ....1 Cor 11:27
For as the *b* is one ....1 Cor 12:12
baptized into one *b* ....1 Cor 12:13
b is not one member ....1 Cor 12:14
are the *b* of Christ ....1 Cor 12:27
though I give my *b* ....1 Cor 13:3
It is sown a natural *b* ....1 Cor 15:44
both to God in one *b* ....Eph 2:16
be magnified in my *b* ....Phil 1:20
in the *b* of His flesh ....Col 1:22
by putting off the *b* ....Col 2:11
and neglect of the *b* ....Col 2:23
were called in one *b* ....Col 3:15
b You have prepared ....Heb 10:5
the offering of the *b* ....Heb 10:10
For as the *b* without ....James 2:26
our sins in His own *b* ....1 Pet 2:24

BOILS

Job with painful *b* ....Job 2:7

BOLD

the righteous are *b* ....Prov 28:1
whatever anyone is *b* ....2 Cor 11:21
are much more *b* ....Phil 1:14

BOLDLY

I may open my mouth *b* ....Eph 6:19
therefore come *b* ....Heb 4:16
So we may *b* say ....Heb 13:6

BOLDNESS

Great is my *b* of ....2 Cor 7:4
in whom we have *b* ....Eph 3:12
but with all *b* ....Phil 1:20
standing and great *b* ....1 Tim 3:13
brethren, having *b* ....Heb 10:19
that we may have *b* ....1 John 4:17

BOND

bring you into the *b* ....Ezek 20:37
of the Spirit in the *b* ....Eph 4:3
love, which is the *b* ....Col 3:14

BONDAGE

because of the *b* ....Ex 2:23
out of the house of *b* ....Ex 13:14
the spirit of *b* ....Rom 8:15
might bring us into *b* ....Gal 2:4
which gives birth to *b* ....Gal 4:24
again with a yoke of *b* ....Gal 5:1
lifetime subject to *b* ....Heb 2:15
he is brought into *b* ....2 Pet 2:19

BONDS

"Let us break Their *b* ....Ps 2:3

BONDSERVANTS

B, be obedient to ....Eph 6:5
Masters, give your *b* ....Col 4:1
for vice, but as *b* ....1 Pet 2:16

BONDWOMAN

"Cast out this *b* ....Gen 21:10
the one by a *b* ....Gal 4:22

BONE

"This is now *b* ....Gen 2:23
b clings to my skin ....Job 19:20
bonds came together, *b* ....Ezek 37:7

BONES

shall carry up my *b* ....Gen 50:25
which made all my *b* ....Job 4:14
His *b* are like beams ....Job 40:18
I can count all My *b* ....Ps 22:17
and my *b* waste away ....Ps 31:10
I kept silent, my *b* ....Ps 32:3
the wind, or how the *b* ....Eccl 11:5
say to them, 'O dry *b* ....Ezek 37:4
b are the whole house ....Ezek 37:11
of dead men's *b* ....Matt 23:27
b shall be broken ....John 19:36
concerning his *b* ....Heb 11:22

BOOK

you will find in the *b* ....Ezra 4:15
distinctly from the *b* ....Neh 8:8
were inscribed in a *b* ....Job 19:23
"Search from the *b* ....Is 34:16
'Write in a *b* for ....Jer 30:2
found written in the *b* ....Dan 12:1
so a *b* of remembrance ....Mal 3:16
are written in the *b* ....Gal 3:10
sprinkled both the *b* ....Heb 9:19
in the Lamb's *B* ....Rev 21:27
the prophecy of this *b* ....Rev 22:18
the words of the *b* ....Rev 22:19

BOOKS

b there is no end ....Eccl 12:12
not contain the *b* ....John 21:25
magic brought their *b* ....Acts 19:19
God, and *b* were opened ....Rev 20:12

BOOTH

b which a watchman ....Job 27:18
of Zion is left as a *b* ....Is 1:8

BORDERS

and enlarge your *b* ....Ex 34:24
makes peace in your *b* ....Ps 147:14
and enlarge the *b* ....Matt 23:5

BORE

conceived and *b* Cain ....Gen 4:1
And to Sarah who *b* ....Is 51:2
b the sin of many ....Is 53:12
and He *b* them and ....Is 63:9
b our sicknesses ....Matt 8:17
who Himself *b* our sins ......1 Pet 2:24
b a male Child who was ....Rev 12:5

BORN

"Every son who is *b* ....Ex 1:22
yet man is *b* to ....Job 5:7
"Man who is *b* ....Job 14:1
'This one was *b* ....Ps 87:4
A time to be *b* ....Eccl 3:2
unto us a Child is *b* ....Is 9:6
Or shall a nation be *b* ....Is 66:8
b Jesus who is called ....Matt 1:16
For there is *b* ....Luke 2:11
unless one is *b* again ....John 3:3

That which is *b* ....John 3:6
For this cause I was *b* ....John 18:37
me also, as by one *b* ....1 Cor 15:8
of the bondwoman was *b* ....Gal 4:23
having been *b* again ....1 Pet 1:23
who loves is *b* of God ....1 John 4:7
is the Christ is *b* ....1 John 5:1
know that whoever is *b* ....1 John 5:18

BORNE

And as we have *b* ....1 Cor 15:49

BORROWER

b is servant to the ....Prov 22:7
lender, so with the *b* ....Is 24:2

BORROWS

The wicked *b* and does ....Ps 37:21

BOSOM

man take fire to his *b* ....Prov 6:27
consolation of her *b* ....Is 66:11
angels to Abraham's *b* ....Luke 16:22
Son, who is in the *b* ....John 1:18
leaning on Jesus' *b* ....John 13:23

BOTTLE

b shall be filled ....Jer 13:12

BOTTOMLESS

given the key to the *b* ....Rev 9:1
ascend out of the *b* ....Rev 17:8
the key to the *b* ....Rev 20:1

BOUGHS

cedars with its *b* ....Ps 80:10
She sent out her *b* ....Ps 80:11

BOUGHT

the hand of him who *b* ....Lev 25:28
not your Father, who *b* ....Deut 32:6
b the threshing floor ....2 Sam 24:24
b the field from ....Jer 32:9
all that he had and *b* ....Matt 13:46
For you were *b* at a ....1 Cor 6:20
denying the Lord who *b* ....2 Pet 2:1

BOUND

of the wicked have *b* ....Ps 119:61
b the waters in a ....Prov 30:4
not been closed or *b* ....Is 1:6
on earth will be *b* ....Matt 16:19
b hand and foot with ....John 11:44
And see, now I go *b* ....Acts 20:22
of Israel I am *b* ....Acts 28:20
who has a husband is *b* ....Rom 7:2
Are you *b* to a wife ....1 Cor 7:27
Devil and Satan, and *b* ....Rev 20:2

BOUNDARY

b that they may not ....Ps 104:9

BOUNTIFUL

the miser said to be *b* ....Is 32:5
you into a *b* country ....Jer 2:7

BOUNTIFULLY

Because He has dealt *b* ....Ps 13:6
and he who sows *b* ....2 Cor 9:6

BOW

b remained in strength ....Gen 49:24
You shall not *b* ....Ex 23:24
to serve them and *b* ....Judg 2:19
b is renewed in my ....Job 29:20
will not trust in my *b* ....Ps 44:6
He breaks the *b* ....Ps 46:9
like a deceitful *b* ....Ps 78:57
let us worship and *b* ....Ps 95:6
B down Your heavens ....Ps 144:5
not save them by *b* ....Hos 1:7
who sat on it had a *b* ....Rev 6:2

BOWED

stood all around and *b* ....Gen 37:7
b the heavens also ....2 Sam 22:10
whose knees have not *b* ....1 Kin 19:18
They have *b* down and ....Ps 20:8
And they *b* the knee ....Matt 27:29
men who have not *b* ....Rom 11:4

BOWL

his hand in the *b* ....Prov 19:24
or the golden *b* ....Eccl 12:6
and poured out his *b* ....Rev 16:2

BOWLS

who drink wine from *b* ....Amos 6:6
a harp, and golden *b* ....Rev 5:8
Go and pour out the *b* ....Rev 16:1
who had the seven *b* ....Rev 21:9

BOWS

"The *b* of the mighty ....1 Sam 2:4

BOX

Judas had the money *b* ....John 13:29

BOYS

Shall be full of *b* ....Zech 8:5

BOZRAH

City of Edom, Gen 36:33
Destruction of, foretold, Amos 1:12
Figurative of Messiah's victory, Is 63:1

BRAIDED

not with *b* hair or ....1 Tim 2:9

BRAMBLE

gather grapes from a *b* ....Luke 6:44

BRANCH

blossoms on one *b* ....Ex 25:33
b will not be green ....Job 15:32
from Israel, palm *b* ....Is 9:14
B shall grow out of ....Is 11:1
raise to David a *B* ....Jer 23:5
grow up to David a *B* ....Jer 33:15
forth My Servant the *B* ....Zech 3:8
whose name is the *B* ....Zech 6:12
b has already become ....Matt 24:32
b that bears fruit He ....John 15:2
b cannot bear fruit ....John 15:4
he is cast out as a *b* ....John 15:6

BRANCHES

in the sun, and his *b* ....Job 8:16
and bring forth *b* ....Job 14:9
and cut down the *b* ....Is 18:5
and its *b* are broken ....Jer 11:16
His *b* shall spread ....Hos 14:6
vine, you are the *b* ....John 15:5
b were broken off ....Rom 11:17

BRASS

become sounding *b* ....1 Cor 13:1
feet were like fine *b* ....Rev 1:15

BRAVE

in the faith, be *b* ....1 Cor 16:13

BREACHES

Heal its *b* ....Ps 60:2

BREAD

face you shall eat *b* ....Gen 3:19
of Salem brought out *b* ....Gen 14:18
"Behold, I will rain *b* ....Ex 16:4
shall eat unleavened *b* ....Ex 23:15
not live by *b* alone ....Deut 8:3
lives, I do not have *b* ....1 Kin 17:12
new wine, a land of *b* ....2 Kin 18:32
that his life abhors *b* ....Job 33:20
people as they eat *b* ....Ps 14:4
Can He give *b* also ....Ps 78:20
up late, to eat the *b* ....Ps 127:2
her poor with *b* ....Ps 132:15
For they eat the *b* ....Prov 4:17
b eaten in secret is ....Prov 9:17
B gained by deceit is ....Prov 20:17
Go, eat your *b* with ....Eccl 9:7
Cast your *b* upon the ....Eccl 11:1
b will be given him ....Is 33:16
for what is not *b* ....Is 55:2
to share your *b* ....Is 58:7
We get our *b* at the ....Lam 5:9
who give me my *b* ....Hos 2:5
For their *b* shall be ....Hos 9:4
And lack of *b* in all ....Amos 4:6
these stones become *b* ....Matt 4:3
not live by *b* alone ....Matt 4:4
this day our daily *b* ....Matt 6:11
eating, Jesus took *b* ....Matt 26:26
no bag, no *b* ....Mark 6:8
is he who shall eat *b* ....Luke 14:15
gives you the true *b* ....John 6:32
I am the *b* of life ....John 6:48
having dipped the *b* ....John 13:26
b which we break ....1 Cor 10:16
He was betrayed took *b* ....1 Cor 11:23
as you eat this *b* ....1 Cor 11:26
did we eat anyone's *b* ....2 Thess 3:8
and eat their own *b* ....2 Thess 3:12

BREADTH

is as great as its *b* ....Rev 21:16

BREAK

b their bones and ....Num 24:6
torment my soul, and *b* ....Job 19:2
They *b* up my path ....Job 30:13
B their teeth in their ....Ps 58:6
And now they *b* down ....Ps 74:6
b My statutes and do ....Ps 89:31
covenant I will not *b* ....Ps 89:34
Remember, do not *b* ....Jer 14:21
together to *b* bread ....Acts 20:7

BREAKING

in the *b* of bread ....Acts 2:42
b bread from house to ....Acts 2:46
weeping and *b* my heart ....Acts 21:13
dishonor God through *b* ....Rom 2:23

BREAKS

He *b* in pieces mighty ....Job 34:24
My soul *b* with longing ....Ps 119:20
Until the day *b* ....Song 2:17
Whoever therefore *b* ....Matt 5:19

BREAST

back on Jesus' *b* ....John 13:25

BREASTPLATE

a *b*, an ephod ....Ex 28:4
righteousness as a *b* ....Is 59:17
having put on the *b* ....Eph 6:14

BREASTS
blessings of the *b* ....Gen 49:25
on My mother's *b* ....Ps 22:9
doe, let her *b* satisfy ....Prov 5:19
Your two *b* are like ....Song 4:5
b which nursed You ....Luke 11:27
done, beat their *b* ....Luke 23:48

BREATH
nostrils the *b* of life ....Gen 2:7
at the blast of the *b* ....2 Sam 22:16
that there was no *b* ....1 Kin 17:17
perish, and by the *b* ....Job 4:9
as long as my *b* ....Job 27:3
has made me, and the *b* ....Job 33:4
You take away their *b* ....Ps 104:29
Man is like a *b* ....Ps 144:4
everything that has *b* ....Ps 150:6
they all have one *b* ....Eccl 3:19
from it, who gives *b* ....Is 42:5
"Surely I will cause *b* ....Ezek 37:5
God who holds your *b* ....Dan 5:23
gives to all life, *b* ....Acts 17:25
consume with the *b* ....2 Thess 2:8
power to give *b* ....Rev 13:15

BREATHE
me, and such as *b* ....Ps 27:12
winds, O breath, and *b* ....Ezek 37:9

BREATHES
indeed he *b* his last ....Job 14:10

BRETHREN
presence of all his *b* ....Gen 16:12
be lifted above his *b* ....Deut 17:20
and you are all *b* ....Matt 23:8
least of these My *b* ....Matt 25:40
Go and tell My *b* ....Matt 28:10
firstborn among many *b* ....Rom 8:29
to judge between his *b* ....1 Cor 6:5
thus sin against the *b* ....1 Cor 8:12
over five hundred *b* ....1 Cor 15:6
perils among false *b* ....2 Cor 11:26
b secretly brought ....Gal 2:4
to be made like His *b* ....Heb 2:17
sincere love of the *b* ....1 Pet 1:22
because we love the *b* ....1 John 3:14
our lives for the *b* ....1 John 3:16
does not receive the *b* ....3 John 10
of your *b* the prophets ....Rev 22:9

BRIBE
you shall take no *b* ....Ex 23:8
b blinds the eyes ....Deut 16:19
b debases the heart ....Eccl 7:7

BRIBERY
consume the tents of *b* ....Job 15:34

BRIBES
hand is full of *b* ....Ps 26:10
but he who hates *b* ....Prov 15:27
but he who receives *b* ....Prov 29:4
everyone loves *b* ....Is 1:23
the just and taking *b* ....Amos 5:12

BRICK
people straw to make *b* ....Ex 5:7
incense on altars of *b* ....Is 65:3
Make strong the *b* ....Nah 3:14

BRICKS
"Come, let us make *b* ....Gen 11:3
b which they made ....Ex 5:8
deliver the quota of *b* ....Ex 5:18
b have fallen down ....Is 9:10

BRIDE
them on you as a *b* ....Is 49:18
He who has the *b* ....John 3:29
I will show you the *b* ....Rev 21:9
the Spirit and the *b* ....Rev 22:17

BRIDEGROOM
righteousness, as a *b* ....Is 61:10
and as the *b* rejoices ....Is 62:5
mourn as long as the *b* ....Matt 9:15
b will be taken away ....Matt 9:15
went out to meet the *b* ....Matt 25:1
b fast while the ....Mark 2:19
the friend of the *b* ....John 3:29

BRIDLE
with bit and *b* ....Ps 32:9
b the whole body ....James 3:2

BRIER
b shall come up the ....Is 55:13
longer be a pricking *b* ....Ezek 28:24
of them is like a *b* ....Mic 7:4

BRIERS
there shall come up *b* ....Is 5:6
their words, though *b* ....Ezek 2:6

BRIGHTER
Her Nazirites were *b* ....Lam 4:7
a light from heaven, *b* ....Acts 26:13

BRIGHTNESS
From the *b* before Him ....2 Sam 22:13
and kings to the *b* ....Is 60:3
goes forth as *b* ....Is 62:1
very dark, with no *b* ....Amos 5:20
who being the *b* ....Heb 1:3

BRIMSTONE
Then the LORD rained *b* ....Gen 19:24
b is scattered on his ....Job 18:15
fire, smoke, and *b* ....Rev 9:17
the lake of fire and *b* ....Rev 20:10

BRING
LORD your God will *b* ....Deut 30:3
b back his soul ....Job 33:30
for they *b* down ....Ps 55:3
Lord said, "I will *b* ....Ps 68:22
B forth your ....Is 41:21
b forth justice ....Is 42:3
b My righteousness ....Is 46:13
Though they *b* up their ....Hos 9:12
And she will *b* ....Matt 1:21
b no fruit to maturity ....Luke 8:14
b this Man's blood ....Acts 5:28
Who shall *b* a charge ....Rom 8:33
b Christ down from ....Rom 10:6
b Christ up from the ....Rom 10:7
even so God will *b* ....1 Thess 4:14

BROAD
set me in a *b* place ....Ps 118:5
b is the way that ....Matt 7:13
their phylacteries *b* ....Matt 23:5

BROKE
b them at the foot of ....Ex 32:19
b open the fountain ....Ps 74:15
covenant which they *b* ....Jer 31:32
He blessed and *b* ....Matt 14:19
b the flask and poured ....Mark 14:3
b the legs of the ....John 19:32

BROKEN
he has *b* My covenant ....Gen 17:14
I am like a *b* vessel ....Ps 31:12
their bows shall be *b* ....Ps 37:15
He has *b* his covenant ....Ps 55:20
heart the spirit is *b* ....Prov 15:13
b spirit dries the ....Prov 17:22
but who can bear a *b* ....Prov 18:14
in the staff of this *b* ....Is 36:6
heart within me is *b* ....Jer 23:9
is oppressed and *b* ....Hos 5:11
this stone will be *b* ....Matt 21:44
Scripture cannot be *b* ....John 10:35
is My body which is *b* ....1 Cor 11:24

BROKENHEARTED
He heals the *b* and ....Ps 147:3

BRONZE
So Moses made a *b* ....Num 21:9
your head shall be *b* ....Deut 28:23
b serpent that Moses ....2 Kin 18:4
Or is my flesh *b* ....Job 6:12
b as rotten wood ....Job 41:27
broken the gates of *b* ....Ps 107:16
b I will bring ....Is 60:17
b walls against the ....Jer 1:18
people a fortified *b* ....Jer 15:20
a third kingdom of *b* ....Dan 2:39
make your hooves *b* ....Mic 4:13
were mountains of *b* ....Zech 6:1

BROOD
The *b* of evildoers ....Is 14:20
B of vipers ....Matt 12:34
hen gathers her *b* ....Luke 13:34

BROOK
stones from the *b* ....1 Sam 17:40
shall drink of the *b* ....Ps 110:7
disciples over the *B* ....John 18:1

BROOKS
good land, a land of *b* ....Deut 8:7
b that pass away ....Job 6:15
for the water *b* ....Ps 42:1

BROTHER
"Where is Abel your *b* ....Gen 4:9
he were my friend or *b* ....Ps 35:14
speak against your *b* ....Ps 50:20
and a *b* is born for ....Prov 17:17
b offended is harder ....Prov 18:19
has neither son nor *b* ....Eccl 4:8
and do not trust any *b* ....Jer 9:4
he pursued his *b* ....Amos 1:11
Was not Esau Jacob's *b* ....Mal 1:2
b will deliver up ....Matt 10:21
how often shall my *b* ....Matt 18:21
"Teacher, tell my *b* ....Luke 12:13
b will rise again ....John 11:23
do you judge your *b* ....Rom 14:10
b goes to law against ....1 Cor 6:6
shall the weak *b* ....1 Cor 8:11
slave—a beloved *b* ....Philem 16
He who loves his *b* ....1 John 2:10
and murdered his *b* ....1 John 3:12
Whoever hates his *b* ....1 John 3:15
b sinning a sin which ....1 John 5:16
I, John, both your *b* ....Rev 1:9

BROTHERHOOD
the covenant of *b* ....Amos 1:9
I might break the *b* ....Zech 11:14

Love the *b* .... 1 Pet 2:17
experienced by your *b* .... 1 Pet 5:9

BROTHERLY

to one another with *b* .... Rom 12:10
b love continue .... Heb 13:1

BROTHER'S

Am I my *b* keeper .... Gen 4:9
at the speck in your *b* .... Matt 7:3

BROTHERS

My *b* have dealt .... Job 6:15
a stranger to my *b* .... Ps 69:8
is My mother, or My *b* .... Mark 3:33
b are these who hear .... Luke 8:21
b did not believe .... John 7:5
love as *b* .... 1 Pet 3:8

BROUGHT

He *b* out His people .... Ps 105:48
The king has *b* me into .... Song 1:4
to heaven, will be *b* .... Luke 10:15

BRUISE

He shall *b* your head .... Gen 3:15
LORD binds up the *b* .... Is 30:26
the LORD to *b* Him .... Is 53:10

BRUISED

b reed He will not .... Is 42:3
He was *b* for our .... Is 53:5
b reed He will not .... Matt 12:20

BRUTAL

b men who are .... Ezek 21:31

BUCKLER

be your shield and *b* .... Ps 91:4

BUD

it bring forth and *b* .... Is 55:10

BUFFET

of Satan to *b* me .... 2 Cor 12:7

BUILD

b ourselves a city .... Gen 11:4
"Would you *b* a house .... 2 Sam 7:5
b a temple for the name .... 1 Kin 8:17
that the LORD will *b* .... 1 Chr 17:10
Solomon who shall *b* .... 1 Chr 28:6
able to *b* Him a temple .... 2 Chr 2:6
labor in vain who *b* .... Ps 127:1
down, and a time to *b* .... Eccl 3:3
house that you will *b* .... Is 66:1
I will *b* them and not .... Jer 24:6
Who *b* up Zion with .... Mic 3:10
b the desolate .... Mal 1:4
'This man began to *b* .... Luke 14:30
What house will you *b* .... Acts 7:49
b you up and give you .... Acts 20:32
named, lest I should *b* .... Rom 15:20
For if I *b* again .... Gal 2:18

BUILDER

me, as a wise master *b* .... 1 Cor 3:10
foundations, whose *b* .... Heb 11:10

BUILDING

field, you are God's *b* .... 1 Cor 3:9
destroyed, we have a *b* .... 2 Cor 5:1
in whom the whole *b* .... Eph 2:21
But you, beloved, *b* .... Jude 20

BUILDS

The LORD *b* up .... Ps 147:2
The wise woman *b* .... Prov 14:1
one take heed how he *b* .... 1 Cor 3:10

BUILT

Wisdom has *b* her house .... Prov 9:1
my works great, I *b* .... Eccl 2:4
Babylon, that I have *b* .... Dan 4:30
to a wise man who *b* .... Matt 7:24
a foolish man who *b* .... Matt 7:26
work which he has *b* .... 1 Cor 3:14
having been *b* on the .... Eph 2:20
rooted and *b* up in Him .... Col 2:7
For every house is *b* .... Heb 3:4
stones, are being *b* .... 1 Pet 2:5

BULL

I will not take a *b* .... Ps 50:9
like an untrained *b* .... Jer 31:18

BULLS

in the blood of *b* .... Is 1:11
For if the blood of *b* .... Heb 9:13

BULWARKS

Mark well her *b* .... Ps 48:13
for walls and *b* .... Is 26:1

BUNDLE

each man's *b* of money .... Gen 42:35
A *b* of myrrh is my .... Song 1:13

BURDEN

You have laid the *b* .... Num 11:11
one knows his own *b* .... 2 Chr 6:29
so that I am a *b* .... Job 7:20
Cast your *b* on the .... Ps 55:22
the grasshopper is a *b* .... Eccl 12:5
in that day that his *b* .... Is 10:27
its reproach is a *b* .... Zeph 3:18
easy and My *b* is light .... Matt 11:30
as it may, I did not *b* .... 2 Cor 12:16
we might not be a *b* .... 1 Thess 2:9
on you no other *b* .... Rev 2:24

BURDENED

but you have *b* Me with .... Is 43:24

BURDENS

and looked at their *b* .... Ex 2:11
For they bind heavy *b* .... Matt 23:4
Bear one another's *b* .... Gal 6:2

BURDENSOME

b task God has given .... Eccl 1:13
his life will be *b* .... Is 15:4
I myself was not *b* .... 2 Cor 12:13
commandments are not *b* .... 1 John 5:3

BURIAL

indeed he has no *b* .... Eccl 6:3
she did it for My *b* .... Matt 26:12
for the day of My *b* .... John 12:7
Stephen to his *b* .... Acts 8:2

BURIED

and there will I be *b* .... Ruth 1:17
I saw the wicked *b* .... Eccl 8:10
away the body and *b* .... Matt 14:12
also died and was *b* .... Luke 16:22
Therefore we were *b* .... Rom 6:4
and that He was *b* .... 1 Cor 15:4
b with Him in baptism .... Col 2:12

BURN

the bush does not *b* .... Ex 3:3
that My wrath may *b* .... Ex 32:10
b their chariots .... Josh 11:6
both will *b* together .... Is 1:31
"Did not our heart *b* .... Luke 24:32
eat her flesh and *b* .... Rev 17:16

BURNED

If anyone's work is *b* .... 1 Cor 3:15
my body to be *b* .... 1 Cor 13:3
whose end is to be *b* .... Heb 6:8
be touched and that *b* .... Heb 12:18
are *b* outside the camp .... Heb 13:11
in it will be *b* .... 2 Pet 3:10
all green grass was *b* .... Rev 8:7

BURNING

b torch that passed .... Gen 15:17
with severe *b* fever .... Deut 28:22
on his lips like a *b* .... Prov 16:27
b fire shut up in my .... Jer 20:9
b jealousy against the .... Ezek 36:5
plucked from the *b* .... Amos 4:11
a great mountain *b* .... Rev 8:8
fell from heaven, *b* .... Rev 8:10

BURNT

lamb for a *b* offering .... Gen 22:7
delight in *b* offering .... Ps 51:16
b offerings are not .... Jer 6:20
Though you offer Me *b* .... Amos 5:22

BURST

it is ready to *b* .... Job 32:19
with doors, when it *b* .... Job 38:8
the new wine will *b* .... Luke 5:37
falling headlong, he *b* .... Acts 1:18

BURY

b your dead in the .... Gen 23:6
was no one to *b* them .... Ps 79:3
go and *b* my father .... Matt 8:21
and let the dead *b* .... Matt 8:22

BUSH

from the midst of a *b* .... Ex 3:2
Him who dwelt in the *b* .... Deut 33:16
to him in the *b* .... Acts 7:35

BUSINESS

in ships, who do *b* .... Ps 107:23
farm, another to his *b* .... Matt 22:5
about My Father's *b* .... Luke 2:49

BUSYBODIES

at all, but are *b* .... 2 Thess 3:11
but also gossips and *b* .... 1 Tim 5:13

BUTLER

b did not remember .... Gen 40:23

BUTTER

So he took *b* and milk .... Gen 18:8
were smoother than *b* .... Ps 55:21
of milk produces *b* .... Prov 30:33

BUY

in Egypt to *b* grain .... Gen 41:57
B the truth .... Prov 23:23
Yes, come, *b* wine and .... Is 55:1
that we may *b* the poor .... Amos 8:6
b food for all these .... Luke 9:18
"*B* those things we .... John 13:29

rejoice, those who *b* ....1 Cor 7:30
spend a year there, *b* ......James 4:13
I counsel you to *b* ....Rev 3:18
and that no one may *b* ....Rev 13:17

BUYER

nothing," cries the *b* ....Prov 20:14
as with the *b* ....Is 24:2
'Let not the *b* ....Ezek 7:12

BUYS

a field and *b* it ....Prov 31:16
has and *b* that field ....Matt 13:44
b their merchandise ....Rev 18:11

BYGONE

b generations ....Acts 14:16

BYWORD

But He has made me a *b* ....Job 17:6
You made us a *b* ....Ps 44:14

—C—

CAESAR

——Augustus Caesar (31 B.C.–A.D. 14):
Decree of brings Joseph and Mary to Bethlehem, Luke 2:1
——Tiberius Caesar (A.D. 14–37):
Christ's ministry dated by, Luke 3:1–23
Tribute paid to, Matt 22:17–21
Jews side with, John 19:12
——Claudius Caesar (A.D. 41–54):
Famine in time of, Acts 11:28
Banished Jews from Rome, Acts 18:2
——Nero Caesar (A.D. 54–68):
Paul appealed to, Acts 25:8–12
Christian converts in household of, Phil 4:22
Paul tried before, 2 Tim 4:16–18
Called Augustus, Acts 25:21

CAESAREA

Roman capital of Palestine, Acts 12:19; 23:33
Paul escorted to, Acts 23:23–33
Paul imprisoned at; appeals to Caesar, Acts 25:4, 8–13
Peter preaches at, Acts 10:34–43
Paul preaches at, Acts 9:26–30; 18:22; 21:8

CAESAREA PHILIPPI

A city in northern Palestine; scene of Peter's great confession, Matt 16:13–20
Probable site of the Transfiguration, Matt 17:1–3

CAGE

c is full of birds ....Jer 5:27
foul spirit, and a *c* ....Rev 18:2

CAIAPHAS

Son-in-law of Annas; high priest, John 18:13
Makes prophecy, John 11:49–52
Jesus appears before, John 18:23, 24
Apostles appear before, Acts 4:1–22

CAIN

Adam's first son, Gen 4:1
His offering rejected, Gen 4:2–7; Heb 11:4
Murders Abel; is exiled; settles in Nod, Gen 4:8–17
A type of evil, Jude 11

CAKE

Ephraim is a *c* ....Hos 7:8

CAKES

Sustain me with *c* ....Song 2:5
and love the raisin *c* ....Hos 3:1

CALAMITIES

refuge, until these *c* ....Ps 57:1

CALAMITY

for the day of their *c* ....Deut 32:35
will laugh at your *c* ....Prov 1:26
c shall come suddenly ....Prov 6:15
If there is *c* in a ....Amos 3:6

CALCULATED

c the dust of the ....Is 40:12

CALDRON

this city is the *c* ....Ezek 11:3

CALEB

Sent as spy; gives good report; rewarded, Num 13:2, 6, 27, 30; 14:5–9, 24–38
Inherits Hebron, Josh 14:6–15
Conquers his territory with Othniel's help, Josh 15:13–19

CALF

and made a molded *c* ....Ex 32:4
They made a *c* in Horeb ....Ps 106:19
is, than a fatted *c* ....Prov 15:17
like a stubborn *c* ....Hos 4:16
Your *c* is rejected ....Hos 8:5
And bring the fatted *c* ....Luke 15:23
creature like a *c* ....Rev 4:7

CALL

I will *c* to the LORD ....1 Sam 12:17
c their lands after ....Ps 49:11
To you, O men, I *c* ....Prov 8:4
c upon Him while He ....Is 55:6
'C to Me ....Jer 33:3
Arise, *c* on your God ....Jon 1:6
They will *c* on My name ....Zech 13:9
c His name JESUS ....Matt 1:21
c the righteous ....Matt 9:13
Lord our God will *c* ....Acts 2:39
c them My people ....Rom 9:25
then shall they *c* ....Rom 10:14
For God did not *c* ....1 Thess 4:7
c and election sure ....2 Pet 1:10

CALLED

c the light Day ....Gen 1:5
c his wife's name Eve ....Gen 3:20
"I, the LORD, have *c* ....Is 42:6
I have *c* you by your ....Is 43:1
The LORD has *c* Me from ....Is 49:1
and out of Egypt I *c* ....Hos 11:1
"Out of Egypt I *c* ....Matt 2:15
a city *c* Nazareth ....Matt 2:23
For many are *c* ....Matt 20:16
to those who are the *c* ....Rom 8:28
these He also *c* ....Rom 8:30
But God has *c* us to ....1 Cor 7:15
praises of Him who *c* ....1 Pet 2:9
knowledge of Him who *c* ....2 Pet 1:3
c children of God ....1 John 3:1

CALLING

the gifts and the *c* ....Rom 11:29
For you see your *c* ....1 Cor 1:26
remain in the same *c* ....1 Cor 7:20
to walk worthy of the *c* ....Eph 4:1
us with a holy *c* ....2 Tim 1:9
of the heavenly *c* ....Heb 3:1

CALLS

c them all by name ....Ps 147:4
there is no one who *c* ....Is 64:7
David himself *c* ....Mark 12:37
c his own sheep ....John 10:3
For "whoever *c* ....Rom 10:13

CALM

the sea will become *c* ....Jon 1:12
there was a great *c* ....Matt 8:26

CALMED

Surely I have *c* ....Ps 131:2

CALVARY

Christ crucified there, Luke 23:33
Same as "Golgotha" in Hebrew, John 19:17

CALVES

made two *c* of gold ....1 Kin 12:28
their cow *c* without ....Job 21:10
like stall-fed *c* ....Mal 4:2
blood of goats and *c* ....Heb 9:12

CAMEL

it is easier for a *c* ....Matt 19:24
and swallow a *c* ....Matt 23:24

CAMP

"This is God's *c* ....Gen 32:2
who went before the *c* ....Ex 14:19
to Him, outside the *c* ....Heb 13:13

CAN

I *c* do all things ....Phil 4:13

CANA

A village of upper Galilee; home of Nathanael, John 21:2
Site of Christ's first miracle, John 2:1–11
Healing at, John 4:46–54

CANAAN

A son of Ham, Gen 10:6
Cursed by Noah, Gen 9:20–25
——Promised Land, Gen 12:5
Boundaries of, Gen 10:19
God's promises concerning, given to Abraham, Gen 12:1–3
to Isaac, Gen 26:2, 3
to Jacob, Gen 28:10–13
to Israel, Ex 3:8
Conquest of, announced, Gen 15:7–21
preceded by spying expedition, Num 13:1–33
delayed by unbelief, Num 14:1–35
accomplished by the Lord, Josh 23:1–16
achieved only in part, Judg 1:21, 27–36

CANAANITES

Israelites commanded to:
drive them out; not serve their gods, Ex 23:23–33

shun their abominations, Lev 18:24–30
not make covenants or intermarry with them, Deut 7:1–3

CANCER

will spread like c ....2 Tim 2:17

CANE

bought Me no sweet c..........Is 43:24
Sheba, and sweet c ....Jer 6:20

CANOPIES

He made darkness c ......2 Sam 22:12

CANOPY

His c around Him was ....Ps 18:11

CAPERNAUM

Simon Peter's home, Mark 1:21, 29
Christ performs healings there, Matt 8:5–17; 9:1–8; Mark 1:21–28; John 4:46–54
preaches there, Mark 9:33–50; John 6:24–71
uses as headquarters, Matt 4:13–17
pronounces judgment upon, Matt 11:23, 24

CAPPADOCIA

Jews from, at Pentecost, Acts 2:1, 9
Christians of, addressed by Peter, 1 Pet 1:1

CAPSTONE

bring forth the c ....Zech 4:7

CAPTAIN

which, having no c ....Prov 6:7

CAPTIVE

have led captivity c ....Ps 68:18
of your neck, O c ....Is 52:2
they shall now go c ....Amos 6:7
and be led away c ....Luke 21:24
He led captivity c ....Eph 4:8

CAPTIVES

will bring back the c ....Amos 9:14
and return their c............Zeph 2:7
make c of gullible women ....2 Tim 3:6

CAPTIVITY

bring you back from c ......Deut 30:3
high, You have led c ....Ps 68:18
Judah has gone into c ....Lam 1:3
from David until the c ....Matt 1:17
and bringing me into c ....Rom 7:23
every thought into c ....2 Cor 10:5
on high, He led c ....Eph 4:8
shall go into c ....Rev 13:10

CARCASS

honey were in the c ....Judg 14:8
For wherever the c ....Matt 24:28

CARE

"Lord, do You not c ....Luke 10:40
you to be without c..........1 Cor 7:32
who will sincerely c...........Phil 2:20
how will he take c ....1 Tim 3:5
casting all your c ....1 Pet 5:7

CARED

he said, not that he c ....John 12:6

CAREFULLY

c keep all these ....Deut 11:22
I shall walk c all my ....Is 38:15

CARELESS

but he who is c ....Prov 19:16

CARES

no one c for my soul ....Ps 142:4
and are choked with c ......Luke 8:14
He who is unmarried c .....1 Cor 7:32
for He c for you ....1 Pet 5:7

CARMEL

City of Judah, Josh 15:55
Site of Saul's victory, 1 Sam 15:12
——A mountain of Palestine, Josh 19:26
Scene of Elijah's triumph, 1 Kin 18:19–45
Elisha visits, 2 Kin 2:25

CARNAL

spiritual, but I am c ....Rom 7:14
c mind is enmity ....Rom 8:7
for you are still c ....1 Cor 3:3
our warfare are not c ....2 Cor 10:4

CARNALLY

we may know them c ....Gen 19:5
that we may know him c ...Judg 19:22
c minded is death ....Rom 8:6

CAROUSE

count it pleasure to c ....2 Pet 2:13

CAROUSING

be weighed down with c ...Luke 21:34

CARPENTER

Is this not the c ....Mark 6:3

CARRIED

the LORD your God c ....Deut 1:31
and c our sorrows ....Is 53:4
parted from them and c ...Luke 24:51
c me away in the ....Rev 17:3

CARRY

their hands cannot c ....Job 5:12
c them away like a ....Ps 90:5
I am not worthy to c ....Matt 3:11
for you to c your bed ....John 5:10
it is certain we can c ....1 Tim 6:7

CARRYING

a man will meet you c .....Mark 14:13
always c about in the ....2 Cor 4:10

CASE

c that is too hard ....Deut 1:17
I have prepared my c ....Job 13:18
I would present my c..........Job 23:4
"Present your c................Is 41:21
Festus laid Paul's c ....Acts 25:14

CASSIA

myrrh and aloes and c ....Ps 45:8

CAST

When they c you down ....Job 22:29
c away Their ....Ps 2:3
Why are you c down ....Ps 42:5
But You have c us off ....Ps 44:9
c me away from Your ....Ps 51:11
He c on them the ....Ps 78:49
the LORD will not c ....Ps 94:14
me up and c me away ......Ps 102:10
and the earth shall c ....Is 26:19
My sight, as I have c ....Jer 7:15
C away from you all ....Ezek 18:31
brought Daniel and c ....Dan 6:16
c all our sins into ....Mic 7:19
whole body to be c ....Matt 5:29
the kingdom will be c ....Matt 8:12
spirits, to c them out ....Matt 10:1
In My name they will c ....Mark 16:17
by no means c out ....John 6:37
c away His people ....Rom 11:1
c away your confidence ....Heb 10:35
c their crowns before ....Rev 4:10
the great dragon was c ....Rev 12:9

CASTING

nation which I am c ....Lev 20:23
Andrew his brother, c ....Matt 4:18
c down arguments ....2 Cor 10:5
c all your care ....1 Pet 5:7

CASTS

If Satan c ....Matt 12:26
perfect love c out ....1 John 4:18

CATCH

in wait to c the poor ....Ps 10:9
c Him in His words ....Mark 12:13
down your nets for a c ....Luke 5:4
From now on you will c .....Luke 5:10

CATCHES

and the wolf c the ....John 10:12
c the wise in their ....1 Cor 3:19

CATERPILLAR

their crops to the c ....Ps 78:46

CATTLE

c you shall take as ....Josh 8:2
does not let their c ....Ps 107:38

CAUGHT

behind him was a ram c ....Gen 22:13
and that night they c ....John 21:3
Spirit of the Lord c ....Acts 8:39
her Child was c up ....Rev 12:5

CAUSE

I would commit my c ....Job 5:8
my enemy without c............Ps 7:4
hate me without a c ....Ps 35:19
c His face to shine ....Ps 67:1
C me to know the way ....Ps 143:8
one to plead his c ....Prov 18:17
God, Who pleads the c ....Is 51:22
He judged the c ....Jer 22:16
brother without a c...........Matt 5:22
hated Me without a c ....John 15:25
For this c I was born ....John 18:37

CAVES

the people hid in c ....1 Sam 13:6
rocks, and into the c ....Is 2:19
in dens and c of the ....Heb 11:38

CEASE

and night shall not c ....Gen 8:22
Why should the work c ....Neh 6:3
There the wicked c.............Job 3:17
He makes wars c ....Ps 46:9

C listening to ....Prov 19:27
C to do evil ....Is 1:16
tongues, they will c ....1 Cor 13:8
do not c to give ....Eph 1:16
do not c to pray for ....Col 1:9

CEASED

c building the city ....Gen 11:8
the sea, and the sea c ....Jon 1:15

CEASES

for the godly man c ....Ps 12:1

CEASING

c your work of faith ....1 Thess 1:3
thank God without c ....1 Thess 2:13
pray without c ....1 Thess 5:17

CEDAR

dwell in a house of c ....2 Sam 7:2
He shall grow like a c ....Ps 92:12
of our houses are c ....Song 1:17
it, paneling it with c ....Jer 22:14
Indeed Assyria was a c .....Ezek 31:3

CEDARS

the LORD breaks the c ....Ps 29:5
c of Lebanon which He ......Ps 104:16

CELESTIAL

but the glory of the c ......1 Cor 15:40

CENCHREA

A harbor of Corinth, Acts 18:18
Home of Phoebe, Rom 16:1

CENSER

Aaron, each took his c ....Lev 10:1
Each man had a c ....Ezek 8:11
which had the golden c ....Heb 9:4
the angel took the c ....Rev 8:5

CEPHAS

Aramaic for Peter, John 1:42

CERTAINTY

make you know the c ....Prov 22:21
you may know the c ....Luke 1:4

CERTIFICATE

a man to write a c ....Mark 10:4

CERTIFIED

His testimony has c ....John 3:33

CHAFF

c that a storm ....Job 21:18
c which the wind ....Ps 1:4
Let them be like c ....Ps 35:5
be chased like the c ....Is 17:13
You shall conceive c ....Is 33:11
the day passes like c ....Zeph 2:2
He will burn up the c ....Matt 3:12

CHAIN

He has made my c ....Lam 3:7
pit and a great c ....Rev 20:1

CHAINED

of God is not c ....2 Tim 2:9
the prisoners as if c ....Heb 13:3

CHAINS

their kings with c ....Ps 149:8
your neck with c ....Song 1:10
And his c fell off ....Acts 12:7
am, except for these c ......Acts 26:29
Remember my c ....Col 4:18
minister to me in my c......Philem 13
delivered them into c ....2 Pet 2:4

CHALDEA

Originally, the southern portion of Babylonia, Gen 11:31
Applied later to all Babylonia, Dan 3:8
Abram came from, Gen 11:28–31

CHALDEANS

Attack Job, Job 1:17
Nebuchadnezzar, king of, 2 Kin 24:1
Jerusalem defeated by, 2 Kin 25:1–21
Babylon, "the glory of," Is 13:19
Predicted captivity of Jews among, Jer 25:1–26
God's agent, Hab 1:6

CHAMBERS

and the c of the south ....Job 9:9
brought me into his c ....Song 1:4
and his c by injustice ....Jer 22:13

CHAMPION

And a c went out from .....1 Sam 17:4

CHANGE

c his countenance ....Job 14:20
c the night into day ....Job 17:12
and who can make Him c....Job 23:13
Because they do not c ....Ps 55:19
a cloak You will c ....Ps 102:26
with those given to c ....Prov 24:21
Can the Ethiopian c ....Jer 13:23
c times and law ....Dan 7:25
c their glory into ....Hos 4:7
the LORD, I do not c ....Mal 3:6
now and to c my tone ....Gal 4:20
there is also a c ....Heb 7:12

CHANGED

But My people have c ....Jer 2:11
c the glory of the ....Rom 1:23
but we shall all be c ....1 Cor 15:51
the priesthood being c ....Heb 7:12

CHANGERS'

and poured out the c ....John 2:15

CHANGES

c the times and the ....Dan 2:21

CHANNELS

c of the sea were seen ....Ps 18:15

CHARACTER

and c, hope ....Rom 5:4

CHARGED

May it not be c ....2 Tim 4:16

CHARIOT

He took off their c ....Ex 14:25
that suddenly a c ....2 Kin 2:11
makes the clouds His c ....Ps 104:3
and overtake this c ....Acts 8:29

CHARIOTS

the clatter of his c ....Judg 5:28
Some trust in c ....Ps 20:7
The c of God are ....Ps 68:17

CHARITABLE

you do not do your c ....Matt 6:1
that your c deed ....Matt 6:4
c deeds which she ....Acts 9:36

CHARM

C is deceitful and ....Prov 31:30

CHARMERS

heed the voice of c ....Ps 58:5

CHARMS

women who sew magic c ...Ezek 13:18

CHASE

Five of you shall c ....Lev 26:8
How could one c ....Deut 32:30
angel of the LORD c ....Ps 35:5

CHASTE

may present you as a c ......2 Cor 11:2
to be discreet, c ....Titus 2:5
c conduct accompanied ....1 Pet 3:2

CHASTEN

C your son while there .....Prov 19:18
is My desire, I will c ....Hos 10:10
a father does not c ....Heb 12:7
I love, I rebuke and c ....Rev 3:19

CHASTENED

c my soul with fasting ....Ps 69:10
c every morning ....Ps 73:14
The LORD has c me ....Ps 118:18
In vain I have c ....Jer 2:30
c us as seemed best ....Heb 12:10

CHASTENING

have not seen the c ....Deut 11:2
do not despise the c ....Job 5:17
'I have borne c ....Job 34:31
a prayer when Your c..............Is 26:16
if you are without c ....Heb 12:8
Now no c seems to be ....Heb 12:11

CHASTENS

the LORD loves He c ....Heb 12:6

CHASTISE

and I, even I, will c ....Lev 26:28
c them according ....Hos 7:12
I will therefore c ....Luke 23:22

CHASTISEMENT

the c for our peace ....Is 53:5

CHATTER

c leads only to ....Prov 14:23

CHEAT

'You shall not c...............Lev 19:13
Beware lest anyone c ....Col 2:8

CHEATED

let yourselves be c ....1 Cor 6:7
we have c no one ....2 Cor 7:2

CHEBAR

River in Babylonia, Ezek 1:3
Site of Ezekiel's visions, Ezek 10:15, 20

CHEDORLAOMER

A king of Elam; invaded Canaan, Gen 14:1–16

CHEEK

Let him give his c ....Lam 3:30
with a rod on the c ....Mic 5:1
on your right c..............Matt 5:39

CHEEKBONE

my enemies on the c ....Ps 3:7

CHEEKS

c are lovely with............Song 1:10
His c are like a bed ....Song 5:13
struck Me, and My c ....Is 50:6

CHEER

and let your heart c..........Eccl 11:9
"Son, be of good c ....Matt 9:2

CHEERFUL

for God loves a c ....2 Cor 9:7
Is anyone c ....James 5:13

CHEERFULNESS

shows mercy, with c ....Rom 12:8

CHEESE

and curdle me like c.........Job 10:10

CHEMOSH

The god of the Moabites, Num 21:29
Children sacrificed to, 2 Kin 3:26, 27
Solomon builds altars to, 1 Kin 11:7
Josiah destroys altars of, 2 Kin 23:13

CHERISHES

but nourishes and c..........Eph 5:29
as a nursing mother c ....1 Thess 2:7

CHERUB

He rode upon a c ....2 Sam 22:11

CHERUBIM

and He placed c ....Gen 3:24
dwell between the c ....Ps 80:1
fire from among the c ....Ezek 10:2
above it were the c ....Heb 9:5

CHIEF

is white and ruddy, c ....Song 5:10
of whom I am c ....1 Tim 1:15
Zion a c cornerstone ....1 Pet 2:6
has become the c ....1 Pet 2:7
C Shepherd appears ....1 Pet 5:4

CHILD

Like a weaned c ....Ps 131:2
c is known by his ....Prov 20:11
Train up a c in the ....Prov 22:6
For unto us a C ....Is 9:6
c shall lead them ....Is 11:6
When Israel was a c ....Hos 11:1
virgin shall be with c ....Matt 1:23
He took a little c ....Mark 9:36
of God as a little c ....Mark 10:15
kind of c will this be ....Luke 1:66
So the c grew and ....Luke 1:80
When I was a c ....1 Cor 13:11
She bore a male C ....Rev 12:5

CHILDBEARING

she will be saved in c ....1 Tim 2:15

CHILDBIRTH

pain as a woman in c ....Is 13:8

CHILDHOOD

from your flesh, for c ....Eccl 11:10

And he said, "From c........Mark 9:21
c you have known..........2 Tim 3:15

CHILDLESS

give me, seeing I go c ....Gen 15:2
this man down as c ....Jer 22:30

CHILDREN

she bore Jacob no c..........Gen 30:1
and all of you are c ....Ps 82:6
c are a heritage ....Ps 127:3
He has blessed your c ....Ps 147:13
let the c of Zion be ....Ps 149:2
c are blessed after ....Prov 20:7
c rise up and call her ....Prov 31:28
c are their oppressors ....Is 3:12
c whom the LORD has ....Is 8:18
be the peace of your c ....Is 54:13
they are My people, c ....Is 63:8
the hearts of the c ....Mal 4:6
c will rise up against ....Matt 10:21
and become as little c ....Matt 18:3
c were brought to Him ....Matt 19:13
"Let the little c ....Matt 19:14
the right to become c.........John 1:12
you were Abraham's c ....John 8:39
spirit that we are c ....Rom 8:16
but as my beloved c ....1 Cor 4:14
Brethren, do not be c ....1 Cor 14:20
c ought not to lay up ....2 Cor 12:14
and were by nature c ....Eph 2:3
should no longer be c.........Eph 4:14
Walk as c of light ....Eph 5:8
and harmless, c...............Phil 2:15
now we are c of God ....1 John 3:2
that we love the c ....1 John 5:2
to hear that my c ....3 John 4

CHILION

Elimelech's son, Ruth 1:2
Orpah's deceased husband, Ruth 1:4, 5
Boaz redeems his estate, Ruth 4:9

CHINNERETH (or Chinneroth)

Fortified city in Naphtali, Deut 3:17
A region bordering the Sea of Galilee, 1 Kin 15:20
Same as the plain of Gennesaret, Matt 14:34
——The OT name for the Sea of Galilee, Num 34:11
Also called Lake of Gennesaret, Luke 5:1

CHOICE

rather than c gold ....Prov 8:10

CHOOSE

therefore c life...............Deut 30:19
c none of his ways ....Prov 3:31
evil and c the good ....Is 7:15
will still c Israel ....Is 14:1
will again c Jerusalem ....Zech 1:17
You did not c.................John 15:16
yet what I shall c ....Phil 1:22

CHOOSES

in the way He c ....Ps 25:12

CHOSE

a good while ago God c......Acts 15:7
just as He c us in Him ....Eph 1:4
from the beginning c ....2 Thess 2:13

CHOSEN

of Jacob, His c ....1 Chr 16:13

people He has c ....Ps 33:12
a covenant with My c...........Ps 89:3
c the way of truth ....Ps 119:30
servant whom I have c.........Is 43:10
c that good part ....Luke 10:42
I know whom I have c .....John 13:18
c you that you should ....Acts 22:14
c the foolish things ....1 Cor 1:27
Has God not c the poor .....James 2:5
But you are a c ....1 Pet 2:9

CHRIST

genealogy of Jesus C ....Matt 1:1
Jesus who is called C.........Matt 1:16
"You are the C ....Matt 16:16
if You are the C ....Matt 26:63
a Savior, who is C ....Luke 2:11
that He Himself is C ....Luke 23:2
the law that the C...........John 12:34
he preached the C ....Acts 9:20
have the Spirit of C ....Rom 8:9
It is C who died ....Rom 8:34
C did not please ....Rom 15:3
Is C divided ....1 Cor 1:13
Him you are in C Jesus .....1 Cor 1:30
to be justified by C............Gal 2:17
been crucified with C ....Gal 2:20
but C lives in me ....Gal 2:20
your Seed," who is C ....Gal 3:16
before by God in C.............Gal 3:17
C may dwell in your ....Eph 3:17
C will give you ....Eph 5:14
C is head of the ....Eph 5:23
to me, to live is C ....Phil 1:21
confess that Jesus C ....Phil 2:11
C who strengthens ....Phil 4:13
which is C in you ....Col 1:27
C who is our ....Col 3:4
C is all and in all ....Col 3:11
and men, the Man C ....1 Tim 2:5
Jesus C is the same ....Heb 13:8
C His Son cleanses us ......1 John 1:7
that Jesus is the C ....1 John 5:1
of His C have come ....Rev 12:10
and reigned with C ....Rev 20:4

CHRISTIAN

me to become a C ....Acts 26:28
anyone suffers as a C ....1 Pet 4:16

CHRISTIANS

were first called C...........Acts 11:26

CHRISTS

For false c and ....Matt 24:24

CHURCH

rock I will build My c ......Matt 16:18
them, tell it to the c.........Matt 18:17
c daily those who were ....Acts 2:47
elders in every c ....Acts 14:23
do you despise the c ....1 Cor 11:22
be made known by the c .....Eph 3:10
also loved the c...............Eph 5:25
Himself a glorious c ....Eph 5:27
as the Lord does the c ....Eph 5:29
body, which is the c ....Col 1:24
and do not let the c ....1 Tim 5:16
general assembly and c .....Heb 12:23
To the angel of the c ....Rev 2:1

CHURCHES

strengthening the c ....Acts 15:41
The c of Christ greet ....Rom 16:16
imitators of the c ....1 Thess 2:14
John, to the seven c ....Rev 1:4

angels of the seven c ....Rev 1:20
these things in the c ....Rev 22:16

CHURNING

For as the c of milk ....Prov 30:33

CHURNS

My heart c within Me ....Hos 11:8

CILICIA

Paul's homeland, Acts 21:39
Students from, argued with Stephen, Acts 6:9
Paul labors in, Gal 1:21

CIRCLE

He walks above the c ....Job 22:14
when He drew a c ....Prov 8:27
who sits above the c ....Is 40:22

CIRCUIT

of heaven, and its c ....Ps 19:6
comes again on its c ....Eccl 1:6

CIRCUMCISE

c the foreskin of your ....Deut 10:16
LORD your God will c ....Deut 30:6
C yourselves to the ....Jer 4:4
is necessary to c them ....Acts 15:5

CIRCUMCISED

among you shall be c ....Gen 17:10
who will justify the c ....Rom 3:30
While he was c ....Rom 4:10
the gospel for the c ....Gal 2:7
if you become c ....Gal 5:2
c the eighth day ....Phil 3:5
In Him you were also c ....Col 2:11

CIRCUMCISION

him the covenant of c ....Acts 7:8
c that which is outward ....Rom 2:28
c is that of the heart ....Rom 2:29
a servant to the c ....Rom 15:8
C is nothing and ....1 Cor 7:19
Christ Jesus neither c ....Gal 5:6
For we are the c ....Phil 3:3
circumcised with the c ....Col 2:11
those of the c ....Titus 1:10

CIRCUMSPECTLY

then that you walk c ....Eph 5:15

CISTERN

waters of his own c ....2 Kin 18:31
from your own c ....Prov 5:15

CITIES

He overthrew those c ....Gen 19:25
repair the ruined c ....Is 61:4
c are a wilderness ....Is 64:10
c will be laid waste ....Jer 4:7
three parts, and the c ....Rev 16:19

CITIZEN

But I was born a c ....Acts 22:28

CITIZENS

But his c hated him ....Luke 19:14
but fellow c with the ....Eph 2:19

CITIZENSHIP

sum I obtained this c ....Acts 22:28
For our c is in heaven ....Phil 3:20

CITY

And he built a c ....Gen 4:17
shall make glad the c ....Ps 46:4
c shall flourish ....Ps 72:16
They found no c ....Ps 107:4
c that is compact ....Ps 122:3
the LORD guards the c ....Ps 127:1
at the entry of the c ....Prov 8:3
c has become a harlot ....Is 1:21
upon Zion, the c ....Is 33:20
after the holy c ....Is 48:2
How lonely sits the c ....Lam 1:1
Nineveh, that great c ....Jon 4:11
c that dwelt securely ....Zeph 2:15
to the oppressing c ....Zeph 3:1
c called Nazareth ....Matt 2:23
c that is set on a ....Matt 5:14
He has prepared a c ....Heb 11:16
Zion and to the c ....Heb 12:22
have no continuing c ....Heb 13:14
will tread the holy c ....Rev 11:2
fallen, that great c ....Rev 14:8
and the beloved c ....Rev 20:9
John, saw the holy c ....Rev 21:2
c was pure gold ....Rev 21:18
c had no need of the ....Rev 21:23
the gates into the c ....Rev 22:14

CLAMOROUS

A foolish woman is c ....Prov 9:13

CLAP

c their hands at him ....Job 27:23
Oh, c your hands ....Ps 47:1
let the rivers c ....Ps 98:8
of the field shall c ....Is 55:12

CLAUDIUS LYSIAS

Roman commander who protected Paul, Acts 24:22–24, 26

CLAY

dwell in houses of c ....Job 4:19
have made me like c ....Job 10:9
are defenses of c ....Job 13:12
been formed out of c ....Job 33:6
takes on form like c ....Job 38:14
pit, out of the miry c ....Ps 40:2
be esteemed as the c ....Is 29:16
Shall the c say to him ....Is 45:9
We are the c ....Is 64:8
"Look, as the c ....Jer 18:6
iron and partly of c ....Dan 2:33
blind man with the c ....John 9:6
have power over the c ....Rom 9:21

CLEAN

seven each of every c ....Gen 7:2
between unclean and c ....Lev 10:10
wash in them and be c ....2 Kin 5:12
Who can bring a c ....Job 14:4
He who has c hands and ....Ps 24:4
make yourselves c ....Is 1:16
Then I will sprinkle c ....Ezek 36:25
c out His threshing ....Matt 3:12
You can make me c ....Matt 8:2
all things are c ....Luke 11:41
but is completely c ....John 13:10
"You are not all c ....John 13:11
You are already c ....John 15:3
in fine linen, c ....Rev 19:8

CLEANSE

You shall c the altar ....Ex 29:36
C me from secret ....Ps 19:12
and c me from my sin ....Ps 51:2
How can a young man c ....Ps 119:9
I will c you from all ....Ezek 36:25
c the lepers, raise ....Matt 10:8
might sanctify and c ....Eph 5:26
c your conscience ....Heb 9:14
C your hands ....James 4:8
us our sins and to c ....1 John 1:9

CLEANSED

Surely I have c ....Ps 73:13
and you were not c ....Ezek 24:13
the lepers are c ....Matt 11:5
"Were there not ten c ....Luke 17:17

CLEANSES

Therefore if anyone c ....2 Tim 2:21
Jesus Christ His Son c ....1 John 1:7

CLEAR

c shining after rain ....2 Sam 23:4
fair as the moon, c ....Song 6:10
yourselves to be c ....2 Cor 7:11
like a jasper stone, c ....Rev 21:11
of life, c as crystal ....Rev 22:1

CLEFTS

to go into the c ....Is 2:21
valleys and in the c ....Is 7:19
you who dwell in the c ....Jer 49:16

CLERK

c had quieted the ....Acts 19:35

CLIFF

secret places of the c ....Song 2:14

CLIMB

go into thickets and c ....Jer 4:29
mighty men, they c ....Joel 2:7
though they c up to ....Amos 9:2

CLIMBS

c up some other way ....John 10:1

CLING

and that you may c ....Deut 30:20
to her, "Do not c ....John 20:17
C to what is good ....Rom 12:9

CLINGS

and My tongue c ....Ps 22:15
My soul c to the dust ....Ps 119:25

CLOAK

c You will change them ....Ps 102:26
let him have your c ....Matt 5:40
c You will fold them ....Heb 1:12
using liberty as a c ....1 Pet 2:16

CLODS

The c of the valley ....Job 21:33

CLOSE

c friends abhor me ....Job 19:19
of Christ he came c ....Phil 2:30

CLOSED

and has c your eyes ....Is 29:10
for the words are c ....Dan 12:9
the deep c around me ....Jon 2:5

CLOTH

a piece of unshrunk c ....Matt 9:16
in a clean linen c ....Matt 27:59

CLOTHE

c them with tunics ....Ex 40:14
c me with skin and..........Job 10:11
c her priests with ....Ps 132:16
His enemies I will c ....Ps 132:18
Though you c yourself ....Jer 4:30
He not much more c ....Matt 6:30

CLOTHED

of skin, and c them ....Gen 3:21
Have you c his neck ....Job 39:19
off my sackcloth and c ....Ps 30:11
The pastures are c ....Ps 65:13
the LORD is c ....Ps 93:1
You are c with honor ....Ps 104:1
c himself with cursing ....Ps 109:18
Let Your priests be c ....Ps 132:9
all her household is c ....Prov 31:21
c you with fine linen ....Ezek 16:10
A man c in soft ....Matt 11:8
I was naked and you c ....Matt 25:36
legion, sitting and c ....Mark 5:15
And they c Him with ....Mark 15:17
rich man who was c ....Luke 16:19
desiring to be c ....2 Cor 5:2
that you may be c ....Rev 3:18
a woman c with the sun ....Rev 12:1
He was c with a robe ....Rev 19:13

CLOTHES

c will abhor me ....Job 9:31
c became shining ....Mark 9:3
many spread their c ....Luke 19:36
laid down their c ....Acts 7:58
and tore off their c ....Acts 22:23
a poor man in filthy c ....James 2:2

CLOTHING

c they cast lots ....Ps 22:18
c is woven with gold ....Ps 45:13
will provide your c ....Prov 27:26
and honor are her c ....Prov 31:25
of vengeance for c ....Is 59:17
the body more than c ....Matt 6:25
do you worry about c ....Matt 6:28
to you in sheep's c ....Matt 7:15
those who wear soft c ....Matt 11:8
c as white as snow ....Matt 28:3
c they cast lots ....John 19:24
before me in bright c ....Acts 10:30

CLOTHS

wrapped in swaddling c ....Luke 2:12
in, saw the linen c ....John 20:5

CLOUD

My rainbow in the c ....Gen 9:13
day in a pillar of c ....Ex 13:21
c covered the mountain ....Ex 24:15
c descended and stood ....Ex 33:9
c did not depart ....Neh 9:19
He led them with the c ....Ps 78:14
his favor is like a c ....Prov 16:15
these who fly like a c ....Is 60:8
like a morning c ....Hos 6:4
behold, a bright c ....Matt 17:5
of Man coming in a c ....Luke 21:27
c received Him out of ....Acts 1:9
were under the c ....1 Cor 10:1
by so great a c ....Heb 12:1

CLOUDS

a morning without c ....2 Sam 23:3
c poured out water ....Ps 77:17
and hail, snow and c ....Ps 148:8
c drop down the dew ....Prov 3:20
he who regards the c ....Eccl 11:4
of Man coming on the c ....Matt 24:30
with them in the c ....1 Thess 4:17
are c without water ....Jude 12
He is coming with c ....Rev 1:7

CLOUDY

them by day with a c ....Neh 9:12
spoke to them in the c ....Ps 99:7

CLOVEN

the hoof, having c ....Lev 11:3
chew the cud or have c ....Deut 14:7

CLUSTER

beloved is to me a c ....Song 1:14
wine is found in the c ....Is 65:8

COAL

in his hand a live c ....Is 6:6
it shall not be a c ....Is 47:14

COALS

wicked He will rain c ....Ps 11:6
c were kindled by it ....Ps 18:8
let burning c fall ....Ps 140:10
Can one walk on hot c ....Prov 6:28
so you will heap c ....Prov 25:22
doing you will heap c ....Rom 12:20

COBRA

it becomes c venom ....Job 20:14
c that stops its ear ....Ps 58:4
the lion and the c ....Ps 91:13

COBRA'S

shall play by the c ....Is 11:8

COFFIN

and he was put in a c ....Gen 50:26
David followed the c ....2 Sam 3:31
touched the open c ....Luke 7:14

COIN

sold for a copper c ....Matt 10:29
if she loses one c ....Luke 15:8

COLD

and harvest, C and ....Gen 8:22
can stand before His c ....Ps 147:17
Like the c of snow in ....Prov 25:13
c water to a weary ....Prov 25:25
c water in the name of ....Matt 10:42
of many will grow c ....Matt 24:12
that you are neither c ....Rev 3:15

COLLECTED

coming I might have c ....Luke 19:23

COLLECTION

from Jerusalem the c ....2 Chr 24:6
concerning the c ....1 Cor 16:1

COLOSSE

A city in Asia Minor, Col 1:2
Evangelized by Epaphras, Col 1:7
Not visited by Paul, Col 2:1
Paul writes against errors of, Col 2:16–23

COLT

and his donkey's c ....Gen 49:11
on a donkey, a c ....Zech 9:9
on a donkey, a c ....Matt 21:5
own clothes on the c ....Luke 19:35

COME

then does wisdom c ....Job 28:20
of glory shall c ....Ps 24:7
Our God shall c ....Ps 50:3
You all flesh will c ....Ps 65:2
C with me from Lebanon ....Song 4:8
He will c and save you ....Is 35:4
who have no money, C ....Is 55:1
Your kingdom c ....Matt 6:10
C to Me ....Matt 11:28
For many will c ....Matt 24:5
Israel, let Him now c ....Matt 27:42
If anyone desires to c ....Luke 9:23
kingdom of God has c ....Luke 10:9
I have c in My ....John 5:43
and I have not c ....John 7:28
thirsts, let him c ....John 7:37
c that they may have ....John 10:10
c as a light into the ....John 12:46
I will c to you ....John 14:18
If I had not c ....John 15:22
savage wolves will c ....Acts 20:29
O Lord, c ....1 Cor 16:22
the door, I will c ....Rev 3:20
the bride say, "C ....Rev 22:17

COMELINESS

He has no form or c ....Is 53:2

COMES

Who is this who c ....Is 63:1
'Come,' and he c ....Matt 8:9
Lord's death till He c ....1 Cor 11:26
Then c the end ....1 Cor 15:24

COMFORT

with him, and to c him ....Job 2:11
and Your staff, they c ....Ps 23:4
When will you c ....Ps 119:82
yes, c My people ....Is 40:1
For the LORD will c ....Is 51:3
c all who mourn ....Is 61:2
she has none to c her ....Lam 1:2
the LORD will again c ....Zech 1:17
and God of all c ....2 Cor 1:3
trouble, with the c ....2 Cor 1:4
in Christ, if any c ....Phil 2:1
c each other and edify ....1 Thess 5:11

COMFORTED

So Isaac was c after ....Gen 24:67
soul refused to be c ....Ps 77:2
For the LORD has c ....Is 49:13
refusing to be c ....Jer 31:15
but now he is c ....Luke 16:25

COMFORTER

She had no c ....Lam 1:9

COMFORTS

the army, as one who c ....Job 29:25
I, even I, am He who c ....Is 51:12
him, and restore c ....Is 57:18
one whom his mother c ....Is 66:13
who c us in all our ....2 Cor 1:4
who c the downcast ....2 Cor 7:6

COMING

your salvation is c ....Is 62:11
behold, the day is c ....Mal 4:1
but He who is c ....Matt 3:11

"Are You the C ....Matt 11:3
be the sign of Your c ....Matt 24:3
is delaying his c ....Matt 24:48
see the Son of Man c ......Mark 13:26
mightier than I is c ....Luke 3:16
are Christ's at His c ....1 Cor 15:23
to you the power and c ......2 Pet 1:16
the promise of His c ....2 Pet 3:4
Behold, I am c ....Rev 3:11
"Behold, I am c ....Rev 22:7
"Surely I am c ....Rev 22:20

COMMAND

in order that he may c ......Gen 18:19
"The LORD will c ....Deut 28:8
in that I c you ....Deut 30:16
c His lovingkindness ....Ps 42:8
c victories for Jacob ....Ps 44:4
to all that I c ....Jer 11:4
if it is You, c ....Matt 14:28
c fire to come down ....Luke 9:54
c I have received ....John 10:18
And I know that His c .....John 12:50
if you do whatever I c ......John 15:14
do the things we c ....2 Thess 3:4

COMMANDED

"Have you c the ....Job 38:12
c His covenant forever ....Ps 111:9
For there the LORD c..........Ps 133:3
it is the God who c ....2 Cor 4:6
not endure what was c ......Heb 12:20

COMMANDMENT

c of the LORD is pure ....Ps 19:8
c is exceedingly broad ....Ps 119:96
For the c is a lamp ....Prov 6:23
Me is taught by the c ....Is 29:13
which is the great c ....Matt 22:36
A new c I give to ....John 13:34
the Father gave Me c ....John 14:31
law, but when the c ....Rom 7:9
the c might become ....Rom 7:13
which is the first c ....Eph 6:2
c is the word which ....1 John 2:7
And this is His c ....1 John 3:23
as we received c ....2 John 4
This is the c ....2 John 6

COMMANDMENTS

covenant, the Ten C ....Ex 34:28
to observe all these c ......Deut 6:25
who remember His c ....Ps 103:18
do not hide Your c ....Ps 119:19
myself in Your c ....Ps 119:47
for I believe Your c ....Ps 119:66
Your c are faithful ....Ps 119:86
c more than gold ....Ps 119:127
as doctrines the c ....Matt 15:9
c hang all the Law ....Matt 22:40
He who has My c ....John 14:21
according to the c ....Col 2:22
Now he who keeps His c ...1 John 3:24

COMMANDS

with authority He c ....Mark 1:27

COMMEND

But food does not c ....1 Cor 8:8

COMMENDABLE

For this is c ....1 Pet 2:19
patiently, this is c ....1 Pet 2:20

COMMENDED

A man will be c ....Prov 12:8

c the unjust steward ....Luke 16:8
where they had been c ....Acts 14:26

COMMENDING

of the truth c ....2 Cor 4:2

COMMENDS

but whom the Lord c ......2 Cor 10:18

COMMIT

"You shall not c ....Ex 20:14
C your works to the ....Prov 16:3
mammon, who will c ......Luke 16:11
into Your hands I c ....Luke 23:46
But Jesus did not c ....John 2:24
c sexual immorality ....1 Cor 10:8
c these to faithful ....2 Tim 2:2
c their souls to Him ....1 Pet 4:19
c sin not leading ....1 John 5:16

COMMITS

to you, whoever c ....John 8:34
sin also c lawlessness ....1 John 3:4

COMMITTED

For My people have c ....Jer 2:13
c things deserving ....Luke 12:48
For God has c them all ......Rom 11:32
Guard what was c ....1 Tim 6:20
"Who c no sin ....1 Pet 2:22
c Himself to Him who ....1 Pet 2:23

COMMON

of the c people sins ....Lev 4:27
poor have this in c ....Prov 22:2
c people heard Him ....Mark 12:37
had all things in c ....Acts 2:44
never eaten anything c ......Acts 10:14
not call any man c ....Acts 10:28
a true son in our c ....Titus 1:4
concerning our c ....Jude 3

COMMOTION

there arose a great c ....Acts 19:23

COMMUNED

I c with my heart ....Eccl 1:16

COMMUNION

bless, is it not the c ....1 Cor 10:16
c has light with ....2 Cor 6:14
c of the Holy Spirit ....2 Cor 13:14

COMPANION

a man my equal, My c ....Ps 55:13
I am a c of all who ....Ps 119:63
the Man who is My C ....Zech 13:7
urge you also, true c ....Phil 4:3
your brother and c ....Rev 1:9

COMPANIONS

are rebellious, and c ....Is 1:23
and calling to their c ....Matt 11:16
more than Your c ....Heb 1:9
while you became c ....Heb 10:33

COMPANY

great was the c ....Ps 68:11
epistle not to keep c ....1 Cor 5:9
c corrupts good habits .....1 Cor 15:33
and do not keep c ....2 Thess 3:14
to an innumerable c ....Heb 12:22

COMPARE

may desire cannot c ....Prov 3:15

c ourselves with those ....2 Cor 10:12

COMPARED

the heavens can be c ....Ps 89:6
may desire cannot be c ....Prov 8:11
are not worthy to be c ....Rom 8:18

COMPASSION

show you mercy, have c ....Deut 13:17
His people and have c .....Deut 32:36
He, being full of c ....Ps 78:38
are a God full of c ....Ps 86:15
will return and have c ....Jer 12:15
yet He will show c ....Lam 3:32
c everyone to his ....Zech 7:9
He was moved with c ....Matt 9:36
also have had c ....Matt 18:33
"I have c on the ....Mark 8:2
whomever I will have c ....Rom 9:15
He can have c on those ....Heb 5:2
of one mind, having c ....1 Pet 3:8
And on some have c ....Jude 22

COMPASSIONATE

c women have cooked ....Lam 4:10
the Lord is very c ....James 5:11

COMPASSIONS

because His c fail not ....Lam 3:22

COMPEL

c them to come in ....Luke 14:23

COMPELLED

Macedonia, Paul was c ....Acts 18:5

COMPELS

the spirit within me c ....Job 32:18
And whoever c ....Matt 5:41
the love of Christ c ....2 Cor 5:14

COMPLACENCY

slay them, and the c ....Prov 1:32
who are settled in c ....Zeph 1:12

COMPLAIN

should a living man c ....Lam 3:39

COMPLAINED

and you c in your ....Deut 1:27
but c in their tents ....Ps 106:25
some of them also c ....1 Cor 10:10

COMPLAINERS

These are grumblers, c ....Jude 16

COMPLAINING

all things without c ....Phil 2:14

COMPLAINT

"Even today my c ....Job 23:2
I pour out my c ....Ps 142:2
for the LORD has a c ....Mic 6:2
if anyone has a c ....Col 3:13

COMPLAINTS

Who has c ....Prov 23:29
laid many serious c ....Acts 25:7

COMPLETE

that you may be made c ....2 Cor 13:9
work in you will c ....Phil 1:6
and you are c in Him ....Col 2:10
of God may be c ....2 Tim 3:17

make you *c* in every ....Heb 13:21
the wrath of God is *c* ....Rev 15:1

COMPLETELY

I made a man *c* well ....John 7:23
Himself sanctify you *c* .....1 Thess 5:23

COMPOSED

But God *c* the body ....1 Cor 12:24

COMPREHEND

which we cannot *c* ....Job 37:5
c my path and my lying ....Ps 139:3
the darkness did not *c* ....John 1:5
may be able to *c* ....Eph 3:18

CONCEAL

Almighty I will not *c* ....Job 27:11
c pride from man ....Job 33:17
of God to *c* a matter ....Prov 25:2

CONCEALED

c Your lovingkindness ....Ps 40:10
than love carefully *c* ....Prov 27:5

CONCEIT

selfish ambition or *c* ....Phil 2:3

CONCEITED

Let us not become *c* ....Gal 5:26

CONCEIVE

the virgin shall *c* ....Is 7:14
And behold, you will *c* ......Luke 1:31

CONCEIVED

in sin my mother *c* ....Ps 51:5
when desire has *c* ....James 1:15

CONCERN

Neither do I *c* myself ....Ps 131:1
the things which *c* ....Acts 28:31
my deep *c* for all the ....2 Cor 11:28

CONCERNED

Is it oxen God is *c* ....1 Cor 9:9

CONCESSION

But I say this as a *c* ....1 Cor 7:6

CONCILIATION

c pacifies great ....Eccl 10:4

CONCLUSION

Let us hear the *c* ....Eccl 12:13

CONDEMN

say to God, 'Do not *c* ....Job 10:2
world to *c* the world ....John 3:17
her, "Neither do I *c* ....John 8:11
judge another you *c* ....Rom 2:1
our heart does not *c* ....1 John 3:21

CONDEMNATION

will receive greater *c* ....Matt 23:14
can you escape the *c* ......Matt 23:33
subject to eternal *c* ....Mark 3:29
And this is the *c* ....John 3:19
the resurrection of *c* ....John 5:29
Their *c* is just ....Rom 3:8
therefore now no *c* ....Rom 8:1
of *c* had glory ....2 Cor 3:9
having *c* because they ......1 Tim 5:12
marked out for this *c* ....Jude 4

CONDEMNED

words you will be *c* ....Matt 12:37
does not believe is *c* ....John 3:18
c sin in the flesh ....Rom 8:3

CONDEMNS

Who is he who *c* ....Rom 8:34
For if our heart *c* ....1 John 3:20

CONDUCT

c yourselves like men ....1 Sam 4:9
who are of upright *c* ....Ps 37:14
c yourself in the ....1 Tim 3:15
c that his works are ....James 3:13
to each one's work, *c* ....1 Pet 1:17
from your aimless *c* ....1 Pet 1:18
may be won by the *c* ....1 Pet 3:1

CONFESS

c my transgressions ....Ps 32:5
that if you *c* with ....Rom 10:9
every tongue shall *c* ....Rom 14:11
C your trespasses ....James 5:16
If we *c* our sins ....1 John 1:9
but I will *c* his name ....Rev 3:5

CONFESSED

c that He was Christ ....John 9:22
c the good confession ......1 Tim 6:12

CONFESSES

prosper, but whoever *c* .....Prov 28:13
c that Jesus is the ....1 John 4:15

CONFESSION

of Israel, and make *c* ....Josh 7:19
with the mouth *c* ....Rom 10:10
confessed the good *c* ....1 Tim 6:12
witnessed the good *c* ....1 Tim 6:13
High Priest of our *c* ....Heb 3:1
let us hold fast our *c* ....Heb 4:14

CONFIDENCE

You who are the *c* ....Ps 65:5
the LORD than to put *c* ....Ps 118:8
c shall be your ....Is 30:15
Jesus, and have no *c* ....Phil 3:3
if we hold fast the *c* ....Heb 3:6
appears, we may have *c* ...1 John 2:28

CONFINED

saying, "I am *c* ....Jer 36:5
the Scripture has *c* ....Gal 3:22

CONFIRM

c the promises ....Rom 15:8
who will also *c* ....1 Cor 1:8

CONFIRMED

covenant that was *c* ....Gal 3:17
by the Lord, and was *c* ....Heb 2:3
c it by an oath ....Heb 6:17
prophetic word *c* ....2 Pet 1:19

CONFIRMING

c the word through the ....Mark 16:20

CONFLICT

having the same *c* ....Phil 1:30
to know what a great *c* ....Col 2:1

CONFLICTS

Outside were *c* ....2 Cor 7:5

CONFORMED

predestined to be *c* ....Rom 8:29

And do not be *c* ....Rom 12:2
sufferings, being *c* ....Phil 3:10
body that it may be *c* ....Phil 3:21

CONFOUNDED

who seek You be *c* ....Ps 69:6

CONFUSE

c their language ....Gen 11:7

CONFUSED

there the LORD *c* ....Gen 11:9
the assembly was *c* ....Acts 19:32

CONFUSION

c who plot my hurt ....Ps 35:4
us drink the wine of *c* ....Ps 60:3

CONGREGATION

Nor sinners in the *c* ....Ps 1:5
the *c* of the wicked ....Ps 22:16
God stands in the *c* ....Ps 82:1

CONIAH

King of Judah, Jer 22:24, 28
Same as Jehoiachin, 2 Kin 24:8

CONQUER

conquering and to *c* ....Rev 6:2

CONQUERORS

we are more than *c* ....Rom 8:37

CONSCIENCE

convicted by their *c* ....John 8:9
strive to have a *c* ....Acts 24:16
I am not lying, my *c* ....Rom 9:1
wrath but also for *c* ....Rom 13:5
no questions for *c* ....1 Cor 10:25
faith with a pure *c* ....1 Tim 3:9
having their own *c* ....1 Tim 4:2
to God, cleanse your *c* ....Heb 9:14
from an evil *c* and our ......Heb 10:22
having a good *c* ....1 Pet 3:16

CONSECRATE

"*C* to Me all the ....Ex 13:2
c himself this day ....1 Chr 29:5
the trumpet in Zion, *c* ....Joel 2:15
c their gain to the ....Mic 4:13

CONSECRATED

c this house which you ....1 Kin 9:3

CONSENT

entice you, do not *c* ....Prov 1:10
and does not *c* to ....1 Tim 6:3

CONSENTED

you saw a thief, you *c* ....Ps 50:18
He had not *c* to their ....Luke 23:51

CONSENTING

Now Saul was *c* to his ....Acts 8:1

CONSIDER

When I *c* Your heavens ....Ps 8:3
c her palaces ....Ps 48:13
c carefully what is ....Prov 23:1
C the work of God ....Eccl 7:13
My people do not *c* ....Is 1:3
c the operation ....Is 5:12
your God will *c* ....Jon 1:6
"*C* your ways ....Hag 1:5

Site of church, 1 Cor 1:2
Visited by Apollos, Acts 19:1

CORNELIUS
A religious Gentile, Acts 10:1–48

CORNER
was not done in a c ....Acts 26:26

CORNERSTONE
Or who laid its c ....Job 38:6
has become the chief c ....Ps 118:22
stone, a precious c ....Is 28:16
become the chief c ....Matt 21:42
in Zion a chief c ....1 Pet 2:6

CORPSE
c was thrown on the ....1 Kin 13:24
c trodden underfoot ....Is 14:19

CORRECT
with rebukes You c ....Ps 39:11
C your son ....Prov 29:17
But I will c you in ....Jer 30:11

CORRECTED
human fathers who c ....Heb 12:9

CORRECTION
nor detest His c ....Prov 3:11
but he who refuses c ....Prov 10:17
but he who hates c ....Prov 12:1
c will drive it ....Prov 22:15
Do not withhold c............Prov 23:13
they received no c ....Jer 2:30
for reproof, for c ....2 Tim 3:16

CORRECTS
is the man whom God c ....Job 5:17
the LORD loves He c ....Prov 3:12

CORRODED
and silver are c ....James 5:3

CORRUPT
have together become c ....Ps 14:3
have together become c ....Ps 53:3
old man which grows c ....Eph 4:22
men of c minds ....2 Tim 3:8
in these things they c ....Jude 10

CORRUPTED
for all flesh had c ....Gen 6:12
we have c no one ....2 Cor 7:2
so your minds may be c ....2 Cor 11:3
Your riches are c ....James 5:2
the great harlot who c ....Rev 19:2

CORRUPTIBLE
For this c must put on .....1 Cor 15:53
redeemed with c things .....1 Pet 1:18

CORRUPTION
Your Holy One to see c ....Ps 16:10
God raised up saw no c.....Acts 13:37
from the bondage of c ....Rom 8:21
The body is sown in c .....1 Cor 15:42
c inherit incorruption ......1 Cor 15:50
of the flesh reap c ....Gal 6:8
having escaped the c ....2 Pet 1:4
perish in their own c ....2 Pet 2:12

COST
and count the c...........Luke 14:28

COULD
has done what she c ....Mark 14:8
c remove mountains ....1 Cor 13:2
which no one c number ....Rev 7:9

COUNCILS
deliver you up to c ....Mark 13:9

COUNSEL
and strength, He has c ......Job 12:13
the c of the wicked is ....Job 21:16
when the friendly c ....Job 29:4
is this who darkens c ....Job 38:2
who walks not in the c ....Ps 1:1
We took sweet c ....Ps 55:14
guide me with Your c ....Ps 73:24
you disdained all my c ......Prov 1:25
have none of my c ....Prov 1:30
Where there is no c ....Prov 11:14
C in the heart of man ....Prov 20:5
by wise c wage war ....Prov 20:18
whom did He take c ....Is 40:14
You are great in c ....Jer 32:19
according to the c ....Eph 1:11
immutability of His c ....Heb 6:17
I c you to buy from ....Rev 3:18

COUNSELOR
be called Wonderful, C ....Is 9:6
but there was no c ....Is 41:28
Has your c perished ....Mic 4:9
who has become His c .....Rom 11:34

COUNSELORS
c there is safety ....Prov 11:14

COUNT
c the people of Israel ....2 Sam 24:4
c my life dear to ....Acts 20:24
c me as a partner ....Philem 17
His promise, as some c ....2 Pet 3:9

COUNTED
Even a fool is c ....Prov 17:28
c as the small dust ....Is 40:15
the wages are not c ....Rom 4:4
He c me faithful ....1 Tim 1:12
who rule well be c ....1 Tim 5:17

COUNTENANCE
The LORD lift up His c ......Num 6:26
c they did not cast ....Job 29:24
up the light of Your c ....Ps 4:6
His c is like Lebanon ....Song 5:15
with a sad c ....Matt 6:16
His c was like..................Matt 28:3
of the glory of his c ....2 Cor 3:7
sword, and His c ....Rev 1:16

COUNTRY
"Get out of your c ....Gen 12:1
good news from a far c .....Prov 25:25
and went into a far c ....Matt 21:33
as in a foreign c ....Heb 11:9
that is, a heavenly c ....Heb 11:16

COUNTRYMEN
for my brethren, my c ....Rom 9:3

COURAGE
strong and of good c ....Deut 31:6
thanked God and took c ....Acts 28:15

COURSE
and sets on fire the c........James 3:6

COURT
appoint my day in c ....Job 9:19
by you or by a human c .....1 Cor 4:3
They zealously c ....Gal 4:17

COURTEOUS
be tenderhearted, be c ....1 Pet 3:8

COURTS
he may dwell in Your c ....Ps 65:4
even faints for the c ....Ps 84:2
flourish in the c ....Ps 92:13
and into His c....................Ps 100:4
drink it in My holy c ....Is 62:9

COVENANT
I will establish My c ....Gen 6:18
the LORD made a c ....Gen 15:18
for Me, behold, My c ....Gen 17:4
as a perpetual c..............Ex 31:16
it is a c of salt ....Num 18:19
Remember His c forever ...1 Chr 16:15
"I have made a c ....Job 31:1
will show them His c ....Ps 25:14
c shall stand firm ....Ps 89:28
sons will keep My c ....Ps 132:12
and give You as a c ....Is 42:6
the words of this c ....Jer 11:2
I will make a new c ....Jer 31:31
'I made a c with your ....Jer 34:13
I might break the c ....Zech 11:10
the Messenger of the c ....Mal 3:1
cup is the new c ....Luke 22:20
c that was confirmed ....Gal 3:17
Mediator of a better c ....Heb 8:6
c had been faultless ....Heb 8:7
He says, "A new c ....Heb 8:13
Mediator of the new c ....Heb 12:24
of the everlasting c ....Heb 13:20

COVENANTED
your kingdom, as I c ....2 Chr 7:18
to the word that I c ....Hag 2:5

COVENANTS
the glory, the c..................Rom 9:4
these are the two c ....Gal 4:24

COVER
the rock, and will c ....Ex 33:22
He shall c you with ....Ps 91:4
c Yourself with light ....Ps 104:2
LORD as the waters c ....Is 11:9
and will no more c ....Is 26:21
from the wind and a c.............Is 32:2
not to c his head ....1 Cor 11:7
c a multitude of sins ....James 5:20

COVERED
The depths have c ....Ex 15:5
c my transgressions as ......Job 31:33
Whose sin is c ....Ps 32:1
the wings of a dove c..........Ps 68:13
c all their sin ....Ps 85:2
You c me in my ....Ps 139:13
with two he c his face ....Is 6:2
of Jacob will be c ....Is 27:9
You have c Yourself ....Lam 3:44
For there is nothing c ......Matt 10:26

COVERING
spread a cloud for a c ....Ps 105:39
make sackcloth their c ....Is 50:3
given to her for a c ....1 Cor 11:15

COVERINGS

and made themselves c ....Gen 3:7

COVET

"You shall not c ....Ex 20:17
c fields and take them ....Mic 2:2
You murder and c ....James 4:2

COVETED

c no one's silver ....Acts 20:33

COVETOUS

nor thieves, nor c ....1 Cor 6:10
trained in c practices ....2 Pet 2:14

COVETOUSNESS

but he who hates c ....Prov 28:16
for nothing but your c ....Jer 22:17
heed and beware of c ......Luke 12:15
would not have known c .....Rom 7:7
all uncleanness or c ....Eph 5:3
conduct be without c ....Heb 13:5

COWARDLY

the c, unbelieving ....Rev 21:8

CRAFTILY

His people, to deal c ....Ps 105:25

CRAFTINESS

wise in their own c ....Job 5:13
not walking in c ....2 Cor 4:2
deceived Eve by his c ....2 Cor 11:3
in the cunning c ....Eph 4:14

CRAFTSMAN

instructor of every c ....Gen 4:22
c encouraged the ....Is 41:7
c stretches out his ....Is 44:13

CRAFTY

Jonadab was a very c ....2 Sam 13:3
the devices of the c ....Job 5:12
They have taken c ....Ps 83:3
of a harlot, and a c ....Prov 7:10
Nevertheless, being c ....2 Cor 12:16

CRANE

Like a c or a swallow ....Is 38:14

CRAVES

and his soul still c ....Is 29:8

CREAM

she brought out c ....Judg 5:25
were bathed with c ....Job 29:6

CREATE

peace and c calamity ....Is 45:7
For behold, I c ....Is 65:17

CREATED

So God c man in His ....Gen 1:27
Spirit, they are c ....Ps 104:30
and they were c ....Ps 148:5
and see who has c ....Is 40:26
of Israel has c ....Is 41:20
For the LORD has c ....Jer 31:22
Has not one God c ....Mal 2:10
Nor was man c for the ......1 Cor 11:9
c in Christ Jesus ....Eph 2:10
hidden in God who c ....Eph 3:9
new man which was c ....Eph 4:24
Him all things were c ....Col 1:16
from foods which God c .....1 Tim 4:3
for You c all things ....Rev 4:11

CREATION

c which God ....Mark 13:19
c was subjected ....Rom 8:20
know that the whole c ....Rom 8:22
Christ, he is a new c ....2 Cor 5:17
anything, but a new c ....Gal 6:15
firstborn over all c ....Col 1:15

CREATOR

Remember now your C ....Eccl 12:1
God, the LORD, the C ....Is 40:28
rather than the C ....Rom 1:25
to a faithful C ....1 Pet 4:19

CREATURE

the gospel to every c ....Mark 16:15
For every c of God is ....1 Tim 4:4
And there is no c ....Heb 4:13
And every c which is ....Rev 5:13
and every living c ....Rev 16:3

CREATURES

created great sea c ....Gen 1:21
firstfruits of His c ....James 1:18
were four living c ....Rev 4:6

CREDIT

who love you, what c ....Luke 6:32
For what c is it if ....1 Pet 2:20

CREDITOR

Every c who has lent ....Deut 15:2
c is coming to take my ....2 Kin 4:1
c seize all that he ....Ps 109:11
There was a certain c ....Luke 7:41

CREEP

of the forest c ....Ps 104:20
sort are those who c ....2 Tim 3:6

CREEPING

c thing and beast of ....Gen 1:24
every sort of c thing ....Ezek 8:10

CREPT

For certain men have c ....Jude 4

CRETE

Paul visits, Acts 27:7–21
Titus dispatched to, Titus 1:5
Inhabitants of, evil and lazy, Titus 1:12

CRIB

donkey its master's c ....Is 1:3

CRIED

the poor who c out ....Job 29:12
They c to You ....Ps 22:5
of the depths I have c ....Ps 130:1

CRIES

your brother's blood c ....Gen 4:10
with vehement c ....Heb 5:7

CRIMES

land is filled with c ....Ezek 7:23

CRIMINALS

also two others, c ....Luke 23:32

CRISPUS

Chief ruler of synagogue of Corinth, Acts 18:8
Baptized by Paul, 1 Cor 1:14

CROOKED

turn aside to their c ....Ps 125:5
whose ways are c ....Prov 2:15
c places shall be made ....Is 40:4
c places straight ....Is 45:2
c places shall be made ....Luke 3:5
in the midst of a c ....Phil 2:15

CROSS

does not take his c ....Matt 10:38
to bear His c ....Matt 27:32
down from the c ....Matt 27:40
lest the c of Christ ....1 Cor 1:17
persecution for the c ....Gal 6:12
boast except in the c ....Gal 6:14
one body through the c ......Eph 2:16
the enemies of the c ....Phil 3:18
Him endured the c ....Heb 12:2

CROWD

shall not follow a c ....Ex 23:2

CROWN

You set a c of pure ....Ps 21:3
c the year with Your ....Ps 65:11
have profaned his c ....Ps 89:39
upon Himself His c ....Ps 132:18
The c of the wise is ....Prov 14:24
head is a c of glory ....Prov 16:31
Woe to the c of pride ....Is 28:1
hosts will be for a c ....Is 28:5
c has fallen from our ....Lam 5:16
they had twisted a c ....Matt 27:29
obtain a perishable c ....1 Cor 9:25
brethren, my joy and c ....Phil 4:1
laid up for me the c ....2 Tim 4:8
he will receive the c ....James 1:12
no one may take your c ......Rev 3:11
on His head a golden c .....Rev 14:14

CROWNED

angels, and You have c ....Ps 8:5
but the prudent are c .....Prov 14:18
athletics, he is not c ....2 Tim 2:5
You have c him with glory ....Heb 2:7

CROWNS

and they had c of gold ....Rev 4:4
on his horns ten c ....Rev 13:1
His head were many c ......Rev 19:12

CRUCIFIED

"Let Him be c ....Matt 27:22
Calvary, there they c ......Luke 23:33
lawless hands, have c ....Acts 2:23
that our old man was c ....Rom 6:6
Was Paul c for you ....1 Cor 1:13
Jesus Christ and Him c ....1 Cor 2:2
they would not have c ....1 Cor 2:8
though He was c ....2 Cor 13:4
I have been c ....Gal 2:20

CRUCIFY

out again, "C Him ....Mark 15:13
I have power to c You ....John 19:10
since they c again ....Heb 6:6

CRUEL

wrath, for it is c ....Gen 49:7
spirit and c bondage ....Ex 6:9
hate me with c hatred ....Ps 25:19
of the wicked are c ....Prov 12:10

CRUELTY

of c are in their ....Gen 49:5

Interprets dreams; honored by king, Dan 2
Interprets handwriting on wall; honored by Belshazzar, Dan 5:10–29
Appointed to high office; conspired against and thrown to lions, Dan 6:1–23
Visions of four beasts, ram and goat, Dan 7; 8
Intercedes for Israel, Dan 9:1–19
Further visions, Dan 9:20—12:13

DARE

someone would even *d* ......Rom 5:7
D any of you ....1 Cor 6:1

DARIUS

Darius the Mede, son of Ahasuerus; made king of the Chaldeans, Dan 9:1
Succeeds Belshazzar, Dan 5:30, 31
Co-ruler with Cyrus, Dan 6:28
—— Darius Hystaspis (522–486 B.C.), king of all Persia; temple work dated by his reign, Ezra 4:5, 24
Confirms Cyrus's royal edict, Ezra 6:1–14
—— Darius the Persian (423–404 B.C.); priestly records kept during his reign, Neh 12:22

DARK

dwell in the *d* cloud ....1 Kin 8:12
I am *d* ....Song 1:5
d place of the earth ....Is 45:19
d places like the dead ....Lam 3:6
and makes the day *d* ....Amos 5:8
and the day shall be *d* ....Mic 3:6
I tell you in the *d* ....Matt 10:27
while it was still *d* ....John 20:1
shines in a *d* place ....2 Pet 1:19

DARKENED

so that the land was *d* ....Ex 10:15
Let their eyes be *d* ....Ps 69:23
their understanding *d* ....Eph 4:18

DARKNESS

d He called Night ....Gen 1:5
shall enlighten my *d* ......2 Sam 22:29
through the deep *d* ....Job 22:13
Those who sat in *d* ....Ps 107:10
d shall not hide ....Ps 139:12
d have seen a ....Is 9:2
I will make *d* light ....Is 42:16
and deep *d* the people ....Is 60:2
Israel, or a land of *d* ....Jer 2:31
body will be full of *d* ....Matt 6:23
cast out into outer *d* ....Matt 8:12
and the power of *d* ....Luke 22:53
d rather than light ....John 3:19
d does not know ....John 12:35
For you were once *d* ....Eph 5:8
the rulers of the *d* ....Eph 6:12
us from the power of *d* ....Col 1:13
of the night nor of *d* ....1 Thess 5:5
and to blackness and *d* .....Heb 12:18
called you out of *d* ....1 Pet 2:9
d is reserved ....2 Pet 2:17
and in Him is no *d* ....1 John 1:5
Him, and walk in *d* ....1 John 1:6
d is passing away ....1 John 2:8
blackness of *d* forever ....Jude 13

DARTS

quench all the fiery *d* ....Eph 6:16

DASH

You shall *d* them to ....Ps 2:9
lest you *d* your foot ....Matt 4:6

DASHED

hand, O LORD, has *d* ....Ex 15:6
also will be *d* to ....Is 13:16
infants shall be *d* ....Hos 13:16

DATHAN

Joins Korah's rebellion, Num 16:1–35
Swallowed up by the earth, Ps 106:17

DAUGHTER

had neither son nor *d* ....Judg 11:34
"Rejoice greatly, O *d* ....Zech 9:9
"Fear not, *d* of Zion ....John 12:15
the son of Pharaoh's *d* ....Heb 11:24

DAUGHTERS

he had sons and *d* ....Gen 5:4
of God saw the *d* ....Gen 6:2
a bird, and all the *d* ....Eccl 12:4
d shall prophesy ....Acts 2:17
man had four virgin *d* ....Acts 21:9
shall be My sons and *d* .....2 Cor 6:18

DAVID

Anointed by Samuel, 1 Sam 16:1–13
Becomes royal harpist, 1 Sam 16:14–23
Defeats Goliath, 1 Sam 17
Makes covenant with Jonathan, 1 Sam 18:1–4
Honored by Saul; loved by the people; Saul becomes jealous, 1 Sam 18:5–16
Wins Michal as wife, 1 Sam 18:17–30
Flees from Saul, 1 Sam 19; 20; 21:10—22:5; 23:14–29
Eats the holy bread, 1 Sam 21:1–6; Matt 12:3, 4
Saves Keilah from Philistines, 1 Sam 23:1–13
Twice spares Saul's life, 1 Sam 24:1–22; 26:1–25
Anger at Nabal appeased by Abigail; marries her, 1 Sam 25:2–42
Allies with the Philistines, 1 Sam 27:1—28:2
Rejected by them, 1 Sam 29
Avenges destruction of Ziklag, 1 Sam 30
Mourns death of Saul and Jonathan, 2 Sam 1
Anointed king of Judah, 2 Sam 2:1–7
War with Saul's house; Abner defects to David, 2 Sam 3:1, 6–21
Mourns Abner's death, 2 Sam 3:28–39
Punishes Ishbosheth's murderers, 2 Sam 4
Anointed king of all Israel, 2 Sam 5:1–5
Conquers Jerusalem; makes it his capital, 2 Sam 5:6–16
Defeats Philistines, 2 Sam 5:17–25
Brings ark to Jerusalem, 2 Sam 6
Receives eternal covenant, 2 Sam 7
Further conquests, 2 Sam 8; 10
Shows mercy to Mephibosheth, 2 Sam 9
Commits adultery and murder, 2 Sam 11
Rebuked by Nathan; repents, 2 Sam 12:1–23; Ps 32; 51
Absalom's rebellion, 2 Sam 15—18
Mourns Absalom's death, 2 Sam 18:33—19:8
Shows himself merciful, 2 Sam 19:18–39
Sheba's rebellion, 2 Sam 19:40—20:22
Avenges the Gibeonites, 2 Sam 21:1–14
Song of deliverance, 2 Sam 22
Sins by numbering the people, 2 Sam 24:1–17
Buys threshing floor to build altar, 2 Sam 24:18–25
Secures Solomon's succession, 1 Kin 1:5–53
Instructions to Solomon, 1 Kin 2:1–11
Last words, 2 Sam 23:1–7
Inspired by Spirit, Matt 22:43
As prophet, Acts 2:29–34
Faith of, Heb 11:32–34

DAY

God called the light *D* ....Gen 1:5
and *d* and night ....Gen 8:22
shall observe this *d* ....Ex 12:17
Remember the Sabbath *d* ......Ex 20:8
and cursed the *d* ....Job 3:1
d utters speech ....Ps 19:2
For a *d* in Your courts ....Ps 84:10
d the LORD has ....Ps 118:24
not strike you by *d* ....Ps 121:6
night shines as the *d* ....Ps 139:12
do not know what a *d* ....Prov 27:1
For the *d* of the LORD ....Joel 2:11
who put far off the *d* ....Amos 6:3
for the *d* of the LORD ....Zeph 1:7
who has despised the *d* .....Zech 4:10
who can endure the *d* ....Mal 3:2
d our daily bread ....Matt 6:11
and Gomorrah in the *d* .....Matt 10:15
sent Me while it is *d* ....John 9:4
great and awesome *d* ....Acts 2:20
person esteems one *d* ....Rom 14:5
D will declare it ....1 Cor 3:13
again the third *d* ....1 Cor 15:4
perfectly that the *d* ....1 Thess 5:2
and sons of the *d* ....1 Thess 5:5
with the Lord one *d* ....2 Pet 3:8

DAYS

d are swifter than a ....Job 7:6
Let me alone, for my *d* ....Job 7:16
of woman is of few *d* ....Job 14:1
blessed the latter *d* ....Job 42:12
The *d* of our lives are ....Ps 90:10
for length of *d* ....Prov 3:2
"Why were the former *d* .....Eccl 7:10
Before the difficult *d* ....Eccl 12:1
and tested them ten *d* ....Dan 1:14
had shortened those *d* .....Mark 13:20
raise it up in three *d* ....John 2:20
You observe *d* and ....Gal 4:10
life and see good *d* ....1 Pet 3:10

DAYSPRING

with which the *D* ....Luke 1:78

DEACONS

with the bishops and *d* ....Phil 1:1
d must be reverent ....1 Tim 3:8
d be the husbands ....1 Tim 3:12

DEAD

"We shall all be *d* ....Ex 12:33
he stood between the *d* .....Num 16:48
work wonders for the *d* ......Ps 88:10
who have long been *d* ....Ps 143:3
But the *d* know nothing ....Eccl 9:5
shall cast out the *d* ....Is 26:19
d bury their own *d* ....Matt 8:22
d are raised up and ....Matt 11:5

not the God of the *d* ....Matt 22:32
for this my son was *d* ......Luke 15:24
d will hear the voice ....John 5:25
was raised from the *d* ....Rom 6:4
yourselves to be *d* ....Rom 6:11
from the law sin was *d* ....Rom 7:8
be Lord of both the *d* ....Rom 14:9
resurrection of the *d* ....1 Cor 15:12
baptized for the *d* ....1 Cor 15:29
made alive, who were *d* ....Eph 2:1
And the *d* in Christ ....1 Thess 4:16
d while she lives ....1 Tim 5:6
without works is *d* ....James 2:26
d did not live again ....Rev 20:5
And the *d* were judged ......Rev 20:12

DEAD SEA

Called the:
Salt Sea, Gen 14:3
Sea of the Arabah, Deut 3:17

DEADLY

they drink anything *d* ......Mark 16:18
evil, full of *d* poison ....James 3:8
d wound was healed ....Rev 13:3

DEADNESS

the *d* of Sarah's womb ....Rom 4:19

DEAF

makes the mute, the *d* ....Ex 4:11
d shall hear the words ....Is 29:18
d shall be unstopped ....Is 35:5
d as My messenger ....Is 42:19
d who have ears ....Is 43:8
their ears shall be *d* ....Mic 7:16
are cleansed and the *d* .....Matt 11:5

DEAL

Do you thus *d* with the ......Deut 32:6
My Servant shall *d* ....Is 52:13

DEATH

Let me die the *d* ....Num 23:10
d parts you and me ....Ruth 1:17
and the shadow of *d* ....Job 10:21
You will bring me to *d* ....Job 30:23
For in *d* there is no ....Ps 6:5
I sleep the sleep of *d* ....Ps 13:3
of the shadow of *d* ....Ps 23:4
my soul from *d* ....Ps 56:13
can live and not see *d* ....Ps 89:48
house leads down to *d* ....Prov 2:18
who hate me love *d* ....Prov 8:36
D and life are in the ....Prov 18:21
swallow up *d* forever ....Is 25:8
no pleasure in the *d* ....Ezek 18:32
redeem them from *d* ....Hos 13:14
turns the shadow of *d* ....Amos 5:8
who shall not taste *d* ......Matt 16:28
but has passed from *d* ....John 5:24
he shall never see *d* ....John 8:51
Nevertheless *d* reigned ......Rom 5:14
as sin reigned in *d* ....Rom 5:21
D no longer has ....Rom 6:9
the wages of sin is *d* ....Rom 6:23
to bear fruit to *d* ....Rom 7:5
proclaim the Lord's *d* ......1 Cor 11:26
since by man came *d* ....1 Cor 15:21
D is swallowed up in ......1 Cor 15:54
The sting of *d* is sin ....1 Cor 15:56
we are the aroma of *d* ......2 Cor 2:16
d is working in us ....2 Cor 4:12
the world produces *d* ....2 Cor 7:10
to the point of *d* ....Phil 2:8
d crowned with glory ....Heb 2:9

who had the power of *d* ....Heb 2:14
that he did not see *d* ....Heb 11:5
brings forth *d* ....James 1:15
to God, being put to *d* ....1 Pet 3:18
is sin leading to *d* ....1 John 5:16
Be faithful until *d* ....Rev 2:10
Over such the second *d* ......Rev 20:6
shall be no more *d* ....Rev 21:4
which is the second *d* ....Rev 21:8

DEBIR

City of Judah; captured by Joshua, Josh 10:38, 39
Recaptured by Othniel; formerly called Kirjath Sepher, Josh 15:15–17; Judg 1:11–13

DEBORAH

A prophetess and judge, Judg 4:4–14
Composed song of triumph, Judg 5:1–31

DEBTOR

I am a *d* both to ....Rom 1:14
that he is a *d* to keep ....Gal 5:3

DEBTORS

as we forgive our *d* ....Matt 6:12
of his master's *d* ....Luke 16:5
brethren, we are *d* ....Rom 8:12
and they are their *d* ....Rom 15:27

DECEIT

spirit there is no *d* ....Ps 32:2
from speaking *d* ....Ps 34:13
d shall not dwell ....Ps 101:7
D is in the heart of ....Prov 12:20
Nor was any *d* in His ....Is 53:9
They hold fast to *d* ....Jer 8:5
in whom is no *d* ....John 1:47
"O full of all *d* ....Acts 13:10
philosophy and empty *d* ....Col 2:8
no sin, nor was *d* ....1 Pet 2:22
mouth was found no *d* ....Rev 14:5

DECEITFUL

deliver me from the *d* ....Ps 43:1
d men shall not ....Ps 55:23
of the wicked are *d* ....Prov 12:5
of an enemy are *d* ....Prov 27:6
"The heart is *d* ....Jer 17:9
are false apostles, *d* ....2 Cor 11:13

DECEITFULLY

an idol, nor sworn *d* ....Ps 24:4
the word of God *d* ....2 Cor 4:2

DECEITFULNESS

this world and the *d* ....Matt 13:22
hardened through the *d* ......Heb 3:13

DECEIVE

'Do not *d* yourselves ....Jer 37:9
rise up and *d* many ....Matt 24:11
wonders to *d* ....Matt 24:24
Let no one *d* himself ....1 Cor 3:18
Let no one *d* you with ....Eph 5:6
we have no sin, we *d* ....1 John 1:8

DECEIVED

"The serpent *d* ....Gen 3:13
d heart has turned him ....Is 44:20
by the commandment, *d* .....Rom 7:11
as the serpent *d* ....2 Cor 11:3
but the woman being *d* ....1 Tim 2:14

deceiving and being *d* ......2 Tim 3:13

DECEIVER

"But cursed be the *d* ....Mal 1:14
how that *d* said ....Matt 27:63
This is a *d* and an ....2 John 7

DECEIVES

heed that no one *d* ....Matt 24:4
d his own heart ....James 1:26

DECENTLY

all things be done *d* ....1 Cor 14:40

DECEPTION

d all the day long ....Ps 38:12

DECEPTIVE

you with *d* words ....2 Pet 2:3

DECISION

but its every *d* ....Prov 16:33
in the valley of *d* ....Joel 3:14

DECLARE

The heavens *d* the ....Ps 19:1
d Your name to My ....Ps 22:22
d what He had done ....Ps 66:16
d that the LORD is ....Ps 92:15
d His generation ....Is 53:8
"I will *d* Your name ....Heb 2:12
seen and heard we *d* ....1 John 1:3

DECLARED

the Father, He has *d* ....John 1:18
and *d* to be the Son of ....Rom 1:4

DECREE

"I will declare the *d* ....Ps 2:7
d which shall not pass ....Ps 148:6
in those days that a *d* ....Luke 2:1

DEDICATED

house and has not *d* ....Deut 20:5
every *d* thing in ....Ezek 44:29
first covenant was *d* ....Heb 9:18

DEDICATION

sacrifices at the *d* ....Ezra 6:17
it was the Feast of *D* ....John 10:22

DEED

d has been done ....Judg 19:30
you do a charitable *d* ....Matt 6:2
you do in word or *d* ....Col 3:17

DEEDS

Declare His *d* among ....Ps 9:11
vengeance on their *d* ....Ps 99:8
harlot by their own *d* ....Ps 106:39
declare His *d* among ....Is 12:4
they surpass the *d* ....Jer 5:28
because their *d* ....John 3:19
You do the *d* ....John 8:41
one according to his *d* ....Rom 2:6
you put to death the *d* ....Rom 8:13
shares in his evil *d* ....2 John 11

DEEP

LORD God caused a *d* ....Gen 2:21
He lays up the *d* ....Ps 33:7
D calls unto *d* ....Ps 42:7
In His hand are the *d* ....Ps 95:4
His wonders in the *d* ....Ps 107:24

put out in *d* darkness ....Prov 20:20
led them through the *d* ....Is 63:13
d closed around me ....Jon 2:5
d uttered its voice ....Hab 3:10
"Launch out into the *d* ....Luke 5:4
I have been in the *d* ....2 Cor 11:25

DEEPER

D than Sheol ....Job 11:8

DEEPLY

Drink, yes, drink *d* ....Song 5:1
But He sighed *d* ....Mark 8:12

DEER

"Naphtali is a *d* ....Gen 49:21
As the *d* pants for the ....Ps 42:1
shall leap like a *d* ....Is 35:6

DEFEATED

and Israel was *d* ....1 Sam 4:10

DEFECT

who has any *d* ....Lev 21:17

DEFEND

'For I will *d* this ....2 Kin 19:34
d my own ways before ......Job 13:15
D the poor and ....Ps 82:3
d the fatherless ....Is 1:17
of hosts *d* Jerusalem ....Is 31:5

DEFENDER

a *d* of widows ....Ps 68:5

DEFENSE

For wisdom is a *d* ....Eccl 7:12
d will be the ....Is 33:16
am appointed for the *d* ....Phil 1:17
d no one stood with me ......2 Tim 4:16
be ready to give a *d* ....1 Pet 3:15

DEFILE

the heart, and they *d* ....Matt 15:18
also these dreamers *d* ....Jude 8

DEFILED

d the dwelling place ....Ps 74:7
For your hands are *d* ....Is 59:3
lest they should be *d* ....John 18:28
to those who are *d* ....Titus 1:15
and conscience are *d* ....Titus 1:15
even the garment *d* ....Jude 23

DEFILES

mouth, this *d* a man ....Matt 15:11
d the temple of God ....1 Cor 3:17
it anything that *d* ....Rev 21:27

DEFRAUD

d his brother in this ....1 Thess 4:6

DEGENERATE

before Me into the *d* ....Jer 2:21
d is your heart ....Ezek 16:30

DEGREES

go forward ten *d* ....2 Kin 20:9

DELAIAH

Son of Shemaiah; urges Jehoiakim not to burn Jeremiah's scroll, Jer 36:12, 25

DELICACIES

let me eat of their *d* ....Ps 141:4
Do not desire his *d* ....Prov 23:3
of the king's *d* ....Dan 1:5

DELICATE

be called tender and *d* ....Is 47:1
a lovely and *d* woman ....Jer 6:2

DELIGHT

the LORD as great *d* ....1 Sam 15:22
And his heart took *d* ....2 Chr 17:6
Will he *d* himself in ....Job 27:10
But his *d* is in the ....Ps 1:2
D yourself also in the ....Ps 37:4
I *d* to do Your will ....Ps 40:8
Your law had been my *d* ....Ps 119:92
d ourselves with love ....Prov 7:18
And I was daily His *d* ....Prov 8:30
truthfully are His *d* ....Prov 12:22
And let your soul *d* ....Is 55:2
call the Sabbath a *d* ....Is 58:13
For I *d* in the law of ....Rom 7:22

DELIGHTED

The LORD *d* only in ....Deut 10:15

DELIGHTS

O love, with your *d* ....Song 7:6
For the LORD *d* in you ....Is 62:4
forever, because He *d* ....Mic 7:18

DELILAH

Deceives Samson, Judg 16:4–22

DELIVER

d them out of the hand ....Ex 3:8
He shall *d* you in six ....Job 5:19
is no one who can *d* ....Job 10:7
'*D* him from going down ......Job 33:24
Let Him *d* Him ....Ps 22:8
d their soul from ....Ps 33:19
I will *d* him and honor ....Ps 91:15
d you from the immoral ......Prov 2:16
wickedness will not *d* ....Eccl 8:8
have I no power to *d* ....Is 50:2
we serve is able to *d* ....Dan 3:17
into temptation, but *d* ....Matt 6:13
let Him *d* Him now if ....Matt 27:43
d such a one to Satan ....1 Cor 5:5
And the Lord will *d* ....2 Tim 4:18
d the godly out of ....2 Pet 2:9

DELIVERANCE

d He gives to His king ....Ps 18:50
but *d* is of the LORD ....Prov 21:31
not accepting *d* ....Heb 11:35

DELIVERED

d the poor who cried ....Job 29:12
for You have *d* my soul ....Ps 56:13
For He has *d* the life ....Jer 20:13
All things have been *d* ....Matt 11:27
who was *d* up because ....Rom 4:25
But now we have been *d* ....Rom 7:6
who *d* us from so great ....2 Cor 1:10
was once for all *d* ....Jude 3

DELIVERER

the LORD raised up a *d* ....Judg 3:9
LORD gave Israel a *d* ....2 Kin 13:5
D will come out of ....Rom 11:26

DELIVERERS

d who saved them ....Neh 9:27

DELIVERS

d the kingdom to God ....1 Cor 15:24
even Jesus who *d* ....1 Thess 1:10

DELUSION

send them strong *d* ....2 Thess 2:11

DEMAS

Follows Paul, Col 4:14
Forsakes Paul, 2 Tim 4:10

DEMETRIUS

A silversmith at Ephesus, Acts 19:24–31
—— A good Christian, 3 John 12

DEMON

Jesus rebuked the *d* ....Matt 17:18
you say, 'He has a *d* ....Luke 7:33
and have a *d* ....John 8:48

DEMONIC

is earthly, sensual, *d* ....James 3:15

DEMONS

They sacrificed to *d* ....Deut 32:17
their daughters to *d* ....Ps 106:37
authority over all *d* ....Luke 9:1
the *d* are subject ....Luke 10:17
Lord and the cup of *d* ....1 Cor 10:21
Even the *d* believe ....James 2:19
a dwelling place of *d* ....Rev 18:2

DEMONSTRATE

faith, to *d* His ....Rom 3:25

DEMONSTRATES

d His own love toward ....Rom 5:8

DEN

in the viper's *d* ....Is 11:8
by My name, become a *d* ....Jer 7:11
cast him into the *d* ....Dan 6:16
it a '*d* of thieves ....Matt 21:13

DENARIUS

the laborers for a *d* ....Matt 20:2
they brought Him a *d* ....Matt 22:19
quart of wheat for a *d* ....Rev 6:6

DENIED

before men will be *d* ....Luke 12:9
Peter then *d* again ....John 18:27
d the Holy One and the ....Acts 3:14
things cannot be *d* ....Acts 19:36
household, he has *d* ....1 Tim 5:8
word, and have not *d* ....Rev 3:8

DENIES

But whoever *d* ....Matt 10:33
d that Jesus is the ....1 John 2:22

DENS

lie down in their *d* ....Ps 104:22
and mountains, in *d* ....Heb 11:38

DENY

lest I be full and *d* ....Prov 30:9
let him *d* himself ....Matt 16:24
He cannot *d* Himself ....2 Tim 2:13
in works they *d* ....Titus 1:16
d the only Lord ....Jude 4
d My faith even ....Rev 2:13

DENYING

but *d* its power ....2 Tim 3:5

d ungodliness and .... Titus 2:12
d the Lord who bought .... 2 Pet 2:1

DEPART

scepter shall not *d* .... Gen 49:10
they say to God, '*D* .... Job 21:14
D from evil .... Ps 34:14
fear the LORD and *d* .... Prov 3:7
the mountains, shall *d* .... Is 54:10
on the left hand, '*D* .... Matt 25:41
will *d* from the faith .... 1 Tim 4:1

DEPARTED

the day that you *d* .... Deut 9:7

DEPARTING

heart of unbelief in *d* .... Heb 3:12

DEPARTURE

d savage wolves will .... Acts 20:29
and the time of my *d* .... 2 Tim 4:6

DEPRESSION

of man causes *d* .... Prov 12:25

DEPRIVE

d myself of good .... Eccl 4:8
d one another except .... 1 Cor 7:5

DEPTH

because they had no *d* ...... Matt 13:5
nor height nor *d* .... Rom 8:39
Oh, the *d* of the .... Rom 11:33
width and length and *d* .... Eph 3:18

DEPTHS

d have covered them .... Ex 15:5
The *d* also trembled .... Ps 77:16
my soul from the *d* .... Ps 86:13
led them through the *d* .... Ps 106:9
go down again to the *d* ...... Ps 107:26
d I was brought forth .... Prov 8:24
our sins into the *d* .... Mic 7:19
have not known the *d* .... Rev 2:24

DERANGED

the nations are *d* .... Jer 51:7

DERBE

Paul visits, Acts 14:6, 20
Paul meets Timothy at, Acts 16:1

DERISION

shall hold them in *d* .... Ps 2:4
I am in *d* daily .... Jer 20:7

DESCEND

His glory shall not *d* .... Ps 49:17
d now from the cross ...... Mark 15:32
Lord Himself will *d* .... 1 Thess 4:16
This wisdom does not *d* .... James 3:15

DESCENDANTS

All you *d* of Jacob .... Ps 22:23
d shall inherit the .... Ps 25:13
In the LORD all the *d* .... Is 45:25
"We are Abraham's *d* ...... John 8:33

DESCENDED

because the LORD *d* .... Ex 19:18
that He also first *d* .... Eph 4:9
He who *d* is also the .... Eph 4:10

DESCENDING

were ascending and *d* ...... Gen 28:12
"I saw the Spirit *d* .... John 1:32
God ascending and *d* .... John 1:51
the holy Jerusalem, *d* .... Rev 21:10

DESERT

d shall rejoice .... Is 35:1
and rivers in the *d* .... Is 43:19
'Look, He is in the *d* ...... Matt 24:26

DESERTED

d place by Himself .... Matt 14:13

DESERTS

led them through the *d* ...... Is 48:21
They wandered in *d* .... Heb 11:38

DESERVE

to them what they *d* .... Ps 28:4
d I will judge them .... Ezek 7:27

DESIGN

with an artistic *d* .... Ex 26:31
may keep its whole *d* ...... Ezek 43:11

DESIRABLE

the eyes, and a tree *d* .... Gen 3:6
d that we should leave .... Acts 6:2

DESIRE

d shall be for your .... Gen 3:16
for we do not *d* .... Job 21:14
him his heart's *d* .... Ps 21:2
Behold, You *d* truth in .... Ps 51:6
upon earth that I *d* .... Ps 73:25
the *d* of the wicked .... Ps 112:10
and satisfy the *d* .... Ps 145:16
The *d* of the lazy .... Prov 21:25
a burden, and *d* fails .... Eccl 12:5
the *d* of our soul is .... Is 26:8
d I have desired .... Luke 22:15
"Father, I *d* that .... John 17:24
all manner of evil *d* .... Rom 7:8
Brethren, my heart's *d* .... Rom 10:1
d the best gifts .... 1 Cor 12:31
d spiritual gifts .... 1 Cor 14:1
the two, having a *d* .... Phil 1:23
passion, evil *d* .... Col 3:5
d has conceived .... James 1:15

DESIRED

d are they than gold .... Ps 19:10
One thing I have *d* .... Ps 27:4
guides them to their *d* ...... Ps 107:30
What is *d* in a man is ...... Prov 19:22
Whatever my eyes *d* .... Eccl 2:10
desire I have *d* .... Luke 22:15

DESIRES

Who is the man who *d* .... Ps 34:12
shall give you the *d* .... Ps 37:4
the devil, and the *d* .... John 8:44
fulfilling the *d* .... Eph 2:3
not come from your *d* .... James 4:1

DESOLATE

on me, for I am *d* .... Ps 25:16
the wilderness in a *d* .... Ps 107:4
my children and am *d* .... Is 49:21
any more be termed *D* .... Is 62:4
to make your land *d* .... Jer 4:7
house is left to you *d* ...... Matt 23:38
one hour she is made *d* ..... Rev 18:19

DESOLATION

the 'abomination of *d* .... Matt 24:15
then know that its *d* .... Luke 21:20

DESOLATIONS

LORD, who has made *d* .... Ps 46:8

DESPAIRED

turned my heart and *d* .... Eccl 2:20
strength, so that we *d* .... 2 Cor 1:8

DESPERATELY

he flees *d* from its .... Job 27:22

DESPISE

if you *d* My statutes .... Lev 26:15
d Me shall be lightly .... 1 Sam 2:30
d your mother when she .... Prov 23:22
d your feast days .... Amos 5:21
to you priests who *d* .... Mal 1:6
one and *d* the other .... Matt 6:24
d the riches of His .... Rom 2:4
d the church of God ...... 1 Cor 11:22
and *d* authority .... 2 Pet 2:10

DESPISED

poor man's wisdom is *d* ...... Eccl 9:16
d the word of the Holy .... Is 5:24
He is *d* and rejected .... Is 53:3
the things which are *d* ...... 1 Cor 1:28

DESPISES

wisdom *d* his neighbor ...... Prov 11:12
d the word will be .... Prov 13:13
d his neighbor sins .... Prov 14:21
but a foolish man *d* .... Prov 15:20
d the scepter of My .... Ezek 21:10

DESPISING

the cross, *d* the shame .... Heb 12:2

DESTINY

did not consider her *d* .... Lam 1:9

DESTITUTE

the prayer of the *d* .... Ps 102:17
of corrupt minds and *d* .... 1 Tim 6:5
sister is naked and *d* .... James 2:15

DESTROY

d the righteous .... Gen 18:23
d all the wicked .... Ps 101:8
of the LORD I will *d* .... Ps 118:10
the wicked He will *d* .... Ps 145:20
Why should you *d* .... Eccl 7:16
shall not hurt nor *d* .... Is 11:9
have mercy, but will *d* .... Jer 13:14
d them with double .... Jer 17:18
I did not come to *d* .... Matt 5:17
Him who is able to *d* .... Matt 10:28
Barabbas and *d* Jesus ...... Matt 27:20
d this temple .... Mark 14:58
to save life or to *d* .... Luke 6:9
d men's lives but to .... Luke 9:56
d the work of God for ...... Rom 14:20
d the wisdom of the .... 1 Cor 1:19
foods, but God will *d* .... 1 Cor 6:13
able to save and to *d* .... James 4:12

DESTROYED

d all living things .... Gen 7:23
d those who hated me ..... 2 Sam 22:41
My people are *d* .... Hos 4:6
"O Israel, you are *d* .... Hos 13:9
house, this tent, is *d* .... 2 Cor 5:1

DESTROYER

the paths of the *d* .... Ps 17:4

him who is a great *d* ....Prov 18:9
destroyed by the *d*..........1 Cor 10:10

DESTRUCTION

not be afraid of *d* ....Job 5:21
D has no covering ....Job 26:6
d come upon him..................Ps 35:8
cast them down to *d*............Ps 73:18
You turn man to *d* ....Ps 90:3
d that lays waste ....Ps 91:6
your life from *d* ....Ps 103:4
d will come to the ....Prov 10:29
Pride goes before *d* ....Prov 16:18
d the heart of a man ....Prov 18:12
called the City of *D* ....Is 19:18
neither wasting nor *d* ....Is 60:18
heifer, but *d* comes ....Jer 46:20
wrath prepared for *d* ....Rom 9:22
one to Satan for the *d*...........1 Cor 5:5
whose end is *d* ....Phil 3:19
then sudden *d* ....1 Thess 5:3
with everlasting *d* ....2 Thess 1:9
which drown men in *d* ....1 Tim 6:9
twist to their own *d* ....2 Pet 3:16

DESTRUCTIVE

bring in *d* heresies ....2 Pet 2:1

DETERMINED

Since his days are *d*...............Job 14:5
of hosts will make a *d* ....Is 10:23
"Seventy weeks are *d*..............Dan 9:24
d their preappointed ....Acts 17:26
For I *d* not to know ....1 Cor 2:2

DETESTABLE

shall not eat any *d* ....Deut 14:3

DEVICE

there is no work or *d* ....Eccl 9:10

DEVICES

not ignorant of his *d*...............2 Cor 2:11

DEVIL

to be tempted by the *d* ....Matt 4:1
prepared for the *d*..................Matt 25:41
forty days by the *d* ....Luke 4:2
then the *d* comes and ....Luke 8:12
and one of you is a *d*................John 6:70
of your father the *d* ....John 8:44
d having already put ....John 13:2
give place to the *d* ....Eph 4:27
the wiles of the *d* ....Eph 6:11
the snare of the *d* ....2 Tim 2:26
Resist the *d* and he ....James 4:7
the works of the *d* ....1 John 3:8
contending with the *d* ....Jude 9
Indeed, the *d* is about ....Rev 2:10

DEVIOUS

crooked, and who are *d* ....Prov 2:15

DEVISE

Do not *d* evil against ....Prov 3:29
Woe to those who *d* ....Mic 2:1

DEVISES

d wickedness on his ....Ps 36:4
he *d* evil continually ....Prov 6:14
d wicked plans to ....Is 32:7
But a generous man *d* ....Is 32:8

DEVOID

He who is *d* of wisdom ....Prov 11:12

DEVOTED

d offering is most ....Lev 27:28
"Every *d* thing in ....Num 18:14
Your servant, who is *d* ....Ps 119:38

DEVOUR

A fire shall *d* before ....Ps 50:3
For you *d* widows' ....Matt 23:14
bite and *d* one another ....Gal 5:15
seeking whom he may *d* ....1 Pet 5:8
d her Child as ....Rev 12:4

DEVOURED

Some wild beast has *d* ....Gen 37:20
rebel, you shall be *d* ....Is 1:20
the curse has *d* ....Is 24:6
Your sword has *d* ....Jer 2:30
For shame has *d*...........................Jer 3:24
have *d* their judges ....Hos 7:7
trees, the locust *d* ....Amos 4:9
birds came and *d* them ....Matt 13:4
of heaven and *d* them ....Rev 20:9

DEVOURER

I will rebuke the *d*.........................Mal 3:11

DEVOURING

You love all *d* words ....Ps 52:4
the flame of *d* fire ....Is 29:6

DEVOUT

man was just and *d* ....Luke 2:25
d men carried ....Acts 8:2
d soldier from among ....Acts 10:7
d proselytes ....Acts 13:43

DEW

God give you of the *d*...................Gen 27:28
shall also drop *d* ....Deut 33:28
his favor is like *d* ....Prov 19:12
your *d* is like the *d* ....Is 26:19
like the early *d* ....Hos 6:4
many peoples, like *d* ....Mic 5:7

DIADEM

LORD, and a royal *d* ....Is 62:3

DIADEMS

ten horns, and seven *d* ....Rev 12:3

DIAMOND

d it is engraved...............................Jer 17:1

DIBON

Amorite town, Num 21:30
Taken by Israel, Num 32:2–5
Destruction of, foretold, Jer 48:18, 22

DICTATES

according to the *d* ....Jer 23:17

DIE

it you shall surely *d*.........................Gen 2:17
but a person shall *d* ....2 Chr 25:4
sees wise men *d* ....Ps 49:10
I shall not *d* ....Ps 118:17
who are appointed to *d* ....Prov 31:8
how does a wise man *d* ....Eccl 2:16
born, and a time to *d* ....Eccl 3:2
why should you *d* ....Eccl 7:17
wicked way, he shall *d* ....Ezek 3:19
"Even if I have to *d* ....Matt 26:35
nor can they *d* ....Luke 20:36
eat of it and not *d* ....John 6:50

to you that you will *d* ....John 8:24
though he may *d* ....John 11:25
that one man should *d* ....John 11:50
that Jesus would *d* ....John 11:51
our law He ought to *d* ....John 19:7
the flesh you will *d* ....Rom 8:13
For as in Adam all *d* ....1 Cor 15:22
and to *d* is gain ....Phil 1:21
for men to *d* once ....Heb 9:27
are the dead who *d* ....Rev 14:13

DIED

And all flesh *d*...............................Gen 7:21
"Oh, that we had *d* ....Ex 16:3
was that the beggar *d* ....Luke 16:22
in due time Christ *d* ....Rom 5:6
Christ *d* for us ....Rom 5:8
For he who has *d* ....Rom 6:7
Now if we *d* with ....Rom 6:8
sin revived and I *d* ....Rom 7:9
that if One *d* for all ....2 Cor 5:14
and He *d* for all ....2 Cor 5:15
through the law *d* ....Gal 2:19
who *d* for us ....1 Thess 5:10
for if we *d* with Him ....2 Tim 2:11
These all *d* in faith ....Heb 11:13
having *d* to sins ....1 Pet 2:24

DIES

made alive unless it *d* ....1 Cor 15:36

DIFFERS

for one star *d* from ....1 Cor 15:41

DIFFUSED

By what way is light *d* ....Job 38:24

DILIGENCE

d is man's ....Prov 12:27
d it produced in you ....2 Cor 7:11
of your love by the *d* ....2 Cor 8:8

DILIGENT

and my spirit makes *d* ....Ps 77:6
d makes rich ....Prov 10:4
of the *d* will rule ....Prov 12:24
d shall be made rich ....Prov 13:4
Let us therefore be *d* ....Heb 4:11

DILIGENTLY

d followed every good ....1 Tim 5:10
d lest anyone fall ....Heb 12:15

DIM

His eyes were not *d* ....Deut 34:7
the windows grow *d* ....Eccl 12:3
the gold has become *d* ....Lam 4:1

DIMLY

we see in a mirror, *d* ....1 Cor 13:12

DINAH

Daughter of Leah, Gen 30:20, 21
Defiled by Shechem, Gen 34:1–24
Avenged by brothers, Gen 34:25–31

DINE

asked Him to *d* with ....Luke 11:37
come in to him and *d* ....Rev 3:20

DINNER

I have prepared my *d* ....Matt 22:4
invites you to *d* ....1 Cor 10:27

DIOTREPHES

Unruly church member, 3 John 9, 10

DIP
d your piece of bread ....Ruth 2:14

DIPPED
d his finger in the ....Lev 9:9
of bread when I have *d* .....John 13:26
clothed with a robe *d* ....Rev 19:13

DIRECT
the morning I will *d* ....Ps 5:3
d their work in truth ....Is 61:8
Now may the Lord *d* ....2 Thess 3:5

DIRT
I cast them out like *d* ....Ps 18:42
cast up mire and *d* ....Is 57:20

DISAPPEARS
As water *d* from the ....Job 14:11

DISARMED
d principalities ....Col 2:15

DISARMS
and *d* the mighty ....Job 12:21

DISASTER
D will come upon ....Ezek 7:26
you shall see *d* ....Zeph 3:15
voyage will end with *d* .....Acts 27:10

DISCERN
Can I *d* between the ....2 Sam 19:35
Then you shall again *d* ....Mal 3:18
d the face of the sky ....Matt 16:3
senses exercised to *d* ....Heb 5:14

DISCERNED
they are spiritually *d* ....1 Cor 2:14

DISCERNER
d of the thoughts ....Heb 4:12

DISCERNMENT
and takes away the *d* ....Job 12:20

DISCERNS
a wise man's heart *d* ....Eccl 8:5

DISCIPLE
d is not above his ....Matt 10:24
in the name of a *d* ....Matt 10:42
he cannot be My *d* ....Luke 14:26
d whom Jesus loved ....John 21:7

DISCIPLES
but Your *d* do not fast ....Matt 9:14
d transgress the ....Matt 15:2
took the twelve *d* ....Matt 20:17
My word, you are My *d* ....John 8:31
to become His *d* ....John 9:27
but we are Moses' *d* ....John 9:28
so you will be My *d* ....John 15:8

DISCIPLINE
Harsh *d* is for him who .....Prov 15:10

DISCIPLINES
but he who loves him *d* ......Prov 13:24

DISCLOSE
d my dark saying ....Ps 49:4

DISCORD
and one who sows *d* ....Prov 6:19

DISCOURAGED
will not fail nor be *d* ....Is 42:4
lest they become *d* ....Col 3:21
you become weary and *d* ....Heb 12:3

DISCRETION
D will preserve you ....Prov 2:11
out knowledge and *d* ....Prov 8:12
woman who lacks *d* ....Prov 11:22
The *d* of a man makes ....Prov 19:11
the heavens at His *d* ....Jer 10:12

DISFIGURE
d their faces that ....Matt 6:16

DISGUISES
and he *d* his face ....Job 24:15
He who hates, *d* ....Prov 26:24

DISHONOR
d who wish me evil ....Ps 40:14
d the pride of all ....Is 23:9
My Father, and you *d* Me ....John 8:49
d their bodies among ....Rom 1:24
and another for *d* ....Rom 9:21
It is sown in *d* ....1 Cor 15:43
honor and some for *d* ....2 Tim 2:20

DISHONORED
But you have *d* the ....James 2:6

DISHONORS
For son *d* father ....Mic 7:6
covered, *d* his head ....1 Cor 11:4

DISOBEDIENCE
d many were made ....Rom 5:19
works in the sons of *d* ....Eph 2:2
d received a just ....Heb 2:2

DISOBEDIENT
out My hands to a *d* ....Rom 10:21
d, deceived, serving ....Titus 3:3
They stumble, being *d* ....1 Pet 2:8
who formerly were *d* ....1 Pet 3:20

DISORDERLY
for this *d* gathering ....Acts 19:40
brother who walks *d* ....2 Thess 3:6

DISPENSATION
d of the fullness of ....Eph 1:10
d of the grace of God ....Eph 3:2

DISPERSE
d them throughout the .....Ezek 20:23

DISPERSION
intend to go to the *D* ....John 7:35
the pilgrims of the *D* ....1 Pet 1:1

DISPLEASE
LORD see it, and it *d* ....Prov 24:18

DISPLEASED
that David had done *d* ....2 Sam 11:27
You have been *d* ....Ps 60:1
they were greatly *d* ....Matt 20:24
it, He was greatly *d* ....Mark 10:14

DISPUTE
Now there was also a *d* ...Luke 22:24

DISPUTER
Where is the *d* of this ....1 Cor 1:20

DISPUTES
d rather than godly ....1 Tim 1:4
but is obsessed with *d* ....1 Tim 6:4
foolish and ignorant *d* ....2 Tim 2:23
But avoid foolish *d* ....Titus 3:9

DISQUALIFIED
myself should become *d* ....1 Cor 9:27
indeed you are *d* ....2 Cor 13:5
though we may seem *d* ....2 Cor 13:7

DISQUIETED
And why are you *d* ....Ps 42:5

DISSENSION
had no small *d* and ....Acts 15:2

DISSENSIONS
selfish ambitions, *d* ....Gal 5:20

DISSIPATION
not accused of *d* ....Titus 1:6
in the same flood of *d* ....1 Pet 4:4

DISSOLVED
of heaven shall be *d* ....Is 34:4
the heavens will be *d* ....2 Pet 3:12

DISTINCTION
and made no *d* ....Acts 15:9
For there is no *d* ....Rom 10:12
compassion, making a *d* ....Jude 22

DISTRESS
me in the day of my *d* ....Gen 35:3
When you are in *d* ....Deut 4:30
my life from every *d* ....1 Kin 1:29
you out of dire *d* ....Job 36:16
keep you from *d* ....Job 36:19
d them in His deep ....Ps 2:5
on the LORD in *d* ....Ps 118:5
a whirlwind, when *d* ....Prov 1:27
and on the earth *d* ....Luke 21:25
tribulation, or *d* ....Rom 8:35
of the present *d* ....1 Cor 7:26

DISTRESSED
heart within me is *d* ....Ps 143:4
troubled and deeply *d* ....Mark 14:33

DISTRESSES
bring me out of my *d* ....Ps 25:17

DISTRIBUTE
that you have and *d* ....Luke 18:22

DISTRIBUTED
and they *d* to each as ....Acts 4:35
But as God has *d* ....1 Cor 7:17

DISTRIBUTING
d to the needs of the ....Rom 12:13

DITCH
will fall into a *d* ....Matt 15:14

DIVERSITIES
There are *d* ....1 Cor 12:4

DIVIDE
D the living child ....1 Kin 3:25
d their tongues ....Ps 55:9
d the spoil with the ....Prov 16:19
d the inheritance ....Luke 12:13

d that was cast ....Matt 13:47

DRAGON

a great, fiery red *d* ....Rev 12:3
fought with the *d* ....Rev 12:7
they worshiped the *d* ....Rev 13:4
He laid hold of the *d* ....Rev 20:2

DRAIN

wicked of the earth *d* ....Ps 75:8

DRAINED

all faces are *d* ....Joel 2:6

DRANK

them, and they all *d* ....Mark 14:23
d the same spiritual ....1 Cor 10:4

DRAW

d honey from the rock ....Deut 32:13
me to *d* near to God ....Ps 73:28
and the years *d* ....Eccl 12:1
D me away ....Song 1:4
Woe to those who *d* ....Is 5:18
with joy you will *d* ....Is 12:3
"*D* some out now ....John 2:8
You have nothing to *d* ....John 4:11
will *d* all peoples ....John 12:32
let us *d* near with a ....Heb 10:22
D near to God and He ....James 4:8

DRAWN

The wicked have *d* ....Ps 37:14
tempted when he is *d* ....James 1:14

DRAWS

and my life *d* near to ....Ps 88:3
your redemption *d* ....Luke 21:28

DREAD

fear of you and the *d* ....Gen 9:2
begin to put the *d* ....Deut 2:25

DREADFUL

of the great and *d* ....Mal 4:5

DREAM

Now Joseph had a *d* ....Gen 37:5
I speak to him in a *d* ....Num 12:6
will fly away like a *d* ....Job 20:8
As a *d* when one awakes ....Ps 73:20
like those who *d* ....Ps 126:1
For a *d* comes through ....Eccl 5:3
her, shall be as a *d* ....Is 29:7
prophet who has a *d* ....Jer 23:28
do not let the *d* ....Dan 4:19
your old men shall *d* ....Joel 2:28
to Joseph in a *d* ....Matt 2:13
things today in a *d* ....Matt 27:19
your old men shall *d* ....Acts 2:17

DREAMERS

d defile the flesh ....Jude 8

DREAMS

in the multitude of *d* ....Eccl 5:7
when a hungry man *d* ....Is 29:8
Nebuchadnezzar had *d* ....Dan 2:1

DREGS

d shall all the wicked ....Ps 75:8
has settled on his *d* ....Jer 48:11

DRIED

My strength is *d* ....Ps 22:15
of her blood was *d* ....Mark 5:29
saw the fig tree *d* ....Mark 11:20
and its water was *d* ....Rev 16:12

DRIFT

have heard, lest we *d* ....Heb 2:1

DRINK

"What shall we *d* ....Ex 15:24
"Do not *d* wine or ....Lev 10:9
and let him *d* of the ....Job 21:20
gave me vinegar to *d* ....Ps 69:21
D water from your own ....Prov 5:15
mocker, strong *d* ....Prov 20:1
lest they *d* and forget ....Prov 31:5
Give strong *d* to him ....Prov 31:6
Let him *d* and forget ....Prov 31:7
d your wine with a ....Eccl 9:7
follow intoxicating *d* ....Is 5:11
mixing intoxicating *d* ....Is 5:22
d the milk of the ....Is 60:16
My servants shall *d* ....Is 65:13
bosom, that you may *d* ....Is 66:11
d water by measure ....Ezek 4:11
"Bring wine, let us *d* ....Amos 4:1
to you of wine and *d* ....Mic 2:11
and you gave Me no *d* ....Matt 25:42
that day when I *d* ....Matt 26:29
mingled with gall to *d* ....Matt 27:34
with myrrh to *d* ....Mark 15:23
to her, "Give Me a *d* ....John 4:7
him come to Me and *d* ....John 7:37
d wine nor do anything ....Rom 14:21
do, as often as you *d* ....1 Cor 11:25
all been made to *d* ....1 Cor 12:13
No longer *d* only water ....1 Tim 5:23
has made all nations *d* ....Rev 14:8

DRINKS

to her, "Whoever *d* ....John 4:13
d My blood has ....John 6:54
For he who eats and *d* ....1 Cor 11:29
For the earth which *d* ....Heb 6:7

DRIPPING

wife are a continual *d* ....Prov 19:13
His lips are lilies, *d* ....Song 5:13

DRIVE

of the wicked *d* ....Ps 36:11
They shall *d* you from ....Dan 4:25
temple and began to *d* ....Mark 11:15

DRIVEN

They were *d* out from ....Job 30:5
Let them be *d* backward ....Ps 40:14
sail and so were *d* ....Acts 27:17
a wave of the sea *d* ....James 1:6

DROP

They *d* on the pastures ....Ps 65:12
the nations are as a *d* ....Is 40:15

DROSS

of the earth like *d* ....Ps 119:119
Take away the *d* ....Prov 25:4
purge away your *d* ....Is 1:25
of Israel has become *d* ....Ezek 22:18

DROUGHT

through a land of *d* ....Jer 2:6
in the year of *d* ....Jer 17:8
For I called for a *d* ....Hag 1:11

DROVE

So He *d* out the man ....Gen 3:24
temple of God and *d* ....Matt 21:12
a whip of cords, He *d* ....John 2:15

DROWN

nor can the floods *d* ....Song 8:7
harmful lusts which *d* ....1 Tim 6:9

DROWSINESS

d will clothe a ....Prov 23:21

DRUNK

of the wine and was *d* ....Gen 9:21
d my wine with my milk ....Song 5:1
you afflicted, and *d* ....Is 51:21
My anger, made them *d* ....Is 63:6
be satiated and made *d* ....Jer 46:10
the guests have well *d* ....John 2:10
For these are not *d* ....Acts 2:15
and another is *d* ....1 Cor 11:21
And do not be *d* ....Eph 5:18
and those who get *d* ....1 Thess 5:7
the earth were made *d* ....Rev 17:2
I saw the woman, *d* ....Rev 17:6

DRUNKARD

d could be included ....Deut 29:19
d is a proverb in the ....Prov 26:9
to and fro like a *d* ....Is 24:20
or a reviler, or a *d* ....1 Cor 5:11

DRUNKEN

I am like a *d* man ....Jer 23:9

DRUNKENNESS

will be filled with *d* ....Ezek 23:33
Jerusalem a cup of *d* ....Zech 12:2
with carousing, *d* ....Luke 21:34
not in revelry and *d* ....Rom 13:13
envy, murders, *d* ....Gal 5:21
lusts, *d* ....1 Pet 4:3

DRUSILLA

Wife of Felix; hears Paul, Acts 24:24, 25

DRY

place, and let the *d* ....Gen 1:9
made the sea into *d* ....Ex 14:21
It was *d* on the fleece ....Judg 6:40
I will *d* up her sea ....Jer 51:36
d tree flourish ....Ezek 17:24
will make the rivers *d* ....Ezek 30:12
will be done in the *d* ....Luke 23:31

DUE

because it is your *d* ....Lev 10:13
their food in *d* season ....Ps 104:27
pay all that was *d* ....Matt 18:34
d time Christ died ....Rom 5:6
to whom taxes are *d* ....Rom 13:7
d season we shall ....Gal 6:9
exalt you in *d* time ....1 Pet 5:6

DULL

heart of this people *d* ....Is 6:10
people have grown *d* ....Matt 13:15
you have become *d* ....Heb 5:11

DUMB

the tongue of the *d* ....Is 35:6
"Deaf and *d* spirit ....Mark 9:25

DUNGHILL

the land nor for the *d* ....Luke 14:35

DUST

formed man of the *d* ....Gen 2:7

d you shall return ....Gen 3:19
descendants as the *d* ....Gen 13:16
now, I who am but *d* ....Gen 18:27
"Who can count the *d* ....Num 23:10
lay your gold in the *d* ....Job 22:24
and repent in *d* ....Job 42:6
Will the *d* praise You ....Ps 30:9
like the whirling *d* ....Ps 83:13
show favor to her *d* ....Ps 102:14
that we are *d* ....Ps 103:14
or the primal *d* ....Prov 8:26
all are from the *d* ....Eccl 3:20
counted as the small *d* ....Is 40:15
They shall lick the *d* ....Mic 7:17
city, shake off the *d* ....Matt 10:14
image of the man of *d* ....1 Cor 15:49

DUTY

done what was our *d* ....Luke 17:10

DWELL

O LORD, make me *d* ....Ps 4:8
Who may *d* in Your holy ....Ps 15:1
He himself shall *d* ....Ps 25:13
d in the land ....Ps 37:3
the LORD God might *d* ....Ps 68:18
of my God than *d* ....Ps 84:10
Him, that glory may *d* ....Ps 85:9
Woe is me, that I *d* ....Ps 120:5
he will *d* on high ....Is 33:16
into Egypt to *d* there ....Is 52:4
"I *d* in the high and ....Is 57:15
"They shall no longer *d* ....Lam 4:15
they enter and *d* there ....Matt 12:45
of Judea and all who *d* ....Acts 2:14
"I will *d* in them ....2 Cor 6:16
that Christ may *d* ....Eph 3:17
the fullness should *d* ....Col 1:19
the word of Christ *d* ....Col 3:16
men, and He will *d* ....Rev 21:3

DWELLER

fled and became a *d* ....Acts 7:29

DWELLING

A people *d* alone ....Num 23:9
is the way to the *d* ....Job 38:19
built together for a *d* ....Eph 2:22
a foreign country, *d* ....Heb 11:9

DWELLS

He who *d* in the secret ....Ps 91:1
but the Father who *d* ....John 14:10
do it, but sin that *d* ....Rom 7:17
the Spirit of God *d* ....Rom 8:9
from the dead *d* ....Rom 8:11
the Spirit of God *d* ....1 Cor 3:16
d all the fullness ....Col 2:9
which righteousness *d* ....2 Pet 3:13
you, where Satan *d* ....Rev 2:13

DWELT

Egypt, and Jacob *d* ....Ps 105:23
became flesh and *d* ....John 1:14
By faith he *d* in the ....Heb 11:9

DYING

I do not object to *d* ....Acts 25:11
in the body the *d* ....2 Cor 4:10
Jacob, when he was *d* ....Heb 11:21

— E —

EAGLE

As an *e* stirs up its ....Deut 32:11
e swooping on its prey ....Job 9:26
fly away like an *e* ....Prov 23:5
The way of an *e* ....Prov 30:19
nest as high as the *e* ....Jer 49:16
had the face of an *e* ....Ezek 1:10
like a flying *e* ....Rev 4:7
two wings of a great *e* ....Rev 12:14

EAGLES

up with wings like *e* ....Is 40:31
are swifter than *e* ....Jer 4:13
e will be gathered ....Matt 24:28

EAGLES'

how I bore you on *e* ....Ex 19:4

EAR

shall pierce his *e* ....Ex 21:6
Does not the *e* test ....Job 12:11
Bow down Your *e* ....Ps 31:2
And the *e* of the wise ....Prov 18:15
He awakens My *e* ....Is 50:4
e is uncircumcised ....Jer 6:10
what you hear in the *e* ....Matt 10:27
cut off his right *e* ....John 18:10
not seen, nor *e* heard ....1 Cor 2:9
if the *e* should say ....1 Cor 12:16
He who has an *e* ....Rev 2:7

EARLY

Very *e* in the morning ....Mark 16:2
arrived at the tomb *e* ....Luke 24:22

EARNEST

must give the more *e* ....Heb 2:1

EARNESTLY

if you *e* obey My ....Deut 11:13
He prayed more *e* ....Luke 22:44
in this we groan, *e* ....2 Cor 5:2
e that it would not ....James 5:17
you to contend *e* ....Jude 3

EARS

both his *e* will tingle ....2 Kin 21:12
Whoever shuts his *e* ....Prov 21:13
And hear with their *e* ....Is 6:10
He who has *e* ....Matt 11:15
e are hard of hearing ....Matt 13:15
they have itching *e* ....2 Tim 4:3
e are open to their ....1 Pet 3:12

EARTH

e which is under you ....Deut 28:23
e are the LORD'S ....1 Sam 2:8
coming to judge the *e* ....1 Chr 16:33
service for man on *e* ....Job 7:1
He hangs the *e* on ....Job 26:7
foundations of the *e* ....Job 38:4
e is the LORD'S ....Ps 24:1
the shields of the *e* ....Ps 47:9
You visit the *e* ....Ps 65:9
You had formed the *e* ....Ps 90:2
let the *e* be moved ....Ps 99:1
glory is above the *e* ....Ps 148:13
wisdom founded the *e* ....Prov 3:19
there was ever an *e* ....Prov 8:23
For three things the *e* ....Prov 30:21
e abides forever ....Eccl 1:4
for the meek of the *e* ....Is 11:4
e is My footstool ....Is 66:1
and the *e* shone with ....Ezek 43:2
I will darken the *e* ....Amos 8:9
e will be filled ....Hab 2:14
shall inherit the *e* ....Matt 5:5
heaven and *e* pass away ....Matt 5:18
e as it is in heaven ....Matt 6:10
treasures on *e* ....Matt 6:19
then shook the *e* ....Heb 12:26
"Do not harm the *e* ....Rev 7:3
from whose face the *e* ....Rev 20:11
new heaven and a new *e* ....Rev 21:1

EARTHLY

If I have told you *e* ....John 3:12
that if our *e* house ....2 Cor 5:1
their mind on *e* things ....Phil 3:19
from above, but is *e* ....James 3:15

EARTHQUAKE

after the wind an *e* ....1 Kin 19:11
as you fled from the *e* ....Zech 14:5
there was a great *e* ....Matt 28:2
there was a great *e* ....Rev 6:12

EARTHQUAKES

And there will be *e* ....Mark 13:8

EASE

I was at *e* ....Job 16:12
you women who are at *e* ....Is 32:9
to you who are at *e* ....Amos 6:1
take your *e* ....Luke 12:19

EASIER

Which is *e*, to say ....Mark 2:9
It is *e* for a camel ....Mark 10:25

EAST

goes toward the *e* ....Gen 2:14
the LORD brought an *e* ....Ex 10:13
e wind scattered ....Job 38:24
As far as the *e* ....Ps 103:12
descendants from the *e* ....Is 43:5
wise men from the *E* ....Matt 2:1
many will come from *e* ....Matt 8:11
will come from the *e* ....Luke 13:29
e might be prepared ....Rev 16:12

EAT

you may freely *e* ....Gen 2:16
'You shall not *e* ....Gen 3:17
my people as they *e* ....Ps 53:4
good to *e* much honey ....Prov 25:27
e this scroll ....Ezek 3:1
on your couches, *e* ....Amos 6:4
e the flesh of My ....Mic 3:3
life, what you will *e* ....Matt 6:25
You to *e* the Passover ....Matt 26:17
give us His flesh to *e* ....John 6:52
one believes he may *e* ....Rom 14:2
e meat nor drink wine ....Rom 14:21
I will never again *e* ....1 Cor 8:13
neither shall he *e* ....2 Thess 3:10
e your flesh like fire ....James 5:3

EATEN

Have you *e* from the ....Gen 3:11
e my honeycomb with my ....Song 5:1
e the fruit of lies ....Hos 10:13
And he was *e* by worms ....Acts 12:23

EATS

The righteous *e* ....Prov 13:25
receives sinners and *e* ....Luke 15:2
Whoever *e* My flesh ....John 6:54
e this bread will live ....John 6:58
e despise him who does ....Rom 14:3
He who *e*, *e* to the ....Rom 14:6
an unworthy manner *e* ....1 Cor 11:29

Taken up to heaven, 2 Kin 2:1–15
Appears with Christ in Transfiguration, Matt 17:1–4
Type of John the Baptist, Mal 4:5, 6; Luke 1:17

ELIMELECH

Naomi's husband, Ruth 1:1–3; 2:1, 3; 4:3–9

ELIPHAZ

One of Job's friends, Job 2:11
Rebukes Job, Job 4:1, 5
Is forgiven, Job 42:7–9

ELISHA

Chosen as Elijah's successor; follows him, 1 Kin 19:16–21
Witnesses Elijah's translation; receives his spirit and mantle, 2 Kin 2:1–18
Performs miracles, 2 Kin 2:19–25; 4:1—6:23
Prophesies victory over Moab; fulfilled, 2 Kin 3:11–27
Prophesies end of siege; fulfilled, 2 Kin 7
Prophesies death of Ben-Hadad, 2 Kin 8:7–15
Sends servant to anoint Jehu, 2 Kin 9:1–3
Last words and death; miracle performed by his bones, 2 Kin 13:14–21

ELIZABETH

Barren wife of Zacharias, Luke 1:5–7
Conceives a son, Luke 1:13, 24, 25
Salutation to Mary, Luke 1:36–45
Mother of John the Baptist, Luke 1:57–60

ELIZAPHAN

Chief of Kohathites, Num 3:30
Heads family, 1 Chr 15:5, 8
Family consecrated, 2 Chr 29:12–16

ELKANAH

Father of Samuel, 1 Sam 1:1–23
—— Son of Korah, Ex 6:24
Escapes judgment, Num 26:11

ELNATHAN

Father of Nehushta, 2 Kin 24:8
Goes to Egypt, Jer 26:22
Entreats with king, Jer 36:25

ELOQUENT

"O my Lord, I am not *e* ....Ex 4:10
an *e* man and mighty ....Acts 18:24

ELYMAS

Arabic name of Bar-Jesus, a false prophet, Acts 13:6–12

EMBALM

to *e* his father ....Gen 50:2

EMBANKMENT

will build an *e* ....Luke 19:43

EMERALDS

for your wares *e* ....Ezek 27:16

EMMAUS

Town near Jerusalem, Luke 24:13–18

EMPTY

appear before Me *e* ....Ex 23:15
e things which ....1 Sam 12:21
not listen to *e* talk ....Job 35:13
LORD makes the earth *e* ....Is 24:1
comes, he finds it *e* ....Matt 12:44
He has sent away *e* ....Luke 1:53
you with *e* words ....Eph 5:6

EMPTY-HEADED

e man will be wise ....Job 11:12

EN GEDI

Occupied by the Amorites, Gen 14:7
Assigned to Judah, Josh 15:62, 63
David's hiding place, 1 Sam 23:29
Noted for vineyards, Song 1:14

EN HAKKORE

Miraculous spring, Judg 15:14–19

EN ROGEL

Fountain outside Jerusalem, 2 Sam 17:17
Seat of Adonijah's plot, 1 Kin 1:5–9

ENABLED

our Lord who has *e* ....1 Tim 1:12

ENCHANTER

and the expert *e* ....Is 3:3

ENCOURAGED

is, that I may be *e* ....Rom 1:12
and all may be *e* ....1 Cor 14:31
their hearts may be *e* ....Col 2:2

END

yet your latter *e* ....Job 8:7
make me to know my *e* ....Ps 39:4
shall keep it to the *e* ....Ps 119:33
e is the way of death ....Prov 14:12
There was no *e* of all ....Eccl 4:16
Declaring the *e* ....Is 46:10
Our *e* was near ....Lam 4:18
whose iniquity shall *e* ....Ezek 21:25
what shall be the *e* ....Dan 12:8
e has come upon my ....Amos 8:2
the harvest is the *e* ....Matt 13:39
to pass, but the *e* ....Matt 24:6
always, even to the *e* ....Matt 28:20
He loved them to the *e* ....John 13:1
For Christ is the *e* ....Rom 10:4
the hope firm to the *e* ....Heb 3:6
but now, once at the *e* ....Heb 9:26
of Job and seen the *e* ....James 5:11
But the *e* of all ....1 Pet 4:7
what will be the *e* ....1 Pet 4:17
the latter *e* is worse ....2 Pet 2:20
My works until the *e* ....Rev 2:26
Beginning and the *E* ....Rev 22:13

ENDEAVORING

e to keep the unity ....Eph 4:3

ENDLESS

and *e* genealogies ....1 Tim 1:4
to the power of an *e* ....Heb 7:16

ENDS

All the *e* of the world ....Ps 22:27
established all the *e* ....Prov 30:4
she came from the *e* ....Matt 12:42
to the *e* of the ....Acts 13:47
their words to the *e* ....Rom 10:18

ENDURANCE

For you have need of *e* ......Heb 10:36
e the race that ....Heb 12:1

ENDURE

But the LORD shall *e* ....Ps 9:7
as the sun and moon *e* ....Ps 72:5
His name shall *e* ....Ps 72:17
nor does a crown *e* ....Prov 27:24
Can your heart *e* ....Ezek 22:14
persecuted, we *e* ....1 Cor 4:12
Therefore I *e* all ....2 Tim 2:10
them blessed who *e* ....James 5:11

ENDURED

what persecutions I *e* ....2 Tim 3:11
he had patiently *e* ....Heb 6:15
e as seeing Him who ....Heb 11:27
For consider Him who *e* ....Heb 12:3

ENDURES

And His truth *e* ....Ps 100:5
For His mercy *e* ....Ps 136:1
But he who *e* to the ....Matt 10:22
e only for a while ....Matt 13:21
for the food which *e* ....John 6:27
he has built on it *e* ....1 Cor 3:14
hopes all things, *e* ....1 Cor 13:7
is the man who *e* ....James 1:12
word of the LORD *e* ....1 Pet 1:25

ENDURING

the LORD is clean, *e* ....Ps 19:9
e possession for ....Heb 10:34

ENEMIES

Your *e* be scattered ....Num 10:35
delivers me from my *e* ....Ps 18:48
the presence of my *e* ....Ps 23:5
Let not my *e* triumph ....Ps 25:2
But my *e* are vigorous ....Ps 38:19
e will lick the dust ....Ps 72:9
me wiser than my *e* ....Ps 119:98
I count them my *e* ....Ps 139:22
e are the men of his ....Mic 7:6
to you, love your *e* ....Matt 5:44
e will be those ....Matt 10:36
be saved from our *e* ....Luke 1:71
e we were reconciled ....Rom 5:10
the gospel they are *e* ....Rom 11:28
till He has put all *e* ....1 Cor 15:25
were alienated and *e* ....Col 1:21
His *e* are made His ....Heb 10:13
and devours their *e* ....Rev 11:5

ENEMY

then I will be an *e* ....Ex 23:22
regard me as Your *e* ....Job 13:24
He counts me as His *e* ....Job 33:10
or have plundered my *e* ....Ps 7:4
You may silence the *e* ....Ps 8:2
e does not triumph ....Ps 41:11
e who reproaches me ....Ps 55:12
e has persecuted my ....Ps 143:3
If your *e* is hungry ....Prov 25:21
e are deceitful ....Prov 27:6
with the wound of an *e* ......Jer 30:14
rejoice over me, my *e* ....Mic 7:8
and hate your *e* ....Matt 5:43
last *e* that will be ....1 Cor 15:26
become your *e* because ....Gal 4:16
not count him as an *e* ....2 Thess 3:15
makes himself an *e* ....James 4:4

ENGRAVE

two onyx stones and *e* ....Ex 28:9

e its inscription ....Zech 3:9

ENJOY

e its sabbaths as long ....Lev 26:34
therefore *e* pleasure ....Eccl 2:1
richly all things to *e* ....1 Tim 6:17
than to *e* the passing ....Heb 11:25

ENJOYMENT

So I commended *e* ....Eccl 8:15

ENLARGES

He *e* nations ....Job 12:23
e his desire as hell ....Hab 2:5

ENLIGHTEN

E my eyes ....Ps 13:3
the LORD my God will *e* ......Ps 18:28

ENLIGHTENED

those who were once *e* ....Heb 6:4

ENMITY

And I will put *e* ....Gen 3:15
the carnal mind is *e* ....Rom 8:7
in His flesh the *e* ....Eph 2:15
putting to death the *e* ....Eph 2:16
with the world is *e* ....James 4:4

ENOCH

Father of Methuselah, Gen 5:21
Walks with God, Gen 5:22
Taken up to heaven, Gen 5:24
Prophecy of, cited, Jude 14, 15

ENOUGH

never say, "*E* ....Prov 30:15
It is *e* ....Mark 14:41
servants have bread *e* ......Luke 15:17

ENRAGED

being exceedingly *e* ....Acts 26:11
And the dragon was *e* ....Rev 12:17

ENRAPTURED

And always be *e* ....Prov 5:19

ENRICHED

that you were *e* ....1 Cor 1:5
while you are *e* ....2 Cor 9:11

ENSNARED

The wicked is *e* ....Prov 12:13

ENSNARES

sin which so easily *e* ....Heb 12:1

ENTANGLE

how they might *e* ....Matt 22:15

ENTANGLES

engaged in warfare *e* ....2 Tim 2:4

ENTER

E into His gates ....Ps 100:4
Do not *e* into judgment ....Ps 143:2
E into the rock ....Is 2:10
He shall *e* into peace ....Is 57:2
you will by no means *e* ......Matt 5:20
"*E* by the narrow ....Matt 7:13
e the kingdom of God ....Matt 19:24
E into the joy of your ....Matt 25:21
and pray, lest you *e* ....Matt 26:41
"Strive to *e* through ....Luke 13:24
you, he who does not *e* ......John 10:1
who have believed do *e* ....Heb 4:3
e the Holiest by the ....Heb 10:19
e the temple till the ....Rev 15:8
e through the gates ....Rev 22:14

ENTERED

Then Satan *e* Judas ....Luke 22:3
through one man sin *e* ....Rom 5:12
ear heard, nor have *e* ....1 Cor 2:9
the forerunner has *e* ....Heb 6:20
e the Most Holy Place ....Heb 9:12

ENTERS

If anyone *e* by Me ....John 10:9
e the Presence behind ....Heb 6:19

ENTHRONED

You are holy, *e* in ....Ps 22:3

ENTICED

his own desires and *e* ....James 1:14

ENTICING

e speech she caused ....Prov 7:21

ENTIRELY

give yourself *e* ....1 Tim 4:15

ENTRANCE

The *e* of Your words ....Ps 119:130
e will be supplied ....2 Pet 1:11

ENTREAT

"*E* me not to leave you ......Ruth 1:16
"But now *e* God's favor ....Mal 1:9
being defamed, we *e* ....1 Cor 4:13

ENTREATED

man of God *e* the LORD .....1 Kin 13:6
e our God for this ....Ezra 8:23

ENVIOUS

For I was *e* of the ....Ps 73:3
Do not be *e* of evil ....Prov 24:1
patriarchs, becoming *e* ....Acts 7:9

ENVY

e slays a simple ....Job 5:2
e the oppressor ....Prov 3:31
e is rottenness ....Prov 14:30
not let your heart *e* ....Prov 23:17
e have now perished ....Eccl 9:6
full of *e* ....Rom 1:29
not in strife and *e* ....Rom 13:13
love does not *e* ....1 Cor 13:4
e, murders ....Gal 5:21
living in malice and *e* ....Titus 3:3
For where *e* and ....James 3:16
deceit, hypocrisy, *e* ....1 Pet 2:1

EPAPHRAS

Leader of the Colossian church, Col 1:7, 8
Suffers as a prisoner in Rome, Philem 23

EPAPHRODITUS

Messenger from Philippi, Phil 2:25–27
Brings a gift to Paul, Phil 4:18

EPHES DAMMIM

Philistine encampment, 1 Sam 17:1
Called Pasdammim, 1 Chr 11:13

EPHESUS

Paul visits, Acts 18:18–21
Miracles done here, Acts 19:11–21
Demetrius stirs up riot in, Acts 19:24–29
Elders of, addressed by Paul at Miletus, Acts 20:17–38
Letter sent to, Eph 1:1
Site of one of seven churches, Rev 1:11

EPHRAIM

Joseph's younger son, Gen 41:52
Obtains Jacob's blessing, Gen 48:8–20
—— Tribe of:
Predictions concerning, Gen 48:20
Territory assigned to, Josh 16:1–10
Assist Deborah, Judg 5:14, 15
Assist Gideon, Judg 7:24, 25
Quarrel with Gideon, Judg 8:1–3
Quarrel with Jephthah, Judg 12:1–4
Leading tribe of kingdom of Israel, Is 7:2–17
Provoke God by sin, Hos 12:7–14
Many of, join Judah, 2 Chr 15:8, 9
Captivity of, predicted, Hos 9:3–17
Messiah promised to, Zech 9:9–13

EPHRATHAH

Ancient name of Bethlehem, Ruth 4:11
Prophecy concerning, Mic 5:2

EPHRON

Hittite who sold Machpelah to Abraham, Gen 23:8–20

EPICUREANS

Sect of pleasure-loving philosophers, Acts 17:18

EPISTLE

You are our *e* written ....2 Cor 3:2
you are an *e* ....2 Cor 3:3
by word or our *e* ....2 Thess 2:15
our word in this *e* ....2 Thess 3:14
is a sign in every *e* ....2 Thess 3:17

EPISTLES

e of commendation to ....2 Cor 3:1
as also in all his *e* ....2 Pet 3:16

EQUAL

it was you, a man my *e* ....Ps 55:13
and you made them *e* ......Matt 20:12
making Himself *e* ....John 5:18
it robbery to be *e* ....Phil 2:6

EQUALITY

that there may be *e* ....2 Cor 8:14

EQUITY

You have established *e* ....Ps 99:4
judgment, and *e* ....Prov 1:3
and *e* cannot enter ....Is 59:14
and pervert all *e* ....Mic 3:9
with Me in peace and *e* ....Mal 2:6

ER

Son of Judah, Gen 38:1–7; 46:12

ERASTUS

Paul's friend at Ephesus, Acts 19:21, 22; 2 Tim 4:20
Treasurer of Corinth, Rom 16:23

ERR

you cause you to *e* ....Is 3:12

My people Israel to *e* ....Jer 23:13

ERROR

God that it was an *e* ....Eccl 5:6
e which was due ....Rom 1:27
a sinner from the *e* ....James 5:20
led away with the *e* ....2 Pet 3:17
and the spirit of *e* ....1 John 4:6
run greedily in the *e* ....Jude 11

ERRORS

can understand his *e* ....Ps 19:12

ESARHADDON

Son of Sennacherib; king of Assyria (681–669 B.C.), 2 Kin 19:36, 37

ESAU

Isaac's favorite son, Gen 25:25–28
Sells his birthright, Gen 25:29–34
Deprived of blessing; seeks to kill Jacob, Gen 27
Reconciled to Jacob, Gen 33:1–17
Descendants of, Gen 36

ESCAPE

E to the mountains ....Gen 19:17
and they shall not *e* ....Job 11:20
Shall they *e* by ....Ps 56:7
speaks lies will not *e* ....Prov 19:5
and how shall we *e* ....Is 20:6
e all these things ....Luke 21:36
same, that you will *e* ....Rom 2:3
also make the way of *e* ....1 Cor 10:13
how shall we *e* if we ....Heb 2:3
e who refused Him who .....Heb 12:25

ESCAPED

my flesh, and I have *e* ....Job 19:20
Our soul has *e* as a ....Ps 124:7
after they have *e* ....2 Pet 2:20

ESH-BAAL

Son of Saul, 1 Chr 8:33

ESHCOL

Valley near Hebron, Num 13:22–27; Deut 1:24

ESTABLISH

to *e* them forever ....2 Chr 9:8
'Your seed I will *e* ....Ps 89:4
e the work of our ....Ps 90:17
E Your word to Your ....Ps 119:38
e an everlasting ....Ezek 16:60
e justice in the gate ....Amos 5:15
seeking to *e* their own ....Rom 10:3
faithful, who will *e* ....2 Thess 3:3
E your hearts ....James 5:8
a while, perfect, *e* ....1 Pet 5:10

ESTABLISHED

also is firmly *e* ....1 Chr 16:30
David my father be *e* ....2 Chr 1:9
a rock, and *e* my steps ....Ps 40:2
e a testimony in Jacob ....Ps 78:5
Your throne is *e* ....Ps 93:2
let all your ways be *e* ....Prov 4:26
e the clouds above ....Prov 8:28
lip shall be *e* forever ....Prov 12:19
house shall be *e* ....Is 2:2
by His power, He has *e* ......Jer 10:12
built up in Him and *e* ....Col 2:7
covenant, which was *e* ....Heb 8:6
that the heart be *e* ....Heb 13:9

ESTABLISHES

The king *e* the land by ....Prov 29:4
Now He who *e* us with ....2 Cor 1:21

ESTEEM

high wall in his own *e* ....Prov 18:11
and we did not *e* ....Is 53:3
e others better than ....Phil 2:3
and hold such men in *e* ....Phil 2:29
e them very highly ....1 Thess 5:13

ESTEEMED

For what is highly *e* ....Luke 16:15
those who are least *e* ....1 Cor 6:4

ESTEEMS

One person *e* one day ....Rom 14:5

ESTHER

Selected for harem, Esth 2:7–16
Chosen to be queen, Esth 2:17, 18
Agrees to intercede for her people, Esth 4
Invites king to banquet, Esth 5:1–8
Denounces Haman; obtains reversal of decree, Esth 7:1—8:8
Establishes Purim, Esth 9:29–32

ESTRANGED

The wicked are *e* ....Ps 58:3
because they are all *e* ....Ezek 14:5
You have become *e* ....Gal 5:4

ETAM

Rock where Samson took refuge, Judg 15:8–19

ETERNAL

e God is your refuge ....Deut 33:27
For man goes to his *e* ....Eccl 12:5
I do that I may have *e* ....Matt 19:16
and inherit *e* life ....Matt 19:29
in the age to come, *e* ....Mark 10:30
not perish but have *e* ....John 3:15
you think you have *e* ....John 5:39
And I give them *e* life ....John 10:28
that He should give *e* ....John 17:2
And this is *e* life ....John 17:3
e life to those who by ....Rom 2:7
the gift of God is *e* ....Rom 6:23
e weight of glory ....2 Cor 4:17
are not seen are *e* ....2 Cor 4:18
not made with hands, *e* ....2 Cor 5:1
lay hold on *e* life ....1 Tim 6:12
e life which God ....Titus 1:2
and of *e* judgment ....Heb 6:2
e life which was ....1 John 1:2
that no murderer has *e* ......1 John 3:15
God has given us *e* ....1 John 5:11
that you have *e* life ....1 John 5:13
Jesus Christ unto *e* ....Jude 21

ETERNITY

Also He has put *e* ....Eccl 3:11
One who inhabits *e* ....Is 57:15

ETHIOPIA

See CUSH
Hostile to Israel and Judah, 2 Chr 12:2, 3; 14:9–15; Is 43:3; Dan 11:43
Prophecies against, Is 20:1–6; Ezek 30:4–9

ETHIOPIANS

Skin of, unchangeable, Jer 13:23

EUNICE

Mother of Timothy, 2 Tim 1:5

EUNUCH

of Ethiopia, a *e* ....Acts 8:27

EUNUCHS

have made themselves *e* ....Matt 19:12

EUPHRATES

River of Eden, Gen 2:14
Boundary of Promised Land, Gen 15:18; 1 Kin 4:21, 24
Scene of battle, Jer 46:2, 6, 10
Angels bound there, Rev 9:14

EUTYCHUS

Sleeps during Paul's sermon, Acts 20:9
Restored to life, Acts 20:12

EVANGELIST

of Philip the *e* ....Acts 21:8
do the work of an *e* ....2 Tim 4:5

EVANGELISTS

some prophets, some *e* ....Eph 4:11

EVEN

E in laughter the ....Prov 14:13
E a child is known ....Prov 20:11
e nature itself teach ....1 Cor 11:14
e denying the Lord who ....2 Pet 2:1

EVENING

At *e* they return ....Ps 59:6
e it is cut down and ....Ps 90:6
of my hands as the *e* ....Ps 141:2
e do not withhold your ....Eccl 11:6
and more fierce than *e* ....Hab 1:8

EVERLASTING

God of Israel from *e* ....1 Chr 16:36
of the LORD is from *e* ....Ps 103:17
righteousness is an *e* ....Ps 119:142
Your kingdom is an *e* ....Ps 145:13
in YAH, the LORD, is *e* ....Is 26:4
will be to you an *e* ....Is 60:19
from *E* is Your name ....Is 63:16
awake, some to *e* life ....Dan 12:2
not perish but have *e* ....John 3:16
Him who sent Me has *e* ....John 5:24
endures to *e* life ....John 6:27
in Him may have *e* ....John 6:40
believes in Me has *e* ....John 6:47
unworthy of *e* life ....Acts 13:46
of the Spirit reap *e* ....Gal 6:8
e destruction from the ....2 Thess 1:9

EVERYONE

said, 'Repent now *e* ....Jer 25:5
e who is born of the ....John 3:8
E who is of the truth ....John 18:37

EVIDENCE

e of things not seen ....Heb 11:1

EVIDENT

the sight of God is *e* ....Gal 3:11
of some are clearly *e* ....1 Tim 5:25
e that our Lord arose ....Heb 7:14

EVIL

of good and *e* ....Gen 2:9
knowing good and *e* ....Gen 3:5

EXIST
things which do not *e* ....Rom 4:17
by Your will they *e* ....Rev 4:11

EXPECT
an hour you do not *e* ......Luke 12:40

EXPECTATION
The *e* of the poor ....Ps 9:18
God alone, for my *e* ....Ps 62:5
the people were in *e* ....Luke 3:15
a certain fearful *e* ....Heb 10:27

EXPERT
and the *e* enchanter ....Is 3:3
those of an *e* warrior ....Jer 50:9
because you are *e* ....Acts 26:3

EXPLAIN
was no one who could *e* ....Gen 41:24
days they could not *e* ......Judg 14:14
"*E* this parable to us ....Matt 15:15
to say, and hard to *e* ....Heb 5:11

EXPLAINED
He *e* all things to His ....Mark 4:34

EXPLOIT
e all your ....Is 58:3
against those who *e* ....Mal 3:5
they will *e* you with ....2 Pet 2:3

EXPOSED
his deeds should be *e* ....John 3:20
all things that are *e* ....Eph 5:13

EXPOUNDED
He *e* to them in all ....Luke 24:27

EXPRESS
man cannot *e* it ....Eccl 1:8
of His glory and the *e* ....Heb 1:3

EXPRESSLY
of the LORD came *e* ....Ezek 1:3
Now the Spirit *e* ....1 Tim 4:1

EXTEND
none to *e* mercy to him ......Ps 109:12
"Behold, I will *e* ....Is 66:12
did not *e* to you ....2 Cor 10:14

EXTINGUISHED
broken, my days are *e* ....Job 17:1
They are *e* ....Is 43:17

EXTOL
I will *e* You ....Ps 30:1
e Him who rides ....Ps 68:4

EXTOLLED
shall be exalted and *e* ....Is 52:13

EXTORTION
e gathers it for him ....Prov 28:8
your neighbors by *e* ....Ezek 22:12
they are full of *e* ....Matt 23:25

EXTORTIONERS
e will inherit ....1 Cor 6:10

EXULT
in anguish I would *e* ....Job 6:10

EYE
e for *e* ....Ex 21:24
the ear, but now my *e* ....Job 42:5
guide you with My *e* ....Ps 32:8
Behold, the *e* of the ....Ps 33:18
He who formed the *e* ....Ps 94:9
and the seeing *e* ....Prov 20:12
who has a generous *e* ....Prov 22:9
A man with an evil *e* ....Prov 28:22
e that mocks his ....Prov 30:17
e is not satisfied ....Eccl 1:8
labors, nor is his *e* ....Eccl 4:8
for they shall see *e* ....Is 52:8
e seen any God besides ....Is 64:4
the apple of His *e* ....Zech 2:8
if your right *e* ....Matt 5:29
it was said, 'An *e* ....Matt 5:38
plank in your own *e* ....Matt 7:3
e causes you to sin ....Matt 18:9
Or is your *e* evil ....Matt 20:15
e causes you to sin ....Mark 9:47
the *e* of a needle ....Luke 18:25
"Because I am not an *e* ....1 Cor 12:16
whole body were an *e* .....1 Cor 12:17
the twinkling of an *e* ......1 Cor 15:52
every *e* will see Him ....Rev 1:7
your eyes with *e* salve ....Rev 3:18

EYELIDS
His eyes behold, His *e* ....Ps 11:4
e look right before ....Prov 4:25

EYES
e will be opened ....Gen 3:5
and you can be our *e* ......Num 10:31
she put paint on her *e* ....2 Kin 9:30
For the *e* of the ....2 Chr 16:9
Do You have *e* of flesh ....Job 10:4
And my *e* shall behold ......Job 19:27
I was *e* to the blind ....Job 29:15
e observe from afar ....Job 39:29
e are secretly fixed ....Ps 10:8
e are ever toward the ....Ps 25:15
The *e* of the LORD are ....Ps 34:15
e fail while I wait ....Ps 69:3
e shall you look ....Ps 91:8
I will lift up my *e* ....Ps 121:1
not give sleep to my *e* ....Ps 132:4
e saw my substance ....Ps 139:16
e look straight ahead ....Prov 4:25
but the *e* of a fool ....Prov 17:24
Will you set your *e* ....Prov 23:5
Who has redness of *e* ....Prov 23:29
be wise in his own *e* ....Prov 26:5
so the *e* of man are ....Prov 27:20
The wise man's *e* ....Eccl 2:14
e than the wandering ....Eccl 6:9
You have dove's *e* ....Song 1:15
e have seen the King ....Is 6:5
of the book, and the *e* ....Is 29:18
e fail from looking ....Is 38:14
O LORD, are not Your *e* ....Jer 5:3
Who have *e* and see ....Jer 5:21
e will weep bitterly ....Jer 13:17
For I will set My *e* ....Jer 24:6
rims were full of *e* ....Ezek 1:18
full of *e* all around ....Ezek 10:12
that horn which had *e* ....Dan 7:20
horn between his *e* ....Dan 8:5
You are of purer *e* ....Hab 1:13
But blessed are your *e* ......Matt 13:16
"He put clay on my *e* ....John 9:15
e they have closed ....Acts 28:27
e that they should not ....Rom 11:8
plucked out your own *e* ....Gal 4:15
have seen with our *e* ....1 John 1:1
the lust of the *e* ....1 John 2:16
as snow, and His *e* ....Rev 1:14
and anoint your *e* ....Rev 3:18
creatures full of *e* ....Rev 4:6
horns and seven *e* ....Rev 5:6
tear from their *e* ....Rev 21:4

EYESERVICE
not with *e* ....Eph 6:6
the flesh, not with *e* ....Col 3:22

EYEWITNESSES
the beginning were *e* ....Luke 1:2
e of His majesty ....2 Pet 1:16

EZEKIEL
Sent to rebellious Israel, Ezek 2; 3
Prophesies by symbolic action:
 siege of Jerusalem, Ezek 4
 destruction of Jerusalem, Ezek 5
 captivity of Judah, Ezek 12:1–20
 destruction of the temple, Ezek 24:15–27
Visions of:
 God's glory, Ezek 1:4–28
 abominations, Ezek 8:5–18
 valley of dry bones, Ezek 37:1–14
 messianic times, Ezek 40—48
 river of life, Ezek 47:1–5
Parables, allegories, dirges of, Ezek 15; 16; 17; 19; 23; 24

EZION GEBER
See ELATH
Town on the Red Sea, 1 Kin 9:26
Israelite encampment, Num 33:35
Seaport of Israel's navy, 1 Kin 22:48

EZRA
Scribe, priest and reformer of postexilic times; commissioned by Artaxerxes, Ezra 7
Returns with exiles to Jerusalem, Ezra 8
Institutes reforms, Ezra 9
Reads the Law, Neh 8
Assists in dedication of wall, Neh 12:27–43

—F—

FABLES
nor give heed to *f* ....1 Tim 1:4
be turned aside to *f* ....2 Tim 4:4
cunningly devised *f* ....2 Pet 1:16

FACE
"For I have seen God *f* ......Gen 32:30
f shone while he ....Ex 34:29
he put a veil on his *f* ....Ex 34:33
the LORD make His *f* ....Num 6:25
Then he turned his *f* ....2 Kin 20:2
curse You to Your *f* ....Job 1:11
me, I will see Your *f* ....Ps 17:15
Why do You hide Your *f* ....Ps 44:24
and cause His *f* ....Ps 67:1
of his *f* is changed ....Eccl 8:1
sins have hidden His *f* ....Is 59:2
I have made your *f* ....Ezek 3:8
but to us shame of *f* ....Dan 9:7
before Your *f* who ....Matt 11:10
f shone like the sun ....Matt 17:2
always before my *f* ....Acts 2:25
dimly, but then *f* ....1 Cor 13:12
look steadily at the *f* ....2 Cor 3:7
with unveiled *f* ....2 Cor 3:18
withstood him to his *f* ....Gal 2:11

its flower *f* ....James 1:11
so that no rain *f* ....Rev 11:6

FALSE

"You shall not bear *f* ....Ex 20:16
I hate every *f* way ....Ps 119:104
gives heed to *f* lips ....Prov 17:4
f witness shall perish ....Prov 21:28
and do not love a *f* ....Zech 8:17
"Beware of *f* prophets ....Matt 7:15
f christs and *f* ....Matt 24:24
and we are found *f* ....1 Cor 15:15
among *f* brethren ....2 Cor 11:26
of *f* brethren ....Gal 2:4
f prophets have gone ....1 John 4:1
mouth of the *f* prophet ....Rev 16:13

FALSEHOOD

those who speak *f* ....Ps 5:6
and brings forth *f* ....Ps 7:14
For their deceit is *f* ....Ps 119:118
remove *f* and lies far ....Prov 30:8
under *f* we have hidden ....Is 28:15
offspring of *f* ....Is 57:4

FALSELY

it, and swears *f* ....Lev 6:3
nor have we dealt *f* ....Ps 44:17
surely they swear *f* ....Jer 5:2
words, swearing *f* ....Hos 10:4
of evil against you *f* ....Matt 5:11
f called knowledge ....1 Tim 6:20

FAME

Sheba heard of the *f* ....1 Kin 10:1
Your *f* went out ....Ezek 16:14
them for praise and *f* ....Zeph 3:19
Then His *f* went ....Matt 4:24

FAMILIES

in you all the *f* ....Gen 12:3
and makes their *f* ....Ps 107:41
the God of all the *f* ....Jer 31:1
f which the LORD has ....Jer 33:24
in your seed all the *f* ....Acts 3:25

FAMILY

shall mourn, every *f* ....Zech 12:12
f were baptized ....Acts 16:33
from whom the whole *f* ....Eph 3:15

FAMINE

Now there was a *f* ....Gen 12:10
keep them alive in *f* ....Ps 33:19
He called for a *f* ....Ps 105:16
send the sword, the *f* ....Jer 24:10
of the fever of *f* ....Lam 5:10
I will increase the *f* ....Ezek 5:16
there arose a severe *f* ....Luke 15:14

FAMINES

And there will be *f* ....Matt 24:7

FAMISH

righteous soul to *f* ....Prov 10:3

FAMISHED

honorable men are *f* ....Is 5:13

FAMOUS

and may his name be *f* ....Ruth 4:14

FAN

not to *f* or to cleanse ....Jer 4:11
His winnowing *f* ....Matt 3:12

FANCIES

with their own *f* ....Prov 1:31

FAR

removed my brothers *f* ....Job 19:13
Your judgments are *f* ....Ps 10:5
Be not *f* from Me ....Ps 22:11
those who are *f* ....Ps 73:27
The LORD is *f* from the ....Prov 15:29
but it was *f* from me ....Eccl 7:23
removed their hearts *f* ....Is 29:13
Those near and those *f* ....Ezek 22:5
their heart is *f* from ....Matt 15:8
going to a *f* country ....Mark 13:34
though He is not *f* ....Acts 17:27
you who once were *f* ....Eph 2:13

FARMER

The hard-working *f* ....2 Tim 2:6
See how the *f* waits ....James 5:7

FASHIONED

have made me and *f* ....Job 10:8

FASHIONS

He *f* their hearts ....Ps 33:15

FAST

f as you do this day ....Is 58:4
f that I have chosen ....Is 58:5
"Moreover, when you *f* ....Matt 6:16
disciples do not *f* ....Matt 9:14
I *f* twice a week ....Luke 18:12

FASTED

'Why have we *f* ....Is 58:3
'When you *f* and ....Zech 7:5
And when He had *f* ....Matt 4:2

FASTENED

were its foundations *f* ....Job 38:6
'the peg that is *f* ....Is 22:25

FASTING

humbled myself with *f* ....Ps 35:13
are weak through *f* ....Ps 109:24
house on the day of *f* ....Jer 36:6
except by prayer and *f* ......Matt 17:21
give yourselves to *f* ....1 Cor 7:5

FASTINGS

in sleeplessness, in *f* ....2 Cor 6:5

FAT

and you will eat the *f* ....Gen 45:18
f is the LORD's ....Lev 3:16
Now Eglon was a very *f* ....Judg 3:17
have closed up their *f* ....Ps 17:10

FATHER

man shall leave his *f* ....Gen 2:24
and you shall be a *f* ....Gen 17:4
'You are my *f* ....Job 17:14
I was a *f* to the poor ....Job 29:16
A *f* of the fatherless ....Ps 68:5
f pities his children ....Ps 103:13
the instruction of a *f* ....Prov 4:1
God, Everlasting *F* ....Is 9:6
You, O LORD, are our *F* ....Is 63:16
time cry to Me, My *F* ....Jer 3:4
for I am a *F* to Israel ....Jer 31:9
"A son honors his *f* ....Mal 1:6
Have we not all one *F* ....Mal 2:10
Our *F* in heaven ....Matt 6:9
He who loves *f* ....Matt 10:37
does anyone know the *F* ....Matt 11:27
'He who curses *f* ....Matt 15:4
for One is your *F* ....Matt 23:9
F will be divided ....Luke 12:53
F loves the Son ....John 3:35
F has been working ....John 5:17
F raises the dead ....John 5:21
F judges no one ....John 5:22
He has seen the *F* ....John 6:46
F who sent Me bears ....John 8:18
we have one *F* ....John 8:41
of your *f* the devil ....John 8:44
I and My *F* are one ....John 10:30
and believe that the *F* ....John 10:38
'I am going to the *F* ....John 14:28
F is the vinedresser ....John 15:1
came forth from the *F* ....John 16:28
that he might be the *f* ....Rom 4:11
"I have made you a *f* ....Rom 4:17
"I will be a *F* ....2 Cor 6:18
one God and *F* of all ....Eph 4:6
but exhort him as a *f* ....1 Tim 5:1
"I will be to Him a *F* ....Heb 1:5
without *f*, without mother ....Heb 7:3
comes down from the *F* ....James 1:17
if you call on the *F* ....1 Pet 1:17
and testify that the *F* ....1 John 4:14

FATHER'S

you in My *F* kingdom ....Matt 26:29
I must be about My *F* ....Luke 2:49
F house are many ....John 14:2
that a man has his *f* ....1 Cor 5:1

FATHERLESS

my hand against the *f* ....Job 31:21
the helper of the *f* ....Ps 10:14
to do justice to the *f* ....Ps 10:18
He relieves the *f* ....Ps 146:9
the fields of the *f* ....Prov 23:10
do not defend the *f* ....Is 1:23
they may rob the *f* ....Is 10:2
You the *f* finds mercy ....Hos 14:3

FATHERS

the LORD God of our *f* ....Ezra 7:27
f trusted in You ....Ps 22:4
our ears, O God, our *f* ....Ps 44:1
have sinned with our *f* ....Ps 106:6
f ate the manna ....John 6:31
of whom are the *f* ....Rom 9:5
you do not have many *f* ....1 Cor 4:15
unaware that all our *f* ....1 Cor 10:1

FATLING

and the *f* together ....Is 11:6

FATNESS

as with marrow and *f* ....Ps 63:5
of the root and *f* ....Rom 11:17

FATTED

f cattle are ....Matt 22:4
has killed the *f* ....Luke 15:27

FATTENED

f your hearts as ....James 5:5

FAULT

find no charge or *f* ....Dan 6:4
I have found no *f* ....Luke 23:14
does He still find *f* ....Rom 9:19
of God without *f* ....Phil 2:15
for they are without *f* ....Rev 14:5

FAULTLESS

covenant had been *f* ....Heb 8:7

to present you *f* .... Jude 24

FAULTS

"I remember my *f* .... Gen 41:9
me from secret *f* .... Ps 19:12
are beaten for your *f* .... 1 Pet 2:20

FAVOR

granted me life and *f* .... Job 10:12
f You will .... Ps 5:12
His *f* is for life .... Ps 30:5
A good man obtains *f* .... Prov 12:2
but his *f* is like dew .... Prov 19:12
and seek the LORD's *f* .... Jer 26:19
and stature, and in *f* .... Luke 2:52
God and having *f* .... Acts 2:47
to do the Jews a *f* .... Acts 24:27

FAVORABLE

And will He be *f* .... Ps 77:7
LORD, You have been *f* .... Ps 85:1

FAVORED

because You *f* them .... Ps 44:3
"Rejoice, highly *f* .... Luke 1:28

FAVORITISM

do not show personal *f* ..... Luke 20:21
God shows personal *f* .... Gal 2:6

FEAR

this and live, for I *f* God ..... Gen 42:18
f the people of the .... Num 14:9
to put the dread and *f* .... Deut 2:25
f Me all the days .... Deut 4:10
f the LORD your God .... Deut 6:2
book, that you may *f* .... Deut 28:58
said, "Does Job *f* .... Job 1:9
Yes, you cast off *f* .... Job 15:4
Surely no *f* of me will .... Job 33:7
He mocks at *f* .... Job 39:22
they are in great *f* .... Ps 14:5
The *f* of the LORD is .... Ps 19:9
of death, I will *f* .... Ps 23:4
whom shall I *f* .... Ps 27:1
Let all the earth *f* .... Ps 33:8
Oh, *f* the LORD .... Ps 34:9
there is no *f* of God .... Ps 36:1
they are in great *f* .... Ps 53:5
hear, all you who *f* .... Ps 66:16
f You as long as the .... Ps 72:5
heart to *f* Your name .... Ps 86:11
The *f* of the LORD is .... Ps 111:10
f You will be glad .... Ps 119:74
f the LORD and depart .... Prov 3:7
The *f* of man brings a ...... Prov 29:25
it, that men should *f* .... Eccl 3:14
F God and keep His .... Eccl 12:13
let Him be your *f* .... Is 8:13
"Be strong, do not *f* .... Is 35:4
Do you not *f* Me .... Jer 5:22
who would not *f* .... Jer 10:7
but I will put My *f* .... Jer 32:40
who *f* My name the Sun .... Mal 4:2
f Him who is able .... Matt 10:28
"Do not *f* .... Luke 12:32
a judge who did not *f* .... Luke 18:2
"Do you not even *f* .... Luke 23:40
And walking in the *f* .... Acts 9:31
the rest also may *f* .... 1 Tim 5:20
given us a spirit of *f* .... 2 Tim 1:7
those who through *f* .... Heb 2:15
His rest, let us *f* .... Heb 4:1
because of His godly *f* .... Heb 5:7
F God .... 1 Pet 2:17
love casts out *f* .... 1 John 4:18

Do not *f* any of .... Rev 2:10

FEARED

But the midwives *f* .... Ex 1:17
He is also to be *f* .... 1 Chr 16:25
f God more than .... Neh 7:2
Yourself, are to be *f* .... Ps 76:7
Then those who *f* .... Mal 3:16

FEARFUL

f in praises, doing .... Ex 15:11
them, "Why are you *f* .... Matt 8:26
It is a *f* thing to .... Heb 10:31

FEARFUL-HEARTED

to those who are *f* .... Is 35:4

FEARFULLY

f and wonderfully made ..... Ps 139:14

FEARFULNESS

F and trembling have .... Ps 55:5
f has seized the .... Is 33:14

FEARING

is devoted to *f* You .... Ps 119:38
sincerity of heart, *f* .... Col 3:22
forsook Egypt, not *f* .... Heb 11:27

FEARS

upright man, one who *f* .... Job 1:8
Who is the man that *f* .... Ps 25:12
me from all my *f* .... Ps 34:4
an oath as he who *f* .... Eccl 9:2
every nation whoever *f* ...... Acts 10:35
f has not been made .... 1 John 4:18

FEAST

Then he made them a *f* .... Gen 19:3
and you shall keep a *f* ...... Num 29:12
f is made for laughter .... Eccl 10:19
f day the terrors that .... Lam 2:22
hate, I despise your *f* .... Amos 5:21
every year at the *F* .... Luke 2:41
when you give a *f* .... Luke 14:13
Now the Passover, a *f* .... John 6:4
great day of the *f* .... John 7:37
let us keep the *f* .... 1 Cor 5:8

FEASTING

go to the house of *f* .... Eccl 7:2

FEASTS

I will turn your *f* .... Amos 8:10
the best places at *f* .... Luke 20:46
spots in your love *f* .... Jude 12

FED

f me all my life long .... Gen 48:15
and *f* you with manna .... Deut 8:3
but the shepherds *f* .... Ezek 34:8
f you with milk and .... 1 Cor 3:2

FEEBLE

strengthened the *f* .... Job 4:4
And there was none *f* .... Ps 105:37
And my flesh is *f* .... Ps 109:24
Every hand will be *f* .... Ezek 7:17
hang down, and the *f* .... Heb 12:12

FEED

ravens to *f* you there .... 1 Kin 17:4
death shall *f* on them .... Ps 49:14
of the righteous *f* .... Prov 10:21

and *f* your flocks .... Is 61:5
to him, "*F* My lambs .... John 21:15
to him, "*F* My sheep .... John 21:17
your enemy hungers, *f* ...... Rom 12:20
my goods to *f* the poor ...... 1 Cor 13:3

FEEDS

"Ephraim *f* on the wind ...... Hos 12:1
your heavenly Father *f* ...... Matt 6:26

FEET

So she lay at his *f* .... Ruth 3:14
so my *f* did not slip .... 2 Sam 22:37
f they hang far .... Job 28:4
I was *f* to the lame .... Job 29:15
all things under his *f* .... Ps 8:6
He makes my *f* like the .... Ps 18:33
You have set my *f* .... Ps 31:8
does not allow our *f* .... Ps 66:9
f had almost stumbled .... Ps 73:2
f have been standing .... Ps 122:2
For their *f* run to .... Prov 1:16
Her *f* go down to death .... Prov 5:5
sandals off your *f* .... Is 20:2
called him to His *f* .... Is 41:2
up the dust of your *f* .... Is 49:23
mountains are the *f* .... Is 52:7
place of My *f* glorious .... Is 60:13
are the dust of His *f* .... Nah 1:3
in that day His *f* .... Zech 14:4
two hands or two *f* .... Matt 18:8
began to wash His *f* .... Luke 7:38
also sat at Jesus' *f* .... Luke 10:39
wash the disciples' *f* .... John 13:5
at the apostles' *f* .... Acts 4:35
f are swift to shed .... Rom 3:15
beautiful are the *f* .... Rom 10:15
all things under His *f* ...... 1 Cor 15:27
and having shod your *f* .... Eph 6:15
fell at His *f* as dead .... Rev 1:17
And I fell at his *f* .... Rev 19:10

FELIX

Governor of Judea; letter addressed to, Acts 23:24–30
Paul's defense before, Acts 24:1–27

FELLOW

f servants who owed .... Matt 18:28
begins to beat his *f* .... Matt 24:49
f worker concerning .... 2 Cor 8:23
f citizens with the .... Eph 2:19
Gentiles should be *f* .... Eph 3:6
rest of my *f* workers .... Phil 4:3
These are my only *f* .... Col 4:11
that we may become *f* .... 3 John 8
I am your *f* servant .... Rev 19:10

FELLOWSHIP

doctrine and *f* .... Acts 2:42
were called into the *f* .... 1 Cor 1:9
not want you to have *f* ..... 1 Cor 10:20
f has righteousness .... 2 Cor 6:14
the right hand of *f* .... Gal 2:9
And have no *f* with the .... Eph 5:11
for your *f* in the .... Phil 1:5
of love, if any *f* .... Phil 2:1
and the *f* of His .... Phil 3:10
also may have *f* .... 1 John 1:3
we say that we have *f* ...... 1 John 1:6
the light, we have *f* .... 1 John 1:7

FENCE

and a tottering *f* .... Ps 62:3

FENCED

He has *f* up my way .... Job 19:8

FERTILIZE
I dig around it and *f* ....Luke 13:8

FERVENT
and being *f* in spirit ....Acts 18:25
f prayer of a ....James 5:16
all things have *f* ....1 Pet 4:8
will melt with *f* ....2 Pet 3:10

FERVENTLY
you, always laboring *f* ....Col 4:12
love one another *f* ....1 Pet 1:22

FESTIVAL
night when a holy *f* ....Is 30:29
or regarding a *f* ....Col 2:16

FESTUS
Governor of Judea, Acts 24:27
Paul's defense made to, Acts 25:1–22

FETCH
f my knowledge from ....Job 36:3

FETTERS
hurt his feet with *f* ....Ps 105:18
their nobles with *f* ....Ps 149:8

FEVER
f which shall ....Lev 26:16
my bones burn with *f* ....Job 30:30
and rebuked the *f* ....Luke 4:39

FEW
f and evil have been ....Gen 47:9
f days and full of ....Job 14:1
Let his days be *f* ....Ps 109:8
let your words be *f* ....Eccl 5:2
and there are *f* ....Matt 7:14
but the laborers are *f* ....Matt 9:37
called, but *f* chosen ....Matt 20:16
"Lord, are there *f* ....Luke 13:23
prepared, in which a *f* ....1 Pet 3:20
I have a *f* things ....Rev 2:20

FIDELITY
but showing all good *f* ......Titus 2:10

FIELD
Let the *f* be joyful ....Ps 96:12
to house; they add *f* ....Is 5:8
becomes a fruitful *f* ....Is 32:15
The *f* is the world ....Matt 13:38
and buys that *f* ....Matt 13:44
f has been called the ....Matt 27:8
you are God's *f* ....1 Cor 3:9

FIELD OF BLOOD
A field bought as a cemetery for Judas's burial, Matt 27:1–10
Predicted in the OT, Zech 11:12, 13

FIELDS
f yield no food ....Hab 3:17
living out in the *f* ....Luke 2:8
eyes and look at the *f* ....John 4:35

FIERCENESS
f has deceived you ....Jer 49:16
the winepress of the *f* ....Rev 19:15

FIERY
the LORD sent *f* serpents ....Num 21:6
right hand came a *f* ....Deut 33:2
shall make them as a *f* ....Ps 21:9
offspring will be a *f* ....Is 14:29
burning *f* furnace ....Dan 3:6
concerning the *f* ....1 Pet 4:12
f red dragon having ....Rev 12:3

FIG
f leaves together ....Gen 3:7
his vine and his *f* ....1 Kin 4:25
fruit falling from a *f* ....Is 34:4
f tree may not blossom ....Hab 3:17
fruit on this *f* ....Luke 13:7
"Look at the *f* ....Luke 21:29
'I saw you under the *f* ....John 1:50
Can a *f* tree ....James 3:12
f tree drops its late ....Rev 6:13

FIGHT
The LORD will *f* ....Ex 14:14
you go with me to *f* ....1 Kin 22:4
Our God will *f* for us ....Neh 4:20
My servants would *f* ....John 18:36
to him, let us not *f* ....Acts 23:9
F the good *f* ....1 Tim 6:12
have fought the good *f* ....2 Tim 4:7
You *f* and war ....James 4:2

FIGHTS
your God is He who *f* ....Josh 23:10
because my lord *f* ....1 Sam 25:28
f come from among ....James 4:1

FIGS
puts forth her green *f* ....Song 2:13
f set before the ....Jer 24:1
from thornbushes or *f* ....Matt 7:16
men do not gather *f* ....Luke 6:44
or a grapevine bear *f* ......James 3:12

FIGURATIVELY
brethren, I have *f* ....1 Cor 4:6

FIGURE
and using no *f* ....John 16:29

FILL
f the earth and subdue ....Gen 1:28
wealth, that I may *f* ....Prov 8:21
"Do I not *f* heaven ....Jer 23:24
f this temple with ....Hag 2:7
"*F* the waterpots ....John 2:7
that He might *f* ....Eph 4:10
so as always to *f* ....1 Thess 2:16

FILLED
the whole earth be *f* ....Ps 72:19
Then our mouth was *f* ....Ps 126:2
for they shall be *f* ....Matt 5:6
"Let the children be *f* ....Mark 7:27
he would gladly have *f* ......Luke 15:16
being *f* with all ....Rom 1:29
full of goodness, *f* ....Rom 15:14
that you may be *f* ....Eph 3:19
but be *f* with the ....Eph 5:18
being *f* with the ....Phil 1:11
peace, be warmed and *f* ....James 2:16

FILTH
has washed away the *f* ....Is 4:4
been made as the *f* ....1 Cor 4:13
the removal of the *f* ....1 Pet 3:21

FILTHINESS
from all your *f* ....Ezek 36:25
ourselves from all *f* ....2 Cor 7:1
lay aside all *f* ....James 1:21
abominations and the *f* ....Rev 17:4

FILTHY
is abominable and *f* ....Job 15:16
with *f* garments ....Zech 3:3
malice, blasphemy, *f* ....Col 3:8
poor man in *f* clothes ....James 2:2
oppressed by the *f* ....2 Pet 2:7
let him be *f* ....Rev 22:11

FIND
sure your sin will *f* ....Num 32:23
Almighty, we cannot *f* ....Job 37:23
life to those who *f* ....Prov 4:22
that no one can *f* ....Eccl 3:11
waters, for you will *f* ....Eccl 11:1
seek, and you will *f* ....Matt 7:7
for My sake will *f* ....Matt 10:39
when he comes, will *f* ....Matt 24:46
f a Babe wrapped ....Luke 2:12
f no fault in this Man ....Luke 23:4
I *f* then a law ....Rom 7:21
f grace to help in ....Heb 4:16

FINDING
great things past *f* ....Jon 9:10
and *f* none ....Luke 11:24
and His ways past *f* ....Rom 11:33

FINDS
f me *f* life ....Prov 8:35
f a wife *f* a good ....Prov 18:22
Whatever your hand *f* ....Eccl 9:10
and he who seeks *f* ....Matt 7:8
f his life will lose ....Matt 10:39
and he who seeks *f* ....Luke 11:10

FINE
Then I beat them as *f* .....2 Sam 22:43
gold, yea, than much *f* ....Ps 19:10
f gold is a wise ....Prov 25:12
set on bases of *f* gold ....Song 5:15
more rare than *f* ....Is 13:12
and for *f* clothing ....Is 23:18
how changed the *f* ....Lam 4:1
rings, in *f* apparel ....James 2:2
for the *f* linen is the ....Rev 19:8

FINGER
written with the *f* ....Ex 31:18
f shall be thicker ....1 Kin 12:10
the pointing of the *f* ....Is 58:9
dip the tip of his *f* ....Luke 16:24
the ground with His *f* ....John 8:6
"Reach your *f* ....John 20:27

FINGERS
the work of Your *f* ....Ps 8:3
he points with his *f* ....Prov 6:13
that which their own *f* ....Is 2:8
with one of their *f* ....Matt 23:4

FINISH
city, to *f* the ....Dan 9:24
he has enough to *f* ....Luke 14:28
has given Me to *f* ....John 5:36
so that I may *f* ....Acts 20:24

FINISHED
f the work which You ....John 17:4
He said, "It is *f* ....John 19:30
I have *f* the race ....2 Tim 4:7
thousand years were *f* ....Rev 20:3

FIRE
rained brimstone and *f* ......Gen 19:24

to him in a flame of *f* ....Ex 3:2
by day, and *f* was over ....Ex 40:38
God, who answers by *f* ....1 Kin 18:24
LORD was not in the *f* .....1 Kin 19:12
I was musing, the *f* ....Ps 39:3
we went through *f* ....Ps 66:12
they have set *f* ....Ps 74:7
f goes before Him ....Ps 97:3
f and hail ....Ps 148:8
burns as the *f* ....Is 9:18
says the LORD, whose *f* ....Is 31:9
you walk through the *f* ....Is 43:2
f that burns all the ....Is 65:5
on whose bodies the *f* ....Dan 3:27
He break out like *f* ....Amos 5:6
for conflict by *f* ....Amos 7:4
like a refiner's *f* ....Mal 3:2
the Holy Spirit and *f* ....Matt 3:11
f is not quenched ....Mark 9:44
"I came to send *f* ....Luke 12:49
tongues, as of *f* ....Acts 2:3
f taking vengeance ....2 Thess 1:8
and that burned with *f* ......Heb 12:18
And the tongue is a *f* ....James 3:6
vengeance of eternal *f* ....Jude 7
f came down from God ....Rev 20:9
into the lake of *f* ....Rev 20:14

FIREBRAND

f plucked from the ....Amos 4:11

FIREBRANDS

a madman who throws *f* ....Prov 26:18
two stubs of smoking *f* ....Is 7:4

FIRM

their strength is *f* ....Ps 73:4
f the feeble knees ....Is 35:3
of the hope *f* to the ....Heb 3:6

FIRMAMENT

Thus God made the *f* ....Gen 1:7
f shows His handiwork ....Ps 19:1
in His mighty *f* ....Ps 150:1
brightness of the *f* ....Dan 12:3

FIRST

The *f* one to plead his ......Prov 18:17
f father sinned ....Is 43:27
desires to be *f* ....Matt 20:27
f shall be slave ....Mark 10:44
And the gospel must *f* ....Mark 13:10
evil, of the Jew *f* ....Rom 2:9
"Or who has *f* ....Rom 11:35
f man Adam became a .....1 Cor 15:45
f a willing mind ....2 Cor 8:12
that we who *f* trusted ....Eph 1:12
For Adam was formed *f* ....1 Tim 2:13
f covenant had been ....Heb 8:7
love Him because He *f* ....1 John 4:19
I am the *F* and the ....Rev 1:17
you have left your *f* ....Rev 2:4
is the *f* resurrection ....Rev 20:5

FIRST-RIPE

f fruit which my soul ....Mic 7:1

FIRSTBORN

LORD struck all the *f* ....Ex 12:29
I will make him My *f* ....Ps 89:27
Shall I give my *f* ....Mic 6:7
brought forth her *f* ....Matt 1:25
that He might be the *f* ....Rom 8:29
invisible God, the *f* ....Col 1:15
the beginning, the *f* ....Col 1:18

witness, the *f* from ....Rev 1:5

FIRSTFRUIT

For if the *f* is holy ....Rom 11:16

FIRSTFRUITS

and with the *f* ....Prov 3:9
also who have the *f* ....Rom 8:23
and has become the *f* ......1 Cor 15:20
Christ the *f* ....1 Cor 15:23
might be a kind of *f* ....James 1:18
among men, being *f* ....Rev 14:4

FISH

f taken in a cruel net ....Eccl 9:12
had prepared a great *f* ....Jon 1:17
do You make men like *f* ......Hab 1:14
Or if he asks for a *f* ....Matt 7:10
belly of the great *f* ....Matt 12:40
five loaves and two *f* ....Matt 14:17
and likewise the *f* ....John 21:13

FISHERMEN

The *f* also will mourn ....Is 19:8
I will send for many *f* ....Jer 16:16

FISHERS

and I will make you *f* ....Matt 4:19

FIT

and looking back, is *f* ....Luke 9:62

FITTING

Is it *f* to say to a ....Job 34:18
Luxury is not *f* ....Prov 19:10
so honor is not *f* ....Prov 26:1
things which are not *f* ....Rom 1:28
a High Priest was *f* ....Heb 7:26

FIVE

f smooth stones ....1 Sam 17:40
about *f* thousand men ......Matt 14:21
and *f* were foolish ....Matt 25:2

FIXED

f My limit for it ....Job 38:10
is a great gulf *f* ....Luke 16:26

FLAME

appeared to him in a *f* ....Ex 3:2
f will dry out his ....Job 15:30
f consumes the chaff ....Is 5:24
and tempest and the *f* ....Is 29:6
nor shall the *f* ....Is 43:2
behind them a *f* ....Joel 2:3
am tormented in this *f* .....Luke 16:24
and His ministers a *f* ....Heb 1:7
and His eyes like a *f* ....Rev 1:14

FLAMES

the LORD divides the *f* ....Ps 29:7

FLAMING

f sword which turned ....Gen 3:24
f fire in their land ....Ps 105:32
in *f* fire taking ....2 Thess 1:8

FLATTER

I do not know how to *f* ......Job 32:22
They *f* with their ....Ps 5:9

FLATTERED

Nevertheless they *f* ....Ps 78:36

FLATTERING

f mouth works ruin ....Prov 26:28

f speech deceive ....Rom 16:18
any time did we use *f* ....1 Thess 2:5
swelling words, *f* ....Jude 16

FLATTERS

with one who *f* with ....Prov 20:19
f his neighbor spreads ....Prov 29:5

FLATTERY

shall corrupt with *f* ....Dan 11:32

FLAVOR

the salt loses its *f* ....Matt 5:13

FLAVORLESS

f food be eaten ....Job 6:6

FLAX

f He will not quench ....Is 42:3
f He will not quench ....Matt 12:20

FLED

The sea saw it and *f* ....Ps 114:3
who have *f* for refuge ....Heb 6:18

FLEE

f away secretly ....Gen 31:27
those who hate You *f* ......Num 10:35
such a man as I *f* ....Neh 6:11
who see me outside *f* ....Ps 31:11
Or where can I *f* ....Ps 139:7
And the shadows *f* ....Song 2:17
who are in Judea *f* ....Matt 24:16
F sexual immorality ....1 Cor 6:18
f these things and ....1 Tim 6:11
devil and he will *f* ....James 4:7

FLESH

bone of my bones and *f* ......Gen 2:23
shall become one *f* ....Gen 2:24
f had corrupted their ....Gen 6:12
f I shall see God ....Job 19:26
My *f* also will rest in ....Ps 16:9
that they were but *f* ....Ps 78:39
my heart and my *f* ....Ps 84:2
f shall bless His holy ....Ps 145:21
is wearisome to the *f* ....Eccl 12:12
And all *f* shall see it ....Is 40:5
"All *f* is grass ....Is 40:6
out My Spirit on all *f* ....Joel 2:28
Simon Bar-Jonah, for *f* .....Matt 16:17
two shall become one *f* ....Matt 19:5
were shortened, no *f* ....Matt 24:22
shall become one *f* ....Mark 10:8
f shall see the ....Luke 3:6
And the Word became *f* .....John 1:14
I shall give is My *f* ....John 6:51
unless you eat the *f* ....John 6:53
f profits nothing ....John 6:63
according to the *f* ....John 8:15
when we were in the *f* ....Rom 7:5
of God, but with the *f* ....Rom 7:25
on the things of the *f* ....Rom 8:5
you are not in the *f* ....Rom 8:9
to the *f* you will die ....Rom 8:13
f should glory in His ....1 Cor 1:29
"shall become one *f* ....1 Cor 6:16
there is one kind of *f* ......1 Cor 15:39
For the *f* lusts ....Gal 5:17
have crucified the *f* ....Gal 5:24
good showing in the *f* ....Gal 6:12
may boast in your *f* ....Gal 6:13
f has ceased from sin ....1 Pet 4:1
of his time in the *f* ....1 Pet 4:2
the lust of the *f* ....1 John 2:16

has come in the *f* ....1 John 4:2
dreamers defile the *f* ....Jude 8

FLESHLY

f wisdom but by the ....2 Cor 1:12
law of a *f* commandment ......Heb 7:16
f lusts which ....1 Pet 2:11

FLIES

will send swarms of *f* ....Ex 8:21
He sent swarms of *f* ....Ps 78:45
Dead *f* putrefy the ....Eccl 10:1

FLIGHT

f shall perish from ....Amos 2:14
And pray that your *f* ....Matt 24:20

FLINT

will seem like *f* ....Is 5:28
set My face like a *f* ....Is 50:7

FLINTY

out of the *f* rock ....Deut 8:15

FLOAT

and he made the iron *f* ....2 Kin 6:6

FLOCK

Your people like a *f* ....Ps 77:20
wilderness like a *f* ....Ps 78:52
lead Joseph like a *f* ....Ps 80:1
the footsteps of the *f* ....Song 1:8
He will feed His *f* ....Is 40:11
you do not feed the *f* ....Ezek 34:3
are My *f*, the *f* ....Ezek 34:31
though the *f* be cut ....Hab 3:17
my God, "Feed the *f* ....Zech 11:4
sheep of the *f* ....Matt 26:31
"Do not fear, little *f* ....Luke 12:32
there will be one *f* ....John 10:16
of the milk of the *f* ....1 Cor 9:7
Shepherd the *f* of God ....1 Pet 5:2
examples to the *f* ....1 Pet 5:3

FLOCKS

are clothed with *f* ....Ps 65:13

FLOOD

the waters of the *f* ....Gen 7:10
sat enthroned at the *F* ....Ps 29:10
them away like a *f* ....Ps 90:5
will you do in the *f* ....Jer 12:5
the days before the *f* ....Matt 24:38
bringing in the *f* ....2 Pet 2:5
of his mouth like a *f* ....Rev 12:15

FLOODS

me, and the *f* of ....Ps 18:4
f on the dry ground ....Is 44:3
rain descended, the *f* ....Matt 7:25

FLOURISH

the righteous shall *f* ....Ps 72:7

FLOURISHED

your care for me has *f* ....Phil 4:10

FLOURISHES

In the morning it *f* ....Ps 90:6

FLOW

f away as waters which ....Ps 58:7
and the waters *f* ....Ps 147:18
that its spices may *f* ....Song 4:16

all nations shall *f* ....Is 2:2
of his heart will *f* ....John 7:38

FLOWER

comes forth like a *f* ....Job 14:2
as a *f* of the field ....Ps 103:15
beauty is a fading *f* ....Is 28:4
is like the *f* of the ....Is 40:6
grass withers, the *f* ....Is 40:7
if she is past the *f* ....1 Cor 7:36
of man as the *f* ....1 Pet 1:24

FLOWERS

f appear on the earth ....Song 2:12

FLOWING

'a land *f* with milk ....Deut 6:3
of wisdom is a *f* ....Prov 18:4
the Gentiles like a *f* ....Is 66:12

FLUTE

play the harp and *f* ....Gen 4:21
sound of the horn, *f* ....Dan 3:5

FLUTES

instruments and *f* ....Ps 150:4

FLUTISTS

harpists, musicians, *f* ....Rev 18:22

FLY

I would *f* ....Ps 55:6
soon cut off, and we *f* ....Ps 90:10
they *f* away like an ....Prov 23:5

FOE

and scattered the *f* ....Ps 18:14

FOES

my enemies and *f* ....Ps 27:2
I will beat down his *f* ....Ps 89:23

FOLD

are not of this *f* ....John 10:16
a cloak You will *f* ....Heb 1:12

FOLDING

slumber, a little *f* ....Prov 6:10

FOLLOW

f what is altogether ....Deut 16:20
to Me, you who *f* ....Is 51:1
f You wherever You go ....Matt 8:19
He said to him, "*F* ....Matt 9:9
up his cross, and *f* ....Mark 8:34
someone who does not *f* ....Mark 9:38
will by no means *f* ....John 10:5
serves Me, let him *f* ....John 12:26
those of some men *f* ....1 Tim 5:24
that you should *f* ....1 Pet 2:21
f the Lamb wherever He ....Rev 14:4
and their works *f* ....Rev 14:13

FOLLOWED

f the LORD my God ....Josh 14:8
LORD took me as I *f* ....Amos 7:15
we have left all and *f* ....Mark 10:28

FOLLOWS

My soul *f* close behind ....Ps 63:8
f Me shall not walk ....John 8:12

FOLLY

taken much notice of *f* ....Job 35:15

not turn back to *f* ....Ps 85:8
F is joy to him who is ....Prov 15:21
of fools is *f* ....Prov 16:22
F is set in great ....Eccl 10:6

FOOD

you it shall be for *f* ....Gen 1:29
that lives shall be *f* ....Gen 9:3
stranger, giving him *f* ....Deut 10:18
He gives *f* in ....Job 36:31
he may bring forth *f* ....Ps 104:14
Who gives *f* to all ....Ps 136:25
Much *f* is in the ....Prov 13:23
night, and provides *f* ....Prov 31:15
f which you eat shall ....Ezek 4:10
the fields yield no *f* ....Hab 3:17
that there may be *f* ....Mal 3:10
to give them *f* ....Matt 24:45
and you gave Me *f* ....Matt 25:35
and he who has *f* ....Luke 3:11
have you any *f* ....John 21:5
they ate their *f* ....Acts 2:46
our hearts with *f* ....Acts 14:17
destroy with your *f* ....Rom 14:15
f makes my brother ....1 Cor 8:13
the same spiritual *f* ....1 Cor 10:3
sower, and bread for *f* ....2 Cor 9:10
And having *f* and ....1 Tim 6:8
and not solid *f* ....Heb 5:12
But solid *f* belongs to ....Heb 5:14
of *f* sold his ....Heb 12:16
destitute of daily *f* ....James 2:15

FOODS

F for the stomach ....1 Cor 6:13
f which God ....1 Tim 4:3

FOOL

f has said in his ....Ps 14:1
is like sport to a *f* ....Prov 10:23
f will be servant ....Prov 11:29
f is right in his own ....Prov 12:15
f lays open his folly ....Prov 13:16
is too lofty for a *f* ....Prov 24:7
whoever says, 'You *f* ....Matt 5:22
I speak as a *f* ....2 Cor 11:23
I have become a *f* ....2 Cor 12:11

FOOLISH

of the *f* women speaks ....Job 2:10
I was so *f* and ....Ps 73:22
f pulls it down with ....Prov 14:1
f man squanders it ....Prov 21:20
"For My people are *f* ....Jer 4:22
Has not God made *f* ....1 Cor 1:20
O *f* Galatians ....Gal 3:1
were also once *f* ....Titus 3:3
But avoid *f* disputes ....Titus 3:9

FOOLISHLY

I speak *f* ....2 Cor 11:21

FOOLISHNESS

O God, You know my *f* ....Ps 69:5
Forsake *f* and live ....Prov 9:6
of fools proclaims *f* ....Prov 12:23
The *f* of a man twists ....Prov 19:3
F is bound up in the ....Prov 22:15
devising of *f* is sin ....Prov 24:9
person will speak *f* ....Is 32:6
of the cross is *f* ....1 Cor 1:18
Because the *f* of God ....1 Cor 1:25

FOOLS

f despise wisdom ....Prov 1:7

folly of *f* is deceit ....Prov 14:8
F mock at sin ....Prov 14:9
has no pleasure in *f* ....Eccl 5:4
We are *f* for Christ's ....1 Cor 4:10

FOOT

will not allow your *f* ....Ps 121:3
f will not stumble ....Prov 3:23
From the sole of the *f* ....Is 1:6
you turn away your *f* ....Is 58:13
f causes you to sin ....Matt 18:8
you dash your *f* ....Luke 4:11
If the *f* should say ....1 Cor 12:15

FOOTMEN

have run with the *f* ....Jer 12:5

FOOTSTEPS

f were not known ....Ps 77:19
and shall make His *f* ....Ps 85:13

FOOTSTOOL

Your enemies Your *f* ....Ps 110:1
Your enemies Your *f* ....Matt 22:44
"Sit here at my *f* ....James 2:3

FORBID

said, "Do not *f* ....Mark 9:39
"Can anyone *f* ....Acts 10:47
prophesy, and do not *f* ....1 Cor 14:39
f that I should boast ....Gal 6:14

FORBIDDING

confidence, no one *f* ....Acts 28:31
f us to speak to the ....1 Thess 2:16
f to marry ....1 Tim 4:3

FORCE

violent take it by *f* ....Matt 11:12
come and take Him by *f* ....John 6:15
a testament is in *f* ....Heb 9:17

FORCEFUL

f are right words ....Job 6:25

FORCES

Though they join *f* ....Prov 11:21

FOREFATHERS

f who refused to hear ....Jer 11:10
and oppressed our *f* ....Acts 7:19
conscience, as my *f* ....2 Tim 1:3

FOREHEADS

against their *f* ....Ezek 3:8
put a mark on the *f* ....Ezek 9:4
seal of God on their *f* ....Rev 9:4
his mark on their *f* ....Rev 20:4

FOREIGNER

"I am a *f* and a ....Gen 23:4
of me, since I am a *f* ....Ruth 2:10
to God except this *f* ....Luke 17:18
who speaks will be a *f* ....1 Cor 14:11

FOREIGNERS

with the children of *f* ....Is 2:6
f shall build up your ....Is 60:10
f who were there ....Acts 17:21
longer strangers and *f* ....Eph 2:19

FOREKNEW

For whom He *f* ....Rom 8:29
His people whom He *f* ....Rom 11:2

FOREKNOWLEDGE

purpose and *f* of God ....Acts 2:23
according to the *f* ....1 Pet 1:2

FOREORDAINED

He indeed was *f* ....1 Pet 1:20

FORERUNNER

f has entered for us ....Heb 6:20

FORESAW

'I *f* the LORD ....Acts 2:25

FORESEEING

f that God would ....Gal 3:8

FORESEES

A prudent man *f* ....Prov 22:3

FOREST

beast of the *f* is Mine ....Ps 50:10
See how great a *f* ....James 3:5

FORESTS

and strips the *f* ....Ps 29:9

FORETOLD

have also *f* these days ....Acts 3:24
killed those who *f* ....Acts 7:52

FOREVER

and eat, and live *f* ....Gen 3:22
to our children *f* ....Deut 29:29
has loved Israel *f* ....1 Kin 10:9
I would not live *f* ....Job 7:16
from this generation *f* ....Ps 12:7
LORD sits as King *f* ....Ps 29:10
Do not cast us off *f* ....Ps 44:23
throne, O God, is *f* ....Ps 45:6
"You are a priest *f* ....Ps 110:4
His mercy endures *f* ....Ps 136:1
will bless Your name *f* ....Ps 145:1
who keeps truth *f* ....Ps 146:6
The LORD shall reign *f* ....Ps 146:10
for riches are not *f* ....Prov 27:24
Trust in the LORD *f* ....Is 26:4
of our God stands *f* ....Is 40:8
My salvation will be *f* ....Is 51:6
will not cast off *f* ....Lam 3:31
be the name of God *f* ....Dan 2:20
Like the stars *f* ....Dan 12:3
of the LORD our God *f* ....Mic 4:5
and the glory *f* ....Matt 6:13
the Christ remains *f* ....John 12:34
who is blessed *f* ....2 Cor 11:31
to whom be glory *f* ....Gal 1:5
generation, *f* and ever ....Eph 3:21
and Father be glory *f* ....Phil 4:20
throne, O God, is *f* ....Heb 1:8
has been perfected *f* ....Heb 7:28
lives and abides *f* ....1 Pet 1:23
of darkness *f* ....Jude 13
power, both now and *f* ....Jude 25
And they shall reign *f* ....Rev 22:5

FOREVERMORE

Blessed be the LORD *f* ....Ps 89:52
this time forth and *f* ....Ps 113:2
behold, I am alive *f* ....Rev 1:18

FOREWARNED

all such, as we also *f* ....1 Thess 4:6

FORGAVE

f the iniquity of my ....Ps 32:5
to repay, he freely *f* ....Luke 7:42
God in Christ *f* ....Eph 4:32
even as Christ *f* ....Col 3:13

FORGED

The proud have *f* ....Ps 119:69

FORGERS

But you *f* of lies ....Job 13:4

FORGET

"For God has made me *f* ....Gen 41:51
yourselves, lest you *f* ....Deut 4:23
f the covenant of your ....Deut 4:31
f the LORD who brought ....Deut 6:12
the paths of all who *f* ....Job 8:13
all the nations that *f* ....Ps 9:17
this, you who *f* ....Ps 50:22
f the works of God ....Ps 78:7
I will not *f* Your word ....Ps 119:16
If I *f* you ....Ps 137:5
My son, do not *f* ....Prov 3:1
f her nursing child ....Is 49:15
f the LORD your Maker ....Is 51:13
f her ornaments ....Jer 2:32
f your work and labor ....Heb 6:10

FORGETFULNESS

in the land of *f* ....Ps 88:12

FORGETS

f the covenant of her ....Prov 2:17
and immediately *f* ....James 1:24

FORGETTING

f those things which ....Phil 3:13

FORGIVE

dwelling place, and *f* ....1 Kin 8:39
f their sin and heal ....2 Chr 7:14
good, and ready to *f* ....Ps 86:5
And *f* us our debts ....Matt 6:12
Father will also *f* ....Matt 6:14
f men their trespasses ....Matt 6:15
his heart, does not *f* ....Matt 18:35
Who can *f* sins but God ....Mark 2:7
f the sins of any ....John 20:23
you ought rather to *f* ....2 Cor 2:7
anything, I also *f* ....2 Cor 2:10
F me this wrong ....2 Cor 12:13
f us our sins and to ....1 John 1:9

FORGIVEN

transgression is *f* ....Ps 32:1
sins be *f* them ....Mark 4:12
to whom little is *f* ....Luke 7:47
indeed I have *f* ....2 Cor 2:10
f you all trespasses ....Col 2:13
sins, he will be *f* ....James 5:15
your sins are *f* ....1 John 2:12

FORGIVENESS

But there is *f* with ....Ps 130:4
God belong mercy and *f* ....Dan 9:9
preached to you the *f* ....Acts 13:38
they may receive *f* ....Acts 26:18
His blood, the *f* ....Eph 1:7

FORGIVES

f all your iniquities ....Ps 103:3
"Who is this who even *f* ....Luke 7:49

FORGIVING

tenderhearted, *f* ....Eph 4:32
and *f* one another ....Col 3:13

FORGOT
remember Joseph, but *f* .....Gen 40:23
f the LORD their God ....Judg 3:7
f His works and His ....Ps 78:11
They soon *f* His works ......Ps 106:13

FORGOTTEN
f the God who fathered .....Deut 32:18
"Why have You *f* ....Ps 42:9
If we had *f* the name ....Ps 44:20
memory of them is *f* ....Eccl 9:5
you will not be *f* ....Is 44:21
And my Lord has *f* ....Is 49:14
I have *f* prosperity ....Lam 3:17
not one of them is *f* ....Luke 12:6
f the exhortation ....Heb 12:5
f that he was cleansed ....2 Pet 1:9

FORM
earth was without *f* ....Gen 1:2
Who would *f* a god or ....Is 44:10
f the light and create ....Is 45:7
descended in bodily *f* ....Luke 3:22
time, nor seen His *f* ....John 5:37
For the *f* of this ....1 Cor 7:31
who, being in the *f* ....Phil 2:6
Abstain from every *f* .....1 Thess 5:22
having a *f* of ....2 Tim 3:5

FORMED
And the LORD God *f* ....Gen 2:7
And His hands *f* ....Ps 95:5
f my inward parts ....Ps 139:13
f everything gives the ......Prov 26:10
say of him who *f* ....Is 29:16
Me there was no God *f* ....Is 43:10
This people I have *f* ....Is 43:21
"Before I *f* you in ....Jer 1:5
Will the thing *f* ....Rom 9:20
say to him who *f* ....Rom 9:20
until Christ is *f* ....Gal 4:19
For Adam was *f* first ....1 Tim 2:13

FORMER
f lovingkindness ....Ps 89:49
f days better than ....Eccl 7:10
f rain to the earth ....Hos 6:3
f prophets preached ....Zech 1:4
f conduct in Judaism ....Gal 1:13
your *f* conduct ....Eph 4:22
f things have passed ....Rev 21:4

FORMS
clay say to him who *f* ....Is 45:9
f the spirit of man ....Zech 12:1

FORNICATION
"We were not born of *f* ....John 8:41
of the wrath of her *f* ....Rev 14:8

FORNICATOR
you know, that no *f* ....Eph 5:5
lest there be any *f* ....Heb 12:16

FORNICATORS
but *f* and adulterers ....Heb 13:4

FORSAKE
but if you *f* Him ....2 Chr 15:2
"If his sons *f* ....Ps 89:30
f His inheritance ....Ps 94:14
But I did not *f* ....Ps 119:87
father, and do not *f* ....Prov 1:8
worthless idols *f* ....Jon 2:8
of you does not *f* ....Luke 14:33
never leave you nor *f* ....Heb 13:5

FORSAKEN
My God, why have You *f* ......Ps 22:1
seen the righteous *f* ....Ps 37:25
you dread will be *f* ....Is 7:16
cities will be as a *f* ....Is 17:9
a mere moment I have *f* ....Is 54:7
no longer be termed *F* ....Is 62:4
they have *f* Me ....Jer 2:13
My God, why have You *f* ...Matt 27:46
persecuted, but not *f* ....2 Cor 4:9
for Demas has *f* ....2 Tim 4:10
f the right way ....2 Pet 2:15

FORSAKING
f the assembling ....Heb 10:25

FORSOOK
f God who made him ....Deut 32:15
all the disciples *f* ....Matt 26:56
with me, but all *f* ....2 Tim 4:16
By faith he *f* Egypt ....Heb 11:27

FORTRESS
LORD is my rock, my *f* .....2 Sam 22:2
my rock of refuge, a *f* ....Ps 31:2

FOUL
My wounds are *f* ....Ps 38:5
f weather today ....Matt 16:3
a prison for every *f* ....Rev 18:2

FOUND
f a helper comparable ....Gen 2:20
where can wisdom be *f* ....Job 28:12
when You may be *f* ....Ps 32:6
f My servant David ....Ps 89:20
a thousand I have *f* ....Eccl 7:28
this only I have *f* ....Eccl 7:29
f the one I love ....Song 3:4
LORD while He may be *f* ....Is 55:6
your fruit is *f* ....Hos 14:8
fruit on it and *f* none ....Luke 13:6
he was lost and is *f* ....Luke 15:24
f the Messiah" (which ....John 1:41
I *f* to bring death ....Rom 7:10
and be *f* in Him ....Phil 3:9
be diligent to be *f* ....2 Pet 3:14

FOUNDATION
he shall lay its *f* ....Josh 6:26
His *f* is in the holy ....Ps 87:1
and justice are the *f* ....Ps 89:14
Of old You laid the *f* ....Ps 102:25
has an everlasting *f* ....Prov 10:25
deep and laid the *f* ....Luke 6:48
the earth without a *f* ....Luke 6:49
loved Me before the *f* ....John 17:24
I have laid the *f* ....1 Cor 3:10
f can anyone lay than ....1 Cor 3:11
us in Him before the *f* ....Eph 1:4
the solid *f* of God ....2 Tim 2:19
not laying again the *f* ....Heb 6:1
Lamb slain from the *f* ....Rev 13:8
the first *f* was jasper ....Rev 21:19

FOUNDATIONS
when I laid the *f* ....Job 38:4
f are destroyed ....Ps 11:3
You who laid the *f* ....Ps 104:5
shall raise up the *f* ....Is 58:12
The *f* of the wall ....Rev 21:19

FOUNDED
For He has *f* it upon ....Ps 24:2
shake it, for it was *f* ....Luke 6:48

FOUNTAIN
will become in him a *f* ....John 4:14

FOUNTAINS
on that day all the *f* ....Gen 7:11
f be dispersed abroad ....Prov 5:16
when there were no *f* ....Prov 8:24
lead them to living *f* ....Rev 7:17

FOX
build, if even a *f* ....Neh 4:3
"Go, tell that *f* ....Luke 13:32

FOXES
caught three hundred *f* ......Judg 15:4
f that spoil the vines ....Song 2:15
F have holes and birds ......Luke 9:58

FRAGMENTS
f that remained ....Matt 14:20
of the leftover *f* ....Luke 9:17
baskets with the *f* ....John 6:13

FRAGRANCE
garments is like the *f* ....Song 4:11
was filled with the *f* ....John 12:3
we are to God the *f* ....2 Cor 2:15

FRAIL
that I may know how *f* ....Ps 39:4

FRAME
For He knows our *f* ....Ps 103:14
f was not hidden ....Ps 139:15

FRAMED
that the worlds were *f* ....Heb 11:3

FREE
and the servant is *f* ....Job 3:19
let the oppressed go *f* ....Is 58:6
'You will be made *f* ....John 8:33
if the Son makes you *f* ....John 8:36
And having been set *f* ....Rom 6:18
now having been set *f* ....Rom 6:22
Jesus has made me *f* ....Rom 8:2
Am I not *f* ....1 Cor 9:1
is neither slave nor *f* ....Gal 3:28
Jerusalem above is *f* ....Gal 4:26
Christ has made us *f* ....Gal 5:1
he is a slave or *f* ....Eph 6:8
poor, *f* and slave ....Rev 13:16

FREED
has died has been *f* ....Rom 6:7

FREEDMAN
slave is the Lord's *f* ....1 Cor 7:22

FREELY
the garden you may *f* ....Gen 2:16
I will love them *f* ....Hos 14:4
F you have received ....Matt 10:8
f give us all ....Rom 8:32
that have been *f* ....1 Cor 2:12
the water of life *f* ....Rev 22:17

FREEWOMAN
the other by a *f* ....Gal 4:22
with the son of the *f* ....Gal 4:30

FRESH
My glory is *f* within ....Job 29:20

They shall be *f* ....Ps 92:14
both salt water and *f* ....James 3:12

FRETS

and his heart *f* ....Prov 19:3

FRIEND

a man speaks to his *f*..........Ex 33:11
of Abraham Your *f* ....2 Chr 20:7
though he were my *f* ....Ps 35:14
f You have put ....Ps 88:18
f loves at all times ....Prov 17:17
f who sticks closer ....Prov 18:24
not forsake your own *f* ....Prov 27:10
a *f* of tax collectors ....Matt 11:19
of you shall have a *f* ....Luke 11:5
f Lazarus sleeps ....John 11:11
you are not Caesar's *f* ....John 19:12
Philemon our beloved *f* ....Philem 1
he was called the *f* ....James 2:23
wants to be a *f* ....James 4:4

FRIENDS

and hate your *f* ....2 Sam 19:6
My *f* scorn me ....Job 16:20
f have forgotten me ....Job 19:14
the rich has many *f* ....Prov 14:20
one's life for his *f* ....John 15:13
You are My *f* ....John 15:14
I have called you *f* ....John 15:15
to forbid any of his *f* ....Acts 24:23

FROGS

your territory with *f*..................Ex 8:2
f coming out of the ....Rev 16:13

FRONTLETS

on your hand and as *f* ....Ex 13:16
and they shall be as *f* ....Deut 6:8

FROZEN

the broad waters are *f* ....Job 37:10

FRUIT

and showed them the *f* .....Num 13:26
Blessed shall be the *f* ....Deut 28:4
brings forth its *f*......................Ps 1:3
f is better than gold ....Prov 8:19
The *f* of the righteous ....Prov 11:30
with good by the *f* ....Prov 12:14
f was sweet to my ....Song 2:3
they shall eat the *f* ....Is 3:10
like the first *f* ....Is 28:4
"I create the *f* ....Is 57:19
f is found in Me ....Hos 14:8
does not bear good *f* ....Matt 3:10
good tree bears good *f* ....Matt 7:17
not drink of this *f* ....Matt 26:29
and blessed is the *f* ....Luke 1:42
life, and bring no *f* ....Luke 8:14
and he came seeking *f* ....Luke 13:6
And if it bears *f* ....Luke 13:9
branch that bears *f* ....John 15:2
that you bear much *f* ....John 15:8
should go and bear *f* ....John 15:16
f did you have then in ....Rom 6:21
God, you have your *f* ....Rom 6:22
that we should bear *f* ....Rom 7:4
But the *f* of the ....Gal 5:22
but I seek the *f* ....Phil 4:17
yields the peaceable *f* ....Heb 12:11
Now the *f* of ....James 3:18
autumn trees without *f* ....Jude 12
tree yielding its *f* ....Rev 22:2

FRUITFUL

them, saying, "Be *f* ....Gen 1:22
a *f* bough, a *f* ....Gen 49:22
wife shall be like a *f* ....Ps 128:3
heaven and *f* seasons ....Acts 14:17
pleasing Him, being *f* ....Col 1:10

FRUITS

Therefore bear *f* ....Matt 3:8
know them by their *f* ....Matt 7:16
and increase the *f* ....2 Cor 9:10
of mercy and good *f* ....James 3:17
which bore twelve *f* ....Rev 22:2

FUEL

people shall be as *f* ....Is 9:19
into the fire for *f* ....Ezek 15:4

FULFILL

the LORD, to *f* his vow ....Lev 22:21
And you shall *f* ....1 Kin 5:9
f all your petitions ....Ps 20:5
f the desire of those ....Ps 145:19
for us to *f* all ....Matt 3:15
f the law of Christ ....Gal 6:2
f my joy by being ....Phil 2:2
and *f* all the good ....2 Thess 1:11
If you really *f* ....James 2:8

FULFILLED

the law till all is *f* ....Matt 5:18
of the Gentiles are *f* ....Luke 21:24
all things must be *f* ....Luke 24:44
of the law might be *f* ....Rom 8:4
loves another has *f* ....Rom 13:8
For all the law is *f* ....Gal 5:14

FULFILLMENT

for there will be a *f* ....Luke 1:45
love is the *f* of the ....Rom 13:10

FULL

I went out *f* ....Ruth 1:21
For I am *f* of words ....Job 32:18
of the LORD is *f* ....Ps 29:4
who has his quiver *f* ....Ps 127:5
Lest I be *f* and deny ....Prov 30:9
yet the sea is not *f* ....Eccl 1:7
the whole earth is *f* ....Is 6:3
and it was *f* of bones ....Ezek 37:1
But truly I am *f* ....Mic 3:8
whole body will be *f* ....Matt 6:22
of the Father, *f* ....John 1:14
your joy may be *f* ....John 15:11
chose Stephen, a man *f* ....Acts 6:5
You are already *f* ....1 Cor 4:8
learned both to be *f* ....Phil 4:12
I am *f*, having received ....Phil 4:18

FULL-GROWN

and sin, when it is *f* ....James 1:15

FULLNESS

satisfied with the *f* ....Ps 36:8
f we have all received ....John 1:16
to Israel until the *f* ....Rom 11:25
But when the *f* of the ....Gal 4:4
dispensation of the *f* ....Eph 1:10
filled with all the *f* ....Eph 3:19
Him dwells all the *f* ....Col 2:9

FUME

Why do you *f* with envy ....Ps 68:16

FUNCTION

do not have the same *f* ....Rom 12:4

FURIOUS

You have been *f* ....Ps 89:38
f man do not go ....Prov 22:24
fury and in *f* rebukes ....Ezek 5:15
LORD avenges and is *f* ....Nah 1:2
this, they were *f* ....Acts 5:33

FURIOUSLY

for he drives *f* ....2 Kin 9:20

FURNACE

you out of the iron *f* ....Deut 4:20
tested you in the *f* ....Is 48:10
of a burning fiery *f* ....Dan 3:6
cast them into the *f* ....Matt 13:42
the smoke of a great *f* ....Rev 9:2

FURNISHED

also *f* her table ....Prov 9:2
a large upper room, *f* ....Mark 14:15

FURY

F is not in Me ....Is 27:4
they are full of the *f* ....Is 51:20
f to His adversaries ....Is 59:18
and My own *f* ....Is 63:5
even in anger and *f* ....Jer 21:5
and I will cause My *f* ....Ezek 5:13
Thus will I spend My *f* ....Ezek 6:12
in anger and *f* on the ....Mic 5:15

FUTILE

For it is not a *f* ....Deut 32:47
of the peoples are *f* ....Jer 10:3
wise, that they are *f* ....1 Cor 3:20
risen, your faith is *f* ....1 Cor 15:17

FUTILITY

allotted months of *f* ....Job 7:3
f have You created all ....Ps 89:47
was subjected to *f* ....Rom 8:20

FUTURE

for the *f* of that man ....Ps 37:37
the *f* of the wicked ....Ps 37:38
to give you a *f* ....Jer 29:11

—G—

GAAL

Son of Ebed; vilifies Abimelech, Judg 9:26–41

GAASH

Hill of Ephraim, Judg 2:9
Joshua buried near, Josh 24:30

GABBATHA

Place of Pilate's court, John 19:13

GABRIEL

Messenger archangel; interprets Daniel's vision, Dan 8:16–27
Reveals the prophecy of 70 weeks, Dan 9:21–27
Announces John's birth, Luke 1:11–22
Announces Christ's birth, Luke 1:26–38
Stands in God's presence, Luke 1:19

GAD

Son of Jacob by Zilpah, Gen 30:10, 11
Blessed by Jacob, Gen 49:19
——Tribe of:
Census of, Num 1:24, 25
Territory of, Num 32:20–36
Captivity of, 1 Chr 5:26

Later references to, Rev 7:5
——— Prophet in David's reign, 1 Sam 22:5
Message of, to David, 2 Sam 24:10–16

GADARENES (or Gergesenes)

People east of the Sea of Galilee, Mark 5:1
Healing of demon-possessed in territory of, Matt 8:28–34

GAIN

g than fine gold ....Prov 3:14
will have no lack of *g* ....Prov 31:11
a time to *g* ....Eccl 3:6
to get dishonest *g* ....Ezek 22:27
him who covets evil *g* ....Hab 2:9
and to die is *g* ....Phil 1:21
rubbish, that I may *g* ....Phil 3:8
is a means of *g* ....1 Tim 6:5
contentment is great *g* ....1 Tim 6:6
for dishonest *g* ....1 Pet 5:2

GAINED

g more wisdom than all ....Eccl 1:16
g five more talents ....Matt 25:20

GAINS

g the whole world ....Matt 16:26

GAIUS

Companion of Paul, Acts 19:29
——— Convert at Derbe, Acts 20:4
——— Paul's host at Corinth, Rom 16:23; 1 Cor 1:14

GALATIA

Paul visits, Acts 16:6; 18:23
Paul writes to Christians in, Gal 1:1
Peter writes to Christians in, 1 Pet 1:1

GALILEANS

Speech of, Mark 14:70
Faith of, John 4:45
Pilate's cruelty toward, Luke 13:1, 2

GALILEE

Prophecies concerning, Deut 33:18–23; Is 9:1, 2
Dialect of, distinctive, Matt 26:73
Herod's jurisdiction over, Luke 3:1
Christ's contacts with, Matt 2:22; 4:12–25; 26:32; 27:55; John 4:1, 3

GALILEE, SEA OF

Scene of many events in Christ's life, Mark 7:31
Called Chinnereth, Num 34:11
Later called Gennesaret, Luke 5:1

GALL

They also gave me *g* ....Ps 69:21
the wormwood and the *g* ....Lam 3:19
turned justice into *g* ....Amos 6:12
wine mingled with *g* ....Matt 27:34

GALLIO

Roman proconsul of Achaia, dismisses charges against Paul, Acts 18:12–17

GAMALIEL

Famous Jewish teacher, Acts 22:3
Respected by people, Acts 5:34–39

GAP

and stand in the *g* ....Ezek 22:30

GARDEN

LORD God planted a *g* ....Gen 2:8
g enclosed is my ....Song 4:12
like a watered *g* ....Is 58:11
Eden, the *g* of God ....Ezek 28:13
raise up for them a *g* ....Ezek 34:29
where there was a *g* ....John 18:1
in the *g* a new tomb ....John 19:41

GARDENER

Him to be the *g* ....John 20:15

GARDENS

I made myself *g* ....Eccl 2:5
plant *g* and eat their ....Jer 29:5

GARLANDS

brought oxen and *g* ....Acts 14:13

GARMENT

beautiful Babylonian *g* ....Josh 7:21
g that is moth-eaten ....Job 13:28
made sackcloth my *g* ....Ps 69:11
with light as with a *g* ....Ps 104:2
one who takes away a *g* .....Prov 25:20
the hem of His *g* ....Matt 9:20
have on a wedding *g* ....Matt 22:11
cloth on an old *g* ....Mark 2:21
all grow old like a *g* ....Heb 1:11
hating even the *g* ....Jude 23

GARMENTS

g did not wear out on ....Deut 8:4
Why are your *g* hot ....Job 37:17
They divide My *g* ....Ps 22:18
g always be white ....Eccl 9:8
g rolled in blood ....Is 9:5
from Edom, with dyed *g* ....Is 63:1
Take away the filthy *g* ....Zech 3:4
man clothed in soft *g* ....Matt 11:8
spread their *g* on the ....Matt 21:8
and divided His *g* ....Matt 27:35
by them in shining *g* ....Luke 24:4
g are moth-eaten ....James 5:2
be clothed in white *g* ....Rev 3:5

GARRISON

gathered the whole *g* ....Matt 27:27
Damascenes with a *g* ......2 Cor 11:32

GATE

This is the *g* of the ....Ps 118:20
by the narrow *g* ....Matt 7:13
by the Sheep *G* a pool ....John 5:2
laid daily at the *g* ....Acts 3:2
suffered outside the *g* ....Heb 13:12
each individual *g* ....Rev 21:21

GATES

possess the *g* of those ....Gen 24:60
g are burned with fire ....Neh 1:3
they go down to the *g* ....Job 17:16
up your heads, O you *g* ....Ps 24:7
The LORD loves the *g* ....Ps 87:2
Open to me the *g* ....Ps 118:19
is known in the *g* ....Prov 31:23
go through the *g* ....Is 62:10
and the *g* of Hades ....Matt 16:18
wall with twelve *g* ....Rev 21:12
g were twelve pearls ....Rev 21:21
g shall not be shut ....Rev 21:25

GATH

Philistine city, 1 Sam 6:17
Ark carried to, 1 Sam 5:8
David takes refuge in, 1 Sam 21:10–15
David's second flight to, 1 Sam 27:3–12
Captured by David, 1 Chr 18:1
Destruction of, prophetic, Amos 6:1–3
Name becomes proverbial, Mic 1:10

GATHER

g my soul with sinners ....Ps 26:9
G My saints ....Ps 50:5
and a time to *g* stones ....Eccl 3:5
g the lambs with His ....Is 40:11
g His wheat into the ....Matt 3:12
sow nor reap nor *g* ....Matt 6:26
Do men *g* grapes from ....Matt 7:16
g where I have not ....Matt 25:26
g together His ....Mark 13:27

GATHERED

g little had no lack ....Ex 16:18
And *g* out of the lands ....Ps 107:3
g some of every kind ....Matt 13:47
the nations will be *g* ....Matt 25:32

GATHERING

g together of the ....Gen 1:10
g together to Him ....2 Thess 2:1

GATHERS

g the waters of the ....Ps 33:7
His heart *g* iniquity ....Ps 41:6
g her food in the ....Prov 6:8
The Lord GOD, who *g* ....Is 56:8
together, as a hen *g* ....Matt 23:37

GAVE

to be with me, she *g* ....Gen 3:12
g You this authority ....Matt 21:23
that He *g* His only ....John 3:16
Those whom You *g* ....John 17:12
but God *g* the increase ....1 Cor 3:6
g Himself for our sins ....Gal 1:4
g Himself for me ....Gal 2:20
g Himself for it ....Eph 5:25
The sea *g* up the dead ....Rev 20:13

GAZA

Philistine city, Josh 13:3
Samson removes the gates of, Judg 16:1–3
Samson taken there as prisoner; his revenge, Judg 16:21–31
Sin of, condemned, Amos 1:6, 7
Philip journeys to, Acts 8:26

GAZED

g into heaven and saw ....Acts 7:55

GAZING

why do you stand *g* ....Acts 1:11

GEDALIAH

Made governor of Judah, 2 Kin 25:22–26
Befriends Jeremiah, Jer 40:5, 6
Murdered by Ishmael, Jer 41:2, 18

GEHAZI

Elisha's servant; seeks reward from Naaman, 2 Kin 5:20–24
Afflicted with leprosy, 2 Kin 5:25–27
Relates Elisha's deeds to Jehoram, 2 Kin 8:4–6

GENEALOGIES

fables and endless *g* ....1 Tim 1:4

GENEALOGY

The book of the *g* ....Matt 1:1
mother, without *g* ....Heb 7:3

GENERATION

perverse and crooked *g* .....Deut 32:5
The *g* of the upright ....Ps 112:2
g shall praise Your ....Ps 145:4
g that curses its ....Prov 30:11
g that is pure in its ....Prov 30:12
One *g* passes away ....Eccl 1:4
g it shall lie ....Is 34:10
who will declare His *g* ....Is 53:8
and adulterous *g* ....Matt 12:39
this *g* will by no ....Matt 24:34
from this perverse *g* ....Acts 2:40
But you are a chosen *g* ....1 Pet 2:9

GENERATIONS

be remembered in all *g* ......Ps 45:17
Your praise to all *g* ....Ps 79:13
for a thousand *g* ....Ps 105:8
g will call me blessed ....Luke 1:48

GENEROUS

g soul will be made ....Prov 11:25
g eye will be blessed ....Prov 22:9
no longer be called *g* ....Is 32:5
g man devises *g* ....Is 32:8

GENTILES

G were separated ....Gen 10:5
as a light to the *G* ....Is 42:6
G shall come to your ....Is 60:3
the riches of the *G* ....Is 61:6
all these things the *G* ....Matt 6:32
into the way of the *G* ....Matt 10:5
revelation to the *G* ....Luke 2:32
G are fulfilled ....Luke 21:24
bear My name before *G* .....Acts 9:15
poured out on the *G* ....Acts 10:45
a light to the *G* ....Acts 13:47
blasphemed among the *G* ....Rom 2:24
also the God of the *G* ....Rom 3:29
even named among the *G* ....1 Cor 5:1
mystery among the *G* ....Col 1:27
a teacher of the *G* ....1 Tim 2:7
nothing from the *G* ....3 John 7

GENTLE

g tongue breaks a bone .....Prov 25:15
from Me, for I am *g* ....Matt 11:29
But we were *g* among ......1 Thess 2:7
to be peaceable, *g* ....Titus 3:2
only to the good and *g* ......1 Pet 2:18
ornament of a *g* ....1 Pet 3:4

GENTLENESS

g has made me great ....Ps 18:35
love and a spirit of *g* ....1 Cor 4:21
g, self-control ....Gal 5:23
all lowliness and *g* ....Eph 4:2
Let your *g* be known to ....Phil 4:5
love, patience, *g* ....1 Tim 6:11

GERAR

Town of Philistia, Gen 10:19
Visited by Abraham, Gen 20:1–18
Visited by Isaac, Gen 26:1–17
Abimelech, king of, Gen 26:1, 26

GERIZIM

See MOUNT GERIZIM

GERSHOM (or Gershon)

Son of Moses, Ex 2:21, 22
Circumcised, Ex 4:25
Founder of Levite family, 1 Chr 23:14–16

GESHUR

Inhabitants of, not expelled by Israel, Josh 13:13
Talmai, king of, grandfather of Absalom, 2 Sam 3:3
Absalom flees to, 2 Sam 13:37, 38

GETHSEMANE

Garden near Jerusalem, Matt 26:30, 36
Often visited by Christ, Luke 22:39
Scene of Christ's agony and betrayal, Matt 26:36–56; John 18:1–12

GEZER

Canaanite city, Josh 10:33
Inhabitants not expelled, Josh 16:10
Given as dowry of Pharaoh's daughter, 1 Kin 9:15–17

GHOST

supposed it was a *g* ....Mark 6:49

GIBEAH

Town of Benjamin; known for wickedness, Judg 19:12–30
Destruction of, Judg 20:1–48
Saul's birthplace, 1 Sam 10:26
Saul's political capital, 1 Sam 15:34
Wickedness of, long remembered, Hos 9:9

GIBEON

Sun stands still at, Josh 10:12
Location of tabernacle, 1 Chr 16:39
Joab struck Amasa at, 2 Sam 20:8–10
Joab killed at, 1 Kin 2:28–34
Site of Solomon's sacrifice and dream, 1 Kin 3:5–15

GIBEONITES

Trick Joshua into making treaty; subjected to forced labor, Josh 9:3–27
Rescued by Joshua, Josh 10
Massacred by Saul; avenged by David, 2 Sam 21:1–9

GIDEON

Called by an angel, Judg 6:11–24
Destroys Baal's altar, Judg 6:25–32
Fleece confirms call from God, Judg 6:36–40
Miraculous victory over the Midianites, Judg 7
Takes revenge on Succoth and Penuel, Judg 8:4–21
Refuses kingship; makes an ephod, Judg 8:22–28
Fathers seventy-one sons; dies, Judg 8:29–35

GIFT

g makes room for him .....Prov 18:16
A *g* in secret pacifies ....Prov 21:14
it is the *g* of God ....Eccl 3:13
is Corban"—'(that is, a *g* ....Mark 7:11
"If you knew the *g* ....John 4:10
But the free *g* is not ....Rom 5:15
but the *g* of God is ....Rom 6:23
each one has his own *g* ....1 Cor 7:7
though I have the *g* ....1 Cor 13:2
it is the *g* of God ....Eph 2:8
Not that I seek the *g* ....Phil 4:17
Do not neglect the *g* ....1 Tim 4:14
you to stir up the *g* ....2 Tim 1:6
tasted the heavenly *g* ....Heb 6:4
Every good *g* and every ......James 1:17
one has received a *g* ....1 Pet 4:10

GIFTED

the women who were *g* ......Ex 35:25
but good-looking, *g* ....Dan 1:4

GIFTS

g you shall offer ....Num 18:29
You have received *g* ....Ps 68:18
and Seba will offer *g* ....Ps 72:10
though you give many *g* .....Prov 6:35
to one who gives *g* ....Prov 19:6
how to give good *g* ....Matt 7:11
rich putting their *g* ....Luke 21:1
g differing ....Rom 12:6
are diversities of *g* ....1 Cor 12:4
and desire spiritual *g* .....1 Cor 14:1
captive, and gave *g* ....Eph 4:8

GIHON

River of Eden, Gen 2:13
——Spring outside Jerusalem, 1 Kin 1:33–45
Source of water supply, 2 Chr 32:30

GILBOA

Range of limestone hills in Issachar, 1 Sam 28:4
Scene of Saul's death, 1 Sam 31:1–9
Under David's curse, 2 Sam 1:17, 21

GILEAD

Plain east of the Jordan; taken from the Amorites and assigned to Gad, Reuben, and Manasseh, Num 21:21–31; 32:33–40; Deut 3:12, 13; Josh 13:24–31
Ishbosheth rules over, 2 Sam 2:8, 9
David takes refuge in, 2 Sam 17:21–26
Conquered by Hazael, 2 Kin 10:32, 33
Balm of, figurative of national healing, Jer 8:22

GILGAL

Site of memorial stones, circumcision, first Passover in the Promised Land, Josh 4:19—5:12
Site of Gibeonite covenant, Josh 9:3–15
One location on Samuel's circuit, 1 Sam 7:15, 16
Saul made king and later rejected, 1 Sam 11:15; 13:4–15
Denounced for idolatry, Hos 9:15

GIRD

G Your sword upon Your ....Ps 45:3
of wrath You shall *g* ....Ps 76:10
I will *g* you ....Is 45:5
and another will *g* ....John 21:18
Therefore *g* up the ....1 Pet 1:13

GIRDED

a towel and *g* Himself ......John 13:4
down to the feet and *g* ......Rev 1:13

GIRGASHITES

Descendants of Canaan, Gen 10:15, 16
Land of, given to Abraham's descendants, Gen 15:18, 21
Delivered to Israel, Josh 24:11

GITTITES

600 follow David, 2 Sam 15:18–23

GIVE

g thanks to the LORD ....1 Chr 16:8
g me wisdom and ....2 Chr 1:10
G ear to my prayer ....Ps 17:1
G to them according ....Ps 28:4
g you the desires ....Ps 37:4
Yes, the LORD will *g* ....Ps 85:12
G me understanding ....Ps 119:34
g me your heart ....Prov 23:26
You will *g* truth to ....Mic 7:20
G to him who asks ....Matt 5:42
G us this day our ....Matt 6:11
what you have and *g* ....Matt 19:21
authority I will *g* ....Luke 4:6
g them eternal life ....John 10:28
A new commandment I *g* ...John 13:34
but what I do have I *g* ....Acts 3:6
g us all things ....Rom 8:32
G no offense ....1 Cor 10:32
So let each one *g* ....2 Cor 9:7
g him who has need ....Eph 4:28
g thanks to God always ...2 Thess 2:13
g yourself entirely ....1 Tim 4:15
good works, ready to *g* .....1 Tim 6:18

GIVEN

to him more will be *g* ......Matt 13:12
has, more will be *g* ....Matt 25:29
to whom much is *g* ....Luke 12:48
g Me I should lose ....John 6:39
Spirit was not yet *g* ....John 7:39
have been freely *g* ....1 Cor 2:12
not *g* to wine ....1 Tim 3:3

GIVES

He who *g* to the poor ....Prov 28:27
For God *g* wisdom and ......Eccl 2:26
g life to the world ....John 6:33
All that the Father *g* ....John 6:37
The good shepherd *g* ....John 10:11
not as the world *g* ....John 14:27
g us richly all things ....1 Tim 6:17
who *g* to all liberally ....James 1:5
But He *g* more grace ....James 4:6
g grace to the humble ....James 4:6

GLAD

I will be *g* and ....Ps 9:2
my heart is *g* ....Ps 16:9
Be *g* in the LORD and ....Ps 32:11
streams shall make *g* ....Ps 46:4
And wine that makes *g* ......Ps 104:15
I was *g* when they said ....Ps 122:1
make merry and be *g* .....Luke 15:32
he saw it and was *g* ....John 8:56

GLADNESS

in the day of your *g* ....Num 10:10
day of feasting and *g* ....Esth 9:17
You have put *g* in my ....Ps 4:7
me hear joy and *g* ....Ps 51:8
Serve the LORD with *g* ....Ps 100:2
shall obtain joy and *g* ....Is 35:10
over you with *g* ....Zeph 3:17
receive it with *g* ....Mark 4:16

GLASS

there was a sea of *g* ....Rev 4:6
like transparent *g* ....Rev 21:21

GLORIFIED

the people I must be *g* ....Lev 10:3
and they *g* the God of ....Matt 15:31
Jesus was not yet *g* ....John 7:39
when Jesus was *g* ....John 12:16
By this My Father is *g* ....John 15:8
I have *g* You on the ....John 17:4
g His Servant Jesus ....Acts 3:13
these He also *g* ....Rom 8:30
things God may be *g* ....1 Pet 4:11

GLORIFY

My altar, and I will *g* ....Is 60:7
g your Father in ....Matt 5:16
"Father, *g* Your name ....John 12:28
He will *g* Me ....John 16:14
And now, O Father, *g* ....John 17:5
what death he would *g* ....John 21:19
God, they did not *g* ....Rom 1:21
therefore *g* God in ....1 Cor 6:20
also Christ did not *g* ....Heb 5:5
ashamed, but let him *g* .....1 Pet 4:16

GLORIOUS

daughter is all *g* ....Ps 45:13
And blessed be His *g* ....Ps 72:19
G things are spoken ....Ps 87:3
is honorable and *g* ....Ps 111:3
g splendor of Your ....Ps 145:5
habitation, holy and *g* ....Is 63:15
it to Himself a *g* ....Eph 5:27
be conformed to His *g* ....Phil 3:21
g appearing of our ....Titus 2:13

GLORY

"Please, show me Your *g* .....Ex 33:18
g has departed from ....1 Sam 4:21
G in His holy name ....1 Chr 16:10
a shield for me, my *g* ....Ps 3:3
who have set Your *g* ....Ps 8:1
Who is this King of *g* ....Ps 24:8
the place where Your *g* ....Ps 26:8
Your power and Your *g* ....Ps 63:2
shall speak of the *g* ....Ps 145:11
wise shall inherit *g* ....Prov 3:35
The *g* of young men is .....Prov 20:29
It is the *g* of God to ....Prov 25:2
"*G* to the righteous ....Is 24:16
g I will not give ....Is 42:8
g will be seen upon ....Is 60:2
then be likened in *g* ....Ezek 31:18
I will change their *g* ....Hos 4:7
and I will be the *g* ....Zech 2:5
He shall bear the *g* ....Zech 6:13
that they may have *g* ....Matt 6:2
the power and the *g* ....Matt 6:13
g was not arrayed ....Matt 6:29
Man will come in the *g* .....Matt 16:27
with power and great *g* ....Matt 24:30
"*G* to God in the ....Luke 2:14
and we beheld His *g* ....John 1:14
and manifested His *g* ....John 2:11
I do not seek My own *g* .....John 8:50
"Give God the *g* ....John 9:24
g which I had with You .....John 17:5
g which You gave Me I .....John 17:22
he did not give *g* ....Acts 12:23
doing good seek for *g* ....Rom 2:7
fall short of the *g* ....Rom 3:23
in faith, giving *g* ....Rom 4:20
the adoption, the *g* ....Rom 9:4
the riches of His *g* ....Rom 9:23
God, alone wise, be *g* ....Rom 16:27
who glories, let him *g* ....1 Cor 1:31
but woman is the *g* ....1 Cor 11:7
of the *g* that excels ....2 Cor 3:10
of the gospel of the *g* ....2 Cor 4:4
eternal weight of *g* ....2 Cor 4:17
who glories, let him *g* ......2 Cor 10:17
to His riches in *g* ....Phil 4:19
appear with Him in *g* ....Col 3:4
For you are our *g* ....1 Thess 2:20
many sons to *g* ....Heb 2:10
grass, and all the *g* ....1 Pet 1:24
to whom belong the *g* ....1 Pet 4:11
for the Spirit of *g* ....1 Pet 4:14
the presence of His *g* ....Jude 24
O Lord, to receive *g* ....Rev 4:11
g of God illuminated ....Rev 21:23

GLORYING

Your *g* is not good ....1 Cor 5:6

GLUTTON

g will come to poverty .....Prov 23:21
you say, 'Look, a *g* ....Luke 7:34

GLUTTONS

g shames his ....Prov 28:7
evil beasts, lazy *g* ....Titus 1:12

GNASHING

will be weeping and *g* ....Matt 8:12

GO

He said, "Let Me *g* ....Gen 32:26
'Let My people *g* ....Ex 5:1
Presence does not *g* ....Ex 33:15
for wherever you *g* ....Ruth 1:16
"Look, I *g* forward ....Job 23:8
For I used to *g* ....Ps 42:4
g astray as soon as ....Ps 58:3
I will *g* in the ....Ps 71:16
Those who *g* down to ....Ps 107:23
Where can I *g* from ....Ps 139:7
G to the ant ....Prov 6:6
All *g* to one place ....Eccl 3:20
of mourning than to *g* ....Eccl 7:2
of Zion shall *g* ....Is 2:3
You wherever You *g* ....Matt 8:19
do not *g* out ....Matt 24:26
He said to them, "*G* ....Mark 16:15
And I say to one, '*G* ....Luke 7:8
also want to *g* away ....John 6:67
to whom shall we *g* ....John 6:68
g you cannot come ....John 8:21
I *g* to prepare a place ....John 14:2
will do, because I *g* ....John 14:12
seek Me, let these *g* ....John 18:8
and he shall *g* out no more ...Rev 3:12

GOADS

of the wise are like *g* ....Eccl 12:11
to kick against the *g* ....Acts 9:5

GOAL

I press toward the *g* ....Phil 3:14

GOATS

drink the blood of *g* ....Ps 50:13
his sheep from the *g* ....Matt 25:32
with the blood of *g* ....Heb 9:12
g could take away ....Heb 10:4

GOD

G created the heavens ....Gen 1:1
Abram of *G* Most High ....Gen 14:19
and I will be their *G* ....Gen 17:8
of the Mighty *G* ....Gen 49:24
the *G* of Abraham ....Ex 3:6
He is my *G* ....Ex 15:2
Stand before *G* for the ....Ex 18:19
"I am the LORD your *G* ....Ex 20:2

"This is your g ....Ex 32:4
G is not a man ....Num 23:19
G is a consuming fire ....Deut 4:24
great and awesome G ....Deut 7:21
my people, and your G ....Ruth 1:16
know that there is a G ....1 Sam 17:46
a rock, except our G ....2 Sam 22:32
If the LORD is G ....1 Kin 18:21
G is greater than all ....2 Chr 2:5
G is greater than ....Job 33:12
"Behold, G is mighty ....Job 36:5
"Behold, G is great ....Job 36:26
You have been My G ....Ps 22:10
"Where is your G ....Ps 42:3
G is our refuge ....Ps 46:1
G is in the midst of ....Ps 46:5
G is the King of all ....Ps 47:7
The Mighty One, G ....Ps 50:1
I am G ....Ps 50:7
me a clean heart, O G ....Ps 51:10
Our G is the G ....Ps 68:20
Who is so great a G ....Ps 77:13
Restore us, O G ....Ps 80:7
You alone are G ....Ps 86:10
Exalt the LORD our G ....Ps 99:9
Yes, our G is merciful ....Ps 116:5
give thanks to the G ....Ps 136:26
For G is in heaven ....Eccl 5:2
Counselor, Mighty G ....Is 9:6
G is my salvation ....Is 12:2
Behold, this is our G ....Is 25:9
"Behold your G ....Is 40:9
Is there a G besides ....Is 44:8
to Zion, "Your G ....Is 52:7
stricken, smitten by G ....Is 53:4
and I will be their G ....Jer 31:33
and I saw visions of G ....Ezek 1:1
Who is a G like You ....Mic 7:18
"G with us ....Matt 1:23
in G my Savior ....Luke 1:47
the Word was with G ....John 1:1
enter the kingdom of G ....John 3:5
For G so loved the ....John 3:16
has certified that G ....John 3:33
G is Spirit ....John 4:24
"My Lord and my G ....John 20:28
Christ is the Son of G ....Acts 8:37
To the Unknown G ....Acts 17:23
Indeed, let G be true ....Rom 3:4
If G is for us ....Rom 8:31
G is faithful ....1 Cor 1:9
us there is one G ....1 Cor 8:6
G shall supply all ....Phil 4:19
and I will be their G ....Heb 8:10
G is a consuming fire ....Heb 12:29
G is greater than our ....1 John 3:20
for G is love ....1 John 4:8
No one has seen G ....1 John 4:12
in the temple of My G ....Rev 3:12
gave glory to the G ....Rev 11:13
G Himself will be ....Rev 21:3
and I will be his G ....Rev 21:7

GODDESS

after Ashtoreth the g ....1 Kin 11:5
of the great g Diana ....Acts 19:35

GODHEAD

eternal power and G ....Rom 1:20
the fullness of the G ....Col 2:9

GODLINESS

is the mystery of g ....1 Tim 3:16
g is profitable ....1 Tim 4:8
Now g with contentment ....1 Tim 6:6
having a form of g ....2 Tim 3:5
pertain to life and g ....2 Pet 1:3
to perseverance g ....2 Pet 1:6

GODLY

Himself him who is g ....Ps 4:3
everyone who is g ....Ps 32:6
who desire to live g ....2 Tim 3:12
righteously, and g ....Titus 2:12
reverence and g fear ....Heb 12:28
to deliver the g ....2 Pet 2:9

GODS

your God is God of g ....Deut 10:17
the household g ....2 Kin 23:24
He judges among the g ....Ps 82:1
I said, "You are g ....Ps 82:6
yourselves with g ....Is 57:5
If He called them g ....John 10:35
g have come down to ....Acts 14:11

GOG

Prince of Rosh, Meshech, and Tubal, Ezek 38:2, 3
——Leader of the final battle, Rev 20:8–15

GOLD

And the g of that land ....Gen 2:12
a mercy seat of pure g ....Ex 25:17
multiply silver and g ....Deut 17:17
"If I have made g ....Job 31:24
yea, than much fine g ....Ps 19:10
is like apples of g ....Prov 25:11
is Mine, and the g ....Hag 2:8
g I do not have ....Acts 3:6
with braided hair or g ....1 Tim 2:9
a man with g rings ....James 2:2
Your g and silver are ....James 5:3
more precious than g ....1 Pet 1:7
like silver or g ....1 Pet 1:18
of the city was pure g ....Rev 21:21

GOLGOTHA

Where Jesus died, Matt 27:33–35

GOLIATH

Giant of Gath, 1 Sam 17:4
Killed by David, 1 Sam 17:50
——Brother of above; killed by Elhanan, 2 Sam 21:19

GOMER

Son of Japheth, Gen 10:2, 3; 1 Chr 1:5, 6
Northern nation, Ezek 38:6
——Wife of Hosea, Hos 1:2, 3

GOMORRAH

With Sodom, defeated by Chedorlaomer; Lot captured, Gen 14:8–12
Destroyed by God, Gen 19:23–29
Later references to, Is 1:10; Amos 4:11; Matt 10:15

GONE

I am g like a shadow ....Ps 109:23
I have g astray like a ....Ps 119:176
the word has g out of ....Is 45:23
like sheep have g ....Is 53:6

GOOD

God saw that it was g ....Gen 1:10
but God meant it for g ....Gen 50:20
LORD has promised g ....Num 10:29
you have spoken is g ....2 Kin 20:19
seeking the g of his ....Esth 10:3
indeed accept g ....Job 2:10
"Who will show us any g ....Ps 4:6
is none who does g ....Ps 14:1
G and upright is the ....Ps 25:8
that he may see g ....Ps 34:12
Truly God is g to ....Ps 73:1
g man deals graciously ....Ps 112:5
Your Spirit is g ....Ps 143:10
g man obtains favor ....Prov 12:2
g word makes it glad ....Prov 12:25
on the evil and the g ....Prov 15:3
A merry heart does g ....Prov 17:22
who knows what is g ....Eccl 6:12
learn to do g ....Is 1:17
Zion, you who bring g ....Is 40:9
tidings of g things ....Is 52:7
talked to me, with g ....Zech 1:13
they may see your g ....Matt 5:16
said, "Be of g cheer ....Matt 9:22
A g man out of the ....Matt 12:35
"G Teacher, what g ....Matt 19:16
No one is g but One ....Matt 19:17
For she has done a g ....Matt 26:10
behold, I bring you g ....Luke 2:10
love your enemies, do g ....Luke 6:35
"Can anything g ....John 1:46
Some said, "He is g ....John 7:12
g works I have shown ....John 10:32
who went about doing g ....Acts 10:38
For he was a g man ....Acts 11:24
in that He did g ....Acts 14:17
g man someone would ....Rom 5:7
in my flesh) nothing g ....Rom 7:18
overcome evil with g ....Rom 12:21
Jesus for g works ....Eph 2:10
fruitful in every g ....Col 1:10
know that the law is g ....1 Tim 1:8
For this is g and ....1 Tim 2:3
bishop, he desires a g ....1 Tim 3:1
for this is g and ....1 Tim 5:4
be rich in g works ....1 Tim 6:18
prepared for every g ....2 Tim 2:21
and have tasted the g ....Heb 6:5
Every g gift and every ....James 1:17
g works which they ....1 Pet 2:12
to suffer for doing g ....1 Pet 3:17

GOODNESS

"I will make all My g ....Ex 33:19
and abounding in g ....Ex 34:6
"You are my Lord, my g ....Ps 16:2
Surely g and mercy ....Ps 23:6
that I would see the g ....Ps 27:13
how great is Your g ....Ps 31:19
The g of God endures ....Ps 52:1
how great is its g ....Zech 9:17
the riches of His g ....Rom 2:4
consider the g and ....Rom 11:22
kindness, g ....Gal 5:22

GOODS

When g increase ....Eccl 5:11
and plunder his g ....Matt 12:29
ruler over all his g ....Matt 24:47
"Soul, you have many g ....Luke 12:19
man was wasting his g ....Luke 16:1
I give half of my g ....Luke 19:8
has this world's g ....1 John 3:17

GOSHEN

District of Egypt where Israel lived; the best of the land, Gen 45:10; 46:28, 29; 47:1–11

GOSPEL

The beginning of the g ....Mark 1:1

and believe in the *g* ....Mark 1:15
g must first be ....Mark 13:10
to testify to the *g* ....Acts 20:24
separated to the *g* ....Rom 1:1
not ashamed of the *g* ....Rom 1:16
should live from the *g* ......1 Cor 9:14
if our *g* is veiled ....2 Cor 4:3
to a different *g* ....Gal 1:6
of truth, the *g* ....Eph 1:13
the mystery of the *g* ....Eph 6:19
g which you heard ....Col 1:23
the everlasting *g* ....Rev 14:6

GOSSIPS

only idle but also *g* ....1 Tim 5:13

GOVERNMENT

and the *g* will be upon ....Is 9:6

GRACE

But Noah found *g* ....Gen 6:8
G is poured upon Your ....Ps 45:2
The LORD will give *g* ....Ps 84:11
the Spirit of *g* ....Zech 12:10
and the *g* of God was ....Luke 2:40
g and truth came ....John 1:17
And great *g* was upon ....Acts 4:33
G to you and peace ....Rom 1:7
receive abundance of *g* ....Rom 5:17
g is no longer *g* ....Rom 11:6
The *g* of our Lord ....Rom 16:20
For you know the *g* ....2 Cor 8:9
g is sufficient ....2 Cor 12:9
The *g* of the Lord ....2 Cor 13:14
you have fallen from *g* ....Gal 5:4
to the riches of His *g* ....Eph 1:7
g you have been ....Eph 2:8
dispensation of the *g* ....Eph 3:2
g was given according ....Eph 4:7
G be with all those ....Eph 6:24
shaken, let us have *g* ....Heb 12:28
But He gives more *g* ....James 4:6
this is the true *g* ....1 Pet 5:12
but grow in the *g* ....2 Pet 3:18

GRACIOUS

he said, "God be *g* ....Gen 43:29
I will be *g* to whom I ....Ex 33:19
then He is *g* to him ....Job 33:24
wise man's mouth are *g* ....Eccl 10:12
of hosts will be *g* ....Amos 5:15
know that You are a *g* ....Jon 4:2
that He may be *g* ....Mal 1:9
at the *g* words which ....Luke 4:22
that the Lord is *g* ....1 Pet 2:3

GRAFTED

in unbelief, will be *g* ....Rom 11:23

GRAIN

Israel went to buy *g* ....Gen 42:5
it treads out the *g* ....Deut 25:4
You provide their *g* ....Ps 65:9
be an abundance of *g* ....Ps 72:16
him who withholds *g* ....Prov 11:26
be revived like *g* ....Hos 14:7
G shall make the young ......Zech 9:17
to pluck heads of *g* ....Matt 12:1
unless a *g* of wheat ....John 12:24
it treads out the *g* ....1 Cor 9:9

GRANT

and *g* us Your ....Ps 85:7
G that these two ....Matt 20:21
who overcomes I will *g* ....Rev 3:21

GRAPES

in the blood of *g* ....Gen 49:11
their *g* are *g* of gall ....Deut 32:32
g give a good smell ....Song 2:13
vines have tender *g* ....Song 2:15
brought forth wild *g* ....Is 5:2
Yet gleaning *g* will be ....Is 17:6
"No *g* shall be ....Jer 8:13
have eaten sour *g* ....Ezek 18:2
Do men gather *g* ....Matt 7:16
g are fully ripe ....Rev 14:18

GRASPING

all is vanity and *g* ....Eccl 1:14

GRASS

they were as the *g* ....2 Kin 19:26
offspring like the *g* ....Job 5:25
g which grows up ....Ps 90:5
his days are like *g* ....Ps 103:15
The *g* withers ....Is 40:7
so clothes the *g* ....Matt 6:30
to sit down on the *g* ....Matt 14:19
"All flesh is as *g* ....1 Pet 1:24

GRASSHOPPERS

inhabitants are like *g* ....Is 40:22
generals like great *g* ....Nah 3:17

GRAVE

g does not come ....Job 7:9
for the *g* as my house ....Job 17:13
my soul up from the *g* ....Ps 30:3
the power of the *g* ....Ps 49:15
or wisdom in the *g* ....Eccl 9:10
And they made His *g* ....Is 53:9
the power of the *g* ....Hos 13:14

GRAVES

there were no *g* ....Ex 14:11
and the *g* were opened ....Matt 27:52
g which are not ....Luke 11:44
g will hear His voice ....John 5:28

GRAY

would bring down my *g* ....Gen 42:38
the man of *g* hairs ....Deut 32:25
of old men is their *g* ....Prov 20:29

GREAT

and make your name *g* ....Gen 12:2
He has done us this *g* ....1 Sam 6:9
For the LORD is *g* ....1 Chr 16:25
I build will be *g* ....2 Chr 2:5
"The work is *g* ....Neh 4:19
Who does *g* things ....Job 5:9
G men are not always ....Job 32:9
in the *g* assembly ....Ps 22:25
g are Your works ....Ps 92:5
my God, You are very *g* ....Ps 104:1
"The LORD has done *g* ....Ps 126:2
g is the sum of them ....Ps 139:17
in the place of the *g* ....Prov 25:6
g is the Holy One ....Is 12:6
And do you seek *g* ....Jer 45:5
g is Your faithfulness ....Lam 3:23
The *g* day of the LORD ....Zeph 1:14
he shall be called *g* ....Matt 5:19
one pearl of *g* price ....Matt 13:46
desires to become *g* ....Matt 20:26
g drops of blood ....Luke 22:44
that he was someone *g* ....Acts 8:9
"*G* is Diana of the ....Acts 19:28
that I have *g* sorrow ....Rom 9:2
without controversy *g* ....1 Tim 3:16

with contentment is *g* ....1 Tim 6:6
But in a *g* house ....2 Tim 2:20
appearing of our *g* ....Titus 2:13
See how *g* a forest ....James 3:5
g men, the rich men ....Rev 6:15
Babylon the *G* ....Rev 17:5
Then I saw a *g* white ....Rev 20:11
the dead, small and *g* ....Rev 20:12

GREATER

the throne will I be *g* ....Gen 41:40
g than all the gods ....Ex 18:11
whose appearance was *g* ....Dan 7:20
kingdom of heaven is *g* ....Matt 11:11
place there is One *g* ....Matt 12:6
g than Jonah is here ....Matt 12:41
g than Solomon is here ....Matt 12:42
g things than these ....John 1:50
g than our father ....John 4:12
a servant is not *g* ....John 13:16
g than he who sent him ....John 13:16
G love has no one ....John 15:13
'A servant is not *g* ....John 15:20
parts have *g* modesty ....1 Cor 12:23
he who prophesies is *g* ....1 Cor 14:5
swear by no one *g* ....Heb 6:13
condemns us, God is *g* ....1 John 3:20
witness of God is *g* ....1 John 5:9

GREATEST

little child is the *g* ....Matt 18:4
be considered the *g* ....Luke 22:24
but the *g* of these is ....1 Cor 13:13

GREATNESS

And in the *g* of Your ....Ex 15:7
According to the *g* ....Ps 79:11
g is unsearchable ....Ps 145:3
I will declare Your *g* ....Ps 145:6
I have attained *g* ....Eccl 1:16
traveling in the *g* ....Is 63:1
is the exceeding *g* ....Eph 1:19

GREECE

Paul preaches in, Acts 17:16–31
Daniel's vision of, Dan 8:21

GREED

part is full of *g* ....Luke 11:39

GREEDINESS

all uncleanness with *g* ....Eph 4:19
the faith in their *g* ....1 Tim 6:10

GREEDY

of everyone who is *g* ....Prov 1:19
not violent, not *g* ....1 Tim 3:3
not violent, not *g* ....Titus 1:7

GREEK

written in Hebrew, *G* ....John 19:20
and also for the *G* ....Rom 1:16
with me, being a *G* ....Gal 2:3
is neither Jew nor *G* ....Gal 3:28

GREEKS

Natives of Greece, Joel 3:6; Acts 16:1
Spiritual state of, Rom 10:12
Some believe, Acts 14:1

GREEN

lie down in *g* pastures ....Ps 23:2

GREET

g your brethren only ....Matt 5:47

G one another with a ......1 Cor 16:20
into your house nor *g* ....2 John 10
G the friends by name ......3 John 14

GREETED

and *g* Elizabeth ....Luke 1:40

GREW

And the Child *g* ....Luke 2:40
But the word of God *g* ......Acts 12:24
the word of the Lord *g* ......Acts 19:20

GRIEF

burden and his own *g* ......2 Chr 6:29
g were fully weighed ....Job 6:2
Though I speak, my *g* ....Job 16:6
observe trouble and *g* ....Ps 10:14
of mirth may be *g* ....Prov 14:13
much wisdom is much *g* .....Eccl 1:18
and acquainted with *g* ....Is 53:3
joy and not with *g* ....Heb 13:17

GRIEVE

g the children of men ....Lam 3:33
g the Holy Spirit ....Eph 4:30

GRIEVED

earth, and He was *g* ....Gen 6:6
Has not my soul *g* ....Job 30:25
forty years I was *g* ....Ps 95:10
a woman forsaken and *g* ....Is 54:6
g His Holy Spirit ....Is 63:10
with anger, being *g* ....Mark 3:5
Peter was *g* because ....John 21:17

GRINDERS

when the *g* cease ....Eccl 12:3

GRINDING

the sound of *g* is low ....Eccl 12:4
g the faces of the ....Is 3:15
Two women will be *g* ......Matt 24:41

GROAN

The dying *g* in the ....Job 24:12
even we ourselves *g* ....Rom 8:23
who are in this tent *g* ....2 Cor 5:4

GROANING

So God heard their *g* ....Ex 2:24
I am weary with my *g* ....Ps 6:6
Then Jesus, again *g* ....John 11:38

GROANINGS

g which cannot ....Rom 8:26

GROPE

And you shall *g* ....Deut 28:29
They *g* in the dark ....Job 12:25
We *g* for the wall like ....Is 59:10
hope that they might *g* .....Acts 17:27

GROUND

"Cursed is the *g* ....Gen 3:17
you stand is holy *g* ....Ex 3:5
up your fallow *g* ....Jer 4:3
give its fruit, the *g* ....Zech 8:12
others fell on good *g* ....Matt 13:8
bought a piece of *g* ....Luke 14:18
God, the pillar and *g* .....1 Tim 3:15

GROUNDED

being rooted and *g* ....Eph 3:17

GROW

they will all *g* ....Ps 102:26
the horn of David *g* ....Ps 132:17
the earth will *g* ....Is 51:6
you shall go out and *g* ....Mal 4:2
truth in love, may *g* ....Eph 4:15
and they will all *g* ....Heb 1:11
but *g* in the grace and ....2 Pet 3:18

GRUDGINGLY

in his heart, not *g* ....2 Cor 9:7

GRUMBLERS

These are *g* ....Jude 16

GUARANTEE

in our hearts as a *g* ....2 Cor 1:22
us the Spirit as a *g* ....2 Cor 5:5
who is the *g* of our ....Eph 1:14

GUARD

g the way to the tree ....Gen 3:24
will be your rear *g* ....Is 52:12
g the doors of your ....Mic 7:5
we were kept under *g* ....Gal 3:23
G what was committed ....1 Tim 6:20

GUARDIANS

but is under *g* and ....Gal 4:2

GUARDS

Unless the LORD *g* ....Ps 127:1
And the *g* shook for ....Matt 28:4

GUIDANCE

and excellent in *g* ....Is 28:29

GUIDE

He will be our *g* ....Ps 48:14
Father, You are the *g* ....Jer 3:4
g our feet into the ....Luke 1:79
has come, He will *g* ....John 16:13
Judas, who became a *g* ......Acts 1:16
you yourself are a *g* ....Rom 2:19

GUIDES

to you, blind *g* ....Matt 23:16
unless someone *g* ....Acts 8:31

GUILT

they accept their *g* ....Lev 26:41
g has grown up to the ....Ezra 9:6
of your fathers' *g* ....Matt 23:32

GUILTLESS

g who takes His name ....Ex 20:7
have condemned the *g* ......Matt 12:7

GUILTY

"We are truly *g* ....Gen 42:21
we have been very *g* ....Ezra 9:7
the world may become *g* .....Rom 3:19
in one point, he is *g* ....James 2:10

GULF

you there is a great *g* ......Luke 16:26

—H—

HABAKKUK

Prophet in Judah just prior to Babylonian invasion, Hab 1:1
Prayer of, in praise of God, Hab 3:1–19

HABITATION

to Your holy *h* ....Ex 15:13
your rightful *h* ....Job 8:6
Is God in His holy *h* ....Ps 68:5
their *h* be desolate ....Ps 69:25
the Most High, your *h* ....Ps 91:9
go to a city for *h* ....Ps 107:7
establish a city for *h* ....Ps 107:36
but He blesses the *h* ....Prov 3:33
in a peaceful *h* ....Is 32:18
Jerusalem, a quiet *h* ....Is 33:20
from His holy *h* ....Zech 2:13
'Let his *h* be ....Acts 1:20
be clothed with our *h* ....2 Cor 5:2

HACHILAH

Hill in the Wilderness of Ziph where David hid, 1 Sam 23:19–26

HADADEZER

King of Zobah, 2 Sam 8:3–13
Defeated by David, 2 Sam 10:6–19

HADASSAH

Esther's Jewish name, Esth 2:7

HADES

be brought down to *H* ......Matt 11:23
H shall not ....Matt 16:18
being in torments in *H* .....Luke 16:23
not leave my soul in *H* ....Acts 2:27
I have the keys of *H* ....Rev 1:18
H were cast into the ....Rev 20:14

HAGAR

Sarah's servant; bears Ishmael to Abraham, Gen 16
Abraham sends her away; God comforts her, Gen 21:9–21
Paul explains symbolic meaning of, Gal 4:22–31

HAGGAI

Postexilic prophet; contemporary of Zechariah, Ezra 5:1, 2; 6:14; Hag 1:1

HAGGITH

One of David's wives, 2 Sam 3:4
Mother of Adonijah, 1 Kin 1:5

HAIL

cause very heavy *h* ....Ex 9:18
seen the treasury of *h* ....Job 38:22
He casts out His *h* ....Ps 147:17
h will sweep away the ....Is 28:17
of the plague of the *h* ....Rev 16:21

HAILSTONES

clouds passed with *h* ....Ps 18:12

HAIR

bring down my gray *h* ......Gen 42:38
the *h* on my body stood ......Job 4:15
Your *h* is like a flock ....Song 4:1
you cannot make one *h* .....Matt 5:36
But not a *h* of your ....Luke 21:18
if a woman has long *h* .....1 Cor 11:15
not with braided *h* ....1 Tim 2:9
h like women's *h* ....Rev 9:8

HAIRS

are more than the *h* ....Ps 40:12
h I will carry you ....Is 46:4
yes, gray *h* are here ....Hos 7:9
But the very *h* ....Matt 10:30

HAIRY

h garment all over ....Gen 25:25

h is one body with ....1 Cor 6:16
h Rahab did not perish ......Heb 11:31
of the great *h* who ....Rev 17:1

HARLOTRIES

the land with your *h* ....Jer 3:2
Let her put away her *h* ....Hos 2:2

HARLOTRY

through her casual *h* ....Jer 3:9
the lewdness of your *h* ....Jer 13:27
let them put their *h* ....Ezek 43:9
are the children of *h* ....Hos 2:4
Ephraim, you commit *h* ....Hos 5:3
for the spirit of *h* ....Hos 5:4

HARLOTS

his blood while the *h* ....1 Kin 22:38
h enter the ....Matt 21:31
Great, The Mother of *H* ....Rev 17:5

HARM

do My prophets no *h* ......1 Chr 16:22
and I will not *h* ....Jer 25:6
and do not *h* the oil ....Rev 6:6

HARMLESS

become blameless and *h* .....Phil 2:15
for us, who is holy, *h* ....Heb 7:26

HARMONIOUS

the harp, with *h* sound ....Ps 92:3

HARP

those who play the *h* ....Gen 4:21
with the lute and *h* ....Ps 150:3
Lamb, each having a *h* ....Rev 5:8

HARPS

We hung our *h* upon the ......Ps 137:2
playing their *h* ....Rev 14:2

HARSH

"Your words have been *h* ....Mal 3:13
but also to the *h* ....1 Pet 2:18

HARVEST

seedtime and *h* ....Gen 8:22
to the joy of *h* ....Is 9:3
shall eat up your *h* ....Jer 5:17
"The *h* is past ....Jer 8:20
of her *h* will come ....Jer 51:33
h truly is plentiful ....Matt 9:37
pray the Lord of the *h* ....Matt 9:38
sickle, because the *h* ....Mark 4:29
already white for *h* ....John 4:35
the *h* of the earth is ....Rev 14:15

HASTE

you shall eat it in *h* ....Ex 12:11
For I said in my *h* ....Ps 31:22
And they came with *h* ......Luke 2:16
"Zacchaeus, make *h* ....Luke 19:5

HASTEN

be multiplied who *h* ....Ps 16:4
Do not *h* in your ....Eccl 7:9
I, the LORD, will *h* ....Is 60:22

HASTENING

h the coming of the ....2 Pet 3:12

HASTENS

and he sins who *h* ....Prov 19:2

with an evil eye *h* ....Prov 28:22
is near and *h* quickly ....Zeph 1:14

HASTILY

utter anything *h* ....Eccl 5:2
lay hands on anyone *h* .....1 Tim 5:22

HASTY

Do you see a man *h* ....Prov 29:20

HATE

'You shall not *h* ....Lev 19:17
h all workers of ....Ps 5:5
h the righteous shall ....Ps 34:21
love the LORD, *h* evil ....Ps 97:10
h every false way ....Ps 119:104
h the double-minded ....Ps 119:113
I *h* and abhor lying ....Ps 119:163
love, and a time to *h* ....Eccl 3:8
h robbery for burnt ....Is 61:8
You who *h* good and ....Mic 3:2
either he will *h* ....Matt 6:24

HATED

Therefore I *h* life ....Eccl 2:17
h all my labor in ....Eccl 2:18
but Esau I have *h* ....Mal 1:3
And you will be *h* ....Matt 10:22
have seen and also *h* ....John 15:24
but Esau I have *h* ....Rom 9:13
For no one ever *h* ....Eph 5:29
and *h* lawlessness ....Heb 1:9

HATEFUL

h woman when she is ....Prov 30:23
in malice and envy, *h* ....Titus 3:3

HATERS

The *h* of the LORD ....Ps 81:15
backbiters, *h* of God ....Rom 1:30

HATES

six things the LORD *h* ......Prov 6:16
lose it, and he who *h* ....John 12:25
"If the world *h* ....John 15:18
h his brother is ....1 John 2:11

HAUGHTY

Your eyes are on the *h* ....2 Sam 22:28
bring down *h* looks ....Ps 18:27
my heart is not *h* ....Ps 131:1
h spirit before a fall ....Prov 16:18
A proud and *h* man ....Prov 21:24
Do not be *h* ....Rom 11:20
age not to be *h* ....1 Tim 6:17

HAUNTS

are full of the *h* ....Ps 74:20

HAVEN

shall dwell by the *h* ....Gen 49:13
to their desired *h* ....Ps 107:30

HAVOC

for Saul, he made *h* ....Acts 8:3

HAZAEL

Anointed king of Syria by Elijah, 1 Kin 19:15–17
Elisha predicts his taking the throne, 2 Kin 8:7–15
Oppresses Israel, 2 Kin 8:28, 29; 10:32, 33; 12:17, 18; 13:3–7, 22

HAZEROTH

Scene of sedition of Miriam and Aaron, Num 11:35—12:16

HAZOR

Royal Canaanite city destroyed by Joshua, Josh 11:1–13
Rebuilt and assigned to Naphtali, Josh 19:32, 36
Army of, defeated by Deborah and Barak, Judg 4:1–24

HEAD

He shall bruise your *h* ....Gen 3:15
my skin, and laid my *h* ....Job 16:15
return upon his own *h* ....Ps 7:16
h is covered with dew ....Song 5:2
The whole *h* is sick ....Is 1:5
it to bow down his *h* ....Is 58:5
could lift up his *h* ....Zech 1:21
you swear by your *h* ....Matt 5:36
having his *h* covered ....1 Cor 11:4
and gave Him to be *h* ....Eph 1:22
For the husband is *h* ....Eph 5:23
His *h* and his hair ....Rev 1:14

HEADS

men to ride over our *h* ....Ps 66:12
Him, wagging their *h* ....Matt 27:39
dragon having seven *h* ....Rev 12:3

HEAL

I wound and I *h* ....Deut 32:39
O LORD, *h* me ....Ps 6:2
sent Me to *h* the ....Is 61:1
h your backslidings ....Jer 3:22
who can *h* you ....Lam 2:13
torn, but He will *h* ....Hos 6:1
H the sick ....Matt 10:8
so that I should *h* ....Matt 13:15
sent Me to *h* the ....Luke 4:18
Physician, *h* yourself ....Luke 4:23

HEALED

His word and *h* them ....Ps 107:20
And return and be *h* ....Is 6:10
His stripes we are *h* ....Is 53:5
h the hurt of My ....Jer 6:14
When I would have *h* ....Hos 7:1
and He *h* them ....Matt 4:24
he had faith to be *h* ....Acts 14:9
that you may be *h* ....James 5:16
his deadly wound was *h* ......Rev 13:3

HEALING

h shall spring forth ....Is 58:8
so that there is no *h* ....Jer 14:19
Your injury has no *h* ....Nah 3:19
shall arise with *h* ....Mal 4:2
and *h* all kinds of ....Matt 4:23
tree were for the *h* ....Rev 22:2

HEALINGS

to another gifts of *h* ....1 Cor 12:9
Do all have gifts of *h* ......1 Cor 12:30

HEALS

h all your diseases ....Ps 103:3
h the stroke of their ....Is 30:26
Jesus the Christ *h* ....Acts 9:34

HEALTH

to the soul and *h* ....Prov 16:24
and for a time of *h* ....Jer 8:15
no recovery for the *h* ....Jer 8:22
all things and be in *h* ....3 John 2

HEAP

I could *h* up words ....Job 16:4

sea together as a *h* ....Ps 33:7
ears, they will *h* ....2 Tim 4:3

HEAPS

Though he *h* up silver ....Job 27:16

HEAR

"*H*, O Israel ....Deut 6:4
Him you shall *h* ....Deut 18:15
H me when I call ....Ps 4:1
O You who *h* prayer ....Ps 65:2
h what God the LORD ....Ps 85:8
ear, shall He not *h* ....Ps 94:9
h the words of the ....Prov 22:17
h rather than to give ....Eccl 5:1
H, O heavens ....Is 1:2
H, you who are afar ....Is 33:13
Let the earth *h* ....Is 34:1
I spoke, you did not *h* ....Is 65:12
'Hearing you will *h* ....Matt 13:14
if he will not *h* ....Matt 18:16
"Take heed what you *h* ....Mark 4:24
ears, do you not *h* ....Mark 8:18
h the sound of it ....John 3:8
that God does not *h* ....John 9:31
And how shall they *h* ....Rom 10:14
man be swift to *h* ....James 1:19
h what the Spirit says ....Rev 2:7

HEARD

h the sound of the ....Gen 3:8
h their cry because of ....Ex 3:7
you only *h* a voice ....Deut 4:12
certainly God has *h* ....Ps 66:19
quietly, should be *h* ....Eccl 9:17
Have you not *h* ....Is 40:21
world men have not *h* ....Is 64:4
Who has *h* such a thing ....Is 66:8
h Ephraim bemoaning ....Jer 31:18
that they will be *h* ....Matt 6:7
h the word believed ....Acts 4:4
I say, have they not *h* ....Rom 10:18
not seen, nor ear *h* ....1 Cor 2:9
h inexpressible ....2 Cor 12:4
things that you have *h* ....2 Tim 2:2
the things we have *h* ....Heb 2:1
the word which they *h* ....Heb 4:2
from death, and was *h* ....Heb 5:7
which we have *h* ....1 John 1:1
Lord's Day, and I *h* ....Rev 1:10

HEARER

if anyone is a *h* ....James 1:23
is not a forgetful *h* ....James 1:25

HEARERS

for not the *h* of the ....Rom 2:13
impart grace to the *h* ....Eph 4:29
of the word, and not *h* ....James 1:22

HEARING

and read in the *h* ....Ex 24:7
Book of Moses in the *h* ....Neh 13:1
Do not speak in the *h* ....Prov 23:9
'Keep on *h* ....Is 6:9
h they do not ....Matt 13:13
h they may hear ....Mark 4:12
If the whole were *h* ....1 Cor 12:17
or by the *h* of faith ....Gal 3:2
have become dull of *h* ....Heb 5:11

HEARS

for Your servant *h* ....1 Sam 3:9
out, and the LORD *h* ....Ps 34:17
He who *h* you *h* Me ....Luke 10:16
of God *h* God's words ....John 8:47

And if anyone *h* ....John 12:47
who is of the truth *h* ....John 18:37
He who knows God *h* ....1 John 4:6
And let him who *h* ....Rev 22:17

HEART

h was only evil ....Gen 6:5
for you know the *h* ....Ex 23:9
great searchings of *h* ....Judg 5:16
h rejoices in the LORD ....1 Sam 2:1
God gave him another *h* ....1 Sam 10:9
LORD looks at the *h* ....1 Sam 16:7
his wives turned his *h* ....1 Kin 11:4
He pierces my *h* ....Job 16:13
How my *h* yearns within ....Job 19:27
For God made my *h* ....Job 23:16
My *h* is in turmoil and ....Job 30:27
My *h* also instructs me ....Ps 16:7
your *h* live forever ....Ps 22:26
h is overflowing ....Ps 45:1
My *h* is steadfast ....Ps 57:7
Thus my *h* was grieved ....Ps 73:21
my *h* and my flesh cry ....Ps 84:2
h shall depart from me ....Ps 101:4
look and a proud *h* ....Ps 101:5
with my whole *h* ....Ps 111:1
h is not haughty ....Ps 131:1
h makes a cheerful ....Prov 15:13
The king's *h* is in the ....Prov 21:1
as he thinks in his *h* ....Prov 23:7
with a wicked *h* ....Prov 26:23
h reveals the man ....Prov 27:19
trusts in his own *h* ....Prov 28:26
The *h* of the wise is ....Eccl 7:4
and a wise man's *h* ....Eccl 8:5
h yearned for him ....Song 5:4
and the whole *h* ....Is 1:5
h shall resound ....Is 16:11
the yearning of Your *h* ....Is 63:15
the mind and the *h* ....Jer 11:20
h is deceitful above ....Jer 17:9
I will give them a *h* ....Jer 24:7
therefore My *h* yearns ....Jer 31:20
and take the stony *h* ....Ezek 11:19
get yourselves a new *h* ....Ezek 18:31
uncircumcised in *h* ....Ezek 44:7
are the pure in *h* ....Matt 5:8
is, there your *h* ....Matt 6:21
of the *h* proceed evil ....Matt 15:19
h will flow rivers ....John 7:38
"Let not your *h* ....John 14:1
believed were of one *h* ....Acts 4:32
Satan filled your *h* ....Acts 5:3
h is not right in the ....Acts 8:21
h that God has raised ....Rom 10:9
in sincerity of *h* ....Eph 6:5
refresh my *h* in the ....Philem 20
and shuts up his *h* ....1 John 3:17
if our *h* condemns us ....1 John 3:20

HEARTILY

you do, do it *h* ....Col 3:23

HEARTS

God tests the *h* ....Ps 7:9
who seek God, your *h* ....Ps 69:32
let the *h* of those ....Ps 105:3
And he will turn the *h* ....Mal 4:6
h failing them from ....Luke 21:26
purifying their *h* ....Acts 15:9
will guard your *h* ....Phil 4:7
of God rule in your *h* ....Col 3:15

HEATHEN

repetitions as the *h* ....Matt 6:7
him be to you like a *h* ....Matt 18:17

HEAVEN

called the firmament *H* ....Gen 1:8
precious things of *h* ....Deut 33:13
LORD looks down from *h* ....Ps 14:2
word is settled in *h* ....Ps 119:89
For God is in *h* ....Eccl 5:2
"*H* is My throne ....Is 66:1
"If *h* above can be ....Jer 31:37
and the birds of the *h* ....Dan 2:38
come to know that *H* ....Dan 4:26
for the kingdom of *h* ....Matt 3:2
your Father in *h* ....Matt 5:16
on earth as it is in *h* ....Matt 6:10
H and earth will ....Matt 24:35
from Him a sign from *h* ....Mark 8:11
have sinned against *h* ....Luke 15:18
you shall see *h* ....John 1:51
one has ascended to *h* ....John 3:13
the true bread from *h* ....John 6:32
a voice came from *h* ....John 12:28
sheet, let down from *h* ....Acts 11:5
the whole family in *h* ....Eph 3:15
laid up for you in *h* ....Col 1:5
and the *h* gave rain ....James 5:18
there was silence in *h* ....Rev 8:1
sign appeared in *h* ....Rev 12:1
Now I saw a new *h* ....Rev 21:1

HEAVENLY

your *h* Father will ....Matt 6:14
h host praising God ....Luke 2:13
if I tell you *h* things ....John 3:12
are those who are *h* ....1 Cor 15:48
blessing in the *h* ....Eph 1:3
and have tasted the *h* ....Heb 6:4
h things themselves ....Heb 9:23
a better, that is, a *h* ....Heb 11:16
the living God, the *h* ....Heb 12:22

HEAVENS

I will make your *h* ....Lev 26:19
and the highest *h* ....Deut 10:14
h cannot contain ....1 Kin 8:27
the LORD made the *h* ....1 Chr 16:26
Till the *h* are no more ....Job 14:12
in the *h* shall laugh ....Ps 2:4
h declare the glory ....Ps 19:1
Let the *h* declare His ....Ps 50:6
h can be compared ....Ps 89:6
The *h* are Yours ....Ps 89:11
For as the *h* are high ....Ps 103:11
When He prepared the *h* ....Prov 8:27
h are higher than the ....Is 55:9
behold, I create new *h* ....Is 65:17
and behold, the *h* ....Matt 3:16
h will be shaken ....Matt 24:29
h are the work of Your ....Heb 1:10
h will pass away ....2 Pet 3:10

HEAVINESS

and I am full of *h* ....Ps 69:20
My soul melts from *h* ....Ps 119:28

HEAVY

the bondage was *h* ....Neh 5:18

HEBREW

Term applied to:
Abram, Gen 14:13
Israelites, 1 Sam 4:6, 9
Jews, Acts 6:1
Paul, Phil 3:5

HEBRON

Abram, Isaac, and Jacob dwell there,
Gen 13:18; 23:2-20; 35:27

Visited by spies, Num 13:21, 22
Defeated by Joshua, Josh 10:1–37
Caleb's inheritance, Josh 14:12–15
David's original capital; sons born there, 2 Sam 2:1–3, 11; 3:2–5
Site of Absalom's rebellion, 2 Sam 15:7–10

HEDGE

behold, I will *h* ....Hos 2:6
sharper than a thorn *h* ....Mic 7:4
a vineyard and set a *h* ....Mark 12:1

HEDGED

and whom God has *h* ....Job 3:23
You have *h* me behind ....Ps 139:5
He has *h* me in so that ....Lam 3:7

HEED

By taking *h* according ....Ps 119:9
if you *h* Me ....Jer 17:24
and let us not give *h* ....Jer 18:18
nor give *h* to fables ....1 Tim 1:4
the more earnest *h* ....Heb 2:1

HEEDS

h counsel is wise ....Prov 12:15

HEEL

you shall bruise His *h* ....Gen 3:15
took hold of Esau's *h* ....Gen 25:26
has lifted up his *h* ....Ps 41:9
Me has lifted up his *h* ....John 13:18

HEIGHT

"Is not God in the *h* ....Job 22:12
looked down from the *h* ....Ps 102:19
nor *h* nor depth ....Rom 8:39
length and depth and *h* ....Eph 3:18

HEIR

Has he no *h* ....Jer 49:1
Now I say that the *h* ....Gal 4:1
if a son, then an *h* ....Gal 4:7
He has appointed *h* ....Heb 1:2
the world and became *h* ....Heb 11:7

HEIRS

if children, then *h* ....Rom 8:17
of God and joint *h* ....Rom 8:17
should be fellow *h* ....Eph 3:6
be rich in faith and *h* ....James 2:5
vessel, and as being *h* ....1 Pet 3:7

HELAM

Place between Damascus and Hamath where David defeated Syrians, 2 Sam 10:16–19

HELL

shall be turned into *h* ....Ps 9:17
go down alive into *h* ....Ps 55:15
house is the way to *h* ....Prov 7:27
his soul from *h* ....Prov 23:14
H and Destruction are ....Prov 27:20
"*H* from beneath is ....Is 14:9
be in danger of *h* fire ....Matt 5:22
to be cast into *h* ....Matt 18:9
the condemnation of *h* ....Matt 23:33
power to cast into *h* ....Luke 12:5
it is set on fire by *h* ....James 3:6

HELLENISTS

Greek-speaking Jews, Acts 6:1
Hostile to Paul, Acts 9:29

Gospel preached to, Acts 11:20

HELMET

a breastplate, and a *h* ....Is 59:17
And take the *h* of ....Eph 6:17
and love, and as a *h* ....1 Thess 5:8

HELP

the shield of your *h* ....Deut 33:29
Is my *h* not within me ....Job 6:13
"There is no *h* ....Ps 3:2
May He send you *h* ....Ps 20:2
He is our *h* and our ....Ps 33:20
yet praise Him, the *h* ....Ps 42:11
A very present *h* ....Ps 46:1
Give us *h* from trouble ....Ps 60:11
God, make haste to *h* ....Ps 71:12
"I have given *h* ....Ps 89:19
the LORD had been my *h* ....Ps 94:17
there was none to *h* ....Ps 107:12
He is their *h* and ....Ps 115:9
Our *h* is in the name ....Ps 124:8
let no one *h* him ....Prov 28:17
h my unbelief ....Mark 9:24
tell her to *h* me ....Luke 10:40
and find grace to *h* ....Heb 4:16

HELPED

far the LORD has *h* ....1 Sam 7:12
fall, but the LORD *h* ....Ps 118:13
of salvation I have *h* ....Is 49:8
h His servant Israel ....Luke 1:54

HELPER

I will make him a *h* ....Gen 2:18
Behold, God is my *h* ....Ps 54:4
give you another *H* ....John 14:16
"But when the *H* ....John 15:26
she has been a *h* ....Rom 16:2
"The LORD is my *h* ....Heb 13:6

HELPFUL

all things are not *h* ....1 Cor 6:12

HELPS

the Spirit also *h* ....Rom 8:26
gifts of healings, *h* ....1 Cor 12:28

HEM

and touched the *h* ....Matt 9:20
might only touch the *h* ....Matt 14:36

HEMAN

Composer of a Psalm, Ps 88:title

HERE

Then I said, "*H* am I ....Is 6:8

HERESIES

dissensions, *h* ....Gal 5:20
in destructive *h* ....2 Pet 2:1

HERITAGE

give it to you as a *h* ....Ex 6:8
have given me the *h* ....Ps 61:5
for that is his *h* ....Eccl 3:22
for it is his *h* ....Eccl 5:18
This is the *h* of the ....Is 54:17
of My people, My *h* ....Joel 3:2
The flock of Your *h* ....Mic 7:14

HERMES

Paul acclaimed as, Acts 14:12

HERMON

Highest mountain (9,166 ft.) in Syria; also called Sirion, Shenir, Deut 3:8, 9

HEROD

——Herod the Great, procurator of Judea (37–4 B.C.), Luke 1:5
Inquires about Jesus' birth, Matt 2:3–8
Slays infants of Bethlehem, Matt 2:12–18
——Herod Antipas, the tetrarch, ruler of Galilee and Perea (4 B.C.–A.D. 39), Luke 3:1
Imprisons John the Baptist, Luke 3:18–21
Has John the Baptist beheaded, Matt 14:1–12
Disturbed about Jesus, Luke 9:7–9
Jesus sent to him, Luke 23:7–11
——Herod Agrippa I (A.D. 37–44), Acts 12:1, 19
Kills James, Acts 12:1, 2
Imprisons Peter, Acts 12:3–11, 19
Slain by an angel, Acts 12:20–23
——Herod Agrippa II (A.D. 53–70); called Agrippa and King Agrippa, Acts 25:22–24, 26
Festus tells him about Paul, Acts 25:13–27
Paul makes a defense before, Acts 26:1–32

HERODIANS

Join Pharisees against Jesus, Mark 3:6
Seek to trap Jesus, Matt 22:15–22
Jesus warns against, Mark 8:15

HERODIAS

Granddaughter of Herod the Great; plots John's death, Matt 14:3–12
Married her uncle, Mark 6:17, 18

HESHBON

Ancient Moabite city; taken by Moses, Num 21:23–34
Assigned to Reubenites, Num 32:1–37
Prophecies concerning, Is 15:1–4; 16:8–14; Jer 48:2, 34, 35

HETH

Son of Canaan, Gen 10:15
Abraham buys field from sons of, Gen 23:3–20
Esau marries daughters of, Gen 27:46

HEWN

in a tomb that was *h* ....Luke 23:53

HEZEKIAH

Righteous king of Judah; reforms temple and worship, 2 Chr 29—31
Wars with Assyria; prayer for deliverance is answered, 2 Kin 18:7—19:37
His sickness and recovery; thanksgiving, 2 Kin 20:1–11; Is 38:9–22
Boasts to Babylonian ambassadors, 2 Kin 20:12–19
Death, 2 Kin 20:20, 21

HID

and I *h* myself ....Gen 3:10

HIDDEKEL

Hebrew name of the river Tigris, Gen 2:14; Dan 10:4

HIDDEN

and the LORD has *h* ....2 Kin 4:27
It is *h* from the eyes ....Job 28:21
h Your righteousness ....Ps 40:10
and my sins are not *h* ....Ps 69:5
Your word I have *h* ....Ps 119:11
h riches of secret ....Is 45:3
there His power was *h*..........Hab 3:4
h that will not ....Matt 10:26
the *h* wisdom which God .....1 Cor 2:7
bring to light the *h* ....1 Cor 4:5
have renounced the *h*..........2 Cor 4:2
rather let it be the *h*............1 Pet 3:4
give some of the *h* ....Rev 2:17

HIDE

H me under the shadow ....Ps 17:8
You shall *h* them in ....Ps 31:20
O God, and do not *h*............Ps 55:1
You *h* Your face ....Ps 104:29
darkness shall not *h*..........Ps 139:12
You are God, who *h* ....Is 45:15
h yourself from your ....Is 58:7
"Fall on us and *h* ....Rev 6:16

HIDES

He *h* His face ....Ps 10:11

HIDING

You are my *h* place ....Ps 32:7
A man will be as a *h* ....Is 32:2

HIEL

Native of Bethel; rebuilds Jericho, 1 Kin 16:34
Fulfills Joshua's curse, Josh 6:26

HIGH

priest of God Most *H* ....Gen 14:18
For the LORD Most *H*.............Ps 47:2
h is Your right ....Ps 89:13
are on *h* forevermore ....Ps 92:8
the LORD is on *h*..................Ps 138:6
"I dwell in the *h*..................Is 57:15
know that the Most *H* ....Dan 4:17
whose habitation is *h*.............Obad 3
up on a *h* mountain by ....Matt 17:1
your mind on *h* things ....Rom 12:16
h thing that exalts ....2 Cor 10:5
and faithful *H* Priest ....Heb 2:17

HIGHER

They are *h* than heaven ......Job 11:8
you, 'Friend, go up *h*.........Luke 14:10
h than the heavens ....Heb 7:26

HIGHWAY

of the upright is a *h*..........Prov 15:19
in the desert a *h* ....Is 40:3
up, build up the *h* ....Is 62:10

HIGHWAYS

h shall be elevated ....Is 49:11
go into the *h* ....Matt 22:9

HILKIAH

Shallum's son, 1 Chr 6:13
High priest in Josiah's reign, 2 Chr 34:9–22
Oversees temple work, 2 Kin 22:4–7
Finds the Book of the Law, 2 Kin 22:8–14
Aids in reformation, 2 Kin 23:4

HILL

My King on My holy *h* ....Ps 2:6
h cannot be hidden ....Matt 5:14
and *h* brought low ....Luke 3:5
to the brow of the *h*............Luke 4:29

HILLS

of the everlasting *h* ....Gen 49:26
possess is a land of *h* ....Deut 11:11
of the *h* are His also ....Ps 95:4
up my eyes to the *h* ....Ps 121:1
settled, before the *h* ....Prov 8:25

HINDER

takes away, who can *h* ....Job 9:12
all things lest we *h* ....1 Cor 9:12

HINDERED

come to you (but was *h*.........Rom 1:13
Who *h* you from obeying ....Gal 5:7
prayers may not be *h* ....1 Pet 3:7

HINNOM, VALLEY OF THE SON OF

See TOPHET
Place near Jerusalem used for human sacrifice, 2 Kin 23:10; 2 Chr 28:3; Jer 7:31, 32; 19:1–15

HIP

socket of Jacob's *h* ....Gen 32:25

HIRAM

King of Tyre; provided for David's palace and Solomon's temple, 2 Sam 5:11; 1 Kin 5:1–12; 9:10–14, 26–28; 10:11; 1 Chr 14:1

HIRE

h laborers for his ....Matt 20:1

HIRED

h man who eagerly ....Job 7:2
h servants have bread ....Luke 15:17

HIRELING

The *h* flees because ....John 10:13

HITTITES

One of seven Canaanite nations, Deut 7:1
Israelites intermarry with, Judg 3:5, 6; 1 Kin 11:1; Ezra 9:1, 2

HIVITES

One of seven Canaanite nations, Deut 7:1
Esau intermarries with, Gen 36:2
Gibeonites belong to, Josh 9:3, 7

HOLD

h my eyelids open ....Ps 77:4
right hand shall *h* ....Ps 139:10
LORD your God, will *h* ....Is 41:13
I cannot *h* my peace ....Jer 4:19
h fast that word ....1 Cor 15:2
h fast our confession ....Heb 4:14
h fast and repent ....Rev 3:3

HOLES

"Foxes have *h* ....Matt 8:20

HOLIER

near me, for I am *h* ....Is 65:5

HOLIEST

the way into the *H*...................Heb 9:8
to enter the *H* by the ....Heb 10:19

HOLINESS

You, glorious in *h* ....Ex 15:11
has spoken in His *h* ....Ps 60:6
I have sworn by My *h* ....Ps 89:35
h adorns Your house ....Ps 93:5
the Highway of *H* ....Is 35:8
to the Spirit of *h* ....Rom 1:4
spirit, perfecting *h* ....2 Cor 7:1
uncleanness, but in *h* ....1 Thess 4:7
be partakers of His *h* ....Heb 12:10

HOLY

where you stand is *h* ....Ex 3:5
priests and a *h* nation ....Ex 19:6
day, to keep it *h* ....Ex 20:8
distinguish between *h* ....Lev 10:10
the LORD your God am *h*.........Lev 19:2
"No one is *h*.......................1 Sam 2:2
h seed is mixed ....Ezra 9:2
h ones will you turn ....Job 5:1
God sits on His *h*....................Ps 47:8
God, in His *h* mountain ....Ps 48:1
my life, for I am *h* ....Ps 86:2
"*H*, *h*, *h* is the LORD ....Is 6:3
child of the *H* Spirit ....Matt 1:18
baptize you with the *H*.........Mark 1:8
who speak, but the *H*........Mark 13:11
H Spirit will come ....Luke 1:35
H Spirit descended............Luke 3:22
Father give the *H* ....Luke 11:13
H Spirit will teach ....Luke 12:12
H Spirit was not ....John 7:39
H Spirit has come ....Acts 1:8
all filled with the *H*..............Acts 2:4
apostles' hands the *H*..........Acts 8:18
to speak, the *H* Spirit ....Acts 11:15
good to the *H* Spirit ....Acts 15:28
receive the *H* Spirit ....Acts 19:2
if the firstfruit is *h* ....Rom 11:16
peace and joy in the *H* ....Rom 14:17
one another with a *h* ....Rom 16:16
H Spirit teaches ....1 Cor 2:13
that we should be *h* ....Eph 1:4
were sealed with the *H*.........Eph 1:13
partakers of the *H* ....Heb 6:4
has not entered the *h* ....Heb 9:24
H Spirit sent from ....1 Pet 1:12
He who called you is *h* ....1 Pet 1:15
it is written, "Be *h* ....1 Pet 1:16
moved by the *H* Spirit ....2 Pet 1:21
anointing from the *H*..........1 John 2:20
says He who is *h* ....Rev 3:7
For You alone are *h* ....Rev 15:4
is *h*, let him be *h*..................Rev 22:11

HOME

LORD has brought me *h* ......Ruth 1:21
sparrow has found a *h* ....Ps 84:3
the stork has her *h* ....Ps 104:17
to his eternal *h* ....Eccl 12:5
said to him, "Go *h* ....Mark 5:19
into an everlasting *h* ....Luke 16:9
to him and make Our *h* ....John 14:23
took her to his own *h* ....John 19:27
let him eat at *h* ....1 Cor 11:34
own husbands at *h* ....1 Cor 14:35
that while we are at *h* ....2 Cor 5:6
to show piety at *h* ....1 Tim 5:4

HOMELESS

and beaten, and *h* ....1 Cor 4:11

HOMEMAKERS

be discreet, chaste, *h*................Titus 2:5

HONEST

we are *h* men ....Gen 42:11

HONEY

"What is sweeter than *h*....Judg 14:18
and with *h* from the ....Ps 81:16
My son, eat *h* because ......Prov 24:13
not good to eat much *h*......Prov 25:27
h and milk are under ....Song 4:11
was locusts and wild *h* ....Matt 3:4

HONEYCOMB

than honey and the *h*.........Ps 19:10
words are like a *h*.........Prov 16:24
fish and some *h* ....Luke 24:42

HONOR

H your father and your ....Ex 20:12
both riches and *h*.............1 Kin 3:13
the king delights to *h* ....Esth 6:6
earth, and lay my *h* ....Ps 7:5
A man who is in *h* ....Ps 49:20
Sing out the *h* of His ....Ps 66:2
will deliver him and *h*...........Ps 91:15
H and majesty are ....Ps 96:6
h have all His saints ....Ps 149:9
H the LORD with your ....Prov 3:9
before *h* is humility ....Prov 15:33
h is not fitting.................Prov 26:1
spirit will retain *h*............Prov 29:23
Father, where is My *h*..........Mal 1:6
is not without *h* ....Matt 13:57
'*H* your father and your ....Matt 15:4
h the Son just as they ....John 5:23
"I do not receive *h* ....John 5:41
but I *h* My Father ....John 8:49
"If I *h* Myself ....John 8:54
him My Father will *h* ....John 12:26
make one vessel for *h* ....Rom 9:21
to whom fear, *h* ....Rom 13:7
we bestow greater *h* ....1 Cor 12:23
sanctification and *h*.........1 Thess 4:4
alone is wise, be *h* ....1 Tim 1:17
worthy of double *h* ....1 Tim 5:17
and clay, some for *h*.........2 Tim 2:20
no man takes this *h* ....Heb 5:4
H the king ....1 Pet 2:17
from God the Father *h* ......2 Pet 1:17
give glory and *h* ....Rev 4:9

HONORABLE

of God, and he is an *h* ......1 Sam 9:6
His work is *h* and ....Ps 111:3
It is *h* for a man to ....Prov 20:3
traders are the *h*.....................Is 23:8
holy day of the LORD *h* ....Is 58:13
providing *h* things ....2 Cor 8:21
Marriage is *h* among ....Heb 13:4
having your conduct *h* ......1 Pet 2:12

HONORABLY

desiring to live *h* ....Heb 13:18

HONORS

h those who fear the ....Ps 15:4
'This people *h* Me ....Mark 7:6
It is My Father who *h* ....John 8:54

HOOKS

will lament who cast *h* ....Is 19:8
spears into pruning *h*............Mic 4:3

HOPE

I should say I have *h* ....Ruth 1:12
are spent without *h*............Job 7:6
so You destroy the *h* ....Job 14:19
where then is my *h* ....Job 17:15
h He has uprooted ....Job 19:10
also will rest in *h* ....Ps 16:9
heart, all you who *h* ....Ps 31:24
My *h* is in You ....Ps 39:7
For You are my *h* ....Ps 71:5
I *h* in Your word ....Ps 119:147
O Israel, *h* in the ....Ps 130:7
h will not be cut ....Prov 23:18
There is more *h* ....Prov 26:12
the living there is *h*............Eccl 9:4
O the *H* of Israel ....Jer 14:8
good that one should *h* ....Lam 3:26
Achor as a door of *h* ....Hos 2:15
you prisoners of *h* ....Zech 9:12
I have *h* in God ....Acts 24:15
to *h*, in *h* believed ....Rom 4:18
and rejoice in *h* ....Rom 5:2
h does not disappoint ....Rom 5:5
were saved in this *h*...........Rom 8:24
h that is seen is ....Rom 8:24
But if we *h* for what ....Rom 8:25
And now abide faith, *h* ....1 Cor 13:13
life only we have *h* ....1 Cor 15:19
may know what is the *h* ....Eph 1:18
were called in one *h* ....Eph 4:4
h which is laid ....Col 1:5
Christ in you, the *h*..............Col 1:27
For what is our *h* ....1 Thess 2:19
others who have no *h* .....1 Thess 4:13
and as a helmet the *h* ....1 Thess 5:8
Jesus Christ, our *h* ....1 Tim 1:1
in *h* of eternal life ....Titus 1:2
for the blessed *h* ....Titus 2:13
to lay hold of the *h* ....Heb 6:18
of a better *h*.......................Heb 7:19
us again to a living *h* ....1 Pet 1:3
you a reason for the *h*.........1 Pet 3:15
who has this *h* in Him ......1 John 3:3

HOPED

substance of things *h* ....Heb 11:1

HOPHNI

Wicked son of Eli, 1 Sam 1:3; 2:12–17, 22–25
Prophecy against, 1 Sam 2:27–36; 3:11–14
Carries ark into battle; killed, 1 Sam 4:1–11

HOR

Mountain of Edom; scene of Aaron's death, Num 20:22–29; 33:37–39

HOREB

See SINAI
God appears to Moses at, Ex 3:1–22
Water flows from, Ex 17:6
Elijah lodged here 40 days, 1 Kin 19:8, 9

HORITES

Inhabitants of Mt. Seir, Gen 36:20
Defeated by Chedorlaomer, Gen 14:5, 6
Driven out by Esau's descendants, Gen 36:20–29; Deut 2:12, 22

HORMAH

Destroyed by Israel, Num 21:1–3

HORN

my shield and the *h* ....Ps 18:2
h will be exalted ....Ps 112:9
goat had a notable *h* ....Dan 8:5
and has raised up a *h* ....Luke 1:69

HORRIBLE

h thing has been ....Jer 5:30
I have seen a *h* ....Hos 6:10

HORROR

and behold, *h* and ....Gen 15:12
sorrow, the cup of *h* ....Ezek 23:33
you will become a *h* ....Ezek 27:36

HORSE

The *h* and its rider He ....Ex 15:1
Have you given the *h*.........Job 39:19
h is a vain hope ....Ps 33:17
the strength of the *h*.........Ps 147:10
h is prepared for the ....Prov 21:31
and behold, a white *h* ....Rev 6:2
and behold, a black *h* ....Rev 6:5
and behold, a pale *h* ....Rev 6:8
and behold, a white *h* ....Rev 19:11

HORSES

seen servants on *h*..............Eccl 10:7
h are swifter than ....Jer 4:13
Do *h* run on rocks ....Amos 6:12
we put bits in *h* ....James 3:3

HOSANNA

H in the highest ....Matt 21:9

HOSEA

Son of Beeri, prophet of the northern kingdom, Hos 1:1

HOSHEA

Original name of Joshua, the son of Nun, Deut 32:44; Num 13:8, 16
——— Israel's last king; usurps throne, 2 Kin 15:30
Reigns wickedly; Israel taken to Assyria during reign, 2 Kin 17:1–23

HOSPITABLE

of good behavior, *h*..........1 Tim 3:2
Be *h* to one another ....1 Pet 4:9

HOST

who brings out their *h* ....Is 40:26
of the heavenly *h* ....Luke 2:13

HOSTILITY

Him who endured such *h*.....Heb 12:3

HOSTS

name of the LORD of *h*....1 Sam 17:45
As the LORD of *h* lives .....1 Kin 18:15
The LORD of *h* is with ....Ps 46:7
LORD, all you His *h* ....Ps 103:21
praise Him, all His *h* ....Ps 148:2
word of the LORD of *h* ....Is 39:5
LORD of *h* is His name ....Is 47:4
against spiritual *h* ....Eph 6:12

HOT

of the LORD was *h* ....Judg 2:14
My heart was *h* within ....Ps 39:3
are neither cold nor *h* ....Rev 3:15

HOUND

My enemies would *h* ....Ps 56:2

HOUR

h what you should ....Matt 10:19

day and *h* no one knows ....Matt 24:36
Man is coming at an *h* .....Matt 24:44
Behold, the *h* is at ....Matt 26:45
But this is your *h* ....Luke 22:53
h has not yet come ....John 2:4
But the *h* is coming ....John 4:23
h has come that the ....John 12:23
save Me from this *h* ....John 12:27
"Father, the *h* ....John 17:1
will not know what *h* ....Rev 3:3
keep you from the *h* ....Rev 3:10

HOURS

Are there not twelve *h* ....John 11:9

HOUSE

from your father's *h* ....Gen 12:1
But as for me and my *h* .....Josh 24:15
h appointed for all ....Job 30:23
with them to the *h* ....Ps 42:4
the goodness of Your *h* ....Ps 65:4
For her *h* leads down ....Prov 2:18
Through wisdom a *h* ....Prov 24:3
better to go to the *h* ....Eccl 7:2
of the *h* tremble ....Eccl 12:3
to the *h* of the God of ....Is 2:3
to those who join *h* ....Is 5:8
h was filled with ....Is 6:4
'Set your *h* in order ....Is 38:1
h shall be called a ....Is 56:7
and beat on that *h* ....Matt 7:25
h divided against ....Matt 12:25
h shall be called a ....Matt 21:13
h may be filled ....Luke 14:23
make My Father's *h* ....John 2:16
h are many mansions ....John 14:2
publicly and from *h* ....Acts 20:20
in his own rented *h* ....Acts 28:30
who rules his own *h* ....1 Tim 3:4
the church in your *h* ....Philem 2
For every *h* is built ....Heb 3:4
His own *h*, whose *h* ....Heb 3:6
him into your *h* ....2 John 1:10

HOUSEHOLD

over the ways of her *h* ...Prov 31:27
If the *h* is worthy ....Matt 10:13
be those of his own *h* ....Matt 10:36
h were baptized ....Acts 16:15
saved, you and your *h* ....Acts 16:31
also baptized the *h* ....1 Cor 1:16
those who are of the *h* ....Gal 6:10
who are of Caesar's *h* ....Phil 4:22

HOUSEHOLDER

h who brings out of ....Matt 13:52

HOUSES

h are safe from fear ....Job 21:9
Yet He filled their *h* ....Job 22:18
is that their *h* ....Ps 49:11
H and riches are an ....Prov 19:14
who has left *h* or ....Matt 19:29
you devour widows' *h* ....Matt 23:14
Do you not have *h* ....1 Cor 11:22

HOVERING

Spirit of God was *h* ....Gen 1:2

HOW

"*H* can this be ....Luke 1:34
H long do You keep ....John 10:24
h you turned to God ....1 Thess 1:9

HULDAH

Wife of Shallum, 2 Kin 22:14
Foretells Jerusalem's ruin, 2 Kin 22:15–17; 2 Chr 34:22–25
Exempts Josiah from trouble, 2 Kin 22:18–20

HUMAN

we have had *h* fathers ....Heb 12:9

HUMBLE

man Moses was very *h* ....Num 12:3
h you and test you ....Deut 8:2
who is proud, and *h* ....Job 40:11
the cry of the *h* ....Ps 9:12
Do not forget the *h* ....Ps 10:12
the desire of the *h* ....Ps 10:17
h He guides in justice ....Ps 25:9
h shall hear of it and ....Ps 34:2
LORD lifts up the *h* ....Ps 147:6
h spirit with the ....Prov 16:19
contrite and *h* spirit ....Is 57:15
a meek and *h* people ....Zeph 3:12
associate with the *h* ....Rom 12:16
gives grace to the *h* ....James 4:6
H yourselves in the ....James 4:10
gives grace to the *h* ....1 Pet 5:5
h yourselves under the ....1 Pet 5:6

HUMBLED

h himself greatly ....2 Chr 33:12
as a man, He *h* Himself ....Phil 2:8

HUMBLES

h Himself to behold ....Ps 113:6

HUMILIATION

to plunder, and to *h* ....Ezra 9:7
h His justice was ....Acts 8:33
but the rich in his *h* ....James 1:10

HUMILITY

By *h* and the fear of ....Prov 22:4
righteousness, seek *h* ....Zeph 2:3
the Lord with all *h* ....Acts 20:19
delight in false *h* ....Col 2:18
mercies, kindness, *h* ....Col 3:12
h correcting those ....2 Tim 2:25
gentle, showing all *h* ....Titus 3:2
and be clothed with *h* ....1 Pet 5:5

HUNGER

you, allowed you to *h* ....Deut 8:3
lack and suffer *h* ....Ps 34:10
They shall neither *h* ....Is 49:10
likely to die from *h* ....Jer 38:9
are those who *h* ....Matt 5:6
for you shall *h* ....Luke 6:25
to Me shall never *h* ....John 6:35
present hour we both *h* .....1 Cor 4:11
They shall neither *h* ....Rev 7:16

HUNGRY

bread from the *h* ....Job 22:7
and fills the *h* ....Ps 107:9
gives food to the *h* ....Ps 146:7
h soul every bitter ....Prov 27:7
your soul to the *h* ....Is 58:10
for I was *h* and you ....Matt 25:35
when did we see You *h* .....Matt 25:37
and one is *h* and ....1 Cor 11:21
But if anyone is *h* ....1 Cor 11:34
to be full and to be *h* ....Phil 4:12

HUNT

Yet you *h* my life to ......1 Sam 24:11
h the violent man ....Ps 140:11
h the souls of My ....Ezek 13:18

HUNTER

Nimrod the mighty *h* ....Gen 10:9
Esau was a skillful *h* ....Gen 25:27

HUR

Man of Judah; of Caleb's house, 1 Chr 2:18–20
Supports Moses' hands, Ex 17:10–12
Aids Aaron, Ex 24:14

HURAM

Master craftsman of Solomon's temple, 1 Kin 7:13–40, 45; 2 Chr 2:13, 14

HURT

h a woman with child ....Ex 21:22
who plot my *h* ....Ps 35:4
but I was not *h* ....Prov 23:35
another to his own *h* ....Eccl 8:9
They shall not *h* ....Is 11:9
of my people I am *h* ....Jer 8:21
Woe is me for my *h* ....Jer 10:19
it will by no means *h* ......Mark 16:18
shall not be *h* by the ....Rev 2:11

HUSBAND

She also gave to her *h* ....Gen 3:6
"Surely you are a *h* ....Ex 4:25
h safely trusts her ....Prov 31:11
your Maker is your *h* ....Is 54:5
though I was a *h* ....Jer 31:32
now have is not your *h* .....John 4:18
woman have her own *h* .....1 Cor 7:2
For the unbelieving *h* ....1 Cor 7:14
you will save your *h* ....1 Cor 7:16
betrothed you to one *h* .....2 Cor 11:2
For the *h* is head of ....Eph 5:23
the *h* of one wife ....1 Tim 3:2

HUSBANDS

them ask their own *h* .....1 Cor 14:35
H, love your wives ....Eph 5:25
Let deacons be the *h* ....1 Tim 3:12

HUSHAI

Archite; David's friend, 2 Sam 15:32–37
Feigns sympathy with Absalom, 2 Sam 16:16–19
Defeats Ahithophel's advice, 2 Sam 17:5–23

HYMENAEUS

False teacher excommunicated by Paul, 1 Tim 1:19, 20

HYMN

they had sung a *h* ....Matt 26:30

HYMNS

praying and singing *h* ......Acts 16:25
in psalms and *h* ....Eph 5:19

HYPOCRISY

you are full of *h* ....Matt 23:28
Pharisees, which is *h* ......Luke 12:1
Let love be without *h* ......Rom 12:9
away with their *h* ....Gal 2:13
and without *h* ....James 3:17
malice, all deceit, *h* ....1 Pet 2:1

HYPOCRITE

of the *h* shall perish ....Job 8:13
and the joy of the *h* ....Job 20:5

is the hope of the *h* ....Job 27:8
for everyone is a *h* ....Is 9:17
also played the *h* ....Gal 2:13

HYPOCRITES

"But the *h* in heart ....Job 36:13
will I go in with *h* ....Ps 26:4
For you were *h* ....Jer 42:20
not be like the *h* ....Matt 6:5
do you test Me, you *h* ....Matt 22:18
and Pharisees, *h* ....Matt 23:13

HYSSOP

Purge me with *h* ....Ps 51:7
sour wine, put it on *h* ....John 19:29

— I —

IBZAN

Judge of Israel; father of 60 children, Judg 12:8, 9

ICE

dark because of the *i* ....Job 6:16

ICHABOD

Son of Phinehas, 1 Sam 4:19–22

ICONIUM

City of Asia Minor; visited by Paul, Acts 13:51
Many converts in, Acts 14:1–6

IDDO

Leader of Jews at Casiphia, Ezra 8:17–20
——— Seer whose writings are cited, 2 Chr 9:29

IDLE

For they are *i* ....Ex 5:8
i person will suffer ....Prov 19:15
i word men may speak ....Matt 12:36
saw others standing *i* ....Matt 20:3
they learn to be *i* ....1 Tim 5:13
both *i* talkers and ....Titus 1:10

IDOL

if he blesses an *i* ....Is 66:3
thing offered to an *i* ....1 Cor 8:7
That an *i* is anything ....1 Cor 10:19

IDOLATER

or covetous, or an *i* ....1 Cor 5:11
man, who is an *i* ....Eph 5:5

IDOLATERS

fornicators, nor *i* ....1 Cor 6:9
immoral, sorcerers, *i* ....Rev 21:8
and murderers and *i* ....Rev 22:15

IDOLATRIES

and abominable *i* ....1 Pet 4:3

IDOLATRY

beloved, flee from *i* ....1 Cor 10:14
i, sorcery ....Gal 5:20

IDOLS

stolen the household *i* ....Gen 31:19
of the peoples are *i* ....Ps 96:5
i are silver and gold ....Ps 115:4
land is also full of *i* ....Is 2:8
insane with their *i* ....Jer 50:38
in the room of his *i* ....Ezek 8:12
from their wooden *i* ....Hos 4:12
who regard worthless *i* ....Jon 2:8
i speak delusion ....Zech 10:2
things polluted by *i* ....Acts 15:20
You who abhor *i* ....Rom 2:22
This was offered to *i* ....1 Cor 10:28
keep yourselves from *i* ....1 John 5:21
worship demons, and *i* ....Rev 9:20

IDUMEA

Name used by Greeks and Romans to designate Edom, Mark 3:8

IGNORANCE

that you did it in *i* ....Acts 3:17
i God overlooked ....Acts 17:30
sins committed in *i* ....Heb 9:7
to silence the *i* ....1 Pet 2:15

IGNORANT

I was so foolish and *i* ....Ps 73:22
though Abraham was *i* ....Is 63:16
not want you to be *i* ....1 Cor 12:1
But if anyone is *i* ....1 Cor 14:38
on those who are *i* ....Heb 5:2

IGNORANTLY

because I did it *i* ....1 Tim 1:13

ILLEGITIMATE

then you are *i* ....Heb 12:8

ILLUMINATED

after you were *i* ....Heb 10:32
and the earth was *i* ....Rev 18:1
for the glory of God *i* ....Rev 21:23

ILLYRICUM

Paul preaches in, Rom 15:19

IMAGE

Us make man in Our *i* ....Gen 1:26
yourselves a carved *i* ....Deut 4:16
shall despise their *i* ....Ps 73:20
the king made an *i* ....Dan 3:1
to them, "Whose *i* ....Matt 22:20
since he is the *i* ....1 Cor 11:7
He is the *i* of the ....Col 1:15
and not the very *i* ....Heb 10:1
the beast and his *i* ....Rev 14:9
who worshiped his *i* ....Rev 19:20

IMAGINATION

the proud in the *i* ....Luke 1:51

IMITATE

I urge you, *i* me ....1 Cor 4:16
as I also *i* Christ ....1 Cor 11:1
i those who through ....Heb 6:12

IMMANUEL

shall call His name *I* ....Is 7:14
shall call His name *I* ....Matt 1:23

IMMEDIATELY

i the Spirit ....Mark 1:12
hear, Satan comes *i* ....Mark 4:15
i forgets what ....James 1:24
I i was in the Spirit ....Rev 4:2

IMMORAL

i woman is a deep pit ....Prov 22:14
murderers, sexually *i* ....Rev 21:8

IMMORALITY

except sexual *i* ....Matt 5:32
i as is not even named ....1 Cor 5:1
abstain from sexual *i* ....1 Thess 4:3

IMMORTAL

to the King eternal, *i* ....1 Tim 1:17

IMMORTALITY

glory, honor, and *i* ....Rom 2:7
mortal must put on *i* ....1 Cor 15:53
who alone has *i* ....1 Tim 6:16
and brought life and *i* ....2 Tim 1:10

IMMOVABLE

be steadfast, *i* ....1 Cor 15:58

IMMUTABLE

that by two *i* things ....Heb 6:18

IMPART

see you, that I may *i* ....Rom 1:11
that it may *i* grace ....Eph 4:29

IMPENITENT

i heart you are ....Rom 2:5

IMPLANTED

with meekness the *i* ....James 1:21

IMPOSSIBLE

and nothing will be *i* ....Matt 17:20
"With men this is *i* ....Matt 19:26
God nothing will be *i* ....Luke 1:37
without faith it is *i* ....Heb 11:6

IMPOSTORS

i will grow worse ....2 Tim 3:13

IMPRISONMENT

and of chains and *i* ....Heb 11:36

IMPRISONMENTS

in stripes, in *i* ....2 Cor 6:5

IMPULSIVE

but he who is *i* ....Prov 14:29

IMPURITY

a woman during her *i* ....Ezek 18:6

IMPUTE

"Do not let my lord *i* ....2 Sam 19:19
the LORD does not *i* ....Ps 32:2
the LORD shall not *i* ....Rom 4:8

IMPUTED

bloodshed shall be *i* ....Lev 17:4
might be *i* to them ....Rom 4:11
alone that it was *i* ....Rom 4:23
but sin is not *i* ....Rom 5:13

IMPUTES

i righteousness apart ....Rom 4:6

INCENSE

golden bowls full of *i* ....Rev 5:8

INCLINE

i your heart to the ....Josh 24:23
i my heart to any evil ....Ps 141:4

INCORRUPTIBLE

the glory of the *i* ....Rom 1:23

dead will be raised *i* ....1 Cor 15:52
to an inheritance *i* ....1 Pet 1:4
corruptible seed but *i*.......1 Pet 1:23

INCORRUPTION

it is raised in *i* ....1 Cor 15:42
corruption inherit *i* ....1 Cor 15:50
must put on *i*..............1 Cor 15:53

INCREASE

if riches *i* ....Ps 62:10
the LORD give you *i* ....Ps 115:14
hear and *i* learning ....Prov 1:5
When goods *i* ....Eccl 5:11
Of the *i* of His ....Is 9:7
and knowledge shall *i* ....Dan 12:4
Lord, "*I* our faith ....Luke 17:5
He must *i* ....John 3:30
but God gave the *i* ....1 Cor 3:6
grows with the *i* ....Col 2:19
for they will *i* ....2 Tim 2:16

INCREASED

The waters *i* and ....Gen 7:17
i your mercy which you .....Gen 19:19
nation and *i* its joy ....Is 9:3
And Jesus *i* in wisdom ......Luke 2:52

INCREASES

i knowledge *i*.....................Eccl 1:18
who have no might He *i*.......Is 40:29

INCREDIBLE

should it be thought *i*........Acts 26:8

INCURABLE

My wound is *i* ....Job 34:6
'Your affliction is *i* ....Jer 30:12
Your sorrow is *i* ....Jer 30:15

INDEBTED

everyone who is *i*.............Luke 11:4

INDEED

i it was very ....Gen 1:31
"But will God *i* ....1 Kin 8:27
"Behold, an Israelite *i* ......John 1:47

INDIA

Eastern limit of Persian Empire, Esth 1:1

INDICATING

the Holy Spirit *i* ....Heb 9:8
who was in them was *i* ......1 Pet 1:11

INDIGNANT

saw it, they were *i* ....Matt 26:8

INDIGNATION

of His anger, wrath, *i*.........Ps 78:49
I has taken hold ....Ps 119:53
in whose hand is My *i*...........Is 10:5
For the *i* of the LORD ....Is 34:2
have filled me with *i* ....Jer 15:17
can stand before His *i*..........Nah 1:6
i which will devour ....Heb 10:27
into the cup of His *i* ....Rev 14:10

INDUCED

O LORD, You *i* me ....Jer 20:7
if the prophet is *i* ....Ezek 14:9
I the LORD have *i* ....Ezek 14:9

INDULGENCE

no value against the *i* ....Col 2:23

INEXCUSABLE

Therefore you are *i* ....Rom 2:1

INEXPRESSIBLE

Paradise and heard *i* ....2 Cor 12:4
you rejoice with joy *i* ....1 Pet 1:8

INFALLIBLE

suffering by many *i* ....Acts 1:3

INFANTS

i who never saw ....Job 3:16
they also brought *i* ....Luke 18:15

INFERIOR

another kingdom *i* ....Dan 2:39
that I am not at all *i* ....2 Cor 11:5

INFIRMITIES

"He Himself took our *i* ......Matt 8:17
boast, except in my *i* ....2 Cor 12:5
and your frequent *i*..........1 Tim 5:23

INFLAMING

i yourselves with gods ....Is 57:5

INHABIT

the wicked will not *i* ....Prov 10:30
cities and *i* them ....Amos 9:14

INHABITANT

Cry out and shout, O *i*..........Is 12:6
And the *i* will not say ....Is 33:24

INHABITANTS

He looks on all the *i* ....Ps 33:14
give ear, all *i* ....Ps 49:1
Let the *i* of Sela sing ....Is 42:11
Woe to the *i* of the ....Rev 12:12

INHABITED

rejoicing in His *i* ....Prov 8:31
'You shall be *i* ....Is 44:26
who formed it to be *i*.............Is 45:18

INHERIT

i the iniquities ....Job 13:26
descendants shall *i* ....Ps 25:13
The righteous shall *i* ....Ps 37:29
The wise shall *i* ....Prov 3:35
love me to *i* wealth ....Prov 8:21
The simple *i* folly ....Prov 14:18
the blameless will *i* ....Prov 28:10
i the kingdom prepared .....Matt 25:34
I do that I may *i* ....Mark 10:17
unrighteous will not *i* ....1 Cor 6:9
you may *i* a blessing ....1 Pet 3:9
who overcomes shall *i*.........Rev 21:7

INHERITANCE

"You shall have no *i* ....Num 18:20
is the place of His *i* ....Deut 32:9
the portion of my *i* ....Ps 16:5
yes, I have a good *i* ....Ps 16:6
i shall be forever ....Ps 37:18
He will choose our *i* ....Ps 47:4
You confirmed Your *i* ....Ps 68:9
the tribe of Your *i* ....Ps 74:2
i gained hastily ....Prov 20:21
right of *i* is yours ....Jer 32:8
i has been turned ....Lam 5:2
will arise to your *i* ....Dan 12:13
And God gave him no *i* ....Acts 7:5
and give you an *i* ....Acts 20:32

For if the *i* is of the ....Gal 3:18
we have obtained an *i*...........Eph 1:11
be partakers of the *i* ....Col 1:12
receive as an *i* ....Heb 11:8
i incorruptible ....1 Pet 1:4

INIQUITIES

How many are my *i* ....Job 13:23
i have overtaken me ....Ps 40:12
I prevail against me ....Ps 65:3
forgives all your *i* ....Ps 103:3
LORD, should mark *i* ....Ps 130:3
was bruised for our *i* ....Is 53:5
He shall bear their *i* ....Is 53:11
i have separated you ....Is 59:2

INIQUITY

God, visiting the *i* of the ....Ex 20:5
He has not observed *i* ....Num 23:21
wicked brings forth *i* ....Ps 7:14
O LORD, pardon my *i* ....Ps 25:11
i I have not hidden ....Ps 32:5
was brought forth in *i* ....Ps 51:5
If I regard *i* in my ....Ps 66:18
Add *i* to their ....Ps 69:27
workers of *i* flourish ....Ps 92:7
i boast in themselves ....Ps 94:4
Shall the throne of *i* ....Ps 94:20
i have dominion ....Ps 119:133
i will reap sorrow ....Prov 22:8
a people laden with *i* ....Is 1:4
i is taken away ....Is 6:7
has laid on Him the *i* ....Is 53:6
will remember their *i*............Hos 9:9
to those who devise *i* ....Mic 2:1
like You, pardoning *i*..........Mic 7:18
all you workers of *i* ....Luke 13:27
a fire, a world of *i* ....James 3:6

INJUSTICE

of truth and without *i* ....Deut 32:4
i shuts her mouth ....Job 5:16
i have your fathers ....Jer 2:5

INK

us, written not with *i* ....2 Cor 3:3
do so with paper and *i* ......2 John 12

INN

room for them in the *i* ....Luke 2:7
brought him to an *i* ....Luke 10:34

INNOCENCE

of my heart and *i* ....Gen 20:5
washed my hands in *i* ....Ps 73:13

INNOCENT

do not kill the *i* ....Ex 23:7
a bribe to slay an *i*..........Deut 27:25
i will divide the ....Job 27:17
a bribe against the *i* ....Ps 15:5
because I was found *i* ....Dan 6:22
saying, "I am *i* ....Matt 27:24
this day that I am *i*............Acts 20:26

INNUMERABLE

i as the sand which is ....Heb 11:12
i company of angels ....Heb 12:22

INQUIRED

children of Israel *i* ....Judg 20:27
Therefore David *i* ....1 Sam 23:2
the LORD, nor *i* of Him ....Zeph 1:6
the prophets have *i*...........1 Pet 1:10

INQUIRY

shall make careful *i*.........Deut 19:18

INSANE

images, and they are *i* ....Jer 50:38
the spiritual man is *i* ....Hos 9:7

INSCRIBED

Oh, that they were *i* ....Job 19:23
See, I have *i* you on ....Is 49:16

INSPIRATION

is given by *i* of God ....2 Tim 3:16

INSTRUCT

good Spirit to *i* them ....Neh 9:20
I will *i* you and teach ....Ps 32:8
the LORD that he may *i* .....1 Cor 2:16

INSTRUCTED

Surely you have *i* ....Job 4:3
counsel, and who *i* ....Is 40:14
This man had been *i* ....Acts 18:25
are excellent, being *i* ....Rom 2:18
Moses was divinely *i* ....Heb 8:5

INSTRUCTION

seeing you hate *i* ....Ps 50:17
despise wisdom and *i* ....Prov 1:7
Take firm hold of *i* ....Prov 4:13
Hear *i* and be wise ....Prov 8:33
Give *i* to a wise man ....Prov 9:9
i loves knowledge ....Prov 12:1
Cease listening to *i* ....Prov 19:27
Apply your heart to *i* ....Prov 23:12
for correction, for *i* ....2 Tim 3:16

INSTRUCTORS

have ten thousand *i* ....1 Cor 4:15

INSTRUCTS

My heart also *i* ....Ps 16:7
He who *i* the nations ....Ps 94:10

INSTRUMENT

to Him with an *i* ....Ps 33:2
on an *i* of ten strings ....Ps 92:3

INSTRUMENTS

i of cruelty are in ....Gen 49:5
with stringed *i* ....Ps 150:4
i of unrighteousness ....Rom 6:13
i of righteousness ....Rom 6:13

INSUBORDINATE

for the lawless and *i* ....1 Tim 1:9
For there are many *i* ....Titus 1:10

INSUBORDINATION

of dissipation or *i* ....Titus 1:6

INSULTED

will be mocked and *i* ......Luke 18:32
i the Spirit of grace ....Heb 10:29

INSULTS

nor be afraid of their *i* ....Is 51:7

INTEGRITY

In the *i* of my heart ....Gen 20:5
he holds fast to his *i* ....Job 2:3
that God may know my *i* .....Job 31:6
I have walked in my *i* ....Ps 26:1
You uphold me in my *i* ....Ps 41:12
The *i* of the upright ....Prov 11:3
in doctrine showing *i* ....Titus 2:7

INTELLIGENT

Sergius Paulus, an *i* ....Acts 13:7

INTERCEDE

the LORD, who will *i* ....1 Sam 2:25

INTERCESSION

of many, and made *i* ....Is 53:12
Spirit Himself makes *i* ....Rom 8:26
always lives to make *i* ....Heb 7:25

INTERCESSOR

that there was no *i* ....Is 59:16

INTEREST

shall not charge him *i* ....Ex 22:25
men lent to me for *i* ....Jer 15:10
collected it with *i* ....Luke 19:23

INTERPRET

Do all *i* ....1 Cor 12:30
pray that he may *i* ....1 Cor 14:13
in turn, and let one *i* ....1 Cor 14:27

INTERPRETATION

"This is the *i* ....Gen 40:12
to another the *i* ....1 Cor 12:10
a revelation, has an *i* ......1 Cor 14:26
of any private *i* ....2 Pet 1:20

INTERPRETATIONS

Do not *i* belong to God ....Gen 40:8
that you can give *i* ....Dan 5:16

INTRIGUE

seize the kingdom by *i* ......Dan 11:21
join with them by *i* ....Dan 11:34

INVISIBLE

of the world His *i* ....Rom 1:20
is the image of the *i* ....Col 1:15
eternal, immortal, *i* ....1 Tim 1:17
as seeing Him who is *i* ......Heb 11:27

INWARD

i part is destruction ....Ps 5:9
Both the *i* thought ....Ps 64:6
You have formed my *i* ....Ps 139:13
God according to the *i* ....Rom 7:22
i man is being renewed .....2 Cor 4:16

INWARDLY

i they are ....Matt 7:15
is a Jew who is one *i* ....Rom 2:29

IRON

He regards *i* as straw ....Job 41:27
i sharpens *i* ....Prov 27:17
and your neck was an *i* ....Is 48:4
its feet partly of *i* ....Dan 2:33

ISAAC

Promised heir of the covenant, Gen 17:16–21
Born and circumcised, Gen 21:1–7
Offered up as a sacrifice, Gen 22:1–19
Marries Rebekah, Gen 24:62–67
Prays for children; prefers Esau, Gen 25:21–28
Dealings with Abimelech, king of Gerar, Gen 26:1–31
Mistakenly blesses Jacob, Gen 27:1–28:5
Dies in his old age, Gen 35:28, 29
NT references to, Luke 3:34; Gal 4:21–31; Heb 11:9, 20

ISAIAH

Prophet during reigns of Uzziah, Jotham, Ahaz and Hezekiah, Is 1:1
Responds to prophetic call, Is 6:1–13
Prophesies to Hezekiah, 2 Kin 19; 20
Writes Uzziah's biography, 2 Chr 26:22
Writes Hezekiah's biography, 2 Chr 32:32
Quoted in NT, Matt 1:22, 23; 3:3; 8:17; 12:17–21; Luke 4:17–19; Acts 13:34; Rom 9:27, 29; 10:16, 20, 21; 11:26, 27; 15:12; 1 Pet 2:22

ISCARIOT, JUDAS

Listed among the Twelve, Mark 3:14, 19; Luke 6:16
Criticizes Mary, John 12:3–6
Identified as betrayer, John 13:21–30
Takes money to betray Christ, Matt 26:14–16
Betrays Christ with a kiss, Mark 14:43–45
Repents and commits suicide, Matt 27:3–10
His place filled, Acts 1:15–26

ISHBOSHETH

One of Saul's sons; made king, 2 Sam 2:8–10
Offends Abner, 2 Sam 3:7–11
Slain; his assassins executed, 2 Sam 4:1–12

ISHMAEL

Abram's son by Hagar, Gen 16:3, 4, 11–16
Circumcised, Gen 17:25
Scoffs at Isaac's feast; exiled with his mother, Gen 21:8–21
His sons; his death, Gen 25:12–18
—— Son of Nethaniah; kills Gedaliah, 2 Kin 25:22–26

ISHMAELITES

Settle at Havilah, Gen 25:17, 18
Joseph sold to, Gen 37:25–28
Sell Joseph to Potiphar, Gen 39:1

ISRAEL

Used to refer to:
Jacob, Gen 32:28
descendants of Jacob, Gen 49:16, 28
ten northern tribes (in contrast to Judah), 1 Sam 11:8
restored nation after exile, Ezra 9:1
true church, Gal 6:16

ISRAEL

be called Jacob, but *I* ....Gen 32:28
"Hear, O *I* ....Deut 6:4
shepherd My people *I* ....2 Sam 7:7
Truly God is good to *I* ....Ps 73:1
helped His servant *I* ....Luke 1:54
For they are not all *I* ....Rom 9:6
and upon the *I* of God ....Gal 6:16

ISRAELITES

Afflicted in Egypt, Ex 1:12–22
Escape from Egypt, Ex 12:29–42, 50; 13:17–22
Receive law at Sinai, Ex 19
Idolatry and rebellion of, Ex 32; Num 13; 14
Wander in the wilderness, Num 14:26–39

Cross Jordan; conquer Canaan, Josh 4; 12
Ruled by judges, Judg 2
Saul chosen as king, 1 Sam 10
Kingdom divided, 1 Kin 12
Northern kingdom carried captive, 2 Kin 17
Southern kingdom carried captive, 2 Kin 24
70 years in exile, 2 Chr 36:20, 21
Return after exile, Ezra 1:1–5
Nation rejects Christ, Matt 27:20–27
Nation destroyed, Luke 21:20–24

ISSACHAR

Jacob's fifth son, Gen 30:17, 18
—— Tribe of:
Genealogy of, 1 Chr 7:1–5
Prophecy concerning, Gen 49:14, 15
Census at Sinai, Num 1:28, 29
Inheritance of, Josh 19:17–23

ITALY

Jews expelled from, Acts 18:2
Paul sails for, Acts 27:1, 6
Christians in, Acts 28:14

ITCHING

they have *i* ears . . . . 2 Tim 4:3

ITHAMAR

Youngest son of Aaron, Ex 6:23
Consecrated as priest, Ex 28:1
Duty entrusted to, Ex 38:21
Jurisdiction over Gershonites and Merarites, Num 4:21–33

ITINERANT

i Jewish exorcists . . . . Acts 19:13

— J —

JABBOK

River entering the Jordan about 20 miles north of the Dead Sea, Num 21:24
Scene of Jacob's conflict, Gen 32:22–32
Boundary marker, Deut 3:16

JABESH GILEAD

Consigned to destruction, Judg 21:8–15
Saul defeats the Ammonites at, 1 Sam 11:1–11
Citizens of, rescue Saul's body, 1 Sam 31:11–13
David thanks citizens of, 2 Sam 2:4–7

JABIN

Canaanite king of Hazor; leads confederacy against Joshua, Josh 11:1–14
—— Another king of Hazor; oppresses Israelites, Judg 4:2
Defeated by Deborah and Barak, Judg 4:3–24
Immortalized in poetry, Judg 5:1–31

JACHIN

One of two pillars in front of Solomon's temple, 1 Kin 7:21, 22

JACOB

Son of Isaac and Rebekah; Rebekah's favorite, Gen 25:21–28
Obtains birthright, Gen 25:29–34
Obtains blessing meant for Esau; flees, Gen 27:1—28:5
Sees vision of ladder, Gen 28:10–22
Serves Laban for Rachel and Leah, Gen 29:1–30
Fathers children, Gen 29:31—30:24
Flees from, makes covenant with Laban, Gen 30:25—31:55
Makes peace with Esau, Gen 32:1–21; 33:1–17
Wrestles with God, Gen 32:22–32
Returns to Bethel; renamed Israel, Gen 35:1–15
Shows preference for Joseph, Gen 37:3
Mourns Joseph's disappearance, Gen 37:32–35
Sends sons to Egypt for food, Gen 42:1–5
Reluctantly allows Benjamin to go, Gen 43:1–15
Moves his household to Egypt, Gen 45:25—47:12
Blesses his sons and grandsons; dies, Gen 48; 49
Buried in Canaan, Gen 50:1–14

JACOB'S WELL

Christ teaches a Samaritan woman at, John 4:5–26

JAEL

Wife of Heber the Kenite; kills Sisera, Judg 4:17–22
Praised by Deborah, Judg 5:24–27

JAIR

Manassite warrior; conquers towns in Gilead, Num 32:41; Deut 3:14
—— Eighth judge of Israel, Judg 10:3–5

JAIRUS

Ruler of the synagogue; Jesus raises his daughter, Mark 5:22–24, 35–43

JAMES

Son of Zebedee, called as disciple, Matt 4:21, 22; Luke 5:10, 11
One of the Twelve, Matt 10:2; Mark 3:17
Zealous for the Lord, Luke 9:52–54
Ambitious for honor, Mark 10:35–45
Witnesses Transfiguration, Matt 17:1–9
Martyred by Herod Agrippa, Acts 12:2
—— Son of Alphaeus; one of the Twelve, Matt 10:3, 4
Called "the Less," Mark 15:40
—— Jesus' half brother, Matt 13:55, 56; Gal 1:19
Becomes leader of Jerusalem Council and Jerusalem church, Acts 15:13–22; Gal 2:9
Author of an epistle, James 1:1

JANNES AND JAMBRES

Two Egyptian magicians; oppose Moses, Ex 7:11–22; 2 Tim 3:8

JAPHETH

One of Noah's three sons, Gen 5:32
Receives blessing, Gen 9:20–27
His descendants occupy Asia Minor and Europe, Gen 10:2–5

JARED

Father of Enoch, Gen 5:15–20
Ancestor of Noah, 1 Chr 1:2
Ancestor of Christ, Luke 3:37

JASHER

Book of, quoted, Josh 10:13

JASON

Welcomes Paul at Thessalonica, Acts 17:5–9
Described as Paul's kinsman, Rom 16:21

JAVAN

Son of Japheth, Gen 10:2, 4
Descendants of, to receive good news, Is 66:19, 20

JEALOUS

your God, am a *j* God . . . . Ex 20:5
LORD, whose name is *J* . . . . . Ex 34:14
a consuming fire, a *j* . . . . Deut 4:24
For I am *j* for you . . . . 2 Cor 11:2

JEALOUSY

They provoked Him to *j* . . . . Deut 32:16
Will Your *j* burn like . . . . Ps 79:5
j is a husband's . . . . Prov 6:34
as strong as death, *j* . . . . Song 8:6
will provoke you to *j* . . . . Rom 10:19
for you with godly *j* . . . . 2 Cor 11:2

JEBUS

Canaanite name of Jerusalem before captured by David, 1 Chr 11:4–8

JEBUSITES

Descendants of Canaan, Gen 15:18–21; Num 13:29
Defeated by Joshua, Josh 11:1–12
Not driven from Jerusalem; later conquered by David, Judg 1:21; 2 Sam 5:6–8
Put to forced labor under Solomon, 1 Kin 9:20, 21

JECONIAH

See JEHOIACHIN
Variant form of Jehoiachin, 1 Chr 3:16, 17
Abbreviated to Coniah, Jer 22:24, 28

JEDIDIAH

Name given to Solomon by Nathan, 2 Sam 12:24, 25

JEDUTHUN

Levite musician appointed by David, 1 Chr 16:41, 42
Heads a family of musicians, 2 Chr 5:12
Name appears in Psalm titles, Ps 39; 62; 77

JEGAR SAHADUTHA

Name given by Laban to memorial stones, Gen 31:46, 47

JEHOAHAZ

Son and successor of Jehu, king of Israel, 2 Kin 10:35
Seeks the Lord in defeat, 2 Kin 13:2–9
—— Son and successor of Josiah, king of Judah, 2 Kin 23:30–34
Called Shallum, 1 Chr 3:15
—— Another form of Ahaziah, youngest son of King Joram, 2 Chr 21:17

JEHOASH

See JOASH

JEHOIACHIN

Son of Jehoiakim; next to the last king of Judah, 2 Kin 24:8
Deported to Babylon, 2 Kin 24:8–16
Liberated by Evil-Merodach, Jer 52:31–34

JEHOIADA

High priest during reign of Joash, 2 Kin 11:4—12:16
Instructs Joash, 2 Kin 12:2

JEHOIAKIM

Wicked king of Judah; son of Josiah; serves Pharaoh and Nebuchadnezzar, 2 Kin 23:34—24:7
Taken captive to Babylon, 2 Chr 36:6–8
Kills prophet Urijah, Jer 26:20–23
Destroys Jeremiah's scroll; cursed by God, Jer 36

JEHORAM (or Joram)

Wicked king of Judah; son of Jehoshaphat, 2 Kin 8:16–24
Marries Athaliah, 2 Kin 8:18, 19
Kills his brothers, 2 Chr 21:2, 4
Elijah prophesies against him; prophecy fulfilled, 2 Chr 21:12–20
—— Wicked king of Israel; son of Ahab, 2 Kin 3:1–3
Counseled by Elisha, 2 Kin 3; 5:8; 6:8–12
Wounded in battle, 2 Kin 8:28, 29
Killed by Jehu, 2 Kin 9:14–26

JEHOSHAPHAT

Righteous king of Judah; son of Asa, 1 Kin 22:41–50
Goes to war with Ahab against Syria, 1 Kin 22:1–36
Institutes reforms; sends out teachers of the Law, 2 Chr 17:6–9; 19
His enemies defeated through his faith, 2 Chr 20:1–30

JEHOZABAD

Son of a Moabitess; assassinates Joash, 2 Kin 12:20, 21
Put to death, 2 Chr 25:3

JEHU

Prophet; denounces Baasha, 1 Kin 16:1–7
Rebukes Jehoshaphat, 2 Chr 19:2, 3
—— Commander under Ahab; anointed king, 1 Kin 19:16; 2 Kin 9:1–13
Destroys the house of Ahab, 2 Kin 9:14—10:30
Turns away from the Lord; dies, 2 Kin 10:31–36

JEHUDI

Reads Jeremiah's scroll, Jer 36:14, 21, 23

JEOPARDY

stand in *j* every hour ...... 1 Cor 15:30

JEPHTHAH

Gilead's son by a harlot, Judg 11:1
Driven out, then brought back to command army against Ammonites, Judg 11:2–28
Sacrifices his daughter to fulfill a vow, Judg 11:29–40
Chastises Ephraim, Judg 12:1–7

JEREMIAH

Prophet under Josiah, Jehoiakim, and Zedekiah, Jer 1:1–3
Called by God, Jer 1:4–9
Forbidden to marry, Jer 16:2
Imprisoned by Pashhur, Jer 20:1–6
Prophecy written, destroyed, rewritten, Jer 36
Accused of defection and imprisoned; released by Zedekiah, Jer 37
Cast into dungeon; rescued; prophesies to Zedekiah, Jer 38
Set free by Nebuchadnezzar, Jer 39:11—40:6
Forcibly taken to Egypt, Jer 43:5–7

JERICHO

City near the Jordan, Num 22:1
Called the city of palm trees, Deut 34:3; 2 Chr 28:15
Miraculously defeated by Joshua, Josh 6
Rebuilt by Hiel, 1 Kin 16:34
Visited by Jesus, Matt 20:29–34; Luke 19:1–10

JEROBOAM

Son of Nebat; receives prophecy that he will be king, 1 Kin 11:26–40
Made king; leads revolt against Rehoboam, 1 Kin 12:1–24
Sets up idols, 1 Kin 12:25–33
Rebuked by a man of God, 1 Kin 13:1–10
Judgment on house of, 1 Kin 13:33—14:20
—— Wicked king of Israel; son of Joash; successful in war, 2 Kin 14:23–29
Prophecy concerning, by Amos, Amos 7:7–13

JERUBBAAL

Name given to Gideon for destroying Baal's altar, Judg 6:32

JERUSALEM

Originally called Salem, Gen 14:18
Jebusite city, Josh 15:8; Judg 1:8, 21
King of, defeated by Joshua, Josh 10:5–23
Conquered by David; made capital, 2 Sam 5:6–9
Ark brought to, 2 Sam 6:12–17; 1 Kin 8:1–13
Saved from plague, 2 Sam 24:16
Temple built and dedicated here, 1 Kin 6; 8:14–66
Suffers in war, 1 Kin 14:25–27; 2 Kin 14:13, 14; Is 7:1
Miraculously saved, 2 Kin 19:31–36
Captured by Babylon, 2 Kin 24:10—25:21; Jer 39:1–8
Exiles return and rebuild temple, Ezra 1:1–4; 2:1
Walls of, dedicated, Neh 12:27–47
Christ enters as king, Matt 21:4–11
Christ laments for, Matt 23:37; Luke 19:41–44
Church born in, Acts 2
Christians of, persecuted, Acts 4

JESHIMON

Wilderness west of the Dead Sea, 1 Sam 23:19, 24

JESHUA (or Joshua)

Postexilic high priest; returns with Zerubbabel, Ezra 2:2
Aids in rebuilding temple, Ezra 3:2–8
Also called Joshua; seen in vision, Zech 3:1–10

JESHURUN

Poetic name of endearment for Israel, Deut 32:15

JESSE

Grandson of Ruth and Boaz, Ruth 4:17–22
Father of David, 1 Sam 16:1–13
Mentioned in prophecy, Is 11:1, 10

JESTING

talking, nor coarse *j* .... Eph 5:4

JESUS

J Christ was as .... Matt 1:18
shall call His name *J* .... Matt 1:21
J was led up by the .... Matt 4:1
These twelve *J* sent .... Matt 10:5
and laid hands on *J* .... Matt 26:50
Barabbas and destroy *J* ..... Matt 27:20
we to do with You, *J* .... Mark 1:24
J withdrew with His .... Mark 3:7
J went into Jerusalem ..... Mark 11:11
as they were eating, *J* ..... Mark 14:22
and he delivered *J* .... Mark 15:15
J rebuked the .... Luke 9:42
truth came through *J* .... John 1:17
J lifted up His eyes .... John 6:5
J wept .... John 11:35
J was crucified .... John 19:20
This *J* God has raised .... Acts 2:32
of Your holy Servant *J* ...... Acts 4:30
believed on the Lord *J* ...... Acts 11:17
baptized into Christ *J* .... Rom 6:3
your mouth the Lord *J* ...... Rom 10:9
among you except *J* .... 1 Cor 2:2
the day of the Lord *J* .... 1 Cor 5:5
perfect in Christ *J* .... Col 1:28
J who is called .... Col 4:11
exhort in the Lord *J* .... 1 Thess 4:1
But we see *J* .... Heb 2:9
looking unto *J* .... Heb 12:2
J Christ the righteous .... 1 John 2:1
Revelation of *J* Christ .... Rev 1:1
so, come, Lord *J* .... Rev 22:20

JETHER

Gideon's oldest son, Judg 8:20, 21

JETHRO

Priest of Midian; becomes Moses' father-in-law, Ex 2:16–22
Blesses Moses' departure, Ex 4:18
Visits and counsels Moses, Ex 18
Also called Reuel, Num 10:29

JEWELS

your thighs are like *j* .... Song 7:1
that I make them My *j* .... Mal 3:17

JEWS

Jesus born King of the, Matt 2:2
Salvation comes through the, John 4:22; Acts 11:19; Rom 1:16; 2:9, 10
Reject Christ, Matt 27:21–25
Reject the gospel, Acts 13:42–46

JEZEBEL

Ahab's idolatrous wife, 1 Kin 16:31

Her abominable acts, 1 Kin 18:4, 13; 19:1, 2; 21:1–16
Death prophesied; prophecy fulfilled, 1 Kin 21:23; 2 Kin 9:7, 30–37
——Type of paganism in the church, Rev 2:20

JEZREEL

Ahab's capital, 1 Kin 18:45; 21:1
Ahab's family destroyed at, 1 Kin 21:23; 2 Kin 9:30–37; 10:1–11

JOAB

David's nephew; commands his army, 2 Sam 2:10–32; 8:16; 10:1–14; 11:1, 14–25; 20:1–23
Kills Abner, 2 Sam 3:26, 27
Intercedes for Absalom, 2 Sam 14:1–33
Remains loyal to David; kills Absalom, 2 Sam 18:1–5, 9–17
Demoted; kills Amasa, 2 Sam 19:13; 20:8–10
Opposes census, 2 Sam 24:1–9; 1 Chr 21:1–6
Supports Adonijah, 1 Kin 1:7
Solomon orders his death in obedience to David's command, 1 Kin 2:1–6, 28–34

JOANNA

Wife of Chuza, Herod's steward, Luke 8:1–3
With others, heralds Christ's resurrection, Luke 23:55, 56

JOASH (or Jehoash)

Son of Ahaziah; saved from Athaliah's massacre and crowned by Jehoiada, 2 Kin 11:1–12
Repairs the temple, 2 Kin 12:1–16
Turns away from the Lord and is killed, 2 Chr 24:17–25
——Wicked king of Israel; son of Jehoahaz, 2 Kin 13:10–25
Defeats Amaziah in battle, 2 Kin 14:8–15; 2 Chr 25:17–24

JOB

Model of righteousness, Job 1:1–5
His faith tested, Job 1:6—2:10
Debates with his three friends; complains to God, Job 3—33
Elihu intervenes, Job 34—37
God's answer, Job 38—41
Humbles himself and repents, Job 42:1–6
Restored to prosperity, Job 42:10–17

JOCHEBED

Daughter of Levi; mother of Miriam, Aaron, and Moses, Ex 6:20

JOEL

Preexilic prophet, Joel 1:1
Quoted in NT, Acts 2:16

JOHANAN

Military leader of Judah; warns Gedaliah of Ishmael's plot, Jer 40:13–16
Avenges Gedaliah; takes the people to Egypt, Jer 41:11–18

JOHN

The apostle, son of Zebedee; called as disciple, Matt 4:21, 22; Luke 5:1–11
Chosen as one of the Twelve, Matt 10:2
Especially close to Christ, Matt 17:1–9; Mark 13:3; John 13:23–25; 19:26, 27; 20:2–8; 21:7, 20
Ambitious and overzealous, Mark 10:35–41; Luke 9:54–56
Sent to prepare the Passover, Luke 22:8–13
With Peter, heals a man and is arrested, Acts 3:1—4:22
Goes on missionary trip with Peter, Acts 8:14–25
Exiled on Patmos, Rev 1:9
Author of Gospel, three epistles, and the Revelation, John 21:23–25; 1 John; 2 John; 3 John; Rev 1:1
——The Baptist; OT prophecy concerning, Is 40:3–5; Mal 4:5
His birth announced and accomplished, Luke 1:11–20, 57–80
Preaches repentance, Luke 3:1–20
Bears witness to Christ, John 1:19–36; 3:25–36
Baptizes Jesus, Matt 3:13–17
Jesus speaks about, Matt 11:7–19
Identified with Elijah, Matt 11:13, 14
Herod imprisons and kills, Matt 14:3–12
——Surnamed Mark: *see* MARK

JOIN

Woe to those who *j* . . . . Is 5:8
'Come and let us *j* . . . . Jer 50:5
of the rest dared *j* . . . . Acts 5:13

JOINED

and mother and be *j* . . . . Gen 2:24
for him who is *j* . . . . Eccl 9:4
"Ephraim is *j* . . . . Hos 4:17
what God has *j* . . . . Matt 19:6
you be perfectly *j* . . . . 1 Cor 1:10
But he who is *j* . . . . 1 Cor 6:17
the whole body, *j* . . . . Eph 4:16

JOINT

j as He wrestled . . . . Gen 32:25
My bones are out of *j* . . . . Ps 22:14
j heirs with Christ . . . . Rom 8:17
by what every *j* . . . . Eph 4:16

JOINTS

and knit together by *j* . . . . Col 2:19
and spirit, and of *j* . . . . Heb 4:12

JONADAB (or Jehonadab)

David's nephew; encourages Amnon in sin, 2 Sam 13:3–5, 32–36
——Son of Rechab; father of the Rechabites, Jer 35:5–19
Helps Jehu overthrow Baal, 2 Kin 10:15–28

JONAH

Prophet sent to Nineveh; rebels and is punished, Jon 1
Repents and is saved, Jon 2
Preaches in Nineveh, Jon 3
Becomes angry at God's mercy, Jon 4
Type of Christ's resurrection, Matt 12:39, 40

JONATHAN

King Saul's eldest son; his exploits in battle, 1 Sam 13:2, 3; 14:1–14, 49
Saved from his father's wrath, 1 Sam 14:24–45
Makes covenant with David; protects him from Saul, 1 Sam 18:1–4; 19:1–7; 20:1–42; 23:15–18
Killed by Philistines, 1 Sam 31:2, 8
Mourned by David; his son provided for, 2 Sam 1:17–27; 9:1–8
——Son of high priest Abiathar; faithful to David, 2 Sam 15:26–36; 17:15–22
Informs Adonijah of Solomon's coronation, 1 Kin 1:41–49

JOPPA

Scene of Peter's vision, Acts 10:5–23, 32

JORAM

See JEHORAM

JORDAN RIVER

Lot dwells near, Gen 13:8–13
Canaan's eastern boundary, Num 34:12
Moses forbidden to cross, Deut 3:27
Miraculous dividing of, for Israel, Josh 3:1–17
by Elijah, 2 Kin 2:5–8
by Elisha, 2 Kin 2:13,14
Naaman healed in, 2 Kin 5:10–14
John baptizes in, Matt 3:6, 13–17

JOSEPH

Son of Jacob by Rachel, Gen 30:22–24
Loved by Jacob; hated by his brothers, Gen 37:3–11
Sold into slavery, Gen 37:12–36
Unjustly imprisoned in Egypt, Gen 39:1–23
Interprets dreams in prison, Gen 40:1–23
Wins Pharaoh's favor, Gen 41:1–44
Prepares Egypt for famine, Gen 41:45–57
Sells grain to his brothers, Gen 42—44
Reveals identity and reconciles with brothers; sends for Jacob, Gen 45:1–28
Settles family in Egypt, Gen 47:1–12
His sons blessed by Jacob, Gen 48:1–22
Blessed by Jacob, Gen 49:22–26
Buries his father; reassures his brothers, Gen 50:1–21
His death, Gen 50:22–26
——Husband of Mary, Jesus' mother, Matt 1:16
Visited by angel, Matt 1:19–25
Takes Mary to Bethlehem, Luke 2:3–7
Protects Jesus from Herod, Matt 2:13–23
Jesus subject to, Luke 2:51
——Secret disciple from Arimathea; donates tomb and assists in Christ's burial, Mark 15:42–46; Luke 23:50–53; John 19:38–42

JOSES

One of Jesus' half brothers, Matt 13:55
——The name of Barnabas, Acts 4:36

JOSHUA

See JESHUA
——Leader of Israel succeeding Moses, Num 27:18–23
Leads battle against Amalek, Ex 17:8–16
Sent as spy into Canaan; reports favorably, Num 13:16–25; 14:6–9

Assumes command, Josh 1:1–18
Sends spies to Jericho, Josh 2:1
Leads Israel across Jordan, Josh 3:1–17
Sets up commemorative stones, Josh 4:1–24
Circumcises the people, Josh 5:2–9
Conquers Jericho, Josh 5:13—6:27
Punishes Achan, Josh 7:10–26
Conquers Canaan, Josh 8—12
Divides the land, Josh 13—19
Addresses rulers, Josh 23:1–16
Addresses the people, Josh 24:1–28
His death, Josh 24:29, 30

JOSIAH

Righteous king of Judah; son of Amon, 2 Kin 22:1, 2
Repairs the temple, 2 Kin 22:3–9
Hears the Law; spared for his humility, 2 Kin 22:10–20
Institutes reforms, 2 Kin 23:1–25
Killed in battle, 2 Chr 35:20–25

JOT

one *j* or one tittle .... Matt 5:18

JOTHAM

Gideon's youngest son; escapes Abimelech's massacre, Judg 9:5
Utters prophetic parable, Judg 9:7–21
—— Righteous king of Judah; son of Azariah, 2 Kin 15:32–38; 2 Chr 27:1–9

JOURNEY

us go three days' *j* .... Ex 3:18
busy, or he is on a *j* ...... 1 Kin 18:27
Nevertheless I must *j* ...... Luke 13:33
wearied from His *j* .... John 4:6

JOY

LORD your God with *j* ..... Deut 28:47
heart to sing for *j* .... Job 29:13
is fullness of *j* .... Ps 16:11
j comes in the morning .... Ps 30:5
To God my exceeding *j* .... Ps 43:4
You according to the *j* .... Is 9:3
j you will draw .... Is 12:3
ashes, the oil of *j* .... Is 61:3
j shall be theirs .... Is 61:7
shall sing for *j* .... Is 65:14
word was to me the *j* .... Jer 15:16
receives it with *j* .... Matt 13:20
Enter into the *j* .... Matt 25:21
in my womb for *j* .... Luke 1:44
there will be more *j* .... Luke 15:7
did not believe for *j* .... Luke 24:41
My *j* may remain in .... John 15:11
they may have My *j* .... John 17:13
fill you with all *j* .... Rom 15:13
that my *j* is the *j* .... 2 Cor 2:3
the Spirit is love, *j* .... Gal 5:22
brethren, my *j* and .... Phil 4:1
longsuffering with *j* .... Col 1:11
are our glory and *j* .... 1 Thess 2:20
j that was set before .... Heb 12:2
count it all *j* .... James 1:2
j inexpressible .... 1 Pet 1:8
with exceeding *j* .... 1 Pet 4:13
I have no greater *j* .... 3 John 4

JOYFUL

And my soul shall be *j* .... Ps 35:9
Make a *j* shout to the .... Ps 100:1
of prosperity be *j* .... Eccl 7:14
and make them *j* .... Is 56:7

I am exceedingly *j* .... 2 Cor 7:4

JOZACHAR

Assassin of Joash, 2 Kin 12:19–21
Called Zabad, 2 Chr 24:26

JUBAL

Son of Lamech, Gen 4:21

JUDAH

Son of Jacob and Leah, Gen 29:30–35
Intercedes for Joseph, Gen 37:26, 27
Fails in duty to Tamar, Gen 38:1–30
Offers himself as Benjamin's ransom, Gen 44:18–34
Jacob bestows birthright on, Gen 49:3–10
Ancestor of Christ, Matt 1:3, 16
—— Tribe of:
Prophecy concerning, Gen 49:8–12
Numbered at Sinai, Num 1:26, 27
Territory assigned to, Josh 15:1–63
Leads in conquest of Canaan, Judg 1:1–19
Makes David king, 2 Sam 2:1–11
Loyal to David and his house, 2 Sam 20:1, 2; 1 Kin 12:20
Becomes leader of southern kingdom, 1 Kin 14:21, 22
Taken to Babylon, 2 Kin 24:1–16
Returns after exile, 2 Chr 36:20–23

JUDAISM

And I advanced in *J* .... Gal 1:14

JUDAS

Judas Lebbaeus, surnamed Thaddaeus, Matt 10:3
One of Christ's apostles, Luke 6:13, 16
Offers a question, John 14:22
—— Judas Barsabas, a chief deputy, Acts 15:22–32
—— Betrayer of Christ: *see* ISCARIOT

JUDE (or Judas)

Half brother of Christ, Matt 13:55
Does not believe in Christ, John 7:5
Becomes Christ's disciple, Acts 1:14
Writes an epistle, Jude 1

JUDEA

Christ born in, Matt 2:1, 5, 6
Hostile toward Christ, John 7:1
Gospel preached in, Acts 8:1, 4
Churches established in, Acts 9:31

JUDGE

The LORD *j* between .... Gen 16:5
For the LORD will *j* .... Deut 32:36
coming to *j* the earth ...... 1 Chr 16:33
Rise up, O *J* of the .... Ps 94:2
sword the LORD will *j* .... Is 66:16
deliver you to the *j* .... Matt 5:25
"*J* not, that you be not .... Matt 7:1
"Man, who made Me a *j* ... Luke 12:14
j who did not fear God ...... Luke 18:2
As I hear, I *j* .... John 5:30
Do not *j* according .... John 7:24
I *j* no one .... John 8:15
j the world but to .... John 12:47
this, O man, you who *j* .... Rom 2:3
then how will God *j* .... Rom 3:6
Therefore let us not *j* .... Rom 14:13
Christ, who will *j* .... 2 Tim 4:1
Lord, the righteous *J* .... 2 Tim 4:8

heaven, to God the *J* .... Heb 12:23
But if you *j* the law .... James 4:11
are you to *j* another .... James 4:12

JUDGES

j who delivered .... Judg 2:16
in the days when the *j* .... Ruth 1:1
Surely He is God who *j* .... Ps 58:11
He *j* among the gods .... Ps 82:1
He makes the *j* of the .... Is 40:23
j are evening wolves .... Zeph 3:3
For the Father *j* .... John 5:22
he who is spiritual *j* .... 1 Cor 2:15
j me is the Lord .... 1 Cor 4:4
Him who *j* righteously ...... 1 Pet 2:23

JUDGMENT

show partiality in *j* .... Deut 1:17
Teach me good *j* .... Ps 119:66
him in right *j* .... Is 28:26
from prison and from *j* .... Is 53:8
I will also speak *j* .... Jer 4:12
j was made in favor of .... Dan 7:22
be in danger of the *j* .... Matt 5:21
will rise up in the *j* .... Matt 12:42
shall not come into *j* .... John 5:24
and My *j* is righteous .... John 5:30
if I do judge, My *j* .... John 8:16
Now is the *j* .... John 12:31
the righteous *j* .... Rom 1:32
j which came from one .... Rom 5:16
all stand before the *j* .... Rom 14:10
eats and drinks *j* .... 1 Cor 11:29
appear before the *j* .... 2 Cor 5:10
after this the *j* .... Heb 9:27
For *j* is without mercy ...... James 2:13
receive a stricter *j* .... James 3:1
time has come for *j* .... 1 Pet 4:17
a long time their *j* .... 2 Pet 2:3
darkness for the *j* .... Jude 6

JUDGMENTS

The *j* of the LORD are .... Ps 19:9
j are a great deep .... Ps 36:6
I dread, for Your *j* .... Ps 119:39
unsearchable are His *j* ..... Rom 11:33
righteous are His *j* .... Rev 19:2

JULIUS

Roman centurion assigned to guard Paul, Acts 27:1–44

JUST

Noah was a *j* man .... Gen 6:9
Hear a *j* cause .... Ps 17:1
It is a joy for the *j* .... Prov 21:15
j man who perishes .... Eccl 7:15
For there is not a *j* .... Eccl 7:20
j is uprightness .... Is 26:7
the blood of the *j* .... Lam 4:13
j shall live by his .... Hab 2:4
He is *j* and having .... Zech 9:9
her husband, being a *j* .... Matt 1:19
resurrection of the *j* .... Luke 14:14
j persons who need no .... Luke 15:7
the Holy One and the *J* ...... Acts 3:14
dead, both of the *j* .... Acts 24:15
j shall live by faith .... Rom 1:17
that He might be *j* .... Rom 3:26
whatever things are *j* .... Phil 4:8
j men made perfect .... Heb 12:23
have murdered the *j* .... James 5:6
He is faithful and *j* .... 1 John 1:9
J and true are Your .... Rev 15:3

JUSTICE

for all His ways are *j* .... Deut 32:4

the Almighty pervert *j* ....Job 8:3
j as the noonday ....Ps 37:6
and Your poor with *j* ....Ps 72:2
He will bring *j* ....Ps 72:4
Do *j* to the afflicted ....Ps 82:3
and *j* are the ....Ps 89:14
revenues without *j* ....Prov 16:8
do not understand *j* ....Prov 28:5
j the measuring line ....Is 28:17
the LORD is a God of *j* ......Is 30:18
He will bring forth *j* ....Is 42:1
No one calls for *j* ....Is 59:4
J is turned back ....Is 59:14
I, the LORD, love *j* ....Is 61:8
you, O home of *j* ....Jer 31:23
plundering, execute *j* ....Ezek 45:9
truth, and His ways *j* ....Dan 4:37
observe mercy and *j* ....Hos 12:6
'Execute true *j* ....Zech 7:9
"Where is the God of *j* ....Mal 2:17
And He will declare *j* ....Matt 12:18
His humiliation His *j* ....Acts 8:33

JUSTIFICATION

because of our *j* ....Rom 4:25
offenses resulted in *j* ....Rom 5:16
men, resulting in *j* ....Rom 5:18

JUSTIFIED

Me that you may be *j* ....Job 40:8
of Israel shall be *j* ....Is 45:25
words you will be *j* ....Matt 12:37
But wisdom is *j* ....Luke 7:35
j rather than the ....Luke 18:14
who believes is *j* ....Acts 13:39
"That You may be *j* ....Rom 3:4
law no flesh will be *j* ....Rom 3:20
j freely by His grace ....Rom 3:24
having been *j* by ....Rom 5:1
these He also *j* ....Rom 8:30
but you were *j* ....1 Cor 6:11
that we might be *j* ....Gal 2:16
no flesh shall be *j* ....Gal 2:16
who attempt to be *j* ....Gal 5:4
j in the Spirit ....1 Tim 3:16
then that a man is *j* ....James 2:24
the harlot also *j* ....James 2:25

JUSTIFIER

be just and the *j* ....Rom 3:26

JUSTIFIES

He who *j* the wicked ....Prov 17:15
It is God who *j* ....Rom 8:33

JUSTIFY

j the wicked for a ....Is 5:23
wanting to *j* himself ....Luke 10:29
"You are those who *j* ....Luke 16:15
is one God who will *j* ....Rom 3:30
that God would *j* ....Gal 3:8

JUSTLY

of you but to do *j* ....Mic 6:8
And we indeed *j* ....Luke 23:41
how devoutly and *j* ....1 Thess 2:10

JUSTUS

Surname of Joseph, a disciple, Acts 1:23
—— Man of Corinth; befriends Paul, Acts 18:7

— K —

KADESH

Spies sent from, Num 13:3, 26
Moses strikes rock at, Num 20:1–13
Boundary in the new Israel, Ezek 47:19

KADESH BARNEA

Boundary of Promised Land, Num 34:1–4
Limit of Joshua's military campaign, Josh 10:41

KEEP

k you wherever you ....Gen 28:15
day, to *k* it holy ....Ex 20:8
and *k* My judgments ....Lev 25:18
k all My commandments .....1 Kin 6:12
and that You would *k* ....1 Chr 4:10
Even he who cannot *k* ....Ps 22:29
K my soul ....Ps 25:20
do not *k* silence ....Ps 35:22
k Your righteous ....Ps 119:106
k them in the midst of ....Prov 4:21
K your heart with all ....Prov 4:23
a time to *k* silence ....Eccl 3:7
Let all the earth *k* ....Hab 2:20
k the commandments ....Matt 19:17
If you love Me, *k* ....John 14:15
k through Your name ....John 17:11
orderly and *k* the law ....Acts 21:24
Let your women *k* ....1 Cor 14:34
k the unity of the ....Eph 4:3
k yourself pure ....1 Tim 5:22
k His commandments ....1 John 2:3
k yourselves in the ....Jude 21
k you from stumbling ....Jude 24
k those things ....Rev 1:3

KEEPER

Am I my brother's *k* ....Gen 4:9
The LORD is your *k* ....Ps 121:5

KEEPERS

in the day when the *k* ....Eccl 12:3

KEEPS

the faithful God who *k* ....Deut 7:9
k truth forever ....Ps 146:6
k his way preserves ....Prov 16:17
k the commandment ....Prov 19:16
Whoever *k* the law is a ....Prov 28:7
none of you *k* the law ....John 7:19
born of God *k* himself ....1 John 5:18
and *k* his garments ....Rev 16:15

KEILAH

Town of Judah; rescued from Philistines by David, 1 Sam 23:1–5
Prepares to betray David; he escapes, 1 Sam 23:6–13

KENITES

Canaanite tribe whose land is promised to Abraham's seed, Gen 15:19
Subjects of Balaam's prophecy, Num 24:20–22
Settle with Judahites, Judg 1:16
Spared by Saul in war with Amalekites, 1 Sam 15:6

KEPT

For I have *k* the ways .....2 Sam 22:22
vineyard I have not *k* ....Song 1:6
these things I have *k* ....Matt 19:20
all these things I have *k* ...Mark 10:20
k all these things ....Luke 2:19
love, just as I have *k* ....John 15:10
k back part of the ....Acts 5:2
I have *k* the faith ....2 Tim 4:7
who are *k* by the power ....1 Pet 1:5
which now exist are *k* ....2 Pet 3:7

KETURAH

Abraham's second wife, Gen 25:1
Sons of:
Listed, Gen 25:1, 2
Given gifts and sent away, Gen 25:6

KEY

The *k* of the house of ....Is 22:22
have taken away the *k* ......Luke 11:52
"He who has the *k* ....Rev 3:7
heaven, having the *k* ....Rev 20:1

KEYS

I will give you the *k* ....Matt 16:19
And I have the *k* ....Rev 1:18

KIBROTH HATTAAVAH

Burial site of Israelites slain by God, Num 11:33–35

KICK

is hard for you to *k* ....Acts 9:5

KIDNAPPERS

for sodomites, for *k* ....1 Tim 1:10

KIDNAPS

"He who *k* a man and ....Ex 21:16

KIDRON

Valley near Jerusalem; crossed by David and Christ, 2 Sam 15:23; John 18:1
Idols dumped there, 2 Chr 29:16

KILL

who finds me will *k* ....Gen 4:14
k the Passover ....Ex 12:21
I *k* and I make alive ....Deut 32:39
"Am I God, to *k* ....2 Kin 5:7
a time to *k* ....Eccl 3:3
to save life or to *k* ....Mark 3:4
of them they will *k* ....Luke 11:49
afraid of those who *k* ....Luke 12:4
Why do you seek to *k* ....John 7:19
"Rise, Peter; *k* and eat ....Acts 10:13

KILLED

Abel his brother and *k* ....Gen 4:8
For I have *k* a man for ....Gen 4:23
LORD *k* all the ....Ex 13:15
Your servant has *k* ....1 Sam 17:36
for Your sake we are *k* ....Ps 44:22
and scribes, and be *k* ....Matt 16:21
Siloam fell and *k* them ....Luke 13:4
k the Prince of life ....Acts 3:15
me, and by it *k* ....Rom 7:11
"For Your sake we are *k* ....Rom 8:36
who *k* both the Lord ....1 Thess 2:15
martyr, who was *k* ....Rev 2:13

KILLS

"The LORD *k* and ....1 Sam 2:6
the one who *k* the ....Matt 23:37
for the letter *k* ....2 Cor 3:6

KIND

animals after their *k* ....Gen 6:20
k can come out by ....Mark 9:29
For He is *k* to the ....Luke 6:35
suffers long and is *k* ....1 Cor 13:4

And be *k* to one ....Eph 4:32

KINDLED

When His wrath is *k* ....Ps 2:12
I, the LORD, have *k* ....Ezek 20:48
wish it were already *k* .....Luke 12:49

KINDLY

The LORD deal *k* ....Ruth 1:8
Julius treated Paul *k* ....Acts 27:3
k affectionate to one ....Rom 12:10

KINDNESS

may the LORD show *k* ......2 Sam 2:6
anger, abundant in *k* ....Neh 9:17
me His marvelous *k* ....Ps 31:21
For His merciful *k* ....Ps 117:2
tongue is the law of *k* ......Prov 31:26
k shall not depart ....Is 54:10
I remember you, the *k* ....Jer 2:2
by longsuffering, by *k* ....2 Cor 6:6
longsuffering, *k* ....Gal 5:22
But when the *k* and the ......Titus 3:4
and to brotherly *k* ....2 Pet 1:7

KING

Then Melchizedek *k* ....Gen 14:18
days there was no *k* ....Judg 17:6
said, "Give us a *k* ....1 Sam 8:6
"Long live the *k* ....1 Sam 10:24
they anointed David *k* ......2 Sam 2:4
Yet I have set My *K* ....Ps 2:6
The LORD is *K* forever ....Ps 10:16
K answer us when we ....Ps 20:9
And the *K* of glory ....Ps 24:7
k is saved by the ....Ps 33:16
k Your judgments ....Ps 72:1
For God is my *K* ....Ps 74:12
do who succeeds the *k* ....Eccl 2:12
out of prison to be *k* ....Eccl 4:14
when your *k* is a child ......Eccl 10:16
In the year that *K* ....Is 6:1
k will reign in ....Is 32:1
the LORD is our *K* ....Is 33:22
Is not her *K* in her ....Jer 8:19
and the everlasting *K* ....Jer 10:10
k of Babylon, *k* ....Ezek 26:7
I gave you a *k* in My ....Hos 13:11
the LORD shall be *K* ....Zech 14:9
He who has been born *K* .....Matt 2:2
This Is Jesus the *K* ....Matt 27:37
by force to make Him *k* .....John 6:15
"Behold your *K* ....John 19:14
there is another *k* ....Acts 17:7
Now to the *K* eternal ....1 Tim 1:17
only Potentate, the *K* ....1 Tim 6:15
this Melchizedek, *k* ....Heb 7:1
Honor the *k* ....1 Pet 2:17
K of kings and Lord of ....Rev 19:16

KINGDOM

you shall be to Me a *k* ....Ex 19:6
LORD has torn the *k* ......1 Sam 15:28
Yours is the *k* ....1 Chr 29:11
k is the LORD's ....Ps 22:28
the scepter of Your *k* ....Ps 45:6
in heaven, and His *k* ....Ps 103:19
is an everlasting *k* ....Ps 145:13
k which shall never be ....Dan 2:44
High rules in the *k* ....Dan 4:17
k shall be the LORD's ....Obad 21
"Repent, for the *k* ....Matt 3:2
for Yours is the *k* ....Matt 6:13
But seek first the *k* ....Matt 6:33
the mysteries of the *k* ....Matt 13:11
are the sons of the *k* ....Matt 13:38
of such is the *k* ....Matt 19:14
up to half of my *k* ....Mark 6:23
are not far from the *k* ......Mark 12:34
back, is fit for the *k* ....Luke 9:62
against nation, and *k* ....Luke 21:10
he cannot see the *k* ....John 3:3
he cannot enter the *k* ....John 3:5
If My *k* were of this ....John 18:36
for the *k* of God is ....Rom 14:17
when He delivers the *k* .....1 Cor 15:24
will not inherit the *k* ....Gal 5:21
the scepter of Your *k* ....Heb 1:8
we are receiving a *k* ....Heb 12:28
into the everlasting *k* ....2 Pet 1:11

KINGDOMS

the *k* were moved ....Ps 46:6
tremble, who shook *k* ....Is 14:16
showed Him all the *k* ....Matt 4:8
have become the *k* ....Rev 11:15

KINGS

The *k* of the earth set ....Ps 2:2
k shall fall down ....Ps 72:11
He is awesome to the *k* ....Ps 76:12
By me *k* reign ....Prov 8:15
He will stand before *k* ....Prov 22:29
k is unsearchable ....Prov 25:3
that which destroys *k* ....Prov 31:3
it is not for *k* ....Prov 31:4
K shall be your foster ....Is 49:23
"They set up *k* ....Hos 8:4
before governors and *k* ....Matt 10:18
k have desired to see ....Luke 10:24
You have reigned as *k* ....1 Cor 4:8
and has made us *k* ....Rev 1:6
that the way of the *k* ....Rev 16:12
may eat the flesh of *k* ....Rev 19:18

KIRJATH ARBA

Ancient name of Hebron, Gen 23:2
Possessed by Judah, Judg 1:10

KIRJATH JEARIM

Gibeonite town, Josh 9:17
Ark taken from, 1 Chr 13:5

KISH

Benjamite of Gibeah; father of King Saul, 1 Sam 9:1–3

KISHON

River of north Palestine; Sisera's army swept away by, Judg 4:7, 13
Elijah executes prophets of Baal at, 1 Kin 18:40

KISS

K the Son ....Ps 2:12
Let him *k* me with the ....Song 1:2
You gave Me no *k* ....Luke 7:45
another with a holy *k* ....Rom 16:16
one another with a *k* ....1 Pet 5:14

KISSED

And they *k* one another ...1 Sam 20:41
and *k* Him ....Matt 26:49
and she *k* His feet and ......Luke 7:38

KNEE

that to Me every *k* ....Is 45:23
And they bowed the *k* ......Matt 27:29
have not bowed the *k* ....Rom 11:4
every *k* shall bow to ....Rom 14:11
of Jesus every *k* ....Phil 2:10

KNEES

make firm the feeble *k* ....Is 35:3
be dandled on her *k* ....Is 66:12
this reason I bow my *k* ....Eph 3:14
and the feeble *k* ....Heb 12:12

KNEW

Adam *k* Eve his wife ....Gen 4:1
in the womb I *k* ....Jer 1:5
to them, 'I never *k* ....Matt 7:23
k what was in man ....John 2:25
For He made Him who *k* ....2 Cor 5:21

KNIT

of Jonathan was *k* ....1 Sam 18:1
k me together with ....Job 10:11
be encouraged, being *k* ....Col 2:2

KNOCK

k, and it will be ....Matt 7:7
at the door and *k* ....Rev 3:20

KNOW

k good and evil ....Gen 3:22
and I did not *k* ....Gen 28:16
k that I am the LORD ....Ex 6:7
k that there is no God ......2 Kin 5:15
you, my son Solomon, *k* .....1 Chr 28:9
Hear it, and *k* for ....Job 5:27
and *k* nothing ....Job 8:9
k that my Redeemer ....Job 19:25
'What does God *k* ....Job 22:13
k Your name will put ....Ps 9:10
k that I am God ....Ps 46:10
make me to *k* wisdom ....Ps 51:6
Who can *k* it ....Jer 17:9
saying, '*K* the LORD ....Jer 31:34
for you to *k* justice ....Mic 3:1
k what hour your Lord .....Matt 24:42
an oath, "I do not *k* ....Matt 26:72
the world did not *k* ....John 1:10
We speak what We *k* ....John 3:11
k what we worship ....John 4:22
k that You are ....John 6:69
hear My voice, and I *k* .....John 10:27
If you *k* these things ....John 13:17
k whom I have chosen ....John 13:18
we are sure that You *k* .....John 16:30
k that I love You ....John 21:15
k times or seasons ....Acts 1:7
and said, "Jesus I *k* ....Acts 19:15
wisdom did not *k* ....1 Cor 1:21
nor can he *k* them ....1 Cor 2:14
For we *k* in part and ....1 Cor 13:9
k a man in Christ who ....2 Cor 12:2
k the love of Christ ....Eph 3:19
k whom I have believed ....2 Tim 1:12
so that they may *k* ....2 Tim 2:25
this we *k* that we *k* Him ......1 John 2:3
He who says, "I *k* ....1 John 2:4
and you *k* all things ....1 John 2:20
By this we *k* love ....1 John 3:16
k that we are of the ....1 John 3:19
k that He abides ....1 John 3:24
k that we are of God ....1 John 5:19
"I *k* your works ....Rev 2:2

KNOWLEDGE

and the tree of the *k* ....Gen 2:9
LORD is the God of *k* ....1 Sam 2:3
Can anyone teach God *k* ....Job 21:22
who is perfect in *k* ....Job 36:4
unto night reveals *k* ....Ps 19:2
k is too wonderful ....Ps 139:6
k the depths were ....Prov 3:20
k rather than ....Prov 8:10

Wise people store up *k* .....Prov 10:14
k is easy to him who ....Prov 14:6
k spares his words ....Prov 17:27
a soul to be without *k* ....Prov 19:2
and he who increases *k* ....Eccl 1:18
k is that wisdom ....Eccl 7:12
no work or device or *k* ....Eccl 9:10
Whom will he teach *k* ....Is 28:9
k shall increase ....Dan 12:4
you have rejected *k* ....Hos 4:6
having more accurate *k*.....Acts 24:22
having the form of *k* ....Rom 2:20
by the law is the *k* of sin ....Rom 3:20
K puffs up ....1 Cor 8:1
whether there is *k* ....1 Cor 13:8
Christ which passes *k* ....Eph 3:19
is falsely called *k* ....1 Tim 6:20
in the grace and *k* ....2 Pet 3:18

KNOWN

In Judah God is *k* ....Ps 76:1
my mouth will I make *k* ....Ps 89:1
If you had *k* Me ....John 8:19
My sheep, and am *k* ....John 10:14
The world has not *k* ....John 17:25
peace they have not *k* ....Rom 3:17
I would not have *k* ....Rom 7:7
"For who has *k* ....Rom 11:34
after you have *k* ....Gal 4:9
requests be made *k* ....Phil 4:6
k the Holy Scriptures ....2 Tim 3:15

KNOWS

For God *k* that in ....Gen 3:5
k the secrets of the ....Ps 44:21
he understands and *k* ....Jer 9:24
k what is in the ....Dan 2:22
k those who trust ....Nah 1:7
k the things you have ....Matt 6:8
and hour no one *k* ....Matt 24:36
k who the Son is ....Luke 10:22
but God *k* your hearts .....Luke 16:15
searches the hearts *k* ....Rom 8:27
k the things of God ....1 Cor 2:11
k those who are His ....2 Tim 2:19
to him who *k* to do ....James 4:17
and *k* all things ....1 John 3:20
written which no one *k* ....Rev 2:17

KOHATH

Second son of Levi, Gen 46:8, 11
Brother of Jochebed, mother of Aaron and Moses, Ex 6:16–20

KOHATHITES

Numbered, Num 3:27, 28
Duties assigned to, Num 4:15–20
Leaders of temple music, 1 Chr 6:31–38; 2 Chr 20:19

KORAH

Leads rebellion against Moses and Aaron; supernaturally destroyed, Num 16:1–35
Sons of, not destroyed, Num 26:9–11

—L—

LABAN

Son of Bethuel; brother of Rebekah; father of Leah and Rachel, Gen 24:15, 24, 29; 29:16
Agrees to Rebekah's marriage to Isaac, Gen 24:50, 51
Entertains Jacob, Gen 29:1–14
Substitutes Leah for Rachel, Gen 29:15–30
Agrees to division of cattle; grows resentful of Jacob, Gen 30:25—31:2
Pursues Jacob and makes covenant with him, Gen 31:21–55

LABOR

Six days you shall *l* ....Ex 20:9
why then do I *l* ....Job 9:29
their boast is only *l* ....Ps 90:10
The *l* of the righteous ......Prov 10:16
l will increase ....Prov 13:11
l there is profit ....Prov 14:23
things are full of *l* ....Eccl 1:8
has man for all his *l* ....Eccl 2:22
He shall see the *l* ....Is 53:11
"Before she was in *l* ....Is 66:7
from the womb to see *l* ....Jer 20:18
to Me, all you who *l* ....Matt 11:28
Do not *l* for the ....John 6:27
knowing that your *l* ......1 Cor 15:58
but rather let him *l* ....Eph 4:28
mean fruit from my *l* ....Phil 1:22
your work of faith, *l* ....1 Thess 1:3
forget your work and *l* ....Heb 6:10
your works, your *l* ....Rev 2:2

LABORED

l more abundantly than ....1 Cor 15:10
for you, lest I have *l* ....Gal 4:11

LABORERS

but the *l* are few ....Matt 9:37

LABORING

of a *l* man is sweet ....Eccl 5:12
l night and day ....1 Thess 2:9

LABORS

The person who *l* ....Prov 16:26
is no end to all his *l* ....Eccl 4:8
entered into their *l* ....John 4:38
creation groans and *l* ....Rom 8:22
l more abundant ....2 Cor 11:23
may rest from their *l* ....Rev 14:13

LACHISH

Defeated by Joshua, Josh 10:3–33
Taken by Sennacherib, 2 Kin 18:13–17; Is 36:1, 2; 37:8

LACK

anyone perish for *l* ....Job 31:19
the LORD shall not *l* ....Ps 34:10
to the poor will not *l* ....Prov 28:27
What do I still *l* ....Matt 19:20
"One thing you *l* ....Mark 10:21

LACKED

among them who *l* ....Acts 4:34

LACKING

the things that are *l* ....Titus 1:5

LADDER

and behold, a *l* ....Gen 28:12

LADEN

nation, a people *l* ....Is 1:4
and are heavy *l* ....Matt 11:28

LADIES

wisest *l* answered her ....Judg 5:29
very day the noble *l* ....Esth 1:18

LADY

'I shall be a *l* ....Is 47:7
To the elect *l* ....2 John 1

LAGGING

not *l* in diligence ....Rom 12:11

LAHAI ROI

Name of a well, Gen 16:7, 14
Same as Beer Lahai Roi, Gen 24:62

LAID

But man dies and is *l* ....Job 14:10
the place where they *l* ....Mark 16:6
"Where have you *l* ....John 11:34

LAISH

Called Leshem, Josh 19:47; Judg 18:29
Taken by Danites, Judg 18:7, 14, 27

LAKE

cast alive into the *l* ....Rev 19:20

LAMB

but where is the *l* ....Gen 22:7
took the poor man's *l* ......2 Sam 12:4
shall dwell with the *l* ....Is 11:6
He was led as a *l* ....Is 53:7
l shall feed together ....Is 65:25
The *L* of God who takes .....John 1:29
of Christ, as of a *l* ....1 Pet 1:19
the elders, stood a *L* ....Rev 5:6
"Worthy is the *L* ....Rev 5:12
by the blood of the *L* ....Rev 12:11
Book of Life of the *L* ....Rev 13:8
supper of the *L* ....Rev 19:9

LAME

l take the prey ....Is 33:23
l shall leap like a ....Is 35:6
when you offer the *l* ....Mal 1:8
blind see and the *l* ....Matt 11:5
And a certain man *l* ....Acts 3:2
so that what is *l* ....Heb 12:13

LAMECH

Son of Methushael, of Cain's race, Gen 4:17, 18
—— Son of Methuselah; father of Noah, Gen 5:25–31

LAMENTATION

was heard in Ramah, *l* ....Jer 31:15
was heard in Ramah, *l* ....Matt 2:18
and made great *l* ....Acts 8:2

LAMP

For You are my *l* ....2 Sam 22:29
"How often is the *l* ....Job 21:17
You will light my *l* ....Ps 18:28
Your word is a *l* ....Ps 119:105
the *l* of the wicked ....Prov 13:9
his *l* will be put out ....Prov 20:20
Nor do they light a *l* ....Matt 5:15
"The *l* of the body ....Matt 6:22
when he has lit a *l* ....Luke 8:16
l gives you light ....Luke 11:36
does not light a *l* ....Luke 15:8
burning and shining *l* ....John 5:35
l shall not shine ....Rev 18:23
They need no *l* nor ....Rev 22:5

LAMPS

he made its seven *l* ....Ex 37:23
Jerusalem with *l* ....Zeph 1:12

and trimmed their *l* .... Matt 25:7
Seven *l* of fire .... Rev 4:5

LAMPSTAND

branches of the *l* .... Ex 25:32
and there is a *l* .... Zech 4:2
a basket, but on a *l* .... Matt 5:15
in which was the *l* .... Heb 9:2
and remove your *l* .... Rev 2:5

LAND

l that I will show you .... Gen 12:1
l flowing with milk .... Ex 3:8
l which I am giving .... Josh 1:2
is heard in our *l* .... Song 2:12
they will see the *l* .... Is 33:17
Bethlehem, in the *l* .... Matt 2:6

LANDMARK

your neighbor's *l* .... Deut 19:14
remove the ancient *l* .... Prov 22:28
those who remove a *l* .... Hos 5:10

LANGUAGE

whole earth had one *l* .... Gen 11:1
is no speech nor *l* .... Ps 19:3
a people of strange *l* .... Ps 114:1
the peoples a pure *l* .... Zeph 3:9
speak in his own *l* .... Acts 2:6
blasphemy, filthy *l* .... Col 3:8

LANGUAGES

according to their *l* .... Gen 10:20
be, so many kinds of *l* .... 1 Cor 14:10

LAODICEA

Paul's concern for, Col 2:1; 4:12–16
Letter to church of, Rev 3:14–22

LAST

He shall stand at *l* .... Job 19:25
First and I am the *L* .... Is 44:6
l man the same as .... Matt 20:14
l will be first .... Matt 20:16
children, it is the *l* .... 1 John 2:18
the First and the *L* .... Rev 1:11

LATTER

former rain, and the *l* .... Joel 2:23
l times some will .... 1 Tim 4:1

LATTICE

I looked through my *l* .... Prov 7:6
gazing through the *l* .... Song 2:9

LAUGH

Why did Sarah *l* .... Gen 18:13
"God has made me *l* .... Gen 21:6
You, O LORD, shall *l* .... Ps 59:8
Woe to you who *l* .... Luke 6:25

LAUGHS

he *l* at the threat of .... Job 41:29
The Lord *l* at him .... Ps 37:13

LAUGHTER

was filled with *l* .... Ps 126:2
your *l* be turned to .... James 4:9

LAW

stones a copy of the *l* .... Josh 8:32
When He made a *l* .... Job 28:26
The *l* of the LORD is .... Ps 19:7
The *l* of his God is in .... Ps 37:31
I delight in Your *l* .... Ps 119:70
The *l* of Your mouth is .... Ps 119:72
l is my delight .... Ps 119:77
Oh, how I love Your *l* .... Ps 119:97
And Your *l* is truth .... Ps 119:142
and the *l* a light .... Prov 6:23
shall go forth the *l* .... Is 2:3
l will proceed from Me .... Is 51:4
in whose heart is My *l* .... Is 51:7
the *L* is no more .... Lam 2:9
The *l* of truth was in .... Mal 2:6
to destroy the *L* .... Matt 5:17
for this is the *L* .... Matt 7:12
hang all the *L* and the .... Matt 22:40
"The *l* and the .... Luke 16:16
l was given through .... John 1:17
"Does our *l* judge a .... John 7:51
l is the knowledge .... Rom 3:20
because the *l* brings .... Rom 4:15
when there is no *l* .... Rom 5:13
you are not under *l* .... Rom 6:14
Is the *l* sin .... Rom 7:7
For we know that the *l* .... Rom 7:14
warring against the *l* .... Rom 7:23
For what the *l* could .... Rom 8:3
who are without *l* .... 1 Cor 9:21
l that I might live .... Gal 2:19
under guard by the *l* .... Gal 3:23
born under the *l* .... Gal 4:4
l is fulfilled in one .... Gal 5:14
l is not made for a .... 1 Tim 1:9
into the perfect *l* .... James 1:25
fulfill the royal *l* .... James 2:8

LAWFUL

doing what is not *l* .... Matt 12:2
Is it *l* to pay taxes .... Matt 22:17
All things are *l* .... 1 Cor 6:12

LAWGIVER

Judah is My *l* .... Ps 60:7
the LORD is our *L* .... Is 33:22
There is one *L* .... James 4:12

LAWLESS

l one will be revealed .... 2 Thess 2:8
and hearing their *l* .... 2 Pet 2:8

LAWLESSNESS

Me, you who practice *l* .... Matt 7:23
l is already at work .... 2 Thess 2:7
and hated *l* .... Heb 1:9
and sin is *l* .... 1 John 3:4

LAWYERS

l rejected the will of .... Luke 7:30
Woe to you also, *l* .... Luke 11:46

LAY

nowhere to *l* His head .... Matt 8:20
l hands may receive .... Acts 8:19
Do not *l* hands on .... 1 Tim 5:22
l aside all .... James 1:21

LAZARUS

Beggar described in a parable, Luke 16:20–25
—— Brother of Mary and Martha; raised from the dead, John 11:1–44
Attends a supper, John 12:1, 2
Jews seek to kill, John 12:9–11

LAZINESS

L casts one into a .... Prov 19:15
l the building decays .... Eccl 10:18

LAZY

l man will be put to .... Prov 12:24
l man does not roast .... Prov 12:27
soul of a *l* man desires .... Prov 13:4
l man buries his hand .... Prov 19:24
by the field of the *l* .... Prov 24:30
l man is wiser in his .... Prov 26:16
wicked and *l* servant .... Matt 25:26
liars, evil beasts, *l* .... Titus 1:12

LEAD

they sank like *l* .... Ex 15:10
L me in Your truth and .... Ps 25:5
L me and guide me .... Ps 31:3
Your hand shall *l* .... Ps 139:10
And do not *l* us into .... Matt 6:13
"Can the blind *l* .... Luke 6:39

LEADS

He *l* me beside the .... Ps 23:2
He *l* me in the paths .... Ps 23:3
And if the blind *l* .... Matt 15:14
by name and *l* them out .... John 10:3
the goodness of God *l* .... Rom 2:4

LEAF

plucked olive *l* .... Gen 8:11
Will You frighten a *l* .... Job 13:25
l will be green .... Jer 17:8

LEAH

Laban's eldest daughter; given to Jacob deceitfully, Gen 29:16–27
Unloved by Jacob, but bears children, Gen 29:30–35; 30:16–21

LEAN

all your heart, and *l* .... Prov 3:5
Yet they *l* on the LORD .... Mic 3:11

LEANING

Then, *l* back on Jesus' .... John 13:25
l on the top of his .... Heb 11:21

LEANNESS

request, but sent *l* .... Ps 106:15
of hosts, will send *l* .... Is 10:16

LEAP

by my God I can *l* .... Ps 18:29
Then the lame shall *l* .... Is 35:6

LEARN

it, may hear and *l* .... Deut 31:13
l Your statutes .... Ps 119:71
lest you *l* his ways .... Prov 22:25
l to do good .... Is 1:17
neither shall they *l* .... Is 2:4
My yoke upon you and *l* .... Matt 11:29
Let a woman *l* in .... 1 Tim 2:11
let our people also *l* .... Titus 3:14

LEARNED

Me the tongue of the *l* .... Is 50:4
who has heard and *l* .... John 6:45
have not so *l* Christ .... Eph 4:20
in all things I have *l* .... Phil 4:12
l obedience by the .... Heb 5:8

LEARNING

hear and increase *l* .... Prov 1:5
l is driving you mad .... Acts 26:24
were written for our *l* .... Rom 15:4

LEAST

Judah, are not the *l* .... Matt 2:6

so, shall be called *l* ....Matt 5:19
For I am the *l* of the ....1 Cor 15:9

LEAVE

a man shall *l* his ....Gen 2:24
He will not *l* you nor ....Deut 31:6
For You will not *l* ....Ps 16:10
do not *l* me nor ....Ps 27:9
"I will never *l* ....Heb 13:5

LEAVEN

day you shall remove *l* ....Ex 12:15
of heaven is like *l* ....Matt 13:33
and beware of the *l* ....Matt 16:6
know that a little *l* ....1 Cor 5:6
l leavens the whole ....Gal 5:9

LEAVES

and they sewed fig *l* ....Gen 3:7
nothing on it but *l* ....Matt 21:19
l the sheep and flees ....John 10:12
The *l* of the tree ....Rev 22:2

LEBANON

Part of Israel's inheritance, Josh 13:5–7
Not completely conquered, Judg 3:1–3
Source of materials for temple, 1 Kin 5:2–18; Ezra 3:7
Mentioned in prophecy, Is 10:34; 29:17; 35:2; Ezek 17:3; Hos 14:5–7

LEBBAEUS

See JUDAS
Surname of Judas (Jude), Matt 10:3

LED

l the people around by ....Ex 13:18
so the LORD alone *l* ....Deut 32:12
l them forth by the ....Ps 107:7
l them by the right ....Is 63:12
For as many as are *l* ....Rom 8:14
l captivity captive ....Eph 4:8
l away by various ....2 Tim 3:6

LEFT

l hand know what your ....Matt 6:3
"See, we have *l* ....Matt 19:27
And everyone who has *l* ...Matt 19:29

LEGACY

shame shall be the *l* ....Prov 3:35

LEGS

Like the *l* of the lame ....Prov 26:7
l are pillars of ....Song 5:15
did not break His *l* ....John 19:33

LEHI

Samson kills Philistines at, Judg 15:9–19

LEMUEL

King taught by his mother, Prov 31:1–31

LEND

"If you *l* money to ....Ex 22:25
l him sufficient ....Deut 15:8
And if you *l* ....Luke 6:34
l me three loaves ....Luke 11:5

LENDER

is servant to the *l* ....Prov 22:7

as with the *l* ....Is 24:2

LENDING

and my servants, am *l* ....Neh 5:10

LENDS

ever merciful, and *l* ....Ps 37:26
deals graciously and *l* ....Ps 112:5
has pity on the poor *l* ....Prov 19:17

LENGTH

The *l* of the ark shall ....Gen 6:15
is your life and the *l* ....Deut 30:20
L of days is in her ....Prov 3:16
l is as great as its ....Rev 21:16

LENGTHENS

a shadow when it *l* ....Ps 109:23

LEOPARD

the *l* shall lie down ....Is 11:6
or the *l* its spots ....Jer 13:23

LEPERS

And when these *l* ....2 Kin 7:8
And many *l* were in ....Luke 4:27

LET

"*L* there be light" ....Gen 1:3
L the little ....Matt 19:14

LETTER

the oldness of the *l* ....Rom 7:6
for the *l* kills ....2 Cor 3:6
you sorry with my *l* ....2 Cor 7:8
or by word or by *l* ....2 Thess 2:2

LETTERS

does this Man know *l* ....John 7:15
or *l* of commendation ....2 Cor 3:1
"For his *l*," they say ....2 Cor 10:10
with what large *l* ....Gal 6:11

LEVI

Third son of Jacob and Leah, Gen 29:34
Avenges rape of Dinah, Gen 34:25–31
Jacob's prophecy concerning, Gen 49:5–7
Ancestor of Moses and Aaron, Ex 6:16–27

LEVIATHAN

"Can you draw out *L* ....Job 41:1
L which You have made .....Ps 104:26

LEVITE

"Is not Aaron the *L* ....Ex 4:14
Likewise a *L* ....Luke 10:32
a *L* of the country of ....Acts 4:36

LEVITES

Rewarded for dedication, Ex 32:26–29
Appointed over tabernacle, Num 1:47–54
Substituted for Israel's firstborn, Num 3:12–45
Consecrated to the Lord's service, Num 8:5–26
Cities assigned to, Num 35:2–8; Josh 14:3, 4; 1 Chr 6:54–81
Organized for temple service, 1 Chr 9:14–34; 23:1—26:28

LEVITICAL

were through the *L* ....Heb 7:11

LEWDNESS

wickedness, deceit, *l* ....Mark 7:22
drunkenness, not in *l* ....Rom 13:13
themselves over to *l* ....Eph 4:19
when we walked in *l* ....1 Pet 4:3

LIAR

for he is a *l* and the ....John 8:44
but every man a *l* ....Rom 3:4
we make Him a *l* ....1 John 1:10
Who is a *l* but he who ....1 John 2:22
his brother, he is a *l* ....1 John 4:20
God has made Him a *l* ....1 John 5:10

LIARS

"All men are *l* ....Ps 116:11
Cretans are always *l* ....Titus 1:12
and have found them *l* ....Rev 2:2
l shall have their ....Rev 21:8

LIBERALITY

he who gives, with *l* ....Rom 12:8
the riches of their *l* ....2 Cor 8:2

LIBERALLY

who gives to all *l* ....James 1:5

LIBERTY

year, and proclaim *l* ....Lev 25:10
And I will walk at *l* ....Ps 119:45
to proclaim *l* to the ....Is 61:1
to proclaim *l* to the ....Luke 4:18
into the glorious *l* ....Rom 8:21
For why is my *l* ....1 Cor 10:29
Lord is, there is *l* ....2 Cor 3:17
therefore in the *l* ....Gal 5:1
l as an opportunity ....Gal 5:13
the perfect law of *l* ....James 1:25
yet not using *l* ....1 Pet 2:16

LIBNAH

Canaanite city, captured by Joshua, Josh 10:29, 30
Given to Aaron's descendants, Josh 21:13

LIBYA

Mentioned in prophecy, Ezek 30:5; Dan 11:43
Jews from, present at Pentecost, Acts 2:1–10

LIE

man, that He should *l* ....Num 23:19
For now I will *l* ....Job 7:21
I will not *l* to David ....Ps 89:35
Do not *l* to one ....Col 3:9
God, who cannot *l* ....Titus 1:2
do not boast and *l* ....James 3:14
know it, and that no *l* ....1 John 2:21
an abomination or a *l* ....Rev 21:27

LIED

They have *l* about the ....Jer 5:12
You have not *l* to men ....Acts 5:4

LIES

sin *l* at the door ....Gen 4:7
and he who speaks *l* ....Prov 19:5
speaking *l* in ....1 Tim 4:2
and the whole world *l* ....1 John 5:19

LIFE

the breath of *l* ....Gen 2:7
l was also in the ....Gen 2:9

then you shall give *l* ....Ex 21:23
For the *l* of the ....Lev 17:11
before you today *l* ....Deut 30:15
You have granted me *l* ......Job 10:12
in whose hand is the *l* ....Job 12:10
God takes away his *l* ....Job 27:8
with the light of *l* ....Job 33:30
He will redeem their *l* ....Ps 72:14
word has given me *l* ....Ps 119:50
regain the paths of *l* ....Prov 2:19
She is a tree of *l* ....Prov 3:18
so they will be *l* ....Prov 3:22
finds me finds *l* ....Prov 8:35
l winds upward for the .....Prov 15:24
thief hates his own *l* ....Prov 29:24
is that wisdom gives *l* ....Eccl 7:12
I have cut off my *l* ....Is 38:12
you the way of *l* ....Jer 21:8
l shall be as a prize ....Jer 39:18
not worry about your *l* ......Matt 6:25
l does not consist ....Luke 12:15
L is more than ....Luke 12:23
l was the light ....John 1:4
so the Son gives *l* ....John 5:21
as the Father has *l* ....John 5:26
spirit, and they are *l* ....John 6:63
have the light of *l* ....John 8:12
and I lay down My *l* ....John 10:15
resurrection and the *l* ....John 11:25
you lay down your *l* ....John 13:38
God, who gives *l* ....Rom 4:17
that pertain to this *l* ....1 Cor 6:3
Lord Jesus, that the *l* ....2 Cor 4:10
l which I now live ....Gal 2:20
l is hidden with ....Col 3:3
of God who gives *l* ....1 Tim 6:13
For what is your *l* ....James 4:14
that pertain to *l* ....2 Pet 1:3
l was manifested ....1 John 1:2
and the pride of *l* ....1 John 2:16
has given us eternal *l* ......1 John 5:11
who has the Son has *l* ......1 John 5:12
the Lamb's Book of *L* ....Rev 21:27
right to the tree of *l* ....Rev 22:14
the water of *l* freely ....Rev 22:17
from the Book of *L* ....Rev 22:19

LIFT

I will *l* up my hands ....Ps 63:4
I will *l* up my eyes to ....Ps 121:1
l up your voice like a ....Is 58:1
l our hearts and hands ....Lam 3:41
Lord, and He will *l* ....James 4:10

LIFTED

O LORD, for You have *l* ....Ps 30:1
your heart is *l* ....Ezek 28:2
in Hades, he *l* up his ....Luke 16:23
the Son of Man be *l* ....John 3:14
And I, if I am *l* ....John 12:32
of Man must be *l* ....John 12:34

LIGHT

"Let there be *l* ....Gen 1:3
"The *l* of the wicked ....Job 18:5
l will shine on your ....Job 22:28
the wicked their *l* ....Job 38:15
to the dwelling of *l* ....Job 38:19
LORD, lift up the *l* ....Ps 4:6
The LORD is my *l* ....Ps 27:1
Oh, send out Your *l* ....Ps 43:3
L is sown for the ....Ps 97:11
and He has given us *l* ....Ps 118:27
and a *l* to my path ....Ps 119:105
The *l* of the righteous ....Prov 13:9
The *l* of the eyes ....Prov 15:30
The LORD gives *l* ....Prov 29:13
Truly the *l* is sweet ....Eccl 11:7
let us walk in the *l* ....Is 2:5
l is darkened by the ....Is 5:30
because there is no *l* ....Is 8:20
moon will be as the *l* ....Is 30:26
l shall break forth ....Is 58:8
for your *l* has come ....Is 60:1
be your everlasting *l* ....Is 60:20
gives the sun for a *l* ....Jer 31:35
l that goes ....Hos 6:5
"You are the *l* ....Matt 5:14
Let your *l* so shine ....Matt 5:16
body will be full of *l* ....Matt 6:22
than the sons of *l* ....Luke 16:8
and the life was the *l* ....John 1:4
That was the true *L* ....John 1:9
darkness rather than *l* ....John 3:19
evil hates the *l* ....John 3:20
truth comes to the *l* ....John 3:21
saying, "I am the *l* ....John 8:12
believe in the *l* ....John 12:36
I have come as a *l* ....John 12:46
l the hidden ....1 Cor 4:5
God who commanded *l* ....2 Cor 4:6
Walk as children of *l* ....Eph 5:8
You are all sons of *l* ....1 Thess 5:5
and immortality to *l* ....2 Tim 1:10
into His marvelous *l* ....1 Pet 2:9
do well to heed as a *l* ....2 Pet 1:19
to you, that God is *l* ....1 John 1:5
l as He is in the ....1 John 1:7
says he is in the *l* ....1 John 2:9
The Lamb is its *l* ....Rev 21:23
Lord God gives them *l* ....Rev 22:5

LIGHTEN

L the yoke which ....1 Kin 12:9
the sea, to *l* the load ....Jon 1:5

LIGHTLY

this, did I do it *l* ....2 Cor 1:17

LIGHTNING

For as the *l* ....Matt 24:27
countenance was like *l* ....Matt 28:3
saw Satan fall like *l* ....Luke 10:18

LIGHTNINGS

were thunderings and *l* ....Ex 19:16
the *l* lit up the world ....Ps 77:18
l light the world ....Ps 97:4
the throne proceeded *l* ....Rev 4:5

LIGHTS

"Let there be *l* ....Gen 1:14
Him who made great *l* ....Ps 136:7
whom you shine as *l* ....Phil 2:15
from the Father of *l* ....James 1:17

LIKE

"Who is *l* You ....Ex 15:11
L a lily among thorns ....Song 2:2
be made *l* His brethren ....Heb 2:17

LIKE-MINDED

grant you to be *l* ....Rom 15:5
For I have no one *l* ....Phil 2:20

LIKENESS

according to Our *l* ....Gen 1:26
carved image—any *l* ....Ex 20:4
when I awake in Your *l* ....Ps 17:15
His own Son in the *l* ....Rom 8:3
and coming in the *l* ....Phil 2:7

LILY

the *l* of the valleys ....Song 2:1
Like a *l* among thorns ....Song 2:2
shall grow like the *l* ....Hos 14:5

LIMIT

Do you *l* wisdom to ....Job 15:8
to the sea its *l* ....Prov 8:29

LIMITED

l the Holy One of ....Ps 78:41

LINE

l has gone out through ....Ps 19:4
upon precept, *l* upon *l* ....Is 28:10
I am setting a plumb *l* ....Amos 7:8

LINEAGE

was of the house and *l* ....Luke 2:4

LINEN

her clothing is fine *l* ....Prov 31:22
wrapped Him in the *l* ......Mark 15:46
l is the righteous ....Rev 19:8

LINGER

Those who *l* long at ....Prov 23:30
salvation shall not *l* ....Is 46:13

LION

he lies down as a *l* ....Gen 49:9
like a fierce *l* ....Job 10:16
l shall eat straw ....Is 11:7
For I will be like a *l* ....Hos 5:14

LIONS

My soul is among *l* ....Ps 57:4
the mouths of *l* ....Heb 11:33

LIPS

of uncircumcised *l* ....Ex 6:12
off all flattering *l* ....Ps 12:3
Let the lying *l* ....Ps 31:18
The *l* of the righteous ....Prov 10:21
but the *l* of knowledge .....Prov 20:15
am a man of unclean *l* ....Is 6:5
asps is under their *l* ....Rom 3:13
other *l* I will speak ....1 Cor 14:21
from evil, and his *l* ....1 Pet 3:10

LISTEN

L carefully to Me ....Is 55:2
O Lord, *l* and act ....Dan 9:19
you are not able to *l* ....John 8:43
Why do you *l* to Him ......John 10:20
you who fear God, *l* ....Acts 13:16

LISTENS

but whoever *l* to me ....Prov 1:33

LITTLE

l foxes that spoil the ....Song 2:15
We have a *l* sister ....Song 8:8
upon line, here a *l* ....Is 28:10
though you are *l* ....Mic 5:2
indeed it came to *l* ....Hag 1:9
for I was a *l* angry ....Zech 1:15
l ones only a cup ....Matt 10:42
"O you of *l* faith ....Matt 14:31
Whoever receives one *l* ......Matt 18:5
to whom *l* is forgiven ....Luke 7:47
faithful in a very *l* ....Luke 19:17
exercise profits a *l* ....1 Tim 4:8

LIVE

eat, and *l* forever ....Gen 3:22

a man does, he shall *l* ....Lev 18:5
I would not *l* forever ....Job 7:16
L joyfully with the ....Eccl 9:9
by these things men *l* ....Is 38:16
sin, he shall surely *l* ....Ezek 3:21
"Seek Me and *l* ....Amos 5:4
but the just shall *l* ....Hab 2:4
l by bread alone ....Matt 4:4
who feeds on Me will *l* ......John 6:57
for in Him we *l* ....Acts 17:28
l peaceably with all ....Rom 12:18
the life which I now *l* ....Gal 2:20
If we *l* in the Spirit ....Gal 5:25
to me, to *l* is Christ ....Phil 1:21
l godly in Christ ....2 Tim 3:12
to *l* honorably ....Heb 13:18
l according to God in ....1 Pet 4:6

LIVED

died and rose and *l* ....Rom 14:9
And they *l* and reigned ....Rev 20:4

LIVES

but man *l* by every ....Deut 8:3
have risked their *l* ....Acts 15:26
He *l* to God ....Rom 6:10
For none of us *l* ....Rom 14:7
but Christ *l* in me ....Gal 2:20
to lay down our *l* ....1 John 3:16
I am He who *l* ....Rev 1:18

LIVING

and man became a *l* ....Gen 2:7
in the light of the *l* ....Ps 56:13
l will take it to ....Eccl 7:2
l know that they will ....Eccl 9:5
Why should a *l* man ....Lam 3:39
the dead, but of the *l* ....Matt 22:32
Why do you seek the *l* ......Luke 24:5
to be Judge of the *l* ....Acts 10:42
who will judge the *l* ....2 Tim 4:1
the word of God is *l* ....Heb 4:12
ready to judge the *l* ....1 Pet 4:5
l creature was like a ....Rev 4:7

LO-AMMI

Symbolic name of Hosea's son,
Hos 1:8, 9

LO-RUHAMAH

Symbolic name of Hosea's daughter,
Hos 1:6

LOAD

shall bear his own *l* ....Gal 6:5

LOATHE

I *l* my life ....Job 7:16
l themselves for the ....Ezek 6:9

LOATHSOME

but a wicked man is *l* ....Prov 13:5

LOAVES

have here only five *l* ....Matt 14:17
He took the seven *l* ....Matt 15:36
lend me three *l* ....Luke 11:5
you ate of the *l* ....John 6:26

LOCUST

What the chewing *l* ....Joel 1:4
left, the swarming *l* ....Joel 1:4

LOCUSTS

as numerous as *l* ....Judg 7:12

He spoke, and *l* came ....Ps 105:34
the *l* have no king ....Prov 30:27
and his food was *l* ....Matt 3:4
waist, and he ate *l* ....Mark 1:6
out of the smoke *l* ....Rev 9:3

LODGED

them in and *l* them ....Acts 10:23
children, if she has *l* ....1 Tim 5:10

LOFTILY

they speak *l* ....Ps 73:8

LOFTY

haughty, nor my eyes *l* ....Ps 131:1
Wisdom is too *l* ....Prov 24:7
l are their eyes ....Prov 30:13
and *L* One who ....Is 57:15

LOINS

gird up the *l* of your ....1 Pet 1:13

LONG

your days may be *l* ....Deut 5:16
who *l* for death ....Job 3:21
me the thing that I *l* ....Job 6:8
I *l* for Your salvation ....Ps 119:174
go around in *l* robes ....Mark 12:38
how greatly I *l* ....Phil 1:8

LONGSUFFERING

and gracious, *l* ....Ps 86:15
is love, joy, peace, *l* ....Gal 5:22
and gentleness, with *l* ....Eph 4:2
for all patience and *l* ....Col 1:11
might show all *l* ....1 Tim 1:16
when once the Divine *l* ......1 Pet 3:20
and consider that the *l* ......2 Pet 3:15

LOOK

Do not *l* behind you ....Gen 19:17
who has a haughty *l* ....Ps 101:5
A proud *l* ....Prov 6:17
that day a man will *l* ....Is 17:7
L upon Zion ....Is 33:20
"*L* to Me ....Is 45:22
we *l* for light ....Is 59:9
we *l* for justice ....Is 59:11
l on Me whom they ....Zech 12:10
say to you, '*L* here ....Luke 17:23
of Israel could not *l* ....2 Cor 3:7
while we do not *l* ....2 Cor 4:18
Let each of you *l* ....Phil 2:4
L to yourselves ....2 John 8

LOOKED

But when I *l* for good ....Job 30:26
They *l* to Him and were ....Ps 34:5
For He *l* down from the .....Ps 102:19
He *l* for justice ....Is 5:7
"We *l* for peace ....Jer 8:15
"You *l* for much ....Hag 1:9
the Lord turned and *l* ....Luke 22:61
for he *l* to the reward ....Heb 11:26

LOOKING

the plow, and *l* back ....Luke 9:62
l for the blessed hope ......Titus 2:13
l unto Jesus ....Heb 12:2
l carefully lest ....Heb 12:15
l for the mercy of ....Jude 21

LOOKS

Absalom for his good *l* ..2 Sam 14:25
Then he *l* at men and ....Job 33:27

God *l* down from heaven ....Ps 53:2
The lofty *l* of man ....Is 2:11
to you that whoever *l* ....Matt 5:28

LOOM

and the web from the *l* .....Judg 16:14
cuts me off from the *l* ....Is 38:12

LOOSE

l the armor of kings ....Is 45:1
and whatever you *l* ....Matt 16:19
said to them, "*L* him ....John 11:44

LOOSED

You have *l* my bonds ....Ps 116:16
the silver cord is *l* ....Eccl 12:6

LORD

L is my strength ....Ex 15:2
L is a man of war ....Ex 15:3
L our God, the *L* ....Deut 6:4
sacrifice to the *L* your God ..Deut 17:1
may know that the *L* ....1 Kin 8:60
If the *L* is God ....1 Kin 18:21
You alone are the *L* ....Neh 9:6
The *L* of hosts ....Ps 24:10
belongs to the *L* ....Ps 89:18
let us sing to the *L* ....Ps 95:1
L is the great God ....Ps 95:3
Gracious is the *L* ....Ps 116:5
L surrounds His people ....Ps 125:2
The *L* is righteous ....Ps 129:4
L is near to all who ....Ps 145:18
L is a God of justice ....Is 30:18
L Our Righteousness ....Jer 23:6
L has done marvelous ....Joel 2:21
L God is my strength ....Hab 3:19
"The *L* is one ....Zech 14:9
shall not tempt the *L* ....Matt 4:7
shall worship the *L* ....Matt 4:10
Son of Man is also *L* ....Mark 2:28
who is Christ the *L* ....Luke 2:11
why do you call Me '*L* ....Luke 6:46
L is risen indeed ....Luke 24:34
call Me Teacher and *L* .....John 13:13
He is *L* of all ....Acts 10:36
'Who are You, *L* ....Acts 26:15
with your mouth the *L* ....Rom 10:9
Greek, for the same *L* ......Rom 10:12
say that Jesus is *L* ....1 Cor 12:3
second Man is the *L* ....1 Cor 15:47
the Spirit of the *L* ....2 Cor 3:17
that Jesus Christ is *L* ....Phil 2:11
and deny the only *L* ....Jude 4
L God Omnipotent ....Rev 19:6

LORDS

many gods and many *l* ....1 Cor 8:5
nor as being *l* over ....1 Pet 5:3
for He is Lord of *l* ....Rev 17:14

LORDSHIP

Gentiles exercise *l* ....Luke 22:25

LOSE

gain, and a time to *l* ....Eccl 3:6
save his life will *l* ....Matt 16:25
reap if we do not *l* ....Gal 6:9
that we do not *l* ....2 John 8

LOSES

but if the salt *l* ....Matt 5:13
and *l* his own soul ....Matt 16:26
if she *l* one coin ....Luke 15:8
l his life will ....Luke 17:33

LOSS

he will suffer *l* ....1 Cor 3:15
count all things *l* ....Phil 3:8

LOST

are dry, our hope is *l* ....Ezek 37:11
save that which was *l* ....Matt 18:11
the one which is *l* ....Luke 15:4
my sheep which was *l* ....Luke 15:6
the piece which I *l* ....Luke 15:9
and none of them is *l* ......John 17:12
You gave Me I have *l* ....John 18:9

LOT

Abram's nephew; accompanies him, Gen 11:27—12:5; 13:1
Separates from Abram, Gen 13:5–12
Rescued by Abram, Gen 14:12–16
Saved from Sodom for his hospitality, Gen 19:1–29
Tricked into committing incest, Gen 19:30–38

LOT

shall be divided by *l* ....Num 26:55
You maintain my *l* ....Ps 16:5
cast in your *l* among ....Prov 1:14
l is cast into the lap ....Prov 16:33

LOT'S WIFE

Disobedient, becomes pillar of salt, Gen 19:26
Event to be remembered, Luke 17:32

LOTS

l causes contentions ....Prov 18:18
garments, casting *l* ....Mark 15:24
And they cast their *l* ....Acts 1:26

LOUD

I cried out with a *l* ....Gen 39:14
Him with *l* cymbals ....Ps 150:5
cried out with a *l* ....Matt 27:46
I heard behind me a *l* ....Rev 1:10

LOVE

l your neighbor as ....Lev 19:18
l the LORD your God ....Deut 6:5
your *l* to me was ....2 Sam 1:26
How long will you *l* ....Ps 4:2
Oh, *l* the LORD ....Ps 31:23
l righteousness ....Ps 45:7
he has set his *l* ....Ps 91:14
Oh, how I *l* Your law ....Ps 119:97
peace have those who *l* .....Ps 119:165
preserves all who *l* ....Ps 145:20
us take our fill of *l* ....Prov 7:18
l covers all sins ....Prov 10:12
a time to *l* ....Eccl 3:8
People know neither *l* ....Eccl 9:1
l is better than wine ....Song 1:2
banner over me was *l* ....Song 2:4
stir up nor awaken *l* ....Song 3:5
I will give you my *l* ....Song 7:12
l is as strong as ....Song 8:6
waters cannot quench *l* ......Song 8:7
time was the time of *l* ....Ezek 16:8
backsliding, I will *l* ....Hos 14:4
do justly, to *l* mercy ....Mic 6:8
to you, *l* your enemies ....Matt 5:44
l those who *l* you ....Matt 5:46
which of them will *l* ....Luke 7:42
you do not have the *l* ....John 5:42
if you have *l* for one ....John 13:35
"If you *l* Me ....John 14:15
and My Father will *l* ....John 14:23
l one another as I ....John 15:12
l has no one than this ......John 15:13
l Me more than these ......John 21:15
of Jonah, do you *l* ....John 21:16
You know that I *l* ....John 21:16
because the *l* of God ....Rom 5:5
Let *l* be without ....Rom 12:9
to *l* one another ....Rom 13:8
L does no harm to a ....Rom 13:10
up, but *l* edifies ....1 Cor 8:1
L suffers long and is ....1 Cor 13:4
l does not envy ....1 Cor 13:4
l does not parade ....1 Cor 13:4
L never fails ....1 Cor 13:8
greatest of these is *l* ....1 Cor 13:13
For the *l* of Christ ....2 Cor 5:14
and the God of *l* ....2 Cor 13:11
of the Spirit is *l* ....Gal 5:22
Husbands, *l* your wives ......Eph 5:25
of the Son of His *l* ....Col 1:13
l your wives and do ....Col 3:19
the commandment is *l* ....1 Tim 1:5
continue in faith, *l* ....1 Tim 2:15
word, in conduct, in *l* ....1 Tim 4:12
For the *l* of money is ....1 Tim 6:10
l their husbands ....Titus 2:4
Let brotherly *l* ....Heb 13:1
having not seen you *l* ....1 Pet 1:8
L the brotherhood ....1 Pet 2:17
for "*l* will cover a ....1 Pet 4:8
with a kiss of *l* ....1 Pet 5:14
brotherly kindness *l* ....2 Pet 1:7
loves the world, the *l* ....1 John 2:15
we *l* the brethren ....1 John 3:14
By this we know *l* ....1 John 3:16
him, how does the *l* ....1 John 3:17
Beloved, let us *l* ....1 John 4:7
know God, for God is *l* .....1 John 4:8
In this is *l* ....1 John 4:10
If we *l* one another ....1 John 4:12
L has been perfected ......1 John 4:17
There is no fear in *l* ....1 John 4:18
l Him because He first .....1 John 4:19
who loves God must *l* ......1 John 4:21
For this is the *l* ....1 John 5:3
have left your first *l* ....Rev 2:4
and they did not *l* ....Rev 12:11

LOVED

Because the LORD has *l* .....1 Kin 10:9
L one and friend You ....Ps 88:18
"I have *l* you ....Mal 1:2
Yet Jacob I have *l* ....Mal 1:2
forgiven, for she *l* ....Luke 7:47
so *l* the world that ....John 3:16
"See how He *l* ....John 11:36
whom Jesus *l* ....John 13:23
"As the Father *l* ....John 15:9
l them as You have ....John 17:23
"Jacob I have *l* ....Rom 9:13
the Son of God, who *l* ....Gal 2:20
l the church and gave ....Eph 5:25
l righteousness ....Heb 1:9
God, but that He *l* ....1 John 4:10
Beloved, if God so *l* ....1 John 4:11
To Him who *l* us and ....Rev 1:5

LOVELY

l is Your tabernacle ....Ps 84:1
l woman who lacks ....Prov 11:22
he is altogether *l* ....Song 5:16
whatever things are *l* ....Phil 4:8

LOVER

a *l* of what is good ....Titus 1:8

LOVERS

For men will be *l* ....2 Tim 3:2

LOVES

l righteousness ....Ps 33:5
life, and *l* many days ....Ps 34:12
A friend *l* at all ....Prov 17:17
He who *l* father or ....Matt 10:37
l his life will lose ....John 12:25
l Me will be loved ....John 14:21
l a cheerful giver ....2 Cor 9:7
who *l* his wife *l* ....Eph 5:28
If anyone *l* the world ......1 John 2:15
l God must love his ....1 John 4:21
l him who is ....1 John 5:1

LOVESICK

apples, for I am *l* ....Song 2:5
you tell him I am *l* ....Song 5:8

LOVINGKINDNESS

not concealed Your *l* ....Ps 40:10
l is better than life ....Ps 63:3
to declare Your *l* ....Ps 92:2
l I have drawn ....Jer 31:3

LOW

He brings *l* and lifts ....1 Sam 2:7
both *l* and high ....Ps 49:2
it *l*, He lays it *l* ....Is 26:5
and hill brought *l* ....Luke 3:5

LOWER

made him a little *l* ....Ps 8:5
shall go into the *l* ....Ps 63:9
made him a little *l* ....Heb 2:7

LOWEST

and sets over it the *l* ....Dan 4:17

LOWLINESS

with all *l* and ....Eph 4:2
or conceit, but in *l* ....Phil 2:3

LOWLY

yet He regards the *l* ....Ps 138:6
for I am gentle and *l* ....Matt 11:29
He has regarded the *l* ....Luke 1:48
and exalted the *l* ....Luke 1:52
in presence am *l* ....2 Cor 10:1
l body that it may be ....Phil 3:21
l brother glory ....James 1:9

LOYAL

or else he will be *l* ....Matt 6:24

LUCIFER

Name applied to Satan, Is 14:12

LUKE

"The beloved physician," Col 4:14
Paul's last companion, 2 Tim 4:11

LUKEWARM

because you are *l* ....Rev 3:16

LUMP

from the same *l* ....Rom 9:21
you may be a new *l* ....1 Cor 5:7

LUST

Do not *l* after her ....Prov 6:25
caught by their *l* ....Prov 11:6
looks at a woman to *l* ....Matt 5:28

not fulfill the *l* ....Gal 5:16
not in passion of *l* ....1 Thess 4:5
You *l* and do not have ......James 4:2
the *l* of the flesh ....1 John 2:16

LUSTS

to fulfill its *l* ....Rom 13:14
l which drown men ....1 Tim 6:9
also youthful *l* ....2 Tim 2:22
and worldly *l* ....Titus 2:12
to the former *l* ....1 Pet 1:14
abstain from fleshly *l* ....1 Pet 2:11
to their own ungodly *l* ....Jude 18

LUTE

Awake, *l* and harp ....Ps 57:8
l I will praise You ....Ps 71:22
harp with the *l* ....Ps 81:2
ten strings, on the *l* ....Ps 92:3
Awake, *l* and harp ....Ps 108:2
Praise Him with the *l* ....Ps 150:3

LUXURY

L is not fitting ....Prov 19:10
l are in kings' courts ....Luke 7:25
in pleasure and *l* ....James 5:5
the abundance of her *l* ....Rev 18:3

LYDDA

Aeneas healed at, Acts 9:32–35

LYDIA

Woman of Thyatira; Paul's first European convert, Acts 16:14, 15, 40
——District of Asia Minor containing Ephesus, Smyrna, Thyatira, and Sardis, Rev 1:11

LYING

I hate and abhor *l* ....Ps 119:163
righteous man hates *l* ....Prov 13:5
not trust in these *l* ....Jer 7:4
in swaddling cloths, *l* ....Luke 2:12
saw the linen cloths *l* ....John 20:5
putting away *l* ....Eph 4:25
signs, and *l* wonders ....2 Thess 2:9

LYSIAS, CLAUDIUS

See CLAUDIUS LYSIAS

LYSTRA

Paul visits; is worshiped by people of and stoned by Jews, Acts 14:6–20
Home of Timothy, Acts 16:1, 2

— M —

MAACAH (or Maachah)

Small Syrian kingdom near Mt. Hermon, Deut 3:14
Not possessed by Israel, Josh 13:13
——David's wife; mother of Absalom, 2 Sam 3:3
——Wife of Rehoboam; mother of King Abijah, 2 Chr 11:18–21
Makes idol; is deposed as queen mother, 1 Kin 15:13

MACEDONIA

Paul preaches in, Acts 16:9—17:14
Paul's troubles in, 2 Cor 7:5
Churches of, generous, Rom 15:26; 2 Cor 8:1–5

MACHIR

Manasseh's only son, Gen 50:23
Founder of the family of Machirites, Num 26:29
Conqueror of Gilead, Num 32:39, 40

MACHPELAH

Field containing a cave; bought by Abraham, Gen 23:9–18
Sarah and Abraham buried here, Gen 23:19; 25:9, 10
Isaac, Rebekah, Leah, and Jacob buried here, Gen 49:29–31

MAD

has a demon and is *m* ......John 10:20
he said, "I am not *m* ....Acts 26:25

MADE

m the stars also ....Gen 1:16
wife the LORD God *m* ....Gen 3:21
hear long ago how I *m* ....Is 37:26
things My hand has *m* ....Is 66:2
All things were *m* ....John 1:3

MADNESS

before them, *m* ....1 Sam 21:13
wisdom and to know *m* ......Eccl 1:17
m is in their hearts ....Eccl 9:3

MAGDALENE

See MARY

MAGIC

women who sew *m* ....Ezek 13:18
m brought their books ....Acts 19:19

MAGNIFICENCE

m I cannot endure ....Job 31:23

MAGNIFIED

So let Your name be *m* .....2 Sam 7:26
"Let the LORD be *m* ....Ps 35:27
for You have *m* Your ....Ps 138:2
the Lord Jesus was *m* ......Acts 19:17
also Christ will be *m* ....Phil 1:20

MAGNIFIES

"My soul *m* the Lord ....Luke 1:46

MAGNIFY

m the LORD with me ....Ps 34:3
m himself above every ....Dan 11:36

MAGOG

People among Japheth's descendants, Gen 10:2
Associated with Gog, Ezek 38:2
Representatives of final enemies, Rev 20:8

MAHANAIM

Name given by Jacob to a sacred site, Gen 32:2
Becomes Ishbosheth's capital, 2 Sam 2:8–29
David flees to, during Absalom's rebellion, 2 Sam 17:24, 27

MAHER-SHALAL-HASH-BAZ

Symbolic name of Isaiah's second son; prophetic of the fall of Damascus and Samaria, Is 8:1–4

MAHLON

Husband of Ruth; without child, Ruth 1:2–5

MAIDENS

Both young men and *m* ......Ps 148:12
She has sent out her *m* ....Prov 9:3

MAIDSERVANT

"I am Ruth, your *m* ....Ruth 3:9
save the son of Your *m* ....Ps 86:16
"Behold the *m* ....Luke 1:38
lowly state of His *m* ....Luke 1:48

MAIDSERVANTS

m shall lead her as ....Nah 2:7
m I will pour out My ....Acts 2:18

MAIMED

to enter into life *m* ....Mark 9:43
the poor and the *m* ....Luke 14:21

MAINTAIN

and *m* their cause ....1 Kin 8:45

MAINTAINED

For You have *m* my ....Ps 9:4

MAJESTY

with God is awesome *m* ......Job 37:22
splendor of Your *m* ....Ps 145:5
right hand of the *M* ....Heb 1:3
eyewitnesses of His *m* ....2 Pet 1:16
wise, be glory and *m* ....Jude 25

MAKE

"Let Us *m* man in Our ....Gen 1:26
let us *m* a name for ....Gen 11:4
m you a great nation ....Gen 12:2
"You shall not *m* ....Ex 20:4
m Our home with him ......John 14:23

MAKER

where is God my *M* ....Job 35:10
man will look to his *M* ....Is 17:7
who strives with his *M* ....Is 45:9
M is your husband ....Is 54:5
has forgotten his *M* ....Hos 8:14
builder and *m* is God ....Heb 11:10

MALACHI

Prophet and writer, Mal 1:1

MALCHISHUA

Son of King Saul, 1 Sam 14:49
Killed at Gilboa, 1 Sam 31:2

MALCHUS

Servant of the high priest, John 18:10

MALICE

in *m* be babes ....1 Cor 14:20
pleasures, living in *m* ....Titus 3:3
laying aside all *m* ....1 Pet 2:1

MALICIOUSNESS

covetousness, *m* ....Rom 1:29

MALIGN

m a servant to his ....Prov 30:10

MALTA

Paul's shipwreck, Acts 28:1–8

MAMRE

Town or district near Hebron, Gen 23:19
Abram dwells by the oaks of, Gen 13:18

MAN

"Let Us make *m* ....Gen 1:26

"You are the *m* ....2 Sam 12:7
"What is *m* ....Job 7:17
For an empty-headed *m* .....Job 11:12
"Are you the first *m* ....Job 15:7
m that You are mindful ....Ps 8:4
What can *m* do to me ....Ps 118:6
coming of the Son of *M* ....Matt 24:27
"Behold the *M* ....John 19:5
m is not from woman ....1 Cor 11:8
since by *m* came death ......1 Cor 15:21
though our outward *m* ......2 Cor 4:16
in Himself one new *m* ....Eph 2:15
that the *m* of God may ......2 Tim 3:17
is the number of a *m* ....Rev 13:18

MANASSEH

Joseph's firstborn son, Gen 41:50, 51
Adopted by Jacob, Gen 48:5, 6
Loses his birthright to Ephraim, Gen 48:13–20
——— Tribe of:
Numbered, Num 1:34, 35
Half-tribe of, settle east of Jordan, Num 32:33–42; Deut 3:12–15
Help Joshua against Canaanites, Josh 1:12–18
Land assigned to western half-tribe, Josh 17:1–13
Eastern half-tribe builds altar, Josh 22:9–34
Some of, help David, 1 Chr 12:19–31
——— Wicked king of Judah; son of Hezekiah, 2 Kin 21:1–18; 2 Chr 33:1–9
Captured and taken to Babylon; repents and is restored, 2 Chr 33:10–13
Removes idols and altars, 2 Chr 33:14–20

MANGER

Will he bed by your *m* ....Job 39:9
and laid Him in a *m* ....Luke 2:7
the Babe lying in a *m* ....Luke 2:16

MANIFEST

m Myself to him ....John 14:21
is it that You will *m* ....John 14:22

MANIFESTATION

But the *m* of the ....1 Cor 12:7
deceitfully, but by *m* ....2 Cor 4:2

MANIFESTED

"I have *m* Your name ....John 17:6
God was *m* in the flesh .....1 Tim 3:16
the life was *m* ....1 John 1:2
the love of God was *m* ......1 John 4:9

MANIFOLD

m are Your works ....Ps 104:24
the *m* wisdom of God ....Eph 3:10
good stewards of the *m* .....1 Pet 4:10

MANNA

of Israel ate *m* ....Ex 16:35
had rained down *m* ....Ps 78:24
Our fathers ate the *m* ....John 6:31
of the hidden *m* ....Rev 2:17

MANNER

Is this the *m* of man ....2 Sam 7:19
in an unworthy *m* ....1 Cor 11:27
sorrowed in a godly *m* ......2 Cor 7:11
as is the *m* of some ....Heb 10:25
what *m* of persons ....2 Pet 3:11

Behold what *m* of love ....1 John 3:1
m worthy of God ....3 John 6

MANOAH

Danite; father of Samson, Judg 13:1–25

MANSIONS

house are many *m* ....John 14:2

MANTLE

Then he took the *m* ....2 Kin 2:14

MARA

Name chosen by Naomi, Ruth 1:20

MARAH

First Israelite camp after passing through the Red Sea, Num 33:8, 9

MARCHED

people, when You *m* ....Ps 68:7

MARK (John)

Son of Mary of Jerusalem; travels with Barnabas and Saul, Acts 12:12, 25
Leaves Paul at Perga, Acts 13:13
Barnabas and Paul separate because of him, Acts 15:37–40
Later approved by Paul, Col 4:10; 2 Tim 4:11
Companion of Peter, 1 Pet 5:13
Author of the second Gospel, Mark 1:1

MARK

And the LORD set a *m* ....Gen 4:15
M the blameless man ....Ps 37:37
slave, to receive a *m* ....Rev 13:16
whoever receives the *m* .....Rev 14:11

MARKET

is sold in the meat *m* ....1 Cor 10:25

MARRED

so His visage was *m* ....Is 52:14
he made of clay was *m* ....Jer 18:4

MARRIAGE

nor are given in *m* ....Matt 22:30
her in *m* does well ....1 Cor 7:38
M is honorable among ....Heb 13:4
the *m* of the Lamb has ....Rev 19:7

MARRIED

"for I am *m* to you ....Jer 3:14
But he who is *m* ....1 Cor 7:33
But she who is *m* ....1 Cor 7:34

MARROW

and of joints and *m* ....Heb 4:12

MARRY

it is better not to *m* ....Matt 19:10
they neither *m* nor are .....Matt 22:30
let them *m* ....1 Cor 7:9
forbidding to *m* ....1 Tim 4:3
the younger widows *m* .....1 Tim 5:14

MARRYING

and drinking, *m* ....Matt 24:38

MARTHA

Sister of Mary and Lazarus; loved by Jesus, John 11:1–5
Affirms her faith, John 11:19–28
Offers hospitality to Jesus, Luke 10:38; John 12:1, 2
Gently rebuked by Christ, Luke 10:39–42

MARTYR

m Stephen was shed ....Acts 22:20
was My faithful *m* ....Rev 2:13

MARTYRS

the blood of the *m* ....Rev 17:6

MARVEL

Do not *m* at this ....John 5:28

MARVELED

Jesus heard it, He *m* ....Matt 8:10
And the multitudes *m* ....Matt 9:33
so that Pilate *m* ....Mark 15:5
And all the world *m* ....Rev 13:3
when I saw her, I *m* ....Rev 17:6

MARVELOUS

m things He did ....Ps 78:12
It is *m* in our eyes ....Ps 118:23
M are Your works ....Ps 139:14
of darkness into His *m* ....1 Pet 2:9

MARVELS

people I will do *m* ....Ex 34:10

MARY

Mother of Christ, Matt 1:16
Visited by angel, Luke 1:26–38
Visits Elizabeth and offers praise, Luke 1:39–56
Gives birth to Jesus, Luke 2:6–20
Flees to Egypt, Matt 2:13–18
Visits Jerusalem with Jesus, Luke 2:41–52
Entrusted to John's care, John 19:25–27
——— Mother of James and Joses; present at crucifixion and burial, Matt 27:55–61
Sees the risen Lord; informs disciples, Matt 28:1–10
——— Magdalene; delivered from seven demons; supports Christ's ministry, Luke 8:2, 3
Present at crucifixion and burial, Matt 27:55–61
First to see the risen Lord, Mark 16:1–10; John 20:1–18
——— Sister of Martha and Lazarus; loved by Jesus, John 11:1–5
Grieves for Lazarus, John 11:19, 20, 28–33
Anoints Jesus, Matt 26:6–13; John 12:1–8
Commended by Jesus, Luke 10:38–42
——— Mark's mother, Acts 12:12–17

MASSAH AND MERIBAH

First, at Rephidim, Israel just out of Egypt, Ex 17:1–7
Second, at Kadesh Barnea, 40 years later, Num 20:1–13

MASTER

of Abraham his *m* ....Gen 24:9
a servant like his *m* ....Matt 10:25
greater than his *m* ....John 15:20
m builder I have laid ....1 Cor 3:10
and useful for the *M* ....2 Tim 2:21

MASTERS

m besides You have ....Is 26:13

can serve two *m* . . . . .Luke 16:13
M, give your bondservants . . . . .Col 4:1
who have believing *m* . . . . . . .1 Tim 6:2

MATTANIAH

King Zedekiah's original name, 2 Kin 24:17

MATTER

m is found in me . . . . .Job 19:28
He who answers a *m* . . . . . . .Prov 18:13

MATTERS

the weightier *m* . . . . .Matt 23:23
judge the smallest *m* . . . . .1 Cor 6:2

MATTHEW

Becomes Christ's follower, Matt 9:9
Chosen as one of the Twelve, Matt 10:2, 3
Called Levi, the son of Alphaeus, Mark 2:14
Author of the first Gospel, Matt (title)

MATTHIAS

Chosen by lot to replace Judas, Acts 1:15–26

MATURE

among those who are *m* . . . . .1 Cor 2:6
understanding be *m* . . . . . . .1 Cor 14:20
us, as many as are *m* . . . . .Phil 3:15

MEAN

What do you *m* . . . . .Ex 12:26

MEANING

'What is the *m* . . . . .Deut 6:20
if I do not know the *m* . . . . .1 Cor 14:11

MEANT

but God *m* it for good . . . . . . .Gen 50:20

MEASURE

a perfect and just *m* . . . . .Deut 25:15
apportion the waters by *m* . . .Job 28:25
and the short *m* . . . . .Mic 6:10
give the Spirit by *m* . . . . .John 3:34
to each one a *m* . . . . .Rom 12:3
m the temple of God . . . . .Rev 11:1

MEASURED

m the waters in the . . . . .Is 40:12
you use, it will be *m* . . . . .Matt 7:2
Then he *m* its wall . . . . .Rev 21:17

MEASURES

your house differing *m* . . . . .Deut 25:14
weights and diverse *m* . . . . .Prov 20:10

MEASURING

the man's hand was a *m* . . . .Ezek 40:5
behold, a man with a *m* . . . . . .Zech 2:1
m themselves by . . . . .2 Cor 10:12
given a reed like a *m* . . . . .Rev 11:1

MEAT

Can He provide *m* . . . . .Ps 78:20
He also rained *m* . . . . .Ps 78:27
good neither to eat *m* . . . . . .Rom 14:21
will never again eat *m* . . . . . .1 Cor 8:13
is sold in the *m* . . . . .1 Cor 10:25

MEDDLE

why should you *m* . . . . .2 Kin 14:10

MEDES, MEDIA

Part of Medo-Persian Empire, Esth 1:19
Israel deported to, 2 Kin 17:6
Babylon falls to, Dan 5:30, 31
Daniel rises high in kingdom of, Dan 6:1–28
Cyrus, king of, allows Jews to return, 2 Chr 36:22, 23
Agents in Babylon's fall, Is 13:17–19

MEDIATE

a mediator does not *m* . . . . .Gal 3:20

MEDIATOR

Nor is there any *m* . . . . .Job 9:33
by the hand of a *m* . . . . .Gal 3:19
is one God and one *M* . . . . . . .1 Tim 2:5
as He is also *M* . . . . .Heb 8:6
to Jesus the *M* of the . . . . . . .Heb 12:24

MEDICINE

does good, like *m* . . . . .Prov 17:22

MEDICINES

you will use many *m* . . . . .Jer 46:11

MEDITATE

Isaac went out to *m* . . . . .Gen 24:63
but you shall *m* . . . . .Josh 1:8
M within your heart on . . . . .Ps 4:4
I *m* within my heart . . . . .Ps 77:6
I will *m* on Your . . . . .Ps 119:15
Your heart will *m* . . . . .Is 33:18
m beforehand on what . . . . . . .Luke 21:14
m on these things . . . . .Phil 4:8

MEDITATES

in His law he *m* . . . . .Ps 1:2

MEDITATION

of my mouth and the *m* . . . . . . .Ps 19:14
m be sweet to Him . . . . .Ps 104:34
It is my *m* all the day . . . . .Ps 119:97

MEDITERRANEAN SEA

Described as:
Sea, Gen 49:13
Great Sea, Josh 1:4; 9:1
Sea of the Philistines, Ex 23:31
Western Sea, Deut 11:24; Joel 2:20; Zech 14:8

MEDIUM

a woman who is a *m* . . . . .Lev 20:27
a woman who is a *m* . . . . . . .1 Sam 28:7

MEDIUM'S

shall be like a *m* . . . . .Is 29:4

MEDIUMS

"Seek those who are *m* . . . . .Is 8:19

MEEK

with equity for the *m* . . . . .Is 11:4
Blessed are the *m* . . . . .Matt 5:5

MEEKNESS

with you by the *m* . . . . .2 Cor 10:1
are done in the *m* . . . . .James 3:13

MEET

For You *m* him with the . . . . .Ps 21:3
prepare to *m* your God . . . . . .Amos 4:12
go out to *m* him . . . . .Matt 25:6

m the Lord in the air . . . . .1 Thess 4:17

MEETING

In the tabernacle of *m* . . . . .Ex 27:21
burned up all the *m* . . . . .Ps 74:8

MEGIDDO

City of Canaan; scene of battles, Judg 5:19–21; 2 Kin 23:29, 30
Fortified by Solomon, 1 Kin 9:15
Possible site of Armageddon, Rev 16:16

MELCHIZEDEK

Priest and king of Salem, Gen 14:18–20
Type of Christ's eternal priesthood, Heb 7:1–22

MELODY

make sweet *m* . . . . .Is 23:16
singing and making *m* . . . . .Eph 5:19

MELT

You make his beauty *m* . . . . . . .Ps 39:11
man's heart will *m* . . . . .Is 13:7
the elements will *m* . . . . .2 Pet 3:10

MEMBER

body is not one *m* . . . . .1 Cor 12:14
tongue is a little *m* . . . . .James 3:5

MEMBERS

you that one of your *m* . . . . . .Matt 5:29
do not present your *m* . . . . .Rom 6:13
that your bodies are *m* . . . . . . .1 Cor 6:15
neighbor, for we are *m* . . . . .Eph 4:25

MEMORIAL

and this is My *m* . . . . .Ex 3:15
also be told as a *m* . . . . .Matt 26:13
be told of as a *m* . . . . .Mark 14:9

MEMORY

The *m* of him perishes . . . . . . .Job 18:17
He may cut off the *m* . . . . .Ps 109:15
The *m* of the righteous . . . . .Prov 10:7

MEMPHIS (or Noph)

Ancient capital of Egypt, Hos 9:6
Prophesied against by Isaiah, Is 19:13
Jews flee to, Jer 44:1
Denounced by the prophets, Jer 46:19

MEN

m began to call on the . . . . . . .Gen 4:26
saw the daughters of *m* . . . . .Gen 6:2
you shall die like *m* . . . . .Ps 82:7
the Egyptians are *m* . . . . .Is 31:3
make you fishers of *m* . . . . . . .Matt 4:19
goodwill toward *m* . . . . .Luke 2:14
from heaven or from *m* . . . . . .Luke 20:4
Likewise also the *m* . . . . .Rom 1:27
let no one boast in *m* . . . . . . .1 Cor 3:21
the Lord, and not to *m* . . . . .Eph 6:7
between God and *m* . . . . .1 Tim 2:5

MENAHEM

Cruel king of Israel, 2 Kin 15:14–18

MENSERVANTS

And also on My *m* . . . . .Joel 2:29
And on My *m* and on My . . . .Acts 2:18

MENTION

I will make *m* of Your . . . . .Ps 71:16

by You only we make *m* ......Is 26:13
You who make *m* of the ....Is 62:6
he was dying, made *m* ......Heb 11:22

MEPHIBOSHETH

Son of King Saul, 2 Sam 21:8
——Grandson of King Saul; crippled son of Jonathan, 2 Sam 4:4–6
Sought out and honored by David, 2 Sam 9:1–13
Accused by Ziba, 2 Sam 16:1–4
Later explains himself to David, 2 Sam 19:24–30
Spared by David, 2 Sam 21:7

MERAB

King Saul's eldest daughter, 1 Sam 14:49
Saul promises her to David, but gives her to Adriel, 1 Sam 18:17–19

MERARI

Third son of Levi, Gen 46:11
——Descendants of, called Merarites:
Duties in the tabernacle, Num 3:35–37
Cities assigned to, Josh 21:7, 34–40
Duties in the temple, 1 Chr 26:10–19
Assist Ezra after exile, Ezra 8:18, 19

MERCHANDISE

perceives that her *m* ......Prov 31:18
house a house of *m* ....John 2:16

MERCHANTS

set it in a city of *m* ....Ezek 17:4
have multiplied your *m* ......Nah 3:16
m were the great men ....Rev 18:23

MERCIES

for His *m* are great ....2 Sam 24:14
and His tender *m* ....Ps 145:9
give you the sure *m* ....Acts 13:34
the Father of *m* ....2 Cor 1:3

MERCIFUL

LORD, the LORD God, *m* ......Ex 34:6
He is ever *m* ....Ps 37:26
God be *m* to us and ....Ps 67:1
Blessed are the *m* ....Matt 5:7
saying, 'God be *m* ....Luke 18:13
For I will be *m* ....Heb 8:12
compassionate and *m* ....James 5:11

MERCY

but showing *m* to ....Ex 20:6
and abundant in *m* ....Num 14:18
m endures forever ....1 Chr 16:34
to Your *m* remember me ....Ps 25:7
I trust in the *m* ....Ps 52:8
shall send forth His *m* ....Ps 57:3
You, O Lord, belongs *m* ......Ps 62:12
m ceased forever ....Ps 77:8
M and truth have met ....Ps 85:10
M shall be built ....Ps 89:2
m and truth go before ....Ps 89:14
m is everlasting ....Ps 100:5
I will sing of *m* ....Ps 101:1
For Your *m* is great ....Ps 108:4
is full of Your *m* ....Ps 119:64
the LORD there is *m* ....Ps 130:7
Let not *m* and truth ....Prov 3:3
who honors Him has *m* ....Prov 14:31
cruel and have no *m* ....Jer 6:23
Lord our God belong *m* ....Dan 9:9
For I desire *m* and not ....Hos 6:6
do justly, to love *m* ....Mic 6:8
'I desire *m* and not ....Matt 9:13
And His *m* is on those ....Luke 1:50
"I will have *m* ....Rom 9:15
of God who shows *m* ....Rom 9:16
that He might have *m* ....Rom 11:32
m has made trustworthy .....1 Cor 7:25
as we have received *m* ....2 Cor 4:1
God, who is rich in *m* ....Eph 2:4
but I obtained *m* ....1 Tim 1:13
that he may find *m* ....2 Tim 1:18
to His *m* He saved us ....Titus 3:5
that we may obtain *m* ....Heb 4:16
judgment is without *m* .....James 2:13
God, looking for the *m* ....Jude 21

MERIB-BAAL

Another name for Mephibosheth, 1 Chr 8:34

MERODACH

Supreme deity of the Babylonians, Jer 50:2
Otherwise called Bel, Is 46:1

MERODACH-BALADAN

Sends ambassadors to Hezekiah, Is 39:1–8
Also called Berodach-Baladan, 2 Kin 20:12

MEROZ

Town cursed for failing to help the Lord, Judg 5:23

MERRY

m heart makes a ....Prov 15:13
eat, drink, and be *m* ....Eccl 8:15
we should make *m* ....Luke 15:32

MESHACH

Name given to Mishael, Dan 1:7
Advanced to high position, Dan 2:49
Remains faithful in testing, Dan 3:13–30

MESHECH

Son of Japheth, Gen 10:2
His descendants, mentioned in prophecy, Ezek 27:13; 32:26; 38:2, 3

MESOPOTAMIA

Home of Abraham's relatives, Gen 24:4, 10, 15
Called Padan Aram and Syria, Gen 25:20; 31:20, 24
Israel enslaved to, Judg 3:8–10
Jews from, present at Pentecost, Acts 2:9

MESSAGE

I have heard a *m* ....Jer 49:14
For the *m* of the cross ......1 Cor 1:18

MESSENGER

is a faithful *m* ....Prov 25:13
"Behold, I send My *m* ....Mal 3:1
'Behold, I send My *m* ......Matt 11:10

MESSIAH

until *M* the Prince ....Dan 9:25
"We have found the *M* ......John 1:41

METHUSELAH

Oldest man on record, Gen 5:27

MICAH

Prophet, contemporary of Isaiah, Is 1:1; Mic 1:1

MICAIAH (or Michaiah)

Prophet who predicts Ahab's death, 1 Kin 22:8–28
——Contemporary of Jeremiah, Jer 36:11–13

MICHAEL

Chief prince, Dan 10:13, 21
Disputes with Satan, Jude 9
Fights the dragon, Rev 12:7–9

MICHAL

Daughter of King Saul, 1 Sam 14:49
Loves and marries David, 1 Sam 18:20–28
Saves David from Saul, 1 Sam 19:9–17
Given to Palti, 1 Sam 25:44
David demands her from Abner, 2 Sam 3:13–16
Ridicules David; becomes barren, 2 Sam 6:16–23

MICHMASH

Site of battle with Philistines, 1 Sam 13:5, 11, 16, 23
Scene of Jonathan's victory, 1 Sam 14:1–16

MIDIAN

Son of Abraham by Keturah, Gen 25:1–4
——Region in the Arabian desert occupied by the Midianites, Gen 25:6; Ex 2:15

MIDIANITES

Descendants of Abraham by Keturah, Gen 25:1, 2
Moses flees to, Ex 2:15
Join Moab in cursing Israel, Num 22:4–7
Intermarriage with incurs God's wrath, Num 25:1–18
Defeated by Israel, Num 31:1–10
Oppress Israel; defeated by Gideon, Judg 6; 7

MIDST

God is in the *m* ....Ps 46:5
that I am in the *m* ....Joel 2:27
I am there in the *m* ....Matt 18:20

MIGHT

'My power and the *m* ....Deut 8:17
shall speak of the *m* ....Ps 145:6
the greatness of His *m* ....Is 40:26
man glory in his *m* ....Jer 9:23
their *m* has failed ....Jer 51:30
'Not by *m* nor by ....Zech 4:6
in the power of His *m* ....Eph 6:10
greater in power and *m* .....2 Pet 2:11
honor and power and *m* ......Rev 7:12

MIGHTIER

coming after me is *m* ....Matt 3:11

MIGHTILY

to shake the earth *m* ....Is 2:19
which works in me *m* ....Col 1:29

MIGHTY

He was a *m* hunter ....Gen 10:9

for they are too *m* ....Num 22:6
How the *m* have fallen .....2 Sam 1:19
is wise in heart and *m* ....Job 9:4
The LORD *m* in battle ....Ps 24:8
their Redeemer is *m* ....Prov 23:11
Woe to men *m* at ....Is 5:22
great in counsel and *m* ....Jer 32:19
m men are made red ....Nah 2:3
m has done great ....Luke 1:49
He has put down the *m* .....Luke 1:52
the flesh, not many *m* .....1 Cor 1:26
the working of His *m* ....Eph 1:19
from heaven with His *m* ...2 Thess 1:7

MILCOM

Solomon went after, 1 Kin 11:5
Altar destroyed by Josiah, 2 Kin 23:12, 13

MILETUS

Paul meets Ephesian elders here, Acts 20:15–38
Paul leaves Trophimus here, 2 Tim 4:20

MILK

for water, she gave *m* ....Judg 5:25
honey and *m* are under .....Song 4:11
come, buy wine and *m* ....Is 55:1
and whiter than *m* ....Lam 4:7
shall flow with *m* ....Joel 3:18
have come to need *m* ....Heb 5:12
m is unskilled in the ....Heb 5:13
desire the pure *m* ....1 Pet 2:2

MILL

be grinding at the *m* ....Matt 24:41

MILLO

Fort at Jerusalem, 2 Sam 5:9
Prepared by Solomon, 1 Kin 9:15
Strengthened by Hezekiah, 2 Chr 32:5
Scene of Joash's death, 2 Kin 12:20, 21

MILLSTONE

m were hung around his .....Matt 18:6
a stone like a great *m* ....Rev 18:21

MIND

put wisdom in the *m* ....Job 38:36
perfect peace, whose *m* ....Is 26:3
nor have an anxious *m* .....Luke 12:29
m I myself serve the ....Rom 7:25
who has known the *m* ....Rom 11:34
Be of the same *m* ....Rom 12:16
convinced in his own *m* .....Rom 14:5
"who has known the *m* .....1 Cor 2:16
you are out of your *m* ......1 Cor 14:23
Let this *m* be in you ....Phil 2:5
to *m* your own ....1 Thess 4:11
love and of a sound *m* ....2 Tim 1:7

MINDFUL

is man that You are *m* ....Ps 8:4
The LORD has been *m* ....Ps 115:12
for you are not *m* ....Matt 16:23
is man that You are *m* ....Heb 2:6

MINDS

people change their *m* ....Ex 13:17
put My law in their *m* ....Jer 31:33
I stir up your pure *m* ....2 Pet 3:1
He who searches the *m* ....Rev 2:23

MINISTER

to make you a *m* ....Acts 26:16
for he is God's *m* ....Rom 13:4
you will be a good *m* ....1 Tim 4:6
a *M* of the sanctuary ....Heb 8:2

MINISTERED

But the child *m* ....1 Sam 2:11
a thousand thousands *m* ......Dan 7:10
As they *m* to the Lord ....Acts 13:2

MINISTERS

angels spirits, His *m* ....Ps 104:4
for they are God's *m* ....Rom 13:6
commend ourselves as *m* .....2 Cor 6:4
Are they *m* of Christ ....2 Cor 11:23
If anyone *m* ....1 Pet 4:11

MINISTRIES

are differences of *m* ....1 Cor 12:5

MINISTRY

I magnify my *m* ....Rom 11:13
But if the *m* of death ....2 Cor 3:7
since we have this *m* ....2 Cor 4:1
and has given us the *m* ......2 Cor 5:18
for the work of *m* ....Eph 4:12
m which you have ....Col 4:17
fulfill your *m* ....2 Tim 4:5
a more excellent *m* ....Heb 8:6

MINT

For you pay tithe of *m* .....Matt 23:23

MIRACLE

saying, 'Show a *m* ....Ex 7:9
no one who works a *m* ......Mark 9:39
that a notable *m* ....Acts 4:16

MIRACLES

God worked unusual *m* .....Acts 19:11
the working of *m* ....1 Cor 12:10
Are all workers of *m* ....1 Cor 12:29
with various *m* ....Heb 2:4

MIRIAM

Sister of Aaron and Moses, Num 26:59
Chosen by God; called a prophetess, Ex 15:20
Punished for rebellion, Num 12:1–16
Buried at Kadesh, Num 20:1

MIRTH

I will test you with *m* ....Eccl 2:1
is in the house of *m* ....Eccl 7:4
joy is darkened, the *m* ....Is 24:11

MISER

eat the bread of a *m* ....Prov 23:6

MISERIES

m that are coming ....James 5:1

MISERY

would forget your *m* ....Job 11:16
and remember his *m* ....Prov 31:7

MISTREATED

But the Egyptians *m* ....Deut 26:6
those who are *m* ....Heb 13:3

MISTREATS

m his father and ....Prov 19:26

MITES

widow putting in two *m* .....Luke 21:2

MIZPAH

Site of covenant between Jacob and Laban, Gen 31:44–53
—— Town of Benjamin; outraged Israelites gather here, Josh 18:21, 26; Judg 20:1, 3
Samuel gathers Israel, 1 Sam 7:5–16; 10:17–25
Residence of Gedaliah, 2 Kin 25:23, 25

MOAB

Son of Lot, Gen 19:33–37
—— Country of the Moabites, Deut 1:5

MOABITES

Descendants of Lot, Gen 19:36, 37
Join Midian in cursing Israel, Num 22:4
Excluded from Israel, Deut 23:3–6
Kindred of Ruth, Ruth 1:4
Subdued by Israel, 1 Sam 14:47; 2 Sam 8:2; 2 Kin 3:4–27
Women of, lead Solomon astray, 1 Kin 11:1–8
Prophecies concerning, Is 11:14; 15:1–9; Jer 48:1–47; Amos 2:1–3

MOAN

m sadly like doves ....Is 59:11

MOCK

I will *m* when your ....Prov 1:26
Fools *m* at sin ....Prov 14:9
to the Gentiles to *m* ....Matt 20:19

MOCKED

at noon, that Elijah *m* .....1 Kin 18:27
"I am one *m* by his ....Job 12:4
knee before Him and *m* .....Matt 27:29
deceived, God is not *m* ....Gal 6:7

MOCKER

Wine is a *m* ....Prov 20:1

MOCKERS

that there would be *m* ....Jude 18

MOCKINGS

others had trial of *m* ....Heb 11:36

MOCKS

He who *m* the poor ....Prov 17:5

MODERATION

with propriety and *m* ....1 Tim 2:9

MOLECH

God of the Ammonites; worshiped by Solomon, 1 Kin 11:7
Human sacrifice made to, Lev 18:21; 2 Kin 23:10

MOMENT

consume them in a *m* ....Num 16:21
In a *m* they die ....Job 34:20
face from you for a *m* ....Is 54:8
in a *m*, in the ....1 Cor 15:52
which is but for a *m* ....2 Cor 4:17

MONEY

does not put out his *m* ....Ps 15:5
m answers every ....Eccl 10:19
be redeemed without *m* ....Is 52:3
and you who have no *m* ....Is 55:1

of the *m* changers ....Matt 21:12
and hid his lord's *m* ....Matt 25:18
promised to give him *m* ...Mark 14:11
Carry neither *m* ....Luke 10:4
I sent you without *m* ......Luke 22:35
the *m* changers doing ......John 2:14
be purchased with *m* ....Acts 8:20
not greedy for *m* ....1 Tim 3:3
m is a root of all ....1 Tim 6:10
not greedy for *m* ....Titus 1:7

MONSTER

me up like a *m* ....Jer 51:34
of Egypt, O great *m* ....Ezek 29:3

MOON

until the *m* is no more ....Ps 72:7
morning, fair as the *m* ....Song 6:10
sun and *m* grow dark ....Joel 2:10
m will not give its ....Mark 13:24

MORDECAI

Esther's guardian; advises her, Esth 2:5–20
Reveals plot to kill the king, Esth 2:21–23
Refuses homage to Haman, Esth 3:1–6
Honored by the king, Esth 6:1–12
Exalted highly, Esth 8:15; 9:4
Institutes feast of Purim, Esth 9:20–31

MORIAH

God commands Abraham to sacrifice Isaac here, Gen 22:1–13
Site of Solomon's temple, 2 Chr 3:1

MORNING

the eyelids of the *m* ....Job 41:18
Evening and *m* and at ....Ps 55:17
the wings of the *m* ....Ps 139:9
looks forth as the *m* ....Song 6:10
Lucifer, son of the *m* ....Is 14:12
established as the *m* ....Hos 6:3
very early in the *m* ....Luke 24:1
the Bright and *M* Star ....Rev 22:16

MORSEL

or eaten my *m* by ....Job 31:17
Better is a dry *m* ....Prov 17:1
Esau, who for one *m* ....Heb 12:16

MORTAL

sin reign in your *m* ....Rom 6:12
and this *m* must put ....1 Cor 15:53

MORTALITY

m may be swallowed ....2 Cor 5:4

MORTALS

with idolatrous *m* ....Ps 26:4

MOSES

Born; hidden by mother; adopted by Pharaoh's daughter, Ex 2:1–10
Kills Egyptian and flees to Midian, Ex 2:11–22
Receives call from God, Ex 3:1—4:17
Returns to Israelites in Egypt, Ex 4:18–31
Wins Israel's deliverance with plagues, Ex 5:1—6:13; 6:28—11:10; 12:29–42
Leads Israel out of Egypt and through the Red Sea, Ex 13:17—14:31
His song of praise, Ex 15:1–18
Provides miraculously for the people, Ex 15:22—17:7
Appoints judges, Ex 18
Receives the law on Mount Sinai, Ex 19—23
Receives instructions for tabernacle, Ex 25—31
Intercedes for Israel's sin, Ex 32
Recommissioned and encouraged, Ex 33; 34
Further instructions and building of the tabernacle, Ex 35—40
Consecrates Aaron, Lev 8:1–36
Takes census, Num 1:1–54
Resumes journey to Canaan, Num 10:11–36
Complains; 70 elders appointed, Num 11:1–35
Intercedes for people when they refuse to enter Canaan, Num 14:11–25
Puts down Korah's rebellion, Num 16
Sins in anger, Num 20:1–13
Makes bronze serpent, Num 21:4–9
Travels toward Canaan, Num 21:10–20
Takes second census, Num 26
Commissions Joshua as his successor, Num 27:12–23
Receives further laws, Num 28—30
Commands conquest of Midian, Num 31
Final instructions, Num 32—36
Forbidden to enter Promised Land, Deut 3:23–28
Gives farewell messages, Deut 32; 33
Sees Promised Land; dies, Deut 34:1–7
Is mourned and extolled, Deut 34:8–12
Appears with Christ at Transfiguration, Matt 17:1–3

MOST

His mouth is *m* sweet ....Song 5:16
on your *m* holy faith ....Jude 20

MOTH

m will eat them ....Is 50:9
where *m* and rust ....Matt 6:19

MOTHER

because she was the *m* ....Gen 3:20
like a joyful *m* ....Ps 113:9
the only one of her *m* ....Song 6:9
m might have been my ......Jer 20:17
leave his father and *m* ....Matt 19:5
"Behold your *m* ....John 19:27
free, which is the *m* ....Gal 4:26
The *M* of Harlots ....Rev 17:5

MOUNT

come up to *M* Sinai ....Ex 19:23
you like *M* Carmel ....Song 7:5
they shall *m* up with ....Is 40:31
for this Hagar is *M* ....Gal 4:25

MOUNT CARMEL

Prophets gather at, 1 Kin 18:19, 20
Elisha journeys to, 2 Kin 2:25
Shunammite woman comes to Elisha at, 2 Kin 4:25

MOUNT EBAL

Cursed by God, Deut 11:29
Joshua builds an altar on, Josh 8:30

MOUNT GERIZIM

Mount of blessing, Deut 11:29; 27:12
Jotham speaks to people of Shechem here, Judg 9:7
Samaritans' sacred mountain, John 4:20, 21

MOUNT GILBOA

Men of Israel slain at, 1 Sam 31:1
Saul and his sons slain at, 1 Sam 31:8

MOUNT GILEAD

Gideon divides the people for battle at, Judg 7:3

MOUNT HOR

Lord speaks to Moses and Aaron on, Num 20:23
Aaron dies on, Num 20:25–28

MOUNT HOREB

Sons of Israel stripped of ornaments at, Ex 33:6
The same as Sinai, Ex 3:1

MOUNT OF OLIVES

See OLIVES, MOUNT OF

MOUNT SINAI

Lord descends upon, in fire, Ex 19:18
Lord calls Moses to the top of, Ex 19:20
The glory of the Lord rests on, for six days, Ex 24:16

MOUNT TABOR

Deborah sends Barak there to defeat Canaanites, Judg 4:6–14

MOUNT ZION

Survivors shall go out from, 2 Kin 19:31

MOUNTAIN

to Horeb, the *m* ....Ex 3:1
"But as a *m* falls ....Job 14:18
You have made my *m* ....Ps 30:7
of many peaks is the *m* ....Ps 68:15
let us go up to the *m* ....Is 2:3
image became a great *m* ......Dan 2:35
Who are you, O great *m* ......Zech 4:7
you will say to this *m* ....Matt 17:20
with Him on the holy *m* .....2 Pet 1:18

MOUNTAINS

He removes the *m* ....Job 9:5
Surely the *m* yield ....Job 40:20
m will bring peace ....Ps 72:3
excellent than the *m* ....Ps 76:4
m were brought forth ....Ps 90:2
m melt like wax at the ....Ps 97:5
m skipped like rams ....Ps 114:4
m surround Jerusalem ....Ps 125:2
m shall depart and the ....Is 54:10
in Judea flee to the *m* ....Matt 24:16
that I could remove *m* ......1 Cor 13:2
m were not found ....Rev 16:20

MOURN

and you *m* at last ....Prov 5:11
a time to *m* ....Eccl 3:4
are those who *m* ....Matt 5:4
Lament and *m* and weep ......James 4:9
of the earth will *m* ....Rev 1:7

MOURNED

we *m* to you ....Matt 11:17
and have not rather *m* ....1 Cor 5:2

MOURNING

This is a deep *m* ....Gen 50:11
m all the day long ....Ps 38:6
m shall be ended ....Is 60:20

men break bread in *m* ....Jer 16:7
I will turn their *m* ....Jer 31:13
shall be a great *m* ....Zech 12:11
be turned to *m* and ....James 4:9

MOURNS

heavily, as one who *m* ....Ps 35:14
The earth *m* and fades ....Is 24:4
for Him as one *m* ....Zech 12:10

MOUTH

"Who has made man's *m* ......Ex 4:11
Out of the *m* of babes ....Ps 8:2
The *m* of the righteous ....Ps 37:30
m shall speak wisdom ....Ps 49:3
iniquity stops its *m* ....Ps 107:42
knowledge, but the *m* ....Prov 10:14
m preserves his life ....Prov 13:3
The *m* of an immoral ....Prov 22:14
and a flattering *m* ....Prov 26:28
m speaking pompous ....Dan 7:8
the doors of your *m* ....Mic 7:5
m defiles a man ....Matt 15:11
m I will judge you ....Luke 19:22
I will give you a *m* ....Luke 21:15
m confession is made ....Rom 10:10
m great swelling words ....Jude 16
vomit you out of My *m* ....Rev 3:16

MOVE

and the earth will *m* ....Is 13:13
the mountain shall *m* ....Zech 14:4
in Him we live and *m* ....Acts 17:28

MOVED

shall never be *m* ....Ps 15:5
she shall not be *m* ....Ps 46:5
spoke as they were *m* ....2 Pet 1:21

MUCH

m study is ....Eccl 12:12
m better than wine is ....Song 4:10
to whom *m* is given ....Luke 12:48
M more then ....Rom 5:9

MULTIPLIED

sorrows shall be *m* ....Ps 16:4
of the disciples *m* ....Acts 6:7
word of God grew and *m* ...Acts 12:24

MULTIPLY

"Be fruitful and *m* ....Gen 1:22
m your descendants ....Gen 16:10
m my days as the ....Job 29:18
m the descendants ....Jer 33:22

MULTITUDE

stars of heaven in *m* ....Deut 1:10
Your house in the *m* ....Ps 5:7
m that kept a pilgrim ....Ps 42:4
In the *m* of words sin ....Prov 10:19
In a *m* of people is a ....Prov 14:28
compassion on the *m* ....Matt 15:32
with the angel a *m* ....Luke 2:13
"love will cover a *m* ....1 Pet 4:8
and behold, a great *m* ....Rev 7:9

MURDER

"You shall not *m* ....Ex 20:13
'You shall not *m* ....Matt 5:21
threats and *m* against ....Acts 9:1
You *m* and covet and ....James 4:2

MURDERED

sons of those who *m* ....Matt 23:31
Jesus whom you *m* ....Acts 5:30
one and *m* his brother .....1 John 3:12

MURDERER

He was a *m* from the ....John 8:44
and asked for a *m* ....Acts 3:14
of you suffer as a *m* ....1 Pet 4:15
his brother is a *m* ....1 John 3:15

MURDERERS

in it, but now *m* ....Is 1:21
and profane, for *m* ....1 Tim 1:9
abominable, *m* ....Rev 21:8

MURDERS

evil thoughts, *m* ....Matt 15:19
envy, *m*, drunkenness ....Gal 5:21

MUSIC

So David played *m* ....1 Sam 18:10
m are brought low ....Eccl 12:4
the house, he heard *m* .....Luke 15:25

MUSING

while I was *m* ....Ps 39:3

MUTE

Or who makes the *m* ....Ex 4:11
m who does not open ....Ps 38:13
I was *m* with silence ....Ps 39:2
I was *m* ....Ps 39:9

MUTILATION

beware of the *m* ....Phil 3:2

MUTUAL

by the *m* faith both ....Rom 1:12

MUZZLE

"You shall not *m* ....Deut 25:4
"You shall not *m* ....1 Tim 5:18

MYSTERIES

to you to know the *m* ....Matt 13:11
and understand all *m* ....1 Cor 13:2
the spirit he speaks *m* ....1 Cor 14:2

MYSTERIOUS

today is not too *m* ....Deut 30:11

MYSTERY

given to know the *m* ....Mark 4:11
wisdom of God in a *m* ....1 Cor 2:7
Behold, I tell you a *m* .....1 Cor 15:51
made known to us the *m* ....Eph 1:9
This is a great *m* ....Eph 5:32
m which has been ....Col 1:26
the *m* of godliness ....1 Tim 3:16

— N —

NAAMAN

Captain in the Syrian army, 2 Kin 5:1–11
Healed of his leprosy, 2 Kin 5:14–17
Referred to by Christ, Luke 4:27

NABAL

Refuses David's request, 1 Sam 25:2–12
Escapes David's wrath but dies of a stroke, 1 Sam 25:13–39

NABOTH

Murdered for his vineyard by King Ahab, 1 Kin 21:1–16
His murder avenged, 1 Kin 21:17–25

NADAB

Eldest of Aaron's four sons, Ex 6:23
Takes part in affirming covenant, Ex 24:1, 9–12
Becomes priest, Ex 28:1
Consumed by fire, Lev 10:1–7
——— King of Israel, 1 Kin 14:20
Killed by Baasha, 1 Kin 15:25–31

NAHASH

King of Ammon; makes impossible demands, 1 Sam 11:1–15

NAHOR

Grandfather of Abraham, Gen 11:24–26
——— Son of Terah, brother of Abraham, Gen 11:17

NAHUM

Inspired prophet to Judah concerning Nineveh, Nah 1:1

NAILED

n it to the cross ....Col 2:14

NAIN

Village south of Nazareth; Jesus raises widow's son here, Luke 7:11–17

NAIOTH

Prophets' school in Ramah, 1 Sam 19:18, 19, 22, 23

NAKED

And they were both *n* ....Gen 2:25
knew that they were *n* ....Gen 3:7
"*N* I came from my ....Job 1:21
Isaiah has walked *n* ....Is 20:3
I was *n* and you ....Matt 25:36
and fled from them *n* ....Mark 14:52
shall not be found *n* ....2 Cor 5:3
but all things are *n* ....Heb 4:13
brother or sister is *n* ....James 2:15
poor, blind, and *n* ....Rev 3:17

NAKEDNESS

of Canaan, saw the *n* ....Gen 9:22
or famine, or *n* ....Rom 8:35
often, in cold and *n* ....2 Cor 11:27
n may not be revealed ....Rev 3:18

NAME

Abram called on the *n* ....Gen 13:4
Israel shall be your *n* ....Gen 35:10
This is My *n* forever ....Ex 3:15
shall not take the *n* ....Ex 20:7
are called by the *n* ....Deut 28:10
glorious and awesome *n* ....Deut 28:58
by My *n* will humble ....2 Chr 7:14
and he has no *n* ....Job 18:17
excellent is Your *n* ....Ps 8:1
n will put their trust ....Ps 9:10
be His glorious *n* ....Ps 72:19
n is great in Israel ....Ps 76:1
do not call on Your *n* ....Ps 79:6
to Your *n* give glory ....Ps 115:1
above all Your *n* ....Ps 138:2
He calls them all by *n* ....Ps 147:4
The *n* of the LORD is a ....Prov 18:10
A good *n* is to be ....Prov 22:1
what is His Son's *n* ....Prov 30:4
make mention of Your *n* ....Is 26:13
the LORD, that is My *n* ....Is 42:8

be to the LORD for a *n* ....Is 55:13
be called by a new *n* ....Is 62:2
Everlasting is Your *n* ....Is 63:16
who calls on Your *n* ....Is 64:7
it shall be to Me a *n* ....Jer 33:9
and made Yourself a *n* ....Dan 9:15
we will walk in the *n* ....Mic 4:5
They will call on My *n* ......Zech 13:9
n shall be great ....Mal 1:11
to you who fear My *n* ....Mal 4:2
you shall call His *n* ....Matt 1:21
hallowed be Your *n* ....Matt 6:9
prophesied in Your *n* ....Matt 7:22
righteous man in the *n* .....Matt 10:41
n Gentiles will trust ....Matt 12:21
together in My *n* ....Matt 18:20
will come in My *n* ....Matt 24:5
"My *n* is Legion ....Mark 5:9
The virgin's *n* was ....Luke 1:27
"His *n* is John ....Luke 1:63
and cast out your *n* ....Luke 6:22
who believe in His *n* ....John 1:12
comes in his own *n* ....John 5:43
his own sheep by *n* ....John 10:3
through faith in His *n* ....Acts 3:16
there is no other *n* ....Acts 4:12
suffer shame for His *n* ....Acts 5:41
which is above every *n* ....Phil 2:9
deed, do all in the *n* ....Col 3:17
a more excellent *n* ....Heb 1:4
blaspheme that noble *n* .....James 2:7
reproached for the *n* ....1 Pet 4:14
you hold fast to My *n* ....Rev 2:13
n that you are alive ....Rev 3:1
having His Father's *n* ....Rev 14:1
and glorify Your *n* ....Rev 15:4
n written that no one ....Rev 19:12

NAME'S

saved them for His *n* ....Ps 106:8
forgiven you for His *n* .....1 John 2:12

NAMED

let my name be *n* ....Gen 48:16
I have *n* you ....Is 45:4

NAOMI

Widow of Elimelech, Ruth 1:1–3
Returns to Bethlehem with Ruth, Ruth 1:14–19
Arranges Ruth's marriage to Boaz, Ruth 3; 4

NAPHTALI

Son of Jacob by Bilhah, Gen 30:1–8
Receives Jacob's blessing, Gen 49:21, 28
——Tribe of:
Numbered, Num 1:42, 43
Territory assigned to, Josh 19:32–39
Joins Gideon's army, Judg 7:23
Attacked by Ben-Hadad and Tiglath-Pileser, 1 Kin 15:20; 2 Kin 15:29
Prophecy of great light in; fulfilled in Christ's ministry, Is 9:1–7; Matt 4:12–16

NARROW

"Enter by the *n* gate ....Matt 7:13
n is the gate and ....Matt 7:14

NATHAN

Son of David, 2 Sam 5:14
Mary's lineage traced through, Zech 12:12
——Prophet under David and Solomon, 1 Chr 29:29
Reveals God's plan to David, 2 Sam 7:2–29
Rebukes David's sin, 2 Sam 12:1–15
Reveals Adonijah's plot, 1 Kin 1:10–46

NATHANAEL

One of Christ's disciples, John 1:45–51

NATION

make you a great *n* ....Gen 12:2
You slay a righteous *n* ....Gen 20:4
priests and a holy *n* ....Ex 19:6
dealt thus with any *n* ....Ps 147:20
exalts a *n* ....Prov 14:34
lift up sword against *n* ....Is 2:4
that the righteous *n* ....Is 26:2
a small one a strong *n* ....Is 60:22
n that was not called ....Is 65:1
n changed its gods ....Jer 2:11
I will make them one *n* .....Ezek 37:22
since there was a *n* ....Dan 12:1
n will rise against ....Matt 24:7
for he loves our *n* ....Luke 7:5
those who are not a *n* ......Rom 10:19
tribe, tongue, and *n* ....Rev 13:7

NATIONS

itself among the *n* ....Num 23:9
Why do the *n* rage ....Ps 2:1
I will give You the *n* ....Ps 2:8
n shall serve Him ....Ps 72:11
n shall call Him ....Ps 72:17
n shall fear the name ....Ps 102:15
is high above all *n* ....Ps 113:4
All *n* before Him are ....Is 40:17
n who do not know ....Is 55:5
the wise men of the *n* ....Jer 10:7
n shall be joined ....Zech 2:11
disciples of all the *n* ....Matt 28:19
who was to rule all *n* ....Rev 12:5
the healing of the *n* ....Rev 22:2

NATURAL

women exchanged the *n* .....Rom 1:26
the men, leaving the *n* ....Rom 1:27
did not spare the *n* ....Rom 11:21
n man does not receive ......1 Cor 2:14
It is sown a *n* body ....1 Cor 15:44
not first, but the *n* ....1 Cor 15:46

NATURE

for what is against *n* ....Rom 1:26
n itself teach you ....1 Cor 11:14
We who are Jews by *n* ....Gal 2:15
by *n* children of wrath ....Eph 2:3
of the divine *n* ....2 Pet 1:4

NAZARENE

Jesus to be called, Matt 2:23
Descriptive of Jesus' followers, Acts 24:5

NAZARETH

Town in Galilee; considered obscure, John 1:46
City of Jesus' parents, Matt 2:23
Early home of Jesus, Luke 2:39–51
Jesus rejected by, Luke 4:16–30

NEAR

that has God so *n* to it ....Deut 4:7
But the word is very *n* .....Deut 30:14
The LORD is *n* to all ....Ps 145:18
upon Him while He is *n* ....Is 55:6
know that it is *n* ....Matt 24:33
kingdom of God is *n* ....Luke 21:31
"The word is *n* ....Rom 10:8
to those who were *n* ....Eph 2:17
for the time is *n* ....Rev 1:3

NEARER

now our salvation is *n* ....Rom 13:11

NEBO

Babylonian god, Is 46:1
—— Summit of Pisgah; Moses dies here, Deut 32:49; 34:1, 5

NEBUCHADNEZZAR

Monarch of the Neo-Babylonian Empire (605–562 B.C.); carries Jews captive to Babylon, Dan 1:1–3
Crushes Jehoiachin's revolt, 2 Kin 24:10–17
Destroys Jerusalem; captures Zedekiah, Jer 39:5–8
Prophecies concerning, Is 14:4–27; Jer 21:7–10; 25:8, 9; 27:4–11; 32:28–36; 43:10–13; Ezek 26:7–12

NEBUZARADAN

Nebuchadnezzar's captain at siege of Jerusalem, 2 Kin 25:8–20
Protects Jeremiah, Jer 39:11–14

NECESSARY

mouth more than my *n* ......Job 23:12
and thus it was *n* ....Luke 24:46
burden than these *n* ....Acts 15:28
I found it *n* to write ....Jude 3

NECESSITIES

have provided for my *n* .....Acts 20:34
and again for my *n* ....Phil 4:16

NECESSITY

n is laid upon me ....1 Cor 9:16
not grudgingly or of *n* ....2 Cor 9:7

NECK

smooth part of his *n* ....Gen 27:16
and grace to your *n* ....Prov 3:22
n was an iron sinew ....Is 48:4
were hung around his *n* .....Matt 18:6
ran and fell on his *n* ....Luke 15:20

NECKS

stiffened their *n* ....Neh 9:29
with outstretched *n* ....Is 3:16
who risked their own *n* ....Rom 16:4

NEED

in nakedness, and in *n* .....Deut 28:48
a prowler, and your *n* ....Prov 24:34
the things you have *n* ....Matt 6:8
'The Lord has *n* ....Matt 21:3
each as anyone had *n* ....Acts 4:35
hand, "I have no *n* ....1 Cor 12:21
who ministered to my *n* ....Phil 2:25
supply all your *n* ....Phil 4:19
to help in time of *n* ....Heb 4:16
sees his brother in *n* ....1 John 3:17
The city had no *n* ....Rev 21:23

NEEDY

your poor and your *n* ......Deut 15:11
They push the *n* ....Job 24:4
n shall not always be ....Ps 9:18
He will deliver the *n* ....Ps 72:12
and lifts the *n* ....Ps 113:7

to rob the *n* of ....Is 10:2
n will lie down in ....Is 14:30
a strength to the *n* ....Is 25:4

NEGLECT

n the gift that is ....1 Tim 4:14
if we *n* so great a ....Heb 2:3

NEGLECTED

n the weightier ....Matt 23:23
their widows were *n* ....Acts 6:1

NEHEMIAH

Jewish cupbearer to King Artaxerxes; prays for restoration of Jerusalem, Neh 1:4–11
King commissions him to rebuild walls, Neh 2:1–8
Overcomes opposition and accomplishes rebuilding, Neh 4—6
Appointed governor, Neh 5:14
Participates with Ezra in restored worship, Neh 8—10
Registers the people and the priests and Levites, Neh 11:1—12:26
Dedicates the wall, Neh 12:27–43
Returns to Jerusalem after absence and institutes reforms, Neh 13:4–31

NEIGHBOR

you shall love your *n* ....Lev 19:18
for better is a *n* ....Prov 27:10
every man teach his *n* ....Jer 31:34
gives drink to his *n* ....Hab 2:15
'You shall love your *n* ....Matt 5:43
"And who is my *n* ....Luke 10:29
"You shall love your *n* ....Rom 13:9

NEST

and make its *n* ....Job 39:27
n is a man who wanders ......Prov 27:8
though you set your *n* ....Obad 4
that he may set his *n* ....Hab 2:9

NET

me with His *n* ....Job 19:6
have hidden their *n* ....Ps 35:7
They have prepared a *n* ....Ps 57:6
an antelope in a *n* ....Is 51:20
catch in their *n* ....Hab 1:15
I will let down the *n* ....Luke 5:5
to them, "Cast the *n* ....John 21:6

NETHINIM

Servants of the Levites, Ezra 8:20
Possible origins of:
Gibeonites, Josh 9:23–27
Solomon's forced laborers, 1 Kin 9:20, 21
Mentioned, 1 Chr 9:2; Ezra 2:43–54; 7:24; 8:17; Neh 3:31; 7:46–60, 73; 10:28, 29; 11:21

NEVER

in Me shall *n* thirst ....John 6:35
in Me shall *n* die ....John 11:26
Love *n* fails ....1 Cor 13:8
n take away sins ....Heb 10:11
"I will *n* leave you ....Heb 13:5
prophecy *n* came by ....2 Pet 1:21

NEW

Now there arose a *n* ....Ex 1:8
the LORD creates a *n* ....Num 16:30
They chose *n* gods ....Judg 5:8
and there is nothing *n* ....Eccl 1:9
Behold, I will do a *n* ....Is 43:19
For behold, I create *n* ....Is 65:17
when I will make a *n* ....Jer 31:31
n every morning ....Lam 3:23
wine into *n* wineskins ....Matt 9:17
of the *n* covenant ....Matt 26:28
n commandment I give ....John 13:34
tell or to hear some *n* ....Acts 17:21
he is a *n* creation ....2 Cor 5:17
n man who is renewed ....Col 3:10
when I will make a *n* ....Heb 8:8
n heavens and a *n* ....2 Pet 3:13
n name written which ....Rev 2:17
And they sang a *n* ....Rev 5:9
And I saw a *n* heaven ....Rev 21:1
I make all things *n* ....Rev 21:5

NEWNESS

also should walk in *n* ....Rom 6:4
should serve in the *n* ....Rom 7:6

NEWS

heard this bad *n* ....Ex 33:4
soul, so is good *n* ....Prov 25:25
him who brings good *n* ....Is 52:7

NICANOR

One of the first seven deacons, Acts 6:1–5

NICODEMUS

Pharisee; converses with Jesus, John 3:1–12
Protests unfairness of Christ's trial, John 7:50–52
Brings gifts to anoint Christ's body, John 19:39, 40

NICOLAITANS

Group teaching moral laxity, Rev 2:6–15

NICOLAS

One of the first seven deacons, Acts 6:5

NIGHT

darkness He called *N* ....Gen 1:5
It is a *n* of solemn ....Ex 12:42
pillar of fire by *n* ....Ex 13:22
and the *n* be ended ....Job 7:4
gives songs in the *n* ....Job 35:10
n reveals knowledge ....Ps 19:2
awake through the *n* ....Ps 119:148
and stars to rule by *n* ....Ps 136:9
desired You in the *n* ....Is 26:9
and perished in a *n* ....Jon 4:10
and continued all *n* ....Luke 6:12
man came to Jesus by *n* ....John 3:2
n is coming when no ....John 9:4
came to Jesus by *n* ....John 19:39
The *n* is far spent ....Rom 13:12
as a thief in the *n* ....1 Thess 5:2
We are not of the *n* ....1 Thess 5:5
there shall be no *n* ....Rev 21:25
there shall be no *n* ....Rev 22:5

NILE

Hebrew children drowned in, Ex 1:22
Moses hidden in, Ex 2:3–10
Water of, turned to blood, Ex 7:14–21
Mentioned in prophecies, Is 19:5–8; 23:3; 27:12; Jer 46:7–9; Amos 9:5

NIMROD

Ham's grandson, Gen 10:6–12

NINE

where are the *n* ....Luke 17:17

NINETY-NINE

he not leave the *n* ....Matt 18:12
n just persons ....Luke 15:7

NINEVEH

Capital of Assyria, 2 Kin 19:36
Jonah preaches to; people repent, Jon 3:1–10; Matt 12:41
Prophecy against, Nah 2:13—3:19; Zeph 2:13–15

NOAH

Son of Lamech, Gen 5:28–32
Finds favor with God; commissioned to build the ark, Gen 6:8–22
Fills ark and survives flood, Gen 7
Leaves ark; builds altar; receives God's promise, Gen 8
God's covenant with, Gen 9:1–17
Blesses and curses his sons; dies, Gen 9:18–29

NO AMON (or Thebes)

Nineveh compared to, Nah 3:8

NOB

City of priests; David flees to, 1 Sam 21:1–9
Priests of, killed by Saul, 1 Sam 22:9–23

NOBLE

whatever things are *n* ....Phil 4:8
not blaspheme that *n* ....James 2:7

NOBLES

voice of *n* was hushed ....Job 29:10
king is the son of *n* ....Eccl 10:17
n have sent their lads ....Jer 14:3
your *n* rest in the ....Nah 3:18

NOD

Place (east of Eden) of Cain's exile, Gen 4:16, 17

NOISE

The *n* of a multitude ....Is 13:4
people who make a *n* ....Is 17:12
of Egypt, is but a *n* ....Jer 46:17
They have made a *n* ....Lam 2:7
away with a great *n* ....2 Pet 3:10

NOSTRILS

n the breath of life ....Gen 2:7
breath of God in my *n* ....Job 27:3
breath is in his *n* ....Is 2:22

NOTE

urge you, brethren, *n* ....Rom 16:17
n those who so walk ....Phil 3:17

NOTHING

For now you are *n* ....Job 6:21
rich, yet has *n* ....Prov 13:7
"It is good for *n* ....Prov 20:14
before Him are as *n* ....Is 40:17
their works are *n* ....Is 41:29
I can of Myself do *n* ....John 5:30
Me you can do *n* ....John 15:5
men, it will come to *n* ....Acts 5:38
bring to *n* the things ....1 Cor 1:28

sitting at the tax *o* ....Matt 9:9

OFFICERS

also make your *o* ....Is 60:17

OFFSCOURING

You have made us an *o* .....Lam 3:45
the *o* of all things ....1 Cor 4:13

OFFSPRING

My blessing on your *o* ....Is 44:3
He seeks godly *o* ....Mal 2:15
wife and raise up *o* ....Matt 22:24
For we are also His *o* ....Acts 17:28
am the Root and the *O* ....Rev 22:16

OFTEN

o I wanted to gather ....Luke 13:34
as *o* as you eat this ....1 Cor 11:26
in sleeplessness *o* ....2 Cor 11:27
should offer Himself *o* ....Heb 9:25

OG

Amorite king of Bashan, Deut 3:1–13
Defeated and killed by Israel, Num 21:32–35

OHOLAH

Symbolic name of Samaria, Ezek 23:4, 5, 36

OIL

for the anointing *o* ....Ex 25:6
I cease giving my *o* ....Judg 9:9
a bin, and a little *o* ....1 Kin 17:12
poured out rivers of *o* ....Job 29:6
anointed with fresh *o* ....Ps 92:10
the heart of man, *o* ....Ps 104:15
like the precious *o* ....Ps 133:2
be as excellent *o* ....Ps 141:5
thousand rivers of *o* ....Mic 6:7
very costly fragrant *o* ....Matt 26:7
o might have been sold ....Matt 26:9
anointing him with *o* ....James 5:14
and do not harm the *o* ....Rev 6:6

OINTMENT

O and perfume delight ....Prov 27:9
your name is *o* ....Song 1:3

OLD

young, and now am *o* ....Ps 37:25
all manner, new and *o* ....Song 7:13
was said to those of *o* ....Matt 5:21
yet fifty years *o* ....John 8:57
but when you are *o* ....John 21:18
Your *o* men shall dream ....Acts 2:17
o man was crucified ....Rom 6:6
of the *O* Testament ....2 Cor 3:14
o things have passed ....2 Cor 5:17
have put off the *o* man ....Col 3:9
obsolete and growing *o* ......Heb 8:13
that serpent of *o* ....Rev 20:2

OLDER

o shall serve the ....Gen 25:23
o than your father ....Job 15:10
"Now his *o* son was ....Luke 15:25
not rebuke an *o* man ....1 Tim 5:1
o women as mothers ....1 Tim 5:2

OLDEST

beginning with the *o* ....John 8:9

OLIVE

a freshly plucked *o* ....Gen 8:11
I am like a green *o* ....Ps 52:8
of the *o* may fail ....Hab 3:17
o tree which is wild ....Rom 11:24

OLIVES, MOUNT OF

David flees to, 2 Sam 15:30
Prophecy concerning, Zech 14:4
Christ's triumphal entry from, Matt 21:1
Prophetic discourse delivered from, Matt 24:3
Christ's ascension from, Acts 1:9–12

OMNIPOTENT

For the Lord God *O* ....Rev 19:6

OMRI

Made king of Israel by army, 1 Kin 16:16, 21, 22
Builds Samaria; reigns wickedly, 1 Kin 16:23–27

ON

City of Lower Egypt; center of sun worship, Gen 41:45, 50
Called Beth Shemesh, Jer 43:13

ONAN

Second son of Judah; slain for failure to give his brother an heir, Gen 38:8–10

ONCE

died, He died to sin *o* ....Rom 6:10
for men to die *o* ....Heb 9:27
also suffered *o* ....1 Pet 3:18

ONE

God may speak in *o* way .....Job 33:14
Two are better than *o* ....Eccl 4:9
you will be gathered *o* ....Is 27:12
"*O* thing you lack ....Mark 10:21
o thing is needed ....Luke 10:42
I and My Father are *o* .....John 10:30
Me, that they may be *o* .....John 17:11
o accord in the temple ....Acts 2:46
for you are all *o* ....Gal 3:28
to create in Himself *o* ....Eph 2:15
o body and *o* Spirit ....Eph 4:4
o hope of your calling ....Eph 4:4
o Lord, *o* faith, *o* ....Eph 4:5
o God and Father of ....Eph 4:6
For there is *o* God and ....1 Tim 2:5
o Mediator between God ......1 Tim 2:5
the husband of *o* wife ....1 Tim 3:2
a thousand years as *o* ....2 Pet 3:8
and these three are *o* ....1 John 5:7

ONESIMUS

Slave of Philemon converted by Paul in Rome, Philem 10–17
With Tychicus, carries Paul's letters to Colosse and to Philemon, Col 4:7–9

ONESIPHORUS

Ephesian Christian commended for his service, 2 Tim 1:16–18

OPEN

o His lips against you ....Job 11:5
You *o* Your hand ....Ps 104:28
O your mouth for the ....Prov 31:8
and no one shall *o* ....Is 22:22
a lamb in *o* country ....Hos 4:16
Can a demon *o* the eyes ....John 10:21
our heart is wide *o* ....2 Cor 6:11
things are naked and *o* ......Heb 4:13
o the scroll and to ....Rev 5:2

OPENED

o not His mouth ....Is 53:7
Then their eyes were *o* ....Luke 24:31
o the Scriptures ....Luke 24:32
o their understanding ......Luke 24:45
effective door has *o* ....1 Cor 16:9
when the Lamb *o* ....Rev 6:1
Now I saw heaven *o* ....Rev 19:11

OPENS

o the ears of men ....Job 33:16
The LORD *o* the eyes of ......Ps 146:8
him the doorkeeper *o* ....John 10:3
and shuts and no one *o* ....Rev 3:7

OPHIR

Famous for gold, 1 Chr 29:4

OPHRAH

Town in Manasseh; home of Gideon, Judg 6:11, 15
Site of Gideon's burial, Judg 8:32

OPINION

dared not declare my *o* ....Job 32:6
be wise in your own *o* ......Rom 11:25

OPINIONS

falter between two *o* ....1 Kin 18:21

OPPORTUNITY

But sin, taking *o* ....Rom 7:8
as we have *o* ....Gal 6:10
but you lacked *o* ....Phil 4:10
they would have had *o* ......Heb 11:15

OPPOSES

who *o* and exalts ....2 Thess 2:4

OPPRESS

you shall not *o* ....Lev 25:17
You that You should *o* ....Job 10:3
He does not *o* ....Job 37:23
he loves to *o* ....Hos 12:7
o the widow or the ....Zech 7:10
Do not the rich *o* ....James 2:6

OPPRESSED

Whom have I *o* ....1 Sam 12:3
For he has *o* and ....Job 20:19
fatherless and the *o* ....Ps 10:18
for all who are *o* ....Ps 103:6
The tears of the *o* ....Eccl 4:1
He was *o* and He was ....Is 53:7
her midst, and the *o* ....Amos 3:9
healing all who were *o* .....Acts 10:38
Lot, who was *o* by ....2 Pet 2:7

OPPRESSES

o the poor reproaches ......Prov 14:31
o the poor to increase ......Prov 22:16
A poor man who *o* ....Prov 28:3

OPPRESSION

have surely seen the *o* ....Ex 3:7
"For the *o* of the ....Ps 12:5
Do not trust in *o* ....Ps 62:10
their life from *o* ....Ps 72:14
brought low through *o* ......Ps 107:39
Redeem me from the *o* ....Ps 119:134
considered all the *o* ....Eccl 4:1
o destroys a wise ....Eccl 7:7

justice, but behold, o ....Is 5:7
surely seen the o ....Acts 7:34

OPPRESSIONS

of o they cry out ....Job 35:9

OPPRESSOR

the voice of the o ....Job 3:18
Do not envy the o ....Prov 3:31
is a great o ....Prov 28:16
of the fury of the o ....Is 51:13
No more shall an o ....Zech 9:8

OPPRESSORS

not leave me to my o ....Ps 119:121
o there is power ....Eccl 4:1

ORACLES

received the living o ....Acts 7:38
were committed the o ....Rom 3:2
principles of the o ....Heb 5:12
let him speak as the o ....1 Pet 4:11

ORDAINED

infants You have o.............Ps 8:2
o you a prophet ....Jer 1:5
the Man whom He has o....Acts 17:31

ORDER

'Set your house in o ....2 Kin 20:1
set your words in o ....Job 33:5
you, and set them in o ....Ps 50:21
swept, and put in o..........Matt 12:44
done decently and in o.....1 Cor 14:40
each one in his own o ....1 Cor 15:23
to see your good o ....Col 2:5
according to the o ....Heb 5:6

ORDERS

o his conduct aright I..........Ps 50:23

ORDINANCE

resists the o of God ....Rom 13:2
yourselves to every o........1 Pet 2:13

ORDINANCES

Do you know the o..........Job 38:33
"If those o depart ....Jer 31:36
not appointed the o ....Jer 33:25
gone away from My o.........Mal 3:7
and fleshly o imposed.........Heb 9:10

ORION

Brilliant constellation, Job 9:9

ORNAMENT

will be a graceful o ....Prov 1:9
of gold and an o ....Prov 25:12
with them all as an o ....Is 49:18

ORNAMENTS

a virgin forget her o..........Jer 2:32

ORPAH

Ruth's sister-in-law, Ruth 1:4, 14

ORPHANS

We have become o............Lam 5:3
I will not leave you o ......John 14:18
to visit o and widows ......James 1:27

OSNAPPER

Called "the great and noble," Ezra 4:10

OSTRICHES

o will dwell there ....Is 13:21

is cruel, like o ....Lam 4:3
a mourning like the o ....Mic 1:8

OTHNIEL

Son of Kenaz, Caleb's youngest brother, Judg 1:13
Captures Kirjath Sepher; receives Caleb's daughter as wife, Josh 15:15–17
First judge of Israel, Judg 3:9–11

OUGHT

what Israel o to do ....1 Chr 12:32
These you o to have ....Matt 23:23
pray for as we o ....Rom 8:26
how you o to conduct ......1 Tim 3:15
which they o not ....1 Tim 5:13
persons o you to be ....2 Pet 3:11

OUTCAST

they called you an o ....Jer 30:17

OUTCASTS

gathers together the o ....Ps 147:2
will assemble the o ....Is 11:12
hide the o ....Is 16:3
Let My o dwell with ....Is 16:4

OUTCRY

that there be no o ....Ps 144:14

OUTGOINGS

You make the o of the ....Ps 65:8

OUTRAGE

lewdness and o in ....Judg 20:6

OUTRAN

the other disciple o...........John 20:4

OUTSIDE

and dish, that the o ....Matt 23:26
Pharisees make the o ......Luke 11:39
toward those who are o ....Col 4:5
to Him, o the camp ....Heb 13:13
But o are dogs and..........Rev 22:15

OUTSTRETCHED

and with an o arm ....Deut 26:8
against you with an o ....Jer 21:5

OUTWARD

at the o appearance ....1 Sam 16:7
adornment be merely o.......1 Pet 3:3

OUTWARDLY

appear beautiful o ....Matt 23:27
not a Jew who is one o ......Rom 2:28

OUTWIT

The enemy shall not o ....Ps 89:22

OVEN

make them as a fiery o ....Ps 21:9
burning like an o ....Mal 4:1
is thrown into the o ....Matt 6:30

OVERCAME

My throne, as I also o ....Rev 3:21
And they o him by ....Rev 12:11

OVERCOME

good cheer, I have o ....John 16:33
o evil with good ....Rom 12:21
because you have o........1 John 2:13

and the Lamb will o ....Rev 17:14

OVERCOMES

of God o the world ....1 John 5:4
o I will give to eat ....Rev 2:7
o shall not be hurt ....Rev 2:11
o shall inherit all ....Rev 21:7

OVERFLOWING

My heart is o with a ....Ps 45:1

OVERSEER

Then he made him o.........Gen 39:4
having no captain, o..........Prov 6:7
to the Shepherd and O ......1 Pet 2:25

OVERSEERS

Spirit has made you o ......Acts 20:28
you, serving as o ....1 Pet 5:2

OVERSHADOW

of the Highest will o ....Luke 1:35

OVERTAKE

does righteousness o ....Is 59:9
you feared shall o ....Jer 42:16
and o this chariot ....Acts 8:29
that this Day should o ......1 Thess 5:4

OVERTAKEN

No temptation has o ....1 Cor 10:13
if a man is o in any ....Gal 6:1

OVERTHREW

So He o those cities.........Gen 19:25
will be as when God o ....Is 13:19
As God o Sodom and ....Jer 50:40
"I o some of you ....Amos 4:11

OVERTHROW

you shall utterly o ....Ex 23:24
o the righteous in ....Prov 18:5
o the throne of ....Hag 2:22
o the faith of some ....2 Tim 2:18

OVERTHROWN

Their judges are o ....Ps 141:6
of Sodom, which was o ....Lam 4:6
I will make it o ....Ezek 21:27
and Nineveh shall be o ....Jon 3:4

OVERTHROWS

and o the mighty ....Job 12:19
o them in the night ....Job 34:25
o the words of the ....Prov 22:12

OVERTURNED

my heart is o within ....Lam 1:20
o the tables of the ....Matt 21:12
money and o the tables .....John 2:15

OVERWHELM

o the fatherless ....Job 6:27
sends them out, they o .....Job 12:15

OVERWHELMED

when my heart is o ....Ps 61:2
and my spirit was o...........Ps 77:3
o their enemies ....Ps 78:53
waters would have o ....Ps 124:4
my spirit is o within..........Ps 143:4

OVERWORK

Do not o to be rich ....Prov 23:4

OWE

'How much do you *o* ....Luke 16:5
O no one anything ....Rom 13:8
o me even your own ....Philem 19

OWED

o him ten thousand ....Matt 18:24
fellow servants who *o* ......Matt 18:28
o five hundred denarii ....Luke 7:41

OWN

He came to His *o* ....John 1:11
having loved His *o* ....John 13:1
world would love its *o* ......John 15:19
and you are not your *o* ......1 Cor 6:19
But each one has his *o* ....1 Cor 7:7
For all seek their *o* ....Phil 2:21
from our sins in His *o* ....Rev 1:5

OX

shall not muzzle an *o* ....Deut 25:4
"Will the wild *o* ....Job 39:9
you bind the wild *o* ....Job 39:10
like a young wild *o* ....Ps 29:6
exalted like a wild *o* ....Ps 92:10
o knows its owner ....Is 1:3
had the face of an *o* ....Ezek 1:10
Sabbath loose his *o* ....Luke 13:15
shall not muzzle an *o* ....1 Cor 9:9

— P —

PACE

are majestic in *p* ....Prov 30:29

PACIFIES

A gift in secret *p* ....Prov 21:14
for conciliation *p* ....Eccl 10:4

PADAN ARAM

Same as Mesopotamia, Gen 24:10; *see* MESOPOTAMIA
Home of Isaac's wife, Gen 25:20
Jacob flees to, Gen 28:2–7
Jacob returns from, Gen 31:17, 18
People of, called Syrians, Gen 31:24
Language of, called Aramaic, 2 Kin 18:26

PAILS

p are full of milk ....Job 21:24

PAIN

p you shall bring ....Gen 3:16
p as a woman in ....Is 13:8
are filled with *p* ....Is 21:3
before her *p* came ....Is 66:7
Why is my *p* perpetual ....Jer 15:18
shall be no more *p* ....Rev 21:4

PAINED

My heart is severely *p* ....Ps 55:4
I am *p* in my very ....Jer 4:19

PAINFUL

this, it was too *p* ....Ps 73:16
for the present, but *p* ....Heb 12:11

PAINS

The *p* of death ....Ps 116:3
having loosed the *p* ....Acts 2:24
upon them, as labor *p* ......1 Thess 5:3

PAINT

and she put *p* on her ....2 Kin 9:30
your eyes with *p* ....Jer 4:30

PAINTING

it with cedar and *p* ....Jer 22:14

PALACE

enter the King's *p* ....Ps 45:15
a *p* of foreigners ....Is 25:2
guards his own *p* ....Luke 11:21
evident to the whole *p* ....Phil 1:13

PALACES

out of the ivory *p* ....Ps 45:8
God is in her *p* ....Ps 48:3
has entered our *p* ....Jer 9:21

PALE

his face now grow *p* ....Is 29:22
and all faces turned *p* ....Jer 30:6
behold, a *p* horse ....Rev 6:8

PALM

of water and seventy *p* ....Ex 15:27
p trees and went out ....John 12:13
p branches in their ....Rev 7:9

PALMS

struck Him with the *p* ....Matt 26:67

PALTI (or Paltiel)

Man to whom Saul gives Michal, David's wife, in marriage, 1 Sam 25:44; 2 Sam 3:15

PAMPERS

p his servant from ....Prov 29:21

PAMPHYLIA

People from, at Pentecost, Acts 2:10
Paul visits; John Mark returns home from, Acts 13:13; 15:38
Paul preaches in cities of, Acts 14:24, 25

PANGS

The *p* of death ....Ps 18:4
P and sorrows will ....Is 13:8
labors with birth *p* ....Rom 8:22

PANICKED

the men of Benjamin *p* ....Judg 20:41

PANT

They *p* after the dust ....Amos 2:7

PANTS

As the deer *p* for the ....Ps 42:1

PAPHOS

Paul blinds Elymas at, Acts 13:6–13

PAPYRUS

"Can the *p* grow up ....Job 8:11

PARABLE

open my mouth in a *p* ....Ps 78:2
p He did not speak ....Matt 13:34
do You speak this *p* ....Luke 12:41

PARABLES

'Does he not speak *p* ....Ezek 20:49
understand all the *p* ....Mark 4:13
rest it is given in *p* ....Luke 8:10

PARADE

love does not *p* ....1 Cor 13:4

PARADISE

will be with Me in *P* ....Luke 23:43
was caught up into *P* ....2 Cor 12:4
in the midst of the *P* ....Rev 2:7

PARAN

Residence of exiled Ishmael, Gen 21:21
Israelites camp in, Num 10:12
Headquarters of spies, Num 13:3, 26
Site of David's refuge, 1 Sam 25:1

PARCHMENTS

especially the *p* ....2 Tim 4:13

PARDON

p your transgressions ....Ex 23:21
O LORD, *p* my iniquity ....Ps 25:11
He will abundantly *p* ....Is 55:7
p all their iniquities ....Jer 33:8

PARDONING

is a God like You, *p* ....Mic 7:18

PARENTS

will rise up against *p* ....Matt 10:21
has left house or *p* ....Luke 18:29
disobedient to *p* ....Rom 1:30
to lay up for the *p* ....2 Cor 12:14

PARMENAS

One of the first seven deacons, Acts 6:5

PART

You have no *p* in the ....Josh 22:25
has chosen that good *p* ......Luke 10:42
you, you have no *p* ....John 13:8
For we know in *p* ....1 Cor 13:9
p has a believer ....2 Cor 6:15
shall take away his *p* ....Rev 22:19

PARTAKE

for we all *p* of that ....1 Cor 10:17
you cannot *p* of the ....1 Cor 10:21

PARTAKER

and have been a *p* ....Ps 50:18
in hope should be *p* ....1 Cor 9:10
Christ, and also a *p* ....1 Pet 5:1

PARTAKERS

Gentiles have been *p* ....Rom 15:27
of the sacrifices *p* ....1 Cor 10:18
know that as you are *p* ....2 Cor 1:7
gospel, you all are *p* ....Phil 1:7
qualified us to be *p* ....Col 1:12
For we have become *p* ....Heb 3:14

PARTED

them, that He was *p* ....Luke 24:51
so sharp that they *p* ....Acts 15:39

PARTIAL

You shall not be *p* ....Lev 19:15

PARTIALITY

You shall not show *p* ....Deut 1:17
unjustly, and show *p* ....Ps 82:2
is not good to show *p* ....Prov 18:5
but have shown *p* ....Mal 2:9
that God shows no *p* ....Acts 10:34
For there is no *p* ....Rom 2:11
doing nothing with *p* ....1 Tim 5:21
but if you show *p* ....James 2:9
good fruits, without *p* ....James 3:17

PEACEFUL
in a *p* habitation ....Is 32:18

PEACEMAKERS
Blessed are the *p* ....Matt 5:9

PEARL
had found one *p* ....Matt 13:46
gate was of one *p* ....Rev 21:21

PEARLS
nor cast your *p* ....Matt 7:6
hair or gold or *p* ....1 Tim 2:9
gates were twelve *p* ....Rev 21:21

PEG
wife, took a tent *p* ....Judg 4:21
will fasten him as a *p* ....Is 22:23

PEKAH
Son of Remaliah; usurps Israel's throne, 2 Kin 15:25–28
Forms alliance with Rezin of Syria against Ahaz, Is 7:1–9
Alliance defeated; captives returned, 2 Kin 16:5–9
Territory of, overrun by Tiglath-Pileser, 2 Kin 15:29
Assassinated by Hoshea, 2 Kin 15:30

PEKAHIAH
Son of Menahem; king of Israel, 2 Kin 15:22–26
Assassinated by Pekah, 2 Kin 15:23–25

PEN
My tongue is the *p* ....Ps 45:1
on it with a man's *p* ....Is 8:1
to write to you with *p* ....3 John 13

PENNY
have paid the last *p* ....Matt 5:26

PENTECOST
P had fully come ....Acts 2:1

PENUEL
Place east of Jordan; site of Jacob's wrestling with angel, Gen 32:24–31
Inhabitants of, slain by Gideon, Judg 8:8, 9, 17

PEOPLE
will take you as My *p* ....Ex 6:7
Who is like you, a *p* ....Deut 33:29
p shall be my *p* ....Ruth 1:16
p who know the joyful ....Ps 89:15
We are His *p* and the ....Ps 100:3
Happy are the *p* ....Ps 144:15
"Blessed is Egypt My *p* ....Is 19:25
this is a rebellious *p* ....Is 30:9
p who provoke Me ....Is 65:3
and they shall be My *p* ....Jer 24:7
for you are not My *p* ....Hos 1:9
like *p*, like priest ....Hos 4:9
to make ready a *p* ....Luke 1:17
take out of them a *p* ....Acts 15:14
who were not My *p* ....Rom 9:25
and they shall be My *p* ....2 Cor 6:16
His own special *p* ....Titus 2:14
LORD will judge His *p* ....Heb 10:30
but are now the *p* ....1 Pet 2:10
tribe and tongue and *p* ....Rev 5:9
they shall be His *p* ....Rev 21:3

PEOR
Mountain of Moab opposite Jericho, Num 23:28
Israel's camp seen from, Num 24:2
—— Moabite god called Baal of Peor, Num 25:3, 5, 18
Israelites punished for worship of, Num 31:16

PERCEIVE
given you a heart to *p* ....Deut 29:4
but I cannot *p* ....Job 23:8
seeing, but do not *p* ....Is 6:9
may see and not *p* ....Mark 4:12

PERDITION
except the son of *p* ....John 17:12
to them a proof of *p* ....Phil 1:28
revealed, the son of *p* ....2 Thess 2:3
who draw back to *p* ....Heb 10:39
day of judgment and *p* ....2 Pet 3:7

PEREZ
One of Judah's twin sons by Tamar, Gen 38:24–30

PERFECT
Noah was a just man, *p* ....Gen 6:9
one who is *p* in ....Job 36:4
for God, His way is *p* ....Ps 18:30
You were *p* in your ....Ezek 28:15
Father in heaven is *p* ....Matt 5:48
"If you want to be *p* ....Matt 19:21
they may be made *p* ....John 17:23
and *p* will of God ....Rom 12:2
when that which is *p* ....1 Cor 13:10
present every man *p* ....Col 1:28
the law made nothing *p* ....Heb 7:19
of just men made *p* ....Heb 12:23
good gift and every *p* ....James 1:17
in word, he is a *p* ....James 3:2
p love casts out fear ....1 John 4:18

PERFECTED
third day I shall be *p* ....Luke 13:32
or am already *p* ....Phil 3:12
the Son who has been *p* ....Heb 7:28
the love of God is *p* ....1 John 2:5

PERFECTION
the *p* of beauty ....Ps 50:2
consummation of all *p* ....Ps 119:96
let us go on to *p* ....Heb 6:1

PERFORM
p Your statutes ....Ps 119:112
am ready to *p* My word ....Jer 1:12
how to *p* what is good ....Rom 7:18

PERGA
Visited by Paul, Acts 13:13, 14; 14:25

PERGAMOS
Site of one of the seven churches, Rev 1:11
Special message to, Rev 2:12–17

PERIL
or nakedness, or *p* ....Rom 8:35

PERILOUS
from the *p* pestilence ....Ps 91:3
in the last days *p* ....2 Tim 3:1

PERILS
journeys often, in *p* ....2 Cor 11:26

PERISH
"Surely we die, we *p* ....Num 17:12
All flesh would *p* ....Job 34:15
they *p* at the rebuke ....Ps 80:16
very day his plans *p* ....Ps 146:4
so that we may not *p* ....Jon 1:6
little ones should *p* ....Matt 18:14
will all likewise *p* ....Luke 13:3
in Him should not *p* ....John 3:16
they shall never *p* ....John 10:28
concern things which *p* ....Col 2:22
among those who *p* ....2 Thess 2:10
that any should *p* ....2 Pet 3:9

PERISHABLE
do it to obtain a *p* ....1 Cor 9:25

PERISHED
p being innocent ....Job 4:7
Truth has *p* and has ....Jer 7:28
The faithful man has *p* ....Mic 7:2

PERISHING
We are *p* ....Matt 8:25
to those who are *p* ....2 Cor 4:3

PERIZZITES
One of seven Canaanite nations, Deut 7:1
Possessed Palestine in Abraham's time, Gen 13:7
Jacob's fear of, Gen 34:30
Many of, slain by Judah, Judg 1:4, 5

PERJURER
p shall be expelled ....Zech 5:3

PERMIT
the Spirit did not *p* ....Acts 16:7
I do not *p* a woman ....1 Tim 2:12

PERMITS
you, if the Lord *p* ....1 Cor 16:7
we will do if God *p* ....Heb 6:3

PERMITTED
p no one to do them ....Ps 105:14

PERPETUATED
Your name shall be *p* ....Nah 1:14

PERPLEXED
at one another, *p* ....John 13:22
we are *p* ....2 Cor 4:8

PERSECUTE
p me as God does ....Job 19:22
p me wrongfully ....Ps 119:86
when they revile and *p* ....Matt 5:11
Bless those who *p* ....Rom 12:14

PERSECUTED
p the poor and needy ....Ps 109:16
p the prophets who ....Matt 5:12
If they *p* Me ....John 15:20
p the church of God ....1 Cor 15:9
p, but not forsaken ....2 Cor 4:9
p us now preaches the ....Gal 1:23

PERSECUTES
wicked in his pride *p* ....Ps 10:2

PERSECUTION
p arises because of ....Matt 13:21

At that time a great *p* . . . . Acts 8:1
do I still suffer *p* . . . . Gal 5:11

PERSECUTOR

a blasphemer, a *p* . . . . 1 Tim 1:13

PERSEVERANCE

tribulation produces *p* . . . . Rom 5:3
to this end will all *p* . . . . Eph 6:18
longsuffering, love, *p* . . . . 2 Tim 3:10
to self-control *p* . . . . 2 Pet 1:6

PERSEVERE

kept My command to *p* . . . . Rev 3:10

PERSISTENCE

p he will rise and . . . . Luke 11:8

PERSON

In whose eyes a vile *p* . . . . Ps 15:4
p will suffer hunger . . . . Prov 19:15
do not regard the *p* . . . . Matt 22:16
express image of His *p* . . . . Heb 1:3
let it be the hidden *p* . . . . 1 Pet 3:4

PERSUADE

"You almost *p* me . . . . Acts 26:28
the Lord, we *p* men . . . . 2 Cor 5:11
For do I now *p* men . . . . Gal 1:10

PERSUADED

a ruler is *p* . . . . Prov 25:15
neither will they be *p* . . . . . . Luke 16:31
p that He is able . . . . 2 Tim 1:12

PERSUASIVE

p words of human . . . . 1 Cor 2:4
you with *p* words . . . . Col 2:4

PERTAINING

Priest in things *p* . . . . Heb 2:17
for men in things *p* . . . . Heb 5:1

PERTURBED

things the earth is *p* . . . . Prov 30:21

PERVERSE

your way is *p* . . . . Num 22:32
for the *p* person is an . . . . Prov 3:32
p lips far from you . . . . Prov 4:24
p heart will be . . . . Prov 12:8
p man sows strife . . . . Prov 16:28
but he who is *p* . . . . Prov 28:18
from this *p* generation . . . . Acts 2:40

PERVERSITY

in oppression and *p* . . . . Is 30:12

PERVERT

You shall not *p* . . . . Deut 16:19
and *p* all equity . . . . Mic 3:9
p the gospel of Christ . . . . Gal 1:7

PERVERTING

We found this fellow *p* . . . . . . Luke 23:2
will you not cease *p* . . . . Acts 13:10

PERVERTS

p the words of the . . . . Ex 23:8
p his ways will become . . . . . . Prov 10:9

PESTILENCE

from the perilous *p* . . . . Ps 91:3
p that walks in . . . . Ps 91:6

Before Him went *p* . . . . Hab 3:5

PESTILENCES

will be famines, *p* . . . . Matt 24:7

PETER

Fisherman; called to discipleship, Matt 4:18–20; John 1:40–42
Called as apostle, Matt 10:2–4
Walks on water, Matt 14:28–33
Confesses Christ's deity, Matt 16:13–19
Rebuked by Christ, Matt 16:21–23
Witnesses Transfiguration, Matt 17:1–8; 2 Pet 1:16–18
Denies Christ three times, Matt 26:69–75
Commissioned to feed Christ's sheep, John 21:15–17
Leads disciples, Acts 1:15–26
Preaches at Pentecost, Acts 2:1–41
Performs miracles, Acts 3:1–11; 5:14–16; 9:32–43
Called to minister to Gentiles, Acts 10
Defends his visit to Gentiles, Acts 11:1–18
Imprisoned and delivered, Acts 12:3–19
Speaks at Jerusalem Council, Acts 15:7–14
Writes epistles, 1 Pet 1:1; 2 Pet 1:1

PETITION

of Israel grant your *p* . . . . . . 1 Sam 1:17

PETITIONS

fulfill all your *p* . . . . Ps 20:5
p that we have asked . . . . . . 1 John 5:15

PHARAOH

Kings of Egypt, contemporaries of:
Abraham, Gen 12:15–20
Joseph, Gen 40; 41
Moses in youth, Ex 1:8–11
the Exodus, Ex 5—14
Solomon, 1 Kin 3:1; 11:17–20
Other Pharaohs, 1 Kin 14:25, 26; 2 Kin 17:4; 18:21; 19:9; 23:29; Jer 44:30

PHARISEE

to pray, one a *P* . . . . Luke 18:10
and brethren, I am a *P* . . . . Acts 23:6

PHILADELPHIA

City of Lydia in Asia Minor; church established here, Rev 1:11

PHILEMON

Christian at Colosse to whom Paul writes, Philem 1
Paul appeals to him to receive Onesimus, Philem 9–21

PHILETUS

False teacher, 2 Tim 2:17, 18

PHILIP

Son of Herod the Great, Matt 14:3
—— One of the twelve apostles, Matt 10:3
Brings Nathanael to Christ, John 1:43–48
Tested by Christ, John 6:5–7
Introduces Greeks to Christ, John 12:20–22
Gently rebuked by Christ, John 14:8–12
—— One of the first seven deacons, Acts 6:5

Called an evangelist, Acts 21:8
Preaches in Samaria, Acts 8:5–13
Leads the Ethiopian eunuch to Christ, Acts 8:26–40

PHILIPPI

City of Macedonia (named after Philip of Macedon); visited by Paul, Acts 16:12; 20:6
Paul writes letter to church of, Phil 1:1

PHILISTIA

The land of the Philistines, Gen 21:32, 34; Josh 13:2; Ps 60:8

PHILISTINES

Not attacked by Joshua, Josh 13:1–3
Left to test Israel, Judg 3:1–4
God delivers Israel to, as punishment, Judg 10:6, 7
Israel delivered from, by Samson, Judg 13—16
Capture, then return the ark of the Lord, 1 Sam 4—6
Wars and dealings with Saul and David, 1 Sam 13:15—14:23; 17:1–52; 18:25–27; 21:10–15; 27:1—28:6; 29:1–11; 31:1–13; 2 Sam 5:17–25
Originally on the island of Caphtor, Jer 47:4
Prophecies concerning, Is 9:11, 12; Jer 25:15–20; 47:1–7; Ezek 25:15–17; Zeph 2:4–6

PHILOSOPHERS

p encountered him . . . . Acts 17:18

PHILOSOPHY

cheat you through *p* . . . . Col 2:8

PHINEHAS

Aaron's grandson; executes God's judgment, Num 25:1–18; Ps 106:30, 31
Settles dispute over memorial altar, Josh 22:11–32
—— Younger son of Eli; abuses his office, 1 Sam 1:3; 2:12–17, 22–36
Killed by Philistines, 1 Sam 4:11, 17

PHOENICIA

Mediterranean coastal region including the cities of Ptolemais, Tyre, Zarephath and Sidon; evangelized by early Christians, Acts 11:19
Jesus preaches here, Matt 15:21

PHRYGIA

Jews from, at Pentecost, Acts 2:1, 10
Visited twice by Paul, Acts 16:6

PHYLACTERIES

They make their *p* . . . . Matt 23:5

PHYSICIAN

Gilead, is there no *p* . . . . Jer 8:22
have no need of a *p* . . . . Matt 9:12
Luke the beloved *p* . . . . Col 4:14

PHYSICIANS

are all worthless *p* . . . . Job 13:4
her livelihood on *p* . . . . Luke 8:43

PI HAHIROTH

Israel camps there before crossing the Red Sea, Ex 14:2, 9; Num 33:7, 8

PIECES
for my wages thirty *p* ......Zech 11:12
they took the thirty *p* ......Matt 27:9
shall be dashed to *p* ....Rev 2:17

PIERCE
and his master shall *p* ....Ex 21:6
a sword will *p* ....Luke 2:35

PIERCED
p My hands and My feet ......Ps 22:16
on Me whom they have *p*...Zech 12:10
of the soldiers *p* ....John 19:34
p themselves through ....1 Tim 6:10
and they also who *p* ....Rev 1:7

PIERCING
p even to the division ....Heb 4:12

PIETY
first learn to show *p* ....1 Tim 5:4

PILATE, PONTIUS
Governor of Judea (A.D. 26–36), Luke 3:1
Questions Jesus and delivers Him to Jews, Matt 27:2, 11–26; John 18:28—19:16

PILGRIMAGE
heart is set on *p* ....Ps 84:5
In the house of my *p* ....Ps 119:54

PILGRIMS
we are aliens and *p* ....1 Chr 29:15
were strangers and *p* ....Heb 11:13

PILLAR
and she became a *p*.........Gen 19:26
and by night in a *p* ....Ex 13:21
the living God, the *p*......1 Tim 3:15

PILLARS
break their sacred *p*..........Ex 34:13
I set up its *p* firmly ....Ps 75:3
out her seven *p* ....Prov 9:1
blood and fire and *p* ....Joel 2:30
and his feet like *p* ....Rev 10:1

PILOT
rudder wherever the *p* ......James 3:4

PINE
cypress tree and the *p* ....Is 41:19
for these *p* away ....Lam 4:9

PINNACLE
set Him on the *p*..................Luke 4:9

PISGAH
Balaam offers sacrifice upon, Num 23:14
Moses views Promised Land from, Deut 3:27
Site of Moses' death, Deut 34:1–7

PISHON
One of Eden's four rivers, Gen 2:10, 11

PISIDIA
Twice visited by Paul, Acts 13:13, 14; 14:24

PITHOM
Egyptian city built by Hebrew slaves, Ex 1:11

PIT
cast him into some *p* ....Gen 37:20
soul draws near the *P* ....Job 33:22
who go down to the *p* ....Ps 28:1
woman is a deep *p* ....Prov 22:14
a harlot is a deep *p* ....Prov 23:27
fall into his own *p* ....Prov 28:10
my life in the *p* ....Lam 3:53
who descend into the *P* ....Ezek 31:16
up my life from the *p* ....Jon 2:6
from the waterless *p* ....Zech 9:11
if it falls into a *p* ....Matt 12:11
into the bottomless *p* ....Rev 20:3

PITCHERS
hand, with empty *p* ....Judg 7:16
the washing of cups, *p*........Mark 7:4

PITIABLE
of all men the most *p* ....1 Cor 15:19

PITS
The proud have dug *p* ....Ps 119:85

PITY
eye shall have no *p* ....Deut 7:16
"Have *p* on me ....Job 19:21
for someone to take *p* ....Ps 69:20
He who has *p* on the ....Prov 19:17
p He redeemed them ....Is 63:9
land, and *p* His people ....Joel 2:18
And should I not *p* ....Jon 4:11
just as I had *p* ....Matt 18:33

PLACE
p know him anymore ....Job 7:10
All go to one *p* ....Eccl 3:20
return again to My *p* ....Hos 5:15
Come, see the *p* ....Matt 28:6
My word has no *p* ....John 8:37
I go to prepare a *p* ....John 14:2
might go to his own *p* ....Acts 1:25

PLACES
set them in slippery *p* ....Ps 73:18
dark *p* of the earth ....Ps 74:20
and the rough *p* ....Is 40:4
They love the best *p* ....Matt 23:6
in the heavenly *p* ....Eph 1:3

PLAGUE
bring yet one more *p* ....Ex 11:1
p come near your ....Ps 91:10
and the *p* was stopped.......Ps 106:30

PLAGUES
I will send all My *p* ....Ex 9:14
I will be your *p* ....Hos 13:14
p that are written ....Rev 22:18

PLAINLY
the Christ, tell us *p* ....John 10:24
now You are speaking *p* ...John 16:29
such things declare *p* ....Heb 11:14

PLAN
p evil things in their ....Ps 140:2
Let none of you *p* ....Zech 7:10

PLANK
First remove the *p* ....Matt 7:5

PLANS
He makes the *p* of the ....Ps 33:10

in that very day his *p* ....Ps 146:4
that devises wicked *p* ....Prov 6:18
A man's heart *p* ....Prov 16:9
P are established ....Prov 20:18

PLANT
A time to *p* ....Eccl 3:2
Him as a tender *p* ....Is 53:2
they shall *p* vineyards ....Is 65:21
p of an alien vine ....Jer 2:21
p which My heavenly ....Matt 15:13

PLANTED
shall be like a tree *p* ....Ps 1:3
Your right hand has *p* ....Ps 80:15
shall they be *p*........................Is 40:24
by the roots and be *p* ....Luke 17:6
I *p*, Apollos watered ....1 Cor 3:6

PLANTS
our sons may be as *p* ....Ps 144:12
down its choice *p* ....Is 16:8
neither he who *p* ....1 Cor 3:7

PLATFORM
scribe stood on a *p* ....Neh 8:4

PLATTER
head here on a *p* ....Matt 14:8

PLAY
and rose up to *p* ....Ex 32:6
p skillfully with a ....Ps 33:3
nursing child shall *p* ....Is 11:8
and rose up to *p* ....1 Cor 10:7

PLEAD
the one who would *p* ....Judg 6:31
Oh, that one might *p* ....Job 16:21
p my cause against an ....Ps 43:1
p with your friend ....Prov 6:3
Behold, I will *p* ....Jer 2:35
p His case with all ....Jer 25:31

PLEADED
Then Moses *p* with the ....Ex 32:11
this thing I *p* with ....2 Cor 12:8

PLEADING
though God were *p*..........2 Cor 5:20

PLEASANT
food, that it was *p* ....Gen 3:6
they despised the *p*...........Ps 106:24
how good and how *p* ....Ps 133:1
and knowledge is *p* ....Prov 2:10
P words are like a ....Prov 16:24
p places of the ....Jer 23:10
Is he a *p* child ....Jer 31:20
I ate no *p* food ....Dan 10:3

PLEASANTNESS
Her ways are ways of *p* .....Prov 3:17

PLEASE
When a man's ways *p* ....Prov 16:7
do those things that *p* ....John 8:29
in the flesh cannot *p* ....Rom 8:8
p his neighbor for his ....Rom 15:2
how he may *p* the Lord ....1 Cor 7:32
Or do I seek to *p* men ....Gal 1:10
is impossible to *p* Him ....Heb 11:6

PLEASED
Then You shall be *p* ....Ps 51:19

The LORD is well *p* ....Is 42:21
Would he be *p* with you .....Mal 1:8
in whom I am well *p* ....Matt 3:17
God was not well *p* ....1 Cor 10:5
testimony, that he *p* ....Heb 11:5
in whom I am well *p* ....2 Pet 1:17

PLEASES

He does whatever He *p* ....Ps 115:3
Whatever the LORD *p* ....Ps 135:6

PLEASING

sacrifice, well *p* ....Phil 4:18
for this is well *p* ....Col 3:20
in you what is well *p* ....Heb 13:21

PLEASURE

not a God who takes *p* ....Ps 5:4
Do good in Your good *p* ....Ps 51:18
Your servants take *p* ....Ps 102:14
p will be a poor man ....Prov 21:17
for He has no *p* ....Eccl 5:4
shall perform all My *p* ....Is 44:28
your fast you find *p* ....Is 58:3
nor finding your own *p* ....Is 58:13
Do I have any *p* ....Ezek 18:23
I have no *p* in you ....Mal 1:10
your Father's good *p* ....Luke 12:32
to the good *p* of His ....Eph 1:5
fulfill all the good *p* ......2 Thess 1:11
p is dead while ....1 Tim 5:6
for sin You had no *p* ....Heb 10:6
back, My soul has no *p* .....Heb 10:38
p that war in your ....James 4:1
on the earth in *p* ....James 5:5

PLEASURES

Your right hand are *p* ....Ps 16:11
cares, riches, and *p* ....Luke 8:14
to enjoy the passing *p* ....Heb 11:25

PLEIADES

Part of God's creation, Job 9:9; Amos 5:8

PLENTIFUL

You, O God, sent a *p* ....Ps 68:9
The harvest truly is *p* ....Matt 9:37

PLENTIFULLY

rich man yielded *p* ....Luke 12:16

PLENTY

p which were in the ....Gen 41:53
LORD will grant you *p* .....Deut 28:11
his land will have *p* ....Prov 28:19

PLIGHT

He laughs at the *p* ....Job 9:23

PLOT

and the people *p* ....Ps 2:1
p became known to Saul .....Acts 9:24

PLOTS

The wicked *p* against ....Ps 37:12

PLOTTED

and *p* to take Jesus by ....Matt 26:4
chief priests *p* ....John 12:10

PLOW

lazy man will not *p* ....Prov 20:4
Does one *p* there with ....Amos 6:12

put his hand to the *p* ....Luke 9:62
he who plows should *p* ....1 Cor 9:10

PLOWED

"Zion shall be *p* ....Jer 26:18
You have *p* wickedness ....Hos 10:13
of you Zion shall be *p* ....Mic 3:12

PLOWMAN

p shall overtake the ....Amos 9:13

PLUCK

grain, you may *p* ....Deut 23:25
who pass by the way *p* ....Ps 80:12
obey, I will utterly *p* ....Jer 12:17
p the heads of grain ....Mark 2:23

PLUCKED

p the victim from his ....Job 29:17
cheeks to those who *p* ....Is 50:6
And His disciples *p* ....Luke 6:1
you would have *p* ....Gal 4:15

PLUMB

a *p* line, with a *p* ....Amos 7:7
rejoice to see the *p* ....Zech 4:10

PLUNDER

p the Egyptians ....Ex 3:22
who pass by the way *p* ....Ps 89:41
The *p* of the poor is ....Is 3:14
p you shall become ....Jer 30:16
house and *p* his goods ....Matt 12:29

PLUNDERED

stouthearted were *p* ....Ps 76:5
a people robbed and *p* ....Is 42:22
"And when you are *p* ....Jer 4:30
Because you have *p* ....Hab 2:8

PLUNDERING

me because of the *p* ....Is 22:4
accepted the *p* of your ....Heb 10:34

POETS

some of your own *p* ....Acts 17:28

POISON

the *p* of asps is under ....Ps 140:3
"The *p* of asps is ....Rom 3:13
evil, full of deadly *p* ....James 3:8

POISONED

p by bitterness ....Acts 8:23
p their minds against ....Acts 14:2

POLLUTIONS

have escaped the *p* ....2 Pet 2:20

POMP

multitude and their *p* ....Is 5:14
p is brought down to ....Is 14:11
had come with great *p* ....Acts 25:23

POMPOUS

and a mouth speaking *p* ....Dan 7:8

PONDER

P the path of your ....Prov 4:26

PONDERED

p them in her heart ....Luke 2:19

PONDERS

p all his paths ....Prov 5:21

PONTUS

Jews from, at Pentecost, Acts 2:5, 9
Home of Aquila, Acts 18:2
Christians of, addressed by Peter, 1 Pet 1:1

POOL

the wilderness a *p* ....Is 41:18
by the Sheep Gate a *p* ....John 5:2

POOLS

also covers it with *p* ....Ps 84:6
a wilderness into *p* ....Ps 107:35
your eyes like the *p* ....Song 7:4

POOR

p shall not give less ....Ex 30:15
be partial to the *p* ....Lev 19:15
p will never cease ....Deut 15:11
So the *p* have hope ....Job 5:16
and forsaken the *p* ....Job 20:19
I delivered the *p* ....Job 29:12
soul grieved for the *p* ....Job 30:25
p shall eat and be ....Ps 22:26
p man cried out ....Ps 34:6
But I am *p* and needy ....Ps 40:17
goodness for the *p* ....Ps 68:10
Let the *p* and needy ....Ps 74:21
yet He sets the *p* ....Ps 107:41
He raises the *p* ....Ps 113:7
a slack hand becomes *p* ....Prov 10:4
p man is hated even ....Prov 14:20
has mercy on the *p* ....Prov 14:21
who oppresses the *p* ....Prov 14:31
p reproaches his Maker ....Prov 17:5
p man is better than a ....Prov 19:22
p have this in common ....Prov 22:2
Do not rob the *p* ....Prov 22:22
p man who oppresses ....Prov 28:3
remembered that same *p* ....Eccl 9:15
for silver, and the *p* ....Amos 2:6
the alien or the *p* ....Zech 7:10
in particular the *p* ....Zech 11:7
"Blessed are the *p* ....Matt 5:3
p have the gospel ....Matt 11:5
For you have the *p* ....Matt 26:11
your sakes He became *p* ....2 Cor 8:9
should remember the *p* ....Gal 2:10
God not chosen the *p* ....James 2:5
have dishonored the *p* ....James 2:6
wretched, miserable, *p* ....Rev 3:17

PORCIUS FESTUS

Paul stands trial before, Acts 25:1–22

PORTION

For the LORD's *p* ....Deut 32:9
This is the *p* from God ....Job 20:29
O LORD, You are the *p* ....Ps 16:5
heart and my *p* forever ....Ps 73:26
You are my *p* ....Ps 119:57
I will divide Him a *p* ....Is 53:12
rejoice in their *p* ....Is 61:7
The *P* of Jacob is not ....Jer 10:16
they have trodden My *p* ....Jer 12:10
"The LORD is my *p* ....Lam 3:24
and appoint him his *p* ....Matt 24:51
to give them their *p* ....Luke 12:42
give me the *p* ....Luke 15:12

PORTRAYED

Christ was clearly *p* ....Gal 3:1

POSITION

If a man desires the *p* ....1 Tim 3:1

POSSESS

descendants shall *p* ... Gen 22:17
p the land which ... Josh 1:11
By your patience *p* ... Luke 21:19
p his own vessel ... 1 Thess 4:4

POSSESSED

much land yet to be *p* ... Josh 13:1
"The LORD *p* me at ... Prov 8:22
of the things he *p* ... Acts 4:32

POSSESSING

and yet *p* all things ... 2 Cor 6:10

POSSESSION

as an everlasting *p* ... Gen 17:8
the rest of their *p* ... Ps 17:14
they did not gain *p* ... Ps 44:3
of the purchased *p* ... Eph 1:14
and an enduring *p* ... Heb 10:34

POSSESSIONS

is full of Your *p* ... Ps 104:24
kinds of precious *p* ... Prov 1:13
Yes, I had greater *p* ... Eccl 2:7
for he had great *p* ... Mark 10:22
and there wasted his *p* ... Luke 15:13
and sold their *p* ... Acts 2:45

POSSIBLE

God all things are *p* ... Matt 19:26
p that the blood ... Heb 10:4

POSTERITY

to preserve a *p* ... Gen 45:7
p shall serve Him ... Ps 22:30
p who approve their ... Ps 49:13

POT

to Aaron, "Take a *p* ... Ex 16:33
from a boiling *p* ... Job 41:20
The refining *p* is for ... Prov 17:3
p that had the manna ... Heb 9:4

POTENTATE

the blessed and only *P* ... 1 Tim 6:15

POTI-PHERAH

Egyptian priest of On (Heliopolis), Gen 41:45–50
Father of Asenath, Joseph's wife, Gen 46:20

POTIPHAR

High Egyptian officer, Gen 39:1
Puts Joseph in jail, Gen 39:20

POTS

when we sat by the *p* ... Ex 16:3
also took away the *p* ... Jer 52:18
are regarded as clay *p* ... Lam 4:2

POTSHERD

for himself a *p* ... Job 2:8
is dried up like a *p* ... Ps 22:15
Let the *p* strive with ... Is 45:9

POTTER'S FIELD

Judas's money used for purchase of, Matt 27:7, 8

POUR

p out your heart ... Ps 62:8
P out Your wrath ... Ps 79:6
p My Spirit on your ... Is 44:3
and let the skies *p* ... Is 45:8
P out Your fury ... Jer 10:25
that I will *p* out My ... Joel 2:28
"And I will *p* ... Zech 12:10
angels, "Go and *p* ... Rev 16:1

POURED

And now my soul is *p* ... Job 30:16
I am *p* out like water ... Ps 22:14
grace is *p* upon Your ... Ps 45:2
name is ointment *p* ... Song 1:3
visited You, they *p* ... Is 26:16
strong, because He *p* ... Is 53:12
and My fury will be *p* ... Jer 7:20
His fury is *p* out like ... Nah 1:6
broke the flask and *p* ... Mark 14:3
of God has been *p* ... Rom 5:5
if I am being *p* ... Phil 2:17
I am already being *p* ... 2 Tim 4:6
whom He *p* out on us ... Titus 3:6

POVERTY

of the poor is their *p* ... Prov 10:15
but it leads to *p* ... Prov 11:24
P and shame will come ... Prov 13:18
leads only to *p* ... Prov 14:23
lest you come to *p* ... Prov 20:13
give me neither *p* ... Prov 30:8
p put in all the ... Luke 21:4
and their deep *p* ... 2 Cor 8:2
p might become rich ... 2 Cor 8:9
tribulation, and *p* ... Rev 2:9

POWER

that I may show My *p* ... Ex 9:16
become glorious in *p* ... Ex 15:6
for God has *p* to help ... 2 Chr 25:8
him who is without *p* ... Job 26:2
p who can understand ... Job 26:14
p belongs to God ... Ps 62:11
p Your enemies shall ... Ps 66:3
gives strength and *p* ... Ps 68:35
a king is, there is *p* ... Eccl 8:4
No one has *p* over the ... Eccl 8:8
the strength of His *p* ... Is 40:26
truly I am full of *p* ... Mic 3:8
anger and great in *p* ... Nah 1:3
'Not by might nor by *p* ... Zech 4:6
the kingdom and the *p* ... Matt 6:13
the Son of Man has *p* ... Matt 9:6
who had given such *p* ... Matt 9:8
Scriptures nor the *p* ... Matt 22:29
And the *p* of the Lord ... Luke 5:17
p went out from Him ... Luke 6:19
you are endued with *p* ... Luke 24:49
I have *p* to lay it ... John 10:18
not know that I have *p* ... John 19:10
"You could have no *p* ... John 19:11
you shall receive *p* ... Acts 1:8
as though by our own *p* ... Acts 3:12
man is the great *p* ... Acts 8:10
"Give me this *p* ... Acts 8:19
for it is the *p* ... Rom 1:16
even His eternal *p* ... Rom 1:20
saved it is the *p* ... 1 Cor 1:18
Greeks, Christ the *p* ... 1 Cor 1:24
be brought under the *p* ... 1 Cor 6:12
that the *p* of Christ ... 2 Cor 12:9
greatness of His *p* ... Eph 1:19
working of His *p* ... Eph 3:7
the Lord and in the *p* ... Eph 6:10
to His glorious *p* ... Col 1:11
the glory of His *p* ... 2 Thess 1:9
of fear, but of *p* ... 2 Tim 1:7
by the word of His *p* ... Heb 1:3
p of death, that ... Heb 2:14
but according to the *p* ... Heb 7:16
as His divine *p* ... 2 Pet 1:3
dominion and *p* ... Jude 25
to him I will give *p* ... Rev 2:26
glory and honor and *p* ... Rev 4:11
honor and glory and *p* ... Rev 5:13

POWERFUL

of the LORD is *p* ... Ps 29:4
of God is living and *p* ... Heb 4:12

POWERS

principalities and *p* ... Col 2:15
word of God and the *p* ... Heb 6:5

PRAETORIUM

Pilate's, in Jerusalem, Mark 15:16; John 18:28; Matt 27:27
—— Herod's palace at Caesarea, Acts 23:35

PRAISE

your brothers shall *p* ... Gen 49:8
He is your *p* ... Deut 10:21
I will sing *p* to the ... Judg 5:3
p shall be of You in ... Ps 22:25
For *p* from the upright ... Ps 33:1
p shall continually be ... Ps 34:1
the people shall *p* ... Ps 45:17
Whoever offers *p* ... Ps 50:23
P is awaiting You ... Ps 65:1
make His *p* glorious ... Ps 66:2
let all the peoples *p* ... Ps 67:3
Let heaven and earth *p* ... Ps 69:34
p shall be continually ... Ps 71:6
And the heavens will *p* ... Ps 89:5
silent, O God of my *p* ... Ps 109:1
Seven times a day I *p* ... Ps 119:164
All Your works shall *p* ... Ps 145:10
shall speak the *p* ... Ps 145:21
P the LORD ... Ps 148:1
that has breath *p* ... Ps 150:6
Let another man *p* ... Prov 27:2
let her own works *p* ... Prov 31:31
And your gates *P* ... Is 60:18
He makes Jerusalem a *p* ... Is 62:7
For You are my *p* ... Jer 17:14
Me a name of joy, a *p* ... Jer 33:9
give you fame and *p* ... Zeph 3:20
You have perfected *p* ... Matt 21:16
of men more than the *p* ... John 12:43
p is not from men but ... Rom 2:29
Then each one's *p* ... 1 Cor 4:5
the brother whose *p* ... 2 Cor 8:18
should be to the *p* ... Eph 1:12
to the glory and *p* ... Phil 1:11
I will sing *p* to You ... Heb 2:12
the sacrifice of *p* ... Heb 13:15
and for the *p* of those ... 1 Pet 2:14
saying, "*P* our God ... Rev 19:5

PRAISED

who is worthy to be *p* ... 2 Sam 22:4
daily He shall be *p* ... Ps 72:15
LORD's name is to be *p* ... Ps 113:3
and greatly to be *p* ... Ps 145:3
where our fathers *p* ... Is 64:11
the Most High and *p* ... Dan 4:34

PRAISES

enthroned in the *p* ... Ps 22:3
it is good to sing *p* ... Ps 147:1
and he *p* her ... Prov 31:28
shall proclaim the *p* ... Is 60:6
you may proclaim the *p* ... 1 Pet 2:9

PRAISEWORTHY
if there is anything *p* ....Phil 4:8

PRAISING
they will still be *p* ....Ps 84:4
of the heavenly host *p* ......Luke 2:13
in the temple *p* ....Luke 24:53

PRATING
p fool will fall ....Prov 10:8

PRAY
LORD in ceasing to *p* .....1 Sam 12:23
at noon I will *p* ....Ps 55:17
who hate you, and *p* ....Matt 5:44
"And when you *p* ....Matt 6:5
But you, when you *p* ....Matt 6:6
manner, therefore, *p* ....Matt 6:9
Watch and *p* ....Matt 26:41
to the mountain to *p* ....Mark 6:46
"Lord, teach us to *p* ....Luke 11:1
men always ought to *p* ....Luke 18:1
And I will *p* ....John 14:16
I do not *p* for the ....John 17:9
"I do not *p* for ....John 17:20
know what we should *p* ....Rom 8:26
I will *p* with the ....1 Cor 14:15
p without ceasing ....1 Thess 5:17
Brethren, *p* for us ....1 Thess 5:25
therefore that the men *p* .....1 Tim 2:8
Let him *p* ....James 5:13
to one another, and *p* ......James 5:16
say that he should *p* ....1 John 5:16
p that you may prosper ....3 John 2

PRAYED
Pharisee stood and *p* ......Luke 18:11
p more earnestly ....Luke 22:44
p earnestly that it ....James 5:17

PRAYER
in heaven their *p* ....1 Kin 8:45
p made in this place ....2 Chr 7:15
fear, and restrain *p* ....Job 15:4
And my *p* is pure ....Job 16:17
p would return to my ....Ps 35:13
A *p* to the God of my ....Ps 42:8
P also will be made ....Ps 72:15
Let my *p* come before ....Ps 88:2
He shall regard the *p* ....Ps 102:17
but I give myself to *p* ....Ps 109:4
to the LORD, but the *p* ....Prov 15:8
not go out except by *p* ....Matt 17:21
all night in *p* to God ....Luke 6:12
continually to *p* ....Acts 6:4
where *p* was ....Acts 16:13
steadfastly in *p* ....Rom 12:12
to fasting and *p* ....1 Cor 7:5
always with all *p* ....Eph 6:18
but in everything by *p* ....Phil 4:6
the word of God and *p* ....1 Tim 4:5
And the *p* of faith ....James 5:15

PRAYERS
though you make many *p* ......Is 1:15
pretense make long *p* .....Matt 23:14
fervently for you in *p* ....Col 4:12
that supplications, *p* ....1 Tim 2:1
p may not be hindered ....1 Pet 3:7
are open to their *p* ....1 Pet 3:12
and watchful in your *p* ....1 Pet 4:7
which are the *p* ....Rev 5:8

PREACH
that great city, and *p* ....Jon 3:2
time Jesus began to *p* ....Matt 4:17
you hear in the ear, *p* ......Matt 10:27
P the gospel to the ....Luke 4:18
p the kingdom of God ....Luke 9:60
And how shall they *p* ......Rom 10:15
p Christ crucified ....1 Cor 1:23
is me if I do not *p* ....1 Cor 9:16
I or they, so we *p* ....1 Cor 15:11
For we do not *p* ....2 Cor 4:5
p Christ even from ....Phil 1:15
P the word ....2 Tim 4:2

PREACHED
p that people ....Mark 6:12
out and *p* everywhere ...Mark 16:20
of sins should be *p* ....Luke 24:47
p Christ to them ....Acts 8:5
through this Man is *p* ......Acts 13:38
lest, when I have *p* ....1 Cor 9:27
whom we have not *p* ....2 Cor 11:4
than what we have *p* ....Gal 1:8
in truth, Christ is *p* ....Phil 1:18
the gospel was *p* ....Heb 4:2
also He went and *p* ....1 Pet 3:19

PREACHER
The words of the P ....Eccl 1:1
they hear without a *p* ....Rom 10:14
I was appointed a *p* ....1 Tim 2:7
of eight people, a *p* ....2 Pet 2:5

PREACHES
the Jesus whom Paul *p* ......Acts 19:13
p another Jesus whom ......2 Cor 11:4
p any other gospel ....Gal 1:9
p the faith which he ....Gal 1:23

PREACHING
p Jesus as the ....Acts 5:42
to my gospel and the *p* .....Rom 16:25
not risen, then our *p* ....1 Cor 15:14

PRECEDE
p those who are asleep ...1 Thess 4:15

PRECEPT
p must be upon *p* ....Is 28:10

PRECEPTS
and commanded them *p* ....Neh 9:14
all His *p* are sure ....Ps 111:7
us to keep Your *p* ....Ps 119:4
how I love Your *p* ....Ps 119:159
and kept all his *p* ....Jer 35:18

PRECIOUS
because my life was *p* .....1 Sam 26:21
P in the sight of the ....Ps 116:15
How *p* also are Your ....Ps 139:17
She is more *p* than ....Prov 3:15
Since you were *p* ....Is 43:4
p things shall not ....Is 44:9
if you take out the *p* ....Jer 15:19
The *p* sons of Zion ....Lam 4:2
farmer waits for the *p* ....James 5:7
more *p* than gold ....1 Pet 1:7
who believe, He is *p* ....1 Pet 2:7
p in the sight of ....1 Pet 3:4

PREDESTINED
He foreknew, He also *p* .....Rom 8:29
having *p* us to ....Eph 1:5
inheritance, being *p* ....Eph 1:11

PREEMINENCE
He may have the *p* ....Col 1:18
loves to have the *p* ....3 John 9

PREFERENCE
in honor giving *p* ....Rom 12:10

PREFERRED
comes after me is *p* ....John 1:15

PREJUDICE
these things without *p* ......1 Tim 5:21

PREMEDITATE
p what you will ....Mark 13:11

PREPARATION
Now it was the P ....John 19:14
your feet with the *p* ....Eph 6:15

PREPARE
p your hearts for the ....1 Sam 7:3
p a table before me in ....Ps 23:5
p mercy and truth ....Ps 61:7
P the way of the LORD ....Is 40:3
P the way for the ....Is 62:10
P the way of the LORD ......Mark 1:3
will, and did not *p* ....Luke 12:47
p a place for you ....John 14:2

PREPARED
place which I have *p* ....Ex 23:20
You *p* room for it ....Ps 80:9
When He *p* the heavens ......Prov 8:27
for the LORD has *p* ....Zeph 1:7
for whom it is *p* ....Matt 20:23
which You have *p* ....Luke 2:31
mercy, which He had *p* ......Rom 9:23
things which God has *p* ......1 Cor 2:9
Now He who has *p* ....2 Cor 5:5
p beforehand that we ....Eph 2:10
God, for He has *p* ....Heb 11:16

PRESENCE
themselves from the *p* ....Gen 3:8
went out from the *p* ....Gen 4:16
we die in your *p* ....Gen 47:15
P will go with you ....Ex 33:14
and honor the *p* ....Lev 19:32
afraid in any man's *p* ....Deut 1:17
am terrified at His *p* ....Job 23:15
p is fullness of joy ....Ps 16:11
shall dwell in Your *p* ....Ps 140:13
not tremble at My *p* ....Jer 5:22
shall shake at My *p* ....Ezek 38:20
Be silent in the *p* ....Zeph 1:7
and drank in Your *p* ....Luke 13:26
full of joy in Your *p* ....Acts 2:28
but his bodily *p* ....2 Cor 10:10
obeyed, not as in my *p* ......Phil 2:12

PRESENT
we are all *p* before ....Acts 10:33
evil is *p* with me ....Rom 7:21
p your bodies a living ....Rom 12:1
or death, or things *p* ....1 Cor 3:22
absent in body but *p* ....1 Cor 5:3
not only when I am *p* ....Gal 4:18
that He might *p* ....Eph 5:27
to *p* yourself ....2 Tim 2:15
p you faultless ....Jude 24

PRESENTED
treasures, they *p* ....Matt 2:11
For just as you *p* ....Rom 6:19

PRESENTS
kings will bring *p* ....Ps 68:29

PRESERVE

before you to p life ....Gen 45:5
You shall p me from ....Ps 32:7
O LORD, You p man and ......Ps 36:6
He shall p your soul ....Ps 121:7
The LORD shall p ....Ps 121:8
children, I will p ....Jer 49:11
pardon those whom I p ......Jer 50:20
loses his life will p.........Luke 17:33
every evil work and p ......2 Tim 4:18

PRESERVED

and my life is p ....Gen 32:30
soul, and body be p.......1 Thess 5:23

PRESERVES

For the LORD p the ....Ps 31:23
p the souls of His ....Ps 97:10
The LORD p the simple ....Ps 116:6
who guards his mouth p.....Prov 13:3
he who keeps his way p.....Prov 16:17

PRESS

I p toward the goal ....Phil 3:14

PRESSED

p her virgin bosom ....Ezek 23:8
We are hard p on every ......2 Cor 4:8
For I am hard p ....Phil 1:23

PRESUMPTUOUS

servant also from p ....Ps 19:13

PRETENDED

before them, p madness ...1 Sam 21:13

PRETENSE

whole heart, but in p ....Jer 3:10
p make long prayers ....Matt 23:14

PREVAIL

no man shall p ....1 Sam 2:9
our tongue we will p ....Ps 12:4
but they shall not p ....Jer 1:19
of Hades shall not p ....Matt 16:18

PREVAILED

hand, that Israel p ....Ex 17:11
with the Angel and p ....Hos 12:4
grew mightily and p ....Acts 19:20

PREY

the mountains of p ....Ps 76:4
has not given us as p ....Ps 124:6
Shall the p be taken ....Is 49:24
evil makes himself a p ....Is 59:15
shall no longer be a p ......Ezek 34:22
when he has no p ....Amos 3:4

PRICE

be weighed for its p ....Job 28:15
a fool the purchase p.......Prov 17:16
one pearl of great p ....Matt 13:46
back part of the p ....Acts 5:3
you were bought at a p ......1 Cor 6:20

PRIDE

p come against me ....Ps 36:11
p serves as.........................Ps 73:6
p and arrogance and ....Prov 8:13
By p comes nothing ....Prov 13:10
P goes before ....Prov 16:18
p will bring him low ....Prov 29:23
and her daughter had p ....Ezek 16:49
p He is able to put down ....Dan 4:37
was hardened in p ....Dan 5:20
has sworn by the p ....Amos 8:7
For the p of the ....Zech 11:3
evil eye, blasphemy, p.........Mark 7:22
p he fall into the ....1 Tim 3:6
eyes, and the p of life ....1 John 2:16

PRIEST

he was the p of God ....Gen 14:18
Myself a faithful p ....1 Sam 2:35
p forever according ....Ps 110:4
the p and the prophet ....Is 28:7
So He shall be a p ....Zech 6:13
of a p should keep ....Mal 2:17
and faithful High P ....Heb 2:17
we have a great High P ....Heb 4:14
p forever according ....Heb 5:6
Christ came as High P ....Heb 9:11

PRIESTHOOD

be an everlasting p ....Ex 40:15
have defiled the p ....Neh 13:29
p being changed ....Heb 7:12
has an unchangeable p ....Heb 7:24
house, a holy p ....1 Pet 2:5
generation, a royal p.........1 Pet 2:9

PRIESTS

to Me a kingdom of p ....Ex 19:6
her p teach for pay ....Mic 3:11
made us kings and p...........Rev 1:6
but they shall be p ....Rev 20:6

PRINCE

"Who made you a p ....Ex 2:14
is the house of the p ....Job 21:28
is the downfall of a p.......Prov 14:28
Everlasting Father, P ....Is 9:6
until Messiah the P ....Dan 9:25
except Michael your p.......Dan 10:21
days without king or p ....Hos 3:4
p asks for gifts ....Mic 7:3
and killed the P ....Acts 3:15
His right hand to be P ....Acts 5:31
the p of the power ....Eph 2:2

PRINCES

He is not partial to p ....Job 34:19
to bind his p at his ....Ps 105:22
He may seat him with p ....Ps 113:8
to put confidence in p ....Ps 118:9
P also sit and speak ....Ps 119:23
p and all judges of ....Ps 148:11
good, nor to strike p ....Prov 17:26
is a child, and your p ....Eccl 10:16
of nobles, and your p ....Eccl 10:17
children to be their p ....Is 3:4
p will rule with ....Is 32:1
He brings the p ....Is 40:23

PRINCIPAL

Wisdom is the p ....Prov 4:7

PRINCIPALITY

far above all p ....Eph 1:21
is the head of all p ....Col 2:10

PRINCIPLES

from the basic p..................Col 2:20
again the first p ....Heb 5:12

PRISCILLA (or Prisca)

Wife of Aquila, Acts 18:1–3
With Aquila, instructs Apollos, Acts 18:26
Mentioned by Paul, Rom 16:3; 1 Cor 16:19; 2 Tim 4:19

PRISON

and put him into the p ......Gen 39:20
Bring my soul out of p ....Ps 142:7
in darkness from the p ....Is 42:7
the opening of the p ....Is 61:1
should put him in p ....Jer 29:26
John had heard in p ....Matt 11:2
I was in p and you ....Matt 25:36
to the spirits in p ....1 Pet 3:19

PRISONER

the groaning of the p ....Ps 79:11
reason I, Paul, the p ....Eph 3:1
Lord, nor of me His p ....2 Tim 1:8

PRISONERS

p rest together ....Job 3:18
does not despise His p ....Ps 69:33
gives freedom to the p ....Ps 146:7
the stronghold, you p ....Zech 9:12
Remember the p as if ....Heb 13:3

PRISONS

the synagogues and p ......Luke 21:12
p more frequently ....2 Cor 11:23

PRIZE

life shall be as a p ....Jer 21:9
but one receives the p ....1 Cor 9:24
the goal for the p ....Phil 3:14

PROCEED

For they p from evil ....Jer 9:3
of the same mouth p ....James 3:10

PROCEEDED

for I p forth ....John 8:42

PROCEEDS

by every word that p ....Deut 8:3
by every word that p ....Matt 4:4
Spirit of truth who p.........John 15:26
back part of the p ....Acts 5:2

PROCESSION

They have seen Your p ....Ps 68:24

PROCHORUS

One of the first seven deacons, Acts 6:5

PROCLAIM

you, and I will p ....Ex 33:19
p the name of the LORD ....Deut 32:3
p it not in the ....2 Sam 1:20
and they shall p ....Is 60:6
began to p it freely ....Mark 1:45
knowing, Him I p ....Acts 17:23
drink this cup, you p ....1 Cor 11:26

PROCLAIMED

p the good news ....Ps 40:9
company of those who p .....Ps 68:11
he went his way and p ....Luke 8:39
inner rooms will be p ....Luke 12:3

PROCLAIMER

"He seems to be a p ....Acts 17:18

PROCLAIMS

good news, who p ....Is 52:7

PROCONSUL

seeking to turn the p............Acts 13:8

When Gallio was *p* ....Acts 18:12

PRODIGAL

with *p* living ....Luke 15:13

PRODUCE

land shall yield its *p* ....Lev 26:4
all kinds of *p* ....Ps 144:13

PROFANE

and offered *p* fire ....Lev 10:1
and priest are *p* ....Jer 23:11
"But you *p* it ....Mal 1:12
tried to *p* the temple ....Acts 24:6
But reject *p* and old ....1 Tim 4:7
p person like Esau ....Heb 12:16

PROFANED

p his crown by casting ....Ps 89:39
and *p* My Sabbaths ....Ezek 22:8
p the LORD's holy ....Mal 2:11

PROFANENESS

of Jerusalem *p* has ....Jer 23:15

PROFANING

p the covenant of the ....Mal 2:10

PROFESS

They *p* to know God ....Titus 1:16

PROFESSING

P to be wise ....Rom 1:22
is proper for women *p* ......1 Tim 2:10

PROFIT

p is there in my blood ....Ps 30:9
p has a man from all ....Eccl 1:3
There was no *p* under ....Eccl 2:11
for they will not *p* ....Is 57:12
words that cannot *p* ....Jer 7:8
p which you have made ....Ezek 22:13
p is it that we have ....Mal 3:14
For what *p* is it to ....Matt 16:26
For what will it *p* ....Mark 8:36
For what *p* is it to ....Luke 9:25
her masters much *p* ....Acts 16:16
hope of *p* was gone ....Acts 16:19
brought no small *p* ....Acts 19:24
what is the *p* of ....Rom 3:1
not seeking my own *p* .....1 Cor 10:33
Christ will *p* you ....Gal 5:2
about words to no *p* ....2 Tim 2:14
them, but He for our *p* ....Heb 12:10
What does it *p* ....James 2:14
and sell, and make a *p* .....James 4:13

PROFITABLE

"Can a man be *p* ....Job 22:2
It is doubtless not *p* ....2 Cor 12:1
of God, and is *p* ....2 Tim 3:16
things are good and *p* ....Titus 3:8
to you, but now is *p* ....Philem 11

PROFITS

p a man nothing that ....Job 34:9
have not love, it *p* ....1 Cor 13:3
exercise *p* a little ....1 Tim 4:8

PROFOUND

with things too *p* ....Ps 131:1

PROLONG

you will not *p* your ....Deut 4:26

p Your anger to all ....Ps 85:5
nor will he *p* his days ....Eccl 8:13

PROLONGED

and his days are *p* ....Eccl 8:12

PROLONGS

The fear of the LORD *p* .....Prov 10:27

PROMISE

of all His good *p* ....1 Kin 8:56
Behold, I send the *P* ....Luke 24:49
but to wait for the *P* ....Acts 1:4
For the *p* is to you ....Acts 2:39
p drew near which God ....Acts 7:17
for the hope of the *p* ....Acts 26:6
is made void and the *p* ......Rom 4:14
p might be sure ....Rom 4:16
it is no longer of *p* ....Gal 3:18
Therefore, since a *p* ....Heb 4:1
to the heirs of *p* ....Heb 6:17
did not receive the *p* ....Heb 11:39
they *p* them liberty ....2 Pet 2:19
p that He has promised ....1 John 2:25

PROMISED

bless you as He has *p* ....Deut 1:11
Him faithful who had *p* .....Heb 11:11

PROMISES

For all the *p* of God ....2 Cor 1:20
his Seed were the *p* ....Gal 3:16
patience inherit the *p* ....Heb 6:12
having received the *p* ....Heb 11:13
great and precious *p* ....2 Pet 1:4

PROMPTLY

him disciplines him *p* ......Prov 13:24

PROOF

which is to them a *p* ....Phil 1:28

PROOFS

by many infallible *p* ....Acts 1:3

PROPER

you, but for what is *p* ....1 Cor 7:35
Is it *p* for a woman to .....1 Cor 11:13
but, which is *p* ....1 Tim 2:10

PROPERLY

Let us walk *p* ....Rom 13:13

PROPHECY

miracles, to another *p* .....1 Cor 12:10
for *p* never came by ....2 Pet 1:21
is the spirit of *p* ....Rev 19:10
of the book of this *p* ....Rev 22:19

PROPHESIED

upon them, that they *p* .....Num 11:25
to them, yet they *p* ....Jer 23:21
Lord, have we not *p* ....Matt 7:22
prophets and the law *p* .....Matt 11:13
virgin daughters who *p* ......Acts 21:9
even more that you *p* ....1 Cor 14:5

PROPHESIES

for the prophet who *p* ....Jer 28:9
woman who prays or *p* ....1 Cor 11:5
p edifies the church ....1 Cor 14:4

PROPHESY

prophets, "Do not *p* ....Is 30:10

The prophets *p* falsely ....Jer 5:31
your daughters shall *p* ....Joel 2:28
Who can but *p* ....Amos 3:8
saying, "*P* to us ....Matt 26:68
your daughters shall *p* ....Acts 2:17
if prophecy, let us *p* ....Rom 12:6
know in part and we *p* .....1 Cor 13:9
desire earnestly to *p* ....1 Cor 14:39

PROPHET

shall be your *p* ....Ex 7:1
raise up for you a *P* ....Deut 18:15
arisen in Israel a *p* ....Deut 34:10
"I alone am left a *p* ....1 Kin 18:22
is no longer any *p* ....Ps 74:9
I ordained you a *p* ....Jer 1:5
p is induced to speak ....Ezek 14:9
The *p* is a fool ....Hos 9:7
nor was I a son of a *p* ....Amos 7:14
send you Elijah the *p* ....Mal 4:5
p shall receive a ....Matt 10:41
p is not without honor ....Matt 13:57
by Daniel the *p* ....Mark 13:14
is not a greater *p* ....Luke 7:28
it cannot be that a *p* ....Luke 13:33
Nazareth, who was a *P* .....Luke 24:19
"Are you the *P* ....John 1:21
"This is truly the *P* ....John 6:14
with him the false *p* ....Rev 19:20

PROPHETIC

p word confirmed ....2 Pet 1:19

PROPHETS

LORD's people were *p* ....Num 11:29
Saul also among the *p* ....1 Sam 10:12
the mouth of all his *p* ......1 Kin 22:22
Where now are your *p* ....Jer 37:19
prophesy against the *p* ......Ezek 13:2
Her *p* are insolent ....Zeph 3:4
the Law or the *P* ....Matt 5:17
is the Law and the *P* ....Matt 7:12
or one of the *p* ....Matt 16:14
the tombs of the *p* ....Matt 23:29
indeed, I send you *p* ....Matt 23:34
one who kills the *p* ....Matt 23:37
Then many false *p* ....Matt 24:11
have Moses and the *p* ......Luke 16:29
You are sons of the *p* ....Acts 3:25
p did your fathers not ....Acts 7:52
To Him all the *p* ....Acts 10:43
do you believe the *p* ....Acts 26:27
before through His *p* ....Rom 1:2
by the Law and the *P* ....Rom 3:21
have killed Your *p* ....Rom 11:3
p are subject to the ....1 Cor 14:32
to be apostles, some *p* ....Eph 4:11
brethren, take the *p* ....James 5:10
this salvation the *p* ....1 Pet 1:10
were also false *p* ....2 Pet 2:1
because many false *p* ....1 John 4:1
blood of saints and *p* ....Rev 16:6
found the blood of *p* ....Rev 18:24
of your brethren the *p* ....Rev 22:9

PROPITIATION

set forth as a *p* ....Rom 3:25
to God, to make *p* ....Heb 2:17
He Himself is the *p* ....1 John 2:2
His Son to be the *p* ....1 John 4:10

PROPORTION

let us prophesy in *p* ....Rom 12:6

PROPRIETY

modest apparel, with *p* ....1 Tim 2:9

PROSECUTOR
answer me, that my *P* ....Job 31:35

PROSELYTE
and sea to win one *p* ....Matt 23:15

PROSELYTES
Rome, both Jews and *p* ......Acts 2:10

PROSPER
made all he did to *p*..........Gen 39:3
you shall not *p* ....Deut 28:29
LORD, God made him *p*.......2 Chr 26:5
they *p* who love you ....Ps 122:6
his sins will not *p* ....Prov 28:13
of the LORD shall *p* ....Is 53:10
against you shall *p* ....Is 54:17
please, and it shall *p* ....Is 55:11
of the wicked *p*..................Jer 12:1
King shall reign and *p* ....Jer 23:5
storing up as he may *p* ....1 Cor 16:2
I pray that you may *p* ....3 John 2

PROSPERED
since the LORD has *p* ....Gen 24:56

PROSPERING
His ways are always *p* ....Ps 10:5

PROSPERITY
p all your days ....Deut 23:6
p exceed the fame ....1 Kin 10:7
p the destroyer.................Job 15:21
spend their days in *p* ....Job 36:11
Now in my *p* I said ....Ps 30:6
has pleasure in the *p* ....Ps 35:27
When I saw the *p* ....Ps 73:3
I pray, send now *p* ....Ps 118:25
the day of *p* be joyful ....Eccl 7:14
that we have our *p* ....Acts 19:25

PROSPEROUS
had made his journey *p* .....Gen 24:21
will make your way *p* ....Josh 1:8

PROSPERS
he turns, he *p* ....Prov 17:8
just as your soul *p* ....3 John 2

PROSTRATE
of the proud lie *p* ....Job 9:13

PROUD
p waves must stop ....Job 38:11
tongue that speaks *p* ....Ps 12:3
and fully repays the *p*...........Ps 31:23
does not respect the *p* ....Ps 40:4
a haughty look and a *p* ....Ps 101:5
p He knows from afar ....Ps 138:6
the house of the *p* ....Prov 15:25
Everyone *p* ....Prov 16:5
p heart stirs up ....Prov 28:25
is better than the *p* ....Eccl 7:8
by wine, he is a *p*...................Hab 2:5
He has scattered the *p* ....Luke 1:51
"God resists the *p* ....1 Pet 5:5

PROVE
p yourself a man ....1 Kin 2:2
does your arguing *p* ....Job 6:25
mind, that you may *p* ....Rom 12:2

PROVERB
an astonishment, a *p* ....Deut 28:37

incline my ear to a *p* ....Ps 49:4
that hang limp is a *p* ....Prov 26:7
of a drunkard is a *p* ....Prov 26:9
one shall take up a *p* ....Mic 2:4
to the true *p* ....2 Pet 2:22

PROVERBS
spoke three thousand *p* ....1 Kin 4:32
in order many *p* ....Eccl 12:9

PROVIDE
"My son, God will *p* ....Gen 22:8
Can He *p* meat for His ....Ps 78:20
prosperity that I *p* ....Jer 33:9
P neither gold nor................Matt 10:9
if anyone does not *p* ....1 Tim 5:8

PROVIDED
these hands have *p* ....Acts 20:34
p something better ....Heb 11:40

PROVIDES
p food for the raven ....Job 38:41
p her supplies in the ....Prov 6:8

PROVISION
abundantly bless her *p* ....Ps 132:15
no *p* for the flesh ....Rom 13:14

PROVOKE
do not *p* Him ....Ex 23:21
p God are secure ....Job 12:6
Do they *p* Me to ....Jer 7:19
p them to jealousy ....Rom 11:11
you, fathers, do not *p* ....Eph 6:4

PROVOKED
How often they *p* ....Ps 78:40
p the Most High ....Ps 78:56
Thus they *p* Him to ....Ps 106:29
his spirit was *p* ....Acts 17:16
seek its own, is not *p* ....1 Cor 13:5

PRUDENCE
To give *p* to the ....Prov 1:4
wisdom, dwell with *p* ....Prov 8:12
us in all wisdom and *p*...............Eph 1:8

PRUDENT
p man covers shame ....Prov 12:16
A *p* man conceals ....Prov 12:23
The wisdom of the *p* ....Prov 14:8
p considers well ....Prov 14:15
heart will be called *p* ....Prov 16:21
p acquires knowledge ....Prov 18:15
p wife is from the ....Prov 19:14
p man foresees evil ....Prov 22:3
perished from the *p* ....Jer 49:7
Therefore the *p* ....Amos 5:13
from the wise and *p* ....Matt 11:25

PRUDENTLY
Servant shall deal *p* ....Is 52:13

PRUNES
that bears fruit He *p* ....John 15:2

PSALM
and the sound of a *p* ....Ps 98:5
in the second *P* ....Acts 13:33
each of you has a *p* ....1 Cor 14:26

PSALMIST
And the sweet *p* ....2 Sam 23:1

PSALMS
Sing to Him, sing *p* ....1 Chr 16:9
to one another in *p* ....Eph 5:19
Let him sing *p* ....James 5:13

PSALTERY
harp, lyre, and *p* ....Dan 3:10

PUBLISHED
to be proclaimed and *p* ....Jon 3:7

PUBLIUS
Roman official; entertains Paul, Acts 28:7, 8

PUFFED
Now some are *p* up ....1 Cor 4:18
itself, is not *p* ....1 Cor 13:4
a novice, lest being *p* ....1 Tim 3:6

PUFFS
Knowledge *p* up ....1 Cor 8:1

PUL
King of Assyria; same as Tiglath-Pileser, 2 Kin 15:19
—— Country and people in Africa, Is 66:19

PULL
P me out of the net ....Ps 31:4
I will *p* down my barns ....Luke 12:18

PUNISH
take that man and *p* ....Deut 22:18
p the righteous is ....Prov 17:26
"I will *p* the world ....Is 13:11
Shall I not *p* them for ....Jer 5:9
p all who oppress them ....Jer 30:20
p your iniquity ....Lam 4:22
So I will *p* them for ....Hos 4:9

PUNISHED
You our God have *p* ....Ezra 9:13
because He has not *p* ....Job 35:15
p them often in every ....Acts 26:11
These shall be *p* ....2 Thess 1:9

PUNISHES
will you say when He *p* ....Jer 13:21

PUNISHMENT
p is greater than I ....Gen 4:13
you do in the day of *p* ....Is 10:3
p they shall be cast ....Jer 8:12
p they shall perish ....Jer 10:15
a man for the *p* ....Lam 3:39
The *p* of the iniquity ....Lam 4:6
days of *p* have come ....Hos 9:7
not turn away its *p* ....Amos 1:3
into everlasting *p* ....Matt 25:46
p which was inflicted ....2 Cor 2:6
Of how much worse *p* ....Heb 10:29
sent by him for the *p* ....1 Pet 2:14
the unjust under *p* ....2 Pet 2:9

PURCHASED
of God could be *p* ....Acts 8:20
of the *p* possession ....Eph 1:14

PURE
a mercy seat of *p* gold ....Ex 25:17
Can a man be more *p* ....Job 4:17
if you were *p* and ....Job 8:6

'My doctrine is *p* ....Job 11:4
that he could be *p* ....Job 15:14
the heavens are not *p* ....Job 15:15
the stars are not *p* ....Job 25:5
of the LORD are *p* ....Ps 12:6
will show Yourself *p* ....Ps 18:26
To such as are *p* ....Ps 73:1
of the *p* are pleasant ....Prov 15:26
ways of a man are *p* ....Prov 16:2
my heart clean, I am *p* ......Prov 20:9
but as for the *p* ....Prov 21:8
a generation that is *p* ......Prov 30:12
Shall I count *p* ....Mic 6:11
things indeed are *p* ....Rom 14:20
whatever things are *p* ....Phil 4:8
keep yourself *p* ....1 Tim 5:22
p all things are *p* ....Titus 1:15
above is first *p* ....James 3:17
babes, desire the *p* ....1 Pet 2:2
just as He is *p* ....1 John 3:3

PURER

p eyes than to behold ....Hab 1:13

PURGE

P me with hyssop ....Ps 51:7
p them as gold and ....Mal 3:3

PURGED

away, and your sin *p* ....Is 6:7
He had by Himself *p* ....Heb 1:3

PURIFICATION

for the water of *p* ....Num 19:9
with the water of *p* ....Num 31:23

PURIFIED

earth, *p* seven times ....Ps 12:6
all things are *p* ....Heb 9:22
Since you have *p* ....1 Pet 1:22

PURIFIES

hope in Him *p* himself ......1 John 3:3

PURIFY

p the sons of Levi ....Mal 3:3
and *p* your hearts ....James 4:8

PURIFYING

thus *p* all foods ....Mark 7:19
p their hearts by ....Acts 15:9
sanctifies for the *p* ....Heb 9:13

PURIM

called these days *P* ....Esth 9:26

PURITY

be delivered by the *p* ....Job 22:30
He who loves *p* of ....Prov 22:11
by *p*, by knowledge ....2 Cor 6:6
spirit, in faith, in *p* ....1 Tim 4:12

PURPLE

who was clothed in *p* ......Luke 16:19
they put on Him a *p* ....John 19:2
She was a seller of *p* ....Acts 16:14

PURPOSE

and fulfill all your *p* ....Ps 20:4
A time for every *p* ....Eccl 3:1
p that is purposed ....Is 14:26
But for this *p* I came ....John 12:27
by the determined *p* ....Acts 2:23
them all that with *p* ....Acts 11:23
to the eternal *p* ....Eph 3:11
Now the *p* of the ....1 Tim 1:5
to fulfill His *p* ....Rev 17:17

PURPOSED

For the LORD had *p* ......2 Sam 17:14
LORD of hosts has *p* ....Is 23:9
But Daniel *p* in his ....Dan 1:8
pleasure which He *p* ....Eph 1:9

PURPOSES

each one give as he *p* ....2 Cor 9:7

PURSE

let us all have one *p* ....Prov 1:14

PURSES

p his lips and brings ....Prov 16:30

PURSUE

And will You *p* dry ....Job 13:25
p my honor as the wind .....Job 30:15
The sword shall *p* ....Jer 48:2
but their hearts *p* ....Ezek 33:31
Let us know, let us *p* ....Hos 6:3
p righteousness ....Rom 9:30
P love, and desire ....1 Cor 14:1
p righteousness ....1 Tim 6:11
him seek peace and *p* ....1 Pet 3:11

PURSUES

Evil *p* sinners ....Prov 13:21
flee when no one *p* ....Prov 28:1

PURSUING

but Israel, *p* the law ....Rom 9:31

PUT

Also He has *p* eternity ....Eccl 3:11
pride He is able to *p* down ...Dan 4:37
what you will *p* on ....Matt 6:25
p my hand into His ....John 20:25
But *p* on the Lord ....Rom 13:14

PUTREFYING

bruises and *p* sores ....Is 1:6

— Q —

QUAIL

and it brought *q* ....Num 11:31
and He brought *q* ....Ps 105:40

QUAKED

the whole mountain *q* ....Ex 19:18
and the earth *q* ....Matt 27:51

QUAKES

The earth *q* before ....Joel 2:10

QUALIFIED

the Father who has *q* ....Col 1:12

QUARREL

see how he seeks a *q* ....2 Kin 5:7
any fool can start a *q* ....Prov 20:3
He will not *q* nor cry ....Matt 12:19
of the Lord must not *q* ....2 Tim 2:24

QUARRELSOME

but gentle, not *q* ....1 Tim 3:3

QUARTZ

be made of coral or *q* ....Job 28:18

QUEEN

Q Vashti also made a ....Esth 1:9
stands the *q* in gold ....Ps 45:9
burn incense to the *q* ....Jer 44:17
The *q* of the South ....Matt 12:42
under Candace the *q* ....Acts 8:27
heart, 'I sit as *q* ....Rev 18:7

QUEENS

There are sixty *q* ....Song 6:8
q your nursing mothers ....Is 49:23

QUENCH

Many waters cannot *q* ....Song 8:7
so that no one can *q* ....Jer 4:4
flax He will not *q* ....Matt 12:20
q all the fiery ....Eph 6:16
Do not *q* the Spirit ....1 Thess 5:19

QUENCHED

LORD, the fire was *q* ....Num 11:2
they were *q* like a ....Ps 118:12
their fire is not *q* ....Is 66:24
that shall never be *q* ....Mark 9:43
and the fire is not *q* ....Mark 9:44
q the violence of fire ....Heb 11:34

QUESTIONS

test him with hard *q* ....1 Kin 10:1
and asking them *q* ....Luke 2:46
market, asking no *q* ....1 Cor 10:25

QUICK-TEMPERED

q man acts foolishly ....Prov 14:17
not self-willed, not *q* ....Titus 1:7

QUICKLY

have turned aside *q* ....Ex 32:8
with your adversary *q* ....Matt 5:25
"What you do, do *q* ....John 13:27
Behold, I am coming *q* ....Rev 3:11
"Surely I am coming *q* ......Rev 22:20

QUIET

lain still and been *q* ....Job 3:13
'Take heed, and be *q* ....Is 7:4
earth is at rest and *q* ....Is 14:7
gladness, He will *q* ....Zeph 3:17
warned him to be *q* ....Mark 10:48
aspire to lead a *q* ....1 Thess 4:11
we may lead a *q* and ....1 Tim 2:2
a gentle and *q* spirit ....1 Pet 3:4

QUIETED

calmed and *q* my soul ....Ps 131:2
the city clerk had *q* ....Acts 19:35

QUIETNESS

will give peace and *q* ....1 Chr 22:9
When He gives *q* ....Job 34:29
a handful with *q* ....Eccl 4:6
in *q* and confidence ....Is 30:15
of righteousness, *q* ....Is 32:17
that they work in *q* ....2 Thess 3:12

QUIETS

q the earth by the ....Job 37:17

QUIVER

q rattles against him ....Job 39:23
the man who has his *q* ....Ps 127:5
q He has hidden Me ....Is 49:2
Their *q* is like an ....Jer 5:16

— R —

RAAMSES

Treasure city built by Hebrew slaves, Ex 1:11

and being *r* to punish ... 2 Cor 10:6
Be *r* in season and out ... 2 Tim 4:2
and always be *r* ... 1 Pet 3:15

REAFFIRM

r your love to him ... 2 Cor 2:8

REAP

in tears shall *r* ... Ps 126:5
r the whirlwind ... Hos 8:7
they neither sow nor *r* ... Matt 6:26
you knew that I *r* ... Matt 25:26
that he will also *r* ... Gal 6:7
due season we shall *r* ... Gal 6:9

REAPED

wheat but *r* thorns ... Jer 12:13
you have *r* iniquity ... Hos 10:13

REAPER

r does not fill his ... Ps 129:7

REAPERS

I will say to the *r* ... Matt 13:30
r are the angels ... Matt 13:39

REAPING

r what I did not ... Luke 19:22

REAPS

One sows and another *r* ... John 4:37

REASON

out wisdom and the *r* ... Eccl 7:25
Come now, and let us *r* ... Is 1:18
faith, why do you *r* ... Matt 16:8
words of truth and *r* ... Acts 26:25
who asks you a *r* ... 1 Pet 3:15

REASONED

for three Sabbaths *r* ... Acts 17:2
r about righteousness ... Acts 24:25

REBEKAH

Great-niece of Abraham, Gen 22:20–23
Becomes Isaac's wife, Gen 24:15–67
Mother of Esau and Jacob, Gen 25:21–28
Encourages Jacob to deceive Isaac, then to flee, Gen 27:1–29, 42–46

REBEL

Only do not *r* ... Num 14:9
Will you *r* against the ... Neh 2:19
There are those who *r* ... Job 24:13
and they did not *r* ... Ps 105:28
if you refuse and *r* ... Is 1:20

REBELLING

more against Him by *r* ... Ps 78:17

REBELLION

r is as the sin ... 1 Sam 15:23
For he adds *r* to his ... Job 34:37
evil man seeks only *r* ... Prov 17:11
you have taught *r* ... Jer 28:16
hearts as in the *r* ... Heb 3:8
and perished in the *r* ... Jude 11

REBELLIOUS

r exalt themselves ... Ps 66:7
but the *r* dwell in a ... Ps 68:6
day long to a *r* people ... Is 65:2

a defiant and *r* heart ... Jer 5:23
their princes are *r* ... Hos 9:15

REBELS

are all stubborn *r* ... Jer 6:28

REBUILD

God, to *r* its ruins ... Ezra 9:9
tombs, that I may *r* ... Neh 2:5
r it as in the days of ... Amos 9:11

REBUKE

He will surely *r* ... Job 13:10
astonished at His *r* ... Job 26:11
they perish at the *r* ... Ps 80:16
At Your *r* they fled ... Ps 104:7
And let him *r* me ... Ps 141:5
Turn at my *r* ... Prov 1:23
r a wise man ... Prov 9:8
R is more effective ... Prov 17:10
r is better than love ... Prov 27:5
better to hear the *r* ... Eccl 7:5
r the oppressor ... Is 1:17
sake I have suffered *r* ... Jer 15:15
r strong nations ... Mic 4:3
sins against you, *r* ... Luke 17:3
r Your disciples ... Luke 19:39
Do not *r* an older man ... 1 Tim 5:1
who are sinning *r* ... 1 Tim 5:20
r them sharply ... Titus 1:13
"The Lord *r* you ... Jude 9
As many as I love, I *r* ... Rev 3:19

REBUKED

r the winds and the ... Matt 8:26
r their unbelief ... Mark 16:14
when you are *r* by Him ... Heb 12:5
but he was *r* for his ... 2 Pet 2:16

REBUKES

with *r* You correct ... Ps 39:11
r a wicked man ... Prov 9:7
ear that hears the *r* ... Prov 15:31
r a man will find more ... Prov 28:23

RECALL

r the former days ... Heb 10:32

RECEIVE

He shall *r* blessing ... Ps 24:5
r us graciously ... Hos 14:2
you are willing to *r* ... Matt 11:14
believing, you will *r* ... Matt 21:22
and His own did not *r* ... John 1:11
"I do not *r* honor ... John 5:41
will come again and *r* ... John 14:3
the world cannot *r* ... John 14:17
Ask, and you will *r* ... John 16:24
"*R* the Holy Spirit ... John 20:22
"Lord Jesus, *r* ... Acts 7:59
r the Holy Spirit ... Acts 19:2
R one who is weak ... Rom 14:1
that each one may *r* ... 2 Cor 5:10
r the grace of God in ... 2 Cor 6:1
r the Spirit by the ... Gal 3:2
R him therefore in the ... Phil 2:29
suppose that he will *r* ... James 1:7
whatever we ask we *r* ... 1 John 3:22

RECEIVED

r your consolation ... Luke 6:24
in your lifetime you *r* ... Luke 16:25
But as many as *r* ... John 1:12
for God has *r* him ... Rom 14:3
For I *r* from the Lord ... 1 Cor 11:23

have *r* Christ Jesus ... Col 2:6
r up in glory ... 1 Tim 3:16
For He *r* from God the ... 2 Pet 1:17

RECEIVES

r correction is prudent ... Prov 15:5
r you *r* Me ... Matt 10:40
r one little child ... Matt 18:5
and whoever *r* Me ... Mark 9:37

RECEIVING

r a kingdom which ... Heb 12:28

RECHAB

Assassin of Ishbosheth, 2 Sam 4:2, 6
—— Father of Jehonadab, founder of the Rechabites, 2 Kin 10:15–23
Related to the Kenites, 1 Chr 2:55

RECHABITES

Kenite clan fathered by Rechab, committed to nomadic life, Jer 35:1–19

RECOMPENSE

He will accept no *r* ... Prov 6:35
not say, "I will *r* ... Prov 20:22
days of *r* have come ... Hos 9:7

RECOMPENSED

of my hands He has *r* ... 2 Sam 22:21
the LORD has *r* me ... 2 Sam 22:25

RECONCILE

and that He might *r* ... Eph 2:16
r all things to ... Col 1:20

RECONCILED

First be *r* to your ... Matt 5:24
were enemies we were *r* ... Rom 5:10
Christ's behalf, be *r* ... 2 Cor 5:20

RECONCILIATION

now received the *r* ... Rom 5:11
to us the word of *r* ... 2 Cor 5:19

RECONCILING

cast away is the *r* ... Rom 11:15
God was in Christ *r* ... 2 Cor 5:19

RECORD

r My name I will come ... Ex 20:24

RED

the first came out *r* ... Gen 25:25
though they are *r* ... Is 1:18
Why is Your apparel *r* ... Is 63:2
for the sky is *r* ... Matt 16:2

RED SEA

Divided for Israelites, Ex 14:15–31
Boundary of Promised Land, Ex 23:31

REDEEM

man you shall surely *r* ... Num 18:15
in our power to *r* them ... Neh 5:5
In famine He shall *r* ... Job 5:20
R me from the hand of ... Job 6:23
can by any means *r* ... Ps 49:7
But God will *r* my soul ... Ps 49:15
r their life from ... Ps 72:14
And He shall *r* Israel ... Ps 130:8
all that it cannot *r* ... Is 50:2
I will *r* them from ... Hos 13:14

was going to *r* Israel ......Luke 24:21
r those who were ....Gal 4:5
us, that He might *r* ....Titus 2:14

REDEEMED

people whom You have *r* .....Ex 15:13
r them from the hand ....Ps 106:10
Let the *r* of the LORD ....Ps 107:2
r shall walk there ....Is 35:9
sea a road for the *r* ....Is 51:10
and you shall be *r* ....Is 52:3
and *r* His people ....Luke 1:68
Christ has *r* us from ....Gal 3:13
that you were not *r* ....1 Pet 1:18
were slain, and have *r* ....Rev 5:9
These were *r* from ....Rev 14:4

REDEEMER

For I know that my *R* ....Job 19:25
Most High God their *R* ....Ps 78:35
for their *R* is mighty ....Prov 23:11
the LORD and your *R* ....Is 41:14
R will come to Zion ....Is 59:20
our *R* from Everlasting ....Is 63:16
Their *R* is strong ....Jer 50:34

REDEEMING

r the time ....Eph 5:16

REDEMPTION

For the *r* of their ....Ps 49:8
with Him is abundant *r* ....Ps 130:7
r is yours to buy it ....Jer 32:7
those who looked for *r* ......Luke 2:38
your *r* draws near ....Luke 21:28
grace through the *r* ....Rom 3:24
the adoption, the *r* ....Rom 8:23
sanctification and *r* ....1 Cor 1:30
In Him we have *r* ....Eph 1:7
for the day of *r* ....Eph 4:30
obtained eternal *r* ....Heb 9:12

REED

r He will not break ....Is 42:3
r shaken by the wind ....Matt 11:7
on the head with a *r* ....Mark 15:19

REEDS

r flourish without ....Job 8:11
the beasts of the *r* ....Ps 68:30

REFINED

where gold is *r* ....Job 28:1
us as silver is *r* ....Ps 66:10

REFINER

He will sit as a *r* ....Mal 3:3

REFORMATION

until the time of *r* ....Heb 9:10

REFRAIN

R from meddling with .....2 Chr 35:21
who have no right to *r* ....1 Cor 9:6
good days, let him *r* ....1 Pet 3:10

REFRESH

bread, that you may *r* ....Gen 18:5
r my heart in the Lord ......Philem 20

REFRESHED

of God, and may be *r* ......Rom 15:32
r my spirit and yours ......1 Cor 16:18
his spirit has been *r* ....2 Cor 7:13
for he often *r* ....2 Tim 1:16

REFRESHES

r the soul of his ....Prov 25:13

REFRESHING

r may come from the ....Acts 3:19

REFUGE

six cities of *r* ....Num 35:6
eternal God is your *r* ....Deut 33:27
you have come for *r* ....Ruth 2:12
but the LORD is his *r* ....Ps 14:6
God is our *r* and ....Ps 46:1
wings I will make my *r* ....Ps 57:1
God is a *r* for us ....Ps 62:8
You are my strong *r* ....Ps 71:7
who have fled for *r* ....Heb 6:18

REFUSE

r the evil and choose ....Is 7:15
through deceit they *r* ....Jer 9:6
hear or whether they *r* ....Ezek 2:5
See that you do not *r* ....Heb 12:25

REFUSED

They *r* to obey ....Neh 9:17

REFUSES

My soul *r* to touch ....Job 6:7
And if he *r* to hear ....Matt 18:17

REGARD

r the rich more than ....Job 34:19
r iniquity in my heart ....Ps 66:18
r the prayer of the ....Ps 102:17
did not fear God nor *r* .....Luke 18:2

REGARDED

my hand and no one *r* ......Prov 1:24
r the lowly state ....Luke 1:48

REGARDS

r a rebuke will be ....Prov 13:18
He no longer *r* them ....Lam 4:16

REGENERATION

to you, that in the *r* ....Matt 19:28
the washing of *r* ....Titus 3:5

REGISTERED

So all went to be *r* ....Luke 2:3
firstborn who are *r* ....Heb 12:23

REGRETTED

but afterward he *r* ....Matt 21:29

REGULATIONS

yourselves to *r* ....Col 2:20

REHOBOAM

Son and successor of Solomon; refuses reform, 1 Kin 11:43—12:15
Ten tribes revolt against, 1 Kin 12:16–24
Reigns over Judah 17 years, 1 Kin 14:21–31; 2 Chr 11:5–23
Apostasizes, then repents, 2 Chr 12:1–16

REHOBOTH

Name of a well dug by Isaac, Gen 26:22

REIGN

but a king shall *r* ....1 Sam 12:12
hypocrite should not *r* ......Job 34:30
so the LORD will *r* ....Mic 4:7
And He will *r* ....Luke 1:33
not have this man to *r* .....Luke 19:14
righteousness will *r* ....Rom 5:17
so grace might *r* ....Rom 5:21
do not let sin *r* ....Rom 6:12
For He must *r* till He ......1 Cor 15:25
and we shall *r* on the ....Rev 5:10
of Christ, and shall *r* ....Rev 20:6

REIGNED

so that as sin *r* ....Rom 5:21
You have *r* as kings ....1 Cor 4:8
And they lived and *r* ....Rev 20:4

REIGNS

God *r* over the nations ....Ps 47:8
The LORD *r* ....Ps 93:1
to Zion, "Your God *r* ....Is 52:7
Lord God Omnipotent *r* ......Rev 19:6

REJECT

will these people *r* ....Num 14:11
r all those who stray ....Ps 119:118
"All too well you *r* ....Mark 7:9
R a divisive man ....Titus 3:10

REJECTED

r has become the chief ......Ps 118:22
He is despised and *r* ....Is 53:3
Israel has *r* the ....Hos 8:3
r has become the chief .....Matt 21:42
many things and be *r* ....Luke 17:25
This Moses whom they *r* .....Acts 7:35
to a living stone, *r* ....1 Pet 2:4
r has become the chief ....1 Pet 2:7

REJECTION

you shall know My *r* ....Num 14:34

REJECTS

he who *r* Me *r* ....Luke 10:16
r this does not reject ....1 Thess 4:8

REJOICE

so the LORD will *r* ....Deut 28:63
let the field *r* ....1 Chr 16:32
and let Your saints *r* ....2 Chr 6:41
r who put their trust ....Ps 5:11
people, let Jacob *r* ....Ps 14:7
R in the LORD ....Ps 33:1
mutual confusion who *r* ......Ps 35:26
The righteous shall *r* ....Ps 58:10
of Your wings I will *r* ....Ps 63:7
But the king shall *r* ....Ps 63:11
Let them *r* before God ....Ps 68:3
In Your name they *r* ....Ps 89:16
Let the heavens *r* ....Ps 96:11
Let the earth *r* ....Ps 97:1
righteous see it and *r* ....Ps 107:42
we will *r* and be glad ....Ps 118:24
who *r* in doing evil ....Prov 2:14
be blessed, and *r* ....Prov 5:18
she shall *r* in time to ....Prov 31:25
R, O young man ....Eccl 11:9
We will be glad and *r* ....Song 1:4
among men shall *r* ....Is 29:19
I will greatly *r* ....Is 61:10
My servants shall *r* ....Is 65:13
your heart shall *r* ....Is 66:14
Yes, I will *r* ....Jer 32:41
Do not *r* over me ....Mic 7:8
He will *r* over you ....Zeph 3:17
do not *r* in this ....Luke 10:20
loved Me, you would *r* ....John 14:28

but the world will *r* ....John 16:20
and your heart will *r* ....John 16:22
R with those who ....Rom 12:15
and in this I *r*................Phil 1:18
faith, I am glad and *r* ....Phil 2:17
R in the Lord always ....Phil 4:4
R always ....1 Thess 5:16
yet believing, you *r* ....1 Pet 1:8

REJOICED

for good as He *r* ....Deut 30:9
for my heart *r* ....Eccl 2:10
and my spirit has *r* ....Luke 1:47
In that hour Jesus *r* ....Luke 10:21
Your father Abraham *r* ......John 8:56
But I *r* in the Lord ....Phil 4:10

REJOICES

glad, and my glory *r* ....Ps 16:9
but *r* in the truth ....1 Cor 13:6

REJOICING

His works with *r*..............Ps 107:22
The voice of *r* and ....Ps 118:15
for they are the *r* ....Ps 119:111
come again with *r*............Ps 126:6
r in His inhabited ....Prov 8:31
he went on his way *r* ....Acts 8:39
yet always *r*..................2 Cor 6:10
or joy, or crown of *r* ......1 Thess 2:19
confidence and the *r* ....Heb 3:6

RELATIVES

r stand afar off ....Ps 38:11

RELEASE

do you want me to *r* ....Matt 27:17
and power to *r* You ....John 19:10
"*R* the four angels ....Rev 9:14

RELENT

sworn and will not *r*...........Ps 110:4
and will not *r* ....Jer 4:28
then the LORD will *r*..........Jer 26:13
if He will turn and *r* ....Joel 2:14
sworn and will not *r* ....Heb 7:21

RELENTED

So the LORD *r* from the ......Ex 32:14
the LORD looked and *r* ....1 Chr 21:15
and God *r* from the ....Jon 3:10

RELENTING

I am weary of *r*...............Jer 15:6

RELIEF

saw that there was *r* ....Ex 8:15
that I may find *r* ....Job 32:20

RELIEVE

of my lips would *r* ....Job 16:5
r those who are really ......1 Tim 5:16

RELIEVED

You have *r* me when I ....Ps 4:1

RELIEVES

r the fatherless ....Ps 146:9

RELIGION

about their own *r* ....Acts 25:19
in self-imposed *r* ....Col 2:23
heart, this one's *r*..........James 1:26
and undefiled *r* ....James 1:27

RELIGIOUS

things you are very *r* ....Acts 17:22
you thinks he is *r* ....James 1:26

RELY

name of the LORD and *r* ......Is 50:10
You *r* on your sword ....Ezek 33:26

REMAIN

shall let none of it *r* ....Ex 12:10
r angry forever ....Jer 3:5
and this city shall *r* ....Jer 17:25
that if ten men *r* ....Amos 6:9
you, that My joy may *r* .....John 15:11
your fruit should *r* ....John 15:16
"If I will that he *r* ....John 21:22
the greater part *r*............1 Cor 15:6
Nevertheless to *r* ....Phil 1:24
we who are alive and *r* ...1 Thess 4:15
the things which *r* ....Rev 3:2

REMAINDER

with the *r* of wrath ....Ps 76:10
I am deprived of the *r* ....Is 38:10

REMAINED

Also my wisdom *r* ....Eccl 2:9
And Mary *r* with her ....Luke 1:56
like a dove, and He *r* ....John 1:32

REMAINS

"While the earth *r* ....Gen 8:22
Therefore your sin *r*..........John 9:41
There *r* therefore a ....Heb 4:9
sin, for His seed *r* ....1 John 3:9

REMEMBER

But *r* me when it is ....Gen 40:14
R the Sabbath day ....Ex 20:8
r that you were a ....Deut 15:15
R His marvelous works ....1 Chr 16:12
but we will *r* the name ....Ps 20:7
r the sins of my youth ....Ps 25:7
r Your name in the ....Ps 119:55
R now your Creator ....Eccl 12:1
r your love more than ....Song 1:4
r the former things ....Is 43:18
"I *r* you, the kindness ....Jer 2:2
and their sin I will *r* ....Jer 31:34
r the covenant of ....Amos 1:9
in wrath *r* mercy ....Hab 3:2
and to *r* His holy ....Luke 1:72
R Lot's wife ....Luke 17:32
r the words of the ....Acts 20:35
R my chains ....Col 4:18
R that Jesus Christ ....2 Tim 2:8
R those who rule ....Heb 13:7

REMEMBERED

Then God *r* Noah ....Gen 8:1
r His covenant with ....Ex 2:24
I *r* God ....Ps 77:3
r His covenant forever ....Ps 105:8
r Your judgments ....Ps 119:52
Who *r* us in our lowly ....Ps 136:23
yea, we wept when we *r* ......Ps 137:1
r that same poor man ....Eccl 9:15
r the days of old ....Is 63:11
And Peter *r* the word ....Matt 26:75
r the word of the Lord ......Acts 11:16

REMEMBERS

My soul still *r* ....Lam 3:20

REMEMBRANCE

in death there is no *r* ....Ps 6:5

I call to *r* my song ....Ps 77:6
There is no *r* of ....Eccl 1:11
Put Me in *r* ....Is 43:26
do this in *r* of Me ....Luke 22:19
do this in *r* of Me ....1 Cor 11:24

REMIND

r you always of these ....2 Pet 1:12
But I want to *r* you ....Jude 5

REMINDER

there is a *r* of sins ....Heb 10:3
you always have a *r* ....2 Pet 1:15
pure minds by way of *r* ......2 Pet 3:1

REMISSION

repentance for the *r* ....Mark 1:4
Jesus Christ for the *r* ....Acts 2:38
where there is *r* ....Heb 10:18

REMNANT

to us a very small *r* ....Is 1:9
The *r* will return ....Is 10:21
be well with your *r* ....Jer 15:11
I will gather the *r*.............Jer 23:3
and all the *r* of Judah ....Jer 44:28
Yet I will leave a *r* ....Ezek 6:8
r whom the LORD calls ....Joel 2:32
I will not treat the *r* ....Zech 8:11
time there is a *r* ....Rom 11:5

REMORSEFUL

been condemned, was *r* .....Matt 27:3

REMOVE

R Your plague from me ......Ps 39:10
R Your gaze from me ....Ps 39:13
r your foot from evil ....Prov 4:27
r falsehood and lies ....Prov 30:8
Therefore *r* sorrow ....Eccl 11:10
r this cup from Me ....Luke 22:42
r your lampstand ....Rev 2:5

REMOVED

Though the earth be *r* ....Ps 46:2
r our transgressions ....Ps 103:12
will never be *r* ....Prov 10:30
and the hills be *r* ....Is 54:10
this mountain, 'Be *r* ....Matt 21:21

REMOVES

r the mountains ....Job 9:5

REND

So *r* your heart ....Joel 2:13

RENDER

What shall I *r* to the ....Ps 116:12
who will *r* to him the ....Matt 21:41
"*R* therefore to Caesar .....Matt 22:21

RENEW

r a steadfast ....Ps 51:10
r the face of the ....Ps 104:30
on the LORD shall *r* ....Is 40:31

RENEWED

that your youth is *r* ....Ps 103:5
inward man is being *r* ....2 Cor 4:16
and be *r* in the spirit ....Eph 4:23
the new man who is *r* ....Col 3:10

RENEWING

transformed by the *r* ....Rom 12:2

of regeneration and *r* ... Titus 3:5

RENOUNCE

Why do the wicked *r* ... Ps 10:13

RENOUNCED

r the covenant of Your ... Ps 89:39
r the hidden things ... 2 Cor 4:2

RENOUNCES

greedy and *r* the LORD ... Ps 10:3

RENOWN

were of old, men of *r* ... Gen 6:4

REPAID

done, so God has *r* ... Judg 1:7
And he has *r* me evil ... 1 Sam 25:21
good shall be *r* ... Prov 13:21
Shall evil be *r* ... Jer 18:20

REPAIR

r the house of your ... 2 Chr 24:5
r the ruined cities ... Is 61:4

REPAY

He will *r* him to his ... Deut 7:10
silence, but will *r* ... Is 65:6
He will surely *r* ... Jer 51:56
again, I will *r* ... Luke 10:35
because they cannot *r* ... Luke 14:14
R no one evil for evil ... Rom 12:17
is Mine, I will *r* ... Rom 12:19
r their parents ... 1 Tim 5:4
I will *r* ... Philem 19

REPAYS

and who *r* him for what ... Job 21:31
r the proud person ... Ps 31:23
shall he be who *r* ... Ps 137:8
the LORD, who fully *r* ... Is 66:6

REPEATS

r a matter separates ... Prov 17:9

REPENT

I abhor myself, and *r* ... Job 42:6
"*R*, for the kingdom ... Matt 3:2
you *r* you will all ... Luke 13:3
said to them, "*R* ... Acts 2:38
men everywhere to *r* ... Acts 17:30
be zealous and *r* ... Rev 3:19

REPENTANCE

you with water unto *r* ... Matt 3:11
a baptism of *r* for the ... Mark 1:4
persons who need no *r* ... Luke 15:7
sorrow produces *r* ... 2 Cor 7:10
will grant them *r* ... 2 Tim 2:25
renew them again to *r* ... Heb 6:6
found no place for *r* ... Heb 12:17
all should come to *r* ... 2 Pet 3:9

REPENTED

No man *r* of his ... Jer 8:6
after my turning, I *r* ... Jer 31:19
it, because they *r* ... Matt 12:41

REPETITIONS

r as the heathen do ... Matt 6:7

REPHAIM

Valley near Jerusalem, 2 Sam 23:13, 14
Scene of Philistine defeats, 2 Sam 5:18–22

REPHIDIM

Israelite camp, Num 33:12–15
Moses strikes rock at, Ex 17:1–7
Amalek defeated at, Ex 17:8–16

REPORT

circulate a false *r* ... Ex 23:1
For it is not a good *r* ... 1 Sam 2:24
r makes the bones ... Prov 15:30
Who has believed our *r* ... Is 53:1
who has believed our *r* ... Rom 10:16
things are of good *r* ... Phil 4:8

REPRIMANDED

And they *r* him sharply ... Judg 8:1

REPROACH

r me as long as I live ... Job 27:6
does he take up a *r* ... Ps 15:3
You make us a *r* ... Ps 44:13
sake I have borne *r* ... Ps 69:7
R has broken my heart ... Ps 69:20
nation, but sin is a *r* ... Prov 14:34
with dishonor comes *r* ... Prov 18:3
do not fear the *r* ... Is 51:7
not remember the *r* ... Is 54:4
bring an everlasting *r* ... Jer 23:40
because I bore the *r* ... Jer 31:19
you shall bear the *r* ... Mic 6:16
these things You *r* ... Luke 11:45
lest he fall into *r* ... 1 Tim 3:7
esteeming the *r* ... Heb 11:26
and without *r* ... James 1:5

REPROACHED

If you are *r* for the ... 1 Pet 4:14

REPROACHES

is not an enemy who *r* ... Ps 55:12
oppresses the poor *r* ... Prov 14:31
curse, and Israel to *r* ... Is 43:28
in infirmities, in *r* ... 2 Cor 12:10

REPROACHFULLY

they strike me *r* ... Job 16:10

REPROOF

for doctrine, for *r* ... 2 Tim 3:16

REPROOFS

R of instruction are ... Prov 6:23

REPUTATION

seven men of good *r* ... Acts 6:3
to those who were of *r* ... Gal 2:2
made Himself of no *r* ... Phil 2:7

REQUEST

not withheld the *r* ... Ps 21:2
He gave them their *r* ... Ps 106:15
the Lord God to make *r* ... Dan 9:3
For Jews *r* a sign ... 1 Cor 1:22
of mine making *r* ... Phil 1:4

REQUESTS

r be made known ... Phil 4:6

REQUIRE

the LORD your God *r* ... Deut 10:12
a foreigner you may *r* ... Deut 15:3
"You will not *r* ... Ps 10:13
offering You did not *r* ... Ps 40:6
what does the LORD *r* ... Mic 6:8

REQUIRED

of the world may be *r* ... Luke 11:50
your soul will be *r* ... Luke 12:20
him much will be *r* ... Luke 12:48
Moreover it is *r* ... 1 Cor 4:2

REQUIREMENTS

keeps the righteous *r* ... Rom 2:26
r that was against us ... Col 2:14

RESCUE

R me from their ... Ps 35:17
and no one shall *r* ... Hos 5:14

RESERVE

r the unjust under ... 2 Pet 2:9

RESERVED

which I have *r* for the ... Job 38:23
"I have *r* for Myself ... Rom 11:4
r in heaven for you ... 1 Pet 1:4
of darkness, to be *r* ... 2 Pet 2:4
habitation, He has *r* ... Jude 6

RESIDUE

The *r* of My people ... Zeph 2:9

RESIST

r an evil person ... Matt 5:39
r the Holy Spirit ... Acts 7:51
R the devil and he ... James 4:7

RESISTED

For who has *r* His will ... Rom 9:19
Jannes and Jambres *r* ... 2 Tim 3:8
for he has greatly *r* ... 2 Tim 4:15
You have not yet *r* ... Heb 12:4

RESISTS

"God *r* the proud ... James 4:6
for "God *r* the proud ... 1 Pet 5:5

RESOLVED

I have *r* what to do ... Luke 16:4

RESORT

to which I may *r* ... Ps 71:3

RESOUND

my heart shall *r* ... Is 16:11

RESPECT

Have *r* to the covenant ... Ps 74:20
his eyes will have *r* ... Is 17:7
saying, 'They will *r* ... Matt 21:37
of the law held in *r* ... Acts 5:34
and we paid them *r* ... Heb 12:9

RESPECTED

And the LORD *r* Abel ... Gen 4:4
little folly to one *r* ... Eccl 10:1

RESPONSE

in whose mouth is no *r* ... Ps 38:14

REST

is the Sabbath of *r* ... Ex 31:15
you shall find no *r* ... Deut 28:65
to build a house of *r* ... 1 Chr 28:2
I would have been at *r* ... Job 3:13
the weary are at *r* ... Job 3:17
R in the LORD ... Ps 37:7
fly away and be at *r* ... Ps 55:6
of the LORD shall *r* ... Is 11:2
whole earth is at *r* ... Is 14:7
"This is the *r* ... Is 28:12

sake I will not *r*..............Is 62:1
is the place of My *r*..............Is 66:1
then you will find *r*..............Jer 6:16
and I will give you *r*........Matt 11:28
and you will find *r*..........Matt 11:29
shall not enter My *r*..........Heb 3:11
remains therefore a *r*..........Heb 4:9
to enter that *r*..............Heb 4:11
And they do not *r*............Rev 4:8
that they should *r*............Rev 6:11
"that they may *r*............Rev 14:13
But the *r* of the dead..........Rev 20:5

RESTED

He had done, and He *r*........Gen 2:2
glory of the LORD *r*..........Ex 24:16
when the Spirit *r*..........Num 11:25
"And God *r* on the............Heb 4:4

RESTING

do not plunder his *r*........Prov 24:15
r place shall be..............Is 11:10
all the earth is *r*............Zech 1:11
still sleeping and *r*..........Matt 26:45

RESTLESS

I am *r* in my complaint..........Ps 55:2

RESTORATION

until the times of *r*..........Acts 3:21

RESTORE

R to me the joy..............Ps 51:12
I still must *r*..............Ps 69:4
r your judges as..............Is 1:26
r them to this place..........Jer 27:22
For I will *r* health to..........Jer 30:17
"So I will *r* to you..........Joel 2:25
declare that I will *r*..........Zech 9:12
and will *r* all things..........Matt 17:11
I *r* fourfold..................Luke 19:8
You at this time *r*............Acts 1:6
who are spiritual *r*............Gal 6:1

RESTORER

may he be to you a *r*..........Ruth 4:15

RESTORES

with joy, for He *r*............Job 33:26
He *r* my soul..................Ps 23:3

RESTRAIN

now *r* Your hand..........2 Sam 24:16
Therefore I will not *r*..........Job 7:11
Will You *r* Yourself............Is 64:12
no one can *r* His hand..........Dan 4:35

RESTRAINED

r my feet from every..........Ps 119:101
Are they *r*....................Is 63:15

RESTRAINS

For nothing *r* the LORD......1 Sam 14:6
r his lips is wise............Prov 10:19
only He who now *r*..........2 Thess 2:7

RESTRAINT

they have cast off *r*..........Job 30:11
they break all *r*..............Hos 4:2

RESTS

r quietly in the heart........Prov 14:33

RESURRECTION

who say there is no *r*........Matt 22:23
Therefore, in the *r*..........Matt 22:28
done good, to the *r*..........John 5:29
to her, "I am the *r*..........John 11:25
them Jesus and the *r*..........Acts 17:18
that there will be a *r*..........Acts 24:15
the likeness of His *r*..........Rom 6:5
say that there is no *r*......1 Cor 15:12
and the power of His *r*........Phil 3:10
that the *r* is already..........2 Tim 2:18
obtain a better *r*..............Heb 11:35
This is the first *r*............Rev 20:5

RETAIN

happy are all who *r*..........Prov 3:18
spirit to *r* the spirit..........Eccl 8:8
r the sins of any..............John 20:23
like to *r* God in their..........Rom 1:28

RETURN

So the LORD will *r*..........1 Kin 2:32
and *r* to our neighbors..........Ps 79:12
R, O LORD......................Ps 90:13
none who go to her *r*..........Prov 2:19
womb, naked shall he *r*..........Eccl 5:15
the clouds do not *r*............Eccl 12:2
let him *r* to the LORD............Is 55:7
it shall not *r* to Me............Is 55:11
"If you will *r*..................Jer 4:1
for they shall *r*................Jer 24:7
me, and I will *r*................Jer 31:18
say, 'I will go and *r*............Hos 2:7
help of your God, *r*............Hos 12:6
"*R* to Me......................Zech 1:3
he says, 'I will *r*............Matt 12:44

RETURNED

and they *r* and sought..........Ps 78:34
yet you have not *r*............Amos 4:6
astray, but have now *r*........1 Pet 2:25

RETURNING

"I am *r* to Jerusalem..........Zech 1:16
r evil for evil or............1 Pet 3:9

RETURNS

spirit departs, he *r*............Ps 146:4
As a dog *r* to his own........Prov 26:11
"A dog *r* to his own..........2 Pet 2:22

REUBEN

Jacob's eldest son, Gen 29:31, 32
Lies with Bilhah; loses preeminence, Gen 35:22; 49:3, 4
Plots to save Joseph, Gen 37:21–30
Offers sons as pledge for Benjamin, Gen 42:37
——Tribe of:
Numbered, Num 1:20, 21; 26:5–11
Settle east of Jordan, Num 32:1–42
Join in war against Canaanites, Josh 1:12–18
Erect memorial altar, Josh 22:10–34

REVEAL

The heavens will *r*............Job 20:27
I will heal them and *r*..........Jer 33:6
the Son wills to *r* Him........Matt 11:27
r His Son in me................Gal 1:16
otherwise, God will *r*..........Phil 3:15

REVEALED

things which are *r*............Deut 29:29
of the LORD shall be *r*..........Is 40:5
righteousness to be *r*............Is 56:1
Then the secret was *r*..........Dan 2:19
the Son of Man is *r*............Luke 17:30
the wrath of God is *r*..........Rom 1:18
glory which shall be *r*..........Rom 8:18
But God has *r* them to........1 Cor 2:10
as it has now been *r*............Eph 3:5
but now has been *r*............Col 1:26
the Lord Jesus is *r*..........2 Thess 1:7
lawless one will be *r*........2 Thess 2:8
ready to be *r* in the..........1 Pet 1:5
when His glory is *r*..........1 Pet 4:13
r what we shall be..........1 John 3:2

REVEALER

Lord of kings, and a *r*..........Dan 2:47

REVEALING

waits for the *r*................Rom 8:19

REVEALS

as a talebearer *r*............Prov 20:19
r deep and secret..............Dan 2:22
r secrets has made............Dan 2:29
r His secret to His............Amos 3:7

REVELATION

Where there is no *r*..........Prov 29:18
the day of wrath and *r*..........Rom 2:5
has a tongue, has a *r*........1 Cor 14:26
it came through the *r*..........Gal 1:12
spirit of wisdom and *r*..........Eph 1:17
r He made known to............Eph 3:3
and glory at the *r*..............1 Pet 1:7

REVELATIONS

come to visions and *r*........2 Cor 12:1

REVELRIES

drunkenness, *r*................Gal 5:21
lusts, drunkenness, *r*..........1 Pet 4:3

REVENGE

and we will take our *r*..........Jer 20:10

REVENUES

than vast *r* without............Prov 16:8

REVERENCE

and *r* My sanctuary............Lev 19:30
and to be held in *r*............Ps 89:7
Master, where is My *r*..........Mal 1:6
submission with all *r*..........1 Tim 3:4
God acceptably with *r*........Heb 12:28

REVERENT

man who is always *r*..........Prov 28:14
their wives must be *r*..........1 Tim 3:11
older men be sober, *r*..........Titus 2:2

REVILE

are you when they *r*............Matt 5:11
r God's high priest............Acts 23:4
evildoers, those who *r*........1 Pet 3:16

REVILED

crucified with Him *r*..........Mark 15:32
who, when He was *r*..........1 Pet 2:23

REVILER

or an idolater, or a *r*..........1 Cor 5:11

REVILERS

nor drunkards, nor *r*..........1 Cor 6:10

REVILING

come envy, strife, *r*..........1 Tim 6:4

REVIVAL
give us a measure of *r* . . . Ezra 9:8

REVIVE
troubles, shall *r* . . . Ps 71:20
Will You not *r* us . . . Ps 85:6
r me according to Your . . . Ps 119:25
r the spirit of the . . . Is 57:15
two days He will *r* . . . Hos 6:2
r Your work in the . . . Hab 3:2

REVIVED
they shall be *r* . . . Hos 14:7
came, sin *r* and I died . . . Rom 7:9

REVOLT
You will *r* more and . . . Is 1:5

REVOLTED
Israel have deeply *r* . . . Is 31:6
they have *r* and . . . Jer 5:23

REVOLTERS
r are deeply involved . . . Hos 5:2

REWARD
exceedingly great *r* . . . Gen 15:1
them there is great *r* . . . Ps 19:11
r me evil for good . . . Ps 35:12
"Surely there is a *r* . . . Ps 58:11
look, and see the *r* . . . Ps 91:8
will a sure *r* . . . Prov 11:18
and the LORD will *r* . . . Prov 25:22
and this was my *r* . . . Eccl 2:10
behold, His *r* is with . . . Is 40:10
r them for their deeds . . . Hos 4:9
You have loved for *r* . . . Hos 9:1
for great is your *r* . . . Matt 5:12
you have no *r* from . . . Matt 6:1
you, they have their *r* . . . Matt 6:2
receive a prophet's *r* . . . Matt 10:41
by no means lose his *r* . . . Matt 10:42
r will be great . . . Luke 6:35
we receive the due *r* . . . Luke 23:41
will receive his own *r* . . . 1 Cor 3:8
cheat you of your *r* . . . Col 2:18
for he looked to the *r* . . . Heb 11:26
may receive a full *r* . . . 2 John 8
quickly, and My *r* . . . Rev 22:12

REWARDED
Thus they have *r* . . . Ps 109:5

REWARDER
and that He is a *r* . . . Heb 11:6

REWARDS
Whoever *r* evil for . . . Prov 17:13
and follows after *r* . . . Is 1:23
and give your *r* . . . Dan 5:17

REZIN
King of Damascus; joins Pekah against Ahaz, 2 Kin 15:37
Confederacy of, inspires Isaiah's great messianic prophecy, Is 7:1—9:12

REZON
Son of Eliadah; establishes Syrian kingdom, 1 Kin 11:23–25

RHODA
Servant girl, Acts 12:13–16

RIBLAH
Headquarters of:
Pharaoh Necho, 2 Kin 23:31–35
Nebuchadnezzar, 2 Kin 25:6, 20, 21
Zedekiah blinded here, Jer 39:5–7

RICH
Abram was very *r* . . . Gen 13:2
makes poor and makes *r* . . . 1 Sam 2:7
r man will lie down . . . Job 27:19
the *r* among the people . . . Ps 45:12
when one becomes *r* . . . Ps 49:16
soul will be made *r* . . . Prov 11:25
who makes himself *r* . . . Prov 13:7
r has many friends . . . Prov 14:20
The *r* and the poor . . . Prov 22:2
r man is wise in his . . . Prov 28:11
do not curse the *r* . . . Eccl 10:20
it is hard for a *r* . . . Matt 19:23
to you who are *r* . . . Luke 6:24
from the *r* man's table . . . Luke 16:21
for he was very *r* . . . Luke 18:23
Lord over all is *r* . . . Rom 10:12
You are already *r* . . . 1 Cor 4:8
though He was *r* . . . 2 Cor 8:9
who desire to be *r* . . . 1 Tim 6:9
but the *r* in his . . . James 1:10
So the *r* man also will . . . James 1:11
of this world to be *r* . . . James 2:5
you say, 'I am *r* . . . Rev 3:17

RICHES
Both *r* and honor come . . . 1 Chr 29:12
He swallows down *r* . . . Job 20:15
he heaps up *r* . . . Ps 39:6
the abundance of his *r* . . . Ps 52:7
if *r* increase . . . Ps 62:10
r will be in his house . . . Ps 112:3
in her left hand *r* . . . Prov 3:16
R and honor are . . . Prov 8:18
R do not profit . . . Prov 11:4
in his *r* will fall . . . Prov 11:28
yet has great *r* . . . Prov 13:7
of the wise is their *r* . . . Prov 14:24
of the LORD are *r* . . . Prov 22:4
r are not forever . . . Prov 27:24
r kept for their owner . . . Eccl 5:13
darkness and hidden *r* . . . Is 45:3
you shall eat the *r* . . . Is 61:6
so is he who gets *r* . . . Jer 17:11
have increased your *r* . . . Ezek 28:5
for those who have *r* . . . Mark 10:23
do you despise the *r* . . . Rom 2:4
might make known the *r* . . . Rom 9:23
what are the *r* . . . Eph 1:18
show the exceeding *r* . . . Eph 2:7
the unsearchable *r* . . . Eph 3:8
trust in uncertain *r* . . . 1 Tim 6:17
r than the treasures . . . Heb 11:26
r are corrupted . . . James 5:2
to receive power and *r* . . . Rev 5:12

RICHLY
Christ dwell in you *r* . . . Col 3:16
God, who gives us *r* . . . 1 Tim 6:17

RIDDLE
"Let me pose a *r* . . . Judg 14:12

RIDDLES
the wise and their *r* . . . Prov 1:6

RIDE
wind and cause me to *r* . . . Job 30:22
in Your majesty *r* . . . Ps 45:4
have caused men to *r* . . . Ps 66:12

RIDER
r He has thrown . . . Ex 15:1
the horse and its *r* . . . Job 39:18

RIDES
Behold, the LORD *r* . . . Is 19:1

RIDGES
You water its *r* . . . Ps 65:10

RIDICULE
those who see Me *r* Me . . . Ps 22:7
Whom do you *r* . . . Is 57:4

RIDICULED
they *r* Him . . . Matt 9:24

RIGHT
you shall do what is *r* . . . Deut 6:18
the *r* of the firstborn . . . Deut 21:17
did what was *r* in his . . . Judg 21:25
"Is your heart *r* . . . 2 Kin 10:15
them forth by the *r* . . . Ps 107:7
Lord, "Sit at My *r* . . . Ps 110:1
is a way which seems *r* . . . Prov 14:12
way of a man is *r* . . . Prov 21:2
things that are *r* . . . Is 45:19
until He comes whose *r* . . . Ezek 21:27
of the LORD are *r* . . . Hos 14:9
do not know to do *r* . . . Amos 3:10
and whatever is *r* . . . Matt 20:4
clothed and in his *r* . . . Mark 5:15
not judge what is *r* . . . Luke 12:57
to them He gave the *r* . . . John 1:12
your heart is not *r* . . . Acts 8:21
Do we have no *r* . . . 1 Cor 9:4
seven stars in His *r* . . . Rev 2:1

RIGHTEOUS
also destroy the *r* . . . Gen 18:23
and they justify the *r* . . . Deut 25:1
"You are more *r* . . . 1 Sam 24:17
that he could be *r* . . . Job 15:14
r will hold to his way . . . Job 17:9
"The *r* see it and . . . Job 22:19
knows the way of the *r* . . . Ps 1:6
LORD, will bless the *r* . . . Ps 5:12
r God tests the hearts . . . Ps 7:9
what can the *r* . . . Ps 11:3
The *r* cry out . . . Ps 34:17
the LORD upholds the *r* . . . Ps 37:17
r shows mercy and . . . Ps 37:21
I have not seen the *r* . . . Ps 37:25
the *r* will be in . . . Ps 112:6
The LORD is *r* in all . . . Ps 145:17
the LORD loves the *r* . . . Ps 146:8
will not allow the *r* . . . Prov 10:3
r is a well of life . . . Prov 10:11
The labor of the *r* . . . Prov 10:16
r will be gladness . . . Prov 10:28
r is delivered from . . . Prov 11:8
r will be delivered . . . Prov 11:21
r will flourish . . . Prov 11:28
r will be recompensed . . . Prov 11:31
r man regards the life . . . Prov 12:10
r should choose his . . . Prov 12:26
r there is much . . . Prov 15:6
the prayer of the *r* . . . Prov 15:29
the *r* run to it and . . . Prov 18:10
r are bold as a lion . . . Prov 28:1
When the *r* are in . . . Prov 29:2
r considers the cause . . . Prov 29:7
Do not be overly *r* . . . Eccl 7:16
event happens to the *r* . . . Eccl 9:2
r that it shall be . . . Is 3:10

ROBBERS
and Israel to the *r* ....Is 42:24
also crucified two *r* ....Mark 15:27
Me are thieves and *r* ....John 10:8
here who are neither *r* ....Acts 19:37
waters, in perils of *r* ....2 Cor 11:26

ROBBERY
nor vainly hope in *r* ....Ps 62:10
I hate *r* for burnt ....Is 61:8
did not consider it *r* ....Phil 2:6

ROBE
justice was like a *r* ....Job 29:14
instead of a rich *r* ....Is 3:24
covered me with the *r* ....Is 61:10
'Bring out the best *r* ....Luke 15:22
on Him a purple *r* ....John 19:2
Then a white *r* was ....Rev 6:11

ROBES
to the King in *r* ....Ps 45:14
have stained all My *r* ....Is 63:3
clothe you with rich *r* ....Zech 3:4
go around in long *r* ....Luke 20:46
clothed with white *r* ....Rev 7:9

ROCK
you shall strike the *r* ....Ex 17:6
and struck the *r* ....Num 20:11
R who begot you ....Deut 32:18
For their *r* is not ....Deut 32:31
nor is there any *r* ....1 Sam 2:2
"The LORD is my *r* ....2 Sam 22:2
Blessed be my *R* ....2 Sam 22:47
away, and as a *r* ....Job 14:18
set me high upon a *r* ....Ps 27:5
For You are my *r* ....Ps 31:3
r that is higher than ....Ps 61:2
and my God the *r* ....Ps 94:22
who turned the *r* ....Ps 114:8
been mindful of the *R* ....Is 17:10
shadow of a great *r* ....Is 32:2
his house on the *r* ....Matt 7:24
r I will build My ....Matt 16:18
Some fell on *r* ....Luke 8:6
stumbling stone and *r* ....Rom 9:33
R that followed them ....1 Cor 10:4

ROCKS
and the *r* were split ....Matt 27:51
to the mountains and *r* ....Rev 6:16

ROD
And Moses took the *r* ....Ex 4:20
chasten him with the *r* ....2 Sam 7:14
Your *r* and Your staff ....Ps 23:4
The *r* and rebuke give ....Prov 29:15
shall come forth a *R* ....Is 11:1
you pass under the *r* ....Ezek 20:37
I come to you with a *r* ....1 Cor 4:21
rule them with a *r* ....Rev 2:27

ROLL
ruinous storm they *r* ....Job 30:14
r away the stone ....Mark 16:3

ROLLED
the heavens shall be *r* ....Is 34:4
the stone had been *r* ....Mark 16:4

ROME
Jews expelled from, Acts 18:2
Paul:
Writes to Christians of, Rom 1:7
Desires to go to, Acts 19:21
Comes to, Acts 28:14
Imprisoned in, Acts 28:16

ROOM
You prepared *r* for it ....Ps 80:9
until no more *r* ....Zech 10:10
you a large upper *r* ....Mark 14:15
no *r* for them in the ....Luke 2:7
still there is *r* ....Luke 14:22
into the upper *r* ....Acts 1:13

ROOMS
make *r* in the ark ....Gen 6:14
He is in the inner *r* ....Matt 24:26

ROOSTER
him, "Before the *r* ....Matt 26:75

ROOT
r bearing bitterness ....Deut 29:18
the foolish taking *r* ....Job 5:3
r may grow old in the ....Job 14:8
day there shall be a *R* ....Is 11:10
shall again take *r* ....Is 37:31
because they had no *r* ....Matt 13:6
and if the *r* is holy ....Rom 11:16
of money is a *r* ....1 Tim 6:10
lest any *r* of ....Heb 12:15
I am the *R* and the ....Rev 22:16

ROOTED
that you, being *r* ....Eph 3:17
r and built up in Him ....Col 2:7

ROOTS
because its *r* reached ....Ezek 31:7
and lengthen his *r* ....Hos 14:5
dried up from the *r* ....Mark 11:20
pulled up by the *r* ....Jude 12

ROSE
I am the *r* of Sharon ....Song 2:1
and blossom as the *r* ....Is 35:1
end Christ died and *r* ....Rom 14:9
buried, and that He *r* ....1 Cor 15:4
that Jesus died and *r* ....1 Thess 4:14

RUBIES
of wisdom is above *r* ....Job 28:18
more precious than *r* ....Prov 3:15
is better than *r* ....Prov 8:11
worth is far above *r* ....Prov 31:10
your pinnacles of *r* ....Is 54:12
ruddy in body than *r* ....Lam 4:7

RUDDY
Now he was *r* ....1 Sam 16:12
beloved is white and *r* ....Song 5:10

RUIN
r those two can bring ......Prov 24:22
have made a city a *r* ....Is 25:2
will not be your *r* ....Ezek 18:30
And the *r* of that ....Luke 6:49
to no profit, to the *r* ....2 Tim 2:14

RUINED
shall be utterly *r* ....Is 60:12
the mighty trees are *r* ....Zech 11:2
wineskins will be *r* ....Luke 5:37

RUINS
rebuild the old *r* ....Is 61:4

RULE
and he shall *r* ....Gen 3:16
r the raging of the ....Ps 89:9
A wise servant will *r* ....Prov 17:2
Yet he will *r* over all ....Eccl 2:19
puts an end to all *r* ....1 Cor 15:24
us walk by the same *r* ....Phil 3:16
let the peace of God *r* ....Col 3:15
Let the elders who *r* ....1 Tim 5:17
Remember those who *r* ......Heb 13:7

RULER
the sheep, to be *r* ....2 Sam 7:8
down to eat with a *r* ....Prov 23:1
bear is a wicked *r* ....Prov 28:15
r pays attention ....Prov 29:12
to Me the One to be *r* ....Mic 5:2
by Beelzebub, the *r* ....Matt 12:24
I will make you *r* ....Matt 25:21
the *r* of this world ....John 12:31
because the *r* of this ....John 16:11
'Who made you a *r* ....Acts 7:27
speak evil of a *r* ....Acts 23:5

RULERS
and the *r* take counsel ....Ps 2:2
r decree justice ....Prov 8:15
"You know that the *r* ......Matt 20:25
Have any of the *r* ....John 7:48
r are not a ....Rom 13:3
which none of the *r* ....1 Cor 2:8
powers, against the *r* ....Eph 6:12
to be subject to *r* ....Titus 3:1

RULES
'He who *r* over men ....2 Sam 23:3
them know that God *r* ....Ps 59:13
He *r* by His power ....Ps 66:7
r his spirit than he ....Prov 16:32
that the Most High *r* ....Dan 4:17
that the Most High *r* ....Dan 4:32
r his own house well ....1 Tim 3:4
according to the *r* ....2 Tim 2:5

RULING
r their children ....1 Tim 3:12

RUMOR
r will be upon *r* ....Ezek 7:26

RUMORS
hear of wars and *r* ....Matt 24:6
you hear of wars and *r* ....Mark 13:7

RUN
I will *r* the course of ....Ps 119:32
r and not be weary ....Is 40:31
many shall *r* to and ....Dan 12:4
Therefore I *r* thus ....1 Cor 9:26
I might *r*, or had *r* ....Gal 2:2
that I have not *r* ....Phil 2:16
us, and let us *r* ....Heb 12:1
that you do not *r* ....1 Pet 4:4

RUNNER
are swifter than a *r* ....Job 9:25
r will run to meet ....Jer 51:31

RUNS
word *r* very swiftly ....Ps 147:15
nor of him who *r* ....Rom 9:16

RUSH
The nations will *r* ....Is 17:13

Anoints David, 1 Sam 16:1–13
Death of, 1 Sam 25:1

SANBALLAT

Influential Samaritan; attempts to thwart Nehemiah's plans, Neh 2:10; 4:7, 8; 6:1–14

SANCTIFICATION

righteousness and *s* ....1 Cor 1:30
will of God, your *s* ....1 Thess 4:3
salvation through *s* ....2 Thess 2:13

SANCTIFIED

I have commanded My *s* ....Is 13:3
you were born I *s* ....Jer 1:5
Him whom the Father *s* ....John 10:36
they also may be *s* ....John 17:19
might be acceptable, *s* ....Rom 15:16
to those who are *s* ....1 Cor 1:2
washed, but you were *s* ....1 Cor 6:11
husband is *s* by the ....1 Cor 7:14
for it is *s* by the ....1 Tim 4:5
those who are being *s* ....Heb 2:11
will we have been *s* ....Heb 10:10
who are called, *s* ....Jude 1

SANCTIFIES

or the temple that *s* ....Matt 23:17
For both He who *s* ....Heb 2:11

SANCTIFY

would send and *s* them ....Job 1:5
s My great name ....Ezek 36:23
that I, the LORD, *s* ....Ezek 37:28
Myself and *s* Myself ....Ezek 38:23
S them by Your ....John 17:17
for their sakes I *s* ....John 17:19
that He might *s* ....Eph 5:26

SANCTUARY

let them make Me a *s* ....Ex 25:8
I went into the *s* ....Ps 73:17
set fire to Your *s* ....Ps 74:7
O God, is in the *s* ....Ps 77:13
He will be as a *s* ....Is 8:14
He has abandoned His *s* ....Lam 2:7
I shall be a little *s* ....Ezek 11:16
to shine on Your *s* ....Dan 9:17
and the earthly *s* ....Heb 9:1

SAND

descendants as the *s* ....Gen 32:12
be heavier than the *s* ....Job 6:3
in number than the *s* ....Ps 139:18
O Israel, be as the *s* ....Is 10:22
innumerable as the *s* ....Heb 11:12

SAPPHIRA

Wife of Ananias; struck dead for lying, Acts 5:1–11

SAPPHIRES

are the source of *s* ....Job 28:6

SARAH (or Sarai)

Barren wife of Abram, Gen 11:29–31
Represented as Abram's sister, Gen 12:10–20
Gives Abram her maid, Gen 16:1–3
Receives promise of a son, Gen 17:15–21
Gives birth to Isaac, Gen 21:1–8

SARDIS

Site of one of the seven churches, Rev 1:11

SAT

of Babylon, there we *s* ....Ps 137:1
I *s* down in his shade ....Song 2:3
s alone because of ....Jer 15:17
into heaven, and *s* ....Mark 16:19
And He who *s* there was ....Rev 4:3

SATAN

S stood up against ....1 Chr 21:1
before the LORD, and *S* ....Job 1:6
And the LORD said to *S* ....Zech 3:2
"Away with you, *S* ....Matt 4:10
"Get behind Me, *S* ....Matt 16:23
"How can *S* cast out ....Mark 3:23
to them, "I saw *S* ....Luke 10:18
S has asked for you ....Luke 22:31
S filled your heart ....Acts 5:3
such a one to *S* ....1 Cor 5:5
For *S* himself ....2 Cor 11:14
to the working of *S* ....2 Thess 2:9
are a synagogue of *S* ....Rev 2:9
you, where *S* dwells ....Rev 2:13
known the depths of *S* ....Rev 2:24
called the Devil and *S* ....Rev 12:9
years have expired, *S* ....Rev 20:7

SATIATED

s the weary soul ....Jer 31:25
It shall be *s* and made ....Jer 46:10

SATISFIED

I shall be *s* when I ....Ps 17:15
his land will be *s* ....Prov 12:11
a good man will be *s* ....Prov 14:14
s soul loathes the ....Prov 27:7
that are never *s* ....Prov 30:15
silver will not be *s* ....Eccl 5:10
left hand and not be *s* ....Is 9:20
of His soul, and be *s* ....Is 53:11
My people shall be *s* ....Jer 31:14
still were not *s* ....Ezek 16:28
but they were not *s* ....Amos 4:8
and cannot be *s* ....Hab 2:5

SATISFIES

s your mouth with good ....Ps 103:5
s the longing soul ....Ps 107:9

SATISFY

s us early with Your ....Ps 90:14
long life I will *s* ....Ps 91:16
s her poor with bread ....Ps 132:15
for what does not *s* ....Is 55:2

SATISFYING

eats to the *s* of his ....Prov 13:25

SAUL

Becomes first king of Israel, 1 Sam 9—11
Sacrifices unlawfully, 1 Sam 13:1–14
Wars with Philistines, 1 Sam 13:15—14:52
Disregards the Lord's command; rejected by God, 1 Sam 15
Suffers from distressing spirits, 1 Sam 16:14–23
Becomes jealous of David; attempts to kill him, 1 Sam 18:5—19:22
Pursues David; twice spared by him, 1 Sam 22—24; 26
Consults medium, 1 Sam 28:7–25
Defeated, commits suicide; buried, 1 Sam 31
——— of Tarsus, apostle to the Gentiles: *see* PAUL

SAVE

the LORD does not *s* ....1 Sam 17:47
there was none to *s* ....2 Sam 22:42
s the humble person ....Job 22:29
Oh, *s* me for Your ....Ps 6:4
S Your people ....Ps 28:9
send from heaven and *s* ....Ps 57:3
s the children of the ....Ps 72:4
s the souls of the ....Ps 72:13
LORD, and He will *s* ....Prov 20:22
He will come and *s* ....Is 35:4
LORD was ready to *s* ....Is 38:20
s your children ....Is 49:25
that it cannot *s* ....Is 59:1
mighty to *s* ....Is 63:1
one who cannot *s* ....Jer 14:9
s you and deliver you ....Jer 15:20
s me, and I shall be ....Jer 17:14
O LORD, *s* Your people ....Jer 31:7
other, That he may *s* ....Hos 13:10
Assyria shall not *s* ....Hos 14:3
the Mighty One, will *s* ....Zeph 3:17
JESUS, for He will *s* ....Matt 1:21
s his life will ....Matt 16:25
s that which was ....Matt 18:11
s life or to kill ....Mark 3:4
let Him *s* Himself if ....Luke 23:35
You are the Christ, *s* ....Luke 23:39
'Father, *s* Me from ....John 12:27
but to *s* the world ....John 12:47
and *s* some of them ....Rom 11:14
the world to *s* sinners ....1 Tim 1:15
doing this you will *s* ....1 Tim 4:16
able to *s* your souls ....James 1:21
Can faith *s* him ....James 2:14

SAVED

like you, a people *s* ....Deut 33:29
But You have *s* us from ....Ps 44:7
and we are not *s* ....Jer 8:20
"Who then can be *s* ....Matt 19:25
"He *s* others ....Matt 27:42
That we should be *s* ....Luke 1:71
"Your faith has *s* ....Luke 7:50
through Him might be *s* ....John 3:17
them, saying, "Be *s* ....Acts 2:40
what must I do to be *s* ....Acts 16:30
For we were *s* in this ....Rom 8:24
is that they may be *s* ....Rom 10:1
all Israel will be *s* ....Rom 11:26
his spirit may be *s* ....1 Cor 5:5
which also you are *s* ....1 Cor 15:2
those who are being *s* ....2 Cor 2:15
grace you have been *s* ....Eph 2:8
all men to be *s* ....1 Tim 2:4
she will be *s* in ....1 Tim 2:15
to His mercy He *s* ....Titus 3:5
eight souls, were *s* ....1 Pet 3:20
of those who are *s* ....Rev 21:24

SAVES

s the needy from the ....Job 5:15
s such as have a ....Ps 34:18
antitype which now *s* ....1 Pet 3:21

SAVIOR

forgot God their *S* ....Ps 106:21
He will send them a *S* ....Is 19:20
of Israel, your *S* ....Is 43:3
Me, a just God and a *S* ....Is 45:21
I, the LORD, am your *S* ....Is 60:16
So He became their *S* ....Is 63:8
for there is no *s* ....Hos 13:4
rejoiced in God my *S* ....Luke 1:47
the city of David a *S* ....Luke 2:11
the Christ, the *S* ....John 4:42

to be Prince and *S* . . . . Acts 5:31
up for Israel a *S* . . . . Acts 13:23
and He is the *S* . . . . Eph 5:23
of God our *S* and the . . . . 1 Tim 1:1
God, who is the *S* . . . . 1 Tim 4:10
of our *S* Jesus Christ . . . . 2 Tim 1:10
God and *S* Jesus Christ . . . . . Titus 2:13

SAVIORS

s shall come to Mount . . . . Obad 21

SAVOR

days, and I do not *s* . . . . Amos 5:21

SAWN

stoned, they were *s* . . . . Heb 11:37

SAY

But I *s* to you that . . . . Matt 5:22
"But who do you *s* . . . . Matt 16:15
s that we have no sin . . . . 1 John 1:8

SAYING

disclose my dark *s* . . . . Ps 49:4
cannot accept this *s* . . . . Matt 19:11
"This is a hard *s* . . . . John 6:60
This is a faithful *s* . . . . 1 Tim 1:15

SAYINGS

I will utter dark *s* . . . . Ps 78:2
whoever hears these *s* . . . . Matt 7:24

SCALES

You shall have honest *s* . . . . . Lev 19:36
be weighed on honest *s* . . . . Job 31:6
deceitful *s* are in his . . . . Hos 12:7
on it had a pair of *s* . . . . Rev 6:5

SCARLET

s cord in the window . . . . Josh 2:18
are like a strand of *s* . . . . Song 4:3
your sins are like *s* . . . . Is 1:18
s beast which was full . . . . Rev 17:3

SCATTER

I will *s* you among the . . . . . . Lev 26:33
S the peoples who . . . . Ps 68:30
s the sheep of My . . . . Jer 23:1
I will *s* to all winds . . . . Jer 49:32

SCATTERED

lest we be *s* abroad . . . . Gen 11:4
of iniquity shall be *s* . . . . Ps 92:9
"You have *s* My flock . . . . Jer 23:2
s Israel will gather . . . . Jer 31:10
"Israel is like *s* sheep . . . . Jer 50:17
they were weary and *s* . . . . . . Matt 9:36
the sheep will be *s* . . . . Mark 14:27
that you will be *s* . . . . John 16:32

SCATTERS

s the frost like ashes . . . . Ps 147:16
There is one who *s* . . . . Prov 11:24
throne of judgment *s* . . . . Prov 20:8
not gather with Me *s* . . . . Matt 12:30

SCEPTER

s shall not depart . . . . Gen 49:10
S shall rise out of . . . . Num 24:17
a *s* of righteousness . . . . Ps 45:6
a *s* of righteousness . . . . Heb 1:8

SCHEME

perfected a shrewd *s* . . . . Ps 64:6

SCHEMER

will be called a *s* . . . . Prov 24:8

SCHEMES

who brings wicked *s* . . . . Ps 37:7
sought out many *s* . . . . Eccl 7:29

SCHISM

there should be no *s* . . . . 1 Cor 12:25

SCHOOL

daily in the *s* of . . . . Acts 19:9

SCOFF

They *s* and speak . . . . Ps 73:8
They *s* at kings . . . . Hab 1:10

SCOFFER

"He who corrects a *s* . . . . Prov 9:7
s does not listen . . . . Prov 13:1
s seeks wisdom and . . . . Prov 14:6
s is an abomination . . . . Prov 24:9

SCOFFERS

S ensnare a city . . . . Prov 29:8
s will come in the . . . . 2 Pet 3:3

SCORCHED

sun was up they were *s* . . . . . . Matt 13:6
And men were *s* with . . . . Rev 16:9

SCORN

My friends *s* me . . . . Job 16:20
to our neighbors, a *s* . . . . Ps 44:13

SCORNED

consider, for I am *s* . . . . Lam 1:11
and princes are *s* . . . . Hab 1:10

SCORNS

He *s* the scornful . . . . Prov 3:34
s obedience to his . . . . Prov 30:17

SCORPIONS

and you dwell among *s* . . . . Ezek 2:6
on serpents and *s* . . . . Luke 10:19
They had tails like *s* . . . . Rev 9:10

SCOURGE

hosts will stir up a *s* . . . . Is 10:26
up to councils and *s* . . . . Matt 10:17
will mock Him, and *s* . . . . Mark 10:34

SCOURGES

s every son whom . . . . Heb 12:6

SCRIBE

"Where is the *s* . . . . Is 33:18

SCRIBES

and not as the *s* . . . . Matt 7:29
"But woe to you, *s* . . . . Matt 23:13
"Beware of the *s* . . . . Mark 12:38

SCRIPTURE

what is noted in the *S* . . . . Dan 10:21
S was fulfilled which . . . . . . Mark 15:28
"Today this *S* . . . . Luke 4:21
S cannot be broken . . . . John 10:35
For what does the *S* . . . . Rom 4:3
S has confined all . . . . Gal 3:22
All *S* is given by . . . . 2 Tim 3:16
that no prophecy of *S* . . . . 2 Pet 1:20

SCRIPTURES

not knowing the *S* . . . . Matt 22:29
S must be fulfilled . . . . Mark 14:49
and mighty in the *S* . . . . Acts 18:24
have known the Holy *S* . . . . . . 2 Tim 3:15
also the rest of the *S* . . . . 2 Pet 3:16

SCROLL

in the *s* of the book . . . . Ps 40:7
and note it on a *s* . . . . Is 30:8
eat this *s* . . . . Ezek 3:1
saw there a flying *s* . . . . Zech 5:1
on the throne a *s* . . . . Rev 5:1
was able to open the *s* . . . . Rev 5:3
the sky receded as a *s* . . . . Rev 6:14

SEA

drowned in the Red *S* . . . . Ex 15:4
this great and wide *s* . . . . Ps 104:25
who go down to the *s* . . . . Ps 107:23
to the *s* its limit . . . . Prov 8:29
rebuke I dry up the *s* . . . . Is 50:2
the waters cover the *s* . . . . Hab 2:14
and the *s* obey Him . . . . Matt 8:27
throne there was a *s* . . . . Rev 4:6
standing on the *s* . . . . Rev 15:2
there was no more *s* . . . . Rev 21:1

SEAL

Set me as a *s* upon . . . . Song 8:6
of circumcision, a *s* . . . . Rom 4:11
stands, having this *s* . . . . 2 Tim 2:19
He opened the second *s* . . . . Rev 6:3

SEALED

My transgression is *s* . . . . Job 14:17
who also has *s* us and . . . . 2 Cor 1:22
by whom you were *s* . . . . Eph 4:30
of those who were *s* . . . . Rev 7:4

SEAM

tunic was without *s* . . . . John 19:23

SÉANCE

"Please conduct a *s* . . . . 1 Sam 28:8

SEARCH

"Can you *s* out the . . . . Job 11:7
would not God *s* . . . . Ps 44:21
glory of kings is to *s* . . . . Prov 25:2
found it by secret *s* . . . . Jer 2:34
I, the LORD, *s* the . . . . Jer 17:10
s the Scriptures . . . . John 5:39

SEARCHED

O LORD, You have *s* . . . . Ps 139:1
s the Scriptures . . . . Acts 17:11
and *s* carefully . . . . 1 Pet 1:10

SEARCHES

for the LORD *s* all . . . . 1 Chr 28:9
s the hearts knows . . . . Rom 8:27
For the Spirit *s* . . . . 1 Cor 2:10
that I am He who *s* . . . . Rev 2:23

SEASON

there is a *s* . . . . Eccl 3:1
Be ready in *s* and out . . . . 2 Tim 4:2

SEASONED

how shall it be *s* . . . . Matt 5:13
"For everyone will be *s* . . . . Mark 9:49

SEASONS

days and months and *s* . . . . Gal 4:10
the times and the *s* . . . . 1 Thess 5:1

SEAT

shall make a mercy *s* . . . . Ex 25:17

I might come to His *s* ....Job 23:3
that He may *s* him with ....Ps 113:8
sit in Moses' *s* ....Matt 23:2
before the judgment *s* ......2 Cor 5:10
the mercy *s* ....Heb 9:5

SEATS

at feasts, the best *s* ....Matt 23:6
you love the best *s* ....Luke 11:43

SECRET

s things belong ....Deut 29:29
The *s* of the LORD is ....Ps 25:14
in the *s* place of His ....Ps 27:5
when I was made in *s* ....Ps 139:15
do not disclose the *s* ....Prov 25:9
I have not spoken in *s* ....Is 45:19
Father who is in the *s* ....Matt 6:6
are done by them in *s* ....Eph 5:12

SECRETLY

"Now a word was *s* ....Job 4:12
He lies in wait *s* ....Ps 10:9

SECRETS

would show you the *s* ....Job 11:6
For He knows the *s* ....Ps 44:21
A talebearer reveals *s* ....Prov 11:13
heaven who reveals *s* ....Dan 2:28
God will judge the *s* ....Rom 2:16
And thus the *s* of his ......1 Cor 14:25

SECT

him (which is the *s* ....Acts 5:17
to the strictest *s* ....Acts 26:5

SECURELY

pleasures, who dwell *s* ....Is 47:8
nation that dwells *s* ....Jer 49:31

SEDUCED

flattering lips she *s* ....Prov 7:21
because they have *s* ....Ezek 13:10

SEE

for no man shall *s* ....Ex 33:20
the LORD does not *s* ....1 Sam 16:7
in my flesh I shall *s* ....Job 19:26
s the works of God ....Ps 66:5
lest they *s* with their ....Is 6:10
for sin, He shall *s* ....Is 53:10
for they shall *s* God ....Matt 5:8
seeing they do not *s* ....Matt 13:13
s greater things than ....John 1:50
rejoiced to *s* My day ....John 8:56
we wish to *s* Jesus ....John 12:21
and the world will *s* ....John 14:19
Him, for we shall *s* ....1 John 3:2
They shall *s* His face ....Rev 22:4

SEED

s shall be called ....Gen 21:12
s shall be its stump ....Is 6:13
He shall see His *s* ....Is 53:10
you a noble vine, a *s* ....Jer 2:21
s is the word of God ....Luke 8:11
had left us a *s* ....Rom 9:29
to each *s* its own body .....1 Cor 15:38
S were the promises ....Gal 3:16
you are Abraham's *s* ....Gal 3:29
Jesus Christ, of the *s* ....2 Tim 2:8
of corruptible *s* ....1 Pet 1:23
not sin, for His *s* ....1 John 3:9

SEEDS

the good *s* are the ....Matt 13:38

not say, "And to *s* ....Gal 3:16

SEEK

will find Him if you *s* ......Deut 4:29
pray and *s* My face ....2 Chr 7:14
your heart to *s* God ....2 Chr 19:3
s your God as you do ....Ezra 4:2
may God above not *s* ....Job 3:4
countenance does not *s* ....Ps 10:4
LORD, that will I *s* ....Ps 27:4
You said, "*S* My face ....Ps 27:8
early will I *s* You ....Ps 63:1
s me diligently will ....Prov 8:17
s one's own glory ....Prov 25:27
s justice, rebuke ....Is 1:17
Should they *s* the dead ....Is 8:19
the Gentiles shall *s* ....Is 11:10
Jacob, '*S* Me in vain ....Is 45:19
S the LORD while He ....Is 55:6
Yet they *s* Me daily ....Is 58:2
s great things for ....Jer 45:5
s what was lost ....Ezek 34:16
"*S* Me and live ....Amos 5:4
and people should *s* ....Mal 2:7
things the Gentiles *s* ....Matt 6:32
s, and you will find ....Matt 7:7
of Man has come to *s* ....Luke 19:10
because I do not *s* ....John 5:30
You will *s* Me and ....John 7:34
in doing good *s* ....Rom 2:7
Because they did not *s* ....Rom 9:32
Let no one *s* his own ....1 Cor 10:24
for I do not *s* yours ....2 Cor 12:14
For all *s* their own ....Phil 2:21
s those things which ....Col 3:1
s the one to come ....Heb 13:14

SEEKING

run to and fro, *s* ....Amos 8:12
and he came *s* fruit ....Luke 13:6
for the Father is *s* ....John 4:23
like a roaring lion, *s* ....1 Pet 5:8

SEEKS

no one *s* her ....Jer 30:17
receives, and he who *s* ....Matt 7:8
There is none who *s* ....Rom 3:11

SEEMS

There is a way which *s* .....Prov 14:12
have, even what he *s* ....Luke 8:18
If anyone among you *s* ....1 Cor 3:18

SEEN

s God face to face ....Gen 32:30
All this I have *s* ....Eccl 8:9
s the one I love ....Song 3:3
Who has *s* such things ....Is 66:8
s strange things today ....Luke 5:26
No one has *s* God at ....John 1:18
time, nor *s* His form ....John 5:37
I speak what I have *s* ....John 8:38
s Me has *s* the ....John 14:9
things which we have *s* ....Acts 4:20
s Jesus Christ our ....1 Cor 9:1
things which are not *s* ....2 Cor 4:18
whom no man has *s* ....1 Tim 6:16
heard, which we have *s* ....1 John 1:1

SEES

here seen Him who *s* ....Gen 16:13
s all the sons of men ....Ps 33:13
s his brother in need ....1 John 3:17
s his brother sinning ....1 John 5:16

SEIR

Home of Esau, Gen 32:3

Horites of, dispossessed by Esau's descendants, Deut 2:12
Desolation of, Ezek 35:15

SELF-CONFIDENT

a fool rages and is *s* ....Prov 14:16

SELF-CONTROL

about righteousness, *s* ....Acts 24:25
they cannot exercise *s* ....1 Cor 7:9
gentleness, *s* ....Gal 5:23
slanderers, without *s* ....2 Tim 3:3
to knowledge *s* ....2 Pet 1:6

SELF-CONTROLLED

just, holy, *s* ....Titus 1:8

SELF-SEEKING

envy and *s* exist ....James 3:16

SELL

said, "*S* me your ....Gen 25:31
s Your people for ....Ps 44:12
s the righteous ....Amos 2:6
s whatever you have ....Mark 10:21
no sword, let him *s* ....Luke 22:36
no one may buy or *s* ....Rev 13:17

SEND

He shall *s* from heaven ....Ps 57:3
"Whom shall I *s* ....Is 6:8
s them a Savior ....Is 19:20
"Behold, I *s* you out ....Matt 10:16
The Son of Man will *s* ....Matt 13:41
s Lazarus that he ....Luke 16:24
whom the Father will *s* ......John 14:26
has sent Me, I also *s* ....John 20:21

SENNACHERIB

Assyrian king (705–681 B.C.); son and successor of Sargon II, 2 Kin 18:13
Death of, by assassination, 2 Kin 19:36, 37

SENSELESS

Understand, you *s* ....Ps 94:8

SENSES

of use have their *s* ....Heb 5:14

SENSIBLY

who can answer *s* ....Prov 26:16

SENSUAL

but is earthly, *s* ....James 3:15
These are *s* persons ....Jude 19

SENT

and His Spirit have *s* ....Is 48:16
s these prophets ....Jer 23:21
As the Father has *s* ....John 20:21
unless they are *s* ....Rom 10:15
s His Son to be the ....1 John 4:10

SEPARATE

he shall *s* himself ....Num 6:3
s yourselves from the ....Ezra 10:11
let not man *s* ....Matt 19:6
Who shall *s* us from ....Rom 8:35
harmless, undefiled, *s* ....Heb 7:26

SEPARATED

but the poor is *s* ....Prov 19:4
"The LORD has utterly *s* ....Is 56:3

to be an apostle, *s* ....Rom 1:1
it pleased God, who *s* ....Gal 1:15

SEPARATES
who repeats a matter *s* ....Prov 17:9

SEPARATION
the middle wall of *s* ....Eph 2:14

SERAPHIM
Above it stood *s* ....Is 6:2

SERGIUS PAULUS
Roman proconsul of Cyprus, converted by Paul, Acts 13:7–12

SERIOUS
therefore be *s* and ....1 Pet 4:7

SERPENT
s was more cunning ....Gen 3:1
"The *s* deceived me ....Gen 3:13
"Make a fiery *s* ....Num 21:8
like the poison of a *s* ....Ps 58:4
s you shall trample ....Ps 91:13
their tongues like a *s* ....Ps 140:3
air, the way of a *s* ....Prov 30:19
s may bite when it is ....Eccl 10:11
be a fiery flying *s* ....Is 14:29
and wounded the *s* ....Is 51:9
will he give him a *s* ....Matt 7:10
Moses lifted up the *s* ....John 3:14
was cast out, that *s* ....Rev 12:9

SERPENTS
is the poison of *s* ....Deut 32:33
be wise as *s* ....Matt 10:16
to trample on *s* ....Luke 10:19

SERVANT
a *s* of servants he ....Gen 9:25
s who earnestly ....Job 7:2
and the fool will be *s* ....Prov 11:29
s will rule over a son ....Prov 17:2
A *s* will not be ....Prov 29:19
Who is blind but My *s* ....Is 42:19
"Is Israel a *s* ....Jer 2:14
and a *s* his master ....Mal 1:6
you, let him be your *s* ....Matt 20:26
good and faithful *s* ....Matt 25:21
'You wicked and lazy *s* ....Matt 25:26
the unprofitable *s* ....Matt 25:30
that *s* who knew his ....Luke 12:47
s does not know what ....John 15:15
against Your holy *S* ....Acts 4:27

SERVANTS
puts no trust in His *s* ....Job 4:18
for all your *s* ....Ps 119:91
on the ground like *s* ....Eccl 10:7
shall call you the *s* ....Is 61:6
S rule over us ....Lam 5:8
are unprofitable *s* ....Luke 17:10
longer do I call you *s* ....John 15:15
so consider us, as *s* ....1 Cor 4:1

SERVE
LORD your God and *s* ....Deut 6:13
land, so you shall *s* aliens ....Jer 5:19
s Him with one accord ....Zeph 3:9
You cannot *s* God and ....Matt 6:24
to be served, but to *s* ....Matt 20:28
the mind I myself *s* ....Rom 7:25
but through love *s* ....Gal 5:13
s the LORD Christ ....Col 3:24

s the living God ....Heb 9:14
s Him day and night in ....Rev 7:15

SERVES
If anyone *s* Me ....John 12:26

SERVICE
do you mean by this *s* ....Ex 12:26
that he offers God *s* ....John 16:2
is your reasonable *s* ....Rom 12:1
with goodwill doing *s* ....Eph 6:7
your works, love, *s* ....Rev 2:19

SERVING
years I have been *s* ....Luke 15:29
s the Lord with all ....Acts 20:19
fervent in spirit, *s* ....Rom 12:11
you, *s* as overseers ....1 Pet 5:2

SET
"See, I have *s* ....Deut 30:15
s the LORD always ....Ps 16:8
I will *s* him on high ....Ps 91:14
s aside the grace ....Gal 2:21

SETH
Third son of Adam, Gen 4:25
In Christ's ancestry, Luke 3:38

SETTLE
Therefore *s* it in ....Luke 21:14

SETTLED
and my speech *s* ....Job 29:22
O LORD, Your word is *s* ....Ps 119:89
the mountains were *s* ....Prov 8:25
s accounts with them ....Matt 25:19

SEVEN
S times a day I praise ....Ps 119:164
s other spirits more ....Luke 11:26
s times in a day ....Luke 17:4
out from among you *s* ....Acts 6:3
s churches which are ....Rev 1:4

SEVENTY
S weeks are ....Dan 9:24
up to *s* times seven ....Matt 18:22
Then the *s* returned ....Luke 10:17

SEVERE
My wound is *s* ....Jer 10:19
not to be too *s* ....2 Cor 2:5

SEVERITY
the goodness and *s* ....Rom 11:22

SHADE
I sat down in his *s* ....Song 2:3
be a tabernacle for *s* ....Is 4:6
may nest under its *s* ....Mark 4:32

SHADOW
May darkness and the *s* ....Job 3:5
He flees like a *s* ....Job 14:2
hide me under the *s* ....Ps 17:8
walks about like a *s* ....Ps 39:6
like a passing *s* ....Ps 144:4
he passes like a *s* ....Eccl 6:12
and to trust in the *s* ....Is 30:2
In the *s* of His hand ....Is 49:2
which are a *s* of ....Col 2:17
the law, having a *s* ....Heb 10:1
is no variation or *s* ....James 1:17

SHADOWS
my members are like *s* ....Job 17:7
and the *s* flee away ....Song 2:17

SHADRACH
Hananiah's Babylonian name, Dan 1:3, 7
Cast into the fiery furnace, Dan 3:1–28

SHAKE
Who is he who will *s* ....Job 17:3
s the earth ....Is 2:19
S yourself from the ....Is 52:2
s their heads at the ....Lam 2:15
and the knees *s* ....Nah 2:10
hiss and *s* his fist ....Zeph 2:15
I will *s* all nations ....Hag 2:7
s not only the earth ....Heb 12:26

SHAKEN
he will never be *s* ....Ps 112:6
together was *s* ....Acts 4:31
not to be soon *s* ....2 Thess 2:2

SHAKES
s the earth out of its ....Job 9:6
s the Wilderness ....Ps 29:8

SHALLUM
King of Israel, 2 Kin 15:10–15

SHALMANESER
Assyrian king, 2 Kin 17:3

SHAME
you turn my glory to *s* ....Ps 4:2
let them be put to *s* ....Ps 83:17
s who serve carved ....Ps 97:7
hate Zion be put to *s* ....Ps 129:5
s shall be the ....Prov 3:35
is a son who causes *s* ....Prov 10:5
hide My face from *s* ....Is 50:6
S has covered our ....Jer 51:51
their glory into *s* ....Hos 4:7
never be put to *s* ....Joel 2:26
the unjust knows no *s* ....Zeph 3:5
worthy to suffer *s* ....Acts 5:41
will not be put to *s* ....Rom 9:33
to put to *s* the wise ....1 Cor 1:27
I say this to your *s* ....1 Cor 6:5
glory is in their *s* ....Phil 3:19
put Him to an open *s* ....Heb 6:6

SHAMEFUL
committing what is *s* ....Rom 1:27
for it is *s* for women ....1 Cor 14:35
For it is *s* even to ....Eph 5:12

SHAMGAR
Judge of Israel; strikes down 600 Philistines, Judg 3:31

SHAMMAH
Son of Jesse, 1 Sam 16:9
Called Shimea, 1 Chr 2:13
——— One of David's mighty men, 2 Sam 23:11
Also called Shammoth the Harorite, 1 Chr 11:27

SHAPHAN
Scribe under Josiah, 2 Kin 22:3–14

SHARE
a stranger does not *s* ....Prov 14:10

s your bread with the ....Is 58:7
is taught the word s ....Gal 6:6
to give, willing to s ....1 Tim 6:18
to do good and to s ....Heb 13:16

SHARING

for your liberal s ....2 Cor 9:13

SHARON

Coastal plain between Joppa and Mt. Carmel, 1 Chr 27:29
Famed for roses, Song 2:1
Inhabitants of, turn to the Lord, Acts 9:35

SHARP

S as a two-edged sword ....Prov 5:4

SHARPEN

s their tongue like a ....Ps 64:3
and one does not s ....Eccl 10:10

SHARPENS

My adversary s His ....Job 16:9

SHARPNESS

I should use s ....2 Cor 13:10

SHATTERED

at ease, but He has s ....Job 16:12

SHEALTIEL

Son of King Jeconiah and father of Zerubbabel, 1 Chr 3:17

SHEAR-JASHUB

Symbolic name given to Isaiah's son, Is 7:3

SHEATH

'Return it to its s ....Ezek 21:30
your sword into the s ....John 18:11

SHEAVES

bringing his s ....Ps 126:6
nor he who binds s ....Ps 129:7
gather them like s ....Mic 4:12

SHEBA

Land of, occupied by Sabeans, famous traders, Job 1:15; Ps 72:10
Queen of, visits Solomon; marvels at his wisdom, 1 Kin 10:1–13
Mentioned by Christ, Matt 12:42

SHEBAH

Name given to a well and town (Beersheba), Gen 26:31–33

SHEBNA

Treasurer under Hezekiah, Is 22:15
Demoted to position of scribe, 2 Kin 19:2
Man of pride and luxury, replaced by Eliakim, Is 22:19–21

SHECHEM

Son of Hamor; rapes Dinah, Jacob's daughter, Gen 34:1–31
——— Ancient city of Ephraim, Gen 33:18
Joshua's farewell address delivered at, Josh 24:1–25
Supports Abimelech; destroyed, Judg 9
Rebuilt by Jeroboam I, 1 Kin 12:25

SHED

which is s for many ....Matt 26:28

SHEDDING

blood, and without s ....Heb 9:22

SHEEP

astray like a lost s ....Ps 119:176
slaughter, and as a s ....Is 53:7
Pull them out like s ....Jer 12:3
have been lost s ....Jer 50:6
will search for My s ....Ezek 34:11
shall judge between s ......Ezek 34:17
s will be scattered ....Zech 13:7
rather to the lost s ....Matt 10:6
I send you out as s ....Matt 10:16
And He will set the s ....Matt 25:33
having a hundred s ....Luke 15:4
and he calls his own s ....John 10:3
and I know My s ....John 10:14
s I have which are not .....John 10:16
"He was led as a s ....Acts 8:32
like s going astray ....1 Pet 2:25

SHEEPFOLDS

lie down among the s ....Ps 68:13

SHEET

object like a great s ....Acts 10:11

SHELTER

I will trust in the s ....Ps 61:4
in You I take s ....Ps 143:9
the LORD will be a s ....Joel 3:16

SHELTERS

s him all the day long ......Deut 33:12
be pastures, with s ....Zeph 2:6

SHEM

Oldest son of Noah, Gen 5:32
Escapes the flood, Gen 7:13
Receives a blessing, Gen 9:23, 26
Ancestor of Semitic people, Gen 10:22–32

SHEMAIAH

Prophet of Judah, 1 Kin 12:22–24
Explains Shishak's invasion as divine punishment, 2 Chr 12:5–8
Records Rehoboam's reign, 2 Chr 12:15

SHEMER

Sells Omri the hill on which Samaria is built, 1 Kin 16:23, 24

SHEOL

down to the gates of S ....Job 17:16
not leave my soul in S ....Ps 16:10
S laid hold of me ....Ps 116:3
S cannot thank ....Is 38:18
the belly of S I cried ....Jon 2:2

SHEPHERD

s is an abomination ....Gen 46:34
s My people Israel ....2 Sam 5:2
The LORD is my s ....Ps 23:1
s Jacob His people ....Ps 78:71
His flock like a s ....Is 40:11
of Cyrus, 'He is My s ....Is 44:28
s who follows You ....Jer 17:16
because there was no s .....Ezek 34:5
I will establish one s ....Ezek 34:23
"As a s takes from ....Amos 3:12
to the worthless s ....Zech 11:17
'I will strike the S ....Matt 26:31
"I am the good s ....John 10:11
s the church of God ....Acts 20:28
the dead, that great S ....Heb 13:20
S the flock of God ....1 Pet 5:2
when the Chief S ....1 Pet 5:4
of the throne will s ....Rev 7:17

SHEPHERDS

your sons shall be s ....Num 14:33
And they are s who ....Is 56:11
And I will give you s ....Jer 3:15
s who destroy and ....Jer 23:1
s who feed My people ....Jer 23:2
s have led them astray ....Jer 50:6
s fed themselves ....Ezek 34:8
in the same country s ....Luke 2:8

SHESHACH

Symbolic of Babylon, Jer 25:26

SHESHBAZZAR

Prince of Judah, Ezra 1:8, 11

SHETHAR-BOZNAI

Official of Persia, Ezra 5:3, 6

SHIELD

I am your s ....Gen 15:1
He is a s to all who ....2 Sam 22:31
my s and the horn of ....Ps 18:2
God is a sun and s ....Ps 84:11
truth shall be your s ....Ps 91:4
all, taking the s ....Eph 6:16

SHIHOR

Name given to the Nile, Is 23:3
Israel's southwestern border, Josh 13:3

SHILOH

Center of worship, Judg 18:31
Headquarters for division of Promised Land, Josh 18:1, 10
Benjamites seize women of, Judg 21:19–23
Ark of the covenant taken from, 1 Sam 4:3–11
Punishment given to, Jer 7:12–15
——— Messianic title, Gen 49:10

SHIMEI

Benjamite; insults David, 2 Sam 16:5–13
Pardoned, but confined, 2 Sam 19:16–23
Breaks agreement; executed by Solomon, 1 Kin 2:39–46

SHIMSHAI

Scribe opposing the Jews, Ezra 4:8–24

SHINAR

Tower built at, Gen 11:2–9

SHINE

LORD make His face s ......Num 6:25
cause His face to s ....Ps 67:1
the cherubim, s ....Ps 80:1
Make Your face s ....Ps 119:135
who are wise shall s ....Dan 12:3
the righteous will s ....Matt 13:43
among whom you s ....Phil 2:15

SHINED

them a light has s ....Is 9:2

SHINES
And the light *s* . . . . .John 1:5

SHINING
the earth, by clear *s* . . . . .2 Sam 23:4
His clothes became *s* . . . . .Mark 9:3
light is already *s* . . . . .1 John 2:8
was like the sun *s* . . . . .Rev 1:16

SHIPHRAH
Hebrew midwife, Ex 1:15

SHIPS
pass by like swift *s* . . . . .Job 9:26
down to the sea in *s* . . . . .Ps 107:23
like the merchant *s* . . . . .Prov 31:14
Look also at *s* . . . . .James 3:4

SHIPWRECK
faith have suffered *s* . . . . .1 Tim 1:19

SHOOT
they *s* out the lip . . . . .Ps 22:7
But God shall *s* . . . . .Ps 64:7

SHORT
have sinned and fall *s* . . . . . . .Rom 3:23
the work and cut it *s* . . . . .Rom 9:28

SHORTENED
his youth You have *s* . . . . .Ps 89:45
the wicked will be *s* . . . . .Prov 10:27
those days were *s* . . . . .Matt 24:22

SHOT
shall be stoned or *s* . . . . .Heb 12:20

SHOUT
s joyfully to the Rock . . . . .Ps 95:1
S joyfully to the LORD . . . . .Ps 98:4
Make a joyful *s* . . . . .Ps 100:1
from heaven with a *s* . . . . .1 Thess 4:16

SHOW
a land that I will *s* . . . . .Gen 12:1
S me Your ways . . . . .Ps 25:4
s yourselves men . . . . .Is 46:8
s Him greater works . . . . .John 5:20
s us the Father . . . . .John 14:8

SHOWBREAD
you shall set the *s* . . . . .Ex 25:30
s which had been taken . . . .1 Sam 21:6
s which was not lawful . . . . . .Matt 12:4

SHOWERS
make it soft with *s* . . . . .Ps 65:10
s have been withheld . . . . .Jer 3:3
can the heavens give *s* . . . . .Jer 14:22
from the LORD, like *s* . . . . .Mic 5:7

SHREWDLY
because he had dealt *s* . . . . . .Luke 16:8

SHRINES
who made silver *s* . . . . .Acts 19:24

SHRIVELED
You have *s* me up . . . . .Job 16:8

SHUFFLES
with his eyes, he *s* . . . . .Prov 6:13

SHULAMITE
Beloved of the bridegroom king, Song 6:13

SHUNAMMITE
Abishag, David's nurse, 1 Kin 1:3, 15
—— Woman who cared for Elisha, 2 Kin 4:8–12

SHUNNED
feared God and *s* evil . . . . .Job 1:1

SHUSHAN
Residence of Persian monarchs, Esth 1:2

SHUT
"Or who *s* in the sea . . . . .Job 38:8
Has He in anger *s* . . . . .Ps 77:9
For you *s* up the . . . . .Matt 23:13

SHUTS
s his ears to the cry . . . . .Prov 21:13
s his eyes from seeing . . . . .Is 33:15
brother in need, and *s* . . . . .1 John 3:17
who opens and no one *s* . . . . .Rev 3:7

SICK
have made him *s* . . . . .Hos 7:5
I was *s* and you . . . . .Matt 25:36
he whom You love is *s* . . . . . .John 11:3
many are weak and *s* . . . . . .1 Cor 11:30
have left in Miletus *s* . . . . .2 Tim 4:20
faith will save the *s* . . . . .James 5:15

SICKLE
Put in the *s* . . . . .Joel 3:13
"Thrust in Your *s* . . . . .Rev 14:15

SICKNESS
will sustain him in *s* . . . . .Prov 18:14
"This *s* is not unto . . . . .John 11:4

SICKNESSES
And bore our *s* . . . . .Matt 8:17

SIDE
The LORD is on my *s* . . . . .Ps 118:6
the net on the right *s* . . . . .John 21:6

SIDON
Canaanite city; inhabitants not expelled, Judg 1:31
Hostile relations with Israel, Judg 10:12; Is 23:12; Joel 3:4–6
Jesus preaches to, Matt 15:21; Luke 6:17

SIFT
s the nations with the . . . . .Is 30:28
s the house of Israel . . . . .Amos 9:9
for you, that he may *s* . . . . .Luke 22:31

SIFTS
A wise king *s* out the . . . . . . .Prov 20:26

SIGH
our years like a *s* . . . . .Ps 90:9
the merry-hearted *s* . . . . .Is 24:7
of the men who *s* . . . . .Ezek 9:4

SIGHING
For my *s* comes before . . . . . . .Job 3:24
s is not hidden . . . . .Ps 38:9

SIGHT
and see this great *s* . . . . .Ex 3:3
seemed good in Your *s* . . . . . .Matt 11:26
by faith, not by *s* . . . . .2 Cor 5:7

SIGN
Show me a *s* for good . . . . .Ps 86:17
will give you a *s* . . . . .Is 7:14
for an everlasting *s* . . . . .Is 55:13
we want to see a *s* . . . . .Matt 12:38
seeks after a *s* . . . . .Matt 12:39
And what will be the *s* . . . . . .Matt 24:3
s which will be spoken . . . . . .Luke 2:34
again is the second *s* . . . . .John 4:54
For Jews request a *s* . . . . .1 Cor 1:22
Now a great *s* appeared . . . . . .Rev 12:1

SIGNS
and let them be for *s* . . . . .Gen 1:14
you not know their *s* . . . . .Job 21:29
They performed His *s* . . . . . . .Ps 105:27
We are for *s* and . . . . .Is 8:18
How great are His *s* . . . . .Dan 4:3
cannot discern the *s* . . . . .Matt 16:3
the accompanying *s* . . . . .Mark 16:20
s Jesus did in Cana of . . . . .John 2:11
no one can do these *s* . . . . .John 3:2
you people see *s* . . . . .John 4:48
because you saw the *s* . . . . . . .John 6:26
is a sinner do such *s* . . . . .John 9:16
this Man works many *s* . . . .John 11:47
Jesus did many other *s* . . . . .John 20:30
demons, performing *s* . . . . .Rev 16:14

SIHON
Amorite king; defeated by Israel, Num 21:21–32
Territory of, assigned to Reuben and Gad, Num 32:1–38

SILAS (or Silvanus)
Leader in Jerusalem church; sent to Antioch, Acts 15:22–35
Travels with Paul, Acts 15:40, 41
Jailed and released, Acts 16:25–40
Mentioned in epistles, 2 Cor 1:19; 1 Thess 1:1; 2 Thess 1:1; 1 Pet 5:12

SILENCE
that You may *s* . . . . .Ps 8:2
I was mute with *s* . . . . .Ps 39:2
soon have settled in *s* . . . . .Ps 94:17
"Sit in *s* . . . . .Is 47:5
seal, there was *s* . . . . .Rev 8:1

SILENT
the wicked shall be *s* . . . . .1 Sam 2:9
season, and am not *s* . . . . .Ps 22:2
Do not be *s* to me . . . . .Ps 28:1
Let them be *s* in the . . . . .Ps 31:17
Be *s* in the presence . . . . .Zeph 1:7
Let your women keep *s* . . . .1 Cor 14:34

SILK
and covered you with *s* . . . . . . .Ezek 16:10

SILLY
They are *s* children . . . . .Jer 4:22

SILOAM
Tower of, falls and kills 18 people, Luke 13:4
Blind man washes in pool of, John 9:1–11

SILVER
and your precious *s* . . . . .Job 22:25
Though he heaps up *s* . . . . .Job 27:16
s tried in a furnace . . . . .Ps 12:6
have refined us as *s* . . . . .Ps 66:10

than the profits of *s* ....Prov 3:14
chosen rather than *s* ....Prov 16:16
refining pot is for *s* ....Prov 17:3
He who loves *s* will ....Eccl 5:10
s has become dross ....Is 1:22
call them rejected *s* ....Jer 6:30
may buy the poor for *s* ......Amos 8:6
him thirty pieces of *s* ....Matt 26:15

SIMEON

Son of Jacob by Leah, Gen 29:32, 33
Avenged his sister's dishonor, Gen 34:25–31
Held hostage by Joseph, Gen 42:18–20, 24
Rebuked by Jacob, Gen 49:5–7
——Tribe of:
Numbered, Num 1:23; 26:12–14
Receive inheritance, Josh 19:1–9
Fight Canaanites with Judah, Judg 1:1–3, 17–20
——Just man; blesses infant Jesus, Luke 2:25–35

SIMILITUDE

been made in the *s* ....James 3:9

SIMON

Simon Peter: *see* PETER
——One of the Twelve; called "the Cananite," Matt 10:4
——One of Jesus' half brothers, Matt 13:55
——Pharisee, Luke 7:36–40
——Man of Cyrene, Matt 27:32
——Sorcerer, Acts 8:9–24
——Tanner in Joppa, Acts 9:43

SIMPLE

making wise the *s* ....Ps 19:7
LORD preserves the *s* ....Ps 116:6
understanding to the *s* .....Ps 119:130
s believes every word ....Prov 14:15
the hearts of the *s* ....Rom 16:18

SIMPLICITY

ones, will you love *s* ....Prov 1:22
in the world in *s* ....2 Cor 1:12
corrupted from the *s* ....2 Cor 11:3

SIN

committed a great *s* ....Ex 32:20
he died in his own *s* ....Num 27:3
and be sure your *s* ....Num 32:23
to death for his own *s* ....Deut 24:16
all this Job did not *s* ....Job 2:10
and search out my *s* ....Job 10:6
Be angry, and do not *s* ....Ps 4:4
my ways, lest I *s* ....Ps 39:1
s is always before me ....Ps 51:3
in *s* my mother ....Ps 51:5
s is a reproach ....Prov 14:34
good and does not *s* ....Eccl 7:20
soul an offering for *s* ....Is 53:10
And He bore the *s* ....Is 53:12
s I will remember no ....Jer 31:34
They eat up the *s* ....Hos 4:8
Now they *s* more and ....Hos 13:2
who believe in Me to *s* ....Matt 18:6
who takes away the *s* ....John 1:29
S no more ....John 5:14
"He who is without *s* ....John 8:7
convict the world of *s* ....John 16:8
they are all under *s* ....Rom 3:9
s entered the world ....Rom 5:12
s is not imputed ....Rom 5:13
s that grace may ....Rom 6:1
died to *s* once for all ....Rom 6:10
s shall not have ....Rom 6:14
Shall we *s* because we ....Rom 6:15
s that dwells in me ....Rom 7:17
Him who knew no *s* ....2 Cor 5:21
man of *s* is revealed ....2 Thess 2:3
we are, yet without *s* ....Heb 4:15
appeared to put away *s* ....Heb 9:26
s willfully after we ....Heb 10:26
it gives birth to *s* ....James 1:15
do it, to him it is *s* ....James 4:17
"Who committed no *s* ....1 Pet 2:22
say that we have no *s* ....1 John 1:8
that you may not *s* ....1 John 2:1
s is lawlessness ....1 John 3:4
in Him there is no *s* ....1 John 3:5
and he cannot *s* ....1 John 3:9
for those who commit *s* ......1 John 5:16
unrighteousness is *s* ....1 John 5:17

SINAI

Mountain (same as Horeb) where the law was given, Ex 19:1–25
Used allegorically by Paul, Gal 4:24, 25

SINCERE

Holy Spirit, by *s* love ....2 Cor 6:6
and from *s* faith ....1 Tim 1:5
s love of the brethren ....1 Pet 1:22

SINCERITY

LORD, serve Him in *s* ....Josh 24:14
unleavened bread of *s* ....1 Cor 5:8
simplicity and godly *s* ....2 Cor 1:12
men-pleasers, but in *s* ....Col 3:22

SINFUL

Alas, *s* nation ....Is 1:4
and *s* generation ....Mark 8:38
from me, for I am a *s* ....Luke 5:8
the hands of *s* men ....Luke 24:7
become exceedingly *s* ....Rom 7:13
likeness of *s* flesh ....Rom 8:3

SING

"*S* to the LORD ....Ex 15:21
the widow's heart to *s* ....Job 29:13
S out the honor ....Ps 66:2
I will *s* of mercy and ....Ps 101:1
"*S* us one of the songs ....Ps 137:3
My servants shall *s* ....Is 65:14
I will *s* with the ....1 Cor 14:15
assembly I will *s* ....Heb 2:12
Let him *s* psalms ....James 5:13

SINGERS

The *s* went before ....Ps 68:25
male and female *s* ....Eccl 2:8

SINGING

His presence with *s* ....Ps 100:2
and our tongue with *s* ....Ps 126:2
the time of *s* has come ....Song 2:12
break forth into *s* ....Is 14:7
even with joy and *s* ....Is 35:2
come to Zion with *s* ....Is 35:10
and spiritual songs, *s* ....Eph 5:19

SINISTER

who understands *s* ....Dan 8:23

SINK

I *s* in deep mire ....Ps 69:2
to *s* he cried out ....Matt 14:30

SINNED

You only, have I *s* ....Ps 51:4
Jerusalem has *s* ....Lam 1:8
Our fathers *s* and are ....Lam 5:7
"Father, I have *s* ....Luke 15:18
"Rabbi, who *s* ....John 9:2
For as many as have *s* ....Rom 2:12
for all have *s* and ....Rom 3:23
marries, she has not *s* ....1 Cor 7:28
say that we have not *s* ....1 John 1:10
for the devil has *s* ....1 John 3:8

SINNER

s He gives the work ....Eccl 2:26
s does evil a hundred ....Eccl 8:12
s destroys much good ....Eccl 9:18
the city who was a *s* ....Luke 7:37
s who repents than ....Luke 15:7
can a man who is a *s* ....John 9:16
the ungodly and the *s* ....1 Pet 4:18

SINNERS

in the path of *s* ....Ps 1:1
therefore He teaches *s* ....Ps 25:8
soul with *s* ....Ps 26:9
s be consumed from the ....Ps 104:35
son, if *s* entice you ....Prov 1:10
The *s* in Zion are ....Is 33:14
the righteous, but *s* ....Matt 9:13
tax collectors and *s* ....Matt 11:19
s love those who love ....Luke 6:32
Galileans were worse *s* ....Luke 13:2
God does not hear *s* ....John 9:31
while we were still *s* ....Rom 5:8
many were made *s* ....Rom 5:19
the ungodly and for *s* ....1 Tim 1:9
the world to save *s* ....1 Tim 1:15
separate from *s* ....Heb 7:26
such hostility from *s* ....Heb 12:3
things which ungodly *s* ....Jude 15

SINS

my iniquities and *s* ....Job 13:23
from presumptuous *s* ....Ps 19:13
You, our secret *s* ....Ps 90:8
but he who *s* against ....Prov 8:36
s have hidden His face ....Is 59:2
the soul who *s* shall ....Ezek 18:4
to make an end of *s* ....Dan 9:24
if your brother *s* ....Matt 18:15
I take away their *s* ....Rom 11:27
s according to the ....1 Cor 15:3
are still in your *s* ....1 Cor 15:17
the forgiveness of *s* ....Eph 1:7
s are clearly evident ....1 Tim 5:24
once to bear the *s* ....Heb 9:28
If we confess our *s* ....1 John 1:9
propitiation for our *s* ....1 John 2:2
s are forgiven you ....1 John 2:12
Whoever *s* has neither ....1 John 3:6
you share in her *s* ....Rev 18:4

SION

See ZION
Name given to all or part of Mt. Hermon, Deut 4:48

SISERA

Canaanite commander of Jabin's army; slain by Jael, Judg 4:2–22

SISTER

are my mother and my *s* ....Job 17:14
We have a little *s* ....Song 8:8
is My brother and *s* ....Matt 12:50

to you Phoebe our *s* ....Rom 16:1
s is not under bondage .....1 Cor 7:15

SIT

Those who *s* in the ....Ps 69:12
"Come down and *s* ....Is 47:1
"Why do we *s* still ....Jer 8:14
but to *s* on My right ....Matt 20:23
and the Pharisees *s*..........Matt 23:2
"*S* at My right hand ....Heb 1:13
say to him, "You *s* ....James 2:3
I will grant to *s* ....Rev 3:21
heart, 'I *s* as queen ....Rev 18:7

SITS

God *s* on His holy ....Ps 47:8
It is He who *s* above ....Is 40:22
so that he *s* as God ....2 Thess 2:4
where the harlot *s* ....Rev 17:15

SITTING

You know my *s* down and ....Ps 139:2
see the Son of Man *s* .....Mark 14:62
where Christ is, *s* ....Col 3:1

SKILL

hand forget its *s* ....Ps 137:5
nor favor to men of *s* ....Eccl 9:11
them knowledge and *s* ....Dan 1:17
forth to give you *s* ....Dan 9:22

SKILLFULNESS

guided them by the *s* ....Ps 78:72

SKIN

God made tunics of *s* ....Gen 3:21
LORD and said, "*S* ....Job 2:4
have escaped by the *s* ....Job 19:20
Ethiopian change his *s* ....Jer 13:23
s is hot as an oven ....Lam 5:10

SKIP

He makes them also *s* ....Ps 29:6

SKIPPING

upon the mountains, *s* ....Song 2:8

SKULL

to say, Place of a *S* ....Matt 27:33

SKY

s receded as a scroll ....Rev 6:14

SLACK

He will not be *s* ....Deut 7:10
s hand becomes poor ....Prov 10:4
The Lord is not *s* ....2 Pet 3:9

SLAIN

s his thousands ....1 Sam 18:7
beauty of Israel is *s* ....2 Sam 1:19
the dead, like the *s* ....Ps 88:5
and all who were *s* ....Prov 7:26
I shall be *s* in the ....Prov 22:13
s men are not *s* ....Is 22:2
no more cover her *s* ....Is 26:21
and the *s* of the LORD ....Is 66:16
and night for the *s* ....Jer 9:1
Those *s* by the sword ....Lam 4:9
the prophets, I have *s* ....Hos 6:5
is the Lamb who was *s* ....Rev 5:12

SLANDER

s your own mother's ....Ps 50:20
and whoever spreads *s* .....Prov 10:18

SLANDERERS

be reverent, not *s* ....1 Tim 3:11
unforgiving, *s* ....2 Tim 3:3
in behavior, not *s* ....Titus 2:3

SLANDEROUSLY

as we are *s* reported ....Rom 3:8

SLAUGHTER

as sheep for the *s* ....Ps 44:22
led as a lamb to the *s* ....Is 53:7
but the Valley of *S* ....Jer 7:32
"Feed the flock for *s* ....Zech 11:4
as sheep for the *s* ....Rom 8:36

SLAVE

that you were a *s* ....Deut 15:15
commits sin is a *s* ....John 8:34
you called while a *s* ....1 Cor 7:21
you are no longer a *s* ....Gal 4:7

SLAVES

should no longer be *s* ....Rom 6:6
though you were *s* ....Rom 6:17
your members as *s* ....Rom 6:19
do not become *s* ....1 Cor 7:23

SLAY

s the righteous ....Gen 18:25
s a righteous nation ....Gen 20:4
Evil shall *s* the ....Ps 34:21
Oh, that You would *s* ....Ps 139:19
s them before me ....Luke 19:27

SLEEP

God caused a deep *s* ....Gen 2:21
the night, when deep *s* ....Job 4:13
my eyes, lest I *s* ....Ps 13:3
Why do You *s* ....Ps 44:23
have sunk into their *s* ....Ps 76:5
they are like a *s* ....Ps 90:5
neither slumber nor *s* ....Ps 121:4
He gives His beloved *s* ....Ps 127:2
I will not give *s* ....Ps 132:4
s will be sweet ....Prov 3:24
For they do not *s* ....Prov 4:16
A little *s* ....Prov 6:10
Do not love *s* ....Prov 20:13
The *s* of a laboring ....Eccl 5:12
the spirit of deep *s* ....Is 29:10
Also his *s* went from ....Dan 6:18
I was in a deep *s* ....Dan 8:18
them, "Why do you *s* ......Luke 22:46
among you, and many *s* ...1 Cor 11:30
We shall not all *s*..........1 Cor 15:51
"Awake, you who *s* ....Eph 5:14
with Him those who *s* .....1 Thess 4:14
Therefore let us not *s* ......1 Thess 5:6

SLEEPERS

gently the lips of *s* ....Song 7:9

SLEEPING

is not dead, but *s* ....Matt 9:24
"Are you still *s* ....Matt 26:45
that night Peter was *s* ....Acts 12:6

SLEEPLESSNESS

in labors, in *s* ....2 Cor 6:5
and toil, in *s* often ....2 Cor 11:27

SLEEPS

wise son; he who *s* ....Prov 10:5
"Our friend Lazarus *s* ......John 11:11

SLEPT

I lay down and *s* ....Ps 3:5
but while men *s* ....Matt 13:25

SLIGHTED

is the one who is *s* ....Prov 12:9

SLING

he had, and his *s* ....1 Sam 17:40
a stone in a *s* is he ....Prov 26:8

SLIP

their foot shall *s* ....Deut 32:35
my footsteps may not *s* ....Ps 17:5

SLIPPERY

way be dark and *s* ....Ps 35:6
set them in *s* places ....Ps 73:18
be to them like *s* ....Jer 23:12

SLOOPS

all the beautiful *s* ....Is 2:16

SLOW

but I am *s* of speech ....Ex 4:10
He who is *s* to wrath ....Prov 14:29
hear, *s* to speak, *s* ....James 1:19

SLUGGARD

will you slumber, O *s* ....Prov 6:9

SLUMBERED

delayed, they all *s* ....Matt 25:5

SLUMBERING

upon men, while *s* ....Job 33:15

SMALL

'The place is too *s* ....Is 49:20
I will make you *s* ....Jer 49:15
may stand, for he is *s* ....Amos 7:2
I will make you *s* ....Obad 2
the day of *s* things ....Zech 4:10
And I saw the dead, *s* ....Rev 20:12

SMELL

and he smelled the *s* ....Gen 27:27
s there will be a ....Is 3:24

SMELLS

s the battle from afar ....Job 39:25

SMITTEN

Him stricken, *s* ....Is 53:4

SMOKE

went up like the *s* ....Gen 19:28
s is driven away ....Ps 68:2
are consumed like *s* ....Ps 102:3
like a wineskin in *s* ....Ps 119:83
like pillars of *s* ....Song 3:6
s shall ascend forever ....Is 34:10
vanish away like *s* ....Is 51:6
fire and vapor of *s* ....Acts 2:19
s arose out of the pit ....Rev 9:2
was filled with *s* ....Rev 15:8
Her *s* rises up ....Rev 19:3

SMOOTH

speak to us *s* things ....Is 30:10
And the rough places *s* ....Is 40:4
though they speak *s* ....Jer 12:6

the rough ways *s* ....Luke 3:5

SMOOTH-SKINNED

man, and I am a *s* ....Gen 27:11

SMYRNA

Site of one of the seven churches, Rev 1:11

SNAIL

s which melts away as.........Ps 58:8

SNARE

it will surely be a *s* ....Ex 23:33
It became a *s* to...............Judg 8:27
that she may be a *s* ....1 Sam 18:21
s snatches their ....Job 5:5
and he walks into a *s*..........Job 18:8
their table become a *s* ....Ps 69:22
as a bird from the *s* ....Ps 124:7
birds caught in a *s* ....Eccl 9:12
and the pit and the *s* ....Is 24:17
I have laid a *s* ....Jer 50:23
s have come upon us ....Lam 3:47
is a fowler's *s* ....Hos 9:8
a bird fall into a *s*.............Amos 3:5
it will come as a *s* ....Luke 21:35
temptation and a *s* ....1 Tim 6:9
and escape the *s* ....2 Tim 2:26

SNARED

The wicked is *s* ....Ps 9:16
and be broken, be *s* ....Is 8:15
all of them are *s* ....Is 42:22

SNARES

the *s* of death ....Ps 18:5
who seek my life lay *s* ....Ps 38:12
and built great *s* ....Eccl 9:14
wait as one who sets *s* ....Jer 5:26

SNATCH

s the fatherless..................Job 24:9
neither shall anyone *s* ....John 10:28

SNATCHES

s away what was ....Matt 13:19

SNEER

and you *s* at it ....Mal 1:13

SNIFFED

they *s* at the wind ....Jer 14:6

SNORTING

s strikes terror ....Job 39:20

SNOW

and heat consume the *s* ....Job 24:19
For He says to the *s* ....Job 37:6
the treasury of *s* ....Job 38:22
shall be whiter than *s*..........Ps 51:7
He gives *s* like wool ....Ps 147:16
As *s* in summer and ....Prov 26:1
She is not afraid of *s* ....Prov 31:21
shall be as white as *s* ....Is 1:18
garment was white as *s* ....Dan 7:9
clothing as white as *s* ....Matt 28:3
wool, as white as *s* ....Rev 1:14

SOAKED

their land shall be *s* ....Is 34:7

SOAP

lye, and use much *s* ....Jer 2:22

SOBER

of the day be *s* ....1 Thess 5:8
the older men be *s* ....Titus 2:2

SOBERLY

think, but to think *s* ....Rom 12:3
we should live *s* ....Titus 2:12

SODA

and like vinegar on *s* ....Prov 25:20

SODOM

Lot chooses to live there, Gen 13:10–13
Plundered by Chedorlaomer, Gen 14:8–24
Abraham intercedes for, Gen 18:16–33
Destroyed by God, Gen 19:1–29
Cited as example of sin and destruction, Deut 29:23; 32:32; Is 1:9, 10; 3:9; Jer 23:14; 49:18; Lam 4:6; Ezek 16:46–63; Matt 11:23, 24; 2 Pet 2:6; Jude 7

SODOMITES

nor homosexuals, nor *s* ......1 Cor 6:9
for fornicators, for *s* ....1 Tim 1:10

SOFTER

his words were *s* ....Ps 55:21

SOJOURNER

But no *s* had to lodge ....Job 31:32

SOJOURNERS

are strangers and *s*...........Lev 25:23
I beg you as *s* ....1 Pet 2:11

SOLD

s his birthright ....Gen 25:33
the house that was *s* ....Lev 25:33
their Rock had *s* ....Deut 32:30
and He *s* them into the ....Judg 2:14
s themselves to do ....2 Kin 17:17
Had we been *s* as male ....Esth 7:4
who was *s* as a slave ....Ps 105:17
s all that he had ....Matt 13:46
they bought, they *s* ....Luke 17:28
s their possessions ....Acts 2:45
but I am carnal, *s* ....Rom 7:14
Eat whatever is *s* ....1 Cor 10:25

SOLDIER

hardship as a good *s* ....2 Tim 2:3
enlisted him as a *s* ....2 Tim 2:4

SOLDIERS

sum of money to the *s*.......Matt 28:12
The *s* also mocked ....Luke 23:36
s twisted a crown ....John 19:2

SOLEMNLY

saying, "The man *s* ....Gen 43:3
s testified of the ....Acts 28:23

SOLITARILY

heritage, who dwell *s* ....Mic 7:14

SOLITARY

God sets the *s* in ....Ps 68:6

SOLOMON

David's son by Bathsheba, 2 Sam 12:24
Becomes king, 1 Kin 1:5–53
Receives and carries out David's instructions, 1 Kin 2
Prays for and demonstrates wisdom, 1 Kin 3:3–28; 4:29–34
Builds and dedicates temple; builds palace, 1 Kin 5–8
Lord appears to, 1 Kin 9:1–9
His fame and glory, 1 Kin 9:10—10:29
Falls into idolatry; warned by God, 1 Kin 11:1–13
Adversaries arise, 1 Kin 11:14–40
Death of, 1 Kin 11:41–43
Writings credited to him, Ps 72; 127; Prov 1:1; 10:1; 25:1; Eccl 1:1; Song 1:1

SOMEBODY

up, claiming to be *s*...........Acts 5:36

SOMETHING

"Simon, I have *s* ....Luke 7:40
thinks himself to be *s* ....Gal 6:3

SON

Me, 'You are My *S* ....Ps 2:7
I was my father's *s* ....Prov 4:3
s makes a glad father ....Prov 10:1
s is a grief to his ....Prov 17:25
And what, *s* of my womb ....Prov 31:2
is born, unto us a *S* ....Is 9:6
heaven, O Lucifer, *s* ....Is 14:12
fourth is like the *S*...........Dan 3:25
He is an unwise *s* ....Hos 13:13
prophet, nor was I a *s* ....Amos 7:14
s honors his father ....Mal 1:6
will bring forth a *S* ....Matt 1:21
"This is My beloved *S* ....Matt 3:17
Jesus, You *S* of God ....Matt 8:29
not the carpenter's *s* ....Matt 13:55
You are the *S* of God ....Matt 14:33
are the Christ, the *S* ....Matt 16:16
of all he sent his *s* ....Matt 21:37
Whose *S* is He ....Matt 22:42
'Lord,' how is He his *S* .....Matt 22:45
as much a *s* of hell ....Matt 23:15
of the *S* of Man ....Matt 24:37
'I am the *S* of God ....Matt 27:43
"Truly this was the *S*.......Matt 27:54
of Jesus Christ, the *S* ....Mark 1:1
called the *S* of the ....Luke 1:32
out, the only *s* ....Luke 7:12
And if a *s* of peace ....Luke 10:6
to be called your *s* ....Luke 15:19
because he also is a *s* ....Luke 19:9
The only begotten *S* ....John 1:18
that this is the *S* ....John 1:34
of the only begotten *S* ....John 3:18
S can do nothing ....John 5:19
s abides forever ....John 8:35
you believe in the *S* ....John 9:35
I said, 'I am the *S* ....John 10:36
"Woman, behold your *s* ....John 19:26
Jesus Christ is the *S* ....Acts 8:37
declared to be the *S* ....Rom 1:4
in the gospel of His *S* ....Rom 1:9
by sending His own *S* ....Rom 8:3
not spare His own *S* ....Rom 8:32
S Himself will also be .....1 Cor 15:28
live by faith in the *S*...........Gal 2:20
God sent forth His *S* ....Gal 4:4
longer a slave but a *s* ....Gal 4:7
the knowledge of the *S*.........Eph 4:13
you for my *s* Onesimus.....Philem 10
"You are My *S* ....Heb 1:5
but Christ as a *S* over His ......Heb 3:6
though He was a *S* ....Heb 5:8
but made like the *S* ....Heb 7:3
to be called the *s* ....Heb 11:24

"This is My beloved *S* ....2 Pet 1:17
Whoever denies the *S* .....1 John 2:23
God has given of His *S* ....1 John 5:10
One like the *S* of Man ....Rev 1:13

SONG

is my strength and *s* ....Ex 15:2
Sing to Him a new *s* ....Ps 33:3
He has put a new *s* ....Ps 40:3
in the night His *s* ....Ps 42:8
me, and I am the *s* ....Ps 69:12
asked of us a *s* ....Ps 137:3
I will sing a new *s* ....Ps 144:9
to my Well-beloved a *s* ....Is 5:1
their taunting *s* ....Lam 3:14
I am their taunting *s* ....Lam 3:63
as a very lovely *s* ....Ezek 33:32
They sang a new *s* ....Rev 5:9
And they sing the *s* ....Rev 15:3

SONGS

my Maker, who gives *s* ......Job 35:10
surround me with *s* ....Ps 32:7
have been my *s* in the ....Ps 119:54
Sing us one of the *s* ....Ps 137:3
is one who sings *s* ....Prov 25:20
and spiritual *s* ....Eph 5:19

SONS

s come to honor ....Job 14:21
shall be Your *s* ....Ps 45:16
my beloved among the *s* .....Song 2:3
s shall come from afar ....Is 60:4
"Has Israel no *s* ....Jer 49:1
The precious *s* of Zion ....Lam 4:2
'You are the *s* ....Hos 1:10
He will purify the *s* ....Mal 3:3
to him, "Then the *s* ....Matt 17:26
and you will be *s* ....Luke 6:35
that you may become *s* .....John 12:36
You are *s* of the ....Acts 3:25
of God, these are *s* ....Rom 8:14
who are of faith are *s* ....Gal 3:7
the adoption as *s* ....Gal 4:5
because you are *s* ....Gal 4:6
You are all *s* of light ....1 Thess 5:5
in bringing many *s* ....Heb 2:10
speaks to you as to *s* ....Heb 12:5
illegitimate and not *s* ....Heb 12:8

SOON

for it is *s* cut off ....Ps 90:10
s forgot His works ....Ps 106:13

SOOTHED

or bound up, or *s* ....Is 1:6

SORCERER

omens, or a *s* ....Deut 18:10
But Elymas the *s* ....Acts 13:8

SORCERERS

soothsayers, or your *s* ....Jer 27:9
outside are dogs and *s* ......Rev 22:15

SORCERESS

shall not permit a *s* ....Ex 22:18

SORCERY

For there is no *s* ....Num 23:23
idolatry, *s* ....Gal 5:20

SORES

and putrefying *s* ....Is 1:6
Lazarus, full of *s* ....Luke 16:20

SORROW

multiply your *s* ....Gen 3:16
s dances before him ....Job 41:22
in my soul, having *s* ....Ps 13:2
s is continually ....Ps 38:17
I found trouble and *s* ....Ps 116:3
And He adds no *s* ....Prov 10:22
the heart may *s* ....Prov 14:13
S is better than ....Eccl 7:3
Therefore remove *s* ....Eccl 11:10
and desperate *s* ....Is 17:11
you shall cry for *s* ....Is 65:14
to see labor and *s* ....Jer 20:18
Your *s* is incurable ....Jer 30:15
added grief to my *s* ....Jer 45:3
gather those who *s* ....Zeph 3:18
them sleeping from *s* ......Luke 22:45
s has filled your ....John 16:6
s will be turned ....John 16:20
that I have great *s* ....Rom 9:2
s produces repentance ......2 Cor 7:10
lest I should have *s* ....Phil 2:27
s as others who have .....1 Thess 4:13
no more death, nor *s* ....Rev 21:4

SORROWFUL

am a woman of *s* spirit .....1 Sam 1:15
But I am poor and *s* ....Ps 69:29
For all his days are *s* ....Eccl 2:23
replenished every *s* ....Jer 31:25
were exceedingly *s* ....Matt 17:23
saying, he went away *s* .....Matt 19:22
soul is exceedingly *s* ....Matt 26:38
and went away *s* ....Mark 10:22
and you will be *s* ....John 16:20
if I make you *s* ....2 Cor 2:2
and I may be less *s* ....Phil 2:28

SORROWS

the *s* of Sheol ....2 Sam 22:6
s God distributes ....Job 21:17
s shall be multiplied ....Ps 16:4
by men, a Man of *s* ....Is 53:3
are the beginning of *s* ....Matt 24:8
through with many *s* ....1 Tim 6:10

SORRY

s that He had made man ......Gen 6:6
who will be *s* for you ....Is 51:19
And the king was *s* ....Matt 14:9
For you were made *s* ....2 Cor 7:9

SOSTHENES

Ruler of the synagogue at Corinth, Acts 18:17
——— Paul's Christian brother, 1 Cor 1:1

SOUGHT

I *s* the LORD ....Ps 34:4
whole heart I have *s* ....Ps 119:10
s the one I love ....Song 3:1
shall be called *S* Out ....Is 62:12
So I *s* for a man ....Ezek 22:30
s what was lost ....Ezek 34:4
s favor from Him ....Hos 12:4
LORD, and have not *s* ....Zeph 1:6
s it diligently ....Heb 12:17

SOUL

s enter their council ....Gen 49:6
with all your *s* ....Deut 6:5
was knit to the *s* ....1 Sam 18:1
your heart and your *s* .....1 Chr 22:19
"My *s* loathes my life ....Job 10:1
as you do, if your *s* ....Job 16:4
s draws near the Pit ....Job 33:22
will not leave my *s* ....Ps 16:10
converting the *s* ....Ps 19:7
He restores my *s* ....Ps 23:3
s shall make its boast ....Ps 34:2
s shall be joyful ....Ps 35:9
you cast down, O my *s* ....Ps 42:5
s silently waits ....Ps 62:1
He has done for my *s* ....Ps 66:16
Let my *s* live ....Ps 119:175
s knows very well ....Ps 139:14
No one cares for my *s* ....Ps 142:4
so destroys his own *s* ....Prov 6:32
me wrongs his own *s* ....Prov 8:36
it is not good for a *s* ....Prov 19:2
A satisfied *s* loathes ....Prov 27:7
When You make His *s* ....Is 53:10
s delight itself ....Is 55:2
and your *s* shall live ....Is 55:3
you have heard, O my *s* ....Jer 4:19
the *s* of the father as ....Ezek 18:4
the proud, his *s* ....Hab 2:4
able to destroy both *s* ......Matt 10:28
and loses his own *s* ....Matt 16:26
with all your *s* ....Matt 22:37
Now My *s* is troubled ......John 12:27
of one heart and one *s* ....Acts 4:32
your whole spirit, *s* ....1 Thess 5:23
to the saving of the *s* ....Heb 10:39
his way will save a *s* ....James 5:20
his righteous *s* ....2 Pet 2:8
health, just as your *s* ....3 John 2

SOULS

and will save the *s* ....Ps 72:13
and he who wins *s* ....Prov 11:30
s shall be like a ....Jer 31:12
who made our very *s* ....Jer 38:16
unsettling your *s* ....Acts 15:24
is able to save your *s* ......James 1:21

SOUND

s heart is life ....Prov 14:30
one rises up at the *s* ....Eccl 12:4
voice was like the *s* ....Ezek 43:2
s an alarm in My holy ....Joel 2:1
do not *s* a trumpet ....Matt 6:2
s words which you ....2 Tim 1:13
that they may be *s* ....Titus 1:13

SOUNDNESS

There is no *s* in my ....Ps 38:3
him this perfect *s* ....Acts 3:16

SOUNDS

Dreadful *s* are in his ....Job 15:21
a distinction in the *s* ....1 Cor 14:7

SOW

s trouble reap ....Job 4:8
then let me *s* ....Job 31:8
s fields and plant ....Ps 107:37
Those who *s* in tears ....Ps 126:5
the wind will not *s* ....Eccl 11:4
Blessed are you who *s* ....Is 32:20
ground, and do not *s* ....Jer 4:3
"They *s* the wind ....Hos 8:7
S for yourselves ....Hos 10:12
s is not made alive ....1 Cor 15:36

SOWER

may give seed to the *s* ....Is 55:10
"Behold, a *s* went ....Matt 13:3

SOWN

shall they be *s* ....Is 40:24

s that we are children .... Rom 8:16
what the mind of the S .... Rom 8:27
to us through His S .... 1 Cor 2:10
also have the S .... 1 Cor 7:40
gifts, but the same S .... 1 Cor 12:4
in a tongue, my s .... 1 Cor 14:14
but the S gives life .... 2 Cor 3:6
Now the Lord is the S .... 2 Cor 3:17
we have the same s .... 2 Cor 4:13
Having begun in the S .... Gal 3:3
has sent forth the S .... Gal 4:6
he who sows to the S .... Gal 6:8
with the Holy S .... Eph 1:13
may give to you the s .... Eph 1:17
the unity of the S .... Eph 4:3
is one body and one S .... Eph 4:4
stand fast in one s .... Phil 1:27
yet I am with you in s .... Col 2:5
and may your whole s .... 1 Thess 5:23
S expressly says that .... 1 Tim 4:1
division of soul and s .... Heb 4:12
through the eternal S .... Heb 9:14
S who dwells in us .... James 4:5
made alive by the S .... 1 Pet 3:18
S whom He has given .... 1 John 3:24
do not believe every s .... 1 John 4:1
By this you know the S .... 1 John 4:2
By this we know the s .... 1 John 4:6
has given us of His S .... 1 John 4:13
S who bears witness .... 1 John 5:6
not having the S .... Jude 19
I was in the S on the .... Rev 1:10
him hear what the S .... Rev 2:7
And the S and the .... Rev 22:17

SPIRITS

God, the God of the s .... Num 16:22
who makes His angels s .... Ps 104:4
the LORD weighs the s .... Prov 16:2
power over unclean s .... Matt 10:1
heed to deceiving s .... 1 Tim 4:1
not all ministering s .... Heb 1:14
to the Father of s .... Heb 12:9
and preached to the s .... 1 Pet 3:19
spirit, but test the s .... 1 John 4:1

SPIRITUAL

s judges all things .... 1 Cor 2:15
s people but as to .... 1 Cor 3:1
to be a prophet or s .... 1 Cor 14:37
However, the s is not .... 1 Cor 15:46
s restore such a one .... Gal 6:1

SPIRITUALLY

s minded is life .... Rom 8:6
because they are s .... 1 Cor 2:14

SPITEFULLY

for those who s .... Matt 5:44

SPITTING

face from shame and s .... Is 50:6

SPLENDOR

on the glorious s .... Ps 145:5
of Zion all her s .... Lam 1:6

SPOIL

hate us have taken s .... Ps 44:10
when they divide the s .... Is 9:3
He shall divide the s .... Is 53:12
Take s of silver .... Nah 2:9
s will be divided .... Zech 14:1

SPOILER

I have created the s .... Is 54:16

SPOKE

s they did not hear .... Is 66:4
who feared the LORD s .... Mal 3:16
"No man ever s .... John 7:46
We know that God s .... John 9:29
I was a child, I s .... 1 Cor 13:11
in various ways s .... Heb 1:1
s as they were moved .... 2 Pet 1:21

SPOKEN

'just as you have s .... Num 14:28
God has s once .... Ps 62:11
I have not s in secret .... Is 45:19
'What have we s .... Mal 3:13
why am I evil s .... 1 Cor 10:30

SPOKESMAN

So he shall be your s .... Ex 4:16

SPONGE

them ran and took a s .... Matt 27:48

SPOT

and there is no s .... Song 4:7
church, not having s .... Eph 5:27
commandment without s .... 1 Tim 6:14
Himself without s .... Heb 9:14

SPOTS

They are s and .... 2 Pet 2:13
These are s in your .... Jude 12

SPREAD

fell on my knees and s .... Ezra 9:5
they have s a net by .... Ps 140:5
Then He s it before me .... Ezek 2:10
Then the word of God s .... Acts 6:7
the Lord was being s .... Acts 13:49
their message will s .... 2 Tim 2:17

SPREADS

He alone s out the .... Job 9:8
s them out like a tent .... Is 40:22
Zion s out her hands .... Lam 1:17

SPRING

Truth shall s out of .... Ps 85:11
is like a murky s .... Prov 25:26
sister, my spouse, a s .... Song 4:12
s forth I tell you .... Is 42:9
of Israel to s forth .... Ezek 29:21
s shall become dry .... Hos 13:15
s send forth fresh .... James 3:11

SPRINGING

a fountain of water s .... John 4:14
of bitterness s .... Heb 12:15

SPRINGS

"Have you entered the s .... Job 38:16
He sends the s into .... Ps 104:10
and the thirsty land s .... Is 35:7
and the dry land s .... Is 41:18

SPRINKLE

He s many nations .... Is 52:15
Then I will s .... Ezek 36:25

SPRINKLED

s dust on his head .... Job 2:12
and hyssop, and s .... Heb 9:19
having our hearts s .... Heb 10:22

SPRINKLING

s that speaks .... Heb 12:24

for obedience and s .... 1 Pet 1:2

SPROUT

down, that it will s .... Job 14:7
and the seed should s .... Mark 4:27

SQUARES

voice in the open s .... Prov 1:20
s I will seek the one .... Song 3:2

STABILITY

will be the s of your .... Is 33:6

STAFF

this Jordan with my s .... Gen 32:10
your feet, and your s .... Ex 12:11
Your rod and Your s .... Ps 23:4
LORD has broken the s .... Is 14:5
'How the strong s .... Jer 48:17
they have been a s .... Ezek 29:6
on the top of his s .... Heb 11:21

STAGGER

and He makes them s .... Job 12:25
they will drink and s .... Jer 25:16

STAGGERS

as a drunken man s .... Is 19:14

STAKES

s will ever be removed .... Is 33:20

STALLS

be no herd in the s .... Hab 3:17

STAMMERERS

s will be ready .... Is 32:4

STAMMERING

For with s lips and .... Is 28:11
s tongue that you .... Is 33:19

STAMPING

At the noise of the s .... Jer 47:3

STAND

one shall be able to s .... Deut 7:24
"Who is able to s .... 1 Sam 6:20
but it does not s .... Job 8:15
lives, and He shall s .... Job 19:25
ungodly shall not s .... Ps 1:5
Why do You s afar off .... Ps 10:1
Or who may s in His .... Ps 24:3
Who will s up for me .... Ps 94:16
and let an accuser s .... Ps 109:6
he will not s before .... Prov 22:29
Do not take your s .... Eccl 8:3
"It shall not s .... Is 7:7
"S in the ways and .... Jer 6:16
not lack a man to s .... Jer 35:19
whose words will s .... Jer 44:28
and it shall s .... Dan 2:44
but she shall not s .... Dan 11:17
Who can s before His .... Nah 1:6
And who can s when He .... Mal 3:2
that kingdom cannot s .... Mark 3:24
he will be made to s .... Rom 14:4
Watch, s fast in the .... 1 Cor 16:13
for by faith you s .... 2 Cor 1:24
having done all, to s .... Eph 6:13
S therefore .... Eph 6:14
s fast in the Lord .... Phil 4:1
now we live, if you s .... 1 Thess 3:8
of God in which you s .... 1 Pet 5:12
Behold, I s at the .... Rev 3:20

STANDARD

LORD will lift up a *s* ....Is 59:19
Set up the *s* toward ....Jer 4:6

STANDING

the LORD, and Satan *s* ....Zech 3:1
they love to pray *s* ....Matt 6:5
and the Son of Man *s* ....Acts 7:56
Then I saw an angel *s* ....Rev 19:17

STANDS

The LORD *s* up to plead ....Is 3:13
him who thinks he *s* ....1 Cor 10:12

STAR

S shall come out of ....Num 24:17
For we have seen His *s* ....Matt 2:2
for one *s* differs from ......1 Cor 15:41
give him the morning *s* ....Rev 2:28
And a great *s* fell ....Rev 8:10
Bright and Morning *S* ....Rev 22:16

STARS

He made the *s* also ....Gen 1:16
s are not pure in His ....Job 25:5
when the morning *s* ....Job 38:7
the moon and the *s* ....Ps 8:3
praise Him, all you *s* ....Ps 148:3
born as many as the *s* .....Heb 11:12
wandering *s* for whom ....Jude 13
a garland of twelve *s* ....Rev 12:1

STARVED

His strength is *s* ....Job 18:12

STATE

man at his best *s* ....Ps 39:5
us in our lowly *s* ....Ps 136:23
and the last *s* of that ....Matt 12:45
learned in whatever *s* ....Phil 4:11

STATURE

add one cubit to his *s* ....Matt 6:27
in wisdom and *s* ....Luke 2:52
the measure of the *s* ....Eph 4:13

STATUTE

shall be a perpetual *s* ....Lev 3:17

STATUTES

the *s* of the LORD are ....Ps 19:8
Teach me Your *s* ....Ps 119:12
s have been my songs ....Ps 119:54
not walked in My *s* ....Ezek 5:6

STAY

her feet would not *s* ....Prov 7:11
S here and watch with .....Matt 26:38
for today I must *s* ....Luke 19:5
the time of your *s* ....1 Pet 1:17

STEADFAST

yes, you could be *s* ....Job 11:15
O God, my heart is *s* ....Ps 57:7
their heart was not *s* ....Ps 78:37
his heart is *s* ....Ps 112:7
God, and *s* forever ....Dan 6:26
brethren, be *s* ....1 Cor 15:58
faith, grounded and *s* ....Col 1:23
angels proved *s* ....Heb 2:2
of our confidence *s* ....Heb 3:14
soul, both sure and *s* ....Heb 6:19
Resist him, *s* in the ....1 Pet 5:9

STEADFASTLY

s set His face to go ....Luke 9:51
And they continued *s* ....Acts 2:42
continuing *s* in ....Rom 12:12

STEADFASTNESS

good order and the *s* ....Col 2:5
from your own *s* ....2 Pet 3:17

STEADILY

could not look *s* ....2 Cor 3:13

STEADY

and his hands were *s* ....Ex 17:12

STEAL

"You shall not *s* ....Ex 20:15
Will you *s* ....Jer 7:9
s My words every one ....Jer 23:30
thieves break in and *s* ....Matt 6:19
night and *s* Him away ....Matt 27:64
murder, 'Do not *s* ....Mark 10:19
not come except to *s* ....John 10:10
a man should not *s* ....Rom 2:21
Let him who stole *s* ....Eph 4:28

STEEP

s places shall fall ....Ezek 38:20
waters poured down a *s* ....Mic 1:4
violently down the *s* ....Matt 8:32

STEM

forth a Rod from the *s* ....Is 11:1

STENCH

there will be a *s* ....Is 3:24
this time there is a *s* ....John 11:39

STEP

there is but a *s* ....1 Sam 20:3
s has turned from the ....Job 31:7

STEPHEN

One of the first seven deacons, Acts 6:1–8
Falsely accused by Jews; gives defense, Acts 6:9—7:53
Becomes first Christian martyr, Acts 7:54–60

STEPS

has held fast to His *s* ....Job 23:11
and count all my *s* ....Job 31:4
and He sees all his *s* ....Job 34:21
Uphold my *s* in Your ....Ps 17:5
The *s* of a good man ....Ps 37:23
of his *s* shall slide ....Ps 37:31
and established my *s* ....Ps 40:2
hide, they mark my *s* ....Ps 56:6
s had nearly slipped ....Ps 73:2
Direct my *s* by Your ....Ps 119:133
s will not be hindered ....Prov 4:12
the LORD directs his *s* ....Prov 16:9
A man's *s* are of the ....Prov 20:24
to direct his own *s* ....Jer 10:23
should follow His *s* ....1 Pet 2:21

STEWARD

faithful and wise *s* ....Luke 12:42
you can no longer be *s* ....Luke 16:2
commended the unjust *s* .....Luke 16:8
be blameless, as a *s* ....Titus 1:7

STEWARDS

of Christ and *s* ....1 Cor 4:1
one another, as good *s* ....1 Pet 4:10

STEWARDSHIP

entrusted with a *s* ....1 Cor 9:17

STICK

and his bones *s* ....Job 33:21
'For Joseph, the *s* ....Ezek 37:16

STICKS

a man gathering *s* ....Num 15:32
And the *s* on which ....Ezek 37:20

STIFF

rebellion and your *s* ....Deut 31:27
do not speak with a *s* ....Ps 75:5

STIFF-NECKED

Now do not be *s* ....2 Chr 30:8
"You *s* and uncircumcised ...Acts 7:51

STILL

on your bed, and be *s* ....Ps 4:4
s the noise of the ....Ps 65:7
earth feared and was *s* ....Ps 76:8
that its waves are *s* ....Ps 107:29
When I awake, I am *s* ....Ps 139:18
time, I have been *s* ....Is 42:14
rest and be *s* ....Jer 47:6
sea, "Peace, be *s* ....Mark 4:39
let him be holy *s* ....Rev 22:11

STILLBORN

hidden like a *s* child ....Job 3:16
as it goes, like a *s* ....Ps 58:8
burial, I say that a *s* ....Eccl 6:3

STINGS

like a serpent, and *s* ....Prov 23:32

STIR

that he would dare *s* ....Job 41:10
S up Yourself ....Ps 35:23
I remind you to *s* ....2 Tim 1:6
another in order to *s* ....Heb 10:24

STIRRED

fulfilled, the LORD *s* ....2 Chr 36:22
and my sorrow was *s* ....Ps 39:2
So the LORD *s* up the ....Hag 1:14

STIRS

and the innocent *s* ....Job 17:8
it *s* up the dead for ....Is 14:9
on Your name, who *s* ....Is 64:7

STOCKS

put my feet in the *s* ....Job 13:27
s that were in the ....Jer 20:2

STOIC

and *S* philosophers ....Acts 17:18

STOMACH

mouth goes into the *s* ....Matt 15:17
his heart but his *s* ....Mark 7:19
Foods for the *s* ....1 Cor 6:13

STOMACH'S

little wine for your *s* ....1 Tim 5:23

STONE

him, a pillar of *s* ....Gen 35:14
to the bottom like a *s* ....Ex 15:5
s shall be a witness ....Josh 24:27
heart is as hard as *s* ....Job 41:24
s which the builders ....Ps 118:22
s is heavy and sand is ....Prov 27:3
I lay in Zion a *s* ....Is 28:16

foundation, a tried *s* ....Is 28:16
take the heart of *s* ....Ezek 36:26
You watched while a *s* ....Dan 2:34
s will cry out from ....Hab 2:11
to silent *s* ....Hab 2:19
will give him a *s* ....Matt 7:9
s will be broken ....Matt 21:44
secure, sealing the *s* ....Matt 27:66
s which the builders ....Luke 20:17
you, let him throw a *s* ....John 8:7
those works do you *s* ....John 10:32
Jews sought to *s* You ....John 11:8
not on tablets of *s* ....2 Cor 3:3
Him as to a living *s* ....1 Pet 2:4
give him a white *s* ....Rev 2:17
angel took up a *s* ....Rev 18:21
like a jasper *s* ....Rev 21:11

STONED

s Stephen as he was ....Acts 7:59
once I was *s* ....2 Cor 11:25
They were *s* ....Heb 11:37

STONES

I will lay your *s* ....Is 54:11
Among the smooth *s* ....Is 57:6
Abraham from these *s* ....Matt 3:9
command that these *s* ....Matt 4:3
see what manner of *s* ....Mark 13:1
also, as living *s* ....1 Pet 2:5
kinds of precious *s* ....Rev 21:19

STONY

them, and take the *s* ....Ezek 11:19
Some fell on *s* ground ....Mark 4:5

STOOPED

And again He *s* down ....John 8:8

STOPPED

speak lies shall be *s* ....Ps 63:11
her flow of blood *s* ....Luke 8:44

STORE

no room to *s* my crops .....Luke 12:17
exist are kept in *s* ....2 Pet 3:7

STORK

s has her home in the ....Ps 104:17
"Even the *s* in the ....Jer 8:7

STORM

from the windy *s* ....Ps 55:8
He calms the *s* ....Ps 107:29
terror comes like a *s* ....Prov 1:27
for a shelter from *s* ....Is 4:6
a refuge from the *s* ....Is 25:4
and a destroying *s* ....Is 28:2
coming like a *s* ....Ezek 38:9
whirlwind and in the *s* ....Nah 1:3

STOUTHEARTED

s were plundered ....Ps 76:5

STRAIGHT

make Your way *s* ....Ps 5:8
for who can make *s* ....Eccl 7:13
make *s* in the desert a ....Is 40:3
Their legs were *s* ....Ezek 1:7
LORD; make His paths *s* .....Luke 3:4
to the street called *S* ....Acts 9:11
and make *s* paths for ....Heb 12:13

STRAIGHTFORWARD

that they were not *s* ....Gal 2:14

STRAIN

Blind guides, who *s* ....Matt 23:24

STRAITS

and desperate *s* ....Deut 28:53

STRANGE

were considered a *s* ....Hos 8:12
"We have seen *s* ....Luke 5:26
are bringing some *s* ....Acts 17:20
these, they think it *s* ....1 Pet 4:4
s thing happened ....1 Pet 4:12

STRANGER

but he acted as a *s* ....Gen 42:7
"I have been a *s* ....Ex 2:22
neither mistreat a *s* ....Ex 22:21
and loves the *s* ....Deut 10:18
I have become a *s* ....Ps 69:8
s will suffer for it ....Prov 11:15
s does not share its ....Prov 14:10
should You be like a *s* ....Jer 14:8
I was a *s* and you took .....Matt 25:35
"Are You the only *s* ....Luke 24:18

STRANGERS

descendants will be *s* ....Gen 15:13
s plunder his labor ....Ps 109:11
watches over the *s* ....Ps 146:9
s devour your land ....Is 1:7
S shall stand and feed ....Is 61:5
know the voice of *s* ....John 10:5
of Israel and *s* ....Eph 2:12
you are no longer *s* ....Eph 2:19
if she has lodged *s* ....1 Tim 5:10
that they were *s* ....Heb 11:13
forget to entertain *s* ....Heb 13:2
the brethren and for *s* ....3 John 5

STRANGLING

that my soul chooses *s* ....Job 7:15

STRAP

than I, whose sandal *s* ....Mark 1:7

STRAW

They are like *s* ....Job 21:18
stones, wood, hay, *s* ....1 Cor 3:12

STRAY

the cursed, who *s* ....Ps 119:21
who make my people *s* ....Mic 3:5

STRAYED

yet I have not *s* ....Ps 119:110
for which some have *s* ....1 Tim 6:10
who have *s* concerning ......2 Tim 2:18

STREAM

like an overflowing *s* ....Is 30:28
of the LORD, like a *s* ....Is 30:33
like a flowing *s* ....Is 66:12

STREAMS

He dams up the *s* ....Job 28:11
He also brought *s* ....Ps 78:16
O LORD, as the *s* ....Ps 126:4

STREET

to be heard in the *s* ....Is 42:2
s called Straight ....Acts 9:11
And the *s* of the city ....Rev 21:21
In the middle of its *s* ....Rev 22:2

STREETS

the corners of the *s* ....Matt 6:5

You taught in our *s* ....Luke 13:26
out quickly into the *s* ......Luke 14:21

STRENGTH

for by *s* of hand the ....Ex 13:3
just as my *s* was then ......Josh 14:11
my soul, march on in *s* ......Judg 5:21
a man is, so is his *s* ....Judg 8:21
s no man shall ....1 Sam 2:9
the God of my *s* ....2 Sam 22:3
have armed me with *s* ....2 Sam 22:40
the LORD glory and *s* .....1 Chr 16:28
Is my *s* the *s* ....Job 6:12
Him are wisdom and *s* ......Job 12:13
him because his *s* ....Job 39:11
You have ordained *s* ....Ps 8:2
love You, O LORD, my *s* ....Ps 18:1
The LORD is the *s* ....Ps 27:1
The LORD is their *s* ....Ps 28:8
The LORD will give *s* ....Ps 29:11
delivered by great *s* ....Ps 33:16
He is their *s* in the ....Ps 37:39
are the God of my *s* ....Ps 43:2
is our refuge and *s* ....Ps 46:1
is He who gives *s* ....Ps 68:35
I will go in the *s* ....Ps 71:16
but God is the *s* ....Ps 73:26
They go from *s* to ....Ps 84:7
the glory of their *s* ....Ps 89:17
s and beauty are in ....Ps 96:6
made me bold with *s* ....Ps 138:3
of the LORD is *s* ....Prov 10:29
knowledge increases *s* ....Prov 24:5
S and honor are her ....Prov 31:25
is better than *s* ....Eccl 9:16
for *s* and not for ....Eccl 10:17
For You have been a *s* ....Is 25:4
him take hold of My *s* ....Is 27:5
of His might and the *s* ....Is 40:26
might He increases *s* ....Is 40:29
works it with the *s* ....Is 44:12
righteousness and *s* ....Is 45:24
Put on your *s* ....Is 52:1
O LORD, my *s* and my ....Jer 16:19
I will destroy the *s* ....Hag 2:22
He has shown *s* with ....Luke 1:51
were still without *s* ....Rom 5:6
s is made perfect ....2 Cor 12:9
you have a little *s* ....Rev 3:8

STRENGTHEN

and He shall *s* ....Ps 27:14
S the weak hands ....Is 35:3
"So I will *s* them in ....Zech 10:12
s your brethren ....Luke 22:32
s the hands ....Heb 12:12
s the things ....Rev 3:2

STRENGTHENED

weak you have not *s* ....Ezek 34:4
unbelief, but was *s* ....Rom 4:20
of His glory, to be *s* ....Eph 3:16
stood with me and *s* ....2 Tim 4:17

STRENGTHENING

s the souls of the ....Acts 14:22

STRENGTHENS

s the wise more than ....Eccl 7:19
through Christ who *s* ....Phil 4:13

STRETCH

will quickly *s* out her ....Ps 68:31
said to the man, "*S* ....Matt 12:13
are old, you will *s* ....John 21:18

STRETCHED

I have *s* out my hands ....Ps 88:9
His wisdom, and has *s* ....Jer 10:12
"All day long I have *s* ....Rom 10:21

STRETCHES

For he *s* out his hand ....Job 15:25

STRICKEN

My heart is *s* and ....Ps 102:4
yet we esteemed Him *s* ....Is 53:4
of My people He was *s* ....Is 53:8
You have *s* them ....Jer 5:3
He has *s*, but He will ....Hos 6:1

STRIFE

let there be no *s* ....Gen 13:8
You have made us a *s* ....Ps 80:6
at the waters of *s* ....Ps 106:32
Hatred stirs up *s* ....Prov 10:12
comes nothing but *s* ....Prov 13:10
man stirs up *s* ....Prov 15:18
transgression loves *s* ....Prov 17:19
borne me, a man of *s* ....Jer 15:10
and lust, not in *s* ....Rom 13:13
even from envy and *s* ....Phil 1:15
which come envy, *s* ....1 Tim 6:4

STRIKE

said, "*S* this people ....2 Kin 6:18
The sun shall not *s* ....Ps 121:6
Let the righteous *s* ....Ps 141:5
S a scoffer ....Prov 19:25
s your hands ....Ezek 21:14
s the waves of the sea ....Zech 10:11
"*S* the Shepherd ....Zech 13:7
s the earth with a ....Mal 4:6
'I will *s* the Shepherd ....Matt 26:31
if well, why do you *s* ....John 18:23
the sun shall not *s* ....Rev 7:16
s the earth with all ....Rev 11:6

STRINGED

of your *s* instruments ....Is 14:11
of your *s* instruments ....Amos 5:23

STRIP

S yourselves ....Is 32:11
s her naked and expose ....Hos 2:3

STRIPES

their iniquity with *s* ....Ps 89:32
s we are healed ....Is 53:5
be beaten with many *s* ....Luke 12:47
I received forty *s* ....2 Cor 11:24
s you were healed ....1 Pet 2:24

STRIVE

"My Spirit shall not *s* ....Gen 6:3
He will not always *s* ....Ps 103:9
Do not *s* with a man ....Prov 3:30
Let the potsherd *s* ....Is 45:9
"*S* to enter through ....Luke 13:24
the Lord not to *s* ....2 Tim 2:14

STRIVING

for a man to stop *s* ....Prov 20:3

STROKE

with a mighty *s* ....Jer 14:17

STRONG

Be *s* and conduct ....1 Sam 4:9
indeed He is *s* ....Job 9:19
The LORD *s* and mighty ....Ps 24:8
bring me to the *s* ....Ps 60:9
s is Your hand ....Ps 89:13
A wise man is *s* ....Prov 24:5
s shall be as tinder ....Is 1:31
"We have a *s* city ....Is 26:1
the weak say, 'I am *s* ....Joel 3:10
When a *s* man ....Luke 11:21
We then who are *s* ....Rom 15:1
I am weak, then I am *s* ....2 Cor 12:10
are weak and you are *s* ....2 Cor 13:9
my brethren, be *s* ....Eph 6:10
weakness were made *s* ....Heb 11:34
s is the Lord God ....Rev 18:8

STRONGHOLD

of my salvation, my *s* ....Ps 18:2
down the trusted *s* ....Prov 21:22

STRUCK

s the rock twice ....Num 20:11
the hand of God has *s* ....Job 19:21
s all my enemies ....Ps 3:7
Behold, He *s* the rock ....Ps 78:20
I was angry and *s* ....Is 57:17
in My wrath I *s* ....Is 60:10
s the head from the ....Hab 3:13
I *s* you with blight ....Hag 2:17
took the reed and *s* ....Matt 27:30
Him, they *s* Him on the ....Luke 22:64

STUBBLE

shall bring forth *s* ....Is 33:11
his sword, as driven *s* ....Is 41:2
they shall be as *s* ....Is 47:14
s that passes ....Jer 13:24
do wickedly will be *s* ....Mal 4:1

STUBBORN

If a man has a *s* ....Deut 21:18
and *s* children ....Ezek 2:4

STUBBORN-HEARTED

"Listen to Me, you *s* ....Is 46:12

STUBBORNNESS

do not look on the *s* ....Deut 9:27

STUDIED

having never *s* ....John 7:15

STUMBLE

causes them to *s* ....Ps 119:165
to make my steps *s* ....Ps 140:4
your foot will not *s* ....Prov 3:23
know what makes them *s* ....Prov 4:19
one will be weary or *s* ....Is 5:27
among them shall *s* ....Is 8:15
we *s* at noonday as at ....Is 59:10
that they might not *s* ....Is 63:13
before your feet *s* ....Jer 13:16
they will *s* and fall ....Jer 46:6
have caused many to *s* ....Mal 2:8
you will be made to *s* ....Matt 26:31
if all are made to *s* ....Matt 26:33
immediately they *s* ....Mark 4:17
who believe in Me to *s* ....Mark 9:42
the day, he does not *s* ....John 11:9
Who is made to *s* ....2 Cor 11:29
whole law, and yet *s* ....James 2:10
For we all *s* in many ....James 3:2

STUMBLED

and those who *s* ....1 Sam 2:4
God, for you have *s* ....Hos 14:1
s that they should ....Rom 11:11

STUMBLES

word, immediately he *s* ....Matt 13:21

STUMBLING

the deaf, nor put a *s* ....Lev 19:14
but a stone of *s* ....Is 8:14
Behold, I will lay *s* ....Jer 6:21
watched for my *s* ....Jer 20:10
it became their *s* ....Ezek 7:19
stumbled at that *s* ....Rom 9:32
I lay in Zion a *s* ....Rom 9:33
this, not to put a *s* ....Rom 14:13
to the Jews a *s* ....1 Cor 1:23
of yours become a *s* ....1 Cor 8:9
and "A stone of *s* ....1 Pet 2:8
is no cause for *s* ....1 John 2:10
to keep you from *s* ....Jude 24

STUPID

and regarded as *s* ....Job 18:3
who hates correction is *s* ....Prov 12:1
Surely I am more *s* ....Prov 30:2

SUBDUE

s the peoples under us ....Ps 47:3
shall *s* three kings ....Dan 7:24
s our iniquities ....Mic 7:19
s all things to ....Phil 3:21

SUBJECT

for it is not *s* ....Rom 8:7
Let every soul be *s* ....Rom 13:1
all things are made *s* ....1 Cor 15:28
Himself will also be *s* ....1 Cor 15:28
Remind them to be *s* ....Titus 3:1
all their lifetime *s* ....Heb 2:15
having been made *s* ....1 Pet 3:22

SUBJECTED

because of Him who *s* ....Rom 8:20

SUBJECTION

put all things in *s* ....Heb 2:8
more readily be in *s* ....Heb 12:9

SUBMISSION

in silence with all *s* ....1 Tim 2:11
his children in *s* ....1 Tim 3:4

SUBMISSIVE

Wives, likewise, be *s* ....1 Pet 3:1
Yes, all of you be *s* ....1 Pet 5:5

SUBMIT

Your enemies shall *s* ....Ps 66:3
Wives, *s* to your own ....Eph 5:22
Therefore *s* to God ....James 4:7
s yourselves to every ....1 Pet 2:13
you younger people, *s* ....1 Pet 5:5

SUBSIDED

and the waters *s* ....Gen 8:1
the king's wrath *s* ....Esth 7:10

SUBSTANCE

Bless his *s* ....Deut 33:11
the LORD, and their *s* ....Mic 4:13

SUCCEED

For this will not *s* ....Num 14:41
you shall not *s* ....Jer 32:5

SUCCESS

please give me *s* ....Gen 24:12

You spoil my *s* ....Job 30:22
but wisdom brings *s* ....Eccl 10:10

SUCCESSFUL

Joseph, and he was a *s* ....Gen 39:2

SUCCOTH

Place east of the Jordan, Judg 8:4, 5
Jacob's residence here, Gen 33:17
——Israel's first camp, Ex 12:37

SUDDENLY

whom you seek, will *s* ....Mal 3:1
s there was with the ....Luke 2:13

SUE

s you and take away ....Matt 5:40

SUFFER

for a stranger will *s* ....Prov 11:15
for the Christ to *s* ....Luke 24:46
Christ, if indeed we *s* ....Rom 8:17
all the members *s* ....1 Cor 12:26
that they may not *s* ....Gal 6:12
in Him, but also to *s* ....Phil 1:29
s trouble as an ....2 Tim 2:9
when you do good and *s* .....1 Pet 2:20
the will of God, to *s* ....1 Pet 3:17
s as a murderer ....1 Pet 4:15
you are about to *s* ....Rev 2:10

SUFFERED

s these things and to ....Luke 24:26
Have you *s* so many ....Gal 3:4
for whom I have *s* ....Phil 3:8
with His own blood, *s* ....Heb 13:12
because Christ also *s* ....1 Pet 2:21
For Christ also *s* ....1 Pet 3:18
since Christ *s* ....1 Pet 4:1
after you have *s* ....1 Pet 5:10

SUFFERING

My eyes bring *s* ....Lam 3:51
Is anyone among you *s* ....James 5:13
forth as an example, *s* ....Jude 7

SUFFERINGS

I consider that the *s* ....Rom 8:18
share with me in the *s* ....2 Tim 1:8
perfect through *s* ....Heb 2:10
great struggle with *s* ....Heb 10:32
beforehand the *s* ....1 Pet 1:11

SUFFERS

Love *s* long and is ....1 Cor 13:4

SUFFICIENCY

but our *s* is from God ....2 Cor 3:5
always having all *s* ....2 Cor 9:8

SUFFICIENT

S for the day is its ....Matt 6:34
by the majority is *s* ....2 Cor 2:6
Not that we are *s* ....2 Cor 3:5

SUITABLE

by the hand of a *s* ....Lev 16:21

SUM

How great is the *s* ....Ps 139:17
s I obtained this ....Acts 22:28

SUMMED

commandment, are all *s* .....Rom 13:9

SUMMER

and heat, winter and *s* ....Gen 8:22
into the drought of *s* ....Ps 32:4
You have made *s* ....Ps 74:17
you know that *s* ....Matt 24:32

SUMPTUOUSLY

fine linen and fared *s* ......Luke 16:19

SUN

So the *s* stood still ....Josh 10:13
love Him be like the *s* ....Judg 5:31
grows green in the *s* ....Job 8:16
a tabernacle for the *s* ....Ps 19:4
the LORD God is a *s* ....Ps 84:11
s shall not strike you ....Ps 121:6
the *s* to rule by day ....Ps 136:8
to behold the *s* ....Eccl 11:7
while the *s* and the ....Eccl 12:2
moon, clear as the *s* ....Song 6:10
s will be sevenfold ....Is 30:26
s returned ten degrees ....Is 38:8
s shall no longer be ....Is 60:19
s has gone down while ....Jer 15:9
LORD, who gives the *s* ....Jer 31:35
the *s* and moon grow ....Joel 2:10
s shall be turned ....Joel 2:31
s shall go down on the ....Mic 3:6
The *s* and moon stood ....Hab 3:11
for He makes His *s* ....Matt 5:45
the *s* was darkened ....Luke 23:45
is one glory of the *s* ....1 Cor 15:41
do not let the *s* ....Eph 4:26
s became black as ....Rev 6:12
s shall not strike ....Rev 7:16
had no need of the *s* ....Rev 21:23

SUPPER

man gave a great *s* ....Luke 14:16
to eat the Lord's *S* ....1 Cor 11:20
took the cup after *s* ....1 Cor 11:25
together for the *s* ....Rev 19:17

SUPPLICATION

s that you have made ....1 Kin 9:3
and make your *s* ....Job 8:5
LORD has heard my *s* ....Ps 6:9
to the LORD I made *s* ....Ps 30:8
Yourself from my *s* ....Ps 55:1
Let my *s* come before ......Ps 119:170
They will make *s* ....Is 45:14
with all prayer and *s* ....Eph 6:18
by prayer and *s* ....Phil 4:6

SUPPLIES

Now may He who *s* ....2 Cor 9:10
Therefore He who *s* ....Gal 3:5
by what every joint *s* ....Eph 4:16

SUPPLY

s what was lacking ....Phil 2:30
And my God shall *s* ....Phil 4:19

SUPPORT

but the LORD was my *s* ...2 Sam 22:19
this, that you must *s* ....Acts 20:35

SUPREME

to the king as *s* ....1 Pet 2:13

SURE

s your sin will find ....Num 32:23
but no man is *s* ....Job 24:22
call and election *s* ....2 Pet 1:10

SURETY

Be *s* for Your servant ......Ps 119:122
one who hates being *s* .....Prov 11:15
Jesus has become a *s* ....Heb 7:22

SURROUND

But you shall *s* ....2 Kin 11:8
LORD, mercy shall *s* ....Ps 32:10

SURROUNDED

the waves of death *s* ....2 Sam 22:5
The pangs of death *s* ....Ps 18:4
The pains of death *s* ....Ps 116:3
All nations *s* me ....Ps 118:10
their own deeds have *s* ....Hos 7:2
and the floods *s* ....Jon 2:3
also, since we are *s* ....Heb 12:1

SURVIVOR

was no refugee or *s* ....Lam 2:22

SUSANNA

Believing woman ministering to Christ, Luke 8:2, 3

SUSPICIONS

reviling, evil *s* ....1 Tim 6:4

SUSTAIN

You will *s* him on his ....Ps 41:3
of a man will *s* ....Prov 18:14
S me with cakes of ....Song 2:5

SWADDLING

thick darkness its *s* ....Job 38:9
Him in *s* cloths ....Luke 2:7

SWALLOW

like a flying *s* ....Prov 26:2
Like a crane or a *s* ....Is 38:14
s observe the time ....Jer 8:7
great fish to *s* Jonah ....Jon 1:17
a gnat and *s* a camel ....Matt 23:24

SWEAR

shall I make you *s* ....1 Kin 22:16
in the earth shall *s* ....Is 65:16
s oaths by the LORD ....Zeph 1:5
'You shall not *s* ....Matt 5:33
began to curse and *s* ....Matt 26:74
because He could *s* ....Heb 6:13
my brethren, do not *s* ....James 5:12

SWEARING

By *s* and lying ....Hos 4:2

SWEARS

he who *s* to his own ....Ps 15:4
everyone who *s* by Him ......Ps 63:11
but whoever *s* by the ....Matt 23:18

SWEAT

In the *s* of your face ....Gen 3:19
Then His *s* became like ....Luke 22:44

SWEET

Though evil is *s* ....Job 20:12
s are Your words ....Ps 119:103
His mouth is most *s* ....Song 5:16
but it will be as *s* ....Rev 10:9

SWEETNESS

'Should I cease my *s* ....Judg 9:11
called prudent, and *s* ....Prov 16:21

mouth like honey in *s* ....Ezek 3:3

SWELLING

they speak great *s* ....2 Pet 2:18

SWIFT

s as the eagle flies ....Deut 28:49
pass by like *s* ships ....Job 9:26
handles the bow, the *s* .....Amos 2:15
let every man be *s* ....James 1:19

SWIFTLY

His word runs very *s* ....Ps 147:15

SWIM

night I make my bed *s* ....Ps 6:6

SWOON

as they *s* like the ....Lam 2:12

SWORD

s which turned every ....Gen 3:24
but not with your *s* ....Josh 24:12
the wicked with Your *s* ....Ps 17:13
land by their own *s* ....Ps 44:3
my bow, nor shall my *s* ....Ps 44:6
their tongue a sharp *s* ....Ps 57:4
shall not lift up *s* ....Is 2:4
s shall be bathed ....Is 34:5
The *s* of the LORD is ....Is 34:6
And I will send a *s* ....Jer 9:16
will die by the *s* ....Ezek 7:15
'A *s*, a *s* is sharpened ....Ezek 21:9
'A *s*, a *s* is drawn ....Ezek 21:28
Bow and *s* of battle I ....Hos 2:18
"Awake, O *s* ....Zech 13:7
to bring peace but a *s* ....Matt 10:34
for all who take the *s* ....Matt 26:52
s will pierce through ....Luke 2:35
he does not bear the *s* ....Rom 13:4
the *s* of the Spirit ....Eph 6:17
than any two-edged *s* ....Heb 4:12
a sharp two-edged *s* ....Rev 1:16
mouth goes a sharp *s* ....Rev 19:15

SWORDS

yet they were drawn *s* ....Ps 55:21
shall beat their *s* ....Is 2:4
look, here are two *s* ....Luke 22:38

SWORE

So I *s* in My wrath ....Ps 95:11
So I *s* in My wrath ....Heb 3:11
and *s* by Him who lives ....Rev 10:6

SWORN

"By Myself I have *s* ....Gen 22:16
The LORD has *s* in ....Ps 132:11
I have *s* by Myself ....Is 45:23
"The LORD has *s* ....Heb 7:21

SYMBOLIC

which things are *s* ....Gal 4:24
It was *s* for the ....Heb 9:9

SYMBOLS

I have given *s* through ....Hos 12:10

SYMPATHIZE

Priest who cannot *s* ....Heb 4:15

SYMPATHY

My *s* is stirred ....Hos 11:8

SYNAGOGUE

He went into the *s* ....Luke 4:16
but are a *s* of Satan ....Rev 2:9

SYRIANS

Abraham's kindred, Gen 22:20–23; 25:20
Hostile to Israel, 2 Sam 8:11–13; 10:6–19; 1 Kin 20:1–34; 22:1–38; 2 Kin 6:8—7:7
Defeated by Assyria, 2 Kin 16:9
Destruction of, foretold, Is 17:1–3
Gospel preached to, Acts 15:23, 41

SYRO-PHOENICIAN

Daughter of, freed of demon, Mark 7:25–31

— T —

TABERAH

Israelite camp; fire destroys many there, Num 11:1–3

TABERNACLE

you shall make the *t* ....Ex 26:1
t He shall hide me ....Ps 27:5
I will abide in Your *t* ....Ps 61:4
In Salem also is His *t* ....Ps 76.2
How lovely is Your *t* ....Ps 84:1
quiet home, a *t* ....Is 33:20
You also took up the *t* ....Acts 7:43
and will rebuild the *t* ....Acts 15:16
and more perfect *t* ....Heb 9:11
Behold, the *t* ....Rev 21:3

TABERNACLES

us make here three *t* ....Matt 17:4
Feast of *T* was at hand ....John 7:2

TABITHA

See DORCAS

TABLE

shall also make a *t* ....Ex 25:23
prepare a *t* before me ....Ps 23:5
t become a snare ....Ps 69:22
dogs under the *t* ....Mark 7:28
t become a snare ....Rom 11:9
of the Lord's *t* ....1 Cor 10:21

TABLES

t are full of vomit ....Is 28:8
and overturned the *t* ....Matt 21:12
of God and serve *t* ....Acts 6:2

TABLET

write them on the *t* ....Prov 3:3
is engraved on the *t* ....Jer 17:1

TABOR

Scene of rally against Sisera, Judg 4:6, 12, 14

TAHPANHES (or Tehaphnehes)

City of Egypt; refuge of fleeing Jews, Jer 2:16; 44:1; Ezek 30:18

TAIL

the head and not the *t* ....Deut 28:13
t drew a third of the ....Rev 12:4

TAKE

T your sandal off your ....Josh 5:15
t Your Holy Spirit ....Ps 51:11
t not the word of ....Ps 119:43
in You I *t* shelter ....Ps 143:9
t words with you ....Hos 14:2
T My yoke upon ....Matt 11:29
T what is yours and ....Matt 20:14
and *t* up his cross ....Mark 8:34
T this cup away ....Mark 14:36
My life that I may *t* ....John 10:17
I urge you to *t* heart ....Acts 27:22

TAKEN

you are *t* by the words ....Prov 6:2
He was *t* from prison ....Is 53:8
one will be *t* and the ....Matt 24:40
what he has will be *t* ....Mark 4:25
He was *t* up ....Acts 1:9
until He is *t* out of ....2 Thess 2:7
By faith Enoch was *t* away ...Heb 11:5

TALEBEARER

not go about as a *t* ....Lev 19:16
t reveals secrets ....Prov 11:13

TALENT

went and hid your *t* ....Matt 25:25

TALK

shall *t* of them when ....Deut 6:7
t be vindicated ....Job 11:2
with unprofitable *t* ....Job 15:3
My tongue also shall *t* ....Ps 71:24
entangle Him in His *t* ....Matt 22:15
I will no longer *t* ....John 14:30
turned aside to idle *t* ....1 Tim 1:6

TALKED

within us while He *t* ....Luke 24:32

TALKERS

both idle *t* and ....Titus 1:10

TALL

to a nation *t* and ....Is 18:2

TAMAR

Wife of Er and mother of Perez and Zerah, Gen 38:6–30
—— Absalom's sister, 2 Sam 13:1–32

TAMBOURINE

They sing to the *t* ....Job 21:12
The mirth of the *t* ....Is 24:8

TARES

the *t* also appeared ....Matt 13:26

TARGET

You set me as Your *t* ....Job 7:20
and set me up as a *t* ....Lam 3:12

TARRY

who turns aside to *t* ....Jer 14:8
come and will not *t* ....Heb 10:37

TARSHISH

City at a great distance from Palestine, Jon 1:3
Ships of, noted in commerce, Ps 48:7

TARSUS

Paul's birthplace, Acts 21:39
Saul sent to, Acts 9:30
Visited by Barnabas, Acts 11:25

TARTAN

Sent to fight against Jerusalem, 2 Kin 18:17

TASK
this burdensome *t* .... Eccl 1:13

TASTE
and its *t* was like the .... Num 11:8
Oh, *t* and see that the .... Ps 34:8
are Your words to my *t* .... Ps 119:103
was sweet to my *t* .... Song 2:3
Do not touch, do not *t* .... Col 2:21
might *t* death for .... Heb 2:9

TASTED
But when He had *t* .... Matt 27:34
t the heavenly gift .... Heb 6:4
t the good word .... Heb 6:5
t that the Lord is .... 1 Pet 2:3

TATTENAI
Persian governor opposing the Jews, Ezra 5:3, 6

TAUGHT
O God, You have *t* .... Ps 71:17
as His counselor has *t* .... Is 40:13
presence, and You *t* .... Luke 13:26
they shall all be *t* .... John 6:45
but as My Father *t* .... John 8:28
from man, nor was I *t* .... Gal 1:12

TAUNT
and a byword, a *t* .... Jer 24:9

TAX
t collectors do the .... Matt 5:46
received the temple *t* .... Matt 17:24
I say to you that *t* .... Matt 21:31
Show Me the *t* .... Matt 22:19

TAXES
take customs or *t* .... Matt 17:25
Is it lawful to pay *t* .... Matt 22:17
forbidding to pay *t* .... Luke 23:2
t to whom *t* .... Rom 13:7

TEACH
t them diligently .... Deut 6:7
t Jacob Your judgments .... Deut 33:10
t you the good and the .... 1 Sam 12:23
"Can anyone *t* .... Job 21:22
"I will *t* you about .... Job 27:11
t me what I do not see .... Job 34:32
t me Your paths .... Ps 25:4
T me Your way .... Ps 27:11
t you the fear of the .... Ps 34:11
t You awesome things .... Ps 45:4
t transgressors Your .... Ps 51:13
So *t* us to number our .... Ps 90:12
He will *t* us His ways .... Is 2:3
"Whom will he *t* .... Is 28:9
a bribe, her priests *t* .... Mic 3:11
t the way of God in .... Matt 22:16
in My name, He will *t* .... John 14:26
even nature itself *t* .... 1 Cor 11:14
permit a woman to *t* .... 1 Tim 2:12
things command and *t* .... 1 Tim 4:11
T and exhort these .... 1 Tim 6:2
t you again the first .... Heb 5:12

TEACHER
for One is your *T* .... Matt 23:8
asked Him, "Good *T* .... Mark 10:17
know that You are a *t* .... John 3:2
You call Me *T* .... John 13:13
named Gamaliel, a *t* .... Acts 5:34
a *t* of babes, having .... Rom 2:20
a *t* of the Gentiles in .... 1 Tim 2:7

TEACHERS
than all my *t* .... Ps 119:99
t will not be moved .... Is 30:20
prophets, third *t* .... 1 Cor 12:28
and some pastors and *t* .... Eph 4:11
desiring to be *t* .... 1 Tim 1:7
time you ought to be *t* .... Heb 5:12
of you become *t* .... James 3:1
there will be false *t* .... 2 Pet 2:1

TEACHES
therefore He *t* sinners .... Ps 25:8
the Holy Spirit *t* .... 1 Cor 2:13
If anyone *t* otherwise .... 1 Tim 6:3
the same anointing *t* .... 1 John 2:27

TEACHING
t them to observe all .... Matt 28:20
they did not cease *t* .... Acts 5:42
he who teaches, in *t* .... Rom 12:7
t every man in all .... Col 1:28
t things which they .... Titus 1:11
t us that .... Titus 2:12

TEAR
t yourself in anger .... Job 18:4
lest they *t* me like a .... Ps 7:2
I, even I, will *t* .... Hos 5:14
feet, and turn and *t* .... Matt 7:6
will wipe away every *t* .... Rev 21:4

TEARS
I have seen your *t* .... 2 Kin 20:5
my couch with my *t* .... Ps 6:6
t have been my food .... Ps 42:3
with the bread of *t* .... Ps 80:5
drench you with my *t* .... Is 16:9
GOD will wipe away *t* .... Is 25:8
eyes may run with *t* .... Jer 9:18
My eyes fail with *t* .... Lam 2:11
His feet with her *t* .... Luke 7:38
night and day with *t* .... Acts 20:31
mindful of your *t* .... 2 Tim 1:4
vehement cries and *t* .... Heb 5:7
it diligently with *t* .... Heb 12:17

TEETH
t whiter than milk .... Gen 49:12
by the skin of my *t* .... Job 19:20
You have broken the *t* .... Ps 3:7
As vinegar to the *t* .... Prov 10:26
you cleanness of *t* .... Amos 4:6

TEKOA
Home of a wise woman, 2 Sam 14:2, 4, 9
Home of Amos, Amos 1:1

TELL
that you may *t* it to .... Ps 48:13
the message that I *t* .... Jon 3:2
Who can *t* if God .... Jon 3:9
t him his fault .... Matt 18:15
whatever they *t* .... Matt 23:3
He comes, He will *t* .... John 4:25

TEMAN
Tribe in northeast Edom, Gen 36:34
Judgment pronounced against, Amos 1:12
God appears from, Hab 3:3

TEMPERATE
for the prize is *t* in all .... 1 Cor 9:25
husband of one wife, *t* .... 1 Tim 3:2

TEMPEST
the windy storm and *t* .... Ps 55:8
one, tossed with *t* .... Is 54:11
And suddenly a great *t* .... Matt 8:24

TEMPLE
So Solomon built the *t* .... 1 Kin 6:14
LORD is in His holy *t* .... Ps 11:4
to inquire in His *t* .... Ps 27:4
suddenly come to His *t* .... Mal 3:1
One greater than the *t* .... Matt 12:6
murdered between the *t* .... Matt 23:35
found Him in the *t* .... Luke 2:46
"Destroy this *t* .... John 2:19
was speaking of the *t* .... John 2:21
one accord in the *t* .... Acts 2:46
that you are the *t* .... 1 Cor 3:16
your body is the *t* .... 1 Cor 6:19
grows into a holy *t* .... Eph 2:21
sits as God in the *t* .... 2 Thess 2:4
Then the *t* of God was .... Rev 11:19
But I saw no *t* in it .... Rev 21:22
and the Lamb are its *t* .... Rev 21:22

TEMPLES
t made with hands .... Acts 7:48

TEMPORARY
which are seen are *t* .... 2 Cor 4:18

TEMPT
Why do you *t* the LORD .... Ex 17:2
they even *t* God .... Mal 3:15
t the LORD your God .... Matt 4:7
that Satan does not *t* .... 1 Cor 7:5
nor let us *t* Christ .... 1 Cor 10:9
nor does He Himself *t* .... James 1:13

TEMPTATION
do not lead us into *t* .... Matt 6:13
lest you enter into *t* .... Matt 26:41
in time of *t* fall away .... Luke 8:13
t has overtaken you .... 1 Cor 10:13
to be rich fall into *t* .... 1 Tim 6:9
the man who endures *t* .... James 1:12

TEMPTED
forty days, *t* by Satan .... Mark 1:13
not allow you to be *t* .... 1 Cor 10:13
lest you also be *t* .... Gal 6:1
has suffered, being *t* .... Heb 2:18
in all points *t* .... Heb 4:15
But each one is *t* .... James 1:14

TEMPTER
Now when the *t* came .... Matt 4:3

TENDER
your heart was *t* .... 2 Kin 22:19
t shoots will not .... Job 14:7
no more be called *t* .... Is 47:1
through the *t* mercy of .... Luke 1:78
put on *t* mercies .... Col 3:12

TENDERHEARTED
to one another, *t* .... Eph 4:32
love as brothers, be *t* .... 1 Pet 3:8

TENDS
t a flock and does not .... 1 Cor 9:7

TENT
shall know that your *t* .... Job 5:24

like a shepherd's *t* ....Is 38:12
the place of your *t* ....Is 54:2
My *t* is plundered ....Jer 10:20
earthly house, this *t* ....2 Cor 5:1
long as I am in this *t* ....2 Pet 1:13
I must put off my *t* ....2 Pet 1:14

TENTMAKERS

occupation they were *t* ....Acts 18:3

TENTS

those who dwell in *t* ....Gen 4:20
"How lovely are your *t* ....Num 24:5
The *t* of robbers ....Job 12:6
than dwell in the *t* ....Ps 84:10
I dwell among the *t* ....Ps 120:5
LORD will save the *t* ....Zech 12:7

TERAH

Father of Abram, Gen 11:26
Idolater, Josh 24:2
Dies in Haran, Gen 11:25–32

TERRESTRIAL

bodies and *t* bodies ....1 Cor 15:40

TERRIBLE

t wilderness ....Deut 1:19
haughtiness of the *t* ....Is 13:11
is great and very *t* ....Joel 2:11

TERRIFIED

to you, 'Do not be *t* ....Deut 1:29
But they were *t* ....Luke 24:37
and not in any way *t* ....Phil 1:28

TERRIFIES

and the Almighty *t* ....Job 23:16

TERRIFY

me with dreams and *t* ....Job 7:14
not let dread of Him *t* ....Job 9:34
are coming to *t* them ....Zech 1:21

TERRIFYING

t was the sight ....Heb 12:21

TERROR

there shall be *t* ....Deut 32:25
are nothing, you see *t* ....Job 6:21
from God is a *t* ....Job 31:23
not be afraid of the *t* ....Ps 91:5
I will make you a *t* ....Jer 20:4
but a great *t* fell ....Dan 10:7

TERRORS

the *t* of God are ....Job 6:4
T frighten him on ....Job 18:11
before the king of *t* ....Job 18:14
T overtake him like a ....Job 27:20
consumed with *t* ....Ps 73:19

TERTULLUS

Orator who accuses Paul, Acts 24:1–8

TEST

God has come to *t* you ....Ex 20:20
t him with hard ....1 Kin 10:1
behold, His eyelids *t* ....Ps 11:4
t them as gold is ....Zech 13:9
said, "Why do you *t* ....Matt 22:18
t the Spirit of the ....Acts 5:9
why do you *t* God by ....Acts 15:10
and the fire will *t* ....1 Cor 3:13
T yourselves ....2 Cor 13:5
T all things ....1 Thess 5:21
but *t* the spirits ....1 John 4:1

TESTAMENT

where there is a *t* ....Heb 9:16
For a *t* is in force ....Heb 9:17

TESTATOR

be the death of the *t* ....Heb 9:16

TESTED

that God *t* Abraham ....Gen 22:1
You have *t* my heart ....Ps 17:3
And they *t* God in ....Ps 78:18
t you at the waters of ....Ps 81:7
When your fathers *t* ....Ps 95:9
t them ten days ....Dan 1:14
also first be *t* ....1 Tim 3:10
Where your fathers *t* ....Heb 3:9
though it is *t* by fire ....1 Pet 1:7
t those who say they ....Rev 2:2

TESTIFIED

Yet the LORD *t* against ....2 Kin 17:13
he who has seen has *t* ....John 19:35
for as you have *t* ....Acts 23:11
t beforehand the ....1 Pet 1:11
of God which He has *t* ....1 John 5:9

TESTIFIES

and heard, that He *t* ....John 3:32
that the Holy Spirit *t* ....Acts 20:23

TESTIFY

yes, your own lips *t* ....Job 15:6
You, and our sins *t* ....Is 59:12
T against Me ....Mic 6:3
t what We have ....John 3:11
these are they which *t* ....John 5:39
t that the Father ....1 John 4:14
sent My angel to *t* ....Rev 22:16

TESTIFYING

was righteous, God *t* ....Heb 11:4
t that this is ....1 Pet 5:12

TESTIMONIES

those who keep His *t* ....Ps 119:2
for I have kept Your *t* ....Ps 119:22
t are my meditation ....Ps 119:99
I love Your *t* ....Ps 119:119
t are wonderful ....Ps 119:129

TESTIMONY

two tablets of the *T* ....Ex 31:18
For He established a *t* ....Ps 78:5
that I may keep the *t* ....Ps 119:88
Bind up the *t* ....Is 8:16
under your feet as a *t* ....Mark 6:11
Now this is the *t* ....John 1:19
no one receives His *t* ....John 3:32
who has received His *t* ....John 3:33
in your law that the *t* ....John 8:17
and we know that his *t* ....John 21:24
declaring to you the *t* ....1 Cor 2:1
obtained a good *t* ....Heb 11:2
he had this *t* ....Heb 11:5
not believed the *t* ....1 John 5:10
And this is the *t* ....1 John 5:11
For the *t* of Jesus is ....Rev 19:10

TESTING

came to Him, *t* Him ....Matt 19:3
knowing that the *t* ....James 1:3

TESTS

the righteous God *t* ....Ps 7:9
gold, but the LORD *t* ....Prov 17:3
men, but God who *t* ....1 Thess 2:4

THADDAEUS

One of the Twelve, Mark 3:18

THANK

"I *t* You and praise ....Dan 2:23
"I *t* You, Father ....Matt 11:25
t that servant because ....Luke 17:9
t You that I am not ....Luke 18:11
First, I *t* my God ....Rom 1:8
t Christ Jesus our ....1 Tim 1:12

THANKFUL

Be *t* to Him ....Ps 100:4
Him as God, nor were *t* ....Rom 1:21

THANKFULNESS

Felix, with all *t* ....Acts 24:3

THANKS

the cup, and gave *t* ....Matt 26:27
t He distributed them ....John 6:11
for he gives God *t* ....Rom 14:6
T be to God for His ....2 Cor 9:15
giving *t* always for ....Eph 5:20
t can we render ....1 Thess 3:9

THANKSGIVING

with the voice of *t* ....Ps 26:7
Offer to God *t* ....Ps 50:14
His presence with *t* ....Ps 95:2
into His gates with *t* ....Ps 100:4
the sacrifices of *t* ....Ps 107:22
supplication, with *t* ....Phil 4:6
vigilant in it with *t* ....Col 4:2
to be received with *t* ....1 Tim 4:3

THEATER

and rushed into the *t* ....Acts 19:29

THEOPHILUS

Luke addresses his writings to, Luke 1:3; Acts 1:1

THESSALONICA

Paul preaches in, Acts 17:1–13
Paul writes letters to churches of, 1 Thess 1:1

THIEF

When you saw a *t* ....Ps 50:18
do not despise a *t* ....Prov 6:30
t hates his own life ....Prov 29:24
t is ashamed when he ....Jer 2:26
the windows like a *t* ....Joel 2:9
t shall be expelled ....Zech 5:3
known what hour the *t* ....Matt 24:43
t approaches nor moth ....Luke 12:33
way, the same is a *t* ....John 10:1
because he was a *t* ....John 12:6
Lord will come as a *t* ....2 Pet 3:10
upon you as a *t* ....Rev 3:3

THIEVES

And companions of *t* ....Is 1:23
destroy and where *t* ....Matt 6:19
before Me and *t* ....John 10:8

THIGH

them hip and *t* with a ....Judg 15:8

good piece, the *t* . . . . . Ezek 24:4

THINGS

in heaven give good *t* . . . . . Matt 7:11
evil, speak good *t* . . . . . Matt 12:34
kept all these *t* . . . . . Luke 2:51
Lazarus evil *t* . . . . . Luke 16:25
the Scriptures the *t* . . . . . Luke 24:27
share in all good *t* . . . . . Gal 6:6

THINK

nor does his heart *t* . . . . . Is 10:7
t that they will be . . . . . Matt 6:7
t you have eternal . . . . . John 5:39
not to *t* of himself . . . . . Rom 12:3
of ourselves to *t* . . . . . 2 Cor 3:5
all that we ask or *t* . . . . . Eph 3:20

THINKS

yet the LORD *t* upon me . . . . . Ps 40:17
for as he *t* in his . . . . . Prov 23:7
t that he knows . . . . . 1 Cor 8:2
t he stands take heed . . . . . 1 Cor 10:12
For if anyone *t* . . . . . Gal 6:3
t he is religious . . . . . James 1:26

THIRST

tongues fail for *t* . . . . . Is 41:17
those who hunger and *t* . . . . . Matt 5:6
in Me shall never *t* . . . . . John 6:35
said, "I *t*!" . . . . . John 19:28
we both hunger and *t* . . . . . 1 Cor 4:11
anymore nor *t* anymore . . . . . Rev 7:16

THIRSTS

My soul *t* for God . . . . . Ps 42:2
saying, "If anyone *t* . . . . . John 7:37
if he *t* . . . . . Rom 12:20
freely to him who *t* . . . . . Rev 21:6
And let him who *t* . . . . . Rev 22:17

THIRSTY

and if he is *t* . . . . . Prov 25:21
as when a *t* man dreams . . . . . Is 29:8
the drink of the *t* . . . . . Is 32:6
t land springs of . . . . . Is 35:7
on him who is *t* . . . . . Is 44:3
but you shall be *t* . . . . . Is 65:13
I was *t* and you gave . . . . . Matt 25:35
we see You hungry or *t* . . . . . Matt 25:44

THISTLES

t grow instead of . . . . . Job 31:40
or figs from *t* . . . . . Matt 7:16

THOMAS

Apostle of Christ, Matt 10:3
Ready to die with Christ, John 11:16
Doubts Christ's resurrection, John 20:24–29

THORN

t that goes into the . . . . . Prov 26:9
t shall come up the . . . . . Is 55:13
a *t* in the flesh was . . . . . 2 Cor 12:7

THORNBUSHES

gather grapes from *t* . . . . . Matt 7:16

THORNS

Both *t* and thistles it . . . . . Gen 3:18
T and snares are . . . . . Prov 22:5
all overgrown with *t* . . . . . Prov 24:31
the crackling of *t* . . . . . Eccl 7:6
Like a lily among *t* . . . . . Song 2:2
and do not sow among *t* . . . . . Jer 4:3
wheat but reaped *t* . . . . . Jer 12:13
And some fell among *t* . . . . . Matt 13:7
wearing the crown of *t* . . . . . John 19:5

THOUGHT

t is that their houses . . . . . Ps 49:11
You *t* that I was . . . . . Ps 50:21
Both the inward *t* . . . . . Ps 64:6
I *t* about my ways . . . . . Ps 119:59
You understand my *t* . . . . . Ps 139:2
"Surely, as I have *t* . . . . . Is 14:24
to man what his *t* . . . . . Amos 4:13
perceiving the *t* . . . . . Luke 9:47
And he *t* within . . . . . Luke 12:17
I *t* as a child . . . . . 1 Cor 13:11

THOUGHTS

the intent of the *t* . . . . . 1 Chr 28:9
is in none of his *t* . . . . . Ps 10:4
t toward us . . . . . Ps 40:5
t are very deep . . . . . Ps 92:5
The LORD knows the *t* . . . . . Ps 94:11
t will be established . . . . . Prov 16:3
unrighteous man his *t* . . . . . Is 55:7
For My *t* are not your . . . . . Is 55:8
long shall your evil *t* . . . . . Jer 4:14
they do not know the *t* . . . . . Mic 4:12
Jesus, knowing their *t* . . . . . Matt 9:4
heart proceed evil *t* . . . . . Matt 15:19
futile in their *t* . . . . . Rom 1:21
The LORD knows the *t* . . . . . 1 Cor 3:20

THREAT

shall flee at the *t* . . . . . Is 30:17

THREATEN

suffered, He did not *t* . . . . . 1 Pet 2:23

THREATENING

to them, giving up *t* . . . . . Eph 6:9

THREATS

Lord, look on their *t* . . . . . Acts 4:29
still breathing *t* . . . . . Acts 9:1

THREE

you will deny Me *t* . . . . . Matt 26:34
hope, love, these *t* . . . . . 1 Cor 13:13
and these *t* are one . . . . . 1 John 5:7

THRESH

he does not *t* it . . . . . Is 28:28
t the mountains . . . . . Is 41:15
it is time to *t* her . . . . . Jer 51:33
"Arise and *t* . . . . . Mic 4:13

THRESHING

t shall last till the . . . . . Lev 26:5
like the dust at *t* . . . . . 2 Kin 13:7
Oh, my *t* and the grain . . . . . Is 21:10

THROAT

t is an open tomb . . . . . Ps 5:9
put a knife to your *t* . . . . . Prov 23:2
unshod, and your *t* . . . . . Jer 2:25
t is an open tomb . . . . . Rom 3:13

THRONE

LORD sitting on His *t* . . . . . 1 Kin 22:19
He has prepared His *t* . . . . . Ps 9:7
temple, the LORD's *t* . . . . . Ps 11:4
Your *t*, O God, is . . . . . Ps 45:6
has established His *t* . . . . . Ps 103:19
he upholds his *t* . . . . . Prov 20:28
Lord sitting on a *t* . . . . . Is 6:1
"Heaven is My *t* . . . . . Is 66:1
shall be called The *T* . . . . . Jer 3:17
do not disgrace the *t* . . . . . Jer 14:21
A glorious high *t* . . . . . Jer 17:12
t was a fiery flame . . . . . Dan 7:9
sit and rule on His *t* . . . . . Zech 6:13
for it is God's *t* . . . . . Matt 5:34
will give Him the *t* . . . . . Luke 1:32
"Your *t*, O God, is . . . . . Heb 1:8
come boldly to the *t* . . . . . Heb 4:16
where Satan's *t* . . . . . Rev 2:13
My Father on His *t* . . . . . Rev 3:21
I saw a great white *t* . . . . . Rev 20:11

THRONES

t are set there . . . . . Ps 122:5
also sit on twelve *t* . . . . . Matt 19:28
mighty from their *t* . . . . . Luke 1:52
invisible, whether *t* . . . . . Col 1:16
t I saw twenty-four . . . . . Rev 4:4

THRONG

house of God in the *t* . . . . . Ps 55:14

THROW

of your land and *t* . . . . . Mic 5:11
t Yourself down . . . . . Matt 4:6
children's bread and *t* . . . . . Matt 15:26

THROWN

their slain shall be *t* . . . . . Is 34:3
neck, and he were *t* . . . . . Mark 9:42

THRUST

and rose up and *t* . . . . . Luke 4:29

THUNDER

But the *t* of His power . . . . . Job 26:14
The voice of Your *t* . . . . . Ps 77:18
the secret place of *t* . . . . . Ps 81:7
t they hastened away . . . . . Ps 104:7
that is, "Sons of *T*" . . . . . Mark 3:17
the voice of loud *t* . . . . . Rev 14:2

THUNDERED

"The LORD *t* from . . . . . 2 Sam 22:14
The LORD *t* . . . . . Ps 18:13

THUNDERINGS

people witnessed the *t* . . . . . Ex 20:18
the sound of mighty *t* . . . . . Rev 19:6

THUNDERS

t marvelously with His . . . . . Job 37:5
The God of glory *t* . . . . . Ps 29:3

THYATIRA

Residence of Lydia, Acts 16:14
Site of one of the seven churches, Rev 2:18–24

TIBERIAS

Sea of Galilee called, John 6:1, 23

TIDINGS

be afraid of evil *t* . . . . . Ps 112:7
I bring you good *t* . . . . . Luke 2:10
who bring glad *t* . . . . . Rom 10:15

TIGLATH-PILESER

Powerful Assyrian king who invades Samaria, 2 Kin 15:29

TILL

no man to *t* the ground . . . . . Gen 2:5

TILLER

but Cain was a *t* ....Gen 4:2

TILLS

t his land will be ....Prov 12:11
t his land will have ....Prov 28:19

TIME

pray to You in a *t* ....Ps 32:6
ashamed in the evil *t*.........Ps 37:19
how short my *t* is ....Ps 89:47
A *t* to be born ....Eccl 3:2
but *t* and chance ....Eccl 9:11
your *t* was the *t* ....Ezek 16:8
you did not know the *t*.....Luke 19:44
t has not yet come ....John 7:6
I have a convenient *t* ....Acts 24:25
for the *t* is near ....Rev 1:3

TIMES

understanding of the *t* .....1 Chr 12:32
t are not hidden ....Job 24:1
t are in Your hand ....Ps 31:15
the signs of the *t* ....Matt 16:3
Gentiles until the *t*........Luke 21:24
not for you to know *t*...........Acts 1:7
their preappointed *t*.........Acts 17:26
last days perilous *t* ....2 Tim 3:1
God, who at various *t* ....Heb 1:1

TIMON

One of the first seven deacons, Acts 6:1–5

TIMOTHY

Paul's companion, Acts 16:1–3; 18:5; 20:4, 5; 2 Cor 1:19; Phil 1:1; 2 Tim 4:9, 21
Ministers independently, Acts 17:14, 15; 19:22; 1 Cor 4:17; Phil 2:19, 23; 1 Thess 3:1–6; 1 Tim 1:1–3; 4:14

TIRZAH

Seat of Jeroboam's rule, 1 Kin 14:17
Capital of Israel until Omri's reign, 1 Kin 16:6–23

TITHE

And he gave him a *t* ....Gen 14:20
LORD, a tenth of the *t* ....Num 18:26
"You shall truly *t* ....Deut 14:22
shall bring out the *t* ....Deut 14:28
laying aside all the *t* ....Deut 26:12
in abundantly the *t* ....2 Chr 31:5
Judah brought the *t* ....Neh 13:12
For you pay *t* of mint........Matt 23:23

TITHES

to redeem any of his *t* ....Lev 27:31
t which you receive ....Num 18:28
and to bring the *t* ....Neh 10:37
firstfruits, and the *t* ....Neh 12:44
the articles, the *t* ....Neh 13:5
Bring all the *t* ....Mal 3:10
I give *t* of all that I ....Luke 18:12
to receive *t* from the ....Heb 7:5
mortal men receive *t* ....Heb 7:8
Levi, who receives *t* ....Heb 7:9

TITHING

the year of *t* ....Deut 26:12

TITLE

Now Pilate wrote a *t* ....John 19:19

TITTLE

away, one jot or one *t* ....Matt 5:18

TITUS

Ministers in Crete, Titus 1:4, 5
Paul's representative in Corinth, 2 Cor 7:6, 7, 13, 14; 8:6–23

TOBIAH

Ammonite servant; ridicules the Jews, Neh 2:10

TODAY

t I have begotten You ....Ps 2:7
of the field, which *t* ....Matt 6:30
the grass, which *t* ....Luke 12:28
t you will be with Me ....Luke 23:43
t I have begotten You ....Heb 1:5
"*T*, if you will hear ....Heb 3:7
the same yesterday, *t* ....Heb 13:8

TOIL

t you shall eat of ....Gen 3:17
they neither *t* nor ....Matt 6:28
our labor and *t* ....1 Thess 2:9

TOILED

"Master, we have *t* ....Luke 5:5

TOLD

Behold, I have *t* ....Matt 28:7
things which were *t* ....Luke 2:18
t me all things that I ....John 4:29
t you the truth which ....John 8:40
so, I would have *t* ....John 14:2
"And now I have *t* ....John 14:29

TOLERABLE

you, it will be more *t* ....Matt 10:15

TOMB

throat is an open *t* ....Ps 5:9
in the garden a new *t* ......John 19:41
throat is an open *t* ....Rom 3:13

TOMBS

like whitewashed *t* ....Matt 23:27
you build the *t* ....Matt 23:29
For you build the *t* ....Luke 11:47

TOMORROW

drink, for *t* we die ....Is 22:13
t will be as today ....Is 56:12
t is thrown into the ....Matt 6:30
do not worry about *t* ....Matt 6:34
drink, for *t* we die ....1 Cor 15:32
what will happen *t* ....James 4:14

TONGUE

the scourge of the *t* ....Job 5:21
hides it under his *t* ....Job 20:12
Keep your *t* from evil ....Ps 34:13
t shall speak of Your ....Ps 35:28
lest I sin with my *t* ....Ps 39:1
to you, you false *t* ....Ps 120:3
laughter, and our *t* ....Ps 126:2
remember you, let my *t* ....Ps 137:6
is not a word on my *t* ....Ps 139:4
but the perverse *t* ....Prov 10:31
forever, but a lying *t* ....Prov 12:19
A wholesome *t* is a ....Prov 15:4
t keeps his soul ....Prov 21:23
t breaks a bone ....Prov 25:15
t shall take an oath ....Is 45:23
GOD has given Me the *t* ....Is 50:4

t should confess that ....Phil 2:11
does not bridle his *t* ....James 1:26
t is a little member ....James 3:5
And the *t* is a fire ....James 3:6
no man can tame the *t* ....James 3:8
love in word or in *t* ....1 John 3:18
every nation, tribe, *t* ....Rev 14:6

TONGUES

From the strife of *t* ....Ps 31:20
speak with new *t*..............Mark 16:17
to them divided *t*, as of fire ...Acts 2:3
and they spoke with *t* ....Acts 19:6
I speak with the *t* ....1 Cor 13:1
Therefore *t* are for a ....1 Cor 14:22

TOOTH

eye for eye, *t* ....Ex 21:24
is like a bad *t* ....Prov 25:19
eye for an eye and a *t* ....Matt 5:38

TOPHET

See HINNOM, VALLEY OF THE SON OF
T was established ....Is 30:33
the high places of *T* ....Jer 7:31
make this city like *T* ....Jer 19:12
like the place of *T* ....Jer 19:13

TORCH

and like a fiery *t* ....Zech 12:6

TORCHES

When he had set the *t*........Judg 15:5
his eyes like *t* ....Dan 10:6
come with flaming *t* ....Nah 2:3

TORMENT

"How long will you *t* ....Job 19:2
shall lie down in *t* ....Is 50:11
You come here to *t* ....Matt 8:29
to this place of *t* ....Luke 16:28
fear involves *t* ....1 John 4:18
t ascends forever ....Rev 14:11

TORMENTED

for I am *t* in this ....Luke 16:24
And they will be *t* ....Rev 20:10

TORMENTS

And being in *t* ....Luke 16:23

TORN

aside my ways and *t* ....Lam 3:11
for He has *t* ....Hos 6:1
of the temple was *t* ....Matt 27:51

TORTURED

Others were *t* ....Heb 11:35

TOSSED

t with tempest ....Is 54:11
t to and fro and ....Eph 4:14

TOTTER

drunkard, and shall *t* ....Is 24:20

TOUCH

seven no evil shall *t* ....Job 5:19
t no unclean thing ....Is 52:11
"If only I may *t* ....Matt 9:21
that they might only *t* ....Matt 14:36
a man not to *t* a woman ....1 Cor 7:1
wicked one does not *t* ....1 John 5:18

TOUCHED

whose hearts God had *t* ......1 Sam 10:26

t my mouth with it ....Is 6:7
hand and *t* my mouth ....Jer 1:9
mountain that may be *t* .....Heb 12:18

TOUCHES

He *t* the hills ....Ps 104:32
t you *t* the ....Zech 2:8

TOWER

t whose top is in the ....Gen 11:4
for me, a strong *t* ....Ps 61:3
my fortress, my high *t* ....Ps 144:2
like an ivory *t* ....Song 7:4
a watchman in the *t* ....Is 21:5
in it and built a *t* ....Matt 21:33

TRACKED

t our steps so that we ....Lam 4:18

TRADERS

are princes, whose *t* ....Is 23:8

TRADITION

transgress the *t* ....Matt 15:2
of no effect by your *t* ....Matt 15:6
according to the *t* ....Col 2:8
t which he received ....2 Thess 3:6
conduct received by *t* ....1 Pet 1:18

TRADITIONS

zealous for the *t* ....Gal 1:14
t which you were ....2 Thess 2:15

TRAIN

T up a child in the ....Prov 22:6
t of His robe filled ....Is 6:1

TRAINED

who is perfectly *t* ....Luke 6:40
those who have been *t* ......Heb 12:11

TRAINING

bring them up in the *t* ....Eph 6:4

TRAITOR

also became a *t* ....Luke 6:16

TRAITORS

t, headstrong ....2 Tim 3:4

TRAMPLE

Your name we will *t* ....Ps 44:5
serpent you shall *t* ....Ps 91:13
hand, to *t* My courts ....Is 1:12
You shall *t* the wicked ....Mal 4:3
swine, lest they *t* ....Matt 7:6
you the authority to *t* ......Luke 10:19

TRAMPLED

t them in My fury ....Is 63:3
now she will be *t* ....Mic 7:10
t the nations in anger ....Hab 3:12
Jerusalem will be *t* ....Luke 21:24
t the Son of God ....Heb 10:29
the winepress was *t* ....Rev 14:20

TRANCE

he fell into a *t* ....Acts 10:10
t I saw a vision ....Acts 11:5

TRANSFIGURED

and was *t* before them ......Matt 17:2

TRANSFORMED

this world, but be *t* ....Rom 12:2

the Lord, are being *t* ....2 Cor 3:18

TRANSGRESS

t the command of the ....Num 14:41
the LORD's people *t* ....1 Sam 2:24
my mouth shall not *t* ....Ps 17:3
his mouth must not *t* ....Prov 16:10
of bread a man will *t* ....Prov 28:21
do Your disciples *t* ....Matt 15:2

TRANSGRESSED

t My covenant ....Josh 7:11
your mediators have *t* ....Is 43:27
the rulers also *t* ....Jer 2:8
their fathers have *t* ....Ezek 2:3
Yes, all Israel has *t* ....Dan 9:11
t your commandment ....Luke 15:29

TRANSGRESSES

"Indeed, because he *t* ....Hab 2:5
Whoever *t* and does not ......2 John 9

TRANSGRESSION

iniquity and *t* and sin ....Ex 34:7
Make me know my *t* ....Job 13:23
t is sealed up in a ....Job 14:17
be innocent of great *t* ....Ps 19:13
because of their *t* ....Ps 107:17
He who covers a *t* ....Prov 17:9
He who loves *t* loves ....Prov 17:19
tell My people their *t* ....Is 58:1
at Gilgal multiply *t* ....Amos 4:4
my firstborn for my *t* ....Mic 6:7
and passing over the *t* ....Mic 7:18
no law there is no *t* ....Rom 4:15
deceived, fell into *t* ....1 Tim 2:14
steadfast, and every *t* ....Heb 2:2

TRANSGRESSIONS

if I have covered my *t* ....Job 31:33
"I will confess my *t* ....Ps 32:5
me from all my *t* ....Ps 39:8
mercies, blot out my *t* ....Ps 51:1
For I acknowledge my *t* ....Ps 51:3
has He removed our *t* ....Ps 103:12
who blots out your *t* ....Is 43:25
was wounded for our *t* ....Is 53:5
for the *t* of My people ....Is 53:8
from you all the *t* ....Ezek 18:31
was added because of *t* ....Gal 3:19
redemption of the *t* ....Heb 9:15

TRANSGRESSOR

and were called a *t* ....Is 48:8
I make myself a *t* ....Gal 2:18

TRANSGRESSORS

Then I will teach *t* ....Ps 51:13
to any wicked *t* ....Ps 59:5
numbered with the *t* ....Is 53:12
numbered with the *t* ....Mark 15:28

TRAP

of Israel, as a *t* ....Is 8:14
where there is no *t* ....Amos 3:5

TRAPS

they have set *t* ....Ps 140:5
for me, and from the *t* ....Ps 141:9

TRAVEL

For you *t* land and sea ......Matt 23:15

TRAVELER

t who turns aside ....Jer 14:8

TRAVELING

lie waste, the *t* ....Is 33:8

TREACHEROUS

the *t* dealer deals ....Is 21:2
an assembly of *t* men ....Jer 9:2
are insolent, *t* ....Zeph 3:4

TREACHEROUSLY

and you who deal *t* ....Is 33:1
happy who deal so *t* ....Jer 12:1
even they have dealt *t* ....Jer 12:6
They have dealt *t* ....Hos 5:7
Why do we deal *t* ....Mal 2:10
that you do not deal *t* ....Mal 2:16
This man dealt *t* ....Acts 7:19

TREAD

t down the wicked in ....Job 40:12
it is He who shall *t* ....Ps 60:12
You shall *t* upon the ....Ps 91:13
shout, as those who *t* ....Jer 25:30
will come down and *t* ....Mic 1:3
And they will *t* ....Rev 11:2

TREADS

like one who *t* in the ....Is 63:2
t the high places ....Amos 4:13
an ox while it *t* ....1 Tim 5:18
t the winepress ....Rev 19:15

TREASURE

to you His good *t* ....Deut 28:12
one who finds great *t* ......Ps 119:162
for His special *t* ....Ps 135:4
there is much *t* ....Prov 15:6
There is desirable *t* ....Prov 21:20
of the LORD is His *t* ....Is 33:6
For where your *t* ....Matt 6:21
t brings forth evil ....Matt 12:35
t things new and old ....Matt 13:52
and you will have *t* ....Matt 19:21
So is he who lays up *t* ......Luke 12:21
But we have this *t* ....2 Cor 4:7
You have heaped up *t* ......James 5:3

TREASURED

t the words of His ....Job 23:12

TREASURER

Erastus, the *t* of the ....Rom 16:23

TREASURES

sealed up among My *t* ......Deut 32:34
it more than hidden *t* ....Job 3:21
her as for hidden *t* ....Prov 2:4
t of wickedness profit ....Prov 10:2
Getting *t* by a lying ....Prov 21:6
is no end to their *t* ....Is 2:7
I will give you the *t* ....Is 45:3
Are there yet the *t* ....Mic 6:10
for yourselves *t* ....Matt 6:19
are hidden all the *t* ....Col 2:3
riches than the *t* ....Heb 11:26

TREATY

Now Solomon made a *t* ......1 Kin 3:1

TREE

but of the *t* ....Gen 2:17
you eaten from the *t* ....Gen 3:11
there is hope for a *t* ....Job 14:7
t planted by the ....Ps 1:3
like a native green *t* ....Ps 37:35
t falls to the south ....Eccl 11:3

Like an apple *t* ....Song 2:3
for as the days of a *t* ....Is 65:22
t planted by the ....Jer 17:8
t bears good fruit ....Matt 7:17
His own body on the *t* ....1 Pet 2:24
give to eat from the *t*..........Rev 2:7
the river, was the *t* ....Rev 22:2

TREES

t once went forth ....Judg 9:8
Also he spoke of *t* ....1 Kin 4:33
Then all the *t* of the ....Ps 96:12
The *t* of the LORD are ....Ps 104:16
all kinds of fruit *t* ....Eccl 2:5
they may be called *t* ....Is 61:3
and on beast, on the *t* ....Jer 7:20
so that all the *t* ....Ezek 31:9
"I see men like *t* ....Mark 8:24
late autumn *t* without ....Jude 12
the sea, or the *t* ....Rev 7:3

TREMBLE

T before Him ....1 Chr 16:30
have made the earth *t* ....Ps 60:2
let the peoples *t* ....Ps 99:1
who made the earth *t* ....Is 14:16
That the nations may *t* ....Is 64:2
'Will you not *t* ....Jer 5:22
wrath the earth will *t* ....Jer 10:10
they shall fear and *t* ....Jer 33:9
my kingdom men must *t* .....Dan 6:26

TREMBLED

of Edom, the earth *t* ....Judg 5:4
for his heart *t* ....1 Sam 4:13
Then everyone who *t* ....Ezra 9:4
the earth shook and *t*...........Ps 18:7
and indeed they *t* ....Jer 4:24

TREMBLES

the earth sees and *t* ....Ps 97:4

TREMBLING

it was a very great *t* ....1 Sam 14:15
your water with *t* ....Ezek 12:18
in fear, and in much *t* ....1 Cor 2:3
t you received ....2 Cor 7:15
flesh, with fear and *t* ....Eph 6:5
with fear and *t* ....Phil 2:12

TRENCH

and he made a *t* ....1 Kin 18:32

TRESPASSES

still goes on in his *t* ....Ps 68:21
forgive men their *t* ....Matt 6:14
not imputing their *t* ....2 Cor 5:19
who were dead in *t* ....Eph 2:1
forgiven you all *t* ....Col 2:13

TRIAL

as in the day of *t* ....Ps 95:8
in the day of *t* ....Heb 3:8
concerning the fiery *t* ....1 Pet 4:12
t which shall come ....Rev 3:10

TRIBE

of old, the *t* of Your ....Ps 74:2
belongs to another *t* ....Heb 7:13
the Lion of the *t* ....Rev 5:5
blood out of every *t* ....Rev 5:9

TRIBES

where the *t* go up ....Ps 122:4
to raise up the *t* ....Is 49:6

promise our twelve *t* ....Acts 26:7
t which are scattered ....James 1:1

TRIBULATION

there will be great *t* ....Matt 24:21
world you will have *t* ....John 16:33
in hope, patient in *t* ....Rom 12:12
joyful in all our *t* ....2 Cor 7:4
that we would suffer *t* ....1 Thess 3:4
t those who ....2 Thess 1:6
and you will have *t* ....Rev 2:10
with her into great *t* ....Rev 2:22
out of the great *t* ....Rev 7:14

TRIBULATIONS

t enter the kingdom ....Acts 14:22
but we also glory in *t* ....Rom 5:3
not lose heart at my *t* ....Eph 3:13
t that you endure ....2 Thess 1:4

TRIED

You have *t* me and have ....Ps 17:3
a *t* stone, a precious ....Is 28:16

TRIMMED

and *t* their lamps ....Matt 25:7

TRIUMPH

Let not my enemies *t* ....Ps 25:2
I will *t* in the works ....Ps 92:4
always leads us in *t* ....2 Cor 2:14

TRIUMPHED

the LORD, for He has *t* ....Ex 15:1

TROAS

Paul receives vision at, Acts 16:8–11

TRODDEN

t the winepress alone ....Is 63:3

TROUBLE

that they were in *t* ....Ex 5:19
no rest, for *t* comes ....Job 3:26
few days and full of *t* ....Job 14:1
for the time of *t* ....Job 38:23
have increased who *t* ....Ps 3:1
under his tongue is *t* ....Ps 10:7
from Me, for *t* is near ....Ps 22:11
t He shall hide me ....Ps 27:5
O LORD, for I am in *t* ....Ps 31:9
not in *t* as other men ....Ps 73:5
will be with him in *t* ....Ps 91:15
walk in the midst of *t* ....Ps 138:7
is delivered from *t* ....Prov 11:8
of the wicked is *t* ....Prov 15:6
t they have ....Is 26:16
also in the time of *t* ....Is 33:2
and there was *t* ....Jer 8:15
Savior in time of *t* ....Jer 14:8
such will have *t* ....1 Cor 7:28
there are some who *t* ....Gal 1:7

TROUBLED

Your face, and I was *t* ....Ps 30:7
Your face, they are *t* ....Ps 104:29
wicked are like the *t* ....Is 57:20
You are worried and *t* .....Luke 10:41
to give you who are *t* ....2 Thess 1:7
shaken in mind or *t* ....2 Thess 2:2

TROUBLES

"What *t* the people ....1 Sam 11:5
deliver you in six *t* ....Job 5:19
The *t* of my heart have ....Ps 25:17

out of all their *t* ....Ps 25:22
my soul is full of *t* ....Ps 88:3
because the former *t* ....Is 65:16
will be famines and *t* ....Mark 13:8
him out of all his *t* ....Acts 7:10

TROUBLING

spirit from God is *t* ....1 Sam 16:15
wicked cease from *t* ....Job 3:17

TRUE

and Your words are *t* ....2 Sam 7:28
But the LORD is the *t* ....Jer 10:10
"Let the LORD be a *t* ....Jer 42:5
we know that You are *t* ....Matt 22:16
He who sent Me is *t* ....John 7:28
about this Man were *t* ....John 10:41
Indeed, let God be *t* ....Rom 3:4
whatever things are *t* ....Phil 4:8
may know Him who is *t* ....1 John 5:20
is holy, He who is *t* ....Rev 3:7
"These are the *t* ....Rev 19:9
for these words are *t* ....Rev 21:5

TRUMPET

Blow the *t* at the time ....Ps 81:3
"Blow the *t* in the ....Jer 4:5
deed, do not sound a *t* ....Matt 6:2
t makes an uncertain ....1 Cor 14:8
For the *t* will sound ....1 Cor 15:52
loud voice, as of a *t* ....Rev 1:10

TRUST

t is a spider's web ....Job 8:14
If God puts no *t* ....Job 15:15
T in the LORD ....Ps 37:3
You are my *t* from my ....Ps 71:5
T in the LORD with all ....Prov 3:5
my salvation, I will *t* ....Is 12:2
Let him *t* in the name ....Is 50:10
Do not *t* in these ....Jer 7:4
Do not *t* in a friend ....Mic 7:5
those who *t* in riches ....Mark 10:24
committed to your *t* ....1 Tim 6:20

TRUSTED

"He *t* in the LORD ....Ps 22:8
He *t* in God ....Matt 27:43
that we who first *t* ....Eph 1:12
the holy women who *t* ....1 Pet 3:5

TRUSTS

But he who *t* in the ....Ps 32:10
He who *t* in his own ....Prov 28:26

TRUTH

led me in the way of *t* ....Gen 24:48
justice, a God of *t* ....Deut 32:4
and speaks the *t* ....Ps 15:2
t continually preserve ....Ps 40:11
Behold, You desire *t* ....Ps 51:6
T shall spring out of ....Ps 85:11
t shall be your shield ....Ps 91:4
t utterly out of my ....Ps 119:43
and Your law is *t* ....Ps 119:142
of Your word is *t* ....Ps 119:160
t is fallen in the ....Is 59:14
not valiant for the *t* ....Jer 9:3
"There is no *t* ....Hos 4:1
called the City of *T* ....Zech 8:3
speak each man the *t* ....Zech 8:16
t was in his mouth ....Mal 2:6
you shall know the *t* ....John 8:32
"I am the way, the *t* ....John 14:6
He, the Spirit of *t*...................John 16:13

to Him, "What is *t* .... John 18:38
speak the words of *t* .... Acts 26:25
who suppress the *t* .... Rom 1:18
of sincerity and *t* .... 1 Cor 5:8
but, speaking the *t* .... Eph 4:15
your waist with *t* .... Eph 6:14
in the word of the *t* .... Col 1:5
the love of the *t* .... 2 Thess 2:10
I am speaking the *t* .... 1 Tim 2:7
they may know the *t* .... 2 Tim 2:25
the knowledge of the *t* .... 2 Tim 3:7
in the present *t* .... 2 Pet 1:12
way of *t* will be .... 2 Pet 2:2
that we are of the *t* .... 1 John 3:19
the Spirit is *t* .... 1 John 5:6
t that is in you .... 3 John 3

TRY

t my mind and my heart .... Ps 26:2
refine them and *t* them .... Jer 9:7
t Me now in this .... Mal 3:10
which is to *t* you .... 1 Pet 4:12

TUBAL

Son of Japheth, Gen 10:2
—— Tribe associated with Javan and Meshech, Is 66:19
In Gog's army, Ezek 38:2, 3
Punishment of, Ezek 32:26, 27

TUBAL-CAIN

Son of Lamech, Gen 4:19–22

TUMULT

their waves, and the *t* .... Ps 65:7
Your enemies make a *t* .... Ps 83:2

TUNIC

Also he made him a *t* .... Gen 37:3
and take away your *t* .... Matt 5:40

TUNICS

the LORD God made *t* .... Gen 3:21
not to put on two *t* .... Mark 6:9
weeping, showing the *t* .... Acts 9:39

TURBAN

like a robe and a *t* .... Job 29:14
"Remove the *t* .... Ezek 21:26

TURN

you shall not *t* .... Deut 17:11
Then we will not *t* .... Ps 80:18
but let them not *t* .... Ps 85:8
yet I do not *t* .... Ps 119:51
T at my rebuke .... Prov 1:23
not let your heart *t* .... Prov 7:25
'*T* now everyone from .... Jer 35:15
"Repent, *t* away from .... Ezek 14:6
yes, let every one *t* .... Jon 3:8
"*T* now from your evil .... Zech 1:4
on your right cheek, *t* .... Matt 5:39
t the hearts of the .... Luke 1:17
you that you should *t* .... Acts 14:15
t them from darkness .... Acts 26:18
Let him *t* away from .... 1 Pet 3:11

TURNED

kept His way and not *t* .... Job 23:11
The wicked shall be *t* .... Ps 9:17
let them be *t* back and .... Ps 70:2
t my feet to Your .... Ps 119:59
of Israel, they have *t* .... Is 1:4
number believed and *t* .... Acts 11:21
and how you *t* to God .... 1 Thess 1:9

TURNING

marvel that you are *t* .... Gal 1:6
or shadow of *t* .... James 1:17

TURNS

of the wicked He *t* .... Ps 146:9
A soft answer *t* .... Prov 15:1
but no one *t* back .... Nah 2:8
that he who *t* .... James 5:20

TURTLEDOVE

the life of Your *t* .... Ps 74:19
t is heard in our land .... Song 2:12

TUTOR

the law was our *t* .... Gal 3:24
no longer under a *t* .... Gal 3:25

TWIST

All day they *t* my .... Ps 56:5
unstable people *t* to .... 2 Pet 3:16

TWO

the ark to Noah, *t* .... Gen 7:15
t young pigeons .... Lev 12:8
T are better than one .... Eccl 4:9
t he covered his .... Is 6:2
t shall become one .... Matt 19:5
t young pigeons .... Luke 2:24
new man from the *t* .... Eph 2:15

TYCHICUS

Paul's companion, Acts 20:1, 4
Paul's messenger, Eph 6:21, 22; Col 4:7–9; 2 Tim 4:12

TYPE

of Adam, who is a *t* .... Rom 5:14

— U —

ULAI

Scene of Daniel's visions, Dan 8:2–16

UNAFRAID

Do you want to be *u* .... Rom 13:3

UNBELIEF

because of their *u* .... Matt 13:58
help my *u* .... Mark 9:24
and He rebuked their *u* .... Mark 16:14
did it ignorantly in *u* .... 1 Tim 1:13
you an evil heart of *u* .... Heb 3:12
enter in because of *u* .... Heb 3:19

UNBELIEVERS

who believe but to *u* .... 1 Cor 14:22
are uninformed or *u* .... 1 Cor 14:23
yoked together with *u* .... 2 Cor 6:14

UNBELIEVING

Do not be *u* .... John 20:27
u Jews stirred up the .... Acts 14:2
For the *u* husband is .... 1 Cor 7:14
u nothing is pure .... Titus 1:15
But the cowardly, *u* .... Rev 21:8

UNCIRCUMCISED

You stiff-necked and *u* .... Acts 7:51
not the physically *u* .... Rom 2:27
by faith and the *u* .... Rom 3:30
u had been committed .... Gal 2:7

UNCLEAN

of animals that are *u* .... Gen 7:2
who touches any *u* .... Lev 7:21
I am a man of *u* lips .... Is 6:5
u shall no longer come .... Is 52:1
He commands even the *u* .... Mark 1:27
He rebuked the *u* .... Mark 9:25
any man common or *u* .... Acts 10:28
there is nothing *u* .... Rom 14:14
Do not touch what is *u* .... 2 Cor 6:17
that no fornicator, *u* .... Eph 5:5

UNCLEANNESS

men's bones and all *u* .... Matt 23:27
members as slaves of *u* .... Rom 6:19
did not call us to *u* .... 1 Thess 4:7
flesh in the lust of *u* .... 2 Pet 2:10

UNCLEANNESSES

from all your *u* .... Ezek 36:29

UNCLOTHED

we want to be *u* .... 2 Cor 5:4

UNCOVER

skirt, *u* the thigh .... Is 47:2

UNCOVERS

u deep things out of .... Job 12:22

UNDEFILED

Blessed are the *u* .... Ps 119:1
all, and the bed *u* .... Heb 13:4
incorruptible and *u* .... 1 Pet 1:4

UNDERMINE

And you *u* your friend .... Job 6:27

UNDERSTAND

u one another's speech .... Gen 11:7
if there are any who *u* .... Ps 14:2
in Egypt did not *u* .... Ps 106:7
is to *u* his way .... Prov 14:8
Evil men do not *u* .... Prov 28:5
hearing, but do not *u* .... Is 6:9
and quick to *u* .... Dan 1:4
set your heart to *u* .... Dan 10:12
u shall instruct many .... Dan 11:33
of the wicked shall *u* .... Dan 12:10
people who do not *u* .... Hos 4:14
Let him *u* these things .... Hos 14:9
Why do you not *u* .... John 8:43
u what you are reading .... Acts 8:30
lest they should *u* .... Acts 28:27
u all mysteries .... 1 Cor 13:2
some things hard to *u* .... 2 Pet 3:16

UNDERSTANDING

asked for yourself *u* .... 1 Kin 3:11
He has counsel and *u* .... Job 12:13
is the place of *u* .... Job 28:12
depart from evil is *u* .... Job 28:28
Almighty gives him *u* .... Job 32:8
not endow her with *u* .... Job 39:17
my heart shall give *u* .... Ps 49:3
Give me *u* .... Ps 119:34
Your precepts I get *u* .... Ps 119:104
His *u* is infinite .... Ps 147:5
apply your heart to *u* .... Prov 2:2
lean not on your own *u* .... Prov 3:5
u He established .... Prov 3:19
and go in the way of *u* .... Prov 9:6
of the Holy One is *u* .... Prov 9:10
a man of *u* has wisdom .... Prov 10:23
U is a wellspring .... Prov 16:22
u will find good .... Prov 19:8
and instruction and *u* .... Prov 23:23

but the poor who has *u* .....Prov 28:11
Spirit of wisdom and *u* ....Is 11:2
His *u* is unsearchable ....Is 40:28
the heaven by His *u* ....Jer 51:15
also still without *u* ....Matt 15:16
And He opened their *u* .....Luke 24:45
also pray with the *u* ......1 Cor 14:15
five words with my *u* ......1 Cor 14:19
and spiritual *u* ....Col 1:9
the Lord give you *u* ....2 Tim 2:7
Who is wise and *u* ....James 3:13
and has given us an *u* .....1 John 5:20

UNDERSTANDS

all plain to him who *u* ....Prov 8:9
is easy to him who *u* ....Prov 14:6
there is none who *u* ....Rom 3:11

UNDERSTOOD

Then I *u* their end ....Ps 73:17
My heart has *u* great ....Eccl 1:16
Have you not *u* from ....Is 40:21
u all these things ....Matt 13:51
clearly seen, being *u* ....Rom 1:20

UNDESIRABLE

gather together, O *u* ....Zeph 2:1

UNDIGNIFIED

I will be even more *u* ......2 Sam 6:22

UNDISCERNING

u, untrustworthy ....Rom 1:31

UNDONE

"Woe is me, for I am *u* ....Is 6:5
leaving the others *u* ....Matt 23:23

UNEDUCATED

that they were *u* ....Acts 4:13

UNFAITHFUL

u will be uprooted ....Prov 2:22
way of the *u* is hard ....Prov 13:15

UNFAITHFULLY

back and acted *u* ....Ps 78:57

UNFORGIVING

unloving, *u* ....Rom 1:31

UNFORMED

substance, being yet *u* ....Ps 139:16

UNFRUITFUL

and it becomes *u* ....Mark 4:19
that they may not be *u* ....Titus 3:14

UNGODLINESS

u made me afraid ....Ps 18:4
heaven against all *u* ....Rom 1:18
He will turn away *u* ....Rom 11:26

UNGODLY

delivered me to the *u* ....Job 16:11
u shall not stand ....Ps 1:5
of the *u* shall perish ....Ps 1:6
my cause against an *u* ....Ps 43:1
u man digs up evil ....Prov 16:27
who justifies the *u* ....Rom 4:5
Christ died for the *u* ....Rom 5:6
and perdition of *u* men ....2 Pet 3:7
convict all who are *u* ....Jude 15

UNHOLY

the holy and *u* ....Ezek 22:26

for sinners, for the *u* ....1 Tim 1:9

UNINFORMED

the place of the *u* ....1 Cor 14:16

UNINTENTIONALLY

kills his neighbor *u* ....Deut 4:42

UNITE

U my heart to fear ....Ps 86:11

UNITY

to dwell together in *u* ....Ps 133:1
to keep the *u* of the ....Eph 4:3
we all come to the *u* ....Eph 4:13

UNJUST

hope of the *u* perishes ....Prov 11:7
u knows no shame ....Zeph 3:5
commended the *u* ....Luke 16:8
extortioners, *u* ....Luke 18:11
of the just and the *u* ....Acts 24:15
u who inflicts wrath ....Rom 3:5
For God is not *u* ....Heb 6:10
the just for the *u* ....1 Pet 3:18
let him be *u* still ....Rev 22:11

UNJUSTLY

long will you judge *u* ....Ps 82:2
he will deal *u* ....Is 26:10

UNKNOWN

not stand before *u* ....Prov 22:29
To The *U* God ....Acts 17:23
And I was *u* by face to ....Gal 1:22

UNLEAVENED

the Feast of *U* Bread ....Ex 12:17
the Feast of *U* Bread ....Mark 14:1
since you truly are *u* ....1 Cor 5:7

UNLOVING

untrustworthy, *u* ....Rom 1:31

UNMERCIFUL

unforgiving, *u* ....Rom 1:31

UNPREPARED

with me and find you *u* ......2 Cor 9:4

UNPRESENTABLE

u parts have greater ....1 Cor 12:23

UNPROFITABLE

And cast the *u* ....Matt 25:30
'We are *u* servants ....Luke 17:10
have together become *u* ......Rom 3:12
who once was *u* to you ....Philem 11
for that would be *u* ....Heb 13:17

UNPROFITABLENESS

of its weakness and *u* ....Heb 7:18

UNPUNISHED

wicked will not go *u* ....Prov 11:21
be rich will not go *u* ....Prov 28:20

UNQUENCHABLE

up the chaff with *u* ....Matt 3:12
He will burn with *u* ....Luke 3:17

UNRESTRAINED

that the people were *u* ....Ex 32:25

UNRIGHTEOUS

u man his thoughts ....Is 55:7

been faithful in the *u* ....Luke 16:11
u will not inherit the ....1 Cor 6:9

UNRIGHTEOUSNESS

and there is no *u* ....Ps 92:15
builds his house by *u* ....Jer 22:13
Him is true, and no *u* ....John 7:18
all ungodliness and *u* ....Rom 1:18
the truth, but obey *u* ....Rom 2:8
Is there *u* with God ....Rom 9:14
cleanse us from all *u* ....1 John 1:9
All *u* is sin ....1 John 5:17

UNRULY

those who are *u* ....1 Thess 5:14
It is an *u* evil ....James 3:8

UNSEARCHABLE

heart of kings is *u* ....Prov 25:3
u are His judgments ....Rom 11:33

UNSKILLED

only of milk is *u* ....Heb 5:13

UNSPOTTED

to keep oneself *u* ....James 1:27

UNSTABLE

U as water ....Gen 49:4

UNSTOPPED

of the deaf shall be *u* ....Is 35:5

UNTAUGHT

which *u* and unstable ....2 Pet 3:16

UNTRUSTWORTHY

undiscerning, *u* ....Rom 1:31

UNWASHED

eat bread with *u* hands ......Mark 7:5

UNWISE

He is an *u* son ....Hos 13:13
Therefore do not be *u* ....Eph 5:17

UNWORTHY

and judge yourselves *u* ......Acts 13:46
u manner will be ....1 Cor 11:27

UPHOLD

u the evildoers ....Job 8:20
U me according to ....Ps 119:116
My Servant whom I *u* ....Is 42:1
there was no one to *u* ....Is 63:5

UPHOLDING

u all things by the ....Heb 1:3

UPHOLDS

Your right hand *u* ....Ps 63:8
LORD *u* all who fall ....Ps 145:14

UPPER

show you a large *u* ....Mark 14:15
went up into the *u* ....Acts 1:13
many lamps in the *u* ....Acts 20:8

UPRIGHT

righteous and *u* is He ....Deut 32:4
where were the *u* ....Job 4:7
Good and *u* is the LORD ....Ps 25:8
u shall have dominion ....Ps 49:14
u will be blessed ....Ps 112:2

u there arises light . . . . Ps 112:4
is strength for the *u* . . . . Prov 10:29
u will guide them . . . . Prov 11:3
u will deliver them . . . . Prov 11:6
u will flourish . . . . Prov 14:11
u is His delight . . . . Prov 15:8
of the *u* is a highway . . . . Prov 15:19
that God made man *u* . . . . Eccl 7:29
and there is no one *u* . . . . Mic 7:2
his soul is not *u* . . . . Hab 2:4

UPRIGHTNESS

to show man His *u* . . . . Job 33:23
me in the land of *u* . . . . Ps 143:10
princes for their *u* . . . . Prov 17:26
of the just is *u* . . . . Is 26:7
land of *u* he will deal . . . . Is 26:10

UPROOT

then I will *u* . . . . 2 Chr 7:20
u you from the land . . . . Ps 52:5
u the wheat with . . . . Matt 13:29

UR OF THE CHALDEANS

City of Abram's early life, Gen 11:28–31; 15:7
Located in Mesopotamia by Stephen, Acts 7:2, 4

URIAH

Hittite; one of David's warriors, 2 Sam 23:39
Husband of Bathsheba; condemned to death by David, 2 Sam 11:1–27

URIJAH

High priest in Ahaz's time, 2 Kin 16:10–16
——— Prophet in Jeremiah's time, Jer 26:20–23

URIM

of judgment of *U* . . . . Ex 28:30
Thummim and Your *U* . . . . . . Deut 33:8

US

"God with *u* . . . . Matt 1:23
who is not against *u* . . . . Mark 9:40
If God is for *u* . . . . Rom 8:31
They went out from *u* . . . . . 1 John 2:19
of them were of *u* . . . . 1 John 2:19

USE

who spitefully *u* you . . . . Matt 5:44
leaving the natural *u* . . . . Rom 1:27
u this world as not . . . . 1 Cor 7:31
u liberty as an . . . . Gal 5:13
u a little wine . . . . 1 Tim 5:23
reason of *u* have their . . . . Heb 5:14

USELESS

all of them are *u* . . . . Is 44:9
are unprofitable and *u* . . . . Titus 3:9
one's religion is *u* . . . . James 1:26

USES

if one *u* it lawfully . . . . 1 Tim 1:8

USING

u no figure of speech . . . . . . John 16:29
perish with the *u* . . . . Col 2:22
u liberty as a . . . . 1 Pet 2:16

USURY

Take no *u* or . . . . Lev 25:36

put out his money at *u* . . . . Ps 15:5

UTTER

u pure knowledge . . . . Job 33:3
u dark sayings of old . . . . Ps 78:2
let not your heart *u* . . . . Eccl 5:2
lawful for a man to *u* . . . . 2 Cor 12:4

UTTERANCE

the Spirit gave them *u* . . . . Acts 2:4
u may be given to me . . . . Eph 6:19

UTTERED

The deep *u* its voice . . . . Hab 3:10
which cannot be *u* . . . . Rom 8:26
the seven thunders *u* . . . . Rev 10:4

UTTERMOST

upon them to the *u* . . . . 1 Thess 2:16
u those who come . . . . Heb 7:25

UTTERS

Day unto day *u* speech . . . . Ps 19:2
u His voice from . . . . Amos 1:2
and the great man *u* . . . . Mic 7:3

UZZAH

Son of Abinadab, struck down for touching the ark of the covenant, 2 Sam 6:3–11

UZZIAH

King of Judah, called Azariah, 2 Kin 14:21; 15:1–7
Reigns righteously, 2 Chr 26:1–15
Usurps priestly function; stricken with leprosy, 2 Chr 26:16–21
Life of, written by Isaiah, 2 Chr 26:22, 23

— V —

VAGABOND

v you shall be on the . . . . Gen 4:12

VAIN

the people plot a *v* . . . . Ps 2:1
v life which he passes . . . . Eccl 6:12
'I have labored in *v* . . . . Is 49:4
you believed in *v* . . . . 1 Cor 15:2

VALIANT

Only be *v* for me . . . . 1 Sam 18:17
They are not *v* for the . . . . Jer 9:3
v men swept away . . . . Jer 46:15

VALIANTLY

while Israel does *v* . . . . Num 24:18
God we will do *v* . . . . Ps 60:12
of the LORD does *v* . . . . Ps 118:15

VALLEY

I walk through the *v* . . . . Ps 23:4
pass through the *V* . . . . Ps 84:6
the verdure of the *v* . . . . Song 6:11
v shall be exalted . . . . Is 40:4
in the midst of the *v* . . . . Ezek 37:1
v shall be filled . . . . Luke 3:5

VALOR

a mighty man of *v* . . . . 1 Sam 16:18

VALUE

does not know its *v* . . . . Job 28:13

of more *v* than they . . . . Matt 6:26
they counted up the *v* . . . . Acts 19:19

VALUED

It cannot be *v* in the . . . . Job 28:16

VANISH

when it is hot, they *v* . . . . Job 6:17
For the heavens will *v* . . . . Is 51:6
knowledge, it will *v* . . . . 1 Cor 13:8
old is ready to *v* away . . . . Heb 8:13

VANISHED

and He *v* from their . . . . Luke 24:31

VANITY

of vanities, all is *v* . . . . Eccl 1:2

VAPOR

best state is but *v* . . . . Ps 39:5
surely every man is *v* . . . . Ps 39:11
It is even a *v* that . . . . James 4:14

VARIATION

whom there is no *v* . . . . James 1:17

VASHTI

Queen of Ahasuerus, deposed and divorced, Esth 1:9–22

VEGETABLES

and let them give us *v* . . . . Dan 1:12
is weak eats only *v* . . . . Rom 14:2

VEHEMENT

of fire, a most *v* . . . . Song 8:6

VEIL

he put a *v* on his face . . . . Ex 34:33
v of the temple was . . . . Matt 27:51
Moses, who put a *v* . . . . 2 Cor 3:13
Presence behind the *v* . . . . Heb 6:19

VENGEANCE

You shall not take *v* . . . . Lev 19:18
V is Mine . . . . Deut 32:35
spare in the day of *v* . . . . Prov 6:34
God will come with *v* . . . . Is 35:4
on the garments of *v* . . . . Is 59:17
let me see Your *v* . . . . Jer 11:20
are the days of *v* . . . . Luke 21:22
written, "*V* is Mine . . . . Rom 12:19
flaming fire taking *v* . . . . 2 Thess 1:8
suffering the *v* . . . . Jude 7

VENOM

It becomes cobra *v* . . . . Job 20:14

VESSEL

like a potter's *v* . . . . Ps 2:9
v that he made of clay . . . . Jer 18:4
like a precious *v* . . . . Jer 25:34
been emptied from *v* . . . . Jer 48:11
for he is a chosen *v* . . . . Acts 9:15
lump to make one *v* . . . . Rom 9:21
to possess his own *v* . . . . 1 Thess 4:4
to the weaker *v* . . . . 1 Pet 3:7

VESSELS

longsuffering the *v* . . . . Rom 9:22
treasure in earthen *v* . . . . 2 Cor 4:7
like the potter's *v* . . . . Rev 2:27

VEXED

grieved, and I was *v* . . . . Ps 73:21

WAVES
and here your proud *w* ...... Job 38:11
all Your *w* and billows ...... Ps 42:7
the noise of their *w* ...... Ps 65:7
the multitude of its *w* ...... Jer 51:42
was covered with the *w* ...... Matt 8:24
sea, tossed by the *w* ...... Matt 14:24
raging *w* of the sea ...... Jude 13

WAX
My heart is like *w* ...... Ps 22:14
w melts before the ...... Ps 68:2
mountains melt like *w* ...... Ps 97:5

WAY
and show them the *w* ...... Ex 18:20
day I am going the *w* ...... Josh 23:14
and the right *w* ...... 1 Sam 12:23
As for God, His *w* ...... 2 Sam 22:31
to a man whose *w* ...... Job 3:23
But He knows the *w* ...... Job 23:10
"Where is the *w* ...... Job 38:19
the LORD knows the *w* ...... Ps 1:6
you perish in the *w* ...... Ps 2:12
Teach me Your *w* ...... Ps 27:11
This is the *w* of those ...... Ps 49:13
w may be known on ...... Ps 67:2
Your *w* was in the sea ...... Ps 77:19
where there is no *w* ...... Ps 107:40
I have chosen the *w* ...... Ps 119:30
I hate every false *w* ...... Ps 119:104
in the *w* everlasting ...... Ps 139:24
and preserves the *w* ...... Prov 2:8
The *w* of the wicked is ...... Prov 4:19
instruction are the *w* ...... Prov 6:23
w that seems right ...... Prov 14:12
not know what is the *w* ...... Eccl 11:5
of terrors in the *w* ...... Eccl 12:5
The *w* of the just is ...... Is 26:7
"This is the *w* ...... Is 30:21
LORD, who makes a *w* ...... Is 43:16
wicked forsake his *w* ...... Is 55:7
O LORD, I know the *w* ...... Jer 10:23
one heart and one *w* ...... Jer 32:39
Israel, is it not My *w* ...... Ezek 18:25
w which is not fair ...... Ezek 33:17
and pervert the *w* ...... Amos 2:7
the LORD has His *w* ...... Nah 1:3
he will prepare the *w* ...... Mal 3:1
and broad is the *w* ...... Matt 7:13
and difficult is the *w* ...... Matt 7:14
will prepare Your *w* ...... Matt 11:10
and teach the *w* ...... Matt 22:16
and the *w* you know ...... John 14:4
to him, "I am the *w* ...... John 14:6
proclaim to us the *w* ...... Acts 16:17
explained to him the *w* ...... Acts 18:26
you a more excellent *w* ...... 1 Cor 12:31
w which He consecrated ...... Heb 10:20
forsaken the right *w* ...... 2 Pet 2:15
to have known the *w* ...... 2 Pet 2:21
have gone in the *w* ...... Jude 11

WAYS
for all His *w* are ...... Deut 32:4
they do not know its *w* ...... Job 24:13
is the first of the *w* ...... Job 40:19
Show me Your *w* ...... Ps 25:4
transgressors Your *w* ...... Ps 51:13
would walk in My *w* ...... Ps 81:13
w were directed ...... Ps 119:5
I thought about my *w* ...... Ps 119:59
righteous in all His *w* ...... Ps 145:17
For the *w* of man are ...... Prov 5:21
w please the LORD ...... Prov 16:7
He will teach us His *w* ...... Is 2:3
nor are your *w* ...... Is 55:8
"Stand in the *w* ...... Jer 6:16
"Amend your *w* ...... Jer 7:3
and examine our *w* ...... Lam 3:40
and owns all your *w* ...... Dan 5:23
w are everlasting ...... Hab 3:6
misery are in their *w* ...... Rom 3:16
judgments and His *w* ...... Rom 11:33
unstable in all his *w* ...... James 1:8
their destructive *w* ...... 2 Pet 2:2
and true are Your *w* ...... Rev 15:3

WEAK
then I shall become *w* ...... Judg 16:7
And I am *w* today ...... 2 Sam 3:39
me, O LORD, for I am *w* ...... Ps 6:2
gives power to the *w* ...... Is 40:29
knee will be as *w* ...... Ezek 7:17
let the *w* say ...... Joel 3:10
not your hands be *w* ...... Zeph 3:16
but the flesh is *w* ...... Matt 26:41
And not being *w* ...... Rom 4:19
Receive one who is *w* ...... Rom 14:1
God has chosen the *w* ...... 1 Cor 1:27
We are *w*, but you are ...... 1 Cor 4:10
to the *w* I became as *w* ...... 1 Cor 9:22
this reason many are *w* ...... 1 Cor 11:30
For when I am *w* ...... 2 Cor 12:10

WEAKENED
w my strength in the ...... Ps 102:23
the ground, you who *w* ...... Is 14:12

WEAKENS
w the hands of the men ...... Jer 38:4

WEAKER
house of Saul grew *w* ...... 2 Sam 3:1
the wife, as to the *w* ...... 1 Pet 3:7

WEAKNESS
than men, and the *w* ...... 1 Cor 1:25
I was with you in *w* ...... 1 Cor 2:3
It is sown in *w* ...... 1 Cor 15:43
is also subject to *w* ...... Heb 5:2
w were made strong ...... Heb 11:34

WEAKNESSES
also helps in our *w* ...... Rom 8:26
sympathize with our *w* ...... Heb 4:15

WEALTH
have gained me this *w* ...... Deut 8:17
a man of great *w* ...... Ruth 2:1
not asked riches or *w* ...... 2 Chr 1:11
who trust in their *w* ...... Ps 49:6
w is his strong city ...... Prov 10:15
W gained by dishonesty ...... Prov 13:11
W makes many friends ...... Prov 19:4
may bring to you the *w* ...... Is 60:11

WEALTHY
w nation that dwells ...... Jer 49:31
rich, have become *w* ...... Rev 3:17

WEANED
w child shall put his ...... Is 11:8
Those just *w* from milk ...... Is 28:9

WEAPON
w formed against you ...... Is 54:17
with a deadly *w* ...... Ezek 9:1

WEAPONS
is better than *w* ...... Eccl 9:18
the LORD and His *w* ...... Is 13:5
For the *w* of our ...... 2 Cor 10:4

WEAR
but the just will *w* ...... Job 27:17
'What shall we *w* ...... Matt 6:31

WEARIED
you have *w* Me with ...... Is 43:24
You are *w* in the ...... Is 57:10
and they have *w* ...... Jer 12:5
You have *w* the LORD ...... Mal 2:17
therefore, being *w* ...... John 4:6

WEARINESS
say, 'Oh, what a *w* ...... Mal 1:13
in *w* and toil ...... 2 Cor 11:27

WEARISOME
and much study is *w* ...... Eccl 12:12

WEARY
to Isaac, "I am *w* ...... Gen 27:46
lest he become *w* ...... Prov 25:17
As cold water to a *w* ...... Prov 25:25
No one will be *w* ...... Is 5:27
you may cause the *w* ...... Is 28:12
shall run and not be *w* ...... Is 40:31
to him who is *w* ...... Is 50:4
I am *w* of holding it ...... Jer 6:11
w themselves to commit ...... Jer 9:5
I was *w* of holding it ...... Jer 20:9
continual coming she *w* ...... Luke 18:5
And let us not grow *w* ...... Gal 6:9
do not grow *w* in ...... 2 Thess 3:13
lest you become *w* ...... Heb 12:3

WEATHER
a garment in cold *w* ...... Prov 25:20
'It will be fair *w* ...... Matt 16:2

WEDDING
were invited to the *w* ...... Matt 22:3
Come to the *w* ...... Matt 22:4
find, invite to the *w* ...... Matt 22:9
in with him to the *w* ...... Matt 25:10
day there was a *w* ...... John 2:1

WEEK
with many for one *w* ...... Dan 9:27
the first day of the *w* ...... Matt 28:1
the first day of the *w* ...... Acts 20:7
the first day of the *w* ...... 1 Cor 16:2

WEEKS
w are determined ...... Dan 9:24
w Messiah shall be cut ...... Dan 9:26

WEEP
"Hannah, why do you *w* ...... 1 Sam 1:8
a time to *w* ...... Eccl 3:4
you shall *w* no more ...... Is 30:19
it, my soul will *w* ...... Jer 13:17
W not for the dead ...... Jer 22:10
to the LORD, *w* between ...... Joel 2:17
this commotion and *w* ...... Mark 5:39
Blessed are you who *w* ...... Luke 6:21
to her, "Do not *w* ...... Luke 7:13
and you did not *w* ...... Luke 7:32
of Jerusalem, do not *w* ...... Luke 23:28
to the tomb to *w* there ...... John 11:31
w with those who *w* ...... Rom 12:15
those who *w* as though ...... 1 Cor 7:30

WEEPING
of Israel, who were *w* ...... Num 25:6

w as they went up ....2 Sam 15:30
the noise of the *w* ....Ezra 3:13
face is flushed from *w* ....Job 16:16
the voice of my *w* ....Ps 6:8
my drink with *w* ....Ps 102:9
of hosts called for *w* ....Is 22:12
w shall no longer ....Is 65:19
They shall come with *w* ....Jer 31:9
w they shall come ....Jer 50:4
were sitting there *w* ....Ezek 8:14
with fasting, with *w* ....Joel 2:12
with tears, with *w* ....Mal 2:13
There will be *w* ....Matt 8:12
outside by the tomb *w* ....John 20:11
"Woman, why are you *w* ...John 20:13
"What do you mean by *w* ...Acts 21:13

WEIGH

You *w* out the violence ....Ps 58:2
O Most Upright, You *w* ....Is 26:7

WEIGHED

nor can silver be *w* ....Job 28:15
W the mountains ....Is 40:12
You have been *w* ....Dan 5:27
lest your hearts be *w* ......Luke 21:34

WEIGHS

eyes, but the LORD *w* ....Prov 16:2
Where is he who *w* ....Is 33:18

WEIGHT

a perfect and just *w* ....Deut 25:15
a just *w* is His delight ....Prov 11:1
and eternal *w* of glory ......2 Cor 4:17
us lay aside every *w* ....Heb 12:1

WEIGHTIER

have neglected the *w* ....Matt 23:23

WELFARE

does not seek the *w* ....Jer 38:4

WELL

If you do *w* ....Gen 4:7
that it may go *w* ....Deut 4:40
you when you do *w* ....Ps 49:18
daughters have done *w* .....Prov 31:29
know that it will be *w* ....Eccl 8:12
wheel broken at the *w* ....Eccl 12:6
that it shall be *w* ....Is 3:10
"Those who are *w* ....Matt 9:12
said to him, '*W* done ....Matt 25:21
faith has made you *w* ....Mark 5:34
Now Jacob's *w* was ....John 4:6
the elders who rule *w* ....1 Tim 5:17

WELL-BEING

them, and their *w* ....Ps 69:22
each one the other's *w* .....1 Cor 10:24

WELLS

draw water from the *w* ....Is 12:3
These are *w* without ....2 Pet 2:17

WENT

They *w* out from us ....1 John 2:19

WEPT

and the man of God *w* ......2 Kin 8:11
for the people *w* ....Ezra 10:1
that I sat down and *w* ....Neh 1:4
Have I not *w* for him ....Job 30:25
down, yea, we *w* ....Ps 137:1
out and *w* bitterly ....Matt 26:75
He saw the city and *w* ....Luke 19:41
Jesus *w* ....John 11:35
So I *w* much ....Rev 5:4

WET

They are *w* with the ....Job 24:8
his body was *w* with ....Dan 4:33

WHEAT

with the finest of *w* ....Ps 81:16
we may trade *w* ....Amos 8:5
even sell the bad *w* ....Amos 8:6
but gather the *w* ....Matt 13:30
w falls into the ....John 12:24
perhaps *w* or some ....1 Cor 15:37
oil, fine flour and *w* ....Rev 18:13

WHEEL

brings the threshing *w* .....Prov 20:26
the fountain, or the *w* ....Eccl 12:6
in the middle of a *w* ....Ezek 1:16

WHEELS

off their chariot *w* ....Ex 14:25
the rumbling of his *w* ....Jer 47:3
appearance of the *w* ....Ezek 1:16
noise of rattling *w* ....Nah 3:2

WHERE

not knowing *w* he was ....Heb 11:8

WHIP

A *w* for the horse ....Prov 26:3
The noise of a *w* ....Nah 3:2

WHIRLWIND

Elijah went up by a *w* ....2 Kin 2:11
Job out of the *w* ....Job 38:1
them away as with a *w* ....Ps 58:9
w will take them away ....Is 40:24
w shall scatter them ....Is 41:16
w shall be raised ....Jer 25:32
has His way in the *w* ....Nah 1:3

WHISPER

my ear received a *w* ....Job 4:12
and wizards, who *w* ....Is 8:19

WHISPERER

w separates the best ....Prov 16:28

WHISPERERS

they are *w* ....Rom 1:29

WHISPERINGS

backbitings, *w* ....2 Cor 12:20

WHITE

My beloved is *w* ....Song 5:10
and make them *w* ....Dan 11:35
be purified, made *w* ....Dan 12:10
for they are already *w* ....John 4:35
walk with Me in *w* ....Rev 3:4
clothed in *w* garments ....Rev 3:5
behold, a *w* horse ....Rev 6:2
and made them *w* ....Rev 7:14
Then I saw a great *w* ....Rev 20:11

WHOLE

w body were an eye ....1 Cor 12:17

WHOLESOME

w tongue is a tree ....Prov 15:4
not consent to *w* words ....1 Tim 6:3

WHOLLY

w followed the LORD ....Deut 1:36
I will not leave you *w* ....Jer 46:28

WICKED

w shall be silent ....1 Sam 2:9
Should you help the *w* ......2 Chr 19:2
Why do the *w* live and ....Job 21:7
w are reserved for the ....Job 21:30
to nobles, 'You are *w* ....Job 34:18
with the *w* every day ....Ps 7:11
w is snared in the ....Ps 9:16
w shall be turned ....Ps 9:17
do the *w* renounce God ....Ps 10:13
w bend their bow ....Ps 11:2
w He will rain coals ....Ps 11:6
Evil shall slay the *w* ....Ps 34:21
w shall be no more ....Ps 37:10
The *w* watches the ....Ps 37:32
how long will the *w* ....Ps 94:3
and the *w* be no more ....Ps 104:35
is far from the *w* ....Ps 119:155
if there is any *w* ....Ps 139:24
w will be cut off from ....Prov 2:22
w will fall by his own ....Prov 11:5
LORD is far from the *w* ....Prov 15:29
w flee when no one ....Prov 28:1
Do not be overly *w* ....Eccl 7:17
not be well with the *w* ....Eccl 8:13
w forsake his way ....Is 55:7
But the *w* are like the ....Is 57:20
and desperately *w* ....Jer 17:9
w shall do wickedly ....Dan 12:10
at all acquit the *w* ....Nah 1:3
w one does not touch ....1 John 5:18
the sway of the *w* ....1 John 5:19

WICKEDLY

Will you speak *w* ....Job 13:7
God will never do *w* ....Job 34:12
Those who do *w* ....Dan 11:32
yes, all who do *w* ....Mal 4:1

WICKEDNESS

LORD saw that the *w* ....Gen 6:5
can I do this great *w* ....Gen 39:9
'*W* proceeds from the ....1 Sam 24:13
w oppress them ....2 Sam 7:10
Is not your *w* great ....Job 22:5
Oh, let the *w* of the ....Ps 7:9
alive into hell, for *w* ....Ps 55:15
in the tents of *w* ....Ps 84:10
I will not know *w* ....Ps 101:4
eat the bread of *w* ....Prov 4:17
w is an abomination ....Prov 8:7
w will not deliver ....Eccl 8:8
w burns as the ....Is 9:18
have trusted in your *w* ....Is 47:10
w will correct you ....Jer 2:19
wells up with her *w* ....Jer 6:7
man repented of his *w* ....Jer 8:6
not turn from his *w* ....Ezek 3:19
You have plowed *w* ....Hos 10:13
and cannot look on *w* ....Hab 1:13
for those who do *w* ....Mal 3:15
is full of greed and *w* ....Luke 11:39
sexual immorality, *w* ....Rom 1:29
spiritual hosts of *w* ....Eph 6:12
and overflow of *w* ....James 1:21

WIDE

shall open your hand *w* ....Deut 15:8
opened their mouth *w* ....Job 29:23
w his lips shall have ....Prov 13:3
will build myself a *w* ....Jer 22:14
w is the gate and ....Matt 7:13

all the treasures of *w* ....Col 2:3
Walk in *w* toward those ....Col 4:5
If any of you lacks *w* ....James 1:5
power and riches and *w* ....Rev 5:12
and glory and *w* ....Rev 7:12

WISE

great nation is a *w* ....Deut 4:6
He catches the *w* ....Job 5:13
God is *w* in heart and ....Job 9:4
men are not always *w* ....Job 32:9
when will you be *w* ....Ps 94:8
w will observe these ....Ps 107:43
Do not be *w* in your ....Prov 3:7
he who wins souls is *w* ......Prov 11:30
The *w* in heart will be ......Prov 16:21
folly, lest he be *w* ....Prov 26:5
they are exceedingly *w* .....Prov 30:24
The words of the *w* ....Eccl 12:11
They are *w* to do evil ....Jer 4:22
Therefore be *w* as ....Matt 10:16
five of them were *w* ....Matt 25:2
barbarians, both to *w* ....Rom 1:14
to God, alone *w* ....Rom 16:27
Where is the *w* ....1 Cor 1:20
sake, but you are *w* ....1 Cor 4:10
not as fools but as *w* ....Eph 5:15
are able to make you *w* .....2 Tim 3:15

WISELY

I will behave *w* ....Ps 101:2
who heeds the word *w* .....Prov 16:20
you do not inquire *w* ....Eccl 7:10

WISER

he was *w* than all men ......1 Kin 4:31
w than the birds ....Job 35:11
w than my enemies ....Ps 119:98
of God is *w* than men ....1 Cor 1:25

WISH

for me to do what I *w* ......Matt 20:15
w it were already ....Luke 12:49

WISHED

Then he *w* death for ....Jon 4:8

WITCHCRAFT

is as the sin of *w* ....1 Sam 15:23

WITHDRAW

God will not *w* His ....Job 9:13
He does not *w* His eyes ....Job 36:7
From such *w* yourself ....1 Tim 6:5

WITHER

also shall not *w* ....Ps 1:3
w as the green ....Ps 37:2
leaves will not *w* ....Ezek 47:12
How did the fig tree *w* .....Matt 21:20

WITHERS

The grass *w* ....Is 40:7
burning heat than it *w* .....James 1:11
The grass *w* ....1 Pet 1:24

WITHHELD

and your sins have *w* ....Jer 5:25

WITHHOLD

w Your tender mercies ....Ps 40:11
good thing will He *w* ....Ps 84:11
Do not *w* good from ....Prov 3:27
your cloak, do not *w* ....Luke 6:29

WITHOUT

having no hope and *w* ....Eph 2:12

pray *w* ceasing ....1 Thess 5:17
w controversy ....1 Tim 3:16
w works is dead ....James 2:26

WITHSTAND

was I that I could *w* ....Acts 11:17
you may be able to *w* ....Eph 6:13

WITHSTOOD

I *w* him to his face ....Gal 2:11

WITNESS

see, God is *w* between ......Gen 31:50
Surely even now my *w* ......Job 16:19
like the faithful *w* ....Ps 89:37
w does not lie ....Prov 14:5
have given him as a *w* ....Is 55:4
a true and faithful *w* ....Jer 42:5
I will be a swift *w* ....Mal 3:5
all the world as a *w* ....Matt 24:14
This man came for a *w* ....John 1:7
do not receive Our *w* ....John 3:11
"If I bear *w* of ....John 5:31
is another who bears *w* ......John 5:32
But I have a greater *w* ....John 5:36
who was bearing *w* ....Acts 14:3
For you will be His *w* ....Acts 22:15
For God is my *w* ....Phil 1:8
are three who bear *w* ....1 John 5:7
If we receive the *w* ....1 John 5:9
who bore *w* to the word ....Rev 1:2
Christ, the faithful *w* ....Rev 1:5
beheaded for their *w* ....Rev 20:4

WITNESSED

is revealed, being *w* ....Rom 3:21
w the good confession ......1 Tim 6:13

WITNESSES

of two or three *w* ....Deut 17:6
for Myself faithful *w* ....Is 8:2
"You are My *w* ....Is 43:10
the presence of many *w* .....1 Tim 6:12
the Holy Spirit also *w* ......Heb 10:15
so great a cloud of *w* ....Heb 12:1
give power to my two *w* ....Rev 11:3

WIVES

Husbands, love your *w* ....Eph 5:25
w must be reverent ....1 Tim 3:11

WIZARDS

who are mediums and *w* ....Is 8:19

WOLF

The *w* and the lamb ....Is 65:25
the sheep, sees the *w* ....John 10:12

WOLVES

they are ravenous *w* ....Matt 7:15
out as lambs among *w* ....Luke 10:3
savage *w* will come in ......Acts 20:29

WOMAN

she shall be called *W* ....Gen 2:23
w builds her house ....Prov 14:1
w who fears the LORD .....Prov 31:30
w shall encompass a ....Jer 31:22
whoever looks at a *w* ....Matt 5:28
"Do you see this *w* ....Luke 7:44
Then the *w* of Samaria ....John 4:9
brought to Him a *w* ....John 8:3
"*W*, behold your ....John 19:26
w was full of good ....Acts 9:36
natural use of the *w* ....Rom 1:27

a man not to touch a *w* ....1 Cor 7:1
w is the glory of man ....1 Cor 11:7
His Son, born of a *w* ....Gal 4:4
Let a *w* learn in ....1 Tim 2:11
I do not permit a *w* ....1 Tim 2:12
w being deceived ....1 Tim 2:14
w clothed with the sun ....Rev 12:1
the earth helped the *w* ......Rev 12:16

WOMB

nations are in your *w* ....Gen 25:23
LORD had closed her *w* .....1 Sam 1:5
took Me out of the *w* ....Ps 22:9
formed you from the *w* ....Is 44:2
called Me from the *w* ....Is 49:1
in the *w* I knew you ....Jer 1:5
is the fruit of your *w* ....Luke 1:42
"Blessed is the *w* ....Luke 11:27

WOMEN

blessed is she among *w* ......Judg 5:24
among Your honorable *w* ....Ps 45:9
O fairest among *w* ....Song 1:8
w rule over them ....Is 3:12
new wine the young *w* ....Zech 9:17
w will be grinding ....Matt 24:41
are you among *w* ....Luke 1:28
w keep silent in the ....1 Cor 14:34
admonish the young *w* ....Titus 2:4
times, the holy *w* ....1 Pet 3:5
not defiled with *w* ....Rev 14:4

WONDER

I have become as a *w* ....Ps 71:7
marvelous work and a *w* ....Is 29:14

WONDERFUL

name, seeing it is *w* ....Judg 13:18
Your love to me was *w* .....2 Sam 1:26
things too *w* for me ....Job 42:3
Your testimonies are *w* .....Ps 119:129
name will be called *W* ....Is 9:6
of hosts, who is *w* ....Is 28:29
and scribes saw the *w* ......Matt 21:15
our own tongues the *w* ....Acts 2:11

WONDERFULLY

fearfully and *w* made ....Ps 139:14

WONDERS

w which I will do ....Ex 3:20
are the God who does *w* ....Ps 77:14
Shall Your *w* be known ....Ps 88:12
who alone does great *w* ....Ps 136:4
Egypt with signs and *w* ....Jer 32:21
and how mighty His *w* ....Dan 4:3
He works signs and *w* ....Dan 6:27
"And I will show *w* ....Joel 2:30
and done many *w* ....Matt 7:22
signs, and lying *w* ....2 Thess 2:9
both with signs and *w* ....Heb 2:4

WONDROUS

and tell of all Your *w* ....Ps 26:7
w works declare that ....Ps 75:1
w works in the land of ....Ps 106:22
for they are a *w* ....Zech 3:8

WONDROUSLY

God, who has dealt *w* ....Joel 2:26

WOOD

precious stones, *w* ....1 Cor 3:12

WOODCUTTERS

but let them be *w* ....Josh 9:21

WOOL

they shall be as *w* ....Is 1:18
head was like pure *w* ....Dan 7:9
hair were white like *w* ....Rev 1:14

WORD

w that proceeds ....Deut 8:3
w is very near you ....Deut 30:14
w I have hidden ....Ps 119:11
w has given me life ....Ps 119:50
w is a lamp to my feet .....Ps 119:105
w makes it glad ....Prov 12:25
w spoken in due season ....Prov 15:23
w fitly spoken is ....Prov 25:11
Every *w* of God is pure ......Prov 30:5
The LORD sent a *w* ....Is 9:8
the *w* of our God ....Is 40:8
w has gone out of My ....Is 45:23
w be that goes forth ....Is 55:11
But His *w* was in my ....Jer 20:9
w will be his oracle ....Jer 23:36
w which I speak will ....Ezek 12:28
But only speak a *w* ....Matt 8:8
for every idle *w* ....Matt 12:36
The seed is the *w* ....Luke 8:11
mighty in deed and *w* ......Luke 24:19
beginning was the *W* ....John 1:1
W became flesh and ....John 1:14
if anyone keeps My *w* ....John 8:51
w which you hear is ....John 14:24
Your *w* is truth ....John 17:17
and glorified the *w* ....Acts 13:48
to one is given the *w* ....1 Cor 12:8
of water by the *w* ....Eph 5:26
holding fast the *w* ....Phil 2:16
Let the *w* of Christ ....Col 3:16
come to you in *w* only .....1 Thess 1:5
in every good *w* ....2 Thess 2:17
by the *w* of His power ....Heb 1:3
w which they heard did ....Heb 4:2
For the *w* of God is ....Heb 4:12
the implanted *w* ....James 1:21
does not stumble in *w* ....James 3:2
through the *w* of God ....1 Pet 1:23
that by the *w* of God ....2 Pet 3:5
whoever keeps His *w* ....1 John 2:5
let us not love in *w* ....1 John 3:18
the Father, the *W* ....1 John 5:7
name is called The *W* ....Rev 19:13

WORDS

Give ear to my *w* ....Ps 5:1
Let the *w* of my mouth ....Ps 19:14
How sweet are Your *w* .....Ps 119:103
pay attention to the *w* ....Prov 7:24
The *w* of the wise are ....Eccl 12:11
And I have put My *w* ....Is 51:16
Take *w* with you ....Hos 14:2
Do not My *w* do good to ....Mic 2:7
pass away, but My *w* ....Matt 24:35
at the gracious *w* ....Luke 4:22
w that I speak to you ....John 6:63
You have the *w* of ....John 6:68
And remember the *w* ....Acts 20:35
not with wisdom of *w* ......1 Cor 1:17
those who hear the *w* ....Rev 1:3
is he who keeps the *w* ....Rev 22:7

WORK

day God ended His *w* ....Gen 2:2
Moses finished the *w* ....Ex 40:33
people had a mind to *w* ....Neh 4:6
You shall desire the *w* ....Job 14:15
for they are all the *w* ....Job 34:19
the *w* of Your fingers ....Ps 8:3
I hate the *w* of those ....Ps 101:3
the heavens are the *w* ....Ps 102:25
Man goes out to his *w* ....Ps 104:23
w is honorable and ....Ps 111:3
man does deceptive *w* ......Prov 11:18
then I saw all the *w* ....Eccl 8:17
for there is no *w* ....Eccl 9:10
God will bring every *w* ......Eccl 12:14
that He may do His *w* ....Is 28:21
and all we are the *w* ....Is 64:8
him nothing for his *w* ....Jer 22:13
and mighty in *w* ....Jer 32:19
For I will *w* a *w* ....Hab 1:5
and said, 'Son, go, *w* ....Matt 21:28
could do no mighty *w* ....Mark 6:5
we do, that we may *w* ....John 6:28
"This is the *w* of God ....John 6:29
I must *w* the works ....John 9:4
w which You have given ......John 17:4
know that all things *w* ....Rom 8:28
He will finish the *w* ....Rom 9:28
w is no longer *w* ....Rom 11:6
Do not destroy the *w* ....Rom 14:20
w will become manifest .....1 Cor 3:13
Are you not my *w* ....1 Cor 9:1
abounding in the *w* ....1 Cor 15:58
without ceasing your *w* ....1 Thess 1:3
every good word and *w* ...2 Thess 2:17
If anyone will not *w* ......2 Thess 3:10
but a doer of the *w* ....James 1:25

WORKED

with one hand they *w* ....Neh 4:17
and wonders God had *w* ...Acts 15:12
which He *w* in Christ ....Eph 1:20

WORKER

w is worthy of his ....Matt 10:10
Timothy, my fellow *w* ......Rom 16:21
w who does not need ....2 Tim 2:15

WORKERS

You hate all *w* of ....Ps 5:5
we are God's fellow *w* ....1 Cor 3:9
dogs, beware of evil *w* ....Phil 3:2

WORKING

everywhere, the Lord *w* ...Mark 16:20
My Father has been *w* ......John 5:17
according to the *w* ....Eph 1:19
through faith in the *w* ....Col 2:12
manner, not *w* at all ......2 Thess 3:11

WORKMANSHIP

For we are His *w* ....Eph 2:10

WORKS

the wondrous *w* of God .....Job 37:14
are Your wonderful *w* ....Ps 40:5
Come and see the *w* ....Ps 66:5
how great are Your *w* ....Ps 92:5
manifold are Your *w* ....Ps 104:24
The *w* of the LORD are ....Ps 111:2
w shall praise You ....Ps 145:10
and let her own *w* ....Prov 31:31
"For I know their *w* ....Is 66:18
of whose *w* are truth ....Dan 4:37
show Him greater *w* ....John 5:20
w that I do in My ....John 10:25
w that I do he will do ......John 14:12
w righteousness ....Acts 10:35
might stand, not of *w* ....Rom 9:11
let us cast off the *w* ....Rom 13:12
is the same God who *w* .....1 Cor 12:6
not justified by the *w* ....Gal 2:16
Now the *w* of the flesh ....Gal 5:19
the spirit who now *w* ....Eph 2:2
not of *w*, lest anyone ....Eph 2:9
with the unfruitful *w* ....Eph 5:11
for it is God who *w* ....Phil 2:13
w they deny Him ....Titus 1:16
zealous for good *w* ....Titus 2:14
repentance from dead *w* ......Heb 6:1
but does not have *w* ....James 2:14
also justified by *w* ....James 2:25
He might destroy the *w* .....1 John 3:8
"I know your *w* ....Rev 2:2
their *w* follow them ....Rev 14:13
according to their *w* ....Rev 20:12

WORLD

He shall judge the *w* ....Ps 9:8
For the *w* is Mine ....Ps 50:12
w is established ....Ps 93:1
The field is the *w* ....Matt 13:38
w are more shrewd ....Luke 16:8
He was in the *w* ....John 1:10
For God so loved the *w* .....John 3:16
His Son into the *w* ....John 3:17
the Savior of the *w* ....John 4:42
w cannot hate you ....John 7:7
You are of this *w* ....John 8:23
Look, the *w* has gone ......John 12:19
w will see Me no more .....John 14:19
"If the *w* hates you ....John 15:18
If you were of the *w* ....John 15:19
I have overcome the *w* .....John 16:33
do not pray for the *w* ....John 17:9
w has not known You ......John 17:25
w may become guilty ....Rom 3:19
be conformed to this *w* ......Rom 12:2
things of the *w* ....1 Cor 1:27
w is foolishness ....1 Cor 3:19
w has been crucified ....Gal 6:14
without God in the *w* ....Eph 2:12
loved this present *w* ....2 Tim 4:10
He has not put the *w* ....Heb 2:5
unspotted from the *w* ......James 1:27
w is enmity with God ....James 4:4
Do not love the *w* ....1 John 2:15
all that is in the *w* ....1 John 2:16
w is passing away ....1 John 2:17
w does not know us ....1 John 3:1
They are of the *w* ....1 John 4:5
so are we in this *w* ....1 John 4:17
And all the *w* marveled ....Rev 13:3

WORLDS

also He made the *w* ....Heb 1:2

WORM

w should feed sweetly ....Job 24:20
But I am a *w* ....Ps 22:6
"Fear not, you *w* ....Is 41:14
their *w* does not die ....Is 66:24
w does not die and the .....Mark 9:44

WORMS

flesh is caked with *w* ....Job 7:5
you, and *w* cover you ....Is 14:11
And he was eaten by *w* ....Acts 12:23

WORMWOOD

end she is bitter as *w* ....Prov 5:4
who turn justice to *w* ....Amos 5:7
of the star is *W* ....Rev 8:11

WORRY

to you, do not *w* ....Matt 6:25
Therefore do not *w* ....Matt 6:31

YES

let your 'Y' be 'Y,' .... Matt 5:37
No, but in Him was Y ...... 2 Cor 1:19

YESTERDAY

For we were born y .... Job 8:9

YOKE

you shall break his y .... Gen 27:40
and He will put a y .... Deut 28:48
Your father made our y ..... 1 Kin 12:4
You have broken the y .... Is 9:4
Take My y upon you .... Matt 11:29

YOKED

Do not be unequally y ...... 2 Cor 6:14

YOUNG

His flesh shall be y .... Job 33:25
I have been y .... Ps 37:25
she may lay her y .... Ps 84:3
y ones shall lie .... Is 11:7
dream dreams, your y .... Joel 2:28
y man followed Him .... Mark 14:51
I write to you, y .... 1 John 2:13

YOUNGER

they mock at me, men y ...... Job 30:1
y son gathered all .... Luke 15:13
let him be as the y .... Luke 22:26
y women as sisters .... 1 Tim 5:2
Likewise you y people .... 1 Pet 5:5

YOURS

all that I have are y .... 1 Kin 20:4
the battle is not y .... 2 Chr 20:15
I am Y, save me .... Ps 119:94
Y is the kingdom .... Matt 6:13
Take what is y .... Matt 20:14
y is the kingdom .... Luke 6:20
And all Mine are Y .... John 17:10
For all things are y .... 1 Cor 3:21
for I do not seek y .... 2 Cor 12:14

YOUTH

for he was only a y .... 1 Sam 17:42
the LORD from my y ...... 1 Kin 18:12
the sins of my y .... Ps 25:7
the companion of her y ...... Prov 2:17
in the days of your y .... Eccl 11:9
the shame of your y .... Is 54:4
speak, for I am a y .... Jer 1:6
I have kept from my y ...... Matt 19:20
no one despise your y ...... 1 Tim 4:12

YOUTHFUL

Flee also y lusts .... 2 Tim 2:22

—Z—

ZACCHAEUS

Wealthy tax collector converted to Christ, Luke 19:1–10

ZACHARIAS

Father of John the Baptist, Luke 1:5–17

ZADOK

Co-priest with Abiathar; remains loyal to David, 2 Sam 15:24–29; 20:25
Rebuked by David, 2 Sam 19:11, 12
Does not follow Adonijah; anoints Solomon, 1 Kin 1:8–45
Takes Abiathar's place, 1 Kin 2:35

ZALMUNNA

Midianite king, Judg 8:4–21

ZAREPHATH

Town of Sidon where Elijah revives widow's son, 1 Kin 17:8–24; Luke 4:26

ZEAL

The z of the LORD of ...... 2 Kin 19:31
z has consumed me .... Ps 119:139
He shall stir up His z .... Is 42:13
have spoken it in My z ...... Ezek 5:13
for Zion with great z .... Zech 8:2
"Z for Your house has ...... John 2:17
that they have a z .... Rom 10:2
z has stirred up the .... 2 Cor 9:2

ZEALOUS

"I have been very z .... 1 Kin 19:10
'I am z for Zion with .... Zech 8:2
since you are z .... 1 Cor 14:12
But it is good to be z .... Gal 4:18
z for good works .... Titus 2:14

ZEBAH

King of Midian killed by Gideon, Judg 8:4–28

ZEBEDEE

Galilean fisherman; father of James and John, Matt 4:21, 22

ZEBULUN

Sixth son of Jacob and Leah, Gen 30:19, 20
Prophecy concerning, Gen 49:13
—— Tribe of:
Numbered, Num 1:30, 31; 26:27
Territory assigned to, Josh 19:10–16
Joins Gideon in battle, Judg 6:34, 35
Some respond to Hezekiah's reforms, 2 Chr 30:10–18
Christ visits territory of, Matt 4:13–16

ZECHARIAH

King of Israel; last ruler of Jehu's dynasty, 2 Kin 15:8–12
—— Postexilic prophet and priest, Ezra 5:1; Zech 1:1, 7

ZEDEKIAH

Last king of Judah; uncle and successor of Jehoiachin; reigns wickedly, 2 Kin 24:17–19; 2 Chr 36:10
Rebels against Nebuchadnezzar, 2 Chr 36:11–13
Denounced by Jeremiah, Jer 34:1–22
Consults Jeremiah, Jer 37; 38
Captured and taken to Babylon, 2 Kin 25:1–7; Jer 39:1–7

ZELOPHEHAD

Manassite whose five daughters secure female rights, Num 27:1–7

ZEPHANIAH

Author of Zephaniah, Zeph 1:1
—— Priest and friend of Jeremiah during Zedekiah's reign, Jer 21:1

ZERUBBABEL

Descendant of David, 1 Chr 3:1–19
Leader of Jewish exiles, Neh 7:6, 7; Hag 2:21–23
Rebuilds the temple, Ezra 3:1–10; Zech 4:1–14

ZIBA

Saul's servant, 2 Sam 9:9
Befriends David, 2 Sam 16:1–4
Accused of deception by Mephibosheth, 2 Sam 19:17–30

ZIKLAG

City on the border of Judah, Josh 15:1, 31
Held by David, 1 Sam 27:6
Overthrown by Amalekites, 1 Sam 30:1–31

ZILPAH

Leah's maid, Gen 29:24
Mother of Gad and Asher, Gen 30:9–13

ZIMRI

Simeonite prince slain by Phinehas, Num 25:6–14
—— King of Israel for seven days, 1 Kin 16:8–20

ZIN

Wilderness through which the Israelites passed, Num 20:1
Border between Judah and Edom, Josh 15:1–3

ZION

Literally, an area in Jerusalem; called the City of David, 2 Sam 5:6–9; 2 Chr 5:2
Used figuratively of God's kingdom, Ps 125:1; Heb 12:22; Rev 14:1

ZIPPORAH

Daughter of Jethro; wife of Moses, Ex 18:1, 2

ZOAR

Ancient city of Canaan originally named Bela, Gen 14:2, 8
Spared destruction at Lot's request, Gen 19:20–23

ZOPHAR

Naamathite; friend of Job, Job 2:11

Index to Maps

Map 1. The Nations of Genesis 10
Map 2. The Exodus from Egypt
Map 3. The Conquest of Canaan
Map 4. The Kingdom Years
Map 6. Palestine in Christ's Time
Map 7. Paul's First and Second Journeys
Map 8. Paul's Third and Fourth Journeys
Map 9. The Holy Land in Modern Times

Index to Maps

Map 5. Jerusalem—From David to Christ

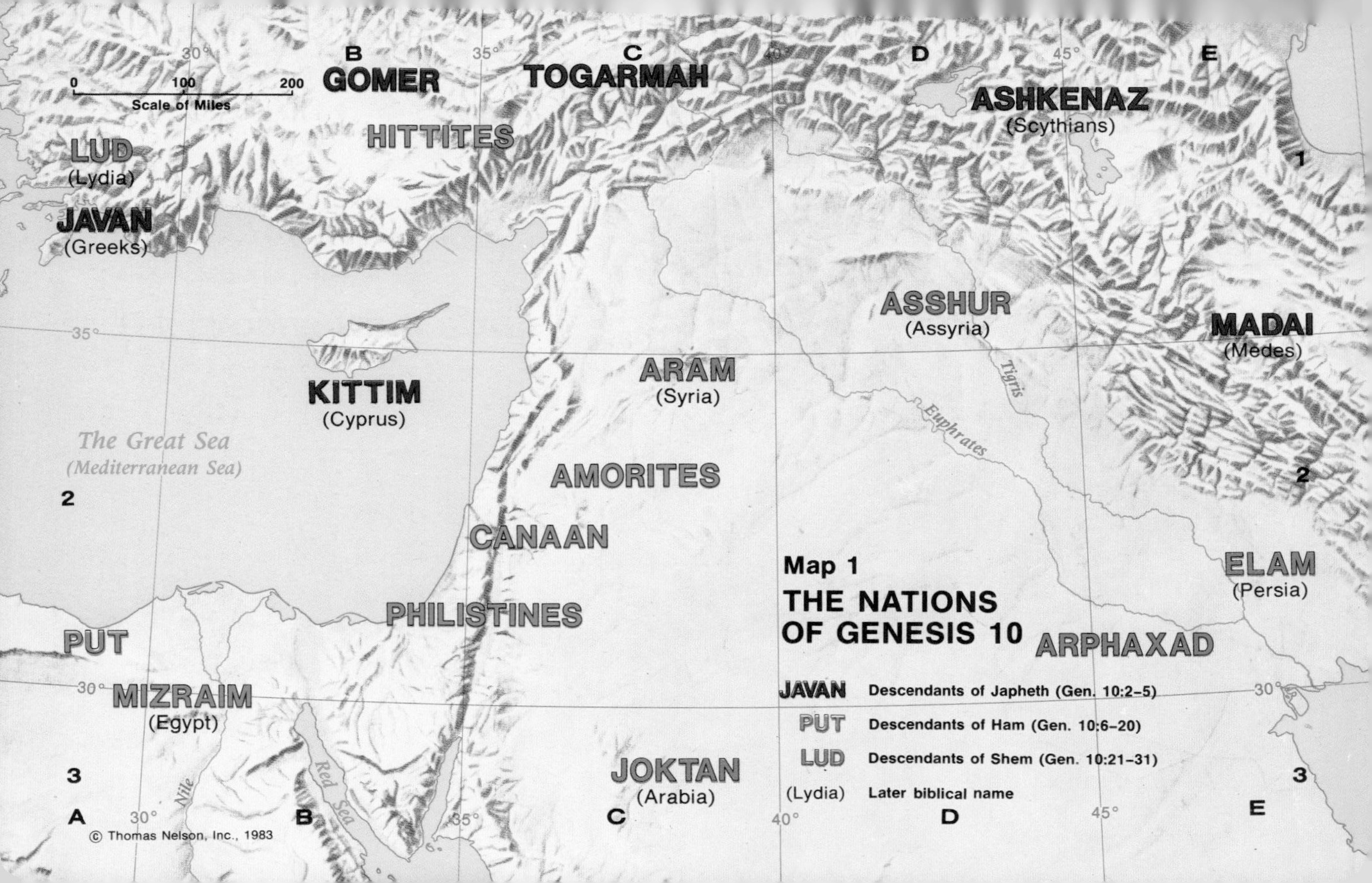

Map 1
THE NATIONS OF GENESIS 10
JAVAN Descendants of Japheth (Gen. 10:2–5)
PUT Descendants of Ham (Gen. 10:6–20)
LUD Descendants of Shem (Gen. 10:21–31)
(Lydia) Later biblical name
0 100 200
Scale of Miles
GOMER
TOGARMAH
ASHKENAZ
(Scythians)
HITTITES
LUD
(Lydia)
JAVAN
(Greeks)
ASSHUR
(Assyria)
MADAI
(Medes)
ARAM
(Syria)
KITTIM
(Cyprus)
The Great Sea
(Mediterranean Sea)
AMORITES
CANAAN
ELAM
(Persia)
PHILISTINES
ARPHAXAD
PUT
MIZRAIM
(Egypt)
JOKTAN
(Arabia)
Tigris
Euphrates
Nile
Red Sea
A
B
C
D
E
1
2
3
30°
35°
40°
45°
© Thomas Nelson, Inc., 1983

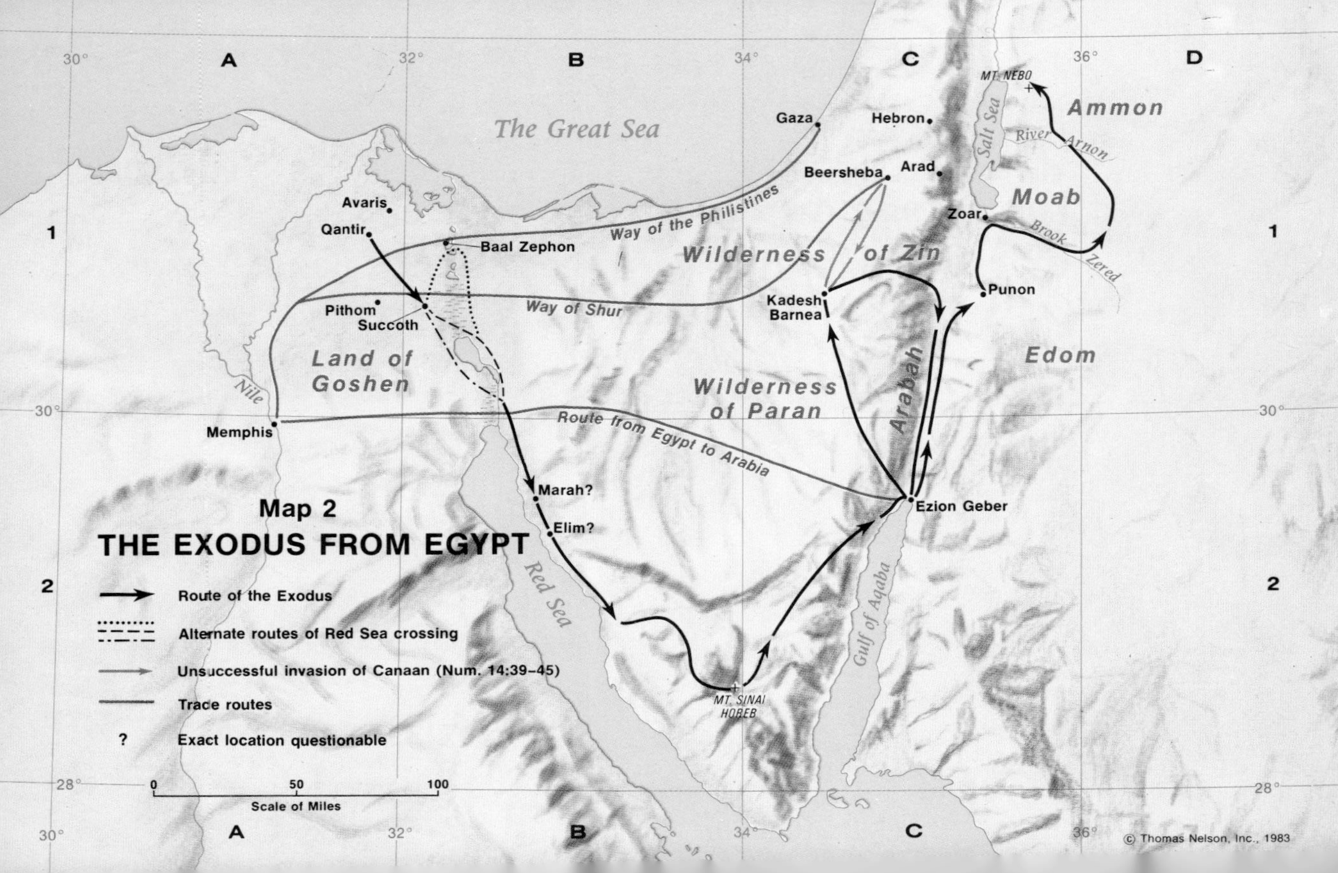
Map 2
THE EXODUS FROM EGYPT
Route of the Exodus
Alternate routes of Red Sea crossing
Unsuccessful invasion of Canaan (Num. 14:39–45)
Trace routes
?
Exact location questionable
0
50
100
Scale of Miles
The Great Sea
Gaza
Hebron
Arad
Beersheba
MT. NEBO
Salt Sea
Ammon
River
Arnon
Moab
Zoar
Brook
Zered
Punon
Edom
Avaris
Qantir
Baal Zephon
Way of the Philistines
Wilderness
of Zin
Kadesh
Barnea
Pithom
Succoth
Way of Shur
Land of
Goshen
Nile
Memphis
Wilderness
of Paran
Arabah
Route from Egypt to Arabia
Marah?
Elim?
Ezion Geber
Red Sea
Gulf of Aqaba
MT. SINAI
HOREB
A
B
C
D
1
2
30°
32°
34°
36°
28°
© Thomas Nelson, Inc., 1983

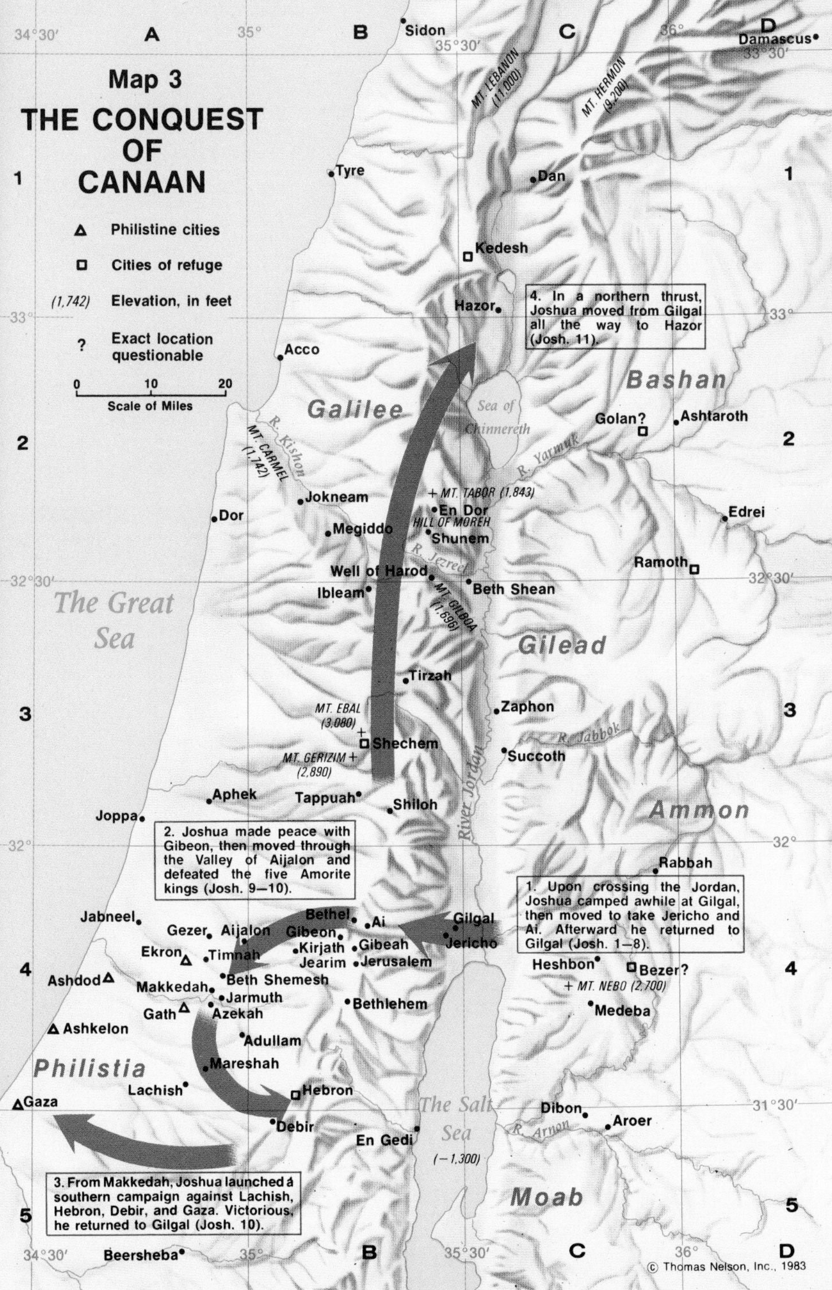

Map 3
THE CONQUEST OF CANAAN
Philistine cities
Cities of refuge
(1,742) Elevation, in feet
? Exact location questionable
0 10 20
Scale of Miles
A
B
C
D
34°30′
35°
35°30′
36°
33°30′
33°
32°30′
32°
31°30′
1
2
3
4
5
Sidon
Damascus
MT. LEBANON (11,000)
MT. HERMON (9,200)
Tyre
Dan
Kedesh
Hazor
4. In a northern thrust, Joshua moved from Gilgal all the way to Hazor (Josh. 11).
Acco
Bashan
Galilee
Sea of Chinnereth
Golan?
Ashtaroth
R. Kishon
MT. CARMEL (1,742)
R. Yarmuk
Jokneam
+ MT. TABOR (1,843)
En Dor
HILL OF MOREH
Dor
Megiddo
Shunem
Edrei
R. Jezreel
Ramoth
Well of Harod
Beth Shean
Ibleam
MT. GILBOA (1,696)
The Great Sea
Gilead
Tirzah
MT. EBAL (3,080)
Zaphon
R. Jabbok
Shechem
MT. GERIZIM (2,890)
Succoth
River Jordan
Aphek
Tappuah
Shiloh
Joppa
Ammon
2. Joshua made peace with Gibeon, then moved through the Valley of Aijalon and defeated the five Amorite kings (Josh. 9—10).
Rabbah
1. Upon crossing the Jordan, Joshua camped awhile at Gilgal, then moved to take Jericho and Ai. Afterward he returned to Gilgal (Josh. 1—8).
Jabneel
Bethel
Ai
Gilgal
Gezer
Aijalon
Gibeon
Jericho
Ekron
Timnah
Kirjath Jearim
Gibeah
Jerusalem
Heshbon
Bezer?
Ashdod
Makkedah
Beth Shemesh
+ MT. NEBO (2,700)
Jarmuth
Gath
Azekah
Bethlehem
Medeba
Ashkelon
Adullam
Philistia
Mareshah
Lachish
Hebron
Gaza
The Salt Sea
(−1,300)
Dibon
Aroer
R. Arnon
Debir
En Gedi
3. From Makkedah, Joshua launched a southern campaign against Lachish, Hebron, Debir, and Gaza. Victorious, he returned to Gilgal (Josh. 10).
Moab
Beersheba

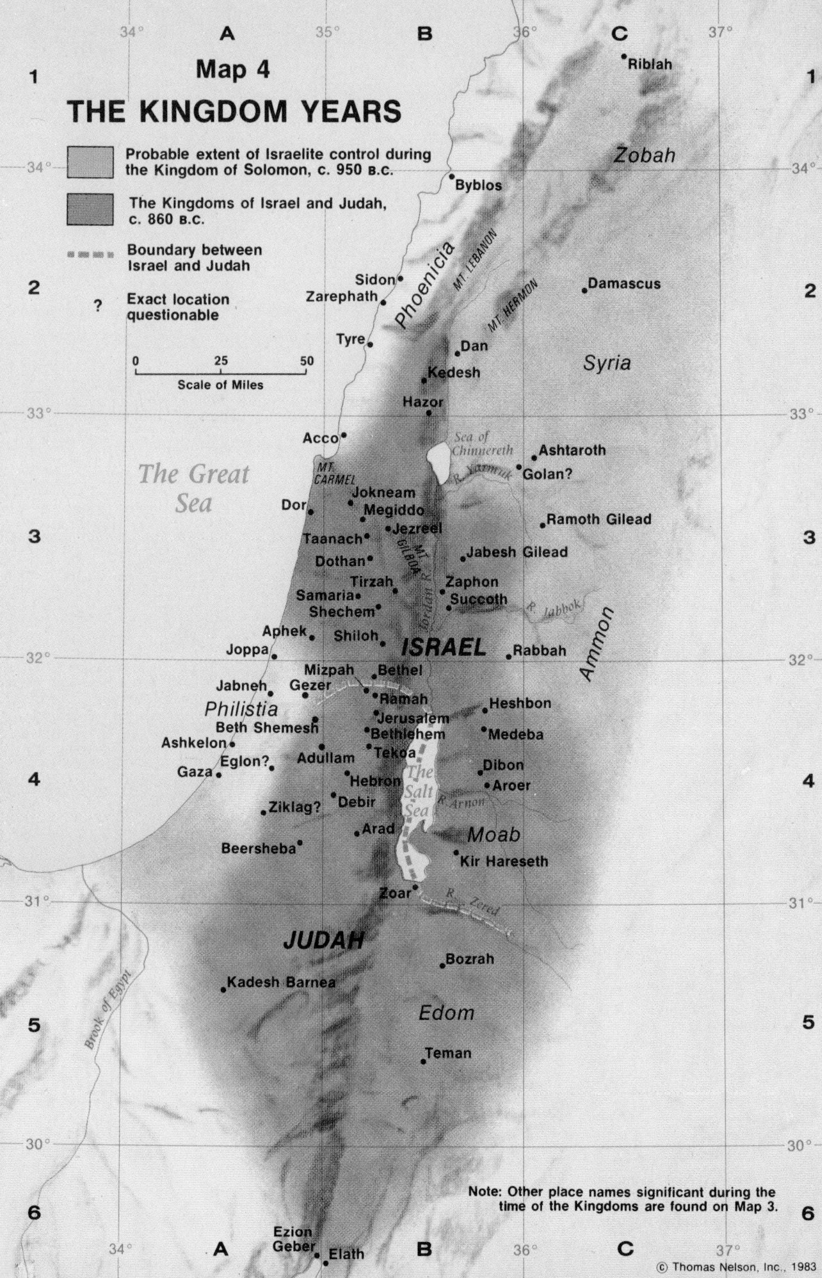
Map 4
THE KINGDOM YEARS
Probable extent of Israelite control during the Kingdom of Solomon, c. 950 B.C.
The Kingdoms of Israel and Judah, c. 860 B.C.
Boundary between Israel and Judah
? Exact location questionable
0 25 50
Scale of Miles
A
B
C
34°
35°
36°
37°
1
2
3
4
5
6
33°
32°
31°
30°
Riblah
Zobah
Byblos
Phoenicia
MT. LEBANON
MT. HERMON
Sidon
Zarephath
Damascus
Tyre
Dan
Kedesh
Syria
Hazor
Acco
Sea of Chinnereth
Ashtaroth
Golan?
R. Yarmuk
MT. CARMEL
The Great Sea
Jokneam
Megiddo
Dor
Jezreel
Ramoth Gilead
Taanach
MT. GILBOA
Dothan
Jabesh Gilead
Tirzah
Zaphon
Samaria
Succoth
Jordan R.
Shechem
R. Jabbok
Ammon
Aphek
Shiloh
ISRAEL
Rabbah
Joppa
Mizpah
Bethel
Jabneh
Gezer
Ramah
Heshbon
Philistia
Jerusalem
Beth Shemesh
Bethlehem
Medeba
Ashkelon
Tekoa
Adullam
Eglon?
Dibon
Gaza
Hebron
The Salt Sea
Aroer
Debir
R. Arnon
Ziklag?
Arad
Moab
Beersheba
Kir Hareseth
Zoar
R. Zered
JUDAH
Bozrah
Kadesh Barnea
Brook of Egypt
Edom
Teman
Note: Other place names significant during the time of the Kingdoms are found on Map 3.
Ezion Geber
Elath
© Thomas Nelson, Inc., 1983

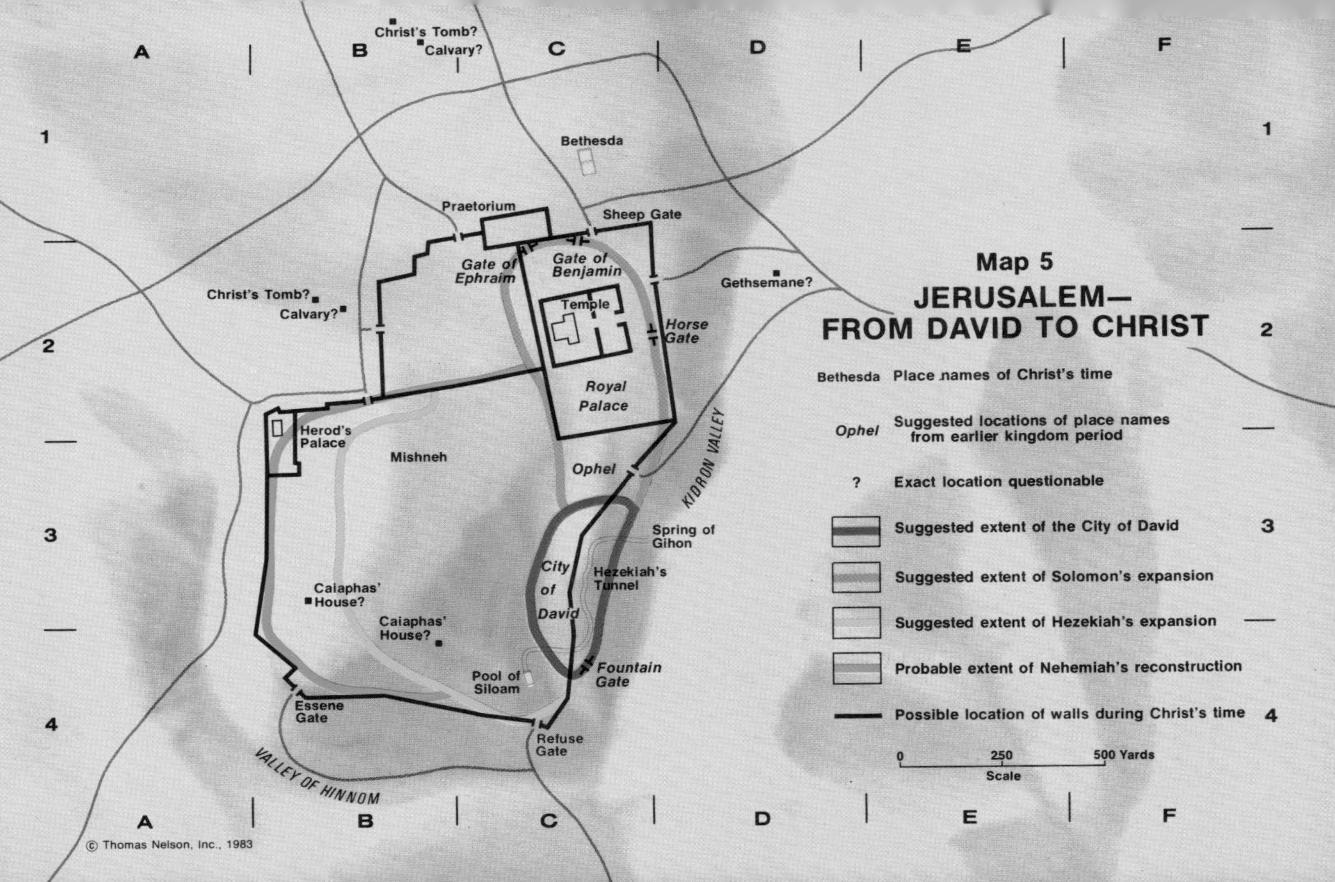
Map 5
JERUSALEM—
FROM DAVID TO CHRIST
Bethesda Place names of Christ's time
Ophel Suggested locations of place names from earlier kingdom period
? Exact location questionable
Suggested extent of the City of David
Suggested extent of Solomon's expansion
Suggested extent of Hezekiah's expansion
Probable extent of Nehemiah's reconstruction
Possible location of walls during Christ's time
0
250
500 Yards
Scale
A
B
C
D
E
F
1
2
3
4
Christ's Tomb?
Calvary?
Bethesda
Praetorium
Sheep Gate
Gate of Ephraim
Gate of Benjamin
Gethsemane?
Temple
Horse Gate
Royal Palace
Herod's Palace
Mishneh
Ophel
KIDRON VALLEY
Spring of Gihon
City of David
Hezekiah's Tunnel
Caiaphas' House?
Caiaphas' House?
Pool of Siloam
Fountain Gate
Essene Gate
Refuse Gate
VALLEY OF HINNOM

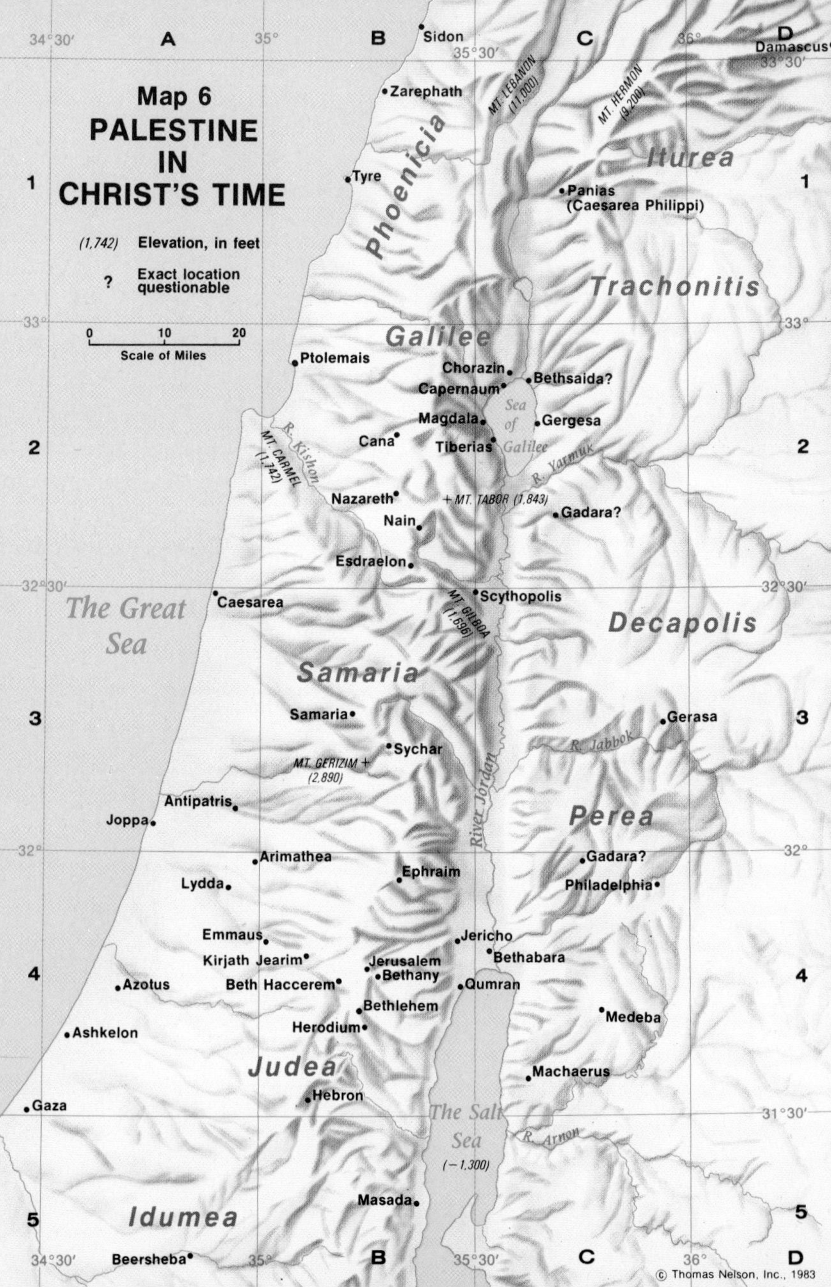

Map 6
PALESTINE IN CHRIST'S TIME
(1,742) Elevation, in feet
? Exact location questionable
0 10 20
Scale of Miles
A
B
C
D
1
2
3
4
5
34°30′
35°
35°30′
36°
33°30′
33°
32°30′
32°
31°30′
Sidon
Damascus
Zarephath
MT. LEBANON (11,000)
MT. HERMON (9,200)
Phoenicia
Iturea
Tyre
Panias (Caesarea Philippi)
Trachonitis
Galilee
Ptolemais
Chorazin
Bethsaida?
Capernaum
Sea of Galilee
Magdala
Gergesa
Cana
Tiberias
R. Kishon
MT. CARMEL (1,742)
R. Yarmuk
Nazareth
+ MT. TABOR (1,843)
Gadara?
Nain
Esdraelon
Scythopolis
MT. GILBOA (1,696)
Caesarea
The Great Sea
Decapolis
Samaria
Samaria
Gerasa
Sychar
R. Jabbok
MT. GERIZIM + (2,890)
River Jordan
Antipatris
Joppa
Perea
Arimathea
Gadara?
Ephraim
Lydda
Philadelphia
Emmaus
Jericho
Kirjath Jearim
Bethabara
Jerusalem
Bethany
Azotus
Beth Haccerem
Qumran
Bethlehem
Medeba
Herodium
Ashkelon
Judea
Machaerus
Hebron
Gaza
The Salt Sea (−1,300)
R. Arnon
Masada
Idumea
Beersheba

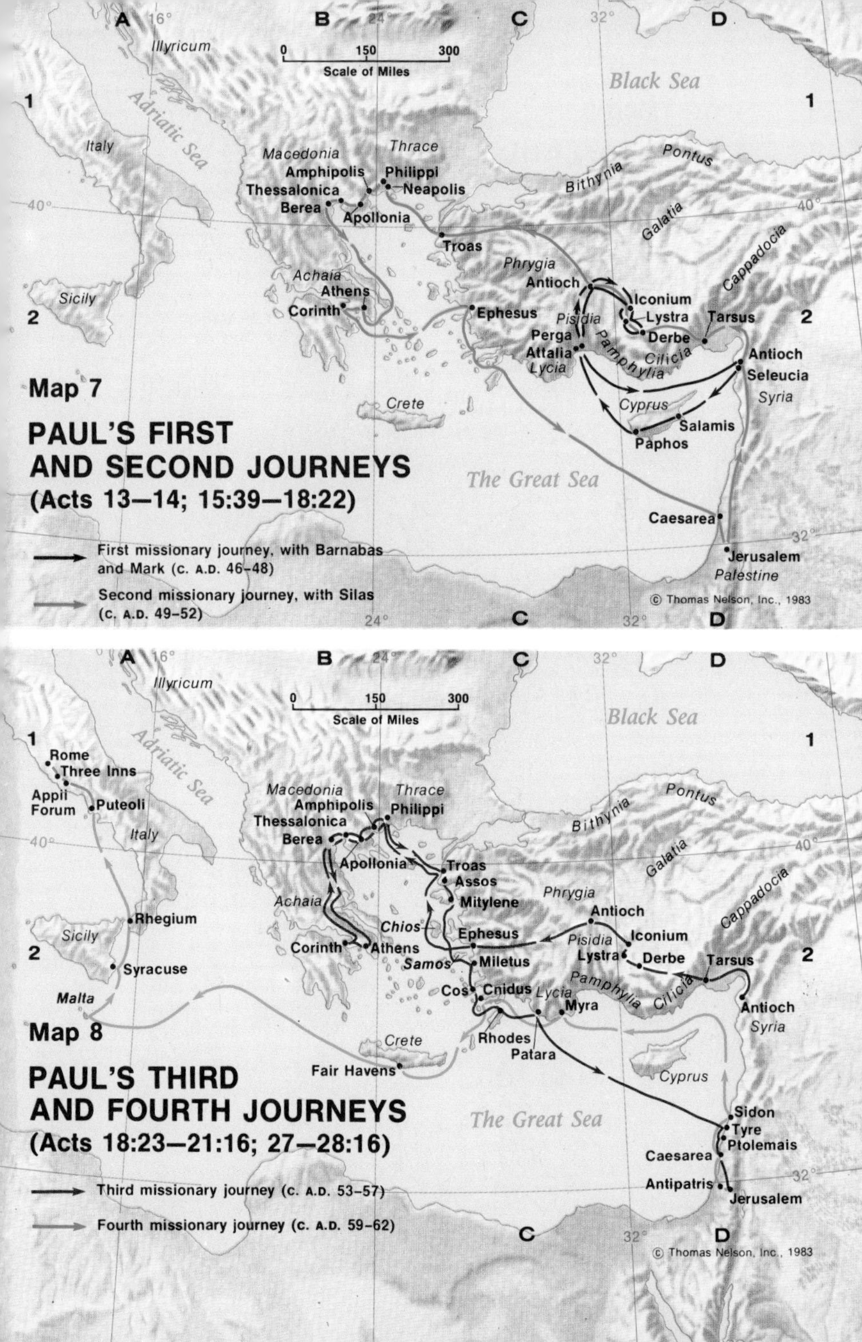

Map 7
PAUL'S FIRST AND SECOND JOURNEYS
(Acts 13–14; 15:39–18:22)
First missionary journey, with Barnabas and Mark (c. A.D. 46–48)
Second missionary journey, with Silas (c. A.D. 49–52)
Scale of Miles
0
150
300
Illyricum
Adriatic Sea
Italy
Sicily
Macedonia
Thrace
Amphipolis
Philippi
Neapolis
Thessalonica
Berea
Apollonia
Troas
Achaia
Athens
Corinth
Ephesus
Black Sea
Pontus
Bithynia
Galatia
Cappadocia
Phrygia
Antioch
Iconium
Lystra
Derbe
Pisidia
Perga
Attalia
Lycia
Pamphylia
Cilicia
Tarsus
Antioch
Seleucia
Syria
Cyprus
Salamis
Paphos
Crete
The Great Sea
Caesarea
Jerusalem
Palestine
© Thomas Nelson, Inc., 1983
Map 8
PAUL'S THIRD AND FOURTH JOURNEYS
(Acts 18:23–21:16; 27–28:16)
Third missionary journey (c. A.D. 53–57)
Fourth missionary journey (c. A.D. 59–62)
Scale of Miles
0
150
300
Illyricum
Adriatic Sea
Rome
Three Inns
Appii Forum
Puteoli
Italy
Rhegium
Sicily
Syracuse
Malta
Macedonia
Thrace
Amphipolis
Philippi
Thessalonica
Berea
Apollonia
Troas
Assos
Mitylene
Achaia
Chios
Corinth
Athens
Samos
Ephesus
Miletus
Cos
Cnidus
Rhodes
Patara
Lycia
Myra
Crete
Fair Havens
Black Sea
Pontus
Bithynia
Galatia
Cappadocia
Phrygia
Antioch
Pisidia
Iconium
Lystra
Derbe
Pamphylia
Cilicia
Tarsus
Antioch
Syria
Cyprus
The Great Sea
Sidon
Tyre
Ptolemais
Caesarea
Antipatris
Jerusalem
© Thomas Nelson, Inc., 1983

Map 9
THE HOLY LAND IN MODERN TIMES
Area occupied by Israel since June, 1967
0 25 50
Scale of Miles
A B C D E
34° 35° 36° 37°
1 2 3 4 5 6
LEBANON
Tripoli
Beirut
BEKAA VALLEY
LEBANON MTS.
ANTI-LEBANON MTS.
Sidon
Damascus
Tyre
Dan
U.N. Buffer Zone
1973 Line
SYRIA
Qiryat Shemona
Quneitra
1967 Cease-Fire Line
Nahariyya
Safad
Akko
Golan Heights
Sea of Galilee
Haifa
Tiberias
Nazareth
Dera
Mediterranean Sea
Afula
Ramtha
Beth Shean
Hadera
Netanya
Tulkarm
Jarash
Nablus
Herzliyya
Tel Aviv
Petah Tiqwa
West Bank
Jordan River
Yafo
Rishon le Zion
Lod
Amman
Ramla
Ramalah
Ashdod
Jericho
Jerusalem
Bethlehem
Madaba
Ashqelon
Qiryat Gat
Hebron
Dead Sea
Gaza
En Gedi
Dhiban
Beersheba
Karak
JORDAN
Al-Arish
ISRAEL
EGYPT
Negev
Arabah
Sinai
Elat
Aqaba
© Thomas Nelson, Inc., 1983